FOOTBALL YEARBOOK 2025–2026

Compiled by
John Anderson

HEADLINE

First published in 2025 by
HEADLINE PUBLISHING GROUP

1

Cover photographs:
Left: Cole Palmer – Chelsea – Visionhaus/Contributor/Getty Images;
Middle: Jude Bellingham – Real Madrid – David Ramos/Staff/Getty Images;
Right: Alessia Russo – Arsenal – Ryan Pierse/Staff/Getty Images

Spine photograph:
Eddie Howe – Newcastle United – Alex Dodd/CameraSport via Getty Images

Cataloguing in Publication Data is available from the British Library

ISBN (Hardback) 978 1 0354 1952 4
ISBN (Trade Paperback) 978 1 0354 1953 1

Typeset by Paperghosts Ltd, Tyne and Wear

Printed and bound in Great Britain by Clays Ltd, Elcograf S.p.A.

MIX
Paper | Supporting
responsible forestry
FSC
www.fsc.org
FSC® C104740

HEADLINE PUBLISHING GROUP
An Hachette UK Company
Carmelite House
50 Victoria Embankment
London
EC4Y 0DZ

The authorised representative in the EEA is Hachette Ireland, 8 Castlecourt Centre,
Dublin 15, D15 XTP3, Ireland (email: info@hbgi.ie)

www.headline.co.uk
www.hachette.co.uk

CONTENTS

INTRODUCTION

The 56th edition of the *Football Yearbook* is sponsored for the fifth time by Utilita. The coverage in this edition is once again full and comprehensive. It includes full coverage of FIFA World Cup 2026 qualifying groups to date. England under new manager Thomas Tuchel began the qualifying campaign with three successive wins to top Group K. Wales lie second in Group J with an impressive start under manager Craig Bellamy. Scotland, Northern Ireland and Republic of Ireland, all being in a four-team group, will begin their campaigns in September 2026.

Coverage of the UEFA Nations League 2024–25 includes the Group and Final stages, with match line-ups and final league tables. Also included are the promotion and relegation play-offs. Other international football at various levels is well covered in this edition.

At European club level, English clubs were once again dominant. So much so, that a fifth Champions League spot was awarded for the 2025–26 season. The Champions League saw Arsenal reach the semi-finals where they were defeated by eventual winners Paris Saint-Germain, 3-1 on aggregate. The French champions also defeated Aston Villa 5-4 on aggregate in the quarter-finals and Liverpool 4-1 on penalties, after the tie finished 1-1 on aggregate, in the Round of 16. Manchester City made it to the league phase play-offs, falling to 6-3 on aggregate to Real Madrid. The Europa League saw Tottenham Hotspur triumph 1-0 over Manchester United in the final in Bilbao. It was the sixth all-English European final. Chelsea won the Conference League with a comprehensive 4-1 win over Real Betis in the final in Wroclaw, Poland. These three European competitions have comprehensive details included. For the preliminary and qualifying rounds all results are included with details of goalscorers, attendances, full line-ups and formations for all matches involving British and Irish clubs. From the group phase onwards, goalscorers, attendances, full line-ups and formations are included for all matches, together with all of the league tables from the respective groups.

The 2024–25 Premier League season saw Liverpool win the top-league title for the 20th time, equalling the record set by Manchester United at the end of the 2012–13 season. Liverpool had the league won on 27 April with four games still to play, and although Arsenal fought hard throughout the season, they were consigned to finishing runners-up for the third season in succession. The fight for the European places went down to the final day of the season. Liverpool, Arsenal and Tottenham (due to winning the Europa League) had already secured their places in the Champions League, leaving five teams to fight it out for the three remaining Champions League places. The English quota has been increased from four to five teams due to the excellent performances in European competition during the season. Manchester City, Newcastle United, Chelsea, Aston Villa and Nottingham Forest were all in the hunt. Manchester City won 2-0 at Fulham to finish third, Chelsea won 1-0 at Nottingham Forest to finish fourth and leave Nottingham Forest in seventh, qualifying for a place in the Conference League. Despite a 1-0 defeat at home to Everton, Newcastle United made it to fifth and secured the final Champions League place. Aston Villa lost 2-0 to Manchester United and finished in sixth place, qualifying for the Europa League. Crystal Palace who won the FA Cup with a 1-0 victory over Manchester City qualified for the Europa League. The three promoted clubs, Ipswich Town, Leicester City and Southampton all had a difficult season. Although some big clubs (Manchester United, Tottenham Hotspur, Everton and West Ham) briefly flirted with relegation, they were never in real danger and the season ended with all three promoted sides being relegated. The dual ownership rule left Crystal Palace wondering whether they would be allowed to compete.

In the Championship, Leeds United returned to the Premier League, followed by Burnley, leaving Sheffield United, Sunderland, Coventry City and Bristol City to contest the play-offs. Sunderland were victorious in the final against Sheffield United. An injury-time goal from Brighton-bound Tommy Watson saw the Black Cats win 2-1 and move into the Premier League after an absence of eight seasons.

In League One, pre-season favourites Birmingham City were promoted automatically, together with Wrexham. The League One Play-off final saw an all-London affair with Charlton Athletic overcoming Leyton Orient 1-0. League Two champions Doncaster Rovers were promoted to League One and were joined by Port Vale and Bradford City. The League Two Play-off final ended with AFC Wimbledon winning 1-0 over Walsall. Carlisle United and Morecambe were relegated to the National League. Oldham Athletic (the first former Premier League club to play non-league football) regained their league status after three seasons by beating Southend United 3-2 after extra-time in the National League Play-off final which attracted a crowd of 52,115, a National League record.

All of these statistics are reproduced in the pages devoted not only to the Premier League, but the three Football League competitions too, as well as the National League and all major allied cup competitions.

Women's football is also featured. Women's Super League, Championship and National Leagues are included, together with the domestic cup competitions: Adobe Women's FA Cup and Subway League Cup. The UEFA Women's Champions League is also covered, together with the UEFA Women's Euro 2025 qualifying and 2025 Finals. England Women's Internationals since 1974 and all of the 2024–25 season's games are included.

In the club-by-club pages that contain the line-ups of all league matches, appearances are split into starting and substitute appearances. In the Players Directory the totals show figures combined.

The Players Directory and its accompanying A to Z index enable the reader to quickly find the club of any specific player. Throughout the book players sent off are designated with ■; substitutes in the club pages are numbered 12–18.

In addition to competitions already mentioned there is full coverage of Scottish Premiership, Scottish Football League and Scottish domestic cup competitions. There are also sections devoted to Welsh and Northern Irish football, Under-21s and various other UEFA youth levels, schools, reserve team, academies and the leading non-league competitions as well as the work of club chaplains. The chief tournaments outside the UK at club and national level are not forgotten. The International Directory features Europe in some depth as well as every FIFA-affiliated country's international results for the year since July 2024; every reigning league and cup champion worldwide is listed.

Naturally, there are international appearances and goals scored by players for England, Scotland, Northern Ireland, Wales and the Republic of Ireland. For easy reference, those players making appearances and scoring goals in the season covered are picked out in **bold** type.

The *Football Yearbook* would like to extend its appreciation to the publishers Headline for excellent support in the preparation of this edition, particularly Louise Rothwell for her continued help and Raiyah Butt for her enthusiasm and determination and for the photographic selections throughout the book.

ACKNOWLEDGEMENTS

In addition the *Football Yearbook* is also keen to thank the following individuals and organisations for their co-operation. Special thanks to Jonathan Wilson for his Review of the Season and Team of the Season and to Stephan Behan for image-sourcing.

Thanks are also due to Ian Nannestad for the Obituaries and the Did You Know? and Fact File features in the club section. Many thanks also to John English for his conscientious proof reading and compilation of the International Directory.

The *Football Yearbook* is grateful to the Football Association, the Scottish Professional Football League, the Football League, Matt Baker for his contribution to the Chaplain's page and Bob Bannister, Paul Anderson, Kenny Holmes and Martin Cooper for their help. Sincere thanks to George Schley and Simon Dunnington for their excellent work on the database, and to Andy Cordiner and the staff at Paperghosts for their much appreciated efforts in the production of the book throughout the year. We thank Utilita for their sponsorship of the *Football Yearbook* over the last five years, and their continued dedication to football and its community.

WELCOME

Welcome to the latest edition of the *Football Yearbook*.

Without a doubt, the 2024–25 season was the year of the underdog as a number of clubs ended their long wait for silverware.

Both English cup winners ended barren spells – a collective trophy drought numbering *186 years* – to climb the famous Wembley steps as victors. Newcastle United overcame Liverpool in March's Carabao Cup final to spark jubilant scenes 56 years after their last major trophy. Eddie Howe has written himself into Geordie folklore. Crystal Palace, a long-term partner of Utilita, edged out Manchester City in May's FA Cup final, the first major trophy in the club's 130-year history.

Ange Postecoglou guided his Tottenham side to Europa League glory, a first trophy in N17 since 2008, only to be sacked 16 days later after a wretched league campaign. Down the Seven Sisters Road, Arsenal Women upset the odds with a 1-0 victory over Barcelona to win the UEFA Champions League for the first time in 18 years. And while Celtic dominated in Scotland – winning their 13th title in 14 years *and* the League Cup – Aberdeen beat them after a penalty shoot-out victory in the Scottish Cup final. It was their first cup success since 1990.

Even Premier League winners Liverpool were celebrating only their second league title in 35 years, although to call Arne Slot's side underdogs would be a stretch. The Reds were worthy champions as their main challengers Arsenal finished runners-up for a third successive season.

Elsewhere, Utilita partner club Sunderland beat favourites Sheffield United in the Championship Play-off final to return to the Premier League after an eight-year absence. The Tyne-Wear derby will be a welcome addition to the topflight in 2025–26.

In fact, the EFL – of which Utilita is a proud partner – celebrated a cumulative record attendance across the three Play-off finals of 211,858. It's worth noting that a further 52,115 watched Oldham beat Southend in the National League Play-off final, underlining the strength in numbers of the English pyramid (it was also the Latics' first promotion for 34 years).

Meanwhile, on the continent there was yet *more* success for the 'unlikely'. In Italy, Bologna's 51 year wait for silverware ended when they lifted the Coppa Italia, ex-Aberdeen midfielder Lewis Ferguson their captain. And in the ancient Dutch town of Deventer, local side Go Ahead Eagles won the KNVB Trophy – their first major trophy since 1933!

As Alex Ferguson once said: 'Football, bloody hell!'

As regards the next generation, at Utilita we are so proud of our continuing support of the EFL Utilita Kids & Girls Cups. It is the biggest schools' football competition in the country with 20,000 children, across 2,500 teams, competing to play at Wembley while representing their local EFL club. A big well done to Salesbury C of E Primary (Blackburn Rovers), St Mary's Catholic (Charlton Athletic) and Higher Bebington Primary (Tranmere Rovers) for winning their respective finals. We are also proud of the growth of our Football Rebooted campaign – British football's biggest environmental movement, lead by David James MBE & former WSL striker Courtney Sweetman-Kirk. We now have nearly a thousand collection points across the country, from grassroots venues to elite football clubs, to major supermarkets (thank you Tesco Fratton). We are unrelenting in our mission to save one million pairs of boots and repurpose them because remember, for every pair of boots made 30lbs of carbon emissions are produced!

Speaking of sustainability, we have also been making big strides off the pitch. We are so proud of our work at Portsmouth FC In The Community where we installed solar panels at its brand-new facility used by both the club's women's team and the local community. In addition, we played a part in AFC Bournemouth's new £32m training centre where our team installed more than 650 solar panels – reducing the club's carbon footprint by 34 tonnes per year. Football is finally waking up to Net Zero and the potential of solar – it is gratifying Utilita is at the centre of this. We are at the start of a long journey, but I believe football's influence can really drive positive change as society becomes less reliant on fossil fuels.

In the meantime, I hope you enjoy reading this book, which meticulously chronicles the Beautiful Game – and all the best to your clubs in 2025–26.

Jem Maidment, Chief Marketing Officer, Utilita Energy

Utilita Kids & Girls Cup competitions, one of the biggest schools' tournaments in Europe, culminate with four finals across two dates at Wembley Stadium each season. (Joe Toth/Shutterstock)

TEAM OF THE SEASON 2024–25

JONATHAN WILSON

Alisson (Liverpool)

Jurrien Timber *(Arsenal)*	**Nikola Milenkovic** *(Nottingham F)*	**Virgil van Dijk** *(Liverpool)*	**Milos Kerkez** *(Bournemouth)*

Ryan Gravenberch *(Liverpool)*   **Youri Tielemans** *(Aston Villa)*   **Alexis Mac Allister** *(Liverpool)*

Mohamed Salah *(Liverpool)*   **Alexander Isak** *(Newcastle U)*   **Eberechi Eze** *(Crystal Palace)*

Manager: Arne Slot *(Liverpool)*

Alisson: Matz Sels and David Raya kept the most clean sheets this season, but Alisson, who was restricted by injury to 28 Premier League starts, remains the most impressive goalkeeper. He's an all-rounder, both shot-stopper and ball-player, agile and blessed with lighting reflexes, and more than capable of sweeping a 40-yard pass to a player in space. The thought that Caoimhín Kelleher might retain his place after an impressive stint deputising for the number one soon disappeared when Alisson returned with charisma and a sense of authority.

Jurrien Timber: Of all the players Arsenal lost to injury this season, the one who was missed the least was probably Ben White, which says much about how well Jurien Timber performed. He started the season at left-back and also had a couple of games in the centre. He's a rugged and tactically astute player, a threat at dead-balls and also extremely adept at tucking in to operate as a deep-lying midfielder.

Nikola Milenković: After two years of apparently scattergun spending, Forest this season were much more focused and in picking up Milenkovic for £10.3m from Fiorentina, they found a remarkable bargain. He thrived in a defence that typically sat deep, forging a formidable partnership with Murillo. Strong in the air and firm in the challenge, he also proved an adept passer of the ball, while weighing in with five goals.

Virgil van Dijk: Composed, elegant and powerful, Van Dijk has an aura about him that seems to discourage opponents even from attempting to take the ball past him. Only six players won more aerials per game than the Dutchman, and none have a pass completion rate anywhere near his 91.2%. A respected leader, he has been probably the best central defender in the world over the past decade.

Milos Kerkez: It's a sign of the strength of the Premier League that Bournemouth could sign a player of the class of Kerkez, not just in being able to afford his wages but even in identifying his talent. A hard-tackling, hard-running left-back, he got forward to register two goals and five assists, a fine exponent of the running game Andoni Iraola has interpolated with positional play.

Youri Tielemans: Tielemans seemed a risky signing for Aston Villa when he arrived from Leicester, where he had been accused of a lack of commitment. There has been no sign of that at Villa, though, where he showed great intelligence in knitting the midfield together, scoring three goals in the league and setting up seven. A pass completion rate of 86% for somebody who plays so many long or risky balls is remarkable.

Ryan Gravenberch: When Liverpool signed nobody but Federico Chiesa last summer, the biggest concern was at the back of midfield. Fabinho had not been replaced, and there seemed an obvious shortfall. But Arne Slot proved a fine solver of problems; none of his solutions were quite so effective as his decision to pair Graven-berch and Alexis Mac Allister at the back of midfield. Together they fulfilled the function of a defensive mid-fielder while also offering passing options, giving Liverpool control.

Alexis Mac Allister: Although they did the holding midfield job as a pair, Gravenberch was the more defen-sive, giving Mac Allister licence to push forwards. As a result he got five goals and five assists (as opposed to Gravenberch's no goals and four assists), including screamers late in the season against Fulham and Totten-ham, the game in which the title was sealed. His contribution, though, was far more than just goals, as his passing and positional sense helped Liverpool dominate games.

Mohamed Salah: Was this his best season in the Premier League? There have been so many good ones it's very hard to tell, but he was an obvious choice for both PFA and FWA Player of the Year awards, while also finishing as the Premier League's top scorer. It was his third FWA Player of the Year award, emulating Thierry Henry. His 29 goals plus 18 assists equalled the record for goal involvements, but what was critical was how important they often were. It began on the opening weekend when he turned an awkward fixture at Ipswich with an assist and a goal, and never really stopped.

Alexander Isak: Chris Wood suggested there is still a role for a target-man, Bryan Mbuemo also got 20 goals as part of a very mobile front three, and Erling Haaland, despite a disappointing season by his own exceptional standards, got 22 goals. But the pick of the central forwards was Alexander Isak. The very model of a modern striker, he is strong, lithe and imaginative, his 23 league goals the best by a Newcastle player since Alan Shearer in 2001–02.

Eberechi Eze: Eze is a throwback to the time when it seemed every club had their own genius. Quick, skilful and direct, he got eight goals and eight assists this season, operating as a sort of inside-left in Oliver Glasner's 3-4-2-1. His most important goal, though, was the delicious first-time sweep to convert a counter-attack against Manchester City in the FA Cup final.

Manager: Arne Slot: Nuno Espírito Santo, Thomas Frank, Andoni Iraola and Oliver Glasner have all had excellent seasons, but nobody has stood out like Slot, who not only seemed entirely unfazed by replacing Jürgen Klopp, but tweaked the style to lead Liverpool to the title in his first season in English football.

THE FA COMMUNITY SHIELD WINNERS 1908–2024

CHARITY SHIELD 1908–2001

1908	Manchester U v QPR	1-1
Replay	Manchester U v QPR	4-0
1909	Newcastle U v Northampton T	2-0
1910	Brighton v Aston Villa	1-0
1911	Manchester U v Swindon T	8-4
1912	Blackburn R v QPR	2-1
1913	Professionals v Amateurs	7-2
1920	WBA v Tottenham H	2-0
1921	Tottenham H v Burnley	2-0
1922	Huddersfield T v Liverpool	1-0
1923	Professionals v Amateurs	2-0
1924	Professionals v Amateurs	3-1
1925	Amateurs v Professionals	6-1
1926	Amateurs v Professionals	6-3
1927	Cardiff C v Corinthians	2-1
1928	Everton v Blackburn R	2-1
1929	Professionals v Amateurs	3-0
1930	Arsenal v Sheffield Wed	2-1
1931	Arsenal v WBA	1-0
1932	Everton v Newcastle U	5-3
1933	Arsenal v Everton	3-0
1934	Arsenal v Manchester C	4-0
1935	Sheffield Wed v Arsenal	1-0
1936	Sunderland v Arsenal	2-1
1937	Manchester C v Sunderland	2-0
1938	Arsenal v Preston NE	2-1
1948	Arsenal v Manchester U	4-3
1949	Portsmouth v Wolverhampton W	1-1*
1950	English World Cup XI v FA Canadian Touring Team	4-2
1951	Tottenham H v Newcastle U	2-1
1952	Manchester U v Newcastle U	4-2
1953	Arsenal v Blackpool	3-1
1954	Wolverhampton W v WBA	4-4*
1955	Chelsea v Newcastle U	3-0
1956	Manchester U v Manchester C	1-0
1957	Manchester U v Aston Villa	4-0
1958	Bolton W v Wolverhampton W	4-1
1959	Wolverhampton W v Nottingham F	3-1
1960	Burnley v Wolverhampton W	2-2*
1961	Tottenham H v FA XI	3-2
1962	Tottenham H v Ipswich T	5-1
1963	Everton v Manchester U	4-0
1964	Liverpool v West Ham U	2-2*
1965	Manchester U v Liverpool	2-2*
1966	Liverpool v Everton	1-0
1967	Manchester U v Tottenham H	3-3*
1968	Manchester C v WBA	6-1
1969	Leeds U v Manchester C	2-1
1970	Everton v Chelsea	2-1
1971	Leicester C v Liverpool	1-0
1972	Manchester C v Aston Villa	1-0
1973	Burnley v Manchester C	1-0
1974	Liverpool v Leeds U	1-1
	Liverpool won 6-5 on penalties.	
1975	Derby Co v West Ham U	2-0
1976	Liverpool v Southampton	1-0
1977	Liverpool v Manchester U	0-0*
1978	Nottingham F v Ipswich T	5-0
1979	Liverpool v Arsenal	3-1
1980	Liverpool v West Ham U	1-0
1981	Aston Villa v Tottenham H	2-2*
1982	Liverpool v Tottenham H	1-0
1983	Manchester U v Liverpool	2-0
1984	Everton v Liverpool	1-0
1985	Everton v Manchester U	2-0
1986	Everton v Liverpool	1-1*
1987	Everton v Coventry C	1-0
1988	Liverpool v Wimbledon	2-1
1989	Liverpool v Arsenal	1-0
1990	Liverpool v Manchester U	1-1*
1991	Arsenal v Tottenham H	0-0*
1992	Leeds U v Liverpool	4-3
1993	Manchester U v Arsenal	1-1
	Manchester U won 5-4 on penalties.	
1994	Manchester U v Blackburn R	2-0
1995	Everton v Blackburn R	1-0
1996	Manchester U v Newcastle U	4-0
1997	Manchester U v Chelsea	1-1
	Manchester U won 4-2 on penalties.	
1998	Arsenal v Manchester U	3-0
1999	Arsenal v Manchester U	2-1
2000	Chelsea v Manchester U	2-0
2001	Liverpool v Manchester U	2-1

COMMUNITY SHIELD 2002–24

Year	Match	Score
2002	Arsenal v Liverpool	1-0
2003	Manchester U v Arsenal	1-1
	Manchester U won 4-3 on penalties.	
2004	Arsenal v Manchester U	3-1
2005	Chelsea v Arsenal	2-1
2006	Liverpool v Chelsea	2-1
2007	Manchester U v Chelsea	1-1
	Manchester U won 3-0 on penalties.	
2008	Manchester U v Portsmouth	0-0
	Manchester U won 3-1 on penalties.	
2009	Chelsea v Manchester U	2-2
	Chelsea won 4-1 on penalties.	
2010	Manchester U v Chelsea	3-1
2011	Manchester U v Manchester C	3-2
2012	Manchester C v Chelsea	3-2
2013	Manchester U v Wigan Ath	2-0
2014	Arsenal v Manchester C	3-0
2015	Arsenal v Chelsea	1-0
2016	Manchester U v Leicester C	2-1
2017	Arsenal v Chelsea	1-1
	Arsenal won 4-1 on penalties.	
2018	Manchester C v Chelsea	2-0
2019	Manchester C v Liverpool	1-1
	Manchester C won 5-4 on penalties.	
2020	Arsenal v Liverpool	1-1
	Arsenal won 5-4 on penalties.	
2021	Leicester C v Manchester C	1-0
2022	Liverpool v Manchester C	3-1
2023	Arsenal v Manchester C	1-1
	Arsenal won 4-1 on penalties.	
2024	Manchester C v Manchester U	1-1
	Manchester C won 7-6 on penalties.	

* Each club retained shield for six months.

THE FA COMMUNITY SHIELD 2024

Saturday, 10 August 2024

(at Wembley Stadium, attendance 78,146)

Manchester C (0) 1   Manchester U (0) 1

Manchester C: (4321) Ederson; Lewis, Akanji, Dias, Gvardiol (Ake 90); O'Reilly (Nunes 63), Kovacic, McAtee (Bernardo Silva 80); Bobb (De Bruyne 90), Doku (Savinho 63); Haaland.
Scorer: Bernardo Silva 89.

Manchester U: (4231) Onana; Dalot, Maguire (Pellistri 58), Evans, Martinez; Casemiro, Mainoo (Collyer 59); Diallo (Garnacho 59), Mount (McTominay 58), Rashford (Sancho 83); Bruno Fernandes.
Scorer: Garnacho 82.

Manchester C won 7-6 on penalties.

Referee: Jarred Gillett.

FOOTBALL AWARDS 2024–25

THE FOOTBALL WRITERS' FOOTBALLER OF THE YEAR 2025

The Football Writers' Association Sir Stanley Matthews Trophy for the Footballer of the Year was awarded to Mohamed Salah of Liverpool and Egypt. Virgil van Dijk (Liverpool and Netherlands) was runner-up and Alexander Isak (Newcastle U and Sweden) came third.

Past Winners
1947–48 Stanley Matthews (Blackpool), 1948–49 Johnny Carey (Manchester U), 1949–50 Joe Mercer (Arsenal), 1950–51 Harry Johnston (Blackpool), 1951–52 Billy Wright (Wolverhampton W), 1952–53 Nat Lofthouse (Bolton W), 1953–54 Tom Finney (Preston NE), 1954–55 Don Revie (Manchester C), 1955–56 Bert Trautmann (Manchester C), 1956–57 Tom Finney (Preston NE), 1957–58 Danny Blanchflower (Tottenham H), 1958–59 Syd Owen (Luton T), 1959–60 Bill Slater (Wolverhampton W), 1960–61 Danny Blanchflower (Tottenham H), 1961–62 Jimmy Adamson (Burnley), 1962–63 Stanley Matthews (Stoke C), 1963–64 Bobby Moore (West Ham U), 1964–65 Bobby Collins (Leeds U), 1965–66 Bobby Charlton (Manchester U), 1966–67 Jackie Charlton (Leeds U), 1967–68 George Best (Manchester U), 1968–69 Dave Mackay (Derby Co) shared with Tony Book (Manchester C), 1969–70 Billy Bremner (Leeds U), 1970–71 Frank McLintock (Arsenal), 1971–72 Gordon Banks (Stoke C), 1972–73 Pat Jennings (Tottenham H), 1973–74 Ian Callaghan (Liverpool), 1974–75 Alan Mullery (Fulham), 1975–76 Kevin Keegan (Liverpool), 1976–77 Emlyn Hughes (Liverpool), 1977–78 Kenny Burns (Nottingham F), 1978–79 Kenny Dalglish (Liverpool), 1979–80 Terry McDermott (Liverpool), 1980–81 Frans Thijssen (Ipswich T), 1981–82 Steve Perryman (Tottenham H), 1982–83 Kenny Dalglish (Liverpool), 1983–84 Ian Rush (Liverpool), 1984–85 Neville Southall (Everton), 1985–86 Gary Lineker (Everton), 1986–87 Clive Allen (Tottenham H), 1987–88 John Barnes (Liverpool), 1988–89 Steve Nicol (Liverpool), 1989–90 John Barnes (Liverpool), 1990–91 Gordon Strachan (Leeds U), 1991–92 Gary Lineker (Tottenham H), 1992–93 Chris Waddle (Sheffield Wed), 1993–94 Alan Shearer (Blackburn R), 1994–95 Jurgen Klinsmann (Tottenham H), 1995–96 Eric Cantona (Manchester U), 1996–97 Gianfranco Zola (Chelsea), 1997–98 Dennis Bergkamp (Arsenal), 1998–99 David Ginola (Tottenham H), 1999–2000 Roy Keane (Manchester U), 2000–01 Teddy Sheringham (Manchester U), 2001–02 Robert Pires (Arsenal), 2002–03 Thierry Henry (Arsenal), 2003–04 Thierry Henry (Arsenal), 2004–05 Frank Lampard (Chelsea), 2005–06 Thierry Henry (Arsenal), 2006–07 Cristiano Ronaldo (Manchester U), 2007–08 Cristiano Ronaldo (Manchester U), 2008–09 Ryan Giggs (Manchester U), 2009–10 Wayne Rooney (Manchester U), 2010–11 Scott Parker (West Ham U), 2011–12 Robin van Persie (Arsenal), 2012–13 Gareth Bale (Tottenham H), 2013–14 Luis Suárez (Liverpool), 2014–15 Eden Hazard (Chelsea), 2015–16 Jamie Vardy (Leicester C), 2016–17 N'Golo Kanté (Chelsea), 2017–18 Mohamed Salah (Liverpool), 2018–19 Raheem Sterling (Manchester C), 2019–20 Jordan Henderson (Liverpool), 2020–21 Ruben Dias (Manchester C), 2021–22 Mohamed Salah (Liverpool), 2022–23 Erling Haaland (Manchester C), 2023–24 Phil Foden (Manchester C and England), 2024–25 Mohamed Salah (Liverpool and Egypt).

THE FOOTBALL WRITERS' WOMEN'S FOOTBALLER OF THE YEAR 2025
Alissia Russo (Arsenal and England)

THE PFA AWARDS 2024
Player of the Year: Phil Foden (Manchester C and England)
Young Player of the Year: Cole Palmer (Chelsea and England)
Women's Player of the Year: Bunny Shaw (Manchester C and Jamaica)
Women's Young Player of the Year: Grace Clinton (Manchester U and England)
Championship Player of the Year: Crysencio Summerville (Leeds U)
League One Player of the Year: Alfie May (Charlton Ath)
League Two Player of the Year: Jodi Jones (Notts Co and Malta)
PFA Merit Award: Dean Lewington
PFA Merit Award: Fara Williams

SCOTTISH AWARDS 2024–25

SCOTTISH PFA PLAYER OF THE YEAR AWARDS 2024–25
Player of the Year: Daizen Maeda (Celtic and Japan)
Young Player of the Year: Lennon Miller (Motherwell and Scotland)
Manager of the Year: John McGlynn (Falkirk)
Championship Player of the Year: Brad Spencer (Falkirk)
League 1 Player of the Year: Fraser Taylor (Arbroath (on loan from St Mirren))
League 2 Player of the Year: Alan Trouten (East Fife)
Women's Player of the Year: Emma Lawton (Celtic and Scotland)
Women's Young Player of the Year: Laura Berry (Rangers and Scotland)
Special Merit Award: Sir Kenny Daglish.

SCOTTISH FOOTBALL WRITERS' ASSOCIATION AWARDS 2025
Manager of the Year: Brendan Rodgers (Celtic)
Player of the Year: Daizen Maeda (Celtic and Japan)
Young Player of the Year: Lennon Miller (Motherwell and Scotland)
International Player of the Year: Scott McTominay (Napoli and Scotland)
Women's International Player of the Year: Erin Cuthbert (Chelsea and Scotland)

PREMIER LEAGUE AWARDS 2024–25

PLAYER OF THE MONTH AWARDS 2024–25		MANAGER OF THE MONTH AWARDS 2024–25
August	Erling Haaland (Manchester C)	Fabian Hurzeler (Brighton & HA)
September	Cole Palmer (Chelsea)	Enzo Maresca (Chelsea)
October	Chris Wood (Nottingham F)	Nuno Espirito Santo (Nottingham F)
November	Mohammed Salah (Liverpool)	Arne Slot (Liverpool)
December	Alexander Isak (Newcastle U)	Nuno Espirito Santo (Nottingham F)
January	Justin Kluivert (Bournemouth)	Andoni Iraola (Bournemouth)
February	Mohamed Salah (Liverpool)	David Moyes (Everton)
March	Bruno Fernandes (Manchester U)	Nuno Espirito Santo (Nottingham F)
April	Alexis Mac Allister (Liverpool)	Vito Pereira (Wolverhampton W)
Season	Mohamed Salah (Liverpool)	Arne Slot (Liverpool)

SKY BET LEAGUE AWARDS 2024–25

SKY BET FOOTBALL LEAGUE PLAYER OF THE MONTH AWARDS 2024–25

	Championship	*League One*	*League Two*
August	Mark Harris (Oxford U)	Louis Barry (Stockport Co)	Luke Molyneux (Doncaster R)
September	Borja Sainz (Norwich C)	Kwame Poku (Peterborough U)	Glenn Morris (Gillingham)
October	Borja Sainz (Norwich C)	Kwame Poku (Peterborough U)	Will Grigg (Chesterfield)
November	Finn Azaz (Middlesbrough)	Louis Barry (Stockport Co)	Alex Gilbey (Milton Keynes Dons)
December	Ephron Mason-Clark (Coventry C)	Miles Leaburn (Charlton Ath)	Nathan Lowe (Walsall)
January	James Trafford (Burnley)	Rumarn Burrell (Burton Alb)	Shaun Whalley (Accrington S)
February	Dan James (Leeds U)	Niall Ennis (Blackpool)	Antoni Sarcevic (Bradford C)
March	Tyrese Campbell (Sheffield U)	Jovan Makama (Lincoln C)	George Lapslie (Bradford C)
April	Josh Brownhill (Burnley)	Charlie Kelman (Leyton Orient)	Lorent Tolaj (Port Vale)
Season	Gustavo Hamer (Sheffield U)	Richard Kone (Wycombe W)	Michael Cheek (Bromley)

SKY BET FOOTBALL LEAGUE MANAGER OF THE MONTH AWARDS 2024–25

	Championship	*League One*	*League Two*
August	Regis Le Bris (Sunderland)	Phil Parkinson (Wrexham)	Mark Bonner (Gillingham)
September	Chris Wilder (Sheffield U)	Steve Bruce (Blackpool)	Darren Moore (Port Vale)
October	Regis Le Bris (Sunderland)	Matt Bloomfield (Wycombe W)	Darren Moore (Port Vale)
November	Chris Wilder (Sheffield U)	Matt Bloomfield (Wycombe W)	Derek Adams (Morecambe)
December	Daniel Farke (Leeds U)	Richie Wellens (Leyton Orient)	Mat Sadler (Walsall)
January	Gary Rowett (Oxford U)	Richie Wellens (Leyton Orient)	Ian Holloway (Swindon T)
February	Daniel Farke (Leeds U)	Chris Davies (Birmingham C)	Graham Alexander (Bradford C)
March	Chris Wilder (Sheffield U)	Phil Parkinson (Wrexham)	Danny Cowley (Colchester U)
April	Scott Parker (Burnley)	Chris Davies (Birmingham C)	Grant McCann (Doncaster R)
Season	Scott Parker (Burnley)	Chris Davies (Birmingham C)	Graham Alexander (Bradford C)

SKY BET CHAMPIONSHIP TEAM OF THE SEASON
Trafford (Burnley); Bogle (Leeds U), Egan-Riley (Burnley), Esteve (Burnley), Burrows (Sheffield U), Tanaka (Leeds U), Bellingham (Sunderland), Hamer (Sheffield U), James (Leeds U), Sainz (Norwich C), Sargent (Norwich C).

SKY BET LEAGUE ONE TEAM OF THE SEASON
Tickle (Wigan Ath); Cleworth (Wrexham), Klarer (Birmingham C), Jones (Charlton Ath), Barnett (Wrexham), Iwata (Birmingham C), Bate (Stockport Co), Cochrane (Birmingham C), Poku (Peterborough U), Keillor-Dunn (Barnsley), Kone (Wycombe W).

SKY BET LEAGUE TWO TEAM OF THE SEASON
Goodman (AFC Wimbledon); Barrett (Walsall), Allen (Walsall), Hall (Port Vale), Hume (Grimsby T), Smallwood (Bradford C), Molyneux (Doncaster R), Payne (Colchester U), McGoldrick (Notts Co), Jatta (Notts Co), Cheek (Bromley).

LEAGUE MANAGERS ASSOCIATION AWARDS 2024–25

SIR ALEX FERGUSON TROPHY FOR LMA MANAGER OF THE YEAR
Arne Slot (Liverpool)

BARCLAYS PREMIER LEAGUE MANAGER OF THE YEAR
Arne Slot (Liverpool)

SKY BET CHAMPIONSHIP MANAGER OF THE YEAR
Daniel Farke (Leeds U)

SKY BET LEAGUE 1 MANAGER OF THE YEAR
Chris Davies (Birmingham C)

SKY BET LEAGUE 2 MANAGER OF THE YEAR
Grant McCann (Doncaster R)

BARCLAYS WSL MANAGER OF THE YEAR
Sonia Bompastor (Chelsea)

BARCLAYS WOMEN'S CHAMPIONSHIP MANAGER OF THE YEAR
Jay Sadler (Portsmouth)

LMA JOHN DUNCAN AWARD
Oliver Glasner (Crystal Palace), Eddie Howe (Newcastle U), Ange Postecoglou (Tottenham H) and Renee Slegers (Arsenal Women)

OTHER AWARDS

2024 BALLON D'OR PRESENTED BY FRANCE FOOTBALL

MEN'S PLAYER OF THE YEAR
Rodri (Manchester C and Spain)

WOMEN PLAYER OF THE YEAR
Aitana Bonmati (Barcelona and Spain)

MEN'S COACH OF THE YEAR
Carlo Ancelotti (Real Madrid)

WOMEN'S COACH OF THE YEAR
Emma Hayes (Chelsea and USA national coach)

THE BEST FIFA FOOTBALL AWARDS 2024

BEST MEN'S PLAYER OF THE YEAR 2024
Vinicius Junior (Real Madrid and Brazil)

BEST WOMEN'S PLAYER OF THE YEAR 2024
Aitana Bonmati (Barcelona and Spain)

BEST MEN'S GOALKEEPER OF THE YEAR 2024
Emiliano Martinez (Aston Villa and Argentina)

BEST WOMEN'S GOALKEEPER OF THE YEAR 2024
Alyssa Naeher (Chicago Red Stars and USA)

BEST MEN'S COACH OF THE YEAR 2024
Carlo Ancelotti (Real Madrid)

BEST WOMEN'S COACH OF THE YEAR 2024
Emma Hayes (Chelsea and USA)

PUSKAS AWARD GOAL OF THE YEAR 2024
Alejandro Garnacho, Everton v Manchester U, Premier League, 26 November 2023.

FAIR PLAY AWARD 2024
Thiago Maia (Internacional and Brazil U23).

MEN'S WORLD XI 2024
(433) Martinez (Aston Villa); Carvajal (Real Madrid), Rudiger (Real Madrid), Dias (Manchester C), Saliba (Arsenal); Bellingham (Real Madrid), Rodri (Manchester C), Kroos (Real Madrid); Yamal (Barcelona), Haaland (Manchester C), Vinicius Junior (Real Madrid).

WOMEN'S WORLD XI 2024
(442) Naeher (Chicago Red Stars); Bronze (Chelsea), Girma (San Diego Wave), Paredes (Barcelona), Batlle (Barcelona); Portilho (Corinthians), Guijarro (Barcelona), Horan (Lyon), Bonmati (Barcelona); Hansen (Barcelona), Paralluelo (Barcelona).

PREMIER LEAGUE 2024–25

(P) Promoted into division at end of 2023–24 season.

			Home					Away					Total						
1	Liverpool[1]	38	14	4	1	42	16	11	5	3	44	25	25	9	4	86	41	45	84
2	Arsenal[1]	38	11	6	2	35	17	9	8	2	34	17	20	14	4	69	34	35	74
3	Manchester C[1]	38	13	3	3	43	23	8	5	6	29	21	21	8	9	72	44	28	71
4	Chelsea[1]	38	12	5	2	35	18	8	4	7	29	25	20	9	9	64	43	21	69
5	Newcastle U[1]	38	12	2	5	40	20	8	4	7	28	27	20	6	12	68	47	21	66
6	Aston Villa[2]	38	11	7	1	34	20	8	2	9	24	31	19	9	10	58	51	7	66
7	Nottingham F[3]	38	9	5	5	26	16	10	3	6	32	30	19	8	11	58	46	12	65
8	Brighton & HA	38	8	8	3	30	26	8	5	6	36	33	16	13	9	66	59	7	61
9	Bournemouth	38	8	4	7	23	16	7	7	5	35	30	15	11	12	58	46	12	56
10	Brentford	38	9	4	6	40	35	7	4	8	26	22	16	8	14	66	57	9	56
11	Fulham	38	7	5	7	27	30	8	4	7	27	24	15	9	14	54	54	0	54
12	Crystal Palace[2]	38	6	7	6	24	26	7	7	5	27	25	13	14	11	51	51	0	53
13	Everton	38	5	9	5	26	23	6	6	7	16	21	11	15	12	42	44	−2	48
14	West Ham U	38	5	5	9	23	34	6	5	8	23	28	11	10	17	46	62	−16	43
15	Manchester U	38	7	3	9	23	28	4	6	9	21	26	11	9	18	44	54	−10	42
16	Wolverhampton W	38	6	3	10	27	32	6	3	10	27	37	12	6	20	54	69	−15	42
17	Tottenham H[4]	38	6	3	10	35	35	5	2	12	29	30	11	5	22	64	65	−1	38
18	Leicester C (P)	38	4	3	12	15	34	2	4	13	18	46	6	7	25	33	80	−47	25
19	Ipswich T (P)	38	1	4	14	14	44	3	6	10	22	38	4	10	24	36	82	−46	22
20	Southampton (P)	38	1	3	15	13	47	1	3	15	13	39	2	6	30	26	86	−60	12

[1] *Liverpool, Arsenal, Manchester C, Chelsea and Newcastle U qualify for Champions League league phase.* [2] *Aston Villa and Crystal Palace (FA Cup winners) qualify for Europa League league phase.* [3] *Nottingham F qualify for UEFA Conference League play-off round.* [4] *Tottenham H qualify for Champions League league phase as Europa League winners.*

PREMIER LEAGUE LEADING GOALSCORERS 2024–25

Qualification 8 League Goals	League	FA Cup	EFL Cup	Other	Total
Mohamed Salah (Liverpool)	29	0	2	3	34
Erling Haaland (Manchester C)	22	1	0	11	34
Alexander Isak (Newcastle U)	23	1	3	0	27
Brian Mbeumo (Brentford)	20	0	0	0	20
Yoane Wissa (Brentford)	19	0	1	0	20
Chris Wood (Nottingham F)	20	0	0	0	20
Bruno Fernandes (Manchester U)	8	2	2	7	19
Cody Gakpo (Liverpool)	10	0	5	3	18
Brennan Johnson (Tottenham H)	11	1	1	5	18
Cole Palmer (Chelsea)	15	0	0	3	18
Matheus Cunha (Wolverhampton W)	15	2	0	0	17
Luis Diaz (Liverpool)	13	0	1	3	17
Jean-Philippe Mateta (Crystal Palace)	14	0	3	0	17
Ollie Watkins (Aston Villa)	16	0	0	1	17
Dominic Solanke (Tottenham H)	9	0	2	5	16
Kai Havertz (Arsenal)	9	0	2	4	15
Jarrod Bowen (West Ham U)	13	1	0	0	14
Eberechi Eze (Crystal Palace)	8	4	2	0	14
Raul Jimenez (Fulham)	12	1	1	0	14
Jorgen Strand Larsen (Wolverhampton W)	14	0	0	0	14
Morgan Rogers (Aston Villa)	8	2	0	4	14
Liam Delap (Ipswich T)	12	0	0	1	13
Includes 1 FIFA Club World Cup goal for Chelsea.					
Nicolas Jackson (Chelsea)	10	0	0	3	13
Justin Kluivert (Bournemouth)	12	1	0	0	13
Joao Pedro (Brighton & HA)	10	0	0	3	13
Includes 3 FIFA Club World Cup goals for Chelsea.					
Antoine Semenyo (Bournemouth)	11	2	0	0	13
Evanilson (Bournemouth)	10	2	0	0	12
Ismaila Sarr (Crystal Palace)	8	3	1	0	12
Kevin Schade (Brentford)	11	0	1	0	12
Amad Diallo (Manchester U)	8	0	1	2	11
Kaoru Mitoma (Brighton & HA)	10	1	0	0	11
Rodrigo Muniz (Fulham)	8	3	0	0	11
Iliman Ndiaye (Everton)	9	1	1	0	11
Danny Welbeck (Brighton & HA)	10	1	0	0	11
Beto (Everton)	8	1	1	0	10
Gabriel Martinelli (Arsenal)	8	0	0	2	10
Leandro Trossard (Arsenal)	8	0	0	2	10
Jamie Vardy (Leicester C)	9	1	0	0	10
Harvey Barnes (Newcastle U)	9	0	0	0	9
Alex Iwobi (Fulham)	9	0	0	0	9
James Maddison (Tottenham H)	9	0	0	0	9
Jacob Murphy (Newcastle U)	8	0	1	0	9
Toma Soucek (West Ham U)	9	0	0	0	9

Other matches consist of UEFA Champions League, UEFA Europa League, UEFA Conference League, FIFA Club World Cup, European Super Cup, FA Community Shield.

SKY BET CHAMPIONSHIP 2024–25

(P) Promoted into division at end of 2023–24 season.   (R) Relegated into division at end of 2023–24 season.

			Home					Away					Total						
		P	W	D	L	F	A	W	D	L	F	A	W	D	L	F	A	GD	Pts
1	Leeds U	46	18	4	1	61	12	11	9	3	34	18	29	13	4	95	30	65	100
2	Burnley (R)	46	14	9	0	35	8	14	7	2	34	8	28	16	2	69	16	53	100
3	Sheffield U* (R)	46	15	4	4	33	17	13	4	6	30	19	28	8	10	63	36	27	90
4	Sunderland¶	46	12	7	4	32	18	9	6	8	26	26	21	13	12	58	44	14	76
5	Coventry C	46	14	3	6	40	24	6	6	11	24	34	20	9	17	64	58	6	69
6	Bristol C	46	13	7	3	36	20	4	10	9	23	35	17	17	12	59	55	4	68
7	Blackburn R	46	12	4	7	34	23	7	5	11	19	25	19	9	18	53	48	5	66
8	Millwall	46	12	4	7	27	19	6	8	9	20	30	18	12	16	47	49	-2	66
9	WBA	46	11	8	4	33	20	4	11	8	24	27	15	19	12	57	47	10	64
10	Middlesbrough	46	11	6	6	31	23	7	4	12	33	33	18	10	18	64	56	8	64
11	Swansea C	46	10	6	7	33	24	7	4	12	18	32	17	10	19	51	56	-5	61
12	Sheffield W	46	6	8	9	30	32	9	5	9	30	37	15	13	18	60	69	-9	58
13	Norwich C	46	10	8	5	52	34	4	7	12	19	34	14	15	17	71	68	3	57
14	Watford	46	12	4	7	27	22	4	5	14	26	39	16	9	21	53	61	-8	57
15	QPR	46	7	8	8	31	34	7	6	10	22	29	14	14	18	53	63	-10	56
16	Portsmouth (P)	46	11	7	5	33	21	3	5	15	25	50	14	12	20	58	71	-13	54
17	Oxford U (P)	46	11	5	7	31	29	2	9	12	18	36	13	14	19	49	65	-16	53
18	Stoke C	46	8	9	6	29	25	4	6	13	16	37	12	15	19	45	62	-17	51
19	Derby C (P)	46	9	5	9	25	18	4	6	13	23	38	13	11	22	48	56	-8	50
20	Preston NE	46	7	12	4	26	22	3	8	12	22	37	10	20	16	48	59	-11	50
21	Hull C	46	5	8	10	24	28	7	5	11	20	26	12	13	21	44	54	-10	49
22	Luton T (R)	46	9	7	7	25	22	4	3	16	20	47	13	10	23	45	69	-24	49
23	Plymouth Arg	46	9	7	7	40	39	2	6	15	11	49	11	13	22	51	88	-37	46
24	Cardiff C	46	7	6	10	24	27	2	11	10	24	46	9	17	20	48	73	-25	44

¶*Sunderland promoted via play-offs. * Sheffield U deducted 2 points.*

SKY BET LEAGUE CHAMPIONSHIP LEADING GOALSCORERS 2024–25

Qualification 8 League Goals	League	FA Cup	EFL Cup	Play-Offs	Total
Joel Piroe (Leeds U)	19	0	0	0	19
Borja Sainz (Norwich C)	18	0	1	0	19
Josh Brownhill (Burnley)	18	0	0	0	18
Milutin Osmajic (Preston NE)	9	3	3	0	15
Josh Sargent (Norwich C)	15	0	0	0	15
Zian Flemming (Burnley)	12	2	0	0	14
On loan from Millwall.					
Tommy Conway (Middlesbrough)	13	0	0	0	13
Wilson Isidor (Sunderland)	12	0	0	1	13
Mihailo Ivanovic (Millwall)	12	1	0	0	13
Josh Windass (Sheffield Wed)	13	0	0	0	13
Finn Azaz (Middlesbrough)	12	0	0	0	12
Tom Cannon (Sheffield U)	10	1	1	0	12
Includes 9 league goals, 1 FA Cup goal and 1 EFL Cup goal at Stoke C on loan from Leicester C.					
Liam Cullen (Swansea C)	11	0	1	0	12
Ryan Hardie (Plymouth Arg)	10	1	1	0	12
Emil Riis Jakobsen (Preston NE)	12	0	0	0	12
Daniel James (Leeds U)	12	0	0	0	12
Josh Maja (WBA)	12	0	0	0	12
Anis Mehmeti (Bristol C)	12	0	0	0	12
Callum Robinson (Cardiff C)	12	0	0	0	12
Haji Wright (Coventry C)	12	0	0	0	12
Colby Bishop (Portsmouth)	11	0	0	0	11
Mustapha Bundu (Plymouth Arg)	10	0	1	0	11
Tyrese Campbell (Sheffield U)	10	0	0	1	11
Emmanuel Latte Lath (Middlesbrough)	11	0	0	0	11
Vakoun Bayo (Watford)	10	0	0	0	10
Gustavo Hamer (Sheffield U)	9	0	0	1	10
Callum Lang (Portsmouth)	10	0	0	0	10
Eliezer Mayenda (Sunderland)	8	0	0	2	10
Yuki Ohashi (Blackburn R)	9	0	1	0	10
Jack Rudoni (Coventry C)	9	0	0	1	10
Manor Solomon (Leeds U)	10	0	0	0	10
On loan from Tottenham H.					
Nahki Wells (Bristol C)	10	0	0	0	10
Jerry Yates (Derby Co)	10	0	0	0	10
On loan from Swansea C.					
Brenden Aaronson (Leeds U)	9	0	0	0	9
Michael Frey (QPR)	8	0	1	0	9
Willy Gnonto (Leeds U)	9	0	0	0	9
Yousef Salech (Cardiff C)	8	1	0	0	9
Jaidon Anthony (Burnley)	8	0	0	0	8
On loan from Bournemouth.					
Edo Kayembe (Watford)	8	0	0	0	8
Carlton Morris (Luton T)	8	0	0	0	8
Michael Smith (Sheffield Wed)	8	0	0	0	8

SKY BET LEAGUE ONE 2024–25

(P) Promoted into division at end of 2023–24 season.   *(R) Relegated into division at end of 2023–24 season.*

			Home					Away					Total						
		P	W	D	L	F	A	W	D	L	F	A	W	D	L	F	A	GD	Pts
1	Birmingham C (R)	46	19	4	0	47	11	15	5	3	37	20	34	9	3	84	31	53	111
2	Wrexham (P)	46	16	5	2	41	15	11	6	6	26	19	27	11	8	67	34	33	92
3	Stockport Co (P)	46	16	4	3	42	22	9	8	6	30	20	25	12	9	72	42	30	87
4	Charlton Ath¶	46	15	6	2	38	16	10	4	9	29	27	25	10	11	67	43	24	85
5	Wycombe W	46	12	6	5	27	18	12	6	5	43	27	24	12	10	70	45	25	84
6	Leyton Orient	46	12	4	7	33	19	12	2	9	39	29	24	6	16	72	48	24	78
7	Reading	46	14	4	5	37	21	7	8	8	31	36	21	12	13	68	57	11	75
8	Bolton W	46	11	4	8	36	32	9	4	10	31	38	20	8	18	67	70	–3	68
9	Blackpool	46	7	11	5	35	29	10	5	8	37	31	17	16	13	72	60	12	67
10	Huddersfield T (R)	46	10	4	9	27	24	9	3	11	31	31	19	7	20	58	55	3	64
11	Lincoln C	46	10	6	7	37	24	6	7	10	27	32	16	13	17	64	56	8	61
12	Barnsley	46	6	8	9	33	36	11	2	10	36	37	17	10	19	69	73	–4	61
13	Rotherham U (R)	46	11	5	7	35	30	5	6	12	19	29	16	11	19	54	59	–5	59
14	Stevenage	46	9	5	9	28	26	6	7	10	14	24	15	12	19	42	50	–8	57
15	Wigan Ath	46	7	7	9	20	23	6	10	7	20	19	13	17	16	40	42	–2	56
16	Exeter C	46	8	6	9	30	33	7	5	11	19	32	15	11	20	49	65	–16	56
17	Mansfield T (P)	46	8	4	11	30	34	7	5	11	30	39	15	9	22	60	73	–13	54
18	Peterborough U	46	8	7	8	38	36	5	5	13	30	45	13	12	21	68	81	–13	51
19	Northampton T	46	7	7	9	24	31	5	8	10	24	35	12	15	19	48	66	–18	51
20	Burton Alb	46	6	6	11	30	34	5	8	10	19	32	11	14	21	49	66	–17	47
21	Crawley T (P)	46	7	6	10	31	35	5	4	14	26	48	12	10	24	57	83	–26	46
22	Bristol R	46	9	4	10	31	33	3	3	17	13	43	12	7	27	44	76	–32	43
23	Cambridge U	46	5	6	12	25	33	4	5	14	20	40	9	11	26	45	73	–28	38
24	Shrewsbury T	46	5	3	15	20	37	3	6	14	21	42	8	9	29	41	79	–38	33

¶Charlton Ath promoted via play-offs.

SKY BET LEAGUE ONE LEADING GOALSCORERS 2024–25

Qualification 9 League Goals	League	FA Cup	EFL Cup	EFL Trophy	Play-Offs	Total
Charlie Kelman (Leyton Orient)	21	1	1	2	2	25
Jay Stansfield (Birmingham C)	19	0	1	4	0	24
Matt Godden (Charlton Ath)	18	2	0	1	1	21
Richard Kone (Wycombe W)	18	1	2	0	0	21
Davis Keillor-Dunn (Barnsley)	18	1	1	0	0	20
Includes 1 EFL Cup goal for Mansfield T.						
Aaron Collins (Bolton W)	12	0	1	6	0	19
Ricky Jade Jones (Peterborough U)	11	4	0	3	0	18
Sam Smith (Wrexham)	18	0	0	0	0	18
Includes 11 league goals for Reading.						
Alfie May (Birmingham C)	16	0	0	1	0	17
Louie Barry (Stockport Co)	15	0	0	1	0	16
On loan from Aston Villa.						
Harvey Knibbs (Reading)	14	0	0	2	0	16
Malik Mothersille (Peterborough U)	12	0	0	4	0	16
Sam Nombe (Rotherham U)	14	0	1	0	0	15
Will Evans (Mansfield T)	14	0	0	0	0	14
Kyle Wootton (Stockport Co)	11	2	0	0	0	13
Millenic Alli (Exeter C)	9	0	1	2	0	12
Also 4 league goals for Luton T in Championship.						
Josh Koroma (Huddersfield T)	11	0	1	0	0	12
John Marquis (Shrewsbury T)	11	1	0	0	0	12
John McAtee (Bolton W)	11	0	0	1	0	12
Issac Olaofe (Stockport Co)	9	1	0	2	1	12
Kwame Poku (Peterborough U)	12	0	0	0	0	12
Rumarn Burrell (Burton Alb)	11	0	0	0	0	11
Kamari Doyle (Crawley T)	10	1	0	0	0	11
On loan from Brighton & HA. Includes 3 league goals for Exeter C on loan from Brighton & HA.						
Ashley Fletcher (Blackpool)	11	0	0	0	0	11
Rushian Hepburn-Murphy (Crawley T)	10	0	0	1	0	11
Daniel Kemp (Stevenage)	10	0	0	1	0	11
Jonathan Russell (Barnsley)	11	0	0	0	0	11
Dale Taylor (Wigan Ath)	11	0	0	0	0	11
On loan from Nottingham F.						
Lewis Wing (Reading)	9	1	1	0	0	11
Jamie Collins (Lincoln C)	10	0	0	0	0	10
Lee Gregory (Mansfield T)	10	0	0	0	0	10
Callum Marshall (Huddersfield T)	9	0	1	0	0	10
On loan from West Ham U.						
Cameron McGeehan (Northampton T)	10	0	0	0	0	10
Adam Phillips (Barnsley)	9	1	0	0	0	10
Mallik Wilks (Rotherham U)	9	1	0	0	0	10
On loan from Sheffield Wed.						

SKY BET LEAGUE TWO 2024–25

(P) *Promoted into division at end of 2023–24 season.*   (R) *Relegated into division at end of 2023–24 season.*

		P	W	D	L	F	A	W	D	L	F	A	W	D	L	F	A	GD	Pts
				Home						**Away**					**Total**				
1	Doncaster R	46	12	7	4	38	23	12	5	6	35	27	24	12	10	73	50	23	84
2	Port Vale (R)	46	12	7	4	34	18	10	7	6	31	28	22	14	10	65	46	19	80
3	Bradford C	46	17	4	2	39	13	5	8	10	25	32	22	12	12	64	45	19	78
4	Walsall	46	12	6	5	46	32	9	8	6	29	22	21	14	11	75	54	21	77
5	AFC Wimbledon¶	46	13	5	5	35	16	7	8	8	21	19	20	13	13	56	35	21	73
6	Notts Co	46	10	5	8	31	21	10	7	6	37	28	20	12	14	68	49	19	72
7	Chesterfield (P)	46	10	10	3	41	27	9	3	11	32	27	19	13	14	73	54	19	70
8	Salford C	46	10	5	8	32	28	8	10	5	32	26	18	15	13	64	54	10	69
9	Grimsby T	46	10	3	10	30	35	10	5	8	31	32	20	8	18	61	67	−6	68
10	Colchester U	46	10	8	5	28	15	6	11	6	24	32	16	19	11	52	47	5	67
11	Bromley (P)	46	9	7	7	35	26	8	8	7	29	33	17	15	14	64	59	5	66
12	Swindon T	46	9	8	6	39	33	6	9	8	32	30	15	17	14	71	63	8	62
13	Crewe Alex	46	9	6	8	30	27	6	11	6	19	21	15	17	14	49	48	1	62
14	Fleetwood T (R)	46	7	12	4	24	21	8	3	12	36	39	15	15	16	60	60	0	60
15	Cheltenham T (R)	46	10	6	7	32	31	6	6	11	28	39	16	12	18	60	70	−10	60
16	Barrow	46	10	7	6	34	22	5	7	11	18	28	15	14	17	52	50	2	59
17	Gillingham	46	10	5	8	24	20	4	11	8	17	26	14	16	16	41	46	−5	58
18	Harrogate T	46	10	4	9	26	31	4	7	12	17	30	14	11	21	43	61	−18	53
19	Milton Keynes D	46	8	6	9	25	25	6	4	13	27	41	14	10	22	52	66	−14	52
20	Tranmere R	46	8	9	6	24	22	4	6	13	21	43	12	15	19	45	65	−20	51
21	Accrington S	46	5	11	7	29	31	7	3	13	24	38	12	14	20	53	69	−16	50
22	Newport Co	46	10	5	8	32	32	3	5	15	20	44	13	10	23	52	76	−24	49
23	Carlisle U (R)	46	5	8	10	25	35	5	4	14	19	36	10	12	24	44	71	−27	42
24	Morecambe	46	6	4	13	24	36	4	2	17	16	36	10	6	30	40	72	−32	36

¶*AFC Wimbledon promoted via play-offs.*

SKY BET LEAGUE LEAGUE TWO LEADING GOALSCORERS 2024–25

Qualification 8 League Goals	League	FA Cup	EFL Cup	EFL Trophy	Play-Offs	Total
Michael Cheek (Bromley)	25	1	0	0	0	26
Alassana Jatta (Notts Co)	19	2	1	0	0	22
Matt Stevens (AFC Wimbledon)	17	2	1	1	0	21
Nathan Lowe (Walsall)	15	0	2	1	0	18
Also 1 league goal for Stoke C in Championship.						
Luke Molyneux (Doncaster R)	16	1	1	0	0	18
Cole Stockton (Salford C)	16	1	0	1	0	18
David McGoldrick (Notts Co)	17	0	0	0	0	17
Harry Smith (Swindon T)	15	0	1	1	0	17
Andy Cook (Bradford C)	12	0	1	2	0	15
Danny Rose (Grimsby T)	14	0	0	1	0	15
Lorent Tolaj (Port Vale)	14	0	0	1	0	15
Will Grigg (Chesterfield)	12	2	0	0	0	14
Hakeem Adelakun (Salford C)	13	0	0	0	0	13
Armado Dobra (Chesterfield)	9	1	1	1	1	13
Ryan Graydon (Fleetwood T)	9	0	3	1	0	13
Calum Kavanagh (Bradford C)	9	1	0	3	0	13
Omari Patrick (Tranmere R)	11	0	1	1	0	13
Rob Street (Doncaster R)	12	0	0	1	0	13
On loan from Lincoln C. Includes 1 EFL Trophy goal for Lincoln C.						
Lyle Taylor (Colchester U)	10	0	0	3	0	13
Kabongo Tshmimanga (Swindon T)	11	1	0	1	0	13
On loan from Peterborough U.						
Jamille Matt (Walsall)	12	0	0	0	0	12
Billy Sharp (Doncaster R)	9	2	1	0	0	12
Taylor Allen (Walsall)	10	0	0	0	1	11
Kristian Dennis (Tranmere R)	9	0	0	2	0	11
Alex Gilbey (Milton Keynes D)	11	0	0	0	0	11
George Miller (Cheltenham T)	9	0	0	2	0	11
Jayden Stockley (Port Vale)	11	0	0	0	0	11
Ronan Coughlan (Fleetwood T)	8	0	1	1	0	10
Scott Hogan (Milton Keynes D)	8	0	1	0	0	9
Bobby Kamwa (Newport Co)	9	0	0	0	0	9
Josh March (Harrogate T)	9	0	0	0	0	9
Kelly N'Mai (Salford C)	9	0	0	0	0	9
Jack Payne (Colchester U)	8	0	1	0	0	9
Jordan Thomas (Cheltenham T)	8	0	0	1	0	9
Matty Virtue (Fleetwood T)	9	0	0	0	0	9
Shaun Whalley (Accrington S)	9	0	0	0	0	9
Ben Woods (Accrington S)	9	0	0	0	0	9

FOOTBALL LEAGUE PLAY-OFFS 2024–25

■ Denotes player sent off.

SKY BET CHAMPIONSHIP SEMI-FINALS FIRST LEG
Thursday, 8 May 2025
Bristol C (0) 0
Sheffield U (1) 3 *(Burrows 45 (pen), Brooks 73, O'Hare 79)*   25,652
Bristol C: (3421) O'Leary; Tanner, Dickie■, Vyner; Hirakawa (Roberts 46), Knight, Williams (Earthy 40), McCrorie; Bird (McGuane 74), Mehmeti (Bell 84); Wells (Armstrong 46).
Sheffield U: (442) Cooper; Choudhury, Ahmedhodzic, Robinson (Holding 81), Burrows; Brewster (Brooks 67), Peck (Davies T 67), Vinicius Souza, Hamer (McCallum 85); Moore, Campbell (O'Hare 67).
Referee: Oliver Langford.

Friday, 9 May 2025
Coventry C (0) 1 *(Rudoni 70)*
Sunderland (0) 2 *(Isidor 68, Mayenda 88)*   31,293
Coventry C: (4231) Wilson; van Ewijk, Thomas, Kitching, Dasilva; Grimes, Sheaf (Allen 82); Sakamoto, Rudoni, Wright; Thomas-Asante (Mason-Clark 71).
Sunderland: (442) Patterson; Hume, Ballard, O'Nien, Cirkin; Roberts (Mepham 86), Neil, Bellingham, Le Fee; Mayenda (Browne 90), Isidor (Rigg 77).
Referee: John Busby.

SKY BET CHAMPIONSHIP SEMI-FINALS SECOND LEG
Monday, 12 May 2025
Sheffield U (1) 3 *(Moore 41, Hamer 52, O'Hare 83)*
Bristol C (0) 0   26,543
Sheffield U: (442) Cooper; Choudhury, Ahmedhodzic, Robinson, Burrows; Brooks (Brewster 62), Peck, Vinicius Souza (Davies T 80), Hamer (Rak-Sakyi 72); Cannon (O'Hare 62), Moore (Campbell 62).
Bristol C: (3421) O'Leary; Tanner, Vyner, Pring (Bell 68); McCrorie, Knight, Bird (McGuane 59), Roberts; Earthy (Hirakawa 59), Twine (Mehmeti 58); Wells (Cornick 80).
Sheffield U won 6-0 on aggregate.
Referee: Peter Bankes.

Tuesday, 13 May 2025
Sunderland (0) 1 *(Ballard 120)*
Coventry C (0) 1 *(Mason-Clark 76)*   46,530
Sunderland: (442) Patterson; Hume, Ballard, O'Nien, Cirkin (Hjelde 120); Roberts (Mundle 95), Neil, Bellingham, Le Fee; Mayenda, Isidor (Rigg 83).
Coventry C: (4231) Wilson; van Ewijk, Thomas, Kitching, Dasilva; Sheaf (Eccles 73 (Allen 117)), Grimes; Sakamoto, Rudoni, Mason-Clark (Thomas-Asante 110); Wright.
aet; Sunderland won 3-2 on aggregate.
Referee: Andrew Madley.

SKY BET CHAMPIONSHIP FINAL
Wembley Stadium, Saturday, 24 May 2025
Sheffield U (1) 1 *(Campbell 25)*
Sunderland (0) 2 *(Mayenda 76, Watson 90)*   82,718
Sheffield U: (442) Cooper; Choudhury, Ahmedhodzic (Seriki 90), Robinson, Burrows; Brewster (Brooks 65), Peck (Davies T 90), Vinicius Souza, Hamer (Brereton Diaz 72 (Cannon 90)); Moore, Campbell (O'Hare 65).
Sunderland: (442) Patterson; Hume, Ballard, O'Nien (Mepham 8), Cirkin; Rigg (Roberts 58), Neil (Watson 73), Bellingham, Mundle (Isidor 73); Le Fee, Mayenda (Hjelde 90).
Referee: Chris Kavanagh.

SKY BET LEAGUE ONE SEMI-FINALS FIRST LEG
Saturday, 10 May 2025
Leyton Orient (1) 2 *(Kelman 30, 88 (pen))*
Stockport Co (0) 2 *(Norwood 60 (pen), Horsfall 65)*   8571
Leyton Orient: (3421) Keeley; Edmonds-Green, Beckles, Cooper (James 67); Galbraith, Donley, Clare, Williams (Currie 66); Agyei, Abdulai (O'Neill 71); Kelman.
Stockport Co: (3142) Addai; Hills (Rydel 84), Horsfall, Pye; Norwood; Fevrier (Bate 83), Collar (Connolly 83), Moxon (Camps 90), Touray; Wootton, Olaofe (Bailey 90).
Referee: Ben Speedie.

Jobe Bellingham of Sunderland lifts the Sky Bet Championship Play-off trophy after his team's victory over Sheffield United at Wembley. (Justin Setterfield/Getty Images)

Sunday, 11 May 2025
Wycombe W (0) 0
Charlton Ath (0) 0 6585
Wycombe W: (4231) Norris; Grimmer, Taylor, Bradley, Reach; Humphreys, Leahy; Onyedinma (McCleary 63), Simons (Westergaard 90), Udoh; Kone.
Charlton Ath: (4231) Mannion; Ramsay, Jones, Gillesphey, Edwards; Coventry, Docherty; Watson (Small 71), Berry (Anderson 71); Campbell T; Godden.
Referee: Farai Hallam.

SKY BET LEAGUE ONE SEMI-FINALS SECOND LEG
Wednesday, 14 May 2025
Stockport Co (0) 1 *(Olaofe 74)*
Leyton Orient (1) 1 *(O'Neill 3)* 10,592
Stockport Co: (3142) Addai; Hills (Knoyle 46), Horsfall, Pye; Norwood; Fevrier (Diamond 62), Collar (Bailey 84), Moxon, Touray (Rydel 46); Wootton, Olaofe (Andresson 106).
Leyton Orient: (3421) Keeley; Beckles, Edmonds-Green (Cooper 106), Currie (James 65); Galbraith, Brown (Ball 91), Clare, O'Neill (Williams 67); Agyei (Abdulai 77), Donley (Markanday 112); Kelman.
aet; Leyton Orient won 4-1 on penalties.
Referee: James Bell.

Thursday, 15 May 2025
Charlton Ath (0) 1 *(Godden 81)*
Wycombe W (0) 0 25,722
Charlton Ath: (3412) Mannion; Ramsay, Jones, Gillesphey; Small (Aneke 71), Docherty, Coventry, Edwards; Gilbert (Anderson 84); Godden, Campbell T (Watson 89).
Wycombe W: (4231) Ravizzoli; Grimmer, Taylor, Bradley, Reach (Kodua 87); Humphreys, Leahy; Udoh, Simons (Sadlier 87), Kone (Onyedinma 73); McCleary (Westergaard 87).
Charlton Ath won 1-0 on aggregate.
Referee: Dean Whitestone.

SKY BET LEAGUE ONE FINAL
Wembley Stadium, Sunday, 25 May 2025
Charlton Ath (1) 1 *(Gillesphey 31)*
Leyton Orient (0) 0 76,193
Charlton Ath: (3421) Mannion; Ramsay, Jones, Gillesphey; Small (Watson 68), Coventry, Docherty, Edwards; Gilbert (Anderson 68), Campbell T (Mbick 81); Godden (Aneke 81).
Leyton Orient: (4231) Keeley; Galbraith, Beckles (Happe 82), Edmonds-Green, Currie; Brown (Ball 74), Clare (James 74); Agyei (Abdulai 82), Donley, O'Neill (Williams 82); Kelman.
Referee: Andrew Kitchen.

SKY BET LEAGUE TWO SEMI-FINALS FIRST LEG
Saturday, 10 May 2025
Notts Co (0) 0
AFC Wimbledon (0) 1 *(Harbottle 59)* 12,385
Notts Co: (3421) Bass; Macari (McDonald 77), Platt, Bedeau; Jones, Abbott, Palmer, Austin (Jarvis 72); Grant, McGoldrick (Traore 90); Jatta■.
AFC Wimbledon: (352) Goodman; Harbottle, Lewis, Johnson (Ogundere 57); Tilley (Furlong 90), Smith, Reeves, Hippolyte (Maycock 74), Neufville; Browne (Kelly 74), Stevens (Bugiel 57).
Referee: Thomas Kirk.

Sunday, 11 May 2025
Chesterfield (0) 0
Walsall (2) 2 *(Allen 28 (pen), Chang 39)* 10,001
Chesterfield: (433) Boot; Mandeville, Palmer, McFadzean, Gordon (Sparkes 88); Metcalfe, Fleck (Jacobs 87), Naylor (Pepple 80); Olakigbe (Dobra 67), Grigg, Colclough (Duffy 79).
Walsall: (3421) Simkin; Okagbue, Williams, Allen; Asiimwe, Chang (Comley 64), Stirk (Lakin 76), Gordon L; Hall (Adomah 82), Jellis (Gordon J 82); Matt (Amantchi 75).
Referee: Martin Coy.

SKY BET LEAGUE TWO SEMI-FINALS SECOND LEG
Friday, 16 May 2025
Walsall (0) 2 *(Lakin 81, Amantchi 90)*
Chesterfield (0) 1 *(Dobra 90)* 9585
Walsall: (3421) Simkin; Okagbue, Williams, Allen; Asiimwe (Daniels 90), Chang (Comley 62), Stirk, Gordon L; Jellis (Adomah 75), Hall (Lakin 75); Matt (Amantchi 62).
Chesterfield: (4231) Boot; Mandeville (Colclough 75), Palmer, McFadzean, Gordon (Sparkes 67); Metcalfe (Grigg 67), Fleck; Banks (Duffy 76), Naylor (Jacobs 82), Dobra; Pepple.
Walsall won 4-1 on aggregate.
Referee: Ben Toner.

Saturday, 17 May 2025
AFC Wimbledon (1) 1 *(Neufville 8)*
Notts Co (0) 0 8501
AFC Wimbledon: (4132) Goodman; Harbottle (Ogundere 46), Lewis, Johnson, Neufville; Reeves; Tilley, Smith, Hippolyte (Maycock 82); Stevens (Sasu 81), Browne (Kelly 63).
Notts Co: (3412) Bass; Macari, Platt, Bedeau; Jones, Abbott, Palmer, Austin (Jarvis 54); Grant (Robertson 70); Traore (Morias 70); Whitaker.
AFC Wimbledon won 2-0 on aggregate.
Referee: Lewis Smith.

SKY BET LEAGUE TWO FINAL
Wembley Stadium, Monday, 26 May 2025
AFC Wimbledon (1) 1 *(Hippolyte 45)*
Walsall (0) 0 50,947
AFC Wimbledon: (352) Goodman; Harbottle (Ogundere 69), Lewis, Johnson; Tilley, Smith, Reeves, Hippolyte (Maycock 90), Neufville; Stevens (Kelly 77), Browne (Sasu 90).
Walsall: (3421) Simkin; Okagbue, Williams (McEntee 34), Allen; Asiimwe (Barrett 74), Chang (Lakin 74), Stirk, Gordon L; Jellis (Adomah 62), Hall; Matt (Amantchi 63).
Referee: Will Finnie.

Myles Hippolyte of AFC Wimbledon celebrates after scoring the only goal of the Sky Bet League 2 Play-off final against Walsall at Wembley.
(Kevin Hodgson/MI News/NurPhoto via Getty Images)

REVIEW OF THE SEASON 2024–25

In some ways, this was an extremely competitive Premier League season, just not at the very top or at the very bottom. Liverpool effectively won the title on the Saturday in January when, having been frustrated for 90 minutes by Brentford, they scored twice in injury-time, then second-placed Arsenal squandered a two-goal lead to draw against Aston Villa. That gave them a six-point lead, with a game in hand, and from that moment Liverpool never looked like surrendering their advantage. They won their 20th title by 10 points, pulling level with Manchester United as the most successful side in English league history. Although their total of 84 is low by recent standards, they won none of their four games after sealing the championship with a 5-1 win over Tottenham.

Beyond the Premier League title race, as Saudi Arabia were awarded the right to host the 2034 World Cup, the FIFA president Gianni Infantino continued to hobnob with authoritarian leaders and Nasser al-Khelaifi tightened his grip on the European game, the sense was of football becoming ever more a tool of politicians, a soft-power weapon losing touch with its truest essence.

Many have struggled to replace a long-serving club legend, but not Arne Slot. It perhaps helped that Jürgen Klopp had led the singing of his name at Anfield after the final game of the previous season, making clear that he was happily passing on the baton. Few managers have ever gone with such good grace, and even fewer have bequeathed such a rich legacy. Liverpool added only one senior player over the summer, Federico Chiesa, who started a single league game, but it didn't matter because the work of rejuvenating the front half of the side had already begun.

The role of Mohamed Salah, who scored 29 goals and set up a further 18, matching the record for goal-involvements jointly held by Andrew Cole and Alan Shearer, was obviously key, but the strength of the side was the midfield. The sense had been that Liverpool had been short of a proper holding player since the departure of Fabinho in 2023 but the combination of Ryan Gravenberch and Alexis Mac Allister more than filled the gap, allowing Liverpool to play with more control than was usual during the Klopp years.

While Liverpool found an early rhythm, other top sides faltered. Most dramatic was the collapse of Manchester City in the autumn after the loss of Rodri to a serious knee injury. Recruitment also came under scrutiny. Julian Alvarez was never adequately replaced and, with Phil Foden out of sorts, the squad was looking old and short of inspiration. Starting the season with 14 games unbeaten, the wheels fell off in an EFL Cup defeat to Tottenham. That was the first in a run of 13 games in all competitions in which they won just once and, although they recovered to finish third, the sense was of an aura lost.

A stellar season: Mohamed Salah of Liverpool celebrates scoring his team's fourth goal during the Premier League match against Tottenham Hotspur at Anfield. (Liverpool FC via Getty Images)

Alexander Isak of Newcastle United showed no signs of slowing down, celebrating scoring his team's first goal during the Premier League match against Ipswich Town. (Alex Livesey/Getty Images)

The other huge issue around City remained unresolved. A verdict on the 130 charges they face for alleged breaches of Financial Fair Play regulations had been widely expected in April, but it has been delayed and, given the probability of an appeal whichever way it goes, it could be several months before a final decision is reached. That uncertainty, inevitably, means another season played out amid doubts of possible points deductions.

Arsenal finished second for the third season running. They suffered a number of injuries in forward areas and had six players sent off in the league, yet their biggest problem was the fact that they dropped 21 points from winning positions this season. Without an orthodox centre-forward – Kai Havertz was their top scorer with nine goals, despite starting only 21 league games – there was a sense they had to really dominate games to win them. A 5-1 home win over Manchester City, and a 3-0 Champions League win against Real Madrid will live in the memory, but this was a fifth straight season without silverware for Mikel Arteta.

But Arsenal were not the only club to suffer a glut of injuries. Almost every Premier League side had spells when they were without half a dozen senior players – that Liverpool avoided that, perhaps in part because of the way Slot managed the season, was one of the reasons they were so dominant. Identifying the cause of injuries is never straightforward, but the consensus view is that given the intensity of modern football, players are being asked to play too many games as tournaments expand. As players protested about that, this was also a season notable for a number of demonstrations by fans about rising ticket prices and a general feeling of alienation.

At the same time, though, with Liverpool prioritising the league and Arsenal and City a little out of sorts, there were opportunities for others to prosper in the domestic cups. Newcastle won their first trophy in 56 years, beating Arsenal in the Carabao Cup semi-final and completing the job against Liverpool in the final, thanks to a remarkable header from Dan Burn and a goal from the persistently dangerous Alexander Isak. Success-starved fans celebrated the trophy as the League Cup has perhaps never been celebrated before, and a fine season was capped by fifth place and qualification for the Champions League.

Crystal Palace's wait for silverware had been even longer; they had never won a trophy in their 119-year history. This was a classic FA Cup season, with a smattering of shocks, including Liverpool losing to Plymouth Argyle in the fourth round, and a semi-final line-up that featured three sides not used to success, plus City who had a season to salvage. Palace beat Aston Villa comprehensively in the semi and then rode their luck to beat City in the final, their goalkeeper Dean Henderson escaping sanction for a handball outside the box and saving an Omar Marmoush penalty to protect a lead given them by Eberechi Eze.

Tottenham Hotspur won their first trophy since 2008, Ange Postecoglou finding a new pragmatism to get them through to the final of the Europa League where they beat a dismal Manchester United in a dire game, the winner an appropriately scruffy affair bundled in by Brennan Johnson via the hand of Luke Shaw. Spurs, though, lost a club record 22 of 38 games to finish fourth bottom of the table.

There was also European silverware for Chelsea, who used their superior financial resources to bludgeon their way to success in the Conference League. A fourth-place finish and Champions League qualification was hailed as vindication by their manager Enzo Maresca, but fans seemed unconvinced by his conservative, possession-heavy football. After the expenditure of more than £1bn over three years, fourth was probably a minimum requirement, even with the youngest side in Premier League history.

Defeat on the final day saw Aston Villa slip to sixth, out of the Champions League slots, but they had enjoyed a fine European campaign, beating Bayern Munich on their way to a narrow defeat to Paris Saint-Germain in the Champions League quarter-final. Nottingham Forest took the Conference League slot, although seventh and defeat in the FA Cup semi felt almost anti-climactic after a brilliant start to the season.

Forest were emblematic of the burgeoning of the middle class; a result, perhaps, of the twin effects of vast broadcast rights enabling Premier League clubs to compete financially with Europe's elites, and of PSR preventing the English elite from pulling away from the pack. Brighton, Bournemouth, Brentford and Fulham all had fine seasons. Brentford, inspired by a front three of Bryan Mbeumo, Yoane Wissa and Kevin Schade, who all got into double figures, were all the more remarkable for having the second-lowest payroll in the league, while Bournemouth were spectacular through December and January when Justin Kluivert was at his peak.

Everton struggled early on, but improved significantly after David Moyes had replaced Sean Dyche as manager, and were able to bid farewell to Goodison Park with their Premier League future long since secured. West Ham United never really got going under either Julen Lopetegui or Graham Potter, while Wolverhampton Wanderers flirted with the drop early on before recovering under Vitor Pereira.

None of the three promoted sides ever looked like staying up, the 59 points they accumulated by far the worst total of any group of three relegated teams. Southampton fared worst, but at least scrabbled together 12 points, one better than the record low set by Derby County in 2008.

The challenge for the three sides going up from the Championship will be enormous. Leeds United at least have the financial backing to suggest they might be able to bridge the gap, while Burnley shouldn't have to adapt their approach very much, having gone up conceding just 16 league goals. Both sides to win automatic promotion accumulated 100 points, the first time that has happened, and

Morgan Rogers of Aston Villa during his team's Premier League match against Everton at Villa Park.
(George Wood/Aston Villa FC via Getty Images)

An emotional goodbye: Everton's final Premier League fixture played at Goodison Park, their home since 1892. (Paul Ellis/AFP)

evidence, perhaps, of an increasingly distinct group of mezzanine clubs that exists between the Premier League and Championship. Sunderland lost form as they rested players over the final weeks of the season but were rewarded with a very late goal in each of their three play-off games, securing promotion with a 2-1 win over Sheffield United.

Parachute payments, though, are no guarantee, and Luton Town suffered a second successive relegation. Plymouth improved after Miron Muslić had replaced Wayne Rooney but not enough to stay up, while the desperate late appointment of Aaron Ramsey could not save Cardiff City.

League One was all about US investment. Birmingham City, backed by a consortium featuring Tom Brady, dominated the division, amassing a mammoth 111 points, and were joined in promotion by Wrexham, backed by Ryan Reynolds and Rob McElhenney. Charlton Athletic beat Leyton Orient in the play-off final. Shrewsbury Town won just eight games in finishing bottom and were joined in relegation by Cambridge United, Bristol Rovers and Crawley Town.

Walsall looked to be flying to promotion from League Two but suffered a startling collapse of form mid-January and ended up losing out in the play-off final to AFC Wimbledon. Doncaster Rovers came through to take the League Two title, with Port Vale second. A scruffy last-minute winner that prompted a gleeful pitch invasion saw Bradford City take the final automatic promotion slot. Carlisle United turned to Mark Hughes in an attempt to escape the drop, but they were relegated out of the league alongside Morecambe.

Barnet amassed over 100 points to take the automatic promotion spot from the National league and, after second-placed York City suffered a shock defeat in the play-offs, they will be joined in League Two by Oldham Athletic.

But even as the season drew to an end with that play-off and Paris Saint-Germain's victory in the Champions League final, it wasn't truly done, with the bloated jamboree of the Club World Cup about to begin in the USA. Nothing, perhaps, could better encapsulate the sense of dislocation between the priorities of those who run the game and those who play and follow it.

Football is beset by complex issues of resource distribution and the calendar, and by the often competing interests of various stakeholders in a globalised world. Yet its leaders ignore them to pursue a needless tournament whose only value is in the political battle between FIFA and UEFA and to generate revenues that will further unbalance leagues that are already struggling under the contradictions of their own iniquity. The needs and wants of players and fans, meanwhile, are ignored.

There has been a lot of joy for a lot of clubs who aren't used to it this season, but that shouldn't disguise the generally gloomy prognosis.

Jonathan Wilson

ACCRINGTON STANLEY

FOUNDATION

Accrington Football Club, founder members of the Football League in 1888, were not connected with Accrington Stanley. In fact both clubs ran concurrently between 1891 when Stanley were formed and 1895 when Accrington FC folded. Actually Stanley Villa was the original name, those responsible for forming the club living in Stanley Street and using the Stanley Arms as their meeting place. They became Accrington Stanley in 1893. In 1894–95 they joined the Accrington & District League, playing at Moorhead Park. Subsequently they played in the North-East Lancashire Combination and the Lancashire Combination before becoming founder members of the Third Division (North) in 1921, two years after moving to Peel Park. In 1962 they resigned from the Football League, were wound up, re-formed in 1963, disbanded in 1966 only to restart as Accrington Stanley (1968), returning to the Lancashire Combination in 1970.

Wham Stadium, Livingstone Road, Accrington, Lancashire BB5 5BX.

Telephone: (01254) 356 950.

Ticket Office: (01254) 356 950.

Website: www.accringtonstanley.co.uk

Email: info@accringtonstanley.co.uk

Ground Capacity: 5,317.

Record Attendance: 17,634 v Blackburn R, Friendly, 15 November 1954; 13,181 v Hull C, Division 3 (N), 28 September 1948 (at Peel Park); 5,397 v Derby Co, FA Cup 4th rd, 26 January 2019 (at Wham Stadium).

Pitch Measurements: 102m × 66m (111.5yd × 72yd).

Vice-Chairman: David Burgess. *Chief Executive:* Warren Eastam.

Manager: John Doolan. *Assistant Manager:* Ged Brannan.

Colours: Red shirts with white trim, red shorts with white trim, red socks.

Year Formed: 1891, reformed 1968. *Turned Professional:* 1919.

Club Nicknames: 'The Owd Reds', 'The Reds'; 'Stanley', 'Accy Stanley'.

Previous Names: 1891, Stanley Villa; 1893, Accrington Stanley.

Grounds: 1891, Moorhead Park; 1897, Bell's Ground; 1919, Peel Park; 1970, Crown Ground (renamed Interlink Express Stadium, Fraser Eagle Stadium, Store First Stadium 2013; Wham Stadium 2015).

First Football League Game: 27 August 1921, Division 3 (N), v Rochdale (a) L 3–6 – Tattersall; Newton, Baines, Crawshaw, Popplewell, Burkinshaw, Oxley, Makin, Green (1), Hosker (2), Hartles.

Record League Victory: 8–0 v New Brighton, Division 3 (N), 17 March 1934 – Maidment; Armstrong (pen), Price, Dodds, Crawshaw, McCulloch, Wyper, Lennox (2), Cheetham (4), Leedham (1), Watson.

Record Cup Victory: 7–0 v Spennymoor U, FA Cup 2nd rd, 8 December 1938 – Tootill; Armstrong, Whittaker, Latham, Curran, Lee, Parry (2), Chadwick, Jepson (3), McLoughlin (2), Barclay; 7–0 v Leeds U U21, Football League Trophy, Northern Section Group G, 8 September 2020 – Savin; Sykes, Hughes, Burgess 1), Conneely, Allan, Sangare, Butcher (Sama), Uwakwe (3); Cassidy (2) (Scully), Charles (1) (Spinelli).

HONOURS

League Champions: FL 2 – 2017–18; Football Conference – 2005–06.
Runners-up: Division 3N – 1954–55, 1957–58.
FA Cup: 4th rd – 1927, 1937, 1959, 2010, 2017, 2019, 2023.
League Cup: 3rd rd – 2016–17.

FOOTBALL YEARBOOK FACT FILE

Accrington Stanley hosted the representative fixture between Division Three North and Division Three South at Peel Park in October 1955. The second half of the match was shown live on BBC Television, with 10,521 fans also turning out to watch the 3-3 draw. John Ryden, Stanley's centre-half, who played for the Northern Section, was sold to Tottenham Hotspur shortly afterwards.

Record Defeat: 1–9 v Lincoln C, Division 3 (N), 3 March 1951.

Most League Points (2 for a win): 61, Division 3 (N), 1954–55.

Most League Points (3 for a win): 93, FL 2, 2017–18.

Most League Goals: 96, Division 3 (N), 1954–55.

Highest League Scorer in Season: George Stewart, 35, Division 3 (N), 1955–56; George Hudson, 35, Division 4, 1960–61.

Most League Goals in Total Aggregate: George Stewart, 136, 1954–58.

Most League Goals in One Match: 5, Billy Harker v Gateshead, Division 3 (N), 16 November 1935; George Stewart v Gateshead, Division 3 (N), 27 November 1954.

Most Capped Player: Romuald Boco, 19 (51), Benin.

Most League Appearances: Sean McConville, 388, 2009–11; 2015–2024.

Youngest League Player: Ian Gibson, 15 years 358 days, v Norwich C, 23 March 1959.

Record Transfer Fee Received: £1,000,000 from Ipswich T for Kayden Jackson, August 2018.

Record Transfer Fee Paid: £85,000 (potentially rising to £150,000) to Swansea C for Ian Craney, January 2008.

Football League Record: 1921 Original Member of Division 3 (N); 1921–58 Division 3 (N); 1958–60 Division 3; 1960–62 Division 4; 1962 Resigned from the league and joined the Lancashire Combination League; 2006 Promoted from Football Conference; 2006–18 FL 2; 2018–23 FL 1; 2023– FL 2.

LATEST SEQUENCES

Longest Sequence of League Wins: 7, 24.2.2018 – 7.4.2018.

Longest Sequence of League Defeats: 9, 8.3.1930 – 21.4.1930.

Longest Sequence of League Draws: 4, 25.8.2018 – 15.9.2018.

Longest Sequence of Unbeaten League Matches: 15, 3.2.2018 – 21.4.2018.

Longest Sequence Without a League Win: 18, 17.9.1938 – 31.12.1938.

Successive Scoring Runs: 24 from 23.12.2017.

Successive Non-scoring Runs: 6 from 29.12.2018.

MANAGERS

William Cronshaw *c.*1894
John Haworth 1897–1910
Johnson Haworth *c.*1916
Sam Pilkingson 1919–24
  (*Tommy Booth p-m 1923–24*)
Ernie Blackburn 1924–32
Amos Wade 1932–35
John Hacking 1935–49
Jimmy Porter 1949–51
Walter Crook 1951–53
Walter Galbraith 1953–58
George Eastham Snr 1958–59
Harold Bodle 1959–60
James Harrower 1960–61
Harold Mather 1962–63
Jimmy Hinksman 1963–64
Terry Neville 1964–65
Ian Bryson 1965
Danny Parker 1965–66
Jimmy Hinksman 1970–75
Don Bramley 1975–78
Dave Baron 1978–82
Mick Finn 1982
Dennis Cook 1982–83
Pat Lynch 1983–84
Gerry Keenan 1984–85
Frank O'Kane 1985–86
Eric Whalley 1986–88
Gary Pierce 1988–89
David Thornley 1989–90
Phil Staley 1990–93
Ken Wright 1993–94
Eric Whalley 1994–95
Stan Allan 1995–96
Tony Greenwood 1996–97
Leighton James 1997–98
Billy Rodaway 1998
Wayne Harrison 1998–99
John Coleman 1999–2012
Paul Cook 2012
Leam Richardson 2012–13
James Beattie 2013–14
John Coleman 2014–24
John Doolan March 2024–

TEN YEAR LEAGUE RECORD

		P	W	D	L	F	A	Pts	Pos
2015-16	FL 2	46	24	13	9	74	48	85	4
2016-17	FL 2	46	17	14	15	59	56	65	13
2017-18	FL 2	46	29	6	11	76	46	93	1
2018-19	FL 1	46	14	13	19	51	67	55	14
2019-20	FL 1	35	10	10	15	47	53	40	17§
2020-21	FL 1	46	18	13	15	63	68	67	11
2021-22	FL 1	46	17	10	19	61	80	61	12
2022-23	FL 1	46	11	11	24	40	77	44	23
2023-24	FL 2	46	16	9	21	63	71	57	17
2024-25	FL 2	46	12	14	20	53	69	50	21

§*Decided on points-per-game (1.14)*

DID YOU KNOW ?

Accrington Stanley returned to the Football League in April 2006, clinching promotion with three games remaining. They were confirmed as Conference champions following the 1-0 win at Woking on 15 April with Paul Mullin scoring the crucial goal, and keeper Robert Elliott saving a second-half penalty.

ACCRINGTON STANLEY – SKY BET LEAGUE TWO 2024–25 LEAGUE RECORD

Match No.	Date	Venue	Opponents	Result	H/T Score	Lg Pos.	Goalscorers	Attendance
1	Aug 10	A	Doncaster R	L	1-4	0-1	23	Walton [47]	6423
2	17	H	Harrogate T	D	3-3	1-2	20	Walton [29], Knowles [60], Mooney [62]	1905
3	24	A	Newport Co	L	1-3	1-1	22	Whalley [38]	4437
4	31	H	Colchester U	D	1-1	1-0	22	Mooney [25]	1956
5	Sept 7	A	Notts Co	L	0-2	0-1	23		10,147
6	14	A	Crewe Alex	L	0-1	0-0	23		2883
7	21	H	Port Vale	D	2-2	2-0	23	Whalley [29], Love [43]	2628
8	Oct 1	A	Cheltenham T	L	1-2	1-0	24	Costelloe [39]	2976
9	5	H	Morecambe	W	2-1	2-0	23	Costelloe 2 (1 pen) [36 (p), 45]	2862
10	12	A	Gillingham	W	2-1	0-0	22	Woods B [60], Costelloe [90]	6622
11	19	H	Barrow	W	1-0	1-0	19	Whalley [8]	2354
12	22	A	Milton Keynes D	L	1-2	0-1	21	Woods J [67]	5084
13	26	H	Walsall	D	0-0	0-0	20		2595
14	Nov 9	A	Chesterfield	W	3-0	1-0	18	Woods J [18], Awe [65], Knowles [69]	8285
15	16	H	Swindon T	D	2-2	2-1	18	Aljofree [16], Rawson [30]	2755
16	19	A	AFC Wimbledon	D	2-2	0-0	16	Khumbeni [58], Costelloe [75]	7020
17	Dec 3	A	Grimsby T	L	2-5	0-4	19	Henderson [63], Woods J [80]	3874
18	7	H	Bromley	L	1-2	1-1	20	Woods B [9]	1816
19	16	A	Fleetwood T	D	1-1	1-0	21	Aljofree [32]	2669
20	21	H	Salford C	L	0-2	0-0	22		2350
21	29	A	Carlisle U	L	1-2	0-1	22	Walton [73]	7130
22	Jan 1	H	Grimsby T	W	3-2	1-2	20	Woods B 2 [9, 82], Whalley (pen) [60]	2675
23	4	A	Colchester U	W	2-0	1-0	19	Whalley 2 (1 pen) [18 (p), 59]	4366
24	18	H	Notts Co	L	0-3	0-2	21		2924
25	25	A	Crewe Alex	W	1-0	1-0	20	Whalley [16]	4965
26	28	H	Cheltenham T	D	0-0	0-0	19		1605
27	Feb 1	A	Port Vale	L	1-2	0-1	21	Walton [51]	6198
28	8	H	AFC Wimbledon	D	0-0	0-0	20		2170
29	11	A	Bradford C	L	0-1	0-1	20		15,263
30	15	A	Morecambe	L	0-2	0-0	21		3473
31	22	H	Doncaster R	L	1-2	0-1	21	Conneely [57]	2258
32	25	A	Tranmere R	W	1-0	0-0	20	Whalley [49]	5613
33	Mar 1	A	Harrogate T	L	1-2	0-1	21	Woods J [50]	3015
34	4	H	Milton Keynes D	W	2-0	2-0	21	Walton [24], O'Brien-Whitmarsh [39]	1596
35	8	A	Barrow	L	0-2	0-1	21		3200
36	11	A	Newport Co	W	5-0	3-0	21	O'Brien-Whitmarsh 2 [4, 53], Mooney 2 [15, 75], Woods B [26]	1503
37	15	H	Gillingham	D	1-1	1-0	20	Ward [45]	2449
38	22	A	Swindon T	D	0-0	0-0	20		7168
39	29	H	Bradford C	D	0-0	0-0	20		4572
40	Apr 1	H	Fleetwood T	L	1-4	0-1	21	Woods B [52]	1987
41	5	A	Bromley	L	0-4	0-1	22		2410
42	12	H	Tranmere R	D	3-3	3-0	22	Woods B [1], Walton [24], Woods J [42]	3197
43	18	A	Salford C	W	2-1	1-0	21	Whalley [36], Woods B [62]	2945
44	21	H	Carlisle U	D	1-1	0-0	21	Aljofree [69]	3380
45	26	A	Walsall	W	1-0	1-0	19	Woods B [33]	8131
46	May 3	H	Chesterfield	L	0-1	0-1	21		3969

Final League Position: 21

GOALSCORERS

League (53): Whalley 9 (2 pens), Woods B 9, Walton 6, Costelloe 5 (1 pen), Woods J 5, Mooney 4, Aljofree 3, O'Brien-Whitmarsh 3, Knowles 2, Awe 1, Conneely 1, Henderson 1, Khumbeni 1, Love 1, Rawson 1, Ward 1.
FA Cup (4): Walton 3, Woods J 1.
Carabao Cup (0).
Vertu Trophy (4): Hunter 1, Popoola 1, Woods J 1, own goal 1.

Kelly M 12	O'Brien Connor 18 + 7	Rawson F 38	Awe Z 21	Quirk S 10 + 6	Conneely S 20 + 6	Love D 39 + 2	Whalley S 32 + 1	Knowles J 9 + 7	Walton T 30 + 11	Mooney K 19 + 11	Costelloe D 14 + 3	Coyle L 26 + 8	Woods J 15 + 16	Martin D 4 + 2	Khumbeni N 13 + 5	Woods B 31 + 5	Batty J 21 + 4	Hunter A 9 + 12	Henderson A 10 + 18	Crellin B 34	Pickles Aaron — +1	Aljofree S 24 + 1	Trickett L — +1	Popoola A — +2	Hall C — +1	Caton C 4 + 8	Ward B 21	Matthews D 19 + 1	Brown C 1 + 11	O'Brien-Whitmarsh J 6 + 7	Grant C 6 + 10	Match No.
1	2	3	4	5	6^2	7	8^4	9^3	10^1	11	12	13	14	15																		1
1	2	3^1	4	5	6^2	7	8	9^3	10	11		13			12	14																2
1	2^1	3	4	5	6^4	7	8	9^2	10^3			15	13		12	14																3
1	2	3	4	5	6^2	7	8	9^1	10^3	11^4	14				12	13	15															4
1	2	4^2	3		6^3	14	7	8		10^1			11^4		15	9	13	5^5	12	16													5
1	2	3	4		6^4	7	8^3	9^2	10^1	11^5	12	16			13		5	14	15													6
1	2	4	5		8	3	7^2	12		11	10^1				9	13	6															7
	2	4	5		8	3	7	14	13	11^3	10^2				9		6^1				1	12										8
	2	4	5		8	6	7		12	11	10^1				9						1	3										9
		3	4	6^1	5	9	10^2	13		11^3	12				7	8		14		1		2										10
	5	3	4		12	9	11^1	14	10^3	7^2					6	8	13	1		1		2										11
	5	3	4		12	9^4	11^3	13	10^1	6^2	14				7	8^5	15	16		1		2										12
		3	4		5	12	11		10^2	6	13				7	8		9^1		1		2										13
	5	3	4	13		12	11		10	6	9^1				7^2	8				1		2										14
		3	4		5	12	10		9	6	11^1				7	8				1		2										15
		3^8	4		5	10			9^2	6	11^1				7	8	13	12		1		2										16
12		3	4	13	5^4	11^3						6^2	10^6		7^1	8	14	9		1		2	15	16								17
12		3		4	5^1	9^2			11			7^1	10		6	8	13	1		1		2		14								18
	5	3	4		8	9^1			11			10	6	12	7					1		2										19
	5	3		4	9^2	12	10^1		11^3	6	13				7	8^4	15	14		1		2										20
		3^1	4	5^3	6	11	15	10^4		7^5	12	13		8^2	9		14	16		1		2										21
		3	4		5	9			10^4	15		6^2	12	7^1	13	8	11	14		1		2^3										22
		3	4	13	2	10			11^1	12		8	6^2	7^5	5		9^1	14		1												23
12		3	4		11^5			9^4	15			6	5^1	7^2	8	13	16	10^3		1		2				14						24
		3		12	5	11			13	10^3		6			7	8^1	9^2	14		1		2				4						25
14		3		12	5^3	10			15	11^4		6			7	8^1	9^2	13		1		2				4						26
15		3^2			5	11			12	10^1		6			7	8^4	9			1		2^3				4	13	14				27
5^2		3			11				10^3	14		6			7	8	9^1			1		12		4		2	13					28
5		3^1		6					11^4	10^5		16			7^3	8^2	9	13		1		12		4		2	15		14			29
				6	5^5	10			11^2	14		7^1			8^3	15	9^4	1		3				13		4	2	16		12		30
8^3				6	5	9^5			10^2			12			7	16	14	1		3^1		11^4		4		2	13		15			31
14			5		2	7^2			13			6^3	11		10	8^1	1			14		4		3		12	9					32
			5	9^3	2	7^2			13			6	11		10^6	8^1	1			14		4	3	15	12							33
		3	8	5					11	12		6			13	9^2	1		10^1		4	2		7								34
		3	8^3	5					10^2	12		6^5			13	15	9^4	1		11^1		4	2	14	7	16						35
		3^3	14	6^1	5				10^5	11		12			7^8	8	15	1		4		2	16		9^4	13						36
		3	14	6^2	5				10	11^4		12	13		7	8^3		1		4		2			9^1	15						37
		3	15	6^1	5				10	11^2		7			8^4	9^3	1		14		4	2	13		12							38
		3		6^2	5				10^4	11^3		7	8		12	1		14		4		2	15	9^1	13							39
5^2		3	12		14				10	11^5		13	16		7	8	1		4		2^1	15	9^3	6^4								40
15		3		6^1	5^3	9			10^5	11^2	12	16			7	8^4	1		2		4	13	14									41
1		3^2	12		5	9^1			10^3	14		6	11^4		7	8				15		4	2		13							42
1					5	9^3			10^1	12		6	11^2		8		14			2		4	3		13	7						43
1					5	9^2			10^1	12		6	11^1		8					2		14	4	3	12	7						44
1		12			5	9^2			10^3	13		6	11		8					2		4	4^1	3	14	7						45
1		2				16			10^5	13	6		8	14	9^4		4	15		11^2		3	5^3	12	7^1								46

FA Cup

First Round	Rushall Olympic	(a)	2-0
Second Round	Swindon T	(h)	2-2
aet; Accrington S won 4-1 on penalties.			
Third Round	Liverpool	(a)	0-4

Carabao Cup

First Round	Tranmere R	(a)	0-3

Vertu Trophy

Group A (N)	Stockport Co	(h)	1-4
Group A (N)	Tranmere R	(a)	1-2
Group A (N)	Everton U21	(h)	2-1

AFC WIMBLEDON

FOUNDATION

While the history of AFC Wimbledon is straightforward since it was a new club formed in 2002, there were in effect two clubs operating for two years with Wimbledon connections. The other club was MK Dons, of course. In August 2001, the Football League had rejected the existing Wimbledon's application to move to Milton Keynes. In May 2002, they rejected local sites and were given permission to move by an independent commission set up by the Football League. AFC Wimbledon was founded in the summer of 2002 and held its first trials on Wimbledon Common. In subsequent years, there was considerable debate over the rightful home of the trophies obtained by the former Wimbledon football club. In October 2006, an agreement was reached between Milton Keynes Dons, its Supporters Association, the Wimbledon Independent Supporters Association and the Football Supporters Federation to transfer such trophies and honours to the London Borough of Merton.

Cherry Red Records Stadium, Plough Lane, London SW17 0NR.

Telephone: (020) 8547 3528.

Ticket Office: (020) 3988 7863.

Website: www.afcwimbledon.co.uk

Email: enquiries@afcwimbledon.ltd.uk

Ground Capacity: 9,300.

Record Attendance: 8,664 v Port Vale, FL 2, 26 April 2025.

Pitch Measurements: 105m × 68m (115yd × 74.5yd).

Chairman: Mick Buckley.

Managing Director: James Woodroof.

Manager: Johnnie Jackson.

Assistant Manager: Terry Skiverton.

Club Nickname: 'The Dons'.

Colours: Blue shirts with yellow trim, blue shorts with yellow trim, blue socks.

Year Formed: 2002.

Turned Professional: 2002.

Grounds: 2002, Kingsmeadow; 2020, Loftus Road (temporary groundshare with QPR); 2020, Plough Lane (renamed Cherry Reds Records Stadium 2021).

First Football League Game: 6 August 2011, FL 2 v Bristol R (h) L 2–3 – Brown; Hatton, Gwillim (Bush), Porter (Minshull), Stuart (1), Johnson B, Moore L, Wellard, Jolley (Ademeno (1)), Midson, Yussuff.

HONOURS

League: Runners-up: FL 2 – (7th) 2015–16 *(promoted to FL 1 via play-offs)*; Football Conference – (2nd) 2010–11 *(promoted to FL 2 via play-offs)*.

FA Cup: 5th rd – 2019.

League Cup: 3rd rd 2022, 2024, 2025.

FOOTBALL YEARBOOK FACT FILE

AFC Wimbledon claimed their first-ever Premier League scalp when they defeated West Ham United 4-2 at Kingsmeadow Stadium in an FA Cup fourth-round tie in January 2019. Kwasi Appiah, Scott Wagstaff (2) and Toby Siddick scored the goals for the Dons, who at the time were rock bottom of the League One table, in front of a crowd of 4,777.

Record League Victory: 5–1 v Bury, FL 2, 19 November 2016 – Shea; Fuller, Robertson, Robinson (Taylor), Owens, Francomb (2 (1 pen)), Reeves, Parrett, Whelpdale (1), Elliott (1) (Nightingale), Poleon (1), (Barrett); 5–1 v Accrington S, FL 1, 10 April 2021 – Tzanev; O'Neill (Alexander), Heneghan[!], Nightingale, Guinness-Walker, Dobson (Oksanen), Woodyard, Rudoni, Assal (2) (Osew), Palmer (2) (McLoughlin), Pigott (1) (Longman).

Record Cup Victory: 5–0 v Bury, FA Cup 1st rd replay, 5 November 2016 – Shea; Fuller (Owens), Robertson, Robinson (1), Francomb. Parrett (1), Reeves, Bulman (Beere), Whelpdale, Barcham (Poleon (2)), Taylor (1); 5–0 v Ramsgate, FA Cup 2nd rd, 4 December 2023 – Bass; Biler (Ogundere), Lewis (Pearce), Johnson, Currie, Neufville (1), Reeves (1) (Ball), Little, Lemonheigh-Evans (1), Al Hamadi (2) (Davison), Bugiel (Sasu).

Record Defeat: 0–5 v Oxford U, FL 2, 18 February 2020.

Most League Points (3 for a win): 75, FL 2, 2015–16.

Most League Goals: 64, FL 2, 2015–16.

Highest League Scorer in Season: Lyle Taylor, 20, 2015–16; Joe Pigott, 20, 2020–21.

Most League Goals in Total Aggregate: Kevin Cooper, 107, 2002–04.

Most League Goals in One Match: 3, Lyle Taylor v Rotherham U, FL 1, 17 October 2017; 3, Joe Pigott v Rochdale, FL 1, 19 February 2019; 3, Marcus Foss v Southend U, FL 1, 12 October 2019; 3, Ali Al-Hamadi v Tranmere R, FL 2, 30 September 2023; 3, Omar Bugiel v Walsall, FL 2, 27 April 2024; 3, Matty Stevens v Carlisle U, FL 2, 12 October 2024.

Most Capped Player: Ali Al-Hamadi, 7 (14), Iraq.

Most League Appearances: Barry Fuller, 205, 2013–18.

Youngest League Player: Alfie Bendle, 17 years 93 days v Accrington S, 30 April 2022.

Record Transfer Fee Received: £1,750,000 from Ipswich T for Ali Al-Hamadi, January 2024.

Record Transfer Fee Paid: Undisclosed to Charlton Ath for Josh Davison, July 2022.

Football League Record: 2011 Promoted from Football Conference; 2011–16 FL 2; 2016–22 FL 1; 2022–25 FL 2; 2025– FL 1.

LATEST SEQUENCES

Longest Sequence of League Wins: 5, 2.4.2016 – 23.4.2016.

Longest Sequence of League Defeats: 8, 2.10.2018 – 17.11.2018.

Longest Sequence of League Draws: 4, 6.4.2019 – 23.4.2019.

Longest Sequence of Unbeaten League Matches: 12, 26.12.2024 – 22.2.2025.

Longest Sequence Without a League Win: 27, 11.12.2021 – 30.4.2022.

Successive Scoring Runs: 11 from 24.10.2020.

Successive Non-scoring Runs: 6 from 1.4.2017.

MANAGERS

Terry Eames 2002–04
Nicky English *(Caretaker)* 2004
Dave Anderson 2004–07
Terry Brown 2007–12
Neal Ardley 2012–18
Wally Downes 2018–19
Glyn Hodges 2019–21
Mark Robinson 2021–22
Mark Bowen 2022
Johnnie Jackson May 2022–

TEN YEAR LEAGUE RECORD

		P	W	D	L	F	A	Pts	Pos
2015-16	FL 2	46	21	12	13	64	50	75	7
2016-17	FL 1	46	13	18	15	52	55	57	15
2017-18	FL 1	46	13	14	19	47	58	53	18
2018-19	FL 1	46	13	11	22	42	63	50	20
2019-20	FL 1	35	8	11	16	39	52	35	20§
2020-21	FL 1	46	12	15	19	54	70	51	19
2021-22	FL 1	46	6	19	21	49	75	37	23
2022-23	FL 2	46	11	15	20	48	60	48	21
2023-24	FL 2	46	17	14	15	64	51	65	10
2024-25	FL 2	46	20	13	13	56	35	73	5

§*Decided on points-per-game (1.00)*

DID YOU KNOW

AFC Wimbledon applied to join the Ryman Isthmian League when they were formed in the summer of 2002. However, as their application was submitted after the required deadline they required 95 per cent of the member clubs to accept them. They were unable to achieve this so began their new life in the Combined Counties League.

AFC WIMBLEDON – SKY BET LEAGUE TWO 2024–25 LEAGUE RECORD

Match No.	Date		Venue	Opponents	Result	H/T Score	Lg Pos.	Goalscorers	Attendance
1	Aug	10	H	Colchester U	W 4-2	3-2	3	Ball [13], Reeves [30], Stevens (pen) [38], Bugiel [54]	7924
2		17	A	Bromley	L 0-2	0-1	11		4102
3		24	A	Cheltenham T	W 1-0	0-0	8	Pigott [67]	4256
4		31	H	Fleetwood T	W 1-0	1-0	6	Neufville [28]	7162
5	Sept	14	H	Milton Keynes D	W 3-0	1-0	4	Hippolyte [11], Maycock 2 [90, 90]	7921
6		21	A	Bradford C	D 0-0	0-0	5		16,344
7	Oct	5	A	Salford C	L 0-1	0-0	12		2627
8		12	H	Carlisle U	W 4-0	3-0	10	Stevens 3 [8, 39, 50], Harper (og) [45]	8331
9		19	A	Notts Co	L 0-1	0-0	11		10,156
10		22	H	Morecambe	W 3-0	0-0	10	Tilley [52], Bugiel [66], Stevens [70]	7651
11		26	A	Port Vale	L 2-3	0-2	12	Neufville [61], Hippolyte [78]	7163
12	Nov	9	H	Grimsby T	L 0-1	0-1	14		8307
13		16	A	Barrow	W 3-1	1-1	10	Pigott [2], Stevens 2 [76, 77]	3227
14		19	H	Accrington S	D 2-2	0-0	8	Smith [89], Tilley [90]	7020
15		23	H	Walsall	L 0-1	0-0	9		7519
16		26	A	Tranmere R	W 2-0	1-0	7	Stevens [37], Bugiel [53]	5007
17	Dec	3	H	Newport Co	D 2-2	2-1	8	Smith [12], Stevens [20]	6519
18		7	A	Harrogate T	W 3-0	2-0	6	Kelly [12], O'Toole [23], Stevens [50]	2506
19		14	A	Doncaster R	W 1-0	1-0	4	Stevens [27]	7862
20		21	A	Chesterfield	L 0-1	0-1	6		8555
21		26	H	Swindon T	D 1-1	0-1	5	Tilley [56]	8304
22		30	H	Gillingham	W 1-0	0-0	2	Stevens [50]	8281
23	Jan	2	A	Newport Co	W 2-1	0-0	2	Kelly [49], Sawyers [77]	4485
24		18	H	Tranmere R	W 2-0	0-0	4	Neufville [48], Stevens (pen) [81]	7975
25		25	A	Milton Keynes D	D 0-0	0-0	5		7693
26		28	A	Crewe Alex	D 1-1	1-1	6	Neufville [45]	4039
27	Feb	1	H	Bradford C	W 1-0	1-0	4	Tilley [13]	8536
28		8	A	Accrington S	D 0-0	0-0	5		2170
29		11	H	Crewe Alex	W 3-0	2-0	4	Stevens 2 (1 pen) [41 (p), 56], Reeves [45]	7662
30		15	A	Salford C	W 1-0	0-0	2	Stevens [65]	7739
31		18	A	Fleetwood T	D 0-0	0-0	2		2106
32		22	H	Colchester U	D 1-1	0-1	3	Browne [39]	6029
33	Mar	1	H	Bromley	L 0-1	0-0	5		8519
34		4	A	Morecambe	L 0-1	0-1	5		2488
35		8	H	Notts Co	W 2-0	2-0	4	Lewis [21], Smith [35]	8659
36		11	A	Cheltenham T	L 1-2	1-1	5	Browne [37]	8114
37		15	A	Carlisle U	W 2-1	1-0	3	Maycock [2], Smith [49]	7050
38		22	H	Barrow	D 2-2	0-0	3	Browne [60], Stevens [85]	8657
39		29	A	Walsall	D 1-1	0-0	5	Bugiel [70]	9203
40	Apr	1	A	Swindon T	L 1-2	0-0	5	Browne [56]	6500
41		5	H	Harrogate T	W 1-0	0-0	5	Smith [77]	8341
42		12	A	Doncaster R	D 1-1	1-0	5	Smith [5]	8733
43		18	H	Chesterfield	D 0-0	0-0	5		8506
44		21	A	Gillingham	L 0-1	0-0	5		7641
45		26	H	Port Vale	L 0-2	0-0	6		8664
46	May	3	A	Grimsby T	W 1-0	0-0	5	Hutchinson [52]	8369

Final League Position: 5

GOALSCORERS

League (56): Stevens 17 (3 pens), Smith 6, Browne 4, Bugiel 4, Neufville 4, Tilley 4, Maycock 3, Hippolyte 2, Kelly 2, Pigott 2, Reeves 2, Ball 1, Hutchinson 1, Lewis 1, O'Toole 1, Sawyers 1, own goal 1.
FA Cup (3): Stevens 2, Bugiel 1.
Carabao Cup (4): Bugiel 1, Kelly 1, Pigott 1, Stevens 1.
Vertu Trophy (5): Bugiel 1, Maycock 1, Pigott 1, Stevens 1, Tilley 1.
League Two Play-offs (3): Harbottle 1, Hippolyte 1, Neufville 1.

Goodman O 46	Lewis J 35 + 1	Ogundere I 24 + 15	Johnson R 38 + 2	Neufville J 46	Reeves J 28	Ball J 11 + 4	Smith A 45	Furlong J 10 + 12	Bugiel O 34 + 5	Stevens M 41 + 5	Kelly A 16 + 24	Pigott J 8 + 20	Maycock C 17 + 10	Hippolyte M 12 + 7	Tilley J 36 + 5	Harbottle R 23 + 2	Biler H — + 6	O'Toole J 7	Sidwell H — + 1	Hutchinson S 13 + 5	Sawyers R 1 + 3	Sasu A 4 + 18	Browne M 10 + 8	Foyo O 1 + 5	Match No.
1	2	3	4	5	6	7[3]	8	9	10[2]	11[1]	12	13	14												1
1	3	2	4	5	6	7[1]	8	9[4]	11[3]	10[2]	12	13		14	15										2
1	3		4	5	7	14	6	9	11[3]	13			10[2]	12	8[1]	2									3
1	3	12	4[1]	5	7		6	9	11	13			10[2]	14	8[3]	2									4
1	3	4		5	7[1]	16	6[5]	15	10[3]	11[2]	13	14	12	8	9[4]	2									5
1	3	4		5		7[2]	6	14	11	10[1]		13	12	8	9[3]	2									6
1	3[1]	4		5	7[5]	12	6	9[4]	11	13	14	10[2]	16	8[3]	15	2									7
1		4[5]	16	5[3]		3	7	15	11[2]	10[1]	12	13	6	8[4]	9	2	14								8
1		4	12	5[3]		3	7	16	11[4]	10[2]	13	15	6[5]	8	9	2[1]	14								9
1	2[1]	12	4	5		3	7		11[2]	10[3]	13	14	6	8	9										10
1	2[4]	14	4[3]	5		3	7		11	10	12		6[1]	8	9[2]	15	13								11
1	2	12	4[1]	5	3[3]	7		11	10[2]	14	13		6[4]	8	9		15								12
1	3	12	4	5	6[2]	7		10	13	11			8	9	2[1]										13
1	13		4[2]	5	3	7	9[1]		10	12	11		8	6	2										14
1	3	12	4	5		7		11	10[3]	14	13		6[2]	8	9	2[1]									15
1	3	14	4[3]	5		7		12	10	11[2]	13		6[1]	8	9	2									16
1	2	4	5[3]		7	13	11[2]	9	10[1]	12			8	6	14	3									17
1	2	4	5		7		11[1]	9	10	12			8	6[2]		3	13								18
1	2	4	5		6	13	11	9	10[2]				8	12		3		7[1]							19
1	2[2]	4	5		7		9	10[2]	11				8	2	14	3	6[1]	12	13						20
1		4	5		7		11[1]	9	10[3]	12			8	2		3	6[2]	13	14						21
1	12	4	5	7		6	15		11	10[4]			9	2[3]		3[1]	14	8[2]	13						22
1	4	3	5	7		8	13		11[3]	10			9[2]	2[1]		6	12	14							23
1	13	2[1]	4	5	7		6		9	11[3]	10[1]		8			3		14	12						24
1	2[1]	12	4	5	7		6		11[3]	9	10[2]		8			3		14	13						25
1	3	2	4	5	6		7	8[3]	13	11[1]	12		15	14						9[4]	10[2]				26
1	3	2	4	5	6		7		10	9[1]	11[2]		8							13	12				27
1	3	2	4	5	6		7	8[3]	11	12	10[2]		14							9[1]	13				28
1	3	2	4	5[2]	6		7	15	10[3]	11[5]		14		13	8[4]					12	9[1]	16			29
1	3	2	4	5	6		7		10	11[2]	13		8							12	9[1]				30
1	3[4]	2	4	5[2]	6		7		9[3]	10	11[1]	15			8					14	13	12			31
1	3	2	4	5	6		7	12	10	11[3]	14			8[1]						13	9[2]				32
1	3	2[5]	4	5[2]	6		7[3]		10[1]	11[4]	16	13	12	8						15	14	9			33
1	3		4	5	7		8[5]	9[1]	15	13	11[4]	10[2]	6[3]	16						2	12	14			34
1	3	2		5	6		7		10[3]	11[2]	13	14	12	8						4		9[1]			35
1	3	2		5	7		6[4]		10[2]	11[1]	12		15	8[3]						4	14	9	13		36
1	3	12	4	5	6		8	9[1]	10	11[3]	14		7[2]	13						2		10[3]			37
1	3	12	4	5	7		6	14		11	13		8	9[2]						2[1]		10[3]			38
1	3	14	4		6	5	15	8		12	11[1]		7[4]	9	2[3]					13	10[2]				39
1	2	4			5	7	6		10	11[1]	13		8[2]		3[4]						12				40
1	3		4	5	6		7		10[3]	9[2]	11[1]	14		13	2					8		12			41
1	3	14	4	5	6[5]		7		9[2]	11[1]	10[4]	12		8	2[3]					15		13			42
1	3		4[1]	5		7			10[4]	9[2]	11[3]	15	6	8	2					12	14		13		43
1	3		4	5		7			12	9[2]	13	14	6[4]	8[3]	2					15	11		10[1]		44
1	3	14	4	5		6			10[1]	11[4]		15	8[5]	13	9	2[3]				7[2]		16	12		45
1	3		4	9		6[3]	8		12	11[2]	13			14	5	2				7			10[1]		46

FA Cup

First Round	Milton Keynes D	(a)	2-0
Second Round	Dagenham & Red	(h)	1-2

Carabao Cup

First Round	Bromley	(a)	2-1
Second Round	Ipswich T	(h)	2-2

AFC Wimbledon won 4-2 on penalties.

Third Round	Newcastle U	(a)	0-1

Vertu Trophy

Group B (S)	Wycombe W	(h)	1-0
Group B (S)	Crawley T	(a)	4-3
Group B (S)	Brighton & HA U21	(h)	0-3
Second Round	Colchester U	(a)	0-2

League Two Play-offs

Semi-Final 1st leg	Notts Co	(a)	1-0
Semi-Final 2nd leg	Notts Co	(h)	1-0
Final	Walsall	(Wembley)	1-0

ARSENAL

FOUNDATION

Formed by workers at the Royal Arsenal, Woolwich in 1886, they began as Dial Square (name of one of the workshops), and included two former Nottingham Forest players, Fred Beardsley and Morris Bates. Beardsley wrote to his old club seeking help and they provided the new club with a full set of red jerseys and a ball. The club became known as the 'Woolwich Reds' although their official title soon after formation was Woolwich Arsenal.

Emirates Stadium, Highbury House, 75 Drayton Park, Islington, London N5 1BU.

Telephone: (020) 7619 5003.

Ticket Office: (020) 7619 5000.

Website: www.arsenal.com

Email: fanservices@arsenal.co.uk

Ground Capacity: 60,704.

Record Attendance: 73,295 v Sunderland, Div 1, 9 March 1935 (at Highbury); 73,707 v RC Lens, UEFA Champions League, 25 November 1998 (at Wembley); 60,383 v Wolverhampton W, Premier League, 2 November 2019; 60,383 v Liverpool, Premier League, 27 October 2024 (at Emirates).

Pitch Measurements: 105m × 68m (115yd × 74.5yd).

Co-Chairmen: Stan Kroenke, Josh Kroenke.

Managing Director: Richard Garlick.

Manager: Mikel Arteta.

Assistant Manager: Albert Stuiverberg.

Colours: Red shirts with white sleeves and blue trim, white shorts with blue trim, red socks with blue trim.

Year Formed: 1886.

Turned Professional: 1891.

Previous Names: 1886, Dial Square; 1886, Royal Arsenal; 1891, Woolwich Arsenal; 1914, Arsenal.

Club Nickname: 'The Gunners', 'Gooners'.

HONOURS

League Champions: Premier League – 1997–98, 2001–02, 2003–04; Division 1 – 1930–31, 1932–33, 1933–34, 1934–35, 1937–38, 1947–48, 1952–53, 1970–71, 1988–89, 1990–91.
Runners-up: Premier League – 1998–99, 1999–2000, 2000–01, 2002–03, 2004–05, 2015–16, 2022–23, 2023–24, 2024–25; Division 1 – 1925–26, 1931–32, 1972–73; Division 2 – 1903–04.
FA Cup Winners: 1930, 1936, 1950, 1971, 1979, 1993, 1998, 2002, 2003, 2005, 2014, 2015, 2017, 2020.
Runners-up: 1927, 1932, 1952, 1972, 1978, 1980, 2001.
League Cup Winners: 1987, 1993.
Runners-up: 1968, 1969, 1988, 2007, 2011, 2018.
Double performed: 1970–71, 1997–98, 2001–02.
European Competitions
European Cup: 1971–72 *(qf)*, 1991–92. *UEFA Champions League:* 1998–99, 1999–2000, 2000–01 *(qf)*, 2001–02, 2002–03, 2003–04 *(qf)*, 2004–05, 2005–06 *(runners-up)*, 2006–07, 2007–08 *(qf)*, 2008–09 *(sf)*, 2009–10 *(qf)*, 2010–11, 2011–12, 2012–13, 2013–14, 2014–15, 2015–16, 2016–17, 2023–24 *(qf)*, 2024–25 *(sf)*.
Fairs Cup: 1963–64, 1969–70 *(winners)*, 1970–71 *(qf)*.
UEFA Cup: 1978–79, 1981–82, 1982–83, 1996–97, 1997–98, 1999–2000 *(runners-up)*.
Europa League: 2017–18 *(sf)*, 2018–19 *(runners-up)*, 2019–20, 2020–21 *(sf)*, 2022–23.
European Cup-Winners' Cup: 1979–80 *(runners-up)*, 1993–94 *(winners)*, 1994–95 *(runners-up)*.
Super Cup: 1994 *(runners-up)*.

Grounds: 1886, Plumstead Common; 1887, Sportsman Ground; 1888, Manor Ground; 1890, Invicta Ground; 1893, Manor Ground; 1913, Highbury; 2006, Emirates Stadium.

FOOTBALL YEARBOOK FACT FILE

Arsenal's Manor Ground was closed to fans for six weeks towards the end of the 1894–95 season after the referee in their home game against Burton Wanderers was attacked by spectators at the end of the match. They played two home Football League games during their enforced exile, defeating Burton Swifts 3-0 at the Priestfield Stadium (home of New Brompton, now Gillingham) and drawing 3-3 with Leicester Fosse at the Essex County Cricket Club ground in Leyton.

First Football League Game: 2 September 1893, Division 2, v Newcastle U (h) D 2–2 – Williams; Powell, Jeffrey; Devine, Buist, Howat; Gemmell, Henderson, Shaw (1), Elliott (1), Booth.

Record League Victory: 12–0 v Loughborough T, Division 2, 12 March 1900 – Orr; McNichol, Jackson; Moir, Dick (2), Anderson (1); Hunt, Cottrell (2), Main (2), Gaudie (3), Tennant (2).

Record Cup Victory: 11–1 v Darwen, FA Cup 3rd rd, 9 January 1932 – Moss; Parker, Hapgood; Jones, Roberts, John; Hulme (2), Jack (3), Lambert (2), James, Bastin (4).

Record Defeat: 0–8 v Loughborough T, Division 2, 12 December 1896.

Most League Points (2 for a win): 66, Division 1, 1930–31.

Most League Points (3 for a win): 90, Premier League, 2003–04.

Most League Goals: 127, Division 1, 1930–31.

Highest League Scorer in Season: Ted Drake, 42, 1934–35.

Most League Goals in Total Aggregate: Thierry Henry, 175, 1999–2007; 2011–12.

Most League Goals in One Match: 7, Ted Drake v Aston Villa, Division 1, 14 December 1935.

Most Capped Player: Thierry Henry, 81 (123), France.

Most League Appearances: David O'Leary, 558, 1975–93.

Youngest League Player: Ethan Nwaneri, 15 years 181 days v Brentford, 18 September 2022.

Record Transfer Fee Received: £40,000,000 from Liverpool for Alex Oxlade-Chamberlain, August 2017.

Record Transfer Fee Paid: £105,000,000 to West Ham U for Declan Rice, July 2023.

Football League Record: 1893 Elected to Division 2; 1904–13 Division 1; 1913–19 Division 2; 1919 Re-elected to Division 1; 1919–92 Division 1; 1992– Premier League.

MANAGERS

Sam Hollis 1894–97
Tom Mitchell 1897–98
George Elcoat 1898–99
Harry Bradshaw 1899–1904
Phil Kelso 1904–08
George Morrell 1908–15
Leslie Knighton 1919–25
Herbert Chapman 1925–34
George Allison 1934–47
Tom Whittaker 1947–56
Jack Crayston 1956–58
George Swindin 1958–62
Billy Wright 1962–66
Bertie Mee 1966–76
Terry Neill 1976–83
Don Howe 1984–86
George Graham 1986–95
Bruce Rioch 1995–96
Arsène Wenger 1996–2018
Unai Emery 2018–19
Mikel Arteta December 2019–

LATEST SEQUENCES

Longest Sequence of League Wins: 14, 10.2.2002 – 18.8.2002.

Longest Sequence of League Defeats: 7, 12.2.1977 – 12.3.1977.

Longest Sequence of League Draws: 6, 4.3.1961 – 1.4.1961.

Longest Sequence of Unbeaten League Matches: 49, 7.5.2003 – 24.10.2004.

Longest Sequence Without a League Win: 23, 28.9.1912 – 1.3.1913.

Successive Scoring Runs: 55 from 19.5.2001.

Successive Non-scoring Runs: 6 from 25.2.1987.

TEN YEAR LEAGUE RECORD

		P	W	D	L	F	A	Pts	Pos
2015-16	PR Lge	38	20	11	7	65	36	71	2
2016-17	PR Lge	38	23	6	9	77	44	75	5
2017-18	PR Lge	38	19	6	13	74	51	63	6
2018-19	PR Lge	38	21	7	10	73	51	70	5
2019-20	PR Lge	38	14	14	10	56	48	56	8
2020-21	PR Lge	38	18	7	13	55	39	61	8
2021-22	PR Lge	38	22	3	13	61	48	69	5
2022-23	PR Lge	38	26	6	6	88	43	84	2
2023-24	PR Lge	38	28	5	5	91	29	89	2
2024-25	PR Lge	38	20	14	4	69	34	74	2

DID YOU KNOW ?

In the 1930–31 season Arsenal established an all-time record for the top flight by scoring 60 goals in their away games. The Gunners scored consistently throughout the campaign, netting in all 21 away games as they won the Football League title. The highlight came with a 7-2 win at Leicester City in February.

ARSENAL – PREMIER LEAGUE 2024–25 LEAGUE RECORD

Match No.	Date	Venue	Opponents	Result	H/T Score	Lg Pos.	Goalscorers	Attendance
1	Aug 17	H	Wolverhampton W	W 2-0	1-0	2	Havertz [25], Saka [74]	60,261
2	24	A	Aston Villa	W 2-0	0-0	3	Trossard [67], Thomas [77]	41,587
3	31	H	Brighton & HA	D 1-1	1-0	3	Havertz [38]	60,326
4	Sept 15	A	Tottenham H	W 1-0	0-0	2	Gabriel [64]	61,645
5	22	A	Manchester C	D 2-2	2-1	4	Calafiori [22], Gabriel [45]	52,846
6	28	H	Leicester C	W 4-2	2-0	3	Martinelli [20], Trossard [45], Ndidi (og) [90], Havertz [90]	60,323
7	Oct 5	A	Southampton	W 3-1	0-0	3	Havertz [58], Martinelli [68], Saka [88]	60,307
8	19	A	Bournemouth	L 0-2	0-0	3		11,235
9	27	H	Liverpool	D 2-2	2-1	3	Saka [9], Merino [43]	60,383
10	Nov 2	A	Newcastle U	L 0-1	0-1	4		52,249
11	10	A	Chelsea	D 1-1	0-0	4	Martinelli [60]	39,780
12	23	H	Nottingham F	W 3-0	1-0	4	Saka [15], Thomas [52], Nwaneri [86]	60,298
13	30	A	West Ham U	W 5-2	5-2	3	Gabriel [19], Trossard [27], Odegaard (pen) [34], Havertz [36], Saka (pen) [45]	62,475
14	Dec 4	H	Manchester U	W 2-0	0-0	3	Timber [54], Saliba [73]	60,256
15	8	A	Fulham	D 1-1	0-1	3	Saliba [52]	26,954
16	14	H	Everton	D 0-0	0-0	3		60,176
17	21	A	Crystal Palace	W 5-1	3-1	3	Gabriel Jesus 2 [6, 15], Havertz [38], Martinelli [60], Rice [84]	25,167
18	27	H	Ipswich T	W 1-0	1-0	3	Havertz [23]	60,271
19	Jan 1	A	Brentford	W 3-1	1-1	2	Gabriel Jesus [29], Merino [50], Martinelli [53]	17,190
20	4	A	Brighton & HA	D 1-1	1-1	2	Nwaneri [16]	31,714
21	15	H	Tottenham H	W 2-1	2-1	2	Solanke (og) [40], Trossard [44]	60,287
22	18	A	Aston Villa	D 2-2	1-0	2	Martinelli [35], Havertz [55]	60,067
23	25	A	Wolverhampton W	W 1-0	0-0	2	Calafiori [74]	31,503
24	Feb 2	H	Manchester C	W 5-1	1-0	2	Odegaard [2], Thomas [56], Lewis-Skelly [62], Havertz [76], Nwaneri [90]	60,355
25	15	A	Leicester C	W 2-0	0-0	2	Merino 2 [81, 87]	31,968
26	22	H	West Ham U	L 0-1	0-1	2		60,262
27	26	A	Nottingham F	D 0-0	0-0	2		30,200
28	Mar 9	A	Manchester U	D 1-1	0-1	2	Rice [74]	73,812
29	16	H	Chelsea	W 1-0	1-0	2	Merino [20]	60,311
30	Apr 1	H	Fulham	W 2-1	1-0	2	Merino [37], Saka [73]	60,256
31	5	A	Everton	D 1-1	1-0	2	Trossard [34]	39,316
32	12	A	Brentford	D 1-1	1-0	2	Thomas [61]	60,184
33	20	A	Ipswich T	W 4-0	2-0	2	Trossard 2 [14, 69], Martinelli [28], Nwaneri [88]	29,549
34	23	H	Crystal Palace	D 2-2	2-1	2	Kiwior [3], Trossard [42]	60,167
35	May 3	H	Bournemouth	L 1-2	1-0	2	Rice [34]	60,110
36	11	A	Liverpool	D 2-2	0-2	2	Martinelli [47], Merino [70]	60,324
37	18	H	Newcastle U	W 1-0	0-0	2	Rice [55]	60,160
38	25	A	Southampton	W 2-1	1-0	2	Tierney [43], Odegaard [90]	31,289

Final League Position: 2

GOALSCORERS

League (69): Havertz 9, Martinelli 8, Trossard 8, Merino 7, Saka 6 (1 pen), Nwaneri 4, Rice 4, Thomas 4, Gabriel Jesus 3, Gabriel 3, Odegaard 3 (1 pen), Calafiori 2, Saliba 2, Kiwior 1, Lewis-Skelly 1, Tierney 1, Timber 1, own goals 2.
FA Cup (1): Gabriel 1.
Carabao Cup (11): Gabriel Jesus 4, Nwaneri 3, Havertz 2, Rice 1, Sterling 1.
(Arsenal U21) Vertu Trophy (4): Butler-Oyedeji 1, Harriman-Annous 1, Kabia 1, Robinson 1.
Champions League (31): Saka 6 (1 pen), Havertz 4, Rice 4, Odegaard 3, Martinelli 2, Merino 2, Nwaneri 2, Trossard 2, Calafiori 1, Gabriel 1, Jorginho 1 (1 pen), Timber 1, Zinchenko 1, own goal 1.

Raya D 38	White B 13+4	Saliba W 35	Gabriel M 28	Zinchenko A 5+10	Odegaard M 26+4	Thomas P 31+4	Rice D 33+2	Saka B 20+5	Havertz K 21+2	Martinelli G 25+8	Timber J 27+3	Trossard L 28+10	Gabriel Jesus F 6+11	Calafiori R 11+8	Nelson R —+1	Jorginho F 9+6	Sterling R 7+10	Nwaneri E 11+15	Kiwior J 10+7	Lewis-Skelly M 15+8	Merino M 17+11	Tomiyasu T —+1	Tierney K 2+11	Butler-Oyedeji N —+1	Match No.
1	2	3	4	5^1	6	7	8^3	9^2	10	11	12	13	14												1
1	2	3	4			6	7	8	9^3	10	11^1	5^2	12	13	14										2
1	2	3	4	14	6^2	7	8^4	9	10	13	5^3	11^1		12											3
1	2	3	4		6		9^3	10	8^2	5	11^1	13				7	12	14							4
1	12	3	4			7	8	6^1	10	9^3	2^4	11^5	14	5^2				13	15						5
1		3	4			7^2	8	6	10	9^1	2	11^3	14	5		12	13								6
1		3	4	2^4	8	6	10	12	13	11^1	5^5	7^3	9^2	16			14	15							7
1	2	3^5	4		6	7	11	13	10^3	14	5			8^1	15	12^3		9^4							8
1	3	4^1		2	7	6^3	10	9^4	5^2	11	15			14	12	13	8								9
1	15	3	4	13	2^6	7	6	10	9^2	5^3	11^4	14		16		12		8^1							10
1	2	3	4		6	7	8^2	9^3	10	11^1	5	13	14				12								11
1		3	4	13	6^3	12		9^4		2^5	11	10	5^2			7^1	15	14	16		8				12
1		3	4^1	13	6^4		8	9^3	10	2	11^5	14		5^2		7	15	16	12						13
1		3		5^2	6^3	7	8	9	10	11^1	2	13				14		4		12					14
1		3		6^4	2	8	9	10^3	12	5	11^1	14		7^2		15	4	13							15
1		3	4		6^1	15	7^2	9	10	11^5	2	16	14	13		12		5^3	8^4						16
1		3	4		6	7	13	9^1	8^3	11	2^4	12	10^5	14			15			5^2	16				17
1		3	4		6	13	7^2		8	9	2	11	10^1					5	12						18
1		3	4	16	6^4	7	12		11		2	14	10^5	5^1	15		9^2		13	8^3					19
1		3	4		13	2	6		12			11	10	5		7^2		9^1		8					20
1		3	4	14	6	7	8^3		10	12	2	11^2				9^1			5^4	15		13			21
1			4		6	2	7		10	9^1	3	11				12			5	8					22
1		3	4			7	8		10	9^2	2	11				6^1		5^4		13					23
1		3	4		6^2	7	8		10^3	9	2	11^1		15		14	12		5^4	13					24
1		3	4		6	7^2	8		2	10^4	14		13	11^1	9		5^3	12		15					25
1	15	3^4	4	13	6	7	8^2		2	11		5^1		14		9^3		12^1	10						26
1	15	3	4	13	6^4	16	8		2^5	11		5^1		7^2	14		9^3		10	12					27
1		3	4		6	7^3	8		13	2	11		5^2			9^1		12	10	14					28
1		3	4		6^2	7	8			9^1	2	11				12		5	10	13					29
1		3	4^1		6	7	8	13		11	2^3	14				9^2	12	5	10						30
1	2^5	3		15		6	13		12	14	10			7^4	11^2	9^1	4	5^5	8	16					31
1		3		6^2	13	2^4	8^5	14	11	15	10			7		9^3	4	12	16	5^1					32
1	2	3		5	6	7^4	9^2		11^3		10^5			15	13	4	12	8^1		14	16				33
1		3		6^2	7	8	12		11	2	10			9^1	13	4	5^3			14					34
1	2^5	3		15	6	7	8^1	9^4		11^2	10			14	13	4	5	12						35
1	2^2	3		14	6	7		9^3	11		10^1	13				4	5	8^8	12						36
1	2	3^1		6^4	7	8	9^2	13	11		10^5		12	15		4	5			14					37
1	2			5^3	16	6	7	12	15	10^4		13				8^1	9^5	3	14	11			4^2		38

FA Cup

Third Round	Manchester U	(h)	1-1

aet; Manchester U won 5-3 on penalties.

Carabao Cup

Third Round	Bolton W	(h)	5-1
Fourth Round	Preston NE	(a)	3-0
Quarter-Final	Crystal Palace	(h)	3-2
Semi-Final 1st leg	Newcastle U	(h)	0-2
Semi-Final 2nd leg	Newcastle U	(a)	0-2

Vertu Trophy (Arsenal U21)

Group E (S)	Leyton Orient	(a)	2-1
Group E (S)	Milton Keynes D	(a)	2-2

Milton Keynes D won 3-1 on penalties.

Group E (S)	Colchester U	(a)	0-3

Champions League

League game	Atalanta	(a)	0-0
League game	Paris Saint-Germain	(a)	2-0
League game	Shakhtar Donetsk	(h)	1-0
League game	Internazionale	(a)	0-1
League game	Sporting Lisbon	(a)	5-1
League game	Monaco	(h)	3-0
League game	Dinamo Zagreb	(h)	3-0
League game	Girona	(a)	2-1
Round of 16 1st leg	PSV Eindhoven	(a)	7-1
Round of 16 2nd leg	PSV Eindhoven	(h)	2-2
Quarter-Final 1st leg	Real Madrid	(h)	3-0
Quarter-Final 2nd leg	Real Madrid	(a)	2-1
Semi-Final 1st leg	Paris Saint-Germain	(h)	0-1
Semi-Final 2nd leg	Paris Saint-Germain	(a)	1-2

ASTON VILLA

FOUNDATION

Cricketing enthusiasts of Villa Cross Wesleyan Chapel, Aston, Birmingham decided to form a football club during the winter of 1874–75. Football clubs were few and far between in the Birmingham area and in their first game against Aston Brook St Mary's rugby team they played one half rugby and the other soccer. In 1876 they were joined by Scottish soccer enthusiast George Ramsay who was immediately appointed captain and went on to lead Aston Villa from obscurity to one of the country's top clubs in a period of less than ten years.

Villa Park, Trinity Road, Birmingham B6 6HE.
Telephone: (0121) 327 2299.
Ticket Office: (0333) 323 1874.
Website: www.avfc.co.uk
Email: postmaster@avfc.co.uk
Ground Capacity: 42,918.
Record Attendance: 76,588 v Derby Co, FA Cup 6th rd, 2 March 1946.
Pitch Measurements: 105m × 68m (115yd × 74.5yd).
Co-Chairmen: Nassef Sawiris, Wesley Edens.
President of Business Operations: Francesco Calvo.
Head Coach: Unai Emery.
Assistant Head Coach: Pako Ayestaran.
Colours: Claret shirts with sky blue sleeves and claret trim, white shorts, sky blue socks with claret trim.
Year Formed: 1874.   *Turned Professional:* 1885.
Club Nickname: 'The Villans'.
Grounds: 1874, Wilson Road and Aston Park (also used Aston Lower Grounds for some matches); 1876, Wellington Road, Perry Barr; 1897, Villa Park.
First Football League Game: 8 September 1888, Football League, v Wolverhampton W (a) D 1–1 – Warner; Cox, Coulton; Yates, Harry Devey, Dawson; Albert Brown, Green (1), Allen, Garvey, Hodgetts.
Record League Victory: 12–2 v Accrington S, Division 1, 12 March 1892 – Warner; Evans, Cox; Harry Devey, Jimmy Cowan, Baird; Athersmith (1), Dickson (2), John Devey (4), Lewis Campbell (4), Hodgetts (1).
Record Cup Victory: 13–0 v Wednesbury Old Ath, FA Cup 1st rd, 30 October 1886 – Warner; Coulton, Simmonds; Yates, Robertson, Burton (2); Richard Davis (1), Albert Brown (3), Hunter (3), Loach (2), Hodgetts (2).

HONOURS

League Champions: Division 1 – 1893–94, 1895–96, 1896–97, 1898–99, 1899–1900, 1909–10, 1980–81; Division 2 – 1937–38, 1959–60; Division 3 – 1971–72.
Runners-up: Premier League – 1992–93; Division 1 – 1902–03, 1907–08, 1910–11, 1912–13, 1913–14, 1930–31, 1932–33, 1989–90; Football League 1888–89; Division 2 – 1974–75, 1987–88.
FA Cup Winners: 1887, 1895, 1897, 1905, 1913, 1920, 1957.
Runners-up: 1892, 1924, 2000, 2015.
League Cup Winners: 1961, 1975, 1977, 1994, 1996.
Runners-up: 1963, 1971, 2010, 2020.
Double Performed: 1896–97.
European Competitions
European Cup: 1981–82 *(winners)*, 1982–83 *(qf)*.
UEFA Champions League: 2024–25 *(qf)*.
UEFA Cup: 1975–76, 1977–78 *(qf)*, 1983–84, 1990–91, 1993–94, 1994–95, 1996–97, 1997–98 *(qf)*, 1998–99, 2001–02, 2008–09.
Europa League: 2009–10, 2010–11.
UEFA Europa Conference League: 2023–24 *(sf)*.
Intertoto Cup: 2000 *(sf)*, 2001 *(winners)*, 2002 *(sf)*, 2008 *(qualified for UEFA Cup)*.
Super Cup: 1982 *(winners)*.
World Club Championship: 1982.

FOOTBALL YEARBOOK FACT FILE

Aston Villa made an amazing comeback playing at White Hart Lane against Tottenham Hotspur on 19 March 1966. Villa found themselves 3-0 down after 15 minutes and trailed 5-1 early in the second half. A great turn around saw them score four goals in the last 35 minutes to earn a point from a 5-5 draw. Centre-forward Tony Hateley netted four of the goals with Alan Deakin also scoring.

Record Defeat: 0–8 v Chelsea, Premier League, 23 December 2012.

Most League Points (2 for a win): 70, Division 3, 1971–72.

Most League Points (3 for a win): 83, FL C, 2017–18.

Most League Goals: 128, Division 1, 1930–31.

Highest League Scorer in Season: 'Pongo' Waring, 49, Division 1, 1930–31.

Most League Goals in Total Aggregate: Harry Hampton, 215, 1904–15.

Most League Goals in One Match: 5, Harry Hampton v Sheffield Wed, Division 1, 5 October 1912; 5, Harold Halse v Derby Co, Division 1, 19 October 1912; 5, Len Capewell v Burnley, Division 1, 29 August 1925; 5, George Brown v Leicester C, Division 1, 2 January 1932; 5, Gerry Hitchens v Charlton Ath, Division 2, 18 November 1959.

Most Capped Player: Olof Mellberg, 69 (117), Sweden.

Most League Appearances: Charlie Aitken, 561, 1961–76.

Youngest League Player: Jimmy Brown, 15 years 349 days v Bolton W, 17 September 1969.

Record Transfer Fee Received: £100,000,000 from Manchester C for Jack Grealish, August 2021.

Record Transfer Fee Paid: £50,000,000 to Everton for Amadou Onana, July 2024.

Football League Record: 1888 Founder Member of the Football League; 1888–92 Football League; 1892–36 Division 1; 1936–38 Division 2; 1938–59 Division 1; 1959–60 Division 2; 1960–67 Division 1; 1967–70 Division 2; 1970–72 Division 3; 1972–75 Division 2; 1975–87 Division 1; 1987–88 Division 2; 1988–92 Division 1; 1992–2016 Premier League; 2016–19 FL C; 2019– Premier League.

LATEST SEQUENCES

Longest Sequence of League Wins: 10, 2.3.2019 – 22.4.2019.

Longest Sequence of League Defeats: 11, 14.2.2016 – 30.4.2016.

Longest Sequence of League Draws: 6, 12.9.1981 – 10.10.1981.

Longest Sequence of Unbeaten League Matches: 15, 12.3.1949 – 27.8.1949.

Longest Sequence Without a League Win: 19, 14.8.2015 – 2.1.2016.

Successive Scoring Runs: 35 from 10.11.1895.

Successive Non-scoring Runs: 6 from 26.12.2014.

MANAGERS

George Ramsay 1884–1926
  (*Secretary-Manager*)
W. J. Smith 1926–34
  (*Secretary-Manager*)
Jimmy McMullan 1934–35
Jimmy Hogan 1936–44
Alex Massie 1945–50
George Martin 1950–53
Eric Houghton 1953–58
Joe Mercer 1958–64
Dick Taylor 1964–67
Tommy Cummings 1967–68
Tommy Docherty 1968–70
Vic Crowe 1970–74
Ron Saunders 1974–82
Tony Barton 1982–84
Graham Turner 1984–86
Billy McNeill 1986–87
Graham Taylor 1987–90
Dr Jozef Venglos 1990–91
Ron Atkinson 1991–94
Brian Little 1994–98
John Gregory 1998–2002
Graham Taylor OBE 2002–03
David O'Leary 2003–06
Martin O'Neill 2006–10
Gerard Houllier 2010–11
Alex McLeish 2011–12
Paul Lambert 2012–15
Tim Sherwood 2015
Remi Garde 2015–16
Roberto Di Matteo 2016
Steve Bruce 2016–18
Dean Smith 2018–21
Steven Gerrard 2021–22
Unai Emery November 2022–

TEN YEAR LEAGUE RECORD

		P	W	D	L	F	A	Pts	Pos
2015-16	PR Lge	38	3	8	27	27	76	17	20
2016-17	FL C	46	16	14	16	47	48	62	13
2017-18	FL C	46	24	11	11	72	42	83	4
2018-19	FL C	46	20	16	10	82	61	76	5
2019-20	PR Lge	38	9	8	21	41	67	35	17
2020-21	PR Lge	38	16	7	15	55	46	55	11
2021-22	PR Lge	38	13	6	19	52	54	45	14
2022-23	PR Lge	38	18	7	13	51	46	61	7
2023-24	PR Lge	38	20	8	10	76	61	68	4
2024-25	PR Lge	38	19	9	10	58	51	66	6

DID YOU KNOW ?

After losing at home to Preston North End in a fifth-round tie in January 1888, Aston Villa did not lose another FA Cup tie on home soil until January 1902, a run of more than 14 years. During that period they played a total of 15 matches and won the coveted trophy on two occasions, 1894–95 and 1896–97.

ASTON VILLA – PREMIER LEAGUE 2024–25 LEAGUE RECORD

Match No.	Date	Venue	Opponents	Result	H/T Score	Lg Pos.	Goalscorers	Attendance
1	Aug 17	A	West Ham U	W 2-1	1-1	4	Onana [4], Duran [79]	62,463
2	24	H	Arsenal	L 0-2	0-0	12		41,587
3	31	A	Leicester C	W 2-1	1-0	6	Onana [28], Duran [63]	31,725
4	Sept 14	H	Everton	W 3-2	1-2	3	Watkins 2 [36, 58], Duran [76]	41,573
5	21	H	Wolverhampton W	W 3-1	0-1	3	Watkins [73], Konsa [88], Duran [90]	39,978
6	29	A	Ipswich T	D 2-2	2-1	5	Rogers [15], Watkins [32]	29,943
7	Oct 6	H	Manchester U	D 0-0	0-0	5		42,682
8	19	A	Fulham	W 3-1	1-1	4	Rogers [9], Watkins [59], Diop (og) [69]	26,743
9	26	H	Bournemouth	D 1-1	0-0	3	Barkley [76]	42,165
10	Nov 3	A	Tottenham H	L 1-4	1-0	6	Rogers [32]	61,253
11	9	A	Liverpool	L 0-2	0-1	8		60,292
12	23	H	Crystal Palace	D 2-2	1-2	8	Watkins [36], Barkley [77]	42,175
13	Dec 1	A	Chelsea	L 0-3	0-2	12		39,689
14	4	H	Brentford	W 3-1	3-0	7	Rogers [21], Watkins (pen) [28], Cash [34]	37,890
15	7	H	Southampton	W 1-0	1-0	6	Duran [24]	42,453
16	14	A	Nottingham F	L 1-2	0-0	6	Duran [63]	30,117
17	21	H	Manchester C	W 2-1	1-0	5	Duran [16], Rogers [65]	42,345
18	26	A	Newcastle U	L 0-3	0-1	9		52,168
19	30	H	Brighton & HA	D 2-2	1-1	9	Watkins (pen) [36], Rogers [47]	41,414
20	Jan 4	H	Leicester C	W 2-1	0-0	8	Barkley [58], Bailey [76]	42,386
21	15	A	Everton	W 1-0	0-0	7	Watkins [51]	39,085
22	18	A	Arsenal	D 2-2	0-1	7	Tielemans [60], Watkins [68]	60,067
23	26	H	West Ham U	D 1-1	1-0	8	Ramsey [8]	41,628
24	Feb 1	A	Wolverhampton W	L 0-2	0-1	8		31,385
25	15	H	Ipswich T	D 1-1	0-0	9	Watkins [69]	42,510
26	19	H	Liverpool	D 2-2	2-1	9	Tielemans [38], Watkins [45]	41,910
27	22	A	Chelsea	W 2-1	0-1	7	Asensio 2 [57, 89]	42,423
28	25	A	Crystal Palace	L 1-4	0-1	10	Rogers [52]	24,712
29	Mar 8	A	Brentford	W 1-0	0-0	7	Watkins [49]	17,171
30	Apr 2	A	Brighton & HA	W 3-0	0-0	7	Rashford [51], Asensio [78], Malen [90]	31,230
31	5	H	Nottingham F	W 2-1	2-0	6	Rogers [13], Malen [15]	42,743
32	12	A	Southampton	W 3-0	0-0	5	Watkins [73], Malen [79], McGinn [90]	30,673
33	19	H	Newcastle U	W 4-1	1-1	6	Watkins [1], Maatsen [64], Burn (og) [73], Onana [75]	42,618
34	22	A	Manchester C	L 1-2	1-1	7	Rashford (pen) [18]	52,192
35	May 3	H	Fulham	W 1-0	1-0	7	Tielemans [12]	42,515
36	10	A	Bournemouth	W 1-0	1-0	6	Watkins [45]	11,248
37	16	H	Tottenham H	W 2-0	0-0	5	Konsa [59], Kamara [73]	42,239
38	25	A	Manchester U	L 0-2	0-0	6		73,839

Final League Position: 6

GOALSCORERS

League (58): Watkins 16 (2 pens), Rogers 8, Duran 7, Asensio 3, Barkley 3, Malen 3, Onana 3, Tielemans 3, Konsa 2, Rashford 2 (1 pen), Bailey 1, Cash 1, Kamara 1, Maatsen 1, McGinn 1, Ramsey 1, own goals 2.
FA Cup (9): Asensio 2, Ramsey 2, Rashford 2 (1 pen), Rogers 2, Onana 1.
Carabao Cup (3): Duran 2 (1 pen), Buendia 1.
(Aston Villa U21) Vertu Trophy (6): Buendia 2, Pierre 2, Jimoh 1, Mulley 1.
Champions League (23): Rogers 4, Asensio 3 (1 pen), Duran 3, McGinn 3, Tielemans 2, Bailey 1, Barkley 1, Konsa 1, Maatsen 1, Onana 1, Ramsey 1, Watkins 1, own goal 1.

Martinez D 37	Cash M 24 + 3	Konsa E 33 + 1	Torres P 23 + 1	Digne L 28 + 4	Onana A 20 + 6	Tielemans Y 35 + 1	Bailey L 14 + 10	Rogers M 37	McGinn J 27 + 7	Watkins O 31 + 7	Duran J 4 + 16	Ramsey J 19 + 10	Philogene-Bidace J 2 + 9	Maatsen I 10 + 19	Nedeljkovic K — + 5	Barkley R 3 + 17	Bogarde L 5 + 3	Emi B — + 12	Diego Carlos S 8 + 2	Kamara B 20 + 6	Olsen R 1 + 3	Mings T 12 + 2	Malen D 2 + 12	Garcia A 5 + 2	Disasi A 5 + 2	Rashford M 4 + 6	Asensio M 9 + 4	Match No.
1	2^5	3	4	5^3	6	7	8^4	9	10^2	11^1	12	13	14	15	16													1
1	2^1	3	4	5^5	7^4	8	6	10	9^5	11^2	13	14		16	12	15												2
1		3	4	5	7^3	8	6^1	10	9	11^2	13	12^5		16	15	14	2^4											3
1		3	4	5^2	6^1	7		9	8^5	11^4	13	10^3	16	14		12	2	15										4
1		2	4	5^1	6^3	7	12	9	8^2	11^5	15	10^4		13		14		16	3									5
1		2	4	5^5	6	7^3	8^2	9^1		11^4	13	10	12	16		14		15	3									6
1	2	3^1	4	5^3		7	8^2	9		11	13	10	14			6			12									7
1	2		4	5	6^3	7	8^1	9^4	15	11^2	14	10^5	12^4		13		16	3										8
1	2	3	4	5^3	7^1	8	14	10^2	6^4	11^5	13	9		15	12				16									9
1	2^1	3	4	5	6	7^5	16	9^2	8^4	11	13	10^3	15					12	14									10
1	2	4	5^4	6^5	7	8^2	9	12	11^3	13	10^1	14	16				3	15										11
1	12		4	14		7	8^4	9^5	10^3	11	13		15	5^2		6	2^1	16	3									12
1^1	2	3	4	5		7	15	9^3	10	11^5	14		8^4		13		16		6^2	12								13
1	2	3		5		7	8^2	10^4	9^5	11^3	13		12	16		14		15	6^3		4							14
1	2	4	15			7^2	8^3	10	9	12	11^1		13	5^4		14			3	6								15
1	8	2	4	5^4	13	7^2		9	10	12	11^1			15		14			3	6^3								16
1	2	3	4	5	7	9		10^2	8	12	11^1			15					13	6								17
1	2^3	3	4	5	7	9^1	15	10^4	8^6	12	11^1			14	13		16		6^2									18
1	2	4^1	5^4	14	7^3	8^2	10	9	11	13		16		15				3	6^5		12							19
1	2	3		5^3		9	8		10^1	11		12		13		7^2		14	6	4								20
1	2	3		5	7	9		8		11		10^1					12		6	4								21
1	2	3		13	7^1	9	15	8		11^3	14	10^4		5^2		12			6	4								22
1	2	3		5		6	8^2	9^4	16	11^3	14	10^6		12			15		7		4^1	13						23
1		3		5^1	12	7	14	8	9	11^3		10^4		15	16		6^5		4		13	2^2						24
1				5^3		7		9	6	11		10^2		14					4^1		12	8^4	2	3	13	15		25
1	12			5^4		7		8	6^5	11		13		15		16					4	14	2^3	3	10^1	9^2		26
1	2^3	3			7	15	8^5	6	11^4		10^1		5	13				4			4^2	16	14		12	9		27
1^1		3		8^6	7	13	9	6	10^4		11^3	16				4				12			5^2	2	14	15		28
	12	3		5		7	8^1	9^4	6^2	11		10^3							13	1	4	15		2	14			29
1	2^4	3	4	5	14	7^3		8^6	9	13		10^1							6			16		15	11^2	12		30
1		12			6^4	7		10	16	11^2	14		5						15		4	8^3	2^1	3	13	9^6		31
1	2^4	3			6^5	7		8^3	14	12		10^1		5					16		4	13	15		11^2	9		32
1	2	3			13	7		8^4	10^3	11^5		12		5	14				6^3		4	15			16	9^1		33
1	2^1	3	4	5	7^4	9		8^6	12	15		10^2							6			16		13	11^3	14		34
1	2	3	4	15	13	7^5		10	8^2	11^3		12		5^4	16				6			14				9^1		35
1	2	3	12	5	7			8^3	13	11		10^4	14						6		4^2					9^1		36
1	2	3	4		7^2		14	8	10^3	11^1				5	13				6			12				9		37
1^1	2	3	4		7^3	13		8^5	10^2	11		14		5	15				6^4	12		16				9^1		38

FA Cup

Third Round	West Ham U	(h)	2-1
Fourth Round	Tottenham H	(h)	2-1
Fifth Round	Cardiff C	(h)	2-0
Quarter-Final	Preston NE	(a)	3-0
Semi-Final	Crystal Palace (Wembley)		0-3

Carabao Cup

Third Round	Wycombe W	(a)	2-1
Fourth Round	Crystal Palace	(h)	1-2

Vertu Trophy (Aston Villa U21)

Group D (N)	Fleetwood T	(a)	3-2
Group D (N)	Bolton W	(a)	1-1

Aston Villa U21 won 4-1 on penalties.

Group D (N)	Barrow	(a)	0-3
Second Round	Blackpool	(a)	1-1

Aston Villa U21 won 18-17 on penalties.

Third Round	Bradford C	(h)	1-3

Champions League

League game	Young Boys	(a)	3-0
League game	Bayern Munich	(h)	1-0
League game	Bologna	(h)	2-0
League game	Club Brugge	(a)	0-1
League game	Juventus	(h)	0-0
League game	RB Leipzig	(a)	3-2
League game	Monaco	(a)	0-1
League game	Celtic	(h)	4-2
Round of 16 1st leg	Club Brugge	(a)	3-1
Round of 16 2nd leg	Club Brugge	(h)	3-0
Quarter-Final 1st leg	Paris Saint-Germain	(a)	1-3
Quarter-Final 2nd leg	Paris Saint-Germain	(h)	3-2

BARNSLEY

FOUNDATION

Many clubs owe their inception to the Church and Barnsley are among them, for they were formed in 1887 by the Rev. T. T. Preedy, curate of Barnsley St Peter's, and went under that name until it was dropped in 1897 a year before being admitted to the Second Division of the Football League.

Oakwell Stadium, Grove Street, Barnsley, South Yorkshire S71 1ET.

Telephone: (01226) 211 211.

Ticket Office: (01226) 211 183.

Website: www.barnsleyfc.co.uk

Email: administration@barnsleyfc.co.uk

Ground Capacity: 23,240.

Record Attendance: 40,255 v Stoke C, FA Cup 5th rd, 15 February 1936.

Pitch Measurements: 100.5m × 68.5m (110yd × 75yd).

Chairman: Neerav Paarekh.

Chief Executive: Jon Flatman.

Head Coach: Conor Hourihane.

Assistant Head Coach: Richard Keogh.

HONOURS

League Champions: Division 3N – 1933–34, 1938–39, 1954–55.
Runners-up: First Division – 1996–97; FL 1 – 2018–19; Division 3 – 1980–81; Division 3N – 1953–54; Division 4 – 1967–68.

FA Cup Winners: 1912.
Runners-up: 1910.

League Cup: quarter-final – 1982.

League Trophy Winners: 2016.

Colours: Red shirts with 21 stars on the chest and white trim, red shorts, red socks with white trim.

Year Formed: 1887.

Turned Professional: 1888.

Previous Name: 1887, Barnsley St Peter's; 1897, Barnsley.

Club Nicknames: 'The Tykes'; 'The Reds'; 'The Colliers'.

Ground: 1887, Oakwell.

First Football League Game: 1 September 1898, Division 2, v Lincoln C (a) L 0–1 – Fawcett; McArtney, Nixon; King, Burleigh, Porteous; Davis, Lees, Murray, McCullough, McGee.

Record League Victory: 9–0 v Loughborough T, Division 2, 28 January 1899 – Greaves; McArtney, Nixon; Porteous, Burleigh, Howard; Davis (4), Hepworth (1), Lees (1), McCullough (1), Jones (2). 9–0 v Accrington S, Division 3 (N), 3 February 1934 – Ellis; Cookson, Shotton; Harper, Henderson, Whitworth; Spence (2), Smith (1), Blight (4), Andrews (1), Ashton (1).

Record Cup Victory: 6–0 v Blackpool, FA Cup 1st rd replay, 20 January 1910 – Mearns; Downs, Ness; Glendinning, Boyle (1), Utley; Bartrop, Gadsby (1), Lillycrop (2), Tufnell (2), Forman. 6–0 v Peterborough U, League Cup 1st rd 2nd leg, 15 September 1981 – Horn; Joyce, Chambers, Glavin (2), Banks, McCarthy, Evans, Parker (2), Aylott (1), McHale, Barrowclough (1).

Record Defeat: 0–9 v Notts Co, Division 2, 19 November 1927.

Most League Points (2 for a win): 67, Division 3 (N), 1938–39.

Most League Points (3 for a win): 91, FL 1, 2018–19.

FOOTBALL YEARBOOK FACT FILE

Barnsley struggled for much of the 2015–16 season and after drawing 1-1 at home to Sheffield United on 28 November they were bottom of the League One table. However, they then went on a run which saw them win eight of the next nine games and they finished the season in sixth place, taking them to the play-offs. Victory over Millwall at Wembley in the play-off final saw them promoted to the Championship.

Most League Goals: 118, Division 3 (N), 1933–34.

Highest League Scorer in Season: Cecil McCormack, 33, Division 2, 1950–51.

Most League Goals in Total Aggregate: Ernest Hine, 123, 1921–26 and 1934–38.

Most League Goals in One Match: 5, Frank Eaton v South Shields, Division 3 (N), 9 April 1927; 5, Peter Cunningham v Darlington, Division 3 (N), 4 February 1933; 5, Beau Asquith v Darlington, Division 3 (N), 12 November 1938; 5, Cecil McCormack v Luton T, Division 2, 9 September 1950.

Most Capped Player: Gerry Taggart, 35 (51), Northern Ireland.

Most League Appearances: Barry Murphy, 514, 1962–78.

Youngest League Player: Reuben Noble-Lazarus, 15 years 45 days v Ipswich T, 30 September 2008.

Record Transfer Fee Received: £3,000,000 (potentially rising to £10,125,000) from Everton for John Stones, January 2013.

Record Transfer Fee Paid: £1,500,000 to Partizan Belgrade for Georgi Hristov, July 1997; £1,500,000 to QPR for Mike Sheron, January 1999.

Football League Record: 1898 Elected to Division 2; 1898–1932 Division 2; 1932–34 Division 3 (N); 1934–38 Division 2; 1938–39 Division 3 (N); 1946–53 Division 2; 1953–55 Division 3 (N); 1955–59 Division 3; 1959–65 Division 3; 1965–68 Division 4; 1968–72 Division 3; 1972–79 Division 4; 1979–81 Division 3; 1981–92 Division 2; 1992–97 First Division; 1997–98 Premier League; 1998–2002 First Division; 2002–04 Second Division; 2004–06 FL 1; 2006–14 FL C; 2014–16 FL 1; 2016–18 FL C; 2018–19 FL 1; 2019–22 FL C; 2022– FL 1.

LATEST SEQUENCES

Longest Sequence of League Wins: 10, 5.3.1955 – 23.4.1955.

Longest Sequence of League Defeats: 9, 14.3.1953 – 25.4.1953.

Longest Sequence of League Draws: 7, 28.3.1911 – 22.4.1911.

Longest Sequence of Unbeaten League Matches: 21, 1.1.1934 – 5.5.1934.

Longest Sequence Without a League Win: 26, 13.12.1952 – 26.8.1953.

Successive Scoring Runs: 44 from 2.10.1926.

Successive Non-scoring Runs: 6 from 27.11.1971.

MANAGERS

Arthur Fairclough 1898–1901 (*Secretary-Manager*)
John McCartney 1901–04 (*Secretary-Manager*)
Arthur Fairclough 1904–12
John Hastie 1912–14
Percy Lewis 1914–19
Peter Sant 1919–26
John Commins 1926–29
Arthur Fairclough 1929–30
Brough Fletcher 1930–37
Angus Seed 1937–53
Tim Ward 1953–60
Johnny Steele 1960–71 (*continued as General Manager*)
John McSeveney 1971–72
Johnny Steele (*General Manager*) 1972–73
Jim Iley 1973–78
Allan Clarke 1978–80
Norman Hunter 1980–84
Bobby Collins 1984–85
Allan Clarke 1985–89
Mel Machin 1989–93
Viv Anderson 1993–94
Danny Wilson 1994–98
John Hendrie 1998–99
Dave Bassett 1999–2000
Nigel Spackman 2001
Steve Parkin 2001–02
Glyn Hodges 2002–03
Gudjon Thordarson 2003–04
Paul Hart 2004–05
Andy Ritchie 2005–06
Simon Davey 2007–09 (*Caretaker from November 2006*)
Mark Robins 2009–11
Keith Hill 2011–12
David Flitcroft 2012–13
Danny Wilson 2013–15
Lee Johnson 2015–16
Paul Heckingbottom 2016–18
Jose Morais 2018
Daniel Stendel 2018–19
Gerhard Struber 2019–20
Valerien Ismael 2020–21
Markus Schopp 2021
Poya Asbaghi 2021–22
Michael Duff 2022–23
Neill Collins 2023–24
Darrell Clarke 2024–25
Conor Hourihane April 2025–

TEN YEAR LEAGUE RECORD

		P	W	D	L	F	A	Pts	Pos
2015-16	FL 1	46	22	8	16	70	54	74	6
2016-17	FL C	46	15	13	18	64	67	58	14
2017-18	FL C	46	9	14	23	48	72	41	22
2018-19	FL 1	46	26	13	7	80	39	91	2
2019-20	FL C	46	12	13	21	49	69	49	21
2020-21	FL C	46	23	9	14	58	50	78	5
2021-22	FL C	46	6	12	28	33	73	30	24
2022-23	FL 1	46	26	8	12	80	47	86	4
2023-24	FL 1	46	21	13	12	82	64	76	6
2024-25	FL 1	46	17	10	19	69	73	61	12

DID YOU KNOW ?

Winger Dickie Jones became the first player to score a Football League hat-trick for Barnsley, achieving the feat on 14 January 1899 when Small Heath were defeated 7-2 at Oakwell. Jones had previously been on the books of Sheffield United but joined the Tykes from Merseyside club White Star Wanderers.

BARNSLEY – SKY BET LEAGUE ONE 2024–25 LEAGUE RECORD

Match No.	Date	Venue	Opponents	Result	H/T Score	Lg Pos.	Goalscorers	Attendance
1	Aug 9	H	Mansfield T	L 1-2	1-2	2	Connell [33]	14,817
2	17	A	Lincoln C	W 2-1	1-0	13	Cosgrove [13], Roberts [47]	9768
3	24	H	Northampton T	D 2-2	1-0	9	Watters [26], Phillips [46]	11,248
4	31	A	Crawley T	W 3-0	3-0	7	Pines [12], Phillips 2 (1 pen) [23, 45 (p)]	4704
5	Sept 7	H	Bristol R	W 2-1	1-1	3	Keillor-Dunn [11], Phillips [65]	11,196
6	14	A	Stevenage	L 0-3	0-0	7		4206
7	21	A	Burton Alb	W 2-1	1-0	3	Connell [36], Humphrys [90]	3711
8	28	H	Stockport Co	D 1-1	1-0	5	Phillips (pen) [4]	14,882
9	Oct 1	H	Wycombe W	D 2-2	0-0	7	Humphrys [58], Roberts [89]	9857
10	5	A	Huddersfield T	L 0-2	0-0	11		19,523
11	19	A	Blackpool	W 2-1	1-0	8	Keillor-Dunn [27], Roberts [90]	10,565
12	22	H	Charlton Ath	D 2-2	1-0	8	Keillor-Dunn [34], Watters [90]	12,441
13	26	A	Shrewsbury T	W 2-0	1-0	7	Russell [45], Watters [47]	6129
14	Nov 8	H	Rotherham U	W 2-0	1-0	4	Russell [32], Humphrys [86]	14,731
15	16	A	Cambridge U	D 1-1	1-1	5	Humphrys [17]	6817
16	23	H	Wigan Ath	L 0-1	0-1	6		11,438
17	26	H	Reading	D 2-2	1-0	6	Keillor-Dunn [7], Earl [72]	10,011
18	Dec 3	A	Wrexham	L 0-1	0-0	8		12,386
19	7	H	Birmingham C	L 1-2	0-0	8	Paik (og) [58]	15,367
20	14	A	Exeter C	W 2-1	0-1	7	Nwakali [49], Keillor-Dunn [58]	5669
21	21	H	Leyton Orient	L 0-4	0-2	9		11,373
22	26	A	Bolton W	W 2-1	0-1	7	Keillor-Dunn [80], Phillips [89]	22,215
23	29	A	Peterborough U	W 3-1	0-0	7	Pines [47], Keillor-Dunn [55], Russell [86]	9404
24	Jan 1	H	Wrexham	W 2-1	2-0	6	Keillor-Dunn [11], Phillips [24]	15,248
25	4	H	Crawley T	W 3-0	1-0	5	Russell [11], Watters [51], Keillor-Dunn [54]	11,016
26	18	A	Bristol R	L 1-3	0-1	5	Earl [67]	7638
27	25	H	Stevenage	L 0-1	0-0	6		10,831
28	28	A	Wycombe W	L 1-2	1-0	9	Russell [10]	3803
29	Feb 1	H	Burton Alb	D 0-0	0-0	10		10,555
30	8	A	Stockport Co	L 1-2	0-2	10	Keillor-Dunn [90]	10,148
31	15	H	Huddersfield T	L 1-2	1-0	10	Russell [14]	15,600
32	22	H	Rotherham U	W 1-0	0-0	10	Phillips (pen) [52]	10,755
33	25	A	Northampton T	W 2-1	1-0	10	Keillor-Dunn 2 [36, 59]	5817
34	Mar 1	H	Lincoln C	W 4-3	2-0	10	Keillor-Dunn [13], Phillips [33], Gent [53], Watters [76]	11,914
35	4	A	Charlton Ath	L 0-1	0-1	10		12,707
36	8	H	Blackpool	L 0-3	0-0	10		11,563
37	15	H	Mansfield T	L 1-2	0-1	10	Benson [54]	8592
38	22	H	Cambridge U	D 1-1	0-1	11	Lewis [90]	10,790
39	29	A	Wigan Ath	D 1-1	1-0	11	Keillor-Dunn [8]	10,942
40	Apr 1	H	Exeter C	L 1-2	0-1	11	Humphrys [58]	10,092
41	5	A	Birmingham C	L 2-6	1-1	12	Keillor-Dunn [35], Humphrys [59]	25,018
42	12	H	Bolton W	W 4-1	2-0	11	Russell 2 [15, 86], Jalo 2 [25, 71]	13,685
43	18	A	Leyton Orient	L 3-4	2-0	12	Humphrys 2 [11, 19], Keillor-Dunn [64]	8410
44	21	H	Peterborough U	D 1-1	1-1	12	Russell [45]	11,049
45	26	H	Shrewsbury T	L 1-2	0-1	12	Russell [78]	11,159
46	May 3	A	Reading	W 4-2	0-0	12	Humphrys [52], Russell [57], Keillor-Dunn 2 [79, 85]	21,481

Final League Position: 12

GOALSCORERS
League (69): Keillor-Dunn 18, Russell 11, Humphrys 9, Phillips 9 (3 pens), Watters 5, Roberts 3, Connell 2, Earl 2, Jalo 2, Pines 2, Benson 1, Cosgrove 1, Gent 1, Lewis 1, Nwakali 1, own goal 1.
FA Cup (3): Keillor-Dunn 1, Phillips 1 (1 pen), Roberts 1.
Carabao Cup (2): Pines 1, Watters 1.
Vertu Trophy (3): Yoganathan 2, Marsh 1.

Killip B 17	Durand de Gevigney M 39	Roberts M 35 + 2	Earl J 34	O'Keeffe C 35 + 6	Craig M 10 + 4	Phillips A 34 + 2	Connell L 37 + 4	Gent G 19 + 6	Watters M 18 + 12	Cosgrove S 8 + 11	Russell J 34 + 6	Marsh A —+7	Hourihane C 1 + 1	Cotter B 14 + 7	Lofthouse K 3 + 15	Slonina G 11	Pines D 17 + 7	Yoganathan V 1 + 4	Keillor-Dunn D 42	Benson J 2 + 12	Humphrys S 26 + 11	Jalo F 5 + 11	Nwakali K 12 + 11	McCarthy C 16 + 4	Farrugia N 6 + 3	Gauci J 7	Rodrigues C 2 + 4	Lembikisa D 3 + 9	Lewis J —+5	Dyer J —+1	Smith J 5 + 1	Barratt C 1 + 4	McCann B —+1	Flavell K 6 + 1	Bland J 6 + 3	Graham K —+1	Match No.
1	2	3	4	5²	6³	7	8⁵	9¹	10⁴	11	12	13	14	15	16																						1
1	2	3	4	5⁵	6⁴	7¹	8	9	10⁵	11	12	13	14	15																							2
1	2	3	4	5⁴	6²	7	8¹	9	10	11³	12	13	14	15																							3
1	2	3³	4	5	6	7	8	9	10¹	11²	12	13	14																								4
1	2	3¹	4	5	6	7³	8²	9	10⁴	11	12	13	14	15																							5
1	2	3¹	4	5	6³	7²	8	9	10⁵	11⁴	12	13	14	15	16																						6
1	2	3	4	5	6	7	8	9³	10²	11¹	12	13⁴	14	15																							7
1	2	3	4	5⁴	6⁵	7	8¹	9	10³	11²	12	13	14	15	16																						8
1	2	3	4¹	5	6	7	8	9²	10³	11	12	13	14																								9
1	2	3	4	5³	6⁵	7	8²	9¹	10⁴	11	12	13	14	15	16																						10
1	2	3	4	5¹	6	7²	8	9³	10⁴	11	12	13	14	15																							11
1	2	3	4	5	6¹	7²	8	9	10³	11⁴	12	13	14	15																							12
1	2	3	4	5	6⁴	7	8²	9³	10	11¹	12	13	14	15																							13
1	2	3	4	5	6	7²	8	9	10	11¹	12	13																									14
1	2	3	4	5	6	7	8	9	10¹	11	12																										15
1	2	3	4	5³	6¹	7⁵	8²	9⁴	10	11	12	13	14	15	16																						16
1	2	3	4	5²	6	7	8	9³	10	11¹	12	13	14																								17
1	2	3	4	5³	6	7	8	9²	10¹	11⁴	12	13	14	15																							18
1	2	3¹	4	5⁴	6⁴	7	8	9	10⁵	11²	12³	13	14	15	16																						19
1	2	3	4	5⁴	6¹	7	8	9	10³	11²	12	13	14																								20
1	2	3	4¹	5³	6	7	8²	9	10	11⁴	12	13	14	15																							21
1	2	3	4	5	6⁴	7²	8	9³	10¹	11	12	13	14	15																							22
1	2	3	4	5	6³	7	8	9²	10¹	11⁴	12	13	14	15																							23
1	2	3	4²	5	6	7	8	9⁴	10¹	11³	12	13	14	15																							24
1	2	3²	4¹	5	6	7	8³	9	10⁴	11⁵	12	13	14	15	16																						25
1	2	3	4	5⁴	6	7²	8	9³	10⁵	11¹	12	13	14	15	16																						26
1	2	3	4	5	6²	7	8³	9¹	10	11	12	13	14																								27
1	2	3⁸	4	5	6	7	8²	9	10³	11¹	12	13	14																								28
1	2	3	4	5	6	7²	8	9¹	10	11	12	13																									29
	2	3	4	5	6	7	8	9		11	12	13							10¹							1											30
1	2	3	4	5²	6	7	8³	9¹		11	12	13	14	15					10⁴																		31
	2	3	4	5	6	7⁴	8	9¹		11²	12	13	14	15			10									1³											32
1	2⁸	3	4	5	6³	7	8	9¹		11⁴	12	13	14	15			10²									5											33
	3	4		6¹		7²	8	9⁵		11⁴	13	14		16			10³			5	2							15			12						34
	3	4¹	6	5		7³	8⁵	9⁴		11	14	13		16			10²				2							15			12						35
	3		5			7²	8⁶	9		11¹	13						10		12	6	4		8⁴	14						1	2³	15					36
	2	3³		9	6	7	8⁶				13						10	5⁴	11²			4	15						16		1¹	14		12			37
	2			8		9⁵	7⁴	10¹		14			3²				11	5¹	13	15	6	4							16					1	12		38
	2	3		8		12	11²	7									9		13	10¹	6	4						14			1	5³				39
	2⁴	3		8		12	13	7									10		11	9	6²	4		15			14			1	5¹					40
	2⁸	3		8³		5²	6⁵	10¹		7							11		9⁴	13	16	4		14	15						1	12					41
	3			5²	12	6	7				8		14				10		11¹	9³	4		13				1	2									42
	3			5	14	9⁴	6				7		13				11	15	10¹	8²	4		12				1	2³									43
	2	3	4			10	7	12		8			9²				11			6¹			5							13							44
	3	4	5			7	8²	12		9			10				11			13			1						6¹			2					45
	3	4	5	12		13	7²	14		8			9³				10⁴			11¹			1						2						6	15	46

BARROW

FOUNDATION

Barrow was home to a number of junior soccer clubs at the start of the twentieth century before a public meeting was called to set up a senior team in the town. Almost 800 people attended the meeting held in the Drill Hall on the night of Tuesday 16 July 1901 which resulted in the formation of Barrow Association Football Club. A team was put together made up, in the main, of seasoned professionals, some of whom were described as 'bordering the veteran stage', and £300 was spent on laying out the club's new ground. The newly formed Barrow AFC were elected to the Lancashire League for the 1901–02 season and after making a promising start they eventually finished 10th out of 14 clubs.

The So Legal Stadium, Wilkie Road, Barrow-in-Furness, Cumbria LA14 5UW.

Telephone: (01229) 666 010.

Ticket Office: (01229) 666 010.

Website: www.barrowafc.com

Email: office@barrowafc.com

Ground Capacity: 6,309.

Record Attendance: 16,854 v Swansea T, FA Cup 3rd rd, 9 January 1954.

Pitch Measurements: 100.5m × 68m (110yd × 74.5yd).

Chairman: Paul Hornby.

Chief Executive: Iain Wood.

Head Coach: Andy Whing.

Assistant Head Coach: Craig Pead.

Colours: White shirts with blue trim, blue shorts with white trim, white socks with blue trim.

Year Formed: 1901.

Turned Professional: 1908.

Club Nickname: 'The Bluebirds'.

Grounds: 1901, The Strawberry Ground; 1904, Ainslie Street; 1905, Little Park, Roose; 1909, Holker Street (renamed The Progression Solicitors Stadium 2019; The Dunes Hotel Stadium 2021; The So Legal Stadium 2022).

First Football League Game (since 2020): 12 September 2020, FL, v Lincoln C (a) L 0–1 – Dixon; Barry, Jones J, Hird, Ntlhe, Brown (Wilson), Jones M, Hardcastle, Beadling (Biggins), Hindle (James), Angus (1 pen).

Record League Victory: 12–1 v Gateshead, Division 3(N), 5 May 1934.

Record Cup Victory: 8–0 v Annfield Plain, FA Cup 3rd qual rd, 1982.

Record League Defeat: 1–10 v Hartlepools U, Division 4, 4 April 1966–67.

HONOURS

League Champions: National League – 2019–20.
FA Cup: 3rd rd – 1946, 1948, 1954, 1956, 1959, 1964, 1967, 1968, 1991, 2009, 2010, 2017, 2022.
League Cup: 3rd rd – 1963, 1968, 2925.
FA Trophy Winners: 1989–90, 2009–10.

FOOTBALL YEARBOOK FACT FILE

Barrow played their first-ever match against Blackpool at the Strawberry Grounds, their original home, on 2 September 1901. The Bluebirds won the exhibition game 3-1 thanks to goals from Thomas Hall (2) and George Hammond in front of a crowd estimated at 4,000. The match was one of a series of friendlies played against Football League sides to boost interest in the new club as it sought to establish itself in a predominantly rugby town.

Most League Points (2 for a win): 59, Division 4, 1966–67.

Most League Points (3 for a win): 69, FL 2, 2023–24.

Most League Goals: 116, Division 3(N), 1933–34.

Highest League Scorer in Season: 39, Jimmy Shankly, Division 3(N), 1933–34.

Most League Goals in One Match: 5, Jimmy Shankly v Gateshead, Division 3(N), 5 May 1934.

Most League Goals in Total Aggregate: Billy Gordon, 145, 1949–58.

Most Capped Player: Harry Panayiotou, 5 (39), St Kitts & Nevis.

Most League Appearances: Brian Arrowsmith, 378, 1952–71.

Youngest League Player (since 2020): Jayden Reid, 19 years 181 days v Bolton W, 20 October 2020.

Record Transfer Fee Received: £100,000 from Rochdale for Jordan Williams, June 2017.

Record Transfer Fee Paid: Undisclosed to Fleetwood T for Gerard Garner, January 2023.

Football League Record: 1921 Original Member of Division 3 (N); 1921–58 Division 3 (N); 1958–67 Division 4; 1967–70 Division 3; 1970–72 Division 4; 1972 Failed to gain re-election to Football League and joined Northern Premier League; 2020 Promoted from National League; 2020– FL 2.

LATEST SEQUENCES

Longest Sequence of League Wins: 7, 31.10.2023 – 22.12.2023.

Longest Sequence of League Defeats: 5, 24.11.2020 – 15.12.2020.

Longest Sequence of League Draws: 3, 7.10.2023 – 21.10.2023.

Longest Sequence of Unbeaten League Matches: 14, 7.10.2023 – 29.12.2023.

Longest Sequence Without a League Win: 9, 12.10.2024 – 14.12.2024.

Successive Scoring Runs: 15 from 31.10.2023.

Successive Non-scoring Runs: 4 from 13.11.2021.

MANAGERS

Jacob Fletcher 1901–04; **E. Freeland** 1904–05; **W. Smith** 1905–06; **Alec Craig** 1906–07; **Roger Charnley** 1907–08; **Jacob Fletcher** 1908–09; **Jas P. Phillips** 1909–13; **John Parker** 1913–20; **William Dickinson** 1920–22; **Jimmy Atkinson** 1922–23; **J. E. Moralee** 1923–26; **Robert Greenhalgh** 1926; **William Dickinson** 1926–27; **John S. Maconnachie** 1927–28; **Andrew Walker** 1929–30; **Thomas Miller** 1930; **John Commins** 1930–32; **Tommy Lowes** 1932–37; **James Y. Bissett** 1937; **Fred Pentland** 1938–40; **John Commins** 1945–47; **Andy Beattie** 1947–49; **Jack Hacking** 1949–55; **Joe Harvey** 1955–57; **Norman Dodgin** 1957–58; **Willie Brown** 1958–59; **Bill Rogers** 1959; **Ron Staniforth** 1959–64; **Don McEvoy** 1964–67; **Colin Appleton** 1967–69; **Fred Else** 1969; **Norman Bodell** 1969–70; **Don McEvoy** 1970–71; **Bill Rogers** 1971; **Jack Crompton** 1971–72; **Peter Kane** 1972–74; **Brian Arrowsmith** 1974–75; **Ron Yeats** 1975–77; **Alan Coglan and Billy McAdams** 1977; **David Hughes** 1977; **Brian McManus** 1977–79; **Micky Taylor** 1979–83; **Vic Halom** 1983–84; **Peter McDonnell** 1984; **Joe Wojciechowicz** 1984; **Brian Kidd** 1984–85; **John Cooke** 1985; **Bob Murphy** 1985; **Maurice Whittle** 1985; **David Johnson** 1985–86; **Glenn Skivington and Neil McDonald** 1986; **Ray Wilkie** 1986; **Neil McDonald** 1991; **John King** 1991–92; **Graham Heathcote** 1992; **Richard Dinnis** 1992–93; **Mick Cloudsdale** 1993–94; **Tony Hesketh** 1994–96; **Neil McDonald and Franny Ventre** 1996; **Mike Walsh** 1996; **Owen Brown** 1996–99; **Shane Westley** 1999; **Greg Challender** 1999; **Kenny Lowe** 1999–2003; **Lee Turnbull** 2003–05; **Darren Edmondson** 2005; **Phil Wilson** 2005–07; **Darren Sheridan and David Bayliss** 2007–12; **David Bayliss** 2012–13; **Alex Meechan** 2013; **Darren Edmondson** 2013–15; **Paul Cox** 2015–17; **Micky Moore** 2017; **Neill Hornby** 2017; **Ady Pennock** 2017–18; **Ian Evatt** 2018–20; **David Dunn** 2020; **Michael Jolly** 2020; **Mark Cooper** 2021–22; **Phil Brown** 2022; **Pete Wild** 2022–24; **Stephen Clemence** 2024–25; **Andy Whing** January 2025–

TEN YEAR LEAGUE RECORD

		P	W	D	L	F	A	Pts	Pos
2015-16	NL	46	17	14	15	64	71	65	11
2016-17	NL	46	20	15	11	72	53	75	7
2017-18	NL	46	11	16	19	51	63	49	20
2018-19	NL	46	17	13	16	52	51	64	11
2019-20	NL	37	21	7	9	68	39	70	1§
2020-21	FL 2	46	13	11	22	53	59	50	21
2021-22	FL 2	46	10	14	22	44	57	44	22
2022-23	FL 2	46	18	8	20	47	53	62	9
2023-24	FL 2	46	18	15	13	62	56	69	8
2024-25	FL 2	46	15	14	17	52	50	59	16

§*Decided on points-per-game (1.89)*

DID YOU KNOW ?

Barrow had a difficult start to life in the Football League after being elected as founder members of Division Three North for the 1921–22 season. The Bluebirds lost their first six games and were rock bottom of the table before gaining their first-ever win at home to Ashington on 8 October. Their fortunes improved and they went on to finish the campaign in a respectable mid-table position.

BARROW – SKY BET LEAGUE TWO 2024–25 LEAGUE RECORD

Match No.	Date	Venue	Opponents	Result	H/T Score	Lg Pos.	Goalscorers	Attendance
1	Aug 10	H	Crewe Alex	W	1-0	1-0	8	Vassell [22]	3585
2	17	A	Carlisle U	L	0-1	0-1	14		9813
3	24	H	Port Vale	W	4-0	0-0	3	Garner [54], Acquah [77], Spence [81], Telford [90]	3481
4	31	A	Harrogate T	W	1-0	0-0	3	Eccleston [74]	2270
5	Sept 7	H	Swindon T	D	1-1	1-0	3	Garner [35]	3763
6	14	A	Grimsby T	W	2-1	2-1	3	Foley [14], Vassell [26]	5496
7	21	H	Newport Co	W	2-0	1-0	1	Newby [27], Vassell [82]	3434
8	28	A	Gillingham	L	0-2	0-1	3		7166
9	Oct 1	A	Doncaster R	L	0-1	0-0	4		5632
10	5	H	Cheltenham T	W	2-1	0-1	3	Acquah [48], Dallas [86]	3518
11	12	H	Morecambe	L	0-1	0-0	6		4665
12	19	A	Accrington S	L	0-1	0-1	7		2354
13	22	H	Notts Co	D	1-1	1-0	8	Feely [7]	3123
14	26	A	Bromley	D	1-1	1-0	9	Garner [21]	3406
15	Nov 9	A	Colchester U	D	1-1	1-0	11	Newby [31]	3179
16	16	H	AFC Wimbledon	L	1-3	1-1	12	Dallas [44]	3227
17	23	A	Chesterfield	L	0-1	0-0	12		· 7701
18	Dec 3	A	Bradford C	D	1-1	0-0	13	Gotts [57]	14,547
19	14	A	Walsall	L	0-1	0-1	15		5109
20	21	H	Fleetwood T	W	2-0	2-0	15	Acquah [4], Vassell [10]	3007
21	26	A	Salford C	L	0-3	0-2	17		2983
22	29	A	Tranmere R	D	1-1	1-1	17	Turnbull (og) [11]	6109
23	Jan 1	H	Bradford C	D	2-2	1-1	15	Dallas (pen) [45], Acquah [78]	3918
24	4	H	Harrogate T	L	0-2	0-0	15		3148
25	18	A	Swindon T	L	0-2	0-1	17		6398
26	25	H	Grimsby T	W	3-0	1-0	16	Gotts [40], Smith [56], Vassell [85]	3661
27	29	H	Doncaster R	L	1-3	1-2	18	Acquah [45]	3009
28	Feb 1	A	Newport Co	L	0-1	0-0	18		4133
29	8	H	Gillingham	W	3-0	0-0	18	Spence 2 [60, 84], Smith [90]	3130
30	11	H	Milton Keynes D	W	2-1	1-1	18	Spence [10], Cameron [61]	2783
31	15	A	Cheltenham T	L	2-3	1-0	18	Foley [32], Whitfield [46]	4404
32	22	A	Crewe Alex	L	0-3	0-1	18		4735
33	27	H	Carlisle U	L	0-1	0-1	18		4213
34	Mar 4	A	Notts Co	W	2-1	1-0	17	Spence [10], Foley [62]	7872
35	8	H	Accrington S	W	2-0	1-0	16	Duru [14], Pressley [78]	3200
36	15	A	Morecambe	D	2-2	0-2	17	Gotts [63], Smith [73]	4351
37	22	A	AFC Wimbledon	D	2-2	0-0	17	Campbell [88], Mahoney [90]	8657
38	25	A	Port Vale	W	1-0	1-0	16	Jackson [36]	5894
39	29	H	Chesterfield	L	0-1	0-0	16		3392
40	Apr 1	H	Salford C	D	1-1	1-0	16	Smith [37]	2818
41	5	A	Milton Keynes D	W	3-0	1-0	15	Pressley 2 [16, 57], Smith [90]	6585
42	12	H	Walsall	W	2-0	1-0	15	Pressley [23], Acquah [90]	3071
43	18	A	Fleetwood T	D	0-0	0-0	15		3256
44	21	H	Tranmere R	D	0-0	0-0	14		3304
45	26	H	Bromley	D	3-3	1-0	16	Whitfield (pen) [42], Fletcher [53], Newby [85]	3137
46	May 3	A	Colchester U	D	0-0	0-0	16		7512

Final League Position: 16

GOALSCORERS

League (52): Acquah 6, Smith 5, Spence 5, Vassell 5, Pressley 4, Dallas 3 (1 pen), Foley 3, Garner 3, Gotts 3, Newby 3, Whitfield 2 (1 pen), Cameron 1, Campbell 1, Duru 1, Eccleston 1, Feely 1, Fletcher 1, Jackson 1, Mahoney 1, Telford 1, own goal 1.
FA Cup (0).
Carabao Cup (3): Acquah 1, Garner 1, Jackson 1.
Vertu Trophy (5): Dallas 2, Foley 1, Telford 1, Vassell 1.

Farman P 29	Feely R 16+3	Vassell T 30+2	Canavan N 35+1	Jackson B 43+2	Campbell D 28+5	Spence K 30+2	Mahoney C 18+11	Garner G 12+4	Newby E 35+9	Acquah E 19+20	Gotts R 39+2	Kouyate K 8+13	Dallas A 6+12	Eccleston N 7+10	Telford D 3+13	Foley S 26+8	Popov C 3+8	Worrall D —+5	Tiensia J 3+5	Stanway W 17	Stokes C 12+1	Weston C —+1	Kirk C 3+4	Ogungbo M —+1	Cameron K 16+1	Fletcher I 6+5	Duru L 7+1	Pressley A 15+6	Smith T 11+10	Williams M 16+2	Whitfield B 13+4	Barnes S —+4	Match No.
1	2	3	4	5	6	7		8^2	9^1	10^4	11^3	12	13	14	15																		1
1		3	4	5	7	9	6	12	10^1	11^2	8^3	13	15		2^4	14																	2
1	2^2	3	4	5	6	9^9	8^1	11^3	12	14	7	10^4			13	15	16																3
1		3	4	5	6	9		11^2		12^3	7	10^1	14	2		8^4	13	15															4
1^*	12	3	4	5	6	9		11^3	8^2		7^4	10^1	13	2		15	14																5
	2	3	4	5	6	9^3		11^2	10	14		12		13	7	8^1			1														6
1	2	3		5	6	9^4		11^1	10^3	12		8^2		13	15	7	14				4												7
	2^1	3		5	7		11^4	10^2	9^3		12		8	14	6	13	15			1	4												8
14	3		5	7		11^1	8^3	12		10^2	16	2		9^4	6	13				1	4^5	15											9
2^4	3		5	7	6		10	11^2		12	13	15	14	9^3	8^1					1	4												10
2^2	3		5	7	9		11^3	8	12	16	10^4	15	13	14	6^1					1	4^5												11
2^3	3		5	6	9		12	13	10^4	8^1		11^2	15	14	7^5	16				1	4												12
	2	3	15	5	7^3	9		11^1	8^4		6	10^2		12	13	14				1	4												13
	2	3	4	5	7	9	13	11^3	8		6^1	10^2		12						1	14												14
15	3	4	5	7	9^3	8^2		10		6		12	2^4	11^1		14				1			13										15
1		3	4	5	7		8^2	10		6	13	11	2	12									9^1										16
1	2	3	5^3	7		9		8		6	12	11^1		14				13		4^2		10											17
1	2	3	4	6	8	12	14		10^2	13	7	11^3								5		9^1											18
1	2^3	3	4	6	9	8	15	10^1	14	11^2	7^4	13						5				12											19
1	2	3		5	7	9^4	8^3		10^2	11^1	6		12		14	13		15		4													20
1	2	3		5^3		9^5	8^2	10^4	11	6		12		14	7^1	13		15		4	16												21
1	2	3		9			6	11	8		12	13	10^1	7		5		4^2															22
1	2^1	3^5		8			9^2	14	5	11^4	7	13	10^3	12	15	6		4						16									23
1		2	3	8		6	9	14	5^4	10^3	7		11^2	12									15		4^1	13							24
1		3	4	9		5	14	13	10^1	8		6^3												7^2	2	11	12						25
1		3	4	6	13	7			12	9													5	2	10^1	11^2	8						26
1		3	2	9^4	15	6	14	13	10	8				12									4^1	5^2	16	11^3	7^5						27
1		3	4	6	9^4	7^1	12	13	11^3	10													5	2^2	14	15	8						28
		3	5	8	9^2		6	12	7		2	13													11^1	14	4	10^3					29
		3	5	9		6	12	8		2												4	11^1	13	7	10^2							30
	14	3	8	9^3	16	5^4	12	7		2^5									4	15	10^1	13	6	11^2									31
	2^3	3^1	8	15	9^4	5^5	12	6		14	16								4		10^1	13	7	11^2									32
1		4	5	8^2		13	10^1	9		2									3		12	11	6	7									33
1		3	12	6		8	14	7		2											5	10^3	11^1	4	9^2	13							34
1		3	13	12	6	8	7		2												5^2	10^1	11^1	4	9^3	14							35
1		3		12	6	14	8	13^3	7		2											5^1	11^3	10	4	9^2								36
1		3	5	12	6^4	15	8	14	7^2		2										4	13	11	10^3		9^1								37
1		3	5	7	6^1	10^2	9	11^3	8		2										4		14	13	12								38
		3	5	7		6^1	14	13	8^5	16	12									1			4^4	15	11^2	10	2	9^3					39
		3	5	7		14	8	11^3	6		2										1			4	12	13	10^1		9^2					40
		3	5	7^5		10^2	9	15	8	16	2^3									1			4	6^1	11^4	14		13	12				41
		3	5	7		10^2	9	14	8^3		2									1			4	6^1	11		12	13					42
		3	5^1	7		10^3		9^4	11^2	6	15	2								1			14	13	12	4	8						43
	2^4	3	5		12		9^2	14	8		15									1			4	6	11^3	10^1	7	13					44
	16	3	8		9^3		13	12	7	14	6									1			4	10^4	11^1	15	2^5	5^1					45
		3	5		9^5		8^1	10^3	6	14	2^2	15								1			13^8	7		11^4	4	12	16					46

FA Cup

First Round	Doncaster R	(h)	0-1

Carabao Cup

First Round	Port Vale	(h)	3-2
Second Round	Derby Co	(h)	0-0

Barrow won 3-2 on penalties.

Third Round	Chelsea	(a)	0-5

Vertu Trophy

Group D (N)	Bolton W	(h)	2-3
Group D (N)	Fleetwood T	(a)	0-3
Group D (N)	Aston Villa U21	(h)	3-0

BIRMINGHAM CITY

In 1875, cricketing enthusiasts who were largely members of Trinity Church, Bordesley, determined to continue their sporting relationships throughout the year by forming a football club which they called Small Heath Alliance. For their earliest games played on waste land in Arthur Street, the team included three Edden brothers and two James brothers.

St Andrew's @ Knighthead Park, Cattell Road, Birmingham B9 4RL.

Telephone: (0121) 772 0101.

Ticket Office: (0121) 772 0101 (option 2).

Website: www.bcfc.com

Email: reception@bcfc.com

Ground Capacity: 28,251.

Record Attendance: 66,844 v Everton, FA Cup 5th rd, 11 February 1939.

Pitch Measurements: 100m × 67.6m (109.5yd × 74.5yd).

Chairman: Tom Wagner.

Chief Executive: Jeremy Dale (interim).

Manager: Chris Davies.

Assistant Manager: Ben Petty.

Colours: Blue shirts with broad white chest panel and white trim, white shorts, blue socks.

Year Formed: 1875.

Turned Professional: 1885.

Previous Names: 1875, Small Heath Alliance; 1888, dropped 'Alliance'; 1905, Birmingham; 1945, Birmingham City.

Club Nickname: 'Blues'.

HONOURS

League Champions: Division 2 – 1892–93, 1920–21, 1947–48, 1954–55; Second Division – 1994–95; FL 1 – 2024–25.
Runners-up: FL C – 2006–07, 2008–09; Division 2 – 1893–94, 1900–01, 1902–03; 1971–72, 1984–85; Division 3 – 1991–92.
FA Cup: Runners-up: 1931, 1956.
League Cup Winners: 1963, 2011. *Runners-up:* 2001.
League Trophy Winners: 1991, 1995. *Runners-up:* 2025.
European Competitions
Fairs Cup: 1955–58, 1958–60 *(runners-up)*, 1960–61 *(runners-up)*, 1961–62.
Europa League: 2011–12.

Grounds: 1875, waste ground near Arthur St; 1877, Muntz St, Small Heath; 1906, St Andrew's (renamed St Andrew's Trillion Trophy Stadium 2018; St Andrew's @ Knighthead Park 2024).

First Football League Game: 3 September 1892, Division 2, v Burslem Port Vale (h) W 5–1 – Charsley; Bayley, Speller; Ollis, Jenkyns, Devey; Hallam (1), Edwards (1), Short (1), Wheldon (2), Hands.

Record League Victory: 12–0 v Walsall T Swifts, Division 2, 17 December 1892 – Charsley; Bayley, Jones; Ollis, Jenkyns, Devey; Hallam (2), Walton (3), Mobley (3), Wheldon (2), Hands (2). 12–0 v Doncaster R, Division 2, 11 April 1903 – Dorrington; Goldie, Wassell; Beer, Dougherty (1), Howard; Athersmith, Leonard (4), McRoberts (1), Wilcox (4), Field (1), (1 og).

Record Cup Victory: 9–2 v Burton W, FA Cup 1st rd, 31 October 1885 – Hedges; Jones, Evetts (1); Fred James, Felton, Arthur James (1); Davenport (2), Stanley (4), Simms, Figures, Morris (1).

Record Defeat: 1–9 v Blackburn R, Division 1, 5 January 1895; 1–9 v Sheffield Wed, Division 1, 13 December 1930; 0–8 v Bournemouth, FLC, 25 October 2014.

FOOTBALL YEARBOOK FACT FILE

Birmingham City were the first English association football club to establish themselves as a limited liability company. Small Heath Football Club Co Limited was registered in August 1888 with £500 capital divided into 10s (50p) shares. The first year's accounts showed a profit of £17 0s 11d, with a total wage bill of £127 7s 6d. Shareholders were rewarded with a dividend of 5 per cent.

Most League Points (2 for a win): 59, Division 2, 1947–48.

Most League Points (3 for a win): 111, FL 1, 2024–25.

Most League Goals: 103, Division 2, 1893–94 (only 28 games).

Highest League Scorer in Season: Walter Abbott, 34, Division 2, 1898–99 (Small Heath); Joe Bradford, 29, Division 1, 1927–28 (Birmingham City).

Most League Goals in Total Aggregate: Joe Bradford, 249, 1920–35.

Most League Goals in One Match: 5, Walter Abbott v Darwen, Division 2, 26 November, 1898; 5, John McMillan v Blackpool, Division 2, 2 March 1901; 5, James Windridge v Glossop, Division 2, 23 January 1915.

Most Capped Player: Maik Taylor, 58 (including 4 on loan at Fulham) (88), Northern Ireland.

Most League Appearances: Frank Womack, 491, 1908–28.

Youngest League Player: Jude Bellingham, 16 years 57 days v Swansea C, 25 August 2019.

Record Transfer Fee Received: £20,000,000 from Borussia Dortmund for Jude Bellingham, July 2020.

Record Transfer Fee Paid: £15,000,000 (potentially rising to £20,000,000) to Fulham for Jay Stansfield, August 2024.

Football League Record: 1892 Elected to Division 2; 1892–94 Division 2; 1894–96 Division 1; 1896–1901 Division 2; 1901–02 Division 1; 1902–03 Division 2; 1903–08 Division 1; 1908–21 Division 2; 1921–39 Division 1; 1946–48 Division 2; 1948–50 Division 1; 1950–55 Division 2; 1955–65 Division 1; 1965–72 Division 2; 1972–79 Division 1; 1979–80 Division 2; 1980–84 Division 1; 1984–85 Division 2; 1985–86 Division 1; 1986–89 Division 2; 1989–92 Division 3; 1992–94 First Division; 1994–95 Second Division; 1995–2002 First Division; 2002–06 Premier League; 2006–07 FL C; 2007–08 Premier League; 2008–09 FL C; 2009–11 Premier League; 2011–24 FL C; 2024–25 FL 1; 2025– FL C.

LATEST SEQUENCES

Longest Sequence of League Wins: 13, 17.12.1892 – 16.9.1893.

Longest Sequence of League Defeats: 8, 28.9.1985 – 23.11.1985.

Longest Sequence of League Draws: 8, 18.9.1990 – 23.10.1990.

Longest Sequence of Unbeaten League Matches: 20, 3.9.1994 – 2.1.1995.

Longest Sequence Without a League Win: 17, 28.9.1985 – 18.1.1986.

Successive Scoring Runs: 24 from 24.9.1892.

Successive Non-scoring Runs: 6 from 18.9.2021.

MANAGERS

Alfred Jones 1892–1908 (*Secretary-Manager*)
Alec Watson 1908–10
Bob McRoberts 1910–15
Frank Richards 1915–23
Billy Beer 1923–27
William Harvey 1927–28
Leslie Knighton 1928–33
George Liddell 1933–39
William Camkin and Ted Goodier 1939–45
Harry Storer 1945–48
Bob Brocklebank 1949–54
Arthur Turner 1954–58
Pat Beasley 1959–60
Gil Merrick 1960–64
Joe Mallett 1964–65
Stan Cullis 1965–70
Fred Goodwin 1970–75
Willie Bell 1975–77
Sir Alf Ramsay 1977–78
Jim Smith 1978–82
Ron Saunders 1982–86
John Bond 1986–87
Garry Pendrey 1987–89
Dave Mackay 1989–91
Lou Macari 1991
Terry Cooper 1991–93
Barry Fry 1993–96
Trevor Francis 1996–2001
Steve Bruce 2001–07
Alex McLeish 2007–11
Chris Hughton 2011–12
Lee Clark 2012–14
Gary Rowett 2014–16
Gianfranco Zola 2016–17
Harry Redknapp 2017
Steve Cotterill 2017–18
Garry Monk 2018–19
Pep Clotet 2019–20
Aitor Karanka 2020–21
Lee Bowyer 2021–22
John Eustace 2022–23
Wayne Rooney 2023–24
Tony Mowbray 2024
Chris Davies June 2024–

TEN YEAR LEAGUE RECORD

		P	W	D	L	F	A	Pts	Pos
2015-16	FL C	46	16	15	15	53	49	63	10
2016-17	FL C	46	13	14	19	45	64	53	19
2017-18	FL C	46	13	7	26	38	68	46	19
2018-19	FL C	46	14	19	13	64	58	52*	17
2019-20	FL C	46	12	14	20	54	75	50	20
2020-21	FL C	46	13	13	20	37	61	52	18
2021-22	FL C	46	11	14	21	50	75	47	20
2022-23	FL C	46	14	11	21	47	58	53	17
2023-24	FL C	46	13	11	22	50	65	50	22
2024-25	FL 1	46	34	9	3	84	31	111	1

* 9 pts deducted.

DID YOU KNOW ❓

Small Heath, as Birmingham City were then known, won all 17 of their home fixtures in 1902–03 to ensure that they were promoted back to the top flight after being relegated the previous season. They equalled the club's record Football League victory in their penultimate home game, beating Doncaster Rovers 12-0.

BIRMINGHAM CITY – SKY BET LEAGUE ONE 2024–25 LEAGUE RECORD

Match No.	Date	Venue	Opponents	Result	H/T Score	Lg Pos.	Goalscorers	Attendance
1	Aug 10	H	Reading	D 1-1	0-1	12	May (pen) [87]	27,985
2	17	A	Wycombe W	W 3-2	1-1	7	May [31], Harris [68], Willumsson [82]	6224
3	24	A	Leyton Orient	W 2-1	2-1	5	Anderson [7], May [20]	8005
4	31	H	Wigan Ath	W 2-1	1-0	3	May [18], Wright [90]	26,136
5	Sept 16	H	Wrexham	W 3-1	1-1	2	Stansfield 2 [22, 52], Iwata [59]	27,980
6	21	A	Rotherham U	W 2-0	2-0	2	Iwata [14], Stansfield [22]	10,335
7	28	A	Peterborough U	W 3-2	1-2	1	Willumsson [24], Wallin (og) [49], Bielik [66]	27,206
8	Oct 1	H	Huddersfield T	W 1-0	0-0	1	May [63]	24,757
9	5	A	Charlton Ath	L 0-1	0-0	1		16,250
10	19	A	Lincoln C	W 3-1	1-1	1	Anderson 2 [14, 79], Willumsson [52]	10,026
11	22	H	Bolton W	W 2-0	1-0	1	Iwata [3], Stansfield (pen) [86]	25,793
12	26	H	Mansfield T	D 1-1	1-0	1	Willumsson [10]	8583
13	Nov 9	H	Northampton T	D 1-1	0-0	2	Stansfield [58]	27,485
14	23	A	Shrewsbury T	L 2-3	1-2	4	Iwata [44], Stansfield (pen) [76]	7887
15	26	A	Exeter C	W 2-0	1-0	3	Iwata [11], Stansfield (pen) [83]	7928
16	Dec 4	H	Stockport Co	W 2-0	2-0	3	May 2 [26, 35]	24,863
17	7	A	Barnsley	W 2-1	0-0	3	Stansfield 2 [60, 79]	15,367
18	14	H	Bristol R	W 2-0	2-0	2	Buchanan [6], Stansfield (pen) [38]	26,459
19	23	A	Crawley T	W 1-0	0-0	1	Stansfield [79]	5530
20	26	A	Burton Alb	W 2-0	1-0	1	Stansfield (pen) [26], Crocombe (og) [56]	27,524
21	29	H	Blackpool	D 0-0	0-0	1		27,340
22	Jan 1	A	Stockport Co	D 1-1	1-0	2	May [5]	10,528
23	4	A	Wigan Ath	W 3-0	2-0	1	May 2 [18, 30], Willumsson [61]	13,485
24	18	A	Exeter C	W 1-0	1-0	1	Laird [45]	25,930
25	23	A	Wrexham	D 1-1	1-1	1	Dykes [18]	13,237
26	28	A	Huddersfield T	W 1-0	0-0	1	Anderson [49]	19,138
27	Feb 1	H	Rotherham U	W 2-1	0-1	1	Stansfield 2 (1 pen) [54, 81 (p)]	34,393
28	11	H	Cambridge U	W 4-0	3-0	1	Stansfield (pen) [23], Bennett (og) [39], Dowell [40], Harris [79]	22,456
29	15	A	Charlton Ath	W 1-0	1-0	1	Stansfield [23]	25,542
30	22	H	Reading	D 0-0	0-0	1		13,919
31	25	H	Leyton Orient	W 2-0	0-0	1	Gardner-Hickman [53], Laird [84]	26,857
32	Mar 1	H	Wycombe W	W 1-0	1-0	1	Gardner-Hickman [21]	27,522
33	4	A	Bolton W	L 1-3	1-1	1	Hansson [23]	23,023
34	8	H	Lincoln C	W 1-0	0-0	1	Dowell (pen) [71]	26,210
35	11	H	Stevenage	W 2-1	1-0	1	Dowell (pen) [27], Paik [47]	25,544
36	15	A	Northampton T	D 1-1	1-1	1	Anderson [45]	7947
37	29	H	Shrewsbury T	W 4-1	1-0	1	Davies [27], Laird [61], May 2 [77, 86]	26,254
38	Apr 1	A	Bristol R	W 2-1	1-1	1	Anderson [3], Stansfield (pen) [85]	8088
39	5	H	Barnsley	W 6-2	1-1	1	Stansfield (pen) [33], May 2 [47, 55], Harris [72], Dowell [82], Jutkiewicz [89]	25,018
40	8	A	Peterborough U	W 2-1	2-1	1	May [19], Gardner-Hickman [37]	10,640
41	18	A	Crawley T	D 0-0	0-0	1		27,325
42	21	A	Burton Alb	W 2-1	2-0	1	Sampsted [44], Stansfield [45]	4928
43	24	A	Stevenage	W 1-0	0-0	1	Cochrane [75]	4135
44	27	H	Mansfield T	W 4-0	2-0	1	Anderson 2 [24], Willumsson [39], Dowell [50], Iwata [57]	27,920
45	30	A	Blackpool	W 2-0	1-0	1	Laird [39], May [51]	9618
46	May 3	A	Cambridge U	W 2-1	1-1	1	Klarer [25], Watts (og) [82]	6764

Final League Position: 1

GOALSCORERS

League (84): Stansfield 19 (9 pens), May 16 (1 pen), Anderson 7, Iwata 6, Willumsson 6, Dowell 5 (2 pens), Laird 4, Gardner-Hickman 3, Harris 3, Bielik 1, Buchanan 1, Cochrane 1, Davies 1, Dykes 1, Hansson 1, Jutkiewicz 1, Klarer 1, Paik 1, Sampsted 1, Wright 1, own goals 4.
FA Cup (7): Dykes 2, Iwata 1, Jutkiewicz 1, Laird 1, Willumsson 1, Yokoyama 1.
Carabao Cup (1): Khela 1.
Vertu Trophy (19): Stansfield 4, Yokoyama 3, Anderson 2, Dykes 2, Wright 2, Hansson 1, Harris 1, Iwata 1, Klarer 1, May 1, own goal 1.

Peacock-Farrell B 8+1	Laird E 27+8	Sanderson D 1+1	Bielik K 20+12	Cochrane A 41+1	Leonard M 14+21	Paik S 36+5	Miyoshi K 1+2	Williumsson W 36+5	Dembele S 1	May A 27+17	Hansson E 12+8	Harris L 10+19	Anderson K 27+10	Jutkiewicz L —+16	Khela B —+2	Klarer C 43	Yokoyama A —+10	Sampsted A 4+13	Gardner-Hickman T 22+11	Wright S 3+10	Dykes L 9+16	Iwata T 38+2	Stansfield J 31+6	Davies B 32+3	Allsop R 38	Buchanan L 3	Dowell K 17+2	Hanley G 3+11	Lee M 2+1	Match No.
1	2⁴	3	4	5	6⁵	7	8³	9²	10¹	11	12	13	14	15	16															1
1	2		4	5	6²	7	12	13		11⁴	10¹	9⁵	8³	15	16	3	14	17												2
1	2		4	5	7¹	6	16	12		11⁵	10²	9³	8⁴	15		3	14		13											3
1	2¹		4	5	14	6		9		11⁴	10⁵	8²				3	16	12	7³	13	15									4
1	4⁸		5		15	7	8	9²		10³		14				3		12	2¹	13	6⁵	11⁴	16							5
1			5	16	7	8		14		10²	12			3	15	2⁴	13	11¹	6⁵	9³	4									6
1	4		5	16	7⁵	8		14		10²	12			3	15	2⁴	13	9¹	6	11³										7
	4		5		7	8		9³		13	10²			3	12	2¹	14	15	6	11⁴	1									8
	3²	4			7		9⁴	10³	13		8¹		2	16	5⁵	14	15	6	11	12	1									9
13			5	15	7		9	11³	10¹		8⁴		3		12	2²	14	6	4	1										10
2²			5	12	7⁴		8	11³	10¹		8⁵		3	16	13	15	6	14	4	1										11
2³			5	15	7	8		12		14	10⁵		3	16	13	11²	6⁴	9¹	4	1									12
2³	16	4⁵	5		7	8⁴		9¹		12	10²		3	13	14		15	6	11	1										13
2³	4⁴	5	14	6		8		13		9²	10¹		3	15		12	7	11	1											14
2	5	13	7²		9	11¹	14	8		3		12	6	10³	4	1														15
13	2	8	15	7		9⁴	11¹	14	5²		3		12	6	10³	4	1													16
5	2	8¹	14	7		11³	9²	13		3		12	6	10	4	1														17
12	2³	16	7	9		10⁴	13	5⁵	15	3	14		6	11²	4	1	8¹													18
12	2	13	7	9²		11³	16	8⁵		3	15		10⁴	7⁴	11⁵	3	1	5¹												19
2	3	5	7⁵	14	9⁵	13	12	15	8¹	16	11³	6	10⁴	4	1															20
12	3	16	7	8	9⁵	10²	13	4⁴	2	11³	6	14	15	1	5¹															21
16	2	5⁵	12	7	9¹	11²	15	3	8³	14	13	6	10⁴	4	1															22
2	5	12	7	8⁴	11²	9¹	15	3	16	10⁵	14	13	6³	4	1															23
2	14	5	6	11³	9	3	12	7	8²	13	10¹	4	1																	24
2	14	5	6	11²	12	13	3	7	8¹	9	10³	4	1																	25
5	14	4	8	15	9¹	3	6⁵	12	10⁴	7²	11³	2	1	13	16															26
5	16	4	14	13	9²	2	8	12	10²	7⁴	11⁵	3	1	6³	15															27
2	12	5	7⁵	9²	16	10³	3⁴	14	13	6¹¹	4	1	8	15																28
2	15	5	6	9¹	13	10³	3	12	7	11²	4	1	8⁴	14																29
2	5	7	12	13	10³	3	14	8¹	11²	6	4	1	9⁴	15																30
2⁴	16	5	7	9¹	11⁵	13	14	12	3	15	10²	6	4	1	8³															31
15	2²	14	5	7	9	11³	12	13	3	10¹	6	4	14	1	8²															32
1	16	5	7	9	11⁴	10¹	13	15	3	12	2²	6⁵	14	4	8³															33
2²	5	7	13	14	10¹	12	3	8	6	11³	4	1	9⁴	15																34
15	5	13	7	9	12⁵	10¹	14	3	2⁴	6²	11³	4	1	8	16															35
15	5	7	9²	14	12	3	2⁴	6	11³	4	1	8																		36
2¹	5	7	9³	14	13	15	10²	3⁵	12	6	11⁴	4	1	8	16															37
2³	5	7¹	12	9	13	10	3	14	6	11⁴	4	1	8²	15																38
2³	5	16	7⁵	9¹	12	14	10²	15	3	13	6	11⁴	4	1	8															39
12	4	5	7²	14	8	11⁴	9⁵	13	3	2³	10¹	6	15	1	16															40
2⁴	5⁵	13	7	9²	11⁵	12	8	16	3	14	6¹	10	4	1	15															41
15	5	7³	14	9	12	16	13	3	2⁴	10²	6	11¹	4	1	8⁵	4														42
15	6²	7	13	11⁵	9³	10¹	16	2	14	12	4	1	8	3	5⁴															43
2²	5	16	7⁵	9³	14	13	10¹	15	3	12	6	11⁴	4	1	8⁴															44
2¹	5	7⁵	14	9	11⁵	15	10³	3	12	6	13	4	1	8⁴	16															45
2³	15	6	7²	8¹	9⁵	14	16	3	10	12	11	1	13	4⁴	5															46

FA Cup

First Round	Sutton U	(a)	1-0
Second Round	Blackpool	(a)	2-1
Third Round	Lincoln C	(h)	2-1
Fourth Round	Newcastle U	(h)	2-3

Carabao Cup

First Round	Charlton Ath	(a)	1-0
Second Round	Fulham	(h)	0-2

Vertu Trophy

Group A (S)	Walsall	(h)	1-1
Walsall won 4-3 on penalties.			
Group A (S)	Shrewsbury T	(a)	4-0
Group A (S)	Fulham U21	(h)	7-1
Second Round	Exeter C	(a)	2-1
Third Round	Swindon T	(a)	2-1
Quarter-Final	Stevenage	(a)	1-0
Semi-Final	Bradford C	(h)	2-1
Final	Peterborough U	(Wembley)	0-2

BLACKBURN ROVERS

FOUNDATION

It was in 1875 that some public school old boys called a meeting at which the Blackburn Rovers club was formed and the colours blue and white adopted. The leading light was John Lewis, later to become a founder of the Lancashire FA, a famous referee who was in charge of two FA Cup finals, and a vice-president of both the FA and the Football League.

Ewood Park, Blackburn, Lancashire BB2 4JF.

Telephone: (01254) 372 001.

Ticket Office: (01254) 372 000.

Website: www.rovers.co.uk

Email: enquiries@rovers.co.uk

Ground Capacity: 31,363.

Record Attendance: 62,522 v Bolton W, FA Cup 6th rd, 2 March 1929.

Pitch Measurements: 105m × 65.84m (115yd × 72yd).

Chief Operating Officer: Suhail Shaikh.

Head Coach: Valerien Ismael.

Assistant Head Coach: Dean Whitehead.

Colours: Blue and white halved shirts with blue and red trim, white shorts with blue and red trim, blue socks with white and red trim.

Year Formed: 1875.

Turned Professional: 1880.

Club Nickname: 'Rovers'.

HONOURS

League Champions: Premier League – 1994–95; Division 1 – 1911–12, 1913–14; Division 2 – 1938–39; Division 3 – 1974–75.
Runners-up: Premier League – 1993–94; FL 1 – 2017–18; First Division – 2000–01; Division 2 – 1957–58; Division 3 – 1979–80.
FA Cup Winners: 1884, 1885, 1886, 1890, 1891, 1928.
Runners-up: 1882, 1960.
League Cup Winners: 2002.
Full Members' Cup Winners: 1987.
European Competitions
European Cup: 1995–96.
UEFA Cup: 1994–95, 1998–99, 2002–03, 2003–04, 2006–07, 2007–08.
Intertoto Cup: 2007.

Grounds: 1875, all matches played away; 1876, Oozehead Ground; 1877, Pleasington Cricket Ground; 1878, Alexandra Meadows; 1881, Leamington Road; 1890, Ewood Park.

First Football League Game: 15 September 1888, Football League, v Accrington (h) D 5–5 – Arthur; Beverley, James Southworth; Douglas, Almond, Forrest; Beresford (1), Walton, John Southworth (1), Fecitt (1), Townley (2).

Record League Victory: 9–0 v Middlesbrough, Division 2, 6 November 1954 – Elvy; Suart, Eckersley; Clayton, Kelly, Bell; Mooney (3), Crossan (2), Briggs, Quigley (3), Langton (1).

Record Cup Victory: 11–0 v Rossendale, FA Cup 1st rd, 13 October 1884 – Arthur; Hopwood, McIntyre; Forrest, Blenkhorn, Lofthouse; Sowerbutts (2), Jimmy Brown (1), Fecitt (4), Barton (3), Birtwistle (1).

Record Defeat: 0–8 v Arsenal, Division 1, 25 February 1933; 0–8 v Lincoln C, Division 2, 29 August 1953.

FOOTBALL YEARBOOK FACT FILE

Blackburn Rovers made their first visit to Europe in the summer of 1910 when they visited Belgium and Germany. During the tour they played two games against Chelsea, winning 3-1 in Brussels in a match played for the Dedecker Cup, then losing 5-3 in an exhibition game played in Frankfurt. Other opponents included Karlsruher, who were coached by former Rovers favourite Billy Townley.

Most League Points (2 for a win): 60, Division 3, 1974–75.

Most League Points (3 for a win): 96, FL 1, 2017–18.

Most League Goals: 114, Division 2, 1954–55.

Highest League Scorer in Season: Ted Harper, 43, Division 1, 1925–26.

Most League Goals in Total Aggregate: Simon Garner, 168, 1978–92.

Most League Goals in One Match: 7, Tommy Briggs v Bristol R, Division 2, 5 February 1955.

Most Capped Player: Morten Gamst Pedersen, 69 (83), Norway.

Most League Appearances: Derek Fazackerley, 596, 1970–86.

Youngest League Player: Harry Dennison, 16 years 155 days v Bristol C, 8 April 1911.

Record Transfer Fee Received: £22,000,000 from Crystal Palace for Adam Wharton, January 2024.

Record Transfer Fee Paid: £3,000,000 (potentially rising to £10,000,000) to Arsenal for David Bentley, January 2006.

Football League Record: 1888 Founder Member of the League; 1888–92 Football League; 1892–1936 Division 1; 1936–39 Division 2; 1946–48 Division 1; 1948–58 Division 2; 1958–66 Division 1; 1966–71 Division 2; 1971–75 Division 3; 1975–79 Division 2; 1979–80 Division 3; 1980–92 Division 2; 1992–99 Premier League; 1999–2001 First Division; 2001–12 Premier League; 2012–17 FL C; 2017–18 FL 1; 2018– FL C.

LATEST SEQUENCES

Longest Sequence of League Wins: 8, 1.3.1980 – 7.4.1980.

Longest Sequence of League Defeats: 7, 12.3.1966 – 16.4.1966.

Longest Sequence of League Draws: 5, 11.10.1975 – 1.11.1975.

Longest Sequence of Unbeaten League Matches: 23, 30.9.1987 – 27.2.1988.

Longest Sequence Without a League Win: 16, 11.11.1978 – 24.3.1979.

Successive Scoring Runs: 32 from 24.4.1954.

Successive Non-scoring Runs: 5 from 29.1.2022.

MANAGERS

Thomas Mitchell 1884–96
  (*Secretary-Manager*)
J. Walmsley 1896–1903
  (*Secretary-Manager*)
R. B. Middleton 1903–25
Jack Carr 1922–26
  (*Team Manager under
  Middleton to 1925*)
Bob Crompton 1926–31
  (*Hon. Team Manager*)
Arthur Barritt 1931–36
  (*had been Secretary from 1927*)
Reg Taylor 1936–38
Bob Crompton 1938–41
Eddie Hapgood 1944–47
Will Scott 1947
Jack Bruton 1947–49
Jackie Bestall 1949–53
Johnny Carey 1953–58
Dally Duncan 1958–60
Jack Marshall 1960–67
Eddie Quigley 1967–70
Johnny Carey 1970–71
Ken Furphy 1971–73
Gordon Lee 1974–75
Jim Smith 1975–78
Jim Iley 1978
John Pickering 1978–79
Howard Kendall 1979–81
Bobby Saxton 1981–86
Don Mackay 1987–91
Kenny Dalglish 1991–95
Ray Harford 1995–96
Roy Hodgson 1997–98
Brian Kidd 1998–99
Graeme Souness 2000–04
Mark Hughes 2004–08
Paul Ince 2008
Sam Allardyce 2008–10
Steve Kean 2010–12
Henning Berg 2012
Michael Appleton 2013
Gary Bowyer 2013–15
Paul Lambert 2015–16
Owen Coyle 2016–17
Tony Mowbray 2017–22
Jon Dahl Tomasson 2022–24
John Eustace 2024–25
Valerien Ismael February 2025–

TEN YEAR LEAGUE RECORD

		P	W	D	L	F	A	Pts	Pos
2015-16	FL C	46	13	16	17	46	46	55	15
2016-17	FL C	46	12	15	19	53	65	51	22
2017-18	FL 1	46	28	12	6	82	40	96	2
2018-19	FL C	46	16	12	18	64	69	60	15
2019-20	FL C	46	17	12	17	66	63	63	11
2020-21	FL C	46	15	12	19	65	54	57	15
2021-22	FL C	46	19	12	15	59	50	69	8
2022-23	FL C	46	20	9	17	52	54	69	7
2023-24	FL C	46	14	11	21	60	74	53	19
2024-25	FL C	46	19	9	18	53	48	66	7

DID YOU KNOW ?

Blackburn Rovers share with Aston Villa the distinction of enjoying the longest continuous run of membership of the top flight of those clubs who were founder members in the 1888–89 season. Coincidentally both were relegated to the Second Division for the first time in 1935–36, with Rovers taking four years to win back their place in the highest division.

BLACKBURN ROVERS – SKY BET CHAMPIONSHIP 2024–25 LEAGUE RECORD

Match No.	Date	Venue	Opponents	Result	H/T Score	Lg Pos.	Goalscorers	Attendance
1	Aug 9	H	Derby Co	W 4-2	1-0	1	Dolan [19], Weimann [72], Szmodics [76], Ohashi [84]	17,975
2	17	A	Norwich C	D 2-2	1-0	3	Hedges [20], Ohashi [87]	26,400
3	24	H	Oxford U	W 2-1	1-1	3	Rankin-Costello [45], Sigurdsson [83]	14,769
4	31	A	Burnley	D 1-1	1-1	5	Weimann [23]	21,042
5	Sept 14	H	Bristol C	W 3-0	1-0	2	Travis [17], Ohashi 2 [55, 70]	14,087
6	22	A	Preston NE	D 0-0	0-0	5		20,945
7	28	H	QPR	W 2-0	0-0	3	Travis [53], Batth [63]	13,789
8	Oct 1	A	Coventry C	L 0-3	0-1	6		24,583
9	5	A	Plymouth Arg	L 1-2	0-1	8	Rankin-Costello [86]	16,635
10	19	H	Swansea C	W 1-0	1-0	6	Dolan [13]	13,550
11	23	H	WBA	D 0-0	0-0	6		13,647
12	26	A	Watford	L 0-1	0-0	6		18,880
13	Nov 2	H	Sheffield U	L 0-2	0-1	7		16,810
14	6	H	Stoke C	L 0-2	0-0	10		13,144
15	9	A	Cardiff C	W 3-1	1-0	9	Weimann 2 [15, 54], Baker [86]	17,188
16	27	A	Middlesbrough	W 1-0	0-0	8	Hyam [77]	22,751
17	30	H	Leeds U	W 1-0	1-0	8	Cantwell (pen) [22]	21,942
18	Dec 7	A	Hull C	W 1-0	1-0	6	McLoughlin (og) [20]	20,544
19	10	A	Sheffield Wed	W 1-0	0-0	5	Gueye [68]	22,703
20	14	H	Luton T	W 2-0	2-0	5	Cozier-Duberry [32], Beck [40]	13,857
21	21	A	Millwall	L 0-1	0-0	5		14,009
22	26	H	Sunderland	D 2-2	1-0	5	Ohashi [13], Leonard [90]	24,961
23	29	H	Hull C	L 0-1	0-0	5		16,245
24	Jan 1	A	Leeds U	D 1-1	0-0	7	Batth [90]	36,645
25	4	H	Burnley	L 0-1	0-0	7		25,909
26	15	H	Portsmouth	W 3-0	0-0	5	Gueye [61], Brittain [71], Weimann [76]	13,703
27	18	A	Oxford U	L 0-1	0-0	5		11,407
28	21	H	Coventry C	L 0-2	0-1	6		12,819
29	25	A	Bristol C	L 1-2	1-1	7	Weimann [40]	20,945
30	31	H	Preston NE	W 2-1	1-0	5	Gueye [39], Cantwell (pen) [78]	21,392
31	Feb 4	A	QPR	L 1-2	0-1	5	Dolan (pen) [53]	13,571
32	12	A	WBA	W 2-0	0-0	5	Gueye 2 [47, 63]	23,305
33	15	H	Plymouth Arg	W 2-0	0-0	5	Forshaw [55], Dolan [78]	14,875
34	22	A	Swansea C	L 0-3	0-2	6		13,788
35	Mar 1	H	Norwich C	D 1-1	0-0	7	Weimann [90]	14,240
36	8	A	Derby Co	L 1-2	1-2	8	Gueye [40]	29,753
37	12	A	Stoke C	L 0-1	0-1	9		20,194
38	15	H	Cardiff C	L 1-2	1-1	9	Ohashi [16]	13,456
39	29	A	Portsmouth	L 0-1	0-1	11		20,342
40	Apr 4	H	Middlesbrough	L 0-2	0-2	11		15,638
41	8	H	Sheffield Wed	D 2-2	0-2	12	Dolan [51], Ohashi [85]	15,575
42	12	A	Luton T	W 1-0	0-0	10	Ohashi [52]	11,552
43	18	H	Millwall	W 4-1	2-1	10	Hyam [42], Tronstad 2 [45, 59], Brittain [50]	14,167
44	21	A	Sunderland	W 1-0	1-0	9	Dolan [33]	40,031
45	26	H	Watford	W 2-1	0-0	8	Cantwell [59], Dolan [74]	15,154
46	May 3	A	Sheffield U	D 1-1	0-0	7	Ohashi [50]	30,556

Final League Position: 7

GOALSCORERS

League (53): Ohashi 9, Dolan 7 (1 pen), Weimann 7, Gueye 6, Cantwell 3 (2 pens), Batth 2, Brittain 2, Hyam 2, Rankin-Costello 2, Travis 2, Tronstad 2, Baker 1, Beck 1, Cozier-Duberry 1, Forshaw 1, Hedges 1, Leonard 1, Sigurdsson 1, Szmodics 1, own goal 1.
FA Cup (1): Weimann 1.
Carabao Cup (7): Gueye 2 (1 pen), Szmodics 2, Ohashi 1, Vale 1, Weimann 1.

Pears A 40	Britain C 30 + 3	Carter H 16	Hyam D 46	Pickering H 12 + 3	Rankin-Costello J 13 + 16	Travis L 37 + 1	Tronstad S 36 + 2	Hedges R 33 + 9	Dolan T 40 + 4	Gueye M 23 + 21	Weimann A 15 + 15	Szmodics S — + 1	Ohashi Y 26 + 10	Batth D 34 + 3	Buckley J 8 + 15	Sigurdsson A — + 5	Beck O 21 + 3	Baker L 7 + 6	Duru L — + 1	Cantwell T 27 + 10	Tyjon I — + 2	Cozier-Duberry A 6 + 16	Leonard H — + 9	McFadzean K — + 1	Forshaw A 5 + 11	Sanderson D 4 + 8	Toth B 6	Kargbo A 2 + 6	Yuri Ribeiro 0 15	Bonaventure E 1 + 5	Woodrow C 2 + 7	Montgomery K 1 + 2	Match No.
1	2	3	4	5	6^3	7	8	9^1	10^4	11^2	12	13	14	15																			1
1	2	3^5	4	5	8^4	7	6	10^1	9^3	11^2	13		12	16	14	15																	2
1	2	3	4	5	8^2	6	7	10^1	9^3	12	13		11		14																		3
1	2^3	3	4		6	7	10^2	9	11^1	8^1	12			5	13	14																	4
1		2	4		7	6^4	8^5	9^2		12			11^3	3	15		5	10^1		13	14	16											5
1		2	4	16	7	6^4	8^3	9^2	12	13			11^5	3			5^1	10^1		15	14												6
1		2	4	5^1	15	6^5	7	10^4	9	13	8		11^2	3	16					12	14												7
1		2	4	5^5		7^2	6^4	12	10^1	16	8		11	3	13					9^3	14												8
1		2	4	5	14	7	6	10^5	9^2	11^1	8^3		12	3^4	16					13	15												9
1	13	3	4		2	6	7	8^2	9^3	11^1	14		12				5	15		10^4													10
1	14	3^1	4		2	6	7	8^2	9^5	16	13		11^3	12			15	5		10^4													11
1	2		4		14	6^4	7^5	8^3	16	11^1	9^2		12	3	15	13	5			10													12
1	12		4	15	2^4	7^3	6	8^2	9^1	16	13		11^5	3	14		5			10													13
1	2		4	5		7^3	6	10^1	12	13	8		11^2	3						9		14											14
1	2		3	5	12	6	7	10^4		15	8^1		11^2	4						9^3													15
1	2		3	5		7	6	10^1	8	14			11^3	4			12	13		9^2													16
1	2		3	5		7	6	13	8	12			11^1	4			10			9^2													17
1	2		3		14		6	10	8^1	13			11^2	4			5	7		9^3	12												18
1		3		2	6	7	10^4	8^3	12	11^1			4				5	14		9^2	13	15											19
1		3	5	2	6	7	12			11^3			9^2	4	13		10			8^1	14												20
1		4	5^4	2	8	7	15	12	10	14			11^3	3			13			9^2		6^1											21
1	2	3			7^5	10^2	8^4	13	15	11^1			4	14			5	6^3		9		12	16										22
1	2	4		15		7^4		10^2	11^1	13			12	3			5	6^3		8^5	16												23
1	2	3		13		6	9	8^2	15	10^3			11^1	4			5	7				14	12^4										24
1	2	3		14		7^5	16	8^4	11^2	12			4	15			5	6^3		9		10^1	13										25
1	2	3		14		7	10^2	8^1	13	11^3			4	6^4			5			9^5		12			15	16							26
1	2	3		16		6^1	13	14	11^4	10^3			4	7	7^5		5			9		8^2	15	12									27
	2^1	3		6			10^2	8^5	11	14			4^4	7^3			5			13	16	12	15	1									28
1	2	5		13	14		6	10^5	11	9^1			4^2	8^4			12					15	16		7^3	3							29
1	2		3		13	6^2		10^3	8^4	11	9^1			4	7		5			12		13			15	14							30
1	2	3		14	6^4			10^5	8^1	11	9^2			4	7		5			12		13			15		16						31
1	2		3			7		10^2	8^4	11	9^3			4^1	6^5					13		14			16	12		15	5				32
1	2		4			6		15	10^4	11	14			13						9^3		8^1			7^2	3		12	5				33
1	2		4	15	6			10^1	8^4	11^5	9^2			14											7^3	3		12	5	13	16		34
1	2	3	4		7	12	15	8^3	11^5	13		16								9^2					6^1			10^4	5	14^b			35
1	2	3	4		7	6^4		8^3	11	9^2			14		15					12					10^5	5		13					36
1	5	4	3		15	7^5	12		9^2	10			13							11^3					6^1	2^4		8	14	16			37
1		3	4		2	7^1	6^2		8	11			9^3							14		12						5	10^1	13			38
1	2^5	3		15	7	6^4	12	9	14				11^3	4	16		10^1			13								5		8^2			39
1		3		2	7			10^2	8	11^1			12	4	6					9								5		13			40
1		3		2^1	7	6	10^2	8	13	11			4							9								5			12		41
		3			7	6	10^2	8	14	11^3			4							9^1					13	12	1	5			2^b		42
	2^4	3	14		7^1	6^5	10^2	8	15	11^3			4	16						9					13	1	1	5		12		43
	2^1	3			7	6	10^2	8^4	15	11^3			4	14						13			16		14	13	1	5		9^5	12	44
	2	3			7	6	10^2	8^4		11^3			4							9^1					13	12	1	14	5	15			45
	2	3			7^4	6^5	10^1	8^2	14	11			4							9^3					16		1	12	5	13	15		46

FA Cup
Third Round   Middlesbrough   (a)   1-0
Fourth Round   Wolverhampton W   (h)   0-2

Carabao Cup
First Round   Stockport Co   (a)   6-1
Second Round   Blackpool   (h)   1-2

BLACKPOOL

FOUNDATION

Old boys of St John's School, who had formed themselves into a football club, decided to establish a club bearing the name of their town and Blackpool FC came into being at a meeting at the Stanley Arms Hotel in the summer of 1887. In their first season playing at Raikes Hall Gardens, the club won both the Lancashire Junior Cup and the Fylde Cup.

Bloomfield Road, Seasiders Way, Blackpool, Lancashire FY1 6JJ.

Telephone: (01253) 599 344.

Ticket Office: (01253) 599 745.

Website: www.blackpoolfc.co.uk

Email: customerservices@blackpoolfc.co.uk

Ground Capacity: 16,332.

Record Attendance: 38,098 v Wolverhampton W, Division 1, 17 September 1955.

Pitch Measurements: 103m × 64m (112.5yd × 70yd).

Chairman: Simon Sadler.

Chief Executive: Julian Winter.

Head Coach: Steve Bruce.

Assistant Head Coach: Steve Agnew.

HONOURS

League Champions: Division 2 – 1929–30.
Runners-up: Division 1 – 1955–56; Division 2 – 1936–37, 1969–70; Division 4 – 1984–85.
FA Cup Winners: 1953.
Runners-up: 1948, 1951.
League Cup: semi-final – 1962.
League Trophy Winners: 2002, 2004.
Anglo-Italian Cup Winners: 1971.
Runners-up: 1972.

Colours: Tangerine shirts with white trim, white shorts with tangerine trim, tangerine socks with white trim.

Year Formed: 1887.

Turned Professional: 1887.

Previous Name: 'South Shore' combined with Blackpool in 1899, twelve years after the latter had been formed on the breaking up of the old 'Blackpool St John's' club.

Club Nickname: 'The Seasiders', 'The Tangerines', 'The Pool'.

Grounds: 1887, Raikes Hall Gardens; 1897, Athletic Grounds; 1899, Raikes Hall Gardens; 1899, Bloomfield Road.

First Football League Game: 5 September 1896, Division 2, v Lincoln C (a) L 1–3 – Douglas; Parr, Bowman; Stuart, Stirzaker, Norris; Clarkin, Donnelly, Robert Parkinson, Mount (1), Jack Parkinson.

Record League Victory: 7–0 v Reading, Division 2, 10 November 1928 – Mercer; Gibson, Hamilton, Watson, Wilson, Grant, Ritchie, Oxberry (2), Hampson (5), Tufnell, Neal. 7–0 v Preston NE (away), Division 1, 1 May 1948 – Robinson; Shimwell, Crosland; Buchan, Hayward, Kelly; Hobson, Munro (1), McIntosh (5), McCall, Rickett (1). 7–0 v Sunderland, Division 1, 5 October 1957 – Farm; Armfield, Garrett, Kelly J, Gratrix, Kelly H, Matthews, Taylor (2), Charnley (2), Durie (2), Perry (1).

Record Cup Victory: 7–1 v Charlton Ath, League Cup 2nd rd, 25 September 1963 – Harvey; Armfield, Martin; Crawford, Gratrix, Cranston; Lea, Ball (1), Charnley (4), Durie (1), Oates (1).

Record Defeat: 1–10 v Small Heath, Division 2, 2 March 1901 and v Huddersfield T, Division 1, 13 December 1930.

FOOTBALL YEARBOOK FACT FILE

In July 1914 Blackpool announced a change of shirts from red, which the directors considered to be unlucky, to black, red and yellow hoops, the colours of the well-known I Zingari Cricket Club. One advantage was that there would be no clash of colours with opposing teams. The Seasiders continued to use the colours in 1915–16 when the hoops changed from narrow to broad, reminiscent of the Belgian flag, with the town hosting some 2,000 refugees from the country.

Most League Points (2 for a win): 58, Division 2, 1929–30 and Division 2, 1967–68.

Most League Points (3 for a win): 86, Division 4, 1984–85.

Most League Goals: 98, Division 2, 1929–30.

Highest League Scorer in Season: Jimmy Hampson, 45, Division 2, 1929–30.

Most League Goals in Total Aggregate: Jimmy Hampson, 248, 1927–38.

Most League Goals in One Match: 5, Jimmy Hampson v Reading, Division 2, 10 November 1928; 5, Jimmy McIntosh v Preston NE, Division 1, 1 May 1948.

Most Capped Player: Jimmy Armfield, 43, England.

Most League Appearances: Jimmy Armfield, 568, 1952–71.

Youngest League Player: Matty Kay, 16 years 32 days v Scunthorpe U, 13 November 2005.

Record Transfer Fee Received: £6,750,000 from Liverpool for Charlie Adam, July 2011.

Record Transfer Fee Paid: £1,250,000 to Leicester C for D.J. Campbell, August 2010.

Football League Record: 1896 Elected to Division 2; 1896–99 Division 2; 1899 Failed re-election; 1900 Re-elected to Division 2; 1900–30 Division 2; 1930–33 Division 1; 1933–37 Division 2; 1937–67 Division 1; 1967–70 Division 2; 1970–71 Division 1; 1971–78 Division 2; 1978–81 Division 3; 1981–85 Division 4; 1985–90 Division 3; 1990–92 Division 4; 1992–2000 Second Division; 2000–01 Third Division; 2001–04 Second Division; 2004–07 FL 1; 2007–10 FL C; 2010–11 Premier League; 2011–15 FL C; 2015–16 FL 1; 2016–17 FL 2; 2017–21 FL 1; 2021–23 FL C; 2023– FL 1.

LATEST SEQUENCES

Longest Sequence of League Wins: 9, 21.11.1936 – 1.1.1937.

Longest Sequence of League Defeats: 8, 26.11.1898 – 7.1.1899.

Longest Sequence of League Draws: 5, 4.12.1976 – 1.1.1977.

Longest Sequence of Unbeaten League Matches: 17, 6.4.1968 – 21.9.1968.

Longest Sequence Without a League Win: 23, 7.2.2015 – 29.8.2015.

Successive Scoring Runs: 33 from 23.2.1929.

Successive Non-scoring Runs: 5 from 25.11.1989.

MANAGERS

Tom Barcroft 1903–33
(*Secretary-Manager*)
John Cox 1909–11
Bill Norman 1919–23
Maj. Frank Buckley 1923–27
Sid Beaumont 1927–28
Harry Evans 1928–33
(*Hon. Team Manager*)
Alex 'Sandy' Macfarlane 1933–35
Joe Smith 1935–58
Ronnie Suart 1958–67
Stan Mortensen 1967–69
Les Shannon 1969–70
Bob Stokoe 1970–72
Harry Potts 1972–76
Allan Brown 1976–78
Bob Stokoe 1978–79
Stan Ternent 1979–80
Alan Ball 1980–81
Allan Brown 1981–82
Sam Ellis 1982–89
Jimmy Mullen 1989–90
Graham Carr 1990
Bill Ayre 1990–94
Sam Allardyce 1994–96
Gary Megson 1996–97
Nigel Worthington 1997–99
Steve McMahon 2000–04
Colin Hendry 2004–05
Simon Grayson 2005–08
Ian Holloway 2009–12
Michael Appleton 2012–13
Paul Ince 2013–14
José Riga 2014
Lee Clark 2014–15
Neil McDonald 2015–16
Gary Bowyer 2016–18
Terry McPhillips 2018–19
Simon Grayson 2019–20
Neil Critchley 2020–22
Michael Appleton 2022–23
Mick McCarthy 2023
Neil Critchley 2023–24
Steve Bruce September 2024–

TEN YEAR LEAGUE RECORD

		P	W	D	L	F	A	Pts	Pos
2015-16	FL 1	46	12	10	24	40	63	46	22
2016-17	FL 2	46	18	16	12	69	46	70	7
2017-18	FL 1	46	15	15	16	60	55	60	12
2018-19	FL 1	46	15	17	14	50	52	62	10
2019-20	FL 1	35	11	12	12	44	43	45	13§
2020-21	FL 1	46	23	11	12	60	37	80	3
2021-22	FL C	46	16	12	18	54	58	60	16
2022-23	FL C	46	11	11	24	48	72	44	23
2023-24	FL 1	46	21	10	15	65	48	73	8
2024-25	FL 1	46	17	16	13	72	60	67	9

§*Decided on points-per-game (1.29)*

DID YOU KNOW ?

Despite leaving out three internationals including Stanley Matthews, Blackpool achieved a 7-0 win away to Preston North End in the final game of the 1947–48 season. Jimmy McIntosh scored five goals, with Alex Munro and Walter Rickett also scoring. This is the Seasiders' highest-ever victory over their local rivals.

BLACKPOOL – SKY BET LEAGUE ONE 2024–25 LEAGUE RECORD

Match No.	Date	Venue	Opponents	Result		H/T Score	Lg Pos.	Goalscorers	Attendance
1	Aug 10	A	Crawley T	L	1-2	0-2	16	Fletcher [74]	4718
2	17	H	Stockport Co	L	0-3	0-0	24		12,567
3	24	A	Cambridge U	D	4-4	3-1	22	Husband 2 [5, 38], Joseph [39], Ballard [53]	6083
4	31	H	Wycombe W	D	2-2	1-1	22	Joseph [32], Beesley [84]	9143
5	Sept 14	H	Exeter C	W	2-1	1-0	19	Hamilton [19], Husband [90]	8813
6	21	A	Charlton Ath	W	2-1	2-0	13	Joseph [27], Morgan [32]	14,149
7	24	A	Huddersfield T	W	2-0	2-0	9	Joseph [31], Hamilton [45]	17,068
8	28	H	Burton Alb	W	3-0	1-0	4	Offiah [19], Apter [50], Evans [75]	9168
9	Oct 1	H	Lincoln C	D	1-1	0-0	6	Joseph [74]	8528
10	5	A	Mansfield T	L	0-2	0-2	10		8121
11	19	H	Barnsley	L	1-2	0-1	14	Casey [68]	10,565
12	22	A	Peterborough U	L	1-5	1-3	16	Joseph [27]	6391
13	28	H	Wigan Ath	D	2-2	1-2	16	Kerr (og) [46], Aimson (og) [90]	10,226
14	Nov 9	A	Leyton Orient	L	0-3	0-1	18		8527
15	16	H	Northampton T	D	0-0	0-0	18		8873
16	23	A	Bolton W	L	1-2	1-0	19	Joseph [32]	22,479
17	26	A	Bristol R	W	2-0	1-0	16	Akono Bilongo (og) [27], Evans (pen) [52]	6342
18	Dec 4	A	Shrewsbury T	W	2-1	0-1	12	Pierre (og) [52], Onomah [57]	5251
19	14	A	Reading	W	3-0	2-0	10	Morgan [24], Apter [37], Fletcher [72]	14,455
20	21	H	Stevenage	D	0-0	0-0	12		8610
21	26	A	Wrexham	L	1-2	1-1	15	Fletcher [3]	13,313
22	29	A	Birmingham C	D	0-0	0-0	15		27,340
23	Jan 1	H	Shrewsbury T	D	1-1	0-1	15	Apter [61]	9433
24	4	A	Wycombe W	D	1-1	0-1	15	Joseph [90]	4936
25	18	H	Huddersfield T	D	2-2	2-0	14	Apter [11], Morgan [45]	10,410
26	25	A	Exeter C	W	3-1	3-0	14	Hamilton [33], Bloxham [43], Fletcher [45]	6325
27	28	A	Lincoln C	W	2-0	1-0	13	Fletcher [32], Casey [57]	7517
28	Feb 1	H	Charlton Ath	D	2-2	0-0	13	Silvera [74], Ennis [87]	9462
29	8	A	Burton Alb	D	1-1	0-1	13	Morgan [90]	2965
30	11	H	Rotherham U	D	0-0	0-0	11		8216
31	15	H	Mansfield T	D	3-3	1-2	11	Carey [19], Fletcher [71], Ennis [77]	10,309
32	22	H	Crawley T	W	3-1	2-1	11	Ennis 2 [10, 18], Evans (pen) [79]	9281
33	Mar 1	A	Stockport Co	L	1-2	1-0	11	Fletcher [7]	10,554
34	4	H	Peterborough U	D	0-0	0-0	13		7873
35	8	A	Barnsley	W	3-0	0-0	11	Carey 2 [56, 73], Fletcher [64]	11,563
36	11	A	Cambridge U	W	2-1	1-1	11	Fletcher [17], Carey [54]	7957
37	15	H	Leyton Orient	L	1-2	0-1	11	Carey [61]	9438
38	22	A	Northampton T	W	2-0	1-0	10	Fletcher [20], Ennis [61]	6714
39	29	H	Bolton W	W	2-1	1-1	10	Fletcher [13], Ennis [59]	11,602
40	Apr 1	H	Reading	W	3-0	0-0	9	Carey 2 [53, 90], Casey [55]	8345
41	5	A	Rotherham U	L	1-2	0-1	10	Carey (pen) [82]	9172
42	18	A	Stevenage	W	3-1	0-0	10	Apter 3 [56, 63, 68]	4161
43	21	H	Wrexham	L	1-2	0-0	10	Apter [90]	12,266
44	26	H	Wigan Ath	D	1-1	0-1	9	Evans (pen) [74]	11,176
45	30	H	Birmingham C	L	0-2	0-1	9		9618
46	May 3	H	Bristol R	W	4-1	1-1	9	Bloxham [40], Morgan [55], Ennis [76], Finnigan [89]	10,534

Final League Position: 9

GOALSCORERS

League (72): Fletcher 11, Apter 8, Carey 8 (1 pen), Joseph 8, Ennis 7, Morgan 5, Evans 4 (3 pens), Casey 3, Hamilton 3, Husband 3, Bloxham 2, Ballard 1, Beesley 1, Finnigan 1, Offiah 1, Onomah 1, Silvera 1, own goals 4.
FA Cup (3): Carey 2, Rhodes 1.
Carabao Cup (6): Pennington 2, Beesley 1, Coulson 1, Evans 1, Finnigan 1.
Vertu Trophy (7): Hamilton 2, Rhodes 2, Carey 1, Embleton 1, Finnigan 1.

Grimshaw D 2	Pennington M 18+3	Casey O 43	Husband J 31+3	Coulson H 26+9	Hamilton C 22+12	Norburn O 6+2	Evans L 40+2	Carey S 23+10	Joseph K 24	Rhodes J 3+18	Embleton E 4+11	Fletcher J 32+9	Beesley J 3+19	Apter R 40+5	Baggott E 15+3	Finnigan R 2+6	Ballard D 10+8	Ashworth Z 1+5	O'Donnell R 6	Lawrence-Gabriel J 13+17	Tyrer H 38	Offiah O 40	Morgan A 36	Onomah J 3+12	Thompson D —+3	Bondo T —+3	Bloxham T 5+9	Silvera S 3+12	Ennis N 17+2	Lyons A —+1	Match No.
1	2	3	4	5¹	6	7¹	8	9	10³	11²	12	13	14	15																	1
1	2		4		9⁵	14	6	8	10⁴	13	12	11²		5³	3	7¹	15	16													2
	2		4	8⁵	5	6³	7	16	9⁴	12	13	10²		15	3		11¹		1	14											3
	3		4		8³	7⁴	6	16	10	12	13	9¹	15	5⁵			11²	14	1	2											4
		4	5	13	9²	8	7	11⁴	12	14		15	6³				10¹			2	1	3									5
12	4	5	15	9		7	16	10²	13	14	6⁵			11³						2¹	1	3	8⁴								6
	4		5	9		7	15	10⁴		13	12	14	6²				11¹			2	1	3	8⁵								7
	4		5	9		7	12	11³	10²	14	13	15	6⁴							2	1	3	8¹								8
	4	12	5¹	9		7	15	11		14	13	10²	6⁴							2	1	3	8³								9
	4	5²		9		7		10	12	13	11¹		6							2	1	3	8								10
12	4	5			7		10	13	9³	15		6	11¹							2²	1	3	8⁴	14							11
	4	5¹			15	10		13	9	6	14	11³	12							2	1	3	7²	8⁴							12
3	4		5		7	8³	10	12	9²	11¹		6	14						1		2	13									13
	4		5	9⁴	7	8²	10	12	14	6³		13	11¹			1	2			3		15									14
	4	5	13	9²	15	7	10¹	11³	14	6	8⁴					1	2			3		12									15
	4	5	8²		7⁴	6	11		10¹	9³	14	12	13	1	2			3				15									16
3	4	5		8⁵	7		10¹	14	9³	12		6⁴	16	11²		1	2			15	13										17
3		5		7	10⁵		11⁴	6¹	14	16	4	12	1	2	8³	9³	13	15													18
3	4	5	13	7²	10⁵	14	11³	6	12	16	15	1	2	8	9¹																19
3	4	5		7		11	12	10	6	9¹	1	2	8																		20
3	4	5	9²	7	13	11	12	10¹	6³	14	1	2	8																		21
3	4	5	9¹	7	12	10³	13	11²	6⁴	14	15	1	2	8																	22
3	4	5³	12	14	7	9¹	10⁴	13	11²	6	15	1	2	8																	23
3	4	5²	14	13	7⁴	9	10	15	11³	6	12	1	2¹	8																	24
3¹	4	5	9³	7	15	14	10²	6	12	1	2	8										11⁴	13								25
3	5	9⁴	8	15	11²	14	6¹	4	1	2	7	13										10³	12								26
3	5	9	8	11²	13	6¹	4	12	1	2	7	14										10³									27
3	5²	9	8	10¹	14	6³	4	15	1	2⁴	7										11	12	13								28
3	5¹	14	9	13	8	10⁴	15	6³	4	1	2²	7										12	11								29
3¹	5	16	6²	15	8	10⁴	11³	13	4	12	1	2	7									9⁵	14								30
3	5	13	14	7	10	12	6³	4¹	15	1	2⁴	8										9²	11								31
3	4	5⁴	8¹	6	9	11⁸	13	15	12	1	2	7³	14									10²									32
3	4	9³	6²	5⁴	8	10¹	15	13	14	1	2	7										12	11								33
3	4	6³	12	8	9	10²	13	5¹	2	1	7⁴	15										14	11								34
3	4	5⁵	7	9	10³	15	6⁴	16	12	1	2¹	8	14									13	11²								35
3	4	15	5	8	9⁴	10²	14	6¹	1	2	7	13										12	11³								36
3³	4	5	13	8	9	11¹	14	6²	1	2	7											12	10								37
3	12	5¹	13	7	9²	11⁵	6²	4	15	1	2	8	16									14	10⁴								38
15	3	4	5⁴	13	7	9	10³	6¹	1	2	8											12	14	11²							39
3	4	5	14	7⁴	9	10³	6²	15	1	2	8											13	12	11¹							40
3	4	5	13	7¹	9	11⁴	15⁵	6²	1	2	8											12	14	10³							41
3		5	13	7	9	11²	6³	4	1	2	8											12	14	10¹							42
3		5¹	13	7	9	11⁴	15	6	4	14	1	2³	8									12	9²	10							43
3	5¹	9	7	11²	6	4	1	2	8	13	12	10																			44
3	5¹	12	9	7³	11²	15	6⁴	4	16	1	2⁵	8	13									14	10								45
2²	3		5	9	7⁴	12	16	6¹	4	15	13	1	8									11³	10⁵	14							46

FA Cup

First Round	Gillingham	(a)	2-0
Second Round	Birmingham C	(h)	1-2

Carabao Cup

First Round	Burton Alb	(a)	4-0
Second Round	Blackburn R	(a)	2-1
Third Round	Sheffield Wed	(h)	0-1

Vertu Trophy

Group E (N)	Crewe Alex	(h)	4-1
Group E (N)	Liverpool U21	(h)	0-0
Liverpool U21 won 8-7 on penalties.			
Group E (N)	Harrogate T	(a)	2-2
Blackpool won 5-4 on penalties.			
Second Round	Aston Villa U21	(h)	1-1
Aston Villa U21 won 18-17 on penalties.			

BOLTON WANDERERS

FOUNDATION

In 1874 boys of Christ Church Sunday School, Blackburn Street, led by their master Thomas Ogden, established a football club which went under the name of the school and whose president was vicar of Christ Church. Membership was 6d (two and a half pence). When their president began to lay down too many rules about the use of church premises, the club broke away and formed Bolton Wanderers in 1877, holding their earliest meetings at the Gladstone Hotel.

The Toughsheet Community Stadium, Burnden Way, Lostock, Bolton BL6 6JW.

Telephone: (01204) 673 673.

Ticket Office: (01204) 328 888.

Website: www.bwfc.co.uk

Email: reception@bwfc.co.uk (or via website).

Ground Capacity: 28,018.

Record Attendance: 69,912 v Manchester C, FA Cup 5th rd, 18 February 1933 (at Burnden Park); 28,353 v Leicester C, Premier League, 23 December 2003 (at The Reebok Stadium).

Pitch Measurements: 105m × 68m (115yd × 74.5yd).

Chairman: Sharon Brittan.

Chief Executive: David Ray.

Head Coach: Steven Schumacher.

Assistant Head Coach: Richie Kyle.

HONOURS

League Champions: First Division – 1996–97; Division 2 – 1908–09, 1977–78; Division 3 – 1972–73.
Runners-up: Division 2 – 1899–1900, 1904–05, 1910–11, 1934–35; Second Division – 1992–93; FL 1 – 2016–17.

FA Cup Winners: 1923, 1926, 1929, 1958.
Runners-up: 1894, 1904, 1953.

League Cup: *Runners-up:* 1995, 2004.

League Trophy Winners: 1989, 2023.
Runners-up: 1986.

European Competitions
UEFA Cup: 2005–06, 2007–08.

Colours: White shirts with red and blue trim, blue shorts with white trim, white socks with red and blue trim.

Year Formed: 1874.

Turned Professional: 1880.

Previous Name: 1874, Christ Church FC; 1877, Bolton Wanderers.

Club Nickname: 'The Trotters'.

Grounds: Park Recreation Ground and Cockle's Field before moving to Pike's Lane ground 1881; 1895, Burnden Park; 1997, Reebok Stadium (renamed Macron Stadium 2014; University of Bolton Stadium 2018; The Toughsheet Community Stadium 2023).

First Football League Game: 8 September 1888, Football League, v Derby Co (h) L 3–6 – Harrison; Robinson, Mitchell; Roberts, Weir, Bullough, Davenport (2), Milne, Coupar, Barbour, Brogan (1).

Record League Victory: 8–0 v Barnsley, Division 2, 6 October 1934 – Jones; Smith, Finney; Goslin, Atkinson, George Taylor; George T. Taylor (2), Eastham, Milsom (1), Westwood (4), Cook, (1 og).

Record Cup Victory: 13–0 v Sheffield U, FA Cup 2nd rd, 1 February 1890 – Parkinson; Robinson (1), Jones; Bullough, Davenport, Roberts; Rushton, Brogan (3), Cassidy (5), McNee, Weir (4).

Record Defeat: 1–9 v Preston NE, FA Cup 2nd rd, 5 November 1887.

FOOTBALL YEARBOOK FACT FILE

Bolton Wanderers goalkeeper John Sutcliffe is the last player to win full international honours for England at both soccer and rugby union. A prominent rugby player with Heckmondwike, he appeared for England against the New Zealand Maori touring team in February 1889. Soon afterwards he was suspended for professionalism and switched codes to sign for the Trotters. He went on to make over 350 appearances for Bolton and won five caps for England, making his debut against Wales in March 1893.

Most League Points (2 for a win): 61, Division 3, 1972–73.

Most League Points (3 for a win): 98, Division 1, 1996–97.

Most League Goals: 100, Division 1, 1996–97.

Highest League Scorer in Season: Joe Smith, 38, Division 1, 1920–21.

Most League Goals in Total Aggregate: Nat Lofthouse, 255, 1946–61.

Most League Goals in One Match: 5, Tony Caldwell v Walsall, Division 3, 10 September 1983.

Most Capped Player: Ricardo Gardner, 72 (111), Jamaica.

Most League Appearances: Eddie Hopkinson, 519, 1956–70.

Youngest League Player: Ray Parry, 15 years 267 days v Wolverhampton W, 13 October 1951.

Record Transfer Fee Received: £15,000,000 from Chelsea for Nicolas Anelka, January 2008.

Record Transfer Fee Paid: £8,250,000 to Toulouse for Johan Elmander, June 2008.

Football League Record: 1888 Founder Member of the League; 1888–92 Football League; 1892–99 Division 1; 1899–1900 Division 2; 1900–03 Division 1; 1903–05 Division 2; 1905–08 Division 1; 1908–09 Division 2; 1909–10 Division 1; 1910–11 Division 2; 1911–33 Division 1; 1933–35 Division 2; 1935–64 Division 1; 1964–71 Division 2; 1971–73 Division 3; 1973–78 Division 2; 1978–80 Division 1; 1980–83 Division 2; 1983–87 Division 3; 1987–88 Division 4; 1988–92 Division 3; 1992–93 Second Division; 1993–95 First Division; 1995–96 Premier League; 1996–97 First Division; 1997–98 Premier League; 1998–2001 First Division; 2001–12 Premier League; 2012–16 FL C; 2016–17 FL 1; 2017–19 FL C; 2019–20 FL 1; 2020–21 FL 2; 2021– FL 1.

LATEST SEQUENCES

Longest Sequence of League Wins: 11, 5.11.1904 – 2.1.1905.

Longest Sequence of League Defeats: 11, 7.4.1902 – 18.10.1902.

Longest Sequence of League Draws: 6, 25.1.1913 – 8.3.1913.

Longest Sequence of Unbeaten League Matches: 23, 13.10.1990 – 9.3.1991.

Longest Sequence Without a League Win: 26, 7.4.1902 – 10.1.1903.

Successive Scoring Runs: 24 from 22.11.1996.

Successive Non-scoring Runs: 11 from 9.4.2019.

MANAGERS

Tom Rawthorne 1874–85
 (Secretary)
J. J. Bentley 1885–86
 (Secretary)
W. G. Struthers 1886–87
 (Secretary)
Fitzroy Norris 1887
 (Secretary)
J. J. Bentley 1887–95
 (Secretary)
Harry Downs 1895–96
 (Secretary)
Frank Brettell 1896–98
 (Secretary)
John Somerville 1898–1910
Will Settle 1910–15
Tom Mather 1915–19
Charles Foweraker 1919–44
Walter Rowley 1944–50
Bill Ridding 1951–68
Nat Lofthouse 1968–70
Jimmy McIlroy 1970
Jimmy Meadows 1971
Nat Lofthouse 1971
 (then Admin. Manager to 1972)
Jimmy Armfield 1971–74
Ian Greaves 1974–80
Stan Anderson 1980–81
George Mulhall 1981–82
John McGovern 1982–85
Charlie Wright 1985
Phil Neal 1985–92
Bruce Rioch 1992–95
Roy McFarland 1995–96
Colin Todd 1996–99
Roy McFarland and Colin Todd 1995–96
Sam Allardyce 1999–2007
Sammy Lee 2007
Gary Megson 2007–09
Owen Coyle 2010–12
Dougie Freedman 2012–14
Neil Lennon 2014–16
Phil Parkinson 2016–19
Keith Hill 2019–20
Ian Evatt 2020–25
Steven Schumacher January 2025–

TEN YEAR LEAGUE RECORD

		P	W	D	L	F	A	Pts	Pos
2015-16	FL C	46	5	15	26	41	81	30	24
2016-17	FL 1	46	25	11	10	68	36	86	2
2017-18	FL C	46	10	13	23	39	74	43	21
2018-19	FL C	46	8	8	30	29	78	32	23
2019-20	FL 1	34	5	11	18	27	66	14	23§
2020-21	FL 2	46	23	10	13	59	50	79	3
2021-22	FL 1	46	21	10	15	74	57	73	9
2022-23	FL 1	46	23	12	11	62	36	81	5
2023-24	FL 1	46	25	12	9	86	51	87	3
2024-25	FL 1	46	20	8	18	67	70	68	8

§*Decided on points-per-game (0.41)*

DID YOU KNOW ❓

Bolton Wanderers did not play a competitive first-team match between 8 December and 16 February during the 'Big Freeze' of 1962–63. On 14 February they travelled to Cork in the Republic of Ireland where they played a friendly game with Manchester United to gain some much-needed match practice. Teenager Francis Lee scored both goals for Wanderers who lost 4-2 in front of a crowd of around 10,000.

BOLTON WANDERERS – SKY BET LEAGUE ONE 2024–25 LEAGUE RECORD

Match No.	Date	Venue	Opponents	Result	H/T Score	Lg Pos.	Goalscorers	Attendance
1	Aug 10	A	Leyton Orient	W 2-1	1-1	5	Charles [8], Adeboyejo [75]	7835
2	18	H	Wrexham	D 0-0	0-0	9		25,957
3	24	A	Charlton Ath	L 0-2	0-1	13		14,365
4	31	H	Exeter C	L 0-2	0-1	18		22,086
5	Sept 14	H	Huddersfield T	L 0-4	0-1	21		22,532
6	21	H	Reading	W 5-2	4-1	18	Sheehan [12], Charles 3 (2 pens) [21 (p), 34, 45 (p)], Dempsey [87]	19,635
7	28	A	Crawley T	W 2-0	1-0	14	Dempsey [5], McAtee [78]	4696
8	Oct 1	A	Northampton T	W 4-2	2-0	11	McAtee [6], Thomason [23], Toal [60], Charles [83]	5730
9	5	H	Shrewsbury T	D 2-2	0-2	13	Dempsey [47], Schon [61]	19,765
10	19	H	Burton Alb	W 2-1	0-0	11	Collins [61], Williams [63]	19,540
11	22	A	Birmingham C	L 0-2	0-1	14		25,793
12	26	H	Peterborough U	W 1-0	0-0	9	Lolos [90]	20,022
13	29	A	Stevenage	W 4-1	2-0	6	Santos [13], McAtee [16], Adeboyejo [61], Charles [88]	3611
14	Nov 9	A	Stockport Co	L 0-5	0-1	10		10,342
15	23	H	Blackpool	W 2-1	0-1	9	Thomason [53], Collins [90]	22,479
16	26	A	Cambridge U	D 1-1	0-0	8	Collins [60]	5266
17	Dec 3	H	Mansfield T	W 3-1	0-1	7	Charles [75], Adeboyejo [80], McAtee [85]	19,823
18	14	H	Wigan Ath	L 0-2	0-1	8		24,448
19	20	A	Wycombe W	D 0-0	0-0	7		6119
20	26	H	Barnsley	L 1-2	1-0	10	Lolos [26]	22,215
21	29	H	Lincoln C	W 3-0	1-0	8	Collins [36], Matete 2 [50, 66]	22,395
22	Jan 1	A	Mansfield T	L 1-2	1-2	10	Collins [40]	8553
23	4	A	Exeter C	W 2-1	0-0	10	Collins [88], Morley [90]	6353
24	11	A	Rotherham U	L 1-3	0-2	10	McAtee [86]	10,258
25	18	H	Cambridge U	D 2-2	1-2	9	McAtee [34], Rossi (og) [90]	19,946
26	21	H	Charlton Ath	L 1-2	0-0	9	Randall [55]	18,477
27	25	A	Huddersfield T	W 1-0	0-0	9	Collins [55]	19,999
28	28	H	Northampton T	W 3-1	2-1	7	Thomason [3], Shaw (og) [44], Collins [83]	18,956
29	Feb 1	A	Reading	L 0-1	0-0	9		11,508
30	8	H	Crawley T	W 4-3	0-0	7	Osei-Tutu [52], Murphy [68], Sheehan [85], Barker (og) [90]	20,384
31	15	A	Shrewsbury T	W 3-2	0-1	8	Toal [59], McAtee 2 [63, 79]	7613
32	22	A	Leyton Orient	W 2-1	0-1	8	McAtee [60], Morley (pen) [75]	20,851
33	Mar 1	A	Wrexham	D 0-0	0-0	7		13,284
34	4	H	Birmingham C	W 3-1	1-1	7	McAtee [39], Thomason [49], Collins [71]	23,023
35	8	A	Burton Alb	W 2-1	1-0	6	Morley [22], Sheehan [60]	4172
36	11	A	Bristol R	L 2-3	1-1	6	Morley [39], McAtee [70]	7644
37	15	H	Stockport Co	L 0-1	0-0	7		24,571
38	29	A	Blackpool	L 1-2	1-1	8	Collins [35]	11,602
39	Apr 1	A	Wigan Ath	W 1-0	0-0	6	Forino-Joseph [90]	15,445
40	5	H	Bristol R	W 1-0	0-0	6	Collins [76]	22,422
41	8	H	Rotherham U	L 0-1	0-1	7		19,218
42	12	A	Barnsley	L 1-4	0-2	8	Collins [74]	13,685
43	18	H	Wycombe W	L 0-2	0-0	8		21,114
44	21	A	Lincoln C	W 2-1	2-2	8	Matete [29], Murphy [38]	10,240
45	26	A	Peterborough U	D 1-1	1-1	8	Forino-Joseph [33]	9231
46	May 3	H	Stevenage	D 1-1	0-0	8	Dacres-Cogley [66]	20,613

Final League Position: 8

GOALSCORERS

League (67): Collins 12, McAtee 11, Charles 7 (2 pens), Morley 4 (1 pen), Thomason 4, Adeboyejo 3, Dempsey 3, Matete 3, Sheehan 3, Forino-Joseph 2, Lolos 2, Murphy 2, Toal 2, Dacres-Cogley 1, Osei-Tutu 1, Randall 1, Santos 1, Schon 1, Williams 1, own goals 3.
FA Cup (1): Sheehan 1.
Carabao Cup (4): Charles 1, Collins 1, Osei-Tutu 1, Thomason 1.
Vertu Trophy (10): Collins 6, Adeboyejo 1, Dempsey 1, Lolos 1, McAtee 1.

Baxter N 26	Toal E 18+1	Santos R 25	Iredale J 1	Dacres-Cogley J 37+5	Arfield S 3+9	Sheehan J 29+5	Thomason G 35+3	Schon S 34+5	Charles D 15+9	Collins A 36+9	McAtee J 31+14	Matete J 18+17	Osei-Tutu J 15+17	Lolos K 8+16	Adeboyejo V 12+15	Johnston G 37+1	Dempsey K 8+7	Forino-Joseph C 12+4	Williams R 7+9	Southwood L 20	Forrester W 18+5	Jones G 16+7	Sharples S 1+2	Mendes Gomes C 2+9	Morley A 18+1	Randall J 10+9	Murphy A 11+2	Etete K —+5	Abimbola D 1+3	Inwood S 2	Lawrence D —+2	Rice H —+1	Match No.
1	2	3	4[3]	5	6[1]	7[2]	8	9	10[5]	11[4]	12	13	14	15	16																		1
1	2	3		5[4]	14	6[5]	7	8	11[2]	10[1]	9[3]	16	15	13		4		12															2
1	2	3		5[1]	16	7[3]	6[4]	8	10[2]	11	9	15	13	12		4[5]		14															3
1		3		5	8[2]	7	9[1]	11	15	10[5]	13	14	12			4	6[4]	2															4
1	4	3		5	13	14	6	8	11[1]	10[4]	15	7		12		9[2]	2[3]																5
1	2	3		5	12	7[2]	8	9[3]	10[4]	16	15	6[1]	11[5]			4	13	14															6
1	2	3		5	15	7	8[4]	9	10[1]	13	12	14	11[2]			4	6[3]																7
1	2	3		5	15	7	8[4]	9[5]	13	10[2]	11[1]	14	12			4	6[3]	16															8
	2	3		5	16	7[3]	8	9	11[4]	13	12	14	10[2]			4	6[5]	15		1													9
		3		2	14	7	8	11[1]	9	10[3]	13	12				4	6[2]	5		1													10
		3		2	10[3]	6	8	11[2]	14	12	7	13				4	9[1]	5[4]	1		15												11
	2	3		5	6	8[3]	12	10	9[2]	7	13	11[1]				4		14		1													12
	2[1]	3		5	16	6	8[6]	13	9[4]	10[3]	7	14	11[2]			4		15		1	12												13
1		4		2[1]		9	6[3]	10	13	7	8	14	11[5]			5					3	12											14
1		3		5[3]		6	7[1]	8	11	10	9[3]	12	14	13		4		2															15
1		3		5[1]		7	8[2]		10[2]	11[4]	14	6	13	12	15	4		9			2												16
1		3		9[4]		7[1]	5[2]	14	11[3]	8[6]	6	15	12	10		4		13			2	16											17
1		3		15		7	8[1]	10	13	9	6[3]	5[4]	14	11[2]		4		12			2												18
1		2		7		8	13	10[2]	12	6	9	11[1]				5		3	4														19
1		3		12	6[1]	7	8[1]	13	10	11[2]	14	9[4]				5		4	2		15												20
1	2[1]	3		5[2]		7	8[3]	14	11	10[4]	6	15	9[5]			4		13	12		16												21
		3		5[2]		7	8[1]	10[4]	11	15	6	13	9[3]			4		12	1		2	14											22
1		3				7[3]	8[1]	12	11	10	14	13	9[2]			4		5	2			6											23
1		3		13			8[2]	9	12	10	11					4		6[1]	2			5	7										24
	3[1]			5[2]	16	6	8	11	10[3]		13	14	15	4				1	12		2[5]			7	9[4]								25
		3		8[1]	9[4]	6		11	13	12	2[2]	15	14	5				1	4					7[3]	10								26
		2		9	6[1]	11[2]	14	12	8[3]	10		5					1	4	3		2	7	13										27
				14	7	8	9[1]	11		5[3]	10[2]	4				1		3	2			6	12	13									28
	2			5[5]	6	7[4]	12	9	14	16	11[2]	4				1		3			15	10[3]	8[1]	13									29
	3			2[3]	8	6[2]	11	16	9	12	15	13				1	4[5]	14			7	10[4]	5[1]										30
	2			13		14	11[2]	9[5]	6[4]	12	16	4[1]	15			1	3	5			7	10[3]	8										31
	2			8	15	6	12	11[2]	9[1]	10[4]	16	13[5]		14		1	3	7				5[3]											32
	13	2		8[4]	15	6[2]	10	11[3]	9	4	1	3						12	7		14	5[1]											33
	2			5	14	7[3]	11	9[2]	15	8	13	4		3	1				10[1]		6[4]	12											34
4		2[4]		7		8	13	9[3]	10[1]	11[2]	14	15	1	3		6			12		5												35
2				7	8[3]	9[1]	10	11	12	15	1	3		5[4]	13	6	14	4[2]															36
1	3[4]	2[5]		7	8	16	11	10[1]	13	5	14	4	15	12	6[2]	9[3]																	37
1		5[5]		13	7[1]	9[3]	10	11[4]	8[2]	4	3	2	16	12	6[1]	14	15																38
1		5		6	7	14	10[2]	11[4]	13	8[3]	4	3	2	15	12	9[1]																	39
1		5[2]		7	12	11	10	15	8	4	14	3	2[1]	13	9[3]	6	4																40
1		5[1]		6	7[3]	10	11[2]	8	4	12	3	2[4]	14	9	13	15																	41
1	3[5]	5[1]		6[4]	7	11	10	14	8	16	4[3]	15	2	12	9[3]	13																	42
1		2[5]		7	10	12	6	8[1]	11[3]	4	9[2]	3	16	15	5[4]	13	14																43
1		5[4]		7	10[2]	14	6	13	4[5]	12	3	2[4]	9[1]	15	8	16	11[3]																44
				9	6[2]	12	11[4]	7	10[1]	3	1	2	8	5[3]	15	4	13	14															45
		13		7	5	11[2]	10[3]	6	15	3	1	2[1]	9[4]	8	14	4	12																46

FA Cup

First Round	Walsall	(a)	1-2	

Carabao Cup

First Round	Mansfield T	(h)	1-1	
Bolton W won 5-4 on penalties.				
Second Round	Shrewsbury T	(a)	2-0	
Third Round	Arsenal	(a)	1-5	

Vertu Trophy

Group D (N)	Barrow	(a)	3-2	
Group D (N)	Aston Villa U21	(h)	1-1	
Aston Villa U21 won 4-1 on penalties.				
Group D (N)	Fleetwood T	(h)	2-1	
Second Round	Huddersfield T	(h)	3-1	
Third Round	Lincoln C	(a)	1-0	
Quarter-Final	Wrexham	(a)	0-1	

AFC BOURNEMOUTH

FOUNDATION

There was a Bournemouth FC as early as 1875, but the present club arose out of the remnants of the Boscombe St John's club (formed 1890). The meeting at which Boscombe FC came into being was held at a house in Gladstone Road in 1899. They began by playing in the Boscombe and District Junior League.

Vitality Stadium, Dean Court, Kings Park, Bournemouth, Dorset BH7 7AF.

Telephone: (01202) 726 300.

Ticket Office: (01202) 726 300.

Website: www.afcb.co.uk

Email: enquiries@afcb.co.uk

Ground Capacity: 11,307.

Record Attendance: 28,799 v Manchester U, FA Cup 6th rd, 2 March 1957.

Pitch Measurements: 105m × 68m (115yd × 74.5yd).

Chairman: Bill Foley.

Chief Executive: Neill Blake.

Head Coach: Andoni Iraola.

Assistant Head Coaches: Tommy Elphick, Shaun Cooper.

Colours: Red and black striped shirts, black shorts with red trim, black socks with red trim.

Year Formed: 1899.

Turned Professional: 1910.

Previous Names: 1890, Boscombe St John's; 1899, Boscombe FC; 1923, Bournemouth & Boscombe Ath FC; 1972, AFC Bournemouth.

Club Nickname: 'The Cherries'.

Grounds: 1899, Castlemain Road, Pokesdown; 1910, Dean Court (renamed Fitness First Stadium 2001; Seward Stadium 2011; Goldsands Stadium 2012; Vitality Stadium 2015).

First Football League Game: 25 August 1923, Division 3 (S), v Swindon T (a) L 1–3 – Heron; Wingham, Lamb; Butt, Charles Smith, Voisey; Miller, Lister (1), Davey, Simpson, Robinson.

Record League Victory: 8–0 v Birmingham C, FL C, 25 October 2014 – Boruc; Francis, Elphick, Cook, Daniels; Ritchie (1), Arter (Gosling), Surman, Pugh (3); Pitman (1) (Rantie 2 (1 pen)), Wilson (1) (Fraser). 10–0 win v Northampton T at start of 1939–40 expunged from the records on outbreak of war.

Record Cup Victory: 11–0 v Margate, FA Cup 1st rd, 20 November 1971 – Davies; Machin (1), Kitchener, Benson, Jones, Powell, Cave (1), Boyer, MacDougall (9 incl. 1p), Miller, Scott (De Garis).

Record Defeat: 0–9 v Lincoln C, Division 3, 18 December 1982; 0–9 v Liverpool, Premier League, 27 August 2022.

HONOURS

League Champions: FL C – 2014–15; Division 3 – 1986–87. *Runners-up:* FL C – 2021–22; FL 1 – 2012–13; Division 3S – 1947–48; FL 2 – 2009–10; Division 4 – 1970–71.

FA Cup: 6th rd – 1957, 2021, 2025.

League Cup: quarter-final – 2015, 2018, 2019.

League Trophy Winners: 1984. *Runners-up:* 1998.

FOOTBALL YEARBOOK FACT FILE

The facilities at Dean Court were rudimentary when AFC Bournemouth were elected to the Football League in 1923. However, the directors purchased the steel framework of a café at the sale of the effects of the Empire Exhibition at Wembley. This was then transformed into a grandstand holding 3,500 in time for the opening fixture of the 1927–28 season against Swindon Town.

Most League Points (2 for a win): 62, Division 3, 1971–72.

Most League Points (3 for a win): 97, Division 3, 1986–87.

Most League Goals: 98, FL C, 2014–15.

Highest League Scorer in Season: Ted MacDougall, 42, 1970–71.

Most League Goals in Total Aggregate: Ron Eyre, 202, 1924–33.

Most League Goals in One Match: 4, Jack Russell v Clapton Orient, Division 3 (S), 7 January 1933; 4, Jack Russell v Bristol C, Division 3 (S), 28 January 1933; 4, Harry Mardon v Southend U, Division 3 (S), 1 January 1938; 4, Jack McDonald v Torquay U, Division 3 (S), 8 November 1947; 4, Ted MacDougall v Colchester U, 18 September 1970; 4, Brian Clark v Rotherham U, 10 October 1972; 4, Luther Blissett v Hull C, 29 November 1988; 4, James Hayter v Bury, Division 2, 21 October 2000.

Most Capped Player: Chris Mepham, 45 (includes 3 on loan at Sunderland) (49) Wales.

Most League Appearances: Steve Fletcher, 628, 1992–2007; 2008–13.

Youngest League Player: Jimmy White, 15 years 321 days v Brentford, 30 April 1958.

Record Transfer Fee Received: £55,000,000 (potentially rising to £65,000,000) from Tottenham H for Dominic Solanke, August 2024.

Record Transfer Fee Paid: £31,700,000 (potentially rising to £40,200,00) to Porto for Evanilson, August 2024.

Football League Record: 1923 Elected to Division 3 (S); 1923–58 Division 3 (S); 1959–70 Division 3 (record number of years); 1970–71 Division 4; 1971–75 Division 3; 1975–82 Division 4; 1982–87 Division 3; 1987–90 Division 2; 1990–92 Division 3; 1992–2002 Second Division; 2002–03 Third Division; 2003–04 Second Division; 2004–08 FL 1; 2008–10 FL 2; 2010–13 FL 1; 2013–15 FL C; 2015–20 Premier League; 2020–22 FL C; 2022– Premier League.

LATEST SEQUENCES

Longest Sequence of League Wins: 8, 12.3.2013 – 20.4.2013.

Longest Sequence of League Defeats: 7, 13.8.1994 – 13.9.1994.

Longest Sequence of League Draws: 5, 25.4.2000 – 19.8.2000.

Longest Sequence of Unbeaten League Matches: 18, 6.3.1982 – 28.8.1982.

Longest Sequence Without a League Win: 14, 6.3.1974 – 27.4.1974.

Successive Scoring Runs: 31 from 28.10.2000.

Successive Non-scoring Runs: 6 from 1.2.1975.

MANAGERS

Vincent Kitcher 1914–23 *(Secretary-Manager)*
Harry Kinghorn 1923–25
Leslie Knighton 1925–28
Frank Richards 1928–30
Billy Birrell 1930–35
Bob Crompton 1935–36
Charlie Bell 1936–39
Harry Kinghorn 1939–47
Harry Lowe 1947–50
Jack Bruton 1950–56
Fred Cox 1956–58
Don Welsh 1958–61
Bill McGarry 1961–63
Reg Flewin 1963–65
Fred Cox 1965–70
John Bond 1970–73
Trevor Hartley 1974–75
John Benson 1975–78
Alec Stock 1979–80
David Webb 1980–82
Don Megson 1983
Harry Redknapp 1983–92
Tony Pulis 1992–94
Mel Machin 1994–2000
Sean O'Driscoll 2000–06
Kevin Bond 2006–08
Jimmy Quinn 2008
Eddie Howe 2008–11
Lee Bradbury 2011–12
Paul Groves 2012
Eddie Howe 2012–20
Jason Tindall 2020–21
Jonathan Woodgate 2021
Scott Parker 2021–22
Gary O'Neil 2022–23
Andoni Iraola June 2023–

TEN YEAR LEAGUE RECORD

		P	W	D	L	F	A	Pts	Pos
2015-16	PR Lge	38	11	9	18	45	67	42	16
2016-17	PR Lge	38	12	10	16	55	67	46	9
2017-18	PR Lge	38	11	11	16	45	61	44	12
2018-19	PR Lge	38	13	6	19	56	70	45	14
2019-20	PR Lge	38	9	7	22	40	65	34	18
2020-21	FL C	46	22	11	13	73	46	77	6
2021-22	FL C	46	25	13	8	74	39	88	2
2022-23	PR Lge	38	11	6	21	37	71	39	15
2023-24	PR Lge	38	13	9	16	54	67	48	12
2024-25	PR Lge	38	15	11	12	58	46	56	9

DID YOU KNOW ?

AFC Bournemouth proved to be the equals of First Division giants in their FA Cup fourth-round tie against Liverpool in January 1968, securing a replay after the teams drew 0-0 at Dean Court before losing the replay 4-1. The first encounter was the first occasion when highlights of a Cherries game had appeared on the BBC's *Match of the Day* programme.

AFC BOURNEMOUTH – PREMIER LEAGUE 2024–25 LEAGUE RECORD

Match No.	Date	Venue	Opponents	Result	H/T Score	Lg Pos.	Goalscorers	Atten-dance
1	Aug 17	A	Nottingham F	D 1-1	0-1	7	Semenyo [86]	29,763
2	25	H	Newcastle U	D 1-1	1-0	14	Tavernier [37]	11,161
3	31	H	Everton	W 3-2	0-0	7	Semenyo [87], Cook [90], Sinisterra [90]	38,805
4	Sept 14	H	Chelsea	L 0-1	0-0	11		11,235
5	21	A	Liverpool	L 0-3	0-3	13		60,347
6	30	H	Southampton	W 3-1	1-0	11	Evanilson [17], Ouattara [32], Semenyo [39]	11,243
7	Oct 5	A	Leicester C	L 0-1	0-1	13		31,706
8	19	H	Arsenal	W 2-0	0-0	10	Christie [70], Kluivert (pen) [79]	11,235
9	26	A	Aston Villa	D 1-1	0-0	11	Evanilson [90]	42,165
10	Nov 2	H	Manchester C	W 2-1	1-0	8	Semenyo [9], Evanilson [64]	11,231
11	9	A	Brentford	L 2-3	1-1	11	Evanilson [17], Kluivert [49]	16,993
12	23	H	Brighton & HA	L 1-2	0-1	13	Brooks [90]	11,196
13	30	A	Wolverhampton W	W 4-2	3-1	11	Kluivert 3 (3 pens) [3, 18, 74], Kerkez [8]	26,685
14	Dec 5	H	Tottenham H	W 1-0	1-0	9	Huijsen [17]	11,234
15	8	A	Ipswich T	W 2-1	0-1	8	Unal [87], Ouattara [90]	29,180
16	16	H	West Ham U	D 1-1	0-0	6	Unal [90]	11,204
17	22	A	Manchester U	W 3-0	1-0	5	Huijsen [29], Kluivert (pen) [61], Semenyo [63]	73,720
18	26	H	Crystal Palace	D 0-0	0-0	6		11,129
19	29	A	Fulham	D 2-2	0-1	6	Evanilson [51], Ouattara [89]	27,301
20	Jan 4	H	Everton	W 1-0	0-0	7	Brooks [77]	11,223
21	14	A	Chelsea	D 2-2	0-1	7	Kluivert (pen) [50], Semenyo [68]	39,092
22	18	A	Newcastle U	W 4-1	2-1	6	Kluivert 3 [6, 44, 90], Kerkez [90]	52,227
23	25	H	Nottingham F	W 5-0	1-0	7	Kluivert [9], Ouattara 3 [55, 61, 87], Semenyo [90]	11,228
24	Feb 1	A	Liverpool	L 0-2	0-1	7		11,239
25	15	H	Southampton	W 3-1	2-0	5	Ouattara [14], Christie [16], Tavernier [83]	31,037
26	22	H	Wolverhampton W	L 0-1	0-1	5		11,206
27	25	A	Brighton & HA	L 1-2	0-1	7	Kluivert [61]	31,138
28	Mar 9	A	Tottenham H	D 2-2	1-0	8	Tavernier [42], Evanilson [65]	61,178
29	15	H	Brentford	L 1-2	1-1	9	Janelt (og) [17]	11,180
30	Apr 2	A	Ipswich T	L 1-2	0-1	10	Evanilson [67]	11,192
31	5	A	West Ham U	D 2-2	1-0	9	Evanilson 2 [38, 79]	62,459
32	14	H	Fulham	W 1-0	1-0	8	Semenyo [1]	11,195
33	19	A	Crystal Palace	D 0-0	0-0	8		25,185
34	27	H	Manchester U	D 1-1	1-0	10	Semenyo [23]	11,241
35	May 3	A	Arsenal	W 2-1	0-1	8	Huijsen [67], Evanilson [75]	60,110
36	10	H	Aston Villa	L 0-1	0-1	10		11,248
37	20	A	Manchester C	L 1-3	0-2	11	Jebbison [90]	52,487
38	25	H	Leicester C	W 2-0	0-0	9	Semenyo 2 [74, 88]	11,238

Final League Position: 9

GOALSCORERS

League (58): Kluivert 12 (6 pens), Semenyo 11, Evanilson 10, Ouattara 7, Huijsen 3, Tavernier 3, Brooks 2, Christie 2, Kerkez 2, Unal 2, Cook 1, Jebbison 1, Sinisterra 1, own goal 1.
FA Cup (9): Evanilson 2, Jebbison 2, Ouattara 2, Semenyo 2 (1 pen), Kluivert 1.
Carabao Cup (0).

Neto M 2	Smith A 19+6	Zabarnyi 35+1	Huijsen D 26+6	Kerkez M 38	Scott A 8+12	Cook L 32+4	Ouattara D 21+11	Tavernier M 20+9	Sinisterra L 1+11	Semenyo A 36+1	Araujo J 7+5	Christie R 27+2	Kluivert J 29+5	Jebbison D —+16	Billing P 1+9	Senesi M 13+4	Evanilson F 28+3	Arrizabalaga K 31	Travers M 5	Unal E 2+15	Brooks D 9+20	Adams T 21+7	Aarons M 1+2	Hill J 6+4	Winterburn B —+4	Rees-Dottin R —+1	Silcott-Duberry Z —+1	Soler J —+3	Match No.
2²	3	4	5	6¹	7⁵	8⁴	9	10³	11	12	13	14	15	16															1
16	3		5	12		6	13	10⁴	14	8	2⁵	7¹	9³	15		4	11²												2
16	3	15	5³	14		6	13	10	12	8	2⁴	7²	9			4⁵	11¹	1											3
2⁴	3		5	12		6		10³	13	8	15	7¹	9³	14		4	11²	1		16									4
13	3	4	5	14		6	12	10	15	8⁴	2²	7³	9¹				11⁵	1		16									5
2	3		5	14		6	10¹	9	15	8⁴		7	12			4	11³	1		13									6
2³	3		5²	14		6	12	10	13	8		7⁴	9¹			4	11⁵	1		15	16								7
12	3		5	6³	7	8²	9⁴	13	10		2¹	14	15			4	11⁵	1		16									8
12	3		5⁴		7	8	14		10	2¹	6⁶	9³				4	13	1	11²	15	16								9
2	3	15	5		6		10⁴		8		7¹	9³				4	11²	1	14	13	12								10
2⁵	3	12	5		6		13		8	16	9³	10⁴				4²	11	1	15	14	7¹								11
2⁴	3	12	5⁴		7	13	8	10		9³						4²	11	1	16	14	6¹	15							12
2	3	15	5		12	10		7		9³	14					4⁴	11²	1		13	8¹	6							13
2	3	4	5	13	12	10⁴		8³		7²		9¹	16				11⁵	1		15	14	6							14
2¹	3	4	5	7	13	8⁴		6⁵		9²	15		11³			12	14			16									15
2¹	3	4	5	7	10		8²		6	9⁴		11³				14	12	13											16
2¹	3	4	5	12	10		8⁵		7	9³	14		11²	1		13	15	6⁴		16									17
	3	4	5	7	10⁴		8		6	9³	14		12	1		11²	15	13	2¹										18
	3	4	5	7	12		10		6	9³		9²	11⁴			13	8¹	15	2³	14									19
	3	4	5	7	10²		8		6	9³	15		11⁴	1		13	12	14	2¹										20
	3	4	5	6	11		10		9	12	13			1		8²	7	2¹											21
	3	4	5	2	11³		10		7	9²	12			1		8¹	6				13	14							22
	3	4	5	2	11³	12	10		6	9²	13			1		8¹	7					14							23
	3	4	5	2	11	12	10		6²	9	13			1		8¹	7												24
	3	4	5	13	2	11³	12	15	10	7⁴		9²	14			8¹	6												25
	3⁴	4	5	14	6	11⁴	8		10	7¹		9³	15			12	13	2²											26
		4	5	12	2	11³	13	15	10	6¹	9		14			8²	7	3⁴											27
		4	5	13	2	12	8³	15	10⁴	6¹	9		11²	1		14	7	3											28
	3⁵	4	5		2	16	8	12⁴	10	6¹	9³	15		11	1		13	7²	14										29
2¹	3⁴	4	5	9²	7	8			10	6³			15		14	11	1			13	12								30
2²	3⁴	4	5	9¹	6	10⁴		8					16		14	11⁵	1		12	7	13	15							31
2	12	3	5	9²	7	10	13	8³							4¹	11	1		6					14				32
2⁴	3	4	5	6¹	12	10³	13		8	15	9					11	1		14	7²									33
2	3	4	5	6²	12	10⁴	13		8³			9¹	15		14	11¹	1		7										34
	3	4	5	13	7	10³	8		12	2¹		9²	15			11⁴	1		14	6									35
2³	3⁵	4	5⁴	6¹	9	8		10	16	12	15		14		11	1		13	7²										36
13	3	4	5⁴	6⁴		10		8	2²			9¹	14			11³	1		12	7							15		37
2	3	13	5	16		7³		10				9⁴	12		4²	11⁵	1		8¹	6		14					15		38

FA Cup

Round	Opponent		Result
Third Round	WBA	(h)	5-1
Fourth Round	Everton	(a)	2-0
Fifth Round	Wolverhampton W	(h)	1-1
aet; Bournemouth won 5-4 on penalties.			
Quarter-Final	Manchester C	(h)	1-2

Carabao Cup

Round	Opponent		Result
Second Round	West Ham U	(a)	0-1

BRADFORD CITY

FOUNDATION

Bradford was a rugby stronghold around the turn of the 20th century but after Manningham RFC held an archery contest to help them out of financial difficulties in 1903, they were persuaded to give up the handling code and turn to soccer. So they formed Bradford City and continued at Valley Parade. Recognising this as an opportunity to spread the dribbling code in this part of Yorkshire, the Football League immediately accepted the new club's first application for membership of the Second Division.

The University of Bradford Stadium, Valley Parade, Bradford, West Yorkshire BD8 7DY.

Telephone: (01274) 773 355.

Ticket Office: (01274) 770 012.

Website: www.bradfordcityafc.com

Email: hello@bradfordcityfc.com

Ground Capacity: 24,459.

Record Attendance: 39,146 v Burnley, FA Cup 4th rd, 11 March 1911.

Pitch Measurements: 100m × 64m (109.5yd × 70yd).

Chairman: Stephan Rupp.

Chief Executive: Ryan Sparks.

Manager: Graham Alexander.

Assistant Manager: Chris Lucketti.

Colours: Amber and claret hooped shirts with black trim, black shorts with amber and claret trim, black socks with amber trim.

Year Formed: 1903.

Turned Professional: 1903.

Club Nickname: 'The Bantams'.

Ground: 1903, Valley Parade (renamed Bradford & Bingley Stadium 1999; Intersonic Stadium 2007; Coral Windows Stadium 2007; Northern Commercials Stadium 2016; The Utilita Energy Stadium 2019; The University of Bradford Stadium 2022).

First Football League Game: 1 September 1903, Division 2, v Grimsby T (a) L 0–2 – Seymour; Wilson, Halliday; Robinson, Millar, Farnall; Guy, Beckram, Forrest, McMillan, Graham.

Record League Victory: 11–1 v Rotherham U, Division 3 (N), 25 August 1928 – Sherlaw; Russell, Watson; Burkinshaw (1), Summers, Bauld; Harvey (2), Edmunds (3), White (3), Cairns, Scriven (2).

Record Cup Victory: 11–3 v Walker Celtic, FA Cup 1st rd (replay), 1 December 1937 – Parker; Rookes, McDermott; Murphy, Mackie, Moore; Bagley (1), Whittingham (1), Deakin (4 incl. 1p), Cooke (1), Bartholomew (4).

Record Defeat: 1–9 v Colchester U, Division 4, 30 December 1961.

HONOURS

League Champions: Division 2 – 1907–08; Division 3 – 1984–85; Division 3N – 1928–29. *Runners-up:* First Division – 1998–99; Division 4 – 1981–82. *FA Cup Winners:* 1911. *League Cup: Runners-up:* 2013. **European Competitions** *Intertoto Cup:* 2000 (*sf*).

FOOTBALL YEARBOOK FACT FILE

Bradford City played two games against Huddersfield Town on the same day during the 1940–41 campaign. The Football League scrapped all Boxing Day fixtures that season, so City played the Terriers twice on Christmas Day, the game at Valley Parade kicking off at 11.15 and the return fixture at 3.00. Huddersfield won the first game 5-0, but the Bantams turned things round in the afternoon to gain a 4-3 victory.

Most League Points (2 for a win): 63, Division 3 (N), 1928–29.

Most League Points (3 for a win): 94, Division 3, 1984–85.

Most League Goals: 128, Division 3 (N), 1928–29.

Highest League Scorer in Season: David Layne, 34, Division 4, 1961–62.

Most League Goals in Total Aggregate: Bobby Campbell, 121, 1981–84, 1984–86.

Most League Goals in One Match: 7, Albert Whitehurst v Tranmere R, Division 3 (N), 6 March 1929.

Most Capped Player: Jamie Lawrence, 19 (24), Jamaica.

Most League Appearances: Cec Podd, 502, 1970–84.

Youngest League Player: Robert Cullingford, 16 years 141 days v Mansfield T, 22 April 1970.

Record Transfer Fee Received: £2,000,000 from Newcastle U for Des Hamilton, March 1997; £2,000,000 from Newcastle U for Andrew O'Brien, March 2001.

Record Transfer Fee Paid: £2,500,000 to Leeds U for David Hopkin, July 2000.

Football League Record: 1903 Elected to Division 2; 1903–08 Division 2; 1908–22 Division 1; 1922–27 Division 2; 1927–29 Division 3 (N); 1929–37 Division 2; 1937–58 Division 3 (N); 1958–61 Division 3; 1961–69 Division 4; 1969–72 Division 3; 1972–77 Division 4; 1977–78 Division 3; 1978–82 Division 4; 1982–85 Division 3; 1985–90 Division 2; 1990–92 Division 3; 1992–96 Second Division; 1996–99 First Division; 1999–2001 Premier League; 2001–04 First Division; 2004–07 FL 1; 2007–13 FL 2; 2013–19 FL 1; 2019–25 FL 2; 2025– FL 1.

LATEST SEQUENCES

Longest Sequence of League Wins: 10, 26.11.1983 – 3.2.1984.

Longest Sequence of League Defeats: 8, 21.1.1933 – 11.3.1933.

Longest Sequence of League Draws: 6, 30.1.1976 – 13.3.1976.

Longest Sequence of Unbeaten League Matches: 21, 11.1.1969 – 2.5.1969.

Longest Sequence Without a League Win: 16, 28.8.1948 – 20.11.1948.

Successive Scoring Runs: 30 from 26.12.1961.

Successive Non-scoring Runs: 7 from 18.4.1925.

MANAGERS

Robert Campbell 1903–05
Peter O'Rourke 1905–21
David Menzies 1921–26
Colin Veitch 1926–28
Peter O'Rourke 1928–30
Jack Peart 1930–35
Dick Ray 1935–37
Fred Westgarth 1938–43
Bob Sharp 1943–46
Jack Barker 1946–47
John Milburn 1947–48
David Steele 1948–52
Albert Harris 1952
Ivor Powell 1952–55
Peter Jackson 1955–61
Bob Brocklebank 1961–64
Bill Harris 1965–66
Willie Watson 1966–69
Grenville Hair 1967–68
Jimmy Wheeler 1968–71
Bryan Edwards 1971–75
Bobby Kennedy 1975–78
John Napier 1978
George Mulhall 1978–81
Roy McFarland 1981–82
Trevor Cherry 1982–87
Terry Dolan 1987–89
Terry Yorath 1989–90
John Docherty 1990–91
Frank Stapleton 1991–94
Lennie Lawrence 1994–95
Chris Kamara 1995–98
Paul Jewell 1998–2000
Chris Hutchings 2000
Jim Jefferies 2000–01
Nicky Law 2001–03
Bryan Robson 2003–04
Colin Todd 2004–07
Stuart McCall 2007–10
Peter Taylor 2010–11
Peter Jackson 2011
Phil Parkinson 2011–16
Stuart McCall 2016–18
Simon Grayson 2018
Michael Collins 2018
David Hopkin 2018–19
Gary Bowyer 2019–20
Stuart McCall 2020
Mark Trueman and Conor Sellars 2021
Derek Adams 2021–22
Mark Hughes 2022–23
Graham Alexander November 2023–

TEN YEAR LEAGUE RECORD

		P	W	D	L	F	A	Pts	Pos
2015-16	FL 1	46	23	11	12	55	40	80	5
2016-17	FL 1	46	20	19	7	62	43	79	5
2017-18	FL 1	46	18	9	19	57	67	63	11
2018-19	FL 1	46	11	8	27	49	77	41	24
2019-20	FL 2	37	14	12	11	44	40	54	9§
2020-21	FL 2	46	16	11	19	48	53	59	15
2021-22	FL 2	46	14	16	16	53	55	58	14
2022-23	FL 2	46	20	16	10	61	43	76	6
2023-24	FL 2	46	19	12	15	61	59	69	9
2024-25	FL 2	46	22	12	12	64	45	78	3

§ *Decided on points-per-game (1.46)*

DID YOU KNOW

Bradford City played their first-ever Football League Cup tie against Manchester United on 2 November 1960. The Valley Paraders, then members of the Third Division, defeated their top-flight opponents 2-1 with goals from Gerry Smith and Bobby Webb. The game was played in the afternoon with a 2.45 kick-off, a factor which restricted the attendance to just 4,670.

BRADFORD CITY – SKY BET LEAGUE TWO 2024–25 LEAGUE RECORD

Match No.	Date	Venue	Opponents	Result	H/T Score	Lg Pos.	Goalscorers	Attendance
1	Aug 10	A	Milton Keynes D	W 2-1	2-1	7	Pattison [2], Sherring (og) [5]	7561
2	17	H	Salford C	D 0-0	0-0	6		16,183
3	24	H	Bromley	W 3-1	2-0	2	Smallwood (pen) [9], Cook [41], Pointon [79]	16,001
4	31	A	Grimsby T	L 1-2	0-1	9	Sanderson [78]	7004
5	Sept 7	H	Carlisle U	W 2-1	1-0	5	Cook 2 [2, 70]	18,041
6	14	A	Walsall	L 1-2	1-1	7	Sanderson [38]	5967
7	21	H	AFC Wimbledon	D 0-0	0-0	8		16,344
8	28	A	Harrogate T	L 1-2	1-2	13	Cook [28]	3059
9	Oct 1	A	Morecambe	D 1-1	0-1	13	Shepherd [88]	3606
10	7	H	Newport Co	W 3-1	1-0	9	Cook [39], Walker J [75], Pointon [85]	15,542
11	12	A	Tranmere R	W 2-0	1-0	7	Cook 2 [23, 72]	8366
12	19	H	Gillingham	W 2-1	2-1	5	Byrne [38], Shepherd [45]	16,471
13	22	A	Cheltenham T	D 1-1	1-1	5	Byrne [8]	3404
14	26	H	Doncaster R	L 1-2	0-0	7	Cook [83]	18,269
15	Nov 9	A	Fleetwood T	L 0-1	0-1	10		3971
16	16	A	Colchester U	D 1-1	1-0	8	Cook [30]	4825
17	Dec 3	H	Barrow	D 1-1	0-0	10	Cook [79]	14,547
18	7	A	Crewe Alex	D 1-1	0-0	11	Pattison [55]	5350
19	14	H	Swindon T	W 1-0	1-0	10	Kavanagh [24]	15,751
20	21	A	Notts Co	L 0-3	0-3	12		11,500
21	26	H	Port Vale	W 2-1	1-0	10	Cook 2 [3, 59]	18,330
22	29	H	Chesterfield	W 2-1	1-1	10	Pointon [42], Sarcevic [52]	18,730
23	Jan 1	A	Barrow	D 2-2	1-1	9	Richards [23], Odour [86]	3918
24	4	H	Grimsby T	W 3-1	1-0	8	Richards [45], Smallwood (pen) [48], Pattison [69]	18,011
25	18	A	Carlisle U	W 1-0	0-0	8	Kavanagh [54]	8399
26	25	H	Walsall	W 3-0	2-0	7	Sarcevic [11], Pattison 2 [43, 53]	17,172
27	28	H	Morecambe	W 1-0	1-0	3	Kavanagh [30]	15,083
28	Feb 1	A	AFC Wimbledon	L 0-1	0-1	7		8536
29	8	H	Harrogate T	W 1-0	1-0	4	Sarcevic [2]	17,126
30	11	H	Accrington S	W 1-0	1-0	3	Pattison [20]	15,263
31	15	A	Newport Co	D 0-0	0-0	3		4760
32	22	H	Milton Keynes D	W 2-0	1-0	5	Sarcevic 2 [11, 60]	17,666
33	25	A	Bromley	W 1-0	0-0	2	Pointon [82]	2442
34	Mar 1	A	Salford C	W 2-1	0-1	2	Halliday [71], Mellon [90]	3656
35	4	H	Cheltenham T	W 3-0	1-0	2	Lapslie 2 [31, 53], Mellon [60]	15,229
36	8	A	Gillingham	L 0-1	0-0	2		6297
37	15	H	Tranmere R	L 0-1	0-0	2		18,845
38	22	H	Colchester U	W 4-1	2-1	2	Kavanagh 2 [31, 70], Lapslie 2 [41, 78]	23,381
39	29	A	Accrington S	D 0-0	0-0	2		4572
40	Apr 1	A	Port Vale	L 0-2	0-2	2		8659
41	5	H	Crewe Alex	W 2-0	1-0	1	Pointon [1], Kavanagh [85]	22,214
42	12	A	Swindon T	L 4-5	3-2	2	Kavanagh 3 [6, 10, 35], Halliday [77]	8051
43	17	H	Notts Co	D 1-1	0-0	2	Kelly [53]	20,392
44	21	A	Chesterfield	D 3-3	2-1	3	Pointon [10], Sarcevic (pen) [19], Pattison [49]	9520
45	26	H	Doncaster R	L 1-2	0-1	3	Crichlow-Noble [90]	12,574
46	May 3	H	Fleetwood T	W 1-0	0-0	3	Sarcevic [90]	24,033

Final League Position: 3

GOALSCORERS
League (64): Cook 12, Kavanagh 9, Pattison 7, Sarcevic 7 (1 pen), Pointon 6, Lapslie 4, Byrne 2, Halliday 2, Mellon 2, Richards 2, Sanderson 2, Shepherd 2, Smallwood 2 (2 pens), Crichlow-Noble 1, Kelly 1, Odour 1, Walker J 1, own goal 1.
FA Cup (3): Kavanagh 1, Oliver 1, own goal 1.
Carabao Cup (1): Cook 1.
Vertu Trophy (13): Kavanagh 3, Cook 2, Pointon 2, Johnson 1, Oduor 1, Oliver 1, Sanderson 1, Shepherd 1, Smallwood 1 (1 pen).

Walker S 46	Baldwin A 30+2	Byrne N 24+3	Kelly C 16+5	Halliday B 39+4	Sarcevic A 20+4	Smallwood R 43	Pattison A 24+6	Wright T 19+9	Kavanagh C 31+7	Cook A 22	Walker J 16+19	Odour C 7+12	Shepherd J 31+8	Oliver V 1+11	Pointon B 27+13	Sanderson O 6+7	Diabate C 10+1	Richards L 17+5	Adams Joe —+1	Benn J 11+1	Smith T 1+4	Evans Corry 1+5	Huntington P 9+10	Lapslie G 7+6	Johnson C 3+8	Leigh T 6+10	Khela B 11+4	Mellon M 5+10	Crichlow-Noble R 8+2	Adaramola T 15+1	Match No.
1	2	3	4	5	6^3	7	8	9^2	10^4	11^1	12	13	14	15																	1
1	2	3	4	5	6	7	8^2	9^1	11^3	10			13		12	14															2
1	2	3	4	5	6		8^1	9^3	11^2	10^4	14	15			12	13															3
1	2^1	3	4	5		6^3	9		11^2	10	14	15	12				8^4	13													4
1		3	4	5		7	13	9^3		10^4	6	8^1	14	15	12	11^2	2														5
1		3^1	4^2	5		7	13	9		11	6	8^4	12	14	15	10^3	2														6
1			2			8	7	9		11			13	4	14	6	10^3	3	5^1	12^2											7
1			2^3			7	8^2	15	12	10	6^5	14	4	16	9^4	11^1	3	5		13											8
1						7		9	10^1	11	6^2	8	4	12			3	5		2	13										9
1	3^3					7		9	11^2	10	8^4	6^1	4		12		2	14		5	13	15									10
1			2			7		9^2	11	10	8^3	6^4	4^1		15		3	12		5		13	14								11
1	3		5			7		9^1	10^5	11^5	6^2	8^3	4	15	13		2	12				16	14								12
1	3		5			7			10^1	11	8		4		6		2	9				12									13
1	3	13				7		9^3	14	10	6^1		4	15	8		2^4	12		5^5	11^{12}	16									14
1	3		2			6			9^2	10	7	12			11^1	8	13			4		5									15
1	3		2			7			11^4	6	12	4	15		8^1	10^2	14	9^3		5		13									16
1	15		2^3			7	8^2		12	10	14	6^4	4		13	11^1		9		5		3									17
1	2^2					12		7	6^4		11^1		9		4	13	10			8		5		3							18
1	2					12	13	7			10^3	11	14		4		9			8		5^1	6^2	3							19
1	2	15	16			7^2	6		10^1	11	13	14	4^4		9^3	12		8		5^5		3									20
1	2	4	5			7	6		9^2	11			12		10	13		8				3^1									21
1	2	3	4	9	6^3		8	10^2		11	13	14	15		12^4					5^1											22
1	2	3^5	15	5	13	7	6^2	9^3	11^1	14	16	4^4			10	12	8														23
1	2		4	5	9	7	6	11^2							3	13	10^1			8			12								24
1	2^1		4	5	9	7	6	11^2							3		10			8			12	13							25
1	2		4	5^5	9^3	7	6	14	11^1						3		10^2			8^4			12	16	13	15					26
1	2		4	5^3	7	6	13	8^1	11^2						3		10			12			14	9							27
1	2	4^2		9	7	6	12	11^3							3			8^1					14	15	5	10^4		13			28
1	2		5^5	9^2	7	6	8	11^1		15					3		10^4						14		16	12		13	4^3		29
1	3		5	14	7		6^3	8	11^1		12		4		10^4								13		2^2	9	15				30
1	2		5	6	7				13		4$^•$				10^1							3		14	9	11^2	12	8^3			31
1	3	13	5	9	7	6^1			14						10								2	15	12	11^3	4^2	8^4			32
1	2	16	5	9^3	6	14			15	4					10^5		8^1					3			13	7^2	11^4		12		33
1	2		5	10^1	7			14		9^4		3			16								13	15	11^5	6^3	12	4^2	8		34
1	3	2	5			6			12		10^3	14	4									15	9^1		13	7	11^2		8^4		35
1	2	13	5^5		7		15	14	9^3	4					3		10^4	16	11^1	6^2	12								8		36
1	3	2	5^3		7		12	13	9	4												10^2	14	6	11				8^1	37
1	3	2^3	13	5		7	15	10^1	11^4	14					12							16	9		6		4^2	8^5		38
1	3	2	15	5		7	13	10	11^5	14					12								9^2		6^1	16	4^4	8^3		39
1	2		4	5^4		7	6	10	11	15			13		12		10					3^1	9^3		14			8^2		40
1	3	2^3		5		7	6^4		11	15	12		10									9^1	14		13		4^2	8		41
1		2	13	5	14	7^4	6^1	16	11						3		10^2						12		9^3	15	4^5	8^4		42
1	12	2	4^4	5	9^1	7			11^3		13		3^2		10							15			6	14		8		43
1	3^3	2		5	9^2	7	16	11^4	12	4			10									14		13	6^1		15	8^5		44
1	3^4	2		5	9^4	6	13	11^3	10^2	12												15		7^1	14	4	8			45
1		2	4	5	9	7^3	6^1	15	11^5				3		10^2							16	14		12		13	8^4		46

BRENTFORD

FOUNDATION

Formed as a small amateur concern in 1889 they were very successful in local circles. They won the championship of the West London Alliance in 1893 and a year later the West Middlesex Junior Cup before carrying off the Senior Cup in 1895. After winning both the London Senior Amateur Cup and the Middlesex Senior Cup in 1898 they were admitted to the Second Division of the Southern League.

Gtech Community Stadium, 166 Lionel Road North, Brentford, Middlesex TW8 9QT.
Telephone: (020) 8847 2511.
Ticket Office: (0333) 005 8521.
Website: www.brentfordfc.com
Email: enquiries@brentfordfc.com
Ground Capacity: 17,250.
Record Attendance: 38,678 v Leicester C, FA Cup 6th rd, 26 February 1949 (at Griffin Park); 17,215 v Liverpool, Premier League, 18 January 2025 (at Gtech Community Stadium).
Pitch Measurements: 105m × 68m (115yd × 74.5yd).
Chairman: Cliff Crown.
Chief Executive: Jon Varney.
Head Coach: Keith Andrews.
Assistant Head Coach: Kevin O'Connor.

HONOURS

League Champions: Division 2 – 1934–35; Division 3 – 1991–92; Division 3S – 1932–33; FL 2 – 2008–09; Third Division – 1998–99; Division 4 – 1962–63.
Runners-up: FL 1 – 2013–14; Second Division – 1994–95; Division 3S – 1929–30, 1957–58.
FA Cup: 6th rd – 1938, 1946, 1949, 1989.
League Cup: semi-final 2021.
League Trophy: *Runners-up:* 1985, 2001, 2011.

Colours: Red and white striped shirts with red and black trim, black shorts with red and white trim, black socks with red and white trim.
Year Formed: 1889. *Turned Professional:* 1899. *Club Nickname:* 'The Bees'.
Grounds: 1889, Clifden Road; 1891, Benns Fields, Little Ealing; 1895, Shotters Field; 1898, Cross Road, S. Ealing; 1900, Boston Park; 1904, Griffin Park; 2020, Brentford Community Stadium (renamed Gtech Community Stadium 2022).
First Football League Game: 28 August 1920, Division 3, v Exeter C (a) L 0–3 – Young; Hodson, Rosier, Jimmy Elliott, Levitt, Amos, Smith, Thompson, Spreadbury, Morley, Henery.
Record League Victory: 9–0 v Wrexham, Division 3, 15 October 1963 – Cakebread; Coote, Jones; Slater, Scott, Higginson; Summers (1), Brooks (2), McAdams (2), Ward (2), Hales (1), (1 og).
Record Cup Victory: 7–0 v Windsor & Eton (a), FA Cup 1st rd, 20 November 1982 – Roche; Rowe, Harris (Booker), McNichol (1), Whitehead, Hurlock (2), Kamara, Joseph (1), Mahoney (3), Bowles, Roberts; 7–0 v Oldham Ath (h), Carabao Cup, 21 September 2021 – Fernandez; Jorgensen, Goode, Thompson, Roerslev (Bidstrup 71), Ghoddos, Jensen, Onyeka (Peart-Harris 72), Fosu (Stevens 71), Wissa (2), Forss (4 (1 pen)), own goal (1). *N.B.* 8–0 v Uxbridge: Frail, Jock Watson, Caie, Bellingham, Parsonage (1), Jay, Atherton, Leigh (1), Bell (2), Buchanan (2), Underwood (2), FA Cup, 3rd Qual rd, 31 October 1903.
Record Defeat: 0–7 v Swansea T, Division 3 (S), 8 November 1924; v Walsall, Division 3 (S), 19 January 1957; v Peterborough U, 24 November 2007.

FOOTBALL YEARBOOK FACT FILE

Brentford won all 21 home games in the 1929–30 season but still didn't gain promotion due to the fact that they finished as runners-up in Division Three South and only the champions went up. The Bees are the only team in Football league history to win all their home games in a season when 42 or more matches have been played.

Most League Points (2 for a win): 62, Division 3 (S), 1932–33 and Division 4, 1962–63.

Most League Points (3 for a win): 94, FL 1, 2013–14.

Most League Goals: 98, Division 4, 1962–63.

Highest League Scorer in Season: Jack Holliday, 38, Division 3 (S), 1932–33.

Most League Goals in Total Aggregate: Jim Towers, 153, 1954–61.

Most League Goals in One Match: 5, Jack Holliday v Luton T, Division 3 (S), 28 January 1933; 5, Billy Scott v Barnsley, Division 2, 15 December 1934; 5, Peter McKennan v Bury, Division 2, 18 February 1949.

Most Capped Player: Christian Norgaard, 35, Denmark.

Most League Appearances: Ken Coote, 514, 1949–64.

Youngest League Player: Danis Salman, 15 years 248 days v Watford, 15 November 1975.

Record Transfer Fee Received: £40,000,000 from Al Ahli for Ivan Toney, August 2024.

Record Transfer Fee Paid: £30,000,000 to Club Brugge for Igor Thiago, July 2024.

Football League Record: 1920 Original Member of Division 3; 1920–21 Division 3; 1921–33 Division 3 (S); 1933–35 Division 2; 1935–47 Division 1; 1947–54 Division 2; 1954–58 Division 3 (S); 1958–62 Division 3; 1962–63 Division 4; 1963–66 Division 3; 1966–72 Division 4; 1972–73 Division 3; 1973–78 Division 4; 1978–92 Division 3; 1992–93 First Division; 1993–98 Second Division; 1998–99 Third Division; 1999–2004 Second Division; 2004–07 FL 1; 2007–09 FL 2; 2009–14 FL 1; 2014–21 FL C; 2021– Premier League.

LATEST SEQUENCES

Longest Sequence of League Wins: 9, 30.4.1932 – 24.9.1932.

Longest Sequence of League Defeats: 9, 20.10.1928 – 25.12.1928.

Longest Sequence of League Draws: 5, 16.3.1957 – 6.4.1957.

Longest Sequence of Unbeaten League Matches: 26, 20.2.1999 – 16.10.1999.

Longest Sequence Without a League Win: 18, 9.9.2006 – 26.12.2006.

Successive Scoring Runs: 26 from 4.3.1963.

Successive Non-scoring Runs: 7 from 7.3.2000.

MANAGERS

Will Lewis 1900–03
(*Secretary-Manager*)
Dick Molyneux 1902–06
W. G. Brown 1906–08
Fred Halliday 1908–12, 1915–21, 1924–26
(*only Secretary to 1922*)
Ephraim Rhodes 1912–15
Archie Mitchell 1921–24
Harry Curtis 1926–49
Jackie Gibbons 1949–52
Jimmy Bain 1952–53
Tommy Lawton 1953
Bill Dodgin Snr 1953–57
Malcolm Macdonald 1957–65
Tommy Cavanagh 1965–66
Billy Gray 1966–67
Jimmy Sirrel 1967–69
Frank Blunstone 1969–73
Mike Everitt 1973–75
John Docherty 1975–76
Bill Dodgin Jnr 1976–80
Fred Callaghan 1980–84
Frank McLintock 1984–87
Steve Perryman 1987–90
Phil Holder 1990–93
David Webb 1993–97
Eddie May 1997
Micky Adams 1997–98
Ron Noades 1998–2000
Ray Lewington 2000–01
Steve Coppell 2001–02
Wally Downes 2002–04
Martin Allen 2004–06
Leroy Rosenior 2006
Scott Fitzgerald 2006–07
Terry Butcher 2007
Andy Scott 2007–11
Nicky Forster 2011
Uwe Rosler 2011–13
Mark Warburton 2013–15
Marinus Dijkhuizen 2015
Dean Smith 2015–18
Thomas Frank 2018–25
Keith Andrews June 2025–

TEN YEAR LEAGUE RECORD

		P	W	D	L	F	A	Pts	Pos
2015-16	FL C	46	19	8	19	72	67	65	9
2016-17	FL C	46	18	10	18	75	65	64	10
2017-18	FL C	46	18	15	13	62	52	69	9
2018-19	FL C	46	17	13	16	73	59	64	11
2019-20	FL C	46	24	9	13	80	38	81	3
2020-21	FL C	46	24	15	7	79	42	87	3
2021-22	PR Lge	38	13	7	18	48	56	46	13
2022-23	PR Lge	38	15	14	9	58	46	59	9
2023-24	PR Lge	38	10	9	19	56	65	39	16
2024-25	PR Lge	38	16	8	14	66	57	56	10

DID YOU KNOW ?

Brentford made their first appearance on the BBC's iconic *Match of the Day* programme on the final Saturday of the 1965–66 season, 28 May. The Bees, already relegated from the Third Division, faced mid-table Gillingham at Griffin Park. The visitors gained a comfortable 2-0 win in front of a crowd of 4,457.

BRENTFORD – PREMIER LEAGUE 2024–25 LEAGUE RECORD

Match No.	Date	Venue	Opponents	Result		H/T Score	Lg Pos.	Goalscorers	Attendance
1	Aug 18	H	Crystal Palace	W	2-1	1-0	5	Mbeumo [29], Wissa [76]	16,988
2	25	A	Liverpool	L	0-2	0-1	12		60,107
3	31	H	Southampton	W	3-1	1-0	5	Mbeumo 2 [43, 65], Wissa [69]	16,955
4	Sept 14	A	Manchester C	L	1-2	1-2	9	Wissa [1]	52,148
5	21	A	Tottenham H	L	1-3	1-2	12	Mbeumo [1]	61,246
6	28	H	West Ham U	D	1-1	1-0	12	Mbeumo [1]	17,050
7	Oct 5	A	Wolverhampton W	W	5-3	4-2	9	Collins [2], Mbeumo (pen) [20], Norgaard [28], Pinnock [45], Carvalho [90]	16,960
8	19	A	Manchester U	L	1-2	1-0	13	Pinnock [45]	73,738
9	26	H	Ipswich T	W	4-3	2-2	9	Wissa 2 [44, 45], Mbeumo 2 (1 pen) [51 (p), 90]	17,109
10	Nov 4	A	Fulham	L	1-2	1-0	12	Janelt [24]	24,931
11	9	H	Bournemouth	W	3-2	1-1	10	Wissa 2 [27, 58], Damsgaard [50]	16,993
12	23	A	Everton	D	0-0	0-0	11		38,915
13	30	H	Leicester C	W	4-1	3-1	7	Wissa [25], Schade 3 [29, 45, 59]	17,084
14	Dec 4	A	Aston Villa	L	1-3	0-3	9	Damsgaard [54]	37,890
15	7	H	Newcastle U	W	4-2	2-2	7	Mbeumo [8], Wissa [28], Collins [56], Schade [90]	17,078
16	15	A	Chelsea	L	1-2	0-1	11	Mbeumo [90]	39,751
17	21	H	Nottingham F	L	0-2	0-1	12		17,115
18	27	A	Brighton & HA	D	0-0	0-0	11		31,548
19	Jan 1	H	Arsenal	L	1-3	1-1	12	Mbeumo [13]	17,190
20	4	A	Southampton	W	5-0	1-0	11	Schade [6], Mbeumo 2 (1 pen) [62, 69 (p)], Lewis-Potter [90], Wissa [90]	31,001
21	14	H	Manchester C	D	2-2	0-0	10	Wissa [82], Norgaard [90]	17,048
22	18	H	Liverpool	L	0-2	0-0	11		17,215
23	26	A	Crystal Palace	W	2-1	0-0	11	Mbeumo (pen) [66], Schade [80]	25,066
24	Feb 2	H	Tottenham H	L	0-2	0-1	11		17,154
25	15	A	West Ham U	W	1-0	1-0	11	Schade [4]	62,467
26	21	H	Leicester C	W	4-0	3-0	10	Wissa [17], Mbeumo [27], Norgaard [32], Carvalho [89]	31,077
27	26	H	Everton	D	1-1	1-0	11	Wissa [45]	17,082
28	Mar 8	A	Aston Villa	L	0-1	0-0	12		17,171
29	15	A	Bournemouth	W	2-1	1-1	11	Wissa [30], Norgaard [71]	11,180
30	Apr 2	A	Newcastle U	L	1-2	0-1	11	Mbeumo (pen) [66]	52,021
31	6	H	Chelsea	D	0-0	0-0	12		17,183
32	12	A	Arsenal	D	1-1	1-0	11	Wissa [74]	60,184
33	19	H	Brighton & HA	W	4-2	1-1	11	Mbeumo 2 [9, 48], Wissa [58], Norgaard [90]	17,083
34	May 1	A	Nottingham F	W	2-0	1-0	11	Schade [44], Wissa [70]	29,040
35	4	H	Manchester U	W	4-3	2-1	9	Shaw (og) [27], Schade 2 [33, 70], Wissa [74]	17,190
36	10	A	Ipswich T	W	1-0	1-0	8	Schade [18]	29,511
37	18	H	Fulham	L	2-3	2-1	8	Mbeumo [22], Wissa [43]	17,136
38	25	A	Wolverhampton W	D	1-1	1-0	10	Mbeumo [20]	31,382

Final League Position: 10

GOALSCORERS

League (66): Mbeumo 20 (5 pens), Wissa 19, Schade 11, Norgaard 5, Carvalho 2, Collins 2, Damsgaard 2, Pinnock 2, Janelt 1, Lewis-Potter 1, own goal 1.
FA Cup (0).
Carabao Cup (6): Carvalho 1, Damsgaard 1, Lewis-Potter 1, Norgaard 1, Schade 1, Wissa 1.

Flekken M 37	Roerslev Rasmussen M 11+8	Collins N 38	Pinnock E 21+1	Ajer K 17+7	Norgaard C 34	Janelt V 27+5	Jensen M 8+16	Mbeumo B 38	Wissa Y 34+1	Schade K 26+12	Lewis-Potter K 36+2	Damsgaard M 34+4	Carvalho F 3+16	Onyeka F —+2	Mee B 2+5	van den Berg S 29+2	Yarmolyuk Y 15+16	Konak Y —+10	Trevitt R —+1	Thiago I 1+7	Maghoma E —+8	Meghoma J —+1	Valdimarsson H 1+1	Kim J —+3	Henry R —+5	Kayode M 6+6	Nunes Gomes G —+3	Match No.
1	2	3	4	5	6	7¹	8⁴	9⁵	10³	11²	12	13	14	15	16													1
1	2	3	4	5	7	8³	6²	10	11⁴	14		9¹	13	12	15													2
1	12	3	4	2¹	7	5³	6	9	10	11²	14	8¹		15		13												3
1	14	5	4	2²	8	9³	11	10¹	12	6	7⁴	13				3	15											4
1	13	5	4	2³		8		11	12	6	9²	10⁴				3	7¹	14	15									5
1		3	4	5		8		11		6¹	9	7	10²			2	12	13										6
1	14	3	4	5³	7¹	6		8	11²	10	9⁴	12				2	13	15										7
1	15	3	4	5	6	7³		9	12	11²	10¹	8	13			2⁴	14											8
1	2	3	4		6²	7	13	8	11	12	10³	9¹	14			5												9
1	2	3	4		6	7⁵	12	8⁴	11¹	13	10³	9²	14			15	5	16										10
1		3	4		7²	8	6¹	9³	10	13	5	11⁴	14			2	12	15										11
1		3	4		7⁸	8³	6	9	10¹	12	5	11²				2	14		13									12
1	16	3	4		6²	12	7¹	8	11	10³	5	9⁴	13			2⁵	14		15									13
1	15	3	4			7		9	10	11²	5⁴	8	13			2	6¹		14	12								14
1		3	4		7			5	9³	12	8	13	10²			14	2	6⁴		11¹	15							15
1	5⁴	4	3	14	7	12		10	11³	15	9⁵	8¹	13			2	6²					16						16
1	12⁴	3		2¹	7	6²		9	10	11³	5	8	14			4		15		13								17
1	2	3			6²	7		8	11	10	5	9				4³	13				12	14						18
1	2	3			7³	6	12	10	11⁴	13	5	9¹				4²	8				15	14						19
1	2	3			6²	12	7¹	9	10	11³	5	8				4	13				14							20
1	2³	3			6	7²	8¹	9	10	12	5	11				4	13					14						21
1	2	3			6	7¹	13	8	11	12	5	9²				4	10					14						22
1	2	3			6¹	7	12	8	11	10²	5	9³				14	4	13										23
		3			2²	6³	7¹	12	8	11	10	5	9	14		4				1						13		24
1		3	12	2	6	7²	13	8	11⁴	10³	5	9⁵	15			4¹	14					16						25
1		3	4	2⁴	6¹	7³		8	11	10⁵	5	9²	13			12	16		14			15						26
1		3	4	2²		7		8	11	10¹	5	9				6	12					13						27
1		3	4	2²	6	7¹²		8	11	10	5	9										13						28
1		3	4	2²	6	7¹		8	11	10⁴	5	9³	14	12	13	15												29
1		3	4²	13	6	7¹		8	11	10	5	12				2	9¹		14									30
1		3		2⁶	6	12	13	8	11	10	5	9³				4	7¹									14		31
1		3		2¹	7⁴	8²	14	6	10	11	5	9³				4	13								12	15		32
1		3		12	6	16	13	8	11	10⁵	5²	9⁴	4	7³	15							14			2¹	17		33
1		3		14	6			13	8	11	10²	5¹	9³	4	7		15					12			2⁴			34
1		3		15	6			13	8	11	10²	5³	9⁴	4	7¹	16	13							2⁵	14			35
1		3			6			12	8	11³	10¹	5	9²	4	7	14								13		2		36
1		3		12	6			13	8	11	10³	5⁴	9	4	7²	15								14		2¹		37
1		3		14	6			12	8	11	10¹	5	9²	4	7	13										2³		38

FA Cup

Third Round   Plymouth Arg   (h)   0-1

Carabao Cup

Second Round   Colchester U   (a)   1-0
Third Round   Leyton Orient   (h)   3-1
Fourth Round   Sheffield Wed   (h)   1-1
Brentford won 5-4 on penalties.
Quarter-Final   Newcastle U   (a)   1-3

BRIGHTON & HOVE ALBION

FOUNDATION

A professional club Brighton United was formed in November 1897 at the Imperial Hotel, Queen's Road, but folded in March 1900 after less than two seasons in the Southern League at the County Ground. An amateur team Brighton & Hove Rangers was then formed by some prominent United supporters and after one season at Withdean, decided to turn semi-professional and play at the County Ground. Rangers were accepted into the Southern League but folded in June 1901. John Jackson, the former United manager, organised a meeting at the Seven Stars public house, Ship Street on 24 June 1901 at which a new third club Brighton & Hove United was formed. They took over Rangers' place in the Southern League and pitch at County Ground. The name was changed to Brighton & Hove Albion before a match was played because of objections by Hove FC.

American Express Community Stadium, Village Way, Falmer, Brighton BN1 9BL.

Telephone: (01273) 668 855.

Ticket Office: (0844) 327 1901.

Website: www.brightonandhovealbion.com

Email: supporter.services@brightonandhovealbion.com

Ground Capacity: 31,876.

Record Attendance: 36,747 v Fulham, Division 2, 27 December 1958 (at Goldstone Ground); 8,691 v Leeds U, FL 1, 20 October 2007 (at Withdean); 31,746 v Chelsea, Premier League, 29 October 2022 (at Amex).

Pitch Measurements: 105m × 68m (115yd × 74.5yd).

Chairman: Tony Bloom MBE.

Chief Executive and Deputy Chairman: Paul Barber.

Head Coach: Fabian Hurzeler.

Assistant Head Coaches: Jonas Scheuermann, Andrew Crofts, Daniel Niedzkowski.

Colours: Blue and white striped shirts with white sleeves and blue trim, blue shorts with yellow trim, white socks.

Year Formed: 1901.

Turned Professional: 1901.

Club Nickname: 'The Seagulls'.

Grounds: 1901, County Ground; 1902, Goldstone Ground; 1997, Priestfield Stadium (groundshare with Gillingham); 1999, Withdean Stadium; 2011, American Express Community Stadium.

First Football League Game: 28 August 1920, Division 3, v Southend U (a) L 0–2 – Hayes; Woodhouse, Little; Hall, Comber, Bentley; Longstaff, Ritchie, Doran, Rodgerson, March.

Record League Victory: 9–1 v Newport Co, Division 3 (S), 18 April 1951 – Ball; Tennant (1p), Mansell (1p), Willard, McCoy, Wilson; Reed, McNichol (4), Garbutt, Bennett (2), Keene (1). 9–1 v Southend U, Division 3, 27 November 1965 – Powney; Magill, Baxter; Leck, Gall, Turner; Gould (1), Collins (1), Livesey (2), Smith (3), Goodchild (2).

HONOURS

League Champions: FL 1 – 2010–11; Second Division – 2001–02; Division 3S – 1957–58; Third Division – 2000–01; Division 4 – 1964–65. *Runners-up:* FL C – 2016–17; Division 2 – 1978–79; Division 3 – 1971–72, 1976–77, 1987–88; Division 3S – 1953–54, 1955–56.

FA Cup: Runners-up: 1983.

League Cup: 5th rd – 1979.

European Competitions
Europa League: 2023–24.

FOOTBALL YEARBOOK FACT FILE

Brighton & Hove Albion's wartime game against Southampton on 21 September 1940 lasted just under five minutes before being abandoned, making it one of the shortest games on record. With the Battle of Britain underway, the FA ruled that in the event of an air raid warning being sounded matches should be immediately suspended and if there was insufficient shelter for spectators then they should be abandoned.

Record Cup Victory: 10–1 v Wisbech, FA Cup 1st rd, 13 November 1965 – Powney; Magill, Baxter; Collins (1), Gall, Turner; Gould, Smith (2), Livesey (3), Cassidy (2), Goodchild (1), (1 og).

Record Defeat: 0–9 v Middlesbrough, Division 2, 23 August 1958.

Most League Points (2 for a win): 65, Division 3 (S), 1955–56 and Division 3, 1971–72.

Most League Points (3 for a win): 95, FL 1, 2010–11.

Most League Goals: 112, Division 3 (S), 1955–56.

Highest League Scorer in Season: Peter Ward, 32, Division 3, 1976–77.

Most League Goals in Total Aggregate: Tommy Cook, 114, 1922–29.

Most League Goals in One Match: 5, Jack Doran v Northampton T, Division 3 (S), 5 November 1921; 5, Adrian Thorne v Watford, Division 3 (S), 30 April 1958.

Most Capped Player: Shane Duffy, 50 (includes 9 on loan at Celtic) (61), Republic of Ireland.

Most League Appearances: Ernie 'Tug' Wilson, 509, 1922–36.

Youngest League Player: Harry Howell, 16 years 232 days v Liverpool, 19 May 2025.

Record Transfer Fee Received: £115,000,000 from Chelsea for Moises Caicedo, August 2023.

Record Transfer Fee Paid: £40,000,000 to Leeds U for Georginio Rutter, August 2024.

Football League Record: 1920 Original Member of Division 3; 1920–21 Division 3; 1921–58 Division 3 (S); 1958–62 Division 2; 1962–63 Division 3; 1963–65 Division 4; 1965–72 Division 3; 1972–73 Division 2; 1973–77 Division 3; 1977–79 Division 2; 1979–83 Division 1; 1983–87 Division 2; 1987–88 Division 3; 1988–92 Division 2; 1992–96 Second Division; 1996–2001 Third Division; 2001–02 Second Division; 2002–03 First Division; 2003–04 Second Division; 2004–06 FL C; 2006–11 FL 1; 2011–17 FL C; 2017– Premier League.

LATEST SEQUENCES

Longest Sequence of League Wins: 9, 2.10.1926 – 20.11.1926.

Longest Sequence of League Defeats: 12, 17.8.2002 – 26.10.2002.

Longest Sequence of League Draws: 6, 16.2.1980 – 15.3.1980.

Longest Sequence of Unbeaten League Matches: 22, 2.5.2015 – 15.12.2015.

Longest Sequence Without a League Win: 15, 21.10.1972 – 27.1.1973.

Successive Scoring Runs: 32 from 4.3.2023.

Successive Non-scoring Runs: 6 from 30.3.2019.

MANAGERS

John Jackson 1901–05
Frank Scott-Walford 1905–08
John Robson 1908–14
Charles Webb 1919–47
Tommy Cook 1947
Don Welsh 1947–51
Billy Lane 1951–61
George Curtis 1961–63
Archie Macaulay 1963–68
Fred Goodwin 1968–70
Pat Saward 1970–73
Brian Clough 1973–74
Peter Taylor 1974–76
Alan Mullery 1976–81
Mike Bailey 1981–82
Jimmy Melia 1982–83
Chris Cattlin 1983–86
Alan Mullery 1986–87
Barry Lloyd 1987–93
Liam Brady 1993–95
Jimmy Case 1995–96
Steve Gritt 1996–98
Brian Horton 1998–99
Jeff Wood 1999
Micky Adams 1999–2001
Peter Taylor 2001–02
Martin Hinshelwood 2002
Steve Coppell 2002–03
Mark McGhee 2003–06
Dean Wilkins 2006–08
Micky Adams 2008–09
Russell Slade 2009
Gus Poyet 2009–13
Óscar Garcia 2013–14
Sammi Hyypia 2014
Chris Hughton 2014–19
Graham Potter 2019–22
Roberto de Zerbi 2022–24
Fabian Hurzeler June 2024–

TEN YEAR LEAGUE RECORD

		P	W	D	L	F	A	Pts	Pos
2015-16	FL C	46	24	17	5	72	42	89	3
2016-17	FL C	46	28	9	9	74	40	93	2
2017-18	PR Lge	38	9	13	16	34	54	40	15
2018-19	PR Lge	38	9	9	20	35	60	36	17
2019-20	PR Lge	38	9	14	15	39	54	41	15
2020-21	PR Lge	38	9	14	15	40	46	41	16
2021-22	PR Lge	38	12	15	11	42	44	51	9
2022-23	PR Lge	38	18	8	12	72	53	62	6
2023-24	PR Lge	38	12	12	14	55	62	48	11
2024-25	PR Lge	38	16	13	9	66	59	61	8

DID YOU KNOW

Brighton & Hove Albion signed their first shirt sponsorship deal with British Caledonian Airways in March 1980 with the Seagulls receiving £60,000 a year through the deal. The agreement ran for three years from the start of the 1980–81 season, and the club switched to all-blue shirts to accommodate the sponsor's name.

BRIGHTON & HOVE ALBION – PREMIER LEAGUE 2024–25 LEAGUE RECORD

Match No.	Date	Venue	Opponents	Result	H/T Score	Lg Pos.	Goalscorers	Atten-dance
1	Aug 17	A	Everton	W 3-0	1-0	1	Mitoma [25], Welbeck [56], Adingra [87]	39,217
2	24	H	Manchester U	W 2-1	1-0	2	Welbeck [32], Joao Pedro [90]	31,537
3	31	A	Arsenal	D 1-1	0-1	2	Joao Pedro [58]	60,326
4	Sept 14	H	Ipswich T	D 0-0	0-0	4		31,573
5	22	H	Nottingham F	D 2-2	2-1	7	Hinshelwood [42], Welbeck [45]	31,444
6	28	A	Chelsea	L 2-4	2-4	8	Rutter [7], Baleba [34]	39,495
7	Oct 6	H	Tottenham H	W 3-2	0-2	6	Minteh [48], Rutter [58], Welbeck [66]	31,487
8	19	A	Newcastle U	W 1-0	1-0	5	Welbeck [35]	52,220
9	26	H	Wolverhampton W	D 2-2	1-0	5	Welbeck [45], Ferguson [85]	31,480
10	Nov 2	A	Liverpool	L 1-2	1-0	7	Kadioglu [14]	60,331
11	9	H	Manchester C	W 2-1	0-1	4	Joao Pedro [78], O'Riley [83]	31,715
12	23	A	Bournemouth	W 2-1	1-0	5	Joao Pedro [4], Mitoma [49]	11,196
13	29	H	Southampton	D 1-1	1-0	3	Mitoma [29]	31,542
14	Dec 5	A	Fulham	L 1-3	0-1	5	Baleba [56]	26,368
15	8	H	Leicester C	D 2-2	1-0	7	Lamptey [37], Minteh [79]	31,647
16	15	H	Crystal Palace	L 1-3	0-2	9	Guehi (og) [87]	30,893
17	21	A	West Ham U	D 1-1	0-0	9	Wieffer [51]	62,460
18	27	H	Brentford	D 0-0	0-0	10		31,548
19	30	A	Aston Villa	D 2-2	1-1	10	Adingra [12], Lamptey [81]	41,414
20	Jan 4	H	Arsenal	D 1-1	0-1	10	Joao Pedro (pen) [61]	31,714
21	16	A	Ipswich T	W 2-0	0-0	9	Mitoma [59], Rutter [82]	29,403
22	19	A	Manchester U	W 3-1	1-1	9	Minteh [5], Mitoma [60], Rutter [76]	73,758
23	25	H	Everton	L 0-1	0-1	9		31,567
24	Feb 1	A	Nottingham F	L 0-7	0-3	10		30,164
25	14	H	Chelsea	W 3-0	2-0	8	Mitoma [27], Minteh 2 [38, 63]	31,503
26	22	A	Southampton	W 4-0	1-0	9	Joao Pedro [23], Rutter [56], Mitoma [71], Hinshelwood [82]	30,775
27	25	H	Bournemouth	W 2-1	1-0	8	Joao Pedro (pen) [12], Welbeck [75]	31,138
28	Mar 8	H	Fulham	W 2-1	1-1	6	Van Hecke [41], Joao Pedro (pen) [90]	31,584
29	15	A	Manchester C	D 2-2	1-2	7	Estupinan [21], Khusanov (og) [48]	52,471
30	Apr 2	H	Aston Villa	L 0-3	0-0	8		31,230
31	5	A	Crystal Palace	L 1-2	1-1	8	Welbeck [31]	24,564
32	12	H	Leicester C	D 2-2	1-1	9	Joao Pedro 2 (2 pens) [31, 55]	31,330
33	19	A	Brentford	L 2-4	1-1	10	Welbeck [45], Mitoma [81]	17,083
34	26	H	West Ham U	W 3-2	1-0	9	Ayari [13], Mitoma [89], Baleba [90]	31,499
35	May 4	A	Newcastle U	D 1-1	1-0	10	Minteh [28]	31,580
36	10	A	Wolverhampton W	W 2-0	1-0	9	Welbeck (pen) [29], Gruda [85]	31,279
37	19	H	Liverpool	W 3-2	1-2	8	Ayari [32], Mitoma [69], Hinshelwood [85]	31,611
38	25	A	Tottenham H	W 4-1	0-1	8	Hinshelwood 2 [51, 64], O'Riley (pen) [88], Gomez [90]	61,449

Final League Position: 8

GOALSCORERS

League (66): Joao Pedro 10 (5 pens), Mitoma 10, Welbeck 10 (1 pen), Minteh 6, Hinshelwood 5, Rutter 5, Baleba 3, Adingra 2, Ayari 2, Lamptey 2, O'Riley 2 (1 pen), Estupinan 1, Ferguson 1, Gomez 1, Gruda 1, Kadioglu 1, Van Hecke 1, Wieffer 1, own goals 2.
FA Cup (8): Rutter 3, Enciso 1, March 1, Minteh 1, Mitoma 1, Welbeck 1.
Carabao Cup (9): Adingra 3, Baleba 1, Kadioglu 1, Lamptey 1, O'Mahony 1, Sarmiento 1, Webster 1.
(Brighton & HA U21) Vertu Trophy (8): Howell 2 (2 pens), Peupion 2, Duffus 1, Ifill 1, Moulton 1, Vickers C 1.

Steele J 2	Veltman J 19+2	Van Hecke J 33+1	Dunk L 23+2	Hinshelwood J 22+4	Milner J 3+1	Wieffer M 10+15	Minteh Y 20+12	Joao Pedro d 23+4	Mitoma K 28+8	Welbeck D 24+6	Adingra S 12+17	Webster A 11+3	Sarmiento J —+1	Gilmour B 1+1	Ayari Y 22+12	Baleba C 31+3	Enciso J 2+10	Rutter G 19+9	Verbruggen B 36	Estupinan P 26+4	Kadioglu F 5+1	Ferguson E 2+11	Igor d 10+3	Gruda B 8+13	Lamptey T 10+5	Moder J —+4	O'Riley M 11+10	March S 1+7	Gomez D 4+12	Cashin E —+2	Howell H —+1	Match No.
1	2	3	4²	5	6⁴	7	8¹	9³	10⁵	11	12	13	14	15	16																	1
1	2	3	4	5	6¹		8⁵	9	10³	11²			14		7¹	15	12	13		16												2
	2³	3	4	5	6¹		8²	9	10⁵	11⁴	15				12	7	16	13	1	14												3
	2	3	4	5²			6³		9	11⁴	14				8	7	13	10¹	1	12	15											4
	2	3	4	6		13	12	14	10	11	8¹				13	8	15	9	1	5⁴	15											5
		4	6			7²	14		11	10⁵		3¹			13	8	15	9⁴	1	5	2⁹	16	12									6
	2		4	7		15	8⁵		10	11		3¹			6⁴	14	9³	1	13	5²	12	16										7
	2	15	3	8		13				12	11⁴				9⁵	7²	16	6³	1	14	5	10¹	4									8
	2	3		14					9⁵	11²					8	7³	16	10⁴	1	5	6¹	13	4	12	15							9
	2¹	3		7⁵		12		9³	11	15					8²	10	1	5	6⁴	16	4	13	14									10
	2	3		7²		–14	9⁵	11	6³						8¹	12	10¹	1	5	4	15	16	13									11
	2	3		13			9³	10	11⁴	12					7³	6⁸	8¹	1	5	15	4	14										12
		3	13			14	16	11¹	9	10⁴	12				8	6⁹	1	5	15	4	2²	7³										13
	2¹	3		7⁵		14	11³	10	5²						6	15	1	8	13	4	16	12	9⁴									14
	3	4		12		14	9²	10⁵	13						7⁴	6¹	8	1	5	11³	16	2	15									15
	3	4		16		8²	11	10	14						7⁴	6⁶	12	9³	1	5	13	15	2¹									16
	2²	3	4	7¹		14	9	10⁵							12	6	15	11⁴	1	5	16	8³	13									17
	2⁵	3	4			13	11	10³	12						14	7	9⁴	15	1	5	8²	6¹	16									18
		3	4			12	11	13		10³					7⁴	6⁵	9¹	14	1	5	8²	2	16	15								19
	2	3				13	11	14	10³	15					7	6	12	1	5	4⁴	8¹	9²										20
	2	3	14			12	11⁴	10	15	7³	4¹				9⁵	6	13	1	5						16	8²							21
	2	3	4			6²	10⁹	9	11¹						8	7⁴	16	12	1	5³						14	13	15				22
	2⁴	3	4	14		13	9	10	11		16				7³	6⁵	12	1						8¹	5²	15							23
	2	3	4	6²		7	9³	10¹	11⁴	12					8	1		15		5	14			13									24
	3	4	9²			2⁵	12	10	11⁴	16	5				15	8³	7¹	1		6	14		13									25
	3		2⁵			16	8	11	10⁴	14	4				7²	6	9³	1	12	15	5¹		13									26
	3		12			15	8	11²	10	14	4				13	6⁴	9⁵	1	5¹	2			16	7³								27
	3		2			16	8²	11	10⁵	13	15	4			7¹	6⁴	9³	1	5				14	12								28
	3		2			16	8³	11	10⁴	13	14	4			12	6⁵	9¹	1	5				15					7²				29
	3	4³	2¹			15	11²	10	13	8					7	14		1	5				9⁵		16		6⁴	12				30
	3⁴	4	2			17	8⁴	13	10²	11	12				16	6		1	5⁵				14		9¹	15	7³					31
	3	2				7¹	9		11	10³					6	4		1	5				14		8²	13	12					32
	3	4	7			2⁵	10⁴	12	11⁴	16					14	6³		1	5				9¹	13	15	17						33
	3	7³	2			12	13	11	10²						6	4		1	5				15	9⁴	8¹	14						34
14	3	4	7³			2¹	8⁴	11	10²						13	6		1	5				15	12	9⁶	16						35
	3		16			2	10⁴	15	11	12	4				7⁵	6³		1	5				13	8¹	9²	14						36
	3		15			2	8⁴	12	11⁵	10¹	4				7³	6		1	5				9²	13	14		16					37
14	3		11	16		2	9⁵	12		6²	4				8¹	7		1					5³	10⁴	15	13						38

FA Cup

Third Round	Norwich C	(a)	4-0
Fourth Round	Chelsea	(h)	2-1
Fifth Round *aet.*	Newcastle U	(a)	2-1
Quarter-Final	Nottingham F	(h)	0-0

aet; Nottingham F won 4-3 on penalties.

Carabao Cup

Second Round	Crawley T	(h)	4-0
Third Round	Wolverhampton W	(h)	3-2
Fourth Round	Liverpool	(h)	2-3

Vertu Trophy (Brighton & HA U21)

Group B (S)	Crawley T	(a)	2-2
Crawley T won 4-3 on penalties.			
Group B (S)	Wycombe W	(a)	3-5
Group B (S)	AFC Wimbledon	(a)	3-0

BRISTOL CITY

FOUNDATION

The name Bristol City came into being in 1897 when the Bristol South End club, formed three years earlier, decided to adopt professionalism and apply for admission to the Southern League after competing in the Western League. The historic meeting was held at the Albert Hall, Bedminster. Bristol City employed Sam Hollis from Woolwich Arsenal as manager and gave him £40 to buy players. In 1900 they merged with Bedminster, another leading Bristol club.

Ashton Gate Stadium, Ashton Road, Bristol BS3 2EJ.

Telephone: (0117) 963 0600.

Ticket Office: (0117) 963 0600.

Website: www.bcfc.co.uk

Email: enquiries@bcfc.co.uk

Ground Capacity: 26,387.

Record Attendance: 43,335 v Preston NE, FA Cup 5th rd, 16 February 1935.

Pitch Measurements: 105m × 68m (115yd × 74.5yd).

Chairman: Jon Lansdown.

Chief Operating Officer: Tom Rawcliffe.

Head Coach: Gerhard Struber.

Assistant Head Coach: Bernd Eibler.

Colours: Red shirts with white and red trim, white shorts with red trim, red socks.

Year Formed: 1894.

Turned Professional: 1897.

Previous Name: 1894, Bristol South End; 1897, Bristol City.

Club Nickname: 'The Robins'.

Grounds: 1894, St John's Lane; 1904, Ashton Gate.

First Football League Game: 7 September 1901, Division 2, v Blackpool (a) W 2–0 – Moles; Tuft, Davies; Jones, McLean, Chambers; Bradbury, Connor, Boucher, O'Brien (2), Flynn.

Record League Victory: 9–0 v Aldershot, Division 3 (S), 28 December 1946 – Eddols; Morgan, Fox; Peacock, Roberts, Jones (1); Chilcott, Thomas, Clark (4 incl. 1p), Cyril Williams (1), Hargreaves (3).

Record Cup Victory: 11–0 v Chichester C, FA Cup 1st rd, 5 November 1960 – Cook; Collinson, Thresher; Connor, Alan Williams, Etheridge; Tait (1), Bobby Williams (1), Atyeo (5), Adrian Williams (3), Derrick, (1 og).

Record Defeat: 0–9 v Coventry C, Division 3 (S), 28 April 1934.

HONOURS

League Champions: Division 2 – 1905–06; FL 1 – 2014–15; Division 3S – 1922–23, 1926–27, 1954–55.
Runners-up: Division 1 – 1906–07; Division 2 – 1975–76; FL 1 – 2006–07; Second Division – 1997–98; Division 3 – 1964–65, 1989–90; Division 3S – 1937–38.
FA Cup: Runners-up: 1909.
League Cup: semi-final – 1971, 1989, 2018.
League Trophy Winners: 1986, 2003, 2015.
Runners-up: 1987, 2000.
Welsh Cup Winners: 1934.
Anglo-Scottish Cup Winners: 1978.

FOOTBALL YEARBOOK FACT FILE

Bristol City almost went out of business in February 1982, only being saved when a group of players who became known as 'The Ashton Gate Eight' agreed to leave the club immediately under a redundancy arrangement. The incident led to the introduction of the Football Creditors' Rule which requires clubs threatened with insolvency or liquidation to pay football-related creditors in full before addressing other debts.

Most League Points (2 for a win): 70, Division 3 (S), 1954–55.

Most League Points (3 for a win): 99, FL 1, 2014–15.

Most League Goals: 104, Division 3 (S), 1926–27.

Highest League Scorer in Season: Don Clark, 36, Division 3 (S), 1946–47.

Most League Goals in Total Aggregate: John Atyeo, 314, 1951–66.

Most League Goals in One Match: 6, Tommy 'Tot' Walsh v Gillingham, Division 3 (S), 15 January 1927.

Most Capped Player: Billy Wedlock, 26, England.

Most League Appearances: John Atyeo, 596, 1951–66.

Youngest League Player: Marvin Brown, 16 years 105 days v Bristol R, 17 October 1999.

Record Transfer Fee Received: £25,000,000 from Bournemouth for Alex Scott, August 2023.

Record Transfer Fee Paid: £8,000,000 to Chelsea for Tomas Kalas, July 2019.

Football League Record: 1901 Elected to Division 2; 1901–06 Division 2; 1906–11 Division 1; 1911–22 Division 2; 1922–23 Division 3 (S); 1923–24 Division 2; 1924–27 Division 3 (S); 1927–32 Division 2; 1932–55 Division 3 (S); 1955–60 Division 2; 1960–65 Division 3; 1965–76 Division 2; 1976–80 Division 1; 1980–81 Division 2; 1981–82 Division 3; 1982–84 Division 4; 1984–90 Division 3; 1990–92 Division 2; 1992–95 First Division; 1995–98 Second Division; 1998–99 First Division; 1999–2004 Second Division; 2004–07 FL 1; 2007–13 FL C; 2013–15 FL 1; 2015– FL C.

LATEST SEQUENCES

Longest Sequence of League Wins: 14, 9.9.1905 – 2.12.1905.

Longest Sequence of League Defeats: 8, 10.12.2016 – 21.1.2017.

Longest Sequence of League Draws: 4, 6.11.1999 – 27.11.1999.

Longest Sequence of Unbeaten League Matches: 24, 9.9.1905 – 10.2.1906.

Longest Sequence Without a League Win: 21, 16.3.2013 – 22.10.2013.

Successive Scoring Runs: 25 from 26.12.1905.

Successive Non-scoring Runs: 6 from 20.12.1980.

MANAGERS

Sam Hollis 1897–99
Bob Campbell 1899–1901
Sam Hollis 1901–05
Harry Thickett 1905–10
Frank Bacon 1910–11
Sam Hollis 1911–13
George Hedley 1913–17
Jack Hamilton 1917–19
Joe Palmer 1919–21
Alex Raisbeck 1921–29
Joe Bradshaw 1929–32
Bob Hewison 1932–49
  (*under suspension 1938–39*)
Bob Wright 1949–50
Pat Beasley 1950–58
Peter Doherty 1958–60
Fred Ford 1960–67
Alan Dicks 1967–80
Bobby Houghton 1980–82
Roy Hodgson 1982
Terry Cooper 1982–88
  (*Director from 1983*)
Joe Jordan 1988–90
Jimmy Lumsden 1990–92
Denis Smith 1992–93
Russell Osman 1993–94
Joe Jordan 1994–97
John Ward 1997–98
Benny Lennartsson 1998–99
Tony Pulis 1999–2000
Tony Fawthrop 2000
Danny Wilson 2000–04
Brian Tinnion 2004–05
Gary Johnson 2005–10
Steve Coppell 2010
Keith Millen 2010–11
Derek McInnes 2011–13
Sean O'Driscoll 2013
Steve Cotterill 2013–16
Lee Johnson 2016–20
Dean Holden 2020–21
Nigel Pearson 2021–23
Liam Manning 2023–25
Gerhard Struber June 2025–

TEN YEAR LEAGUE RECORD

		P	W	D	L	F	A	Pts	Pos
2015-16	FL C	46	13	13	20	54	71	52	18
2016-17	FL C	46	15	9	22	60	66	54	17
2017-18	FL C	46	17	16	13	67	58	67	11
2018-19	FL C	46	19	13	14	59	53	70	8
2019-20	FL C	46	17	12	17	60	65	63	12
2020-21	FL C	46	15	6	25	46	68	51	19
2021-22	FL C	46	15	10	21	62	77	55	17
2022-23	FL C	46	15	14	17	55	56	59	14
2023-24	FL C	46	17	11	18	53	51	62	11
2024-25	FL C	46	17	17	12	59	55	68	6

DID YOU KNOW ?

Bristol City recorded their highest-ever win in a senior competitive match against local rivals Bristol Rovers at Eastville in the 1926–27 season on their way to winning the Division Three South title. City won 5-0 on 9 October with goals from Albert Keating, Tot Walsh (2), Arthur Rankin and John Paul. The attendance was 28,581.

BRISTOL CITY – SKY BET CHAMPIONSHIP 2024–25 LEAGUE RECORD

Match No.	Date	Venue	Opponents	Result		H/T Score	Lg Pos.	Goalscorers	Attendance
1	Aug 10	A	Hull C	D	1-1	0-0	11	Mayulu [84]	21,011
2	17	H	Millwall	W	4-3	2-0	6	Mehmeti [3], Armstrong [12], Mayulu [78], Twine [88]	20,733
3	24	H	Coventry C	D	1-1	1-0	8	Tanner [45]	21,545
4	31	A	Derby Co	L	0-3	0-1	14		29,270
5	Sept 14	A	Blackburn R	L	0-3	0-1	17		14,087
6	21	H	Oxford U	W	2-1	0-0	13	Armstrong [57], Wells (pen) [76]	24,807
7	29	A	Swansea C	D	1-1	0-1	14	Knight [76]	16,328
8	Oct 2	H	Sheffield Wed	D	0-0	0-0	13		20,293
9	6	H	Cardiff C	D	1-1	0-0	16	McNally [73]	22,664
10	19	A	Middlesbrough	W	2-0	2-0	10	Mehmeti [27], Hirakawa [45]	24,438
11	22	H	Stoke C	D	2-2	0-2	9	Wells 2 [50, 52]	19,679
12	26	H	Leeds U	D	0-0	0-0	11		25,283
13	Nov 2	A	Preston NE	W	3-1	1-0	8	Hirakawa [6], Wells [51], Bird [81]	14,261
14	5	H	Sheffield U	L	1-2	0-1	11	Mehmeti (pen) [75]	18,736
15	9	A	Norwich C	W	2-0	1-0	10	Mehmeti [16], Wells [63]	26,423
16	23	H	Burnley	L	0-1	0-1	10		20,800
17	26	A	Watford	L	0-1	0-0	11		17,579
18	30	H	Plymouth Arg	W	4-0	0-0	11	Twine [57], Mehmeti 2 [62, 70], Armstrong [90]	24,317
19	Dec 7	A	Portsmouth	L	0-3	0-1	12		20,415
20	10	A	Sunderland	D	1-1	0-0	11	McNally [62]	35,421
21	14	H	QPR	D	1-1	0-0	11	Twine [60]	20,925
22	22	L	WBA	L	0-2	0-2	12		25,910
23	26	H	Luton T	W	1-0	0-0	11	Twine [47]	21,828
24	29	H	Portsmouth	W	3-0	3-0	10	Mehmeti 2 [15, 32], Dickie [35]	24,560
25	Jan 1	A	Plymouth Arg	D	2-2	1-0	10	Mehmeti [32], Knight [56]	17,005
26	4	H	Derby Co	W	1-0	1-0	8	McNally [19]	22,040
27	18	A	Coventry C	L	0-1	0-0	9		26,695
28	22	A	Sheffield Wed	D	2-2	0-1	9	Wells [51], McCrorie [86]	22,774
29	25	H	Blackburn R	W	2-1	1-1	8	Twine [12], Wells [77]	20,945
30	Feb 1	A	Oxford U	D	1-1	0-0	9	Sykes [65]	11,430
31	9	H	Swansea C	L	0-1	0-0	9		21,554
32	12	H	Stoke C	W	2-0	1-0	7	Mehmeti 2 [11, 73]	18,457
33	15	A	Cardiff C	D	1-1	0-0	8	Knight [60]	22,433
34	21	H	Middlesbrough	W	2-1	0-1	6	Earthy 2 [72, 82]	21,894
35	Mar 4	A	Millwall	W	2-0	0-0	7	Vyner [53], Cornick [83]	12,380
36	8	H	Hull C	D	1-1	0-1	7	Mehmeti (pen) [54]	21,754
37	11	A	Sheffield U	D	1-1	0-0	7	Sykes [90]	25,070
38	14	H	Norwich C	W	2-1	2-0	5	Sykes [6], Wells [23]	21,237
39	29	A	Burnley	L	0-1	0-1	8		20,523
40	Apr 5	H	Watford	W	2-1	2-0	6	McCrorie [24], Wells [29]	22,505
41	8	H	WBA	W	2-1	0-0	5	Wells [56], Roberts [90]	24,734
42	12	A	QPR	D	1-1	1-1	5	Earthy [30]	16,867
43	18	H	Sunderland	W	2-1	0-1	5	Dickie [55], McCrorie [76]	25,915
44	21	A	Luton T	L	1-3	0-0	5	Tanner [52]	11,874
45	28	A	Leeds U	L	0-4	0-1	5		36,310
46	May 3	H	Preston NE	D	2-2	0-1	6	McCrorie 2 [69, 74]	24,987

Final League Position: 6

GOALSCORERS

League (59): Mehmeti 12 (2 pens), Wells 10 (1 pen), McCrorie 5, Twine 5, Armstrong 3, Earthy 3, Knight 3, McNally 3, Sykes 3, Dickie 2, Hirakawa 2, Mayulu 2, Tanner 2, Bird 1, Cornick 1, Roberts 1, Vyner 1.
FA Cup (1): Twine 1.
Carabao Cup (0).
Championship Play-offs (0).

O'Leary M 46	Tanner G 23 + 9	Vyner Z 46	Dickie R 35 + 1	Pring C 27 + 5	Williams J 18 + 6	Knight J 46	Sykes M 21 + 6	Bird M 43 + 3	Mehmeti A 29 + 13	Armstrong S 17 + 19	Mayulu F 3 + 12	Bell S — + 20	Wells N 26 + 13	Naismith K 2 + 4	Twine S 26 + 9	Earthy G 11 + 26	Hirakawa Y 17 + 19	McNally L 26	Roberts H 15 + 15	McCrorie R 18 + 5	McGuane M 11 + 10	Morrison E — + 3	Cornick H — + 3	Match No.
1	2	3	4	5	6	7	8[2]	9[3]	10[4]	11[1]	12	13	14	15										1
1	2	3	4	5	6	7	8[3]	9	10[1]	11[2]		13			12	14								2
1	2	3	4[1]	5	6	7	8[4]	9[5]	14	11[2]	13		16		12	10[3]	15							3
1	2	3		5	6	7	8[4]	9[2]	12	11[1]	13		15			4	10[3]		14					4
1	2	3		5[3]	6[2]	7	8[4]	9	15	12	11[1]		10			13	4		14					5
1	2	3		14	6[1]	9		7	8[3]	11[2]		13	10		12	4	5							6
1	2	3		12	13	7	14	6[3]	10	11[4]	16		15		8[5]		9[2]	4	5[1]					7
1	2	3		5	6	7	13	14	10[2]	11[1]		12	8[3]			9	4							8
1	2	3		5[1]	6	7	13	14	10[2]	11[4]	15		9[5]	16	8[3]	4		12						9
1	2	3			6	9		7[3]	10[2]	12		11[1]	14		13	8[4]	4		5	15				10
1	2	3			6	9	8[3]	7	10[1]	13		11[2]		12	14	4		5						11
1	2	3			7	5[5]	10		14	15		11[2]	12		13	9[4]	4		8[1]	6[3]	16			12
1	5[1]	2	3		6[2]	7	8	10	15	14		11[4]			9[3]	4	12		13					13
1		3	15[8]	5[3]		8	2[1]	11	12	13		10[2]	4[4]		6[9]	9		14		7	16			14
1		2		4		7		9	11	13		10[2]		5[1]	12	3	8		6					15
1		2	3	13		7		9[5]	10[4]	14	16	11[3]		15	5[1]	12	4	8[2]		6				16
1		2	3	8		7		9[4]	11[2]	14		10[3]	13	15	5[1]	4	12		6					17
1		2	3	5		7		6	10	13	14	11[2]		9[1]	12	8[3]	4							18
1		2	3	5[3]		7		9	10[4]	13	15	11[2]		12	8	4	14		6[1]					19
1		2	3	5		7		9[1]	10[4]	11[3]		13	14	12	8[2]	4	15		6					20
1		2	3	5		7		6	10	13	14	11[2]	12	9[3]	8[1]	4								21
1		2	3	5		6		9[1]	8[9]	11[2]	13	10[4]	14	15	4	12	7							22
1	14	2	3	8		6		7[5]	13	11[1]	12	10[4]	15	9[4]	4	5[2]	16							23
1	13	2	3	8		7		6[4]	10[5]	12	11[1]	9[3]	14	16	4	5[2]	15							24
1	5[2]	2	3	8[1]		6		7	10[5]	15	11[4]	9[3]	16	13	4	12	14							25
1	13	2	3		6	7		7	11	12	10[1]	9[3]	14	4	8	5[2]								26
1		2	3	15	6	12	7[5]	11[1]	14	13	10[3]	9[6]	4	8[4]	5[2]									27
1	16	2	3		7	5[5]	6	13	14	10[2]	9[3]	12	11[1]	4	15	8[4]								28
1	5[1]	2	3	14	7	13	6[3]	9[4]	10[2]	12	11	15	4	8[5]	16									29
1	15	2	3	6[8]	7	5	13	12[4]	11[1]	10[2]	9[3]	4	8[8]	14										30
1		2	3	7	5[5]	6	10[2]	13	14	11[1]	9[4]	12	15	4[3]	8	16								31
1	16	2	3	7	5[2]	6[4]	11	10[3]	13	9[1]	12	14	4	8[5]	15									32
1	14	2	3	7	8[1]	6	9[5]	10[4]	12	15	11[2]	16	13	4	5[3]									33
1	2	4	3	13	16	7	5[3]	6	11[1]	10[4]	15	9[5]	12	14	8[2]									34
1	2	4	3	8[3]	15	7	5[1]	6	10[2]	14	11[4]	9	12	13										35
1	2[1]	4	3	8[1]	6	5[3]	7	11[4]	10[5]	13	9	14	15	12	16									36
1	2	4	3	16	5	6	12	8[1]	14	11[2]	13	9[3]	15	7[4]	10[5]									37
1		2	3	4	6[2]	7	5[5]	9[4]	11[3]	13	16	10[1]	14	12	8	15								38
1		2	3	4	6	5[4]	7	11[3]	10[2]	16	14	9[5]	12	15	8[1]	13								39
1		2	3	4	7[3]	6	5[5]	9[4]	15	12	16	10[1]	11	13	8[2]	14								40
1	16	2	3	4	12	7	5[3]	9[5]	13	11[4]	10	14	15	8[2]	6[1]									41
1	13	2	3	4	6	7	9[3]	12	16	15	11[5]	14	10[4]	5[1]	8[2]									42
1	2[1]	4	3	8	6[2]	7	9[3]	14	11	13	10[4]	12	16	5[5]	15									43
1	5	2	3	4[1]	6	9[3]	10[4]	14	13	12	8[5]	6	16											44
1	2	4	3	6	9[2]	13	12	15	11[1]	14	10[4]	8	5[3]	7										45
1	2[3]	4	3	6[4]	7	9[1]	13	16	11[5]	10[2]	12	5	14	8	15									46

FA Cup
Third Round　　Wolverhampton W　(h)　1-2

Carabao Cup
First Round　　Coventry C　(h)　0-1

Championship Play-offs
Semi-Final 1st leg　Sheffield U　(h)　0-3
Semi-Final 2nd leg　Sheffield U　(a)　0-3

BRISTOL ROVERS

FOUNDATION

Bristol Rovers were formed at a meeting in Stapleton Road, Eastville, in 1883. However, they first went under the name of the Black Arabs (wearing black shirts). Changing their name to Eastville Rovers in their second season in 1888–89, they won the Gloucestershire Senior Cup. Original members of the Bristol & District League in 1892, this eventually became the Western League and Eastville Rovers adopted professionalism in 1897.

The Memorial Stadium, Filton Avenue, Horfield, Bristol BS7 0BF.
Telephone: (0117) 909 6648.
Ticket Office: (0117) 909 6648.
Website: www.bristolrovers.co.uk
Email: info@bristolrovers.co.uk
Ground Capacity: 12,565.
Record Attendance: 38,472 v Preston NE, FA Cup 4th rd, 30 January 1960 (at Eastville); 9,464 v Liverpool, FA Cup 4th rd, 8 February 1992 (at Twerton Park); 12,011 v WBA, FA Cup 6th rd, 9 March 2008 (at Memorial Stadium).
Pitch Measurements: 100m × 68m (109.5yd × 74.5yd).
Chairman: Hussain AlSaeed.
Director of Football: Ricky Martin.
Head Coach: Darrell Clarke.
Assistant Head Coaches: Jon Stead, Rhys Carr.
Colours: Blue and white quartered shirts with blue sleeves and blue and white trim, blue shorts with white trim, blue socks with white trim.
Year Formed: 1883.   *Turned Professional:* 1897.
Previous Names: 1883, Black Arabs; 1884, Eastville Rovers; 1897, Bristol Eastville Rovers; 1898, Bristol Rovers. *Club Nicknames:* 'The Pirates'; 'The Gas'.
Grounds: 1883, Purdown; Three Acres, Ashley Hill; Rudgeway, Fishponds; 1897, Eastville; 1986, Twerton Park; 1996, The Memorial Stadium.
First Football League Game: 28 August 1920, Division 3, v Millwall (a) L 0–2 – Stansfield; Bethune, Panes; Boxley, Kenny, Steele; Chance, Bird, Sims, Bell, Palmer.
Record League Victory: 7–0 v Brighton & HA, Division 3 (S), 29 November 1952 – Hoyle; Bamford, Fox; Pitt, Warren, Sampson; McIlvenny, Roost (2), Lambden (1), Bradford (1), Petherbridge (2), (1 og). 7–0 v Swansea T, Division 2, 2 October 1954 – Radford; Bamford, Watkins; Pitt, Muir, Anderson; Petherbridge, Bradford (2), Meyer, Roost (1), Hooper (2), (2 og). 7–0 v Shrewsbury T, Division 3, 21 March 1964 – Hall; Hillard, Gwyn Jones; Oldfield, Stone (1), Mabbutt; Jarman (2), Brown (1), Biggs (1p), Hamilton, Bobby Jones (2); 7–0 v Scunthorpe U (h), FL 2, 7 May 2022 – Belshaw; Anderson H, Taylor (1), Connolly, Clarke T (Nicholson), Whelan, Thomas, Evans (2) (Clarke L), Finley, Anderson E (1), Collins (2), own goal 1.
Record Cup Victory: 7–1 v Dorchester, FA Cup 4th qualifying rd, 25 October 2014 – Midenhall; Locyer, Trotman (McChrystal), Parkes, Monkhouse (2), Clarke, Mansell (1) (Thomas), Brown, Gosling, Harrison (3), Taylor (1) (White).
Record Defeat: 0–12 v Luton T, Division 3 (S), 13 April 1936.

HONOURS

League Champions: Division 3 – 1989–90; Division 3S – 1952–53.
Runners-up: Division 3 – 1973–74; Football Conference – (2nd) 2014–15 *(promoted to FL 2 via play-offs).*
FA Cup: 6th rd – 1951, 1958, 2008.
League Cup: 5th rd – 1971, 1972.
League Trophy: Runners-up: 1990, 2007.

FOOTBALL YEARBOOK FACT FILE

Bristol Rovers played Southampton on two consecutive days in different countries in 1909. On Saturday 20 March the teams met in a Southern League fixture with Saints winning 1-0. Later that evening the teams travelled by boat from Southampton to Le Havre and on the following day they played an exhibition game at the Parc des Princes in Paris, the match finishing as a 5-5 draw.

Most League Points (2 for a win): 64, Division 3 (S), 1952–53.
Most League Points (3 for a win): 93, Division 3, 1989–90.
Most League Goals: 92, Division 3 (S), 1952–53.
Highest League Scorer in Season: Geoff Bradford, 33, Division 3 (S), 1952–53.
Most League Goals in Total Aggregate: Geoff Bradford, 242, 1949–64.
Most League Goals in One Match: 4, Sidney Leigh v Exeter C, Division 3 (S), 2 May 1921; 4, Jonah Wilcox v Bournemouth, Division 3 (S), 12 December 1925; 4, Bill Culley v QPR, Division 3 (S), 5 March 1927; 4, Frank Curran v Swindon T, Division 3 (S), 25 March 1939; 4, Vic Lambden v Aldershot, Division 3 (S), 29 March 1947; 4, George Petherbridge v Torquay U, Division 3 (S), 1 December 1951; 4, Vic Lambden v Colchester U, Division 3 (S), 14 May 1952; 4, Geoff Bradford v Rotherham U, Division 2, 14 March 1959; 4, Robin Stubbs v Gillingham, Division 2, 10 October 1970; 4, Alan Warboys v Brighton & HA, Division 3, 1 December 1973; 4, Jamie Cureton v Reading, Division 2, 16 January 1999; 4, Ellis Harrison v Northampton T, FL 1, 7 January 2017.
Most Capped Player: Vitalijs Astafjevs, 30 (167), Latvia.
Most League Appearances: Stuart Taylor, 546, 1966–80.
Youngest League Player: Ronnie Dix, 15 years 173 days v Charlton Ath, 25 February 1928.
Record Transfer Fee Received: £2,000,000 from Fulham for Barry Hayles, November 1998; £2,000,000 from WBA for Jason Roberts, July 2000.
Record Transfer Fee Paid: £500,000 to Fleetwood T for Promise Omochere, July 2024.
Football League Record: 1920 Original Member of Division 3; 1920–21 Division 3; 1921–53 Division 3 (S); 1953–62 Division 2; 1962–74 Division 3; 1974–81 Division 2; 1981–90 Division 3; 1990–92 Division 2; 1992–93 First Division; 1993–2001 Second Division; 2001–04 Third Division; 2004–07 FL 2; 2007–11 FL 1; 2011–14 FL 2; 2014–15 Football Conference; 2015–16 FL 2; 2016–21 FL 1; 2021–22 FL 2; 2022–25 FL 1; 2025– FL 2.

LATEST SEQUENCES

Longest Sequence of League Wins: 12, 18.10.1952 – 17.1.1953.
Longest Sequence of League Defeats: 8, 26.10.2002 – 21.12.2002.
Longest Sequence of League Draws: 6, 4.2.2017 – 28.2.2017.
Longest Sequence of Unbeaten League Matches: 32, 7.4.1973 – 27.1.1974.
Longest Sequence Without a League Win: 20, 5.4.1980 – 1.11.1980.
Successive Scoring Runs: 26 from 26.3.1927.
Successive Non-scoring Runs: 7 from 9.3.2024.

MANAGERS

Alfred Homer 1899–1920
  (*continued as Secretary to 1928*)
Ben Hall 1920–21
Andy Wilson 1921–26
Joe Palmer 1926–29
Dave McLean 1929–30
Albert Prince-Cox 1930–36
Percy Smith 1936–37
Brough Fletcher 1938–49
Bert Tann 1950–68 (*continued as General Manager to 1972*)
Fred Ford 1968–69
Bill Dodgin Snr 1969–72
Don Megson 1972–77
Bobby Campbell 1978–79
Harold Jarman 1979–80
Terry Cooper 1980–81
Bobby Gould 1981–83
David Williams 1983–85
Bobby Gould 1985–87
Gerry Francis 1987–91
Martin Dobson 1991
Dennis Rofe 1992
Malcolm Allison 1992–93
John Ward 1993–96
Ian Holloway 1996–2001
Garry Thompson 2001
Gerry Francis 2001
Garry Thompson 2001–02
Ray Graydon 2002–04
Ian Atkins 2004–05
Paul Trollope 2005–10
Dave Penney 2011
Paul Buckle 2011–12
Mark McGhee 2012
John Ward 2012–14
Darrell Clarke 2014–18
Graham Coughlan 2018–19
Ben Garner 2019–20
Paul Tisdale 2020–21
Joey Barton 2021–23
Matt Taylor 2023–24
Inigo Calderon 2024–25
Darrell Clarke May 2025–

TEN YEAR LEAGUE RECORD

		P	W	D	L	F	A	Pts	Pos
2015-16	FL 2	46	26	7	13	77	46	85	3
2016-17	FL 1	46	18	12	16	68	70	66	10
2017-18	FL 1	46	16	11	19	60	66	59	13
2018-19	FL 1	46	13	15	18	47	50	54	15
2019-20	FL 1	35	12	9	14	38	49	45	14§
2020-21	FL 1	46	10	8	28	40	70	38	24
2021-22	FL 2	46	23	11	12	71	49	80	3
2022-23	FL 1	46	14	11	21	58	73	53	17
2023-24	FL 1	46	16	9	21	52	68	57	15
2024-25	FL 1	46	12	7	27	44	76	43	22

§*Decided on points-per-game (1.29)*

DID YOU KNOW ?

Bristol Rovers centre-forward Vic Lambden scored four times in the first half of the 6-0 home win against Colchester United on Easter Monday in 1952. His tally included a hat-trick in the opening 15 minutes, the quickest hat-trick from the start of a Football League match in the club's history.

BRISTOL ROVERS – SKY BET LEAGUE ONE 2024–25 LEAGUE RECORD

Match No.	Date		Venue	Opponents	Result		H/T Score	Lg Pos.	Goalscorers	Attendance
1	Aug	10	H	Northampton T	W	1-0	0-0	8	Akono Bilongo [90]	8529
2		17	A	Rotherham U	D	0-0	0-0	8		9414
3		24	A	Stockport Co	L	0-2	0-1	14		9423
4		31	H	Cambridge U	W	2-0	1-0	9	Omochere 2 [30, 48]	7893
5	Sept	7	A	Barnsley	L	1-2	1-1	9	Sotiriou [37]	11,196
6		14	H	Wigan Ath	L	0-4	0-2	14		7925
7		21	A	Peterborough U	L	2-3	0-2	19	McCormick [74], O'Donkor [76]	8006
8		28	H	Wycombe W	L	1-2	1-0	21	Sinclair [17]	7814
9	Oct	1	H	Charlton Ath~	W	3-2	1-0	18	Sinclair [30], Lindsay [57], Wilson [67]	6638
10		5	A	Burton Alb	W	3-1	0-1	18	Forde [52], Mola [59], Ward G [90]	2832
11		19	A	Huddersfield T	L	1-3	0-2	18	Hutchinson [69]	18,179
12		22	H	Shrewsbury T	W	1-0	0-0	15	Lindsay [52]	6361
13		26	A	Reading	L	0-1	0-0	16		12,843
14	Nov	9	H	Lincoln C	D	1-1	1-0	16	Forde [35]	7262
15		16	H	Crawley T	D	0-0	0-0	14		7411
16		23	A	Mansfield T	W	1-0	0-0	13	McCormick [49]	7357
17		26	H	Blackpool	L	0-2	0-1	14		6342
18	Dec	3	A	Leyton Orient	L	0-3	0-3	15		7422
19		14	A	Birmingham C	L	0-2	0-2	20		26,459
20		21	H	Wrexham	D	1-1	0-1	19	Omochere [86]	9471
21		26	A	Exeter C	L	1-3	0-0	19	Omochere [61]	8192
22		29	A	Stevenage	L	0-3	0-1	20		3768
23	Jan	1	H	Leyton Orient	L	2-3	1-2	20	Martin 2 (1 pen) [32 (p), 74]	7887
24		4	A	Cambridge U	W	1-0	1-0	20	Thomas [26]	6467
25		18	H	Barnsley	W	3-1	1-0	18	O'Donkor [41], Hutchinson [52], Sotiriou [85]	7638
26		25	A	Wigan Ath	L	0-2	0-1	18		10,112
27		28	A	Charlton Ath	L	0-2	0-2	19		11,149
28	Feb	2	H	Peterborough U	W	3-1	1-0	18	Wilson [16], Hutchinson [62], Sotiriou [83]	7461
29		11	H	Stockport Co	D	1-1	0-0	19	Swinkels [90]	6643
30		15	H	Burton Alb	W	3-1	1-0	17	Martin [13], Thomas [87], Hutchinson [90]	7938
31		18	A	Wycombe W	L	0-2	0-0	18		4419
32		22	A	Northampton T	L	1-2	0-0	19	Sinclair [46]	6996
33	Mar	1	H	Rotherham U	L	2-3	1-1	20	Sotiriou [5], Swinkels [72]	7799
34		4	A	Shrewsbury T	D	0-0	0-0	20		5257
35		8	H	Huddersfield T	W	1-0	1-0	20	Sotiriou [10]	7705
36		11	H	Bolton W	W	3-2	1-1	17	Martin 2 (1 pen) [6 (p), 63], Taylor [88]	7644
37		15	A	Lincoln C	L	0-5	0-1	20		8506
38		22	A	Crawley T	L	0-1	0-1	20		4421
39		29	H	Mansfield T	L	1-2	1-1	20	Sawyers [26]	9067
40	Apr	1	H	Birmingham C	L	1-2	1-1	20	O'Donkor [19]	8088
41		5	A	Bolton W	L	0-1	0-0	20		22,422
42		12	H	Exeter C	L	1-2	0-2	21	Sotiriou [70]	9508
43		18	A	Wrexham	D	1-1	1-0	21	Moore [32]	12,740
44		21	H	Stevenage	L	0-1	0-1	21		9192
45		26	H	Reading	L	0-2	0-0	22		9035
46	May	3	A	Blackpool	L	1-4	1-1	22	O'Donkor [18]	10,534

Final League Position: 22

GOALSCORERS

League (44): Sotiriou 6, Martin 5 (2 pens), Hutchinson 4, O'Donkor 4, Omochere 4, Sinclair 3, Forde 2, Lindsay 2, McCormick 2, Swinkels 2, Thomas 2, Wilson 2, Akono Bilongo 1, Mola 1, Moore 1, Sawyers 1, Taylor 1, Ward G 1.
FA Cup (3): Lindsay 1, Taylor 1, Ward 1.
Carabao Cup (0).
Vertu Trophy (5): Hutchinson 2, McCormick 1, Shaw 1, Taylor 1.

Griffiths J 28	Moore T 25 + 8	Wilson J 46	Mola C 29 + 5	Thomas L 20 + 16	Conteh K 18 + 1	Ward G 22 + 13	Akono Bilongo B 11 + 3	Hutchinson J 22 + 15	Sinclair S 20 + 21	Omochere P 16 + 6	McCormick L 8 + 11	Lindsay J 18 + 10	Forbes M 2 + 5	Senior J 7 + 12	Sotiriou R 32 + 5	Martin C 16 + 7	Taylor C 38 + 4	Garrett J 3 + 4	O'Donkor G 14 + 14	Sousa L 14 + 11	Shaw K 12 + 3	Forde S 14 + 17	Hunt J 16 + 4	Sawyers R 9 + 4	Butcher M 17 + 1	Ward J 18	Reindorf M — + 4	Swinkels S 10 + 4	Dewsbury O 1 + 5	Match No.
1	2	3	4	5	6	7^2	8	9^3	10^1	11^4	12	13	14	15																1
1	2	3	4	5	6	8^6	9^4	7^3	16	11^4	12	14			10^1	13	15													2
1	2^3	3	4	5	6	8^2	9^5	7^4	16	11				15	12	10^1	13	14												3
1	2^5	3	4	5	6	8^3	9^4		15	11^2	12				10^1		14	7	13	16										4
1	2	3	4	6^4		7^3	9^2		15	11	8^5				10^1		5	12	13	14	16									5
1	2^4	3	4	6	5	7	13	10^5					14		11^4		12	8^3	16	9^2		15								6
1		2	4	14	7	15	8^1			11^2	13	6^4			10^5		3		12	5	9^3	16								7
1		4	5	6	14	7^3		9^5	12	15	8				10^4		3		11^1	2^2		16	13							8
1		2	4		7		8	10^4	11^5	13	6^1	14			9^2		3	12	15			16	5^3							9
1	14	2	4		7	12	8^2	10	11^5	16	6^1				9^4		3		15			13	5^3							10
1	3	2	4		5	8^3	9^4	14	11^2	10		7^5			13		16		12			15	6^1							11
1	2	4	12	16		7	14	13	10^2	11	15	6^3			9^4		3		5^1			8^5								12
1	2	4	5		7	6^4	15	12	10^3	11^1		14			9^2		3					8^4	13							13
1	2	4	5		7	14	13	10		9^1	6^3	12			15	11^2	3					8^4								14
1		4	2	15		7^1	12	5	10^2	13	14	9^4	6			11^3	3					8								15
1	2	4	5		7	13		10^4	15		9^1	6	14		11^2	3			12			8^3								16
1	2	4	13	15		7	16	5^3	10^2	14		9^4	6^5		11^3	3			12			8								17
1	2^2	4	5^1			7^4		10		15	6^5	12	13		9^3	11	3	16	14			8								18
1	13	2	8		7	14		15	16	11^5	6^4	4^1	5^2		12	3			10^4			9								19
1	5^2	2	8^5	12	6		15	9^3	13	10^4	7	4^1	14		11	3						16								20
1	12	2	4	8^1	7		11	13	10^4	15	6^3				5^2	16	3		14			9^6								21
1		4	5^3	13		15		9^5	10^2	11	6^4	7^8		2	16	3			12	14		8^1								22
1	2	4		8		7		6^4	15	11^5	13				16	9^3	12	3^5		10	5^2	14								23
1	2	3	8^2		7		13	10^3		6^4					15	9^1	11	4	12	5		14								24
1	2	3	14	8^4	6		9^2	10^1		15		16	12	13	4	11^3	5					7^5								25
1		3	16	8^1		7^5		9^3	12		15				2	10	14	4	11	5^4		13			6^2					26
1	2	3	5^1	16		7^3		8^4		6^2					9^5	11	4	13	12	10		14								27
1		3	8^2		6		9	13		15	10	12	4		11^1	5			2^4	14	7^3									28
	3	8^3	6		9^1	15		16	13	10^5	11	4			5^4			2^2		7	1	12	14							29
14	3	8^3	6^1		15	10^2		12		9^5	11	4			5		13	2^4		7	1		16							30
12	3	8^2			9^1	10^1		7^3		2	6^4	11	4		5	16	15^8			1	14	13								31
	3	8^2			6	10		12		9^1	11	4			5			2		7	1	13								32
	12	3	14	6^3		9	8^1	13		10	11				5^2		2		7	1		4								33
14	2	8^2	6^1		9	12		15	10	11	3				13		5^4		7	1		4^3								34
12	4	6^5	16		9	10	11^1		7^4	3	13	14	2		8	1			5^2	15										35
7^5	2	8^3	15		13	12		5^2	11	10^1	3			14	9^4	16		6	1		4									36
6^3	2	8^1	12		14	11		16	10^2	3				15	9^5	5		7	1		4^4	13								37
	3	5^4	8^2		7^5	11^1	10^3		4		12	15	9	13	2	14	6	1		16										38
	3		8^1	14	15		2^2	11		4	10^5		6	9^3	12	7^4	13	1		5	16									39
2^3	3	5	14	12	16	13		15	10		4	11^2		8^1	7^4		6	9^5	1		5									40
2^5	3	14	13	15	12		10		4	11^3		8^4	7^1	16	6^2	9	1		5											41
	3	12	9^2	13	15		10		4	11^3	8		2	6	7^1	1		5^4	14											42
2	3	12	8^2	14	15	16		10^4		4	11^1		9^3	13	5	6^5	7	1												43
2^2	3	8	12	14		11^1		4	10		9	13	5	7	6^3	1														44
2	8^1	13	14	15		11		3	10^3		9^2	5	7	6	1		4^4	12												45
5	2	8^1	15	7^5	14		3	10^2	12	9		13	6	1	16	4^4	11^3													46

FA Cup

First Round	Weston-super-Mare	(h)	3-1
aet.			
Second Round	Barnsley	(a)	0-0
aet; Bristol R won 4-3 on penalties.			
Third Round	Ipswich T	(a)	0-3

Carabao Cup

First Round	Cardiff C	(a)	0-2

Vertu Trophy

Group G (S)	Tottenham H U21	(h)	3-3
Tottenham H U21 won 6-5 on penalties.			
Group G (S)	Swindon T	(a)	0-4
Group G (S)	Exeter C	(h)	2-3

BROMLEY

FOUNDATION

Bromley Football Club were founded in 1892, but initially did not join a league or cup competition, playing only local friendly fixtures. They joined the South London League and played their first competitive match on 14 October 1893, a 5-1 victory away to Anerley. In that first season Bromley went on to be league champions and also won the Kent Junior Cup. Bromley switched leagues a number of times, joining the London League, Kent League, Spartan League and Isthmian League before joining the Athenian League for the 1919–20 season. In 1938 they moved to the current stadium at Hayes Lane. They were to remain in the Athenian League until 1952 when they joined the Isthmian League. In 2007 they joined the Blue Square Conference South Division as runner-up of the Isthmian Premier Division. In 2015 they were promoted to the National League, where they remained until their promotion to EFL Two after a play-off final victory on penalties over Solihull Moors at Wembley. Bromley became the 147th club to play in the Football League and their first game was on 10 August 2024 when they won 2-0 at Harrogate Town to record their first Football League victory.

The Stadium, Hayes Lane, Bromley, Kent BR2 9EF.

Telephone: (020) 8460 5291.

Ticket Office: (020) 8460 5291.

Website: www.bromleyfc.co.uk

Email: enquiries@bromleyfc.co.uk

Ground Capacity: 5,150.

Record Attendance: 10,978 v Nigeria XI, Friendly, 24 September 1948.

Pitch Measurements: 100.5m × 65.8m (110yd × 72yd).

Chairman: Robin Stanton-Gleaves.

Chief Executive: Mark Hammond.

Manager: Andy Woodman.

Assistant Manager: Steve Aris.

Colours: White shirts with black and gold trim, white shorts with black and gold trim, white socks.

Year Formed: 1892.

Turned Professional: 2023.

Club Nickname: 'The Ravens'.

HONOURS

League: Champions: Conference – South 2014–15; National League (3rd) 2023–24 (*promoted to FL 2 via play-offs*).

FA Cup: 3rd rd – 2024–25.

League Cup: 1st rd – 2024–25.

FA Trophy Winners: 2021–22. *Runners-up:* 2017–18.

FA Amateur Cup Winners: 1910–11, 1937–38, 1948–49.

FOOTBALL YEARBOOK FACT FILE

Bromley won the first-ever FA Amateur Cup final to be played at Wembley Stadium, defeating Romford 1-0 with a goal from Tommy Hopper in front of a crowd of 95,000 in April 1949. The full match was shown live on BBC television while radio commentary of the second half was available on the BBC's Light Programme.

Grounds: 1892, Queensmead Recreation Ground; 1897, Glebe Road; 1904, Plaistow Cricket Ground; 1904, Hayes Lane; 1938, Hayes Lane.

First Football League Game: 10 August 2024, FL 2, v Harrogate T (a) W 2–0 – Smith; Grant (1), Webster, Reynolds, Passley (Imray), Arthurs, Charles, Congreve (Dinanga), Odutayo, Whiteley (Amantchi), Cheek (1) (Leigh).

Record League Victory: 13–1 v Redhill, Athenian League, 1945–46.

Record Cup Victory: 12–1 v Chertsey T, FA Cup Preliminary rd, 4 September 1982.

Record Defeat: 1–11 v Barking, Athenian League, 1933–34.

Most League Points (3 for a win): 66, FL 2, 2024–25.

Most League Goals: 64, FL 2, 2024–25.

Highest League Scorer in Season: Michael Check, 25, FL 2, 2024–25.

Most League Goals in Total Aggregate: Michael Cheek, 25, 2024–25.

Most Capped Player: Antonio Morgan, 8, Antigua & Barbuda.

Most League Appearances: Michael Cheek, 45, 2024–25.

Youngest League Player: Nathan Paul-Lavely, 18 years 163 days v Doncaster R, 4 March 2025.

Record Transfer Fee Received: £200,000 from Brentford for Ben Krauhaus, January 2024.

Football League Record: 2024 Promoted from National League; 2024– FL 2.

MANAGERS

(Since 2008)
Simon Osborne 2008
Mark Goldberg 2008–16
Neil Smith 2016–21
Alan Dunne 2021
Andy Woodman March 2021–

LATEST SEQUENCES

Longest Sequence of League Wins: 3, 8.2.2025 – 22.2.2025.

Longest Sequence of League Defeats: 2, 22.3.2025 – 29.03.2025.

Longest Sequence of League Draws: 4, 26.10.2024 – 26.11.2024.

Longest Sequence of Unbeaten League Matches: 12, 22.10.2024 – 2.1.2025.

Longest Sequence Without a League Win: 9, 24.8.2024 – 19.10.2024.

Successive Scoring Runs: 8 from 1.3.2025.

Successive Non-scoring Runs: 2 from 28.1.2025.

TEN YEAR LEAGUE RECORD

		P	W	D	L	F	A	Pts	Pos
2015-16	NL	46	17	9	20	67	72	60	14
2016-17	NL	46	18	8	20	59	66	62	10
2017-18	NL	46	19	13	14	75	57	70	9
2018-19	NL	46	16	12	18	68	69	60	12
2019-20	NL	38	14	10	14	57	52	52	13§
2020-21	NL	42	19	12	11	63	53	69	7
2021-22	NL	44	18	13	13	61	53	67	10
2022-23	NL	46	18	17	11	68	53	71	7
2023-24	NL	46	22	15	9	73	49	81	3
2024-25	FL 2	46	17	15	14	64	59	66	11

§*Decided on points-per-game (1.37)*

DID YOU KNOW ?

Bromley moved to Hayes Lane in 1938, playing their first match at their new ground on 3 September when the FA secretary Stanley Rous performed the opening honours. The Ravens, then members of the Athenian League, went down to a 6-1 defeat to Walthamstow Avenue in front of an attendance of 4,200.

BROMLEY – SKY BET LEAGUE TWO 2024–25 LEAGUE RECORD

Match No.	Date	Venue	Opponents	Result	H/T Score	Lg Pos.	Goalscorers	Attendance
1	Aug 10	A	Harrogate T	W 2-0	0-0	4	Cheek [62], Grant [71]	2236
2	17	H	AFC Wimbledon	W 2-0	1-0	3	Cheek [35], Whitely [60]	4102
3	24	A	Bradford C	L 1-3	0-2	7	Webster [86]	16,001
4	31	H	Crewe Alex	L 1-2	1-0	10	Leigh [2]	3322
5	Sept 7	A	Colchester U	D 1-1	1-0	11	Cheek (pen) [23]	4877
6	14	H	Notts Co	L 2-4	2-1	15	Cheek [4], Thompson [6]	3322
7	21	A	Grimsby T	L 0-1	0-0	18		6115
8	28	H	Milton Keynes D	D 1-1	1-1	18	Cheek [23]	3522
9	Oct 1	H	Chesterfield	D 2-2	1-2	19	Olomola [14], Cheek [50]	2057
10	5	A	Fleetwood T	D 0-0	0-0	19		2605
11	19	H	Tranmere R	L 1-2	0-0	22	Dennis [90]	3376
12	22	A	Doncaster R	W 1-0	1-0	19	Thompson [20]	6309
13	26	H	Barrow	D 1-1	0-1	18	Cheek (pen) [90]	3406
14	Nov 9	A	Cheltenham T	D 1-1	0-0	19	Sowunmi [82]	3786
15	16	H	Carlisle U	D 1-1	0-0	20	Cheek [54]	3741
16	26	A	Walsall	D 2-2	0-1	19	Cheek [59], Imray [77]	4424
17	Dec 4	H	Gillingham	W 2-1	0-0	19	Congreve [54], Arthurs [71]	3438
18	7	A	Accrington S	W 2-1	1-1	14	Cheek [7], Odutayo [63]	1816
19	14	D	Port Vale	D 0-0	0-0	14		3697
20	21	A	Morecambe	W 2-0	1-0	13	Sowunmi [19], Cheek (pen) [84]	3515
21	26	H	Newport Co	W 5-2	2-0	12	Sowunmi [27], Reynolds [35], Cheek [53], Arthurs [70], Thompson [90]	3320
22	29	H	Swindon T	D 1-1	0-0	12	Sowunmi [69]	3833
23	Jan 2	A	Gillingham	W 3-0	2-0	11	Dennis [7], Arthurs [26], Grant [76]	7454
24	5	A	Crewe Alex	L 1-4	1-3	12	Cheek (pen) [36]	4462
25	18	H	Colchester U	L 0-1	0-1	11		3907
26	25	A	Notts Co	D 1-1	0-0	11	Congreve [80]	9947
27	28	A	Chesterfield	L 0-3	0-1	13		7192
28	Feb 1	H	Grimsby T	L 0-2	0-0	16		3857
29	4	A	Salford C	D 3-3	2-0	16	Congreve 2 [13, 51], Cheek [38]	2112
30	8	A	Milton Keynes D	W 1-0	0-0	13	Thompson [60]	6972
31	15	H	Fleetwood T	W 1-0	0-0	11	Cheek [46]	2474
32	22	H	Harrogate T	W 2-0	2-0	10	Cheek [30], Arthurs [45]	2518
33	25	H	Bradford C	L 0-1	0-0	10		2442
34	Mar 1	A	AFC Wimbledon	W 1-0	0-0	10	Whitely [76]	8519
35	4	H	Doncaster R	W 1-0	1-0	9	Elerewe [10]	2433
36	8	A	Tranmere R	L 1-2	1-1	10	Cheek [27]	5615
37	13	H	Walsall	D 2-2	1-1	10	Thompson [7], McKirdy [55]	2512
38	22	A	Carlisle U	L 1-2	1-1	12	McKirdy [28]	6515
39	29	H	Salford C	L 2-3	1-2	13	Ashley (og) [8], Cheek [74]	2658
40	Apr 1	A	Newport Co	D 1-1	0-1	13	Cheek [72]	3465
41	5	H	Accrington S	W 4-0	1-0	12	Congreve [29], Cheek 2 (2 pens) [56, 76], Thompson [69]	2410
42	12	A	Port Vale	L 0-5	0-2	14		10,864
43	18	H	Morecambe	W 1-0	0-0	13	Cheek (pen) [48]	2382
44	21	A	Swindon T	W 1-0	0-0	12	Wright (og) [88]	8884
45	26	A	Barrow	D 3-3	0-1	11	Cheek [50], Kabamba [75], Sowunmi [90]	3137
46	May 3	H	Cheltenham T	W 3-0	2-0	11	Cheek 2 (1 pen) [26 (p), 53], Kabamba [45]	2818

Final League Position: 11

GOALSCORERS

League (64): Cheek 25 (9 pens), Thompson 6, Congreve 5, Sowunmi 5, Arthurs 4, Dennis 2, Grant 2, Kabamba 2, McKirdy 2, Whitely 2, Elerewe 1, Imray 1, Leigh 1, Odutayo 1, Olomola 1, Reynolds 1, Webster 1, own goals 2.
FA Cup (7): Whitely 2, Amantchi 1, Cheek 1, Congreve 1, Imray 1, Sowunmi 1.
Carabao Cup (1): Amantchi 1.
Vertu Trophy (5): Dinanga 2, Amantchi 1, Charles 1, Olomola 1.

Smith G 45	Grant K 34+6	Webster B 27+1	Reynolds C 17+3	Passley J 1+3	Arthurs J 37+4	Charles A 25+3	Congreve C 32+8	Odutayo I 32+2	Whitely C 36+8	Cheek M 44+1	Imray D 37+2	Dinanga M 1+6	Leigh L 3+14	Amanchi L 2+12	Sowunmi O 29+5	Dennis L 6+11	Thompson B 38+4	Topalloj B 2+1	Thomas J —+3	Olomola O 6+10	Jenkinson C 9+2	Elerewe A 17	Kabamba N 3+16	Ilunga B 4+13	Mayor A 15+2	Kacurri M 1+2	McKirdy H 2+7	Ifil M —+6	Paul-Lavely N —+3	Long S 1	Kader S —+1	Match No.
1	2	3	4	5¹	6	7	8²	9	10⁴	11³	12	13	14	15																		1
1	2	3	4		6	7	8¹	9	11	10³	5²	12	14	13																		2
1	2	3	4		6	7⁴	8²	9	11³	10⁴	5¹	12	13	15	14																	3
1	2	3	4		6		8¹	9	11	10	5³		7²		14	12	13															4
1	2	3	14		6²	7		4	9³	10	5	11¹		12				13	8⁶														5
1	2	3	4			7²	9³	8	11¹	10	5	12	13				6		14													6
1	2		3		6¹		9²	4⁴	11	10	5	13	12	14	15		7	8³														7
1	4¹		3			7²	9³	8	11	10	5	14	13				2			6	12											8
1	4		3		13	7		8	9	11	5						2			6²		12	10¹									9
1	4		3		7		8	9	10	5		12		2			6			11¹												10
1	4		3		7¹	15	8	9	10³	5		12	13	2	14		6⁴			11²												11
1	4	3			13		8	11		5¹		7²	10³	2	14	6		9	12													12
1	4	3⁴			12	8	9	14	5		7¹	10³	2	13	6		11²	15														13
1	5	4			7³	9¹	6		10			14	13	3	11²	8		12	2⁶													14
1	4	3			6	8¹	9		10	5	12⁶		2	11²	7	13																15
1	4	3			6	12	8	11	9	5		2		7			10¹															16
1	4	12			7		9²	5	10	11	6		3		8			13	2¹													17
1	2	4			7	8²	9¹	5	10	11	6	13		3			12															18
1	4	3			6		9¹	8	10	11	5			2			7			12												19
1	2	4	13		6		10¹	5	9	11³	8²		14	3			7			12												20
1	2	4			6		10²	5	9³	11¹	8	13	12	3			7			14												21
1	2	4³			6²		10¹	5	9	11	8	13		3			7		14	12												22
1	2		14		8³	13		5	9	11⁴	6		12	3	10¹		7			15		4²										23
1	2⁴	16	4¹	14	6		13	8	9⁵	10⁴	5³		12	3	11²	7				15												24
1	2⁴		13	12		7¹		5	9²	10	6			3	14	8							4	11³	15							25
1	16	3			6		9	8⁴	10²	11³	5⁵	13		2	15	7¹							4	14	12							26
1	4		3		6²	7³	9¹	8²	12	11⁵	5		14	2⁴	10	13								16	15							27
1	2	3³			6		15	9	10	5	12			11⁴	7¹								4	14	13		8²					28
1	12	4			7	6	10		13	11³	8				9						2¹		14		5		3²					29
1	14	4			6	7	10¹		12	11³	8				9²						2		3	13	5							30
1	15	4			6	7	10¹		12	11³	8²				9⁴						2		3	14	13	5						31
1		4			6	7	10		12	11²					9³						2		3	13	14	5⁴		8¹				32
1		4			6	7³	10¹		8⁴	11				12	15	9					2		3		13	5²			14			33
1	13	4			6		7		9	11³					8						2²		3	14	10¹	5		12				34
1		4			6		7		9	11³				12	8						2		3¹	14	10²	5			13			35
1	2	4			6	12	8²	14	9³	11⁴				3	13	7							15	10⁵	5¹	16						36
1	2¹	4			6	7¹	10²		8	11³				15	9						3		14	13	5		12					37
1		4			6	7²			2	11	12				9						3		13	10³	5		8¹	14				38
1	2¹	4			6⁵	15	10²	14	7	11	8			3	9⁴								16	13	5³		12					39
	2				6¹	7	12	5¹	10⁵	11	8			3	9						4²			15	13	14				1		40
1	2				6	7	10¹		12	11⁴	8²			3	9²								4	15	14	5		13				41
1	2	4			6	7	10²		15	11⁴	8³			3	9								14	13	5		12					42
1	2				6	7	10¹	5	13	11	8³			3	9²						4			12			14					43
1	16	3			6²	7	12	4	9⁴	10	5⁵			2	14								11³		8¹		13	15				44
1		3			6¹	7⁴	13	8²	10	11	5³			2	9						4		12					15	14			45
1					14	5	9¹	4⁵	8⁴	10	6²			3	7³						2		11	12	16			15	13		17	46

FA Cup

First Round	Rochdale	(a)	4-3
Second Round	Solihull Moors	(a)	2-1
Third Round	Newcastle U	(a)	1-3

Carabao Cup

First Round	AFC Wimbledon	(h)	1-2

Vertu Trophy

Group C (S)	Cambridge U	(h)	3-3
	Bromley won 5-4 on penalties.		
Group C (S)	Chelsea U21	(h)	2-3
Group C (S)	Charlton Ath	(a)	0-1

BURNLEY

FOUNDATION

On 18 May 1882 Burnley (Association) Football Club was still known as Burnley Rovers as members of that rugby club had decided on that date to play Association Football in the future. It was only a matter of days later that the members met again and decided to drop Rovers from the club's name.

Turf Moor, Harry Potts Way, Burnley, Lancashire BB10 4BX.

Telephone: (01282) 446 800.

Ticket Office: (0844) 807 1882.

Website: www.burnleyfc.com

Email: info@burnleyfc.com

Ground Capacity: 21,744.

Record Attendance: 54,775 v Huddersfield T, FA Cup 3rd rd, 23 February 1924.

Pitch Measurements: 105m × 68m (115yd × 74.5yd).

Chairman: Alan Pace.

Chief Executive: James Holroyd.

Head Coach: Scott Parker.

Assistant Head Coach: Henrik Jensen.

Colours: Claret shirts with sky blue sleeves and trim, white shorts with sky blue trim, sky blue socks with claret trim.

Year Formed: 1882.

Turned Professional: 1883.

Previous Name: 1882, Burnley Rovers; 1882, Burnley.

Club Nickname: 'The Clarets'.

Grounds: 1882, Calder Vale; 1883, Turf Moor.

HONOURS

League Champions: Division 1 – 1920–21, 1959–60; FL C – 2015–16, 2022–23; Division 2 – 1897–98, 1972–73; Division 3 – 1981–82; Division 4 – 1991–92.
Runners-up: Division 1 – 1919–20, 1961–62; FL C – 2013–14, 2024–25; Division 2 – 1912–13, 1946–47; Second Division – 1999–2000.
FA Cup Winners: 1914.
Runners-up: 1947, 1962.
League Cup: semi-final – 1961, 1969, 1983, 2009.
League Trophy: Runners-up: 1988.
Anglo–Scottish Cup Winners: 1979.
European Competitions
European Cup: 1960–61 *(qf)*.
Fairs Cup: 1966–67 *(qf)*.
Europa League: 2018–19.

First Football League Game: 8 September 1888, Football League, v Preston NE (a) L 2–5 – Smith; Lang, Bury, Abrahams, Friel, Keenan, Brady, Tait, Poland (1), Gallocher (1), Yates.

Record League Victory: 9–0 v Darwen, Division 1, 9 January 1892 – Hillman; Walker, McFettridge, Lang, Matthews, Keenan, Nicol (3), Bowes, Espie (1), McLardie (3), Hill (2).

Record Cup Victory: 9–0 v Crystal Palace, FA Cup 2nd rd (replay), 10 February 1909 – Dawson; Barron, McLean; Cretney (2), Leake, Moffat; Morley, Ogden, Smith (3), Abbott (2), Smethams (1). 9–0 v New Brighton, FA Cup 4th rd, 26 January 1957 – Blacklaw; Angus, Winton; Seith, Adamson, Miller; Newlands (1), McIlroy (3), Lawson (3), Cheesebrough (1), Pilkington (1). 9–0 v Penrith, FA Cup 1st rd, 17 November 1984 – Hansbury; Miller, Hampton, Phelan, Overson (Kennedy), Hird (3 incl. 1p), Grewcock (1), Powell (2), Taylor (3), Biggins, Hutchison.

Record Defeat: 0–11 v Darwen, FA Cup 1st rd, 17 October 1885.

Most League Points (2 for a win): 62, Division 2, 1972–73.

Most League Points (3 for a win): 101, FL C, 2022–23.

FOOTBALL YEARBOOK FACT FILE

Burnley's opening game of the 1920–21 season on Saturday 28 August was scheduled for a 6.00pm kick-off to allow neighbours Burnley Cricket Club to play their Lancashire League fixture with Enfield. The Clarets took the field in their usual claret and blue shirts only to be required to change to white with light blue sleeves after a few minutes as the referee decided there was a colour clash with opponents Bradford City, who won the game 4-1.

Most League Goals: 102, Division 1, 1960–61.

Highest League Scorer in Season: George Beel, 35, Division 1, 1927–28.

Most League Goals in Total Aggregate: George Beel, 179, 1923–32.

Most League Goals in One Match: 6, Louis Page v Birmingham C, Division 1, 10 April 1926.

Most Capped Player: Jimmy McIlroy, 51 (55), Northern Ireland.

Most League Appearances: Jerry Dawson, 522, 1907–28.

Youngest League Player: Tommy Lawton, 16 years 174 days v Doncaster R, 28 March 1936.

Record Transfer Fee Received: £25,000,000 (potentially rising to £30,000,000) from Everton for Michael Keane, July 2017; £25,000,000 from Newcastle U for Chris Wood, January 2022.

Record Transfer Fee Paid: £16,100,000 to FC Basel for Zeki Amdouni, July 2023.

Football League Record: 1888 Original Member of the Football League; 1888–92 Football League; 1892–97 Division 1; 1897–98 Division 2; 1898–1900 Division 1; 1900–13 Division 2; 1913–30 Division 1; 1930–47 Division 2; 1947–71 Division 1; 1971–73 Division 2; 1973–76 Division 1; 1976–80 Division 2; 1980–82 Division 3; 1982–83 Division 2; 1983–85 Division 3; 1985–92 Division 4; 1992–94 Second Division; 1994–95 First Division; 1995–2000 Second Division; 2000–04 First Division; 2004–09 FL C; 2009–10 Premier League; 2010–14 FL C; 2014–15 Premier League; 2015–16 FL C; 2016–22 Premier League; 2022–23 FL C; 2023–24 Premier League; 2024–25 FL C; 2025– Premier League.

LATEST SEQUENCES

Longest Sequence of League Wins: 10, 13.11.2022 – 11.2.2023.

Longest Sequence of League Defeats: 8, 2.1.1995 – 25.2.1995.

Longest Sequence of League Draws: 6, 21.2.1931 – 28.3.1931.

Longest Sequence of Unbeaten League Matches: 33, 7.11.2024 – 3.5.2025.

Longest Sequence Without a League Win: 24, 16.4.1979 – 17.11.1979.

Successive Scoring Runs: 31 from 16.8.2022.

Successive Non-scoring Runs: 6 from 21.3.2015.

MANAGERS

Harry Bradshaw 1894–99
  (*Secretary-Manager from 1897*)
Club Directors 1899–1900
J. Ernest Mangnall 1900–03
  (*Secretary-Manager*)
Spen Whittaker 1903–10
  (*Secretary-Manager*)
John Haworth 1910–24
  (*Secretary-Manager*)
Albert Pickles 1925–31
  (*Secretary-Manager*)
Tom Bromilow 1932–35
Selection Committee 1935–45
Cliff Britton 1945–48
Frank Hill 1948–54
Alan Brown 1954–57
Billy Dougall 1957–58
Harry Potts 1958–70
  (*General Manager to 1972*)
Jimmy Adamson 1970–76
Joe Brown 1976–77
Harry Potts 1977–79
Brian Miller 1979–83
John Bond 1983–84
John Benson 1984–85
Martin Buchan 1985
Tommy Cavanagh 1985–86
Brian Miller 1986–89
Frank Casper 1989–91
Jimmy Mullen 1991–96
Adrian Heath 1996–97
Chris Waddle 1997–98
Stan Ternent 1998–2004
Steve Cotterill 2004–07
Owen Coyle 2007–10
Brian Laws 2010
Eddie Howe 2011–12
Sean Dyche 2012–22
Vincent Kompany 2022–24
Scott Parker July 2024–

TEN YEAR LEAGUE RECORD

		P	W	D	L	F	A	Pts	Pos
2015-16	FL C	46	26	15	5	72	35	93	1
2016-17	PR Lge	38	11	7	20	39	55	40	16
2017-18	PR Lge	38	14	12	12	36	39	54	7
2018-19	PR Lge	38	11	7	20	45	68	40	15
2019-20	PR Lge	38	15	9	14	43	50	54	10
2020-21	PR Lge	38	10	9	19	33	55	39	17
2021-22	PR Lge	38	7	14	17	34	53	35	18
2022-23	FL C	46	29	14	3	87	35	101	1
2023-24	PR Lge	38	5	9	24	41	78	24	19
2024-25	FL C	46	28	16	2	69	16	100	2

DID YOU KNOW ?

Burnley visited Central Europe in 1914 where they played six games including one against Celtic in Budapest for a trophy donated by a local newspaper proprietor. The match ended 1-1 with the Clarets then being successful on the toss of a coin only for the donor of the trophy to refuse to release it until a replay had taken place. In September Celtic visited Turf Moor, winning 2-1, although it is unclear whether they then received the trophy.

BURNLEY – SKY BET CHAMPIONSHIP 2024–25 LEAGUE RECORD

Match No.	Date	Venue	Opponents	Result	H/T Score	Lg Pos.	Goalscorers	Atten-dance
1	Aug 12	A	Luton T	W 4-1	2-0	2	Brownhill [6], Odobert [37], O'Shea [72], Vitinho [80]	11,777
2	17	H	Cardiff C	W 5-0	2-0	1	Horvath (og) [9], Koleosho [31], Brownhill [51], Amdouni [98], Gudmundsson [90]	19,759
3	24	A	Sunderland	L 0-1	0-1	5		40,096
4	31	H	Blackburn R	D 1-1	1-1	6	Foster [10]	21,042
5	Sept 14	A	Leeds U	W 1-0	1-0	4	Koleosho [18]	36,405
6	21	H	Portsmouth	W 2-1	0-1	4	Sarmiento [63], Brownhill [90]	20,476
7	28	A	Oxford U	D 0-0	0-0	5		11,517
8	Oct 1	H	Plymouth Arg	W 1-0	1-0	2	Brownhill (pen) [26]	18,779
9	5	H	Preston NE	D 0-0	0-0	3		20,816
10	19	A	Sheffield Wed	W 2-0	0-0	1	Anthony [37], Brownhill [50]	28,105
11	23	H	Hull C	D 1-1	0-1	2	Flemming [77]	20,168
12	26	H	QPR	D 0-0	0-0	3		19,187
13	Nov 3	A	Millwall	L 0-1	0-0	4		14,245
14	7	A	WBA	D 0-0	0-0	4		23,443
15	10	H	Swansea C	W 1-0	0-0	4	Rodriguez (pen) [90]	18,717
16	23	A	Bristol C	W 1-0	1-0	3	Anthony [23]	20,800
17	26	H	Coventry C	W 2-0	0-0	2	Sarmiento [47], Egan-Riley [80]	18,293
18	30	A	Stoke C	W 2-0	0-0	2	Rodriguez [52], Brownhill (pen) [78]	22,994
19	Dec 6	H	Middlesbrough	D 1-1	1-1	2	Roberts [37]	20,543
20	10	A	Derby Co	D 0-0	0-0	3		18,813
21	15	A	Norwich C	W 2-1	0-1	3	Flemming [68], Brownhill [76]	26,218
22	21	H	Watford	W 2-1	1-0	3	Anthony [9], Brownhill [62]	19,601
23	26	A	Sheffield U	W 2-0	1-0	3	Brownhill [43], Flemming [53]	30,580
24	29	A	Middlesbrough	D 0-0	0-0	3		27,686
25	Jan 1	H	Stoke C	D 0-0	0-0	3		20,119
26	4	A	Blackburn R	W 1-0	0-0	3	Flemming [60]	25,909
27	17	H	Sunderland	D 0-0	0-0	3		21,014
28	22	A	Plymouth Arg	W 5-0	5-0	3	Flemming 2 [11, 31], Laurent 2 [34, 45], Cullen [45]	15,509
29	27	H	Leeds U	D 0-0	0-0	3		21,329
30	Feb 1	A	Portsmouth	D 0-0	0-0	3		20,381
31	4	A	Oxford U	W 1-0	0-0	3	Helik (og) [33]	18,187
32	12	H	Hull C	W 2-0	2-0	3	Humphreys [3], Flemming [21]	18,987
33	15	A	Preston NE	D 0-0	0-0	3		19,864
34	21	H	Sheffield Wed	W 4-0	1-0	3	Edwards [43], Brownhill [62], Roberts [70], Benson [90]	20,675
35	Mar 4	A	Cardiff C	W 2-1	2-1	3	Brownhill [19], Esteve [40]	15,713
36	8	H	Luton T	W 4-0	2-0	3	McGuinness (og) [30], Foster [39], Brownhill [53], Barnes [90]	19,453
37	11	A	WBA	D 1-1	1-1	3	Flemming [23]	18,843
38	15	A	Swansea C	W 2-0	2-0	3	Brownhill [4], Anthony [22]	13,679
39	29	H	Bristol C	W 1-0	1-0	3	Flemming [16]	20,523
40	Apr 5	A	Coventry C	W 2-1	1-1	2	Anthony 2 [16, 46]	28,704
41	8	A	Derby Co	D 0-0	0-0	2		27,584
42	11	H	Norwich C	W 2-1	2-0	1	Mejbri [14], Anthony [24]	19,030
43	18	A	Watford	W 2-1	1-1	2	Flemming [43], Brownhill [58]	20,523
44	21	H	Sheffield U	W 2-1	2-1	2	Brownhill 2 (1 pen) [28, 44 (p)]	21,486
45	26	A	QPR	W 5-0	3-0	1	Cullen [9], Flemming 2 [20, 28], Sarmiento 2 [62, 90]	16,977
46	May 3	H	Millwall	W 3-1	1-1	2	Brownhill 2 [13, 90], Anthony [65]	21,485

Final League Position: 2

GOALSCORERS

League (69): Brownhill 18 (3 pens), Flemming 12, Anthony 8, Sarmiento 4, Cullen 2, Foster 2, Koleosho 2, Laurent 2, Roberts 2, Rodriguez 2 (1 pen), Amdouni 1, Barnes 1, Benson 1, Edwards 1, Egan-Riley 1, Esteve 1, Gudmundsson 1, Humphreys 1, Mejbri 1, O'Shea 1, Odobert 1, Vitinho 1, own goals 3.
FA Cup (4): Flemming 2, Edwards 1, Foster 1.
Carabao Cup (0).

Trafford J 45	Roberts C 40+1	O'Shea D 2	Esteve M 46	Lucas Pires S 32+2	Cullen J 43+1	Brownhill J 39+3	Vitinho d 3	Odobert W 1	Koleosho L 20+8	Foster L 17+11	Zaroury A —+1	Weghorst W —+2	Massengo H 1+7	McNally L —+2	Hladky V 1	Rodriguez J 8+12	Gudmundsson J —+1	Amdouni Z —+2	Hountondji A 2+7	Egan-Riley C 40+1	Sambo S —+1	Worrall J 3+6	Laurent J 25+17	Mejbri H 23+14	Anthony J 42+1	Sarmiento J 11+24	Benson M —+3	Humphreys B 20+5	Flemming Z 28+7	Egan J 1+6	Agyei E —+3	Sonne O —+2	Barnes A 1+12	Shelvey J —+2	Edwards M 12+2	Redmond N —+2	Ramsey A —+1	Match No.
1	2	3	4	5^4	6	7	8	9^4	10^1	11^2	12	13	14	15																								1
	2	3	4	5	7^4	8	6^1		9^3	11^2		13	16		1	10^5	12	14	15																			2
1	2		4	5	7	6^2			11			8^1	14			10		12	9^3	3		13																3
1	2		4^4	5	7	8^3			11			14	15							3		6^2	9^1	10	12	13												4
1			4	5	13	7^3			8^1			14							15	3		6	9^2	10	12			2^8	11^4									5
1			4	5	6^3	7			8	11^4			15						2	3	14		9^1	10^2	12		13											6
1			4	5	6	7			8	11^3			14						13	3				9^2	12	10^1	2											7
1			4	5	6^4	9			7^1	11^2			15						14	3		13		8^3	10	12	2											8
1	12		4	5	6^4	7			8	11									3		15		9^2	10^3	14		2^1	13									9
1	2		4		6^2	7			8^1			13							3		9			10^3	12	5	11	14										10
1	2		4	5^4	6^3	9			7^2				16						14	3		13		8^1	10		15	11^5	12									11
1	2		4	12	6^1	7			8				13						15	3		9^4		10^3			5^2	11	14									12
1	2		4		7	9			8				14						11^3	3		6^1	12	10	13	5^2												13
1	2		4	5	7	6			10^2										3		12	13	8	9^1		11											14
1	2		4	5	6^4	7			10^2				16						3		14	15	8	9^5		12	11^3	13									15
1	2		4	5^1	6	7^4			10^2			15						11^5	3		13	9^1	8	12	14	16												16
1	2		4	5^2	6				12			13						11^4	14	3		7	9^3	8	10^1	15												17
1	2		4		6^3	12			10									11^1	3		7	14	8	9^2	5	13											18
1	2		4	14	6	7			10^3				11^1						3		15	12	9^2	5	13	3^4											19
1	2		4	5	7	6			13				12					14		3		8^2		9^3	11	3	10^1											20
1			4^1	5^3	6	7			8^5				11^4						3	16	13	14	10	9^2		2	15	12										21
1	2^2		4		6	9			12				14						3		7	10^1	8		5	11^3	13											22
1	2		4		6	9			12										3		7	10^2	8		5	11^1	13											23
1	2		4		6	9^4			13	15			14						3		7	10^1	8^2	12	5	11^3												24
1	2		4	5	6^4	7			9^2	15			11^1						3		13	14^4	10	8^3	16	12												25
1	2		4		6	9			12										3		7		8	10^1	5	11^2	13											26
1	2^3		4		6	9^2			13	10^4									3		7	8	12	5	11^1		14	15										27
1	2		4	5	6	9^2			12	10^3			15						3^5	16	7	14	8^1	13		11^4												28
1	2		4		6	9^2			10^1										3		7	13	8	12	5	11												29
1	2		4	5	6				10										3		7	12	8	9^1		11^2		13									30
1	2		4		6				10^3										3		7	9^1	8	12	5	11^2		13	14									31
1	2		4		7				10^4										3	15	6	9^2	8^3	13	5	11^1		14	12									32
1	2		4		7	12			10^1										3		6	9^2	8		5	11			13									33
1	2		4	5	7	12			13										3		6^3	9^1	10^5	15	16	11^2		14	8^4									34
1	2		4	5^4	7	6			12										3	15	13	9	10^4	14		11^2			8^3									35
1	2		4	5^4	7	6^1			10^5										3		8		11^3	13	12		15	14	9^2	16								36
1	2		4	5	7	6			14	12^4									3^8		13	9^1	10^5	16		11^1		15	8^3									37
1	2		4	5	7	10			12										3		8	13	9^3		11^1		14	6^2										38
1	2		4	5	7	10^2			14	12									3		8	13	9		11^1			6^3										39
1	2		4	5	7	10^2			11^3										3		8	13	9	14		12			6^1									40
1	2		4	5	7	10			12^2										3		8^1	13	9		11		14	6^3										41
1	2		4	5	7	6			13										3	15	12	9^2	10^3	13		11^4		14	8^1									42
1	2		4	5	7	6^3													3		12	9	10	14		11^2		13	8^1									43
1	2		4	5	7	6^4													3	15	12	9	13	14		11^3		14	8^1									44
1	2		4	5	7	6^4		8^3											3		13	9^1	10^2	12		11^5		15								14	16	45
1	2		4	5	7	6			12										3		14	9^3	10	13		11^2			8^1									46

FA Cup

Third Round *aet.*	Reading	(a)	3-1
Fourth Round	Southampton	(a)	1-0
Fifth Round	Preston NE	(a)	0-3

Carabao Cup

Second Round	Wolverhampton W	(a)	0-2

BURTON ALBION

FOUNDATION

Once upon a time there were three Football League clubs bearing the name Burton. Then there were none. In reality it had been two. Originally Burton Swifts and Burton Wanderers competed in it until 1901 when they amalgamated to form Burton United. This club disbanded in 1910. There was no senior club representing the town until 1924 when Burton Town, formerly known as Burton All Saints, played in the Birmingham & District League, subsequently joining the Midland League in 1935–36. When the Second World War broke out the club fielded a team in a truncated version of the Birmingham & District League taking over from the club's reserves. But it was not revived in peacetime. So it was not until a further decade that a club bearing the name of Burton reappeared. Founded in 1950 Burton Albion made progress from the Birmingham & District League, too, then into the Southern League and because of its geographical situation later had spells in the Northern Premier League. In April 2009 Burton Albion restored the name of the town to the Football League competition as champions of the Blue Square Premier League.

Pirelli Stadium, Princess Way, Burton-on-Trent, Staffordshire DE13 0AR.

Telephone: (01283) 565 938.

Ticket Office: (01283) 565 938.

Website: www.burtonalbionfc.co.uk

Email: bafc@burtonalbionfc.co.uk

Ground Capacity: 6,972.

Record Attendance: 5,806 v Weymouth, Southern League Cup final 2nd leg, 1964 (at Eton Park); 6,746 v Derby Co, FL C, 26 August 2016 (at Pirelli Stadium).

Pitch Measurements: 100m × 67m (109.5yd × 73.5yd).

Chairman: Ole Jakob Strandhagen.

Chief Executive: Walter Gudde (interim).

Head Coach: Gary Bowyer.

Assistant Head Coach: Pat Lyons.

Colours: Yellow shirts with thin black stripes and black trim, black shorts with yellow trim, yellow socks with black trim.

Year Formed: 1950.

Turned Professional: 1950.

Club Nickname: 'The Brewers'.

Grounds: 1950, Eton Park; 2005, Pirelli Stadium.

First Football League Game: 8 August 2009, FL 2, v Shrewsbury T (a) L 1–3 – Redmond; Edworthy, Boertien, Austin, Branston, McGrath, Maghoma, Penn, Phillips (Stride), Walker, Shroot (Pearson) (1).

HONOURS

League Champions: FL 2 – 2014–15; Football Conference – 2008–09.
Runners-up: FL 1 – 2015–16.
FA Cup: 4th rd – 2011.
League Cup: semi-final 2019.

FOOTBALL YEARBOOK FACT FILE

Burton Albion took no chances when travelling to Weymouth for the first leg of the Southern League Cup final in April 1964. The club chartered a 36-seater plane to fly from Burnaston Airport, Derby, to Hurn, near Bournemouth. Although they lost the first leg 2-1, they fought back to win the return tie at Eton Park 4-0 in front of a record attendance of more than 5,800.

Record League Victory: 6–1 v Aldershot T, FL 2, 12 December 2009 – Krysiak; James, Boertien, Stride, Webster, McGrath, Jackson, Penn, Kabba (2), Pearson (3) (Harrad) (1), Gilroy (Maghoma).

Record Cup Victory: 12–1 v Coalville T, Birmingham Senior Cup, 6 September 1954.

Record Defeat: 0–10 v Barnet, Southern League, 7 February 1970.

Most League Points (3 for a win): 94, FL 2, 2014–15.

Most League Goals: 71, FL 2, 2009–10; 2012–13.

Highest League Scorer in Season: Shaun Harrad, 21, 2009–10.

Most League Goals in Total Aggregate: Lucas Akins, 65, 2014–22.

Most League Goals in One Match: 3, Greg Pearson v Aldershot T, FL 2, 12 December 2009; 3, Shaun Harrad v Rotherham U, FL 2, 11 September 2010; 3, Lucas Akins v Colchester U, FL 1, 23 April 2016; 3, Marcus Harness v Rochdale, FL 1, 5 January 2019; 3, Scott Fraser v Oxford U, FL 1, 20 August 2019; 3, Kane Hemmings v Crewe Alex, FL 1, 13 March 2021; 3, Davis Keillor-Dunn v Accrington S, FL 1, 13 August 2022; 3, Victor Adeboyejo v Forest Green R, FL 1, 1 October 2022.

Most Capped Player: Max Crocombe, 14 (17), New Zealand.

Most League Appearances: Lucas Akins, 307, 2014–22.

Youngest League Player: Romelle Donovan, 17 years 289 days v Rotherham U, 14 September 2024.

Record Transfer Fee Received: £2,000,000 from Hull C for Jackson Irvine, August 2017.

Record Transfer Fee Paid: £500,000 to Ross Co for Liam Boyce, June 2017.

Football League Record: 2009 Promoted from Football Conference; 2009–15 FL 2; 2015–16 FL 1; 2016–18 FL C; 2018– FL 1.

MANAGERS

Reg Weston 1953–57
Sammy Crooks 1957
Eddie Shimwell 1958
Bill Townsend 1959–62
Peter Taylor 1962–65
Alex Tait 1965–70
Richie Norman 1970–73
Ken Gutteridge 1973–74
Harold Bodle 1974–76
Ian Storey-Moore 1978–81
Neil Warnock 1981–86
Brian Fidler 1986–88
Vic Halom 1988
Bobby Hope 1988
Chris Wright 1988–89
Ken Blair 1989–90
Steve Powell 1990–91
Brian Fidler 1991–92
Brian Kenning 1992–94
John Barton 1994–98
Nigel Clough 1998–2009
Roy McFarland 2009
Paul Peschisolido 2009–12
Gary Rowett 2012–14
Jimmy Floyd Hasselbaink 2014–15
Nigel Clough 2015–20
Jake Buxton 2020
Jimmy Floyd Hasselbaink 2021–22
Dino Maamria 2022–23
Martin Paterson 2024
Mark Robinson 2024
Gary Bowyer December 2024–

LATEST SEQUENCES

Longest Sequence of League Wins: 6, 23.2.2021 – 13.3.2021.
Longest Sequence of League Defeats: 8, 25.2.2012 – 24.3.2012.
Longest Sequence of League Draws: 6, 25.4.2011 – 16.8.2011.
Longest Sequence of Unbeaten League Matches: 13, 7.3.2015 – 8.8.2015.
Longest Sequence Without a League Win: 16, 31.12.2011 – 24.3.2012.
Successive Scoring Runs: 18 from 16.4.2011 – 8.10.2011.
Successive Non-scoring Runs: 5 from 19.3.2022.

TEN YEAR LEAGUE RECORD

		P	W	D	L	F	A	Pts	Pos
2015-16	FL 1	46	25	10	11	57	37	85	2
2016-17	FL C	46	13	13	20	49	63	52	20
2017-18	FL C	46	10	11	25	38	81	41	23
2018-19	FL 1	46	17	12	17	66	57	63	9
2019-20	FL 1	35	12	12	11	50	50	48	12§
2020-21	FL 1	46	15	12	19	61	73	57	16
2021-22	FL 1	46	14	11	21	51	67	53	16
2022-23	FL 1	46	15	11	20	57	79	56	15
2023-24	FL 1	46	12	10	24	39	67	46	20
2024-25	FL 1	46	11	14	21	49	66	47	20

§*Decided on points-per-game (1.37)*

DID YOU KNOW ?

The first live television match to feature Burton Albion was the FA Trophy quarter-final tie away to Hereford United played on 10 March 2001. The game was shown on Sky Sports with a noon kick-off. The financial rewards were minimal, each team receiving just £2,500, and the Brewers went down to a 1-0 defeat.

BURTON ALBION – SKY BET LEAGUE ONE 2024–25 LEAGUE RECORD

Match No.	Date	Venue	Opponents	Result	H/T Score	Lg Pos.	Goalscorers	Attendance
1	Aug 10	H	Lincoln C	L 2-3	2-2	14	Godwin-Malife [5], Bodin [41]	5027
2	17	A	Mansfield T	D 3-3	1-2	17	Bodin 2 [7, 81], Whitfield [69]	7781
3	24	H	Stevenage	D 0-0	0-0	19		2378
4	31	A	Northampton T	D 0-0	0-0	19		5909
5	Sept 14	A	Rotherham U	D 2-2	1-1	20	Orsi-Dadomo [25], Cooper-Love [71]	8704
6	21	H	Barnsley	L 1-2	0-1	22	Cooper-Love [88]	3711
7	28	A	Blackpool	L 0-3	0-1	22		9168
8	Oct 1	A	Reading	L 1-3	0-2	22	Orsi-Dadomo [84]	8774
9	5	H	Bristol R	L 1-3	1-0	23	Orsi-Dadomo [15]	2832
10	19	A	Bolton W	L 1-2	0-0	24	Orsi-Dadomo [66]	19,540
11	22	H	Wycombe W	L 2-3	1-1	24	Orsi-Dadomo [34], Webster [63]	1993
12	26	A	Cambridge U	L 0-1	0-0	24		6706
13	Nov 5	H	Crawley T	D 0-0	0-0	24		1810
14	9	H	Shrewsbury T	W 2-0	1-0	23	Kalinauskas [10], Orsi-Dadomo [51]	2935
15	23	H	Stockport Co	L 0-3	0-2	24		3564
16	26	H	Charlton Ath	L 0-1	0-0	24		1749
17	Dec 4	A	Peterborough U	W 1-0	0-0	23	Bennett [64]	6043
18	7	H	Wrexham	L 0-1	0-0	24		3644
19	14	A	Leyton Orient	D 0-0	0-0	23		7267
20	21	H	Exeter C	L 1-2	1-1	23	Bodin [8]	2690
21	26	A	Birmingham C	L 0-2	0-1	24		27,524
22	29	A	Huddersfield T	D 1-1	1-0	24	Webster [13]	18,842
23	Jan 1	H	Peterborough U	D 2-2	2-1	24	Chauke [6], Burrell [26]	2821
24	4	A	Northampton T	L 0-1	0-0	24		2837
25	18	A	Crawley T	D 1-1	1-0	24	Burrell [25]	3521
26	21	A	Wigan Ath	W 2-1	1-1	23	Bodvarsson [34], Burrell [59]	7553
27	25	A	Rotherham U	W 4-2	3-1	21	Bodvarsson 2 [8, 41], Sweeney [39], McKiernan [47]	3733
28	28	H	Reading	W 3-2	2-0	21	Burrell 2 [10, 90], Bodvarsson [29]	2358
29	Feb 1	A	Barnsley	D 0-0	0-0	21		10,555
30	8	H	Blackpool	D 1-1	1-0	21	Burrell [19]	2965
31	15	A	Bristol R	L 1-3	0-1	23	Tavares [82]	7938
32	18	A	Stevenage	W 1-0	1-0	21	Webster [45]	2801
33	22	A	Lincoln C	W 1-0	0-0	21	Webster [90]	8507
34	Mar 1	H	Mansfield T	D 1-1	1-0	21	Dodgson [13]	5007
35	4	A	Wycombe W	L 0-2	0-1	21		3456
36	8	H	Bolton W	L 1-2	0-1	21	Sweeney [53]	4172
37	15	A	Shrewsbury T	W 2-0	0-0	21	Burrell [72], Vancooten [86]	5807
38	29	A	Stockport Co	L 1-2	0-1	21	Larsson [89]	9554
39	Apr 1	H	Leyton Orient	W 2-1	0-1	21	Webster [60], Burrell [64]	2367
40	5	A	Wrexham	L 0-3	0-0	21		12,829
41	12	H	Huddersfield T	W 3-0	2-0	20	Burrell 2 [9, 55], Larsson [45]	4278
42	18	A	Exeter C	D 0-0	0-0	20		6972
43	21	H	Birmingham C	L 1 2	0 2	20	Tavares [90]	4928
44	26	A	Cambridge U	W 2-1	0-0	20	Bodvarsson [48], Williams [90]	3540
45	29	H	Wigan Ath	D 1-1	0-0	20	Burrell [57]	3506
46	May 3	A	Charlton Ath	L 1-3	1-2	20	Bennett (pen) [13]	20,971

Final League Position: 20

GOALSCORERS

League (49): Burrell 11, Orsi-Dadomo 6, Bodvarsson 5, Webster 5, Bodin 4, Bennett 2 (1 pen), Cooper-Love 2, Larsson 2, Sweeney 2, Tavares 2, Chauke 1, Dodgson 1, Godwin-Malife 1, Kalinauskas 1, McKiernan 1, Vancooten 1, Whitfield 1, Williams 1.
FA Cup (2): Bennett 1, Kalinauskas 1.
Carabao Cup (0).
Vertu Trophy (9): Whitfield 2, Akoto 1, Bennett 1, Donovan 1, Orsi-Dadomo 1, Sweeney 1, Webster 1, Williams 1.

Isted H 3	Vancooten T 29 + 1	Sweeney R 42	Williams D 15 + 11	Godwin-Malife U 39 + 3	Watt E 24 + 1	Gilligan C 8 + 4	Kalinauskas T 18 + 21	Whitfield B 13 + 10	Bodin B 7 + 5	Orsi-Dadomo D 18 + 9	Chauke K 32 + 6	Armer J 33 + 5	Bennett M 15 + 19	Akoto N 6 + 8	Crocombe M 43	Bajrami G — + 1	Cooper-Love J 6 + 8	Donovan R 1 + 5	Burrell R 26 + 4	Bannon A 9	Webster C 26 + 6	Stutter R — + 1	Sraha J 12 + 4	Bran A — + 1	Hazlehurst J 1 + 1	Dodgson O 21 + 1	McKiernan J 19	Bodvarsson J 11 + 2	Tavares F 1 + 9	Jones J 1 + 3	Lofthouse K 14 + 2	Larsson J 6 + 5	Forde A 4 + 7	Stretton J — + 3	Delap F 3 + 2	Taroni J — + 2	Newall J — + 1	Match No.
2⁴	3	4	5	6	7¹	8²	9	10³	11	12	13	14	15																									1
	3	12	2	7		8	9⁴	10	11³	6²	4	14	5¹	1	13	15																						2
	2	3	8⁴	5⁵	7	6³	13	9²	10	11¹	14	4	12	16	1		15																					3
	2	3	14	8³	7		5²	9	11¹	10	6	4			13	1	12																					4
	2¹	3	8	5	7	16	14	9²		11³	6⁴		12	1	10⁵	13	15																					5
	2	3	8¹	5²	7		14	9³		11⁴	6	4	12	1	10	13	15																					6
	2⁴	4	8	5	7		12	9²		11³	6	3¹	14	15	1	10	13																					7
		4	5	14	6	12	10	8		13	7¹			2	1	11³	9²	3																				8
14ᵇ		4	5⁵	6		8	10⁴	11³	7			2	1	13	12	3²	9¹	15	16																			9
1		3	5²	6	9¹	8	14	11⁵	7	15	10³	13			12	2	16		4⁴																			10
1	2	3	14	6		12	8²		11	13		10³	5¹		9		4	7																				11
	3	4		6		8³	13	9¹	11	7	5	10²	14	1	12		2⁴	15																				12
	3	4	14	6		10	8²	12	11³		5			1	9¹	13		2	7																			13
	3	4	12	6		10	13	8²	11⁴		5	9		1			2³	7¹		15	14																	14
	3	4	8³	6		10	15	13	11⁴		5	9¹		1	14		2²	7		12																		15
	3	4	2			12	10	8³	11²		5	13		1		14	7	6ᵇ		9¹																		16
	3	4	13	2	6	8	9²	12		7		10¹	1		11		5																					17
	3	4		2	7³	6²	10	12	14	13	8	9		1	11¹		5																					18
	3	4	14	2	7	8	9³	6		13		11²		1	10¹		12	5																				19
	3	4	14	2	7⁵	6⁴	9²	12	11¹	13	8			1		16			15		5																	20
	3	4		2	8	7⁴	15	14		12	9²	6	10¹	1			11³		13		5																	21
3ᵇ		4	12	2	8	13	14		11	9	6			1		10³		7²		5¹																		22
	3	9	2	7		14	12	11²	6	4	13	5³	1		10		8¹																					23
	3	9	2	7		14	12	11²	6³	4	13	5	1		10		8¹																					24
	3	4		2	6	10²		15	7	14	8⁴			1	11³		12				5		9¹	13														25
	3	4		2	14	12		15	8³	5	13			1	10²		7				6		9¹	11⁴														26
	2	3	5				14	13	7	4	12			1	10²		6				9		8¹	11¹														27
	2	3	5			13			8	4	12			1	10		6				9		7²	11¹														28
	2	3	5					15		14	8³	4		1	11¹		6²				9		7	10⁴	12	13												29
	2	3	5							9	4			1	11		6¹				8		7²	10³	14	12	13											30
	2	3	5					15		7	4	12		1	11²		6				9⁴		8³	10¹	13⁵		14	16										31
2ᵇ	3		5					12			4	13		1	11¹		6				9		8	10²		7												32
	3		2					8⁴			6²	4	12	1	11³		7				9			10¹		13	5	14	15									33
	3	15	2					9¹			4	10²		1			7				8		11³			6⁴	5	14	13	12								34
	3		2					14			13	4	10³	1	12		6				9		8			5		11¹	7²									35
	2	3	5					14			13	4	10¹	1	11²		7				8		9³			6			12									36
	2	3	5								13	4	12	1	10		9³				8		7²	11¹			6		14									37
	3³	16	2					12			7⁴	4		1	11⁵		9	15			8		10¹			5		14	6²	13								38
	3¹		2					13			7	12		1	11		6	4²			8		9			5		10										39
		12	3					15			8	5⁴		1	11²		9ᵇ	4			6		7¹		13		2	10³	14									40
		12	2					13			7⁴		14	1	11³			4⁵			8		9			15	5	10²	6¹		3	16						41
	3	7	2					15			6	12	13	1	11²			4¹			8		9⁴		14	5	10³											42
	3	7	2¹					6²			4	16		1	11⁵			8			10³	14	15			5		9¹	13	12								43
	3	7	2					6			4	14		1	11³			8¹			9ᵇ	10¹	15			5²		12	13									44
	3²	7	5					6			4	12		1	11⁴		9³	13			8		10¹	15				14	2									45
		7	2					13			8	10³		1	9⁵		4	12						11⁴				5	14	6¹	3²	16	15					46

FA Cup

First Round	Scarborough Ath	(h)	1-0
Second Round	Tamworth	(h)	1-1

aet; Tamworth won 4-3 on penalties.

Carabao Cup

First Round	Blackpool	(h)	0-4

Vertu Trophy

Group F (S)	Leicester C U21	(h)	3-1
Group F (S)	Notts Co	(h)	1-2
Group F (S)	Northampton T	(a)	5-2
Second Round	Stevenage	(h)	0-4

CAMBRIDGE UNITED

FOUNDATION

The football revival in Cambridge began soon after World War II when the Abbey United club (formed 1912) decided to turn professional in 1949. In 1951 they changed their name to Cambridge United. They were competing in the United Counties League before graduating to the Eastern Counties League in 1951 and the Southern League in 1958.

The Abbey Stadium, Newmarket Road, Cambridge CB5 8LN.

Telephone: (01223) 566 500.

Ticket Office: (01223) 566 500 (option 1).

Website: www.cambridgeunited.com

Email: info@cambridge-united.co.uk

Ground Capacity: 7,916.

Record Attendance: 14,000 v Chelsea, Friendly, 1 May 1970.

Pitch Measurements: 100m × 65m (109.5yd × 71yd).

Chairman: Shaun Grady.

Chief Executive: Alex Tunbridge.

Head Coach: Neil Harris.

Assistant Head Coaches: Adam Barrett, Barry Corr.

HONOURS

League Champions: Division 3 – 1990–91; Division 4 – 1976–77.
Runners-up: FL 2 – 2020–21; Division 3 – 1977–78; Fourth Division – (6th) 1989–90 *(promoted to Third Division via play-offs)*; Third Division – 1998–99; Football Conference – *Runners-up:* 2007–08, 2008–09, (2nd) 2013–14 *(promoted to FL 2 via play-offs)*.
FA Cup: 6th rd – 1990, 1991.
League Cup: quarter-final – 1993.
League Trophy: Runners-up: 2002.

Colours: Amber shirts with black and white trim, black shorts with amber and white trim, black socks with amber trim.

Year Formed: 1912.

Turned Professional: 1949.

Ltd Co.: 1948.

Previous Name: 1919, Abbey United; 1951, Cambridge United.

Club Nickname: The 'U's'.

Grounds: 1932, Abbey Stadium (renamed R Costings Abbey Stadium 2009; Cambs Glass Stadium 2016; The Abbey Stadium 2017).

First Football League Game: 15 August 1970, Division 4, v Lincoln C (h) D 1–1 – Roberts; Thompson, Meldrum (1), Slack, Eades, Hardy, Leggett, Cassidy, Lindsey, McKinven, Harris.

Record League Victory: 7–0 v Morecambe, FL 2, 19 April 2016 – Norris; Roberts (1), Coulson, Clark, Dunne (Williams), Ismail (1), Berry (2 pens), Ledson (Spencer), Dunk (2), Williamson (1) (Simpson).

Record Cup Victory: 5–1 v Bristol C, FA Cup 5th rd second replay, 27 February 1990 – Vaughan; Fensome, Kimble, Bailie (O'Shea), Chapple, Daish, Cheetham (Robinson), Leadbitter (1), Dublin (2), Taylor (1), Philpott (1).

Record Defeat: 0–7 v Sunderland, League Cup 2nd rd, 1 October 2002; 0–7 v Luton T, FL 2, 18 November 2017.

FOOTBALL YEARBOOK FACT FILE

Cambridge United, then members of the Eastern Counties League, signed former England international Wilf Mannion in August 1956 and he spent two seasons at the Abbey Stadium as a regular in the team. Mannion had previously been suspended by the Football League in June 1955 as a result of controversial comments made in his Sunday newspaper column.

Most League Points (2 for a win): 65, Division 4, 1976–77.

Most League Points (3 for a win): 86, Division 3, 1990–91.

Most League Goals: 87, Division 4, 1976–77.

Highest League Scorer in Season: Paul Mullin, 32, FL 2, 2020–21.

Most League Goals in Total Aggregate: John Taylor, 86, 1988–92; 1996–2001.

Most League Goals in One Match: 5, Steve Butler v Exeter C, Division 2, 4 April 1994.

Most Capped Player: Reggie Lambe, 12 (60), Bermuda.

Most League Appearances: Steve Spriggs, 416, 1975–87.

Youngest League Player: Andy Sinton, 16 years 228 days v Wolverhampton W, 2 November 1982.

Record Transfer Fee Received: £1,300,000 from Leicester C for Trevor Benjamin, July 2000.

Record Transfer Fee Paid: £190,000 to Luton T for Steve Claridge, November 1992.

Football League Record: 1970 Elected to Division 4; 1970–73 Division 4; 1973–74 Division 3; 1974–77 Division 4; 1977–78 Division 3; 1978–84 Division 2; 1984–85 Division 3; 1985–90 Division 4; 1990–91 Division 3; 1991–92 Division 2; 1992–93 First Division; 1993–95 Second Division; 1995–99 Third Division; 1999–2002 Second Division; 2002–04 Third Division; 2004–05 FL 2; 2005–14 Football Conference; 2014–21 FL 2; 2021–25 FL 1; 2025– FL 2.

LATEST SEQUENCES

Longest Sequence of League Wins: 7, 19.2.1977 – 1.4.1977.

Longest Sequence of League Defeats: 7, 8.4.1985 – 30.4.1985.

Longest Sequence of League Draws: 6, 6.9.1986 – 30.9.1986.

Longest Sequence of Unbeaten League Matches: 14, 9.9.1972 – 10.11.1972.

Longest Sequence Without a League Win: 31, 8.10.1983 – 23.4.1984.

Successive Scoring Runs: 26 from 9.4.2002.

Successive Non-scoring Runs: 5 from 29.9.1973.

MANAGERS

Bill Whittaker 1949–55
Gerald Williams 1955
Bert Johnson 1955–59
Bill Craig 1959–60
Alan Moore 1960–63
Roy Kirk 1964–66
Bill Leivers 1967–74
Ron Atkinson 1974–78
John Docherty 1978–83
John Ryan 1984–85
Ken Shellito 1985
Chris Turner 1985–90
John Beck 1990–92
Ian Atkins 1992–93
Gary Johnson 1993–95
Tommy Taylor 1995–96
Roy McFarland 1996–2001
John Beck 2001
John Taylor 2001–04
Claude Le Roy 2004
Herve Renard 2004
Steve Thompson 2004–05
Rob Newman 2005–06
Jimmy Quinn 2006–08
Gary Brabin 2008–09
Martin Ling 2009–11
Jez George 2011–12
Richard Money 2012–15
Shaun Derry 2015–18
Joe Dunne 2018
Colin Calderwood 2018–20
Mark Bonner 2020–23
Neil Harris 2023–24
Garry Monk 2024–25
Neil Harris February 2025–

TEN YEAR LEAGUE RECORD

		P	W	D	L	F	A	Pts	Pos
2015-16	FL 2	46	18	14	14	66	55	68	9
2016-17	FL 2	46	19	9	18	58	50	66	11
2017-18	FL 2	46	17	13	16	56	60	64	12
2018-19	FL 2	46	12	11	23	40	66	47	21
2019-20	FL 2	37	12	9	16	40	48	45	16§
2020-21	FL 2	46	24	8	14	73	49	80	2
2021-22	FL 1	46	15	13	18	56	74	58	14
2022-23	FL 1	46	13	7	26	41	68	46	20
2023-24	FL 1	46	12	12	22	39	61	48	18
2024-25	FL 1	46	9	11	26	45	73	38	23

§*Decided on points-per-game (1.22)*

DID YOU KNOW ?

Harvey Cornwell was one of the legendary figures in the early history of Cambridge United, in the days when they were known as Abbey United. He first appeared for the U's in 1922 and played his last game at the age of 49 in 1945–46, featuring in over 500 games. During the 1938–39 season he turned out for the club alongside his sons Sam and Harvey junior.

CAMBRIDGE UNITED – SKY BET LEAGUE ONE 2024–25 LEAGUE RECORD

Match No.	Date	Venue	Opponents	Result	H/T Score	Lg Pos.	Goalscorers	Attendance
1	Aug 10	A	Stockport Co	L	0-2	0-1	23		9457
2	17	H	Crawley T	L	0-1	0-0	21		6720
3	24	H	Blackpool	D	4-4	1-3	20	Lavery 2 [28, 75], Andrew [59], Njoku [72]	6083
4	31	A	Bristol R	L	0-2	0-1	23		7893
5	Sept 14	A	Mansfield T	L	1-2	0-1	24	Emmanuel [50]	7294
6	21	A	Wycombe W	L	1-2	1-1	24	N'Lundulu [19]	4189
7	28	H	Lincoln C	L	0-1	0-1	24		6969
8	Oct 1	H	Rotherham U	L	0-1	0-0	24		5085
9	5	A	Exeter C	L	0-1	0-1	24		6406
10	19	H	Wigan Ath	W	2-0	2-0	23	Kachunga [5], Tickle (og) [22]	7000
11	22	A	Stevenage	W	2-0	1-0	23	Smith [31], KaiKai [90]	4574
12	26	H	Burton Alb	W	1-0	0-0	21	Cousins [84]	6706
13	Nov 9	A	Peterborough U	L	1-6	0-4	22	KaiKai [84]	12,370
14	16	H	Barnsley	D	1-1	1-1	22	N'Lundulu [4]	6817
15	23	A	Northampton T	D	0-0	0-0	22		6654
16	26	H	Bolton W	D	1-1	0-0	22	KaiKai [89]	5266
17	Dec 3	A	Reading	L	0-3	0-0	22		8333
18	7	H	Shrewsbury T	W	4-1	2-0	22	Lavery 2 [1, 30], N'Lundulu [46], Kachunga [53]	6167
19	14	A	Wrexham	D	2-2	1-1	22	Kachunga [20], N'Lundulu (pen) [89]	11,698
20	20	H	Huddersfield T	L	0-4	0-3	22		6949
21	26	A	Charlton Ath	L	1-2	0-2	22	Kachunga [51]	14,369
22	29	A	Leyton Orient	L	0-2	0-1	22		8914
23	Jan 1	H	Reading	L	1-3	0-1	23	Kachunga [48]	6878
24	4	H	Bristol R	L	0-1	0-1	23		6467
25	18	A	Bolton W	D	2-2	2-1	23	Stokes [4], Kachunga [36]	19,946
26	25	H	Mansfield T	W	3-2	2-0	22	Morrison [1], Stokes (pen) [7], Loft [47]	6687
27	28	A	Rotherham U	L	1-2	0-0	23	Loft [49]	8162
28	Feb 1	H	Wycombe W	D	1-1	0-1	24	Stokes [83]	6866
29	8	H	Lincoln C	D	1-1	1-1	24	Gibbons [42]	8606
30	11	A	Birmingham C	L	0-4	0-3	24		22,456
31	15	H	Exeter C	L	0-1	0-0	24		5455
32	22	A	Stockport Co	W	2-0	2-0	24	Stokes 2 [9, 43]	6905
33	Mar 1	H	Crawley T	W	2-0	1-0	22	Doyle (og) [33], Digby [64]	4955
34	4	H	Stevenage	L	0-1	0-0	22		6338
35	8	A	Wigan Ath	L	0-1	0-0	23		10,052
36	11	A	Blackpool	L	1-2	1-1	23	Ballard [3]	7957
37	15	H	Peterborough U	L	0-1	0-0	23		7359
38	22	A	Barnsley	D	1-1	1-0	23	Brophy [9]	10,790
39	29	H	Northampton T	D	1-1	0-1	23	Brophy [52]	7252
40	Apr 1	H	Wrexham	D	2-2	1-1	23	Bennett [40], Stokes (pen) [47]	6871
41	5	A	Shrewsbury T	W	1-0	0-0	23	Ballard [76]	5952
42	12	H	Charlton Ath	L	0-1	0-1	23		6707
43	18	A	Huddersfield T	W	2-1	0-0	22	Brophy [69], KaiKai [90]	18,289
44	21	H	Leyton Orient	L	1-2	0-1	23	Stokes [19]	7414
45	26	A	Burton Alb	L	1-2	0-0	23	Kachunga [84]	3540
46	May 3	H	Birmingham C	L	1-2	1-1	23	Lavery [36]	6764

Final League Position: 23

GOALSCORERS

League (45): Kachunga 7, Stokes 7 (2 pens), Lavery 5, KaiKai 4, N'Lundulu 4 (1 pen), Brophy 3, Ballard 2, Loft 2, Andrew 1, Bennett 1, Cousins 1, Digby 1, Emmanuel 1, Gibbons 1, Morrison 1, Njoku 1, Smith 1, own goals 2.
FA Cup (2): Brophy 1, Njoku 1.
Carabao Cup (1): Digby 1.
Vertu Trophy (6): Barton 1, Bennett 1, Kaunda 1, Longelo 1, N'Lundulu 1 (1 pen), Stokes 1 (1 pen).

Reyes Vicente 20	Okedina J 23+4	Rossi Z 12+3	Watts K 26+3	Andrew D 25+7	Smith K 23	Gibbons J 23+6	Brophy J 43+3	Kachunga E 31+12	KaiKai S 11+14	Lavery S 10+5	Digby P 27+4	Richards T —+5	Morrison M 40+1	Bennett L 34+7	Barton D 6+10	O'Riordan C 3+1	Stokes J 26+6	Emmanuel M 3+12	Njoku B 8+17	N'Lundulu D 17+8	Cousins J 23+5	Loft R 18+14	Stephens J 11+1	Kaunda A —+1	Marosi M 2	Ballard D 11+6	Esapa D —+2	Hoddle G —+2	Stevenson B 11+6	Bishop N 13+1	Malone S 6+2	Match No.
1	2^1	3^3	4^5	5	6^4	7	8^2	9	10	11	12	13	14	15	16																	1
1	3		4	7	5	8^1	12	10^2	11	6	14		13	9^3	2																	2
1	3		4	6		8^1		9^2	11	7			5	10^3	2	12	13	14														3
1	4		8^4	6	5^3	13		10^1	11	7		3^2		12	2	9	14	15														4
1	2		4^1	6	15	7		14	10^3	3			5	9^2	12	11	8^4	13														5
1	8	2	4	6	5	7^3	14	9^2		3			12				11^1	15	10^4	13												6
1	2		4	7	5^2	9^1	15	12		6		3	13				8^4	10^3	11		14											7
1	2		4	8	9	6	12			7		3	5				10^2	11^1			13											8
1	2		4	6^4	8^3	13	11^2	15		7		3	5				14	12	10		9^1											9
1	2		4	7	14	8^2	9^4	13		6		3	5				12	11^3	15		10^1											10
1	2	13		7^3	4	8	11^2	12		6		3	5				14	10^1	9^4	15												11
1	2		4	7	15	8^2	9	12		6^3		3	5				13	11^1	10^2		14											12
1	2	12		7	4^1	8	9	13				3	5				11^3	10^2	6		14											13
	2	14		4	8	9^3	6		13			3	5				10^1	11^2	7	12	1											14
	2		4	8		9	6		12			3	5				10^1	11	7													15
1	2^1	13	15	4	7		8^4	14	9	12		3	5				11^1		6^3	10^2												16
1	2	13		4	7		8^2	9^4		11^1		3	5				12	10^3	6	14		15										17
1	2		4	13	7		8^2	9^4		11^3		3	5				14	15	10^1	6	12											18
1	2	12	4^5	16	7		8^4	9^2	13	11^2		3	5				15	14	10		6											19
1	2		4	8		7		9^2	12	11^3		3	5^1	14			13	15	10^4		6											20
1	2	3^2	5^1	13	7	10	8^4	11				4	12				9^3		14		6	15										21
3			5^2	6		12	8	10^1		15		4	2				9		13	11^3	7^4	14	1									22
2			4	7^2		8^3	11^1			14		3	5	13			9		10		6	12	1									23
	2^3		4	7		8^2	10^4			15		3^6	5				9	12	14	11^1	6	13	1									24
	2	3	4			7	9^2						5	8		10	13	12			6	11^1			1							25
15	2	4		8^3	14	7	9^5			13		3	5^4	10	16		6		11^2	12				1^1								26
2^1	4		8	12		7^3	9		13			3	5^5	16	10^2		6		11^4							14	15	17				27
2			4	8		13			6^2			3	5				9			7^3	10	1				11^1	14		12			28
2	4		8	5^3		7	9^1		14	3							10				6	11^2				12			13^3	1		29
3	5		12	8^5	10^4		6			4			2^2	9	13		14				15	11^1						16	7^3	1		30
2^4	4		8^5	7^1	9					3		14	5^3	10	16	15					6	11^2				13			12	1		31
12	4		5	10		7^2					8	3	2	9							6	11^1							13	1		32
12	4		5^6	10^4	8^3		7					3	9^1	15			14				6	11^2							13	1		33
5^2	4					9	6^3				8	4	2	14			10				12	11^1				13			7	1		34
13	4					6	11^4	8^5		3		2^3	16	9	14	15	12	7				10^1							1	5^2		35
	4			8		9^2	13	6^1		3		2		10	15		14	7^4			11					12			1	5^3		36
	4		2^3	6^1	13	12		8		3	14		9				15	7	11^2		10^4					1			5			37
	4		2	10	9	12		7		3			8^2	13			11			6					1			5			38
	4		2	10	8			6		3		13	9^3	14			12			7					1			5^1			39
	5		3	6^2	12		8	4	2	7			11				10¹			9			1			13					40
	5		3	6^1	13		8	4	2	7^3	14			11	1						10^2				9				12		41
	5	13	3^2	9^4	12	14		4	2		7		15				11^3	1			10				8			6^1			42
	4	13	5	10	8^1	12		3	2^2		9			14	1						11^3	7									43
	4		5^1	8	14	10^2	12	6^4		3		13					9			11	1				15			7			44
	4^5	16	5	8	13	10	15	6^4		3		2^2					9^1		12^5	1^3		11						7	14			45
	4		5	10	9^4	8^3	11^1	6		3		2^2					13			14					12			7	1		46

FA Cup
First Round — Woking — (a) 1-0
Second Round — Wigan Ath — (h) 1-2
aet.

Carabao Cup
First Round — QPR — (h) 1-2

Vertu Trophy
Group C (S) — Bromley — (a) 3-3
Bromley won 5-4 on penalties.
Group C (S) — Charlton Ath — (h) 1-2
Group C (S) — Chelsea U21 — (h) 1-0
Second Round — Cheltenham T — (a) 1-2

CARDIFF CITY

FOUNDATION

Credit for the establishment of a first class professional football club in such a rugby stronghold as Cardiff is due to members of the Riverside club formed in 1899 out of a cricket club of that name. Cardiff became a city in 1905 and in 1908 the South Wales and Monmouthshire FA granted Riverside permission to call themselves Cardiff City. The club turned professional under that name in 1910.

Cardiff City Stadium, Leckwith Road, Cardiff CF11 8AZ.

Telephone: (0845) 365 1115.

Ticket Office: (0333) 311 1920.

Website: www.cardiffcityfc.co.uk

Email: club@cardiffcityfc.co.uk

Ground Capacity: 33,280.

Record Attendance: 57,893 v Arsenal, Division 1, 22 April 1953 (at Ninian Park); 33,028 v Manchester U, Premier League, 22 December 2018 (at Cardiff City Stadium).

Ground Record Attendance: 62,634, Wales v England, 17 October 1959 (at Ninian Park); 33,280, Wales v Belgium, 12 June 2015 (at Cardiff City Stadium).

Pitch Measurements: 105m × 68m (115yd × 74.5yd).

Chairman: Mehmet Dalman.

Chief Executive: Ken Choo.

Head Coach: Brian Barry-Murphy.

Assistant Head Coach: Lee Riley.

Colours: Blue shirts with white trim, white shorts with blue trim, blue socks with white trim.

Year Formed: 1899.

Turned Professional: 1910.

Previous Names: 1899, Riverside; 1902, Riverside Albion; 1908, Cardiff City.

Club Nickname: 'The Bluebirds'.

Grounds: Riverside, Sophia Gardens, Old Park and Fir Gardens; 1910, Ninian Park; 2009, Cardiff City Stadium.

First Football League Game: 28 August 1920, Division 2, v Stockport Co (a) W 5–2 – Kneeshaw; Brittan, Leyton; Keenor (1), Smith, Hardy; Grimshaw (1), Gill (2), Cashmore, West, Evans (1).

Record League Victory: 9–2 v Thames, Division 3 (S), 6 February 1932 – Farquharson; Eric Morris, Roberts; Galbraith, Harris, Ronan; Emmerson (1), Keating (1), Jones (1), McCambridge (1), Robbins (5).

Record Cup Victory: 8–0 v Enfield, FA Cup 1st rd, 28 November 1931 – Farquharson; Smith, Roberts; Harris (1), Galbraith, Ronan; Emmerson (2), Keating (3); O'Neill (2), Robbins, McCambridge.

HONOURS

League Champions: FL C – 2012–13; Division 3S – 1946–47; Third Division – 1992–93.

Runners-up: FL C – 2017–18; Division 1 – 1923–24; Division 2 – 1920–21, 1951–52, 1959–60; Division 3 – 1975–76, 1982–83; Third Division – 2000–01; Division 4 – 1987–88.

FA Cup Winners: 1927. *Runners-up:* 1925, 2008.

League Cup: Runners-up: 2012.

Welsh Cup Winners: 22 times.

European Competitions *European Cup-Winners' Cup:* 1964–65 *(qf)*, 1965–66, 1967–68 *(sf)*, 1968–69, 1969–70, 1970–71 *(qf)*, 1971–72, 1973–74, 1974–75, 1976–77, 1977–78, 1988–89, 1992–93, 1993–94.

FOOTBALL YEARBOOK FACT FILE

Cardiff City's first-ever shirt sponsorship deal was agreed with Whitbread Wales in November 1983. The club received an undisclosed four-figure sum for allowing the company's logo to appear on shirts for just three matches. Later that season further deals were made with the creator of the Welsh-language cartoon *SuperTed*, and with a local roofing company.

Record Defeat: 2–11 v Sheffield U, Division 1, 1 January 1926.

Most League Points (2 for a win): 66, Division 3 (S), 1946–47.

Most League Points (3 for a win): 90, FL C, 2017–18.

Most League Goals: 95, Division 3, 2000–01.

Highest League Scorer in Season: Robert Earnshaw, 31, Division 2, 2002–03.

Most League Goals in Total Aggregate: Len Davies, 128, 1920–31.

Most League Goals in One Match: 5, Hugh Ferguson v Burnley, Division 1, 1 September 1928; 5, Walter Robbins v Thames, Division 3 (S), 6 February 1932; 5, William Henderson v Northampton T, Division 3 (S), 22 April 1933.

Most Capped Player: Aron Gunnarsson, 62 (107), Iceland.

Most League Appearances: Phil Dwyer, 471, 1972–85.

Youngest League Player: Bob Adams, 15 years 355 days v Southend U, 18 February 1933.

Record Transfer Fee Received: £10,000,000 from Internazionale for Gary Medel, August 2014.

Record Transfer Fee Paid: £15,000,000 to Nantes for Emiliano Sala, January 2019.

Football League Record: 1920 Elected to Division 2; 1920–21 Division 2; 1921–29 Division 1; 1929–31 Division 2; 1931–47 Division 3 (S); 1947–52 Division 2; 1952–57 Division 1; 1957–60 Division 2; 1960–62 Division 1; 1962–75 Division 2; 1975–76 Division 3; 1976–82 Division 2; 1982–83 Division 3; 1983–85 Division 2; 1985–86 Division 3; 1986–88 Division 4; 1988–90 Division 3; 1990–92 Division 4; 1992–93 Third Division; 1993–95 Second Division; 1995–99 Third Division; 1999–2000 Second Division; 2000–01 Third Division; 2001–03 Second Division; 2003–04 First Division; 2004–13 FL C; 2013–14 Premier League; 2014–18 FL C; 2018–19 Premier League; 2019–25 FL C; 2025– FL 1.

LATEST SEQUENCES

Longest Sequence of League Wins: 9, 26.10.1946 – 28.12.1946.

Longest Sequence of League Defeats: 8, 15.9.2021 – 23.10.2021.

Longest Sequence of League Draws: 6, 29.11.1980 – 17.1.1981.

Longest Sequence of Unbeaten League Matches: 21, 21.9.1946 – 1.3.1947.

Longest Sequence Without a League Win: 15, 21.11.1936 – 6.3.1937.

Successive Scoring Runs: 24 from 25.8.2012.

Successive Non-scoring Runs: 8 from 20.12.1952.

MANAGERS

Davy McDougall 1910–11
Fred Stewart 1911–33
Bartley Wilson 1933–34
B. Watts-Jones 1934–37
Bill Jennings 1937–39
Cyril Spiers 1939–46
Billy McCandless 1946–48
Cyril Spiers 1948–54
Trevor Morris 1954–58
Bill Jones 1958–62
George Swindin 1962–64
Jimmy Scoular 1964–73
Frank O'Farrell 1973–74
Jimmy Andrews 1974–78
Richie Morgan 1978–81
Graham Williams 1981–82
Len Ashurst 1982–84
Jimmy Goodfellow 1984
Alan Durban 1984–86
Frank Burrows 1986–89
Len Ashurst 1989–91
Eddie May 1991–94
Terry Yorath 1994–95
Eddie May 1995
Kenny Hibbitt (*Chief Coach*) 1995–96
Phil Neal 1996
Russell Osman 1996–97
Kenny Hibbitt 1997–98
Frank Burrows 1998–2000
Billy Ayre 2000
Bobby Gould 2000
Alan Cork 2000–02
Lennie Lawrence 2002–05
Dave Jones 2005–11
Malky Mackay 2011–13
Ole Gunnar Solskjaer 2014
Russell Slade 2014–16
Paul Trollope 2016
Neil Warnock 2016–19
Neil Harris 2019–21
Mick McCarthy 2021
Steve Morison 2021–22
Mark Hudson 2022–23
Sabri Lamouchi 2023
Erol Bulut 2023–24
Omer Riza 2024–25
Brian Barry-Murphy June 2025–

TEN YEAR LEAGUE RECORD

		P	W	D	L	F	A	Pts	Pos
2015-16	FL C	46	17	17	12	56	51	68	8
2016-17	FL C	46	17	11	18	60	61	62	12
2017-18	FL C	46	27	9	10	69	39	90	2
2018-19	PR Lge	38	10	4	24	34	69	34	18
2019-20	FL C	46	19	16	11	68	58	73	5
2020-21	FL C	46	18	14	14	66	49	68	8
2021-22	FL C	46	15	8	23	50	68	53	18
2022-23	FL C	46	13	10	23	41	58	49	21
2023-24	FL C	46	19	5	22	53	70	62	12
2024-25	FL C	46	9	17	20	48	73	44	24

DID YOU KNOW

After changing their name from Riverside to Cardiff City in the summer of 1908 the club played their first game under their new title on 5 September. They travelled to Weston-Super-Mare where they met the local Christ Church Old Boys club in a friendly match that ended 2-2. Goalscorers for City were Sheppard and Meaker.

CARDIFF CITY – SKY BET CHAMPIONSHIP 2024–25 LEAGUE RECORD

Match No.	Date	Venue	Opponents	Result	H/T Score	Lg Pos.	Goalscorers	Atten-dance
1	Aug 10	H	Sunderland	L	0-2	0-1	22		21,401
2	17	A	Burnley	L	0-5	0-2	24		19,759
3	25	A	Swansea C	D	1-1	0-1	24	Robinson [79]	20,174
4	31	H	Middlesbrough	L	0-2	0-0	24		18,000
5	Sept 14	A	Derby Co	L	0-1	0-1	24		28,985
6	21	H	Leeds U	L	0-2	0-1	24		23,207
7	28	A	Hull C	L	1-4	1-2	24	Robinson [18]	22,665
8	Oct 1	H	Millwall	W	1-0	1-0	24	Ng [39]	15,687
9	6	A	Bristol C	D	1-1	0-0	24	Tanner [54]	22,664
10	19	H	Plymouth Arg	W	5-0	2-0	22	Robertson [16], Colwill R [24], El Ghazi [52], Robinson [75], Willock [80]	20,634
11	22	H	Portsmouth	W	2-0	2-0	19	Poole (og) [5], Robinson [13]	18,534
12	26	A	WBA	D	0-0	0-0	20		25,312
13	Nov 2	H	Norwich C	W	2-1	0-0	17	Robinson [89], O'Dowda [90]	19,032
14	6	A	Luton T	L	0-1	0-0	21		10,656
15	9	H	Blackburn R	L	1-3	0-1	22	Turnbull [73]	17,188
16	23	A	Sheffield Wed	D	1-1	1-1	21	Tanner [34]	23,974
17	27	H	QPR	L	0-2	0-1	21		16,205
18	30	A	Coventry C	D	2-2	1-1	20	Meite [4], Robertson [48]	27,137
19	Dec 11	H	Preston NE	L	0-2	0-0	22		15,006
20	14	A	Stoke C	D	2-2	1-1	21	El Ghazi [32], Gibson (og) [72]	20,847
21	21	H	Sheffield U	L	0-2	0-0	22		18,312
22	26	A	Oxford U	L	2-3	0-1	23	Ashford [82], Robinson [90]	11,494
23	29	A	Watford	W	2-1	2-1	22	Robinson 2 [1, 42]	19,916
24	Jan 1	H	Coventry C	D	1-1	1-0	23	Robertson [6]	19,045
25	4	A	Middlesbrough	D	1-1	1-1	23	Chambers [21]	24,634
26	14	A	Watford	D	1-1	0-0	21	Ashford [65]	16,942
27	18	H	Swansea C	W	3-0	0-0	20	Robinson 2 [47, 51], Goutas [67]	26,536
28	21	A	Millwall	D	2-2	1-2	19	Willock [45], Salech [90]	12,041
29	25	H	Derby Co	W	2-1	0-0	18	Robinson [62], El Ghazi [64]	19,548
30	Feb 1	A	Leeds U	L	0-7	0-2	19		35,810
31	11	A	Portsmouth	L	1-2	1-2	20	O'Dowda [22]	20,251
32	15	H	Bristol C	D	1-1	0-0	20	Salech [90]	22,433
33	22	A	Plymouth Arg	D	1-1	1-0	21	Salech [12]	16,981
34	25	H	Hull C	W	1-0	0-0	19	Robinson [52]	16,622
35	Mar 4	H	Burnley	L	1-2	1-2	21	Salech [42]	15,713
36	8	A	Sunderland	L	1-2	1-1	21	Davies I [41]	40,066
37	11	H	Luton T	L	1-2	0-0	21	Chambers [50]	16,641
38	15	H	Blackburn R	W	2-1	1-1	21	Salech [4], Meite [73]	13,456
39	29	H	Sheffield Wed	D	1-1	1-0	21	Davies I [21]	20,460
40	Apr 5	A	QPR	D	0-0	0-0	22		17,066
41	8	A	Preston NE	D	2-2	0-1	22	Alves [52], Meite [90]	13,293
42	12	H	Stoke C	L	0-1	0-0	22		20,658
43	18	A	Sheffield U	L	0-2	0-1	23		28,201
44	21	H	Oxford U	D	1-1	0-0	23	Salech [56]	23,407
45	26	H	WBA	D	0-0	0-0	24		23,710
46	May 3	A	Norwich C	L	2-4	0-3	24	Salech 2 (1 pen) [56 (p), 84]	26,581

Final League Position: 24

GOALSCORERS

League (48): Robinson 12, Salech 8 (1 pen), El Ghazi 3, Meite 3, Robertson 3, Ashford 2, Chambers 2, Davies I 2, O'Dowda 2, Tanner 2, Willock 2, Alves 1, Colwill R 1, Goutas 1, Ng 1, Turnbull 1, own goals 2.
FA Cup (4): Colwill R 2, Ashford 1, Salech 1.
Carabao Cup (5): Colwill R 2, McGuinness 1, Robertson 1, own goal 1.

Horvath E 17	Ng P 31 + 4	Chambers C 41	Goutas D 33 + 1	O'Dowda C 41 + 1	Siopis M 16 + 5	Ralls J 15 + 6	Tanner O 15 + 14	Ramsey A 6 + 2	Willock C 17 + 15	Robinson C 24 + 10	Meite Y 11 + 23	Kanga W 5 + 10	Turnbull D 10 + 9	Colwill R 24 + 19	Bagan J 17 + 14	Walcott M — + 1	Daland J 16 + 4	Robertson A 29 + 6	El Ghazi A 14 + 11	Alnwick J 29	Fish W 14 + 7	Ashford C 17 + 11	Collins J 2 + 1	Rinomhota A 24 + 6	Reindorf M — + 2	Kpakio R 1 + 2	Salech Y 14 + 6	Mannsverk S 12 + 2	Alves W 8 + 6	Davies I 3 + 6	Lawlor D — + 1	Nyakuhwa T — + 1	Match No.
1	2	3	4	5	6	7^3	8^1	9	10^4	11^2	12	13	14	15																			1
1	2	3^3	4	5^2	6	7^1	15	9	10	16	8^5	11^4		12	13	14																	2
1	2	3		5	6		13	9	10^3	15	8^2	11^4		12				4	7^1		14												3
1	2	3	12	5	6		13	9	10^4	16	8^2	11^5		15				4^1	7^3		14												4
	2^1	3	4	10	6	7^4	13	14	11^5	9	5^2	16							8^3	1	12	15											5
	2	4	10^5	6^4	7^3	8^2	16	11^1	9	5^4	14	13								1	3	15	12										6
	2	3	8^4		7	14	13	11^3	16	15	9	6	10^5					4^1	5^2	1		12											7
	2	4	3		7	8^3	12	11^1	13	15	9^4	5	6	10^2						1	14												8
	2	4	3	12	16	7^4	8^3	11^2	17	14	9	5	13	6^5	10^1					1	15												9
	2	4	3	5^5		8^3	12	11	14	15	7^2	9^1	16	6	10^4					1	13												10
	2	4	3	5	12	8^3	15	11^5	14	16	7^1	9		6^2	10^4					1	13												11
	2	4	3	5	12	8^5	15	11^3	13	14	7^1	9^4	16	6	10^2					1													12
		4	3	5	6	8				9^2	12		7	11	14		10^1			1	13	2^3											13
	2	4	3	5	6^4	8^1	13	11^2	12	15	7	9		10^3						1	14												14
	2	3	5		8		11	12			7	9		4	6		10^1			1													15
	2	3	5	14	12	8		11^4	10^2	15	7^3	9	13	4	6^1		1																16
	2	4	3^3	10		7^2	8^1	12	11	14	13	9	5	6		1																	17
	2	4	3	10	6^5		15	11^3	8^4	9^1	12	13	7	1				5^2	16	14													18
	2	4	3	10		12		13	11^4	8^2	9	5^1	7	14	1			6^3	15														19
		4	3	8	6	7		11^3		10^2	13	12		2^5	14	9^1	1	5															20
		4	3		6			11^1	13	10^3	14	12	8	2^5	7^4	9^2	1	16	5		15												21
	2	3	8^3	6^2				11^1	12	10^4	9	4		7	14	1	15	5		13													22
		7^2	3	5^4	6	12				10^1	11	14		15	13	4	9			8^3	2												23
	12	7	3	5	6^4	15	13		10^3	11^8	14			16			4^1	9^6			8^2	2											24
		7	3	5	6	15	10^1		12		14	11^2	13				4	9^4			8^3	2											25
	2	7	3	5			14	12	10^1		13		11^2	15			4	9^4			8^3	6											26
	6^2	3	5^1	13	7	10^4			11^5	15		14	12				4	9^2			8	2		16									27
	12	7	3		6^1				10^5	11	8^2			9^1	5		4^4	15				2		14									28
	5	6	3			7			10^1	11^4	15					4	9^2	12	1	14	8^3	2		13									29
	15	7	3	5^5		8^3			10						12		4^1	6	11^2	1	16	9^4		2			13	14					30
	16	6	2	9		7^1			11					13	4^2			15		1	3	10^5		5^4			14	8^3	12				31
	2		3	5			12	13	11^2					9	4			8^3	1		15		6^1			14	7^4	10					32
	2	3^4	8			6			14					11^3	4^1				1	12	13		5			10^4	7	9^2	15				33
1	4	7^3	5				8^1	9^2		16	15		13	14			13	14			3	10^5	2			11^4	6		12				34
1	2	5	3	9			15		16					13	4^5			7^1	14		12	11^3	6^2			10	8^4						35
1	2	6^2	3	5					9^3					10	4			14			13	15			11	7^4	12	8^1					36
1	2	6	3^5	5			7^1	13	15	16				10^2				9^3			4				11	12	8^4	14					37
1	2	5		9		8^1				11^4	16	15	12	4			13				3			6^3			10^2	7^5	13	14			38
1	2^5	7		5			14			15		12	16	4				13			3	9					11^4	6^1	10^2	8^3			39
1			5				14			13	15		6	4^1			12				3^9	9^4	2			11	7	10^2	8^3				40
		6	3^1	8						14	15		11^4			4	13				2	9^9		5^2			10^3	7	12	16			41
1	2	7^5	9			13			10^1	14			12	16			4	6			3	5^2					11^3		8^4	15			42
1		4	5			8^1	12		9			14	15^5	16			6^3				3	13	2				11	7^4	10^2				43
1	2	4	5				16		10^2		12	15^5	14					9^3			3	8^1	6				11^5	7^4	13				44
1	2^1	4	5		13	15	10^2					7^3	16			12		9^4			3	8^5	6				11		14				45
1		4^1	5		7^3		15					6^1	14	12				9^5			3	8					2^4	11		10^2	13	16	46

FA Cup
Third Round	Sheffield U	(a)	1-0
Fourth Round	Stoke C	(a)	3-3

aet; Cardiff C won 4-2 on penalties.

Fifth Round	Aston Villa	(a)	0-2

Carabao Cup
First Round	Bristol R	(h)	2-0
Second Round	Southampton	(h)	3-5

CARLISLE UNITED

FOUNDATION

Carlisle United came into being when members of Shaddongate United voted to change its name on 17 May 1904. The new club was admitted to the Second Division of the Lancashire Combination in 1905–06, winning promotion the following season. Devonshire Park was officially opened on 2 September 1905, when St Helens Town were the visitors. Despite defeat in a disappointing 3–2 start, a respectable mid-table position was achieved.

Brunton Park, Warwick Road, Carlisle, Cumbria
CA1 1LL.

Telephone: (0330) 094 5930.

Ticket Office: (0330) 094 5930 (option 1).

Website: www.carlisleunited.co.uk

Email: enquiries@carlisleunited.co.uk

Ground Capacity: 17,030.

Record Attendance: 27,500 v Birmingham C, FA Cup 3rd rd, 5 January 1957 and v Middlesbrough, FA Cup 5th rd, 7 February 1970.

Pitch Measurements: 102m × 68m (111.5yd × 74.5yd).

Chairman: Tom Piatak.

Chief Executive: Nigel Clibbens.

Head Coach: Mark Hughes.

First-Team Coaches: Frank McAvoy, Gavin Skelton.

Colours: Blue shirts with white front panel and thin red stripes, blue shorts, blue socks with white and red trim.

Year Formed: 1904. *Turned Professional:* 1921.

Previous Name: 1904, Shaddongate United; 1904, Carlisle United.

Club Nicknames: 'The Cumbrians'; 'The Blues'.

Grounds: 1904, Milholme Bank; 1905, Devonshire Park; 1909, Brunton Park.

First Football League Game: 25 August 1928, Division 3 (N), v Accrington S (a) W 3–2 – Prout; Coulthard, Cook; Harrison, Ross, Pigg; Agar (1), Hutchison, McConnell (1), Ward (1), Watson.

Record League Victory: 8–0 v Hartlepool U, Division 3 (N), 1 September 1928 – Prout; Smiles, Cook; Robinson (1) Ross, Pigg; Agar (1), Hutchison (1), McConnell (4), Ward (1), Watson. 8–0 v Scunthorpe U, Division 3 (N), 25 December 1952 – MacLaren; Hill, Scott; Stokoe, Twentyman, Waters; Harrison (1), Whitehouse (5), Ashman (2), Duffett, Bond.

Record Cup Victory: 6–0 v Shepshed Dynamo, FA Cup 1st rd, 16 November 1996 – Caig; Hopper, Archdeacon (pen), Walling, Robinson, Pounewatchy, Peacock (1), Conway (1) (Jansen), Smart (McAlindon (1)), Hayward, Aspinall (Thorpe), (2 og). 6–0 v Tipton T, FA Cup 1st rd, 6 November 2010 – Collin; Simek, Murphy, Chester, Cruise, Robson (McKenna), Berrett, Taiwo (Hurst), Marshall, Zoko (Curran) (2), Madine (4).

HONOURS

League Champions: Division 3 – 1964–65; FL 2 – 2005–06; Third Division – 1994–95.
Runners-up: Division 3 – 1981–82; Division 4 – 1963–64; Football Conference – (3rd) 2004–05 *(promoted to FL 2 via play-offs).*
FA Cup: 6th rd – 1975.
League Cup: semi-final – 1970.
League Trophy Winners: 1997, 2011. *Runners-up:* 1995, 2003, 2006, 2010.

FOOTBALL YEARBOOK FACT FILE

Wing-half Bill Blyth captained the Carlisle United team that won the Lancashire Combination Division Two title in 1906–07 and after several seasons as a player with the club retired to become a local licensee. He went on to serve the Cumbrians as a director and, briefly, chairman, being instrumental in bringing his nephew Bill Shankly to the club as a player. Later Shankly returned to Brunton Park as manager, going on to become one of the greatest managers in British football.

Record Defeat: 1–11 v Hull C, Division 3 (N), 14 January 1939.

Most League Points (2 for a win): 62, Division 3 (N), 1950–51.

Most League Points (3 for a win): 91, Division 3, 1994–95.

Most League Goals: 113, Division 4, 1963–64.

Highest League Scorer in Season: Jimmy McConnell, 42, Division 3 (N), 1928–29.

Most League Goals in Total Aggregate: Jimmy McConnell, 124, 1928–32.

Most League Goals in One Match: 5, Hugh Mills v Halifax T, Division 3 (N), 11 September 1937; 5, Jim Whitehouse v Scunthorpe U, Division 3 (N), 25 December 1952.

Most Capped Player: Reggie Lambe, 6 (60), Bermuda; Hallam Hope, 6 (13), Barbados.

Most League Appearances: Allan Ross, 466, 1963–79.

Youngest League Player: John Slaven, 16 years 162 days v Scunthorpe U, 16 March 2002.

Record Transfer Fee Received: £1,000,000 from Crystal Palace for Matt Jansen, February 1998.

Record Transfer Fee Paid: £500,000 to Harrogate T for Luke Armstrong, January 2024.

Football League Record: 1928 Elected to Division 3 (N); 1928–58 Division 3 (N); 1958–62 Division 4; 1962–63 Division 3; 1963–64 Division 4; 1964–65 Division 3; 1965–74 Division 2; 1974–75 Division 1; 1975–77 Division 2; 1977–82 Division 3; 1982–86 Division 2; 1986–87 Division 3; 1987–92 Division 4; 1992–95 Third Division; 1995–96 Second Division; 1996–97 Third Division; 1997–98 Second Division; 1998–2004 Third Division; 2004–05 Football Conference; 2005–06 FL 2; 2006–14 FL 1; 2014–23 FL 2; 2023–24 FL 1; 2024–25 FL 2; 2025– National League.

LATEST SEQUENCES

Longest Sequence of League Wins: 7, 18.2.2006 – 8.4.2006.

Longest Sequence of League Defeats: 12, 27.9.2003 – 13.12.2003.

Longest Sequence of League Draws: 6, 11.2.1978 – 11.3.1978.

Longest Sequence of Unbeaten League Matches: 19, 1.10.1994 – 11.2.1995.

Longest Sequence Without a League Win: 15, 12.4.2014 – 20.9.2014.

Successive Scoring Runs: 26 from 23.8.1947.

Successive Non-scoring Runs: 7 from 25.2.2017.

MANAGERS

Harry Kirkbride 1904–05 (*Secretary-Manager*); **McCumiskey** 1905–06 (*Secretary-Manager*); **Jack Houston** 1906–08 (*Secretary-Manager*); **Bert Stansfield** 1908–10; **Jack Houston** 1910–12; **Davie Graham** 1912–13; **George Bristow** 1913–30; **Billy Hampson** 1930–33; **Bill Clarke** 1933–35; **Robert Kelly** 1935–36; **Fred Westgarth** 1936–38; **David Taylor** 1938–40; **Howard Harkness** 1940–45; **Bill Clark** 1945–46 (*Secretary-Manager*); **Ivor Broadis** 1946–49; **Bill Shankly** 1949–51; **Fred Emery** 1951–58; **Andy Beattie** 1958–60; **Ivor Powell** 1960–63; **Alan Ashman** 1963–67; **Tim Ward** 1967–68; **Bob Stokoe** 1968–70; **Ian MacFarlane** 1970–72; **Alan Ashman** 1972–75; **Dick Young** 1975–76; **Bobby Moncur** 1976–80; **Martin Harvey** 1980; **Bob Stokoe** 1980–85; **Bryan 'Pop' Robson** 1985; **Bob Stokoe** 1985–86; **Harry Gregg** 1986–87; **Cliff Middlemass** 1987–91; **Aidan McCaffery** 1991–92; **David McCreery** 1992–93; **Mick Wadsworth** (*Director of Coaching*) 1993–96; **Mervyn Day** 1996–97; **David Wilkes and John Halpin** (*Directors of Coaching*), and **Michael Knighton** 1997–99; **Nigel Pearson** 1998–99; **Keith Mincher** 1999; **Martin Wilkinson** 1999–2000; **Ian Atkins** 2000–01; **Roddy Collins** 2001–02; 2002–03; **Paul Simpson** 2003–06; **Neil McDonald** 2006–07; **John Ward** 2007–08; **Greg Abbott** 2008–13; **Graham Kavanagh** 2013–14; **Keith Curle** 2014–18; **John Sheridan** 2018–19; **Steven Pressley** 2019; **Chris Beech** 2019–21; **Keith Millen** 2021–22; **Paul Simpson** 2022–24; **Mike Williamson** 2024–25; **Mark Hughes** February 2025–

TEN YEAR LEAGUE RECORD

		P	W	D	L	F	A	Pts	Pos
2015-16	FL 2	46	17	16	13	67	62	67	10
2016-17	FL 2	46	18	17	11	69	68	71	6
2017-18	FL 2	46	17	16	13	62	54	67	10
2018-19	FL 2	46	20	8	18	67	62	68	11
2019-20	FL 2	37	10	12	15	39	56	42	18§
2020-21	FL 2	46	18	12	16	60	51	66	10
2021-22	FL 2	46	14	11	21	39	62	53	20
2022-23	FL 2	46	20	16	10	66	43	76	5
2023-24	FL 1	46	7	9	30	41	81	30	24
2024-25	FL 2	46	10	12	24	44	71	42	23

§*Decided on points-per-game (1.14)*

DID YOU KNOW ?

Carlisle United hosted the first modern floodlit rugby union match played in the North West of England. The North of England representative team played an exhibition game against the South of Scotland on 11 October 1955, the match ending in a 16-16 draw. The attendance at Brunton Park was 4,000, around half of the average soccer attendance, but considered very large by rugby union standards.

CARLISLE UNITED – SKY BET LEAGUE TWO 2024–25 LEAGUE RECORD

Match No.	Date	Venue	Opponents	Result		H/T Score	Lg Pos.	Goalscorers	Attendance
1	Aug 10	A	Gillingham	L	1-4	0-1	23	Mellish [65]	7037
2	17	H	Barrow	W	1-0	1-0	15	Adu-Adjei [35]	9813
3	24	A	Milton Keynes D	L	0-3	0-2	19		6399
4	31	H	Tranmere R	L	1-2	1-2	20	Davies [7]	8003
5	Sept 7	A	Bradford C	L	1-2	0-1	22	Neal [58]	18,041
6	14	H	Fleetwood T	L	2-3	1-2	22	Wyke 2 (1 pen) [42 (p), 52]	7090
7	21	A	Swindon T	W	2-0	1-0	22	Lavelle [42], Armstrong [72]	6878
8	28	H	Grimsby T	L	2-3	2-1	22	Lavelle [12], Sadi [27]	7510
9	Oct 1	H	Notts Co	L	0-2	0-2	22		5594
10	5	A	Colchester U	D	0-0	0-0	22		4392
11	12	A	AFC Wimbledon	L	0-4	0-3	24		8331
12	19	H	Harrogate T	D	1-1	1-1	23	Armstrong [44]	8297
13	22	A	Walsall	L	1-3	0-1	23	Mellish [82]	4939
14	26	H	Cheltenham T	L	0-1	0-1	23		6064
15	Nov 9	A	Salford C	W	1-0	0-0	23	Barclay [88]	3737
16	16	A	Bromley	D	1-1	0-0	23	Adu-Adjei [90]	3741
17	23	H	Doncaster R	D	0-0	0-0	24		6837
18	30	H	Crewe Alex	D	1-1	1-0	22	Sadi [2]	5839
19	Dec 14	A	Chesterfield	L	0-2	0-1	24		6586
20	21	A	Port Vale	D	0-0	0-0	23		6920
21	26	H	Morecambe	L	0-1	0-0	24		9225
22	29	A	Accrington S	W	2-1	1-0	23	Harris [11], Armstrong [54]	7130
23	Jan 1	A	Crewe Alex	L	2-3	1-1	24	Ellis [21], Harris [78]	6345
24	4	A	Tranmere R	L	0-1	0-1	24		6886
25	18	H	Bradford C	L	0-1	0-0	24		8399
26	25	A	Fleetwood T	W	2-1	1-0	23	Scott [19], Lavelle [85]	3517
27	28	A	Notts Co	L	0-1	0-1	23		8521
28	Feb 1	H	Swindon T	L	1-5	0-1	24	Hugill [88]	7457
29	8	A	Grimsby T	L	1-2	1-0	24	Lavelle [5]	5788
30	11	A	Newport Co	L	0-1	0-0	24		3932
31	15	H	Colchester U	D	0-0	0-0	24		7021
32	22	H	Gillingham	D	0-0	0-0	24		6976
33	27	A	Barrow	W	1-0	1-0	24	Dennis [19]	4213
34	Mar 4	H	Walsall	D	1-1	1-1	24	Hayden [22]	6378
35	8	A	Harrogate T	L	0-1	0-0	24		4136
36	15	H	AFC Wimbledon	L	1-2	0-1	24	Dennis [67]	7050
37	22	H	Bromley	W	2-1	1-1	24	Wearne [13], Whelan [54]	6515
38	25	H	Milton Keynes D	D	2-2	2-2	23	Dennis [26], Harris [45]	6679
39	29	A	Doncaster R	L	0-3	0-1	24		8299
40	Apr 1	A	Chesterfield	L	1-2	0-0	24	Hugill [89]	7508
41	5	H	Newport Co	W	3-2	1-2	24	Kelly 2 [33, 59], Hayden [84]	5889
42	12	A	Morecambe	W	2-0	1-0	23	Kelly [28], Thomas [60]	4901
43	18	H	Port Vale	W	3-2	1-0	23	Kelly [36], Dennis [43], Hayden [49]	12,305
44	21	A	Accrington S	D	1-1	0-0	23	Whelan [90]	3380
45	26	A	Cheltenham T	L	2-3	1-2	23	Dennis [29], Kelly [73]	4963
46	May 3	H	Salford C	D	2-2	2-1	23	Wearne [16], Dennis [17]	8128

Final League Position: 23

GOALSCORERS

League (44): Dennis 6, Kelly 5, Lavelle 4, Armstrong 3, Harris 3, Hayden 3, Adu-Adjei 2, Hugill 2, Mellish 2, Sadi 2, Wearne 2, Whelan 2, Wyke 2 (1 pen), Barclay 1, Davies 1, Ellis 1, Neal 1, Scott 1, Thomas 1.
FA Cup (0).
Carabao Cup (0).
Vertu Trophy (3): Allen 1, O'Donoghue 1, Williams 1.

Note: In the appearance grid below each value is a shirt number; a superscript indicates goals scored (e.g. 6^{2} = shirt 6, 2 goals). Because of the very dense layout, column alignment for some substitute entries is approximate.

Lewis H 14	Davies A 21	Hayden A 23+1	Thomas T 29+3	Melish J 21+2	Williams B 8	Vela J 17+12	Barclay B 14+8	Neal H 13+8	Adu-Adjei D 11+3	Dummett P 1+2	Wyke C 10+3	Williams J 6	Butterworth D —+3	Ellis J 9+12	Armstrong L 13+7	Kelly G 7+11	Lavelle S 35+2	Sadi D 17+5	Jones J 17+4	Bevan J 3+11	Biggins H 13+4	Harper C 30+6	McGeouch D 3+3	O'Donoghue F —+2	Robinson J —+3	Dennis M 11+3	Charters T 2+4	Guy C 12+8	Burey T 5+5	Robson E 1+6	Breeze G 32	Harris K 26+4	Whelan C 22+1	Embleton E 11+7	Dudik A —+1	McArthur C 8+2	Patching W 6+4	Wearne S 13+5	Hugill J 9+8	Scott C 5+6	Fusire S 8+6	Match No.
1	2	3	4	5	6^{2}	7	8^{1}	9	10^{3}	11^{4}	12	13	14	15																												1
1	2	3	4^{1}	5	6^{3}	7	8	9	10^{4}	11^{2}	15	13		14	12																											2
1	2	3		5	6^{3}	7	8^{1}	9	10^{2}	11^{1}	16	14	13	15^{5}	4		12																									3
1	2	3^{2}	4	5	6^{3}	7^{1}	13	9		11	10			15	14		12		8^{4}																							4
1	2		3^{2}	4	5^{1}	7		6^{3}		11				14			13	8	10^{4}	9	12	15																				5
1	2	3^{4}					8				13		14		10		12	4	9^{1}	11	6^{3}	5	7^{2}	15																		6
1	5			4			12	2						10^{3}			9	3	13	11^{1}	6	8	7^{2}	14																		7
1	5		13	12			6	2						11			10	3	8^{2}	9	7^{1}	4																				8
1	2		4	5			8^{1}		12					13			11^{2}	3	7	9	6	10																				9
1	5^{1}		3	4^{3}			9	14	6					10			11^{2}	2	12		7	8		13																		10
1	5^{2}		4				11^{3}	2	7					10^{1}			12	3	9^{4}		6	8		13	14	15																11
1		2	4				7						14				10^{4}	3	9^{3}		5	8		15	11^{1}	6^{2}	12	13														12
1		2^{1}	4	8			9^{4}	16	7						11		3^{5}	12			10	5^{3}			15	6^{2}	14	13														13
1		5	14				16	3^{4}	15		12^{3}			11			4	2			7	6			10^{1}	9^{5}	13	8^{2}														14
	2^{4}	4	8				15	6	11					10^{3}			3	9			13	12				7^{2}	5^{1}				1	14									15
		4	8^{2}	14	2		11							12	15		3	9			7^{4}					13	6	5^{1}			1	10^{3}										16
	2^{3}	4	8^{1}	12			13	11						14			16	3	9		7	15				6^{5}	5^{4}				1	10^{2}									17
	2^{5}		8				4	14	11					16			15	3	9	13		6^{4}	12				7^{2}	5^{1}			1	10^{3}										18
	2	4					9^{1}		13	11				12			3	5	10^{3}	14	6	7^{4}				15	8^{2}				1											19
	2	8					4	7	12					5^{3}	11		3	9^{1}	10^{2}	13	6						14				1										20
	2	8^{4}					4	6	12					5	11		3^{3}	9^{1}	10^{2}	14	7										1	13									21
	2^{2}	4					3	12	10					13	11		8	5	6	7											1	9^{1}									22
		4					2	5	10^{4}					9^{1}	11		3	8^{3}	13	6	7^{2}										1	12									23
	2	4					12	13							11		3	5			6^{1}	8^{2}									1	10	7		9^{3}	14					24
	2^{3}							2^{3}						14	3		8	15													1	5	7	9^{4}		4	6^{2}	10^{1}	11	12	13	25
		12										3^{1}		5^{4}			2		8	15											1	9	7	9^{4}	4	6^{3}		11	10^{2}	6^{3}	13	26
	2^{1}	12												5			3		8										15		1	13	7	9^{4}	4	14		11	10^{2}	6^{3}	27
		3												5			2	13	8^{4}										14		1	9^{4}	7^{3}	10^{1}	4	6^{2}		11	12	15	28
		4					15							2			3^{4}	12				7^{4}							13		1	10	6	9^{3}	5	7^{2}	8^{1}	11	14		29
		3												5^{5}			2	13				16						14			1	8	7	10^{1}	4	6^{4}	9^{1}	11^{2}	12	15	30
	14	4												2^{1}			3	15			12							16		1	10	7	9^{4}	5^{2}	6^{5}	8	11^{2}				31
	2^{3}	4												14			3	8^{2}			5				11^{4}		6^{1}				1	10	7	9^{5}		12	15	16	13		32
	2	4					13							15			3	16			5				11^{5}		6^{3}				1	10^{4}	7^{2}	9^{1}		14	12		8			33
	2	3	5				12							4				13			10^{4}				8^{3}						1	6	9^{2}	7^{1}		14	15		11			34
	2	3	5				12							14	4		16				9				6^{5}						1	10^{4}	8^{1}	7^{2}		15	13		11^{3}			35
	2	4					6^{3}							16	3		8^{1}	10^{5}			5				11^{4}		7^{2}				1	9	13	15		14	12					36
	2	4					6^{1}							13	3		14	10			5				11^{2}		12				1	8	7			9^{3}						37
	2	4					6^{1}							12	3		13	10^{2}			5				11		15				1	8	7^{3}			9^{4}				14		38
	2	4					6^{3}							13	3		10				5^{5}				11^{2}						1	8	7	14		9^{5}				12		39
	5	3					6^{5}	16						13			11^{3}	2^{6}	10^{4}		15										1	9	7^{4}	12^{8}	4		10			8^{1}	40
	2^{1}	3	4				7^{2}							5	10	14		13								13					1	11	6		12		9^{5}	15		8^{3}		41
		3	4				12							2	11	14		5							10^{5}		15				1	8	6^{3}			9^{8}	13				7^{1}	42
		3	4				14							2	11			5							10^{4}		12				1	8	6			9^{3}	13				7^{1}	43
		3	4				12	15						2^{4}	11	14		5							1						1	8	6	13		9^{1}	10^{10}				7^{2}	44
		3	4				12		14					2^{1}	11			5^{4}							10						1	8	7	13		9^{5}	15				6^{3}	45
		3	4				16	15						2	10			5							11^{2}		14				1	8^{4}	6^{3}	12		9^{5}	13				7^{1}	46

FA Cup
First Round *aet.* — Wigan Ath (h) 0-2

Carabao Cup
First Round — Stoke C (h) 0-2

Vertu Trophy
Group C (N) — Nottingham F U21 (h) 1-2
Group C (N) — Wigan Ath (h) 0-2
Group C (N) — Morecambe (a) 2-1

CHARLTON ATHLETIC

FOUNDATION

The club was formed on 9 June 1905, by a group of 14- and 15-year-old youths living in streets by the Thames in the area which now borders the Thames Barrier. The club's progress through local leagues was so rapid that after the First World War they joined the Kent League where they spent a season before turning professional and joining the Southern League in 1920. A year later they were elected to the Football League's Division 3 (South).

The Valley, Floyd Road, Charlton, London SE7 8BL.
Telephone: (020) 8333 4000.
Ticket Office: (03330) 144 444.
Website: www.charltonafc.com
Email: info@cafc.co.uk
Ground Capacity: 27,111.
Record Attendance: 75,031 v Aston Villa, FA Cup 5th rd, 12 February 1938 (at The Valley).
Pitch Measurements: 103m × 68m (112.5yd × 74.5yd).
Non-Executive Chairman: Gavin Carter.
Managing Director: James Rodwell.
Manager: Nathan Jones.
Assistant Manager: Curtis Fleming.
Colours: Red shirts with white and black trim, white shorts with red trim, red socks with white trim.
Year Formed: 1905.
Turned Professional: 1920.
Club Nickname: 'The Addicks'.
Grounds: 1906, Siemen's Meadow; 1907, Woolwich Common; 1909, Pound Park; 1913, Horn Lane; 1920, The Valley; 1923, Catford (The Mount); 1924, The Valley; 1985, Selhurst Park (groundshare with Crystal Palace); 1991, Upton Park (groundshare with West Ham U); 1992, The Valley.
First Football League Game: 27 August 1921, Division 3 (S), v Exeter C (h) W 1–0 – Hughes; Johnny Mitchell, Goodman; Dowling (1), Hampson, Dunn; Castle, Bailey, Halse, Green, Wilson.
Record League Victory: 8–1 v Middlesbrough, Division 1, 12 September 1953 – Bartram; Campbell, Ellis; Fenton, Ufton, Hammond; Hurst (2), O'Linn (2), Leary (1), Firmani (3), Kiernan.
Record Cup Victory: 8–0 v Stevenage, FL Trophy, 9 October 2018 – Phillips; Marshall, Dijksteel, Sarr, Stevenson (3) (Reeves), Lapslie (1), Maloney, Ward (Morgan), Pratley (1), Vetokele (2), Ajose (1).
Record Defeat: 1–11 v Aston Villa, Division 2, 14 November 1959.
Most League Points (2 for a win): 61, Division 3 (S), 1934–35.
Most League Points (3 for a win): 101, FL 1, 2011–12.

HONOURS

League Champions: First Division – 1999–2000; FL 1 – 2011–12; Division 3S – 1928–29, 1934–35.
Runners-up: Division 1 – 1936–37; Division 2 – 1935–36, 1985–86.
FA Cup Winners: 1947.
Runners-up: 1946.
League Cup: quarter-final – 2007, 2023.
Full Members' Cup:
Runners-up 1987.

FOOTBALL YEARBOOK FACT FILE

Match attendances in London were particularly badly affected by daytime bombing raids during the early years of the Second World War, with the FA ruling that play must be stopped whenever an air raid siren was sounded. Charlton Athletic's home game with West Ham United on 30 November 1940 attracted a crowd of just 249. The Addicks were only able to turn out 10 men, fielding centre-half John Oakes in goal, as they went down to a 2-1 defeat.

Most League Goals: 107, Division 2, 1957–58.

Highest League Scorer in Season: Ralph Allen, 32, Division 3 (S), 1934–35.

Most League Goals in Total Aggregate: Stuart Leary, 153, 1953–62.

Most League Goals in One Match: 5, Wilson Lennox v Exeter C, Division 3 (S), 2 February 1929; 5, Eddie Firmani v Aston Villa, Division 1, 5 February 1955; 5, John Summers v Huddersfield T, Division 2, 21 December 1957; 5, John Summers v Portsmouth, Division 2, 1 October 1960.

Most Capped Player: Jonatan Johansson, 44 (includes 1 while on loan at Norwich C) (105), Finland.

Most League Appearances: Sam Bartram, 579, 1934–56.

Youngest League Player: Jonjo Shelvey, 16 years 59 days v Burnley, 26 April 2008.

Record Transfer Fee Received: £16,500,000 from Tottenham H for Darren Bent, June 2007.

Record Transfer Fee Paid: £4,750,000 to Wimbledon for Jason Euell, January 2001.

Football League Record: 1921 Elected to Division 3 (S); 1921–29 Division 3 (S); 1929–33 Division 2; 1933–35 Division 3 (S); 1935–36 Division 2; 1936–57 Division 1; 1957–72 Division 2; 1972–75 Division 3; 1975–80 Division 2; 1980–81 Division 3; 1981–86 Division 2; 1986–90 Division 1; 1990–92 Division 2; 1992–98 First Division; 1998–99 Premier League; 1999–2000 First Division; 2000–07 Premier League; 2007–09 FL C; 2009–12 FL 1; 2012–16 FL C; 2016–19 FL 1; 2019–20 FL C; 2020–25 FL 1; 2025– FL C.

LATEST SEQUENCES

Longest Sequence of League Wins: 12, 26.12.1999 – 7.3.2000.

Longest Sequence of League Defeats: 10, 11.4.1990 – 15.9.1990.

Longest Sequence of League Draws: 6, 13.12.1992 – 16.1.1993.

Longest Sequence of Unbeaten League Matches: 15, 4.10.1980 – 20.12.1980.

Longest Sequence Without a League Win: 18, 18.10.2008 – 17.1.2009.

Successive Scoring Runs: 25 from 26.12.1935.

Successive Non-scoring Runs: 5 from 17.10.2015.

MANAGERS

Walter Rayner 1920–25
Alex Macfarlane 1925–27
Albert Lindon 1928
Alex Macfarlane 1928–32
Albert Lindon 1932–33
Jimmy Seed 1933–56
Jimmy Trotter 1956–61
Frank Hill 1961–65
Bob Stokoe 1965–67
Eddie Firmani 1967–70
Theo Foley 1970–74
Andy Nelson 1974–79
Mike Bailey 1979–81
Alan Mullery 1981–82
Ken Craggs 1982
Lennie Lawrence 1982–91
Steve Gritt and Alan Curbishley 1991–95
Alan Curbishley 1995–2006
Iain Dowie 2006
Les Reed 2006
Alan Pardew 2006–08
Phil Parkinson 2008–11
Chris Powell 2011–14
José Riga 2014
Bob Peeters 2014–15
Guy Luzon 2015
Karel Fraeye 2015–16
José Riga 2016
Russell Slade 2016
Karl Robinson 2016–18
Lee Bowyer 2018–21
Nigel Adkins 2021
Johnny Jackson 2021–22
Ben Garner 2022
Dean Holden 2022–23
Michael Appleton 2023–24
Nathan Jones February 2024–

TEN YEAR LEAGUE RECORD

		P	W	D	L	F	A	Pts	Pos
2015-16	FL C	46	9	13	24	40	80	40	22
2016-17	FL 1	46	14	18	14	60	53	60	13
2017-18	FL 1	46	20	11	15	58	51	71	6
2018-19	FL 1	46	26	10	10	73	40	88	3
2019-20	FL C	46	12	12	22	50	65	48	22
2020-21	FL 1	46	20	14	12	70	56	74	7
2021-22	FL 1	46	17	8	21	55	59	59	13
2022-23	FL 1	46	16	14	16	70	66	62	10
2023-24	FL 1	46	11	20	15	64	65	53	16
2024-25	FL 1	46	25	10	11	67	43	85	4

DID YOU KNOW ?

Wing-half Seth Plum became the first Charlton Athletic player to win full international honours when he appeared for England against France in Paris in May 1923. Plum was one of four amateurs and six debutants in an inexperienced England team that won comfortably 4-1. Shortly afterwards he joined the professional ranks, signing for Chelsea.

CHARLTON ATHLETIC – SKY BET LEAGUE ONE 2024–25 LEAGUE RECORD

Match No.	Date	Venue	Opponents	Result	H/T Score	Lg Pos.	Goalscorers	Attendance
1	Aug 10	A	Wigan Ath	W 1-0	0-0	8	Jones [81]	9564
2	17	H	Leyton Orient	W 1-0	0-0	4	Berry [90]	15,126
3	24	H	Bolton W	W 2-0	1-0	3	Docherty [10], Godden [88]	14,365
4	31	A	Reading	L 0-2	0-0	6		14,778
5	Sept 7	H	Rotherham U	D 1-1	0-0	5	Aneke [72]	13,569
6	14	A	Shrewsbury T	W 1-0	0-0	2	Ahadme [49]	6171
7	21	H	Blackpool	L 1-2	0-2	4	Berry [90]	14,149
8	28	A	Stevenage	L 0-1	0-0	8		4701
9	Oct 1	A	Bristol R	L 2-3	0-1	13	Mitchell A [79], Godden [90]	6638
10	5	H	Birmingham C	W 1-0	0-0	8	Godden [54]	16,250
11	19	H	Stockport Co	D 1-1	0-1	12	Edmonds-Green [66]	13,711
12	22	A	Barnsley	D 2-2	0-1	11	Berry 2 [77, 90]	12,441
13	26	H	Wrexham	D 2-2	1-1	11	Gillesphey [23], Godden (pen) [90]	24,692
14	Nov 9	A	Exeter C	L 0-1	0-0	13		7347
15	23	A	Huddersfield T	L 1-2	1-1	14	Godden (pen) [32]	18,550
16	26	A	Burton Alb	W 1-0	0-0	12	Coventry [82]	1749
17	Dec 3	H	Crawley T	L 1-2	0-1	12	Kanu [68]	11,427
18	7	A	Lincoln C	D 0-0	0-0	12		8307
19	14	H	Mansfield T	D 0-0	0-0	14		14,132
20	21	A	Northampton T	W 5-0	3-0	11	Docherty 2 [9, 68], Campbell T [12], Leaburn [36], Hylton [90]	7015
21	26	H	Cambridge U	W 2-1	2-0	11	Campbell T [1], Leaburn [20]	14,369
22	29	H	Wycombe W	W 2-1	0-0	9	Leaburn 2 [46, 52]	15,544
23	Jan 4	A	Reading	D 0-0	0-0	11		15,526
24	18	A	Rotherham U	L 2-4	1-3	12	Leaburn [45], Godden [90]	8911
25	21	A	Bolton W	W 2-1	0-0	10	Jones [71], Anderson [86]	18,477
26	25	H	Shrewsbury T	W 1-0	0-0	10	Small [90]	12,999
27	28	H	Bristol R	W 2-0	2-0	8	Godden [13], Edwards [36]	11,149
28	Feb 1	A	Blackpool	D 2-2	0-0	7	Godden [52], Casey (og) [54]	9462
29	8	H	Stevenage	W 2-0	1-0	6	Godden [44], Berry [48]	14,093
30	11	H	Peterborough U	W 2-1	0-0	5	Godden (pen) [54], Gillesphey [89]	11,653
31	15	A	Birmingham C	L 0-1	0-1	7		25,542
32	22	H	Exeter C	W 3-0	1-0	7	MacDonald A (og) [20], Campbell T [68], Leaburn [84]	14,864
33	Mar 1	A	Leyton Orient	W 2-1	0-0	6	Ramsay [90], Gillesphey [90]	8942
34	4	H	Barnsley	W 1-0	1-0	5	Gillesphey [12]	12,707
35	8	A	Stockport Co	D 0-0	0-0	5		10,338
36	11	A	Crawley T	W 1-0	1-0	4	Small [37]	5489
37	15	H	Wigan Ath	W 2-1	2-0	4	Godden 2 [11, 38]	16,491
38	22	A	Peterborough U	L 0-3	0-2	4		10,231
39	29	H	Huddersfield T	W 4-0	2-0	4	Godden [1], Campbell T 2 [17, 53], Nicholls (og) [60]	17,278
40	Apr 1	A	Mansfield T	W 2-1	1-1	4	Godden [22], Campbell T [74]	7517
41	5	H	Lincoln C	D 2-2	0-1	5	Gillesphey [56], Docherty [75]	15,611
42	12	A	Cambridge U	W 1-0	1-0	5	Campbell T [14]	6707
43	18	A	Northampton T	W 2-1	1-1	4	Berry [9], Godden [71]	20,198
44	21	A	Wycombe W	W 4-0	2-0	4	Jones [11], Berry [24], Godden [58], Anderson [62]	8084
45	26	A	Wrexham	L 0-3	0-2	5		12,774
46	May 3	H	Burton Alb	W 3-1	2-1	4	Godden 2 [24, 34], Mitchell A [51]	20,971

Final League Position: 4

GOALSCORERS
League (67): Godden 18 (3 pens), Berry 7, Campbell T 7, Leaburn 6, Gillesphey 5, Docherty 4, Jones 3, Anderson 2, Mitchell A 2, Small 2, Ahadme 1, Aneke 1, Coventry 1, Edmonds-Green 1, Edwards 1, Hylton 1, Kanu 1, Ramsay 1, own goals 3.
FA Cup (9): Ahadme 3, Godden 2, Berry 1, Campbell T 1, Leaburn 1, Mitchell Z 1.
Carabao Cup (0).
Vertu Trophy (6): Leaburn 3, Campbell T 1, Edun 1, Godden 1.
League One Play-offs (2): Gillesphey 1, Godden 1.

Mamion W 27+1	Mitchell A 26+5	Jones L 35+1	Gillesphey M 43+1	Ramsay K 30+2	Docherty G 37+3	Coventry C 44	Anderson K 16+22	Edwards J 38	Ahadme G 11+8	Campbell T 37+7	Aneke C —+26	Watson T 6+10	Kanu D 5+12	Berry L 32+9	Small T 32+7	Godden M 29+12	Campbell A 6+6	Edmonds-Green R 5+6	Potts D 1	Leaburn M 14+13	Taylor T 6+2	Dixon K —+3	Hylton D —+6	Maynard-Brewer A 19	Mitchell Z 1	Laqeretabua Joshua —+2	Gilbert A 2+10	McIntyre T 4+6	Mbick M —+4	Fullah I —+1	Enslin K —+1	Match No.
1	2	3	4	5[3]	6[4]	7	8	9	10[2]	11[1]	12	13	14	15																		1
1	2	3	4	5	6	7		9[1]	10[3]	11[2]		13			8	12	14															2
1	2	3	4	5	7	6	14		10[2]	11[1]	12				8[3]	9	13															3
1	2	3	4	5	6	7	12		10[3]	11[12]		13		15	8[1]	9[4]	14															4
1	2	3	4	5	6	7		11[2]	14	12					8[3]	9	10[1]	13														5
1	2	3	4	5	6	7			10[1]	11[12]				12	8[3]	9	14	13														6
1		3	4	5	6[3]	7	14		10[5]	12	16			11[4]	13	9[1]	15	8[2]	2													7
1	2	3	14	5	16	7	6[5]	9[3]		8	12	15	10[4]	13		11[1]				4[2]						'						8
1	2	3	4	16	15	7[5]	6	9[4]	10[1]	11	12	5[3]		8[2]	14			13														9
1		3	4		2	6	7	8	5[3]		12	13		10[1]	14	15	11[2]	9[4]														10
1		3		4	2[1]	6[3]		8	5	10		13			11	9[2]	12			14	7[4]	15										11
1		3		4		6	8[1]	5[3]	15		12			13	14	11	9	2		10[4]	7[2]											12
1		3		4	6[3]	7[5]	8[2]	5		10		2[1]		9[4]		11	15	12		13	14		16									13
		3		4		6	8[3]		5	12				14	13	11	9[2]			10	7[1]		1	2								14
		4		5		7[1]	8	9[4]	6	13	12			14	2	10[2]		3[1]		11[3]			15	1								15
		3		4		7	6[1]	5	10[2]	13				8	14	9[4]		2[3]		11[5]	12		16	1		15						16
	3	16	4[5]		6[3]			5	11	13			14		12	9[4]	8	2[2]		10[1]	7			1		15						17
	2	3	4		7		8[4]	9[3]	10[2]	6				11[1]		15	12	14		13	5			1								18
	2	3	4		8	7[3]		14	6				11	13	9	10[1]		12	5[2]					1								19
	2	3	4		8[1]	5[5]	12	9	13	11[12]				7[4]	6		15	16		10[3]		14		1								20
	2	3	4		7	6	12	5	13	8[3]				9[1]	10			14		11[2]				1								21
	2	3	4		7	6	12	5	13	10				9[1]	8					11[2]				1								22
	3	4	5		9	8		8		6				11[2]	12					7	2	13		10[1]								23
	2	3	4		8[4]	7[5]	14	9		11	12		15	6[2]	5[1]	13	16			10[3]				1								24
	2[1]	3	4		7	6	12	5[5]		10	14			9[2]	8	13		15		11[4]				1								25
	2[4]	3	4	14	7[3]	6	13	5		10	12			9[2]	8	15				11[1]				1								26
		3	4	2	7	6	12	5[4]		10[2]	13	14		9[1]	8	11[3]	15							1								27
		3	4	2	8	5[4]	14	9		11[2]	12			13	7[3]	6	10[1]			15				1								28
		3	4	2	7	6		5		10[1]				13	9[2]	8	11[3]			12				1		14						29
15		3	4	2	7	6		5[1]		10[4]	13			9[3]	8	11[2]				12				1		14						30
12		3	4	2	7	6[4]	13	5		14				9[3]	8[2]	11[5]				15				1[1]		16						31
1		3	4	2		6[1]	7	5[6]		10[3]		16	15	9[1]	8	11[2]				12							13	14				32
1		3	4	2	14	6[4]	7[3]	5[2]		10	15			9[1]	8	11				13							12					33
1		3	4	2	6[5]	7	13	5		10[3]	14	16		9[2]	8[4]	11[1]				12								15				34
1		3	4	2	6	7	13	5		10	12			9[2]	8[1]					11												35
1	15	3	4	2		6	7	5[1]		10[4]				8	12					11[3]	14						9[2]	13				36
1	13	3	4	2	7	6	14			10		8[2]		9[4]	5[3]	11[1]				12								15				37
1		3	4	2	7	6[4]	15		16	10[6]	12	8[1]		9[2]	5	11[3]						13					14	13				38
1		3	4	2	7	6[5]	15			10[3]	12	14		9[4]	8	11[2]				13								16				39
1	15		4	2	7	6	13	5[2]		10[3]	12	14		9[1]	8[4]	11												3				40
1	14		4	2	7[5]	6	10[1]	5	15	12				9[2]	8[4]	11						13					16	3[3]				41
1		4	2	7	6	13	5			10[1]	12	14		9[2]	8[3]	11[4]												3	15			42
1	3		2	7[2]	6	16	5		10[4]	12	15			9[5]	8	11[3]											13	4[1]	14			43
1	3[4]	4	2	7	6	12	5		10[2]	13[4]	14			9[1]	8[5]	11[3]				15							16					44
1	3[1]	4	2	7	6	9[2]	5		10					8[3]	13			11									14	12				45
	3		4	2	7	6[2]	13	5[5]		10[1]				8	14			11[3]									1	9[4]		12	15 16	46

FA Cup

First Round	Southend U	(a)	4-3
aet.			
Second Round	Walsall	(a)	4-0
Third Round	Preston NE	(a)	1-2

Carabao Cup

First Round	Birmingham C	(h)	0-1

Vertu Trophy

Group C (S)	Cambridge U	(a)	2-1
Group C (S)	Chelsea U21	(h)	3-0
Group C (S)	Bromley	(h)	1-0
Second Round	Leyton Orient	(h)	0-2

League One Play-offs

Semi-Final 1st leg	Wycombe W	(a)	0-0
Semi-Final 2nd leg	Wycombe W	(h)	1-0
Final	Leyton Orient	(Wembley)	1-0

CHELSEA

FOUNDATION

Chelsea may never have existed but for the fact that Fulham rejected an offer to rent the Stamford Bridge ground from Mr H. A. Mears who had owned it since 1904. Fortunately he was determined to develop it as a football stadium rather than sell it to the Great Western Railway and got together with Frederick Parker, who persuaded Mears of the financial advantages of developing a major sporting venue. Chelsea FC was formed in 1905 and applications made to join both the Southern League and Football League. The latter competition was decided upon because of its comparatively meagre representation in the south of England.

Stamford Bridge, Fulham Road, London SW6 1HS.
Telephone: (0371) 811 1955.
Ticket Office: (0371) 811 1905.
Website: www.chelseafc.com
Email: enquiries@chelseafc.com
Ground Capacity: 40,173.
Record Attendance: 82,905 v Arsenal, Division 1, 12 October 1935.
Pitch Measurements: 103m × 67.5m (112.5yd × 74yd).
Chairman: Todd Boehly.
President and Chief Operating Officer: Jason Gannon.
Head Coach: Enzo Maresca.
Assistant Head Coach: Willy Cabellero.
Colours: Rush blue patterned shirts with red and white trim, rush blue patterned shorts with red and white trim, white socks with blue trim.
Year Formed: 1905. *Turned Professional:* 1905.
Club Nickname: 'The Blues'.
Ground: 1905, Stamford Bridge.
First Football League Game: 2 September 1905, Division 2, v Stockport Co (a) L 0–1 – Foulke; Mackie, McEwan; Key, Harris, Miller; Moran, Jack Robertson, Copeland, Windridge, Kirwan.
Record League Victory: 8–0 v Wigan Ath, Premier League, 9 May 2010 – Cech; Ivanovic (Belletti), Ashley Cole (1), Ballack (Matic), Terry, Alex, Kalou (1) (Joe Cole), Lampard (pen), Anelka (2), Drogba (3, 1 pen), Malouda; 8–0 v Aston Villa, Premier League, 23 December 2012 – Cech; Azpilicueta, Ivanovic (1), Cahill, Cole, Luiz (1), Lampard (1) (Ramirez (2)), Moses, Mata (Piazon), Hazard (1), Torres (1) (Oscar (1)).

HONOURS

League Champions: Premier League – 2004–05, 2005–06, 2009–10, 2014–15, 2016–17; Division 1 – 1954–55; Division 2 – 1983–84, 1988–89.
Runners-up: Premier League – 2003–04, 2006–07, 2007–08, 2010–11; Division 2 – 1906–07, 1911–12, 1929–30, 1962–63, 1976–77.
FA Cup Winners: 1970, 1997, 2000, 2007, 2009, 2010, 2012, 2018.
Runners-up: 1915, 1967, 1994, 2002, 2017, 2020, 2021, 2022.
League Cup Winners: 1965, 1998, 2005, 2007, 2015.
Runners-up: 1972, 2008, 2019, 2022, 2024.
Full Members' Cup Winners: 1986, 1990.
European Competitions
Champions League: 1999–2000 *(qf)*, 2003–04 *(sf)*, 2004–05 *(sf)*, 2005–06, 2006–07 *(sf)*, 2007–08 *(runners-up)*, 2008–09 *(sf)*, 2009–10, 2010–11 *(qf)*, 2011–12 *(winners)*, 2012–13, 2013–14 *(sf)*, 2014–15, 2015–16, 2017–18, 2019–20, 2020–21 *(winners)*, 2021–22 *(qf)*, 2022–23 *(qf)*.
Fairs Cup: 1958–60 *(qf)*, 1965–66 *(sf)*, 1968–69.
UEFA Cup: 2000–01, 2001–02, 2002–03.
Europa League: 2012–13 *(winners)*, 2018–19 *(winners)*. *European Cup-Winners' Cup:* 1970–71 *(winners)*, 1971–72, 1994–95 *(sf)*, 1997–98 *(winners)*, 1998–99 *(sf)*.
Super Cup: 1998 *(winners)*, 2012, 2013, 2019, 2021 *(winners)*.
Club World Cup: 2012 *(runners-up)*, 2022 *(winners)*, 2025 *(winners)*.

FOOTBALL YEARBOOK FACT FILE

Chelsea introduced a number of innovations for their friendly match with Los Angeles Aztecs in September 1979. A band played on the pitch before the game, there were plans for a USA-style shoot-out if the match finished level, and red and yellow cards were issued to fans to hold in the air when they felt a foul deserved further punishment. The Blues won 2-0 in front of a crowd of just 10,575.

Record Cup Victory: 13–0 v Jeunesse Hautcharage, ECWC, 1st rd 2nd leg, 29 September 1971 – Bonetti; Boyle, Harris (1), Hollins (1p), Webb (1), Hinton, Cooke, Baldwin (3), Osgood (5), Hudson (1), Houseman (1).

Record Defeat: 1–8 v Wolverhampton W, Division 1, 26 September 1953; 0–7 v Nottingham F, Division 1, 20 April 1991.

Most League Points (2 for a win): 57, Division 2, 1906–07.

Most League Points (3 for a win): 99, Division 2, 1988–89.

Most League Goals: 103, Premier League, 2009–10.

Highest League Scorer in Season: Jimmy Greaves, 41, 1960–61.

Most League Goals in Total Aggregate: Bobby Tambling, 164, 1958–70.

Most League Goals in One Match: 5, George Hilsdon v Glossop, Division 2, 1 September 1906; 5, Jimmy Greaves v Wolverhampton W, Division 1, 30 August 1958; 5, Jimmy Greaves v Preston NE, Division 1, 19 December 1959; 5, Jimmy Greaves v WBA, Division 1, 3 December 1960; 5, Bobby Tambling v Aston Villa, Division 1, 17 September 1966; 5, Gordon Durie v Walsall, Division 2, 4 February 1989.

Most Capped Player: Frank Lampard, 104 (106), England.

Most League Appearances: Ron Harris, 655, 1962–80.

Youngest League Player: Ian Hamilton, 16 years 138 days v Tottenham H, 18 March 1967.

Record Transfer Fee Received: £88,500,000 from Real Madrid for Eden Hazard, June 2019.

Record Transfer Fee Paid: £115,000,000 to Brighton & HA for Moises Caicedo, August 2023.

Football League Record: 1905 Elected to Division 2; 1905–07 Division 2; 1907–10 Division 1; 1910–12 Division 2; 1912–24 Division 1; 1924–30 Division 2; 1930–62 Division 1; 1962–63 Division 2; 1963–75 Division 1; 1975–77 Division 2; 1977–79 Division 1; 1979–84 Division 1; 1984–88 Division 1; 1988–89 Division 2; 1989–92 Division 1; 1992– Premier League.

LATEST SEQUENCES

Longest Sequence of League Wins: 13, 1.10.2016 – 31.12.2016.

Longest Sequence of League Defeats: 7, 1.11.1952 – 20.12.1952.

Longest Sequence of League Draws: 6, 20.8.1969 – 13.9.1969.

Longest Sequence of Unbeaten League Matches: 40, 23.10.2004 – 29.10.2005.

Longest Sequence Without a League Win: 21, 3.11.1987 – 2.4.1988.

Successive Scoring Runs: 27 from 29.10.1988.

Successive Non-scoring Runs: 9 from 14.3.1981.

MANAGERS

John Tait Robertson 1905–07
David Calderhead 1907–33
Leslie Knighton 1933–39
Billy Birrell 1939–52
Ted Drake 1952–61
Tommy Docherty 1961–67
Dave Sexton 1967–74
Ron Suart 1974–75
Eddie McCreadie 1975–77
Ken Shellito 1977–78
Danny Blanchflower 1978–79
Geoff Hurst 1979–81
John Neal 1981–85 (*Director to 1986*)
John Hollins 1985–88
Bobby Campbell 1988–91
Ian Porterfield 1991–93
David Webb 1993
Glenn Hoddle 1993–96
Ruud Gullit 1996–98
Gianluca Vialli 1998–2000
Claudio Ranieri 2000–04
Jose Mourinho 2004–07
Avram Grant 2007–08
Luiz Felipe Scolari 2008–09
Guus Hiddink 2009
Carlo Ancelotti 2009–11
Andre Villas-Boas 2011–12
Roberto Di Matteo 2012
Rafael Benitez 2012–13
Jose Mourinho 2013–15
Guus Hiddink 2015–16
Antonio Conte 2016–18
Maurizio Sarri 2018–19
Frank Lampard 2019–21
Thomas Tuchel 2021–22
Graham Potter 2022–23
Frank Lampard 2023
Mauricio Pochettino 2023–24
Enzo Maresca July 2024–

TEN YEAR LEAGUE RECORD

		P	W	D	L	F	A	Pts	Pos
2015-16	PR Lge	38	12	14	12	59	53	50	10
2016-17	PR Lge	38	30	3	5	85	33	93	1
2017-18	PR Lge	38	21	7	10	62	38	70	5
2018-19	PR Lge	38	21	9	8	63	39	72	3
2019-20	PR Lge	38	20	6	12	69	54	66	4
2020-21	PR Lge	38	19	10	9	58	36	67	4
2021-22	PR Lge	38	21	11	6	76	33	74	3
2022-23	PR Lge	38	11	11	16	38	47	44	12
2023-24	PR Lge	38	18	9	11	77	63	63	6
2024-25	PR Lge	38	20	9	9	64	43	69	4

DID YOU KNOW ?

Chelsea visited Algeria in May 1951 where they played four games as part of the events to mark the 30th anniversary of the regional football leagues in Algiers and Oran, which at the time were part of the national pyramid of French football. The Blues played against representative teams of both leagues as well as against touring teams Austria Vienna and Real Valladolid (Spain).

CHELSEA – PREMIER LEAGUE 2024–25 LEAGUE RECORD

Match No.	Date	Venue	Opponents	Result	H/T Score	Lg Pos.	Goalscorers	Attendance
1	Aug 18	H	Manchester C	L	0-2	0-1	17		39,818
2	25	A	Wolverhampton W	W	6-2	2-2	8	Jackson [2], Palmer [45], Madueke 3 [49, 58, 63], Joao Felix [80]	31,235
3	Sept 1	H	Crystal Palace	D	1-1	1-0	11	Jackson [25]	39,298
4	14	A	Bournemouth	W	1-0	0-0	7	Nkunku [86]	11,235
5	21	A	West Ham U	W	3-0	2-0	4	Jackson 2 [4, 18], Palmer [47]	62,473
6	28	H	Brighton & HA	W	4-2	4-2	4	Palmer 4 (1 pen) [21, 28 (p), 31, 41]	39,495
7	Oct 6	A	Nottingham F	D	1-1	0-0	4	Madueke [57]	39,501
8	20	A	Liverpool	L	1-2	0-1	6	Jackson [48]	60,277
9	27	H	Newcastle U	W	2-1	1-1	5	Jackson [18], Palmer [47]	39,526
10	Nov 3	A	Manchester U	D	1-1	0-0	4	Caicedo [74]	73,813
11	10	H	Arsenal	D	1-1	0-0	3	Pedro Neto [70]	39,780
12	23	A	Leicester C	W	2-1	1-0	3	Jackson [15], Fernandez [75]	31,880
13	Dec 1	A	Aston Villa	W	3-0	2-0	2	Jackson [7], Fernandez [36], Palmer [83]	39,689
14	4	A	Southampton	W	5-1	3-1	2	Disasi [7], Nkunku [17], Madueke [34], Palmer [76], Sancho [87]	31,193
15	8	A	Tottenham H	W	4-3	1-2	2	Sancho [17], Palmer 2 (2 pens) [61, 84], Fernandez [73]	61,184
16	15	H	Brentford	W	2-1	1-0	2	Cucurella [43], Jackson [80]	39,751
17	22	A	Everton	D	0-0	0-0	2		39,308
18	26	H	Fulham	L	1-2	1-0	2	Palmer [16]	39,687
19	30	A	Ipswich T	L	0-2	0-1	4		29,968
20	Jan 4	A	Crystal Palace	D	1-1	1-0	4	Palmer [14]	25,179
21	14	H	Bournemouth	D	2-2	1-0	4	Palmer [13], James [90]	39,092
22	20	H	Wolverhampton W	W	3-1	1-1	4	Adarabioyo [24], Cucurella [60], Madueke [65]	39,221
23	25	A	Manchester C	L	1-3	0-1	6	Madueke [3]	52,793
24	Feb 3	H	West Ham U	W	2-1	0-1	4	Pedro Neto [64], Wan Bissaka (og) [74]	39,459
25	14	A	Brighton & HA	L	0-3	0-2	4		31,503
26	22	A	Aston Villa	L	1-2	1-0	6	Fernandez [9]	42,423
27	25	H	Southampton	W	4-0	3-0	4	Nkunku [24], Pedro Neto [36], Colwill [44], Cucurella [78]	39,485
28	Mar 9	A	Leicester C	W	1-0	0-0	4	Cucurella [60]	39,750
29	16	H	Arsenal	L	0-1	0-1	4		60,311
30	Apr 3	H	Tottenham H	W	1-0	0-0	4	Fernandez [50]	39,852
31	6	A	Brentford	D	0-0	0-0	4		17,183
32	13	H	Ipswich T	D	2-2	0-2	6	Tuanzebe (og) [46], Sancho [79]	39,805
33	20	H	Fulham	W	2-1	0-1	5	George [83], Pedro Neto [90]	27,712
34	26	H	Everton	W	1-0	1-0	5	Jackson [27]	39,894
35	May 4	H	Liverpool	W	3-1	1-0	5	Fernandez [3], Quansah (og) [56], Palmer (pen) [90]	39,829
36	11	A	Newcastle U	L	0-2	0-1	5		52,231
37	16	H	Manchester U	W	1-0	0-0	4	Cucurella [71]	39,849
38	25	A	Nottingham F	W	1-0	0-0	4	Colwill [50]	30,263

Final League Position: 4

GOALSCORERS

League (64): Palmer 15 (4 pens), Jackson 10, Madueke 7, Fernandez 6, Cucurella 5, Pedro Neto 4, Nkunku 3, Sancho 3, Colwill 2, Adarabioyo 1, Caicedo 1, Disasi 1, George 1, James 1, Joao Felix 1, own goals 3.
FA Cup (6): Adarabioyo 2, Joao Felix 2, Nkunku 1, own goal 1.
Carabao Cup (5): Nkunku 3, Pedro Neto 1, own goal 1.
(Chelsea U21) Vertu Trophy (3): Vale 2, McNeilly 1.
UEFA Conference League (45): Nkunku 7 (4 pens), Guiu 6, Dewsbury-Hall 4, Joao Felix 4, Madueke 4, Jackson 3, Mudryk 3, Cucurella 2, Fernandez 2, Sancho 2, Veiga 2, Adarabioyo 1, Caicedo 1, Disasi 1, George 1, James 1, Pedro Neto 1.
FIFA Club World Cup (17): Neto 3, Palmer 3, Joao Pedro 3, Adarabioyo 1, Delap 1, Dewsbury-Hall 1, Fernandez 1, George 1, James 1, Nkunku 1, own goal 1.

Sanchez R 32	Gusto M 19+13	Fofana W 14	Colwill L 35	Cucurella M 33+3	Caicedo M 38	Lavia R 11+5	Palmer C 36+1	Fernandez E 32+4	Nkunku C 9+18	Jackson N 28+2	Pedro Neto L 24+11	Dewsbury-Hall K 2+11	Guiu M —+3	Veiga M R 1+6	Madueke N 27+5	Mudryk M 1+6	Joao Felix S 3+9	Disasi A 4+2	Sancho J 19+12	Adarabioyo T 15+7	James R 12+7	Badiashile B 3+2	Jorgensen F 6	Acheampong J 2+2	Chalobah T 11+2	George T 1+7	Amougou M —+1	Mheuka S —+1	Match No.
1	2	3	4	5^4	6	7^3	8	9	10^1	11^2	12	13	14	15															1
1	2	3	4	5^4	6^3		9^5	7	15	11^2	12	14	16		8	10^1	13												2
1	2^2	3	4	5	6		9	7	14	11	10^1				8^3	13	12												3
1		3	4	5	6		9	15	11^4	10^1					7	8^2	13	2^3	12	14									4
1	2^2		4	5	6	9^4	7^5	15	11^3	13	16				8	14	12		10^1	3									5
1	2	3	4	5^2	6	16	9	7^4	15	11^5	12	13			8^1	14	10^3												6
1	2	3	4^4	5	6		9	7^2	13	11^1	15				8^3	14	12		10^5	16									7
1	5		4		6	7^2	9	15	16	11	12		14		8^5				10^1	3^4	2^3	13							8
1	2^3	3	4	15	6	7^2	9	13	14	11^4	10				8^1			12				5							9
1	2^3	3	4	12	6	7^3	9	11	10						8^2			13				5							10
1	2^3	3	4	12	6	7^3	9	13	15	11^4	10				8^1			12				5							11
1	2		4	5	6^2	13	9	7	12	11^4	15				8^3				10^1	14	3								12
1	16	3^1	4	5	2	6^4	9^5	7	13	11^3	8				14		15		10^2	12									13
	2			5^2	7		9^3	6	11			13			8	10^1	3	12	14		1								14
1	12		4	5^5	2	6^1	9	7	13	11^2	8^3				16	14			10^1	5	3								15
1	2		4	5^4	6		9	7	12	11^1					8				10^1	3									16
1	5		4		6		9	7	12	11^1	8^2				13			2	10	3									17
1	2		4	5	7		9	6	12	11^1	8								10^3	3									18
	14		4	5	7		9	6	11^2	12	15				8^4		10^1	2^3	13	3		1							19
1	2		4	5	7		9	6		11^1	8	12			13				10^2					3					20
1			4	5	2^3	6^1	9	7		11	15				8^4	14		10	13	12				3^2					21
1	14			5	7		9^5			11	10^1	6^3			8^4	16	13	12	3	2^2					4	15			22
1	13		4	5	6		9	7	12	11^1	14				8^4		10^3	2^2		3									23
	15		4	5	7		9^5	6	14	11^1	13			12	8^4		10^2	3	2^3	1					16				24
	2^2		4	5	6^3		9	7	11		10^4	15			8^1				12		13		1		3	14			25
	2		4	5	7		8	9	10^2		11								13	12	6		1		3^1				26
	2		4	5	7^3		9	6		10^4	11^2	13			8^1		3			1		15			12	14	16		27
1		2^2	4	5	7		9^1	6	10^3		11				8		3				14	13	12						28
1	15	2^4	3	5	7	14		9	10^1		11	13			8^2	16	6^3	4^5							12				29
1	2		4	5	6		9^4	7^3		11^2	8	14			12				10^1	15	13				3				30
1	2		15	7		13	6	11	11^1	12	14	9^3			8^2				10	4	5^4				3				31
1	12		4	5	2		9	6	14	11^3	10				8^2				13	3^1					2				32
1	13^4		4	5	7		9	6		11^3	10				8^2				12	15	2^1				3	14			33
1		3	4	6	7^1	9^4	10		11^3	5	15				8^2				13		12				2	14			34
1	13		4	5	2		6	9	7^3	11^1	8				10				12	14					3				35
1	14		4	5	2		6^2	9	7	11^1	8				10^1				13	12					3^3				36
1	13		4	5	7	12	9	6		8^2					10				3	2						11^1			37
1	13		4	5	7	12	9	6		11^2	14				8^3				10^1	3	2								38

FA Cup

Third Round	Morecambe	(h)	5-0
Fourth Round	Brighton & HA	(a)	1-2

Carabao Cup

Third Round	Barrow	(h)	5-0
Fourth Round	Newcastle U	(a)	0-2

Vertu Trophy (Chelsea U21)

Group C (S)	Bromley	(a)	3-2
Group C (S)	Charlton Ath	(a)	0-3
Group C (S)	Cambridge U	(a)	0-1

FIFA Club World Cup

Group D	Los Angeles	(n)	2-0
Group D	Flamengo	(n)	1-3
Group D	Esperance de Tunis	(n)	3-0
Round of 16	Benfica	(n)	4-1
aet.			
Quarter-finals	Palmeiras	(n)	2-1
Semi-finals	Fluminense	(n)	2-0
Final	Paris Saint-Germain	(n)	3-0

UEFA Conference League

Qualifying Play-off 1st leg	Servette	(h)	2-0
Qualifying Play-off 2nd leg	Servette	(a)	1-2
League game	Gent	(h)	4-2
League game	Panathinaikos	(a)	4-1
League game	Noah	(h)	8-0
League game	1.FC Heidenheim	(a)	2-0
League game	Astana	(a)	3-1
League game	Shamrock R	(h)	5-1
Round of 16 1st leg	FC Copenhagen	(a)	2-1
Round of 16 2nd leg	FC Copenhagen	(h)	1-0
Quarter-Final 1st leg	Legia Warsaw	(a)	3-0
Quarter-Final 2nd leg	Legia Warsaw	(h)	1-2
Semi-Final 1st leg	Djurgarden	(a)	4-1
Semi-Final 2nd leg	Djurgarden	(h)	1-0
Final	Real Betis (Wroclaw)		4-1

CHELTENHAM TOWN

FOUNDATION

The origins of Cheltenham Town date back to around 1887. A key figure in the development of football in the town was Albert Close White who had learnt the game while studying at St Mark's Teacher Training College in Chelsea. He returned to Cheltenham in 1884 and for the next 40 years he was a teacher at Cheltenham Parish Boys' School, where he introduced a range of sporting activities including association football. He later recalled the formation of the Cheltenham Town club: 'The club was started somewhere between 1884–7, and its first matches were more or less practice or scratch games, and were played on the East Gloucestershire Cricket Ground.' A fixture list from 1894–95 gave the club's ground as Eldorado Road, with team colours of chocolate and blue.

The EV Charger Points Stadium, Whaddon Road, Cheltenham, Gloucestershire GL52 5NA.

Telephone: (01242) 573 558.

Ticket Office: (01242) 573 558 (option 1).

Website: www.ctfc.com

Email: info@ctfc.com

Ground Capacity: 6,868.

Record Attendance: 10,389 v Blackpool, FA Cup 3rd rd, 13 January 1934 (at Cheltenham Athletic Ground); 8,326 v Reading, FA Cup 1st rd, 17 November 1956 (at Whaddon Road).

Pitch Measurements: 100m × 65m (109.5yd × 71yd).

Chairman: David Bloxham.

Head of Commercial: Linton Brown.

Manager: Michael Flynn.

Assistant Manager: Aaron Downes.

Colours: Red and white striped shirts with black trim, black shorts with red trim, red socks with black trim.

Year Formed: 1887.

Turned Professional: 1932.

Club Nickname: 'The Robins'.

Grounds: Pre-1932, Agg-Gardner's Recreation Ground; Whaddon Lane; Carter's Lane; 1932, Whaddon Road (renamed The Abbey Business Stadium 2009; World of Smile Stadium 2015; LCI Rail Stadium 2016; The Jonny-Rocks Stadium 2019; The Completely Suzuki Stadium 2022; The EV Charger Points Stadium 2024).

First Football League Game: 7 August 1999, Division 3, v Rochdale (h) L 0–2 – Book; Griffin, Victory, Banks, Freeman, Brough (Howarth), Howells, Bloomer (Devaney), Grayson, Watkins (McAuley), Yates.

Record League Victory: 5–0 v Mansfield T, FL 2, 6 May 2006 – Higgs; Gallinagh, Bell, McCann (1) (Connolly), Caines, Duff, Wilson, Bird (1p), Gillespie (1) (Spencer), Guinan (Odejayi (1)), Vincent (1).

HONOURS

League Champions: FL 2 – 2020–21; Football Conference – 1998–99; National League 2015–16.
Runners-up: Football Conference – 1997–98.
FA Cup: 5th rd – 2002.
League Cup: 3rd rd – 2022.

FOOTBALL YEARBOOK FACT FILE

Cheltenham Town took part in the FA Trophy every season from the competition's formation in 1969–70 through to 1998–99 and again in 2015–16, but their highest-ever victory came in their first game in the competition. The Robins were drawn at home to South Western League club St Blazey and romped to an 8-0 victory. Four players scored two goals each: Gerald Horlick, Tony Cooper, Ralph Norton and Keith Wiggan.

Record Cup Victory: 12–0 v Chippenham R, FA Cup 3rd qual. rd, 2 November 1935 – Bowles; Whitehouse, Williams; Lang, Devonport (1), Partridge (2); Perkins, Hackett, Jones (4), Black (4), Griffiths (1).

Record Defeat: 1–8 v Crewe Alex, FL 2, 2 April 2011; 0–7 v Crystal Palace, League Cup 2nd rd, 2 October 2002; 0–7 v Exeter C, League Cup 1st rd, 9 August 2022.
N.B. 1–10 v Merthyr T, Southern League, 8 March 1952.

Most League Points (2 for a win): 60, Southern League Division 1, 1963–64.

Most League Points (3 for a win): 82, FL 2, 2020–21.

Most League Goals: 67, FL 2, 2017–18.

Highest League Scorer in Season: Mo Eisa, 23, FL 2, 2017–18; Alfie May, 23, FL 1, 2021–22.

Most League Goals in Total Aggregate: Alfie May, 58, 2019–23.

Most League Goals in One Match: 4, Alfie May v Wycombe W, FL 1, 19 February 2022.

Most Capped Player: Grant McCann, 9 (39), Northern Ireland.

Most League Appearances: David Bird, 288, 2001–11.

Youngest League Player: Kyle Haynes, 17 years 85 days v Oldham Ath, 24 March 2009.

Record Transfer Fee Received: £1,400,000 from Bristol C for Mo Eisa, July 2018.

Record Transfer Fee Paid: £75,000 to Sligo R for Aidan Keena, January 2023.

Football League Record: 1999 Promoted from Football Conference; 1999–2002 Third Division; 2002–03 Second Division; 2003–04 Third Division; 2004–06 FL 2; 2006–09 FL 1; 2009–15 FL 2; 2015–16 National League; 2016–21 FL 2; 2021–24 FL 1; 2024– FL 2.

LATEST SEQUENCES

Longest Sequence of League Wins: 5, 11.2.2020 – 29.2.2020.

Longest Sequence of League Defeats: 7, 26.8.2023 – 3.10.2023.

Longest Sequence of League Draws: 5, 5.4.2003 – 21.4.2003.

Longest Sequence of Unbeaten League Matches: 16, 1.12.2001 – 12.3.2002.

Longest Sequence Without a League Win: 14, 20.12.2008 – 7.3.2009.

Successive Scoring Runs: 17 from 16.2.2008.

Successive Non-scoring Runs: 11 from 5.8.2023.

MANAGERS

George Blackburn 1932–34
George Carr 1934–37
Jimmy Brain 1937–48
Cyril Dean 1948–50
George Summerbee 1950–52
William Raeside 1952–53
Arch Anderson 1953–58
Ron Lewin 1958–60
Peter Donnelly 1960–61
Tommy Cavanagh 1961
Arch Anderson 1961–65
Harold Fletcher 1965–66
Bob Etheridge 1966–73
Willie Penman 1973–74
Dennis Allen 1974–79
Terry Paine 1979
Alan Grundy 1979–82
Alan Wood 1982–83
John Murphy 1983–88
Jim Barron 1988–90
John Murphy 1990
Dave Lewis 1990–91
Ally Robertson 1991–92
Lindsay Parsons 1992–95
Chris Robinson 1995–97
Steve Cotterill 1997–2002
Graham Allner 2002–03
Bobby Gould 2003
John Ward 2003–07
Keith Downing 2007–08
Martin Allen 2008–09
Mark Yates 2009–14
Paul Buckle 2014–15
Gary Johnson 2015–18
Michael Duff 2018–22
Wade Elliott 2022–23
Darrell Clarke 2023–24
Michael Flynn May 2024–

TEN YEAR LEAGUE RECORD

		P	W	D	L	F	A	Pts	Pos
2015-16	NL	46	30	11	5	87	30	101	1
2016-17	FL 2	46	12	14	20	49	69	50	21
2017-18	FL 2	46	13	12	21	67	73	51	17
2018-19	FL 2	46	15	12	19	57	68	57	16
2019-20	FL 2	36	17	13	6	52	27	64	4§
2020-21	FL 2	46	24	10	12	61	39	82	1
2021-22	FL 1	46	13	17	16	66	80	56	15
2022-23	FL 1	46	14	12	20	45	61	54	16
2023-24	FL 1	46	12	8	26	41	65	44	21
2024-25	FL 2	46	16	12	18	60	70	60	15

§*Decided on points-per-game (1.78)*

DID YOU KNOW ?

The England Semi-Professional squad that defeated Netherlands at Crawley on 3 March 1998 included five Cheltenham Town players. Dale Watkins, Chris Banks, Lee Howells and Neil Grayson were all in the starting line-up, while Jamie Victory came off the bench with 18 minutes remaining. Grayson, who scored one of England's goals, had recently signed from Hereford United and had yet to make his debut for the Robins.

CHELTENHAM TOWN – SKY BET LEAGUE TWO 2024–25 LEAGUE RECORD

Match No.	Date		Venue	Opponents	Result		H/T Score	Lg Pos.	Goalscorers	Attendance
1	Aug	10	H	Newport Co	W	3-2	2-2	6	Colwill 2 [22, 90], Dulson [27]	4613
2		17	A	Grimsby T	L	2-3	0-1	10	Young [61], Taylor [82]	5885
3		24	H	AFC Wimbledon	L	0-1	0-0	16		4256
4		31	A	Walsall	L	1-2	0-0	19	Miller [85]	5760
5	Sept	7	H	Harrogate T	W	1-0	0-0	15	Bradbury [90]	3594
6		14	A	Salford C	L	1-2	0-0	19	Archer [48]	2347
7		21	A	Chesterfield	D	1-1	0-1	17	Jude-Boyd [53]	7652
8		28	H	Fleetwood T	L	0-2	0-1	20		3928
9	Oct	1	H	Accrington S	W	2-1	0-1	16	Norkett [69], Bowman [80]	2976
10		5	A	Barrow	L	1-2	1-0	20	Bowman [41]	3518
11		12	H	Swindon T	L	2-3	0-2	21	Miller [63], Archer [78]	5561
12		19	A	Colchester U	W	2-1	2-1	17	Thomas 2 [5, 45]	4031
13		22	H	Bradford C	D	1-1	1-1	17	Young [15]	3404
14		26	A	Carlisle U	W	1-0	1-0	16	Archer [17]	6064
15	Nov	9	H	Bromley	W	1-0	0-0	16	Archer [50]	3786
16		16	A	Milton Keynes D	L	2-3	2-1	16	Young [6], Miller [13]	7333
17		22	H	Tranmere R	W	1-0	0-0	14	Colwill [89]	3939
18	Dec	3	H	Port Vale	D	1-1	0-0	15	Miller [53]	3245
19		7	A	Doncaster R	D	2-2	1-0	15	Bailey (og) [15], Archer [56]	6259
20		14	H	Morecambe	W	2-0	1-0	13	Jude-Boyd [33], Miller [74]	3371
21		20	A	Gillingham	D	2-2	1-1	13	Young [36], Miller [60]	5938
22		26	H	Crewe Alex	W	2-1	0-0	14	Colwill 2 [70, 83]	5261
23		29	A	Notts Co	L	3-5	1-2	14	Stubbs [4], Bowman [47], Colwill [60]	5430
24	Jan	1	A	Port Vale	D	0-0	0-0	13		5873
25		17	A	Harrogate T	L	0-2	0-1	13		2522
26		25	H	Salford C	W	2-1	1-0	14	Backwell [31], Thomas [80]	4187
27		28	A	Accrington S	D	0-0	0-0	14		1605
28	Feb	1	H	Chesterfield	W	1-0	0-0	12	Jude-Boyd [90]	3869
29		8	H	Fleetwood T	L	0-2	0-1	16		2257
30		15	H	Barrow	W	3-2	0-1	13	Taylor 2 [60, 70], Hay [76]	4404
31		22	A	Newport Co	W	3-0	1-0	11	Taylor [30], Williams [53], Archer [82]	4987
32		25	H	Walsall	D	2-2	0-1	11	Thomas [90], Miller [90]	4454
33	Mar	1	H	Grimsby T	D	1-1	1-0	12	Williams [26]	4473
34		4	A	Bradford C	L	0-3	0-1	13		15,229
35		8	H	Colchester U	L	0-1	0-0	14		3954
36		11	A	AFC Wimbledon	W	2-1	1-1	13	Hay [24], Taylor [79]	8114
37		15	A	Swindon T	D	3-3	1-1	13	Thomas [8], Wright (og) [54], Dieng [48]	8556
38		22	H	Milton Keynes D	L	0-1	0-1	14		4283
39		28	A	Tranmere R	L	0-2	0-1	14		6650
40	Apr	1	A	Morecambe	L	0-2	0-0	15		2502
41		5	H	Doncaster R	L	0-2	0-0	16		3897
42		10	A	Crewe Alex	W	3-2	1-1	15	Miller [22], Thomas [78], Dulson [86]	4939
43		18	H	Gillingham	D	1-1	1-1	16	Stubbs [22]	4702
44		21	A	Notts Co	W	2-1	0-0	16	Thomas [75], Archer [89]	10,642
45		26	H	Carlisle U	W	3-2	2-1	15	Thomas (pen) [33], Hay [45], Miller [90]	4963
46	May	3	A	Bromley	L	0-3	0-2	15		2818

Final League Position: 15

GOALSCORERS

League (60): Miller 9, Thomas 8 (1 pen), Archer 7, Colwill 6, Taylor 5, Young 4, Bowman 3, Hay 3, Jude-Boyd 3, Dulson 2, Stubbs 2, Williams 2, Backwell 1, Bradbury 1, Dieng 1, Norkett 1, own goals 2.
FA Cup (3): Colwill 2, Archer 1.
Carabao Cup (0).
Vertu Trophy (12): Miller 2, Pett 2, Taylor 2 (1 pen), Colwill 1, Dulson 1, Jude-Boyd 1, King 1, Sohna 1, Thomas 1.

Evans O 11	Laing L 3+3	Bennett S 25+1	Bakare I 18+12	Payne L 12+5	Kinsella L 33+4	Sohna H 6+2	Haynes R 11+2	Colwill J 20+2	Dulson L 8+21	Bowman R 8+9	Taylor M 10+27	Pett T 5+15	Archer E 42+4	Thomas J 32+8	Miller G 26+14	Jude-Boyd A 29+5	Young L 33+1	Stubbs S 41	Willcox F —+2	Bradbury T 38+1	Shipley L 5+3	Norkett M 2+3	Day J 35	Power D 5+7	Adedokun V 11+4	Hay A 10+11	Backwell T 10+3	Williams E 8+9	Dieng T 9+6	King T —+4	Tustin H —+1	Match No.
1	2	3	4	5	6³	7¹	8⁴	9	10²	11⁵	12	13	14	15	16																	1
1	2⁴	3	4		6¹		5²	9	7	10³	11	14	8⁵	15	16		12	13														2
1	2	7⁴	4³					8⁵	9	13	11	10¹	16	14	15	12		5	6²	3												3
1		4	2²				5⁴	7	11	10³		14	9¹	12	13	6		8	3	15												4
1	3		5⁴		7⁵	8³		11²	13	10		9¹	12	14			6	2		4	15	16										5
1	4		2	14⁵	6¹	9³	13	16	11⁴		10		7²	8	3		5	12	15													6
1	4	2		14			9	13		11²	12	10		7¹	8	3		5	6³													7
1	4²		2³				9	14	12	11	13	7		10¹		8	3		5	6												8
1	13	6¹		2			10²		11		9	8			7	3		4	5	12												9
1			2				8²	13	11		9³	6		14		7	3	12	4	5	10¹											10
1		3²	14	5⁵	15		16	10		7¹	8	12	13	6⁴	10³	8	3		4	9⁴	11³											11
12		4¹	14	2²	7⁵	9		15	13			16	11	6⁴	10³	8	3	5		1												12
		3	12	2¹	6	5		9²		14	13		10	8	11³		7			4			1									13
		3	13	5	6	8²		15		14		12	10	9³	11⁴		7¹	2		4			1									14
		4	14	2³	6⁵			9²		15	16	12	10	8¹	11⁴	13	7	3		5			1									15
		2	3⁴	5⁵	6			9¹	12	15	16	14	10	8³	11²		7			4	13		1									16
		4		2¹	6			9			12	14	10³	8	11²	13	7	3		5			1									17
	14		3		6			8³			12	13	9²	10	11¹	2	7	4		5			1									18
		3	13	7				9¹			14	12	10	8²	11³	2	6	4		5			1									19
		3	15	7				9³	12		13	14	10⁴	8²	11¹	2	6	4		5			1									20
		3	12	6				9¹	14		13		10	8	11²	2³	7	4		5			1									21
		3		7¹				9		12		13	10	8	11²	2	6	4		5			1									22
		3¹	13	7⁴				9	14	12	16	15	10³	8	11²	2	6⁵	4		5			1									23
		4¹		2	7			9	14	11²	12		10³	8		13	6	3		5			1									24
		4			6¹						12		9	8⁵	15	10	7	3					1		2	5⁴	11³	13	14			25
		4	15		6						12		10	8⁴	11¹	2³	7	3		5			1		14		13	9²				26
		4			7						13		10	8³	11²	2	6	3		5			1			14	9¹	12				27
		4¹	16		6								10	8	13	2⁵	7	3		5		1	15	12	11²	9³	14					28
					6¹				10²		14		9	8	11³	2⁴	7⁵	3		4			1	15	5	16		12	13			29
		6²	14								12		9	8⁴	11¹	2	7	3		4			1	15	5	13		10³				30
		12			13						14		9		15	2	7⁵	3		4			1	6¹	5	8⁴		10¹	16			31
			15						16				8	12	14	6	7⁵	3		4			1	2²	5⁴	10³		9	13			32
					13				14		15		9⁴	8³	11²	2	7	3		4			1		5	12		10	6¹			33
		3		16					15		11³		8	12	14	6	7⁴			4			1	2	5¹	10⁹		9²	13			34
					6				15				9	8	11³	2¹	7⁴	3		4			1	12	5	14		10²	13			35
		3			6				13				9	8	10¹		4	5		1	2¹	12	11			14	7					36
		2			8				12				9	6³	11¹			3		4⁸			1		5	10²	13	14	7			37
		3⁵			2				13				11³	10	8	16	12			4			1		5⁴	14	7¹	9⁴	6	15		38
					6²				15				9	8	13	2		3		4			1		5⁴	11³	12	10¹	7	14		39
		2			6		15		13		11⁵		9³	8	10¹	5		3		4²			1		14	12		16	7			40
		4			6		14		12				10	8	11¹	2⁴		3		5³			1			13	9²		7⁸	15		41
		7²	15		6		9¹		13		14		8	5⁴	11³	2		3		4			1	12		10						42
		4¹	16		6		5⁵		10⁴		13		9³	8	11²	2		3		12			1		15	7	14					43
		13			6		5¹		12		14		10	8	11⁴	2		3		4			1		15	9²		7³				44
		16			6		5²		10¹		15		9	8	14	2		3		4⁹			1	12	11⁴	7³		13				45
		3⁴			5		9⁵		16				10	8	12	2		4					1	13	11³	7¹	15	6²	17	14		46

FA Cup

First Round	Rotherham U		(a)	3-1
Second Round	Salford C		(a)	0-2

Carabao Cup

First Round	Plymouth Arg		(a)	0-3

Vertu Trophy

Group H (S)	Newport Co		(a)	2-1
Group H (S)	West Ham U U21		(h)	3-1
Group H (S)	Reading		(h)	1-0
Second Round	Cambridge U		(h)	2-1
Third Round	Colchester U		(h)	2-1
Quarter-Final	Peterborough U		(a)	2-3

CHESTERFIELD

The SMH Group Stadium, 1866 Sheffield Road, Whittington Moor, Chesterfield, Derbyshire S41 8NZ.
Telephone: (01246) 269 300.
Ticket Office: (01246) 269 300.
Website: www.chesterfield-fc.co.uk
Email: hello@chesterfield-fc.co.uk
Ground Capacity: 10,558.
Record Attendance: 30,968 v Newcastle U, Division 2, 7 April 1939 (at Saltergate); 10,108 v Maidenhead U, National League, 20 April 2024 (at the SMH Group Stadium).
Pitch Measurements: 103.2m × 67.5m (112.5yd × 74yd).
Chairman: Mike Goodwin.
Chief Executive: John Croot.
Manager: Paul Cook.
Assistant Manager: Danny Webb.
Colours: Blue shirts with dark blue patterned stripes and white trim, white shorts with blue trim, blue socks with white trim.
Year Formed: 1866.
Turned Professional: 1891.
Previous Name: 1867, Chesterfield Town; 1919, Chesterfield.
Club Nicknames: 'The Blues', 'The Spireites'.
Grounds: 1867, Drill Field; 1871, Recreation Ground, Saltergate; 2010, b2net Stadium (renamed The Proact Stadium 2012; The SMH Group Stadium 2023).
First Football League Game: 2 September 1899, Division 2, v Sheffield W (a) L 1–5 – Hancock; Pilgrim, Fletcher; Ballantyne, Bell, Downie; Morley, Thacker, Gooing, Munday (1), Geary.
Record League Victory: 10–0 v Glossop NE, Division 2, 17 January 1903 – Clutterbuck; Thorpe, Lerper; Haig, Banner, Thacker; Tomlinson (2), Newton (1), Milward (3), Munday (2), Steel (2).
Record Cup Victory: 6–0 v Braintree T (a), FA Cup 1st rd, 8 November 2014 – Lee; Darikwa, Evatt, Raglan, Jones (Humpreys), Morsy, Ryan, O'Shea (1) (Gardner), Clucas (1), Roberts (1) (Boco), Doyle (2), own goal (1).
Record Defeat: 0–10 v Gillingham, Division 3, 5 September 1987.
Most League Points (2 for a win): 64, Division 4, 1969–70.

Most League Points (3 for a win): 91, Division 4, 1984–85.

Most League Goals: 102, Division 3 (N), 1930–31.

Highest League Scorer in Season: Jimmy Cookson, 44, Division 3 (N), 1925–26.

Most League Goals in Total Aggregate: Ernie Moss, 162, 1969–76, 1979–81 and 1984–86.

Most League Goals in One Match: 4, Jimmy Cookson v Accrington S, Division 3 (N), 16 January 1926; 4, Jimmy Cookson v Ashington, Division 3 (N), 1 May 1926; 4, Jimmy Cookson v Wigan Borough, Division 3 (N), 4 September 1926; 4, Tommy Lyon v Southampton, Division 2, 3 December 1938.

Most Capped Player: Walter McMillen, 4 (7), Northern Ireland; Mark Williams, 4 (36), Northern Ireland; Liam Graham, 4, New Zealand.

Most League Appearances: Dave Blakey, 617, 1948–67.

Youngest League Player: Dennis Thompson, 16 years 160 days v Notts Co, 26 December 1950.

Record Transfer Fee Received: £1,300,000 from Hull C for Sam Clucas, July 2015.

Record Transfer Fee Paid: £250,000 to Watford for Jason Lee, August 1998.

Football League Record: 1899 Elected to Division 2; 1909 failed re-election; 1921–31 Division 3 (N); 1931–33 Division 2; 1933–36 Division 3 (N); 1936–51 Division 2; 1951–58 Division 3 (N); 1958–61 Division 3; 1961–70 Division 4; 1970–83 Division 3; 1983–85 Division 4; 1985–89 Division 3; 1989–92 Division 4; 1992–95 Division 3; 1995–2000 Division 2; 2000–01 Division 3; 2001–04 Division 2; 2004–07 FL 1; 2007–11 FL 2; 2011–12 FL 1; 2012–14 FL 2; 2014–17 FL 1; 2017–18 FL 2; 2018–24 National League; 2024– FL2.

LATEST SEQUENCES

Longest Sequence of League Wins: 10, 6.9.1933 – 4.11.1933.

Longest Sequence of League Defeats: 9, 22.10.1960 – 27.12.1960.

Longest Sequence of League Draws: 8, 26.11.2005 – 2.1.2006.

Longest Sequence of Unbeaten League Matches: 21, 26.12.1994 – 29.4.1995.

Longest Sequence Without a League Win: 18, 11.9.1999 – 3.1.2000.

Successive Scoring Runs: 46 from 25.12.1929.

Successive Non-scoring Runs: 7 from 23.9.1977.

MANAGERS

E. Russell Timmeus 1891–95
  (*Secretary-Manager*)
Gilbert Gillies 1895–1901
E. F. Hind 1901–02
Jack Hoskin 1902–06
W. Furness 1906–07
George Swift 1907–10
G. H. Jones 1911–13
R. L. Weston 1913–17
T. Callaghan 1919
J. J. Caffrey 1920–22
Harry Hadley 1922
Harry Parkes 1922–27
Alec Campbell 1927
Ted Davison 1927–32
Bill Harvey 1932–38
Norman Bullock 1938–45
Bob Brocklebank 1945–48
Bobby Marshall 1948–52
Ted Davison 1952–58
Duggie Livingstone 1958–62
Tony McShane 1962–67
Jimmy McGuigan 1967–73
Joe Shaw 1973–76
Arthur Cox 1976–80
Frank Barlow 1980–83
John Duncan 1983–87
Kevin Randall 1987–88
Paul Hart 1988–91
Chris McMenemy 1991–93
John Duncan 1993–2000
Nicky Law 2000–01
Dave Rushbury 2002–03
Roy McFarland 2003–07
Lee Richardson 2007–09
John Sheridan 2009–12
Paul Cook 2012–15
Dean Saunders 2015
Danny Wilson 2015–17
Gary Caldwell 2017
Jack Lester 2017–18
Martin Allen 2018–19
John Sheridan 2019–20
John Pemberton 2020
James Rowe 2020–22
Paul Cook February 2022–

TEN YEAR LEAGUE RECORD

		P	W	D	L	F	A	Pts	Pos
2015-16	FL 1	46	15	8	23	58	70	53	18
2016-17	FL 1	46	9	10	27	43	78	37	24
2017-18	FL 2	46	10	8	28	47	83	38	24
2018-19	NL	46	14	17	15	55	53	59	14
2019-20	NL	38	11	11	16	55	65	44	20§
2020-21	NL	42	21	6	15	60	43	69	6
2021-22	NL	44	20	14	10	69	51	74	7
2022-23	NL	46	25	9	12	81	52	84	3
2023-24	NL	46	31	5	10	106	65	98	1
2024-25	FL 2	46	19	13	14	73	54	70	7

§*Decided on points-per-game (1.16)*

DID YOU KNOW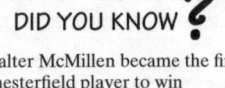

Walter McMillen became the first Chesterfield player to win international recognition when he appeared at centre-half for Northern Ireland against Scotland in November 1937. McMillen, who made almost 90 appearances for the Spireites after signing in December 1936, went on to win three more caps while on the Derbyshire club's books.

CHESTERFIELD – SKY BET LEAGUE TWO 2024–25 LEAGUE RECORD

Match No.	Date	Venue	Opponents	Result	H/T Score	Lg Pos.	Goalscorers	Attendance
1	Aug 9	H	Swindon T	D 1-1	1-0	1	Dobra [15]	9262
2	17	A	Crewe Alex	W 5-0	4-0	4	Berry 2 [1, 12], Grigg [10], Naylor [28], Dobra [49]	5626
3	24	H	Salford C	D 1-1	0-0	9	Berry [69]	8334
4	31	A	Gillingham	L 0-1	0-1	12		6954
5	Sept 7	H	Grimsby T	W 2-1	2-0	9	Berry [28], Markanday [45]	9325
6	14	A	Port Vale	L 0-1	0-1	11		7976
7	21	H	Cheltenham T	D 1-1	1-0	10	Markanday [27]	7652
8	28	A	Doncaster R	W 3-0	1-0	9	Dunkley [31], Madden (pen) [59], Berry [90]	10,790
9	Oct 1	A	Bromley	D 2-2	2-1	10	Grigg 2 [19, 37]	2057
10	5	H	Walsall	D 2-2	1-1	11	Oldaker [45], Markanday [67]	9035
11	12	H	Notts Co	D 2-2	1-1	12	Madden [6], Grigg [74]	10,032
12	18	A	Newport Co	W 3-0	1-0	7	Markanday [1], Grigg 2 [84, 87]	4570
13	22	H	Colchester U	D 1-1	0-1	9	Grigg [64]	7465
14	26	H	Morecambe	W 5-2	1-1	6	Markanday [8], Oldaker [48], Berry [74], Dobra [81], Grimes [89]	3666
15	Nov 9	H	Accrington S	L 0-3	0-1	9		8285
16	16	A	Harrogate T	L 1-2	0-0	11	Berry [77]	3686
17	23	H	Barrow	W 1-0	0-0	7	Grimes [89]	7701
18	Dec 3	A	Milton Keynes D	L 0-3	0-2	9		5903
19	7	H	Tranmere R	W 3-0	2-0	8	Colclough [29], Dobra [44], Drummond [86]	7923
20	14	A	Carlisle U	W 2-0	1-0	6	Markanday [25], Grigg [75]	6586
21	21	H	AFC Wimbledon	W 1-0	1-0	5	Dobra [3]	8555
22	26	A	Fleetwood T	L 0-2	0-1	6		3469
23	29	A	Bradford C	L 1-2	1-1	9	Dobra [35]	18,730
24	Jan 1	H	Milton Keynes D	L 1-2	0-2	10	Oldaker [76]	9119
25	18	A	Grimsby T	D 1-1	1-1	10	Naylor [34]	6706
26	25	H	Port Vale	D 1-1	0-1	10	Dobra [76]	9077
27	28	H	Bromley	W 3-0	1-0	9	Dobra [36], Colclough [82], Madden [90]	7192
28	Feb 1	A	Cheltenham T	L 0-1	0-0	10		3869
29	6	H	Doncaster R	W 5-2	2-1	9	Duffy [11], Pepple 2 [37, 59], Olakigbe [54], Banks [90]	8707
30	15	A	Walsall	L 1-3	1-0	10	Grimes [8]	6830
31	22	A	Swindon T	L 0-1	0-0	13		7531
32	Mar 1	H	Crewe Alex	L 1-3	0-2	15	Duffy [87]	8919
33	4	A	Colchester U	L 0-1	0-0	16		3774
34	8	H	Newport Co	W 2-1	2-1	15	Banks [42], Pepple [44]	7692
35	11	A	Salford C	W 4-0	2-0	14	Mandeville 2 [40, 90], Pepple [43], Dobra [59]	2289
36	15	A	Notts Co	W 2-1	0-0	12	Pepple [70], Naylor [88]	13,229
37	22	H	Harrogate T	D 0-0	0-0	11		8540
38	29	A	Barrow	W 1-0	0-0	11	Jacobs [78]	3392
39	Apr 1	H	Carlisle U	W 2-1	0-0	10	Mandeville [73], Madden [81]	7508
40	5	H	Tranmere R	L 0-4	0-0	10		6316
41	8	H	Gillingham	D 1-1	0-1	10	Grigg [77]	7810
42	12	H	Fleetwood T	W 3-0	0-0	9	Colclough [55], Palmer [69], Madden [78]	7739
43	18	A	AFC Wimbledon	D 0-0	0-0	9		8506
44	21	H	Bradford C	D 3-3	1-2	10	Metcalfe [45], Grigg [71], Mandeville [90]	9520
45	26	H	Morecambe	W 4-1	1-0	9	Grigg [45], Palmer [61], Olakigbe [75], Naylor [80]	8725
46	May 3	A	Accrington S	W 1-0	1-0	7	Grigg [32]	3969

Final League Position: 7

GOALSCORERS
League (73): Grigg 12, Dobra 9, Berry 7, Markanday 6, Madden 5 (1 pen), Pepple 5, Mandeville 4, Naylor 4, Colclough 3, Grimes 3, Oldaker 3, Banks 2, Duffy 2, Olakigbe 2, Palmer 2, Drummond 1, Dunkley 1, Jacobs 1, Metcalfe 1.
FA Cup (3): Grigg 2, Dobra 1.
Carabao Cup (1): Dobra 1.
Vertu Trophy (8): Berry-McNally 3 (1 pen), Cook 1, Dobra 1, Madden 1, Markanday 1, Oldaker 1.
League Two Play-offs (1): Dobra 1.

Boot R 28	Tanton D 8	Naylor T 37 + 3	Dunkley C 9	Gordon L 29 + 4	Banks O 25 + 14	Oldaker D 26 + 6	Jacobs M 2 + 15	Dobra A 36 + 6	Colclough R 13 + 23	Grigg W 21 + 9	Berry J 11 + 11	Mandeville L 33 + 9	Drummond K 4 + 10	Quigley J — + 3	Palmer A 15	Daley-Campbell V 6 + 3	Markanday D 22	Hobson B 4 + 7	Araujo H 15 + 5	Jessop L 1 + 1	Metcalfe J 20 + 8	Williams T 9 + 1	Grimes J 24 + 11	Jones M — + 2	Madden P 9 + 18	Thompson M 18	Cook C — + 2	Horton B 2 + 5	Sheckelford R 15 + 2	Elliott G — + 1	Akinola T — + 2	Pepple A 14 + 6	Fleck J 7 + 9	Donacien J 4 + 3	McFadzean K 8	Sparkes J 10	Duffy D 8 + 10	Olakigbe M 13 + 4	Match No.
1	2	3	4	5	6	7	8²	9³	10¹	11⁴	12	13	14	15																									1
1		3	4	5	6		7	12	9²		11⁴	10³			15	2⁵	8¹	13	14	16																			2
1		3	4	5	6	7	12	9		11³	10²				14	2	8¹	13																					3
1		3	4⁸	5	6⁴	7	12	9		11²	10		14			2¹	8³				13	15																	4
1	2⁶	3		5	6¹	7⁸	15	9⁴		11	10²	13			16	8³		14			12		4																5
1	2	3	4	5	6⁵		14	9		11¹	10²	13	12			8³		15			7⁴		16																6
1	2	3	4	5		6		9	13		10¹	14	11³			8⁴		12			7²		15																7
1	2¹	7	3	5	12	6		9⁸	16	13	15	10				8⁶		4³					14		11²														8
1		7	3	5	16	6⁵	9²	14	10	11⁴	12	8			2³						13		4		15														9
	6	3	5	9		7³		10	12	11²	13	2¹			16	8⁵		4⁴			14				15	1													10
	3		5	14	6⁵	15	8	12	13	10¹	2					9⁴		4			7³			16	11²	1													11
		5	15	7	12	8⁸	10¹	14		2²						13	9	4			6	3⁵	16		11³	1													12
	3	8	7	16	13	14	11⁴	10²	12			2¹	9⁵				4				6³				15	1													13
	3	5	16	7		13	10³	15	14	8			2¹	9⁵			4²				6		12		11⁴	1													14
1	2¹	4		5	6	7	15	9⁸	14	11	10³	12			8⁶		3²		13	16																			15
1	2¹	3		5³	7	6⁴		10	15	11	12	9			8²	14		4	13																				16
1	2	7		5	15	6⁴		16	13	14	10²	9⁵			8		4¹		3	12	11³																		17
		5	7	6⁸			10⁶	16	11²	14	9	13			8³		4⁵	2¹	3	12			1	15															18
		5	7				9	10¹	11⁴	12	6	15			8	13	4³		3	14		1	2																19
	13		5¹	6			9⁴	10³	11⁵	15	8	16			7	14	4		3²	12		1	2																20
	3		6⁴	14			9³	10¹	11²	12	8	13			7	15	5⁵			4		1	16	2															21
	3		6¹	12		9		10³	8	11²					7⁵	13	5⁴			4		1	16	15	2	14													22
	3		6	12	9			8	11¹						7	10	5²			4		1		13	2														23
	3			6	9	12		8	11¹						7	10	4			1			5²	2	13														24
	3			6³	9	10⁶	13	8⁵	15						7²		4	12	1	5	2	14	11¹	16															25
	6			7³	10	8²		9	15			14			4	13	1	16	12		11⁴		2¹	3	5⁵														26
	6		15	7⁵	9¹³	8						14			4		1		2	11¹	16		3³	5	10²														27
	6		14	7	9	13									3	4	11¹	1		2	12		5²	10	8³														28
	6		13	7⁴	9⁸	16		12							15	3	4	14	1		2	11³		5	10¹	8²													29
	6⁴		14	7³	9	12		16							15	3	4	13	1		2	11¹		5	10²	8⁵													30
1	12		13		9			6³	15						7	3¹	4	14			16	11	2⁶	5	10²	8⁴													31
1		13	6⁵	16	10		12	3							7⁴	4	9²	11	15	2¹			5	14	8³														32
1	6⁴		7³		12	13		10⁵	3					9²		4	11⁸		2	15	14		5	8¹	16														33
1	6	15	9³	7²		10⁴	16	8	3							4		2¹	11	12	13		5⁵	14															34
1	6	13	9⁵			10³	14	8	3				7			4		2¹	11⁴	12		5²	15	16															35
1	6	5²	9⁴			10¹⁵		8	3		14		7			4		2¹	11	16	12		13																36
1	6⁵	5	9			10¹	14	13	8				7⁴			4	15		11²	16	2¹			12															37
1	6⁴	5	8⁵		14	9²	10¹	12	2	3			7			4			11³	16		13	15																38
1		5	9⁵	12	15	10³	16	11²	2	3			6			4	13		7¹			14	8⁴																39
1	7¹	5	8²		15	9		12	2	3			6⁵			4	16		11³	14		13	10⁴																40
1		5	15			13	14	11⁵	2	3			6³			12	9⁴		16	7	4²		10¹	8															41
1	16	5	12			9¹	10²	11³	2	3			6⁵			15			14	7⁴	4		13	8															42
1	7	13	8¹			14	15		2	3			5³	9			12		11²	6	4		10⁴																43
1	7	13	15			10³	11	2	3⁵				5¹	9		12	16		6⁴		4²	14	8																44
1	8	5⁵		13	12	14	10³	2	3				6¹	16			15	7	4²	11⁴	9																		45
1	8	5		13		11¹	10³	2	3				6⁴	15			14	7	4	12	9²																		46

FA Cup

First Round	Horsham	(h)	3-1
Second Round	Exeter C	(a)	0-2

Carabao Cup

First Round	Derby Co	(a)	1-2

League Two Play-offs

Semi-Final 1st leg	Walsall	(h)	0-2
Semi-Final 2nd leg	Walsall	(a)	1-2

Vertu Trophy

Group G (N)	Manchester C U21	(h)	1-1
Chesterfield won 4-2 on penalties.			
Group G (N)	Lincoln C	(a)	1-0
Group G (N)	Grimsby T	(h)	3-2
Second Round	Wigan Ath	(h)	3-2
Third Round	Rotherham U	(h)	0-0
Rotherham U won 4-3 on penalties.			

COLCHESTER UNITED

FOUNDATION

Colchester United was formed in 1937 when a number of
enthusiasts of the much older Colchester Town club decided to
establish a professional concern as a limited liability company.
The new club continued at Layer Road which had been the
amateur club's home since 1909.

*JobServe Community Stadium, United Way, Colchester,
Essex CO4 5UP.*

Telephone: (01206) 755 100.

Ticket Office: (01206) 755 161.

Website: www.cu-fc.com

Email: media@colchesterunited.net

Ground Capacity: 10,105.

Record Attendance: 19,072 v Reading, FA Cup 1st rd,
27 November 1948 (at Layer Road); 10,064 v Norwich C,
FL 1, 16 January 2010 (at Community Stadium).

Pitch Measurements: 102m × 64m (111.5yd × 70yd).

Executive Chairman: Robbie Cowling.

General Manager: Tim Waddington.

Head Coach: Danny Cowley.

Assistant Head Coach: Nicky Cowley.

HONOURS

League Champions: Football
Conference – 1991–92.
Runners-up: FL 1 – 2005–06; Division
4 – 1961–62; Football Conference –
1990–91.
FA Cup: 6th rd – 1971.
League Cup: 5th rd – 1975, 2020.
League Trophy: Runners-up: 1997.

Colours: Blue and white striped shirts with blue sleeves and white trim, white shorts with blue trim,
white socks.

Year Formed: 1937.

Turned Professional: 1937.

Club Nickname: 'The U's'.

Grounds: 1937, Layer Road; 2008, Weston Homes Community Stadium (renamed JobServe
Community Stadium 2018).

First Football League Game: 19 August 1950, Division 3 (S), v Gillingham (a) D 0–0 – Wright; Kettle,
Allen; Bearryman, Stewart, Elder; Jones, Curry, Turner, McKim, Church.

Record League Victory: 9–1 v Bradford C, Division 4, 30 December 1961 – Ames; Millar, Fowler;
Harris, Abrey, Ron Hunt; Foster, Bobby Hunt (4), King (4), Hill (1), Wright.

Record Cup Victory: 9–1 v Leamington, FA Cup 1st rd, 5 November 2005 – Davison; Stockley
(Garcia), Duguid, Brown (1), Chilvers, Watson (1), Halford (1), Izzet (Danns) (2), Iwelumo (1)
(Williams), Cureton (2), Yeates (1).

FOOTBALL YEARBOOK FACT FILE

Colchester United installed floodlights at their Layer Road ground shortly after the
start of the 1959–60 season. On 21 October the lights were officially opened with a
friendly against Ipswich Town. The U's won the match 3-1 with goals from Neil
Langman, Peter Hill and Tommy Williams in front of a crowd of 8,198.

Record Defeat: 0–8 v Leyton Orient, Division 4, 15 October 1988.

Most League Points (2 for a win): 60, Division 4, 1973–74.

Most League Points (3 for a win): 81, Division 4, 1982–83.

Most League Goals: 104, Division 4, 1961–62.

Highest League Scorer in Season: Bobby Hunt, 38, Division 4, 1961–62.

Most League Goals in Total Aggregate: Martyn King, 130, 1956–64.

Most League Goals in One Match: 4, Bobby Hunt v Bradford C, Division 4, 30 December 1961; 4, Martyn King v Bradford C, Division 4, 30 December 1961; 4, Bobby Hunt v Doncaster R, Division 4, 30 April 1962.

Most Capped Player: Tommy Smith, 13 (includes 1 while on loan from Ipswich T) (56), New Zealand.

Most League Appearances: Micky Cook, 613, 1969–84.

Youngest League Player: Todd Miller, 16 years 166 days v Exeter C, 16 March 2019.

Record Transfer Fee Received: £2,500,000 from Reading for Greg Halford, January 2007.

Record Transfer Fee Paid: £400,000 to Cheltenham T for Steve Gillespie, July 2008.

Football League Record: 1950 Elected to Division 3 (S); 1950–58 Division 3 (S); 1958–61 Division 3; 1961–62 Division 4; 1962–65 Division 3; 1965–66 Division 4; 1966–68 Division 3; 1968–74 Division 4; 1974–76 Division 3, 1976–77 Division 4; 1977–81 Division 3; 1981–90 Division 4; 1990–92 Football Conference; 1992–98 Third Division; 1998–2004 Second Division; 2004–06 FL 1; 2006–08 FL C; 2008–16 FL 1; 2016– FL 2.

LATEST SEQUENCES

Longest Sequence of League Wins: 7, 31.12.2005 – 7.2.2006.

Longest Sequence of League Defeats: 9, 31.10.2015 – 28.12.2015.

Longest Sequence of League Draws: 6, 21.3.1977 – 11.4.1977.

Longest Sequence of Unbeaten League Matches: 20, 22.12.1956 – 19.4.1957.

Longest Sequence Without a League Win: 20, 2.3.1968 – 31.8.1968.

Successive Scoring Runs: 24 from 15.9.1962.

Successive Non-scoring Runs: 5 from 14.2.2023.

MANAGERS

Ted Fenton 1946–48
Jimmy Allen 1948–53
Jack Butler 1953–55
Benny Fenton 1955–63
Neil Franklin 1963–68
Dick Graham 1968–72
Jim Smith 1972–75
Bobby Roberts 1975–82
Allan Hunter 1982–83
Cyril Lea 1983–86
Mike Walker 1986–87
Roger Brown 1987–88
Jock Wallace 1989
Mick Mills 1990
Ian Atkins 1990–91
Roy McDonough 1991–94
George Burley 1994
Steve Wignall 1995–99
Mick Wadsworth 1999
Steve Whitton 1999–2003
Phil Parkinson 2003–06
Geraint Williams 2006–08
Paul Lambert 2008–09
Aidy Boothroyd 2009–10
John Ward 2010–12
Joe Dunne 2012–14
Tony Humes 2014–15
Kevin Keen 2015–16
John McGreal 2016–20
Steve Ball 2020–21
Hayden Mullins 2021–22
Wayne Brown 2022
Matt Bloomfield 2022–23
Ben Garner 2023
Matthew Etherington 2023–24
Danny Cowley January 2024–

TEN YEAR LEAGUE RECORD

		P	W	D	L	F	A	Pts	Pos
2015-16	FL 1	46	9	13	24	57	99	40	23
2016-17	FL 2	46	19	12	15	67	57	69	8
2017-18	FL 2	46	16	14	16	53	52	62	13
2018-19	FL 2	46	20	10	16	65	53	70	8
2019-20	FL 2	37	15	13	9	52	37	58	6§
2020-21	FL 2	46	11	18	17	44	61	51	20
2021-22	FL 2	46	14	13	19	48	60	55	15
2022-23	FL 2	46	12	13	21	44	51	49	20
2023-24	FL 2	46	11	12	23	59	80	45	22
2024-25	FL 2	46	16	19	11	52	47	67	10

§*Decided on points-per-game (1.57)*

DID YOU KNOW ?

Colchester United's home fixture with Manchester City on 20 March 1999 was one of a handful of games shown on Sky Sports as 'pay-per-view'. Sky estimated that around 15–20,000 viewers paid to watch the match, which kicked off at 6pm on the Saturday evening. The visitors won 1-0, with a 'live' attendance of 6,554 turning out.

COLCHESTER UNITED – SKY BET LEAGUE TWO 2024–25 LEAGUE RECORD

Match No.	Date	Venue	Opponents	Result	H/T Score	Lg Pos.	Goalscorers	Attendance
1	Aug 10	A	AFC Wimbledon	L 2-4	2-3	20	Goodliffe 2 [1, 9]	7924
2	17	H	Milton Keynes D	W 2-0	0-0	12	Read [81], Payne [90]	4521
3	24	H	Harrogate T	L 0-1	0-0	17		3883
4	31	A	Accrington S	D 1-1	0-1	14	Goodliffe [85]	1956
5	Sept 7	H	Bromley	D 1-1	0-1	18	Edwards O [60]	4877
6	14	A	Morecambe	D 3-3	1-1	17	Edwards O [43], Tovide [49], Taylor [64]	2754
7	21	A	Tranmere R	W 3-0	2-0	11	Taylor 2 [7, 38], Tovide [78]	4243
8	28	A	Walsall	L 0-4	0-1	15		5140
9	Oct 1	A	Port Vale	D 1-1	0-0	15	Tovide [90]	4533
10	5	H	Carlisle U	D 0-0	0-0	16		4392
11	19	H	Cheltenham T	L 1-2	1-2	20	Taylor [27]	4031
12	22	A	Chesterfield	D 1-1	1-0	20	Payne [6]	7465
13	26	H	Salford C	L 1-2	0-0	21	Anderson [70]	3936
14	Nov 9	A	Barrow	D 1-1	0-1	21	Taylor [90]	3179
15	16	H	Bradford C	D 1-1	0-1	21	McDonnell [90]	4825
16	23	A	Grimsby T	W 1-0	0-0	19	Gordon [78]	4952
17	30	A	Fleetwood T	D 0-0	0-0	18		3202
18	Dec 3	H	Swindon T	W 4-0	4-0	17	Smith (og) [9], Tovide 2 [12, 26], Payne [38]	3401
19	14	H	Newport Co	D 0-0	0-0	18		4046
20	20	A	Crewe Alex	D 0-0	0-0	16		9288
21	26	H	Gillingham	W 2-0	1-0	15	Taylor [6], Gordon [85]	5934
22	29	H	Doncaster R	D 1-1	0-1	15	Taylor [51]	5729
23	Jan 1	A	Swindon T	L 2-3	1-1	16	Payne 2 (2 pens) [44, 61]	7680
24	4	A	Accrington S	L 0-2	0-1	17		4366
25	18	A	Bromley	W 1-0	1-0	15	Edwards O [4]	3907
26	21	A	Harrogate T	D 0-0	0-0	14		2284
27	25	H	Morecambe	W 1-0	0-0	13	Egbo [65]	4238
28	Feb 1	A	Tranmere R	W 3-1	2-0	13	Taylor 2 (1 pen) [9 ipl, 33], Edwards O [63]	5166
29	8	H	Walsall	W 2-1	0-0	11	Bishop [69], Edwards O [74]	4734
30	15	A	Carlisle U	D 0-0	0-0	12		7021
31	18	A	Notts Co	D 1-1	0-1	11	Simpson [48]	9467
32	22	H	AFC Wimbledon	D 1-1	0-1	12	Tovide [89]	6029
33	Mar 1	A	Milton Keynes D	W 1-0	0-0	11	Payne (pen) [87]	8002
34	4	H	Chesterfield	W 1-0	0-0	10	Gordon [59]	3774
35	8	A	Cheltenham T	W 1-0	0-0	9	Anderson [69]	3954
36	11	H	Port Vale	W 2-1	1-0	9	Tovide [34], Kelleher [86]	4055
37	15	H	Fleetwood T	W 3-0	0-0	7	Taylor [55], Edwards O [59], Payne [85]	5636
38	22	A	Bradford C	L 1-4	1-2	8	Anderson [36]	23,381
39	28	H	Grimsby T	L 1-2	0-0	8	Edwards O [51]	6986
40	Apr 1	A	Gillingham	D 1-1	1-0	9	Payne [20]	5924
41	5	H	Notts Co	W 1-0	1-0	8	Simpson [44]	6172
42	12	A	Newport Co	W 2-0	0-0	8	Kelleher [88], Scully [90]	3899
43	18	H	Crewe Alex	D 0-0	0-0	7		7623
44	21	A	Doncaster R	L 0-3	0-2	8		8936
45	26	A	Salford C	L 1-4	0-3	10	Iandolo [66]	3150
46	May 3	H	Barrow	D 0-0	0-0	10		7512

Final League Position: 10

GOALSCORERS

League (52): Taylor 10 (1 pen), Payne 8 (3 pens), Edwards O 7, Tovide 7, Anderson 3, Goodliffe 3, Gordon 3, Kelleher 2, Simpson 2, Bishop 1, Egbo 1, Iandolo 1, McDonnell 1, Read 1, Scully 1, own goal 1.
FA Cup (1): Anderson 1.
Carabao Cup (2): Hopper 1, Payne 1 (1 pen).
Vertu Trophy (9): Taylor 3, Anderson 1, Egbo 1, Goodliffe 1, Hopper 1, Kelleher 1, Scully 1 (1 pen).

	Macey M 46	Hunt R 16+6	Goodliffe B 8+3	Flanagan T 41	Iandolo E 44	Payne J 39+3	Read A 23+16	Ihionvien B 1+1	Gordon J 17+24	Tovide S 23+6	Hopper T 9+7	Kelleher F 24+4	Edwards O 30+7	Bishop T 22+5	Egbo M 38+7	Woodyard A 11+3	Anderson H 20+11	Oni M —+1	Taylor L 27+10	Scully A 2+13	Donnelly A 14+3	McDonnell J 29+3	Thorn O 11+15	Terry F 1	Simpson T 6+14	Tucker J 3+7	Vincent-Young K —+10	Aboh K —+2	Jolliffe M —+2	Lisbie K 1+3	Match No.
1	1	2^6	3^1	4	5	6	7	8^3	9	10^2	11	12	13	14	15																1
1	1	2		3	4	8	12		9^1	11^4	10		14	7^1	6^3	5	13	15													2
1	1	2		3	4	8	15	14	9^1	11	10		13	7^4	6^2	5^3	12														3
1	1	2^4	16	3	4	7	13		9^1	11	10^1		14	8^6	6	5^3	15	12													4
1	1	4^1		3	9	6	7^5	13	11	15	12	8^3	2	14	5^2	10^4	16														5
1	1	2^3		3	4	7	13	15	10^5	16	9^4	8^2	6	5	14	11^1	12														6
1	1	14		4	3	5	6	13	15	11^5	9^3	8^2	2^4	7	10^1	12	16														7
1	1	14		4	3	5^5	6	13	15	11^4	9^1	8^2	2	7	10^3	12	16														8
1	1	2^4		3	6	13	7	16	10	11^5	4	15	8^3		12	9^1	5^2	14													9
1	1	2		4	5	6	8	13	11	9^5	12	3^1	7^3	10	14																10
1	1	2^4		4	5	6	7^3	9	10^1	12	3^2	15	8^5	14	11	13	16														11
1	1	2	3		5	9			10^1	11		14	6	12	13		4	7^2	8^3												12
1	1	2^3	3		5	6	12		10^1	9^4		14	13	11	15	4	7	8^2													13
1	1	2^1		3	5	9			10	13			12	6^2	8^3	11	4	7	14												14
1	1				3	4	5	9	7	10^1	12	15		13	2	8^3	11	4	6	14											15
1	1		3		5	13	7^3		12	11		9^2		2	14	8	10^1	4	6												16
1	1		3^2		5	9	7		12	11	13	10^3		2	8^1		4	6	14												17
1	1	15		3	5	9	7^2		8^5	11^3		10^1	12	2^4	16	14	4	6	13												18
1	1		3		5	9^2	7^3		15	11		10^4	14	2	8^1	13	4	6	12												19
1	1	16		5	12	7		14	11^1	15	3	10^5	2^2		8^3	9^4	4	6	13												20
1	1		3	5	9	7^3		14		13		10^4	15	2		12	11^2	4	6	8^1											21
1	1		3	5	9				12			10	7	2		11	4	6	8^1												22
1	1		4	5^1	9				10		11^1	14	13	7^3	2		8^2	12	3	6											23
1	1		3		9^2	12		13			10	7	2^3	14	11	4	6	8	5^1												24
1	1	14	4	5	9^3			13	3	10^1	7	2	8		11^2		6	12													25
1	1		4	5	9	12		14		3	10^3	6^1	2	8^4	11^2		7	15	13												26
1	1		4	5	9	15		16		3^1	10^5	7^4	2	8^2	12		6	13	11^3	14											27
1	1		4	5	9				12^3	3	10^1	7	2	8	11^2		6	14	13												28
1	1		4	5	9^2	13			3	10^1	7^4	2	8	11^3		6			15	14	12										29
1	1		4	5	9	14		13		3	10^2	7^3	2^1	8	11^4		6			15	12										30
1	1		4	5	9	15		14		3	10^2	6^4	2	8^3	13		7			11^1	12										31
1	1		4	5	9	14		8	13	3^1	10^4	7^3	2^2		11^4		6				15	12									32
1	1		4	5	8	15		9^5	11^2	3			2^4	6^1	10^3		7	12		13		14	16								33
1	1		4	5	9	7^1		8^4	13	3	10^3	2^5	14		12		6	15		11^2	16										34
1	1	16		4	5	8^5	15		7^1	11^2		9^3	2		12	10^4		6	14		13	3									35
1	1	5		4	7	9^2	6		11^1	3	10^1	2	8	12				14	13												36
1	1	5		4	7^3	9	6^4	13		3	10^2	2	8	11^1				12	14			15									37
1	1	5^1		4	7	9^4	6	12		3	10^2	2	8	11^3	14			15	13												38
1	1	5^2		4		9	7^5	12^4		3^3	10	2	8^1	11	16		6	15	14		13										39
1	1	13		4	5	9^2	7			3	10^1	2			12^3		8^4	11	6		15	14									40
1	1	13		4	5		7			12	3	10^2	2		9	14	6	8^3	11^1												41
1	1			4	5		7	15	11^2	3	10	2		9^1	13	6	8^3	12^4			14										42
1	1			4	5		7	14	11	3^2	10	13	2		9^1	6	8^3	12													43
1	1			4	5	9		16	13	3^3	10^4	7^5	2		14	6^1	11^2	12	15	8^4											44
1	1			4	5	9^2	7		10^4	11^1	3^5	6	2		12		8	13	16	15	14										45
1	1	2^1		4	5	9		10^2	11^4	3	7	13	14		8^5	16		6^3	12	15											46

FA Cup
First Round   Swindon T   (a)   1-2
aet.

Carabao Cup
First Round   Reading   (h)   2-2
Colchester U won 4-3 on penalties.
Second Round   Brentford   (h)   0-1

Vertu Trophy
Group E (S)   Milton Keynes D   (h)   2-1
Group E (S)   Leyton Orient   (a)   1-1
Leyton Orient won 4-2 on penalties.
Group E (S)   Arsenal U21   (h)   3-0
Second Round   AFC Wimbledon   (h)   2-0
Third Round   Cheltenham T   (a)   1-2

COVENTRY CITY

FOUNDATION

Workers at Singers' cycle factory formed a club in 1883. The first success of Singers FC was to win the Birmingham Junior Cup in 1891 and this led in 1894 to their election to the Birmingham & District League. Four years later they changed their name to Coventry City and joined the Southern League in 1908 at which time they were playing in blue and white quarters.

The Coventry Building Society Arena, Jimmy Hill Way, Foleshill, Coventry CV6 6GE.

Telephone: (024) 7699 1987.

Ticket Office: (024) 7699 1987.

Website: www.ccfc.co.uk

Email: info@ccfc.co.uk

Ground Capacity: 32,604.

Record Attendance: 51,455 v Wolverhampton W, Division 2, 29 April 1967 (at Highfield Road); 31,452 v Middlesbrough, FL C, 3 May 2025 (at Ricoh Arena).

Pitch Measurements: 105m × 68m (115yd × 74.5yd).

Executive Chairman: Doug King.

Chief Operating Officer: John Taylor.

Manager: Frank Lampard.

Assistant Manager: Joe Edwards.

Colours: Sky blue shirts with white trim, white shorts with sky blue trim, sky blue socks with white trim.

Year Formed: 1883.

Turned Professional: 1893.

Previous Name: 1883, Singers FC; 1898, Coventry City.

Club Nickname: 'The Sky Blues'.

Grounds: 1883, Binley Road; 1887, Stoke Road; 1899, Highfield Road; 2005, Ricoh Arena; 2013, Sixfields Stadium (groundshare with Northampton T); 2014, Ricoh Arena; 2019, St Andrew's Trillion Trophy Stadium (groundshare with Birmingham C); 2021, The Coventry Building Society Arena.

First Football League Game: 30 August 1919, Division 2, v Tottenham H (h) L 0–5 – Lindon; Roberts, Chaplin, Allan, Hawley, Clarke, Sheldon, Mercer, Sambrooke, Lowes, Gibson.

Record League Victory: 9–0 v Bristol C, Division 3 (S), 28 April 1934 – Pearson; Brown, Bisby; Perry, Davidson, Frith; White (2), Lauderdale, Bourton (5), Jones (2), Lake.

Record Cup Victory: 8–0 v Rushden & D, League Cup 2nd rd, 2 October 2002 – Debec; Caldwell, Quinn, Betts (1p), Konjic (Shaw), Davenport, Pipe, Safri (Stanford), Mills (2) (Bothroyd (2)), McSheffery (3), Partridge.

Record Defeat: 2–10 v Norwich C, Division 3 (S), 15 March 1930.

Most League Points (2 for a win): 60, Division 4, 1958–59 and Division 3, 1963–64.

Most League Points (3 for a win): 75, FL 2, 2017–18.

HONOURS

League Champions: Division 2 – 1966–67; FL 1 – 2019–20. Division 3 – 1963–64; Division 3S – 1935–36.
Runners-up: Division 3S – 1933–34; Division 4 – 1958–59.
FA Cup Winners: 1987.
League Cup: semi-final – 1981, 1990.
League Trophy Winners: 2017.
European Competitions
Fairs Cup: 1970–71.

FOOTBALL YEARBOOK FACT FILE

Coventry City were restricted to playing friendly matches for the first three seasons during the First World War, but when Chesterfield Town were closed down by the football authorities a vacancy for another club became available. City applied for this and were co-opted into the Midland Section of the Football League for 1918–19, seen as a significant step towards gaining election to the peacetime League for the following season.

Most League Goals: 108, Division 3 (S), 1931–32.

Highest League Scorer in Season: Clarrie Bourton, 49, Division 3 (S), 1931–32.

Most League Goals in Total Aggregate: Clarrie Bourton, 173, 1931–37.

Most League Goals in One Match: 5, Clarrie Bourton v Bournemouth, Division 3 (S), 17 October 1931; 5, Arthur Bacon v Gillingham, Division 3 (S), 30 December 1933.

Most Capped Player: Magnus Hedman, 44 (58), Sweden.

Most League Appearances: Steve Ogrizovic, 507, 1984–2000.

Youngest League Player: Ben Mackey, 16 years 167 days v Ipswich T, 12 April 2003.

Record Transfer Fee Received: £20,000,000 from Sporting Lisbon for Viktor Gyokeres, July 2023.

Record Transfer Fee Paid: £7,700,000 to Antalyaspor for Haji Wright, August 2023.

Football League Record: 1919 Elected to Division 2; 1919–25 Division 2; 1925–26 Division 3 (N); 1926–36 Division 3 (S); 1936–52 Division 2; 1952–58 Division 3 (S); 1958–59 Division 4; 1959–64 Division 3; 1964–67 Division 2; 1967–92 Division 1; 1992–2001 Premier League; 2001–04 First Division; 2004–12 FL C; 2012–17 FL 1; 2017–18 FL 2; 2018–20 FL 1; 2020– FL C.

LATEST SEQUENCES

Longest Sequence of League Wins: 6, 25.4.1964 – 5.9.1964.

Longest Sequence of League Defeats: 9, 30.8.1919 – 11.10.1919.

Longest Sequence of League Draws: 6, 1.11.2003 – 29.11.2003.

Longest Sequence of Unbeaten League Matches: 25, 26.11.1966 – 13.5.1967.

Longest Sequence Without a League Win: 19, 30.8.1919 – 20.12.1919.

Successive Scoring Runs: 25 from 10.9.1966.

Successive Non-scoring Runs: 11 from 11.10.1919.

MANAGERS

H. R. Buckle 1909–10
Robert Wallace 1910–13
  (*Secretary-Manager*)
Frank Scott-Walford 1913–15
William Clayton 1917–19
H. Pollitt 1919–20
Albert Evans 1920–24
Jimmy Kerr 1924–28
James McIntyre 1928–31
Harry Storer 1931–45
Dick Bayliss 1945–47
Billy Frith 1947–48
Harry Storer 1948–53
Jack Fairbrother 1953–54
Charlie Elliott 1954–55
Jesse Carver 1955–56
George Raynor 1956
Harry Warren 1956–57
Billy Frith 1957–61
Jimmy Hill 1961–67
Noel Cantwell 1967–72
Bob Dennison 1972
Joe Mercer 1972–75
Gordon Milne 1972–81
Dave Sexton 1981–83
Bobby Gould 1983–84
Don Mackay 1985–86
George Curtis 1986–87
  (*became Managing Director*)
John Sillett 1987–90
Terry Butcher 1990–92
Don Howe 1992
Bobby Gould 1992–93
  (*with Don Howe, June 1992*)
Phil Neal 1993–95
Ron Atkinson 1995–96
  (*became Director of Football*)
Gordon Strachan 1996–2001
Roland Nilsson 2001–02
Gary McAllister 2002–04
Eric Black 2004
Peter Reid 2004–05
Micky Adams 2005–07
Iain Dowie 2007–08
Chris Coleman 2008–10
Aidy Boothroyd 2010–11
Andy Thorn 2011–12
Mark Robins 2012–13
Steven Pressley 2013–15
Tony Mowbray 2015–16
Russell Slade 2016–17
Mark Robins 2017–24
Frank Lampard November 2024–

TEN YEAR LEAGUE RECORD

		P	W	D	L	F	A	Pts	Pos
2015-16	FL 1	46	19	12	15	67	49	69	8
2016-17	FL 1	46	9	12	25	37	68	39	23
2017-18	FL 2	46	22	9	15	64	47	75	6
2018-19	FL 1	46	18	11	17	54	54	65	8
2019-20	FL 1	34	18	13	3	48	30	67	1§
2020-21	FL C	46	14	13	19	49	61	55	16
2021-22	FL C	46	17	13	16	60	59	64	12
2022-23	FL C	46	18	16	12	58	46	70	5
2023-24	FL C	46	17	13	16	70	59	64	9
2024-25	FL C	46	20	9	17	64	58	69	5

§*Decided on points-per-game (1.97)*

DID YOU KNOW ?

Coventry City hosted a World Cup qualifier between Northern Ireland and Portugal at their former home Highfield Road on 28 March 1973. The game was switched as a result of security concerns preventing matches being played on home soil during the Troubles. The match ended in a 1-1 draw in front of a crowd of 11,273, around half the average attendance at Sky Blues home games that season.

COVENTRY CITY – SKY BET CHAMPIONSHIP 2024–25 LEAGUE RECORD

Match No.	Date	Venue	Opponents	Result	H/T Score	Lg Pos.	Goalscorers	Attendance
1	Aug 10	A	Stoke C	L	0-1	0-0	18		25,037
2	16	H	Oxford U	W	3-2	2-1	11	Wright 2 [15, 90], van Ewijk [31]	28,051
3	24	A	Bristol C	D	1-1	0-1	9	Palmer [76]	21,545
4	31	H	Norwich C	L	0-1	0-0	17		27,353
5	Sept 14	A	Watford	D	1-1	1-0	14	Simms [4]	19,441
6	21	H	Swansea C	L	1-2	1-2	19	Ronald (og) [34]	26,273
7	28	A	Leeds U	L	0-3	0-1	21		36,625
8	Oct 1	H	Blackburn R	W	3-0	1-0	16	Bidwell [11], Wright [48], Thomas-Asante [84]	24,583
9	5	H	Sheffield Wed	L	1-2	1-1	20	Rudoni [26]	28,571
10	19	A	Preston NE	L	0-1	0-0	21		15,907
11	22	A	QPR	D	1-1	1-0	22	Wright [4]	14,173
12	26	H	Luton T	W	3-2	0-2	18	Simms [59], Overgaard [76], Wright [90]	26,409
13	Nov 2	A	Middlesbrough	W	3-0	1-0	13	Thomas [42], Wright [76], Eccles [81]	24,921
14	6	H	Derby Co	L	1-2	0-1	17	Sakamoto [77]	27,243
15	9	A	Sunderland	D	2-2	0-2	17	Wright [62], Rudoni [84]	43,374
16	23	H	Sheffield U	D	2-2	1-2	17	Bassette [22], Thomas [80]	28,057
17	26	A	Burnley	L	0-2	0-0	17		18,293
18	30	H	Cardiff C	D	2-2	1-1	16	Mason-Clark [7], Overgaard (pen) [88]	27,137
19	Dec 7	A	Millwall	W	1-0	0-0	14	Mason-Clark [63]	16,460
20	11	A	WBA	L	0-2	0-1	16		24,859
21	14	H	Hull C	W	2-1	0-1	15	Mason-Clark [52], Rudoni [72]	25,528
22	21	A	Portsmouth	L	1-4	1-2	17	Bassette [3]	20,330
23	26	H	Plymouth Arg	W	4-0	4-0	15	Sakamoto [5], Eccles 2 [20, 45], Mason-Clark [39]	29,420
24	29	A	Millwall	D	0-0	0-0	15		28,216
25	Jan 1	A	Cardiff C	D	1-1	0-1	14	Sakamoto [46]	19,045
26	4	A	Norwich C	L	1-2	1-0	15	van Ewijk [24]	26,682
27	18	H	Bristol C	W	1-0	0-0	14	Thomas-Asante [62]	26,695
28	21	H	Blackburn R	W	2-0	1-0	13	Simms [41], Thomas-Asante [48]	12,819
29	25	H	Watford	W	2-1	1-0	12	Overgaard 2 [32, 75]	27,078
30	Feb 1	A	Swansea C	W	2-0	2-0	11	Simms [17], Thomas-Asante [44]	15,189
31	5	H	Leeds U	L	0-2	0-2	11		28,008
32	11	H	QPR	W	1-0	0-0	8	Thomas [90]	24,600
33	15	A	Sheffield Wed	W	2-1	1-0	7	Simms 2 [16, 90]	28,121
34	22	H	Preston NE	W	2-1	2-0	7	Rudoni [30], Thomas [37]	26,493
35	Mar 1	A	Oxford U	W	3-2	1-0	5	Rudoni [7], Mason-Clark [58], Sakamoto [71]	11,405
36	8	H	Stoke C	W	3-2	2-0	5	Overgaard 2 [22, 31], Thomas [90]	30,011
37	11	H	Derby Co	L	0-2	0-1	6		28,879
38	15	A	Sunderland	W	3-0	2-0	5	Wright 3 (1 pen) [21, 29 (p), 73]	30,219
39	28	A	Sheffield U	L	1-3	0-2	5	Rudoni [90]	30,803
40	Apr 5	H	Burnley	L	1-2	1-1	7	Wright [5]	28,704
41	9	H	Portsmouth	W	1-0	0-0	6	Paterson [90]	28,411
42	14	A	Hull C	D	1-1	0-0	6	Grimes [46]	21,659
43	18	H	WBA	W	2-0	1-0	6	Rudoni [6], Grimes [48]	31,167
44	21	A	Plymouth Arg	L	1-3	1-2	6	Wright [45]	16,974
45	26	A	Luton T	L	0-1	0-0	6		11,965
46	May 3	H	Middlesbrough	W	2-0	1-0	5	Rudoni 2 [44, 87]	31,452

Final League Position: 5

GOALSCORERS

League (64): Wright 12 (1 pen), Rudoni 9, Overgaard 6 (1 pen), Simms 6, Mason-Clark 5, Thomas 5, Sakamoto 4, Thomas-Asante 4, Eccles 3, Bassette 2, Grimes 2, van Ewijk 2, Bidwell 1, Palmer 1, Paterson 1, own goal 1.
FA Cup (2): Kitching 1, Latibeaudiere 1.
Carabao Cup (3): Thomas-Asante 2, Simms 1.
Championship Play-offs (2): Mason-Clark 1, Rudoni 1.

Dovin O 28	van Ewijk M 45	Thomas B 37 + 1	Binks L 21 + 1	Bidwell J 23 + 6	Rudoni J 40 + 3	Allen J 12 + 9	Overgaard V 25 + 11	Sakamoto T 30 + 12	Simms E 26 + 17	Mason-Clark E 17 + 13	Eccles J 25 + 14	Wright H 21 + 6	Thomas-Asante B 14 + 22	Palmer K — + 3	Latibeaudiere J 29 + 4	Dasilva J 20 + 11	Bassette N 11 + 14	Kitching L 26 + 1	Wilson B 4	Sheaf B 23 + 6	Collins B 14 + 1	Tavares F — + 1	Borges Rodrigues R — + 3	Grimes M 15 + 1	Paterson J — + 8	Match No.
1	2	3	4	5	6	7	8³	9⁴	10²	11¹	12	13	14	15												1
1	2		4	5⁴	9		7⁴	8²	11¹	13	6	10	12	15	3	14										2
1	2		4	5⁴	9		6²	8¹	11³	13	7	10	14	12	3	15										3
1	2		4	5³	9	15	7⁵	8¹	11²	12	6	10⁴	16		3	14	13									4
1	2	4		8		9		10	11²	7	12	13			3¹	6	5									5
1	2	3	4	5⁵	9	7¹	12	15	14	13	6	10²	8⁴		16	11³										6
8	3			9⁴			15	12	11¹	10³	6	13	14		2	5		4	1	7²						7
	2	3		5	9		14	8¹	15	12	6³	10	11⁴	13				4	1	7²						8
	2	3		5²	9			12	8¹	7	10	11			13			4	1	6						9
1	2⁴	3	5		9³		14	15	10²		7	12	13		4	6	11¹			8						10
1	5	3	4		8⁴		12	15	13		7¹	10³	11²		2	9	14			6						11
1	5	3	4		12		13	9²	11		6	10			2			8¹		7						12
1	5	3	4		8²		9¹	12		13	6	10³	11⁴		2	14	15			7						13
1	5	3	4		8³		13	9		14	6	10	11²		2¹	12				7						14
	5	2	3		7		9	13		14		11³	10¹		6	8²	12	4				1				15
	5	3	4	16	8		10¹	12	15	13	6⁴		14		2³	9⁵	11²			7	1					16
	5	3	4⁵	15	14		10³	8	12	13	6		16		2	9¹	11²			7⁴	1					17
	2	3	4		9		13	8³	12	10	6²		14			5	11¹			7	1					18
	2	3		5³	9		6²	8⁵	11¹	10⁴	12		15		4	14	13			7	1	16				19
	2	3		5	9		12	8³	14	10²	6¹		13		4		11			7	1					20
	2	3	4	13	9		6⁴	8	12	10³	14		15		5²	11¹				7	1					21
	2	3²	4		9	16	6³	8	13	10¹	14		12		15	5	11⁴			7⁵	1					22
1	2⁴	3		5	9⁵	15	12	8²	13	10¹	6		14		4	11³	16			7						23
1	2	3		5	10		9²	8	12		6		13		4	11¹				7						24
1	2	3		5	10		9²	8³	11		6¹		12		4	13				7		14				25
1	2	4		6	9	8		13			12		10		3	11²	5			7¹						26
1	5		3		8¹	7	6		11		12		10²		2	9	13	4								27
1	5	12	3¹	9	8	7	6²	14	11⁴		13		10³		2		15	4								28
1	5	3		8	9	7²	6	12	11³		13		10¹		2		14	4								29
1	5	3		9	8¹	7	6⁴	12	11³		13		10²		2		14	4					15			30
1	5	3		9⁴	8⁵	7²	6³	12	11		14		10¹		2	15		4					16	13		31
1	5	2	3		10		6³	9	11²	14	12		13		8		4¹			7						32
1	5	3		13	11³	14		12	10	15	6⁴		9¹		2	8²		4		7						33
1	5	2		4	8	13		9³	11	10¹	6²							3		14			7	12		34
1	5	2		4	8¹	14		9	11²	10⁴	6³	13						3		12			7	15		35
1	2⁴	3			14		6³	9	10²	11¹	8⁵	13	12		15	5		4		16			7			36
1	2	3		5¹			6	9	10²	13	8³	11				12	14	4					7			37
1	2	3			8		6²	9	13	11¹	14	10³				5		4					7	12		38
1¹	2	3	4	5	13	7³	9²	8	15	10⁵	11⁴				14	12							6	16		39
	2	3			9	7¹	12	8³	13	10		11			5			4		1			6			40
	2	3			9		7¹	8²	13	10³		11⁴			5	14		4		12	1		6	15		41
	2				9			8	11¹			10²			3	5	12	4		6	1		7	13		42
	2	16	12		9	13		8	11³			10⁵			3	5¹	14	4⁴		6	1		7²	15		43
	2			5¹	9	7²		8¹	11³			10	15		3	12		4		14	1		6	13		44
		3³	12	9		8¹	11²		13	10	14				2	5⁸		4		7	1		6			45
	2	3⁴		5	9	13		8³	11¹		14	10	12	15				4	1	7²			6			46

FA Cup
Third Round   Sheffield Wed   (h)   1-1
aet; Coventry C won 4-3 on penalties.
Fourth Round   Ipswich T   (h)   1-4

Carabao Cup
First Round   Bristol C   (a)   1-0
Second Round   Oxford U   (h)   1-0
Third Round   Tottenham H   (h)   1-2

Championship Play-offs
Semi-Final 1st leg   Sunderland   (h)   1-2
Semi-Final 2nd leg   Sunderland   (a)   1-1
aet.

CRAWLEY TOWN

FOUNDATION

Formed in 1896, Crawley Town initially entered the West Sussex League before switching to the mid-Sussex League in 1901, winning the Second Division in its second season. The club remained at such level until 1951 when it became members of the Sussex County League and five years later moved to the Metropolitan League while remaining as an amateur club. It was not until 1962 that the club turned semi-professional and a year later, joined the Southern League. Many honours came the club's way, but the most successful run was achieved in 2010–11 when they reached the fifith round of the FA Cup and played before a crowd of 74,778 spectators at Old Trafford against Manchester United. Crawley Town spent 48 years at the Town Mead ground before a new site was occupied at Broadfield in 1997, ideally suited to access from the neighbouring motorway. History was also made on 9 April when the team won promotion to the Football League after beating Tamworth 3-0 to stretch their unbeaten League record to 26 games. They finished the season with a Conference record points total of 105 and at the same time, established another milestone for the longest unbeaten run, having extended it to 30 matches by the end of the season.

Broadfield Stadium, Winfield Way, Crawley, West Sussex RH11 9RX.

Telephone: (01293) 410 000.

Ticket Office: (01293) 410 000.

Website: www.crawleytownfc.com

Email: feedback@crawleytownfc.com

Ground Capacity: 5,836.

Record Attendance: 5,880 v Reading, FA Cup 3rd rd, 5 January 2013.

Pitch Measurements: 102m × 66m (111.5yd × 72yd).

Chairman: Preston Johnson.

General Manager: Tom Allman.

Manager: Scott Lindsey.

Assistant Manager: Neil Smith.

Colours: Red shirts with dark red pattern and trim, red shorts with dark red trim, red socks with dark red trim.

Year Formed: 1896. *Turned Professional:* 1962.

Club Nickname: 'The Reds', 'The Red Devils'.

Grounds: Up to 1997, Town Mead; 1997 Broadfield Stadium (renamed Checkatrade.com Stadium 2013; The People's Pension Stadium 2018; Broadfield Stadium 2022).

First Football League Game: 6 August 2011, FL 2 v Port Vale (a) D 2–2 – Shearer; Hunt, Howell, Bulman, McFadzean (1), Dempster (Thomas), Simpson, Torres, Tubbs (Neilson), Barnett (1) (Wassmer), Smith.

HONOURS

League Champions: Football Conference – 2010–11.

FL 2 – (3rd) 2011–12 *(promoted to FL 1).*

FA Cup: 5th rd – 2011, 2012.

League Cup: 4th rd – 2020.

FOOTBALL YEARBOOK FACT FILE

It was not until the 1971–72 season that Crawley Town were drawn to face a Football League team in the FA Cup. After battling through the qualifying rounds the then Southern League club faced Exeter City at Town Meadow in the first round. The game finished in a goalless draw in front of a crowd of 3,053, with the Grecians winning the replay 2-0.

Record League Victory: 5–1 v Barnsley, FL 1, 14 February 2015 – Price; Dickson, Bradley (1), Ward, Fowler (Smith); Young, Elliott (1), Edwards, Wordsworth (Morgan), Pogba (Tomlin); McLeod (3); 5–1 v Milton Keynes D, FL 2 Play-off Semi-Final, 11 May 2024 – Addai; Wright (Mukena), Conroy, Maguire, Forster (Gordon), Williams (1) (Tsaroulla), Kelly L, Kelly J, Lolos (Roles (1)), Campbell (Darcy), Orsi-Dadomo (3).

Record Cup Victory: 8–0 v Droylsen, FA Trophy 3rd rd, 2 February 2008 – Bayes; Watson, Stevens, Thompson, Vieira (3, 1 pen), Bulman (1), Wilson, Cook (3, 1 pen), Murphy, Carayol, Pittman (1). *Substitutes:* Blackburn, Lovegrove, Joseph-Dubois, Krause, Thomas.

Record Defeat: 0–6 v Morecambe, FL 2, 10 September 2011; 0–6 v Swindon T, FL 2, 26 August 2023.

Most League Points (3 for a win): 84, FL 2, 2011–12.

Most League Goals: 76, FL 2, 2011–12.

Highest League Scorer in Season: James Collins, 20, FL 2, 2016–17.

Most League Goals in Total Aggregate: Ollie Palmer, 27, 2018–20.

Most League Goals in One Match: 3, Izale McLeod v Barnsley, FL 1, 14 February 2015; 3, Jimmy Smith v Colchester U, FL 2, 14 February 2017; 3, Max Watters v Barrow, FL 2, 12 December 2020.

Most Capped Player: Ricky German, 3, Grenada.

Most League Appearances: Glenn Morris, 257, 2016–22.

Youngest League Player: Brian Galach, 17 years 353 days v Tranmere R, 4 May 2019.

MANAGERS
John Maggs 1978–90
Brian Sparrow 1990–92
Steve Wicks 1992–93
Ted Shepherd 1993–95
Colin Pates 1995–96
Billy Smith 1997–99
Cliff Cant 1999–2000
Billy Smith 2000–03
Francis Vines 2003–05
John Hollins 2005–06
David Woozley, Ben Judge and John Yems 2006–07
Steve Evans 2007–12
Sean O'Driscoll 2012
Richie Barker 2012–13
John Gregory 2013–14
Dean Saunders 2014–15
Mark Yates 2015–16
Dermot Drummy 2016–17
Harry Kewell 2017–18
Gabriele Cioffi 2018–19
John Yems 2019–22
Kevin Betsy 2022
Matthew Etherington 2022
Scott Lindsey 2023–24
Rob Elliot 2024–25
Scott Lindsey March 2025–

Record Transfer Fee Received: £1,100,000 from Peterborough U for Tyrone Barnett, July 2012.

Record Transfer Fee Paid: £650,000 to Singida Black Stars for Benjamin Tanimu, September 2024.

Football League Record: 2011 Promoted from Football Conference; 2011–12 FL 2; 2012–15 FL 1; 2015–24 FL 2; 2024–25 FL 1; 2025– FL 2.

LATEST SEQUENCES

Longest Sequence of League Wins: 7, 17.9.2011 – 25.10.2011.

Longest Sequence of League Defeats: 8, 28.3.2016 – 7.5.2016.

Longest Sequence of League Draws: 5, 25.10.2014 – 29.11.2014.

Longest Sequence of Unbeaten League Matches: 13, 17.9.2011 – 17.12.2011.

Longest Sequence Without a League Win: 13, 25.10.2014 – 27.1.2015.

Successive Scoring Runs: 21 from 6.4.2019.

Successive Non-scoring Runs: 4 from 14.10.2017.

TEN YEAR LEAGUE RECORD		P	W	D	L	F	A	Pts	Pos
2015-16	FL 2	46	13	8	25	45	78	47	20
2016-17	FL 2	46	13	12	21	53	71	51	19
2017-18	FL 2	46	16	11	19	58	66	59	14
2018-19	FL 2	46	15	8	23	51	68	53	19
2019-20	FL 2	37	11	15	11	51	47	48	13§
2020-21	FL 2	46	16	13	17	56	62	61	12
2021-22	FL 2	46	17	10	19	56	66	61	12
2022-23	FL 2	46	11	13	22	48	71	46	22
2023-24	FL 2	46	21	7	18	73	67	70	7
2024-25	FL 1	46	12	10	24	57	83	46	21

§*Decided on points-per-game (1.30)*

DID YOU KNOW ?

The highest attendance to watch Crawley Town was 74,778 for the FA Cup fifth-round tie against Manchester United on 19 February 2011. Over 9,000 fans travelled up from Sussex, well in excess of the club's home capacity, to watch Crawley go down 1-0 to a 28th minute goal from Wes Brown.

CRAWLEY TOWN – SKY BET LEAGUE ONE 2024–25 LEAGUE RECORD

Match No.	Date	Venue	Opponents	Result	H/T Score	Lg Pos.	Goalscorers	Attendance
1	Aug 10	H	Blackpool	W 2-1	2-0	5	Hepburn-Murphy [16], Quitirna [33]	4718
2	17	A	Cambridge U	W 1-0	0-0	3	Adeyemo [86]	6720
3	24	A	Wigan Ath	L 0-1	0-1	8		8432
4	31	H	Barnsley	L 0-3	0-3	12		4704
5	Sept 14	H	Stockport Co	D 1-1	0-1	13	Quitirna (pen) [68]	4538
6	21	A	Wrexham	L 1-2	0-1	17	Quitirna [54]	12,732
7	28	H	Bolton W	L 0-2	0-1	20		4696
8	Oct 1	H	Mansfield T	L 0-2	0-1	21		3351
9	5	A	Wycombe W	L 0-1	0-1	21		4472
10	12	H	Shrewsbury T	L 3-5	1-1	22	Swan [33], Quitirna [62], Kelly [90]	4215
11	19	A	Reading	L 1-4	1-2	22	Forster [30]	13,243
12	22	H	Lincoln C	W 3-0	0-0	21	Swan [46], Darcy [73], Hepburn-Murphy [90]	3221
13	26	A	Northampton T	L 0-3	0-2	22		6445
14	Nov 5	A	Burton Alb	D 0-0	0-0	21		1810
15	9	H	Huddersfield T	D 2-2	1-0	21	Hepburn-Murphy [42], Anderson [65]	4752
16	16	A	Bristol R	D 0-0	0-0	21		7411
17	23	H	Rotherham U	W 1-0	1-0	20	Swan [21]	3631
18	Dec 3	A	Charlton Ath	W 2-1	1-0	19	Showunmi [33], Anderson [80]	11,427
19	14	A	Peterborough U	L 3-4	1-2	21	Adeyemo [38], Swan [53], Showunmi [55]	7874
20	23	H	Birmingham C	L 0-1	0-0	21		5530
21	26	A	Leyton Orient	L 0-3	0-1	21		8195
22	29	A	Exeter C	D 4-4	4-1	21	Camara [15], Swan [37], Showunmi [42], Quitirna [45]	6805
23	Jan 4	A	Barnsley	L 0-3	0-1	21		11,016
24	18	H	Burton Alb	D 1-1	0-1	21	Showunmi [72]	3521
25	25	A	Stockport Co	L 0-2	0-2	23		8960
26	28	A	Mansfield T	W 1-0	0-0	22	Adeyemo [81]	6836
27	Feb 1	H	Wrexham	L 1-2	0-1	22	Ibrahim [90]	5049
28	8	A	Bolton W	L 3-4	0-0	23	Hepburn-Murphy 2 [50, 62], Swan [54]	20,384
29	11	H	Stevenage	W 3-1	0-0	22	Forster [50], Quitirna [87], Doyle [90]	3220
30	15	H	Wycombe W	D 1-1	1-1	21	Swan [5]	4330
31	18	H	Wigan Ath	D 1-1	1-1	22	Barker [42]	3733
32	22	A	Blackpool	L 1-3	1-2	22	Doyle [30]	9281
33	Mar 1	H	Cambridge U	L 0-2	0-1	23		4955
34	4	A	Lincoln C	L 1-4	1-3	23	Doyle [6]	7253
35	8	H	Reading	D 1-1	0-1	22	Camara [90]	4526
36	11	H	Charlton Ath	L 0-1	0-1	22		5489
37	15	A	Huddersfield T	L 1-5	0-4	22	Adeyemo [90]	18,516
38	22	H	Bristol R	W 1-0	1-0	22	Doyle [19]	4421
39	29	A	Rotherham U	W 4-0	1-0	22	Doyle 2 [23, 52], Holohan [84], Camara [87]	8177
40	Apr 1	A	Peterborough U	L 3-4	2-3	22	Quitirna [12], Kelly [32], Hepburn-Murphy [49]	4111
41	5	A	Stevenage	L 1-3	0-1	22	Ibrahim [70]	4403
42	12	H	Leyton Orient	L 1-3	0-0	22	Quitirna (pen) [49]	4793
43	18	A	Birmingham C	D 0-0	0-0	23		27,325
44	21	H	Exeter C	W 3-1	3-1	22	Hepburn-Murphy 2 [7, 23], Camara [9]	4441
45	26	A	Northampton T	W 3-0	0-0	21	Hepburn-Murphy [39], Kelly [66], Doyle [88]	5105
46	May 3	A	Shrewsbury T	W 2-1	0-0	21	Hepburn-Murphy (pen) [50], Anderson [60]	5599

Final League Position: 21

GOALSCORERS

League (57): Hepburn-Murphy 10 (1 pen), Quitirna 8 (2 pens), Doyle 7, Swan 7, Adeyemo 4, Camara 4, Showunmi 4, Anderson 3, Kelly 3, Forster 2, Ibrahim 2, Barker 1, Darcy 1, Holohan 1.
FA Cup (5): Showunmi 2, Kelly 1, Mullarkey 1, Roles 1.
Carabao Cup (4): Roles 2, Adeyemo 1, Khaleel 1.
Vertu Trophy (6): Barker 1, Darcy 1 (1 pen), Flint 1, Hepburn-Murphy 1, Papadopoulos 1, Showunmi 1.

Wollacott J 33	Mullarkey T 31	Mukena J 16 + 3	Flint J 15 + 1	Malone S 2	Williams J 12	Anderson M 32 + 7	Oyitirna J 21 + 13	Kelly J 32 + 5	Darcy R 19 + 2	Hepburn-Murphy R 27 + 15	Bragg C 2 + 4	Camara P 28 + 14	Adeyemo A 11 + 18	Roles J 5 + 15	Barker C 37 + 2	Swan W 31 + 6	Forster H 16 + 9	Ibrahim B 24 + 9	Showunmi T 11 + 13	Trueman C 4	Holohan G 4 + 17	Tanimu B 1 + 6	Fish S — + 1	John-Jules T 10 + 15	Khaleel R — + 1	Conroy D 21	Radcliffe B 16 + 3	Papadopoulos A — + 5	Cox M 3	Doyle K 15 + 6	Feely R 2 + 5	Fraser L 15 + 1	Watson L 4 + 3	Lo-Tutala T 1	Hutchinson L 1	Steward T 4	Match No.
1	2	3	4	5	6	7[2]	8[1]	9	10[4]	11[3]	12	13	14	15																							1
1	2	3	4	5[1]	6[5]	7[2]	8[1]	9	10	11[4]	13	14	12	15	16																						2
1	2	3	4		6[3]	7[1]	9	8	10	11	12	13	5[2]	14																							3
1	2	3	4			7	9[1]	8	10	11[3]	6[2]	5	14				12	13																			4
1	2	3	4		6[2]	7	13	8	10	9[3]	5	12					11[1]	14																			5
1	2	3	4		6	7[1]	8	10[4]	12	13	5	14					11[2]	15																			6
1	2	3	4		6[5]		5[4]	8	10	15		7[2]	9	12	16		11[1]	14	13																		7
1	2	3	4		7	15	5	13	9	14		11[1]	12			10[8]	8[3]	6[4]																			8
1	2	3[1]	4		7		9[6]	5	10	15		14	13	12	11[4]	8[2]	6[3]	16																			9
	3	14	4		7	12	5[1]	15	9[2]	11[3]		13			2	10	8[4]	6[5]		1	16																10
1	2		4[1]			6[2]	8[5]	10	9	12		3			11[4]	5[1]	7	15			16	14															11
1	3		4		7	8[3]	5[1]	9	11[4]	13		14			2	10	12	6			15																12
1	4		5[2]		8	9[1]	6	11[4]	13	12		3			10[5]	2	7[3]	16		14	15																13
	2	3			7		8[3]	10	13	12	15	4	11[2]	5[4]	6	14				1	9[1]																14
	2	3			7		13	10[4]	8[2]	9[3]		4	11[1]	5	6	12				1	15			14													15
	2	3			7[1]		5[1]	11	8[3]			9	13	15	4	10[2]				6	12	1		14													16
1	2	3			7		8	9[3]				6[5]	5[2]	15	4	10[4]				11[1]		16	13	12	14												17
1		3			6		7	5[3]	16			8[5]	9	15	4	11[4]	13	12	10[1]			2[2]		14													18
1		4	3		6[5]		7	5[1]	13			8[4]	9	15	2	11[3]	14	16	10[2]					12													19
1	2				8[3]	17	7	12	15			6[4]	9[1]	16	4	10	5	14	11[2]					13				3[5]									20
1	2	15			8	13	7[3]		9[2]			12		6[1]	4	11		5	16			14		10[4]				3[5]									21
1	2	12			8[4]	6[1]	7		14			9		15	4	10[3]		5	11[2]					13				3									22
1	2				6[2]	5	7[4]	12	9			4			11[3]	13	10							8[1]				3	14	15							23
1	4[1]				7[2]	6	6[5]	13	8			9[5]			2	10[4]	16	15	11					14				3	12								24
1					14		7[3]	13	9			6[5]	5[4]	15	4	10[3]	12	8[3]	11					16				3	2								25
					8[5]			11				6[3]	12		4	9[4]	5[1]	7	13	15	16			10[2]				3	2	1	14						26
					8[4]		12	10				6[1]	14		4	9[5]	5[3]	7	13					11[2]				3	2	1	16	15					27
							15					8[4]	14		4	9[3]	5[2]	7	12					10				3	2	1	6[1]	13					28
1					6[5]	14		10[4]				8[2]	16		2	5[3]	9	7	11[1]		15			12				3	4		13						29
1					8[2]	14		11[5]				13			2	5[1]	9	7	15					10[4]				3	4		6[3]	16	12				30
1					6[1]	13		10[3]				8[5]	15		2	14	9	11[12]						16				3	4		5[4]		7				31
1					8[1]	12		11				14			-4	9	5[2]							13				3	10[5]	3	2[3]			6[4]	15	7	16	32
1					15	5[3]		11				16	14		2	13	9[2]	7[1]	12					10				3			8[5]	4	6[4]				33
1					7	5						8[4]			6	9					14	13		11		3[2]	4	15		10[3]	2[1]		12				34
1	3				8[2]	13						12	5[4]		4	9		14			16			11[5]				2[3]		10	15	7	6[1]				35
1	3[5]				6[1]	5	14					10[2]	8[3]		2	11	15				16			13				4		9		7[4]	12				36
1	3	14			16	15	9[4]		13			8[1]	12		2	5[2]			11[5]					4				10			7[3]	6					37
	3		4		16	5[3]	9[1]	11[4]	12			2	15	13	6[5]						14							10			7	8[2]	1				38
1	3		4			5	9[4]	11	12			2	13[3]	8	15	14												10[2]			7	6[1]					39
1	3		4			5	9[2]	11	6[13]	12		2	12	8		14												10[3]			7						40
1	2[3]					5	9	11	6[1]	12	4		8		14				13		3	15						10[4]			7[2]						41
	2					5[2]	9	10	6	13	4	12	8			14			3									11[1]			7[3]		1				42
					13	9	10	6[2]		5[3]	4		8			12											3	2	14		11[1]	7	1				43
					8	13	9	10	6[1]	5[2]	4		11			3											2	12			7	1				44
					8	12	9	10	6[2]	5[1]	4		11[3]			3											2	14		13	7	1				45
					8	12	9[1]	11	6	5[3]	2		10[2]			3											4	14		13	7	1				46

FA Cup

First Round	Maidenhead U	(a)	2-1	
aet.				
Second Round	Lincoln C	(h)	3-4	

Carabao Cup

First Round	Swindon T	(h)	4-2
Second Round	Brighton & HA	(a)	0-4

Vertu Trophy

Group B (S)	Brighton & HA U21	(h)	2-2
Crawley T won 4-3 on penalties.			
Group B (S)	AFC Wimbledon	(h)	3-4
Group B (S)	Wycombe W	(a)	1-2

CREWE ALEXANDRA

FOUNDATION

The first match played at Crewe was on 1 December 1877 against Basford, the leading North Staffordshire team of that time. During the club's history they have also played in a number of other leagues including the Football Alliance, Football Combination, Lancashire League, Manchester League, Central League and Lancashire Combination. Two former players, Aaron Scragg in 1899 and Jackie Pearson in 1911, had the distinction of refereeing FA Cup finals. Pearson was also capped for England against Ireland in 1892.

The Mornflake Stadium, Gresty Road, Crewe, Cheshire CW2 6EB.

Telephone: (01270) 213 014.

Ticket Office: (01270) 252 610.

Website: www.crewealex.net

Email: info@crewealex.net

Ground Capacity: 10,109.

Record Attendance: 20,000 v Tottenham H, FA Cup 4th rd, 30 January 1960.

Pitch Measurements: 101m × 68m (110.5yd × 74.5yd).

Chairman: Charles Grant.

Head of Commercial: James Beckett.

Manager: Lee Bell.

Assistant Manager: Ryan Dicker.

Colours: Red shirts with white and blue trim, white shorts with blue trim, red socks with white trim.

Year Formed: 1877. *Turned Professional:* 1893. *Club Nickname:* 'The Railwaymen'.

Ground: 1898, Gresty Road (renamed The Mornflake Stadium 2021).

First Football League Game: 3 September 1892, Division 2, v Burton Swifts (a) L 1–7 – Hickton; Moore, Cope; Linnell, Johnson, Osborne; Bennett, Pearson (1), Bailey, Barnett, Roberts.

Record League Victory: 8–0 v Rotherham U, Division 3 (N), 1 October 1932 – Foster; Pringle, Dawson; Ward, Keenor (1), Turner (1); Gillespie, Swindells (1), McConnell (2), Deacon (2), Weale (1).

Record Cup Victory: 8–0 v Hartlepool U, Auto Windscreens Shield 1st rd, 17 October 1995 – Gayle; Collins (1), Booty, Westwood (Unsworth), Macauley (1), Whalley (1), Garvey (1), Murphy (1), Savage (1) (Rivers (1p)), Lennon, Edwards, (1 og). 8–0 v Doncaster R, LDV Vans Trophy 3rd rd, 10 November 2002 – Bankole; Wright, Walker, Foster, Tierney; Lunt (1), Brammer, Sorvel, Vaughan (1) (Bell); Ashton (3) (Miles), Jack (2) (Jones (1)).

HONOURS

League: Runners-up: Second Division – 2002–03; FL 2 – 2019–20.

FA Cup: semi-final – 1888.

League Cup: 3rd rd – 1975, 1976, 1979, 1993, 1999, 2000, 2002, 2005, 2009, 2020.

League Trophy Winners: 2013.

Welsh Cup Winners: 1936, 1937.

FOOTBALL YEARBOOK FACT FILE

Crewe Alexandra scored a remarkable 8-1 win over top-of-the-table Lincoln City in their Division Three North fixture at Gresty Road on 5 December 1931. Centre-forward Bert Swindells netted a hat-trick and other goals came from Jack Maddock, Mick Murray, Eric Sweeney and Harry Deacon (2). The Railwaymen established a new club record Football League win, but this lasted less than 12 months as they went on to beat Rotherham United 8-0 the following October.

Record Defeat: 2–13 v Tottenham H, FA Cup 4th rd replay, 3 February 1960.

Most League Points (2 for a win): 59, Division 4, 1962–63.

Most League Points (3 for a win): 86, Division 2, 2002–03.

Most League Goals: 95, Division 3 (N), 1931–32.

Highest League Scorer in Season: Terry Harkin, 35, Division 4, 1964–65.

Most League Goals in Total Aggregate: Bert Swindells, 126, 1928–37.

Most League Goals in One Match: 5, Tony Naylor v Colchester U, Division 3, 24 April 1993.

Most Capped Player: Clayton Ince, 40 (79), Trinidad & Tobago.

Most League Appearances: Tommy Lowry, 436, 1966–78.

Youngest League Player: Steve Walters, 16 years 119 days v Peterborough U, 6 May 1988.

Record Transfer Fee Received: £3,000,000 (potentially rising to £6,000,000) from Manchester U for Nick Powell, June 2012.

Record Transfer Fee Paid: £650,000 to Torquay U for Rodney Jack, July 1998.

Football League Record: 1892 Original Member of Division 2; 1892–96 Division 2; 1896 Failed re-election; 1921–58 Division 3 (N); 1921 Re-entered Division (N); 1958–63 Division 4; 1963–64 Division 3; 1964–68 Division 4; 1968–69 Division 3; 1969–89 Division 4; 1989–91 Division 3; 1991–92 Division 4; 1992–94 Third Division; 1994–97 Second Division; 1997–2002 First Division; 2002–03 Second Division; 2003–04 First Division; 2004–06 FL C; 2006–09 FL 1; 2009–12 FL 2; 2012–16 FL 1; 2016–20 FL 2; 2020–22 FL 1; 2022– FL 2.

LATEST SEQUENCES

Longest Sequence of League Wins: 7, 30.4.1994 – 3.9.1994.

Longest Sequence of League Defeats: 10, 16.4.1979 – 22.8.1979.

Longest Sequence of League Draws: 5, 18.9.2010 – 9.10.2010.

Longest Sequence of Unbeaten League Matches: 17, 25.3.1995 – 16.9.1995.

Longest Sequence Without a League Win: 30, 22.9.1956 – 6.4.1957.

Successive Scoring Runs: 26 from 7.4.1934.

Successive Non-scoring Runs: 9 from 6.11.1974.

MANAGERS

W. C. McNeill 1892–94 *(Secretary-Manager)*
J. G. Hall 1895–96 *(Secretary-Manager)*
R. Roberts (*1st team Secretary-Manager*) 1897
J. B. Blomerley 1898–1911 *(Secretary-Manager, continued as Hon. Secretary to 1925)*
Tom Bailey (*Secretary only*) 1925–38
George Lillycrop (*Trainer*) 1938–44
Frank Hill 1944–48
Arthur Turner 1948–51
Harry Catterick 1951–53
Ralph Ward 1953–55
Maurice Lindley 1956–57
Willie Cook 1957–58
Harry Ware 1958–60
Jimmy McGuigan 1960–64
Ernie Tagg 1964–71 *(continued as Secretary to 1972)*
Dennis Viollet 1971
Jimmy Melia 1972–74
Ernie Tagg 1974
Harry Gregg 1975–78
Warwick Rimmer 1978–79
Tony Waddington 1979–81
Arfon Griffiths 1981–82
Peter Morris 1982–83
Dario Gradi 1983–2007
Steve Holland 2007–08
Gudjon Thordarson 2008–09
Dario Gradi 2009–11
Steve Davis 2011–17
David Artell 2017–22
Alex Morris 2022
Lee Bell November 2022–

TEN YEAR LEAGUE RECORD

		P	W	D	L	F	A	Pts	Pos
2015-16	FL 1	46	7	13	26	46	83	34	24
2016-17	FL 2	46	14	13	19	58	67	55	17
2017-18	FL 2	46	17	5	24	62	75	56	15
2018-19	FL 2	46	19	8	19	60	59	65	12
2019-20	FL 2	37	20	9	8	67	43	69	2§
2020-21	FL 1	46	18	12	16	56	61	66	12
2021-22	FL 1	46	7	8	31	37	83	29	24
2022-23	FL 2	46	14	16	16	48	60	58	13
2023-24	FL 2	46	19	14	13	69	65	71	6
2024-25	FL 2	46	15	17	14	49	48	62	13

§*Decided on points-per-game (1.86)*

DID YOU KNOW ?

James Hall was one of the most important figures in the history of Crewe Alexandra and a key figure in the development of both the Football Combination (1888–89) and the Football Alliance (1889–1892). A founder member of the club, he captained the team in their first-ever match and was heavily involved in the administration of the club, serving at various times as secretary, treasurer, director and vice-president up until his death in December 1922.

CREWE ALEXANDRA – SKY BET LEAGUE TWO 2024–25 LEAGUE RECORD

Match No.	Date	Venue	Opponents	Result	H/T Score	Lg Pos.	Goalscorers	Attendance
1	Aug 10	A	Barrow	L	0-1	0-1	17		3585
2	17	H	Chesterfield	L	0-5	0-4	24		5626
3	24	H	Swindon T	D	0-0	0-0	23		4402
4	31	A	Bromley	W	2-1	0-1	17	Demetriou [83], Long [90]	3322
5	Sept 7	H	Morecambe	W	1-0	1-0	13	Hemmings (pen) [43]	4868
6	14	A	Accrington S	W	1-0	0-0	9	Williams [85]	2883
7	21	H	Harrogate T	W	3-0	2-0	7	Hemmings 2 [7, 88], Lankester [31]	4320
8	28	A	Newport Co	L	1-2	0-1	8	Thibaut [71]	4273
9	Oct 5	H	Gillingham	W	2-0	1-0	8	Tracey 2 [17, 60]	5000
10	12	A	Doncaster R	D	1-1	0-0	9	Conway [56]	7472
11	19	H	Salford C	D	1-1	1-1	9	Cooney [26]	4936
12	22	A	Fleetwood T	W	1-0	0-0	6	Cooney (pen) [87]	2725
13	26	H	Tranmere R	W	3-1	1-1	5	Tracey 2 [39, 54], Tabiner [84]	5957
14	Nov 9	A	Walsall	D	1-1	0-0	5	Bogle [66]	8105
15	16	H	Notts Co	W	2-0	1-0	2	Tracey [40], Cooney (pen) [62]	6127
16	25	A	Port Vale	D	1-1	0-1	3	Lankester [90]	10,222
17	30	A	Carlisle U	D	1-1	0-1	3	Lankester (pen) [82]	5839
18	Dec 7	H	Bradford C	D	1-1	0-0	4	Bogle [47]	5350
19	14	A	Grimsby T	W	2-0	0-0	3	Lankester [55], Tabiner [63]	5745
20	20	H	Colchester U	D	0-0	0-0	3		9288
21	26	A	Cheltenham T	L	1-2	0-0	4	Lankester [56]	5261
22	29	A	Milton Keynes D	D	1-1	0-1	6	Knight-Lebel [56]	7508
23	Jan 1	A	Carlisle U	W	3-2	1-1	4	Long [32], Lankester [90], Bogle [90]	6345
24	5	H	Bromley	W	4-1	3-1	2	Bogle 2 [28, 32], Lankester [38], Knight-Lebel [82]	4462
25	11	A	Swindon T	D	0-0	0-0	2		6638
26	18	A	Morecambe	W	1-0	0-0	2	Long [68]	3648
27	25	H	Accrington S	L	0-1	0-1	2		4965
28	28	H	AFC Wimbledon	D	1-1	1-1	4	Knight-Lebel [14]	4039
29	Feb 1	A	Harrogate T	D	1-1	0-1	5	Long [58]	2704
30	8	H	Newport Co	L	0-3	0-2	8		4472
31	11	A	AFC Wimbledon	L	0-3	0-2	8		7662
32	15	H	Gillingham	D	0-0	0-0	7		5663
33	22	H	Barrow	W	3-0	1-0	7	O'Riordan [37], Lowery (pen) [50], Holicek [85]	4735
34	Mar 1	A	Chesterfield	W	3-1	2-0	7	Tracey [11], Conway [22], Lowery [90]	8919
35	4	H	Fleetwood T	L	1-4	0-2	7	Long [90]	3881
36	8	A	Salford C	D	1-1	0-0	7	O'Riordan [79]	3524
37	15	H	Doncaster R	D	1-1	1-0	8	O'Riordan [10]	5142
38	22	A	Notts Co	D	0-0	0-0	9		10,225
39	29	H	Port Vale	L	0-1	0-0	9		8365
40	Apr 1	H	Grimsby T	W	2-0	1-0	8	Long [14], Demetriou [90]	4512
41	5	A	Bradford C	L	0-2	0-1	9		22,214
42	10	H	Cheltenham T	L	2-3	1-1	9	Hemmings (pen) [45], Agius [90]	4939
43	18	A	Colchester U	D	0-0	0-0	11		7623
44	21	H	Milton Keynes D	L	0-1	0-1	11		4954
45	26	A	Tranmere R	L	0-2	0-1	12		9496
46	May 3	H	Walsall	L	0-1	0-0	13		7112

Final League Position: 13

GOALSCORERS
League (49): Lankester 7 (1 pen), Long 6, Tracey 6, Bogle 5, Hemmings 4 (2 pens), Cooney 3 (2 pens), Knight-Lebel 3, O'Riordan 3, Conway 2, Demetriou 2, Lowery 2 (1 pen), Tabiner 2, Agius 1, Holicek 1, Thibaut 1, Williams 1.
FA Cup (0).
Carabao Cup (1): Holicek 1.
Vertu Trophy (7): Long 2, Agius 1, Bogle 1, Cooney 1 (1 pen), Roberts 1, Thibaut 1.

Marshall F 46	Billington L 16 + 7	Connolly J 14 + 7	Demetriou M 35	Williams Z 41	Thomas C 13 + 6	Sanders M 31 + 10	Lankester J 16 + 7	Tabiner J 36 + 5	Hemmings K 14 + 6	Conway M 44 + 2	Holicek M 31 + 7	Cooney R 31 + 7	Long C 8 + 17	Knight-Lebel J 29 + 4	Breckin K 3 + 10	Finney C — + 10	Bogle O 13 + 17	Thibaut A 6 + 12	Roberts Finley — + 4	Agius C 1 + 13	Lunt O 5 + 12	Powell J 11 + 11	O'Riordan C 19 + 1	Lowery T 15 + 2	Moore L — + 1	Match No.
1	2^2	3^4	4	5	6^1	7	8	9	10^3	11	12	13	14	15												1
1		3^1	4	5	6^2	7^3	10^4	9	14	11	12	8	2		13	15										2
1	5		3	4	6	7^4	12	9^2	10^4	11	8^3	15		13	2	14										3
1	5^2		3	4	7^1	8	13	12	10^4	11	9^5	6^3	16	14		15										4
1	15		3	4	5	8^2	12	7^5	11^3	10^4	9^1	14	6	2	16	13										5
1	15		3	4	6	7^3	10^4	9^2	12	11	8^1	13	5	2	14											6
1	15		3	4	6^2	13	10^1	7^3	9	11	8^4	12	5	2	14											7
1			3	4		6	10	7^1	9^4	11^2	8^3		5	2	12		13	14	15							8
1	16	2	4	9			11^1	7^3	10^5		8^2	13	5	3	6^4		12		15	14						9
1	14	3	4	5		8^1		9	11	6	10^2	2		7^3		13		12								10
1	3	5	6	14	8^2		11^4		9^3	10	2		4	7^1		15	12		13							11
1	2		4	14	6^3		7^1	11		8	9^4	5		3	15		13	10^2		12						12
1	14	4	5	13	8^3		9	11		6^4		2		3	15		12	10^1		7^2						13
1	12	3	4		7		8	10^4		9^2	6^3	5		2	15		11^1	13		14						14
1	2	3	4		7^3	12	8	11^2		9	6^4	5	14^4		15		10^1			13						15
1	2	3	4^3		7	12	8	11		9	6^2	5					10^1	13			14					16
1	5^1	2^3	3	4		7^3	9^4	10^4	11	8	6^5		12	16	14		13			15						17
1		2	3	4		6^3	9	7^4	11	8^1	12	5		14	10^2	15				13						18
1		2	4	9		5^4	10^2	7^3		8^5	11^1	6	3		16	13		14		12	15					19
1		2	3	4		5^1	10^2	7	11	9	8^3	6	13			12				14						20
1		2^3	3	4		13	11	8	10	9	6^2	5	14			12				7^1						21
1			3	4			7^3		8	11^4		9^2	6^1	5	12	2		15	10		13	14				22
1		12	3	4^1			7	13	8^3	10^2		9	6	5^3	11^4	2		14	15			16				23
1	12	2^1	4				7^3	11^2	14	13		9	8	5	16	3		10^4			15	6^5				24
1			3	4			5	11^4	12^2	13		9	8^1	6	15	2		10			14	7^3				25
1			3	4			5^1	11^2	8	10^3		9	7	6	13	2		15^2	12		14					26
1			4	5			8^1		13	12	15	6^3	7	2^4	11^1	3		10			9^2	14				27
1			4	9		14			7^2	11	12	8^3	6	5	13	2		10^1				3				28
1			4	9		5^3			8^1	10^4		6^5	7	16	11	2^2		15^{12}			14	3	13			29
1	15		5		9^2			7	11		6^1	10^5	2		4^3	13^4	14		16		8	3	12			30
1	12		5		13			7^1	11^3		6^1	10^1	2		3^{8}				14		8	4	9^2			31
1	3			7					9	11^1		5^1	10	2^{8}				12		13	6	4	8^2			32
1	2			7^2				8		5^1	10^3		3					11^1	12^2	13	6	4	9	14		33
1	2^5		5	14	12			7^3	11^2	6	10^4	15		3			13		16		9^1	4	8			34
1			4	14	6^4			9^1	11^1	8	10	5	15	2^2				13			12	3	7^3			35
1	2^5		5	14			15		13	6^3	9	16	12	4				10^1	11^4		7^2	3	8			36
1	5		4	9			7^3		11^2	8	10	14	12	2			13					3^1	6			37
1	4	3		6	12		9^4		11^3	8	10^2	5^1	13				14				15	2	7			38
1	5^3	3	4^4		12	13	7^1		11	8	10	14	9^2				15					2	6			39
1	14	3	4		12	6^9			16	8	10^1	5^4	9^5	15			11^5		13			2	7			40
1	12		4	8^4		6^5			14	10		5^1	9	3^2			11		15		13	2	7			41
1	5		3	4		7			11	9							10^1	14		13	12	8^2	2	6^1		42
1	2		4	5	6^1	12		7^2		11^4	10		14	15				13	8^{8}			3	9^3			43
1	2		4	5^1	7^2			8		11^3	10		12				14			13	9		3	6		44
1	2		4^{8}	7	14			9^1		13	5		11^2					10			12	6^3	3	8^{8}		45
1	2	14		6^2	7				5				11^4	3^3		15	12	10^1	13	9	8		4			46

FA Cup
First Round　　Dagenham & Red　(h)　0-1

Carabao Cup
First Round　　Rotherham U　(a)　1-2

Vertu Trophy
Group E (N)　Liverpool U21　(h)　5-1
Group E (N)　Blackpool　(a)　1-4
Group E (N)　Harrogate T　(h)　1-0
Second Round　Wrexham　(a)　0-1

CRYSTAL PALACE

FOUNDATION

There was a Crystal Palace club as early as 1861 but the present organisation was born in 1905 after the formation of a club by the company that controlled the Crystal Palace (building) had been rejected by the FA, who did not like the idea of the Cup Final hosts running their own club. A separate company had to be formed and they had their home on the old Cup Final ground until 1915.

Selhurst Park Stadium, Holmesdale Road, London SE25 6PU.

Telephone: (020) 8768 6000.

Ticket Office: (0871) 200 0071.

Website: www.cpfc.co.uk

Email: info@cpfc.co.uk

Ground Capacity: 25,194.

Record Attendance: 51,482 v Burnley, Division 2, 11 May 1979 (at Selhurst Park).

Pitch Measurements: 101m × 68m (110.5yd × 74.5yd).

Chairman: Steve Parish.

President: Martin Long.

Manager: Oliver Glasner.

Assistant Manager: Paddy McCarthy.

Colours: Red and blue striped shirts with red and white trim, blue shorts with red trim, blue socks with red and white trim.

Year Formed: 1905.

Turned Professional: 1905.

Club Nickname: 'The Eagles'.

Grounds: 1905, Crystal Palace; 1915, Herne Hill; 1918, The Nest; 1924, Selhurst Park.

First Football League Game: 28 August 1920, Division 3, v Merthyr T (a) L 1–2 – Alderson; Little, Rhodes; McCracken, Jones, Feebury; Bateman, Conner, Smith, Milligan (1), Whibley.

Record League Victory: 9–0 v Barrow, Division 4, 10 October 1959 – Rouse; Long, Noakes; Truett, Evans, McNichol; Gavin (1), Summersby (4 incl. 1p), Sexton, Byrne (2), Colfar (2).

Record Cup Victory: 8–0 v Southend U, Rumbelows League Cup 2nd rd (1st leg), 25 September 1990 – Martyn; Humphrey (Thompson (1)), Shaw, Pardew, Young, Thorn, McGoldrick, Thomas, Bright (3), Wright (3), Barber (Hodges (1)).

Record Defeat: 0–9 v Burnley, FA Cup 2nd rd replay, 10 February 1909; 0–9 v Liverpool, Division 1, 12 September 1990.

Most League Points (2 for a win): 64, Division 4, 1960–61.

HONOURS

League Champions: First Division – 1993–94; Division 2 – 1978–79; Division 3S – 1920–21.
Runners-up: Division 2 – 1968–69; Division 3 – 1963–64; Division 3S – 1928–29, 1930–31, 1938–39; Division 4 – 1960–61.
FA Cup Winners: 2025.
Runners-up: 1990, 2016.
League Cup: semi-final – 1993, 1995, 2001, 2012.
Full Members' Cup Winners: 1991.
European Competition
Intertoto Cup: 1998.

FOOTBALL YEARBOOK FACT FILE

Crystal Palace attracted record Division Four attendances in the 1960–61 season when they were runners-up, winning promotion to Division Three. The Eagles twice created new record match attendances for the competition, with 28,491 attending the Boxing Day game against Exeter City, and 37,774 turning out on Good Friday to see Millwall. The club's seasonal average attendance of 19,089 was also a new divisional record.

Most League Points (3 for a win): 90, Division 1, 1993–94.

Most League Goals: 110, Division 4, 1960–61.

Highest League Scorer in Season: Peter Simpson, 46, Division 3 (S), 1930–31.

Most League Goals in Total Aggregate: Peter Simpson, 153, 1930–36.

Most League Goals in One Match: 6, Peter Simpson v Exeter C, Division 3 (S), 4 October 1930.

Most Capped Player: Wayne Hennessey, 55 (109), Wales.

Most League Appearances: Jim Cannon, 571, 1973–88.

Youngest League Player: John Bostock, 15 years 287 days v Watford, 29 October 2007.

Record Transfer Fee Received: £50,800,000 from Bayern Munich for Michael Olise, July 2024.

Record Transfer Fee Paid: £27,000,000 to Liverpool for Christian Benteke, August 2016; £25,000,000 (potentially rising to £30,000,000) to Arsenal for Eddie Nketiah, August 2024.

Football League Record: 1920 Original Members of Division 3; 1920–21 Division 3; 1921–25 Division 2; 1925–58 Division 3 (S); 1958–61 Division 4; 1961–64 Division 3; 1964–69 Division 2; 1969–73 Division 1; 1973–74 Division 2; 1974–77 Division 3; 1977–79 Division 2; 1979–81 Division 1; 1981–89 Division 2; 1989–92 Division 1; 1992–93 Premier League; 1993–94 First Division; 1994–95 Premier League; 1995–97 First Division; 1997–98 Premier League; 1998–2004 First Division; 2004–05 Premier League; 2005–13 FL C; 2013– Premier League.

LATEST SEQUENCES

Longest Sequence of League Wins: 8, 21.5.2017 – 30.9.2017.

Longest Sequence of League Defeats: 8, 10.1.1998 – 14.3.1998.

Longest Sequence of League Draws: 5, 21.9.2002 – 19.10.2002.

Longest Sequence of Unbeaten League Matches: 18, 22.2.1969 – 13.8.1969.

Longest Sequence Without a League Win: 20, 3.3.1962 – 8.9.1962.

Successive Scoring Runs: 24 from 27.4.1929.

Successive Non-scoring Runs: 9 from 19.11.1994.

MANAGERS

John T. Robson 1905–07
Edmund Goodman 1907–25
  (*Secretary 1905–33*)
Alex Maley 1925–27
Fred Mavin 1927–30
Jack Tresadern 1930–35
Tom Bromilow 1935–36
R. S. Moyes 1936
Tom Bromilow 1936–39
George Irwin 1939–47
Jack Butler 1947–49
Ronnie Rooke 1949–50
Charlie Slade and Fred Dawes (*Joint Managers*) 1950–51
Laurie Scott 1951–54
Cyril Spiers 1954–58
George Smith 1958–60
Arthur Rowe 1960–62
Dick Graham 1962–66
Bert Head 1966–72 (*continued as General Manager to 1973*)
Malcolm Allison 1973–76
Terry Venables 1976–80
Ernie Walley 1980
Malcolm Allison 1980–81
Dario Gradi 1981
Steve Kember 1981–82
Alan Mullery 1982–84
Steve Coppell 1984–93
Alan Smith 1993–95
Steve Coppell (*Technical Director*) 1995–96
Dave Bassett 1996–97
Steve Coppell 1997–98
Attilio Lombardo 1998
Terry Venables (*Head Coach*) 1998–99
Steve Coppell 1999–2000
Alan Smith 2000–01
Steve Bruce 2001
Trevor Francis 2001–03
Steve Kember 2003
Iain Dowie 2003–06
Peter Taylor 2006–07
Neil Warnock 2007–10
Paul Hart 2010
George Burley 2010–11
Dougie Freedman 2011–12
Ian Holloway 2012–13
Tony Pulis 2013–14
Neil Warnock 2014
Alan Pardew 2015–16
Sam Allardyce 2016–17
Frank de Boer 2017
Roy Hodgson 2017–21
Patrick Vieira 2021–23
Roy Hodgson 2023–24
Oliver Glasner February 2024–

TEN YEAR LEAGUE RECORD

		P	W	D	L	F	A	Pts	Pos
2015-16	PR Lge	38	11	9	18	39	51	42	15
2016-17	PR Lge	38	12	5	21	50	63	41	14
2017-18	PR Lge	38	11	11	16	45	55	44	11
2018-19	PR Lge	38	14	7	17	51	53	49	12
2019-20	PR Lge	38	11	10	17	31	50	43	14
2020-21	PR Lge	38	12	8	18	41	66	44	14
2021-22	PR Lge	38	11	15	12	50	46	48	12
2022-23	PR Lge	38	11	12	15	40	49	45	11
2023-24	PR Lge	38	13	10	15	57	58	49	10
2024-25	PR Lge	38	13	14	11	51	51	53	12

DID YOU KNOW ?

In January 1939 Crystal Palace travelled to Brussels to play a floodlit friendly match against the Belgian national team who were preparing for their forthcoming fixture against Germany. Palace went down to a 5-4 defeat at the home of local club Union Saint-Gilloise in front of a crowd of about 8,000. Goalscorers were Bert Robson (2), Bert Dawes and George Daniels.

CRYSTAL PALACE – PREMIER LEAGUE 2024–25 LEAGUE RECORD

Match No.	Date	Venue	Opponents	Result	H/T Score	Lg Pos.	Goalscorers	Attendance
1	Aug 18	A	Brentford	L	1-2	0-1	13	Pinnock (og) [57]	16,988
2	24	H	West Ham U	L	0-2	0-0	18		25,099
3	Sept 1	A	Chelsea	D	1-1	0-1	16	Eze [53]	39,298
4	14	H	Leicester C	D	2-2	0-1	16	Mateta 2 (1 pen) [47, 90 (p)]	25,124
5	21	H	Manchester U	D	0-0	0-0	16		25,172
6	28	A	Everton	L	1-2	1-0	17	Guehi [10]	38,954
7	Oct 5	H	Liverpool	L	0-1	0-1	18		25,185
8	21	A	Nottingham F	L	0-1	0-0	18		29,443
9	27	H	Tottenham H	W	1-0	1-0	17	Mateta [31]	25,108
10	Nov 2	A	Wolverhampton W	D	2-2	0-0	17	Chalobah [60], Guehi [77]	29,505
11	9	H	Fulham	L	0-2	0-1	17		25,142
12	23	A	Aston Villa	D	2-2	2-1	18	Sarr [4], Devenny [45]	42,175
13	30	H	Newcastle U	D	1-1	0-0	17	Munoz [90]	25,101
14	Dec 3	A	Ipswich T	W	1-0	0-0	16	Mateta [59]	29,533
15	7	H	Manchester C	D	2-2	1-1	16	Munoz [4], Lacroix [56]	25,142
16	15	A	Brighton & HA	W	3-1	2-0	15	Chalobah [27], Sarr 2 [33, 82]	30,893
17	21	H	Arsenal	L	1-5	1-3	15	Sarr [11]	25,167
18	26	A	Bournemouth	D	0-0	0-0	16		11,129
19	29	H	Southampton	W	2-1	1-1	15	Chalobah [31], Eze [52]	25,130
20	Jan 4	H	Chelsea	D	1-1	0-1	15	Mateta [82]	25,179
21	15	A	Leicester C	W	2-0	0-0	14	Mateta [52], Guehi [78]	29,766
22	18	A	West Ham U	W	2-0	0-0	12	Mateta 2 (1 pen) [48, 89 (p)]	62,469
23	26	H	Brentford	L	1-2	0-0	13	Esse [85]	25,066
24	Feb 2	A	Manchester U	W	2-0	0-0	12	Mateta 2 [64, 89]	73,751
25	15	H	Everton	L	1-2	0-1	12	Mateta [47]	25,108
26	22	A	Fulham	W	2-0	1-0	13	Andersen (og) [37], Munoz [66]	26,777
27	25	H	Aston Villa	W	4-1	1-0	12	Sarr 2 [29, 71], Mateta [59], Nketiah [90]	24,712
28	Mar 8	H	Ipswich T	W	1-0	0-0	11	Sarr [82]	25,155
29	Apr 2	A	Southampton	D	1-1	0-1	12	Matheus Franca [90]	29,366
30	5	H	Brighton & HA	W	2-1	1-1	11	Mateta [3], Munoz [55]	24,564
31	12	A	Manchester C	L	2-5	2-2	12	Eze [8], Richards [21]	52,489
32	16	A	Newcastle U	L	0-5	0-4	12		52,197
33	19	H	Bournemouth	D	0-0	0-0	12		25,185
34	23	A	Arsenal	D	2-2	1-2	12	Eze [27], Mateta [83]	60,167
35	May 5	H	Nottingham F	D	1-1	0-0	12	Eze (pen) [60]	25,096
36	11	A	Tottenham H	W	2-0	1-0	12	Eze 2 [45, 48]	60,254
37	20	H	Wolverhampton W	W	4-2	2-1	12	Nketiah 2 [27, 32], Chilwell [50], Eze [86]	24,766
38	25	A	Liverpool	D	1-1	1-0	12	Sarr [9]	60,382

Final League Position: 12

GOALSCORERS

League (51): Mateta 14 (2 pens), Eze 8 (1 pen), Sarr 8, Munoz 4, Chalobah 3, Guehi 3, Nketiah 3, Chilwell 1, Devenny 1, Esse 1, Lacroix 1, Matheus Franca 1, Richards 1, own goals 2.
FA Cup (13): Eze 4, Sarr 3, Munoz 2, Nketiah 2, Devenny 1, own goal 1.
Carabao Cup (10): Mateta 3, Eze 2, Kamada 2, Nketiah 2, Sarr 1.
(Crystal Palace U21) Vertu Trophy (4): Marsh 1, Mustapha 1, Umeh 1, Umolu 1.

Henderson D 38	Richards C 22 + 2	Andersen J 1	Guehi M 34	Munoz D 37	Wharton A 16 + 4	Hughes W 24 + 9	Mitchell T 37	Kamada D 15 + 19	Eze E 31 + 3	Mateta J 33 + 4	Edouard O 1 + 1	Ayew J — + 1	Lerma J 26 + 7	Doucoure C 4 + 9	Sarr I 30 + 8	Riad C 1	Schlupp J — + 12	Clyne N 5 + 8	Lacroix M 35	Nketiah E 9 + 20	Chalobah T 12	Agbinone A — + 2	Devenny J 4 + 19	Kporha C — + 2	Esse R 1 + 6	Chilwell B 1 + 7	Matheus Franca d — + 4	Ward J 1 + 1	Match No.
1	2^5	3	4	5	6^3	7^4	8	9^2	10	11^1	12	13	14	15	16														1
1	2^3		3	5	6		8	12	10	11	9^2		7^1		13	4	14												2
1	4		3	5	6	7^1	8	9^3	10	11^2					12	13	14	2											3
1			3	5^3	6	12	8^4	13	10	11			7^1				15		2^2	4	9								4
1	4		3	5	6^2	14	8	7	10^4	11^1			12		13		15		2	9^3									5
1			3	5	6^3	14	8	7^1	11	10			4		12		13		2	9^2									6
1			3	5^1	6^3	13	8^2	15	11	14			7		12		2	10	4^4										7
1			4	5	6^2		8	9^3	10^1	9	12		7		13		14		3	11^1	2	15							8
1			4	5	6^3	12	8	14	10	11			7^1		9^2				3	13	2								9
1			4	5	6^1		8	7		11					12	9	14	13	3	10^2	2								10
1	7		5^4				8	9^4		11					12		10^3	13	4^1	2	14	6^2	15						11
1	14		4	5	6^3	8			11		12	7^1	9^4	13	15	3			2	10^2									12
1			4	5	6^2	8		10^1	11				7		9	14	3	13	2^3		12								13
1	14		4	5	6	8		10^2	11				12	7^1	9^4		3	15	2^3		13								14
1			4	5	6	8		10^1	11				7		9^2		3	13	2		12								15
1			4	5	6^3	8^4	12	10^2	11^1				7	14	9^5		15	3	13	2		16							16
1	2		4		6^2	8	10^1		11^5				7^3	14	9	16	5^4	3	12		13	15							17
1			4	5	6^1	8	13	10^3	11^2				7	12	9		3		2	14									18
1	4		5		6^1	8	13	10^2	11				7	12	9^3		3	14	2										19
1	2		4	5		8	12	10^2	11				7	6^1	9		3	13											20
1	2		4	5	6^2	8^5	13	10^4	11^3				7^1	12	9		15	3	16		14								21
1	2		4	5	6^4	8	7	10^2	11^3					9^1		15	14	3	13		12								22
1	2^3		4	5	6^2	8	14	10	11				7	9^1			3	12			13								23
1	2		4	5	14	6^3	8^2	10^1	12	11			7	9^4		13	3			15									24
1	2		4	5	13	6^5	8^3	15	12	11			7^2	9		3^4	16	10^1		14									25
1	2		4	5	13	6^3	8	12	10^4	11			7^2	9^1		3		14		15									26
1	2		4	5	6^2	7^1	8	13	10	11			12	9^3		3	14												27
1	2		4	5	6^3		8^2	12	10	4			7	9		3	11^1		14	15	13								28
1			4	5^4	6^5		8^1	13	10	11^2			7	9		2^3	3	14		16		12	15						29
1			4^8	5	6^3	15	8^1	7	10^4	11^2			2	9			3^5	13^8	14		12		16						30
1	2			5	6^4	12	8^3	7	10^5	11^1			4	9			14	3^2	15		13	16							31
1	2		4	5	14	7^2	8	13	10^3	11^1			6^5	9^4		3	12	16	15										32
1	2^8		4	5	6^2	7	8	13	10^1	11^3			12	9^4		3	14		15										33
1			4	5	6^2	12	8	7	10^1	15			2	13		3	11^3		9^4	14									34
1			4	5	6^1	12	8	7^3	10	11^2			14	9		3	13												35
1	2		4	5	6^5	8^3	13	10	11^1				7^2	9^4		3	12		16	15	14								36
1	4		5	6^1		14	15	16					7	9^2		3	11^4		12	10^5	8	13	2^3						37
1	2		5	6^3	8	7	10^1	11^2				4	9		3	13		12	14^4	15									38

FA Cup

Third Round	Stockport Co	(h)	1-0
Fourth Round	Doncaster R	(a)	2-0
Fifth Round	Millwall	(h)	3-1
Quarter-Final	Fulham	(a)	3-0
Semi-Final	Aston Villa	(Wembley)	3-0
Final	Manchester C	(Wembley)	1-0

Carabao Cup

Second Round	Norwich C	(h)	4-0
Third Round	QPR	(a)	2-1
Fourth Round	Aston Villa	(a)	2-1
Quarter-Final	Arsenal	(a)	2-3

Vertu Trophy (Crystal Palace U21)

Group D (S)	Stevenage	(a)	0-1
Group D (S)	Gillingham	(a)	3-1
Group D (S)	Peterborough U	(a)	1-4

DERBY COUNTY

FOUNDATION

Derby County was formed by members of the Derbyshire County Cricket Club in 1884, when football was booming in the area and the cricketers thought that a football club would help boost finances for the summer game. To begin with, they sported the cricket club's colours of amber, chocolate and pale blue, and went into the game at the top immediately entering the FA Cup.

Pride Park Stadium, Pride Park, Derby DE24 8XL.

Telephone: (0871) 472 1884.

Ticket Office: (0871) 472 1884 (option 1).

Website: www.dcfc.co.uk

Email: derby.county@dcfc.co.uk

Ground Capacity: 32,944.

Record Attendance: 41,826 v Tottenham H, Division 1, 20 September 1969 (at Baseball Ground); 33,378 v Liverpool, Premier League, 18 March 2000 (at Pride Park).

Stadium Record Attendance: 33,597, England v Mexico, 25 May 2001 (at Pride Park).

Pitch Measurements: 105m × 68m (115yd × 74.5yd).

Chairman: David Clowes.

Chief Executive Officer: Stephen Pearce.

Head Coach: John Eustace.

Assistant Head Coach: Matt Gardiner.

Colours: White shirts with black side panel and patterned trim, black shorts with white trim, black socks.

Year Formed: 1884.

Turned Professional: 1884.

Club Nickname: 'The Rams'.

Grounds: 1884, Racecourse Ground; 1895, Baseball Ground; 1997, Pride Park (renamed The iPro Stadium 2013; Pride Park Stadium 2016).

First Football League Game: 8 September 1888, Football League, v Bolton W (a) W 6–3 – Marshall; Latham, Ferguson, Williamson; Monks, Walter Roulstone; Bakewell (2), Cooper (2), Higgins, Harry Plackett, Lol Plackett (2).

Record League Victory: 9–0 v Wolverhampton W, Division 1, 10 January 1891 – Bunyan; Archie Goodall, Roberts; Walker, Chalmers, Walter Roulstone (1); Bakewell, McLachlan, Johnny Goodall (1), Holmes (2), McMillan (5). 9–0 v Sheffield Wed, Division 1, 21 January 1899 – Fryer; Methven, Staley; Cox, Archie Goodall, May; Oakden (1), Bloomer (6), Boag, McDonald (1), Allen, (1 og).

Record Cup Victory: 12–0 v Finn Harps, UEFA Cup 1st rd 1st leg, 15 September 1976 – Moseley; Thomas, Nish, Rioch (1), McFarland, Todd (King), Macken, Gemmill, Hector (5), George (3), James (3).

Record Defeat: 2–11 v Everton, FA Cup 1st rd, 1889–90.

HONOURS

League Champions: Division 1 – 1971–72, 1974–75; Division 2 – 1911–12, 1914–15, 1968–69, 1986–87; Division 3N – 1956–57.
Runners-up: Division 1 – 1895–96, 1929–30, 1935–36; First Division – 1995–96; FL 1 – 2023–24; Division 2 – 1925–26; Division 3N – 1955–56.

FA Cup Winners: 1946.
Runners-up: 1898, 1899, 1903.

League Cup: semi-final – 1968, 2009.

Texaco Cup Winners: 1972.

Anglo-Italian Cup: Runners-up: 1992–93, 1993–94, 1994–95.

European Competitions
European Cup: 1972–73 *(sf)*, 1975–76.
UEFA Cup: 1974–75, 1976–77.

FOOTBALL YEARBOOK FACT FILE

In January 1990 a new railway station named Ramsline Halt was opened by England manager Bobby Robson adjacent to Derby County's Baseball Ground stadium. The station, which was for visiting fans, was first used for the match against Nottingham Forest on 20 January. However, the Rams were relegated at the end of the following season, and reduced numbers of away fans arriving by train meant that it was used on just a handful of occasions before being mothballed.

Most League Points (2 for a win): 63, Division 2, 1968–69 and Division 3 (N), 1955–56 and 1956–57.

Most League Points (3 for a win): 92, FL 1, 2023–24.

Most League Goals: 111, Division 3 (N), 1956–57.

Highest League Scorer in Season: Jack Bowers, 37, Division 1, 1930–31; Ray Straw, 37 Division 3 (N), 1956–57.

Most League Goals in Total Aggregate: Steve Bloomer, 292, 1892–1906 and 1910–14.

Most League Goals in One Match: 6, Steve Bloomer v Sheffield Wed, Division 1, 2 January 1899.

Most Capped Player: Deon Burton, 42 (61), Jamaica.

Most League Appearances: Kevin Hector, 486, 1966–78 and 1980–82.

Youngest League Player: Mason Bennett, 15 years 99 days v Middlesbrough 22 October 2011.

Record Transfer Fee Received: £9,000,000 from Brighton & HA for Eiran Cashin, January 2025.

Record Transfer Fee Paid: £7,500,000 (potentially rising to £10,000,000) to Arsenal for Krystian Bielik, August 2019.

Football League Record: 1888 Founder Member of the Football League; 1988–92 Football League; 1892–1907 Division 1; 1907–12 Division 2; 1912–14 Division 1; 1914–15 Division 2; 1915–21 Division 1; 1921–26 Division 2; 1926–53 Division 1; 1953–55 Division 2; 1955–57 Division 3 (N); 1957–69 Division 2; 1969–80 Division 1; 1980–84 Division 2; 1984–86 Division 3; 1986–87 Division 2; 1987–91 Division 1; 1991–92 Division 2; 1992–96 First Division; 1996–2002 Premier League; 2002–04 First Division; 2004–07 FL C; 2007–08 Premier League; 2008–22 FL C; 2022–24 FL 1; 2024– FL C.

LATEST SEQUENCES

Longest Sequence of League Wins: 9, 15.3.1969 – 19.4.1969.

Longest Sequence of League Defeats: 8, 12.12.1987 – 10.2.1988.

Longest Sequence of League Draws: 6, 26.3.1927 – 18.4.1927.

Longest Sequence of Unbeaten League Matches: 22, 8.3.1969 – 20.9.1969.

Longest Sequence Without a League Win: 36, 22.9.2007 – 30.8.2008.

Successive Scoring Runs: 29 from 3.12.1960.

Successive Non-scoring Runs: 8 from 30.10.1920.

MANAGERS

W. D. Clark 1896–1900
Harry Newbould 1900–06
Jimmy Methven 1906–22
Cecil Potter 1922–25
George Jobey 1925–41
Ted Magner 1944–46
Stuart McMillan 1946–53
Jack Barker 1953–55
Harry Storer 1955–62
Tim Ward 1962–67
Brian Clough 1967–73
Dave Mackay 1973–76
Colin Murphy 1977
Tommy Docherty 1977–79
Colin Addison 1979–82
Johnny Newman 1982
Peter Taylor 1982–84
Roy McFarland 1984
Arthur Cox 1984–93
Roy McFarland 1993–95
Jim Smith 1995–2001
Colin Todd 2001–02
John Gregory 2002–03
George Burley 2003–05
Phil Brown 2005–06
Billy Davies 2006–07
Paul Jewell 2007–08
Nigel Clough 2009–13
Steve McClaren 2013–15
Paul Clement 2015–16
Darren Wassall 2016
Nigel Pearson 2016
Steve McClaren 2016–17
Gary Rowett 2017–18
Frank Lampard 2018–19
Phillip Cocu 2019–20
Wayne Rooney 2020–22
Liam Rosenior 2022
Paul Warne 2022–25
John Eustace February 2025–

TEN YEAR LEAGUE RECORD

		P	W	D	L	F	A	Pts	Pos
2015-16	FL C	46	21	15	10	66	43	78	5
2016-17	FL C	46	18	13	15	54	50	67	9
2017-18	FL C	46	20	15	11	70	48	75	6
2018-19	FL C	46	20	14	12	69	54	74	6
2019-20	FL C	46	17	13	16	62	64	64	10
2020-21	FL C	46	11	11	24	36	58	44	21
2021-22	FL C	46	14	13	19	45	53	34*	23
2022-23	FL 1	46	21	13	12	67	46	76	7
2023-24	FL 1	46	28	8	10	78	37	92	2
2024-25	FL C	46	13	11	22	48	56	50	19

*21 pts deducted.

DID YOU KNOW ?

Brothers John and Archie Goodall both played over 200 games for Derby County in the Victorian era. However, they gained international honours for different countries, John winning 14 caps for England, and Archie appearing 10 times for Ireland. Their father had served in the army and as a result John was born in Westminster, Archie in Belfast.

DERBY COUNTY – SKY BET CHAMPIONSHIP 2024–25 LEAGUE RECORD

Match No.	Date	Venue	Opponents	Result	H/T Score	Lg Pos.	Goalscorers	Attendance
1	Aug 9	A	Blackburn R	L 2-4	0-1	23	Nelson [67], Wilson [88]	17,975
2	17	H	Middlesbrough	W 1-0	1-0	13	Jackson [14]	29,443
3	24	A	Watford	L 1-2	1-1	15	Adams [2]	18,911
4	31	H	Bristol C	W 3-0	1-0	9	Goudmijn [28], Jackson [60], Ozoh [89]	29,270
5	Sept 14	H	Cardiff C	W 1-0	1-0	8	Goudmijn [28]	28,985
6	21	A	Sheffield U	L 0-1	0-0	10		28,685
7	28	H	Norwich C	L 2-3	0-1	13	Forsyth [60], Blackett-Taylor [90]	28,915
8	Oct 1	A	Sunderland	L 0-2	0-1	13		39,017
9	5	H	QPR	W 2-0	0-0	12	Nelson [54], Harness [55]	29,305
10	19	A	Millwall	D 1-1	1-0	12	Yates [78]	17,321
11	22	A	Oxford U	D 1-1	0-1	12	Mendez-Laing [55]	11,423
12	26	H	Hull C	D 1-1	0-0	12	Brown [66]	29,877
13	Nov 2	A	Stoke C	L 1-2	0-1	14	Johansson (og) [68]	24,511
14	6	A	Coventry C	W 2-1	1-0	13	Yates [11], Thomas (og) [73]	27,243
15	9	H	Plymouth Arg	D 1-1	1-1	12	Yates [8]	29,652
16	23	A	Preston NE	D 1-1	1-1	11	Yates [29]	16,646
17	27	H	Swansea C	L 1-2	0-2	15	Mendez-Laing (pen) [65]	25,141
18	Dec 1	H	Sheffield Wed	L 1-2	1-0	15	Adams [9]	29,212
19	7	A	Leeds U	L 0-2	0-2	16		36,468
20	10	H	Burnley	D 0-0	0-0	16		18,813
21	13	H	Portsmouth	W 4-0	3-0	14	Wilson [8], Cashin [23], Adams [29], Pack (og) [65]	26,980
22	20	A	Luton T	L 1-2	0-0	15	Jackson [58]	11,667
23	26	H	WBA	W 2-1	1-0	14	Yates [28], Holgate (og) [68]	31,267
24	29	H	Leeds U	L 0-1	0-0	16		32,240
25	Jan 1	A	Sheffield Wed	L 2-4	0-1	17	Yates [68], Adams [90]	31,056
26	4	A	Bristol C	L 0-1	0-1	18		22,040
27	18	H	Watford	L 0-2	0-1	19		29,040
28	21	H	Sunderland	L 0-1	0-1	20		27,441
29	25	A	Cardiff C	L 1-2	0-0	22	Salvesen [70]	19,548
30	Feb 1	H	Sheffield U	L 0-1	0-0	22		29,472
31	8	A	Norwich C	D 1-1	0-0	22	Yates (pen) [90]	26,584
32	11	A	Oxford U	D 0-0	0-0	21		25,999
33	14	A	QPR	L 0-4	0-2	22		16,591
34	22	H	Millwall	L 0-1	0-0	23		28,321
35	Mar 1	A	Middlesbrough	L 0-1	0-0	24		25,839
36	8	H	Blackburn R	W 2-1	2-1	22	Forsyth [3], Adams [7]	29,753
37	11	H	Coventry C	W 2-0	1-0	22	Clarke [23], Harness [48]	28,879
38	15	A	Plymouth Arg	W 3-2	2-1	22	Harness 2 [11, 88], Armstrong [26]	16,978
39	Apr 2	H	Preston NE	W 2-0	0-0	20	Forsyth [48], Yates [52]	26,014
40	5	A	Swansea C	L 0-1	0-0	21		16,501
41	8	H	Burnley	D 0-0	0-0	21		27,584
42	12	A	Portsmouth	D 2-2	0-0	21	Yates [70], Atkinson (og) [75]	20,412
43	18	H	Luton T	L 0-1	0-1	21		32,159
44	21	A	WBA	W 3-1	2-0	21	Adams [7], Yates [30], Mendez-Laing [87]	25,750
45	26	H	Hull C	W 1-0	0-0	19	Phillips [84]	24,451
46	May 3	H	Stoke C	D 0-0	0-0	19		32,471

Final League Position: 19

GOALSCORERS
League (48): Yates 10 (1 pen), Adams 6, Harness 4, Forsyth 3, Jackson 3, Mendez-Laing 3 (1 pen), Goudmijn 2, Nelson 2, Wilson 2, Armstrong 1, Blackett-Taylor 1, Brown 1, Cashin 1, Clarke 1, Ozoh 1, Phillips 1, Salvesen 1, own goals 5.
FA Cup (1): Brown 1.
Carabao Cup (2): Jackson 1, Thompson 1.

Vickers J 6	Wilson K 26 + 7	Nelson C 27	Cashin E 21	Elder C 24 + 5	Osborn B 18 + 7	Ozoh D 9 + 1	Goudmijn K 29 + 12	Barkhuizen T 2 + 17	Jackson K 28 + 18	Mendez-Laing N 26 + 15	Collins J 1 + 16	Adams E 42 + 2	Fornah T — + 1	Forsyth C 26 + 13	Thompson L 18 + 10	Bradley S 3 + 4	Nyambe R 14 + 3	Zetterstrom J 40	Yates J 40 + 2	Ward J 2 + 5	Brown D 3 + 12	Harness M 26 + 15	Phillips N 24 + 8	Blackett-Taylor C 4 + 8	Chirewa T 1 + 4	Salvesen L 6 + 2	Clarke M 15 + 1	Langas S 13 + 1	Armstrong H 12 + 3	Roofe K — + 3	Wheeldon L — + 1	Pieters E — + 1	Match No.
1	2	3	4	5^3	6^4	7^5	8^2	9^1	10	11	12	13	14	15	16																		1
1	2^2	3	4^1	5	8	7^5	6^3	16	9	11	10^4	14		15	17	12	13																2
		3		5^1		6	9^2	14	8	10^3	15	7		13	12	4		2^5	1	11^4	16												3
	3	4	5		6	9^3	12	8^5	10^1		7			13	14			2^4	1	11^2	16	15											4
	3	4	5^4	12	7^1	6^3		9	11^2		8	15						2	1	10			13	14									5
	3	4	5^5	7^1		6^4		9	11^2		8							2^3	1	10	16	13	12	14	15								6
13	3	4		7^1	6		9	11^3	15	8^5		5						2^2	1	10^4			12		16	14							7
2	3	5		6^2	8		14	15		9		12			16			1	11^3			7^4	4^5	13	10^1								8
12	3	4			6		9^3	11^1	15	7		5						2	1	10^4			8^2	13	14								9
12	3	4		14			6^3	9^4	13	16		7						2^1	1	10^4			8^5	15	11^2								10
2	3	4	5	8		7^1		13	9^4	15	6								1	10^3			12	14	11^2								11
2	3	4		14		6^3		9	11^2		7			5	16				1	10^1		12^5	8^5	15	13								12
	3	4	13	8		15		9	11^5	16	7			5^1					1	10^3	2^2	14	6^4	12									13
14	3	5	6^1		7		2	13	16	8		12		9^4	15				1	10^5		11^2			4^3								14
2^1	3			13		8^2		7	10^3		6			5	9				1	11		14	12	4									15
12	3	4		8			6^2	14	15	5		9		7^3					1	11^4		10^1	13	2									16
2	3	4	5^2		6^1	13	11^5	8	16	7		12	14						1			15	9^4		10^3								17
2	3	4	15	6^4		14	13	12	7^2	16	8			5	9^3				1	11^5			10^1										18
2^5	4	5		9		13	16	7^2	10^1	15		6		8^4					1	11^3	14		12	3									19
13	4	5	6		7^4		14	15		9				8	16				1	11^2	2^3	10^1	12	3^5									20
2	3	4^1	13	7			6		14	10^3	15	9^4		5	16				1	11^5			8^3	12									21
2	4		6	8			7^4		10^2	14	13	9		12		5^1			1	11^3			15	3									22
2	3		5^2		6			8^1	10^2		7	13			14				1	11^4		15	9	4	12								23
2	3		5				6^5	14	10^2	8^1	16	7							1	11^4		15	9^3	4	12	13							24
5^5	3		13				7^4	16	11^2	15		6		8	14	4^1			1	10		12	9^2	2									25
2	3		5	12			6^2		8^1	10^5	16			15	7^3				1	11		14	9^4	4		13							26
2^5	3	4	5	7^1			9^2		8^1	10^4	6			15					1	11	16	14	13		12								27
9^4			4	14		7	16	5^1	11^2		2	3		6^3					1	10^5		15	8		12	13							28
	4		5^1	8^4	14		9^3	16	15	12		7		3			2	1	11^5			13		6^1		10							29
				9		7^2	6^4	15	5^3	14		8		4	13		2^1	1	11			12				10	3					30
				14		6^3	9^5	10^4		16	7^2	8			2			1	12		15	4			11^1	5	3	13					31
				9			7^3	8^1	16	5^5	10^2	6					14^1	1	13			12	2^4		11	3	4	15					32
				5		7^3		13	12	14	8^2	6^4						2	1	9			10			11^1	4	3	15				33
				5				7^5	10^3	13	8^1	14		6				2	1	11^4			9			11^2	4^4	3		16			34
				5		15		13	10^1	8^5		6		4	12		2	1	11^4			9^1			14		3	7^2	16				35
	5			9			14	13			6	4		8				1	11			10^2	3				12	2^1	7^3				36
				9			13		12		6	4		8^2	5	1		10^1			11	2					3		7				37
	5^2			9				12			6	4		8^1			1	10			11	2					3	13	7				38
	12			9			14	13			6	4		8^2	5^1	1		10^2			11	2					3		7				39
	2						12	13	11^4	14		7^3		6	9^1			1			10	4					5	3^2	8		15		40
	6						14		$13^{}$	12		8		9	7^3			1	10			11^3	3				4	2^2	5				41
	5							13		12	11^1	6		8				1	9			10^2	3				4	2	7				42
1	5						13	14	12	9^1	7	8							10			11	3				4	2^2	6^3				43
1	5							12	13		8	9		6					10^2			11^1	3				4	2	7				44
1	5							14	13	12	8	9		6^1					10^3			11^2	3				4	2	7				45
1	5							14	12		8	9^4		6^2					10^3			11^1	3				4	2	7	13		15	46

FA Cup

Third Round   Leyton Orient   (a)   1-1
aet; Leyton Orient won 6-5 on penalties.

Carabao Cup

First Round   Chesterfield   (h)   2-1
Second Round   Barrow   (a)   0-0
Barrow won 3-2 on penalties.

DONCASTER ROVERS

FOUNDATION

In 1879, Mr Albert Jenkins assembled a team to play a match against the Yorkshire Institution for the Deaf. The players remained together as Doncaster Rovers, joining the Midland Alliance in 1889 and the Midland Counties League in 1891.

The Eco-Power Stadium, Stadium Way, Lakeside, Doncaster, South Yorkshire DN4 5JW.

Telephone: (01302) 764 664.

Ticket Office: (01302) 762 576.

Website: www.doncasterroversfc.co.uk

Email: reception@clubdoncaster.co.uk

Ground Capacity: 15,148.

Record Attendance: 37,149 v Hull C, Division 3 (N), 2 October 1948 (at Belle Vue); 15,001 v Leeds U, FL 1, 1 April 2008 (at Keepmoat Stadium).

Pitch Measurements: 100m × 66m (111.5yd × 72yd).

Chairman: Terry Bramall.

Chief Executive: Gavin Baldwin.

Head Coach: Grant McCann.

Assistant Head Coach: Cliff Byrne.

HONOURS

League Champions: FL 1 – 2012–13; FL 2 – 2024–25. Division 3N – 1934–35, 1946–47, 1949–50; Third Division – 2003–04; Division 4 – 1965–66, 1968–69.
Runners-up: Division 3N – 1937–38, 1938–39; Division 4 – 1983–84; Football Conference – (3rd) 2002–03 *(promoted via play-offs (and golden goal)).*
FA Cup: 5th rd – 1952, 1954, 1955, 1956, 2019.
League Cup: 5th rd – 1976, 2006.
League Trophy Winners: 2007.

Colours: Red shirts with white hoops and black trim, black shorts, red socks with white trim.

Year Formed: 1879.

Turned Professional: 1885.

Club Nicknames: 'The Rovers'; 'Donny'.

Grounds: 1880–1916, Intake Ground; 1920, Benetthorpe Ground; 1922, Low Pasture, Belle Vue; 2007, Keepmoat Stadium (renamed The Eco-Power Stadium 2021).

First Football League Game: 7 September 1901, Division 2, v Burslem Port Vale (h) D 3–3 – Eggett; Simpson, Layton; Longden, Jones, Wright, Langham, Murphy, Price, Goodson (2), Bailey (1).

Record League Victory: 10–0 v Darlington, Division 4, 25 January 1964 – Potter; Raine, Meadows, Windross (1), White, Ripley (2), Robinson, Booth (2), Hale (4), Jeffrey, Broadbent (1).

Record Cup Victory: 7–0 v Blyth Spartans, FA Cup 1st rd, 27 November 1937 – Imrie; Shaw, Rodgers, McFarlane, Bycroft, Cyril Smith, Burton (1), Killourhy (4), Morgan (2), Malam, Dutton; 7–0 v Chorley, FA Cup 1st rd replay, 20 November 2018 – Lawlor; Mason, Butler, Anderson T*, Andrew, Whiteman (Rowe), Coppinger (Taylor), Kane (1) (Crawford), May (4), Marquis (1), Blair (1).

Record Defeat: 0–12 v Small Heath, Division 2, 11 April 1903.

FOOTBALL YEARBOOK FACT FILE

The original Doncaster Rovers club was wound up in May 1917 and when a meeting was held in April 1920 to revive senior football in the town the title of the new club was discussed. Although the name of Doncaster Town was suggested by some it was agreed to revert to the old name of Rovers and a new limited liability company, The Doncaster Rovers Football Club (1920), Ltd was established with £10,000 capital made up of 10s (50p) shares.

Most League Points (2 for a win): 72, Division 3 (N), 1946–47.

Most League Points (3 for a win): 92, Division 3, 2003–04.

Most League Goals: 123, Division 3 (N), 1946–47.

Highest League Scorer in Season: Clarrie Jordan, 42, Division 3 (N), 1946–47.

Most League Goals in Total Aggregate: Tom Keetley, 180, 1923–29.

Most League Goals in One Match: 6, Tom Keetley v Ashington, Division 3 (N), 16 February 1929.

Most Capped Player: Len Graham, 14, Northern Ireland.

Most League Appearances: James Coppinger, 614, 2004–21.

Youngest League Player: Alick Jeffrey, 15 years 229 days v Fulham, 15 September 1954.

Record Transfer Fee Received: £2,000,000 from Reading for Matthew Mills, July 2009.

Record Transfer Fee Paid: £1,150,000 to Sheffield U for Billy Sharp, August 2010.

Football League Record: 1901 Elected to Division 2; 1901–03 Division 2; 1903 Failed re-election; 1904 Re-elected to Division 2; 1905 Failed re-election; 1923 Re-elected to Division 3 (N); 1923–35 Division 3 (N); 1935–37 Division 2; 1937–47 Division 3 (N); 1947–48 Division 2; 1948–50 Division 3 (N); 1950–58 Division 2; 1958–59 Division 3; 1959–66 Division 4; 1966–67 Division 3; 1967–69 Division 4; 1969–71 Division 3; 1971–81 Division 4; 1981–83 Division 3; 1983–84 Division 4; 1984–88 Division 3; 1988–92 Division 4; 1992–98 Third Division; 1998–2003 Football Conference; 2003–04 Third Division; 2004–08 FL 1; 2008–12 FL C; 2012–13 FL 1; 2013–14 FL C; 2014–16 FL 1; 2016–17 FL 2; 2017–22 FL 1; 2022–25 FL 2; 2025– FL 1.

LATEST SEQUENCES

Longest Sequence of League Wins: 10, 9.3.2024 –23.4.2024.

Longest Sequence of League Defeats: 9, 14.1.1905 – 1.4.1905.

Longest Sequence of League Draws: 4, 1.1.2018 – 23.1.2018.

Longest Sequence of Unbeaten League Matches: 20, 26.12.1968 – 12.4.1969.

Longest Sequence Without a League Win: 20, 9.8.1997 – 29.11.1997.

Successive Scoring Runs: 27 from 10.11.1934.

Successive Non-scoring Runs: 7 from 27.9.1947.

MANAGERS

Arthur Porter 1920–21
Harry Tufnell 1921–22
Arthur Porter 1922–23
Dick Ray 1923–27
David Menzies 1928–36
Fred Emery 1936–40
Bill Marsden 1944–46
Jackie Bestall 1946–49
Peter Doherty 1949–58
Jack Hodgson and Sid Bycroft (*Joint Managers*) 1958
Jack Crayston 1958–59 (*continued as Secretary-Manager to 1961*)
Jackie Bestall 1959–60
Norman Curtis 1960–61
Danny Malloy 1961–62
Oscar Hold 1962–64
Bill Leivers 1964–66
Keith Kettleborough 1966–67
George Raynor 1967–68
Lawrie McMenemy 1968–71
Maurice Setters 1971–74
Stan Anderson 1975–78
Billy Bremner 1978–85
Dave Cusack 1985–87
Dave Mackay 1987–89
Billy Bremner 1989–91
Steve Beaglehole 1991–93
Ian Atkins 1994
Sammy Chung 1994–96
Kerry Dixon (*Player-Manager*) 1996–97
Dave Cowling 1997
Mark Weaver 1997–98
Ian Snodin 1998–99
Steve Wignall 1999–2001
Dave Penney 2002–06
Sean O'Driscoll 2006–11
Dean Saunders 2011–13
Brian Flynn 2013
Paul Dickov 2013–15
Darren Ferguson 2015–18
Grant McCann 2018–19
Darren Moore 2019–21
Andy Butler 2021
Richie Wellens 2021
Gary McSheffrey 2021–22
Danny Schofield 2022–23
Grant McCann May 2023–

TEN YEAR LEAGUE RECORD

		P	W	D	L	F	A	Pts	Pos
2015-16	FL 1	46	11	13	22	48	64	46	21
2016-17	FL 2	46	25	10	11	85	55	85	3
2017-18	FL 1	46	13	17	16	52	52	56	15
2018-19	FL 1	46	20	13	13	76	58	73	6
2019-20	FL 1	34	15	9	10	51	33	54	9§
2020-21	FL 1	46	19	7	20	63	67	64	14
2021-22	FL 1	46	10	8	28	37	82	38	22
2022-23	FL 2	46	16	7	23	46	65	55	18
2023-24	FL 2	46	21	8	17	73	68	71	5
2024-25	FL 2	46	24	12	10	73	50	84	1

§*Decided on points-per-game (1.59)*

DID YOU KNOW ❓

Doncaster Rovers travelled to Rotterdam to play the Dutch National XI on 21 October 1936. Rovers faced a team that included seven men who had played against England the previous year and went down to a 7-2 defeat in front of a crowd of 18,000 at the Sparta Stadium. Rovers' scorers were Albert Malam and Ronnie Dodd.

DONCASTER ROVERS – SKY BET LEAGUE TWO 2024–25 LEAGUE RECORD

Match No.	Date	Venue	Opponents	Result	H/T Score	Lg Pos.	Goalscorers	Attendance
1	Aug 10	H	Accrington S	W 4-1	1-0	1	Molyneux 2 [43, 62], Gibson [68], Sharp [87]	6423
2	17	A	Newport Co	L 1-3	1-0	7	Bailey [30]	4755
3	24	H	Morecambe	W 1-0	1-0	6	Clifton [20]	6832
4	31	A	Port Vale	W 3-2	1-1	5	Molyneux 2 [16, 58], Sharp [46]	5454
5	Sept 7	H	Gillingham	W 1-0	1-0	1	Sharp [30]	7546
6	12	A	Harrogate T	L 0-2	0-2	1		3123
7	21	A	Milton Keynes D	D 1-1	0-1	6	Anderson [82]	7838
8	28	H	Chesterfield	L 0-3	0-1	7		10,790
9	Oct 1	H	Barrow	W 1-0	0-0	5	Clifton [81]	5632
10	5	A	Grimsby T	W 3-0	3-0	4	Gibson 2 [2, 44], Molyneux [10]	7693
11	12	H	Crewe Alex	D 1-1	0-0	2	Hurst [73]	7472
12	19	A	Swindon T	W 2-1	0-0	2	Olowu [58], Ironside (pen) [90]	6837
13	22	H	Bromley	L 0-1	0-1	4		6309
14	26	A	Bradford C	W 2-1	0-0	4	Molyneux [57], Sharp [66]	18,269
15	Nov 9	H	Notts Co	D 1-1	0-0	4	Ironside [73]	10,988
16	16	A	Salford C	D 1-1	0-0	3	Sharp [77]	7280
17	23	A	Carlisle U	D 0-0	0-0	3		6837
18	Dec 4	A	Fleetwood T	W 4-2	3-2	3	Hurst [13], Bailey [39], Sharp [45], Bolton (og) [68]	2205
19	7	A	Cheltenham T	D 2-2	0-1	3	Broadbent [55], Molyneux [75]	6259
20	14	A	AFC Wimbledon	L 0-1	0-1	5		7862
21	21	H	Tranmere R	W 3-1	1-0	2	Olowu [38], Kelly [66], Hurst [77]	7201
22	26	A	Walsall	L 0-2	0-0	3		7220
23	29	A	Colchester U	D 1-1	1-1	3	Gibson [40]	5729
24	Jan 1	H	Fleetwood T	W 2-1	1-0	2	Bailey [44], Sharp [90]	7290
25	4	H	Port Vale	L 1-2	0-1	6	Street [84]	8438
26	18	A	Gillingham	W 1-0	1-0	6	Molyneux [33]	5814
27	25	H	Harrogate T	W 1-0	0-0	3	Clifton [86]	7241
28	29	A	Barrow	W 3-1	2-1	2	Olowu [28], Molyneux 2 [29, 78]	3009
29	Feb 1	H	Milton Keynes D	W 2-1	1-0	2	Ironside [31], Street [73]	6871
30	6	A	Chesterfield	L 2-5	1-2	2	Molyneux [45], Ironside [90]	8707
31	15	H	Grimsby T	L 1-2	0-1	6	Street [85]	9961
32	18	A	Morecambe	W 1-0	1-0	3	Street [3]	2951
33	22	A	Accrington S	W 2-1	1-0	2	Clifton [2], Ward (og) [61]	2258
34	Mar 1	H	Newport Co	W 3-0	1-0	3	Street 2 [34, 46], Molyneux [78]	8007
35	4	A	Bromley	L 0-1	0-1	3		2433
36	8	H	Swindon T	D 2-2	1-0	3	Street [1], Sbarra [22]	7440
37	15	A	Crewe Alex	D 1-1	0-1	4	Bailey [75]	5142
38	29	H	Carlisle U	W 3-0	1-0	4	Bailey [36], Gibson [68], Clifton [73]	8299
39	Apr 1	H	Walsall	D 2-2	1-1	4	Molyneux [16], Sharp [84]	7796
40	5	A	Cheltenham T	W 2-0	0-0	4	Sterry [89], Street [90]	3897
41	12	H	AFC Wimbledon	D 1-1	0-1	4	Sterry [79]	8733
42	15	A	Salford C	D 1-1	1-1	4	Street [21]	3030
43	18	A	Tranmere R	W 3-0	1-0	2	Molyneux 3 (1 pen) [23, 51 (p), 77]	8814
44	21	H	Colchester U	W 3-0	2-0	1	Clifton [9], Gibson [22], Kelly [90]	8936
45	26	H	Bradford C	W 2-1	1-0	1	Street [33], Sharp [90]	12,574
46	May 3	A	Notts Co	W 2-1	2-0	1	Street 2 [18, 28]	15,427

Final League Position: 1

GOALSCORERS

League (73): Molyneux 16 (1 pen), Street 12, Sharp 9, Clifton 6, Gibson 6, Bailey 5, Ironside 4 (1 pen), Hurst 3, Olowu 3, Kelly 2, Sterry 2, Anderson 1, Broadbent 1, Sbarra 1, own goals 2.
FA Cup (4): Sharp 2, Kelly 1, Molyneux 1.
Carabao Cup (2): Molyneux 1, Sharp 1.
Vertu Trophy (8): Ironside 2 (1 pen), Yeboah 2, Broadbent 1, Clifton 1, Hurst 1, Sbarra 1.

Sharman-Lowe T 46	Sterry J 40+1	Anderson T 24+5	Wood R 7+1	Maxwell J 20+4	Bailey O 46	Gibson J 32+10	Molyneux L 44+1	Broadbent G 28+10	Hurst K 9+12	Ironside J 17+22	Sbarra J 7+20	Clifton H 27+14	Yeboah E 1+10	Sharp B 19+24	Nixon T 2+7	Senior J 15+6	Fleming B 12+5	Kelly P 15+15	Olowu J 27+4	McGrath J 30+3	Westbrooke Z 2+5	Close B 3+4	Emmanuel J 3+2	Street R 16+6	Crew C 11+2	Ennis E 3+12	Match No.
1	2	3	4	5⁵	6	7³	8	9⁴	10¹	11²	12	13	14	15	16												1
1	2	3	4		6⁵	10²	8	7¹		11	12	9⁴	13	15		5³	14	16									2
1	2	4			6	10²	8⁰			13	12	14		9	15	11¹		5	7⁴	3							3
1	2	3			6	10²	8⁵	15		12		9³	13	11¹			5	14	16	4	7⁴						4
1	2	3			6	10²	8⁴			14	12	9		11¹			5		15	4	7²	13					5
1	2⁴	3			8	10¹	7			13	12	9		11¹			5		4		6²	15					6
1	2¹	3			6	10²	8⁵			11	15	9⁵	14	13		5³	16	12	4	7⁴							7
1	2¹	3⁴			6	10²	8⁴			16	11	9⁵		14	13	5³	15	12	4	7⁴							8
1	2				7	12		15	13	14	10²	9	8¹	11³		16	5³	6⁴	3	4							9
1	2²				3	10	8⁵	7		14		9	16	11³		12	5¹	6⁴		4		15	13				10
1	2¹				6	10	8	7	14	12	13	9³		11			5²		3	4							11
1	15			14	3	8⁴	5	6	12	10		9³		11¹				7²	2	4		13					12
1	2		5⁴	6	10	8	15	13	11¹		9² 14	12					7³	3	4								13
1	5		8¹	6		9	7	10⁴	15		13		11³		4²	12	14	3	2								14
1	2				7	14	8			10	12	9¹		11³		5¹	13	6	3	4							15
1	2²			14	6	10¹	8	16		9⁵	11	12		15	13		5³	7⁴	3	4							16
1	5⁴	16			8¹	7	13	9		10²	12	15⁵		11³	14	4		6	2	3⁴							17
1	5	3			8²	6		12	7	10¹	9		14	11³		13			2	4							18
1	2⁴	15		5¹	6	13	8	7	9³	11	14	16		10²		12		3⁵	4								19
1	3				6	15	9	7¹	11³	12	14	13		10		8		2⁴	4		5²						20
1				15	6	10¹	8	9³	13	12	14			11²		5⁴	7³	3	4	16	2						21
1					6	15	9³	7⁴	14	10				11		12	5²	8¹	3	4	2						22
1	2	14		5³	6	10⁵	8²	7⁴	13	11¹		9		12		15		13	3	4							23
1	2				5	6		8	7²	10¹	11³	12		9		14		13	3	4							24
1	2			5²	6	10⁵	8¹	15	13	16		9⁴		11		14	7³	3	4				12				25
1	2	16		5	6		8⁵	12		14	9²	13		11⁴				3	4					10³	7¹	15	26
1	2			5	6	15	8			11²	10¹	12		14				3	4					13	7⁴	9³	27
1	2			5	6	14	8⁴	12		11³		9¹		16				13	3	4				15	7²	10⁵	28
1	2			5	6	16	8⁵	14		11³		13		15			9⁴	3	4					12	7²	10¹	29
1	2²			5⁵	6	16	8	14		11		13		15			9¹	3	4					10³	7⁴	12	30
1	2	4		5¹	6	10³	8	15		11⁵		9²		16		12	13	3						14	7⁴		31
1	2	4			6	10³	8²	7¹		13		9		15	12	5⁴		14	3					11⁴			32
1	2	4	15		6	10³	8⁵	7¹		12		9		16			13⁴	3	5					11²		14⁴	33
1	2			5	6²	10⁵	8³	7		16	12	9¹		15				3	4					11⁴	13	14	34
1	2³	13		5⁴	6	10	8	7		14	12	9¹		15				3⁵	4²					11		16	35
1		4			3	10	8	7		12	9¹	13		14	2	5								11²	6³		36
1		4	3⁵		6	10¹	8	7		12	13	9³		16	2⁴	5		14						11²		15	37
1	2⁵	3	4⁴		6	10	8³	7		9²	12	13	16	5		15			17					11¹		14	38
1	2	3	4		6	10	8	7		9¹	12	13		5										11²			39
1	2	3⁵	4¹		6	10⁴	8	7		16	15	13		11³		5		9²	12					14			40
1	2	3²	4¹		6	10⁴	8	7		15	13	9²		16⁴		5		14	12					11⁵			41
1	5	3		8¹	2	10³	9	7						14	4	6²								11	13	12	42
1	2⁵	4			3	10²	8⁴	7		15		9³		16	5		12			14				11	6¹	13	43
1	2	4	14		3	10²	8¹	7		15		9¹				5³		12		16				11⁴	6⁵	13	44
1	2	4		5	3	10⁵	8¹	7		12		9¹		14					16	15				11²	6⁴	13	45
1	2	4		5¹	3	10¹	8⁵	6		12		9		15	13				14					11³	7⁴	16	46

FA Cup

First Round	Barrow	(a)	1-0
Second Round	Kettering T	(a)	2-1
aet.			
Third Round	Hull C	(a)	1-1
aet; Doncaster R won 5-4 on penalties.			
Fourth Round	Crystal Palace	(h)	0-2

Carabao Cup

First Round	Salford C	(a)	2-0
Second Round	Everton	(a)	0-3

Vertu Trophy

Group F (N)	Huddersfield T	(h)	2-1
Group F (N)	Manchester U U21	(h)	3-3
Manchester U U21 won 5-3 on penalties.			
Group F (N)	Barnsley	(a)	3-1
Second Round	Port Vale	(h)	0-1

EVERTON

FOUNDATION

St Domingo Church Sunday School formed a football club in 1878 which played at Stanley Park. Enthusiasm was so great that in November 1879 they decided to expand membership and changed the name to Everton, playing in black shirts with a scarlet sash and nicknamed the 'Black Watch'. After wearing several other colours, royal blue was adopted in 1901.

Hill Dickinson Stadium, Bramley-Moore Dock, Liverpool L5 9SR.

Telephone: (0151) 556 1878.

Ticket Office: (0151) 556 1878.

Website: www.evertonfc.com

Email: everton@evertonfc.com

Ground Capacity: 52,769.

Record Attendance: 78,299 v Liverpool, Division 1, 18 September 1948.

Pitch Measurements: 100.48m × 68m (110yd × 74.5yd).

Executive Chairman: Mark Watts.

Chief Executive: Angus Kinnear.

Manager: David Moyes.

Assistant Managers: Alan Irvine, Billy McKinlay, Leighton Baines.

Colours: Blue shirts with white trim, white shorts with blue trim, white socks with blue trim.

Year Formed: 1878.

Turned Professional: 1885.

Previous Name: 1878, St Domingo FC; 1879, Everton.

Club Nickname: 'The Toffees'.

Grounds: 1878, Stanley Park; 1882, Priory Road; 1884, Anfield Road; 1892, Goodison Park; 2025, Everton Stadium (renamed Hill Dickinson Stadium 2025).

HONOURS

League Champions: Division 1 – 1914–15, 1927–28, 1931–32, 1938–39, 1962–63, 1969–70, 1984–85, 1986–87; Football League 1890–91; Division 2 – 1930–31.
Runners-up: Division 1 – 1894–95, 1901–02, 1904–05, 1908–09, 1911–12, 1985–86; Football League 1889–90; Division 2 – 1953–54.
FA Cup Winners: 1906, 1933, 1966, 1984, 1995.
Runners-up: 1893, 1897, 1907, 1968, 1985, 1986, 1989, 2009.
League Cup: Runners-up: 1977, 1984.
League Super Cup: Runners-up: 1986.
Full Members' Cup: Runners-up: 1989, 1991.
European Competitions
European Cup: 1963–64, 1970–71 *(qf).*
Champions League: 2005–06.
Fairs Cup: 1962–63, 1964–65, 1965–66.
UEFA Cup: 1975–76, 1978–79, 1979–80, 2005–06, 2007–08, 2008–09.
Europa League: 2009–10, 2014–15, 2017–18.
European Cup-Winners' Cup: 1966–67, 1984–85 *(winners),* 1995–96.

First Football League Game: 8 September 1888, Football League, v Accrington (h) W 2–1 – Smalley; Dick, Ross; Holt, Jones, Dobson; Fleming (2), Waugh, Lewis, Edgar Chadwick, Farmer.

Record League Victory: 9–1 v Manchester C, Division 1, 3 September 1906 – Scott; Balmer, Crelley; Booth, Taylor (1), Abbott (1); Sharp, Bolton (1), Young (4), Settle (2), George Wilson; 9–1 v Plymouth Arg, Division 2, 27 December 1930 – Coggins; Williams, Cresswell; McPherson, Griffiths, Thomson; Critchley, Dunn, Dean (4), Johnson (1), Stein (4).

FOOTBALL YEARBOOK FACT FILE

Everton were the first Football League club to host an FA Cup final. Goodison Park was chosen in preference to Molineux to host the 1894 final between Notts County and Bolton Wanderers. Two new stands were erected, raising the capacity to an estimated 50,000, while a press box with space for 100 reporters was also installed. However, the attendance was widely regarded as disappointing with some suggesting a figure as low as 23,000.

Record Cup Victory: 11–2 v Derby Co, FA Cup 1st rd, 18 January 1890 – Smalley; Hannah, Doyle (1); Kirkwood, Holt (1), Parry; Latta, Brady (3), Geary (3), Edgar Chadwick, Millward (3).

Record Defeat: 4–10 v Tottenham H, Division 1, 11 October 1958.

Most League Points (2 for a win): 66, Division 1, 1969–70.

Most League Points (3 for a win): 90, Division 1, 1984–85.

Most League Goals: 121, Division 2, 1930–31.

Highest League Scorer in Season: William Ralph 'Dixie' Dean, 60, Division 1, 1927–28 (All-time League record).

Most League Goals in Total Aggregate: William Ralph 'Dixie' Dean, 349, 1925–37.

Most League Goals in One Match: 6, Jack Southworth v WBA, Division 1, 30 December 1893.

Most Capped Player: Tim Howard, 93 (121), USA.

Most League Appearances: Neville Southall, 578, 1981–98.

Youngest League Player: Jose Baxter, 16 years 191 days v Blackburn R, 16 August 2008.

Record Transfer Fee Received: £75,000,000 from Manchester U for Romelu Lukaku, July 2017.

Record Transfer Fee Paid: £40,000,000 (potentially rising to £45,000,000) to Swansea C for Gylfi Sigurdsson, August 2017.

Football League Record: 1888 Founder Member of the Football League; 1888–1930 Division 1; 1930–31 Division 2; 1931–51 Division 1; 1951–54 Division 2; 1954–92 Division 1; 1992– Premier League.

LATEST SEQUENCES

Longest Sequence of League Wins: 12, 24.3.1894 – 13.10.1894.

Longest Sequence of League Defeats: 6, 27.8.2005– 15.10.2005.

Longest Sequence of League Draws: 5, 4.5.1977 – 16.5.1977.

Longest Sequence of Unbeaten League Matches: 20, 29.4.1978 – 16.12.1978.

Longest Sequence Without a League Win: 14, 6.3.1937 – 4.9.1937.

Successive Scoring Runs: 40 from 15.3.1930.

Successive Non-scoring Runs: 6 from 27.8.2005.

MANAGERS

W. E. Barclay 1888–89
(Secretary-Manager)
Dick Molyneux 1889–1901
(Secretary-Manager)
William C. Cuff 1901–18
(Secretary-Manager)
W. J. Sawyer 1918–19
(Secretary-Manager)
Thomas H. McIntosh 1919–35
(Secretary-Manager)
Theo Kelly 1936–48
Cliff Britton 1948–56
Ian Buchan 1956–58
Johnny Carey 1958–61
Harry Catterick 1961–73
Billy Bingham 1973–77
Gordon Lee 1977–81
Howard Kendall 1981–87
Colin Harvey 1987–90
Howard Kendall 1990–93
Mike Walker 1994
Joe Royle 1994–97
Howard Kendall 1997–98
Walter Smith 1998–2002
David Moyes 2002–13
Roberto Martinez 2013–16
Ronald Koeman 2016–17
Sam Allardyce 2017–18
Marco Silva 2018–19
Carlo Ancelotti 2019–21
Rafael Benitez 2021–22
Frank Lampard 2022–23
Sean Dyche 2023–25
David Moyes January 2025–

TEN YEAR LEAGUE RECORD

		P	W	D	L	F	A	Pts	Pos
2015-16	PR Lge	38	11	14	13	59	55	47	11
2016-17	PR Lge	38	17	10	11	62	44	61	7
2017-18	PR Lge	38	13	10	15	44	58	49	8
2018-19	PR Lge	38	15	9	14	54	46	54	8
2019-20	PR Lge	38	13	10	15	44	56	49	12
2020-21	PR Lge	38	17	8	13	47	48	59	10
2021-22	PR Lge	38	11	6	21	43	66	39	16
2022-23	PR Lge	38	8	12	18	34	57	36	17
2023-24	PR Lge	38	13	9	16	40	51	40*	15
2024-25	PR Lge	38	11	15	12	42	44	48	13

* 8 pts deducted.

DID YOU KNOW ?

Everton were the first club to win a European Cup tie on penalties. The Toffees drew both legs of their second-round tie with Borussia Moenchengladbach in 1970–71, the second leg going to extra time and then penalties. Although Joe Royle missed with the first kick in the sequence, the remaining four Everton players were successful and after Andy Rankin saved the final Borussia kick they were left as 4-3 winners.

EVERTON – PREMIER LEAGUE 2024–25 LEAGUE RECORD

Match No.	Date	Venue	Opponents	Result		H/T Score	Lg Pos.	Goalscorers	Attendance
1	Aug 17	H	Brighton & HA	L	0-3	0-1	20		39,217
2	24	A	Tottenham H	L	0-4	0-2	20		61,357
3	31	H	Bournemouth	L	2-3	0-0	20	Keane [50], Calvert-Lewin [57]	38,805
4	Sept 14	A	Aston Villa	L	2-3	2-1	20	McNeil [16], Calvert-Lewin [27]	41,573
5	21	A	Leicester C	D	1-1	1-0	20	Ndiaye [12]	31,765
6	28	H	Crystal Palace	W	2-1	0-1	15	McNeil 2 [47, 54]	38,954
7	Oct 5	H	Newcastle U	D	0-0	0-0	16		39,265
8	19	A	Ipswich T	W	2-0	2-0	16	Ndiaye [17], Keane [40]	29,862
9	26	H	Fulham	D	1-1	0-0	15	Beto [90]	38,742
10	Nov 2	A	Southampton	L	0-1	0-0	16		31,143
11	9	A	West Ham U	D	0-0	0-0	16		62,463
12	23	H	Brentford	D	0-0	0-0	15		38,915
13	Dec 1	A	Manchester U	L	0-4	0-2	15		73,817
14	4	H	Wolverhampton W	W	4-0	2-0	15	Young [10], Mangala [33], Dawson 2 (2 ogs) [49, 72]	38,820
15	14	A	Arsenal	D	0-0	0-0	15		60,176
16	22	H	Chelsea	D	0-0	0-0	15		39,308
17	26	A	Manchester C	D	1-1	1-1	15	Ndiaye [36]	52,527
18	29	H	Nottingham F	L	0-2	0-1	16		39,352
19	Jan 4	A	Bournemouth	L	0-1	0-0	16		11,223
20	15	H	Aston Villa	L	0-1	0-0	16		39,085
21	19	H	Tottenham H	W	3-2	3-0	16	Calvert-Lewin [13], Ndiaye [30], Gray (og) [45]	39,326
22	25	A	Brighton & HA	W	1-0	1-0	16	Ndiaye (pen) [42]	31,567
23	Feb 1	A	Leicester C	W	4-0	3-0	15	Doucoure [1], Beto 2 [6, 45], Ndiaye [90]	39,376
24	12	H	Liverpool	D	2-2	1-1	15	Beto [11], Tarkowski [90]	39,280
25	15	A	Crystal Palace	W	2-1	1-0	13	Beto [42], Alcaraz [80]	25,108
26	22	H	Manchester U	D	2-2	2-0	14	Beto [19], Doucoure [33]	39,290
27	26	A	Brentford	D	1-1	0-1	15	O'Brien [77]	17,082
28	Mar 8	A	Wolverhampton W	D	1-1	1-1	14	Harrison [33]	30,738
29	15	H	West Ham U	D	1-1	0-0	14	O'Brien [90]	39,343
30	Apr 2	A	Liverpool	L	0-1	0-0	15		60,331
31	5	A	Arsenal	D	1-1	0-1	14	Ndiaye (pen) [49]	39,316
32	12	A	Nottingham F	W	1-0	0-0	14	Doucoure [90]	30,199
33	19	H	Manchester C	L	0-2	0-0	13		39,332
34	26	A	Chelsea	L	0-1	0-1	14		39,894
35	May 3	H	Ipswich T	D	2-2	2-1	14	Beto [26], McNeil [35]	39,305
36	10	H	Fulham	W	3-1	1-1	13	Mykolenko [45], Keane [70], Beto [74]	27,653
37	18	H	Southampton	W	2-0	2-0	13	Ndiaye 2 [6, 45]	39,201
38	25	A	Newcastle U	W	1-0	0-0	13	Alcaraz [65]	52,221

Final League Position: 13

GOALSCORERS

League (42): Ndiaye 9 (2 pens), Beto 8, McNeil 4, Calvert-Lewin 3, Doucoure 3, Keane 3, Alcaraz 2, O'Brien 2, Harrison 1, Mangala 1, Mykolenko 1, Tarkowski 1, Young 1, own goals 3.
FA Cup (2): Beto 1, Ndiaye 1 (1 pen).
Carabao Cup (4): Beto 1, Doucoure 1, McNeil 1, Ndiaye 1.
(Everton U21) Vertu Trophy (5): Beto 2, Armstrong 1, Benjamin 1, Sherif 1.

Pickford J 38	Young A 19 + 13	Tarkowski J 33	Keane M 11 + 3	Mykolenko V 35	Iroegbunam T 5 + 13	Gana J 35 + 2	Harrison J 24 + 10	McNeil D 15 + 6	Doucoure A 31 + 2	Calvert-Lewin D 19 + 7	Ndiaye I 29 + 4	Beto N 15 + 15	Holgate M — + 1	Dixon R 1	Lindstrom J 15 + 10	Armstrong H — + 3	Coleman S 3 + 2	Garner J 17 + 4	O'Brien J 17 + 3	Mangala O 14 + 5	Branthwaite J 28 + 2	Patterson N 3 + 7	Broja A 4 + 6	Alcaraz C 7 + 8	Chermiti Y — + 4	Match No.
1	2	3	4	5	6	7	8^3	9^1	10	11^2	12	13	14													1
1		3	4	5	6	7^4	8^1	9^2	10	11^3	13	14		2	12	15										2
1		3	4	5	6	7	8	12	9	11^2	10^1	13					2									3
1	2	3	4	5^1	7^4	6^2	8^3	9	11	10^5	16				15			12	13	14						4
1	5	3	4		13		12	7	9	11	10^2				8^1			2		6						5
1	2	3		5			14	12	6	9^2	11	10			8^1			13		7^3	4					6
1	5	3	4		13	12	8^2	6	9	11	10						2			7^1						7
1	2	3	4	5		7	8	6	9	11	10^1									12						8
1	2	3	4	5		7	8^1	6^2	9^4	11^3	10	14			12				13	15						9
1	2	3	4	5		6	12		9	11^2	10^1	10			8^3			7	14							10
1	2	3		5		6	13	9^2	11^1	10	12				8			7			4					11
1	2	3		5		7		6^2	9	11	10	13			8^1			12			4					12
1	2^4	3^5		5		7^1	13	6	9	14	10	11^3			8^2			16	12		4	15				13
1	2	3		5		6	12	9^2	10^1	11^3	8				13	15				7^4	4			14		14
1	2	3		5		7	9^1	8	10^2	11					12					6	4			13		15
1	2^2	3		5		7	9^3	8	10^1	11	12				14	13				6	4					16
1		3		5		7	9	8	10^1	11^2					13	2^3				6	4	14	12			17
1	2^3	3		5		7^2	9^1	8	14	11	15				12					6	4	13	10^4			18
1	2	3		5		7^4	9	12	10	15					8^3	14				6	4	13	11^1			19
1	2^2	3		5		7	8^1	9^3	11	10	14				12				13	6	4					20
1	12	3	14	5		7		9	11	10^2					8^1				2^3	6	4	13				21
1	14	3		5		7		9^4	11^1	10^3	12				8^2		15		2	6	4	13				22
1	12	3		5^3	13	7	15	9		10	11^4				8^1			6^2	2		4	14				23
1	15	3		5	13	7^2	12	9		10^1	11				8^3			6^4	2		4			14		24
1	12	3		5	13	7	10			11					8^1			6	2		4			9^2		25
1	12	3		5	13	7	10	9^2		11					8^1			6^3	2		4			14		26
1	13	3		5	12	6^2	10			11					8^1			7	2		4			9		27
1	14	3		5	12	6	10	9^2		11					8^1			7^3	2		4			13		28
1		3		5	13	6	8^3	9^1		11^4					12			7^2	2		4	15	10	14		29
1	14	3		5	13	6	8^1	9^5		12	11^4							7^3	2		4	15	10^2	16		30
1	14	3		7^2	6	8^5	9	16		10^3	11^1				13				2		4	5^4	12	15		31
1		3		5	6	8^3	9	14		10^2	12							7	2		4		11^1	13		32
1	3^1	12		5	14	6^4	8^5	9	15	10^3	13							7	2		4		11^2	16		33
1	14			5		7	8^2	9	13	10^1	11^3							6	3		4	2^4	12	15		34
1	14			5	15	6^4	13	8^2	12	9	11^1							7	3		4	2^3	10^5	16		35
1	2	3	5	14	6^5	8^1	9^2	12	15	13	11^4					16		7			4			10^3		36
1	12		15	5		7	13	9^3	8^2	16	10^5	11					2^1	6	3		4^4			14		37
1	2		4	5		7	8	13	12	14	10^2	11^3						6	3					9^1		38

FA Cup

Third Round	Peterborough U	(h)	2-0
Fourth Round	Bournemouth	(h)	0-2

Carabao Cup

Second Round	Doncaster R	(h)	3-0
Third Round	Southampton	(h)	1-1

Southampton won 6-5 on penalties.

Vertu Trophy (Everton U21)

Group A (N)	Tranmere R	(a)	3-1
Group A (N)	Stockport Co	(a)	1-4
Group A (N)	Accrington S	(a)	1-2

EXETER CITY

FOUNDATION

Exeter City was formed in 1904 by the amalgamation of St Sidwell's United and Exeter United. The club first played in the East Devon League and then the Plymouth & District League. After an exhibition match between West Bromwich Albion and Woolwich Arsenal, which was held to test interest as Exeter was then a rugby stronghold, it was decided to form Exeter City. At a meeting at the Red Lion Hotel in 1908, the club turned professional.

St James Park, Stadium Way, Exeter, Devon EX4 6PX.

Telephone: (01392) 411 243.

Ticket Office: (01392) 411 243.

Website: www.exetercityfc.co.uk

Email: reception@ecfc.co.uk

Ground Capacity: 8,720.

Record Attendance: 20,984 v Sunderland, FA Cup 6th rd (replay), 4 March 1931.

Pitch Measurements: 104m × 64m (114yd × 70yd).

Chairman: Clive Harrison (interim).

Manager: Gary Caldwell.

Assistant Manager: Kevin Nicholson.

HONOURS

League Champions: Division 4 – 1989–90.
Runners-up: Division 3S – 1932–33; FL 2 – 2008–09, 2021–22; Division 4 – 1976–77; Football Conference – (4th) 2007–08 *(promoted to FL 2 via play-offs)*.
FA Cup: 6th rd replay – 1931; 6th rd – 1981.
League Cup: 4th rd – 1974, 1979, 1980, 1990, 2024.

Colours: Red and white striped shirts with red sleeves and black trim, black shorts with white trim, red socks with white trim.

Year Formed: 1904.

Turned Professional: 1908.

Club Nickname: 'The Grecians'.

Ground: 1904, St James Park.

First Football League Game: 28 August 1920, Division 3, v Brentford (h) W 3–0 – Pym; Coleburne, Feebury (1p); Crawshaw, Carrick, Mitton; Appleton, Makin, Wright (1), Vowles (1), Dockray.

Record League Victory: 8–1 v Coventry C, Division 3 (S), 4 December 1926 – Bailey; Pollard, Charlton; Pullen, Pool, Garrett; Purcell (2), McDevitt, Blackmore (2), Dent (2), Compton (2). 8–1 v Aldershot, Division 3 (S), 4 May 1935 – Chesters; Gray, Miller; Risdon, Webb, Angus; Jack Scott (1), Wrightson (1), Poulter (3), McArthur (1), Dryden (1), (1 og).

Record Cup Victory: 14–0 v Weymouth, FA Cup 1st qual rd, 3 October 1908 – Fletcher; Craig, Bulcock; Ambler, Chadwick, Wake; Parnell (1), Watson (1), McGuigan (4), Bell (6), Copestake (2).

Record Defeat: 0–9 v Notts Co, Division 3 (S), 16 October 1948; 0–9 v Northampton T, Division 3 (S), 12 April 1958; 0–9 v Reading, EFL Trophy Group G (S), 19 September 2023

Most League Points (2 for a win): 62, Division 4, 1976–77.

FOOTBALL YEARBOOK FACT FILE

On 4 March 1953 the Barnsley wing-half Tim Ward was announced as the new player-manager of Exeter City, and he accompanied the team to their game at Ipswich Town three days later. However, Barnsley still held his playing registration and after refusing to release him, Ward returned to Oakwell where he was appointed as manager of the Tykes at the end of the month. His eight-day spell in charge of the Grecians is one of the shortest of any Football League manager.

Most League Points (3 for a win): 89, Division 4, 1989–90.

Most League Goals: 88, Division 3 (S), 1932–33.

Highest League Scorer in Season: Fred Whitlow, 33, Division 3 (S), 1932–33.

Most League Goals in Total Aggregate: Tony Kellow, 129, 1976–78, 1980–83, 1985–88.

Most League Goals in One Match: 4, Harold 'Jazzo' Kirk v Portsmouth, Division 3 (S), 3 March 1923; 4, Fred Dent v Bristol R, Division 3 (S), 5 November 1927; 4, Fred Whitlow v Watford, Division 3 (S), 29 October 1932.

Most Capped Player: Ilmari Niskanen, 11 (25), Finland.

Most League Appearances: Arnold Mitchell, 495, 1952–66.

Youngest League Player: Ethan Ampadu, 15 years 337 days v Crawley T, 16 August 2016.

Record Transfer Fee Received: £1,800,000 (potentially rising to £5,730,000) from Brentford for Ollie Watkins, July 2017.

Record Transfer Fee Paid: £100,000 to Aberdeen for Jayden Stockley, August 2017.

Football League Record: 1920 Elected to Division 3; 1920–21 Division 3; 1921–58 Division 3 (S); 1958–64 Division 4; 1964–66 Division 3; 1966–77 Division 4; 1977–84 Division 3; 1984–90 Division 4; 1990–92 Division 3; 1992–94 Second Division; 1994–2003 Third Division; 2003–08 Football Conference; 2008–09 FL 2; 2009–12 FL 1; 2012–22 FL 2; 2022– FL 1.

LATEST SEQUENCES

Longest Sequence of League Wins: 7, 31.12.2016 – 4.2.2017.

Longest Sequence of League Defeats: 7, 14.1.1984 – 25.2.1984.

Longest Sequence of League Draws: 6, 13.9.1986 – 4.10.1986.

Longest Sequence of Unbeaten League Matches: 15, 17.8.2021 – 20.11.2021.

Longest Sequence Without a League Win: 18, 21.2.1995 – 19.8.1995.

Successive Scoring Runs: 22 from 15.9.1958.

Successive Non-scoring Runs: 6 from 17.1.1986.

MANAGERS

Arthur Chadwick 1910–22
Fred Mavin 1923–27
Dave Wilson 1928–29
Billy McDevitt 1929–35
Jack English 1935–39
George Roughton 1945–52
Norman Kirkman 1952–53
Norman Dodgin 1953–57
Bill Thompson 1957–58
Frank Broome 1958–60
Glen Wilson 1960–62
Cyril Spiers 1962–63
Jack Edwards 1963–65
Ellis Stuttard 1965–66
Jock Basford 1966–67
Frank Broome 1967–69
Johnny Newman 1969–76
Bobby Saxton 1977–79
Brian Godfrey 1979–83
Gerry Francis 1983–84
Jim Iley 1984–85
Colin Appleton 1985–87
Terry Cooper 1988–91
Alan Ball 1991–94
Terry Cooper 1994–95
Peter Fox 1995–2000
Noel Blake 2000–01
John Cornforth 2001–02
Neil McNab 2002–03
Gary Peters 2003
Eamonn Dolan 2003–04
Alex Inglethorpe 2004–06
Paul Tisdale 2006–18
Matt Taylor 2018–22
Gary Caldwell October 2022–

TEN YEAR LEAGUE RECORD

		P	W	D	L	F	A	Pts	Pos
2015-16	FL 2	46	17	13	16	63	65	64	14
2016-17	FL 2	46	21	8	17	75	56	71	5
2017-18	FL 2	46	24	8	14	64	54	80	4
2018-19	FL 2	46	19	13	14	60	49	70	9
2019-20	FL 2	37	18	11	8	53	43	65	5§
2020-21	FL 2	46	18	16	12	71	50	70	9
2021-22	FL 2	46	23	15	8	65	41	84	2
2022-23	FL 1	46	15	11	20	64	68	56	14
2023-24	FL 1	46	17	10	19	46	61	61	13
2024-25	FL 1	46	15	11	20	49	65	56	16

§*Decided on points-per-game (1.76)*

DID YOU KNOW ❓

Exeter City's fourth-round FA Cup tie at Manchester United in January 2005 attracted a crowd of 67,551, the highest ever to watch a Grecians match. Exeter were members of the Football Conference that season but held the Premier League side 0-0 at Old Trafford before going out in the replay. The income from the tie and the televised replay helped put the club's finances on solid ground after they had entered into a CVA the previous season.

EXETER CITY – SKY BET LEAGUE ONE 2024–25 LEAGUE RECORD

Match No.	Date	Venue	Opponents	Result	H/T Score	Lg Pos.	Goalscorers	Attendance
1	Aug 10	H	Rotherham U	W 1-0	0-0	8	Watts [71]	7458
2	17	A	Northampton T	L 1-2	1-0	14	Crama [8]	5981
3	24	H	Peterborough U	L 1-2	1-2	17	Cole [4]	6343
4	31	A	Bolton W	W 2-0	1-0	10	Doyle [34], Alli [49]	22,086
5	Sept 14	A	Blackpool	L 1-2	0-1	16	Francis [88]	8813
6	21	H	Stevenage	W 2-0	1-0	11	Francis [9], Doyle [50]	5612
7	28	A	Wigan Ath	D 0-0	0-0	13		8837
8	Oct 1	A	Leyton Orient	W 1-0	1-0	10	Richards A [40]	6439
9	5	H	Cambridge U	W 1-0	1-0	7	Woods [23]	6406
10	17	A	Shrewsbury T	W 2-0	1-0	4	Doyle [9], Magennis [64]	4965
11	22	H	Reading	L 1-2	0-2	6	Niskanen [58]	6807
12	26	A	Huddersfield T	L 0-2	0-1	10		17,890
13	Nov 9	H	Charlton Ath	W 1-0	0-0	11	Crama [59]	7347
14	16	A	Lincoln C	D 0-0	0-0	9		5950
15	23	H	Wrexham	L 0-3	0-2	11		12,484
16	26	H	Birmingham C	L 0-2	0-1	11		7928
17	Dec 3	H	Wycombe W	D 2-2	2-1	11	Alli [2], McMillan [22]	5073
18	7	A	Stockport Co	L 0-2	0-0	11		9192
19	14	H	Barnsley	L 1-2	1-0	15	Magennis [13]	5669
20	21	A	Burton Alb	W 2-1	1-1	13	Magennis [45], Alli [71]	2690
21	26	H	Bristol R	W 3-1	0-0	12	Fitzwater [72], Alli [78], Richards J [90]	8192
22	29	H	Crawley T	D 4-4	1-4	13	Alli [35], Harper [60], Woods [82], Mitchell [90]	6805
23	Jan 1	A	Wycombe W	L 1-2	0-0	13	Crama [86]	5829
24	4	H	Bolton W	L 1-2	1-0	14	Mitchell [54]	6353
25	18	A	Birmingham C	L 0-1	0-1	16		25,930
26	21	A	Peterborough U	D 1-1	0-1	14	Alli [90]	5913
27	25	H	Blackpool	L 1-3	0-3	17	Alli [82]	6325
28	28	H	Leyton Orient	L 2-6	0-4	17	Alli 2 [47, 56]	5022
29	Feb 1	A	Stevenage	L 1-4	1-2	17	Magennis (pen) [2]	3094
30	15	A	Cambridge U	W 1-0	0-0	16	Magennis [73]	5455
31	22	A	Charlton Ath	L 0-3	0-1	18		14,864
32	Mar 1	H	Northampton T	D 1-1	0-1	19	Cox [87]	6834
33	4	A	Reading	D 0-0	0-0	19		7955
34	8	H	Shrewsbury T	W 2-0	1-0	18	Watts [29], Mitchell [48]	6197
35	11	H	Mansfield T	W 2-0	1-0	16	Mitchell [8], MacDonald [49]	5214
36	15	A	Rotherham U	D 1-1	0-1	16	Hartridge [56]	8438
37	22	A	Lincoln C	D 0-0	0-0	16		8971
38	29	H	Wrexham	L 0-2	0-1	17		8084
39	Apr 1	A	Barnsley	W 2-1	1-0	16	Trevitt [13], Magennis [81]	10,092
40	5	A	Stockport Co	L 0-2	0-2	16		6541
41	8	H	Wigan Ath	D 1-1	0-0	15	Cole [69]	5382
42	12	A	Bristol R	W 2-1	2-0	15	Watts [11], Cole [42]	9508
43	18	H	Burton Alb	D 0-0	0-0	14		6972
44	21	A	Crawley T	L 1-3	1-3	16	Watts [25]	4441
45	26	H	Huddersfield T	W 3-1	1-1	13	Niskanen [39], McMillan [56], Oluwabori [90]	7276
46	May 3	A	Mansfield T	L 0-3	0-2	16		7494

Final League Position: 16

GOALSCORERS

League (49): Alli 9, Magennis 6 (1 pen), Mitchell 4, Watts 4, Cole 3, Crama 3, Doyle 3, Francis 2, McMillan 2, Niskanen 2, Woods 2, Cox 1, Fitzwater 1, Harper 1, Hartridge 1, MacDonald 1, Oluwabori 1, Richards A 1, Richards J 1, Trevitt 1.
FA Cup (12): Magennis 6 (2 pens), Mitchell 2, Bird 1, Crama 1, Doyle 1, Harper 1.
Carabao Cup (1): Alli 1.
Vertu Trophy (8): Alli 2, Aitchison 1, Bird 1, Francis 1, Mitchell 1, Richards J 1, Sweeney 1.

Whitworth J 46	Sweeney P 18	Crama T 22	Yfeko J 11+1	Niskanen J 35+5	McMillan J 43	Francis E 34+8	Harper V 10+12	Cole R 8+14	Aitchison J 22+6	Magennis J 35+5	Alli M 19+6	Watts C 20+11	Borges P —+1	Purrington B 12+9	Doyle K 10+10	Woods R 26+11	Richards A 2+4	Cox S 7+16	Carayol M 1+5	Fitzwater J 13+3	Bird J 2+12	Mitchell D 12+11	McDonald K 9+2	Richards J 9+4	Jones P 6+11	Colwill J 9+9	Diabate C 2+2	Yogane T 5+13	Hartridge A 18	Trevitt R 10+1	MacDonald A 14+1	Oluwabori A 1+5	Turns E 13	Dean T 2+1	Oakes L —+1	Match No.
1	2	3	4^4	5	6	7	8^1	9^2	10^3	11	12	13	14	15																						1
1	3	4	5	2	7^2	6	8^1	9	11	10					13	12																				2
1	2	3	4	6	9	14		7	8^1	10^3	11				13	12	5^2																			3
1	2	3	4	8	5			12	9^2	10^3	11^4				13	6^1	7	14	15																	4
1	2^4	3	4	5	8	15		12	9	10^2	11^3					7^1	6	14	13																	5
1	2	3	4	5	8^2	7		10^4	11^3	12				15	9^1	6		13	14																	6
1	2	3	4	9	5	12		8^1	11^4	13					6^3	7	10^2	15	14																	7
1	2	3	4	9	5	6^4			11^3	12	13^4				8^2	7	10^1	14	15																	8
1	2		4	8	5	6^4			10^3	11^1	9				14	7	12^2	13	15	3																9
1	2	3	4	8	5	6			13	12	9^3				11^1	7		10^2	14																	10
1	3	4	5	8	2	7^3			9	13	12				14	6^4		11	10^2	15																11
1	3	4	6^3	2	12			16	7^4	11	10^1			5	9^2	8^5		13	15	14																12
1	3	4*	6	2	7^3				9^2	10^4	11^1			5	15	8				14	12	13														13
1	2	3		5	7	8^1			10^3		11	9^2	4		6^4					14	12	13														14
1	2	3		5	6	7	16		9^3	11^5		8^2	4^1		10^4			12		14	13	15														15
1	2	3		5	6	4	8^3		9^4	11		15			13	7^2	14	12		10^1																16
1		4		7	2	5			9^4	10^2	11	14	12			15				3	13				6^1	8^3										17
1	2	3	5^3	6	4	8^1	13		10	12	11	9^2			15	7^4						14														18
1	2	3	5	8	4	15	12		9^5	10^3	11^4	6^1				7^3				13	14		16													19
1	3^1	10	2	4		13		8^2	11	7	16				14	6^5				12		9^4	5^3	15												20
1			8	2	4	14			11	10	5^3			15	12	6^4				3		9^2	7^1	13												21
1	2		8^3	5	4	12			14	10	15				9^4	6				3^2	11^1	13		7^5	16											22
1	3	16	5^5	6	4	8^3			11		9^2				13	7				2^4	15	12		10^1	14											23
1	3	13	5	4	10^3				12	11	14	8^1				6				2		9^2		7^4	15											24
1		16	5^4	4	8^5				14	12	11^4	10				6				2		9^3	3^1	7^3	15	13										25
1		5^3	4						9	10^5	11				3^4	7^1	6^2			2	15	12	13		14	8	16									26
1		14	8	4					16	11	10				12					2^1	9	3^2	6^4	5^3	7^3	13	15									27
1		10	2	4					8^1	11^4	7	9^3				5				15	14		6^2		13	3	12									28
1		8^2	2	7		5^3			11^4		9^1					6				15	13			16	14	3	10^5	4	12							29
1		2	3		9^3	6^1	13		11		7^4	16				14				12				8^5		15	5	10^2	4							30
1		6^1	3		2	14			11						12					7^3		10^2	16	9^5		13	5	8^4	4	15						31
1		12	2^1			13	8^2		11		16	5			7		14			6^3		15	17		9^4	4	10^5	3								32
1			7^5		16	9^1	10^4		5^3		8					14				11^2		15	13		12	4	6	3		2						33
1			6^4	12		13	11		9^1		8				15					10^3		5^2			14	4	7	3		2						34
1			5^4	7^3		16	11^5		12		8				15					10^2		9^1	14		13	4	6	3		2						35
1		13	5	7^1		15	11		14											9^2		8^3	10^4		12	4	6	3		2						36
1			5	7		11			9^1	8				12					10^2		13			4	6	3	2									37
1		7	13	14	12	11^5			15	6^2				16								2^4	8^1	10^5	5	9	4		3							38
1		8^3	5	7	14				11	10^2	15			13							9^1			12	4	6^4	3		2							39
1		5	7	6^3	15	13			11	9	8^1		12	16							14^4		10^4	4	3				2^5							40
1		8	5	15	13	7^3			11	14				6		10^1	3^2				9^4			4		2	12									41
1		7	2	15	12	8^3			9^4			13		11^5		3		6^2		14		10^1	5		16		4									42
1		8	5	7^3	16	10^2			9^5			12		11^4		6^1				14		13	4		3	15	2									43
1		8^5	5	6^4	13	15			9^3			14		11		3^4				7					12	4			10^2	2^1	16					44
1		8	5		6^5				9^3			15		11^2		3^4				7^3	12	13			14	4			3	16	2	9^4				45
1		8	5^4	13		6						14				3				7^2	10^3			11^5	12	4			15	2	9^1	16				46

FA Cup

First Round	Barnet	(h)	5-3
Second Round	Chesterfield	(h)	2-0
Third Round	Oxford U	(h)	3-1
Fourth Round	Nottingham F	(h)	2-2

aet; Nottingham F won 4-2 on penalties.

Carabao Cup

First Round	Walsall	(a)	1-1

Walsall won 4-3 on penalties.

Vertu Trophy

Group G (S)	Swindon T	(h)	2-1
Group G (S)	Tottenham H U21	(h)	2-0
Group G (S)	Bristol R	(a)	3-2
Second Round	Birmingham C	(h)	1-2

FLEETWOOD TOWN

FOUNDATION

Originally formed in 1908 as Fleetwood FC, it was liquidated in 1976. Re-formed as Fleetwood Town in 1977, it folded again in 1996. Once again, it was re-formed a year later as Fleetwood Wanderers, but a sponsorship deal saw the club's name immediately changed to Fleetwood Freeport through the local retail outlet centre. This sponsorship ended in 2002, but since then local energy businessman Andy Pilley took charge and the club has risen through the non-league pyramid until finally achieving Football League status in 2012 as Fleetwood Town.

Highbury Stadium, Park Avenue, Fleetwood, Lancashire FY7 6TX.

Telephone: (01253) 775 080.

Ticket Office: (01253) 775 080.

Website: www.fleetwoodtownfc.com

Email: info@fleetwoodtownfc.com

Ground Capacity: 5,137.

HONOURS

League Champions: Football Conference – 2011–12.
FA Cup: 5th rd – 2023.
League Cup: 3rd rd – 2021, 2025.

Record Attendance: (Before 1997) 6,150 v Rochdale, FA Cup 1st rd, 13 November 1965; (Since 1997) 5,194 v York C, FL 2 Play-Off semi-final 2nd leg, 16 May 2014.

Pitch Measurements: 101m × 64m (110.5yd × 70yd).

Chairman: Jamie Pilley.

Chief Executive: Steve Curwood.

Head Coach: Pete Wild.

Assistant Head Coach: Adam Temple.

Colours: Red shirts with white sleeves and black trim, white shorts with black trim, red socks with white trim.

Year Formed: 1908 (re-formed 1997).

Previous Names: 1908, Fleetwood FC; 1977, Fleetwood Town; 1997, Fleetwood Wanderers; 2002 Fleetwood Town.

Club Nicknames: 'The Trawlermen'; 'The Cod Army'.

Grounds: 1908, North Euston Hotel; 1934, Memorial Park (now Highbury Stadium).

First Football League Game: 18 August 2012, FL 2, v Torquay U (h) D 0–0 – Davies; Beeley, Mawene, McNulty, Howell, Nicolson, Johnson, McGuire, Ball, Parkin, Mangan.

Record League Victory: 13–0 v Oldham T, North West Counties Div 2, 5 December 1998.

FOOTBALL YEARBOOK FACT FILE

Striker Jon Parkin became the first Fleetwood Town player to score a hat-trick in senior football when he achieved the feat in the 4-0 away win over Morecambe in what was only the club's fifth Football League game. Parkin, who finished the 2012–13 campaign as the Cod Army's top scorer with 12 League and Cup goals, added a further hat-trick away to Accrington Stanley later in the season.

Record Cup Victory: 4–0 v Leicester C U21, EFL Trophy Group D (N), 7 November 2023 – McMullan; Teale (Glenfeld), Holgate, Lawal (Johnson (1)), Armstrong; Robertson, Simons; Graydon (1), Broom (2), Brown (Macadam); Tshimanga.

Record Defeat: 0–7 v Billingham T, FA Cup 1st qual rd, 15 September 2001.

Most League Points (3 for a win): 82, FL 1, 2016–17.

Most League Goals: 66, FL 2, 2013–14.

Highest League Scorer in Season: Ched Evans, 17, FL 1, 2018–19.

Most League Goals in Total Aggregate: Paddy Madden, 43, 2018–21.

Most League Goals in One Match: 3, Steven Schumacher v Newport Co, FL 2, 2 November 2013; 3, Paddy Madden v Burton Alb, FL 1, 19 October 2019; 3, Jack Marriott v Accrington S, FL 1, 15 April 2023.

Most Capped Player: Conor McLaughlin, 25 (43), Northern Ireland.

Most League Appearances: Alex Cairns, 209, 2016–22.

Youngest League Player: Pele Smith, 15 years 304 days v Barrow, 21 December 2024.

Record Transfer Fee Received: £1,000,000 (potentially rising to £1,700,000) from Leicester C for Jamie Vardy, May 2012; £1,000,000 from Bournemouth for James Hill, January 2022.

Record Transfer Fee Paid: £300,000 to Kidderminster H for Jamille Matt, January 2013; £300,000 to Huddersfield T for Kyle Dempsey, May 2017.

Football League Record: 2012 Promoted from Football Conference; 2012–14 FL 2; 2014–24 FL 1; 2024– FL 2.

MANAGERS

Alan Tinsley 1997
Mark Hughes 1998
Brian Wilson 1998–99
Mick Hoyle 1999–2001
Les Attwood 2001
Mark Hughes 2001
Alan Tinsley 2001–02
Mick Hoyle 2002–03
Tony Greenwood 2003–08
Micky Mellon 2008–12
Graham Alexander 2012–15
Steven Pressley 2015–16
Uwe Rosler 2016–18
John Sheridan 2018
Joey Barton 2018–21
Simon Grayson 2021
Stephen Crainey 2021–22
Scott Brown 2022–23
Lee Johnson 2023
Charlie Adam 2023–24
Pete Wild December 2024–

LATEST SEQUENCES

Longest Sequence of League Wins: 5, 1.2.2020 – 22.2.2020.

Longest Sequence of League Defeats: 6, 12.8.2023 – 16.9.2023.

Longest Sequence of League Draws: 5, 13.8.2022 – 3.9.2022.

Longest Sequence of Unbeaten League Matches: 18, 19.11.2016 – 4.3.2017.

Longest Sequence Without a League Win: 13, 22.1.2022 – 19.3.2022.

Successive Scoring Runs: 24 from 2.5.2016.

Successive Non-scoring Runs: 4 from 25.11.2023.

TEN YEAR LEAGUE RECORD

		P	W	D	L	F	A	Pts	Pos
2015-16	FL 1	46	12	15	19	52	56	51	19
2016-17	FL 1	46	23	13	10	64	43	82	4
2017-18	FL 1	46	16	9	21	59	68	57	14
2018-19	FL 1	46	16	13	17	58	52	61	11
2019-20	FL 1	35	16	12	7	51	38	60	6§
2020-21	FL 1	46	16	12	18	49	46	60	15
2021-22	FL 1	46	8	16	22	62	82	40	20
2022-23	FL 1	46	14	16	16	53	51	58	13
2023-24	FL 1	46	10	13	23	49	72	43	22
2024-25	FL 2	46	15	15	16	60	60	60	14

§*Decided on points-per-game (1.71)*

DID YOU KNOW ?

Fleetwood, as the club was then known, became the first team to win the Lancashire Combination League Cup in three consecutive seasons. They beat Darwen 5-0 in the 1931–32 final, Lancaster Town 3-0 the following season and Chorley 2-1 in 1933–34. They came close to making it four in a row but lost out to Clitheroe in the 1934–35 final.

FLEETWOOD TOWN – SKY BET LEAGUE TWO 2024–25 LEAGUE RECORD

Match No.	Date	Venue	Opponents	Result	H/T Score	Lg Pos.	Goalscorers	Atten-dance
1	Aug 10	H	Grimsby T	W 1-0	1-0	8	Helm [18]	3525
2	18	A	Notts Co	D 2-2	1-0	6	Graydon [30], Sarpeng-Wiredu [46]	10,057
3	24	H	Gillingham	D 0-0	0-0	11		3157
4	31	A	AFC Wimbledon	L 0-1	0-1	13		7162
5	Sept 14	H	Carlisle U	W 3-2	2-1	12	Mayor 2 [10, 68], Coughlan [19]	7090
6	23	H	Morecambe	D 2-2	2-0	12	Graydon [34], Coughlan [45]	4025
7	28	A	Cheltenham T	W 2-0	1-0	10	Virtue 2 [5, 51]	3928
8	Oct 1	A	Walsall	W 6-2	1-2	6	Coughlan 2 (1 pen) [25, 51 (p)], Hughes 2 [57, 67], Virtue [85], Helm [90]	4237
9	5	H	Bromley	D 0-0	0-0	7		2605
10	19	A	Port Vale	L 1-3	1-1	12	Johnston [36]	6643
11	22	H	Crewe Alex	L 0-1	0-0	14		2725
12	26	A	Newport Co	D 0-0	0-0	15		4244
13	29	H	Salford C	D 2-2	1-1	15	Coughlan [33], Helm [61]	2549
14	Nov 9	H	Bradford C	W 1-0	1-0	12	Coughlan (pen) [8]	3971
15	30	A	Colchester U	D 0-0	0-0	12		3202
16	Dec 4	H	Doncaster R	L 2-4	2-3	14	Helm [34], Graydon [42]	2205
17	7	A	Swindon T	L 1-3	0-2	16	Virtue [67]	5819
18	16	H	Accrington S	D 1-1	0-1	15	Broom [52]	2669
19	21	A	Barrow	L 0-2	0-2	18		3007
20	26	H	Chesterfield	W 2-0	1-0	16	Virtue [28], Harratt [87]	3469
21	29	H	Harrogate T	D 1-1	1-1	16	Bolton [2]	2468
22	Jan 1	A	Doncaster R	L 1-2	0-1	17	Virtue [62]	7290
23	18	A	Salford C	W 2-0	2-0	14	Coughlan [2], Sarpeng-Wiredu [11]	3216
24	21	H	Milton Keynes D	W 2-1	1-0	13	Broom [33], Rooney [68]	2150
25	25	H	Carlisle U	L 1-2	0-1	15	Coughlan [70]	3517
26	28	A	Walsall	W 2-0	0-0	12	Rooney [12], Bolton [17]	2307
27	Feb 1	A	Morecambe	L 2-4	1-1	15	Bolton [41], Virtue [75]	3522
28	8	H	Cheltenham T	W 2-0	1-0	12	Virtue [44], Helm [90]	2257
29	11	A	Tranmere R	D 0-0	0-0	12		5166
30	15	A	Bromley	L 0-1	0-0	14		2474
31	18	A	AFC Wimbledon	D 0-0	0-0	13		2106
32	22	A	Grimsby T	L 1-2	0-1	14	Graydon [61]	5996
33	25	A	Gillingham	W 2-1	1-1	12	Helm [45], Graydon [50]	5370
34	Mar 1	H	Notts Co	D 2-2	0-1	13	Graydon 2 (1 pen) [68 (p), 70]	3555
35	4	A	Crewe Alex	W 4-1	2-0	12	Graydon [11], Marsh [33], Bennett [79], Patterson [89]	3881
36	8	H	Port Vale	D 1-1	0-0	12	Graydon [81]	3501
37	15	A	Colchester U	L 0-3	0-0	14		5636
38	22	H	Tranmere R	D 0-0	0-0	13		3421
39	29	A	Milton Keynes D	W 4-2	1-1	12	Virtue [45], Bolton [49], Marsh [59], Devonport [71]	6273
40	Apr 1	A	Accrington S	W 4-1	1-0	12	Helm [9], Patterson [62], Grant (og) [85], Hunt [90]	1987
41	5	H	Swindon T	L 0-4	0-1	13		2742
42	12	A	Chesterfield	L 0-3	0-0	13		7739
43	18	H	Barrow	D 0-0	0-0	14		3256
44	21	A	Harrogate T	L 1-3	0-0	15	Moore [51]	3081
45	26	H	Newport Co	W 2-0	0-0	14	Patterson [52], Medley [74]	2469
46	May 3	A	Bradford C	L 0-1	0-0	14		24,033

Final League Position: 14

GOALSCORERS

League (60): Graydon 9 (1 pen), Virtue 9, Coughlan 8 (2 pens), Helm 7, Bolton 4, Patterson 3, Broom 2, Hughes 2, Marsh 2, Mayor 2, Rooney 2, Sarpeng-Wiredu 2, Bennett 1, Devonport 1, Harratt 1, Hunt 1, Johnston 1, Medley 1, Moore 1, own goal 1.
FA Cup (0).
Carabao Cup (5): Graydon 3, Bennett 1, Coughlan 1.
Vertu Trophy (6): Harratt 2, Coughlan 1, Graydon 1, Odubeko 1, Smith 1.

Harrington D 20	Sarpeng-Wiredu B 34	Holgate H 5	Medley Z 4+3	Johnston C 19	Mayor D 29+10	Bonds E 30+3	Hunt M 29+10	Helm M 32+12	Lonergan T 2+4	Coughlan R 21+2	Graydon R 33+1	Patterson P 22+17	Virtue M 33+8	Broom R 10+17	Bolton J 35+3	Odubeko A —+5	Hughes K 7+1	Harratt K 2+18	Bennett R 26+9	Potter F 19+9	Shaw L 6+5	Devonport D 11+13	Smith P —+1	Lynch J 26+1	Rooney S 18+1	Neal H 14+7	Cover B 4+4	Marsh L 11+5	Moore K 2+8	Lane M —+1	Morrison G 1+6	Cross-Adair F —+1	Johnson W 1+1	Match No.
1	2	3	4	5	6	7	8	9²	10¹	11³	12	13	14																					1
1	2¹	3	4	6	8³	5	9²	7⁴	14	11⁵	12	15	10	13	16																			2
1	2	3	4¹	6	8	5⁴	9⁶	7²	10³	11	15	16	13	12	14																			3
1	2	3		6	8	5	9⁴	10²		11³		15	7¹	14		13		4⁵	12	16														4
1	2	3		5	7	12	8²	9³		11	10¹	13	6⁵	16	15		14	4⁴																5
1	2		6	8¹	5	14	7³	11²	10	9⁴	12	15	3		13	4																		6
1	2		6	8	5	9	13	11¹	10²	7³		3	14	4	12																			7
1	2¹		6	7²	5	9	13	10³	11	8		3	4	14	12																			8
1	2		6	7⁵	5	9²	15	16	10³	11	14	8⁴	3¹	4	13	12																		9
1	2		6⁵	8	5	14	12	10²	11⁴	9	7¹	16	13	4³	15	3																		10
1	2		6²	8¹	12	4	7	10³	11	9	5	13	14	3																				11
1	2		6	8	5	9	10³	14	12	11¹	7²		4	3	13																			12
1	2¹		6⁴	8³	5	9	12	16	10²	11⁵	15	7	13	4	3	14																		13
1			6	8		9	7²	10¹	11	5	13	3	12	4	2																			14
1			6	8¹		9³	7	11²	10	13	5	14	3	12	4	2																		15
1			6¹	13	14	7	11³	10⁵	9⁴	8	12	3	15	2	4²	5	16																	16
1			9		6	7²	10	11⁴	14	8	2³	4	13	5	12	3¹	15																	17
1			8³		9¹	6	10	11⁴	5	7	14	3	13	4	12	2²	15																	18
1			8²			6¹	11	10	9	5	3⁴	15	2	4	13	14	12																	19
1²	2¹		6	8	5³		10⁵	11⁴	9	7		3	16	12	4	14	15	13																20
	2²		6	8	5⁵	13	11¹	10⁴	9	7³		3	12	14	4	16	15	1																21
	2⁵		6	8²	5⁴	12	14	10	9	13	15	3	11³	4	16	7¹	1																	22
			8²	5	13		11¹	10³	9	7	14	3	12	2	4		1	6																23
	8¹		15	6³	12	10²	11⁴	7	9		13	3	5		1	2	14																	24
	8		16	6	14	9	10⁴	11	7²	2³	4	12	3⁵	5¹	1	15	13																	25
	2		13	7	9	8²	10³	12	3	11	4	14	1	5	6¹																			26
	10²		8	5	9³	11	6¹	7	3	4	13	1	2	14	12																			27
4			7	9	13	11⁴	15	6²	3	14	12	2	8	5³	10¹																			28
4			12	8	9⁶	14	11⁴	15	7¹	13	16	1	2	6	5²	10³																		29
9			13	8¹	6⁴	7	11⁵	10	4	3²	5	16		2³	12	14	15																	30
3			9¹	6	8³	12	11	14	4	2	12	1	5	7	10²	13																		31
4			8²	6⁴	14	13	11	9	2³	12	1	5	7	10¹	15																			32
4			8	9	7	11		3	12	10²	1	2	5	6¹	13																			33
4			7⁴	5	9²	8	10	14	15	3	13	11¹	1	2	6²	12																		34
4			8²	6	9	7	11³	13	12	5	3	2	1	10¹	14																			35
5			7²	8	6¹	9⁴	10	13	12	2	4	3	14	1	15	11³																		36
4			13	7	9²	8³	10¹	14	6⁴	5⁵	3	2	11	1	15	16	12																	37
4			13		8³		9	6²	16	3	2	14	11⁴	1	5⁵	7	12	10¹	15															38
4			14	8		9⁶	6	12	3	2	13	10⁴	1	5³	7²	15	11¹	16																39
4²			13	8¹	9³	6		3	2	12	10	1	5	7	11¹		14	15																40
4			14	12	8⁵	9	6⁴	3³	2	15	10²	1	5	7	11¹	13	16																	41
	14		11	5	8	6³		3	4	10²	1	2	7	9¹	13	12																		42
			8	10		9	6	3	2	4	11²	1	5	7¹	13	12																		43
	14	15		9	8⁴	16	6	5	3	2²	4⁵	1	12	11	10³	7¹	13																	44
	4⁵		12	5	9¹	10	8³	7	3	15	16	11²	1	6	14	13	2⁴																	45
	12		8	14	9	10³	7⁴	13	4	3²	5¹	11	1	2	6	15																		46

FA Cup

First Round	Reading	(a)	0-2

Carabao Cup

First Round	WBA	(h)	2-1
Second Round	Rotherham U	(h)	2-1
Third Round	Stoke C	(a)	1-1

Stoke C won 2-1 on penalties.

Vertu Trophy

Group D (N)	Aston Villa U21	(h)	2-3
Group D (N)	Barrow	(h)	3-0
Group D (N)	Bolton W	(a)	1-2

FULHAM

FOUNDATION

Churchgoers were responsible for the foundation of Fulham, which first saw the light of day as Fulham St Andrew's Church Sunday School FC in 1879. They won the West London Amateur Cup in 1887 and the championship of the West London League in its initial season of 1892–93. The name Fulham had been adopted in 1888.

Craven Cottage, Stevenage Road, London SW6 6HH.

Telephone: (0843) 208 1222.

Ticket Office: (020) 3871 0810.

Website: www.fulhamfc.com

Email: enquiries@fulhamfc.com

Ground Capacity: 24,500.

Record Attendance: 49,335 v Millwall, Division 2, 8 October 1938.

Pitch Measurements: 100m × 65m (109.5yd × 71yd).

Chairman: Shahid Khan.

Chief Executive: Alistair Mackintosh.

Head Coach: Marco Silva.

Assistant Head Coach: Goncalo Santos.

Colours: White shirts with black and red trim, black shorts with red trim, white socks with red and black trim.

Year Formed: 1879.

Turned Professional: 1898.

Reformed: 1987.

Previous Name: 1879, Fulham St Andrew's; 1888, Fulham.

Club Nickname: 'The Cottagers'.

HONOURS

League Champions: First Division – 2000–01; FL C – 2021–22; Division 2 – 1948–49; Second Division – 1998–99; Division 3S – 1931–32.
Runners-up: Division 2 – 1958–59; Division 3 – 1970–71; Third Division – 1996–97.

FA Cup: Runners-up: 1975.

League Cup: semi-final – 2024.

European Competitions
UEFA Cup: 2002–03.
Europa League: 2009–10 *(runners-up)*, 2011–12.
Intertoto Cup: 2002 *(winners)*.

Grounds: 1879, Star Road, Fulham; c.1883, Eel Brook Common, 1884, Lillie Road; 1885, Putney Lower Common; 1886, Ranelagh House, Fulham; 1888, Barn Elms, Castelnau; 1889, Purser's Cross (Roskell's Field), Parsons Green Lane; 1891, Eel Brook Common; 1891, Half Moon, Putney; 1895, Captain James Field, West Brompton; 1896, Craven Cottage; 2002, Loftus Road (groundshare with QPR); 2004, Craven Cottage.

First Football League Game: 3 September 1907, Division 2, v Hull C (h) L 0–1 – Skene; Ross, Lindsay; Collins, Morrison, Goldie; Dalrymple, Freeman, Bevan, Hubbard, Threlfall.

Record League Victory: 10–1 v Ipswich T, Division 1, 26 December 1963 – Macedo; Cohen, Langley; Mullery (1), Keetch, Robson (1); Key, Cook (1), Leggat (4), Haynes, Howfield (3).

Record Cup Victory: 7–0 v Swansea C, FA Cup 1st rd, 11 November 1995 – Lange; Jupp (1), Herrera, Barkus (Brooker (1)), Moore, Angus, Thomas (1), Morgan, Brazil (Hamill), Conroy (3) (Bolt), Cusack (1).

Record Defeat: 0–10 v Liverpool, League Cup 2nd rd 1st leg, 23 September 1986.

Most League Points (2 for a win): 60, Division 2, 1958–59 and Division 3, 1970–71.

FOOTBALL YEARBOOK FACT FILE

The dangers posed by daytime bombing raids brought havoc to football in the South East in the 1940–41 season, with matches regularly being suspended or abandoned. Fulham's home game with Charlton Athletic was the only London game out of the five scheduled for 9 November to be played to completion without stoppage. The Cottagers went down to a 2-1 defeat in front of an estimated 150 fans, the smallest number to watch a game in the club's history.

Most League Points (3 for a win): 101, Division 2, 1998–99.
101, Division 1, 2000–01.

Most League Goals: 111, Division 3 (S), 1931–32.

Highest League Scorer in Season: Frank Newton, 43,
Division 3 (S), 1931–32; Aleksandar Mitrovic, 43, FL C,
2021–22.

Most League Goals in Total Aggregate: Gordon Davies,
159, 1978–84, 1986–91.

Most League Goals in One Match: 5, Fred Harrison v
Stockport Co, Division 2, 5 September 1908; 5, Bedford
Jezzard v Hull C, Division 2, 8 October 1955; 5, Jimmy Hill
v Doncaster R, Division 2, 15 March 1958; 5, Steve Earle v
Halifax T, Division 3, 16 September 1969.

Most Capped Player: Johnny Haynes, 56, England.

Most League Appearances: Johnny Haynes, 594, 1952–70.

Youngest League Player: Harvey Elliott, 16 years 30 days
v Wolverhampton W, 4 May 2019.

Record Transfer Fee Received: £50,000,000 from Al-Hilal
for Aleksandar Mitrovic, August 2023.

Record Transfer Fee Paid: £27,000,000 to Nice for Jean
Michael Seri, July 2018; £27,000,000 (potentially rising to
£34,000,000) to Arsenal for Emile Smith Rowe, July 2024.

Football League Record: 1907 Elected to Division 2;
1907–28 Division 2; 1928–32 Division 3 (S);
1932–49 Division 2; 1949–52 Division 1; 1952–59 Division 2;
1959–68 Division 1; 1968–69 Division 2; 1969–71 Division 3;
1971–80 Division 2; 1980–82 Division 3; 1982–86 Division 2;
1986–92 Division 3; 1992–94 Second Division; 1994–97
Third Division; 1997–99 Second Division; 1999–2001 First
Division; 2001–14 Premier League; 2014–18 FL C; 2018–19
Premier League; 2019–20 FL C; 2020–21 Premier League;
2021–22 FL C; 2022– Premier League.

LATEST SEQUENCES

Longest Sequence of League Wins: 12, 7.5.2000 – 18.10.2000.
Longest Sequence of League Defeats: 11, 2.12.1961 –
24.2.1962.
Longest Sequence of League Draws: 6, 23.12.2006 –
20.1.2007.
Longest Sequence of Unbeaten League Matches: 23,
23.12.2017 – 27.4.2018.
Longest Sequence Without a League Win: 15, 25.2.1950 –
23.8.1950.
Successive Scoring Runs: 26 from 28.3.1931.
Successive Non-scoring Runs: 6 from 21.8.1971.

MANAGERS

Harry Bradshaw 1904–09
Phil Kelso 1909–24
Andy Ducat 1924–26
Joe Bradshaw 1926–29
Ned Liddell 1929–31
Jim McIntyre 1931–34
Jimmy Hogan 1934–35
Jack Peart 1935–48
Frank Osborne 1948–64
*(was Secretary-Manager or
General Manager for most of
this period and Team Manager
1953–56)*
Bill Dodgin Snr 1949–53
Duggie Livingstone 1956–58
Bedford Jezzard 1958–64
*(General Manager for last two
months)*
Vic Buckingham 1965–68
Bobby Robson 1968
Bill Dodgin Jnr 1968–72
Alec Stock 1972–76
Bobby Campbell 1976–80
Malcolm Macdonald 1980–84
Ray Harford 1984–96
Ray Lewington 1986–90
Alan Dicks 1990–91
Don Mackay 1991–94
Ian Branfoot 1994–96
(continued as General Manager)
Micky Adams 1996–97
Ray Wilkins 1997–98
Kevin Keegan 1998–99
(Chief Operating Officer)
Paul Bracewell 1999–2000
Jean Tigana 2000–03
Chris Coleman 2003–07
Lawrie Sanchez 2007
Roy Hodgson 2007–10
Mark Hughes 2010–11
Martin Jol 2011–13
Rene Muelenstein 2013–14
Felix Magath 2014
Kit Symons 2014–15
Slavisa Jokanovic 2015–18
Claudio Ranieri 2018–19
Scott Parker 2019–21
Marco Silva July 2021–

TEN YEAR LEAGUE RECORD

		P	W	D	L	F	A	Pts	Pos
2015-16	FL C	46	12	15	19	66	79	51	20
2016-17	FL C	46	22	14	10	85	57	80	6
2017-18	FL C	46	25	13	8	79	46	88	3
2018-19	PR Lge	38	7	5	26	34	81	26	19
2019-20	FL C	46	23	12	11	64	48	81	4
2020-21	PR Lge	38	5	13	20	27	53	28	18
2021-22	FL C	46	27	9	10	106	43	90	1
2022-23	PR Lge	38	15	7	16	55	53	52	10
2023-24	PR Lge	38	13	8	17	55	61	47	13
2024-25	PR Lge	38	15	9	14	54	54	54	11

DID YOU KNOW

Leslie Skene signed professional
forms for Fulham in July 1907 after
winning a full international cap for
Scotland. He was the Cottagers'
first-choice goalkeeper for their
initial three seasons as a Football
League club, combining soccer with
his studies as a medical student. He
later qualified as a doctor and
psychiatrist and was for many years
the medical superintendent at the
Isle of Man Mental Hospital.

FULHAM – PREMIER LEAGUE 2024–25 LEAGUE RECORD

Match No.	Date	Venue	Opponents	Result		H/T Score	Lg Pos.	Goalscorers	Attendance
1	Aug 16	A	Manchester U	L	0-1	0-0	20		73,297
2	24	H	Leicester C	W	2-1	1-1	11	Smith Rowe [18], Iwobi [70]	25,401
3	31	A	Ipswich T	D	1-1	1-1	11	Traore [32]	29,517
4	Sept 14	H	West Ham U	D	1-1	1-0	12	Jimenez [24]	26,528
5	21	H	Newcastle U	W	3-1	2-0	8	Jimenez [5], Smith Rowe [22], Nelson [90]	25,700
6	28	A	Nottingham F	W	1-0	0-0	6	Jimenez (pen) [51]	30,139
7	Oct 5	A	Manchester C	L	2-3	1-1	7	Pereira [26], Rodrigo Muniz [88]	52,719
8	19	H	Aston Villa	L	1-3	1-1	9	Jimenez [5]	26,743
9	26	A	Everton	D	1-1	0-0	10	Iwobi [61]	38,742
10	Nov 4	H	Brentford	W	2-1	0-1	9	Wilson 2 [90, 90]	24,931
11	9	A	Crystal Palace	W	2-0	1-0	7	Smith Rowe [45], Wilson [83]	25,142
12	23	H	Wolverhampton W	L	1-4	1-1	10	Iwobi [20]	26,685
13	Dec 1	A	Tottenham H	D	1-1	0-0	10	Cairney [67]	61,141
14	5	H	Brighton & HA	W	3-1	1-0	6	Iwobi 2 [4, 87], O'Riley (og) [79]	26,368
15	8	H	Arsenal	D	1-1	1-0	10	Jimenez [11]	26,954
16	14	A	Liverpool	D	2-2	1-0	9	Pereira [11], Rodrigo Muniz [76]	60,333
17	22	H	Southampton	D	0-0	0-0	9		26,819
18	26	A	Chelsea	W	2-1	0-1	8	Wilson [82], Rodrigo Muniz [90]	39,687
19	29	H	Bournemouth	D	2-2	1-0	8	Jimenez [40], Wilson [72]	27,301
20	Jan 5	H	Ipswich T	D	2-2	0-1	9	Jimenez 2 (2 pens) [69, 90]	27,042
21	14	A	West Ham U	L	2-3	0-2	9	Iwobi 2 [51, 78]	62,456
22	18	A	Leicester C	W	2-0	0-0	9	Smith Rowe [48], Traore [68]	31,500
23	26	H	Manchester U	L	0-1	0-1	10		27,288
24	Feb 1	A	Newcastle U	L	2-1	0-1	9	Jimenez [61], Rodrigo Muniz [82]	52,173
25	15	H	Nottingham F	W	2-1	1-1	8	Smith Rowe [15], Bassey [62]	27,164
26	22	H	Crystal Palace	L	0-2	0-1	10		26,777
27	25	A	Wolverhampton W	W	2-1	1-1	9	Sessegnon [1], Rodrigo Muniz [47]	28,708
28	Mar 8	A	Brighton & HA	L	1-2	1-1	10	Jimenez [35]	31,584
29	16	H	Tottenham H	W	2-0	0-0	8	Rodrigo Muniz [78], Sessegnon [88]	27,182
30	Apr 1	A	Arsenal	L	1-2	0-1	8	Rodrigo Muniz [90]	60,256
31	6	H	Liverpool	W	3-2	3-1	8	Sessegnon [23], Iwobi [32], Rodrigo Muniz [37]	27,770
32	14	A	Bournemouth	L	0-1	0-1	9		11,195
33	20	H	Chelsea	L	1-2	1-0	9	Iwobi [20]	27,712
34	26	A	Southampton	W	2-1	0-1	8	Smith Rowe [72], Sessegnon [90]	28,946
35	May 3	A	Aston Villa	L	0-1	0-1	9		42,515
36	10	H	Everton	L	1-3	1-1	11	Jimenez [17]	27,653
37	18	A	Brentford	W	3-2	1-2	10	Jimenez [16], Cairney [68], Wilson [70]	17,136
38	25	H	Manchester C	L	0-2	0-1	11		27,671

Final League Position: 11

GOALSCORERS

League (54): Jimenez 12 (3 pens), Iwobi 9, Rodrigo Muniz 8, Smith Rowe 6, Wilson 6, Sessegnon 4, Cairney 2, Pereira 2, Traore 2, Bassey 1, Nelson 1, own goal 1.
FA Cup (7): Rodrigo Muniz 3, Andersen 1, Bassey 1, Castagne 1, Jimenez 1 (pen).
Carabao Cup (3): Jimenez 1 (1 pen), Nelson 1, Stansfield 1.
(Fulham U21) Vertu Trophy (3): Godo 1, Gordon 1, Osmand 1.

Leno B 38	Tete K 21+1	Diop I 15+6	Bassey C 34+1	Robinson A 35+1	Pereira A 25+8	Lukic S 28+2	Traore A 18+18	Smith Rowe E 25+9	Iwobi A 35+3	Rodrigo Muniz C 8+23	Cairney T 3+22	Jimenez R 30+8	Wilson H 12+13	Reed H —+12	Stansfield J —+1	Berge S 26+5	Andersen J 29	Nelson R 5+6	Castagne T 17+7	Cuenca J 4+4	Sessegnon R 7+9	King J 1+7	Godo M —+2	Vinicius C —+3	Willian d 2+8	Match No.
1	2	3	4	5	6^4	7^5	8^2	9^1	10	11^3	12	13	14	15	16											1
1	2	3	4	5	6^4	7	8^2	9^1	10	11^3	13	14	12	15												2
1	2	3	4	5	6^3	7^4	9	8^1	11^5	10^2	16	13	14	15		12										3
1	2		4	5	6^5	7^1	8	9^4	10^2	15	14	11^3			16	12	3	13								4
1	2	16	4	5	6^2	7^1	8^3	9^9	10	15	11^4	13				12	3	14								5
1	2	16	4	5	6^2	7^3	8^1	9^9	10	15	11^4	14				12	3	13								6
1	3^3		5	6	7^2	9	10	13	2^5	14	12	11^4				8^1	4	16	15							7
1	2	12	4	5	6^1		8^2	9^1	10	15	11	14				7^4	3^4	13								8
1	2	3	4	5	6^2		8^1	9^3	10^5	16		11^4	14	13		7	12		15							9
1	2^3		4	5	6^1		12	9^9	8	14	16	11^2	15			7	3	10^4	13							10
1	2		4	5	6^3		16	9^9	8^4	12	14	11^1	13	15		7	3	10^2								11
1	2^3		4	5	6^2	7	14	9^1	8	15	12	11^5	13				3	10^4	16							12
1	2	3	4	5		6^1		9^4	8^5	14	12^*	11^3	13			7		10^2	16		15					13
1		3	4	5	12		13	9^1	6	11^3		15	8^4			7^5		10^2	2	16		14				14
1	2	3	4	5	13	7^4	10^2	9^1	8	14		11^3	12			6			15							15
1	2^1	3		5	9^3	7	15	14	8	13		11^2	10^4			6			12	4						16
1		3	4	5		14	13		10	11^2	7^4	12	8^5			6^3		2			9^1	15	16			17
1		3	5	10	7^2	8	6^1		9^4	14	13	11^3	12				4	2	15							18
1		3	5	10	7^2	8^4	14	16	9^5	13	12	11^1	6^3				4	2	15							19
1	2^1	4	8	13	6^4	15	12	11^2	14		7^3	10	9			3		5								20
1		4	5	7^1	6	12	9^2	10^4	15	13	11	8^3				3		2	14							21
1	16	4	5		6^5	12	9^3	10^1	13	14	11^2	8^4				7	3	2	15							22
1		4	5	14	6^4	12	9^3	10	13	15	11^2	8^1				7	3	2								23
1	15		4	5	12	6	8^4	9^1	10^3	13		11^2				7	3	2	14							24
1		4	5	13	6^2	8^4	9^3	10^5	12		11^1	14				7	3	2	16		15					25
1	15	4	5	12	6	8	9^2	10^3	16	13^5	11					7^1	3	2^4			14					26
1	2	16	10	6^1	9^2	·	13	11^4	14				7^3	3	5	4^5	8^3	12								27
1	2	4	8	6^2		10^3	9^4	12	11^1		13			7	3	5	15	14								28
1		4	5	6	12	9^3	8^2	13	14	11^1			7	3	2	15	10^4									29
1	2^4		8	13	6^2	9^3	10^1	14	16	11^5			7	3	5	4^1	15	12								30
1	15		4	5	9^3	7^2	16	14	10^4	11^1	12		13		6	3	2	8^6								31
1		4	5	9^4	7^5	13	15	10	11^1	14	12			6^3	3	2^7	16									32
1	2^2	4	5	9	7^1	15	10^4		12	11^{15}	14		6	3	13	8^3		16								33
1	2	4		6^1	12	13	14	8^5	16	10	9^4		7^2	3	5		15	11^3								34
1	2^3	4		7	14	12	10^5	11	9^2	15	16	8^1	3	13												35
1	2	4	6^3		12	9^1	10	14	11	8^2	7^4	3		5^5	15	16	13									36
1	2	4	5^5	6	8^4	9^3	10^2	12	11	14	7^1	3		16	15	13										37
1	2	5	9^1	7^5	10^4	13	12	6^3	11	8^2	16	3		4	15	14										38

FA Cup

Third Round	Watford	(h)	4-1
Fourth Round	Wigan Ath	(a)	2-1
Fifth Round	Manchester U	(a)	1-1

aet; Fulham won 4-3 on penalties.

Quarter-Final	Crystal Palace	(h)	0-3

Carabao Cup

Second Round	Birmingham C	(a)	2-0
Third Round	Preston NE	(a)	1-1

Preston NE won 16-15 on penalties.

Vertu Trophy (Fulham U21)

Group A (S)	Shrewsbury T	(a)	2-1
Group A (S)	Walsall	(a)	0-1
Group A (S)	Birmingham C	(a)	1-7

GILLINGHAM

FOUNDATION

The success of the pioneering Royal Engineers of Chatham excited the interest of the residents of the Medway Towns and led to the formation of many clubs including Excelsior. After winning the Kent Junior Cup and the Chatham District League in 1893, Excelsior decided to go for bigger things and it was at a meeting in the Napier Arms, Brompton, in 1893 that New Brompton FC came into being, buying and developing the ground which is now Priestfield Stadium. They changed their name to Gillingham in 1913, when they also changed their strip from black and white stripes to predominantly blue.

Priestfield Stadium, Redfern Avenue, Gillingham, Kent ME7 4DD.

Telephone: (01634) 300 000.

Ticket Office: (01634) 300 000.

Website: www.gillinghamfootballclub.com

Email: enquiries@priestfield.com

Ground Capacity: 10,018.

Record Attendance: 23,002 v QPR, FA Cup 3rd rd, 10 January 1948.

Pitch Measurements: 104.2m × 68.6m (114yd × 75yd).

Chairman: Brad Galinson.

Managing Director: Joe Comper.

Manager: Gareth Ainsworth.

Assistant Manager: Richard Dobson.

Colours: Blue shirts with white sleeves and blue trim, white shorts with blue trim, white socks with blue trim.

Year Formed: 1893.

Turned Professional: 1894.

Previous Name: 1893, New Brompton; 1913, Gillingham.

Club Nickname: 'The Gills'.

Ground: 1893, Priestfield Stadium (renamed KRBS Priestfield Stadium 2009; MEMS Priestfield Stadium 2011; Priestfield Stadium 2023).

First Football League Game: 28 August 1920, Division 3, v Southampton (h) D 1–1 – Branfield; Robertson, Sissons; Battiste, Baxter, Wigmore; Holt, Hall, Gilbey (1), Roe, Gore.

Record League Victory: 10–0 v Chesterfield, Division 3, 5 September 1987 – Kite; Haylock, Pearce, Shipley (2) (Lillis), West, Greenall (1), Pritchard (2), Shearer (2), Lovell, Elsey (2), David Smith (1).

Record Cup Victory: 10–1 v Gorleston, FA Cup 1st rd, 16 November 1957 – Brodie; Parry, Hannaway; Riggs, Boswell, Laing; Payne, Fletcher (2), Saunders (5), Morgan (1), Clark (2).

Record Defeat: 2–9 v Nottingham F, Division 3 (S), 18 November 1950.

HONOURS

League Champions: FL 2 – 2012–13; Division 4 – 1963–64.
Runners-up: Third Division – 1995–96; Division 4 – 1973–74.
FA Cup: 6th rd – 2000.
League Cup: 4th rd – 1964, 1997, 2023.

FOOTBALL YEARBOOK FACT FILE

Gillingham came close to closing down in the summer of 1939. Faced with significant debts and falling attendances, a meeting of shareholders held a vote as to whether the club should be wound up at a meeting in July 1939. Interest was minimal and apart from the directors only 15 shareholders showed up. The decision to enter voluntary liquidation was tied 3-3 and only the casting vote of the chairman ensured the club survived.

Most League Points (2 for a win): 62, Division 4, 1973–74.

Most League Points (3 for a win): 85, Division 2, 1999–2000.

Most League Goals: 90, Division 4, 1973–74.

Highest League Scorer in Season: Ernie Morgan, 31, Division 3 (S), 1954–55; Brian Yeo, 31, Division 4, 1973–74.

Most League Goals in Total Aggregate: Brian Yeo, 135, 1963–75.

Most League Goals in One Match: 6, Fred Cheesmur v Merthyr T, Division 3 (S), 26 April 1930.

Most Capped Player: Andrew Crofts, 13 (includes 1 on loan from Brighton & HA) (29), Wales.

Most League Appearances: John Simpson, 571, 1957–72.

Youngest League Player: Luke Freeman, 15 years 247 days v Hartlepool U, 24 November 2007.

Record Transfer Fee Received: £1,500,000 from Manchester C for Robert Taylor, November 1999.

Record Transfer Fee Paid: £600,000 to Reading for Carl Asaba, August 1998.

Football League Record: 1920 Original Member of Division 3; 1920–21 Division 3; 1921–38 Division 3 (S); 1938 Failed re-election; Southern League 1938–44; Kent League 1944–46; Southern League 1946–50; 1950 Re-elected to Division 3 (S); 1950–58 Division 3 (S); 1958–64 Division 4; 1964–71 Division 4; 1971–74 Division 4; 1974–89 Division 3; 1989–92 Division 4; 1992–96; Third Division; 1996–2000 Second Division; 2000–04 First Division; 2004–05 FL C; 2005–08 FL 1; 2008–09 FL 2; 2009–10 FL 1; 2010–13 FL 2; 2013–22 FL 1; 2022– FL 2.

LATEST SEQUENCES

Longest Sequence of League Wins: 7, 18.12.1954 – 29.1.1955.

Longest Sequence of League Defeats: 10, 20.9.1988 – 5.11.1988.

Longest Sequence of League Draws: 6, 15.3.2025 – 8.4.2025.

Longest Sequence of Unbeaten League Matches: 20, 13.10.1973 – 10.2.1974.

Longest Sequence Without a League Win: 15, 1.4.1972 – 2.9.1972.

Successive Scoring Runs: 20 from 31.10.1959.

Successive Non-scoring Runs: 7 from 25.10.2022.

MANAGERS

W. Ironside Groombridge
 1896–1906 *(Secretary-Manager)*
 (previously Financial Secretary)
Steve Smith 1906–08
W. I. Groombridge 1908–19
 (Secretary-Manager)
George Collins 1919–20
John McMillan 1920–23
Harry Curtis 1923–26
Albert Hoskins 1926–29
Dick Hendrie 1929–31
Fred Mavin 1932–37
Alan Ure 1937–38
Bill Harvey 1938–39
Archie Clark 1939–58
Harry Barratt 1958–62
Freddie Cox 1962–65
Basil Hayward 1966–71
Andy Nelson 1971–74
Len Ashurst 1974–75
Gerry Summers 1975–81
Keith Peacock 1981–87
Paul Taylor 1988
Keith Burkinshaw 1988–89
Damien Richardson 1989–92
Glenn Roeder 1992–93
Mike Flanagan 1993–95
Neil Smillie 1995
Tony Pulis 1995–99
Peter Taylor 1999–2000
Andy Hessenthaler 2000–04
Stan Ternent 2004–05
Neale Cooper 2005
Ronnie Jepson 2005–07
Mark Stimson 2007–10
Andy Hessenthaler 2010–12
Martin Allen 2012–13
Peter Taylor 2013–14
Justin Edinburgh 2015–17
Adrian Pennock 2017
Steve Lovell 2017–19
Steve Evans 2019–22
Neil Harris 2022–23
Stephen Clemence 2023–24
Mark Bonner 2024–25
John Coleman 2025
Gareth Ainsworth March 2025–

TEN YEAR LEAGUE RECORD

		P	W	D	L	F	A	Pts	Pos
2015-16	FL 1	46	19	12	15	71	56	69	9
2016-17	FL 1	46	12	14	20	59	79	50	20
2017-18	FL 1	46	13	17	16	50	55	56	17
2018-19	FL 1	46	15	10	21	61	72	55	13
2019-20	FL 1	35	12	15	8	42	34	51	10§
2020-21	FL 1	46	19	10	17	63	60	67	10
2021-22	FL 1	46	8	16	22	35	69	40	21
2022-23	FL 2	46	14	13	19	36	49	55	17
2023-24	FL 2	46	18	10	18	46	57	64	12
2024-25	FL 2	46	14	16	16	41	46	58	17

§*Decided on points-per-game (1.46)*

DID YOU KNOW ?

Striker Robert Taylor became the first Gillingham player to score five goals in an away match in the Football League, achieving this when he scored all the goals in the Gills' 5-0 win away to Burnley in February 1999. Taylor netted three times in a seven-minute spell either side of the break, having earlier scored after 14 and 27 minutes.

GILLINGHAM – SKY BET LEAGUE TWO 2024–25 LEAGUE RECORD

Match No.	Date	Venue	Opponents	Result	H/T Score	Lg Pos.	Goalscorers	Attendance
1	Aug 10	H	Carlisle U	W 4-1	1-0	1	Dieng 2, Wakeling 48, Nolan 77, Williams J 87	7037
2	17	A	Morecambe	W 1-0	0-0	2	Lapslie 76	3611
3	24	A	Fleetwood T	D 0-0	0-0	1		3157
4	31	H	Chesterfield	W 1-0	1-0	1	McKenzie 8	6954
5	Sept 7	A	Doncaster R	L 0-1	0-1	4		7546
6	14	H	Tranmere R	W 3-0	0-0	2	Little 48, Clarke 2 82, 89	6660
7	21	A	Notts Co	W 1-0	1-0	2	Nevitt 38	14,747
8	28	H	Barrow	W 2-0	1-0	1	Clarke 17, McKenzie 62	7166
9	Oct 1	H	Grimsby T	L 0-1	0-1	1		5652
10	5	A	Crewe Alex	L 0-2	0-1	2		5000
11	12	H	Accrington S	L 1-2	0-0	5	Little 49	6622
12	19	A	Bradford C	L 1-2	1-2	6	Clarke 11	16,471
13	22	H	Newport Co	L 0-2	0-2	11		5262
14	26	A	Swindon T	D 1-1	1-0	11	Dieng 16	7325
15	Nov 9	H	Port Vale	W 1-0	0-0	8	Clarke 79	6267
16	23	H	Harrogate T	L 1-2	0-0	11	Dieng 51	5611
17	Dec 4	A	Bromley	L 1-2	0-0	12	McKenzie 56	3438
18	7	H	Salford C	W 1-0	0-0	10	Clarke 48	5296
19	14	A	Milton Keynes D	W 1-0	0-0	9	McKenzie 59	7191
20	20	H	Cheltenham T	D 2-2	1-1	9	Clarke 24, Lapslie 68	5938
21	26	A	Colchester U	L 0-2	0-1	13		5934
22	30	A	AFC Wimbledon	L 0-1	0-0	13		8281
23	Jan 2	H	Bromley	L 0-3	0-2	14		7454
24	18	H	Doncaster R	L 0-1	0-1	16		5814
25	25	A	Tranmere R	D 1-1	1-1	17	Turnbull (og) 44	7325
26	28	A	Grimsby T	D 1-1	1-0	17	Tharme (og) 35	4239
27	Feb 1	H	Notts Co	L 1-2	0-2	17	Gbode 80	6031
28	8	A	Barrow	L 0-3	0-0	19		3130
29	11	A	Walsall	D 1-1	0-0	19	McKenzie 68	6229
30	15	H	Crewe Alex	D 0-0	0-0	19		5663
31	22	A	Carlisle U	D 0-0	0-0	19		6976
32	25	H	Fleetwood T	L 1-2	1-1	19	Nevitt 39	5370
33	Mar 1	H	Morecambe	W 1-0	0-0	18	McKenzie 79	5612
34	4	A	Newport Co	L 1-3	0-3	19	Morgan 69	3589
35	8	H	Bradford C	W 1-0	0-0	19	Masterson 56	6297
36	15	A	Accrington S	D 1-1	0-1	19	Clark 90	2449
37	22	H	Walsall	D 0-0	0-0	19		6153
38	29	A	Harrogate T	D 1-1	0-1	19	Clark (pen) 68	3253
39	Apr 1	H	Colchester U	D 1-1	0-1	19	Clark (pen) 77	5924
40	5	A	Salford C	D 2-2	2-2	18	Nevitt 2, Hutton 24	2914
41	8	A	Chesterfield	D 1-1	1-0	19	Nevitt 14	7810
42	12	H	Milton Keynes D	W 1-0	0-0	17	Dack 90	6080
43	18	A	Cheltenham T	D 1-1	1-1	17	Morgan 2	4702
44	21	A	AFC Wimbledon	W 1-0	0-0	17	Gbode 64	7641
45	26	H	Swindon T	D 1-1	0-0	17	Gbode 61	7667
46	May 3	A	Port Vale	W 1-0	0-0	17	Rowe 56	13,661

Final League Position: 17

GOALSCORERS
League (41): Clarke 7, McKenzie 6, Nevitt 4, Clark 3 (2 pens), Dieng 3, Gbode 3, Lapslie 2, Little 2, Morgan 2, Dack 1, Hutton 1, Masterson 1, Nolan 1, Rowe 1, Wakeling 1, Williams J 1, own goals 2.
FA Cup (0).
Carabao Cup (1): Hawkins 1.
Vertu Trophy (3): Andrews 1, Nevitt 1, Wyllie 1.

Turner J 9	Hutton R 40 + 4	Ehmer M 33 + 2	Masterson C 24	Clark M 39 + 1	McKenzie R 37 + 2	Dieng T 8 + 5	Nolan J 20 + 11	Little A 30 + 3	Rowe A 10 + 6	Wakeling J 5 + 11	Williams J 8 + 18	Clarke J 20 + 13	Gbode J 18 + 16	Ogie S 26 + 8	Lapsie G 8 + 7	Hawkins O 9 + 16	Morris G 35 + 1	Wyllie M 7 + 5	Andrews J 2 + 10	Coleman E 16 + 5	Nevitt E 31 + 5	Dack B 5 + 14	Ashby-Hammond L — + 1	Williams E 5 + 5	Webster H 2	Gale S 22	Agbinone A 5 + 1	Khumbeni N 4 + 6	Morgan J 10 + 6	Smith A 12	Corness D 4 + 2	Holtam T 2	Match No.
1	2	3	4⁴	5	6	7¹	8	9	10²	11³	12	13	14	15																			1
1	2	3		5	6		8³	7		11¹	9²	10	14		4	12	13																2
1	2	3		5	6	7³	8²	9	13	11¹	15	10⁴	12		4	14																3
	2	3⁸		5	6		8	7	10¹		14	12		4	9³		1	11²	13													4
	2		5			8⁵	7		14	13	10³	16	4	9⁴	3	1	11¹	15	6²	12												5
	2	3	5			8²	7		13		12	10¹	4	9⁴	15	1	14		6⁴	11³												6
	2	3	5	6⁵		13	7		12	15	10¹	8²	4	9⁴	16	1	14		11³													7
	2	3	5	6²		8³	7		12	10⁴	15	4	9¹		1	16		13	11⁵	14												8
	3		5	2	14	8	7		9¹	10³	13	4⁴	12	15	1		6²	11														9
2⁵	3		5	6¹	15	8³	7²		13		10	16	4	9⁴	14	1		12	11													10
2	3		5			8²	7		14	10¹	12	4	15	16	1³	9⁴		6⁵	11	13												11
1	2	3	4	5		7⁵	15		13	14	8³	10²		9	11¹		12		6⁴		16												12
1	2	3	4⁵	5²		6⁴	10³		16	12	8	14	13	9¹	15		11		7														13
1	2	4	3			8³		12	10²	14	6		5	11⁴		13	15	7		9¹													14
1	2	3	4	6		7⁵	16	8¹	10⁴	14	13		5		11³	15	12		9²														15
1	2	4	3	6	16	7³	14		15		5⁴	13		11	12	8²	10¹		9⁵														16
1¹	2	4	3			7³		6⁵		15		9		5	13		12	10²	14	8	11⁴		16										17
13	4	3	5	7		12			14	6²	9¹	16		1		10²	8	11⁵	15		2⁴												18
12	3	4	5	6		9²		10³		8⁴	14		1		16	7	11⁵	15		13	2¹												19
2⁴	3	4	5	6		9²		10¹		8			15	12	1		14	7³	11	13													20
2	3	4⁴	5²	6		15		9¹	13	10³			8		12		1	16	7³	11	14												21
	3	4¹	9⁵	7	14	16	6	12		5	15	13		1		8	11⁴	10³		2²													22
13	3		5²	2	6¹	8³	14		9⁵	12	10	4		1		11	7⁴	15		16													23
	2	4		3		10	7	12		8³	14	5		1		6	11²	13		9¹													24
5	3		12	2		8³	7		14		4		13	1		10	9		6¹	11²													25
2	4		6	12	7²	9		15		11	5		13	1		14		3⁴	10³	8¹													26
2	4		6		8	14			13	12	5		1		11⁴	15		3	10¹	9²	7³												27
13	4		6		12	7³		11	5²			1		10⁴	9⁵		3	8¹	16	14	2	15											28
5	3		8	6		13	7		11¹		12	1		10³		4		14	2	9²													29
2⁴	4		6³	8		15	7		14		13	1		10	12	5		11²	3	9¹													30
2	4		6	7		9			11²		13	1		10³	12	5		14		3	8¹												31
5³	3		8¹	6		12	7		13	10²		11⁴	1		9	14		4		15	2												32
5	3		8	7		6			10²		11¹	1		9		4		13	12	2													33
5	3		8	6		7			11			1		9		4		10	2														34
5	15	3³	8	6⁴		7			14	10		11¹	1		12		4		13	9²	2												35
5	16	3⁵	8	6⁴		7			13	15	10²	11¹	1		12		4		14	9³	2												36
5		3	8	6		7			13	12	11²		1		10		4		9¹	2													37
5		3	8	6		15	7³	14	11²			12	1		10⁴		13	4		9¹	2												38
5		3	8	6		13	14	7	9²	11¹		12	1		10³		2			4													39
5		3	8	6		7			12	9¹	13	4	11²	1		10³			2	14													40
5		3	8	13		12	7	11¹	6²		9³	4		1		10			2		14												41
5³		3	8	6		7	11²		14	12⁴	4	15		10	13		9¹		2			1											42
5		3	8	6		9²	14	13		4	15		11⁴	12		2		7³	10¹			1											43
5		3	8	6		10³		9	13	12	4	11¹	1		14	7²		2															44
5		3	8	6³		10⁴		7⁸	12⁴	4		1		15	11¹	9²		2		14		13											45
2		4	5	7		11⁴			15			-1	16	13	12		6¹		3	9⁵	14	10²		8³									46

FA Cup
First Round   Blackpool   (h)   0-2

Carabao Cup
First Round   Swansea C   (a)   1-3

Vertu Trophy
Group D (S)   Peterborough U   (h)   1-2
Group D (S)   Crystal Palace U21   (h)   1-3
Group D (S)   Stevenage   (a)   1-1
Gillingham won 5-4 on penalties.

GRIMSBY TOWN

FOUNDATION

Grimsby Pelham FC, as they were first known, came into being at a meeting held at the Wellington Arms in September 1878. Pelham is the family name of big landowners in the area, the Earls of Yarborough. The receipts for their first game amounted to 6s. 9d. (equivalent to approx. £25 today). After a year, the club name was changed to Grimsby Town.

Blundell Park, Cleethorpes, North East Lincolnshire DN35 7PY.

Telephone: (01472) 605 050.

Ticket Office: (01472) 605 050 (option 4).

Website: www.gtfc.co.uk

Email: enquiries@gtfc.co.uk

Ground Capacity: 9,031.

Record Attendance: 31,651 v Wolverhampton W, FA Cup 5th rd, 20 February 1937.

Pitch Measurements: 105m × 66m (115yd × 72yd).

Chairman: Andrew Petit.

Chief Executive: Polly Bancroft.

Head Coach: David Artell.

Assistant Head Coach: Shaun Pearson.

Colours: Black and white striped shirts with white sleeves and red trim, black shorts with red and white trim, white socks with red and black trim.

Year Formed: 1878. *Turned Professional:* 1890. *Ltd Co.:* 1890.

Previous Name: 1878, Grimsby Pelham; 1879, Grimsby Town.

Club Nickname: 'The Mariners'.

Grounds: 1880, Clee Park; 1889, Abbey Park; 1899, Blundell Park.

First Football League Game: 3 September 1892, Division 2, v Northwich Victoria (h) W 2–1 – Whitehouse; Lundie, T. Frith; C. Frith, Walker, Murrell; Higgins, Henderson, Brayshaw, Riddoch (2), Ackroyd.

Record League Victory: 9–2 v Darwen, Division 2, 15 April 1899 – Bagshaw; Lockie, Nidd; Griffiths, Bell (1), Nelmes; Jenkinson (3), Richards (1), Cockshutt (3), Robinson, Chadburn (1).

Record Cup Victory: 8–0 v Darlington, FA Cup 2nd rd, 21 November 1885 – G. Atkinson; J. H. Taylor, H. Taylor; Hall, Kimpson, Hopewell; H. Atkinson (1), Garnham, Seal (3), Sharman, Monument (4).

Record Defeat: 1–9 v Arsenal, Division 1, 28 January 1931.

Most League Points (2 for a win): 68, Division 3 (N), 1955–56.

HONOURS

League Champions: Division 2 – 1900–01, 1933–34; Division 3 – 1979–80; Division 3N – 1925–26, 1955–56; Division 4 – 1971–72. *Runners-up:* Division 2 – 1928–29; Division 3 – 1961–62; Division 3N – 1951–52; Division 4 – 1978–79, 1989–90. Conference – (4th) 2015–16 *(promoted to FL 2 via play-offs)*; (6th) 2021–22 *(promoted to FL 2 via play-offs)*.

FA Cup: semi-final – 1936, 1939.

League Cup: 5th rd – 1980, 1985.

League Trophy Winners: 1998. *Runners-up:* 2008.

FOOTBALL YEARBOOK FACT FILE

Grimsby Town are recognised as the team that has won the most Football League promotions. The Mariners have three promotions to the top tier, six to tier two, three to tier three, and a further two from the National League back to the Football League (tier four). In addition, after being ejected from the League in 1909–10 they were voted back in the following season as champions of the Midland League.

Most League Points (3 for a win): 83, Division 3, 1990–91.

Most League Goals: 103, Division 2, 1933–34.

Highest League Scorer in Season: Pat Glover, 42, Division 2, 1933–34.

Most League Goals in Total Aggregate: Pat Glover, 180, 1930–39.

Most League Goals in One Match: 6, Tommy McCairns v Leicester Fosse, Division 2, 11 April 1896.

Most Capped Player: Otis Khan, 9, Pakistan.

Most League Appearances: John McDermott, 647, 1987–2007.

Youngest League Player: Louis Boyd, 15 years 326 days v Walsall, 12 September 2020.

Record Transfer Fee Received: £1,500,000 from Everton for John Oster, July 1997.

Record Transfer Fee Paid: £500,000 to Preston NE for Lee Ashcroft, August 1998.

Football League Record: 1892 Original Member of Division 2; 1892–1901 Division 2; 1901–03 Division 1; 1903 Division 2; 1910 Failed re-election; 1911 Re-elected Division 2; 1920–21 Division 3; 1921–26 Division 3 (N); 1926–29 Division 2; 1929–32 Division 1; 1932–34 Division 2; 1934–48 Division 1; 1948–51 Division 2; 1951–56 Division 3 (N); 1956–59 Division 2; 1959–62 Division 3; 1962–64 Division 2; 1964–68 Division 3; 1968–72 Division 4; 1972–77 Division 3; 1977–79 Division 4; 1979–80 Division 3; 1980–87 Division 2; 1987–88 Division 3; 1988–90 Division 4; 1990–91 Division 3; 1991–92 Division 2; 1992–97 First Division; 1997–98 Second Division; 1998–2003 First Division; 2003–04 Second Division; 2004–10 FL 2; 2010–15 Football Conference; 2015–16 National League; 2016–21 FL 2; 2021–22 National League; 2022– FL 2.

LATEST SEQUENCES

Longest Sequence of League Wins: 11, 19.1.1952 – 29.3.1952.

Longest Sequence of League Defeats: 9, 30.11.1907 – 18.1.1908.

Longest Sequence of League Draws: 5, 6.2.1965 – 6.3.1965.

Longest Sequence of Unbeaten League Matches: 19, 16.2.1980 – 30.8.1980.

Longest Sequence Without a League Win: 22, 24.3.2008 – 1.11.2008.

Successive Scoring Runs: 33 from 6.10.1928.

Successive Non-scoring Runs: 7 from 19.10.2019.

MANAGERS

H. N. Hickson 1902–20
 (Secretary-Manager)
Haydn Price 1920
George Fraser 1921–24
Wilf Gillow 1924–32
Frank Womack 1932–36
Charles Spencer 1937–51
Bill Shankly 1951–53
Billy Walsh 1954–55
Allenby Chilton 1955–59
Tim Ward 1960–62
Tom Johnston 1962–64
Jimmy McGuigan 1964–67
Don McEvoy 1967–68
Bill Harvey 1968–69
Bobby Kennedy 1969–71
Lawrie McMenemy 1971–73
Ron Ashman 1973–75
Tom Casey 1975–76
Johnny Newman 1976–79
George Kerr 1979–82
David Booth 1982–85
Mike Lyons 1985–87
Bobby Roberts 1987–88
Alan Buckley 1988–94
Brian Laws 1994–96
Kenny Swain 1997
Alan Buckley 1997–2000
Lennie Lawrence 2000–01
Paul Groves 2001–04
Nicky Law 2004
Russell Slade 2004–06
Graham Rodger 2006
Alan Buckley 2006–08
Mike Newell 2008–09
Neil Woods 2009–11
Rob Scott and Paul Hurst 2011–13
Paul Hurst 2013–16
Marcus Bignot 2016–17
Russell Slade 2017–18
Michael Jolley 2018–19
Ian Holloway 2019–20
Paul Hurst 2020–23
David Artell November 2023–

TEN YEAR LEAGUE RECORD

		P	W	D	L	F	A	Pts	Pos
2015-16	NL	46	22	14	10	82	45	80	4
2016-17	FL 2	46	17	11	18	59	63	62	14
2017-18	FL 2	46	13	12	21	42	66	51	18
2018-19	FL 2	46	16	8	22	45	56	56	17
2019-20	FL 2	37	12	11	14	45	51	47	15§
2020-21	FL 2	46	10	13	23	37	69	43	24
2021-22	NL	46	23	8	13	68	46	77	6
2022-23	FL 2	46	16	13	17	49	56	61	11
2023-24	FL 2	46	11	16	19	57	74	49	21
2024-25	FL 2	46	20	8	18	61	67	68	9

§ *Decided on points-per-game (1.27)*

DID YOU KNOW ?

After a period of exile at Scunthorpe, Grimsby Town returned to Blundell Park for a wartime fixture against Doncaster Rovers on 1 January 1944. The game was level at 1-1 when the referee controversially ended proceedings with five minutes remaining. Newspaper reports suggests that he ordered Mariners captain Alec Hall off, but the player had refused to leave the field.

GRIMSBY TOWN – SKY BET LEAGUE TWO 2024–25 LEAGUE RECORD

Match No.	Date	Venue	Opponents	Result	H/T Score	Lg Pos.	Goalscorers	Attendance
1	Aug 10	A	Fleetwood T	L 0-1	0-1	17		3525
2	17	H	Cheltenham T	W 3-2	1-0	13	Davies 2 [44, 90], Vernam [51]	5885
3	22	A	Notts Co	L 1-4	1-3	16	Rodgers [45]	10,046
4	31	H	Bradford C	W 2-1	1-0	11	Rose [28], Svanthorsson [47]	7004
5	Sept 7	A	Chesterfield	L 1-2	0-2	16	Vernam [50]	9325
6	14	H	Barrow	L 1-2	1-2	21	Green [45]	5496
7	21	H	Bromley	W 1-0	0-0	12	Rose (pen) [51]	6115
8	28	A	Carlisle U	W 3-2	1-2	11	Barrington [24], Cass [81], Rodgers [90]	7510
9	Oct 1	A	Gillingham	W 1-0	1-0	8	Green [21]	5652
10	5	H	Doncaster R	L 0-3	0-3	10		7693
11	12	A	Salford C	W 2-1	2-1	8	Barrington 2 [1, 45]	3608
12	19	H	Walsall	L 1-4	0-0	10	Wilson [87]	5984
13	22	A	Tranmere R	W 1-0	0-0	7	Obikwu [59]	5428
14	26	H	Milton Keynes D	L 1-3	1-0	10	Rose [16]	5853
15	Nov 9	A	AFC Wimbledon	W 1-0	1-0	7	Rose [30]	8307
16	16	A	Newport Co	D 0-0	0-0	7		4298
17	23	H	Colchester U	L 0-1	0-0	8		4952
18	Dec 3	H	Accrington S	W 5-2	4-0	7	Rodgers [2], Luker [11], Obikwu [19], Davies (pen) [33], Aljofree (og) [68]	3874
19	7	A	Morecambe	W 3-0	2-0	5	Obikwu 2 [25, 39], Rose [90]	2995
20	14	H	Crewe Alex	L 0-2	0-0	7		5745
21	21	A	Swindon T	L 1-3	0-2	8	Rose (pen) [72]	7453
22	26	H	Harrogate T	W 2-1	0-0	8	Khouri [55], Svanthorsson [74]	6514
23	29	H	Port Vale	W 3-0	1-0	5	McJannet [29], Tharme [81], Svanthorsson [90]	7045
24	Jan 1	A	Accrington S	L 2-3	2-1	8	Green [5], Khouri [39]	2675
25	4	A	Bradford C	L 1-3	0-1	9	McJannet [51]	18,011
26	18	H	Chesterfield	D 1-1	1-1	9	Davies [17]	6706
27	25	A	Barrow	L 0-3	0-0	9		3661
28	28	H	Gillingham	D 1-1	0-1	10	Rose [90]	4239
29	Feb 1	A	Bromley	W 2-0	0-0	9	Rose [46], Obikwu [70]	3857
30	8	H	Carlisle U	W 2-1	0-1	9	Obikwu [62], Rose (pen) [83]	5788
31	15	A	Doncaster R	W 2-1	1-0	9	Obikwu [38], Olowu (og) [47]	9961
32	22	H	Fleetwood T	W 2-1	1-0	8	McEachran [23], Rose [64]	5996
33	Mar 1	A	Cheltenham T	D 1-1	0-1	8	Rodgers [53]	4473
34	4	H	Tranmere R	D 1-1	0-1	8	Rose (pen) [68]	4854
35	8	A	Walsall	W 3-1	2-1	8	Luker 2 [21, 66], Rose (pen) [44]	6255
36	11	H	Notts Co	L 0-2	0-0	8		6270
37	15	H	Salford C	L 0-1	0-0	9		6398
38	22	H	Newport Co	W 1-0	0-0	7	McEachran [64]	5339
39	28	A	Colchester U	W 2-1	0-0	7	Green [46], Khouri [76]	6986
40	Apr 1	A	Crewe Alex	L 0-2	0-1	7		4512
41	5	H	Morecambe	W 3-1	1-1	7	Green 2 [24, 80], Barrington [48]	5807
42	12	A	Harrogate T	D 2-2	2-0	7	Green [39], Svanthorsson [45]	3881
43	18	H	Swindon T	L 0-4	0-2	8		7624
44	21	A	Port Vale	D 2-2	1-0	7	Rose 2 (1 pen) [24, 52 (p)]	11,829
45	26	A	Milton Keynes D	D 0-0	0-0	8		10,244
46	May 3	H	AFC Wimbledon	L 0-1	0-0	9		8369

Final League Position: 9

GOALSCORERS

League (61): Rose 14 (6 pens), Green 7, Obikwu 7, Barrington 4, Davies 4 (1 pen), Rodgers 4, Svanthorsson 4, Khouri 3, Luker 3, McEachran 2, McJannet 2, Vernam 2, Cass 1, Tharme 1, Wilson 1, own goals 2.
FA Cup (0).
Carabao Cup (2): McJannet 1, Wilson 1.
Vertu Trophy (4): Cass 1, Gardner 1, Rose 1, Svanthorsson 1.

Wright J 34	Cass L 18+8	Rodgers H 44	McJannet C 38+3	Hume D 43+2	McEachran G 40+4	Khouri E 41+5	Svanthorsson J 36+7	Green K 36+3	Vernam C 10+7	Wilson D 4+8	Barrington L 21+17	Davies J 8+10	Gardner C 3+8	Rose D 35+10	Ainley C 4+22	Warren T 19+13	Carson M —+9	Eastwood J 6	Tharme D 22+6	Auton S —+1	Smith J 6	Pyke R 1+6	Obikwu J 12+7	Luker J 15+7	Thompson C 6+13	Burns D 2+7	Turi G 2+2	Brown H —+1	Match No.
1	2	3	4	5	6^3	7	8^1	9^2	10^5	11^4	12	13	14	15	16														1
1	2	3	4	12	6	5		9^2	10^3	11^4	8^1	7		15	13	14													2
1	2	3	4	14	7^3	5	13	9	10	11^4	8^2	6^1		15	12														3
1	12	3	4	5	6^4	9^2	7^3	8	10^1					15		11	13		2	14									4
1		3	4	5^2	6	9^1	7	8^4	10^3	13	14					11	15		2	12									5
		3	4	5^4	6	9	7^2	8	10^3	12	14				16	11^1	13	1	2	15									6
13		3	4	5	6	9	7^3	8^8	10^1		12				11	2^2		1		14									7
13		3	5	6	8	9	15		11^4	7^3		16	10	14	2^2			1^1	4^5	12									8
	2	3	4	5	6	9	7^2	8^4		14	10^1			12	11^3			15		1	13								9
	2	3^4	4	5^5	6	9	7^2	8^1		10^5		13	11^4		14	12		1	15	16									10
	2		4	5	6^1	9	7^2		15	8^5		10^4	11^3	12	13	14		3	1	16									11
	2	3^3	4	5	6^1	9	7^5		13	8^4		10^2	11	12	16	15		14	1										12
14		3	5	6	13	8			7^2		12	11	9^3	2		4		1	10^1										13
		3^5	5	6	9^2	8	16		14	7^1		15	10^4	12	2		4	1	11^3	13									14
1	12	3	4	5	6^3	7	8	9^1		10^2		11^4	13	2		15			14										15
1		3	4	5	6^2	9	7^1	8^4		10	15	11^3		2		14	12	13											16
1		3	4	5		9	14		10^3	13	11^1	8	2		12	7	6^2												17
1	2	3^2	4	5^5	6	16	10	8^4		9^3		12	15		13		11^1	7	14										18
1	2	3	4	5	9^2	13	10^4	8		16	14		12	15		11^1	7^5	6^3											19
1	2		4	5	13	14	10^5	8		16	9^3		12		3		15	11^1	7^4	6^2									20
1	2	3	4^4	5	6	12		8^1		10^3	9^2	13	11		15		14	7											21
1	2	3	4	5	6	9	13	8^4		14	15	11^1	12	10^2				7^3											22
1	2^1	3	4	5	6	9	13	14		8^3		11	10^2	12		15			7^4										23
1	2	3	4	5	6	9	10^3	8^1		15	12	13	14			11^2		7^4											24
1	12	3	4	5	6^3	7^4	10^5		15	8^2	9	11	13	2^1		16		14											25
1	2	3	4	5	6	7^2	10^3	13	14		9	12				11^1	8												26
1	2	3	4^1	6^4	7	10^3	9	14		15			12		11	8^2	13												27
1	2	3		7^3	5	10	9	8^1		11		14	4		13	12	6^2												28
1	13^8	2	4	9	12	8^4	5^5	7	14		11	15	3		10^2		6^1												29
1	2	4^1	8	6	7^4	5	9^9	13		15		10	12		3	11^2	14												30
1	2^1	4	8	6^3	7	5	9^2		15		10^5	13	12		3	11^4	14	16											31
1	2	4	8	6	7	5^4	9^2	12	10^1		11^3	14	15		3	13													32
1	15	2^3	4	8	6^1	7	5	9^4		11		14	3		13	12	10^2												33
1	2	4	8	6	14	5	15	13		11	12	3^1		10^2	9^4	7^3													34
1	3^1	2	4	8	6^2	7	5^4	9^5	14		10	16	12		11^3	13	15												35
1		3	4^3	5		7	8^1	9^4	14		11	15	2		10	13	12	6^2											36
1	4		8	6^3	7^4	5^1	9^2	13		10	2		3		11		12	14	15										37
1	2		9	5^2	8	6	7	11^1		10	4		3		12	13													38
1	2		9	5^2	8	6	7^1	11^3	12	10	4		3		14	13													39
1	2	13	9	5^2	8	6	7	11^4	14		4^1		3		10^3	12	15												40
1	2	4	9	12	8	13	7^3	11^4	14	10	15		3											6^2	5^1				41
1	2	4	9	5	8^5	6^5	7^3	13	10^2	12	11	15	3^4											14	16				42
1	2	4	9^2	5^1	7^3	6	8	12	11		10^4	14	3											15	13				43
	2	13	9	5^4	7	6^2	8^3	11^1	15		10	14	4	1	3			12											44
	2		9	5	8	6	7	10^1			11	4	1	3				12											45
	2^2	12	9	5	8^3	6	7	13	14		10	4^1	1	3				11											46

FA Cup

First Round	Wealdstone	(h)	0-1

Carabao Cup

First Round	Bradford C	(h)	1-1

Grimsby T won 9-8 on penalties.

Second Round	Sheffield Wed	(h)	1-5

Vertu Trophy

Group G (N)	Lincoln C	(h)	1-2
Group G (N)	Manchester C U21	(h)	1-1

Manchester C U21 won 5-4 on penalties.

Group G (N)	Chesterfield	(a)	2-3

HARROGATE TOWN

FOUNDATION

An earlier club, Harrogate AFC, was formed in 1914, but did not start the 1914–15 season and was reformed in 1919. They competed in the Midland, Yorkshire and Northern Leagues before folding in 1932. The current club was established in the summer of 1935 as Harrogate Hotspurs, several of the players having previously played for Harrogate YMCA. Harry Lunn, the club's first secretary, had previously been secretary of the YMCA team. Hotspurs began life in the Harrogate & District League in 1935–36 when they finished in fourth position, gaining their first trophy when they won the Harrogate Charity Cup. By 1948 they had reached the West Yorkshire League and they changed their name to Harrogate Town to reflect their status as the town's leading club.

The Exercise Stadium, Wetherby Road, Harrogate, North Yorkshire HG2 7SA.

Telephone: (01423) 210 600.

Ticket Office: (01423) 210 600.

Website: www.harrogatetownafc.com

Email: enquiries@harrogatetownafc.com

Ground Capacity: 5,065.

Record Attendance: 4,280 v Harrogate Railway Ath, Whitworth Cup Final, May 1950.

Pitch Measurements: 100m × 66m (109.5yd × 72yd).

Chairman: Irving Weaver.

Chief Executive: Sarah Barry.

Manager: Simon Weaver.

Assistant Manager: Paul Thirlwell.

HONOURS

League: National League (2nd) 2019–20 *(promoted to FL 2 via play-offs).*

FA Cup: 3rd rd – 2022.

League Cup: 2nd rd – 2021, 2024, 2025.

FA Trophy Winners: 2019–20 (final played in 2021).

Colours: Yellow shirts with black patterned stripes and black trim, black shorts with yellow trim, black socks with yellow trim.

Year Formed: 1914. *Turned Professional:* 2017.

Previous Names: 1914, Harrogate AFC; 1935, Harrogate Hotspurs; 1948, Harrogate Town.

Club Nicknames: 'Town'; 'Sulphurites'.

Grounds: 1919, Starbeck Lane; 1920, Wetherby Lane; 1935, Christ Church Stray; 1937, Old Showground; 1946, Wetherby Road (renamed The EnviroVent Stadium 2020; The Exercise Stadium 2024).

First League Game: (As Harrogate AFC) 30 August 1919, West Riding League v Horsforth (h) (at Starbeck Lane) W 1–0 – Middleton; Deans, Bell, Goodall, Carroll, Jenkinson H (Capt), Day, O'Rourke, Priestley, Craven (1), Codd.

First Football League Game: 12 September 2020, FL 2 v Southend U (a) W 4–0 – Cracknell; Fallowfield, Falkingham, Smith, Burrell, Thomson, Beck (Stead 58), Martin (1) (Walker 75), Kerry (1), Muldoon (2), Hall.

FOOTBALL YEARBOOK FACT FILE

After reaching the FA Cup first round in 2005–06, Harrogate Town were drawn to play against Torquay United, their first competitive match against a Football League club. The Sulphurites drew 1-1 at Torquay thanks to Danny Holland's 20th minute goal but went out on penalties in the replay after the match finished goalless after extra time.

Record League Victory: 6–1 v Scunthorpe U (h), FL 2, 9 October 2021 – Oxley; Fallowfield, Smith, Hall, Burrell, Thomson, Falkingham (Kerry), Pattison (2) (Power), Diamond (1), Muldoon (2) (Orsi-Dadomo (1 pen)), Armstrong.

Record Cup Victory: 11–2 v Yeadon Celtic, West Riding County Challenge Cup, 5 November 1938 – McLaren; Hebblethwaite, Keogan, Atha, Harker, Clelland, Annakin (4), Sibson, Stanley (7), Everitt C, Richardson.

Record Defeat: 1–10, v Methley U (h), West Yorkshire League Division One, 20 August 1956.

Most League Points in a Season (3 for a win): 63, FL 2, 2023–24.

Most League Goals in a Season: 64, FL 2, 2021–22.

Highest League Scorer in Season: Luke Armstrong, 16, FL 2, 2022–23; George Thomson, 16, FL 2, 2023–24.

Most League Goals in Total Aggregate: Jack Muldoon, 44, 2020–25.

Most League Goals in One Match: 3, Brendan Kiernan v Cambridge U, FL 2, 30 April 2021; 3, Jack Muldoon v Oldham Ath, FL 2, 22 January 2022.

Most Capped Player: Stephen Duke-McKenna, 6 (28), Guyana.

Most League Appearances: Jack Muldoon, 202, 2018–25.

Youngest League Player: Emmanuel Ilesanmi, 17 years 136 days v Colchester U, 2 April 2022.

Record Transfer Fee Received: £500,000 from Carlisle U for Luke Armstrong, January 2024.

Record Transfer Fee Paid: £23,000 to Huddersfield T for Adam Porritt, January 2017.

Football League Record: 2020 Promoted from National League; 2020– FL 2.

LATEST SEQUENCES

Longest Sequence of League Wins: 3, 6.1.2024 – 30.1.2024.

Longest Sequence of League Defeats: 5, 3.12.2024 – 26.12.2024.

Longest Sequence of League Draws: 4, 31.3.2023 – 15.4.2023.

Longest Sequence of Unbeaten League Matches: 6, 1.1.2024 – 10.2.2024.

Longest Sequence Without a League Win: 8, 13.2.2024 – 16.3.2024.

Successive Scoring Runs: 13 from 7.3.2023.

Successive Non-scoring Runs: 4 from 20.3.2021.

MANAGERS

Tommy Codd 1919–20
J. C. Field 1920–21
Jimmy Dyer 1921–23
Mr Gill 1923–24
Mr Sixton 1924–29
C. Edwards 1929–30
Selection Committee 1930–31
Tom Bell 1931–32
Eddie Smith 1935–46
Selection Committee 1946–50
Walter Cook 1950–53
Bernard Cross 1953–55
Jack (Boss) Townrow 1955–67
Selection Committee 1967–69
Stan Hall 1969–70
Thomas (Chick) Farr 1970–71
Peter Gunby 1971–77
Alan Milburn 1977–78
Reg Taylor 1978–79
Alan Smith 1979–88
Denis Metcalf 1988–89
Alan Smith 1989–90
John Reed 1990–91
Alan Smith 1991–93
Mick Doig and John Deacey 1993
Frank Gray 1994
John Deacey then Alan Smith 1994–96
Mick Doig 1996–97
Paul Marshall 1997–98
Gavin Liddle 1998–99
Alan Smith (caretaker) 1999
Paul Ward 1999
Dave Fell 1999–2000
Mick Hennigan 2000–01
John Reed 2001–05
Neil Aspin 2005–09
Simon Weaver 2009–

TEN YEAR LEAGUE RECORD

		P	W	D	L	F	A	Pts	Pos
2015-16	NLN	42	21	9	12	73	46	72	4
2016-17	NLN	42	16	11	15	71	63	59	11
2017-18	NLN	42	26	7	9	100	49	85	2
2018-19	NL	46	21	11	14	78	57	74	6
2019-20	NL	37	19	9	9	61	44	66	2§
2020-21	FL 2	46	16	9	21	52	61	57	17
2021-22	FL 2	46	14	11	21	64	75	53	19
2022-23	FL 2	46	12	16	18	59	68	52	19
2023-24	FL 2	46	17	12	17	60	69	63	13
2024-25	FL 2	46	14	11	21	43	61	53	18

§*Decided on points-per-game (1.78).*

DID YOU KNOW

Harrogate Town stepped up to the Football Conference for the 2004–05 season after the competition expanded to add Divisions One North and One South. They played their first game in the competition on 14 August when they defeated Barrow 2-1 with two goals from Colin Hunter in front of a crowd of 771.

HARROGATE TOWN – SKY BET LEAGUE TWO 2024–25 LEAGUE RECORD

Match No.	Date	Venue	Opponents	Result		H/T Score	Lg Pos.	Goalscorers	Attendance
1	Aug 10	H	Bromley	L	0-2	0-0	21		2236
2	17	A	Accrington S	D	3-3	2-1	18	Daly J [16], Taylor [33], Folarin [90]	1905
3	24	A	Colchester U	W	1-0	0-0	13	Folarin [68]	3883
4	31	H	Barrow	L	0-1	0-0	15		2270
5	Sept 7	A	Cheltenham T	L	0-1	0-0	20		3594
6	12	H	Doncaster R	W	2-0	2-0	13	Taylor [27], March [45]	3123
7	21	A	Crewe Alex	L	0-3	0-2	20		4320
8	28	H	Bradford C	W	2-1	2-1	14	Dooley [11], Taylor [23]	3059
9	Oct 1	H	Milton Keynes D	L	1-5	0-3	18	Offord (og) [73]	1694
10	5	A	Swindon T	D	0-0	0-0	18		6333
11	12	H	Newport Co	W	1-0	1-0	14	Sims [40]	2564
12	19	A	Carlisle U	D	1-1	1-1	14	Daly M [39]	8297
13	22	H	Port Vale	L	0-1	0-0	16		2780
14	26	A	Notts Co	L	0-1	0-0	17		9427
15	Nov 9	H	Morecambe	L	1-2	0-1	20	Daly J [86]	2982
16	16	H	Chesterfield	W	2-1	0-0	17	Sims [57], Cornelius [90]	3686
17	23	A	Gillingham	W	2-1	0-0	17	O'Connor [59], March [71]	5611
18	Dec 3	A	Salford C	L	0-2	0-1	18		1838
19	7	H	AFC Wimbledon	L	0-3	0-2	19		2506
20	14	A	Tranmere R	L	1-2	1-1	20	Daly J [14]	5122
21	21	H	Walsall	L	0-2	0-1	20		2843
22	26	A	Grimsby T	L	1-2	0-0	20	Duke-McKenna [82]	6514
23	29	A	Fleetwood T	D	1-1	1-1	20	March [8]	2468
24	Jan 1	H	Salford C	L	0-2	0-1	22		2814
25	4	A	Barrow	W	2-0	0-0	21	Muldoon [56], March [61]	3148
26	17	A	Cheltenham T	W	2-0	1-0	16	Young (og) [34], Bennett (og) [56]	2522
27	21	H	Colchester U	D	0-0	0-0	17		2284
28	25	A	Doncaster R	L	0-1	0-0	19		7241
29	28	H	Milton Keynes D	L	1-2	0-1	20	Asare [90]	5101
30	Feb 1	A	Crewe Alex	D	1-1	1-0	20	March [28]	2704
31	8	A	Bradford C	L	0-1	0-1	21		17,126
32	15	H	Swindon T	W	1-0	0-0	20	Moon [53]	2909
33	22	A	Bromley	L	0-2	0-2	20		2518
34	Mar 1	H	Accrington S	W	2-1	1-0	20	Moon [19], March [58]	3015
35	4	A	Port Vale	D	0-0	0-0	20		5107
36	8	H	Carlisle U	W	1-0	0-0	20	Vela (og) [90]	4136
37	15	A	Newport Co	L	0-3	0-2	21		3756
38	22	A	Chesterfield	D	0-0	0-0	21		8540
39	29	H	Gillingham	D	1-1	1-0	21	March (pen) [40]	3253
40	Apr 1	H	Tranmere R	W	3-2	1-0	20	Taylor [33], Cursons [58], Fox [75]	3325
41	5	A	AFC Wimbledon	L	0-1	0-0	20		8341
42	12	H	Grimsby T	D	2-2	0-2	20	Taylor [85], Rose (og) [87]	3881
43	18	A	Walsall	D	2-2	1-1	20	March [22], Taylor [62]	7408
44	21	H	Fleetwood T	W	3-1	0-0	19	Moon [56], Taylor [61], Cursons [90]	3081
45	26	H	Notts Co	L	1-3	1-1	20	Muldoon [37]	4136
46	May 3	A	Morecambe	W	2-1	2-1	18	Akono Bilongo [19], March [22]	3043

Final League Position: 18

GOALSCORERS

League (43): March 9 (1 pen), Taylor 7, Daly J 3, Moon 3, Cursons 2, Folarin 2, Muldoon 2, Sims 2, Akono Bilongo 1, Asare 1, Cornelius 1, Daly M 1, Dooley 1, Duke-McKenna 1, Fox 1, O'Connor 1, own goals 5.
FA Cup (2): Cornelius 1, Muldoon 1.
Carabao Cup (2): Daly J 1, Folarin 1.
Vertu Trophy (3): Burrell 1, Muldoon 1, Nto 1.

Belshaw J 45	Asare Z 16 + 10	O'Connor A 45	Sims T 38 + 2	Thomson G 1	Cornelius D 30 + 5	Sutton L 19 + 8	Daly J 32 + 6	Daly M 13 + 2	Muldoon J 28 + 11	Duke-McKenna S 12 + 6	Oxley M 1 + 1	Folarin S 6 + 13	March J 29 + 5	Taylor E 33 + 3	Foulds M 14 + 1	Burrell W 19 + 8	Gibson L 6 + 3	Dooley S 18 + 5	Moon J 40	Falkingham J 6 + 2	Nto E — + 2	Muskwe A — + 1	Bray J — + 1	Morris B 21 + 1	Sanderson O 4 + 4	Solomon E — + 3	Akono Bilongo B 9 + 7	Hill T 2 + 4	Cursons T 6 + 10	Fox B 13 + 1	Barnes L — + 1	Match No.
1^1	2	3	4	5^4	6	7	8	9	10^3	11^2	12	13	14	15																		1
1	5	3	2				7	10^1	8	12		11		9	4	6																2
1	5^1	3	2				7	10	9	12		11^2	14	8	4^3	6	13															3
1	5^4	3	2		13		7^2	11^1	9^3	14	12	10		8	4^5	6	15	16														4
1	12	4	2^2		7		8^1	10				11^1	13	9		14	5^3	6	3	15												5
1	13	3	2^2		7		9		10			12	11^1	6			5	8	4													6
1		4	2^3		7^4	15	9		10^2	13		14	11	6		12	5^1	8	3													7
1	15	3	2		8^1	12	10^4		11			14		7^2		13	5	9	9	4	6^3											8
1		4	2		8^3	13	10		11	14			7			12	5^1	9	3	6^2												9
1		3	2		7		10		11	9^1		12		8	5			6	4													10
1		3	2		7		9	10	11					6	5			8	4													11
1		3	2		7		9	10	11^1			12		6	5			8	4													12
1	14	3	2^3		7^4		9^2	10	11^1	13		12		6	5			8	4	15												13
1	2^4	3			7^3	14	12	10	13	9^1		11^2		6	5	15		8	4													14
1	2	3			7		13		11	9^1		12	10^2	6	5			8	4													15
1	5	3	2		8		10		11	9			12			7	4	6^1														16
1	5	3	2		7		9		10	6^2			11^1		13	8	4		12													17
1	5	3	2		6		10^3	14	9^1	8^4		13	11^2		7		4		15	12												18
1	5^3	3	2		9	8	10	12	13	7		11^2		14			4	6^1														19
1	12	3	2^2		6	7	10^3	9^1	11	8		14	13	5			4															20
1	9^3	3	5^2		7	6		10	12	14		13	11$^■$	4			8^1	2														21
1	2^2	3	14		8^3	6	11^1	9	12	10			5			7	4		13													22
1	13	3	12		6	7^1	9	10		5		11	4^2			8	2															23
1	5	3	2		6^2	13	8	10^3	12	9		14	11^1		4	7																24
1		3	5		6	7	8		10			12	11^1		4		2							9								25
1		3	2		6^2	8^3	9^4		10^1			11	13		5		4							7	12	14	15					26
1		3	2^4		6^3	8^5	9^1		10^2	15		11	13		5		4							7	12	16	14					27
1		3	2		13	8	9^1		12			11	6		5		4							7	10^2		5					28
1	15	3	2		6^3	8^2			12			11	9		5		4							7	10^1		5^4	13	14			29
1		3	2		6^4	8	15		12			11^3	9	13	5		4							7	10^1		5^2		14			30
1		3	2		6^2	8^1			8			11	9	15	5		4							7	10		5^4	14	13	12		31
1		3	2			12	9^1		10			11^2	6^3	5		4							7				14	13	8		32
1		3	2^1			15	10^2		7^5			11^4	9	5		4							8^3	16		13	12	14	6		33
1		3	2		14	12			11^4			10^2	9^3	5	15	4							6			8	13	7^1			34
1			2		6	8						9		3	12	4							7		13	5	10^1	11^2			35
1		3	2		8	9^1						11	10	5	12	4							7		13			6^2			36
1		3	2		9^1	10						11	8	5		4							6				12	7			37
1	12	3			13	10^2	9					11^3	8	2		4							7		5^1		14	6			38
1		3	2			10^1	9					11	8	5		4							6				12	7			39
1	13	3	2	12			8					9^1	10	5		4							7				11	6^2			40
1		3	2^1			8						9	10	5		4							7	13		12	11^2	6			41
1		3	2		12		8					9	10	5^3	13	4							7		14		11^1	6^2			42
1	12	3	2			10	9					11	8			4							6		5^1			7			43
1	2	3			12	9						11^2	10			4							6		5	13	7				44
1	2	3			15	8						9	10	5^2	14	4	6^3						12		13	11^4	7^1				45
	2	3			10			1				9	8	4		6^1							7		5	11		12			46

FA Cup

First Round	Wrexham	(h)	1-0
Second Round	Gainsborough Trinity	(h)	1-0
Third Round	Leeds U	(a)	0-1

Carabao Cup

First Round	Lincoln C	(a)	2-1
Second Round	Preston NE	(h)	0-5

Vertu Trophy

Group E (N)	Liverpool U21	(h)	1-1
Harrogate T won 4-2 on penalties.			
Group E (N)	Crewe Alex	(a)	0-1
Group E (N)	Blackpool	(h)	2-2
Blackpool won 5-4 on penalties.			

HUDDERSFIELD TOWN

FOUNDATION

A meeting, attended largely by members of the Huddersfield & District FA, was held at the Imperial Hotel in 1906 to discuss the feasibility of establishing a football club in this rugby stronghold. However, it was not until a man with both the enthusiasm and the money to back the scheme came on the scene that real progress was made. This benefactor was Mr Hilton Crowther and it was at a meeting at the Albert Hotel in 1908 that the club formally came into existence with an investment of £2,000 and joined the North-Eastern League.

The John Smith's Stadium, Stadium Way, Leeds Road, Huddersfield, West Yorkshire HD1 6PX.
Telephone: (01484) 960 600.
Ticket Office: (01484) 960 606.
Website: www.htafc.com
Email: info@htafc.com
Ground Capacity: 24,436.
Record Attendance: 67,037 v Arsenal, FA Cup 6th rd, 27 February 1932 (at Leeds Road); 24,169 v Tottenham H, Premier League, 30 September 2017; 24,169 v Manchester U, Premier League, 21 October 2017; 24,169 v WBA, Premier League, 4 November 2017; 24,169 v Chelsea, Premier League, 12 December 2017 (at John Smith's Stadium).
Pitch Measurements: 106m × 68m (116yd × 74.5yd).
Chairman: Kevin M. Nagle.
Chief Executive: Jake Edwards.
Manager: Lee Grant.
Assistant Managers: Paul McShane, Marc Bridge-Wilkinson, Jonathan Robinson.
Colours: Blue and white striped shirts with white trim, white shorts with blue trim, black socks with blue and white trim.
Year Formed: 1908.
Turned Professional: 1908.
Club Nickname: 'The Terriers'.
Grounds: 1908, Leeds Road; 1994, The Alfred McAlpine Stadium (renamed The Galpharm Stadium 2004; The John Smith's Stadium 2012).
First Football League Game: 3 September 1910, Division 2, v Bradford PA (a) W 1–0 – Mutch; Taylor, Morris; Beaton, Hall, Bartlett; Blackburn, Wood, Hamilton (1), McCubbin, Jee.
Record League Victory: 10–1 v Blackpool, Division 1, 13 December 1930 – Turner; Goodall, Spencer; Redfern, Wilson, Campbell; Bob Kelly (1), McLean (4), Robson (3), Davies (1), Smailes (1).
Record Cup Victory: 7–0 v Lincoln U, FA Cup 1st rd, 16 November 1991 – Clarke; Trevitt, Charlton, Donovan (2), Mitchell, Doherty, O'Regan (1), Stapleton (1) (Wright), Roberts (2), Onuora (1), Barnett (Ireland). *N.B.* 11–0 v Heckmondwike (a), FA Cup pr rd, 18 September 1909 – Doggart; Roberts, Ewing; Hooton, Stevenson, Randall; Kenworthy (2), McCreadie (1), Foster (4), Stacey (4), Jee.

HONOURS

League Champions: Division 1 – 1923–24, 1924–25, 1925–26; Division 2 – 1969–70; Division 4 – 1979–80.
Runners-up: Division 1 – 1926–27, 1927–28, 1933–34; Division 2 – 1919–20, 1952–53.
FA Cup Winners: 1922.
Runners-up: 1920, 1928, 1930, 1938.
League Cup: semi-final – 1968.
League Trophy: Runners-up – 1994.

FOOTBALL YEARBOOK FACT FILE

Inside-forward Karl Hansen signed for Huddersfield Town as an amateur in January 1949 at a time when they were bottom of the old First Division and in danger of relegation. His performances over the next few months helped the Terriers turn their fortunes around and they narrowly retained their top-flight place. Hansen was an established international for Denmark and had previously featured in their team in the 1948 Olympic Games tournament.

Record Defeat: 1–10 v Manchester C, Division 2, 7 November 1987.

Most League Points (2 for a win): 66, Division 4, 1979–80.

Most League Points (3 for a win): 87, FL 1, 2010–11.

Most League Goals: 101, Division 4, 1979–80.

Highest League Scorer in Season: Sam Taylor, 35, Division 2, 1919–20; George Brown, 35, Division 1, 1925–26; Jordan Rhodes, 35, 2011–12.

Most League Goals in Total Aggregate: George Brown, 142, 1921–29; Jimmy Glazzard, 142, 1946–56.

Most League Goals in One Match: 5, Dave Mangnall v Derby Co, Division 1, 21 November 1931; 5, Alf Lythgoe v Blackburn R, Division 1, 13 April 1935; 5, Jordan Rhodes v Wycombe W, FL 1, 6 January 2012.

Most Capped Player: Jimmy Nicholson, 31 (41), Northern Ireland.

Most League Appearances: Billy Smith, 521, 1914–34.

Youngest League Player: Denis Law, 16 years 303 days v Notts Co, 24 December 1956.

Record Transfer Fee Received: £15,000,000 from AFC Bournemouth for Philip Billing, July 2019; £15,000,000 from WBA for Karlan Grant, October 2020.

Record Transfer Fee Paid: £17,500,000 to Monaco for Terence Kongolo, June 2018.

Football League Record: 1910 Elected to Division 2; 1910–20 Division 2; 1920–52 Division 1; 1952–53 Division 2; 1953–56 Division 1; 1956–70 Division 2; 1970–72 Division 1; 1972–73 Division 2; 1973–75 Division 3; 1975–80 Division 4; 1980–83 Division 3; 1983–88 Division 2; 1988–92 Division 3; 1992–95 Second Division; 1995–2001 First Division; 2001–03 Second Division; 2003–04 Third Division; 2004–12 FL 1; 2012–17 FL C; 2017–19 Premier League; 2019–24 FL C; 2024– FL 1.

LATEST SEQUENCES

Longest Sequence of League Wins: 11, 5.4.1920 – 4.9.1920.

Longest Sequence of League Defeats: 8, 2.3.2019 – 26.4.2019.

Longest Sequence of League Draws: 6, 3.3.1987 – 3.4.1987.

Longest Sequence of Unbeaten League Matches: 43, 1.1.2011 – 19.11.2011.

Longest Sequence Without a League Win: 22, 4.12.1971 – 29.4.1972.

Successive Scoring Runs: 27 from 12.3.2005.

Successive Non-scoring Runs: 7 from 14.10.2000.

MANAGERS

Fred Walker 1908–10
Richard Pudan 1910–12
Arthur Fairclough 1912–19
Ambrose Langley 1919–21
Herbert Chapman 1921–25
Cecil Potter 1925–26
Jack Chaplin 1926–29
Clem Stephenson 1929–42
Ted Magner 1942–43
David Steele 1943–47
George Stephenson 1947–52
Andy Beattie 1952–56
Bill Shankly 1956–59
Eddie Boot 1960–64
Tom Johnston 1964–68
Ian Greaves 1968–74
Bobby Collins 1974
Tom Johnston 1975–78
    (had been General Manager since 1975)
Mike Buxton 1978–86
Steve Smith 1986–87
Malcolm Macdonald 1987–88
Eoin Hand 1988–92
Ian Ross 1992–93
Neil Warnock 1993–95
Brian Horton 1995–97
Peter Jackson 1997–99
Steve Bruce 1999–2000
Lou Macari 2000–02
Mick Wadsworth 2002–03
Peter Jackson 2003–07
Andy Ritchie 2007–08
Stan Ternent 2008
Lee Clark 2008–12
Simon Grayson 2012–13
Mark Robins 2013–14
Chris Powell 2014–15
David Wagner 2015–19
Jan Siewert 2019
Danny Cowley 2019–20
Carlos Corberán 2020–22
Danny Schofield 2022
Mark Fotheringham 2022–23
Neil Warnock 2023
Darren Moore 2023–24
Andre Breitenreiter 2024
Michael Duff 2024–25
Lee Grant May 2025–

TEN YEAR LEAGUE RECORD

		P	W	D	L	F	A	Pts	Pos
2015-16	FL C	46	13	12	21	59	70	51	19
2016-17	FL C	46	25	6	15	56	58	81	5
2017-18	PR Lge	38	9	10	19	28	58	37	16
2018-19	PR Lge	38	3	7	28	22	76	16	20
2019-20	FL C	46	13	12	21	52	70	51	18
2020-21	FL C	46	12	13	21	50	71	49	20
2021-22	FL C	46	23	13	10	64	47	82	3
2022-23	FL C	46	14	11	21	47	62	53	18
2023-24	FL C	46	9	18	19	48	77	45	23
2024-25	FL 1	46	19	7	20	58	55	64	10

DID YOU KNOW ?

Veteran winger Joe Hulme ended his playing career with a six-month spell at Huddersfield Town in 1938. Although not always a first choice he appeared for the Terriers in their FA Cup final defeat by Preston North End that year, creating a piece of history by becoming the first man to appear in five Wembley FA Cup finals.

HUDDERSFIELD TOWN – SKY BET LEAGUE ONE 2024–25 LEAGUE RECORD

Match No.	Date	Venue	Opponents	Result	H/T Score	Lg Pos.	Goalscorers	Attendance
1	Aug 10	A	Peterborough U	W 2-0	2-0	1	Evans [36], Wiles [45]	10,627
2	17	H	Stevenage	W 2-1	1-0	2	Koroma [26], Wiles [52]	18,529
3	24	H	Shrewsbury T	W 1-0	1-0	2	Marshall [20]	18,205
4	31	A	Rotherham U	L 1-2	0-0	5	Joe Hodge [74]	10,404
5	Sept 14	A	Bolton W	W 4-0	1-0	3	Koroma 2 (1 pen) [44, 59 (p)], Wiles [68], Evans [81]	22,532
6	21	H	Northampton T	L 1-3	0-2	5	Koroma [80]	18,417
7	24	H	Blackpool	L 0-2	0-2	5		17,068
8	28	A	Reading	L 1-2	1-1	10	Pearson [21]	11,181
9	Oct 1	A	Birmingham C	L 0-1	0-0	15		24,757
10	5	H	Barnsley	W 2-0	0-0	9	Wiles [83], Kasumu [90]	19,523
11	19	H	Bristol R	W 3-1	2-0	6	Pearson [34], Marshall [38], Radulovic [52]	18,179
12	22	A	Wrexham	D 0-0	0-0	5		12,894
13	26	H	Exeter C	W 2-0	1-0	5	Pearson [16], Wiles [63]	17,890
14	Nov 9	A	Crawley T	D 2-2	0-1	8	Healey [59], Kane [68]	4752
15	23	H	Charlton Ath	W 2-1	1-1	5	Pearson [13], Kasumu [63]	18,550
16	26	A	Leyton Orient	W 2-0	1-0	5	Helik [26], Marshall [90]	7819
17	Dec 3	H	Wigan Ath	W 1-0	0-0	4	Turton [53]	17,036
18	7	A	Mansfield T	W 2-1	2-1	4	Wiles [8], Koroma [33]	8568
19	14	H	Lincoln C	D 2-2	0-2	4	Spencer [49], Marshall [89]	18,675
20	20	A	Cambridge U	W 4-0	3-0	4	Kasumu [12], Spencer [32], Marshall 2 [38, 72]	6949
21	26	H	Stockport Co	W 1-0	1-0	4	Bate (og) [1]	21,657
22	29	H	Burton Alb	D 1-1	0-1	4	Helik [88]	18,842
23	Jan 4	H	Rotherham U	D 0-0	0-0	4		18,353
24	7	A	Wycombe W	W 1-0	1-0	4	Kane [15]	4095
25	18	A	Blackpool	D 2-2	0-2	4	Taylor [47], Spencer [50]	10,410
26	25	H	Bolton W	L 0-1	0-0	4		19,999
27	28	H	Birmingham C	L 0-1	0-0	4		19,138
28	Feb 1	A	Northampton T	L 2-3	0-2	5	Kane [70], Hogg [82]	6933
29	8	H	Reading	D 0-0	0-0	5		18,385
30	15	A	Barnsley	W 2-1	0-1	5	Koroma [59], Wiles [61]	15,600
31	18	A	Shrewsbury T	W 1-0	0-0	5	Koroma [82]	6762
32	22	H	Peterborough U	L 0-1	0-1	5		18,977
33	25	A	Wigan Ath	L 1-2	0-2	5	Marshall [50]	10,049
34	Mar 1	A	Stevenage	W 2-1	2-1	5	Marshall [3], Lonwijk [24]	4373
35	4	H	Wrexham	L 0-1	0-0	6		20,502
36	8	H	Bristol R	L 0-1	0-1	7		7705
37	15	H	Crawley T	W 5-1	4-0	6	Taylor [3], Barker (og) [8], Marshall [16], Pearson [29], Roosken [76]	18,516
38	29	A	Charlton Ath	L 0-4	0-2	7		17,278
39	Apr 1	A	Lincoln C	L 0-1	0-1	8		8755
40	5	H	Mansfield T	W 2-1	0-0	8	Roosken [69], Wiles [80]	19,986
41	8	H	Wycombe W	L 0-1	0-0	8		17,297
42	12	A	Burton Alb	L 0-3	0-2	9		4278
43	18	H	Cambridge U	L 1-2	0-0	9	Koroma [89]	18,289
44	21	A	Stockport Co	L 1-2	0-0	9	Koroma [61]	10,336
45	26	A	Exeter C	L 1-3	1-1	10	Koroma [20]	7276
46	May 3	H	Leyton Orient	L 1-4	1-2	10	Koroma [41]	20,774

Final League Position: 10

GOALSCORERS

League (58): Koroma 11 (1 pen), Marshall 9, Wiles 8, Pearson 5, Kane 3, Kasumu 3, Spencer 3, Evans 2, Helik 2, Roosken 2, Taylor 2, Healey 1, Joe Hodge 1, Hogg 1, Lonwijk 1, Radulovic 1, Turton 1, own goals 2.
FA Cup (0).
Carabao Cup (5): Headley 1, Koroma 1, Marshall 1, Ruffels 1, Ward 1.
Vertu Trophy (8): Ward 2, Healey 1, Kasumu 1, Ladapo 1, Lees 1, Wiles 1, own goal 1.

Nicholls L 23	Lees T 28+1	Helik M 15+2	Spencer B 28+5	Hogg J 19+15	Sorenson L 22+10	Evans A 21+13	Wiles B 39+6	Miller M 15+3	Healey R 2+7	Koroma J 27+10	Kane H 21+7	Headley J 3+4	Ward D 9+4	Kasumu D 27+5	Harratt K —+2	Marshall C 31+12	Pearson M 25+4	Iorpenda T —+5	Lonwijk N 21	Hodge Joe 13+14	Turton O 18+10	Ruffels J 14+8	Ladapo F 1+20	Radulovic B 9+8	Chapman J 23	Falls C —+1	Roosken R 11+3	Balker R 10+4	Charles D 13+5	Taylor J 8+7	Chirewa T 8+5	Eccleston N 2+1	Match No.
1	2	3	4	5⁴	6	7¹	8	9³	10⁵	11²	12	13	14	15	16																		1
1	2	3	4	5	6	7³	8⁵	9¹		11²	13	12		10⁴	16	15	14																2
1	2	3	4¹		7	5	6³	8⁵	9	15	13			10⁴	14		11²	12	16														3
1	2	3		5	6	7²	8	9		10⁴				13⁴		11¹				4³	12	14	15										4
1	2	3		5²	6	7	8⁴	9¹		10⁵	12			11³		16			4	14				13	15								5
1	2	3	16	5⁵	6⁴	7²	8			11	14	9³		10¹					4	13				12	15								6
1	2	3¹	12		6²	14	8			10	7³	9		13					4	5			11⁴	15									7
		3		6⁴	5⁵	15	7	12	13	11		9²		8¹		10³	2		4	16			14	1									8
		4⁴		5	14	2	7	9	6	13				8³		11¹	3			15			12	10²	1								9
		14		2		6		7	9	12				5		11³	3		4	8²			10	1									10
		3		16	6¹	14	8	9		7³		13	5	11²			4			12⁵		15	10⁴	1									11
		3	13			15	7	9	14	8³		12	5	11¹		2	4			6²			10⁴	1									12
		3	6	13		14	7²	9	12	8³		10¹	5	11⁴		2	4						15	1									13
		4⁴	15	5			6	9	12	13	7			8³		11¹	3	14	2				10²	1									14
		3	12	5³			6	9	10²	11⁴	7			8		15	2¹		4	14			13	1									15
		2	3	16	14			9³	8¹	11⁴	7			6		15			4	5⁵	12	13	10²	1									16
		3	4		14		8			10	7³			11¹	6	9²			5	2	12	13		1									17
		4	3		13		9			8⁴	7³			10²	6	11¹	2			5	12	14	15	1									18
		3	12		13⁴		6			11	8	15	10⁵	7		14	2¹		4	5³	9²	16		1									19
	2	3	4			6				9³	8		10¹	7²		11		13		5		12		1	14								20
	2	3	5			6				9³	8		10¹	7		11	13		4²	12		14		1									21
	2²	3	5⁴			6				9	8		10¹	7⁵		11	15		4	16	13	12³	14	1									22
	2³	3	5			14	6			9⁴	8					10	13		4¹	7²	12			11	1	15⁸							23
		3		4³	15		13	6⁵		9¹	7					11	2			8⁵	5	12	16	10⁴	1		14						24
		3		4	12		13	6	16	9⁴	8¹					14	2			7²	5				1		15	10⁵	11³				25
		3		9	7⁴	13	8	6¹		15	12					14	2			16	5³				1		4⁵	11	10²				26
		3		4	7	5²	8			16	14	6¹				10⁵	2			12	13		15	1		9³	17	11⁴					27
		4	7	5	15	6⁴		14		12						13	2			8²	16		10	1		9¹	3⁵	11³					28
1	4		5	6²	2³		9			12	7		13			8					14	15					3	11⁴		10¹			29
1	4		5	14	2		6			12	8³					7⁴			11⁵		15		13	16			3	10¹		9²			30
1	4			6²	2	12	9¹			11						7			8⁴		14		5	15			3	13		10³			31
1			8	2	13	6²				11						7	10⁵			4⁴	15	12	5	16			3¹	14		9³			32
1		3		2		6⁴	9			10²						7¹	8			4³	12	13	5	16			15	11⁵		14			33
1			2	12	13	7⁴	15			11³						10				3	6	5	4				8²			14	9¹		34
1			2	15	13	7	14			11¹						10				3²	6	5	4⁵				8⁴		12	16	9³		35
1			3	14	5	6	13									11				7³	2	4⁴	15				8		10¹	12	9²		36
1			4	14	13	7	8									10	3¹			6²	2	5					9⁴		11²	12	15		37
1			5	12		9³	6			15						13	8	3		7¹	2	14					10⁵	4²	11⁴	16			38
1			7	12	13	6				11⁴						8⁵	9²	3		16	2¹	5					14	4³		10	15		39
1			15	2	16	9⁵	13									6	14	4		7⁴		5					10	3³	12	11¹	8²		40
1			6⁴	2	9³	8	5²			13						7	14	3			4						10		11¹	12	15		41
1			7	2	14	8	5³									6²	13	3			4						10	12	11	9¹			42
1			6⁸	14	9	8	12			13						2³	7²	4			5						10	3¹	11	15			43
1			4⁵	7²	16	9	8⁴			10¹	13					6	12⁸	3		15	2	5							11³	14			44
			4¹		12		9³	14		10	6					8		3		7	5					1			11²	13		2	45
			6¹	5		9²	12			10	7					8		3	13	4						1			14	11³		2	46

FA Cup

First Round	Tamworth	(a)	0-1

Carabao Cup

First Round	Morecambe	(h)	3-0
Second Round	Walsall	(a)	2-3

Vertu Trophy

Group F (N)	Doncaster R	(a)	1-2
Group F (N)	Barnsley	(h)	2-0
Group F (N)	Manchester U U21	(h)	4-1
Second Round	Bolton W	(a)	1-3

HULL CITY

FOUNDATION

The enthusiasts who formed Hull City in 1904 were brave men indeed. More than that, they were audacious for they immediately put the club on the map in this Rugby League fortress by obtaining a three-year agreement with the Hull Rugby League club to rent their ground! They had obtained quite a number of conversions to the dribbling code, before the Rugby League forbade the use of any of their club grounds by Association Football clubs. By that time, Hull City were well away, having entered the FA Cup in their initial season and the Football League, Second Division after only a year.

The MKM Stadium, West Park, Hull, East Yorkshire HU3 6HU.

Telephone: (01482) 504 600.

Ticket Office: (01482) 505 600.

Website: www.wearehullcity.co.uk

Email: info@wearehullcity.co.uk

Ground Capacity: 24,983.

Record Attendance: 55,019 v Manchester U, FA Cup 6th rd, 26 February 1949 (at Boothferry Park); 25,030 v Liverpool, Premier League, 9 May 2010 (at KC Stadium).

Stadium Record Attendance: 25,280, England U21s v Netherlands U21, 17 February 2004 (at Kingston Community Stadium).

Pitch Measurements: 104m × 74m (113.5yd × 81yd).

Chairman: Acun Ilicali.

Head Coach: Sergej Jakirovic.

Assistant Head Coach: Marko Salatovic.

HONOURS

League Champions: FL 1 2020–21; Division 3 – 1965–66; Division 3N – 1932–33, 1948–49.
Runners-up: FL C – 2012–13; FL 1 – 2004–05; Division 3 – 1958–59; Third Division – 2003–04; Division 4 – 1982–83.

FA Cup: Runners-up: 2014.

League Cup: semi-final – 2017.

League Trophy: Runners-up: 1984.

European Competitions
Europa League: 2014–15.

Colours: Black and amber striped shirts with amber trim, black shorts with amber trim, black socks with amber trim.

Year Formed: 1904.   *Turned Professional:* 1905.

Club Nickname: 'The Tigers'.

Grounds: 1904, Boulevard Ground (Hull RFC); 1905, Anlaby Road (Hull CC); 1944, Boulevard Ground; 1946, Boothferry Park; 2002, Kingston Communications Stadium (renamed The KCOM Stadium 2016; The MKM Stadium 2021).

First Football League Game: 2 September 1905, Division 2, v Barnsley (h) W 4–1 – Spendiff; Langley, Jones; Martin, Robinson, Gordon (2); Rushton, Spence (1), Wilson (1), Howe, Raisbeck.

Record League Victory: 11–1 v Carlisle U, Division 3 (N), 14 January 1939 – Ellis; Woodhead, Dowen; Robinson (1), Blyth, Hardy; Hubbard (2), Richardson (2), Dickinson (2), Davies (2), Cunliffe (2).

Record Cup Victory: 8–2 v Stalybridge Celtic (a), FA Cup 1st rd, 26 November 1932 – Maddison; Goldsmith, Woodhead; Gardner, Hill (1), Denby; Forward (1), Duncan, McNaughton (1), Wainscoat (4), Sargeant (1).

FOOTBALL YEARBOOK FACT FILE

Hull City played Tampa Bay Rowdies over two legs for the Arrow Air Anglo-American Cup in 1984. The Tigers won the first leg at Boothferry Park 3-0, with goals from Garreth Roberts, Steve McClaren and Steve Massey in front of a crowd 5,861. The second leg was played in Fort Lauderdale in June, attracting an attendance of around 15,000. Hull went down to a 1-0 defeat, taking the trophy 3-1 on aggregate.

Record Defeat: 0–8 v Wolverhampton W, Division 2, 4 November 1911; 0–8 v Wigan Ath, FL C, 14 July 2020.

Most League Points (2 for a win): 69, Division 3, 1965–66.

Most League Points (3 for a win): 90, Division 4, 1982–83.

Most League Goals: 109, Division 3, 1965–66.

Highest League Scorer in Season: Bill McNaughton, 39, Division 3 (N), 1932–33.

Most League Goals in Total Aggregate: Chris Chilton, 193, 1960–71.

Most League Goals in One Match: 5, Ken McDonald v Bristol C, Division 2, 17 November 1928; 5, Simon 'Slim' Raleigh v Halifax T, Division 3 (N), 26 December 1930.

Most Capped Player: Theo Whitmore, 28 (119), Jamaica.

Most League Appearances: Andy Davidson, 520, 1952–67.

Youngest League Player: Matthew Edeson, 16 years 63 days v Fulham, 10 October 1992.

Record Transfer Fee Received: £17,000,000 (potentially rising to £26,450,000) from Leicester C for Harry McGuire, June 2017.

Record Transfer Fee Paid: £13,000,000 to Tottenham H for Ryan Mason, August 2016.

Football League Record: 1905 Elected to Division 2; 1905–30 Division 2; 1930–33 Division 3 (N); 1933–36 Division 2; 1936–49 Division 3 (N); 1949–56 Division 2; 1956–58 Division 3 (N); 1958–59 Division 3; 1959–60 Division 2; 1960–66 Division 3; 1966–78 Division 2; 1978–81 Division 3; 1981–83 Division 4; 1983–85 Division 3; 1985–91 Division 2; 1991–92 Division 2; 1992–96 Second Division; 1996–2004 Third Division; 2004–05 FL 1; 2005–08 FL C; 2008–10 Premier League; 2010–13 FL C; 2013–15 Premier League; 2015–16 FL C; 2016–17 Premier League; 2017–20 FL C; 2020–21 FL 1; 2021– FL C.

LATEST SEQUENCES

Longest Sequence of League Wins: 10, 23.2.1966 – 20.4.1966.

Longest Sequence of League Defeats: 8, 7.4.1934 – 8.9.1934.

Longest Sequence of League Draws: 5, 14.2.2012 – 10.3.2012.

Longest Sequence of Unbeaten League Matches: 19, 13.3.2001 – 22.9.2001.

Longest Sequence Without a League Win: 27, 27.3.1989 – 4.11.1989.

Successive Scoring Runs: 26 from 10.4.1990.

Successive Non-scoring Runs: 6 from 14.8.2021.

MANAGERS

James Ramster 1904–05 *(Secretary-Manager)*
Ambrose Langley 1905–13
Harry Chapman 1913–14
Fred Stringer 1914–16
David Menzies 1916–21
Percy Lewis 1921–23
Bill McCracken 1923–31
Haydn Green 1931–34
John Hill 1934–36
David Menzies 1936
Ernest Blackburn 1936–46
Major Frank Buckley 1946–48
Raich Carter 1948–51
Bob Jackson 1952–55
Bob Brocklebank 1955–61
Cliff Britton 1961–70
    (continued as General Manager to 1971)
Terry Neill 1970–74
John Kaye 1974–77
Bobby Collins 1977–78
Ken Houghton 1978–79
Mike Smith 1979–82
Bobby Brown 1982
Colin Appleton 1982–84
Brian Horton 1984–88
Eddie Gray 1988–89
Colin Appleton 1989
Stan Ternent 1989–91
Terry Dolan 1991–97
Mark Hateley 1997–98
Warren Joyce 1998–2000
Brian Little 2000–02
Jan Molby 2002
Peter Taylor 2002–06
Phil Parkinson 2006
Phil Brown *(after caretaker role December 2006)* 2007–10
Ian Dowie *(consultant)* 2010
Nigel Pearson 2010–11
Nick Barmby 2011–12
Steve Bruce 2012–16
Mike Phelan 2016–17
Marco Silva 2017
Leonid Slutsky 2017
Nigel Adkins 2017–19
Grant McCann 2019–22
Shota Arveladze 2022
Liam Rosenior 2022–24
Tim Walter 2024
Rueben Selles 2024–25
Sergej Jakirovic June 2025–

TEN YEAR LEAGUE RECORD

		P	W	D	L	F	A	Pts	Pos
2015-16	FL C	46	24	11	11	69	35	83	4
2016-17	PR Lge	38	9	7	22	37	80	34	18
2017-18	FL C	46	11	16	19	70	70	49	18
2018-19	FL C	46	17	11	18	66	68	62	13
2019-20	FL C	46	12	9	25	57	87	45	24
2020-21	FL 1	46	27	8	11	80	38	89	1
2021-22	FL C	46	14	9	23	41	54	51	19
2022-23	FL C	46	14	16	16	51	61	58	15
2023-24	FL C	46	19	13	14	68	60	70	7
2024-25	FL C	46	12	13	21	44	54	49	21

DID YOU KNOW ❓

Hull City signed their first professionals in August 1904, shortly after the club was formed. The very first player to be registered with the FA was defender Tom Jones who was appointed as club captain. Jones spent two seasons on the Tigers' books before joining Wigan County for the 1906–07 season. He was also a talented cricketer who played professionally and appeared for Shropshire.

HULL CITY – SKY BET CHAMPIONSHIP 2024–25 LEAGUE RECORD

Match No.	Date	Venue	Opponents	Result	H/T Score	Lg Pos.	Goalscorers	Attendance
1	Aug 10	H	Bristol C	D 1-1	0-0	11	Estupinan (pen) [90]	21,011
2	17	A	Plymouth Arg	D 1-1	0-0	17	Coyle L [63]	16,306
3	24	H	Millwall	D 0-0	0-0	14		20,009
4	31	A	Leeds U	L 0-2	0-0	19		36,517
5	Sept 13	H	Sheffield U	L 0-2	0-1	19		22,403
6	20	H	Stoke C	W 3-1	0-1	13	Wilmot (og) [79], Palmer [63], Slater [77]	23,366
7	28	H	Cardiff C	W 4-1	2-1	12	Belloumi 2 [22, 35], Zambrano [51], Bedia (pen) [90]	22,665
8	Oct 1	A	QPR	W 3-1	2-1	9	Drameh [25], Bedia [36], Millar [71]	13,407
9	5	A	Norwich C	L 0-4	0-2	13		26,326
10	20	A	Sunderland	L 0-1	0-0	14		23,072
11	23	H	Burnley	D 1-1	1-0	15	Simons [45]	20,168
12	26	A	Derby Co	D 1-1	0-0	15	Simons [57]	29,877
13	Nov 2	H	Portsmouth	D 1-1	1-0	15	Joao Pedro [11]	21,904
14	5	A	Oxford U	L 0-1	0-0	18		10,213
15	10	H	WBA	L 1-2	1-2	19	Joao Pedro [40]	20,538
16	23	A	Luton T	L 0-1	0-1	22		11,386
17	26	H	Sheffield Wed	L 0-2	0-1	22	-	21,297
18	30	A	Middlesbrough	L 1-3	0-2	22	Burstow [70]	24,121
19	Dec 7	A	Blackburn R	L 0-1	0-1	24		20,544
20	11	H	Watford	D 1-1	0-0	24	Bedia [82]	18,694
21	14	A	Coventry C	L 1-2	1-0	24	Joao Pedro [43]	25,528
22	21	H	Swansea C	W 2-1	1-1	21	Joao Pedro [34], Burstow [80]	20,024
23	26	A	Preston NE	L 0-1	0-0	22		16,521
24	29	A	Blackburn R	W 1-0	0-0	21	Longman [77]	16,245
25	Jan 1	H	Middlesbrough	L 0-1	0-0	22		21,585
26	4	H	Leeds U	D 3-3	1-0	22	Kamara 2 [5, 89], Joao Pedro [81]	24,463
27	18	A	Millwall	W 1-0	0-0	21	Cooper (og) [58]	14,579
28	21	H	QPR	L 1-2	0-0	21	Gelhardt [84]	19,180
29	24	A	Sheffield U	W 3-0	1-0	18	Crooks [6], Jacob [63], Burrows (og) [88]	27,448
30	Feb 1	H	Stoke C	L 1-2	1-1	21	Matazo [6]	21,709
31	12	A	Burnley	L 0-2	0-2	22		18,987
32	15	H	Norwich C	D 1-1	1-0	21	Crooks [14]	22,141
33	22	A	Sunderland	W 1-0	1-0	20	Patterson (og) [18]	44,009
34	25	A	Cardiff C	L 0-1	0-0	21		16,622
35	Mar 4	H	Plymouth Arg	W 2-0	0-0	19	Gelhardt [48], Kamara [61]	18,772
36	8	A	Bristol C	D 1-1	0-0	19	Joao Pedro [13]	21,754
37	12	H	Oxford U	W 2-1	0-0	18	Gelhardt [73], Puerta [76]	19,024
38	15	A	WBA	D 1-1	0-0	19	Kamara [79]	24,870
39	29	H	Luton T	L 0-1	0-0	20		23,005
40	Apr 5	A	Sheffield Wed	W 1-0	0-0	19	Hughes [90]	27,342
41	8	A	Watford	L 0-1	0-0	19		17,268
42	14	H	Coventry C	D 1-1	0-0	20	Kamara [82]	21,659
43	18	A	Swansea C	L 0-1	0-0	20		18,775
44	21	H	Preston NE	W 2-1	0-1	20	Gelhardt 2 (2 pens) [50, 67]	22,103
45	26	H	Derby Co	L 0-1	0-0	22		24,451
46	May 3	A	Portsmouth	D 1-1	1-0	21	Crooks [18]	20,420

Final League Position: 21

GOALSCORERS

League (44): Joao Pedro 6, Gelhardt 5 (2 pens), Kamara 5, Bedia 3 (1 pen), Crooks 3, Belloumi 2, Burstow 2, Simons 2, Coyle L 1, Drameh 1, Estupinan 1 (1 pen), Hughes 1, Jacob 1, Longman 1, Matazo 1, Millar 1, Palmer 1, Puerta 1, Slater 1, Zambrano 1, own goals 4.
FA Cup (1): Puerta 1.
Carabao Cup (1): Mehlem 1.

Pandur I 44	Coyle L 42 + 2	Jones A 37 + 4	McLoughlin S 37	Jacob M 4 + 4	Simons X 13 + 7	Omur A 12 + 8	Slater R 36 + 8	Mehlem M 9 + 7	Giles R 11 + 5	Estupinan O 2	Millar L 6 + 5	Jarvis W — + 6	Sellars-Fleming T — + 4	Burns F 4 + 5	Burstow M 8 + 23	Zambrano O 5 + 3	Bedia C 9 + 12	Drameh C 17 + 11	Palmer K 11 + 15	Belloumi M 10	Kamara A 25 + 11	Alzate S 21 + 7	Hughes C 26 + 1	Joao Pedro G 25 + 10	Puerta G 22 + 8	Longman R 6 + 3	Vaughan H 1 + 2	Rushworth C 2	Gelhardt J 19 + 1	Amrabat N 2 + 8	Crooks M 9 + 9	Joseph K 13 + 3	Matazo E 4 + 2	Barry L 2 + 2	Egan J 8 + 3	Lincoln d 4 + 7	Match No.
1	2	3	4	5³	6	7	8²	9⁴	10¹	11	12	13	14	15																							1
1	2	3	4		6	8³	7¹	9	5	11²	10⁴	12	15	14	13																						2
1	2	3	4		12	7³	8	9	5⁴		10⁵	14	16		11²	6¹	13	15																			3
1	2	3	4		13	7³	8¹	9	5⁵		10	12			15	6²	11⁴	16	14																	4
1	2	3	4		8	15	9	5²		13				6³				11	12	14	7⁴	10¹															5
1	2	3	4		13	11¹	14	6²		12					15	16	7³	10⁵	5	8⁴	9															6
1	2	3	4		15	11²	6³	8⁵		12							7⁴	10	5	14	9¹	13	16													7
1	2	3	4			6	7	13		11⁴					14	12	10³	5	8¹	9⁵																8
1	2	3	4¹			6	7	13		11⁵					8³	10⁴	5³		9	16	14	12	15													9
1	2	3			7⁵		13	6³		12					15	10	5	14	9	11¹			4⁴	16	8²											10
1	2	3			7	13	6⁵			15		11¹				14	5	16	9⁴	12			4	10²	8³												11
1	2	3			7	12	6¹								15		10³	5	13	9⁴	11		4	14	8²											12
1	2	3			6²	14	9³					15				12	16	5	13	8	10⁴		4	11⁵	7¹											13
1	2	3			6³	10²	9		5¹			13			15		16	12	7⁵	8⁴		4	11	14													14
1	2	3			6²	10	7								8¹		14	5	13			4	11	9³	12											15
1	2	3			6³	8²	7										14	5	13		10		4	11	9¹	12										16
1	2	3			6³	12	9¹	13							16		15	5	8		10⁵		4⁴	11	14	7²										17
1	2	4	3		6¹	7⁵	8	16	13						14		15	5⁹	9⁴		10			11³	12											18
1	2		4			14	7	16	5						12		11⁴		9³		8⁵	13	3	15	6²	10¹										19
1	2		4			15	6	12	5						13		14		9		8⁴	7²	3	11³		10¹										20
1	2		4	14			6	13	5³						12		14		9²		8¹	7⁴	3	11	15	10⁵										21
1	2³	3			12		6	15	5						13		14				9	7²	4	10	8⁴	11										22
1	2⁵	3	4	12		14	6³		5¹						9		15	16			13	7		10⁴	8	11²										23
1	14	3	4	5³	7¹		6								15	11²			2		9⁴	12		10	8	13										24
1	5	3	4		13	9³	6		12						11⁵		15	2²			14	7		10⁴	8¹		16									25
1	2	3	4	5	13		6					15	14	10¹							8⁴	7²		11	9³	12										26
	2¹	4	5			6						3	11²		12				9³	7		10	8⁴			1	13	14	15							27
	4	5	14			6						3³	13			2				7		11	9²		10¹	1	8	12								28
1	4	5	13			6⁵						3¹	16			2				9	7	14	15			11⁴		8²	10³	12						29
1	13	3	4	5		6									14			2³			8²	7	11¹				10⁵	16	15	12	9⁴	14				30
1	2	4	5			16								12						9¹	7	13				11⁴	15	8³	10²	6²	12	3				31
1	2	4	5			7								12		15	6³		11²					8		9¹	13	14	10¹	3						32
1	2	3	5			16											6	4⁴	14	13				8		11³	10²	7⁵	9¹	15	12					33
1	2	3	5⁵			6⁴											13	15	4	14	12			9	16	11	10²	7¹				8³				34
1	2	3	5			13								15			14	12		8³	7²	4	11	6			9⁴		10¹						35
1	2⁴	3	5			13										15				8¹	7	4	11⁸	6⁵			9²		14	10³			12	16		36
1	2	3	5			13								14			12		8⁴	6³	4		7⁸				9		11²	10¹			15			37
1	2	3	5			8³								9²			13	12	7	4						10		6¹	11²					14		38
1	2	3	5														9¹		8	6	4		7³				10	14	13	11²				12		39
1	2		5			6⁵								12			14		8⁴	13	4	11	7³				9²		16	10¹			3	15		40
1	2⁴	3	5			6											14		12	7	4	11²				8¹	15	9³	13			10			41
1	2⁵	14	5			7										15	9²		13	6⁴	4	11				8	12	16				3³	10¹		42
1	2⁵		5¹			6								16			12	9²		15		4	11	7³			8	14	13⁸				3	10⁴		43
1	2	16	5			7								13						8³	6¹	4	15	12				9⁵	10²	11⁴			3	14		44
1	2	13	5			6¹								16						8⁵	12	4	15	7				9	10⁴	14	11³			3²		45
1	2	15	5											14			13			8¹		4	11⁴	7				9²		6	10³			3	12	46

IPSWICH TOWN

FOUNDATION

Considering that Ipswich Town only reached the Football League in 1938, many people outside of East Anglia may be surprised to learn that this club was formed at a meeting held in the Town Hall as far back as 1878 when Mr T. C. Cobbold, MP, was voted president. Originally it was the Ipswich Association FC to distinguish it from the older Ipswich Football Club which played rugby. These two amalgamated in 1888 and the handling game was dropped in 1893.

Portman Road, Ipswich, Suffolk IP1 2DA.

Telephone: (01473) 400 500.

Ticket Office: (0333) 005 0503.

Website: www.itfc.co.uk

Email: supporter.service@itfc.co.uk

Ground Capacity: 29,813.

Record Attendance: 38,010 v Leeds U, FA Cup 6th rd, 8 March 1975.

Pitch Measurements: 105m × 66m (115yd × 72yd).

Chairman: Mark Ashton.

Chief Operating Officer: Luke Werhun.

Manager: Kieran McKenna.

Assistant Manager: Martyn Pert.

Colours: Blue shirts with thin white stripes and dark blue trim, white shorts with blue trim, blue socks with dark blue trim.

Year Formed: 1878.

Turned Professional: 1936.

HONOURS

League Champions: Division 1 – 1961–62; Division 2 – 1960–61, 1967–68, 1991–92; Division 3S – 1953–54, 1956–57.
Runners-up: Division 1 – 1980–81, 1981–82; FL C – 2023–24; FL 1 – 2022–23.
FA Cup Winners: 1978.
League Cup: semi-final – 1982, 1985, 2001, 2011.
Texaco Cup Winners: 1973.
European Competitions
European Cup: 1962–63.
UEFA Cup: 1973–74 *(qf)*, 1974–75, 1975–76, 1977–78, 1979–80, 1980–81 *(winners)*, 1981–82, 1982–83, 2001–02, 2002–03.
European Cup-Winners' Cup: 1978–79 *(qf)*.

Previous Name: 1878, Ipswich Association FC; 1888, Ipswich Town.

Club Nicknames: 'The Blues'; 'Town'; 'The Tractor Boys'.

Grounds: 1878, Broom Hill and Brook's Hall; 1884, Portman Road.

First Football League Game: 27 August 1938, Division 3 (S), v Southend U (h) W 4–2 – Burns; Dale, Parry; Perrett, Fillingham, McLuckie; Williams, Davies (1), Jones (2), Alsop (1), Little.

Record League Victory: 7–0 v Portsmouth, Division 2, 7 November 1964 – Thorburn; Smith, McNeil; Baxter, Bolton, Thompson; Broadfoot (1), Hegan (2), Baker (1), Leadbetter, Brogan (3). 7–0 v Southampton, Division 1, 2 February 1974 – Sivell; Burley, Mills (1), Morris, Hunter, Beattie (1), Hamilton (2), Viljoen, Johnson, Whymark (2), Lambert (1) (Woods). 7–0 v WBA, Division 1, 6 November 1976 – Sivell; Burley, Mills, Talbot, Hunter, Beattie (1), Osborne, Wark (1), Mariner (1) (Bertschin), Whymark (4), Woods.

FOOTBALL YEARBOOK FACT FILE

Ipswich Town made their first shirt sponsorship deal with Pioneer High Fidelity, the car audio and hi-fi business in August 1981. The three-year deal was said to be worth £400,000 to the club and some of the money was used towards the redevelopment of the west stand at Portman Road, which subsequently bore the sponsorship title the Pioneer Stand.

Record Cup Victory: 10–0 v Floriana, European Cup prel. rd, 25 September 1962 – Bailey; Malcolm, Compton; Baxter, Laurel, Elsworthy (1); Stephenson, Moran (2), Crawford (5), Phillips (2), Blackwood.

Record Defeat: 1–10 v Fulham, Division 1, 26 December 1963.

Most League Points (2 for a win): 64, Division 3 (S), 1953–54 and 1955–56.

Most League Points (3 for a win): 98, FL 1, 2022–23.

Most League Goals: 106, Division 3 (S), 1955–56.

Highest League Scorer in Season: Ted Phillips, 41, Division 3 (S), 1956–57.

Most League Goals in Total Aggregate: Ray Crawford, 204, 1958–63 and 1966–69.

Most League Goals in One Match: 5, Alan Brazil v Southampton, Division 1, 16 February 1981.

Most Capped Player: Allan Hunter, 47 (53), Northern Ireland.

Most League Appearances: Mick Mills, 591, 1966–82.

Youngest League Player: Connor Wickham, 16 years 11 days, v Doncaster R, 11 April 2009.

MANAGERS
Mick O'Brien 1936–37
Scott Duncan 1937–55
(continued as Secretary)
Alf Ramsey 1955–63
Jackie Milburn 1963–64
Bill McGarry 1964–68
Bobby Robson 1969–82
Bobby Ferguson 1982–87
Johnny Duncan 1987–90
John Lyall 1990–94
George Burley 1994–2002
Joe Royle 2002–06
Jim Magilton 2006–09
Roy Keane 2009–11
Paul Jewell 2011–12
Mick McCarthy 2012–18
Paul Hurst 2018
Paul Lambert 2018–21
Paul Cook 2021
Kieran McKenna December 2021–

Record Transfer Fee Received: £30,000,000 from Chelsea for Liam Delap, June 2025.

Record Transfer Fee Paid: £20,000,000 (potentially rising to £22,500,000) to Chelsea for Omari Hutchinson, June 2024; £20,000,000 to Aston Villa for Jaden Philogene, January 2025.

Football League Record: 1938 Elected to Division 3 (S); 1938–54 Division 3 (S); 1954–55 Division 2; 1955–57 Division 3 (S); 1957–61 Division 2; 1961–64 Division 1; 1964–68 Division 2; 1968–86 Division 1; 1986–92 Division 2; 1992–95 Premier League; 1995–2000 First Division; 2000–02 Premier League; 2002–04 First Division; 2004–19 FL C; 2019–23 FL 1; 2023–24 FL C; 2024–25 Premier League; 2025– FL C.

LATEST SEQUENCES

Longest Sequence of League Wins: 8, 18.2.2023 – 7.4.2023.

Longest Sequence of League Defeats: 10, 4.9.1954 – 16.10.1954.

Longest Sequence of League Draws: 7, 10.11.1990 – 21.12.1990.

Longest Sequence of Unbeaten League Matches: 23, 8.12.1979 – 26.4.1980.

Longest Sequence Without a League Win: 21, 28.8.1963 – 14.12.1963.

Successive Scoring Runs: 31 from 18.2.2023.

Successive Non-scoring Runs: 7 from 28.2.1995.

TEN YEAR LEAGUE RECORD

		P	W	D	L	F	A	Pts	Pos
2015-16	FL C	46	18	15	13	53	51	69	7
2016-17	FL C	46	13	16	17	48	58	55	16
2017-18	FL C	46	17	9	20	57	60	60	12
2018-19	FL C	46	5	16	25	36	77	31	24
2019-20	FL 1	36	14	10	12	46	36	52	11§
2020-21	FL 1	46	19	12	15	46	46	69	9
2021-22	FL 1	46	18	16	12	67	46	70	11
2022-23	FL 1	46	28	14	4	101	35	98	2
2023-24	FL C	46	28	12	6	92	57	96	2
2024-25	PR Lge	38	4	10	24	36	82	22	19

§*Decided on points-per-game (1.44)*

DID YOU KNOW ?

Ipswich Town took part in the very first series of Football League play-offs after finishing in fifth place in Division Two in 1986–87. In the semi-final stage they faced Charlton Athletic who were fourth from bottom of the First Division, drawing 0-0 at Portman Road before going down to a 2-1 defeat in the second leg.

IPSWICH TOWN – PREMIER LEAGUE 2024–25 LEAGUE RECORD

Match No.	Date	Venue	Opponents	Result	H/T Score	Lg Pos.	Goalscorers	Attendance
1	Aug 17	H	Liverpool	L	0-2	0-0	18		30,014
2	24	A	Manchester C	L	1-4	1-3	19	Szmodics [7]	53,147
3	31	H	Fulham	D	1-1	1-1	16	Delap [15]	29,517
4	Sept 14	A	Brighton & HA	D	0-0	0-0	17		31,573
5	21	A	Southampton	D	1-1	0-1	17	Morsy [90]	31,117
6	29	A	Aston Villa	D	2-2	1-2	15	Delap 2 [8, 72]	29,943
7	Oct 5	A	West Ham U	L	1-4	1-2	17	Delap [6]	62,467
8	19	H	Everton	L	0-2	0-2	17		29,862
9	26	A	Brentford	L	3-4	2-2	17	Szmodics [28], Hirst [31], Delap [86]	17,109
10	Nov 2	H	Leicester C	D	1-1	0-0	18	Davis [55]	29,874
11	10	A	Tottenham H	W	2-1	2-0	17	Szmodics [31], Delap [43]	61,505
12	24	H	Manchester U	D	1-1	1-1	18	Hutchinson [43]	30,017
13	30	A	Nottingham F	L	0-1	0-0	19		30,237
14	Dec 3	H	Crystal Palace	L	0-1	0-0	19		29,533
15	8	H	Bournemouth	L	1-2	1-0	18	Chaplin [21]	29,180
16	14	A	Wolverhampton W	W	2-1	1-0	18	Doherty (og) [15], Taylor J [90]	30,866
17	21	H	Newcastle U	L	0-4	0-3	18		29,774
18	27	A	Arsenal	L	0-1	0-1	19		60,271
19	30	H	Chelsea	W	2-0	1-0	18	Delap (pen) [12], Hutchinson [53]	29,968
20	Jan 5	A	Fulham	D	2-2	1-0	18	Szmodics [38], Delap (pen) [71]	27,042
21	16	H	Brighton & HA	L	0-2	0-0	18		29,403
22	19	H	Manchester C	L	0-6	0-3	18		29,841
23	25	A	Liverpool	L	1-4	0-3	18	Greaves [90]	60,420
24	Feb 1	H	Southampton	L	1-2	1-1	19	Delap [31]	29,902
25	15	A	Aston Villa	D	1-1	0-0	18	Delap [56]	42,510
26	22	H	Tottenham H	L	1-4	1-2	18	Hutchinson [36]	30,003
27	26	A	Manchester U	L	2-3	2-2	18	Philogene-Bidace 2 [4, 45]	73,827
28	Mar 8	A	Crystal Palace	L	0-1	0-0	18		25,155
29	15	H	Nottingham F	L	2-4	0-3	18	Cajuste [82], Hirst [90]	29,878
30	Apr 2	A	Bournemouth	W	2-1	1-0	18	Broadhead [34], Delap [60]	11,192
31	5	H	Wolverhampton W	L	1-2	1-0	18	Delap [16]	29,549
32	13	A	Chelsea	D	2-2	2-0	18	Enciso [19], Johnson [31]	39,805
33	20	H	Arsenal	L	0-4	0-2	18		29,549
34	26	A	Newcastle U	L	0-3	0-1	18		52,171
35	May 3	A	Everton	D	2-2	1-2	18	Enciso [41], Hirst [79]	39,305
36	10	H	Brentford	L	0-1	0-1	18		29,511
37	18	A	Leicester C	L	0-2	0-1	19		31,986
38	25	H	West Ham U	L	1-3	0-1	19	Broadhead [52]	29,771

Final League Position: 19

GOALSCORERS

League (36): Delap 12 (2 pens), Szmodics 4, Hirst 3, Hutchinson 3, Broadhead 2, Enciso 2, Philogene-Bidace 2, Cajuste 1, Chaplin 1, Davis 1, Greaves 1, Johnson 1, Morsy 1, Taylor J 1, own goal 1.
FA Cup (8): Clarke J 3, Hirst 2 (1 pen), Phillips 1, Philogene-Bidace 1, Taylor J 1.
Carabao Cup (2): Al Hamadi 1, Chaplin 1.

Walton C 7	Tuanzebe A 20+2	Woolfenden L 12+3	Greaves J 25	Davis L 32+1	Morsy S 31+2	Luongo M 2+9	Burns W 12+6	Chaplin C 10+12	Hutchinson O 30+1	Delap L 32+5	Johnson B 14+9	Harness M —+2	Taylor J 4+28	Szmodics S 13+7	Al-Hamadi A —+11	Muric A 18	Edmundson S —+1	Phillips K 14+5	Ogbene C 3+2	Cajuste J 25+5	Clarke J 12+20	O'Shea D 35	Hirst G 5+21	Burgess C 16+2	Clarke H 4+3	Townsend C 3+3	Broadhead N 7+11	Godfrey B 2+1	Philogene-Bidace J 5+5	Enciso J 12+1	Palmer A 13	Match No.
2^5	3	4	5	6	7^2	8^1	9^3	10	11^4	12	13	14	15	16																		1
	3^4	4	5	6	8	9^2		16	7^5	11^3	2	12	13	10^1	14	1	15															2
	2	3	4	5	6			15	9	11^3				10^2	13	1		7^1	8^4	12	14											3
	2		4	5	6^4	15	8^3	16	9^5	11^1				10^2		1		7	13		14	3	12									4
	2^5		4	5	6			8^3	15	9	11^4	16		12	10^1	1		7^2	13		3	14										5
	2		4	5	6^5	16	13		9	11^3			12	15		1		7^2	8^1	10^4	3	14										6
		4	5	6				8^2	16	9^4	11^5	2	14	12		1		7^3	13		10^1	3	15									7
	3		5	6				8^2	12	9	11^5		15	14		1		7^3			10^4	2^1	16	4^5	13							8
	14		5				12	9^3		13			15			10^2	1	7	8^1	6^5	15	3^1	11^4	4	2^4	16						9
			5	6			15	9^3	8^4	11^2	2			10^1		1	7^4			14	12	3	13	4								10
	2		5	6	14				9^1	11^3	8			10^2		1		7^3	13		3	12	4									11
	2		5	6			8^4	15	9	11^3				12	10^2	14^1	1	7^1	13		3		4									12
	2^5		5	6			14	9^2	8^4	11				13	10^1	1		7^3	12		3		4	15		16						13
		4	5	6			8^3	14	9	11^4			12		15	1		7^2	10^1	3			2	13								14
			5	6			15	9	8^3	11^2	2		7^4	10^1	13	1		14	12	3			4									15
			5	6			8^3	9^2	10	11^4	15		12		14	1		7^1	13	3			4	2								16
			5	6			8^5	11^2	9^1		15		13	10^4	12	1		14	7^3	3			4	2	16							17
	4^5	5	6					7	11^2	2^3		14	10^1	13	1	8		9^4	12	3			16	15								18
1	3	4	5	6			8^3		9^4	11^5	14	16	12	15	13		7	2			10^2											19
1		4	5	6	8		14			11^5	2^3		12	7^1	16	13		9^2	15	3			10⁴									20
1		3	4	5	13		8^1		9	11^3			12			6^4		7^2	15	2	14		10									21
1	14			6	9	12			7^5	11^4	2	16						8^1	10^2	4	15	5							3^3	13		22
1	2		4	5^2	6		8^1		9^5	11^4	12			7						3	14			13	16		10^3	15				23
	2	4	5^3	6				8	11		13							7^2	14	3	15				10^1	12	9^4					24
	2^*	13	4		15			9^5	11^4	8	16				6			7^3	12^2	3	14		5				10^1	1				25
	12	4	5	16				9^5	11^4	13					6^5			7^2	10^3	3	15		14	2^1	8			1				26
	2^3	4	8^4	6^1				9^2	11	15	12	16						7^5	10	3	14		13	5			8^2	9^3	1			27
	3	4	5				12	11^5	13	16					6			7^4	10^1	2	15		14				8^2	9^3	1			28
	3	4^1	5					9	11^2	16					6^5			7	14	2	13	12		15			8^3	10^4	1			29
	2			6^4					11^2	8^5	12				15			7	14	3	13	4		5	9^3		16	10^1	1			30
	2^2		14	6		16			11^3	8	12							7^5		3	13	4	5^4	9^1		15	10	1				31
	2		5^1	6				14	8	15					13			7	10^3	3	11^2	4	12	16	13^5	9^4		1				32
	2	4	5^*	7^5	15		16		14^6	6				13				8^4	9^1	3	11^3	12					10^2	1				33
	3	5		7	15		14		11^2	6^*				8^4						9^1	2	13	4			12		10^3	1			34
16	3	5		6^1				9^3	8	11^2				7^4			13	15	14	2	12	4						10^5	1			35
	2^4	5		6				9^1	8	11^3	15			7^2			13	12	3	14	4							10	1			36
	2		4	5	6^5	16		15	8	12							7^4	10^3	3	11^2			14					9^1	1			37
1	2		4	5	6^5	16		9^3	8	12				15	14			7^3	13	3	11^1			10^4								38

FA Cup

Third Round	Bristol R	(h)	3-0
Fourth Round	Coventry C	(a)	4-1
Fifth Round	Nottingham F	(a)	1-1

  aet; Nottingham F won 5-4 on penalties.

Carabao Cup

Second Round	AFC Wimbledon	(a)	2-2

  AFC Wimbledon won 4-2 on penalties.

LEEDS UNITED

FOUNDATION

Immediately the Leeds City club (founded in 1904) was wound up by the FA in October 1919, following allegations of illegal payments to players, a meeting was called by a Leeds solicitor, Mr Alf Masser, at which Leeds United was formed. They joined the Midland League, playing their first game in that competition in November 1919. It was in this same month that the new club had discussions with the directors of a virtually bankrupt Huddersfield Town who wanted to move to Leeds in an amalgamation. But Huddersfield survived even that crisis.

Elland Road Stadium, Elland Road, Leeds, West Yorkshire LS11 0ES.

Telephone: (0871) 334 1919.

Ticket Office: (0371) 334 1992.

Website: www.leedsunited.com

Email: tickets@leedsunited.com

Ground Capacity: 37,645.

Record Attendance: 57,892 v Sunderland, FA Cup 5th rd (replay), 15 March 1967.

Pitch Measurements: 105m × 68m (115yd × 74.5yd).

Chairman: Paraag Marathe.

Sporting Director: Adam Underwood.

Manager: Daniel Farke.

Assistant Coach: Eddie Riemer.

Colours: White shirts with blue and limellow trim, white shorts with blue and limellow trim, white socks with blue and limellow trim.

Year Formed: 1919, as Leeds United after disbandment (by FA order) of Leeds City (formed in 1904).

Turned Professional: 1920.

Club Nickname: 'The Whites'.

Ground: 1919, Elland Road.

First Football League Game: 28 August 1920, Division 2, v Port Vale (a) L 0–2 – Down; Duffield, Tillotson; Musgrove, Baker, Walton; Mason, Goldthorpe, Thompson, Lyon, Best.

HONOURS

League Champions: Division 1 – 1968–69, 1973–74, 1991–92; FL C – 2019–20, 2024–25. Division 2 – 1923–24, 1963–64, 1989–90. *Runners-up:* Division 1 – 1964–65, 1965–66, 1969–70, 1970–71, 1971–72; Division 2 – 1927–28, 1931–32, 1955–56; FL 1 – 2009–10.

FA Cup Winners: 1972. *Runners-up:* 1965, 1970, 1973.

League Cup Winners: 1968. *Runners-up:* 1996.

European Competitions *European Cup:* 1969–70 *(sf)*, 1974–75 *(runners-up).* *Champions League:* 1992–93, 2000–01 *(sf).* *Fairs Cup:* 1965–66 *(sf)*, 1966–67 *(runners-up)*, 1967–68 *(winners)*, 1968–69 *(qf)*, 1970–71 *(winners).* *UEFA Cup:* 1971–72, 1973–74, 1979–80, 1995–96, 1998–99, 1999–2000 *(sf)*, 2001–02, 2002–03. *European Cup-Winners' Cup:* 1972–73 *(runners-up).*

Record League Victory: 8–0 v Leicester C, Division 1, 7 April 1934 – Moore; George Milburn, Jack Milburn; Edwards, Hart, Copping; Mahon (2), Firth (2), Duggan (2), Furness (2), Cochrane.

Record Cup Victory: 10–0 v Lyn (Oslo), European Cup 1st rd 1st leg, 17 September 1969 – Sprake; Reaney, Cooper, Bremner (2), Charlton, Hunter, Madeley, Clarke (2), Jones (3), Giles (2) (Bates), O'Grady (1).

FOOTBALL YEARBOOK FACT FILE

Leeds United appeared to have been eliminated from the European Cup at the first-round stage in 1992–93 at the hands of VfB Stuttgart after the teams finished 4-4 on aggregate with the Germans going through on the away goals rule. However, it was discovered that Stuttgart had exceeded the limit of foreign players allowed in line-ups and UEFA ordered a replay. The teams met at Barcelona's Nou Camp Stadium where Leeds won 2-1 thanks to goals from Gordon Strachan and Carl Shutt.

Record Defeat: 1–8 v Stoke C, Division 1, 27 August 1934.

Most League Points (2 for a win): 67, Division 1, 1968–69.

Most League Points (3 for a win): 100, FL C, 2024–25.

Most League Goals: 98, Division 2, 1927–28.

Highest League Scorer in Season: John Charles, 42, Division 2, 1953–54.

Most League Goals in Total Aggregate: Peter Lorimer, 168, 1965–79 and 1983–86.

Most League Goals in One Match: 5, Gordon Hodgson v Leicester C, Division 1, 1 October 1938.

Most Capped Player: Lucas Radebe, 58 (70), South Africa.

Most League Appearances: Jack Charlton, 629, 1953–73.

Youngest League Player: Peter Lorimer, 15 years 289 days v Southampton, 29 September 1962.

Record Transfer Fee Received: £49,000,000 (potentially rising to £55,000,000) from Barcelona for Raphina, July 2022.

Record Transfer Fee Paid: £35,500,000 to TSG 1899 Hoffenheim for Georginio Rutter, January 2023.

Football League Record: 1920 Elected to Division 2; 1920–24 Division 2; 1924–27 Division 1; 1927–28 Division 2; 1928–31 Division 1; 1931–32 Division 2; 1932–47 Division 1; 1947–56 Division 2; 1956–60 Division 1; 1960–64 Division 2; 1964–82 Division 1; 1982–90 Division 2; 1990–92 Division 1; 1992–2004 Premier League; 2004–07 FL C; 2007–10 FL 1; 2010–20 FL C; 2020–23 Premier League; 2023–25 FL C; 2025– Premier League.

LATEST SEQUENCES

Longest Sequence of League Wins: 9, 1.1.2024 – 23.2.2024.

Longest Sequence of League Defeats: 6, 12.2.2022 – 10.3.2022.

Longest Sequence of League Draws: 5, 2.5.2015 – 22.8.2015.

Longest Sequence of Unbeaten League Matches: 34, 26.10.1968 – 26.8.1969.

Longest Sequence Without a League Win: 17, 1.2.1947 – 26.5.1947.

Successive Scoring Runs: 30 from 27.8.1927.

Successive Non-scoring Runs: 6 from 30.1.1982.

MANAGERS

Dick Ray 1919–20
Arthur Fairclough 1920–27
Dick Ray 1927–35
Bill Hampson 1935–47
Willis Edwards 1947–48
Major Frank Buckley 1948–53
Raich Carter 1953–58
Bill Lambton 1958–59
Jack Taylor 1959–61
Don Revie OBE 1961–74
Brian Clough 1974
Jimmy Armfield 1974–78
Jock Stein CBE 1978
Jimmy Adamson 1978–80
Allan Clarke 1980–82
Eddie Gray MBE 1982–85
Billy Bremner 1985–88
Howard Wilkinson 1988–96
George Graham 1996–98
David O'Leary 1998–2002
Terry Venables 2002–03
Peter Reid 2003
Eddie Gray *(Caretaker)* 2003–04
Kevin Blackwell 2004–06
Dennis Wise 2006–08
Gary McAllister 2008
Simon Grayson 2008–12
Neil Warnock 2012–13
Brian McDermott 2013–14
Dave Hockaday 2014
Darko Milanic 2014
Neil Redfearn 2014–15
Uwe Rosler 2015
Steve Evans 2015–16
Garry Monk 2016–17
Thomas Christiansen 2017–18
Paul Heckingbottom 2018
Marcelo Bielsa 2018–22
Jesse Marsch 2022–23
Javi Gracia 2023
Sam Allardyce 2023
Daniel Farke July 2023–

TEN YEAR LEAGUE RECORD

		P	W	D	L	F	A	Pts	Pos
2015-16	FL C	46	14	17	15	50	58	59	13
2016-17	FL C	46	22	9	15	61	47	75	7
2017-18	FL C	46	17	9	20	59	64	60	13
2018-19	FL C	46	25	8	13	73	50	83	3
2019-20	FL C	46	28	9	9	77	35	93	1
2020-21	PR Lge	38	18	5	15	62	54	59	9
2021-22	PR Lge	38	9	11	18	42	79	38	17
2022-23	PR Lge	38	7	10	21	48	78	31	19
2023-24	FL C	46	27	9	10	81	43	90	3
2024-25	FL C	46	29	13	4	95	30	100	1

DID YOU KNOW ?

Luciano Becchio came off the bench after 60 minutes for Leeds United to score a hat-trick in the 3-1 home win over Bristol City on 13 November 2010. He remains the only Leeds substitute to score a hat-trick in an EFL or Premier League match. Becchio holds a second club record as the scorer of the most goals as a substitute, netting 11 times, nine in Football League games and one each in the League Cup and EFL Trophy.

LEEDS UNITED – SKY BET CHAMPIONSHIP 2024–25 LEAGUE RECORD

Match No.	Date	Venue	Opponents	Result		H/T Score	Lg Pos.	Goalscorers	Attendance
1	Aug 10	H	Portsmouth	D	3-3	1-2	9	Struijk (pen) [10], Gnonto [46], Aaronson [90]	36,432
2	17	A	WBA	D	0-0	0-0	15		25,329
3	23	A	Sheffield Wed	W	2-0	1-0	4	Aaronson [24], James [48]	28,800
4	31	H	Hull C	W	2-0	0-0	4	Fernandez [63], Piroe [81]	36,517
5	Sept 14	H	Burnley	L	0-1	0-1	9		36,405
6	21	A	Cardiff C	W	2-0	1-0	6	Ramazani [30], Piroe [87]	23,207
7	28	H	Coventry C	W	3-0	1-0	6	Gnonto [16], Bogle [49], Piroe [79]	36,625
8	Oct 1	A	Norwich C	D	1-1	0-1	4	Ramazani [60]	26,261
9	4	A	Sunderland	D	2-2	1-1	4	Piroe [22], Firpo [56]	41,769
10	18	H	Sheffield U	W	2-0	0-0	3	Struijk [69], Fernandez [90]	36,695
11	22	H	Watford	W	2-1	2-0	2	Ramazani [4], Aaronson [7]	34,968
12	26	A	Bristol C	D	0-0	0-0	2		25,283
13	Nov 2	H	Plymouth Arg	W	3-0	3-0	3	James [30], Piroe [33], Aaronson [38]	36,066
14	6	A	Millwall	L	0-1	0-1	3		16,693
15	9	H	QPR	W	2-0	1-0	3	Bogle [19], Piroe [90]	36,011
16	24	A	Swansea C	W	4-3	1-2	2	Solomon 2 [20, 73], Cabango (og) [55], Gnonto [90]	17,125
17	27	H	Luton T	W	3-0	2-0	2	Byram [10], Piroe [45], James [81]	35,340
18	30	A	Blackburn R	L	0-1	0-1	3		21,942
19	Dec 7	H	Derby Co	W	2-0	2-0	2	Rodon [39], Wober [44]	36,468
20	10	H	Middlesbrough	W	3-1	1-0	1	Gnonto [14], James [74], Aaronson [90]	36,422
21	14	A	Preston NE	D	1-1	0-1	2	Whatmough (og) [90]	19,508
22	21	H	Oxford U	W	4-0	1-0	2	James [9], Bogle [57], Aaronson [67], Solomon [73]	36,646
23	26	A	Stoke C	W	2-0	1-0	2	Piroe 2 [42, 63]	24,738
24	29	A	Derby Co	W	1-0	0-0	1	Aaronson [79]	32,240
25	Jan 1	H	Blackburn R	D	1-1	0-0	1	Struijk (pen) [88]	36,645
26	4	A	Hull C	D	3-3	0-1	2	Tanaka [46], James [62], Piroe [72]	24,463
27	19	H	Sheffield Wed	W	3-0	1-0	2	Solomon [3], Ramazani [88], Tanaka [90]	36,685
28	22	H	Norwich C	W	2-0	1-0	2	Solomon [1], James [65]	35,157
29	27	A	Burnley	D	0-0	0-0	1		21,329
30	Feb 1	H	Cardiff C	W	7-0	2-0	1	Aaronson [6], Solomon [13], James [50], Piroe 2 (1 pen) [65 (p), 90], Gnonto [67], Fernandez [88]	35,810
31	5	A	Coventry C	W	2-0	2-0	1	Piroe [17], Bogle [26]	28,008
32	11	A	Watford	W	4-0	3-0	1	James 2 [20, 28], Solomon [35], Piroe [62]	19,582
33	17	H	Sunderland	W	2-1	0-1	1	Struijk 2 [78, 90]	36,804
34	24	A	Sheffield U	W	3-1	0-1	1	Firpo [72], Tanaka [89], Piroe [90]	29,702
35	Mar 1	H	WBA	D	1-1	1-1	1	Firpo [9]	36,705
36	9	A	Portsmouth	L	0-1	0-0	2		20,314
37	12	H	Millwall	W	2-0	1-0	1	Cooper (og) [3], Tanaka [85]	34,401
38	15	A	QPR	D	2-2	1-2	1	Fox (og) [40], Bogle [51]	17,457
39	29	H	Swansea C	D	2-2	1-0	2	Aaronson [1], Gnonto [86]	35,574
40	Apr 5	A	Luton T	D	1-1	1-1	3	James [28]	11,867
41	8	A	Middlesbrough	W	1-0	1-0	1	James [2]	28,729
42	12	H	Preston NE	W	2-1	2-1	1	Solomon [4], Bogle [13]	35,747
43	18	A	Oxford U	W	1-0	1-0	1	Solomon [33]	11,537
44	21	H	Stoke C	W	6-0	5-0	1	Piroe 4 [6, 8, 20, 41], Firpo [26], Gnonto [59]	36,644
45	28	H	Bristol C	W	4-0	1-0	1	Tanaka [21], Gnonto [55], Ramazani 2 [82, 90]	36,310
46	May 3	A	Plymouth Arg	W	2-1	0-1	1	Gnonto [53], Solomon [90]	16,758

Final League Position: 1

GOALSCORERS

League (95): Piroe 19 (1 pen), James 12, Solomon 10, Aaronson 9, Gnonto 9, Bogle 6, Ramazani 6, Struijk 5 (2 pens), Tanaka 5, Firpo 4, Fernandez 3, Byram 1, Rodon 1, Wober 1, own goals 4.
FA Cup (1): Ramazani 1.
Carabao Cup (0).

Meslier I 39	Bogle J 44	Rodon J 46	Struijk P 31 + 4	Firpo J 30 + 2	Ampadu E 26 + 3	Gruev I 20 + 3	James D 30 + 6	Rutter G 1	Gnonto W 26 + 17	Fernandez M 11 + 28	Rothwell J 24 + 12	Piroe J 36 + 10	Aaronson B 43 + 3	Bamford P — + 17	Byram S 16 + 20	Gelhardt J — + 2	Solomon M 30 + 9	Ramazani L 7 + 22	Tanaka A 37 + 6	Schmidt I — + 12	Chambers S — + 1	Guilavogui J — + 16	Crew C — + 1	Wober M 2 + 6	Debayo J — + 1	Darlow K 7	Gray H — + 1	Match No.
1	2	3	4	5	6	7[1]	8[3]	9	10[2]	11[4]	12	13	14	15														1
1	2	3	4	5	6	7	8[2]		10	11[3]	13	9[1]	12	14														2
1	2	3	4	5	6	7	8[4]		10[2]	11[1]	13	12	9[3]		14	15												3
1	2[3]	3	4	5		7	6[4]		8[2]	11[5]	15	12	9		14		10[1]		13	16								4
1	2	3[6]	4	5[4]	7[1]	6		8	11	12	13	9[2]		14		10[3]	15	16										5
1	2[1]	3	4	5	6	7[4]		8[5]	11[3]	15	13	9		12		10[2]	16	14										6
1	2	3	4	5[3]	6[1]	7		8[4]	11[5]	16	13	9		14		10[2]	12	15										7
1	2	3	4	5[5]		6[1]		8[4]	11[2]	12	14	9	13	16	15	10[3]	7											8
1	2	3	4	5				8[3]	12	7	11[1]	9		13		10[2]	6	14										9
1	2	3	4	5[5]		13		8[2]	14	7	11[4]	9[1]	16	15		12	10[3]	6										10
1	2	3	4	5		14		8[3]	13	7	11[2]	9		15		12[4]	10[1]	6										11
1	2	3	4					8[2]	10[3]	12	6	11[1]	9	14	5		13	7										12
1		3	4	5				8[2]	10[3]	12	6[4]	11[5]	9[1]		2	13	7		14	15	16							13
1	2[3]	3	4	5				8	10[2]	13	7[1]	11	9	14		12	6											14
1	2	3	4			13			8[4]	11	6[3]	12	9		5	10[2]	6	7	15	14								15
1	2	3	4					8[5]	13	12	7[3]	11[2]	9	5[4]	10[1]	6	14		15	16								16
1	2	3	4			13			8[1]	14	6[5]	11[3]	9[4]	5[1]	10	16	7	15	12									17
1	2	3	4	5		10			8[2]	15	7[4]	11[1]	9[3]	13	12	14	6											18
1	2	3	4	5[1]				8[4]	14	13	7[5]	11	9[3]		10[6]	6	15	12										19
1		3	4		14			8[4]	10[2]	11[1]	7[5]	13	9		2[3]	12	6	15	16	5								20
1	2[5]	3	4		16			8	10[1]	15	7[3]	11	9[2]	12	5[4]	14	13	6										21
1	2	3			4			8	13	12	7[5]	11[3]	9[1]		5[4]	10[2]	14	6	15	16								22
1	2	3	4			6			8[1]	12	14	7[4]	11[3]	9		5[5]	10[2]	13	15	16								23
1	2	3	4		6			14	8[3]	11[2]		13	9[4]	15	5	12	10[1]	7[5]			16							24
1	2[2]	3	4		13			8	15	14	7[3]	11[4]	9	16	5[1]	10[5]	6				12							25
1	2	3			4			8		13	7[3]	11[2]	9		12	10	6		14	5[1]								26
1	2	3			4	13		8[4]	14	12	7[2]	11[1]	9[6]		5	10[3]	15	6		16								27
1	2	3		12	4	13		8[3]	14		7[5]	11	9		5[1]	10[4]	15	6[2]		16								28
1	2	3			4	7[3]		8		12		11[1]	9		5	10[2]	13	6		14								29
1	2[2]	3	16	5	4			8[1]	13	14	7	11	9[4]		12	10[3]	15	6[5]										30
1	2	3	15	5	4	7		8[3]	14	13		11[2]	9[6]			10[1]	12	6[4]		16								31
1	2	3	16	5	4[5]	7		8[2]	12	14	15	11[3]	9			10[1]	13	6[4]										32
1	2	3	12	5[5]	4	7[1]		8		14	13	11	9[3]		16	10[4]	15	6[2]										33
1	2[4]	3	4	5		7[1]		8	14	12	13	11	9[2]		15	10[3]	6											34
1	2	3	4	5				8	13	12	6	11	9[1]		10[2]	7												35
1	2[4]	3	4	5		7[5]	8		16	12	13	11	9[1]		15	10[3]	14	6[2]										36
1	2[1]	3	4	5		14	8[4]		13	15	7[2]	11[5]	9		12	10[3]	16	6										37
1	2	3	4	5			8		12		7	11	9[1]			10[2]	13	6										38
1	2	3	4	13	6[1]		8[5]		16	15	7	11	9[4]		5[2]	10[3]	14	12										39
	2[5]	3	4[3]	5	6	8			9[1]		11[2]	13	12	15		10[4]		7	16			14				1		40
	2	3		5[2]	4	7	8[3]		13		11[4]	9[5]	15	12		10[1]		6	14		16					1		41
	2	3		5	4	7			8[2]		11	9[1]	13	14		10[3]		6	12							1		42
	2[3]	3		5	4	7	12		8[1]		11[2]	9[4]	13			10[3]		6	14		15					1		43
	2[3]	3		5[4]	4	7			8[2]		11[1]	9[5]	12	15		10	13	6	14							1	16	44
	2	3		5[5]	4	7			8[2]	14	11[1]	9[4]	12	16		10	13	6[3]			15					1		45
	2[4]	3			4	7			8	15	11	9[3]	13	5[1]		10	14	6[2]					12			1		46

FA Cup
Third Round — Harrogate T (h) 1-0
Fourth Round — Millwall (h) 0-2

Carabao Cup
First Round — Middlesbrough (h) 0-3

LEICESTER CITY

FOUNDATION

In 1884 a number of young footballers, who were mostly old boys of Wyggeston School, held a meeting at a house on the Roman Fosse Way and formed Leicester Fosse FC. They collected 9d (less than 4p) towards the cost of a ball, plus the same amount for membership. Their first professional, Harry Webb from Stafford Rangers, was signed in 1888 for 2s 6d (12p) per week, plus travelling expenses.

King Power Stadium, Filbert Way, Leicester LE2 7FL.
Telephone: (0344) 815 5000.
Ticket Office: (0344) 815 5000 (option 1).
Website: www.lcfc.com
Email: help@lcfc.co.uk
Ground Capacity: 32,259.
Record Attendance: 47,298 v Tottenham H, FA Cup 5th rd, 18 February 1928 (at Filbert Street); 32,242 v Sunderland, Premier League, 8 August 2015 (at King Power Stadium).
Pitch Measurements: 105m × 68m (115yd × 74.5yd).
Chairman: Aiyawatt 'Top' Srivaddhanaprabha.
Chief Executive: Susan Whelan OBE.
Manager: Marti Cifuentes.
Assistant Manager: Xavi Calm.
Colours: Blue shirts with white and gold trim, blue shorts with white trim, blue socks with white trim.
Year Formed: 1884.
Turned Professional: 1888.
Previous Name: 1884, Leicester Fosse; 1919, Leicester City.
Club Nickname: 'The Foxes'.

HONOURS

League Champions: Premier League – 2015–16; FL C – 2013–14, 2023–24; Division 2 – 1924–25, 1936–37, 1953–54, 1956–57, 1970–71, 1979–80; FL 1 – 2008–09.
Runners-up: Division 1 – 1928–29; First Division – 2002–03; Division 2 – 1907–08.
FA Cup Winners: 2021.
Runners-up: 1949, 1961, 1963, 1969.
League Cup Winners: 1964, 1997, 2000.
Runners-up: 1965, 1999.
European Competitions
UEFA Champions League: 2016–17 (*qf*).
UEFA Cup: 1997–98, 2000–01.
Europa League: 2020–21, 2021–22.
UEFA Europa Conference League: 2021–22 (*sf*).
European Cup-Winners' Cup: 1961–62.

Grounds: 1884, Victoria Park; 1887, Belgrave Road; 1888, Victoria Park; 1891, Filbert Street; 2002, Walkers Stadium (renamed King Power Stadium 2011).
First Football League Game: 1 September 1894, Division 2, v Grimsby T (a) L 3–4 – Thraves; Smith, Bailey; Seymour, Brown, Henrys; Hill, Hughes, McArthur (1), Skea (2), Priestman.
Record League Victory: 10–0 v Portsmouth, Division 1, 20 October 1928 – McLaren; Black, Brown; Findlay, Carr, Watson; Adcock, Hine (3), Chandler (6), Lochhead, Barry (1).
Record Cup Victory: 8–1 v Coventry C (a), League Cup 5th rd, 1 December 1964 – Banks; Sjoberg, Norman (2); Roberts, King, McDerment; Hodgson (2), Cross, Goodfellow, Gibson (1), Stringfellow (2), (1 og).
Record Defeat: 0–12 (as Leicester Fosse) v Nottingham F, Division 1, 21 April 1909.

FOOTBALL YEARBOOK FACT FILE

Leicester City provided three players in the England starting line-up on two occasions in May 1974. Peter Shilton, Keith Weller and Frank Worthington all appeared against Scotland and Argentina, the only occasions that this has happened, although in the previous game against Northern Ireland Shilton and Weller started, with Worthington coming off the bench in the second half.

Most League Points (2 for a win): 61, Division 2, 1956–57.

Most League Points (3 for a win): 102, FL C, 2013–14.

Most League Goals: 109, Division 2, 1956–57.

Highest League Scorer in Season: Arthur Rowley, 44, Division 2, 1956–57.

Most League Goals in Total Aggregate: Arthur Chandler, 259, 1923–35.

Most League Goals in One Match: 6, John Duncan v Port Vale, Division 2, 25 December 1924; 6, Arthur Chandler v Portsmouth, Division 1, 20 October 1928.

Most Capped Player: Kasper Schmeichel, 84 (113), Denmark.

Most League Appearances: Adam Black, 528, 1920–35.

Youngest League Player: Jeremy Monga, 15 years 271 days v Newcastle U, 7 April 2025.

Record Transfer Fee Received: £80,000,000 from Manchester U for Harry Maguire, August 2019.

Record Transfer Fee Paid: £40,000,000 to Monaco for Youri Tielemans, July 2019.

Football League Record: 1894 Elected to Division 2; 1894–1908 Division 2; 1908–09 Division 1; 1909–25 Division 2; 1925–35 Division 1; 1935–37 Division 2; 1937–39 Division 1; 1946–54 Division 2; 1954–55 Division 1; 1955–57 Division 2; 1957–69 Division 1; 1969–71 Division 2; 1971–78 Division 1; 1978–80 Division 2; 1980–81 Division 1; 1981–83 Division 2; 1983–87 Division 1; 1987–92 Division 2; 1992–94 First Division; 1994–95 Premier League; 1995–96 First Division; 1996–2002 Premier League; 2002–03 First Division; 2003–04 Premier League; 2004–08 FL C; 2008–09 FL 1; 2009–14 FL C; 2014–23 Premier League; 2023–24 FL C; 2024–25 Premier League; 2025– FL C.

LATEST SEQUENCES

Longest Sequence of League Wins: 9, 15.9.2023 – 28.10.2023.

Longest Sequence of League Defeats: 8, 1.2.2025 – 7.4.2025.

Longest Sequence of League Draws: 6, 2.10.2004 – 2.11.2004.

Longest Sequence of Unbeaten League Matches: 23, 1.11.2008 – 7.3.2009.

Longest Sequence Without a League Win: 18, 12.4.1975 – 1.11.1975.

Successive Scoring Runs: 32 from 23.11.2013.

Successive Non-scoring Runs: 8 from 1.2.2025.

MANAGERS

Frank Gardner 1884–92
Ernest Marson 1892–94
J. Lee 1894–95
Henry Jackson 1895–97
William Clark 1897–98
George Johnson 1898–1912
Jack Bartlett 1912–14
Louis Ford 1914–15
Harry Linney 1915–19
Peter Hodge 1919–26
Willie Orr 1926–32
Peter Hodge 1932–34
Arthur Lochhead 1934–36
Frank Womack 1936–39
Tom Bromilow 1939–45
Tom Mather 1945–46
John Duncan 1946–49
Norman Bullock 1949–55
David Halliday 1955–58
Matt Gillies 1958–68
Frank O'Farrell 1968–71
Jimmy Bloomfield 1971–77
Frank McLintock 1977–78
Jock Wallace 1978–82
Gordon Milne 1982–86
Bryan Hamilton 1986–87
David Pleat 1987–91
Gordon Lee 1991
Brian Little 1991–94
Mark McGhee 1994–95
Martin O'Neill 1995–2000
Peter Taylor 2000–01
Dave Bassett 2001–02
Micky Adams 2002–04
Craig Levein 2004–06
Robert Kelly 2006–07
Martin Allen 2007
Gary Megson 2007
Ian Holloway 2007–08
Nigel Pearson 2008–10
Paulo Sousa 2010
Sven-Göran Eriksson 2010–11
Nigel Pearson 2011–15
Claudio Ranieri 2015–17
Craig Shakespeare 2017
Claude Puel 2017–19
Brendan Rodgers 2019–23
Dean Smith 2023
Enzo Maresca 2023–24
Steve Cooper 2024
Ruud van Nistelrooy 2024–25
Marti Cifuentes July 2025–

TEN YEAR LEAGUE RECORD

		P	W	D	L	F	A	Pts	Pos
2015-16	PR Lge	38	23	12	3	68	36	81	1
2016-17	PR Lge	38	12	8	18	48	63	44	12
2017-18	PR Lge	38	12	11	15	56	60	47	9
2018-19	PR Lge	38	15	7	16	51	48	52	9
2019-20	PR Lge	38	18	8	12	67	41	62	5
2020-21	PR Lge	38	20	6	12	68	50	66	5
2021-22	PR Lge	38	14	10	14	62	59	52	8
2022-23	PR Lge	38	9	7	22	51	68	34	18
2023-24	FL C	46	31	4	11	89	41	97	1
2024-25	PR Lge	38	6	7	25	33	80	25	18

DID YOU KNOW ?

Leicester City defeated Carlisle United 6-0 at Filbert Street in a Division Two match on 11 September 1982 with Steve Lynex and Gary Lineker netting hat-tricks. Three of the goals were penalty kicks, with Lynex slotting home on 23 and 83 minutes, and Lineker completing his hat-trick with the final spot kick three minutes from time.

LEICESTER CITY – PREMIER LEAGUE 2024–25 LEAGUE RECORD

Match No.	Date	Venue	Opponents	Result	H/T Score	Lg Pos.	Goalscorers	Attendance
1	Aug 19	H	Tottenham H	D	1-1	0-1	9	Vardy [57]	31,977
2	24	A	Fulham	L	1-2	1-1	14	Faes [38]	25,401
3	31	H	Aston Villa	L	1-2	0-1	15	Buonanotte [73]	31,725
4	Sept 14	A	Crystal Palace	D	2-2	1-0	15	Vardy [21], Mavididi [46]	25,124
5	21	H	Everton	D	1-1	0-1	15	Mavididi [73]	31,765
6	28	A	Arsenal	L	2-4	0-2	16	Justin 2 [47, 63]	60,323
7	Oct 5	H	Bournemouth	W	1-0	1-0	15	Buonanotte [16]	31,706
8	19	A	Southampton	W	3-2	0-2	14	Buonanotte [64], Vardy (pen) [74], Ayew [90]	31,145
9	25	H	Nottingham F	L	1-3	1-1	14	Vardy [23]	31,879
10	Nov 2	A	Ipswich T	D	1-1	0-0	15	Ayew [90]	29,874
11	10	A	Manchester U	L	0-3	0-2	15		73,829
12	23	H	Chelsea	L	1-2	0-1	16	Ayew (pen) [90]	31,880
13	30	A	Brentford	L	1-4	1-3	16	Buonanotte [21]	17,084
14	Dec 3	H	West Ham U	W	3-1	1-0	15	Vardy [2], El Khannous [61], Daka [90]	30,947
15	8	A	Brighton & HA	D	2-2	0-1	16	Vardy [86], Decordova-Reid [90]	31,647
16	14	H	Newcastle U	L	0-4	0-1	16		52,235
17	22	H	Wolverhampton W	L	0-3	0-3	17		31,818
18	26	A	Liverpool	L	1-3	1-1	18	Ayew [6]	60,300
19	29	H	Manchester C	L	0-2	0-1	18		32,057
20	Jan 4	A	Aston Villa	L	1-2	0-0	19	Mavididi [63]	42,386
21	15	H	Crystal Palace	L	0-2	0-0	19		29,766
22	18	H	Fulham	L	0-2	0-0	19		31,500
23	26	A	Tottenham H	W	2-1	0-1	17	Vardy [46], El Khannous [50]	61,295
24	Feb 1	A	Everton	L	0-4	0-3	18		39,376
25	15	H	Arsenal	L	0-2	0-0	18		31,968
26	21	H	Brentford	L	0-4	0-3	19		31,077
27	27	H	West Ham U	L	0-2	0-2	19		62,455
28	Mar 9	A	Chelsea	L	0-1	0-0	19		39,750
29	16	H	Manchester U	L	0-3	0-1	19		31,773
30	Apr 2	A	Manchester C	L	0-2	0-2	19		51,983
31	7	H	Newcastle U	L	0-3	0-3	19		30,403
32	12	A	Brighton & HA	D	2-2	1-1	19	Mavididi [38], Okoli [74]	31,330
33	20	H	Liverpool	L	0-1	0-0	19		30,402
34	26	A	Wolverhampton W	L	0-3	0-1	19		31,518
35	May 3	H	Southampton	W	2-0	2-0	19	Vardy [17], Ayew [44]	31,240
36	11	A	Nottingham F	D	2-2	1-1	19	Coady [16], Buonanotte [81]	30,245
37	18	H	Ipswich T	W	2-0	1-0	18	Vardy [28], McAteer [69]	31,986
38	25	A	Bournemouth	L	0-2	0-0	18		11,238

Final League Position: 18

GOALSCORERS

League (33): Vardy 9 (1 pen), Ayew 5 (1 pen), Buonanotte 5, Mavididi 4, El Khannous 2, Justin 2, Coady 1, Daka 1, Decordova-Reid 1, Faes 1, McAteer 1, Okoli 1.
FA Cup (7): Justin 2, Buonanotte 1, De Cordova-Reid 1, Faes 1, Mavididi 1, Vardy 1 (1 pen).
Carabao Cup (6): Ayew 1, Coady 1, El Khannous 1, Mavididi 1 (1 pen), Ndidi 1, Winks 1.
(Leicester C U21) Vertu Trophy (1): Richards 1.

Hermansen M 27	Justin J 34 + 2	Vestergaard J 16 + 2	Faes W 30 + 4	Kristiansen V 29 + 1	Winks H 17 + 5	Ndidi O 28	Fatawu I 6 + 5	Buonanotte F 14 + 17	Decordova-Reid B 9 + 14	Vardy J 35	Soumare B 25 + 6	Mavididi S 16 + 14	McAteer K 9 + 9	Ayew J 19 + 11	Skipp O 10 + 14	Okoli C 12 + 7	El Khannous B 27 + 5	Choudhury H 1 + 3	Coady C 19 + 3	Edouard O — + 4	Ricardo Pereira D 4 + 6	Daka P 6 + 17	Thomas L 13 + 1	Ward D 1 + 1	Stolarczyk J 10	Alves W — + 1	Couibaly W 1 + 3	Monga J — + 7	Evans J — + 4	Golding M — + 1	Aluko O — + 1	Match No.
1	2	3	4	5	6	7	8	9^2	10^3	11^1	12	13	14																			1
1	2	3	4	8^4	6	7	5	9^3	11^1	10^2		13	15	12	14																	2
1	2		3	5	6	9^4	8^2	13	15	11		12	16	10^1	7^3	4^5	14															3
1	2		3	5	6	9^2	12			11				10^1		8^3	7	4		13	14											4
1	2		3	5	6	7	14	12		11^2				10^3		8		4	9^1		13											5
1	2		3	5	7	9^2	13	8^1	16	11				10^3		12	6^5	4^4	14		15											6
1	2		3	5		6	14	8^2	13	11^1	15	10^3				9^4	7	4		12												7
1	2		3	5^2	12	6	13	8	15	11				10^4		14	7^1	4	9^3													8
1	5		3		7	6^3	8	9		11	14	10^1		12			4	13			2^2											9
1		4	3	5^4	7	6^2	8	9		11	13	10^1	12	15			14				2^3											10
2^2		4	3	5	7	8^1	11	9			6			13	10^3		12		14													11
1	2		3	5	9^1	7^3			16	11^4	8	14		6^2	13	12	4	10^5			15											12
1	5	12	2		7		9^2	16	11^3	6^4	14			10^5	15	4^1			3		13	8										13
1	2	4^2	13	5		6		9^5	15	11^1	7	14	8^2	16			10^4		3		12											14
1	2	4^4	16	5		6^1			14	11	7	13	8^3	10^2	12		9^5		3		15											15
1^1	2	4		5				13	16	11^3			10^4	8		6	14		9^5	7^2	3		15		12							16
	2^3	4^2	13	5	12			16	15	11	7	10		8^5	6^1		9^4	14	3				1									17
	2	4		5	6^2			12	14	7	10^3			8	13	15	9^1	3^4			11			1								18
	2^1	4		5	6^2			8	11	7	10^4			14	9	12	3^3				13		1	15								19
	2	4^1	12		6			15	16	11	7	10		8^4		14	9^2	3^3			13	5^5		1								20
	2^4	4	3	5	6^2			8^3		11	7	10	13	15	14		9^1				12		1									21
	2	4	3	5	6^2			14		11	7	10^3	12	8^4	13		9^1				15		1									22
	2^5	4	3	5	6			12	10^3	11^2	7			8^{14}			9^1		15		13		1	16								23
	2^4	4^1	3	5	6				10^3	11^2	7	14		8		13	9				12		1	15								24
1	2^1		3	5		6^4		14	8^0	11	7	13		10^2		4	9				15		1					12				25
1		12	3	5		6^4		14	8^1	11	7	13		10^3	15	4^5	9	16					1					2^2				26
1	2	4^3	3	5^4	12	6		8	10^1	11	7^2	13		9							14	15										27
1	5^4		2	8^3	12	6		13	14	11	7^1	15				10^2		3		16	9^5	4										28
1	5^2		2	8^1	13	6		12		11	7^1	14	15	16			10^5		3			9^2	4									29
1	5		2	8^3		6		13		11^1	7^4			16	12	14	10^2		3		15	9^5	4									30
1	5^4		2	8^2		6		12		11^1	7^3					14	15						16	14								31
1	2					6^3			16	11^1	7	10^5	8^4		14	3	9	4		13	12	5^2								15		32
1	15	3				6^3		12		8^1	11^2	7	10^5		14		9	4		2^4	13	5						16				33
1	15	3				6				8^4	10^1	11	7^2		13	12	14	9^5		4	2^3	5						16				34
	2	4				6				11^4	14			8^2	9^1	7^5	10^3		3		15	5		1				12	13	16		35
	2		4	15		6		13		11	12			8^3	9^2	7^1	16	10^5	3			5		5^4	1			14				36
	2^2		4			6^5				11^4	7			8^3	9^1	16	10		3		13	15	5	1				12	14			37
	2		3	10^5		12				7				8^4	9	6^3			4		14	11^1	5^2	1				13	15	16		38

FA Cup

Third Round	QPR	(h)	6-2
Fourth Round	Manchester U	(a)	1-2

Carabao Cup

Second Round	Tranmere R	(h)	4-0
Third Round	Walsall	(a)	0-0
Leicester C won 3-0 on penalties.			
Fourth Round	Manchester U	(a)	2-5

Vertu Trophy (Leicester C U21)

Group F (S)	Burton Alb	(a)	1-3
Group F (S)	Northampton T	(a)	0-3
Group F (S)	Notts Co	(a)	0-1

LEYTON ORIENT

FOUNDATION

There is some doubt about the foundation of Leyton Orient, and, indeed, some confusion with clubs like Leyton and Clapton over their early history. As regards the foundation, the most favoured version is that Leyton Orient was formed originally by members of Homerton Theological College who established Glyn Cricket Club in 1881 and then carried on through the following winter playing football. Eventually many employees of the Orient Shipping Line became involved and so the name Orient was chosen in 1888.

Brisbane Road, Leyton, London E10 5NF.
Telephone: (020) 8926 1111.
Ticket Office: (020) 8926 1010.
Website: www.leytonorient.com
Email: enquiries@leytonorient.net
Ground Capacity: 9,253.
Record Attendance: 34,345 v West Ham U, FA Cup 4th rd, 25 January 1964.
Pitch Measurements: 100m × 67m (109.5yd × 73.5yd).
Chairman: Nigel Travis.
Chief Executive: Mark Devlin.
Director of Football: Martin Ling.
Head Coach: Richie Wellens.
Assistant Head Coach: Paul Terry.
Colours: Red shirts with two white stripes, red shorts, red socks with white trim.
Year Formed: 1881. *Turned Professional:* 1903.

HONOURS

League Champions: Division 3 – 1969–70; Division 3S – 1955–56; FL 2 – 2022–23; National League – 2018–19.
Runners-up: Division 2 – 1961–62; Division 3S – 1954–55.
FA Cup: semi-final – 1978.
League Cup: 5th rd – 1963.

Previous Names: 1881, Glyn Cricket and Football Club; 1886, Eagle Football Club; 1888, Orient Football Club; 1898, Clapton Orient; 1946, Leyton Orient; 1966, Orient; 1987, Leyton Orient.
Club Nickname: 'The O's'.
Grounds: 1884, Glyn Road; 1896, Whittles Athletic Ground; 1900, Millfields Road; 1930, Lea Bridge Road; 1937, Brisbane Road (renamed Matchroom Stadium 1995; The Breyer Group Stadium 2018; Brisbane Road 2022).
First Football League Game: 2 September 1905, Division 2, v Leicester Fosse (a) L 1–2 – Butler; Holmes, Codling; Lamberton, Boden, Boyle; Kingaby (1), Wootten, Leigh, Evenson, Bourne.
Record League Victory: 8–0 v Crystal Palace, Division 3 (S), 12 November 1955 – Welton; Lee, Earl; Blizzard, Aldous, McKnight; White (1), Facey (3), Burgess (2), Heckman, Hartburn (2). 8–0 v Rochdale, Division 4, 20 October 1987 – Wells; Howard, Dickenson (1), Smalley (1), Day, Hull, Hales (2), Castle (Sussex), Shinners (2), Godfrey (Harvey), Comfort (2). 8–0 v Colchester U, Division 4, 15 October 1988 – Wells; Howard, Dickenson, Hales (1p), Day (1), Sitton (1), Baker (1), Ward, Hull (3), Juryeff, Comfort (1). 8–0 v Doncaster R, Division 3, 28 December 1997 – Hyde; Channing, Naylor, Smith (1p), Hicks, Clark, Ling, Roger Joseph, Griffiths (3) (Harris), Richards (2) (Baker (1)), Inglethorpe (1) (Simpson).

FOOTBALL YEARBOOK FACT FILE

The Leyton Orient board of directors voted to change the name of the club to 'Orient Football Club' at their annual general meeting in November 1966 when it was agreed that the new name would be used from the start of the 1967–68 season. The O's played their first match as Orient away to Grimsby Town on 19 August 1967, the game ending in a 0-0 draw.

Record Cup Victory: 9–2 v Chester, League Cup 3rd rd, 15 October 1962 – Robertson; Charlton, Taylor; Gibbs, Bishop, Lea; Deeley (1), Waites (3), Dunmore (2), Graham (3), Wedge.

Record Defeat: 0–8 v Aston Villa, FA Cup 4th rd, 30 January 1929.

Most League Points (2 for a win): 66, Division 3 (S), 1955–56.

Most League Points (3 for a win): 91, FL 2, 2022–23.

Most League Goals: 106, Division 3 (S), 1955–56.

Highest League Scorer in Season: Tom Johnston, 35, Division 2, 1957–58.

Most League Goals in Total Aggregate: Tom Johnston, 121, 1956–58, 1959–61.

Most League Goals in One Match: 4, Wally Leigh v Bradford C, Division 2, 13 April 1906; 4, Albert Pape v Oldham Ath, Division 2, 1 September 1924; 4, Peter Kitchen v Millwall, Division 3, 21 April 1984.

Most Capped Player: Jobi McAnuff, 22 (32), Jamaica.

Most League Appearances: Peter Allen, 432, 1965–78.

Youngest League Player: Paul Went, 15 years 327 days v Preston NE, 4 September 1965.

Record Transfer Fee Received: £1,000,000 (potentially rising to £1,500,000) from Fulham for Gabriel Zakuani, July 2006; £1,500,000 from Swansea C for Ethan Galbraith, July 2025.

Record Transfer Fee Paid: £200,000 to Oldham Ath for Liam Kelly, July 2016.

Football League Record: 1905 Elected to Division 2; 1905–29 Division 2; 1929–56 Division 3 (S); 1956–62 Division 2; 1962–63 Division 1; 1963–66 Division 2; 1966–70 Division 3; 1970–82 Division 2; 1982–85 Division 3; 1985–89 Division 4; 1989–92 Division 3; 1992–95 Second Division; 1995–2004 Third Division; 2004–06 FL 2; 2006–15 FL 1; 2015–17 FL 2; 2017–19 National League; 2019–23 FL 2; 2023– FL 1.

LATEST SEQUENCES

Longest Sequence of League Wins: 10, 21.1.1956 – 30.3.1956.

Longest Sequence of League Defeats: 9, 1.4.1995 – 6.5.1995.

Longest Sequence of League Draws: 6, 30.11.1974 – 28.12.1974.

Longest Sequence of Unbeaten League Matches: 15, 13.4.2013 – 19.10.2013.

Longest Sequence Without a League Win: 23, 6.10.1962 – 13.4.1963.

Successive Scoring Runs: 22 from 12.3.1927.

Successive Non-scoring Runs: 8 from 19.11.1994.

MANAGERS

Sam Omerod 1905–06
Ike Ivenson 1906
Billy Holmes 1907–22
Peter Proudfoot 1922–29
Arthur Grimsdell 1929–30
Peter Proudfoot 1930–31
Jimmy Seed 1931–33
David Pratt 1933–34
Peter Proudfoot 1935–39
Tom Halsey 1939
Bill Wright 1939–45
Willie Hall 1945
Bill Wright 1945–46
Charlie Hewitt 1946–48
Neil McBain 1948–49
Alec Stock 1949–59
Les Gore 1959–61
Johnny Carey 1961–63
Benny Fenton 1963–64
Dave Sexton 1965
Dick Graham 1966–68
Jimmy Bloomfield 1968–71
George Petchey 1971–77
Jimmy Bloomfield 1977–81
Paul Went 1981
Ken Knighton 1981–83
Frank Clark 1983–91
(Managing Director)
Peter Eustace 1991–94
Chris Turner and John Sitton 1994–95
Pat Holland 1995–96
Tommy Taylor 1996–2001
Paul Brush 2001–03
Martin Ling 2003–09
Geraint Williams 2009–10
Russell Slade 2010–14
Kevin Nugent 2014
Mauro Milanese 2014
Fabio Liverani 2014–15
Ian Hendon 2015–16
Kevin Nolan 2016
Andy Hessenthaler 2016
Alberto Cavasin 2016
Andy Edwards 2016–17
Danny Webb 2017
Martin Ling 2017
Omer Riza 2017
Steve Davis 2017
Justin Edinburgh 2017–19
Carl Fletcher 2019
Ross Embleton 2019–21
Kenny Jackett 2021–22
Richie Wellens March 2022–

TEN YEAR LEAGUE RECORD

		P	W	D	L	F	A	Pts	Pos
2015-16	FL 2	46	19	12	15	60	61	69	8
2016-17	FL 2	46	10	6	30	47	87	36	24
2017-18	NL	46	16	12	18	58	56	60	13
2018-19	NL	46	25	14	7	73	35	89	1
2019-20	FL 2	36	10	12	14	47	55	42	17§
2020-21	FL 2	46	17	10	19	53	55	61	11
2021-22	FL 2	46	14	16	16	62	47	58	13
2022-23	FL 2	46	26	13	7	61	34	91	1
2023-24	FL 1	46	18	11	17	53	55	65	11
2024-25	FL 1	46	24	6	16	72	48	78	6

§*Decided on points-per-game (1.17)*

DID YOU KNOW ?

Floodlights were erected at Leyton Orient's Brisbane Road ground in the summer of 1960, and they were first used in the Division Two fixture against Brighton & Hove Albion on 31 August. The O's won 2-1 with goals from Sid Bishop and Ken Facey in front of a crowd of 12,937.

LEYTON ORIENT – SKY BET LEAGUE ONE 2024–25 LEAGUE RECORD

Match No.	Date	Venue	Opponents	Result	H/T Score	Lg Pos.	Goalscorers	Attendance
1	Aug 10	H	Bolton W	L	1-2	1-1	16	Kelman [38]	7835
2	17	A	Charlton Ath	L	0-1	0-0	20		15,126
3	24	H	Birmingham C	L	1-2	1-2	23	Galbraith [14]	8005
4	31	A	Shrewsbury T	L	0-3	0-1	24		5602
5	Sept14	A	Reading	W	1-0	1-0	22	Kelman [27]	12,952
6	21	A	Stockport Co	W	4-1	2-0	20	Galbraith 2 [12, 17], Agyei [57], Clare [81]	9473
7	24	H	Peterborough U	D	2-2	1-2	16	James [20], Kelman [53]	6416
8	28	H	Wrexham	D	0-0	0-0	18		8705
9	Oct 1	H	Exeter C	L	0-1	0-1	20		6439
10	5	A	Lincoln C	L	1-2	0-0	19	Agyei [80]	9511
11	19	A	Northampton T	L	0-1	0-0	20		7015
12	22	H	Rotherham U	W	1-0	0-0	20	Happe [68]	6314
13	26	A	Wycombe W	L	0-3	0-2	20		5400
14	Nov 9	H	Blackpool	W	3-0	1-0	20	Perkins [34], Kelman [71], James [76]	8527
15	23	A	Stevenage	D	0-0	0-0	21		4259
16	26	H	Huddersfield T	L	0-2	0-1	21		7819
17	Dec 3	H	Bristol R	W	3-0	3-0	20	Happe [17], O'Neill [29], Agyei [45]	7422
18	7	A	Wigan Ath	W	2-0	1-0	16	Sweeney [41], Jaiyesimi [90]	8306
19	14	H	Burton Alb	D	0-0	0-0	18		7267
20	21	A	Barnsley	W	4-0	2-0	15	Donley [6], Beckles [28], Kelman [51], Perkins [90]	11,373
21	26	H	Crawley T	W	3-0	1-0	13	Kelman [33], Agyei [50], Beckles [55]	8195
22	29	H	Cambridge U	W	2-0	1-0	10	O'Neill [32], Donley [70]	8914
23	Jan 1	A	Bristol R	W	3-2	2-1	8	Galbraith [9], Donley [39], Kelman [53]	7887
24	4	A	Shrewsbury T	W	1-0	0-0	8	Donley [63]	7552
25	18	A	Peterborough U	D	0-0	0-0	8		8235
26	25	H	Reading	W	2-0	1-0	7	Markanday [29], Kelman [51]	8774
27	28	A	Exeter C	W	6-2	4-0	6	Abdulai 3 [5, 7, 64], Clare [14], Markanday [34], Donley [78]	5022
28	Feb 1	A	Stockport Co	L	0-1	0-1	6		8485
29	11	H	Mansfield T	W	3-0	3-0	7	Brown [6], Williams [17], Galbraith [32]	6597
30	15	H	Lincoln C	W	3-2	2-1	6	Perkins 2 [17, 28], Kelman [90]	7967
31	18	A	Wrexham	W	2-1	1-1	6	Kelman [30], Donley [50]	11,703
32	22	A	Bolton W	L	1-2	1-0	6	Kelman [40]	20,851
33	25	A	Birmingham C	L	0-2	0-0	6		26,857
34	Mar 1	H	Charlton Ath	L	1-2	0-0	8	Brown [50]	8942
35	4	A	Rotherham U	L	0-1	0-0	9		8106
36	8	H	Northampton T	L	1-2	0-2	9	Kelman [60]	8911
37	15	A	Blackpool	W	2-1	1-0	9	Kelman 2 [29, 63]	9438
38	27	H	Stevenage	W	1-0	1-0	8	Kelman [12]	7305
39	Apr 1	A	Burton Alb	L	1-2	1-0	10	Agyei [10]	2367
40	5	A	Wigan Ath	D	0-0	0-0	9		3069
41	8	H	Mansfield T	W	3-2	1-1	9	Markanday [39], Kelman 2 [54, 69]	6980
42	12	A	Crawley T	W	3-1	0-0	7	Kelman 2 (1 pen) [52, 53 (p)], Donley [90]	4793
43	18	H	Barnsley	W	4-3	0-2	6	Galbraith [51], Kelman [68], Clare [72], Beckles [74]	8410
44	21	A	Cambridge U	W	2-1	0-1	6	Kelman [67], Donley [78]	7414
45	26	H	Wycombe W	W	1-0	0-0	6	Williams [66]	8935
46	May 3	A	Huddersfield T	W	4-1	2-1	6	Agyei 2 [2, 48], Chapman (og) [24], Abdulai [79]	20,774

Final League Position: 6

GOALSCORERS

League (72): Kelman 21 (1 pen), Donley 8, Agyei 7, Galbraith 6, Abdulai 4, Perkins 4, Beckles 3, Clare 3, Markanday 3, Brown 2, Happe 2, James 2, O'Neill 2, Williams 2, Jaiyesimi 1, Sweeney 1, own goal 1.
FA Cup (6): Agyei 2, Keeley 1, Kelman 1, Perkins 1, own goal 1.
Carabao Cup (6): Agyei 2, Cooper 2, Jaiyesimi 1, Kelman 1.
Vertu Trophy (7): Agyei 2, Kelman 2, Happe 1, Obiero 1, Perkins 1.
League One Play-offs (3): Kelman 2 (1 pen), O'Neill 1.

Hemming Z 10	Clare S 19+10	Beckles O 29+3	Happe D 24+1	Sweeney J 9+10	Brown J 38+6	Obiero Z 4+6	Galbraith E 37+2	Kelman C 37+9	O'Neill O 21+5	Agyei D 31+10	Perkins S 11+19	James T 17+5	Jaiyesimi D 4+24	Cooper B 16+14	Pratley D 21+10	Donley J 31+8	Warrington L 4+4	Currie J 34+2	Simpson J 10+7	Ball D 11+20	Graham J —+8	Keeley J 36	Markanday D 13+3	Abdulai A 11+10	Edmonds-Green R 16+1	Williams R 12+2	Match No.
1	2	3⁴	4	5²	6	7³	8⁶	9	10	11¹	12	13	14	15	16												1
1	2	12	4	16	7	6¹		8	10³	11	14	5⁶	15	3²		9⁴	13										2
1	2		4	5	6⁴	9¹	7	11²	10³	12	14			15	3	13	8										3
1	2	12	4¹	5⁴	6²		7	11	10³	8	15		14		3	13	9										4
1	7	3	4²		6³		9	11	8⁴	10¹	12	2						5	13	14	15						5
1	7⁴	3	4		6⁵		9	11	8¹	10³		2²		12	16	15		5	13	14							6
1	7⁴	3	4		6¹		9	11	8²	10³		2	13	15		5	12	14									7
1	7¹	2			12		11	10		13		5		3²	9³	8	4	6	14								8
1	13	3		2			11	10⁴	8³	16		12	15	7¹	5	4⁵	6²	14									9
1	8¹	3		12	15		11	7⁴	10		2	14	13	16	9⁵	5	4²	6³									10
	3	4⁵		7²	15		9	11	10¹	8		2³		16	14		5	12	6⁴	13		1					11
	3	4	13	7			9	8	10	11²		2		6¹			5		12			1					12
	3	4		7⁵	13		9	11⁴	10	8⁹	15		12			6²		5	2¹	14		1					13
	3	4			15		9⁶	12	10⁴	11³	8¹	2	14			6	16	7²	5	13		1					14
	3	4					9	13	10	11	8²	2				6		7¹	5	12		1					15
	3	4²		6⁴			9	10		11		8³	2	2⁵	13	15		7¹	5	14	12	16	1				16
	3	4²	16	12			14	10⁴	11³	8		2	15			7¹	9		5⁵	13	6	1					17
	3	4	5	6			12	13	10	11³	8¹	2	14			9²			7			1					18
	3	4	5³	6⁵			12	13	10⁴	11	8²	2¹	15			14	9		16	7		1					19
	3	4²		7	16		2	11	10⁴	8⁵	14		12	15	6	9¹		5³	13			1					20
15	3	4¹		7⁴			2	11	10²	8³	14	13				6⁵	9	5	12	16		1					21
13	3		15	7²			2	11⁴	10³	8	14					12	9	5	4	6		1					22
14	3	4		7			2	12	13	11	8⁴		10²			6³	9	5		15		1					23
13	3		14	7			2	11	10¹		8³		12			6²	9	5	4			1					24
	3		15	13	10¹	7	11			2	12	14	6³	9²		5	4					1	8⁴				25
12	3		15	7			2	11⁴			13	14	4	6	6²	9		5				1	8¹	10¹			26
7³	3²	13	16	14			2⁵	11⁴			12	15	4	6	9		5					1	8¹	10			27
		4		7³			2	11		13	12	14	3	6¹	9		5					1	8²	10			28
		4		6²			2	13		16	15	14		7	9³		5		12			1	8¹	11⁴	3	10⁵	29
				6			7	11		15	8²	2¹	16	12⁵	14		5	4	13			1		9⁴	3	10³	30
		4	5	7			2	11⁴		14	8³			6¹	9			3¹	15			1		13	12	10²	31
		12		6⁴	15		2	11		14	13			4¹	9		5		7⁵			1	16	10³	3	8²	32
		13		7			2⁴	11²			8³	16		4	6	9⁵		5⁸	12			1	10¹	14	3	15	33
14		5		7			2	11		12	8¹			4	6	9³						1	10³	13	3		34
16		5		6			2	11³		8²	14		12	3		9			7⁴			1	10¹	15	4	13	35
13		5¹		7⁴			2	12		11	16		14			6²	9³		4	15		1	10⁵	3	8		36
2²			6				7	11		8⁵	16			10³	12	13	14	5	4¹	15		1	9⁴	3			37
2			7¹				11⁴	13		8⁵	15			10³	3	6	14	5		12		1	9⁵	16	4		38
2³	4		7				11	13		8⁴	15			10²		6¹	9⁵	5		12		1	16	14	3		39
6	4		12				7	13		10²			2¹	14	3		15	5				1	9	11⁴		8³	40
6⁴	12		7¹				11	14					4	13	9			5		14		1	8²	10³	3	2	41
2	3		6¹				11⁴	13		15	12			9			5	14				1	8³	10²	4	7	42
12	3		7				2	11³		10²				15	6¹	9		5				1	13	14	4	8⁴	43
6³	3		7				2	11⁴	16	13		12	15			9		5⁵				1	8²	14	4	10¹	44
7	3		6³				5	11		9²				4¹	12	10				14		1	13	2	8		45
7	3		6⁴				5	11²	14	9³				16	4¹		10		15	12		1	13	2	8⁵		46

FA Cup

First Round	Boreham Wood	(a)	2-2

aet; Leyton Orient won 3-1 on penalties.

Second Round	Oldham Ath	(h)	2-1

aet.

Third Round	Derby Co	(h)	1-1

aet; Leyton Orient won 6-5 on penalties.

Fourth Round	Manchester C	(h)	1-2

Carabao Cup

First Round	Newport Co	(h)	4-1
Second Round	Millwall	(a)	1-0
Third Round	Brentford	(a)	1-3

Vertu Trophy

Group E (S)	Arsenal U21	(h)	1-2
Group E (S)	Colchester U	(h)	1-1

Leyton Orient won 4-2 on penalties.

Group E (S)	Milton Keynes D	(a)	3-1
Second Round	Charlton Ath	(a)	2-0
Third Round	Stevenage	(h)	0-1

League One Play-offs

Semi-Final 1st leg	Stockport Co	(h)	2-2
Semi-Final 2nd leg	Stockport Co	(a)	1-1

aet; Leyton Orient won 4-1 on penalties.

Final	Charlton Ath	(Wembley)	0-1

LINCOLN CITY

FOUNDATION

The original Lincoln Football Club was established in the early 1860s and was one of the first provisional clubs to affiliate to the Football Association. In their early years, they regularly played matches against the famous Sheffield Football Club and later became known as Lincoln Lindum. The present organisation was formed at a public meeting held in the Monson Arms Hotel in June 1884 and won the Lincolnshire Cup in only their third season. They were founder members of the Midland League in 1889 and that competition's first champions.

LNER Stadium, Sincil Bank, Lincoln LN5 8LD.
Telephone: (01522) 880 011.
Ticket Office: (01522) 458 884.
Website: www.weareimps.com
Email: feedback@theredimps.com
Ground Capacity: 10,669.
Record Attendance: 23,196 v Derby Co, League Cup 4th rd, 15 November 1967.
Pitch Measurements: 100m × 64m (109.5yd × 70yd).
Chairman: Clive Nates.
Chief Executive Officer: Liam Scully.
Head Coach: Michael Skubala.
Assistant Head Coaches: Tom Shaw, Chris Cohen.
Colours: Red shirts with thin white stripes, white sleeves and black trim, black shorts, red socks with black and white trim.
Year Formed: 1884.   *Turned Professional:* 1885.
Ltd Co.: 1895.
Club Nickname: 'The Imps', 'The Red Imps'.
Grounds: 1884, John O'Gaunt's; 1894, Sincil Bank (renamed LNER Stadium 2019).
First Football League Game: 3 September 1892, Division 2, v Sheffield U (a) L 2–4 – William Gresham; Coulton, Neill; Shaw, Mettam, Moore; Smallman, Irving (1), Cameron (1), Kelly, James Gresham.
Record League Victory: 11–1 v Crewe Alex, Division 3 (N), 29 September 1951 – Jones; Green (1p); Varney; Wright, Emery, Grummett (1); Troops (1), Garvey, Graver (6), Whittle (1), Johnson (1).
Record Cup Victory: 13-0 v Peterborough, FA Cup 1st qual rd, 12 October 1895 – Shaw, McFarlane, Eyre, Richardson, Neaves (1), Burke (2), Frettingham (2), Smith (1), Gillespie W (2), Gillespie M (3), Hulme (2).
Record Defeat: 3–11 v Manchester C, Division 2, 23 March 1895.
Most League Points (2 for a win): 74, Division 4, 1975–76.
Most League Points (3 for a win): 85, FL 2, 2018–19.
Most League Goals: 121, Division 3 (N), 1951–52.
Highest League Scorer in Season: Allan Hall, 41, Division 3 (N), 1931–32.
Most League Goals in Total Aggregate: Andy Graver, 143, 1950–55 and 1958–61.

HONOURS

League Champions: Division 3N – 1931–32, 1947–48, 1951–52; FL 2 – 2018–19; Division 4 – 1975–76; Football Conference – 1987–88; National League 2016–17.
Runners-up: Division 3N – 1927–28, 1930–31, 1936–37; Division 4 – 1980–81.
FA Cup: quarter-final – 2017.
League Cup: 4th rd – 1968, 2023.
League Trophy Winners: 2018.

FOOTBALL YEARBOOK FACT FILE

Lincoln City's game at Wrexham on 9 April 1927 was abandoned after an hour's play with the home team leading 2-0. Heavy rain and hail had fallen throughout the game and early in the second half the Imps' left-half Alf Hale collapsed and was carried from the field unconscious. Shortly afterwards Alf Bassnett, Joe Robson and Tom Maidment all staggered off 'numbed with cold', and with City reduced to just seven men the referee called the proceedings to a halt.

Most League Goals in One Match: 6, Frank Keetley v Halifax T, Division 3 (N), 16 January 1932; 6, Andy Graver v Crewe Alex, Division 3 (N), 29 September 1951.

Most Capped Player: Delroy Facey, 8 (15) Grenada.

Most League Appearances: Grant Brown, 407, 1989–2002.

Youngest League Player: Jack Hobbs, 16 years 150 days v Bristol R, 15 January 2005.

Record Transfer Fee Received: £640,000 from Huddersfield T for Harry Toffolo, January 2020.

Record Transfer Fee Paid: £325,000 to Barnet for John Akinde, July 2018.

Football League Record: 1892 Founder member of Division 2; 1892–1907 Division 2; 1908 Failed re-election; 1908–09 Midland League; 1909 Re-elected to Division 2; 1909–11 Division 2; 1911 Failed re-election; 1911–12 Central League; 1912 Re-elected to Division 2; 1912–20 Division 2; 1920 Failed re-election; 1920–21 Midland League; 1921 Elected to Division 3 (N); 1921–32 Division 3 (N); 1932–34 Division 2; 1934–48 Division 3 (N); 1948–49 Division 2; 1949–52 Division 3 (N); 1952–61 Division 2; 1961–62 Division 3; 1962–76 Division 4; 1976–79 Division 3; 1979–81 Division 4; 1981–86 Division 3; 1986–87 Division 4; 1987–88 Football Conference; 1988–92 Division 4; 1992–98 Third Division; 1998–99 Second Division; 1999–2004 Third Division; 2004–11 FL 2; 2011–15 Football Conference; 2015–17 National League; 2017–19 FL 2; 2019– FL 1.

LATEST SEQUENCES

Longest Sequence of League Wins: 10, 1.9.1930 – 18.10.1930.

Longest Sequence of League Defeats: 12, 21.9.1896 – 9.1.1897.

Longest Sequence of League Draws: 5, 21.2.1981 – 7.3.1981.

Longest Sequence of Unbeaten League Matches: 19, 29.12.2018 – 13.4.2019.

Longest Sequence Without a League Win: 19, 22.8.1978 – 23.12.1978.

Successive Scoring Runs: 37 from 1.3.1930.

Successive Non-scoring Runs: 5 from 15.11.1913.

MANAGERS

Jack Strawson 1884–96 *(hon. secretary)*
Alf Martin 1896–97 *(sec.-manager)*
James West 1897–1900 *(hon. secretary)*
David Calderhead, snr 1900–07 *(sec.-manager)*
Jack Strawson 1907–08 *(managing director & secretary)*
Jack Strawson 1908–19 *(secretary)*
Clem Jackson 1919–20 *(player-manager)*
George Fraser 1919–21 *(sec.-manager)*
David Calderhead, jnr 1921–24 *(sec.-manager)*
Horace Henshall 1924–27 *(sec.-manager)*
Harry Parkes 1927–36 *(sec.-manager)*
Joe McClelland 1936–47 *(sec.-manager)*
Bill Anderson 1947–65
Con Moulson 1965–65
Roy Chapman 1965–66
Ron Gray 1966–70
Bert Loxley 1970–71
David Herd 1971–72
Graham Taylor 1972–77
George Kerr 1977
Willie Bell 1977–78
Colin Murphy 1978–85
John Pickering 1985
George Kerr 1985–87
Peter Daniel 1987 *(caretaker)*
Colin Murphy 1987–90
Allan Clarke 1990
Steve Thompson 1990–93
Keith Alexander 1993–94
Sam Ellis 1994–95
Steve Wicks 1995 *(head coach)*
John Beck 1995–98
Shane Westley 1998
John Reames 1998–2000 *(chairman-manager)*
Phil Stant 2000–01
Alan Buckley 2001–02
Keith Alexander 2002–06
John Schofield 2006–07
Peter Jackson 2007–09
Chris Sutton 2009–10
Steve Tilson 2010–11
David Holdsworth 2011–13
Gary Simpson 2013–14
Chris Moyses 2014–16
Danny Cowley 2016–19
Michael Appleton 2019–22
Mark Kennedy 2022–23
Michael Skubala November 2023–

TEN YEAR LEAGUE RECORD

		P	W	D	L	F	A	Pts	Pos
2015-16	NL	46	16	13	17	69	68	61	13
2016-17	NL	46	30	9	7	83	40	99	1
2017-18	FL 2	46	20	15	11	64	48	75	7
2018-19	FL 2	46	23	16	7	73	43	85	1
2019-20	FL 1	35	12	6	17	44	46	42	16§
2020-21	FL 1	46	22	11	13	69	50	77	5
2021-22	FL 1	46	14	10	22	55	63	52	17
2022-23	FL 1	46	14	20	12	47	47	62	11
2023-24	FL 1	46	20	14	12	65	40	74	7
2024-25	FL 1	46	16	13	17	64	56	61	11

§*Decided on points-per-game (1.20)*

DID YOU KNOW ?

Lincoln City, already confirmed as finishing bottom of the League in 1966–67, had to wait until 26 May before playing their final game of the season away to Fourth Division champions Stockport County. The Imps fielded a team with an average age of just 22 years and 173 days, one of their youngest on record, and were allowed to use two men signed after the transfer deadline. They gained a remarkable 5-4 victory, ending a run of 15 games without a win.

LINCOLN CITY – SKY BET LEAGUE ONE 2024–25 LEAGUE RECORD

Match No.	Date	Venue	Opponents	Result	H/T Score	Lg Pos.	Goalscorers	Attendance
1	Aug 10	A	Burton Alb	W 3-2	2-2	3	O'Connor 2 [9, 86], Darikwa [22]	5027
2	17	H	Barnsley	L 1-2	0-1	12	House [70]	9768
3	24	H	Mansfield T	W 4-1	2-0	6	Jackson 2 [29, 47], Roughan [45], House [51]	9809
4	31	A	Stevenage	W 1-0	0-0	4	Moylan (pen) [72]	4017
5	Sept 14	A	Peterborough U	D 1-1	1-0	5	House [33]	9537
6	21	H	Wigan Ath	D 0-0	0-0	6		8534
7	28	A	Cambridge U	W 2-0	1-0	3	Draper [26], Cadamarteri [68]	6969
8	Oct 1	A	Blackpool	D 1-1	0-0	4	Hamer [90]	8528
9	5	H	Leyton Orient	W 2-1	0-0	4	Makama [47], Draper [77]	9511
10	19	H	Birmingham C	L 1-3	1-1	7	Cadamarteri [1]	10,026
11	22	A	Crawley T	L 0-3	0-0	10		3221
12	26	H	Stockport Co	W 2-1	1-1	8	House [42], Cadamarteri [66]	9513
13	29	H	Northampton T	W 2-1	1-1	5	Hamer [18], Ring [88]	8219
14	Nov 9	A	Bristol R	D 1-1	0-1	5	Moylan [64]	7262
15	16	A	Exeter C	D 0-0	0-0	6		5950
16	23	H	Wycombe W	L 2-3	1-2	7	Darikwa 2 [14, 87]	8558
17	26	A	Wrexham	L 0-1	0-0	9		11,786
18	Dec 3	A	Rotherham U	L 1-2	0-1	9	Makama [50]	8995
19	7	H	Charlton Ath	D 0-0	0-0	9		8307
20	14	A	Huddersfield T	D 2-2	2-0	9	House [15], Cadamarteri [25]	18,675
21	21	H	Reading	W 2-0	1-0	6	Cadamarteri [8], Hackett-Fairchild [72]	9396
22	26	A	Shrewsbury T	L 0-1	0-1	9		6369
23	29	A	Bolton W	L 0-3	0-1	12		22,395
24	Jan 1	H	Rotherham U	L 0-1	0-0	12		9222
25	4	H	Stevenage	D 0-0	0-0	12		8220
26	18	A	Northampton T	W 1-0	1-0	11	Darikwa [38]	6094
27	25	A	Peterborough U	W 5-1	2-0	11	Jefferies [12], Bayliss [33], Draper (pen) [55], Hayes (og) [66], Collins [82]	10,014
28	28	H	Blackpool	L 0-2	0-1	11		7517
29	Feb 1	A	Wigan Ath	D 1-1	0-1	12	Collins [88]	8606
30	8	H	Cambridge U	D 1-1	1-1	11	Draper [17]	8606
31	15	A	Leyton Orient	L 2-3	1-2	13	Montsma [45], Collins [75]	7967
32	18	A	Mansfield T	W 3-0	1-0	10	O'Connor [9], Clucas [83], Jefferies [89]	8326
33	22	H	Burton Alb	L 0-1	0-0	13		8507
34	Mar 1	A	Barnsley	L 3-4	0-2	13	Darikwa [67], Hackett-Fairchild [84], Makama [90]	11,914
35	4	H	Crawley T	W 4-1	3-1	12	Collins [14], Makama [24], Jefferies [32], Gardner [88]	7253
36	8	A	Birmingham C	L 0-1	0-0	13		26,210
37	15	H	Bristol R	W 5-0	1-0	12	Makama 3 [31, 65, 81], Bayliss [49], Collins [52]	8506
38	22	A	Exeter C	D 0-0	0-0	12		8971
39	29	A	Wycombe W	L 0-1	0-0	12		4939
40	Apr 1	H	Huddersfield T	W 1-0	0-0	12	Hackett-Fairchild [35]	8755
41	5	A	Charlton Ath	D 2-2	1-0	11	Collins 2 [17, 49]	15,611
42	12	H	Shrewsbury T	D 1-1	1-1	12	Bayliss [4]	9282
43	18	A	Reading	W 1-0	0-0	11	Collins [65]	16,388
44	21	H	Bolton W	W 4-2	2-2	11	Ring [10], Collins 2 (1 pen) [18 ipl, 53], Hackett-Fairchild [61]	10,240
45	26	A	Stockport Co	L 2-3	2-0	11	House [24], Ring [43]	9717
46	May 3	H	Wrexham	L 0-2	0-0	11		10,347

Final League Position: 11

GOALSCORERS

League (64): Collins 10 (1 pen), Makama 7, House 6, Cadamarteri 5, Darikwa 5, Draper 4 (1 pen), Hackett-Fairchild 4, Bayliss 3, Jefferies 3, O'Connor 3, Ring 3, Hamer 2, Jackson 2, Moylan 2 (1 pen), Clucas 1, Gardner 1, Montsma 1, Roughan 1, own goal 1.
FA Cup (9): Makama 3 (1 pen), Moylan 2, McGrandles 1, O'Connor 1, Ring 1, own goal 1.
Carabao Cup (1): Makama 1 (1 pen).
Vertu Trophy (8): Cadamarteri 3, Draper 1, McKiernan 1, Moylan 1, Okoro 1, Street 1.

Wickens G 36	Jackson A 26 + 1	O'Connor P 38 + 1	Roughan S 46	Darikwa T 44	Erhahon E 28 + 3	McKiernan J 2 + 10	Bayliss T 22 + 12	Duffy D 3 + 5	Makama J 29 + 9	House B 34 + 7	Moylan J 11 + 17	Draper F 10 + 28	Street R — + 6	Hamer T 14 + 9	McGrandles C 36 + 6	Jefferies D 24 + 10	Cadamarteri B 13 + 10	Ring E 9 + 15	Jeacock Z 10 + 1	Hamilton E 16 + 16	Hackett-Fairchild R 23 + 10	Montsma L 12 + 4	Collins J 14 + 6	Gardner J 4 + 7	Clucas S 2 + 6	Okoro Z — + 2	Match No.
1	2	3	4	5	6	7¹	8	9	10³	11²	12	13	14														1
1	2³	3	4	6	5	7¹	8	9	11²	10⁴	12	13	15	14													2
1	2	3	4	6	5	15	8⁴		11⁵	10¹	14	12	16	13	7³	9²											3
1	2	3¹	4	6	5	13	8²		11¹	10³	7	12		15		9⁴	14										4
1⁴	3		4	6	5		7³		11²	10⁶	12	16		2	8	9¹	13	14	15								5
	2	3	4	6	5	13	8³		12	10	14	16			7²	9⁴	11¹	15	1								6
1	2	3	4	6	5	16	14		11²	10¹	7³	12⁵		15	8		13	9⁴									7
1	2	3	4	6	5	15	12		11⁵		7³	13		14	8¹	9⁴	10²	16									8
1		3	4	6	5		7¹		11²		12	10⁴		2	8	9³	13	14		15							9
1		3	5	2⁶	6				9⁴	8²12				4	7	10³	11¹	14		13	15	16					10
1		3	4	9	7	14			11	15	10²			14	7	8	10²			12	9³	2					11
1		3	4	6	5¹				11⁴	15	13			14	7	8	10²			12	9³	2					12
1		3	4	6					14	11³	13	15		2¹	5	8²	10⁴	16		7	9⁵	12					13
1		3	4	6		15			10²	11³	12	14			5	7¹	13			8⁴	9	2					14
1		3¹	4	6	12	15			14	13	11³	9			5	7	10²			8⁴		2					15
1		3	4	6	5	15			9¹	11²	10⁶	8⁵		16	7³		13	12		14		2					16
1		4	3	2	7	14			11³		9	12	15		6⁴	8	10¹	5⁴		13							17
1	3¹	4	5	2	7				9⁴	10³	11⁵	14			8	12	15	16		6²13							18
1	3	4		5					10		8³	11²			7	12	13	6¹		14	9	2					19
1		4	5	2	7				9¹	10³		13			6	14	11²			12	8	3					20
1		4	5	2	7		15		8³	9¹	12	13			6⁵		11²14			16	10⁴	3					21
1		4	5	3	6	12	14		8¹	9⁵	13	16	15		7²	2³	11⁴				10						22
1	14	4	5⁵	7¶		12			15	10⁴	13				6	16	11			8³	9²	2					23
1	3	4	5	2			13	14	8	9²	10³	12			6		11¹			7							24
1		4	5	2	8		6¹	14	10²		12	13			7		11				9³	3					25
	2	3	4	6	5		12		14	10	8¹	11³			7	13			1		9²						26
	2	3⁵	4	6	5		7¹		15	10⁴		11²			8	9³			1	13	14	16	12				27
	2	3	4	6⁴	5		8		15	10¹		11⁵			7³	9²		16	1	14	13		12				28
	2	3	4	6⁵	5¹		8		10³	14		15			12	9²		16	1	7⁴	13		11				29
	2	3	4	6²			7		12	14		10¹			5	13			1	8³	9		11⁴	15¶			30
		4	5				13		6	10³		11¹			7	2			1	14	9	3	12		8²		31
	2	3	4	6			7²		10³	8⁴		16			5	12		14	1	15	9¹		11⁵		13		32
	2	3	4	6¹			12		10³	7⁴		14			5	9			1	15	13		11		8²		33
	3		4	6⁵			8		13	10¹		11²		16	5⁴	9			1	7¹	12	2	14	15			34
1	4		5	2			6³		8¹	12				3	7	10²15				16	9⁴		11⁵13	14			35
1	2⁵		4	6⁴			7²		10¹	8		14		16	5	9					13		11³15	12			36
1		4	5	2			6³		8⁵	12				3	7	10²		13		14	9⁴		11¹15	16			37
1		4	5	2			7²		8	14				3	6	10¹		12			9³		11		13		38
1	4¶	5	2³				6⁴		8	11²				3	7⁵	12		10¹		16	9		13	14	15		39
1	4		5	2			7⁴		8	13		12		3	15	14				6	9²		11¹	10³			40
1	4		5	2			13		10¹	9⁵		16		3	6	12³		8²		7	14	15	11⁴				41
1	4		5	2	13		7			12		15		16	6³			8¹		9	3⁵	11⁴	10²			14	42
1	4		5	2	13		7²			9⁴		11³		3	15			12		6	8		14	10¹			43
1	4	16	5	2	6¹		14		9⁴	13	15			3	12			10²		7	8³		11⁵				44
1	4	3	5	2	6		12		9⁴	13	15			14			10¹			7⁵	8²		11³	16			45
1		4	5	2	7⁵		13		9²	12	15			3	14					6⁴	8³		11	10¹		16	46

FA Cup

First Round	Chesham U	(a)	4-0
Second Round	Crawley T	(a)	4-3
Third Round	Birmingham C	(a)	1-2

Carabao Cup

First Round	Harrogate T	(h)	1-2

Vertu Trophy

Group G (N)	Chesterfield	(h)	0-1
Group G (N)	Grimsby T	(a)	2-1
Group G (N)	Manchester C U21	(h)	5-0
Second Round	Morecambe	(a)	1-0
Third Round	Bolton W	(h)	0-1

LIVERPOOL

FOUNDATION

But for a dispute between Everton FC and their landlord at Anfield in 1892, there may never have been a Liverpool club. This dispute persuaded the majority of Evertonians to quit Anfield for Goodison Park, leaving the landlord, Mr John Houlding, to form a new club. He originally tried to retain the name 'Everton' but when this failed, he founded Liverpool Association FC on 15 March 1892.

Anfield Stadium, Anfield Road, Anfield, Liverpool L4 0TH.

Telephone: (0151) 263 2361.

Ticket Office: (0843) 170 5000.

Website: www.liverpoolfc.com

Email: customerservices@liverpoolfc.com

Ground Capacity: 61,276.

Record Attendance: 61,905 v Wolverhampton W, FA Cup 4th rd, 2 February 1952.

Pitch Measurements: 101m × 68m (110.5yd × 74.5yd).

Chairman: Tom Werner.

Chief Executive: Billy Hogan.

Manager: Arne Slot.

Assistant Manager: Sipke Hulshoff.

Colours: Red shirts with thin yellow stripes, red shorts with yellow trim, red socks with yellow trim.

Year Formed: 1892.

Turned Professional: 1892.

Club Nicknames: 'The Reds'; 'Pool'.

Ground: 1892, Anfield.

First Football League Game: 2 September 1893, Division 2, v Middlesbrough Ironopolis (a) W 2–0 – McOwen; Hannah, McLean; Henderson, McQue (1), McBride; Gordon, McVean (1), Matt McQueen, Stott, Hugh McQueen.

Record League Victory: 10–1 v Rotherham T, Division 2, 18 February 1896 – Storer; Goldie, Wilkie; McCartney, McQue, Holmes; McVean (3), Ross (2), Allan (4), Becton (1), Bradshaw.

HONOURS

League Champions: Premier League – 2019–20, 2024–25; Division 1 – 1900–01, 1905–06, 1921–22, 1922–23, 1946–47, 1963–64, 1965–66, 1972–73, 1975–76, 1976–77, 1978–79, 1979–80, 1981–82, 1982–83, 1983–84, 1985–86, 1987–88, 1989–90; Division 2 – 1893–94, 1895–96, 1904–05, 1961–62.
Runners-up: Premier League – 2001–02, 2008–09, 2013–14, 2018–19, 2021–22; Division 1 – 1898–99, 1909–10, 1968–69, 1973–74, 1974–75, 1977–78, 1984–85, 1986–87, 1988–89, 1990–91.
FA Cup Winners: 1965, 1974, 1986, 1989, 1992, 2001, 2006, 2022.
Runners-up: 1914, 1950, 1971, 1977, 1988, 1996, 2012.
League Cup Winners: 1981, 1982, 1983, 1984, 1995, 2001, 2003, 2012, 2022, 2024.
Runners-up: 1978, 1987, 2005, 2016, 2025.
League Super Cup Winners: 1986.

European Competitions
European Cup: 1964–65 *(sf)*, 1966–67, 1973–74, 1976–77 *(winners)*, 1977–78 *(winners)*, 1978–79, 1979–80, 1980–81 *(winners)*, 1981–82 *(qf)*, 1982–83 *(qf)*, 1983–84 *(winners)*, 1984–85 *(runners-up)*.
Champions League: 2001–02 *(qf)*, 2002–03, 2004–05 *(winners)*, 2005–06, 2006–07 *(runners-up)*, 2007–08 *(sf)*, 2008–09 *(qf)*, 2009–10, 2014–15, 2017–18 *(runners-up)*, 2018–19 *(winners)*, 2019–20, 2020–21 *(qf)*, 2021–22 *(runners-up)*, 2022–23, 2024–25.
Fairs Cup: 1967–68, 1968–69, 1969–70, 1970–71 *(sf)*.
UEFA Cup: 1972–73 *(winners)*, 1975–76 *(winners)*, 1991–92 *(qf)*, 1995–96, 1997–98, 1998–99, 2000–01 *(winners)*, 2002–03 *(qf)*, 2003–04.
Europa League: 2009–10 *(sf)*, 2010–11, 2012–13, 2014–15, 2015–16 *(runners-up)*, 2023–24 *(qf)*.
European Cup-Winners' Cup: 1965–66 *(runners-up)*, 1971–72, 1974–75, 1992–93, 1996–97 *(sf)*.
Super Cup: 1977 *(winners)*, 1978, 1984, 2001 *(winners)*, 2005 *(winners)*, 2019 *(winners)*.
World Club Championship: 1981, 1984.
FIFA Club World Cup: 2005, 2019 *(winners)*.

FOOTBALL YEARBOOK FACT FILE

South African Berry Nieuwenhuys made over 250 appearances for Liverpool between 1933 and 1947. He was talented at many sports, notably golf. Towards the end of his football career he was appointed as the assistant professional at West Derby Golf Club on Merseyside, and in July 1946 he achieved a top-12 placing in the Irish Open. He was elected to membership of the Professional Golfers Association while still a Liverpool player.

Record Cup Victory: 11–0 v Stromsgodset Drammen, ECWC 1st rd 1st leg, 17 September 1974 – Clemence; Smith (1), Lindsay (1p), Thompson (2), Cormack (1), Hughes (1), Boersma (2), Hall, Heighway (1), Kennedy (1), Callaghan (1).

Record Defeat: 1–9 v Birmingham C, Division 2, 11 December 1954.

Most League Points (2 for a win): 68, Division 1, 1978–79.

Most League Points (3 for a win): 99, Premier League, 2019–20.

Most League Goals: 106, Division 2, 1895–96.

Highest League Scorer in Season: Roger Hunt, 41, Division 2, 1961–62.

Most League Goals in Total Aggregate: Roger Hunt, 245, 1959–69.

Most League Goals in One Match: 5, Andy McGuigan v Stoke C, Division 1, 4 January 1902; 5, John Evans v Bristol R, Division 2, 15 September 1954; 5, Ian Rush v Luton T, Division 1, 29 October 1983.

Most Capped Player: Steven Gerrard, 114, England.

Most League Appearances: Ian Callaghan, 640, 1960–78.

Youngest League Player: Jack Robinson, 16 years 250 days v Hull C, 9 May 2010.

MANAGERS
W. E. Barclay 1892–96
Tom Watson 1896–1915
David Ashworth 1920–23
Matt McQueen 1923–28
George Patterson 1928–36
(continued as Secretary)
George Kay 1936–51
Don Welsh 1951–56
Phil Taylor 1956–59
Bill Shankly 1959–74
Bob Paisley 1974–83
Joe Fagan 1983–85
Kenny Dalglish 1985–91
Graeme Souness 1991–94
Roy Evans 1994–98
(then Joint Manager)
Gerard Houllier 1998–2004
Rafael Benitez 2004–10
Roy Hodgson 2010–11
Kenny Dalglish 2011–12
Brendan Rodgers 2012–15
Jürgen Klopp 2015–24
Arne Slot June 2024–

Record Transfer Fee Received: £142,000,000 from Barcelona for Philippe Coutinho, January 2018.

Record Transfer Fee Paid: £100,000,000 (potentially rising to £116,000,000) to Bayer Leverkusen for Florian Wirtz, June 2025.

Football League Record: 1893 Elected to Division 2; 1893–94 Division 2; 1894–95 Division 1; 1895–96 Division 2; 1896–1904 Division 1; 1904–05 Division 2; 1905–54 Division 1; 1954–62 Division 2; 1962–92 Division 1; 1992– Premier League.

LATEST SEQUENCES

Longest Sequence of League Wins: 18, 27.10.2019 – 24.2.2020.

Longest Sequence of League Defeats: 9, 29.4.1899 – 14.10.1899.

Longest Sequence of League Draws: 6, 19.2.1975 – 19.3.1975.

Longest Sequence of Unbeaten League Matches: 44, 12.1.2019 – 24.2.2020.

Longest Sequence Without a League Win: 14, 12.12.1953 – 20.3.1954.

Successive Scoring Runs: 36 from 10.3.2019.

Successive Non-scoring Runs: 5 from 21.4.2000.

TEN YEAR LEAGUE RECORD

		P	W	D	L	F	A	Pts	Pos
2015-16	PR Lge	38	16	12	10	63	50	60	8
2016-17	PR Lge	38	22	10	6	78	42	76	4
2017-18	PR Lge	38	21	12	5	84	38	75	4
2018-19	PR Lge	38	30	7	1	89	22	97	2
2019-20	PR Lge	38	32	3	3	85	33	99	1
2020-21	PR Lge	38	20	9	9	68	42	69	3
2021-22	PR Lge	38	28	8	2	94	26	92	2
2022-23	PR Lge	38	19	10	9	75	47	67	5
2023-24	PR Lge	38	24	10	4	86	41	82	3
2024-25	PR Lge	38	25	9	4	86	41	84	1

DID YOU KNOW ?

Liverpool's opening game of the 1906–07 season against Stoke was played during a heatwave. The temperature in the sun was said to have been 104 degrees Fahrenheit (39°C) around kick-off time, although later in the game a light breeze appeared. The only concession to the heat was that the referee allowed an extended half-time break of 15 minutes. The Reds won the game 1-0 with a goal from Joe Hewitt.

LIVERPOOL – PREMIER LEAGUE 2024–25 LEAGUE RECORD

Match No.	Date	Venue	Opponents	Result	H/T Score	Lg Pos.	Goalscorers	Attendance
1	Aug 17	A	Ipswich T	W 2-0	0-0	2	Jota [60], Salah [65]	30,014
2	25	H	Brentford	W 2-0	1-0	3	Diaz [13], Salah [70]	60,107
3	Sept 1	A	Manchester U	W 3-0	2-0	2	Diaz 2 [35, 42], Salah [56]	73,738
4	14	H	Nottingham F	L 0-1	0-0	2		60,344
5	21	H	Bournemouth	W 3-0	3-0	1	Diaz 2 [26, 28], Nunez [37]	60,347
6	28	A	Wolverhampton W	W 2-1	1-0	1	Konate [45], Salah (pen) [61]	31,413
7	Oct 5	A	Crystal Palace	W 1-0	1-0	1	Jota [9]	25,185
8	20	H	Chelsea	W 2-1	1-0	1	Salah (pen) [29], Jones [51]	60,277
9	27	A	Arsenal	D 2-2	1-2	2	van Dijk [18], Salah [81]	60,383
10	Nov 2	H	Brighton & HA	W 2-1	0-1	1	Gakpo [70], Salah [72]	60,331
11	9	H	Aston Villa	W 2-0	1-0	1	Nunez [20], Salah [84]	60,292
12	24	A	Southampton	W 3-2	1-1	1	Szoboszlai [30], Salah 2 (1 pen) [65, 83 (p)]	31,278
13	Dec 1	H	Manchester C	W 2-0	1-0	1	Gakpo [12], Salah (pen) [78]	60,248
14	4	A	Newcastle U	D 3-3	0-1	1	Jones [50], Salah 2 [68, 83]	52,237
15	14	H	Fulham	D 2-2	0-1	1	Gakpo [47], Jota [86]	60,333
16	22	A	Tottenham H	W 6-3	3-1	1	Diaz 2 [23, 85], Mac Allister [36], Szoboszlai [45], Salah 2 [54, 61]	61,439
17	26	H	Leicester C	W 3-1	1-1	1	Gakpo [45], Jones [48], Salah [82]	60,300
18	29	H	West Ham U	W 5-0	3-0	1	Diaz [30], Gakpo [40], Salah [44], Alexander-Arnold [54], Jota [84]	62,476
19	Jan 5	A	Manchester U	D 2-2	0-0	1	Gakpo [59], Salah (pen) [70]	60,275
20	14	A	Nottingham F	D 1-1	0-1	1	Jota [66]	30,249
21	18	A	Brentford	W 2-0	0-0	1	Nunez 2 [90, 90]	17,215
22	25	H	Ipswich T	W 4-1	3-0	1	Szoboszlai [11], Salah [35], Gakpo 2 [44, 65]	60,420
23	Feb 1	A	Bournemouth	W 2-0	1-0	1	Salah 2 (1 pen) [30 (p), 75]	11,239
24	12	A	Everton	D 2-2	1-1	1	Mac Allister [16], Salah [73]	39,280
25	16	H	Wolverhampton W	W 2-1	2-0	1	Diaz [15], Salah (pen) [37]	60,401
26	19	A	Aston Villa	D 2-2	1-2	1	Salah [29], Alexander-Arnold [61]	41,910
27	23	A	Manchester C	W 2-0	2-0	1	Salah [14], Szoboszlai [37]	52,803
28	26	H	Newcastle U	W 2-0	1-0	1	Szoboszlai [11], Mac Allister [63]	60,374
29	Mar 8	H	Southampton	W 3-1	0-1	1	Nunez [51], Salah 2 (2 pens) [55, 88]	60,399
30	Apr 2	A	Everton	W 1-0	0-0	1	Jota [57]	60,331
31	6	A	Fulham	L 2-3	1-3	1	Mac Allister [14], Diaz [72]	27,770
32	13	H	West Ham U	W 2-1	1-0	1	Diaz [18], van Dijk [89]	60,376
33	20	A	Leicester C	W 1-0	0-0	1	Alexander-Arnold [76]	30,402
34	27	H	Tottenham H	W 5-1	3-1	1	Diaz [16], Mac Allister [24], Gakpo [34], Salah [63], Udogie (og) [69]	60,415
35	May 4	A	Chelsea	L 1-3	0-1	1	van Dijk [85]	39,829
36	11	H	Arsenal	D 2-2	2-0	1	Gakpo [20], Diaz [21]	60,324
37	19	A	Brighton & HA	L 2-3	2-1	1	Elliott [9], Szoboszlai [45]	31,611
38	25	H	Crystal Palace	D 1-1	0-1	1	Salah [84]	60,382

Final League Position: 1

GOALSCORERS

League (86): Salah 29 (9 pens), Diaz 13, Gakpo 10, Jota 6, Szoboszlai 6, Mac Allister 5, Nunez 5, Alexander-Arnold 3, Jones 3, van Dijk 3, Elliott 1, Konate 1, own goal 1.
FA Cup (4): Alexander-Arnold 1, Chiesa 1, Danns 1, Jota 1.
Carabao Cup (15): Gakpo 5, Jota 2, Salah 2 (1 pen), Chiesa 1, Diaz 1, Elliott 1, Nunez 1, Szoboszlai 1, van Dijk 1.
(Liverpool U21) Vertu Trophy (2): Corness 1 (1 pen), Norris 1.
Champions League (18): Diaz 3, Elliott 3, Gakpo 3 (1 pen), Salah 3 (1 pen), Mac Allister 2, Konate 1, Nunez 1, Szoboszlai 1, van Dijk 1.

Alisson R 28	Alexander-Arnold T 28+5	Quansah J 4+9	van Dijk V 37	Robertson A 29+4	Gravenberch R 37	Mac Allister A 30+5	Salah M 38	Szoboszlai D 29+7	Diaz L 28+8	Jota D 14+12	Konate I 30+1	Bradley C 7+12	Tsimikas K 9+9	Gakpo C 23+12	Nunez D 8+22	Elliott H 2+16	Endo W 1+19	Jones C 19+14	Kelleher C 10	Chiesa F 1+5	Gomez J 6+3	Jaros V —+1	Danns J —+1	Match No.
1	2^2	3^1	4	5^3	6	7	8	9	10	11^4	12	13	14	15										1
1	2^3		4	5	6^5	7	8^4	9	10^1	11^2	3	14		13	12	15	16							2
1	2^2		4	5^4	6	7	8	9	10^1	11^3	3	13	15	12	14									3
1	2		4	5^5	6	7^2	8	9	10^5	11^1	3^4	12	16	14	13			15						4
	2		4	5	6	7	8	9^1	10^2		3			14	11^3			12	1	13				5
1	2		4	5^3	6	7	8	9^2	10^1	11^1	3			13				12		14				6
1^3	2		4	15	6	7^1	8^2	12	13	11	3		5^4	10			16	9^6			14			7
	2^4		4	5	6	14	8	9	13	11^1	3			10^2	12			7^3	1	15				8
	2		4	5^2	6	7^3	8	12	10^1		3		13	14	11	15		9^4	1					9
	2		4		6	7^2	8^5	9^3	14		3^1	16	5	10	11^4			15	13	1	12			10
	2^1		4		5	6	7^4	8	13	10	3	12			14	11^2		15	9^3	1				11
			4	5	6	13	8	9	12		3	2			10^1	11^3		14	7^2	1				12
	2^2	13	4	5	6	7	8^3	9	11^4			10^1	12	15				14	1	3				13
	14	2	4	5	6^1	7	8	12	13			10^3	11					9	1	3^2				14
1	2^3	13	4	5^4	7		9	8^4	10	14		11^1	12	15	6^2			3						15
1	2		4	5	6	7^1	8^3	9	11^4	12		10^2	15	14	13			3						16
1	2		4	5^3	6^4	7^5	8	12	13		14	10	11^2	16	15	9^1		3						17
1	2	12	4	5^5	6^2	7	8		11	14		16	10^3		15	13	9^4	3^1						18
1	2^4		4	5	6	7	8		11^1	13	3	14		10^2	12	15		9^2						19
1	2		4	5^1	6	7	8	9	11^3	13	3^2		12	10				14						20
1	2		4	13	6	7^4	8	9^3	11^2		3		5^1	10^6	12	14		15		16				21
1	2		4	5	6^3	7^4	8	9^1	11^5		3			10^2	13	12	14			16			15	22
1	2^2		4	5	6	7^1	8^4	9	11		3	13		10^3	14			15		12				23
1	12		4	5^3	6^2	7	8	9	11^5	16	3	2^1	15	10^4	14			13^4						24
1	2^2	12	4	5	6	7	8	9	10^4	11^3	3^1	13			14	15								25
1	2^1	15	4	5	6	7^3	8	9	14	11^2	3	12^4			13			10						26
1	2^5	16	4	5^2	6	7	8^4	10	9^3			13	14	15	12	11^1								27
1	2^3	13	4		6^2	7^4	8	9	10^5	11^1	3		5	12	15	14	16							28
1	2	17	4	14	7^5	13	9	6^3	11	15	3		5^1	10^4	12	16	8^2							29
			4	5	6	7	8	8^3	9	10^2	11^1	3			13	12		14	2	1				30
			4	5^3	6	7	8	9^1	13	11^3	3^4	14		10^2	15	12		2	1	16				31
1		15	4	13	6	7	8	9^5	14	10	11^2	3	2^9	5^1	12			16	9^4					32
1	14		4		6	7	8	9^3	11^4	12	3	2^2	5	10^1		13		15						33
1	2^4		4	5	6	7^5	8	9	11^3	13	3			10^2	16	14	15	12						34
1	2^1	3	4			15	8	14		11^2		12	5^5	10	13	9^4	6^3	7		16				35
1	14		4	5	6^5	12	8	9	11^4	15	3	2^2		10^1	13	16				7^3				36
1		4			6		8	7^3	12		3	2^4	5	10^1	13	9	15	14		11^2				37
1	12		4	5^5	6^4		8	9^2	11^4	14	3^3	2^1		10	13	16	15	7						38

FA Cup

Third Round	Accrington S	(h)	4-0
Fourth Round	Plymouth Arg	(a)	0-1

Carabao Cup

Third Round	West Ham U	(h)	5-1
Fourth Round	Brighton & HA	(a)	3-2
Quarter-Final	Southampton	(a)	2-1
Semi-Final 1st leg	Tottenham H	(a)	0-1
Semi-Final 2nd leg	Tottenham H	(h)	4-0
Final	Newcastle U	(Wembley)	1-2

Vertu Trophy (Liverpool U21)

Group E (N)	Crewe Alex	(a)	1-5
Group E (N)	Harrogate T	(a)	1-1

Harrogate T won 4-2 on penalties.

Group E (N)	Blackpool	(a)	0-0

Liverpool U21 won 8-7 on penalties.

Champions League

League game	AC Milan	(a)	3-1
League game	Bologna	(h)	2-0
League game	RB Leipzig	(a)	1-0
League game	Bayer Leverkusen	(h)	4-0
League game	Real Madrid	(h)	2-0
League game	Girona	(a)	1-0
League game	Lille	(h)	2-1
League game	PSV Eindhoven	(a)	2-3
Round of 16 1st leg	Paris Saint-Germain	(a)	1-0
Round of 16 2nd leg	Paris Saint-Germain	(h)	0-1

aet; Paris Saint-Germain won 4-1 on penalties.

LUTON TOWN

FOUNDATION

Formed by an amalgamation of two leading local clubs, Wanderers and Excelsior a works team, at a meeting in Luton Town Hall in April 1885. The Wanderers had three months earlier changed their name to Luton Town Wanderers and did not take too kindly to the formation of another Town club but were talked around at this meeting. Wanderers had already appeared in the FA Cup and the new club entered in its inaugural season.

Kenilworth Road Stadium, 1 Maple Road, Luton, Bedfordshire LU4 8AW.

Telephone: (01582) 411 622.

Ticket Office: (01582) 416 976.

Website: www.lutontown.co.uk

Email: info@lutontown.co.uk

Ground Capacity: 10,640.

Record Attendance: 30,069 v Blackpool, FA Cup 6th rd replay, 4 March 1959.

Pitch Measurements: 100.6m × 65.8m (110yd × 72yd).

Chairman: David Wilkinson.

Chief Executive: Gary Sweet.

Manager: Matt Bloomfield.

Assistant Manager: Richard Thomas.

Colours: Orange shirts with white patterned stripe and navy blue trim, navy blue shorts with white trim, orange socks with black and white trim.

Year Formed: 1885.

Turned Professional: 1890. *Ltd Co.:* 1897.

Club Nickname: 'The Hatters'.

Grounds: 1885, Excelsior, Dallow Lane; 1897, Dunstable Road; 1905, Kenilworth Road.

First Football League Game: 4 September 1897, Division 2, v Leicester Fosse (a) D 1–1 – Williams; McCartney, McEwen; Davies, Stewart, Docherty; Gallacher, Coupar, Birch, McInnes, Ekins (1).

Record League Victory: 12–0 v Bristol R, Division 3 (S), 13 April 1936 – Dolman; Mackey, Smith; Finlayson, Nelson, Godfrey; Rich, Martin (1), Payne (10), Roberts (1), Stephenson.

Record Cup Victory: 9–0 v Clapton, FA Cup 1st rd (replay after abandoned game), 30 November 1927 – Abbott; Kingham, Graham; Black, Rennie, Fraser; Pointon, Yardley (4), Reid (2), Woods (1), Dennis (2).

Record Defeat: 0–9 v Small Heath, Division 2, 12 November 1898.

Most League Points (2 for a win): 66, Division 4, 1967–68.

Most League Points (3 for a win): 98, FL 1 2004–05.

HONOURS

League Champions: Division 2 – 1981–82; FL 1 – 2004–05, 2018–19; Division 3S – 1936–37; Division 4 – 1967–68; Football Conference – 2013–14.
Runners-up: FL 2 – 2017–18; Division 2 – 1954–55, 1973–74; Division 3 – 1969–70; Division 3S – 1935–36; Third Division – 2001–02; National League 2009–10.
FA Cup: Runners-up: 1959.
League Cup Winners: 1988.
Runners-up: 1989.
League Trophy Winners: 2009.
Full Members' Cup: Runners-up: 1988.

FOOTBALL YEARBOOK FACT FILE

Luton Town had the unique experience of winning a Wembley final and being relegated out of the Football League in the same season. The Hatters received a 30-point deduction at the start of the 2008–09 season, making relegation almost inevitable. However, they battled away in the Johnstone's Paint Trophy to reach the final against Scunthorpe United. Around 40,000 Luton fans turned out to see them win 3-2 thanks to an extra-time goal from Claude Gnakpa.

Most League Goals: 103, Division 3 (S), 1936–37.

Highest League Scorer in Season: Joe Payne, 55, Division 3 (S), 1936–37.

Most League Goals in Total Aggregate: Gordon Turner, 243, 1949–64.

Most League Goals in One Match: 10, Joe Payne v Bristol R, Division 3 (S), 13 April 1936.

Most Capped Player: Mal Donaghy, 58 (91), Northern Ireland.

Most League Appearances: Bob Morton, 495, 1948–64.

Youngest League Player: Mike O'Hara, 16 years 32 days v Stoke C, 1 October 1960.

Record Transfer Fee Received: £8,000,000 from Ipswich T for Chiedozie Ogbene, August 2024.

Record Transfer Fee Paid: £10,000,000 to Cardiff C for Mark McGuinness, August 2024.

Football League Record: 1897 Elected to Division 2; 1897–1900 Division 2; 1900 Failed re-election; 1920 Re-elected to Division 3; 1920–21 Division 3; 1921–37 Division 3 (S); 1937–55 Division 2; 1955–60 Division 1; 1960–63 Division 2; 1963–65 Division 3; 1965–68 Division 4; 1968–70 Division 3; 1970–74 Division 2; 1974–75 Division 1; 1975–82 Division 2; 1982–92 Division 1; 1992–96 First Division; 1996–2001 Second Division; 2001–02 Third Division; 2002–04 Second Division; 2004–05 FL 1; 2005–07 FL C; 2007–08 FL 1; 2008–09 FL 2; 2009–14 Football Conference; 2014–18 FL 2; 2018–19 FL 1; 2019–23 FL C; 2023–24 Premier League; 2024–25 FL C; 2025– FL 1.

LATEST SEQUENCES

Longest Sequence of League Wins: 12, 19.2.2002 – 6.4.2002.

Longest Sequence of League Defeats: 8, 11.11.1899 – 6.1.1900.

Longest Sequence of League Draws: 5, 28.8.1971 – 18.9.1971.

Longest Sequence of Unbeaten League Matches: 28, 20.10.2018 – 6.4.2019.

Longest Sequence Without a League Win: 16, 9.9.1964 – 6.11.1964.

Successive Scoring Runs: 25 from 24.10.1931.

Successive Non-scoring Runs: 5 from 10.4.1973.

MANAGERS

Charlie Green 1901–28
(Secretary-Manager)
George Thomson 1925
John McCartney 1927–29
George Kay 1929–31
Harold Wightman 1931–35
Ted Liddell 1936–38
Neil McBain 1938–39
George Martin 1939–47
Dally Duncan 1947–58
Syd Owen 1959–60
Sam Bartram 1960–62
Bill Harvey 1962–64
George Martin 1965–66
Allan Brown 1966–68
Alec Stock 1968–72
Harry Haslam 1972–78
David Pleat 1978–86
John Moore 1986–87
Ray Harford 1987–89
Jim Ryan 1990–91
David Pleat 1991–95
Terry Westley 1995
Lennie Lawrence 1995–2000
Ricky Hill 2000
Lil Fuccillo 2000
Joe Kinnear 2001–03
Mike Newell 2003–07
Kevin Blackwell 2007–08
Mick Harford 2008–09
Richard Money 2009–11
Gary Brabin 2011–12
Paul Buckle 2012–13
John Still 2013–15
Nathan Jones 2016–19
Mick Harford 2019
(caretaker)
Graeme Jones 2019–20
Nathan Jones 2020–22
Rob Edwards 2022–25
Matt Bloomfield January 2025–

TEN YEAR LEAGUE RECORD

		P	W	D	L	F	A	Pts	Pos
2015-16	FL 2	46	19	9	18	63	61	66	11
2016-17	FL 2	46	20	17	9	70	43	77	4
2017-18	FL 2	46	25	13	8	94	46	88	2
2018-19	FL 1	46	27	13	6	90	42	94	1
2019-20	FL C	46	14	9	23	54	82	51	19
2020-21	FL C	46	17	11	18	41	52	62	12
2021-22	FL C	46	21	12	13	63	55	75	6
2022-23	FL C	46	21	17	8	57	39	80	3
2023-24	PR Lge	38	6	8	24	52	85	26	18
2024-25	FL C	46	13	10	23	45	69	49	22

DID YOU KNOW ?

Inside-forward George Martin played over 100 games for Luton Town between 1933 and 1937 before becoming trainer and then manager of the Hatters. Martin was a man of many talents. In his earlier days he was recognised as an accomplished sculptor and he produced a bust of Julius Caesar that won a prize at an Edinburgh exhibition, while he was also a tenor singer who passed an audition for BBC Radio.

LUTON TOWN – SKY BET CHAMPIONSHIP 2024–25 LEAGUE RECORD

Match No.	Date	Venue	Opponents	Result	H/T Score	Lg Pos.	Goalscorers	Attendance
1	Aug 12	H	Burnley	L 1-4	0-2	23	Chong [55]	11,777
2	17	A	Portsmouth	D 0-0	0-0	20		20,293
3	24	A	Preston NE	L 0-1	0-1	23		15,245
4	30	H	QPR	L 1-2	1-0	23	Dunne (og) [18]	11,798
5	Sept 14	A	Millwall	W 1-0	1-0	19	Mengi [10]	14,804
6	21	H	Sheffield Wed	W 2-1	0-0	15	Morris 2 (1 pen) [77 (p), 88]	11,805
7	27	A	Plymouth Arg	L 1-3	0-1	16	Moses [70]	16,616
8	Oct 1	H	Oxford U	D 2-2	2-1	18	Clark [10], Krauss [37]	11,397
9	5	A	Sheffield U	L 0-2	0-1	21		27,925
10	19	H	Watford	W 3-0	1-0	17	Clark [11], Morris [47], Brown [90]	11,758
11	23	H	Sunderland	L 1-2	0-0	19	Adebayo [63]	11,332
12	26	A	Coventry C	L 2-3	2-0	22	Morris (pen) [15], Adebayo [37]	26,409
13	Nov 1	H	WBA	D 1-1	0-1	20	Chong [60]	11,665
14	6	H	Cardiff C	W 1-0	0-0	19	Brown [57]	10,656
15	9	A	Middlesbrough	L 1-5	0-2	21	Clark [77]	23,692
16	23	H	Hull C	W 1-0	1-0	16	McGuinness [33]	11,386
17	27	A	Leeds U	L 0-3	0-2	16		35,340
18	30	A	Norwich C	L 2-4	1-2	19	Adebayo [20], Brown [48]	26,719
19	Dec 7	A	Swansea C	D 1-1	1-0	18	Adebayo [17]	11,264
20	10	H	Stoke C	W 2-1	1-1	14	Morris [24], Adebayo [90]	10,537
21	14	A	Blackburn R	L 0-2	0-2	19		13,857
22	20	H	Derby Co	W 2-1	0-0	14	Holmes [89], Morris [90]	11,667
23	26	A	Bristol C	L 0-1	0-0	18		21,828
24	29	A	Swansea C	L 1-2	1-1	19	Morris [5]	16,414
25	Jan 1	H	Norwich C	L 0-1	0-0	20		11,828
26	6	A	QPR	L 1-2	1-1	20	McGuinness [45]	14,025
27	18	H	Preston NE	D 0-0	0-0	23		11,540
28	21	A	Oxford U	L 2-3	2-1	23	Krauss [11], McGuinness [26]	11,035
29	25	H	Millwall	L 0-1	0-0	23		11,418
30	Feb 1	A	Sheffield Wed	D 1-1	1-0	23	Doughty [31]	27,437
31	12	A	Sunderland	L 0-2	0-1	24		37,929
32	15	H	Sheffield U	L 0-1	0-0	24		11,461
33	19	H	Plymouth Arg	D 1-1	0-0	24	Brown [55]	11,752
34	23	A	Watford	L 0-2	0-2	24		20,252
35	Mar 1	H	Portsmouth	W 1-0	1-0	22	Clark [25]	11,662
36	8	A	Burnley	L 0-4	0-2	23		19,453
37	11	A	Cardiff C	W 2-1	0-0	23	Clark [57], Aasgaard [80]	16,641
38	15	H	Middlesbrough	D 0-0	0-0	23		11,815
39	29	A	Hull C	W 1-0	0-0	23	Jones (og) [46]	23,005
40	Apr 5	H	Leeds U	D 1-1	1-1	23	Jones [15]	11,867
41	8	A	Stoke C	D 1-1	0-0	23	Alli [90]	21,226
42	12	A	Blackburn R	L 0-1	0-0	23		11,552
43	18	A	Derby Co	W 1-0	1-0	22	Alli [10]	32,159
44	21	H	Bristol C	W 3-1	0-0	22	Aasgaard [49], Morris [59], Jones [72]	11,874
45	26	H	Coventry C	W 1-0	0-0	21	Baptiste [90]	11,965
46	May 3	A	WBA	L 3-5	1-3	22	Alli 2 [9, 88], Clark [65]	25,615

Final League Position: 22

GOALSCORERS

League (45): Morris 8 (2 pens), Clark 6, Adebayo 5, Alli 4, Brown 4, McGuinness 3, Aasgaard 2, Chong 2, Jones 2, Krauss 2, Baptiste 1, Doughty 1, Holmes 1, Mengi 1, Moses 1, own goals 2.
FA Cup (0).
Carabao Cup (1): Nelson 1.

Kaminski T 45	Walters R 11+3	Mengi T 17+3	Johnson J 5+3	Ogbene C 3	Baptiste S 7+9	Nelson Z 7+14	Doughty A 25+1	Morris C 37+4	Chong T 24+6	Adebayo E 31+8	Townsend A —+1	Ruddock P 1+9	Bell A 31	Clark J 37+3	Shea J 1+1	Holmes T 15+3	Taylor J —+13	McGuinness M 41+2	Walsh L 18+8	Woodrow C 1+14	Burke R 10+1	Nakamba M 15+6	Krauss T 20+3	Moses V 12+6	Andersen M 5+3	Brown J 11+18	Hashioka D 12+5	Phillips J —+1	Dabo L 6+6	Jones I 16+1	Aasgaard T 17	Bowler J —+8	Alli M 6+10	Naismith K 5+5	Nordas L 2+8	Makosso C 12+1	Match No.
1	2	3	4^1	5	6^2	7	8	9	10	11	12	13																									1
1^*	2	3			5	7^4	8	9^1	10	11^3			15	4^2	6	12	13	14^1																			2
1		13	2		5^1	6^5	16	8	9^3	10^2	11			4	7^4	1		14	3	12	15																3
1	5	12			6^4	15	8	9	10^3	11				4	7			14	3^2	13		2^1															4
1		4				5	12	10	11^1	13	8	9		14		3	6^3		2	7^2																	5
1	5^2	4			13	8	14	10^4	11^5				9			15	3	6^3		2	7^1	12	16														6
1	5	4^1			9^5	8		11^2	10^4			7		16	3		15	2		6	14	12^3	13														7
1	13	4			8				11	12			9^4			3	14^3	15	2	7^3	6^1	5		10^2													8
1	8^3	3			14	16	5		10^1				9^5		15	4		13	2	7^2	6^4	11		12													9
1		13			8	11^5	9^3	10	15			7		4^1	3			2^2	14	6^4	5	16	12														10
1					13	8	11	9^3	10^2			7		4	15	3		14		6^3	5	12	2^4														11
1						8	10^1	9^2	11^4			7		$4^∎$	3	14	15		13	6^3	5	12	2														12
1	2		12			11	9	10^2			4	7		3	13			6^3	8^1		14	5															13
1	2		13		8	10	9^2	12			4	7		3				14	6^3		11^1	5															14
1	2		6^2			14	9	11^5			8^1	16		4		3	7^4	10^3	15	13	12		5														15
1	4		6^1			11	9	10^2	15			2		3	12		5^3	7	8^4		14	13															16
1	2		15			10^3	16	14			4	8		13	3		5^1	7^4	6	9^5	11^2	12															17
1	2		7^4			11^3	9^1	10			4^5	8	16	15^3	3		13		14	12	6^2	5															18
1						10		11^1			4^2	8		3			7	6	9	13	12	5															19
1						11	5	9			7	4		3			6	8	10	2																	20
1		14			15	10^6	8	11			7		2	16	$3^{12∎}$	13		6^1	5^4	9^2	4^3																21
1	15			13	10	5	11		12		7^5		4	16	2		14		6^2	8^1	3^4	9^3															22
1	4^3			13	10	9	11		6^1		7		2	15^3	3		12		8^4	5^2		14															23
1	13	$9^∎$			12	11	5	10^2	14	4	7		2	3			8^1	6^3																			24
1	5^5			6^4	11	9	10^3		4	7^1	2	14	3		15		12	8^2	16	13																	25
1	2^5			10^2	11	8	12	5	16	4^4		3	7	14	6^1			13	15	9^3																	26
1				12	11	13^3	14	5	8	4		3	15	6	9^4	13		10^1	2	7^2																	27
1				10^4	15^3	13	11^1	12	5	9^6	4	3	16	6	8^2		14	2	7^3																		28
1				13	10^3	11		12	5	9		3	15		6^4	8^1	4	7^2	2	14																	29
1	2^3	5			10^2	11			9			3					4	7^1	14	6	8^4	12	13	15													30
1	2	5			10	11^4	15		9			3					4^3	13	6^2		8^5	12	7^1	14	16												31
1			13		9	10	11^1	4				2	6^4		7^2		12	5	8	15	14	3^4															32
1			13		9		11^1	4				2^4	6^2		7	15	12	5	8		14	3	10^3														33
1	2		12^4		9	10^5	16	4				6		7^3		3^2	14	5	8	15				11^1	13												34
1			14		9^2	10^4	15	4	7			13	6^3		11^1		5	8	12	3			2														35
1			7		6^4		11^3	5	9^2			12	8^1		15		13	5	2^5	10	16	14	$4^∎$		3												36
1			14		9^3	10^4	11^2	4	7			3	6^1	16		13		5	8^5	15	12		2														37
1					9^4	10		11^1	4	7			3	6^3			12^2	15	5	8		14		13	2												38
1					9^5	10^4	12	11^3	4	6			3	7^2	5^1		13		8		14	15	16	2													39
1					9^{10}	12	11^1	4	8			3	6^4				15	5^3	7		13	14	2														40
1					9^1	11^3	10^5	4	7			3	6^2	14			13	5	8	16	12		15	2^4													41
1	13			16	11^5	10^2	4	8			3	6^4	14				5^1	7	12	9	15		2^3														42
1	12				10^3	16	4	8^4	3			13	14			11^1	5^2	7	9^5	6	15	2															43
1	4		13		10	8	3	7	12			6^2	5	11	9		2^1																				44
1	4^5		14		10	15	8^3	13	3	$7^∎$	16	6^2	5	11	9^4	12	2^1																				45
1	4^5			11^1	12	5	6	3	7^3	13		14	8^4	9	10	16	15	2^2																			46

FA Cup
Third Round   Nottingham F   (a)   0-2

Carabao Cup
Second Round   QPR   (a)   1-1
QPR won 4-1 on penalties.

MANCHESTER CITY

FOUNDATION

Manchester City was formed as a limited company in 1894 after their predecessors Ardwick had been forced into bankruptcy. However, many historians like to trace the club's lineage as far back as 1880 when St Mark's Church, West Gorton added a football section to their cricket club. They amalgamated with Belle Vue for one season before splitting again under the name Gorton Association FC in 1884–85. In 1887 Gorton AFC turned professional and moved ground to Hyde Road under the new name Ardwick AFC.

Etihad Stadium, Etihad Campus, Manchester M11 3FF.
Telephone: (0161) 444 1894.
Ticket Office: (0161) 444 1894.
Website: www.mancity.com
Email: mancity@mancity.com
Ground Capacity: 52,900.
Record Attendance: 84,569 v Stoke C, FA Cup 6th rd, 3 March 1934 (at Maine Road; British record for any game outside London or Glasgow); 54,693 v Leicester C, Premier League, 6 February 2016 (at Etihad Stadium).
Pitch Measurements: 105m × 68m (115yd × 74.5yd).
Chairman: Khaldoon Al Mubarak.
Chief Executive: Ferran Soriano.
Manager: Pep Guardiola.
Assistant Manager: Pep Lijnders.
Colours: Light blue shirts with dark blue trim, white shorts, dark blue socks with light blue and white trim.
Year Formed: 1887 as Ardwick FC; 1894 as Manchester City.
Turned Professional: 1887 as Ardwick FC.
Previous Names: 1880, St Mark's Church, West Gorton; 1884, Gorton; 1887, Ardwick; 1894, Manchester City.
Club Nicknames: 'The Blues'; 'The Citizens'.
Grounds: 1880, Clowes Street; 1881, Kirkmanshulme Cricket Ground; 1882, Queens Road; 1884, Pink Bank Lane; 1887, Hyde Road (1894–1923 as City); 1923, Maine Road; 2003, City of Manchester Stadium (renamed Etihad Stadium 2011).
First Football League Game: 3 September 1892, Division 2, v Bootle (h) W 7–0 – Douglas; McVickers, Robson; Middleton, Russell, Hopkins; Davies (3), Morris (2), Angus (1), Weir (1), Milarvie.
Record League Victory: 10–1 v Huddersfield T, Division 2, 7 November 1987 – Nixon; Gidman, Hinchcliffe, Clements, Lake, Redmond, White (3), Stewart (3), Adcock (3), McNab (1), Simpson.
Record Cup Victory: 10–1 v Swindon T, FA Cup 4th rd, 29 January 1930 – Barber; Felton, McCloy; Barrass, Cowan, Heinemann; Toseland, Marshall (5), Tait (3), Johnson (1), Brook (1).

HONOURS

League Champions: Premier League – 2011–12, 2013–14, 2017–18, 2018–19, 2020–21, 2021–22, 2022–23, 2023–24; Division 1 – 1936–37, 1967–68; First Division – 2001–02; Division 2 – 1898–99, 1902–03, 1909–10, 1927–28, 1946–47, 1965–66.
Runners-up: Premier League – 2012–13, 2014–15, 2019–20; Division 1 – 1903–04, 1920–21, 1976–77; First Division – 1999–2000; Division 2 – 1895–96, 1950–51, 1988–89.
FA Cup Winners: 1904, 1934, 1956, 1969, 2011, 2019, 2023.
Runners-up: 1926, 1933, 1955, 1981, 2013, 2024, 2025.
League Cup Winners: 1970, 1976, 2014, 2016, 2018, 2019, 2020, 2021.
Runners-up: 1974.
Full Members Cup: Runners-up: 1986.
European Competitions
European Cup: 1968–69.
Champions League: 2011–12, 2012–13, 2013–14, 2014–15, 2015–16 (sf), 2016–17, 2017–18 (qf), 2018–19 (qf), 2019–20 (qf), 2020–21 (runners-up), 2021–22 (sf), 2022–23 (winners), 2023–24 (qf), 2024–25.
UEFA Cup: 1972–73, 1976–77, 1977–78, 1978–79 (qf), 2003–04, 2008–09 (qf).
Europa League: 2010–11, 2011–12.
European Cup-Winners' Cup: 1969–70 (winners), 1970–71 (sf).
Super Cup: 2023 (winners).
FIFA Club World Cup: 2023 (winners), 2025.

FOOTBALL YEARBOOK FACT FILE

Manchester City struggled with the intense heat during their game with Woolwich Arsenal on 1 September 1906 and finished the match with just six players on the field. Irvine Thornley and Bob Grieve failed to reappear after the half-time break, and Jimmy Conlin, George Dorsett and Tommy Kelso all departed during the second half. The Gunners, who kept 11 men on the field, won 4-1.

Record Defeat: 1–9 v Everton, Division 1, 3 September 1906.

Most League Points (2 for a win): 62, Division 2, 1946–47.

Most League Points (3 for a win): 100, Premier League, 2017–18.

Most League Goals: 108, Division 2, 1926–27, 108, Division 1, 2001–02.

Highest League Scorer in Season: Tommy Johnson, 38, Division 1, 1928–29.

Most League Goals in Total Aggregate: Sergio Aguero, 184, 2011–21.

Most League Goals in One Match: 5, Fred Williams v Darwen, Division 2, 18 February 1899; 5, Tom Browell v Burnley, Division 2, 24 October 1925; 5, Tom Johnson v Everton, Division 1, 15 September 1928; 5, George Smith v Newport Co, Division 2, 14 June 1947; 5, Sergio Aguero v Newcastle U, Premier League, 3 October 2015.

Most Capped Player: David Silva, 87 (125), Spain; Bernardo Silva, 87 (102), Portugal.

Most League Appearances: Alan Oakes, 564, 1959–76.

Youngest League Player: Glyn Pardoe, 15 years 314 days v Birmingham C, 11 April 1962.

Record Transfer Fee Received: £64,400,000 (potentially rising to £81,500,000) from Atletico Madrid for Julian Alvarez, August 2024.

Record Transfer Fee Paid: £100,000,000 to Aston Villa for Jack Grealish, August 2021.

Football League Record: 1892 Ardwick elected founder member of Division 2; 1894 Newly formed Manchester C elected to Division 2; 1899–1902 Division 1; 1902–03 Division 2; 1903–09 Division 1; 1909–10 Division 2; 1910–26 Division 1; 1926–28 Division 2; 1928–38 Division 1; 1938–47 Division 2; 1947–50 Division 1; 1950–51 Division 2; 1951–63 Division 1; 1963–66 Division 2; 1966–83 Division 1; 1983–85 Division 2; 1985–87 Division 1; 1987–89 Division 2; 1989–92 Division 1; 1992–96 Premier League; 1996–98 First Division; 1998–99 Second Division; 1999–2000 First Division; 2000–01 Premier League; 2001–02 First Division; 2002– Premier League.

LATEST SEQUENCES

Longest Sequence of League Wins: 18, 26.8.2017 – 27.12.2017.

Longest Sequence of League Defeats: 8, 23.8.1995 – 14.10.1995.

Longest Sequence of League Draws: 7, 5.10.2009 – 28.11.2009.

Longest Sequence of Unbeaten League Matches: 32, 10.12.2023 – 26.10.2024.

Longest Sequence Without a League Win: 17, 26.12.1979 – 7.4.1980.

Successive Scoring Runs: 44 from 3.10.1936.

Successive Non-scoring Runs: 6 from 30.1.1971.

MANAGERS

Joshua Parlby 1893–95
  (Secretary-Manager)
Sam Omerod 1895–1902
Tom Maley 1902–06
Harry Newbould 1906–12
Ernest Magnall 1912–24
David Ashworth 1924–25
Peter Hodge 1926–32
Wilf Wild 1932–46
  (continued as Secretary to 1950)
Sam Cowan 1946–47
John 'Jock' Thomson 1947–50
Leslie McDowall 1950–63
George Poyser 1963–65
Joe Mercer 1965–71
  (continued as General Manager to 1972)
Malcolm Allison 1972–73
Johnny Hart 1973
Ron Saunders 1973–74
Tony Book 1974–79
Malcolm Allison 1979–80
John Bond 1980–83
John Benson 1983
Billy McNeill 1983–86
Jimmy Frizzell 1986–87
  (continued as General Manager)
Mel Machin 1987–89
Howard Kendall 1989–90
Peter Reid 1990–93
Brian Horton 1993–95
Alan Ball 1995–96
Steve Coppell 1996
Frank Clark 1996–98
Joe Royle 1998–2001
Kevin Keegan 2001–05
Stuart Pearce 2005–07
Sven-Göran Eriksson 2007–08
Mark Hughes 2008–09
Roberto Mancini 2009–13
Manuel Pellegrini 2013–16
Pep Guardiola June 2016–

TEN YEAR LEAGUE RECORD

		P	W	D	L	F	A	Pts	Pos
2015-16	PR Lge	38	19	9	10	71	41	66	4
2016-17	PR Lge	38	23	9	6	80	39	78	3
2017-18	PR Lge	38	32	4	2	106	27	100	1
2018-19	PR Lge	38	32	2	4	95	23	98	1
2019-20	PR Lge	38	26	3	9	102	35	81	2
2020-21	PR Lge	38	27	5	6	83	32	86	1
2021-22	PR Lge	38	29	6	3	99	26	93	1
2022-23	PR Lge	38	28	5	5	94	33	89	1
2023-24	PR Lge	38	28	7	3	96	34	91	1
2024-25	PR Lge	38	21	8	9	72	44	71	3

DID YOU KNOW ?

Centre-forward Fred Howard is one of a very small number of players to have scored four goals on his Football League debut. Howard achieved his feat playing for Manchester City against Liverpool on 18 January 1913, netting three times in the first 13 minutes and a fourth after half-time as City went on to win 4-1.

MANCHESTER CITY – PREMIER LEAGUE 2024–25 LEAGUE RECORD

Match No.	Date	Venue	Opponents	Result	H/T Score	Lg Pos.	Goalscorers	Attendance
1	Aug 18	A	Chelsea	W 2-0	1-0	2	Haaland [18], Kovacic [84]	39,818
2	24	H	Ipswich T	W 4-1	3-1	1	Haaland 3 (1 pen) [12 (p), 16, 88], De Bruyne [14]	53,147
3	31	A	West Ham U	W 3-1	2-1	1	Haaland 3 [10, 30, 83]	62,469
4	Sept 14	H	Brentford	W 2-1	2-1	1	Haaland 2 [19, 32]	52,148
5	22	H	Arsenal	D 2-2	1-2	1	Haaland [9], Stones [90]	52,846
6	28	A	Newcastle U	D 1-1	1-0	2	Gvardiol [35]	52,248
7	Oct 5	H	Fulham	W 3-2	1-1	2	Kovacic 2 [32, 47], Doku [82]	52,719
8	20	A	Wolverhampton W	W 2-1	1-1	2	Gvardiol [33], Stones [90]	31,319
9	26	H	Southampton	W 1-0	1-0	1	Haaland [5]	52,844
10	Nov 2	A	Bournemouth	L 1-2	0-1	2	Gvardiol [82]	11,231
11	9	A	Brighton & HA	L 1-2	1-0	2	Haaland [23]	31,715
12	23	H	Tottenham H	L 0-4	0-2	2		52,478
13	Dec 1	A	Liverpool	L 0-2	0-1	5		60,248
14	4	H	Nottingham F	W 3-0	2-0	4	Bernardo Silva [8], De Bruyne [31], Doku [57]	51,764
15	7	A	Crystal Palace	D 2-2	1-1	4	Haaland [30], Lewis [68]	25,142
16	15	H	Manchester U	L 1-2	1-0	5	Gvardiol [36]	52,788
17	21	A	Aston Villa	L 1-2	0-1	6	Foden [90]	42,345
18	26	H	Everton	D 1-1	1-1	7	Bernardo Silva [14]	52,527
19	29	A	Leicester C	W 2-0	1-0	5	Savio [21], Haaland [74]	32,057
20	Jan 4	H	West Ham U	W 4-1	2-0	6	Coufal (og) [10], Haaland 2 [42, 55], Foden [58]	52,737
21	14	A	Brentford	D 2-2	0-0	6	Foden 2 [66, 78]	17,048
22	19	A	Ipswich T	W 6-0	3-0	4	Foden 2 [27, 42], Kovacic [30], Doku [49], Haaland [57], McAtee [69]	29,841
23	25	H	Chelsea	W 3-1	1-1	4	Gvardiol [42], Haaland [68], Foden [87]	52,793
24	Feb 2	A	Arsenal	L 1-5	0-1	4	Haaland [55]	60,355
25	15	H	Newcastle U	W 4-0	3-0	4	Marmoush 3 [19, 24, 33], McAtee [84]	52,432
26	23	H	Liverpool	L 0-2	0-2	4		52,803
27	26	A	Tottenham H	W 1-0	1-0	4	Haaland [12]	60,820
28	Mar 8	A	Nottingham F	L 0-1	0-0	4		30,252
29	15	H	Brighton & HA	D 2-2	2-1	5	Haaland (pen) [11], Marmoush [39]	52,471
30	Apr 2	H	Leicester C	W 2-0	2-0	4	Grealish [2], Marmoush [29]	51,983
31	6	A	Manchester U	D 0-0	0-0	5		73,738
32	12	H	Crystal Palace	W 5-2	2-2	4	De Bruyne [33], Marmoush [36], Kovacic [47], McAtee [56], O'Reilly [79]	52,489
33	19	H	Everton	W 2-0	0-0	4	O'Reilly [84], Kovacic [90]	39,332
34	22	H	Aston Villa	W 2-1	1-1	3	Bernardo Silva [7], Matheus Luiz [90]	52,192
35	May 2	A	Wolverhampton W	W 1-0	1-0	3	De Bruyne [35]	53,282
36	10	A	Southampton	D 0-0	0-0	3		30,937
37	20	H	Bournemouth	W 3-1	2-0	3	Marmoush [14], Bernardo Silva [38], Gonzalez [89]	52,487
38	25	A	Fulham	W 2-0	1-0	3	Gundogan [21], Haaland (pen) [72]	27,671

Final League Position: 3

GOALSCORERS

League (72): Haaland 22 (3 pens), Foden 7, Marmoush 7, Kovacic 6, Gvardiol 5, Bernardo Silva 4, De Bruyne 4, Doku 3, McAtee 3, O'Reilly 2, Stones 2, Gonzalez 1, Grealish 1, Gundogan 1, Lewis 1, Matheus Luiz 1, Savio 1, own goal 1.
FA Cup (17): McAtee 3, O'Reilly 3, De Bruyne 2, Doku 2 (1 pen), Grealish 1 (1 pen), Gvardiol 1, Haaland 1, Khusanov 1, Lewis 1, Marmoush 1, Mubama 1.
Carabao Cup (3): Matheus Luiz 2, Doku 1.
(Manchester C U21) Vertu Trophy (2): Heskey R 1, Wright 1.
Champions League (21): Haaland 8 (2 pens), Foden 3, Gundogan 2, Gonzalez 1, Grealish 1, Kovacic 1, Matheus Luiz 1 (1 pen), McAtee 1, Savio 1, Stones 1, own goal 1.
FIFA Club World Cup (16): Foden 3, Haaland 3, Doku 2, Gundogan 2, Bobb 1, Cherki 1, Echeverri 1, Savinho 1, Bernardo Silva 1, own goal 1.

Ederson d 26	Akanji M 23+3	Dias R 25+2	Gvardiol J 36+1	Lewis R 21+7	Kovacic M 25+6	Doku J 16+13	Bernardo Silva M 29+4	De Bruyne K 19+9	Savio d 21+8	Haaland E 31	Foden P 20+8	Stones J 6+5	Grealish J 7+13	Gundogan I 25+8	Matheus Luiz N 19+7	McAtee J 3+12	Ake N 8+2	Walker K 9+6	Rodri R 1+2	Simpson-Pusey J 1+1	Ortega S 12+1	Mubama D —+1	O'Reilly N 6+3	Khusanov A 6	Marmoush O 14+2	Gonzalez N 9+2	Bobb O —+3	Vitor Reis d —+1	Echeverri C —+1	Match No.
1	2	3	4	5	6	7	8	9	10^1	11	12																			1
1	2	3	4	5	6^1	10^2	8	7^3		11^5	12	13	14	15	16															2
1	2	3	4^4	5	6	7^1	8	9^3		11	10^2			12	13			14	15											3
1	4	15	13	5^1	6^2	14	9	8^5		11		3^3	10^4	7	16			2	12											4
1	4	3	5		12	11^2	6	9^3	10	13	15	14	8					2^4	7^1											5
1	4	3	5	6^3	7	14	8	13		11	12			10^2	9^1			2												6
1	3^1	4	5	2	6	13	7			11	8^3	14		10^2	9^1	15		12												7
1		4	5	2	6^3	10^1	9	7^2		11	12	3		13	8			14												8
1	3	4	5	2^2	6		9	7		11	8	13		12	10^1															9
1	3		5		12		6	13	8	11	7	9^2		10				4^1	2											10
1		4	5	6	12	13	7^2			11	8	9^1		10					2	3										11
1	4		5	6^2		8	13	11^3	10	9		3^1	14		7			12	2											12
	4	3			8^4	12	6	14	13	11	9^3	15	7^2	10^1				5	2		1									13
	2^1	3	5	13	10^5	12	6	9^2		14	11	7^4		15	16			4^3			1		12							14
	3	4	5^4	12	6	9^2	8^1			11	13	7		10				2			1									15
1		3	4	12	10^2	7	8^1	14		11	9	13		6^3				5	2											16
	3	5	2	7^3	14	8	13			11	9	4^1		10	6^2	12					1									17
	3	5	2	6^3	10^1	9	12	7		11	8	13		4^2		14					1									18
	3	5	2	6	9	8	10			11	7^1	12		4^2		13					1									19
	3	5	2	6^1	9	8	10^3	11^4		7	15	13	14	4^2		12					1									20
	3	5		7^1	6	9	10			11	8^2	12		2	13	4					1									21
1	3^5	4	5	15	7^4	10	9^3	11^1	8^2	13	6	2	14										12	16						22
1	4	5		7	6	13	10	9	12		8	2						3^1							11^2					23
	3	5		7	6	12	10	11	8^2		4	2		13							1				9^1					24
1	5^5	2	16	12		8	11^4	9^1	4		7^3	15	13	14				3							10^2	6				25
1	14	5	2	15	10	8^1	7	11			13	12		4^2									3		9^3	6^4				26
1	4	5	6^4	10^5	12	8^3	11	13	14	16					2^2								15	3	9^1	7^2				27
1	4	5	12	13	10	8	14	7^3		11				2^2									3	15	9^4	6^1				28
	4	5	2	10	12^2	14	8^1	11	13	6											1		3		9^3	7				29
1	3	4^3	15	10^1	8^2	9	7^4	2		12	5								11						6	13	14			30
	3	4	14	6	12	7	9	10^1	13	8^2								2			1		5^3		11					31
1^1	3	4	2	6^5	16	11^4	13	15		9	8^3							5					12		10^2	7	14			32
	14	3	4		12	13	8	9^3	10^1		7							2			1		5		11	6^2				33
	13	3	4	6	12	8	11^2	9	2		7^1										1		5		10					34
1	12	3	4	13	7^5	10	6	11^3	14	9^4								2					15		5^1	8^2	16			35
1	4	3	5	2^2	7^4	12	6	9	14	11	10^3												15		8^1	13				36
1	4	3	5	6^4	15	8^4	9^1	11^2	14	7^5	2	13													10^3	12	16			37
1	4	3	5	10^1	6	15	12	11^3	13	9^4	2														8^2	7			14	38

FA Cup

Third Round	Salford C	(h)	8-0
Fourth Round	Leyton Orient	(a)	2-1
Fifth Round	Plymouth Arg	(h)	3-1
Quarter-Final	Bournemouth	(a)	2-1
Semi-Final	Nottingham F	(Wembley)	2-0
Final	Crystal Palace	(Wembley)	0-1

Carabao Cup

Third Round	Watford	(h)	2-1
Fourth Round	Tottenham H	(a)	1-2

Vertu Trophy (Manchester C U21)

Group G (N)	Chesterfield	(a)	1-1
Chesterfield won 4-2 on penalties.			
Group G (N)	Grimsby T	(a)	1-1
Manchester C U21 won 5-4 on penalties.			
Group G (N)	Lincoln C	(a)	0-5

Champions League

League game	Internazionale	(h)	0-0
League game	Slovan Bratislava	(a)	4-0
League game	Sparta Prague	(h)	5-0
League game	Sporting Lisbon	(a)	1-4
League game	Feyenoord	(h)	3-3
League game	Juventus	(a)	0-2
League game	Paris Saint-Germain	(a)	2-4
League game	Club Brugge	(h)	3-1
Knockout 1st leg	Real Madrid	(h)	2-3
Knockout 2nd leg	Real Madrid	(a)	1-3

FIFA Club World Cup

Group G	Wydad AC	(n)	2-0
Group G	Al Ain	(n)	6-0
Group G	Juventus	(n)	5-2
Round of 16	Al-Hilal	(n)	3-4
aet.			

MANCHESTER UNITED

FOUNDATION

Manchester United was formed as comparatively recently as 1902 after their predecessors, Newton Heath, went bankrupt. However, it is usual to give the date of the club's foundation as 1878 when the dining room committee of the carriage and waggon works of the Lancashire and Yorkshire Railway Company formed Newton Heath L and YR Cricket and Football Club. They won the Manchester Cup in 1886 and as Newton Heath FC were admitted to the Second Division in 1892.

Old Trafford, Sir Matt Busby Way, Manchester M16 0RA.

Telephone: (0161) 676 7770.

Ticket Office: (0161) 676 7770 (option 1).

Website: www.manutd.co.uk

Email: enquiries@manutd.co.uk

Ground Capacity: 72,197.

Record Attendance: 76,098 v Blackburn R, Premier League, 31 March 2007. 83,260 v Arsenal, First Division, 17 January 1948 (at Maine Road – United shared City's ground after Old Trafford suffered World War II bomb damage).

Ground Record Attendance: 76,962 Wolverhampton W v Grimsby T, FA Cup semi-final, 25 March 1939.

Pitch Measurements: 105m × 68m (115yd × 74.5yd).

Executive Co-Chairmen: Joel Glazer, Avram Glazer.

Chief Executive: Omar Berrada.

Head Coach: Ruben Amorim.

Assistant Head Coach: Carlos Fernandes.

Colours: Red shirts with white trim, white shorts with red trim, black socks with red and white trim.

Year Formed: 1878 as Newton Heath LYR; 1902, Manchester United.

Turned Professional: 1885.

Previous Name: 1880, Newton Heath; 1902, Manchester United.

Club Nickname: 'Red Devils'.

Grounds: 1880, North Road, Monsall Road; 1893, Bank Street; 1910, Old Trafford (played at Maine Road 1941–49).

HONOURS

League Champions: Premier League – 1992–93, 1993–94, 1995–96, 1996–97, 1998–99, 1999–2000, 2000–01, 2002–03, 2006–07, 2007–08, 2008–09, 2010–11, 2012–13; Division 1 – 1907–08, 1910–11, 1951–52, 1955–56, 1956–57, 1964–65, 1966–67; Division 2 – 1935–36, 1974–75.
Runners-up: Premier League – 1994–95, 1997–98, 2005–06, 2009–10, 2011–12, 2017–18, 2020–21; Division 1 – 1946–47, 1947–48, 1948–49, 1950–51, 1958–59, 1963–64, 1967–68, 1979–80, 1987–88, 1991–92; Division 2 – 1896–97, 1905–06, 1924–25, 1937–38.
FA Cup Winners: 1909, 1948, 1963, 1977, 1983, 1985, 1990, 1994, 1996, 1999, 2004, 2016, 2024.
Runners-up: 1957, 1958, 1976, 1979, 1995, 2005, 2007, 2018, 2023.
League Cup Winners: 1992, 2006, 2009, 2010, 2017 2023. *Runners-up:* 1983, 1991, 1994, 2003.
European Competitions
European Cup: 1956–57 (sf), 1957–58 (sf), 1965–66 (sf), 1967–68 (winners), 1968–69 (sf).
Champions League: 1993–94, 1994–95, 1996–97 (sf), 1997–98 (qf), 1998–99 (winners), 1999–2000 (qf), 2000–01 (qf), 2001–02 (sf), 2002–03 (qf), 2003–04, 2004–05, 2005–06, 2006–07 (sf), 2007–08 (winners), 2008–09 (runners-up), 2009–10 (qf), 2010–11 (runners-up), 2011–12, 2012–13, 2013–14 (qf), 2015–16, 2017–18, 2018–19 (qf), 2020–21, 2021–22, 2023–24.
Fairs Cup: 1964–65 (sf).
UEFA Cup: 1976–77, 1980–81, 1982–83, 1984–85 (qf), 1992–93, 1995–96. *Europa League:* 2011–12, 2015–16, 2016–17 (winners), 2019–20 (sf), 2020–21 (runners-up), 2022–23 (qf). 2024–25 (runners-up).
European Cup-Winners' Cup: 1963–64 (qf), 1977–78, 1983–84 (sf), 1990–91 (winners). 1991–92.
Super Cup: 1991 (winners), 1999, 2008.
World Club Championship: 1968, 1999 (winners), 2000.
FIFA Club World Cup: 2008 (winners).
NB: In 1958–59 FA refused permission to compete in European Cup.

FOOTBALL YEARBOOK FACT FILE

Manchester United underwent a lengthy tour of Continental Europe in May 1908 after winning the Football League championship. They opened with a 4-2 win over a representative team from Zurich, becoming the first British professional team to play in Switzerland. Scorers for United in the game were Jimmy Turnbull, John Picken, George Wall and Jimmy Bannister.

First Football League Game: 3 September 1892, Division 1, v Blackburn R (a) L 3–4 – Warner; Clements, Brown; Perrins, Stewart, Erentz; Farman (1), Coupar (1), Donaldson (1), Carson, Mathieson.
Record League Victory (as Newton Heath): 10–1 v Wolverhampton W, Division 1, 15 October 1892 – Warner; Mitchell, Clements; Perrins, Stewart (3), Erentz; Farman (1), Hood (1), Donaldson (3), Carson (1), Hendry (1).
Record League Victory (as Manchester U): 9–0 v Ipswich T, Premier League, 4 March 1995 – Schmeichel; Keane (1) (Sharpe), Irwin, Bruce (Butt), Kanchelskis, Pallister, Cole (5), Ince (1), McClair, Hughes (2), Giggs; 9–0 v Southampton, Premier League, 2 February 2021 – De Gea, Wan Bissaka (1), Lindelof, Maguire, Shaw (Martial (2)), McTominay (1), Fred, Rashford (1) (James (1)), Bruno Fernandes (1 pen), Greenwood, Cavani (1) (van der Beek), 1 own goal.
Record Cup Victory: 10–0 v RSC Anderlecht, European Cup prel. rd 2nd leg, 26 September 1956 – Wood; Foulkes, Byrne; Colman, Jones, Edwards; Berry (1), Whelan (2), Taylor (3), Viollet (4), Pegg.
Record Defeat: 0–7 v Blackburn R, Division 1, 10 April 1926; 0–7 v Aston Villa, Division 1, 27 December 1930; 0–7 v Wolverhampton W, Division 2, 26 December 1931; 0–7 v Liverpool, Premier League, 5 March 2023.
Most League Points (2 for a win): 64, Division 1, 1956–57.
Most League Points (3 for a win): 92, Premier League, 1993–94.
Most League Goals: 103, Division 1, 1956–57 and 1958–59.
Highest League Scorer in Season: Dennis Viollet, 32, 1959–60.
Most League Goals in Total Aggregate: Bobby Charlton, 199, 1956–73.
Most League Goals in One Match: 5, Andrew Cole v Ipswich T, Premier League, 3 March 1995; 5, Dimitar Berbatov v Blackburn R, Premier League, 27 November 2010.
Most Capped Player: Bobby Charlton, 106, England.
Most League Appearances: Ryan Giggs, 672, 1991–2014.
Youngest League Player: Jeff Whitefoot, 16 years 105 days v Portsmouth, 15 April 1950.
Record Transfer Fee Received: £80,000,000 from Real Madrid for Cristiano Ronaldo, July 2009.
Record Transfer Fee Paid: £89,300,000 to Juventus for Paul Pogba, August 2016.
Football League Record: 1892 Newton Heath elected to Division 1; 1892–94 Division 1; 1894–1906 Division 2; 1906–22 Division 1; 1922–25 Division 2; 1925–31 Division 1; 1931–36 Division 2; 1936–37 Division 1; 1937–38 Division 2; 1938–74 Division 1; 1974–75 Division 2; 1975–92 Division 1; 1992– Premier League.

MANAGERS

J. Ernest Mangnall 1903–12
John Bentley 1912–14
John Robson 1914–21
(Secretary-Manager from 1916)
John Chapman 1921–26
Clarence Hilditch 1926–27
Herbert Bamlett 1927–31
Walter Crickmer 1931–32
Scott Duncan 1932–37
Walter Crickmer 1937–45
(Secretary-Manager)
Matt Busby 1945–69
(continued as General Manager then Director)
Wilf McGuinness 1969–70
Sir Matt Busby 1970–71
Frank O'Farrell 1971–72
Tommy Docherty 1972–77
Dave Sexton 1977–81
Ron Atkinson 1981–86
Sir Alex Ferguson 1986–2013
David Moyes 2013–14
Louis van Gaal 2014–16
Jose Mourinho 2016–18
Ole Gunnar Solskjaer 2018–21
Ralf Rangnick 2021–22
Erik ten Hag 2022–24
Ruben Amorim November 2024–

LATEST SEQUENCES

Longest Sequence of League Wins: 14, 15.10.1904 – 3.1.1905.
Longest Sequence of League Defeats: 14, 26.4.1930 – 25.10.1930.
Longest Sequence of League Draws: 6, 30.10.1988 – 27.11.1988.
Longest Sequence of Unbeaten League Matches: 29, 11.4.2010 – 1.2.2011.
Longest Sequence Without a League Win: 16, 19.4.1930 – 25.10.1930.
Successive Scoring Runs: 36 from 3.12.2007.
Successive Non-scoring Runs: 5 from 7.2.1981.

TEN YEAR LEAGUE RECORD

		P	W	D	L	F	A	Pts	Pos
2015-16	PR Lge	38	19	9	10	49	35	66	5
2016-17	PR Lge	38	18	15	5	54	29	69	6
2017-18	PR Lge	38	25	6	7	68	28	81	2
2018-19	PR Lge	38	19	9	10	65	54	66	6
2019-20	PR Lge	38	18	12	8	66	36	66	3
2020-21	PR Lge	38	21	11	6	73	44	74	2
2021-22	PR Lge	38	16	10	12	57	57	58	6
2022-23	PR Lge	38	23	6	9	58	43	75	3
2023-24	PR Lge	38	18	6	14	57	58	60	8
2024-25	PR Lge	38	11	9	18	44	54	42	15

DID YOU KNOW ?

Manchester United lost the first 12 games of the 1930–31 season, by which time they were rock bottom of the First Division, seven points adrift of the closest team. Their 13th game proved lucky as they beat Birmingham 2-0, but they remained bottom of the table for the remainder of the campaign and were relegated to Division Two.

MANCHESTER UNITED – PREMIER LEAGUE 2024–25 LEAGUE RECORD

Match No.	Date	Venue	Opponents	Result	H/T Score	Lg Pos.	Goalscorers	Attendance
1	Aug 16	H	Fulham	W 1-0	0-0	1	Zirkzee [87]	73,297
2	24	A	Brighton & HA	L 1-2	0-1	10	Diallo [60]	31,537
3	Sept 1	H	Liverpool	L 0-3	0-2	14		73,738
4	14	A	Southampton	W 3-0	2-0	10	de Ligt [35], Rashford [41], Garnacho [90]	31,144
5	21	A	Crystal Palace	D 0-0	0-0	11		25,172
6	29	H	Tottenham H	L 0-3	0-1	12		73,587
7	Oct 6	A	Aston Villa	D 0-0	0-0	14		42,682
8	19	H	Brentford	W 2-1	0-1	11	Garnacho [47], Hojlund [62]	73,738
9	27	A	West Ham U	L 1-2	0-0	14	Casemiro [81]	62,474
10	Nov 3	H	Chelsea	D 1-1	0-0	13	Bruno Fernandes (pen) [70]	73,813
11	10	H	Leicester C	W 3-0	2-0	13	Bruno Fernandes [17], Kristiansen (og) [38], Garnacho [82]	73,829
12	24	A	Ipswich T	D 1-1	1-1	12	Rashford [2]	30,017
13	Dec 1	H	Everton	W 4-0	2-0	9	Rashford 2 [34, 46], Zirkzee 2 [41, 64]	73,817
14	4	A	Arsenal	L 0-2	0-0	11		60,256
15	7	H	Nottingham F	L 2-3	1-1	13	Hojlund [18], Bruno Fernandes [61]	73,778
16	15	A	Manchester C	W 2-1	0-1	13	Bruno Fernandes (pen) [88], Diallo [90]	52,788
17	22	H	Bournemouth	L 0-3	0-1	13		73,720
18	26	A	Wolverhampton W	L 0-2	0-0	14		31,407
19	30	H	Newcastle U	L 0-2	0-2	14		73,809
20	Jan 5	A	Liverpool	D 2-2	0-0	13	Martinez [52], Diallo [80]	60,275
21	16	H	Southampton	W 3-1	0-1	12	Diallo 3 [82, 90, 90]	73,722
22	19	A	Brighton & HA	L 1-3	1-1	13	Bruno Fernandes (pen) [23]	73,758
23	26	A	Fulham	W 1-0	0-0	12	Martinez [78]	27,288
24	Feb 2	H	Crystal Palace	L 0-2	0-1	13		73,751
25	16	A	Tottenham H	L 0-1	0-1	15		61,383
26	22	A	Everton	D 2-2	0-2	15	Bruno Fernandes [72], Ugarte [80]	39,290
27	26	H	Ipswich T	W 3-2	2-2	14	Morsy (og) [22], de Ligt [26], Maguire [47]	73,827
28	Mar 9	H	Arsenal	D 1-1	1-0	14	Bruno Fernandes [45]	73,812
29	16	A	Leicester C	W 3-0	1-0	13	Hojlund [28], Garnacho [67], Bruno Fernandes [90]	31,773
30	Apr 1	A	Nottingham F	L 0-1	0-1	13		30,249
31	6	H	Manchester C	D 0-0	0-0	13		73,738
32	13	A	Newcastle U	L 1-4	1-1	14	Garnacho [37]	52,252
33	20	H	Wolverhampton W	L 0-1	0-0	14		73,819
34	27	A	Bournemouth	D 1-1	0-1	14	Hojlund [90]	11,241
35	May 4	A	Brentford	L 3-4	1-2	15	Mount [14], Garnacho [82], Diallo [90]	17,190
36	11	H	West Ham U	L 0-2	0-0	16		73,804
37	16	A	Chelsea	L 0-1	0-0	16		39,849
38	25	H	Aston Villa	W 2-0	0-0	15	Diallo [76], Eriksen (pen) [87]	73,839

Final League Position: 15

GOALSCORERS

League (44): Bruno Fernandes 8 (3 pens), Diallo 8, Garnacho 6, Hojlund 4, Rashford 4, Zirkzee 3, de Ligt 2, Martinez 2, Casemiro 1, Eriksen 1 (1 pen), Maguire 1, Mount 1, Ugarte 1, own goals 2.
FA Cup (4): Fernandes 2, Maguire 1, Zirkzee 1.
Carabao Cup (15): Garnacho 3, Casemiro 2, Eriksen 2, Fernandes 2, Rashford 2, Antony 1 (1 pen), Diallo 1, Evans 1, Zirkzee 1.
(Manchester U U21) Vertu Trophy (7): Ennis 2, Fletcher 2, Jackson 1, Mather 1, Musa 1.
Europa League (35): Fernandes 7 (4 pens), Hojlund 6, Dalot 3, Casemiro 2, Diallo 2, Eriksen 2, Maguire 2, Mainoo 2, Mount 2, Zirkzee 2, Garnacho 1, Rashford 1, Ugarte 1, Yoro 1, own goal 1.

Onana A 34	Mazraoui N 34+3	Maguire H 19+8	Martinez L 20	Dalot D 31+2	Casemiro C 18+6	Mainoo K 19+6	Diallo A 20+6	Mount M 8+9	Rashford M 12+3	Bruno Fernandes M 35+1	Garnacho A 23+13	Zirkzee J 14+18	de Ligt M 25+4	Evans J 3+4	McTominay S —+2	Antony d —+8	Collyer T —+6	Eriksen C 11+12	Ugarte M 22+7	Hojlund R 23+9	Lindelof V 6+10	Shaw L 4+3	Malacia T 2+1	Yoro L 12+9	Dorgu P 10+2	Obi-Martin C 1+6	Heaven A 2+2	Amass H 4+1	Bayindir A 4	Fredricson T 2	Match No.
1	2^3	3^4	4	5	6	7^5	8^1	9^2		10	11	12	13	14	15	16															1
1	2	3^3	4	5	6	7	8^5	9^1	10^2	11^4	13	12	14		15	16															2
1	2	13	4	5	6^1	7	14		10	9	8^2	11^4	3^3					12	15												3
1	2^3	14	4^4	5	16	7	8		10^1	9	12	11	3^5	15					6^2	13											4
1	2		4	5		6	8^3		12	9	10	11^1	3					7^2	13	14											5
1	2		4	5	13	6^1	16	12	10^4	9^8	8	11^2	3					14	7^3	15											6
1	2^1	3^2		5	16	6^5			10^4	9	8	15	12	4		14		7		11^3	13										7
1	15		5	2	7^2				8	9	10^4	12	3	4^3				6	13	11^1	14										8
1	5^3		4	2	7		12		8^1	9	10	13	3					6^2		11	14										9
1	5		4	2	6		12		10^1	9	8	13	3					7^3	11^2	14											10
1	5		4	2^1	6^4				10^2	9	12	14	3	13				15	7	11^3											11
1	2			8	6^1		5	16	11^4	9	10^5	14	3	4^2				7^3	12	15	13										12
1	2^1	12	4	8	7^3	6^5	5	16	9	10^4	14	11	3^2					15			13										13
1	4	3^4		5			12		9^3	13	7	10^2	14	2		16		6	11^5			8^1	15								14
1	14	13	4	8		6	5	15	12	9^9	10^1	16	3^2					7^4	11			2^3									15
1	5^3	3	4	8		12	9^5	11^1		6		14	2^4		13			7	10^2	16		15									16
1	2	3	4	5		7	9			10	14	11^2						6^3	13			8^1	12								17
1	5	3	4	8	12	7^2	9^5		10^1	15	16				13		14	6^3	11^4			2^1									18
1	5	3	4^3	8	6^2	12	9			13	10^1	2^4		15	7			11				14									19
1	5	3	4	8		7^1	9			10	12	14	2^2					6	11^3			13									20
1	8^3	15	4		7^1	5			9	10	13	3		12	14	16		6^2	11^3			2^4									21
1	5^4	3		8		7^2	9			10	12	11^3	2		14	13		6^1	15			4									22
1	8^3	3	4	5		16	9			7	10^4	12	2^1			14		6^3	11^2			15	13								23
1	5^1	3	4^3	8		10^2	9			7	11	12	14					15	6^4	13			2								24
1	2	3		5	7^1				6	10	9	4							11					8	12						25
1	2^3	3		5	7^1				10	12	9	4						6^1	11^2					13	8	14					26
1	12	3		5	13				7	10^1	9^8	2						14	6	11^2	15			4^3	8^1						27
1	5			8	7				6	9	11^2	2			14	10^3		13	3					4^1		12					28
1	5			8	13				6	9^3	14	2			12	10^4	7^2	11^5	3					16	4^1	15					29
1	4	15		5	7^2			14		10	9	11^3	3					13	6^1	12				2^4	8						30
1	2	3^1		5	6			13		9	10	14						7^3	11^2	12				4	8						31
	2^4			5		16		12		10^5	9^1	11^2						7	6	13	3	15		4	14		8^3	1			32
1	2		14		10^1		12		13	9								7	6^2	11^4	3^5			16	5^3	15	8		4		33
1	5^4	3^3			7^1	6^2		12		10	9							16	13	11	14	4		2	8^9	15					34
	12				7	14	9^4		10		3^1							15	6		16	4^3		13	5^2	11		8	1	2^6	35
2	12				9	5^5	10^4		7	14								16	6^3	11	13	4^1		3^2	15		8	1			36
1	5	3			7^1	15	9		10^2		6^3	12							13	11	2	4^4			8		14				37
	5^1	3			12^2	7	13		10^4		6					14			15	11^5	2				8	16	4^3		1		38

FA Cup

Third Round	Arsenal	(a)	1-1
aet; Manchester U won 5-3 on penalties.			
Fourth Round	Leicester C	(h)	2-1
Fifth Round	Fulham	(h)	1-1
aet; Fulham won 4-3 on penalties.			

Carabao Cup

Third Round	Barnsley	(h)	7-0
Fourth Round	Leicester C	(h)	5-2
Quarter-Final	Tottenham H	(a)	3-4

Vertu Trophy (Manchester U U21)

Group F (N)	Barnsley	(a)	3-2
Group F (N)	Doncaster R	(a)	3-3
Manchester U U21 won 5-3 on penalties.			
Group F (N)	Huddersfield T	(a)	1-4

Europa League

League game	FC Twente	(h)	1-1
League game	Porto	(a)	3-3
League game	Fenerbahce	(a)	1-1
League game	PAOK	(h)	2-0
League game	Bodo/Glimt	(h)	3-2
League game	Viktoria Plzen	(a)	2-1
League game	Rangers	(h)	2-1
League game	FCSB	(a)	2-0
Round of 16 1st leg	Real Sociedad	(a)	1-1
Round of 16 2nd leg	Real Sociedad	(h)	4-1
Quarter-Final 1st leg	Lyon	(a)	2-2
Quarter-Final 2nd leg	Lyon	(h)	5-4
aet.			
Semi-Final 1st leg	Athletic Bilbao	(a)	3-0
Semi-Final 2nd leg	Athletic Bilbao	(h)	4-1
Final	Tottenham H	(Bilbao)	0-1

MANSFIELD TOWN

FOUNDATION

The club was formed as Mansfield Wesleyans in 1897, and changed their name to Mansfield Wesley in 1906 and Mansfield Town in 1910. This was after the Mansfield Wesleyan Chapel trustees had requested that the club change its name as 'it has no longer had any connection with either the chapel or school'. The new club participated in the Notts and Derby District League, but in the following season 1911–12 joined the Central Alliance.

One Call Stadium, Quarry Lane, Mansfield, Nottinghamshire NG18 5DA.

Telephone: (01623) 482 482.

Ticket Office: (01623) 482 482 (option 1).

Website: www.mansfieldtown.net

Email: info@mansfieldtown.net

Ground Capacity: 9,348.

Record Attendance: 24,467 v Nottingham F, FA Cup 3rd rd, 10 January 1953.

Pitch Measurements: 104.5m × 66.5m (114yd × 73yd).

Chairman: John Radford.

Chief Executive: Carolyn Radford.

Manager: Nigel Clough.

Assistant Manager: Gary Crosby.

Colours: Yellow shirts with darker yellow stripes and blue trim, blue shorts, yellow socks with blue trim.

Year Formed: 1897.

Turned Professional: 1906.

Ltd Co.: 1922.

Previous Name: 1897, Mansfield Wesleyans; 1906, Mansfield Wesley; 1910, Mansfield Town.

Grounds: 1897–99, Westfield Lane; 1899–1901, Ratcliffe Gate; 1901–12, Newgate Lane; 1912–16, Ratcliffe Gate; 1916, Field Mill (renamed One Call Stadium 2012).

Club Nickname: 'The Stags'.

First Football League Game: 29 August 1931, Division 3 (S), v Swindon T (h) W 3–2 – Wilson; Clifford, England; Wake, Davis, Blackburn; Gilhespy, Readman (1), Johnson, Broom (2), Baxter.

Record League Victory: 9–2 v Rotherham U, Division 3 (N), 27 December 1932 – Wilson; Anthony, England; Davies, S. Robinson, Slack; Prior, Broom, Readman (3), Hoyland (3), Bowater (3); 9–2 v Harrogate T (h), FL 2, 13 February 2024 – Pym; Bowery, Flint (Lewis), Brunt, Cargill, Reed (Maris), Boateng (3), Quinn (McLaughlin), Keillor-Dunn (1) (Williams), Akins (2), Nichols (1), (Swan (2)).

Record Cup Victory: 8–0 v Scarborough (a), FA Cup 1st rd, 22 November 1952 – Bramley; Chessell, Bradley; Field, Plummer, Lewis; Scott, Fox (3), Marron (2), Sid Watson (1), Adam (2).

HONOURS

League Champions: Division 3 – 1976–77; Division 4 – 1974–75; Football Conference – 2012–13. *Runners-up:* Division 3N – 1950–51, Third Division – (3rd) 2001–02 *(promoted to Second Division).*

FA Cup: 6th rd – 1969.

League Cup: 5th rd – 1976.

League Trophy Winners: 1987.

FOOTBALL YEARBOOK FACT FILE

All 10 Mansfield Town outfield players were booked in their FA Cup first-round tie away to Crystal Palace in November 1962. When the referee awarded a last-minute penalty to Palace, resulting in the equaliser, the players expressed their feelings by applauding the official off the pitch, all except goalkeeper Colin Treharne going into the book. The Stags had the last laugh, winning the replay 7-2.

Record Defeat: 1–8 v Walsall, Division 3 (N), 19 January 1933.

Most League Points (2 for a win): 68, Division 4, 1974–75.

Most League Points (3 for a win): 86, FL 2, 2023–24.

Most League Goals: 108, Division 4, 1962–63.

Highest League Scorer in Season: Ted Harston, 55, Division 3 (N), 1936–37.

Most League Goals in Total Aggregate: Harry Johnson, 104, 1931–36.

Most League Goals in One Match: 7, Ted Harston v Hartlepools U, Division 3N, 23 January 1937.

Most Capped Player: Luke Dimech, 10 (78), Malta.

Most League Appearances: Rod Arnold, 440, 1970–83.

Youngest League Player: Cyril Poole, 15 years 351 days v New Brighton, 27 February 1937.

Record Transfer Fee Received: £30,000 (potentially rising to £655,000) from Swindon T for Colin Calderwood, July 1985.

Record Transfer Fee Paid: £200,000 to Newport Co for Will Evans, August 2024.

Football League Record: 1931 Elected to Division 3 (S); 1931–32 Division 3 (S); 1932–37 Division 3 (N); 1937–47 Division 3 (S); 1947–58 Division 3 (N); 1958–60 Division 3; 1960–63 Division 4; 1963–72 Division 3; 1972–75 Division 4; 1975–77 Division 3; 1977–78 Division 2; 1978–80 Division 3; 1980–86 Division 4; 1986–91 Division 3; 1991–92 Division 4; 1992–93 Second Division; 1993–2002 Third Division; 2002–03 Second Division; 2003–04 Third Division; 2004–08 FL 2; 2008–13 Football Conference; 2013–24 FL 2; 2024– FL 1.

LATEST SEQUENCES

Longest Sequence of League Wins: 8, 27.11.2021 – 29.1.2022.

Longest Sequence of League Defeats: 7, 18.1.1947 – 15.3.1947.

Longest Sequence of League Draws: 5, 18.10.1986 – 22.11.1986.

Longest Sequence of Unbeaten League Matches: 20, 14.2.1976 – 21.8.1976.

Longest Sequence Without a League Win: 14, 25.3.2000 – 2.9.2000.

Successive Scoring Runs: 27 from 1.10.1962.

Successive Non-scoring Runs: 8 from 25.3.2000.

MANAGERS

John Baynes 1922–25
Ted Davison 1926–28
Jack Hickling 1928–33
Henry Martin 1933–35
Charlie Bell 1935
Harold Wightman 1936
Harold Parkes 1936–38
Jack Poole 1938–44
Lloyd Barke 1944–45
Roy Goodall 1945–49
Freddie Steele 1949–51
George Jobey 1952–53
Stan Mercer 1953–55
Charlie Mitten 1956–58
Sam Weaver 1958–60
Raich Carter 1960–63
Tommy Cummings 1963–67
Tommy Eggleston 1967–70
Jock Basford 1970–71
Danny Williams 1971–74
Dave Smith 1974–76
Peter Morris 1976–78
Billy Bingham 1978–79
Mick Jones 1979–81
Stuart Boam 1981–83
Ian Greaves 1983–89
George Foster 1989–93
Andy King 1993–96
Steve Parkin 1996–99
Billy Dearden 1999–2002
Stuart Watkiss 2002
Keith Curle 2002–04
Carlton Palmer 2004–05
Peter Shirtliff 2005–06
Billy Dearden 2006–08
Paul Holland 2008
Billy McEwan 2008
David Holdsworth 2008–10
Duncan Russell 2010–11
Paul Cox 2011–14
Adam Murray 2014–16
Steve Evans 2016–18
David Flitcroft 2018–19
John Dempster 2019
Graham Coughlan 2019–20
Nigel Clough November 2020–

TEN YEAR LEAGUE RECORD

		P	W	D	L	F	A	Pts	Pos
2015-16	FL 2	46	17	13	16	61	53	64	12
2016-17	FL 2	46	17	15	14	54	50	66	12
2017-18	FL 2	46	18	18	10	67	52	72	8
2018-19	FL 2	46	20	16	10	69	41	76	4
2019-20	FL 2	36	9	11	16	48	55	38	21§
2020-21	FL 2	46	13	19	14	57	55	58	16
2021-22	FL 2	46	22	11	13	67	52	77	7
2022-23	FL 2	46	21	12	13	72	55	75	8
2023-24	FL 2	46	24	14	8	90	47	86	3
2024-25	FL 1	46	15	9	22	60	73	54	17

§*Decided on points-per-game (1.06)*

DID YOU KNOW ?

John McClelland became the first Mansfield Town player to gain full international honours when he came off the bench after 50 minutes for Northern Ireland in their 1-0 win over Scotland in a Home International Championship match on 16 May 1980. McClelland went on to win seven full caps during his time with the Stags before being sold to Rangers in May 1981.

MANSFIELD TOWN – SKY BET LEAGUE ONE 2024–25 LEAGUE RECORD

Match No.	Date	Venue	Opponents	Result	H/T Score	Lg Pos.	Goalscorers	Attendance
1	Aug 9	A	Barnsley	W 2-1	2-1	1	Quinn S [13], Gregory [18]	14,817
2	17	H	Burton Alb	D 3-3	2-1	6	Evans [4], Armer (og) [45], Gregory (pen) [90]	7781
3	24	A	Lincoln C	L 1-4	0-2	15	Oshilaja [69]	9809
4	31	H	Stockport Co	D 1-1	1-1	14	Boateng [22]	8293
5	Sept 14	H	Cambridge U	W 2-1	1-0	8	Gregory 2 [39, 68]	7294
6	21	H	Shrewsbury T	W 2-1	0-1	8	Gregory (pen) [49], Lewis [86]	7313
7	28	A	Northampton T	W 2-0	0-0	5	Evans [47], Lewis [89]	7024
8	Oct 1	A	Crawley T	W 2-0	1-0	3	Gregory [12], Waine [90]	3351
9	5	H	Blackpool	W 2-0	2-0	3	Evans 2 [8, 39]	8121
10	19	H	Stevenage	L 0-1	0-1	4		7135
11	22	A	Wigan Ath	W 2-1	1-0	4	Evans [29], Baccus [62]	9460
12	26	A	Birmingham C	D 1-1	0-1	4	Gregory [63]	8583
13	Nov 9	A	Wrexham	L 0-1	0-1	7		13,278
14	23	A	Bristol R	L 0-1	0-0	10		7357
15	26	A	Wycombe W	L 0-1	0-0	10		4670
16	Dec 3	A	Bolton W	L 1-3	1-0	10	Boateng [34]	19,823
17	7	H	Huddersfield T	L 1-2	1-2	10	Evans [31]	8568
18	14	A	Charlton Ath	D 0-0	0-0	11		14,132
19	21	H	Rotherham U	W 1-0	1-0	10	Oshilaja [27]	8401
20	26	A	Peterborough U	W 3-0	3-0	8	Cargill [6], Evans 2 [9, 31]	9985
21	29	A	Reading	L 1-2	1-1	11	Evans [45]	13,626
22	Jan 1	H	Bolton W	W 2-1	2-1	9	McLaughlin [20], Gregory [36]	8553
23	4	A	Stockport Co	W 2-1	2-1	9	Gregory [12], Evans [39]	10,012
24	18	H	Wycombe W	L 1-2	0-0	10	Akins [68]	7459
25	25	A	Cambridge U	L 2-3	0-2	12	Maris [61], Gregory (pen) [90]	6687
26	28	H	Crawley T	L 0-1	0-0	12		6836
27	Feb 1	H	Shrewsbury T	L 1-2	1-0	14	Evans [5]	7376
28	7	H	Northampton T	L 0-1	0-0	14		7320
29	11	A	Leyton Orient	L 0-3	0-3	15		6597
30	15	A	Blackpool	D 3-3	2-1	15	Evans [24], Baccus [29], Akins [64]	10,309
31	18	A	Lincoln C	L 0-3	0-1	15		8326
32	23	H	Wrexham	L 1-2	1-1	15	MacDonald [16]	8122
33	Mar 1	A	Burton Alb	D 1-1	0-1	16	Sweeney (og) [52]	5007
34	4	H	Wigan Ath	D 0-0	0-0	16		6884
35	8	H	Stevenage	D 1-1	0-1	16	Rhodes [81]	3675
36	11	A	Exeter C	L 0-2	0-1	18		5214
37	15	H	Barnsley	W 2-1	1-0	15	Vickers [11], Oshilaja [90]	8592
38	29	A	Bristol R	W 2-1	1-1	14	Vickers [1], Dwyer [59]	9067
39	Apr 1	H	Charlton Ath	L 1-2	1-1	17	Craig [40]	7517
40	5	A	Huddersfield T	L 1-2	0-0	17	Dwyer [84]	19,986
41	8	H	Leyton Orient	L 2-3	1-1	17	Dwyer [3], Maris [62]	6980
42	18	A	Rotherham U	D 3-3	1-2	18	Maris [8], Flint [77], Bowery [86]	10,665
43	21	H	Reading	L 1-5	0-1	19	Baccus [62]	8377
44	27	A	Birmingham C	L 0-4	0-2	19		27,920
45	30	H	Peterborough U	W 4-2	3-0	18	Maris [4], Baccus [7], Evans 2 [34, 59]	7373
46	May 3	H	Exeter C	W 3-0	2-0	17	McLaughlin [25], Dwyer [38], Waine [82]	7494

Final League Position: 17

GOALSCORERS

League (60): Evans 14, Gregory 10 (3 pens), Baccus 4, Dwyer 4, Maris 4, Oshilaja 3, Akins 2, Boateng 2, Lewis 2, McLaughlin 2, Vickers 2, Waine 2, Bowery 1, Cargill 1, Craig 1, Flint 1, MacDonald 1, Quinn S 1, Rhodes 1, own goals 2.
FA Cup (5): Akins 1 (1 pen), McLaughlin 1, Quinn B 1, Quinn S 1, Waine 1.
Carabao Cup (1): Keillor-Dunn 1.
Vertu Trophy (3): Quinn B 2, Akins 1.

Pym C 38	Bowery J 29+15	Flint A 14+22	Oshilaja A 38+1	Blake-Tracy F 14+4	Reed L 39+2	Baccus K 32+7	Keillor-Dunn D 3	Quinn S 13+17	Akins L 29+5	Gregory L 17+3	Evans W 35+5	Boateng H 19+22	Lewis A 22+20	Nichols T 1+4	Swan W —+1	McLaughlin S 27+14	Hewitt E 30+4	Quinn B —+1	Cargill B 34	MacDonald C 3+3	Waine B 2+23	Maris G 17+10	Williams G 8+3	Kilgour A 7+10	Flinders S 7+1	Oates R 1+3	Craig M 4+1	Vickers C 14+5	Rhodes J 3+11	Dwyer D 5+4	Mason O 1	Anderson T —+1	Kokkinos R —+1	Match No.
1	2	3	4	5	6	7^3	8^4	9^2	10	11^1	12	13	14	15																				1
1	5^3	3	4		7	6^4	9	8^1	2	11	10^3	13	15		12	14																		2
1	5	3^3	4		7^5	6^4	9^3	8^1	2	10	11	12	15			14	13	16																3
1	12		4		8			9^3	2	10	11^4	7	14			6^2	3^1		5	13	15													4
1	14		3		7	12	8^4	13	10	11^5	6^2	15	9^3			5	2^1		4	16														5
1	13		3		7	6^4	8^1	10^5	11	9^2	12	15				5^3	2		4	14	16													6
1	12		3		5	6^4	8^1	10		11^3	7^2	13				9	2		4	14	15													7
1	2		3		7	5^1		16	10^2	11^4	9^5	6	15			8	12		4^3	13	14													8
1	2		3	14	6	12		7^1	10^4	9^2	13	16				8	5				11^5	4^3	15											9
1	15		3	12	6	13		7^2	11	10^4	9	14				8	5^5		4^1		16	2^3												10
1	2	16	3		9^3	7^5	6	5^1	15		10^4	8				13	12		4		11^{12}	14												11
1	2	12	3	13	6^5		16	14	11	10	15	9^4				8	5^3		4^1		7^2													12
1^1	17		3	2	9^3	7^5	6^2	14	15	11	10	13	8^4			5			4	16		12												13
1	16	3	2	4^5	7	6^4	8^1	10^2	11	12	14					9^3	5		13	15														14
1	12	3	2	9^4	13			10		11^3	6	8^5				14	5		4^1		15	7^2	16											15
1	6	12	4	5^3	9^4	8		2^5		11^2	7^8	13				15	3		16		10^1	14												16
1	14	3^2	2	9^3	7^5	8^1	12	5^4	11		6					13			4	16		10	15											17
1	2	15	3	9	7^2	8^1		11	10^3	12	6^4					5			4		13	14												18
1	2	12	3	9		8^4		10		11^3	13	7^2				14	5		4		15	6^1												19
1	2		3	9^2	8^3	6		14	10	11^5	15	7^4				12	5		4^1		13	16												20
1	2^5	16	3	9	7^4	6^2		14	10	15	11	13	8			12	5^3		4^1															21
1	5	16	3	14	7	8^3		10^2	12	6^4	13					9^5			4		15	2		11^1										22
1	2	13	3^1	9	14	15		11^5	10^3		7^4	8				16	6		4		5^2	12												23
	3	15	4		6^1	16	14	10^3		11^5	7^2	8				12	2		5			9^4		1	13									24
1	3		4	9	7^1	6		10^5	16	11^4	12	8^3				14	5^2		15		13	2												25
1	2	15	3^1	7	8^2	12		11^3	10^4		13	6^5				9	5		4		16	14												26
1	2		3		8^2	12	5	11	10		6^5	13				9^4			4^3		16	15		7^1	14									27
1	3		4		6^4	15	5	10^1			14	7^3				9	2		8^2		13							11	12					28
1	2		3^1		7^5	13	5	15			6	8				14	12	9	16			4^2						10^4	11^3					29
1	15	13			7	6	5	10^5			14					8^1	3		4		12			16				9^3	2^2	11^4				30
1	13	12	4^3		7	6^4		14	5		10	16				9	3^1		8									2^2	11^5	15				31
1	5		3	12	7	6^2		10	15		14								4^5		9^1	16	8^4	2^3	1			11	13					32
1	2				7	6^5		16	10		11^3	12				9	5^4		4		8^1	15	3^2		1			13	14					33
	13	16	3		6	8^2		14	7^1		11^4	12	9			5	2^3		4			15			1			10^5						34
	7	14	3		6^5	15		13	8^3		9^4					5			4		2^1	16			1			10	12	11^2				35
	12	14	3		6^5	16		11^4	7		8	9				5^1			4^3		2				1			10^2	13	15				36
1	2	15	4		6	9^4		7	11		8^2	13				5	3^1		14									10^3	12					37
1	14	15	3		7^5	6	5	10^4		8^1	12					9	2^3		4		16							11^2	13					38
1	2	15	3		7^4	12	5	13	16		6^5					9^3			4		14		8^1					11	10^2					39
1	2	14			8	7	6	10^4	16		12						3^2		5				4^5	9^3				11^4	15	13				40
1	2		3		7^5	8^2		10			13	6^4				9	5^3		4		14		12	16				15	11^1					41
1	15	16	2		7	12		10			13					9^4	5^5		4		6^2	3		8^1				14	11^3					42
1	9	14	2		7	8		11	15		6^5						5^2		4^3		10^4	13		3^1				12	16					43
1	7		4	3	12	8		15			9^4					16	5^5		14		13	2^2		6^1				10	11^3					44
	2	13	3^1		7	6		12			11^3	14				9	5^2		4			8^4	16	15				10^5		1				45
	2	3			7^5	5		8^1			12					9			4		14	6^3			1			11^4	13	10^2		15	16	46

FA Cup

First Round	Curzon Ashton	(a)	4-0
Second Round	Stevenage	(a)	1-0
Third Round	Wigan Ath	(h)	0-2

Carabao Cup

First Round	Bolton W	(a)	1-1

Bolton W won 5-4 on penalties.

Vertu Trophy

Group H (N)	Rotherham U	(a)	0-2
Group H (N)	Bradford C	(h)	0-3
Group H (N)	Newcastle U U21	(h)	3-0

MIDDLESBROUGH

FOUNDATION

A previous belief that Middlesbrough Football Club was founded at a tripe supper at the Corporation Hotel has proved to be erroneous. In fact, members of Middlesbrough Cricket Club were responsible for forming it at a meeting in the gymnasium of the Albert Park Hotel in 1875.

Riverside Stadium, Middlehaven Way, Middlesbrough TS3 6RS.

Telephone: (01642) 929 420.

Ticket Office: (01642) 929 421.

Website: www.mfc.co.uk

Email: enquiries@mfc.co.uk

Ground Capacity: 33,931.

Record Attendance: 53,802 v Newcastle U, Division 1, 27 December 1949 (at Ayresome Park); 34,814 v Newcastle U, Premier League, 5 March 2003 (at Riverside Stadium); 35,000, England v Slovakia, Euro 2004 qualifier, 11 June 2003.

Pitch Measurements: 105m × 68m (115yd × 74.5yd).

Chairman: Steve Gibson.

Chief Executive: Neil Bausor.

Head Coach: Rob Edwards.

Assistant Head Coach: Adi Viveash.

Colours: Red shirts with white trim, red shorts with white and black trim, red socks with white trim.

Year Formed: 1876; re-formed 1986.

Turned Professional: 1889; became amateur 1892, and professional again, 1899.

Club Nickname: 'The Boro'; 'The Smoggies'.

Grounds: 1877, Old Archery Ground, Albert Park; 1879, Breckon Hill; 1882, Linthorpe Road Ground; 1903, Ayresome Park; 1995, Cellnet Riverside Stadium (renamed BT Cellnet Riverside Stadium 1995; Riverside Stadium 2002).

First Football League Game: 2 September 1899, Division 2, v Lincoln C (a) L 0–3 – Smith; Shaw, Ramsey; Allport, McNally, McCracken; Wanless, Longstaffe, Gettins, Page, Pugh.

Record League Victory: 9–0 v Brighton & HA, Division 2, 23 August 1958 – Taylor; Bilcliff, Robinson; Harris (2p), Phillips, Walley; Day, McLean, Clough (5), Peacock (2), Holliday.

Record Cup Victory: 7–0 v Hereford U, Coca-Cola Cup 2nd rd, 1st leg, 18 September 1996 – Miller; Fleming (1), Branco (1), Whyte, Vickers, Whelan, Emerson (1), Mustoe, Stamp, Juninho, Ravanelli (4).

Record Defeat: 0–9 v Blackburn R, Division 2, 6 November 1954.

HONOURS

League Champions: First Division – 1994–95; Division 2 – 1926–27, 1928–29, 1973–74.
Runners-up: FL C – 2015–16; First Division – 1997–98; Division 2 – 1901–02, 1991–92; Division 3 – 1966–67, 1986–87.
FA Cup: Runners-up: 1997.
League Cup Winners: 2004. *Runners-up:* 1997, 1998.
Amateur Cup Winners: 1895, 1898.
Anglo-Scottish Cup Winners: 1976.
Full Members' Cup: Runners-up: 1990.
European Competitions
UEFA Cup: 2004–05, 2005–06 *(runners-up).*

FOOTBALL YEARBOOK FACT FILE

Middlesbrough entered league football for the first time in the 1889–90 season as founder members of the Northern League. Their first game in the competition came on 14 August when they faced Elswick Rangers at Linthorpe Road in front of a crowd of 4,000. The game was scheduled to kick off at 4.30 but was delayed until 5.00 due to the late arrival of the visitors. Boro won 3-2 with goals from Dennis (2) and Wynn.

Most League Points (2 for a win): 65, Division 2, 1973–74.

Most League Points (3 for a win): 94, Division 3, 1986–87.

Most League Goals: 122, Division 2, 1926–27.

Highest League Scorer in Season: George Camsell, 59, Division 2, 1926–27 (Second Division record).

Most League Goals in Total Aggregate: George Camsell, 325, 1925–39.

Most League Goals in One Match: 5, John Wilkie v Gainsborough T, Division 2, 2 March 1901; 5, Andy Wilson v Nottingham F, Division 1, 6 October 1923; 5, George Camsell v Manchester C, Division 2, 25 December 1926; 5, George Camsell v Aston Villa, Division 1, 9 September 1935; 5, Brian Clough v Brighton & HA, Division 2, 22 August 1958.

Most Capped Player: Mark Schwarzer, 52 (109), Australia.

Most League Appearances: Tim Williamson, 563, 1902–23.

Youngest League Player: Luke Williams, 16 years 200 days v Barnsley, 18 December 2009.

Record Transfer Fee Received: £22,500,000 from Atlanta U for Emmanuel Latte Lath, February 2025.

Record Transfer Fee Paid: £15,000,000 to Nottingham F for Britt Assombalonga, July 2017.

Football League Record: 1899 Elected to Division 2; 1899–1902 Division 2; 1902–24 Division 1; 1924–27 Division 2; 1927–28 Division 1; 1928–29 Division 2; 1929–54 Division 1; 1954–66 Division 2; 1966–67 Division 3; 1967–74 Division 2; 1974–82 Division 1; 1982–86 Division 2; 1986–87 Division 3; 1987–88 Division 2; 1988–89 Division 1; 1989–92 Division 2; 1992–93 Premier League; 1993–95 First Division; 1995–97 Premier League; 1997–98 First Division; 1998–2009 Premier League; 2009–16 FL C; 2016–17 Premier League; 2017– FL C.

LATEST SEQUENCES

Longest Sequence of League Wins: 9, 16.2.1974 – 6.4.1974.

Longest Sequence of League Defeats: 8, 26.12.1995 – 17.2.1996.

Longest Sequence of League Draws: 8, 3.4.1971 – 1.5.1971.

Longest Sequence of Unbeaten League Matches: 24, 8.9.1973 – 19.1.1974.

Longest Sequence Without a League Win: 19, 3.10.1981 – 6.3.1982.

Successive Scoring Runs: 26 from 21.9.1946.

Successive Non-scoring Runs: 7, 25.1.2014 – 1.3.2014.

MANAGERS

John Robson 1899–1905
Alex Mackie 1905–06
Andy Aitken 1906–09
J. Gunter 1908–10
 (Secretary-Manager)
Andy Walker 1910–11
Tom McIntosh 1911–19
Jimmy Howie 1920–23
Herbert Bamlett 1923–26
Peter McWilliam 1927–34
Wilf Gillow 1934–44
David Jack 1944–52
Walter Rowley 1952–54
Bob Dennison 1954–63
Raich Carter 1963–66
Stan Anderson 1966–73
Jack Charlton 1973–77
John Neal 1977–81
Bobby Murdoch 1981–82
Malcolm Allison 1982–84
Willie Maddren 1984–86
Bruce Rioch 1986–90
Colin Todd 1990–91
Lennie Lawrence 1991–94
Bryan Robson 1994–2001
Steve McClaren 2001–06
Gareth Southgate 2006–09
Gordon Strachan 2009–10
Tony Mowbray 2010–13
Aitor Karanka 2013–17
Garry Monk 2017
Tony Pulis 2017–19
Jonathan Woodgate 2019–20
Neil Warnock 2020–21
Chris Wilder 2021–22
Michael Carrick 2022–25
Rob Edwards June 2025–

TEN YEAR LEAGUE RECORD

		P	W	D	L	F	A	Pts	Pos
2015-16	FL C	46	26	11	9	63	31	89	2
2016-17	PR Lge	38	5	13	20	27	53	28	19
2017-18	FL C	46	22	10	14	67	45	76	5
2018-19	FL C	46	20	13	13	49	41	73	7
2019-20	FL C	46	13	14	19	48	61	53	17
2020-21	FL C	46	18	10	18	55	53	64	10
2021-22	FL C	46	20	10	16	59	50	70	7
2022-23	FL C	46	22	9	15	84	56	75	4
2023-24	FL C	46	20	9	17	71	62	69	8
2024-25	FL C	46	18	10	18	64	56	64	10

DID YOU KNOW ❓

Middlesbrough won the Division Two title with ease in 1973–74, clinching top spot following their 1-0 win at Luton Town on 30 March. Boro finished 15 points clear of their closest rivals, thus creating a new Football League record for the gap between the winners and runners-up in a league table. This remained intact for the remainder of the period when two points were awarded for a win.

MIDDLESBROUGH – SKY BET CHAMPIONSHIP 2024–25 LEAGUE RECORD

Match No.	Date	Venue	Opponents	Result		H/T Score	Lg Pos.	Goalscorers	Attendance
1	Aug 10	H	Swansea C	W	1-0	1-0	7	Latte Lath (pen) [25]	26,610
2	17	A	Derby Co	L	0-1	0-1	12		29,443
3	24	H	Portsmouth	D	2-2	1-2	10	Clarke [11], Conway (pen) [90]	26,270
4	31	A	Cardiff C	W	2-0	0-0	7	Clarke [55], Ramsey (og) [82]	18,000
5	Sept 14	H	Preston NE	D	1-1	1-1	10	Conway [16]	25,116
6	21	H	Sunderland	L	0-1	0-1	12		42,871
7	28	H	Stoke C	W	2-0	1-0	8	Doak [34], Hackney [73]	24,610
8	Oct 1	A	WBA	W	1-0	0-0	7	Hackney [73]	23,769
9	5	A	Watford	L	1-2	0-0	9	Edmundson [54]	20,002
10	19	H	Bristol C	L	0-2	0-2	9		24,438
11	23	H	Sheffield U	W	1-0	0-0	8	Latte Lath [80]	24,303
12	27	A	Norwich C	D	3-3	3-1	9	Conway 2 [13, 40], Azaz [45]	26,487
13	Nov 2	H	Coventry C	L	0-3	0-1	10		24,921
14	5	A	QPR	W	4-1	2-0	7	McGree [31], Conway [35], Latte Lath [87], Barlaser [90]	14,054
15	9	H	Luton T	W	5-1	2-0	6	Burgzorg 2 [30, 54], Latte Lath [42], Azaz 2 [51, 87]	23,692
16	23	A	Oxford U	W	6-2	3-1	5	Latte Lath 3 (1 pen) [37 (p), 45, 49], Azaz 2 [42, 83], Conway [80]	11,442
17	27	H	Blackburn R	L	0-1	0-0	6		22,751
18	30	H	Hull C	W	3-1	2-0	5	Azaz [24], Conway 2 [41, 79]	24,121
19	Dec 6	A	Burnley	D	1-1	1-1	5	Dijksteel [13]	20,543
20	10	A	Leeds U	L	1-3	0-1	6	Wober (og) [54]	36,422
21	14	H	Millwall	W	1-0	1-0	6	Latte Lath [10]	23,445
22	21	A	Plymouth Arg	D	3-3	0-1	6	Howson [50], Hackney [77], Latte Lath [84]	16,550
23	26	H	Sheffield Wed	D	3-3	3-0	7	Doak [5], Azaz 2 [15, 30]	32,147
24	29	A	Burnley	D	0-0	0-0	6		27,686
25	Jan 1	A	Hull C	W	1-0	0-0	5	Gilbert [90]	21,585
26	4	H	Cardiff C	D	1-1	1-1	5	Latte Lath [11]	24,634
27	18	A	Portsmouth	L	1-2	1-0	7	Latte Lath [30]	20,389
28	21	H	WBA	W	2-0	1-0	5	Hackney [29], Doak [83]	22,323
29	25	A	Preston NE	L	1-2	0-1	6	Burgzorg [52]	18,474
30	Feb 3	H	Sunderland	L	2-3	1-1	7	Burgzorg [11], Hackney [59]	29,161
31	12	A	Sheffield U	L	1-3	1-1	9	Burgzorg (pen) [45]	27,124
32	15	A	Watford	L	0-1	0-1	11		24,326
33	21	A	Bristol C	L	1-2	1-0	11	Conway [37]	21,894
34	25	A	Stoke C	W	3-1	1-1	11	Forss [20], Azaz [52], Conway [73]	20,141
35	Mar 1	H	Derby Co	W	1-0	0-0	8	Azaz [80]	25,839
36	8	A	Swansea C	L	0-1	0-1	9		13,986
37	11	H	QPR	W	2-1	1-0	8	Conway [11], Dijksteel [58]	22,177
38	15	A	Luton T	D	0-0	0-0	8		11,815
39	29	H	Oxford U	W	2-1	0-1	7	Iheanacho [48], Borges [80]	24,624
40	Apr 4	A	Blackburn R	W	2-0	2-0	5	Conway [2], Iling-Junior [8]	15,638
41	8	A	Leeds U	L	0-1	0-1	6		28,729
42	12	A	Millwall	L	0-1	0-0	8		17,523
43	18	H	Plymouth Arg	W	2-1	1-1	7	Azaz [12], Conway (pen) [90]	26,276
44	21	A	Sheffield Wed	L	1-2	1-0	7	Azaz [11]	27,668
45	26	A	Norwich C	D	0-0	0-0	9		26,374
46	May 3	A	Coventry C	L	0-2	0-1	10		31,452

Final League Position: 10

GOALSCORERS

League (64): Conway 13 (2 pens), Azaz 12, Latte Lath 11 (2 pens), Burgzorg 5 (1 pen), Hackney 5, Doak 3, Clarke 2, Dijksteel 2, Barlaser 1, Borges 1, Edmundson 1, Forss 1, Gilbert 1, Howson 1, Iheanacho 1, Iling-Junior 1, McGree 1, own goals 2.
FA Cup (0).
Carabao Cup (3): Burgzorg 1, Coburn 1, Dijksteel 1.

Dieng T 17	Ayling L 23 + 3	van den Berg R 23 + 4	Clarke M 12 + 2	Engel L 4 + 5	Morris A 33 + 2	Hackney H 43	Jones I 8 + 13	Azaz F 43 + 2	McGree R 11 + 6	Latte Lath E 20 + 9	Burgzorg D 23 + 19	Coburn J — + 2	Howson J 15 + 6	Barlaser D 12 + 11	Hamilton M 2 + 11	Conway T 27 + 9	Dijksteel A 27 + 6	Borges N 34 + 1	Gilbert A — + 7	Simpson N — + 1	Edmundson S 24	Doak B 21 + 3	McCormick G — + 1	Forss M 6 + 18	Fry D 15 + 6	Brynn S 6	Glover T 6 + 1	Giles R 3 + 9	Travers M 17	Whittaker M 11 + 5	Iling-Junior S 11 + 5	Iheanacho K 9 + 6	Match No.
1	2	3	4	5	6	7	8	9¹	10³	11²	12	13	14																				1
1	2	3	4	5	7¹	6⁴	8²	9³		11	10	15	12	13	14																		2
1	3		4	5²	6³	7	8	9¹		11	10			13	14	12	2																3
1	3		4		6	7	8⁴	10³		12	11²			15		9¹	2	5	13	14													4
1	2		4		14	7	8¹	10³		11²	13				6⁴	15	9	5			3	12											5
1	2		4		6	7	8¹	10²		11³	14				12	9		5			3	13											6
1	3	13			6	7⁵	12	9	10⁴	11³	14			16	15			2²	5			4	8¹											7
1	2	3			6	7	13	9	10³	11¹	12							5			4	8²	14										8
1	2	3			6⁴	7	13	9	12	11³	14				10¹			5			4	8²		15									9
1	2⁵	3			6³	7	15	9¹	14	11⁴	12					10²		5			4	8		16									10
1	2	3	15		6	7	13	9⁴	10²	12		14				11¹		5			4	8³											11
1	15	3			6⁵	7	12	9	10⁴	13		14			16	11¹	2³	5			4	8²											12
1	2²		4		6	7⁸	8³	9¹	10⁴	14	16	12	15			11⁵	13	5			3												13
1	2		4		7			9	10	13		6³	14	15	11²	12	5¹				3	8⁴											14
1	5		4		6¹	7	16	9		11³	10²			12	14	13	2				3⁴	8⁶		15									15
		2⁵	4					9⁴	14	11²	10³		6	7	16	13	15	5			3	8¹		12		1							16
		2²	4					10¹	11⁴				6³	7	12	9	13	5	14		3	8		15		1							17
1					7³	14	9		12	10¹	13	6		11²	2	5		4	8			3	1										18
1					7	14	9	13	12	10²		6		11¹	2	5		4	8³			3											19
1		4			7			9²	10¹	11	12	6		13	2	5		4	8			3	8										20
	2¹	3			7	13	9⁴		11²	10		6		14	12	5		4	8³			15	1										21
	3				7		9⁵	10¹	13	12		6³	14	11²	2	5	16	4⁴	8			15	1										22
	4⁸	13	16		7	14	9²		12	10		6		11¹	2	5⁵		8³	3		1⁴	15											23
		14			6	12	9	13	11	10¹		7			2	5³	4	8²	3		1												24
	4	5²			7	8¹	9⁴	10³	11	12		6			2	13	15	14	3		1												25
	4	14			7	12	9²	11	10¹			6			2	5³	13	8	3		1												26
15	2⁴	12	13		7		9⁵	11	10³	6²				5¹	14	4	8	16	3		1												27
2	4	13	6		7		9¹	11	10³	12				5		8²	14	3	1														28
2	4		6		7		9³	11¹	10					5²	14	8	12	3	1	13													29
2	3		6		7		9¹		10					13			4	11²				5	1	8	12								30
2	3		6⁴		7		9¹		10	12				14			4	15				5	1	13	8³	11²							31
2³	3		8		9		13		12			7¹		11	14	5⁵	4	16				1		6¹	15	10²							32
	4				7	8	12		9					11	2	5		13	3	1					6²	10¹							33
12			6		7		10³		13	11⁴	2	5				4¹		8²	3			14	1	9	15								34
4¹			6		7		10³	14	11⁴	2	5					8²	3	12	1		9	15	15	13									35
			6		7		10		14	15	11	2	4			8¹	3⁴	5²	1	9³	13	12											36
			6		7		10⁴	8³	3	14	9²	2	4		13		15	1	12	5	11¹												37
			6		7		10	8	3		11¹	2	4		12		1	5	9														38
	15		6		7		10	8¹	3	11⁴	2	4		13	14	1	12	5³	9²														39
12			6		7		10⁴	8²	3	14	11⁵	2	4¹	16		15	1	13	5	9³													40
	4		7³	8	9		6²		3	11	2		13	14		1	12	5	10¹														41
	4		6	7	10	12	9²	3	11	2³		13				1	8¹	5	14														42
	4		6	7	10	15	3	11	2¹			8³	12	14		1	9⁴	5³	13														43
	4		6	7	10	12	3³	11	2			8¹	13			1	9	5	14														44
			7	6	10	14	4	11	2			12	3			13	1	8²	5³	9¹													45
	15		7³	6	9	12	4⁴	11	2²	5¹		14	3			16	1	8	10⁵	13													46

FA Cup
Third Round — Blackburn R — (h) — 0-1

Carabao Cup
First Round — Leeds U — (a) — 3-0
Second Round — Stoke C — (h) — 0-5

MILLWALL

The Den, John Berylson Way, Bermondsey, London SE16 3LN.

Telephone: (020) 7232 1222.

Ticket Office: (020) 7231 9999.

Website: www.millwallfc.co.uk

Email: slo@millwallplc.com

Ground Capacity: 19,500.

Record Attendance: 48,672 v Derby Co, FA Cup 5th rd, 20 February 1937 (at The Den, Cold Blow Lane); 20,093 v Arsenal, FA Cup 3rd rd, 10 January 1994 (at The Den, Bermondsey).

Pitch Measurements: 106m × 68m (116yd × 74.5yd).

Chairman: James Berylson.

Managing Director: Mark Fairbrother.

Head Coach: Alex Neil.

Assistant Head Coach: Martin Canning.

HONOURS

League Champions: Division 2 – 1987–88; Second Division – 2000–01; Division 3S – 1927–28, 1937–38; Division 4 – 1961–62.
Runners-up: Division 3 – 1965–66, 1984–85; Division 3S – 1952–53; Division 4 – 1964–65.

FA Cup: Runners-up: 2004.

League Cup: 5th rd – 1974, 1977, 1995.

League Trophy: Runners-up: 1999.

European Competitions
UEFA Cup: 2004–05.

Colours: Navy blue shirts with white horizontal lines and white trim, navy blue shorts with white trim, navy blue socks with white trim.

Year Formed: 1885.

Turned Professional: 1893.

Previous Names: 1885, Millwall Rovers; 1889, Millwall Athletic; 1899, Millwall; 1985, Millwall Football & Athletic Company.

Club Nickname: 'The Lions'.

Grounds: 1885, Glengall Road, Millwall; 1886, Back of 'Lord Nelson'; 1890, East Ferry Road; 1901, North Greenwich; 1910, The Den, Cold Blow Lane; 1993, The Den, Bermondsey.

First Football League Game: 28 August 1920, Division 3, v Bristol R (h) W 2–0 – Lansdale; Fort, Hodge; Voisey (1), Riddell, McAlpine; Waterall, Travers, Broad (1), Sutherland, Dempsey.

Record League Victory: 9–1 v Torquay U, Division 3 (S), 29 August 1927 – Lansdale, Tilling, Hill, Amos, Bryant (3), Graham, Chance, Hawkins (3), Landells (1), Phillips (2), Black. 9–1 v Coventry C, Division 3 (S), 19 November 1927 – Lansdale, Fort, Hill, Amos, Collins (1), Graham, Chance, Landells (4), Cock (2), Phillips (2), Black.

Record Cup Victory: 7–0 v Gateshead, FA Cup 2nd rd, 12 December 1936 – Yuill; Ted Smith, Inns; Brolly, Hancock, Forsyth; Thomas (1), Mangnall (1), Ken Burditt (2), McCartney (2), Thorogood (1).

Record Defeat: 1–9 v Aston Villa, FA Cup 4th rd, 28 January 1946.

FOOTBALL YEARBOOK FACT FILE

Millwall scored 87 home goals from their 21 matches in the 1927–28 season, creating a Football League record that has never been broken. The Lions scored five or more goals on 11 occasions, including 9-1 wins over Torquay United and Coventry City, which remain the club's joint-highest victories. They finished the campaign as champions of Division Three South, winning promotion to the Second Division for the first time.

Most League Points (2 for a win): 65, Division 3 (S), 1927–28 and Division 3, 1965–66.

Most League Points (3 for a win): 93, Division 2, 2000–01.

Most League Goals: 127, Division 3 (S), 1927–28.

Highest League Scorer in Season: Richard Parker, 37, Division 3 (S), 1926–27.

Most League Goals in Total Aggregate: Neil Harris, 124, 1995–2004; 2006–11.

Most League Goals in One Match: 5, Richard Parker v Norwich C, Division 3 (S), 28 August 1926.

Most Capped Player: George Saville, 34 (60), Northern Ireland.

Most League Appearances: Barry Kitchener, 523, 1967–82.

Youngest League Player: Moses Ashikodi, 15 years 240 days v Brighton & HA, 22 February 2003.

Record Transfer Fee Received: £14,000,000 from Crystal Palace for Romain Esse, January 2025.

Record Transfer Fee Paid: £5,000,000 to Middlesbrough for Josh Coburn, June 2025.

Football League Record: 1920 Original Members of Division 3; 1920–21 Division 3; 1921–28 Division 3 (S); 1928–34 Division 2; 1934–38 Division 3 (S); 1938–48 Division 2; 1948–58 Division 3 (S); 1958–62 Division 4; 1962–64 Division 3; 1964–65 Division 4; 1965–66 Division 3; 1966–75 Division 2; 1975–76 Division 3; 1976–79 Division 2; 1979–85 Division 3; 1985–88 Division 2; 1988–90 Division 1; 1990–92 Division 2; 1992–96 First Division; 1996–2001 Second Division; 2001–04 First Division; 2004–06 FL C; 2006–10 FL 1; 2010–15 FL C; 2015–17 FL 1; 2017– FL C.

LATEST SEQUENCES

Longest Sequence of League Wins: 10, 10.3.1928 – 25.4.1928.

Longest Sequence of League Defeats: 11, 10.4.1929 – 16.9.1929.

Longest Sequence of League Draws: 5, 3.11.2020 – 28.11.2020.

Longest Sequence of Unbeaten League Matches: 19, 22.8.1959 – 31.10.1959.

Longest Sequence Without a League Win: 20, 26.12.1989 – 5.5.1990.

Successive Scoring Runs: 22 from 27.11.1954.

Successive Non-scoring Runs: 6 from 27.4.2013.

MANAGERS

F. B. Kidd 1894–99
(Hon. Treasurer/Manager)
E. R. Stopher 1899–1900
(Hon. Treasurer/Manager)
George Saunders 1900–11
(Hon. Treasurer/Manager)
Herbert Lipsham 1911–19
Robert Hunter 1919–33
Bill McCracken 1933–36
Charlie Hewitt 1936–40
Bill Voisey 1940–44
Jack Cock 1944–48
Charlie Hewitt 1948–56
Ron Gray 1956–57
Jimmy Seed 1958–59
Reg Smith 1959–61
Ron Gray 1961–63
Billy Gray 1963–66
Benny Fenton 1966–74
Gordon Jago 1974–77
George Petchey 1978–80
Peter Anderson 1980–82
George Graham 1982–86
John Docherty 1986–90
Bob Pearson 1990
Bruce Rioch 1990–92
Mick McCarthy 1992–96
Jimmy Nicholl 1996–97
John Docherty 1997
Billy Bonds 1997–98
Keith Stevens 1998–2000
(then Joint Manager)
(plus **Alan McLeary** 1999–2000)
Mark McGhee 2000–03
Dennis Wise 2003–05
Steve Claridge 2005
Colin Lee 2005
David Tuttle 2005–06
Nigel Spackman 2006
Willie Donachie 2006–07
Kenny Jackett 2007–13
Steve Lomas 2013
Ian Holloway 2014–15
Neil Harris 2015–19
Gary Rowett 2019–23
Joe Edwards 2023–24
Neil Harris 2024
Alex Neil December 2024–

TEN YEAR LEAGUE RECORD

		P	W	D	L	F	A	Pts	Pos
2015-16	FL 1	46	24	9	13	73	49	81	4
2016-17	FL 1	46	20	13	13	66	57	73	6
2017-18	FL C	46	19	15	12	56	45	72	8
2018-19	FL C	46	10	14	22	48	64	44	21
2019-20	FL C	46	17	17	12	57	51	68	8
2020-21	FL C	46	15	17	14	47	52	62	11
2021-22	FL C	46	15	15	13	53	45	69	9
2022-23	FL C	46	19	11	16	57	50	68	8
2023-24	FL C	46	16	11	19	45	55	59	13
2024-25	FL C	46	18	12	16	47	49	66	8

DID YOU KNOW ?

Herbert Banks became the first Millwall player to win full international honours for England when he appeared in the line-up against Ireland at Southampton in March 1901. Banks, who was often referred to as 'The Penalty King' by contemporaries, spent three seasons with the Lions in their Southern League days.

MILLWALL – SKY BET CHAMPIONSHIP 2024–25 LEAGUE RECORD

Match No.	Date	Venue	Opponents	Result		H/T Score	Lg Pos.	Goalscorers	Attendance
1	Aug 10	H	Watford	L	2-3	0-1	17	Watmore 2 [74, 88]	16,456
2	17	A	Bristol C	L	3-4	0-2	22	Esse [51], Bradshaw (pen) [54], Watmore [64]	20,733
3	24	A	Hull C	D	0-0	0-0	22		20,009
4	31	H	Sheffield Wed	W	3-0	0-0	15	Coburn [58], Watmore [71], Cooper [88]	14,905
5	Sept 14	L	Luton T	L	0-1	0-1	18		14,804
6	21	A	QPR	D	1-1	1-1	18	Watmore [34]	15,350
7	28	H	Preston NE	W	3-1	2-0	14	Honeyman [24], Esse [38], Langstaff [47]	13,674
8	Oct 1	A	Cardiff C	L	0-1	0-1	15		15,687
9	5	A	WBA	D	0-0	0-0	18		24,158
10	19	H	Derby Co	D	1-1	0-0	20	Ivanovic [85]	17,321
11	23	H	Plymouth Arg	W	1-0	1-0	13	Esse [13]	13,954
12	26	A	Swansea C	W	1-0	0-0	10	De Norre [90]	15,119
13	Nov 3	H	Burnley	W	1-0	0-0	7	Cooper [52]	14,245
14	6	H	Leeds U	W	1-0	1-0	5	Tanganga [40]	16,693
15	9	A	Stoke C	D	1-1	1-0	7	Coburn [42]	21,060
16	23	H	Sunderland	D	1-1	0-1	8	Azeez [90]	18,385
17	30	A	Oxford U	D	1-1	1-0	10	Tanganga [45]	10,990
18	Dec 7	A	Coventry C	L	0-1	0-0	11		16,460
19	11	H	Sheffield U	L	0-1	0-1	13		12,734
20	14	A	Middlesbrough	L	0-1	0-1	13		23,445
21	21	H	Blackburn R	W	1-0	0-0	10	Ivanovic [90]	14,009
22	26	A	Norwich C	L	1-2	0-2	13	Esse [65]	26,060
23	29	A	Coventry C	D	0-0	0-0	13		28,216
24	Jan 1	H	Oxford U	L	0-1	0-0	13		14,964
25	4	A	Sheffield Wed	D	2-2	0-1	13	Honeyman [65], Wintle [83]	25,208
26	18	H	Hull C	L	0-1	0-0	17		14,579
27	21	H	Cardiff C	D	2-2	2-1	17	Scanlon [2], De Norre [19]	12,041
28	25	A	Luton T	W	1-0	0-0	16	Ivanovic [61]	11,418
29	28	A	Portsmouth	W	1-0	1-0	14	Ivanovic [40]	19,815
30	Feb 1	H	QPR	W	2-1	2-1	13	Connolly [1], Cundle [25]	17,914
31	12	A	Plymouth Arg	L	1-5	0-2	14	Bryan [80]	15,453
32	15	A	WBA	D	1-1	1-1	14	Cooper [19]	15,842
33	18	A	Preston NE	D	1-1	1-0	14	Ivanovic [40]	13,290
34	22	A	Derby Co	W	1-0	0-0	10	Coburn [90]	28,321
35	Mar 4	A	Bristol C	L	0-2	0-0	12		12,380
36	8	A	Watford	W	2-1	0-1	12	De Norre [59], Coburn [81]	20,031
37	12	A	Leeds U	L	0-2	0-1	13		34,401
38	15	H	Stoke C	W	1-0	0-0	11	Ivanovic (pen) [90]	16,799
39	29	A	Sunderland	L	0-1	0-1	13		41,762
40	Apr 5	H	Portsmouth	W	2-1	0-0	9	Ivanovic 2 [57, 87]	16,913
41	8	A	Sheffield U	W	1-0	1-0	9	Coburn [21]	25,775
42	12	H	Middlesbrough	W	1-0	0-0	9	Neghli [65]	17,523
43	18	A	Blackburn R	L	1-4	1-2	9	Ivanovic [44]	14,167
44	21	H	Norwich C	W	3-1	2-1	8	Ivanovic 2 [8, 69], Azeez [39]	16,426
45	26	A	Swansea C	W	1-0	1-0	7	Saville [38]	17,239
46	May 3	A	Burnley	L	1-3	1-1	8	Ivanovic [11]	21,485

Final League Position: 8

GOALSCORERS

League (47): Ivanovic 12 (1 pen), Coburn 5, Watmore 5, Esse 4, Cooper 3, De Norre 3, Azeez 2, Honeyman 2, Tanganga 2, Bradshaw 1 (1 pen), Bryan 1, Connolly 1, Cundle 1, Langstaff 1, Neghli 1, Saville 1, Scanlon 1, Wintle 1.
FA Cup (6): Azeez 2, Bangura-Williams 1, De Norre 1, Harding 1, Ivanovic 1.
Carabao Cup (1): Esse 1.

Jensen L 41	Leonard R 29+4	Hutchinson S 4+5	Cooper J 36	Bryan J 37+2	Saville G 36+9	De Norre C 44+2	Esse R 24	Honeyman G 28+12	Watmore D 19+7	Bradshaw T 4+7	Emakhu A 6+19	Langstaff M 14+20	Nisbet K —+1	McNamara D 7+6	Leahy T —+1	Tanganga J 40	Azeez F 21+13	Coburn J 14+6	Wintle R 3+19	Scanlon C 3+1	Ivanovic M 23+14	Wallace M 8+3	Kelly D —+2	Mitchell B 9+10	Connolly A 6+8	Bangura-Williams R 7+3	Crama T 18+2	Roberts L 1+1	Cundle L 13+3	Neghli C 2+2	Sturge Z 3+2	Harding W 2+3	Evans G 4	Match No.
1	2[4]	3	4	5	6	7	8[1]	9[2]	10	11[3]	12	13	14	15																				1
1	2	3[4]	4	5	7	6	8[1]	9	10[2]	11[3]	12	14		13	15																			2
1	2		4	5	7	6	8	9	10[1]	11[2]		13				3	12																	3
1	2		4	5	7	6	8[2]	9[4]	10[3]	15	12					3	14	11[1]	13															4
1	2	13	3[2]	5[4]	4	6	7	8[5]	9[3]	10	16	12				4	14	11[1]	15															5
1	2	3		5	6	7	8	9[3]	10[2]	11[1]						4	12	14	13															6
1	2[2]		4	5	7	6	8[4]	9[6]	10[2]	15[4]	11[1]	14				3	13	12	16															7
1	2		4	5	7[2]	6	8	9[1]	10	11						3	13	12																8
1	2		4	15	7	6[3]	10	9	13	11[1]	5[4]					3	8[2]	14	12															9
1	2		4	15	7[4]	6[3]	8	9	10[1]	11[2]						3	12	14	13	15														10
1	2		4	5	7	6[3]	8[4]	9	14	15						3	10[1]	12	11[2]	13														11
1	2		4	15	7	12	8[4]	9[3]	10[1]	11[2]	5					3	13	6	14															12
1	2	16	4	5[1]	7	6	10[4]	9[5]	15	11[2]	12					3	8[3]	13	14															13
1	2	15	4	7	12	8[3]	9	10[1]	11[2]	5						3	14	13	6[4]															14
1	2	15	4	13	6	8[2]	12	11[1]	5							3	10[4]	9[3]	7	14														15
1	2	3[5]		5	6[4]	7	8	9[1]	10[2]	12	15	16				4	13	11[3]	14															16
1	2	3[2]		5	6	7	8	9	12	14						4	10[3]	11[1]	13															17
1		3		5	7[3]	6[4]		9[2]	10[1]	16	12	11				8	15	13	4	14														18
1				5	7	6[2]	8	9[3]	13	12	2					3	10[1]	14	11	4														19
1	2			7	6[4]	8[6]	9[2]	13	16	12	11[3]	5				3	10[1]	15	4	14														20
1	2			5	6	7[2]	10	14	9	11[3]						3	8[1]	13	12	4														21
1	2			5	7[5]	6[4]	9	14	12	16	10[1]	13				3	8[3]	15	11[2]	4														22
1	2			5	7	6	8	9	12	11[1]						3	10		4															23
1	2			5	7[4]	6[3]	8	13	10[1]	14	9[2]					3	12	15	11	4														24
1	2	14		5	7[1]	6[2]	8	9	13							3	10	12	11[3]	4														25
1	5	3	4	7[3]	6	10		9[2]	13							2	8[1]							11[4]	15	12	14							26
1	2[1]		4	5	6	7	15	8[5]	11		12[2]					3					10[4]	14	16			9[3]	13							27
1[3]			4	5	7	6	13	8[2]								3					10[1]	11		12	9	2	14							28
1	4	5	6[5]	7[4]	12	9[1]	15									3	13	11[3]	16		14	10		8[2]			2							29
1	4	5	6	7[2]	14	13	16									3	12	11	15		10[4]	8[5]					2		9[1]					30
1	4	5	6	7[3]	15											3	13	11	14		10[4]	12					2		9[2]	8[1]				31
1	4	5	13	6[3]	14	7[2]										3	10	11				8[1]					2		9	12				32
1	4	8	13	6[5]	14	7[2]	15									3	5	12	16		11[4]					9[1]	2		10[3]					33
1	4	5[1]		7	6[5]		14	15	13							3	10[1]	16			11					9[2]	2		8	12				34
1	4	5	14	7[4]	15	12			13							3	10[1]	11			6[3]					9[2]	2		8					35
1	4	5	16	6[1]	8	7[5]	13	10[3]								3	14	11[4]	15		12					9[2]	2							36
1	4	5	7	6[3]	8[1]		13									3	10[6]	15			11[4]	12	16			9	2[2]		14					37
1	4	5	7			9[2]										3	11				10	8		13	6[2]	14	2[1]		12					38
1	14	4	5	13	7[4]			9[1]	15							3	11	12			8			10[5]		6[3]	2[2]		16					39
1	12	4	5	6[2]	7		8	13	15							3[1]	11[3]	9	14		10[4]						2							40
1	2	4	5	13	7[3]	6[4]	12	14	11									16			10[2]			8[5]		3	9[1]		15					41
1	2	4	5	13	7[2]	6[3]	9[4]	12	14								14				10			8		3	11[1]		15[5]		16			42
	5	4	12	8[2]	6		13	9[4]	11								10[3]				7[1]	15				3	14		2				1	43
	15	4	7	6[1]			16	14								3	10[5]	11	12		9[3]			13			2		8[2]	5[4]		1	1	44
		4	7	6[3]	12		13									3	10	11[2]	14		9						2		8[1]	5		1	1	45
	15	4	7[5]	6[1]	8[3]		13	16								3	10	11	14		9[2]						2[4]		12	5		1	1	46

FA Cup

Third Round	Dagenham & Red	(h)	3-0
Fourth Round	Leeds U	(a)	2-0
Fifth Round	Crystal Palace	(a)	1-3

Carabao Cup

First Round	Portsmouth	(a)	1-0
Second Round	Leyton Orient	(h)	0-1

MILTON KEYNES DONS

FOUNDATION

In July 2004 Wimbledon became MK Dons and relocated to Milton Keynes. In 2007 it recognised itself as a new club with no connection to the old Wimbledon FC. In August of that year the replica trophies and other Wimbledon FC memorabilia were returned to the London Borough of Merton.

Stadium MK, Stadium Way West, Milton Keynes, Buckinghamshire MK1 1ST.

Telephone: (01908) 622 933.

Ticket Office: (01908) 622 933.

Website: www.mkdons.com

Email: info@mkdons.com

Ground Capacity: 30,303.

Record Attendance: 28,521 v Liverpool, EFL Cup 3rd rd, 25 September 2019.

Pitch Measurements: 105m × 68m (115yd × 74.5yd).

Chairman: Fahad Al Ghanim.

Sporting Director: Neil Hart.

Head Coach: Paul Warne.

Assistant Head Coach: Richie Barker.

Colours: White shirts with black and gold trim, white shorts with black and gold trim, white socks with black and gold trim.

Year Formed: 2004.

Turned Professional: 2004.

Club Nickname: 'The Dons'.

Grounds: 2004, The National Hockey Stadium; 2007, Stadium MK.

First Football League Game: 7 August 2004, FL 1, v Barnsley (h) D 1–1 – Rachubka; Palmer, Lewington, Harding, Williams, Oyedele, Kamara, Smith, Smart (Herve), McLeod (1) (Hornuss), Small.

Record League Victory: 7–0 v Oldham Ath, FL 1, 20 December 2014 – Martin; Spence, McFadzean, Kay (Baldock), Lewington; Potter (1), Alli (1); Baker C (1), Carruthers (Green), Bowditch (1) (Afobe (1)); Grigg (2).

HONOURS

League Champions: FL 2 – 2007–08.
Runners-up: FL 1 – 2014–15.
FA Cup: 5th rd – 2013.
League Cup: 4th rd – 2015, 2023.
League Trophy Winners: 2008.

FOOTBALL YEARBOOK FACT FILE

Milton Keynes Dons defeated Blackpool 4-3 at Stadium MK in the Football League Cup second round on 24 August 2010, providing the club with their first-ever win against Premier League opposition in a competitive match. Goals from Sam Baldock and Jermaine Easter (2) enabled the Dons to level the tie 3-3 after 90 minutes before Lewis Guy clinched the victory in extra time.

Record Cup Victory: 6–0 v Nantwich T, FA Cup 1st rd, 12 November 2011 – Martin; Chicksen, Baldock G, Doumbe (1), Flanagan, Williams S, Powell (1) (O'Shea (1), Chadwick (Galloway), Bowditch (2), MacDonald (Williams G (1)), Balanta; 6–0 v Norwich C U21, EFL Trophy Southern Section 2nd rd, 8 December 2020 – Nicholls; Poole (2), Williams (Davies), Cargill, Harvie; Sorensen (1), Kasumu (Surman), Freeman (Johnson), Sorinola; Walker S (1), Agard (2); 6–0 v Taunton T, FA Cup 1st rd, 5 November 2022 – Ravizzoli; Tucker, O'Hora, Lewington; Lawrence, McEachran, Devoy (1), Harvie (Watson 59); Barry (Holland 59), Grigg (1) (Eisa 60 (1)), Burns (1) (Grant 72 (2)).

Record Defeat: 0–6 v Southampton, Capital One Cup 3rd rd, 23 September 2015.

Most League Points (3 for a win): 97, FL 2, 2007–08.

Most League Goals: 101, FL 1, 2014–15.

Highest League Scorer in Season: Izale McLeod, 21, 2006–07.

Most League Goals in Total Aggregate: Izale McLeod, 62, 2004–07; 2012–14.

Most Capped Player: Simon Church, 9 (38) including 5 on loan at Aberdeen, Wales; also Troy Parrott, 9 (23), Republic of Ireland (on loan from Tottenham H).

Most League Goals in One Match: 4, Will Grigg v Swindon T, FL 1, 24 April 2021; 4, Scott Twine v Plymouth Arg, FL 1, 30 April 2022.

Most League Appearances: Dean Lewington, 791, 2004–25.

Youngest League Player: Brendon Galloway, 16 years 42 days v Rochdale, 28 April 2012.

Record Transfer Fee Received: £5,000,000 from Tottenham H for Dele Alli, February 2015.

Record Transfer Fee Paid: £1,300,000 to Peterborough U for Mo Eisa, July 2021.

Football League Record: 2004–06 FL 1; 2006–08 FL 2; 2008–15 FL 1; 2015–16 FL C; 2016–18 FL 1; 2018–19 FL 2; 2019–23 FL 1; 2023– FL 2.

MANAGERS

Stuart Murdock 2004
Danny Wilson 2004–06
Martin Allen 2006–07
Paul Ince 2007–08
Roberto Di Matteo 2008–09
Paul Ince 2009–10
Karl Robinson 2010–16
Robbie Neilson 2016–18
Dan Micciche 2018
Paul Tisdale 2018–19
Russell Martin 2019–21
Liam Manning 2021–22
Mark Jackson 2022–23
Graham Alexander 2023
Mike Williamson 2023–24
Scott Lindsey 2024–25
Paul Warne April 2025–

LATEST SEQUENCES

Longest Sequence of League Wins: 8, 7.9.2007 – 20.10.2007.

Longest Sequence of League Defeats: 6, 2.4.2018 – 28.4.2018.

Longest Sequence of League Draws: 4, 1.4.2023 – 15.4.2023.

Longest Sequence of Unbeaten League Matches: 18, 29.1.2008 – 3.5.2008.

Longest Sequence Without a League Win: 12, 17.9.2019 – 7.12.2019.

Successive Scoring Runs: 18 from 21.8.2018.

Successive Non-scoring Runs: 5 from 5.10.2019.

TEN YEAR LEAGUE RECORD

		P	W	D	L	F	A	Pts	Pos
2015-16	FL C	46	9	12	25	39	69	39	23
2016-17	FL 1	46	16	13	17	60	58	61	12
2017-18	FL 1	46	11	12	23	43	69	45	23
2018-19	FL 2	46	23	10	13	71	49	79	3
2019-20	FL 1	35	10	7	18	36	47	37	19§
2020-21	FL 1	46	18	11	17	64	62	65	13
2021-22	FL 1	46	26	11	9	78	44	89	3
2022-23	FL 1	46	11	12	23	44	66	45	21
2023-24	FL 2	46	23	9	14	83	68	78	4
2024-25	FL 2	46	14	10	22	52	66	52	19

§*Decided on points-per-game (1.06)*

DID YOU KNOW ?

Milton Keynes Dons played their first game at the new Stadium MK on 18 July 2007. A young Chelsea XI provided the opposition and with a restricted capacity of 5,000 the attendance was recorded as 4,777. Both teams made significant changes to their line-ups during the match with the Dons winning 4-3.

MILTON KEYNES DONS FC – SKY BET LEAGUE TWO 2024–25 LEAGUE RECORD

Match No.	Date	Venue	Opponents	Result	H/T Score	Lg Pos.	Goalscorers	Attendance
1	Aug 10	H	Bradford C	L 1-2	1-2	16	Gilbey [20]	7561
2	17	A	Colchester U	L 0-2	0-0	23		4521
3	24	H	Carlisle U	W 3-0	2-0	15	Hendry [18], Gilbey [31], Harrison [90]	6399
4	Sept 2	A	Salford C	L 0-1	0-1	19		2227
5	7	H	Walsall	W 1-0	1-0	14	Hendry [18]	6547
6	14	A	AFC Wimbledon	L 0-3	0-1	20		7921
7	21	H	Doncaster R	D 1-1	1-0	19	Harrison [34]	7838
8	28	A	Bromley	D 1-1	1-1	19	Tomlinson [8]	3522
9	Oct 1	A	Harrogate T	W 5-1	3-0	14	Leigh [35], White [45], Gilbey [45], Lemonheigh-Evans [87], Finch [90]	1694
10	5	H	Tranmere R	D 1-1	1-0	13	White [23]	6047
11	12	H	Port Vale	L 0-1	0-0	15		2427
12	19	A	Morecambe	W 3-1	2-1	13	Tomlinson (pen) [2], Hogan [22], Kelly [49]	3448
13	22	H	Accrington S	W 2-1	1-0	12	Gilbey [1], Tomlinson [58]	5084
14	26	A	Grimsby T	W 3-1	0-1	8	Gilbey [49], Hogan [53], Lemonheigh-Evans [90]	5853
15	Nov 9	H	Swindon T	W 3-1	1-1	6	Thompson-Sommers [45], Williams M [57], Gilbey [64]	7407
16	16	H	Cheltenham T	W 3-2	1-2	5	Gilbey [22], Harrison [75], Maguire [86]	7333
17	Dec 3	H	Chesterfield	W 3-0	2-0	3	Hogan [1], Gilbey 2 [26, 82]	5903
18	14	H	Gillingham	L 0-1	0-0	8		7191
19	21	A	Newport Co	L 3-6	1-4	9	Offord 2 [45, 75], White [71]	4382
20	26	H	Notts Co	L 0-2	0-0	11		9249
21	29	H	Crewe Alex	D 1-1	1-0	11	White [9]	7508
22	Jan 1	A	Chesterfield	W 2-1	2-0	11	Hendry [18], White [44]	9119
23	4	A	Salford C	L 0-1	0-1	12		5934
24	18	A	Walsall	L 2-4	1-1	12	Hogan [14], Thompson-Sommers [85]	6144
25	21	A	Fleetwood T	L 1-2	0-1	12	O'Reilly [81]	2150
26	25	H	AFC Wimbledon	D 0-0	0-0	12		7693
27	28	A	Harrogate T	W 2-1	1-0	11	White [27], Gilbey [90]	5101
28	Feb 1	A	Doncaster R	L 1-2	0-1	11	Hogan [58]	6871
29	8	H	Bromley	L 0-1	0-0	14		6972
30	11	A	Barrow	L 1-2	1-1	15	Hogan [8]	2783
31	15	A	Tranmere R	D 1-1	1-0	16	Orsi-Dadomo [32]	5699
32	22	A	Bradford C	L 0-2	0-0	17		17,666
33	Mar 1	H	Colchester U	L 0-1	0-0	17		8002
34	4	A	Accrington S	L 0-2	0-2	18		1596
35	8	H	Morecambe	W 2-1	1-1	18	Offord [42], Orsi-Dadomo [64]	5718
36	15	A	Port Vale	L 0-3	0-1	18		6773
37	22	A	Cheltenham T	W 1-0	1-0	18	Sanders [9]	4283
38	25	A	Carlisle U	D 2-2	2-2	17	Tomlinson [6], Gilbey [37]	6679
39	29	H	Fleetwood T	L 2-4	1-1	17	Orsi-Dadomo [27], Hogan [83]	6273
40	Apr 2	A	Notts Co	L 0-3	0-0	18		8920
41	5	H	Barrow	L 0-3	0-1	19		6585
42	12	A	Gillingham	L 0-1	0-0	19		6080
43	18	H	Newport Co	D 0-0	0-0	19		8135
44	21	A	Crewe Alex	W 1-0	1-0	18	Hogan [28]	4954
45	26	H	Grimsby T	D 0-0	0-0	18		10,244
46	May 3	A	Swindon T	D 0-0	0-0	19		9503

Final League Position: 19

GOALSCORERS
League (52): Gilbey 11, Hogan 8, White 6, Tomlinson 4 (1 pen), Harrison 3, Hendry 3, Offord 3, Orsi-Dadomo 3, Lemonheigh-Evans 2, Thompson-Sommers 2, Finch 1, Kelly 1, Leigh 1, Maguire 1, O'Reilly 1, Sanders 1, Williams M 1.
FA Cup (0).
Carabao Cup (0).
Vertu Trophy (4): Harrison 2, Hendry 1, Wearne 1.

McGill T 25	Sherring S 9+1	Tucker J 7+2	Lawrence N 22	Nemane A 36+4	Kelly L 31+6	Offord L 42	Tomlinson J 38+2	Wearne S 9+2	Gilbey A 42	Hendry C 15+14	Dennis M —+2	Leigh T 7+5	Tripp C 5+2	Carroll T 3+11	Lewington D 2+4	Lemonheigh-Evans C 29+5	Harrison E 3+16	Maguire L 29+1	Williams M 4+9	Finch S —+6	Thompson-Sommers K 11+12	White J 23+11	Ilunga B —+3	Hogan S 25+8	Pritchard J 3+1	Williams J 9+1	Crowley D 18	MacGillivray C 8	O'Reilly T 3+13	Thompson N 2	Waller C 4+4	Sanders J 13	Trueman C 13	Patterson T 4+3	Orsi-Dadomo D 10+8	Leko J 2+7	Match No.
1	2	3	4	5^3	6	7^4	8	9^2	10	11^1	12	13	14	15																							1
1	2	3		5^1		6^3	8	9	10	11^2				14		7		4	12	13																	2
1	2	12		5^4		3^1	8	9^3	10	11^2				14	15	7		6^5	13	4	16																3
1				5	7^1	3	8	9^2	11	10^3			12	2		6	14	4	15	13^4																	4
1		14		5^1	7^4	3	8	12	10	11^5	15		9^3	2		6		4^2	16		13																5
1				5^4	7	3	8	12	10^3	11^2			9^1	2		6	15	4		13	14																6
1	2			5^2	9^1	3	8		11							6^3	10^6	4	7	12		14	13														7
1	2			5^1	9^2	3	8^3		11			10^4		13		6		4	7	15		14	12														8
1	2			5	7^3	3	8		10			11^2		12		6		4	14	13		9^1															9
1	2			5	7^3	3	8		10			11^1		12		6		4	14	13		9^2															10
1	2			5	7	3	8		10			11^2				6	13	4				9^1	12														11
1			2	5^3	7	3	8		10					13	15	6	12	4^4	14			9^1	11^2														12
1		3		5^1	7	2	8		10					12^4	15	6	13	4	14			9^1	11^2														13
1	2			5	7^3	3	8		10					9^1		6	13	4	14	14		12	11^2														14
1				5^2		2	8		9^1	10	12							4	3		7	6		11^2													15
1				5	13	2	8^3		9^4	10	14					12		15	4	3^1		7^2	6	11													16
1		3		5^5	7^4	2			9^2	10	12			15		13		14	4		16	6		11^3	8^1												17
1		3		5	6	2			9^1	10	13					14			12	4^3			7		11	8^2											18
1		3		5	7^3	2			9^1	10	13					12		14	4			6		11	8^2												19
1	13		3	12	9	2	8^3		10					6^4			5^1	14	4^2			15	7	11													20
1	4		3	5	6^3	2	8^2		10	12				14				13				7	9^1	11													21
1	4		3	5	7^4	2	8		10	11^2				14				12	9^1		15		6^3	13													22
1	4		3	5^1	7^2	2	8		10	9								11					6	13	12												23
1	4		3	5	6^2	2	8^4		10	15								14			12	13		11^3		7^1	9										24
	4		3	5^4		2	12		10	13						14					7^2	8^3		11^1		6	9	1	15								25
	4	5				2^1	8		10												13	7^2		11		6	9	1		3	12						26
	2	5					8		10	14						13					12	6^4		11		7	9	1	15	3^1	4						27
1		4			13		5		9	10^3						2	14					8^1		11		6^2	7		12			3					28
	4	12		7^3		5^2	8		11^4							2^1					16			10		6^5	9		15			3	1	13	14		29
	4			9		5	8		11^1							2^3								10		6^2	7		13			3	1	14	12		30
	4			8^2	3		9		14							2					13			11		6^3	7			12		1	5	10^1			31
	3			5^2	7	2			10	14											12			9^1		6	13	4		4		1	8	11^3			32
				5^3	7^4	3			10	13^8				2							15	9^2		12		6	14	4		1		8	11^1				33
	3	5		7^3		2	13		10							15					12			11		6^2	9		4^4		1	8^1	14				34
	3	5	15		2	8			10							7^1		4^2				9^3		16	12	6^5	14	13			1		11^4				35
	3^9			2	8		10							7^1		5	4			13	9	14		6	12				1		11^2					36
				14	13	2	9		5	10^1						7	4				8^3			6^2				3	1		11	12					37
				2^2	12	3	6		10							8	5				9^1			7^3	14			4	1		11^3	13					38
				5^1	8^2	2	9		10							7	4			14		13		6^4	12			3	1		11^3	15					39
				5		2	9		10							7	4			8^2		12		6				3	1		11^1	13					40
		12				3	8^1		10							6		7^2			11			9		5^3		2	1		13	14					41
		13				2	8		10^3	9^1						6		4			7^2 12	11					1	5	3		14						42
		9^3				2	5			11^1						6		4			7	13		10				1	8^2	3		12	14				43
	5^2	9^3			3	8			13							7	4			6	12		11^4			1		14	2		15	10^1				44
	5^5	7^4			2	8			13					4^3	9	14					6	15		11^2			1	16		3		13	10^1				45
		6		5^3	2	9^1			10^4					16	8	4^5					7	14					1	12		3		15	11^2 13				46

FA Cup
First Round   AFC Wimbledon   (h)   0-2

Carabao Cup
First Round   Watford   (a)   0-5

Vertu Trophy
Group E (S)   Colchester U   (a)   1-2
Group E (S)   Arsenal U21   (h)   2-2
Milton Keynes D won 3-1 on penalties.
Group E (S)   Leyton Orient   (h)   1-3

MORECAMBE

FOUNDATION

Several attempts to start a senior football club in a rugby stronghold finally succeeded on 7 May 1920 at the West View Hotel, Morecambe and a team competed in the Lancashire Combination for 1920–21. The club shared with a local cricket club at Woodhill Lane for the first season and a crowd of 3,000 watched the first game. The club moved to Roseberry Park, the name of which was changed to Christie Park after J.B. Christie who as President had purchased the ground.

The Mazuma Mobile Stadium, Christie Way, Westgate, Morecambe, Lancashire LA4 4TB.

Telephone: (01524) 411 797.

Ticket Office: (01524) 411 797.

Website: www.morecambefc.com

Email: reception@morecambefc.com

Ground Capacity: 6,241.

Record Attendance: 9,383 v Weymouth, FA Cup 3rd rd, 6 January 1962 (at Christie Park); 5,831 v Sunderland, FL 1, 30 April 2022 (at Mazuma Stadium).

Pitch Measurements: 101m × 66m (110.5yd × 72yd).

Co-Chairmen: Graham Howse, Rod Taylor.

Director of Football Operations: Mick Horton.

Manager: Derek Adams.

Assistant Manager: Danny Grainger.

Colours: Red shirts with black, white and red trim, white shorts with red trim, black socks with white trim.

Year Formed: 1920.

Turned Professional: 1920.

Club Nickname: 'The Shrimps'.

Grounds: 1920, Woodhill Lane; 1921, Christie Park; 2010, Globe Arena (renamed Mazuma Stadium 2020; The Mazuma Mobile Stadium 2023).

First Football League game: 11 August 2007, FL 2, v Barnet (h) D 0–0 – Lewis; Yates, Adams, Artell, Bentley, Stanley, Baker (Burns), Sorvel, Twiss (Newby), Curtis, Hunter (Thompson).

HONOURS

League: *Runners-up:* Football Conference – 2002–03, (3rd) 2006–07 *(promoted to FL 2 via play-offs)*.
FA Cup: 3rd rd – 1962, 2001, 2003, 2021, 2022, 2024, 2025.
League Cup: 3rd rd – 2008, 2021, 2023.

FOOTBALL YEARBOOK FACT FILE

Fred Warburton was a well-known professional player before the First World War, including a spell with a previous incarnation of Morecambe FC. He later spent over 25 years coaching in the Netherlands, including a four-year spell in charge of the national team, guiding them to the bronze medal at the 1920 Olympics. In September 1936 he returned to the North West and served Morecambe as trainer through until the outbreak of the Second World War.

Record League Victory: 6–0 v Crawley T, FL 2, 10 September 2011 – Roche; Reid, Wilson (pen), McCready, Haining (Parrish), Fenton (1), Drummond, McDonald, Price (Jevons), Carlton (3) (Alessandra), Ellison (1).

Record Cup Victory: 6–2 v Nelson (a), Lancashire Trophy, 27 January 2004.

Record Defeat: 0–7 v Cambridge U, FL 2, 19 April 2016; 0–7 v Newcastle U, League Cup 3rd rd, 23 September 2020.

Most League Points (3 for a win): 78, FL 2, 2020–21.

Most League Goals: 73, FL 2, 2009–10.

Highest League Scorer in Season: Cole Stockton, 23, 2021–22.

Most League Goals in Total Aggregate: Kevin Ellison, 81, 2011–20.

Most League Goals in One Match: 3, Jon Newby v Rotherham U, FL 2, 29 March 2008; 3, JJ McKiernan v Colchester U, FL 2, 7 October 2023; 3, Michael Mellon v AFC Wimbledon, FL 2, 28 October 2023.

Most Capped Player: Greg Leigh, 6 (25), Jamaica.

Most League Appearances: Barry Roche, 436, 2008–20.

Youngest League Player: Aaron McGowan, 16 years 263 days, 20 April 2013.

Record Transfer Fee Received: £225,000 from Stockport Co for Carl Baker, July 2008.

Record Transfer Fee Paid: £50,000 to Southport for Carl Baker, July 2007.

Football League Record: 2007 Promoted from Football Conference; 2007–21 FL 2; 2021–23 FL 1; 2023–25 FL 2; 2025– National League.

MANAGERS

Jimmy Milne 1947–48
Albert Dainty 1955–56
Ken Horton 1956–61
Joe Dunn 1961–64
Geoff Twentyman 1964–65
Ken Waterhouse 1965–69
Ronnie Clayton 1969–70
Gerry Irving and
    Ronnie Mitchell 1970
Ken Waterhouse 1970–72
Dave Roberts 1972–75
Alan Spavin 1975–76
Johnny Johnson 1976–77
Tommy Ferber 1977–78
Mick Hogarth 1978–79
Don Curbage 1979–81
Jim Thompson 1981
Les Rigby 1981–84
Sean Gallagher 1984–85
Joe Wojciechowicz 1985–88
Eric Whalley 1988
Billy Wright 1988–89
Lawrie Milligan 1989
Bryan Griffiths 1989–93
Leighton James 1994
Jim Harvey 1994–2006
Sammy McIlroy 2006–11
Jim Bentley 2011–19
Derek Adams 2019–21
Stephen Robinson 2021–22
Derek Adams 2022–23
Ged Brannan 2023–24
Derek Adams June 2024–

LATEST SEQUENCES

Longest Sequence of League Wins: 7, 31.10.2009 – 12.12.2009.

Longest Sequence of League Defeats: 7, 4.3.2017 – 1.4.2017.

Longest Sequence of League Draws: 5, 3.1.2015 – 31.1.2015.

Longest Sequence of Unbeaten League Matches: 12, 31.1.2009 – 21.3.2009.

Longest Sequence Without a League Win: 15, 6.4.2024 – 5.10.2024.

Successive Scoring Runs: 17 from 13.8.2011.

Successive Non-scoring Runs: 7 from 21.4.2018.

TEN YEAR LEAGUE RECORD

		P	W	D	L	F	A	Pts	Pos
2015-16	FL 2	46	12	10	24	69	91	46	21
2016-17	FL 2	46	14	10	22	53	73	52	18
2017-18	FL 2	46	9	19	18	41	56	46	22
2018-19	FL 2	46	14	12	20	54	70	54	18
2019-20	FL 2	37	7	11	19	35	60	32	22§
2020-21	FL 2	46	23	9	14	69	58	78	4
2021-22	FL 1	46	10	12	24	57	88	42	19
2022-23	FL 1	46	10	14	22	47	78	44	22
2023-24	FL 2	46	17	10	19	67	81	58*	15
2024-25	FL 2	46	10	6	30	40	72	36	24

*3 pts deducted. §Decided on points-per-game (0.86)

DID YOU KNOW ?

Morecambe's home fixture with neighbours Lancaster City on New Year's Day 1947 attracted a new record attendance of 5,777 to Christie Park for the Lancashire Combination fixture. The attendance remained a record for a league game at the ground until the club moved to the Globe Arena in 2010, although the figure was exceeded on several occasions for FA Cup ties.

MORECAMBE – SKY BET LEAGUE TWO 2024–25 LEAGUE RECORD

Match No.	Date	Venue	Opponents	Result	H/T Score	Lg Pos.	Goalscorers	Attendance
1	Aug 10	A	Walsall	L	0-1	0-1	17		5226
2	17	H	Gillingham	L	0-1	0-0	22		3611
3	24	A	Doncaster R	L	0-1	0-1	24		6832
4	31	H	Newport Co	L	0-1	0-1	24		2724
5	Sept 7	A	Crewe Alex	L	0-1	0-1	24		4868
6	14	H	Colchester U	D	3-3	1-1	24	Tollitt [17], Jones (pen) [83], Flanagan (og) [88]	2754
7	23	A	Fleetwood T	D	2-2	0-2	24	Songo'o [74], Hope [86]	4025
8	28	H	Notts Co	D	1-1	1-0	23	Angol [2]	3595
9	Oct 1	H	Bradford C	D	1-1	1-0	23	Diabate (og) [5]	3606
10	5	A	Accrington S	L	1-2	0-2	24	Tollitt [86]	2862
11	12	A	Barrow	W	1-0	0-0	23	Tollitt [82]	4665
12	19	H	Milton Keynes D	L	1-3	1-2	24	Stott [44]	3448
13	22	A	AFC Wimbledon	L	0-3	0-0	24		7651
14	26	H	Chesterfield	L	2-5	1-1	24	Tollitt [10], Naylor (og) [61]	3666
15	Nov 9	A	Harrogate T	W	2-1	1-0	24	Williams [37], Macadam [90]	2982
16	16	H	Port Vale	L	0-1	0-0	24		4150
17	23	A	Swindon T	W	3-2	2-1	23	Stott [6], Tollitt [14], Hope [78]	6494
18	Dec 3	A	Tranmere R	D	2-2	1-0	22	Tollitt [12], Lewis A [50]	4968
19	7	H	Grimsby T	L	0-3	0-2	23		2995
20	14	A	Cheltenham T	L	0-2	0-1	23		3371
21	21	H	Bromley	L	0-2	0-1	24		3515
22	26	A	Carlisle U	W	1-0	0-0	23	Edwards [61]	9225
23	29	A	Salford C	L	0-1	0-0	24		3179
24	Jan 1	H	Tranmere R	W	2-0	0-0	23	Songo'o [72], Stott [84]	3577
25	18	H	Crewe Alex	L	0-1	0-0	23		3648
26	25	A	Colchester U	L	0-1	0-0	24		4238
27	28	A	Bradford C	L	0-1	0-1	24		15,083
28	Feb 1	H	Fleetwood T	W	4-2	1-1	23	Cooke (pen) [13], Dallas 2 [52, 59], Dackers [86]	3522
29	4	A	Newport Co	L	1-2	0-1	23	Edwards [79]	3831
30	8	A	Notts Co	L	0-2	0-0	23		9909
31	15	H	Accrington S	W	2-0	0-0	23	Angol [54], Garner [88]	3473
32	18	H	Doncaster R	L	0-1	0-1	23		2951
33	22	H	Walsall	L	0-2	0-0	23		3457
34	Mar 1	A	Gillingham	L	0-1	0-0	23		5612
35	4	H	AFC Wimbledon	W	1-0	1-0	23	Angol [20]	2488
36	8	A	Milton Keynes D	L	1-2	1-1	23	Angol (pen) [37]	5718
37	15	H	Barrow	D	2-2	2-0	23	Edwards [9], Angol [45]	4351
38	22	A	Port Vale	L	0-1	0-0	23		7038
39	29	H	Swindon T	W	1-0	1-0	23	Angol [38]	3419
40	Apr 1	H	Cheltenham T	W	2-0	0-0	23	Garner [66], Angol [74]	2502
41	5	A	Grimsby T	L	1-3	1-1	23	Dallas [30]	5807
42	12	H	Carlisle U	L	0-2	0-1	24		4901
43	18	A	Bromley	L	0-1	0-0	24		2382
44	21	H	Salford C	L	1-3	0-2	24	Songo'o [52]	3027
45	26	A	Chesterfield	L	1-4	0-1	24	Slew [59]	8725
46	May 3	H	Harrogate T	L	1-2	1-2	24	Taylor [12]	3043

Final League Position: 24

GOALSCORERS

League (40): Angol 7 (1 pen), Tollitt 6, Dallas 3, Edwards 3, Songo'o 3, Stott 3, Garner 2, Hope 2, Cooke 1 (pen), Dackers 1, Jones 1 (pen), Lewis A 1, Macadam 1, Slew 1, Taylor 1, Williams 1, own goals 3.
FA Cup (3): Slew 2, Williams 1.
Carabao Cup (0).
Vertu Trophy (7): Hope 2, Tollitt 2, Angol 1, Brown 1, Macadam 1.

Moore S 15	Hendrie L 34	Ray G 1+1	Stott J 43+2	Tutonda D 34+8	Harrack K 4+4	Jones C 31+3	Tollit B 28+11	Macadam H 22+7	Edwards G 19+6	Hope H 14+15	White T 27+7	Songo'o Y 26+10	Angol L 21+5	Slew J 8+23	Millen R 5+12	Lewis A 31+13	Williams R 32+1	Lewis P 17+12	Dackers M 21+15	Taylor M 14+6	Brown C —+4	Dobson L —+1	Burgoyne H 26+2	Cooke C 11+7	Fairclough A —+5	Dallas A 14+3	Schofield R 5	Garner G 3+5	Whaite B —+1	Match No.
1	2^5	3^2	4	5	6^1	7	8	9	10^3	11^4	12	13	14	15	16															1
1	2^3		4	5^4		7	8^2	9	10	11	6^1	3	13	12	15	14														2
1	2		4	5^4		7	13	9	8^2	11^1	15	6^3	12	10		14	3													3
1	2		4	5^4		7	14	9^3	8	11	16	6^3	13	10^2		15	3	12												4
1	2^4		4	5^3		7	16	9	8^1			6^5	11	10^3	15	13	3	12	14											5
1	$2^■$		4	15	16	9	10^3	8^1				6^4	11^2	14	12	5^5	3	7	13											6
1			4	12	13	7^1	10	9^3		16		3	11^4	15		5^5	8	2^2	6	14										7
1	2	3	4		$6^■$	7		9^3				11^1	12		5^2	8			13	10	14									8
1	5	3	4			9	10^1	14		13		6		12		8^3	2	7	11^2											9
1	5^4	3	4^2			7^3	10	12		13			6^1	14		8	2	9	11					15						10
1	5	3	4			7	10				12	6^2		13		8^3	2	9^1	11	14										11
1	5	3	4	6^2		7		9^3		11^1	13			14		8^4	2		10				12	15						12
1	2	3	5	7^4				9	8^1		12	13	6^3		16	10^2		4^5	11				15	14						13
1	2		4	5		7^1	8	9	12		6					10	3	11												14
1^2	2		4	5	12	7	8	14	10			6^4		15		9^1	3	11^3						13						15
	2		4	5^1		6^4	8	12	10^2	14	7			15		9	3	13	11^3				1							16
	2	15	4	5^1		6^3	8	12		14	7	13	10^4			9	3	11^2					1							17
	2		4	12	14		8	9^2			6^3	13	10^1	15		5^4	3	7	11				1							18
	2^5		4	13		8	9	12	7^3	14	10^5			15		5	6^1	11	16				1							19
	2		4	12		7^2	8	9	11^3		6^4	10		15		5^1	3	14	13				1							20
	2^2		4	5		8	9		12		7	6		13		10^1	3	11					1							21
	2		4	5		7^2	8	9^1	10^3		6	14		13		3	12	11					1							22
	2		4	5		9	8		10^3	12	6^1	7		11^2		13	3	14					1							23
	2		4	5		7	8^1		10^2	14	6	9		13		12	3	11^3					1							24
	2		4	5^1		9^4	8^5	16	10^3	14	7	6		13		12	3	11^2					1	15						25
	2		4	5		16	12	14	10^5	7^4	6^3	$11^■$	13			8^2	3	15					1	9^1						26
	2		4	5^5			8^1	9	10^2	11^3	6^4		12		7		14	15	3				1		13	16				27
	2		4	5^2					9	14	10^1	13	6		12	15	11	3					1	7^4	8^3					28
	2		4^3	5^2			15		6	12	10^1		7^4			13	14	11	3				1	8	9					29
	2			5			13	6	9						11^1		4	7	12	3				8^2	10	1				30
	2		12	15			7	8^2		16	11^1				5^4	4	6	13	3					9^4	10^3	1	14			31
	2		4	5^3			15	7	13		16		14	3	6	11				12	9^2		10^5	1^1	8^4					32
	2^2		12	5^4			6	16		7	11^3		15	$4^■$	8^9	9	3			1	14		10^1	13						33
	2^5		4	5^4			6	12		7	11^3	14	16	13		9	3			1	8^2		10^1	15						34
	5^2		4				6^3	9	12	3	11^5	13	8		7^1	16	2			1	15		14	10^4						35
	4		13				9^3		7	3	11^4	14	5	8	12	15	2^2			1	6^5		16	10^4						36
	4	12	14				9		7	3	10^3	13	5	8^1	15	$2^■$		1	6^4	11^2										37
	4	5	6^3	8^4			10^2		7	12	11	13	2	9^1	3			1	15				14							38
	4	5	6				11^2	8	7	10^3	14		2	3	13	12		1					9^1							39
	4	5	6^4	14			11^3	7	13	10		2	3	8^2				1	15				9^1	12						40
	4^5	5^3	6	13			11^2	8^1	15	10		2	3	7	12	14		1	16				9^4							41
	4	5^3	8	15			11^1	6^5	7	10		2	3^2	13	16	12		1		14	9^4									42
	4^1	$12^■$	8^3	7			13	6	3	10^4	15	5		9	14	2		1				11^2								43
	4		8	7^3			13	6	3	11^4	12	5		9^2		2		1		14	10^1		15							44
	4	5	2	8^1			13	7	6^3	11^2	12	10		14	3			9^4	15	1										45
	4	12	2	7^2			11^4	6	13	10	14	5^5	9		3^3			8^1	16	15	1									46

FA Cup

First Round	Worthing	(a)	2-0
Second Round	Bradford C	(h)	1-0
Third Round	Chelsea	(a)	0-5

Carabao Cup

First Round	Huddersfield T	(a)	0-3

Vertu Trophy

Group C (N)	Wigan Ath	(a)	2-1
Group C (N)	Nottingham F U21	(h)	4-2
Group C (N)	Carlisle U	(h)	1-2
Second Round	Lincoln C	(h)	0-1

NEWCASTLE UNITED

FOUNDATION

In October 1882 a club called Stanley, which had been formed in 1881, changed its name to Newcastle East End to avoid confusion with two other local clubs, Stanley Nops and Stanley Albion. Shortly afterwards another club, Rosewood, merged with them. Newcastle West End had been formed in August 1882 and they played on a pitch which was part of the Town Moor. They moved to Brandling Park in 1885 and St James' Park 1886 (home of Newcastle Rangers). West End went out of existence after a bad run and the remaining committee men invited East End to move to St James' Park. They accepted and, at a meeting in Bath Lane Hall in 1892, changed their name to Newcastle United.

St James' Park, Newcastle-upon-Tyne NE1 4ST.
Telephone: (0344) 372 1892.
Ticket Office: (0344) 372 1892 (option 1).
Website: www.nufc.co.uk
Email: admin@nufc.co.uk
Ground Capacity: 52,258.
Record Attendance: 68,386 v Chelsea, Division 1, 3 September 1930.
Pitch Measurements: 105m × 68m (115yd × 74.5yd).
Chairman: Yasir O. Al-Rumayyan.
Chief Executive: Darren Eales.
Head Coach: Eddie Howe.
Assistant Head Coach: Jason Tindall.
Colours: Black and white striped shirts, black shorts, black socks with white trim.
Year Formed: 1881.
Turned Professional: 1889.
Previous Names: 1881, Stanley; 1882, Newcastle East End; 1892, Newcastle United.
Club Nicknames: 'The Magpies'; 'The Toon'.
Grounds: 1881, South Byker; 1886, Chillingham Road, Heaton; 1892, St James' Park.
First Football League Game: 2 September 1893, Division 2, v Royal Arsenal (a) D 2–2 – Ramsay; Jeffery, Miller; Crielly, Graham, McKane; Bowman, Crate (1), Thompson, Sorley (1), Wallace. Graham not Crate scored according to some reports.
Record League Victory: 13–0 v Newport Co, Division 2, 5 October 1946 – Garbutt; Cowell, Graham; Harvey, Brennan, Wright; Milburn (2), Bentley (1), Wayman (4), Shackleton (6), Pearson.

HONOURS

League Champions: Division 1 – 1904–05, 1906–07, 1908–09, 1926–27; FL C – 2009–10, 2016–17; First Division – 1992–93; Division 2 – 1964–65.
Runners-up: Premier League – 1995–96, 1996–97; Division 2 – 1897–98, 1947–48.

FA Cup Winners: 1910, 1924, 1932, 1951, 1952, 1955.
Runners-up: 1905, 1906, 1908, 1911, 1974, 1998, 1999.

League Cup Winners: 2025.
Runners-up: 1976, 2023.

Texaco Cup Winners: 1974, 1975.
Anglo-Italian Cup Winners: 1972–73.

European Competitions
Champions League: 1997–98, 2002–03, 2003–04, 2023–24.
Fairs Cup: 1968–69 *(winners)*, 1969–70 *(qf)*, 1970–71.
UEFA Cup: 1977–78, 1994–95, 1996–97 *(qf)*, 1999–2000, 2003–04 *(sf)*, 2004–05 *(qf)*, 2006–07.
Europa League: 2012–13 *(qf)*.
European Cup Winners' Cup: 1998–99.
Intertoto Cup: 2001 *(runners-up)*, 2005, 2006 *(winners)*.

FOOTBALL YEARBOOK FACT FILE

Striker Micky Quinn enjoyed an explosive start to his career with Newcastle United after signing from Portsmouth in the summer of 1989. After getting off the mark with an early penalty he scored three more in a 5-2 opening day win over Leeds United. Quinn went on to net in each of his first five appearances for the Magpies and finished the season as the Football League's leading scorer with 32 goals.

Record Cup Victory: 9–0 v Southport (at Hillsborough), FA Cup 4th rd, 1 February 1932 – McInroy; Nelson, Fairhurst; McKenzie, Davidson, Weaver (1); Boyd (1), Jimmy Richardson (3), Cape (2), McMenemy (1), Lang (1).

Record Defeat: 0–9 v Burton Wanderers, Division 2, 15 April 1895.

Most League Points (2 for a win): 57, Division 2, 1964–65.

Most League Points (3 for a win): 102, FL C, 2009–10.

Most League Goals: 98, Division 1, 1951–52.

Highest League Scorer in Season: Hughie Gallacher, 36, Division 1, 1926–27.

Most League Goals in Total Aggregate: Jackie Milburn, 177, 1946–57.

Most League Goals in One Match: 6, Len Shackleton v Newport Co, Division 2, 5 October 1946.

Most Capped Player: Shay Given, 82 (134), Republic of Ireland.

Most League Appearances: Jim Lawrence, 432, 1904–22.

Youngest League Player: Steve Watson, 16 years 223 days v Wolverhampton W, 10 November 1990.

Record Transfer Fee Received: £35,000,000 from Liverpool for Andy Carroll, January 2011; £35,000,000 from Nottingham F for Elliott Anderson, June 2024.

Record Transfer Fee Paid: £59,000,000 (potentially rising to £63,000,000) to Real Sociedad for Alexander Isak, July 2022.

Football League Record: 1893 Elected to Division 2; 1893–98 Division 2; 1898–1934 Division 1; 1934–48 Division 2; 1948–61 Division 1; 1961–65 Division 2; 1965–78 Division 1; 1978–84 Division 2; 1984–89 Division 1; 1989–92 Division 2; 1992–93 First Division; 1993–2009 Premier League; 2009–10 FL C; 2010–16 Premier League; 2016–17 FL C; 2017– Premier League.

LATEST SEQUENCES

Longest Sequence of League Wins: 13, 25.4.1992 – 18.10.1992.

Longest Sequence of League Defeats: 10, 23.8.1977 – 15.10.1977.

Longest Sequence of League Draws: 4, 15.11.2008 – 6.12.2008.

Longest Sequence of Unbeaten League Matches: 17, 3.9.2022 – 11.2.2023.

Longest Sequence Without a League Win: 21, 14.1.1978 – 23.8.1978.

Successive Scoring Runs: 25 from 15.4.1939.

Successive Non-scoring Runs: 6 from 29.10.1988.

MANAGERS

Frank Watt 1895–32
(Secretary-Manager)
Andy Cunningham 1930–35
Tom Mather 1935–39
Stan Seymour 1939–47
(Hon. Manager)
George Martin 1947–50
Stan Seymour 1950–54
(Hon. Manager)
Duggie Livingstone 1954–56
Stan Seymour 1956–58
(Hon. Manager)
Charlie Mitten 1958–61
Norman Smith 1961–62
Joe Harvey 1962–75
Gordon Lee 1975–77
Richard Dinnis 1977
Bill McGarry 1977–80
Arthur Cox 1980–84
Jack Charlton 1984
Willie McFaul 1985–88
Jim Smith 1988–91
Ossie Ardiles 1991–92
Kevin Keegan 1992–97
Kenny Dalglish 1997–98
Ruud Gullit 1998–99
Sir Bobby Robson 1999–2004
Graeme Souness 2004–06
Glenn Roeder 2006–07
Sam Allardyce 2007–08
Kevin Keegan 2008
Joe Kinnear 2008–09
Alan Shearer 2009
Chris Hughton 2009–10
Alan Pardew 2010–15
John Carver 2015
Steve McClaren 2015–16
Rafael Benitez 2016–19
Steve Bruce 2019–21
Eddie Howe November 2021–

TEN YEAR LEAGUE RECORD

		P	W	D	L	F	A	Pts	Pos
2015-16	PR Lge	38	9	10	19	44	65	37	18
2016-17	FL C	46	29	7	10	85	40	94	1
2017-18	PR Lge	38	12	8	18	39	47	44	10
2018-19	PR Lge	38	12	9	17	42	48	45	13
2019-20	PR Lge	38	11	11	16	38	58	44	13
2020-21	PR Lge	38	12	9	17	46	62	45	12
2021-22	PR Lge	38	13	10	15	44	62	49	11
2022-23	PR Lge	38	19	14	5	68	33	71	4
2023-24	PR Lge	38	18	6	14	85	62	60	7
2024-25	PR Lge	38	20	6	12	68	47	66	5

DID YOU KNOW ?

When the members of Newcastle East End met in December 1892 three alternative names were proposed for a new title for the club: Newcastle, Newcastle City and Newcastle United. The meeting was almost unanimous in support of adopting the name Newcastle United and they played their first match under their new identity on 24 December, resulting in a 2-1 win over Middlesbrough.

NEWCASTLE UNITED – PREMIER LEAGUE 2024–25 LEAGUE RECORD

Match No.	Date	Venue	Opponents	Result	H/T Score	Lg Pos.	Goalscorers	Attendance
1	Aug 17	H	Southampton	W 1-0	1-0	5	Joelinton [45]	52,196
2	25	A	Bournemouth	D 1-1	0-1	6	Gordon [77]	11,161
3	Sept 1	H	Tottenham H	W 2-1	1-0	5	Barnes [37], Isak [78]	52,211
4	15	A	Wolverhampton W	W 2-1	0-1	3	Schar [75], Barnes [80]	30,255
5	21	A	Fulham	L 1-3	0-2	6	Barnes [46]	25,700
6	28	H	Manchester C	D 1-1	0-1	7	Gordon (pen) [58]	52,248
7	Oct 5	A	Everton	D 0-0	0-0	6		39,265
8	19	H	Brighton & HA	L 0-1	0-1	8		52,220
9	27	A	Chelsea	L 1-2	1-1	12	Isak [32]	39,526
10	Nov 2	H	Arsenal	W 1-0	1-0	9	Isak [12]	52,249
11	10	A	Nottingham F	W 3-1	0-1	8	Isak [54], Joelinton [72], Barnes [83]	30,145
12	25	H	West Ham U	L 0-2	0-1	10		52,094
13	30	A	Crystal Palace	D 1-1	0-0	10	Guehi (og) [53]	25,101
14	Dec 4	H	Liverpool	D 3-3	1-0	10	Isak [35], Gordon [62], Schar [90]	52,237
15	7	A	Brentford	L 2-4	2-2	12	Isak [11], Barnes [32]	17,078
16	14	H	Leicester C	W 4-0	1-0	11	Murphy J [30, 60], Bruno Guimaraes [47], Isak [50]	52,235
17	21	A	Ipswich T	W 4-0	3-0	7	Isak 3 [1, 45, 54], Murphy J [32]	29,774
18	26	H	Aston Villa	W 3-0	1-0	5	Gordon [2], Isak [59], Joelinton [90]	52,168
19	30	A	Manchester U	W 2-0	2-0	5	Isak [4], Joelinton [19]	73,809
20	Jan 4	A	Tottenham H	W 2-1	2-1	5	Gordon [6], Isak [38]	61,293
21	15	H	Wolverhampton W	W 3-0	1-0	4	Isak 2 [34, 57], Gordon [74]	51,975
22	18	H	Bournemouth	L 1-4	1-2	4	Bruno Guimaraes [25]	52,227
23	25	A	Southampton	W 3-1	2-1	5	Isak 2 (1 pen) [26 (p), 30], Tonali [51]	31,141
24	Feb 1	H	Fulham	L 1-2	1-0	5	Murphy J [37]	52,173
25	15	A	Manchester C	L 0-4	0-3	7		52,432
26	23	H	Nottingham F	W 4-3	4-1	5	Miley [23], Murphy J [25], Isak 2 (1 pen) [33 (p), 34]	52,223
27	26	A	Liverpool	L 0-2	0-1	6		60,374
28	Mar 10	A	West Ham U	W 1-0	0-0	6	Bruno Guimaraes [63]	62,463
29	Apr 2	H	Brentford	W 2-1	1-0	5	Isak [45], Tonali [74]	52,021
30	7	A	Leicester C	W 3-0	3-0	5	Murphy J 2 [2, 11], Barnes [34]	30,403
31	13	H	Manchester U	W 4-1	1-1	4	Tonali [24], Barnes 2 [49, 64], Bruno Guimaraes [77]	52,252
32	16	H	Crystal Palace	W 5-0	4-0	3	Murphy J [14], Guehi (og) [38], Schar [45], Barnes [45], Isak [58]	52,197
33	19	A	Aston Villa	L 1-4	1-1	3	Schar [18]	42,618
34	26	H	Ipswich T	W 3-0	1-0	3	Isak (pen) [45], Burn [56], Osula [80]	52,171
35	May 4	A	Brighton & HA	D 1-1	0-1	4	Isak (pen) [89]	31,580
36	11	H	Chelsea	W 2-0	1-0	3	Tonali [2], Bruno Guimaraes [90]	52,231
37	18	A	Arsenal	L 0-1	0-0	3		60,160
38	25	H	Everton	L 0-1	0-0	5		52,221

Final League Position: 5

GOALSCORERS

League (68): Isak 23 (4 pens), Barnes 9, Murphy J 8, Gordon 6 (1 pen), Bruno Guimaraes 5, Joelinton 4, Schar 4, Tonali 4, Burn 1, Miley 1, Osula 1, own goals 2.
FA Cup (7): Willock 2, Gordon 1 (1 pen), Isak 1 (1 pen), Miley 1, Osula 1, Wilson 1.
Carabao Cup (13): Isak 3, Gordon 2, Schar 2 (1 pen), Tonali 2, Burn 1, Murphy 1, Willock 1, own goal 1.
(Newcastle U U21) Vertu Trophy (3): Donaldson 1, Emerson 1, Parkinson 1.

Pope N 28	Livramento V 32 + 5	Schär F 33 + 1	Burn D 37	Hall L 24 + 3	Longstaff S 8 + 17	Bruno Guimarães M 38	Joelinton d 29	Murphy J 31 + 4	Isak A 34	Gordon A 28 + 6	Krafth E 2 + 10	Kelly L 4 + 6	Barnes H 17 + 16	Trippier K 14 + 11	Willock J 11 + 21	Almiron M 1 + 8	Tonali S 28 + 8	Osula W — + 14	Wilson C 2 + 16	Dubravka M 10	Miley L 1 + 13	Targett M — + 2	Botman S 6 + 2	Match No.
1	2	3⁴	4	5²	6	7	8	9¹	10	11³	12	13	14											1
1	2⁵		4	15	6³	7	8	9	10	11⁵	3	5⁴	13	12	14	16								2
1	2		4	13	6³	7	8	12	10	9⁴	3	5²	11¹		15	14								3
1	2⁴	3	4	5	6³	7⁵	8²	9	10¹	11			16	12	15	13	14							4
1	14	3	4	12		7	8⁴	13	10	9⁵			5²	11	2³	6¹	15		16					5
1	13	3	4	5	14	7	8	9	10				11¹	2³	12	6²								6
1	14	3	4	5	15	7	8	9	10				11¹	2⁴	13	12	6³							7
1	2	3	4	5⁵	15	7⁴	8	9	10	11³	12	13	14		16		6²							8
1	2	3	4	5⁵	12	7	8⁴	13	10	15			11³	14	9¹	16	6²							9
1	2	3	4	5	6	7³	11		10	9²			14	13	12		8¹							10
1	2	3	4	5	6	7	11		10³	9²			13	14	12		8¹							11
1	2	3		5	6²	7⁵	9⁴	15	10	11³	4	12	16		13	14	8¹							12
1	2	3	4	5	13	7	11		10¹	9³		12	14	6			8²							13
1	2	3	4	5	13	7	8⁴	9¹	10	11²		12	15	14			6³							14
1	2	3	4	5⁵	6³	7	8²	9¹	10	12		11⁴	16	14	13		15							15
	2³	3	4	5	14	7²	8	9¹	10⁴	11⁵		12	13	6	16		15			1				16
	2³	3	4	5	14	7⁵	9²	10⁴	11	12		13	8¹	15	6	16				1				17
		3	4	5	6⁴		8	9³	10⁵	11¹		12	14	2³	7	16	15			1	13			18
	12	3	4	5	6		8	9²	10	11³		13	14	2¹	7					1				19
	2	4	5	13	6		8	9³	10²	11¹		15	12	14	7					1			3⁴	20
	2⁶	4	5		6		8⁴	9¹	10²	11³		13	16	14	12	7	15			1			3	21
	2	12	4	5²	6⁴		8	9³	10	11		13	14		7		15			1			3¹	22
	2	3	4	5	6²	15	8	9⁴	10¹	11³		13	14	7			12			1				23
	2¹	3	4	5⁵	6³		8²	9⁴	10	11		14	12	13	7	16	15			1				24
	12	3	4	5	14	6³		9	10⁵	11⁴			16	2²	7		8¹	15		1	13			25
1	2	3	4	5		7		9¹	10³	11		12	13	14	6		8²							26
1	2³	3	4	5	16	6⁵	8	9	10¹	11⁴	12	13	14		7²		15							27
1	5	3	4	14	6³		8	9²	10²	11⁴		13	12	2	7									28
1	5	3	4	14	6		8	9²	10¹	11⁴		13	12	2³	7		15							29
1	5	3	4	13	6¹		8²	9⁴	10³	16	11		14	2⁵	7		15				12			30
1	5	3	4	16	6⁵		8⁴	9²	10³	12	13	11	14	2¹	7		15							31
1	5	3	4	14	6³		8	9²	10⁴	12	16	11	13	2⁶	7		15							32
1	5	3⁵	4		6		8	9¹	10⁴	12	13	11²	15	2³	7		14	16						33
1	5	3⁵	4		6			9¹	10³	12		11⁴	14	2	7		8²	15			13		16	34
1	5	3⁴	4		6			9¹	10	12		14	11	2³	7		8²	15			13			35
1	8	2	4	14	6⁴	5	11³	10²	13	9			12		7		15						3¹	36
1	8	2	4		6	5¹	13	15	10	9⁴			14		7		11²				12		3³	37
1	8	2	4		6	5³	13	9⁴	10	11¹		12	14		7		15						3²	38

FA Cup

Third Round	Bromley	(h)	3-1
Fourth Round	Birmingham C	(a)	3-2
Fifth Round	Brighton & HA	(h)	1-2
aet.			

Carabao Cup

Second Round	Nottingham F	(a)	1-1
Newcastle U won 4-3 on penalties.			
Third Round	AFC Wimbledon	(h)	1-0
Fourth Round	Chelsea	(h)	2-0
Quarter-Final	Brentford	(h)	3-1
Semi-Final 1st leg	Arsenal	(a)	2-0
Semi-Final 2nd leg	Arsenal	(h)	2-0
Final	Liverpool	(Wembley)	2-1

Vertu Trophy (Newcastle U U21)

Group H (N)	Bradford C	(a)	2-2
Newcastle U U21 won 4-3 on penalties.			
Group H (N)	Rotherham U	(a)	1-3
Group H (N)	Mansfield T	(a)	0-3

NEWPORT COUNTY

FOUNDATION

In 1912 Newport County were formed following a meeting at The Tredegar Arms Hotel. A professional football club had existed in the town called Newport FC, but they ceased to exist in 1907. The first season as Newport County was in the second division of the Southern League. They started life playing at Somerton Park where they remained through their League years. They were elected to the Football League for the beginning of the 1920–21 season as founder members of Division 3. At the end of the 1987–88 season, they were relegated from the Football League and replaced by Lincoln City. On 27 February 1989, Newport County went out of business and from the ashes Newport AFC was born. Starting down the pyramid in the Hellenic League, they eventually gained promotion to the Football Conference in 2011 and were promoted to the Football League after a play-off with Wrexham in 2013.

Rodney Parade, Rodney Road, Newport, South Wales NP19 0UU.

Telephone: (01633) 302 012.

Ticket Office: (01633) 302 012.

Website: www.newport-county.co.uk

Email: office@newport-county.co.uk

Ground Capacity: 8,722.

Record Attendance: 24,268 v Cardiff C, Division 3 (S), 16 October 1937 (Somerton Park); 4,660 v Swansea C, FA Cup 1st rd, 11 November 2006 (Newport Stadium); 9,836 v Tottenham H, FA Cup 4th rd, 27 January 2018 (Rodney Parade).

Pitch Measurements: 100m × 68m (109.5yd × 74.5yd).

Chairman: Huw Jenkins OBE.

Chief Operating Officer: Jonathan Wilsher.

Manager: David Hughes.

Assistant Manager: Wayne Hatswell.

Colours: Amber shirts with black trim, black shorts with amber trim, amber socks with black trim.

Year Formed: 1912.

Turned Professional: 1912.

Previous Names: Newport County, 1912; Newport AFC, 1989; Newport County, 1999.

Club Nicknames: 'The Exiles'; 'The Ironsides'; 'The Port'; 'The County'.

Grounds: 1912–89, 1990–92, Somerton Park; 1992–94, Meadow Park Stadium; 1994, Newport Stadium; 2012, Rodney Parade.

First Football League Game: 28 August 1920, Division 3, v Reading (h) L 0–1.

Record League Victory: 10–0 v Merthyr T, Division 3(S), 10 April 1930 – Martin (5), Gittins (2), Thomas (1), Bagley (1), Lawson (1).

HONOURS

League Champions: Division 3S – 1938–39.

Runners-up: Football Conference – (3rd) 2012–13 *(promoted to FL 2 via play-offs)*.

FA Cup: 5th rd – 1949, 2019.

League Cup: 4th rd – 2021.

Welsh Cup Winners: 1980.

Runners-up: 1963, 1987.

European Competitions
European Cup Winners' Cup: 1980–81 *(qf)*.

FOOTBALL YEARBOOK FACT FILE

Jack Nicholls became the first Newport County player to gain full international honours when he appeared for Wales against Scotland in March 1924. Nicholls was an amateur and had previously been capped by Wales Amateurs. In his brief stay with County he scored four goals from 11 appearances before joining Cardiff City, where his father was on the board of directors, for the 1924–25 season.

Record Cup Victory: 7–0 v Working, FA Cup 1st rd, 24 November 1928 – Young (3), Pugh (2) Gittins (1), Reid (1).

Record Defeat: 0–13 v Newcastle U, Division 2, 5 October 1946.

Most League Points (2 for a win): 61, Division 4, 1979–80.

Most League Points (3 for a win): 78, Division 3, 1982–83.

Most League Goals: 85, Division 4, 1964–65.

Highest League Scorer in Season: Tudor Martin, 34, Division 3 (S), 1929–30.

Most League Goals in Total Aggregate: Reg Parker, 99, 1948–54.

Most League Goals in One Match: 5, Tudor Martin v Merthyr T, Dvision 3 (S), 10 April 1930.

Most Capped Player: Keanu Marsh-Brown, 11 (16), Guyana; Nick Townsend, 11, Antigua & Barbuda.

Most League Appearances: Len Weare, 527, 1955–70.

Youngest League Player: Regan Poole, 16 years 94 days v Shrewsbury T, 20 September 2014.

Record Transfer Fee Received: £500,000 (potentially rising to £1,000,000) from Peterborough U for Conor Washington, January 2014.

Record Transfer Fee Paid: £80,000 to Swansea C for Alan Waddle, January 1981.

Football League Record: 1920 Original member of Division 3; 1920–21 Division 3; 1921–31 Division 3 (S); 1931 Failed re-election; 1931–32 Southern League; 1932 Re-elected to Division 3 (S); 1932–39 Division 3 (S); 1946–47 Division 2; 1947–58 Division 3 (S); 1958–62 Division 3; 1962–80 Division 4; 1980–87 Division 3; 1987–88 Division 4 (relegated from Football League); 2013 Promoted from Football Conference; 2013– FL 2.

LATEST SEQUENCES

Longest Sequence of League Wins: 5, 17.10.2020 – 31.10.2020.

Longest Sequence of League Defeats: 9, 23.3.2024 – 10.8.2024.

Longest Sequence of League Draws: 4, 16.11.2024 – 14.12.2024.

Longest Sequence of Unbeaten League Matches: 17, 15.3.2019 – 7.9.2019.

Longest Sequence Without a League Win: 12, 15.3.2016 – 6.8.2017.

Successive Scoring Runs: 20 from 12.9.2020.

Successive Non-scoring Runs: 4 from 12.4.2025.

MANAGERS

Davy McDougle 1912–13
(Player-Manager)
Sam Hollis 1913–17
Harry Parkes 1919–22
Jimmy Hindmarsh 1922–35
Louis Page 1935–36
Tom Bromilow 1936–37
Billy McCandless 1937–45
Tom Bromilow 1945–50
Fred Stansfield 1950–53
Billy Lucas 1953–61
Bobby Evans 1961–62
Billy Lucas 1962–67
Leslie Graham 1967–69
Bobby Ferguson 1969–70
(Player-Manager)
Billy Lucas 1970–74
Brian Harris 1974–75
Dave Elliott 1975–76
(Player-Manager)
Jimmy Scoular 1976–77
Colin Addison 1977–78
Len Ashurst 1978–82
Colin Addison 1982–85
Bobby Smith 1985–86
John Relish 1986
Jimmy Mullen 1986–87
John Lewis 1987
Brian Eastick 1987–88
David Williams 1988
Eddie May 1988
John Mahoney 1988–89
John Relish 1989–93
Graham Rogers 1993–96
Chris Price 1997
Tim Harris 1997–2002
Peter Nicholas 2002–04
John Cornforth 2004–05
Peter Beadle 2005–08
Dean Holdsworth 2008–11
Anthony Hudson 2011
Justin Edinburgh 2011–15
Jimmy Dack 2015
Terry Butcher 2015
John Sheridan 2015–16
Warren Feeney 2016
Graham Westley 2016–17
Michael Flynn 2017–21
James Rowberry 2021–22
Graham Coughlan 2022–24
Nelson Jadim 2024–25
David Hughes May 2025–

TEN YEAR LEAGUE RECORD

		P	W	D	L	F	A	Pts	Pos
2015-16	FL 2	46	10	13	23	43	64	43	22
2016-17	FL 2	46	12	12	22	51	73	48	22
2017-18	FL 2	46	16	16	14	56	58	64	11
2018-19	FL 2	46	20	11	15	59	59	71	7
2019-20	FL 2	36	12	10	14	32	39	46	14§
2020-21	FL 2	46	20	13	13	57	42	73	5
2021-22	FL 2	46	19	12	15	67	58	69	11
2022-23	FL 2	46	14	15	17	53	56	57	15
2023-24	FL 2	46	16	7	23	62	76	55	18
2024-25	FL 2	46	13	10	23	52	76	49	22

§*Decided on points-per-game (1.28)*

DID YOU KNOW

When Newport County moved to Rodney Parade for the 2012–13 season the pitch had to be relaid and was unavailable for use in the opening weeks of the campaign. County had to play their first three League One matches away from home, while they were drawn at home in the League Cup to both Southend United and Leeds United, both games taking place on their opponents' grounds.

NEWPORT COUNTY – SKY BET LEAGUE TWO 2024–25 LEAGUE RECORD

Match No.	Date	Venue	Opponents	Result	H/T Score	Lg Pos.	Goalscorers	Attendance
1	Aug 10	A	Cheltenham T	L	2-3	2-2	15	Baker-Richardson (pen) [31], Greaves [43]	4613
2	17	H	Doncaster R	W	3-1	0-1	8	Kamwa [47], Whitmore [66], Baker [69]	4755
3	24	H	Accrington S	W	3-1	1-1	5	Quirk (og) [12], Baker-Richardson (pen) [52], Wildig [63]	4437
4	31	A	Morecambe	W	1-0	1-0	4	Wildig [9]	2724
5	Sept 7	H	Port Vale	L	1-4	1-2	8	Wildig [24]	4851
6	14	H	Swindon T	L	0-4	0-4	10		6857
7	21	A	Barrow	L	0-2	0-1	13		3434
8	28	H	Crewe Alex	W	2-1	1-0	12	Evans C [33], Baker [74]	4273
9	Oct 1	H	Salford C	W	3-1	2-0	9	Hudlin [10], Wildig [26], Spellman [67]	3552
10	7	A	Bradford C	L	1-3	0-1	10	Hudlin [65]	15,542
11	12	A	Harrogate T	L	0-1	0-1	13		2564
12	18	H	Chesterfield	L	0-3	0-1	13		4570
13	22	A	Gillingham	W	2-0	2-0	13	Baker [16], Hudlin [33]	5262
14	26	H	Fleetwood T	D	0-0	0-0	14		4244
15	Nov 9	A	Tranmere R	L	1-2	0-1	15	Hudlin [84]	5805
16	16	H	Grimsby T	D	0-0	0-0	15		4298
17	23	A	Notts Co	D	0-0	0-0	16		9408
18	Dec 3	A	AFC Wimbledon	D	2-2	1-2	16	Spellman [26], McLoughlin (pen) [90]	6519
19	14	A	Colchester U	D	0-0	0-0	16		4046
20	21	H	Milton Keynes D	W	6-3	4-1	16	Morris 3 (1 pen) [12, 16, 36 (p)], Kamwa 3 [23, 47, 81]	4382
21	26	A	Bromley	L	2-5	0-2	18	Evans K [72], Whitmore [79]	3320
22	29	A	Walsall	L	0-2	0-0	18		6706
23	Jan 2	H	AFC Wimbledon	L	1-2	0-0	18	Greaves [90]	4485
24	18	A	Port Vale	L	2-3	2-1	20	Kamwa [12], Evans C [33]	6354
25	24	H	Swindon T	L	1-2	1-1	20	Hudlin [12]	5244
26	28	A	Salford C	D	1-1	1-1	21	McLoughlin (pen) [11]	1952
27	Feb 1	H	Barrow	W	1-0	0-0	19	Cameron (og) [70]	4133
28	4	H	Morecambe	W	2-1	1-0	17	Thomas [8], Ajiboye [82]	3831
29	8	A	Crewe Alex	W	3-0	2-0	17	Antwi [33], Ajiboye [45], Baker-Richardson [82]	4472
30	11	H	Carlisle U	W	1-0	0-0	14	Hudlin [76]	3932
31	15	H	Bradford C	D	0-0	0-0	15		4760
32	22	A	Cheltenham T	L	0-3	0-1	16		4987
33	Mar 1	A	Doncaster R	L	0-3	0-1	16		8007
34	4	H	Gillingham	W	3-1	3-0	15	Kamwa 3 [9, 27, 30]	3589
35	8	A	Chesterfield	L	1-2	1-2	17	Baker [40]	7692
36	11	A	Accrington S	L	0-5	0-3	17		1503
37	15	H	Harrogate T	W	3-0	2-0	16	Evans C [2], Baker-Richardson [15], Clarke [61]	3756
38	22	A	Grimsby T	L	0-1	0-0	16		5339
39	29	H	Notts Co	L	0-2	0-1	18		4691
40	Apr 1	H	Bromley	D	1-1	1-0	17	Evans C [32]	3465
41	5	A	Carlisle U	L	2-3	2-1	17	Evans K [26], Kamwa [28]	5889
42	12	A	Colchester U	L	0-2	0-0	18		3899
43	18	A	Milton Keynes D	D	0-0	0-0	18		8135
44	21	H	Walsall	D	0-0	0-0	20		4578
45	26	A	Fleetwood T	L	0-2	0-0	21		2469
46	May 3	H	Tranmere R	L	1-4	1-1	22	McLoughlin [23]	5465

Final League Position: 22

GOALSCORERS

League (52): Kamwa 9, Hudlin 6, Baker-Richardson 4 (2 pens), Baker 4, Evans C 4, Wildig 4, McLoughlin 3 (2 pens), Morris 3 (1 pen), Ajiboye 2, Evans K 2, Greaves 2, Spellman 2, Whitmore 2, Antwi 1, Clarke 1, Thomas 1, own goals 2.
FA Cup (2): Driscoll-Glennon 1, Whitmore 1.
Carabao Cup (1): Clarke 1.
Vertu Trophy (2): Evans K 1, Greaves 1.

Townsend N 43	McLoughlin S 34 + 2	Clarke J 24	Jameson K 15 + 9	Driscoll-Glennon A 34 + 5	Brennan C 26 + 1	Wildig A 15	Antwi C 31 + 9	Greaves O 6 + 10	Baker-Richardson C 24 + 12	Kamwa B 41 + 2	Wood N — + 1	Whitmore K 14 + 14	Jephcott L 2 + 10	Kargbo H — + 2	Baker M 41	Evans C 26 + 5	Rai K 1 + 3	Morris B 19	Evans K 21 + 13	Mawene N 4 + 10	Sanca N — + 1	Hudin K 16 + 11	Spellman M 12 + 19	Carney J 3	Miley J 3 + 3	Thomas J 21 + 2	Bony G 2 + 4	Ajiboye D 16 + 5	Davies T 2 + 2	Martin J 6 + 9	Patten K 1 + 5	Warner J 3 + 2	Alexander-Walker M — + 1	Match No.
1	2	3	4	5	6	7	8²	9¹	10⁴	11³	12	13	14	15																				1
1	2		4		6	5	9¹	8		10²	11³		7	12		14		3	13	14														2
1	2		4		6	5	8⁴	9		10³	11²		14		3	12	13	7¹	15														3
1	2		4	6	5	9³	7		11	10²		3	14		8¹	13	12																4
1	2¹		4⁸	6	5⁸	9	7²	15	10³	11⁴			3		8	14		12	13														5
1				6		9³	8¹	10²	11	13		12		4	5	14	3	2	7														6
1		3	5			13	14	10¹	9		12	4	4	2	6²	8	7³		11															7
1			4	5		9¹	7⁴	12	11³	10²		3	2	8	6	14	15	13															8
1			4	5		7¹	12	14	15	11²		3	2	8	9³	6	10⁴	13															9
1			4	5	3	9	12		13	10³		2	7	8	6¹	11³	14																10
		3	4	2	9		14	12	10¹			5²		7	8	6³	11	13	1														11
1		3	4	5	2	9³	8¹		11	10		12		6	7²	13⁴	14	15															12
1			4	10⁵	3	9	15	13	8³	12		2	5	7¹	14	11²	16	6⁴															13
1			4	10	3	9²	13	8⁴	14	2	5¹	7	12	11³	15	6																	14
1	14		4⁸	3	8²		12	11	13	2³	5		6	15	10	9¹	7⁴																15
1	5			3	7²	13		14	11¹	8		4	2	6	9³	10	12																16
1	5		3	12	9⁶	13		8⁴	14	4	2	6²	7	10¹	11³	15	16																17
1	5	16	12	3	6³	14	13	15	4	8	7	14	10⁴	9⁶	2⁹	11²																	18
1	5	16	12	3	6³	13	15	4	8	7	14	10⁴	9⁶	2²	11¹																		19
1	2	14	5⁴	3	6¹	11	10²	4	8	7	12	13	9³	15																			20
1	2	5	3	6³	15	9	14	13	4	8⁴	7	10²	11¹¹	12																			21
1	2	15	5	3	8¹	14	9⁵	6⁴	10³	13	4	7	16	11²	12																		22
2⁴		15	5	3	8	14	10	9²	12	4	6	11¹	7³	1	13																		23
5	12⁸	3¹	6	10⁴	11	7³	4	2	8	14	13	1	9²	15																			24
1	7	3	13	10	9²	4	2	6	11¹	14	8³	5	12																				25
1	8	4	13	12	14	10	9¹	3	2	7	15	11³	5²	6⁴																			26
1	5	3	8	12	13	8²	4	2	14⁴	15	6	11³	7¹																				27
1	6	3	14	8	7	10¹	11²	4	2	13	5³	9	12																				28
1	6	3	14	8	7¹	11	10⁴	4	2³	15	5²	9³	12	13																			29
1	6	3	8	7	10¹	11	4	2	13	5²	9³	12	14																				30
1	6	3⁵	15	8	7	10	11³	4	2⁴	14	5¹	13	9²	12	16																		31
1	6	3	9	8	12	10⁸	11	13	4	2¹	5³	14	7²																				32
1	6	3²	2	14	10	9³	13	4	8⁴	12	15	5	11	7¹																			33
1	7	3	8	6	10	9	4	12	13	5	11²	2¹																					34
1	6	3	8	7³	10	11⁴	14	4	15	13	5	9¹	12	2²																			35
1	6⁵	3	8	13	10²	11¹	7³	4	15	16	9	5	14	12	2⁴																		36
1	8	3	9	6	10	7	4	2	12	5	11¹																						37
1	6	3	9	7	14	10	13	4	2³	5¹	8	11²	12																				38
1	2		5	4	7	10	11	12	3	8	13	9	6²																				39
1	15	3	9	7	11⁵	10²	4	2	12	14	16	5⁴	13	6³	8¹																		40
1	6	3	9	7	10	13	4	2	8²	5	11¹	12																					41
1		3	5¹	7	8²	10	11	6	4	12	13	14	2	9³																			42
1	5	3⁴		7	6	10¹	11	8²	4	13	12	9³	2	14	15																		43
1	5	3¹	14	6⁸	7	15	10	9³	4	11⁴	8²	2	16	13⁵	12																		44
1	6		3	5	7	9⁴	10¹	11	13	4	8²	12³	2	14	15																		45
1	6	4³	5⁵	8¹	9²	10	7⁸	3	15	11⁴	16	2	14	13	12																		46

FA Cup
First Round   Peterborough U   (h)   2-4

Carabao Cup
First Round   Leyton Orient   (a)   1-4

Vertu Trophy
Group H (S)   Cheltenham T   (h)   1-2
Group H (S)   West Ham U U21   (h)   1-0
Group H (S)   Reading   (a)   0-3

NORTHAMPTON TOWN

FOUNDATION

Formed in 1897 by schoolteachers connected with the Northampton & District Elementary Schools' Association, they survived a financial crisis at the end of their first year when they were £675 in the red and became members of the Midland League – a fast move indeed for a new club. They achieved Southern League membership in 1901.

Sixfields Stadium, Upton Way, Northampton NN5 5QA.

Telephone: (01604) 683 700.

Ticket Office: (01604) 683 777.

Website: www.ntfc.co.uk

Email: secretary@ntfc.co.uk

Ground Capacity: 7,972.

Record Attendance: 24,523 v Fulham, Division 1, 23 April 1966 (at County Ground); 7,798 v Manchester U, EFL Cup 3rd rd, 21 September 2016; 7,798 v Derby Co, FA Cup 4th rd, 24 January 2019 (at Sixfields Stadium).

Pitch Measurements: 106m × 66m (116yd × 72yd).

Executive Chairman: Kelvin Thomas.

Chief Executive: James Whiting.

Manager: Kevin Nolan.

Assistant Manager: Ian Sampson.

Colours: Claret shirts with white trim, white shorts with claret trim, claret socks with white trim.

Year Formed: 1897.

Turned Professional: 1901.

Grounds: 1897, County Ground; 1994, Sixfields Stadium (renamed PTS Academy Stadium 2018; Sixfields Stadium 2021).

Club Nickname: 'The Cobblers'.

First Football League Game: 28 August 1920, Division 3, v Grimsby T (a) L 0–2 – Thorpe; Sproston, Hewison; Jobey, Tomkins, Pease; Whitworth, Lockett, Thomas, Freeman, MacKechnie.

Record League Victory: 10–0 v Walsall, Division 3 (S), 5 November 1927 – Hammond; Watson, Jeffs; Allen, Brett, Odell; Daley, Smith (3), Loasby (3), Hoten (1), Wells (3).

Record Cup Victory: 10–0 v Sutton T, FA Cup prel rd, 7 December 1907 – Cooch; Drennan, Lloyd Davies, Tirrell (1), McCartney, Hickleton, Badenock (3), Platt (3), Lowe (1), Chapman (2), McDiarmid.

Record Defeat: 0–11 v Southampton, Southern League, 28 December 1901.

Most League Points (2 for a win): 68, Division 4, 1975–76.

Most League Points (3 for a win): 99, Division 4, 1986–87; FL 2, 2015–16.

HONOURS

League Champions: Division 3 – 1962–63; FL 2 – 2015–16; Division 4 – 1986–87.
Runners-up: Division 2 – 1964–65; Division 3S – 1927–28, 1949–50; FL 2 – 2005–06; Division 4 – 1975–76.
FA Cup: 5th rd – 1934, 1950, 1970.
League Cup: 5th rd – 1965, 1967.

FOOTBALL YEARBOOK FACT FILE

Northampton Town's home game with Fulham on 5 November 1994 was delayed for almost 25 minutes after a deep hole appeared in one of the penalty areas. The foundations for one of the rugby league posts, which had recently been installed, were identified as the problem. The hole was filled in by the groundsman and the game went ahead with the visitors winning 1-0, the Cobblers' first defeat at their Sixfields Stadium.

Most League Goals: 109, Division 3, 1962–63 and Division 3 (S), 1952–53.

Highest League Scorer in Season: Cliff Holton, 36, Division 3, 1961–62.

Most League Goals in Total Aggregate: Jack English, 135, 1947–60.

Most League Goals in One Match: 5, Ralph Hoten v Crystal Palace, Division 3 (S), 27 October 1928.

Most Capped Player: Edwin Lloyd Davies, 12 (16), Wales.

Most League Appearances: Tommy Fowler, 521, 1946–61.

Youngest League Player: Fran Obiagwu, 16 years 170 days v Charlton Ath, 21 December 2024.

Record Transfer Fee Received: £1,000,000 (potentially rising to £1,500,000) from Brentford for Charlie Goode, August 2020.

Record Transfer Fee Paid: £165,000 to Oldham Ath for Josh Low, July 2003.

Football League Record: 1920 Original Member of Division 3; 1920–21 Division 3; 1921–58 Division 3 (S); 1958–61 Division 4; 1961–63 Division 3; 1963–65 Division 2; 1965–66 Division 1; 1966–67 Division 2; 1967–69 Division 3; 1969–76 Division 4; 1976–77 Division 3; 1977–87 Division 4; 1987–90 Division 3; 1990–92 Division 4; 1992–97 Third Division; 1997–99 Second Division; 1999–2000 Third Division; 2000–03 Second Division; 2003–04 Third Division; 2004–06 FL 2; 2006–09 FL 1; 2009–16 FL 2; 2016–18 FL 1; 2018–20 FL 2; 2020–21 FL 1; 2021–23 FL 2; 2023– FL 1.

LATEST SEQUENCES

Longest Sequence of League Wins: 10, 28.12.2015 – 23.2.2016.

Longest Sequence of League Defeats: 8, 26.10.1935 – 21.12.1935.

Longest Sequence of League Draws: 6, 5.2.2011 – 26.2.2011.

Longest Sequence of Unbeaten League Matches: 31, 28.12.2015 – 10.9.2016.

Longest Sequence Without a League Win: 18, 5.2.2011 – 25.4.2011.

Successive Scoring Runs: 28 from 29.8.2015.

Successive Non-scoring Runs: 7 from 7.4.1939.

MANAGERS

Arthur Jones 1897–1907 *(Secretary-Manager)*
Herbert Chapman 1907–12
Walter Bull 1912–13
Fred Lessons 1913–19
Bob Hewison 1920–25
Jack Tresadern 1925–30
Jack English 1931–35
Syd Puddefoot 1935–37
Warney Cresswell 1937–39
Tom Smith 1939–49
Bob Dennison 1949–54
Dave Smith 1954–59
David Bowen 1959–67
Tony Marchi 1967–68
Ron Flowers 1968–69
Dave Bowen 1969–72
(continued as General Manager and Secretary 1972–85 when joined the board)
Billy Baxter 1972–73
Bill Dodgin Jnr 1973–76
Pat Crerand 1976–77
By committee 1977
Bill Dodgin Jnr 1977
John Petts 1977–78
Mike Keen 1978–79
Clive Walker 1979–80
Bill Dodgin Jnr 1980–82
Clive Walker 1982–84
Tony Barton 1984–85
Graham Carr 1985–90
Theo Foley 1990–92
Phil Chard 1992–93
John Barnwell 1993–94
Ian Atkins 1995–99
Kevin Wilson 1999–2001
Kevan Broadhurst 2001–03
Terry Fenwick 2003
Martin Wilkinson 2003
Colin Calderwood 2003–06
John Gorman 2006
Stuart Gray 2007–09
Ian Sampson 2009–11
Gary Johnson 2011
Aidy Boothroyd 2011–13
Chris Wilder 2014–16
Rob Page 2016–17
Justin Edinburgh 2017
Jimmy Floyd Hasselbaink 2017–18
Dean Austin 2018
Keith Curle 2018–21
Jon Brady 2021–24
Kevin Nolan December 2024–

TEN YEAR LEAGUE RECORD

		P	W	D	L	F	A	Pts	Pos
2015-16	FL 2	46	29	12	5	82	46	99	1
2016-17	FL 1	46	14	11	21	60	73	53	16
2017-18	FL 1	46	12	11	23	43	77	47	22
2018-19	FL 2	46	14	19	13	64	63	61	15
2019-20	FL 2	37	17	7	13	54	40	58	7§
2020-21	FL 1	46	11	12	23	41	67	45	22
2021-22	FL 2	46	23	11	12	60	38	80	4
2022-23	FL 2	46	23	14	9	62	42	83	3
2023-24	FL 1	46	17	9	20	57	66	60	14
2024-25	FL 1	46	12	15	19	48	66	51	19

§*Decided on points-per-game (1.57)*

DID YOU KNOW ?

Northampton Town started their wartime match against Arsenal on 23 November 1940 with just eight men after a carload of players failed to arrive from Birmingham. The Cobblers trailed 7-0 at half-time but managed to recruit a further three men during the break to even things out. They eventually went down to an 8-1 defeat in front of a crowd of 7,000, the biggest attendance of the day.

NORTHAMPTON TOWN – SKY BET LEAGUE ONE 2024–25 LEAGUE RECORD

Match No.	Date	Venue	Opponents	Result	H/T Score	Lg Pos.	Goalscorers	Attendance
1	Aug 10	A	Bristol R	L	0-1	0-0	19		8529
2	17	H	Exeter C	W	2-1	0-1	16	Morton [65], McGeehan [77]	5981
3	24	A	Barnsley	D	2-2	0-1	10	McCarron [72], Baldwin [78]	11,248
4	31	H	Burton Alb	D	0-0	0-0	13		5909
5	Sept 14	H	Wycombe W	L	1-2	1-1	18	Hoskins (pen) [4]	5995
6	21	H	Huddersfield T	W	3-1	2-0	12	Helik (og) [18], McGeehan [25], Fosu [58]	18,417
7	28	H	Mansfield T	L	0-2	0-0	17		7024
8	Oct 1	H	Bolton W	L	2-4	0-2	19	Guthrie [90], Eaves [90]	5730
9	5	A	Wrexham	L	1-4	1-2	20	McGeehan [27]	13,324
10	19	A	Leyton Orient	W	1-0	0-0	19	McGeehan [48]	7015
11	22	A	Stockport Co	D	1-1	0-0	19	Magliore [90]	8585
12	26	H	Crawley T	W	3-0	2-0	17	Fosu [16], Williams (og) [29], Pinnock [55]	6445
13	29	A	Lincoln C	L	1-2	1-1	18	Fosu [2]	8219
14	Nov 9	A	Birmingham C	D	1-1	0-0	17	Pinnock [90]	27,485
15	16	A	Blackpool	D	0-0	0-0	16		8873
16	23	H	Cambridge U	D	0-0	0-0	16		6654
17	26	A	Wigan Ath	L	1-2	0-2	18	Eaves [56]	7754
18	Dec 3	A	Stevenage	L	0-2	0-0	21		2767
19	9	H	Peterborough U	W	2-1	1-1	17	McGeehan 2 [28, 84]	7098
20	14	A	Rotherham U	L	0-3	0-2	19		8745
21	21	H	Charlton Ath	L	0-5	0-3	20		7015
22	26	A	Reading	L	1-4	0-2	20	Eaves [81]	12,283
23	29	A	Shrewsbury T	D	1-1	0-0	19	McGeehan [63]	6894
24	Jan 1	H	Stevenage	D	0-0	0-0	19		6294
25	4	A	Burton Alb	W	1-0	0-0	18	Hoskins [86]	2837
26	18	H	Lincoln C	L	0-1	0-1	20		6094
27	25	A	Wycombe W	D	0-0	0-0	20		5446
28	28	A	Bolton W	L	1-3	1-2	20	Shaw [8]	18,956
29	Feb 1	H	Huddersfield T	W	3-2	2-0	19	Hoskins [32], Eaves [40], Shaw [51]	6933
30	7	A	Mansfield T	W	1-0	0-0	17	McGeehan [55]	7320
31	15	H	Wrexham	L	0-2	0-2	19		7685
32	22	H	Bristol R	W	2-1	0-0	17	Costelloe [61], Guinness-Walker [78]	6996
33	25	H	Barnsley	L	1-2	0-1	17	Hoskins [78]	5817
34	Mar 1	A	Exeter C	D	1-1	1-0	18	Costelloe [42]	6834
35	4	H	Stockport Co	D	1-1	1-0	18	Taylor [31]	5559
36	8	A	Leyton Orient	W	2-1	2-0	17	Roberts [11], McGeehan [45]	8911
37	15	H	Birmingham C	D	1-1	1-1	19	Iwata (og) [17]	7947
38	22	H	Blackpool	L	0-2	0-1	19		6714
39	29	A	Cambridge U	D	1-1	1-0	19	Hoskins [26]	7252
40	Apr 1	A	Rotherham U	L	0-2	0-1	19		5720
41	5	A	Peterborough U	W	4-0	3-0	18	Hoskins 2 (1 pen) [15, 34 (p)], Costelloe [41], Eaves [90]	9782
42	12	H	Reading	D	0-0	0-0	19		7614
43	18	A	Charlton Ath	L	1-2	1-1	19	Costelloe (pen) [15]	20,198
44	21	H	Shrewsbury T	W	4-1	2-0	18	McGowan [26], Costelloe 2 [44, 83], McGeehan [70]	6632
45	26	A	Crawley T	L	0-3	0-0	18		5105
46	May 3	H	Wigan Ath	D	1-1	1-0	19	Fosu [33]	7591

Final League Position: 19

GOALSCORERS

League (48): McGeehan 10, Hoskins 7 (2 pens), Costelloe 6 (1 pen), Eaves 5, Fosu 4, Pinnock 2, Shaw 2, Baldwin 1, Guinness-Walker 1, Guthrie 1, Magliore 1, McCarron 1, McGowan 1, Morton 1, Roberts 1, Taylor 1, own goals 3.
FA Cup (1): own goal 1.
Carabao Cup (0).
Vertu Trophy (7): Dobson 3, Eyoma 1, Fox 1, McCarron 1, Waghorn 1.

Burge L 30	McGowan A 30+5	Willis J 11+4	Guthrie J 24	Koiki A 2+3	Pinnock M 45+1	Fox B 10+3	Hondermarck W 12+21	McGeehan C 40	Morton C 5+2	Hoskins S 32+5	Magiore T 6+15	Fosu T 17+17	Wilson J —+9	Odimayo A 32+9	Mbebe-Tabu L 9+4	Dibhey-Dias M 1+1	Baldwin J 11+11	Chouchane S 17+5	McCarron L 4+12	Sowerby J 8+2	Brough P 1+4	Roberts T 21+6	Tzanev N 16+1	Eaves T 14+9	Guinness-Walker N 23+4	Eyoma T 17+7	Waghorn M —+6	Dobson N —+4	Lintott H —+1	Obiagwu F —+2	Licorish Mullings K —+1	Shaw L 8	Dyche M 13+7	Taylor T 19	Perry B 14+3	Costelloe D 14+1	Dadge J —+1	Match No.
1	2^4	3^1	4	5	6	7	8^2	9	10^3	11	12	13	14	15																								1
1	2^2	3^3	4		8	6	11	10	9	12				5	7^1		14																					2
1	2	3^1	4		9		14	11	10	6		8^2		5			12	7^3	13																			3
1	2^5		4	5^2	8		6^3	9	11^4	10			16	15			3	7^1	14	12	13																	4
1^2	2		4		6^4			7	11	9			16				12	3	15	14	8^3	5^1	10^5	13														5
1					6^3			10	12		15	9^2		2			5					3	7^4	14	8	13	11^1											6
1	2^1	12	4		10^2	16		7				13	14	9^1			5					3	8	15	6^5	11^3												7
1	15	16	4		8		7		13	10^1				2^2	5^4		3	6^3	14	9		11^5	12															8
1	2^1		4		15		6	14	10			5^5	12				3	16	8^2	7^4	9	11^3	13															9
1		3			10	9^2	14	6	8	12		2^3		4			7					13	11	5^1														10
1		4			9^5	8^3	14	10		7^4	16	15		2			3	13		6^1		12	11^2	5														11
1		4	8		7	15	9		14	13		10^3		2^1			3	6^4	16			11^2	12	5^5														12
1		4	8		6^1	13	9		16	10^4		2^6		3			7^3	15	14	11		12^2	5															13
1		5	9		8^6	13	7		11^3	3^1		2		4^2	15		10^4					6	12	14	16													14
1		4	8		9	12			10^3		13	2		9^1			6				7	11^2	5	3	14													15
1		4	8^3		7^4	15	9		10^1		12	2		6^2			11					14	5	3	13													16
1	12	4	8		7	9	14	10^5		2^4		6^3		15			11^2					13	5	3^1	16													17
	3		4		8	7^2	12	6	10			2							13			9^1	1	11^1	5^3				14									18
	2^1		4		9	13	7^2	8				11^3	14		16		7^1					10^5	1	4	12	15												19
	3^2		4		8^3	15	6^4	9				11^5		2				7^1	14	10		1	13	5	12	16												20
	3^2		4^5		9	7^3	8							2			14	13				11^1	1	10^4	6	5	12		15	16								21
	2^4		4		8	6^2	9					12					15	7	10^1			1	11	5	3^3	13	14											22
	2	14	4		8	6	9					10^1		13^3			7	12^2				1	11	5	3													23
	2	4^3	5^1		7	8			12			13		6			9	11^2				1	10	3	14													24
	2	3			8	7			10			12		5			9^1					1	11	4								6						25
	2^3	3			8	7^2			10			12	13	5			9^1					1	11	4								6	14					26
	2	3^3			8	12	9^1		10^4	15		14		2^4								1	11^2	4								6	13	7				27
	2^3				9	7^2	11^1	10				14	13	5^4			15					1	12	4								6	3	8				28
	2^1	3			8	13	5^4	9				10^2		14			15					1	11	4^3								6	12	7				29
	3				8	9						5^6	13	11^1			2					14	1	10^3								6	4	7	12			30
	12	3^1			8	5	14	11^2	13			2^3		15								1										4	7	6^4	10		31
	2^3				8	9	5	10^1	4			14										1	12									6	3	7	13	11^2		32
	13	3^3			9	15	5	14	10			2^1										1	8^2									6^4	4	7	12	11		33
1	2^2	14	13	9	15	5	3^4	10^1	16								12					8											4	7	6^3	11^5		34
1	13				5^2	9	8^3	14	10^1	2							12					4											3	7	6	11		35
1	4^2			16	8	15	9^4	5^5	12	14		2^1					11^3					13											3	7	6	10		36
1	4^3			14	8	13	9	11	3			5^1					12																2	7	6^2	10		37
1	4^1				8^3	9	5	2^2		12							11					14	13										3	7	6^4			38
1	2^3				8^1	15	9	5	13	12							11					10^2	4	14									3	7	6^4			39
1					8	9	11		5	4^2							10^1	13	14	2^3													3	7	6	12		40
1	3^1				8	10^2	9^4	15	12	4^5							14	13	5	2		16											7	6	11^3			41
1	5^1				8^3	16	10^2	9^4	13	12	3						14	4	2			15											7	6^5	11			42
1	5				8	14	7	13	10^2	15		4^3	3^1				9^4		2			12											6	11				43
1	5^4				8	15	9	3^1	13	2		14					11^2		4			12											7	6^3	10			44
1					8^6	15	9	3	13	14		2^1	12				16	11^2				4^3	5										7^4	6	10			45
1^5	5^1				8	13	11	12	9	2^3	14						16	4				3										3	7^4	6^2	10	15		46

FA Cup
First Round   Kettering T   (h)   1-2
aet.

Carabao Cup
First Round   Wycombe W   (h)   0-2

Vertu Trophy
Group F (S)   Notts Co   (a)   2-0
Group F (S)   Leicester C U21   (h)   3-0
Group F (S)   Burton Alb   (h)   2-5
Second Round Peterborough U   (a)   0-3

NORWICH CITY

FOUNDATION

Formed in 1902, largely through the initiative of two local schoolmasters who called a meeting at the Criterion Cafe, they were shocked by an FA Commission which in 1904 declared the club professional and ejected them from the FA Amateur Cup. However, this only served to strengthen their determination. New officials were appointed and a professional club established at a meeting in the Agricultural Hall in March 1905.

Carrow Road, Norwich, Norfolk NR1 1JE.
Telephone: (01603) 721 902.
Ticket Office: (01603) 721 902.
Website: www.canaries.co.uk
Email: reception@canaries.co.uk
Ground Capacity: 27,359.
Record Attendance: 25,037 v Sheffield Wed, FA Cup 5th rd, 16 February 1935 (at The Nest); 43,984 v Leicester C, FA Cup 6th rd, 30 March 1963 (at Carrow Road).
Pitch Measurements: 105m × 68m (115yd × 74.5yd).
Chairman: Mark Attanasio.
Sporting Director: Ben Knapper.
Head Coach: Liam Manning.
Assistant Head Coach: Chris Hogg.
Colours: Yellow shirts with green trim, green shorts with yellow trim, yellow socks with green trim.
Year Formed: 1902.
Turned Professional: 1905.
Club Nickname: 'The Canaries'.
Grounds: 1902, Newmarket Road; 1908, The Nest, Rosary Road; 1935, Carrow Road.
First Football League Game: 28 August 1920, Division 3, v Plymouth Arg (a) D 1–1 – Skermer; Gray, Gadsden; Wilkinson, Addy, Martin; Laxton, Kidger, Parker, Whitham (1), Dobson.
Record League Victory: 10–2 v Coventry C, Division 3 (S), 15 March 1930 – Jarvie; Hannah, Graham; Brown, O'Brien, Lochhead (1); Porter (1), Anderson, Hunt (5), Scott (2), Slicer (1).
Record Cup Victory: 8–0 v Sutton U, FA Cup 4th rd, 28 January 1989 – Gunn; Culverhouse, Bowen, Butterworth, Linighan, Townsend (Crook), Gordon, Fleck (3), Allen (4), Phelan, Putney (1).
Record Defeat: 2–10 v Swindon T, Southern League, 5 September 1908.
Most League Points (2 for a win): 64, Division 3 (S), 1950–51.
Most League Points (3 for a win): 97, FL C, 2020–21.
Most League Goals: 99, Division 3 (S), 1952–53.
Highest League Scorer in Season: Ralph Hunt, 31, Division 3 (S), 1955–56.

HONOURS

League Champions: FL C – 2018–19, 2020–21; First Division – 2003–04; Division 2 – 1971–72, 1985–86; FL 1 – 2009–10; Division 3S – 1933–34.
Runners-up: FL C – 2010–11; Division 3 – 1959–60; Division 3S – 1950–51.
FA Cup: semi-final – 1959, 1989, 1992.
League Cup Winners: 1962, 1985.
Runners-up: 1973, 1975.
European Competitions
UEFA Cup: 1993–94.

FOOTBALL YEARBOOK FACT FILE

Norwich City scored 31 goals in a run of three consecutive games in the emergency wartime competitions in December 1940. A 10-1 win over Aldershot was followed by a 3-0 victory against Southend United and then 18-0 against Brighton & Hove Albion. Fred Chadwick, a guest player from Ipswich Town, netted four against Aldershot and six against Brighton.

Most League Goals in Total Aggregate: Johnny Gavin, 122, 1945–54, 1955–58.

Most League Goals in One Match: 5, Tommy Hunt v Coventry C, Division 3 (S), 15 March 1930; 5, Roy Hollis v Walsall, Division 3 (S), 29 December 1951.

Most Capped Player: Teemu Pukki, 48 (130), Finland; Kenny McLean, 48 (including 1 on loan at Aberdeen) (50), Scotland.

Most League Appearances: Ron Ashman, 592, 1947–64.

Youngest League Player: Ryan Jarvis, 16 years 282 days v Walsall, 19 April 2003.

Record Transfer Fee Received: £38,000,000 from Aston Villa for Emiliano Buendia, June 2021.

Record Transfer Fee Paid: £11,500,000 to Sao Paulo for Gabriel Sara, July 2022.

Football League Record: 1920 Original Member of Division 3; 1920–21 Division 3; 1921–34 Division 3 (S); 1934–39 Division 2; 1946–58 Division 3 (S); 1958–60 Division 3; 1960–72 Division 2; 1972–74 Division 1; 1974–75 Division 2; 1975–81 Division 1; 1981–82 Division 2; 1982–85 Division 1; 1985–86 Division 2; 1986–92 Division 1; 1992–95 Premier League; 1995–2004 Division 1; 2004–05 Premier League; 2005–09 FL C; 2009–10 FL 1; 2010–11 FL C; 2011–14 Premier League; 2014–15 FL C; 2015–16 Premier League; 2016–19 FL C; 2019–20 Premier League; 2020–21 FL C; 2021–22 Premier League; 2022– FL C.

LATEST SEQUENCES

Longest Sequence of League Wins: 10, 23.11.1985 – 25.1.1986.

Longest Sequence of League Defeats: 10, 7.3.2020 – 26.7.2020.

Longest Sequence of League Draws: 7, 15.1.1994 – 26.2.1994.

Longest Sequence of Unbeaten League Matches: 20, 31.8.1950 – 30.12.1950.

Longest Sequence Without a League Win: 25, 22.9.1956 – 23.2.1957.

Successive Scoring Runs: 30 from 1.12.2018.

Successive Non-scoring Runs: 6 from 5.12.2021.

MANAGERS

John Bowman 1905–07
James McEwen 1907–08
Arthur Turner 1909–10
Bert Stansfield 1910–15
Major Frank Buckley 1919–20
Charles O'Hagan 1920–21
Albert Gosnell 1921–26
Bert Stansfield 1926
Cecil Potter 1926–29
James Kerr 1929–33
Tom Parker 1933–37
Bob Young 1937–39
Jimmy Jewell 1939
Bob Young 1939–45
Duggie Lochhead 1945–46
Cyril Spiers 1946–47
Duggie Lochhead 1947–50
Norman Low 1950–55
Tom Parker 1955–57
Archie Macaulay 1957–61
Willie Reid 1961–62
George Swindin 1962
Ron Ashman 1962–66
Lol Morgan 1966–69
Ron Saunders 1969–73
John Bond 1973–80
Ken Brown 1980–87
Dave Stringer 1987–92
Mike Walker 1992–94
John Deehan 1994–95
Martin O'Neill 1995
Gary Megson 1995–96
Mike Walker 1996–98
Bruce Rioch 1998–2000
Bryan Hamilton 2000
Nigel Worthington 2000–06
Peter Grant 2006–07
Glenn Roeder 2007–09
Bryan Gunn 2009
Paul Lambert 2009–12
Chris Hughton 2012–14
Neil Adams 2014–15
Alex Neil 2015–17
Daniel Farke 2017–21
Dean Smith 2021–22
David Wagner 2023–24
Johannes Hoff Thorup 2024–25
Liam Manning June 2025–

TEN YEAR LEAGUE RECORD

		P	W	D	L	F	A	Pts	Pos
2015-16	PR Lge	38	9	7	22	39	67	34	19
2016-17	FL C	46	20	10	16	85	69	70	8
2017-18	FL C	46	15	15	16	49	60	60	14
2018-19	FL C	46	27	13	6	93	57	94	1
2019-20	PR Lge	38	5	6	27	26	75	21	20
2020-21	FL C	46	29	10	7	75	36	97	1
2021-22	PR Lge	38	5	7	26	23	84	22	20
2022-23	FL C	46	17	11	18	57	54	62	13
2023-24	FL C	46	21	10	15	79	64	73	6
2024-25	FL C	46	14	15	17	71	68	57	13

DID YOU KNOW ?

After joining Norwich City from Sunderland in the summer of 1933, centre-forward Jack Vinall went on to make 164 consecutive League and Cup appearances before injury finally brought the run to an end in January 1937. Vinall scored a total of 81 goals for the Canaries, leading the scoring charts in his first three seasons before moving on to Luton Town in October 1937.

NORWICH CITY – SKY BET CHAMPIONSHIP 2024–25 LEAGUE RECORD

Match No.	Date	Venue	Opponents	Result	H/T Score	Lg Pos.	Goalscorers	Attendance
1	Aug 10	A	Oxford U	L	0-2	0-1	22		11,333
2	17	H	Blackburn R	D	2-2	0-1	19	Sargent [65], Sainz [73]	26,400
3	24	H	Sheffield U	D	1-1	1-1	20	Sargent [22]	26,373
4	31	A	Coventry C	W	1-0	0-0	13	Sainz [49]	27,353
5	Sept 14	A	Swansea C	L	0-1	0-1	15		14,097
6	21	H	Watford	W	4-1	2-1	11	Doyle [3], Sainz [45], Nunez [54], Chrisene [89]	26,438
7	28	A	Derby Co	W	3-2	1-0	9	Sainz 3 [45, 65, 87]	28,915
8	Oct 1	H	Leeds U	D	1-1	1-0	10	Sargent (pen) [15]	26,261
9	5	H	Hull C	W	4-0	2-0	7	Nunez [16], Sargent [20], Gordon [66], Sainz [78]	26,326
10	19	A	Stoke C	D	1-1	1-1	7	Crnac [45]	23,002
11	22	A	Preston NE	L	1-2	1-2	7	Sainz [45], Duffy [61]	13,677
12	27	H	Middlesbrough	D	3-3	1-3	8	Sainz 2 [9, 71], Dieng (og) [80]	26,487
13	Nov 2	A	Cardiff C	L	1-2	0-0	9	Sainz [52]	19,032
14	5	A	Sheffield Wed	L	0-2	0-2	12		22,731
15	9	H	Bristol C	L	0-2	0-1	14		26,423
16	23	A	WBA	D	2-2	2-2	13	Marcondes [20], Heggem (og) [41]	25,673
17	26	H	Plymouth Arg	W	6-1	2-1	9	Sainz 3 [2, 17, 72], Duffy [51], Ben Slimane [80], Crnac [82]	25,893
18	30	H	Luton T	W	4-2	2-1	9	Crnac 2 [25, 33], Marcondes [81], Sainz [86]	26,719
19	Dec 7	A	QPR	L	0-3	0-2	10		15,688
20	10	A	Portsmouth	D	0-0	0-0	10		20,151
21	15	H	Burnley	L	1-2	1-0	12	Cordoba [2]	26,218
22	21	A	Sunderland	L	1-2	1-0	13	Ben Slimane [21]	40,114
23	26	H	Millwall	W	2-1	2-0	12	Marcondes [4], Schwartau [39]	26,060
24	29	H	QPR	D	1-1	0-1	12	Nunez [89]	26,563
25	Jan 1	A	Luton T	W	1-0	0-0	11	Nunez [73]	11,828
26	4	H	Coventry C	W	2-1	0-1	11	Forson 2 [90, 90]	26,682
27	18	A	Sheffield U	L	0-2	0-1	11		28,239
28	22	A	Leeds U	L	0-2	0-1	12		35,157
29	25	H	Swansea C	W	5-1	1-0	11	Sargent 2 [44, 63], Dobbin [76], Crnac [84], Marcondes [86]	25,713
30	Feb 1	A	Watford	W	1-0	1-0	8	Sargent [41]	19,774
31	8	H	Derby Co	D	1-1	0-0	8	Sargent [68]	26,584
32	11	H	Preston NE	L	0-1	0-1	9		25,910
33	15	A	Hull C	D	1-1	0-1	12	Sargent [47]	22,141
34	22	H	Stoke C	W	4-2	1-1	9	Dobbin [32], Sargent 2 [48, 71], Tchamadeu (og) [78]	26,267
35	Mar 1	A	Blackburn R	D	1-1	0-0	11	Crnac [90]	14,240
36	7	H	Oxford U	D	1-1	1-0	10	Sargent [5]	25,996
37	11	H	Sheffield Wed	L	2-3	2-0	11	Sainz [16], Crnac [35]	25,498
38	14	A	Bristol C	L	1-2	0-2	12	Sainz [82]	21,237
39	29	H	WBA	W	1-0	0-0	10	Sargent [90]	26,707
40	Apr 5	A	Plymouth Arg	L	1-2	0-2	10	Sargent [46]	16,560
41	8	H	Sunderland	D	0-0	0-0	11		26,320
42	11	A	Burnley	L	1-2	0-2	11	Stacey [76]	19,030
43	18	H	Portsmouth	L	3-5	1-3	13	Sargent [21], Stacey [64], Marcondes [90]	26,838
44	21	A	Millwall	L	1-3	1-2	14	Duffy [45]	16,426
45	26	A	Middlesbrough	D	0-0	0-0	14		26,374
46	May 3	H	Cardiff C	W	4-2	3-0	13	Nunez 2 [13, 17], Sainz [23], Duffy [67]	26,581

Final League Position: 13

GOALSCORERS

League (71): Sainz 18, Sargent 15 (1 pen), Crnac 7, Nunez 6, Marcondes 5, Duffy 4, Ben Slimane 2, Dobbin 2, Forson 2, Stacey 2, Chrisene 1, Cordoba 1, Doyle 1, Gordon 1, Schwartau 1, own goals 3.
FA Cup (0).
Carabao Cup (4): Hernandez 2, Kamara 1, Sainz 1.

Gunn A 35	Stacey J 20+21	Hanley G 1+2	Duffy S 45	Doyle C 38+2	Nunez M 27+5	McLean K 33+1	Gibbs L 1+8	Fassnacht C 1+2	Sargent J 28+4	Sainz B 41	Forson A 8+13	Sorensen J 14+13	Idah A —+1	Kamara A —+2	Forsyth G 2+3	Chrisene B 12+14	Cordoba J 24+10	Hernandez O 5+18	Fisher K 34+4	Crnac A 29+9	Schwartau O 17+23	Ben Slimane A 25+8	Gordon K 1+9	Long G 8+1	Marcondes E 25+8	Barnes A 1+7	Hills B —+3	Dobbin L 8+2	Mahovo L 6+2	Myles E —+3	Wright J 10+5	Jurasek M 1+1	McConville R 3+5	Reyes Vicente 3+1	Match No.
1	2	3^2	4	5	6^4	7	8^1	9^3	10	11^5	12	13	14	15	16																				1
1	2		3	4	6	7	14		11^5	10^4	9^3			15	8^1	5^2	12	13	16																2
1	2		3	4	6	7	12		11	10	9^1				5		13		8^2																3
1	2		3	4	6^3	7	14		11	10^5	9^1				5^4	15	16		8^2	12	13														4
1	2^4		3	4	6^5	7	16		11	10	9^2		13		5^3	14	15		12	8^1															5
1	14		3	5	6	7			11	10^5	12				16	4	13^4	2^2	8^3	9^1		15													6
1	14	16	3	5^5	6	7			11	10^4	15				13	4		2^3	8^2	9^1	12														7
1	12		3	5	6^4	7			11	10	15					4^1		2	8^3	13	9^3	14													8
1^1	15		3	5	6	7			11^5	10^4						4		2	8^2	14	9^3	13	12	16											9
	15		3	5	6^1	7			11	10	13				16	4^5		2^4	8^2	9^3		1	14												10
	15		3	5		7			10	11			14	13	4			2^1	9^2		8^4	12	1	6^3											11
	14		3	5		7^8			10^4	11^5	13	15			4			2	9^1	12	6^2	16	1	8^3											12
	12	15	3	5					11	14	7^4	6^1			13	4		2^2	9^5	10^3		16	1	8											13
			3	5						13	11	12	7			4		2^2	10	8		9^1	1	6											14
	13		3	5						15	11	14	7^2				4^1	2	9	8^3	6^4		1	10											15
1	2		3	4			13			11	9^2	7^3					12	5	10^1	14	6^4	15		8											16
1	2		3	4		7	12^3			11^5	9^2	6^1			5^4			10	14	13				8	15	16									17
1	2		3	4	13	7				11^5	9^1	16					12	5	10^4		8^2			9	13										18
1	2		3	4	4^5	6^3	7			11		14		12	16	15	5^1	10^4		14			9	13											19
1	2^1		3	5	6^3					11		7				4	12	13	9^5	15	14		8	10^2											20
1	13		3	5^5	7					11					16	4	12	2^4	10^5	9^1	6^3	15	8	14											21
1	2		3^4	5	7					11		14				13	4^8	10^1	16	9^3	12	8^5		6^2	15										22
1	12		3	4	7	7^1				11						5^2	13	2	10	9	6	8													23
1	13		3	4	8	7				11						5^3	14	15	2^2	10^4	9^5	6^1		12	16										24
1	2		3	4	7^4	8				11^5						5^3	16	10^1	15	12	14	6^1		9	13										25
1			3	4	6	7				11	14					5^4		13	2^3	10^2	9^1		15	8			12								26
1	2		3	4		7				13						5^1	10^3	6^4	9^2	14			8			11	12	15							27
1	2		3	4		7				13						5^4		9^1	6^3	12	10^2			8		16	11^5	14	15						28
1	13		3	4		7				10^4		14				15	16	9^1	2^2	12	6			8			11^5	5^3							29
1	13		3	4		8				10^3			7^2			14		2	12	6				11	15	9^1	5^4								30
1	13		3	4	6^2	7				10						15		2^1	9^4	14	12			8^5			11	5^4	16						31
1			3	4	14					11^1	10		13				16	2	12	9^3	6^4			8^5			8	5^5		7^2	15				32
1	13		3	4						10^3	11	7				16		2^2	14	15	8						12	5^4		6^5	9^1				33
1			3		6^2					10^3	11^4	7				15	4		2	12	14	8						9^1	5^5		13		16		34
1	13		3		6					10	11	7				5^4	4	2^2	12		8^3			14			9^1		15						35
	5^4		3				12			10	11	7				4	13	2	9^3	15	8^1		14				6^2					1			36
			3	5		7				12	11	13				4	15	2^3	9	14	8^4		10^2				6^1					1			37
	15		3	5	12	6				10	11	7^5				4^1		2^3	9^2	13	14	1	8^4								16				38
1	5^5		3	13	7					10	11^4	2^3				4	8	9^2	15	6^1		12					14				16				39
1	2^2		3	6^1	7					11	10					4^5	15	5^4	8	14	9^3						13				16				40
1	15		3	6^5	5					11	9	13	14			4		2^4		8^1	10^2		12				7^3				16				41
1	14		4	12	6					13	11		9^1			5	2	15	10^5		7^3					16	8^4				3^2				42
	12			2	14	8^2	4			10^1	11	16	15			3^4	6^5	9^3	7		1	13					5								43
	2		3	15	6^4	5	12			10^1	10	10^1				4	13	8^2	14		9^3						7^5					1			44
1	8		3	4^2	9^4	5	12			11	10	16	14			15		13	7^1								6^5				2^3				45
1^4	6^1		3^5	4	9	5				11	10	8^3	12				15	13		14							7				2^2	16			46

NOTTINGHAM FOREST

FOUNDATION

One of the oldest football clubs in the world, Nottingham Forest was formed at a meeting in the Clinton Arms in 1865. Known originally as the Forest Football Club, the game which first drew the founders together was 'shinney', a form of hockey. When they determined to change to football in 1865, one of their first moves was to buy a set of red caps to wear on the field.

The City Ground, Pavilion Road, West Bridgford, Nottingham NG2 5FJ.

Telephone: (0115) 982 4444.

Ticket Office: (0115) 982 4388.

Website: www.nottinghamforest.co.uk

Email: press@nottinghamforest.co.uk

Ground Capacity: 30,404.

Record Attendance: 49,946 v Manchester U, Division 1, 28 October 1967.

Pitch Measurements: 105m × 68m (115yd × 74.5yd).

Chairman: Nicholas Randall KC.

Chief Executive: Lina Souloukou.

Head Coach: Nuno Espirito Santo.

Assistant Head Coaches: Rui Pedro Silva, Julio Figueroa.

Colours: Red shirts with white trim, white shorts with red trim, red socks with white trim.

Year Formed: 1865.   *Turned Professional:* 1889.

Previous Name: Forest Football Club.

Club Nickname: 'The Reds'.

Grounds: 1865, Forest Racecourse; 1879, The Meadows; 1880, Trent Bridge Cricket Ground; 1882, Parkside, Lenton; 1885, Gregory, Lenton; 1890, Town Ground; 1898, City Ground.

First Football League Game: 3 September 1892, Division 1, v Everton (a) D 2–2 – Brown; Earp, Scott; Hamilton, Albert Smith, McCracken; McCallum, 'Tich' Smith, Higgins (2), Pike, McInnes.

Record League Victory: 12–0 v Leicester Fosse, Division 1, 12 April 1909 – Iremonger; Dudley, Maltby; Hughes (1), Needham, Armstrong; Hooper (3), Marrison, West (3), Morris (2), Spouncer (3 incl. 1p).

Record Cup Victory: 14–0 v Clapton (away), FA Cup 1st rd, 17 January 1891 – Brown; Earp, Scott; Albert Smith, Russell, Jeacock; McCallum (2), 'Tich' Smith (1), Higgins (5), Lindley (4), Shaw (2).

Record Defeat: 1–9 v Blackburn R, Division 2, 10 April 1937.

Most League Points (2 for a win): 70, Division 3 (S), 1950–51.

Most League Points (3 for a win): 94, Division 1, 1997–98.

Most League Goals: 110, Division 3 (S), 1950–51.

Highest League Scorer in Season: Wally Ardron, 36, Division 3 (S), 1950–51.

HONOURS

League Champions: Division 1 – 1977–78; First Division – 1997–98; Division 2 – 1906–07, 1921–22; Division 3S – 1950–51.
Runners-up: Division 1 – 1966–67, 1978–79; First Division – 1993–94; Division 2 – 1956–57; FL 1 – 2007–08.
FA Cup Winners: 1898, 1959.
Runners-up: 1991.
League Cup Winners: 1978, 1979, 1989, 1990.
Runners-up: 1980, 1992.
Anglo-Scottish Cup Winners: 1977.
Full Members' Cup Winners: 1989, 1992.

European Competitions
European Cup: 1978–79 *(winners)*, 1979–80 *(winners)*, 1980–81.
Fairs Cup: 1961–62, 1967–68.
UEFA Cup: 1983–84 *(sf)*, 1984–85, 1995–96 *(qf)*.
Super Cup: 1979 *(winners)*, 1980.
World Club Championship: 1980.

FOOTBALL YEARBOOK FACT FILE

Nottingham Forest's home match with local rivals Notts County on 5 February 1927 was one of the first football matches to be broadcast live on radio. Coverage of the match, which was on the BBC's Nottingham station 5NG, included the community singing before kick-off, with live commentary provided by Arthur Hayes. Forest won 2-0 in front of a crowd of 25,578.

Most League Goals in Total Aggregate: Grenville Morris, 199, 1898–1913.

Most League Goals in One Match: 4, Enoch West v Sunderland, Division 1, 9 November 1907; 4, Tommy Gibson v Burnley, Division 2, 25 January 1913; 4, Tom Peacock v Port Vale, Division 2, 23 December 1933; 4, Tom Peacock v Barnsley, Division 2, 9 November 1935; 4, Tom Peacock v Port Vale, Division 2, 23 November 1935; 4, Tom Peacock v Doncaster R, Division 2, 26 December 1935; 4, Tommy Capel v Gillingham, Division 3 (S), 18 November 1950; 4, Wally Ardron v Hull C, Division 2, 26 December 1952; 4, Tommy Wilson v Barnsley, Division 2, 9 February 1957; 4, Peter Withe v Ipswich T, Division 1, 4 October 1977; 4, Marlon Harewood v Stoke C, Division 1, 22 February 2003; Gareth McCleary v Leeds U, FL C, 20 March 2012.

Most Capped Player: Stuart Pearce, 76 (78), England.

Most League Appearances: Bob McKinlay, 614, 1951–70.

Youngest League Player: Craig Westcarr, 16 years 257 days v Burnley, 13 October 2001.

Record Transfer Fee Received: £55,000,000 from Newcastle U for Anthony Elanga, July 2025.

Record Transfer Fee Paid: £35,000,000 to Newcastle U for Elliott Anderson, June 2024.

Football League Record: 1892 Elected to Division 1; 1892–1906 Division 1; 1906–07 Division 2; 1907–11 Division 1; 1911–22 Division 2; 1922–25 Division 1; 1925–49 Division 2; 1949–51 Division 3 (S); 1951–57 Division 2; 1957–72 Division 1; 1972–77 Division 2; 1977–92 Division 1; 1992–93 Premier League; 1993–94 First Division; 1994–97 Premier League; 1997–98 First Division; 1998–99 Premier League; 1999–2004 First Division; 2004–05 FL C; 2005–08 FL 1; 2008–22 FL C; 2022– Premier League.

LATEST SEQUENCES

Longest Sequence of League Wins: 7, 9.5.1979 – 1.9.1979.

Longest Sequence of League Defeats: 14, 21.3.1913 – 27.9.1913.

Longest Sequence of League Draws: 7, 29.4.1978 – 2.9.1978.

Longest Sequence of Unbeaten League Matches: 42, 26.11.1977 – 25.11.1978.

Longest Sequence Without a League Win: 19, 8.9.1998 – 16.1.1999.

Successive Scoring Runs: 22 from 28.3.1931.

Successive Non-scoring Runs: 7 from 26.11.2011.

MANAGERS

Harry Radford 1889–97
(Secretary-Manager)
Harry Haslam 1897–1909
(Secretary-Manager)
Fred Earp 1909–12
Bob Masters 1912–25
John Baynes 1925–29
Stan Hardy 1930–31
Noel Watson 1931–36
Harold Wightman 1936–39
Billy Walker 1939–60
Andy Beattie 1960–63
Johnny Carey 1963–68
Matt Gillies 1969–72
Dave Mackay 1972
Allan Brown 1973–75
Brian Clough 1975–93
Frank Clark 1993–96
Stuart Pearce 1996–97
Dave Bassett 1997–99
(previously General Manager)
Ron Atkinson 1999
David Platt 1999–2001
Paul Hart 2001–04
Joe Kinnear 2004
Gary Megson 2005–06
Colin Calderwood 2006–08
Billy Davies 2009–11
Steve McClaren 2011
Steve Cotterill 2011–12
Sean O'Driscoll 2012
Alex McLeish 2012–13
Billy Davies 2013–14
Stuart Pearce 2014–15
Dougie Freedman 2015–16
Philippe Montanier 2016–17
Mark Warburton 2017
Aitor Karanka 2018–19
Martin O'Neill 2019
Sabri Lamouchi 2019–20
Chris Hughton 2020–21
Steve Cooper 2021–23
Nuno Espírito Santo December 2023–

TEN YEAR LEAGUE RECORD

		P	W	D	L	F	A	Pts	Pos
2015-16	FL C	46	13	16	17	43	47	55	16
2016-17	FL C	46	14	9	23	62	72	51	21
2017-18	FL C	46	15	8	23	51	65	53	17
2018-19	FL C	46	17	15	14	61	54	66	9
2019-20	FL C	46	18	16	12	58	50	70	7
2020-21	FL C	46	12	16	18	37	45	52	17
2021-22	FL C	46	23	11	12	73	40	80	4
2022-23	PR Lge	38	9	11	18	38	68	38	16
2023-24	PR Lge	38	9	9	20	49	67	32*	17
2024-25	PR Lge	38	19	8	11	58	46	65	7

* 4 pts deducted.

DID YOU KNOW ?

Nottingham Forest entertained local rivals Notts Rangers in an experimental match played under floodlights at the Gregory Ground in Lenton on 25 March 1889. The pitch was lit up by 14 portable Wells' Lights and the ball was painted white to aid visibility. The game attracted an estimated attendance of 5,000 who saw Forest go down to a 2-0 defeat.

NOTTINGHAM FOREST – PREMIER LEAGUE 2024–25 LEAGUE RECORD

Match No.	Date	Venue	Opponents	Result	H/T Score	Lg Pos.	Goalscorers	Attendance
1	Aug 17	H	Bournemouth	D 1-1	1-0	7	Wood[23]	29,763
2	24	A	Southampton	W 1-0	0-0	5	Gibbs-White[70]	31,150
3	31	H	Wolverhampton W	D 1-1	1-1	8	Wood[10]	29,918
4	Sept14	A	Liverpool	W 1-0	0-0	5	Hudson-Odoi[72]	60,344
5	22	A	Brighton & HA	D 2-2	1-2	8	Wood (pen)[13], Sosa[70]	31,444
6	28	H	Fulham	L 0-1	0-0	9		30,139
7	Oct 6	A	Chelsea	D 1-1	1-0	10	Wood[49]	39,501
8	21	H	Crystal Palace	W 1-0	0-0	8	Wood[65]	29,443
9	25	A	Leicester C	W 3-1	1-1	5	Yates[16], Wood 2[47,60]	31,879
10	Nov 2	H	West Ham U	W 3-0	1-0	3	Wood[27], Hudson-Odoi[65], Aina[78]	30,112
11	10	A	Newcastle U	L 1-3	1-0	5	Murillo[22]	30,145
12	23	H	Arsenal	L 0-3	0-1	7		60,298
13	30	H	Ipswich T	W 1-0	0-0	6	Wood (pen)[49]	30,237
14	Dec 4	A	Manchester C	L 0-3	0-2	6		51,764
15	7	A	Manchester U	W 3-2	1-1	5	Milenkovic[2], Gibbs-White[47], Wood[54]	73,778
16	14	H	Aston Villa	W 2-1	0-0	4	Milenkovic[87], Elanga[90]	30,117
17	21	A	Brentford	W 2-0	1-0	4	Aina[38], Elanga[51]	17,115
18	26	H	Tottenham H	W 1-0	1-0	3	Elanga[28]	30,200
19	29	A	Everton	W 2-0	1-0	2	Wood[15], Gibbs-White[61]	39,352
20	Jan 6	A	Wolverhampton W	W 3-0	2-0	3	Gibbs-White[7], Wood[44], Awoniyi[90]	29,940
21	14	H	Liverpool	D 1-1	1-0	2	Wood[8]	30,249
22	19	H	Southampton	W 3-2	3-0	3	Anderson[11], Hudson-Odoi[28], Wood[41]	30,180
23	25	A	Bournemouth	L 0-5	0-1	3		11,228
24	Feb 1	H	Brighton & HA	W 7-0	3-0	3	Dunk (og)[12], Gibbs-White[25], Wood 3 (1 pen)[32,64,69(p)], Williams[89], Jota Silva[90]	30,164
25	15	A	Fulham	L 1-2	1-1	3	Wood[37]	27,164
26	23	H	Newcastle U	L 3-4	1-4	3	Hudson-Odoi[6], Milenkovic[63], Yates[90]	52,223
27	26	A	Arsenal	D 0-0	0-0	3		30,200
28	Mar 8	H	Manchester C	W 1-0	0-0	3	Hudson-Odoi[83]	30,252
29	15	A	Ipswich T	W 4-2	3-0	3	Milenkovic[35], Elanga 2[37,41], Jota Silva[87]	29,878
30	Apr 1	H	Manchester U	W 1-0	1-0	3	Elanga[5]	30,249
31	5	A	Aston Villa	L 1-2	0-2	3	Jota Silva[57]	42,743
32	12	A	Everton	L 0-1	0-0	3		30,199
33	21	H	Tottenham H	W 2-1	2-0	3	Anderson[5], Wood[16]	59,314
34	May 1	H	Brentford	L 0-2	0-1	6		29,040
35	5	A	Crystal Palace	D 1-1	0-0	6	Murillo[64]	25,096
36	11	H	Leicester C	D 2-2	0-0	7	Gibbs-White[25], Wood[56]	30,245
37	18	A	West Ham U	W 2-1	1-0	7	Gibbs-White[11], Milenkovic[61]	62,466
38	25	H	Chelsea	L 0-1	0-0	7		30,263

Final League Position: 7

GOALSCORERS

League (58): Wood 20 (3 pens), Gibbs-White 7, Elanga 6, Hudson-Odoi 5, Milenkovic 5, Jota Silva 3, Aina 2, Anderson 2, Murillo 2, Yates 2, Awoniyi 1, Sosa 1, Williams 1, own goal 1.
FA Cup (5): Sosa 2, Yates 2, Awoniyi 1.
Carabao Cup (1): Jota Silva 1.
(Nottingham F U21) Vertu Trophy (4): Back 1, Gardner 1, Whitehall 1, own goal 1.

Sels M 38	Williams N 28 + 7	Boly W 1 + 5	Murillo d 36	Aina O 35	Sangare 17 + 6	Danilo d 5 + 3	Elanga A 31 + 7	Gibbs-White M 34	Hudson-Odoi C 25 + 6	Wood C 35 + 1	Yates R 18 + 17	Toffolo H 1 + 3	Dominguez N 23 + 11	Awoniyi T 3 + 23	Anderson E 33 + 4	Milenkovic N 37	Jota Silva P 5 + 26	Sosa R 1 + 18	Alex Moreno L 11 + 4	Ward-Prowse J 5 + 4	Morato F 6 + 20	Moreira E — + 2	Match No.
1	2	3	4	5²	6	7¹	8³	9	10⁴	11⁵	12	13	14	15	16								1
1	2	16	4	5	6¹		8	9⁴	10⁵	11²	12		14	13	7³	3	15						2
1	2		4	5	6¹		8³	9	10²	11	12		15		7⁴	3	14	13	·				3
1	14		4	2			13	9⁴	12	11⁵	6		8¹		10²	3	16		5³	7	15		4
1	14		4	2			10¹	9⁸	8	11⁵	12		7⁴		3	13	15	5²	6²	16			5
1	16		4	2			12	13	11	8	9³	10¹	6²	3	14	15	5⁵	7⁴					6
1	15		4	2			16	9²	8⁴	11³	6	13	10¹	3	12	5⁵	7⁸	14					7
1	14		4	2			8¹		10⁵	11⁴	6		7	16	9²	3	12	15	5³		13		8
1	13		4	2			8³		10⁴	11⁵	6		7	16	9¹	3	15	14	5²		12		9
1			4	2⁹			8¹	9²	10⁴	11³	6		7	14	12	3	13	15	5			16	10
1			4	2			8⁴	9²	10¹	11	6		7³	15	12	3	13	14	5⁵	16			11
1	15		4	2			8¹		10	14	9		7²	11³		3	12	13	5⁴	6			12
1	5²		4	2			15	9³	10⁵	11	7		12		6¹	3	8⁴	16	13		14		13
1			4	2³			8	9⁴		11²	6		7	13	14	3	10⁵	16	5		12	15	14
1	5		4	2			14	9³	10⁴	11²	7		13	15	6	3	8¹				12		15
1	5	15	4¹	2			14	9	10⁴	11	6²		8³		7	3	13				12		16
1	8⁴		3	5			9¹	6³	10	11⁵	12	15	13	16	7²	2	14			4			17
1	5		4	2			8¹	9²	10⁴	11⁵	6			16	7³	3	14	15		13	12		18
1	5⁵	12	4	2			8	9²		11³		15	6	14	7⁸	3	13	10¹					19
1	5		4	2			8²	9⁵	10	11⁴	13		6¹	15	7³	3	14			16	12		20
1	5⁴		4	2			8	9⁵	10¹	11³	6³		12	15	7	3	13		16		14		21
1	5		4	2			8²	9⁴	10¹	11³	15		6⁵	16	7	3	12	14			13		22
1	5³		4	2⁴			10	9⁵		11	6¹		12	16	7	3	8²	15	14		13		23
1	8	14	4²	5	16	7¹	10	9³		11⁵			12	15	6⁴	3	13				2		24
1	9		4	5	12	7¹	11	6	13	10					8³	3	14				2²		25
1	5		4	2	13		8	9	10	11	12		6¹		7²	3							26
1	5		4	2	13		8¹	9	10	11³	12		6²	14	7	3							27
1	5		4	2	13		8²	9	10⁴	11³	12		6¹	15	7	3		14					28
1	5		4	2	16		8¹	9⁵	10⁴	11³	12		6²	14	7	3	15			13			29
1	5		4	2¹	16	10²	8⁴	9		6			14	11⁵	7³	3		15	13		12		30
1	8	14	4				10¹	9	11		6		5²		7	3	12	13			2³		31
1	2		4		12		9	10	11	13			6²		7	3	8¹	5					32
1	2		4		7³	11¹	8⁵	13	10⁴	14	5	6²	15	9	3		16				12		33
1	5		4	2⁴	15		8	9²	10¹	11	6⁵		12	13	7²	3	14	16					34
1	5		4³	2	6²		10	9		11	13		8¹		7	3	12			14			35
1	5			2	6²		8	9		11	12		10¹	13	7³	3	14			4			36
1	5		4	2	7¹	14	11⁴	9³	12	10	15		6⁵		8²	3	16				13		37
1	5		4	2³	7¹		10	9	12	11	13		6²		8	3	14						38

FA Cup

Third Round	Luton T	(h)	2-0
Fourth Round	Exeter C	(a)	2-2

aet; Nottingham F won 4-2 on penalties.

Fifth Round	Ipswich T	(h)	1-1

aet; Nottingham F won 5-4 on penalties.

Quarter-Final	Brighton & HA	(a)	0-0

aet; Nottingham F won 4-3 on penalties.

Semi-Final	Manchester C	(Wembley)	0-2

Carabao Cup

Second Round	Newcastle U	(h)	1-1

Newcastle U won 4-3 on penalties.

Vertu Trophy (Nottingham F U21)

Group C (N)	Carlisle U	(a)	2-1
Group C (N)	Morecambe	(a)	2-4
Group C (N)	Wigan Ath	(a)	0-0

Wigan Ath won 3-0 on penalties.

NOTTS COUNTY

FOUNDATION

According to the official history of Notts County 'the true date of Notts' foundation has to be the meeting at the George Hotel on 7 December 1864'. However, there is documented evidence of continuous play from 1862, when club members played organised matches amongst themselves in The Park in Nottingham. They are the world's oldest professional football club.

Meadow Lane Stadium, Meadow Lane, Nottingham NG2 3HJ.

Telephone: (0115) 952 9000.

Ticket Office: (0115) 955 7210.

Website: www.nottscountyfc.co.uk

Email: office@nottscountyfc.co.uk

Ground Capacity: 19,841.

Record Attendance: 47,310 v York C, FA Cup 6th rd, 12 March 1955.

Pitch Measurements: 105m × 68m (115yd × 74.5yd).

Chairman: Christoffer Reedtz.

Chief Executive: Joe Palmer.

Manager: Martin Paterson.

Assistant Manager: Andy Edwards.

HONOURS

League Champions: Division 2 – 1896–97, 1913–14, 1922–23; Division 3S – 1930–31, 1949–50; FL 2 – 2009–10; Third Division – 1997–98; Division 4 – 1970–71.
Runners-up: Division 2 – 1894–95, 1980–81; Division 3 – 1972–73; Division 3S – 1936–37; Division 4 – 1959–60.
FA Cup Winners: 1894.
Runners-up: 1891.
League Cup: 5th rd – 1964, 1973, 1976.
Anglo-Italian Cup Winners: 1995.
Runners-up: 1994.

Colours: Black shirts with faded white stripes and black trim, black shorts with white trim, black socks with white trim.

Year Formed: 1862* (*see Foundation*).

Turned Professional: 1885.

Club Nickname: 'The Magpies'.

Grounds: 1862, The Park; 1864, The Meadows; 1877, Beeston Cricket Ground; 1880, Castle Ground; 1883, Trent Bridge; 1910, Meadow Lane.

First Football League Game: 15 September 1888, Football League, v Everton (a) L 1–2 – Holland; Guttridge, McLean; Brown, Warburton, Shelton; Hodder, Harker, Jardine, Albert Moore (1), Wardle.

Record League Victory: 11–1 v Newport Co, Division 3 (S), 15 January 1949 – Smith; Southwell, Purvis; Gannon, Baxter, Adamson; Houghton (1), Sewell (4), Lawton (4), Pimbley, Johnston (2).

Record Cup Victory: 15–0 v Rotherham T (at Trent Bridge), FA Cup 1st rd, 24 October 1885 – Sherwin; Snook, Henry Thomas Moore; Dobson (1), Emmett (1), Chapman; Gunn (1), Albert Moore (2), Jackson (3), Daft (2), Cursham (4), (1 og).

Record Defeat: 1–9 v Blackburn R, Division 1, 16 November 1889. 1–9 v Aston Villa, Division 1, 29 September 1888. 1–9 v Portsmouth, Division 2, 9 April 1927.

Most League Points (2 for a win): 69, Division 4, 1970–71.

Most League Points (3 for a win): 99, Division 3, 1997–98.

FOOTBALL YEARBOOK FACT FILE

Notts County took part in one of the earliest games played under artificial lighting, entertaining Derbyshire on the evening of 30 November 1878 in front of a crowd of nearly 5,000. Although the event was a commercial success, the game was beset by difficulties. The pitch was illuminated by just two lights and with fog descending spectators struggled to see what was happening. Notts claimed a 1-0 victory, although some sources suggest the teams agreed that the game should be counted as a draw.

Most League Goals: 107, Division 4, 1959–60.

Highest League Scorer in Season: Tom Keetley, 39, Division 3 (S), 1930–31.

Most League Goals in Total Aggregate: Les Bradd, 125, 1967–78.

Most League Goals in One Match: 5, Robert Jardine v Burnley, Division 1, 27 October 1888; 5, Daniel Bruce v Port Vale, Division 2, 26 February 1895; 5, Bertie Mills v Barnsley, Division 2, 19 November 1927.

Most Capped Player: Aki Lahtinen, 17 (56), Finland.

Most League Appearances: Albert Iremonger, 564, 1904–26.

Youngest League Player: Tony Bircumshaw, 16 years 54 days v Brentford, 3 April 1961.

Record Transfer Fee Received: £2,500,000 from Derby Co for Craig Short, September 1992.

Record Transfer Fee Paid: £800,000 to Manchester C for Kasper Schmeichel, July 2009.

Football League Record: 1888 Founder Member of the Football League; 1893–97 Division 2; 1897–1913 Division 1; 1913–14 Division 2; 1914–20 Division 1; 1920–23 Division 2; 1923–26 Division 1; 1926–30 Division 2; 1930–31 Division 3 (S); 1931–35 Division 2; 1935–50 Division 3 (S); 1950–58 Division 2; 1958–59 Division 3; 1959–60 Division 4; 1960–64 Division 3; 1964–71 Division 4; 1971–73 Division 3; 1973–81 Division 2; 1981–84 Division 1; 1984–85 Division 2; 1985–90 Division 3; 1990–91 Division 2; 1991–95 Division 1; 1995–97 Division 2; 1997–98 Division 3; 1998–2004 Division 2; 2004–10 FL 2; 2010–15 FL 1; 2015–19 FL 2; 2019–23 National League; 2023– FL 2.

LATEST SEQUENCES

Longest Sequence of League Wins: 10, 3.12.1997 – 31.1.1998.

Longest Sequence of League Defeats: 10, 12.11.2016 – 7.1.2017.

Longest Sequence of League Draws: 6, 16.8.2008 – 20.9.2008.

Longest Sequence of Unbeaten League Matches: 19, 26.4.1930 – 6.12.1930.

Longest Sequence Without a League Win: 20, 3.12.1996 – 31.3.1997.

Successive Scoring Runs: 35 from 10.10.1959.

Successive Non-scoring Runs: 5 from 15.3.2011.

MANAGERS

Edwin Browne 1883–93; **Tom Featherstone** 1893; **Tom Harris** 1893–1913; **Albert Fisher** 1913–27; **Horace Henshall** 1927–34; **Charlie Jones** 1934; **David Pratt** 1935; **Percy Smith** 1935–36; **Jimmy McMullan** 1936–37; **Harry Parkes** 1938–39; **Tony Towers** 1939–42; **Frank Womack** 1942–43; **Major Frank Buckley** 1944–46; **Arthur Stollery** 1946–49; **Eric Houghton** 1949–53; **George Poyser** 1953–57; **Tommy Lawton** 1957–58; **Frank Hill** 1958–61; **Tim Coleman** 1961–63; **Eddie Lowe** 1963–65; **Tim Coleman** 1965–66; **Jack Burkitt** 1966–67; **Andy Beattie** *(General Manager)* 1967; **Billy Gray** 1967–68; **Jack Wheeler** *(Caretaker Manager)* 1968–69; **Jimmy Sirrel** 1969–75; **Ron Fenton** 1975–77; **Jimmy Sirrel** 1978–82 *(continued as General Manager to 1984)*; **Howard Wilkinson** 1982–83; **Larry Lloyd** 1983–84; **Richie Barker** 1984–85; **Jimmy Sirrel** 1985–87; **John Barnwell** 1987–88; **Neil Warnock** 1989–93; **Mick Walker** 1993–94; **Russell Slade** 1994–95; **Howard Kendall** 1995; **Colin Murphy** 1995–96 *(General Manager)*; **Steve Thompson** 1995–96; **Sam Allardyce** 1997–99; **Gary Brazil** 1999–2000; **Jocky Scott** 2000–01; **Gary Brazil** 2001–02; **Billy Dearden** 2002–04; **Gary Mills** 2004; **Ian Richardson** 2004–05; **Gudjon Thordarson** 2005–06; **Steve Thompson** 2006–07; **Ian McParland** 2007–09; **Hans Backe** 2009; **Sven-Göran Eriksson** 2009–10 *(Director of Football)*; **Steve Cotterill** 2010; **Craig Short** 2010; **Paul Ince** 2010–11; **Martin Allen** 2011–12; **Keith Curle** 2012–13; **Chris Kiwomya** 2013; **Shaun Derry** 2013–15; **Ricardo Moniz** 2015; **Jamie Fullarton** 2016; **Mark Cooper** 2016; **John Sheridan** 2016–17; **Kevin Nolan** 2017–18; **Harry Kewell** 2018; **Neal Ardley** 2018–21; **Ian Burchnall** 2021–22; **Luke Williams** 2022–24; **Stuart Maynard** 2024–25; **Martin Paterson** June 2025–

TEN YEAR LEAGUE RECORD

		P	W	D	L	F	A	Pts	Pos
2015-16	FL 2	46	14	9	23	54	83	51	17
2016-17	FL 2	46	16	8	22	54	76	56	16
2017-18	FL 2	46	21	14	11	71	48	77	5
2018-19	FL 2	46	9	14	23	48	84	41	23
2019-20	NL	38	17	12	9	61	38	63	3§
2020-21	NL	42	20	10	12	62	41	70	5
2021-22	NL	44	24	10	10	81	52	82	5
2022-23	NL	46	32	11	3	117	42	107	2
2023-24	FL 2	46	18	7	21	89	86	61	14
2024-25	FL 2	46	20	12	14	68	49	72	6

§*Decided on points-per-game (1.66)*

DID YOU KNOW ?

Notts County were forced to change their kit at half-time during their visit to Huddersfield Town on 25 November 1989 after the referee decided that the Magpies' black and white stripes clashed with the home team's blue and white stripes. Notts played the second half in the Terriers' second strip shirts with black and yellow checks, but it made no difference to the score as they wound up 2-1 winners.

NOTTS COUNTY – SKY BET LEAGUE TWO 2024–25 LEAGUE RECORD

Match No.	Date	Venue	Opponents	Result	H/T Score	Lg Pos.	Goalscorers	Attendance
1	Aug 10	A	Tranmere R	D	0-0	0-0	13		8198
2	18	H	Fleetwood T	D	2-2	0-1	16	Jatta [57], Jones (pen) [90]	10,057
3	22	H	Grimsby T	W	4-1	3-1	4	Jatta [6], Crowley 2 [15, 57], Jones [45]	10,046
4	31	A	Swindon T	W	2-1	1-1	7	McGoldrick 2 [30, 80]	7326
5	Sept 7	H	Accrington S	W	2-0	1-0	2	McGoldrick 2 [18, 67]	10,147
6	14	A	Bromley	W	4-2	1-2	1	Jones 2 (1 pen) [13 (p), 89], Crowley [47], Jatta [56]	3322
7	21	H	Gillingham	L	0-1	0-1	4		14,747
8	28	A	Morecambe	D	1-1	0-1	4	Platt [79]	3595
9	Oct 1	A	Carlisle U	W	2-0	2-0	2	Jatta [10], Robertson [34]	5594
10	5	H	Port Vale	L	0-1	0-1	5		11,974
11	12	A	Chesterfield	D	2-2	1-1	3	Jatta [14], McGoldrick [90]	10,032
12	19	H	AFC Wimbledon	W	1-0	0-0	4	Platt [67]	10,156
13	22	A	Barrow	D	1-1	0-1	3	McGoldrick (pen) [90]	3123
14	26	H	Harrogate T	W	1-0	0-0	3	Jatta [58]	9427
15	Nov 9	A	Doncaster R	D	1-1	1-0	3	Jatta [13]	10,988
16	16	H	Crewe Alex	L	0-2	0-1	6		6127
17	23	H	Newport Co	D	0-0	0-0	4		9408
18	Dec 3	A	Walsall	L	2-3	0-0	6	McGoldrick (pen) [74], Hinchy [90]	5720
19	14	A	Salford C	L	0-3	0-2	11		2768
20	21	H	Bradford C	W	3-0	3-0	7	Jatta 2 [28, 32], McGoldrick [31]	11,500
21	26	A	Milton Keynes D	W	2-0	0-0	7	Abbott [57], Crowley [71]	9249
22	29	A	Cheltenham T	W	5-3	2-1	2	Jatta 2 [26, 90], Martin [39], Abbott [58], Austin [62]	5430
23	Jan 1	A	Walsall	L	1-2	1-0	7	Jatta [26]	4610
24	4	H	Swindon T	W	2-0	2-0	5	McGoldrick 2 [17, 36]	9296
25	18	A	Accrington S	W	3-0	2-0	5	Abbott [16], McGoldrick 2 [27, 63]	2924
26	25	H	Bromley	D	1-1	0-0	6	Jones (pen) [56]	9947
27	28	H	Carlisle U	W	1-0	1-0	2	Jatta [19]	8521
28	Feb 1	A	Gillingham	W	2-1	2-0	3	Tsaroulla [17], McGoldrick [20]	6031
29	8	H	Morecambe	W	2-0	0-0	2	Whitaker [66], Jatta [75]	9909
30	13	A	Port Vale	L	0-1	0-0	2		7213
31	18	A	Colchester U	D	1-1	1-0	4	Grant [3]	9467
32	22	H	Tranmere R	W	2-1	0-0	4	Whitaker [80], Jatta [83]	9476
33	Mar 1	A	Fleetwood T	D	2-2	1-0	4	Abbott [16], Jatta [89]	3555
34	4	H	Barrow	L	1-2	0-1	4	Grant [64]	7872
35	8	A	AFC Wimbledon	L	0-2	0-2	5		8659
36	11	A	Grimsby T	W	2-0	0-0	4	Jatta [56], McGoldrick [88]	6270
37	15	H	Chesterfield	L	1-2	0-0	5	Jarvis [81]	13,229
38	22	H	Crewe Alex	D	0-0	0-0	6		10,225
39	29	A	Newport Co	W	2-0	1-0	6	Whitaker 2 [6, 63]	4691
40	Apr 2	H	Milton Keynes D	W	3-0	1-0	4	McGoldrick [47], Tsaroulla [54], Jarvis [74]	8920
41	5	A	Colchester U	L	0-1	0-1	6		6172
42	11	H	Salford C	L	1-3	0-1	6	McGoldrick [67]	9643
43	17	A	Bradford C	D	1-1	0-0	6	McGoldrick [69]	20,392
44	21	H	Cheltenham T	L	1-2	1-0	6	Jatta [45]	10,642
45	26	H	Harrogate T	W	3-1	1-1	5	Abbott [33], Grant 2 [51, 76]	4136
46	May 3	H	Doncaster R	L	1-2	0-2	6	Jatta [90]	15,427

Final League Position: 6

GOALSCORERS

League (68): Jatta 19, McGoldrick 17 (2 pens), Abbott 5, Jones 5 (3 pens), Crowley 4, Grant 4, Whitaker 4, Jarvis 2, Platt 2, Tsaroulla 2, Austin 1, Hinchy 1, Martin 1, Robertson 1.
FA Cup (8): Brown 2 (1 pen), Jatta 2, Platt 2, Abbott 1, Scott 1.
Carabao Cup (3): Austin 1, Grant 1, Jatta 1.
Vertu Trophy (3): Austin 1, Gordon 1, Scott 1.
League Two Play-offs (0).

Bass A 39	Macari L 26 + 5	Platt M 45	Bedeau J 43 + 1	Jones J 13 + 7	Hinchy J 12 + 13	Crowley D 18	Chicksen A 2	Austin S 18 + 5	Scott C 3 + 7	Jatta A 38 + 1	Cundy R 2 + 5	Grant C 23 + 9	Edwards C 6 + 10	McGoldrick D 28 + 7	Robertson S 5 + 2	Palmer M 39 + 4	Tsaroulla N 28 + 10	Gordon K 18 + 12	Abbott G 37 + 3	Brown J 4 + 10	Martin J 4 + 4	McDonald R 14 + 4	Ness L 6 + 1	Cisse M 1 + 1	Whitaker C 13 + 7	Jarvis W 7 + 14	Johnson Z 5 + 5	Traore M 2 + 10	Slocombe S 7 + 1	Match No.
1	2	3	4	5	6[1]	7	8[2]	9[3]	10	11[4]	12	13	14	15																1
1	2	3	4	5	6[1]	7	8[2]		10[4]	11		9[3]		15	12	13	14													2
1	2	3	4	5	12	8		14	16	11[3]		10[4]	6[5]	13	7[1]	15	9[2]													3
1	2	3	4		7	6[1]	8[4]		14			10	9[3]	11		13	5[2]	12	15											4
1	2	3	4			7[1]			8	13		10[3]	9	11[2]		12	5[4]	15		6	14									5
1	2	4	5	8	15	9[4]		13		12	3[1]	10[3]		11[5]		6[2]	14			7	16									6
1	2	3	4	5[4]		7		14			15	10[3]		11		6[2]	8[1]	13	9	12										7
1	12	3	4			8		9		2[1]	10[3]		11	14	5[4]	7[2]	6	15	13											8
1	2	3	4			7[3]		5	14	11[2]			10[1]	6	12	8	9	13												9
1	2	3	4			9		10[3]	13	11	15		6[2]	7[4]	8[1]	5	12	14												10
1	2	3	4			9		10	11			13	6[2]	7	12	8[1]	5[3]	14												11
1	2[3]	3	4		6	12		10		11		8[1]	7	13	9[2]	5			14											12
1	2	3	14		6[1]	9		10		11		7	5	8[2]		12	13	4[3]												13
1	2	3	4	13				11		10[2]		7	5	12	6	9	8[1]													14
1	2	3	4			9		11		7		5	8	6	10															15
1	2	4	5			10	11[1]	12		7		8	13	6	9			3[2]												16
1	4	3		8[2]	13	11		10		7		5[3]	12	6	9[1]		2	14												17
1	2		4	6	8[2]	13	11	9		5		7	12				3	10[1]												18
1		3	4	13	6[2]	8		11		10[1]		7	5	9		12	2													19
1	12	3	4		9[1]	5		10[2]		11		7	8	6	13	2														20
1	2[1]	3	4	13	9[2]	5		10[3]		11		7	8	6	14	12														21
1		3	4	6	9	5		11	12[2]	13	10	7		8[3]	14	2[1]														22
1		3	4	12	9	5[1]		10	13	11	7		6	8[2]	2															23
1		3	4	12	16	9[1]	5	10[2]	15	13	11[5]	7			6	14	8[3]	2[4]												24
1		3	4	12	15	5		10[3]	9[1]	16	11[9]	7	8[2]		6[4]		2				13	14								25
1		3	4	5[1]	7	8		11		9[3]	10[2]		12	6		2			13	14										26
1		3	4	5[3]	7			11[4]		9[2]	12	10		8	14	6		2[1]			15	13								27
1		3	4	5[3]				11		13	10	7	8[1]	12	6		2			9[2]	14									28
1		3	4	8[1]	15			11[4]		13	10[2]	7		5[3]	6		2			9	12	14								29
1		3	8	13				10	11[3]	9[2]		7	12	5[1]	6	4					2	14							30
1		3			10	15	11[3]	9[2]	7		8[1]	5	6	4[4]		12	13	2	14									31
1		3	4	15				11		10[1]	14	7	13	5[2]	6[4]		2			9[3]	8	2	12							32
1	15	3	4	14				11		10[1]		7	8[2]	5[3]	6					9	12	2[4]	13							33
1	2[2]	3	4					11		12		7	14	5	6					9	8[1]	13	10[3]							34
1	13	3	4		5[2]			10		9[4]	16	8	6[5]	15	7		12			11[3]	14	2[1]							35
1[1]	2	3	4					10		8[3]	14	13	5	9[4]	6	7				11[2]	15			12					36
	2	3	4					10		8[1]		11	5	9[2]	6	7				12	13			1					37
	2	3	4					9[1]	14	11	7	13	5[2]	6						10[3]	8		12	1					38
	2[4]	3	4					9		14		10[1]	7	5[2]	12	6				11	8[3]	15	13	1					39
	2[4]	3	4		15			11[3]	14	10[5]	7	5[2]	12	6					9[1]	8	16	13	1					40
	2	3	4	12	6			11		14		10	7	5[1]					8[2]	9[3]		13	1					41
	2	3	4	12	7[3]			11[4]	16	10		6	5[2]	14		13			9[1]	8[5]		15	1					42
		3	4	5[2]				10		9[1]		11	7	8	6		2			12	13		1					43
1		3	4	12				9		8[1]		7		5[2]	6		2			13	14		10[3]					44
1		3	4	8[2]	15			11[1]		9		10	7	5[3]	6[4]		2			12	14	13						45
1	12	3	4	8	16			14		11		9[3]	15	7		5[2]	6[5]		2[1]			10[4]	13					46

FA Cup

| First Round | Alfreton T | (h) | 5-1 |
| Second Round | Peterborough U | (a) | 3-4 |

Carabao Cup

First Round Shrewsbury T (a) 3-3
Shrewsbury T won 4-3 on penalties.

Vertu Trophy

Group F (S)	Burton Alb	(a)	2-1
Group F (S)	Northampton T	(h)	0-2
Group F (S)	Leicester C U21	(h)	1-0

League Two Play-offs

| Semi-Final 1st leg | AFC Wimbledon | (h) | 0-1 |
| Semi-Final 2nd leg | AFC Wimbledon | (a) | 0-1 |

OXFORD UNITED

FOUNDATION

There had been an Oxford United club around the time of World War I but only in the Oxfordshire Thursday League and there is no connection with the modern club which began as Headington in 1893, adding 'United' a year later. Playing first on Quarry Fields and subsequently Wootten's Fields, they owe much to a Dr Hitchings for their early development.

The Kassam Stadium, Grenoble Road, Oxford OX4 4XP.
Telephone: (01865) 337 500.
Ticket Office: (01865) 337 533.
Website: www.oufc.co.uk
Email: feedback@oufc.co.uk
Ground Capacity: 12,553.
Record Attendance: 22,750 v Preston NE, FA Cup 6th rd, 29 February 1964 (at Manor Ground); 12,243 v Leyton Orient, FL 2, 6 May 2006 (at The Kassam Stadium).
Pitch Measurements: 100m × 66m (109.5yd × 72yd).
Chairman: Grant Ferguson.
Chief Executive: Tim Williams.
Head Coach: Gary Rowett.
First-Team Coaches: Craig Short, Mark Sale, Chris Hackett.
Colours: Yellow shirts with navy blue trim, navy blue shorts with yellow trim, yellow socks.
Year Formed: 1893.
Turned Professional: 1949.
Previous Names: 1893, Headington; 1894, Headington United; 1960, Oxford United.
Club Nickname: 'The U's'.
Grounds: 1893, Headington Quarry; 1894, Wootten's Fields; 1898, Sandy Lane Ground; 1902, Britannia Field; 1909, Sandy Lane; 1910, Quarry Recreation Ground; 1914, Sandy Lane; 1922, The Paddock Manor Road; 1925, Manor Ground; 2001, The Kassam Stadium.
First Football League Game: 18 August 1962, Division 4, v Barrow (a) L 2–3 – Medlock; Beavon, Quartermain; Ron Atkinson, Kyle, Jones; Knight, Graham Atkinson (1), Houghton (1), Cornwell, Colfar.
Record League Victory: 7–0 v Barrow, Division 4, 19 December 1964 – Fearnley; Beavon, Quartermain; Ron Atkinson (1), Kyle, Jones; Morris, Booth (3), Willey (1), Graham Atkinson (1), Harrington (1).
Record Cup Victory: 9–1 v Dorchester T, FA Cup 1st rd, 11 November 1995 – Whitehead; Wood (2), Mike Ford (1), Smith, Elliott, Gilchrist, Rush (1), Massey (Murphy), Moody (3), Bobby Ford (1), Angel (Beauchamp (1)).
Record Defeat: 0–7 v Sunderland, Division 1, 19 September 1998; 0–7 v Wigan Ath, FL 1, 23 December 2017.

HONOURS

League Champions: Division 2 – 1984–85; Division 3 – 1967–68, 1983–84.
Runners-up: Second Division – 1995–96; FL 2 – 2015–16; Football Conference – 2006–07, (3rd) 2009–10 *(promoted to FL 2 via play-offs).*
FA Cup: 6th rd – 1964.
League Cup Winners: 1986.
League Trophy: Runners-up: 2016, 2017.

FOOTBALL YEARBOOK FACT FILE

After deciding to turn professional early in 1949, Headington United, as the club was then called, were elected to the Southern League for the 1949–50 campaign. This was a big step up from their former competition, the Spartan League, and the U's struggled in their early season matches. It was not until their fifth match, on 22 September, that they gained their first win, defeating Guildford City 4-2 at the Manor Ground.

Most League Points (2 for a win): 61, Division 4, 1964–65.

Most League Points (3 for a win): 95, Division 3, 1983–84.

Most League Goals: 91, Division 3, 1983–84.

Highest League Scorer in Season: John Aldridge, 30, Division 2, 1984–85.

Most League Goals in Total Aggregate: Graham Atkinson, 77, 1962–73.

Most League Goals in One Match: 4, Tony Jones v Newport Co, Division 4, 22 September 1962; 4, Arthur Longbottom v Darlington, Division 4, 26 October 1963; 4, Richard Hill v Walsall, Division 2, 26 December 1988; 4, John Durnin v Luton T, 14 November 1992; 4, Tom Craddock v Accrington S, FL 2, 20 October 2011; 4, Cameron Brannagan v Gillingham, FL 1, 29 January 2022.

Most Capped Player: Jim Magilton, 18 (52), Northern Ireland; Ciaron Brown, 18 (25), Northern Ireland.

Most League Appearances: John Shuker, 478, 1962–77.

Youngest League Player: Jason Seacole, 16 years 149 days v Mansfield T, 7 September 1976.

Record Transfer Fee Received: £3,000,000 from Leeds U for Kemar Roofe, July 2016.

Record Transfer Fee Paid: £1,600,000 to Heracles for Brian De Keersmaeker, July 2025.

Football League Record: 1962 Elected to Division 4; 1962–65 Division 4; 1965–68 Division 3; 1968–76 Division 2; 1976–84 Division 3; 1984–85 Division 2; 1985–88 Division 1; 1988–92 Division 2; 1992–94 First Division; 1994–96 Second Division; 1996–99 First Division; 1999–2001 Second Division; 2001–04 Third Division; 2004–06 FL 2; 2006–10 Football Conference; 2010–16 FL 2; 2016–24 FL 1; 2024– FL C.

LATEST SEQUENCES

Longest Sequence of League Wins: 7, 15.12.2020 – 30.1.2021.

Longest Sequence of League Draws: 5, 28.9.2024 – 22.10.2024.

Longest Sequence of League Draws: 5, 7.10.1978 – 28.10.1978.

Longest Sequence of Unbeaten League Matches: 20, 17.3.1984 – 29.9.1984.

Longest Sequence Without a League Win: 27, 14.11.1987 – 27.8.1988.

Successive Scoring Runs: 17 from 22.4.2006.

Successive Non-scoring Runs: 6 from 26.3.1988.

MANAGERS

Harry Thompson 1949–58
(Player-Manager) 1949-51
Arthur Turner 1959–69
(continued as General Manager to 1972)
Ron Saunders 1969
Gerry Summers 1969–75
Mick Brown 1975–79
Bill Asprey 1979–80
Ian Greaves 1980–82
Jim Smith 1982–85
Maurice Evans 1985–88
Mark Lawrenson 1988
Brian Horton 1988–93
Denis Smith 1993–97
Malcolm Crosby 1997–98
Malcolm Shotton 1998–99
Micky Lewis 1999–2000
Denis Smith 2000
David Kemp 2000–01
Mark Wright 2001
Ian Atkins 2001–04
Graham Rix 2004
Ramon Diaz 2004–05
Brian Talbot 2005–06
Darren Patterson 2006
Jim Smith 2006–07
Darren Patterson 2007–08
Chris Wilder 2008–14
Gary Waddock 2014
Michael Appleton 2014–17
Pep Clotet 2017–18
Karl Robinson 2018–23
Liam Manning 2023
Des Buckingham 2023–24
Gary Rowett December 2024–

TEN YEAR LEAGUE RECORD

		P	W	D	L	F	A	Pts	Pos
2015-16	FL 2	46	24	14	8	84	41	86	2
2016-17	FL 1	46	20	9	17	65	52	69	8
2017-18	FL 1	46	15	11	20	61	66	56	16
2018-19	FL 1	46	15	15	16	58	60	60	12
2019-20	FL 1	35	17	9	9	61	37	60	4§
2020-21	FL 1	46	22	8	16	77	56	74	6
2021-22	FL 1	46	22	10	14	82	59	76	8
2022-23	FL 1	46	11	14	21	49	56	47	19
2023-24	FL 1	46	22	11	13	79	56	77	5
2024-25	FL C	46	13	14	19	49	65	53	17

§*Decided on points-per-game (1.71)*

DID YOU KNOW ?

Oxford United became the first Fourth Division Club to reach the FA Cup quarter-finals in 1963–64 by defeating Blackburn Rovers at the Manor Ground. Tony Jones (2) and Bill Calder scored the goals in a 3-2 win in front of a new ground record crowd of 21,700. This was also the first time they had knocked a top-flight club out of the FA Cup.

OXFORD UNITED – SKY BET CHAMPIONSHIP 2024–25 LEAGUE RECORD

Match No.	Date	Venue	Opponents	Result	H/T Score	Lg Pos.	Goalscorers	Attendance
1	Aug 10	H	Norwich C	W 2-0	1-0	3	Harris [28], Brannagan [58]	11,333
2	16	A	Coventry C	L 2-3	1-2	7	Brown [22], Harris [55]	28,051
3	24	A	Blackburn R	L 1-2	1-1	12	Harris [44]	14,769
4	31	H	Preston NE	W 3-1	1-1	8	Harris [20], Goodrham [53], Leigh [71]	11,403
5	Sept 14	H	Stoke C	W 1-0	0-0	7	El Mizouni [48]	11,507
6	21	A	Bristol C	L 1-2	1-0	9	Rodrigues [28]	24,807
7	28	H	Burnley	D 0-0	0-0	11		11,517
8	Oct 1	A	Luton T	D 2-2	1-2	12	Goodrham [45], Rodrigues [54]	11,397
9	5	A	Portsmouth	D 1-1	0-0	10	Sibley [72]	20,125
10	19	H	WBA	D 1-1	0-1	11	Scarlett [90]	11,453
11	22	H	Derby Co	D 1-1	1-0	10	Scarlett [12]	11,423
12	26	A	Sunderland	L 0-2	0-1	14		40,654
13	Nov 2	H	Swansea C	L 1-2	0-1	19	Scarlett [88]	11,454
14	5	H	Hull C	W 1-0	0-0	14	ter Avest [55]	10,213
15	8	A	Watford	L 0-1	0-0	16		20,268
16	23	H	Middlesbrough	L 2-6	1-3	18	Leigh [24], Scarlett [72]	11,442
17	26	A	Sheffield U	L 0-3	0-2	18		25,574
18	30	H	Millwall	D 1-1	0-1	17	Goodrham [85]	10,990
19	Dec 11	A	QPR	L 0-2	0-0	20		14,440
20	14	H	Sheffield Wed	L 1-3	1-1	20	Leigh [17]	11,567
21	21	A	Leeds U	L 0-4	0-1	23		36,646
22	26	H	Cardiff C	W 3-2	1-0	20	Harris [41], Brown [53], Placheta [57]	11,494
23	29	H	Plymouth Arg	W 2-0	1-0	20	Brown [14], Placheta [61]	11,438
24	Jan 1	A	Millwall	W 1-0	0-0	18	Rodrigues [57]	14,964
25	4	A	Preston NE	D 1-1	1-0	17	Rodrigues [21]	14,749
26	14	A	Plymouth Arg	D 1-1	1-0	17	Vaulks [44]	15,933
27	18	H	Blackburn R	W 1-0	0-0	15	Brannagan [67]	11,407
28	21	H	Luton T	W 3-2	1-2	14	Helik [22], Brown [59], Leigh [69]	11,035
29	25	A	Stoke C	D 0-0	0-0	15		22,911
30	Feb 1	H	Bristol C	D 1-1	0-0	16	Leigh [59]	11,430
31	4	A	Burnley	L 0-1	0-1	16		18,187
32	11	A	Derby Co	D 0-0	0-0	16		25,999
33	15	H	Portsmouth	L 0-2	0-0	16		11,423
34	22	A	WBA	L 0-2	0-1	18		25,951
35	Mar 1	H	Coventry C	L 2-3	0-1	18	Romeny [53], Moore [62]	11,405
36	7	A	Norwich C	D 1-1	1-1	18	Harris [18]	25,996
37	12	A	Hull C	L 1-2	0-0	20	Helik [66]	19,024
38	15	H	Watford	W 1-0	0-0	18	Dembele [82]	11,535
39	29	A	Middlesbrough	L 1-2	1-0	19	Helik [38]	24,624
40	Apr 5	H	Sheffield U	W 1-0	1-0	18	Dembele [38]	11,496
41	9	H	QPR	L 1-3	0-2	18	Mills [62]	11,509
42	12	A	Sheffield Wed	W 1-0	0-0	17	Long [79]	25,646
43	18	H	Leeds U	L 0-1	0-1	19		11,537
44	21	A	Cardiff C	D 1-1	0-0	19	Brannagan [79]	23,407
45	26	H	Sunderland	W 2-0	1-0	17	Nelson [29], Helik [48]	11,431
46	May 3	A	Swansea C	D 3-3	1-1	17	Leigh [40], Helik [62], Placheta [90]	19,672

Final League Position: 17

GOALSCORERS

League (49): Harris 6, Leigh 6, Helik 5, Brown 4, Rodrigues 4, Scarlett 4, Brannagan 3, Goodrham 3, Placheta 3, Dembele 2, El Mizouni 1, Long 1, Mills 1, Moore 1, Nelson 1, Romeny 1, Sibley 1, ter Avest 1, Vaulks 1.
FA Cup (1): Phillips 1.
Carabao Cup (2): Goodrham 1, Phillips 1.

Cumming J 45	Long S 18 + 6	Moore E 24 + 2	Brown C 41	Bennett J 8 + 4	Vaulks W 38 + 6	Goodrham T 33 + 8	Rodrigues R 28 + 11	Brannagan C 33	Placheta P 27 + 5	Harris M 34 + 12	El Mizouni I 12 + 16	Leigh G 24 + 10	O'Donkor G — + 1	Phillips M 10 + 18	Sibley L 1 + 10	Scarlett D 7 + 13	Kioso P 26 + 4	Dale O 4 + 7	McEachran J 6 + 6	Dembele S 15 + 10	Ebiowei M — + 4	Edwards K 1 + 6	Nelson B 16 + 1	ter Avest H 10 + 11	Goodwin W — + 3	Thorniley J — + 2	Matos A 10 + 10	Helik M 20	Bradshaw T 4 + 7	Romeny O 7 + 7	Mills S 3 + 8	Ingram M 1	Ferdinan M — + 1	Match No.
1	2	3	4	5	6	7	8^2	9	10^1	11^3	12	13	14																					1
1	2	3	4	5	6	7^3		9	10^1	11^4	13			12	14	15																		2
1		3		4	5	6	10	8^1		12^4	11	9^3	13			7^2	15		2	14														3
1		3		4	5^2	14	10	8^3	9		11	15	13			7^1			2			6^4	12											4
1		3	4			13	7	12	9^1		11	8	5							2			6^2	10^3	14									5
1		3	4		12	7^3	8^2			11	9	5					13	2			6^1	10^4	14	15										6
1		3	5		6	7	8^1			11^3	9						14	2	13				10^2		12	4								7
1	15	3^4	5		6	10	8^2			11^3	9						14	2	7^1			13		12	4									8
1	3		5		6	10	8^4			11^3	9	12			15	14	2				13		7^2	4^1									9
1		3	5		6	7	8^2			11^1	9^4				13	12	2	15			10^3	14		4										10
1		3	5		6^3	7	8^5			13	9^4	16			15	11^2	2	12	14		10^1			4										11
1		3	5		6^4	7	8^3			10	9^1	12			14	11^5	2^2		15				4	13	16									12
1		3	5		15	10	8^5			11^3	12	16			9^1	13	2	7^2	6^4		14		4											13
1	12	4	5		6	8	15			13	9^4	10			11^2	14		7					3^1	2^3										14
1	2	3	4		6	10	9^4			13	12	8			11^2	5^3		7^1					14	15										15
1	2	3^2	4		6^5	10	9^3	7^4	13	11^1	16	8		14		12			15				5											16
1	3		4		7^4	6^5	10^1	8	9^2	15	13	5		12		11^3		14	16				2											17
1	2	3	4		7^1	10	13	8	9^2	14	12	5^5		6^4		11^3		15							16									18
1		3	4			8	13	6	10^1	11^4	9^3	5		7^2		14	2^5	16	15				12											19
1		3	4		12	6^4	10^2	7		14	8^3	5		13		11	2	9^1					15											20
1	16	3	4		8^3	7	12	9	6^2	11^4		5				15	2^5	10^1	14				13											21
1	2	3	4		7	9^3	10^1	8	6^2	11		5		12	14					13														22
1	2	3	4		6	10^3	9^2	7	8^1	11^4	13	5		12		15							14											23
1	2	3^1	4		6	10^5	9^2	7	8^3	11^4	15	5		13	16			12					14											24
1	3		4		6	10^4	9^5	7		11^1		5		8^3	15	12	2^2			16				14	13									25
1	3^1		4		6		9^5	7	8^2	11^3		10^4		13	2					14				16	12	15								26
1			4		6		9^2	7	8^4	11^1	15	5		14		2				10^3						12	3	13						27
1			4		6		16	7^5	8^3	11^2		5		9^1	15		2			10^4			14			12	3	13						28
1			4		6^4	14	9^5	7	8^5	12		5		16			2			10^2						13	3	11^1	15					29
1			4		6^3	12	9^2	7	8^4	11^5		5					2^1			10			13			15	3	16	14					30
1	2^5		4		6^1	10^3	7	8^4	13	15	5	14					12									9	3	11^2	16					31
1			4		6	14	13	7	8^2	11^4		5		15			2			10^3						9^1	3		12					32
1	12		4		6	15	9^4	7	8	11^2		5^1		16			2^5			10^3						3		14	13					33
1		4	5	12	9		7		6	8^2	10^4			14			2^3			16			15			6^1	3	11^5	13					34
1		3	5		7^1	9		6		8^2	10^4			14			2^3			16			15			13	4	11^3	12					35
1	14	4	5		8		13	9	6^2	11^5	15	12					2^3									7^4	3	10^1	16					36
1		4^1	5		6		9^4		13	11	16			10^3					15			12	2			7^5	3	14	8^2					37
1		5			7	13		6	11^3	10				14		12			8^4			4^1	2			15	3	9^2						38
1		5			8	14			10^2	11^4				6^1		12						9^3		3	2^5		7	4	15	16	13			39
1		5	14		7	13			6^5	8^2	11^4	15										10^3	2		12	4	16	9^1						40
1			5^1	12	6^5	13	15	7	8	11^4												10	3	2^3		17	4	16	9^2	14				41
1	2				5^5	6	10^4	13	7	15	14		16		12								4			9^3	3	11^2		8^1				42
1	2				5^1	6	10^5		7	8^4	11^2	16	13										4			9^3	3	15	12	14				43
1		16			5^5	7	9	14	8	6^1	15		12		13		2^2						4			10^4	3	11^3						44
1	2^3	16			15	6	10	9^1	7	8^2	11^5		5^4		12								4	14		13	3							45
	16	3			15		9	10^2	7	12	13		5^3										2^5				8	4	11^4	6^1	1	14	46

FA Cup
Third Round   Exeter C   (a) 1-3

Carabao Cup
First Round   Peterborough U   (h) 2-0
Second Round   Coventry C   (a) 0-1

PETERBOROUGH UNITED

FOUNDATION

The old Peterborough & Fletton club, founded in 1923, was suspended by the FA during season 1932–33 and disbanded. Local enthusiasts determined to carry on and in 1934 a new professional club, Peterborough United, was formed and entered the Midland League the following year. Peterborough's first success came in 1939–40, but from 1955–56 to 1959–60 they won five successive titles. During the 1958–59 season they were undefeated in the Midland League. They reached the third round of the FA Cup, won the Northamptonshire Senior Cup, the Maunsell Cup and were runners-up in the East Anglian Cup.

Weston Homes Stadium, London Road, Peterborough PE2 8AL.

Telephone: (01733) 563 947.

Ticket Office: (01733) 865 674.

Website: www.theposh.com

Email: info@theposh.com

Ground Capacity: 13,350.

Record Attendance: 30,096 v Swansea T, FA Cup 5th rd, 20 February 1965.

Pitch Measurements: 102m × 69m (111.5yd × 75.5yd).

Chairman: Darragh MacAnthony.

Chief Executive: Dawn Gore.

Manager: Darren Ferguson.

First-Team Coach: Kieran Scarff.

Colours: Blue shirts with white trim, blue shorts, white socks with blue trim.

Year Formed: 1934.

Turned Professional: 1934.

Club Nickname: 'The Posh'.

Ground: 1934, London Road Stadium (renamed ABAX Stadium 2014; Weston Homes Stadium 2019).

First Football League Game: 20 August 1960, Division 4, v Wrexham (h) W 3–0 – Walls; Stafford, Walker; Rayner, Rigby, Norris; Hails, Emery (1), Bly (1), Smith, McNamee (1).

Record League Victory: 9–1 v Barnet (a) Division 3, 5 September 1998 – Griemink; Hooper (1), Drury (Farell), Gill, Bodley, Edwards, Davies, Payne, Grazioli (5), Quinn (2) (Rowe), Houghton (Etherington) (1).

Record Cup Victory: 9–1 v Rushden T, FA Cup 1st qual rd, 6 October 1945 – Hilliard; Bryan, Parrott, Warner, Hobbs, Woods, Polhill (1), Fairchild, Laxton (6), Tasker (1), Rodgers (1); 9–1 v Kingstonian, FA Cup 1st rd, 25 November 1992. Match ordered to be replayed by FA. Peterborough won replay 1–0.

HONOURS

League Champions: Division 4 – 1960–61, 1973–74.
Runners-up: FL 1 – 2008–09, 2020–21; FL 2 – 2007–08.
FA Cup: 6th rd – 1965.
League Cup: semi-final – 1966.
League Trophy Winners: 2014, 2024, 2025.

FOOTBALL YEARBOOK FACT FILE

Peterborough United were formed too late to enter the FA Cup in their first season, so their first entry to the competition came in 1935–36. It proved to be an inauspicious debut as the Posh, then members of the Midland League, went down to a 3-0 home defeat to Rushden Town in the first qualifying round of the competition. The attendance of 4,254 included around 1,000 travelling supporters from Rushden.

Record Defeat: 1–8 v Northampton T, FA Cup 2nd rd (2nd replay), 18 December 1946.

Most League Points (2 for a win): 66, Division 4, 1960–61.

Most League Points (3 for a win): 92, FL 2, 2007–08.

Most League Goals: 134, Division 4, 1960–61.

Highest League Scorer in Season: Terry Bly, 52, Division 4, 1960–61.

Most League Goals in Total Aggregate: Jim Hall, 122, 1967–75.

Most League Goals in One Match: 5, Guiliano Grazioli v Barnet, Division 3, 5 September 1999.

Most Capped Player: Craig Morgan, 19 (23), Wales.

Most League Appearances: Tommy Robson, 482, 1968–81.

Youngest League Player: Matthew Etherington, 15 years 262 days v Brentford, 3 May 1997.

Record Transfer Fee Received: £10,000,000 from Brentford for Ivan Toney, April 2020.

Record Transfer Fee Paid: £1,250,000 (in excess of) to Bristol C for Mo Eisa, June 2019.

Football League Record: 1960 Elected to Division 4; 1960–61 Division 4; 1961–68 Division 3, when they were demoted for financial irregularities; 1968–74 Division 4; 1974–79 Division 3; 1979–91 Division 4; 1991–92 Division 3; 1992–94 First Division; 1994–97 Second Division; 1997–2000 Third Division; 2000–04 Second Division; 2004–05 FL 1; 2005–08 FL 2; 2008–09 FL 1; 2009–10 FL C; 2010–11 FL 1; 2011–13 FL C; 2013–21 FL 1; 2021–22 FL C; 2022– FL 1.

LATEST SEQUENCES

Longest Sequence of League Wins: 9, 1.2.1992 – 14.3.1992.

Longest Sequence of League Defeats: 8, 16.12.2006 – 27.1.2007.

Longest Sequence of League Draws: 8, 18.12.1971 – 12.2.1972.

Longest Sequence of Unbeaten League Matches: 17, 15.1.2008 – 5.4.2008.

Longest Sequence Without a League Win: 17, 23.9.1978 – 30.12.1978.

Successive Scoring Runs: 33 from 20.9.1960.

Successive Non-scoring Runs: 6 from 13.8.2002.

MANAGERS

Jock Porter 1934–36
Fred Taylor 1936–37
Vic Poulter 1937–38
Sam Haden 1938–48
Jack Blood 1948–50
Bob Gurney 1950–52
Jack Fairbrother 1952–54
George Swindin 1954–58
Jimmy Hagan 1958–62
Jack Fairbrother 1962–64
Gordon Clark 1964–67
Norman Rigby 1967–69
Jim Iley 1969–72
Noel Cantwell 1972–77
John Barnwell 1977–78
Billy Hails 1978–79
Peter Morris 1979–82
Martin Wilkinson 1982–83
John Wile 1983–86
Noel Cantwell 1986–88 *(continued as General Manager)*
Mick Jones 1988–89
Mark Lawrenson 1989–90
Dave Booth 1990–91
Chris Turner 1991–92
Lil Fuccillo 1992–93
Chris Turner 1993–94
John Still 1994–95
Mick Halsall 1995–96
Barry Fry 1996–2005
Mark Wright 2005–06
Steve Bleasdale 2006
Keith Alexander 2006–07
Darren Ferguson 2007–09
Mark Cooper 2009–10
Jim Gannon 2010
Gary Johnson 2010–11
Darren Ferguson 2011–15
Dave Robertson 2015
Graham Westley 2015–16
Grant McCann 2016–18
Steve Evans 2018–19
Darren Ferguson 2019–22
Grant McCann 2022–23
Darren Ferguson January 2023–

TEN YEAR LEAGUE RECORD

		P	W	D	L	F	A	Pts	Pos
2015-16	FL 1	46	19	6	21	82	73	63	13
2016-17	FL 1	46	17	11	18	62	62	62	11
2017-18	FL 1	46	17	13	16	68	60	64	9
2018-19	FL 1	46	20	12	14	71	62	72	7
2019-20	FL 1	35	17	8	10	68	40	59	7§
2020-21	FL 1	46	26	9	11	83	46	87	2
2021-22	FL C	46	9	10	27	43	87	37	22
2022-23	FL 1	46	24	5	17	75	54	77	6
2023-24	FL 1	46	25	9	12	89	61	84	4
2024-25	FL 1	46	13	12	21	68	81	51	18

§*Decided on points-per-game (1.69)*

DID YOU KNOW ?

Peterborough United's 1967–68 campaign effectively ended in November when the Football League announced they would be relegated to the Fourth Division following a breach of the rules regarding payments to players. Posh continued to fight for every point and finished the season in sixth place in the Third Division table, just seven points behind champions Oxford United.

PETERBOROUGH UNITED – SKY BET LEAGUE ONE 2024–25 LEAGUE RECORD

Match No.	Date	Venue	Opponents	Result	H/T Score	Lg Pos.	Goalscorers	Attendance
1	Aug 10	H	Huddersfield T	L 0-2	0-2	23		10,627
2	17	A	Shrewsbury T	W 4-1	1-1	9	Adubofour-Poku 2 [23, 58], Randall 2 [87, 88]	6015
3	24	A	Exeter C	W 2-1	2-1	7	Mothersille [7], Fernandez [45]	6343
4	31	H	Wrexham	L 0-2	0-2	11		12,104
5	Sept 14	H	Lincoln C	D 1-1	0-1	11	Adubofour-Poku [65]	9537
6	21	H	Bristol R	W 3-2	2-0	10	Adubofour-Poku [10], Jade-Jones [33], Mothersille [63]	8006
7	24	A	Leyton Orient	D 2-2	2-1	8	Adubofour-Poku [42], Mothersille (pen) [45]	6416
8	28	A	Birmingham C	L 2-3	2-1	12	Jade-Jones [4], Fernandez [16]	27,206
9	Oct 1	A	Wigan Ath	L 0-3	0-1	16		7894
10	5	H	Stevenage	W 2-1	1-0	14	O'Brien-Brady [5], Adubofour-Poku [90]	8018
11	12	H	Rotherham U	D 3-3	1-3	12	Dornelly [17], Rafferty (og) [50], Fernandez [53]	8859
12	19	A	Wycombe W	L 1-3	0-0	15	Jade-Jones [50]	4345
13	22	H	Blackpool	W 5-1	3-1	12	Mothersille [8], Randall 2 [17, 73], Adubofour-Poku [28], Jade-Jones [70]	6391
14	26	A	Bolton W	L 0-1	0-0	13		20,022
15	Nov 9	H	Cambridge U	W 6-1	4-0	12	Jade-Jones [25], Adubofour-Poku 3 [32, 38, 90], Mothersille (pen) [44], De Havilland [50]	12,370
16	23	H	Reading	L 1-2	0-2	12	Fernandez [90]	10,008
17	Dec 4	H	Burton Alb	L 0-1	0-0	15		6043
18	9	A	Northampton T	L 1-2	1-1	15	Mothersille [39]	7098
19	14	H	Crawley T	W 4-3	2-1	13	Jade-Jones [20], Hayes 2 [23, 61], Kyprianou [47]	7874
20	20	A	Stockport Co	L 1-2	1-1	13	Randall [34]	9745
21	26	H	Mansfield T	L 0-3	0-3	17		9985
22	29	H	Barnsley	L 1-3	0-0	18	Mothersille (pen) [74]	9404
23	Jan 1	A	Burton Alb	D 2-2	1-2	18	Collins [42], Fernandez [77]	2821
24	4	A	Wrexham	L 0-1	0-0	19		13,060
25	18	H	Leyton Orient	D 0-0	0-0	19		8235
26	21	H	Exeter C	D 1-1	1-0	19	Kyprianou [34]	5913
27	25	A	Lincoln C	L 1-5	0-0	19	Jade-Jones [60]	10,014
28	28	A	Wigan Ath	W 1-0	1-0	18	Susoho [19]	6136
29	Feb 2	A	Bristol R	L 1-3	0-1	19	Jade-Jones [90]	7461
30	11	A	Charlton Ath	L 1-2	0-0	20	Mothersille (pen) [63]	11,653
31	15	A	Stevenage	D 1-1	0-0	20	Hayes [67]	4476
32	22	A	Huddersfield T	W 1-0	1-0	20	Kyprianou [45]	18,977
33	Mar 1	H	Shrewsbury T	W 3-1	2-1	17	Edun [8], Mothersille [35], Conn-Clarke [90]	11,578
34	4	A	Blackpool	D 0-0	0-0	17		7873
35	8	H	Wycombe W	D 1-1	1-0	19	Mothersille (pen) [16]	8260
36	15	A	Cambridge U	W 1-0	0-0	18	Edun [72]	7359
37	22	H	Charlton Ath	W 3-0	2-0	15	Hughes [38], Odoh [43], Mothersille [79]	10,231
38	29	A	Reading	L 1-3	0-1	15	Adubofour-Poku [66]	12,108
39	Apr 1	A	Crawley T	W 4-3	3-2	14	Odoh 3 [22, 29, 42], Jade-Jones (pen) [90]	4111
40	5	A	Northampton T	L 0-4	0-3	15		9782
41	8	H	Birmingham C	L 1-2	1-2	16	Adubofour-Poku [22]	10,640
42	18	H	Stockport Co	D 1-1	1-0	17	Jade-Jones [43]	11,241
43	21	A	Barnsley	D 1-1	1-1	17	Jade-Jones [17]	11,049
44	26	H	Bolton W	D 1-1	1-1	17	Mothersille (pen) [20]	9231
45	30	A	Mansfield T	L 2-4	0-3	17	De Havilland [51], Lindgren [87]	7373
46	May 3	A	Rotherham U	L 1-2	1-1	18	Odoh [1]	9994

Final League Position: 18

GOALSCORERS

League (68): Adubofour-Poku 12, Mothersille 12 (6 pens), Jade-Jones 11 (1 pen), Fernandez 5, Odoh 5, Randall 5, Hayes 3, Kyprianou 3, De Havilland 2, Edun 2, Collins 1, Conn-Clarke 1, Dornelly 1, Hughes 1, Lindgren 1, O'Brien-Brady 1, Susoho 1, own goal 1.
FA Cup (8): Jones 4, Odoh 2, Randall 2.
Carabao Cup (0).
Vertu Trophy (22): Mothersille 4 (1 pen), Odoh 4, Jones 3, Ihionvien 2, Kyprianou 2, Lindgren 2, Mills 2, De Havilland 1, Hayes 1, Sparkes 1.

Steer J 25	Curtis S 10+7	Fernandez E 27+3	Wallin O 32+2	Sparkes J 18+3	Susoho M 7+8	Collins A 40	Adubofour-Poku K 25+2	Randall J 16+2	Conn-Clarke R 12+11	Jade-Jones R 34+12	Mothersille M 37+8	Ajiboye D 2+4	Hayes C 14+20	O'Brien-Brady D 9+11	Odoh A 23+15	Dornelly J 19+8	Kyprianou H 27+7	Nevett G 10+6	Katongo J 13+4	Ihionvien B 5+6	De Havilland R 15+12	Bilokapic N 18	Rose O —+1	Mills H 8+3	Adebisi R —+1	Johnston C 13+7	Hughes S 19	Edun T 17	Lindgren G 8+5	Blackmore W 3	Shofowoke B —+1	Changunda A —+1	Andrews J —+1	Match No.
1	2^2	3	4	5	6^3	7	8^4	9	10^1	11	12	13	14	15																				1
1	2	3	4	5^1		7	8	9		13	11^2				6	10	12																	2
1	2	3	4	5		7	8	9^2		12	11^1	13				10		6																3
1	2^4	3	4	5^3		7	8	9^1	12	13	11^2		14			10		6	15															4
1	2	12	3^1	5	6^5	8		9^2	13	11^4	14				16	10^3	7		4	15														5
1	14	3	5	6		9	7		11^1	10^1	12	2^3			13	8	4																	6
1	12	2	4^1	8		6^3	9	13		10	11	5^2	14			7	3																	7
1	13	3	4	5^2		6	8		11^4	10	14		9^3	15	12	7		2^1																8
1	5^3	3		14		7	8		11^4	10	13	12	9	15	2^2	6^1	4																	9
1	2^2	3	4	5		7	8	12		11	10		9^1	6^3	13						14													10
1		3	4	5		8	9			11	10^2	12		6		2^1					13	7												11
1	13	3^4	4^5	5		7	8^4	9		11	10^3		15	6^1	16	2^2					14				12									12
	2		3^5	5		7	8^3	9		11^1	10^4		14	12	15		4		13	6^2	1	16												13
	12	4	3	5		7	8	9^3		11^2	10		14		2^1		15		13	6	1													14
	4^4	3	5		6	8	9^6	16	11^3	10^1		14	13	12	2		15			7^2	1													15
	12	4	3	5^4		6	8	9	14	11	10^3		15			13	2^1			7^2	1													16
	5^2		3	13		6	8^1	9		11	12		14		10^3	15	16	4	2^5		7^4	1												17
	4		5^2			7			9	13	11	10	8		2	6^1	3		12		1													18
	4		5^1			7		9^3	12	11^5	10		8		16	2^4	6^2	15	3		13	1	14											19
	4		3^1			9	15		11^3	10	8^4	13	14		7^2	12	2		6	1		5^9	16											20
		14				7		9^2	12	11^3	10		8^4	16	15	2^1	13	3^4	4		6^5	1		5										21
13	4	3	5^3			7		9^4	10	11		12		15		6		2^2		8^1	1	14												22
5^2	3	2	14			7		9	11	10^1		8		13		6	4^3					1												23
	3	2				7		9	10	12		8				6		4	11^1		1			5										24
	4					7		9	13	10		8^1	12		6^3				14		1				2	3	5	11^2						25
	4					7				11	2^1	10		8^1	14	13	6				9^3	1			2	3	5	12						26
	4^5		13	7^2				15	14	10^3		8	16			6	12				9^4	1			2^1	3	5	11						27
			6^1	7				9	10^3	14		13		8		12	4		4^5	16	15	1			2	3	5	11^2						28
			6^3	7^4				9	10	12		13		8^1		14			15	1				2	3	5	11^2						29
1	5^4	3		8^2	9				10	12			13	7										2	4	6	11^1							30
1		3		13	7^2				9^1	11	10		12	8										2	4	5								31
1		3	13	7					11^1	10^2	9		8	2	6			12							4	5								32
1		3	12	7^1			13	15	9		8^2		10	2^4	6	14	11^3								4	5								33
1		3	15	6^4	13			12	9		8^2		10	2^3	7	11^1									4	5								34
1		3		15	6^4	13		12	9		8^2		10	2^3	7	11^1									14	4	5							35
1	14	3			7	8^1			13	9^4		12	10^3	2^6		11^2									15	4	5^1							36
1	14	3	6^4	7	8^1			11	9^3		12		10	2^2			15				5				13	4								37
1	3^2		6^5	7^4	8			11	9		12		10^3	2^1	13	14	16								15	4	5							38
1		3	14	7^3	8^4			11	9^2		13	10	6	12	15										2	4^1	5							39
1		3	13	7^4	8^2			11^5	9^1		15	10	2	6^3	4		14								12		5^4	16						40
	3				7^1	6^5	8		11^4	9^3		12	10	13	14		16	1		5	2^3	4			15									41
1	4	3			7^1	8		11	9^2		13^3	10	2^4	6		12			5			15			14									42
1		3				8^2	13	11^1	9^3		15	10	14	6		7			5			2^4	4		12									43
				12		9^4	13	10^5		6	8^1	14	15	4		7			5^3		2	3	5	11^2	1	16								44
	13				9^3	15	10^4		6	8	2^2		4^1		7		12		14	3	5	11	1											45
					10^1	13		7	9	12		4	3^4	8			5^3		2		6	11^2	1						14	15				46

FA Cup

First Round	Newport Co	(a)	4-2
Second Round	Notts Co	(h)	4-3
Third Round	Everton	(a)	0-2

Carabao Cup

First Round	Oxford U	(a)	0-2

Vertu Trophy

Group D (S)	Gillingham	(a)	2-1
Group D (S)	Stevenage	(h)	2-0
Group D (S)	Crystal Palace U21	(h)	4-1
Second Round	Northampton T	(h)	3-0
Third Round	Walsall	(h)	4-2
Quarter-Final	Cheltenham T	(h)	3-2
Semi-Final	Wrexham	(a)	2-2

Peterborough U won 4-2 on penalties.

Final	Birmingham C	(Wembley)	2-0

PLYMOUTH ARGYLE

FOUNDATION

The club was formed in September 1886 as the Argyle Athletic Club by former public and private school pupils who wanted to continue playing the game. The meeting was held in a room above the Borough Arms (a coffee house), Bedford Street, Plymouth. It was common then to choose a local street/terrace as a club name and Argyle or Argyll was a fashionable name throughout the land due to Queen Victoria's great interest in Scotland.

Home Park, Plymouth, Devon PL2 3DQ.

Telephone: (01752) 562 561.

Ticket Office: (01752) 907 700.

Website: www.pafc.co.uk

Email: argyle@pafc.co.uk

Ground Capacity: 17,494.

Record Attendance: 43,596 v Aston Villa, Division 2, 10 October 1936.

Pitch Measurements: 103m × 66m (112.5yd × 72yd).

Chairman: Simon Hallett.

Chief Executive: Andrew Parkinson.

Head Coach: Tom Cleverley.

Assistant Head Coach: Damon Lathrope.

Colours: Green shirts with white trim, white shorts with green trim, black socks with green trim.

Year Formed: 1886.

Turned Professional: 1903.

Previous Name: 1886, Argyle Athletic Club; 1903, Plymouth Argyle.

Club Nickname: 'The Pilgrims'.

Ground: 1886, Home Park.

HONOURS

League Champions: Second Division – 2003–04; Division 3 – 1958–59; Division 3S – 1929–30, 1951–52; Third Division – 2001–02; FL 1 – 2022–23. *Runners-up:* FL 2 – 2016–17; Division 3 – 1974–75, 1985–86; Division 3S – 1921–22, 1922–23, 1923–24, 1924–25, 1925–26, 1926–27.

FA Cup: semi-final – 1984.

League Cup: semi-final – 1965, 1974.

League Trophy: Runners-up: 2023.

First Football League Game: 28 August 1920, Division 3, v Norwich C (h) D 1–1 – Craig; Russell, Atterbury; Logan, Dickinson, Forbes; Kirkpatrick, Jack, Bowler, Heeps (1), Dixon.

Record League Victory: 8–1 v Millwall, Division 2, 16 January 1932 – Harper; Roberts, Titmuss; Mackay, Pullan, Reed; Grozier, Bowden (2), Vidler (3), Leslie (1), Black (1), (1 og). 8–1 v Hartlepool U (a), Division 2, 7 May 1994 – Nicholls; Patterson (Naylor), Hill, Burrows, Comyn, McCall (1), Barlow, Castle (1), Landon (2), Marshall (1), Dalton (2).

Record Cup Victory: 6–0 v Corby T, FA Cup 3rd rd, 22 January 1966 – Leiper; Book, Baird; Williams, Nelson, Newman; Jones (1), Jackson (1), Bickle (3), Piper (1), Jennings.

Record Defeat: 0–9 v Stoke C, Division 2, 17 December 1960.

Most League Points (2 for a win): 68, Division 3 (S), 1929–30.

FOOTBALL YEARBOOK FACT FILE

Plymouth Argyle toured around the United States in the summer of 1954 after crossing the Atlantic Ocean by ship. They won all eight games against local opposition, including a 16-2 demolition of Colorado All Stars in Denver. They played two games against Borussia Dortmund from West Germany who were also visiting, losing 4-0 in Chicago and 3-1 in Los Angeles.

Most League Points (3 for a win): 102, Division 3, 2001–02.

Most League Goals: 107, Division 3 (S), 1925–26 and 1951–52.

Highest League Scorer in Season: Jack Cock, 32, Division 3 (S), 1926–27.

Most League Goals in Total Aggregate: Sammy Black, 174, 1924–38.

Most League Goals in One Match: 5, Wilf Carter v Charlton Ath, Division 2, 27 December 1960.

Most Capped Player: Tony Capaldi, 21 (22), Northern Ireland.

Most League Appearances: Kevin Hodges, 530, 1978–92.

Youngest League Player: Lee Phillips, 16 years 43 days v Gillingham, 29 October 1996.

Record Transfer Fee Received: £2,000,000 from Hull C for Peter Halmosi, July 2008; £2,000,000 (potentially rising to £4,000,000) from Sheffield U for Michael Cooper, August 2024.

Record Transfer Fee Paid: £1,000,000 to Swansea C for Morgan Whittaker, July 2023; £1,000,000 to Norwich C for Bali Mumba July 2023.

Football League Record: 1920 Original Member of Division 3; 1920–21 Division 3; 1921–30 Division 3 (S); 1930–50 Division 2; 1950–52 Division 3 (S); 1952–56 Division 2; 1956–58 Division 3 (S); 1958–59 Division 3; 1959–68 Division 2; 1968–75 Division 3; 1975–77 Division 2; 1977–86 Division 3; 1986–92 Division 2; 1992–95 Second Division; 1995–96 Third Division; 1996–98 Second Division; 1998–2002 Third Division; 2002–04 Second Division; 2004–10 FL C; 2010–11 FL 1; 2011–17 FL 2; 2017–19 FL 1; 2019–20 FL 2; 2020–23 FL 1; 2023–25 FL C; 2025– FL 1.

LATEST SEQUENCES

Longest Sequence of League Wins: 9, 8.3.1986 – 12.4.1986.

Longest Sequence of League Defeats: 9, 12.10.1963 – 7.12.1963.

Longest Sequence of League Draws: 5, 26.2.2000 – 14.3.2000.

Longest Sequence of Unbeaten League Matches: 22, 20.4.1929 – 21.12.1929.

Longest Sequence Without a League Win: 15, 9.11.2024 – 25.1.2025.

Successive Scoring Runs: 39 from 15.4.1939.

Successive Non-scoring Runs: 5 from 21.11.2009.

MANAGERS

Frank Brettell	1903–05
Bob Jack	1905–06
Bill Fullerton	1906–07
Bob Jack	1910–38
Jack Tresadern	1938–47
Jimmy Rae	1948–55
Jack Rowley	1955–60
Neil Dougall	1961
Ellis Stuttard	1961–63
Andy Beattie	1963–64
Malcolm Allison	1964–65
Derek Ufton	1965–68
Billy Bingham	1968–70
Ellis Stuttard	1970–72
Tony Waiters	1972–77
Mike Kelly	1977–78
Malcolm Allison	1978–79
Bobby Saxton	1979–81
Bobby Moncur	1981–83
Johnny Hore	1983–84
Dave Smith	1984–88
Ken Brown	1988–90
David Kemp	1990–92
Peter Shilton	1992–95
Steve McCall	1995
Neil Warnock	1995–97
Mick Jones	1997–98
Kevin Hodges	1998–2000
Paul Sturrock	2000–04
Bobby Williamson	2004–05
Tony Pulis	2005–06
Ian Holloway	2006–07
Paul Sturrock	2007–09
Paul Mariner	2009–10
Peter Reid	2010–11
Carl Fletcher	2011–13
John Sheridan	2013–15
Derek Adams	2015–19
Ryan Lowe	2019–21
Steven Schumacher	2021–23
Ian Foster	2024
Wayne Rooney	2024
Miron Muslic	2025
Tom Cleverley	June 2025–

TEN YEAR LEAGUE RECORD

		P	W	D	L	F	A	Pts	Pos
2015-16	FL 2	46	24	9	13	72	46	81	5
2016-17	FL 2	46	26	9	11	71	46	87	2
2017-18	FL 1	46	19	11	16	58	59	68	7
2018-19	FL 1	46	13	11	22	56	80	50	21
2019-20	FL 2	37	20	8	9	61	39	68	3§
2020-21	FL 1	46	14	11	21	53	80	53	18
2021-22	FL 1	46	23	11	12	68	48	80	7
2022-23	FL 1	46	31	8	7	82	47	101	1
2023-24	FL C	46	13	12	21	59	70	51	21
2024-25	FL C	46	11	13	22	51	88	46	23

§*Decided on points-per-game (1.84)*

DID YOU KNOW ❓

Centre-forward Luigi Cevenini joined Plymouth Argyle on amateur forms in October 1924 and played a few games for the club's reserve team, scoring in a 4-1 Southern League win over Bridgend Town, before returning to Italy. Cevenini was an established international player and enjoyed a successful playing career in Italy with AC Milan, Internazionale and Juventus.

PLYMOUTH ARGYLE – SKY BET CHAMPIONSHIP 2024–25 LEAGUE RECORD

Match No.	Date	Venue	Opponents	Result	H/T Score	Lg Pos.	Goalscorers	Attendance
1	Aug 11	A	Sheffield Wed	L 0-4	0-1	24		29,535
2	17	H	Hull C	D 1-1	0-0	21	Cissoko [52]	16,306
3	24	A	QPR	D 1-1	1-1	21	Whittaker [28]	15,285
4	31	H	Stoke C	L 0-1	0-0	22		16,934
5	Sept 14	H	Sunderland	W 3-2	0-1	16	Ballard (og) [54], Hardie (pen) [73], Edwards [90]	16,967
6	21	H	WBA	L 0-1	0-0	20		25,754
7	27	H	Luton T	W 3-1	1-0	13	Al Hajj [8], Cissoko 2 [69, 90]	16,616
8	Oct 1	A	Burnley	L 0-1	0-1	17		18,779
9	5	H	Blackburn R	W 2-1	1-0	14	Obafemi [15], Whittaker [90]	16,635
10	19	A	Cardiff C	L 0-5	0-2	19		20,634
11	23	A	Millwall	L 0-1	0-1	21		13,954
12	26	H	Preston NE	D 3-3	0-2	21	Issaka [55], Gray [82], Whittaker [90]	16,443
13	Nov 2	A	Leeds U	L 0-3	0-3	22		36,066
14	5	H	Portsmouth	W 1-0	0-0	20	Obafemi [82]	16,647
15	9	A	Derby Co	D 1-1	1-1	18	Randell [41]	29,652
16	22	H	Watford	D 2-2	1-2	17	Gray 2 [23, 90]	16,400
17	26	A	Norwich C	L 1-6	1-2	20	Bundu [39]	25,893
18	30	A	Bristol C	L 0-4	0-0	21		24,317
19	Dec 10	H	Swansea C	L 1-2	0-1	23	Bundu [79]	15,305
20	14	A	Sheffield U	L 0-2	0-1	23		27,237
21	21	H	Middlesbrough	D 3-3	1-0	24	Gibson [38], Gyabi [72], Bundu [81]	16,550
22	26	A	Coventry C	L 0-4	0-4	24		29,420
23	29	A	Oxford U	L 0-2	0-1	24		11,438
24	Jan 1	H	Bristol C	D 2-2	0-1	24	Al Hajj [50], Pleguezuelo [90]	17,005
25	4	A	Stoke C	D 0-0	0-0	24		26,168
26	14	H	Oxford U	D 1-1	0-1	24	Al Hajj [63]	15,933
27	18	H	QPR	L 0-1	0-0	24		16,988
28	22	H	Burnley	L 0-5	0-5	24		15,509
29	25	A	Sunderland	D 2-2	0-0	24	Patterson (og) [58], Ogbeta [90]	41,097
30	Feb 1	H	WBA	W 2-1	0-0	24	Hardie 2 (1 pen) [77 (p), 88]	16,870
31	12	H	Millwall	W 5-1	2-0	23	Bryan (og) [6], Hardie 2 (1 pen) [10 (p), 56], Bundu [53], Katic [86]	15,453
32	15	A	Blackburn R	L 0-2	0-0	23		14,875
33	19	H	Luton T	D 1-1	0-0	23	Taloverov [70]	11,752
34	22	H	Cardiff C	D 1-1	0-1	22	Tijani [67]	16,981
35	Mar 4	A	Hull C	L 0-2	0-0	23		18,772
36	8	H	Sheffield Wed	L 0-3	0-2	24		16,981
37	12	A	Portsmouth	W 2-1	1-0	24	Bundu [44], Hardie [49]	20,394
38	15	H	Derby Co	L 2-3	1-2	24	Bundu [38], Phillips (og) [46]	16,978
39	29	A	Watford	D 0-0	0-0	24		19,545
40	Apr 5	H	Norwich C	W 2-1	2-0	24	Hardie 2 [24, 29]	16,560
41	9	A	Swansea C	L 0-3	0-3	24		14,978
42	12	A	Sheffield U	W 2-1	0-1	24	Hardie [81], Tijani [88]	16,565
43	18	H	Middlesbrough	L 1-2	1-1	24	Bundu [17]	26,276
44	21	A	Coventry C	W 3-1	2-1	24	Bundu 2 [40, 65], Hardie [43]	16,974
45	26	A	Preston NE	W 2-1	1-0	24	Bundu [14], Wright [75]	19,198
46	May 3	H	Leeds U	L 1-2	1-0	23	Byram (og) [18]	16,758

Final League Position: 23

GOALSCORERS

League (51): Bundu 10, Hardie 10 (3 pens), Al Hajj 3, Cissoko 3, Gray 3, Whittaker 3, Obafemi 2, Tijani 2, Edwards 1, Gibson 1, Gyabi 1, Issaka 1, Katic 1, Ogbeta 1, Pleguezuelo 1, Randell 1, Taloverov 1, Wright 1, own goals 5.
FA Cup (3): Hardie 1 (1 pen), Taloverov 1, Whittaker 1.
Carabao Cup (3): Bundu 1, Hardie 1, Waine 1.

Hazard C 25	Paisson V 19 + 6	Gibson L 18	Galloway B 11 + 2	Ogbeta N 9 + 8	Forshaw A 7 + 9	Gyabi D 34 + 9	Whittaker M 20	Bundu M 27 + 10	Cissoko I 9 + 4	Tijani M 4 + 9	Mumba B 37 + 6	Hardie R 28 + 9	Wright C 14 + 21	Issaka F 3 + 16	Edwards J 12 + 5	Randell A 39	Waine B — + 1	Houghton J 15 + 15	Obafemi M 14 + 15	Szucs K 31 + 5	Grimshaw D 21	Al Hajj R 18 + 10	Sorinola M 19 + 6	Hatch J — + 1	Gray A 5 + 8	Pleguezuelo J 23 + 1	Roberts C 2 + 3	Finn T 1 + 3	Puchacz T 12 + 3	Baidoo M 4 + 7	Taloverov M 10 + 1	Katic N 14 + 1	Boateng M 1 + 6	Match No.
1	2	3	4		5²	6	7	8	9³	10⁴	11¹	12	13	14	15																			1
1		3	4	7⁴	13	8	9²	10¹			5	11³	15	12	2	6⁵	14	16																2
1		3	4⁵	16	7⁸	8		10³			5⁴	11²		14⁸	2	6		12	13	15														3
1			4	14		9²	8	15	10³	13	5	11¹			2	7		6⁴	12	3														4
		4	14	16	7⁵	8		10³			5	13	9¹		2	6⁴		15	11²	3	1	12												5
		4			9¹	8⁴	7	14	10²		5	11³	15		2	6			13	3	1	12												6
		4	12	14	7⁴	8		13	16		5¹	11⁵			2	6		15	10³	3	1	9²												7
2⁴	4		5²		7⁵	6	13	10¹			12	11	15		8			3	1	9³	14	16												8
		4			7⁴	8	13	10⁰			5	12	14		2	6		15	11¹	3	1	9¹												9
		4		15	6³	8⁴		10⁸			5	13	16	14	2	7⁵		12	11²	3	1	9¹												10
		4			6⁴	8	10³				5	11²	9¹	13	2	7			15	3	1	14			12									11
4					6²	14	8	15			5	16			10⁴	2¹	7		11⁵	3	1	9³			13	12								12
2		10¹	9			13					6	11³				8		3	1		5		12	4	7²	14								13
15			7	8⁴	12			5			13	10¹			6	14		3	1	9²	2		11³	4										14
15			14	7	8	10²		5	13	9¹	12				6			11³	3	1		2⁴		4										15
		4			7	9¹	14	8				12	13		6			10²	2	1		5³		11	3									16
4				14	7⁴		9¹	8				10³	13		6			12	2	1	15	5²		11⁵	3	16								17
2	4		5	8							10	11¹		7²	9			6³	13		1			12	3	14								18
	3	4	5¹		7		8³				10	13	9		6			12	2	1	14			11²										19
	4	5		13	6²		8⁴				2	11	15	14		7			10³	3	1	9		12										20
	4	5³	14		7		8				2	11²		12		6			10¹	3	1	9		13										21
	4	5⁴	14	9⁰		7¹					2		12⁸	13		6		15		3	1	8³	16	11²		10								22
1	4	5²			9	7³					10	11				6				3		8¹	2	14		12	13							23
1		4			7	9	13				8³	11¹				6			12	2		10⁵	5	14	3									24
1		4	15	13	6²	9					8		12		2	7		14	11¹	2		10⁵	5⁴		3									25
	3²		4	15		7³	9			13	5					6		14	12		1	10¹			2		8⁴	11						26
	4				7¹	8	14	15			2⁴	11³	13			6			12		1	10²	16		3		5	9⁰						27
	3		8¹		7		12				5	11²	14		6⁴			15			1	10³	13		2		16	4	9⁰					28
1	4		13		15		7³	16			6	11¹	10²			8			9⁴			14	2		3⁵			5	12					29
1	15				16		11²					14	10³			6			7⁵	13		12	5		4			8	9¹	2	3⁴			30
1	4		8³		14		11⁵				13	9¹	10			6²		7		15		16	5⁴						12	2	3			31
1	4⁵				7²		11			15		9¹	10³			6		13	14		16	5²						8	12	2	3			32
1	4				14		11		13			9³				6		7	12			10¹	5²						8		2	3		33
1	4³				16		11			15	12	9¹				6⁵		7²		5		10⁴	14						8		2	3	13	34
1			14		7		11				9⁶		15			6²	13					10¹	5		4				8³	16	2⁴	3	12	35
1	12		8²		7		11⁴			10	13	9¹		16			15						5⁵		4³		14		2	3	6			36
1			15		7		11⁴				14	9³	12					6	10¹	13			5⁸		4²		8		2	3				37
1			15		7²		11				5⁴	9	10¹	14			6	12	2⁵		16						8³		4	3	13			38
1					7²		10¹			16	12	9⁵	15			6		13	11³	2		5⁴			4		8	14		3				39
1	14				12		1				8	9⁴	13	15	16	6		7²	10¹	2		5⁵			4						3³			40
1	16				7		10				8	9⁴	14	15		6³		12	11²	2¹		5			4⁵		13			3				41
1	3		8¹		14		11³			13	5	9	10²		12	6		7		2			4											42
1	4				7¹		11²			13	6	10⁴	12		2⁸	8		9⁶	16	3					5³		14				15			43
1	2				6⁴		10³			11	8	9²	12	13		7						5			4			14		3	15			44
1	2				6⁵		10			11²	8	9⁴	14	16	13	7			15		5				4¹				12	3³			45
1	3						10⁵			11¹	8	9	13		5⁴	6					2³		15			7²			16	4	14	12		46

FA Cup

Third Round	Brentford	(a)	1-0
Fourth Round	Liverpool	(h)	1-0
Fifth Round	Manchester C	(a)	1-3

Carabao Cup

First Round	Cheltenham T	(h)	3-0
Second Round	Watford	(a)	0-2

PORTSMOUTH

Fratton Park, Frogmore Road, Portsmouth, Hampshire PO4 8RA.

Telephone: (0345) 646 1898.

Ticket Office: (0345) 646 1898.

Website: www.portsmouthfc.co.uk

Email: info@pompeyfc.co.uk

Ground Capacity: 28,899.

Record Attendance: 51,385 v Derby Co, FA Cup 6th rd, 26 February 1949.

Pitch Measurements: 100m × 66m (109.5yd × 72yd).

Chairman: Michael Eisner.

Chief Executive: Andrew Cullen.

Head Coach: John Mousinho.

Assistant Head Coach: Jon Harley.

Colours: Blue shirts with thin dark blue stripes and dark blue trim, white shorts with blue trim, red socks.

Year Formed: 1898.

Turned Professional: 1898.

Club Nickname: 'Pompey'.

Ground: 1898, Fratton Park.

HONOURS

League Champions: Division 1 – 1948–49, 1949–50; First Division – 2002–03; FL 1 – 2023–24; Division 3 – 1961–62, 1982–83; Division 3S – 1923–24;
FL 2 – 2016–17.
Runners-up: Division 2 – 1926–27, 1986–87.

FA Cup Winners: 1939, 2008.
Runners-up: 1929, 1934, 2010.

League Cup: 5th rd – 1961, 1986, 1994, 2005, 2010.

League Trophy Winners: 2019.
Runners-up: 2020.

European Competitions
UEFA Cup: 2008–09.

First Football League Game: 28 August 1920, Division 3, v Swansea T (h) W 3–0 – Robson; Probert, Potts; Abbott, Harwood, Turner; Thompson, Stringfellow (1), Reid (1), James (1), Beedie.

Record League Victory: 9–1 v Notts Co, Division 2, 9 April 1927 – McPhail; Clifford, Ted Smith; Reg Davies (1), Foxall, Moffat; Forward (1), Mackie (3), Haines (3), Watson, Cook (2).

Record Cup Victory: 7–0 v Stockport Co, FA Cup 3rd rd, 8 January 1949 – Butler; Rookes, Ferrier; Scoular, Flewin, Dickinson; Harris (3), Barlow, Clarke (2), Phillips (2), Froggatt.

Record Defeat: 0–10 v Leicester C, Division 1, 20 October 1928.

Most League Points (2 for a win): 65, Division 3, 1961–62.

FOOTBALL YEARBOOK FACT FILE

Portsmouth's visit to Newcastle United on 5 December 1931 was reported to be the first Football League game in which there were no corners recorded. The match was played in windy conditions with few goalmouth incidents and ended in a 0-0 draw. Pompey keeper Jock Gilfillan saved a penalty to earn his side the point.

Most League Points (3 for a win): 98, Division 1, 2002–03.

Most League Goals: 97, Division 1, 2002–03.

Highest League Scorer in Season: Guy Whittingham, 42, Division 1, 1992–93.

Most League Goals in Total Aggregate: Peter Harris, 194, 1946–60.

Most League Goals in One Match: 5, Alf Strange v Gillingham, Division 3, 27 January 1923; 5, Peter Harris v Aston Villa, Division 1, 3 September 1958.

Most Capped Player: Jimmy Dickinson, 48, England.

Most League Appearances: Jimmy Dickinson, 764, 1946–65.

Youngest League Player: Clive Green, 16 years 259 days v Wrexham, 21 August 1976.

Record Transfer Fee Received: £18,800,000 from Real Madrid for Lassana Diarra, January 2009.

Record Transfer Fee Paid: £9,000,000 (potentially rising to £11,000,000) to Liverpool for Peter Crouch, July 2008.

Football League Record: 1920 Original Member of Division 3; 1920–21 Division 3; 1921–24 Division 3 (S); 1924–27 Division 2; 1927–59 Division 1; 1959–61 Division 2; 1961–62 Division 3; 1962–76 Division 2; 1976–78 Division 3; 1978–80 Division 4; 1980–83 Division 3; 1983–87 Division 2; 1987–88 Division 1; 1988–92 Division 2; 1992–2003 First Division; 2003–10 Premier League; 2010–12 FL C; 2012–13 FL 1; 2013–17 FL 2; 2017–24 FL 1; 2024– FL C.

LATEST SEQUENCES

Longest Sequence of League Wins: 7, 12.3.2019 – 22.4.2019.

Longest Sequence of League Defeats: 9, 26.12.2012 – 9.2.2013.

Longest Sequence of League Draws: 5, 2.2.2019 – 23.2.2019.

Longest Sequence of Unbeaten League Matches: 27, 14.3.2023 – 11.11.2023.

Longest Sequence Without a League Win: 25, 29.11.1958 – 22.8.1959.

Successive Scoring Runs: 23 from 30.8.1930.

Successive Non-scoring Runs: 6 from 27.12.1993.

MANAGERS

Frank Brettell 1898–1901
Bob Blyth 1901–04
Richard Bonney 1905–08
Bob Brown 1911–20
John McCartney 1920–27
Jack Tinn 1927–47
Bob Jackson 1947–52
Eddie Lever 1952–58
Freddie Cox 1958–61
George Smith 1961–70
Ron Tindall 1970–73
  (General Manager to 1974)
John Mortimore 1973–74
Ian St John 1974–77
Jimmy Dickinson 1977–79
Frank Burrows 1979–82
Bobby Campbell 1982–84
Alan Ball 1984–89
John Gregory 1989–90
Frank Burrows 1990–91
Jim Smith 1991–95
Terry Fenwick 1995–98
Alan Ball 1998–99
Tony Pulis 2000
Steve Claridge 2000–01
Graham Rix 2001–02
Harry Redknapp 2002–04
Velimir Zajec 2004–05
Alain Perrin 2005
Harry Redknapp 2005–08
Tony Adams 2008–09
Paul Hart 2009
Avram Grant 2009–10
Steve Cotterill 2010–11
Michael Appleton 2011–12
Guy Whittingham 2012–13
Richie Barker 2013–14
Andy Awford 2014–15
Paul Cook 2015–17
Kenny Jackett 2017–21
Danny Cowley 2021–23
John Mousinho January 2023–

TEN YEAR LEAGUE RECORD

		P	W	D	L	F	A	Pts	Pos
2015-16	FL 2	46	21	15	10	75	44	78	6
2016-17	FL 2	46	26	9	11	79	40	87	1
2017-18	FL 1	46	20	6	20	57	56	66	8
2018-19	FL 1	46	25	13	8	83	51	88	4
2019-20	FL 1	35	17	9	9	53	36	60	5§
2020-21	FL 1	46	21	9	16	65	51	72	8
2021-22	FL 1	46	20	13	13	68	51	73	10
2022-23	FL 1	46	19	11	16	61	50	70	8
2023-24	FL 1	46	28	13	5	78	41	97	1
2024-25	FL C	46	14	12	20	58	71	54	16

§Decided on points-per-game (1.71)

DID YOU KNOW ?

Portsmouth arranged their first shirt sponsorship deal midway through the 1987–88 season. Motor dealers South Coast Fiat were the selected company, and the deal lasted until the end of the campaign. Shirts bearing the sponsors' name were first worn during the home match with Manchester United on 19 December 1987.

PORTSMOUTH – SKY BET CHAMPIONSHIP 2024–25 LEAGUE RECORD

Match No.	Date	Venue	Opponents	Result	H/T Score	Lg Pos.	Goalscorers	Attendance
1	Aug 10	A	Leeds U	D	3-3	2-1	9	Sorensen [23], Lang 2 (1 pen) [41, 90 (p)]	36,432
2	17	H	Luton T	D	0-0	0-0	15		20,293
3	24	A	Middlesbrough	D	2-2	2-1	12	Saydee 2 [2, 25]	26,270
4	31	H	Sunderland	L	1-3	0-1	18	O'Nien (og) [90]	20,231
5	Sept 15	H	WBA	L	0-3	0-1	23		20,205
6	21	A	Burnley	L	1-0	1-0	23	Lang [42]	20,476
7	28	H	Sheffield U	D	0-0	0-0	23		20,330
8	Oct 2	A	Stoke C	L	1-6	1-3	23	O'Mahony [29]	20,824
9	5	H	Oxford U	D	1-1	0-0	23	O'Mahony [58]	20,125
10	19	A	QPR	W	2-1	1-1	23	Potts [18], Lang (pen) [57]	17,438
11	22	A	Cardiff C	L	0-2	0-2	24		18,534
12	25	H	Sheffield Wed	L	1-2	1-0	24	Ogilvie [44]	20,262
13	Nov 2	A	Hull C	D	1-1	0-1	24	Murphy [46]	21,904
14	5	A	Plymouth Arg	L	0-1	0-0	24		16,647
15	9	H	Preston NE	W	3-1	2-0	23	Murphy [36], Ogilvie [45], Bishop (pen) [89]	20,295
16	30	A	Swansea C	D	2-2	2-1	24	Ritchie [25], Murphy [45]	15,404
17	Dec 7	H	Bristol C	W	3-0	1-0	23	Bishop [20], Murphy [62], Lang [71]	20,415
18	10	H	Norwich C	D	0-0	0-0	21		20,151
19	13	A	Derby Co	L	0-4	0-3	21		26,980
20	21	H	Coventry C	W	4-1	2-1	20	Lang 4 [14, 43, 48, 55]	20,330
21	26	A	Watford	L	1-2	1-0	21	Swanson [10]	20,696
22	29	A	Bristol C	L	0-3	0-3	23		24,560
23	Jan 1	A	Swansea C	W	4-0	2-0	21	Murphy [22], Lane [29], Towler [61], Bishop [78]	20,427
24	5	A	Sunderland	L	0-1	0-1	21		39,846
25	15	A	Blackburn R	L	0-3	0-0	23		13,703
26	18	H	Middlesbrough	W	2-1	0-1	22	Ritchie 2 [54, 82]	20,389
27	22	H	Stoke C	W	3-1	2-1	18	Bishop (pen) [5], Lang [9], Ogilvie [49]	19,388
28	25	A	WBA	L	1-5	0-4	21	Waddingham [90]	25,261
29	28	H	Millwall	L	0-1	0-1	21		19,815
30	Feb 1	H	Burnley	D	0-0	0-0	20		20,381
31	8	A	Sheffield U	L	1-2	1-1	20	Ogilvie [27]	29,104
32	11	H	Cardiff C	W	2-1	2-1	18	Bishop [9], Shaughnessy [17]	20,251
33	15	A	Oxford U	W	2-0	0-0	18	Dozzell [47], O'Mahony [90]	11,423
34	22	H	QPR	W	2-1	0-0	17	Murphy [48], Ritchie [51]	20,426
35	Mar 1	A	Luton T	L	0-1	0-1	17		11,662
36	9	H	Leeds U	W	1-0	0-0	17	Bishop [61]	20,314
37	12	H	Plymouth Arg	L	1-2	0-1	17	Aouchiche [89]	20,394
38	15	A	Preston NE	L	1-2	0-0	17	Bishop [83]	17,240
39	29	H	Blackburn R	W	1-0	1-0	17	Murphy [20]	20,342
40	Apr 5	A	Millwall	L	1-2	0-0	17	Dozzell [80]	16,913
41	9	A	Coventry C	L	0-1	0-0	17		28,411
42	12	H	Derby Co	D	2-2	0-0	19	Atkinson 2 [71, 90]	20,412
43	18	A	Norwich C	W	5-3	3-1	18	Bishop 3 (1 pen) [15, 45 (p), 51], Ritchie [39], Poole [71]	26,838
44	21	H	Watford	W	1-0	1-0	16	Bishop [25]	20,451
45	26	A	Sheffield Wed	D	1-1	1-1	16	Blair [23]	28,346
46	May 3	H	Hull C	D	1-1	0-1	16	Saydee [55]	20,420

Final League Position: 16

GOALSCORERS

League (58): Bishop 11 (3 pens), Lang 10 (2 pens), Murphy 7, Ritchie 5, Ogilvie 4, O'Mahony 3, Saydee 3, Atkinson 2, Dozzell 2, Aouchiche 1, Blair 1, Lane 1, Poole 1, Potts 1, Shaughnessy 1, Sorensen 1, Swanson 1, Towler 1, Waddingham 1, own goal 1.
FA Cup (0).
Carabao Cup (0).

	Norris W 8	Williams J 15+5	Shaughnessy C 7+2	Towler R 10+2	Ogilvie C 45	Pack M 30+11	Dozzell A 32+7	Lane P 13+9	Lang C 28+4	Silvera S 5+6	Sorensen E 4+8	Devlin T 13+21	Saydee C 10+19	Moxon O 2+10	Ritchie M 28+11	Stevenson B —+1	Swanson Z 23+7	Blair H 3+9	Yengi K 4+10	Kamara A —+5	O'Mahony M 5+8	McIntyre T 11+1	Murphy J 40+2	Poole R 23+4	Potts F 35+2	Farrell J 1	Schmid N 35	Archer J 1+1	Bishop C 31+1	Atkinson R 13+1	Hayden I 12+5	Waddingham T 1+4	Matthews H 3+3	Bramall C 4+8	Aouchiche A 9+3	Gordon K —+5	Killip B 2	Match No.
1	1	2	3	4	5	6	7³	8⁴	9	10¹	11¹²	12	13	14	15																							1
2	1	2	3	4	5	7⁴	6²	8¹	9	10	14	11³	13	12	15																							2
3	1		3	4	5	7	6⁴	9³	8⁵	10¹	14	11²	16		15		2	12	13																			3
4	1		3	4	5	6	7¹	15	9⁵	10²		11⁴			8³		2	16	13		12	14																4
5	1		3		5	6	7¹	8²	9	14	15				11⁴		2		13		12		4⁵	10³	16													5
6	1	15			5	8	12	9²	7³		14		13		11⁵	16	2⁴						4	10	3		6¹											6
7	1					6		9²	8¹		12						2		13		11		4	10	3	7	5											7
8	1	15			5	7¹		9		13	16		14				2		8²		12		11⁵	4	10³	3⁴	6											8
9		2²			5	6		15			8⁴		9³		13		14	12			11¹		4	10	3	7	1											9
10		2			5	6		12	8⁴		14	15	9¹				13				11²		4	10³	3	7	1											10
11		2³			5	6		9¹	8		11⁴	15	14		16		12						4	10⁵	3	7	1²	13										11
12					5	14	7³	8	13		2	9¹	15				12				11⁴		4	10²	3	6	1											12
13		13			5	7⁴		9	14		2¹	15	8³				11²		12				4	10	3	6	1											13
14		2¹			5	7⁴		9	13	12	16	15	8²				11³	14					4	10⁵	3	6	1											14
15				5	4	7	15	9			2	12	13		8¹		11³				10⁴	3	6²				1	14										15
16				5	4	7	15	9			2	14	8²		13		12³				10⁴	3	6				1	11¹										16
17				5	4	6²	13	9		15	2	12	8¹		14		10⁴	3	7								1	11³										17
18				5	4		9⁴			15	2	13	7⁵	8³	14		16		12		10	3¹	6				1	11²										18
19				5	3	7	15	9		16	2²	12	8¹		13		14		4		10⁴	6³					1	11⁵										19
20				4	5	3	6	12	9²			13	10		2		8¹										1	7										20
21				4	5	3	7	12	9³		13	14	10¹		2²		8		6								1	11										21
22				4	5	3	7	9	13	10²	2	15	6³	8¹			14		12								1	11⁴										22
23				4	5	3	7	8¹	9⁴	15	13	14	2		10²		6										1	11³										23
24				4	5	3¹	7⁴	8²	9		13	15	14	2¹	10		6³										1	11	12									24
25		14		4	5	3	7³	9¹	8⁴		16	13	15	2	10⁵		6										1	11	4²	12								25
26		2³	13	4	5	3	12	9			8	14	10	7													1	11	4²	6¹								26
27		2³		4	5	3	12	9		14	8²	13	10	7													1	11	4	6²								27
28	16			4	5⁵	3	7	15		8	9	10³	2⁴	14	13												1	11¹	6²	12								28
29		13			5	4	12	9	15		8³	2⁴	10	7													1	11	6¹	14	3²							29
30		3²			5		7	9	15		8³	2⁴	10	6¹													1	11	4	12	13	14						30
31		3³			5	15	7²	9	8¹		2⁴	10	6⁴														1	11	4	13	12	14						31
32		3²			5	15	7	9³	12		8⁴	2¹	10														1	11	4	6³	13	16	14					32
33					5	16	7	9³	15		8²	2⁴	12		10									12			1	11¹	4	6⁵	3	14	13					33
34					5	13	7	14	16		8⁵	2³			10		12							10	12		1	11	4¹	6²	3	15	9⁴					34
35					5	4	7	16	15		8¹	2⁴	13		10²			13						10	3	7	1	11	6⁵			14	9³	12				35
36					5	4	6³	12			8¹	2⁴	14					14						10	3	7	1	11	15			13	9¹					36
37					5	4²	6		8¹		2	14								14				10	3	7³	1	11				12	9	13				37
38				4	15	7³		2⁴													11²	13		10	3	6	1	9		14		5		8¹	12			38
39		13		4	14	7		12			8²		2											10	3	6	1	11					5³	9¹				39
40		2³		4	14	7		9⁴	13		8¹		12											10	3	6	1	11			15		5²					40
41		2¹		4		8⁴		13			14				12		9							3	7	1	11			15	10²		5	6³				41
42					5	16	13		14	9¹	8⁴	2³	15		12									10	3	6⁵	1	11	4	7²								42
43		2			5	16	12		15		8⁵	14	13		10		3										1	11²	4³	7¹					9⁴			43
44		2²	15		5	16		13	12		8	14	10⁵		3⁴		6										1	11³	4	7					9¹			44
45			3¹		5	15	9⁵	14			2						8²							10⁵	12	6	1	11	4	7⁴				16	13	1	1	45
46			3³		5	7⁴	16	9²			2	13	12		8¹		10				14		6⁵					11	4	15						1	1	46

FA Cup
Third Round   Wycombe   W   (a)   0-2

Carabao Cup
First Round   Millwall   (h)   0-1

PORT VALE

Vale Park, Hamil Road, Burslem, Stoke-on-Trent, Staffordshire ST6 1AW.

Telephone: (01782) 655 800.

Ticket Office: (01782) 655 821.

Website: www.port-vale.co.uk

Email: enquiries@port-vale.co.uk

Ground Capacity: 15,389.

Record Attendance: 22,993 v Stoke C, Division 2, 6 March 1920 (at Recreation Ground); 49,768 v Aston Villa, FA Cup 5th rd, 20 February 1960 (at Vale Park).

Pitch Measurements: 103.5m × 70.4m (113yd × 77yd).

Chair: Carol Shanahan OBE.

Chief Executive: Matt Hancock.

Manager: Darren Moore.

First-Team Coach: Jamie Smith.

Colours: White shirts with black patterned trim, white shorts, white socks with black trim.

Year Formed: 1876.

Turned Professional: 1885.

Previous Names: 1876, Port Vale; 1884, Burslem Port Vale; 1909, Port Vale.

Club Nickname: 'The Valiants'.

Grounds: 1876, Limekin Lane, Longport; 1881, Westport; 1884, Moorland Road, Burslem; 1886, Athletic Ground, Cobridge; 1913, Recreation Ground, Hanley; 1950, Vale Park.

First Football League Game: 3 September 1892, Division 2, v Small Heath (a) L 1–5 – Frail; Clutton, Elson; Farrington, McCrindle, Delves; Walker, Scarratt, Bliss (1), Jones. (Only 10 men).

Record League Victory: 9–1 v Chesterfield, Division 2, 24 September 1932 – Leckie; Shenton, Poyser; Sherlock, Round, Jones; McGrath, Mills, Littlewood (6), Kirkham (2), Morton (1).

Record Cup Victory: 7–1 v Irthlingborough, FA Cup 1st rd, 12 January 1907 – Matthews; Dunn, Hamilton; Eardley, Baddeley, Holyhead; Carter, Dodds (2), Beats, Mountford (2), Coxon (3).

Record Defeat: 0–10 v Sheffield U, Division 2, 10 December 1892. 0–10 v Notts Co, Division 2, 26 February 1895.

Most League Points (2 for a win): 69, Division 3 (N), 1953–54.

Most League Points (3 for a win): 89, Division 2, 1992–93.

HONOURS

League Champions: Division 3N – 1929–30, 1953–54; Division 4 – 1958–59.
Runners-up: Second Division – 1993–94; Division 3N – 1952–53. FL 2 – 2024–25.

FA Cup: semi-final – 1954.

League Cup: quarter-final – 2024.

League Trophy Winners: 1993, 2001.

Anglo-Italian Cup: *Runners-up:* 1996.

FOOTBALL YEARBOOK FACT FILE

Half-back Lucien Boullemier made almost 200 appearances for Burslem Port Vale, as the club was then known, between 1897 and 1906, a highlight coming in February 1898 when he scored the goal that knocked Sheffield United out of the FA Cup. Outside football he was renowned as a talented ceramic artist, producing his own Boumier range in the 1930s. He was also well known in local amateur dramatics and appeared on the BBC's Stoke radio station, 5ST, in the 1920s delivering 'humorous and dramatic recitals'

Most League Goals: 110, Division 4, 1958–59.

Highest League Scorer in Season: Wilf Kirkham 38, Division 2, 1926–27.

Most League Goals in Total Aggregate: Wilf Kirkham, 153, 1923–29, 1931–33.

Most League Goals in One Match: 6, Stewart Littlewood v Chesterfield, Division 2, 24 September 1922.

Most Capped Player: Chris Birchall, 27 (44), Trinidad & Tobago.

Most League Appearances: Roy Sproson, 760, 1950–72.

Youngest League Player: Malcolm McKenzie, 15 years 347 days v Newport Co, 12 April 1966.

Record Transfer Fee Received: £2,000,000 from Wimbledon for Gareth Ainsworth, October 1998.

Record Transfer Fee Paid: £500,000 to Lincoln C for Gareth Ainsworth, September 1997.

Football League Record: 1892 Original Member of Division 2; 1896 Failed re-election; 1898 Re-elected to Division 2; club liquidated and resigned from the league; October 1919 returned to Division 2 to take over the league record of Leeds City who were expelled due to financial irregularities 8 games into the season; 1919–29 Division 2; 1929–30 Division 3 (N); 1930–36 Division 2; 1936–38 Division 3 (N); 1938–52 Division 3 (S); 1952–54 Division 3 (N); 1954–57 Division 2; 1957–58 Division 3 (S); 1958–59 Division 4; 1959–65 Division 3; 1965–70 Division 4; 1970–78 Division 3; 1978–83 Division 4; 1983–84 Division 3; 1984–86 Division 4; 1986–89 Division 3; 1989–92 Division 2; 1992–94 Second Division; 1994–2000 First Division; 2000–04 Second Division; 2004–08 FL 1; 2008–13 FL 2; 2013–17 FL 1; 2017–22 FL 2; 2022–24 FL 1; 2024–25 FL 2; 2025– FL 1.

LATEST SEQUENCES

Longest Sequence of League Wins: 8, 8.4.1893 – 30.9.1893.

Longest Sequence of League Defeats: 9, 9.3.1957 – 20.4.1957.

Longest Sequence of League Draws: 6, 26.4.1981 – 12.9.1981.

Longest Sequence of Unbeaten League Matches: 19, 5.5.1969 – 8.11.1969.

Longest Sequence Without a League Win: 17, 7.12.1991 – 21.3.1992.

Successive Scoring Runs: 22 from 12.9.1992.

Successive Non-scoring Runs: 5 from 30.9.2023.

MANAGERS

Sam Gleaves 1896–1905
(Secretary-Manager)
Tom Clare 1905–11
A. S. Walker 1911–12
H. Myatt 1912–14
Tom Holford 1919–24
(continued as Trainer)
Joe Schofield 1924–30
Tom Morgan 1930–32
Tom Holford 1932–35
Warney Cresswell 1936–37
Tom Morgan 1937–38
Billy Frith 1945–46
Gordon Hodgson 1946–51
Ivor Powell 1951
Freddie Steele 1951–57
Norman Low 1957–62
Freddie Steele 1962–65
Jackie Mudie 1965–67
Sir Stanley Matthews
(General Manager) 1965–68
Gordon Lee 1968–74
Roy Sproson 1974–77
Colin Harper 1977
Bobby Smith 1977–78
Dennis Butler 1978–79
Alan Bloor 1979
John McGrath 1980–83
John Rudge 1983–99
Brian Horton 1999–2004
Martin Foyle 2004–07
Lee Sinnott 2007–08
Dean Glover 2008–09
Micky Adams 2009–10
Jim Gannon 2011
Micky Adams 2011–14
Robert Page 2014–16
Bruno Ribeiro 2016
Michael Brown 2017
Neil Aspin 2017–19
John Askey 2019–21
Darrell Clarke 2021–23
Andy Crosby 2023–24
Darren Moore February 2024–

TEN YEAR LEAGUE RECORD

		P	W	D	L	F	A	Pts	Pos
2015-16	FL 1	46	18	11	17	56	58	65	12
2016-17	FL 1	46	12	13	21	45	70	49	21
2017-18	FL 2	46	11	14	21	49	67	47	20
2018-19	FL 2	46	12	13	21	39	55	49	20
2019-20	FL 2	37	14	15	8	50	44	57	8§
2020-21	FL 2	46	17	9	20	57	57	60	13
2021-22	FL 2	46	22	12	12	67	46	78	5
2022-23	FL 1	46	13	10	23	48	71	49	18
2023-24	FL 1	46	10	11	25	41	74	41	23
2024-25	FL 2	46	22	14	10	65	46	80	2

§*Decided on points-per-game (1.54)*

DID YOU KNOW ?

Port Vale hosted a 10-hour heavy metal concert headlined by Motorhead and Ozzy Osbourne at Vale Park on 1 August 1989. The PA system delivered 117,000 Watts, making it one of the loudest outdoor concerts ever. Estimates of the attendance range from 20–25,000, well in excess of the average football crowds of the time of around 6,700. The event was a commercial success, raising £20,000 for the football club and providing a huge boost to their finances.

PORT VALE – SKY BET LEAGUE TWO 2024–25 LEAGUE RECORD

Match No.	Date	Venue	Opponents	Result	H/T Score	Lg Pos.	Goalscorers	Attendance
1	Aug 10	A	Salford C	W 2-0	1-0	4	Garrity 2 [45, 69]	3318
2	17	H	Tranmere R	D 0-0	0-0	5		8102
3	24	A	Barrow	L 0-4	0-0	14		3481
4	31	H	Doncaster R	L 2-3	1-1	16	Croasdale [30], Chislett (pen) [87]	5454
5	Sept 7	A	Newport Co	W 4-1	2-1	12	Stockley 2 [6, 36], Chislett [48], Tolaj [54]	4851
6	14	H	Chesterfield	W 1-0	1-0	8	Chislett [11]	7976
7	21	A	Accrington S	D 2-2	0-2	9	Stockley [90], Hackford [90]	2628
8	28	H	Swindon T	W 2-1	0-0	5	Byers [61], Cover [85]	6747
9	Oct 1	H	Colchester U	D 1-1	0-0	7	Debrah [55]	4533
10	5	A	Notts Co	W 1-0	1-0	6	Tolaj [23]	11,974
11	12	A	Milton Keynes D	W 1-0	0-0	1	Hackford [77]	2427
12	19	H	Fleetwood T	W 3-1	1-1	1	Richards [33], Croasdale [67], Curtis [73]	6643
13	22	A	Harrogate T	W 1-0	0-0	1	Paton [54]	2780
14	26	H	AFC Wimbledon	W 3-2	2-0	1	Cover [9], Richards [11], Stockley [62]	7163
15	Nov 9	A	Gillingham	L 0-1	0-0	1		6267
16	16	A	Morecambe	W 1-0	0-0	1	Chislett [83]	4150
17	25	H	Crewe Alex	D 1-1	1-0	1	Shorrock [3]	10,222
18	Dec 3	A	Cheltenham T	D 1-1	0-0	1	Curtis [90]	3245
19	7	H	Walsall	L 0-1	0-0	2		9142
20	14	A	Bromley	D 0-0	0-0	2		3697
21	21	H	Carlisle U	D 0-0	0-0	2		6920
22	26	A	Bradford C	L 1-2	0-1	2	Hackford [50]	18,330
23	29	A	Grimsby T	L 0-3	0-1	4		7045
24	Jan 1	H	Cheltenham T	D 0-0	0-0	5		5873
25	4	A	Doncaster R	W 2-1	1-0	3	Croasdale [33], Tolaj [61]	8438
26	18	H	Newport Co	W 3-2	1-2	3	Garrity [29], Stockley [62], Headley [77]	6354
27	25	A	Chesterfield	D 1-1	1-0	4	Stockley [2]	9077
28	Feb 1	H	Accrington S	W 2-1	1-0	6	Stockley [7], Tolaj [56]	6198
29	8	A	Swindon T	D 3-3	2-2	6	Headley [31], Tolaj 2 [40, 87]	7606
30	13	H	Notts Co	W 1-0	0-0	6	Curtis [85]	7213
31	22	H	Salford C	W 2-1	1-0	6	Hackford [43], Harper [52]	6823
32	Mar 1	A	Tranmere R	D 1-1	1-1	6	Curtis [29]	6974
33	4	H	Harrogate T	D 0-0	0-0	6		5107
34	8	A	Fleetwood T	D 1-1	0-0	6	Tolaj (pen) [90]	3501
35	11	A	Colchester U	L 1-2	0-1	6	Richards [85]	4055
36	15	H	Milton Keynes D	W 3-0	1-0	6	Tolaj [27], Stockley [52], Garrity [90]	6773
37	22	H	Morecambe	W 1-0	0-0	4	Curtis [89]	7038
38	25	H	Barrow	L 0-1	0-1	4		5894
39	29	A	Crewe Alex	W 1-0	0-0	3	Stockley [86]	8365
40	Apr 1	H	Bradford C	W 2-0	2-0	3	Tolaj [11], Clark [32]	8659
41	5	A	Walsall	W 3-2	3-2	2	Tolaj 2 (1 pen) [4, 45 (p)], Garrity [41]	8446
42	12	H	Bromley	W 5-0	2-0	1	Shorrock [5], Tolaj 2 [28, 68], Byers [66], Croasdale [82]	10,864
43	18	A	Carlisle U	L 2-3	0-2	1	Stockley [61], Hart [70]	12,305
44	21	H	Grimsby T	D 2-2	0-1	2	Tolaj [78], Debrah [90]	11,829
45	26	A	AFC Wimbledon	W 2-0	0-0	2	Stockley [64], Headley [67]	8664
46	May 3	H	Gillingham	L 0-1	0-0	2		13,661

Final League Position: 2

GOALSCORERS

League (65): Tolaj 14 (2 pens), Stockley 11, Curtis 5, Garrity 5, Chislett 4 (1 pen), Croasdale 4, Hackford 4, Headley 3, Richards 3, Byers 2, Cover 2, Debrah 2, Shorrock 2, Clark 1, Harper 1, Hart 1, Paton 1.
FA Cup (1): Curtis 1.
Carabao Cup (2): Paton 1, Sang 1.
Vertu Trophy (7): Curtis 2, Edwards 1, Harper 1, Paton 1, Richards 1, Tolaj 1.

Ripley C 23	Sang T 19+9	Debrah J 33+2	Heneghan B 18+7	Hall C 44	Hart S 12+10	Tolaj L 30+7	Croasdale R 39+6	Garrity B 27+2	Curtis R 20+22	Paton R 9+10	Dipepa B —+3	Boaitey B 3+7	Ojo F —+1	Chislett E 16+9	Stockley J 29+9	John K 24+4	Byers G 14+9	Plant J —+1	Cover B 17+2	Richards R 8+19	Lowe J 3+8	Hackford A 11+13	Shorrock J 12+5	Grant C 4	Smith N 22+2	Harper R 12+6	Edwards D —+1	Clark M 16+4	Amos B 23	Headley J 7+1	Umolu J —+9	Walters R 11+2	Match No.
1	2	3	4	5	6	7²	8	9³	10	11¹	12	13	14																				1
1	2	3	4	5	6³	9	8	10	11²	12				7¹	13	14																	2
1	2	3	4		5⁵		9	8	7³	11¹		15	14	10²	13	6⁴	12		16														3
1	13	3	4		8²	9³	6	7	11¹	10⁴	12			14	15	2	16		5⁵														4
1	14	3	4		9		7	15		8¹				10⁶	11⁴	5	6²		2³	12	13	16											5
1	15	3¹	12	4		9	16	7		14				8²	10¹¹	5⁴	6⁵		2	13													6
1		3	12	4		9⁵	13	6	14	16				8¹	10²	11	5		7³	2⁴		15											7
1	2	15	3	4		9²	13	6	14					12	11³	8	7		5⁴			10¹											8
1	2⁴	15	3²	4		16	12	6	14					9⁵	10	8	7¹		5	13		11³											9
1	15	3	12	4		9⁴	7	6	10²	11³				14	2⁵				5	13	16		8¹										10
1	12	2	3	4		9¹	7⁴	6	10³					11					5²	14	15	13	8										11
1	2	3		4		7⁴	6	13		12				11¹	10³				5	9²	15	14	8										12
1	5	2	3	4		10²	7	6	8	11¹				12				14			13		9³										13
1	2	3	15	4		7	6³	13		12				12	10²				5	9²	14	16	8⁵										14
1	2	6³	3	4		16	7		11³	15				12	10²				5	9¹		14	13	8⁴									15
1	2		3	4	13		6		11²	9³			12	7¹	10				5⁴	14	16			8¹	15								16
1	2		12	3	4		6		13					10⁴	11¹				5	9³	15	14	8²			7⁸							17
1	6		3	4	14	11¹	7		13	15			16	9	10⁵	5⁴			12			15			8²	2³							18
1	2	3		4	8		6³		11	12				10²	16	14			5¹	13	15	9³				7⁵							19
1		2	3	4	8¹		6		10²	14				11	5				12	13	15	9³				7⁴							20
1	12	3		4		13	7		14	11³				9	10				2²	6¹		5			8⁴	15							21
1	9⁸	4⁴	2	3		15	7³		14					8	10				6²	12	5¹	11			13								22
1		3	4	5		14	8		13	11				9		12			7²	10	6¹				2³								23
		3	4	14	10¹	6	7²	11⁴	15					12	8				5	9		13			2³			1					24
		3	4	14	10⁴	6	8⁵	13	16					15	12				7	11²		2			5¹	1	9³						25
14				4³	11⁴	6	8	15						13	2				7¹	10²		3	12		5	1	9						26
12			4		10	6	8	14						11³	2	2	13		3	7²		5⁸	1	9									27
2⁸		14	4		11³	6	8							10²	5	12			3	7¹		1		9	13								28
		3	4		10	6²	8	12						11¹	5	13			2	7³		1		9	14								29
	2		4	13	11³	6	9	12						10¹	5⁴	7			8²			3	14			1	15						30
	2	15	4	9²		6		11⁸						14	5⁴	7			10¹	13		3	8²			1	12						31
	2		4	9	12	6		11						13	5³	7⁴			15	10¹		3	8²		14	1		14					32
			4	12	10	6		11							2³	7			13			9¹			3	8²		5	1	14			33
6⁵	2		4	9²	11	7⁴		12						15		5				10¹		3	14	13	1		16	8³					34
15	2		4		10	6³		11						9¹	12	5²			14			3	16	8⁴	1		13	7⁵					35
	2	3	4		9³	12	14	10						11²	8	6				5		1		13				7¹					36
	2	3	4		9⁵	6	13	11						10	8				12⁴	15		14		5²				7¹					37
5⁴	2		4		12	14	6	10²						11	8⁵				15	9¹		3		8¹				7¹					38
5²	2		4		10³	6	9	14						11					12			13	3	8		1		7¹					39
	2		4	12	10	7	8	14						13	11³					9¹		3			6	1		5²					40
	2		4	12	10³	7	8	13						11²	6¹	14			15			3	9	1				5⁴					41
	2		4	14	10⁵	7	8⁴	12						11¹	13				15			9³	3		6	1	16	5²					42
	2		4⁴	13	10	7	8³	14						11	12				15			9²	3		6	1		5¹					43
	2		4	9³	10	7⁴	13							11	5				15			3¹	8²		6	1	12	14					44
	2		4	10³	7²	11³								11	5				13			3	12		6	1	9²	8¹					45
	2		4	10	7²	11³								13	5				12		15 16	3¹	14		6	1	9⁵	8⁴					46

FA Cup

First Round	Barnsley		(h)	1-3

Carabao Cup

First Round	Barrow		(a)	2-3

Vertu Trophy

Group B (N)	Salford C		(a)	2-0
Group B (N)	Wolverhampton W U21		(h)	2-2
	Port Vale won 5-4 on penalties.			
Group B (N)	Wrexham		(h)	1-1
	Port Vale won 3-1 on penalties.			
Second Round	Doncaster R		(a)	1-0
Third Round	Wrexham		(h)	1-4

PRESTON NORTH END

FOUNDATION

North End Cricket and Rugby Club, which was formed in 1863, indulged in most sports before taking up soccer in about 1879. In 1881 they decided to stick to football to the exclusion of other sports and even a 16–0 drubbing by Blackburn Rovers in an invitation game at Deepdale, a few weeks after taking this decision, did not deter them for they immediately became affiliated to the Lancashire FA.

Deepdale Stadium, Sir Tom Finney Way, Deepdale, Preston, Lancashire PR1 6RU.

Telephone: (0344) 856 1964.

Ticket Office: (0344) 856 1966.

Website: www.pnefc.net

Email: enquiries@pne.com

Ground Capacity: 23,404.

Record Attendance: 42,684 v Arsenal, Division 1, 23 April 1938.

Pitch Measurements: 100m × 68m (109.5yd × 74.5yd).

Chairman: Craig Hemmings.

Chief Executive: Peter Ridsdale.

Manager: Paul Heckingbottom.

Assistant Manager: Stuart McCall.

Colours: White shirts with blue trim, blue shorts with white trim, white socks with blue hoops.

Year Formed: 1880.

Turned Professional: 1885.

Club Nicknames: 'The Lilywhites'; 'North End', 'PNE'.

Ground: 1881, Deepdale.

First Football League Game: 8 September 1888, Football League, v Burnley (h) W 5–2 – Trainer; Howarth, Holmes; Robertson, William Graham, Johnny Graham; Gordon (1), Jimmy Ross (2), Goodall, Dewhurst (2), Drummond.

Record League Victory: 10–0 v Stoke, Division 1, 14 September 1889 – Trainer; Howarth, Holmes; Kelso, Russell (1), Johnny Graham; Gordon, Jimmy Ross (2), Nick Ross (3), Thomson (2), Drummond (2).

Record Cup Victory: 26–0 v Hyde, FA Cup 1st rd, 15 October 1887 – Addision; Howarth, Nick Ross; Russell (1), Thomson (5), Johnny Graham (1); Gordon (5), Jimmy Ross (8), John Goodall (1), Dewhurst (3), Drummond (2).

Record Defeat: 0–7 v Nottingham F, Division 2, 9 April 1927; 0–7 v Blackpool, Division 1, 1 May 1948.

Most League Points (2 for a win): 61, Division 3, 1970–71.

Most League Points (3 for a win): 95, Division 2, 1999–2000.

Most League Goals: 100, Division 2, 1927–28 and Division 1, 1957–58.

Highest League Scorer in Season: Ted Harper, 37, Division 2, 1932–33.

HONOURS

League Champions: Football League 1888–89, 1889–90; Division 2 – 1903–04, 1912–13, 1950–51; Second Division – 1999–2000; Division 3 – 1970–71; Third Division – 1995–96.
Runners-up: Football League 1890–91, 1891–92; Division 1 – 1892–93, 1905–06, 1952–53, 1957–58; Division 2 – 1914–15, 1933–34; Division 4 – 1986–87.

FA Cup Winners: 1889, 1938.
Runners-up: 1888, 1922, 1937, 1954, 1964.

League Cup: 4th rd – 1963, 1966, 1972, 1981, 2003, 2017, 2021, 2022, 2025.
Double Performed: 1888–89.

FOOTBALL YEARBOOK FACT FILE

Preston North End's Deepdale ground was requisitioned by the government for use in the war in July 1940, leaving the club without a home. After briefly considering a move to share with Blackburn Rovers, the club opted to play home games for 1940–41 at the ground of Leyland Motors, four miles away. They remained there until February 1941 when they were once again allowed to play at Deepdale.

Most League Goals in Total Aggregate: Tom Finney, 187, 1946–60.

Most League Goals in One Match: 4, Jimmy Ross v Stoke, Division 1, 6 October 1888; 4, Nick Ross v Derby Co, Division 1, 11 January 1890; 4, George Drummond v Notts Co, Division 1, 12 December 1891; 4, Frank Becton v Notts Co, Division 1, 31 March 1893; 4, George Harrison v Grimsby T, Division 2, 3 November 1928; 4, Alex Reid v Port Vale, Division 2, 23 February 1929; 4, James McClelland v Reading, Division 2, 6 September 1930; 4, Dick Rowley v Notts Co, Division 2, 16 April 1932; 4, Ted Harper v Burnley, Division 2, 29 August 1932; 4, Ted Harper v Lincoln C, Division 2, 11 March 1933; 4, Charlie Wayman v QPR, Division 2, 25 December 1950; 4, Alex Bruce v Colchester U, Division 3, 28 February 1978; 4, Joe Garner v Crewe Alex, FL 1, 14 March 2015.

Most Capped Player: Tom Finney, 76, England.

Most League Appearances: Alan Kelly, 447, 1961–75.

Youngest League Player: Ethan Walker, 16 years 154 days v Aston Villa, 29 December 2018.

Record Transfer Fee Received: £10,000,000 from West Ham U for Jordan Hugill, January 2018.

Record Transfer Fee Paid: £2,000,000 to Cadiz for Milutin Osmajic, September 2023.

Football League Record: 1888 Founder Member of League; 1888–92 Football League; 1892–1901 Division 1; 1901–04 Division 2; 1904–12 Division 1; 1912–13 Division 2; 1913–14 Division 1; 1914–15 Division 2; 1919–25 Division 1; 1925–34 Division 2; 1934–49 Division 1; 1949–51 Division 2; 1951–61 Division 1; 1961–70 Division 2; 1970–71 Division 3; 1971–74 Division 2; 1974–78 Division 3; 1978–81 Division 2; 1981–85 Division 3; 1985–87 Division 4; 1987–92 Division 3; 1992–93 Second Division; 1993–96 Third Division; 1996–2000 Second Division; 2000–04 First Division; 2004–11 FL C; 2011–15 FL 1; 2015– FL C.

LATEST SEQUENCES

Longest Sequence of League Wins: 14, 25.12.1950 – 27.3.1951.

Longest Sequence of League Defeats: 8, 22.9.1984 – 27.10.1984.

Longest Sequence of League Draws: 6, 24.2.1979 – 20.3.1979.

Longest Sequence of Unbeaten League Matches: 23, 8.9.1888 – 14.9.1889.

Longest Sequence Without a League Win: 15, 14.4.1923 – 20.10.1923.

Successive Scoring Runs: 30 from 15.11.1952.

Successive Non-scoring Runs: 7 from 13.4.2024.

MANAGERS

Charlie Parker 1906–15
Vincent Hayes 1919–23
Jim Lawrence 1923–25
Frank Richards 1925–27
Alex Gibson 1927–31
Lincoln Hayes 1931–32
Run by committee 1932–36
Tommy Muirhead 1936–37
Run by committee 1937–49
Will Scott 1949–53
Scot Symon 1953–54
Frank Hill 1954–56
Cliff Britton 1956–61
Jimmy Milne 1961–68
Bobby Seith 1968–70
Alan Ball Snr 1970–73
Bobby Charlton 1973–75
Harry Catterick 1975–77
Nobby Stiles 1977–81
Tommy Docherty 1981
Gordon Lee 1981–83
Alan Kelly 1983–85
Tommy Booth 1985–86
Brian Kidd 1986
John McGrath 1986–90
Les Chapman 1990–92
Sam Allardyce 1992 (*Caretaker*)
John Beck 1992–94
Gary Peters 1994–98
David Moyes 1998–2002
Kelham O'Hanlon 2002 (*Caretaker*)
Craig Brown 2002–04
Billy Davies 2004–06
Paul Simpson 2006–07
Alan Irvine 2007–09
Darren Ferguson 2010
Phil Brown 2011
Graham Westley 2012–13
Simon Grayson 2013–17
Alex Neil 2017–21
Frankie McAvoy 2021
Ryan Lowe 2021–24
Paul Heckingbottom August 2024–

TEN YEAR LEAGUE RECORD

		P	W	D	L	F	A	Pts	Pos
2015-16	FL C	46	15	17	14	45	45	62	11
2016-17	FL C	46	16	14	16	64	63	62	11
2017-18	FL C	46	19	16	11	57	46	73	7
2018-19	FL C	46	16	13	17	67	67	61	14
2019-20	FL C	46	18	12	16	59	54	66	9
2020-21	FL C	46	18	7	21	49	56	61	13
2021-22	FL C	46	16	16	14	52	56	64	13
2022-23	FL C	46	17	12	17	45	59	63	12
2023-24	FL C	46	18	9	19	56	67	63	10
2024-25	FL C	46	10	20	16	48	59	50	20

DID YOU KNOW ?

Preston North End missed out on the Football League title in 1952–53 by 0.099 on goal average. North End finished their matches two points clear of Arsenal, with the Gunners still having to play their final game against Burnley. However, Arsenal beat the Clarets 3-2, surviving a late penalty claim to become League champions.

PRESTON NORTH END – SKY BET CHAMPIONSHIP 2024–25 LEAGUE RECORD

Match No.	Date		Venue	Opponents	Result	H/T Score	Lg Pos.	Goalscorers	Attendance
1	Aug	9	H	Sheffield U	L	0-2	0-1	24		17,948
2		17	A	Swansea C	L	0-3	0-1	23		14,037
3		24	H	Luton T	W	1-0	1-0	18	Keane [39]	15,245
4		31	A	Oxford U	L	1-3	1-1	21	Jakobsen [3]	11,403
5	Sept	14	A	Middlesbrough	D	1-1	1-1	21	Frokjaer-Jensen [43]	25,116
6		22	H	Blackburn R	D	0-0	0-0	21		20,945
7		28	A	Millwall	L	1-3	0-2	22	Storey [87]	13,674
8	Oct	2	H	Watford	W	3-0	0-0	21	Osmajic 2 [53, 65], McCann [75]	13,602
9		5	A	Burnley	D	0-0	0-0	19		20,816
10		19	H	Coventry C	W	1-0	0-0	15	Jakobsen [72]	15,907
11		22	H	Norwich C	D	2-2	2-1	14	Greenwood (pen) [6], Holmes [12]	13,677
12		26	A	Plymouth Arg	D	3-3	2-0	16	Greenwood [16], Frokjaer-Jensen [45], Potts [48]	16,443
13	Nov	2	H	Bristol C	L	1-3	0-1	20	Greenwood [48]	14,261
14		6	H	Sunderland	D	0-0	0-0	20		18,064
15		9	A	Portsmouth	L	1-3	0-0	20	Jakobsen [50]	20,295
16		23	H	Derby Co	D	1-1	1-1	20	Greenwood [23]	16,646
17		26	A	Stoke C	D	0-0	0-0	19		19,805
18		30	H	WBA	D	1-1	0-1	18	Jakobsen [55]	16,124
19	Dec	7	A	Sheffield Wed	D	1-1	1-0	17	Jakobsen [14]	23,927
20		11	A	Cardiff C	W	2-0	0-0	14	Chambers (og) [48], Osmajic [90]	15,006
21		14	H	Leeds U	D	1-1	1-0	16	Potts [23]	19,508
22		21	A	QPR	L	1-2	1-0	18	Osmajic [21]	15,323
23		26	H	Hull C	W	1-0	0-0	16	Potts [60]	16,521
24		29	H	Sheffield Wed	W	3-1	1-0	14	Jakobsen 2 [29, 79], Greenwood (pen) [64]	19,950
25	Jan	1	A	WBA	L	1-3	0-3	15	Ledson [70]	24,320
26		4	H	Oxford U	D	1-1	0-1	14	Keane [69]	14,749
27		18	A	Luton T	D	0-0	0-0	16		11,540
28		21	A	Watford	W	2-1	1-0	16	Osmajic 2 [17, 56]	16,397
29		25	H	Middlesbrough	W	2-1	1-0	14	Thordarson [28], Jakobsen [78]	18,474
30		31	A	Blackburn R	L	1-2	0-1	15	Potts [90]	21,392
31	Feb	11	A	Norwich C	W	1-0	1-0	15	Osmajic [5]	25,910
32		15	H	Burnley	D	0-0	0-0	15		19,864
33		18	H	Millwall	D	1-1	0-1	15	Jakobsen [47]	13,290
34		22	A	Coventry C	L	1-2	0-2	15	Keane [82]	26,493
35	Mar	4	H	Swansea C	D	0-0	0-0	15		12,838
36		8	A	Sheffield U	L	0-1	0-0	16		27,136
37		11	H	Sunderland	D	1-1	0-0	15	Jakobsen [65]	37,731
38		15	H	Portsmouth	W	2-1	0-0	14	Porteous [76], Thordarson [87]	17,240
39	Apr	2	A	Derby Co	L	0-2	0-0	14		26,014
40		5	A	Stoke C	D	1-1	1-0	14	Hayden [10]	17,341
41		8	H	Cardiff C	D	2-2	1-0	14	Osmajic [19], Thordarson [72]	13,293
42		12	A	Leeds U	L	1-2	1-2	16	Hayden [6]	35,747
43		18	H	QPR	L	1-2	1-0	17	Lindsay [45]	14,922
44		21	A	Hull C	L	1-2	1-0	18	Gibson [34]	22,103
45		26	H	Plymouth Arg	L	1-2	0-1	20	Jakobsen [90]	19,198
46	May	3	A	Bristol C	D	2-2	1-0	20	Jakobsen [28], Osmajic [60]	24,987

Final League Position: 20

GOALSCORERS

League (48): Jakobsen 12, Osmajic 9, Greenwood 5 (2 pens), Potts 4, Keane 3, Thordarson 3, Frokjaer-Jensen 2, Hayden 2, Gibson 1, Holmes 1, Ledson 1, Lindsay 1, McCann 1, Porteous 1, Storey 1, own goal 1.
FA Cup (5): Osmajic 3, Brady 1, Keane 1.
Carabao Cup (8): Osmajic 3, Greenwood 2 (1 pen), Ledson 2, Frokjaer-Jensen 1.

Woodman F 37	Whatmough J 12 + 4	Lindsay L 29 + 6	Hughes A 36 + 4	Potts B 22 + 7	Thordarson S 29 + 10	Whiteman B 27 + 8	Greenwood S 29 + 9	Brady R 17 + 12	Jakobsen E 29 + 16	Keane W 13 + 14	Hayden K 41 + 3	Osmajic M 20 + 14	Frokjaer-Jensen M 27 + 11	Best K — + 1	Storey J 35	Ledson R 14 + 12	Okkels J 1 + 6	Holmes D 6 + 23	McCann A 28 + 1	Bowler J 6 + 4	Cornell D 9 + 1	Gibson L 19	Meghoma J 11 + 1	Evans C — + 8	Porteous R 9 + 2	Bauer P — + 1	Carroll T — + 1	Match No.
1	2	3	4	5	6^3	7	8^1	9^4	10	11^{12}	12	13	14	15														1
1		4	5	2	6	7	13	11^1	10^2		12		9^4		3	8^3	14	15										2
1		3	4	6	7^3	5	14		11	10^2	9		8^1		2	12		13										3
1	3^4	4	6	7^4	5	8^3	12	11^{12}	10^5	9^1	13				2			16	14	15								4
1	4^4		5	2		6	10	16	11^5				15	9^3	3	13		8^1	14	7^2	12							5
1		4	5	2		6	9^4		11^3		12	13	8^2		3				14	7	10^1							6
1		4	5^2	2^3	12	7		13	11^1	9^4	14	15	16		3				10	6	8^5							7
1		3	4	12	8^1	7		9^2	16		5^3	11^5	10^4		2	13	14	15	6									8
1	14	2	3^3	7	13	5		9^2	10		6^4		11^1		4	15		12	8									9
1		4	5		8^2		12	10	11		2		9		3	6^1		13	7									10
1		4	5		13	6	9^1	10	11		2		12		3			8^2	7									11
1		3	4	12	14	7	10	9^1	11		5^3		6^2		2			13	8									12
1		3	4	5^2		7^3	11		10		9		6^1		2		14	13	8	12								13
1	12	3^1	4	5	14	7	11^2		10		9		6		2			13	8^3									14
1	3		4	5^2	12	7^3	11^4		10		9		14		2	13	15	6^1	8^5	16								15
1	3		4	5		7^4	10^3		11^2	14	9	12	13		2	8^1		15	6									16
1*	3		4	6	7	5	10		12	13	9^3	11^1			2			8^2		14								17
1		3	4	13	8^4	7^1	11		10^3	12	5	14			2			15	6	9^2	1							18
1	3		4	5	7^2	13	9		11^3		8	14	10^1		2			12	6									19
1	3	4		12	7^3	13	10	15	11^5		8^4	14	9^1		2			16	6	5^2								20
1	16	4		2	12	7^1		10^3	13	9^2	5	11^4	8^5		3	15		14	6									21
1	3^2	4^4		5^1	7		10^4	12	14	15	8	9^3	11^5		2		16	13	6									22
1	3		4	5		6	11^3		12	13	8	10^1	9^2		2			14	7									23
1	3		4		6^2	13	11		10^4	9^1	8	15	12		2			14	7	5^3								24
1	3	4		7^1	12	11^3		10	16	8	15	9^5			2	14		13	6^4	5^2								25
1		3	4		12	7	9^1		11^3	10	8	14	13		2			5^4	6^2	15								26
1		3	8		11		13	9^1	5	10^2	12		2	6		7			4									27
1	16	4		7^5		14	13	15		5	11^4	9^3			2	6^1		12	10			3	8^2					28
1		4		6^1		9^3	13	14	16		5	11^4	10^5		2	12		15	7			3	8^2					29
1	12		4	13	14		9^5		11		5		10^4		2^1	7^2		16	6			3	8^3	15				30
1		14	4	12	7		13				5	11^{10}			6^2		9^1					3	8	15	2^3			31
1		4	7	9		12	15	13	14		5	10^2	11^3		6^1							3	8^4		2			32
1	3	8^2	10^1	7^5		9^3	13	11^4	16	5	12	14			15			6				4			2			33
1	14	4	12	7		10^5	15	13	16	5^4	11				6^2			8				3^3	9^1		2			34
1	3	15	5		8	9^2	14	11^3	2	10					6^1			7^4				4	13		12			35
1	4	14	7	8^3	15	9	6^4	10	11^2	2					12							5	13	3^1				36
1	15	6	9^5	8^3	13	11^1		10	12	2^3		14			7							4	5^4	3	16			37
1	4^2	13		8	14	12^4	15	11	10^5	2		9^4			7^1							5	6^3	16	3			38
1		3		7^1	13		14	12	10^3	5	11	8			6						1	4^4	9^2	15	2			39
1		3		8^2	7	6^3	9	10^1	14	5	11	13			2	12					1	4						40
	14	4^1	6	7	12	9	13	10^2	5	11^3	8				1	3						2						41
	16	4^5	7^4	5		8^2	13	14	6	10	11	2^1			1	3	9^3					12			15			42
	3	4	8^2	5	7^1	9	12	13	6	10	11	2			1													43
	3	12	6	7		8	14		5	11	10^3	2			1							4^2	9^1	13				44
	3	9^2	7^1	5		8	10		6	11	2	12			1	4							13					45
	3	9	12	5	13	8^3	11		6	10^2	2	7^1			1	4							14					46

FA Cup

Third Round	Charlton Ath	(h)	2-1
Fourth Round	Wycombe W	(h)	0-0
aet; Preston NE won 4-2 on penalties.			
Fifth Round	Burnley	(h)	3-0
Quarter-Final	Aston Villa	(h)	0-3

Carabao Cup

First Round	Sunderland	(h)	2-0
Second Round	Harrogate T	(a)	5-0
Third Round	Fulham	(h)	1-1
Preston NE won 16-15 on penalties.			
Fourth Round	Arsenal	(h)	0-3

QUEENS PARK RANGERS

FOUNDATION

There is an element of doubt about the date of the foundation of this club, but it is believed that in either 1885 or 1886 it was formed through the amalgamation of Christchurch Rangers and St Jude's Institute FC. The leading light was George Wodehouse, whose family maintained a connection with the club until comparatively recent times. Most of the players came from the Queen's Park district so this name was adopted after a year as St Jude's Institute.

MATRADE Loftus Road Stadium, South Africa Road, Shepherds Bush, London W12 7PJ.

Telephone: (020) 8743 0262.

Ticket Office: (020) 8740 2613.

Website: www.qpr.co.uk

Email: customerservices@qpr.co.uk

Ground Capacity: 17,600.

Record Attendance: 41,097 v Leeds U, FA Cup 3rd rd, 9 January 1932 (at White City); 35,353 v Leeds U, Division 1, 27 April 1974 (at Loftus Road).

Pitch Measurements: 100m × 66m (109.5yd × 72yd).

Chairman: Lee Hoos.

Chief Executive: Christian Nourry.

Head Coach: Julien Stephan.

First-Team Coach: Alou Diarra.

Colours: Blue and white hooped shirts with white sleeves and blue trim, white shorts with blue trim, white socks with blue trim.

Year Formed: 1885* (*see Foundation*).

Turned Professional: 1898.

Previous Name: 1885, St Jude's; 1887, Queens Park Rangers. *Club Nicknames:* 'Rangers'; 'The Hoops'; 'R's'.

Grounds: 1885* (*see Foundation*), Welford's Fields; 1888–99, London Scottish Ground, Brondesbury, Home Farm, Kensal Rise Green, Gun Club Wormwood Scrubs, Kilburn Cricket Ground; 1899, Kensal Rise Athletic Ground; 1901, Latimer Road, Notting Hill; 1904, Agricultural Society, Park Royal; 1907, Park Royal Ground; 1917, Loftus Road; 1931, White City; 1933, Loftus Road; 1962, White City; 1963, Loftus Road (renamed The Kiyan Prince Foundation Stadium 2019; Loftus Road 2022; MATRADE Loftus Road Stadium 2023).

First Football League Game: 28 August 1920, Division 3, v Watford (h) L 1–2 – Price; Blackman, Wingrove; McGovern, Grant, O'Brien; Faulkner, Birch (1), Smith, Gregory, Middlemiss.

Record League Victory: 9–2 v Tranmere R, Division 3, 3 December 1960 – Drinkwater; Woods, Ingham; Keen, Rutter, Angell; Lazarus (2), Bedford (2), Evans (2), Andrews (1), Clark (2).

Record Cup Victory: 8–1 v Bristol R (a), FA Cup 1st rd, 27 November 1937 – Gilfillan; Smith, Jefferson; Lowe, James, March; Cape, Mallett, Cheetham (3), Fitzgerald (3) Bott (2). 8–1 v Crewe Alex, Milk Cup 1st rd, 3 October 1983 – Hucker; Neill, Dawes, Waddock (1), McDonald (1), Fenwick, Micklewhite (1), Stewart (1), Allen (1), Stainrod (3), Gregory.

HONOURS

League Champions: FL C – 2010–11; Division 2 – 1982–83; Division 3 – 1966–67; Division 3S – 1947–48. *Runners-up:* Division 1 – 1975–76; Division 2 – 1967–68, 1972–73; Second Division – 2003–04; Division 3S – 1946–47.

FA Cup: Runners-up: 1982.

League Cup Winners: 1967. *Runners-up:* 1986.

European Competitions *UEFA Cup:* 1976–77 (*qf*), 1984–85.

FOOTBALL YEARBOOK FACT FILE

Queens Park Rangers switched their fixtures for Easter 1912 from their Park Royal ground to The Stadium, Shepherd's Bush (White City) due to transport problems. The Good Friday game against Southampton attracted a crowd widely estimated as 62,000 by contemporaries. This was a new record attendance for Southern League matches.

Record Defeat: 1–8 v Mansfield T, Division 3, 15 March 1965. 1–8 v Manchester U, Division 1, 19 March 1969.

Most League Points (2 for a win): 67, Division 3, 1966–67.

Most League Points (3 for a win): 88, FL C, 2010–11.

Most League Goals: 111, Division 3, 1961–62.

Highest League Scorer in Season: George Goddard, 37, Division 3 (S), 1929–30.

Most League Goals in Total Aggregate: George Goddard, 174, 1926–34.

Most League Goals in One Match: 4, George Goddard v Merthyr T, Division 3 (S), 9 March 1929; 4, George Goddard v Swindon T, Division 3 (S), 12 April 1930; 4, George Goddard v Exeter C, Division 3 (S), 20 December 1930; 4, George Goddard v Watford, Division 3 (S), 19 September 1931; 4, Tom Cheetham v Aldershot, Division 3 (S), 14 September 1935; 4, Tom Cheetham v Aldershot, Division 3 (S), 12 November 1938.

Most Capped Player: Alan McDonald, 52, Northern Ireland.

Most League Appearances: Tony Ingham, 514, 1950–63.

Youngest League Player: Frank Sibley, 16 years 97 days v Bristol C, 10 March 1964.

Record Transfer Fee Received: £19,500,000 from Crystal Palace for Eberechi Eze, August 2020.

Record Transfer Fee Paid: £12,500,000 to Anzhi Makhachkala for Chris Samba, January 2013.

Football League Record: 1920 Original Members of Division 3; 1920–21 Division 3; 1921–48 Division 3 (S); 1948–52 Division 2; 1952–58 Division 3 (S); 1958–67 Division 3; 1967–68 Division 2; 1968–69 Division 1; 1969–73 Division 2; 1973–79 Division 1; 1979–83 Division 2; 1983–92 Division 1; 1992–96 Premier League; 1996–2001 First Division; 2001–04 Second Division; 2004–11 FL C; 2011–13 Premier League; 2013–14 FL C; 2014–15 Premier League; 2015– FL C.

LATEST SEQUENCES

Longest Sequence of League Wins: 8, 7.11.1931 – 28.12.1931.

Longest Sequence of League Defeats: 9, 25.2.1969 – 5.4.1969.

Longest Sequence of League Draws: 6, 29.1.2000 – 5.3.2000.

Longest Sequence of Unbeaten League Matches: 20, 11.3.1972 – 23.9.1972.

Longest Sequence Without a League Win: 20, 7.12.1968 – 7.4.1969.

Successive Scoring Runs: 33 from 9.12.1961.

Successive Non-scoring Runs: 6 from 18.3.1939.

MANAGERS

James Cowan 1906–13
Jimmy Howie 1913–20
Ned Liddell 1920–24
Will Wood 1924–25
 (had been Secretary since 1903)
Bob Hewison 1925–31
John Bowman 1931
Archie Mitchell 1931–33
Mick O'Brien 1933–35
Billy Birrell 1935–39
Ted Vizard 1939–44
Dave Mangnall 1944–52
Jack Taylor 1952–59
Alec Stock 1959–65
 (General Manager to 1968)
Bill Dodgin Jnr 1968
Tommy Docherty 1968
Les Allen 1968–71
Gordon Jago 1971–74
Dave Sexton 1974–77
Frank Sibley 1977–78
Steve Burtenshaw 1978–79
Tommy Docherty 1979–80
Terry Venables 1980–84
Gordon Jago 1984
Alan Mullery 1984
Frank Sibley 1984–85
Jim Smith 1985–88
Trevor Francis 1988–89
Don Howe 1989–91
Gerry Francis 1991–94
Ray Wilkins 1994–96
Stewart Houston 1996–97
Ray Harford 1997–98
Gerry Francis 1998–2001
Ian Holloway 2001–06
Gary Waddock 2006
John Gregory 2006–07
Luigi Di Canio 2007–08
Iain Dowie 2008
Paulo Sousa 2008–09
Jim Magilton 2009
Paul Hart 2009–10
Neil Warnock 2010–12
Mark Hughes 2012
Harry Redknapp 2012–15
Chris Ramsey 2015
Jimmy Floyd Hasselbaink 2015–16
Ian Holloway 2016–18
Steve McClaren 2018–19
Mark Warburton 2019–22
Michael Beale 2022
Neil Critchley 2022–23
Gareth Ainsworth 2023
Marti Cifuentes 2023–25
Julien Stephan June 2025–

TEN YEAR LEAGUE RECORD

		P	W	D	L	F	A	Pts	Pos
2015-16	FL C	46	14	18	14	54	54	60	12
2016-17	FL C	46	15	8	23	52	66	53	18
2017-18	FL C	46	15	11	20	58	70	56	16
2018-19	FL C	46	14	9	23	53	71	51	19
2019-20	FL C	46	16	10	20	67	76	58	13
2020-21	FL C	46	19	11	16	57	55	68	9
2021-22	FL C	46	19	9	18	60	59	66	11
2022-23	FL C	46	13	11	22	44	71	50	20
2023-24	FL C	46	15	11	20	47	58	56	18
2024-25	FL C	46	14	14	18	53	63	56	15

DID YOU KNOW

Queens Park Rangers announced their first shirt sponsorship deal in August 1983. The arrangement with the Guinness brewery was part of a larger sponsorship package said to be worth £450,000 over three years. The R's were the local club for Guinness, whose head office was nearby at Park Royal.

QUEENS PARK RANGERS – SKY BET CHAMPIONSHIP 2024–25 LEAGUE RECORD

Match No.	Date	Venue	Opponents	Result	H/T Score	Lg Pos.	Goalscorers	Attendance
1	Aug 10	H	WBA	L	1-3	1-1	21	Andersen [16]	16,587
2	17	A	Sheffield U	D	2-2	0-2	18	Dunne [55], Dykes [88]	27,527
3	24	H	Plymouth Arg	D	1-1	1-1	19	Frey [3]	15,285
4	30	A	Luton T	W	2-1	0-1	9	Madsen [59], Frey [62]	11,798
5	Sept 14	A	Sheffield Wed	D	1-1	0-0	12	Lloyd [90]	26,283
6	21	H	Millwall	D	1-1	1-1	14	Frey [40]	15,350
7	28	A	Blackburn R	L	0-2	0-0	17		13,789
8	Oct 1	H	Hull C	L	1-3	1-2	19	Madsen (pen) [44]	13,407
9	5	A	Derby Co	L	0-2	0-0	22		29,305
10	19	H	Portsmouth	L	1-2	1-1	24	Dembele [9]	17,438
11	22	H	Coventry C	D	1-1	0-1	23	Morgan [63]	14,173
12	26	A	Burnley	D	0-0	0-0	23		19,187
13	Nov 2	H	Sunderland	D	0-0	0-0	23		16,383
14	5	H	Middlesbrough	L	1-4	0-2	23	Dijksteel (og) [69]	14,054
15	9	A	Leeds U	L	0-2	0-1	24		36,011
16	23	H	Stoke C	D	1-1	0-1	24	Gibson (og) [62]	15,688
17	27	A	Cardiff C	W	2-0	1-0	23	Celar 2 [40, 90]	16,205
18	30	A	Watford	D	0-0	0-0	23		20,413
19	Dec 7	H	Norwich C	W	3-0	2-0	20	Dunne [22], Kolli 2 [45, 49]	15,688
20	11	A	Oxford U	W	2-0	0-0	19	Field 2 [53, 68]	14,440
21	14	A	Bristol C	D	1-1	0-0	18	Smyth [65]	20,925
22	21	H	Preston NE	W	2-1	0-1	14	Kolli [50], Dunne [89]	15,323
23	26	A	Swansea C	L	0-3	0-3	17		15,843
24	29	A	Norwich C	D	1-1	0-1	17	Crnac (og) [45]	26,563
25	Jan 1	H	Watford	W	3-1	2-0	15	Frey [5], Dunne [37], Field [56]	17,268
26	6	H	Luton T	W	2-1	1-1	13	Frey [24], Fox [62]	14,025
27	18	A	Plymouth Arg	W	1-0	0-0	12	Kolli [65]	16,988
28	21	H	Hull C	W	2-1	0-0	9	Paal [64], Saito [70]	19,180
29	25	H	Sheffield Wed	L	0-2	0-0	13		17,352
30	Feb 1	A	Millwall	L	1-2	1-2	14	Lloyd [3]	17,914
31	4	H	Blackburn R	W	2-1	1-0	13	Frey [5], Colback [76]	13,571
32	11	A	Coventry C	L	0-1	0-0	13		24,600
33	14	H	Derby Co	W	4-0	2-0	11	Chair 2 [21, 57], Saito [35], Edwards [66]	16,591
34	22	A	Portsmouth	L	1-2	0-0	14	Dunne [74]	20,426
35	Mar 1	H	Sheffield U	L	1-2	0-1	14	Frey (pen) [72]	17,346
36	8	A	WBA	L	0-1	0-1	14		25,310
37	11	A	Middlesbrough	L	1-2	0-1	14	Cook [80]	22,177
38	15	H	Leeds U	D	2-2	2-1	15	Saito [17], Cook [30]	17,457
39	29	A	Stoke C	L	1-3	0-2	15	Yang [78]	23,192
40	Apr 5	H	Cardiff C	D	0-0	0-0	16		17,066
41	9	A	Oxford U	W	3-1	2-0	15	Edwards [7], Romeny (og) [42], Yang [90]	11,509
42	12	H	Bristol C	D	1-1	1-1	15	Dembele [21]	16,867
43	18	A	Preston NE	W	2-1	0-1	14	Frey [80], Andersen [90]	14,922
44	21	H	Swansea C	L	1-2	0-1	15	Dembele [72]	16,351
45	26	H	Burnley	L	0-5	0-3	15		16,977
46	May 3	A	Sunderland	W	1-0	1-0	15	Madsen [5]	41,917

Final League Position: 15

GOALSCORERS

League (53): Frey 8 (1 pen), Dunne 5, Kolli 4, Dembele 3, Field 3, Madsen 3 (1 pen), Saito 3, Andersen 2, Celar 2, Chair 2, Cook 2, Edwards 2, Lloyd 2, Yang 2, Colback 1, Dykes 1, Fox 1, Morgan 1, Paal 1, Smyth 1, own goals 4.
FA Cup (2): Kolli 1, Varane 1.
Carabao Cup (4): Field 1, Frey 1, Hevertton 1, Smyth 1.

Nardi P 45	Dunne J 45	Cook S 31	Clarke-Salter J 8 + 3	Paal K 34 + 5	Field S 35	Colback J 16 + 8	Smyth P 30 + 13	Andersen L 13 + 20	Kolli R 9 + 11	Celar Z 10 + 9	Lloyd A 4 + 23	Frey M 21 + 8	Varane J 29 + 10	Bennie D 1 + 11	Dembele K 15 + 8	Saito K 25 + 14	Dykes L — + 1	Madsen N 20 + 11	Heverton S 4 + 2	Ashby H 17 + 12	Chair I 20 + 8	Dixon-Bonner E — + 3	Fox M 12 + 14	Morgan K 19 + 11	Morrison L 14 + 5	Edwards R 20 + 1	Yang M 8 + 6	Sutton E — + 2	Walsh J 1	Match No.
1	2	3	4	5	6	7³	8⁴	9	10¹	11²	12	13	14	15																1
1	2	3	4	5	7	13⁴	12	9¹		15	10³	11⁵	6²		8⁴	14	16													2
1	2	3	4	5	7		8			13	12	15	11²	14		9⁴	10¹	6³												3
1	2	3	4	5	7	6²	12	13		16	10¹	11⁵	14		8⁴	15		9³												4
1	3	4		5	7¹	6	12	9³		14	16	11²	15		8⁶	13		10⁴	2											5
1	2	3	4	5	7		12	9³		15	13	11	14		8⁴	10¹		6²												6
1	4	3		5	9⁵		7	14		15		11⁴	6⁶	16	8²	10³		13	2¹	12										7
1	4	3		5	6		13	9²		12	16	11¹			8³	10⁴		7⁵	2	14	15									8
1	4	3		5⁵	6		12	9²		13		11		16	8	10¹		7³		2⁴	15		14							9
1	2	3		8⁴	7³		12	16		14		11			10⁵	15		6		5²	9¹		4	13						10
1	3	4	5	6¹	9		2⁵	14		11⁴	16				8	7³		12		15	10²			13						11
1	2	3	4		8		6³	14		11¹	15		7	12	9⁴			5		10²			13							12
1	2	3		4			5²	14		11		6			13			9³	12	8¹	10		7							13
1	2	3		4			12	13	14	11	15		6⁵		8			9⁴	5¹		10²	16		7³						14
1	2	3		4			9⁵	11²		10	14		7³	13	8			12	16	5⁴				6¹	15					15
1	2	3	14	7⁴			8³	16		11²	13		6		10			9¹		5			15	12	4⁵					16
1	2	3	12	7			8¹	14	16	11⁵		6			10⁴			9³		5			13	15	4²					17
1	2	3	5³	7			8²	15		11		12			10⁶			6¹		14		16	13	9⁴	4					18
1	2	3	5²				8⁶	15	12	11¹		6			16			10		9³	13		14	7	4⁴					19
1	2	3		8³			13	11¹		12		6⁴			10			9²		5	16		14	15	4⁴					20
1	2	3	15	7			8⁵	9³	11¹		12		6	16	10²			13		5⁴	14				4					21
1	2	3¹	15	5⁵	6		8⁴		11²		13	7	16	10³				14			12	9	4							22
1	2		3	5²	7		8⁵	16	11⁴		15	6			10³			15	13		2	10⁵	4	9¹						23
1	3			5	6¹		7⁴	8³	11²		12	14	16		15			13		2	10⁵		4	9						24
1	3		12	5	8⁵	16	9	13				10²	7		14			15		2	11³		4¹	6⁴						25
1	3		16	5	7	14	8²				15	11³	6¹		13					2⁴	10		4	9⁵		12				26
1	2			5	7	12	8³		13		15	11	6²		14			13	15	16	10⁵		4	9⁴		3				27
1	2			5	6	16	8⁴		11¹		12	7			13	15		14³	10²		4	9³		3						28
1	2			5	7	14	8		15		12	11²	6¹		13					10³		4	9⁴		3					29
1		3²		5	7			8³		16		11⁵	14	6		13			12	10⁴		4	9¹		2	15				30
1	2	3		5	6	14	7¹					13	11²	16		10⁶				9⁴		15	8³		4	12				31
1	2	3		5	8	6¹	7³					12	11²	13		10⁴				9		15			4	11⁴				32
1	2	3⁵		5	6¹		12					15	11³	7		10		14		9⁴			13	16	4	8²				33
1	2	3		5⁵	6²	12	8³					14	11¹	7		16	10⁴			15	9				4	13				34
1	2	3⁵		5²			9⁴	13				14	11	6		16	12			10		15	8¹		4	7²				35
1	2	3¹		5⁵			7	11²	16			12			14	10		15	9			6³	13		4	8⁴				36
1	2	3		5			7³	12	15			11⁴			13	10⁵		16		9²		14	6		4	8¹				37
1	2	3¹		5			6	8²	9³			11			13	10⁴		14				4		12	7					38
1	2			5⁴			7	8	10²		14		6⁵		11³			12		15		4	9¹	16	3	13				39
1	2			5			7²	8	9	6³		10¹		14	13	12				15		3	4		11⁴					40
1	2			5³	9¹	7	8⁴	12				6	11²	15		10⁵		16		14	17		3	4	13					41
1	2						7³	12	16	15		6	14		8¹	10⁴		9²		5		13		3	4	11⁵				42
1	2		14			7	13	16	12			15	6		8²	10¹		9⁶		5⁴			3	4	11³					43
1	2	12			7			9¹	11³		13		14		10⁶			5²	16	4		3	6	8⁴	15					44
1	2		5		7		16	11³				12	6		10²			9¹		8⁶	13		15		3	4¹		14		45
	2					7²		14	12			11	6		10³			9⁴		5	8¹		13	15	3	4			1	46

FA Cup
Third Round   Leicester C   (a)   2-6

Carabao Cup
First Round   Cambridge U   (a)   2-1
Second Round   Luton T   (h)   1-1
   QPR won 4-1 on penalties.
Third Round   Crystal Palace   (h)   1-2

READING

FOUNDATION

Reading was formed as far back as 1871 at a public meeting held at the Bridge Street Rooms. They first entered the FA Cup as early as 1877 when they amalgamated with the Reading Hornets. The club was further strengthened in 1889 when Earley FC joined them. They were the first winners of the Berks & Bucks Cup in 1878–79.

Select Car Leasing Stadium, Junction 11, M4 Motorway, Reading, Berkshire RG2 0FL.

Telephone: (0118) 968 1313.

Ticket Office: (0118) 968 1313.

Website: www.readingfc.co.uk

Email: supporterservices@readingfc.co.uk

Ground Capacity: 24,376.

Record Attendance: 33,042 v Brentford, FA Cup 5th rd, 19 February 1927 (at Elm Park); 24,184 v Everton, Premier League, 17 November 2012 (at Madejski Stadium).

Pitch Measurements: 103m × 68m (112.5yd × 74.5yd).

Chairman: Rob Couhig.

Chief Executive: Joe Jacobson.

Manager: Noel Hunt.

First-Team Coach: Scott Marshall.

Colours: Blue and white hooped shirts with blue sleeves and red trim, blue shorts with red trim, blue socks with red and white trim.

Year Formed: 1871.

Turned Professional: 1895.

Club Nickname: 'The Royals'.

Grounds: 1871, Reading Recreation; Reading Cricket Ground; 1882, Coley Park; 1889, Caversham Cricket Ground; 1896, Elm Park; 1998, Madejski Stadium (renamed Select Car Leasing Stadium 2021).

First Football League Game: 28 August 1920, Division 3, v Newport Co (a) W 1–0 – Crawford; Smith, Horler; Christie, Mavin, Getgood; Spence, Weston, Yarnell, Bailey (1), Andrews.

Record League Victory: 10–2 v Crystal Palace, Division 3 (S), 4 September 1946 – Groves; Glidden, Gulliver; McKenna, Ratcliffe, Young; Chitty, Maurice Edelston (3), McPhee (4), Barney (1), Deverell (2).

Record Cup Victory: 9–0 v Exeter C, EFL Trophy Group G (S), 19 September 2023 – Boyce-Clarke; Salif (Abrefa), Dean, McIntyre (1)(Dorsett), Carson, Elliott (1) (Harris (1)), Rushesha, Craig, Mukairu (2) (Knibbs), Wareham (Ballard (2)), Vickers (1), own goal (1).

Record Defeat: 0–18 v Preston NE, FA Cup 1st rd, 1893–94.

Most League Points (2 for a win): 65, Division 4, 1978–79.

HONOURS

League Champions: FL C – 2005–06, 2011–12; Second Division – 1993–94; Division 3 – 1985–86; Division 3S – 1925–26; Division 4 – 1978–79.
Runners-up: First Division – 1994–95; Second Division – 2001–02; Division 3S – 1931–32, 1934–35, 1948–49, 1951–52.
FA Cup: semi-final – 1927, 2015.
League Cup: 5th rd – 1996, 1998.
Full Members' Cup Winners: 1988.

FOOTBALL YEARBOOK FACT FILE

Reading adopted professionalism in May 1895 following a heated debate at the club's annual general meeting, although only 21 of around 150 members present opposed the move. Early professional signings included Phil Bach (Middlesbrough) and three Scotsmen: Peter Davie (Third Lanark), Sandy Graham (Renton) and George Reid (Dundee).

Most League Points (3 for a win): 106, Championship, 2005–06 (Football League Record).

Most League Goals: 112, Division 3 (S), 1951–52.

Highest League Scorer in Season: Ronnie Blackman, 39, Division 3 (S), 1951–52.

Most League Goals in Total Aggregate: Ronnie Blackman, 158, 1947–54.

Most League Goals in One Match: 6, Arthur Bacon v Stoke C, Division 2, 3 April 1931.

Most Capped Player: Chris Gunter, 59 (109), Wales.

Most League Appearances: Martin Hicks, 500, 1978–91.

Youngest League Player: Peter Castle, 16 years 49 days v Watford, 30 April 2003.

Record Transfer Fee Received: £8,000,000 from Crystal Palace for Michael Olise, July 2021.

Record Transfer Fee Paid: £7,500,000 to Internazionale for George Puscas, August 2019.

Football League Record: 1920 Original Member of Division 3; 1920–21 Division 3; 1921–26 Division 3 (S); 1926–31 Division 2; 1931–58 Division 3 (S); 1958–71 Division 3; 1971–76 Division 4; 1976–77 Division 3; 1977–79 Division 4; 1979–83 Division 3; 1983–84 Division 4; 1984–86 Division 3; 1986–88 Division 2; 1988–92 Division 3; 1992–94 Second Division; 1994–98 First Division; 1998–2002 Second Division; 2002–04 First Division; 2004–06 FL C; 2006–08 Premier League; 2008–12 FL C; 2012–13 Premier League; 2013–23 FL C; 2023– FL 1.

LATEST SEQUENCES

Longest Sequence of League Wins: 13, 17.8.1985 – 19.10.1985.

Longest Sequence of League Defeats: 8, 29.12.2007 – 24.2.2008.

Longest Sequence of League Draws: 6, 23.3.2002 – 20.4.2002.

Longest Sequence of Unbeaten League Matches: 33, 9.8.2005 – 14.2.2006.

Longest Sequence Without a League Win: 15, 4.3.2023 – 12.8.2023.

Successive Scoring Runs: 32 from 1.10.1932.

Successive Non-scoring Runs: 6 from 29.3.2008.

MANAGERS

Thomas Sefton 1897–1901
(Secretary-Manager)
James Sharp 1901–02
Harry Matthews 1902–20
Harry Marshall 1920–22
Arthur Chadwick 1923–25
H. S. Bray 1925–26
(Secretary only since 1922 and 1926–35)
Andrew Wylie 1926–31
Joe Smith 1931–35
Billy Butler 1935–39
John Cochrane 1939
Joe Edelston 1939–47
Ted Drake 1947–52
Jack Smith 1952–55
Harry Johnston 1955–63
Roy Bentley 1963–69
Jack Mansell 1969–71
Charlie Hurley 1972–77
Maurice Evans 1977–84
Ian Branfoot 1984–89
Ian Porterfield 1989–91
Mark McGhee 1991–94
Jimmy Quinn and Mick Gooding 1994–97
Terry Bullivant 1997–98
Tommy Burns 1998–99
Alan Pardew 1999–2003
Steve Coppell 2003–09
Brendan Rodgers 2009
Brian McDermott 2009–13
Nigel Adkins 2013–14
Steve Clarke 2014–15
Brian McDermott 2015–16
Jaap Stam 2016–18
Paul Clement 2018
José Gomes 2018–19
Mark Bowen 2019–20
Veljko Paunović 2020–22
Paul Ince 2022–23
Ruben Selles 2023–24
Noel Hunt December 2024–

TEN YEAR LEAGUE RECORD

		P	W	D	L	F	A	Pts	Pos
2015-16	FL C	46	13	13	20	52	59	52	17
2016-17	FL C	46	26	7	13	68	64	85	3
2017-18	FL C	46	10	14	22	48	70	44	20
2018-19	FL C	46	10	17	19	49	66	47	20
2019-20	FL C	46	15	11	20	59	58	56	14
2020-21	FL C	46	19	13	14	62	54	70	7
2021-22	FL C	46	13	8	25	54	87	41*	21
2022-23	FL C	46	13	11	22	46	68	44*	22
2023-24	FL 1	46	16	11	19	68	70	53*	17
2024-25	FL 1	46	21	12	13	68	57	75	7

*6 pts deducted.

DID YOU KNOW ?

In June 1912 Reading travelled to the Netherlands to play a friendly game against a local representative team, The Swallows, effectively the Dutch Olympic team. The game was played at the RAP Stadium in Amsterdam, with the Royals winning 3-2 in front of a crowd of 5,000. Goalscorers were James Morris, Allen Foster and Ted Mitchell.

READING – SKY BET LEAGUE ONE 2024–25 LEAGUE RECORD

Match No.	Date	Venue	Opponents	Result	H/T Score	Lg Pos.	Goalscorers	Attendance
1	Aug 10	A	Birmingham C	D 1-1	1-0	12	Ehibhationham [42]	27,985
2	17	H	Wigan Ath	W 2-0	1-0	5	Savage [7], Ehibhationham [57]	12,689
3	24	A	Wrexham	L 0-3	0-2	12		13,322
4	31	H	Charlton Ath	W 2-0	0-0	8	Savage [66], Smith [76]	14,778
5	Sept 14	H	Leyton Orient	L 0-1	0-1	12		12,952
6	21	A	Bolton W	L 2-5	1-4	16	Elliott [41], Smith (pen) [57]	19,635
7	28	H	Huddersfield T	W 2-1	1-1	14	Knibbs [30], Elliott [57]	11,181
8	Oct 1	H	Burton Alb	W 3-1	2-0	12	Campbell 2 [23, 42], Smith [82]	8774
9	5	A	Rotherham U	L 1-2	1-0	16	Wing [26]	8907
10	19	H	Crawley T	W 4-1	2-1	13	Salif [20], Wing [40], Savage [65], Smith [73]	13,243
11	22	A	Exeter C	W 2-1	2-0	7	Wareham [1], Craig [36]	6807
12	26	H	Bristol R	W 1-0	0-0	6	Smith [66]	12,843
13	29	A	Stockport Co	L 1-4	1-3	9	Campbell [30]	8128
14	Nov 9	A	Stevenage	D 1-1	0-1	9	Knibbs [82]	4562
15	23	H	Peterborough U	W 2-1	2-0	8	Knibbs 2 [9, 23]	10,008
16	26	A	Barnsley	D 2-2	0-1	7	Smith 2 [50, 66]	10,011
17	Dec 3	H	Cambridge U	W 3-0	0-0	6	Wing 2 [49, 63], Camara [60]	8333
18	7	A	Wycombe W	D 1-1	1-1	6	Knibbs [30]	7651
19	14	H	Blackpool	L 0-3	0-2	6		14,455
20	21	A	Lincoln C	L 0-2	0-1	7		9396
21	26	H	Northampton T	W 4-1	2-0	6	Knibbs [5], Smith [28], Savage [75], Camara [87]	12,283
22	29	H	Mansfield T	W 2-1	1-1	6	Camara [17], Bindon [55]	13,626
23	Jan 1	A	Cambridge U	W 3-1	1-0	5	Knibbs 2 [40, 53], Smith [83]	6878
24	4	A	Charlton Ath	D 0-0	0-0	6		15,526
25	18	H	Stockport Co	L 1-3	0-2	7	Smith [61]	11,019
26	25	A	Leyton Orient	L 0-2	0-1	8		8774
27	28	A	Burton Alb	L 2-3	0-2	10	Craig [69], Smith [71]	2358
28	Feb 1	H	Bolton W	W 1-0	0-0	8	Knibbs (pen) [89]	11,508
29	8	A	Huddersfield T	D 0-0	0-0	8		18,385
30	11	H	Shrewsbury T	D 1-1	1-0	9	Wareham [28]	7975
31	15	H	Rotherham U	W 2-1	1-0	9	Knibbs 2 (1 pen) [24, 90 (p)]	10,034
32	22	H	Birmingham C	D 0-0	0-0	9		13,919
33	Mar 1	A	Wigan Ath	W 2-1	0-0	9	Wareham [71], Bindon [85]	9402
34	4	H	Exeter C	D 0-0	0-0	8		7955
35	8	A	Crawley T	D 1-1	1-1	8	Ehibhationham [29]	4526
36	11	H	Wrexham	W 2-0	0-0	8	Knibbs (pen) [51], Wing [55]	11,557
37	15	H	Stevenage	D 1-1	0-0	8	Piergianni (og) [49]	13,984
38	29	H	Peterborough U	W 3-1	1-0	6	Hughes (og) [7], Knibbs [58], Savage [63]	12,108
39	Apr 1	A	Blackpool	L 0-3	0-0	7		8345
40	5	H	Wycombe W	W 1-0	0-0	7	Knibbs (pen) [77]	15,228
41	8	A	Shrewsbury T	W 3-1	1-0	6	Wing [34], Ehibhationham [53], Campbell [72]	4956
42	12	A	Northampton T	D 0-0	0-0	6		7614
43	18	H	Lincoln C	L 0-1	0-0	7		16,388
44	21	A	Mansfield T	W 5-1	1-0	7	Wareham 2 [35, 74], Williams (og) [49], Wing [57], Bodin [90]	8377
45	26	A	Bristol R	W 2-0	0-0	7	Wing [67], Campbell [90]	9035
46	May 3	H	Barnsley	L 2-4	0-0	7	Wing [67], Bodin [90]	21,481

Final League Position: 7

GOALSCORERS

League (68): Knibbs 14 (4 pens), Smith 11 (1 pen), Wing 9, Campbell 5, Savage 5, Wareham 5, Ehibhationham 4, Camara 3, Bindon 2, Bodin 2, Craig 2, Elliott 2, Salif 1, own goals 3.
FA Cup (8): Campbell 2, Akande 1, Bindon 1, Camara 1, Savage 1, Wing 1, own goal 1.
Carabao Cup (2): Savage 1, Wing 1.
Vertu Trophy (7): Knibbs 2, Sackey 2, Wareham 2, Abrefa 1.

Castro J 40	Craig M 29+1	Salif A 33+1	Bindon T 44	Dorsett J 11+3	Elliott B 17+2	Wing L 46	Knibbs H 41+2	Smith S 24+1	Camara M 19+14	Ehibhationham K 27+6	Abrefa K 11+16	Savage C 40+5	Garcia A 29+9	Wareham J 15+22	Azeez F —+1	Akande A 4+11	Rushesha T 9+9	Tuma B —+4	Dean H 7+12	Boyce-Clarke C 1	Campbell C 36+3	Button D 5	Spencer S —+1	Ahmed A —+5	Kanu A 4+6	Holzman L 3+6	Osho E —+1	Bodin B 3+13	Yiadom A 4+10	Stickland M 4+1	Carroll T —+9	Match No.
1	2	3	4	5^1	6^2	7	8	9	10^3	11^4	12	13	14	15																		1
1	2	3	4	5^2	6	7			10^4	9^3	11^1	15	8	13	14	12																2
1	2	3	4	5^1	6^5	7		10^2		11	16	8^3	15	13			9^1	12	14													3
1	2	3	4^2	5^1	6	7		10		11	12	8					9^3	14	13													4
	2^4	3	4	5^5	8	7	12	10		11^3		15	6^2	16	14	13				1	9^1											5
	2	3	4	5^1	6	7	8	10		11^{12}		12			13						9	1										6
	2	3	4		6^2	7	8	10		11		5^5	13			12		14			9^1	1										7
	2^1	3	4		6	7	8	10		11^2		12	13			5^3	15	14			9^4	1										8
	2^4	3	4		6^3	7	8	10		11^4		5^1	14	12^5	13	16	15				9^2	1										9
	2	4	3		6^5	7	11^1	10^4		8		5^2	15	9	14	13	12					1	16									10
1	2	4	3		14	7	6	12	16	11^5		8^4	5^3	10^2	13	15																11
1	2	3	4		6^2	7	8	10	9^1	11		13	5			12																12
1	2	3^5	4		13	7	6		14	12		8^2	5	10^4		9^1	15	16	11^3													13
1	2^3	3	4	12	6	7	10			11^2		8					9															14
1	2	3^1	4	5	6	7	11	10^2		8							9									12						15
1	2^3		4	5^1	6	7	11	10	14			8^2	12				9							13		3						16
1	2	3^2	4	5	6	7	12	10	11^4			8^1		14					13		9^3							15				17
1	2	3	4	5	6	7	11	10	12			8^1									9											18
1	2^4	3^1	4		6^2	7	11	10	13			8^3	5	14							9		15		12							19
1	2		4			7	6	10	11^1			8	5^2	14					12		9^3					13		3^4				20
1	2	3	4	5^1		7	6	10^3	11^1			8	13	12		14	15				9^4		16	5^2								21
1	2	3	4			7	6	10^3	11^1			8	13	12		14	9				5^2											22
1			4			7	6	10^4	11^1	13		8^3	5	15		14	3		9					12	2^2							23
1		2	4			7	6	10		9^1	8	11^2	13				3						12	5								24
1	14		4	12		7	6	10		13	15	8	11^2			2^3	3		9^4					5^1								25
1	2		4	5^1		7	6	10	14	13		8^4	11				15		3		9^3			12^2								26
1	2		4			7	6		11^1	12	13	8	5^2	10			14		3		9^3											27
1	2		4			7	6		11^1	12	13	8	5^2	10			3				9^3					14						28
1	2	12	4			7	6		11^3	13	14	8	5^4	10^2			3^1				9							15				29
1	2	3	4			7	6		13	11^4	12	8	5^3	10^1							9^2							15	14			30
1	2	3	4			7	6		12	11^3	13	8	5^4	10^1							9^2							15	14			31
1	2	3	4			7	8		11^2	10^1		6	5	12							9							13				32
1		3	4			7	8		11^4		14	6	5^3	10	13	2^1												15	9^2	12		33
1		3	4			7	8		11^3	13		6	5	10	14	2^1												15	9^2	12		34
1			4			7	6		11^2	10^1	2^5	8	5^4	12		16			13		9^3							15	3	14		35
1			4			8	6		14	11^1	2	7	5	10^2				12			9^3							13	3^4			36
1			4			7	6		14	11	2	8^5	5^1	10^2	15	12					9^4				13			3^3	16			37
1						7	8^5		11^1	10^5	5	6^3	12		13	2					9^4			15	16	4		3	14			38
1						7	6		12	11^1	5	8	15	10^5	2^4		9^1	14						16	4^2			3	13			39
1		3	4			7	6		11^3	10^1	2	8	5^2	13		12					9^4							14	15			40
1		3	4			7	6^4		9^1	10^3	13	8	5^2	12		11												14	2	15		41
1		3	4			7	6		12	11^1	5	8		10^2			2^3				9^4							13	14	15		42
1		3	4			7	6		11^2	10^3	2^1	8	5^4	13		14					9^5							16	12	15		43
1		3	4			7	6		11^2		8	5^1	10^4	15	2						9^3							13	12	14		44
1		3	4			7	6		11^{12}		8	5	10^3	2^1							9							13	12	14		45
1		3	4	14		7	6		15	11^2		8^5	5^4	10	2^1						9^3							13	12		16	46

FA Cup

First Round	Fleetwood T	(h)	2-0	
Second Round *aet.*	Harborough T	(h)	5-3	
Third Round *aet.*	Burnley	(h)	1-3	

Carabao Cup

First Round   Colchester U   (a)   2-2
Colchester U won 4-3 on penalties.

Vertu Trophy

Group H (S)	West Ham U U21	(h)	3-1
Group H (S)	Cheltenham T	(a)	0-1
Group H (S)	Newport Co	(h)	3-0
Second Round	Walsall	(a)	1-1

Walsall won 4-2 on penalties.

ROTHERHAM UNITED

FOUNDATION

Rotherham were formed in 1870 before becoming Town in the late 1880s. Thornhill United were founded in 1877 and changed their name to Rotherham County in 1905. The Town amalgamated with Rotherham County to form Rotherham United in 1925.

The AESSEAL New York Stadium, New York Way, Rotherham, South Yorkshire S60 1AH.
Telephone: (01709) 827 760.
Ticket Office: (01709) 827 768.
Website: www.themillers.co.uk
Email: office@rotherhamunited.net
Ground Capacity: 12,088.
Record Attendance: 25,170 v Sheffield U, Division 2, 13 December 1952 (at Millmoor); 7,082 v Aldershot T, FL 2 Play-offs semi-final 2nd leg, 19 May 2010 (at Don Valley); 11,758 v Sheffield U, FL 1, 7 September 2013 (at New York Stadium).
Pitch Measurements: 102m × 65m (111.5yd × 71yd).
Chairman: Tony Stewart OBE.
Chief Operating Officer: Paul Douglas.
Manager: Matt Hanshaw.
Assistant Manager: Dale Tonge.

HONOURS

League Champions: Division 3 – 1980–81; Division 3N – 1950–51; Division 4 – 1988–89.
Runners-up: Second Division – 2000–01; FL 1 – 2019–20, 2021–22; Division 3N – 1946–47, 1947–48, 1948–49; FL 2 – 2012–13; Third Division – 1999–2000; Division 4 – 1991–92.
FA Cup: 5th rd – 1953, 1968.
League Cup: Runners-up: 1961.
League Trophy Winners: 1996, 2022.

Colours: Red shirts with white sleeves and cross-patterned trim, white shorts with red trim, red socks.
Year Formed: 1870 (reformed as Rotherham United 1925). *Turned Professional:* 1905.
Club Nickname: 'The Millers'.
Previous Names: 1877, Thornhill United; 1905, Rotherham County; 1925, amalgamated with Rotherham Town under Rotherham United.
Grounds: 1870, Red House Ground; 1907, Millmoor; 2008, Don Valley Stadium; 2012, New York Stadium (renamed The AESSEAL New York Stadium 2014).
First Football League Game: 2 September 1893, Division 2, Rotherham T v Lincoln C (a) D 1–1 – McKay; Thickett, Watson; Barr, Brown, Broadhead; Longden, Cutts, Leatherbarrow, McCormick, Pickering, (1 og). 30 August 1919, Division 2, Rotherham Co v Nottingham F (h) W 2–0 – Branston; Alton, Baines; Bailey, Coe, Stanton; Lee (1), Cawley (1), Glennon, Lees, Lamb.
Record League Victory: 8–0 v Oldham Ath, Division 3 (N), 26 May 1947 – Warnes; Selkirk, Ibbotson; Edwards, Horace Williams, Danny Williams; Wilson (2), Shaw (1), Ardron (3), Guest (1), Hainsworth (1).
Record Cup Victory: 6–0 v Spennymoor U, FA Cup 2nd rd, 17 December 1977 – McAlister; Forrest, Breckin, Womble, Stancliffe, Green, Finney, Phillips (3), Gwyther (2) (Smith), Goodfellow, Crawford (1). 6–0 v Wolverhampton W, FA Cup 1st rd, 16 November 1985 – O'Hanlon; Forrest, Dungworth, Gooding (1), Smith (1), Pickering, Birch (2), Emerson, Tynan (1), Simmons (1), Pugh. 6–0 v King's Lynn, FA Cup 2nd rd, 6 December 1997 – Mimms; Clark, Hurst (Goodwin), Garner (1) (Hudson) (1), Warner (Bass), Richardson (1), Berry (1), Thompson, Druce (1), Glover (1), Roscoe; 6–0 v Doncaster R (a), Papa John's Trophy Northern Group E, 7 September 2021 – Vickers; Edmonds-Green, Hull (1), Mattock (1), Miller (1), Barlaser, Odofin, Bola, Sadlier (Rathbone 46), Grigg (1) (Gratton 65), Ladapo (1) (Smith 65), own goal 1.
Record Defeat: 1–11 v Bradford C, Division 3 (N), 25 August 1928.
Most League Points (2 for a win): 71, Division 3 (N), 1950–51.

FOOTBALL YEARBOOK FACT FILE

Rotherham United's New York Stadium was used for a public match for the first time on 21 July 2012. In line with protocols, the maximum attendance was restricted to 50 per cent of the ground capacity and a sell-out crowd of 6,000 saw the Millers defeat Barnsley 2-1 in a pre-season friendly fixture. Jacob Mellis scored the first-ever goal at the stadium for the visitors before Rotherham fought back with goals from David Noble and Kayode Odejayi.

Most League Points (3 for a win): 91, Division 2, 2000–01.

Most League Goals: 114, Division 3 (N), 1946–47.

Highest League Scorer in Season: Wally Ardron, 38, Division 3 (N), 1946–47.

Most League Goals in Total Aggregate: Gladstone Guest, 130, 1946–56.

Most League Goals in One Match: 4, Roland Bastow v York C, Division 3 (N), 9 November 1935; 4, Roland Bastow v Rochdale, Division 3 (N), 7 March 1936; 4, Wally Ardron v Crewe Alex, Division 3 (N), 5 October 1946; 4, Wally Ardron v Carlisle U, Division 3 (N), 13 September 1947; 4, Wally Ardron v Hartlepools U, Division 3 (N), 13 October 1948; 4, Ian Wilson v Liverpool, Division 2, 2 May 1955; 4, Carl Gilbert v Swansea C, Division 3, 28 September 1971; 4, Carl Airey v Chester, Division 3, 31 August 1987; 4, Shaun Goater v Hartlepool U, Division 3, 9 April 1994; 4, Lee Glover v Hull C, Division 3, 28 December 1997; 4, Darren Byfield v Millwall, Division 1, 10 August 2002; 4, Adam Le Fondre v Cheltenham T, FL 2, 21 August 2010.

Most Capped Player: Kari Arnason, 20 (90), Iceland.

Most League Appearances: Danny Williams, 461, 1946–62.

Youngest League Player: Kevin Eley, 16 years 72 days v Scunthorpe U, 15 May 1984.

Record Transfer Fee Received: £2,100,000 (potentially rising to £3,500,000) from Cardiff C for Will Vaulks, June 2019.

Record Transfer Fee Paid: £1,000,000 to Exeter C for Sam Nombe, August 2023.

Football League Record: 1893 Rotherham Town elected to Division 2; 1893–96 Division 2; 1896 Failed re-election; 1919 Rotherham County elected to Division 2; 1923–25 Division 2; 1925 Rotherham T and Rotherham Co merge to form Rotherham U; 1925–51 Division 3 (N); 1951–68 Division 2; 1968–73 Division 3; 1973–75 Division 4; 1975–81 Division 3; 1981–83 Division 2; 1983–88 Division 3; 1988–89 Division 4; 1989–91 Division 3; 1991–92 Division 4; 1992–97 Second Division; 1997–2000 Third Division; 2000–01 Second Division; 2001–04 First Division; 2004–05 FL C; 2005–07 FL 1; 2007–13 FL 2; 2013–14 FL 1; 2014–17 FL C; 2017–18 FL 1; 2018–19 FL C; 2019–20 FL 1; 2020–21 FL C; 2021–22 FL 1; 2022–24 FL C; 2024– FL 1.

LATEST SEQUENCES

Longest Sequence of League Wins: 9, 2.2.1982 – 6.3.1982.

Longest Sequence of League Defeats: 10, 14.2.2017 – 8.4.2017.

Longest Sequence of League Draws: 6, 13.10.1969 – 22.11.1969.

Longest Sequence of Unbeaten League Matches: 18, 13.10.1969 – 7.2.1970.

Longest Sequence Without a League Win: 21, 9.5.2004 – 20.11.2004.

Successive Scoring Runs: 30 from 3.4.1954.

Successive Non-scoring Runs: 6 from 21.8.2004.

MANAGERS

Billy Heald 1925–29 *(Secretary only for several years)*
Stanley Davies 1929–30
Billy Heald 1930–33
Reg Freeman 1934–52
Andy Smailes 1952–58
Tom Johnston 1958–62
Danny Williams 1962–65
Jack Mansell 1965–67
Tommy Docherty 1967–68
Jimmy McAnearney 1968–73
Jimmy McGuigan 1973–79
Ian Porterfield 1979–81
Emlyn Hughes 1981–83
George Kerr 1983–85
Norman Hunter 1985–87
Dave Cusack 1987–88
Billy McEwan 1988–91
Phil Henson 1991–94
Archie Gemmill and John McGovern 1994–96
Danny Bergara 1996–97
Ronnie Moore 1997–2005
Mick Harford 2005
Alan Knill 2005–07
Mark Robins 2007–09
Ronnie Moore 2009–11
Andy Scott 2011–12
Steve Evans 2012–15
Neil Redfearn 2015–16
Neil Warnock 2016
Alan Stubbs 2016
Kenny Jackett 2016
Paul Warne 2016–22
Matt Taylor 2022–23
Liam Richardson 2023–24
Steve Evans 2024–25
Matt Hanshaw April 2025–

TEN YEAR LEAGUE RECORD

		P	W	D	L	F	A	Pts	Pos
2015-16	FL C	46	13	10	23	53	71	49	21
2016-17	FL C	46	5	8	33	40	98	23	24
2017-18	FL 1	46	24	7	15	73	53	79	4
2018-19	FL C	46	8	16	22	52	83	40	22
2019-20	FL 1	35	18	8	9	61	38	62	2§
2020-21	FL C	46	11	9	26	44	60	42	23
2021-22	FL 1	46	27	9	10	70	33	90	2
2022-23	FL C	46	11	17	18	49	60	50	19
2023-24	FL C	46	5	12	29	37	89	27	24
2024-25	FL 1	46	16	11	19	54	59	59	13

§*Decided on points-per-game (1.77)*

DID YOU KNOW ?

Amateur centre-forward Tom Hall created a sensation by scoring four goals for the Millers in his Football League debut against Wigan Borough in November 1927. He was promptly signed up on professional forms but struggled to win a regular place in the line-up and scored only two more goals during his stay at Millmoor before departing at the end of the season.

ROTHERHAM UNITED – SKY BET LEAGUE ONE 2024–25 LEAGUE RECORD

Match No.	Date	Venue	Opponents	Result	H/T Score	Lg Pos.	Goalscorers	Attendance
1	Aug 10	A	Exeter C	L	0-1	0-0	19		7458
2	17	H	Bristol R	D	0-0	0-0	18		9414
3	24	A	Wycombe W	L	0-2	0-0	21		4272
4	31	H	Huddersfield T	W	2-1	0-0	17	Clarke-Harris (pen) [77], Wilks [90]	10,404
5	Sept 7	A	Charlton Ath	D	1-1	0-0	15	Kelly [58]	13,569
6	14	H	Burton Alb	D	2-2	1-1	17	Clarke-Harris [39], Humphreys [57]	8704
7	21	H	Birmingham C	L	0-2	0-2	21		10,335
8	28	A	Shrewsbury T	D	1-1	0-1	19	Clarke-Harris (pen) [70]	6001
9	Oct 1	A	Cambridge U	W	1-0	0-0	17	Nombe [90]	5085
10	5	H	Reading	W	2-1	0-1	17	Nombe [49], Odofin [56]	8907
11	12	A	Peterborough U	D	3-3	3-1	15	Nombe [19], Wilks [23], Clarke-Harris [45]	8859
12	19	H	Wrexham	L	0-1	0-1	16		11,235
13	22	A	Leyton Orient	L	0-1	0-0	17		6314
14	26	H	Stevenage	W	2-0	0-0	14	Hugill [70], Wilks [72]	8896
15	Nov 8	A	Barnsley	L	0-2	0-1	14		14,731
16	23	A	Crawley T	L	0-1	0-1	18		3631
17	Dec 3	H	Lincoln C	W	2-1	1-0	17	Nombe [21], Raggett [77]	8995
18	14	H	Northampton T	W	3-0	2-0	17	Clarke-Harris 2 [3, 34], Green [49]	8745
19	21	A	Mansfield T	L	0-1	0-1	18		8401
20	26	H	Wigan Ath	L	0-1	0-1	18		9509
21	29	H	Stockport Co	D	1-1	1-1	17	Odofin [19]	10,194
22	Jan 1	A	Lincoln C	W	1-0	0-0	17	Powell [85]	9222
23	4	A	Huddersfield T	D	0-0	0-0	16		18,353
24	11	H	Bolton W	W	3-1	2-0	13	Wilks (pen) [34], James [45], Nombe [76]	10,258
25	18	H	Charlton Ath	W	4-2	3-1	13	Green [9], MacDonald [14], Jules [45], Wilks [53]	8911
26	25	A	Burton Alb	L	2-4	1-3	13	Sibley [2], Green [61]	3733
27	28	H	Cambridge U	W	2-1	0-0	14	Wilks [53], Odofin [69]	8162
28	Feb 1	A	Birmingham C	L	1-2	1-0	15	Nombe [44]	34,393
29	8	H	Shrewsbury T	L	1-2	0-0	15	Odofin [76]	8820
30	11	A	Blackpool	D	0-0	0-0	14		8216
31	15	A	Reading	L	1-2	0-1	14	Nombe (pen) [57]	10,034
32	22	H	Barnsley	L	0-1	0-0	14		10,755
33	Mar 1	A	Bristol R	W	3-2	1-1	14	Nombe 2 [36, 90], Jules [52]	7799
34	4	H	Leyton Orient	W	1-0	0-0	14	Sweeney (og) [60]	8106
35	8	A	Wrexham	L	0-1	0-0	14		13,245
36	15	H	Exeter C	D	1-1	1-0	14	James [45]	8438
37	18	H	Wycombe W	L	2-3	0-0	14	Sibley [66], Clarke-Harris (pen) [90]	7798
38	29	H	Crawley T	L	0-4	0-1	16		8177
39	Apr 1	A	Northampton T	W	2-0	1-0	15	Ruddock [22], Nombe [65]	5720
40	5	H	Blackpool	W	2-1	1-0	14	Odofin [26], Rafferty [90]	9172
41	8	A	Bolton W	W	1-0	1-0	12	Nombe [11]	19,218
42	12	A	Stockport Co	L	1-3	1-1	13	Wilks [9]	10,390
43	18	H	Mansfield T	D	3-3	2-1	13	Wilks 2 [17, 66], Nombe [36]	10,665
44	21	A	Wigan Ath	L	0-1	0-1	13		9391
45	27	A	Stevenage	D	1-1	1-0	13	Nombe [8]	4012
46	May 3	H	Peterborough U	W	2-1	1-1	13	Nombe [36], Humphreys [66]	9994

Final League Position: 13

GOALSCORERS

League (54): Nombe 14 (1 pen), Wilks 9 (1 pen), Clarke-Harris 7 (3 pens), Odofin 5, Green 3, Humphreys 2, James 2, Jules 2, Sibley 2, Hugill 1, Kelly 1, MacDonald 1, Powell 1, Rafferty 1, Raggett 1, Ruddock 1, own goal 1.
FA Cup (1): Wilks 1.
Carabao Cup (3): McCart 1, Nombe 1, Odofin 1.
Vertu Trophy (9): Hugill 4, Clarke-Harris 1 (1 pen), Esapa Osong 1, Jules 1, McWilliams 1, Odofin 1.

Phillips D 32+1	Humphreys C 39+1	Raggett S 6+3	McCart J 13+3	Rafferty J 38+1	Odofin H 44	Tiehi C 13+3	Bramall C 5+11	Hungbo J 5+8	Hugill J 7+21	Clarke-Harris J 19+10	Nombe S 40+3	Powell J 44+2	Holmes D 32+25	Esapa D 1+5	MacDonald A 8+7	James R 42+1	Kelly L 15+3	McWilliams S 12+12	Wilks M 39+2	Dawson C 14	Jules Z 22	McGuckin C 1+2	Green A 8+5	Sibley L 16+5	Gore D 1+2	Ruddock P 18	Kayode J 1+11	Douglas H —+2	Match No.
1	2	3	4^2	5	6	7	8	9^4	10^3	11^1	12	13	14	15															1
1	3		4		9	6^1		14	11^4	10^3	8		15			2	5	7^2	12	13									2
1	3		4	2				14	10^2	13	11	8^3	12			5	7	6^1	9										3
1	3		4	2	6^3					12	11	10^2	8	14		5	7	13	9										4
1	3		4	2	6					13	11^1	10^2	8	15	12	5	7^3	14	9^4										5
1	3		4	2	6	7^1		14		13	11	10^2	8^3		12	5			9										6
1	3^1	4	5	2	9	7^4		14	13	15	10	11	12			6^2			8^3										7
	3		4	2		7	13	12	11^3	14	10^1	8	15		6^4	5^2			9	1									8
	3		4	2			13	9	6^1	14	10^4	12	8	15		5	7^2	11^3		1									9
	3		4	2	6^4	7^3		12	13	10^2	11	8	16	15		5		14	9^5	1									10
	3		4	2	6	7^4			13	12	10^1	11^3	8	14	15	5			9^2	1									11
	3		4	2	9^2	6			10	13	14	11	7		12	5^1			8^3	1									12
	3			2	6	6^3		12		14	11	7	13			5	10^1		8	1	4^2								13
	3			2	6	7^1	5		11^2	12	10	8^3	13	14	15				9^4	1	4								14
	3			2		7	13		12	10^3	9	8^2	14			5	6			1	4		11^1						15
1	2^1	3		5		13	8	9^2	15	10^4		7	14	11^5	12	6^3					4		16						16
1		3	14	2	6	7			10	9^2		8			12	5^3		13	11^1		4								17
1		16		2	3	6^1		14		11	10^4	7^5		15		5^3	12	13	8		4		9^2						18
1		13		2^1	3				15	10	11^4	7	14			5	6^2	12	9^5		4		16	8^3					19
1		13	4^1	2	3				15	12	14	11^3	10^5	7		5	6^4	16	8				9^2						20
1				2	3				9^1		11	6^3	8	14		5	7	13	10^2		4		12						21
1	6			2	3			12			9	10			8^1	5		7	11		4								22
1	6			2	3			12		13		10	8		7^1	5		9^3	11^2		4		14						23
1	6			2	3			12			11		7		9^1	5		10	8		4								24
1	7	13		2	3			12					8	14	6	5^2		9^1	10^3		4		11						25
1	6	12		2^1	3			13		15			8	14	7^2	5^1			10		4		11	9^4					26
1	7	12		2	3			13					8		6^1	5			10		4		11^2	9					27
1	8	3		2				13			10		7	14		5			11^1		4		9^2	6^3	12				28
1	7			2	3			12			11		10	13		5					4		8^1	9^2		6			29
1	7			2	3					10^2	11		9			5	6^1				4		13	12		8			30
1	7			2	3					10^1	12		11^3	8		5					4		13	9^2		6	14		31
1	7			2	3					9^1	13		10	8^3		5			11		4		12	7^2		6	14		32
1	7				3					10^1	11		8	13		5	2^3		9^2		4		14			6	12		33
1	7				3						11^2	10	8	14		5	2		9^3		4^1		12			6	13		34
1	4	15			3					10^2	11		8^4	14		5	2		9^3				13	6^1		7	12		35
1	4			2	3						11		9^2			5	7	6^1	10				13	8		12			36
1	7			2	3					13	11		8			5			9^2	10^3	4^1		12			6	14		37
1	4			2	3					10	11		8	13		5	12		9		1			7^2		6^1			38
	4			2	3				12	13	11^3	9		14		5	6		10^2		1			7^1		8			39
	4			2	3				12	14	11^3	7	13			8	6^2		10^1		1			9		5			40
	4			2	3				12		11		8	9^1		5			10^2		1		6			7		13	41
	4			2	3				12		11		7	5^2		8	13		10^3		1		9^1			6	14		42
13	4			2	3						11^3		7	5^1		8			10		1^2		9			6	14	12	43
1	2		5^3		3					12	10		7	13		4		14	9				6^1	11^2					44
1	4			2	3					12	11^1		7	8			6^2	13	10^4				9^3	14		5	15		45
1	4			2	3						11		7	13	8		6	12	10^3				9^2	5^1		14			46

FA Cup
First Round   Cheltenham T   (h)   1-3

Carabao Cup
First Round   Crewe Alex   (h)   2-1
Second Round   Fleetwood T   (a)   1-2

Vertu Trophy
Group H (N)   Mansfield T   (h)   2-0
Group H (N)   Newcastle U U21   (h)   3-1
Group H (N)   Bradford C   (a)   1-0
Second Round   Tranmere R   (h)   3-2
Third Round   Chesterfield   (a)   0-0
Rotherham U won 4-3 on penalties.
Quarter-Final   Bradford C   (h)   0-1

SALFORD CITY

FOUNDATION

The club was formed as Salford Central Mission in 1940 and in 1947 changed its name to Salford Central. The club competed in local junior leagues including the Eccles and District League until 1963 when the name was changed to Salford Amateurs and they entered the Manchester League. In 1980 this club merged with another local club, Anson Villa, and adopted the name Salford. They were members of the Cheshire County League and then the North West Counties League. In 1990 Salford became Salford City and after gaining promotion to the Northern Premier League for 2008–09 they made rapid progress and went on to achieve Football League status.

The Peninsula Stadium, Moor Lane, Salford, Greater Manchester M7 3PZ.

Telephone: (0161) 241 9772.

Ticket Office: tickets@salfordcityfc.co.uk

Website: www.salfordcityfc.co.uk

Email: fans@salfordcityfc.co.uk

Ground Capacity: 5,032.

Record Attendance: 4,591 v Wrexham, FL 2, 3 February 2024.

Pitch Measurements: 100m × 64m (109.5yd × 70yd).

Co-Chairmen: Declan Kelly, Lord Mervyn Davies.

Chief Executive: Jonathan Jackson (interim).

Head Coach: Karl Robinson.

Assistant Head Coach: Alex Bruce.

Colours: Red shirts with black and white trim, white shorts with black trim, white socks with black trim.

Year Formed: 1940.

Turned Professional: 2017.

Previous Names: 1940, Salford Central; 1963, Salford Amateurs; 1989, Salford City.

Club Nickname: 'The Ammies'.

Grounds: 1979, Moor Lane (renamed The Peninsula Stadium 2017).

First Football League Game: 3 August 2019, FL 2, v Stevenage (h) W 2–0 – Neal; Maynard, Pond, Piergianni, Wiseman, Towell (Armstrong), Smith, Shelton, Touray, Rooney (Beesley), Dieseruwe (2) (Threlkeld).

Record League Victory: 5–1 v Scunthorpe U (h), FL 2, 19 March 2022 – King; Lowe, Vassell, Ndaba, Touray I, Kelly (1), Lund (Love), Watson, Thomas-Asante (3), Smith M (1) (Loughlin), Hunter (Bolton).

HONOURS

League: Runners-up: National League – (3rd) 2018–19 *(promoted to FL 2 via play-offs).*
FA Cup: 3rd rd – 2025.
League Cup: 3rd rd – 2024.
League Trophy: Winners: 2020 (final played in 2021).

FOOTBALL YEARBOOK FACT FILE

Salford Amateurs merged with Anson Villa the summer of 1980 with the intention of taking over Anson's place in Division Two of the Cheshire League. However, Anson had finished bottom of the table and had to seek re-election at the league AGM in June. They were successful, and the new club took their place in the competition under the name of Salford for the 1980–81 season.

Record Cup Victory: 5–0 v Kennek Ryhope, FA Cup Preliminary rd, 2000–01; 5–0 v Atherton Laburnum R, FA Cup 1st Qualifying rd, 2008–09; 5–0 v Whitby T, FA Cup 1st Qualifying rd, 2015–16.

Record Cup Defeat: 1–7 v St Helen's T, FA Cup prel rd, 2001–02.

Most League Points (3 for a win): 75, FL 2, 2022–23.

Most League Goals: 72, FL 2, 2022–23.

Highest League Scorer in Season: Matt Smith, 24, FL 2, 2023–24.

Most League Goals in Total Aggregate: Matt Smith, 41, 2021–24.

Most League Goals in One Match: 3, Ian Henderson v Grimsby T, FL 2, 19 September 2020; 3, Brandon Thomas-Asante v Scunthorpe U, FL 2, 19 March 2022; 3, Matt Smith v Grimsby T, FL 2, 29 December 2022; 3, Callum Hendry v Tranmere R, FL 2, 19 August 2023; 3, Matt Smith v Doncaster R, FL 2, 24 October 2023; 3, Matt Smith v Crewe Alex, FL 2, 27 January 2024.

Most Capped Player: Ibou Touray, 17 (27), Gambia.

Most League Appearances: Ibou Touray, 153, 2019–23.

Youngest League Player: Kyrell Malcolm, 16 years 260 days v Colchester U, 27 February 2024.

Record Transfer Fee Received: £300,000 from WBA for Brandon Thomas-Asante, August 2022.

Record Transfer Fee Paid: £7,000 to Ramsbottom U for Jordan Hulme, January 2015.

Football League Record: 2019 Promoted from National League; 2019– FL 2.

MANAGERS

John Torkington 1983–84
David Entwhistle 1984–87
Alf Murphy 1987–89
Steve Canaghan 1989–92
Billy Garton 1992–93
Syd White 1993–96
Alan Lord 1996–99
Tom Foster and Matt Wardrop 1999–2001
Andy Brown 2001–03
Chris Willcock 2003–04
Mark Molyneaux 2004–05
Darren Lyons 2005
John Foster 2005
Gary Fellows 2005–08
Ashley Berry 2008
Paul Wright 2009–10
Rhodri Giggs 2010–12
Darren Sheridan 2012–13
Andy Heald 2013
Barry Massey and Phil Power 2013
Phil Power 2013–15
Anthony Johnson and Bernard Morley 2015–18
Graham Alexander 2018–20
Richie Wellens 2020–21
Gary Bowyer 2021–22
Neil Wood 2022–23
Karl Robinson January 2024–

LATEST SEQUENCES

Longest Sequence of League Wins: 6, 14.12.2024 – 4.1.2025.

Longest Sequence of League Defeats: 5, 26.8.2023 – 23.9.2023.

Longest Sequence of League Draws: 5, 17.8.2019 – 7.9.2019.

Longest Sequence of Unbeaten League Matches: 11, 1.2.2022 – 2.4.2022.

Longest Sequence Without a League Win: 11, 28.10.2023 – 6.1.2024.

Successive Scoring Runs: 12 from 23.10.2021.

Successive Non-scoring Runs: 4 from 9.3.2021.

TEN YEAR LEAGUE RECORD

		P	W	D	L	F	A	Pts	Pos
2015–16	NPLP	46	27	9	10	94	48	90	3
2016–17	NLN	42	22	11	9	79	44	77	4
2017–18	NLN	42	28	7	7	80	45	91	1
2018–19	NL	46	25	10	11	77	45	85	3
2019-20	FL 2	37	13	11	13	49	46	50	11§
2020-21	FL 2	46	19	14	13	54	34	71	8
2021-22	FL 2	46	19	13	14	60	46	70	10
2022-23	FL 2	46	22	9	15	72	54	75	7
2023-24	FL 2	46	13	12	21	66	82	51	20
2024-25	FL 2	46	18	15	13	64	54	69	8

§*Decided on points-per-game (1.35)*

DID YOU KNOW ?

Salford City got off to a great start to the 2022–23 season, dropping just two points from their first four games. On 16 August they won 3-2 away to Newport County thanks to goals from Luke Bolton, Ryan Leak and an own goal. The win took them to the top of the League Two table on goal difference, the highest position they have reached in the history of the club.

SALFORD CITY – SKY BET LEAGUE TWO 2024–25 LEAGUE RECORD

Match No.	Date	Venue	Opponents	Result		H/T Score	Lg Pos.	Goalscorers	Attendance
1	Aug 10	H	Port Vale	L	0-2	0-1	21		3318
2	17	A	Bradford C	D	0-0	0-0	19		16,183
3	24	A	Chesterfield	D	1-1	0-0	20	N''Mai [86]	8334
4	Sept 2	H	Milton Keynes D	W	1-0	1-0	14	Okoronkwo [42]	2227
5	14	H	Cheltenham T	W	2-1	0-0	13	Adelakun 2 [60, 86]	2347
6	21	H	Walsall	L	0-2	0-0	15		2860
7	27	A	Tranmere R	D	0-0	0-0	13		7281
8	Oct 1	A	Newport Co	L	1-3	0-2	20	Stockton [81]	3552
9	5	H	AFC Wimbledon	W	1-0	0-0	15	Luamba [84]	2627
10	12	H	Grimsby T	L	1-2	1-2	16	Stockton [15]	3608
11	19	A	Crewe Alex	D	1-1	1-1	18	Woodburn [12]	4936
12	22	A	Swindon T	W	2-1	1-0	15	N''Mai [3], Taylor [69]	2145
13	26	A	Colchester U	W	2-1	0-0	13	N''Mai [61], Kouassi [76]	3936
14	29	H	Fleetwood T	D	2-2	1-1	12	Woodburn [18], Okoronkwo [90]	2549
15	Nov 9	H	Carlisle U	L	0-1	0-0	13		3737
16	16	A	Doncaster R	D	1-1	0-0	14	Kouassi [50]	7280
17	Dec 3	H	Harrogate T	W	2-0	1-0	11	Woodburn [10], Stockton [72]	1838
18	7	A	Gillingham	L	0-1	0-0	12		5296
19	14	H	Notts Co	W	3-0	2-0	12	McAleny [14], Stockton 2 [31, 54]	2768
20	21	A	Accrington S	W	2-0	0-0	11	Mnoga [48], Stockton [85]	2350
21	26	H	Barrow	W	3-0	2-0	9	Garbutt [21], Fornah [33], Kouassi [80]	2983
22	29	H	Morecambe	W	1-0	0-0	6	Lund [47]	3179
23	Jan 1	A	Harrogate T	W	2-0	1-0	3	Stockton [39], Lund [56]	2814
24	4	A	Milton Keynes D	W	1-0	1-0	2	Adelakun [34]	5934
25	18	H	Fleetwood T	L	0-2	0-2	7		3216
26	25	A	Cheltenham T	L	1-2	0-1	8	Tilt [90]	4187
27	28	H	Newport Co	D	1-1	1-1	8	Adelakun (pen) [31]	1952
28	Feb 1	A	Walsall	D	2-2	1-0	8	Stockton [4], Adelakun [75]	5970
29	4	H	Bromley	D	3-3	0-2	8	Warrington [62], Lund [77], Stockton [90]	2112
30	8	H	Tranmere R	W	2-0	0-0	7	Adelakun 2 [51, 61]	3097
31	15	A	AFC Wimbledon	L	0-1	0-0	8		7739
32	22	A	Port Vale	L	1-2	0-1	9	Adelakun (pen) [77]	6823
33	Mar 1	H	Bradford C	L	1-2	1-0	9	Okoronkwo [30]	3656
34	4	A	Swindon T	D	2-2	1-1	11	Adelakun [27], N''Mai [72]	6465
35	8	H	Crewe Alex	D	1-1	0-0	11	N''Mai [68]	3524
36	11	H	Chesterfield	L	0-4	0-2	11		2289
37	15	A	Grimsby T	W	1-0	0-0	10	Lund [82]	6398
38	29	A	Bromley	W	3-2	2-1	10	Stockton 2 [16, 62], N''Mai [28]	2658
39	Apr 1	A	Barrow	D	1-1	0-1	11	Stanway (og) [69]	2818
40	5	H	Gillingham	D	2-2	2-2	11	Stockton [8], N''Mai [15]	2914
41	11	A	Notts Co	W	3-1	1-0	9	Stockton [45], N''Mai [53], Garbutt [77]	9643
42	15	H	Doncaster R	D	1-1	1-1	10	Garbutt [27]	3030
43	18	A	Accrington S	L	1-2	0-1	10	Adelakun (pen) [70]	2945
44	21	H	Morecambe	W	3-1	2-0	9	Ashley [3], Stockton [41], N''Mai [86]	3027
45	26	H	Colchester U	W	4-1	3-0	7	Adelakun 2 (2 pens) [2, 56], Shephard [21], Stockton [24]	3150
46	May 3	A	Carlisle U	D	2-2	1-2	8	Stockton [36], Adelakun [62]	8128

Final League Position: 8

GOALSCORERS

League (64): Stockton 16, Adelakun 13 (5 pens), N''Mai 9, Lund 4, Garbutt 3, Kouassi 3, Okoronkwo 3, Woodburn 3, Ashley 1, Fornah 1, Luamba 1, McAleny 1, Mnoga 1, Shephard 1, Taylor 1, Tilt 1, Warrington 1, own goal 1.
FA Cup (4): Lund 2, Okoronkwo 1, Stockton 1 (1 pen).
Carabao Cup (0).
Vertu Trophy (4): Davies 2, McAleny 1, Stockton 1.

Jones J 26	Olopade T 1	Negru S 26+4	Tilt C 32+5	Garbutt L 40+1	Ashley O 31+2	Humbles L 1	Taylor J 13+15	N'Mai K 28+4	McAleny C 11+16	Stockton C 32+6	Chesters D 5+2	Dackers M —+3	Woodburn B 27+6	Lund M 14+23	Luamba J 3+7	Fornah T 39+1	Edwards T 10+9	Austerfield J 12+9	Okoronkwo F 11+11	Adelakun R 23+7	Watson R 8+10	Kouassi K 16+11	Mnoga H 33+6	Shephard L 20+2	Malcolm K —+2	Berkoe K 8+7	Young M 20	Longelo R 8+8	Warrington L 8+8	Wright W —+2	Curran-Nicholls J —+1	Match No.
1	2	3	4	5	6^4	7	8^1	9^5	10^3	11^2	12	13	14	15	16																	1
1		3	4	5	6^5		14	10^1	12	11^3	2	15	9^2	13	8^4	7	16															2
1		3	4^4	5	6^1		13	16	10^2	11^4	14	15	9			8^3	7	2^5	12													3
1		3			8	6				11^3	5^4		9^2			7	2	4	10^1	12	13	14	15									4
1		3			8	7^1		12	16	11^2	5		9^5			6	2^4	4	10^3	14		13	15									5
1		3	4^4	5			12	14	16	6^2			9^3			8		7^5	13	11		10	15	2^1								6
1		2	3	4	13			8	11^3				14			7		6	12		9^1	10	5^2									7
1		3^4	4	5	16		15	10	8^1	14			12			13	9		6^2	7^3		11^5	2									8
1		3	15	8	6^3		5^2	9^4	14	11^1			13	7		4	12			10		2										9
1		3		4	6		5^1	8	9^2	11^3			14	15	13		7^4	12			10	2										10
1		3	8	7			5	13					9^1	14	12	6		4^3	11^2			10	2									11
1		3	4	6			12	8	14	10^4	5^1		9^2	15		7^5	2		11^3			13	16									12
1		14	4	5	7^2		13	6^5					10^3	12	16	9		8	15			11^4	2	3^1								13
1		3	4	12	6^4		5^3	8		10^1			9	14		7	2^2	13	15			11	2									14
1		2^5	3	4	7		9^1			13	16			15		8		5^3	10^2		11	6^4	14	12								15
1		2	3	4	9		8^4	13					11^2	6^3			7	15			10	5^1	12		14							16
		3	4	7				9^3	15	13			11^2	6^4		8	12				10	5	2^1		14	1						17
		3	4	7				9	13	10			11^1	6		8	2				12	5^2				1						18
		3		4	6		15	8^1	10^2	11^3			9		14^7			13				5^4	2		12	1						19
		3		4	6		15	8^1	10^2	11^4			9^3			7				12	14	13	5	2		1						20
		3^2	13	4	6		12		10	11^4				9^3		7^4	16			14	17	15	5^1	2		8^5	1					21
		14	3	4	6		5^3	13	11^4				12	8^1			9		7^2	10		2		15	1							22
		3	14	4	7^4		9^2			11^5			10^1	6		8	2^3			13	15	12	5		16	1						23
		15	3	4	5		13		16	11^2			12	8			10^5	7^1	14	6^3	2	9^4	1									24
		3	4		5^3			9^2	10				6	7				13	11^8	12	2	14			1	8^1						25
		12	3	4			13	10^3	11				15	8			14	7^4		6^1	2			1	9^2	5						26
1		3	4				9^1		13				6	8^4			11	14	10^2	15	2		5^4		12	7^3						27
1		3	4				17		13	10^4			7			12		16	11^5	8	15	6	2^1		14		9^3	5^2				28
1		3	4^4				5		9^1	10			6					15	11	7^3	14	2			8^2		13	12				29
1		3	15	4			6^4		16	10^3			7^2	8				12	9^5	14	11^1	2		13			5					30
1		3	4				6^3			10^1			7^4	8	16		13	11	15	12	2			9^2		14	5^5					31
1		2	3	4^2			6^3			10^1			7	8			9		11	5				13				12	14			32
1		4	3				12	13					15	7		8		10^3	11	6^4	2			5^3		9^1		14				33
1		3						9					7^1	12		13	14	15	10	11	8^2	2			4^3		6^4	5				34
1		3		4	6^2								9^1	12		7	2		10	11							5	13				35
1		3	15	4			16	9^5	14				7^1	12		8	2^4	13	11^3	10^8							6	5^2				36
		3	4					9					7^2	12		8	14	10^1	11^3		6	2			1	13	5					37
		3	4	6				8		10			9^1	12		7^2			11^3		5	2			1	13	14					38
		3	4	6^1				8		10			13	9^2		7			11		5	2			1		12					39
		3	4	6				11					9^1	12		7	13		8		5	2^2			1							40
		3	4	6^2				11		10^4			9^1	13		7		14	8^3		5	2^1			1	15	12					41
		3^3	4	6				10^2		11			9^3	13		7	12	14	8		5	2^1			1							42
		4	6				14	10		11^3			9^2	7	3^1		8		2			1			5	13						43
		3	6^5				15	11		10^3			9^4	14		7	13	2		8^2	16		5^1		4	1	12					44
		3	4	6^1				11^3	16	10			9^5	13		7		15	8	14		5^2	2^4			1		12				45
		3	4^2	6^1				10	14	11			9^3	15		7		13^4	8			5	2			1		12				46

FA Cup
First Round — Shrewsbury T — (h) 2-1
Second Round — Cheltenham T — (h) 2-0
Third Round — Manchester C — (a) 0-8

Carabao Cup
First Round — Doncaster R — (h) 0-2

Vertu Trophy
Group B (N) — Port Vale — (h) 0-2
Group B (N) — Wrexham — (a) 1-2
Group B (N) — Wolverhampton W U21 — (h) 3-2

SHEFFIELD UNITED

FOUNDATION

In March 1889, Yorkshire County Cricket Club formed Sheffield United six days after an FA Cup semi-final between Preston North End and West Bromwich Albion had finally convinced Charles Stokes, a member of the cricket club, that the formation of a professional football club would prove successful at Bramall Lane. The United's first secretary, Mr J. B. Wostinholm, was also secretary of the cricket club.

Bramall Lane Ground, Cherry Street, Bramall Lane, Sheffield, South Yorkshire S2 4SU.

Telephone: (0114) 253 7200.

Ticket Office: (0114) 253 7200 (option 1).

Website: www.sufc.co.uk

Email: info@sufc.co.uk

Ground Capacity: 32,050.

Record Attendance: 68,287 v Leeds U, FA Cup 5th rd, 15 February 1936.

Pitch Measurements: 101m × 68m (110.5yd × 74.5yd).

Co-Chairmen: Steven Rosen, Helmy Eltoukhy.

Chief Executive Officer: Stephen Bettis.

Manager: Ruben Selles.

Assistant Manager: James Oliver-Pearce.

Colours: Red and white striped shirts with black pinstripes and black and yellow trim, black shorts with red and yellow trim, black socks with red and yellow trim.

Year Formed: 1889.

Turned Professional: 1889.

Club Nickname: 'The Blades'.

Ground: 1889, Bramall Lane.

First Football League Game: 3 September 1892, Division 2, v Lincoln C (h) W 4–2 – Lilley; Witham, Cain; Howell, Hendry, Needham (1); Wallace, Dobson, Hammond (3), Davies, Drummond.

Record League Victory: 10–0 v Burslem Port Vale (a), Division 2, 10 December 1892 – Howlett; Witham, Lilley; Howell, Hendry, Needham; Drummond (1), Wallace (1), Hammond (4), Davies (2), Watson (2). 10–0 v Burnley, Division 1 (h), 19 January 1929.

Record Cup Victory: 6–0 v Leyton Orient (h), FA Cup 1st rd, 6 November 2016 – Ramsdale; Basham (1), O'Connell, Wright, Freeman (1), Coutts (Whiteman), Duffy (Brooks), Fleck, Lafferty, Scougall (1) (Lavery), Chapman (3).

Record Defeat: 0–13 v Bolton W, FA Cup 2nd rd, 1 February 1890.

Most League Points (2 for a win): 60, Division 2, 1952–53.

Most League Points (3 for a win): 100, FL 1, 2016–17.

HONOURS

League Champions: Division 1 – 1897–98; Division 2 – 1952–53; FL 1 – 2016–17; Division 4 – 1981–82. *Runners-up:* Division 1 – 1896–97, 1899–1900; FL C – 2005–06, 2018–19, 2022–23; Division 2 – 1892–93, 1938–39, 1960–61, 1970–71, 1989–90; Division 3 – 1988–89.

FA Cup Winners: 1899, 1902, 1915, 1925. *Runners-up:* 1901, 1936.

League Cup: semi-final – 2003, 2015.

FOOTBALL YEARBOOK FACT FILE

Sheffield United pulled off something of a coup by signing attacking midfield player Alejandro (Alex) Sabella from Argentinian club River Plate in the summer of 1978. Part of the deal was that the clubs should play each other in a friendly match at Bramall Lane and this took place on 30 August. The visitors, who included four members of the Argentina team that had recently won the World Cup, won 2-1. Alan Woodward scored for the Blades in front of a crowd of 22,244.

Most League Goals: 102, Division 1, 1925–26.

Highest League Scorer in Season: Jimmy Dunne, 41, Division 1, 1930–31.

Most League Goals in Total Aggregate: Harry Johnson, 201, 1919–30.

Most League Goals in One Match: 5, Harry Hammond v Bootle, Division 2, 26 November 1892; 5, Harry Johnson v West Ham U, Division 1, 26 December 1927.

Most Capped Player: John Egan, 34 (36), Republic of Ireland.

Most League Appearances: Joe Shaw, 632, 1948–66.

Youngest League Player: Louis Reed, 16 years 257 days v Rotherham U, 8 April 2014.

Record Transfer Fee Received: £24,000,000 (potentially rising to £30,000,000) from Arsenal for Aaron Ramsdale, August 2021.

Record Transfer Fee Paid: £23,500,000 to Liverpool for Rhian Brewster, October 2020.

Football League Record: 1892 Elected to Division 2; 1892–93 Division 2; 1893–1934 Division 1; 1934–39 Division 2; 1946–49 Division 1; 1949–53 Division 2; 1953–56 Division 1; 1956–61 Division 2; 1961–68 Division 1; 1968–71 Division 2; 1971–76 Division 1; 1976–79 Division 2; 1979–81 Division 3; 1981–82 Division 4; 1982–84 Division 3; 1984–88 Division 2; 1988–89 Division 3; 1989–90 Division 2; 1990–92 Division 1; 1992–94 Premier League; 1994–2004 First Division; 2004–06 FL C; 2006–07 Premier League; 2007–11 FL C; 2011–17 FL 1; 2017–19 FL C; 2019–21 Premier League; 2021–23 FL C; 2023–24 Premier League; 2024– FL C.

LATEST SEQUENCES

Longest Sequence of League Wins: 8, 28.3.2017 – 5.8.2017.

Longest Sequence of League Defeats: 8, 24.10.2020 – 17.12.2020.

Longest Sequence of League Draws: 6, 6.5.2001 – 8.9.2001.

Longest Sequence of Unbeaten League Matches: 22, 2.9.1899 – 13.1.1900.

Longest Sequence Without a League Win: 20, 16.7.2020 – 2.1.2021.

Successive Scoring Runs: 34 from 30.3.1956.

Successive Non-scoring Runs: 6 from 4.12.1993.

MANAGERS

J. B. Wostinholm 1889–99
  (Secretary-Manager)
John Nicholson 1899–1932
Ted Davison 1932–52
Reg Freeman 1952–55
Joe Mercer 1955–58
Johnny Harris 1959–68
  *(continued as General Manager
  to 1970)*
Arthur Rowley 1968–69
Johnny Harris *(General Manager
  resumed Team Manager duties)*
  1969–73
Ken Furphy 1973–75
Jimmy Sirrel 1975–77
Harry Haslam 1978–81
Martin Peters 1981
Ian Porterfield 1981–86
Billy McEwan 1986–88
Dave Bassett 1988–95
Howard Kendall 1995–97
Nigel Spackman 1997–98
Steve Bruce 1998–99
Adrian Heath 1999
Neil Warnock 1999–2007
Bryan Robson 2007–08
Kevin Blackwell 2008–10
Gary Speed 2010
Micky Adams 2010–11
Danny Wilson 2011–13
David Weir 2013
Nigel Clough 2013–15
Nigel Adkins 2015–16
Chris Wilder 2016–21
Paul Heckingbottom 2021
Slavisa Jokanovic 2021
Paul Heckingbottom 2021–23
Chris Wilder 2023–25
Ruben Selles June 2025–

TEN YEAR LEAGUE RECORD

		P	W	D	L	F	A	Pts	Pos
2015-16	FL 1	46	18	12	16	64	59	66	11
2016-17	FL 1	46	30	10	6	92	47	100	1
2017-18	FL C	46	20	9	17	62	55	69	10
2018-19	FL C	46	26	11	9	78	41	89	2
2019-20	PR Lge	38	14	12	12	39	39	54	9
2020-21	PR Lge	38	7	2	29	20	63	23	20
2021-22	FL C	46	21	12	13	63	45	75	5
2022-23	FL C	46	28	7	11	73	39	91	2
2023-24	PR Lge	38	3	7	28	35	104	16	20
2024-25	FL C	46	28	8	10	63	36	90*	3

*2 pts deducted.

DID YOU KNOW ?

Sheffield United wore the city's coat of arms on their shirts for the first time in the home game against Sunderland on 5 February 1966. The badge remained in place through until the end of the 1976–77 season before being replaced by a newly designed club crest.

SHEFFIELD UNITED – SKY BET CHAMPIONSHIP 2024–25 LEAGUE RECORD

Match No.	Date	Venue	Opponents	Result		H/T Score	Lg Pos.	Goalscorers	Attendance
1	Aug 9	A	Preston NE	W	2-0	1-0	2	Arblaster [12], Hamer [55]	17,948
2	17	H	QPR	D	2-2	2-0	4	Hamer [6], Moore [13]	27,527
3	24	A	Norwich C	D	1-1	1-1	6	Arblaster [31]	26,373
4	Sept 1	H	Watford	W	1-0	1-0	6	Bachmann (og) [2]	26,914
5	13	A	Hull C	W	2-0	1-0	2	Hamer [15], McCallum [66]	22,403
6	21	H	Derby Co	W	1-0	0-0	3	Hamer [53]	28,685
7	28	A	Portsmouth	D	0-0	0-0	4		20,330
8	Oct 2	H	Swansea C	W	1-0	1-0	2	Tymon (og) [44]	25,112
9	5	H	Luton T	W	2-0	1-0	1	Rak-Sakyi 2 [12, 52]	27,925
10	18	A	Leeds U	L	0-2	0-0	1		36,695
11	23	A	Middlesbrough	L	0-1	0-0	4		24,303
12	26	H	Stoke C	W	2-0	1-0	2	Moore [14], Campbell [50]	28,575
13	Nov 2	A	Blackburn R	W	2-0	1-0	2	Burrows [16], Campbell [64]	16,810
14	5	A	Bristol C	W	2-1	0-0	1	One [86], Burrows [90]	18,736
15	10	H	Sheffield Wed	W	1-0	0-0	1	Campbell [50]	31,127
16	23	A	Coventry C	D	2-2	2-1	1	Campbell [13], Rak-Sakyi [34]	28,057
17	26	H	Oxford U	W	3-0	2-0	1	O'Hare [10], Campbell [26], Rak-Sakyi [58]	25,574
18	29	H	Sunderland	W	1-0	0-0	1	Davies T [83]	28,465
19	Dec 8	A	WBA	D	2-2	2-1	1	O'Hare [35], Campbell [37]	24,930
20	11	A	Millwall	W	1-0	1-0	1	Brewster [42]	12,734
21	14	H	Plymouth Arg	W	2-0	1-0	1	Hamer [19], Moore (pen) [88]	27,237
22	21	A	Cardiff C	W	2-0	0-0	1	Moore 2 [65, 73]	18,312
23	26	H	Burnley	L	0-2	0-1	1		30,580
24	29	H	WBA	D	1-1	1-1	2	Brooks [23]	29,123
25	Jan 1	A	Sunderland	L	1-2	1-2	2	O'Nien (og) [32]	42,276
26	4	A	Watford	W	2-1	1-1	1	Hamer [13], Brooks [53]	19,937
27	18	H	Norwich C	W	2-0	1-0	1	Burrows 2 (1 pen) [22, 59 (p)]	28,239
28	21	A	Swansea C	W	2-1	0-1	1	Brewster [47], Burrows (pen) [68]	13,373
29	24	H	Hull C	L	0-3	0-1	1		27,448
30	Feb 1	A	Derby Co	W	1-0	0-0	2	Brereton [49]	29,472
31	8	H	Portsmouth	W	3-1	1-1	2	Hamer [24], Rak-Sakyi [73]	29,104
32	12	H	Middlesbrough	W	3-1	1-1	2	Rak-Sakyi [32], Brereton [75], Ahmedhodzic [87]	27,124
33	15	A	Luton T	W	1-0	0-0	1	Ahmedhodzic [79]	11,461
34	24	H	Leeds U	L	1-3	1-0	2	Meslier (og) [14]	29,702
35	Mar 1	A	QPR	W	2-1	1-0	2	Brereton [10], Campbell [54]	17,346
36	8	H	Preston NE	W	1-0	0-0	1	Campbell [56]	27,136
37	11	H	Bristol C	D	1-1	0-0	1	Campbell [61]	25,070
38	16	A	Sheffield Wed	W	1-0	0-0	1	Brewster [64]	33,827
39	28	H	Coventry C	W	3-1	2-0	1	Hamer [19], Campbell [30], Brewster [62]	30,803
40	Apr 5	A	Oxford U	L	0-1	0-1	1		11,496
41	8	H	Millwall	L	0-1	0-1	3		25,775
42	12	A	Plymouth Arg	L	1-2	1-0	3	Rak-Sakyi [44]	16,565
43	18	H	Cardiff C	W	2-0	1-0	3	Hamer [33], Brereton [87]	28,201
44	21	A	Burnley	L	1-2	1-2	3	Cannon [37]	21,486
45	25	A	Stoke C	W	2-0	1-0	3	McCallum [38], Brooks [87]	24,460
46	May 3	H	Blackburn R	D	1-1	0-0	3	Ahmedhodzic [59]	30,556

Final League Position: 3

GOALSCORERS

League (63): Campbell 10, Hamer 9, Rak-Sakyi 7, Burrows 5 (2 pens), Moore 5 (1 pen), Brereton 4, Brewster 4, Ahmedhodzic 3, Brooks 3, Arblaster 2, McCallum 2, O'Hare 2, Cannon 1, Davies T 1, One 1, own goals 4.
FA Cup (0).
Carabao Cup (4): Ben Slimane 1, Marsh 1, Trusty 1, own goal 1.
Championship Play-offs (7): O'Hare 2, Brooks 1, Burrows 1 (1 pen), Campbell 1, Hamer 1, Moore 1.

Davies A 3	Gilchrist A 27+3	Robinson J 31+3	Ahmedhodzic A 35+3	Burrows H 39+4	O'Hare C 38+6	Arblaster O 11+1	Hamer G 36+5	Brooks A 10+12	Vinicius Souza C 32+3	Moore K 18+9	Seriki F 8+17	Ben Slimane A —+3	Brewster R 16+20	Peck S 32+10	Soutar H 20+1	Rak-Sakyi J 22+12	Cooper M 43	Trusty A 1	Campbell T 20+13	Sachdev S —+1	Shackleton J 2+10	McCallum S 9+24	Norrington-Davies R 2+12	One R 2+10	Davies T 6+7	Baptiste J —+1	Brereton B 13+4	Blacker B —+1	Cannon T 7+8	Clarke H 6	Choudhury H 13+3	Holding R 4+6	Match No.
1	2^1	3	4	5	6^4	7	8^2	9^3	10	11	12		13	14	15																		1
1	2^1	4	3^4	5	10^2	7	9	6^3	8^5	11		13	15	14	12	16																	2
	2^4			5	10^1	8	9^3	6^2	7	11	13			3	12	1		4	14	15													3
	2^1	4	5	10^3	8	9	7	11^4		14	15	3	6^2	1			12	13															4
	2^4	4	5	10^2	8	9^3	12	7	11^5	15	13	3	6^1	1			16	14															5
	2^1	4	5	9^3		10^4	13	6	11^5	12	14	7	3	8^2	1			15	16														6
	2^3	4	5	9^2	10	12	6	11^4	14	13	7	3	8^1	1		15																	7
13		4	5	9^5		10^4	8^2	7	12		15	6	3	14	1		11^1		2^3		16												8
	2^5	4		10	7	13	12	6	11^4		9^1	3	8^2	1			15	16	5^5	14													9
12		2	9	10^1	8	7^3		5^5	11			16	14	3			13		6^2		4^4												10
	2^5	4		10^2	7	12	16		11^4			9	8^1	3	6		1		10^1	15	14	5^5	13										11
	2^3	4	5	9^4	8		13	7	11^5		12	16	3	6^2	1		10^1		15	14													12
	2^5	4		5	9^2	8	14	13	7	11^4	15	10^1	3	6^3	1		12		16														13
	2^5	4	5	9	12	10	6^2	7	13^4	16		8^3	3	14	1		11^1		15														14
	2^1	16	4	5^5	9	7^2	10	6		12		13	3	8^2	1		11^3		15		14												15
	2	12	4^4	5^3	9^4		10^5	6		13		7	3	8^2	1		11^1		16	14	15												16
		4			9		10^3	12	7		2		6^4	3	8^2	1		11^1	15	5^5	14	13	16										17
	2	4		5^4	9^1		10^6	7		12			6	3^3	8^2	1		11^3		16	15	14	13										18
3	4		5	9^4	10	6		2^3	13	7		11^3	7	8^2	1		11^1		15	14	12												19
	2	4	5	9	10^4		6^1	13		11^3	7	3	8^2	1		15	14		12														20
	2	4	5^2	9^4	10		14		15	6	3	8^1	1	13	12	16	11^3	7^5															21
	2^3	4^4	5	9	10		11^2	12	7	3	8^1	1	13	14		6	15																22
	2^2	4	13	5^4	8^5	10	14	6^1	11	9^3	7	3		1	16	15	12																23
	2	4	3	5	9	10	8^2	11	12	7^1		1	13		6																		24
	2^1	4	3	13	8^4	10	12	11	9	7^2		1	5^3	15	14	6																	25
	2	4	3	5	9	10^2	8^3			12	7		1	13	14	11^1	6																26
	2^1	4	3	5	8	9		12	11	7		1	14	10^2	13	6^3																	27
	2^1	4	3	7	9^5	10	8^2		13	11^4	6		1	14^5	5^3		15	16															28
	2^4	4	3	7	9	8^3	13		12	6	15	1	14	5^1		10^2	11																29
		4	3	5	9^1		6		8^3	15	13	1	12	14	10^2	11^4	2	7															30
		4	3	5^3	9		10	8		15	14	13	1	11^1	12	6^4	10^5	2	7^2	16													31
		4	3	5	9		10^3	7		6^4	8^2	1	12	14		15	13	11^1	2	16													32
		4	3	15	16		6			9^2	13	8^1	1	11^4	5^3	14	10^5		2	7	12												33
		4	3	5	9^5	14		7	16	6		8^2	1	11^3		15	10^4	13	2^1	12													34
		4	3	5	9^4	10^1	7		12	13	6	1	11^3	15		8^5	14	2^2	16														35
		4	3	5	9^5	10^4		6^1	12	7		14^1	11^3	15		8^2	13	2	16														36
		4	16	5	9^1	13		14	2^4	12	7	8^2	1	11^3	15	10	6	3^6															37
		4	3	5	13	10^3		2	9^2	7		1	11^1	14	8^4	12	6	15															38
15		4	3	5	12	10	14		2^4	9^1	6	1	11^2	16	8^3	13	7^5																39
		4	3	5	16	10		12	14	2	9^6	7^4	13	1	11^3	8^2	15	6^1															40
		4	3	5	13	10		14	2^5	9^4	7	12	1	11^2	8^1	15	6^3	16															41
		4	3	5	10	9	7^4	13	14	6^6		8^1	1	16	12	11^3	2^2	15															42
	16	3	5	13	10^6		7	12	15	9^1	6	8^3	1	11^2	14		2	4^4															43
		4	3	5^4	9		8^3	11	14	16	7^5	13	1	12	15	6^1	10^2	2															44
	4	16	12	9^6		15	7	11	2^1	6^4	14		1	10^2	5^3	13	8	3															45
1	2^1		4	16	9		10^2	8	6^3		12	13	7		5^5	15	14	11^4	3														46

FA Cup

Third Round	Cardiff C	(h)	0-1

Carabao Cup

First Round	Wrexham	(h)	4-2
Second Round	Barnsley	(a)	0-1

Championship Play-offs

Semi-Final 1st leg	Bristol C	(a)	3-0
Semi-Final 2nd leg	Bristol C	(h)	3-0
Final	Sunderland	(Wembley)	1-2

SHEFFIELD WEDNESDAY

FOUNDATION

Sheffield being one of the principal centres of early Association Football, this club was formed as long ago as 1867 by the Sheffield Wednesday Cricket Club (formed 1825) and their colours from the start were blue and white. The inaugural meeting was held at the Adelphi Hotel and the original committee included Charles Stokes who was subsequently a founder member of Sheffield United.

Hillsborough Stadium, Hillsborough, Sheffield, South Yorkshire S6 1SW.

Telephone: (0370) 020 1867.

Ticket Office: (0370) 020 1867.

Website: www.swfc.co.uk

Email: enquiries@swfc.co.uk

Ground Capacity: 34,945.

Record Attendance: 72,841 v Manchester C, FA Cup 5th rd, 17 February 1934.

Pitch Measurements: 105m × 68m (115yd × 74.5yd).

Chairman: Dejphon Chansiri.

General Manager: Alastair Wilson.

Manager: Danny Rohl.

Assistant Manager: Henrik Pedersen.

Colours: Blue and white striped shirts with blue trim, black shorts, black socks with blue and yellow trim.

Year Formed: 1867 (fifth oldest League club).

Turned Professional: 1887.

Previous Name: The Wednesday until 1929.

Club Nickname: 'The Owls'.

Grounds: 1867, Highfield; 1869, Myrtle Road; 1877, Sheaf House; 1887, Olive Grove; 1899, Owlerton (since 1912 known as Hillsborough). Some games were played at Endcliffe in the 1880s. Until 1895 Bramall Lane was used for some games.

First Football League Game: 3 September 1892, Division 1, v Notts Co (a) W 1–0 – Allan; Tom Brandon (1), Mumford; Hall, Betts, Harry Brandon; Spiksley, Brady, Davis, Bob Brown, Dunlop.

Record League Victory: 9–1 v Birmingham, Division 1, 13 December 1930 – Brown; Walker, Blenkinsop; Strange, Leach, Wilson; Hooper (3), Seed (2), Ball (2), Burgess (1), Rimmer (1).

Record Cup Victory: 12–0 v Halliwell, FA Cup 1st rd, 17 January 1891 – Smith; Thompson, Brayshaw; Harry Brandon (1), Betts, Cawley (2); Winterbottom, Mumford (2), Bob Brandon (1), Woolhouse (5), Ingram (1).

Record Defeat: 0–10 v Aston Villa, Division 1, 5 October 1912.

Most League Points (2 for a win): 62, Division 2, 1958–59.

HONOURS

League Champions: Division 1 – 1902–03, 1903–04, 1928–29, 1929–30; Division 2 – 1899–1900, 1925–26, 1951–52, 1955–56, 1958–59.
Runners-up: Division 1 – 1960–61; Division 2 – 1949–50, 1983–84; FL 1 – 2011–12.
FA Cup Winners: 1896, 1907, 1935.
Runners-up: 1890, 1966, 1993.
League Cup Winners: 1991.
Runners-up: 1993.

European Competitions
Fairs Cup: 1961–62 *(qf)*, 1963–64.
UEFA Cup: 1992–93.
Intertoto Cup: 1995.

FOOTBALL YEARBOOK FACT FILE

England played their first-ever European Championship fixture at Sheffield Wednesday's Hillsborough ground in October 1962. The ground was chosen as Wembley was undergoing extensive refurbishment at the time. England, including the Owls' goalkeeper Ron Springett, drew 1-1 with France in front of a crowd of 35,380.

Most League Points (3 for a win): 96, FL 1, 2022–23.

Most League Goals: 106, Division 2, 1958–59.

Highest League Scorer in Season: Derek Dooley, 46, Division 2, 1951–52.

Most League Goals in Total Aggregate: Andrew Wilson, 199, 1900–20.

Most League Goals in One Match: 6, Doug Hunt v Norwich C, Division 2, 19 November 1938.

Most Capped Player: Nigel Worthington, 50 (66), Northern Ireland.

Most League Appearances: Andrew Wilson, 501, 1900–20.

Youngest League Player: Peter Fox, 15 years 269 days v Orient, 31 March 1973.

Record Transfer Fee Received: £5,000,000 from Reading for Lucas Joao, August 2019.

Record Transfer Fee Paid: £10,000,000 to Middlesbrough for Jordan Rhodes, July 2017.

Football League Record: 1892 Elected to Division 1; 1892–99 Division 1; 1899–1900 Division 2; 1900–20 Division 1; 1920–26 Division 2; 1926–37 Division 1; 1937–50 Division 2; 1950–51 Division 1; 1951–52 Division 2; 1952–55 Division 1; 1955–56 Division 2; 1956–58 Division 1; 1958–59 Division 2; 1959–70 Division 1; 1970–75 Division 2; 1975–80 Division 3; 1980–84 Division 2; 1984–90 Division 1; 1990–91 Division 2; 1991–92 Division 1; 1992–2000 Premier League; 2000–03 First Division; 2003–04 Second Division; 2004–05 FL 1; 2005–10 FL C; 2010–12 FL 1; 2012–21 FL C; 2021–23 FL 1; 2023– FL C.

LATEST SEQUENCES

Longest Sequence of League Wins: 9, 23.4.1904 – 15.10.1904.

Longest Sequence of League Defeats: 8, 9.9.2000 – 17.10.2000.

Longest Sequence of League Draws: 7, 15.3.2008 – 14.4.2008.

Longest Sequence of Unbeaten League Matches: 23, 8.10.2022 – 17.3.2023.

Longest Sequence Without a League Win: 20, 11.1.1975 – 30.8.1975.

Successive Scoring Runs: 40 from 14.11.1959.

Successive Non-scoring Runs: 8 from 8.3.1975.

MANAGERS

Arthur Dickinson 1891–1920
(Secretary-Manager)
Robert Brown 1920–33
Billy Walker 1933–37
Jimmy McMullan 1937–42
Eric Taylor 1942–58
(continued as General Manager to 1974)
Harry Catterick 1958–61
Vic Buckingham 1961–64
Alan Brown 1964–68
Jack Marshall 1968–69
Danny Williams 1969–71
Derek Dooley 1971–73
Steve Burtenshaw 1974–75
Len Ashurst 1975–77
Jackie Charlton 1977–83
Howard Wilkinson 1983–88
Peter Eustace 1988–89
Ron Atkinson 1989–91
Trevor Francis 1991–95
David Pleat 1995–97
Ron Atkinson 1997–98
Danny Wilson 1998–2000
Peter Shreeves *(Acting)* 2000
Paul Jewell 2000–01
Peter Shreeves 2001
Terry Yorath 2001–02
Chris Turner 2002–04
Paul Sturrock 2004–06
Brian Laws 2006–09
Alan Irvine 2010–11
Gary Megson 2011–12
Dave Jones 2012–13
Stuart Gray 2013–15
Carlos Carvalhal 2015–18
Jos Luhukay 2018
Steve Bruce 2019
Garry Monk 2019–20
Tony Pulis 2020
Darren Moore 2021–23
Xisco Muñoz 2023
Danny Rohl October 2023–

TEN YEAR LEAGUE RECORD

		P	W	D	L	F	A	Pts	Pos
2015-16	FL C	46	19	17	10	66	45	74	6
2016-17	FL C	46	24	9	13	60	45	81	4
2017-18	FL C	46	14	15	17	59	60	57	15
2018-19	FL C	46	16	16	14	60	62	64	12
2019-20	FL C	46	15	11	20	58	66	56	16
2020-21	FL C	46	12	11	23	40	61	41*	24
2021-22	FL 1	46	24	13	9	78	50	85	4
2022-23	FL 1	46	28	12	6	81	37	96	3
2023-24	FL C	46	15	8	23	44	68	53	20
2024-25	FL C	46	15	13	18	60	69	58	12

*6 pts deducted.

DID YOU KNOW ?

Sheffield Wednesday did not enter the Football League Cup until the 1966–67 season. After receiving a bye in the first round they were drawn at home to Rotherham United. The Owls went down to a 1-0 defeat thanks to a last-minute goal in front of a crowd of 20,943, the vast majority of whom chose to sit in the stands.

SHEFFIELD WEDNESDAY – SKY BET CHAMPIONSHIP 2024–25 LEAGUE RECORD

Match No.	Date	Venue	Opponents	Result	H/T Score	Lg Pos.	Goalscorers	Attendance
1	Aug 11	H	Plymouth Arg	W 4-0	1-0	1	Lowe J [35], Galloway (og) [52], Windass [82], Smith [90]	29,535
2	18	A	Sunderland	L 0-4	0-3	10		40,022
3	23	H	Leeds U	L 0-2	0-1	14		28,800
4	31	A	Millwall	L 0-3	0-0	20		14,905
5	Sept 14	H	QPR	D 1-1	0-0	20	Bannan [90]	26,283
6	21	A	Luton T	L 1-2	0-0	21	Bannan [52]	11,805
7	28	H	WBA	W 3-2	2-0	18	Furlong (og) [9], Windass [23], Musaba [86]	26,308
8	Oct 2	A	Bristol C	D 0-0	0-0	19		20,293
9	5	A	Coventry C	W 2-1	1-1	15	Gassama [45], Charles S [90]	28,571
10	19	H	Burnley	L 0-2	0-1	18		28,105
11	22	H	Swansea C	D 0-0	0-0	17		22,452
12	25	A	Portsmouth	W 2-1	0-1	11	Windass [55], Smith [70]	20,262
13	Nov 2	H	Watford	L 2-6	1-1	18	Smith [34], Valentin [82]	25,693
14	5	H	Norwich C	W 2-0	2-0	13	Windass [12], Iorfa [34]	22,731
15	10	A	Sheffield U	L 0-1	0-0	15		31,127
16	23	H	Cardiff C	D 1-1	1-1	15	Bernard [36]	23,974
17	26	A	Hull C	W 2-0	1-0	12	Windass (pen) [37], Smith [81]	21,297
18	Dec 1	A	Derby Co	W 2-1	1-0	12	Bannan [64], Lowe J [90]	29,212
19	7	H	Preston NE	D 1-1	0-1	9	Smith [76]	23,927
20	10	H	Blackburn R	L 0-1	0-0	12		22,703
21	14	A	Oxford U	W 3-1	1-1	9	Windass [28], Lowe J [49], Gassama [61]	11,567
22	21	H	Stoke C	W 2-0	0-0	9	Windass [52], Paterson [76]	26,743
23	26	A	Middlesbrough	D 3-3	0-3	9	Ingelsson [47], Windass [54], Valery [61]	32,147
24	29	A	Preston NE	L 1-3	0-1	11	Windass [59]	19,950
25	Jan 1	H	Derby Co	W 4-2	1-0	9	Bannan [8], Windass [61], Gassama [63], Musaba [74]	31,056
26	4	H	Millwall	D 2-2	1-0	10	Valery [6], Otegbayo [85]	25,208
27	19	A	Leeds U	L 0-3	0-1	10		36,685
28	22	H	Bristol C	D 2-2	1-0	11	Gassama [16], Bernard [53]	22,774
29	25	A	QPR	W 2-0	0-0	10	Smith [72], Paterson [88]	17,352
30	Feb 1	H	Luton T	D 1-1	0-1	10	Smith (pen) [60]	27,437
31	8	A	WBA	L 1-2	0-0	11	Paterson [90]	25,462
32	12	A	Swansea C	W 1-0	0-0	8	Smith [66]	14,149
33	15	A	Coventry C	L 1-2	0-1	9	Latibeaudiere (og) [62]	28,121
34	21	A	Burnley	L 0-4	0-1	10		20,675
35	28	A	Sunderland	L 1-2	0-1	13	Paterson [48]	27,954
36	Mar 8	H	Plymouth Arg	W 3-0	2-0	13	Ogbeta (og) [15], Paterson [41], Gassama [68]	16,981
37	11	A	Norwich C	W 3-2	0-2	10	Ihiekwe [64], Windass [72], Gassama [76]	25,498
38	16	H	Sheffield U	L 0-1	0-0	12		33,827
39	29	A	Cardiff C	D 1-1	0-1	12	Ihiekwe [61]	20,460
40	Apr 5	H	Hull C	L 0-1	0-0	13		27,342
41	8	A	Blackburn R	D 2-2	2-0	13	Valery [16], Gassama [38]	15,575
42	12	H	Oxford U	L 0-1	0-0	14		25,646
43	18	A	Stoke C	L 0-2	0-1	15		29,163
44	21	H	Middlesbrough	W 2-1	0-1	13	Windass [54], Musaba [89]	27,668
45	26	H	Portsmouth	D 1-1	1-1	12	Paterson [9]	28,346
46	May 3	A	Watford	D 1-1	1-1	12	Windass [29]	20,657

Final League Position: 12

GOALSCORERS
League (60): Windass 13 (1 pen), Smith 8 (1 pen), Gassama 7, Paterson 6, Bannan 4, Lowe J 3, Musaba 3, Valery 3, Bernard 2, Ihiekwe 2, Charles S 1, Ingelsson 1, Iorfa 1, Otegbayo 1, Valentin 1, own goals 4.
FA Cup (1): Musaba 1.
Carabao Cup (9): McNeill 2, Paterson 2, Bernard 1, Gassama 1, Lowe J 1, Ugbo 1, Valentin 1.

Beadle J 38	Valery Y 38 + 1	Iorfa D 17 + 5	Bernard D 26 + 1	Lowe M 31 + 3	Ingelsson S 19 + 16	Bannan B 40 + 1	Gassama D 36 + 7	Windass A 38 + 6	Musaba A 12 + 17	Lowe J 12 + 12	Kobacki O 4 + 8	Johnson M 30 + 11	Valentin P 13 + 21	Smith M 16 + 25	Palmer L 7 + 16	Ugbo I 15 + 19	Ihiekwe M 20 + 2	Charles S 42 + 1	Famewo A 11 + 2	Paterson C 14 + 13	Otegbayo G 4 + 7	Chalobah N 4 + 12	McNeill C — + 4	Armstrong S 6 + 5	Cissoko I — + 5	Hatsuse R 5 + 1	Charles P 8	Match No.
1	2³	3	4	5¹	6⁵	7	8²	9⁴	10	11	12	13	14	15	16													1
1	2³	3	4	5⁵	6	7	8¹	9²	10	11⁴		16	13	12	14	15												2
1	2	3	4	5⁵	6⁴	7	12	9²	10	11³		16	8¹	14	15	13												3
1	2		4	5	15	6	8³	13	10⁵	9²	12	16	14		11¹			3		7⁴								4
1	5⁴	13	16		7	9	12					11¹		8⁵	14	15	2	10³		3	6	4²						5
1	5	3⁸	13		7²	12⁴	9	16		11¹	8			10²			14	15			6	4						6
1	5	12	15		7	9⁴	13	11¹		8²			14	2		10³	3	6		4								7
1	5	3		7	14	11²	9³	16	13	13⁵	8	12	15	2¹	10⁴			6		4								8
1	2	3	8⁴	10²	7	9³		12⁵	11¹			14	5		15	13			6	4	16							9
1	2	3		13	7³	9		12	14	10²	8		5¹	16		11⁵		6⁴	4									10
1	2	3		10¹	7	9³	12		11²	15	8		5⁴	14	13			6	4	16								11
1	14	12	3	8		7		9⁴	10³	13				5²	11⁵	2	16			6	4¹	15						12
1	8	3⁴	4	16		7	10¹	9⁵	15	13			5	12	11³	2	14			6²								13
1	2	3¹	4	5	9⁴	8	14	7³				10²	15	16			11⁵			6		13	12					14
1	2⁵	3	4	5	9⁹	8	13	7⁴	14	16		10⁵	15	12¹			11⁵			6								15
1	2¹	3	4		7	5³	9⁵	14	15			8	12	10¹	13	11²				6		16						16
1	3	16	4	5	14	9⁵	10³	7¹	12			6	2⁴	13	15	11²	8											17
1	2	3²		4		8	11³	12	9⁴	14		5	6¹	10⁵	13		7			16		15						18
1	2³		3	4	13		5	9⁴	12	15		8	14	11	7²	10	6⁵					16						19
1	5¹	2⁵	3	4		7	14	9²	10⁴	11³		8	12	13		16		6		15								20
1	2⁴	14	3	4	15	8	9⁵	6¹	12	10²		5	13	11⁵		16		7										21
1	5	2	3⁸	4		7⁴	10³	9²				8		11¹		15		6⁵		13	12	14	16					22
1	5³	2		4	12	7	10⁵	9⁴		11¹		8	14	15	16			6					3²	13				23
1	2⁴	3³		4	15	11	12	9⁵		16		8	5	10²		13		6						7¹	14			24
1		2	3	4	10	8³	6⁵	12	14			9¹		15		11⁴		7		16	13	5²						25
1	2³	3¹	4	5		7	10	9	8⁵	16			14	12		11²		6⁴			13	15						26
1	2		4	5	9¹	6	10	11⁴	8³			12	13					14										27
1	5³		2	4	15	7	10²	9⁴	13			8	14		12	11⁵	3	6¹		16								28
1	2		4	5		8³	9³	11		10¹			12	13			3	7		6	14							29
1	2		4³			8	9	10		11¹		14		13			3	7		6²			12					30
1	2⁵		4¹	5	13		11	9				12	14	10⁴			3	6		15	7³		8²					31
1	2			4	8⁴		9³	6		5			13		11¹	3	7			10²	15		12	14				32
1	2			4	7¹	11	9⁴	12		14		5			13		10²	3	6					8³	15			33
1	2			4	16	7⁴	8	10⁵				5¹		11²		14	3	6			12			9³	13	15		34
1			4¹	9⁴	8	10	11³		14		16	2		12	13	3	6	7²							15	5⁵		35
1			4	10¹	7³	8	9⁵			16		12	13	15		3	6	11²		14				5				36
1	15		5	9¹	8¹	10⁵	7⁴			16		6	2	12	14	4	3²	11		13						5		37
1	2		4¹	13	7	8⁵	9	16		14	12	11				3	6³	10²		15			5⁴					38
	3⁹		13	7	10	9		11³		14	2	15		4	12	16	8⁴		6²					5¹	1		1	39
	15			10²	7	8⁵	9³	14		16		5	2	11¹		3	6	4⁴	13				12		1		1	40
	3⁴			9		7³	13	10⁵	16	6	2	14		4	8	12	11¹	5²		15					1		1	41
	2³			13		8⁵	9	10²		5	14		16	3	6	4	11⁴		12	7¹	15				1		1	42
	2	3³		7²	13	10⁵	8		12	15	16			6	4	11	14		9⁴			5¹	1				1	43
	6			7²	8⁴	9¹	10	12		5	11	14		2	4³	15		13							1		1	44
	6⁴			13	8	9¹	10	12		5		11³	14	4	3	2⁵		15	16	7²					1		1	45
	2			7²	8¹	9	10⁴		15	5		11⁵	14	16	12	3		6	4³	13					1		1	46

FA Cup
Third Round   Coventry C   (a)   1-1
aet; Coventry C won 4-3 on penalties.

Carabao Cup
First Round   Hull C   (a)   2-1
Second Round   Grimsby T   (a)   5-1
Third Round   Blackpool   (a)   1-0
Fourth Round   Brentford   (a)   1-1
Brentford won 5-4 on penalties.

SHREWSBURY TOWN

FOUNDATION

Shrewsbury School having provided a number of the early England and Wales international players it is not surprising that there was a Town club as early as 1876 which won the Birmingham Senior Cup in 1879. However, the present Shrewsbury Town club was formed in 1886 and won the Welsh FA Cup as early as 1891.

The Croud Meadow, Oteley Road, Shrewsbury, Shropshire SY2 6ST.

Telephone: (01743) 289 177.

Ticket Office: (01743) 273 943.

Website: www.shrewsburytown.com

Email: info@shrewsburytown.co.uk

Ground Capacity: 9,875.

Record Attendance: 18,917 v Walsall, Division 3, 26 April 1961 (at Gay Meadow); 10,210 v Chelsea, League Cup 4th rd, 28 October 2014 (at New Meadow).

Pitch Measurements: 100m × 66m (109.5yd × 72yd).

Chairman: Roland Wycherley MBE.

Chief Executive: Liam Dooley.

Head Coach: Michael Appleton.

Assistant Head Coach: Richard O'Donnell.

Colours: Blue and yellow striped shirts, blue shorts, blue socks.

Year Formed: 1886.

Turned Professional: 1896.

Club Nicknames: 'The Town'; 'The Blues'; 'Salop'. The name 'Salop' is a colloquialism for the county of Shropshire. Since Shrewsbury is the only club in Shropshire, cries of 'Come on Salop' are frequently used!

Grounds: 1886, Old Racecourse Ground; 1889, Ambler's Field; 1893, Sutton Lane; 1895, Barracks Ground; 1910, Gay Meadow; 2007, New Meadow (renamed ProStar Stadium 2008; Greenhous Meadow 2010; Montgomery Waters Meadow 2017; The Croud Meadow 2023).

First Football League Game: 19 August 1950, Division 3 (N), v Scunthorpe U (a) D 0–0 – Egglestone; Fisher, Lewis; Wheatley, Depear, Robinson; Griffin, Hope, Jackson, Brown, Barker.

Record League Victory: 7–0 v Swindon T, Division 3 (S), 6 May 1955 – McBride; Bannister, Skeech; Wallace, Maloney, Candlin; Price, O'Donnell (1), Weigh (4), Russell, McCue (2); 7–0 v Gillingham, FL 2, 13 September 2008 – Daniels; Herd, Tierney, Davies (2), Jackson (1) (Langmead), Coughlan (1), Cansdell-Sherriff (1), Thornton, Hibbert (1) (Hindmarch), Holt (pen), McIntyre (Ashton).

Record Cup Victory: 11–2 v Marine, FA Cup 1st rd, 11 November 1995 – Edwards; Seabury (Dempsey (1)), Withe (1), Evans (1), Whiston (2), Scott (1), Woods, Stevens (1), Spink (3) (Anthrobus), Walton, Berkley, (1 og).

Record Defeat: 1–8 v Norwich C, Division 3 (S), 13 September 1952; 1–8 v Coventry C, Division 3, 22 October 1963.

HONOURS

League Champions: Division 3 – 1978–79; Third Division – 1993–94.
Runners-up: FL 2 – 2011–12, 2014–15; Division 4 – 1974–75; Football Conference – (3rd) 2003–04 *(promoted to FL 2 via play-offs).*
FA Cup: 6th rd – 1979, 1982.
League Cup: semi-final – 1961.
League Trophy: Runners-up: 1996, 2018.
Welsh Cup Winners: 1891, 1938, 1977, 1979, 1984, 1985.
Runners-up: 1931, 1948, 1980.

FOOTBALL YEARBOOK FACT FILE

Shrewsbury Town player-manager Arthur Rowley created a piece of history on 26 September 1962 when he scored in the 44th minute of the home game with Millwall. This was his 411th Football League goal, taking him past Jimmy McGrory to establish a new league goalscoring record in senior British football. His final tally of 433 goals, achieved in a career spanning the period 1947 to 1965, has yet to be beaten.

Most League Points (2 for a win): 62, Division 4, 1974–75.

Most League Points (3 for a win): 89, FL 2, 2014–15.

Most League Goals: 101, Division 4, 1958–59.

Highest League Scorer in Season: Arthur Rowley, 38, Division 4, 1958–59.

Most League Goals in Total Aggregate: Arthur Rowley, 152, 1958–65 (thus completing his League record of 434 goals).

Most League Goals in One Match: 5, Alf Wood v Blackburn R, Division 3, 2 October 1971.

Most Capped Player: Aaron Pierre, 18 (25), Grenada.

Most League Appearances: Mickey Brown, 418, 1986–91; 1992–94; 1996–2001.

Youngest League Player: Graham French, 16 years 177 days v Reading, 30 September 1961.

Record Transfer Fee Received: £600,000 (potentially rising to £1,500,000) from Manchester C for Joe Hart, May 2006.

Record Transfer Fee Paid: £200,000 to Tranmere R for Oliver Norburn, August 2018.

Football League Record: 1950 Elected to Division 3 (N); 1950–51 Division 3 (N); 1951–58 Division 3 (S); 1958–59 Division 4; 1959–74 Division 3; 1974–75 Division 4; 1975–79 Division 3; 1979–89 Division 2; 1989–94 Division 3; 1994–97 Second Division; 1997–2003 Third Division; 2003–04 Football Conference; 2004–12 FL 2; 2012–14 FL 1; 2014–15 FL 2; 2015–25 FL 1; 2025– FL 2.

LATEST SEQUENCES

Longest Sequence of League Wins: 7, 28.10.1995 – 16.12.1995.

Longest Sequence of League Defeats: 11, 9.4.2003 – 14.8.2004. (Spread over 2 periods in Football League. 2003–04 season in Football Conference.)

Longest Sequence of League Draws: 6, 30.10.1963 – 14.12.1963.

Longest Sequence of Unbeaten League Matches: 16, 30.10.1993 – 26.2.1994.

Longest Sequence Without a League Win: 18, 8.3.2003 – 14.8.2004.

Successive Scoring Runs: 28 from 7.9.1960.

Successive Non-scoring Runs: 6 from 1.1.1991.

MANAGERS

W. Adams 1905–12
  (Secretary-Manager)
A. Weston 1912–34
  (Secretary-Manager)
Jack Roscamp 1934–35
Sam Ramsey 1935–36
Ted Bousted 1936–40
Leslie Knighton 1945–49
Harry Chapman 1949–50
Sammy Crooks 1950–54
Walter Rowley 1955–57
Harry Potts 1957–58
Johnny Spuhler 1958
Arthur Rowley 1958–68
Harry Gregg 1968–72
Maurice Evans 1972–73
Alan Durban 1974–78
Richie Barker 1978
Graham Turner 1978–84
Chic Bates 1984–87
Ian McNeill 1987–90
Asa Hartford 1990–91
John Bond 1991–93
Fred Davies 1994–97
  (previously Caretaker-Manager 1993–94)
Jake King 1997–99
Kevin Ratcliffe 1999–2003
Jimmy Quinn 2003–04
Gary Peters 2004–08
Paul Simpson 2008–10
Graham Turner 2010–14
Mike Jackson 2014
Micky Mellon 2014–16
Paul Hurst 2016–18
John Askey 2018
Sam Ricketts 2018–20
Steve Cotterill 2020–23
Matty Taylor 2023–24
Paul Hurst 2024
Gareth Ainsworth 2024–25
Michael Appleton March 2025–

TEN YEAR LEAGUE RECORD

		P	W	D	L	F	A	Pts	Pos
2015-16	FL 1	46	13	11	22	58	79	50	20
2016-17	FL 1	46	13	12	21	46	63	51	18
2017-18	FL 1	46	25	12	9	60	39	87	3
2018-19	FL 1	46	12	16	18	51	59	52	18
2019-20	FL 1	34	10	11	13	31	42	41	15§
2020-21	FL 1	46	13	15	18	50	57	54	17
2021-22	FL 1	46	12	14	20	47	51	50	18
2022-23	FL 1	46	17	8	21	52	61	59	12
2023-24	FL 1	46	13	9	24	35	67	48	19
2024-25	FL 1	46	8	9	29	41	79	33	24

§*Decided on points-per-game (1.21)*

DID YOU KNOW ?

After defeating Bury on Boxing Day 2002, Shrewsbury Town were in 18th position in Division Three, 10 points clear of bottom club Swansea City. The Shrews then went on to beat Everton in the FA Cup, but their League form collapsed, and they gained just two wins from the final 23 games. They finished the season seven points adrift of the nearest club and were relegated to the Football Conference.

SHREWSBURY TOWN – SKY BET LEAGUE ONE 2024–25 LEAGUE RECORD

Match No.	Date	Venue	Opponents	Result	H/T Score	Lg Pos.	Goalscorers	Atten- dance
1	Aug 10	A	Stevenage	L 0-1	0-0	19		3357
2	17	H	Peterborough U	L 1-4	1-1	23	Winchester [21]	6015
3	24	A	Huddersfield T	L 0-1	0-1	24		18,205
4	31	H	Leyton Orient	W 3-0	1-0	20	Castledine [22], Bloxham 2 [82, 90]	5602
5	Sept 7	A	Wrexham	L 0-3	0-2	21		13,341
6	14	H	Charlton Ath	L 0-0	0-0	23		6171
7	21	A	Mansfield T	L 1-2	1-0	23	Castledine [2]	7313
8	28	H	Rotherham U	D 1-1	1-0	23	Lloyd [22]	6001
9	Oct 1	H	Stockport Co	L 0-2	0-1	23		5600
10	5	A	Bolton W	D 2-2	2-0	22	Feeney J [20], Shipley [28]	19,765
11	12	A	Crawley T	W 5-3	1-1	21	Marquis 2 (1 pen) [26, 76 (p)], Nsiala [72], Lloyd 2 [86, 90]	4215
12	17	H	Exeter C	L 0-2	0-1	21		4965
13	22	A	Bristol R	L 0-1	0-0	22		6361
14	26	A	Barnsley	L 0-2	0-1	23		6129
15	Nov 9	A	Burton Alb	L 0-2	0-1	24		2935
16	23	H	Birmingham C	W 3-2	2-1	23	Pierre [31], Marquis [38], Bloxham [55]	7887
17	Dec 4	H	Blackpool	L 1-2	1-0	24	Benning [4]	5251
18	7	A	Cambridge U	L 1-4	0-2	24	Marquis (pen) [70]	6167
19	14	H	Wycombe W	L 1-4	0-2	24	Shipley [72]	5737
20	21	A	Wigan Ath	D 2-2	0-1	24	Aimson (og) [67], Lloyd [87]	8752
21	26	H	Lincoln C	W 1-0	1-0	23	Feeney M [9]	6369
22	29	H	Northampton T	D 1-1	0-0	23	Pierre [60]	6894
23	Jan 1	A	Blackpool	D 1-1	0-0	22	Bloxham [80]	9433
24	4	A	Leyton Orient	L 0-1	0-0	22		7552
25	16	H	Wrexham	W 2-1	1-1	21	Marquis 2 [17, 48]	8789
26	25	A	Charlton Ath	L 0-1	0-0	24		12,999
27	28	A	Stockport Co	L 0-1	0-1	24		8862
28	Feb 1	H	Mansfield T	W 2-1	0-1	23	Marquis [54], Lloyd [63]	7376
29	8	A	Rotherham U	W 2-1	0-0	22	Perry [68], Marquis [77]	8820
30	11	A	Reading	D 1-1	0-1	21	Perry [56]	7975
31	15	H	Bolton W	L 2-3	1-2	22	Oliver [20], Hoole [90]	7613
32	18	A	Huddersfield T	L 0-1	0-0	23		6762
33	22	H	Stevenage	L 0-1	0-1	23		5694
34	Mar 1	A	Peterborough U	L 1-3	1-2	24	Benning (pen) [14]	11,578
35	4	H	Bristol R	D 0-0	0-0	24		5257
36	8	A	Exeter C	L 0-2	0-1	24		6197
37	15	H	Burton Alb	L 0-2	0-0	24		5807
38	29	A	Birmingham C	L 1-4	0-1	24	Oliver [87]	26,254
39	Apr 1	A	Wycombe W	D 0-0	0-0	24		3806
40	5	H	Cambridge U	L 0-1	0-0	24		5952
41	8	H	Reading	L 1-3	0-1	24	Perry [48]	4956
42	12	A	Lincoln C	D 1-1	1-1	24	Pierre [23]	9282
43	18	A	Wigan Ath	L 0-1	0-0	24		6338
44	21	A	Northampton T	L 1-4	0-2	24	Marquis [90]	6632
45	26	A	Barnsley	W 2-1	1-0	24	Marquis 2 [18, 67]	11,159
46	May 3	H	Crawley T	L 1-2	0-0	24	Benning [87]	5599

Final League Position: 24

GOALSCORERS

League (41): Marquis 11 (2 pens), Lloyd 5, Bloxham 4, Benning 3 (1 pen), Perry 3, Pierre 3, Castledine 2, Oliver 2, Shipley 2, Feeney J 1, Feeney M 1, Hoole 1, Nsiala 1, Winchester 1, own goal 1.
FA Cup (1): Marquis 1.
Carabao Cup (3): Shipley 2, Kayode 1.
Vertu Trophy (1): Nsiala 1.

Savin T 19	Hoole L 36+3	Nsiala A 16+4	Pierre A 27+6	Benning M 39+5	Winchester C 12+3	Rossiter J 10+5	Bloxham T 14+8	O'Reilly T 6+6	Shipley J 14+19	Marquis J 34+6	Kayode J 1+4	Biggins H 7+10	Lloyd G 34+10	Feeney M 34+2	Sagoe Junior C 5+8	Perry T 20+14	Gillead A 37+5	Castledine L 18+5	Nurse G 14+8	Ojo F 22+9	Feeney J 35+2	Blackman J 27	Gape D 14+2	Stewart C 3+12	Oliver V 4+9	Dinanga R —+1	Wheeler D 4+6	England 1 —+2	Loughran J —+1	Match No.
1	2	3	4	5	6	7²	8¹	9	10	11³	12	13	14																	1
1	2	3	12	5	6		10³	7	9	11²	15	8⁴	14	4¹	13															2
1	2	3	4	5	6		10	7²	9³	11¹		14	13	12	8															3
1	2	4		5			12	8¹	10	13			11	3		7	6³	9²	14											4
1		3²		5	2		8³	12	10				11	4	13		6	9¹		7	14									5
1	2			5	6³		12		13	14			11	3	10¹		8	9²		7	4									6
1	2	4³	14	5	7		13						11	3	10²	12	8	9¹		6										7
1	2		15	5	6⁴		13		12				11	3	10¹	14	8	9²		7	4³									8
1	2³			5		6⁴	8¹	13			14		11	3	12	15	10	9²		7	4									9
1		3	13		6				9¹	10³		11	2		14	5	12	8²	7	4										10
1		3			6	13				11			10	2	12	14	5	9³		7¹	4²									11
1		3		8⁴	6³		12			11			10	2	13	15	5	9¹	14	7	4²									12
1	15		3	12	16	6⁵	14			11			10	2	13		5⁴	9²	8¹	7	4³									13
1	2	3¹				7³	10		13				11	4		9²	5	14	8	6	12									14
1		3	8	5³	7⁵	9	12	14	10¹				15			13	6	11¹	4²	16	2									15
1	2	3³	4	5	7²	12	10⁴		13	11			14			8¹	6	9	15											16
1	2	3	4	5	6	7¹	13	14	11				12			9³	8	10²												17
1	2			7¹	12	10²	9⁴	8	11			13	3	15		8¹	4													18
1	2		4	5	7²	10	15	12	11⁴	14	3		8³	6	9¹	13														19
	2	15	5			12		9²	10	11³			14	4⁴	8¹	6	13				7	3	1							20
	5	3	8		15	10³	7⁴	13	11²			2	6¹	14	9			12	4	1										21
	5	4	8		12	14	11¹	13	10³			2		7²	6	9			3	1										22
	2	5	6		8³	9	7⁴	13	12	11¹			3	10²		15	14	4	1											23
	2	5²	6	15	12	7	10⁴	11³	13			14	3		9¹	8⁵	16	4	1											24
	5	12	4¹	8⁴	13			14	11	10	2		6²	9³	15	7	3	1												25
	5	3³		8			12	11	10	4		13	6	9¹	14	7²	2	1												26
		3	8			9²	11	14	10	4¹	12	5		7	2	1	6³	13												27
	5	3⁵	4	8			11³	13	10			9	6²	14	12	2	1	7¹												28
	5	4	8			10	12	11²	2			9³	7¹	14	3	1	6	13												29
	5	14	8		15	10⁶	6³	11¹	3			9⁴	13	4²	2	1	7	16	12											30
	2	16	5		12	10⁶	13	4	9¹	7⁴			6	3	1	8³	14	11²	15											31
	2	5	6		13	11²	10¹	3	7²	9	4	1	8	14	12															32
	5	4	8³	13	11⁴	16	9	2	6²	14	3	1	7⁵	15	10¹	12														33
	5	4⁴	8	13	10⁸	14	11⁵	2	9³	12	6¹	3	1	7²	16	15														34
	5	8	14	13	11⁴	2	9¹	12	4	7²	3	1	6³	15	16	10⁵														35
	5	8	15	7	11⁴	2²	12	9¹	4	3	1	6³	13	10	14															36
	2	4	5	10²	7¹	11⁴	9³	12	13	3	1	6	14	15	8															37
	2¹	4	6	13	10	11	15	9²	7	5⁴	3	1	8³	14	12															38
	15	3	8	12	10	11	2	14	6²	7³	4	1	13	9¹	5⁴															39
	12	3	8³	9¹	11	10	2	13	7	14	6⁴	4	1	15	5²															40
	5¹	4	13	15	11	10⁶	2	6⁴	7	9³	8²	3	1	14	16	12														41
	5⁴	15	4	13	11	10³	2	6¹	7	9²	3	1	8	14	12															42
	5	3	12	9²	13	10	8	7	4¹	2	1	6³	14																	43
	2¹	4	5²	11	8⁴	10	12	6	7	13	3	1	9³														14	15		44
	5	3	14	8	9	7	11²	12	6	4³	2	1	10¹	13																45
	5	3	15	8	9	7³	11¹	12	6⁴	4	2⁸	1	10²	13									14							46

FA Cup

First Round	Salford C	(a)	1-2

Carabao Cup

First Round	Notts Co	(h)	3-3

Shrewsbury T won 4-3 on penalties,

Second Round	Bolton W	(h)	0-2

Vertu Trophy

Group A (S)	Fulham U21	(h)	1-2
Group A (S)	Birmingham C	(h)	0-4
Group A (S)	Walsall	(a)	0-3

SOUTHAMPTON

FOUNDATION

The club was formed by members of the St Mary's Church of England Young Men's Association at a meeting of the Y.M.A. in November 1885 and it was named as such. For the sake of brevity this was usually shortened to St Mary's Y.M.A. The rector Canon Albert Basil Orme Wilberforce was elected president. The name was changed to plain St Mary's during 1887–88 and did not become Southampton St Mary's until 1894, the inaugural season in the Southern League.

St Mary's Stadium, Britannia Road, Southampton, Hampshire SO14 5FP.

Telephone: (023) 8072 7700.

Ticket Office: (023) 8178 0780.

Website: www.southamptonfc.com

Email: contactsaints@saintsfc.com

Ground Capacity: 32,384.

Record Attendance: 31,044 v Manchester U, Division 1, 8 October 1969 (at The Dell); 32,363 v Coventry C, FL C, 28 April 2012 (at St Mary's).

Pitch Measurements: 105m × 68m (115yd × 74.5yd).

Chairman: Dragan Solak.

Chief Executive: Phil Parsons.

Manager: Will Still.

Assistant Manager: Paul Trollope.

Colours: Red and white striped shirts with black trim, black shorts, white socks with red trim.

Year Formed: 1885. *Turned Professional:* 1894.

Previous Names: 1885, St Mary's Young Men's Association; 1887–88, St Mary's; 1894–95, Southampton St Mary's; 1897, Southampton.

Club Nickname: 'The Saints'.

Grounds: 1885, 'The Common' (from 1887 also used the County Cricket Ground and Antelope Cricket Ground); 1889, Antelope Cricket Ground; 1896, The County Cricket Ground; 1898, The Dell; 2001, St Mary's Stadium (renamed Provident St Mary's Stadium 2001; St Mary's Stadium 2006).

First Football League Game: 28 August 1920, Division 3, v Gillingham (a) D 1–1 – Allen; Parker, Titmuss; Shelley, Campbell, Turner; Barratt, Dominy (1), Rawlings, Moore, Foxall.

Record League Victory: 8–0 v Sunderland, Premier League, 18 October 2014 – Forster; Clyne, Fonte, Alderweireld, Bertrand; Davis S (Mané), Schneiderlin, Cork (1); Long (Wanyama (1)), Pelle (2) (Mayuka), Tadic (1) (plus 3 Sunderland own goals).

HONOURS

League Champions: Division 3 – 1959–60; Division 3S – 1921–22.
Runners-up: Division 1 – 1983–84; FL C – 2011–12; Division 2 – 1965–66, 1977–78; FL 1 – 2010–11; Division 3 – 1920–21.

FA Cup Winners: 1976.
Runners-up: 1900, 1902, 2003.

League Cup: Runners-up: 1979, 2017.

League Trophy Winners: 2010.

Full Members' Cup: Runners-up: 1992.

European Competitions
Fairs Cup: 1969–70.
UEFA Cup: 1971–72, 1981–82, 1982–83, 1984–85, 2003–04.
Europa League: 2015–16, 2016–17.
European Cup-Winners' Cup: 1976–77 *(qf).*

FOOTBALL YEARBOOK FACT FILE

Southampton have hosted two full England international matches a century apart. In March 1901 England defeated Ireland in a Home International Championship fixture at The Dell, comfortably winning 3-0. Then in October 2002 England drew 2-2 with FYR Macedonia at the St Mary's Stadium. The goals came from David Beckham and Steven Gerrard in front of a crowd of 32,095.

Record Cup Victory: 8–0 v Newport Co, Carabao Cup 2nd rd, 25 August 2021 – Forster; Valery, Stephens, Bednarek, Walker-Peters (1), Elyounoussi (3), Diallo, Ward-Prowse (Walcott), Tella (1) (Obafemi), Redmond (1), Broja (2) (Long).

Record Defeat: 0–9 v Leicester C, Premier League, 25 October 2019; 0–9 v Manchester U, Premier League, 2 February 2021.

Most League Points (2 for a win): 61, Division 3 (S), 1921–22 and Division 3, 1959–60.

Most League Points (3 for a win): 92, FL 1, 2010–11.

Most League Goals: 112, Division 3 (S), 1957–58.

Highest League Scorer in Season: Derek Reeves, 39, Division 3, 1959–60.

Most League Goals in Total Aggregate: Mike Channon, 185, 1966–77, 1979–82.

Most League Goals in One Match: 5, Charlie Wayman v Leicester C, Division 2, 23 October 1948.

Most Capped Player: Maya Yoshida, 83 (126), Japan.

Most League Appearances: Terry Paine, 713, 1956–74.

Youngest League Player: Theo Walcott, 16 years 143 days v Wolverhampton W, 6 August 2005.

Record Transfer Fee Received: £75,000,000 from Liverpool for Virgil van Dijk, January 2018.

Record Transfer Fee Paid: £22,000,000 to Rennes for Kamaldeen Sulemana, January 2023.

Football League Record: 1920 Original Member of Division 3; 1920–21 Division 3; 1921–22 Division 3 (S); 1922–53 Division 2; 1953–58 Division 3 (S); 1958–60 Division 3; 1960–66 Division 2; 1966–74 Division 1; 1974–78 Division 2; 1978–92 Division 1; 1992–2005 Premier League; 2005–09 FL C; 2009–11 FL 1; 2011–12 FL C; 2012–23 Premier League; 2023–24 FL C; 2024–25 Premier League; 2025– FL C.

LATEST SEQUENCES

Longest Sequence of League Wins: 10, 16.4.2011 – 20.8.2011.

Longest Sequence of League Defeats: 6, 26.12.2024 – 25.1.2025.

Longest Sequence of League Draws: 8, 29.8.2005 – 15.10.2005.

Longest Sequence of Unbeaten League Matches: 22, 30.9.2023 – 10.2.2024.

Longest Sequence Without a League Win: 20, 30.8.1969 – 27.12.1969.

Successive Scoring Runs: 31 from 23.9.2023.

Successive Non-scoring Runs: 5 from 22.9.2018.

MANAGERS

Cecil Knight 1894–95
(Secretary-Manager)
Charles Robson 1895–97
Ernest Arnfield 1897–1911
(Secretary-Manager)
(continued as Secretary)
George Swift 1911–12
Ernest Arnfield 1912–19
Jimmy McIntyre 1919–24
Arthur Chadwick 1925–31
George Kay 1931–36
George Gross 1936–37
Tom Parker 1937–43
J. R. Sarjantson stepped down from the board to act as Secretary-Manager 1943–47 with the next two listed being Team Managers during this period
Arthur Dominy 1943–46
Bill Dodgin Snr 1946–49
Sid Cann 1949–51
George Roughton 1952–55
Ted Bates 1955–73
Lawrie McMenemy 1973–85
Chris Nicholl 1985–91
Ian Branfoot 1991–94
Alan Ball 1994–95
Dave Merrington 1995–96
Graeme Souness 1996–97
Dave Jones 1997–2000
Glenn Hoddle 2000–01
Stuart Gray 2001
Gordon Strachan 2001–04
Paul Sturrock 2004
Steve Wigley 2004
Harry Redknapp 2004–05
George Burley 2005–08
Nigel Pearson 2008
Jan Poortvliet 2008–09
Mark Wotte 2009
Alan Pardew 2009–10
Nigel Adkins 2010–13
Mauricio Pochettino 2013–14
Ronald Koeman 2014–16
Claude Puel 2016–17
Mauricio Pellegrino 2017–18
Mark Hughes 2018
Ralph Hasenhüttl 2018–22
Nathan Jones 2022–23
Ruben Selles 2023
Russell Martin 2023–24
Ivan Juric 2024–25
Will Still May 2025–

TEN YEAR LEAGUE RECORD

		P	W	D	L	F	A	Pts	Pos
2015-16	PR Lge	38	18	9	11	59	41	63	6
2016-17	PR Lge	38	12	10	16	41	48	46	8
2017-18	PR Lge	38	7	15	16	37	56	36	17
2018-19	PR Lge	38	9	12	17	45	65	39	16
2019-20	PR Lge	38	15	7	16	51	60	52	11
2020-21	PR Lge	38	12	7	19	47	68	43	15
2021-22	PR Lge	38	9	13	16	43	67	40	15
2022-23	PR Lge	38	6	7	25	36	73	25	20
2023-24	FL C	46	26	9	11	87	63	87	4
2024-25	PR Lge	38	2	6	30	26	86	12	20

DID YOU KNOW ?

Defender Tom Parker both saved and missed a penalty playing for Southampton against Northampton Town in a Southern League fixture in October 1919 as Saints went down to a 6-2 home defeat. Parker hit the crossbar with his own effort, then, temporarily having taken over in goal, he saved a Cobblers penalty.

SOUTHAMPTON – PREMIER LEAGUE 2024–25 LEAGUE RECORD

Match No.	Date	Venue	Opponents	Result	H/T Score	Lg Pos.	Goalscorers	Attendance
1	Aug 17	A	Newcastle U	L 0-1	0-1	16		52,196
2	24	H	Nottingham F	L 0-1	0-0	15		31,150
3	31	A	Brentford	L 1-3	0-1	19	Sugawara [90]	16,955
4	Sept 14	H	Manchester U	L 0-3	0-2	19		31,144
5	21	H	Ipswich T	D 1-1	1-0	18	Dibling [5]	31,117
6	30	A	Bournemouth	L 1-3	0-3	19	Harwood-Bellis [51]	11,243
7	Oct 5	A	Arsenal	L 1-3	0-0	19	Archer [55]	60,307
8	19	H	Leicester C	L 2-3	2-0	20	Archer [8], Aribo [28]	31,145
9	26	A	Manchester C	L 0-1	0-1	20		52,844
10	Nov 2	H	Everton	W 1-0	0-0	19	Armstrong [85]	31,143
11	9	A	Wolverhampton W	L 0-2	0-1	20		31,403
12	24	H	Liverpool	L 2-3	1-1	20	Armstrong [42], Fernandes [56]	31,278
13	29	A	Brighton & HA	D 1-1	0-1	20	Downes [59]	31,542
14	Dec 4	H	Chelsea	L 1-5	1-3	20	Aribo [11]	31,193
15	7	A	Aston Villa	L 0-1	0-1	20		42,453
16	15	H	Tottenham H	L 0-5	0-5	20		31,090
17	22	A	Fulham	D 0-0	0-0	20		26,819
18	26	H	West Ham U	L 0-1	0-0	20		31,059
19	29	A	Crystal Palace	L 1-2	1-1	20	Dibling [15]	25,130
20	Jan 4	H	Brentford	L 0-5	0-1	20		31,001
21	16	A	Manchester U	L 1-3	1-0	20	Ugarte (og) [43]	73,722
22	19	A	Nottingham F	L 2-3	0-3	20	Bednarek [60], Onuachu [90]	30,180
23	25	H	Newcastle U	L 1-3	1-2	20	Bednarek [10]	31,141
24	Feb 1	A	Ipswich T	W 2-1	1-1	20	Aribo [21], Onuachu [87]	29,902
25	15	H	Bournemouth	L 1-3	0-2	20	Sulemana [72]	31,037
26	22	H	Brighton & HA	L 0-4	0-1	20		30,775
27	25	A	Chelsea	L 0-4	0-3	20		39,485
28	Mar 8	A	Liverpool	L 1-3	1-0	20	Smallbone [45]	60,399
29	15	H	Wolverhampton W	L 1-2	0-1	20	Onuachu [75]	30,950
30	Apr 2	H	Crystal Palace	D 1-1	1-0	20	Onuachu [20]	29,366
31	6	A	Tottenham H	L 1-3	0-2	20	Fernandes [90]	60,984
32	12	A	Aston Villa	L 0-3	0-0	20		30,673
33	19	A	West Ham U	D 1-1	0-0	20	Ugochukwu [90]	62,461
34	26	H	Fulham	L 1-2	1-0	20	Stephens [14]	28,946
35	May 3	A	Leicester C	L 0-2	0-2	20		31,240
36	10	H	Manchester C	D 0-0	0-0	20		30,937
37	18	A	Everton	L 0-2	0-2	20		39,201
38	25	H	Arsenal	L 1-2	0-1	20	Stewart [56]	31,289

Final League Position: 20

GOALSCORERS

League (26): Onuachu 4, Aribo 3, Archer 2, Armstrong 2, Bednarek 2, Dibling 2, Fernandes 2, Downes 1, Harwood-Bellis 1, Smallbone 1, Stephens 1, Stewart 1, Sugawara 1, Sulemana 1, Ugochukwu 1, own goal 1.
FA Cup (3): Dibling 2, Sulemana 1.
Carabao Cup (10): Archer 3, Bree 2, Harwood-Bellis 2, Amo-Ameyaw 1, Armstrong 1 (1 pen), Fernandes 1.

McCarthy A 5	Harwood-Bellis T 32+2	Bednarek J 30	Stephens J 17+2	Sugawara Y 16+14	Smallbone W 6+12	Downes F 25+2	Aribo J 21+11	Walker-Peters K 33	Armstrong A 15+5	Brereton B 4+6	Edozie S —+2	Dibling T 20+13	Archer C 13+22	Amo-Ameyaw S —+2	Alcaraz C —+1	Fernandes M 34+2	Taylor C 3+5	Ramsdale A 30	Lallana A 5+9	Ugochukwu L 18+8	Stewart R 4+8	Fraser R 4+1	Cornet M 1+1	Manning R 18+6	Onuachu E 11+14	Sulemana K 17+9	Bree J 13+4	Lumley J 3	Wood-Gordon N 9+2	Edwards R —+1	Welington S 6+4	Gronbaek A 2+2	Kotchap A 2+2	Robinson J 1+3	Sanda J —+2	Match No.
1	2	3[4]	4	5[1]	6	7	8[2]	9[5]	10	11[3]	12	13	14	15	16																					1
	2[3]	3	4	5[2]	6[5]	7	8[4]	9	10[1]	11	12	16	13			14	15																			2
	2[3]	3	4	5	6[1]	7	8[4]	9	10[2]	11		14	13			12		1	15																	3
16	4	3[8]	2		6		5		10[3]			8[2]	11[1]			9[5]		1	13	7[4]	12	14	15													4
	3	4		2		6	16		15	14		8[4]	11[2]			9[5]		1		7[3]	13	12	10[1]													5
	3	4		2		6	14			13		11[5]	16			9[4]	5	1	15	7[3]	12	10[1]	8[2]													6
	3	4		2[4]		9	8	5	13			7	12			10[3]	15	1		11[1]			6[2]	14												7
	3	4		2[1]	13	8	7	5				6[4]	11[2]			9[3]	15	1			12[8]			10[5]	14	16										8
	3	4	5			8[4]	13	2	12			7	11[5]			10		1		9[2]			6[3]	16	15	14										9
	3	4	5[3]	14		8	12	2	7			13	11[5]			10[4]		1		9[1]	15		6[2]	16												10
	3	4	5[3]	14			8[5]	2	7	15		12	11[4]			10		1		9[2]	13		6[1]	16												11
1	3		5	14		4	12	2	10[4]			7	15			8				9[1]	13		6[3]		11[2]											12
	3		4	2[1]		8[2]	13	5	10[4]	15		7	11[3]			9					12		6	14	1											13
		4[8]	14			7	5	10[1]	12			11[3]				8[6]	16			9[2]			6	13	2[4]	1	3	15								14
3						8[3]	12	5	10	14		7	11[2]	13		9					6[4]		15	2[1]	1	4										15
1	3	4		13		7	6	2	10[3]			9	14			8					5[2]			11[1]		12										16
	2	3		5[3]		6	7[2]	8	11[4]			10[1]	12			9		1		13				15	14	4										17
	2	3		5[1]		6[2]	13	8[9]	10[3]			14				9[4]		1	17	7			16	11	15	12	4									18
	2	3					7[1]	8[4]	10[3]			9[6]	14			6		1	15	12			16	11[2]	13	5	4									19
	2	3		12			7[5]	8	14			9	15			13	1	16	6					10[3]	11[4]	5[2]	4[1]									20
	4	3[6]		5	12	14	7[2]	8	13			10[1]				9[3]		1		6[4]				16	11	2	15									21
	4	3		5[2]	16	6[1]	7	8	11[3]			10[4]				9	1			12				13	15	14	2[5]									22
1	4	3		12	14		7[5]	5	11[1]			13				9			16	6[3]		15		8[2]	10	2[4]										23
4[1]	3	12[2]	16	13		7	5					9				1	15	6[5]						11	14	2			8[4]	10[3]						24
	3		13	6[3]		7[4]	5					14	16			9	1			12				15	10	11[5]	2		4[2]	8[1]						25
	3[1]		13	14		4	5					9	10[4]			7[5]	1			6[3]				15	11	2			8[2]	16	12					26
12			2[9]	8[4]	5	6[2]						13	15			7	1			1				14	11[3]	10	3[1]			16	4					27
	4	3[1]		13	7[4]		16	2				8[2]	14			9		1	15	6				5[8]	17	10					11[3]	12				28
	4	16	5[2]		14	7[5]	2					9	13			10[1]		1		6[3]				8	12	11[4]					15	3				29
	2	3	4	15		6[9]	12	5				13	16			9		1		7[1]				8[3]	11[4]	10[2]			14							30
	4	3	14	12			7[1]	2				8[4]	11[3]			9		1		6[5]	16			5[2]	15	10			13							31
	2	3	4	15	14			5				12	9[2]			6[6]		1		7	13			8[4]	10[1]	11[3]								16		32
	2[4]	3	4				6	5				13	12			9		1		7	14			8[3]	11[1]	10[2]			15							33
	2	3	4				6	5				13	12			9[3]		1		7	11[1]			8		10[2]	14									34
	2	3	4[1]			15	6	5				12	16			9[4]		1		7[5]	11[2]			8	13	10[3]							14			35
	2	3	4		16	6	12					9[2]	13			10[5]		1		7[1]	14			15		11[3]	5			8[4]						36
	2[5]	4		13	6	7[2]						9[1]	14			10		1			12					11[3]	5		3[1]		8			15	16	37
			2	13	3								14			8	5	1		9[4]	11[1]					12	10[2]				4		6		7[3] 15	38

FA Cup

Third Round	Swansea C	(h)	3-0
Fourth Round	Burnley	(h)	0-1

Carabao Cup

Second Round	Cardiff C	(a)	5-3
Third Round	Everton	(a)	1-1
	Southampton won 6-5 on penalties.		
Fourth Round	Stoke C	(h)	3-2
Quarter-Final	Liverpool	(h)	1-2

STEVENAGE

FOUNDATION

There have been several clubs associated with the town of Stevenage. Stevenage Town was formed in 1884. They absorbed Stevenage Rangers in 1955 and later played at Broadhall Way. The club went into liquidation in 1968 and Stevenage Athletic was formed, but they, too, followed a similar path in 1976. Then Stevenage Borough was founded. The Broadhall Way pitch was dug up and remained unused for three years. Thus the new club started its life in the modest surrounds of the King George V playing fields with a roped-off ground in the Chiltern League. A change of competition followed to the Wallspan Southern Combination and by 1980 the club returned to the council-owned Broadhall Way when 'Borough' was added to the name. Entry into the United Counties League was so successful the league and cup were won in the first season. On to the Isthmian League Division Two and the climb up the pyramid continued. In 1995–96 Stevenage Borough won the Football Conference but was denied a place in the Football League as the ground did not measure up to the competition's standards. Subsequent improvements changed this and the 7,100 capacity venue became one of the best appointed grounds in non-league football. After winning elevation to the Football League the club dropped Borough from its title.

Lamex Stadium, Broadhall Way, Stevenage, Hertfordshire SG2 8RH.

Telephone: (01438) 223 223.

Ticket Office: (01438) 223 223.

Website: www.stevenagefc.com

Email: info@stevenagefc.com

Ground Capacity: 6,861.

Record Attendance: 8,040 v Newcastle U, FA Cup 4th rd, 25 January 1998.

Pitch Measurements: 104.2m × 64m (114yd × 70yd).

Chairman: Phil Wallace.

Chief Executive: Mike Pink.

Manager: Alex Revell.

Assistant Manager: Neil Banfield.

Colours: White shirts with red pattern and trim, red shorts with white trim, white socks with red trim.

Year Formed: 1976.

Turned Professional: 1976.

Club Nickname: 'The Boro'.

Previous Name: 1976, Stevenage Borough; 2010, Stevenage.

Grounds: 1976, King George V playing fields; 1980, Broadhall Way (renamed Lamex Stadium 2009).

HONOURS

League Champions: Football Conference – 1995–96, 2009–10.
Runners-up: FL 2 – 2022–23.
FA Cup: 5th rd – 2012.
League Cup: 3rd rd – 2023.

FOOTBALL YEARBOOK FACT FILE

Stevenage had the narrowest of escapes to avoid relegation in the Covid-hit 2019–20 season. With the EFL having determined that only one club would be relegated that season due to the demise of Bury, the Boro finished the campaign with just three wins from the 36 games played and in bottom place. However, rivals Macclesfield Town were subsequently hit by a series of points deductions which ultimately led to their relegation by the margin of 0.1 points per game.

First Football League Game: 7 August 2010, FL 2, v Macclesfield T (h) D 2–2 – Day; Henry, Laird, Bostwick, Roberts, Foster, Wilson (Sinclair), Byrom, Griffin (1), Winn (Odubade), Vincenti (1) (Beardsley).

Record League Victory: 6–0 v Yeovil T, FL 2, 14 April 2012 – Day; Lascelles (1), Laird, Roberts (1), Ashton (1), Shroot (Mousinho), Wilson (Myrie-Williams), Long, Agyemang (1), Reid (Slew), Freeman (2).

Record Victory: 11–1 v British Timken Ath 1980–81.

Record Defeat: 0–8 v Charlton Ath, FL Trophy, 9 October 2018.

Most League Points (3 for a win): 85, FL 2, 2022–23.

Most League Goals: 69, FL 1, 2011–12.

Highest League Scorer in Season: Matthew Godden, 20, FL 2, 2016–17.

Most League Goals in Total Aggregate: Jamie Reid, 43, 2021–25.

Most League Goals in One Match: 3, Chris Holroyd v Hereford U, FL 2, 28 September 2010; 3, Dani Lopez v Sheffield U, FL 1, 16 March 2013; 3, Chris Whelpdale v Morecambe, FL 2, 28 November 2015; 3, Matthew Godden v Newport Co, FL 2, 7 January 2017; 3, Alex Revell v Exeter C, FL 2, 28 April 2018.

Most Capped Player: Terence Vancooten, 18 (21), Guyana.

Most League Appearances: Luther Wildin, 235, 2018–25.

Youngest League Player: Makise Evans, 16 years 245 days v Mansfield T, 22 April 2023.

MANAGERS

Derek Montgomery 1976–83
Frank Cornwell 1983–87
John Bailey 1987–88
Brian Wilcox 1988–90
Paul Fairclough 1990–98
Richard Hill 1998–2000
Steve Wignall 2000
Paul Fairclough 2000–02
Wayne Turner 2002–03
Graham Westley 2003–06
Mark Stimson 2006–07
Peter Taylor 2007–08
Graham Westley 2008–12
Gary Smith 2012–13
Graham Westley 2013–15
Teddy Sheringham 2015–16
Darren Sarll 2016–18
Dino Maamria 2018–19
Graham Westley 2019–20
Alex Revell 2020–21
Paul Tisdale 2021–22
Steve Evans 2022–24
Alex Revell May 2024–

Record Transfer Fee Received: £1,500,000 from Watford for Ben Wilmot, May 2018.

Record Transfer Fee Paid: £125,000 to Exeter C for James Dunne, May 2012.

Football League Record: 2010 Promoted from Football Conference; 2010–11 FL 2; 2011–14 FL 1; 2014–23 FL 2; 2023– FL 1.

LATEST SEQUENCES

Longest Sequence of League Wins: 6, 25.4.2023 – 15.8.2023.

Longest Sequence of League Defeats: 8, 25.1.2020 – 7.3.2020.

Longest Sequence of League Draws: 5, 17.3.2012 – 31.3.2012.

Longest Sequence of Unbeaten League Matches: 17, 9.4.2012 – 5.10.2012.

Longest Sequence Without a League Win: 12, 3.8.2019 – 5.10.2019.

Successive Scoring Runs: 17 from 9.4.2012.

Successive Non-scoring Runs: 7 from 3.10.2020.

TEN YEAR LEAGUE RECORD

		P	W	D	L	F	A	Pts	Pos
2015-16	FL 2	46	11	15	20	52	67	48	18
2016-17	FL 2	46	20	7	19	67	63	67	10
2017-18	FL 2	46	14	13	19	60	65	55	16
2018-19	FL 2	46	20	10	16	59	55	70	10
2019-20	FL 2	36	3	13	20	24	50	22	23§
2020-21	FL 2	46	14	18	14	41	41	60	14
2021-22	FL 2	46	11	14	21	45	68	47	21
2022-23	FL 2	46	24	13	9	61	39	85	2
2023-24	FL 1	46	19	14	13	57	46	71	9
2024-25	FL 1	46	15	12	19	42	50	57	14

§*Decided on points-per-game (0.61)*

DID YOU KNOW ?

Midfielder Stuart Beevor hit a first-half hat-trick for Stevenage Borough, as the club was then known, in their Vauxhall Conference game at home to Hayes on 28 December, netting after 10, 36 and 41 minutes. However, with the weather conditions worsening the referee abandoned the game at half-time and his feat was removed from the record books.

STEVENAGE – SKY BET LEAGUE ONE 2024–25 LEAGUE RECORD

Match No.	Date	Venue	Opponents	Result		H/T Score	Lg Pos.	Goalscorers	Attendance
1	Aug 10	H	Shrewsbury T	W	1-0	0-0	8	List [58]	3357
2	17	A	Huddersfield T	L	1-2	0-1	14	White (pen) [90]	18,529
3	24	A	Burton Alb	D	0-0	0-0	11		2378
4	31	H	Lincoln C	L	0-1	0-0	16		4017
5	Sept 14	H	Barnsley	W	3-0	0-0	9	List 2 [54, 89], Piergianni [59]	4206
6	21	A	Exeter C	L	0-2	0-1	15		5612
7	24	A	Wigan Ath	D	0-0	0-0	15		7419
8	28	H	Charlton Ath	W	1-0	0-0	11	Roberts [67]	4701
9	Oct 1	H	Wrexham	W	1-0	1-0	9	Thompson L [10]	5704
10	5	A	Peterborough U	L	1-2	0-1	12	Thompson L [64]	8018
11	19	A	Mansfield T	W	1-0	1-0	12	Young [32]	7135
12	22	H	Cambridge U	L	0-2	0-1	13		4574
13	26	A	Rotherham U	L	0-2	0-0	15		8896
14	29	H	Bolton W	L	1-4	0-2	15	Kemp [70]	3611
15	Nov 9	H	Reading	D	1-1	1-0	14	Kemp [29]	4562
16	23	H	Leyton Orient	D	0-0	0-0	15		4259
17	Dec 3	H	Northampton T	W	2-0	0-0	13	Kemp [89], Reid [90]	2767
18	14	H	Stockport Co	W	2-1	1-1	12	Kemp [22], Reid (pen) [55]	3513
19	21	A	Blackpool	D	0-0	0-0	14		8610
20	26	H	Wycombe W	L	0-3	0-2	16		4430
21	29	H	Bristol R	W	3-0	1-0	14	List [34], Roberts [54], Reid [88]	3768
22	Jan 1	A	Northampton T	D	0-0	0-0	14		6294
23	4	A	Lincoln C	D	0-0	0-0	13		8220
24	18	H	Wigan Ath	L	1-2	0-0	15	Kemp [83]	3580
25	25	A	Barnsley	W	1-0	0-0	15	Kemp [90]	10,831
26	28	A	Wrexham	W	3-2	2-0	15	Kemp [13], Reid [18], Young [71]	10,670
27	Feb 1	H	Exeter C	W	4-1	2-1	11	King [11], Roberts 2 [17, 80], Kemp [76]	3094
28	8	A	Charlton Ath	L	0-2	0-1	12		14,093
29	11	A	Crawley T	L	1-3	0-0	13	Hanlan [53]	3220
30	15	H	Peterborough U	D	1-1	0-0	12	Kemp [55]	4476
31	18	H	Burton Alb	L	0-1	0-1	13		2801
32	22	A	Shrewsbury T	W	1-0	1-0	12	Pierre (og) [8]	5694
33	Mar 1	H	Huddersfield T	L	1-2	1-2	12	Hanlan [11]	4373
34	4	A	Cambridge U	W	1-0	0-0	11	Reid [64]	6338
35	8	H	Mansfield T	D	1-1	1-0	12	Reid [44]	3675
36	11	A	Birmingham C	L	1-2	0-1	12	Young [90]	25,544
37	15	A	Reading	D	1-1	0-0	13	Piergianni [60]	13,984
38	27	A	Leyton Orient	L	0-1	0-1	13		7305
39	Apr 1	A	Stockport Co	L	0-3	0-1	13		8427
40	5	H	Crawley T	W	3-1	1-0	13	White [20], Reid [89], Kemp [90]	4403
41	12	A	Wycombe W	L	0-1	0-0	14		4827
42	18	H	Blackpool	L	1-3	0-0	15	Piergianni [77]	4161
43	21	A	Bristol R	W	1-0	1-0	14	Reid [12]	9192
44	24	H	Birmingham C	L	0-1	0-0	14		4135
45	27	H	Rotherham U	D	1-1	0-0	14	Sweeney [90]	4012
46	May 3	A	Bolton W	D	1-1	0-0	14	Young [76]	20,613

Final League Position: 14

GOALSCORERS

League (42): Kemp 10, Reid 8 (1 pen), List 4, Roberts 4, Young 4, Piergianni 3, Hanlan 2, Thompson L 2, White 2 (1 pen), King 1, Sweeney 1, own goal 1.
FA Cup (1): Reid 1.
Carabao Cup (3): Appere 1, Goode 1, own goal 1.
Vertu Trophy (7): Simpson 2, Aboh 1, Freestone 1, Kemp 1, White 1, own goal 1.

Mahoney M 37	Wildin L 29	Sweeney D 14+7	Piergianni C 44	Freestone L 20+6	Phillips D 31+11	White H 23+18	Kemp D 33+7	List E 15+24	Thompson L 34+6	Simpson T 7+12	Appere L 7+10	Thompson N 14+1	Freeman N 13+16	Thompson B —+1	Butler D 28+4	Goode C 17+4	Roberts J 38+4	Smith K 13+1	Aboh K —+3	King E 16+12	Reid J 35+7	Young J 11+18	Pressley A —+4	Ashby-Hammond T 9	Hanlan B 12+4	Edwards K 5+3	Forster-Caskey J 1+2	Bates E —+1	Match No.
1	2	3	4	5	6	7^4	8	9^3	10^2	11^1	12	13	14	15															1
1	2	3	4		6^3	14	13	11^4	8	10^2	12				5	7^1	9	15											2
1		3	4		9	7^2	8	13	6	11^1	12				5	10	2												3
1		3^1	4		6^5	14	9	10^3	7^4	11^2			16		5	12	8	2	13	15									4
1	2		4	5	13	8^2	16	12	14	15					6^3		3	9^5			7	10^4	11^1						5
1	2		4	5	14	8	13	11^5		16			6		12	3^1	9^2		15	7^3	10^4								6
1	2		4		9	7	8		6	12		3			5	10					11^1								7
1	2		4		14	6^5	9^3	10^2	7	11^1		3	15		5	8^4				16	12	13							8
1	2		4		9	14	12		6	13		3			5	8				7^3	10^2	11^1							9
1	2		4	12	9^4	13	15		6^5	14		3^1	16		5	8				7^2	10	11^3							10
1	3		4	5	9	14	15	12	6^5						16		8^3	2		7^4	11^2	10^1	13						11
1		3	4		6^5	12	10^3	16	7^1				15		5		8	2^4		13	9	11^2	14						12
	3			4	9	7		12			15		13		5		8	2^3		6^1	11^4	10^2	14	1					13
	3		4	15	6^3	12	9	10^4	7				13		5		8^2	2^1		11			14	1					14
1			4		6	7	9	12		10^1		3	8^2		5			2		13	11^3	14							15
1	2		4			7	9	12	6	13		3	8^1		5		10			11^2									16
1	2		4		7^1	9	8^2	6	14			3	12		5					13	11	10^3							17
1	2		4		12	7	9^3	8^1	6	13		3	14		5	10^2				11									18
1	2		4		12	7^2	9^4	10^1	6^3	15		3	14		5	8				11	13								19
	2		4		6^3	7	9	12		13		3	14		5	8^1		15		11^4	10^2		1						20
1	2	15	4	12	7^3	13	9^2	10	6	16		3^5	14		5^1	8				11^4									21
1	2		4	5	7	12	9^1	10	6			3			8					11									22
1	2		4		15	8^4	14	12	7	10^2		3	6^3		9	5				13	11^1								23
1	2	13	4		7^3		9	8^2	6^6		12	3^1	14		10	5^4				11	15								24
1	2		4	5	6	7^1	9	13		14				3	8^3		12	11	10^2										25
1		3^4	4	5	6		9	14	15	11^2		12		16	8^3	2^1		7^5	10	13									26
1		3	4	5	6	14	9^3	12	13	11^1		2		8^4			7^2	10	15										27
1		3	4	5	6^1	15	9^5	12	13	11^3		2		3	8^2		7^4	10					14	16					28
1		3	4	5	6^2		9	14	7^3	12				8	2		13	10^4		11^1	15								29
1			4	5	15	16	9	13	6^3			12		3	8^2	2		7^5	14		11^4	10^1							30
1			4	5	6^1		9	12	13			14		3	8^3	2^4		7^2	10^5	16	11	15							31
1		3	4	5	13	7	9^2		6^3			2		14	8			12	11	10^1									32
1		3	4	5	14	7^4	9		6^3			2		13	10^2		15	12	16	11^5	8^1								33
1		3	4		8	12		7				2		5	11		6^1	9^2	13	10									34
1		3	4		7^2	13	9^4	6				2		5	15	8^1	12	10	14	11^3									35
1	15	4^5		6	14	9	13	7^3			2	2	5	3	8^1	11^4	16	10^1											36
1		4	12		13	9	16	6^3		15		2^1	5	3	8^4	7	10^5	14	11^2										37
1	2	16	4		13	9	12	6^5	15			5	3	8^3	7^2	10^4	14	11^1											38
1	2	14	4	16	12		9	13	6			5^3	3	8^4	7^2	10^5	15	11^1											39
1	2		4	5	6^4	8	10^1	9		11^2		3	12	15	14	13													40
	2		4		8	7	9^3	13	6^4	10^1	5	3	14		11^2	12		1		15									41
	2	3	4	16	8^2	6^6	9	14	7		5^4	13			12	11^3		1	10^1		15								42
	2	16	4	5^5	13	12		10^2	6		15	3	9		11^4			1	14	8^3	7^1								43
	2	3		5^4	7	8		12	13	10^3		6	4	9^1		11^2	15	1	14										44
	16	2	4^5	5	7		10^2	6^1	15		8	3	14		12	11^4	13	1		9^3									45
	5	2	4^4		6	7^3	13			11^1		8	3	9		14	10^2	12	1		15								46

FA Cup

First Round	Guiseley	(h)	1-1
aet; Stevenage won 5-4 on penalties.			
Second Round	Mansfield T	(h)	0-1

Carabao Cup

First Round	Norwich C	(a)	3-4

Vertu Trophy

Group D (S)	Crystal Palace U21	(h)	1-0
Group D (S)	Peterborough U	(a)	0-2
Group D (S)	Gillingham	(h)	1-1
Gillingham won 5-4 on penalties.			
Second Round	Burton Alb	(a)	4-0
Third Round	Leyton Orient	(a)	1-0
Quarter-Final	Birmingham C	(h)	0-1

STOCKPORT COUNTY

Edgeley Park, Hardcastle Road, Edgeley, Stockport, Cheshire SK3 9DD.

Telephone: (0161) 266 2700.

Ticket Office: (0161) 266 2700.

Website: www.stockportcounty.com

Email: tickets@stockportcounty.com

Ground Capacity: 10,797.

Record Attendance: 27,833 v Liverpool, FA Cup 5th rd, 11 February 1950.

Pitch Measurements: 104m × 65m (113.5 × 71yd).

Chairman: Ken Knott.

Chief Executive: Simon Wilson.

Manager: Dave Challinor.

First-Team Coach: Clint Hill.

Colours: Royal blue shirts with white trim, white shorts with royal blue trim, royal blue socks with white trim.

Year Formed: 1883.

Turned Professional: 1891.

Ltd Co.: 1908.

Previous Names: 1883, Heaton Norris Rovers; 1888, Heaton Norris; 1890, Stockport County.

Club Nicknames: 'County'; 'The Hatters'.

Grounds: 1883, Heaton Norris Recreation Ground; 1884, Heaton Norris Wanderers Cricket Ground; 1885, Chorlton's Farm, Chorlton's Lane; 1886, Heaton Norris Cricket Ground; 1887, Wilkes' Field, Belmont Street; 1889, Nursery Inn, Green Lane; 1902, Edgeley Park.

First Football League Game: 1 September 1900, Division 2, v Leicester Fosse (a) D 2–2 – Moores; Earp, Wainwright; Pickford, Limond, Harvey; Stansfield, Smith (1), Patterson, Foster, Betteley (1).

Record League Victory: 13–0 v Halifax T, Division 3 (N), 6 January 1934 – McGann; Vincent (1p); Jenkinson; Robinson, Stevens, Len Jones; Foulkes (1), Hill (3), Lythgoe (2), Stevenson (2), Downes (4).

Record Cup Victory: 5–0 v Lincoln C, FA Cup 1st rd, 11 November 1995 – Edwards; Connelly, Todd, Bennett, Flynn, Gannon (Dinning), Beaumont, Oliver (Ware), Eckhardt (3), Armstrong (1) (Mike), Chalk, (1 og).

Record Defeat: 1–8 v Chesterfield, Division 2, 19 April 1902.

Most League Points (2 for a win): 64, Division 4, 1966–67.

HONOURS

League Champions: Division 3N – 1921–22, 1936–37; Division 4 – 1966–67; FL 2 – 2023–24; National League – 2021–22.

Runners-up: Division 2 – 1996–97; Division 3N – 1928–29, 1929–30. Division 4 – 1990–91.

FA Cup: 5th rd, 1935, 1950, 2001.

League Cup: Semi-final 1997.

League Trophy: *Runners-up* 1992, 1993.

FOOTBALL YEARBOOK FACT FILE

Frank Beaumont became the first substitute to be used by Stockport County in a Football League game when he replaced the injured Dennis Hoggart five minutes from the end of their Fourth Division fixture at Chester on the opening day of the 1965–66 season. Chester had earlier used their own substitute, and this was the only game on that day in which both teams used their replacement players.

Most League Points (3 for a win): 92, FL 2, 2023–24.

Most League Goals: 115, Division 3 (N), 1933–34.

Highest League Scorer in Season: Alf Lythgoe, 46, Division 3 (N), 1933–34.

Most League Goals in Total Aggregate: Jack Connor, 132, 1951–56.

Most League Goals in One Match: 5, Joe Smith v Southport, Division 3 (N), 7 January 1928; 5, Joe Smith v Lincoln C, Division 3 (N), 15 September 1928; 5, Frank Newton v Nelson, Division 3 (N), 21 September 1929; 5, Alf Lythgoe v Southport, Division 3 (N), 25 August 1934; 5, Billy McNaughton v Mansfield T, Division 3 (N), 14 December 1935; 5, Jack Connor v Workington, Division 3 (N), 8 November 1952; 5, Jack Connor v Carlisle U, Division 3 (N), 7 April 1956.

Most Capped Player: Jarkko Wiss, 9 (45), Finland.

Most League Appearances: Andy Thorpe, 489, 1978–86, 1988–92.

Youngest League Player: Paul Turnbull, 16 years 97 days v Wrexham, 30 April 2005.

Record Transfer Fee Received: £1,600,000 from Middlesbrough for Alun Armstrong, February 1998.

Record Transfer Fee Paid: £800,000 to Nottingham F for Ian Moore, July 1998.

Football League Record: 1900 Elected to Division 2; 1900–04 Division 2; 1904 Failed re-election; 1905–21 Division 2; 1921–22 Division 3 (N); 1922–26 Division 2; 1926–37 Division 3 (N); 1937–38 Division 2; 1938–58 Division 3 (N); 1958–59 Division 3; 1959–67 Division 4; 1967–70 Division 3; 1970–91 Division 4; 1991–92 Division 3; 1992–97 Second Division; 1997–2002 First Division; 2002–04 Second Division; 2004–05 FL 1; 2005–08 FL 2; 2008–10 FL 1; 2010–11 FL 2; 2011–15 Football Conference; 2015–22 National League; 2022–24 FL 2; 2024– FL 1.

LATEST SEQUENCES

Longest Sequence of League Wins: 12, 9.9.2023 – 18.11.2023.

Longest Sequence of League Defeats: 10, 24.11.2001 – 13.01.2002.

Longest Sequence of League Draws: 7, 17.3.1989 – 14.4.1989.

Longest Sequence of Unbeaten League Matches: 18, 28.1.1933 – 28.8.1933.

Longest Sequence Without a League Win: 19, 28.12.1999 – 22.4.2000.

Successive Scoring Runs: 27 from 20.10.2007.

Successive Non-scoring Runs: 7 from 10.3.1923.

MANAGERS

Fred Stewart 1894–1911
Harry Lewis 1911–14
David Ashworth 1914–19
Albert Williams 1919–24
Fred Scotchbrook 1924–26
Lincoln Hyde 1926–31
Andrew Wilson 1932–33
Fred Westgarth 1934–36
Bob Kelly 1936–38
George Hunt 1938–39
Bob Marshall 1939–49
Andy Beattie 1949–52
Dick Duckworth 1952–56
Billy Moir 1956–60
Reg Flewin 1960–63
Trevor Porteous 1963–65
Bert Trautmann
 (General Manager) 1965–66
Eddie Quigley *(Team Manager)*
 1965–66
Jimmy Meadows 1966–69
Wally Galbraith 1969–70
Matt Woods 1970–71
Brian Doyle 1972–74
Jimmy Meadows 1974–75
Roy Chapman 1975–76
Eddie Quigley 1976–77
Alan Thompson 1977–78
Mike Summerbee 1978–79
Jimmy McGuigan 1979–82
Eric Webster 1982–85
Colin Murphy 1985
Les Chapman 1985–86
Jimmy Melia 1986
Colin Murphy 1986–87
Asa Hartford 1987–89
Danny Bergara 1989–95
Dave Jones 1995–97
Gary Megson 1997–99
Andy Kilner 1999–2001
Carlton Palmer 2001–03
Sammy McIlroy 2003–04
Chris Turner 2004–05
Jim Gannon 2005–09
Gary Ablett 2009–10
Paul Simpson 2010–11
Ray Mathias 2011
Dietmar Hamman 2011
Jim Gannon 2011–13
Darije Kalezic 2013
Ian Bogie 2013
Alan Lord 2013–15
Neil Young 2015–16
Jim Gannon 2016–21
Simon Rusk 2021
Dave Challinor November 2021–

TEN YEAR LEAGUE RECORD

		P	W	D	L	F	A	Pts	Pos
2015–16	NLN	42	15	14	13	50	49	59	9
2016–17	NLN	42	19	16	7	59	41	73	8
2017–18	NLN	42	20	9	13	75	57	69	5
2018–19	NLN	42	24	10	8	77	36	82	1
2019–20	NL	39	16	10	13	51	54	58	8
2020–21	NL	42	21	14	7	69	32	77	3
2021–22	NL	44	30	4	10	87	38	94	1
2022-23	FL 2	46	22	13	11	65	37	79	4
2023-24	FL 2	46	27	11	8	96	48	92	1
2024-25	FL 1	46	25	12	9	72	42	87	3

DID YOU KNOW ?

Goalkeeper Harry Hardy became Stockport County's first-ever international player when he was capped for England against Belgium. Hardy kept a clean sheet as England won 4-0 and went on to make over 200 first-team appearances for the Hatters. He remains the only player to have won full England international honours while on the club's books.

STOCKPORT COUNTY – SKY BET LEAGUE ONE 2024–25 LEAGUE RECORD

Match No.	Date	Venue	Opponents	Result	H/T Score	Lg Pos.	Goalscorers	Attendance
1	Aug 10	H	Cambridge U	W 2-0	1-0	1	Barry [5], Wootton [76]	9457
2	17	A	Blackpool	W 3-0	0-0	1	Barry [67], Fevrier [84], Olaofe [90]	12,567
3	24	H	Bristol R	W 2-0	1-0	1	Barry [39], Wootton [63]	9423
4	31	A	Mansfield T	D 1-1	1-1	1	Wootton [37]	8293
5	Sept 14	A	Crawley T	D 1-1	1-0	4	Barry [6]	4538
6	21	H	Leyton Orient	L 1-4	0-2	7	Diamond [50]	9473
7	28	A	Barnsley	D 1-1	0-1	9	Barry [90]	14,882
8	Oct 1	A	Shrewsbury T	W 2-0	1-0	5	Pye [44], Wootton [86]	5600
9	5	H	Wigan Ath	D 0-0	0-0	6		9995
10	19	A	Charlton Ath	D 1-1	1-0	9	Barry (pen) [12]	13,711
11	22	H	Northampton T	D 1-1	0-0	9	Barry (pen) [87]	8585
12	26	A	Lincoln C	L 1-2	1-1	12	Olaofe [9]	9513
13	29	H	Reading	W 4-1	3-1	10	Collar [18], Wootton [33], Barry 2 (1 pen) [42 (p), 68]	8128
14	Nov 5	H	Wycombe W	L 0-5	0-3	10		8305
15	9	H	Bolton W	W 5-0	1-0	6	Collar [30], Wootton [47], Horsfall [55], Barry [62], Bailey [90]	10,342
16	16	A	Wrexham	W 1-0	1-0	4	Barry [24]	10,327
17	23	A	Burton Alb	W 3-0	2-0	3	Bate [30], Barry 2 [42, 59]	3564
18	Dec 4	A	Birmingham C	L 0-2	0-2	5		24,863
19	7	H	Exeter C	W 2-0	0-0	5	Crama (og) [67], Barry (pen) [89]	9192
20	14	A	Stevenage	L 1-2	1-1	5	Camps [26]	3513
21	20	H	Peterborough U	W 2-1	1-1	5	Bailey [11], Olaofe [75]	9745
22	26	A	Huddersfield T	L 0-1	0-1	5		21,657
23	29	A	Rotherham U	D 1-1	1-1	5	Barry [13]	10,194
24	Jan 1	H	Birmingham C	D 1-1	0-1	7	Southam [78]	10,528
25	4	H	Mansfield T	L 1-2	1-2	7	Collar [20]	10,012
26	18	A	Reading	W 3-1	2-0	6	Olaofe [5], Connolly [13], Diamond [68]	11,019
27	25	H	Crawley T	W 2-0	2-0	5	Collar [25], Southam [34]	8960
28	28	H	Shrewsbury T	W 1-0	1-0	5	Norwood [37]	8862
29	Feb 1	A	Leyton Orient	W 1-0	1-0	4	Wootton [14]	8485
30	8	A	Barnsley	W 2-1	2-0	4	Olaofe [31], Collar (pen) [35]	10,148
31	11	A	Bristol R	D 1-1	0-0	4	Olaofe [53]	6643
32	15	A	Wigan Ath	W 2-0	0-0	4	Bate [79], Collar [82]	12,347
33	22	A	Cambridge U	L 0-2	0-2	4		6905
34	Mar 1	H	Blackpool	W 2-1	0-1	4	Andresson 2 [47, 81]	10,554
35	4	A	Northampton T	D 1-1	0-1	4	Andresson [79]	5559
36	8	H	Charlton Ath	D 0-0	0-0	4		10,338
37	15	A	Bolton W	W 1-0	0-0	5	Olaofe [72]	24,571
38	22	A	Wrexham	L 0-1	0-1	5		13,317
39	29	A	Burton Alb	W 2-1	0-0	5	Wootton [8], Olaofe [76]	9554
40	Apr 1	H	Stevenage	W 3-0	1-0	5	Fevrier [25], Wildin (og) [50], Diamond [72]	8427
41	5	A	Exeter C	W 2-0	2-0	4	Wootton 2 [2, 22]	6541
42	12	H	Rotherham U	W 3-1	1-1	4	Diamond [42], Hills [60], Wootton [73]	10,390
43	18	A	Peterborough U	D 1-1	0-1	5	Diamond [90]	11,241
44	21	H	Huddersfield T	W 2-1	0-0	5	Horsfall [74], Norwood (pen) [87]	10,336
45	26	H	Lincoln C	W 3-2	0-2	3	Fevrier [48], Collar [78], Olaofe [81]	9717
46	May 3	A	Wycombe W	W 3-1	0-1	3	Andresson [70], Norwood (pen) [77], Collar [81]	7561

Final League Position: 3

GOALSCORERS

League (72): Barry 15 (4 pens), Wootton 11, Olaofe 9, Collar 8 (1 pen), Diamond 5, Andresson 4, Fevrier 3, Norwood 3 (2 pens), Bailey 2, Bate 2, Horsfall 2, Southam 2, Camps 1, Connolly 1, Hills 1, Pye 1, own goals 2.
FA Cup (5): Wootton 2, Collar 1, Horsfall 1, Olaofe 1.
Carabao Cup (1): Mapengu 1.
Vertu Trophy (10): Olaofe 2, Stretton 2, Bailey 1, Barry 1, Camps 1, Fevrier 1, Norwood 1, Powell 1.
League One Play-offs (3): Horsfall 1, Norwood 1 (1 pen), Olaofe 1.

	Addai C 28 + 1	Mingi J 8 + 3	Horsfall F 26 + 3	Pye E 42	Touray I 38 + 5	Bate L 28 + 4	Camps C 19 + 8	Diamond J 16 + 17	Collar W 36 + 4	Barry L 22 + 1	Wootton K 40 + 6	Fevrier J 11 + 14	Onyango T 4 + 3	Bailey O 8 + 22	Hughes C — + 1	Gardner C — + 1	Olaofe I 26 + 16	Norwood O 32 + 10	Adaramola T 3 + 3	Connolly C 29 + 9	Fiorini L 4 + 7	Powell N 3 + 4	Mellon M — + 2	Hinchliffe B 18 + 1	Southam M 14 + 3	Rydel R 8 + 9	Knoyle K 15 + 8	Stretton J — + 2	Hamilton M — + 5	Hills B 15 + 1	Moxon O 7 + 10	Andresson B 2 + 9	Cosgrove S 1 + 6	Match No.
1	1	2^2	3	4	5	6^4	7	8^1	9^5	10^3	11	12	13	14	15	16																		1
2	1	2^3	3	4	5	7	6	8^2	9^4	10^1	11	12	13	15			14																	2
3	1	2	3	4	5		6	8^1	9^4	10^2	11^3	12	15	14			13	7																3
4	1		3	4	5		6		9	10^1	11	8	2				12	7																4
5	1		3	4	5		6	13	9^3	11^1	10^2	12	2	16			14	7^5	8^4	15														5
6	1		3	4	16	12	7^1	8	9	10	11^3	14					13	6^2	5^4	2	15													6
7	1		3	4	5	8^2	14	16	6	9	10^4	15	2^1				11^5	7^3	12	13														7
8	1	16	3	4	12	8	7	6^5	15	14	9^3						11^1	13	5^2	2	10^4													8
9	1	2^3	3	4	5	7^4	6	8^2	10	11		12					15			13	9^1	14												9
10	1	2^2	3^4	4	8	7		16	11^4	10^5	13		14				6^3		5	15	9^1													10
11	1			4	8	6		14	11^5	15	9^1		5^2	3			10^3	13	2	16	7^4	12												11
12	1^4	13		4	8	6^3			11	14	5^2		9	3			10^5	12	2		7^1	16	15											12
13	1		3	4	8	6^5		5^4	7^2	11^1	10	15	2	14			12	13	16	9^3														13
14	1		3	4	5^1		7	8^3	6	10^5	11		15				14	16	2^2	9^1							12	13						14
15			3	4		7		9^4	11^3	10	14		15	12			6	13	2					1		5^1	8^2							15
16			3	4		7		9	11^1	10	13		14				12	6^2	15	2				1		5^3	8^4							16
17			3	4	15	7	12		9^1	10^3	11^2		13	16			14	6						1		5^5	8^4							17
18			3	4		7^3	14	12	9	10	11						13	6^2	15	2				1		5	8^1							18
19		5^2	3^1	4	8	7		6^4	15	9^5	10^3	11		14	13		16^1	12	2					1		5								19
20			3	4	8^3	7^2		6^4	16	9	11^5	10		15			14	12	2^1					1		5	13							20
21			3	4	5	6	7^1		9^2	10^3	11			8^4			12	15						1		2		14						21
22			3	4		6^4	16	12	7	10	13			9^1			11^5	15	2^2					1		5^3	8	14						22
23			3^3	4	8			12	13	11^2	10			7^4	14		9^1	6	2					1	15		5^4							23
24		2^1		4	8^3		13	10^4	9		11			7^5			6^2		3	16					1	5	15	12	14					24
25				4	14		7	12	9		11			10^4	3^1		6^2		2	16				1	13	8^5	5^3	15						25
26				4	8		6	12	9^2		10						11^1	7	3	13				1	5		2							26
27				4	8	14	7^3	13	9^1		11						10^6	6	3					1	5	15	5^4	12						27
28				4	8	12	7^1	14	9		10			13			11^2	6^4	3					1	5	15	2^3							28
29				4	8	7^2		12	9^3		10			13			11^1	6	3					1	5		2	14						29
30				4	8	7^3			9		11			14			10^3	6	3					1		2^1			5	12	13			30
31				4	8			5^4	9		11^1			14			10^7	7	3					1		12	15	2^2	8	13				31
32	12			4	8	13	14	5^3	9^4		11						10	7	3							11^1	2		15	6^2				32
33	1				5^1	7^2	15	13	10		11						9	6^5	3^4						8^1	12	2^4		4	16	14			33
34	1			4	5	7	14		9^4		11	8^2					10^5	6^3	3						14	5^4	2	15	3	12	13	16		34
35	1		4	9^3	7	8^5		12	15		11	13					13	3								2^1	5^4		2	6^1	16	10^2		35
36	1			4		6	10		8^4		11^3						9	7^2							2^1	5	12		3	13	14	15		36
37	1		4	12	6	9^4		8			14	15					10	7^5	13							5^2	2^1		3	16	11^3			37
38	1		4	8^1	7	6^1	13	9^4		10	14		15				11		3^2							5		2^4	12					38
39	1	12	4^1	5	7^4		13	9^2			11^1	8^3					10^5	6	3	14						2			15	16				39
40	1		3		5	7^3		9^2			11^5	8^1					10^4	6	4	14						12		15	2	13	16			40
41	1		3	4	5			9^4	12		11^5	8^2	14				10^3	7			16					13			2	6^1		15		41
42	1	15	3	4	9			8	12		10^5	5^1	13				11^4	7	14										2^3	6^2		16		42
43	1	13	3^1	4	5^4			9	8		11	12		7^2			10^6	6											2	15	14			43
44	1	2^1	3		5			9	8^2		11	7^3		12			10^6	6	15										4	13	14			44
45	1		4^3	5	6^1				7		11	12					13	8	15							14	2^4		3	9	10^2			45
46	1		16	4	5^1				8		11	7^5		15			10^5	6	2^2							13	12		3	9^4	14			46

FA Cup

First Round aet.	Forest Green R	(h)	2-1
Second Round	Brackley T	(h)	3-1
Third Round	Crystal Palace	(a)	0-1

Carabao Cup

First Round	Blackburn R	(h)	1-6

Vertu Trophy

Group A (N)	Accrington S	(a)	4-1
Group A (N)	Everton U21	(h)	4-1
Group A (N)	Tranmere R	(h)	0-2
Second Round	Bradford C	(h)	2-3

League One Play-offs

Semi-Final 1st leg	Leyton Orient	(a)	2-2
Semi-Final 2nd leg	Leyton Orient	(h)	1-1

aet; Leyton Orient won 4-1 on penalties.

STOKE CITY

FOUNDATION

The date of the formation of this club has long been in doubt. The year 1863 was claimed, but more recent research by local club historian Wade Martin has uncovered nothing earlier than 1868, when a couple of Old Carthusians, who were apprentices at the local works of the old North Staffordshire Railway Company, met with some others from that works, to form Stoke Ramblers. It should also be noted that the old Stoke club went bankrupt in 1908 when a new club was formed.

bet365 Stadium, Stanley Matthews Way, Stoke-on-Trent, Staffordshire ST4 4EG.

Telephone: (01782) 367 598.

Ticket Office: (01782) 367 599.

Website: www.stokecityfc.com

Email: info@stokecityfc.com

Ground Capacity: 30,360.

Record Attendance: 51,380 v Arsenal, Division 1, 29 March 1937 (at Victoria Ground); 30,022 v Everton, Premier League, 17 March 2018 (at bet365 Stadium).

Pitch Measurements: 105m × 68m (115yd × 74.5yd).

Chairman: John Coates.

Managing Director: Richard Smith.

Manager: Mark Robins.

Assistant Managers: Paul Nevin, James Rowberry.

Colours: Red and white striped shirts with red and black trim, white shorts with red trim, white socks with red and black trim.

Year Formed: 1863* (*see Foundation*).

Turned Professional: 1885.

Previous Names: 1868, Stoke Ramblers; 1870, Stoke; 1925, Stoke City.

Club Nickname: 'The Potters'.

Grounds: 1875, Sweeting's Field; 1878, Victoria Ground (previously known as the Athletic Club Ground); 1997, Britannia Stadium (renamed bet365 Stadium 2016).

First Football League Game: 8 September 1888, Football League, v WBA (h) L 0–2 – Rowley; Clare, Underwood; Ramsey, Shutt, Smith; Sayer, McSkimming, Staton, Edge, Tunnicliffe.

Record League Victory: 10–3 v WBA, Division 1, 4 February 1937 – Doug Westland; Brigham, Harbot; Tutin, Turner (1p), Kirton; Matthews, Antonio (2), Freddie Steele (5), Jimmy Westland, Johnson (2).

Record Cup Victory: 7–1 v Burnley, FA Cup 2nd rd (replay), 20 February 1896 – Clawley; Clare, Eccles; Turner, Grewe, Robertson; Willie Maxwell, Dickson, Alan Maxwell (3), Hyslop (4), Schofield.

Record Defeat: 0–10 v Preston NE, Division 1, 14 September 1889.

Most League Points (2 for a win): 63, Division 3 (N), 1926–27.

HONOURS

League Champions: Division 2 – 1932–33, 1962–63; Second Division – 1992–93; Division 3N – 1926–27.
Runners-up: FL C – 2007–08; Division 2 – 1921–22.

FA Cup: Runners-up: 2011.

League Cup Winners: 1972. *Runners-up:* 1964.

League Trophy Winners: 1992, 2000.

European Competitions
UEFA Cup: 1972–73, 1974–75.
Europa League: 2011–12.

FOOTBALL YEARBOOK FACT FILE

Stoke, as the club was then named, were one of five teams who finished level on 24 points at the foot of the First Division table in 1898–99, the Potters taking bottom position due to goal average. They then played off in a mini-league of Test Matches to determine the relegated clubs, with Stoke topping the table. However, the Football League then voted to expand the First Division for 1899–1900 and all the play-off clubs were automatically included.

Most League Points (3 for a win): 93, Division 2, 1992–93.

Most League Goals: 92, Division 3 (N), 1926–27.

Highest League Scorer in Season: Freddie Steele, 33, Division 1, 1936–37.

Most League Goals in Total Aggregate: Freddie Steele, 142, 1934–49.

Most League Goals in One Match: 7, Neville Coleman v Lincoln C, Division 2, 23 February 1957.

Most Capped Player: Glenn Whelan, 81 (91), Republic of Ireland.

Most League Appearances: Eric Skeels, 507, 1958–76.

Youngest League Player: Peter Bullock, 16 years 163 days v Swansea C, 19 April 1958.

Record Transfer Fee Received: £20,000,000 (potentially rising to £25,000,000) from West Ham U for Marko Arnautovic, July 2017.

Record Transfer Fee Paid: £18,300,000 to Porto for Giannelli Imbula, February 2016.

Football League Record: 1888 Founder Member of Football League; 1888–90 Football League; 1890 Failed re-election; 1891 Re-elected to Football League; 1891–92 Football League; 1892–1907 Division 1; 1907–08 Division 2; 1908 resigned due to financial reasons; 1919 Re-elected to Division 2; 1919–22 Division 2; 1922–23 Division 1; 1923–26 Division 2; 1926–27 Division 3 (N); 1927–33 Division 2; 1933–53 Division 1; 1953–63 Division 2; 1963–77 Division 1; 1977–79 Division 2; 1979–85 Division 1; 1985–90 Division 2; 1990–92 Division 3; 1992–93 Second Division; 1993–98 First Division; 1998–2002 Second Division; 2002–04 First Division; 2004–08 FL C; 2008–18 Premier League; 2018– FL C.

LATEST SEQUENCES

Longest Sequence of League Wins: 8, 30.3.1895 – 21.9.1895.

Longest Sequence of League Defeats: 11, 6.4.1985 – 17.8.1985.

Longest Sequence of League Draws: 5, 13.5.2012 – 15.9.2012.

Longest Sequence of Unbeaten League Matches: 25, 5.9.1992 – 20.2.1993.

Longest Sequence Without a League Win: 17, 22.4.1989 – 14.10.1989.

Successive Scoring Runs: 21 from 24.12.1921.

Successive Non-scoring Runs: 8 from 29.12.1984.

MANAGERS

Tom Slaney 1874–83
(Secretary-Manager)
Walter Cox 1883–84
(Secretary-Manager)
Harry Lockett 1884–90
Joseph Bradshaw 1890–92
Arthur Reeves 1892–95
William Rowley 1895–97
H. D. Austerberry 1897–1908
A. J. Barker 1908–14
Peter Hodge 1914–15
Joe Schofield 1915–19
Arthur Shallcross 1919–23
John 'Jock' Rutherford 1923
Tom Mather 1923–35
Bob McGrory 1935–52
Frank Taylor 1952–60
Tony Waddington 1960–77
George Eastham 1977–78
Alan A'Court 1978
Alan Durban 1978–81
Richie Barker 1981–83
Bill Asprey 1984–85
Mick Mills 1985–89
Alan Ball 1989–91
Lou Macari 1991–93
Joe Jordan 1993–94
Lou Macari 1994–97
Chic Bates 1997–98
Chris Kamara 1998
Brian Little 1998–99
Gary Megson 1999
Gudjon Thordarson 1999–2002
Steve Cotterill 2002
Tony Pulis 2002–05
Johan Boskamp 2005–06
Tony Pulis 2006–13
Mark Hughes 2013–18
Paul Lambert 2018
Gary Rowett 2018–19
Nathan Jones 2019
Michael O'Neill 2019–22
Alex Neill 2022–23
Steven Schumacher 2023–24
Narcis Pelach 2024
Mark Robins January 2025–

TEN YEAR LEAGUE RECORD

		P	W	D	L	F	A	Pts	Pos
2015-16	PR Lge	38	14	9	15	41	55	51	9
2016-17	PR Lge	38	11	11	16	41	56	44	13
2017-18	PR Lge	38	7	12	19	35	68	33	19
2018-19	FL C	46	11	22	13	45	52	55	16
2019-20	FL C	46	16	8	22	62	68	56	15
2020-21	FL C	46	15	15	16	50	52	60	14
2021-22	FL C	46	17	11	18	57	52	62	14
2022-23	FL C	46	14	11	21	55	54	53	16
2023-24	FL C	46	15	11	20	49	60	56	17
2024-25	FL C	46	12	15	19	45	62	51	18

DID YOU KNOW ?

Keith Bebbington became the first substitute to be used in top-flight English football when he replaced Dennis Viollet after 78 minutes of the game away to Arsenal on the opening day of the 1965–66 season, the day substitutes were introduced to the Football League. The home fans were unhappy about the change and booed the replacement whenever he touched the ball.

STOKE CITY – SKY BET CHAMPIONSHIP 2024–25 LEAGUE RECORD

Match No.	Date	Venue	Opponents	Result	H/T Score	Lg Pos.	Goalscorers	Attendance
1	Aug 10	H	Coventry C	W 1-0	0-0	7	Baker [78]	25,037
2	17	A	Watford	L 0-3	0-0	14		18,789
3	24	H	WBA	L 1-2	1-2	17	Koumas [29]	24,371
4	31	A	Plymouth Arg	W 1-0	0-0	10	Manhoef [83]	16,934
5	Sept 14	A	Oxford U	L 0-1	0-0	13		11,507
6	20	H	Hull C	L 1-3	1-0	14	Wilmot [30]	23,366
7	28	A	Middlesbrough	L 0-2	0-1	20		24,610
8	Oct 2	H	Portsmouth	W 6-1	3-1	15	Cannon 4 (1 pen) [13, 43, 48 (p), 51], Gallagher [45], Moran [53]	20,824
9	5	A	Swansea C	D 0-0	0-0	16		14,546
10	19	H	Norwich C	D 1-1	1-1	16	Manhoef [45]	23,002
11	22	A	Bristol C	D 2-2	2-0	15	Koumas [2], Moran [14]	19,679
12	26	A	Sheffield U	L 0-2	0-1	19		28,575
13	Nov 2	H	Derby Co	W 2-1	1-0	16	Cannon (pen) [9], Gibson [82]	24,511
14	6	A	Blackburn R	W 2-0	0-0	14	Manhoef [57], Cannon (pen) [85]	13,144
15	9	H	Millwall	D 1-1	0-1	13	Gibson [60]	21,060
16	23	A	QPR	D 1-1	1-0	12	Cannon [24]	15,688
17	26	H	Preston NE	D 0-0	0-0	13		19,805
18	30	H	Burnley	L 0-2	0-0	14		22,994
19	Dec 7	A	Sunderland	L 1-2	1-1	15	Koumas [6]	39,311
20	10	A	Luton T	L 1-2	1-1	17	Cannon [6]	10,537
21	14	H	Cardiff C	D 2-2	1-1	17	Moran [17], Gibson [90]	20,847
22	21	A	Sheffield Wed	L 0-2	0-0	19		26,743
23	26	H	Leeds U	L 0-2	0-1	19		24,738
24	29	H	Sunderland	W 1-0	0-0	18	Cannon [90]	23,654
25	Jan 1	A	Burnley	D 0-0	0-0	19		20,119
26	4	H	Plymouth Arg	D 0-0	0-0	19		26,168
27	18	A	WBA	D 1-1	1-0	18	Lowe [9]	25,679
28	22	A	Portsmouth	L 1-3	1-2	19	Wilmot [27]	19,388
29	25	H	Oxford U	D 0-0	0-0	20		22,911
30	Feb 1	H	Hull C	W 2-1	1-1	18	Al-Hamadi [43], Moran [74]	21,709
31	12	A	Bristol C	L 0-2	0-1	19		18,457
32	15	H	Swansea C	W 3-1	0-0	19	Burger [64], Bae [73], Baker [90]	21,256
33	22	A	Norwich C	L 2-4	1-1	19	Baker 2 (1 pen) [45, 90 (p)]	26,267
34	25	H	Middlesbrough	L 1-3	1-1	20	Bae [45]	20,141
35	Mar 1	A	Watford	D 0-0	0-0	19		21,894
36	8	A	Coventry C	L 2-3	0-2	20	Gallagher 2 [65, 86]	30,011
37	12	H	Blackburn R	W 1-0	1-0	19	Al-Hamadi [19]	20,194
38	15	A	Millwall	L 0-1	0-0	20		16,799
39	29	H	QPR	W 3-1	2-0	18	Bae [21], Tchamadeu [44], Manhoef [54]	23,192
40	Apr 5	A	Preston NE	D 1-1	0-1	20	Baker (pen) [75]	17,341
41	8	H	Luton T	D 1-1	0-0	20	Baker [74]	21,226
42	12	A	Cardiff C	W 1-0	0-0	18	Fish (og) [85]	20,658
43	18	H	Sheffield Wed	W 2-0	1-0	16	Manhoef [21], Wilmot [61]	29,163
44	21	A	Leeds U	L 0-6	0-5	17		36,644
45	25	H	Sheffield U	L 0-2	0-1	17		24,460
46	May 3	A	Derby Co	D 0-0	0-0	18		32,471

Final League Position: 18

GOALSCORERS

League (45): Cannon 9 (3 pens), Baker 6 (2 pens), Manhoef 5, Moran 4, Bae 3, Gallagher 3, Gibson 3, Koumas 3, Wilmot 3, Al-Hamadi 2, Burger 1, Lowe 1, Tchamadeu 1, own goal 1.
FA Cup (5): Koumas 2, Baker 1 (1 pen), Cannon 1 (1 pen), Ennis 1.
Carabao Cup (10): Manhoef 2, Tezgel 2, Anderson 1, Cannon 1, Koumas 1, Mmaee 1, Phillips 1, Rose 1.

Johansson V 46	Tchamadeu J 35 + 6	Wilmot B 36 + 3	Gibson B 22 + 2	Bocat E 23 + 7	Laurent J 3	Thompson J 13 + 10	Manhoef M 28 + 6	Burger W 37 + 2	Gooch L 12 + 8	Tezgel E 2 + 10	Ennis N 1 + 8	Baker L 16 + 3	Johnson D — + 1	Moran A 26 + 9	Bae J 37 + 8	Koumas L 26 + 17	Mnaee R 1 + 2	Dixon J — + 2	Phillips A 35	Sidibe S 3 + 5	Cannon T 22	Rose M 13 + 9	Seko T 18 + 7	Stevens E 13 + 5	Gallagher S 9 + 13	Andre Vidigal F — + 10	Lawal B 1 + 6	Lowe N 5 + 5	Wilson-Esbrand J 4 + 2	Al-Hamadi A 11 + 4	Pearson B 8 + 5	Match No.
1	2	3	4	5	6	7	8^3	9^2	10	11^1	12	13	14																			1
1	2	3	4	5	6	7^4	8^5	9^1	10^2	11^3				12	13	14	15	16														2
1	2^1	3	4	5	6	7^3	8^4	14	10^5			15	16	12	9^2 11	13																3
1	2	4	13	5		9	7	15			14			6^5	8^4 11^3	10^1 16			3^2 12													4
1	2	3	4	5		14	8	7^5	9^1 15	16	12	10^4	13		6^2	11^3																5
1	2^3	3	4	5^5		8^2	10	7		12	16			9	6^1	11^4 13 14			15													6
1	2^3	3	4	5		8	10^2	7^4		12				9	6^5	14 11^1 15						13	16									7
1	15	2^4	4	16		13		7		12				6^3	10 8^2	11 3			5^5			9^1 14										8
1		2	4	5		12	13	8^2		15				7	9^3 6^1	10 3						11^4 14										9
1	14	2	4			12	8^3	7^1						6	10^4 9^2	11 3 15 5			13													10
1	13	2	4	5^1		7	8^4			14				6	10^2 9^3	11 3			12			15										11
1	2^4	3	5^2	13		7	9^3			8	12	10		4		11^1			14 6			15										12
1	2		4	13		8^3	7	9	10^2	12				3	11				6^1 5			14										13
1	2		4	14		6^4	8			16				7^2 11^5	9^1	3	10^3 13 12 5		15													14
1	2^3	13	4	5^5		16	8	7^1						9^4 10	14			3^2 15 11 12 6														15
1		2	4	5		13	8^3			12				9	10^1	3	7^2 11 14 6															16
1	2^1	13	4	14		8^5	7^2	9^1	10	15				3	12 11			6			5^3	16										17
1	5	2^2	4	8		9	7^1			12				11	13	3			10			6										18
1	2	13		5		9^1		7	10^2	8				3	11 4 6				12													19
1		2		5		10	8^3	13	14	12				9^1 6^2	3	11 4 7																20
1		2	4	5		8^2		13	12	7				9^3 10^1	3^4	11			6			15	14									21
1	5	2	4	8^3		7^4	13	9^2	12 10	15				11	3^1 6			14														22
1	2	3^4	5^1	14		9^5	6^3	7	13 10	4				8^2 11 12				15 16														23
1	2	4				7	5^2	9^1	10 8					3^3	11 14 6 13 12																	24
1	2	4				7^1	5 13	9	10 8					3	11^2			6 12														25
1	2	4				12	5	7	9 8					3	11			6	10^1													26
1	2	4				9^1		12	6	8	13 10			3	7 5				11^2													27
1	2^3	4^6				9		11	6	8^2	14 10			3	13 7^1 15			16 12	5^4													28
1	2					7	10	6		9	12 8^1			3	4 5				11													29
1	12					7^4	2^1 15	13	8 14					3	4 6 5				9	10^5 11^2												30
1	12	5^2				8	15 7^5	9	14 13					3	4 2^1				11^3	6	10^4 16											31
1	2		5^5	12		7^3	13	9	8 10^1					3	4 14				15 16	11^4 6^2												32
1	2		14	12		9		8	10^3 13					3	4 6 5^4 15				11^2 7^1													33
1	14	2^3	16			8^2		6	9 10 13					3	4^5 7^4 5 12				11^1	15												34
1	2	4				7^2	13	9^3	10 8					3	14 5 12				11^1 6													35
1	2	4				12 13	7	9^2	10 8^3					3	5 14				15 11^4 6^1													36
1	2	4	5^2			6	8^1 7	9	10 12					3	15 13^1 14				11^3													37
1	2	4	5			6	14 7	9^2	13 10^3 8					3	12				11^1													38
1	2	4	5			13	8 7	9	10^3 14					3	11^1				12	6^2												39
1	2	4	5			6	8^3 7^4 14	9	10 13					3	11^2				12 15													40
1	2	4	5			6^1	8^2 7	9	10 14					3	11^3				12 13													41
1	2	4	5			6^4	8^3 7 14	9	10^2 13					3	12				11^1 15													42
1	2	4	5^1			12^2	8 7 13	9^4	10					3	11^3				14 6													43
1	2	4	13			8^1	7^5 12	9	10^3 14					3	16				15	5^2 11^4 6												44
1	2^4	4				8^3	7 5	9	10^2 15					3	11				12	14 13 6^1												45
1		4	5			8	6	7	13 9^2					3	11				2 12	10^1												46

FA Cup

Round	Opponent		Result
Third Round	Sunderland	(a)	2-1
aet.			
Fourth Round	Cardiff C	(h)	3-3
aet; Cardiff C won 4-2 on penalties.			

Carabao Cup

Round	Opponent		Result
First Round	Carlisle U	(a)	2-0
Second Round	Middlesbrough	(a)	5-0
Third Round	Fleetwood T	(h)	1-1
Stoke C won 2-1 on penalties.			
Fourth Round	Southampton	(a)	2-3

SUNDERLAND

FOUNDATION

A Scottish schoolmaster named James Allan, working at Hendon Board School, took the initiative in the foundation of Sunderland in 1879 when they were formed as The Sunderland and District Teachers' Association FC at a meeting in the Adults School, Norfolk Street. Due to financial difficulties, they quickly allowed members from outside the teaching profession and so became Sunderland AFC in October 1880.

Stadium of Light, Sunderland, Tyne and Wear SR5 1SU.
Telephone: (0371) 911 1200.
Ticket Office: (0371) 911 1973.
Website: www.safc.com
Email: enquiries@safc.com
Ground Capacity: 48,095.
Record Attendance: 75,118 v Derby Co, FA Cup 6th rd replay, 8 March 1933 (at Roker Park); 48,335 v Liverpool, Premier League, 13 April 2002 (at Stadium of Light).
Pitch Measurements: 105m × 68m (115yd × 74.5yd).
Chairman: Kyril Louis-Dreyfus.
Chief Operating Officer: Paul Kingsmore.
Head Coach: Regis Le Bris.
Assistant Head Coach: Luciano Vulcano.
Colours: Red and white striped shirts with red and white trim, black shorts with red and white trim, red socks with white trim.
Year Formed: 1879.
Turned Professional: 1886.
Previous Names: 1879, Sunderland and District Teachers AFC; 1880, Sunderland.
Club Nickname: 'The Black Cats'.
Grounds: 1879, Blue House Field, Hendon; 1882, Groves Field, Ashbrooke; 1883, Horatio Street; 1884, Abbs Field, Fulwell; 1886, Newcastle Road; 1898, Roker Park; 1997, Stadium of Light.
First Football League Game: 13 September 1890, Football League, v Burnley (h) L 2–3 – Kirtley; Porteous, Oliver; Wilson, Auld, Gibson; Spence (1), Miller, Campbell (1), Scott, Davy Hannah.
Record League Victory: 9–1 v Newcastle U (a), Division 1, 5 December 1908 – Roose; Forster, Melton; Daykin, Thomson, Low; Mordue (1), Hogg (3), Brown, Holley (3), Bridgett (2).
Record Cup Victory: 11–1 v Fairfield, FA Cup 1st rd, 2 February 1895 – Doig; McNeill, Johnston; Dunlop, McCreadie (1), Wilson; Gillespie (1), Millar (5), Campbell, Jimmy Hannah (3), Scott (1).
Record Defeat: 0–8 v Sheff Wed, Division 1, 26 December 1911; 0–8 v West Ham U, Division 1, 19 October 1968; 0–8 v Watford, Division 1, 25 September 1982; 0–8 v Southampton, Premier League, 18 October 2014.

HONOURS

League Champions: Division 1 – 1892–93, 1894–95, 1901–02, 1912–13, 1935–36; Football League 1891–92; FL C – 2004–05, 2006–07; First Division – 1995–96, 1998–99; Division 2 – 1975–76; Division 3 – 1987–88. *Runners-up:* Division 1 – 1893–94, 1897–98, 1900–01, 1922–23, 1934–35; Division 2 – 1963–64, 1979–80.

FA Cup Winners: 1937, 1973. *Runners-up:* 1913, 1992.

League Cup: Runners-up: 1985, 2014.

League Trophy Winners: 2021. *Runners-up:* 2019.

European Competitions
European Cup-Winners' Cup: 1973–74.

FOOTBALL YEARBOOK FACT FILE

Sunderland missed out on promotion at the very end of both 1961–62 and 1962–63 in heartbreaking fashion, failing to win the last game of the season on both occasions to deny themselves a place back in the top flight. Undaunted, they finished as runners-up in Division Two in 1963–64 to secure their return to the First Division.

Most League Points (2 for a win): 61, Division 2, 1963–64.

Most League Points (3 for a win): 105, Division 1, 1998–99.

Most League Goals: 109, Division 1, 1935–36.

Highest League Scorer in Season: Dave Halliday, 43, Division 1, 1928–29.

Most League Goals in Total Aggregate: Charlie Buchan, 209, 1911–25.

Most League Goals in One Match: 5, Charlie Buchan v Liverpool, Division 1, 7 December 1919; 5, Bobby Gurney v Bolton W, Division 1, 7 December 1935; 5, Dominic Sharkey v Norwich C, Division 2, 20 February 1962.

Most Capped Player: Seb Larsson, 59 (133), Sweden.

Most League Appearances: Jim Montgomery, 537, 1962–77.

Youngest League Player: Derek Forster, 15 years 184 days v Leicester C, 22 August 1964.

Record Transfer Fee Received: £28,000,000 (potentially rising to £33,000,000 from Borussia Dortmund for Jobe Bellingham, June 2025.

Record Transfer Fee Paid: £30,000,000 to Strasbourg for Habib Diarra, July 2025.

Football League Record: 1890 Elected to Division 1; 1890–58 Division 1; 1958–64 Division 2; 1964–70 Division 1; 1970–76 Division 2; 1976–77 Division 1; 1977–80 Division 2; 1980–85 Division 1; 1985–87 Division 2; 1987–88 Division 3; 1988–90 Division 2; 1990–91 Division 1; 1991–92 Division 2; 1992–96 First Division; 1996–97 Premier League; 1997–99 First Division; 1999–2003 Premier League; 2003–04 First Division; 2004–05 FL C; 2005–06 Premier League; 2006–07 FL C; 2007–17 Premier League; 2017–18 FL C: 2018–22 FL 1; 2022–25 FL C; 2025– Premier League.

LATEST SEQUENCES

Longest Sequence of League Wins: 13, 14.11.1891 – 2.4.1892.

Longest Sequence of League Defeats: 17, 18.1.2003 – 16.8.2003.

Longest Sequence of League Draws: 6, 26.3.1949 – 19.4.1949.

Longest Sequence of Unbeaten League Matches: 19, 26.12.2018 – 9.4.2019

Longest Sequence Without a League Win: 22, 21.12.2002 – 16.8.2003.

Successive Scoring Runs: 43 from 30.3.2018.

Successive Non-scoring Runs: 10 from 27.11.1976.

MANAGERS

Tom Watson 1888–96
Bob Campbell 1896–99
Alex Mackie 1899–1905
Bob Kyle 1905–28
Johnny Cochrane 1928–39
Bill Murray 1939–57
Alan Brown 1957–64
George Hardwick 1964–65
Ian McColl 1965–68
Alan Brown 1968–72
Bob Stokoe 1972–76
Jimmy Adamson 1976–78
Ken Knighton 1979–81
Alan Durban 1981–84
Len Ashurst 1984–85
Lawrie McMenemy 1985–87
Denis Smith 1987–91
Malcolm Crosby 1991–93
Terry Butcher 1993
Mick Buxton 1993–95
Peter Reid 1995–2002
Howard Wilkinson 2002–03
Mick McCarthy 2003–06
Niall Quinn 2006
Roy Keane 2006–08
Ricky Sbragia 2008–09
Steve Bruce 2009–11
Martin O'Neill 2011–13
Paolo Di Canio 2013
Gus Poyet 2013–15
Dick Advocaat 2015
Sam Allardyce 2015–16
David Moyes 2016–17
Simon Grayson 2017
Chris Coleman 2017–18
Jack Ross 2018–19
Phil Parkinson 2019–20
Lee Johnson 2020–22
Alex Neill 2022
Tony Mowbray 2022–23
Michael Beale 2023–24
Regis Le Bris July 2024–

TEN YEAR LEAGUE RECORD

		P	W	D	L	F	A	Pts	Pos
2015-16	PR Lge	38	9	12	17	48	62	39	17
2016-17	PR Lge	38	6	6	26	29	69	24	20
2017-18	FL C	46	7	16	23	52	80	37	24
2018-19	FL 1	46	22	19	5	80	47	85	5
2019-20	FL 1	36	16	11	9	48	32	59	8§
2020-21	FL 1	46	20	17	9	70	42	77	4
2021-22	FL 1	46	24	12	10	79	53	84	5
2022-23	FL C	46	18	15	13	68	55	69	6
2023-24	FL C	46	16	8	22	52	54	56	16
2024-25	FL C	46	21	13	12	58	44	76	4

§*Decided on points-per-game (1.64)*

DID YOU KNOW ?

Sunderland have hosted five full England internationals at three different grounds: Newcastle Road, Roker Park and the Stadium of Light. The most recent game took place on 2 April 2003 when England beat Turkey 2-0 in a European Championship qualifier in front of a crowd of 47,667.

SUNDERLAND – SKY BET CHAMPIONSHIP 2024–25 LEAGUE RECORD

Match No.	Date	Venue	Opponents	Result		H/T Score	Lg Pos.	Goalscorers	Attendance
1	Aug 10	A	Cardiff C	W	2-0	1-0	3	O'Nien [18], Clarke [89]	21,401
2	18	H	Sheffield Wed	W	4-0	3-0	2	Cirkin [11], Mayenda 2 [15, 47], O'Nien [24]	40,022
3	24	H	Burnley	W	1-0	1-0	1	Mundle [26]	40,096
4	31	A	Portsmouth	W	3-1	1-0	1	Swanson (og) [31], Browne [51], Mundle [56]	20,231
5	Sept 14	A	Plymouth Arg	L	2-3	1-0	1	Roberts (pen) [24], Mundle [86]	16,967
6	21	H	Middlesbrough	W	1-0	1-0	2	Rigg [24]	42,871
7	28	A	Watford	L	1-2	0-1	2	Isidor [49]	20,335
8	Oct 1	H	Derby Co	W	2-0	1-0	1	Bellingham [40], Isidor [55]	39,017
9	4	H	Leeds U	D	2-2	1-1	1	Rigg [9], Firpo (og) [90]	41,769
10	20	A	Hull C	W	1-0	0-0	1	Isidor [63]	23,072
11	23	A	Luton T	W	2-1	0-0	1	Rigg [55], Mundle [66]	11,332
12	26	H	Oxford U	W	2-0	1-0	1	Bellingham [16], Isidor [63]	40,654
13	Nov 2	A	QPR	D	0-0	0-0	1		16,383
14	6	A	Preston NE	D	0-0	0-0	1		18,064
15	9	H	Coventry C	D	2-2	2-0	1	Isidor [17], Cirkin [35]	43,374
16	23	A	Millwall	D	1-1	1-0	2	Connolly [10]	18,385
17	26	H	WBA	D	0-0	0-0	3		36,733
18	29	A	Sheffield U	L	0-1	0-0	4		28,465
19	Dec 7	H	Stoke C	W	2-1	1-1	4	Watson 2 [7, 86]	39,311
20	10	H	Bristol C	D	1-1	0-0	4	Roberts [90]	35,421
21	14	A	Swansea C	W	3-2	1-2	3	Ballard [28], Neil [73], Bellingham [75]	15,791
22	21	H	Norwich C	W	2-1	0-1	4	Ballard [47], Bellingham [72]	40,114
23	26	A	Blackburn R	D	2-2	0-1	4	Rigg [51], Isidor [55]	24,961
24	29	A	Stoke C	L	0-1	0-0	4		23,654
25	Jan 1	H	Sheffield U	W	2-1	2-1	4	Mayenda [27], Isidor [35]	42,276
26	5	H	Portsmouth	W	1-0	1-0	4	Isidor [7]	39,846
27	17	A	Burnley	D	0-0	0-0	4		21,014
28	21	A	Derby Co	W	1-0	1-0	3	Mayenda [28]	27,441
29	25	H	Plymouth Arg	D	2-2	0-0	4	Isidor [60], Hume [72]	41,097
30	Feb 3	A	Middlesbrough	W	3-2	1-1	4	Neil [33], Isidor [51], Giles (og) [67]	29,161
31	8	H	Watford	D	2-2	1-1	4	O'Nien [16], Cirkin [89]	41,329
32	12	H	Luton T	W	2-0	1-0	4	Le Fee [13], Isidor [58]	37,929
33	17	A	Leeds U	L	1-2	1-0	4	Isidor [32]	36,804
34	22	H	Hull C	L	0-1	0-1	4		44,009
35	28	A	Sheffield Wed	W	2-1	1-0	4	Mayenda 2 [34, 71]	27,954
36	Mar 8	H	Cardiff C	W	2-1	1-1	4	Mayenda [2], Mepham [77]	40,066
37	11	H	Preston NE	D	1-1	0-0	4	Mundle [86]	37,731
38	15	A	Coventry C	L	0-3	0-2	4		30,219
39	29	H	Millwall	W	1-0	1-0	4	Hume [20]	41,762
40	Apr 5	A	WBA	W	1-0	1-0	4	Hume [35]	25,918
41	8	A	Norwich C	D	0-0	0-0	4		26,320
42	12	H	Swansea C	L	0-1	0-0	4		42,362
43	18	A	Bristol C	L	1-2	1-0	4	Mayenda [31]	25,915
44	21	H	Blackburn R	L	0-1	0-1	4		40,031
45	26	A	Oxford U	L	0-2	0-1	4		11,431
46	May 3	H	QPR	L	0-1	0-1	4		41,917

Final League Position: 4

GOALSCORERS

League (58): Isidor 12, Mayenda 8, Mundle 5, Bellingham 4, Rigg 4, Cirkin 3, Hume 3, O'Nien 3, Ballard 2, Neil 2, Roberts 2 (1 pen), Watson 2, Browne 1, Clarke 1, Connolly 1, Le Fee 1, Mepham 1, own goals 3.
FA Cup (1): Aleksic 1.
Carabao Cup (0).
Championship Play-offs (5): Mayenda 2, Ballard 1, Isidor 1, Watson 1.

Patterson A 42	Hume T 43 + 1	O'Nien L 44 + 1	Alese A 8 + 4	Cirkin D 30 + 6	Browne A 13 + 9	Neil D 44	Roberts P 38 + 7	Bellingham J 39 + 1	Clarke J 2	Mayenda E 22 + 15	Rusyn N — + 8	Rigg C 36 + 6	Mundle R 17 + 5	Aouchiche A 3 + 5	Ballard D 12 + 8	Triantis N — + 1	Isidor W 34 + 9	Poveda-Ocampo I — + 6	Mepham C 37 + 1	Watson T 11 + 9	Connolly A 2 + 8	Hjelde I 5 + 10	Moore S 4	Aleksic M 3 + 5	Le Fee E 11 + 4	Abdul Samed S 3 + 7	Jones H 2 + 2	Seelt J — + 1	Anderson J 1 + 1	Match No.
1	2	3	4	5	6	7	8²	9		10³		11¹	12		13		14													1
1	2	3	4	5	6	8³	7	10		11²	13	9¹	14	12																2
1	2	3	4	5	12	6⁶	8⁴	11²	13	9¹	10⁵	14	15																	3
1	2	4		5	9	7¹	6	11³	14	8	10²	3	12	13																4
1	2	4		5	12	7	9	8	10²	6¹	11		3	13																5
1	2	4		5	6	8¹	7	11	9²	10	13	12	3																	6
1	2	4		5	7	9¹	8	12	6	11³	10²	13	3	14																7
1	2	4		5	12	7	9²	8	14	6¹	11	10³	13⁴	3	15															8
1	2	4		5	12	7	9²	8	6¹	11	10	3	13																	9
1	2	4		5	13	7	9²	8	6	11	10¹	3	12																	10
1	2	4		5	6	7	13	8	9³	11²	10¹	3	12	14																11
	2	4		5	12	7	9	8	6¹	11²	10⁴	3³	15	13	14	1														12
	2	4		5	9	6	8	7⁸	10¹	11²	3	8²	11¹	1																13
	2	4		5	7	6	13	14	9	12	10³	3	8²	11¹	1															14
	2	4		5	7²	6	8	9	10¹	13	11	3	12	1																15
1		2	5			7		8	6		4	11			3	10	9¹	12												16
1	5	2³	13			6	8	7	12	9	4	11	3	10¹																17
1	2	5	13			6	8²	7	12	9¹	14	4	11⁴	3⁸	10¹	15														18
1	2	4	5²	13		6	8	7	12	9¹	3	11³	10	14																19
1	2	5²	13			6	12	7	8	9²	14	4	11⁴	3	10¹	15														20
1	2	12	5¹			6	8	7	10	9	4	11	3																	21
1	12	2¹	14	5³		6	8	7	10	9	13	4⁴	11²	3	15															22
1	2	4		5		6	8	7	10	9¹	12	11	3																	23
1	2	4	13	5²		6	12	7	8³	10	11	3	14	9¹																24
1	2	4	5			6	8	7	9	13	10¹	11²	3	12																25
1	2	4	5¹	12		6	8	7	9³	14	10²	11	3	13																26
1	2	4		5	7	6	8	12	10¹	13	11	3²	9																	27
1	2	4	5¹		7	13	8	10²	6²	12	11	3	15	9⁴	14														28
1	2	4	5²		6	8³	9	12	14	13	11⁴	3	15	10	7¹														29
1	2	4	5		6	8³	7	13	9¹	11²	14	3	12	10																30
1	2	4	5		7	8²	14	9³	15	11	13	3⁴	12	10	6¹														31
1	2	4	5		6	8	7	12	9¹	3	11²	10	13																	32
1	2	4	5		6	8³	7	13	9¹	3	11²	14	10	12																33
1	2	4	5		7	8	6	14	9³	12	3²	11	13	10¹																34
1	2	4	13	6¹	7	8	9	11⁴	14	10²	12	3	5	15																35
1	2	4	14	6³	7	9¹	8	10	12	11⁴	13	3	15	5²																36
1	2	4	5		7	6	8	10¹	13	12	11	3	9²																	37
1	2	4	5³	15	7²	6⁴	8	11	10	9¹	12	3	13	14																38
1	5	4	2		7	6	8	12	10	9²	11¹	3	13																	39
1	5	4	2³		7	6²	8	12	10	9¹	11⁴	3	13	15	14														40
1	2	4	10	7	12	11	8⁴	13	3	9²	5³	6¹	14	15																41
1	5	4	2⁵	6⁴	8	12	7²	11	3	10³	16	14	13	15	9¹														42
1	2⁶	4	15	6	8²	14	11⁴	9³	12	3	10	5⁵	7¹	13	16														43
1		4	2	15	7	13	12	11	3	8⁴	10²	14	6³	9¹	5														44
1	2	4	12	14	6⁴	8¹	7	9	11	3	13	5²	10³	15																45
1	2	4	5	7²	8	6	11	9³	12	13	3¹	14	10																	46

FA Cup

Third Round   Stoke C   (h)   1-2
aet.

Carabao Cup

First Round   Preston NE   (a)   0-2

Championship Play-offs

Semi-Final 1st leg   Coventry C   (a)   2-1
Semi-Final 2nd leg   Coventry C   (h)   1-1
aet.
Final   Sheffield U   (Wembley)   2-1

SWANSEA CITY

FOUNDATION

The earliest Association Football in Wales was played in the northern part of the country and no international took place in the south until 1894, when a local paper still thought it necessary to publish an outline of the rules and an illustration of the pitch markings. There had been an earlier Swansea club, but this has no connection with Swansea Town (now City) formed at a public meeting in June 1912.

Swansea.com Stadium, Morfa, Landore, Swansea SA1 2FA.

Telephone: (01792) 616 400.

Ticket Office: (01792) 616 400.

Website: www.swanseacity.com

Email: info@swanseacity.com

Ground Capacity: 20,996.

Record Attendance: 32,796 v Arsenal, FA Cup 4th rd, 17 February 1968 (at Vetch Field); 20,972 v Liverpool, Premier League, 1 May 2016 (at Liberty Stadium).

Pitch Measurements: 105m × 68m (115yd × 74.5yd).

Chairman: Andy Coleman.

Chief Executive: Tom Corringe.

Head Coach: Alan Sheehan.

Assistant Head Coach: Darren O'Dea.

HONOURS

League Champions: FL 1 – 2007–08; Division 3S – 1924–25, 1948–49; Third Division – 1999–2000.

FA Cup: semi-final – 1926, 1964.

League Cup Winners: 2013.

League Trophy Winners: 1994, 2006.

Welsh Cup Winners: 10 times; *Runners-up:* 8 times.

European Competitions
Europa League: 2013–14.
European Cup-Winners' Cup: 1961–62, 1966–67, 1981–82, 1982–83, 1983–84, 1989–90, 1991–92.

Colours: White shirts with orange, grey and black trim, white shorts with orange, grey and black trim, white socks with orange and black trim.

Year Formed: 1912.

Turned Professional: 1912.

Previous Name: 1912, Swansea Town; 1970, Swansea City.

Club Nicknames: 'The Swans'; 'The Jacks'.

Grounds: 1912, Vetch Field; 2005, Liberty Stadium (renamed Swansea.com Stadium 2021).

First Football League Game: 28 August 1920, Division 3, v Portsmouth (a) L 0–3 – Crumley; Robson, Evans; Smith, Holdsworth, Williams; Hole, Ivor Jones; Edmundson, Rigsby, Spottiswood.

Record League Victory: 8–0 v Hartlepool U, Division 4, 1 April 1978 – Barber; Evans, Bartley, Lally (1) (Morris), May, Bruton, Kevin Moore, Robbie James (3 incl. 1p), Curtis (3), Toshack (1), Chappell.

Record Cup Victory: 12–0 v Sliema W (Malta), ECWC 1st rd 1st leg, 15 September 1982 – Davies; Marustik, Hadziabdic (1), Irwin (1), Kennedy, Rajkovic (1), Loveridge (2) (Leighton James), Robbie James, Charles (2), Stevenson (1), Latchford (1) (Walsh (3)).

Record Defeat: 0–8 v Liverpool, FA Cup 3rd rd, 9 January 1990; 0–8 v Monaco, ECWC, 1st rd 2nd leg, 1 October 1991.

Most League Points (2 for a win): 62, Division 3 (S), 1948–49.

Most League Points (3 for a win): 92, FL 1, 2007–08.

FOOTBALL YEARBOOK FACT FILE

Swansea Town, as the club was then named, won 20 or their 21 home fixtures in the 1948–49 season as they went on to win the Division Three South title. The only game they failed to win at the Vetch Field was against Southend United on 2 April. The Swans' wing-half Roy Paul missed a first-half penalty but later atoned for his error by creating the equaliser on the stroke of full time.

Most League Goals: 90, Division 2, 1956–57.

Highest League Scorer in Season: Cyril Pearce, 35, Division 2, 1931–32.

Most League Goals in Total Aggregate: Ivor Allchurch, 166, 1949–58, 1965–68.

Most League Goals in One Match: 5, Jack Fowler v Charlton Ath, Division 3S, 27 December 1924.

Most Capped Player: Ashley Williams, 64 (86), Wales.

Most League Appearances: Wilfred Milne, 587, 1919–37.

Youngest League Player: Nigel Dalling, 15 years 289 days v Southport, 6 December 1974.

Record Transfer Fee Received: £40,000,000 (potentially rising to £45,000,000) from Everton for Gylfi Sigurdsson, August 2017.

Record Transfer Fee Paid: £18,000,000 to West Ham U for André Ayew, January 2018.

Football League Record: 1920 Original Member of Division 3; 1920–21 Division 3; 1921–25 Division 3 (S); 1925–47 Division 2; 1947–49 Division 3 (S); 1949–65 Division 2; 1965–67 Division 3; 1967–70 Division 4; 1970–73 Division 3; 1973–78 Division 4; 1978–79 Division 3; 1979–81 Division 2; 1981–83 Division 1; 1983–84 Division 2; 1984–86 Division 3; 1986–88 Division 4; 1988–92 Division 3; 1992–96 Second Division; 1996–2000 Third Division; 2000–01 Second Division; 2001–04 Third Division; 2004–05 FL 2; 2005–08 FL 1; 2008–11 FL C; 2011–18 Premier League; 2018– FL C.

LATEST SEQUENCES

Longest Sequence of League Wins: 9, 27.11.1999 – 22.1.2000.

Longest Sequence of League Defeats: 9, 26.1.1991 – 19.3.1991.

Longest Sequence of League Draws: 8, 25.11.2008 – 28.12.2008.

Longest Sequence of Unbeaten League Matches: 19, 19.10.1970 – 9.3.1971.

Longest Sequence Without a League Win: 15, 25.3.1989 – 2.9.1989.

Successive Scoring Runs: 27 from 28.8.1947.

Successive Non-scoring Runs: 6 from 6.2.1996.

MANAGERS

Walter Whittaker 1912–14
William Bartlett 1914–15
Joe Bradshaw 1919–26
Jimmy Thomson 1927–31
Neil Harris 1934–39
Haydn Green 1939–47
Bill McCandless 1947–55
Ron Burgess 1955–58
Trevor Morris 1958–65
Glyn Davies 1965–66
Billy Lucas 1967–69
Roy Bentley 1969–72
Harry Gregg 1972–75
Harry Griffiths 1975–77
John Toshack 1978–83
   (resigned October re-appointed in December) 1983–84
Colin Appleton 1984
John Bond 1984–85
Tommy Hutchison 1985–86
Terry Yorath 1986–89
Ian Evans 1989–90
Terry Yorath 1990–91
Frank Burrows 1991–95
Bobby Smith 1995
Kevin Cullis 1996
Jan Molby 1996–97
Micky Adams 1997
Alan Cork 1997–98
John Hollins 1998–2001
Colin Addison 2001–02
Nick Cusack 2002
Brian Flynn 2002–04
Kenny Jackett 2004–07
Roberto Martinez 2007–09
Paulo Sousa 2009–10
Brendan Rodgers 2010–12
Michael Laudrup 2012–14
Garry Monk 2014–15
Francesco Guidolin 2016
Bob Bradley 2016
Paul Clement 2017
Carlos Carvalhal 2017–18
Graham Potter 2018–19
Steve Cooper 2019–21
Russell Martin 2021–23
Michael Duff 2023
Luke Williams 2024–25
Alan Sheehan February 2025–

TEN YEAR LEAGUE RECORD

		P	W	D	L	F	A	Pts	Pos
2015-16	PR Lge	38	12	11	15	42	52	47	12
2016-17	PR Lge	38	12	5	21	45	70	41	15
2017-18	PR Lge	38	8	9	21	28	56	33	18
2018-19	FL C	46	18	11	17	65	62	65	10
2019-20	FL C	46	18	16	12	62	53	70	6
2020-21	FL C	46	23	11	12	56	39	80	4
2021-22	FL C	46	16	13	17	58	68	61	15
2022-23	FL C	46	18	12	16	68	64	66	10
2023-24	FL C	46	15	12	19	59	65	57	14
2024-25	FL C	46	17	10	19	51	56	61	11

DID YOU KNOW ?

When Swansea City defeated Reading to win the Championship play-off final at Wembley in May 2011 they became the first team from Wales to enter the Premier League. They made their Premier League debut at Manchester City the following August, losing 4-0, but recovered and went on to spend a total of seven seasons in the top flight.

SWANSEA CITY – SKY BET CHAMPIONSHIP 2024–25 LEAGUE RECORD

Match No.	Date	Venue	Opponents	Result	H/T Score	Lg Pos.	Goalscorers	Attendance
1	Aug 10	A	Middlesbrough	L	0-1	0-1	18		26,610
2	17	H	Preston NE	W	3-0	1-0	8	Grimes (pen) [40], Abdulai [61], Vipotnik [83]	14,037
3	25	H	Cardiff C	D	1-1	1-0	9	Cullen [10]	20,174
4	31	A	WBA	L	0-1	0-1	16		24,975
5	Sept 14	H	Norwich C	W	1-0	1-0	11	Forson (og) [4]	14,097
6	21	A	Coventry C	W	2-1	2-1	7	Cullen [8], Cooper [32]	26,273
7	29	H	Bristol C	D	1-1	1-0	8	Cabango [15]	16,328
8	Oct 2	A	Sheffield U	L	0-1	0-1	12		25,112
9	5	H	Stoke C	D	0-0	0-0	11		14,546
10	19	A	Blackburn R	L	0-1	0-1	13		13,550
11	22	A	Sheffield Wed	D	0-0	0-0	13		22,452
12	26	H	Millwall	L	0-1	0-0	17		15,119
13	Nov 2	A	Oxford U	W	2-1	1-0	12	Vipotnik [38], Bianchini [80]	11,454
14	5	H	Watford	W	1-0	1-0	10	Peart-Harris [35]	12,869
15	10	A	Burnley	L	0-1	0-0	11		18,717
16	24	H	Leeds U	L	3-4	2-1	14	Darling [8], Cullen [45], Bianchini [90]	17,125
17	27	A	Derby Co	W	2-1	2-0	11	Vipotnik [2], Ronald [14]	25,141
18	30	H	Portsmouth	D	2-2	1-2	12	Ogilvie (og) [45], Cullen [53]	15,404
19	Dec 7	A	Luton T	D	1-1	0-1	13	Grimes [64]	11,264
20	10	A	Plymouth Arg	W	2-1	1-0	9	Fulton [44], Cullen [60]	15,305
21	14	H	Sunderland	L	2-3	2-1	10	Vipotnik [5], Cullen [17]	15,791
22	21	A	Hull C	L	1-2	1-1	12	Darling [42]	20,024
23	26	H	QPR	W	3-0	3-0	10	Cullen 2 [12, 28], Goncalo Franco [33]	15,843
24	29	H	Luton T	W	2-1	1-1	9	Goncalo Franco [38], Peart-Harris [90]	16,414
25	Jan 1	A	Portsmouth	L	0-4	0-2	12		20,427
26	4	H	WBA	D	1-1	0-0	12	Allen [90]	14,729
27	18	A	Cardiff C	L	0-3	0-0	13		26,536
28	21	H	Sheffield U	L	1-2	1-0	15	Bianchini [7]	13,373
29	25	A	Norwich C	L	1-5	0-1	17	Cullen [62]	25,713
30	Feb 1	H	Coventry C	L	0-2	0-2	17		15,189
31	9	A	Bristol C	W	1-0	0-0	16	Tymon [55]	21,554
32	12	H	Sheffield Wed	L	0-1	0-0	17		14,149
33	15	A	Stoke C	L	1-3	0-0	17	Tymon [61]	21,256
34	22	H	Blackburn R	W	3-0	2-0	16	Vipotnik [39], Peart-Harris [45], Cullen [62]	13,788
35	Mar 4	A	Preston NE	D	0-0	0-0	16		12,838
36	8	H	Middlesbrough	W	1-0	1-0	15	Eom [26]	13,986
37	12	A	Watford	L	0-1	0-1	16		16,739
38	15	H	Burnley	L	0-2	0-2	16		13,679
39	29	A	Leeds U	D	2-2	0-1	16	Darling [64], Vipotnik [90]	35,574
40	Apr 5	H	Derby Co	W	1-0	0-0	15	Eom [79]	16,501
41	9	H	Plymouth Arg	W	3-0	3-0	14	O'Brien [4], Darling [22], Key [35]	14,978
42	12	A	Sunderland	W	1-0	0-0	12	Cabango [58]	42,362
43	18	H	Hull C	W	1-0	0-0	11	Vipotnik (pen) [51]	18,775
44	21	A	QPR	W	2-1	1-0	11	Fox (og) [29], Darling [55]	16,351
45	26	A	Millwall	L	0-1	0-1	11		17,239
46	May 3	H	Oxford U	D	3-3	1-1	11	Eom [23], Ronald [57], Cullen [82]	19,672

Final League Position: 11

GOALSCORERS

League (51): Cullen 11, Vipotnik 7 (1 pen), Darling 5, Bianchini 3, Eom 3, Peart-Harris 3, Cabango 2, Goncalo Franco 2, Grimes 2 (1 pen), Ronald 2, Tymon 2, Abdulai 1, Allen 1, Cooper 1, Fulton 1, Key 1, O'Brien 1, own goals 3.
FA Cup (0).
Carabao Cup (3): Abdulai 1, Cullen 1, Ronald 1.

Vigouroux L 46	Key J 39 + 6	Cabango B 45	Darling H 38 + 1	Tymon J 44 + 1	Fulton J 13 + 18	Grimes M 29	Eom J 28 + 9	Goncalo Franco B 39 + 1	Abdulai A 2 + 15	Cullen L 35 + 7	Ronald M 43 + 3	Naughton K 9 + 14	Vipotnik Z 24 + 18	Cooper O 10 + 18	Thomas J — + 1	Tjoe-A-On N — + 1	Allen J 8 + 17	Bianchini F 8 + 28	Peart-Harris M 18 + 11	Christie C 2 + 9	Lloyd B — + 2	Parker S — + 7	Delcroix H 10 + 2	Ginnelly J — + 3	O'Brien L 16	Match No.
1	2[2]	3	4	5	6[3]	7	8[5]	9[4]	10[1]	11	12	13	14	15	16											1
1	2[2]	3	4	5[5]	14	7	8[1]	6[3]	12	11[4]	10	13	15	9[3]			16									2
1	2[5]	3	4	5	13	7	8[1]	6[2]	12	11[4]	10	16	14	9[3]				15								3
1	2	3	4	5		7	10[2]	6		8	11[1]	9						12	13							4
1	2	3	4	12		7	10[2]	6[4]		11[5]	8	5[1]	16	9[3]			14	13	15							5
1	2	3	4	5[5]	16	8	9[1]	7[4]	12	11[2]	6	14		10[3]			15	13								6
1	12	3	4	5		8	9[4]	7[2]	15	6	2[1]	11[3]	10				13	14								7
1	2	3	4	5[5]	6[4]	7	10[3]		14	8[1]	16	12	9[2]				15	13	11							8
1	2	3	4	5	16	7	10[4]	6[5]	14	12	8[3]		11[1]	9[2]			15	13								9
1	2	3	4	5		7		6[4]	12	10[3]	9		13	8[2]			14	11[1]	15							10
1	12	3	4	5	6[2]	7		10[3]	14	8	2[1]	11[4]	15				13	9								11
1	2	3	4	5		6	7[3]	9[1]		8	11[2]	14					12	13	10							12
1	2	3	4	5[5]		6	7[4]	14	12	8	16	11[2]					9[1]	13	10[3]	15						13
1	2	3	4			6	7[2]		9	10	5[3]	11[1]					13	12	8	14						14
1	2	3	4	5		6	7		13	10[4]	14	11[1]					9[2]	12	8[3]	15						15
1	2	3	4	5	12	7		6[2]	14	11	10[3]						9[1]	13	8							16
1	14	3	4[1]	5	16	7		6[4]	15	9	10	2[3]	11[2]				13	8[5]	12							17
1	2	3	4	5		7	12		14	9	10[3]		11[2]				6[1]	13	8							18
1	2	3	4	5		7	13	6[3]	15	9	8[1]		11[2]				14	12	10[4]							19
1	2[5]	3	4	5[3]	6[4]	7	10[2]	15		9	13	14	12				11[1]	8	16							20
1	2	3	4	5		7	13	6		9	10		11[1]				12	8[2]								21
1	2	3	4	5	6	7	10[2]			9	13		11[1]				12	8								22
1	2	3	4	5	16	7	10[1]	6[5]	14	9[3]	8[4]		13				11[2]	12		15						23
1	2	3	4	5	12	7	10[2]	6[1]	15	9	8[4]		13				11[3]	14								24
1	15	3[4]	4	5	6[2]	7	10			9	8	2[1]	14				11[3]	12	13							25
1	2		4	5		7	10[3]	6[4]	15	9[5]	8	14	11[1]				16	12	13	3[2]						26
1	2[3]	3	4	5		7	11[1]	6		10	9[4]	14	13				8[2]	12		15						27
1	2	3	4[4]	5		7		6		9[1]	10	12					11	8[2]								28
1	2	3		5	16	7	14	6[5]		9[3]	10[4]		12				11[1]	8[2]	13	4	15					29
1	5[1]	3		8	6[3]		14	7		10[4]	9		12	13			11[2]	15	2		4					30
1	13	3		6	14		7[3]	8		10[4]	2	4[2]	11[1]	15			12						5		9	31
1		3	4	6	8		7[4]			13	2[3]	11[1]	15				12	10[2]				14	5		9	32
1	15	3	13	6	14		7[4]	9		11[1]	2	4[3]	10[2]				12						5		8	33
1	2	3	4	5	15		16	6[4]		9[2]	8[5]		11[3]	14			12	10[1]					13		7	34
1	2	3	4	5	14		12	6		9[3]	8		11[2]	15			13	10[1]							7[4]	35
1	2	3	4[1]	5	15		10[3]	6		9[4]	8		11[2]	14			13					12			7	36
1	2	3		5	14		10[1]	6[3]		9[4]	8		11[2]	15			12					4	13		7	37
1	2	4		5	13		10[1]	6[2]		9	8[3]	3[5]	11	12			14		16			15			7[4]	38
1	2	3	4	9	8[2]		12	7[3]		10[4]	6[5]		16	13			14	15					5[1]		11	39
1	2	3	4	6	8[3]		13	7[1]		11	10[4]		12				14					15	5[2]		9	40
1	2[5]	3	4	5	12		10[4]	6[3]		8[2]	15	11	13				7[1]	14				16			9	41
1	2	3	4	5	7[2]		10[5]	6[3]		11[1]	8[4]	16	12	13			15	14							9	42
1	2	3	4	5	12		10[3]	8		13	7[4]		11[2]	15			6[1]	14							9	43
1	2	3[3]	4	5	7		10[2]	6[4]		11[1]	8[5]		12	13			15					16	14		9	44
1	2	3		5	7[3]		10	6[1]		11[2]	8[4]		12	14			13	15					4		9	45
1	2[1]	3		5			10[5]	6		14	8[4]	13	11[3]	12			7[2]					16	15	4	9	46

FA Cup
Third Round   Southampton   (a)   0-3

Carabao Cup
First Round   Gillingham   (h)   3-1
Second Round   Wycombe W   (h)   0-1

SWINDON TOWN

FOUNDATION

It is generally accepted that Swindon Town came into being in 1881, although there is no firm evidence that the club's founder, Rev. William Pitt, captain of the Spartans (an offshoot of a cricket club), changed his club's name to Swindon Town before 1883, when the Spartans amalgamated with St Mark's Young Men's Friendly Society.

The County Ground, County Road, Swindon, Wiltshire SN1 2ED.

Telephone: (0330) 002 1879.

Ticket Office: (0330) 002 1879.

Website: www.swindontownfc.co.uk

Email: reception@swindontownfc.co.uk

Ground Capacity: 15,547.

Record Attendance: 32,000 v Arsenal, FA Cup 3rd rd, 15 January 1972.

Pitch Measurements: 100m × 64m (109.5yd × 70yd).

Chairman: Clem Morfuni.

Chief Executive: Anthony Hall.

Manager: Ian Holloway.

Assistant Manager: Marcus Bignot.

Colours: Red shirts with white trim, red shorts with white trim, red socks with white trim.

Year Formed: 1881* (*see Foundation*).

Turned Professional: 1894.

Club Nickname: 'The Robins'.

Grounds: 1881, The Croft; 1896, County Ground (renamed The Energy Check County Ground 2017; The County Ground 2023).

First Football League Game: 28 August 1920, Division 3, v Luton T (h) W 9–1 – Nash; Kay, Macconachie; Langford, Hawley, Wareing; Jefferson (1), Fleming (4), Rogers, Batty (2), Davies (1), (1 og).

Record League Victory: 9–1 v Luton T, Division 3 (S), 28 August 1920 – Nash; Kay, Macconachie; Langford, Hawley, Wareing; Jefferson (1), Fleming (4), Rogers, Batty (2), Davies (1), (1 og).

Record Cup Victory: 10–1 v Farnham U Breweries (a), FA Cup 1st rd (replay), 28 November 1925 – Nash; Dickenson, Weston, Archer, Bew, Adey; Denyer (2), Wall (1), Richardson (4), Johnson (3), Davies.

Record Defeat: 1–10 v Manchester C, FA Cup 4th rd (replay), 25 January 1930.

Most League Points (2 for a win): 64, Division 3, 1968–69.

Most League Points (3 for a win): 102, Division 4, 1985–86.

Most League Goals: 100, Division 3 (S), 1926–27.

HONOURS

League Champions: Second Division – 1995–96; FL 2 – 2011–12, 2019–20; Division 4 – 1985–86.
Runners-up: Division 3 – 1962–63, 1968–69.

FA Cup: semi-final – 1910, 1912.

League Cup Winners: 1969.

League Trophy: Runners-up: 2012.

Anglo-Italian Cup Winners: 1970.

FOOTBALL YEARBOOK FACT FILE

After dispensing with Maurice Lindley for financial reasons, Swindon Town spent the whole of the 1955–56 season without a manager, line-ups being selected by a team selection committee from the directors with assistance from the trainer. The move was not a success, and the Robins struggled throughout the campaign, eventually finishing bottom of Division Three South and having to apply for re-election to the Football League.

Highest League Scorer in Season: Harry Morris, 47, Division 3 (S), 1926–27.

Most League Goals in Total Aggregate: Harry Morris, 216, 1926–33.

Most League Goals in One Match: 5, Harry Morris v QPR, Division 3 (S), 18 December 1926; 5, Harry Morris v Norwich C, Division 3 (S), 26 April 1930; 5, Keith East v Mansfield T, Division 3, 20 November 1965.

Most Capped Player: Rod Thomas, 30 (50), Wales.

Most League Appearances: John Trollope, 770, 1960–80.

Youngest League Player: Paul Rideout, 16 years 107 days v Hull C, 29 November 1980.

Record Transfer Fee Received: A combined £4,000,000 from QPR for Ben Gladwin and Massimo Luongo, May 2015.

Record Transfer Fee Paid: £800,000 to West Ham U for Joey Beauchamp, August 1994.

Football League Record: 1920 Original Member of Division 3; 1920–21 Division 3; 1921–58 Division 3 (S); 1958–63 Division 3; 1963–65 Division 2; 1965–69 Division 3; 1969–74 Division 2; 1974–82 Division 3; 1982–86 Division 4; 1986–87 Division 3; 1987–92 Division 2; 1992–93 First Division; 1993–94 Premier League; 1994–95 First Division; 1995–96 Second Division; 1996–2000 First Division; 2000–04 Second Division; 2004–06 FL 1; 2006–07 FL 2; 2007–11 FL 1; 2011–12 FL 2; 2012–17 FL 1; 2017–20 FL 2; 2020–21 FL 1; 2021– FL 2.

LATEST SEQUENCES

Longest Sequence of League Wins: 10, 31.12.2011 – 28.2.2012.

Longest Sequence of League Defeats: 8, 29.8.2005 – 8.10.2005.

Longest Sequence of League Draws: 6, 22.11.1991 – 28.12.1991.

Longest Sequence of Unbeaten League Matches: 22, 12.1.1986 – 23.8.1986.

Longest Sequence Without a League Win: 19, 30.10.1999 – 4.3.2000.

Successive Scoring Runs: 31 from 17.4.1926.

Successive Non-scoring Runs: 5 from 5.4.1997.

MANAGERS

Sam Allen 1902–33
Ted Vizard 1933–39
Neil Harris 1939–41
Louis Page 1945–53
Maurice Lindley 1953–55
Bert Head 1956–65
Danny Williams 1965–69
Fred Ford 1969–71
Dave Mackay 1971–72
Les Allen 1972–74
Danny Williams 1974–78
Bobby Smith 1978–80
John Trollope 1980–83
Ken Beamish 1983–84
Lou Macari 1984–89
Ossie Ardiles 1989–91
Glenn Hoddle 1991–93
John Gorman 1993–94
Steve McMahon 1994–98
Jimmy Quinn 1998–2000
Colin Todd 2000
Andy King 2000–01
Roy Evans 2001
Andy King 2001–05
Iffy Onuora 2005–06
Dennis Wise 2006
Paul Sturrock 2006–07
Maurice Malpas 2008
Danny Wilson 2008–11
Paul Hart 2011
Paolo Di Canio 2011–13
Kevin MacDonald 2013
Mark Cooper 2013–15
Martin Ling 2015
Luke Williams 2015–17
David Flitcroft 2017–18
Phil Brown 2018
Richie Wellens 2018–20
John Sheridan 2020–21
John McGreal 2021
Ben Garner 2021–22
Scott Lindsey 2022–23
Jody Morris 2023
Michael Flynn 2023
Mark Kennedy 2024
Ian Holloway October 2024–

TEN YEAR LEAGUE RECORD

		P	W	D	L	F	A	Pts	Pos
2015-16	FL 1	46	16	11	19	64	71	59	15
2016-17	FL 1	46	11	11	24	44	66	44	22
2017-18	FL 2	46	20	8	18	67	65	68	9
2018-19	FL 2	46	16	16	14	59	56	64	13
2019-20	FL 2	36	21	6	9	62	39	69	1§
2020-21	FL 1	46	13	4	29	55	89	43	23
2021-22	FL 2	46	22	11	13	77	54	77	6
2022-23	FL 2	46	16	13	17	61	55	61	10
2023-24	FL 2	46	14	12	20	77	83	54	19
2024-25	FL 2	46	15	17	14	71	63	62	12

§*Decided on points-per-game (1.92)*

DID YOU KNOW ?

Swindon Town won the Anglo Italian Cup in 1969–70 defeating Napoli in the final in Italy. They were leading 3-0 through goals from Peter Noble (2) and Arthur Horsfield before the match was abandoned after 79 minutes due to crowd trouble, with the Robins subsequently declared winners of the trophy. Earlier in the competition they had defeated Juventus in home and away fixtures.

SWINDON TOWN – SKY BET LEAGUE TWO 2024–25 LEAGUE RECORD

Match No.	Date	Venue	Opponents	Result	H/T Score	Lg Pos.	Goalscorers	Atten-dance
1	Aug 9	A	Chesterfield	D	1-1	0-1	1	Wright [64]	9262
2	17	H	Walsall	L	0-4	0-2	21		7786
3	24	A	Crewe Alex	D	0-0	0-0	21		4402
4	31	H	Notts Co	L	1-2	1-1	23	Kilkenny [21]	7326
5	Sept 7	A	Barrow	D	1-1	0-1	21	Butterworth [90]	3763
6	14	A	Newport Co	W	4-0	4-0	18	Tshimanga [4], Glatzel [18], Baker (og) [21], Cotterill [45]	6857
7	21	H	Carlisle U	L	0-2	0-1	21		6878
8	28	A	Port Vale	L	1-2	0-0	21	Wright [89]	6747
9	Oct 1	A	Tranmere R	D	1-1	0-1	21	Merrie (og) [54]	5120
10	5	H	Harrogate T	D	0-0	0-0	21		6333
11	12	A	Cheltenham T	W	3-2	2-0	18	Cox [30], Wright [34], McGregor [47]	5561
12	19	H	Doncaster R	L	1-2	0-0	21	Smith [75]	6837
13	22	A	Salford C	L	1-2	0-1	22	Smith [50]	2145
14	26	H	Gillingham	D	1-1	0-0	22	Smith [90]	7325
15	Nov 9	A	Milton Keynes D	L	1-3	1-1	22	Smith [1]	7407
16	16	H	Accrington S	D	2-2	1-2	22	Smith [11], Butterworth [69]	2755
17	23	H	Morecambe	L	2-3	1-2	22	Drinan [32], Delaney [49]	6494
18	Dec 3	A	Colchester U	L	0-4	0-4	24		3401
19	7	H	Fleetwood T	W	3-1	2-0	22	Smith 3 [8, 28, 58]	5819
20	14	A	Bradford C	L	0-1	0-1	22		15,751
21	21	H	Grimsby T	W	3-1	2-0	21	Clarke [3], Tshimanga 2 [41, 61]	7453
22	26	A	AFC Wimbledon	D	1-1	1-0	21	Smith [10]	8304
23	29	A	Bromley	D	1-1	0-0	21	Longelo [72]	3833
24	Jan 1	H	Colchester U	W	3-2	1-1	19	Clarke [15], Drinan [82], Cox (pen) [90]	7680
25	4	A	Notts Co	L	0-2	0-2	22		9296
26	11	H	Crewe Alex	D	0-0	0-0	20		6638
27	18	H	Barrow	W	2-0	1-0	18	Ofoborh [8], Smith [87]	6398
28	24	A	Newport Co	W	2-1	1-1	16	Smith [15], Westley [75]	5244
29	28	H	Tranmere R	W	3-1	0-1	16	Glatzel [87], Smith [90], Tshimanga (pen) [90]	6180
30	Feb 1	A	Carlisle U	W	5-1	1-0	14	Butterworth [45], Drinan [47], Westley [83], Wright [90], Glatzel [90]	7457
31	8	H	Port Vale	D	3-3	2-2	15	Wright (pen) [20], Butterworth [45], Cotterill [63]	7606
32	15	A	Harrogate T	L	0-1	0-0	17		2909
33	22	H	Chesterfield	W	1-0	0-0	15	Tshimanga (pen) [61]	7531
34	Mar 1	A	Walsall	W	1-0	0-0	14	Cotterill [59]	6910
35	4	H	Salford C	D	2-2	1-1	14	Nichols [7], Smith [71]	6465
36	8	A	Doncaster R	D	2-2	0-2	13	Butterworth [50], Westley [51]	7440
37	15	A	Cheltenham T	D	3-3	1-1	15	Wright [45], Tshimanga (pen) [67], Clarke [88]	8556
38	22	H	Accrington S	D	0-0	0-0	15		7168
39	29	A	Morecambe	L	0-1	0-1	15		3419
40	Apr 1	H	AFC Wimbledon	W	2-1	0-0	14	Tshimanga 2 (2 pens) [90, 90]	6500
41	5	A	Fleetwood T	W	4-0	1-0	14	Tshimanga (pen) [38], Freckleton [47], Bennett (og) [75], Ofoborh [88]	2742
42	12	H	Bradford C	W	5-4	2-3	12	Byrne (og) [22], Tshimanga [45], Smith 2 [62, 90], Shepherd (og) [90]	8051
43	18	A	Grimsby T	W	4-0	2-0	12	Nichols [8], Clarke [32], Tshimanga [65], Ameen [90]	7624
44	21	H	Bromley	L	0-1	0-0	13		8884
45	26	A	Gillingham	D	1-1	0-0	13	Wright [67]	7667
46	May 3	H	Milton Keynes D	D	0-0	0-0	12		9503

Final League Position: 12

GOALSCORERS

League (71): Smith 15, Tshimanga 11 (6 pens), Wright 7 (1 pen), Butterworth 5, Clarke 4, Cotterill 3, Drinan 3, Glatzel 3, Westley 3, Cox 2 (1 pen), Nichols 2, Ofoborh 2, Ameen 1, Delaney 1, Freckleton 1, Kilkenny 1, Longelo 1, McGregor 1, own goals 5.
FA Cup (4): Cotterill 1, Hall 1, McGregor 1, Tshimanga 1.
Carabao Cup (2): Ofoborh 1, Smith 1.
Vertu Trophy (10): Glatzel 2, Ameen 1, Butterworth 1, Cotterill 1, Kirkman 1, McGregor 1, McGurk 1, Smith 1, Tshimanga 1.

Bycroft J 20 + 1	Wright W 45 + 1	Hall G 11 + 3	Freckleton M 25 + 3	King J 8	Clarke O 26 + 4	Oloborh N 23 + 14	Longelo R 6 + 10	Cotterill J 30 + 11	Smith H 37 + 2	Drinan A 16 + 12	Glatzel P 20 + 19	Sobowale O 27 + 10	Cain J 9 + 10	Mitchell D — + 2	Kilkenny G 39 + 3	Tshimanga K 25 + 14	Butterworth D 20 + 14	Delaney R 19 + 2	Cox G 21 + 5	Minturn H 3 + 5	McGurk S 1 + 7	McGregor J 14 + 5	Barden D 12	Ameen B 3 + 11	Brown J 2 + 1	Kirkman B 11 + 3	Nichols T 16 + 4	Westley J 3 + 14	Ripley C 14	Hart S — + 1	Foye O — + 1	Alston G — + 1	Match No.
1	2	3	4	5¹	6	7³	8	9	10	11²	12	13	14																				1
1	3	4	5	2	7⁴	9¹	6²	8	10	12	11³	13	14	15																			2
1	3	4	5	2	7¹	13	6³	8	10	12	11²	14	9⁴	15																			3
1	2	3	4	9⁴	6³			8	11²	12	10¹	5	15		7	13	14																4
1	2	3²	4	5	6¹			11⁸	16	15⁵	12³	9⁴			7	10	8	13	14														5
1	3		4	5⁵		13		6²		14	11	2	15		7	10³	8⁴		9¹	12	16												6
1	3		4	5				6²		12	11¹	2			7	10	8		9		13												7
1	3			12		6		11³	13	5					7⁴	10	9²		8	2¹	15	14											8
	3		4	5¹		13		6⁴		11	14	2	15		7	10²	9³		8		12	1											9
	3		4			14	16	6		11	12	2⁵			7²	10¹	8⁴		9	13	15	5³	1										10
	3		4	6¹	8²	15			10	2					7		11⁴	14	9³	12		5	1	13									11
	3		4	6³	14	13	8⁴	12		11²	2				7	15	10		9¹		5	1											12
	3	16	4	8²	12	6³	11	14		2					7	13	10⁴		9¹		15	5⁵	1										13
1	4	3⁸	12	6²		14	16	10	11⁴		2				7	15	9⁵		8³	13		5¹											14
1	3		6	15	5³	16	10²	9⁵	14	2					7	11	8¹	4⁴			13	12											15
1	3		7⁴		6²	11	14	9							15	13	8	4	12	2	10¹	5³											16
1	2	3²	6³		14	10	12	15							7	9⁵	11⁴	4	8		16	5¹		13									17
1	3	2⁴	16	15	6	11²	9	12	5³						7⁵	10		4¹	8	13		14											18
5	13		3³	14	12	10	11	9²	15						7		8⁴	4		2	1	6¹											19
14			13		11	8	10²	3	7		6	12			4		2	1		9¹	5												20
	3	4⁴	7²	13	15	9	10³		14	2		8	11		5	6¹		1		12													21
	3	4	7		15	9³	11	12		2⁴		8	10²	14	5	6¹		1		13													22
	3		12	8	6	14	13	11⁴	10²	2		7¹	15	9³	4			1		5													23
	3		7²	8	15	9³	10¹	12	16	2⁵		13	11⁴	14	4	6		1		5													24
15	2		12		5	7		11	9³	13		6²	10⁴	14	3	8¹		1⁴	16		4												25
1	3		2	7²		13	11	10³		5		6		14	4			12		8	9¹												26
1	3		2	7		11	10		5	14		6	12		4	8²		13³	9¹														27
1	3		6	8²		13	11³	9		2	14	7	15		4	5⁴		10¹	12														28
1	3		6		10	11	9³	14	2		7⁴	15	12	4	5¹			13	8²														29
1	3		7¹	6³		13	11⁴	12	16	2	5		8	15	10⁵	4		9²	14														30
1	3		6		7	11	8³	14	2	5		10²	4		12			9¹	13														31
	3	4⁴	15	12	7	8¹	11		13	2	5		6	14	10³			9⁵	16	1													32
	4		5	3	7	8	11		9¹		6	10²	13		2			12		1													33
	4		5	3²	6	8¹	11		12	13	14	7	10³		2			9		1													34
	3		5		6	8⁴	11		13	14	7	10¹	15	4⁵	2²			16		9³	12	1											35
	3		5	6¹		8⁵	11		15	16	7	10¹⁴	4	2²			13			9⁴	12	1											36
	4		5	3	13	15	11	14		6¹	10³	7	2²		8			9⁴	12	1													37
	4		3	7		11		8¹	2	5⁴	6	10³	14		15			12		9²	13	1											38
	3	4	6⁵		15	11		14	2	5¹	7⁴	16	13	12		10²		9³	8	1													39
	2	13	6⁴		7³	3	9		16	12	11	5¹	8		15		4²	14	10³	1													40
1	3		4		12	5¹	11		9	2⁴	14	6	10²		8¹	7⁵	13			15	16												41
	3		4	2³	16	5	11		9⁵		6²	10	14	15		12	8¹	7⁴	13	1													42
	3		4	2²		5	11		9	13	6	10³		14	8	7	12	1															43
	2		4	13	7⁵	5	11		9⁴		6²	10	12	3³	8¹	16		14	15	1													44
	3		4	2	15	5⁴	11		9		6	10²	13		14	8³	7¹	12	1														45
	3	15	4	2⁴	7³	14	11²	9		6	12	10⁵		5	8¹	13	1												16				46

FA Cup

First Round	Colchester U	(h)	2-1

aet.

Second Round	Accrington S	(a)	2-2

aet; Accrington S won 4-1 on penalties.

Carabao Cup

First Round	Crawley T	(a)	2-4

Vertu Trophy

Group G (S)	Exeter C	(a)	1-2
Group G (S)	Bristol R	(h)	4-0
Group G (S)	Tottenham H U21	(h)	2-1
Second Round	Wycombe W	(a)	2-1
Third Round	Birmingham C	(h)	1-2

TOTTENHAM HOTSPUR

FOUNDATION

The Hotspur Football Club was formed from an older cricket club in 1882. Most of the founders were old boys of St John's Presbyterian School and Tottenham Grammar School. The Casey brothers were well to the fore as the family provided the club's first goalposts (painted blue and white) and their first ball. They soon adopted the local YMCA as their meeting place, but after a couple of moves settled at the Red House.

Tottenham Hotspur Stadium, Lilywhite House, 782 High Road, Tottenham, London N17 0BX.

Telephone: (0344) 499 5000.

Ticket Office: (0344) 844 0102.

Website: www.tottenhamhotspur.com

Email: supporterservices@tottenhamhotspur.com

Ground Capacity: 62,850.

Record Attendance: 75,038 v Sunderland, FA Cup 6th rd, 5 March 1938 (at White Hart Lane); 85,512 v Bayer Leverkusen, UEFA Champions League Group E, 2 November 2016 (at Wembley); 62,027 v Arsenal, Premier League, 12 May 2022 (at Tottenham Hotspur Stadium).

Pitch Measurements: 105m × 68m (115yd × 74.5yd).

Executive Chairman: Daniel Levy.

Chief Executive: Vinai Venkatesham.

Head Coach: Thomas Frank.

Assistant Head Coach: Justin Cochrane.

Colours: White shirts with navy blue sleeves and trim, navy blue shorts with white trim, white socks with navy blue trim.

Year Formed: 1882. *Turned Professional:* 1895.

Previous Names: 1882, Hotspur Football Club; 1884, Tottenham Hotspur.

Club Nickname: 'Spurs', 'The Lillywhites'.

Grounds: 1882, Tottenham Marshes; 1888, Northumberland Park; 1899, White Hart Lane; 2018, Tottenham Hotspur Stadium.

HONOURS

League Champions: Division 1 – 1950–51, 1960–61; Division 2 – 1919–20, 1949–50. *Runners-up:* Premier League – 2016–17; Division 1 – 1921–22, 1951–52, 1956–57, 1962–63; Division 2 – 1908–09, 1932–33.

FA Cup Winners: 1901 (as non-league club), 1921, 1961, 1962, 1967, 1981, 1982, 1991. *Runners-up:* 1987.

League Cup Winners: 1971, 1973, 1999, 2008. *Runners-up:* 1982, 2002, 2009, 2015, 2021.

European Competitions
European Cup: 1961–62 (*sf*).
Champions League: 2010–11 (*qf*), 2016–17, 2017–18, 2018–19 (*runners-up*), 2019–20, 2022–23.
UEFA Cup: 1971–72 (*winners*), 1972–73 (*sf*), 1973–74 (*runners-up*), 1983–84 (*winners*), 1984–85 (*qf*), 1999–2000, 2006–07 (*qf*), 2007–08, 2008–09.
Europa League: 2011–12, 2012–13 (*qf*), 2013–14, 2014–15, 2015–16, 2016–17, 2020–21, 2024–25 (*winners*).
UEFA Europa Conference League: 2021–22.
European Cup-Winners' Cup: 1962–63 (*winners*), 1963–64, 1967–68, 1981–82 (*sf*), 1982–83, 1991–92 (*qf*).
Intertoto Cup: 1995.

First Football League Game: 1 September 1908, Division 2, v Wolverhampton W (h) W 3–0 – Hewitson; Coquet, Burton; Morris (1), Danny Steel, Darnell; Walton, Woodward (2), Macfarlane, Bobby Steel, Middlemiss.

Record League Victory: 9–0 v Bristol R, Division 2, 22 October 1977 – Daines; Naylor, Holmes, Hoddle (1), McAllister, Perryman, Pratt, McNab, Moores (3), Lee (4), Taylor (1).

FOOTBALL YEARBOOK FACT FILE

Clive Allen scored 49 League and Cup goals for Tottenham Hotspur in 1986–87 when he was also voted Footballer of the Year by the PFA and the Football Writers Association. His goal tally comprised 33 in the Football League, four in the FA Cup and 12 in the Football League Cup. He remains the all-time leading scorer in a season in the League Cup.

Record Cup Victory: 13–2 v Crewe Alex, FA Cup 4th rd (replay), 3 February 1960 – Brown; Hills, Henry; Blanchflower, Norman, Mackay; White, Harmer (1), Smith (4), Allen (5), Jones (3 incl. 1p).

Record Defeat: 0–8 v Cologne, UEFA Intertoto Cup, 22 July 1995.

Most League Points (2 for a win): 70, Division 2, 1919–20.

Most League Points (3 for a win): 86, Premier League, 2016–17.

Most League Goals: 115, Division 1, 1960–61.

Highest League Scorer in Season: Jimmy Greaves, 37, Division 1, 1962–63.

Most League Goals in Total Aggregate: Jimmy Greaves, 220, 1961–70.

Most League Goals in One Match: 5, Ted Harper v Reading, Division 2, 30 August 1930; 5, Alf Stokes v Birmingham C, Division 1, 18 September 1957; 5, Bobby Smith v Aston Villa, Division 1, 29 March 1958; 5, Jermain Defoe v Wigan Ath, Premier League, 22 November 2009.

Most Capped Player: Hugo Lloris, 107 (145), France.

Most League Appearances: Steve Perryman, 655, 1969–86.

Youngest League Player: Mikey Moore, 16 years 277 days v Manchester C, 14 May 2024.

Record Transfer Fee Received: £85,300,000 from Real Madrid for Gareth Bale, September 2013.

Record Transfer Fee Paid: £55,500,000 (potentially rising to £63,000,000) to Lyon for Tanguy Ndombele, July 2019; £55,000,000 (potentially rising to £65,000,000) to Bournemouth for Dominic Solanke, August 2024.

Football League Record: 1908 Elected to Division 2; 1908–09 Division 2; 1909–15 Division 1; 1919–20 Division 2; 1920–28 Division 1; 1928–33 Division 2; 1933–35 Division 1; 1935–50 Division 2; 1950–77 Division 1; 1977–78 Division 2; 1978–92 Division 1; 1992– Premier League.

LATEST SEQUENCES

Longest Sequence of League Wins: 13, 23.4.1960 – 1.10.1960.

Longest Sequence of League Defeats: 7, 1.1.1994 – 27.2.1994.

Longest Sequence of League Draws: 6, 9.1.1999 – 27.2.1999.

Longest Sequence of Unbeaten League Matches: 22, 31.8.1949 – 31.12.1949.

Longest Sequence Without a League Win: 16, 29.12.1934 – 13.4.1935.

Successive Scoring Runs: 39 from 11.3.2023.

Successive Non-scoring Runs: 6 from 28.12.1985.

MANAGERS

Frank Brettell 1898–99
John Cameron 1899–1906
Fred Kirkham 1907–08
Peter McWilliam 1912–27
Billy Minter 1927–29
Percy Smith 1930–35
Jack Tresadern 1935–38
Peter McWilliam 1938–42
Arthur Turner 1942–46
Joe Hulme 1946–49
Arthur Rowe 1949–55
Jimmy Anderson 1955–58
Bill Nicholson 1958–74
Terry Neill 1974–76
Keith Burkinshaw 1976–84
Peter Shreeves 1984–86
David Pleat 1986–87
Terry Venables 1987–91
Peter Shreeves 1991–92
Doug Livermore 1992–93
Ossie Ardiles 1993–94
Gerry Francis 1994–97
Christian Gross (*Head Coach*) 1997–98
George Graham 1998–2001
Glenn Hoddle 2001–03
David Pleat (*Caretaker*) 2003–04
Jacques Santini 2004
Martin Jol 2004–07
Juande Ramos 2007–08
Harry Redknapp 2008–12
Andre Villas-Boas 2012–13
Tim Sherwood 2013–14
Mauricio Pochettino 2014–19
Jose Mourinho 2019–21
Nuno Espirito Santo 2021
Antonio Conte 2021–23
Ange Postecoglou 2023–25
Thomas Frank June 2025–

TEN YEAR LEAGUE RECORD

		P	W	D	L	F	A	Pts	Pos
2015-16	PR Lge	38	19	13	6	69	35	70	3
2016-17	PR Lge	38	26	8	4	86	26	86	2
2017-18	PR Lge	38	23	8	7	74	36	77	3
2018-19	PR Lge	38	23	2	13	67	39	71	4
2019-20	PR Lg	38	16	11	11	61	47	59	6
2020-21	PR Lge	38	18	8	12	68	45	62	7
2021-22	PR Lge	38	22	5	11	69	40	71	4
2022-23	PR Lge	38	18	6	14	70	63	60	8
2023-24	PR Lge	38	20	6	12	74	61	66	5
2024-25	PR Lge	38	11	5	22	64	65	38	17

DID YOU KNOW ?

Tottenham Hotspur met Arsenal in the first-ever FA Cup semi-final to be played at Wembley in April 1991. Spurs were 2-0 up after 10 minutes and went on to win 3-1 with goals from Paul Gascoigne and Gary Lineker (2). The game kicked off at midday to allow for it to be shown live on television. Spurs went on to win the trophy, defeating Nottingham Forest in the final.

TOTTENHAM HOTSPUR – PREMIER LEAGUE 2024–25 LEAGUE RECORD

Match No.	Date	Venue	Opponents	Result	H/T Score	Lg Pos.	Goalscorers	Attendance
1	Aug 19	A	Leicester C	D	1-1	1-0	9	Porro [29]	31,977
2	24	H	Everton	W	4-0	2-0	4	Bissouma [14], Son 2 [25, 77], Romero [71]	61,357
3	Sept 1	A	Newcastle U	L	1-2	0-1	10	Burn (og) [56]	52,211
4	15	H	Arsenal	L	0-1	0-0	13		61,645
5	21	H	Brentford	W	3-1	2-1	10	Solanke [8], Johnson [28], Maddison [85]	61,246
6	29	A	Manchester U	W	3-0	1-0	8	Johnson [3], Kulusevski [47], Solanke [77]	73,587
7	Oct 6	A	Brighton & HA	L	2-3	2-0	9	Johnson [23], Maddison [37]	31,487
8	19	H	West Ham U	W	4-1	1-1	7	Kulusevski [36], Bissouma [52], Areola (og) [55], Son [60]	61,381
9	27	A	Crystal Palace	L	0-1	0-1	8		25,108
10	Nov 3	A	Aston Villa	W	4-1	0-1	7	Johnson [49], Solanke 2 [75, 79], Maddison [90]	61,253
11	10	H	Ipswich T	L	1-2	0-2	10	Bentancur [69]	61,505
12	23	A	Manchester C	W	4-0	2-0	6	Maddison 2 [13, 20], Porro [52], Johnson [90]	52,478
13	Dec 1	H	Fulham	D	1-1	0-0	7	Johnson [54]	61,141
14	5	A	Bournemouth	L	0-1	0-1	10		11,234
15	8	H	Chelsea	L	3-4	2-1	11	Solanke [5], Kulusevski [11], Son [90]	61,184
16	15	A	Southampton	W	5-0	5-0	10	Maddison 2 [1, 45], Son [12], Kulusevski [14], Sarr [25]	31,090
17	22	H	Liverpool	L	3-6	1-3	11	Maddison [41], Kulusevski [72], Solanke [83]	61,439
18	26	A	Nottingham F	L	0-1	0-1	11		30,200
19	29	H	Wolverhampton W	D	2-2	2-1	11	Bentancur [12], Johnson [45]	61,284
20	Jan 4	H	Newcastle U	L	1-2	1-2	12	Solanke [4]	61,293
21	15	A	Arsenal	L	1-2	1-2	13	Son [25]	60,287
22	19	A	Everton	L	2-3	0-3	15	Kulusevski [77], Richarlison [90]	39,326
23	26	H	Leicester C	L	1-2	1-0	15	Richarlison [33]	61,295
24	Feb 2	A	Brentford	W	2-0	1-0	14	Janelt (og) [29], Sarr [87]	17,154
25	16	H	Manchester U	W	1-0	1-0	12	Maddison [13]	61,383
26	22	A	Ipswich T	W	4-1	2-1	12	Johnson 2 [18, 26], Spence [77], Kulusevski [84]	30,003
27	26	H	Manchester C	L	0-1	0-1	13		60,820
28	Mar 9	H	Bournemouth	D	2-2	0-1	13	Sarr [67], Son (pen) [84]	61,178
29	16	A	Fulham	L	0-2	0-0	14		27,182
30	Apr 3	A	Chelsea	L	0-1	0-0	14		39,852
31	6	A	Southampton	W	3-1	2-0	14	Johnson 2 [13, 42], Tel (pen) [90]	60,984
32	13	H	Wolverhampton W	L	2-4	0-2	15	Tel [59], Richarlison [85]	31,463
33	21	H	Nottingham F	L	1-2	0-2	16	Richarlison [87]	59,314
34	27	A	Liverpool	L	1-5	1-3	16	Solanke [12]	60,415
35	May 4	H	West Ham U	D	1-1	1-0	16	Odobert [15]	62,468
36	11	H	Crystal Palace	L	0-2	0-1	17		60,254
37	16	A	Aston Villa	L	0-2	0-0	17		42,239
38	25	H	Brighton & HA	L	1-4	1-0	17	Solanke (pen) [17]	61,449

Final League Position: 17

GOALSCORERS

League (64): Johnson 11, Maddison 9, Solanke 9 (1 pen), Kulusevski 7, Son 7 (1 pen), Richarlison 4, Sarr 3, Bentancur 2, Bissouma 2, Porro 2, Tel 2 (1 pen), Odobert 1, Romero 1, Spence 1, own goals 3.
FA Cup (4): Johnson 1, Kulusevski 1, Tel 1, own goal 1.
Carabao Cup (9): Solanke 2, Bergvall 1, Johnson 1, Kulusevski 1, Sarr 1, Son 1, Spence 1, Werner 1.
(Tottenham H U21) Vertu Trophy (4): Ajayi 1, Hall 1, Lankshear 1, Moore 1.
Europa League (28): Johnson 5, Solanke 5 (2 pens), Maddison 3, Son 3 (1 pen), Odobert 2, Porro 2, Sarr 2, Ajayi 1, Kulusevski 1, Lankshear 1, Moore 1, Richarlison 1 (1 pen), Scarlett 1.

Vicario G 24	Porro P 28 + 5	Romero C 18	van de Ven M 12 + 1	Udogie I 24 + 1	Sarr P 22 + 14	Bentancur R 21 + 5	Maddison J 21 + 10	Johnson B 24 + 9	Solanke D 25 + 2	Son H 24 + 6	Werner T 4 + 14	Bergvall L 11 + 16	Gray A 19 + 9	Kulusevski D 27 + 5	Spence D 19 + 6	Richarlison d 4 + 11	Bissouma Y 16 + 12	Odobert W 9 + 7	Dragusin R 14 + 2	Moore M 3 + 7	Davies B 14 + 3	Forster F 7	Lankshear W — + 3	Dorrington A — + 1	Reguilon S 1 + 3	Austin B 1	Kinsky A 6	Scarlett D — + 3	Danso K 9 + 1	Tel M 11 + 2	Match No.
1	2⁵	3	4	5	6²	7¹	8⁴	9³	10	11	12	13	14	15	16	17															1
1	2	3	4	5⁴	13		8⁵	9		10			16	14	6²	15	12	7³	11¹												2
1	2	4		5	6¹	15	8⁴	12		11	13	14		10				7³	9²	3											3
1	2	3	4	5	13	7²	8³	9¹	10	11	14			6			12														4
1	2²	3	4	5	13	7¹	8⁵	9²	10⁴	11		16	15	6			12			14											5
1	2	3	4⁵	5¹	15	7	8⁴	9²	10			11³	14	6	12		16	13													6
1	2	3	4	5	13	7²	8³	9	10	11¹				6			12			14											7
1	2	3	4	5⁵	12	15	8¹	9	10³	11²	13		16	6			14	7⁴													8
1	2	3	4	5	13	15	8³	9	10		12			6²			14	7⁴	11¹												9
1	2	3¹		5⁵	8	7¹	16	9	10	11²			15	6			13⁴	12	4	14											10
1	2	3		5	8¹	7³	13	9²	10	11	12			6			14	4													11
1	2			5¹	6⁴		8²	12	10	11¹	13	14		9	15		7	3	4												12
	2			5	6³		8²	9		10	11¹	13	14⁴	12			7	3	4	1	15										13
	13			5	6¹		8⁴	11	10	12	14	15	2	9			7³	3	4²	1											14
	2	3¹	4³	5	8		16	9	10	11	13	15	14	6⁴			7⁵	12		1											15
	12			5¹	6		9⁴	13	11⁵	10²	14	7	4	8	2³			3		1	16	15									16
	2			6²			9¹	13	11	10³	14	12	4	8	5		7	3		1											17
	14			5⁴	7¹	6²	13	8	11	10³	15	12	4	9	2¹		16	3⁵		1											18
	2			5¹	15	7	14	8⁴	11	10²	13		4	9			6³	3		1			12								19
	2			7³			14	8	11	13	10⁴	6²	4	9	5		15	3¹					12	1							20
	2			6²		12	13	10	11³		8	4	9	5	14		7¹	3								1					21
	5			6²		10		11		7	2	9	8	12			3¹	13	4							1					22
	2			8²	7		11	6	5³	9	10¹			3	12	14	13	4								1					23
	2			13	7		10	12	3	9	5	11³	6²				8¹	4					1	14							24
1	2			13	7⁴	8¹	12	11⁵			6²	14	9	5	15	16		4									3³	10			25
1	13		5²		7	12	9¹	11⁴		8⁵	3	6	2	16	15								14	4	10³						26
1	2		5²	15	7⁴	8⁵	13	16	6	3	12	14					11³							4	10¹						27
1	2⁵	3⁴	15	16	8	6³	14	9	10	13		12		5			7²¹	11						4							28
1	3³		5		6⁵	14	9	10	13		12	7		2	8¹⁵				4					16				11⁴			29
1	15	3	4⁴	5	12	7	8³	13	10	11			6²			2		9¹						4					14		30
1	2	3		13	7²	8³	9	10⁵	11¹			6⁴	14	5	15	12			4										16		31
1	3			6²	13	8³	9	10⁴				12	2	14	5	15		7¹						4					11		32
1	2	3¹	4²	8⁵	7		14	15		16			6³	5	10			9⁴		13								12	11		33
1			5	13		8²	9	10³		6	7¹	12	2	14			15		4									3	11⁴		34
1			8							2	6	5	10¹	7	9		12	4										3	11		35
	2³			8	7²			14		6	10¹	5		13	9		12	4						1				3	11		36
			7¹	14		15	13	10²		6		2	16	12	9⁴		8⁵	4					5³	1				3	11		37
1	2		4⁴	5	8¹	7²		9	10³			6	16	15	13	12		14										3	11⁵		38

FA Cup

Third Round	Tamworth	(a)	3-0
aet.			
Fourth Round	Aston Villa	(a)	1-2

Carabao Cup

Third Round	Coventry C	(a)	2-1
Fourth Round	Manchester C	(h)	2-1
Quarter-Final	Manchester U	(h)	4-3
Semi-Final 1st leg	Liverpool	(h)	1-0
Semi-Final 2nd leg	Liverpool	(a)	0-4

Vertu Trophy (Tottenham H U21)

Group G (S)	Bristol R	(a)	3-3
Tottenham H U21 won 6-5 on penalties.			
Group G (S)	Exeter C	(a)	0-2
Group G (S)	Swindon T	(a)	1-2

Europa League

League game	Qarabag	(h)	3-0
League game	Ferencvaros	(a)	2-1
League game	AZ Alkmaar	(h)	1-0
League game	Galatasaray	(a)	2-3
League game	Roma	(h)	2-2
League game	Rangers	(a)	1-1
League game	TSG 1899 Hoffenheim	(a)	3-2
League game	Elfsborg	(h)	3-0
Round of 16 1st leg	AZ Alkmaar	(a)	0-1
Round of 16 2nd leg	AZ Alkmaar	(h)	3-1
Quarter-Final 1st leg	Eintracht Frankfurt	(h)	1-1
Quarter-Final 2nd leg	Eintracht Frankfurt	(a)	1-0
Semi-Final 1st leg	Bodo/Glimt	(h)	3-1
Semi-Final 2nd leg	Bodo/Glimt	(a)	2-0
Final	Manchester U (Bilbao)		1-0

TRANMERE ROVERS

FOUNDATION

Formed in 1884 as Belmont they adopted their present title the following year and eventually joined their first league, the West Lancashire League, in 1889–90, the same year as their first success in the Wirral Challenge Cup. The club almost folded in 1899–1900 when all the players left en bloc to join a rival club, but they survived the crisis and went from strength to strength, winning the 'Combination' title in 1907–08 and the Lancashire Combination in 1913–14. They joined the Football League in 1921 from the Central League.

Prenton Park, Prenton Road West, Birkenhead, Merseyside CH42 9PY.

Telephone: (0333) 014 4452.

Ticket Office: (0333) 014 4452.

Website: www.tranmererovers.co.uk

Email: tellus@tranmererovers.co.uk

Ground Capacity: 16,582.

Record Attendance: 24,424 v Stoke C, FA Cup 4th rd, 5 February 1972.

Pitch Measurements: 100m × 64m (109.5yd × 70yd).

Chairman: Mark Palios.

Vice-Chairman: Nicola Palios.

Manager: Andy Crosby.

First-Team Coach: Andy Parkinson.

HONOURS

League Champions: Division 3N – 1937–38.
Runners-up: Division 4 – 1988–89; National League – 2016–17, 2017–18. (2nd) *(promoted to FL 2 via play-offs).*
FA Cup: quarter-final – 2000, 2001, 2004.
League Cup: Runners-up: 2000.
Welsh Cup Winners: 1935. *Runners-up:* 1934.
League Trophy Winners: 1990. *Runners-up:* 1991, 2021.

Colours: White shirts with blue and red trim, white shorts with blue trim, white socks with red trim.

Year Formed: 1884.

Turned Professional: 1912.

Previous Name: 1884, Belmont AFC; 1885, Tranmere Rovers.

Club Nickname: 'The Rovers'.

Grounds: 1884, Steeles Field; 1887, Ravenshaws Field/Old Prenton Park; 1912, Prenton Park.

First Football League Game: 27 August 1921, Division 3 (N), v Crewe Alex (h) W 4–1 – Bradshaw; Grainger, Stuart (1); Campbell, Milnes (1), Heslop; Moreton, Groves (1), Hyam, Ford (1), Hughes.

Record League Victory: 13–4 v Oldham Ath, Division 3 (N), 26 December 1935 – Gray; Platt, Fairhurst; McLaren, Newton, Spencer; Eden, MacDonald (1), Bell (9), Woodward (2), Urmson (1).

Record Cup Victory: 13–0 v Oswestry U, FA Cup 2nd prel. rd, 10 October 1914 – Ashcroft; Stevenson, Bullough, Hancock, Taylor, Holden (1), Moreton (1), Cunningham (2), Smith (5), Leck (3), Gould (1).

FOOTBALL YEARBOOK FACT FILE

The rise of Tranmere Rovers to the Football League owed much to the demise of Leeds City shortly after the start of the 1919–20 season. Rovers successfully applied to replace the Leeds club's reserve team in the Central League and after finishing in fourth position in the table they were one of 14 clubs selected as a group to join the new Division Three North in March 1921 without having to go to a vote.

Record Defeat: 1–9 v Tottenham H, FA Cup 3rd rd (replay), 14 January 1953.

Most League Points (2 for a win): 60, Division 4, 1964–65.

Most League Points (3 for a win): 80, Division 4, 1988–89; Division 3, 1989–90; Division 2, 2002–03.

Most League Goals: 111, Division 3 (N), 1930–31.

Highest League Scorer in Season: Bunny Bell, 35, Division 3 (N), 1933–34.

Most League Goals in Total Aggregate: Ian Muir, 142, 1985–95.

Most League Goals in One Match: 9, Bunny Bell v Oldham Ath, Division 3 (N), 26 December 1935.

Most Capped Player: John Aldridge, 30 (69), Republic of Ireland.

Most League Appearances: Harold Bell, 595, 1946–64 (incl. League record 401 consecutive appearances).

Youngest League Player: Iain Hume, 16 years 167 days v Swindon T, 15 April 2000.

Record Transfer Fee Received: £2,250,000 from WBA for Jason Koumas, August 2002.

Record Transfer Fee Paid: £450,000 to Aston Villa for Shaun Teale, August 1995.

Football League Record: 1921 Original Member of Division 3 (N): 1921–38 Division 3 (N); 1938–39 Division 2; 1946–58 Division 3 (N); 1958–61 Division 3; 1961–67 Division 4; 1967–75 Division 3; 1975–76 Division 4; 1976–79 Division 3; 1979–89 Division 4; 1989–91 Division 3; 1991–92 First Division; 1992–2001 First Division; 2001–04 Second Division; 2004–14 FL 1; 2014–15 FL 2; 2015–18 National League; 2018–19 FL 2; 2019–20 FL 1; 2020– FL 2.

LATEST SEQUENCES

Longest Sequence of League Wins: 9, 9.2.1990 – 19.3.1990.

Longest Sequence of League Defeats: 8, 29.10.1938 – 17.12.1938.

Longest Sequence of League Draws: 5, 26.12.1997 – 31.1.1998.

Longest Sequence of Unbeaten League Matches: 18, 16.3.1970 – 4.9.1970.

Longest Sequence Without a League Win: 16, 8.11.1969 – 14.3.1970.

Successive Scoring Runs: 32 from 24.2.1934.

Successive Non-scoring Runs: 7 from 20.12.1997.

MANAGERS

Bert Cooke 1912–35
Jackie Carr 1935–36
Jim Knowles 1936–39
Bill Ridding 1939–45
Ernie Blackburn 1946–55
Noel Kelly 1955–57
Peter Farrell 1957–60
Walter Galbraith 1961
Dave Russell 1961–69
Jackie Wright 1969–72
Ron Yeats 1972–75
John King 1975–80
Bryan Hamilton 1980–85
Frank Worthington 1985–87
Ronnie Moore 1987
John King 1987–96
John Aldridge 1996–2001
Dave Watson 2001–02
Ray Mathias 2002–03
Brian Little 2003–06
Ronnie Moore 2006–09
John Barnes 2009
Les Parry 2009–12
Ronnie Moore 2012–14
Robert Edwards 2014
Micky Adams 2014–15
Gary Brabin 2015–16
Paul Cardin 2016
Micky Mellon 2016–20
Mike Jackson 2020
Keith Hill 2020–21
Micky Mellon 2021–23
Ian Dawes 2023
Nigel Adkins 2023–25
Andy Crosby February 2025–

TEN YEAR LEAGUE RECORD

		P	W	D	L	F	A	Pts	Pos
2015-16	NL	46	22	12	12	61	44	78	6
2016-17	NL	46	29	8	9	79	39	95	2
2017-18	NL	46	24	10	12	78	46	82	2
2018-19	FL 2	46	20	13	13	63	50	73	6
2019-20	FL 1	34	8	8	18	36	60	32	21§
2020-21	FL 2	46	20	13	13	55	50	73	7
2021-22	FL 2	46	21	12	13	53	40	75	9
2022-23	FL 2	46	15	13	18	45	48	58	12
2023-24	FL 2	46	17	6	23	67	70	57	16
2024-25	FL 2	46	12	15	19	45	65	51	20

§*Decided on points-per-game (0.94)*

DID YOU KNOW ?

Tranmere Rovers beat Liverpool and Everton at Prenton Park on consecutive days in the emergency wartime competitions in the 1942–43 season. On Christmas Day Rovers beat Liverpool 3-2 thanks to goals from Danny Glidden and Arthur Frost (2). On Boxing Day they beat Everton 2-1, with Pat Jackson and Frost scoring, the attendance of 11,088 establishing a new wartime record for the club.

TRANMERE ROVERS – SKY BET LEAGUE TWO 2024–25 LEAGUE RECORD

Match No.	Date	Venue	Opponents	Result		H/T Score	Lg Pos.	Goalscorers	Attendance
1	Aug 10	H	Notts Co	D	0-0	0-0	13		8198
2	17	A	Port Vale	D	0-0	0-0	16		8102
3	24	H	Walsall	W	1-0	1-0	12	Patrick [13]	6145
4	31	A	Carlisle U	W	2-1	2-1	8	Patrick 2 [6, 37]	8003
5	Sept 14	A	Gillingham	L	0-3	0-0	14		6660
6	21	A	Colchester U	L	0-3	0-2	16		4243
7	27	D	Salford C	D	0-0	0-0	15		7281
8	Oct 1	H	Swindon T	D	1-1	1-0	17	Dennis [17]	5120
9	5	A	Milton Keynes D	D	1-1	0-1	17	Hendry [90]	6047
10	12	H	Bradford C	L	0-2	0-1	19		8366
11	19	A	Bromley	W	2-1	0-0	16	Patrick [75], Saunders [80]	3376
12	22	H	Grimsby T	L	0-1	0-0	18		5428
13	26	A	Crewe Alex	L	1-3	1-1	19	Jennings [8]	5957
14	Nov 9	H	Newport Co	W	2-1	1-0	17	Jennings [41], Morris [58]	5805
15	22	A	Cheltenham T	L	0-1	0-0	19		3939
16	26	H	AFC Wimbledon	L	0-2	0-1	21		5007
17	Dec 3	H	Morecambe	D	2-2	0-1	20	Turnbull [48], Jennings [75]	4968
18	7	A	Chesterfield	L	0-3	0-2	21		7923
19	14	H	Harrogate T	W	2-1	1-1	19	Dennis [25], Patrick [67]	5122
20	21	A	Doncaster R	L	1-3	0-1	19	Solomon [83]	7201
21	29	H	Barrow	D	1-1	1-1	19	Patrick (pen) [35]	6109
22	Jan 1	A	Morecambe	L	0-2	0-0	21		3577
23	4	H	Carlisle U	W	1-0	1-0	20	Norman [23]	6886
24	11	A	Walsall	L	1-5	1-2	22	Jennings [44]	5614
25	18	A	AFC Wimbledon	L	0-2	0-0	22		7975
26	25	H	Gillingham	D	1-1	1-1	22	Solomon [17]	7325
27	28	A	Swindon T	L	1-3	1-0	22	Davison [7]	6180
28	Feb 1	A	Colchester U	L	1-3	0-2	22	Dennis [50]	5166
29	8	A	Salford C	L	0-2	0-0	22		3097
30	11	H	Fleetwood T	D	0-0	0-0	22		5166
31	15	H	Milton Keynes D	D	1-1	0-1	22	Norris (pen) [79]	5699
32	22	A	Notts Co	L	1-2	0-0	22	Dennis [88]	9476
33	25	H	Accrington S	L	0-1	0-0	22		5613
34	Mar 1	H	Port Vale	D	1-1	1-1	22	Dennis [18]	6974
35	4	A	Grimsby T	D	1-1	1-0	22	Finley [10]	4854
36	8	H	Bromley	W	2-1	1-1	22	Hawkes [32], Patrick [70]	5615
37	15	A	Bradford C	W	1-0	0-0	22	Hawkes (pen) [56]	18,845
38	22	A	Fleetwood T	D	0-0	0-0	22		3421
39	28	H	Cheltenham T	W	2-0	1-0	22	Dennis [25], Norman [90]	6650
40	Apr 1	A	Harrogate T	L	2-3	0-1	22	Hendry [61], Patrick [78]	3325
41	5	H	Chesterfield	W	4-0	0-0	21	Norman [46], Hendry [54], Davison [85], Finley [89]	6316
42	12	A	Accrington S	D	3-3	0-3	21	Patrick 2 [78, 90], Dennis [87]	3197
43	18	H	Doncaster R	L	0-3	0-1	22		8814
44	21	A	Barrow	D	0-0	0-0	22		3304
45	26	H	Crewe Alex	W	2-0	1-0	22	Davies [22], Dennis [87]	9496
46	May 3	A	Newport Co	W	4-1	1-1	20	Garrett [41], Dennis [48], Patrick [70], Davison [78]	5465

Final League Position: 20

GOALSCORERS

League (45): Patrick 11 (1 pen), Dennis 9, Jennings 4, Davison 3, Hendry 3, Norman 3, Finley 2, Hawkes 2 (1 pen), Solomon 2, Davies 1, Garrett 1, Morris 1, Norris 1 (1 pen), Saunders 1, Turnbull 1.
FA Cup (1): Jennings 1.
Carabao Cup (3): Patrick 1, Saunders 1, Williams 1.
Vertu Trophy (7): Dennis 2, Hawkes 2, Davison 1, Patrick 1, Taylor 1.

McGee L 46	Norman C 36+5	Davies T 31+3	Walker B 6+2	Wood C 29+5	Morris K 20+8	O'Connor L 39+3	Hendry R 20+6	Jennings C 32+12	Norris L 8+5	Davison J 13+19	Patrick D 40+6	Saunders H 16+21	Bradshaw Z 11+16	Dennis K 22+15	Turnbull J 44	Solomon S 7+7	Merrie C 25+7	Khan S 6+4	Williams J —+2	Taylor S 2+9	Finley S 29+4	Hawkes J 11+12	Drysdale D 7+1	Garrett J 6+5	Mather Sam —+2	Match No.
1	2	3	4	5	6^2	7^3	8	9	10	11^1	12	13	14													1
1	2	3	4	5		7	8	6	11^1	10^3	9^2	13	12	14												2
1	2	3	4			7	8	6		11^2	9	10^1		12	5	13										3
1	2	3		5		7		10		11^1	6	12	9		4		8									4
1	2	3		5	9^4	7^2	8	10	12	11^1	6^3	13	16	15		4^5		14								5
1	2^1			5					12	8^5	6	11	9^3	10^2	3	13	4	16	15	7^4	14					6
1		3		5	13	2	8	6	10^1	12	9	11^2			4	7										7
1	15	3		5^3		2^4	9	8		13	7	10^1	14	11^4	4		6			12						8
1	5	3			9^3	2	13			14	10^2	12	8	11^1	4		7	6								9
1	5	3	2		9^4	6	15	12			10	14	8^1	11^2	4^5		7^3				16	13				10
1	5	3	2			6	12	9^2	11	10^1	8^3	14	13		4		15					7^4				11
1	2	3		5	9^3	6^4	15	14	11		10^1	12		4						8^2	7	13				12
1	5	3	2		13	6^1	12	10^4	14	16	11	9^5	8^3		4		7^2			15						13
1	2^1	3		5	6	12	8	10	11^2	13	9^3				4							7	14			14
1	2	3		5	6^3	8		10	11^2		9^1	12		13	4		15					7^4	14			15
1	2	3		5^4				10	14	6^1	13	15	11^3		4		8			12	7	9^2				16
1	2			5	6		11			13	12		10^1		4		8				7	9^2	3			17
1	2^3			5^4	6^2	13		10		9^1	11	15			4	14	7			12	8		3			18
1		3		5	12		9			10	11^1		8	4		7				6						19
1	14	3^8		5^3		2		9		13	10^1	8^5		11^4	4	15	7				6^2	16	12			20
1	12		15	14	7	2^1		11		10	8	5^3	13		4	9^2					6^4	3				21
1	14	3	15		7	2^3		11		13	10	8^2	5^4	16	4	9^1		12			6^5					22
1	5	3			7^3	2		9		12	11^1	10^2	8	14	4			13			6					23
1	5	3		15	7^5	2^3		9		12	14	11^2	8^4	10^1	4	16		13			6^8					24
1	2	4			9			7		13	12	10^1	6^4	11^2	5	15	14	8^3			3^8					25
1	2	3		5	7^1			9		11^2	10^4	14		13	4	8		6^3			12	15				26
1	2^4	4		6^2		8^8		9		10^1	14	12	13	15	5	11^3				7			3^8			27
1		3		5^4		2		9^5		11^1	10	12	14	13	4	8^2		7			6^3	16		15		28
1	2^5	4		6^3		3		10^4	15	12	14	11^1		16	5	13	8				7			9^2		29
1	12	3			6^3			14	11	9			10^2	4	5	7					13		2	8^1		30
1	5		12		2		10	14	11^2	9	13			4	6^4	7		15					3^1	8^3		31
1	5	3			2		11			10^4	9^2		15	4		7	12	6^1	13			8^3		14		32
1	5	3		13		2^3	15	10		11^1	9			12	4		7^4				6^5	14		8^2	16	33
1	5	14		4^8		2	8^2	12		9			11	3^3	7		6	10^1			13					34
1	2				4	10^2	9^3	14	8	13		11^1	3	7		6	5			12						35
1	2		5	10^1	3	7	13		8	14		11^3	4	12			6	9^2								36
1	5		4	10^1	2	7^4	15		8^5	13	14	11^2	3	12			6	9^3		16						37
1	5			14	2	10^3	12		8^4	11^1	4	13	3	7			15	6	9^2							38
1	5		4	13	2	6^2	12		9^4	14	15	10^3	3	8			7	11^1								39
1	5^1		4^4	13	2	6	12		14	9^5		15	10^3	3	7^2			16	8	11						40
1	5	16	4	14	2^5	8^3	10^1		15	9^2		13	11^4	3	6			7	12							41
1	12		4^1	14	2	10	9^3		13	8	15	11	3^5		6^2			16	7	5^4						42
1	5		4	10^1	2^4	7^5	14	12	8		3	13		15	6^3	9^2		16								43
1	5^1	3^4	8		2	10	14		9^2	13	15	11^3	4	7			6	12								44
1		3	8	9^2	2	7^8	13	12	5^3	11^1	15	10^4	4	6			14									45
1	5^5	3	14	10	2		15		12	9^3	13		11^2	4	6			8¹	16			7^4				46

FA Cup

First Round	Oldham Ath	(h)	1-2	

Carabao Cup

First Round	Accrington S	(h)	3-0
Second Round	Leicester C	(a)	0-4

Vertu Trophy

Group A (N)	Everton U21	(h)	1-3
Group A (N)	Accrington S	(h)	2-1
Group A (N)	Stockport Co	(a)	2-0
Second Round	Rotherham U	(a)	2-3

WALSALL

FOUNDATION

Two of the leading clubs around Walsall in the 1880s were Walsall Swifts (formed 1877) and Walsall Town (formed 1879). The Swifts were winners of the Birmingham Senior Cup in 1881, while the Town reached the 4th round (5th round modern equivalent) of the FA Cup in 1883. These clubs amalgamated as Walsall Town Swifts in 1888, becoming simply Walsall in 1895.

Poundland Bescot Stadium, Bescot Crescent, Walsall WS1 4SA.
Telephone: (01922) 622 791.
Ticket Office: (01922) 651 414/416.
Website: www.saddlers.co.uk
Email: info@walsallfc.co.uk
Ground Capacity: 10,862.
Record Attendance: 25,453 v Newcastle U, Division 2, 29 August 1961 (at Fellows Park); 11,049 v Rotherham U, Division 1, 9 May 2004 (at Bescot Stadium).
Pitch Measurements: 100m × 67m (109.5yd × 73yd).
Co-Chairmen: Benjamin Boycott, Leigh Pomlett.
Chief Executive: Ben Sadler.
Head Coach: Mat Sadler.
Assistant Head Coach: Gary Waddock.
Colours: Red shirts with thin black and white stripes and black trim, white shorts with black trim, white socks.
Year Formed: 1888.
Turned Professional: 1888.
Previous Names: Walsall Swifts (founded 1877) and Walsall Town (founded 1879) amalgamated in 1888 as Walsall Town Swifts; 1895, Walsall.
Club Nickname: 'The Saddlers'.
Grounds: 1888, Hillary Street (renamed Fellows Park 1930); 1990, Bescot Stadium (renamed Banks's Stadium 2007; Poundland Bescot Stadium 2022).
First Football League Game: 3 September 1892, Division 2, v Darwen (h) L 1–2 – Hawkins; Withington, Pinches; Robinson, Whitrick, Forsyth; Marshall, Holmes, Turner, Gray (1), Pangbourn.
Record League Victory: 10–0 v Darwen, Division 2, 4 March 1899 – Tennent; Ted Peers (1), Davies; Hickinbotham, Jenkyns, Taggart; Dean (3), Vail (2), Aston (4), Martin, Griffin.
Record Cup Victory: 7–0 v Macclesfield T (a), FA Cup 2nd rd, 6 December 1997 – Walker; Evans, Marsh, Viveash (1), Ryder, Peron, Boli (2 incl. 1p) (Ricketts), Porter (2), Keates, Watson (Platt), Hodge (2 incl. 1p).
Record Defeat: 0–12 v Small Heath, 17 December 1892; 0–12 v Darwen, 26 December 1896, both Division 2.
Most League Points (2 for a win): 65, Division 4, 1959–60.
Most League Points (3 for a win): 89, FL 2, 2006–07.
Most League Goals: 102, Division 4, 1959–60.

HONOURS

League Champions: FL 2 – 2006–07; Division 4 – 1959–60.
Runners-up: Second Division – 1998–99; Division 3 – 1960–61; Third Division – 1994–95; Division 4 – 1979–80.
FA Cup: last 16 – 1889; 5th rd – 1939, 1975, 1978, 1987, 2002, 2003.
League Cup: semi-final – 1984.
League Trophy: Runners-up: 2015.

FOOTBALL YEARBOOK FACT FILE

Walsall Town Swifts, as the club was then known, played an experimental match under electric lights on the evening of 24 September 1888. The match, which was arranged as part of the celebrations to mark the opening of the Walsall Science and Art Institute, was played in misty conditions and lasted just 30 minutes each way. The Saddlers drew 2-2 with local rivals West Bromwich Albion in front of a crowd estimated at nearly 7,000.

Highest League Scorer in Season: Gilbert Alsop, 40, Division 3 (N), 1933–34 and 1934–35.

Most League Goals in Total Aggregate: Tony Richards, 184, 1954–63; Colin Taylor, 184, 1958–63, 1964–68, 1969–73.

Most League Goals in One Match: 5, Gilbert Alsop v Carlisle U, Division 3 (N), 2 February 1935; 5, Bill Evans v Mansfield T, Division 3 (N), 5 October 1935; 5, Johnny Devlin v Torquay U, Division 3 (S), 1 September 1949.

Most Capped Player: Liam Gordon, 19 (26), Guyana.

Most League Appearances: Colin Harrison, 473, 1964–82.

Youngest League Player: Geoff Morris, 16 years 218 days v Scunthorpe U, 14 September 1965.

Record Transfer Fee Received: £1,500,000 (potentially rising to £5,000,000) from Brentford for Rico Henry, August 2016.

Record Transfer Fee Paid: £300,000 to Anorthosis Famagusta for Andreas Makris, August 2016.

Football League Record: 1892 Elected to Division 2; 1892–95 Division 2; 1895 Failed re-election; 1895–96 Midland League; 1896 Re-elected to Division 2; 1896–1901 Division 2; 1901 Failed re-election; 1921 Original Member of Division 3 (N); 1921–27 Division 3 (N); 1927–31 Division 3 (S); 1931–36 Division 3 (N); 1936–58 Division 3 (S); 1958–60 Division 4; 1960–61 Division 3; 1961–63 Division 2; 1963–79 Division 3; 1979–80 Division 4; 1980–88 Division 3; 1988–89 Division 2; 1989–90 Division 3; 1990–92 Division 4; 1992–95 Third Division; 1995–99 Second Division; 1999–2000 First Division; 2000–01 Second Division; 2001–04 First Division; 2004–06 FL 1; 2006–07 FL 2; 2007–19 FL 1; 2019– FL 2.

LATEST SEQUENCES

Longest Sequence of League Wins: 9, 3.12.2024 – 18.1.2025.

Longest Sequence of League Defeats: 15, 29.10.1988 – 4.2.1989.

Longest Sequence of League Draws: 6, 4.2.2023 – 25.2.2023.

Longest Sequence of Unbeaten League Matches: 21, 6.11.1979 – 22.3.1980.

Longest Sequence Without a League Win: 18, 15.10.1988 – 4.2.1989.

Successive Scoring Runs: 27 from 6.11.1979.

Successive Non-scoring Runs: 5 from 10.4.2004.

MANAGERS

H. Smallwood 1888–91 *(Secretary-Manager)*
A. G. Burton 1891–93
J. H. Robinson 1893–95
C. H. Ailso 1895–96 *(Secretary-Manager)*
A. E. Parsloe 1896–97 *(Secretary-Manager)*
L. Ford 1897–98 *(Secretary-Manager)*
G. Hughes 1898–99 *(Secretary-Manager)*
L. Ford 1899–1901 *(Secretary-Manager)*
J. E. Shutt 1908–13 *(Secretary-Manager)*
Haydn Price 1914–20
Joe Burchell 1920–26
David Ashworth 1926–27
Jack Torrance 1927–28
James Kerr 1928–29
Sid Scholey 1929–30
Peter O'Rourke 1930–32
Bill Slade 1932–34
Andy Wilson 1934–37
Tommy Lowes 1937–44
Harry Hibbs 1944–51
Tony McPhee 1951
Brough Fletcher 1952–53
Major Frank Buckley 1953–55
John Love 1955–57
Billy Moore 1957–64
Alf Wood 1964
Reg Shaw 1964–68
Dick Graham 1968
Ron Lewin 1968–69
Billy Moore 1969–72
John Smith 1972–73
Ronnie Allen 1973
Doug Fraser 1973–77
Dave Mackay 1977–78
Alan Ashman 1978
Frank Sibley 1979
Alan Buckley 1979–86
Neil Martin *(Joint with Buckley)* 1981–82
Tommy Coakley 1986–88
John Barnwell 1989–90
Kenny Hibbitt 1990–94
Chris Nicholl 1994–97
Jan Sorensen 1997–98
Ray Graydon 1998–2002
Colin Lee 2002–04
Paul Merson 2004–06
Kevin Broadhurst 2006
Richard Money 2006–08
Jimmy Mullen 2008–09
Chris Hutchings 2009–11
Dean Smith 2011–15
Sean O'Driscoll 2015–16
Jon Whitney 2016–18
Dean Keates 2018–19
Martin O'Connor 2019
Darrell Clarke 2019–21
Brian Dutton 2021
Matthew Taylor 2021–22
Michael Flynn 2022–23
Mat Sadler May 2023–

TEN YEAR LEAGUE RECORD

		P	W	D	L	F	A	Pts	Pos
2015-16	FL 1	46	24	12	10	71	49	84	3
2016-17	FL 1	46	14	16	16	51	58	58	14
2017-18	FL 1	46	13	13	20	53	66	52	19
2018-19	FL 1	46	12	11	23	49	71	47	22
2019-20	FL 2	36	13	8	15	40	49	47	12§
2020-21	FL 2	46	11	20	15	45	53	53	19
2021-22	FL 2	46	14	12	20	47	60	54	16
2022-23	FL 2	46	12	19	15	46	49	55	16
2023-24	FL 2	46	18	11	17	69	73	65	11
2024-25	FL 2	46	21	14	11	75	54	77	4

§*Decided on points-per-game (1.31)*

DID YOU KNOW ?

After drawing at home to Reading on 11 March 1961, Walsall were in sixth position in the Third Division table, eight points behind the promotion places. However, they went on to win 10 of their last 12 games, dropping just three points to clinch promotion for the second season in a row. For good measure, the Saddlers were also unbeaten at home in a Football League campaign for the first time since 1898–99.

WALSALL – SKY BET LEAGUE TWO 2024–25 LEAGUE RECORD

Match No.	Date	Venue	Opponents	Result	H/T Score	Lg Pos.	Goalscorers	Attendance
1	Aug 10	H	Morecambe	W 1-0	1-0	8	Allen [20]	5226
2	17	A	Swindon T	W 4-0	2-0	1	Gordon J [33], Matt [40], Allen [49], Adomah [64]	7786
3	24	A	Tranmere R	L 0-1	0-1	3		6145
4	31	H	Cheltenham T	W 2-1	0-0	2	Lowe [48], Matt [66]	5760
5	Sept 7	A	Milton Keynes D	L 0-1	0-1	6		6547
6	14	H	Bradford C	W 2-1	1-1	4	Allen (pen) [19], Johnson [88]	5967
7	21	A	Salford C	W 2-0	0-0	3	Lowe [51], Lakin [57]	2860
8	28	H	Colchester U	W 4-0	1-0	2	Jellis [39], Adomah [79], Earing 2 [89, 90]	5140
9	Oct 1	H	Fleetwood T	L 2-6	2-1	3	Williams [14], Matt [45]	4237
10	5	A	Chesterfield	D 2-2	1-1	1	Lowe 2 [33, 46]	9035
11	19	A	Grimsby T	W 4-1	0-0	3	Matt [56], Jellis [69], Lowe [74], Johnson [90]	5984
12	22	H	Carlisle U	W 3-1	1-0	2	Lowe [2], Jellis [49], Matt [56]	4939
13	26	A	Accrington S	D 0-0	0-0	2		2595
14	Nov 9	H	Crewe Alex	D 1-1	0-0	2	Lowe [85]	8105
15	23	A	AFC Wimbledon	W 1-0	0-0	2	Lowe [52]	7519
16	26	H	Bromley	D 2-2	1-0	2	Gordon L [40], Okagbue [90]	4424
17	Dec 3	H	Notts Co	W 3-2	0-0	2	Allen [57], Hall [64], Lowe [86]	5720
18	7	A	Port Vale	W 1-0	0-0	1	Matt [51]	9142
19	14	H	Barrow	W 1-0	1-0	1	Allen [28]	5109
20	21	A	Harrogate T	W 2-0	1-0	1	Lowe [34], Adomah [69]	2843
21	26	H	Doncaster R	W 2-0	0-0	1	Lowe [47], Williams [79]	7220
22	29	H	Newport Co	W 2-0	0-0	1	Lowe 2 [73, 90]	6706
23	Jan 1	A	Notts Co	W 2-1	0-1	1	Matt [65], Lowe [82]	4610
24	11	A	Tranmere R	W 5-1	2-1	1	Matt 2 [15, 49], Stirk [22], Jellis [72], Lowe [80]	5614
25	18	H	Milton Keynes D	W 4-2	1-1	1	Okagbue [32], Gordon L [46], Williams [66], Adomah [81]	6144
26	25	A	Bradford C	L 0-3	0-2	1		17,172
27	28	A	Fleetwood T	L 0-2	0-2	1		2307
28	Feb 1	A	Salford C	D 2-2	0-1	1	Johnson 2 [78, 87]	5970
29	8	A	Colchester U	L 1-2	0-0	1	Lakin [65]	4734
30	11	H	Gillingham	D 1-1	0-0	1	Matt [49]	6229
31	15	H	Chesterfield	W 3-1	0-1	1	Matt [52], Harrison [55], Amantchi [90]	6830
32	22	A	Morecambe	W 2-0	0-0	1	Allen [53], Jellis [87]	3457
33	25	A	Cheltenham T	D 2-2	1-0	1	Harrison [1], Adomah [79]	4454
34	Mar 1	H	Swindon T	L 0-1	0-0	1		6910
35	4	A	Carlisle U	D 1-1	1-1	1	Allen [7]	6378
36	8	A	Grimsby T	L 1-3	1-2	1	Harrison [6]	6255
37	13	A	Bromley	D 2-2	1-1	1	Amantchi [45], Matt [70]	2512
38	22	A	Gillingham	D 0-0	0-0	1		6153
39	29	H	AFC Wimbledon	D 1-1	0-0	1	Allen [87]	9203
40	Apr 1	A	Doncaster R	D 2-2	1-1	1	Allen [18], Johnson [90]	7796
41	5	A	Port Vale	L 2-3	2-3	3	Allen (pen) [7], Amantchi [11]	8446
42	12	A	Barrow	L 0-2	0-1	3		3071
43	18	H	Harrogate T	D 2-2	1-1	4	O'Connor (og) [16], Gordon L [88]	7408
44	21	A	Newport Co	D 0-0	0-0	4		4578
45	26	H	Accrington S	L 0-1	0-1	4		8131
46	May 3	A	Crewe Alex	W 1-0	0-0	4	Hall [59]	7112

Final League Position: 4

GOALSCORERS

League (75): Lowe 15, Matt 12, Allen 10 (2 pens), Adomah 5, Jellis 5, Johnson 5, Amantchi 3, Gordon L 3, Harrison 3, Williams 3, Earing 2, Hall 2, Lakin 2, Okagbue 2, Gordon J 1, Stirk 1, own goal 1.
FA Cup (2): Gordon L 1, Jellis 1.
Carabao Cup (4): Lowe 2, Jellis 1, own goal 1.
Vertu Trophy (8): Johnson 3, Cleary 1, Gordon J 1, Hall 1, Lakin 1, Lowe 1.
League Two Play-offs (4): Allen 1 (1 pen), Amantchi 1, Chang 1, Lakin 1.

Simkin T 40	McEntee O 21 + 10	Farquharson P 3	Allen T 44 + 1	Barrett C 39 + 4	Jellis J 39 + 4	Stirk R 43 + 1	Lakin C 30 + 6	Gordon L 44	Matt J 38 + 5	Gordon J 6 + 2	Adomah A 10 + 32	Earing J 4 + 16	Okagbue D 41 + 3	Maher R — + 2	Lowe N 20 + 2	Williams H 29 + 1	Hornby S 6	Weir E 7 + 7	Hall G 7 + 7	Cleary R — + 3	Johnson D 1 + 23	Comley B 5 + 13	Daniels D 4 + 3	Wheatley E 2 + 2	Asiimwe N 7 + 3	Amantchi L 4 + 14	Harrison E 9 + 3	Chang A 3 + 2	Match No.
1	2	3	4	5^3	6	7	8^2	9	10^1	11	12	13	14																1
1	2	3	4	5	6^2	7	8	9	10^3	11^1	12	13		14															2
1	2	3^1	4	5^4	6^5	7	8^2	9	10	11^3	15	13	12	16	14														3
1	2^2		4	5	6	7	8	9^1	10	11^1		14	3		12	13													4
	5	2^3	7^5	8	13		14		15	9	3		10^4	4	1	6^2	11^1	12	16										5
1			5^4	6	7	8^2	9	11^3		15	12	2	10^1	3				13	14										6
1			4	5	6	7	8^2	9	11^1		12	13	2	10	3														7
1			4	5	6	7^3	8^1	9	10^2		13	12	2	11^4	3			15	14										8
1			4	5^3	6^4	7	8^2	9	10^1		13	12	2	11	3			14	15										9
1			4	5	12	7	8	9	10^3		13	6^1	2	11	3														10
1			4	5	6^5	7^3	8^1	9	10^2		13	12	2	11^4	3		15	16	14										11
1			4	5	6^4	7^3	8^1	9	10^2		12	13	2	11^5	3		15	16	14										12
1			4	5	6	7	8^1	9	10		12		2	11^2	3			13											13
1			4	5^4	6^5	7	8^1	9	11^3		14	12	2	10			15	16	13	3									14
1			4	5	6	7	8^1	9	11^2		13		2	10					12	3									15
1			4	5^3	13	7^4		9	10		14	8^2	2	11		6^1		15	12	3									16
1			4	5		7	8	9	10^1		12	13	2	11	3			6^2											17
1			4	5		7	8	9	10^1		12		2	11	3			6											18
1	13		4	5	12	7	8	9	11^2		14	6^3	2	10	3														19
1	13		4^4	5	6^1	7^3	8	9			10	12	11^2	3		15		14											20
1	12		4	5	6^1	7	8^3	9	10^2		13	14	2	11	3														21
1	14		4	5	6^2	7	8^3	9	11^1		12	13^4	2	10	3				15										22
1	13		14	5	5^3	6	7	8^2	9	12	10^1		2	11	3		4^4		15										23
1	6^1		4	5	8	7^3	12	9	10^2		13		2			3^5			16	15	14								24
1	6^1		4	5	8	7	12	9	10^2	13	11		2			3													25
1	6		4	5^3		7^2	8^4	9	10^1		11^3		2			3		13			12	15		14	16				26
1	6		4	5	8^3	7	13	9		12	10^1		2			3		14						11^2					27
1	16		4	5^4	8	7^5	6^3	9			10^2	13	2			3		14			15			11^1	12				28
1	2		4^8	5	6	7^4	8^3	9	10^1		12		3					14	13						15	11^2			29
1	6			5	8^2	7		9	10^3	11^1			2			3		4			13				14	12			30
1	12		4	5^6	6	7	8^4	9	10^2		13		2			3^1		16				14			15	11^3			31
1	2		4	5^4	8	7		9^2	10^2		12		3					15				6			14	13	11^1		32
1	2		4	5	8	7		9	10^1		13		3									6			12	11^2			33
1	2		4	5^4	6	8	12	9	10^2		13		3					15	7^1						14	11^3			34
1	2		4	5	6	7	8	9	10^2		11^1		3					13							12				35
1	13		4	5	6^5	7^4	8^1	9	12		11^2		2			3		16	15							10^3			36
	2		7	5	6			9	11				3		1	4			8						12	10^1			37
	2		9		6^3	7	8^2		10^1	11^4			3		1	4		14	13			5	12		15				38
	2		4		6^4	7	8^1	9	10^3	13			3		1	15	12	11^2				5	14						39
	2		8	14	6	7^2		9	10	12			3		1	4		13				5^3	11^1						40
	2		8	12	6^3	7		9	10^4	14			3		1	4^1	13	16			15	5^2	11^5						41
1	2		4	5^5	6^4		8^2	9	10^1	13	16					14		15	7	3					12	11^1			42
1			4	5^2	8^3	7		9	10	13			2			3		6^4							14	12	11^1	15	43
1	15		4	13	7^1	8		9	12	10^5			2			3		14					5		11^2	16	6^4		44
1	6^3		4	16^8	13	14		8^5	10^2	11			2			3		9^1					5		12	15	7^4		45
1	13		4		10^4	6	14	8	12				15			2		3				9^3	5		11^1		7^2		46

FA Cup

First Round	Bolton W	(h)	2-1	
Second Round	Charlton Ath	(h)	0-4	

Carabao Cup

First Round	Exeter C	(h)	1-1

Walsall won 4-3 on penalties.

Second Round	Huddersfield T	(h)	3-2
Third Round	Leicester C	(h)	0-0

Leicester C won 3-0 on penalties.

Vertu Trophy

Group A (S)	Birmingham C	(a)	1-1

Walsall won 4-3 on penalties.

Group A (S)	Fulham U21	(h)	1-0
Group A (S)	Shrewsbury T	(h)	3-0
Second Round	Reading	(h)	1-1

Walsall won 4-2 on penalties.

Third Round	Peterborough U	(a)	2-4

League Two Play-offs

Semi-Final 1st leg	Chesterfield	(a)	2-0
Semi-Final 2nd leg	Chesterfield	(h)	2-1
Final	AFC Wimbledon	(Wembley)	0-1

WATFORD

FOUNDATION

The club was formed as Watford Rovers in 1881. The name was changed to West Herts in 1893 and then the name Watford was adopted after rival club Watford St Mary's was absorbed in 1898.

Vicarage Road Stadium, Vicarage Road, Watford, Hertfordshire WD18 0ER.

Telephone: (01923) 496 000.

Ticket Office: (01923) 223 023.

Website: www.watfordfc.com

Email: yourvoice@watfordfc.com

Ground Capacity: 21,593.

Record Attendance: 34,099 v Manchester U, FA Cup 4th rd (replay), 3 February 1969.

Pitch Measurements: 102m × 69m (111.5yd × 75.5yd).

Chairman and Chief Executive: Scott Duxbury.

Head Coach: Paulo Pezzolano.

Assistant Head Coaches: Alberto Garrido, Camilo Speranza.

Colours: Yellow shirts with thin red and black alternating stripes and red and black trim, red shorts, red socks with yellow trim.

Year Formed: 1881.

Turned Professional: 1897.

Previous Names: 1881, Watford Rovers; 1893, West Herts; 1898, Watford.

Club Nickname: 'The Hornets'.

Grounds: 1883, Vicarage Meadow, Rose and Crown Meadow; 1889, Colney Butts; 1890, Cassio Road; 1922, Vicarage Road.

First Football League Game: 28 August 1920, Division 3, v QPR (a) W 2–1 – Williams; Horseman, Fred Gregory; Bacon, Toone, Wilkinson; Bassett, Ronald (1), Hoddinott, White (1), Waterall.

Record League Victory: 8–0 v Sunderland, Division 1, 25 September 1982 – Sherwood; Rice, Rostron, Taylor, Terry, Bolton, Callaghan (2), Blissett (4), Jenkins (2), Jackett, Barnes.

Record Cup Victory: 10–1 v Lowestoft T, FA Cup 1st rd, 27 November 1926 – Yates; Prior, Fletcher (1); Frank Smith, Bert Smith, Strain; Stephenson, Warner (3), Edmonds (3), Swan (1), Daniels (1), (1 og).

Record Defeat: 0–10 v Wolverhampton W, FA Cup 1st rd (replay), 24 January 1912.

Most League Points (2 for a win): 71, Division 4, 1977–78.

Most League Points (3 for a win): 91, FL C, 2020–21.

HONOURS

League Champions: Second Division – 1997–98; Division 3 – 1968–69; Division 4 – 1977–78.
Runners-up: Division 1 – 1982–83; FL C – 2014–15, 2020–21; Division 2 – 1981–82; Division 3 – 1978–79.

FA Cup: Runners-up: 1984, 2019.

League Cup: semi-final – 1979, 2005.

European Competitions
UEFA Cup: 1983–84.

FOOTBALL YEARBOOK FACT FILE

Bomb threats were issued to all 11 First Division games played on 7 December 1985, but the only ground evacuated was St Andrew's, where Birmingham City were playing Watford. The proceedings were halted after 62 minutes with the game tied at 1-1 and the crowd of 7,043 were asked to leave. Play resumed some 65 minutes later after a thorough search had yielded nothing. Shortly afterwards Worrell Sterling netted what proved to be the winner for the Hornets.

Most League Goals: 92, Division 4, 1959–60.

Highest League Scorer in Season: Cliff Holton, 42, Division 4, 1959–60.

Most League Goals in Total Aggregate: Luther Blissett, 148, 1976–83, 1984–88, 1991–92.

Most League Goals in One Match: 5, Eddie Mummery v Newport Co, Division 3 (S), 5 January 1924.

Most Capped Player: Craig Cathcart, 54 (73), Northern Ireland.

Most League Appearances: Luther Blissett, 415, 1976–83, 1984–88, 1991–92.

Youngest League Player: Keith Mercer, 16 years 125 days v Tranmere R, 16 February 1973.

Record Transfer Fee Received: £35,000,000 from Everton for Richarlison, July 2018.

Record Transfer Fee Paid: £30,000,000 to Rennes for Ismaila Sarr, August 2019.

Football League Record: 1920 Original Member of Division 3; 1920–21 Division 3; 1921–58 Division 3 (S); 1958–60 Division 4; 1960–69 Division 3; 1969–72 Division 2; 1972–75 Division 3; 1975–78 Division 2; 1978–79 Division 3; 1979–82 Division 2; 1982–88 Division 1; 1988–92 Division 2; 1992–96 First Division; 1996–98 Second Division; 1998–99 First Division; 1999–2000 Premier League; 2000–04 First Division; 2004–06 FL C; 2006–07 Premier League; 2007–15 FL C; 2015–20 Premier League; 2020–21 FL C; 2021–22 Premier League; 2022– FL C.

LATEST SEQUENCES

Longest Sequence of League Wins: 7, 28.8.2000 – 14.10.2000.

Longest Sequence of League Defeats: 9, 26.12.1972 – 27.2.1973.

Longest Sequence of League Draws: 7, 16.2.2008 – 22.3.2008.

Longest Sequence of Unbeaten League Matches: 22, 1.10.1996 – 1.3.1997.

Longest Sequence Without a League Win: 19, 27.11.1971 – 8.4.1972.

Successive Scoring Runs: 22 from 20.8.1985.

Successive Non-scoring Runs: 7 from 18.12.1971.

MANAGERS

John Goodall 1903–10
Harry Kent 1910–26
Fred Pagnam 1926–29
Neil McBain 1929–37
Bill Findlay 1938–47
Jack Bray 1947–48
Eddie Hapgood 1948–50
Ron Gray 1950–51
Haydn Green 1951–52
Len Goulden 1952–55
 (*General Manager to 1956*)
Johnny Paton 1955–56
Neil McBain 1956–59
Ron Burgess 1959–63
Bill McGarry 1963–64
Ken Furphy 1964–71
George Kirby 1971–73
Mike Keen 1973–77
Graham Taylor 1977–87
Dave Bassett 1987–88
Steve Harrison 1988–90
Colin Lee 1990
Steve Perryman 1990–93
Glenn Roeder 1993–96
Graham Taylor 1996
Kenny Jackett 1996–97
Graham Taylor 1997–2001
Gianluca Vialli 2001–02
Ray Lewington 2002–05
Adrian Boothroyd 2005–08
Brendan Rodgers 2008–09
Malky Mackay 2009–11
Sean Dyche 2011–12
Gianfranco Zola 2012–13
Beppe Sannino 2013–14
Oscar Garcia 2014
Billy McKinlay 2014
Slavisa Jokanovic 2014–15
Quique Sanchez Flores 2015–16
Walter Mazzarri 2016–17
Marco Silva 2017–18
Javi Gracia 2018–19
Quique Sanchez Flores 2019
Nigel Pearson 2019–20
Vladimir Ivić 2020
Xisco Muñoz 2020–21
Claudio Ranieri 2021–22
Roy Hodgson 2022
Rob Edwards 2022
Slavan Bilic 2022–23
Chris Wilder 2023
Valerien Ismael 2023–24
Tom Cleverley 2024–25
Paulo Pezzolano May 2025–

TEN YEAR LEAGUE RECORD

		P	W	D	L	F	A	Pts	Pos
2015-16	PR Lge	38	12	9	17	40	50	45	13
2016-17	PR Lge	38	11	7	20	40	68	40	17
2017-18	PR Lge	38	11	8	19	44	64	41	14
2018-19	PR Lge	38	14	8	16	52	59	50	11
2019-20	PR Lge	38	8	10	20	36	64	34	19
2020-21	FL C	46	27	10	9	63	30	91	2
2021-22	PR Lge	38	6	5	27	34	77	23	19
2022-23	FL C	46	16	15	15	56	53	63	11
2023-24	FL C	46	13	17	16	61	61	56	15
2024-25	FL C	46	16	9	21	53	61	57	14

DID YOU KNOW ?

Watford were the draw specialists of the Second Division in 1996–97. Between October and February they drew 15 out of 18 League matches played, establishing a new Football League record of nine consecutive away draws. Outside of this period they managed only four draws during the season, leaving them with a total of 19 draws from 46 games.

WATFORD – SKY BET CHAMPIONSHIP 2024–25 LEAGUE RECORD

Match No.	Date	Venue	Opponents	Result	H/T Score	Lg Pos.	Goalscorers	Attendance
1	Aug 10	A	Millwall	W 3-2	1-0	6	Kayembe [22], Chakvetadze [55], Rajovic [90]	16,456
2	17	H	Stoke C	W 3-0	0-0	2	Kayembe 2 [47, 73], Andrews [49]	18,789
3	24	H	Derby Co	W 2-1	1-1	2	Bayo [31], Sissoko [76]	18,911
4	Sept 1	A	Sheffield U	L 0-1	0-1	3		26,914
5	14	H	Coventry C	D 1-1	0-1	5	Dele-Bashiru [67]	19,441
6	21	H	Norwich C	L 1-4	1-2	8	Andrews [26]	26,438
7	28	H	Sunderland	W 2-1	1-0	7	Ebosele [28], Dele-Bashiru (pen) [84]	20,335
8	Oct 2	A	Preston NE	L 0-3	0-0	8		13,602
9	5	H	Middlesbrough	W 2-1	0-0	6	Kayembe [75], Baah [87]	20,002
10	19	A	Luton T	L 0-3	0-1	8		11,758
11	22	A	Leeds U	L 1-2	0-2	8	Baah [47]	34,968
12	26	H	Blackburn R	W 1-0	0-0	7	Kayembe (pen) [71]	18,880
13	Nov 2	H	Sheffield Wed	W 6-2	1-1	5	Porteous [29], Ince (pen) [52], Bayo 4 (1 pen) [58 (p), 67, 85, 88]	25,693
14	5	A	Swansea C	L 0-1	0-1	5		12,869
15	8	H	Oxford U	W 1-0	0-0	4	Bayo [54]	20,268
16	22	A	Plymouth Arg	D 2-2	2-1	5	Bayo [8], Porteous [41]	16,400
17	26	H	Bristol C	W 1-0	0-0	5	Andrews [53]	17,579
18	30	H	QPR	D 0-0	0-0	6		20,413
19	Dec 11	A	Hull C	D 1-1	0-0	8	Vata [88]	18,694
20	15	A	WBA	W 2-1	1-0	7	Bayo 2 [35, 50]	19,774
21	21	A	Burnley	L 1-2	0-1	7	Baah [80]	19,601
22	26	H	Portsmouth	W 2-1	0-1	6	Kayembe (pen) [57], Vata [90]	20,696
23	29	H	Cardiff C	L 1-2	1-2	7	Chakvetadze [38]	19,916
24	Jan 1	A	QPR	L 1-3	0-2	8	Baah [55]	17,268
25	4	H	Sheffield U	L 1-2	1-1	9	Ngakia [20]	19,937
26	14	A	Cardiff C	D 1-1	0-0	8	Bayo [87]	16,942
27	18	A	Derby Co	W 2-0	1-0	8	Louza [4], Kayembe [66]	29,040
28	21	H	Preston NE	L 1-2	0-1	8	Vata [90]	16,397
29	25	A	Coventry C	L 1-2	0-1	9	Kitching (og) [82]	27,078
30	Feb 1	H	Norwich C	L 0-1	0-1	12		19,774
31	8	A	Sunderland	D 2-2	1-1	10	Dele-Bashiru (pen) [43], Louza [46]	41,329
32	11	H	Leeds U	L 0-4	0-3	12		19,582
33	15	A	Middlesbrough	W 1-0	1-0	10	Sissoko [40]	24,326
34	23	H	Luton T	W 2-0	2-0	9	Dele-Bashiru (pen) [11], Kayembe [23]	20,252
35	Mar 1	A	Stoke C	D 0-0	0-0	10		21,894
36	8	H	Millwall	L 1-2	1-0	11	Pollock [30]	20,031
37	12	H	Swansea C	W 1-0	1-0	10	Sissoko [27]	16,739
38	15	A	Oxford U	L 0-1	0-0	10		11,535
39	29	A	Plymouth Arg	D 0-0	0-0	9		19,545
40	Apr 5	A	Bristol C	L 1-2	0-2	10	Doumbia [80]	22,505
41	8	A	Hull C	W 1-0	0-0	10	Sissoko [55]	17,268
42	12	A	WBA	L 1-2	0-1	11	Sissoko [76]	24,768
43	18	A	Burnley	L 1-2	1-1	12	Doumbia [8]	20,523
44	21	H	Portsmouth	L 0-1	0-1	12		20,451
45	26	A	Blackburn R	L 1-2	0-0	13	Pollock [47]	15,154
46	May 3	H	Sheffield Wed	D 1-1	1-1	14	Sissoko [45]	20,657

Final League Position: 14

GOALSCORERS

League (53): Bayo 10 (1 pen), Kayembe 8 (2 pens), Sissoko 6, Baah 4, Dele-Bashiru 4 (3 pens), Andrews 3, Vata 3, Chakvetadze 2, Doumbia 2, Louza 2, Pollock 2, Porteous 2, Ebosele 1, Ince 1 (1 pen), Ngakia 1, Rajovic 1, own goal 1.
FA Cup (1): Vata 1.
Carabao Cup (8): Ince 4, Rajovic 2, Baah 1, Pollock 1.

Bachmann D 22	Porteous R 18 + 4	Sierralta F 21 + 12	Pollock M 42 + 3	Andrews R 21 + 17	Sissoko M 33 + 7	Dele-Bashiru A 25 + 2	Ngakia J 23 + 6	Kayembe E 37 + 7	Bayo V 25 + 16	Chakvetadze G 37 + 2	Rajovic M — + 3	Sema K 4 + 10	Ince T 13 + 19	Morris J 13 + 5	Larouci Y 26 + 13	Baah K 16 + 11	Louza I 30 + 3	Jebbison D 3 + 10	E.Losele F 7 + 11	Vata R 15 + 18	Bond J 8 + 1	Ogbonna A 5 + 1	Doumbia M 12 + 7	Dwomoh P 6 + 3	Keben K 3 + 3	Abankwah J 17 + 2	Adu-Poku M — + 1	Selvik E 16	Nabizada A — + 1	Wiley C 8 + 2	Massiah-Edwards Z — + 4	Match No.
1	2	3	4	5	6	7	8²	9	10¹	11³	12	13	14																			1
1		3	2	5	6	7⁴	8¹	9	11²	10¹	13			4	12	14	15															2
1	14		3	2	5	7	6		9⁵	11⁴	10	15	12		4³	8¹	13															3
1		3	2	5	6	7		9	11²	10⁴		12	15		4³	8¹	14	13														4
1	2	3⁵	4	5⁵	7	6		9	10¹	11⁴		13		16	8²		12	14	15													5
1²	12	3¹	2	5	7	6		16	9			8⁴		4	15	14		11⁵	10³	13												6
	12		2		6	7		9¹	11⁴	10⁶		13	14	4	8²	16		15	5³		1	3										7
	2	13	6					9⁵	12	10		14	16	4	8³	11⁴	7		5¹	15	1	3²										8
	4		2	5	6³	7		14	13	9		8⁴	10²		15	12		11¹			1	3										9
1	4		2	5⁵	7	8⁴		6²	11¹	10		9³	15		13	12	14	16		3												10
1	12	3¹	2	14	7⁴			8	11			13	6	9³	10⁵		5²	16		15												11
1	4	3	2²	15	7			8	12	11		13	6¹	9³	10⁵		5	14														12
1	2¹	3	4					9	11⁵	10		13	8⁴	5	7³	14	15	12				6²	16									13
1		3	4	14				9	11⁵	10		7²	8⁴	5¹	12	13	16	2				15	6³									14
1	2		3	5				6³	11⁵	10		16	4	12	9²	7⁴	15	8¹	13				14									15
1	2	14	3	5	6			12	10	11¹		13	15	4⁴	8²	9³	7															16
1	2	3³	4	5	12			7⁴	10⁵	11		16	14	13	9¹	6	8²			15												17
1	2	3²	4	5³	6⁵	14		9¹	10	11		16		8⁴	12	7	15	13														18
1	2	3	4	13				5¹	7⁵	11		10		9²	8³	12	6	15	14													19
1	3	13	4		8			2	12	11⁴	9			5¹	14	7²	6	15		10¹												20
1	3	12	4	13	8			2²	16	11⁴	9			5³	7		15	14		10¹			6⁵									21
1	2		3	13	15			5²	6⁸	14	10			4¹	8	9⁸	7	11¹³		12												22
1	3¹	12	4	2	8			9		11¹³		10		15	5		6⁴	14	13	7²												23
1	2	3	4		6²			5	12	11	10			7¹	8³		9	14	13													24
1		4	2	5³	14			9²	6⁴	12	8			13	10	7	15	11		3¹												25
3¹	4	5		7²				2	13	11	9			6³	10	8	14	12	1													26
	3	4	14	12	7¹			8²	9	11				13	5⁴	6	10	1	15				2³									27
	3	4		6	15			8	9⁴	11	14			13	5¹	7⁵	12³	10	1	16			2²									28
	2⁴	3	12	13	7²	5¹	6	11⁵	9			16	4	8			10³	1		14			15									29
	15	4	2	8³	7¹			9	11⁸	10	13			5²	6		12	1		14			3⁴	14								30
	14	4	2	8³	7	12		9	10	13				5¹	6		11²			3	1		4⁴									31
		4⁵	2	8³	7⁴	5²	9		10					13		6	13			11¹	16	3	4	1	15							32
	15	2³	8¹	7	14	9			10⁴			12		5	6		13			11²⁴	3	4	1									33
	14	13	12		7	2	9	15	10⁶			8		16	5¹	6				11⁴	3²	4³	1									34
	3	15	13	7	2	9		12	10³			8¹		5⁴	6		14			11²	4	1										35
	4	13	8⁶	2²	9³	12	10	16				5⁴	7	15			11¹			3	1	14										36
	15	3	2³	8	7¹	13	11	12	10⁶			9⁴		5²	6		16			4	1	14										37
	3		14	8²	6	2⁴	11	12	10³			9¹	13	5	7		15			4⁸	1											38
	4	3	2¹	8	7²	12	16	11³	9			15	13	6	10⁶					1			5⁶	14								39
	3	15	6²	2⁸	8	10³	13	12				16	9¹	7	11		14			4	1		5⁵									40
	15	3		8	7²	2	9					13	14	6	10³		11¹			4⁴	1		5	12								41
	13	3		8	7³	2	9	14				10¹		6	12		11⁴	15		4²	1		5									42
	16	3	13	8⁵	15	2³	9⁸	12				14		6⁵	10¹		11²			7	4⁴	1	5									43
	4²	12	2³	9	13	15		8				6		10¹	11		7⁴	3⁸	14	1	5											44
	12	3	14	7	5³	9	15	4¹				6²		11	10⁶		13	2⁶		1	8	16										45
	3	14	8	2³	9	15		13				6		10⁶	11⁴	7	12	4¹		1	5²	16										46

FA Cup
Third Round   Fulham   (a)   1-4

Carabao Cup
First Round   Milton Keynes D   (h)   5-0
Second Round   Plymouth Arg   (h)   2-0
Third Round   Manchester C   (a)   1-2

WEST BROMWICH ALBION

FOUNDATION

There is a well known story that when employees of Salter's Spring Works in West Bromwich decided to form a football club, they had to send someone to the nearby Association Football stronghold of Wednesbury to purchase a football. A weekly subscription of 2d (less than 1p) was imposed and the name of the new club was West Bromwich Strollers.

The Hawthorns, West Bromwich, West Midlands B71 4LF.

Telephone: (0871) 271 1100.

Ticket Office: (0121) 227 2227.

Website: www.wba.co.uk

Email: enquiries@wbafc.co.uk

Ground Capacity: 26,702.

Record Attendance: 64,815 v Arsenal, FA Cup 6th rd, 6 March 1937.

Pitch Measurements: 105m × 68m (115yd × 74.5yd).

Chairman: Shilen Patel.

Managing Director: Mark Miles.

Head Coach: Ryan Mason.

Assistant Head Coach: Nigel Gibbs.

Colours: Navy blue and white striped shirts with navy blue trim, white shorts with navy blue and red trim, white socks with navy blue and red trim.

Year Formed: 1878.

Turned Professional: 1885.

Previous Name: 1878, West Bromwich Strollers; 1879, West Bromwich Albion.

Club Nicknames: 'The Throstles'; 'The Baggies'; 'Albion'.

Grounds: 1878, Coopers Hill; 1879, Dartmouth Park; 1881, Bunns Field, Walsall Street; 1882, Four Acres (Dartmouth Cricket Club); 1885, Stoney Lane; 1900, The Hawthorns.

First Football League Game: 8 September 1888, Football League, v Stoke (a) W 2–0 – Roberts; Jack Horton, Green; Ezra Horton, Perry, Bayliss; Bassett, Woodhall (1), Hendry, Pearson, Wilson (1).

Record League Victory: 12–0 v Darwen, Division 1, 4 April 1892 – Reader; Jack Horton, McCulloch; Reynolds (2), Perry, Groves; Bassett (3), McLeod, Nicholls (1), Pearson (4), Geddes (1), (1 og).

Record Cup Victory: 10–1 v Chatham (away), FA Cup 3rd rd, 2 March 1889 – Roberts; Jack Horton, Green; Timmins (1), Charles Perry, Ezra Horton; Bassett (2), Walter Perry (1), Bayliss (2), Pearson, Wilson (3), (1 og).

Record Defeat: 3–10 v Stoke C, Division 1, 4 February 1937.

League Champions: Division 1 – 1919–20; FL C – 2007–08; Division 2 – 1901–02, 1910–11.
Runners-up: Division 1 – 1924–25, 1953–54; FL C – 2009–10, 2019–20; First Division – 2001–02, 2003–04; Division 2 – 1930–31, 1948–49.
FA Cup Winners: 1888, 1892, 1931, 1954, 1968.
Runners-up: 1886, 1887, 1895, 1912, 1935.
League Cup Winners: 1966.
Runners-up: 1967, 1970.
European Competitions
Fairs Cup: 1966–67.
UEFA Cup: 1978–79 *(qf)*, 1979–80, 1981–82.
European Cup-Winners' Cup: 1968–69 *(qf)*.

FOOTBALL YEARBOOK FACT FILE

West Bromwich Albion travelled to Brussels in October 1954 to play against the crack Hungarian team Honved under floodlights at the Heysel Stadium. Albion led 2-1 at half-time before succumbing to a 5-3 defeat against a team that included six men who had appeared for Hungary when they had thrashed England a few months before. Goalscorers were Johnny Nicholls (2) and Ronnie Allen in front of a crowd of 55,000.

Most League Points (2 for a win): 60, Division 1, 1919–20.

Most League Points (3 for a win): 91, FL C, 2009–10.

Most League Goals: 105, Division 2, 1929–30.

Highest League Scorer in Season: William 'Ginger' Richardson, 39, Division 1, 1935–36.

Most League Goals in Total Aggregate: Tony Brown, 218, 1963–79.

Most League Goals in One Match: 6, Jimmy Cookson v Blackpool, Division 2, 17 September 1927.

Most Capped Player: Chris Brunt, 55 (65), Northern Ireland.

Most League Appearances: Tony Brown, 574, 1963–80.

Youngest League Player: Charlie Wilson, 16 years 73 days v Oldham Ath, 1 October 1921.

Record Transfer Fee Received: £16,500,000 from Dalian Yifang for Salomon Rondon, July 2019.

Record Transfer Fee Paid: £12,000,000 (potentially rising to £18,000,000) to West Ham U for Grady Diangana, September 2020.

Football League Record: 1888 Founder Member of Football League; 1888–92 Football League; 1892–1901 Division 1; 1901–02 Division 2; 1902–04 Division 1; 1904–11 Division 2; 1911–27 Division 1; 1927–31 Division 2; 1931–38 Division 1; 1938–49 Division 2; 1949–73 Division 1; 1973–76 Division 2; 1976–86 Division 1; 1986–91 Division 2; 1991–92 Division 3; 1992–93 Second Division; 1993–2002 First Division; 2002–03 Premier League; 2003–04 First Division; 2004–06 Premier League; 2006–08 FL C; 2008–09 Premier League; 2009–10 FL C; 2010–18 Premier League; 2018–20 FL C; 2020–21 Premier League; 2021– FL C.

LATEST SEQUENCES

Longest Sequence of League Wins: 11, 5.4.1930 – 8.9.1930.

Longest Sequence of League Defeats: 11, 28.10.1995 – 26.12.1995.

Longest Sequence of League Draws: 6, 5.10.2024 – 7.11.2024.

Longest Sequence of Unbeaten League Matches: 17, 7.9.1957 – 7.12.1957.

Longest Sequence Without a League Win: 20, 27.8.2017 – 2.1.2018.

Successive Scoring Runs: 36 from 26.4.1958.

Successive Non-scoring Runs: 5 from 26.1.2022.

MANAGERS

Louis Ford 1890–92
(Secretary-Manager)
Henry Jackson 1892–94
(Secretary-Manager)
Edward Stephenson 1894–95
(Secretary-Manager)
Clement Keys 1895–96
(Secretary-Manager)
Frank Heaven 1896–1902 *(Secretary-Manager)*
Fred Everiss 1902–48
Jack Smith 1948–52
Jesse Carver 1952
Vic Buckingham 1953–59
Gordon Clark 1959–61
Archie Macaulay 1961–63
Jimmy Hagan 1963–67
Alan Ashman 1967–71
Don Howe 1971–75
Johnny Giles 1975–77
Ronnie Allen 1977
Ron Atkinson 1978–81
Ronnie Allen 1981–82
Ron Wylie 1982–84
Johnny Giles 1984–85
Nobby Stiles 1985–86
Ron Saunders 1986–87
Ron Atkinson 1987–88
Brian Talbot 1988–91
Bobby Gould 1991–92
Ossie Ardiles 1992–93
Keith Burkinshaw 1993–94
Alan Buckley 1994–97
Ray Harford 1997
Denis Smith 1997–1999
Brian Little 1999–2000
Gary Megson 2000–04
Bryan Robson 2004–06
Tony Mowbray 2006–09
Roberto Di Matteo 2009–11
Roy Hodgson 2011–12
Steve Clarke 2012–13
Pepe Mel 2014
Alan Irvine 2014
Tony Pulis 2015–17
Alan Pardew 2017–18
Darren Moore 2018–19
Slaven Bilic 2019–20
Sam Allardyce 2020–21
Valerien Ismael 2021–22
Steve Bruce 2022
Carlos Corberan 2022–24
Tony Mowbray 2025
Ryan Mason June 2025–

TEN YEAR LEAGUE RECORD

		P	W	D	L	F	A	Pts	Pos
2015-16	PR Lge	38	10	13	15	34	48	43	14
2016-17	PR Lge	38	12	9	17	43	51	45	10
2017-18	PR Lge	38	6	13	19	31	56	31	20
2018-19	FL C	46	23	11	12	87	62	80	4
2019-20	FL C	46	22	17	7	77	45	83	2
2020-21	PR Lge	38	5	11	22	35	76	26	19
2021-22	FL C	46	18	13	15	52	45	67	10
2022-23	FL C	46	18	12	16	59	53	66	9
2023-24	FL C	46	21	12	13	70	47	75	5
2024-25	FL C	46	15	19	12	57	47	64	9

DID YOU KNOW ?

After finishing bottom of the First Division in 1895–96, West Bromwich Albion had to take part in the end-of-season Test Matches to determine whether they would be relegated. The Baggies won two and drew one of the four games played which proved enough for them to retain their First Division place. Small Heath, who had finished above Albion in the table, were relegated.

WEST BROMWICH ALBION – SKY BET CHAMPIONSHIP 2024–25 LEAGUE RECORD

Match No.	Date	Venue	Opponents	Result	H/T Score	Lg Pos.	Goalscorers	Attendance
1	Aug 10	A	QPR	W 3-1	1-1	2	Maja 3 [26, 51, 65]	16,587
2	17	H	Leeds U	D 0-0	0-0	5		25,329
3	24	A	Stoke C	W 2-1	2-1	4	Ahearne-Grant [18], Maja [31]	24,371
4	31	H	Swansea C	W 1-0	1-0	2	Molumby [45]	24,975
5	Sept 15	A	Portsmouth	W 3-0	1-0	1	Maja [1], Mowatt 2 [51, 90]	20,205
6	21	H	Plymouth Arg	W 1-0	0-0	1	Maja [62]	25,754
7	28	A	Sheffield Wed	L 2-3	0-2	1	Maja [65], Mowatt [84]	26,308
8	Oct 1	H	Middlesbrough	L 0-1	0-0	3		23,769
9	5	H	Millwall	D 0-0	0-0	4		24,158
10	19	A	Oxford U	D 1-1	1-0	5	Ahearne-Grant [29]	11,453
11	23	A	Blackburn R	D 0-0	0-0	5		13,647
12	26	H	Cardiff C	D 0-0	0-0	5		25,312
13	Nov 1	A	Luton T	D 1-1	1-0	5	Maja [45]	11,665
14	7	H	Burnley	D 0-0	0-0	5		23,443
15	10	A	Hull C	W 2-1	2-1	5	Ahearne-Grant [12], Maja [17]	20,538
16	23	H	Norwich C	D 2-2	2-2	6	Holgate [11], Maja [43]	25,673
17	26	A	Sunderland	D 0-0	0-0	7		36,733
18	30	A	Preston NE	D 1-1	1-0	7	Ahearne-Grant [13]	16,124
19	Dec 8	H	Sheffield U	D 2-2	1-2	8	Heggem [24], Fellows [62]	24,930
20	11	H	Coventry C	W 2-0	1-0	6	Mowatt [11], Ahearne-Grant [74]	24,859
21	15	A	Watford	L 1-2	0-1	8	Molumby [67]	19,774
22	22	H	Bristol C	W 2-0	2-0	7	Johnston 2 [34, 43]	25,910
23	26	A	Derby Co	L 1-2	0-1	8	Diangana [81]	31,267
24	29	A	Sheffield U	D 1-1	1-1	8	Ahearne-Grant [45]	29,123
25	Jan 1	H	Preston NE	W 3-1	3-0	6	Maja 2 [18, 40], Styles [35]	24,320
26	4	A	Swansea C	D 1-1	0-0	6	Fellows [66]	14,729
27	18	H	Stoke C	D 1-1	0-1	6	Diangana [71]	25,679
28	21	A	Middlesbrough	L 0-2	0-1	7		22,323
29	25	H	Portsmouth	W 5-1	4-0	5	Mowatt [25], Diangana 2 [32, 44], Wallace [37], Swift [56]	25,261
30	Feb 1	A	Plymouth Arg	L 1-2	0-0	6	Molumby [74]	16,870
31	8	H	Sheffield Wed	W 2-1	0-0	5	Armstrong [74], Molumby [90]	25,452
32	12	H	Blackburn R	L 0-2	0-0	6		23,305
33	15	A	Millwall	D 1-1	1-1	6	Bryan (og) [26]	15,842
34	22	H	Oxford U	W 2-0	1-0	5	Mowatt [11], Swift [90]	25,951
35	Mar 1	A	Leeds U	D 1-1	1-1	6	Furlong [39]	36,705
36	8	H	QPR	W 1-0	1-0	6	Armstrong (pen) [40]	25,310
37	11	A	Burnley	D 1-1	1-1	5	Swift [20]	18,843
38	15	H	Hull C	D 1-1	0-0	6	Price [67]	24,870
39	29	A	Norwich C	L 0-1	0-0	6		26,707
40	Apr 5	H	Sunderland	L 0-1	0-1	8		25,918
41	8	A	Bristol C	L 1-2	0-0	8	Mowatt [62]	24,734
42	12	H	Watford	W 2-1	1-0	7	Ahearne-Grant [11], Johnston [60]	24,768
43	18	A	Coventry C	L 0-2	0-0	8		31,167
44	21	H	Derby Co	L 1-3	0-2	10	Armstrong [70]	25,750
45	26	A	Cardiff C	D 0-0	0-0	10		23,710
46	May 3	H	Luton T	W 5-3	3-1	9	Fellows 2 [7, 33], Dike [30], Styles 2 [57, 61]	25,615

Final League Position: 9

GOALSCORERS

League (57): Maja 12, Ahearne-Grant 7, Mowatt 7, Diangana 4, Fellows 4, Molumby 4, Armstrong 3 (1 pen), Johnston 3, Styles 3, Swift 3, Dike 1, Furlong 1, Heggem 1, Holgate 1, Price 1, Wallace 1, own goal 1.
FA Cup (1): Taylor 1.
Carabao Cup (1): Faal 1.

Palmer A 30	Furlong D 42	Ajayi S 14 + 1	Bartley K 30 + 1	Heggem T 45	Molumby J 30 + 7	Mowatt A 39 + 4	Fellows T 35 + 10	Swift J 19 + 17	Ahearne-Grant K 34 + 9	Maja J 26	Cole D — + 14	Diakite O 9 + 13	Dobbin L 1 + 16	Frabotta G — + 6	Wallace J 6 + 23	Diangana G 14 + 20	Racic U 9 + 12	Styles C 29 + 5	Johnston M 25 + 15	McNair P 2	Holgate M 21 + 5	Price I 13 + 2	Wildsmith J 10	Armstrong A 12 + 4	Lankshear W 4 + 7	Dike D 1 + 10	Bany T — + 4	Griffiths J 6	Whitwell H — + 1	Match No
1	2	3	4	5⁴	6¹	7	8³	9	10	11²	12	13	14	15																1
1	2	3	4	5	6⁴	7	10	9²	8¹	11³		15	13					12	14											2
1	2	3	4	5	6⁵	7	8²	9⁴	10¹	11					16	14	15	13	12³											3
1	2	3	4	5⁵	6¹	7	8³	9	10⁴	11²		13			16	14		12	15											4
1	2	3	4	5	6³	7	8¹	9²	10⁴	11⁵				15	12	13		14	16											5
1	2	3	4	5	6⁴	7	8³	9²	10¹	11⁵				15	16	14	13	12												6
1	2	3⁵	4	5	12	8⁴	9	10³	11	7¹					16	15	14	6²	13											7
1	2	3	4	5⁴	13	7	12	9³	10⁵	11				15			8¹	6²	16		14									8
1	2	3	4	5	6²	7	8³	14	15	11⁵	12	16	9⁴	13	10¹															9
1	2	3		5	14	7	8²	12	10	11³	13	9¹	6⁴	15																10
1	2	3		5	6⁵	7	8¹	12	10³	11⁴	16	13	15	9²	14					4										11
1	2	3⁴		5		7	13	9	15	11	8³	6	12	10²						4¹	14									12
			4	14	7	13	16	10⁵	11⁴	12		9²	8¹	6³	5	15					3									13
			4	6	7³	8²	9⁵	10⁵	11⁴	16		12	15	14	5	13					3									14
			4	7	6³	8²	9⁵	11¹	16	12		15	13	14	5	10⁴					3									15
			4	8	7²	6¹	16	10⁵	11⁴	15		12	14	13	5	9³					3									16
		3²	4	6	7	5	14	10⁴	11³	15		12		13	9	8¹					2									17
			4	5	12	8¹	6³	15	11	10⁵		9²	16	7⁴							14		3							18
			3	4	7	8¹	6	14	11	10³	15	12			5²	9⁴		13												19
		14	4	7⁵	8	6²	12	11	10¹	15		13		16	5³	9⁴		3												20
		4³	5	7⁵	13	6	14	11	10⁴	15		16		8²	9¹	12		3												21
			4	5	7¹	6	8²	9⁴	11⁵	16		15	13	14	12	10³		3												22
			4	5	12	7	8	9³	13	11		14		6¹	15	10²		3⁴												23
1	2	3	4	6		8³	16	9¹	11⁴	13	7⁵	15			12	14		5	10²											24
1	2	3	4	6		8¹		9⁴	11³	14	7	16	12	13	15			5⁵	10²											25
			4	6	12	13	14	9⁴	11⁵	15		7¹		8²	16			5	10²		3									26
			4	7		8	6²		11	13		12			10¹			5	9		3									27
			4	8¹	7	6	12	11²	14			13			10			5	9³		3									28
1	2		4		7¹	6	8³	15		13	12				11⁴	10⁵	16	5	9²		3	14								29
1	2		4	12	7	6¹	8²	14		16	15				11⁴	10⁵		5	9³		3	13								30
	2	3⁴	4	6	7⁴	14		11¹		15		16	9²		5	12			8³	1	10⁵	13								31
	2		4	7	6³	8¹	14					15	12	5	10²	3		9⁴	1	11	13									32
	2	3	4	6			13	16	12		7			8³	9⁵	5²		14	1	10⁴	11¹	15								33
	2	3¹	4	7	6	8²	15					13		5	10⁵	12	9³	1	11⁴	14	16									34
	2	3	4	6	7	15	9¹	12				13		5	10⁴	8³	1	11²	14											35
	2⁵	3	4	6	7	8¹	13		15					5	10²	12	9⁴	1	11³	14										36
			4	6		7	11		3			9²	8	12		2	5	1	10¹	13										37
		4	5	6	7⁴	13	8²	11¹		12	9			3	2	1	10³	15	14											38
		3	4	10⁴	7	6²	8	9¹				13		5	12	2	1	11³	14						15					39
	2	3	4⁴	7	8²	13	11			15		6¹		5	9³	1	10⁵	16	12	14										40
	2	4	6⁴	7³	14	9²	10⁵	13						5	16	3	11¹	8⁴	12	15	1									41
	2	3	4	7	8³	9	13							5	10²	6	12	11¹	14	1										42
	2	3	4	7³	8	13	9⁴	14	12					5⁴	10⁵	6¹	16	11²	15	1										43
	2³	4	5	16	8	15	7⁵	14		6		10²		3¹	9	12	11⁴	13	1											44
	2	3	4	7	8³	10		6	12		5	14	9¹	11²	13	1														45
	2	12	3¹	4	13	7	8⁴	11		6³	15	5	10⁵	14	9²	1	16													46

WEST HAM UNITED

FOUNDATION

Thames Ironworks FC was formed by employees of this famous shipbuilding company in 1895 and entered the FA Cup in their initial season at Chatham and the London League in their second. The committee wanted to introduce professional players, so Thames Ironworks was wound up in June 1900 and relaunched a month later as West Ham United.

London Stadium, Queen Elizabeth Olympic Park, London E20 2ST.

Telephone: (020) 8548 2748.

Ticket Office: (0333) 030 1966.

Website: www.whufc.com

Email: supporterservices@westhamunited.co.uk

Ground Capacity: 62,500.

Record Attendance: 42,322 v Tottenham H, Division 1, 17 October 1970 (at Boleyn Ground); 62,478 v Leeds U, Premier League, 21 May 2023 (at London Stadium).

Pitch Measurements: 105m × 68m (115yd × 74.5yd).

Joint Chair: David Sullivan, Vanessa Gold.

Vice-Chair: Baroness Karren Brady CBE.

Head Coach: Graham Potter.

Assistant Head Coach: Bruno Saltor.

Colours: Claret shirts with sky blue sleeves and claret trim, white shorts, white socks with claret trim.

Year Formed: 1895.

Turned Professional: 1900.

Previous Name: 1895, Thames Ironworks FC; 1900, West Ham United.

Club Nicknames: 'The Hammers'; 'The Irons'.

Grounds: 1895, Memorial Recreation Ground, Canning Town; 1904, Boleyn Ground, Upton Park; 2016, London Stadium.

First Football League Game: 30 August 1919, Division 2, v Lincoln C (h) D 1–1 – Hufton; Cope, Lee; Lane, Fenwick, McCrae; David Smith, Moyes (1), Puddefoot, Morris, Bradshaw.

Record League Victory: 8–0 v Rotherham U, Division 2, 8 March 1958 – Gregory; Bond, Wright; Malcolm, Brown, Lansdowne; Grice, Smith (2), Keeble (2), Dick (4), Musgrove. 8–0 v Sunderland, Division 1, 19 October 1968 – Ferguson; Bonds, Charles; Peters, Stephenson, Moore (1); Redknapp, Boyce, Brooking (1), Hurst (6), Sissons.

HONOURS

League Champions: Division 2 – 1957–58, 1980–81.
Runners-up: First Division – 1992–93; Division 2 – 1922–23, 1990–91.

FA Cup Winners: 1964, 1975, 1980.
Runners-up: 1923, 2006.

League Cup: Runners-up: 1966, 1981.

European Competitions
UEFA Cup: 1999–2000; 2006–07.
Europa League: 2015–16, 2016–17, 2021–22 *(sf)*, 2023–24 *(qf)*.
UEFA Europa Conference League: 2022–23 *(winners)*.
European Cup-Winners' Cup: 1964–65 *(winners)*, 1965–66 *(sf)*, 1975–76 *(runners-up)*, 1980–81 *(qf)*.
Intertoto Cup: 1999 *(winners)*.

FOOTBALL YEARBOOK FACT FILE

West Ham United completed a remarkable double over Manchester City in the 1962–63 season, winning both the home and away games by a 6-1 margin. The Hammers thrashed the Mancunians at Maine Road in September with goals from Malcolm Musgrove (2), Tony Scott, Johnny Byrne, Martin Peters and Geoff Hurst. They then repeated the score at the Boleyn Ground in their final game of the season when Hurst (2), Alan Sealey (2), Ronnie Boyce and Peter Brabrook provided the goals.

Record Cup Victory: 10–0 v Bury, League Cup 2nd rd (2nd leg), 25 October 1983 – Parkes; Stewart (1), Walford, Bonds (Orr), Martin (1), Devonshire (2), Allen, Cottee (4), Swindlehurst, Brooking (2), Pike.

Record Defeat: 0–7 v Barnsley, Division 1, 1 September 1919; 0–7 v Everton, Division 1, 22 October 1927; 0–7 v Sheffield Wed, Division 1, 28 November 1959.

Most League Points (2 for a win): 66, Division 2, 1980–81.

Most League Points (3 for a win): 88, Division 1, 1992–93.

Most League Goals: 101, Division 2, 1957–58.

Highest League Scorer in Season: Vic Watson, 42, Division 1, 1929–30.

Most League Goals in Total Aggregate: Vic Watson, 298, 1920–35.

Most League Goals in One Match: 6, Vic Watson v Leeds U, Division 1, 9 February 1929; 6, Geoff Hurst v Sunderland, Division 1, 19 October 1968.

Most Capped Player: Bobby Moore, 108, England.

Most League Appearances: Billy Bonds, 663, 1967–88.

Youngest League Player: Billy Williams, 16 years 221 days v Blackpool, 6 May 1922.

MANAGERS

Syd King 1902–32
Charlie Paynter 1932–50
Ted Fenton 1950–61
Ron Greenwood 1961–74
(continued as General Manager to 1977)
John Lyall 1974–89
Lou Macari 1989–90
Billy Bonds 1990–94
Harry Redknapp 1994–2001
Glenn Roeder 2001–03
Alan Pardew 2003–06
Alan Curbishley 2006–08
Gianfranco Zola 2008–10
Avram Grant 2010–11
Sam Allardyce 2011–15
Slaven Bilic 2015–17
David Moyes 2017–18
Manuel Pellegrini 2018–19
David Moyes 2019–24
Julen Lopetegui 2024–25
Graham Potter January 2025–

Record Transfer Fee Received: £105,000,000 from Arsenal for Declan Rice, July 2023.

Record Transfer Fee Paid: £51,000,000 to Lyon for Lucas Paqueta, August 2022.

Football League Record: 1919 Elected to Division 2; 1919–23 Division 2; 1923–32 Division 1; 1932–58 Division 2; 1958–78 Division 1; 1978–81 Division 2; 1981–89 Division 1; 1989–91 Division 2; 1991–92 Division 1; 1992–93 First Division; 1993–2003 Premier League; 2003–04 First Division; 2004–05 FL C; 2005–11 Premier League; 2011–12 FL C; 2012– Premier League.

LATEST SEQUENCES

Longest Sequence of League Wins: 9, 19.10.1985 – 14.12.1985.

Longest Sequence of League Defeats: 9, 28.3.1932 – 29.8.1932.

Longest Sequence of League Draws: 5, 29.11.2015 – 26.12.2015.

Longest Sequence of Unbeaten League Matches: 27, 27.12.1980 – 10.10.1981.

Longest Sequence Without a League Win: 17, 31.1.1976 – 21.8.1976.

Successive Scoring Runs: 27 from 5.10.1957.

Successive Non-scoring Runs: 5 from 17.9.2006.

TEN YEAR LEAGUE RECORD

		P	W	D	L	F	A	Pts	Pos
2015-16	PR Lge	38	16	14	8	65	51	62	7
2016-17	PR Lge	38	12	9	17	47	64	45	11
2017-18	PR Lge	38	10	12	16	48	68	42	13
2018-19	PR Lge	38	15	7	16	52	55	52	10
2019-20	PR Lge	38	10	9	19	49	62	39	16
2020-21	PR Lge	38	19	8	11	62	47	65	6
2021-22	PR Lge	38	16	8	14	60	51	56	7
2022-23	PR Lge	38	11	7	20	42	55	40	14
2023-24	PR Lge	38	14	10	14	60	74	52	9
2024-25	PR Lge	38	11	10	17	46	62	43	14

DID YOU KNOW ?

West Ham United completed an amazing comeback in their European Cup Winners' Cup tie against ADO Den Haag in the 1975–76 season. The Hammers were 4-0 down at half-time in the first leg before making the score a more respectable 4-2. The second leg was a near mirror image of the first, with West Ham scoring three times before the break to take a 5-4 aggregate lead. The visitors then netted an equaliser with the Hammers going through on away goals.

WEST HAM UNITED – PREMIER LEAGUE 2024–25 LEAGUE RECORD

Match No.	Date	Venue	Opponents	Result		H/T Score	Lg Pos.	Goalscorers	Attendance
1	Aug 17	H	Aston Villa	L	1-2	1-1	15	Lucas Paqueta (pen) [37]	62,463
2	24	A	Crystal Palace	W	2-0	0-0	7	Soucek [67], Bowen [72]	25,099
3	31	H	Manchester C	L	1-3	1-2	14	Dias (og) [19]	62,469
4	Sept 14	A	Fulham	D	1-1	0-1	14	Ings [90]	26,528
5	21	H	Chelsea	L	0-3	0-2	14		62,473
6	28	A	Brentford	D	1-1	0-1	14	Soucek [54]	17,050
7	Oct 5	H	Ipswich T	W	4-1	2-1	12	Antonio [1], Kudus [44], Bowen [49], Lucas Paqueta [69]	62,467
8	19	A	Tottenham H	L	1-4	1-1	15	Kudus [18]	61,381
9	27	H	Manchester U	W	2-1	0-0	13	Summerville [74], Bowen (pen) [90]	62,474
10	Nov 2	A	Nottingham F	L	0-3	0-1	14		30,112
11	9	H	Everton	D	0-0	0-0	14		62,463
12	25	A	Newcastle U	W	2-0	1-0	14	Soucek [10], Wan Bissaka [53]	52,094
13	30	H	Arsenal	L	2-5	2-5	14	Wan Bissaka [38], Emerson [40]	62,475
14	Dec 1	A	Leicester C	L	1-3	0-1	14	Fullkrug [90]	30,947
15	9	H	Wolverhampton W	W	2-1	0-0	14	Soucek [54], Bowen [72]	62,435
16	16	A	Bournemouth	D	1-1	0-0	14	Lucas Paqueta (pen) [87]	11,204
17	21	H	Brighton & HA	D	1-1	0-0	14	Kudus [58]	62,460
18	26	A	Southampton	W	1-0	0-0	13	Bowen [59]	31,059
19	29	H	Liverpool	L	0-5	0-3	13		62,476
20	Jan 4	A	Manchester C	L	1-4	0-2	13	Fullkrug [71]	52,737
21	14	H	Fulham	W	3-2	2-0	12	Soler [31], Soucek [33], Lucas Paqueta [67]	62,456
22	18	H	Crystal Palace	L	0-2	0-0	14		62,469
23	26	A	Aston Villa	D	1-1	0-1	14	Emerson [70]	41,268
24	Feb 3	A	Chelsea	L	1-2	1-0	15	Bowen [42]	39,459
25	15	H	Brentford	L	0-1	0-1	16		62,467
26	22	A	Arsenal	W	1-0	1-0	16	Bowen [44]	60,262
27	27	A	Leicester C	W	2-0	2-0	15	Soucek [21], Vestergaard (og) [43]	62,455
28	Mar 10	H	Newcastle U	L	0-1	0-0	16		62,463
29	15	A	Everton	D	1-1	0-0	16	Soucek [67]	39,343
30	Apr 1	A	Wolverhampton W	L	0-1	0-1	16		30,537
31	5	H	Bournemouth	D	2-2	0-1	15	Fullkrug [61], Bowen [68]	62,459
32	13	A	Liverpool	L	1-2	0-1	17	Robertson (og) [86]	60,376
33	19	H	Southampton	D	1-1	0-0	16	Bowen [47]	62,461
34	26	A	Brighton & HA	L	2-3	0-1	17	Kudus [48], Soucek [83]	31,499
35	May 4	H	Tottenham H	D	1-1	1-1	17	Bowen [28]	62,468
36	11	A	Manchester U	W	2-0	1-0	15	Soucek [26], Bowen [57]	73,804
37	18	H	Nottingham F	L	1-2	0-1	15	Bowen [86]	62,466
38	25	A	Ipswich T	W	3-1	1-0	14	Ward-Prowse [43], Bowen [55], Kudus [87]	29,771

Final League Position: 14

GOALSCORERS

League (46): Bowen 13 (1 pen), Soucek 9, Kudus 5, Lucas Paqueta 4 (2 pens), Fullkrug 3, Emerson 2, Wan Bissaka 2, Antonio 1, Ings 1, Soler 1, Summerville 1, Ward-Prowse 1, own goals 3.
FA Cup (1): Lucas Paqueta 1.
Carabao Cup (2): Bowen 1, own goal 1.
(West Ham U U21) Vertu Trophy (2): Robinson 1, Swyer 1.

Areola A 25 + 1	Coufal V 11 + 11	Mavropanos K 21 + 12	Kilman M 38	Emerson d 26 + 5	Rodriguez G 16 + 7	Bowen J 34	Soucek T 30 + 5	Lucas Paqueta d 27 + 6	Kudus M 31 + 1	Antonio M 11 + 3	Fullkrug N 6 + 12	Summerville C 7 + 12	Ward-Prowse J 12 + 3	Todibo J 20 + 7	Ings D 1 + 14	Wan Bissaka A 35 + 1	Alvarez E 20 + 8	Cresswell A 10 + 8	Fabianski L 13 + 1	Soler C 14 + 17	Irving Andrew 1 + 9	Luis Guilherme d 1 + 11	Scarles O 7 + 8	Casey K — + 1	Orford L — + 2	Ferguson E 1 + 7	Match No.
1	2^5	3	4	5	6^4	7^1	8	9^3	10	11^2	12	13	14	15	16												1
1	2^2	3	4	5^5	6	7	8^3	9	10^4	11^1	13			15			12	14	16								2
1^1	13	3	4	5^2	6	8^5	15	9	10	11^3	14	16				2	7^4	12		15							3
1	14	3	4	5^3	7^4	8	9^1	12	10	11^2	13				16	2	6^5			15							4
1		2	4	8^5	6^1	10	12	7^4	9	13	11^2					5	3^3	16		14	15						5
1	12	4	5^1	6	7^5	8	9^4	10^2	11^3	15		3	14			2	13	16									6
1		4	5^4	6^2	7	9	8^3	10^5	11^1	15		3				2	13	14		12		16					7
1	15	4	5	6^4	7	8^3	9^1	10^4	11^2	14		3				2	12	13									8
		3^4	4	5	7^5	8	12	9^2		11^4	13		14	15			6	16	1	10^1							9
	2	4	8^3	6^1	11		9		12	10^2	3		5	7^8		1	13	14									10
	14	4	5	6^1	7	8	9		11^2	10^4	3	13	2^3				1	12	15								11
	14	12	4	5^3 15	8	6	7		11^2	10^4	3^1	13	2				1	9^5	16								12
	14		4	5^3 15	8	6	7^4		11^2	10^1	3	13	2	12			1	9^5	16								13
	2^3	3	4	13		8	7^2 15	10^5	14	16	12					5	6		1	9^4							14
	3	4	5^4 14	11	7	12	8^3		10^2		16	13	2			6^5 15	1	9^1									15
	2	3	4		11	8	7	10^2	12	14						5^4	6^3	1	9^1			13	15				16
15	3^1	4	5^4 16	7	9	8^3 10	11^2 13	12								2	6^5	1			14						17
13	17	3	4^1	5	6^4	7	8	11^5 16	12							2	14	15	1^2	9^3							18
1	2^2	3	4	10			11^3	6	8^5	12	14	13				5	7^1			9^4 15	16						19
1	2	12	4		6	9	8^2	11	10				3^1 14	5	7^3					13							20
	3	4	5^3	7^4		9	11	8^1					12	2	6	15	1	10^2 13		14							21
	2^4	3	8^3	7^1		10	9^4 11						15	5	6^5	4^2	1	12	16	14	13						22
1	2		3	8^2 15	6	11	9						13	5	7^3	4	10^1 14	12									23
1	2^2	13	3	8^1		11	6	9					15	5		4^5	10^3	7^4 16	12	14							24
1	3^4	4	5^2		8	7^1 11	9		14				2	6		10^3		15	13			12					25
1	12	4		10^2	7	11	8	3^1		2	9^5	5		14			6				13						26
1	13	3	12	10	6^5	11^4	7	2^2		5	8^3	4		14	16		9^1			15							27
1	12	3		10	6^3 14	11	7^5	2^1 16		5	8^2	4^4		13			9			15							28
1	3	4	9	14	11	8	6^1 10²	7	2^3	5				12						13							29
1	2	3	15	9	16	6	13		7^4	5	14		4^3	12	10^1	8^5				11^2							30
	15	4	12	11	9^3 10	8^4	14	7	3^5	2	6^2		13	16	5^1												31
1	12	3	4		10		8	11	13	7	2^2	5				6^3	14	9^1									32
1	2	16	4	5^3	8^4 13	10	9^1	11^2	7^5	3	5					6	12	14				15					33
1	13	3	4	9^2	11	8	6	10	12	7^1	2	5															34
1	15	16	3	8	9	6^1	7^3 10	11^4	14	2^2	5			13						12							35
1	5^4 16	3	15	7^1 10²	9		11^3	14	6	2^5		8	12	4		13											36
1	5		3	7^1 10	9^3 14	11^5		12	6^4	2		8	13	4^2		15		16									37
	12	3	4		14	10	8	15	13		11^2		7^3	2^5		6	5^4 16	1				9^1					38

FA Cup

Third Round	Aston Villa	(a)	1-2

Carabao Cup

Second Round	Bournemouth	(h)	1-0
Third Round	Liverpool	(a)	1-5

Vertu Trophy (West Ham U U21)

Group H (S)	Reading	(a)	1-3
Group H (S)	Newport Co	(a)	0-1
Group H (S)	Cheltenham T	(a)	1-3

WIGAN ATHLETIC

FOUNDATION

Following the demise of Wigan Borough and their resignation from the Football League in 1931, a public meeting was called in Wigan at the Queen's Hall in May 1932 at which a new club, Wigan Athletic, was founded in the hope of carrying on in the Football League. With this in mind, they bought Springfield Park for £2,250, but failed to gain admission to the Football League until 46 years later.

The Brick Community Stadium, Loire Drive, Newtown, Wigan, Lancashire WN5 0UZ.

Telephone: (01942) 774 000.

Ticket Office: (01942) 311 111.

Website: www.wiganathletic.com

Email: feedback@wiganathletic.com

Ground Capacity: 24,925.

Record Attendance: 27,526 v Hereford U, 12 December 1953 (at Springfield Park); 25,133 v Manchester U, Premier League, 11 May 2008 (at DW Stadium).

Pitch Measurements: 105m × 68m (115yd × 74.5yd).

Chairman/Chief Executive: Ben Goodburn.

Sporting Director: Gregor Rioch.

Head Coach: Ryan Lowe.

Assistant Head Coaches: Glenn Whelan, Graham Barrow, Frankie Bunn.

Colours: Blue and white striped shirts with blue sleeves, blue shorts with white trim, blue socks with white trim.

Year Formed: 1932.

Turned Professional: 1932.

Club Nickname: 'The Latics'.

Grounds: 1932, Springfield Park; 1999, JJB Stadium (renamed DW Stadium 2009; The Brick Community Stadium 2024).

First Football League Game: 19 August 1978, Division 4, v Hereford U (a) D 0–0 – Brown; Hinnigan, Gore, Gillibrand, Ward, Davids, Corrigan, Purdie, Houghton, Wilkie, Wright.

Record League Victory: 8–0 v Hull C, FL C, 14 July 2020 – Marshall; Byrne, Kipre, Balogun (Dobre), Robinson (Evans), Williams (1) (Massey), Morsy, Naismith (1), Dowell (3) (Roberts), Lowe (1), Moore (2) (Pearce).

Record Cup Victory: 8–1 v Fleetwood T (h), FA Cup 2nd qualifying rd, 22 September 1962 – Swindells; Houghton, Briars, Hennin, Higgins, Edmondson, Morgans 2, Kinsella 1, Lyon 2, Bradbury 2, O'Loughlin 1.

Record Defeat: 1–9 v Tottenham H, Premier League, 22 November 2009; 0–8 v Chelsea, Premier League, 9 May 2010.

HONOURS

League Champions: FL 1 – 2015–16, 2017–18, 2021–22; Second Division – 2002–03; Third Division – 1996–97. *Runners-up:* FL C – 2004–05.

FA Cup Winners: 2013.

League Cup: Runners-up: 2006.

League Trophy Winners: 1985, 1999.

European Competitions
Europa League: 2013–14.

FOOTBALL YEARBOOK FACT FILE

Wigan Athletic had to wait until their fourth Football League match before scoring a goal. The honour of scoring the club's first-ever goal in the competition went to defender Joe Hinnigan who netted in the 61st minute of the home game with Newport County. The Latics were experiencing hard times following their election to the League and lost 3-2 but recovered to finish in sixth position in the Fourth Division table.

Most League Points (2 for a win): 55, Division 4, 1978–79 and 1979–80.

Most League Points (3 for a win): 100, Division 2, 2002–03.

Most League Goals: 89, FL 1, 2017–18.

Highest League Scorer in Season: Graeme Jones, 31, Division 3, 1996–97.

Most League Goals in Total Aggregate: Andy Liddell, 70, 1998–2004.

Most League Goals in One Match: Not more than three goals by one player.

Most Capped Players: James McClean, 35 (103), Republic of Ireland.

Most League Appearances: Kevin Langley, 317, 1981–86, 1990–94.

Youngest League Player: Steve Nugent, 16 years 132 days v Leyton Orient, 16 September 1989.

Record Transfer Fee Received: £15,250,000 from Manchester U for Antonio Valencia, June 2009.

Record Transfer Fee Paid: £7,000,000 to Newcastle U for Charles N'Zogbia, January 2009.

Football League Record: 1978 Elected to Division 4 (replacing Southport); 1978–82 Division 4; 1982–92 Division 3; 1992–93 Second Division; 1993–97 Third Division; 1997–2003 Second Division; 2003–04 First Division; 2004–05 FL C; 2005–13 Premier League; 2013–15 FL C; 2015–16 FL 1; 2016–17 FL C; 2017–18 FL 1; 2018–20 FL C; 2020–22 FL 1; 2022–23 FL C; 2023– FL 1.

LATEST SEQUENCES

Longest Sequence of League Wins: 11, 2.11.2002 – 18.1.2003.

Longest Sequence of League Defeats: 8, 10.9.2011 – 6.11.2011.

Longest Sequence of League Draws: 6, 11.12.2001 – 5.1.2002.

Longest Sequence of Unbeaten League Matches: 25, 8.5.1999 – 3.1.2000.

Longest Sequence Without a League Win: 14, 9.5.1989 – 17.10.1989.

Successive Scoring Runs: 31 from 10.4.2021.

Successive Non-scoring Runs: 4 from 8.12.2018.

MANAGERS

Charlie Spencer 1932–37
Jimmy Milne 1946–47
Bob Pryde 1949–52
Ted Goodier 1952–54
Walter Crook 1954–55
Ron Suart 1955–56
Billy Cooke 1956
Sam Barkas 1957
Trevor Hitchen 1957–58
Malcolm Barrass 1958–59
Jimmy Shirley 1959
Pat Murphy 1959–60
Allenby Chilton 1960
Johnny Ball 1961–63
Allan Brown 1963–66
Alf Craig 1966–67
Harry Leyland 1967–68
Alan Saunders 1968
Ian McNeill 1968–70
Gordon Milne 1970–72
Les Rigby 1972–74
Brian Tiler 1974–76
Ian McNeill 1976–81
Larry Lloyd 1981–83
Harry McNally 1983–85
Bryan Hamilton 1985–86
Ray Mathias 1986–89
Bryan Hamilton 1989–93
Dave Philpotts 1993
Kenny Swain 1993–94
Graham Barrow 1994–95
John Deehan 1995–98
Ray Mathias 1998–99
John Benson 1999–2000
Bruce Rioch 2000–01
Steve Bruce 2001
Paul Jewell 2001–07
Chris Hutchings 2007
Steve Bruce 2007–09
Roberto Martinez 2009–13
Owen Coyle 2013
Uwe Rosler 2013–14
Malky Mackay 2014–15
Gary Caldwell 2015–16
Warren Joyce 2016–17
Paul Cook 2017–20
John Sheridan 2020
Leam Richardson 2020–22
Kolo Toure 2022–23
Shaun Maloney 2023–25
Ryan Lowe March 2025–

TEN YEAR LEAGUE RECORD

		P	W	D	L	F	A	Pts	Pos
2015-16	FL 1	46	24	15	7	82	45	87	1
2016-17	FL C	46	10	12	24	40	57	42	23
2017-18	FL 1	46	29	11	6	89	29	98	1
2018-19	FL C	46	13	13	20	51	64	52	18
2019-20	FL C	46	15	14	17	57	56	47*	23
2020-21	FL 1	46	13	9	24	54	77	48	20
2021-22	FL 1	46	27	11	8	82	44	92	1
2022-23	FL C	46	10	15	21	38	65	42†	24
2023-24	FL 1	46	20	10	16	63	56	62‡	12
2024-25	FL 1	46	13	17	16	40	42	56	15

12 pts deducted; †3 pts deducted; ‡8 pts deducted.

DID YOU KNOW ?

Wigan Athletic enjoyed a tremendous season in 1965–66, winning the Cheshire League and League Cup, the Liverpool Non-League Senior Cup and reaching the final of the Lancashire Junior Cup. The League title was secured following a run of 15 consecutive victories, while Harry Lyon created a new club record in scoring 66 goals in League and Cup games.

WIGAN ATHLETIC – SKY BET LEAGUE ONE 2024–25 LEAGUE RECORD

Match No.	Date	Venue	Opponents	Result		H/T Score	Lg Pos.	Goalscorers	Attendance
1	Aug 10	H	Charlton Ath	L	0-1	0-0	19		9564
2	17	A	Reading	L	0-2	0-1	21		12,689
3	24	H	Crawley T	W	1-0	1-0	18	Mukena (og) [30]	8432
4	31	A	Birmingham C	L	1-2	0-1	21	Aasgaard [66]	26,136
5	Sept 14	A	Bristol R	W	4-0	2-0	15	Hugill 2 [20, 40], Aasgaard [50], Chambers [71]	7925
6	21	H	Lincoln C	D	0-0	0-0	14		8534
7	24	H	Stevenage	D	0-0	0-0	14		7419
8	28	H	Exeter C	D	0-0	0-0	16		8837
9	Oct 1	H	Peterborough U	W	3-0	1-0	14	Taylor 2 [11, 49], McManaman [81]	7894
10	5	A	Stockport Co	D	0-0	0-0	15		9995
11	19	A	Cambridge U	L	0-2	0-2	17		7000
12	22	H	Mansfield T	L	1-2	0-1	18	Aasgaard [53]	9460
13	28	A	Blackpool	D	2-2	2-1	19	Rankine [20], Smith M [41]	10,226
14	Nov 9	H	Wycombe W	L	0-1	0-1	19		8958
15	23	A	Barnsley	W	1-0	1-0	17	Aasgaard [42]	11,438
16	26	H	Northampton T	W	2-1	2-0	15	Aasgaard [11], Smith J [18]	7754
17	Dec 3	A	Huddersfield T	L	0-1	0-0	16		17,036
18	7	H	Leyton Orient	L	0-2	0-1	18		8306
19	14	H	Bolton W	W	2-0	1-0	16	Taylor [18], Aasgaard [67]	24,448
20	21	H	Shrewsbury T	D	2-2	1-0	17	Taylor 2 [9, 53]	8752
21	26	A	Rotherham U	W	1-0	1-0	14	Adeeko [45]	9509
22	29	A	Wrexham	L	1-2	0-0	16	Hugill [79]	13,332
23	Jan 4	H	Birmingham C	L	0-3	0-2	17		13,485
24	18	A	Stevenage	W	2-1	0-0	17	Taylor [55], Aasgaard [90]	3580
25	21	H	Burton Alb	L	1-2	1-1	17	Aasgaard [32]	7553
26	25	H	Bristol R	W	2-0	1-0	16	Carragher [6], Smith J [70]	10,112
27	28	A	Peterborough U	L	0-1	0-1	16		6136
28	Feb 1	H	Lincoln C	D	1-1	1-0	16	Smith J [36]	8606
29	15	H	Stockport Co	L	0-2	0-0	18		12,347
30	18	A	Crawley T	D	1-1	1-1	16	Taylor [39]	3733
31	22	A	Wycombe W	D	0-0	0-0	16		5445
32	25	H	Huddersfield T	W	2-1	2-0	14	Taylor [15], Dale [42]	10,049
33	Mar 1	H	Reading	L	1-2	0-0	15	Kerr [59]	9402
34	4	A	Mansfield T	D	0-0	0-0	15		6884
35	8	H	Cambridge U	W	1-0	0-0	15	Robinson L [77]	10,052
36	15	A	Charlton Ath	L	1-2	0-2	17	Sze [84]	16,491
37	29	H	Barnsley	D	1-1	0-1	18	Asamoah [77]	10,942
38	Apr 1	H	Bolton W	L	0-1	0-0	18		15,445
39	5	A	Leyton Orient	D	0-0	0-0	19		3069
40	8	A	Exeter C	D	1-1	1-0	18	Taylor (pen) [51]	5382
41	12	H	Wrexham	D	0-0	0-0	17		14,819
42	18	A	Shrewsbury T	W	1-0	0-0	16	Taylor [71]	6338
43	21	H	Rotherham U	W	1-0	1-0	15	Carragher [36]	9391
44	26	A	Blackpool	D	1-1	1-0	16	Mellish [3]	11,176
45	29	A	Burton Alb	D	1-1	0-0	16	Darcy [90]	3506
46	May 3	A	Northampton T	D	1-1	0-1	15	Taylor [90]	7591

Final League Position: 15

GOALSCORERS

League (40): Taylor 11 (1 pen), Aasgaard 8, Hugill 3, Smith J 3, Carragher 2, Adeeko 1, Asamoah 1, Chambers 1, Dale 1, Darcy 1, Kerr 1, McManaman 1, Mellish 1, Rankine 1, Robinson L 1, Smith M 1, Sze 1, own goal 1.
FA Cup (7): Aasgaard 3, Smith J 3, Smith S 1.
Carabao Cup (1): Aasgaard 1 (1 pen).
Vertu Trophy (5): Hugill 2 (1 pen), McManaman 1, Olakigbe 1, Stones 1 (1 pen).

Tickle S 46	Sessegnon S 12 + 1	Kerr J 44	Aimson W 42 + 1	Chambers L 12	Adeeko B 23 + 8	Smith M 17 + 2	Rankine D 13 + 7	Sze C 2 + 10	Aasgaard T 23 + 3	Hugill J 8 + 5	Jones J — + 2	Ramsay C 3 + 5	Hughes C — + 1	Stones J — + 3	Smith S 18 + 20	Thomas S 20 + 4	McManaman C 2 + 24	Carragher J 26 + 7	Payne K — + 2	Sibbick T 22 + 9	Taylor D 36 + 7	Weir J 24 + 9	Asamoah M 10 + 6	Olakigbe M 7 + 6	Smith J 19 + 17	Miller K — + 2	Francois T 4 + 1	Robinson L 12 + 11	Dummett P — + 3	Hungbo J 5 + 6	Goodwin W 2 + 4	Norburn O 12 + 2	McHugh H 4 + 10	Mellish J 15 + 6	Darcy R 8 + 5	Dale O 15 + 2	Match No.
1	2²	3	4⁴	5	6	7⁵	8		9¹	10	11³	12	13	14	15	16																					1
1	2¹	3	4	5	6	7⁵	8⁴	14	9²	11	14	12			16		10³	13																			2
1		3	4	5	6	7¹	8⁴	14	9	11³						13	10²	16	2⁵	12	15																3
1	12	3	4	5	6³	7⁴			10⁵	9	11²					16	8	15	2¹		13	14															4
1		3	4	5	13	7³	8¹		9²	11					16		10⁴	12	2⁵		14	6	15														5
1		3	4	5	16		6	7¹	9³	11²		15				14	10	12	2⁵		13	8⁴															6
1		3	4	5¹	8	16				13	14					6⁵	10²	7³	12		2	11	9⁴	15													7
1		3	4	5	15		6⁵	7¹		9	11²					14	10⁴	16	2		12	8³	13														8
1		3	4	5	8	6³			9			2²				14	10⁴	15	13		16	11⁵				7¹	12										9
1		3	4	5	15		6	7³		9²						14	10¹	2⁵		16	11	8⁴		12 · 13													10
1		3	4		6⁵	13			12			5²		14		8	10		2⁴		11	9¹	7³		15 · 16												11
1	5⁵	3	4	6¹	12	8			9	11⁴	13					10²		2³		14			15 · 16		7												12
1	5⁴	3	4	6	7⁵				9		2³					13 · 12		14 · 11		10² · 16			8¹ · 15														13
1		3	4	6¹	14		11									8² · 10⁴		2³ · 12 · 13 · 15		7		9 · 5⁵ · 16															14
1	5⁵	3	4		6		8³	9²		12						12 · 10⁴		2 · 11 · 13		14		7¹ · 15															15
1	5²	3	4		6	12			9							14 · 10⁴		13		2 · 11⁵ · 8³ · 16		7¹	15														16
1		3	4		6 · 12 · 14		9									15		13		2⁵ · 11³ · 8 · 10¹		7²	5⁴ · 16														17
1	5⁵	3	4⁴		6²		8¹			13						7 · 10³ · 14		2 · 11 · 9 · 15		12			16														18
1	5¹	3	4		6	7³			9 · 16							14 · 10⁵		2 · 11⁴ · 15		13 · 8²																	19
1	5²	3	4		6	8⁴			9 · 15							14 · 12		13		2 · 11³		10 · 7¹															20
1	5	3	4	8	6¹				9² · 16							12 · 10⁴		15		2 · 11⁵ · 13		14 · 7³															21
1	5⁴	3	4	8¹					9 · 15							6 · 13 · 14		2 · 11 · 12		10³ · 7²																	22
1	5²	3	4³						9 · 16							7		15	14	2 · 11⁴ · 6		10¹ · 8⁵	13	12													23
1			4						9							6³ · 10⁵		3		2 · 12 · 8⁸			14⁴		5		7² · 11¹ · 13 · 15 · 16										24
1		3	4						9							6³ · 12		2⁴ · 11		10¹ · 8²			13 · 14 · 7 · 15 · 5														25
1		4							11							8 · 9³		3		2 · 10⁴		12		5		6¹ · 14 · 7² · 13 · 15											26
1		4 · 16							7							9⁴ · 15 · 3⁵		2 · 11		14		5³		6² · 10 · 8¹ · 12 · 13													27
1		4							7 · 10¹							3⁵		2 · 11³ · 9		8⁴		12 · 15 · 13 · 6² · 5 · 14															28
1		4			6³				7⁴								3⁵	2 · 11 · 9 · 10²		8¹		12 · 15	16	5 · 14 · 13													29
1		4 · 3	13						15							13		2 · 10 · 7²		12	15	6¹	8¹ · 7³ · 5 · 9 · 10⁴														30
1		3 · 4	14													13		2 · 10 · 7²		12	15		6¹ · 8³ · 5⁴ · 11 · 9														31
1		4 · 3	6	12												15		2 · 11 · 14		8¹	13		7⁴ · 16 · 5 · 9² · 10⁵													32
1		4 · 3	6	12												14	15	2⁵ · 11 · 13		8¹			7³ · 16 · 5 · 9² · 10⁵													33
1		4 · 3	12	8¹												6³		2 · 11⁴ · 14		13		15	7 · 5 · 9 · 10²													34
1		4 · 3	5² · 6		15											14		16 · 2 · 11⁴		8⁵	13		7³ · 9 · 10¹ · 12													35
1		4 · 3⁵	10³		13											6		11 · 9¹		14	15		7 · 5² · 12 · 8⁴													36
1		3 · 4		10²												6		12 · 2		11	13	8⁴	14 · 7 · 15 · 9³ · 5¹													37
1		3 · 4														8		14 · 2		10³	9¹		15 · 12 · 7² · 6 · 13 · 5⁴													38
1		3 · 4														8		14 · 2		15 · 11 · 6 · 12		9¹	5³ · 7² · 13 · 10⁴														39
1		3 · 4	12													7¹		2 · 15 · 11		6 · 10	14	8²	9⁴ · 13 · 5³													40
1		3 · 4	6															2 · 11 · 9¹ · 10		5			12 · 8 · 7													41
1		3 · 4	6		15											14		13 · 2 · 16 · 11 · 9¹ · 10⁴		12		5	8⁹ · 7⁵													42
1		3 · 4	6		13											15 · 2		14 · 11⁴ · 9³ · 10²		12		5	8 · 7¹													43
1		3 · 4	6		13											12 · 2		14 · 11¹ · 9¹ · 10²		5³			8 · 7⁴													44
1		4⁴	5		16											15 · 2		3 · 11 · 7¹ · 10		6²		13	12 · 8³ · 14 · 9⁶													45
1		3 · 4⁸	6		14											15 · 2		11 · 8¹ · 10		7⁴ · 13		5³	12 · 9²													46

FA Cup

First Round	Carlisle U	(a)	2-0
aet.			
Second Round	Cambridge U	(a)	2-1
aet.			
Third Round	Mansfield T	(a)	2-0
Fourth Round	Fulham	(h)	1-2

Carabao Cup

First Round	Barnsley	(h)	1-1

Barnsley won 4-2 on penalties.

Vertu Trophy

Group C (N)	Morecambe	(h)	1-2
Group C (N)	Carlisle U	(a)	2-0
Group C (N)	Nottingham F U21	(h)	0-0

Wigan Ath won 3-0 on penalties.

Second Round	Chesterfield	(a)	2-3

WOLVERHAMPTON WANDERERS

FOUNDATION

Enthusiasts of the game at St Luke's School, Blakenhall formed a club in 1877. In the same neighbourhood a cricket club called Blakenhall Wanderers had a football section. Several St Luke's footballers played cricket for them and shortly before the start of the 1879–80 season the two amalgamated and Wolverhampton Wanderers FC was brought into being.

Molineux Stadium, Waterloo Road, Wolverhampton, West Midlands WV1 4QR.

Telephone: (01902) 810 485.

Ticket Office: (0371) 222 1877.

Website: www.wolves.co.uk

Email: fanservices@wolves.co.uk

Ground Capacity: 31,750.

Record Attendance: 61,315 v Liverpool, FA Cup 5th rd, 11 February 1939.

Pitch Measurements: 105m × 68m (115yd × 74.5yd).

Executive Chairman: Jeff Shi.

Sporting Director: Matt Hobbs.

Head Coach: Vitor Pereira.

Assistant Head Coach: Luis Miguels.

Colours: Gold shirts with black trim, black shorts with gold trim, gold socks with black trim.

Year Formed: 1877* (*see Foundation*).

Turned Professional: 1888.

Previous Names: 1879, St Luke's combined with Wanderers Cricket Club to become Wolverhampton Wanderers (1923) Ltd. New limited companies followed in 1982 and 1986 (current).

HONOURS

League Champions: Division 1 – 1953–54, 1957–58, 1958–59; FL C – 2008–09, 2017–18; Division 2 – 1931–32, 1976–77; FL 1 – 2013–14; Division 3 – 1988–89; Division 3N – 1923–24; Division 4 – 1987–88.
Runners-up: Division 1 – 1937–38, 1938–39, 1949–50, 1954–55, 1959–60; Division 2 – 1966–67, 1982–83.
FA Cup Winners: 1893, 1908, 1949, 1960.
Runners-up: 1889, 1896, 1921, 1939.
League Cup Winners: 1974, 1980.
League Trophy Winners: 1988.
Texaco Cup Winners: 1971.
European Competitions
European Cup: 1958–59, 1959–60 (*qf*).
UEFA Cup: 1971–72 (*runners-up*), 1973–74, 1974–75, 1980–81.
Europa League: 2019–20 (*qf*).
European Cup-Winners' Cup: 1960–61 (*sf*).

Club Nickname: 'Wolves', 'The Old Gold'.

Grounds: 1877, Windmill Field; 1879, John Harper's Field; 1881, Dudley Road; 1889, Molineux.

First Football League Game: 8 September 1888, Football League, v Aston Villa (h) D 1–1 – Baynton; Baugh, Mason; Fletcher, Allen, Lowder; Hunter, Cooper, Anderson, White, Cannon, (1 og).

Record League Victory: 10–1 v Leicester C, Division 1, 15 April 1938 – Sidlow; Morris, Dowen; Galley, Cullis, Gardiner; Maguire (1), Horace Wright, Westcott (4), Jones (1), Dorsett (4).

Record Cup Victory: 14–0 v Crosswell's Brewery, FA Cup 2nd rd, 13 November 1886 – Ike Griffiths; Baugh, Mason; Pearson, Allen (1), Lowder; Hunter (4), Knight (2), Brodie (4), Bernie Griffiths (2), Wood. Plus one goal 'scrambled through'.

Record Defeat: 1–10 v Newton Heath, Division 1, 15 October 1892.

FOOTBALL YEARBOOK FACT FILE

After being dropped from the starting line-up striker John Richards provided a brilliant response for Wolverhampton Wanderers in their FA Cup fifth-round tie against Charlton Athletic in February 1976. Richards came off the bench to replace the injured Dave Wagstaffe after 21 minutes and went on to score a hat-trick as Wolves progressed to the quarter-finals with a 3-1 victory.

Most League Points (2 for a win): 64, Division 1, 1957–58.

Most League Points (3 for a win): 103, FL 1, 2013–14.

Most League Goals: 115, Division 2, 1931–32.

Highest League Scorer in Season: Dennis Westcott, 38, Division 1, 1946–47.

Most League Goals in Total Aggregate: Steve Bull, 250, 1986–99.

Most League Goals in One Match: 5, Joe Butcher v Accrington, Division 1, 19 November 1892; 5, Tom Phillipson v Barnsley, Division 2, 26 April 1926; 5, Tom Phillipson v Bradford C, Division 2, 25 December 1926; 5, Billy Hartill v Notts Co, Division 2, 12 October 1929; 5, Billy Hartill v Aston Villa, Division 1, 3 September 1934.

Most Capped Player: Billy Wright, 105, England (70 consecutive).

Most League Appearances: Derek Parkin, 501, 1967–82.

Youngest League Player: Jimmy Mullen, 16 years 43 days v Leeds U, 18 February 1939.

Record Transfer Fee Received: £62,500,000 from Manchester U for Matheus Cunha, June 2025.

Record Transfer Fee Paid: £43,000,000 to Atletico Madrid for Matheus Cunha, July 2023.

Football League Record: 1888 Founder Member of Football League: 1888–92 Football League; 1892–1906 Division 1; 1906–23 Division 2; 1923–24 Division 3 (N); 1924–32 Division 2; 1932–65 Division 1; 1965–67 Division 2; 1967–76 Division 1; 1976–77 Division 2; 1977–82 Division 1; 1982–83 Division 2; 1983–84 Division 1; 1984–85 Division 2; 1985–86 Division 3; 1986–88 Division 4; 1988–89 Division 3; 1989–92 Division 2; 1992–2003 First Division; 2003–04 Premier League; 2004–09 FL C; 2009–12 Premier League; 2012–13 FL C; 2013–14 FL 1; 2014–18 FL C; 2018– Premier League.

LATEST SEQUENCES

Longest Sequence of League Wins: 9, 11.1.2014 – 11.3.2014.

Longest Sequence of League Defeats: 8, 5.12.1981 – 13.2.1982.

Longest Sequence of League Draws: 6, 22.4.1995 – 20.8.1995.

Longest Sequence of Unbeaten League Matches: 21, 15.1.2005 – 13.8.2005.

Longest Sequence Without a League Win: 19, 1.12.1984 – 6.4.1985.

Successive Scoring Runs: 41 from 20.12.1958.

Successive Non-scoring Runs: 7 from 2.2.1985.

MANAGERS

George Worrall 1877–85 *(Secretary-Manager)*
John Addenbrooke 1885–1922
George Jobey 1922–24
Albert Hoskins 1924–26 *(had been Secretary since 1922)*
Fred Scotchbrook 1926–27
Major Frank Buckley 1927–44
Ted Vizard 1944–48
Stan Cullis 1948–64
Andy Beattie 1964–65
Ronnie Allen 1966–68
Bill McGarry 1968–76
Sammy Chung 1976–78
John Barnwell 1978–81
Ian Greaves 1982
Graham Hawkins 1982–84
Tommy Docherty 1984–85
Bill McGarry 1985
Sammy Chapman 1985–86
Brian Little 1986
Graham Turner 1986–94
Graham Taylor 1994–95
Mark McGhee 1995–98
Colin Lee 1998–2000
Dave Jones 2001–04
Glenn Hoddle 2004–06
Mick McCarthy 2006–12
Stale Solbakken 2012–13
Dean Saunders 2013
Kenny Jackett 2013–16
Walter Zenga 2016
Paul Lambert 2016–17
Nuno Espirito Santo 2017–21
Bruno Lage 2021–22
Julen Lopetegui 2022–23
Gary O'Neil 2023–24
Vitor Pereira December 2024–

TEN YEAR LEAGUE RECORD

		P	W	D	L	F	A	Pts	Pos
2015-16	FL C	46	14	16	16	53	58	58	14
2016-17	FL C	46	16	10	20	54	58	58	15
2017-18	FL C	46	30	9	7	82	39	99	1
2018-19	PR Lge	38	16	9	13	47	46	57	7
2019-20	PR Lge	38	15	14	9	51	40	59	7
2020-21	PR Lge	38	12	9	17	36	52	45	13
2021-22	PR Lge	38	15	6	17	38	43	51	10
2022-23	PR Lge	38	11	8	19	31	58	41	13
2023-24	PR Lge	38	13	7	18	50	65	46	14
2024-25	PR Lge	38	12	6	20	54	69	42	16

DID YOU KNOW ?

Wolverhampton Wanderers announced their first-ever shirt sponsorship deal in October 1982, after signing an agreement with the Taiwan-based television and video company Tatung who had recently opened a factory nearby at Bridgnorth. The initial deal ran until the end of the 1982–83 season but was later renewed for a further two years.

WOLVERHAMPTON WANDERERS – PREMIER LEAGUE 2024–25 LEAGUE RECORD

Match No.	Date	Venue	Opponents	Result	H/T Score	Lg Pos.	Goalscorers	Attendance
1	Aug 17	A	Arsenal	L 0-2	0-1	18		60,261
2	25	H	Chelsea	L 2-6	2-2	19	Matheus Cunha [27], Larsen [45]	31,235
3	31	A	Nottingham F	D 1-1	1-1	17	Bellegarde [12]	29,918
4	Sept 15	H	Newcastle U	L 1-2	1-0	18	Lemina [36]	30,255
5	21	A	Aston Villa	L 1-3	1-0	19	Matheus Cunha [25]	39,978
6	28	H	Liverpool	L 1-2	0-1	20	Ait Nouri [56]	31,413
7	Oct 5	A	Brentford	L 3-5	2-4	20	Matheus Cunha [4], Larsen [26], Ait Nouri [90]	16,960
8	20	H	Manchester C	L 1-2	1-1	20	Larsen [7]	31,319
9	26	A	Brighton & HA	D 2-2	0-1	19	Ait Nouri [88], Matheus Cunha [90]	31,480
10	Nov 2	H	Crystal Palace	D 2-2	0-0	20	Larsen [67], Joao Gomes [72]	29,505
11	9	H	Southampton	W 2-0	1-0	18	Sarabia [2], Matheus Cunha [51]	31,403
12	23	A	Fulham	W 4-1	1-1	17	Matheus Cunha 2 [31, 87], Joao Gomes [53], Goncalo Guedes [90]	26,685
13	30	H	Bournemouth	L 2-4	1-3	18	Larsen 2 [5, 69]	26,685
14	Dec 4	A	Everton	L 0-4	0-2	19		38,820
15	9	A	West Ham U	L 1-2	0-0	19	Doherty [69]	62,435
16	14	H	Ipswich T	L 1-2	0-1	19	Matheus Cunha [72]	30,866
17	22	A	Leicester C	W 3-0	3-0	18	Goncalo Guedes [19], Gomes R [36], Matheus Cunha [44]	31,818
18	26	H	Manchester U	W 2-0	0-0	17	Matheus Cunha [58], Hwang [90]	31,407
19	29	A	Tottenham H	D 2-2	1-2	17	Hwang [7], Larsen [87]	61,284
20	Jan 6	H	Nottingham F	L 0-3	0-2	17		29,940
21	15	A	Newcastle U	L 0-3	0-1	18		51,975
22	20	A	Chelsea	L 1-3	1-1	17	Doherty [45]	39,221
23	25	H	Arsenal	L 0-1	0-0	17		31,503
24	Feb 1	H	Aston Villa	W 2-0	1-0	17	Bellegarde [12], Matheus Cunha [90]	31,385
25	16	A	Liverpool	L 1-2	0-2	17	Matheus Cunha [67]	60,401
26	22	A	Bournemouth	W 1-0	1-0	17	Matheus Cunha [36]	11,206
27	25	H	Fulham	L 1-2	1-1	17	Joao Gomes [18]	28,708
28	Mar 8	H	Everton	D 1-1	1-1	17	Munetsi [40]	30,738
29	15	A	Southampton	W 2-1	1-0	17	Larsen 2 [19, 47]	30,950
30	Apr 1	H	West Ham U	W 1-0	1-0	17	Larsen [21]	30,537
31	5	A	Ipswich T	W 2-1	0-1	17	Sarabia [72], Larsen [84]	29,549
32	13	H	Tottenham H	W 4-2	2-0	16	Ait Nouri [2], Spence (og) [38], Larsen [64], Matheus Cunha [86]	31,463
33	20	A	Manchester U	W 1-0	0-0	15	Sarabia [77]	73,819
34	26	H	Leicester C	W 3-0	1-0	13	Matheus Cunha [33], Larsen [56], Gomes R [85]	31,518
35	May 2	A	Manchester C	L 0-1	0-1	13		53,282
36	10	H	Brighton & HA	L 0-2	0-1	14		31,279
37	20	A	Crystal Palace	L 2-4	1-2	14	Agbadou [24], Larsen [62]	24,766
38	25	H	Brentford	D 1-1	0-1	16	Munetsi [75]	31,382

Final League Position: 16

GOALSCORERS

League (54): Matheus Cunha 15, Larsen 14, Ait Nouri 4, Joao Gomes 3, Sarabia 3, Bellegarde 2, Doherty 2, Gomes R 2, Goncalo Guedes 2, Hwang 2, Munetsi 2, Agbadou 1, Lemina 1, own goal 1.
FA Cup (5): Cunha 2, Ait Nouri 1, Gomes R 1, Joao Gomes 1.
Carabao Cup (4): Goncalo Guedes 3, Doyle 1.
(Wolverhampton W U21) Vertu Trophy (4): Barnett 1, Edozie 1, Holman 1, Voice 1.

Note: superscript figures denote goals scored; figures 12–17 denote substitutes used.

Jose Sa P 29	Doherty M 25+5	Mosquera Y 5	Gomes T 30+1	Ait Nouri R 37	Joao Gomes d 35+1	Lemina M 15+2	Hwang H 5+16	Bellegarde J 20+15	Gomes R 7+18	Larsen J 30+5	Matheus Cunha S 29+4	Daniel Podence C —+2	Sarabia P 7+16	Chiquinho O —+1	Dawson C 10+5	Doyle T 3+21	Johnstone S 7	Nelson Semedo C 32+2	Goncalo Guedes M 10+19	Andre Trindade N 31+2	Forbs C 1+9	Bueno S 18+11	Pond A —+1	Pedro Lima C 1+2	Agbadou E 16	Munetsi M 12+2	Diga N 1+4	Traore B —+1	Bentley D 2	Mane M —+1	King T —+1	Match No.
1	2	3	4	5[4]	6[5]	7	8	9[1]	10[2]	11[3]	12	13	14	15	16																	1
1	2	3	4	5[4]	6	7[5]	8[1]	10[5]	15	11	9[3]	12	13	14	16																	2
	14	3	5	9[2]	7[1]	8	13	6[4]	11[5]	10					4	12	1	2[3]	15	16												3
	14	3	5[4]	8	6	12	9[1]	11[5]	10						4	13	1	2[3]	16	7[2]	15											4
	3[4]		5	8[3]	9		7[2]	13	11[1]	10					4	14	1	2	12	6	15											5
			4	5	9	8	13	10[1]	11[2]	7						14	1	2	6	12	3[3]											6
			4	5	9[3]	8	12	14	11	10					3		1	2	13	6[1]	7[2]											7
1			4	9	6[4]	8		15	10[3]	11[2]		3	12		5	14		7[1]	13	2												8
1			4[2]	8	9[3]	7[1]		14	11[4]	10	12	3	6		5	16		2	15	13[5]												9
1			4[3]	8	7	12		14	11	10	9[1]	3	6[2]		5			2	13													10
1	14		4	8[3]	7	6	12	15	11[2]	10[4]	9[1]	3			5			2	13													11
1	12	3	4	7[4]	2	14	9[1]	8[5]	11	10[3]	13				5[2]	16			6		15											12
1			4[3]	5	7	3	15	8[2]	10[1]	11	9	12						2	14	6[4]	13											13
1	5[2]	13	8	7[4]	2	12	14	11	10	3					15			9[1]	6	4[3]												14
			5	4	8[4]	9[3]	7	12	15	11[2]	10					14	1	2	13	6[1]	3											15
			5[2]	4	8[4]	7	14	9[3]	11	10	12						1	2	13	6[1]	3											16
1	2		4		6[5]	12	16	8[2]	11[3]	10	13	14			5[4]			9[1]	7	15	3											17
1	2		4		8[3]	7[1]	13	16	14	11[4]	10	15	12		5[5]			9[2]	6		3											18
1	2				8	7	11[5]	9[1]	16	12	10[2]				4[4]	14		5	13	6[3]	3											19
1	2		4		7	12	10[3]	13	8	11			14		5[1]			6[2]	9[4]	15	3											20
1	2				8	7[5]	10[1]	14	5[2]	11	12	16			15			13	9[3]	6[4]	3			4								21
1	2				8[1]	7	12	14	11	10	9[3]				5			13	6[2]		3			4								22
1	2[3]				8[5]	7	12	13	15	11[1]	10	9[2]	14		5	16			6[4]		3			4								23
1	2		4		8[1]	14	7[4]	13	10	9[3]	12				5			11[2]	6	15	3											24
1	2		4		8	7[4]		13	10	9[2]		15			5[5]			11[1]	6	14				16	3[3]	12						25
1	2		4		8[4]	7[1]	9[3]	12	10[5]	14		16			5			6			3[2]			15	11	13						26
1	2		4		8	9	7[1]	12	10	14		13			5			6[2]			3[3]				11							27
1	2		4		8	7	13	10[3]	11[2]	12		15			5[5]	14		6[4]	9[1]		3			16								28
1	2		4		8[3]	6		10[2]	11[5]	12		15			5[4]	13		7	14		3			9[1]		16						29
1	2		4		8[2]	6		10[3]	11	12					5			7[1]	13		3	9		14								30
1	2[2]		4		8[3]	6		10[1]	13	11[4]	12				5			7	14		3	9		15								31
1	2[2]		4		8[3]	7[5]	16	10[1]	14	11[4]		15	12		5			6	13		3	9										32
	14		4		8[3]	6	13	11[2]	10[4]	12					5[1]	7		2			3	9		15					1			33
1	2[3]		4		8[1]	6	15	13	11[2]	10	12				5[5]	17		7[4]	16	14	3	9										34
1	2[1]		4		8	6	15	10[2]	13	11[4]	12				5[5]	14		7[3]	16		3	9										35
1	2[2]		4		8	6[4]	15	14	12	10[1]		13			5			11[3]	7[5]		3	9		16								36
	2[1]		4		8	13	16	6		10	12				5[5]			11[3]	15	9[4]	7[2]				3	14			1			37
1[5]	2[4]		4		8[2]	7	15	13	12	10					5			11[1]	6		14	3		9[3]	16							38

FA Cup

Third Round	Bristol C	(a)	2-1
Fourth Round	Blackburn R	(a)	2-0
Fifth Round	Bournemouth	(a)	1-1

aet; Bournemouth won 5-4 on penalties.

Carabao Cup

Second Round	Burnley	(h)	2-0
Third Round	Brighton & HA	(a)	2-3

Vertu Trophy (Wolverhampton W U21)

Group B (N)	Port Vale	(a)	2-2

Port Vale won 5-4 on penalties.

Group B (N)	Wrexham	(a)	0-3
Group B (N)	Salford C	(a)	2-3

WREXHAM

FOUNDATION

The club was formed on 28 September 1872 by members of Wrexham Cricket Club, so they could continue playing a sport during the winter months. This meeting was held at the Turf Hotel, which although rebuilt since, still stands at one corner of the present ground. Their first game was a few weeks later and matches often included 17 players on either side! By 1875 team formations were reduced to 11 men and a year later the club was among the founder members of the Cambrian Football Association, which quickly changed its title to the Football Association of Wales.

The SToK Racecourse Ground, Mold Road, Wrexham LL11 2AH.

Telephone: (01978) 891 864.

Ticket Office: (01978) 891 864.

Website: www.wrexhamafc.co.uk

Email: info@wrexhamafc.co.uk

Ground Capacity: 10,539 +2,329 temporary seats.

Record Attendance: 34,445 v Manchester U, FA Cup 4th rd, 26 January 1957.

Pitch Measurements: 102.5m × 66m (112yd × 72yd).

Co-Chairmen: Rob McElhenney, Ryan Reynolds.

Chief Executive: Michael Williamson.

Manager: Phil Parkinson.

Assistant Manager: Steve Parkin.

Colours: Red shirts with white trim, white shorts with red trim, white socks with red trim.

Year Formed: 1872 (oldest club in Wales).

Turned Professional: 1912.

Club Nickname: 'Red Dragons'.

Grounds: 1872, Racecourse Ground; 1883, Rhosddu Recreation Ground; 1887, Racecourse Ground (renamed The SToK Racecourse Ground 2023).

HONOURS

League Champions: Division 3 – 1977–78.

Runners-up: FL 1 – 2024–25; Division 3 – 1992–93; (3rd) *(promoted to Championship)* 2002–03; Division 3N – 1932–33; Division 4 – 1969–70; FL 2 – 2023–24.

FA Cup: 6th rd, 1974, 1978, 1997.

League Cup: 5th rd, 1961, 1978.

Welsh Cup Winners: 22 times (joint record).

Runners-up: 22 times (record).

FAW Premier Cup Winners: 1998, 2000, 2001, 2003.

League Trophy Winners: 2005.

European Competition: European Cup-Winners' Cup: 1972–73, 1975–76, 1978–79, 1979–80, 1984–85, 1986–87, 1990–91, 1995–96.

First Football League Game: 27 August 1921, Division 3 (N), v Hartlepools U (h) L 0–2 – Godding; Ellis, Simpson; Matthias, Foster, Griffiths; Burton, Goode, Cotton, Edwards, Lloyd.

Record League Victory: 10–1 v Hartlepool U, Division 4, 3 March 1962 – Keelan; Peter Jones, McGavan; Tecwyn Jones, Fox, Ken Barnes; Ron Barnes (3), Bennion (1), Davies (3), Ambler (3), Ron Roberts.

Record Cup Victory: 11–1 v New Brighton, Football League Northern Section Cup 1st rd, 3 January 1934 – Foster; Alfred Jones, Hamilton, Bulling, McMahon, Lawrence, Bryant (3), Findlay (1), Bamford (5), Snow, Waller (1), (o.g. 1).

Record Defeat: 0–9 v Brentford, Division 3, 15 October 1963.

FOOTBALL YEARBOOK FACT FILE

Wrexham were reformed in the summer of 1884, using the name Wrexham Olympic, and played their inaugural fixture under a form of electric lighting on 30 August 1884. The game was played on the Flower Show Field, adjoining Grosvenor Road, and was in association with the local horticultural society show. The match kicked off at 7.30pm with Wrexham Olympic winning 4-3.

Most League Points (2 for a win): 61, Division 4, 1969–70 and Division 3, 1977–78.

Most League Points (3 for a win): 92, FL 1, 2024–25.

Most League Goals: 106, Division 3 (N), 1932–33.

Highest League Scorer in Season: Tom Bamford, 44, Division 3 (N), 1933–34.

Most League Goals in Total Aggregate: Tom Bamford, 175, 1928–34.

Most League Goals in One Match: 5, Tom Bamford v Carlisle U, Division 3N, 17 March 1934; 5, Lee Jones v Cambridge U, Division 2, 6 April 2002; 5 Juan Ugarte v Hartlepool U, League Championship 1, 5 March 2005.

Most Capped Player: Dennis Lawrence, 49 (89), Trinidad & Tobago.

Most League Appearances: Arfon Griffiths, 592, 1959–61, 1962–79.

Youngest League Player: Ken Roberts, 15 years 158 days v Bradford PA, 1 September 1951.

Record Transfer Fee Received: £800,000 from Birmingham C for Bryan Hughes, March 1997.

Record Transfer Fee Paid: £2,000,000 to Reading for Sam Smith, January 2025.

Football League Record: 1921 Original Member of Division 3 (N); 1958–60 Division 3; 1960–62 Division 4; 1962–64 Division 3; 1964–70 Division 4; 1970–78 Division 3; 1978–82 Division 2; 1982–83 Division 3; 1983–92 Division 4; 1992–93 Division 3; 1993–2002 Division 2; 2002–03 Division 3; 2003–04 Division 2; 2004–05 FL 1; 2005–08 FL 2; 2008–2023 National League; 2023–24 FL 2; 2024–25 FL 1; 2025– FL C.

LATEST SEQUENCES

Longest Sequence of League Wins: 8, 5.4.2003 – 3.5.2003.

Longest Sequence of League Defeats: 9, 2.10.1963 – 30.10.1963.

Longest Sequence of League Draws: 6, 12.11.1999 – 26.12.1999.

Longest Sequence of Unbeaten League Matches: 18, 8.3.2003 – 25.8.2003.

Longest Sequence Without a League Win: 16, 25.9.1999 – 3.1.2000.

Successive Scoring Runs: 25 from 5.5.1928.

Successive Non-scoring Runs: 6 from 12.9.1973.

MANAGERS

Selection Committee 1872–1924
Charlie Hewitt 1924–25
Selection Committee 1925–29
Jack Baynes 1929–31
Ernest Blackburn 1932–37
James Logan 1937–38
Arthur Cowell 1938
Tom Morgan 1938–42
Tom Williams 1942–49
Les McDowell 1949–50
Peter Jackson 1950–55
Cliff Lloyd 1955–57
John Love 1957–59
Cliff Lloyd 1959–60
Billy Morris 1960–61
Ken Barnes 1961–65
Billy Morris 1965
Jack Rowley 1966–67
Alvan Williams 1967–68
John Neal 1968–77
Arfon Griffiths 1977–81
Mel Sutton 1981–82
Bobby Roberts 1982–85
Dixie McNeil 1985–89
Brian Flynn 1989–2001
Denis Smith 2001–07
Brian Carey 2007
Brian Little 2007–08
Dean Saunders 2008–11
Andy Morrell 2011–14
Kevin Wilkin 2014–15
Gary Mills 2015–16
Dean Keates 2016–18
Sam Ricketts 2018
Graham Barrow 2018–19
Bryan Hughes 2019
Dean Keates 2019–21
Phil Parkinson July 2021–

TEN YEAR LEAGUE RECORD

		P	W	D	L	F	A	Pts	Pos
2015-16	NL	46	20	9	17	71	56	69	8
2016-17	NL	46	15	13	18	47	61	58	13
2017-18	NL	46	17	19	10	49	39	70	10
2018-19	NL	46	25	9	12	58	39	84	4
2019-20	NL	37	11	10	16	46	49	43	19§
2020-21	NL	42	19	11	12	64	43	68	8
2021-22	NL	44	26	10	8	91	46	88	2
2022-23	NL	46	34	9	3	116	43	111	1
2023-24	FL 2	46	26	10	10	89	52	88	2
2024-25	FL 1	46	27	11	8	67	34	92	2

§*Decided on points-per-game (1.16)*

DID YOU KNOW ?

The first Football League hat-tricks were scored for Wrexham in their 6-1 home win over Chesterfield on 5 November 1921. Both Billy Cotton and Ted Regan achieved the feat, with Cotton the first to hit three. However, it was winger Matt Burton who topped the club's scoring charts that season with a total of 10 goals.

WREXHAM – SKY BET LEAGUE ONE 2024–25 LEAGUE RECORD

Match No.	Date	Venue	Opponents	Result	H/T Score	Lg Pos.	Goalscorers	Attendance
1	Aug 10	H	Wycombe W	W 3-2	2-0	3	Cleworth 9, Marriott 29, Fletcher 83	13,214
2	18	A	Bolton W	D 0-0	0-0	8		25,957
3	24	H	Reading	W 3-0	2-0	4	Palmer 23, Lee 33, Cannon 49	13,322
4	31	A	Peterborough U	W 2-0	2-0	2	Marriott 28, Cleworth 39	12,104
5	Sept 7	H	Shrewsbury T	W 3-0	2-0	1	Palmer 15, Lee 42, Marriott 59	13,341
6	16	A	Birmingham C	L 1-3	1-1	1	Marriott 3	27,980
7	21	H	Crawley T	W 2-1	1-0	1	Lee 24, Cleworth 79	12,732
8	28	A	Leyton Orient	D 0-0	0-0	2		8705
9	Oct 1	A	Stevenage	L 0-1	0-1	2		5704
10	5	H	Northampton T	W 4-1	2-1	2	McClean 2 8, 67, Marriott 38, Lee 56	13,324
11	19	A	Rotherham U	W 1-0	1-0	2	Mullin 1	11,235
12	22	H	Huddersfield T	D 0-0	0-0	2		12,894
13	26	A	Charlton Ath	D 2-2	1-1	3	Coventry (og) 16, Cannon 72	24,692
14	Nov 9	H	Mansfield T	W 1-0	1-0	3	Barnett 6	13,278
15	16	A	Stockport Co	L 0-1	0-1	3		10,327
16	23	H	Exeter C	W 3-0	2-0	2	Cleworth 7, Palmer 25, Rathbone 72	12,484
17	26	H	Lincoln C	W 1-0	0-0	2	Darikwa (og) 67	11,786
18	Dec 3	A	Barnsley	W 1-0	0-0	2	Rathbone 90	12,386
19	7	A	Burton Alb	W 1-0	0-0	2	Lee 65	3644
20	14	H	Cambridge U	D 2-2	1-1	3	McClean 27, Fletcher 65	11,698
21	21	A	Bristol R	D 1-1	1-0	3	Lee 18	9471
22	26	H	Blackpool	W 2-1	1-1	3	Mullin 24, Fletcher (pen) 88	13,313
23	29	H	Wigan Ath	W 2-1	0-0	2	Barnett 60, Fletcher 90	13,332
24	Jan 1	A	Barnsley	L 1-2	0-2	3	Cleworth 80	15,248
25	4	H	Peterborough U	W 1-0	0-0	3	Fletcher 87	13,060
26	16	A	Shrewsbury T	L 1-2	1-1	3	Fletcher 23	8789
27	23	H	Birmingham C	D 1-1	1-1	3	Rathbone 9	13,237
28	28	H	Stevenage	L 2-3	0-2	3	Mullin 55, Cleworth 90	10,670
29	Feb 1	A	Crawley T	W 2-1	1-0	3	James M 2, Lee 90	5049
30	15	A	Northampton T	W 2-0	2-0	3	Smith 19, Rathbone 22	7685
31	18	A	Leyton Orient	L 1-2	1-1	3	Rathbone 15	11,703
32	23	A	Mansfield T	W 2-1	1-1	3	MacDonald (og) 2, Cleworth 58	8122
33	Mar 1	H	Bolton W	D 0-0	0-0	3		13,284
34	4	A	Huddersfield T	W 1-0	0-0	3	Fletcher 73	20,502
35	8	H	Rotherham U	W 1-0	0-0	3	Smith 48	13,245
36	11	A	Reading	L 0-2	0-0	3		11,557
37	15	A	Wycombe W	W 1-0	0-0	2	Smith 78	9333
38	22	H	Stockport Co	W 1-0	1-0	2	Rodriguez 29	13,317
39	29	A	Exeter C	W 2-0	1-0	2	Rathbone 23, Rodriguez (pen) 60	8084
40	Apr 1	A	Cambridge U	D 2-2	1-1	2	Dobson 4, Smith 57	6871
41	5	H	Burton Alb	W 3-0	0-0	2	Fletcher (pen) 71, Smith 74, Marriott 87	12,829
42	12	A	Wigan Ath	D 0-0	0-0	2		14,819
43	18	A	Bristol R	D 1-1	0-1	3	James M 76	12,740
44	21	A	Blackpool	W 2-1	0-0	2	McClean 61, Rathbone 64	12,266
45	26	H	Charlton Ath	W 3-0	2-0	2	Rathbone 15, Smith 2 18, 81	12,774
46	May 3	A	Lincoln C	W 2-0	0-0	2	Lee 53, Longman 61	10,347

Final League Position: 2

GOALSCORERS

League (67): Fletcher 8 (2 pens), Lee 8, Rathbone 8, Cleworth 7, Smith 7, Marriott 6, McClean 4, Mullin 3, Palmer 3, Barnett 2, Cannon 2, James M 2, Rodriguez 2 (1 pen), Dobson 1, Longman 1, own goals 3.
FA Cup (0).
Carabao Cup (2): Boyle 1, Revan 1.
Vertu Trophy (14): Faal 3, Cannon 2, Mullin 2, Ashfield 1, Boyle 1, Brunt 1, Cleworth 1, Dobson 1, James A 1, Lee 1.

Okonkwo A 33	Barnett R 31 + 9	Cleworth M 42	O'Connell E 38 + 1	O'Connor T 25 + 6	McClean J 39 + 3	Cannon A 17 + 7	Dobson G 38 + 4	Lee E 26 + 12	Marriott J 9 + 17	Palmer O 26 + 1	Fletcher S 2 + 38	Evans G 1 + 6	Dalby S — + 1	Revan S 9 + 10	Rathbone O 34 + 7	Mullin P 9 + 17	Jones J — + 2	Mendy J 1 + 3	Scarr D 12 + 2	Brunt L 21 + 1	Faal M — + 8	Bodvarsson J 1 + 3	Burton C 4	James M 30 + 2	Howard M 9 + 1	Longman R 14 + 5	Smith S 18	Rodriguez J 17	Match No.
1	2	3	4	5	6	7³	8	9⁴	10²	11¹	12	13	14	15															1
1		3	4	5	6	7	8	9³	10²	11¹	12		14	2	13														2
1	2³	3	4	5	6	7⁴	8	9	10²	11¹	12			15	13	14													3
1	2⁴	3	4	5	6	7¹	8	9	11²	10³	14			15	12	13													4
1	2	3	4	5	6⁴		8	9	10¹	11²	13			15	7³	12	14												5
1	2⁵	3	4	5	6⁴	14	8	9	10¹	11²	12			16	7³	13		15											6
1	2	3	4	5	6³	7⁴	8	9	13	11¹	12	15			14	10²													7
1	2	3⁴	4	5	6	7¹	8	9	11³	10²	14	12			13	15													8
1	2		4	5³	9²	12	7	13	10	15	11⁴	8¹		6⁵	14	16	3												9
1	2⁵		3¹	5	6	7⁴	8	9	11³	10²	12			16	15	13		4	14										10
1	2		3	5	6	7¹	8	9		10²	13	12		11	4														11
1	2		3	5	6	7¹	8	9		11²	12			10	4		13												12
1	2²	3		5	6	12	8	9		10³	13	7¹		11	4		14												13
1	2	3		5	6	7¹	8	9³	10	12	11²	14		4	13														14
	2	3	14	6	7¹	8⁵	9	10⁴	12		13	4²		15	11³	1	16												15
	5	2	3	3	9		6	10¹	11³	15	8²	12			4	14		1	7⁴										16
	5	2	3	14	9	13	6	10¹	11		8³	12			4			1	7²										17
	5	2	3		9	15	6⁴	10²	11³	14	8	13			4			1¹	7	12									18
	5	2	3	14		6²		10³	11¹	12	9	8	13		4				7	1									19
	5	2	3		9		6²	10	11¹	12	8	13			4				7	1									20
	5	2	3		9	6³	14	10¹	11²	13	8	12			4				7	1									21
	2	3	4		6	7²	13	11¹	12		9	10³			5	14			8	1									22
	5⁴	2	3		9	6	13	10²	11¹	15	8³	11¹			4	14			7	1									23
	5	2	3³	4	9	13	6²	10¹	12		8	11			14				7	1									24
1		2	3	4	13	6⁴	15	11¹	12		5	8	10³		9²		14		7										25
1	5	2	3²	4	9	6¹		10	13		11			8³	12		3		14	7									26
1	5	2		4	9		6	10¹		11²	12			8	13			3	7										27
1	5⁴	2	3		9		6	10	14	11²	12			8	13			3³	7¹	15									28
	5³	2	3		9		6	15	13		12			8			4		7⁴	1	14	10²	11¹						29
	2³	3	4		6		7		13		12			9			5		8	1	14	10²	11¹						30
	5	2	3⁴		9³	13	6¹		15		12			8			4		7	1	14	11	10²						31
1	14	3	4	5		7¹	8		15	13	12			6					12		2²	10⁴	11³						32
1	12	2	3	4		6	15	14	13		9	8⁴			7						5¹	11²	10³						33
1	14	2	3	4		6¹	12	15	13		9	8			7						5²	11⁴	10³						34
1		2	3	4	13		8²	15		12	14			9	6³				7		5	11⁴	10¹						35
1	5	2	3⁴	4	8³		6		12		13	15		9¹	6⁵				16		7	14	11	10²					36
1		2	3	14	9		6	13		12				8²					4		7	5	11³	10¹					37
1	12	2	3		9	6³	14	15	13		8								4		7	5¹	11⁴	10²					38
1	13	2	3		9	6	14		12		8								4		7	5²	11³	10¹					39
1	13	2	3		9³	6	14		12		8²								4		7	5	11	10¹					40
1	13	2	3		9⁵	6²	14	15		12	8								4		7	5	11⁴	10¹					41
1	13	2	3		9¹	6²	14	15		12	8								4		7	5	11⁴	10³					42
1	5²	2	3¹		13		15	6⁵	16		14			8				12	4⁴		7	9	11	10³					43
1		2		14	9		6		13		12			8³					3	4		7	5	11²	10¹				44
1		2			9		6		13		12			8					3	4		7	5	11²	10¹				45
1	12	2		14	9		6	10²	15		13			8³					3	4		7	5¹	11⁴					46

FA Cup

First Round	Harrogate T	(a)	0-1

Carabao Cup

First Round	Sheffield U	(a)	2-4

Vertu Trophy

Group B (N)	Salford C	(h)	2-1
Group B (N)	Wolverhampton W U21	(h)	3-0
Group B (N)	Port Vale	(a)	1-1

Port Vale won 3-1 on penalties.

Second Round	Crewe Alex	(h)	1-0
Third Round	Port Vale	(a)	4-1
Quarter-Final	Bolton W	(h)	1-0
Semi-Final	Peterborough U	(h)	2-2

Peterborough U won 4-2 on penalties.

WYCOMBE WANDERERS

FOUNDATION

In 1887 a group of young furniture trade workers called a meeting at the Steam Engine public house with the aim of forming a football club and entering junior football. It is thought that they were named after the famous FA Cup winners, The Wanderers, who had visited the town in 1877 for a tie with the original High Wycombe club. It is also possible that they played informally before their formation, although there is no proof of this.

Adams Park, Hillbottom Road, High Wycombe, Buckinghamshire HP12 4HJ.

Telephone: (01494) 472 100.

Ticket Office: (01494) 441 118.

Website: www.wwfc.com   *Email:* wwfc@wwfc.com

Ground Capacity: 9,446.

Record Attendance: 15,850 v St Albans C, FA Amateur Cup 4th rd, 25 February 1950 (at Loakes Park); 9,921 v Fulham, FA Cup 3rd rd, 9 January 2002 (at Adams Park).

Pitch Measurements: 100m × 64m (109.5yd × 70yd).

Chairman and Chief Executive: Dan Rice (interim).

Director of Football Operations & Administration: Tom Holder.

Head Coach: Mike Dodds.   *First-Team Coaches:* Tom Housell, Pete Shuttleworth.

Colours: Light blue and dark blue quartered shirts with white and dark blue trim, dark blue shorts with white trim, dark blue socks with light blue trim.

Year Formed: 1887. *Turned Professional:* 1974.

Club Nicknames: 'The Chairboys' (after High Wycombe's tradition of furniture making); 'The Blues'.

Grounds: 1887, The Rye; 1893, Spring Meadow; 1895, Loakes Park; 1899, Daws Hill Park; 1901, Loakes Park; 1990, Adams Park.

First Football League Game: 14 August 1993, Division 3 v Carlisle U (a) D 2–2: Hyde; Cousins, Horton (Langford), Kerr, Crossley, Ryan, Carroll, Stapleton, Thompson, Scott, Guppy (1) (Hutchinson), (1 og).

Record League Victory: 5–0 v Burnley, Division 2, 15 April 1997 – Parkin; Cousins, Bell, Kavanagh, McCarthy, Forsyth, Carroll (2p) (Simpson), Scott (Farrell), Stallard (1), McGavin (1) (Read (1)), Brown; 5–0 v Northampton T, Division 2, 4 January 2003 – Talia; Senda, Ryan, Thomson, McCarthy, Johnson, Bulman, Simpson (1), Faulconbridge (Harris), Dixon (1) (Roberts 3), Brown (Currie); 5–0 v Hartlepool U, FL 1, 25 February 2012 – Bull; McCoy, Basey, Eastmond (Bloomfield), Laing, Doherty (1), Hackett, Lewis, Bevon (2) (Strevons), Hayes (2) (McClure), McNamee; 5–0 v Stockport Co, FL 1, 5 November 2024 – Ravizzoli; Pattenden, Low, Taylor, Harvie, Morley (1), Scowen (Butcher), Onyedinma (2) (Wheeler), Humphreys (Bakinson), Udoh (Leahy), Kone (2) (Lubula).

Record Cup Victory: 5–0 v Hitchin T (a), FA Cup 2nd rd, 3 December 1994 – Hyde; Cousins, Brown, Crossley, Evans, Ryan (1), Carroll, Bell (1), Thompson, Garner (3) (Hemmings), Stapleton (Langford). 5–0 v Chesterfield (a), FA Cup 2nd rd, 3 December 2017 – Blackman; Harriman, Stewart (1), Pierre, Jacobson, Bloomfield (Wood), O'Nien, Gape (Bean), Kashket (3) (Cowan-Hall), Hayes (1), Akinfenwa.

HONOURS

League Champions: Football Conference – 1992–93.
Runners-up: Football Conference – 1991–92.
FA Cup: semi-final – 2001.
League Cup: semi-final – 2007.
League Trophy: *Runners-up:* 2024.
FA Amateur Cup Winners: 1931.

FOOTBALL YEARBOOK FACT FILE

Wycombe Wanderers hosted four England Amateur international matches at their former ground at Loakes Park. The first of these took place in October 1958, resulting in a 2-2 draw with South Africa in front of a crowd of 6,000. Other games featured Northern Ireland (September 1960), Iceland (September 1961) and the Republic of Ireland (February 1970).

Record Defeat: 0–7 v Shrewsbury T, Johnstone's Paint Trophy, 7 October 2008.

Most League Points (3 for a win): 84, FL 2, 2014–15; 84, FL 2, 2017–18; 84, FL 1, 2024–25.

Most League Goals: 79, FL 2, 2017–18.

Highest League Scorer in Season: Scott McGleish, 25, 2007–08.

Most League Goals in Total Aggregate: Adebayo Akinfenwa, 52, 2016–22.

Most League Goals in One Match: 3, Miquel Desouza v Bradford C, Division 2, 2 September 1995; 3, John Williams v Stockport Co, Division 2, 24 February 1996; 3, Mark Stallard v Walsall, Division 2, 21 October 1997; 3, Sean Devine v Reading, Division 2, 2 October 1999; 3, Sean Divine v Bury, Division 2, 26 February 2000; 3, Stuart Roberts v Northampton T, Division 2, 4 January 2003; 3, Nathan Tyson v Lincoln C, FL 2, 5 March 2005; 3, Nathan Tyson v Kidderminster H, FL 2, 2 April 2005; 3, Nathan Tyson v Stockport Co, FL 2, 10 September 2005; 3, Kevin Betsy v Mansfield T, FL 2, 24 September 2005; 3, Scott McGleish v Mansfield T, FL 2, 8 January 2008; 3, Stuart Beavon v Bury, FL 1, 17 March 2012; 3, Craig Mackail-Smith v Crawley T, FL 2, 18 November 2017; 3, Joe Jacobson v Lincoln C, FL 1, 7 September 2019; 3, Richard Kone v Peterborough U, FL 1, 19 October 2024.

Most Capped Player: Tjay de Barr, 14 (52), Gibraltar.

Most League Appearances: Matt Bloomfield, 486, 2003–21.

Youngest League Player: Jordon Ibe, 15 years 311 days v Hartlepool U, 15 October 2011.

Record Transfer Fee Received: £750,000 (potentially rising to £1,000,000) from Middlesbrough for Uche Ikpeazu, July 2021.

Record Transfer Fee Paid: £800,000 to Viborg for Magnus Westergaard, January 2025.

Football League Record: 1993 Promoted from Football Conference; 1993–94 Third Division; 1994–2004 Second Division; 2004–09 FL 2; 2009–10 FL 1; 2010–11 FL 2; 2011–12 FL 1; 2012–18 FL 2; 2018–20 FL 1; 2020–21 FL C; 2021– FL 1.

MANAGERS

First coach appointed 1951.
Prior to Brian Lee's appointment in 1969 the team was selected by a Match Committee which met every Monday evening.
James McCormack 1951–52
Sid Cann 1952–61
Graham Adams 1961–62
Don Welsh 1962–64
Barry Darvill 1964–68
Brian Lee 1969–76
Ted Powell 1976–77
John Reardon 1977–78
Andy Williams 1978–80
Mike Keen 1980–84
Paul Bence 1984–86
Alan Gane 1986–87
Peter Suddaby 1987–88
Jim Kelman 1988–90
Martin O'Neill 1990–95
Alan Smith 1995–96
John Gregory 1996–98
Neil Smillie 1998–99
Lawrie Sanchez 1999–2003
Tony Adams 2003–04
John Gorman 2004–06
Paul Lambert 2006–08
Peter Taylor 2008–09
Gary Waddock 2009–12
Gareth Ainsworth 2012–23
Matt Bloomfield 2023–25
Mike Dodds February 2025–

LATEST SEQUENCES

Longest Sequence of League Wins: 8, 5.10.2024 – 26.11.2024.

Longest Sequence of League Defeats: 8, 29.2.2020 – 24.10.2020.

Longest Sequence of League Draws: 5, 24.1.2004 – 21.2.2004.

Longest Sequence of Unbeaten League Matches: 21, 6.8.2005 – 10.12.2005.

Longest Sequence Without a League Win: 13, 10.1.2004 – 20.3.2004.

Successive Scoring Runs: 24 from 13.4.2024.

Successive Non-scoring Runs: 5 from 15.10.1996.

TEN YEAR LEAGUE RECORD

		P	W	D	L	F	A	Pts	Pos
2015-16	FL 2	46	17	13	16	45	44	64	13
2016-17	FL 2	46	19	12	15	58	53	69	9
2017-18	FL 2	46	24	12	10	79	60	84	3
2018-19	FL 1	46	14	11	21	55	67	53	17
2019-20	FL 1	34	17	8	9	45	40	59	3§
2020-21	FL C	46	11	10	25	39	69	43	22
2021-22	FL 1	46	23	14	9	75	51	83	6
2022-23	FL 1	46	20	9	17	59	51	69	9
2023-24	FL 1	46	17	14	15	60	55	65	10
2024-25	FL 1	46	24	12	10	70	45	84	5

§*Decided on points-per-game (1.74)*

DID YOU KNOW ?

Defender Mark Rogers became the first Wycombe Wanderers player to win full international honours when he came on as a late substitute for Canada in a World Cup qualifying match against Panama in October 2000. He won a total of seven caps while on the club's books between 1998 and 2004.

WYCOMBE WANDERERS – SKY BET LEAGUE ONE 2024–25 LEAGUE RECORD

Match No.	Date	Venue	Opponents	Result		H/T Score	Lg Pos.	Goalscorers	Attendance
1	Aug 10	A	Wrexham	L	2-3	0-2	14	Kone 58, Vokes 89	13,214
2	17	H	Birmingham C	L	2-3	1-1	19	Bielik (og) 22, Vokes 90	6224
3	24	H	Rotherham U	W	2-0	0-0	16	Humphreys 70, Sadlier (pen) 87	4272
4	31	A	Blackpool	D	2-2	1-1	15	McCleary 10, Udoh 78	9143
5	Sept 14	A	Northampton T	W	2-1	1-1	10	Udoh 11, Kone 52	5995
6	21	H	Cambridge U	W	2-1	1-1	9	McCleary 8, Humphreys 85	4189
7	28	A	Bristol R	W	2-1	0-1	7	Harvie 77, Low 90	7814
8	Oct 1	A	Barnsley	D	2-2	0-0	8	Lubula 47, Kone 85	9857
9	5	H	Crawley T	W	1-0	1-0	5	Onyedinma 23	4472
10	19	H	Peterborough U	W	3-1	0-0	3	Kone 3 (1 pen) 63, 67, 72 (p)	4345
11	22	A	Burton Alb	W	3-2	1-1	3	Kodua 16, Leahy 53, Sweeney (og) 81	1993
12	26	H	Leyton Orient	W	3-0	2-0	2	Onyedinma 5, Udoh 45, Humphreys 59	5400
13	Nov 5	A	Stockport Co	W	5-0	3-0	1	Kone 2 (1 pen) 10 (p), 18, Onyedinma 2 11, 70, Morley 77	8305
14	9	A	Wigan Ath	W	1-0	1-0	1	Low 11	8958
15	23	A	Lincoln C	W	3-2	2-1	1	Kone 35, Onyedinma 43, Low 72	8558
16	26	H	Mansfield T	W	1-0	0-0	1	Leahy 90	4670
17	Dec 3	A	Exeter C	D	2-2	1-2	1	Low 27, Humphreys 54	5073
18	7	H	Reading	D	1-1	1-1	1	Lubula 18	7651
19	14	A	Shrewsbury T	W	4-1	2-0	1	Lubula 15, Taylor 45, Onyedinma 69, Udoh 74	5737
20	20	H	Bolton W	D	0-0	0-0	1		6119
21	26	A	Stevenage	W	3-0	2-0	2	Kone 2 8, 43, Lubula 66	4430
22	29	A	Charlton Ath	L	1-2	0-0	3	Kone 84	15,544
23	Jan 1	H	Exeter C	W	2-1	0-0	1	Leahy 66, Morley (pen) 90	5829
24	4	H	Blackpool	D	1-1	1-0	2	Kone (pen) 40	4936
25	7	H	Huddersfield T	L	0-1	0-1	2		4095
26	18	A	Mansfield T	W	2-1	0-0	2	Kone 57, McCleary 87	7459
27	25	H	Northampton T	D	0-0	0-0	2		5446
28	28	H	Barnsley	W	2-1	0-1	2	Kone 2 (1 pen) 65 (p), 90	3803
29	Feb 1	A	Cambridge U	D	1-1	1-0	2	Humphreys 35	6866
30	15	A	Crawley T	D	1-1	1-1	2	Udoh 20	4330
31	18	H	Bristol R	W	2-0	0-0	2	Humphreys 51, Udoh 59	4419
32	22	H	Wigan Ath	D	0-0	0-0	2		5445
33	Mar 1	A	Birmingham C	L	0-1	0-1	2		27,522
34	4	H	Burton Alb	W	2-0	1-0	2	Udoh 16, Armer (og) 59	3456
35	8	A	Peterborough U	D	1-1	0-1	2	Kone 90	8260
36	15	H	Wrexham	L	0-1	0-0	3		9333
37	18	A	Rotherham U	W	3-2	0-0	2	Kone 69, Bradley 90, Kodua 90	7798
38	29	H	Lincoln C	W	1-0	0-0	3	Humphreys 66	4939
39	Apr 1	H	Shrewsbury T	D	0-0	0-0	3		3806
40	5	A	Reading	L	0-1	0-0	3		15,228
41	8	A	Huddersfield T	W	1-0	0-0	3	Udoh 63	17,297
42	12	H	Stevenage	W	1-0	0-0	3	Taylor 90	4827
43	18	A	Bolton W	W	2-0	0-0	2	Taylor 58, Leahy 90	21,114
44	21	H	Charlton Ath	L	0-4	0-2	3		8084
45	26	A	Leyton Orient	L	0-1	0-0	4		8935
46	May 3	H	Stockport Co	L	1-3	1-0	5	McCleary 31	7561

Final League Position: 5

GOALSCORERS

League (70): Kone 18 (4 pens), Udoh 8, Humphreys 7, Onyedinma 6, Leahy 4, Low 4, Lubula 4, McCleary 4, Taylor 3, Kodua 2, Morley 2 (1 pen), Vokes 2, Bradley 1, Harvie 1, Sadlier 1 (1 pen), own goals 3.
FA Cup (7): Leahy 2 (1 pen), Bradley 1, Hanlan 1, Kodua 1, Kone 1, Lubula 1.
Carabao Cup (4): Kone 2, Udoh 1, own goal 1.
Vertu Trophy (8): Lubula 5, Hanlan 1, Leahy 1, Sadlier 1.
League One Play-offs (0).

Bishop N 2	Grimmer J 32 + 5	Hartridge A 5 + 1	Low J 36 + 2	Harvie D 30	Bakinson T 10 + 15	Leahy L 30 + 9	McCleary G 24 + 19	Scowen J 34 + 4	Sadlier K 5 + 5	Kone R 32 + 9	Udoh D 27 + 14	Bartolo J — + 2	Vokes S — + 7	Pattenden J 10 + 3	Tafazolli R 1	Butcher M 3 + 10	McCarthy J — + 2	Ravizzoli F 27	Humphreys C 40 + 2	Morley A 18 + 1	Kodua G 2 + 18	Skura D 5 + 3	Taylor C 35 + 1	Lubala B 13 + 14	Wheeler D 1 + 4	Onyedinma F 28 + 11	Hanlan B 1 + 7	Bradley S 16 + 1	Hagelskjaer A — + 2	Westergaard M — + 5	Norris W 17	Simons X 12 + 2	Back F 1 + 1	Lowry A 2 + 7	Reach A 7 + 5	Berry J — + 3	Match No.
1	2	3	4	5^4	6^1	7		8^3	9	10^2	11	12	13	14	15																						1
1	2		3	5	12	8^4	9^5	6	11	10^1	13	16	15	14		4^2	7^3	17																			2
	2^1	4	3	5	16	11^4	7	8^5	10^3	9								6^2	12	1	13	14	15														3
	2^2	4	3	5	16	7^4	8	10^1	13	11^5		12						1	9^3	6	15	14															4
	2	15	3	5	14	9^2	6		10	11^4			16				1	8^3	7^5		4^1	12	13														5
	2		4	5				10³	8	7	12	11^2	9^1		14			1	6		3	13															6
	2		3	5	14		10	8		11^2								1	9^3	6		4	12	7^1	13												7
	2		3	5	6^3		13	8	10^2	14	11^4							1	15	9		4	7^1	12													8
	2		3	5		14	7^4	8	15	11^2	13					6		1	9^3			4	12	10^1													9
	2		3	5	15	13	7^3	9^4		12	11					16		1	8^2	6^5	14		4	10^1													10
	2		3	5		9^4	13	8		11^3	14					15		1		6	7^2		4	10^1	12												11
	2^1		3	5	6	14	8^2		13	11^4						15		1	9^5	7	16	12	4			10^3											12
		3	5	13	12		7^5		11^4	10^1		2		16				1	9^2	6		4	15	14	8^3												13
16		3	5		12		7^2		11^1	10^3	2							1	9^5	6		4	13	14	8^4	15											14
16		3	5		7	12			11^3	10^4	2		15					1	9^1	6^5		4	13	8^2	14												15
		3	5		8		7^2			11^3	12							1	9	6		4	13	10^1	14												16
		3	5	14	9^4	7^1			11^2	12		2						1	8	6		4	15	10^3	13												17
2		3	5	6^3	14	13				12	11^1							1	9	7		4	10^2	8^4	15												18
	3	5	14	9	13			11^3	12		2							1	8^1	6^5		4	10^2	16	7^4												19
14	5	3		6	7	12			11^3		2³							1	9			4	10^1	8^2													20
2		3	5	16	6	13	15			11^3	12							1	9^4	7^5	14		4	10^1		8^2											21
2		3	5	6^3		8^1	15			13	11^4							1	9	7	14		4	10^2	12												22
2		3	5		7^1	14	12			11	15							1	9^4	6	13		4	10^3	8^2												23
2	4^8	3	5		9	10^3	8			11^2	13							1	6^1	14	12			7^4	15												24
	2	8	7	4^2	13	6		10^1	11^4									1	9			15		5^3	12	3											25
2^2		5		7	12	6		11^4	15									1	9^3			13	3	10^4		8^1		4	14								26
13	3	5^1		7	8	6		14					12					1	9	2^3			10^4		15	11^{12}	4										27
2^4			6^2	5	12	7		11	10^3							16		1	9^5		14	3		15		8^1	4		13								28
		6	5	13	7			11										1	9^1			2	3	10^3		8^2	4^8	12	14								29
		3	5		6^3	8^2	7			11^4	15								9^1	14	2		12	10	4			1	13								30
		3	5	16	14	13	6			11^4								9^5	12		4	10	8^1					1	7^3	2^2	15						31
		3	5	15	8^3	6^4		13		11^1	2								9^5	14		4	10^2	12					1	7		16					32
15		3	5^1	14	8^6	6			16	11			2^4						9^3			4		10^2	13		1		7^8			12					33
	2		3	14	7^3	13	6			11^1	10^5								9^4			4	12	8^2			15	1			16	5					34
	2^4		3	14	8	9^2	7^3			11	10								6			4	13	12			1					5^1	15			35
	2		3	7		8^2	6			11	13								9			4		10^1		14	1					5^3	12			36
5	2^2			9	13	8^1		11^3		14									6	12		4			3		1			7			10			37
5^1	2			8	13	7		11^3											9			4			12	3		1	6				10^2			38
2^5				8	7^2	14		10			16	5^1							9	12		4		13	3		1	6^4			11^3	15				39
	2			5^1	10^2	7		11	12										9	13	3		15	4			1	6^1	14			8^9				40
	3	13		14	6		9			11^1	10								7^2	15		5		2^4	4		1				8^3		12			41
	2^2			5	12	6			11	10									9							8^1	3		1	7^3			14	13		42
	3	12			6^5	13	8	16		11^1	10^4								7^3			5	15	2^2	4		1			9				14		43
	2	3		9^1	6	10^3	8^2			14			11^3						7			5		14	4		1		12	15						44
	2			8^2	14	7^1	15			11	10								9^4			4		5^2	3		1			6			12	13		45
	2^4			15	8^5	9^2		12		11			16						4			10^3		3		13	1			6	14		7^1	5		46

FA Cup

First Round	York C	(h)	3-2	
Second Round	Wealdstone	(a)	2-0	
Third Round	Portsmouth	(h)	2-0	
Fourth Round	Preston NE	(a)	0-0	
aet; Preston NE won 4-2 on penalties.				

Carabao Cup

First Round	Northampton T	(a)	2-0
Second Round	Swansea C	(a)	1-0
Third Round	Aston Villa	(h)	1-2

Vertu Trophy

Group B (S)	AFC Wimbledon	(a)	0-1
Group B (S)	Brighton & HA U21	(h)	5-3
Group B (S)	Crawley T	(h)	2-1
Second Round	Swindon T	(h)	1-2

League One Play-offs

Semi-Final 1st leg	Charlton Ath	(h)	0-0
Semi-Final 2nd leg	Charlton Ath	(a)	0-1

ENGLISH LEAGUE PLAYERS DIRECTORY

Players listed represent those with their clubs during the 2024–25 season. The position codes after each player's name are as follows: G: Goalkeeper; D: Defender; M: Midfielder: F: Forward. Height (H) and weight (W) are stated in imperial measurements. Club names in *italic* indicate loans.

Players are listed alphabetically on pages 537–544 where the number alongside each player corresponds to the team number heading. (Aarons, Maximillian 11 = team 11 (Bournemouth).)

ACCRINGTON S (1)

ALSTON, Rio (D) — 0 0
Season	Club			Tot	
2024–25	Accrington S	0	0		

BROWN, Charlie (F) — 93 10
H: 6 0 W: 12 04 b.Ipswich 23-9-99
Season	Club			Tot	
2018–19	Chelsea	0	0		
2019–20	Chelsea	0	0		
2019–20	*Union SG*	3	0	3	0
2020–21	Milton Keynes D	20	3		
2021–22	Milton Keynes D	6	0	26	3
2021–22	Cheltenham T	3	0		
2022–23	Cheltenham T	20	1	23	1
2023–24	Morecambe	25	6		
2024–25	Morecambe	4	0	29	6
2024–25	Accrington S	12	0	12	0

CATON, Charlie (F) — 16 0
H: 5 11 W: 11 11 b.Bodelwyddan 25-11-02
Season	Club			Tot	
2019–20	Shrewsbury T	0	0		
2020–21	Shrewsbury T	3	0		
2021–22	Shrewsbury T	0	0		
2022–23	Shrewsbury T	1	0	4	0
From Chester.					
2024–25	Accrington S	12	0	12	0

CONNEELY, Seamus (D) — 475 18
H: 5 9 W: 10 10 b.Galway 9-7-88
Internationals: Republic of Ireland U21, U23.
Season	Club			Tot	
2008	Galway U	20	0		
2009	Galway U	34	2		
2010	Galway U	32	0	86	2
2010–11	Sheffield U	0	0		
2011–12	Sheffield U	0	0		
2012	Sligo R	13	1		
2013	Sligo R	21	1		
2014	Sligo R	25	1	59	3
2014–15	Accrington S	16	3		
2015–16	Accrington S	46	3		
2016–17	Accrington S	38	1		
2017–18	Accrington S	33	2		
2018–19	Accrington S	27	1		
2019–20	Accrington S	31	1		
2020–21	Accrington S	38	1		
2021–22	Accrington S	22	0		
2022–23	Accrington S	26	0		
2023–24	Accrington S	27	0		
2024–25	Accrington S	26	1	330	13

COYLE, Liam (M) — 98 2
H: 5 9 W: 10 08 b.Liverpool 6-12-99
Season	Club			Tot	
2016–17	Liverpool	0	0		
2017–18	Liverpool	0	0		
2018–19	Liverpool	0	0		
2019–20	Liverpool	0	0		
2020–21	Liverpool	0	0		
2021–22	Accrington S	19	1		
2022–23	Accrington S	33	1		
2023–24	Accrington S	12	0		
2024–25	Accrington S	34	0	98	2

GRANT, Conor (M) — 236 18
H: 5 9 W: 12 08 b.Fazakerley 18-4-95
Internationals: England U18.
Season	Club			Tot	
2013–14	Everton	0	0		
2014–15	Everton	0	0		
2014–15	*Motherwell*	11	1	11	1
2015–16	Everton	0	0		
2015–16	*Doncaster R*	19	2		
2016–17	Everton	0	0		
2016–17	*Ipswich T*	6	0	6	0
2016–17	*Doncaster R*	21	1	40	3
2017–18	Everton	0	0		
2017–18	*Crewe Alex*	17	0	17	0
2018–19	Plymouth Arg	19	2		
2019–20	Plymouth Arg	17	2		
2020–21	Plymouth Arg	38	4		
2021–22	Plymouth Arg	38	7		
2022–23	Plymouth Arg	9	1	112	14
2023–24	Port Vale	30	0		
2024–25	Port Vale	4	0	34	0
2024–25	Accrington S	16	0	16	0

HALL, Charlie (M) — 1 0
H: 5 10 W: 11 09 b.Manchester 1-1-06
Season	Club			Tot	
2024–25	Accrington S	1	0	1	0

HENDERSON, Alex (M) — 48 5
H: 6 0 W: 11 11 b.Accrington 25-9-04
Season	Club			Tot	
2023–24	Accrington S	20	4		
2024–25	Accrington S	28	1	48	5

HUNTER, Ashley (F) — 313 45
H: 5 10 W: 10 08 b.Derby 29-9-93
From Ilkeston.
Season	Club			Tot	
2014–15	Fleetwood T	12	1		
2015–16	Fleetwood T	24	5		
2016–17	Fleetwood T	44	8		
2017–18	Fleetwood T	44	9		
2018–19	Fleetwood T	43	8		
2019–20	Fleetwood T	14	0	181	31
2019–20	*Salford C*	11	5		
2020–21	Salford C	41	7		
2021–22	Salford C	33	1	85	13
2022–23	Morecambe	20	1		
2023–24	Milton Keynes D	6	0	6	0
2024–25	Accrington S	21	0	21	0

ISHERWOOD, Liam (G) — 5 0
H: 6 4 W: 12 00 b.Clitheroe 13-7-02
From Portsmouth, Baffins Milton R, Bognor Regis T.
Season	Club			Tot	
2020–21	Accrington S	0	0		
2021–22	Accrington S	4	0		
2022–23	Accrington S	1	0		
2023–24	Accrington S	0	0		
2024–25	Accrington S	0	0	5	0

KELLY, Michael (G) — 126 0
H: 6 5 W: 12 08 b.Dublin 13-7-96
Season	Club			Tot	
2014	Shamrock R	0	0		
2015	Shamrock R	0	0		
2016	Cabinteely	25	0		
2017	Cabinteely	25	0		
2018	Longford T	26	0		
2019	Bohemians	0	0		
2020	Cabinteely	6	0	56	0
2021	Longford T	9	0	35	0
2022	Bray W	8	0	8	0
2022–23	Carlisle U	0	0		
2023–24	Milton Keynes D	15	0	15	0
2024–25	Accrington S	12	0	12	0

KNOWLES, Jimmy (F) — 33 3
H: 6 0 W: 12 08 b.Sutton 27-2-01
Season	Club			Tot	
2018–19	Mansfield T	0	0		
2019–20	Mansfield T	5	1		
2020–21	Mansfield T	0	0		
2021–22	Mansfield T	0	0		
2021–22	*Greenock Morton*	11	0	11	0
2022–23	Mansfield T	1	0	6	1
From Boston U.					
2024–25	Accrington S	16	2	16	2

LOVE, Donald (D) — 195 3
H: 5 10 W: 11 05 b.Rochdale 2-12-94
Internationals: Scotland U17, U19, U21.
Season	Club			Tot	
2015–16	Manchester U	1	0	1	0
2015–16	*Wigan Ath*	7	0	7	0
2016–17	Sunderland	12	0		
2017–18	Sunderland	11	0		
2018–19	Sunderland	4	0	27	0
2019–20	Shrewsbury T	28	0		
2020–21	Shrewsbury T	14	0	42	0
2021–22	Salford C	25	0	25	0
2022–23	Morecambe	36	2		
2023–24	Morecambe	16	0	52	2
2024–25	Accrington S	41	1	41	1

MARTIN, Dan (M) — 59 0
H: 5 11 W: 9 11 b.Trafford 19-4-02
Season	Club			Tot	
2019–20	Accrington S	0	0		
2020–21	Accrington S	0	0		
2021–22	Accrington S	0	0		
2022–23	Accrington S	21	0		
2023–24	Accrington S	32	0		
2024–25	Accrington S	6	0	59	0

MATTHEWS, Devon (D) — 20 0
H: 6 3 W: 12 08 b.Oldham 4-1-00
Season	Club			Tot	
2024–25	Accrington S	20	0	20	0

MOONEY, Kelsey (F) — 38 5
H: 6 3 W: 12 06 b.Hemel Hempsted 5-2-99
Season	Club			Tot	
2018–19	Aston Villa	0	0		
2018–19	*Cheltenham T*	8	1	8	1
From Hereford.					
2020–21	Scunthorpe U	0	0		
From Leamington, Boston U.					
2024–25	Accrington S	30	4	30	4

O'BRIEN, Connor (D) — 51 0
H: 5 11 W: 12 02 b.Accrington 15-2-05
Internationals: Republic of Ireland U21.
Season	Club			Tot	
2022–23	Accrington S	2	0		
2023–24	Accrington S	24	0		
2024–25	Accrington S	25	0	51	0

PATRICK, Oliver (M) — 3 0
H: 5 11 W: 10 12 b.Oldham 2-2-03
From Rochdale.
Season	Club			Tot	
2021–22	Accrington S	0	0		
2022–23	Accrington S	0	0		
2023–24	Accrington S	3	0		
2024–25	Accrington S	0	0	3	0

PICKLES, Aaron (D) — 18 0
H: 6 3 W: 9 11 b.Keighley 20-3-05
Season	Club			Tot	
2022–23	Accrington S	5	0		
2023–24	Accrington S	12	0		
2024–25	Accrington S	1	0	18	0

POILLY, Emerich (M) — 0 0
H: 5 10 W: 12 02 b. 26-2-05
From Stoke C.
Season	Club			Tot	
2022–23	Accrington S	0	0		
2023–24	Accrington S	0	0		
2024–25	Accrington S	0	0		

POPOOLA, Anjola (F) — 4 0
H: 6 1 W: 12 04 b. 8-11-06
Season	Club			Tot	
2023–24	Accrington S	2	0		
2024–25	Accrington S	2	0	4	0

QUIRK, Sebastian (M) — 41 0
H: 6 0 W: 11 00 b.Liverpool 5-12-01
From Everton.
Season	Club			Tot	
2022–23	Accrington S	13	0		
2023–24	Accrington S	12	0		
2024–25	Accrington S	16	0	41	0

RAWSON, Farrend (D) — 315 11
H: 6 1 W: 11 07 b.Nottingham 11-7-96
Season	Club			Tot	
2014–15	Derby Co	0	0		
2014–15	*Rotherham U*	4	0		
2015–16	Derby Co	0	0		
2015–16	*Rotherham U*	16	2	20	2
2016–17	*Coventry C*	14	0	14	0
2016–17	Derby Co	0	0		
2017–18	*Accrington S*	12	0		
2017–18	Forest Green R	18	1		
2018–19	Forest Green R	38	0		
2019–20	Forest Green R	30	3	86	4
2020–21	Mansfield T	43	0		
2021–22	Mansfield T	30	1	73	1
2022–23	Morecambe	41	1		
2023–24	Morecambe	31	2	72	3
2024–25	Accrington S	38	1	50	1

RICH-BAGHUELOU, Jay (D) — 33 2
H: 6 5 W: 14 02 b.Sydney 22-10-99
Internationals: Australia U23.
From Crystal Palace.
Season	Club			Tot	
2021–22	Accrington S	13	2		
2022–23	Accrington S	2	0		
2023–24	Accrington S	18	0		
2024–25	Accrington S	0	0	33	2

RIVA, Oliver (G) — 0 0
H: 6 4 b. 1-12-05
Season	Club			Tot	
2023–24	Accrington S	0	0		
2024–25	Accrington S	0	0		

ROGERSON, James (G) — 0 0
H: 6 0 W: 11 05 b. 30-6-04
Season	Club			Tot	
2024–25	Accrington S	0	0		

SMITH, Josh (D) — 0 0
b.Blackburn 17-9-05
Season	Club			Tot	
2024–25	Accrington S	0	0		

SOHNA, Sheikh (F) — 0 0
b. 2-3-07
Season	Club			Tot	
2024–25	Accrington S	0	0		

TRICKETT, Lewis (M) — 6 0
H: 5 10 W: 11 03 b.Blackburn 27-4-05
Internationals: Northern Ireland U18.
Season	Club			Tot	
2022–23	Accrington S	0	0		
2023–24	Accrington S	5	0		
2024–25	Accrington S	1	0	6	0

TUNSTALL, Finlay (M) — 0 0
b. 26-2-07
Season	Club			Tot	
2024–25	Accrington S	0	0		

WALTON, Tyler (M) 41 6
H: 6 1 W: 11 11 b. 23-9-98
2024–25 Accrington S 41 6 41 6

WARD, Benn (D) 24 1
H: 5 10 W: 12 04 b. 20-1-04
From Hastings U.
2023–24 Burnley 0 0
2023–24 *Swindon T* 3 0 3 0
2024–25 Burnley 0 0
2024–25 Accrington S 21 1 21 1

WHALLEY, Shaun (M) 397 60
H: 5 9 W: 10 08 b. Whiston 7-8-87
2004–05 Chester C 3 0 3 0
From Runcorn, Witton Alb.
2006–07 Accrington S 20 2
2007–08 Accrington S 31 3
From Wrexham, Droylsden, Hyde U, Southport.
2014–15 Luton T 18 3 18 3
2015–16 Shrewsbury T 24 6
2016–17 Shrewsbury T 32 3
2017–18 Shrewsbury T 44 8
2018–19 Shrewsbury T 32 2
2019–20 Shrewsbury T 23 2
2020–21 Shrewsbury T 38 9
2021–22 Shrewsbury T 21 4 214 34
2022–23 Accrington S 42 2
2023–24 Accrington S 36 7
2024–25 Accrington S 33 9 162 23

WILKINSON, Finlay (F) 0 0
H: 5 9 W: 11 00 b. 23-10-07
2024–25 Accrington S 0 0

WILLIAMS, Lennox (D) 0 0
b. 28-9-07
2024–25 Accrington S 0 0

WOODS, Ben (M) 77 11
H: 5 10 W: 11 09 b. Wigan 27-9-02
From Manchester U, Burnley.
2022–23 Inverness CT 7 0 7 0
2023–24 Accrington S 34 2
2024–25 Accrington S 36 9 70 11

WOODS, Josh (F) 76 7
H: 5 10 W: 11 00 b. 5-7-00
From Clay Brow.
2021–22 Accrington S 3 0
2022–23 Accrington S 10 1
2023–24 Accrington S 32 1
2024–25 Accrington S 31 5 76 7

Scholars
Al-Abbas, Yasin Sabah Husam; Alston, Rio Matthew; Bentley-Waite, Thomas Harvey; Broughton, Oliver Michael; Butler, Rohan William; De Melo Dias, Diego; Hanson, Jacob Oliver; Kemp, James Jeremy Harvey; Knight, Lucas Thomas Grant; Robinson, Malakai Bailey; Rogerson, James Gordon; Sohna, Sheikh Omar; Tunstall, Finlay James; Warbrick, Calum Hatton; Wilkinson, Finlay Joseph McEwan; Williams, Lennox Lloyd.

AFC WIMBLEDON (2)

AMISSAH, Reuben (D) 0 0
b. London --
2024–25 AFC Wimbledon 0 0

BALL, James (M) 101 10
H: 6 2 W: 12 08 b. Bolton 1-12-95
From Bolton W, Northwich Vic, Staybridge Celtic, Stockport Co.
2018–19 Stevenage 18 3 18 3
From Ebbsfleet U, Solihull Moors.
2021–22 Rochdale 11 3
2022–23 Rochdale 32 2 43 5
2023–24 AFC Wimbledon 25 1
2024–25 AFC Wimbledon 15 1 40 2

BILER, Huseyin (D) 30 0
H: 5 9 W: 10 03 b. Enfield 26-2-02
2019–20 AFC Wimbledon 0 0
2020–21 AFC Wimbledon 0 0
2021–22 AFC Wimbledon 0 0
2022–23 AFC Wimbledon 13 0
2023–24 AFC Wimbledon 11 0
2024–25 AFC Wimbledon 6 0 30 0

BROWNE, Marcus (M) 132 21
H: 5 10 W: 11 09 b. Tower Hamlets 18-12-97
2015–16 West Ham U 0 0
2016–17 West Ham U 0 0
2016–17 *Wigan Ath* 0 0
2017–18 West Ham U 0 0
2018–19 West Ham U 0 0
2018–19 *Oxford U* 34 6
2019–20 Middlesbrough 13 0
2019–20 *Oxford U* 11 4
2020–21 Middlesbrough 5 2
2021–22 Middlesbrough 0 0 18 2
2021–22 Oxford U 5 1

2022–23 Oxford U 34 4
2023–24 Oxford U 12 0 96 15
2024–25 AFC Wimbledon 18 4 18 4

BUGIEL, Omar (F) 173 30
H: 6 0 W: 12 02 b. Berlin 3-1-94
Internationals: Lebanon Full caps.
From Worthing.
2017–18 Forest Green R 19 3 19 3
From Bromley, Sutton U.
2021–22 Sutton U 39 4
2022–23 Sutton U 35 6 74 10
2023–24 AFC Wimbledon 41 13
2024–25 AFC Wimbledon 39 4 80 17

FOYO, Osman (M) 6 0
H: 6 0 W: 11 00 b. Utrecht 16-10-04
2024–25 Ipswich T 0 0
2024–25 AFC Wimbledon 6 0 6 0

HARBOTTLE, Riley (D) 69 6
H: 6 2 W: 12 08 b. Nottingham 26-9-00
2021–22 Nottingham F 0 0
2022–23 Nottingham F 0 0
2022–23 *Mansfield T* 32 6 32 6
2023–24 *Hibernian* 0 0
2023–24 *Colchester U* 12 0 12 0
2024–25 AFC Wimbledon 25 0 25 0

HEDGES, Harry (M) 0 0
H: 5 9 b. 17-3-08
2024–25 AFC Wimbledon 0 0

HIPPOLYTE, Myles (M) 270 27
H: 6 0 W: 11 09 b. Harrow 9-11-94
Internationals: Grenada Full caps.
2012–13 Brentford 0 0
From Southall, Tamworth, Hayes & Yeading U, Burnham.
2014–15 Livingston 33 2
2015–16 Livingston 17 1 50 3
2015–16 Falkirk 12 1
2016–17 Falkirk 30 7
2017–18 Falkirk 10 2 52 10
2017–18 St Mirren 8 1 8 1
2018–19 Dunfermline Ath 31 2 31 2
From Yeovil T.
2020–21 Scunthorpe U 26 1
2021–22 Scunthorpe U 22 4 48 5
2022–23 Stockport Co 44 4
2023–24 Stockport Co 18 0 62 4
2024–25 AFC Wimbledon 19 2 19 2

HUTCHINSON, Sam (M) 254 8
H: 6 0 W: 11 07 b. Windsor 3-8-89
Internationals: England U18, U19.
2006–07 Chelsea 1 0
2007–08 Chelsea 0 0
2008–09 Chelsea 0 0
2009–10 Chelsea 2 0
2010–11 Chelsea 0 0
2011–12 Chelsea 2 0
2012–13 Chelsea 0 0
2012–13 *Nottingham F* 9 1 9 1
2013–14 Chelsea 0 0 5 0
2013–14 *Vitesse* 1 0 1 0
2013–14 Sheffield Wed 10 1
2014–15 Sheffield Wed 20 0
2015–16 Sheffield Wed 25 0
2016–17 Sheffield Wed 33 2
2017–18 Sheffield Wed 8 0
2018–19 Sheffield Wed 24 0
2019–20 Sheffield Wed 23 1
2020–21 Pafos 5 0 5 0
2020–21 Sheffield Wed 22 1
2021–22 Sheffield Wed 28 1 193 6
2022–23 Reading 11 0
2023–24 Reading 12 0 23 0
2024–25 AFC Wimbledon 18 1 18 1

JENNINGS, Kai (M) 0 0
b. Kingston upon Thames --
2023–24 AFC Wimbledon 0 0
2024–25 AFC Wimbledon 0 0

JOHNSON, Ryan (D) 115 1
H: 6 2 W: 13 05 b. Birmingham 2-10-96
Internationals: Northern Ireland U21.
2013–14 Stevenage 1 0
2014–15 Stevenage 4 0
2015–16 Stevenage 7 0
2016–17 Stevenage 0 0
2017–18 Stevenage 1 0 13 0
From Kidderminster H, Rushall Olympic, Hartlepool U.
2021–22 Port Vale 4 0 4 0
2022–23 Stockport Co 27 0 27 0
2023–24 Stockport Co 31 1
2024–25 AFC Wimbledon 40 0 71 1

JUNIOR NKENG, Robert (M) 0 0
H: 5 6 b. London 14-3-07
2023–24 AFC Wimbledon 0 0
2024–25 AFC Wimbledon 0 0

KELLY, Josh (F) 57 4
H: 5 9 W: 11 05 b. Windsor 19-12-98
Internationals: Northern Ireland U21.
2023–24 AFC Wimbledon 17 2
2024–25 AFC Wimbledon 40 2 57 4

LEACH, Edward (F)
b. 1-3-07
2023–24 AFC Wimbledon 0 0
2024–25 AFC Wimbledon 0 0

LEWIS, Joe (D) 83 5
H: 6 2 W: 13 05 b. Neath 20-9-99
From Swansea C, Torquay U.
2022–23 Stockport Co 16 0
2023–24 Stockport Co 0 0 16 0
2023–24 AFC Wimbledon 31 4
2024–25 AFC Wimbledon 36 1 67 5

LOCK, Paris (F) 0 0
H: 5 11 W: 11 11 b. London 18-10-04
2024–25 AFC Wimbledon 0 0

MAYCOCK, Callum (D) 58 3
H: 6 0 W: 11 03 b. Birmingham 23-12-97
Internationals: England C.
2016–17 Coventry C 3 0
2017–18 Coventry C 1 0
2018–19 Coventry C 0 0
2018–19 *Macclesfield T* 27 0 27 0
2019–20 Coventry C 0 0 4 0
From Solihull Moors.
2024–25 AFC Wimbledon 27 3 27 3

McLEAN, Ryan (F) 8 0
H: 5 9 W: 11 00 b. 3-5-00
2023–24 AFC Wimbledon 8 0
2024–25 AFC Wimbledon 0 0 8 0

MORAN, Riley (M) 0 0
2024–25 AFC Wimbledon 0 0

NEUFVILLE, Josh (F) 114 7
H: 6 0 W: 11 09 b. Luton 22-3-01
2017–18 Luton T 0 0
2018–19 Luton T 0 0
2019–20 Luton T 0 0
2020–21 Luton T 0 0
2021–22 Luton T 0 0
2022–23 Luton T 0 0
2022–23 *Sutton U* 30 2 30 2
2023–24 AFC Wimbledon 38 1
2024–25 AFC Wimbledon 46 4 84 5

O'TOOLE, John (M) 479 66
H: 6 2 W: 12 13 b. Harrow 30-9-88
Internationals: Republic of Ireland U21.
2007–08 Watford 35 3
2008–09 Watford 22 7
2008–09 *Sheffield U* 9 1 9 1
2009–10 Watford 0 0 57 10
2009–10 Colchester U 31 2
2010–11 Colchester U 11 0
2011–12 Colchester U 15 0
2012–13 Colchester U 15 0 72 2
2012–13 *Bristol R* 18 3
2013–14 Bristol R 41 13 59 16
2014–15 Northampton T 35 2
2014–15 *Southend U* 2 0 2 0
2015–16 Northampton T 38 12
2016–17 Northampton T 40 10
2017–18 Northampton T 29 6
2018–19 Northampton T 31 3 173 33
2019–20 Burton Alb 25 0
2020–21 Burton Alb 16 1 41 1
2021–22 Mansfield T 27 2
2022–23 Mansfield T 16 0
2023–24 Mansfield T 2 0 45 2
2023–24 *AFC Wimbledon* 14 0
2024–25 AFC Wimbledon 7 1 21 1

OGUNDERE, Isaac (D) 85 0
H: 5 10 W: 10 12 b. Hilingdon 6-11-02
2022–23 AFC Wimbledon 15 0
2023–24 AFC Wimbledon 31 0
2024–25 AFC Wimbledon 39 0 85 0

REEVES, Jake (M) 336 16
H: 5 8 W: 11 00 b. Lewisham 30-6-93
2010–11 Brentford 1 0
2011–12 Brentford 8 0
2012–13 Brentford 6 0
2012–13 *AFC Wimbledon* 5 0
2013–14 Brentford 20 0 35 0
2014–15 Swindon T 10 1 10 1
2014–15 AFC Wimbledon 23 2
2015–16 AFC Wimbledon 40 1
2016–17 AFC Wimbledon 46 1
2017–18 Bradford C 25 0
2018–19 Bradford C 0 0
2019–20 Bradford C 18 1 43 1
From Notts Co.
2021–22 Stevenage 27 2
2022–23 Stevenage 41 4 68 6
2023–24 Stevenage 38 2
2024–25 AFC Wimbledon 28 2 180 8

SASU, Aron (F)   42 0
H: 6 1   W: 12 08   b.Croyden 5-3-05

2021–22	AFC Wimbledon	0	0
2022–23	AFC Wimbledon	0	0
2023–24	AFC Wimbledon	20	0
2024–25	AFC Wimbledon	22	0 42 0

SIDWELL, Harry (M)   1 0
H: 6 0   b.Basingstoke 31-8-06

2024–25	AFC Wimbledon	1	0 1 0

STEVENS, Mathew (F)   204 58
H: 5 11   W: 11 09   b.Frimley 12-2-98

2015–16	Barnet	10	1 10 1
2016–17	Peterborough U	1	0
2017–18	Peterborough U	0	0
2018–19	Peterborough U	3	0 4 0
2019–20	Forest Green R	29	4
2020–21	Forest Green R	10	2
2020–21	*Stevenage*	18	1 18 1
2021–22	Forest Green R	37	23
2022–23	Forest Green R	5	0
2022–23	*Walsall*	17	1 17 1
2023–24	Forest Green R	28	9 109 38
2024–25	AFC Wimbledon	46	17 46 17

SUTCLIFFE, Ethan (D)   1 0
H: 6 2   W: 12 13   b.Lambeth 20-2-04

2020–21	AFC Wimbledon	0	0
2021–22	AFC Wimbledon	0	0
2022–23	AFC Wimbledon	0	0
2023–24	AFC Wimbledon	1	0
2024–25	AFC Wimbledon	0	0 1 0

TILLEY, James (F)   207 24
H: 5 6   W: 9 04   b.Billingshurst 13-6-98

2014–15	Brighton & HA	1	0
2015–16	Brighton & HA	0	0
2016–17	Brighton & HA	0	0
2017–18	Brighton & HA	0	0
2018–19	Brighton & HA	0	0
2019	*Cork C*	19	0 19 0
2019–20	Brighton & HA	0	0 1 0
2019–20	Grimsby T	10	0
2020–21	Grimsby T	14	2 24 2
2020–21	Crawley T	18	3
2021–22	Crawley T	30	3
2022–23	Crawley T	35	5 83 11
2023–24	AFC Wimbledon	39	7
2024–25	AFC Wimbledon	41	4 80 11

WARD, Lewis (G)   63 0
H: 6 5   W: 12 11   b.5-3-97
Internationals: England U16.

2014–15	Reading	0	0
2015–16	Reading	0	0
2016–17	Reading	0	0
2017–18	Reading	0	0
2018–19	Reading	0	0
2018–19	*Northampton T*	0	0
2018–19	*Forest Green R*	12	0 12 0
2019–20	Exeter C	20	0
2020–21	Exeter C	8	0 28 0
2020–21	Portsmouth	0	0
2021–22	Swindon T	9	0
2022–23	Swindon T	0	0
2022–23	*Sutton U*	9	0 9 0
2023–24	Swindon T	5	0 14 0
2023–24	Charlton Ath	0	0
2024–25	AFC Wimbledon	0	0

WILLIAMS, Morgan (M)   3 0
H: 6 2   W: 11 09   b.Aylesbury 11-12-04
Internationals: Wales U16, U18, U19.

2021–22	AFC Wimbledon	0	0
2022–23	AFC Wimbledon	1	0
2023–24	AFC Wimbledon	2	0
2024–25	AFC Wimbledon	0	0 3 0

YOUNG, Leo (D)   0 0
H: 6 2   b.London 26-11-05

2024–25	AFC Wimbledon	0	0

Scholars
Cavvalhu-Nvrris, Tom Manny; Cotton, Bailey Joseph; Djedje, Eterne El-Elyon; Forzah Nkeng, Robert Junior; Goma Weinberg, Sam; Harris, Connor David; Hedges, Harry Robert; Horan, Riley; Kirby, Joe Paul; Lawrence, Jake Matthew; McGrath, Ethan Michael; McKenzie, Kai Richard; Moore, Kiayon Alexander Naeem; Sealey, Amaari Kacper; Soukou, Oro Shaun.

ARSENAL (3)

ALENCAR, Marquinhos (F)   81 2
H: 5 9   W: 13 05   b.Sao Paulo 7-4-03
Internationals: Brazil U16, U17, U20, U23.

2021	Sao Paulo	21	0
2022	Sao Paulo	1	0 22 0
2022–23	Arsenal	1	0
2022–23	*Norwich C*	11	1 11 1
2023–24	Arsenal	0	0
2023–24	*Nantes*	7	0 7 0
2024	*Fluminense*	23	0 23 0
2024–25	Arsenal	0	0 1 0
2025	*Cruzeiro*	17	1 17 1

BANDEIRA, Mauro (M)   9 0
H: 5 10   b.Loures 18-11-03
From QPR.

2022–23	Arsenal	0	0
2023–24	Arsenal	0	0
2023–24	*Colchester U*	9	0 9 0
2024–25	Arsenal	0	0

BUTLER-OYEDEJI, Nathan (M)   25 0
H: 5 10   W: 10 12   b.London 4-1-03

2022–23	Arsenal	0	0
2022–23	*Accrington S*	11	0 11 0
2023–24	Arsenal	0	0
2023–24	*Cheltenham T*	13	0 13 0
2024–25	Arsenal	1	0

CALAFIORI, Riccardo (D)   88 4
H: 6 2   W: 13 08   b.Rome 19-5-02
Internationals: Italy U16, U17, U19, U21, Full caps.

2019–20	Roma	1	0
2020–21	Roma	3	0
2021–22	Roma	6	0 10 0
2021–22	Genoa	3	0 3 0
2022–23	FC Basel	23	0
2023–24	FC Basel	3	0 26 0
2023–24	Bologna	30	2 30 2
2024–25	Arsenal	19	2 19 2

CLARKE, Brayden (D)   0 0
b.Oldbury 3-7-07
Internationals: Wales U16, U17.

GABRIEL, Magalhaes (D)   222 20
H: 6 3   W: 12 04   b.Sao Paulo 19-12-97
Internationals: Brazil U20, U23, Full caps.

2016	Avai	21	1 21 1
2016–17	Lille	1	0
2017–18	Lille	0	0
2017–18	*Troyes*	1	0 1 0
2017–18	*Dinamo Zagreb*	1	0 1 0
2018–19	Lille	14	1
2019–20	Lille	24	1
2020–21	Lille	0	0 39 2
2020–21	Arsenal	23	2
2021–22	Arsenal	35	5
2022–23	Arsenal	38	3
2023–24	Arsenal	36	4
2024–25	Arsenal	28	3 160 17

GABRIEL JESUS, Fernando (F)   276 92
H: 5 9   W: 11 07   b.Sao Paulo 3-4-97
Internationals: Brazil U20, U23, Full caps.

2015	Palmeiras	2	0
2016	Palmeiras	27	12 47 16
2016–17	Manchester C	10	7
2017–18	Manchester C	29	13
2018–19	Manchester C	29	7
2019–20	Manchester C	34	14
2020–21	Manchester C	29	9
2021–22	Manchester C	28	8 159 58
2022–23	Arsenal	26	11
2023–24	Arsenal	27	4
2024–25	Arsenal	17	3 70 18

GOWER, Jimi (M)   0 0
H: 5 11   W: 11 00   b.London 1-10-04

2023–24	Arsenal	0	0
2024–25	Arsenal	0	0

HAVERTZ, Kai (M)   269 77
H: 6 2   W: 11 11   b.Aachen 11-6-99
Internationals: Germany U16, U17, U19, Full caps.

2016–17	Bayer Leverkusen	24	4
2017–18	Bayer Leverkusen	30	3
2018–19	Bayer Leverkusen	34	17
2019–20	Bayer Leverkusen	30	12
2020–21	Bayer Leverkusen	0	0 118 36
2020–21	Chelsea	27	4
2021–22	Chelsea	29	8
2022–23	Chelsea	35	7 91 19
2023–24	Arsenal	37	13
2024–25	Arsenal	23	9 60 22

HEIN, Karl Jakob (G)   36 0
H: 6 4   W: 12 02   b.Polva 13-4-02
Internationals: Estonia U16, U17, U19, U21, Full caps.
From Nomme U.

2019–20	Arsenal	0	0
2020–21	Arsenal	0	0
2021–22	Arsenal	0	0
2021–22	*Reading*	5	0 5 0
2022–23	Arsenal	0	0
2023–24	Arsenal	0	0
2024–25	Arsenal	0	0
2024–25	*Valladolid*	31	0 31 0

HENRY-FRANCIS, Jack (M)   11 0
H: 5 11   W: 11 00   b.London 23-9-03
Internationals: Republic of Ireland U19, U21.

2021–22	Arsenal	0	0
2022–23	Arsenal	0	0
2023–24	Arsenal	0	0
2024	*Sligo R*	11	0 11 0
2024–25	Arsenal	0	0
2024–25	*Sligo Rovers*	0	0

JORGINHO, Filho Jorge (M)   449 35
H: 5 11   W: 11 03   b.Imbituba 20-12-91
Internationals: Italy Full caps.

2010–11	Verona	0	0
2010–11	*Sambonifacese*	31	1 31 1
2011–12	Verona	30	2
2012–13	Verona	41	2
2013–14	Verona	18	7 89 11
2013–14	Napoli	15	0
2014–15	Napoli	23	0
2015–16	Napoli	35	0
2016–17	Napoli	27	0
2017–18	Napoli	33	2 133 2
2018–19	Chelsea	37	2
2019–20	Chelsea	31	4
2020–21	Chelsea	28	7
2021–22	Chelsea	29	6
2022–23	Chelsea	18	2 143 21
2022–23	Arsenal	14	0
2023–24	Arsenal	24	0
2024–25	Arsenal	15	0 53 0

KABIA, Ismeal (F)   0 0
H: 5 9   W: 10 10   b.Hengelo 10-12-05

2024–25	Arsenal	0	0

KACURRI, Maldini (D)   3 0
H: 6 2   W: 13 03   b.Lewisham 4-11-05
Internationals: Albania U17, U19.

2024–25	Arsenal	0	0
2024–25	*Bromley*	3	0 3 0

KIWIOR, Jakub (D)   145 7
H: 6 2   W: 9 11   b.Tychy 15-2-00
Internationals: Poland U16, U17, U18, U19, U20, U21, Full caps.
From Anderlecht.

2018–19	Zeleziame Podbrezova	14	1
2019–20	Zeleziame Podbrezova	2	0 16 1
2019–20	Zilina	13	0
2020–21	Zilina	30	2
2021–22	Zilina	3	1 46 3
2021–22	Spezia	22	0
2022–23	Spezia	17	0 39 0
2023–24	Arsenal	7	1
2023–24	Arsenal	20	1
2024–25	Arsenal	17	1 44 3

LEWIS-SKELLY, Myles (M)   23 1
H: 5 10   W: 11 05   b.Islington 26-9-06
Internationals: England U16, U17, U18, U19, Full caps.

2022–23	Arsenal	0	0
2023–24	Arsenal	0	0
2024–25	Arsenal	23	1 23 1

MARTINELLI, Gabriel (F)   161 40
H: 5 11   W: 11 11   b.Guarulhos 18-6-01
Internationals: Brazil U23, Full caps.
From Ituano.

2019–20	Arsenal	14	3
2020–21	Arsenal	14	2
2021–22	Arsenal	29	6
2022–23	Arsenal	36	15
2023–24	Arsenal	35	6
2024–25	Arsenal	33	8 161 40

MERINO, Mikel (M)   317 36
H: 6 2   W: 12 04   b.Pamplona 22-6-96
Internationals: Spain U19, U21, U23, Full caps.

2013–14	Osasuna	0	0
2014–15	Osasuna	29	1
2015–16	Osasuna	38	7 67 8
2016–17	Borussia Dortmund	8	0
2017–18	Borussia Dortmund	0	0 8 0
2017–18	Newcastle U	24	1 24 1
2018–19	Real Sociedad	29	3
2019–20	Real Sociedad	36	5
2020–21	Real Sociedad	26	2
2021–22	Real Sociedad	34	3
2022–23	Real Sociedad	33	2
2023–24	Real Sociedad	32	5 190 20
2024–25	Arsenal	28	7 28 7

MONLOUIS, Zane (D)   1 0
H: 6 1   W: 11 11   b.Lewisham 16-10-03
Internationals: England U17.

2023–24	Arsenal	0	0
2023–24	*Reading*	1	0 1 0
2024–25	Arsenal	0	0

Transferred to Toronto, February 2025.

NELSON, Reiss (F)   105 14
H: 5 9   W: 11 00   b.Lambeth 10-12-99
Internationals: England U16, U17, U18, U19, U20, U21.
From Lewisham Bor.

2017–18	Arsenal	3	0
2018–19	Arsenal	0	0
2018–19	*TSG 1899 Hoffenheim*	23	7 23 7
2019–20	Arsenal	17	1

2020–21	Arsenal	2	0		
2021–22	Arsenal	1	0		
2021–22	*Feyenoord*	21	2	21	2
2022–23	Arsenal	11	3		
2023–24	Arsenal	15	0		
2024–25	Arsenal	1	0	50	4
2024–25	Fulham	11	1	11	1

NICHOLS, Josh (D) 0 0
H: 5 5 W: 8 11 b.London 26-7-06

| 2024–25 | Arsenal | 0 | 0 |

NWANERI, Ethan (F) 28 4
H: 5 5 W: 11 05 b.London 21-3-07
Internationals: England U16, U17, U19, U21.

2022–23	Arsenal	1	0		
2023–24	Arsenal	1	0		
2024–25	Arsenal	26	4	28	4

ODEGAARD, Martin (M) 283 54
H: 5 7 W: 9 06 b.Drammen 17-12-98
Internationals: Norway U16, U17, U21, Full caps.

2014	Stromsgodset	23	5	23	5
2014–15	Real Madrid	1	0		
2015–16	Real Madrid	0	0		
2016–17	Real Madrid	0	0		
2016–17	*Heerenveen*	14	1		
2017–18	Real Madrid	0	0		
2017–18	*Heerenveen*	24	2	38	3
2018–19	Real Madrid	0	0		
2018–19	Vitesse	31	8	31	8
2019–20	Real Madrid	0	0		
2019–20	*Real Sociedad*	31	4	31	4
2020–21	Real Madrid	7	0	8	0
2020–21	*Arsenal*	14	1		
2021–22	Arsenal	36	7		
2022–23	Arsenal	37	15		
2023–24	Arsenal	35	8		
2024–25	Arsenal	30	3	152	34

OULAD M'HAND, Salah (M) 19 3
H: 5 10 W: 10 12 b.Den Haag 20-8-03
Internationals: Netherlands U17.
From Feyenoord.

2020–21	Arsenal	0	0		
2021–22	Arsenal	0	0		
2022–23	Arsenal	0	0		
2022–23	*Hull C*	0	0		
2023–24	Arsenal	0	0		
2023–24	*Den Bosch*	19	3	19	3
2024–25	Arsenal	0	0		

PORTER, Jack (G) 0 0
H: 6 1 W: 11 11 b.Harlow 15-7-08
Internationals: England U16, U17.

| 2024–25 | Arsenal | 0 | 0 |

RAYA, David (G) 318 0
H: 6 0 W: 12 08 b.Barcelona 15-9-95
Internationals: Spain Full caps.

2013–14	Blackburn R	0	0		
2014–15	Blackburn R	2	0		
2015–16	Blackburn R	5	0		
2016–17	Blackburn R	5	0		
2017–18	Blackburn R	45	0		
2018–19	Blackburn R	41	0	98	0
2019–20	Brentford	46	0		
2020–21	Brentford	42	0		
2021–22	Brentford	24	0		
2022–23	Brentford	38	0		
2023–24	Brentford	0	0	150	0
2023–24	*Arsenal*	32	0		
2024–25	Arsenal	38	0	70	0

RICE, Declan (M) 277 21
H: 6 1 W: 12 00 b.Kingston-upon-Thames 14-1-99
Internationals: Republic of Ireland U16, U17, U19, U21, Full caps.
From Chelsea.

2016–17	West Ham U	1	0		
2017–18	West Ham U	26	0		
2018–19	West Ham U	34	2		
2019–20	West Ham U	38	1		
2020–21	West Ham U	32	2		
2021–22	West Ham U	36	1		
2022–23	West Ham U	37	4	204	10
2023–24	Arsenal	38	7		
2024–25	Arsenal	35	4	73	11

ROJAS, Alexei (G) 0 0
H: 6 2 W: 12 02 b.Basildon 28-9-05

| 2024–25 | Arsenal | 0 | 0 |

ROSIAK, Michal (M) 0 0
H: 5 9 W: 9 13 b.Bialogard 12-10-05
Internationals: Poland U18, U19, U21.

| 2024–25 | Arsenal | 0 | 0 |

SAGOE JUNIOR, Charles (M) 15 0
H: 5 7 W: 10 03 b.London 24-7-04

2022–23	Arsenal	0	0		
2023–24	Arsenal	0	0		
2023–24	*Swansea C*	2	0	2	0
2024–25	Arsenal	0	0		
2024–25	*Shrewsbury T*	13	0	13	0

SAKA, Bukayo (M) 195 53
H: 5 10 W: 10 03 b.Ealing 5-9-01
Internationals: England U16, U17, U18, U19, U21, Full caps.

2018–19	Arsenal	1	0		
2019–20	Arsenal	26	1		
2020–21	Arsenal	32	5		
2021–22	Arsenal	38	11		
2022–23	Arsenal	38	14		
2023–24	Arsenal	35	16		
2024–25	Arsenal	25	6	195	53

SALIBA, William Alain Andre Gabriel (D) 184 7
H: 6 4 W: 13 05 b.Bondy 24-3-01
Internationals: France U16, U17, U18, U19, U20, U21, Full caps.

2018–19	Saint-Etienne	16	0		
2019–20	Arsenal	0	0		
2019–20	*Saint-Etienne*	12	0	28	0
2020–21	Arsenal	0	0		
2020–21	*Nice*	20	1	20	1
2021–22	Arsenal	0	0		
2021–22	*Marseille*	36	0	36	0
2022–23	Arsenal	27	2		
2023–24	Arsenal	38	2		
2024–25	Arsenal	35	2	100	6

SAMBI LOKONGA, Albert-Mboyo (M) 142 4
H: 5 11 W: 11 03 b.Verviers 22-10-99
Internationals: Belgium U17, U19, U21, Full caps.

2017–18	Anderlecht	7	0		
2018–19	Anderlecht	6	0		
2019–20	Anderlecht	23	0		
2020–21	Anderlecht	33	3		
2021–22	Anderlecht	0	0	69	3
2021–22	*Arsenal*	19	0		
2022–23	Arsenal	6	0		
2022–23	*Crystal Palace*	9	0	9	0
2023–24	Arsenal	0	0		
2023–24	*Luton T*	17	1	17	1
2024–25	Arsenal	0	0	25	0
2024–25	*Sevilla*	22	0	22	0

SETFORD, Tommy (G) 0 0
H: 6 1 W: 12 00 b.Haarlem 13-3-06
Internationals: England U16, U17, U18, U19.

| 2024–25 | Arsenal | 0 | 0 |

THOMAS, Partey (M) 327 30
H: 6 1 W: 11 07 b.Odumase Krobo 13-6-93
Internationals: Ghana Full caps.

2011–12	Atletico Madrid	0	0		
2012–13	Atletico Madrid	0	0		
2013–14	Atletico Madrid	0	0		
2013–14	*Mallorca*	37	5	37	5
2014–15	Atletico Madrid	0	0		
2014–15	*Almeria*	31	4	31	4
2015–16	Atletico Madrid	13	2		
2016–17	Atletico Madrid	16	1		
2017–18	Atletico Madrid	33	3		
2018–19	Atletico Madrid	32	3		
2019–20	Atletico Madrid	35	3		
2020–21	Atletico Madrid	0	0	129	12
2020–21	*Arsenal*	24	0		
2021–22	Arsenal	24	2		
2022–23	Arsenal	33	3		
2023–24	Arsenal	14	0		
2024–25	Arsenal	35	4	130	9

TIERNEY, Kieran (D) 226 9
H: 5 10 W: 11 00 b.Douglas 5-6-97
Internationals: Scotland U18, U19, Full caps.

2014–15	Celtic	23	1		
2015–16	Celtic	24	1		
2016–17	Celtic	32	3		
2017–18	Celtic	32	3		
2018–19	Celtic	21	0	102	5
2019–20	Arsenal	15	1		
2020–21	Arsenal	27	1		
2021–22	Arsenal	22	1		
2022–23	Arsenal	27	0		
2023–24	Arsenal	0	0		
2023–24	*Real Sociedad*	20	0	20	0
2024–25	Arsenal	13	1	104	4

TIMBER, Jurrien (D) 117 7
H: 5 10 W: 12 02 b.Utrecht 17-6-01
Internationals: Netherlands U16, U17, U19, U21, Full caps.

2018–19	Ajax	0	0		
2019–20	Ajax	1	0		
2020–21	Ajax	20	1		
2021–22	Ajax	30	3		
2022–23	Ajax	34	2	85	6
2023–24	Arsenal	2	0		
2024–25	Arsenal	30	1	32	1

TOMIYASU, Takehiro (D) 209 7
H: 6 2 W: 13 03 b.Fukuoka 5-11-98
Internationals: Japan U16, U20, U23, Full caps.

2015	Avispa Fukuoka	0	0		
2016	Avispa Fukuoka	10	0		
2017	Avispa Fukuoka	35	1	45	1
2017–18	Sint-Truidense	1	0		
2018–19	Sint-Truidense	37	1	38	1
2019–20	Bologna	29	1		
2020–21	Bologna	31	2		
2021–22	Bologna	1	0	61	3
2021–22	*Arsenal*	21	0		
2022–23	Arsenal	21	0		
2023–24	Arsenal	22	2		
2024–25	Arsenal	1	0	65	2

TROSSARD, Leandro (M) 380 107
H: 5 8 W: 9 08 b.Waterschei 4-12-94
Internationals: Belgium U16, U17, U18, U19, U21, Full caps.

2011–12	Genk	1	0		
2012–13	Genk	0	0		
2012–13	*Lommel U*	12	7		
2013–14	Genk	0	0		
2013–14	*Westerlo*	17	3	17	3
2014–15	Genk	0	0		
2014–15	*Lommel U*	30	16	42	23
2015–16	Genk	0	0		
2015–16	*OH Leuven*	30	8	30	8
2016–17	Genk	31	6		
2017–18	Genk	17	7		
2018–19	Genk	34	14	83	27
2019–20	Brighton & HA	31	5		
2020–21	Brighton & HA	35	5		
2021–22	Brighton & HA	34	8		
2022–23	Brighton & HA	16	7	116	25
2022–23	*Arsenal*	20	1		
2023–24	Arsenal	34	12		
2024–25	Arsenal	38	8	92	21

VIEIRA, Fabio (M) 113 14
H: 5 9 W: 9 13 b.Saint Maria 30-5-00
Internationals: Portugal U18, U19, U20, U21.

2019–20	Porto	8	2		
2020–21	Porto	19	0		
2021–22	Porto	27	6		
2022–23	Arsenal	22	1		
2023–24	Arsenal	11	1		
2024–25	Arsenal	0	0	33	2
2024–25	*Porto*	26	4	80	12

WHITE, Ben (D) 263 9
H: 6 0 W: 12 04 b.Poole 8-11-97
Internationals: England Full caps.

2016–17	Brighton & HA	0	0		
2017–18	Brighton & HA	0	0		
2017–18	*Newport Co*	42	1	42	1
2018–19	Brighton & HA	0	0		
2018–19	*Peterborough U*	15	1	15	1
2019–20	Brighton & HA	0	0		
2019–20	*Leeds U*	46	1	46	1
2020–21	Brighton & HA	36	0	36	0
2021–22	Arsenal	32	0		
2022–23	Arsenal	38	2		
2023–24	Arsenal	37	4		
2024–25	Arsenal	17	0	124	6

ZINCHENKO, Alexander (D) 188 4
H: 5 9 W: 9 08 b.Radomyshl 15-12-96
Internationals: Ukraine U16, U17, U18, U19, U21, Full caps.

2014–15	Ufa	7	0		
2015–16	Ufa	24	2	31	2
2016–17	Manchester C	0	0		
2016–17	*PSV Eindhoven*	12	0	12	0
2017–18	Manchester C	8	0		
2018–19	Manchester C	14	0		
2019–20	Manchester C	20	0		
2020–21	Manchester C	20	0		
2021–22	Manchester C	15	0	76	0
2022–23	Arsenal	27	1		
2023–24	Arsenal	27	1		
2024–25	Arsenal	15	0	69	2

Players retained or with offer of contract
Dudziak, Harrison James Edward; Ferdinand, Sebastian Reece; Julienne, Theo Devon; Kamara, Osman; Nygaard, Lucas Martin; O'Neill, Ceadach Liam.

Scholars
Casey, Daniel John; Chapman, Samuel Thomas; Chinedu, Samuel Onyekachukwu; Copley, Louie George; Harriman-Annous, Andre Ryan; Ibrahim, Ifeoluwa David; Ismail, Cam'Ron Harry; Lannin-Sweet, William Robert; Marciniak, Aleksander Dominik; Ogunnaike, Oluwatoyosi Joshua Adewale; Oyetunde, Daniel Olaniyi Oluwaseun; Porter, Jack Kenny; Ranson, Khari Bolaji Mawuvi; Zecevic John, Louis Alexander.

ASTON VILLA (4)

ALEX MORENO, Lopera (M) 376 21
H: 5 10 W: 10 12 b.Sant Sadurni d'Anoia 8-6-93

2012–13	Llagostera	27	2	27	2
2013–14	Mallorca	31	2	31	2
2014–15	Rayo Vallecano	11	0		
2015–16	Rayo Vallecano	0	0		

2015–16 *Elche* 40 2 **40 2**
2016–17 Rayo Vallecano 37 4
2017–18 Rayo Vallecano 40 3
2018–19 Rayo Vallecano 36 1
2019–20 Rayo Vallecano 0 0 **124 8**
2019–20 Real Betis 31 0
2020–21 Real Betis 23 0
2021–22 Real Betis 30 5
2022–23 Real Betis 15 0 **99 5**
2022–23 Aston Villa 19 0
2023–24 Aston Villa 21 2
2024–25 Aston Villa 0 0 **40 2**
2024–25 *Nottingham F* 15 0 **15 0**

ASENSIO, Marco (M) 325 57
H: 5 10 W: 11 00 b.Palma 21-1-96
Internationals: Spain U16, U19, U21, U23, Full caps.
2013–14 Real Mallorca 20 1
2014–15 Real Mallorca 36 6
2015–16 Real Mallorca 0 0 **56 7**
2015–16 *Espanyol* 34 4 **34 4**
2016–17 Real Madrid 23 3
2017–18 Real Madrid 32 6
2018–19 Real Madrid 30 1
2019–20 Real Madrid 9 3
2020–21 Real Madrid 35 5
2021–22 Real Madrid 31 10
2022–23 Real Madrid 31 9 **191 37**
2023–24 Paris Saint-Germain 19 4
2024–25 Paris Saint-Germain 12 2 **31 6**
On loan from Paris Saint-Germain.
2024–25 Aston Villa 13 3 **13 3**

BAILEY, Leon (F) 285 52
H: 5 11 W: 11 00 b.Kingston 9-8-97
Internationals: Jamaica U23, Full caps.
From Trencin.
2015–16 Genk 37 6
2016–17 Genk 19 2 **56 8**
2016–17 Bayer Leverkusen 8 0
2017–18 Bayer Leverkusen 30 9
2018–19 Bayer Leverkusen 29 5
2019–20 Bayer Leverkusen 22 5
2020–21 Bayer Leverkusen 30 9 **119 28**
2021–22 Aston Villa 18 1
2022–23 Aston Villa 33 4
2023–24 Aston Villa 35 10
2024–25 Aston Villa 24 1 **110 16**

BARKLEY, Ross (M) 328 45
H: 6 1 W: 12 00 b.Liverpool 5-12-93
Internationals: England U16, U17, U19, U20, U21, Full caps.
2010–11 Everton 0 0
2011–12 Everton 6 0
2012–13 Everton 7 0
2012–13 *Sheffield Wed* 13 4 **13 4**
2012–13 *Leeds U* 4 0 **4 0**
2013–14 Everton 34 6
2014–15 Everton 29 2
2015–16 Everton 38 8
2016–17 Everton 36 5
2017–18 Everton 0 0 **150 21**
2017–18 Chelsea 2 0
2018–19 Chelsea 27 3
2019–20 Chelsea 21 1
2020–21 Chelsea 2 0
2020–21 *Aston Villa* 24 3
2021–22 Chelsea 6 1 **58 5**
2022–23 Nice 27 4 **27 4**
2023–24 Luton T 32 5 **32 5**
2024–25 Aston Villa 20 3 **44 6**

BARRENECHEA, Enzo (M) 69 1
H: 6 1 W: 12 04 b.Villa Maria 25-1-01
2020–21 Juventus 0 0
2021–22 Juventus 0 0
2022–23 Juventus 3 0
2023–24 Juventus 0 0 **3 0**
2023–24 *Frosinone* 36 0 **36 0**
2024–25 Aston Villa 0 0
2024–25 *Valencia* 30 1 **30 1**

BARRY, Louie (F) 104 33
H: 5 7 W: 10 03 b.Aston 21-6-03
Internationals: Republic of Ireland U16. England U16, U17, U18.
From WBA, Barcelona.
2020–21 Aston Villa 0 0
2021–22 Aston Villa 0 0
2021–22 *Ipswich T* 2 0 **2 0**
2021–22 *Swindon T* 14 6 **14 6**
2022–23 Aston Villa 0 0
2022–23 *Milton Keynes D* 22 1 **22 1**
2022–23 *Salford C* 19 2 **19 2**
2023–24 Aston Villa 0 0
2023–24 *Stockport Co* 20 9
2024–25 Aston Villa 0 0
2024–25 *Stockport Co* 23 15 **43 24**
2024–25 *Hull C* 4 0 **4 0**

BOGARDE, Lamar (M) 40 0
H: 6 0 W: 11 14 b.Rotterdam 5-1-04
Internationals: Netherlands U16, U18, U20, U21.
From Feyenoord.
2020–21 Aston Villa 0 0
2021–22 Aston Villa 0 0
2022–23 Aston Villa 0 0
2022–23 *Bristol R* 18 0
2023–24 Aston Villa 0 0
2023–24 *Bristol R* 14 0 **32 0**
2024–25 Aston Villa 8 0 **8 0**

BORLAND, Aidan (M) 0 0
H: 5 10 W: 10 03 b.Glasgow 25-4-07
Internationals: Scotland U16, U17, U19.
2024–25 Aston Villa 0 0

BROGGIO, Ben (M) 0 0
H: 5 11 W: 11 11 b.Sutton Coldfield 29-1-07
Internationals: England U16, U18.
2023–24 Aston Villa 0 0
2024–25 Aston Villa 0 0

BURROWES, Bradley (M) 0 0
H: 5 10 W: 11 00 b. 4-3-08
Internationals: England U17.
2024–25 Aston Villa 0 0

CASH, Matty (M) 289 21
H: 6 2 W: 10 01 b.Slough 7-8-97
Internationals: Poland Full caps.
2015–16 Nottingham F 0 0
2015–16 *Dagenham & Red* 12 3 **12 3**
2016–17 Nottingham F 28 0
2017–18 Nottingham F 23 2
2018–19 Nottingham F 36 6
2019–20 Nottingham F 42 3
2020–21 Nottingham F 0 0 **129 11**
2020–21 Aston Villa 28 0
2021–22 Aston Villa 38 4
2022–23 Aston Villa 26 0
2023–24 Aston Villa 29 2
2024–25 Aston Villa 27 1 **148 7**

COUTINHO, Phillippe (M) 371 81
H: 5 7 W: 10 10 b.Rio de Janeiro 12-6-92
Internationals: Brazil U17, U20, Full caps.
2009–10 Vasco da Gama 7 1
2010–11 Internazionale 12 1
2011–12 Internazionale 5 1
2011–12 *Espanyol* 16 5 **16 5**
2012–13 Internazionale 10 1 **27 3**
2012–13 Liverpool 13 3
2013–14 Liverpool 33 5
2014–15 Liverpool 35 5
2015–16 Liverpool 26 8
2016–17 Liverpool 31 13
2017–18 Liverpool 14 7 **152 41**
2018–19 Barcelona 34 5
2019–20 Barcelona 0 0
2019–20 *Bayern Munich* 23 8 **23 8**
2020–21 Barcelona 12 2
2021–22 Barcelona 12 2 **58 9**
2021–22 *Aston Villa* 19 5
2022–23 Aston Villa 20 1
2023–24 Aston Villa 2 0
2023–24 *Al Duhail* 16 3 **16 3**
2024–25 Aston Villa 0 0 **41 6**
2024–25 *Vasco da Gama* 31 5 **38 6**

DENDONCKER, Leander (M) 310 21
H: 6 2 W: 12 02 b.Passendale 15-4-95
Internationals: Belgium U16, U17, U19, U21, Full caps.
2013–14 Anderlecht 0 0
2014–15 Anderlecht 26 2
2015–16 Anderlecht 23 1
2016–17 Anderlecht 40 5
2017–18 Anderlecht 36 1
2018–19 *Wolverhampton W* 19 2
2019–20 Wolverhampton W 38 4
2020–21 Wolverhampton W 33 1
2021–22 Wolverhampton W 30 2
2022–23 Wolverhampton W 4 0 **124 9**
2022–23 Aston Villa 20 0
2023–24 Aston Villa 8 1
2023–24 *Napoli* 3 0 **3 0**
2024–25 Aston Villa 0 0 **28 1**
2024–25 *Anderlecht* 30 2 **155 11**

DIEGO CARLOS, Silva (D) 272 12
H: 6 0 W: 12 06 b.Barra Bonita 15-3-93
Internationals: Brazil U23.
2013 Sao Paulo 0 0
2014 Sao Paulo 0 0
2014 *Paulista* 0 0
2014 *Madureira* 2 0 **2 0**
2014–15 Estoril 0 0
2014–15 *Porto* 0 0
2015–16 Estoril 31 2 **31 2**
2016–17 Nantes 34 2
2017–18 Nantes 28 1
2018–19 Nantes 35 1 **97 4**
2019–20 Sevilla 35 2
2020–21 Sevilla 33 1
2021–22 Sevilla 34 3 **102 6**
2022–23 Aston Villa 3 0
2023–24 Aston Villa 27 0
2024–25 Aston Villa 10 0 **40 0**
Transferred to Fenerbache, January 2025.

DIGNE, Lucas (D) 363 11
H: 5 10 W: 11 11 b.Meaux 20-7-93
Internationals: France U16, U17, U18, U19, U21, Full caps.
2011–12 Lille 16 0
2012–13 Lille 33 2 **49 2**
2013–14 Paris Saint-Germain 15 0
2014–15 Paris Saint-Germain 15 0
2014–15 Paris Saint-Germain 0 0
2015–16 Paris Saint-Germain 0 0 **30 0**
2015–16 *Roma* 33 3 **33 3**
2016–17 Barcelona 17 0
2017–18 Barcelona 12 0 **29 0**
2018–19 Everton 35 4
2019–20 Everton 35 0
2020–21 Everton 30 0
2021–22 Everton 13 0 **113 4**
2021–22 Aston Villa 16 0
2022–23 Aston Villa 28 1
2023–24 Aston Villa 33 1
2024–25 Aston Villa 32 0 **109 2**

DOBBIN, Lewis (F) 85 6
H: 5 9 W: 11 03 b.Stoke-on-Trent 3-1-03
Internationals: England U16, U17, U19.
2021–22 Everton 3 0
2022–23 Everton 0 0
2022–23 *Derby Co* 43 3 **43 3**
2023–24 Everton 12 1 **15 1**
2024–25 Aston Villa 0 0
2024–25 *WBA* 17 0 **17 0**
2024–25 *Norwich C* 10 2 **10 2**

DURAN, Jhon (F) 129 29
H: 6 1 W: 11 07 b.Medellin 13-12-03
Internationals: Colombia U17, Full caps.
2019 Envigado 10 1
2020 Envigado 13 1
2021 Envigado 24 7 **47 9**
2022 Chicago Fire 27 8 **27 8**
2022–23 Aston Villa 12 0
2023–24 Aston Villa 23 5
2024–25 Aston Villa 20 7 **55 12**
Transferred to Al-Nassr, January 2025.

EMERY, Lander (G) 0 0
b. 29-3-03
2023–24 Aston Villa 0 0
2024–25 Aston Villa 0 0

EMI, Buendia (M) 284 44
H: 5 7 W: 11 05 b.Mar del Plata 25-12-96
Internationals: Spain U19. Argentina U20, Full caps.
2013–14 Getafe 0 0
2014–15 Getafe 6 0
2015–16 Getafe 17 1
2016–17 Getafe 12 2
2017–18 Getafe 0 0 **35 3**
2017–18 *Cultural Leonesa* 40 6 **40 6**
2018–19 Norwich C 38 8
2019–20 Norwich C 36 1
2020–21 Norwich C 39 15 **113 24**
2021–22 Aston Villa 35 4
2022–23 Aston Villa 38 5
2023–24 Aston Villa 0 0
2024–25 Aston Villa 12 0 **85 9**
2024–25 *Bayer Leverkusen* 11 2 **11 2**

FEENEY, Josh (D) 45 1
H: 6 4 W: 12 00 b.Blackpool 6-5-05
Internationals: England U16, U17, U18.
2020–21 Fleetwood T 0 0
2021–22 Aston Villa 0 0
2022–23 Aston Villa 0 0
2023–24 Aston Villa 0 0
2023–24 *Real Union* 8 0 **8 0**
2024–25 Aston Villa 0 0
2024–25 *Shrewsbury T* 37 1 **37 1**

GARCIA, Andres (D) 54 4
H: 6 1 W: 12 04 b.Valencia 7-2-03
Internationals: Spain U21.
2022–23 Levante 1 0
2023–24 Levante 24 1
2024–25 Levante 22 3 **47 4**
2024–25 Aston Villa 7 0 **7 0**

GAUCI, Joe (G) 86 0
H: 6 4 W: 13 10 b.Adelaide 4-7-00
Internationals: Australia U23, Full caps.
2018–19 Central Coast Mariners 0 0
2018–19 Adelaide C 8 0 **8 0**
2019–20 Melbourne C 0 0
2020–21 Adelaide U 10 0
2021–22 Adelaide U 22 0
2022–23 Adelaide U 29 0
2023–24 Adelaide U 10 0 **71 0**
2023–24 Aston Villa 0 0

2024–25 Aston Villa	0	0	
2024–25 *Barnsley*	7	0	7 0

HAUSE, Kortney (D)   150   9
H: 6 2   W: 13 03   b.Goodmayes 16-7-95
Internationals: England U20, U21.

2012–13 Wycombe W	9	1	
2013–14 *Wycombe W*	14	1	23 2
2013–14 Wolverhampton W	0	0	
2014–15 Wolverhampton W	17	0	
2014–15 *Gillingham*	14	1	14 1
2015–16 Wolverhampton W	25	0	
2016–17 Wolverhampton W	24	2	
2017–18 Wolverhampton W	1	0	
2018–19 Wolverhampton W	0	0	67 2
2018–19 *Aston Villa*	11	1	
2019–20 Aston Villa	18	1	
2020–21 Aston Villa	7	1	
2021–22 Aston Villa	7	1	
2022–23 Aston Villa	0	0	
2022–23 *Watford*	3	0	3 0
2023–24 Aston Villa	0	0	
2024–25 Aston Villa	0	0	43 4

HAYDEN, Kaine (D)   118   4
H: 5 9   W: 9 11   b.Birmingham 23-10-02
Internationals: England U20.

2019–20 Aston Villa	0	0	
2020–21 Aston Villa	0	0	
2021–22 Aston Villa	0	0	
2021–22 *Swindon T*	18	0	18 0
2021–22 *Milton Keynes D*	15	1	15 1
2022–23 Aston Villa	0	0	
2022–23 *Huddersfield T*	14	1	14 1
2023–24 Aston Villa	3	0	
2023–24 *Plymouth Arg*	24	0	24 0
2024–25 Aston Villa	0	0	3 0
2024–25 *Preston NE*	44	2	44 2

ILING-JUNIOR, Samuel (M)   59   4
H: 6 0   W: 11 09   b.Islington 4-10-03
Internationals: England U16, U17, U19, U20, U21.

2020–21 Juventus	0	0	
2021–22 Juventus	0	0	
2022–23 Juventus	12	1	
2023–24 Juventus	24	1	36 2
2024–25 Aston Villa	0	0	
2024–25 *Bologna*	7	1	7 1
2024–25 *Middlesbrough*	16	1	16 1

JIMOH, Jamaldeen (M)   0   0
H: 6 0   W: 11 03   b.Birmingham 2-10-06
Internationals: England U16, U17, U18.

2024–25 Aston Villa	0	0	

KAMARA, Boubacar (D)   200   4
H: 6 0   W: 10 10   b.Marseille 23-11-99
Internationals: France U17, U19, U20, U21, Full caps.

2015–16 Marseille	0	0	
2016–17 Marseille	0	0	
2017–18 Marseille	6	0	
2018–19 Marseille	31	1	
2019–20 Marseille	24	1	
2020–21 Marseille	35	0	
2021–22 Marseille	34	1	130 3
2022–23 Aston Villa	24	0	
2023–24 Aston Villa	20	0	
2024–25 Aston Villa	26	1	70 1

KONSA, Ezri (D)   310   9
H: 6 0   W: 12 02   b.Newham 23-10-97
Internationals: England U20, U21, Full caps.

2015–16 Charlton Ath	0	0	
2016–17 Charlton Ath	32	0	
2017–18 Charlton Ath	39	0	71 0
2018–19 Brentford	42	1	42 1
2019–20 Aston Villa	25	1	
2020–21 Aston Villa	36	2	
2021–22 Aston Villa	29	2	
2022–23 Aston Villa	38	0	
2023–24 Aston Villa	35	1	
2024–25 Aston Villa	34	2	197 8

MAATSEN, Ian (D)   170   11
H: 5 6   W: 9 11   b.Vlaardingen 10-3-02
Internationals: Netherlands U16, U17, U18, U21, Full caps.
From PSV Eindhoven.

2019–20 Chelsea	0	0	
2020–21 Chelsea	0	0	
2020–21 *Charlton Ath*	34	1	34 1
2021–22 Chelsea	0	0	
2021–22 *Coventry C*	40	3	40 3
2022–23 Chelsea	0	0	
2022–23 *Burnley*	39	4	39 4
2023–24 Chelsea	12	0	12 0
2023–24 *Borussia Dortmund*	16	2	16 2
2024–25 Aston Villa	29	1	29 1

MALEN, Donyell (F)   189   73
H: 5 9   W: 10 10   b.Wieringen 19-1-99
Internationals: Netherlands U16, U17, U18, U19, U21, Full caps.

2016–17 Arsenal	0	0	
2017–18 Arsenal	0	0	

2017–18 PSV Eindhoven	4	0	
2018–19 PSV Eindhoven	31	10	
2019–20 PSV Eindhoven	14	11	
2020–21 PSV Eindhoven	32	19	81 40
2021–22 Borussia Dortmund	27	5	
2022–23 Borussia Dortmund	26	9	
2023–24 Borussia Dortmund	27	13	
2024–25 Borussia Dortmund	14	3	94 30
2024–25 Aston Villa	14	3	14 3

MARSCHALL, Filip (G)   52   0
H: 6 5   W: 13 10   b.Bedford 24-4-03
Internationals: England U19.

2021–22 Aston Villa	0	0	
2022–23 Aston Villa	0	0	
2023–24 Aston Villa	0	0	
2023–24 *Milton Keynes D*	6	0	6 0
2024–25 Aston Villa	0	0	
2024–25 *Crewe Alex*	46	0	46 0

MARTINEZ, Damian (G)   252   0
H: 6 4   W: 13 05   b.Mar del Plata 2-9-92
Internationals: Argentina U17, U20, Full caps.
From Independiente.

2010–11 Arsenal	0	0	
2011–12 Arsenal	0	0	
2011–12 *Oxford U*	1	0	1 0
2012–13 Arsenal	0	0	
2013–14 Arsenal	0	0	
2013–14 *Sheffield Wed*	11	0	11 0
2014–15 Arsenal	4	0	
2014–15 *Rotherham U*	8	0	8 0
2015–16 Arsenal	0	0	
2015–16 *Wolverhampton W*	13	0	13 0
2016–17 Arsenal	2	0	
2017–18 Arsenal	0	0	
2017–18 *Getafe*	5	0	5 0
2018–19 Arsenal	0	0	
2018–19 *Reading*	18	0	
2019–20 Arsenal	9	0	
2019–20 *Reading*	0	0	18 0
2020–21 Arsenal	0	0	15 0
2020–21 Aston Villa	38	0	
2021–22 Aston Villa	36	0	
2022–23 Aston Villa	36	0	
2023–24 Aston Villa	34	0	
2024–25 Aston Villa	37	0	181 0

McGINN, John (M)   431   39
H: 5 8   W: 10 08   b.Glasgow 18-10-94
Internationals: Scotland U19, U21, Full caps.

2012–13 St Mirren	22	1	
2013–14 St Mirren	35	3	
2014–15 St Mirren	30	0	87 4
2015–16 Hibernian	36	3	
2016–17 Hibernian	29	4	
2017–18 Hibernian	35	5	
2018–19 Hibernian	0	0	101 12
2018–19 *Aston Villa*	40	6	
2019–20 Aston Villa	28	3	
2020–21 Aston Villa	37	3	
2021–22 Aston Villa	35	3	
2022–23 Aston Villa	34	1	
2023–24 Aston Villa	35	6	
2024–25 Aston Villa	34	1	243 23

MINGS, Tyrone (D)   244   9
H: 6 3   W: 12 02   b.Bath 13-3-93
Internationals: England Full caps.
From Southampton.

2012–13 Ipswich T	1	0	
2013–14 Ipswich T	16	0	
2014–15 Ipswich T	40	1	57 1
2015–16 Bournemouth	1	0	
2016–17 Bournemouth	7	0	
2017–18 Bournemouth	4	0	
2018–19 Bournemouth	5	0	17 0
2018–19 *Aston Villa*	15	2	
2019–20 Aston Villa	33	2	
2020–21 Aston Villa	36	2	
2021–22 Aston Villa	36	1	
2022–23 Aston Villa	35	1	
2023–24 Aston Villa	3	0	
2024–25 Aston Villa	14	0	170 8

MOORE, Kobei (M)   10   1
H: 6 0   W: 11 00   b. 30-11-04

2024–25 Aston Villa	0	0	
2024–25 *Fleetwood T*	10	1	10 1

MUNROE, Finley (D)   25   1
H: 8-2-05

2023–24 Aston Villa	1	0	
2024–25 Aston Villa	0	0	1 0
2024–25 *Real Union*	24	1	24 1

NEDELJKOVIC, Kosta (D)   50   1
H: 6 0   W: 11 05   b.Smederevo, Serbia and Montenegro 16-12-05
Internationals: Serbia U17, U18, U19, Full caps.

2022–23 Red Star Belgrade	0	0	
2022–23 *Grafičar*	21	1	21 1
2023–24 Red Star Belgrade	12	0	14 0
2023–24 Aston Villa	0	0	
2023–24 *Red Star Belgrade*	2	0	

2024–25 Aston Villa	5	0	5 0
2024–25 *RB Leipzig*	10	0	10 0

O'REILLY, Tommi (M)   30   1
H: 5 7   W: 9 13   b.Birmingham 15-12-03

2021–22 Aston Villa	0	0	
2022–23 Aston Villa	0	0	
2023–24 Aston Villa	0	0	
2023–24 *Real Union*	2	0	2 0
2024–25 Aston Villa	0	0	
2024–25 *Shrewsbury T*	12	0	12 0
2024–25 *Milton Keynes D*	16	1	16 1

OLSEN, Robin (G)   256   0
H: 6 5   W: 14 00   b.Malmo 8-1-90
Internationals: Sweden Full caps.

2007 Limhamn Bunkeflo	0	0	
2008 Limhamn Bunkeflo	0	0	
2009 Limhamn Bunkeflo	8	0	8 0
2010 Bunkeflo	18	0	18 0
2011 Klagshamn	19	0	19 0
2012 Malmo	1	0	
2013 Malmo	10	0	
2014 Malmo	29	0	
2015 Malmo	13	0	53 0
2015–16 PAOK	11	0	11 0
2015–16 *FC Copenhagen*	14	0	
2016–17 FC Copenhagen	33	0	
2017–18 FC Copenhagen	24	0	71 0
2018–19 Roma	27	0	
2019–20 Roma	0	0	
2019–20 *Cagliari*	17	0	17 0
2020–21 Roma	0	0	
2020–21 *Everton*	7	0	7 0
2021–22 Roma	0	0	27 0
2021–22 *Sheffield U*	11	0	11 0
2021–22 *Aston Villa*	1	0	
2022–23 Aston Villa	4	0	
2023–24 Aston Villa	5	0	
2024–25 Aston Villa	4	0	14 0

ONANA, Amadou (M)   146   9
H: 6 4   W: 12 00   b.Dakar 16-8-01
Internationals: Belgium U17, U18, U19, U21, Full caps.

2018–19 TSG 1899 Hoffenheim	0	0	
2019–20 Hamburger SV	0	0	
2020–21 Hamburger SV	25	2	25 2
2021–22 Lille	32	1	32 1
2022–23 Everton	33	1	
2023–24 Everton	30	2	63 3
2024–25 Aston Villa	26	3	26 3

PATTERSON, Travis (D)   7   0
H: 5 10   W: 10 01   b.Wolverhampton 6-10-05
Internationals: England U16, U17, U18, U19.

2022–23 Aston Villa	0	0	
2023–24 Aston Villa	0	0	
2024–25 Aston Villa	0	0	
2024–25 *Milton Keynes D*	7	0	7 0

PROCTOR, Sam (G)   0   0
H: 6 2   W: 11 11   b.Boston 21-12-06
Internationals: England U17, U18, U19.

2023–24 Aston Villa	0	0	
2024–25 Aston Villa	0	0	

RAMSEY, Jacob (M)   144   17
H: 5 11   W: 11 05   b.Birmingham 28-5-01
Internationals: England U18, U19, U20, U21.

2018–19 Aston Villa	0	0	
2019–20 Aston Villa	0	0	
2019–20 *Doncaster R*	7	3	7 3
2020–21 Aston Villa	22	0	
2021–22 Aston Villa	34	6	
2022–23 Aston Villa	35	6	
2023–24 Aston Villa	16	1	
2024–25 Aston Villa	29	1	137 14

RICHARDS, Rico (M)   39   4
H: 5 9   W: 10 10   b.Birmingham 27-9-03
Internationals: England U16, U17, U18.

2019–20 WBA	0	0	
2020–21 WBA	0	0	
2021–22 WBA	0	0	
2022–23 WBA	1	0	1 0
2023–24 Aston Villa	0	0	
2023–24 *Stockport Co*	11	1	11 1
2024–25 Aston Villa	0	0	
2024–25 *Port Vale*	27	3	27 3

ROGERS, Morgan (M)   134   21
H: 6 2   W: 12 08   b.Halesowen 26-7-02
Internationals: England U16, U17, U18, U20, U21, Full caps.

2018–19 WBA	0	0	
2019–20 Manchester C	0	0	
2020–21 Manchester C	0	0	
2020–21 *Lincoln C*	25	6	25 6
2021–22 Bournemouth	15	1	15 1
2022–23 Manchester C	0	0	
2022–23 *Blackpool*	20	1	20 1
2023–24 *Middlesbrough*	26	2	26 2
2023–24 Aston Villa	11	3	
2024–25 Aston Villa	37	8	48 11

ROWE, Triston (D)   0   0
H: 6 0   W: 11 00   b.18-5-06
Internationals: England U16, U18, U19.
2024–25 Aston Villa   0   0

SMITH, Kerr (D)   13 0
b.Montrose 12-12-04
Internationals: Scotland U19.
2020–21 Dundee U   5   0
2021–22 Dundee U   5   0   10 0
2021–22 Aston Villa   0   0
2021–22 Aston Villa   0   0
2022–23 Aston Villa   0   0
2023–24 Aston Villa   0   0
2023–24 St Johnstone   3   0   3   0
2024–25 Aston Villa   0   0

SOUSA, Lino (D)   33 0
H: 6 1   W: 12 08   b.Lisboa 19-1-05
Internationals: England U16, U17, U18, U19.
From WBA.
2022–23 Arsenal   0   0
2023–24 Arsenal   0   0
2023–24 Aston Villa   0   0
2023–24 Plymouth Arg   8   0   8   0
2024–25 Aston Villa   0   0
2024–25 Bristol R   25 0   25 0

SWINKELS, Sil (D)   14 2
H: 6 3   W: 12 04   b.Sint-Oedenrode 6-1-04
Internationals: Netherlands U18.
From Vitesse.
2020–21 Aston Villa   0   0
2021–22 Aston Villa   0   0
2022–23 Aston Villa   0   0
2024–25 Aston Villa   0   0
2024–25 Bristol R   14 2   14 2

TAYLOR, Kane (M)   0   0
H: 5 10   W: 10 03   b.Birmingham 15-9-05
Internationals: England U17, U18, U19.
2024–25 Aston Villa   0   0

TIELEMANS, Youri (M)   405 57
H: 5 9   W: 10 08   b.Sint-Pieters-Leeuw
7-5-97
Internationals: Belgium U16, U21, Full caps.
2013–14 Anderlecht   29 1
2014–15 Anderlecht   39 6
2015–16 Anderlecht   34 6
2016–17 Anderlecht   37 13 139 26
2017–18 Monaco   27 0
2018–19 Monaco   20 5   47 5
2018–19 Leicester C   13 3
2019–20 Leicester C   37 3
2020–21 Leicester C   38 6
2021–22 Leicester C   32 6
2022–23 Leicester C   31 3   151 21
2023–24 Aston Villa   32 2
2024–25 Aston Villa   36 3   68 5

TORRES, Pau (D)   227 13
H: 6 1   W: 12 00   b.Capellades 16-1-97
Internationals: Spain U21, U23, Full caps.
2016–17 Villarreal   0   0
2017–18 Villarreal   2   0
2018–19 Villarreal   0   0
2018–19 Malaga   38 1   38 1
2019–20 Villarreal   34 2
2020–21 Villarreal   33 2
2021–22 Villarreal   33 5
2022–23 Villarreal   34 1   136 10
2023–24 Aston Villa   29 2
2024–25 Aston Villa   0   0   53 2

WATKINS, Ollie (F)   384 141
H: 5 10   W: 11 00   b.Torbay 30-12-95
Internationals: England Full caps.
2013–14 Exeter C   1   0
2014–15 Exeter C   2   0
2015–16 Exeter C   20 8
2016–17 Exeter C   45 13 68 21
2017–18 Brentford   45 10
2018–19 Brentford   41 10
2019–20 Brentford   46 25
2020–21 Brentford   0   0   132 45
2020–21 Aston Villa   37 14
2021–22 Aston Villa   35 11
2022–23 Aston Villa   37 15
2023–24 Aston Villa   37 19
2024–25 Aston Villa   38 16 184 75

WRIGHT, James (G)   33 0
H: 6 2   W: 12 04   b.2-12-04
From Manchester C.
2022–23 Aston Villa   0   0
2023–24 Aston Villa   0   0
2024–25 Aston Villa   0   0
2024–25 Real Union   33 0   33 0

YOUNG, Finley (F)   7   0
H: 5 9   W: 9 11   b.Erdington 19-1-06
Internationals: England U16, U17, U18, U19.
2022–23 Aston Villa   0   0
2023–24 Aston Villa   0   0
2024–25 Aston Villa   0   0
2024–25 Antwerp   7   0   7   0

ZYCH, Oliwier (G)   26 0
H: 5 9   W: 12 11   b.Gdansk 28-6-04
Internationals: Poland U18, U19, U20, U21.
From Lubin.
2020–21 Aston Villa   0   0
2021–22 Aston Villa   0   0
2022–23 Aston Villa   0   0
2023–24 Aston Villa   0   0
2023–24 Puszcza Niepolomice 26 0   26 0
2024–25 Aston Villa   0   0

Players retained with offer of contract
Amundsen-Day, Ethan; Asemota;
Aimuamwonnsa Presley; Brannigan, Cole
Patrick; Burgess, Woody Jack Robert;
Cotcher, Mason Lee; Edwards, I-Lani;
Hamdin, Omar Khedr Ismail Ahmed;
Hayward, Vinnie Brendan Sean; Hemmings,
George Lawrence; Jenner, Max Daniel;
Katsukunya, Thierry Alfred Farai; Lewis,
Samuel Jack; Lynch, Luka John; Lynskey,
Alfie Tomas; Monteiro Fortes, Rodrigo;
Moreland, Calum Francis; Mosquera, Yeimar
Jesus; Pavey, Charlie James; Quinn, Keilan
James; Routh, Leon George; Simpson, Ewan
Mark; Wilson, Rory.

Scholars
Allan, Jack Richard; Bloomfield, Teddie
Arthur; Briscoe, Elijah Brandon; Carroll,
Theodore James; Duerden, Archie; Green,
Jacob Raymond; McWilliams, Ashton Tyler;
Mulley, Trai-Varn Divinche; Ramsey, Cole
Paul; Wilson, Junior John.

BARNSLEY (5)

ALKER, Luke (F)   0   0
b.12-12-06
2024–25 Barnsley   0   0

ATKINSON, Aaron (M)   0   0
H: 5 9   W: 11 07   b.15-11-04
From Oldham Ath.
2023–24 Barnsley   0   0
2024–25 Barnsley   0   0

BARRATT, Connor (D)   5   0
H: 6 1   W: 12 04   b.5-4-04
Internationals: Republic of Ireland U21.
2024–25 Barnsley   5   0   5   0

BENSON, Josh (M)   97 6
H: 5 9   W: 11 03   b.Thurrock 5-12-99
From Arsenal.
2018–19 Burnley   0   0
2019–20 Burnley   0   0
2019–20 Grimsby T   11 2   11 2
2020–21 Burnley   6   0   6   0
2021–22 Barnsley   25 0
2022–23 Barnsley   35 3
2023–24 Barnsley   6   0
2024–25 Barnsley   14 1   80 4

BLAND, Jonathan (M)   9   0
H: 6 0   W: 12 02   b.Shrewsbury 24-10-05
Internationals: Wales U16, U18, U19, U21.
2023–24 Barnsley   0   0
2024–25 Barnsley   9   0   9   0

CHAPMAN, Theo (M)   4   0
H: 5 10   W: 11 09   b.Leeds 31-3-05
2022–23 Barnsley   0   0
2023–24 Barnsley   4   0
2024–25 Barnsley   0   0   4   0

CONNELL, Luca (M)   152 15
H: 5 10   W: 10 12   b.Liverpool 20-4-01
Internationals: Republic of Ireland U17, U18,
U19, U21.
2018–19 Bolton W   10 0   10 0
2019–20 Celtic   0   0
2020–21 Celtic   0   0
2020–21 Queen's Park   11 3
2021–22 Celtic   0   0
2021–22 Queen's Park   27 7   38 10
2022–23 Barnsley   39 2
2023–24 Barnsley   24 1
2024–25 Barnsley   41 2   104 5

COSGROVE, Sam (F)   224 47
H: 6 4   W: 10 08   b.Beverley 2-12-96
2014–15 Wigan Ath   0   0
2015–16 Wigan Ath   0   0
2016–17 Wigan Ath   0   0
2017–18 Carlisle U   8   1   8   1
2017–18 Aberdeen   5   0
2018–19 Aberdeen   35 17
2019–20 Aberdeen   25 11
2020–21 Aberdeen   14 3   79 31
2020–21 Birmingham C   12 0
2021–22 Birmingham C   0   0
2021–22 Shrewsbury T   17 2   17 2
2021–22 AFC Wimbledon   15 1   15 1
2022–23 Birmingham C   2   0
2022–23 Plymouth Arg   33 8   33 8

2023–24 Birmingham C   0   0   14 0
2023–24 Barnsley   32 3
2024–25 Barnsley   19 1   51 4
2024–25 Stockport Co   7   0   7   0

COTTER, Barry (D)   99 6
H: 5 9   W: 10 10   b.Ennis 4-12-98
Internationals: Republic of Ireland U19.
From Limerick.
2017–18 Ipswich T   2   0
2018–19 Ipswich T   0   0
2019–20 Ipswich T   0   0
2020–21 Ipswich T   0   0   2   0
2021   Shamrock R   9   0
2022   Shamrock R   15 1   24 1
2022   St Patrick's Ath 11 2   11 2
2022–23 Barnsley   6   0
2023–24 Barnsley   35 3
2024–25 Barnsley   21 0   62 3

DALLAS, Andrew (F)   94 12
H: 5 10   W: 12 06   b.Glasgow 22-7-99
2017–18 Rangers   0   0
2017–18 Stenhousemuir   6   3   6   3
2018–19 Rangers   0   0
2018–19 Greenock Morton   12 0   12 0
2019–20 Cambridge U   22 2
2020–21 Cambridge U   1   0   23 2
From Solihull Moors.
2023–24 Barnsley   4   1
2023–24 Kilmarnock   14 0   14 0
2024–25 Barnsley   0   0   4   1
2024–25 Barrow   18 3   18 3
2024–25 Morecambe   17 3   19 3

DURAND DE GEVIGNEY, Mael (D)   165 2
H: 6 1   W: 12 02   b.Feucherolles 21-9-99
2018–19 Versailles   9   0
2019–20 Versailles   17 0
2020–21 Versailles   9   0
2021–22 Versailles   20 0   55 0
2022–23 Nimes   31 0   31 0
2023–24 Barnsley   40 2
2024–25 Barnsley   39 0   79 2

DYER, Josiah (F)   1   0
H: 6 0   W: 11 07   b.Hammersmith 29-4-04
Internationals: Montserrrat Full caps.
2022–23 Barnsley   0   0
2023–24 Barnsley   0   0
2024–25 Barnsley   1   0   1   0

EARL, Joshua (D)   204 6
H: 6 4   W: 12 04   b.Southport 24-10-98
2017–18 Preston NE   19 0
2018–19 Preston NE   14 0
2019–20 Preston NE   0   0
2019–20 Bolton W   9   0   9   0
2019–20 Ipswich T   7   0   7   0
2020–21 Preston NE   5   0
2020–21 Burton Alb   8   0   8   0
2021–22 Preston NE   29 1   67 1
2022–23 Fleetwood T   37 1
2023–24 Fleetwood T   24 2   61 3
2023–24 Barnsley   18 0
2024–25 Barnsley   34 2   52 2

FARRELL, Leo (F)   0   0
b.30-12-05
2024–25 Barnsley   0   0

FARRUGIA, Neil (M)   143 12
H: 6 2   W: 13 01   b.Paris, France 19-5-99
Internationals: Republic of Ireland U9, U21.
2017   UCD   5   0
2018   UCD   11 1
2019   UCD   18 1   34 2
2019   Shamrock R   3   0
2020   Shamrock R   14 1
2021   Shamrock R   11 0
2022   Shamrock R   23 3
2023   Shamrock R   27 4
2024   Shamrock R   22 2   100 10
2024–25 Barnsley   9   0   9   0

FLAVELL, Kieran (G)   7   0
H: 6 6   W: 12 04   b.Pontefract 21-9-03
2021–22 Barnsley   0   0
2022–23 Barnsley   0   0
2023–24 Barnsley   0   0
2024–25 Barnsley   7   0   7   0

GENT, Georgie (D)   54 2
H: 6 0   W: 11 07   b.Manchester 23-9-03
2023–24 Blackburn R   0   0
2023–24 Motherwell   29 1   29 1
2024–25 Blackburn R   0   0
2024–25 Barnsley   25 1   25 1

GRAHAM, Kieran (M)   1   0
b.31-8-07
2024–25 Barnsley   1   0   1   0

HAYTON, Adam (G)   0   0
H: 6 2   W: 12 04   b.Luton 28-4-04
From Tottenham H.
2022–23 Barnsley   0   0

Season	Club			
2023–24	Barnsley	0	0	
2024–25	Barnsley	0	0	

HICKENBOTTOM, Charlie (M) — 0 0
b.Derby 6-12-04

| 2023–24 | Barnsley | 0 | 0 | |
| 2024–25 | Barnsley | 0 | 0 | |

HOURIHANE, Conor (M) — 504 85
H: 5 11 W: 9 11 b.Cork 2-2-91
Internationals: Republic of Ireland U19, U21, Full caps.

2008–09	Sunderland	0	0		
2009–10	Sunderland	0	0		
2010–11	Ipswich T	0	0		
2011–12	Plymouth Arg	38	2		
2012–13	Plymouth Arg	42	5		
2013–14	Plymouth Arg	45	8	125	15
2014–15	Barnsley	46	13		
2015–16	Barnsley	41	10		
2016–17	Barnsley	25	6		
2016–17	Aston Villa	17	1		
2017–18	Aston Villa	41	11		
2018–19	Aston Villa	43	7		
2019–20	Aston Villa	27	3		
2020–21	Aston Villa	4	1		
2020–21	Swansea C	19	5	19	5
2021–22	Aston Villa	0	0	132	23
2021–22	Sheffield U	29	1	29	1
2022–23	Derby Co	44	7		
2023–24	Derby Co	41	5	85	12
2024–25	Barnsley	2	0	114	29

HUMPHRYS, Stephen (F) — 242 55
H: 6 1 W: 10 12 b.Oldham 15-9-97

2016–17	Fulham	2	0		
2016–17	Shrewsbury T	14	2	14	2
2017–18	Fulham	0	0		
2017–18	Rochdale	16	2		
2018–19	Fulham	0	0	2	0
2018–19	Scunthorpe U	16	4	16	4
2018–19	Southend U	10	5		
2019–20	Southend U	21	5		
2020–21	Southend U	0	0	31	10
2020–21	Rochdale	29	11		
2021–22	Rochdale	0	0	45	13
2021–22	Wigan Ath	38	5		
2022–23	Wigan Ath	2	0		
2022–23	Hearts	19	3	19	3
2023–24	Wigan Ath	38	9	78	14
2024–25	Barnsley	37	9	37	9

JALO, Fabio (M) — 37 3
H: 5 10 W: 11 00 b.Lisbon 18-11-05
Internationals: Portugal U18, U19.
From Benfica.

2022–23	Barnsley	7	0		
2023–24	Barnsley	14	1		
2024–25	Barnsley	16	2	37	3

JAMES, Nathan (D) — 0 0
H: 6 2 b.Coventry 28-9-04
Internationals: Thailand U20.

| 2023–24 | Barnsley | 0 | 0 | |
| 2024–25 | Barnsley | 0 | 0 | |

KEILLOR-DUNN, Davis (M) — 267 83
H: 5 11 W: 10 10 b.Sunderland 2-11-97

2016–17	Ross Co	0	0		
2017–18	Ross Co	29	3		
2018–19	Ross Co	11	1	40	4
2018–19	Falkirk	11	3	11	3

From Wrexham.

2020–21	Oldham Ath	41	10		
2021–22	Oldham Ath	46	15	87	25
2022–23	Burton Alb	19	5	19	5
2022–23	Mansfield T	19	6		
2023–24	Mansfield T	46	22		
2024–25	Mansfield T	3	0	68	28
2024–25	Barnsley	42	18	42	18

KOZLUK, Ziggy (M) — 0 0
b. 10-11-05

| 2024–25 | Barnsley | 0 | 0 | |

LEWIS, Jonathan (M) — 185 30
H: 5 7 W: 10 10 b.Atlanta 4-6-97
Internationals: USA U20, U23, Full caps.

2015–16	Bradford C	0	0		
2017	New York City	11	2		
2018	New York City	14	1		
2018	Louisville C	5	0	5	0
2019	New York City	6	0	31	3
2019	Colorado Rapids	16	5		
2020	Colorado Rapids	18	5		
2021	Colorado Rapids	27	7		
2022	Colorado Rapids	33	5		
2023	Colorado Rapids	26	1		
2024	Colorado Rapids	24	3	144	26
2024–25	Barnsley	5	1	5	1

LOFTHOUSE, Kyran (F) — 56 1
H: 5 11 W: 10 03 b.Oxford 21-10-00

2018–19	Oxford U	0	0		
2019–20	Oxford U	0	0		
2020–21	Oxford U	0	0		

From Woking.

2023–24	Barnsley	1	0		
2023–24	Milton Keynes D	21	1	21	1
2024–25	Barnsley	18	0	19	0
2024–25	Burton Alb	16	0	16	0

LOPATA, Kacper (D) — 56 0
H: 6 2 W: 12 08 b.Krakow 27-8-01
Internationals: Poland U18, U19, U20, U21.
From Bristol C.

2019–20	Brighton & HA	0	0		
2019–20	Zaglebie Sosnowiec	7	0	7	0
2020–21	Sheffield U	0	0		
2021–22	Sheffield U	0	0		
2022–23	Sheffield U	0	0		

From Southend U, Woking.

2023–24	Barnsley	13	0		
2023–24	Port Vale	6	0	6	0
2024–25	Barnsley	0	0	13	0
2024–25	Ross Co	30	0	30	0

MAKIESSI, Jean-Claude (M) — 0 0
H: 5 6 W: 9 00 b.Newham 7-9-04

| 2023–24 | Barnsley | 0 | 0 | |
| 2024–25 | Barnsley | 0 | 0 | |

MARSH, Aiden (F) — 39 4
H: 5 8 W: 9 06 b.Barnsley 5-5-03

2019–20	Barnsley	0	0		
2020–21	Barnsley	0	0		
2021–22	Barnsley	4	1		
2022–23	Barnsley	4	0		
2023–24	Barnsley	9	0		
2024–25	Barnsley	7	0	24	1
2024–25	Raith R	15	3	15	3

McCANN, Bayley (D) — 1 0
H: 6 0 W: 11 05 b. 8-12-05
Internationals: Northern Ireland U16.

2022–23	Peterborough U	0	0		
2023–24	Barnsley	0	0		
2024–25	Barnsley	1	0	1	0

McCARTHY, Conor (D) — 179 8
H: 6 0 W: 11 11 b.Cork 11-4-98
Internationals: Republic of Ireland U18.

2016	Cork C	2	1		
2017	Cork C	7	0		
2018	Cork C	22	1		
2019	Cork C	35	4	66	6
2019–20	St Mirren	9	1		
2020–21	St Mirren	37	0		
2021–22	St Mirren	22	1	68	2
2022–23	Barnsley	7	0		
2023–24	Barnsley	0	0		
2023–24	Swindon T	18	0	18	0
2024–25	Barnsley	20	0	27	0

NEJMAN, Harrison (M) — 0 0
H: 5 10 W: 10 08 b.Halifax 8-9-03

2022–23	Barnsley	0	0	
2023–24	Barnsley	0	0	
2024–25	Barnsley	0	0	

NWAKALI, Kelechi (M) — 192 14
H: 5 11 W: 12 00 b.Imo State 5-6-98
Internationals: Nigeria U17, U23, Full caps.

2016–17	MVV Maastricht	29	2		
2017–18	Arsenal	0	0		
2017–18	MVV Maastricht	16	4	45	6
2017–18	VVV Venlo	9	1	9	1
2018–19	Arsenal	0	0		
2018–19	Porto	0	0		
2019–20	Huesca	5	0		
2020–21	Huesca	5	0		
2020–21	Alcorcon	18	4	18	4
2021–22	Huesca	19	0	29	0
2022–23	Ponferradina	36	1	36	1
2023–24	Chaves	32	1	32	1
2023–24	Barnsley	23	1	23	1

NZONDO, Emmaisa (F) — 0 0
H: 6 2 b.Leeds 21-1-06

| 2023–24 | Barnsley | 0 | 0 | |
| 2024–25 | Barnsley | 0 | 0 | |

O'KEEFFE, Corey (M) — 209 5
H: 6 1 W: 11 00 b.Birmingham 5-6-98
Internationals: Republic of Ireland U17, U18, U19.

2016–17	Birmingham C	1	0		
2017–18	Birmingham C	0	0		
2018–19	Birmingham C	0	0		
2019–20	Birmingham C	0	0	1	0
2019–20	Macclesfield T	31	0	31	0
2020–21	Mansfield T	13	0		
2021–22	Mansfield T	0	0	13	0
2021–22	Rochdale	43	2	43	2
2022–23	Forest Green R	41	0	41	0
2023–24	Barnsley	39	3		
2024–25	Barnsley	41	0	80	3

PHILLIPS, Adam (M) — 213 48
H: 5 11 W: 12 00 b.Garstang 15-1-98
Internationals: England U16, U17.

2014–15	Liverpool	0	0	
2015–16	Liverpool	0	0	
2016–17	Liverpool	0	0	
2017–18	Norwich C	0	0	

2017–18	Cambridge U	4	0	4	0
2018–19	Norwich C	0	0		
2018–19	Hamilton A	0	0		
2019–20	Burnley	0	0		
2019–20	Morecambe	11	4		
2020–21	Burnley	0	0		
2020–21	Morecambe	25	8		
2020–21	Accrington S	22	2	22	2
2021–22	Burnley	0	0		
2021–22	Morecambe	38	6	74	18
2022–23	Burnley	0	0		
2022–23	Barnsley	35	8		
2023–24	Barnsley	42	11		
2024–25	Barnsley	36	9	113	28

PICKARD, Hayden (D) — 0 0
H: 5 10 W: 10 06 b.Pontefract 23-8-05

2022–23	Barnsley	0	0	
2023–24	Barnsley	0	0	
2024–25	Barnsley	0	0	

PINES, Donovan (D) — 115 0
H: 6 5 W: 14 05 b.Columbia, MD 7-3-98
Internationals: USA U23, Full caps.

2019	DC United	10	0		
2020	DC United	16	3		
2021	DC United	18	0		
2022	DC United	21	0		
2023	DC United	22	3	87	6
2023–24	Barnsley	4	2		
2024–25	Barnsley	24	2	28	4

RAVENHILL, Rogan (G) — 0 0
H: 5 10 b.Barnsley 25-10-05

| 2023–24 | Barnsley | 0 | 0 | |
| 2024–25 | Barnsley | 0 | 0 | |

ROBERTS, Marc (D) — 295 15
H: 6 0 W: 12 11 b.Wakefield 26-7-90
Internationals: England C.
From FC Halifax T.

2014–15	Barnsley	0	0		
2015–16	Barnsley	32	1		
2016–17	Barnsley	40	4		
2017–18	Birmingham C	30	1		
2018–19	Birmingham C	8	0		
2019–20	Birmingham C	34	0		
2020–21	Birmingham C	36	4		
2021–22	Birmingham C	39	2		
2022–23	Birmingham C	25	0		
2023–24	Birmingham C	14	0	186	7
2024–25	Barnsley	37	3	109	8

RODRIGUES, Clement (F) — 49 7
H: 6 0 W: 12 06 b.L'Isle-D'Espagnac 4-12-00

2022–23	Concarneau	4	1		
2023–24	Concarneau	22	3	26	4
2024–25	Bastia	17	3	17	3

On loan from Bastia.

| 2024–25 | Barnsley | 6 | 0 | 6 | 0 |

RUSSELL, Jonathan (M) — 132 18
H: 6 4 W: 12 11 b.Hounslow 9-10-00
Internationals: Jamaica Full caps.

2020–21	Chelsea	0	0		
2020–21	Accrington S	25	2	25	2
2021–22	Huddersfield T	17	2		
2022–23	Huddersfield T	7	0	24	2
2022–23	Barnsley	12	0		
2023–24	Barnsley	31	3		
2024–25	Barnsley	40	11	83	14

SHEPHERD, Jack (D) — 60 3
H: 6 2 W: 11 00 b. 6-3-01

2023–24	Barnsley	9	0		
2023–24	Cheltenham T	12	1	12	1
2024–25	Barnsley	0	0	9	0
2024–25	Bradford C	39	2	39	2

SMITH, Jackson (G) — 37 0
H: 6 2 W: 12 00 b.Telford 14-10-01

2022–23	Wolverhampton W	0	0		
2022–23	Walsall	2	0		
2023–24	Walsall	23	0	25	0
2024–25	Grimsby T	6	0	6	0

WATTERS, Max (F) — 126 31
H: 6 2 W: 12 08 b.Camden 23-3-99
From Thurrock, Barking, Ashford U.

2019–20	Doncaster R	5	0		
2020–21	Crawley T	15	13	15	13
2020–21	Cardiff C	3	0		
2021–22	Cardiff C	8	1		
2021–22	Milton Keynes D	11	5	11	5
2022–23	Cardiff C	11	0	22	1
2022–23	Barnsley	19	4		
2023–24	Barnsley	24	3		
2024–25	Barnsley	30	5	73	12

WEST, Callum (M) — 0 0
b. 28-10-05

| 2024–25 | Barnsley | 0 | 0 | |

WILKINSON, Oliver (D)   0   0
b. 24-1-09
Internationals: England U16.
| 2024–25 | Barnsley | 0 | 0 | | |

WILSON, Aston (G)   0   0
| 2024–25 | Barnsley | 0 | 0 | | |

WOLFE, Matthew (M)   46   1
H: 6 1   W: 11 11   b.Wakefield 12-6-00
2017–18	Barnsley	0	0		
2018–19	Barnsley	0	0		
2019–20	Barnsley	1	0		
2020–21	Barnsley	0	0		
2021–22	Barnsley	16	0		
2021–22	Esbjerg	16	1	16	1
2022–23	Barnsley	13	0		
2023–24	Barnsley	0	0		
2024–25	Barnsley	0	0	30	0
Transferred to Sligo R, January 2025.

YOGANATHAN, Vimal (M)   5   0
H: 5 6   W: 11 11   b.Trelawnyd 13-1-06
Internationals: Wales U19.
| 2023–24 | Barnsley | 0 | 0 | | |
| 2024–25 | Barnsley | 5 | 0 | 5 | 0 |

Scholars
Afuape, Oluwafeyisayomi Sean; Alker, Luke William; Andrassy, Jake; Cutler, Euan Thomas; Daniel, Kalaab; Graham, Kieran Jack; Kay, Arley Wayne; Kozluk, Ziggy Bob; Lundoloki, Geoffrey Sala; McCann, Bayley; Ogbu, Chrysolite Ikechukwu; Price, Charles Nicholas; Probert, Elliott James; Rayner, Max; Reid, Kallum Nathaniel; Senior, Tom Lawrence; Swift, Maxwell; Thompson, William Alan; Tommy-Mbogba, Malachi Moisa Asare; Warburton, Owen Conner; Ward, Noah Richard Garth; Wilson, Aston Craig; Woodcock, Jack Owen; Woodcock, Robson Luke.

BARROW (6)

ACQUAH, Emile (F)   124   17
H: 6 3   W: 13 03   b.Hackney 13-7-00
Internationals: England C.
2018–19	Southend U	3	0		
2019–20	Southend U	7	1		
2020–21	Southend U	31	2	41	3
From Maidenhead U.
2023–24	Barrow	44	8		
2024–25	Barrow	39	6	83	14

BARNES, Samuel (D)   4   0
H: 5 11   W: 10 01   b.Blackburn 10-3-01
2020–21	Blackburn R	0	0		
2021–22	Blackburn R	0	0		
2022–23	Blackburn R	0	0		
2023–24	Blackburn R	0	0		
2024–25	Barrow	4	0	4	0

CAMPBELL, Dean (M)   157   6
H: 5 11   W: 10 03   b.Bridge of Don 18-5-01
Internationals: Scotland U16, U17, U18, U19.
2016–17	Aberdeen	1	0		
2017–18	Aberdeen	1	0		
2018–19	Aberdeen	8	1		
2019–20	Aberdeen	15	0		
2020–21	Aberdeen	20	0		
2021–22	Aberdeen	12	0		
2021–22	Kilmarnock	8	0	8	0
2022–23	Aberdeen	0	0	57	1
2022–23	Stevenage	14	0	14	0
2023–24	Barrow	45	4		
2024–25	Barrow	33	1	78	5

CANAVAN, Niall (D)   446   29
H: 6 3   W: 12 00   b.Guiseley 11-4-91
Internationals: Republic of Ireland U21.
2009–10	Scunthorpe U	7	1		
2010–11	Scunthorpe U	8	0		
2010–11	Shrewsbury T	3	0	3	0
2011–12	Scunthorpe U	12	1		
2012–13	Scunthorpe U	40	6		
2013–14	Scunthorpe U	45	4		
2014–15	Scunthorpe U	32	3		
2015–16	Scunthorpe U	10	0	154	15
2015–16	Rochdale	11	1		
2016–17	Rochdale	25	2		
2017–18	Rochdale	3	0	39	3
2018–19	Plymouth Arg	33	2		
2019–20	Plymouth Arg	33	2		
2020–21	Plymouth Arg	12	1	78	5
2020–21	Bradford C	16	0		
2021–22	Bradford C	17	1	33	1
2021–22	Barrow	18	0		
2022–23	Barrow	46	2		
2023–24	Barrow	39	3		
2024–25	Barrow	36	0	139	5

DANIELS, Luke (G)   246   0
H: 6 5   W: 14 02   b.Bolton 5-1-88
Internationals: England U18, U19.
| 2006–07 | WBA | 0 | 0 | | |

2007–08	Motherwell	2	0	2	0
2007–08	WBA	0	0		
2008–09	WBA	0	0		
2008–09	Shrewsbury T	38	0	38	0
2009–10	WBA	0	0		
2009–10	Tranmere R	37	0	37	0
2010–11	WBA	0	0		
2010–11	Charlton Ath	0	0		
2010–11	Rochdale	1	0	1	0
2010–11	Bristol R	9	0	9	0
2011–12	WBA	0	0		
2011–12	Southend U	9	0	9	0
2012–13	WBA	0	0		
2013–14	WBA	1	0		
2014–15	WBA	0	0		
2014–15	Scunthorpe U	23	0		
2015–16	Scunthorpe U	39	0		
2016–17	Scunthorpe U	39	0	101	0
2016–17	Brentford	0	0		
2017–18	Brentford	1	0		
2018–19	Brentford	12	0		
2019–20	Brentford	0	0		
2020–21	Brentford	4	0	17	0
2021–22	Middlesbrough	12	0		
2022–23	Middlesbrough	0	0	12	0
2023–24	Forest Green R	19	0	19	0
2024–25	Barrow	0	0		

ETALUKU, Sean (F)   1   0
H: 5 9   W: 11 03   b.Denton 5-12-03
| 2023–24 | Barrow | 1 | 0 | | |
| 2024–25 | Barrow | 0 | 0 | 1 | 0 |
Transferred to Macclesfield, October 2024.

FARMAN, Paul (G)   285   0
H: 6 5   W: 14 07   b.North Shields 2-11-89
From Blyth Spartans, Gateshead.
2017–18	Lincoln C	13	0	13	0
2018–19	Stevenage	33	0		
2019–20	Stevenage	35	0	68	0
2020–21	Carlisle U	42	0	42	0
2021–22	Barrow	46	0		
2022–23	Barrow	43	0		
2023–24	Barrow	44	0		
2024–25	Barrow	29	0	162	0

FLETCHER, Isaac (M)   25   2
H: 6 4   b.Middlesbrough 1-6-02
2020–21	Middlesbrough	0	0		
2021–22	Middlesbrough	0	0		
2021–22	Hartlepool U	14	1	14	1
2022–23	Middlesbrough	0	0		
From Spennymoor T.
2024–25	Barrow	11	1	11	1

FOLEY, Sam (M)   431   27
H: 6 0   W: 11 09   b.St Albans 17-10-86
Internationals: Republic of Ireland U18.
2012–13	Yeovil T	41	5		
2013–14	Yeovil T	7	0		
2013–14	Shrewsbury T	9	0	9	0
2014–15	Yeovil T	40	2	88	7
2015–16	Port Vale	45	6		
2016–17	Port Vale	32	1	77	7
2016–17	Northampton T	0	0		
2017–18	Northampton T	24	2		
2018–19	Northampton T	36	2	60	4
2019–20	St Mirren	27	1		
2020–21	St Mirren	11	0	38	1
2020–21	Motherwell	4	0	4	0
2021–22	Tranmere R	39	1	39	1
2022–23	Barrow	39	0		
2023–24	Barrow	43	4		
2024–25	Barrow	34	3	116	7

GARNER, Gerard (F)   133   24
H: 5 11   W: 11 07   b.Liverpool 2-11-98
2017–18	Fleetwood	0	0		
2018–19	Fleetwood T	1	0		
2019–20	Fleetwood T	0	0		
2020–21	Fleetwood T	17	3		
2021–22	Fleetwood T	28	7		
2022–23	Fleetwood T	13	1	59	11
2022–23	Barrow	16	2		
2023–24	Barrow	18	2		
2023–24	Morecambe	16	4		
2024–25	Barrow	16	3	50	7
2024–25	Morecambe	8	2	24	6

GOTTS, Robbie (M)   185   11
H: 5 10   W: 11 03   b.Harrogate 9-11-99
2018–19	Leeds U	1	0		
2019–20	Leeds U	1	0		
2020–21	Leeds U	0	0	1	0
2020–21	Lincoln C	7	0	7	0
2020–21	Salford C	23	3	23	3
2021–22	Barrow	35	2		
2022–23	Barrow	37	1		
2023–24	Barrow	41	2		
2024–25	Barrow	41	3	154	8

JACKSON, Ben (M)   110   4
H: 5 10   W: 11 00   b.Stockport 22-2-01
2019–20	Huddersfield T	0	0		
2020–21	Huddersfield T	1	0		
2020–21	Bolton W	5	1	5	1

2021–22	Huddersfield T	0	0		
2021–22	Doncaster R	15	0	15	0
2022–23	Huddersfield T	19	1		
2023–24	Huddersfield T	25	1	45	2
2024–25	Barrow	45	1	45	1

KIRK, Charlie (M)   258   34
H: 5 9   W: 11 00   b.Winsford 24-12-97
2015–16	Crewe Alex	14	0		
2016–17	Crewe Alex	22	0		
2017–18	Crewe Alex	25	5		
2018–19	Crewe Alex	42	11		
2019–20	Crewe Alex	36	7		
2020–21	Crewe Alex	42	6		
2021–22	Charlton Ath	8	0		
2021–22	Blackpool	9	0	9	0
2022–23	Charlton Ath	21	3		
2022–23	Burton Alb	14	2	14	2
2023–24	Charlton Ath	4	0	33	3
2023–24	Crewe Alex	14	0	195	29
2024–25	Barrow	7	0	7	0

KOUYATE, Katia (F)   21   0
H: 6 0   W: 11 11   b.Manchester 9-9-03
| 2024–25 | Barrow | 21 | 0 | 21 | 0 |

MAHONEY, Connor (M)   195   13
H: 5 9   W: 10 08   b.Blackburn 12-2-97
Internationals: England U17, U18, U20.
2013–14	Accrington S	4	0	4	0
2013–14	Blackburn R	0	0		
2014–15	Blackburn R	0	0		
2015–16	Blackburn R	0	0		
2016–17	Blackburn R	14	0	16	0
2017–18	Bournemouth	0	0		
2017–18	Barnsley	8	0	8	0
2018–19	Bournemouth	0	0		
2018–19	Birmingham C	30	2	30	2
2019–20	Millwall	38	2		
2020–21	Millwall	14	1		
2021–22	Millwall	8	0	60	3
2022–23	Huddersfield T	9	0		
2023–24	Huddersfield T	0	0	9	0
2023–24	Gillingham	39	7	39	7
2024–25	Barrow	29	1	29	1

NEWBY, Elliot (M)   107   3
H: 5 10   W: 11 07   b.Barrow-in-Furness 21-11-95
2022–23	Stockport Co	2	0	2	0
2022–23	Barrow	17	0		
2023–24	Barrow	45	0		
2024–25	Barrow	44	3	105	3

OGUNGBO, Mazeed (D)   32   1
H: 6 2   W: 13 10   b. 20-10-02
Internationals: Republic of Ireland U16, U19.
2021–22	Arsenal	0	0		
2022–23	Arsenal	0	0		
2022–23	Crawley T	23	1	23	1
2023–24	Barrow	8	0		
2024–25	Barrow	1	0	9	0

SPENCE, Kian (M)   77   14
H: 5 10   W: 11 11   b.Harrogate 9-1-01
| 2023–24 | Barrow | 45 | 9 | | |
| 2024–25 | Barrow | 32 | 5 | 77 | 14 |

STANWAY, Wyll (G)   17   0
H: 6 4   W: 13 05   b.Barrow-in-Furness 21-5-01
Internationals: England C.
| 2024–25 | Barrow | 17 | 0 | 17 | 0 |

STOKES, Chris (M)   262   15
H: 6 1   W: 13 01   b.Trowbridge 8-3-91
Internationals: England U17, C.
| 2009–10 | Bolton W | 0 | 0 | | |
| 2009–10 | Crewe Alex | 2 | 0 | 2 | 0 |
From Swindon Supermarine, Forest Green R.
2014–15	Coventry C	16	1		
2015–16	Coventry C	36	2		
2016–17	Coventry C	7	0		
2017–18	Coventry C	29	0	88	3
2018–19	Bury	37	4	37	4
2019–20	Stevenage	25	0	25	0
2019–20	Forest Green R	0	0		
2020–21	Forest Green R	34	2	39	2
2021–22	Kilmarnock	19	2		
2022–23	Kilmarnock	15	2	34	4
2023–24	Morecambe	24	2	24	2
2024–25	Barrow	13	0	13	0
Transferred to AFC Fylde, January 2025.

TELFORD, Dominic (F)   259   56
H: 5 9   W: 11 05   b.Burnley 5-12-96
2014–15	Blackpool	14	1		
2015–16	Blackpool	0	0	14	1
2016–17	Stoke C	0	0		
2017–18	Stoke C	0	0		
2017–18	Bristol R	19	3	19	3
2018–19	Bury	38	6	38	6
2019–20	Plymouth Arg	19	2		
2020–21	Plymouth Arg	16	1	35	3
2020–21	Newport Co	5	0		
2021–22	Newport Co	37	25	52	26
2022–23	Crawley T	43	12		

2023–24 Crawley T	4	0	47	12
2023–24 Barrow	38	4		
2024–25 Barrow	16	1	54	5

TIENSIA, Junior (D) 17 0
H: 5 10 W: 12 00 b. 25-12-00

2019–20 Millwall	0	0		
2020–21 Millwall	0	0		
2021–22 Millwall	0	0		

From Gloucester C, Solihull Moors.

2023–24 Barrow	9	0		
2024–25 Barrow	8	0	17	0

VASSELL, Theo (D) 164 12
H: 6 0 W: 10 10 b.Stoke 2-1-97

2014–15 Stoke C	0	0		
2015–16 Oldham Ath	0	0		
2016–17 Walsall	0	0		

From Gateshead.

2018–19 Port Vale	15	0	15	0
2019–20 Macclesfield T	17	2	17	2

From Wrexham.

2021–22 Salford C	27	1		
2022–23 Salford C	45	3		
2023–24 Salford C	28	1	100	5
2024–25 Barrow	32	5	32	5

WESTON, Charlie (M) 1 0
H: 5 10 W: 11 09 b.Oldham 13-7-04
Internationals: England U16.

2023–24 Blackburn R	0	0		
2024–25 Barrow	1	0	1	0

Transferred to Rochdale, December 2024.

WILLIAMS, M Jordan (M) 252 3
H: 6 0 W: 12 02 b.Bangor 6-11-95
Internationals: Wales U17, U21.

2014–15 Liverpool	0	0		
2014–15 Notts Co	8	0	8	0
2015–16 Liverpool	0	0		
2015–16 Swindon T	9	0		
2016–17 Liverpool	0	0		
2016–17 Swindon T	0	0	9	0
2017–18 Liverpool	0	0		
2017–18 Rochdale	12	0		
2018–19 Rochdale	28	0		
2019–20 Rochdale	28	0	68	0
2020–21 Blackpool	10	0	10	0
2020–21 Bolton W	21	0		
2021–22 Bolton W	40	1		
2022–23 Bolton W	28	0	89	1
2023–24 Milton Keynes D	37	1		
2024–25 Milton Keynes D	13	1	50	2
2024–25 Barrow	18	0	18	0

WORRALL, David (M) 554 42
H: 6 0 W: 11 02 b.Manchester 12-6-90

2006–07 Bury	1	0		
2007–08 Bury	0	0		
2007–08 WBA	0	0		
2008–09 Accrington S	4	0	4	0
2008–09 Shrewsbury T	9	0	9	0
2009–10 WBA	0	0		
2009–10 Bury	40	4		
2010–11 Bury	40	2		
2011–12 Bury	41	3		
2012–13 Bury	41	2	163	11
2013–14 Rotherham U	3	1	3	1
2013–14 Oldham Ath	18	1	18	1
2014–15 Southend U	38	6		
2015–16 Southend U	35	3	73	9
2016–17 Millwall	33	1	33	1
2017–18 Port Vale	40	4		
2018–19 Port Vale	25	1		
2019–20 Port Vale	34	4		
2020–21 Port Vale	37	5		
2021–22 Port Vale	41	4		
2022–23 Port Vale	39	1	216	19
2023–24 Barrow	30	0		
2024–25 Barrow	5	0	35	0

Players retained or with offer of contract
Shamalo, John Shongo Ndjova.

BIRMINGHAM C (7)

ALLSOP, Ryan (G) 379 2
H: 6 2 W: 12 08 b.Birmingham 17-6-92
Internationals: England U17.

2009–10 WBA	0	0		
2010–11 WBA	0	0		
2011–12 Millwall	0	0		
2012 Hottur	8	2	8	2
2012–13 Leyton Orient	20	0	20	0
2012–13 Bournemouth	10	0		
2013–14 Bournemouth	12	0		
2014–15 Bournemouth	0	0		
2014–15 Coventry C	24	0	24	0
2015–16 Bournemouth	1	0		
2015–16 Wycombe W	18	0		
2015–16 Portsmouth	0	0		
2016–17 Bournemouth	1	0		
2017–18 Bournemouth	0	0	24	0
2017–18 Blackpool	22	0	22	0
2017–18 Lincoln C	16	0	16	0
2018–19 Wycombe W	38	0		
2019–20 Wycombe W	32	0		
2019–20 Wycombe W	29	0	117	0
2020–21 Northampton T	30	0	30	0
2021–22 Derby Co	30	0	30	0
2022–23 Cardiff C	43	0	43	0
2023–24 Hull C	37	0	37	0
2024–25 Birmingham C	38	0	38	0

ANDERSON, Keshi (F) 244 35
H: 5 9 W: 10 10 b.Luton 15-11-95

2014–15 Crystal Palace	0	0		
2015–16 Crystal Palace	0	0		
2015–16 Doncaster R	7	3	7	3
2016–17 Crystal Palace	0	0		
2016–17 Bolton W	8	1	8	1
2016–17 Northampton T	14	3	14	3
2017–18 Swindon T	37	5		
2018–19 Swindon T	43	4		
2019–20 Swindon T	20	6	100	15
2020–21 Blackpool	17	2		
2021–22 Blackpool	32	4		
2022–23 Blackpool	9	0	58	6
2023–24 Birmingham C	20	0		
2024–25 Birmingham C	37	7	57	7

BETTEKA, Zaid (M) 0 0
H: 5 4 W: 7 12 b. 7-2-07

2024–25 Birmingham C	0	0		

BIELIK, Krystian (M) 197 8
H: 5 10 W: 11 00 b.Vrinnevi 4-1-98
Internationals: Poland U16, U17, U18, U19, U21, Full caps.

2014–15 Legia Warsaw	5	0	5	0
2014–15 Arsenal	0	0		
2015–16 Arsenal	0	0		
2016–17 Arsenal	0	0		
2016–17 Birmingham C	10	0		
2017–18 Arsenal	0	0		
2017–18 Walsall	0	0		
2018–19 Arsenal	0	0		
2018–19 Charlton Ath	31	3	31	3
2019–20 Derby Co	20	0		
2020–21 Derby Co	13	2		
2021–22 Derby Co	15	1		
2022–23 Derby Co	0	0	48	3
2022–23 Birmingham C	35	1		
2023–24 Birmingham C	36	0		
2024–25 Birmingham C	32	1	113	2

BUCHANAN, Lee (D) 126 2
H: 5 9 W: 10 08 b.Mansfield 7-3-01
Internationals: England U19, U20, U21.

2018–19 Derby Co	0	0		
2019–20 Derby Co	5	0		
2020–21 Derby Co	35	0		
2021–22 Derby Co	30	0	70	0
2022–23 Werder Bremen	21	1	21	1
2023–24 Birmingham C	32	0		
2024–25 Birmingham C	3	1	35	1

CHANG, Alfie (M) 18 0
H: 6 1 W: 10 10 b.Worcester 4-9-02

2021–22 Birmingham C	0	0		
2022–23 Birmingham C	13	0		
2023–24 Birmingham C	0	0		
2024–25 Birmingham C	0	0	13	0
2024–25 Walsall	5	0	5	0

COCHRANE, Alex (M) 145 5
H: 6 0 W: 12 00 b.Brighton 21-4-00
Internationals: England U16, U20.

2019–20 Brighton & HA	0	0		
2020–21 Brighton & HA	0	0		
2020–21 Union SG	7	0	7	0
2021–22 Brighton & HA	0	0		
2021–22 Hearts	32	2		
2022–23 Hearts	33	2		
2023–24 Hearts	31	0	96	4
2024–25 Birmingham C	42	1	42	1

DAVIES, Ben (D) 317 6
H: 6 1 W: 11 09 b.Barrow 11-8-95

2012–13 Preston NE	3	0		
2013–14 Preston NE	0	0		
2013–14 York C	44	0	44	0
2014–15 Preston NE	4	0		
2014–15 Tranmere R	3	0	3	0
2015–16 Preston NE	0	0		
2015–16 Newport Co	19	0	19	0
2016–17 Preston NE	0	0		
2016–17 Fleetwood T	22	1	22	1
2017–18 Preston NE	34	1		
2018–19 Preston NE	40	1		
2019–20 Preston NE	36	0		
2020–21 Preston NE	19	0	136	2
2020–21 Liverpool	0	0		
2021–22 Liverpool	0	0		
2021–22 Sheffield U	22	1	22	1
2022–23 Rangers	27	0		
2023–24 Rangers	8	1		

On loan from Rangers.

2024–25 Birmingham C	35	1	35	1

DIXON, Junior (F) 0 0
H: 6 1 b.London 24-10-04

2023–24 Birmingham C	0	0		
2024–25 Birmingham C	0	0		

DONOVAN, Romelle (M) 13 0
H: 5 9 W: 11 03 b.Birmingham 30-11-06
Internationals: England U18, U19.

2022–23 Birmingham C	0	0		
2023–24 Birmingham C	7	0		
2024–25 Birmingham C	0	0	7	0
2024–25 Burton Alb	6	0	6	0
2024–25 Brentford	0	0		

DOWELL, Kieran (F) 187 34
H: 5 9 W: 9 04 b.Ormskirk 10-10-97
Internationals: England U16, U17, U18, U20, U21.

2014–15 Everton	0	0		
2015–16 Everton	2	0		
2016–17 Everton	0	0		
2017–18 Everton	0	0		
2017–18 Nottingham F	38	9	38	9
2018–19 Everton	0	0		
2018–19 Sheffield U	16	2	16	2
2019–20 Everton	0	0	2	0
2019–20 Derby Co	10	0	10	0
2020–21 Wigan Ath	12	5	12	5
2020–21 Norwich C	24	5		
2021–22 Norwich C	19	1		
2022–23 Norwich C	23	5	66	11
2023–24 Rangers	12	2		
2024–25 Rangers	12	0	24	2

On loan from Rangers.

2024–25 Birmingham C	19	5	19	5

DYKES, Lyndon (F) 309 58
H: 6 2 W: 13 03 b.Queensland, Australia 7-10-95
Internationals: Scotland Full caps.
From Mudgeeraba, Merrimac, Redlands U, Gold Cost C, Surfers Paradise Apollo.

2016–17 Queen of the South	30	2		
2017–18 Queen of the South	34	7		
2018–19 Queen of the South	36	2	100	11
2019–20 Livingston	25	9		
2020–21 Livingston	3	2	28	11
2020–21 QPR	42	12		
2021–22 QPR	33	8		
2022–23 QPR	39	8		
2023–24 QPR	41	6		
2024–25 QPR	1	1	156	35
2024–25 Birmingham C	25	1	25	1

EMMANUEL, Mbule (D) 55 2
H: 6 0 W: 11 00 b.Barking 27-12-00

2020–21 West Ham U	0	0		
2021–22 West Ham U	0	0		
2022–23 Birmingham C	23	1		
2023–24 Birmingham C	17	0		
2024–25 Birmingham C	0	0	40	1
2024–25 Cambridge U	15	1	15	1

FOGARTY, Tom (D) 19 0
b. 15-3-04
Internationals: Northern Ireland U21.

2023–24 Birmingham C	0	0		
2024–25 Birmingham C	0	0		
2024–25 Dunfermline Ath	19	0	19	0

HALL, George (M) 54 4
H: 5 9 W: 11 00 b.Redditch 15-7-04
Internationals: England U18, U19.

2021–22 Birmingham C	2	0		
2022–23 Birmingham C	30	2		
2023–24 Birmingham C	8	0		
2024–25 Birmingham C	0	0	40	2
2024–25 Walsall	14	2	14	2

HANLEY, Grant (D) 388 13
H: 6 3 W: 12 00 b.Dumfries 20-11-91
Internationals: Scotland U19, U21, Full caps.
From Rangers.

2008–09 Blackburn R	0	0		
2009–10 Blackburn R	1	0		
2010–11 Blackburn R	7	0		
2011–12 Blackburn R	23	1		
2012–13 Blackburn R	39	2		
2013–14 Blackburn R	38	1		
2014–15 Blackburn R	31	1		
2015–16 Blackburn R	44	2	183	7
2016–17 Newcastle U	10	1		
2017–18 Newcastle U	0	0	10	1
2017–18 Norwich C	32	1		
2018–19 Norwich C	9	1		
2019–20 Norwich C	15	0		
2020–21 Norwich C	42	1		
2021–22 Norwich C	33	1		
2022–23 Norwich C	39	1		
2023–24 Norwich C	8	0		
2024–25 Norwich C	3	0	181	5
2024–25 Birmingham C	14	0	14	0

HANSSON, Emil (F) **197 37**
H: 5 8 W: 10 03 b.Bergen 15-6-98
Internationals: Sweden U17. Norway U165, U17, U18, U19, U21.

2015	Brann	2	0	**2**	**0**
2016–17	Feyenoord	2	0		
2017–18	Feyenoord	1	0		
2018–19	Feyenoord	0	0	**3**	**0**
2018–19	*RKC Waalwijk*	35	12		
2019–20	Hannover 96	14	0	**14**	**0**
2019–20	*RKC Waalwijk*	7	1	**42**	**13**
2020–21	Fortuna Sittard	32	2		
2021–22	Fortuna Sittard	11	0	**43**	**2**
2021–22	Heracles	13	0		
2022–23	Heracles	36	16		
2023–24	Heracles	24	5	**73**	**21**
2024–25	Birmingham C	20	1	**20**	**1**

HOME, Josh (M) **0 0**
H: 5 8 W: 10 08 b.Newcastle 21-6-05

2023–24	Birmingham C	0	0		
2024–25	Birmingham C	0	0		

IWATA, Tomoki (M) **251 16**
H: 5 10 W: 11 07 b.Oita 7-4-97
Internationals: Japan U18, U19, U23, Full caps.

2015	Oita Trinita	0	0		
2016	Oita Trinita	24	1		
2017	Oita Trinita	12	0		
2018	Oita Trinita	20	0		
2019	Oita Trinita	27	4		
2020	Oita Trinita	30	2	**113**	**7**
2021	Yokohama F Marinos	34	0		
2022	Yokohama F Marinos	32	2	**66**	**2**
2022–23	*Celtic*	13	0		
2023–24	Celtic	19	1	**32**	**1**
2024–25	Birmingham C	40	6	**40**	**6**

JUTKIEWICZ, Lucas (F) **596 117**
H: 6 1 W: 11 08 b.Southampton 28-3-89

2005–06	Swindon T	5	0		
2006–07	Swindon T	33	5	**38**	**5**
2006–07	Everton	0	0		
2007–08	Everton	0	0		
2007–08	*Plymouth Arg*	3	0	**3**	**0**
2008–09	Everton	1	0		
2008–09	*Huddersfield T*	7	0	**7**	**0**
2009–10	Everton	0	0	**1**	**0**
2009–10	*Motherwell*	33	12	**33**	**12**
2010–11	Coventry C	42	9		
2011–12	Coventry C	25	9	**67**	**18**
2011–12	Middlesbrough	19	2		
2012–13	Middlesbrough	24	8		
2013–14	Middlesbrough	22	1	**65**	**11**
2013–14	*Bolton W*	20	7	**20**	**7**
2014–15	Burnley	25	0		
2015–16	Burnley	5	0		
2016–17	Burnley	2	0	**32**	**0**
2016–17	Birmingham C	38	11		
2017–18	Birmingham C	35	5		
2018–19	Birmingham C	46	14		
2019–20	Birmingham C	46	15		
2020–21	Birmingham C	42	8		
2021–22	Birmingham C	36	2		
2022–23	Birmingham C	43	5		
2023–24	Birmingham C	28	3		
2024–25	Birmingham C	16	1	**330**	**64**

KHELA, Brandon (M) **32 0**
H: 5 11 W: 11 11 b.Coventry 19-1-05
Internationals: England U17.

2021–22	Birmingham C	0	0		
2022–23	Birmingham C	0	0		
2023–24	Birmingham C	1	0		
2023–24	*Ross Co*	14	0	**14**	**0**
2024–25	Birmingham C	2	0	**3**	**0**
2024–25	*Bradford C*	15	0	**15**	**0**

KLARER, Christoph (D) **160 8**
H: 6 3 W: 12 13 b.Boheimkirchen 14-6-00
Internationals: Austria U16, U17, U18, U19, U21.

2017–18	Southampton	0	0		
2018–19	Southampton	0	0		
2019–20	Southampton	0	0		
2019–20	*St Polten*	13	0	**13**	**0**
2020–21	Fortuna Dusseldorf	13	0		
2021–22	Fortuna Dusseldorf	31	3		
2022–23	Fortuna Dusseldorf	30	2	**74**	**5**
2023–24	Darmstadt 98	30	2	**30**	**2**
2024–25	Birmingham C	43	1	**43**	**1**

LAIRD, Ethan (D) **142 5**
H: 5 10 W: 10 06 b.Basingstoke 5-8-01
Internationals: England U17, U18, U19.

2019–20	Manchester U	0	0		
2020–21	Manchester U	0	0		
2020–21	*Milton Keynes D*	24	0	**24**	**0**
2021–22	Manchester U	0	0		
2021–22	*Swansea C*	20	0	**20**	**0**
2021–22	*Bournemouth*	6	0	**6**	**0**
2022–23	Manchester U	0	0		
2022–23	*QPR*	32	1	**32**	**1**
2023–24	Birmingham C	25	0		
2024–25	Birmingham C	35	4	**60**	**4**

LEE, Myung-Jae (D) **209 1**
H: 6 0 W: 10 10 b.Seoul 4-11-93
Internationals: South Korea U20, U23, Full caps.

2014	Ulsan HD	2	0		
2014	*Albirex Niigata*	5	0	**5**	**0**
2015	Ulsan HD	19	0		
2016	Ulsan HD	5	0		
2017	Ulsan HD	32	1		
2018	Ulsan HD	32	0		
2019	Ulsan HD	24	0		
2020	Sangju Sangmu	0	0		
2021	Gimcheon Sangmu	8	0	**8**	**0**
2021	Ulsan HD	2	0		
2022	Ulsan HD	19	0		
2023	Ulsan HD	30	0		
2024	Ulsan HD	28	0	**193**	**1**
2024–25	Birmingham C	3	0	**3**	**0**

LEONARD, Marc (M) **126 6**
H: 5 11 W: 12 00 b.Glasgow 19-12-01
Internationals: Scotland U17, U18, U19, U21.
From Hearts.

2020–21	Brighton & HA	0	0		
2021–22	Brighton & HA	0	0		
2022–23	Brighton & HA	0	0		
2022–23	*Northampton T*	45	1		
2023–24	Brighton & HA	0	0		
2023–24	*Northampton T*	46	5	**91**	**6**
2024–25	Birmingham C	35	0	**35**	**0**

MAY, Alfie (F) **320 107**
H: 5 9 W: 11 05 b.Gravesend 2-7-93
From Billericay T, Chatham T, VCD Ath, Erith & Belvedere, Farnborough, Hythe T.

2016–17	Doncaster R	16	3		
2017–18	Doncaster R	27	4		
2018–19	Doncaster R	34	2		
2019–20	Doncaster R	15	1	**92**	**10**
2019–20	Cheltenham T	12	6		
2020–21	Cheltenham T	44	9		
2021–22	Cheltenham T	46	23		
2022–23	Cheltenham T	39	20	**141**	**58**
2023–24	Charlton Ath	43	23	**43**	**23**
2024–25	Birmingham C	44	16	**44**	**16**

MAYO, Bradley (G) **0 0**
H: 6 0 W: 11 11 b.Birmingham 15-9-04

2023–24	Birmingham C	0	0		
2024–25	Birmingham C	0	0		

MIYOSHI, Koji (M) **194 19**
H: 5 6 W: 10 01 b.Kawasaki 26-3-97
Internationals: Japan U17, U18, U19, U20, U21, U23, Full caps.

2015	Kawasaki Frontale	3	0		
2016	Kawasaki Frontale	15	0		
2017	Kawasaki Frontale	13	1		
2018	Kawasaki Frontale	0	0		
2018	*Consadole Sapporo*	26	3	**26**	**3**
2019	Kawasaki Frontale	0	0	**31**	**1**
2019	*Yokohama F Marinos*	19	3	**19**	**3**
2019–20	Royal Antwerp	14	1		
2020–21	Royal Antwerp	23	3		
2021–22	Royal Antwerp	25	1		
2022–23	Royal Antwerp	10	1	**72**	**6**
2023–24	Birmingham C	43	6		
2024–25	Birmingham C	3	0	**46**	**6**

Transferred to Bochum, August 2024.

NEUMANN, Phil (D) **157 4**
H: 6 3 W: 12 04 b.Herten 8-7-97
Internationals: Germany U19, U20.

2014–15	Schalke 04	0	0		
2015–16	Schalke 04	0	0		
2016–17	Schalke 04	0	0		
2017–18	Ingolstad	4	0		
2018–19	Ingolstad	20	1	**24**	**1**
2019–20	Holstein Kiel	25	0		
2020–21	Holstein Kiel	18	0		
2021–22	Holstein Kiel	29	0	**72**	**0**
2022–23	Hannover 96	29	1		
2023–24	Hannover 96	32	2	**61**	**3**
2024–25	Birmingham C	0	0		

PAIK, Seung Ho (M) **240 15**
H: 5 11 W: 12 04 b.Seoul 17-3-97
Internationals: South Korea U20, U23, Full caps.

2015–16	Barcelona	0	0		
2016–17	Barcelona	0	0		
2017–18	Peralada	34	1		
2018–19	Peralada	21	1	**55**	**2**
2018–19	Girona	3	0	**3**	**0**
2019–20	Darmstadt 98	28	2		
2020–21	Darmstadt 98	13	0	**41**	**2**
2021	Jeonbuk Hyundai Motors	25	4		
2022	Jeonbuk Hyundai Motors	30	2		
2023	Jeonbuk Hyundai Motors	27	3	**82**	**9**
2023–24	Birmingham C	18	1		
2024–25	Birmingham C	41	1	**59**	**2**

PEACOCK-FARRELL, Bailey (G) **125 0**
H: 6 4 W: 11 07 b.Darlington 29-10-96
Internationals: Northern Ireland U21, Full caps.
From Middlesbrough.

2015–16	Leeds U	1	0		
2016–17	Leeds U	0	0		
2017–18	Leeds U	11	0		
2018–19	Leeds U	28	0		
2019–20	Leeds U	0	0	**40**	**0**
2019–20	Burnley	0	0		
2020–21	Burnley	4	0		
2021–22	Burnley	0	0		
2021–22	*Sheffield Wed*	43	0	**43**	**0**
2022–23	Burnley	8	0		
2023–24	Burnley	0	0	**12**	**0**
2023–24	*AGF*	21	0	**21**	**0**
2024–25	Birmingham C	9	0	**9**	**0**

PENDLETON, Byron (D) **0 0**
H: 5 11 W: 10 12 b. 15-12-05

2024–25	Birmingham C	0	0		

PENNINGTON, Cody (M) **0 0**
b.Preston 13-6-06

2024–25	Birmingham C	0	0		

ROBERTS, Tyler (F) **208 22**
H: 5 11 W: 11 11 b.Gloucester 12-1-98
Internationals: Wales U16, U17, U19, U20, U21, Full caps.

2014–15	WBA	0	0		
2015–16	WBA	1	0		
2016–17	WBA	0	0	**1**	**0**
2016–17	*Oxford U*	14	0	**14**	**0**
2016–17	*Shrewsbury T*	13	4	**13**	**4**
2017–18	Leeds U	0	0		
2017–18	*Walsall*	17	5	**17**	**5**
2018–19	Leeds U	28	3		
2019–20	Leeds U	23	4		
2020–21	Leeds U	27	1		
2021–22	Leeds U	23	1		
2022–23	Leeds U	0	0	**101**	**9**
2022–23	*QPR*	18	3	**18**	**3**
2023–24	Birmingham C	17	0		
2024–25	Birmingham C	0	0	**17**	**0**
2024–25	*Northampton T*	27	1	**27**	**1**

SAMPSTED, Alfons (D) **206 5**
H: 5 11 W: 11 05 b.Kopavogur 6-4-98
Internationals: Iceland U16, U17, U19, U21, Full caps.

2015	Breidablik	0	0		
2015	*Por Akureyri*	9	0	**9**	**0**
2016	Breidablik	17	0		
2017	Norrkoping	2	0		
2018	Norrkoping	0	0		
2018	*Landskrona*	12	1	**12**	**1**
2019	Norrkoping	0	0	**2**	**0**
2019	*Sylvia*	16	1	**16**	**1**
2019	*Breidablik*	8	1	**25**	**1**
2020	Bodo/Glimt	29	0		
2021	Bodo/Glimt	29	0		
2022	Bodo/Glimt	30	1	**88**	**1**
2022–23	FC Twente	13	0		
2023–24	FC Twente	24	0		
2024–25	FC Twente	0	0	**37**	**0**

On loan from FC Twente.

2024–25	Birmingham C	17	1	**17**	**1**

SANDERSON, Dion (D) **144 4**
H: 6 2 W: 12 04 b.Wolverhampton 15-12-99

2019–20	Wolverhampton W	0	0		
2019–20	*Cardiff C*	10	0	**10**	**0**
2020–21	Wolverhampton W	0	0		
2020–21	*Sunderland*	26	1	**26**	**1**
2021–22	Wolverhampton W	0	0		
2021–22	*Birmingham C*	15	0		
2021–22	*QPR*	11	0	**11**	**0**
2022–23	Wolverhampton W	0	0		
2022–23	*Birmingham C*	31	2		
2023–24	Birmingham C	37	1		
2024–25	Birmingham C	2	0	**85**	**3**
2024–25	*Blackburn R*	12	0	**12**	**0**

STANSFIELD, Jay (F) **122 40**
H: 5 11 W: 10 12 b.Exeter 24-11-02
Internationals: England U18, U20, U21.
From Exeter C.

2019–20	Fulham	1	0		
2020–21	Fulham	0	0		
2021–22	Fulham	1	0		
2022–23	Fulham	3	0		
2022–23	*Exeter C*	36	9	**36**	**9**
2023–24	Fulham	0	0		
2023–24	*Birmingham C*	43	12		
2024–25	Fulham	1	0	**6**	**0**
2024–25	Birmingham C	37	19	**80**	**31**

WILLUMSSON, Willum (M) **183 36**
H: 6 4 W: 13 03 b.Reykjavik 23-10-98
Internationals: Iceland U19, U21, Full caps.

2016	Breidablik	1	0		
2017	Breidablik	8	0		
2018	Breidablik	19	6	**28**	**6**

2019	BATE Borisov	19	1	
2020	BATE Borisov	18	3	
2021	BATE Borisov	9	1	
2022	BATE Borisov	10	4	56 9
2022–23	Go Ahead Eagles	27	8	
2023–24	Go Ahead Eagles	31	7	58 15
2024–25	Birmingham C	41	6	41 6

WRIGHT, Scott (F)   **161 17**
H: 5 9   W: 10 03   b.Aberdeen 8-8-97
Internationals: Scotland U17, U19, U20, U21.

2014–15	Aberdeen	1	0
2015–16	Aberdeen	4	0
2016–17	Aberdeen	5	3
2017–18	Aberdeen	16	1
2018–19	Aberdeen	13	0
2018–19	*Dundee*	13 3	13 3
2019–20	Aberdeen	3	0
2020–21	Aberdeen	17 2	59 6
2020–21	Rangers	9	1
2021–22	Rangers	19	4
2022–23	Rangers	23	0
2023–24	Rangers	23	2
2024–25	Rangers	2 0	76 7
2024–25	Birmingham C	13 1	13 1

YOKOYAMA, Ayumu (F)   **96 16**
H: 5 7   W: 10 03   b.Tokyo 4-3-03
Internationals: Japan U20.

2021	Matsumoto Yamaga16	0	
2022	Matsumoto Yamaga29	11	45 11
2023	Sagan Tosu	17	0
2024	Sagan Tosu	24 5	41 5
2024–25	Birmingham C	10	10 0
2024–25	*Genk*	9	

Players retained or with offer of contract
Boakye, Godfred; Ellis, O'Shea James;
Eubank, Cameron Paul Joseph; Havenhand,
Kurtis Ryan; Isichei, Daniel Francis;
Maphosa Mazwi, Menzi Brayden; O'Sullivan,
William Joseph; Ruiz Rente, Alvaro; Tattum,
Frank Peter Arthur; Willis, Zachary James;
Wodskou, Benjamin Michael Martin.

Scholars
Ahmed, Mohammed Yusuf; Bamba Biol,
Salif; Bateman, Bria; Brannigan, Liam
Joseph; Briscoe, Trae Anthony Rion; Burrell,
William Harvey; Carvalho Santos Da Silva,
Alezandro De Pedro; Flavell, Benjamin
Oliver; Guernier, Aurelien Alexandre Max;
Maddox, Cobi Joel; Martin-Moore, Dynaeo
Dieago; McCusker, Kian Matthew James;
Okpapi, Dylan James Kweku; Quirk, Jack
William; Rea, Louie; Robinson, Kaidon
Rahvaun; Sanders, Caleb Stewart;
Terenowicz, Szymon Simon; Thompson-
Jones, Riquelme Nathan Reece; Ugorji,
Tobechwukwu Ogadima; Warmington,
Tyrese Karl; Wynne, Loughlin George.

BLACKBURN R (8)

ATCHESON, Tom (D)   **0 0**
H: 6 3   W: 13 05   b.22-9-06
Internationals: Northern Ireland U17, U18, U19.

2023–24	Blackburn R	0	0
2024–25	Blackburn R	0	0

BARRETT, Jack (G)   **1 0**
H: 6 3   W: 12 08   b. 4-6-02

2020–21	Everton	0	0
2021–22	Everton	0	0
2022–23	Everton	0	0
2023–24	Everton	0	0
2024	*Cavalry*	1 0	1 0
2024–25	Blackburn R	0	0

BATTH, Danny (D)   **479 26**
H: 6 3   W: 14 02   b.Brierley Hill 21-9-90

2009–10	Wolverhampton W	0	0
2009–10	*Colchester U*	17 1	17 1
2010–11	Wolverhampton W	0	0
2010–11	*Sheffield U*	1 0	1 0
2010–11	*Sheffield Wed*	10 0	
2011–12	Wolverhampton W	0	0
2011–12	*Sheffield Wed*	42 2	54 2
2012–13	Wolverhampton W	12	1
2013–14	Wolverhampton W	46	2
2014–15	Wolverhampton W	44	4
2015–16	Wolverhampton W	38	2
2016–17	Wolverhampton W	39	4
2017–18	Wolverhampton W	16	1
2018–19	Wolverhampton W	0 0	195 14
2018–19	*Middlesbrough*	10 0	10 0
2018–19	Stoke C	17	0
2019–20	Stoke C	43	4
2020–21	Stoke C	29	1
2021–22	Stoke C	11 0	100 5
2021–22	Sunderland	9	1
2022–23	Sunderland	40	0
2023–24	Sunderland	0 0	49 1

2023–24	Norwich C	16 1	16 1	
2024–25	Blackburn R	37 2	37 2	

BATTY, Jake (D)   **25 0**
H: 5 9   W: 11 00   b.Liverpool 5-4-05
Internationals: England U17.

2022–23	Blackburn R	0	0
2023–24	Blackburn R	0	0
2023–24	Blackburn R	0	0
2024–25	*Accrington S*	25 0	25 0

BLOXHAM, Thomas (F)   **6 0**
H: 5 10   W: 11 00   b.Welwyn Garden City
30-4-05
Internationals: England U17. Republic of
Ireland U18, U19.

2023–24	Blackburn R	1	0
2023–24	*Harrogate T*	5 0	5 0
2024–25	Blackburn R	0 0	1 0

BRITTAIN, Callum (D)   **287 7**
H: 5 10   W: 10 10   b.Bedford 12-3-98
Internationals: England U20.

2015–16	Milton Keynes D	0	0
2016	*Prottur Reykjavik*	6 0	6 0
2016–17	Milton Keynes D	6	0
2017–18	Milton Keynes D	29	2
2018–19	Milton Keynes D	31	1
2019–20	Milton Keynes D	31	1
2020–21	Milton Keynes D	4 0	101 4
2020–21	Barnsley	40	0
2021–22	Barnsley	36 0	76 0
2022–23	Blackburn R	27	0
2023–24	Blackburn R	44	1
2024–25	Blackburn R	33 2	104 3

BUCKLEY, John (M)   **160 6**
H: 5 9   W: 9 13   b.Manchester 13-10-99

2018–19	Blackburn R	7	0
2019–20	Blackburn R	20	2
2020–21	Blackburn R	28	1
2021–22	Blackburn R	42	3
2022–23	Blackburn R	21	0
2023–24	*Sheffield Wed*	13 0	13 0
2024–25	Blackburn R	23 0	147 6

CANTWELL, Todd (M)   **208 25**
H: 5 10   W: 10 06   b.Norwich 27-2-98
Internationals: England U17, U21.

2017–18	Norwich C	0	0
2017–18	*Fortuna Sittard*	10 2	10 2
2018–19	Norwich C	24	1
2019–20	Norwich C	37	6
2020–21	Norwich C	33	6
2021–22	Norwich C	8	0
2021–22	Bournemouth	11 0	11 0
2022–23	Norwich C	18 0	120 13
2023–24	Rangers	30 7	30 7
2024–25	Blackburn R	37 3	37 3

CARTER, Hayden (D)   **135 6**
H: 6 2   W: 10 08   b.Stockport 17-12-99
From Manchester C.

2019–20	Blackburn R	2	0
2020–21	Blackburn R	1	0
2020–21	*Burton Alb*	24 4	24 4
2021–22	Blackburn R	9	0
2021–22	Portsmouth	22 1	22 1
2022–23	Blackburn R	30	1
2023–24	Blackburn R	31	0
2024–25	Blackburn R	16 0	89 6

DAM, Isaac (M)   **0 0**
2024–25	Blackburn R	0	0

DOHERTY, Aodhan (F)   **9 0**
b.Belfast 3-5-06
Internationals: Northern Ireland U17, U18, U19.

2022–23	Linfield	0	0
2023–24	Linfield	9 0	9 0
2024–25	Blackburn R	0	0

DOHERTY, Rhys (D)   **0 0**
b. 30-12-05

2023–24	Blackburn R	0	0
2024–25	Blackburn R	0	0

DOLAN, Tyrhys (M)   **191 23**
H: 5 7   W: 8 09   b.Manchester 28-12-98
Internationals: England U20.

2020–21	Blackburn R	37	3
2021–22	Blackburn R	34	4
2022–23	Blackburn R	40	4
2023–24	Blackburn R	36	5
2024–25	Blackburn R	44 7	191 23

DUNN, Isaac (M)   **0 0**
2024–25	Blackburn R	0	0

DURU, Leo (D)   **9 1**
H: 5 9   W: 10 10   b.Manchester 12-1-05
Internationals: USA U20.

2023–24	Blackburn R	0	0
2024–25	Blackburn R	1 0	1 0
2024–25	*Barrow*	8 1	8 1

EDMONDSON, James (M)   **0 0**
b. 1-11-05

2023–24	Blackburn R	0	0
2024–25	Blackburn R	0	0

FINNERAN, Rory (M)   **0 0**
H: 5 10   W: 11 09   b. 29-2-08
Internationals: Republic of Ireland U17.

2023–24	Blackburn R	0	0
2024–25	Blackburn R	0	0

FORSHAW, Adam (M)   **332 15**
H: 5 9   W: 11 03   b.Liverpool 8-10-91

2009–10	Everton	0	0
2010–11	Everton	1	0
2011–12	Everton	0 0	1 0
2011–12	*Brentford*	7	0
2012–13	Brentford	43	3
2013–14	Brentford	39 8	89 11
2014–15	Wigan Ath	16 1	16 1
2014–15	Middlesbrough	18	0
2015–16	Middlesbrough	29	2
2016–17	Middlesbrough	34	0
2017–18	Middlesbrough	11 0	92 2
2017–18	Leeds U	12	0
2018–19	Leeds U	30	0
2020–21	Leeds U	7	0
2021–22	Leeds U	22	0
2022–23	Leeds U	12 0	83 0
2023–24	Norwich C	6 0	6 0
2023–24	Plymouth Arg	13	0
2024–25	Plymouth Arg	16 0	29 0
2024–25	Blackburn R	16 1	16 1

GAMBLE, Patrick (D)   **0 0**
H: 6 3   W: 12 13   b.Liverpool 5-10-03

2023–24	Blackburn R	0	0
2024–25	Blackburn R	0	0

GARRETT, Jake (D)   **47 2**
H: 6 2   W: 11 11   b.Liverpool 10-3-03
Internationals: England U16.

2020–21	Blackburn R	0	0
2021–22	Blackburn R	0	0
2022–23	Blackburn R	8	0
2023–24	Blackburn R	21	1
2023–24	Blackburn R	0 0	29 1
2024–25	*Bristol R*	7 0	7 0
2024–25	*Tranmere R*	11 1	11 1

GILSENAN, Zak (M)   **2 0**
H: 5 10   W: 9 11   b.Joondalup 8-5-03
Internationals: Republic of Ireland U19, U21.

2023–24	Blackburn R	2	0
2024–25	Blackburn R	0 0	2 0

GUEYE, Makhtar (F)   **191 46**
H: 6 5   W: 14 02   b.Dakar 4-12-97

2017–18	Saint-Etienne	0	0
2018–19	Saint-Etienne	5	1
2019–20	Saint-Etienne	0 0	5 1
2019–20	*Nancy*	20 5	20 5
2020–21	Oostende	33	11
2021–22	Oostende	31	12
2022–23	Oostende	4 0	68 23
2022–23	*Real Zaragoza*	22 0	22 0
2023–24	RWD Molenbeek	32 11	32 11
2024–25	Blackburn R	44 6	44 6

HEDGES, Ryan (M)   **275 26**
H: 6 1   W: 10 03   b.Swansea 7-9-95
Internationals: Wales U19, U21, Full caps.

2013–14	Swansea C	0	0
2014–15	Swansea C	0	0
2014–15	*Leyton Orient*	17 2	17 2
2015–16	Swansea C	0	0
2015–16	*Stevenage*	6 0	6 0
2016–17	Swansea C	0	0
2016–17	*Yeovil T*	21 4	21 4
2016–17	Barnsley	8	0
2017–18	Barnsley	23	2
2018–19	Barnsley	21 0	52 2
2019–20	Aberdeen	22	4
2020–21	Aberdeen	28	5
2021–22	Aberdeen	16 2	66 11
2021–22	Blackburn R	11	0
2022–23	Blackburn R	43	4
2023–24	Blackburn R	17	2
2024–25	Blackburn R	42 1	113 7

HYAM, Dominic (D)   **303 12**
H: 6 2   W: 11 00   b.Leuchars 20-12-95
Internationals: Scotland U19, U21, Full caps.

2014–15	Reading	0	0
2015–16	Reading	0	0
2015–16	*Dagenham & Red*	16 0	16 0
2016–17	Reading	0	0
2016–17	*Portsmouth*	0	0
2017–18	Coventry C	14	0
2018–19	Coventry C	38	1
2019–20	Coventry C	29	2
2020–21	Coventry C	43	3
2021–22	Coventry C	43	2
2022–23	Coventry C	2 0	169 8
2022–23	Blackburn R	37	1

2023–24	Blackburn R	35	1	
2024–25	Blackburn R	46	2	118 4

KARGBO, Augustus (F) 202 41
H: 5 8 W: 10 10 b.Freetown 24-8-99
Internationals: Sierra Leone Full caps.

2017–18	Campobasso	20	6	20 6
2018–19	Crotone	5	0	
2018–19	Roccella	11	3	11 3
2019–20	Crotone	0	0	
2019–20	Reggiana	24	11	
2020–21	Crotone	1	0	
2020–21	Reggiana	20	2	44 13
2021–22	Crotone	32	3	
2022–23	Crotone	30	3	68 6
2023–24	Cesena	33	10	
2024–25	Cesena	18	3	51 13
2024–25	Blackburn R	8	0	8 0

LEONARD, Harry (F) 32 4
H: 6 2 W: 11 00 b.Rochdale 12-9-03

2022–23	Blackburn R	4	0	
2023–24	Blackburn R	19	3	
2024–25	Blackburn R	9	1	32 4

LITHERLAND, Matty (D) 0 0

2024–25	Blackburn R	0	0	

M'BADINGA, Exauce (F) 0 0
H: 5 7 W: 10 03 b. 26-3-05

2023–24	Nantes	0	0	
2024–25	Blackburn R	0	0	
2024–25	Lierse	0	0	

MARKANDAY, Dilan (M) 65 10
H: 5 10 W: 10 01 b.Barnet 20-8-01

2020–21	Tottenham H	0	0	
2021–22	Tottenham H	0	0	
2021–22	Blackburn R	2	0	
2022–23	Blackburn R	1	0	
2022–23	Aberdeen	3	0	3 0
2023–24	Blackburn R	21	1	
2024–25	Blackburn R	0	0	24 1
2024–25	Chesterfield	22	6	22 6
2024–25	Leyton Orient	16	3	16 3

MICHALSKI, Nicholas (G) 0 0
b. 14-3-07
Internationals: England U17, U18.

2023–24	Blackburn R	0	0	
2024–25	Blackburn R	0	0	

MONTGOMERY, Kristi (M) 3 0
b. 31-5-04
Internationals: Scotland U16, U20.

2023–24	Blackburn R	0	0	
2024–25	Blackburn R	3	0	3 0

O'GRADY-MACKEN, Harley (M) 0 0
b.Manchester 9-12-04

2024–25	Blackburn R	0	0	

O'RIORDAN, Connor (D) 96 9
H: 6 4 W: 13 03 b.Crewe 19-10-03
Internationals: Republic of Ireland U20, U21.

2021–22	Crewe Alex	11	0	
2022–23	Crewe Alex	18	3	
2022–23	Raith R	18	0	18 0
2023–24	Crewe Alex	23	3	
2023–24	Blackburn R	2	0	
2024–25	Blackburn R	0	0	2 0
2024–25	Cambridge U	4	0	4 0
2024–25	Crewe Alex	20	3	72 9

OHASHI, Yuki (F) 148 39
H: 5 11 W: 12 00 b.Matsudo 27-7-96
Internationals: Japan Full caps.

2018	Shonan Bellmare	1	0	
2019	Shonan Bellmare	5	1	
2020	Shonan Bellmare	7	0	
2021	Shonan Bellmare	31	4	
2022	Shonan Bellmare	23	2	
2023	Shonan Bellmare	23	3	90 20
2024	Sanfrecce Hiroshima	22	10	22 10
2024–25	Blackburn R	36	9	36 9

PEARS, Aynsley (G) 114 0
H: 6 1 W: 12 08 b.Durham 23-4-98
Internationals: England U19.

2017–18	Middlesbrough	0	0	
2018–19	Middlesbrough	0	0	
2019–20	Middlesbrough	24	0	24 0
2020–21	Blackburn R	3	0	
2021–22	Blackburn R	0	0	
2022–23	Blackburn R	18	0	
2023–24	Blackburn R	26	0	
2024–25	Blackburn R	40	0	90 0

PICKERING, Harry (D) 269 13
H: 6 1 W: 12 04 b.Chester 29-12-98

2017–18	Crewe Alex	35	3	
2018–19	Crewe Alex	32	0	
2019–20	Crewe Alex	35	3	
2020–21	Crewe Alex	0	0	
2020–21	Crewe Alex	44	3	146 9
2021–22	Blackburn R	32	2	
2022–23	Blackburn R	40	1	
2023–24	Blackburn R	36	1	
2024–25	Blackburn R	15	0	123 4

POWELL, Brandon (D) 0 0
b.Huddersfield 17-10-05

2024–25	Blackburn R	0	0	

PRATT, George (D) 0 0
b. 17-9-03

2024–25	Blackburn R	0	0	

RANKIN-COSTELLO, Joe (M) 115 6
H: 5 10 W: 11 00 b.Stockport 26-7-99
From Manchester U.

2017–18	Blackburn R	0	0	
2018–19	Blackburn R	0	0	
2019–20	Blackburn R	11	0	
2020–21	Blackburn R	14	0	
2021–22	Blackburn R	10	0	
2022–23	Blackburn R	24	2	
2023–24	Blackburn R	27	2	
2024–25	Blackburn R	29	2	115 6

SIGURDSSON, Arnor (M) 165 34
H: 5 10 W: 11 11 b.Akranes 15-5-99
Internationals: Iceland U17, U19, U21, Full caps.

2015	IA	1	0	
2016	IA	6	0	7 0
2017	Norrkoping	8	0	
2017	Sylvia	3	3	3 3
2018	Norrkoping	17	3	
2018–19	CSKA Moscow	21	5	
2019–20	CSKA Moscow	22	4	
2020–21	CSKA Moscow	23	2	
2020–21	CSKA Moscow	0	0	
2021–22	Venezia	9	0	9 0
2022	Norrkoping	11	6	
2022–23	CSKA Moscow	0	0	66 11
2023	Norrkoping	10	5	46 14
2023–24	Blackburn R	29	5	
2024–25	Blackburn R	5	1	34 6

Transferred to Malmo, February 2025.

TOTH, Balazs (G) 142 0
H: 6 2 W: 12 06 b.Kazincbarcika 4-9-97
Internationals: Hungary U17, U19, U21.

2015–16	Puskas Akademia	0	0	
2016–17	Puskas Akademia	0	0	
2017–18	Puskas Akademia	0	0	
2018–19	Puskas Akademia	0	0	
2018–19	Csakvar	25	0	25 0
2019–20	Puskas Akademia	9	0	
2020–21	Puskas Akademia	30	0	
2021–22	Puskas Akademia	17	0	
2022–23	Puskas Akademia	20	0	76 0
2023–24	Fehervar	30	0	
2024–25	Fehervar	5	0	35 0
2024–25	Blackburn R	6	0	6 0

TRAVIS, Lewis (D) 247 8
H: 6 0 W: 13 01 b.Whiston 16-10-97

2016–17	Blackburn R	0	0	
2017–18	Blackburn R	5	0	
2018–19	Blackburn R	26	1	
2019–20	Blackburn R	43	2	
2020–21	Blackburn R	19	0	
2021–22	Blackburn R	45	1	
2022–23	Blackburn R	42	2	
2023–24	Blackburn R	20	0	
2023–24	Ipswich T	9	0	9 0
2024–25	Blackburn R	38	2	238 8

TRONSTAD, Sondre (M) 298 15
H: 5 8 W: 11 00 b.Kristiansund 26-8-95
Internationals: Norway U16, U17, U18, Full caps.

2012	IK Start	12	0	
2013	IK Start	9	1	21 1
2013–14	Huddersfield T	0	0	
2014–15	Huddersfield T	0	0	
2015–16	Huddersfield T	0	0	
2016	Haugesund	23	2	
2017	Haugesund	29	0	
2018	Haugesund	29	1	
2019	Haugesund	29	1	110 4
2019–20	Vitesse	6	0	
2020–21	Vitesse	23	2	
2021–22	Vitesse	36	4	
2022–23	Vitesse	28	2	93 8
2023–24	Blackburn R	36	0	
2024–25	Blackburn R	38	2	74 2

TYJON, Igor (F) 2 0
H: 5 11 W: 12 04 b.Southport 20-3-08
Internationals: Poland U16. England U16, U17.

2023–24	Blackburn R	0	0	
2024–25	Blackburn R	2	0	2 0

VALE, Jack (F) 54 3
H: 6 1 W: 11 00 b.Wrexham 3-3-01
Internationals: Wales U17, U19, U21.
From The New Saints.

2019–20	Blackburn R	1	0	
2020–21	Blackburn R	0	0	
2020–21	Rochdale	3	0	3 0
2021–22	Blackburn R	2	0	
2022–23	Blackburn R	15	0	

2023–24	Blackburn R	0	0	
2023–24	Lincoln C	14	1	14 1
2023–24	Motherwell	13	2	
2024–25	Blackburn R	0	0	18 0
2024–25	Motherwell	6	0	19 2

VARE, Frank (M) 0 0
b. 12-9-07

2024–25	Blackburn R	0	0	

WEIMANN, Andreas (F) 481 91
H: 6 2 W: 12 00 b.Vienna 5-8-91
Internationals: Austria U17, U19, U20, U21, Full caps.
From Rapid Vienna.

2008–09	Aston Villa	0	0	
2009–10	Aston Villa	0	0	
2010–11	Aston Villa	1	0	
2010–11	Watford	18	4	
2011–12	Aston Villa	14	2	
2011–12	Watford	3	0	21 4
2012–13	Aston Villa	30	7	
2013–14	Aston Villa	37	5	
2014–15	Aston Villa	31	3	113 17
2015–16	Derby Co	30	4	
2016–17	Derby Co	11	0	
2016–17	Wolverhampton W	19	2	19 2
2017–18	Derby Co	40	5	81 9
2018–19	Bristol C	44	10	
2019–20	Bristol C	45	9	
2020–21	Bristol C	7	2	
2021–22	Bristol C	46	22	
2022–23	Bristol C	43	6	
2023–24	Bristol C	20	1	205 50
2023–24	WBA	12	2	12 2
2024–25	Blackburn R	30	7	30 7

WHARTON, Scott (D) 170 14
H: 6 0 W: 11 11 b.Blackburn 3-10-97

2015–16	Blackburn R	0	0	
2016–17	Blackburn R	2	0	
2016–17	Cambridge U	9	1	9 1
2017–18	Blackburn R	0	0	
2017–18	Lincoln C	14	2	
2018–19	Blackburn R	0	0	
2018–19	Lincoln C	11	1	25 3
2018–19	Bury	15	2	15 2
2019–20	Blackburn R	0	0	
2019–20	Northampton T	32	3	32 3
2020–21	Blackburn R	7	0	
2021–22	Blackburn R	30	2	
2022–23	Blackburn R	22	1	
2023–24	Blackburn R	28	2	
2024–25	Blackburn R	0	0	89 6

YURI RIBEIRO, Oliveira (D) 165 3
H: 5 9 W: 10 10 b.Vieira do Minho 24-1-97
Internationals: Portugal U16, U17, U18, U19, U20, U21.

2014–15	Benfica	0	0	
2015–16	Benfica	0	0	
2016–17	Benfica	0	0	
2017–18	Benfica	0	0	
2017–18	Rio Ave	25	1	25 1
2018–19	Benfica	0	0	
2019–20	Nottingham F	27	0	
2020–21	Nottingham F	25	1	52 1
2021–22	Legia Warsaw	12	0	
2022–23	Legia Warsaw	24	1	
2023–24	Legia Warsaw	27	0	63 1
2024–25	Braga	10	0	10 0
2024–25	Blackburn R	15	0	15 0

Players retained or with offer of contract
Baker, Alexander John William; Boggan, Joseph Francis; Davies, Max Adam; Dlamini, Nathan Mpho; Farkas, Csaba Patrik; Goddard, Felix Benjamin; Honor, Solomon Lindsay Birch; Houghton, Lucas; Khan, Adam Najeeb Ahmed; Olson, Charles Kamel; Stritch, Zack Jacob; Wood, Harrison Jack.

Scholars
Decandia, Michael Stanley; Dunn, Isaac Joseph; Edmondson, Stephen Daniel; Joseph, Valentin Ifeanyi Chukwu; Kelley-Quinn, Leon Barry; Leatherbarrow, Freddie Andrew; Leeming, Bruce George; Mansbridge, Tyler Jake; Mullarkey-Matthews, Lorenze; Pates, Harvey Jack Daniel; Potter, Aaron Lynden; Ramwell, Edward Alexander; Sergeant, Jayden Thomas; Shorrocks, Jackson James; Taylor, Bradley Ryan; Thompson, Luke Andrew; Tyjon, Igor Justin; Vare, Frank Peter; Willis, Nathan Graham; Wolsoncroft, Blake Craig.

BLACKPOOL (9)

APTER, Robert (M) 84 20
H: 5 8 W: 8 09 b.Liverpool 16-1-03
Internationals: Scotland U19, U21.

2020–21	Blackpool	1	0	
2021–22	Blackpool.	0	0	
2022–23	Blackpool	1	0	

2023–24 Blackpool 0 0
2023–24 *Tranmere R* 37 12 **37 12**
2024–25 Blackpool 45 8 **47 8**

ASHWORTH, Zachary (D) 52 2
H: 5 11 W: 11 11 b.King's Lynn 6-9-02
Internationals: Wales U21.
2021–22 WBA 2 0
2022–23 WBA 0 0
2022–23 *Burton Alb* 18 0 **18 0**
2023–24 WBA 0 0 **2 0**
2023–24 *Bolton W* 16 2 **16 2**
2024–25 Blackpool 6 0 **6 0**
2024–25 *Ross Co* 10 0 **10 0**

BEESLEY, Jake (F) 124 27
H: 6 1 W: 10 08 b.Sheffield 2-12-96
2013–14 Chesterfield 0 0
2014–15 Chesterfield 0 0
2015–16 Chesterfield 0 0
2016–17 Chesterfield 7 0 **7 0**
From Chesterfield.
2019–20 Salford C 7 2 **7 2**
2020–21 Rochdale 27 6
2021–22 Rochdale 21 9 **48 15**
2021–22 Blackpool 6 2
2022–23 Blackpool 5 0
2023–24 Blackpool 29 7
2024–25 Blackpool 22 1 **62 10**

BLOXHAM, Tom (F) 144 10
H: 6 5 W: 12 13 b.Leicester 1-11-03
2020–21 Shrewsbury T 4 0
2021–22 Shrewsbury T 34 2
2022–23 Shrewsbury T 28 0
2023–24 Shrewsbury T 18 2
2023–24 *Morecambe* 24 0 **24 0**
2024–25 Shrewsbury T 22 4 **106 8**
2024–25 Blackpool 14 2 **14 2**

BONDO, Terry (F) 3 0
b. 8-2-07
From Oldham Ath.
2024–25 Blackpool 3 0 **3 0**

CAREY, Sonny (M) 116 17
H: 6 0 W: 11 07 b.Norwich 20-1-01
From King's Lynn T.
2021–22 Blackpool 11 1
2022–23 Blackpool 37 3
2023–24 Blackpool 35 5
2024–25 Blackpool 33 8 **116 17**

CASEY, Oliver (D) 118 5
H: 6 2 W: 12 06 b.Leeds 14-10-00
2019–20 Leeds U 1 0
2020–21 Leeds U 0 0 **1 0**
2021–22 Blackpool 6 1
2022–23 Blackpool 0 0
2022–23 *Forest Green R* 39 0 **39 0**
2023–24 Blackpool 29 1
2024–25 Blackpool 43 3 **78 5**

CHAPMAN, Mackenzie (G) 1 0
H: 6 4 W: 13 03 b.Bury 13-9-02
2020–21 Oldham Ath 1 0 **1 0**
2021–22 Oxford U 0 0
2022–23 Bolton W 0 0
2023–24 Blackpool 0 0
2024–25 Blackpool 0 0

COULSON, Hayden (D) 160 3
H: 5 8 W: 11 00 b.Gateshead 17-6-98
Internationals: England U16, U17, U18.
2018–19 Middlesbrough 0 0
2018–19 *St Mirren* 6 0 **6 0**
2018–19 *Cambridge U* 14 0 **14 0**
2019–20 Middlesbrough 29 1
2020–21 Middlesbrough 17 0
2021–22 Middlesbrough 0 0
2021–22 *Ipswich T* 6 0 **6 0**
2021–22 *Peterborough U* 6 0 **6 0**
2022–23 Middlesbrough 0 0
2022–23 *Aberdeen* 28 0 **28 0**
2023–24 Middlesbrough 2 0 **48 1**
2023–24 *Blackpool* 17 2
2024–25 Blackpool 35 0 **52 2**

DANIELS, Jake (F) 1 0
H: 5 9 W: 11 00 b.Blackpool 8-1-05
2021–22 Blackpool 1 0
2022–23 Blackpool 0 0
2023–24 Blackpool 0 0
2024–25 Blackpool 0 0 **1 0**

DONKOR, Kwaku (D) 0 0
H: 6 1 b. 15-9-04
2023–24 Blackpool 0 0
2024–25 Blackpool 0 0

EVANS, Lee (M) 320 25
H: 6 1 W: 13 12 b.Newport 24-7-94
Internationals: Wales U21, Full caps.
From Newport Co.
2012–13 Wolverhampton W 0 0
2013–14 Wolverhampton W 26 2
2014–15 Wolverhampton W 18 1
2015–16 Wolverhampton W 0 0
2015–16 *Bradford C* 35 4 **35 4**
2016–17 Wolverhampton W 15 0
2017–18 Wolverhampton W 0 0 **59 3**
2017–18 *Wigan Ath* 20 1
2017–18 Sheffield U 19 2
2018–19 Sheffield U 2 0 **21 2**
2018–19 *Wigan Ath* 34 1
2019–20 Wigan Ath 32 2
2020–21 Wigan Ath 21 2 **107 6**
2021–22 Ipswich T 27 3
2022–23 Ipswich T 23 3
2023–24 Ipswich T 2 0 **52 6**
2023–24 Portsmouth 4 0 **4 0**
2024–25 Blackpool 42 4 **42 4**

FINNIGAN, Ryan (M) 25 2
H: 5 10 W: 10 12 b.Poole 23-9-03
2020–21 Southampton 0 0
2021–22 Southampton 0 0
2022–23 Southampton 0 0
2022–23 *Crewe Alex* 16 1 **16 1**
2023–24 Southampton 0 0
2023–24 *Shrewsbury T* 1 0 **1 0**
2023–24 Blackpool 0 0
2024–25 Blackpool 8 1 **8 1**

FLETCHER, Ashley (F) 245 39
H: 6 1 W: 12 04 b.Keighley 2-10-95
Internationals: England U19, U20, U21.
2015–16 Manchester U 0 0
2015–16 *Barnsley* 21 5 **21 5**
2016–17 West Ham U 16 0 **16 0**
2017–18 Middlesbrough 16 1
2017–18 *Sunderland* 16 2 **16 2**
2018–19 Middlesbrough 21 5
2019–20 Middlesbrough 43 11
2020–21 Middlesbrough 12 2 **92 19**
2021–22 Watford 3 0
2022 *New York Red Bulls* 7 0 **7 0**
2022–23 Watford 0 0
2022–23 *Wigan Ath* 26 2 **26 2**
2023–24 Watford 0 0 **3 0**
2023–24 *Sheffield Wed* 23 0 **23 0**
2024–25 Blackpool 41 11 **41 11**

HAMILTON, CJ (M) 305 30
H: 5 7 W: 11 09 b.Harrow 23-3-95
Internationals: Republic of Ireland Full caps.
2015–16 Sheffield U 0 0
2016–17 Mansfield T 29 0
2017–18 Mansfield T 33 2
2018–19 Mansfield T 46 11
2019–20 Mansfield T 34 2 **142 15**
2019–20 Blackpool 0 0
2020–21 Blackpool 22 5
2021–22 Blackpool 24 2
2022–23 Blackpool 39 1
2023–24 Blackpool 44 4
2024–25 Blackpool 34 3 **163 15**

HUSBAND, James (D) 336 10
H: 5 11 W: 10 02 b.Leeds 3-1-94
2011–12 Doncaster R 3 0
2012–13 Doncaster R 33 3
2013–14 Doncaster R 28 1 **64 4**
2014–15 Middlesbrough 3 0
2014–15 *Fulham* 5 0
2015–16 Middlesbrough 0 0
2015–16 *Fulham* 12 0 **17 0**
2015–16 *Huddersfield T* 11 0 **11 0**
2016–17 Middlesbrough 1 0 **4 0**
2017–18 Norwich C 18 0
2018–19 Norwich C 1 0 **19 0**
2018–19 *Fleetwood T* 33 1 **33 1**
2019–20 Blackpool 28 0
2020–21 Blackpool 27 0
2021–22 Blackpool 31 1
2022–23 Blackpool 29 0
2023–24 Blackpool 39 1
2024–25 Blackpool 34 3 **188 5**

JONES, Jaden (F) 0 0
2023–24 Blackpool 0 0
2024–25 Blackpool 0 0

KNIGHT, Spencer (D) 0 0
2024–25 Blackpool 0 0

KOUASSI, Kylian (F) 86 6
H: 5 9 W: 11 00 b.Tresor Kouassi 18-6-03
2021–22 Sutton U 4 0
2022–23 Sutton U 36 2 **40 2**
2023–24 Blackpool 19 1
2024–25 Blackpool 0 0 **19 1**
2024–25 *Salford C* 27 3 **27 3**

LANKSHEAR, Alex (M) 1 0
b. 8-9-02
From St Albans C.
2022–23 Blackpool 1 0
2023–24 Blackpool 0 0
2024–25 Blackpool 0 0 **1 0**

LAWRENCE-GABRIEL, Jordan (D) 133 2
H: 5 10 W: 10 12 b.London 25-9-98
From Southend U.
2019–20 Nottingham F 0 0
2019–20 *Scunthorpe U* 9 0 **9 0**
2020–21 Nottingham F 1 0
2020–21 *Blackpool* 27 0
2021–22 Nottingham F 4 0 **5 0**
2021–22 Blackpool 21 0
2022–23 Blackpool 20 0
2023–24 Blackpool 21 2
2024–25 Blackpool 30 0 **119 2**

LELIENDAL, Ky-Mani (D) 0 0
2024–25 Blackpool 0 0

LYONS, Andy (D) 122 13
H: 5 10 W: 11 00 b.Naas 2-8-00
Internationals: Republic of Ireland U18, U19, U21.
2018 Bohemians 5 0
2019 Bohemians 14 0
2020 Bohemians 14 0
2021 Bohemians 25 1 **58 1**
2022 Shamrock R 31 7 **31 7**
2022–23 Blackpool 17 4
2023–24 Blackpool 15 1
2024–25 Blackpool 1 0 **33 5**

MOORE, Jack (D) 0 0
H: 5 11 b.Keighley 19-11-03
2021–22 Blackpool 0 0
2022–23 Blackpool 0 0
2023–24 Blackpool 0 0
2024–25 Blackpool 0 0

MORGAN, Albie (M) 185 13
H: 5 11 W: 10 10 b.Portsmouth 2-2-00
2018–19 Charlton Ath 8 0
2019–20 Charlton Ath 21 0
2020–21 Charlton Ath 28 1
2021–22 Charlton Ath 22 1
2022–23 Charlton Ath 35 3 **114 5**
2023–24 Blackpool 35 3
2024–25 Blackpool 36 5 **71 8**

NORBURN, Oliver (M) 275 20
H: 6 1 W: 12 13 b.Leicester 26-10-92
Internationals: Grenada Full caps.
2011–12 Leicester C 0 0
2011–12 *Bristol R* 5 0
2012–13 Bristol R 35 3
2013–14 Bristol R 16 0 **56 3**
2014–15 Plymouth Arg 14 0 **14 0**
From Guiseley, Macclesfield T, Tranmere R.
2018–19 Shrewsbury T 41 9
2019–20 Shrewsbury T 17 3
2020–21 Shrewsbury T 39 4 **97 16**
2021–22 Peterborough U 36 0
2022–23 Peterborough U 16 0 **52 0**
2023–24 Blackpool 34 1
2024–25 Blackpool 8 0 **42 1**
2024–25 *Wigan Ath* 14 0 **14 0**

NWANKWO, Oluchi (D) 0 0
2024–25 Blackpool 0 0

NYAME, Josh (D) 0 0
b. 8-9-04
2023–24 Blackpool 0 0
2024–25 Blackpool 0 0

O'DONNELL, Richard (G) 383 0
H: 6 2 W: 13 05 b.Sheffield 12-9-88
2007–08 Sheffield Wed 0 0
2007–08 *Rotherham U* 0 0
2007–08 *Oldham Ath* 4 0 **4 0**
2008–09 Sheffield Wed 0 0
2009–10 Sheffield Wed 0 0
2010–11 Sheffield Wed 9 0
2011–12 Sheffield Wed 6 0 **15 0**
2011–12 *Macclesfield T* 11 0 **11 0**
2012–13 Chesterfield 14 0 **14 0**
2013–14 Walsall 46 0
2014–15 Walsall 44 0 **90 0**
2015–16 Wigan Ath 10 0 **10 0**
2015–16 Bristol C 21 0
2016–17 Bristol C 8 0 **29 0**
2016–17 Rotherham U 12 0
2017–18 Rotherham U 10 0 **22 0**
2017–18 Northampton T 19 0 **19 0**
2018–19 Bradford C 42 0
2019–20 Bradford C 33 0
2020–21 Bradford C 28 0
2021–22 Bradford C 19 0 **122 0**
2022–23 Rochdale 40 0 **40 0**
2023–24 Blackpool 1 0
2024–25 Blackpool 6 0 **7 0**

ONOMAH, Joshua (M) 153 9
H: 5 11 W: 10 01 b.Enfield 27-4-97
Internationals: England U16, U17, U18, U19, U20, U21.
2013–14 Tottenham H 0 0
2014–15 Tottenham H 0 0
2015–16 Tottenham H 8 0
2016–17 Tottenham H 5 0
2017–18 Tottenham H 0 0
2017–18 *Aston Villa* 33 4 **33 4**
2018–19 Tottenham H 0 0 **13 0**
2018–19 *Sheffield Wed* 15 0 **15 0**

2019–20 Fulham	31	3		
2020–21 Fulham	11	0		
2021–22 Fulham	20	1		
2022–23 Fulham	2	0	64	4
2022–23 Preston NE	13	0	13	0
2024–25 Blackpool	15	1	15	1

OPAWOLE, Johnson (D) — 0 0
b. 16-4-06

2023–24 Blackpool	0	0		
2024–25 Blackpool	0	0		

PENNINGTON, Matthew (D) — 278 15
H: 6 1   W: 12 02   b.Warrington 6-10-94
Internationals: England U19.

2013–14 Everton	0	0		
2013–14 *Tranmere R*	17	2	17	2
2014–15 Everton	0	0		
2014–15 *Coventry C*	24	0	24	0
2015–16 Everton	4	0		
2015–16 *Walsall*	5	0	5	0
2016–17 Everton	3	1		
2017–18 Everton	0	0		
2017–18 *Leeds U*	24	0	24	0
2018–19 Everton	0	0		
2018–19 *Ipswich T*	30	1	30	1
2019–20 Everton	0	0		
2019–20 *Hull C*	14	0	14	0
2020–21 Everton	0	0	7	1
2020–21 Shrewsbury T	19	2		
2021–22 Shrewsbury T	45	3		
2022–23 Shrewsbury T	37	4	101	9
2023–24 Blackpool	35	2		
2024–25 Blackpool	21	0	56	2

RHODES, Jordan (F) — 592 219
H: 6 1   W: 11 03   b.Oldham 5-2-90
Internationals: Scotland U21, Full caps.

2007–08 Ipswich T	8	1		
2008–09 Ipswich T	2	0	10	1
2008–09 *Rochdale*	5	2	5	2
2008–09 *Brentford*	14	7	14	7
2009–10 Huddersfield T	45	19		
2010–11 Huddersfield T	37	16		
2011–12 Huddersfield T	40	35		
2012–13 Huddersfield T	2	2		
2012–13 Blackburn R	43	27		
2013–14 Blackburn R	46	25		
2014–15 Blackburn R	45	21		
2015–16 Blackburn R	25	10	159	83
2015–16 Middlesbrough	18	6		
2016–17 Middlesbrough	6	0	24	6
2016–17 *Sheffield Wed*	18	3		
2017–18 Sheffield Wed	31	5		
2018–19 Sheffield Wed	0	0		
2018–19 *Norwich C*	36	6	36	6
2019–20 Sheffield Wed	16	3		
2020–21 Huddersfield T	36	7	101	18
2021–22 Huddersfield T	21	3		
2022–23 Huddersfield T	34	5		
2023–24 Huddersfield T	0	0	179	80
2023–24 *Blackpool*	29	15		
2024–25 Blackpool	21	0	50	15
2024–25 *Mansfield T*	14	1	14	1

RICHARDSON, Jack (D) — 0 0

2024–25 Blackpool	0	0

SASSI, Dan (D) — 0 0
H: 6 1   b.Uttoxeter 8-12-03
From Stoke C.

2022–23 Burnley	0	0
2023–24 Blackpool	0	0
2024–25 Blackpool	0	0

SCHLUTER, Gabriel (F) — 0 0
H: 5 10   b. 10-1-09

2024–25 Blackpool	0	0

THOMPSON, Dominic (M) — 105 1
H: 6 0   W: 11 11   b.London Borough of
Brent 26-7-00

2018–19 Arsenal	0	0		
2019–20 Brentford	2	0		
2020–21 Brentford	4	0		
2020–21 *Swindon T*	25	0	25	0
2021–22 Brentford	2	0	8	2
2021–22 *Ipswich T*	17	0	17	0
2022–23 Blackpool	28	0		
2023–24 Blackpool	5	0		
2023–24 *Forest Green R*	19	1	19	1
2024–25 Blackpool	3	0	36	0
Transferred to Motherwell, January 2025.

UPTON, Theo (D) — 0 0
H: 6 0   W: 11 11   b.

2024–25 Blackpool	0	0

Players retained or with offer of contract
Bardsley, Harvey Lucas Shaw; Miles, Joshua
Francis.

Scholars
Amadi-Emina, Chelojo Ezra; Bowen, Taylor
James Nigel; Brier, Charlie Harry;
Butterworth, James Paul; Cox, Charlie;
Crowe, Kai Lewis; Findlow, Luke Joshua;
Leliendal, Ky-Mani Donnatello; Madu, Rhys
Tayte; McVeigh-McDonald, Conor Kevin;

Norris, Harry; Nwankwo, Oluchukwu Joshua
Chukwu; Oshodi, Derek Ayomide Timileyin;
Richardson, Jack Conor; Scholes, Lennon
Thomas; Williamson, Harry David.

BOLTON W (10)

ABIMBOLA, Dave (F) — 4 0
b. 19-5-07

2024–25 Bolton W	4	0	4	0

ADEBOYEJO, Victor (F) — 228 36
H: 5 10   W: 9 13   b.Ibadan 12-1-98
From Arsenal, AFC Wimbledon, Charlton
Ath.

2014–15 Leyton Orient	1	0		
2015–16 Leyton Orient	1	0		
2016–17 Leyton Orient	13	1	15	1
2017–18 Barnsley	0	0		
2018–19 Barnsley	25	2		
2019–20 *Bristol R*	18	1	18	1
2019–20 *Cambridge U*	8	0	8	0
2020–21 Barnsley	32	2		
2021–22 Barnsley	26	3	83	7
2022–23 Burton Alb	26	11	26	11
2022–23 Bolton W	16	3		
2023–24 Bolton W	35	10		
2024–25 Bolton W	27	3	78	16

ANDREUCCI, Ben (F) — 0 0
b.Bedford 5-10-04
From Leeds U.

2023–24 Bolton W	0	0
2024–25 Bolton W	0	0

ARFIELD, Scott (M) — 564 72
H: 5 10   W: 10 01   b.Livingston 1-11-88
Internationals: Scotland U19, U21, B. Canada
Full caps.

2007–08 Falkirk	35	3		
2008–09 Falkirk	37	7		
2009–10 Falkirk	36	3	108	13
2010–11 Huddersfield T	40	4		
2011–12 Huddersfield T	35	2		
2012–13 Huddersfield T	21	1	96	7
2013–14 Burnley	39	4		
2014–15 Burnley	37	2		
2015–16 Burnley	46	8		
2016–17 Burnley	31	1		
2017–18 Burnley	18	2	177	21
2018–19 Rangers	29	11		
2019–20 Rangers	26	5		
2020–21 Rangers	28	4		
2021–22 Rangers	29	4		
2022–23 Rangers	31	5	143	29
2023 Charlotte	14	2		
2024 Charlotte	14	0	28	2
2024–25 Bolton W	12	0	12	0
Transferred to Falkirk, February 2025.

BAXTER, Nathan (G) — 150 0
H: 6 3   W: 12 00   b.Westminster 8-11-98

2018–19 Chelsea	0	0		
2018–19 *Yeovil T*	34	0	34	0
2019–20 Chelsea	0	0		
2019–20 *Ross Co*	13	0	13	0
2020–21 Chelsea	0	0		
2020–21 *Accrington S*	16	0	16	0
2021–22 Chelsea	0	0		
2021–22 *Hull C*	16	0		
2022–23 Chelsea	0	0		
2022–23 *Hull C*	12	0	28	0
2023–24 Bolton W	33	0		
2024–25 Bolton W	26	0	59	0

COLEMAN, Joel (G) — 100 0
H: 6 6   W: 12 13   b.Bolton 26-9-95

2013–14 Oldham Ath	0	0		
2014–15 Oldham Ath	11	0		
2015–16 Oldham Ath	32	0	43	0
2016–17 Huddersfield T	5	0		
2017–18 Huddersfield T	0	0		
2018–19 Huddersfield T	1	0		
2018–19 *Shrewsbury T*	16	0	16	0
2019–20 Huddersfield T	3	0	9	0
2020–21 Fleetwood T	0	0		
2021–22 Fleetwood T	0	0		
2021–22 *Rochdale*	19	0	19	0
2022–23 Ipswich T	0	0		
2023–24 Bolton W	13	0		
2024–25 Bolton W	0	0	13	0

COLLINS, Aaron (F) — 324 81
H: 6 1   W: 11 09   b.Newport 27-5-97
Internationals: Wales U19.

2014–15 Newport Co	2	0		
2015–16 Newport Co	18	2		
2015–16 Wolverhampton W	0	0		
2016–17 Wolverhampton W	0	0		
2016–17 *Notts Co*	18	2	18	2
2017–18 Wolverhampton W	0	0		
2017–18 *Newport Co*	10	0	30	2
2018–19 Wolverhampton W	0	0		
2018–19 *Colchester U*	7	0	7	0
2018–19 Morecambe	15	8	15	8

2019–20 Forest Green R	28	4		
2020–21 Forest Green R	44	10	72	14
2021–22 Bristol R	45	16		
2022–23 Bristol R	46	16		
2023–24 Bristol R	27	3	118	35
2023–24 Bolton W	19	8		
2024–25 Bolton W	45	12	64	20

CONWAY, Max (M) — 46 2
H: 5 10   W: 11 00   b.Manchester 5-9-03

2020–21 Bolton W	0	0		
2021–22 Bolton W	0	0		
2022–23 Bolton W	0	0		
2023–24 Bolton W	0	0		
2024–25 Bolton W	0	0		
2024–25 *Crewe Alex*	46	2	46	2

DACRES-COGLEY, Josh (D) — 216 6
H: 5 9   W: 10 10   b.Coventry 12-3-96

2016–17 Birmingham C	14	0		
2017–18 Birmingham C	3	0		
2018–19 Birmingham C	1	0		
2019–20 Birmingham C	0	0		
2019–20 *Crawley T*	16	0	16	0
2020–21 Birmingham C	5	0	23	0
2021–22 Tranmere R	45	1		
2022–23 Tranmere R	46	1	91	2
2023–24 Bolton W	44	3		
2024–25 Bolton W	42	1	86	4

DALLIMORE, Jack (D) — 0 0
b. 3-1-04
Internationals: Scotland U18, U19.

2024–25 Bolton W	0	0

DEMPSEY, Kyle (M) — 364 36
H: 5 10   W: 11 11   b.Whitehaven 17-9-95

2013–14 Carlisle U	4	0		
2014–15 Carlisle U	43	10	47	10
2015–16 Huddersfield T	21	1		
2016–17 Huddersfield T	0	0	21	1
2016–17 *Fleetwood T*	38	2		
2017–18 Fleetwood T	45	1		
2018–19 Fleetwood T	14	0		
2018–19 *Peterborough T*	11	0	11	0
2019–20 Fleetwood T	21	2	118	5
2020–21 Gillingham	40	8		
2021–22 Gillingham	21	1	61	9
2021–22 Bolton W	11	0		
2022–23 Bolton W	39	5		
2023–24 Bolton W	41	3		
2024–25 Bolton W	15	3	106	11

EZE, Dubem (M) — 0 0
b.London 8-3-05

2024–25 Bolton W	0	0

FORINO-JOSEPH, Chris (D) — 16 2
H: 6 3   W: 13 01   b.Islington 26-4-00
Internationals: Saint Lucia Full caps.
From Wingate & Finchley, Loughborough
University.

2022–23 Wycombe W	0	0		
2023–24 Wycombe W	0	0		
2024–25 Bolton W	16	2	16	2

FORRESTER, William (D) — 80 3
H: 5 11   W: 11 07   b.Stoke-on-Trent 29-6-01

2020–21 Stoke C	1	1		
2021–22 Stoke C	3	0	4	1
2021–22 *Mansfield T*	4	0	4	0
2022–23 Port Vale	35	2	35	2
2023–24 Bolton W	14	0		
2024–25 Bolton W	23	0	37	0

HALFORD, Noah (M) — 0 0
H: 6 4   b.Voiron 2-1-05

2023–24 Bolton W	0	0
2024–25 Bolton W	0	0

HOGAN, Sean (D) — 0 0
H: 5 10   b.Bury 1-9-02

2024–25 Bolton W	0	0

HUTCHINSON, Luke (G) — 1 0
H: 6 1   W: 12 06   b.Bury 1-9-02

2019–20 Bolton W	0	0		
2020–21 Bolton W	0	0		
2021–22 Bolton W	0	0		
2022–23 Bolton W	0	0		
2023–24 Bolton W	0	0		
2024–25 Bolton W	0	0		
2024–25 *Crawley T*	1	0	1	0

INWOOD, Sam (D) — 2 0
H: 6 1   W: 11 00   b. 17-9-05

2023–24 Bolton W	0	0		
2024–25 Bolton W	2	0	2	0

IREDALE, Jack (D) — 219 17
H: 6 0   W: 9 13   b.Greenock 2-5-96
Internationals: Australia U17.

2016–17 Perth Glory	23	2	23	2
2017 ECU Joondalup	4	1	4	1
2017–18 Greenock Morton	9	2		
2017–18 *Queen's Park*	14	1	14	1
2018–19 Greenock Morton	23	1	32	3
2019–20 Carlisle U	22	2	22	2
2020–21 Cambridge U	38	4		
2021–22 Cambridge U	35	1	73	5

2022–23 Bolton W 19 0
2023–24 Bolton W 31 3
2024–25 Bolton W 1 0 51 3
Transferred to Hibernian, August 2024.

IRWIN, Harley (D) 0 0
2024–25 Bolton W 0 0

ISONG, Mark (F) 3 1
b.Dublin 26-1-06
2024 Shelbourne 3 1 3 1
2024–25 Bolton W 0 0

JOHNSTON, George (D) 143 4
H: 5 11 W: 12 04 b.Manchester 1-9-98
Internationals: Scotland U20, U21.
2019–20 Feyenoord 0 0
2020–21 Feyenoord 4 0 4 0
2020–21 Liverpool 0 0
2020–21 *Wigan Ath* 22 1 22 1
2021–22 Bolton W 43 2
2022–23 Bolton W 36 1
2023–24 Bolton W 0 0
2024–25 Bolton W 38 0 117 3

JONES, Gethin (D) 244 6
H: 5 10 W: 11 09 b.Perth, Australia 13-10-95
Internationals: Wales U17, U19, U21. Australia Full caps.
2014–15 Everton 0 0
2014–15 *Plymouth Arg* 6 0 6 0
2015–16 Everton 0 0
2016–17 Everton 0 0
2016–17 *Barnsley* 17 0 17 0
2017–18 Fleetwood T 10 0
2018–19 Fleetwood T 3 0 13 0
2018–19 *Mansfield T* 15 0 15 0
2019–20 Carlisle U 30 0
2020–21 Carlisle U 0 0 30 0
2020–21 Bolton W 38 3
2021–22 Bolton W 29 0
2022–23 Bolton W 39 2
2023–24 Bolton W 34 1
2024–25 Bolton W 23 0 163 6

LAWRENCE, Daeshon (F) 2 0
2024–25 Bolton W 2 0 2 0

LEWIS, Conor (M) 0 0
2023–24 Bolton W 0 0
2024–25 Bolton W 0 0

LOLOS, Klaidi (F) 82 15
H: 6 2 W: 12 04 b.Athens 6-10-00
Internationals: Greece U19.
2017–18 Plymouth Arg 0 0
2018–19 Plymouth Arg 0 0
2019–20 Plymouth Arg 4 0
2020–21 Plymouth Arg 8 0 12 0
From Torquay U, Crawley T.
2023–24 *Crawley T* 46 13 46 13
2024–25 Bolton W 24 2 24 2

MATHESON, Luke (D) 48 1
H: 5 5 W: 11 00 b.Manchester 3-10-02
Internationals: England U17, U18.
2018–19 Rochdale 3 0
2019–20 Wolverhampton W 0 0
2019–20 *Rochdale* 20 1 23 1
2020–21 Wolverhampton W 0 0
2020–21 *Ipswich T* 2 0 2 0
2021–22 Wolverhampton W 0 0
2021–22 *Hamilton A* 0 0
2021–22 *Scunthorpe U* 13 0 13 0
2022–23 Wolverhampton W 0 0
2023–24 Bolton W 0 0
2023–24 *Bohemians* 10 0 10 0
2024–25 Bolton W 0 0

McATEE, John (F) 161 31
H: 5 11 W: 11 11 b.Salford 23-7-99
2016–17 Shrewsbury T 1 0
2017–18 Shrewsbury T 0 0
2018–19 Shrewsbury T 0 0 1 0
2019–20 Scunthorpe U 19 3
2020–21 Scunthorpe U 30 1 49 4
From Grimsby T.
2022–23 Luton T 0 0
2022–23 *Grimsby T* 26 4 26 4
2023–24 *Barnsley* 40 12 40 12
2024–25 Luton T 0 0
2024–25 Bolton W 45 11 45 11

MENDES GOMES, Carlos (F) 142 26
H: 5 10 W: 10 06 b.Yeumbeul 14-11-98
Internationals: Guinea-Bissau Full caps.
From Atletico Madrid, West Didsbury & Chorlton.
2018–19 Morecambe 15 0
2019–20 Morecambe 16 2
2020–21 Morecambe 43 15
2021–22 Morecambe 0 0 74 17
2021–22 Luton T 9 0
2022–23 Luton T 0 0 9 0
2022–23 *Fleetwood T* 32 7 32 7
2023–24 Bolton W 16 2
2024–25 Bolton W 11 0 27 2

MORLEY, Aaron (M) 230 20
H: 5 9 W: 10 08 b.Bury 27-2-00
2016–17 Rochdale 2 0
2017–18 Rochdale 0 0
2018–19 Rochdale 3 0
2019–20 Rochdale 23 3
2020–21 Rochdale 44 2
2021–22 Rochdale 21 1 93 6
2021–22 Bolton W 21 1
2022–23 Bolton W 41 4
2023–24 Bolton W 37 3
2024–25 Bolton W 19 4 118 12
2024–25 *Wycombe W* 19 2 19 2

N'LUNDULU, Daniel (F) 115 12
H: 6 2 W: 11 11 b.France 5-2-99
Internationals: England U16.
2016–17 Southampton 0 0
2017–18 Southampton 0 0
2018–19 Southampton 0 0
2019–20 Southampton 0 0
2020–21 Southampton 13 0
2020–21 Southampton 0 0
2021–22 *Lincoln C* 16 1 16 1
2021–22 *Cheltenham T* 4 1
2022–23 Southampton 0 0 13 0
2022–23 *Cheltenham T* 23 4 27 5
2023–24 *Bolton W* 13 1
2023–24 Bolton W 21 1
2024–25 Bolton W 0 0 34 2
2024–25 *Cambridge U* 25 4 25 4

OSEI-TUTU, Jordi (D) 101 8
H: 5 9 W: 11 03 b.Slough 2-10-98
2017–18 Arsenal 0 0
2018–19 Arsenal 0 0
2019–20 Arsenal 0 0
2019–20 *Bochum* 21 5 21 5
2020–21 Arsenal 0 0
2020–21 *Cardiff C* 8 0
2021–22 *Cardiff C* 0 0 8 0
2021–22 *Nottingham F* 4 0 4 0
2021–22 Arsenal 0 0
2021–22 *Rotherham U* 14 0 14 0
2022–23 VfL Bochum 14 0
2023–24 VfL Bochum 0 0 14 0
2023–24 *PAS Giannina* 8 2 8 2
2024–25 Bolton W 32 1 32 1

RANDALL, Joel (M) 133 24
H: 5 10 W: 10 06 b.Salisbury 29-10-99
2017–18 Exeter C 0 0
2018–19 Exeter C 0 0
2019–20 Exeter C 2 0
2020–21 Exeter C 30 8 32 8
2021–22 Peterborough U 11 0
2022–23 Peterborough U 10 0
2023–24 Peterborough U 43 10
2024–25 Peterborough U 18 5 82 15
2024–25 Bolton W 19 1 19 1

RICE, Harrison (M) 1 0
b. 18-4-07
2024–25 Bolton W 1 0 1 0

SANTOS, Ricardo (D) 292 10
H: 6 5 W: 12 02 b.Almada 18-6-95
Internationals: Cape Verde Full caps.
2012–13 Dagenham & Red 0 0
2013–14 Dagenham & Red 0 0
2013–14 Peterborough U 1 0
2014–15 Peterborough U 24 0
2015–16 Peterborough U 37 0
2016–17 Peterborough U 1 0 63 0
2016–17 *Barnet* 15 2
2017–18 *Barnet* 42 3 57 5
From Barnet.
2020–21 Bolton W 46 0
2021–22 Bolton W 37 0
2022–23 Bolton W 30 3
2023–24 Bolton W 34 0
2024–25 Bolton W 25 1 172 4

SCHON, Szabolcs (M) 165 18
H: 5 8 W: 10 08 b.Budapest 27-9-00
Internationals: Hungary U16, U17, U18, U19, U21, Full caps.
2018–19 Ajax 0 0
2018–19 MTK Budapest 5 0
2019–20 MTK Budapest 17 4
2020–21 MTK Budapest 27 9 49 13
2021 FC Dallas 24 0
2022 FC Dallas 0 0 24 0
2022–23 Fehervar 21 4
2023–24 Fehervar 31 0
2023–24 *Fehervar* 1 0 53 4
2024–25 Bolton W 39 1 39 1

SHARPLES, Sonny (M) 3 0
H: 6 0 W: 12 00 b.Salford 24-3-05
Internationals: Egypt U23.
2023–24 Bolton W 0 0
2024–25 Bolton W 3 0 3 0

SHEEHAN, Josh (M) 284 26
H: 6 0 W: 11 11 b.Pembrey 30-3-95
Internationals: Wales U19, U21, Full caps.
2013–14 Swansea C 0 0
2014–15 Swansea C 0 0
2014–15 *Yeovil T* 13 0
2015–16 Swansea C 0 0
2015–16 *Yeovil T* 13 2 26 2
2016–17 Swansea C 0 0
2016–17 *Newport Co* 20 5
2017–18 *Newport Co* 13 2
2018–19 Newport Co 33 1
2019–20 Newport Co 33 2
2020–21 Newport Co 43 3 142 13
2021–22 Bolton W 15 4
2022–23 Bolton W 24 2
2023–24 Bolton W 43 2
2024–25 Bolton W 34 3 116 11

SOUTHWOOD, Luke (G) 153 0
H: 6 1 W: 11 05 b.Oxford 6-12-97
Internationals: England U19, U20. Northern Ireland Full caps.
2019–20 Reading 0 0
2019–20 *Hamilton A* 15 0 15 0
2020–21 Reading 1 0
2021–22 Reading 25 0
2022–23 Reading 0 0 26 0
2022–23 *Cheltenham T* 46 0
2023–24 *Cheltenham T* 46 0 92 0
2024–25 Bolton W 20 0 20 0

THOMASON, George (M) 134 12
H: 5 10 W: 10 12 b.Barrow-in-Furness 12-1-01
From Longridge T.
2019–20 Bolton W 0 0
2020–21 Bolton W 24 1
2021–22 Bolton W 13 1
2022–23 Bolton W 20 0
2023–24 Bolton W 39 6
2024–25 Bolton W 38 4 134 12

TOAL, Eoin (D) 221 14
H: 6 3 W: 12 08 b.Armagh 15-2-99
Internationals: Northern Ireland U17, U19, U21, Full caps.
2017 Derry C 3 0
2018 Derry C 30 1
2019 Derry C 35 2
2020 Derry C 18 0
2021 Derry C 34 1
2022 Derry C 20 1 140 5
2022–23 Bolton W 22 3
2023–24 Bolton W 40 4
2024–25 Bolton W 19 2 81 9

WESTON, Ajay (D) 0 0
b. 20-6-05
2024–25 Bolton W 0 0

Players retained or with offer of contract
Grayson, Jamie John Coutts; Leigh, Harry Patrick Ellis; Oliver, Emile Wesley James; Smith, Oliver Adam; Tarzan, Mark Ndungu; Tutte, Andrew William.

Scholars
Barlow, George Heath; Cutler, Ethan William; Lewis, Everton Latrell Elijah; Lomax, Luke Ronald; Mawditt, Jack Joseph; Nuttall, Corey Jack; O'Neill, Samuel James; Ritchie, Tobias Luca; Shakespear, Yestin; Sixsmith, Jack; Taylor, Xander; Thomas, Corey Lea.

BOURNEMOUTH (11)

AARONS, Maximillian (D) 228 5
H: 5 10 W: 11 07 b.Hammersmith 4-1-00
Internationals: England U21.
From Luton T.
2018–19 Norwich C 41 2
2019–20 Norwich C 36 0
2020–21 Norwich C 45 2
2021–22 Norwich C 34 0
2022–23 Norwich C 45 1 201 5
2023–24 Bournemouth 20 0
2024–25 Bournemouth 3 0 23 0
2024–25 *Valencia* 4 0 4 0

ADAMS, Tyler (M) 189 3
H: 5 9 W: 11 05 b.New York 14-2-99
Internationals: USA U17, U20, Full caps.
2015 New York Red Bulls 0 0
2016 New York Red Bulls 1 0
2017 New York Red Bulls 27 2
2018 New York Red Bulls 31 0 59 2
2018–19 RB Leipzig 10 0
2019–20 RB Leipzig 14 0
2020–21 RB Leipzig 27 1
2021–22 RB Leipzig 24 0 75 1
2022–23 Leeds U 24 0 24 0
2023–24 Bournemouth 3 0
2024–25 Bournemouth 28 0 31 0

ADU-ADJEI, Daniel (F) **24** **3**
H: 5 11 W: 11 11 b.Hammersmith 21-6-05

2022–23	Bournemouth	0	0		
2023–24	Bournemouth	0	0		
2023–24	*Leyton Orient*	10	1	**10**	**1**
2024–25	Bournemouth	0	0		
2024–25	*Carlisle U*	14	2	**14**	**2**

AKINMBONI, Matai (D) **13** **0**
H: 6 3 W: 12 02 b.Upper Marlboro 17-10-06
Internationals: USA U19.

2022	DC United	2	0		
2023	DC United	3	0		
2024	DC United	8	0	**13**	**0**
2024–25	Bournemouth	0	0		

ANTHONY, Jaidon (F) **157** **20**
H: 5 9 W: 9 11 b.Hackney 1-12-99
From Arsenal.

2019–20	Bournemouth	0	0		
2020–21	Bournemouth	5	0		
2021–22	Bournemouth	45	8		
2022–23	Bournemouth	30	3		
2023–24	Bournemouth	3	0		
2023–24	*Leeds U*	31	1	**31**	**1**
2024–25	Bournemouth	0	0	**83**	**11**
2024–25	*Burnley*	43	8	**43**	**8**

ARAUJO, Julian (D) **137** **2**
H: 5 10 W: 11 00 b.Lompoc 13-8-01
Internationals: USA U16, U18, U19, U20, U23, Full caps. Mexico Full caps.

2018	LA Galaxy	0	0		
2019	LA Galaxy	18	0		
2020	LA Galaxy	17	1		
2021	LA Galaxy	32	0		
2022	LA Galaxy	33	0	**100**	**1**
2022–23	Barcelona	0	0		
2023–24	Barcelona	0	0		
2023–24	*Las Palmas*	25	1	**25**	**1**
2024–25	Bournemouth	12	0	**12**	**0**

BEVAN, Owen (D) **14** **0**
H: 6 1 W: 12 02 b.Winchester 20-12-02
Internationals: Wales U17, U19, U21.

2022–23	Bournemouth	1	0		
2023–24	Bournemouth	0	0		
2023–24	*Cheltenham T*	13	0	**13**	**0**
2023–24	*Hibernian*	0	0		
2024–25	Bournemouth	0	0	**1**	**0**

BILLING, Phillip (M) **274** **34**
H: 6 4 W: 12 08 b.Copenhagen 11-6-96
Internationals: Denmark U19, U21, Full caps.
From Esbjerg.

2013–14	Huddersfield T	1	0		
2014–15	Huddersfield T	0	0		
2015–16	Huddersfield T	13	1		
2016–17	Huddersfield T	24	2		
2017–18	Huddersfield T	16	0		
2018–19	Huddersfield T	27	2	**81**	**5**
2019–20	Bournemouth	34	1		
2020–21	Bournemouth	34	8		
2021–22	Bournemouth	40	10		
2022–23	Bournemouth	36	7		
2023–24	Bournemouth	29	2		
2024–25	Bournemouth	10	0	**183**	**28**
2024–25	*Napoli*	10	1	**10**	**1**

BROOKS, David (M) **173** **22**
H: 5 10 W: 11 09 b.Warrington 8-7-97
Internationals: England U20. Wales U21, Full caps.
From Manchester C.

2015–16	Sheffield U	0	0		
2016–17	Sheffield U	0	0		
2017–18	Sheffield U	30	3	**30**	**3**
2018–19	Bournemouth	30	7		
2019–20	Bournemouth	9	1		
2020–21	Bournemouth	32	5		
2021–22	Bournemouth	7	1		
2022–23	Bournemouth	6	0		
2023–24	Bournemouth	13	1		
2023–24	*Southampton*	17	2	**17**	**2**
2024–25	Bournemouth	29	2	**126**	**17**

CHRISTIE, Ryan (M) **339** **53**
H: 5 10 W: 11 00 b.Inverness 22-2-95
Internationals: Scotland U21, Full caps.

2013–14	Inverness CT	15	3		
2014–15	Inverness CT	35	4		
2015–16	Inverness CT	13	3	**63**	**10**
2015–16	Celtic	5	1		
2016–17	Celtic	5	1		
2016–17	*Aberdeen*	13	6		
2017–18	Celtic	0	0		
2017–18	*Aberdeen*	32	4	**45**	**10**
2018–19	Celtic	23	9		
2019–20	Celtic	24	11		
2020–21	Celtic	34	5		
2021–22	Celtic	4	0	**95**	**27**
2021–22	Bournemouth	38	3		
2022–23	Bournemouth	32	1		
2023–24	Bournemouth	37	0		
2024–25	Bournemouth	29	2	**136**	**6**

COOK, Lewis (M) **311** **4**
H: 5 9 W: 11 03 b.York 3-2-97
Internationals: England U16, U17, U18, U19, U20, U21, Full caps.

2014–15	Leeds U	37	0		
2015–16	Leeds U	43	1	**80**	**1**
2016–17	Bournemouth	6	0		
2017–18	Bournemouth	29	0		
2018–19	Bournemouth	13	0		
2019–20	Bournemouth	27	0		
2020–21	Bournemouth	31	1		
2021–22	Bournemouth	28	1		
2022–23	Bournemouth	28	0		
2023–24	Bournemouth	33	0		
2024–25	Bournemouth	36	1	**231**	**3**

DENNIS, William (G) **36** **0**
H: 6 4 W: 12 06 b.Watford 10-7-00
From Watford.

2019–20	Bournemouth	0	0		
2020–21	Bournemouth	0	0		
2021–22	Bournemouth	0	0		
2022–23	Bournemouth	0	0		
2023–24	Bournemouth	0	0		
2023–24	*Kilmarnock*	36	0	**36**	**0**
2024–25	Bournemouth	0	0		

EVANILSON, Francisco (F) **142** **54**
H: 6 0 W: 12 08 b.Fortaleza 6-10-99
Internationals: Brazil U23, Full caps.

2018	Fluminense	0	0		
2018	*Samorin*	6	3	**6**	**3**
2019	Fluminense	3	2		
2020	Tombense	0	0		
2020	*Fluminense*	6	2	**9**	**4**
2020–21	Porto	15	3		
2021–22	Porto	30	14		
2022–23	Porto	23	7		
2023–24	Porto	27	13		
2024–25	Porto	1	0	**96**	**37**
2024–25	Bournemouth	31	10	**31**	**10**

FAIVRE, Romain (M) **110** **26**
H: 5 11 W: 10 12 b.Asnieres-sur-Seine 14-7-98
Internationals: France U21.

2018–19	Monaco	1	0		
2019–20	Monaco	0	0	**1**	**0**
2020–21	Brest	36	6		
2021–22	Brest	21	7		
2021–22	Lyon	14	3		
2022–23	Lyon	0	0	**14**	**3**
2022–23	*Lorient*	16	5		
2023–24	Bournemouth	5	0		
2023–24	*Lorient*	17	5	**33**	**10**
2024–25	Bournemouth	0	0	**5**	**0**
2024–25	*Brest*	0	0	**57**	**13**

GONZALEZ, Michael (M) **0** **0**
H: 6 1 b.Alicante 5-3-05

2022–23	Bournemouth	0	0		
2023–24	Bournemouth	0	0		
2024–25	Bournemouth	0	0		
2024–25	*Crawley T*	0	0		

HARRIS, Archie (D) **0** **0**
H: 5 5 W: 9 00 b.Liverpool 27-12-04
Internationals: Wales U21.

2024–25	Bournemouth	0	0		

HILL, James (D) **91** **2**
H: 6 0 W: 11 07 b.Bristol 10-1-02
Internationals: England U20, U21.

2018–19	Fleetwood T	2	0		
2019–20	Fleetwood T	0	0		
2020–21	Fleetwood T	28	0		
2021–22	Fleetwood T	13	1	**43**	**1**
2021–22	Bournemouth	1	0		
2022–23	Bournemouth	0	0		
2022–23	*Hearts*	14	0	**14**	**0**
2023–24	Bournemouth	5	0		
2023–24	*Blackburn R*	18	1	**18**	**1**
2024–25	Bournemouth	10	0	**16**	**0**

HUIJSEN, Dean (D) **46** **5**
H: 6 6 W: 12 08 b.Amsterdam 14-4-05
Internationals: Netherlands U17, U18, U19. Spain U21, Full caps.

2022–23	Juventus	0	0		
2023–24	Juventus	1	0	**1**	**0**
2023–24	*Roma*	13	2	**13**	**2**
2024–25	Bournemouth	32	3	**32**	**3**

JEBBISON, Daniel (F) **78** **10**
H: 6 3 W: 10 12 b.Oakville, Canada 11-7-03
Internationals: England U18, U19, U20. Canada Full caps.

2020–21	Sheffield U	4	1		
2021–22	Sheffield U	8	0		
2021–22	*Burton Alb*	20	7	**20**	**7**
2022–23	Sheffield U	16	1		
2023–24	Sheffield U	1	0	**29**	**2**
2024–25	Bournemouth	16	1	**16**	**1**
2024–25	*Watford*	13	0	**13**	**0**

JUNIOR KROUPI, Eli (F) **61** **27**
b.Lorient 23-6-06
Internationals: France U16, U17, U18, U19, U20.

2021–22	Lorient	0	0		
2022–23	Lorient	1	0		
2023–24	Lorient	30	5		
2024–25	Bournemouth	0	0		
2024–25	*Lorient*	30	22	**61**	**27**

KERKEZ, Milos (D) **119** **5**
H: 5 11 W: 11 03 b.Vrbas 7-11-03
Internationals: Hungary U17, U21, Full caps.

2020–21	Gyor	16	0	**16**	**0**
2020–21	AC Milan	0	0		
2021–22	AC Milan	0	0		
2021–22	AZ Alkmaar	4	0		
2022–23	AZ Alkmaar	33	3	**37**	**3**
2023–24	Bournemouth	28	0		
2024–25	Bournemouth	38	2	**66**	**2**

KINSEY-WELLINGS, Max (D) **0** **0**
H: 6 0 W: 12 00 b.Guildford 2-2-05

2022–23	Bournemouth	0	0		
2023–24	Bournemouth	0	0		
2024–25	Bournemouth	0	0		

KLUIVERT, Justin (M) **235** **49**
H: 5 8 W: 10 06 b.Zaandam 5-5-99
Internationals: Netherlands U17, U19, U21, Full caps.

2016–17	Ajax	14	2		
2017–18	Ajax	30	10	**44**	**12**
2018–19	Roma	29	1		
2019–20	Roma	22	4		
2020–21	Roma	2	0		
2020–21	*RB Leipzig*	19	3	**19**	**3**
2021–22	Roma	0	0		
2021–22	*Nice*	27	4	**27**	**4**
2022–23	Roma	0	0	**53**	**5**
2022–23	*Valencia*	26	6	**26**	**6**
2023–24	Bournemouth	32	7		
2024–25	Bournemouth	34	12	**66**	**19**

McKENNA, Callan (G) **7** **0**
H: 6 2 W: 12 00 b.Fernhill 22-12-06
Internationals: Scotland U17, U18, U19, U21.

2023–24	Queen's Park	7	0	**7**	**0**
2023–24	Bournemouth	0	0		
2024–25	Bournemouth	0	0		

MEPHAM, Chris (D) **188** **4**
H: 6 3 W: 11 11 b.Hammersmith 5-11-97
Internationals: Wales U20, U21, Full caps.

2016–17	Brentford	0	0		
2017–18	Brentford	21	1		
2018–19	Brentford	22	0	**43**	**1**
2018–19	Bournemouth	13	0		
2019–20	Bournemouth	12	1		
2020–21	Bournemouth	24	1		
2021–22	Bournemouth	22	0		
2022–23	Bournemouth	26	0		
2023–24	Bournemouth	10	0		
2024–25	Bournemouth	0	0	**107**	**2**
2024–25	*Sunderland*	38	1	**38**	**1**

MOTTOH, Koby (F) **0** **0**
b. 31-8-06

2022–23	Portsmouth	0	0		
2023–24	Portsmouth	0	0		
2024–25	Bournemouth	0	0		

NETO, Murara (G) **259** **0**
H: 6 3 W: 13 01 b.Araxa 19-7-89
Internationals: Brazil U23, Full caps.

2009	Athletico Paranaense	2	0		
2010	Athletico Paranaense	34	0	**36**	**0**
2010–11	Fiorentina	0	0		
2011–12	Fiorentina	2	0		
2012–13	Fiorentina	6	0		
2013–14	Fiorentina	35	0		
2014–15	Fiorentina	29	0	**72**	**0**
2015–16	Juventus	3	0		
2016–17	Juventus	8	0	**11**	**0**
2017–18	Valencia	33	0		
2018–19	Valencia	34	0	**67**	**0**
2019–20	Barcelona	2	0		
2020–21	Barcelona	7	0		
2021–22	Barcelona	3	0	**12**	**0**
2022–23	Bournemouth	27	0		
2023–24	Bournemouth	32	0		
2024–25	Bournemouth	2	0	**61**	**0**
2024–25	*Arsenal*	0	0		

OUATTARA, Dango (M) **135** **21**
H: 5 10 W: 11 03 b.Ouagadougou 11-2-02
Internationals: Burkino Faso Full caps.

2019–20	Majestic	11	5	**11**	**5**
2020–21	Lorient	0	0		
2021–22	Lorient	25	1		
2022–23	Lorient	18	6	**43**	**7**
2022–23	Bournemouth	19	1		
2023–24	Bournemouth	30	1		
2024–25	Bournemouth	32	7	**81**	**9**

PAULSEN, Alex (G) 61 0
H: 6 4 b.Auckland 4-7-02
Internationals: New Zealand U17, U23, Full caps.
2021–22 Wellington Phoenix 4 0
2022–23 Wellington Phoenix 0 0
2023–24 Wellington Phoenix 29 0 33 0
2024–25 Bournemouth 0 0
2024–25 Auckland 28 0 28 0

REES-DOTTIN, Remy (F) 1 0
H: 5 11 W: 12 00 b.6-3-06
2024–25 Bournemouth 1 0 1 0

ROTHWELL, Joe (M) 308 20
H: 6 1 W: 12 02 b.Manchester 11-1-95
Internationals: England U16, U17, U19, U20.
2014–15 Manchester U 0 0
2014–15 *Blackpool* 3 0 3 0
2015–16 Manchester U 0 0
2015–16 *Barnsley* 4 0 4 0
2016–17 Oxford U 33 1
2017–18 Oxford U 36 5 69 6
2018–19 Blackburn R 33 2
2019–20 Blackburn R 36 2
2020–21 Blackburn R 39 3
2021–22 Blackburn R 41 3 149 10
2022–23 Bournemouth 20 0
2023–24 Bournemouth 11 0
2023–24 *Southampton* 16 4 16 4
2024–25 Bournemouth 0 0 31 0
2024–25 *Leeds U* 36 0 36 0

SADI, Dominic (M) 23 2
H: 5 9 W: 10 03 b.Enfield 2-9-03
2021–22 West Ham U 0 0
2022–23 Bournemouth 0 0
2023–24 Bournemouth 1 0
2024–25 Bournemouth 0 0 1 0
2024–25 *Carlisle U* 22 2 22 2

SCOTT, Alex (M) 126 6
H: 5 11 W: 11 09 b.Guernsey 28-8-03
Internationals: England U18, U19, U20, U21.
From Guernsey.
2020–21 Bristol C 3 0
2021–22 Bristol C 38 4
2022–23 Bristol C 42 1 83 5
2023–24 Bristol C 23 1
2024–25 Bournemouth 20 0 43 1

SEMENYO, Antoine (F) 221 39
H: 5 10 W: 9 13 b.Chelsea 7-1-00
Internationals: Ghana Full caps.
2017–18 Bristol C 1 0
2018–19 Bristol C 4 0
2018–19 *Newport Co* 21 3 21 3
2019–20 Bristol C 9 0
2019–20 *Sunderland* 7 0 7 0
2020–21 Bristol C 44 2
2021–22 Bristol C 31 8
2022–23 Bristol C 23 6 112 16
2022–23 Bournemouth 11 1
2023–24 Bournemouth 33 8
2024–25 Bournemouth 37 11 81 20

SENESI, Marcos (D) 212 13
H: 6 1 W: 12 08 b.Concordia 10-5-97
Internationals: Argentina U20, U23, Full caps.
2016–17 San Lorenzo 11 0
2017–18 San Lorenzo 13 1
2018–19 San Lorenzo 23 0
2019–20 San Lorenzo 4 0 51 1
2019–20 Feyenoord 16 1
2020–21 Feyenoord 34 3
2021–22 Feyenoord 32 2 82 6
2022–23 Feyenoord 31 2
2023–24 Bournemouth 31 4
2024–25 Bournemouth 17 0 79 6

SILCOTT-DUBERRY, Zain (M) 1 0
H: 5 10 W: 11 11 b.London 9-7-05
Internationals: England U16, U17.
2024–25 Bournemouth 1 0 1 0

SINISTERRA, Luis (M) 172 34
H: 5 8 W: 9 06 b.Santander de Quilichao 17-6-99
Internationals: Colombia U20, Full caps.
2016 Once Caldas 2 0
2017 Once Caldas 22 1
2018 Once Caldas 19 4 43 5
2018–19 Feyenoord 5 0
2019–20 Feyenoord 21 5
2020–21 Feyenoord 20 3
2021–22 Feyenoord 30 12 76 20
2022–23 Leeds U 19 5
2023–24 Leeds U 2 1 21 6
2023–24 Bournemouth 20 2
2024–25 Bournemouth 12 1 32 3

SMITH, Adam (D) 439 9
H: 5 11 W: 12 04 b.Leytonstone 29-4-91
Internationals: England U16, U17, U19, U20, U21.
2007–08 Tottenham H 0 0
2008–09 Tottenham H 0 0

2009–10 Tottenham H 0 0
2009–10 *Wycombe W* 3 0 3 0
2009–10 *Torquay U* 16 0 16 0
2010–11 Tottenham H 0 0
2010–11 *Bournemouth* 38 1
2011–12 Tottenham H 1 0
2011–12 *Milton Keynes D* 17 2 17 2
2011–12 *Leeds U* 3 0 3 0
2012–13 Tottenham H 0 0
2012–13 *Millwall* 25 1 25 1
2013–14 Tottenham H 0 0 1 0
2013–14 *Derby Co* 8 0 8 0
2014–15 Bournemouth 5 0
2014–15 Bournemouth 29 0
2015–16 Bournemouth 31 2
2016–17 Bournemouth 36 1
2017–18 Bournemouth 27 1
2018–19 Bournemouth 25 1
2019–20 Bournemouth 24 0
2020–21 Bournemouth 41 0
2021–22 Bournemouth 20 0
2022–23 Bournemouth 37 0
2023–24 Bournemouth 28 0
2024–25 Bournemouth 25 0 366 6

SOLER, Julio (D) 49 0
H: 5 7 W: 9 13 b.Asuncion 16-2-05
Internationals: Argentina U20, U23.
2022 Lanus 3 0
2023 Lanus 12 0
2024 Lanus 31 0 46 0
2024–25 Bournemouth 3 0 3 0

TAVERNIER, Marcus (M) 224 26
H: 5 10 W: 11 00 b.Leeds 22-3-99
Internationals: England U19, U20.
2017–18 Middlesbrough 5 1
2017–18 *Milton Keynes D* 7 0 7 0
2018–19 Middlesbrough 20 3
2019–20 Middlesbrough 37 3
2020–21 Middlesbrough 29 3
2021–22 Middlesbrough 44 5 135 15
2022–23 Bournemouth 30 3
2023–24 Bournemouth 29 3 82 11

TRAORE, Hamed (M) 195 28
H: 6 0 W: 12 02 b.Abidjan 16-2-00
Internationals: Ivory Coast U23, Full caps.
2017–18 Empoli 10 0
2018–19 Empoli 32 2
2019–20 Empoli 0 0
2019–20 Sassuolo 31 4
2020–21 Empoli 0 0 42 2
2020–21 Sassuolo 35 5
2021–22 Sassuolo 31 7
2022–23 Sassuolo 11 0 108 16
2022–23 Bournemouth 7 0
2023–24 Bournemouth 3 0
2023–24 *Napoli* 9 0 9 0
2024–25 Bournemouth 0 0 10 0
2024–25 *Auxerre* 26 10 26 10

TRAVERS, Mark (G) 108 0
H: 6 3 W: 12 13 b.Maynooth 18-5-99
Internationals: Republic of Ireland U16, U17, U18, U19, U21, Full caps.
From Shamrock R.
2018–19 Bournemouth 2 0
2019–20 Bournemouth 1 0
2020–21 Bournemouth 1 0
2020–21 *Swindon T* 8 0 8 0
2021–22 Bournemouth 45 0
2022–23 Bournemouth 12 0
2023–24 Bournemouth 4 0
2023–24 *Stoke C* 13 0 13 0
2024–25 Bournemouth 5 0 70 0
2024–25 *Middlesbrough* 17 0 17 0

UNAL, Enes (F) 324 87
H: 6 1 W: 11 11 b.Bursa 10-5-97
Internationals: Turkey U16, U17, U19, U21, Full caps.
2013–14 Bursaspor 16 3
2014–15 Bursaspor 19 1 35 4
2015–16 Manchester C 0 0
2015–16 Genk 12 1 12 1
2015–16 NAC Breda 11 8 11 8
2016–17 Villarreal 0 0
2016–17 FC Twente 32 18 32 18
2017–18 Villarreal 23 5
2017–18 Levante 7 1 7 1
2018–19 Villarreal 0 0
2018–19 Villarreal 33 6
2019–20 Villarreal 0 0 23 5
2019–20 Valladolid 35 6 68 12
2020–21 Getafe 28 4
2021–22 Getafe 37 16
2022–23 Getafe 35 14
2023–24 Getafe 3 0 103 34
2023–24 *Bournemouth* 16 2
2024–25 Bournemouth 17 2 33 4

WINTERBURN, Ben (M) 4 0
H: 6 1 W: 11 11 b.4-9-04
2024–25 Bournemouth 4 0 4 0

ZABARNYI, Illia (D) 128 2
H: 6 2 W: 12 08 b.Kyiv 1-9-02
Internationals: Ukraine U17, U21, Full caps.
2020–21 Dynamo Kyiv 21 1
2021–22 Dynamo Kyiv 15 0
2022–23 Dynamo Kyiv 14 0 50 1
2022–23 Bournemouth 5 0
2023–24 Bournemouth 37 1
2024–25 Bournemouth 36 0 78 1

Players retained or with offer of contract
Boutin, Noa; Crampton, Kai Barry; Dacosta Gonzalez, Malcom; Day, Jonny Raye; Landa, Balraj Jorawar Singh; Osborne, Charlie Henry; Tonks, Finn Robert John.

Scholars
Ali, Ameer Salah-Al'Din; Allan, Mack William; Campbell, Zhaviah Nasir James; Chubinidze, George Manuel Goncalves; Clarke, Ashley Donovan; Davies, James Christopher; Gregory, Karlos Antonio Martin; McGhan, Hayden Michael; Merritt, Alfie Michael Patrick; Morgan, Ollie Luke; Ogunleye, Malachi Solomon Olamide; Purches, Benjamin; Rees-Dottin, Remy William James; Sills, Ethan Philip; Stevens, Charlie George; Stuttle, Jonathon Edward; William, Harold Ikenna.

BRADFORD C (12)

BALDWIN, Aden (D) 86 1
H: 6 0 W: 11 00 b.Gloucester 10-6-97
2018–19 Bristol C 0 0
2018–19 *Cheltenham T* 4 0 4 0
2019–20 Bristol C 0 0
2020–21 Bristol C 0 0
2021–22 *Milton Keynes D* 9 0 9 0
From Notts Co.
2023–24 Notts Co 41 1 41 1
2024–25 Bradford C 32 0 32 0

BYRNE, Neil (D) 118 4
H: 5 7 W: 8 09 b.Dublin 2-2-93
Internationals: Republic of Ireland U19.
2010–11 Nottingham F 0 0
2011–12 Nottingham F 0 0
2011–12 Rochdale 3 0
2012–13 Rochdale 0 0 3 0
From AFC Telford U, Macclesfield T, Gateshead, AFC Fylde, FC Halifax T.
2021–22 Hartlepool U 40 1 40 1
2022–23 Tranmere R 13 0 13 0
2023–24 Stockport Co 19 0
2024–25 Stockport Co 16 1 35 1
2024–25 Bradford C 27 2 27 2

COOK, Andy (F) 260 100
H: 6 1 W: 11 05 b.Bishop Auckland 18-10-90
Internationals: England C.
From Carlisle U, Barrow, Grimsby T, Barrow, Tranmere R.
2018–19 Walsall 43 13 43 13
2019–20 Mansfield T 23 7
2019–20 *Tranmere R* 5 0 5 0
2020–21 Mansfield T 20 3 43 10
2020–21 *Bradford C* 21 8
2021–22 Bradford C 39 12
2022–23 Bradford C 46 28
2023–24 Bradford C 41 17
2024–25 Bradford C 22 12 169 77

CRICHLOW-NOBLE, Romoney (D) 91 3
H: 6 0 W: 11 09 b.Luton 3-6-99
From Enfield Bor.
2017–18 Huddersfield T 0 0
2018–19 Huddersfield T 0 0
2019–20 Huddersfield T 0 0
2020–21 Huddersfield T 4 0
2021–22 Huddersfield T 0 0
2021–22 *Swindon T* 18 1 18 1
2021–22 *Plymouth Arg* 3 0 3 0
2022–23 Huddersfield T 0 0 4 0
2022–23 *Bradford C* 34 1
2023–24 Peterborough U 22 0
2024–25 Peterborough U 0 0 22 0
2024–25 *Bradford C* 10 1 44 2

DOYLE, Colin (G) 171 0
H: 6 5 W: 14 05 b.Cork 12-8-85
Internationals: Republic of Ireland U21, B, Full caps.
2004–05 Birmingham C 0 0
2004–05 *Chester C* 0 0
2004–05 *Nottingham F* 3 0 3 0
2005–06 Birmingham C 0 0
2005–06 *Millwall* 14 0 14 0
2006–07 Birmingham C 19 0
2007–08 Birmingham C 3 0

2008–09 Birmingham C 2 0
2009–10 Birmingham C 0 0
2010–11 Birmingham C 1 0
2011–12 Birmingham C 5 0
2012–13 Birmingham C 0 0
2013–14 Birmingham C 0 0
2014–15 Birmingham C 1 0 **31 0**
2015–16 Blackpool 33 0 **33 0**
2016–17 Bradford C 44 0
2017–18 Bradford C 35 0
2018–19 Hearts 0 0
2019–20 Hearts 0 0
2020–21 Hearts 0 0
2020–21 *Kilmarnock* 11 0
2021–22 Kilmarnock 0 0 **11 0**
2022–23 Bradford C 0 0
2023–24 Bradford C 0 0
2024–25 Bradford C 0 0 **79 0**

EVANS, Corry (M) 366 12
H: 5 8 W: 11 00 b.Belfast 30-7-90
Internationals: Northern Ireland U16, U17, U19, U21, B, Full caps.
2007–08 Manchester U 0 0
2008–09 Manchester U 0 0
2009–10 Manchester U 0 0
2010–11 Manchester U 0 0
2010–11 *Carlisle U* 1 0 **1 0**
2010–11 *Hull C* 18 3
2011–12 Hull C 43 2
2012–13 Hull C 32 1
2013–14 Hull C 0 0 **93 6**
2013–14 Blackburn R 21 1
2014–15 Blackburn R 38 1
2015–16 Blackburn R 30 1
2016–17 Blackburn R 19 0
2017–18 Blackburn R 32 0
2018–19 Blackburn R 35 0
2019–20 Blackburn R 13 1
2020–21 Blackburn R 18 0 **206 4**
2021–22 Sunderland 33 2
2022–23 Sunderland 24 0
2023–24 Sunderland 3 0 **60 2**
2024–25 Bradford C 6 0 **6 0**
Transferred to Oldham Ath, January 2025.

GOODMAN, George (D) 0 0
b. 1-12-06
Internationals: Northern Ireland U19.
2024–25 Bradford C 0 0

HADI, Zachariah (G) 0 0
H: 6 5 W: 12 08 b. 7-4-06
2023–24 Bradford C 0 0
2024–25 Bradford C 0 0

HALLIDAY, Bradley (D) 378 11
H: 5 11 W: 10 10 b.Redcar 10-7-95
2013–14 Middlesbrough 0 0
2014–15 Middlesbrough 0 0
2014–15 *York C* 24 1 **24 1**
2015–16 Middlesbrough 0 0
2015–16 *Hartlepool U* 6 0 **6 0**
2015–16 *Accrington S* 32 0 **32 0**
2016–17 Middlesbrough 0 0
2016–17 Cambridge U 30 1
2017–18 Cambridge U 43 1
2018–19 Cambridge U 38 0 **111 2**
2019–20 Doncaster R 34 0
2020–21 Doncaster R 37 1
2021–22 Doncaster R 0 0 **71 1**
2021–22 Fleetwood T 3 0 **3 0**
2022–23 Bradford C 44 1
2023–24 Bradford C 44 4
2024–25 Bradford C 43 2 **131 7**

HILTON, Joe (G) 18 0
H: 6 5 W: 14 09 b.Sale 11-10-99
From Manchester C.
2018–19 Everton 0 0
2019–20 Blackburn R 0 0
2020–21 Blackburn R 0 0
2020–21 *Fleetwood T* 2 0 **2 0**
2020–21 *Ross Co* 0 0
2021–22 Blackburn R 0 0
2021–22 *Hamilton A* 16 0 **16 0**
2022–23 Blackburn R 0 0
2023–24 Blackburn R 0 0
2024–25 Blackburn R 0 0
2024–25 Bradford C 0 0

HUNTINGTON, Paul (D) 474 25
H: 6 3 W: 12 08 b.Carlisle 17-9-87
Internationals: England U18.
2005–06 Newcastle U 0 0
2006–07 Newcastle U 11 1
2007–08 Newcastle U 0 0 **11 1**
2007–08 Leeds U 17 2
2008–09 Leeds U 4 0
2009–10 Leeds U 0 0 **21 2**
2009–10 Stockport Co 26 0 **26 0**
2010–11 Yeovil T 40 5
2011–12 Yeovil T 37 2 **77 7**
2012–13 Preston NE 37 3
2013–14 Preston NE 23 2
2014–15 Preston NE 32 5
2015–16 Preston NE 38 0
2016–17 Preston NE 33 1
2017–18 Preston NE 44 1
2018–19 Preston NE 22 0
2019–20 Preston NE 9 0
2020–21 Preston NE 21 0
2021–22 Preston NE 1 0 **260 12**
2022–23 Carlisle U 40 2
2023–24 Carlisle U 20 1 **60 3**
2024–25 Bradford C 19 0 **19 0**

IBBITSON, Harry (F) 0 0
H: 6 1 W: 11 11 b. 2-1-06
2024–25 Bradford C 0 0

JOHNSON, Callum (M) 240 6
H: 6 2 W: 11 03 b.Yarm 23-10-96
From Middlesbrough.
2017–18 Accrington S 31 1
2018–19 Accrington S 41 0
2019–20 Accrington S 33 0 **105 1**
2020–21 Portsmouth 40 0
2021–22 Portsmouth 1 0 **41 0**
2021–22 *Fleetwood T* 35 4 **35 4**
2022–23 Ross Co 18 0 **18 0**
2022–23 Mansfield T 13 0
2023–24 Mansfield T 17 1 **30 1**
2024–25 Bradford C 11 0 **11 0**

KAVANAGH, Calum (F) 86 17
H: 6 0 W: 13 05 b.Cardiff 5-9-03
Internationals: Republic of Ireland U17, U21.
2020–21 Middlesbrough 0 0
2021–22 Middlesbrough 0 0
2021–22 *Harrogate T* 12 1 **12 1**
2022–23 Middlesbrough 0 0
2022–23 *Newport Co* 19 2 **19 2**
2023–24 Middlesbrough 2 0 **2 0**
2023–24 Bradford C 15 5
2024–25 Bradford C 38 9 **53 14**

KELLY, Ciaran (D) 189 10
H: 6 3 W: 12 06 b.Lucan 4-7-98
2015 St Patrick's Ath 0 0
2016 St Patrick's Ath 1 0
2017 St Patrick's Ath 0 0
2018 Drogheda U 31 6 **31 6**
2019 St Patrick's Ath 25 1 **26 1**
2020 Bohemians 2 0
2020–21 *Ballymena U* 12 1 **12 1**
2021 Bohemians 25 0
2022 Bohemians 34 1 **61 1**
2022–23 Bradford C 4 0
2023–24 Bradford C 34 0
2024–25 Bradford C 21 1 **59 1**

LAPSLIE, George (M) 212 30
H: 5 11 W: 11 09 b.Waltham Forest 5-9-97
2016–17 Charlton Ath 0 0
2017–18 Charlton Ath 1 0
2018–19 Charlton Ath 27 0
2019–20 Charlton Ath 10 1
2020–21 Charlton Ath 2 0 **40 1**
2020–21 Mansfield T 29 8
2021–22 Mansfield T 32 4
2022–23 Mansfield T 25 5 **86 17**
2022–23 Gillingham 22 3
2023–24 Gillingham 36 3
2024–25 Gillingham 15 2 **73 8**
2024–25 Bradford C 13 4 **13 4**

LEIGH, Tommy (M) 130 22
H: 6 1 W: 11 11 b.Portsmouth 13-4-00
From Baffins Milton R, Bognor Regis T.
2021–22 Accrington S 24 6
2022–23 Accrington S 39 7
2023–24 Accrington S 39 8 **102 21**
2024–25 Milton Keynes D 12 1 **12 1**
2024–25 Bradford C 16 0 **16 0**

ODOUR, Clarke (F) 111 6
H: 5 9 W: 11 00 b.Siaya 25-6-99
Internationals: Kenya Full caps.
2018–19 Leeds U 0 0
2019–20 Leeds U 0 0
2019–20 Barnsley 16 1
2020–21 Barnsley 11 0
2021–22 Barnsley 20 0
2022–23 Barnsley 2 0 **49 1**
2022–23 *Hartlepool U* 11 1 **11 1**
2023–24 Bradford C 32 3
2024–25 Bradford C 19 1 **51 4**

OLIVER, Vadaine (F) 371 61
H: 6 2 W: 12 04 b.Sheffield 21-10-91
2010–11 Sheffield Wed 0 0
2011–12 Sheffield Wed 0 0
From Lincoln C.
2013–14 Crewe Alex 25 2
2014–15 Crewe Alex 9 1 **34 3**
2014–15 *Mansfield T* 30 7 **30 7**
2015–16 York C 37 7 **37 7**
2016–17 Notts Co 19 1 **19 1**
2017–18 Morecambe 34 3
2018–19 Morecambe 30 4 **64 7**
2019–20 Northampton T 30 4 **30 4**
2020–21 Gillingham 43 17
2021–22 Gillingham 39 10 **82 27**
2022–23 Bradford C 30 3
2023–24 Bradford C 6 0
2023–24 *Stevenage* 14 0 **14 0**
2024–25 Bradford C 12 0 **48 3**
2024–25 *Shrewsbury T* 13 2 **13 2**

PATTISON, Alex (F) 168 27
H: 5 8 W: 11 00 b.Darlington 6-9-97
2016–17 Middlesbrough 0 0
2017–18 Middlesbrough 0 0
2018–19 Middlesbrough 0 0
2018–19 *Yeovil T* 29 0 **29 0**
2019–20 Wycombe W 17 0
2020–21 Wycombe W 6 0 **23 0**
2021–22 Harrogate T 41 9
2022–23 Harrogate T 36 9 **77 18**
2023–24 Bradford C 9 2
2024–25 Bradford C 30 7 **39 9**

POINTON, Bobby (F) 64 10
H: 5 7 W: 10 06 b.Bradford 4-1-04
2023–24 Bradford C 24 4
2024–25 Bradford C 40 6 **64 10**

RICHARDS, Lewis (D) 65 2
H: 6 0 W: 10 08 b.Liverpool 15-10-01
Internationals: Republic of Ireland U19, U21.
2019–20 Wolverhampton W 0 0
2020–21 Wolverhampton W 0 0
2021–22 Wolverhampton W 0 0
2021–22 *Harrogate T* 8 0
2022–23 Wolverhampton W 0 0
2022–23 *Harrogate T* 9 0 **17 0**
2023–24 Bradford C 26 0
2024–25 Bradford C 22 2 **48 2**

SARCEVIC, Antoni (M) 389 66
H: 6 1 W: 13 05 b.Manchester 13-3-92
Internationals: England C.
2009–10 Crewe Alex 0 0
2010–11 Crewe Alex 6 1
2011–12 Crewe Alex 6 0 **12 1**
From Chester.
2013–14 Fleetwood T 42 13
2014–15 Fleetwood T 37 2
2015–16 Fleetwood T 39 3 **118 18**
2016–17 Shrewsbury T 12 0 **12 0**
2016–17 Plymouth Arg 17 2
2017–18 Plymouth Arg 30 3
2018–19 Plymouth Arg 37 3
2019–20 Plymouth Arg 32 10 **116 18**
2020–21 Bolton W 32 7
2021–22 Bolton W 14 3 **46 10**
2022–23 Stockport Co 28 4
2023–24 Stockport Co 33 8 **61 12**
2024–25 Bradford C 24 7 **24 7**

SMALLWOOD, Richard (M) 481 17
H: 5 11 W: 11 05 b.Redcar 29-12-90
Internationals: England U19.
2008–09 Middlesbrough 0 0
2009–10 Middlesbrough 0 0
2010–11 Middlesbrough 13 1
2011–12 Middlesbrough 13 0
2012–13 Middlesbrough 22 2
2013–14 Middlesbrough 13 0
2013–14 *Rotherham U* 18 0
2014–15 Middlesbrough 0 0 **61 3**
2014–15 *Rotherham U* 41 1
2015–16 Rotherham U 43 1
2016–17 Scunthorpe U 16 1 **16 1**
2016–17 Rotherham U 25 1 **127 3**
2017–18 Blackburn R 46 2
2018–19 Blackburn R 32 0
2019–20 Blackburn R 0 0 **78 2**
2020–21 Hull C 27 0
2021–22 Hull C 42 2 **69 2**
2022–23 Bradford C 45 3
2023–24 Bradford C 42 1
2024–25 Bradford C 43 2 **130 6**

SMITH, Tyler (F) 169 27
H: 5 10 W: 10 08 b.Sheffield 4-12-98
2018–19 Sheffield U 0 0
2018–19 *Doncaster R* 14 2 **14 2**
2019–20 Sheffield U 0 0
2019–20 *Bristol R* 20 3 **20 3**
2019–20 *Rochdale* 4 1 **4 1**
2020–21 Sheffield U 0 0
2020–21 *Swindon T* 23 7 **23 7**
2021–22 Hull C 23 1
2022–23 Hull C 14 3 **37 4**
2022–23 *Oxford U* 7 0 **7 0**
2023–24 Bradford C 38 5
2024–25 Bradford C 5 0 **43 5**
2024–25 *Barrow* 21 5 **21 5**

STUBBS, Sam (D) 159 6
H: 6 0 W: 10 01 b.Liverpool 20-11-98
From Everton.
2016–17 Wigan Ath 0 0
2017–18 Wigan Ath 0 0
2017–18 *Crewe Alex* 5 0 **5 0**
2018–19 Middlesbrough 0 0

2018–19	*Notts Co*	17	0	**17**	**0**
2019–20	Middlesbrough	0	0		
2019–20	*Hamilton A*	19	0		
2019–20	*ADO Den Haag*	3	0	**3**	**0**
2020–21	Hamilton A	0	0	**19**	**0**
2020–21	Middlesbrough	0	0		
2020–21	Fleetwood T	5	1	**5**	**1**
2020–21	Exeter C	0	0		
2021–22	Exeter C	22	2		
2022–23	Exeter C	2	0	**24**	**2**
2022–23	Bradford C	19	1		
2023–24	Bradford C	26	0		
2024–25	Bradford C	0	0	**45**	**1**
2024–25	*Cheltenham T*	41	2	**41**	**2**

THIRKILL, Ben (M) **0** **0**
H: 6 0 b.Bradford 12-11-05

2024–25	Bradford C	0	0		

WADSWORTH, Gabriel (M) **0** **0**
H: 5 11 W: 11 00 b. 23-9-05

2024–25	Bradford C	0	0		

WALKER, Jamie (M) **347** **68**
H: 5 11 W: 12 00 b.Edinburgh 25-6-93
Internationals: Scotland U16, U17, U19, U21.

2011–12	Hearts	0	0		
2011–12	*Raith R*	23	3	**23**	**3**
2012–13	Hearts	24	2		
2013–14	Hearts	26	3		
2014–15	Hearts	33	11		
2015–16	Hearts	23	7		
2016–17	Hearts	34	12		
2017–18	Hearts	16	2		
2017–18	Wigan Ath	8	0		
2018–19	Wigan Ath	0	0	**8**	**0**
2018–19	*Peterborough U*	12	1	**12**	**1**
2019–20	Hearts	15	3		
2020–21	Hearts	21	7		
2021–22	Hearts	4	0	**196**	**47**
2021–22	Bradford C	19	4		
2022–23	Bradford C	24	4		
2023–24	Bradford C	30	8		
2024–25	Bradford C	35	1	**108**	**17**

WALKER, Sam (G) **375** **0**
H: 6 6 W: 12 04 b.Gravesend 2-10-91

2009–10	Chelsea	0	0		
2010–11	Chelsea	0	0		
2010–11	*Barnet*	7	0	**7**	**0**
2011–12	Chelsea	0	0		
2011–12	*Northampton T*	21	0	**21**	**0**
2011–12	*Yeovil T*	20	0	**20**	**0**
2012–13	Chelsea	0	0		
2012–13	*Bristol R*	11	0	**11**	**0**
2012–13	*Colchester U*	19	0		
2013–14	Colchester U	46	0		
2014–15	Colchester U	45	0		
2015–16	Colchester U	0	0		
2016–17	Colchester U	46	0		
2017–18	Colchester U	44	0	**200**	**0**
2018–19	Reading	7	0		
2019–20	Reading	0	0		
2020–21	Reading	0	0	**7**	**0**
2020–21	*Blackpool*	2	0	**2**	**0**
2020–21	*AFC Wimbledon*	12	0	**12**	**0**
2021–22	Kilmarnock	1	0		
2022–23	Kilmarnock	28	0	**29**	**0**
2023–24	Charlton Ath	0	0		
2023–24	Bradford C	20	0		
2024–25	Bradford C	46	0	**66**	**0**

WILSON, Adam (F) **55** **17**
H: 5 10 W: 11 00 b.Ashington 10-4-00
Internationals: England U18.

2020–21	Newcastle U	0	0		
2021–22	Newcastle U	0	0		
2022–23	The New Saints	19	7		
2023–24	Bradford C	10	1		
2024–25	Bradford C	0	0	**10**	**1**
2024–25	*The New Saints*	26	9	**45**	**16**

WRIGHT, Tyreik (M) **112** **8**
H: 5 10 W: 11 05 b.Cork 22-9-01
Internationals: Republic of Ireland U17, U18, U19, U21.

2020–21	Aston Villa	0	0		
2020–21	*Walsall*	16	0	**16**	**0**
2021–22	Aston Villa	0	0		
2021–22	*Salford C*	16	1	**16**	**1**
2021–22	*Colchester U*	12	1	**12**	**1**
2022–23	Aston Villa	0	0		
2022–23	*Bradford C*	15	4		
2022–23	Plymouth Arg	6	0		
2023–24	Plymouth Arg	5	0	**11**	**0**
2023–24	*Bradford C*	14	2		
2024–25	Bradford C	28	0	**57**	**6**

Scholars
Ayub, Hassan; Boney, Lewis Aaron; Brooks, Leon Smith; Denison, Franklin Leo; Goodman, George Christopher; Hussain, Bilal Ali; Lunn, Oscar Joseph Ghiggini; Martin, Joel Padraig; Mboma, Kieran Nzasi; Mohamad, Mahmod; Murray, Maxwell Jo; Paul, Cameron James; Robinson, Jack William; Rotimi, Eniolorunda Joseph; Thompson, Oliver; White, Brandon Gedd.

BRENTFORD (13)

ADEDOKUN, Valintino (F) **18** **0**
H: 5 7 W: 11 00 b.Dublin 14-2-03
Internationals: Republic of Ireland U19.

2023–24	Brentford	0	0		
2024–25	Brentford	0	0		
2024–25	*Diosgyor*	3	0	**3**	**0**
2024–25	*Cheltenham T*	15	0	**15**	**0**

AJER, Kristoffer (D) **270** **17**
H: 6 5 W: 13 03 b.Raelingen 17-4-98
Internationals: Norway U16, U17, U18, U19, U21, Full caps.

2013	Lillestrom	0	0		
2014	Lillestrom	0	0		
2014	Start	13	1		
2015	Start	30	8		
2016	Start	11	0	**54**	**9**
2016–17	Celtic	0	0		
2016–17	*Kilmarnock*	16	0	**16**	**0**
2017–18	Celtic	24	0		
2018–19	Celtic	28	0		
2019–20	Celtic	28	3		
2020–21	Celtic	35	2	**115**	**5**
2021–22	Brentford	24	1		
2022–23	Brentford	9	0		
2023–24	Brentford	28	2		
2024–25	Brentford	24	0	**85**	**3**

ANGELINI, Vincent (G) **0** **0**
H: 6 1 W: 12 08 b.Glasgow 12-9-03
From Celtic.

2021–22	Watford	0	0		
2022–23	Watford	0	0		
2022–23	Brentford	0	0		
2023–24	Brentford	0	0		
2024–25	Brentford	0	0		

ARTHUR, Benjamin (D) **0** **0**
H: 6 2 W: 7 12 b. 9-10-05
Internationals: England U18, U19.

2023–24	Peterborough U	0	0		
2023–24	Brentford	0	0		
2024–25	Brentford	0	0		

BALCOMBE, Ellery (G) **74** **0**
H: 6 0 W: 12 00 b.Watford 15-10-99
Internationals: England U18, U19, U20, U21.

2016–17	Brentford	0	0		
2017–18	Brentford	0	0		
2018–19	Brentford	0	0		
2019–20	Brentford	0	0		
2019–20	*Viborg*	8	0	**8**	**0**
2020–21	Brentford	0	0		
2020–21	*Doncaster R*	15	0	**15**	**0**
2021–22	Brentford	0	0		
2021–22	*Burton Alb*	0	0		
2022–23	Brentford	0	0		
2022–23	*Crawley T*	10	0	**10**	**0**
2022–23	*Bristol R*	8	0	**8**	**0**
2023–24	Brentford	0	0		
2024–25	Brentford	0	0		
2024–25	*St Mirren*	21	0	**21**	**0**
2024–25	*Motherwell*	12	0	**12**	**0**

BRIERLEY, Ethan (M) **31** **2**
H: 5 6 W: 10 03 b.Rochdale 23-11-03

2019–20	Rochdale	0	0		
2020–21	Rochdale	5	0		
2021–22	Rochdale	2	0		
2022–23	Rochdale	24	2	**31**	**2**
2023–24	Brentford	0	0		
2024–25	Brentford	0	0		

CARVALHO, Fabio (M) **101** **24**
H: 5 7 W: 9 13 b.Lisbon 30-8-02
Internationals: England U16, U17, U18. Portugal U21.

2020–21	Oliveirense	0	0		
2020–21	Fulham	4	1		
2021–22	Fulham	36	10	**40**	**11**
2022–23	Liverpool	13	2		
2023–24	Liverpool	0	0	**13**	**2**
2023–24	*RB Leipzig*	9	0	**9**	**0**
2023–24	*Hull C*	20	9	**20**	**9**
2024–25	Brentford	19	2	**19**	**2**

COLLINS, Nathan (D) **154** **7**
H: 6 4 W: 11 05 b.Leixlip 30-4-01
Internationals: Republic of Ireland U17, U19, U21, Full caps.

2018–19	Stoke C	3	0		
2019–20	Stoke C	14	0		
2020–21	Stoke C	22	2		
2021–22	Stoke C	0	0	**39**	**2**
2021–22	Burnley	19	2	**19**	**2**
2022–23	Wolverhampton W	26	0	**26**	**0**
2023–24	Brentford	32	1		
2024–25	Brentford	38	2	**70**	**3**

COX, Matthew (G) **31** **0**
H: 6 0 W: 10 01 b.London Borough of Sutton 2-5-03
Internationals: England U17, U19, U20, U21.

2020–21	AFC Wimbledon	0	0		
2021–22	Brentford	0	0		
2022–23	Brentford	0	0		
2023–24	Brentford	0	0		
2023–24	*Bristol R*	28	0	**28**	**0**
2024–25	Brentford	0	0		
2024–25	*Crawley T*	3	0	**3**	**0**

DA SILVA, Josh (M) **137** **20**
H: 5 11 W: 11 11 b.London Borough of Redbridge 23-10-98
Internationals: England U19, U20, U21.

2016–17	Arsenal	0	0		
2017–18	Arsenal	0	0		
2018–19	Brentford	17	1		
2019–20	Brentford	42	10		
2020–21	Brentford	30	5		
2021–22	Brentford	9	0		
2022–23	Brentford	36	4		
2023–24	Brentford	3	0		
2024–25	Brentford	0	0	**137**	**20**

DAMSGAARD, Mikkel (F) **217** **17**
H: 5 11 W: 11 03 b.Jyllinge 3-7-00
Internationals: Denmark U18, U19, U21, Full caps.

2017–18	Nordsjaelland	17	1		
2018–19	Nordsjaelland	32	1		
2019–20	Nordsjaelland	35	11	**84**	**13**
2020–21	Sampdoria	35	2		
2021–22	Sampdoria	11	0	**46**	**2**
2022–23	Brentford	26	0		
2023–24	Brentford	23	0		
2024–25	Brentford	38	2	**87**	**2**

EYESTONE, Julian (G) **0** **0**
H: 6 6 W: 15 04 b.Dallas 21-4-06
Internationals: USA U17, U19, U20.

2024–25	Brentford	0	0		

FLEKKEN, Mark (G) **240** **1**
H: 6 4 W: 13 08 b.Kerkrade 13-6-93
Internationals: Netherlands Full caps.

2012–13	Aachen	15	0	**15**	**0**
2013–14	Greuther Furth	0	0		
2014–15	Greuther Furth	2	0		
2015–16	Greuther Furth	1	0	**3**	**0**
2016–17	Duisburg	37	1		
2017–18	Duisburg	31	0	**68**	**1**
2018–19	SC Freiburg	1	0		
2019–20	SC Freiburg	10	0		
2020–21	SC Freiburg	3	0		
2021–22	SC Freiburg	32	0		
2022–23	SC Freiburg	34	0	**80**	**0**
2023–24	Brentford	37	0		
2024–25	Brentford	37	0	**74**	**0**

FREDRICK, Benjamin (D) **0** **0**
H: 6 2 W: 12 08 b. 28-5-05
Internationals: Nigeria U20, Full caps.
From Simoiben.

2023–24	Brentford	0	0		
2024–25	Brentford	0	0		

HAY, Ashley (F) **21** **3**
H: 5 11 W: 11 11 b. 10-7-03

2024–25	Brentford	0	0		
2024–25	*Cheltenham T*	21	3	**21**	**3**

HENRY, Rico (D) **237** **7**
H: 5 7 W: 10 06 b.Birmingham 8-7-97
Internationals: England U19, U20.

2014–15	Walsall	9	0		
2015–16	Walsall	35	2		
2016–17	Walsall	2	0	**46**	**2**
2016–17	Brentford	12	0		
2017–18	Brentford	8	0		
2018–19	Brentford	14	1		
2019–20	Brentford	46	0		
2020–21	Brentford	30	1		
2021–22	Brentford	34	3		
2022–23	Brentford	37	0		
2023–24	Brentford	5	0		
2024–25	Brentford	5	0	**191**	**5**

HICKEY, Aaron (D) **106** **6**
H: 5 9 W: 11 05 b.Glasgow 10-6-02
Internationals: Scotland U17, Full caps.

2018–19	Hearts	2	0		
2019–20	Hearts	22	1	**24**	**1**
2020–21	Bologna	11	0		
2021–22	Bologna	36	5	**47**	**5**
2022–23	Brentford	26	0		
2023–24	Brentford	9	0		
2024–25	Brentford	0	0	**35**	**0**

JANELT, Vitaly (M) **230** **14**
H: 6 0 W: 12 06 b.Hamburg 10-5-98
Internationals: Germany U17, U19, U20, U21.

2016–17	RB Leipzig	0	0		
2016–17	*VfL Bochum*	7	0		
2017–18	RB Leipzig	0	0		
2017–18	*VfL Bochum*	13	0		

2018–19	VfL Bochum	9	1		
2019–20	VfL Bochum	24	1		
2020–21	VfL Bochum	0	0	**53**	**2**
2020–21	Brentford	41	3		
2021–22	Brentford	31	4		
2022–23	Brentford	35	3		
2023–24	Brentford	38	1		
2024–25	Brentford	32	1	**177**	**12**

JENSEN, Mathias (M) 277 26
H: 5 8 W: 10 10 b.Horsens 1-1-96
Internationals: Denmark U18, U19, U20, U21, Full caps.

2015–16	Nordsjaelland	5	1		
2016–17	Nordsjaelland	22	2		
2017–18	Nordsjaelland	35	12		
2018–19	Nordsjaelland	1	0	**63**	**15**
2018–19	Celta Vigo	6	0	**6**	**0**
2019–20	Brentford	39	1		
2020–21	Brentford	45	2		
2021–22	Brentford	31	0		
2022–23	Brentford	37	5		
2023–24	Brentford	32	3		
2024–25	Brentford	24	0	**208**	**11**

KAYODE, Michael (D) 77 3
H: 5 10 W: 11 00 b.Borgomanero 10-7-04
Internationals: Italy U18, U19, U21.

2020–21	Gozzano	34	2	**34**	**2**
2021–22	Fiorentina	0	0		
2022–23	Fiorentina	0	0		
2023–24	Fiorentina	26	1		
2024–25	Fiorentina	5	0	**31**	**1**

On loan from Fiorentina.

2024–25	Brentford	12	0	**12**	**0**

KIM, Ji-Soo (D) 23 0
H: 6 4 W: 13 03 b.Bucheon 24-12-04
Internationals: South Korea U16, U20.

2022	Seongnam	19	0		
2023	Seongnam	1	0	**20**	**0**
2023–24	Brentford	0	0		
2024–25	Brentford	3	0	**3**	**0**

KONAK, Yunus Emre (M) 27 0
H: 5 11 W: 11 05 b.Batman 10-1-06
Internationals: Turkey U18, U21.

2023–24	Sivasspor	17	0	**17**	**0**
2023–24	Brentford	0	0		
2024–25	Brentford	10	0	**10**	**0**

LEWIS-POTTER, Keane (F) 188 31
H: 5 7 W: 10 08 b.Kingston upon Hull 22-2-01
Internationals: England U21.

2018–19	Hull C	0	0		
2019–20	Hull C	21	2		
2020–21	Hull C	43	13		
2021–22	Hull C	46	12	**110**	**27**
2022–23	Brentford	10	0		
2023–24	Brentford	30	3		
2024–25	Brentford	38	1	**78**	**4**

MAGHOMA, Edmond-Paris (M) 83 9
H: 5 11 W: 11 00 b.Enfield 8-5-01
Internationals: England U18, U19, U20.
From Tottenham H.

2020–21	Brentford	0	0		
2021–22	Brentford	0	0		
2022–23	Brentford	0	0		
2022–23	*AFC Wimbledon*	18	0	**18**	**0**
2022–23	*Milton Keynes D*	20	1	**20**	**1**
2023–24	Brentford	0	0		
2023–24	*Bolton W*	37	8	**37**	**8**
2024–25	Brentford	8	0	**8**	**0**

MBEUMO, Bryan (M) 263 76
H: 5 7 W: 11 11 b.Avallon 7-8-99
Internationals: France U17, U20, U21. Cameroon Full caps.

2016–17	Troyes	0	0		
2017–18	Troyes	4	0		
2018–19	Troyes	35	10		
2019–20	Troyes	2	1	**41**	**11**
2019–20	Brentford	42	15		
2020–21	Brentford	44	8		
2021–22	Brentford	35	4		
2022–23	Brentford	38	9		
2023–24	Brentford	25	9		
2024–25	Brentford	38	20	**222**	**65**

MEE, Ben (D) 426 17
H: 5 11 W: 11 09 b.Sale 21-9-89
Internationals: England U19, U20, U21.

2007–08	Manchester C	0	0		
2008–09	Manchester C	0	0		
2009–10	Manchester C	0	0		
2010–11	Manchester C	0	0		
2010–11	*Leicester C*	15	0	**15**	**0**
2011–12	Manchester C	0	0		
2011–12	Burnley	31	0		
2012–13	Burnley	19	1		
2013–14	Burnley	38	0		
2014–15	Burnley	33	2		
2015–16	Burnley	46	2		
2016–17	Burnley	34	1		
2017–18	Burnley	29	0		
2018–19	Burnley	38	0		
2019–20	Burnley	32	1		
2020–21	Burnley	30	2		
2021–22	Burnley	21	3	**351**	**12**
2022–23	Brentford	37	3		
2023–24	Brentford	16	2		
2024–25	Brentford	7	0	**60**	**5**

MEGHOMA, Jayden (D) 13 0
H: 5 9 W: 11 03 b. 28-6-06
Internationals: England U16, U17, U18.

2023–24	Southampton	0	0		
2024–25	Brentford	1	0	**1**	**0**
2024–25	*Preston NE*	12	0	**12**	**0**

MORGAN, Iwan (F) 0 0
H: 6 0 W: 11 11 b.Wales 29-1-06
Internationals: Wales U17, U18, U19

2023–24	Brentford	0	0		
2024–25	Brentford	0	0		

NORGAARD, Christian (M) 304 19
H: 6 1 W: 11 11 b.Copenhagen 10-3-94
Internationals: Denmark U16, U17, U19, U20, U21, Full caps.

2011–12	Lyngby	1	0	**1**	**0**
2012–13	Hamburger SV	0	0		
2013–14	Brondby	13	0		
2014–15	Brondby	21	3		
2015–16	Brondby	16	0		
2016–17	Brondby	31	4		
2017–18	Brondby	34	1		
2018–19	Brondby	1	0	**116**	**8**
2018–19	Fiorentina	6	0	**6**	**0**
2019–20	Brentford	42	0		
2020–21	Brentford	17	0		
2021–22	Brentford	35	3		
2022–23	Brentford	22	1		
2023–24	Brentford	31	2		
2024–25	Brentford	34	5	**181**	**11**

NUNES GOMES, Gustavo (M) 23 3
H: 5 8 W: 11 00 b.Sao Vicente do Sul 20-11-05

2023	Gremio	0	0		
2024	Gremio	20	3	**20**	**3**
2024–25	Brentford	3	0	**3**	**0**

OLAKIGBE, Michael (F) 43 2
H: 5 11 W: 11 07 b.Lambeth 25-4-04
Internationals: England U18, U20.
From QPR, Fulham.

2022–23	Brentford	0	0		
2023–24	Brentford	8	0		
2023–24	*Peterborough U*	5	0	**5**	**0**
2024–25	Brentford	0	0	**8**	**0**
2024–25	*Wigan Ath*	13	0	**13**	**0**
2024–25	*Chesterfield*	17	2	**17**	**2**

ONYEKA, Frank (M) 195 16
H: 6 0 W: 11 00 b.Abuja 1-1-98
Internationals: Nigeria Full caps.
From Ebedei.

2017–18	Midtjylland	15	4		
2018–19	Midtjylland	21	4		
2019–20	Midtjylland	32	4		
2020–21	Midtjylland	27	3	**95**	**15**
2021–22	Brentford	20	0		
2022–23	Brentford	21	0		
2023–24	Brentford	26	1		
2024–25	Brentford	2	0	**69**	**1**
2024–25	*Augsburg*	31	0	**31**	**0**

PEART-HARRIS, Myles (M) 84 10
H: 6 2 W: 11 00 b.Isleworth 18-9-02
Internationals: Englang U16.
From Chelsea.

2021–22	Brentford	0	0		
2022–23	Brentford	0	0		
2022–23	*Forest Green R*	40	5	**40**	**5**
2023–24	Brentford	3	0		
2023–24	*Portsmouth*	12	2	**12**	**2**
2024–25	Brentford	0	0	**3**	**0**
2024–25	*Swansea C*	29	3	**29**	**3**

PINNOCK, Ethan (D) 246 14
H: 6 2 W: 12 06 b.Lambeth 29-5-93
Internationals: England C. Jamaica Full caps.
From Dulwich Hamlet.

2017–18	Barnsley	12	2		
2018–19	Barnsley	46	1	**58**	**3**
2019–20	Brentford	36	2		
2020–21	Brentford	39	1		
2021–22	Brentford	32	1		
2022–23	Brentford	30	3		
2023–24	Brentford	29	2		
2024–25	Brentford	22	2	**188**	**11**

ROERSLEV RASMUSSEN, Mads (D) 139 2
H: 5 11 W: 10 08 b.Copenhagen 24-6-99
Internationals: Denmark U17, U18, U19, U20, U21.

2016–17	FC Copenhagen	3	0		
2016–17	*Halmstads*	1	0	**1**	**0**
2017–18	FC Copenhagen	2	0		
2018–19	FC Copenhagen	0	0	**5**	**0**
2018–19	*Vendsyssel*	4	0	**4**	**0**
2019–20	Brentford	11	0		
2020–21	Brentford	17	0		
2021–22	Brentford	21	1		
2022–23	Brentford	20	0		
2023–24	Brentford	34	1		
2024–25	Brentford	19	0	**122**	**2**
2024–25	*Wolfsburg*	7	0	**7**	**0**

SCHADE, Kevin (F) 96 18
H: 6 1 W: 11 09 b.Potsdam 27-11-01
Internationals: Germany U18, U19, U20, U21, Full caps.

2019–20	SC Freiburg	0	0		
2020–21	SC Freiburg	0	0		
2021–22	SC Freiburg	21	4		
2022–23	SC Freiburg	8	1	**29**	**5**
2022–23	*Brentford*	18	0		
2023–24	Brentford	11	2		
2024–25	Brentford	38	11	**67**	**13**

THIAGO, Igor (F) 119 38
H: 6 2 W: 13 12 b.Gama, Federal District, Brazil 26-6-01

2020	Cruzeiro	18	0		
2021	Cruzeiro	25	4		
2021–22	Ludogorets Razgrad	2	1		
2022	Cruzeiro	0	0	**43**	**4**
2022–23	Ludogorets Razgrad	32	15	**34**	**16**
2023–24	Club Brugge	34	18	**34**	**18**
2024–25	Brentford	8	0	**8**	**0**

TREVITT, Ryan (M) 31 4
H: 5 7 W: 10 03 b.Leatherhead 12-3-03

2020–21	Brentford	0	0		
2021–22	Brentford	0	0		
2022–23	Brentford	0	0		
2023–24	Brentford	0	0		
2023–24	*Exeter C*	19	3		
2024–25	Brentford	1	0	**1**	**0**
2024–25	*Exeter C*	11	1	**30**	**4**

VALDIMARSSON, Hakon (G) 115 0
H: 6 4 W: 14 00 b.Reykjavik 13-10-01
Internationals: Iceland U18, U19, U21, Full caps.

2017	Grotta	1	0		
2018	Grotta	15	0		
2019	Grotta	22	0		
2020	Grotta	18	0		
2021	Grotta	9	0	**65**	**0**
2021	Elfsborg	5	0		
2022	Elfsborg	14	0		
2023	Elfsborg	29	0	**48**	**0**
2023–24	Brentford	0	0		
2024–25	Brentford	2	0	**2**	**0**

VAN DEN BERG, Sepp (D) 156 5
H: 6 2 W: 12 04 b.Zwolle 20-12-01
Internationals: Netherlands U19, U21.

2017–18	PEC Zwolle	7	0		
2018–19	PEC Zwolle	15	0	**22**	**0**
2019–20	Liverpool	0	0		
2020–21	Liverpool	0	0		
2020–21	*Preston NE*	16	0		
2021–22	Liverpool	0	0		
2021–22	*Preston NE*	45	1	**61**	**1**
2022–23	Liverpool	0	0		
2022–23	*Schalke 04*	9	1	**9**	**1**
2023–24	Liverpool	0	0		
2023–24	*Mainz 05*	33	3	**33**	**3**
2024–25	Brentford	31	0	**31**	**0**

WINTERBOTTOM, Ben (G) 0 0
H: 6 2 W: 10 06 b.Preston 16-7-01
From Blackburn R.

2019–20	Liverpool	0	0		
2020–21	Brentford	0	0		
2021–22	Brentford	0	0		
2022–23	Brentford	0	0		
2024–25	Brentford	0	0		

WISSA, Yoane (F) 314 97
H: 5 11 W: 11 11 b.Epinay-sous-Senart 3-9-96
Internationals: DR Congo Full caps.

2013–14	Chateauroux	0	0		
2014–15	Chateauroux	0	0		
2015–16	Chateauroux	23	7	**23**	**7**
2016–17	Angers	2	0		
2016–17	*Stade Laval*	15	2	**15**	**2**
2017–18	Angers	0	0	**2**	**0**
2017–18	*Ajaccio*	20	8	**20**	**8**
2017–18	Lorient	15	4		
2018–19	Lorient	36	6		
2019–20	Lorient	28	15		
2020–21	Lorient	38	10	**117**	**35**
2021–22	Brentford	30	7		
2022–23	Brentford	38	7		
2023–24	Brentford	34	12		
2024–25	Brentford	35	19	**137**	**45**

YARMOLYUK, Yegor (M) 76 0
H: 5 11 W: 11 05 b.Verkhnyodniprovsk 1-3-04
Internationals: Ukraine U16, U19, U21, U23.

2019–20	Dnipro-1	2	0		
2020–21	Dnipro-1	9	0		

2021–22	Dnipro-1	7	0	**18**	**0**
2022–23	Brentford	0	0		
2023–24	Brentford	27	0		
2024–25	Brentford	31	0	**58**	**0**

YOGANE, Tony (M)   **18 0**
H: 5 10 W: 10 10 b.Croydon 24-9-05

2024–25	Brentford	0	0		
2024–25	Exeter C	18	0	**18**	**0**

Players retained or with offer of contract
Asemokhai, Gregory Oshogbeh; Avenell, Caelan; Grey, Andre Everett; Headman, Chanse Allan; Holland, Isaac Joel; Krauhaus, Ben Carl; Laidlaw, Ethan James; McManus, Conor James; McSorley, Michael Joseph; Owen, Riley Jay; Rose, Reginald; Shield, Oliver George; Stephenson, Joshua James; Tavazira, Marley Joseph; Wolfheimer, Connor.

Scholars
Allen, Bobb-Semple Domeiro Dominic JR Davies; Bentt, Luka Maxine Deyne; Boni, Gbenankpon Michel Destiny; Bowen, Staitham Michael; Giscombe, Naeem Umar Alexander Dita; Golding, Aidan Martin; Honor, Otis Samuel Birch; Ouattara, Yerime Ty Ethan; Owusu, Nedved Amankwaa; Peters, Emeka Okwunna; Powis, Isaiah Hindowa; Roca, Enrique Jose; Trimboli, Archie Ian McBlain.

BRIGHTON & HA (14)

ADINGRA, Simon (M)   **96 19**
H: 5 9 W: 10 10 b.Abidjan 1-1-02
Internationals: Ivory Coast Full caps.

2022–23	Brighton & HA	0	0		
2022–23	Union SG	36	11	**36**	**11**
2023–24	Brighton & HA	31	6		
2024–25	Brighton & HA	29	2	**60**	**8**

ATOM, Noel (D)   **0 0**
H: 6 4 W: 12 04 b.5-1-05
Internationals: Germany U17.

2023–24	Brighton & HA	0	0		
2024–25	Brighton & HA	0	0		

AYARI, Yasin (M)   **97 7**
H: 5 8 W: 10 12 b.Solna 6-10-03
Internationals: Sweden U17, U19, U21, Full caps.

2020	AIK	1	0		
2021	AIK	12	0		
2022	AIK	24	4	**37**	**4**
2022–23	Brighton & HA	3	0		
2023–24	Brighton & HA	0	0		
2023–24	Coventry C	13	1	**13**	**1**
2023–24	Blackburn R	10	0	**10**	**0**
2024–25	Brighton & HA	34	2	**37**	**2**

BALEBA, Carlos (M)   **82 3**
H: 5 10 W: 11 11 b.Douala 3-1-04
Internationals: Cameroon Full caps.

2021–22	Lille	0	0		
2022–23	Lille	19	0		
2023–24	Lille	2	0	**21**	**0**
2023–24	Brighton & HA	27	0		
2024–25	Brighton & HA	34	3	**61**	**3**

BARCO, Valentin (D)   **50 1**
H: 5 7 W: 10 10 b.25 de Mayo 23-7-04
Internationals: Argentina U20, U23, Full caps.

2021	Boca Juniors	3	0		
2022	Boca Juniors	0	0		
2023	Boca Juniors	20	1	**23**	**1**
2023–24	Brighton & HA	6	0		
2024–25	Brighton & HA	0	0	**6**	**0**
2024–25	Sevilla	7	0	**7**	**0**
2024–25	Strasbourg	14	0	**14**	**0**

BARRINGTON, Luca (F)   **38 4**
H: 5 10 W: 11 03 b.Manchester 12-12-04
From Manchester C.

2022–23	Brighton & HA	0	0		
2023–24	Brighton & HA	0	0		
2024–25	Brighton & HA	0	0		
2024–25	Grimsby T	38	4	**38**	**4**

BEADLE, James (G)   **91 0**
b. 16-7-04
Internationals: England U16, U18, U19, U20, U21.

2021–22	Charlton Ath	0	0		
2021–22	Brighton & HA	0	0		
2022–23	Brighton & HA	0	0		
2022–23	Crewe Alex	9	0	**9**	**0**
2023–24	Brighton & HA	0	0		
2023–24	Oxford U	25	0	**25**	**0**
2023–24	Sheffield Wed	19	0		
2024–25	Brighton & HA	0	0		
2024–25	Sheffield Wed	38	0	**57**	**0**

BUONANOTTE, Facundo (M)   **95 13**
H: 5 9 W: 10 06 b.Perez 23-12-04
Internationals: Argentina U20, Full caps.

2022	Rosario Central	24	4	**24**	**4**
2022–23	Brighton & HA	13	1		
2023–24	Brighton & HA	27	3		
2024–25	Brighton & HA	0	0	**40**	**4**
2024–25	Leicester C	31	5	**31**	**5**

CAHILL, Killian (G)   **0 0**
W: 10 08 b.Skyrne, Meath 3-11-03

2024–25	Brighton & HA	0	0		

CASHIN, Eiran (D)   **128 6**
H: 6 2 W: 13 12 b.Mansfield 9-11-01
Internationals: Republic of Ireland U18, U21.

2020–21	Derby Co	0	0		
2021–22	Derby Co	18	1		
2022–23	Derby Co	43	1		
2023–24	Derby Co	44	3		
2024–25	Derby Co	21	1	**126**	**6**
2024–25	Brighton & HA	2	0	**2**	**0**

COZIER-DUBERRY, Amario (F)   **22 1**
H: 5 7 W: 9 00 b.London 29-5-05
Internationals: England U16, U17, U18, U19, U20.

2022–23	Arsenal	0	0		
2023–24	Arsenal	0	0		
2024–25	Brighton & HA	22	1	**22**	**1**

DOYLE, Kamari (M)   **42 10**
H: 5 10 W: 10 01 b.1-8-05
Internationals: England U17, U18, U19, U20.

2022–23	Southampton	1	0		
2023–24	Southampton	0	0	**1**	**0**
2024–25	Brighton & HA	0	0		
2024–25	Exeter C	20	3	**20**	**3**
2024–25	Crawley T	21	7	**21**	**7**

DUFFUS, Joshua (M)   **0 0**
H: 6 2 W: 12 02 b.London 31-5-05
Internationals: England U17, U19.

2023–24	Brighton & HA	0	0		
2024–25	Brighton & HA	0	0		

DUNK, Lewis (D)   **438 26**
H: 6 4 W: 13 11 b.Brighton 1-12-91
Internationals: England Full caps.

2009–10	Brighton & HA	1	0		
2010–11	Brighton & HA	5	0		
2011–12	Brighton & HA	31	0		
2012–13	Brighton & HA	8	0		
2013–14	Brighton & HA	6	0		
2013–14	Bristol C	2	0	**2**	**0**
2014–15	Brighton & HA	38	5		
2015–16	Brighton & HA	38	3		
2016–17	Brighton & HA	43	2		
2017–18	Brighton & HA	38	1		
2018–19	Brighton & HA	36	3		
2019–20	Brighton & HA	36	3		
2020–21	Brighton & HA	33	5		
2021–22	Brighton & HA	29	1		
2022–23	Brighton & HA	36	1		
2023–24	Brighton & HA	33	3		
2024–25	Brighton & HA	25	0	**436**	**26**

ENCISO, Julio (F)   **112 24**
H: 5 6 W: 10 01 b.Caaguazu 22-1-04
Internationals: Paraguay Full caps.

2018	Libertad	0	0		
2019	Libertad	3	0		
2020	Libertad	8	1		
2021	Libertad	30	6		
2022	Libertad	14	11	**55**	**18**
2022–23	Brighton & HA	20	4		
2023–24	Brighton & HA	12	0		
2024–25	Brighton & HA	12	0	**44**	**4**
2024–25	Ipswich T	13	2	**13**	**2**

ESTUPINAN, Pervis (D)   **253 7**
H: 5 9 W: 11 07 b.Esmeraldas 21-1-98
Internationals: Ecuador U17, U20, Full caps.

2015	LDU Quito	32	0		
2016	LDU Quito	8	0	**40**	**0**
2016–17	Watford	0	0		
2016–17	Granada	2	0	**2**	**0**
2017–18	Watford	0	0		
2017–18	Almeria	26	0	**26**	**0**
2018–19	Watford	0	0		
2018–19	Mallorca	12	2	**12**	**2**
2019–20	Watford	0	0		
2019–20	Osasuna	36	1	**36**	**1**
2020–21	Villarreal	25	0		
2021–22	Villarreal	28	0	**53**	**0**
2022–23	Brighton & HA	35	1		
2023–24	Brighton & HA	19	2		
2024–25	Brighton & HA	30	1	**84**	**4**

FERGUSON, Evan (F)   **71 13**
H: 5 10 W: 11 09 b.Bettystown 19-10-04
Internationals: Republic of Ireland U17, U21, Full caps.
From St Kevin's Boys.

2019	Bohemians	1	0		
2020	Bohemians	2	0	**3**	**0**

2021–22	Brighton & HA	1	0		
2022–23	Brighton & HA	19	6		
2023–24	Brighton & HA	27	6		
2024–25	Brighton & HA	13	1	**60**	**13**
2024–25	West Ham U	8	0	**8**	**0**

GILMOUR, Billy (M)   **81 0**
H: 5 6 W: 9 06 b.Glasgow 11-6-01
Internationals: Scotland U16, U17, U19, U21, Full caps.
From Rangers.

2019–20	Chelsea	6	0		
2020–21	Chelsea	5	0		
2021–22	Chelsea	0	0	**11**	**0**
2021–22	Norwich C	24	0	**24**	**0**
2022–23	Brighton & HA	14	0		
2023–24	Brighton & HA	30	0		
2024–25	Brighton & HA	2	0	**46**	**0**

Transferred to Napoli, August 2024.

GOMEZ, Diego (M)   **83 10**
H: 6 0 W: 12 02 b.San Juan Bautista 27-3-03
Internationals: Paraguay U20, U23, Full caps.

2022	Libertad	21	2		
2023	Libertad	19	3	**40**	**5**
2023	Inter Miami	5	1		
2024	Inter Miami	22	3	**27**	**4**
2024–25	Brighton & HA	16	1	**16**	**1**

GRUDA, Brajan (M)   **51 5**
H: 5 10 W: 11 07 b.Speyer 31-5-04
Internationals: Germany U16, U18, U19, U21.

2022–23	Mainz 05	2	0		
2023–24	Mainz 05	28	4	**30**	**4**
2024–25	Brighton & HA	21	1	**21**	**1**

HINSHELWOOD, Jack (D)   **39 8**
H: 5 11 W: 11 07 b.Worthing 11-4-05
Internationals: England U18, U19, U21.

2022–23	Brighton & HA	1	0		
2023–24	Brighton & HA	12	3		
2024–25	Brighton & HA	26	5	**39**	**8**

HOWELL, Harry (M)   **1 0**
b. 29-9-08
Internationals: England U16, U17.

2024–25	Brighton & HA	1	0	**1**	**0**

IGOR, de Paulo (D)   **221 0**
H: 6 2 W: 13 01 b.Bom Sucesso 7-2-98
From Red Bull Brasil.

2016–17	Red Bull Salzburg	0	0		
2016–17	Liefering	25	0		
2017–18	Red Bull Salzburg	1	0		
2017–18	Liefering	11	0	**36**	**0**
2017–18	Wolfsberg	15	0	**15**	**0**
2018–19	Red Bull Salzburg	0	0	**2**	**0**
2018–19	Austria Vienna	27	0	**27**	**0**
2019–20	SPAL	17	0		
2019–20	Fiorentina	9	0		
2020–21	SPAL	0	0	**17**	**0**
2020–21	Fiorentina	21	0		
2021–22	Fiorentina	30	0		
2022–23	Fiorentina	27	0	**87**	**0**
2023–24	Brighton & HA	24	0		
2024–25	Brighton & HA	13	0	**37**	**0**

JACKSON, Ben (D)   **0 0**
H: 6 3 W: 12 04 b.Hillingdon 3-9-03

2023–24	Brighton & HA	0	0		
2024–25	Brighton & HA	0	0		
2024–25	Queen's Park	0	0		

JOAO PEDRO, de Jesus (F)   **187 46**
H: 6 0 W: 11 00 b.Ribeirao Preto 26-9-01
Internationals: Brazil U23, Full caps.

2019	Fluminense	25	4	**25**	**4**
2019–20	Watford	3	0		
2020–21	Watford	38	9		
2021–22	Watford	28	3		
2022–23	Watford	35	11	**104**	**23**
2023–24	Brighton & HA	31	9		
2024–25	Brighton & HA	27	10	**58**	**19**

KADIOGLU, Ferdi (M)   **215 23**
H: 5 8 W: 10 01 b.Arnhem 7-10-99
Internationals: Netherlands U16, U17, U18, U19, U21. Turkey Full caps.

2016–17	NEC	27	4		
2017–18	NEC	34	7	**61**	**11**
2018–19	Fenerbahce	0	0		
2019–20	Fenerbahce	23	4		
2020–21	Fenerbahce	26	1		
2021–22	Fenerbahce	28	2		
2022–23	Fenerbahce	32	3		
2023–24	Fenerbahce	37	1		
2024–25	Fenerbahce	2	0	**148**	**11**
2024–25	Brighton & HA	6	1	**6**	**1**

KNIGHT, Joe (M)   **0 0**
b. 21-9-05

2024–25	Brighton & HA	0	0		

LAMPTEY, Tariq (D) 104 3
H: 5 9 W: 10 12 b.Hillingdon 30-9-00
Internationals: England U18, U19, U20, Full caps.

2019–20	Chelsea	1	0	**1**	**0**
2019–20	Brighton & HA	8	0		
2020–21	Brighton & HA	11	1		
2021–22	Brighton & HA	30	0		
2022–23	Brighton & HA	20	0		
2023–24	Brighton & HA	19	0		
2024–25	Brighton & HA	15	2	**103**	**3**

MARCH, Solly (M) 265 21
H: 5 11 W: 12 02 b.Lewes 26-7-94
Internationals: England U20, U21.
From Lewes.

2012–13	Brighton & HA	0	0		
2013–14	Brighton & HA	23	0		
2014–15	Brighton & HA	11	1		
2015–16	Brighton & HA	16	3		
2016–17	Brighton & HA	25	3		
2017–18	Brighton & HA	36	1		
2018–19	Brighton & HA	35	1		
2019–20	Brighton & HA	19	0		
2020–21	Brighton & HA	21	2		
2021–22	Brighton & HA	31	0		
2022–23	Brighton & HA	33	7		
2023–24	Brighton & HA	7	3		
2024–25	Brighton & HA	8	0	**265**	**21**

MAZILU, Adrian (F) 38 7
H: 6 1 W: 11 09 b.Constanta 13-9-05
Internationals: Romania U16, U17, U18, U19, U21.

2022–23	Farul Constanta	19	6		
2023–24	Farul Constanta	16	1	**35**	**7**
2023–24	Brighton & HA	0	0		
2023–24	*Vitesse*	3	0	**3**	**0**
2024–25	Brighton & HA	0	0		

McGILL, Thomas (G) 26 0
H: 6 1 W: 12 08 b.Haywards Heath 25-3-00
Internationals: England U16, U17, U20.

2019–20	Brighton & HA	0	0		
2019–20	*Crawley T*	0	0		
2020–21	Brighton & HA	0	0		
2020–21	*Crawley T*	1	0	**1**	**0**
2021–22	Brighton & HA	0	0		
2022–23	Brighton & HA	0	0		
2023–24	Brighton & HA	0	0		
2024–25	Brighton & HA	0	0		
2024–25	*Milton Keynes D*	25	0	**25**	**0**

MILNER, James (M) 644 57
H: 5 9 W: 11 00 b.Leeds 4-1-86
Internationals: England U16, U17, U19, U20, U21, Full caps.

2002–03	Leeds U	18	2		
2003–04	Leeds U	30	3	**48**	**5**
2003–04	*Swindon T*	6	2	**6**	**2**
2004–05	Newcastle U	25	1		
2005–06	Newcastle U	3	0		
2005–06	*Aston Villa*	27	1		
2006–07	Newcastle U	35	3		
2007–08	Newcastle U	29	2		
2008–09	Newcastle U	2	0	**94**	**6**
2008–09	Aston Villa	36	3		
2009–10	Aston Villa	36	7		
2010–11	Aston Villa	1	1	**100**	**12**
2010–11	Manchester C	32	0		
2011–12	Manchester C	26	3		
2012–13	Manchester C	26	4		
2013–14	Manchester C	31	1		
2014–15	Manchester C	32	5	**147**	**13**
2015–16	Liverpool	28	5		
2016–17	Liverpool	36	7		
2017–18	Liverpool	32	0		
2018–19	Liverpool	31	5		
2019–20	Liverpool	22	2		
2020–21	Liverpool	26	0		
2021–22	Liverpool	24	0		
2022–23	Liverpool	31	0	**230**	**19**
2023–24	Brighton & HA	15	0		
2024–25	Brighton & HA	4	0	**19**	**0**

MINTEH, Yankuba (F) 76 20
H: 5 11 W: 10 03 b.Bakoteh 22-7-04
Internationals: Gambia Full caps.

2022–23	OB	17	4	**17**	**4**
2023–24	Newcastle U	0	0		
2023–24	*Feyenoord*	27	10	**27**	**10**
2024–25	Brighton & HA	32	6	**32**	**6**

MITOMA, Kaoru (F) 165 48
H: 5 10 W: 11 09 b.Kanagawa 20-5-97
Internationals: Japan U21, U23, Full caps.

2018	Kawasaki Frontale	0	0		
2019	Kawasaki Frontale	0	0		
2020	Kawasaki Frontale	30	13		
2021–22	Kawasaki Frontale	20	8	**50**	**21**
2021–22	Brighton & HA	0	0		
2021–22	*Union SG*	27	7	**27**	**7**
2022–23	Brighton & HA	33	7		
2023–24	Brighton & HA	19	3		
2024–25	Brighton & HA	36	10	**88**	**20**

MODER, Jakub (M) 119 9
H: 6 3 W: 12 04 b.Szczecinek 7-4-99
Internationals: Poland U17, U18, U19, U20, Full caps.

2016–17	Lech Poznan	0	0		
2017–18	Lech Poznan	1	0		
2018–19	Lech Poznan	0	0		
2018–19	*Odra Opole*	31	4	**31**	**4**
2019–20	Lech Poznan	26	5		
2020–21	Lech Poznan	0	0	**27**	**5**
2020–21	Brighton & HA	12	0		
2021–22	Brighton & HA	28	0		
2022–23	Brighton & HA	0	0		
2023–24	Brighton & HA	17	0		
2024–25	Brighton & HA	4	0	**61**	**0**

Transferred to Feyenoord, January 2025.

MORAN, Andrew (M) 74 7
H: 5 10 W: 11 07 b.Dublin 15-10-03
Internationals: Republic of Ireland U16, U17, U19, U21, Full caps.
From St Joseph's Boys.

2019	Bray W	2	0		
2020	Bray W	1	1	**3**	**1**
2021–22	Brighton & HA	0	0		
2022–23	Brighton & HA	1	0		
2023–24	Brighton & HA	0	0		
2023–24	*Blackburn R*	35	2	**35**	**2**
2024–25	Brighton & HA	0	0	**1**	**0**
2024–25	*Stoke C*	35	4	**35**	**4**

O'MAHONY, Mark (F) 16 3
b.Cork 14-1-05
Internationals: Republic of Ireland U16, U17, U18, U19, U21.
From Cork C.

2022–23	Brighton & HA	0	0		
2023–24	Brighton & HA	3	0		
2024–25	Brighton & HA	0	0	**3**	**0**
2024–25	*Portsmouth*	13	3	**13**	**3**

O'RILEY, Matt (M) 164 37
H: 6 2 W: 12 02 b.Hounslow 21-11-00
Internationals: England U16, U18. Denmark U21, Full caps.

2017–18	Fulham	0	0		
2018–19	Fulham	0	0		
2019–20	Fulham	1	0	**1**	**0**
2020–21	Milton Keynes D	23	3		
2021–22	Milton Keynes D	26	7	**49**	**10**
2021–22	Celtic	16	4		
2022–23	Celtic	38	3		
2023–24	Celtic	37	18		
2024–25	Celtic	2	0	**93**	**25**
2024–25	Brighton & HA	21	2	**21**	**2**

OFFIAH, Odel (D) 51 1
H: 5 11 W: 12 02 b.Camden 26-10-02

2020–21	Brighton & HA	0	0		
2021–22	Brighton & HA	0	0		
2022–23	Brighton & HA	2	0		
2023–24	Brighton & HA	4	0		
2023–24	*Hearts*	5	0	**5**	**0**
2024–25	Brighton & HA	0	0	**6**	**0**
2024–25	*Blackpool*	40	1	**40**	**1**

OSMAN, Ibrahim (M) 57 9
b.Accra 29-11-04
Internationals: Ghana Full caps.

2022–23	Nordsjaelland	6	0		
2023–24	Nordsjaelland	29	6	**35**	**6**
2024–25	Brighton & HA	0	0		
2024–25	*Feyenoord*	22	3	**22**	**3**

PEUPION, Cameron (M) 7 0
H: 5 9 W: 11 00 b.Sydney 23-9-02
Internationals: Australia U17, U23.
From Sydney FC.

2020–21	Brighton & HA	0	0		
2021–22	Brighton & HA	0	0		
2022–23	Brighton & HA	1	0		
2023–24	Brighton & HA	0	0		
2023–24	*Cheltenham T*	6	0	**6**	**0**
2024–25	Brighton & HA	0	0	**1**	**0**

RUSHWORTH, Carl (G) 133 0
H: 6 2 W: 13 08 b.Halifax 2-7-01
Internationals: England U21.
From Halifax T.

2021–22	Brighton & HA	0	0		
2021–22	*Walsall*	43	0	**43**	**0**
2022–23	Brighton & HA	0	0		
2022–23	*Lincoln C*	42	0	**42**	**0**
2023–24	Brighton & HA	0	0		
2023–24	*Swansea C*	46	0	**46**	**0**
2024–25	Brighton & HA	0	0		
2024–25	*Hull C*	2	0	**2**	**0**

RUTTER, Georginio (F) 146 22
H: 6 0 W: 12 02 b.Plescop 20-4-02
Internationals: France U16, U17, U18, U20, U21.

2020–21	Rennes	4	0	**4**	**0**
2020–21	TSG 1899 Hoffenheim	9	1		
2021–22	TSG 1899 Hoffenheim	33	8		
2022–23	TSG 1899 Hoffenheim	15	2	**57**	**11**
2022–23	Leeds U	11	0		
2023–24	Leeds U	45	6		
2024–25	Leeds U	1	0	**57**	**6**
2024–25	Brighton & HA	28	5	**28**	**5**

SAMUELS, Imari (D) 4 0
H: 6 2 W: 11 07 b.Hammersmith 5-2-03
Internationals: England U16, U17, U20.

2020–21	Reading	0	0		
2021–22	Reading	0	0		
2022–23	Reading	0	0		
2022–23	Brighton & HA	0	0		
2023–24	Brighton & HA	0	0		
2023–24	*Fleetwood T*	4	0	**4**	**0**
2024–25	Brighton & HA	0	0		

Transferred to Dundee, January 2025.

SARMIENTO, Jeremy (F) 90 9
H: 6 0 W: 11 07 b.Madrid 16-6-02
Internationals: England U16, U17, U18. Ecuador Full caps.
From Charlton Ath, Benfica.

2021–22	Brighton & HA	5	0		
2022–23	Brighton & HA	9	0		
2023–24	Brighton & HA	0	0		
2023–24	*WBA*	20	2	**20**	**2**
2023–24	*Ipswich T*	20	3	**20**	**3**
2024–25	Brighton & HA	1	0	**15**	**0**
2024–25	*Burnley*	35	4	**35**	**4**

SCHERPEN, Kjell (G) 116 0
H: 6 8 W: 13 05 b.Emmen 23-1-00
Internationals: Netherlands U19, U21, Full caps.

2017–18	Emmen	1	0		
2018–19	Emmen	34	0	**35**	**0**
2019–20	Ajax	0	0		
2020–21	Ajax	2	0	**2**	**0**
2021–22	Brighton & HA	0	0		
2021–22	*Oostende*	7	0	**7**	**0**
2022–23	Brighton & HA	0	0		
2022–23	*Vitesse*	26	0	**26**	**0**
2023–24	Brighton & HA	0	0		
2023–24	*Stum Graz*	16	0	**16**	**0**
2024–25	Brighton & HA	0	0		
2024–25	*Sturm Graz*	30	0	**30**	**0**

SIMA, Abdallah (F) 78 29
H: 6 2 W: 11 09 b.Dakar 17-6-01
Internationals: Senegal Full caps.

2020–21	Slavia Prague	21	11		
2021–22	Slavia Prague	3	0	**24**	**11**
2021–22	Brighton & HA	0	0		
2021–22	*Stoke C*	2	0	**2**	**0**
2022–23	Brighton & HA	0	0		
2023–24	Brighton & HA	0	0		
2023–24	*Rangers*	25	11	**25**	**11**
2024–25	Brighton & HA	0	0		
2024–25	*Brest*	27	7	**27**	**7**

SIMMONDS, Freddie (D) 0 0
Internationals: England U16, U17.

2024–25	Brighton & HA	0	0		

SLATER, Jacob (D) 1 0
H: 5 10 W: 11 00 b. 5-10-04
Internationals: Republic of Ireland U21.

2022–23	Preston NE	1	0	**1**	**0**
2023–24	Brighton & HA	0	0		
2024–25	Brighton & HA	0	0		

STEELE, Jason (G) 307 0
H: 6 2 W: 12 06 b.Newton Aycliffe 18-8-90
Internationals: England U16, U17, U19, U21. Great Britain.

2007–08	Middlesbrough	0	0		
2008–09	Middlesbrough	0	0		
2009–10	Middlesbrough	0	0		
2009–10	*Northampton T*	13	0	**13**	**0**
2010–11	Middlesbrough	35	0		
2011–12	Middlesbrough	34	0		
2012–13	Middlesbrough	46	0		
2013–14	Middlesbrough	16	0		
2014–15	Middlesbrough	0	0	**131**	**0**
2014–15	*Blackburn R*	31	0		
2015–16	Blackburn R	41	0		
2016–17	Blackburn R	41	0	**113**	**0**
2017–18	Sunderland	15	0	**15**	**0**
2018–19	Brighton & HA	0	0		
2019–20	Brighton & HA	0	0		
2020–21	Brighton & HA	0	0		
2021–22	Brighton & HA	1	0		
2022–23	Brighton & HA	15	0		
2023–24	Brighton & HA	17	0		
2024–25	Brighton & HA	2	0	**35**	**0**

TASKER, Charlie (D) 0 0
b. 24-2-06

2024–25	Brighton & HA	0	0		

TZIMAS, Stefanos (F) 43 16
b. 6-1-06
Internationals: Greece U16, U17, U19, U21.

2022–23	PAOK	4	1		
2023–24	PAOK	16	3	**20**	**4**
2024–25	Brighton & HA	0	0		
2024–25	*Nuremberg*	23	12	**23**	**12**

VAN HECKE, Jan (D) 112 5
H: 6 2 W: 12 04 b.Amemuiden 8-6-00
Internationals: Netherlands U21, Full caps.

Season	Club				
2019–20	NAC Breda	11	3	11	3
2020–21	Brighton & HA	0	0		
2021–22	Brighton & HA	0	0		
2021–22	*Blackburn R*	31	1	31	1
2022–23	Brighton & HA	8	0		
2023–24	Brighton & HA	28	0		
2024–25	Brighton & HA	34	1	70	1

VELTMAN, Joel (D) 320 14
H: 6 0 W: 11 07 b.Velsen 15-1-92
Internationals: Netherlands U17, U19, U20, Full caps.

Season	Club				
2011–12	Ajax	0	0		
2012–13	Ajax	7	0		
2013–14	Ajax	25	2		
2014–15	Ajax	25	4		
2015–16	Ajax	34	2		
2016–17	Ajax	30	0		
2017–18	Ajax	30	1		
2018–19	Ajax	9	1		
2019–20	Ajax	19	0	179	10
2020–21	Brighton & HA	28	1		
2021–22	Brighton & HA	34	1		
2022–23	Brighton & HA	31	1		
2023–24	Brighton & HA	27	1		
2024–25	Brighton & HA	20	1	141	4

VERBRUGGEN, Bart (G) 81 0
H: 6 4 W: 11 11 b.Breda 30-5-00
Internationals: Netherlands U18, U21, Full caps.

Season	Club				
2019–20	NAC Breda	0	0		
2020–21	Anderlecht	6	0		
2021–22	Anderlecht	1	0		
2022–23	Anderlecht	17	0	24	0
2023–24	Brighton & HA	21	0		
2024–25	Brighton & HA	36	0	57	0

VICKERS, Caylon (M) 33 3
H: 5 8 W: 10 03 b.Windsor 22-12-04

Season	Club				
2023–24	Reading	14	1	14	1
2023–24	Brighton & HA	0	0		
2024–25	Brighton & HA	0	0		
2024–25	*Mansfield T*	19	2	19	2

WEBSTER, Adam (D) 300 15
H: 6 1 W: 11 11 b.West Wittering 4-1-95
Internationals: England U18, U19.

Season	Club				
2011–12	Portsmouth	3	0		
2012–13	Portsmouth	18	0		
2013–14	Portsmouth	4	2		
2014–15	Portsmouth	15	1		
2015–16	Portsmouth	27	2	67	5
2016–17	Ipswich T	23	1		
2017–18	Ipswich T	28	0	51	1
2018–19	Bristol C	44	3		
2019–20	Bristol C	0	0	44	3
2019–20	Brighton & HA	31	3		
2020–21	Brighton & HA	29	1		
2021–22	Brighton & HA	22	2		
2022–23	Brighton & HA	27	0		
2023–24	Brighton & HA	15	0		
2024–25	Brighton & HA	14	0	138	6

WELBECK, Danny (F) 371 79
H: 6 0 W: 11 07 b.Manchester 26-11-90
Internationals: England U17, U18, U19, U21, Full caps.

Season	Club				
2007–08	Manchester U	0	0		
2008–09	Manchester U	3	1		
2009–10	Manchester U	5	0		
2009–10	*Preston NE*	8	2	8	2
2010–11	Manchester U	0	0		
2010–11	*Sunderland*	26	6	26	6
2011–12	Manchester U	30	9		
2012–13	Manchester U	27	1		
2013–14	Manchester U	25	9		
2014–15	Manchester U	2	0	92	20
2014–15	Arsenal	25	4		
2015–16	Arsenal	11	4		
2016–17	Arsenal	16	2		
2017–18	Arsenal	28	5		
2018–19	Arsenal	8	1	88	16
2019–20	Watford	18	2		
2020–21	Watford	0	0	18	2
2020–21	Brighton & HA	24	6		
2021–22	Brighton & HA	25	6		
2022–23	Brighton & HA	31	6		
2023–24	Brighton & HA	29	5		
2024–25	Brighton & HA	30	10	139	33

WIEFFER, Mats (M) 145 12
H: 6 2 W: 11 09 b.Borne 18-11-99

Season	Club				
2018–19	FC Twente	1	0		
2019–20	FC Twente	0	0	1	0
2020–21	Excelsior	31	1		
2021–22	Excelsior	34	4	65	5
2022–23	Feyenoord	25	1		
2023–24	Feyenoord	29	5	54	6
2024–25	Brighton & HA	25	1	25	1

YALCOUYE, Malick (M) 39 5
b.Bandiagara 18-11-05
Internationals: Ivory Coast U23.

Season	Club				
2023–24	Gothenborg	11	1	11	1
2024–25	Brighton & HA	0	0		
2024–25	*Sturm Graz*	28	4	28	4

Players retained or with offer of contract
Albarus, Zane Jerome Joseph; Belmont, Joe; Hall, Steven James; Jensen, Sebastian Paldan; Lane, Darius Jefferson Ahamada; Mackley, Callum Luke; Mills, Harry Thomas; Mullins, Jamie Anthony; Penman, Charlie Jai; Robertson, Joshua; West, Aidan Luke.

Scholars
Ademola, Sebastian Adebola; Alakiu, Isaiah Fariq; Brett, Adam Caesar; Cullinane, Billy-Ray; Ferdinand, Lorenz; Ferdinand, Tate; Hayden, Matthew Isaac Tal; Howell, Harry John; Ibrahim, Younes Ahmed; Kasvosve, Henry Tinashe; Middleton, Jesse Gene; Nti, Shane Kojo; Oriola II, Nehemiah Said; Outen, Theo Angelo Ronald; Owusu, Yussif Moro; Rutter, William John; Silsby, Tyler Michael; Simmonds, Freddie James; Taylor, Finley Baxter.

BRISTOL C (15)

ARAOYE, Raphael (D) 0 0
b. 22-4-04

Season	Club				
2023–24	Bristol C	0	0		
2024–25	Bristol C	0	0		

ARMSTRONG, Sinclair (F) 97 6
H: 6 0 W: 12 13 b.Dublin 22-6-03
Internationals: Republic of Ireland U17, U19, U21, Full caps.

Season	Club				
2021–22	QPR	0	0		
2022–23	QPR	22	0		
2023–24	QPR	39	3	61	3
2024–25	Bristol C	36	3	36	3

ATKINSON, Robert (D) 113 9
H: 6 4 W: 13 05 b.Chesterfield 13-7-98
From Basingstoke T.

Season	Club				
2017–18	Fulham	0	0		
2018–19	Fulham	0	0		

From Eastleigh.

Season	Club				
2019–20	Oxford U	0	0		
2020–21	Oxford U	39	1	39	1
2021–22	Bristol C	34	2		
2022–23	Bristol C	26	4		
2023–24	Bristol C	0	0		
2024–25	Bristol C	0	0	60	6
2024–25	*Portsmouth*	14	2	14	2

BAJIC, Stefan (G) 35 0
H: 6 3 W: 13 03 b.Saint-Etienne 23-12-01
Internationals: France U16, U17, U18, U19, U21.

Season	Club				
2018–19	Saint-Etienne	0	0		
2019–20	Saint-Etienne	1	0		
2020–21	Saint-Etienne	1	0		
2021–22	Saint-Etienne	7	0	9	0
2021–22	Pau	15	0	15	0
2022–23	Bristol C	0	0		
2022–23	*Valenciennes*	11	0	11	0
2023–24	Bristol C	0	0		
2024–25	Bristol C	0	0		

BELL, Sam (F) 86 8
H: 5 11 W: 11 11 b.Bristol 23-5-02
Internationals: England U20.

Season	Club				
2018–19	Bristol C	0	0		
2019–20	Bristol C	0	0		
2020–21	Bristol C	4	0		
2021–22	Bristol C	5	0		
2022–23	Bristol C	24	3		
2023–24	Bristol C	33	5		
2024–25	Bristol C	20	0	86	8

BIRD, Max (M) 218 10
H: 6 0 W: 10 10 b.Burton 18-9-00

Season	Club				
2017–18	Derby Co	0	0		
2018–19	Derby Co	4	0		
2019–20	Derby Co	22	0		
2020–21	Derby Co	33	0		
2021–22	Derby Co	42	2		
2022–23	Derby Co	38	1		
2023–24	*Derby Co*	33	6	172	9
2024–25	Bristol C	41	1	46	1

CAMPBELL-SLOWEY, Josh (D) 0 0
H: 6 0 W: 10 08 b.11-11-05

Season	Club				
2023–24	Bristol C	0	0		
2024–25	Bristol C	0	0		

CORNICK, Harry (F) 323 46
H: 5 11 W: 13 03 b.Poole 6-3-95
From Christchurch.

Season	Club				
2013–14	Bournemouth	0	0		
2014–15	Bournemouth	0	0		
2015–16	Bournemouth	0	0		
2015–16	*Yeovil T*	36	7	36	7
2016–17	Bournemouth	0	0		
2016–17	*Leyton Orient*	11	1	11	1
2016–17	*Gillingham*	6	0	6	0
2017–18	Luton T	37	5		
2018–19	Luton T	32	6		
2019–20	Luton T	45	9		
2020–21	Luton T	40	1		
2021–22	Luton T	38	12		
2022–23	Luton T	19	1	211	34
2022–23	Bristol C	17	1		
2023–24	Bristol C	39	2		
2024–25	Bristol C	3	1	59	4

DICKIE, Rob (D) 321 17
H: 6 0 W: 11 09 b.Wokingham 3-3-96
Internationals: England U18, U19.

Season	Club				
2015–16	Reading	1	0		
2016–17	Reading	0	0		
2016–17	*Cheltenham T*	20	2	20	2
2017–18	Reading	0	0	1	0
2017–18	*Lincoln C*	18	0	18	0
2018–19	Oxford U	15	1		
2018–19	Oxford U	37	1		
2019–20	Oxford U	34	0	86	2
2020–21	QPR	43	3		
2021–22	QPR	38	3		
2022–23	QPR	38	0	119	6
2023–24	Bristol C	41	5		
2024–25	Bristol C	36	2	77	7

GARDNER-HICKMAN, Taylor (D) 121 6
H: 6 2 W: 11 11 b.Telford 30-12-01
Internationals: England U20.

Season	Club				
2020–21	WBA	0	0		
2021–22	WBA	19	0		
2022–23	WBA	31	2		
2023–24	WBA	2	0	52	2
2023–24	Bristol C	36	1		
2024–25	Bristol C	0	0	36	1
2024–25	*Birmingham C*	33	3	33	3

HIRAKAWA, Yu (M) 95 11
H: 5 7 W: 10 10 b.Kashima 3-1-01
Internationals: Japan U22, UK23, Full caps.

Season	Club				
2021	Machida Zelvia	0	0		
2022	Machida Zelvia	16	2		
2023	Machida Zelvia	35	6		
2024	Machida Zelvia	7	1	59	9

On loan from Machida Zelvia.

Season	Club				
2024–25	Bristol C	36	2	36	2

JAMES, Joseph (D) 2 0
H: 5 10 W: 11 09 b. 27-6-06

Season	Club				
2023–24	Bristol C	2	0		
2024–25	Bristol C	0	0	2	0

KNIGHT, Jason (M) 242 19
H: 5 9 W: 11 07 b.Dublin 13-2-01
Internationals: Republic of Ireland U17, U18, U19, U21, Full caps.

Season	Club				
2018–19	Derby Co	0	0		
2019–20	Derby Co	31	6		
2020–21	Derby Co	43	2		
2021–22	Derby Co	38	2		
2022–23	Derby Co	38	2	150	12
2023–24	Bristol C	46	4		
2024–25	Bristol C	46	3	92	7

KNIGHT-LEBEL, Jamie (D) 35 3
H: 6 2 W: 10 12 b.Montreal 24-12-04
Internationals: Canada U20, Full caps.

Season	Club				
2023–24	Bristol C	0	0		
2024–25	Bristol C	0	0	2	0
2024–25	*Crewe Alex*	33	3	33	3

MAYULU, Fally (F) 88 22
H: 6 4 W: 12 08 b. 15-7-02

Season	Club				
2020–21	VfL Wolfsburg	0	0		
2021–22	Linz	13	3		
2022–23	Linz	30	11	43	14
2023–24	Rapid Vienna	28	6	28	6
2024–25	Bristol C	15	2	15	2
2024–25	*Sturm Graz*	2	0	2	0

McCRORIE, Ross (M) 193 12
H: 6 1 W: 11 00 b.Dailly 18-3-98
Internationals: Scotland U16, U17, U19, U20, U21, Full caps.

Season	Club				
2015–16	Rangers	0	0		
2015–16	*Ayr U*	11	2	11	2
2016–17	Rangers	0	0		
2016–17	*Dumbarton*	9	0	9	0
2017–18	Rangers	21	2		
2018–19	Rangers	20	0		
2019–20	Rangers	0	0		
2019–20	*Portsmouth*	17	0	17	0
2020–21	Rangers	0	0	41	2
2020–21	Aberdeen	10	0		
2021–22	Aberdeen	30	1		
2022–23	Aberdeen	33	2	73	3
2023–24	Bristol C	19	0		
2024–25	Bristol C	23	5	42	5

McGUANE, Marcus (M) 163 2
H: 5 10 W: 11 07 b.Greenwich 2-2-99
Internationals: Republic of Ireland U17.
England U17, U18, U19.

2017–18	Arsenal	0	0	
2018–19	Barcelona	0	0	
2019–20	Barcelona	0	0	
2019–20	*Telstar*	14	1	14 1
2019–20	Nottingham F	0	0	
2020–21	Nottingham F	0	0	
2020–21	*Oxford U*	15	0	
2021–22	Oxford U	30	0	
2022–23	Oxford U	44	0	
2023–24	Oxford U	39	1	128 1
2024–25	Bristol C	21	0	21 0

McNALLY, Luke (D) 117 9
H: 6 4 W: 13 08 b.County Meath 20-9-99
Internationals: Republic of Ireland U19.
From Drogheda U, St Patricks Ath.

2020–21	Oxford U	0	0	
2021–22	Oxford U	30	4	30 4
2022–23	Burnley	2	0	
2022–23	*Coventry C*	19	0	19 0
2023–24	Burnley	0	0	
2023–24	*Stoke C*	38	2	38 2
2024–25	Burnley	2	0	4 0
2024–25	Bristol C	26	3	26 3

MEHMETI, Anis (M) 183 36
H: 5 11 W: 9 13 b.Islington 9-1-01
Internationals: Albania U19, U21, Full caps.

2019–20	Norwich C	0	0	
2020–21	Wycombe W	29	3	
2021–22	Wycombe W	32	7	
2022–23	Wycombe W	27	9	88 19
2022–23	Bristol C	15	1	
2023–24	Bristol C	38	4	
2024–25	Bristol C	42	12	95 17

MORRISON, Elijah (D) 4 0
H: 5 9 W: 10 03 b.Bristol 18-3-06
Internationals: England U18.

2022–23	Bristol C	0	0	
2023–24	Bristol C	1	0	
2024–25	Bristol C	3	0	4 0

NAISMITH, Kal (F) 390 45
H: 5 7 W: 13 03 b.Glasgow 18-2-92
Internationals: Scotland U16, U17.

2011–12	Rangers	0	0	
2011–12	*Cowdenbeath*	9	2	9 2
2011–12	*Partick Thistle*	8	0	8 0
2012–13	Rangers	17	1	17 1
2013–14	Accrington S	38	10	
2014–15	Accrington S	35	4	73 14
2015–16	Portsmouth	19	3	
2015–16	*Hartlepool U*	4	0	4 0
2016–17	Portsmouth	37	13	
2017–18	Portsmouth	26	2	82 18
2018–19	Wigan Ath	30	1	
2019–20	Wigan Ath	37	3	
2020–21	Wigan Ath	12	2	79 6
2020–21	Luton T	22	1	
2021–22	Luton T	42	2	
2022–23	Bristol C	25	0	
2023–24	Bristol C	13	1	
2024–25	Bristol C	6	0	44 1
2024–25	*Luton T*	10	0	74 3

NELSON, Raekwon (F) 0 0
H: 5 9 W: 10 10 b. 26-10-05

2023–24	Bristol C	0	0	
2024–25	Bristol C	0	0	

O'LEARY, Max (G) 182 0
H: 6 1 W: 12 04 b.Bath 10-10-96

2013–14	Bristol C	0	0	
2014–15	Bristol C	0	0	
2015–16	Bristol C	0	0	
2016–17	Bristol C	0	0	
2017–18	Bristol C	0	0	
2018–19	Bristol C	15	0	
2019–20	Bristol C	0	0	
2019–20	*Shrewsbury T*	30	0	30 0
2020–21	Bristol C	3	0	
2021–22	Bristol C	9	0	
2022–23	Bristol C	33	0	
2023–24	Bristol C	46	0	
2024–25	Bristol C	46	0	152 0

PECOVER, Leo (M) 0 0
H: 5 9 W: 10 10 b.Bristol 10-7-06

2024–25	Bristol C	0	0	

PHILLIPS, Billy (F) 0 0
H: 5 9 W: 10 03 b.Bristol 22-1-98

2024–25	Bristol C	0	0	

PRING, Cameron (D) 183 3
H: 6 1 W: 11 03 b.Bristol 22-1-98

2018–19	Bristol C	0	0	
2018–19	*Newport Co*	7	1	7 1
2018–19	*Cheltenham T*	8	0	8 0
2019–20	Bristol C	0	0	
2019–20	*Walsall*	21	0	21 0
2020–21	Bristol C	0	0	
2020–21	*Portsmouth*	9	0	9 0

ROBERTS, Haydon (D) 116 4
H: 5 11 W: 10 12 b.Brighton 10-5-02
Internationals: England U16, U17, U18.

2021–22	Bristol C	32	0	
2022–23	Bristol C	32	1	
2023–24	Bristol C	42	1	
2024–25	Bristol C	32	0	138 2

2019–20	Brighton & HA	0	0	
2020–21	Brighton & HA	0	0	
2020–21	*Rochdale*	26	0	26 0
2021–22	Brighton & HA	0	0	
2022–23	Brighton & HA	0	0	
2022–23	*Derby Co*	37	2	37 2
2023–24	Bristol C	23	1	
2024–25	Bristol C	30	1	53 2

STOKES, Joshua (M) 32 7
H: 5 10 W: 11 09 b.Shotley 29-4-04

2023–24	Bristol C	0	0	
2024–25	Bristol C	0	0	
2024–25	*Cambridge U*	32	7	32 7

SYKES, Mark (M) 207 22
H: 6 0 W: 12 04 b.Belfast 4-8-97
Internationals: Northern Ireland U19, U21.
Republic of Ireland Full caps.
From Glenavon.

2018–19	Oxford U	9	0	
2019–20	Oxford U	23	1	
2020–21	Oxford U	32	0	
2021–22	Oxford U	40	8	104 9
2022–23	Bristol C	36	5	
2023–24	Bristol C	40	5	
2024–25	Bristol C	27	3	103 13

TANNER, George (D) 173 6
H: 5 11 W: 11 03 b.Blackpool 16-11-99
Internationals: England U17, U18.

2019–20	Manchester U	0	0	
2019–20	*Morecambe*	23	0	23 0
2019–20	*Salford C*	0	0	
2020–21	Carlisle U	37	3	
2021–22	Carlisle U	5	0	42 3
2021–22	Bristol C	13	1	
2022–23	Bristol C	26	0	
2023–24	Bristol C	37	0	
2024–25	Bristol C	32	2	108 3

THOMAS, Lewis (G) 33 0
H: 6 0 W: 11 00 b.Mancelton 20-9-97
Internationals: Wales U17, U19.
From Swansea C.

2018–19	Forest Green R	0	0	
2019–20	Forest Green R	15	0	
2020–21	Forest Green R	13	0	
2021–22	Forest Green R	0	0	
2022–23	Forest Green R	5	0	
2023–24	Forest Green R	0	0	33 0
2023–24	Bristol C	0	0	
2024–25	Bristol C	0	0	

TWINE, Scott (F) 198 48
H: 5 9 W: 10 12 b.Swindon 14-7-99

2015–16	Swindon T	0	0	
2016–17	Swindon T	1	0	
2017–18	Swindon T	4	0	
2018–19	Swindon T	14	1	
2019–20	Swindon T	6	0	
2020–21	Swindon T	25	7	50 8
2020–21	*Newport Co*	19	6	19 6
2021–22	Milton Keynes D	45	20	45 20
2022–23	Burnley	14	3	
2023–24	Burnley	0	0	14 3
2023–24	*Hull C*	25	4	25 4
2023–24	*Bristol C*	10	2	
2024–25	Bristol C	35	5	45 7

VYNER, Zak (D) 288 6
H: 5 10 W: 10 10 b.Bath 14-5-97

2015–16	Bristol C	4	0	
2016–17	Bristol C	3	0	
2016–17	*Accrington S*	16	0	16 0
2017–18	Bristol C	1	0	
2017–18	*Plymouth Arg*	17	1	17 1
2018–19	Bristol C	0	0	
2018–19	*Rotherham U*	31	0	31 0
2019–20	Bristol C	8	0	
2019–20	*Aberdeen*	16	1	16 1
2020–21	Bristol C	43	2	
2021–22	Bristol C	22	0	
2022–23	Bristol C	45	1	
2023–24	Bristol C	36	0	
2024–25	Bristol C	46	1	208 4

WELLS, Nahki (F) 527 153
H: 5 7 W: 10 12 b.Bermuda 1-6-90
Internationals: Bermuda Full caps.

2010–11	Carlisle U	3	0	3 0
2011–12	Bradford C	33	10	
2012–13	Bradford C	39	18	
2013–14	Bradford C	19	14	91 42
2013–14	Huddersfield T	22	7	
2014–15	Huddersfield T	35	11	
2015–16	Huddersfield T	44	17	
2016–17	Huddersfield T	43	10	
2017–18	Huddersfield T	0	0	144 45

ILLIAMS

WILLIAMS, Joe (M) 222 4
H: 5 10 W: 10 06 b.Liverpool 8-12-96
Internationals: England U20.

2017–18	Burnley	9	0	
2018–19	Burnley	0	0	
2018–19	*QPR*	40	7	
2019–20	Burnley	0	0	9 0
2019–20	*QPR*	26	13	66 20
2019–20	Bristol C	17	5	
2020–21	Bristol C	46	10	
2021–22	Bristol C	32	3	
2022–23	Bristol C	45	11	
2023–24	Bristol C	35	7	
2024–25	Bristol C	39	10	214 46

WILLIAMS, Joe (M) 222 4
H: 5 10 W: 10 06 b.Liverpool 8-12-96
Internationals: England U20.

2014–15	Everton	0	0	
2015–16	Everton	0	0	
2016–17	Everton	0	0	
2017–18	Everton	0	0	
2017–18	*Barnsley*	34	1	34 1
2018–19	Everton	0	0	
2018–19	*Bolton W*	30	0	30 0
2019–20	Wigan Ath	38	1	38 1
2020–21	Bristol C	1	0	
2021–22	Bristol C	22	0	
2022–23	Bristol C	33	2	
2023–24	Bristol C	40	0	
2024–25	Bristol C	24	0	120 2

YEBOAH, Ephraim (F) 35 0
H: 5 10 W: 9 13 b.Montirone 21-7-06

2023–24	Bristol C	10	0	
2024–25	Bristol C	0	0	10 0
2024–25	*Doncaster R*	11	0	11 0
2024–25	*Dunfermline Ath*	14	0	14 0

Players retained or with offer of contract
Ali, Zack Asghar; Anderson, Taine Charlie; Casa-Grande, Josey Brian; Duncan, Joseph William Alan; Hewlett, Calum Matthew; Meerholz, Jed; Murphy, Adam; Palmer Houlden, Sebastian; Skinner, Luke Alan; Taylor, Archie Philip.

Scholars
Ababio, Derrick Worlanyo; Akinbo, Oluwanifemi Tolulope Victor; Chaplin, Thomas Lloyd; Clark, Ben Samuel; Davies, Max Charlie; Derrick, Louie Leonard George; Filer, Charlie David; Finch, Isaac John Alexander; Foxwell, Jaiden; Gibbs, Tomos George Steven; Godden, Freddie Scotford; Griffin, Jack Richard Gordon; Hogg, Harry James; Hooper, Jack Clive; Ikpeama, Excellent; Inman, MacKenzie Edward; Jackson, Trayvion You; King-Phillips, Zac Alexander; Pecover, Leo James; Sheppard, Ruehin Lee; Thelwell, Marley Ricardo Romaine; Walker, Cavalli Emile; Walker-Brown, Rushon Nakia Erroll; Witchard, Jack William.

BRISTOL R (16)

AKONO BILONGO, Bryant (D) 30 2
H: 5 11 W: 12 08 b.Wandsworth 15-9-01
From Hanworth Villa, Kingstonian.

2021–22	Middlesbrough	0	0	
2022–23	Middlesbrough	0	0	
2023–24	Middlesbrough	0	0	
2024–25	Bristol R	14	1	14 1
2024–25	*Harrogate T*	16	1	16 1

ANTHONY, Micah (F) 0 0
H: 5 9 W: 11 00 b.Camden 26-3-04

2023–24	QPR	0	0	
2024–25	Bristol R	0	0	

BROWN, Jevani (F) 257 40
H: 5 9 W: 11 11 b.Letchworth 16-10-94
Internationals: Jamaica U21.

2013–14	Peterborough U	0	0	
2014–15	Peterborough U	0	0	
	From Barton R, Arlesey T, Kettering T, Stamford, St Neots T.			
2017–18	Cambridge U	41	6	
2018–19	Cambridge U	43	7	84 13
2019–20	Colchester U	11	0	
2019–20	*Forest Green R*	5	0	5 0
2020–21	Colchester U	40	7	51 7
2021–22	Exeter C	43	7	
2022–23	Exeter C	27	12	70 19
2023–24	Bristol R	33	1	
2024–25	Bristol R	0	0	33 1
2024–25	*Notts Co*	14	0	14 0

CONTEH, Kamil (M) 61 0
H: 5 10 W: 11 00 b.Lambeth 26-12-02
Internationals: Sierra Leone Full caps.
From Crystal Palace.

2021–22	Watford	0	0	
2022–23	Middlesbrough	0	0	
2023–24	*Grimsby T*	25	0	25 0
2023–24	Bristol R	17	0	
2024–25	Bristol R	19	0	36 0

DEWSBURY, Ollie (M) 6 0
b.Wales 22-2-08
Internationals: Wales U16, U17.

2023–24	Bristol R	0	0	
2024–25	Bristol R	6	0	6 0

DIXON, Quincy (M) 0 0

2024–25	Bristol R	0	0

EDWARDS, Max (M) 0 0
H: 6 2 b. 19-9-05
Internationals: Wales U19.

2021–22	Bristol R	0	0

From Bristol R.

2024–25	Bristol R	0	0

ELLISON, Dan (D) 0 0
H: 6 1 W: 13 05 b. 30-3-05
Internationals: England C.

2024–25	Bristol R	0	0

FORDE, Shaqai (F) 71 11
H: 5 9 W: 11 03 b.Watford 5-5-04

2021–22	Watford	0	0	
2022–23	Watford	0	0	
2023–24	Watford	0	0	
2023–24	*Leyton Orient*	40	9	40 9
2024–25	Bristol R	31	2	31 2

HALL, Matt (G) 0 0
H: 6 5 W: 11 09 b.Southampton 24-4-03

2023–24	Bristol R	0	0
2024–25	Bristol R	0	0

HILL, Kian (M) 0 0

2024–25	Bristol R	0	0

HUNT, Jack (D) 472 10
H: 5 9 W: 11 02 b.Rothwell 6-12-90

2009–10	Huddersfield T	0	0	
2010–11	Huddersfield T	19	1	
2010–11	*Chesterfield*	20	0	20 0
2011–12	Huddersfield T	43	1	
2012–13	Huddersfield T	40	0	
2013–14	Huddersfield T	2	0	104 2
2013–14	Crystal Palace	0	0	
2013–14	*Barnsley*	11	0	11 0
2014–15	Crystal Palace	0	0	
2014–15	*Nottingham F*	17	0	17 0
2014–15	*Rotherham U*	16	0	16 0
2015–16	Sheffield Wed	34	0	
2016–17	Sheffield Wed	32	0	
2017–18	Sheffield Wed	29	0	
2018–19	Bristol C	33	1	
2019–20	Bristol C	35	0	
2020–21	Bristol C	41	2	109 3
2021–22	Sheffield Wed	39	2	
2022–23	Sheffield Wed	10	0	150 2
2023–24	Bristol R	25	3	
2024–25	Bristol R	20	0	45 3

HUTCHINSON, Isaac (M) 189 26
H: 5 10 W: 11 00 b.Eastbourne 10-4-00
From Brighton & HA.

2018–19	Southend U	8	0	
2019–20	Southend U	22	1	
2020–21	Southend U	2	0	32 1
2020–21	Derby Co	0	0	
2020–21	*Forest Green R*	10	0	10 0
2021–22	Derby Co	1	0	1 0
2021–22	*Crawley T*	19	2	19 2
2022–23	Walsall	44	7	
2023–24	Walsall	46	12	90 19
2024–25	Bristol R	37	4	37 4

KORSWAGEN, Mattijs (G) 0 0

2024–25	Bristol R	0	0

LEIPUS, Brooklyn (M) 0 0
b. 8-8-07
Internationals: Lithuania U16, U17.

2024–25	Bristol R	0	0

LINDSAY, Jamie (M) 285 18
H: 5 10 W: 10 08 b.Rutherglen 11-10-95
Internationals: Scotland U16, U17, U19.

2015–16	Celtic	0	0	
2015–16	*Dumbarton*	23	0	23 0
2016–17	Celtic	0	0	
2016–17	*Greenock Morton*	31	0	31 0
2017–18	Celtic	0	0	
2017–18	Ross Co	26	2	
2018–19	Ross Co	35	6	61 8
2019–20	Rotherham U	22	1	
2020–21	Rotherham U	35	3	
2021–22	Rotherham U	28	1	
2022–23	Rotherham U	36	2	
2023–24	Rotherham U	21	1	142 8
2024–25	Bristol R	28	2	28 2

MARTIN, Chris (F) 612 164
H: 5 10 W: 11 07 b.Beccles 4-11-88
Internationals: England U19. Scotland Full caps.

2006–07	Norwich C	18	4	
2007–08	Norwich C	7	0	
2008–09	Norwich C	0	0	
2008–09	*Luton T*	40	11	40 11
2009–10	Norwich C	42	17	
2010–11	Norwich C	30	4	
2011–12	Norwich C	4	0	
2011–12	*Crystal Palace*	26	7	26 7
2012–13	Norwich C	1	0	102 25
2012–13	*Swindon T*	12	1	12 1
2012–13	Derby Co	13	2	
2013–14	Derby Co	44	20	
2014–15	Derby Co	35	18	
2015–16	Derby Co	45	15	
2016–17	Derby Co	5	0	
2016–17	*Fulham*	31	10	31 10
2017–18	Derby Co	23	1	
2017–18	*Reading*	10	1	10 1
2018–19	Derby Co	0	0	
2018–19	*Hull C*	30	2	30 2
2019–20	Derby Co	35	11	200 67
2020–21	Bristol C	26	2	
2021–22	Bristol C	45	12	
2022–23	Bristol C	17	1	88 15
2022–23	*QPR*	16	4	16 4
2023–24	Bristol R	34	16	
2024–25	Bristol R	23	5	57 21

McCORMICK, Luke (M) 140 17
H: 5 11 W: 11 09 b.Bury St Edmunds 21-1-99

2019–20	Chelsea	0	0	
2019–20	*Shrewsbury T*	5	0	5 0
2020–21	Chelsea	0	0	
2020–21	*Bristol R*	39	6	
2021–22	AFC Wimbledon	40	7	40 7
2022–23	Bristol R	21	0	
2023–24	Bristol R	16	2	
2024–25	Bristol R	19	2	95 10

MOLA, Clinton (D) 79 1
H: 6 0 W: 12 04 b.Camden 15-3-01
Internationals: England U16, U17, U18, U19, U20, U21.

2018–19	Chelsea	0	0	
2019–20	VfB Stuttgart	8	0	
2020–21	VfB Stuttgart	8	0	
2021–22	VfB Stuttgart	3	0	
2022–23	VfB Stuttgart	0	0	11 0
2022–23	*Blackburn R*	4	0	4 0
2023–24	Reading	30	0	30 0
2024–25	Bristol R	34	1	34 1

MOORE, Taylor (D) 262 3
H: 6 0 W: 12 08 b.Walthamstow 12-5-97
Internationals: England U17, U18, U19, U20.
From West Ham U.

2014–15	Lens	4	0	
2015–16	Lens	5	0	9 0
2016–17	Bristol C	5	0	
2016–17	*Bury*	19	0	19 0
2017–18	Bristol C	0	0	
2017–18	*Cheltenham T*	36	0	36 0
2018–19	Bristol C	0	0	
2018–19	*Southend U*	34	1	34 1
2019–20	Bristol C	21	1	
2019–20	*Blackpool*	8	0	8 0
2020–21	Bristol C	22	0	
2021–22	Bristol C	0	0	
2021–22	*Hearts*	16	0	16 0
2022–23	Bristol C	0	0	48 1
2022–23	*Shrewsbury T*	42	0	42 0
2023–24	Valenciennes	17	0	17 0
2024–25	Bristol R	33	1	33 1

OMOCHERE, Promise (F) 132 25
H: 6 2 W: 12 06 b.Dublin 18-10-00

2018	Bohemians	2	0	
2019	Bohemians	0	0	
2020	Bohemians	6	0	
2021	Bohemians	18	5	
2022	Bohemians	22	5	48 10
2022–23	Fleetwood T	28	5	
2023–24	Fleetwood T	34	6	62 11
2024–25	Bristol R	22	4	22 4

SAVAGE, Taelan (F) 0 0
b.9-4-08

2024–25	Bristol R	0	0

SAWYERS, Romaine (M) 413 30
H: 5 9 W: 10 08 b.Birmingham 2-11-91
Internationals: St Kitts and Nevis U23, Full caps.

2009–10	WBA	0	0	
2010–11	WBA	0	0	
2010–11	*Port Vale*	1	0	1 0
2011–12	WBA	0	0	
2012–13	*Shrewsbury T*	7	0	7 0
2012–13	WBA	0	0	
2012–13	Walsall	4	0	
2013–14	Walsall	44	6	
2014–15	Walsall	42	4	
2015–16	Walsall	46	6	136 16
2016–17	Brentford	43	2	
2017–18	Brentford	42	4	
2018–19	Brentford	42	0	127 6
2019–20	WBA	42	1	
2020–21	WBA	19	0	
2021–22	WBA	0	0	61 1
2021–22	*Stoke C*	25	2	25 2
2022–23	Cardiff C	37	3	
2023–24	Cardiff C	2	0	39 3
2024–25	AFC Wimbledon	4	1	4 1
2024–25	Bristol R	13	1	13 1

SENIOR, Joel (D) 79 2
H: 5 11 W: 11 00 b.Manchester 24-6-99
From FC United of Manchester, Curzon Ath, Burnley, Altrincham.

2021–22	Carlisle U	4	0	
2022–23	Carlisle U	13	1	17 1
2023–24	Morecambe	43	1	43 1
2024–25	Bristol R	19	0	19 0

SHAW, Kofi (M) 16 0
H: 5 9 W: 11 09 b.Takoradi 3-8-83

2023–24	Bristol R	1	0	
2024–25	Bristol R	15	0	16 0

SINCLAIR, Scott (F) 492 101
H: 5 10 W: 10 12 b.Bath 26-3-89
Internationals: England U17, U18, U19, U20, U21. Great Britain.

2004–05	Bristol R	2	0	
2005–06	Chelsea	0	0	
2006–07	Chelsea	2	0	
2006–07	*Plymouth Arg*	15	2	15 2
2007–08	Chelsea	1	0	
2007–08	*QPR*	9	1	9 1
2007–08	*Charlton Ath*	3	0	3 0
2007–08	*Crystal Palace*	6	2	6 2
2008–09	Chelsea	2	0	
2008–09	*Birmingham C*	14	0	14 0
2009–10	Chelsea	0	0	5 0
2009–10	*Wigan Ath*	18	1	18 1
2010–11	Swansea C	43	19	
2011–12	Swansea C	38	8	
2012–13	Swansea C	1	1	82 28
2012–13	Manchester C	11	0	
2013–14	Manchester C	0	0	
2013–14	*WBA*	8	0	8 0
2014–15	Manchester C	2	0	13 0
2014–15	*Aston Villa*	9	1	
2015–16	Aston Villa	27	2	36 3
2016–17	Celtic	35	21	
2017–18	Celtic	35	10	
2018–19	Celtic	33	9	
2019–20	Celtic	2	0	105 40
2019–20	Preston NE	18	3	
2020–21	Preston NE	37	9	
2021–22	Preston NE	23	0	78 12
2022–23	Bristol R	30	5	
2023–24	Bristol R	27	4	
2024–25	Bristol R	41	3	100 12

SOTIRIOU, Ruel (F) 187 41
H: 5 11 W: 11 03 b.Edmonton 24-8-00
Internationals: Cyprus U19, U21, Full caps.

2019–20	Leyton Orient	0	0	
2020–21	Leyton Orient	22	1	
2021–22	Leyton Orient	34	9	
2022–23	Leyton Orient	42	9	
2023–24	Leyton Orient	42	11	150 35
2024–25	Bristol R	37	6	37 6

TAYLOR, Connor (D) 132 4
H: 6 0 W: 13 08 b.Stoke-on-Trent 25-10-01
From Stafford R.

2020–21	Stoke C	1	0	
2021–22	Stoke C	0	0	
2021–22	*Bristol R*	42	3	
2022–23	Stoke C	14	0	15 0
2023–24	Bristol R	33	0	
2024–25	Bristol R	42	1	117 4

THOMAS, Luke (F) 236 14
H: 5 7 W: 10 08 b.Gloucester 19-2-99
Internationals: England U20.
From Cheltenham T.

2015–16	Derby Co	0	0	
2016–17	Derby Co	0	0	
2017–18	Derby Co	2	0	
2018–19	Derby Co	0	0	2 0
2018–19	*Coventry C*	43	4	43 4
2019–20	Barnsley	39	1	
2020–21	Barnsley	19	0	
2020–21	*Ipswich T*	5	0	5 0
2021–22	Barnsley	0	0	
2021–22	*Bristol R*	28	0	
2022–23	Barnsley	27	2	85 3
2023–24	Bristol R	37	5	
2024–25	Bristol R	36	2	101 7

VAUGHAN, Lucas (F) 1 0
H: 5 10 W: 10 08 b. 9-3-04

2021–22	Bristol R	0	0	
2022–23	Bristol R	1	0	
2023–24	Bristol R	0	0	
2024–25	Bristol R	0	0	1 0

WARD, Grant (M) 289 15
H: 5 10 W: 11 07 b.Lewisham 5-12-94

2013–14	Tottenham H	0	0	
2014	*Chicago Fire*	23	1	23 1
2014–15	Tottenham H	0	0	
2014–15	*Coventry C*	11	0	11 0

2015–16	Tottenham H	0	0	
2015–16	*Rotherham U*	40	2	40　2
2016–17	Ipswich T	43	6	
2017–18	Ipswich T	37	2	
2018–19	Ipswich T	14	0	94　8
2019–20	Blackpool	5	0	
2020–21	Blackpool	36	1	
2021–22	Blackpool	4	0	
2022–23	Blackpool	2	0	47　1
2022–23	Bristol R	19	1	
2023–24	Bristol R	20	1	
2024–25	Bristol R	35	1	74　3

WARD, Jed (G) 　38　0
H: 6 2　W: 12 11　b.Bristol 20-5-03
Internationals: England U20.

2020–21	Bristol R	1	0	
2021–22	Bristol R	0	0	
2022–23	Bristol R	1	0	
2023–24	Bristol R	18	0	
2024–25	Bristol R	18	0	38　0

WHITE, Charlie (D) 　0　0
H: 6 3　W: 13 01　b. 2-7-04

2022–23	Bristol R	0	0
2023–24	Bristol R	0	0
2024–25	Bristol R	0	0

WILSON, James (D) 　402　11
H: 6 2　W: 12 13　b.Chepstow 26-2-89
Internationals: Wales U19. U21, Full caps.

2005–06	Bristol C	0	0	
2006–07	Bristol C	0	0	
2007–08	Bristol C	0	0	
2008–09	Bristol C	2	0	
2008–09	*Brentford*	14	0	
2009–10	Bristol C	0	0	
2009–10	*Brentford*	13	0	27　0
2010–11	Bristol C	2	0	
2011–12	Bristol C	21	0	
2012–13	Bristol C	6	0	
2013–14	Bristol C	0	0	31　0
2013–14	*Cheltenham T*	4	0	4　0
2013–14	Oldham Ath	16	1	
2014–15	Oldham Ath	41	1	
2015–16	Oldham Ath	43	0	100　2
2016–17	Sheffield U	7	1	
2017–18	Sheffield U	0	0	7　1
2017–18	*Walsall*	19	1	19　1
2017–18	Lincoln C	8	1	
2018–19	Lincoln C	11	1	
2019–20	Lincoln C	0	0	19　2
2019–20	Ipswich T	23	0	
2020–21	Ipswich T	17	2	40　2
2020–21	Plymouth Arg	0	0	
2021–22	Plymouth Arg	42	0	
2022–23	Plymouth Arg	41	1	83　1
2023–24	Bristol R	26	0	
2024–25	Bristol R	46	2	72　2

Scholars
Bishop, Jaydon David; Cadette, Trey Anthony; Dewsbury, Ollie Joseph; Edwards Stryjewski, Max Oliver; English, Thomas Christopher Robert; Hill, Kian James; Korswagen, Mattijs Thomas; Leipus, Brooklyn; Moggeridge, Reuben Saul; Moody, Charlie Jack; Savage, Taelan John; Sughayer, Rocco Naseef; Sutherland, Jay; Turner, Wil Joseph.

BROMLEY (17)

ARTHURS, Jude (M) 　41　4
H: 6 3　W: 12 11　b.Greenwich 6-8-01
From Gillingham, Bromley.

2024–25	Bromley	41	4	41　4

AZIAYA, David (G) 　10　0
H: 6 6　W: 14 07　b.London 3-8-04

2022–23	Norwich C	0	0	
From Bromley.				
2024–25	Bromley	0	0	
2024–25	*Finn Harps*	10	0	10　0

CHARLES, Ashley (M) 　28　0
H: 5 10　W: 11 09　b.Watford 15-5-99
Internationals: Grenada Full caps.
From Watford, Wealdstone, Bromley.

2024–25	Bromley	28	0	28　0

CHEEK, Michael (F) 　45　25
H: 5 10　W: 11 09　b.Nuneaton 23-8-91
From Chelmsford C, Braintree T, Dagenham & Red, Ebbsfleet U, Bromley.

2024–25	Bromley	45	25	45　25

CORBIN, Callum (M) 　0　0
H: 5 11　W: 12 00
From Bromley.

2024–25	Bromley	0	0

DENNIS, Louis (F) 　66　4
H: 6 1　W: 10 12　b.Hendon 9-10-92

2011–12	Dagenham & Red	0	0
2012–13	Dagenham & Red	6	0
2013–14	Dagenham & Red	2	0	8　0
From Bromley.			
2018–19	Portsmouth	1	0	1　0
2019–20	Leyton Orient	16	1
2020–21	Leyton Orient	24	1	40　2
From Bromley.			
2024–25	Bromley	17	2	17　2

DINANGA, Marcus (F) 　13　1
H: 5 11　W: 12 04　b.Gravesend 30-6-97

2016–17	Burton Alb	0	0	
2017–18	Burton Alb	0	0	
2018–19	Burton Alb	0	0	
From Hartlepool U, AFC Telford U.				
2020–21	Stevenage	6	1	6　1
From Altrincham, Gateshead.				
2024–25	Bromley	7	0	7　0

ELEREWE, Ayodeji (D) 　22　1
H: 6 2　W: 10 10　b.Croydon 14-9-03

2021–22	Charlton Ath	3	0	
2022–23	Charlton Ath	0	0	
2023–24	Charlton Ath	2	0	5　0
2024–25	Bromley	17	1	17　1

EVANS, George (F) 　0　0
From Bromley.

2024–25	Bromley	0	0

FORAN, Taylor (D) 　11　0
H: 6 5　W: 13 08　b.London 14-10-03

2021–22	Arsenal	0	0	
2022–23	Arsenal	0	0	
2022–23	Hartlepool U	11	0	11　0
2023–24	Arsenal	0	0	
2024–25	Bromley	0	0	

HAINES, Harry (G) 　0　0

2024–25	Bromley	0	0

HILDEN, Alfie (F) 　0　0
From Bromley.

2024–25	Bromley	0	0

IFILL, Markus (M) 　6　0
H: 5 11　W: 11 11　b. 2-11-03
From Swindon T.

2019–20	Brighton & HA	0	0	
2020–21	Brighton & HA	0	0	
2021–22	Brighton & HA	0	0	
2022–23	Brighton & HA	0	0	
2023–24	Brighton & HA	0	0	
2024–25	Bromley	6	0	6　0

ILUNGA, Brooklyn (F) 　25　0
H: 5 10　W: 10 08　b.Croydon 21-11-03

2020–21	Milton Keynes D	1	0	
2021–22	Milton Keynes D	1	0	
2022–23	Milton Keynes D	0	0	
2023–24	Milton Keynes D	3	0	
2024–25	Milton Keynes D	3	0	8　0
2024–25	Bromley	17	0	17　0

JENKINSON, Carl (D) 　184　5
H: 6 1　W: 12 02　b.Harlow 8-2-92
Internationals: Finland U19, U21. England U17, U21, Full caps.

2010–11	Charlton Ath	8	0	8　0
2010–11	Arsenal	0	0	
2011–12	Arsenal	9	0	
2012–13	Arsenal	14	0	
2013–14	Arsenal	14	1	
2014–15	Arsenal	0	0	
2014–15	*West Ham U*	32	0	
2015–16	Arsenal	0	0	
2015–16	*West Ham U*	20	2	52　2
2016–17	Arsenal	1	0	
2017–18	Arsenal	0	0	
2017–18	*Birmingham C*	7	0	7　0
2018–19	Arsenal	3	0	
2019–20	Arsenal	0	0	41　1
2019–20	Nottingham F	8	0	
2020–21	Nottingham F	3	0	
2021–22	Nottingham F	0	0	11　0
2022	*Melbourne C*	22	2	22　2
2022–23	Newcastle Jets	23	0	
2023–24	Newcastle Jets	9	0	32　0
2024–25	Bromley	11	0	11　0

KABAMBA, Nicke (F) 　95　9
H: 6 3　W: 11 11　b.Brent 1-2-93
From Uxbridge, Hayes, Burnham, Hampton & Richmond.

2016–17	Portsmouth	4	0	
2017–18	Portsmouth	1	0	5　0
2017–18	*Colchester U*	8	0	8　0
From Havant & Waterlooville, Hartlepool U.				
2019–20	Kilmarnock	9	2	
2020–21	Kilmarnock	33	5	42　7
2021–22	Northampton T	21	0	21　0
From Barnet.				
2024–25	Bromley	19	2	19　2

KADER, Saul (M) 　1　0
H: 5 9　W: 11 00　b. 31-1-04
From Bromley.

2024–25	Bromley	1	0	1　0

LEIGH, Lewis (M) 　32　1
H: 5 8　W: 12 02　b.Preston 5-12-03

2020–21	Preston NE	0	0
2021–22	Preston NE	0	0
2022–23	Preston NE	1	0
2023–24	Preston NE	0	0	1　0
2023–24	*Crewe Alex*	14	0	14　0
2024–25	Bromley	17	1	17　1

LONG, Sam (G) 　17　0
H: 6 0　W: 12 00　b.Redbridge 12-11-02

2020–21	Lincoln C	0	0	
2021–22	Lincoln C	1	0	
2022	*Drogheda U*	15	0	15　0
2022–23	Lincoln C	0	0	
2023–24	Lincoln C	0	0	
2024–25	Bromley	1	0	1　0

McKIRDY, Harry (M) 　163　35
H: 5 9　W: 11 00　b.Stoke-on-Trent 29-3-97
From Stoke C.

2016–17	Aston Villa	0	0	
2016–17	*Stevenage*	11	1	11　1
2017–18	Aston Villa	0	0	
2017–18	*Crewe Alex*	16	3	16　3
2018–19	Aston Villa	0	0	
2018–19	*Newport Co*	12	1	12　1
2019–20	*Carlisle U*	28	5	28　5
2020–21	Port Vale	8	0	8　0
2021–22	Swindon T	35	20	
2022–23	Swindon T	5	2	
2022–23	Hibernian	22	0	
2023–24	Hibernian	2	0	
2023–24	*Swindon T*	9	1	49　23
2024–25	Hibernian	6	0	30　0
2024–25	Bromley	9	2	9　2

MORALEE, Frankie (D) 　0　0
H: 6　b. 6-9-05
From Bromley.

2024–25	Bromley	0	0

ODUTAYO, Idris (D) 　34　1
H: 6 1　W: 12 04　b.Lambeth 26-10-02

2022–23	Fulham	0	0	
2023–24	Fulham	0	0	
2024–25	Bromley	34	1	34　1

OLOMOLA, Olufela (F) 　104　16
H: 5 7　W: 10 08　b.Harrow 5-9-97
From Huddersfield T.

2015–16	Southampton	0	0	
2016–17	Southampton	0	0	
2017–18	Southampton	0	0	
2017–18	*Yeovil T*	21	7	
2018–19	Scunthorpe U	6	0	
2018–19	*Yeovil T*	17	3	38　10
2019–20	Scunthorpe U	0	0	
2019–20	*Carlisle U*	27	5	27　5
2020–21	Scunthorpe U	5	0	11　0
2021–22	Hartlepool U	12	0	12　0
From Wealdstone.				
2024–25	Bromley	16	1	16　1

PASSLEY, Josh (D) 　60　1
H: 6 0　W: 12 06　b.Chelsea 21-9-93

2013–14	Fulham	0	0	
2014–15	Fulham	0	0	
2014–15	*Shrewsbury T*	6	0	6　0
2014–15	*Portsmouth*	12	0	12　0
2015–16	*Dagenham & Red*	38	1	38　1
From Whitehawk, Dover Ath, Havant & Waterlooville, Bromley.				
2024–25	Bromley	4	0	4　0

Transferred to Ebbsfleet U, February 2025.

PAUL-LAVELY, Nathan (M) 　3　0
b. 22-9-06
From Bromley.

2024–25	Bromley	3	0	3　0

PAYE, Charlie (D) 　0　0

2024–25	Bromley	0	0

PENN, George (M) 　0　0

2024–25	Bromley	0	0

REYNOLDS, Callum (D) 　20　1
H: 6 2　W: 13 01　b.Luton 10-11-89
From Portsmouth, Basingstoke T, Tamworth, Boreham Wood, Aldershot T, Barnet, Dagenham & Red, Bromley.

2024–25	Bromley	20	1	20　1

Transferred to Boreham Wood, January 2025.

SMITH, Grant (G) 　61　0
H: 6 1　W: 12 06　b.Reading 20-11-93

2012–13	Brighton & HA	0	0	
2013–14	Brighton & HA	0	0	
From Farnborough, Hayes & Yeading, Bognor Regis T, Boreham Wood.				
2018–19	Lincoln C	16	0	
2019–20	Lincoln C	0	0	16　0
From Wealdstone, Chesterfield, Yeovil T, Bromley.				
2024–25	Bromley	45	0	45　0

SOWUNMI, Omar (D) 　160　12
H: 6 6　W: 14 09　b.Colchester 7-11-95

2014–15	Ipswich T	0	0
2015–16	Yeovil T	5	1
2016–17	Yeovil T	11	0

2017–18 Yeovil T 36 2
2018–19 Yeovil T 17 0 69 3
2019–20 Colchester U 7 0
2020–21 Colchester U 15 0 22 0
From Bromley.
2023–24 Sutton U 35 4 35 4
2024–25 Bromley 34 5 34 5

TOBIN, Joshua (D) 0 0
From Chelsea, Cray W, Margate, Walton & Hersham.
2024–25 Bromley 0 0

TOPALLOJ, Besart (D) 3 0
H: 6 1 W: 12 04 b.Bromley 16-5-01
2021–22 Millwall 0 0
2022–23 Millwall 0 0
From Bromley.
2024–25 Bromley 3 0 3 0

WEBSTER, Byron (D) 335 22
H: 6 5 W: 12 07 b.Sherburn-in-Elmet 31-3-87
2007–08 Siad Most 23 4
2008–09 Siad Most 0 0 23 4
2009–10 Doncaster R 5 0
2010–11 Doncaster R 7 0 12 0
2010–11 Hereford U 2 0 2 0
2010–11 Northampton T 8 0
2011–12 Northampton T 13 0 21 0
2012–13 Yeovil T 44 5
2013–14 Yeovil T 41 3
2014–15 Millwall 11 0
2014–15 Yeovil T 14 0 99 8
2015–16 Millwall 40 6
2016–17 Millwall 44 2
2017–18 Millwall 10 0
2018–19 Millwall 4 0 109 8
2018–19 Scunthorpe U 9 0 9 0
2019–20 Carlisle U 32 1 32 1
From Bromley.
2024–25 Bromley 28 1 28 1

WESTON, Myles (M) 327 30
H: 5 11 W: 12 05 b.Lewisham 12-3-88
Internationals: England U16, U17, U18, U19. Antigua and Barbuda Full caps.
2006–07 Charlton Ath 0 0
2006–07 Notts Co 4 0
2007–08 Notts Co 25 0
2008–09 Notts Co 44 3 73 3
2009–10 Brentford 40 8
2010–11 Brentford 42 3
2011–12 Brentford 26 1 108 12
2012–13 Gillingham 37 8
2013–14 Gillingham 39 2 76 10
2014–15 Southend U 34 2
2015–16 Southend U 17 0 51 2
2016–17 Wycombe W 19 3 19 3
From Ebbsfleet U, Dagenham & Red, Bromley.
2024–25 Bromley 0 0

WHITELY, Corey (M) 54 2
H: 5 10 W: 11 00 b.Enfield 11-7-91
From Waltham Forest, Enfield T, Dagenham & Red, Ebbsfleet U.
2019–20 Newport Co 10 0 10 0
2024–25 Bromley 44 2 44 2

WOODS, Sam (D) 12 0
H: 6 1 W: 12 06 b.Bromley 11-9-98
2018–19 Crystal Palace 0 0
2019–20 Crystal Palace 0 0
2019–20 Hamilton A 3 1 3 1
2020–21 Crystal Palace 0 0
2020–21 Plymouth Arg 9 1 9 1
From Barnet.
2024–25 Bromley 0 0
Transferred to Croydon Ath, November 2024.

WYBORN, Rhys (D) 0 0
H: 5 9 b.London 17-8-05
2024–25 Bromley 0 0

Players retained or with offer of contract
German, Samuel Jesse; Thompson, Ben Rhys.

Scholars
Cassidy, Archie John; Cockerill, Brody Glenn; Haines, Harry John; Hards, Samuel Palapol; Hilden, Alfie Thomas; Hobbs, Jedd William; Mann, Yuvraj Sohan Singh; Patten, Nathan Robert; Paye, Charles Henry; Przybylo, Dawid Jakub; Rees, George Anthony.

BURNLEY (18)

ADEWUMI, Oluwaseun (F) 51 4
H: 6 0 W: 11 05 b.Wien 23-2-05
Internationals: Austria U19, U21.
2021–22 Floridsdorfer 1 0
2022–23 Floridsdorfer 16 0
2023–24 Floridsdorfer 30 3
2024–25 Burnley 0 0

2024–25 Floridsdorfer 4 1 51 4
2024–25 Dundee 0 0

AGYEI, Enock (F) 11 0
H: 5 8 W: 10 06 b. 13-1-05
Internationals: Belgium U17, U18.
2022–23 Anderlecht 0 0
2022–23 Burnley 0 0
2022–23 Mechelen 8 0 8 0
2023–24 Burnley 0 0
2024–25 Burnley 3 0 3 0

AMDOUNI, Zeki (F) 220 65
H: 6 1 W: 12 06 b.Geneve 4-12-00
Internationals: Turkey U21. Switzerland U20, U21, Full caps.
2017–18 Etoile Carouge 13 4
2018–19 Etoile Carouge 25 10 38 14
2019–20 Stade Lausanne 24 3
2020–21 Stade Lausanne 32 11 56 14
2021–22 Lausanne-Sport 34 12
2022–23 Lausanne-Sport 0 0 34 12
2022–23 FC Basel 32 12 32 12
2023–24 Burnley 34 5
2024–25 Burnley 2 1 36 6
2024–25 Benfica 24 7 24 7

BANEL, Jaydon (F) 6 0
H: 5 9 W: 11 00 b.Amsterdam 19-10-04
Internationals: Netherlands U18, U19.
2021–22 Ajax 0 0
2022–23 Ajax 0 0
2023–24 Ajax 5 0
2024–25 Ajax 1 0 6 0
2024–25 Burnley 0 0

BAURESS, Joe (M) 0 0
H: 5 9 W: 11 05 b.Liverpool 1-1-06
Internationals: England U18.
2022–23 Burnley 0 0
2023–24 Burnley 0 0
2024–25 Burnley 0 0

BENSON, Manuel (M) 213 30
H: 5 6 W: 10 10 b.Lokeren 28-3-97
Internationals: Belgium U19, U21. Angola Full caps.
2013–14 Lierse 1 0
2014–15 Lierse 9 0
2015–16 Lierse 21 2
2016–17 Lierse 37 7 68 9
2017–18 Genk 8 0
2018–19 Genk 0 0
2018–19 Mouscron 26 4 26 4
2019–20 Genk 3 0 11 0
2019–20 Antwerp 11 0
2020–21 Antwerp 5 0
2020–21 PEC Zwolle 13 0 13 0
2021–22 Antwerp 34 5
2022–23 Antwerp 1 0 51 5
2022–23 Burnley 33 11
2023–24 Burnley 8 0
2024–25 Burnley 3 1 44 12

BEVAN, Joe (F) 31 0
H. b. 1-1-05
2022–23 Albion R 17 0 17 0
2023–24 Burnley 0 0
2024–25 Burnley 0 0
2024–25 Carlisle U 14 0 14 0

BEYER, Jordan (D) 89 1
H: 6 2 W: 12 08 b.Kempen 19-5-00
Internationals: Germany U16, U17, U18, U19, U20, U21.
2017–18 Borussia M'gladbach 0 0
2018–19 Borussia M'gladbach 9 0
2019–20 Borussia M'gladbach 3 0
2019–20 Hamburger SV 11 0 11 0
2020–21 Borussia M'gladbach 4 0
2021–22 Borussia M'gladbach 17 0
2022–23 Borussia M'gladbach 0 0 33 0
2022–23 Burnley 30 1
2023–24 Burnley 15 0
2024–25 Burnley 0 0 45 1

BROWNHILL, Josh (M) 406 54
H: 5 10 W: 10 12 b.Warrington 19-12-95
2013–14 Preston NE 24 3
2014–15 Preston NE 18 2
2015–16 Preston NE 3 0 45 5
2015–16 Barnsley 22 2 22 2
2016–17 Bristol C 27 1
2017–18 Bristol C 45 5
2018–19 Bristol C 45 5
2019–20 Bristol C 28 5 145 16
2019–20 Burnley 10 0
2020–21 Burnley 33 0
2021–22 Burnley 35 2
2022–23 Burnley 41 7
2023–24 Burnley 33 4
2024–25 Burnley 42 18 194 31

CHURLINOV, Darko (M) 87 9
H: 5 11 W: 11 11 b.Skopje 11-7-00
Internationals: Macedonia U17, U19. North Macedonia U21, Full caps.
2017–18 Cologne 0 0
2018–19 Cologne 0 0
2019–20 Cologne 1 0 1 0
2019–20 VfB Stuttgart 6 1
2020–21 VfB Stuttgart 14 0
2021–22 VfB Stuttgart 0 0
2021–22 Schalke 04 22 2
2021–22 VfB Stuttgart 1 0 21 1
2022–23 Burnley 7 0
2023–24 Burnley 0 0
2023–24 Schalke 04 10 1 32 3
2024–25 Burnley 0 0 7 0
2024–25 Jagiellonia Bialystock 26 5 26 5

COSTELLOE, Dara (F) 75 12
H: 5 9 W: 11 09 b.Limerick 11-12-02
Internationals: Republic of Ireland U21.
2021–22 Burnley 0 0
2022–23 Burnley 4 0
2022–23 Bradford C 11 0 11 0
2023–24 Burnley 0 0
2023–24 St Johnstone 12 1 12 1
2023–24 Dundee 16 0 16 0
2024–25 Burnley 0 0 4 0
2024–25 Accrington S 17 5 17 5
2024–25 Northampton T 15 6 15 6

CULLEN, Josh (M) 312 9
H: 5 8 W: 11 00 b.Southend-on-Sea 4-7-96
Internationals: England U16. Republic of Ireland U19, U20, U21, Full caps.
2014–15 West Ham U 0 0
2015–16 West Ham U 1 0
2015–16 Bradford C 15 0
2016–17 West Ham U 0 0
2016–17 Bradford C 40 1 55 1
2017–18 West Ham U 2 0
2017–18 Bolton W 12 0 12 0
2018–19 West Ham U 0 0
2018–19 Charlton Ath 29 1
2019–20 West Ham U 0 0
2019–20 Charlton Ath 34 1 63 2
2020–21 West Ham U 0 0 3 0
2020–21 Anderlecht 27 0
2021–22 Anderlecht 40 1 67 1
2022–23 Burnley 43 1
2023–24 Burnley 25 2
2024–25 Burnley 44 2 112 5

DELCROIX, Hannes (D) 98 1
b.Grande Hatte 28-2-99
Internationals: Belgium U16, U17, U18, U19, U21, Full caps.
2016–17 Anderlecht 0 0
2017–18 Anderlecht 0 0
2018–19 Anderlecht 1 0
2019–20 Anderlecht 0 0
2019–20 RKC Waalwijk 23 1 23 1
2020–21 Anderlecht 23 0
2021–22 Anderlecht 10 0
2022–23 Anderlecht 16 0
2023–24 Anderlecht 1 0 51 0
2023–24 Burnley 12 0
2024–25 Burnley 0 0 12 0
2024–25 Swansea C 12 0 12 0

DODGSON, Owen (D) 66 2
H: 5 10 W: 10 06 b.Lancaster 19-3-03
From Manchester U.
2021–22 Burnley 0 0
2022–23 Burnley 0 0
2022–23 Rochdale 18 1 18 1
2023–24 Burnley 0 0
2023–24 Barnsley 10 0 10 0
2023–24 Dundee 16 0 16 0
2024–25 Burnley 0 0
2024–25 Burton Alb 22 1 22 1

EDWARDS, Marcus (M) 194 35
H: 5 9 W: 12 04 b.London 3-12-98
Internationals: England U16, U17, U18, U19, U20.
2016–17 Tottenham H 0 0
2017–18 Tottenham H 0 0
2017–18 Norwich C 1 0 1 0
2018–19 Tottenham H 0 0
2018–19 Excelsior 25 2 25 2
2019–20 Vitoria de Guimaraes 27 3
2020–21 Vitoria de Guimaraes 33 3
2021–22 Vitoria de Guimaraes 18 7 77 17
2021–22 Sporting Lisbon 12 3
2022–23 Sporting Lisbon 33 7
2023–24 Sporting Lisbon 26 4
2024–25 Sporting Lisbon 6 1 77 15
On loan from Sporting Lisbon.
2024–25 Burnley 14 1 14 1

EGAN-RILEY, CJ (D)   59   1
H: 6 0   W: 11 00   b.Manchester 2-1-03
Internationals: Republic of Ireland U16.
England U16, U17, U18, U19, U21.

2021–22	Manchester C	1	0	1	0
2022–23	Burnley	3	0		
2022–23	Hibernian	14	0	14	0
2023–24	Burnley	0	0		
2024–25	Burnley	41	1	44	1

EKDAL, Hjalmar (D)   153   11
H: 6 2   W: 12 00   b.Stockholm 21-10-98
Internationals: Sweden U19, U21, Full caps.

2017	Brommapojkarna	0	0		
2018	Frej	15	1		
2018	Assyriska	1	0	1	0
2019	Frej	30	2	45	3
2019	Hammarby	0	0		
2020	Hammarby	0	0		
2020	Sirius	26	0	26	0
2021	Djurgarden	26	4		
2022	Djurgarden	24	3	50	7
2022–23	Burnley	9	1		
2023–24	Burnley	8	0		
2024–25	Burnley	0	0	17	1
2024–25	Groningen	14	0	14	0

ESTEVE, Maxime (D)   109   1
H: 6 4   W: 13 10   b.Montpellier 26-5-02
Internationals: France U20, U21, U23.

2020–21	Montpellier	0	0		
2021–22	Montpellier	24	0		
2022–23	Montpellier	23	0		
2023–24	Burnley	0	0	47	0
2023–24	Burnley	16	0		
2024–25	Burnley	41	1	62	1

FOSTER, Lyle (F)   141   22
H: 6 1   W: 11 11   b.Soweto 3-9-00
Internationals: South Africa U17, U20, U23, Full caps.

2017–18	Orlando Pirates	9	1	9	1
2018–19	Monaco	0	0		
2019–20	Monaco	2	0	2	0
2019–20	Cercle Brugge	18	1	18	1
2020–21	Vitoria de Guimaraes	5	0		
2021–22	Vitoria de Guimaraes	0	0	5	0
2021–22	Westerlo	23	4		
2022–23	Westerlo	21	8	44	12
2022–23	Burnley	11	1		
2023–24	Burnley	24	5		
2024–25	Burnley	28	2	63	8

GREEN, Etienne (G)   37   0
H: 6 3   W: 12 00   b.Colchester 19-7-00
Internationals: England U21.

2019–20	Saint-Etienne	0	0		
2020–21	Saint-Etienne	8	0		
2021–22	Saint-Etienne	15	0		
2022–23	Saint-Etienne	8	0		
2023–24	Saint-Etienne	6	0	37	0
2024–25	Burnley	0	0		

GUDMUNDSSON, Johann Berg (M)   400   40
H: 6 1   W: 12 06   b.Reykjavik 27-10-90
Internationals: Iceland U19, U21, Full caps.

2009–10	AZ Alkmaar	0	0		
2010–11	AZ Alkmaar	23	1		
2011–12	AZ Alkmaar	30	3		
2012–13	AZ Alkmaar	31	2		
2013–14	AZ Alkmaar	35	3	119	9
2014–15	Charlton Ath	41	10		
2015–16	Charlton Ath	40	6	81	16
2016–17	Burnley	20	1		
2017–18	Burnley	35	2		
2018–19	Burnley	29	3		
2019–20	Burnley	12	1		
2020–21	Burnley	22	2		
2021–22	Burnley	18	0		
2022–23	Burnley	37	4		
2023–24	Burnley	26	1		
2024–25	Burnley	1	1	200	15

Transferred to Al-Orobah, August 2024.

HLADKY, Vaclav (G)   226   0
H: 6 2   W: 12 08   b.Brno 14-11-90
Internationals: Czech Republic U16, U17, U18, U19, U20.

2010–11	Zbrojovka Brno	0	0		
2011–12	Zbrojovka Brno	0	0		
2012–13	Zbrojovka Brno	1	0		
2013–14	Zbrojovka Brno	25	0		
2014–15	Zbrojovka Brno	6	0	42	0
2015–16	Slovan Liberec	5	0		
2016–17	Slovan Liberec	2	0		
2017–18	Slovan Liberec	15	0		
2018–19	Slovan Liberec	9	0	31	0
2018–19	St Mirren	17	0		
2019–20	St Mirren	30	0	47	0
2020–21	Salford C	46	0	46	0
2021–22	Ipswich T	12	0		
2022–23	Ipswich T	1	0		
2023–24	Ipswich T	46	0	59	0
2024–25	Burnley	1	0	1	0

HOUNTONDJI, Andreas (F)   114   26
b.Montry 11-7-02
Internationals: Benin Full caps.

2019–20	Caan	0	0		
2020–21	Caan	6	1		
2021–22	Caan	25	1		
2022–23	Caan	0	0		
2022–23	Quevilly-Rouen	7	0	7	0
2022–23	Orleans	15	6	15	6
2023–24	Caan	0	0		
2023–24	Rodez	34	14	34	14
2024–25	Burnley	9	0	9	0
2024–25	Standard Liege	18	4	18	4

HUGILL, Will (M)   0   0
b. 27-6-04

| 2024–25 | Burnley | 0 | 0 | | |

KOLEOSHO, Luca (M)   48   4
H: 5 9   W: 10 10   b.Trumbull 15-9-04
Internationals: Italy U19, U20, U21.

2021–22	Espanyol	0	0		
2022–23	Espanyol	4	1	5	1
2023–24	Burnley	15	1		
2024–25	Burnley	28	2	43	3

LAURENT, Josh (M)   327   18
H: 6 0   W: 11 01   b.Leytonstone 6-5-95
From Wycombe W.

2013–14	QPR	0	0		
2014–15	QPR	0	0		
2015–16	Brentford	0	0		
2015–16	Newport Co	3	0	3	0
2015–16	Hartlepool U	3	0		
2016–17	Hartlepool U	25	1	28	1
2016–17	Wigan Ath	1	0		
2017–18	Wigan Ath	0	0	1	0
2017–18	Bury	22	1	22	1
2018–19	Shrewsbury T	42	2		
2019–20	Shrewsbury T	31	2	73	4
2020–21	Reading	45	3		
2021–22	Reading	41	2	86	5
2022–23	Stoke C	32	4		
2023–24	Stoke C	37	1		
2024–25	Stoke C	3	0	72	5
2024–25	Burnley	42	2	42	2

LUCAS PIRES, Silva (D)   91   1
H: 6 0   W: 12 00   b.Sao Paulo 24-3-01

2021	Santos	0	0		
2022	Santos	20	0		
2023	Santos	9	0	29	0
2023–24	Cadiz	28	1	28	1
2024–25	Burnley	34	0	34	0

MASARA, Vernon (F)   0   0
H: 5 11   W: 12 04   b. 18-4-07

| 2024–25 | Burnley | 0 | 0 | | |

MASSENGO, Han-Noah (M)   144   0
H: 5 9   W: 10 06   b.Villepinte 7-7-01
Internationals: France U17, U18, U19, U21.

2018–19	Monaco	3	0	3	0
2019–20	Bristol C	25	0		
2020–21	Bristol C	27	0		
2021–22	Bristol C	37	0	99	0
2022–23	Auxerre	14	0		
2023–24	Burnley	3	0		
2023–24	Auxerre	8	0	11	0
2024–25	Auxerre	17	0	31	0

McDERMOTT, Tommy (M)   0   0
H: 5 10   W: 11 09   b.Manchester 1-6-05

2021–22	Port Vale	0	0		
2022–23	Port Vale	2	0		
2023–24	Port Vale	0	0	2	0
2023–24	Burnley	0	0		
2024–25	Burnley	0	0		

MEJBRI, Hannibal (M)   89   3
H: 6 0   W: 11 00   b.Ivry-sur-Seine 21-1-03
Internationals: France U16, U17. Tunisia Full caps.

2020–21	Manchester U	1	0		
2021–22	Manchester U	2	0		
2022–23	Manchester U	0	0		
2022–23	Birmingham C	38	1	38	1
2023–24	Manchester U	5	1		
2023–24	Sevilla	6	0	6	0
2024–25	Manchester U	0	0	8	1
2024–25	Burnley	37	1	37	1

MELLON, Michael (F)   61   18
H: 6 1   b.Blackpool 5-12-03
Internationals: Scotland U17, U21.
From Manchester U.

2022–23	Burnley	0	0		
2022–23	Morecambe	8	0		
2023–24	Burnley	0	0		
2023–24	Morecambe	22	13	30	13
2023–24	Dundee	14	3	14	3
2024–25	Burnley	0	0		
2024–25	Stockport Co	2	0	2	0
2024–25	Bradford C	15	2	15	2

NDAYISHIMIYE, Mike Tresor (M)   166   23
H: 5 8   W: 10 12   b.Lembeek 28-5-99
Internationals: Belgium U17, U18, U19, U21, Full caps.
From Anderlecht.

2018–19	NEC	23	6		
2019–20	NEC	2	0	25	6
2019–20	Willem II	20	5		
2020–21	Willem II	34	4	54	9
2021–22	Genk	30	0		
2022–23	Genk	39	8		
2023–24	Genk	2	0	71	8
2023–24	Burnley	16	0		
2024–25	Burnley	0	0	16	0

OBAFEMI, Michael (F)   140   25
H: 5 7   W: 11 03   b.Dublin 6-7-00
Internationals: Republic of Ireland U19, Full caps.
From Leyton Orient.

2017–18	Southampton	1	0		
2018–19	Southampton	6	1		
2019–20	Southampton	21	3		
2020–21	Southampton	4	0		
2021–22	Southampton	0	0	32	4
2021–22	Swansea C	32	12		
2022–23	Swansea C	19	3	51	15
2022–23	Burnley	12	2		
2023–24	Burnley	2	0		
2023–24	Millwall	14	2	14	2
2024–25	Burnley	0	0	14	2
2024–25	Plymouth Arg	29	2	29	2

RAMSEY, Aaron (M)   59   9
H: 5 11   W: 12 02   b.Birmingham 21-1-03
Internationals: England U16, U17, U18, U19, U20.

2020–21	Aston Villa	0	0		
2021–22	Aston Villa	0	0		
2021–22	Cheltenham T	15	1	15	1
2022–23	Aston Villa	0	0		
2022–23	Norwich C	3	0	18	3
2022–23	Middlesbrough	11	5	11	5
2023–24	Burnley	14	0		
2024–25	Burnley	0	0	15	0

REDMOND, Nathan (M)   383   39
H: 5 8   W: 11 11   b.Birmingham 6-3-94
Internationals: England U16, U17, U18, U19, U20, U21, Full caps.

2011–12	Birmingham C	24	5		
2012–13	Birmingham C	38	2	62	7
2013–14	Norwich C	34	1		
2014–15	Norwich C	43	4		
2015–16	Norwich C	35	6	112	11
2016–17	Southampton	37	7		
2017–18	Southampton	31	1		
2018–19	Southampton	38	6		
2019–20	Southampton	32	4		
2020–21	Southampton	29	2		
2021–22	Southampton	27	1		
2022–23	Southampton	1	0	195	21
2023–24	Burnley	12	0		
2024–25	Burnley	2	0	14	0

ROBERTS, Connor (D)   312   19
H: 5 9   W: 11 03   b.Neath 23-9-95
Internationals: Wales U19, U21, Full caps.

2014–15	Swansea C	0	0		
2015–16	Swansea C	0	0		
2015–16	Yeovil T	45	0	45	0
2016–17	Swansea C	0	0		
2016–17	Bristol R	2	0	2	0
2017–18	Swansea C	4	0		
2017–18	Middlesbrough	1	0	1	0
2018–19	Swansea C	45	5		
2019–20	Swansea C	38	1		
2020–21	Swansea C	46	5	133	11
2021–22	Burnley	21	1		
2022–23	Burnley	14	0		
2023–24	Leeds U	12	1	12	1
2024–25	Burnley	41	2	119	7

SAMBO, Shurandy (D)   43   2
H: 5 9   W: 11 00   b.Geldrop 19-8-01
Internationals: Netherlands U16, U17, U21.

2019–20	PSV Eindhoven	0	0		
2020–21	PSV Eindhoven	1	0		
2021–22	PSV Eindhoven	0	0		
2022–23	Sparta Rotterdam	30	2	30	2
2023–24	PSV Eindhoven	11	0	12	0
2024–25	Burnley	1	0	1	0

SHELVEY, Jonjo (M)   412   44
H: 5 9   W: 12 04   b.Romford 27-2-92
Internationals: England U16, U17, U19, U21, Full caps.

2007–08	Charlton Ath	1	0		
2008–09	Charlton Ath	16	3		
2009–10	Charlton Ath	24	4	42	7
2010–11	Liverpool	15	0		
2011–12	Liverpool	13	1		
2011–12	Blackpool	10	6	10	6

2012–13 Liverpool 19 1 **47 2**
2013–14 Swansea C 32 6
2014–15 Swansea C 31 3
2015–16 Swansea C 16 1 **79 10**
2015–16 Newcastle U 15 0
2016–17 Newcastle U 42 5
2017–18 Newcastle U 30 1
2018–19 Newcastle U 16 1
2019–20 Newcastle U 26 6
2020–21 Newcastle U 30 1
2021–22 Newcastle U 24 2
2022–23 Newcastle U 3 0 **186 16**
2022–23 Nottingham F 8 0
2023–24 Nottingham F 0 0 **8 0**
2023–24 *Rizespor* 32 3 **32 3**
2024–25 Eyupspor 6 0 **6 0**
2024–25 Burnley 2 0 **2 0**

SONNE, Oliver (D) 123 9
H: 6 0 W: 11 05 b.Herfolge 10-11-00
Internationals: Peru Full caps.
2019–20 HB Koge 10 0
2020–21 HB Koge 20 1 **30 1**
2021–22 Silkeborg 15 0
2022–23 Silkeborg 29 4
2023–24 Silkeborg 31 1
2024–25 Silkeborg 16 3 **91 8**
2024–25 Burnley 2 0 **2 0**

TRAFFORD, James (G) 151 0
H: 6 6 W: 13 01 b.Cockermouth 10-10-02
Internationals: England U17, U18, U19, U20, U21.
2020–21 Manchester C 0 0
2021–22 Manchester C 0 0
2021–22 *Accrington S* 11 0 **11 0**
2021–22 *Bolton W* 22 0
2022–23 Manchester C 0 0
2022–23 *Bolton W* 45 0 **67 0**
2023–24 Burnley 28 0
2024–25 Burnley 45 0 **73 0**

TWEEDY, Tom (F) 0 0
b. 15-9-04
Internationals: Wales U21.
2024–25 Burnley 0 0

VEEVERS, Charlie (M) 0 0
H: 5 8 b. 13-2-05
2024–25 Burnley 0 0

VITINHO, da Silva (D) 143 6
H: 5 9 W: 11 05 b.Belo Horizonte 23-7-99
Internationals: Brazil U20.
2017 Cruzeiro 0 0
2018 Cruzeiro 1 0 **1 0**
2018–19 Cercle Brugge 12 0
2019–20 Cercle Brugge 0 0
2020–21 Cercle Brugge 28 1
2021–22 Cercle Brugge 32 1 **72 2**
2022–23 Burnley 35 3
2023–24 Burnley 32 0
2024–25 Burnley 3 1 **70 4**
Transferred to Botafogo, August 2024.

WALLER, Sam (G) 0 0
b. 9-9-03
2021–22 Burnley 0 0
2022–23 Burnley 0 0
2024–25 Burnley 0 0

WEGHORST, Wouter (F) 387 146
H: 6 6 W: 13 03 b.Borne 8-7-92
Internationals: Netherlands U21, Full caps.
From Willem II.
2012–13 Emmen 28 8
2013–14 Emmen 34 11 **62 19**
2014–15 Heracles 31 8
2015–16 Heracles 33 12 **64 20**
2016–17 AZ Alkmaar 29 13
2017–18 AZ Alkmaar 31 18 **60 31**
2018–19 VfL Wolfsburg 34 17
2019–20 VfL Wolfsburg 32 16
2020–21 VfL Wolfsburg 34 20
2021–22 VfL Wolfsburg 18 6 **118 59**
2021–22 Burnley 20 2
2022–23 Burnley 0 0
2022–23 *Besiktas* 16 8 **16 8**
2022–23 *Manchester U* 17 0 **17 0**
2023–24 Burnley 0 0
2023–24 *TSG 1899 Hoffenheim* 28 7 **28 7**
2024–25 Burnley 2 0 **22 2**
Transferred to Ajax, August 2024.

WESTLEY, Joe (F) 17 3
b.Kingston upon Thames 18-10-04
2024–25 Burnley 0 0
2024–25 *Swindon T* 17 3 **17 3**

WORRALL, Joe (D) 256 6
H: 6 3 W: 10 01 b.Hucknall 10-1-97
Internationals: England U20, U21.
2015–16 Nottingham F 0 0
2015–16 *Dagenham & Red* 14 1 **14 1**
2016–17 Nottingham F 21 0
2017–18 Nottingham F 31 1
2018–19 Nottingham F 0 0
2018–19 *Rangers* 22 0 **22 0**
2019–20 Nottingham F 46 1
2020–21 Nottingham F 31 1
2021–22 Nottingham F 39 0
2022–23 Nottingham F 30 1
2023–24 Nottingham F 7 0 **205 4**
2023–24 *Besiktas* 6 1 **6 1**
2024–25 Burnley 9 0 **9 0**

ZAROURY, Anass (F) 126 23
H: 5 9 W: 11 05 b.Mechelen 7-11-00
Internationals: Belgium U17, U18, U21. Morocco Full caps.
2019–20 Lommel 5 0
2020–21 Lommel 25 7 **30 7**
2021–22 Charleroi 38 5
2022–23 Charleroi 5 2 **43 7**
2022–23 Burnley 34 7
2023–24 Burnley 6 0
2023–24 *Hull C* 12 2 **12 2**
2024–25 Burnley 1 0 **41 7**
Transferred to Lens, August 2024.

Players retained or with offer of contract
Ashton, Joe David; Balogun, Hamzat Alamu; Campbell, Murray Craig; Casper, Charlie; Forshaw, Lewis Dean; Grant, Bradley George; Leuluai, Marley Johannes; McEvilly, Jack Angus; Pouani Siewe, Brandon Ellison; Pye, Logan; Ryan, Kamarni Anthony; Vetro, Julien Gael; Williams, Jesse Okonofua.

Scholars
Abbas, Adam Ibrahim Khalil; Abbott, Ben Richard; Adekoya, Noah Jonathan Francis; Blackie, Albert Francis; Brierley, George Alexander; Carlin, Logan Owen; Chester, Felix Joseph Redmond; Derbyshire, Braidin Francis Tadhg; Edwards, Connor Jack; Jackson, Luca Daniel; Johnson, Zachary David; King, Corey Mikel; Ly, Brandon Michael; Mamadu Sadjo So, Fabio; McCoy, Adam Lee; McMahon-Brown, Frankie; McMahon-Brown, Kian; Murtesa, Anwar Ahsaro; Pimlott, Oliver Edmund David; Savage, Troy Greig Samuel; Stanley, Michael Ray; Tioffo, Ryan Jefferson; Wetshi, Benjamin Nsenga; Wilcock, Joseph Samuel.

BURTON ALB (19)

AKOTO, Nicholas (D) 14 0
H: 6 2 W: 11 11 b.Miami 16-9-98
From Maldon & Tiptree, Whyteleafe, Ocean C, South Georgia Tormenta.
2024–25 Burton Alb 14 0 **14 0**

ARMER, Jack (D) 190 4
H: 6 1 W: 12 04 b.Preston 16-4-01
Internationals: Scotland U17, U18, U19.
2019–20 Preston NE 0 0
2020–21 Carlisle U 24 1
2021–22 Carlisle U 41 0
2022–23 Carlisle U 46 2
2023–24 Carlisle U 41 1 **152 4**
2024–25 Burton Alb 38 0 **38 0**

BAJRAMI, Geraldo (D) 3 0
H: 6 2 W: 12 04 b.Birmingham 24-9-99
Internationals: Albania U21.
2019–20 Birmingham C 2 0
2020–21 Birmingham C 0 0 **2 0**
From Kidderminster H, Notts Co.
2023–24 Notts Co 0 0
2024–25 Burton Alb 1 0 **1 0**

BANNON, Alex (M) 66 1
H: 5 10 W: 11 07 b.Bishopton 16-9-03
2021–22 Queen's Park 0 0
2022–23 Queen's Park 15 0
2023–24 Queen's Park 30 1 **45 1**
2024–25 Burton Alb 9 0 **9 0**
2024–25 *Airdrieonians* 12 0 **12 0**

BENNETT, Mason (F) 270 23
H: 5 10 W: 10 01 b.Shirebrook 15-7-96
Internationals: England U16, U17, U19.
2011–12 Derby Co 9 0
2012–13 Derby Co 6 0
2013–14 Derby Co 13 1
2013–14 *Chesterfield* 5 0 **5 0**
2014–15 Derby Co 2 0
2014–15 *Bradford C* 11 1 **11 1**
2015–16 Derby Co 0 0
2015–16 *Burton Alb* 16 1
2016–17 Derby Co 2 0
2017–18 Derby Co 3 0
2017–18 *Notts Co* 2 1 **2 1**
2018–19 Derby Co 30 3
2019–20 Derby Co 7 0 **72 4**
2019–20 *Millwall* 9 2
2020–21 Millwall 37 6
2021–22 Millwall 29 3
2022–23 Millwall 21 0 **96 11**
2023–24 Burton Alb 34 3
2024–25 Burton Alb 34 2 **84 6**

BODIN, Billy (M) 366 75
H: 5 11 W: 11 00 b.Swindon 24-3-92
Internationals: Wales U17, U19, U21, Full caps.
2009–10 Swindon T 0 0
2010–11 Swindon T 5 0
2011–12 Swindon T 11 3 **16 3**
2011–12 *Torquay U* 17 5
2011–12 *Crewe Alex* 8 0 **8 0**
2012–13 Torquay U 43 5
2013–14 Torquay U 27 1 **87 11**
2014–15 Northampton T 4 0 **4 0**
2015–16 Bristol R 38 13
2016–17 Bristol R 36 13
2017–18 Bristol R 21 9 **95 35**
2017–18 Preston NE 17 1
2018–19 Preston NE 0 0
2019–20 Preston NE 18 2
2020–21 Preston NE 4 0 **39 3**
2021–22 Oxford U 21 6
2022–23 Oxford U 32 6
2023–24 Oxford U 36 5 **89 17**
2024–25 Burton Alb 12 4 **12 4**
2024–25 *Reading* 16 2 **16 2**

BODVARSSON, Jon Dadi (F) 435 76
H: 6 3 W: 13 05 b.Selfoss 25-5-92
Internationals: Iceland U19, U21, Full caps.
2008 Selfoss 0 0
2009 Selfoss 16 1
2010 Selfoss 21 3
2011 Selfoss 21 7
2012 Selfoss 22 7 **80 18**
2013 Viking 23 1
2014 Viking 29 5
2015 Viking 29 9 **81 15**
2015–16 Kaiserslautern 15 2 **15 2**
2016–17 Wolverhampton W 42 3 **42 3**
2017–18 Reading 33 7
2018–19 Reading 20 7 **53 14**
2019–20 Millwall 31 4
2020–21 Millwall 38 1
2021–22 Millwall 0 0 **69 5**
2021–22 Bolton W 21 7
2022–23 Bolton W 21 3
2023–24 Bolton W 36 4 **78 14**
2024–25 Wrexham 4 0 **4 0**
2024–25 Burton Alb 13 5 **13 5**

BRAN, Alejandro (M) 80 3
H: 5 9 W: 11 11 b.San JosÈ 5-3-01
Internationals: Costa Rica Full caps.
2020–21 Jicaral 14 0
2021–22 Jicaral 0 0 **14 0**
2021–22 *Municipal Grecia* 3 0 **3 0**
2021–22 Herediano 19 0
2022–23 Herediano 0 0
2022–23 *Guanacasteca* 26 0 **26 0**
2023–24 Herediano 17 3 **36 3**
2024 Minnesota U 0 0
On loan from Minnesota U.
2024–25 Burton Alb 1 0 **1 0**

BRAYFORD, John (D) 557 28
H: 5 8 W: 11 03 b.Stoke 29-12-87
Internationals: England C.
From Burton Alb.
2008–09 Crewe Alex 36 2
2009–10 Crewe Alex 45 0 **81 2**
2010–11 Derby Co 46 1
2011–12 Derby Co 23 0
2012–13 Derby Co 40 1 **109 2**
2013–14 Cardiff C 0 0
2013–14 *Sheffield U* 15 1
2014–15 Cardiff C 26 0 **26 0**
2014–15 Sheffield U 22 1
2015–16 Sheffield U 19 1
2016–17 Sheffield U 3 0
2016–17 *Burton Alb* 33 0
2017–18 Sheffield U 0 0 **59 3**
2017–18 Burton Alb 28 0
2018–19 Burton Alb 41 3
2019–20 Burton Alb 32 2
2020–21 Burton Alb 41 4
2021–22 Burton Alb 33 6
2022–23 Burton Alb 43 3
2023–24 Burton Alb 31 3
2024–25 Burton Alb 0 0 **282 21**

BURRELL, Rumarn (F) 119 41
H: 6 0 W: 11 05 b.Birmingham 16-12-00
Internationals: Jamaica Full caps.
2018–19 Grimsby T 4 0 **4 0**
2019–20 Middlesbrough 0 0
2020–21 Middlesbrough 0 0
2020–21 *Bradford C* 2 0 **2 0**
2021–22 Middlesbrough 0 0
2021–22 *Kilmarnock* 19 0 **19 0**
2022–23 Falkirk 30 9 **30 9**
2023–24 Cove Rangers 34 21 **34 21**
2024–25 Burton Alb 30 11 **30 11**

CHAUKE, Kgaogelo (M) **63 1**
H: 5 10 W: 10 03 b.Pretoria 8-1-03
Internationals: South Africa U23.
From Thatcham T.

2020–21	Southampton	0	0		
2021–22	Southampton	0	0		
2022–23	Southampton	0	0		
2022–23	*Exeter C*	20	0	**20**	**0**
2023–24	Burton Alb	5	0		
2024–25	Burton Alb	38	1	**43**	**1**

COOPER-LOVE, Jack (F) **125 38**
H: 5 10 W: 11 05 b.Aneby, Sweden 25-12-01

2020	Aneby	21	10	**21**	**10**
2021	Elfsborg	6	0		
2021	*Orgryte*	9	0	**9**	**0**
2022	Elfsborg	2	0		
2022	*Skovde AIK*	27	14	**27**	**14**
2023	Elfsborg	11	1		
2023	*Halmstads*	16	2	**16**	**2**
2024	Elfsborg	0	0	**19**	**1**
2024	*GAIS*	9	4	**9**	**4**
2024–25	Burton Alb	14	2	**14**	**2**
2024–25	*De Graafschap*	10	5	**10**	**5**

CROCOMBE, Max (G) **157 0**
H: 6 4 W: 13 12 b.Auckland 12-8-93
Internationals: New Zealand U20, U23, Full caps.

2012–13	Oxford U	4	0		
2013–14	Oxford U	0	0		
2014–15	Oxford U	0	0		
2015–16	Oxford U	0	0	**4**	**0**
2015–16	*Barnet*	5	0	**5**	**0**
2016–17	Carlisle U	0	0		
From Salford C.					
2019–20	Brisbane Roar	6	0	**6**	**0**
2020–21	Melbourne Victory	10	0	**10**	**0**
From Grimsby T.					
2022–23	Grimsby T	46	0	**46**	**0**
2023–24	Burton Alb	43	0		
2024–25	Burton Alb	43	0	**86**	**0**

DELAP, Finn (D) **7 0**
H: 5 9 W: 13 01 b.Winchester 10-6-05

2022–23	Burton Alb	0	0		
2023–24	Burton Alb	2	0		
2024–25	Burton Alb	5	0	**7**	**0**

DUDEK, Kamil (D) **0 0**
b. 17-4-06

2024–25	Burton Alb	0	0		

FORDE, Anthony (M) **299 16**
H: 5 9 W: 10 10 b.Limerick 16-11-93
Internationals: Republic of Ireland U19, U21.

2011–12	Wolverhampton W	6	0		
2012–13	Wolverhampton W	12	0		
2012–13	*Scunthorpe U*	8	0	**8**	**0**
2013–14	Wolverhampton W	3	0	**21**	**0**
2014–15	Walsall	37	3		
2015–16	Walsall	41	4	**78**	**7**
2016–17	Rotherham U	32	2		
2017–18	Rotherham U	41	2		
2018–19	Rotherham U	28	1	**101**	**5**
2019–20	Oxford U	18	1		
2020–21	Oxford U	35	1		
2021–22	Oxford U	13	1	**66**	**3**
From Wrexham.					
2023–24	Wrexham	14	1		
2024–25	Wrexham	0	0	**14**	**1**
2024–25	Burton Alb	11	0	**11**	**0**

GILBERT, Cameron (D) **0 0**
H: 6 0 W: 11 09 b. 19-7-07

2024–25	Burton Alb	0	0		

GILLIGAN, Ciaran (M) **59 1**
H: 5 11 W: 12 06 b.Derby 5-2-02
Internationals: Republic of Ireland U19, U20.

2020–21	Burton Alb	18	0		
2021–22	Burton Alb	8	0		
2022–23	Burton Alb	6	0		
2023–24	Burton Alb	15	1		
2024–25	Burton Alb	12	0	**59**	**1**

GODWIN-MALIFE, Udoka (D) **196 2**
H: 5 11 W: 12 06 b.Oxford 9-5-00
From Oxford C.

2018–19	Forest Green R	5	0		
2019–20	Forest Green R	12	0		
2020–21	Forest Green R	44	0		
2021–22	Forest Green R	26	0		
2022–23	Forest Green R	25	0		
2023–24	Forest Green R	0	0	**112**	**0**
2023–24	Swindon T	42	1	**42**	**1**
2024–25	Burton Alb	42	1	**42**	**1**

HAZLEHURST, Jack (M) **2 0**
H: 5 8 W: 11 00 b.Liverpool 25-11-99

2024–25	Burton Alb	2	0	**2**	**0**

INZOUDINE, Ivan (F) **105 1**
H: 5 9 W: 11 05 b.Bobigny 10-12-96

2014–15	Lens	0	0		
2015–16	Lens	0	0		
2016–17	Guingamp	0	0		
2017–18	Guingamp	0	0		
2017–18	Messina	9	0	**9**	**0**
2018–19	Cavese	13	0	**13**	**0**
2019–20	Marsala	9	0	**9**	**0**
2020–21	Marina di Ragusa	11	0	**11**	**0**
2021–22	Saint-Malo	25	1	**25**	**1**
2022–23	Chambly	15	0		
2023–24	Chambly	19	0	**34**	**0**
2024–25	Burton Alb	0	0		
2024–25	*Kalmar*	4	0	**4**	**0**

ISTED, Harry (G) **46 0**
H: 6 1 W: 11 00 b.Chichester 5-3-97
From Southampton, Stoke C.

2017–18	Luton T	0	0		
2018–19	Luton T	0	0		
2019–20	Luton T	0	0		
2020–21	Luton T	0	0		
2021–22	Luton T	2	0		
2022–23	Luton T	1	0	**3**	**0**
2022–23	*Barnsley*	19	0	**19**	**0**
2023–24	Charlton Ath	21	0	**21**	**0**
2024–25	Burton Alb	3	0	**3**	**0**

JONES, James (M) **232 24**
H: 5 9 W: 10 10 b.Winsford 1-2-96
Internationals: Scotland U19, U21.

2014–15	Crewe Alex	24	1		
2015–16	Crewe Alex	31	0		
2016–17	Crewe Alex	45	10		
2017–18	Crewe Alex	6	1		
2018–19	Crewe Alex	38	5		
2019–20	Crewe Alex	23	2	**167**	**19**
2019–20	Lincoln C	0	0		
2020–21	Lincoln C	36	1		
2021–22	Lincoln C	0	0	**36**	**1**
From Wrexham.					
2023–24	Wrexham	23	4		
2024–25	Wrexham	2	0	**25**	**4**
2024–25	Burton Alb	4	0	**4**	**0**

KALINAUSKAS, Tomas (F) **74 2**
H: 5 10 W: 11 00 b.Lithuania 27-4-00
Internationals: Lithuania U19, U21, Full caps.
From Windsor, Hayes & Yeading U, Farnborough.

2021–22	Barnsley	0	0		
2021–22	*AFC Wimbledon*	2	0	**2**	**0**
2022–23	Barnsley	0	0		
2022–23	Den Bosch	17	1		
2023–24	Den Bosch	16	0	**33**	**1**
2024–25	Burton Alb	39	1	**39**	**1**

LARSSON, Julian (F) **24 2**
H: 5 10 W: 11 05 b. 21-4-01
Internationals: Sweden U16, U17, U18, U19, U20.
From AIK Solna.

2020–21	Nottingham F	0	0		
2021–22	Nottingham F	0	0		
2022–23	Nottingham F	0	0		
2023–24	Nottingham F	0	0		
2023–24	*Morecambe*	13	0	**13**	**0**
2024–25	Burton Alb	11	2	**11**	**2**

MOON, Jasper (M) **114 3**
H: 6 1 W: 11 11 b.Coventry 24-11-00
From Leicester C.

2018–19	Barnsley	0	0		
2019–20	Barnsley	0	0		
2020–21	Barnsley	3	0		
2021–22	Barnsley	25	0		
2022–23	Barnsley	0	0	**28**	**0**
2022–23	*Burton Alb*	18	0		
2023–24	Burton Alb	28	0		
2024–25	Burton Alb	0	0	**46**	**0**
2024–25	*Harrogate T*	40	3	**40**	**3**

NEWALL, Jack (F) **1 0**
b. 15-3-07

2024–25	Burton Alb	1	0	**1**	**0**

NIEMcZYK, Jakub (M) **0 0**
H: 5 10 W: 11 11 b.Zielona Gora 22-1-04

2020–21	Burton Alb	0	0		
2022–23	Burton Alb	0	0		
2023–24	Burton Alb	0	0		
2024–25	Burton Alb	0	0		

OAKES, Toby (D) **0 0**
H: 6 0 W: 12 00 b. 1-1-06

2022–23	Burton Alb	0	0		
2023–24	Burton Alb	0	0		
2024–25	Burton Alb	0	0		

ORSI-DADOMO, Danilo (F) **124 31**
H: 6 2 W: 11 07 b.Camden 19-4-96
From Cockfosters, East Thurrock U, Hungerford T, Hampton & Richmond Bor, Maidenhead U.

2021–22	Harrogate T	10	1	**10**	**1**
2022–23	Grimsby T	24	2	**24**	**2**
2023–24	Crawley T	45	19	**45**	**19**
2024–25	Burton Alb	27	6	**27**	**6**
2024–25	*Milton Keynes D*	18	3	**18**	**3**

SCOTT, Dylan (F) **3 0**
b. 16-5-06

2022–23	Burton Alb	0	0		
2023–24	Burton Alb	3	0		
2024–25	Burton Alb	0	0	**3**	**0**

SRAHA, Jason (D) **35 1**
H: 6 2 W: 11 03 b.Lambeth 19-11-02
From Chelsea, Arsenal.

2021–22	Barnsley	2	0		
2022–23	Barnsley	0	0	**2**	**0**
2023–24	Shrewsbury T	17	1	**17**	**1**
2024–25	Burton Alb	16	0	**16**	**0**

STRETTON, Jack (F) **52 5**
H: 6 0 W: 11 09 b.Newell 6-9-01
Internationals: Scotland U19.
From Nottingham F.

2020–21	Derby Co	4	0		
2021–22	Derby Co	9	1		
2022–23	Derby Co	0	0	**13**	**1**
2022–23	*Carlisle U*	18	2	**18**	**2**
2022–23	Stockport Co	16	2		
2023–24	Stockport Co	0	0		
2024–25	Stockport Co	2	0	**18**	**2**
2024–25	Burton Alb	3	0	**3**	**0**

SWEENEY, Ryan (D) **306 19**
H: 6 4 W: 13 10 b.Kingston upon Thames 15-4-97
Internationals: Republic of Ireland U19, U21.

2014–15	AFC Wimbledon	3	0		
2015–16	AFC Wimbledon	10	0	**13**	**0**
2016–17	Stoke C	0	0		
2016–17	*Bristol R*	16	0		
2017–18	Stoke C	0	0		
2017–18	*Bristol R*	23	3	**39**	**3**
2018–19	Stoke C	0	0		
2018–19	*Mansfield T*	38	1		
2019–20	Mansfield T	33	1		
2020–21	Mansfield T	36	3	**107**	**5**
2021–22	Dundee	35	3		
2022–23	Dundee	32	5	**67**	**8**
2023–24	Burton Alb	38	1		
2024–25	Burton Alb	42	2	**80**	**3**

TAMEN, William (D) **1 0**
b. 3-9-05

2022–23	Burton Alb	0	0		
2023–24	Burton Alb	1	0		
2024–25	Burton Alb	0	0	**1**	**0**

TARONI, Josh (D) **2 0**
b. 1-3-07

2024–25	Burton Alb	2	0	**2**	**0**

VANCOOTEN, Terence (D) **206 3**
H: 6 1 W: 12 04 b.Kingston upon Thames 29-12-97
Internationals: Guyana Full caps.
From Staines T.

2016–17	Reading	0	0		
2017–18	Stevenage	22	0		
2018–19	Stevenage	12	0		
2019–20	Stevenage	16	0		
2020–21	Stevenage	29	0		
2021–22	Stevenage	38	0		
2022–23	Stevenage	27	0		
2023–24	Stevenage	32	2	**176**	**2**
2024–25	Burton Alb	30	1	**30**	**1**

WAKELIN, Ronny (M) **0 0**
b. 16-6-06

2022–23	Burton Alb	0	0		
2023–24	Burton Alb	0	0		
2024–25	Burton Alb	0	0		

WATT, Elliot (M) **212 9**
H: 5 9 W: 11 05 b.Preston 11-3-00
Internationals: Scotland U17, U19, U21.
From Preston NE.

2018–19	Wolverhampton W	0	0		
2019–20	Wolverhampton W	0	0		
2019–20	*Carlisle U*	12	1	**12**	**1**
2020–21	Bradford C	46	3		
2021–22	Bradford C	41	2	**87**	**5**
2022–23	Salford C	44	0		
2023–24	Salford C	36	1	**80**	**1**
2024–25	Burton Alb	25	0	**25**	**0**
2024–25	*St Johnstone*	8	2	**8**	**2**

WEBSTER, Charlie (M) **45 6**
H: 5 9 W: 10 08 b.Kingston 31-1-04
Internationals: England U16, U17, U18, U19, U20.

2021–22	Chelsea	0	0		
2022–23	Chelsea	0	0		
2023–24	Chelsea	0	0		
2023–24	*Heerenveen*	13	1	**13**	**1**
2024–25	Burton Alb	32	5	**32**	**5**

WHITFIELD, Ben (M) **222 26**
H: 5 5 W: 9 11 b.Bingley 28-2-96

2013–14	Bournemouth	0	0		
2014–15	Bournemouth	0	0		
2015–16	Bournemouth	0	0		
2016–17	Bournemouth	0	0		
2016–17	*Yeovil T*	34	2	**34**	**2**

2017–18 Bournemouth	0	0		
2017–18 *Port Vale*	37	4		
2018–19 Port Vale	30	4	67	8
From Torquay U, Stockport Co.				
2022–23 Barrow	45	5		
2023–24 Barrow	36	8		
2024–25 Burton Alb	23	1	23	1
2024–25 *Barrow*	17	2	98	15

WILLIAMS, Dylan (D) 32 1
H: 5 10 W: 10 10 b.Telford 3-12-03

2020–21 Derby Co	0	0		
2021–22 Derby Co	6	0	6	0
2021–22 Chelsea	0	0		
2022–23 Chelsea	0	0		
2023–24 Chelsea	0	0		
2024–25 Chelsea	0	0		
2024–25 Burton Alb	26	1	26	1

Scholars
Bilton, Kye; Cleland, Lewis Oliver; Cook,
Spencer; Jones, Daniel Lee; Krubally
Sankareh, Sulyman; Lay, Matthew Junior;
Matthews, Daniel Jack; Mtenga, Cyprian
Oscar; Newall, Jack John; Scutt, Zachariah
Benjamin; Svarc, Kiarhys Kevin; Taroni,
Joshua John; Thistleton, Bodi James; Tootell,
Spencer Rodger; Williamson, Jamal; Willow,
Jack Anthony.

CAMBRIDGE U (20)

ANDREW, Danny (D) 404 22
H: 5 11 W: 11 07 b.Holbeach 23-12-90

2009–10 Peterborough U	2	0	2	0
2009–10 *Cheltenham T*	10	0		
2010–11 Cheltenham T	43	4		
2011–12 Cheltenham T	10	0		
2012–13 Cheltenham T	1	0	64	4
From Gloucester C, Macclesfield T.				
2014–15 Fleetwood T	7	0		
2015–16 Fleetwood T	9	0		
2016–17 Grimsby T	46	0	46	0
2017–18 Doncaster R	4	0		
2018–19 Doncaster R	46	4	50	4
2019–20 Fleetwood T	35	2		
2020–21 Fleetwood T	45	2		
2021–22 Fleetwood T	39	6		
2022–23 Fleetwood T	30	1	165	11
2023–24 Cambridge U	45	2		
2024–25 Cambridge U	32	1	77	3

BARTON, Daniel (M) 16 0
H: 6 0 W: 12 02 b. 28-1-05

2023–24 Cambridge U	0	0		
2024–25 Cambridge U	16	0	16	0

BENNETT, Liam (D) 135 2
H: 5 8 W: 12 04 b.Bury St Edmunds
30-11-01

2021–22 Cambridge U	5	0		
2022–23 Cambridge U	23	0		
2022–23 *Walsall*	20	1	20	1
2023–24 Cambridge U	46	0		
2024–25 Cambridge U	41	1	115	1

BRIGGS, Jasper (G) 0 0

2023–24 Cambridge U	0	0		
2024–25 Cambridge U	0	0		

BROPHY, James (M) 321 8
H: 5 10 W: 10 10 b.Brent 25-7-94
From Harrow Bor, Woodlands U,
Broadfields U.

2015–16 Swindon T	28	0		
2016–17 Swindon T	30	0		
2017–18 Swindon T	6	0	64	0
2018–19 Leyton Orient	0	0		
2019–20 Leyton Orient	34	2		
2020–21 Leyton Orient	44	2	78	4
2021–22 Cambridge U	43	1		
2022–23 Cambridge U	44	0		
2023–24 Cambridge U	46	0		
2024–25 Cambridge U	46	3	179	4

BULAKIO, Randy (D) 0 0

2024–25 Cambridge U	0	0		

CHADWICK, Louis (D) 0 0
H: 6 1 W: 12 04 b. 23-2-03

2020–21 Cambridge U	0	0		
2022–23 Cambridge U	0	0		
2023–24 Cambridge U	0	0		
2024–25 Cambridge U	0	0		

COUSINS, Jordan (D) 314 10
H: 5 10 W: 11 05 b.Greenwich 6-3-94
Internationals: England U16, U17, U18, U20.
Jamaica Full caps.

2011–12 Charlton Ath	0	0		
2012–13 Charlton Ath	0	0		
2013–14 Charlton Ath	42	2		
2014–15 Charlton Ath	44	3		
2015–16 Charlton Ath	39	2	125	7
2016–17 QPR	18	0		
2017–18 QPR	15	0		

2018–19 QPR	28	1	61	1
2019–20 Stoke C	20	0		
2020–21 Stoke C	19	0	39	0
2021–22 Wigan Ath	16	0		
2022–23 Wigan Ath	10	0	26	0
2023–24 Cambridge U	35	1		
2024–25 Cambridge U	28	1	63	2

CRACE, Dempsey (D) 0 0

2024–25 Cambridge U	0	0		

DIGBY, Paul (M) 296 5
H: 6 5 W: 11 00 b.Sheffield 2-2-95
Internationals: England U19, U20.

2011–12 Barnsley	4	0		
2012–13 Barnsley	0	0		
2013–14 Barnsley	5	0		
2014–15 Barnsley	11	0		
2015–16 Barnsley	1	0	21	0
2015–16 *Ipswich T*	4	0		
2016–17 Ipswich T	4	0	8	0
2016–17 Mansfield T	0	0		
2017–18 Mansfield T	15	0	15	0
2018–19 Forest Green R	37	1	37	1
2019–20 Stevenage	17	0	17	0
2021–22 Cambridge U	35	0		
2021–22 Cambridge U	44	1		
2022–23 Cambridge U	46	1		
2023–24 Cambridge U	42	1		
2024–25 Cambridge U	31	1	198	4

EWENS-FINDLAY, Ty (D) 0 0

2023–24 Cambridge U	0	0		
2024–25 Cambridge U	0	0		

GARDNER, Gary (M) 304 27
H: 6 1 W: 12 13 b.Solihull 29-6-92
Internationals: England U17, U19, U20, U21.

2009–10 Aston Villa	0	0		
2010–11 Aston Villa	0	0		
2011–12 Aston Villa	14	0		
2011–12 *Coventry C*	4	1	4	1
2012–13 Aston Villa	2	0		
2013–14 Aston Villa	0	0		
2013–14 *Sheffield Wed*	3	0	3	0
2014–15 Aston Villa	0	0		
2014–15 *Brighton & HA*	17	2	17	2
2014–15 Nottingham F	18	4		
2015–16 Aston Villa	0	0		
2015–16 *Nottingham F*	20	2	38	6
2016–17 Aston Villa	26	1		
2017–18 Aston Villa	0	0		
2017–18 *Barnsley*	29	2	29	2
2018–19 Aston Villa	0	0	42	1
2018–19 *Birmingham C*	40	2		
2019–20 Birmingham C	35	4		
2020–21 Birmingham C	37	2		
2021–22 Birmingham C	35	6		
2022–23 Birmingham C	8	0		
2023–24 Birmingham C	16	1	171	15
2024–25 Cambridge U	0	0		

GIBBONS, James (D) 190 4
H: 5 9 W: 9 11 b.Stoke-on-Trent 16-3-98

2016–17 Port Vale	0	0		
2017–18 Port Vale	30	0		
2018–19 Port Vale	15	0		
2019–20 Port Vale	32	1		
2020–21 Port Vale	11	0		
2021–22 Port Vale	23	2	111	3
2022–23 Bristol R	28	0		
2023–24 Bristol R	9	0	37	0
2023–24 *Cambridge U*	13	0		
2024–25 Cambridge U	29	1	42	1

HAUNSTRUP, Brandon (D) 84 0
H: 5 8 W: 11 11 b.Waterlooville 26-10-96

2015–16 Portsmouth	1	0		
2016–17 Portsmouth	0	0		
2017–18 Portsmouth	16	0		
2018–19 Portsmouth	5	0		
2019–20 Portsmouth	10	0	32	0
2020–21 Kilmarnock	27	0		
2021–22 Kilmarnock	17	0	44	0
2022–23 Cambridge U	5	0		
2023–24 Cambridge U	3	0		
2024–25 Cambridge U	0	0	8	0

HODDLE, George (M) 4 0
H: 5 8 W: 10 03 b.Bishop Stortford 27-9-05

2022–23 Cambridge U	0	0		
2023–24 Cambridge U	2	0		
2024–25 Cambridge U	2	0	4	0

HOLMES, Pete (M) 0 0

2024–25 Cambridge U	0	0		

JOBE, Mamadou (D) 5 0
H: 6 1 W: 12 02 b.Harlow 2-3-03

2021–22 Cambridge U	0	0		
2022–23 Cambridge U	0	0		
2023–24 Cambridge U	5	0		
2024–25 Cambridge U	0	0	5	0

KACHUNGA, Elias (F) 402 55
H: 5 9 W: 10 01 b.Cologne 22-4-92
Internationals: Germany U19, U21, DR
Congo Full caps.

2009–10 Borussia M'gladbach	0	0		
2010–11 Borussia M'gladbach	2	0		
2011–12 Borussia M'gladbach	0	0		
2011–12 Osnabruck	17	10	17	10
2012–13 Borussia M'gladbach	0	0	2	0
2012–13 Hertha Berlin	2	0	2	0
2012–13 Paderborn	13	3		
2013–14 Paderborn	33	6		
2014–15 Paderborn	32	6	78	15
2015–16 Ingolstadt 04	10	0		
2016–17 Ingolstadt 04	0	0	10	0
2016–17 Huddersfield T	42	12		
2017–18 Huddersfield T	19	1		
2018–19 Huddersfield T	20	0		
2019–20 Huddersfield T	36	3	117	16
2020–21 Sheffield Wed	27	0	27	0
2021–22 Bolton W	32	2		
2022–23 Bolton W	38	0	70	2
2023–24 Cambridge U	36	5		
2024–25 Cambridge U	43	7	79	12

KAIKAI, Sullay (F) 257 42
H: 6 0 W: 11 07 b.Southwark 26-8-95
Internationals: Sierra Leone Full caps.

2013–14 Crystal Palace	0	0		
2013–14 *Crawley T*	5	0	5	0
2014–15 Crystal Palace	0	0		
2014–15 *Cambridge U*	25	5		
2015–16 Crystal Palace	1	0		
2015–16 *Shrewsbury T*	26	12	26	12
2016–17 Brentford	18	3	18	3
2017–18 Crystal Palace	1	0		
2017–18 Crystal Palace	10	0		
2017–18 *Charlton Ath*	14	0	14	0
2018–19 Crystal Palace	0	0	3	0
2018–19 NAC Breda	6	0	6	0
2019–20 Blackpool	22	4		
2020–21 Blackpool	36	7		
2021–22 Blackpool	0	0	58	11
2021–22 Wycombe W	17	2		
2022–23 Wycombe W	7	0	24	2
2022–23 Milton Keynes D	14	2	14	2
2023–24 Cambridge U	39	3		
2024–25 Cambridge U	25	4	89	12

KAUNDA, Amaru (D) 1 0
H: 6 1 W: 11 07 b.London 27-11-05

2023–24 Cambridge U	0	0		
2024–25 Cambridge U	1	0	1	0

LAVERY, Shayne (F) 172 53
H: 6 0 W: 11 07 b.Aghagallon 8-12-98
Internationals: Northern Ireland U17, U19,
U21, Full caps.
From Glenavon.

2017–18 Everton	0	0		
2018–19 Everton	0	0		
2018–19 *Falkirk*	6	0	6	0
2019–20 Linfield	25	10		
2020–21 Linfield	31	23	56	33
2021–22 Blackpool	37	8		
2022–23 Blackpool	27	2		
2023–24 Blackpool	31	5	95	15
2024–25 Cambridge U	25	5	15	5

LOFT, Ryan (F) 200 24
H: 6 3 W: 11 07 b.Gravesend 14-9-97

2016–17 Tottenham H	0	0		
2016–17 *Stevenage*	9	0	9	0
2017–18 Tottenham H	0	0		
2017–18 *Exeter C*	1	0	1	0
2018–19 Leicester C	0	0		
2019–20 Leicester C	0	0		
2019–20 *Carlisle U*	26	4	26	4
2020–21 Scunthorpe U	41	8		
2021–22 Scunthorpe U	15	4	56	12
2021–22 Bristol R	13	1		
2022–23 Bristol R	34	4		
2023–24 Bristol R	3	0	50	5
2023–24 Port Vale	26	1	26	1
2024–25 Cambridge U	32	2	32	2

MALONE, Scott (D) 467 34
H: 6 2 W: 11 11 b.Rowley Regis 25-3-91
Internationals: England U19, U20.

2008–09 Wolverhampton W	0	0		
2008–09 *Ujpest*	7	1	7	1
2009–10 Wolverhampton W	0	0		
2009–10 *Southend C*	17	0	17	0
2010–11 Wolverhampton W	0	0		
2010–11 *Burton Alb*	22	1	22	1
2011–12 Wolverhampton W	0	0		
2011–12 *Bournemouth*	32	5	32	5
2012–13 Millwall	15	1		
2013–14 Millwall	33	3		
2014–15 Millwall	20	1		
2014–15 Cardiff C	13	0		
2015–16 Cardiff C	41	2	54	2
2016–17 Fulham	36	6	36	6
2017–18 Huddersfield T	22	0	22	0
2018–19 Derby Co	27	2		

2019–20	Derby Co	18	1	
2020–21	Derby Co	0	0	45 3
2020–21	*Millwall*	41	5	
2021–22	*Millwall*	39	2	
2022–23	*Millwall*	33	0	181 12
2023–24	Gillingham	41	4	41 4
2024–25	Crawley T	2	0	
2024–25	Cambridge U	8	0	8 0

MAROSI, Marko (G)   267   0
H: 6 3   W: 12 08   b.Michalovce 23-10-93
Internationals: Slovakia U21.
From Barnoldswick T.

2013–14	Wigan Ath	0	0	
2014–15	Doncaster R	3	0	
2015–16	Doncaster R	1	0	
2016–17	Doncaster R	25	0	
2017–18	Doncaster R	13	0	
2018–19	Doncaster R	36	0	78 0
2019–20	Coventry C	34	0	
2020–21	Coventry C	20	0	54 0
2021–22	Shrewsbury T	46	0	
2022–23	Shrewsbury T	44	0	
2023–24	Shrewsbury T	43	0	133 0
2024–25	Plymouth Arg	0	0	
2024–25	Cambridge U	2	0	2 0

McCONNELL, Glenn (M)   3   0
H: 5 10   W: 11 00   b.Salvador, Bahia. Brasil 26-4-05
Internationals: Republic of Ireland U18.

2021–22	Cambridge U	0	0	
2022–23	Cambridge U	0	0	
2023–24	Cambridge U	3	0	
2024–25	Cambridge U	0	0	3 0

MORRISON, Michael (D)   627   35
H: 6 0   W: 12 00   b.Bury St Edmunds 3-3-88
Internationals: England U19.
From Cambridge U.

2008–09	Leicester C	35	3	
2009–10	Leicester C	31	2	
2010–11	Leicester C	11	0	77 5
2010–11	Sheffield Wed	12	0	12 0
2011–12	Charlton Ath	45	4	
2012–13	Charlton Ath	44	1	
2013–14	Charlton Ath	45	1	
2014–15	Charlton Ath	2	0	136 6
2014–15	Birmingham C	21	0	
2015–16	Birmingham C	46	3	
2016–17	Birmingham C	31	3	
2017–18	Birmingham C	33	1	
2018–19	Birmingham C	43	7	174 14
2019–20	Reading	44	2	
2020–21	Reading	35	4	
2021–22	Reading	29	2	108 8
2022–23	Portsmouth	22	0	22 0
2022–23	Cambridge U	19	0	
2023–24	Cambridge U	38	1	
2024–25	Cambridge U	41	1	98 2

MUNDAY, George (D)   0   0
H: 6 4

2024–25	Cambridge U	0	0	

NJOKU, Brandon (M)   28   1
H: 5 11   W: 11 11   b.London 29-1-05

2023–24	Cambridge U	3	0	
2024–25	Cambridge U	25	1	28 1

OKEDINA, Jubril (D)   108   0
H: 6 0   W: 12 00   b.Woolwich 26-10-00
Internationals: Malawi full caps.

2020–21	Tottenham H	0	0	
2021–22	*Cambridge U*	14	0	
2021–22	Cambridge U	30	0	
2022–23	Cambridge U	25	0	
2023–24	Cambridge U	12	0	
2024–25	Cambridge U	27	0	108 0

RICHARDS, Taylor (M)   73   10
H: 5 11   W: 12 08   b.Hammersmith 4-12-00
Internationals: England U17, U20.

2018–19	Manchester C	0	0	
2019–20	Brighton & HA	0	0	
2020–21	Brighton & HA	0	0	
2020–21	*Doncaster R*	41	10	41 10
2021–22	Brighton & HA	2	0	
2021–22	*Birmingham C*	6	0	6 0
2022–23	Brighton & HA	0	0	2 0
2022–23	*QPR*	15	0	
2023–24	*QPR*	4	0	19 0
2024–25	Cambridge U	5	0	5 0

ROSSI, Zeno (D)   53   0
H: 6 4   W: 12 04   b.Streatham 28-10-00
From Brentford, Southampton.

2020–21	Bournemouth	0	0	
2020–21	*Kilmarnock*	14	0	14 0
2021–22	Bournemouth	4	0	4 0
2021–22	*Dundee*	3	0	3 0
2022–23	Cambridge U	6	0	
2023–24	Cambridge U	11	0	
2024–25	Cambridge U	15	0	32 0

SMITH, Korey (M)   490   8
H: 6 0   W: 12 04   b.Hatfield 31-1-91

2008–09	Norwich C	2	0	
2009–10	Norwich C	37	4	
2010–11	Norwich C	28	0	
2011–12	Norwich C	0	0	
2011–12	Barnsley	12	0	12 0
2012–13	Norwich C	0	0	67 4
2012–13	*Yeovil T*	17	0	17 0
2012–13	*Oldham Ath*	10	0	
2013–14	Oldham Ath	42	1	52 1
2014–15	Bristol C	44	0	
2015–16	Bristol C	36	0	
2016–17	Bristol C	23	0	
2017–18	Bristol C	45	1	
2018–19	Bristol C	5	0	
2019–20	Bristol C	22	0	
2020–21	Bristol C	0	0	175 1
2020–21	Swansea C	37	0	
2021–22	Swansea C	35	0	72 0
2022–23	Derby Co	40	0	
2023–24	Derby Co	32	1	72 1
2024–25	Cambridge U	8	0	8 0

STEPHENS, Jack (G)   137   0
H: 6 2   W: 12 02   b.Ealing 2-8-97
Internationals: England U18, U19, U20, U21.

2014–15	Oxford U	0	0	
2015–16	Oxford U	0	0	
2016–17	Oxford U	0	0	
2017–18	Oxford U	0	0	
2018–19	Oxford U	0	0	
2019–20	Oxford U	0	0	
2020–21	Oxford U	33	0	
2021–22	Oxford U	30	0	
2022–23	Oxford U	0	0	65 0
2022–23	*Port Vale*	27	0	27 0
2023–24	Cambridge U	33	0	
2024–25	Cambridge U	12	0	45 0

STEVENSON, Ben (M)   212   8
H: 5 10   W: 10 08   b.Leicester 23-3-97

2015–16	Coventry C	0	0	
2016–17	Coventry C	28	2	
2017–18	Coventry C	5	0	33 2
2017–18	Wolverhampton W	0	0	
2017–18	*Colchester U*	13	2	
2018–19	*Colchester U*	14	0	
2018–19	Colchester U	28	2	
2019–20	Colchester U	32	2	
2021–22	Colchester U	0	0	87 6
2021–22	Forest Green R	41	0	
2022–23	Forest Green R	29	0	70 0
2023–24	Portsmouth	4	0	
2024–25	Portsmouth	1	0	5 0
2024–25	Cambridge U	17	0	17 0

THOMAS, George (M)   163   10
H: 5 8   W: 12 00   b.Leicester 24-3-97
Internationals: Wales U17, U19, U20, U21, Full caps.

2013–14	Coventry C	1	0	
2014–15	Coventry C	6	0	
2015–16	Coventry C	7	0	
2015–16	*Yeovil T*	5	0	5 0
2016–17	Coventry C	28	5	42 5
2017–18	Leicester C	0	0	
2018–19	Leicester C	0	0	
2018–19	*Scunthorpe U*	37	3	37 3
2019–20	Leicester C	0	0	
2019–20	*ADO Den Haag*	2	0	2 0
2020–21	QPR	17	0	
2021–22	QPR	20	0	
2022–23	QPR	3	0	40 0
2022–23	*Cambridge U*	6	1	
2023–24	*Cambridge U*	31	1	
2024–25	Cambridge U	0	0	37 2

WATTS, Kelland (D)   144   3
H: 6 4   W: 11 11   b.Alnwick 3-11-99
Internationals: England U19.

2018–19	Newcastle U	0	0	
2019–20	*Stevenage*	16	0	16 0
2019–20	Newcastle U	1	0	
2019–20	*Mansfield T*	7	1	7 1
2020–21	Newcastle U	0	0	
2020–21	*Plymouth Arg*	44	2	44 2
2021–22	*Wigan Ath*	26	0	
2021–22	Newcastle U	0	0	
2022–23	*Peterborough U*	7	0	7 0
2023–24	*Wigan Ath*	0	0	1 0
2023–24	Wigan Ath	14	0	40 0
2024–25	Cambridge U	29	0	29 0

Scholars
Briggs, Jasper Jon; Bulakio, Randy Blessing Bakandesha; Costley, Jahkyah Sean; Crace, Dempsy; Dawson, Harry David; Earley, Blade Owen; Ewens-Findlay, Ty Joseph; Gray, Ryan William; Hipwell, Reece Owen; Holmes, Peter John; King, Lennon Gary; McKoy, Jahrel Jayden; Munday, George Alexander Norman; Okolie, Samuel Ebube Henrie; Sowden-Fletcher, Zak Nicholas Tasker; Tyler-Cowlin, Danny David.

CARDIFF C (21)

ALNWICK, Jak (G)   267   0
H: 6 2   W: 12 13   b.Hexham 17-6-93
Internationals: England U17, U18.

2010–11	Newcastle U	0	0	
2011–12	Newcastle U	0	0	
2012–13	Newcastle U	0	0	
2013–14	Newcastle U	0	0	
2014–15	Newcastle U	6	0	6 0
2014–15	*Bradford C*	1	0	1 0
2015–16	Port Vale	41	0	
2016–17	Port Vale	26	0	67 0
2016–17	Rangers	1	0	
2017–18	Rangers	5	0	
2018–19	Rangers	0	0	
2018–19	*Scunthorpe U*	41	0	41 0
2019–20	Rangers	0	0	6 0
2019–20	*Blackpool*	22	0	22 0
2020–21	St Mirren	34	0	
2021–22	St Mirren	33	0	67 0
2022–23	Cardiff C	4	0	
2023–24	Cardiff C	24	0	
2024–25	Cardiff C	29	0	57 0

ASHFORD, Cian (F)   33   3
H: 5 10   W: 11 05   b.Rhondda 24-9-04
Internationals: Wales U16, U18, U21.

2023–24	Cardiff C	5	1	
2024–25	Cardiff C	28	2	33 3

BAGAN, Joel (D)   86   3
H: 6 4   W: 12 00   b.Basingstoke 3-9-01
Internationals: Scotland U16. Republic of Ireland U21.
From Southampton.

2019–20	Cardiff C	0	0	
2020–21	Cardiff C	7	0	
2021–22	Cardiff C	26	3	
2022–23	Cardiff C	1	0	
2023–24	Cardiff C	0	0	
2023–24	*Zulte-Waregem*	21	0	21 0
2024–25	Cardiff C	31	0	65 3

BEECHER, Joshua (D)   12   0
b. 16-3-06
Internationals: Wales U16, U17, U19.

2023–24	Cardiff C	0	0	
2024–25	Cardiff C	0	0	
2024–25	*Barry Town U*	12	0	12 0

CHAMBERS, Calum (D)   222   9
H: 6 0   W: 10 05   b.Petersfield 20-1-95
Internationals: England U17, U19, U21, Full caps.

2011–12	Southampton	0	0	
2012–13	Southampton	0	0	
2013–14	Southampton	22	0	22 0
2014–15	Arsenal	23	1	
2015–16	Arsenal	12	0	
2016–17	Arsenal	1	1	
2016–17	*Middlesbrough*	24	1	24 1
2017–18	Arsenal	12	0	
2018–19	Arsenal	0	0	
2018–19	*Fulham*	31	2	31 2
2019–20	Arsenal	14	1	
2020–21	Arsenal	10	0	
2021–22	Arsenal	2	0	74 3
2022–23	Aston Villa	11	1	
2022–23	Aston Villa	14	0	
2023–24	Aston Villa	5	0	30 1
2024–25	Cardiff C	22	1	49 2

COLLINS, Jamilu (D)   249   5
H: 5 10   W: 10 12   b.Kaduna 5-8-94
Internationals: Nigeria full caps.

2013–14	*Rijeka*	0	0	
2013–14	*Pomorac*	29	0	29 0
2014–15	*Rijeka*	0	0	
2015–16	*Krka*	13	0	13 0
2015–16	*Sibenik*	14	0	
2016–17	*Rijeka*	0	0	
2016–17	*Istra 1961*	11	0	11 0
2016–17	*Sibenik*	12	2	26 2
2017–18	*Paderborn*	19	0	
2018–19	*Paderborn*	34	0	
2019–20	*Paderborn*	30	1	
2020–21	*Paderborn*	24	0	
2021–22	*Paderborn*	20	1	127 2
2022–23	Cardiff C	4	0	
2023–24	Cardiff C	36	1	
2024–25	Cardiff C	3	0	43 1

COLWILL, Joel (M)   42   6
H: 5 10   W: 10 08   b.Neath 27-10-04
Internationals: Wales U16, U18, U19, U21.

2022–23	Cardiff C	0	0	
2023–24	Cardiff C	2	0	
2024–25	Cardiff C	0	0	2 0
2024–25	*Cheltenham T*	22	6	22 6
2024–25	*Exeter C*	18	0	18 0

COLWILL, Rubin (M) **139** **7**
H: 6 0 W: 11 11 b.Neath 27-4-02
Internationals: Wales U17, U21, Full caps.

2020–21	Cardiff C	6	0		
2021–22	Cardiff C	34	5		
2022–23	Cardiff C	20	0		
2023–24	Cardiff C	36	1		
2024–25	Cardiff C	43	1	**139**	**7**

CONTE, Raheem (M) **3** **0**
b.London 11-11-02

2023–24	Cardiff C	3	0		
2024–25	Cardiff C	0	0	**3**	**0**

DALAND, Jesper (D) **160** **5**
H: 6 2 W: 11 03 b.Kristiansand 6-1-00

2020	Start	30	1	**30**	**1**
2021–22	Cercle Brugge	32	2		
2022–23	Cercle Brugge	37	1		
2023–24	Cercle Brugge	39	1		
2024–25	Cercle Brugge	2	0	**110**	**4**
2024–25	Cardiff C	20	0	**20**	**0**

DAVIES, Isaak (F) **79** **17**
H: 5 9 W: 10 03 b.Aberdare 25-9-01
Internationals: Wales U17, U19, U21.

2020–21	Cardiff C	0	0		
2021–22	Cardiff C	28	2		
2022–23	Cardiff C	10	1		
2023–24	Cardiff C	0	0		
2023–24	*Kortrijk*	32	12	**32**	**12**
2024–25	Cardiff C	9	2	**47**	**5**

EL GHAZI, Anwar (F) **265** **66**
H: 6 2 W: 12 00 b.Barendrecht 3-5-95
Internationals: Netherlands U17, U18, U21, Full caps.

2014–15	Ajax	31	9		
2015–16	Ajax	27	11		
2016–17	Ajax	12	0	**70**	**20**
2016–17	Lille	12	1		
2017–18	Lille	27	4	**39**	**5**
2018–19	*Aston Villa*	31	5		
2019–20	Aston Villa	34	4		
2020–21	Aston Villa	28	10		
2021–22	Aston Villa	9	1	**102**	**20**
2021–22	*Everton*	2	0	**2**	**0**
2022–23	PSV Eindhoven	23	8		
2023–24	PSV Eindhoven	1	10	**24**	**18**
2023–24	Mainz 05	3	0	**3**	**0**
2024–25	Cardiff C	25	3	**25**	**3**

ETETE, Kion (F) **96** **12**
H: 6 6 W: 14 02 b.Derby 28-11-01

2018–19	Notts Co	4	0	**4**	**0**
2019–20	Tottenham H	0	0		
2020–21	Tottenham H	0	0		
2021–22	Tottenham H	0	0		
2021–22	*Northampton T*	18	3	**18**	**3**
2021–22	*Cheltenham T*	13	3	**13**	**3**
2022–23	Cardiff C	28	3		
2023–24	Cardiff C	28	3		
2024–25	Cardiff C	0	0	**56**	**6**
2024–25	*Bolton W*	5	0	**5**	**0**

EVANS, Kieron (M) **44** **2**
H: 5 10 W: 10 10 b.Caerphilly 19-12-01
Internationals: Wales U17, U29, U20.

2020–21	Cardiff C	0	0		
2021–22	Cardiff C	5	0		
2021–22	*Linfield*	5	0	**5**	**0**
2022–23	Cardiff C	0	0		
2023–24	Cardiff C	0	0		
2024–25	Cardiff C	0	0	**5**	**0**
2024–25	*Newport Co*	34	2	**34**	**2**

FISH, William (D) **77** **4**
H: 6 1 W: 11 07 b.Manchester 17-2-03
Internationals: England U17, U18, U19.

2020–21	Manchester U	1	0		
2021–22	Manchester U	0	0		
2022–23	Manchester U	0	0		
2022–23	*Hibernian*	21	3		
2023–24	Manchester U	0	0	**1**	**0**
2023–24	*Hibernian*	34	1	**55**	**4**
2024–25	Cardiff C	21	0	**21**	**0**

GBADEHAN, Adeteye (M) **0** **0**
b. 13-11-03

2024–25	Cardiff C	0	0		

GILES, Luey (D) **2** **0**
H: 5 9 W: 11 05 b.Cardiff 4-8-06
Internationals: Wales U16, U17, U19.

2023–24	Cardiff C	2	0		
2024–25	Cardiff C	0	0	**2**	**0**

GOUTAS, Dimitrios (D) **344** **22**
H: 6 4 W: 12 11 b.Kavala 4-4-94
Internationals: Greece U18, U19, U20, U20, Full caps.

2012–13	Xanthi	22	2		
2013–14	Xanthi	31	3		
2014–15	Xanthi	23	2		
2015–16	Olympiacos	0	0		
2015–16	*Xanthi*	7	0	**83**	**7**
2016–17	Olympiacos	0	0		
2016–17	*Kortrijk*	26	0	**26**	**0**
2017–18	Olympiacos	0	0		
2017–18	*Sint-Truidense*	21	1	**21**	**1**
2018–19	Olympiacos	0	0		
2018–19	*Lech Poznan*	9	0	**9**	**0**
2019–20	Atromitos	30	1		
2020–21	Atromitos	32	3	**62**	**4**
2021–22	Sivasspor	32	5		
2022–23	Sivasspor	31	0	**63**	**5**
2023–24	Cardiff C	46	4		
2024–25	Cardiff C	34	1	**80**	**5**

HORVATH, Ethan (G) **173** **0**
H: 6 4 W: 12 06 b.Highlands Ranch, Colorado 9-6-95
Internationals: USA U18, U20, U23, Full caps.
From Real Colorado.

2013	Molde	0	0		
2014	Molde	0	0		
2015	Molde	17	0		
2016	Molde	22	0	**39**	**0**
2016–17	Club Brugge	4	0		
2017–18	Club Brugge	15	0		
2018–19	Club Brugge	28	0		
2019–20	Club Brugge	2	0		
2020–21	Club Brugge	2	0	**51**	**0**
2021–22	Nottingham F	6	0		
2022–23	Nottingham F	0	0		
2022–23	*Luton T*	44	0	**44**	**0**
2023–24	Nottingham F	0	0	**6**	**0**
2023–24	Cardiff C	16	0		
2024–25	Cardiff C	17	0	**33**	**0**

JEFFERIES, Isaac (F) **0** **0**
H: 5 7 b. 6-5-05
Internationals: Wales U18, U19.

2024–25	Cardiff C	0	0		

KANGA, Wilfried (F) **178** **38**
H: 6 2 b.Montreuil-sous-Bois 21-2-98
Internationals: France U20.

2016–17	Angers	0	0		
2016–17	*Creteil*	24	5	**24**	**5**
2017–18	Angers	9	0		
2018–19	Angers	18	2		
2019–20	Angers	4	0		
2020–21	Angers	2	0	**33**	**2**
2020–21	Kayserispor	14	2	**14**	**2**
2021–22	Young Boys	31	12		
2022–23	Young Boys	2	3	**33**	**15**
2022–23	Hertha Berlin	23	2		
2023–24	Hertha Berlin	0	0		
2023–24	*Standard Liege*	36	12	**36**	**12**
2024–25	Hertha Berlin	0	0	**23**	**2**

On loan from Hertha Berlin.

2024–25	Cardiff C	15	0	**15**	**0**

KING, Eli (M) **83** **2**
H: 6 2 W: 12 08 b. 23-12-02
Internationals: Wales U17, U21.

2021–22	Cardiff C	4	0		
2022–23	Cardiff C	1	0		
2022–23	*Crewe Alex*	15	0	**15**	**0**
2023–24	Cardiff C	0	0		
2023–24	*Morecambe*	20	1	**20**	**1**
2023–24	*Ross Co*	15	0	**15**	**0**
2024–25	Cardiff C	0	0	**5**	**0**
2024–25	*Stevenage*	28	1	**28**	**1**

KPAKIO, Ronan (D) **3** **0**
H: 5 10 W: 11 00 b. 25-5-07
Internationals: Wales U16, U17, U19.

2024–25	Cardiff C	3	0	**3**	**0**

LAWLOR, Dylan (D) **1** **0**
H: 6 2 b.Caerphilly 1-1-06
Internationals: Wales U16, U17, U19.

2023–24	Cardiff C	0	0		
2024–25	Cardiff C	1	0	**1**	**0**

MAFICO, Dakarai (D) **0** **0**
H: 6 0 b.Swansea 7-12-06
Internationals: Wales U16, U17, U19.

2023–24	Cardiff C	0	0		
2024–25	Cardiff C	0	0		

MANNSVERK, Sivert (M) **133** **10**
H: 6 1 W: 12 02 b.Ovre Ardal 8-5-02
Internationals: Norway U18, U21.

2019	Sogndal	16	1		
2020	Sogndal	28	4		
2021	Sogndal	7	1	**51**	**6**
2021	Molde	14	0		
2022	Molde	25	1		
2023	Molde	16	3	**55**	**4**
2023–24	Ajax	13	0		
2024–25	Ajax	0	0	**13**	**0**

On loan from Ajax.

2024–25	Cardiff C	14	0	**14**	**0**

MEITE, Yakou (M) **260** **50**
H: 6 0 W: 11 05 b.Paris 11-2-96
Internationals: Ivory Coast U17, U20, U23, Full caps.

2013–14	Paris Saint-Germain	0	0		
2014–15	Paris Saint-Germain	0	0		
2015–16	Paris Saint-Germain	1	0	**1**	**0**
2016–17	Reading	14	1		
2017–18	Reading	0	0		
2017–18	*Sochaux*	31	3	**31**	**3**
2018–19	Reading	37	12		
2019–20	Reading	40	13		
2020–21	Reading	25	12		
2021–22	Reading	13	0		
2022–23	Reading	27	4	**156**	**42**
2023–24	Cardiff C	38	2		
2024–25	Cardiff C	34	3	**72**	**5**

NG, Perry (D) **330** **16**
H: 5 11 W: 12 02 b.Liverpool 24-6-94

2014–15	Crewe Alex	0	0		
2015–16	Crewe Alex	6	0		
2016–17	Crewe Alex	16	0		
2017–18	Crewe Alex	38	4		
2018–19	Crewe Alex	44	0		
2019–20	Crewe Alex	36	2		
2020–21	Crewe Alex	15	1	**155**	**7**
2020–21	Cardiff C	19	0		
2021–22	Cardiff C	39	0		
2022–23	Cardiff C	43	2		
2023–24	Cardiff C	39	6		
2024–25	Cardiff C	35	1	**175**	**9**

NYAKUHWA, Tanatswa (F) **1** **0**
H: 5 9 b. 17-9-05
Internationals: Wales U17, U18, U19.

2024–25	Cardiff C	1	0	**1**	**0**

O'DOWDA, Callum (M) **339** **26**
H: 5 11 W: 11 11 b.Oxford 23-4-95
Internationals: Republic of Ireland U21, Full caps.

2012–13	Oxford U	0	0		
2013–14	Oxford U	10	0		
2014–15	Oxford U	39	4		
2015–16	Oxford U	38	8	**87**	**12**
2016–17	Bristol C	34	0		
2017–18	Bristol C	24	1		
2018–19	Bristol C	31	4		
2019–20	Bristol C	32	1		
2020–21	Bristol C	19	1		
2021–22	Bristol C	20	1	**160**	**8**
2022–23	Cardiff C	39	3		
2023–24	Cardiff C	11	1		
2024–25	Cardiff C	42	2	**92**	**6**

PEARCE, Luke (F) **11** **2**
H: 5 11 W: 11 11 b. 8-6-04
Internationals: Republic of Ireland U18, U19.

2019–20	Walsall	0	0		
2020–21	Southampton	0	0		
2021–22	Southampton	0	0		
2022–23	Southampton	0	0		
2024–25	Cardiff C	0	0		
2024–25	*Sligo R*	11	2	**11**	**2**

PERRETT, Troy (M) **0** **0**
H: 5 10 b.Cardiff 28-10-06
Internationals: Wales U17, U19.

2024–25	Cardiff C	0	0		

RALLS, Joe (M) **421** **35**
H: 5 10 W: 11 00 b.Aldershot 12-10-93
Internationals: England U19.
From Aldershot T, Farnborough.

2011–12	Cardiff C	10	1		
2012–13	Cardiff C	4	0		
2013–14	Cardiff C	0	0		
2013–14	*Yeovil T*	37	3	**37**	**3**
2014–15	Cardiff C	28	2		
2015–16	Cardiff C	43	1		
2016–17	Cardiff C	42	6		
2017–18	Cardiff C	37	7		
2018–19	Cardiff C	28	0		
2019–20	Cardiff C	27	7		
2020–21	Cardiff C	39	5		
2021–22	Cardiff C	29	1		
2022–23	Cardiff C	41	1		
2023–24	Cardiff C	35	1		
2024–25	Cardiff C	21	0	**384**	**32**

RAMSEY, Aaron (M) **393** **53**
H: 5 10 W: 12 00 b.Caerphilly 26-12-90
Internationals: Wales U17, U21, Full caps. Great Britain.

2006–07	Cardiff C	1	0		
2007–08	Cardiff C	15	1		
2008–09	Arsenal	9	0		
2009–10	Arsenal	18	3		
2010–11	Arsenal	7	1		
2010–11	*Nottingham F*	5	0	**5**	**0**
2010–11	*Cardiff C*	6	1		
2011–12	Arsenal	34	2		
2012–13	Arsenal	36	1		
2013–14	Arsenal	23	10		
2014–15	Arsenal	29	6		
2015–16	Arsenal	31	5		
2016–17	Arsenal	23	1		
2017–18	Arsenal	24	7		
2018–19	Arsenal	28	4	**262**	**40**
2019–20	Juventus	24	3		
2020–21	Juventus	22	2		
2021–22	Juventus	3	0	**49**	**5**

2021–22 *Rangers* 7 2 **7 2**
2022–23 Nice 27 1 **27 1**
2023–24 Cardiff C 13 3
2024–25 Cardiff C 8 0 **43 5**

REINDORF, Michael (M) 6 0
b. 10-5-05
2024–25 Cardiff C 2 0 **2 0**
2024–25 *Bristol R* 4 0 **4 0**

RINOMHOTA, Andy (M) 213 3
H: 5 9 W: 10 01 b.Leeds 21-4-97
Internationals: Zimbabwe Full caps.
From AFC Portchester.
2017–18 Reading 0 0
2018–19 Reading 26 1
2019–20 Reading 37 1
2020–21 Reading 42 1
2021–22 Reading 20 0 **125 3**
2022–23 Cardiff C 39 0
2023–24 Cardiff C 3 0
2023–24 *Rotherham U* 16 0 **16 0**
2024–25 Cardiff C 30 0 **72 0**

ROBERTSON, Alexander (M) 61 4
H: 6 0 W: 10 06 b.Dundee 17-4-03
Internationals: England U16, U17, U18. Australia full caps.
2020–21 Manchester C 0 0
2021–22 Manchester C 0 0
2021–22 *Ross Co* 3 0 **3 0**
2022–23 Manchester C 0 0
2023–24 Manchester C 0 0
2023–24 *Portsmouth* 23 1 **23 1**
2024–25 Cardiff C 35 3 **35 3**

ROBINSON, Callum (F) 345 69
H: 5 10 W: 11 11 b.Northampton 2-2-95
Internationals: England U16, U17, U19, U20. Republic of Ireland Full caps.
2013–14 Aston Villa 4 0
2014–15 Aston Villa 0 0
2014–15 *Preston NE* 25 4
2015–16 Aston Villa 0 0 **4 0**
2015–16 *Bristol C* 6 0 **6 0**
2015–16 *Preston NE* 14 2
2016–17 Preston NE 42 10
2017–18 Preston NE 41 7
2018–19 Preston NE 27 12 **149 35**
2019–20 Sheffield U 16 1 **16 1**
2019–20 *WBA* 16 3
2020–21 WBA 28 5
2021–22 WBA 43 7
2022–23 WBA 4 0 **91 15**
2022–23 Cardiff C 22 5
2023–24 Cardiff C 23 1
2024–25 Cardiff C 34 12 **79 18**

ROMEO, Mahlon (M) 282 3
H: 5 10 W: 11 07 b.Westminster 19-9-95
Internationals: Antigua and Barbuda Full caps.
2012–13 Gillingham 1 0
2013–14 Gillingham 0 0
2014–15 Gillingham 0 0 **1 0**
2015–16 Millwall 18 1
2016–17 Millwall 32 0
2017–18 Millwall 27 1
2018–19 Millwall 41 0
2019–20 Millwall 43 0
2020–21 Millwall 35 1
2021–22 Millwall 2 0 **198 3**
2021–22 *Portsmouth* 35 0 **35 0**
2022–23 Cardiff C 33 0
2023–24 Cardiff C 15 0
2024–25 Cardiff C 0 0 **48 0**

SALECH, Yousef (F) 117 42
H: 6 5 W: 14 07 b.Hellerup 17-1-02
Internationals: Denmark U21.
2020–21 HIK 25 7 **25 7**
2021–22 Brondby 2 0
2022–23 Brondby 4 0
2022–23 *HB Koge* 24 15 **24 15**
2023–24 Brondby 3 0 **9 0**
2023–24 *Beveren* 12 1 **12 1**
2024–25 Sirius 27 11 **27 11**
2024–25 Cardiff C 20 8 **20 8**

SIMIC, Roko (F) 107 31
H: 6 3 W: 11 09 b.Milano 10-9-03
Internationals: Croatia U16, U17, U21.
2020–21 Lokomotiva Zagreb 25 3 **25 3**
2021–22 Red Bull Salzburg 1 0
2021–22 *Liefering* 24 19 **24 19**
2022–23 Red Bull Salzburg 9 0
2022–23 *Zurich* 16 4 **16 4**
2023–24 Red Bull Salzburg 28 5 **38 5**
2024–25 Cardiff C 0 0
2024–25 *Kortrijk* 4 0 **4 0**

SIOPIS, Manolis (M) 324 1
H: 5 7 W: 10 12 b.Tychero 14-5-94
Internationals: Greece U17, U18, U19, U21, Full caps.
2013–14 Olympiacos 0 0
2013–14 *Platanias* 16 0 **16 0**
2014–15 Panionios 21 0
2015–16 Panionios 29 0
2016–17 Panionios 28 0
2017–18 Olympiacos 1 0 **1 0**
2017–18 *Panionios* 16 0 **94 0**
2018–19 Aris 25 1 **25 1**
2019–20 Alanyaspor 27 0
2020–21 Alanyaspor 35 0
2021–22 Alanyaspor 1 0 **63 0**
2021–22 Trabzonspor 32 0
2022–23 Trabzonspor 30 0 **62 0**
2023–24 Cardiff C 42 0
2024–25 Cardiff C 21 0 **63 0**
Transferred to Panathinaikos, January 2025.

TANNER, Ollie (F) 65 4
H: 6 1 W: 10 12 b.Bromley 13-5-02
From Bromley, Lewes.
2022–23 Cardiff C 0 0
2023–24 Cardiff C 36 2
2024–25 Cardiff C 29 2 **65 4**

TURNBULL, David (M) 175 42
H: 5 10 W: 11 07 b.Wishaw 7-10-99
Internationals: Scotland U16, U19, U20, U21, Full caps.
2016–17 Motherwell 0 0
2017–18 Motherwell 2 0
2018–19 Motherwell 30 15
2019–20 Motherwell 2 0
2020–21 Motherwell 5 1 **39 16**
2020–21 Celtic 31 8
2021–22 Celtic 25 6
2022–23 Celtic 28 4
2023–24 Celtic 16 7 **100 25**
2023–24 Cardiff C 17 0
2024–25 Cardiff C 19 1 **36 1**

TURNER, Matthew (G) 22 1
H: 6 4 W: 12 11 b.Pembrey 27-3-02
Internationals: USA Full caps.
2020–21 Haverfordwest Co 9 0 **9 0**
2021–22 Leeds U 0 0
2022–23 Cardiff C 0 0
2022–23 *Aberystwyth T* 13 1 **13 1**
2023–24 Cardiff C 0 0
2024–25 Cardiff C 0 0

TWOSE, Cody (M) 0 0
H: 5 8 b.Merthyr Tydfil 27-6-06
Internationals: Wales U17, U19.
2023–24 Cardiff C 0 0
2024–25 Cardiff C 0 0

WALCOTT, Malachi (D) 18 3
H: 6 2 b.Edmonton 11-3-02
Internationals: England U16, U17.
2019–20 Tottenham H 0 0
2020–21 Tottenham H 0 0
2020–21 *Dundee* 2 0 **2 0**
2021–22 Tottenham H 0 0
2022–23 Tottenham H 0 0
2023–24 Cardiff C 0 0
2023–24 *Dunfermline Ath* 15 3 **15 3**
2024–25 Cardiff C 1 0 **1 0**
Transferred to York C, December 2024.

WIGLEY, Morgan (F) 0 0
H: 5 11 W: 10 12 b. 10-9-04
Internationals: Wales U18, U19.
2022–23 Cardiff C 0 0
2023–24 Cardiff C 0 0
2024–25 Cardiff C 0 0

WILLOCK, Chris (M) 186 24
H: 5 10 W: 10 08 b.Waltham Forest 31-1-98
Internationals: England U16, U17, U18, U19, U20.
2015–16 Arsenal 0 0
2016–17 Arsenal 0 0
2017–18 Arsenal 0 0
2018–19 Arsenal 0 0
2019–20 Arsenal 0 0
2019–20 *WBA* 0 0
2019–20 *Huddersfield T* 14 2 **14 2**
2020–21 QPR 38 3
2021–22 QPR 35 7
2022–23 QPR 28 6
2023–24 QPR 39 4 **140 20**
2024–25 Cardiff C 32 2 **32 2**

WINTLE, Ryan (M) 314 14
H: 5 5 W: 10 01 b.Newcastle-under-Lyme 13-6-97
2015–16 Crewe Alex 3 0
2016–17 Crewe Alex 17 1
2017–18 Crewe Alex 18 2
2018–19 Crewe Alex 46 1
2019–20 Crewe Alex 37 3
2020–21 Crewe Alex 43 2 **164 9**
2021–22 *Blackpool* 18 0 **18 0**
2021–22 Cardiff C 23 0
2022–23 Cardiff C 45 2
2023–24 Cardiff C 42 2
2024–25 Cardiff C 0 0 **110 4**
2024–25 *Millwall* 22 1 **22 1**

Players retained or with offer of contract
Armstrong, Luke; Dennis, Jacob Rees; George, Trey Ellis; Griffiths, Ewan Henri; Kaba, Sekou; Spiers, William McKenzie; Tsunoda, Ryotaro.

Scholars
Allmark, Hayden Ian Slocombe; Barton, Mannie; Davies, Jake Thomas; Debono, Alyas Tony Kyle; Edwards, Joseff Michael; Foggarty, Corey; Higgs, Daniel Evan; Hilaire-Clarke, Riley; Hobson, Jacob James Theill; Jones, Samual Lloyd; Okoli-Parfitt, T-Jay Chibuzo; Ola, Daniel Olutayo Olatimeyin; Phelan, Leeyon Jayden; Rees, Osian Michael Carmody; Reynolds, Oliver Lloyd; Talbot, Lennon Paul; Thomas, Jac Edward; Walsh, Oliver Jack; Watts, Harry Oscar; Williams, Noah Elliot.

CARLISLE U (22)

ALLEN, Jake (M) 0 0
b. 7-11-06
2024–25 Carlisle U 0 0

ARMSTRONG, Luke (F) 205 43
H: 6 1 W: 11 00 b.Durham 2-7-96
Internationals: Wales U17.
2015–16 Cowdenbeath 6 0 **6 0**
From Blyth Spartans.
2017–18 Middlesbrough 0 0
2018–19 Middlesbrough 0 0
2018–19 *Accrington S* 16 3 **16 3**
2019–20 Salford C 21 1
2020–21 Salford C 4 0 **25 1**
2021–22 Harrogate T 45 12
2022–23 Harrogate T 46 16
2023–24 Harrogate T 12 1 **103 29**
2023–24 Carlisle U 21 3
2024–25 Carlisle U 20 3 **41 6**
2024–25 *Motherwell* 14 4 **14 4**

ATKINSON, Hayden (D) 0 0
2024–25 Carlisle U 0 0

BARCLAY, Ben (D) 105 4
H: 6 2 W: 12 04 b.Manchester 7-10-96
2018–19 Brighton & HA 0 0
2018–19 *Notts Co* 13 1 **13 1**
2019–20 Accrington S 8 0
2020–21 Accrington S 26 1 **34 1**
From Stockport Co.
2022–23 Stockport Co 0 0
2022–23 *Carlisle U* 13 1
2023–24 Carlisle U 23 0
2024–25 Carlisle U 22 1 **58 2**

BREEZE, Gabriel (G) 36 0
H: 6 2 W: 12 06 b.Carlisle 30-12-03
2020–21 Carlisle U 0 0
2021–22 Carlisle U 0 0
2022–23 Carlisle U 0 0
2023–24 Carlisle U 4 0
2024–25 Carlisle U 32 0 **36 0**

BUREY, Tyler (M) 84 6
H: 6 2 b.Hillingdon 9-1-01
2018–19 AFC Wimbledon 3 0 **3 0**
2019–20 Millwall 1 0
2020–21 Millwall 13 0
2021–22 Millwall 15 2
2021–22 *Hartlepool U* 7 3 **7 3**
2022–23 Millwall 24 1 **53 3**
2023–24 OB 6 0 **6 0**
2023–24 *Oxford U* 5 0 **5 0**
2024–25 Carlisle U 10 0 **10 0**
Transferred to Igman Konjic, February 2025.

CHARTERS, Taylor (M) 73 2
H: 6 1 W: 11 11 b.Whitehaven 2-10-01
2019–20 Carlisle U 7 0
2020–21 Carlisle U 9 0
2021–22 Carlisle U 9 0
2022–23 Carlisle U 11 1
2023–24 Carlisle U 19 1
2024–25 Carlisle U 6 0 **61 2**
2024–25 *Queen of the South* 12 0 **12 0**

DAVIES, Archie (M) 145 1
H: 6 1 W: 12 06 b.Hastings 7-10-98
2019–20 Brighton & HA 0 0
2020–21 Brighton & HA 0 0
2020–21 Crawley T 34 0
2021–22 Crawley T 33 0 **67 0**
From Aldershot T.
2023 Dundalk 35 0
2024 Dundalk 22 0 **57 0**
2024–25 Carlisle U 21 1 **21 1**

DENNIS, Matthew (M) 58 11
H: 5 10 W: 11 09 b.London 15-4-02
Internationals: England U16.
From Arsenal.
2020–21 Norwich C 0 0
2021–22 Norwich C 0 0

2022–23	Milton Keynes D	18	1	
2022–23	Sutton U	10	0	**10** **0**
2023–24	Milton Keynes D	14	4	
2024–25	Milton Keynes D	2	0	**34** **5**
2024–25	Carlisle U	14	6	**14** **6**

DUDIK, Anton (F) 　　**3** **0**
H: 6 2　W: 12 11　b.Lutsk 10-1-05
| 2023–24 | Carlisle U | 2 | 0 | |
| 2024–25 | Carlisle U | 1 | 0 | **3** **0** |

DUMMETT, Paul (D) 　　**232** **5**
H: 5 10　W: 10 03　b.Newcastle upon Tyne 26-9-91
Internationals: Wales U21, Full caps.
2010–11	Newcastle U	0	0	
2011–12	Newcastle U	0	0	
2012–13	Newcastle U	0	0	
2012–13	*St Mirren*	30	2	**30** **2**
2013–14	Newcastle U	18	1	
2014–15	Newcastle U	25	0	
2015–16	Newcastle U	23	1	
2016–17	Newcastle U	45	0	
2017–18	Newcastle U	20	0	
2018–19	Newcastle U	26	0	
2019–20	Newcastle U	16	0	
2020–21	Newcastle U	15	1	
2021–22	Newcastle U	3	0	
2022–23	Newcastle U	0	0	
2023–24	Newcastle U	5	0	**196** **6**
2024–25	*Wigan Ath*	3	0	**3** **0**
2024–25	Carlisle U	3	0	**3** **0**

ELLIS, Jack (D) 　　**51** **1**
H: 6 0　W: 12 02　b.Kendal 24-10-03
2021–22	Carlisle U	2	0	
2022–23	Carlisle U	12	0	
2023–24	Carlisle U	16	0	
2024–25	Carlisle U	21	1	**51** **1**

EMBLETON, Elliot (M) 　　**154** **14**
H: 5 8　W: 10 01　b.Durham 2-4-99
Internationals: England U17, U18, U19, U20.
2016–17	Sunderland	0	0	
2017–18	Sunderland	2	0	
2018–19	Sunderland	0	0	
2018–19	*Grimsby T*	27	3	**27** **3**
2019–20	Sunderland	3	0	
2020–21	Sunderland	9	0	
2020–21	*Blackpool*	18	1	
2021–22	*Blackpool*	38	8	
2021–22	*Blackpool*	0	0	
2022–23	Sunderland	23	2	
2023–24	Sunderland	0	0	
2023–24	*Derby Co*	1	0	**1** **0**
2024–25	Sunderland	0	0	**75** **10**
2024–25	*Blackpool*	15	0	**33** **1**
2024–25	Carlisle U	18	0	**18** **0**

FITZPATRICK, Aran (D) 　　**1** **0**
H: 5 10　W: 11 09　b.Whitehaven 7-2-06
| 2023–24 | Carlisle U | 1 | 0 | |
| 2024–25 | Carlisle U | 0 | 0 | **1** **0** |

GUY, Callum (M) 　　**219** **3**
H: 5 10　W: 10 01　b.Nottingham 25-11-96
2015–16	Derby Co	0	0	
2016–17	Derby Co	0	0	
2016–17	*Port Vale*	11	0	**11** **0**
2017–18	Derby Co	0	0	
2017–18	*Bradford C*	17	0	**17** **0**
2018–19	Blackpool	15	0	
2019–20	Blackpool	15	0	**30** **0**
2019–20	Carlisle U	3	0	
2020–21	Carlisle U	43	0	
2021–22	Carlisle U	34	0	
2022–23	Carlisle U	45	3	
2023–24	Carlisle U	16	0	
2024–25	Carlisle U	20	0	**161** **3**

HARPER, Cameron (D) 　　**157** **9**
H: 6 0　W: 11 03　b.Inverness 10-11-01
Internationals: Scotland U21.
2017–18	Inverness CT	1	0	
2018–19	Inverness CT	0	0	
2019–20	Inverness CT	3	0	
2019–20	*Elgin C*	4	0	**4** **0**
2020–21	Inverness CT	23	0	
2021–22	Inverness CT	24	1	
2022–23	Inverness CT	31	5	
2023–24	Inverness CT	36	3	**117** **9**
2024–25	Carlisle U	36	0	**36** **0**

HARRIS, Kedeem (M) 　　**284** **20**
H: 5 9　W: 10 08　b.Westminster 8-6-93
2009–10	Wycombe W	2	0	
2010–11	Wycombe W	0	0	
2011–12	Wycombe W	17	0	**19** **0**
2011–12	Cardiff C	0	0	
2012–13	Cardiff C	0	0	
2013–14	Cardiff C	0	0	
2013–14	*Brentford*	10	1	**10** **1**
2014–15	Cardiff C	14	1	
2015–16	Cardiff C	3	0	
2015–16	*Barnsley*	11	0	**11** **0**
2016–17	Cardiff C	37	4	
2017–18	Cardiff C	3	0	
2018–19	Cardiff C	13	1	**70** **6**
2019–20	Sheffield Wed	43	3	
2020–21	Sheffield Wed	38	0	**81** **3**
2021–22	Metalist Kharkiv	11	1	**11** **1**
2021–22	Tuzlaspor	6	3	**6** **3**
2022–23	Samsunspor	24	2	**24** **2**
2023–24	Sanliurfaspor	11	1	**11** **1**
2023–24	Bandirmaspor	11	0	**11** **0**
2024–25	Carlisle U	30	3	**30** **3**

HAYDEN, Aaron (D) 　　**106** **11**
H: 6 1　W: 12 06　b.Croydon 16-1-97
Internationals: England C.
From Chelsea.
2015–16	Wolverhampton W	0	0	
2015–16	*Newport Co*	5	0	**5** **0**
2016–17	Wolverhampton W	0	0	
2017–18	Wolverhampton W	0	0	
2018–19	Wolverhampton W	0	0	
2019–20	Carlisle U	18	2	
2020–21	Carlisle U	44	5	

From Wrexham.
| 2023–24 | Wrexham | 15 | 1 | **15** **1** |
| 2024–25 | Carlisle U | 24 | 3 | **86** **10** |

HETHERINGTON, Sam (M)
b. 6-2-06
| 2024–25 | Carlisle U | 0 | 0 | |

HOPPER, Dan (M) 　　**0** **0**
H: 6 4　b. 17-5-07
| 2024–25 | Carlisle U | 0 | 0 | |

JONES, Jordan (M) 　　**229** **18**
H: 5 9　W: 9 08　b.Redcar 24-10-94
Internationals: Northern Ireland U19, Full caps.
2012–13	Middlesbrough	0	0	
2014–15	Middlesbrough	0	0	
2014–15	Middlesbrough	0	0	
2014–15	*Hartlepool U*	11	0	**11** **0**
2015–16	Middlesbrough	0	0	
2015–16	*Cambridge U*	1	0	**1** **0**
2016–17	Kilmarnock	37	3	
2017–18	Kilmarnock	32	4	
2018–19	Kilmarnock	28	4	
2019–20	Rangers	7	0	
2020–21	Rangers	3	1	**10** **1**
2020–21	*Sunderland*	19	3	**19** **3**
2021–22	Wigan Ath	9	0	
2021–22	*St Mirren*	11	0	**11** **0**
2022–23	Wigan Ath	0	0	
2022–23	*Kilmarnock*	22	0	**119** **11**
2023–24	Wigan Ath	26	3	
2024–25	Wigan Ath	2	0	**37** **3**
2024–25	Carlisle U	21	0	**21** **0**

KELLY, Georgie (F) 　　**155** **43**
H: 6 2　W: 12 02　b.Donegal 12-11-96
| 2015 | *Derry C* | 3 | 0 | **3** **0** |

From University College Dublin.
2018	Dundalk	2	0	
2019	Dundalk	27	8	
2020	Dundalk	12	0	**36** **8**
2020	*St Patrick's Ath*	12	3	**12** **3**
2021	Bohemians	31	21	**31** **21**
2021–22	Rotherham U	1	1	
2022–23	Rotherham U	29	4	
2023–24	Rotherham U	18	1	**48** **6**
2023–24	Carlisle U	7	0	
2024–25	Carlisle U	18	5	**25** **5**

LAVELLE, Sam (D) 　　**256** **13**
H: 6 2　W: 12 00　b.Blackpool 3-10-96
Internationals: Scotland U18, U19.
2015–16	Blackburn R	1	0	
2016–17	Bolton W	0	0	
2017–18	Morecambe	27	1	
2018–19	Morecambe	31	1	
2019–20	Morecambe	31	1	
2020–21	Morecambe	45	1	
2021–22	Morecambe	5	0	**139** **4**
2021–22	Charlton Ath	19	2	
2022–23	Charlton Ath	13	0	**32** **2**
2022–23	*Burton Alb*	2	0	**2** **0**
2023–24	Carlisle U	46	3	
2024–25	Carlisle U	37	4	**83** **7**

LEWIS, Harry (G) 　　**136** **0**
H: 6 3　W: 12 02　b.Shrewsbury 20-12-97
Internationals: England U18.
2015–16	Shrewsbury T	0	0	
2016–17	Shrewsbury T	0	0	
2016–17	Southampton	0	0	
2017–18	Southampton	0	0	
2017–18	*Dundee U*	30	0	**30** **0**
2018–19	Southampton	0	0	
2019–20	Southampton	0	0	
2020–21	Southampton	0	0	
2021–22	Southampton	0	0	
2022–23	Bradford C	46	0	
2023–24	Bradford C	26	0	**72** **0**
2023–24	Carlisle U	20	0	
2024–25	Carlisle U	14	0	**34** **0**

LOWES, Jonah (D) 　　**0** **0**
| 2024–25 | Carlisle U | 0 | 0 | |

MASON, Seb (M) 　　**0** **0**
| 2024–25 | Carlisle U | 0 | 0 | |

McGEOUCH, Dylan (M) 　　**211** **2**
H: 5 10　W: 10 12　b.Glasgow 15-1-93
Internationals: Scotland U16, U17, U19, U21, Full caps.
2011–12	Celtic	6	1	
2012–13	Celtic	12	1	
2013–14	Celtic	1	0	**19** **2**
2013–14	*Coventry C*	8	0	**8** **0**
2014–15	Hibernian	2	0	
2015–16	Hibernian	19	0	
2016–17	Hibernian	18	0	
2017–18	Hibernian	35	0	**74** **0**
2018–19	Sunderland	22	0	
2019–20	Sunderland	8	0	**30** **0**
2019–20	Aberdeen	7	0	
2020–21	Aberdeen	15	0	
2021–22	Aberdeen	14	0	
2022–23	Aberdeen	0	0	**36** **0**
2022–23	*Forest Green R*	24	0	**24** **0**
2023–24	Carlisle U	14	0	
2024–25	Carlisle U	6	0	**20** **0**

O'BRIEN, Josh (D) 　　**0** **0**
H: 6 2　W: 13 01　b. 24-4-06
| 2023–24 | Carlisle U | 0 | 0 | |
| 2024–25 | Carlisle U | 0 | 0 | |

O'DONOGHUE, Freddie (M) 　　**2** **0**
b. 3-2-07
| 2024–25 | Carlisle U | 2 | 0 | **2** **0** |

PARK, Romeo (F) 　　**0** **0**
H: 5 10　b.Whitehaven 16-9-05
| 2023–24 | Carlisle U | 0 | 0 | |
| 2024–25 | Carlisle U | 0 | 0 | |

PATCHING, William (M) 　　**117** **20**
H: 6 1　W: 11 00　b.Manchester 18-10-98
Internationals: England U16, U17, U18.
From Manchester C.
2018–19	Notts Co	6	0	**6** **0**
2020	Dundalk	7	0	
2021	Dundalk	16	0	**23** **0**
2021	*Derry C*	16	6	
2022	*Derry C*	29	7	
2024	*Derry C*	33	7	**78** **20**
2024–25	Carlisle U	10	0	**10** **0**

RANDALL, Thomas (G) 　　**0** **0**
b. 2-2-07
| 2024–25 | Carlisle U | 0 | 0 | |

ROBINSON, Jack (D) 　　**34** **0**
H: 6 3　W: 12 06　b.Middlesbrough 21-6-01
2020–21	Middlesbrough	1	0	
2021–22	Middlesbrough	0	0	
2022–23	Middlesbrough	0	0	**1** **0**
2022–23	*Carlisle U*	7	0	
2023–24	Carlisle U	23	0	
2024–25	Carlisle U	3	0	**33** **0**
Transferred to Hartlepool U, February 2025.

ROBSON, Ethan (M) 　　**144** **7**
H: 5 11　W: 10 10　b.Durham 25-10-96
2016–17	Sunderland	0	0	
2017–18	Sunderland	9	0	
2018–19	Sunderland	0	0	
2018–19	*Dundee*	13	2	**13** **2**
2019–20	Sunderland	0	0	**9** **0**
2019–20	*Grimsby T*	16	3	**16** **3**
2020–21	Blackpool	28	0	
2021–22	Blackpool	2	0	**30** **0**
2021–22	*Milton Keynes D*	18	1	
2022–23	Milton Keynes D	18	1	
2023–24	Milton Keynes D	33	0	**69** **2**
2024–25	Carlisle U	7	0	**7** **0**

SCOTT, Cedwyn (F) 　　**51** **4**
H: 5 10　W: 11 11　b.Hexham 6-12-97
2017–18	Dundee	3	0	
2018–19	Dundee	0	0	**3** **0**
2018–19	*Berwick Rangers*	7	3	**7** **3**
2018–19	*Forfar Ath*	4	0	**4** **0**
From Dunston UTS, Hebburn T.
2020–21	Carlisle U	7	0	
From Gateshead, Notts Co.
2023–24	Notts Co	9	0	
2024–25	Notts Co	10	0	**19** **0**
2024–25	Carlisle U	11	1	**18** **1**

SIMONS, Scott (G) 　　**0** **0**
H: 6 0　W: 12 06　b.Whitehaven 26-10-03
2021–22	Carlisle U	0	0	
2022–23	Carlisle U	0	0	
2023–24	Carlisle U	0	0	
2024–25	Carlisle U	0	0	

SMITH, Jude (G) 　　**25** **0**
H: 6 2　W: 12 06　b.Coatbridge 29-5-03
2021–22	East Fife	25	0	**25** **0**
2022–23	Newcastle U	0	0	
2023–24	Newcastle U	0	0	
2024–25	Carlisle U	0	0	

THOMAS, Terell (D) **178 3**
H: 6 0 W: 11 03 b.Rainham 18-10-97
Internationals: Saint Lucia Full caps.
From Arsenal.

2014–15	Charlton Ath	0	0		
2015–16	Charlton Ath	0	0		
2016–17	Charlton Ath	0	0		
2017–18	Wigan Ath	3	0	**3**	**0**
2018–19	AFC Wimbledon	23	0		
2019–20	AFC Wimbledon	31	1		
2020–21	AFC Wimbledon	19	0		
2021–22	AFC Wimbledon	0	0	**73**	**1**
2021–22	Crewe Alex	13	0	**13**	**0**
2021–22	Reading	2	0	**2**	**0**
2022–23	Charlton Ath	15	1		
2023–24	Charlton Ath	40	0	**55**	**1**
2024–25	Carlisle U	32	1	**32**	**1**

VELA, Joshua (M) **363 21**
H: 5 11 W: 11 07 b.Salford 14-12-93

2010–11	Bolton W	0	0		
2011–12	Bolton W	3	0		
2012–13	Bolton W	4	0		
2013–14	Bolton W	0	0		
2013–14	*Notts Co*	7	0	**7**	**0**
2014–15	Bolton W	29	0		
2015–16	Bolton W	31	2		
2016–17	Bolton W	46	9		
2017–18	Bolton W	30	1		
2018–19	Bolton W	17	0	**160**	**12**
2019–20	Hibernian	9	0	**9**	**0**
2019–20	Shrewsbury T	4	0		
2020–21	Shrewsbury T	44	3		
2021–22	Shrewsbury T	36	2	**84**	**5**
2022–23	Fleetwood T	44	1		
2023–24	Fleetwood T	23	1	**67**	**2**
2023–24	Carlisle U	7	2		
2024–25	Carlisle U	29	0	**36**	**2**

WEARNE, Stephen (M) **54 6**
H: 5 11 W: 12 00 b.Stockton-on-Tees 16-12-00
From Newcastle U.

2020–21	Middlesbrough	0	0		
2020–21	Sunderland	0	0		
2021–22	Sunderland	0	0		
2022–23	Grimsby T	8	0	**8**	**0**
2023–24	Milton Keynes D	17	4		
2024–25	Milton Keynes D	11	0	**28**	**4**
2024–25	Carlisle U	18	2	**18**	**2**

WHELAN, Callum (M) **97 3**
H: 5 9 W: 11 03 b.Barnsley 24-9-98

2018–19	Manchester U	0	0		
2018–19	*Port Vale*	0	0		
2019–20	Watford	0	0		
2020–21	Oldham Ath	31	0		
2021–22	Oldham Ath	43	1	**74**	**1**

From Solihull Moors, Gateshead.

2024–25	Carlisle U	23	2	**23**	**2**

WILLIAMS, Ben (D) **112 3**
H: 5 10 W: 11 00 b.Preston 31-3-99
Internationals: Wales U17, U19, U21.
From Blackburn R.

2017–18	Barnsley	0	0		
2018–19	Barnsley	11	0		
2019–20	Barnsley	20	0		
2020–21	Barnsley	0	0		
2021–22	Barnsley	5	0	**36**	**0**
2021–22	Cheltenham T	11	1		
2022–23	Cheltenham T	30	1		
2023–24	Cheltenham T	27	1	**68**	**3**
2024–25	Carlisle U	8	0	**8**	**0**

WILLIAMS, Josh (M) **18 0**
H: 6 0 W: 11 07 b.Wolverhampton 24-11-02

2021–22	Birmingham C	0	0		
2022–23	Birmingham C	7	0		
2023–24	Birmingham C	0	0		
2023–24	*Cheltenham T*	5	0	**5**	**0**
2024–25	Birmingham C	0	0	**7**	**0**
2024–25	Carlisle U	6	0	**6**	**0**

WYKE, Charlie (F) **358 113**
H: 5 11 W: 11 09 b.Middlesbrough 6-12-92

2011–12	Middlesbrough	0	0		
2012–13	Middlesbrough	0	0		
2012–13	*Hartlepool U*	25	2		
2013–14	Middlesbrough	0	0		
2013–14	*AFC Wimbledon*	17	2	**17**	**2**
2014–15	Middlesbrough	0	0		
2014–15	*Hartlepool U*	13	4	**38**	**6**
2014–15	Carlisle U	17	6		
2015–16	Carlisle U	34	12		
2016–17	Carlisle U	26	14		
2016–17	Bradford C	16	7		
2017–18	Bradford C	40	15	**56**	**22**
2018–19	Sunderland	24	4		
2019–20	Sunderland	27	5		
2020–21	Sunderland	43	25	**94**	**34**
2021–22	Wigan Ath	15	5		
2022–23	Wigan Ath	18	2		
2023–24	Wigan Ath	18	7	**51**	**14**
2023–24	*Rotherham U*	12	1	**12**	**1**
2024–25	Carlisle U	13	2	**90**	**34**

Scholars
Allan, Jake Lee; Atkinson, Hayden Paul; Chapman, Trent John; Fitzpatrick, Aran; Fleming, Mason Lewis Stephen; Hetherington, Sam; Hodgson, Jamie; Hopper, Daniel Joseph; Lambert, Lewis Harry; Lowes, Jonah Robin; Mason, Sebastian Graeme; Murray, James Irvine; Nicholson, Stevyn William; O'Brien, Joshua James; O'Donoghue, Freddie James; Porter, Jack Emil; Randall, Thomas Kieran; Rigby, Simon David; Sillitoe, Casey John; Skinner, Bobby Stephen.

CHARLTON ATH (23)

AHADME, Gassan (F) **86 19**
H: 6 2 W: 12 02 b.Vic 17-11-00
Internationals: Morocco U23.

2020–21	Norwich C	0	0		
2021–22	*Portsmouth*	5	0	**5**	**0**
2021–22	Burton Alb	14	3		
2022–23	Ipswich T	6	0		
2022–23	*Burton Alb*	13	4	**27**	**7**
2023–24	Ipswich T	0	0	**6**	**0**
2023–24	*Cambridge U*	29	11	**29**	**11**
2024–25	Charlton Ath	19	1	**19**	**1**

ANDERSON, Karoy (M) **63 4**
H: 5 11 W: 12 00 b.London 1-10-04
Internationals: Jamaica Full caps.

2022–23	Charlton Ath	0	0		
2023–24	Charlton Ath	25	2		
2024–25	Charlton Ath	38	2	**63**	**4**

ANEKE, Chuks (M) **349 82**
H: 6 3 W: 15 10 b.Newham 3-7-93
Internationals: England U16, U17, U18, U19.

2010–11	Arsenal	0	0		
2011–12	Arsenal	0	0		
2011–12	*Stevenage*	6	0	**6**	**0**
2011–12	*Preston NE*	7	1	**7**	**1**
2012–13	Arsenal	0	0		
2012–13	*Crewe Alex*	30	6		
2013–14	Arsenal	0	0		
2013–14	*Crewe Alex*	40	15	**70**	**21**
2014–15	Arsenal	0	0		
2014–15	Zulte-Waregem	30	2		
2015–16	Zulte-Waregem	11	2	**41**	**4**
2016–17	Milton Keynes D	15	4		
2017–18	Milton Keynes D	31	9		
2018–19	Milton Keynes D	38	17	**84**	**30**
2019–20	Charlton Ath	20	1		
2020–21	Charlton Ath	38	15		
2021–22	Birmingham C	18	2	**18**	**2**
2021–22	Charlton Ath	9	4		
2022–23	Charlton Ath	13	1		
2023–24	Charlton Ath	17	2		
2024–25	Charlton Ath	26	1	**123**	**24**

ASIIMWE, Nathan (D) **28 0**
H: 6 0 W: 12 04 b. 29-12-04

2022–23	Charlton Ath	1	0		
2023–24	Charlton Ath	17	0		
2024–25	Charlton Ath	0	0	**18**	**0**
2024–25	*Walsall*	10	0	**10**	**0**

BERRY, Luke (M) **324 61**
H: 5 10 W: 11 05 b.Bassingbourn 12-7-92
From Cambridge U.

2014–15	Barnsley	31	1	**31**	**1**
2015–16	Cambridge U	46	12		
2016–17	Cambridge U	45	17		
2017–18	Cambridge U	3	0	**94**	**29**
2017–18	Luton T	34	7		
2018–19	Luton T	21	3		
2019–20	Luton T	21	1		
2020–21	Luton T	31	2		
2021–22	Luton T	13	6		
2022–23	Luton T	21	3		
2023–24	Luton T	17	2	**158**	**24**
2024–25	Charlton Ath	41	7	**41**	**7**

BOUZANIS, Dean (G) **184 0**
H: 6 0 W: 12 08 b.Sydney 2-10-90
Internationals: Greece U19. Australia U17, U20, U23.

2007–08	Liverpool	0	0		
2008–09	Liverpool	0	0		
2009–10	Liverpool	0	0		
2009–10	*Accrington S*	14	0	**14**	**0**
2010–11	Liverpool	0	0		
2011–12	Oldham Ath	9	0		
2012–13	Oldham Ath	36	0	**45**	**0**
2013–14	Aris	0	0		
2013–14	Carlisle U	0	0		
2014–15	Western Sydney W	6	0		
2015–16	Western Sydney W	0	0	**6**	**0**
2015–16	Melbourne C	1	0		
2016–17	Melbourne C	22	0		
2017–18	Melbourne C	21	0		
2018–19	Melbourne C	0	0	**44**	**0**
2018–19	*PEC Zwolle*	0	0		

From Sutton U.

2021–22	Sutton U	44	0		
2022–23	Reading	5	0		
2023–24	Reading	1	0		
2023–24	*Sutton U*	25	0	**69**	**0**
2024–25	Reading	0	0	**6**	**0**
2024–25	*Stevenage*	0	0		
2024–25	Charlton Ath	0	0		

BOWER, Toby (D) **0 0**
H: 5 9 W: 10 08 b. 17-4-05

2023–24	Charlton Ath	0	0		
2024–25	Charlton Ath	0	0		

CAMPBELL, Tyreece (M) **101 11**
H: 5 10 W: 10 08 b.Southwark 14-9-03
Internationals: Jamaica Full caps.

2021–22	Charlton Ath	2	0		
2022–23	Charlton Ath	22	2		
2023–24	Charlton Ath	33	2		
2024–25	Charlton Ath	44	7	**101**	**11**

CASEY, Patrick (F) **1 0**
H: 6 2 W: 12 11 b. 19-12-05
Internationals: Republic of Ireland U19.

2022–23	Charlton Ath	0	0		
2023–24	Charlton Ath	1	0		
2024–25	Charlton Ath	0	0	**1**	**0**

COVENTRY, Conor (M) **117 2**
H: 5 9 W: 10 03 b.Waltham Forest 25-3-00
Internationals: Republic of Ireland U16, U17, U18, U19, U21.

2018–19	West Ham U	0	0		
2019–20	West Ham U	0	0		
2019–20	*Lincoln C*	7	0	**7**	**0**
2020–21	West Ham U	0	0		
2021–22	West Ham U	0	0		
2021–22	*Peterborough U*	12	0	**12**	**0**
2021–22	*Milton Keynes D*	20	1	**20**	**1**
2022–23	West Ham U	1	0		
2022–23	*Rotherham U*	16	0	**16**	**0**
2023–24	West Ham U	0	0	**1**	**0**
2023–24	Charlton Ath	17	0		
2024–25	Charlton Ath	44	1	**61**	**1**

DIXON, Kaheim (F) **14 4**
H: 5 11 W: 11 05 b.Kingston 4-10-04
Internationals: Jamaica Full caps.

2022–23	Chapelton Maroons	3	0	**3**	**0**
2023–24	Arnett Gardens	8	4	**8**	**4**
2024–25	Charlton Ath	3	0	**3**	**0**

DOCHERTY, Greg (M) **326 23**
H: 5 10 W: 11 05 b.Glasgow 10-9-96
Internationals: Scotland U17, U21.

2013–14	Hamilton A	3	0		
2014–15	Hamilton A	7	1		
2015–16	Hamilton A	34	1		
2016–17	Hamilton A	29	1		
2017–18	Hamilton A	21	3	**94**	**6**
2017–18	Rangers	11	0		
2018–19	Rangers	0	0		
2018–19	*Shrewsbury T*	41	7	**41**	**7**
2019–20	Rangers	0	0	**11**	**0**
2019–20	*Hibernian*	6	0	**6**	**0**
2020–21	Hull C	44	5		
2021–22	Hull C	40	0		
2022–23	Hull C	35	1		
2023–24	Hull C	15	0	**134**	**6**
2024–25	Charlton Ath	40	4	**40**	**4**

EDWARDS, Josh (D) **219 8**
H: 5 9 W: 10 10 b.Kilmarnock 27-5-00
Internationals: Wales U17, U19.

2017–18	Airdrieonians	12	0		
2018–19	Airdrieonians	22	0	**34**	**0**
2019–20	Dunfermline Ath	15	0		
2020–21	Dunfermline Ath	25	0		
2021–22	Dunfermline Ath	36	2		
2022–23	Dunfermline Ath	35	2		
2023–24	Dunfermline Ath	36	3	**147**	**7**
2024–25	Charlton Ath	38	1	**38**	**1**

ENSLIN, Kai (D) **1 0**
H: 6 0 b. 22-10-05

2024–25	Charlton Ath	1	0	**1**	**0**

FULLAH, Ibrahim (M) **1 0**
b. 5-4-07

2024–25	Charlton Ath	1	0	**1**	**0**

GILLESPHEY, Macaulay (D) **269 14**
H: 5 11 W: 11 00 b.Ashington 24-11-95

2015–16	Newcastle U	0	0		
2015–16	*Carlisle U*	23	2		
2016–17	Newcastle U	0	0		
2016–17	*Carlisle U*	32	0		
2017–18	Newcastle U	0	0		
2018–19	Carlisle U	24	0	**79**	**2**
2019–20	Brisbane Roar	27	1		
2020–21	Brisbane Roar	23	3	**50**	**4**
2021–22	Plymouth Arg	40	1		
2022–23	Plymouth Arg	35	2		
2023–24	Plymouth Arg	4	0	**79**	**3**
2023–24	Charlton Ath	17	0		
2024–25	Charlton Ath	44	5	**61**	**5**

GODDEN, Matthew (F)   311 108
H: 6 1 W: 12 04 b.Canterbury 29-7-91

Season	Club				
2009-10	Scunthorpe U	0	0		
2010-11	Scunthorpe U	5	0		
2011-12	Scunthorpe U	1	0		
2012-13	Scunthorpe U	8	0		
2013-14	Scunthorpe U	4	0		
2014-15	Scunthorpe U	0	0	18	0
From Ebbsfleet U.					
2016-17	Stevenage	38	20		
2017-18	Stevenage	38	10	76	30
2018-19	Peterborough U	38	14		
2019-20	Peterborough U	0	0	38	14
2019-20	Coventry C	26	14		
2020-21	Coventry C	23	6		
2021-22	Coventry C	24	12		
2022-23	Coventry C	30	8		
2023-24	Coventry C	35	6	138	46
2024-25	Charlton Ath	41	18	41	18

HENRY, Aaron (M)   27 0
H: 5 9 W: 10 03 b.Basildon 31-8-03
Internationals: England U16.

Season	Club				
2019-20	Charlton Ath	0	0		
2020-21	Charlton Ath	0	0		
2021-22	Charlton Ath	0	0		
2022-23	Charlton Ath	14	0		
2023-24	Charlton Ath	0	0		
2023-24	Crawley T	13	0	13	0
2024-25	Charlton Ath	0	0	14	0

HYLTON, Danny (F)   447 116
H: 6 0 W: 11 03 b.Camden 25-2-89

Season	Club				
2008-09	Aldershot T	29	5		
2009-10	Aldershot T	21	3		
2010-11	Aldershot T	33	5		
2011-12	Aldershot T	44	13		
2012-13	Aldershot T	27	4	154	30
2013-14	Rotherham U	1	0	1	0
2013-14	Bury	7	2	7	2
2013-14	AFC Wimbledon	17	3	17	3
2014-15	Oxford U	44	14		
2015-16	Oxford U	41	12	85	26
2016-17	Luton T	39	21		
2017-18	Luton T	39	21		
2018-19	Luton T	25	8		
2019-20	Luton T	11	0		
2020-21	Luton T	16	0		
2021-22	Luton T	17	4	147	54
2022-23	Northampton T	26	0		
2023-24	Northampton T	4	0	30	0
2024-25	Charlton Ath	6	1	6	1

JONES, Lloyd (D)   229 13
H: 6 3 W: 12 04 b.Plymouth 7-10-95
Internationals: Wales U17, U19. England U19, U20.

Season	Club				
2012-13	Liverpool	0	0		
2013-14	Liverpool	0	0		
2014-15	Liverpool	0	0		
2014-15	Cheltenham T	6	0	6	0
2014-15	Accrington S	11	1	11	1
2015-16	Liverpool	0	0		
2015-16	Blackpool	10	0	10	0
2016-17	Liverpool	0	0		
2016-17	Swindon T	24	2	24	2
2017-18	Liverpool	1	0		
2018-19	Luton T	1	0		
2018-19	Plymouth Arg	9	1	9	1
2019-20	Luton T	4	0	6	0
2019-20	Northampton T	7	0		
2020-21	Northampton T	27	0	34	0
2021-22	Cambridge U	25	0		
2022-23	Cambridge U	36	4	61	4
2023-24	Charlton Ath	32	2		
2024-25	Charlton Ath	36	3	68	5

KANU, Daniel (M)   59 7
H: 5 11 W: 11 09 b.Lambeth 14-11-04
Internationals: Sierre Leone Full caps.

Season	Club				
2021-22	Charlton Ath	2	0		
2022-23	Charlton Ath	10	0		
2023-24	Charlton Ath	30	6		
2024-25	Charlton Ath	17	1	59	7

LAQERETABUA, Joshua (D)   2 0
H: 6 1 b: 26-9-05
Internationals: Fiji U20.

Season	Club				
2023-24	Charlton Ath	0	0		
2024-25	Charlton Ath	2	0	2	0

LEABURN, Miles (F)   75 21
H: 6 5 W: 12 08 b.Bromley 28-11-03
From Chelsea.

Season	Club				
2022-23	Charlton Ath	35	12		
2023-24	Charlton Ath	13	3		
2024-25	Charlton Ath	27	6	75	21

MANNION, Will (G)   57 0
H: 6 1 W: 11 09 b.Hillingdon 5-5-98
Internationals: England U19.
From AFC Wimbledon.

Season	Club				
2016-17	Hull C	0	0		
2017-18	Hull C	0	0		
2017-18	Plymouth Arg				
2018-19	Hull C	0	0		
2019-20	Hull C	0	0		
2020-21	Pafos	0	0		
2021-22	Cambridge U	2	0		
2022-23	Cambridge U	13	0		
2023-24	Cambridge U	14	0	29	0
2024-25	Charlton Ath	28	0	28	0

MAYNARD-BREWER, Ashley (G)   87 0
H: 6 2 W: 11 07 b.Joondalup 25-6-99
Internationals: Australia U23.

Season	Club				
2017-18	Charlton Ath	0	0		
2018-19	Charlton Ath	0	0		
2019-20	Charlton Ath	0	0		
2020-21	Charlton Ath	0	0		
2021-22	Charlton Ath	0	0		
2021-22	Ross Co	17	0	17	0
2022-23	Charlton Ath	26	0		
2022-23	Gillingham	0	0		
2023-24	Charlton Ath	25	0		
2024-25	Charlton Ath	19	0	70	0

MBICK, Micah (F)   6 0
H: 6 1 W: 12 06 b.Newham 8-11-06

Season	Club				
2023-24	Charlton Ath	2	0		
2024-25	Charlton Ath	4	0	6	0

MITCHELL, Alex (D)   122 4
H: 6 3 W: 11 11 b.Slough 7-10-01

Season	Club				
2020-21	Millwall	0	0		
2021-22	Millwall	0	0		
2021-22	Leyton Orient	26	0	26	0
2022-23	Millwall	0	0		
2022-23	St Johnstone	29	1	29	1
2023-24	Millwall	0	0		
2023-24	Lincoln C	36	1	36	1
2024-25	Charlton Ath	31	2	31	2

MITCHELL, Zach (D)   38 1
H: 6 1 W: 12 13 b.Bromley 9-1-05

Season	Club				
2022-23	Charlton Ath	6	0		
2023-24	Charlton Ath	0	0		
2023-24	Colchester U	23	1	23	1
2024-25	Charlton Ath	1	0	7	0
2024-25	St Johnstone	8	0	8	0

NWAMBA, Alan (D)   0 0
b. 15-9-06

Season	Club				
2024-25	Charlton Ath	0	0		

POTTS, Danny (D)   211 10
H: 5 8 W: 11 00 b.Barking 13-4-94
Internationals: USA U20. England U18, U19, U20.

Season	Club				
2011-12	West Ham U	3	0		
2012-13	West Ham U	2	0		
2012-13	Colchester U	5	0	5	0
2013-14	West Ham U	1	0		
2013-14	Portsmouth	5	0	5	0
2014-15	West Ham U	0	0	5	0
2015-16	Luton T	14	0		
2016-17	Luton T	23	0		
2017-18	Luton T	42	6		
2018-19	Luton T	24	1		
2019-20	Luton T	33	1		
2020-21	Luton T	24	1		
2021-22	Luton T	10	0		
2022-23	Luton T	25	1		
2023-24	Luton T	0	0	195	10
2024-25	Charlton Ath	1	0	1	0

RAMSAY, Kayne (D)   119 2
H: 5 10 W: 12 13 b.Hackney 10-10-00
From Chelsea.

Season	Club				
2018-19	Southampton	1	0		
2019-20	Southampton	0	0		
2019-20	Shrewsbury T	5	0	5	0
2020-21	Southampton	1	0		
2021-22	Southampton	0	0	2	0
2021-22	Crewe Alex	15	0	15	0
2021-22	Ross Co	8	1	8	1
2022-23	Harrogate T	26	0		
2023-24	Harrogate T	24	0	50	0
2023-24	Charlton Ath	7	0		
2024-25	Charlton Ath	32	1	39	1

REID, Tommy (G)   0 0
b.Hastings 18-1-05

Season	Club				
2024-25	Charlton Ath	0	0		

RYLAH, Henry (M)   3 0
H: 5 11 W: 11 09 b. 18-11-05

Season	Club				
2022-23	Charlton Ath	1	0		
2023-24	Charlton Ath	2	0		
2024-25	Charlton Ath	0	0	3	0

SMALL, Thierry (D)   71 3
H: 5 9 W: 10 10 b.Solihull 8-1-04
Internationals: England U16, U17, U18, U19.
From WBA.

Season	Club				
2020-21	Everton	0	0		
2021-22	Southampton	0	0		
2022-23	Port Vale	4	0	4	0
2022-23	St Mirren	14	0	14	0
2023-24	Charlton Ath	14	1		
2024-25	Charlton Ath	39	2	53	3

TAYLOR, Terry (M)   103 1
H: 6 1 W: 11 00 b.Aberdeen 29-6-01
Internationals: Scotland U17. Wales U21.
From Aberdeen.

Season	Club				
2019-20	Wolverhampton W	0	0		
2020-21	Wolverhampton W	0	0		
2020-21	Grimsby T	13	0	13	0
2020-21	Burton Alb	16	0		
2021-22	Burton Alb	16	0		
2022-23	Burton Alb	26	0	58	0
2023-24	Charlton Ath	5	0		
2024-25	Charlton Ath	8	0	13	0
2024-25	Northampton T	19	1	19	1

WATSON, Tennai (M)   139 3
H: 6 0 W: 11 07 b.Hillington 4-3-97
Internationals: England U18.

Season	Club				
2015-16	Reading	0	0		
2016-17	Reading	3	0		
2017-18	Reading	0	0		
2018-19	Reading	0	0		
2018-19	AFC Wimbledon	24	0	24	0
2019-20	Reading	0	0		
2019-20	Coventry C	3	0	3	0
2020-21	Reading	1	0	4	0
2021-22	Milton Keynes D	28	2		
2022-23	Milton Keynes D	30	0	58	2
2023-24	Charlton Ath	34	1		
2024-25	Charlton Ath	16	0	50	1

Players retained or with offer of contract
Gough, Keenan Blue; Hobden, Oliver Henry; Hunter, Mason Ronald; MacLorg, Lennon Jack; Sol-Loza, Emmanuel-Mary Hadriel.

Scholars
Belton, Jack; Brown, Ethan Marcel Solomon; Burnham, Shia-Lee Wayne; Cann, Ethan James; Davis, Dionte Tyler; Elliott, Tate Levi; McMillan, Ellis Solomon Laurel; Ogunnowo, Joshua Itiayo Adegbaite; Olatunji, Olanrewaju Opeyemi; Rayment-Dawkins, Marley Skye; Reid, Reuben Raheme; Sadler, Jude Thomas; Safa, Jacob Ruhy; Tagoe, Bradley Nii-Aryee; Valentine, Phoenix Vincenzo Adekunle; Wales, Manu Isaac Thomas; Washington-Amoah, Samuel Yawson; Woodham, Finley James.

CHELSEA (24)

ACHEAMPONG, Josh (D)   5 0
H: 6 1 W: 11 11 b.London 5-5-06
Internationals: England U16, U17, U18, U19, U20.

Season	Club				
2023-24	Chelsea	1	0		
2024-25	Chelsea	4	0	5	0

ADARABIOYO, Tosin (D)   204 9
H: 6 3 W: 12 08 b.Manchester 24-9-97
Internationals: England U16, U17, U18, U19.

Season	Club				
2014-15	Manchester C	0	0		
2015-16	Manchester C	0	0		
2016-17	Manchester C	0	0		
2017-18	Manchester C	0	0		
2018-19	Manchester C	0	0		
2018-19	WBA	29	0	29	0
2019-20	Manchester C	0	0		
2019-20	Blackburn R	34	3	34	3
2020-21	Fulham	33	0		
2021-22	Fulham	41	2		
2022-23	Fulham	25	1		
2023-24	Fulham	20	2	119	5
2024-25	Chelsea	22	1	22	1

AMOUGOU, Mathis (M)   19 0
H: 5 10 W: 10 12 b.Le Blanc-Mesnil 18-1-06
Internationals: France U16, U17, U18, U19.

Season	Club				
2022-23	Saint-Etienne	0	0		
2023-24	Saint-Etienne	1	0		
2024-25	Saint-Etienne	17	0	18	0
2024-25	Chelsea	1	0	1	0

AMPAH, Ato (M)   0 0
H: 5 9 W: 11 00 b.Accra 22-4-06
Internationals: England U18.

Season	Club				
2024-25	Chelsea	0	0		

ANSELMINO, Aaron (D)   14 0
H: 6 1 W: 12 04 b.Bernardo Larroude 29-4-05
Internationals: Argentina U20.

Season	Club				
2023	Boca Juniors	2	0		
2024	Boca Juniors	12	0	14	0
2024-25	Chelsea	0	0		

ANTWI, Genesis (D)   0 0
b.Stockholm 11-5-07
Internationals: England U16. Sweden U16, U17, U19/

Season	Club				
2024-25	Chelsea	0	0		

ARRIZABALAGA, Kepa (G) 347 0
H: 6 1 W: 12 11 b.Ondorroa 3-10-94
Internationals: Spain U18, U19, U21, Full caps.

2011–12	Basconia	12	0		
2012–13	Basconia	19	0	**31**	**0**
2012–13	Athletic Bilbao	7	0		
2013–14	Athletic Bilbao	26	0		
2014–15	Athletic Bilbao	17	0		
2014–15	*Ponferradina*	20	0	**20**	**0**
2015–16	Athletic Bilbao	0	0		
2015–16	*Vallodolid*	39	0	**39**	**0**
2016–17	Athletic Bilbao	23	0		
2017–18	Athletic Bilbao	30	0	**103**	**0**
2018–19	Chelsea	36	0		
2019–20	Chelsea	33	0		
2020–21	Chelsea	7	0		
2021–22	Chelsea	4	0		
2022–23	Chelsea	29	0		
2023–24	Chelsea	0	0		
2023–24	*Real Madrid*	14	0	**14**	**0**
2024–25	Chelsea	0	0	**109**	**0**
2024–25	*Bournemouth*	31	0	**31**	**0**

BADIASHILE, Benoit (D) 140 7
H: 6 4 W: 11 11 b.Limoges 26-3-01
Internationals: France U16, U17, U18, U19, U21, Full caps.

2017–18	Monaco	0	0		
2018–19	Monaco	20	1		
2019–20	Monaco	16	0		
2020–21	Monaco	35	2		
2021–22	Monaco	24	1		
2022–23	Monaco	11	2	**106**	**6**
2022–23	Chelsea	11	1		
2023–24	Chelsea	18	0		
2024–25	Chelsea	5	0	**34**	**1**

BEACH, Eddie (G) 0 0
H: 6 5 W: 13 03 b.Lymington 14-11-03
Internationals: Wales U19, U21.

2023–24	Chelsea	0	0
2024–25	Chelsea	0	0
2024–25	*Crawley T*	0	0

BERGSTROM, Lucas (G) 24 0
H: 6 7 W: 13 03 b.Paragas 5-9-02
Internationals: Finland U16, U17, U21, Full caps.

2020–21	Chelsea	0	0		
2021–22	Chelsea	0	0		
2022–23	Chelsea	0	0		
2022–23	*Peterborough U*	21	0	**21**	**0**
2023–24	Chelsea	0	0		
2023–24	*Brommapojkarna*	3	0	**3**	**0**
2024–25	Chelsea	0	0		

BETTINELLI, Marcus (G) 183 0
H: 6 4 W: 12 13 b.Camberwell 24-5-92
Internationals: England U21.

2010–11	Fulham	0	0		
2011–12	Fulham	0	0		
2012–13	Fulham	0	0		
2013–14	Fulham	0	0		
2013–14	*Accrington S*	39	0	**39**	**0**
2014–15	Fulham	39	0		
2015–16	Fulham	11	0		
2016–17	Fulham	6	0		
2017–18	Fulham	26	0		
2018–19	Fulham	7	0		
2019–20	Fulham	14	0		
2020–21	Fulham	0	0	**103**	**0**
2020–21	*Middlesbrough*	41	0	**41**	**0**
2021–22	Chelsea	0	0		
2022–23	Chelsea	0	0		
2023–24	Chelsea	0	0		
2024–25	Chelsea	0	0		

BROJA, Armando (F) 106 18
H: 6 0 W: 11 00 b.Slough 10-9-01
Internationals: Albania U19, U21, Full caps.

2019–20	Chelsea	1	0		
2020–21	Chelsea	0	0		
2020–21	*Vitesse*	30	10	**30**	**10**
2021–22	Chelsea	0	0		
2021–22	*Southampton*	32	6	**32**	**6**
2022–23	Chelsea	12	1		
2023–24	Chelsea	13	1		
2023–24	*Fulham*	8	0	**8**	**0**
2024–25	Chelsea	0	0	**26**	**2**
2024–25	*Everton*	10	0	**10**	**0**

CAICEDO, Moises (M) 155 9
H: 5 9 W: 11 03 b.Santo Domingo 2-11-01
Internationals: Ecuador Full caps.

2019	Independiente del Valle	3	0		
2020	Independiente del Valle	22	4		
2020–21	Independiente del Valle	0	0	**25**	**4**
2020–21	Brighton & HA	0	0		
2021–22	Brighton & HA	8	1		
2021–22	*Beerschot*	12	1	**12**	**1**
2022–23	Brighton & HA	37	1	**45**	**2**
2023–24	Chelsea	35	1		
2024–25	Chelsea	38	1	**73**	**2**

CASADEI, Cesare (M) 48 3
H: 6 1 W: 10 03 b.Ravenna 10-1-03
Internationals: Italy U16, U17, U18, U19, U20, U21.

2021–22	Internazionale	0	0		
2022–23	Chelsea	0	0		
2022–23	*Reading*	15	1	**15**	**1**
2023–24	Chelsea	11	0		
2023–24	*Leicester C*	22	2	**22**	**2**
2024–25	Chelsea	0	0	**11**	**0**

Transferred to Torino, February 2025.

CASTLEDINE, Leo (M) 23 2
H: 5 9 W: 10 03 b.Kingston 20-8-05
Internationals: England U16, U7, U18, U19.

2023–24	Chelsea	0	0		
2024–25	Chelsea	0	0		
2024–25	*Shrewsbury T*	23	2	**23**	**2**

CHALOBAH, Trevor (D) 191 12
H: 6 3 W: 11 11 b.Freetown 5-7-99
Internationals: England U16, U17, U19, U20, U21, Full caps.

2017–18	Chelsea	0	0		
2018–19	Chelsea	0	0		
2018–19	*Ipswich T*	43	2	**43**	**2**
2019–20	Chelsea	0	0		
2019–20	*Huddersfield T*	36	1	**36**	**1**
2020–21	Chelsea	0	0		
2020–21	*Lorient*	29	2	**29**	**2**
2021–22	Chelsea	20	3		
2022–23	Chelsea	25	0		
2023–24	Chelsea	13	1		
2024–25	Chelsea	13	0	**71**	**4**
2024–25	*Crystal Palace*	12	3	**12**	**3**

CHILWELL, Ben (D) 185 13
H: 5 10 W: 11 03 b.Milton Keynes 21-12-96
Internationals: England U18, U19, U20, U21, Full caps.

2015–16	Leicester C	0	0		
2015–16	*Huddersfield T*	8	0	**8**	**0**
2016–17	Leicester C	12	1		
2017–18	Leicester C	24	0		
2018–19	Leicester C	36	0		
2019–20	Leicester C	27	3	**99**	**4**
2020–21	Chelsea	27	3		
2021–22	Chelsea	7	3		
2022–23	Chelsea	23	2		
2023–24	Chelsea	13	0		
2024–25	Chelsea	0	0	**70**	**8**
2024–25	*Crystal Palace*	8	1	**8**	**1**

CHUKWUEMEKA, Carney (M) 47 2
H: 6 0 W: 12 02 b.Eisenstadt 20-10-03
Internationals: England U17, U18, U19, U20.

2020–21	Aston Villa	2	0		
2021–22	Aston Villa	12	0	**14**	**0**
2022–23	Chelsea	14	0		
2023–24	Chelsea	9	1		
2024–25	Chelsea	0	0	**23**	**1**
2024–25	*Borussia Dortmund*	10	1	**10**	**1**

COLWILL, Levi (D) 104 5
H: 6 3 W: 13 01 b.Southampton 26-2-99
Internationals: England U16, U17, U19, U21, Full caps.

2021–22	Chelsea	0	0		
2021–22	*Huddersfield T*	29	2	**29**	**2**
2022–23	Chelsea	0	0		
2022–23	*Brighton & HA*	17	0	**17**	**0**
2023–24	Chelsea	23	1		
2024–25	Chelsea	35	2	**58**	**3**

CUCURELLA, Marc (D) 222 11
H: 5 8 W: 10 10 b.Alella 22-7-98
Internationals: Spain U16, U17, U18, U19, U20, U21, U23, Full caps.
From Espanyol.

2016–17	Barcelona	0	0		
2017–18	Barcelona	0	0		
2018–19	Barcelona	0	0		
2018–19	*Eibar*	31	1	**31**	**1**
2019–20	Barcelona	0	0		
2019–20	*Getafe*	37	1		
2020–21	Getafe	37	3		
2021–22	Getafe	1	0	**75**	**4**
2021–22	Brighton & HA	35	1	**35**	**1**
2022–23	Chelsea	24	0		
2023–24	Chelsea	21	0		
2024–25	Chelsea	36	5	**81**	**5**

CURD, Ted (G) 0 0
H: 6 3 W: 11 03 b.Kingston upon Thames 14-2-6
Internationals: England U17, U18, U19.

2023–24	Chelsea	0	0
2024–25	Chelsea	0	0

DEIVID WASHINGTON, Eugenio (F) 22 3
H: 6 2 W: 11 07 b.Itumbiara 5-6-05
Internationals: Brazil U20.

2023	Santos	9	2		
2023–24	Chelsea	2	0		
2024–25	Chelsea	0	0	**2**	**0**
2025	*Santos*	11	1	**20**	**3**

DEWSBURY-HALL, Kiernan (M) 165 22
H: 5 10 W: 11 00 b.Nottingham 6-9-98

2019–20	Leicester C	0	0		
2019–20	*Blackpool*	10	4	**10**	**4**
2020–21	Leicester C	0	0		
2020–21	*Luton T*	39	3	**39**	**3**
2021–22	Leicester C	28	1		
2022–23	Leicester C	31	2		
2023–24	Leicester C	44	12	**103**	**15**
2024–25	Chelsea	13	0	**13**	**0**

DISASI, Axel (D) 191 13
H: 6 3 W: 13 08 b.Gonesse 11-3-98
Internationals: France U20, Full caps.

2015–16	Paris FC	3	1	**3**	**1**
2016–17	Reims	1	0		
2017–18	Reims	13	1		
2018–19	Reims	4	0		
2019–20	Reims	27	1	**45**	**2**
2020–21	Monaco	29	3		
2021–22	Monaco	32	1		
2022–23	Monaco	38	3	**99**	**7**
2023–24	Chelsea	31	2		
2024–25	Chelsea	6	1	**37**	**3**
2024–25	*Aston Villa*	7	0	**7**	**0**

DYER, Kiano (M) 0 0
H: 5 10 W: 10 03 b.Sutton Coldfield 21-11-06
Internationals: England U16, U17, U18, U19.

2023–24	Chelsea	0	0
2024–25	Chelsea	0	0

EMENALO, Landon (M) 0 0
H: 5 11 b.Arizona 18-1-08
Internationals: USA U17. England U16, U17.

2024–25	Chelsea	0	0

FERNANDEZ, Enzo (M) 152 19
H: 5 10 W: 12 00 b.San Martin 17-1-01
Internationals: Argentina U18, Full caps.

2020	River Plate	0	0		
2020–21	*Defensa y Justicia*	14	0	**14**	**0**
2021	River Plate	20	2		
2022	River Plate	19	7	**39**	**9**
2022–23	Benfica	17	1	**17**	**1**
2022–23	Chelsea	18	0		
2023–24	Chelsea	28	3		
2024–25	Chelsea	36	6	**82**	**9**

FOFANA, David Datro (F) 81 22
H: 5 11 W: 12 13 b.Ouragahio 22-12-02
Internationals: Ivory Coast U23, Full caps.

2021	Molde	18	0		
2022	Molde	24	15	**42**	**15**
2022–23	Chelsea	3	0		
2023–24	Chelsea	0	0		
2023–24	*Union Berlin*	12	1	**12**	**1**
2023–24	*Burnley*	15	4	**15**	**4**
2024–25	Chelsea	0	0	**3**	**0**
2024–25	*Goztepe*	9	2	**9**	**2**

FOFANA, Wesley (D) 82 2
H: 6 3 W: 14 09 b.Marseille 17-12-00
Internationals: France U21, Full caps.

2018–19	Saint-Etienne	2	0		
2019–20	Saint-Etienne	14	1	**16**	**1**
2020–21	St Etienne	0	0		
2020–21	Leicester C	28	0		
2021–22	Leicester C	7	0		
2022–23	Leicester C	2	0	**37**	**0**
2022–23	Chelsea	15	1		
2023–24	Chelsea	0	0		
2024–25	Chelsea	14	0	**29**	**1**

GEORGE, Tyrique (F) 8 1
H: 5 11 W: 10 06 b.London 4-2-06
Internationals: England U16, U17, U18, U19.

2023–24	Chelsea	0	0		
2024–25	Chelsea	8	1	**8**	**1**

GILCHRIST, Alfie (D) 41 1
H: 6 0 W: 11 05 b.London 28-11-03

2022–23	Chelsea	0	0		
2023–24	Chelsea	11	1		
2024–25	Chelsea	0	0	**11**	**1**
2024–25	*Sheffield U*	30	0	**30**	**0**

GUIU, Marc (F) 6 1
H: 6 2 W: 12 00 b.Granollers 4-1-06
Internationals: Spain U17, U19.

2022–23	Barcelona	0	0		
2023–24	Barcelona	3	1	**3**	**1**
2024–25	Chelsea	3	0	**3**	**0**

GUSTO, Malo (D) 112 0
H: 5 10 W: 10 08 b.Decines-Charpieu 19-5-03
Internationals: France U16, U17, U19, U21, Full caps.

2020–21	Lyon	2	0		
2021–22	Lyon	30	0		
2022–23	Lyon	21	0	**53**	**0**
2022–23	Chelsea	0	0		
2023–24	Chelsea	27	0		
2024–25	Chelsea	32	0	**59**	**0**

HARRISON, Ollie (M) 0 0
H: 6 2 W: 11 03 b. 7-8-07
Internationals: England U17, U18.

2023–24	Chelsea	0	0		
2024–25	Chelsea	0	0		

HUMPHREYS, Bashir (D) 61 2
H: 6 1 W: 12 06 b.Exeter 15-3-03
Internationals: England U16, U19, U20, U21.

2020–21	Chelsea	0	0		
2021–22	Chelsea	0	0		
2022–23	Chelsea	0	0		
2022–23	*Paderborn*	12	0	**12**	**0**
2023–24	Chelsea	0	0		
2023–24	*Swansea C*	24	1	**24**	**1**
2024–25	Chelsea	0	0		
2024–25	*Burnley*	25	1	**25**	**1**

JACKSON, Nicolas (F) 116 37
H: 6 1 W: 12 04 b.Banjul 20-6-01
Internationals: Senegal U20, Full caps.
From Casa Sports.

2020–21	Villarreal	0	0		
2020–21	*Mirandes*	16	1	**16**	**1**
2021–22	Villarreal	9	0		
2022–23	Villarreal	26	12	**35**	**12**
2023–24	Chelsea	35	14		
2024–25	Chelsea	30	10	**65**	**24**

JAMES, Reece (D) 172 11
H: 5 11 W: 12 13 b.Redbridge 8-12-99
Internationals: England U18, U19, U20, U21, Full caps.

2018–19	Chelsea	0	0		
2018–19	*Wigan Ath*	45	3	**45**	**3**
2019–20	Chelsea	24	0		
2020–21	Chelsea	32	1		
2021–22	Chelsea	26	5		
2022–23	Chelsea	16	1		
2023–24	Chelsea	10	0		
2024–25	Chelsea	19	1	**127**	**8**

JOAO FELIX, Sequeira (F) 151 43
H: 5 11 W: 10 01 b.Viseu 10-11-99
Internationals: Portugal U18, U19, U21, Full caps.

2016–17	Benfica	0	0		
2017–18	Benfica	0	0		
2018–19	Benfica	26	15	**26**	**15**
2019–20	Atletico Madrid	27	6		
2020–21	Atletico Madrid	31	7		
2021–22	Atletico Madrid	24	8		
2022–23	Atletico Madrid	0	0	**82**	**21**
2022–23	Chelsea	16	4		
2024–25	Chelsea	12	1	**28**	**5**
2024–25	*AC Milan*	15	2	**15**	**2**

JORGENSEN, Filip (G) 44 0
H: 6 3 W: 12 13 b.Lomma 16-4-02
Internationals: Sweden U16, U17. Denmark U21, Full caps.

2020–21	Villareal	0	0		
2021–22	Villareal	0	0		
2022–23	Villareal	2	0		
2023–24	Villareal	36	0	**38**	**0**
2024–25	Chelsea	6	0	**6**	**0**

KELLYMAN, Omari (F) 2 0
H: 6 3 W: 13 03 b.Derby 25-9-05
Internationals: Northern Ireland U17, U18. England U19.

2021–22	Derby Co	0	0		
2022–23	Aston Villa	0	0		
2023–24	Aston Villa	2	0	**2**	**0**
2024–25	Chelsea	0	0		

LAVIA, Romeo (M) 46 1
H: 5 11 W: 12 00 b.Brussels 6-1-04
Internationals: Belgium U16, U19, U21, Full caps.
From Anderlecht.

2021–22	Manchester C	0	0		
2022–23	Southampton	29	1	**29**	**1**
2023–24	Chelsea	1	0		
2024–25	Chelsea	16	0	**17**	**0**

MADUEKE, Noni (M) 118 24
H: 5 9 W: 11 11 b.London 10-3-02
Internationals: England U16, U17, U18, U21, Full caps.

2019–20	PSV Eindhoven	4	0		
2020–21	PSV Eindhoven	24	7		
2021–22	PSV Eindhoven	18	3		
2022–23	PSV Eindhoven	5	1	**51**	**11**
2022–23	Chelsea	12	1		
2023–24	Chelsea	23	5		
2024–25	Chelsea	32	7	**67**	**13**

MATOS, Alex (M) 40 1
H: 5 8 W: 10 08 b.Bedford 3-10-04
Internationals: England U20.

2023–24	Chelsea	1	0		
2023–24	*Huddersfield T*	19	1	**19**	**1**
2024–25	Chelsea	0	0	**1**	**0**
2024–25	*Oxford U*	20	0	**20**	**0**

MERRICK, Max (G) 0 0
H: 5 9 W: 11 00 b.High Wycombe 10-11-05
Internationals: England U19, U20.

2023–24	Chelsea	0	0		
2024–25	Chelsea	0	0		

MHEUKA, Shumaira (F) 1 0
H: 6 1 W: 11 11 b.Birmingham 20-10-07
Internationals: England U16, U17, U18, U19.

2024–25	Chelsea	1	0	**1**	**0**

MORGAN, Jimmy-Jay (M) 16 2
b. 21-1-06
Internationals: England U16, U17, U18.
From Southampton.

2022–23	Southampton	0	0		
2022–23	Chelsea	0	0		
2023–24	Chelsea	0	0		
2024–25	Chelsea	0	0		
2024–25	*Gillingham*	16	2	**16**	**2**

MUDRYK, Mykhailo (M) 102 14
H: 5 9 W: 9 08 b.Krasnograd 5-1-01
Internationals: Ukraine U16, U17, U19, U21, Full caps.

2018–19	Shakhtar Donetsk	0	0		
2018–19	*Arsenal Kyiv*	10	0	**10**	**0**
2019–20	Shakhtar Donetsk	3	0		
2020–21	Shakhtar Donetsk	3	0		
2020–21	*Desna Chernihiv*	10	0	**10**	**0**
2021–22	Shakhtar Donetsk	11	2		
2022–23	Shakhtar Donetsk	12	7	**29**	**9**
2022–23	Chelsea	15	0		
2023–24	Chelsea	31	5		
2024–25	Chelsea	7	0	**53**	**5**

MURRAY-CAMPBELL, Harrison (D) 0 0
H: 6 0 W: 11 11 b.Luton 4-8-06
Internationals: England U17, U18, U19.

2023–24	Chelsea	0	0		
2024–25	Chelsea	0	0		

NKUNKU, Christopher (M) 212 61
H: 5 9 W: 11 00 b.Lagny-sur-Marne 14-11-97
Internationals: France U16, U19, U20, U21, Full caps.

2015–16	Paris Saint-Germain	5	0		
2016–17	Paris Saint-Germain	8	1		
2017–18	Paris Saint-Germain	20	4		
2018–19	Paris Saint-Germain	22	3	**55**	**8**
2019–20	RB Leipzig	32	5		
2020–21	RB Leipzig	28	6		
2021–22	RB Leipzig	34	20		
2022–23	RB Leipzig	25	16	**119**	**47**
2023–24	Chelsea	11	3		
2024–25	Chelsea	27	3	**38**	**6**

OLISE, Richard (D) 0 0
H: 5 7 W: 9 06 b.London 9-9-04
Internationals: England U18.

2024–25	Chelsea	0	0		

PALMER, Cole (M) 89 37
H: 6 2 W: 11 05 b.Wythenshawe 6-5-02
Internationals: England U16, U17, U18, U21, Full caps.

2019–20	Manchester C	0	0		
2020–21	Manchester C	0	0		
2021–22	Manchester C	4	0		
2022–23	Manchester C	14	0		
2023–24	Manchester C	1	0	**19**	**0**
2023–24	Chelsea	33	22		
2024–25	Chelsea	37	15	**70**	**37**

PEDRO NETO, Lomba (M) 153 16
H: 5 8 W: 10 12 b.Viana do Castelo 9-3-00
Internationals: Portugal U17, U18, U19, U20, U21, Full caps.

2016–17	Braga	2	1		
2017–18	Braga	1	0		
2018–19	Braga	0	0	**3**	**1**
2018–19	*Lazio*	4	0	**4**	**0**
2019–20	Wolverhampton W	29	3		
2020–21	Wolverhampton W	31	5		
2021–22	Wolverhampton W	13	1		
2022–23	Wolverhampton W	18	0		
2023–24	Wolverhampton W	20	2	**111**	**11**
2024–25	Chelsea	35	4	**35**	**4**

PENDERS, Mike (G) 21 0
b. 31-7-05
Internationals: Belgium U17, U18, U19.

2021–22	Genk	0	0		
2022–23	Genk	0	0		
2023–24	Genk	0	0		
2024–25	Genk	21	0	**21**	**0**
2024–25	Chelsea	0	0		

PETROVIC, Djordje (G) 175 0
H: 6 4 W: 14 00 b.Pozarevac 8-10-99
Internationals: Serbia U21, Full caps.

2019–20	Cukaricki	21	0		
2020–21	Cukaricki	34	0		
2021–22	Cukaricki	23	0	**78**	**0**
2022	NE Revolution	21	0		
2023	NE Revolution	22	0	**43**	**0**
2023–24	Chelsea	23	0		
2024–25	Chelsea	0	0	**23**	**0**
2024–25	*Strasbourg*	31	0	**31**	**0**

RAK-SAKYI, Samuel (M) 0 0
H: 5 11 W: 12 08 b.London 27-3-05
Internationals: England U17, U18.

2023–24	Chelsea	0	0		
2024–25	Chelsea	0	0		

SAMUELS-SMITH, Ishe (D) 0 0
H: 6 3 W: 9 11 b.Manchester 5-6-05
Internationals: England U16, U17, U18, U19.

2022–23	Everton	0	0		
2023–24	Chelsea	0	0		
2024–25	Chelsea	0	0		

SANCHEZ, Robert (G) 178 0
H: 6 6 W: 14 02 b.Cartagena 18-11-97
Internationals: Spain Full caps.
From Levante.

2018–19	Brighton & HA	0	0		
2018–19	*Forest Green R*	17	0	**17**	**0**
2019–20	Brighton & HA	0	0		
2019–20	*Rochdale*	26	0	**26**	**0**
2020–21	Brighton & HA	27	0		
2021–22	Brighton & HA	37	0		
2022–23	Brighton & HA	23	0	**87**	**0**
2023–24	Chelsea	16	0		
2024–25	Chelsea	32	0	**48**	**0**

SANTOS, Andrey (M) 88 20
b.Rio de Janeiro 3-5-04
Internationals: Brazil U20, Full caps.

2021	Vasco da Gama	1	0		
2022	Vasco da Gama	33	8		
2023	Vasco da Gama	10	1	**44**	**9**
2023–24	Chelsea	0	0		
2023–24	*Nottingham F*	1	0	**1**	**0**
2023–24	*Strasbourg*	11	1		
2024–25	Chelsea	0	0		
2024–25	*Strasbourg*	32	10	**43**	**11**

SHARMAN-LOWE, Teddy (G) 46 0
H: 6 2 W: 11 07 b.Leicester 3-3-03
Internationals: England U17, U19, U20, U21.

2019–20	Burton Alb	0	0		
2020–21	Chelsea	0	0		
2020–21	*Burton Alb*	0	0		
2021–22	Chelsea	0	0		
2022–23	Chelsea	0	0		
2023–24	Chelsea	0	0		
2024–25	Chelsea	0	0		
2024–25	*Doncaster R*	46	0	**46**	**0**

SLONINA, Gabriel (G) 54 0
H: 6 5 W: 13 10 b.Addison, Illinois 15-5-04
Internationals: USA U16, U17, U20, Full caps.

2021	Chicago Fire	11	0		
2022	Chicago Fire	23	0		
2022–23	Chelsea	0	0		
2023	*Chicago Fire*	9	0	**43**	**0**
2024–25	Chelsea	0	0		
2024–25	*Barnsley*	11	0	**11**	**0**

STERLING, Raheem (F) 396 123
H: 5 7 W: 10 12 b.Kingston 8-12-94
Internationals: England U16, U17, U19, U21, Full caps.
From QPR.

2011–12	Liverpool	3	0		
2012–13	Liverpool	24	2		
2013–14	Liverpool	33	9		
2014–15	Liverpool	35	7	**95**	**18**
2015–16	Manchester C	31	6		
2016–17	Manchester C	33	7		
2017–18	Manchester C	33	18		
2018–19	Manchester C	34	17		
2019–20	Manchester C	33	20		
2020–21	Manchester C	31	10		
2021–22	Manchester C	30	13	**225**	**91**
2022–23	Chelsea	28	6		
2023–24	Chelsea	31	8		
2024–25	Chelsea	0	0	**59**	**14**
2024–25	*Arsenal*	17	0	**17**	**0**

STURGE, Zak (D) 13 0
H: 6 2 W: 11 00 b.Hillingdon 15-1-04
Internationals: England U18.

2023–24	Chelsea	0	0		
2023–24	*Peterborough U*	8	0	**8**	**0**
2024–25	Chelsea	0	0		
2024–25	*Millwall*	5	0	**5**	**0**

STUTTER, Ronnie (F) 1 0
H: 5 10 W: 11 00 b.London 6-1-05
Internationals: England U16, U17, U19.

2023–24	Chelsea	0	0		
2024–25	Chelsea	0	0		
2024–25	*Burton Alb*	1	0	**1**	**0**

TAURIAINEN, Jimi (F) 1 0
H: 6 1 W: 10 12 b.Helsinki 8-3-04
Internationals: Finland U16, U18, U19.
From Helsinki.

2020–21	Chelsea	0	0		
2021–22	Chelsea	0	0		

2022–23 Chelsea	0	0		
2023–24 Chelsea	1	0		
2024–25 Chelsea	0	0	1	0

UGOCHUKWU, Lesley (M) 85 2
H: 6 3 W: 13 12 b.Rennes 26-3-04
Internationals: France U18, U19, U21, U23.

2020–21 Rennes	3	0		
2021–22 Rennes	18	1		
2022–23 Rennes	26	0		
2023–24 Rennes	0	0	47	1
2023–24 Chelsea	12	0		
2024–25 Chelsea	0	0	12	0
2024–25 Southampton	26	1	26	1

VEIGA, Renato (M) 56 2
H: 6 3 W: 13 01 b.Lisboa 29-7-03
Internationals: Portugal U19, U20, U21, Full caps.

2021–22 Sporting Lisbon	0	0		
2022–23 Sporting Lisbon	0	0		
2022–23 Augsburg	13	0	13	0
2023–24 FC Basel	23	2	23	2
2024–25 Chelsea	7	0	7	0
2024–25 Juventus	13	0	13	0

WALSH, Reggie (M) 0 0
b. 20-10-08
Internationals: England U16, U17.

2024–25 Chelsea	0	0

WILEY, Caleb (D) 93 6
b.Atlanta 22-12-04
Internationals: USA U17, U20, U23, Full caps.

2020 Atlanta U	0	0		
2021 Atlanta U	0	0		
2022 Atlanta U	26	1		
2023 Atlanta U	30	4		
2024 Atlanta U	21	1	77	6
2024–25 Chelsea	0	0		
2024–25 Strasbourg	6	0	6	0
2024–25 Watford	10	0	10	0

WILSON, Kaiden (D) 0 0
H: 6 3 W: 12 08 b.Bristol 2-9-05

2024–25 Chelsea	0	0

Players retained or with offer of contract
Austin, Jack Edward; Barbour, Kobe Zane Liston Jr; Gordon, Sol Diego Neville; Hughes, Brodi; Idrissi-Regragui, Yahya; McGlinchey, Harry Daniel; McMahon, Harrison; McNeilly, Donnell Ocarriel; Menezes, Trovoada Cardoso, Leonardo; Richards, Dujuan Odile; Runham, Frankie Leonard; Sands, Hudson; Subuloye, Olutayo Peter Gabriel; Wade, Shaun Charlie; Wheeler, Henry Joseph Roy.

Scholars
Rodda, Harry Mark Peter.

CHELTENHAM T (25)

ARCHER, Ethon (M) 46 7
H: 6 2 W: 12 04 b. 28-8-02

2024–25 Cheltenham T	46	7	46	7

BACKWELL, Tommy (M) 13 1
H: 5 10 W: 11 03 b.Bristol 22-6-03

2023–24 Bristol C	0	0		
2024–25 Bristol C	0	0		
2024–25 Cheltenham T	13	1	13	1

BAKARE, Ibrahim (D) 55 0
H: 5 11 W: 12 02 b. 7-5-02

2019–20 Morecambe	0	0		
2020–21 Cardiff C	0	0		
2021–22 Cardiff C	0	0		
2022–23 Cardiff C	0	0		
2023 Vancouver	25	0	25	0
2024–25 Cheltenham T	30	0	30	0

BENNETT, Scott (D) 475 27
H: 5 10 W: 12 11 b.Newquay 30-11-90

2008–09 Exeter C	0	0		
2009–10 Exeter C	0	0		
2010–11 Exeter C	1	0		
2011–12 Exeter C	15	3		
2012–13 Exeter C	43	6		
2013–14 Exeter C	45	6		
2014–15 Exeter C	28	3	132	18
2015–16 Notts Co	6	0	6	0
2015–16 York C	11	0	11	0
2016–17 Newport Co	39	0		
2017–18 Newport Co	28	2		
2018–19 Newport Co	38	2		
2019–20 Newport Co	28	1		
2020–21 Newport Co	38	2		
2021–22 Newport Co	33	1		
2022–23 Newport Co	39	1		
2023–24 Newport Co	45	0	300	9
2024–25 Cheltenham T	26	0	26	0

BOWMAN, Ryan (F) 349 68
H: 6 2 W: 12 00 b.Carlisle 30-11-91
Internationals: England U18.

2009–10 Carlisle U	6	0		
2010–11 Carlisle U	3	0	9	0
From Darlington, Hereford U				
2013–14 York C	37	8	37	8
From York C, Gateshead.				
2016–17 Motherwell	24	2		
2017–18 Motherwell	32	7		
2018–19 Motherwell	16	1	72	10
2018–19 Exeter C	18	5		
2019–20 Exeter C	37	13		
2020–21 Exeter C	42	14	97	32
2021–22 Shrewsbury T	42	10		
2022–23 Shrewsbury T	38	4		
2023–24 Shrewsbury T	37	1	117	15
2024–25 Cheltenham T	17	3	17	3

BRADBURY, Tom (D) 74 2
H: 6 3 W: 13 08 b.Aylesbury 27-2-98
From Ware, Banbury U, Dundee U, Yeovil T, FC Halifax T.

2022–23 Cheltenham T	13	1		
2023–24 Cheltenham T	22	0		
2024–25 Cheltenham T	39	1	74	2

DAY, Joe (G) 333 0
H: 6 1 W: 12 00 b.Brighton 13-8-90
From Rushden & D.

2011–12 Peterborough U	0	0		
2012–13 Peterborough U	0	0		
2013–14 Peterborough U	4	0		
2014–15 Peterborough U	0	0	4	0
2014–15 Newport Co	36	0		
2015–16 Newport Co	41	0		
2016–17 Newport Co	45	0		
2017–18 Newport Co	46	0		
2018–19 Newport Co	43	0		
2019–20 Cardiff C	1	0		
2019–20 AFC Wimbledon	9	0	9	0
2020–21 Cardiff C	0	0	1	0
2020–21 Bristol R	18	0	18	0
2021–22 Newport Co	27	0		
2022–23 Newport Co	28	0		
2023–24 Newport Co	0	0	266	0
2024–25 Cheltenham T	35	0	35	0

DIALLO, Mamadou (D) 0 0
H: 6 1 W: 12 13

2024–25 Cheltenham T	0	0

DULSON, Liam (F) 29 2
H: 5 10 W: 11 11 b. 1-1-02

2024–25 Cheltenham T	29	2	29	2

EVANS, Owen (G) 144 0
H: 6 0 W: 11 00 b.Newport 28-11-96
Internationals: Wales U19, U21.
From Hereford U.

2016–17 Wigan Ath	0	0		
2017–18 Wigan Ath	0	0		
2018–19 Wigan Ath	0	0		
2019–20 Wigan Ath	0	0		
2019–20 Macclesfield T	24	0	24	0
2019–20 Cheltenham T	11	0		
2020–21 Wigan Ath	1	0		
2021–22 Wigan Ath	0	0	1	0
2021–22 Cheltenham T	27	0		
2022–23 Walsall	45	0		
2023–24 Walsall	25	0	70	0
2024–25 Cheltenham T	11	0	49	0

FRANKS, Jude (G) 0 0

2023–24 Cheltenham T	0	0
2024–25 Cheltenham T	0	0

HARRIS, Max (G) 0 0
H: 6 2 W: 12 04 b.Gloucester 14-9-99

2018–19 Oxford U	0	0
2019–20 Oxford U	0	0
2020–21 Cheltenham T	0	0
2021–22 Cheltenham T	0	0
2022–23 Cheltenham T	0	0
2023–24 Cheltenham T	0	0
2024–25 Cheltenham T	0	0

HAYNES, Ryan (D) 250 7
H: 5 7 W: 10 10 b.Northampton 27-9-95

2012–13 Coventry C	1	0		
2013–14 Coventry C	2	0		
2014–15 Coventry C	26	1		
2015–16 Coventry C	9	0		
2015–16 Cambridge U	10	0	10	0
2016–17 Coventry C	19	0		
2017–18 Coventry C	21	0	78	1
2018–19 Shrewsbury T	16	0	16	0
2019–20 Newport Co	32	1		
2020–21 Newport Co	37	1		
2021–22 Newport Co	34	3	103	5
2022–23 Northampton T	27	1		
2023–24 Northampton T	3	0	30	1
2024–25 Cheltenham T	13	0	13	0

JUDE-BOYD, Arkell (M) 34 3
H: 6 0 W: 11 09 b.Hillingdon 22-1-03
Internationals: Saint Lucia Full caps.

2024–25 Cheltenham T	34	3	34	3

KING, Tom (M) 4 0
H: 5 7 W: 9 08 b.Gloucester 20-9-06
Internationals: England U18.

2023–24 Cheltenham T	0	0		
2024–25 Cheltenham T	4	0	4	0

KINSELLA, Liam (M) 291 2
H: 5 9 W: 11 11 b.Colchester 23-2-96
Internationals: Republic of Ireland U19, U21.

2013–14 Walsall	0	0		
2014–15 Walsall	4	0		
2015–16 Walsall	7	1		
2016–17 Walsall	8	0		
2017–18 Walsall	19	0		
2018–19 Walsall	31	0		
2019–20 Walsall	31	0		
2020–21 Walsall	43	0		
2021–22 Walsall	32	0		
2022–23 Walsall	37	1	212	2
2023–24 Swindon T	22	0	22	0
2023–24 Cheltenham T	20	0		
2024–25 Cheltenham T	37	0	57	0

LIGGETT, Brandon (M) 0 0
H: 5 9 W: 11 00 b. 6-4-06

2022–23 Cheltenham T	0	0
2023–24 Cheltenham T	0	0
2024–25 Cheltenham T	0	0

MILLER, George (F) 225 51
H: 5 10 W: 10 01 b.Bolton 11-8-98

2015–16 Bury	1	0		
2016–17 Bury	28	7		
2017–18 Middlesbrough	0	0		
2017–18 Bury	19	8	48	15
2018–19 Middlesbrough	0	0		
2018–19 Bradford C	39	3	39	3
2018–19 Barnsley	0	0		
2019–20 Barnsley	1	0		
2019–20 Scunthorpe U	15	1	15	1
2020–21 Barnsley	5	0		
2021–22 Barnsley	0	0	6	0
2021–22 Walsall	41	12	41	12
2022–23 Doncaster R	34	11		
2023–24 Doncaster R	2	0	36	11
2024–25 Cheltenham T	40	9	40	9

OBIERI, Sopuruchukwu (F) 0 0
H: 6 1 W: 11 11 b. 8-1-08

2023–24 Cheltenham T	0	0
2024–25 Cheltenham T	0	0

OLATEJU, Ibrahim (F) 0 0
b. 27-9-06

2024–25 Cheltenham T	0	0

PAYNE, Lewis (D) 48 1
H: 5 11 W: 11 07 b. 30-5-04

2021–22 Southampton	0	0		
2022–23 Southampton	0	0		
2023–24 Southampton	0	0		
2023–24 Newport Co	31	1	31	1
2024–25 Cheltenham T	17	0	17	0

PELL, Harry (M) 355 42
H: 6 4 W: 13 05 b.Tilbury 21-10-91

2009–10 Charlton Ath	0	0		
2010–11 Bristol R	10	0	10	0
2010–11 Hereford U	7	0		
2011–12 Hereford U	30	3	37	3
2012–13 AFC Wimbledon	17	2		
2013–14 AFC Wimbledon	33	4		
2014–15 AFC Wimbledon	9	0		
From Eastleigh.				
2016–17 Cheltenham T	42	7		
2017–18 Cheltenham T	37	5		
2018–19 Colchester U	31	6		
2019–20 Colchester U	22	3		
2020–21 Colchester U	25	2	78	11
2021–22 Accrington S	37	6		
2022–23 Accrington S	1	0	38	6
2022–23 AFC Wimbledon	28	3		
2023–24 AFC Wimbledon	26	1	113	10
2024–25 Cheltenham T	0	0	79	0

PETT, Tom (M) 344 29
H: 5 8 W: 11 00 b.Potters Bar 3-12-91
Internationals: England C.
From Potters Bar T, Wealdstone.

2014–15 Stevenage	34	7		
2015–16 Stevenage	40	1		
2016–17 Stevenage	40	6		
2017–18 Stevenage	27	6		
2017–18 Lincoln C	9	1		
2018–19 Lincoln C	44	3		
2019–20 Lincoln C	2	0	55	4
2020–21 Stevenage	31	2		
2021–22 Stevenage	0	0	172	22
2021–22 Port Vale	39	2		
2022–23 Port Vale	30	1	69	3
2023–24 Cheltenham T	28	0		
2024–25 Cheltenham T	20	0	48	0

POWER, Darragh (D) 136 4
H: 5 10 W: 11 07 b.Dublin 29-12-00

2019 Waterford	0	0
2020 Waterford	8	0

2021 Waterford 31 0
2022 Waterford 31 1
2023 Waterford 18 1
2024 Waterford 35 2 **124 4**
2024–25 Cheltenham T 12 0 **12 0**

SOHNA, Harrison (M) 8 0
H: 5 10 W: 9 08 b.Gloucester 1-7-02
Internationals: England U16.
2020–21 Aston Villa 0 0
2021–22 Sunderland 0 0
2022–23 Sunderland 0 0
From unattached.
2024–25 Cheltenham T 8 0 **8 0**

TAYLOR, Matty (F) 359 122
H: 5 9 W: 11 05 b.Oxford 30-3-90
Internationals: England C.
From Oxford U, North Leigh, Forest Green R.
2015–16 Bristol R 46 27
2016–17 Bristol R 27 16 **73 43**
2016–17 Bristol C 15 2
2017–18 Bristol C 18 1
2018–19 Bristol C 33 4
2019–20 Bristol C 1 0 **67 7**
2019–20 *Oxford U* 26 13
2020–21 Oxford U 46 18
2021–22 Oxford U 44 20
2022–23 Oxford U 22 3 **138 54**
2022–23 *Port Vale* 14 4 **14 4**
2023–24 Forest Green R 17 2 **17 2**
2023–24 Cheltenham T 13 7
2024–25 Cheltenham T 37 5 **50 12**

THOMAS, Jordan (M) 54 8
H: 5 10 W: 11 07 b. 2-5-01
2023–24 Cheltenham T 14 0
2024–25 Cheltenham T 40 8 **54 8**

TUSTIN, Harry (F) 1 0
b. 29-9-06
2024–25 Cheltenham T 1 0 **1 0**

WALTERS, Cameron (D) 0 0
b. 9-10-06
2022–23 Cheltenham T 0 0
2023–24 Cheltenham T 0 0
2024–25 Cheltenham T 0 0

WILLCOX, Freddie (M) 4 0
H: 5 9 W: 10 06 b. 11-12-05
2022–23 Cheltenham T 1 0
2023–24 Cheltenham T 1 0
2024–25 Cheltenham T 2 0 **4 0**

YOUNG, Luke (M) 158 13
H: 5 8 W: 11 05 b.Ivybridge 22-2-93
2010–11 Plymouth Arg 5 0
2011–12 Plymouth Arg 28 2
2012–13 Plymouth Arg 32 2
2013–14 Plymouth Arg 34 4
2014–15 Plymouth Arg 0 0 **99 8**
2014–15 Torquay U 0 0
From Wrexham.
2023–24 Wrexham 25 1 **25 1**
2024–25 Cheltenham T 34 4 **34 4**

Scholars
Bailey, Ieuan James; Barber, Mark Andrew; Burgess, Bradley Thomas; Caple, Charlie Lewis Douglas; Franks, Jude William; King, Fredrick David Ian; Olateju, Ibrahim Adio Olayinka; Rexworthy, Isaac; Shumba, Tinomudaishe Christian; Tustin, Harry James; Wainwright, Tyler Lee; Walters, Cameron Robert; Way, Thomas Bradley.

CHESTERFIELD (26)

AKINOLA, Tim (M) 10 0
H: 5 10 W: 11 07 b.Lokoja 8-5-01
2018–19 Lincoln C 0 0
2019–20 Huddersfield T 0 0
2020–21 Arsenal 0 0
2021–22 Arsenal 0 0
2021–22 *Dundee U* 1 0 **1 0**
2022–23 Arsenal 0 0
2023–24 Al Bidda 7 0 **7 0**
2024–25 Chesterfield 2 0 **2 0**
Transferred to Gateshead, March 2025.

BANKS, Oliver (M) 296 32
H: 6 3 W: 11 11 b.Rotherham 21-9-92
2010–11 Rotherham U 1 1
2011–12 Rotherham U 0 0 **1 1**
From FC United of Manchester.
2013–14 Chesterfield 25 7
2014–15 Chesterfield 24 0
2014–15 *Northampton T* 3 0 **3 0**
2015–16 Chesterfield 32 2
2016–17 Oldham Ath 33 2
2017–18 Oldham Ath 7 0 **40 2**
2017–18 *Swindon T* 17 3 **17 3**
2018–19 Tranmere R 33 3
2019–20 Tranmere R 11 3
2020–21 Tranmere R 12 0 **56 6**
2020–21 Barrow 20 0
2021–22 Barrow 39 9 **59 9**
From Chesterfield.
2024–25 Chesterfield 39 2 **120 11**

BOOT, Ryan (G) 51 0
H: 6 1 W: 11 03 b.Rocester 9-11-94
Internationals: England C.
2012–13 Port Vale 0 0
2013–14 Port Vale 0 0
2014–15 Port Vale 0 0
2015–16 Port Vale 0 0
2016–17 Port Vale 1 0
2017–18 Port Vale 22 0 **23 0**
From Solihull Moors, Chesterfield.
2024–25 Chesterfield 28 0 **28 0**

COLCLOUGH, Ryan (F) 197 28
H: 6 3 W: 13 01 b.Budapest 27-12-94
2012–13 Crewe Alex 18 1
2013–14 Crewe Alex 8 2
2014–15 Crewe Alex 7 2
2015–16 Crewe Alex 27 7 **60 12**
2015–16 Wigan Ath 10 2
2016–17 Wigan Ath 10 0
2016–17 *Milton Keynes D* 18 5 **18 5**
2017–18 Wigan Ath 26 4 **46 6**
2018–19 Scunthorpe U 17 2
2019–20 Scunthorpe U 20 0
2020–21 Scunthorpe U 0 0 **37 2**
From Altrincham, Chesterfield.
2024–25 Chesterfield 36 3 **36 3**

COOK, Connor (M) 2 0
H: 5 10 W: 11 11 b. 14-7-05
From Chesterfield.
2024–25 Chesterfield 2 0 **2 0**

DALEY-CAMPBELL, Vontae (D) 19 0
H: 5 9 W: 11 00 b.Lambeth 2-4-01
Internationals: England U16, U17, U18, U19.
From Arsenal.
2020–21 Leicester C 0 0
2021–22 Leicester C 0 0
2021–22 *Dundee* 9 0 **9 0**
2022–23 Cardiff C 1 0
2023–24 Cardiff C 0 0 **1 0**
2023–24 Peterborough U 0 0
2024–25 Chesterfield 9 0 **9 0**

DOBRA, Armando (M) 75 10
H: 5 9 W: 11 00 b.Redbridge 14-4-01
Internationals: Albania U19, U21.
2019–20 Ipswich T 3 0
2020–21 Ipswich T 17 0
2021–22 Ipswich T 2 0 **22 0**
2021–22 *Colchester U* 11 1 **11 1**
From Chesterfield.
2024–25 Chesterfield 42 9 **42 9**

DONACIEN, Janoi (D) 294 1
H: 6 0 W: 11 11 b.St Lucia 3-11-93
Internationals: St Lucia Full caps.
2011–12 Aston Villa 0 0
2012–13 Aston Villa 0 0
2013–14 Aston Villa 0 0
2014–15 Aston Villa 0 0
2014–15 *Tranmere R* 31 0 **31 0**
2015–16 Aston Villa 0 0
2015–16 *Wycombe W* 2 0 **2 0**
2015–16 *Newport Co* 29 0 **29 0**
2016–17 Accrington S 35 1
2017–18 Accrington S 45 0
2018–19 Ipswich T 10 0
2018–19 *Accrington S* 19 0 **99 1**
2019–20 Ipswich T 13 0
2020–21 Ipswich T 0 0
2020–21 *Fleetwood T* 19 0 **19 0**
2021–22 Ipswich T 43 0
2022–23 Ipswich T 38 0
2023–24 Ipswich T 3 0
2024–25 Ipswich T 0 0 **107 0**
2024–25 Chesterfield 7 0 **7 0**

DRUMMOND, Kane (F) 14 1
b. 19-12-00
From Macclesfield.
2024–25 Chesterfield 14 1 **14 1**

DUFFY, Dylan (F) 98 8
H: 5 6 W: 11 00 b.Dublin 28-11-02
Internationals: Republic of Ireland U21.
2022 UCD 31 3 **31 3**
2022–23 Lincoln C 7 1
2023–24 Lincoln C 34 2
2024–25 Lincoln C 8 0 **49 3**
2024–25 Chesterfield 18 2 **18 2**

DUNKLEY, Cheyenne (D) 318 32
H: 6 2 W: 13 05 b.Wolverhampton 13-2-92
Internationals: England C.
From Crewe Alex, Hednesford T, Kidderminster H.
2014–15 Oxford U 9 0
2015–16 Oxford U 29 4
2016–17 Oxford U 40 3 **78 7**
2017–18 Wigan Ath 43 7
2018–19 Wigan Ath 38 0
2019–20 Wigan Ath 26 6 **107 13**
2020–21 Sheffield Wed 12 0
2021–22 Sheffield Wed 21 2 **33 2**
2022–23 Shrewsbury T 46 5
2023–24 Shrewsbury T 45 4 **91 9**
2024–25 Chesterfield 9 1 **9 1**

ELLIOTT, Gunner (F) 1 0
b. 18-7-08
Internationals: Malta U17, U21.
2024–25 Chesterfield 1 0 **1 0**

FLECK, John (M) 483 25
H: 5 7 W: 11 05 b.Glasgow 24-8-91
Internationals: Scotland U17, U19, U21, Full caps.
2007–08 Rangers 1 0
2008–09 Rangers 8 1
2009–10 Rangers 15 1
2010–11 Rangers 13 0
2011–12 Rangers 4 0 **41 2**
2011–12 *Blackpool* 7 0 **7 0**
2012–13 Coventry C 35 3
2013–14 Coventry C 43 1
2014–15 Coventry C 44 0
2015–16 Coventry C 40 4 **162 8**
2016–17 Sheffield U 44 4
2017–18 Sheffield U 41 2
2018–19 Sheffield U 45 2
2019–20 Sheffield U 30 5
2020–21 Sheffield U 31 0
2021–22 Sheffield U 35 1
2022–23 Sheffield U 26 1
2023–24 Sheffield U 4 0 **256 15**
2023–24 Blackburn R 1 0 **1 0**
2024–25 Chesterfield 16 0 **16 0**

GORDON, Lewis (D) 94 0
H: 5 9 W: 10 01 b.London 12-2-01
Internationals: Scotland U17, U19.
2018–19 Watford 0 0
2019–20 Watford 0 0
2020–21 Brentford 0 0
2021–22 Brentford 0 0
2022–23 Bristol R 39 0
2023–24 Bristol R 22 0 **61 0**
2024–25 Chesterfield 33 0 **33 0**

GRIGG, Will (M) 468 137
H: 5 11 W: 11 00 b.Solihull 3-7-91
Internationals: Northern Ireland U19, U21, Full caps.
From Stratford T.
2008–09 Walsall 1 0
2009–10 Walsall 0 0
2010–11 Walsall 28 4
2011–12 Walsall 29 4
2012–13 Walsall 41 19 **99 27**
2013–14 Brentford 34 5
2014–15 Brentford 0 0 **34 5**
2014–15 *Milton Keynes D* 44 20
2015–16 Wigan Ath 40 25
2016–17 Wigan Ath 33 5
2017–18 Wigan Ath 43 19
2018–19 Wigan Ath 17 4 **133 53**
2018–19 Sunderland 18 4
2019–20 Sunderland 20 1
2020–21 Sunderland 9 0
2020–21 *Milton Keynes D* 20 8
2021–22 Sunderland 0 0 **47 5**
2021–22 *Rotherham U* 19 2 **19 2**
2022–23 Milton Keynes D 42 5 **106 33**
From Chesterfield.
2024–25 Chesterfield 30 12 **30 12**

GRIMES, Jamie (D) 91 7
H: 6 2 W: 12 10 b.Nottingham 22-12-90
Internationals: England C.
From Swansea C, Redditch U, Bedford T, Kidderminster H, Dover Ath.
2017–18 Cheltenham T 43 3 **43 3**
2018–19 Macclesfield T 13 1 **13 1**
From Ebbsfleet U, Hereford, Chesterfield.
2024–25 Chesterfield 35 3 **35 3**

HOBSON, Bailey (F) 11 0
H: 5 10 W: 11 07 b.Pontefract 1-8-02
2024–25 Chesterfield 11 0 **11 0**

HORTON, Branden (D) 38 2
H: 5 10 W: 11 11 b.Doncaster 9-9-00
2017–18 Doncaster R 0 0
2018–19 Doncaster R 0 0
2019–20 Doncaster R 0 0
2020–21 Doncaster R 11 0
2021–22 Doncaster R 20 2 **31 2**
From Chesterfield.
2024–25 Chesterfield 7 0 **7 0**
Transferred to Gateshead, February 2025.

JACOBS, Michael (M) 444 67
H: 5 9 W: 11 09 b.Rothwell 4-11-91
2009–10 Northampton T 0 0
2010–11 Northampton T 41 5
2011–12 Northampton T 46 6 **87 11**

2012–13 Derby Co 38 2
2013–14 Derby Co 3 0 **41 2**
2013–14 Wolverhampton W 30 8
2014–15 Wolverhampton W 12 0 **42 8**
2014–15 *Blackpool* 5 1 **5 1**
2015–16 Wigan Ath 35 10
2016–17 Wigan Ath 43 3
2017–18 Wigan Ath 44 12
2018–19 Wigan Ath 22 4
2019–20 Wigan Ath 32 3 **176 32**
2020–21 Portsmouth 20 2
2021–22 Portsmouth 24 6
2022–23 Portsmouth 32 4 **76 12**
From Chesterfield.
2024–25 Chesterfield 17 1 **17 1**

JESSOP, Liam (F) 2 0
H: 6 1 W: 11 11 b. 13-8-05
Internationals: Gibraltar U17, U19, U21, Full caps.
From Chesterfield.
2024–25 Chesterfield 2 0 **2 0**

JONES, Mike (M) 498 38
H: 6 0 W: 12 04 b.Birkenhead 15-8-87
2005–06 Tranmere R 1 0
2006–07 Tranmere R 0 0
2006–07 *Shrewsbury T* 13 1 **13 1**
2007–08 Tranmere R 9 1 **10 1**
2008–09 Bury 46 4
2009–10 Bury 41 5
2010–11 Bury 42 8
2011–12 Bury 24 3 **153 20**
2011–12 Sheffield Wed 10 0
2012–13 Sheffield Wed 0 0 **10 0**
2012–13 Crawley T 40 1
2013–14 Crawley T 42 3 **82 4**
2014–15 Oldham Ath 45 6
2015–16 Oldham Ath 35 3 **80 9**
2016–17 Carlisle U 28 0
2017–18 Carlisle U 43 0
2018–19 Carlisle U 24 1
2019–20 Carlisle U 37 0 **132 1**
2020–21 Barrow 13 2
2021–22 Barrow 3 0 **16 2**
2024–25 Chesterfield 2 0 **2 0**

MADDEN, Patrick (F) 547 171
H: 6 0 W: 12 00 b.Dublin 4-3-90
Internationals: Republic of Ireland U19, U21, U23, Full caps.
2008 Bohemians 18 4
2009 Bohemians 2 0
2009 Shelbourne 13 6 **13 6**
2010 Bohemians 34 10 **54 14**
2010–11 Carlisle U 13 0
2011–12 Carlisle U 18 1
2012–13 Carlisle U 1 1 **32 2**
2012–13 *Yeovil T* 35 22
2013–14 Yeovil T 9 0 **44 22**
2013–14 Scunthorpe U 21 5
2014–15 Scunthorpe U 46 14
2015–16 Scunthorpe U 46 20
2016–17 Scunthorpe U 34 11
2017–18 Scunthorpe U 20 2 **167 52**
2017–18 Fleetwood T 20 6
2018–19 Fleetwood T 44 15
2019–20 Fleetwood T 35 15
2020–21 Fleetwood T 32 7 **131 43**
From Stockport Co.
2022–23 Stockport Co 37 10
2023–24 Stockport Co 42 17 **79 27**
2024–25 Chesterfield 27 5 **27 5**

MANDEVILLE, Liam (F) 140 16
H: 5 11 W: 12 02 b.Lincoln 17-2-97
Internationals: England C.
2014–15 Doncaster R 3 0
2015–16 Doncaster R 8 1
2016–17 Doncaster R 21 7
2017–18 Doncaster R 17 1
2017–18 *Colchester U* 7 0 **7 0**
2018–19 Doncaster R 0 0 **49 9**
2018–19 *Morecambe* 42 3 **42 3**
From Chesterfield.
2024–25 Chesterfield 42 4 **42 4**

MARSHALL, Thomas (F) 0 0
2024–25 Chesterfield 0 0

McFADZEAN, Kyle (D) 460 22
H: 6 1 W: 13 05 b.Sheffield 20-2-87
Internationals: England C.
2004–05 Sheffield U 0 0
2005–06 Sheffield U 0 0
2006–07 Sheffield U 0 0
From Alfreton T.
2011–12 Crawley T 37 2
2012–13 Crawley T 17 3
2013–14 Crawley T 42 1 **96 6**
2014–15 Milton Keynes D 41 3
2015–16 Milton Keynes D 39 0 **80 3**
2016–17 Burton Alb 31 1
2017–18 Burton Alb 42 0
2018–19 Burton Alb 35 4 **108 5**
2018–19 Coventry C 0 0
2019–20 Coventry C 30 0
2020–21 Coventry C 38 2
2021–22 Coventry C 37 3
2022–23 Coventry C 35 2
2023–24 Coventry C 15 1 **155 8**
2023–24 Blackburn R 12 0
2024–25 Blackburn R 1 0 **13 0**
2024–25 Chesterfield 8 0 **8 0**

MITCHELL, Luke (M) 0 0
From Chesterfield.
2024–25 Chesterfield 0 0

MOHIUDDIN, Ali (M) 0 0
b. 24-4-05
From Chesterfield.
2024–25 Chesterfield 0 0

NAYLOR, Tom (D) 419 33
H: 5 11 W: 11 05 b.Kirkby-in-Ashfield 28-6-91
From Mansfield T.
2011–12 Derby Co 8 0
2012–13 Derby Co 0 0
2012–13 *Bradford C* 5 0 **5 0**
2013–14 Derby Co 0 0
2013–14 *Newport Co* 33 1 **33 1**
2014–15 Derby Co 0 0 **8 0**
2014–15 *Cambridge U* 8 0 **8 0**
2014–15 *Burton Alb* 17 0
2015–16 Burton Alb 41 6
2016–17 Burton Alb 33 3
2017–18 Burton Alb 33 3 **124 12**
2018–19 Portsmouth 43 4
2019–20 Portsmouth 33 1
2020–21 Portsmouth 46 6 **122 11**
2021–22 Wigan Ath 43 3
2022–23 Wigan Ath 36 2 **79 5**
From Chesterfield.
2024–25 Chesterfield 40 4 **40 4**

OLDAKER, Darren (M) 53 3
H: 5 9 W: 12 04 b.London 4-1-99
Internationals: England C.
2015–16 Gillingham 0 0
2016–17 Gillingham 5 0
2017–18 Gillingham 3 0
2018–19 Gillingham 13 0 **21 0**
From Billericay T, Westfield, Hythe T, Welling U, Dorking W, Chesterfield.
2024–25 Chesterfield 32 3 **32 3**

PALMER, Ashley (D) 19 2
H: 6 1 W: 11 13 b.Pontefract 9-11-92
Internationals: England C.
2010–11 Scunthorpe U 0 0
2011–12 Scunthorpe U 1 0 **1 0**
2022–23 Stockport Co 3 0 **3 0**
From Chesterfield.
2024–25 Chesterfield 15 2 **15 2**

QUIGLEY, Joe (F) 15 1
H: 6 4 W: 13 01 b.Hayes 12-10-96
Internationals: Republic of Ireland U21.
2016–17 Bournemouth 0 0
2016–17 *Gillingham* 10 1 **10 1**
2017–18 Bournemouth 0 0
2017–18 *Newport Co* 2 0 **2 0**
From Maidstone U, Bromley, Dagenham & Red, Yeovil T, Chesterfield.
2024–25 Chesterfield 3 0 **3 0**
Transferred to Forest Green R, August 2024.

RINALDO, Ashton (G) 0 0
b. 25-10-05
2024–25 Chesterfield 0 0

SHECKELFORD, Ryheem (D) 17 0
H: 5 9 W: 11 05 b.London 20-5-97
From Fulham, Maidenhead U.
2024–25 Chesterfield 17 0 **17 0**

SIMMONITE, James (F) 0 0
From Chesterfield.
2024–25 Chesterfield 0 0

SMITH, Barnaby (D) 0 0
2024–25 Chesterfield 0 0

THOMAS, Harvey (D) 0 0
From Chesterfield.
2024–25 Chesterfield 0 0

WILLIAMS, Tyrone (D) 10 0
H: 6 2 W: 12 11 b.Birmingham 21-10-94
From Kidderminster H, Solihull Moors, Chesterfield.
2024–25 Chesterfield 10 0 **10 0**

Scholars
Elliott, Gunner Jack; Hague, Joshua Jon; Hardy, Ethan Lucius; McKernan, Marcus Anthony; Shone, Finlay; Whitney, Alexander James; Wright, Bailey Lee.

COLCHESTER U (27)

ANDERSON, Harry (F) 272 30
H: 5 10 W: 9 11 b.Slouth 9-1-97
From Crawley T.
2014–15 Peterborough U 10 0
2015–16 Peterborough U 5 0
2016–17 Peterborough U 1 0 **16 0**
2017–18 Lincoln C 40 6
2018–19 Lincoln C 43 5
2019–20 Lincoln C 30 5
2020–21 Lincoln C 29 3 **142 19**
2021–22 Bristol R 44 6
2022–23 Bristol R 28 0 **72 6**
2023–24 Stevenage 1 0 **1 0**
2023–24 *Colchester U* 10 2
2024–25 Colchester U 31 3 **41 5**

BENDLE, Alfie (M) 14 0
H: 5 10 W: 12 02 b.Eastbourne 27-1-05
2021–22 AFC Wimbledon 1 0
2022–23 AFC Wimbledon 8 0 **9 0**
2023–24 Forest Green R 5 0 **5 0**
2024–25 Colchester U 0 0

BISHOP, Teddy (M) 243 17
H: 5 11 W: 10 03 b.Cambridge 15-7-96
2013–14 Ipswich T 0 0
2014–15 Ipswich T 33 1
2015–16 Ipswich T 4 0
2016–17 Ipswich T 19 0
2017–18 Ipswich T 4 0
2018–19 Ipswich T 18 0
2019–20 Ipswich T 9 0
2020–21 Ipswich T 36 4 **123 5**
2021–22 Lincoln C 36 4
2022–23 Lincoln C 24 3
2023–24 Lincoln C 33 4 **93 11**
2024–25 Colchester U 27 1 **27 1**

CHAMBERLAIN, Harrison (G) 0 0
b. 9-4-06
2024–25 Colchester U 0 0

CONNOLLY, Kien (F) 0 0
H: 6 3 b.London 2-9-05
2024–25 Colchester U 0 0

DRYSDALE, Rashaad (D) 0 0
2024–25 Colchester U 0 0

EDWARDS, Frankie (D) 0 0
H: 6 5 b. 8-2-06
2024–25 Colchester U 0 0

EDWARDS, Owura (F) 115 14
H: 5 8 W: 10 10 b.Bristol 10-4-01
2020–21 Grimsby T 17 1 **17 1**
2020–21 Bristol C 3 0
2021–22 Bristol C 0 0
2021–22 *Exeter C* 10 0 **10 0**
2021–22 *Colchester U* 13 3
2022–23 Bristol C 0 0 **3 0**
2022–23 *Ross Co* 29 3 **29 3**
2023–24 Colchester U 6 0
2024–25 Colchester U 37 7 **56 10**

EGBO, Mandela (D) 138 4
H: 5 11 W: 11 00 b.Brent 17-8-97
Internationals: England U16, U17, U18.
2018–19 Borussia M'gladbach 1 0 **1 0**
2019–20 Darmstadt 98 5 0 **5 0**
2020 New York Red Bulls 9 1
2021 New York Red Bulls 29 2 **38 3**
2021–22 Swindon T 9 0 **9 0**
2022–23 Charlton Ath 15 0 **15 0**
2023–24 Colchester U 25 0
2024–25 Colchester U 45 1 **70 1**

EMERY, Lennox (F) 0 0
b. 30-9-08
2024–25 Colchester U 0 0

FLANAGAN, Tom (D) 345 12
H: 6 2 W: 11 05 b.Hammersmith 21-10-91
Internationals: Northern Ireland U21, Full caps.
2009–10 Milton Keynes D 1 0
2010–11 Milton Keynes D 2 0
2011–12 Milton Keynes D 21 3
2012–13 Milton Keynes D 0 0
2012–13 *Gillingham* 13 1 **13 1**
2012–13 *Barnet* 9 0 **9 0**
2013–14 Milton Keynes D 7 0
2013–14 *Stevenage* 2 0 **2 0**
2014–15 Milton Keynes D 6 0 **37 3**
2014–15 *Plymouth Arg* 4 0 **4 0**
2015–16 Burton Alb 18 0
2016–17 Burton Alb 30 0
2017–18 Burton Alb 27 2 **75 2**
2018–19 Sunderland 32 2
2019–20 Sunderland 18 1
2020–21 Sunderland 16 0
2021–22 Sunderland 25 1 **91 4**
2021–22 Shrewsbury T 14 1
2022–23 Shrewsbury T 38 1

| 2023–24 | Shrewsbury T | 21 | 0 | 73 | 2 |
| 2024–25 | Colchester U | 41 | 0 | 41 | 0 |

GODZIEMSKI, Ollie (F)   0   0

| 2024–25 | Colchester U | 0 | 0 | | |

GOODLIFFE, Ben (D)   107   8
H: 6 2 W: 12 08 b.Watford 19-6-99
From Boreham Wood, Wolverhampton W, Sutton U.

2021–22	Sutton U	43	3		
2022–23	Sutton U	23	0		
2023–24	Sutton U	30	2	96	5
2024–25	Colchester U	11	3	11	3

GORDON, John-Kymani (F)   88   6
H: 5 11 W: 10 10 b.London 13-2-03
Internationals: England U16.

2019–20	Crystal Palace	0	0		
2020–21	Crystal Palace	0	0		
2021–22	Crystal Palace	0	0		
2022–23	*Carlisle U*	15	2	15	2
2023–24	Crystal Palace	0	0		
2023–24	*Cambridge U*	14	0	14	0
2023–24	*AFC Wimbledon*	18	1	18	1
2024–25	Colchester U	41	3	41	3

GREENIDGE, Will (D)   29   0
H: 5 9 W: 11 03 b.Redbridge 15-5-02
From West Ham U.

2022–23	Colchester U	10	0		
2023–24	Colchester U	19	0		
2024–25	Colchester U	0	0	29	0

Transferred to Hornchurch, January 2025.

HOPPER, Tom (F)   316   55
H: 6 1 W: 12 00 b.Boston 14-12-93
Internationals: England U18.
From Boston U.

2011–12	Leicester C	0	0		
2012–13	Leicester C	0	0		
2012–13	*Bury*	22	3	22	3
2013–14	Leicester C	0	0		
2014–15	Leicester C	0	0		
2014–15	Scunthorpe U	12	4		
2015–16	Scunthorpe U	34	8		
2016–17	Scunthorpe U	31	5		
2017–18	Scunthorpe U	38	7	115	24
2018–19	Southend U	14	7		
2019–20	Southend U	14	2	28	9
2019–20	Lincoln C	8	2		
2020–21	Lincoln C	39	8		
2021–22	Lincoln C	20	2		
2022–23	Lincoln C	16	2	83	14
2022–23	Colchester U	17	1		
2023–24	Colchester U	35	4		
2024–25	Colchester U	16	0	68	5

Transferred to Southend U, January 2025.

HUNT, Robert (D)   261   3
H: 5 7 W: 10 08 b.Dagenham 7-7-95

2013–14	Brighton & HA	0	0		
2014–15	Brighton & HA	0	0		
2015–16	Brighton & HA	0	0		
2016–17	Brighton & HA	1	0	1	0
2016–17	Oldham Ath	10	0		
2017–18	Oldham Ath	33	0		
2018–19	Oldham Ath	38	1	81	1
2019–20	Swindon T	34	1		
2020–21	Swindon T	19	0		
2021–22	Swindon T	37	0	90	1
2022–23	Leyton Orient	32	0		
2023–24	Leyton Orient	35	1	67	1
2024–25	Colchester U	22	0	22	0

IANDOLO, Ellis (D)   204   5
H: 6 4 W: 14 00 b.Chatham 22-8-97
From Maidstone U.

2015–16	Swindon T	12	0		
2016–17	Swindon T	10	0		
2017–18	Swindon T	12	1		
2018–19	Swindon T	15	0		
2019–20	Swindon T	13	0		
2020–21	Swindon T	8	0		
2021–22	Swindon T	44	1		
2022–23	Swindon T	23	1	137	3
2023–24	Colchester U	23	1		
2024–25	Colchester U	44	1	67	2

JAY, Matt (F)   198   42
H: 5 10 W: 10 12 b.Torbay 27-2-96

2013–14	Exeter C	2	0		
2014–15	Exeter C	3	0		
2015–16	Exeter C	0	0		
2016–17	Exeter C	2	0		
2017–18	Exeter C	17	1		
2018–19	Exeter C	18	4		
2019–20	Exeter C	14	4		
2020–21	Exeter C	44	18		
2021–22	Exeter C	45	14		
2022–23	Exeter C	18	0	163	41
2022–23	Colchester U	18	0		
2023–24	Colchester U	17	1		
2024–25	Colchester U	0	0	35	1

Tansferred to Torquay U, January 2025.

JOLLIFFE, Max (M)   2   0
b. 13-9-05

| 2024–25 | Colchester U | 2 | 0 | 2 | 0 |

KELLEHER, Fiacre (D)   147   7
H: 6 3 W: 12 08 b.Cork 10-3-96

2016–17	Celtic	0	0		
2016–17	Peterhead	0	0		
2017–18	Oxford U	0	0		
2018–19	Oxford U	0	0		
2018–19	*Macclesfield T*	42	1		
2019–20	*Macclesfield T*	37	1	79	2

From Wrexham.

2021–22	Bradford C	9	0		
2022–23	Bradford C	0	0	9	0
2023–24	Colchester U	20	2		
2023–24	Colchester U	11	1		
2024–25	Colchester U	28	2	59	5

LISBIE, Kyreece (F)   4   0
b. 1-12-03

| 2024–25 | Colchester U | 4 | 0 | 4 | 0 |

MACEY, Matt (G)   154   0
H: 6 7 W: 14 05 b.Bristol 9-9-94

2011–12	Bristol R	0	0		
2012–13	Bristol R	0	0		
2013–14	Arsenal	0	0		
2014–15	Arsenal	0	0		
2014–15	*Accrington S*	4	0	4	0
2015–16	Arsenal	0	0		
2016–17	Arsenal	0	0		
2016–17	*Luton T*	11	0		
2017–18	Arsenal	0	0		
2018–19	Arsenal	0	0		
2018–19	*Plymouth Arg*	34	0	34	0
2019–20	Arsenal	0	0		
2020–21	Arsenal	0	0		
2020–21	Hibernian	3	0		
2021–22	Hibernian	35	0	38	0
2022–23	Luton T	0	0	11	0
2022–23	Portsmouth	21	0		
2023–24	Portsmouth	0	0	21	0
2024–25	Colchester U	46	0	46	0

ONI, Milton (M)   1   0
H: 5 7 W: 13 03 b. 21-3-06

| 2024–25 | Colchester U | 1 | 0 | 1 | 0 |

PAYNE, Jack (M)   410   67
H: 5 5 W: 9 06 b.Tower Hamlets 25-10-94

2013–14	Southend U	11	0		
2014–15	Southend U	34	6		
2015–16	Southend U	32	9	77	15
2016–17	Huddersfield T	23	2		
2017–18	Huddersfield T	0	0		
2017–18	*Oxford U*	28	3	28	3
2017–18	*Blackburn R*	18	1	18	1
2018–19	Huddersfield T	0	0	23	2
2018–19	*Bradford C*	39	9	39	9
2019–20	Lincoln C	23	2	23	2
2020–21	Swindon T	43	4		
2021–22	Swindon T	35	13	78	17
2022–23	Charlton Ath	39	4		
2023–24	Charlton Ath	3	0	42	4
2023–24	*Milton Keynes D*	40	6	40	6
2024–25	Colchester U	42	8	42	8

READ, Arthur (M)   162   9
H: 5 10 W: 10 01 b.Leighton Buzzard 3-11-99

2018–19	Luton T	0	0		
2019–20	Brentford	0	0		
2020–21	Brentford	0	0		
2020–21	*Stevenage*	32	2		
2021–22	Stevenage	19	1		
2022–23	Stevenage	11	0	62	3
2022–23	Colchester U	20	0		
2023–24	Colchester U	41	5		
2024–25	Colchester U	39	1	100	6

SANDAH, Hakeem (D)   0   0
H: 5 9 b. 15-3-05

| 2024–25 | Colchester U | 0 | 0 | | |

SASERE, James (M)   0   0
b. 7-11-07

| 2024–25 | Colchester U | 0 | 0 | | |

SMITH, Tom (G)   9   0
H: 6 2 W: 12 04 b.Inglaterra 30-1-02
Internationals: England U16.

2019–20	Arsenal	0	0		
2020–21	Arsenal	0	0		
2021–22	Arsenal	0	0		
2022–23	Arsenal	0	0		
2022–23	*Colchester U*	6	0		
2023–24	Colchester U	3	0		
2024–25	Colchester U	0	0	9	0

TAYLOR, Lyle (F)   467   142
H: 6 2 W: 12 06 b.Greenwich 29-3-90
Internationals: Montserrat Full caps.

| 2007–08 | Millwall | 0 | 0 | | |
| 2008–09 | Millwall | 0 | 0 | | |

From Concord R.

2010–11	Bournemouth	11	0		
2011–12	Bournemouth	18	0	29	0
2011–12	*Hereford U*	8	2	8	2
2012–13	Falkirk	34	24	34	24
2013–14	Sheffield U	20	2	20	2
2013–14	*Partick Thistle*	20	7		
2014–15	*Scunthorpe U*	18	3	18	3
2014–15	*Partick Thistle*	15	3	35	10
2015–16	AFC Wimbledon	42	20		
2016–17	AFC Wimbledon	43	10		
2017–18	AFC Wimbledon	46	14	131	44
2018–19	Charlton Ath	41	21		
2019–20	Charlton Ath	22	11	63	32
2020–21	Nottingham F	39	4		
2021–22	Nottingham F	18	3		
2021–22	*Birmingham C*	14	5	14	5
2022–23	Nottingham F	0	0	57	7
2023–24	*Wycombe W*	7	0	7	0
2023–24	*Cambridge U*	14	3	14	3
2024–25	Colchester U	37	10	37	10

TERRY, Frankie (D)   1   0
b. 30-1-04

2021–22	Colchester U	0	0		
2022–23	Colchester U	0	0		
2023–24	Colchester U	0	0		
2024–25	Colchester U	1	0	1	0

THOMPSON, Joel (M)   6   0
H: 6 1 W: 11 00 b.Carrickfergus 25-7-05
Internationals: Northern Ireland U16, U17, U19.

2020–21	Crusaders	1	0		
2021–22	Crusaders	5	0	6	0
2022–23	Nottingham F	0	0		
2023–24	Nottingham F	0	0		
2024–25	Colchester U	0	0		

Transferred to Finn Harps, February 2025.

THORN, Oscar (F)   26   0
H: 6 1 W: 11 00 b.Southend-on-Sea 22-3-04
From Norwich C.

2022–23	Colchester U	0	0		
2023–24	Colchester U	0	0		
2024–25	Colchester U	26	0	26	0

TOVIDE, Samson (F)   84   13
H: 6 2 W: 12 04 b.Hackney 4-1-04

2020–21	Colchester U	0	0		
2021–22	Colchester U	6	0		
2022–23	Colchester U	28	2		
2023–24	Colchester U	21	4		
2024–25	Colchester U	29	7	84	13

VINCENT-YOUNG, Kane (D)   188   6
H: 5 11 W: 11 00 b.Camden Town 15-3-96
Internationals: Grenada Full caps.
From Tottenham H, Banbury U.

2014–15	Colchester U	0	0		
2015–16	Colchester U	14	0		
2016–17	Colchester U	18	0		
2017–18	Colchester U	38	1		
2018–19	Colchester U	40	3		
2019–20	Colchester U	2	0		
2019–20	Ipswich T	9	2		
2020–21	Ipswich T	7	0		
2021–22	Ipswich T	15	0		
2022–23	Ipswich T	18	0	49	2
2023–24	*Wycombe W*	17	0	17	0
2024–25	Colchester U	10	0	122	4

WOODYARD, Alex (M)   246   5
H: 5 9 W: 9 02 b.Gravesend 3-5-93
Internationals: England C.
From Charlton Ath.

2010–11	Southend U	3	0		
2011–12	Southend U	0	0		
2012–13	Southend U	5	0		
2013–14	Southend U	0	0	8	0

From Dartford, Concord Rangers, Braintree T.

2017–18	Lincoln C	46	2	46	2
2018–19	Peterborough U	43	0		
2019–20	Peterborough U	14	0	57	0
2019–20	*Tranmere R*	11	1	11	1
2020–21	AFC Wimbledon	40	1		
2021–22	AFC Wimbledon	36	1		
2022–23	AFC Wimbledon	34	0	110	2

From York C.

| 2024–25 | Colchester U | 14 | 0 | 14 | 0 |

Transferred to Sutton U, January 2025.

Players retained or with offer of contract
Kuffour, Samuel Osei Junior.

Scholars
Abidekun, Olufela Moyosoreoluwa; Akor, Elkanah Adakole Aibe; Banjoko, Daniel Oluwanifemi; Campina Do Vale, Dwayne Ricardo; Drysdale, Rashaad Kijani; Harvey, Ronnie David; Kokoshi, Alexander; Kosoko, Alamin Adeshina Ayobami; Makatta, Leo Mensa Michael; Moore, Owen Michael; Newby, Alfie Stephen; Nkrumah Junior, David Frank Kwadwo Apraku; O'Flynn Martin, Kai Haydon; Sabah, Burak; Sasere, James Olaoluwa Phillip; Sexton, Jack; Shaw, Herbie Tope.

COVENTRY C (28)

ALLEN, Jamie (M) 355 29
H: 5 11 W: 11 05 b.Rochdale 29-1-95

2012–13	Rochdale	0	0		
2013–14	Rochdale	25	6		
2014–15	Rochdale	35	0		
2015–16	Rochdale	38	3		
2016–17	Rochdale	31	2		
2017–18	Rochdale	4	0	**133**	**11**
2017–18	Burton Alb	29	1		
2018–19	Burton Alb	42	7	**71**	**8**
2019–20	Coventry C	11	1		
2020–21	Coventry C	22	1		
2021–22	Coventry C	38	1		
2022–23	Coventry C	37	6		
2023–24	Coventry C	22	1		
2024–25	Coventry C	21	0	**151**	**10**

ANDREWS, Kai (M) 13 0
H: 5 11 W: 10 08 b. 6-8-06
Internationals: Wales U19, U21.

2023–24	Coventry C	2	0		
2024–25	Coventry C	0	0	**2**	**0**
2024–25	*Motherwell*	11	0	**11**	**0**

BASSETTE, Norman (F) 70 8
H: 6 1 W: 11 09 b.Arlon 11-11-04
Internationals: Belgium UU18, U19, U20, U21, Full caps.

2021–22	Caen	10	0		
2022–23	Caen	12	1		
2023–24	Caen	1	0	**23**	**1**
2023–24	*Mechelen*	22	5	**22**	**5**
2024–25	Coventry C	25	2	**25**	**2**

BELL, Luke (G) 0 0
H: 6 1 W: 11 00 b. 26-10-03

2023–24	Coventry C	0	0
2024–25	Coventry C	0	0

BIDWELL, Jake (D) 527 11
H: 6 0 W: 11 00 b.Southport 21-3-93
Internationals: England U16, U17, U18, U19.

2009–10	Everton	0	0		
2010–11	Everton	0	0		
2011–12	Everton	0	0		
2011–12	*Brentford*	24	0		
2012–13	Everton	0	0		
2012–13	*Brentford*	40	0		
2013–14	Brentford	38	0		
2014–15	Brentford	43	0		
2015–16	Brentford	45	3	**190**	**3**
2016–17	QPR	36	0		
2017–18	QPR	46	2		
2018–19	QPR	40	0	**122**	**2**
2019–20	Swansea C	37	0		
2020–21	Swansea C	39	1		
2021–22	Swansea C	16	2	**92**	**3**
2021–22	Coventry C	16	0		
2022–23	Coventry C	45	1		
2023–24	Coventry C	33	1		
2024–25	Coventry C	29	1	**123**	**3**

BINKS, Luis (D) 107 0
H: 6 2 W: 13 08 b.Gillingham 2-9-01
Internationals: Scotland U18. England U16, U17, U18, U19.

2020	*Montreal*	19	0	**19**	**0**

From Tottenham H.

2020–21	Bologna	0	0		
2021–22	Bologna	15	0		
2022–23	Bologna	0	0		
2022–23	*Como 1907*	33	0	**33**	**0**
2023–24	Bologna	0	0	**15**	**0**
2023–24	*Coventry C*	18	0		
2024–25	Coventry C	22	0	**40**	**0**

BORGES RODRIGUES, Raphael (M) 41 5
H: 5 8 W: 10 08 b.Maastricht 11-9-03
Internationals: Australia U20, U23.

2018–19	Melbourne C	0	0		
2019–20	Melbourne C	1	0		
2020–21	Melbourne C	4	0		
2021–22	Melbourne C	5	1		
2022–23	Melbourne C	2	0	**12**	**1**
2023–24	Macarthur	26	4	**26**	**4**
2024–25	Coventry C	3	0	**3**	**0**

BROAD, Harvey (D) 0 0
H: 5 10 W: 10 08 b. 15-9-05

2024–25	Coventry C	0	0

BURROUGHS, Jack (M) 60 0
H: 6 2 W: 12 08 b.Coventry 21-3-01
Internationals: Scotland U19, U21.

2018–19	Coventry C	0	0		
2019–20	Coventry C	0	0		
2020–21	Coventry C	2	0		
2021–22	Coventry C	0	0		
2021–22	*Ross Co*	17	0	**17**	**0**
2022–23	Coventry C	12	0		
2023–24	Coventry C	0	0		
2023–24	*Lincoln C*	29	0	**29**	**0**
2024–25	Coventry C	0	0	**14**	**0**
2024–25	*Kilmarnock*	0	0		

COLLINS, Bradley (G) 220 0
H: 6 0 W: 10 12 b.Southampton 18-2-97

2017–18	Chelsea	0	0		
2017–18	*Forest Green R*	39	0	**39**	**0**
2018–19	Chelsea	0	0		
2018–19	*Burton Alb*	31	0	**31**	**0**
2019–20	Barnsley	19	0		
2020–21	Barnsley	22	0		
2021–22	Barnsley	40	0		
2022–23	Barnsley	26	0	**107**	**0**
2023–24	Coventry C	28	0		
2024–25	Coventry C	15	0	**43**	**0**

DASILVA, Jay (D) 249 2
H: 5 7 W: 10 01 b.Luton 22-4-98
Internationals: England U16, U17, U18, U19, U20, U21. Wales Full caps.

2016–17	Chelsea	0	0		
2016–17	*Charlton Ath*	10	0		
2017–18	Chelsea	0	0		
2017–18	*Charlton Ath*	38	0	**48**	**0**
2018–19	Chelsea	0	0		
2018–19	*Bristol C*	28	0		
2019–20	Bristol C	24	0		
2020–21	Bristol C	11	1		
2021–22	Bristol C	36	1		
2022–23	Bristol C	34	0	**133**	**2**
2023–24	Coventry C	37	0		
2024–25	Coventry C	31	0	**68**	**0**

DAUSCH, Aidan (F) 2 0
H: 6 1 b. 1-6-06
Internationals: USA U20.

2023–24	Coventry C	2	0		
2024–25	Coventry C	0	0	**2**	**0**

DOVIN, Oliver (G) 120 0
H: 6 2 W: 11 11 b.London 11-7-02
Internationals: Sweden U17, U19, U21, Full caps.

2019	Hammarby IF	0	0		
2020	Hammarby IF	1	0		
2020	*IK Frej*	23	0	**23**	**0**
2021	Hammarby IF	8	0		
2022	Hammarby IF	17	0		
2022	*Hammarby TFF*	1	0	**1**	**0**
2023	Hammarby IF	29	0		
2024	Hammarby IF	13	0	**68**	**0**
2024–25	Coventry C	28	0	**28**	**0**

ECCLES, Josh (D) 144 5
H: 5 11 W: 10 06 b.Coventry 6-4-00

2018–19	Coventry C	0	0		
2019–20	Coventry C	3	0		
2020–21	Coventry C	7	0		
2020–21	*Gillingham*	12	0	**12**	**0**
2021–22	Coventry C	5	0		
2022–23	Coventry C	34	1		
2023–24	Coventry C	44	1		
2024–25	Coventry C	39	3	**132**	**5**

EGHOSA, Evan (F) 0 0
b. 5-8-05
Internationals: Austria U17.

2023–24	Coventry C	0	0
2024–25	Coventry C	0	0

GRIMES, Matt (M) 443 21
H: 5 10 W: 11 00 b.Exeter 15-7-95
Internationals: England U20, U21.

2013–14	Exeter C	35	1		
2014–15	Exeter C	23	4	**58**	**5**
2014–15	Swansea C	3	0		
2015–16	Swansea C	1	0		
2015–16	*Blackburn R*	13	0	**13**	**0**
2016–17	Swansea C	0	0		
2016–17	*Leeds U*	7	0	**7**	**0**
2017–18	Swansea C	0	0		
2017–18	*Northampton T*	44	4	**44**	**4**
2018–19	Swansea C	45	1		
2019–20	Swansea C	46	0		
2020–21	Swansea C	45	2		
2021–22	Swansea C	46	0		
2022–23	Swansea C	44	1		
2023–24	Swansea C	46	4		
2024–25	Swansea C	29	2	**305**	**10**
2024–25	Coventry C	16	2	**16**	**2**

HOWLEY, Ryan (M) 28 0
H: 5 9 W: 11 07 b.Nuneaton 23-11-03
Internationals: Wales U19, U21.

2021–22	Coventry C	1	0		
2022–23	Coventry C	4	0		
2023–24	Coventry C	0	0		
2023–24	*Dundee*	13	0	**13**	**0**
2024–25	Coventry C	0	0	**5**	**0**
2024–25	*Ayr U*	10	0	**10**	**0**

KITCHING, Liam (D) 181 6
H: 6 3 W: 12 08 b.Harrogate 1-10-99

2017–18	Leeds U	0	0		
2018–19	Leeds U	0	0		
2019–20	Forest Green R	29	0		
2020–21	Forest Green R	15	0	**44**	**0**
2020–21	Barnsley	1	0		
2021–22	Barnsley	32	0		
2022–23	Barnsley	45	4		
2023–24	Barnsley	4	1	**82**	**5**
2023–24	Coventry C	28	1		
2024–25	Coventry C	27	0	**55**	**1**

LATIBEAUDIERE, Joel (D) 150 5
H: 5 11 W: 11 03 b.Doncaster 6-1-00
Internationals: England U16, U17, U18, U20. Jamaica Full caps.

2017–18	Manchester C	0	0		
2018–19	Manchester C	0	0		
2019–20	Manchester C	0	0		
2019–20	*FC Twente*	5	1	**5**	**1**
2020–21	Swansea C	8	0		
2021–22	Swansea C	29	0		
2022–23	Swansea C	34	2	**71**	**2**
2023–24	Coventry C	41	2		
2024–25	Coventry C	33	0	**74**	**2**

MASON-CLARK, Ephron (M) 126 28
H: 5 10 W: 12 00 b.Lambeth 25-8-99
Internationals: England C.

2016–17	Barnet	6	0		
2017–18	Barnet	8	0	**14**	**0**

From Barnet.

2022–23	Peterborough U	39	9		
2023–24	Coventry C	0	0		
2023–24	*Peterborough U*	43	14	**82**	**23**
2024–25	Coventry C	30	5	**30**	**5**

MOORE, Isaac (M) 0 0
b. 15-4-06

2024–25	Coventry C	0	0

OBIKWU, Justin (M) 35 10
H: 6 4 W: 12 02 b.Brent 8-2-04
Internationals: Trinidad & Tobago Full caps.

2023–24	Coventry C	0	0		
2023–24	*Grimsby T*	16	3		
2024–25	Coventry C	0	0		
2024–25	*Grimsby T*	19	7	**35**	**10**

OVERGAARD, Victor (M) 168 27
H: 5 10 W: 9 06 b.Lemvig 30-7-99
Internationals: Denmark U17, U18, U19, U20.

2016–17	Midtjylland	0	0		
2017–18	Midtjylland	0	0		
2018–19	Midtjylland	0	0		
2018–19	*Fredericia*	19	4		
2019–20	Midtjylland	0	0		
2019–20	*Fredericia*	15	5	**34**	**9**
2020–21	Midtjylland	0	0		
2020–21	*Lyngby*	30	4	**30**	**4**
2021–22	Midtjylland	1	0	**1**	**0**
2021–22	*Kortrijk*	9	0	**9**	**0**
2022	Sarpsborg 08	13	2		
2023	Sarpsborg 08	30	6	**43**	**8**
2023–24	Coventry C	15	0		
2024–25	Coventry C	36	6	**51**	**6**

PATERSON, Jamie (F) 453 71
H: 5 9 W: 10 08 b.Coventry 20-12-91

2010–11	Walsall	14	0		
2011–12	Walsall	34	3		
2012–13	Walsall	46	12	**94**	**15**
2013–14	Nottingham F	32	8		
2014–15	Nottingham F	21	1		
2015–16	Nottingham F	1	0	**54**	**9**
2015–16	*Huddersfield T*	34	6	**34**	**6**
2016–17	Bristol C	22	4		
2017–18	Bristol C	41	5		
2018–19	Bristol C	40	5		
2019–20	Bristol C	21	6		
2019–20	*Derby Co*	10	1	**10**	**1**
2020–21	Bristol C	20	3	**144**	**23**
2021–22	Swansea C	38	9		
2022–23	Swansea C	23	0		
2023–24	Swansea C	44	7	**105**	**16**
2024	Charlotte	4	0	**4**	**0**
2024–25	Coventry C	8	1	**8**	**1**

PERRY, Callum (D) 0 0
H: 6 1 W: 12 04 b. 5-10-05

2023–24	Coventry C	0	0
2024–25	Coventry C	0	0

RACHEL, Daniel (G) 0 0
H: 5 10 W: 11 09 b. 15-7-06

2024–25	Coventry C	0	0

RUDONI, Jack (M) 215 32
H: 6 1 W: 11 03 b.Wandsworth 26-5-01

2018–19	AFC Wimbledon	0	0		
2019–20	AFC Wimbledon	11	0		
2020–21	AFC Wimbledon	39	4		
2021–22	AFC Wimbledon	41	12	**91**	**16**
2022–23	Huddersfield T	46	2		
2023–24	Huddersfield T	35	5	**81**	**7**
2024–25	Coventry C	43	9	**43**	**9**

SAKAMOTO, Tatsuhiro (M) 221 26
H: 5 7 W: 9 13 b.Tokyo 22-10-96
Internationals: Japan Full caps.

2019	Montedio Yamagata	42	7	**42**	**7**
2020	Cerezo Osaka	33	2		
2021	Cerezo Osaka	33	6	**66**	**8**

2021–22	Oostende	12	0	
2022–23	Oostende	30	0	42 0
2023–24	Coventry C	29	7	
2024–25	Coventry C	42	4	71 11

SANDIFORD, Greg (D) 0 0
H: 6 0 W: 11 07 b.Luton 7-5-05
Internationals: Grenada Full caps.

2023–24	Cambridge U	0	0
2024–25	Coventry C	0	0

SHEAF, Ben (M) 202 8
H: 5 10 W: 10 01 b.Dartford 5-2-98
Internationals: England U16, U18.

2015–16	Arsenal	0	0	
2016–17	Arsenal	0	0	
2017–18	Arsenal	0	0	
2017–18	Stevenage	10	0	10 0
2018–19	Arsenal	0	0	
2019–20	Doncaster R	32	1	32 1
2020–21	Arsenal	0	0	
2020–21	Coventry C	30	0	
2021–22	Coventry C	35	2	
2022–23	Coventry C	35	2	
2023–24	Coventry C	31	3	
2024–25	Coventry C	29	0	160 7

SIMMS, Ellis (F) 156 40
H: 6 0 W: 11 07 b.Oldham 5-1-01
From Manchester C.

2019–20	Everton	0	0	
2020–21	Everton	0	0	
2020–21	Blackpool	21	8	21 8
2021–22	Everton	1	0	
2021–22	Hearts	17	5	17 5
2022–23	Everton	11	1	12 1
2022–23	Sunderland	17	7	17 7
2023–24	Coventry C	46	13	
2024–25	Coventry C	43	6	89 19

TAVARES, Fabio (F) 58 6
H: 5 11 W: 11 00 b.Matosinhos 22-1-01

2018–19	Rochdale	0	0	
2019–20	Rochdale	14	1	
2020–21	Rochdale	12	1	26 2
2020–21	Coventry C	0	0	
2021–22	Coventry C	7	1	
2022–23	Coventry C	9	0	
2023–24	Coventry C	5	1	
2024–25	Coventry C	1	0	22 2
2024–25	Burton Alb	10	2	10 2

THOMAS, Bobby (D) 144 14
H: 6 1 W: 12 02 b.Chester 30-1-01

2019–20	Burnley	0	0	
2020–21	Burnley	0	0	
2020–21	Barrow	21	1	21 1
2021–22	Burnley	0	0	
2022–23	Burnley	0	0	
2022–23	Bristol R	19	3	19 3
2022–23	Barnsley	22	3	22 3
2023–24	Coventry C	44	2	
2024–25	Coventry C	38	5	82 7

THOMAS-ASANTE, Brandon (F) 237 48
H: 5 11 W: 13 01 b.Milton Keynes 29-12-98
Internationals: Ghana Full caps.

2016–17	Milton Keynes D	6	0	
2017–18	Milton Keynes D	15	0	
2018–19	Milton Keynes D	1	0	22 0
2019–20	Salford C	20	6	
2020–21	Salford C	42	5	
2021–22	Salford C	39	11	
2022–23	Salford C	4	2	107 26
2022–23	WBA	33	7	
2023–24	WBA	39	11	72 18
2024–25	Coventry C	36	4	36 4

VAN EWIJK, Milan (D) 235 14
H: 5 10 W: 11 00 b.Amsterdam 8-9-00
Internationals: Netherlands U21.

2017–18	Excelsior Maassluis	2	0	
2018–19	Excelsior Maassluis	32	2	34 2
2019–20	ADO Den Haag	12	0	
2019–20	Cambuur	2	0	
2020–21	ADO Den Haag	33	1	45 1
2021–22	Heerenveen	33	1	
2022–23	Heerenveen	34	6	67 7
2023–24	Coventry C	42	2	
2024–25	Coventry C	45	2	87 4

WILSON, Ben (G) 125 1
H: 6 1 W: 11 09 b.Stanley 9-8-92

2010–11	Sunderland	0	0	
2011–12	Sunderland	0	0	
2012–13	Sunderland	0	0	
2013–14	Accrington S	0	0	
2013–14	Cardiff C	0	0	
2014–15	Cardiff C	0	0	
2015–16	Cardiff C	0	0	
2015–16	AFC Wimbledon	8	0	8 0
2016–17	Cardiff C	3	0	
2016–17	Rochdale	8	0	8 0
2017–18	Cardiff C	0	0	3 0
2017–18	Oldham Ath	5	0	5 0
2018–19	Bradford C	4	0	4 0
2019–20	Coventry C	0	0	
2020–21	Coventry C	27	0	
2021–22	Coventry C	5	0	
2022–23	Coventry C	43	1	
2023–24	Coventry C	18	0	
2024–25	Coventry C	4	0	97 1

WRIGHT, Haji (F) 207 70
H: 6 3 W: 12 08 b.Los Angeles 27-4-98
Internationals: USA U17, U18, U19, U23, Full caps.

2015	New York Cosmos	3	0	3 0
2015–16	Schalke 04	0	0	
2016–17	Schalke 04	0	0	
2017–18	Schalke 04	0	0	
2017–18	Sandhausen	15	1	15 1
2018–19	Schalke 04	7	1	7 1
2019–20	VVV Venlo	22	0	22 0
2020–21	SonderjyskE	29	11	
2021–22	SonderjyskE	0	0	29 11
2021–22	Antalyaspor	32	14	
2022–23	Antalyaspor	28	15	60 29
2023–24	Coventry C	44	16	
2024–25	Coventry C	27	12	71 28

Players retained or with offer of contract
Batanwi, Tristen Vyss; Betjemann, Elliot George Joshua; Di Trolio, Riccardo Antonio; Finney, Charles Christopher; Siddall, Rylie James; Yearn, Kai.

Scholars
Ambursley, Conrad Jacob; Blakely, Ben Michael Joseph; Critchlow-Woyo, Tionne David Winston; Gordon, Joshua David; James, Jack Stephen; Mantle, David Michael; Marshall, Jay Francis; McBride, Caleb William; McCallum, Joseph Lloyd; Meredith, Eliot Boyd; Nidjebu, Success Ogheneochico; Osaghae, Leon Osalumese Emobome; Panayiotou, Constantine; Russon, William Eric; Stretton, MacKenzie Jake; Toluwaloju, Joshua Ayotunde; Witts, Callum Paul; Wright Smith, Alfie Jack.

CRAWLEY T (29)

ADEYEMO, Ade (F) 51 5
H: 6 0 W: 11 11 b.Ibadan 13-7-98

2023–24	Crawley T	22	1	
2024–25	Crawley T	29	4	51 5

ANDERSON, Max (D) 138 11
H: 5 6 W: 9 13 b. 17-5-01
Internationals: Scotland U21.

2017–18	Dundee	0	0	
2018–19	Dundee	0	0	
2019–20	Dundee	0	0	
2020–21	Dundee	19	4	
2021–22	Dundee	33	1	
2022–23	Dundee	16	1	
2023–24	Dundee	0	0	68 6
2023–24	Inverness CT	31	2	31 2
2024–25	Crawley T	39	3	39 3

BARKER, Charlie (D) 42 1
H: 5 11 W: 11 06 b.Rotherham 12-2-03

2020–21	Charlton Ath	3	0	
2021–22	Charlton Ath	0	0	
2022–23	Charlton Ath	0	0	3 0

From Wealdstone.

2024–25	Crawley T	39	1	39 1

CAMARA, Panutche (F) 240 16
H: 6 1 W: 9 13 b.Canchungo 28-2-97
Internationals: Guinea-Bissau Full caps.
From Dulwich Hamlet.

2017–18	Crawley T	30	2	
2018–19	Crawley T	45	3	
2019–20	Crawley T	29	1	
2020–21	Plymouth Arg	41	2	
2021–22	Plymouth Arg	40	4	
2022–23	Plymouth Arg	0	0	81 6
2022–23	Ipswich T	1	0	
2023–24	Ipswich T	0	0	1 0
2023–24	Charlton Ath	12	0	12 0
2024–25	Crawley T	42	4	146 10

CONROY, Dion (D) 191 5
H: 6 2 W: 11 07 b.Redhill 11-12-95
From Chelsea.

2016–17	Swindon T	14	0	
2017–18	Swindon T	7	0	
2018–19	Swindon T	27	1	
2019–20	Swindon T	11	0	
2020–21	Swindon T	19	0	
2021–22	Swindon T	35	1	113 2
2022–23	Crawley T	25	2	
2023–24	Crawley T	32	1	
2024–25	Crawley T	21	0	78 3

FEELY, Rory (D) 233 10
H: 5 7 W: 12 00 b.Dublin 3-1-97
Internationals: Republic of Ireland U21.

2014	St Patrick's Ath	0	0
2015	St Patrick's Ath	0	0
2016	St Patrick's Ath	13	0
2017	St Patrick's Ath	17	1
2018	Waterford	30	2
2019	Waterford	32	2 62 4
2020	St Patrick's Ath	17	1 48 2
2021	Bohemians	30	0
2022	Bohemians	27	2 57 2
2022–23	Barrow	10	0
2023–24	Barrow	30	1
2024–25	Barrow	19	1 59 2
2024–25	Crawley T	7	0 7 0

FISH, Sonny (F) 1 0
H: 6 2 W: 11 00 b.Southend-on-Sea 9-1-04
Internationals: Wales U18.

2021–22	Leyton Orient	0	0	
2022–23	Leyton Orient	0	0	
2023–24	Crawley T	0	0	
2024–25	Crawley T	1	0	1 0

FLINT, Josh (M) 73 2
H: 6 1 W: 10 10 b.Waterlooville 13-10-00

2018–19	Portsmouth	0	0	
2019–20	Portsmouth	0	0	
2020–21	Volendam	2	0	
2021–22	Volendam	15	1	
2022–23	Volendam	12	0	
2023–24	Volendam	28	1	57 2
2024–25	Crawley T	16	0	16 0

FORSTER, Harry (M) 55 5
H: 5 8 W: 10 06 b.Hillingdon 11-5-00

2023–24	Crawley T	30	3	
2024–25	Crawley T	25	2	55 5

FRASER, Liam (M) 137 1
H: 6 1 W: 12 11 b.Toronto 13-2-98
Internationals: Canada U20, Full caps.

2015	Toronto	0	0	
2016	Toronto	0	0	
2017	Toronto	10	0	
2018	Toronto	10	0	
2019	Toronto	9	0	
2020	Toronto	14	0	
2021	Toronto	1	0	34 0
2021	Columbus Crew	23	0	23 0
2021–22	Deinze	10	0	
2022–23	Deinze	26	0	36 0
2023	Dallas	10	0	
2024	Dallas	18	1	28 1
2024–25	Crawley T	16	0	16 0

HEPBURN-MURPHY, Rushian (F) 138 26
H: 5 8 W: 9 04 b.Birmingham 19-9-98
Internationals: England U16, U17, U18, U19, U20.

2014–15	Aston Villa	1	0	
2015–16	Aston Villa	1	0	
2016–17	Aston Villa	3	0	
2017–18	Aston Villa	3	0	
2018–19	Aston Villa	5	0	
2018–19	Cambridge U	16	2	16 2
2019–20	Aston Villa	0	0	13 0
2019–20	Tranmere R	17	4	17 4
2019–20	Derby Co	0	0	
2023–24	Swindon T	23	5	
2024–25	Swindon T	27	5	50 10
2024–25	Crawley T	42	10	42 10

HOLOHAN, Gavan (M) 244 31
H: 5 11 W: 11 11 b.Dublin 15-12-91

2010–11	Hull C	0	0	
2011–12	Hull C	0	0	

From Alfreton T.

2013	Drogheda U	4	0	
2014	Drogheda U	27	5	31 5
2015	Cork C	18	1	
2016	Cork C	20	2	38 3
2017	Galway U	27	6	27 6
2018	Waterford	30	5	30 5

From Hartlepool U.

2021–22	Hartlepool U	18	2	18 2
2022–23	Grimsby T	39	6	
2023–24	Grimsby T	40	3	79 9
2024–25	Crawley T	21	1	21 1

IBRAHIM, Bradley (M) 33 2
H: 6 1 W: 12 02 b.London 21-10-04
Internationals: England U18.
From QPR.

2022–23	Arsenal	0	0	
2023–24	Arsenal	0	0	
2024–25	Hertha Berlin	0	0	

On loan from Hertha Berlin.

2024–25	Crawley T	33	2	33 2

JOHN-JULES, Tyreece (F) 91 10
H: 6 0 W: 11 11 b.Westminster 14-2-01
Internationals: England U16, U17, U18, U19, U21.

2018–19	Arsenal	0	0	
2019–20	Arsenal	0	0	
2019–20	Lincoln C	7	1	7 1
2020–21	Arsenal	0	0	
2020–21	Doncaster R	18	5	18 5
2021–22	Arsenal	0	0	
2021–22	Blackpool	0	0	11 0

2021–22 *Sheffield Wed* 1 0 **1 0**
2022–23 Arsenal 0 0
2022–23 *Ipswich T* 17 3 **17 3**
2023–24 Arsenal 0 0
2023–24 *Derby Co* 12 1 **12 1**
2024–25 Crawley T 25 0 **25 0**

KELLY, Jeremy (M) 135 15
H: 5 9 W: 11 00 b.Prague 21-10-97
Internationals: USA U20.
2020 Colorado Rapids 8 0
2021 Colorado Rapids 0 0 **8 0**
2021 Phoenix Rising 5 0 **5 0**
2022 Memphis 901 34 8
2023 Memphis 901 33 3 **67 11**
2023–24 Crawley T 18 1
2024–25 Crawley T 37 3 **55 4**

KHALEEL, Rafiq (M) 23 1
H: 5 10 W: 10 01 b.Camden 24-2-03
2020–21 Crawley T 0 0
2021–22 Crawley T 0 0
2022–23 Crawley T 14 1
2023–24 Crawley T 8 0
2024–25 Crawley T 1 0 **23 1**
Transferred to Dagenham & Red, February 2025.

MUKENA, Joy (D) 30 0
H: 5 10 W: 9 11 b.Enfield 3-7-99
From Tottenham H.
2017–18 Watford 0 0
From Bracknell T, St Albans C.
2023–24 Crawley T 11 0
2024–25 Crawley T 19 0 **30 0**

MULLARKEY, Toby (M) 85 2
H: 5 8 W: 10 01 b.Warrington 4-11-96
2015–16 Crewe Alex 0 0
From Nantwich T, Altrincham.
2022–23 Rochdale 12 0 **12 0**
2023–24 Grimsby T 42 2 **42 2**
2024–25 Crawley T 31 0 **31 0**

PAPADOPOULOS, Antony (M) 5 0
H: 5 7 W: 11 00 b. 12-11-02
From Tottenham H.
2021–22 Leyton Orient 0 0
From Welling U.
2024–25 Crawley T 5 0 **5 0**

QUITIRNA, Junior (M) 106 28
H: 5 7 W: 10 01 b.Guinea-Bissau 1-1-01
2019–20 Charlton Ath 0 0
2020–21 Charlton Ath 0 0
2021 Waterford 16 6
2022 Waterford 27 9 **43 15**
2022–23 Fleetwood T 5 1
2023–24 Fleetwood T 24 4 **29 5**
2024–25 Crawley T 34 8 **34 8**

RADCLIFFE, Ben (M) 20 0
b.Nottingham 15-9-03
2021–22 Burton Alb 0 0
2022–23 Burton Alb 1 0 **1 0**
2023–24 Derby Co 0 0
2024–25 Derby Co 0 0
2024–25 Crawley T 19 0 **19 0**

ROLES, Jack (M) 86 7
H: 6 0 W: 10 08 b.London 26-2-99
Internationals: Cyprus U19, U21, Full caps.
2019–20 Tottenham H 0 0
2019–20 *Cambridge U* 23 5 **23 5**
2020–21 Tottenham H 0 0
2020–21 *Burton Alb* 2 0 **2 0**
2020–21 *Stevenage* 2 0 **2 0**
From Woking.
2022–23 Crawley T 9 0
2023–24 Crawley T 30 2
2024–25 Crawley T 20 0 **59 2**

SANDFORD, Ryan (G) 0 0
H: 6 2 W: 11 11 b.Lambeth 21-2-99
Internationals: England U16, U17, U18.
2019–20 Millwall 0 0
2020–21 Millwall 0 0
2021–22 Millwall 0 0
2022–23 Millwall 0 0
2023–24 AFC Wimbledon 0 0
2023–24 Crawley T 0 0
2024–25 Crawley T 0 0

SHEIK, Jasper (G) 0 0
H: 6 0 W: 11 11 b.Haywards Heath 27-2-05
2024–25 Crawley T 0 0

SHOWUNMI, Tola (F) 24 4
H: 6 3 W: 14 05 b.Enfield 3-7-00
2024–25 Crawley T 24 4 **24 4**

SWAN, Will (F) 113 27
H: 5 11 W: 11 11 b.Mansfield 26-10-00
2020–21 Nottingham F 2 0
2020–21 *Port Vale* 10 1 **10 1**
2021–22 Nottingham F 0 0
2022–23 Nottingham F 0 0 **2 0**
2022–23 *Mansfield T* 28 10
2023–24 Mansfield T 35 9
2024–25 Mansfield T 1 0 **64 19**
2024–25 Crawley T 37 7 **37 7**

TANIMU, Benjamin (D) 68 2
H: 6 0 W: 11 11 b.Benin City 24-7-02
Internationals: Nigeria Full caps.
2018–19 Bendel Insurance 15 0
2019–20 Bendel Insurance 0 0
2020–21 Bendel Insurance 0 0
2021–22 Bendel Insurance 0 0
2022–23 Bendel Insurance 16 0
2023–24 Bendel Insurance 19 2 **50 2**
2023–24 Ihefu 11 0 **11 0**
2024–25 Crawley T 7 0 **7 0**

WATSON, Louis (M) 46 0
H: 5 9 W: 9 06 b.Croydon 7-6-01
Internationals: Republic of Ireland U18, U21.
From West Ham U.
2020–21 Derby Co 9 0
2021–22 Derby Co 4 0
2022–23 Derby Co 0 0 **13 0**
2022–23 Luton T 5 0
2023–24 Luton T 0 0 **5 0**
2023–24 *Charlton Ath* 21 0 **21 0**
2024–25 Crawley T 7 0 **7 0**

WOLLACOTT, Jojo (G) 98 0
H: 6 3 W: 12 08 b.Bristol 8-9-96
Internationals: Ghana Full caps.
2015–16 Bristol C 0 0
2016–17 Bristol C 0 0
2017–18 Bristol C 0 0
2018–19 Bristol C 0 0
2019–20 Bristol C 0 0
2019–20 *Forest Green R* 10 0 **10 0**
2020–21 Bristol C 0 0
2020–21 *Swindon T* 2 0
2021–22 Bristol C 0 0
2021–22 Swindon T 37 0 **39 0**
2022–23 Charlton Ath 16 0 **16 0**
2024–25 Crawley T 33 0 **33 0**

CREWE ALEX (30)

AGIUS, Calum (F) 17 1
H: 5 10 W: 10 10 b.Chester 5-9-05
Internationals: Wales U19, U21.
2023–24 Crewe Alex 3 0
2024–25 Crewe Alex 14 1 **17 1**

ALLPORT, Rhys (F) 0 0
H: 5 9 W: 10 10 b. 2-8-06
2023–24 Crewe Alex 0 0
2024–25 Crewe Alex 0 0

ARMSTRONG, Oliver (M) 0 0
2024–25 Crewe Alex 0 0

BILLINGTON, Lewis (D) 48 1
H: 6 1 W: 12 08 b.Crewe 17-2-04
2021–22 Crewe Alex 1 0
2022–23 Crewe Alex 0 0
2023–24 Crewe Alex 24 1
2024–25 Crewe Alex 23 0 **48 1**

BOGLE, Omar (F) 268 72
H: 6 3 W: 12 08 b.Birmingham 26-7-92
Internationals: England C.
From Celtic, Hinckley U, Solihull Moors.
2016–17 Grimsby T 27 19 **27 19**
2016–17 Wigan Ath 14 3 **14 3**
2017–18 Cardiff C 10 3
2017–18 *Peterborough U* 9 1 **9 1**
2018–19 Cardiff C 0 0
2018–19 *Birmingham C* 15 1 **15 1**
2018–19 *Portsmouth* 12 4 **12 4**
2019–20 Cardiff C 11 1 **21 4**
2019–20 *ADO Den Haag* 5 1 **5 1**
2020–21 Charlton Ath 17 2 **17 2**
2020–21 Doncaster R 17 2
2021–22 Doncaster R 10 1 **27 3**
2021–22 Hartlepool U 20 5 **20 5**
2022–23 Newport Co 46 17
2023–24 Newport Co 25 7 **71 24**
2024–25 Crewe Alex 30 5 **30 5**

BOOTH, Tom (G) 21 0
H: 6 3 W: 12 00 b.Crewe 2-8-04
2022–23 Crewe Alex 4 0
2023–24 Crewe Alex 17 0
2024–25 Crewe Alex 0 0 **21 0**

COLLINS, Joe (M) 0 0
2023–24 Crewe Alex 0 0
2024–25 Crewe Alex 0 0

CONNOLLY, James (D) 99 4
H: 6 1 W: 13 03 b.Liverpool 2-11-01
Internationals: Wales U21.
From Blackburn R.
2020–21 Cardiff C 0 0
2021–22 Cardiff C 0 0
2021–22 *Bristol R* 24 1
2022–23 Bristol R 30 1
2023–24 Bristol R 11 0 **65 2**
2023–24 *Morecambe* 13 2 **13 2**
2024–25 Crewe Alex 21 0 **21 0**

COONEY, Ryan (D) 203 3
H: 5 10 W: 12 02 b.Manchester 26-2-00
2016–17 Bury 0 0
2017–18 Bury 12 0
2018–19 Bury 9 0 **21 0**
2019–20 Burnley 0 0
2019–20 *Morecambe* 11 0
2020–21 Burnley 0 0
2020–21 *Morecambe* 36 0
2021–22 Morecambe 32 0
2022–23 Morecambe 27 0 **106 0**
2023–24 Crewe Alex 38 0
2024–25 Crewe Alex 38 3 **76 3**

DANCEY, Stan (D) 0 0
b. 8-3-07
2023–24 Crewe Alex 0 0
2024–25 Crewe Alex 0 0

DEMETRIOU, Mickey (D) 397 39
H: 6 2 W: 12 06 b.Durrington 12-3-90
Internationals: England C.
From Bognor Regis T, Eastbourne Bor, Kidderminster H.
2014–15 Shrewsbury T 42 3
2015–16 Shrewsbury T 1 0
2015–16 *Cambridge U* 15 0 **15 0**
2016–17 Shrewsbury T 0 0 **43 3**
2016–17 Newport Co 17 4
2017–18 Newport Co 46 7
2018–19 Newport Co 45 4
2019–20 Newport Co 21 0
2020–21 Newport Co 45 4
2021–22 Newport Co 39 4
2022–23 Newport Co 45 3 **258 26**
2023–24 Crewe Alex 46 8
2024–25 Crewe Alex 35 2 **81 10**

FINNEY, Charlie (M) 29 0
H: 5 9 W: 11 05 b.Crewe 28-10-03
2022–23 Crewe Alex 9 0
2023–24 Crewe Alex 10 0
2024–25 Crewe Alex 10 0 **29 0**

HEMMINGS, Kane (F) 415 136
H: 6 1 W: 12 04 b.Burton-upon-Trent 8-4-92
From Tamworth.
2010–11 Rangers 0 0
2011–12 Rangers 4 0
2012–13 Rangers 5 1 **9 1**
2012–13 *Cowdenbeath* 7 4
2013–14 Cowdenbeath 31 18 **38 22**
2014–15 Barnsley 23 3 **23 3**
2015–16 Dundee 37 21
2016–17 Oxford U 40 6
2017–18 Oxford U 0 0 **40 6**
2017–18 *Mansfield T* 37 15 **37 15**
2018–19 Notts Co 36 14 **36 14**
2019–20 Dundee 25 10 **62 31**
2020–21 Burton Alb 36 15
2021–22 Burton Alb 18 4 **54 19**
2021–22 Tranmere R 22 8
2022–23 Tranmere R 39 8
2023–24 Tranmere R 1 0 **62 16**
2023–24 Stevenage 34 5 **34 5**
2024–25 Crewe Alex 20 4 **20 4**

HOLICEK, Matus (M) 66 2
H: 6 0 W: 9 06 b.Slovakia 25-1-05
Internationals: Slovakia U17, U18, U19.
2022–23 Crewe Alex 2 0
2023–24 Crewe Alex 26 1
2024–25 Crewe Alex 38 1 **66 2**

LANKESTER, Jack (F) 151 16
H: 5 10 W: 10 03 b.Bury St Edmunds 19-1-00
2018–19 Ipswich T 11 1
2019–20 Ipswich T 0 0
2020–21 Ipswich T 17 2 **28 3**
2021–22 Cambridge U 18 1
2022–23 Cambridge U 42 4
2023–24 Cambridge U 40 1 **100 6**
2024–25 Crewe Alex 23 7 **23 7**

LENARCIK, Mikolaj (G) 0 0
H: 6 2 W: 12 11 b. 18-9-06
2023–24 Crewe Alex 0 0
2024–25 Crewe Alex 0 0

LONG, Chris (F) 263 60
H: 5 7 W: 12 02 b.Huyton 25-2-95
Internationals: England U16, U17, U18, U19, U20.
2013–14 Everton 0 0
2013–14 *Milton Keynes D* 4 1 **4 1**
2014–15 Everton 0 0
2014–15 *Brentford* 10 4 **10 4**
2015–16 Burnley 10 0
2016–17 Burnley 0 0
2016–17 *Fleetwood T* 18 4
2016–17 *Bolton W* 10 1 **10 1**
2017–18 Burnley 0 0 **10 0**

2017–18 *Northampton T*	38	9	**38** 9
2018–19 Fleetwood T	8	0	**26** 4
2018–19 Blackpool	17	2	**17** 2
2019–20 Motherwell	25	7	
2020–21 Motherwell	29	4	**54** 11
2021–22 Crewe Alex	32	10	
2022–23 Crewe Alex	10	3	
2023–24 Crewe Alex	27	9	
2024–25 Crewe Alex	25	6	**94** 28

LUNT, Owen (M) **20** 0
H: 5 6   W: 9 13   b.Prescot 2-9-04
2022–23 Crewe Alex	0	0	
2023–24 Crewe Alex	3	0	
2024–25 Crewe Alex	17	0	**20** 0

MOORE, Luca (M) **1** 0
b. 28-9-05
| 2024–25 Crewe Alex | 1 | 0 | **1** 0 |

NOLAN, Lewis (M) **0** 0
b. 6-9-05
| 2023–24 Crewe Alex | 0 | 0 | |
| 2024–25 Crewe Alex | 0 | 0 | |

PERRY, Will (M) **0** 0
| 2024–25 Crewe Alex | 0 | 0 | |

POWELL, Jack (M) **175** 9
H: 5 10   W: 9 11   b.Canning Town 29-1-94
Internationals: England C.
2013–14 Millwall	0	0	
2014–15 Millwall	5	0	
2015–16 Millwall	1	0	**6** 0
From Ebbsfleet U, Maidstone U.
2019–20 Crawley T	6	0	
2020–21 Crawley T	44	3	
2021–22 Crawley T	37	1	
2022–23 Crawley T	45	4	**132** 8
2023–24 Crewe Alex	15	1	
2024–25 Crewe Alex	22	0	**37** 1

ROBERTS, Finley (F) **4** 0
H: 5 10   b. 31-1-04
| 2024–25 Crewe Alex | 4 | 0 | **4** 0 |

ROBINSON, Nathan (D) **1** 0
H: 6 1   W: 12 00   b. 4-2-06
| 2023–24 Crewe Alex | 1 | 0 | |
| 2024–25 Crewe Alex | 0 | 0 | **1** 0 |

SANDERS, Max (M) **145** 3
H: 5 9   W: 12 08   b.Horsham 4-1-99
Internationals: England U19.
2017–18 Brighton & HA	0	0	
2018–19 Brighton & HA	0	0	
2019–20 Brighton & HA	0	0	
2019–20 *AFC Wimbledon*	20	1	**20** 1
2020–21 Brighton & HA	0	0	
2020–21 Lincoln C	5	0	
2021–22 Lincoln C	19	0	
2022–23 Lincoln C	33	1	**57** 1
2023–24 Leyton Orient	27	1	**27** 1
2024–25 Crewe Alex	41	0	**41** 0

SANT, Lucas (D) **0** 0
H: 5 7   W: 10 03   b. 7-2-06
| 2023–24 Crewe Alex | 0 | 0 | |
| 2024–25 Crewe Alex | 0 | 0 | |

SENIOR, Matthew (M) **0** 0
b. 3-9-05
Internationals: Wales U17.
| 2023–24 Crewe Alex | 0 | 0 | |
| 2024–25 Crewe Alex | 0 | 0 | |

TABINER, Joel (F) **94** 5
H: 5 10   W: 10 06   b.Liverpool 30-11-03
2021–22 Crewe Alex	1	0	
2022–23 Crewe Alex	30	2	
2023–24 Crewe Alex	22	1	
2024–25 Crewe Alex	41	2	**94** 5

THIBAUT, Adrien (F) **18** 1
H: 5 11   W: 11 07   b.Slough 11-7-04
Internationals: Republic of Ireland U21.
| 2024–25 Crewe Alex | 18 | 1 | **18** 1 |

THOMAS, Conor (M) **343** 22
H: 6 1   W: 11 05   b.Coventry 29-10-93
Internationals: England U17, U18.
2010–11 Coventry C	0	0	
2010–11 *Liverpool*	0	0	
2011–12 Coventry C	27	1	
2012–13 Coventry C	11	0	
2013–14 Coventry C	43	0	
2014–15 Coventry C	16	0	
2015–16 Coventry C	3	0	**100** 1
2016–17 Swindon T	33	1	
2017–18 Swindon T	2	0	**35** 1
2018–19 Cheltenham T	32	6	
2019–20 Cheltenham T	26	6	
2020–21 Cheltenham T	38	5	
2021–22 Cheltenham T	24	1	**120** 18
2022–23 Crewe Alex	44	1	
2023–24 Crewe Alex	25	1	
2024–25 Crewe Alex	19	0	**88** 2

TRACEY, Shilow (M) **171** 14
H: 5 10   W: 12 00   b.Newham 29-4-98
From Ebbsfleet U.
2016–17 Tottenham H	0	0	
2017–18 Tottenham H	0	0	
2018–19 Tottenham H	0	0	
2019–20 Tottenham H	0	0	
2019–20 *Macclesfield T*	7	1	**7** 1
2020–21 Tottenham H	0	0	
2020–21 Shrewsbury T	8	0	**8** 0
2020–21 *Cambridge U*	17	1	
2021–22 Cambridge U	26	2	
2022–23 Cambridge U	37	1	**80** 4
2023–24 Crewe Alex	43	3	
2024–25 Crewe Alex	33	6	**76** 9

WESTWOOD, Keiren (G) **475** 0
H: 6 2   W: 14 07   b.Manchester 23-10-84
Internationals: Republic of Ireland Full caps.
2001–02 Manchester C	0	0	
2002–03 Manchester C	0	0	
2003–04 Manchester C	0	0	
2003–04 *Oldham Ath*	0	0	
2004–05 Manchester C	0	0	
2005–06 Manchester C	0	0	
2005–06 Carlisle U	35	0	
2006–07 Carlisle U	46	0	
2007–08 Carlisle U	46	0	**127** 0
2008–09 Coventry C	46	0	
2009–10 Coventry C	44	0	
2010–11 Coventry C	41	0	**131** 0
2011–12 Sunderland	9	0	
2012–13 Sunderland	0	0	
2013–14 Sunderland	10	0	**19** 0
2014–15 Sheffield Wed	43	0	
2015–16 Sheffield Wed	34	0	
2016–17 Sheffield Wed	43	0	
2017–18 Sheffield Wed	18	0	
2018–19 Sheffield Wed	20	0	
2019–20 Sheffield Wed	14	0	
2020–21 Sheffield Wed	20	0	**192** 0
2021–22 QPR	6	0	**6** 0
2023–24 Crewe Alex	0	0	
2024–25 Crewe Alex	0	0	

WILLIAMS, Zac (D) **109** 3
H: 6 0   W: 12 04   b.Denbighshire 27-3-04
Internationals: Wales U16, U18, U19, U21.
2020–21 Crewe Alex	19	0	
2022–23 Crewe Alex	18	0	
2023–24 Crewe Alex	31	2	
2024–25 Crewe Alex	41	1	**109** 3

Scholars
Armstrong, Oliver; Ashe, Joshua Francis; Baker, Billy George; Calder, Benjamin Jonathan; Church, Francis Anthony; Collins, Joseph Robert; Dancey, Stanley Robert; Drummond, Sebastian; Furlong, Ben Anthony; Hardy, Callum Sean; Hodkin, Jordan Ellis; Irwin, Isaac Peter; James, Dominic Theodor; Jones-Mellor, Alfie; Leather, Francis James Lawrence; Lenarcik, Mikolaj Pawel; Mlynarski, Patrick Krystian; Moore, Luca Jack; Perry, William Michael; Roberts, Ethan Jayden Samuel; Scott Abel, Iago; Smith, Xavier James; Thorpe, Ayden Xchyler Olorutony; Vaughan-Evans, Ffranc Dafydd.

CRYSTAL PALACE (31)

ADARAMOLA, Tayo (D) **36** 0
H: 5 11   W: 10 12   b.Dublin 13-11-03
Internationals: Republic of Ireland U17, U19, U21.
2021–22 Crystal Palace	0	0	
2022–23 Crystal Palace	0	0	
2022–23 *Coventry C*	0	0	
2023–24 Crystal Palace	0	0	
2023–24 *RWD Molenbeek*	14	0	**14** 0
2024–25 Crystal Palace	0	0	
2024–25 *Stockport Co*	6	0	**6** 0
2024–25 *Bradford C*	16	0	**16** 0

AGBINONE, Asher (F) **8** 0
H: 5 10   W: 10 03   b. 28-9-05
| 2024–25 Crystal Palace | 2 | 0 | **2** 0 |
| 2024–25 *Gillingham* | 6 | 0 | **6** 0 |

AHAMADA, Naouirou (M) **57** 2
H: 6 0   W: 11 07   b.Marseille 29-3-02
Internationals: France U16, U17, U18.
2020–21 Juventus	0	0	
2020–21 *VfB Stuttgart*	6	0	
2021–22 VfB Stuttgart	3	0	
2022–23 *VfB Stuttgart*	17	2	**26** 2
2022–23 Crystal Palace	8	0	
2023–24 Crystal Palace	20	0	
2024–25 Crystal Palace	0	0	**28** 0
2024–25 *Rennes*	3	0	**3** 0

CLYNE, Nathaniel (D) **390** 5
H: 5 9   W: 10 08   b.Stockwell 5-4-91
Internationals: England U19, U21, Full caps.
2008–09 Crystal Palace	26	0	
2009–10 Crystal Palace	22	1	
2010–11 Crystal Palace	46	0	
2011–12 Crystal Palace	28	0	
2012–13 Southampton	34	1	
2013–14 Southampton	25	0	
2014–15 Southampton	35	2	**94** 3
2015–16 Liverpool	33	1	
2016–17 Liverpool	37	0	
2017–18 Liverpool	3	0	
2018–19 Liverpool	4	0	
2018–19 *Bournemouth*	14	0	**14** 0
2019–20 Liverpool	0	0	**77** 1
2020–21 Crystal Palace	13	0	
2021–22 Crystal Palace	16	0	
2022–23 Crystal Palace	22	0	
2023–24 Crystal Palace	19	0	
2024–25 Crystal Palace	13	0	**205** 1

DEVENNY, Justin (M) **56** 2
H: 5 10   W: 11 09   b. 11-10-03
Internationals: Northern Ireland U21, Full caps.
2021–22 Kilmarnock	0	0	
2022–23 Kilmarnock	0	0	
2022–23 *Airdrieonians*	33	1	**33** 1
2023–24 Crystal Palace	0	0	
2024–25 Crystal Palace	23	1	**23** 1

DOUCOURE, Cheick (M) **175** 6
H: 5 11   W: 11 07   b.Bamakp 8-1-00
Internationals: Mali U17, Full caps.
2017–18 Lens			
2018–19 Lens	29	2	
2019–20 Lens	21	1	
2020–21 Lens	33	2	
2021–22 Lens	34	1	**117** 6
2022–23 Crystal Palace	34	0	
2023–24 Crystal Palace	11	0	
2024–25 Crystal Palace	13	0	**58** 0

EBIOWEI, Malcolm (F) **40** 1
H: 6 1   W: 12 08   b.Lambeth 4-9-03
Internationals: England U16, U20.
From Arsenal.
2019–20 Rangers	0	0	
2020–21 Rangers	0	0	
2021–22 Derby Co	16	1	**16** 1
2022–23 Crystal Palace	3	0	
2022–23 *Hull C*	12	0	**12** 0
2023–24 Crystal Palace	0	0	
2023–24 *RWD Molenbeek*	5	0	**5** 0
2024–25 Crystal Palace	0	0	**3** 0
2024–25 *Oxford U*	4	0	**4** 0

EDOUARD, Odsonne (F) **231** 85
H: 6 0   W: 11 09   b.Kourou 16-1-98
Internationals: France U17, U18, U19, U21.
From AF Bobigny.
2015–16 Paris Saint-Germain	0	0	
2016–17 Paris Saint-Germain	0	0	
2016–17 *Toulouse*	16	1	**16** 1
2017–18 *Celtic*	22	9	
2018–19 *Celtic*	32	15	
2019–20 Celtic	27	22	
2020–21 Celtic	31	18	
2021–22 Celtic	4	2	**116** 66
2021–22 Crystal Palace	28	6	
2022–23 Crystal Palace	35	5	
2023–24 Crystal Palace	30	7	
2024–25 Crystal Palace	2	0	**95** 18
2024–25 *Leicester C*	4	0	**4** 0

ESSE, Romain (M) **68** 7
H: 5 9   W: 10 08   b. 13-5-05
Internationals: England U18, U19, U20.
2022–23 Millwall	12	0	
2023–24 Millwall	25	2	
2024–25 Millwall	24	4	**61** 6
2024–25 Crystal Palace	7	1	**7** 1

EZE, Eberechi (M) **270** 59
H: 5 8   W: 10 08   b.Greenwich 29-6-98
Internationals: England U20, U21, Full caps.
From Millwall.
2016–17 QPR	0	0	
2017–18 *Wycombe W*	20	5	**20** 5
2017–18 QPR	16	2	
2018–19 QPR	42	4	
2019–20 QPR	46	14	**104** 20
2020–21 Crystal Palace	34	4	
2021–22 Crystal Palace	13	1	
2022–23 Crystal Palace	38	10	
2023–24 Crystal Palace	27	11	
2024–25 Crystal Palace	34	8	**146** 34

GOODMAN, Owen (G) **84** 0
H: 6 4   W: 13 03   b.Alliston 27-11-03
Internationals: Canada U20. England U20.
2022–23 Crystal Palace	0	0	
2023–24 Crystal Palace	0	0	
2023–24 *Colchester U*	38	0	**38** 0

2024–25 Crystal Palace 0 0
2024–25 *AFC Wimbledon* 46 0 **46 0**

GREHAN, Sean (D) 21 3
b. 8-1-04
Internationals: Republic of Ireland U19, U21.
2021 Bohemians 0 0
2022 Bohemians 0 0
2023–24 Crystal Palace 0 0
2023–24 *Carlisle U* 3 0 **3 0**
2024–25 Crystal Palace 0 0
2024–25 *Bohemians* 18 3 **18 3**

GUEHI, Marc (D) 184 6
H: 6 0 W: 12 13 b.Abidjan 13-7-00
Internationals: England U16, U17, U18, U19, U20, U21, Full caps.
2018–19 Chelsea 0 0
2019–20 Chelsea 0 0
2019–20 *Swansea C* 12 0
2020–21 Chelsea 0 0
2020–21 *Swansea C* 40 0
2021–22 Chelsea 0 0
2021–22 *Swansea C* 0 0 **52 0**
2021–22 Crystal Palace 36 2
2022–23 Crystal Palace 37 1
2023–24 Crystal Palace 25 0
2024–25 Crystal Palace 34 3 **132 6**

HENDERSON, Dean (G) 214 0
H: 6 3 W: 12 13 b.Whitehaven 12-3-97
Internationals: England U16, U17, U20, U21, Full caps.
2015–16 Manchester U 0 0
2016–17 Manchester U 0 0
2016–17 *Grimsby T* 7 0 **7 0**
2017–18 Manchester U 0 0
2017–18 *Shrewsbury T* 38 0 **38 0**
2018–19 Manchester U 0 0
2018–19 *Sheffield U* 46 0
2019–20 Manchester U 0 0
2019–20 *Sheffield U* 36 0 **82 0**
2020–21 Manchester U 13 0
2021–22 Manchester U 0 0
2022–23 Manchester U 0 0 **13 0**
2022–23 *Nottingham F* 18 0 **18 0**
2023–24 Crystal Palace 18 0
2024–25 Crystal Palace 38 0 **56 0**

HOLDING, Rob (D) 135 3
H: 6 2 W: 11 11 b.Stalybridge 20-9-95
Internationals: England U21.
2014–15 Bolton W 0 0
2014–15 *Bury* 1 0 **1 0**
2015–16 Bolton W 26 1 **26 1**
2016–17 Arsenal 9 0
2017–18 Arsenal 12 0
2018–19 Arsenal 10 0
2019–20 Arsenal 8 0
2020–21 Arsenal 30 0
2021–22 Arsenal 15 1
2022–23 Arsenal 14 1 **98 2**
2023–24 Crystal Palace 0 0
2024–25 Crystal Palace 0 0
2024–25 *Sheffield U* 10 0 **10 0**

HUGHES, Will (M) 378 17
H: 6 1 W: 11 09 b.Weybridge 7-4-95
Internationals: England U17, U21.
2011–12 Derby Co 3 0
2012–13 Derby Co 35 2
2013–14 Derby Co 41 3
2014–15 Derby Co 42 2
2015–16 Derby Co 6 0
2016–17 Derby Co 38 2 **165 9**
2017–18 Watford 15 2
2018–19 Watford 32 2
2019–20 Watford 30 1
2020–21 Watford 30 2
2021–22 Watford 0 0 **107 7**
2021–22 Crystal Palace 16 0
2022–23 Crystal Palace 27 1
2023–24 Crystal Palace 30 0
2024–25 Crystal Palace 33 0 **106 1**

IMRAY, Daniel (D) 39 1
H: 5 10 W: 10 06 b.Harold Wood 27-7-03
From Chelmsford.
2020–21 Crystal Palace 0 0
2021–22 Crystal Palace 0 0
2022–23 Crystal Palace 0 0
2023–24 Crystal Palace 0 0
2024–25 Crystal Palace 0 0
2024–25 *Bromley* 39 1 **39 1**

KAMADA, Daichi (M) 289 50
H: 6 0 W: 11 05 b.Ehime 5-8-96
Internationals: Japan U21, U23, Full caps.
2015 Sagan Tosu 21 3
2016 Sagan Tosu 28 7
2017 Sagan Tosu 16 3 **65 13**
2017–18 Eintracht Frankfurt 3 0
2018–19 Eintracht Frankfurt 0 0
2018–19 *St Truiden* 34 15 **34 15**
2019–20 Eintracht Frankfurt 28 2
2020–21 Eintracht Frankfurt 32 5
2021–22 Eintracht Frankfurt 32 4
2022–23 Eintracht Frankfurt 32 9 **127 20**
2023–24 Lazio 29 2 **29 2**
2024–25 Crystal Palace 34 0 **34 0**

KPORHA, Caleb (D) 2 0
H: 5 10 W: 9 11 b. 15-7-06
Internationals: England U17, U19.
2024–25 Crystal Palace 2 0 **2 0**

LACROIX, Maxence (D) 173 7
H: 6 3 W: 13 12
b.Villeneuve-Saint-Georges 6-4-00
Internationals: France U16, U17, U18, U20.
2017–18 Sochaux 0 0
2018–19 Sochaux 7 0
2019–20 Sochaux 20 0 **27 0**
2020–21 VfL Wolfsburg 30 1
2021–22 VfL Wolfsburg 29 0
2022–23 VfL Wolfsburg 24 1
2023–24 VfL Wolfsburg 28 4 **111 6**
2024–25 Crystal Palace 35 1 **35 1**

LERMA, Jefferson (M) 410 22
H: 5 10 W: 11 00 b.El Cerrito 25-10-94
Internationals: Colombia Full caps.
2013 Atletico Huila 24 0
2014 Atletico Huila 37 4
2015 Atletico Huila 23 2 **84 6**
2015–16 *Levante* 33 1
2016–17 Levante 30 2
2017–18 Levante 26 0 **89 3**
2018–19 Bournemouth 30 2
2019–20 Bournemouth 33 1
2020–21 Bournemouth 42 3
2021–22 Bournemouth 34 1
2022–23 Bournemouth 37 5 **176 12**
2023–24 Crystal Palace 28 1
2024–25 Crystal Palace 33 0 **61 1**

MARSH, Zach (F) 0 0
H: 5 9 W: 11 09 b. 6-10-05
Internationals: England U18.
2024–25 Crystal Palace 0 0

MATETA, Jean-Philippe (F) 262 94
H: 6 4 W: 13 03 b.Clamart 28-6-97
Internationals: France U19, U21, U23.
2015–16 Chateauroux 22 11
2016–17 Chateauroux 4 2 **26 13**
2016–17 Lyon 2 0
2017–18 Lyon 0 0 **2 0**
2017–18 *Le Havre* 37 19 **37 19**
2018–19 Mainz 05 34 14
2019–20 Mainz 05 18 3
2020–21 Mainz 05 15 7 **67 24**
2020–21 *Crystal Palace* 7 1
2021–22 Crystal Palace 22 5
2022–23 Crystal Palace 29 2
2023–24 Crystal Palace 35 16
2024–25 Crystal Palace 37 14 **130 38**

MATHEUS FRANCA, de Oliveira (M) 42 6
H: 6 0 W: 10 08 b.Rio de Janeiro 1-4-01
Internationals: Brazil U16, U20.
2021 Flamengo 2 0
2022 Flamengo 17 4
2023 Flamengo 9 1 **28 5**
2023–24 Crystal Palace 10 0
2024–25 Crystal Palace 4 1 **14 1**

MATHURIN, Roshaun (F) 0 0
b.London 23-1-04
2023–24 Crystal Palace 0 0
2024–25 Crystal Palace 0 0

MATTHEWS, Remi (G) 146 0
H: 6 4 W: 12 04 b.Gorleston 10-2-94
2014–15 Norwich C 0 0
2014–15 *Burton Alb* 0 0
2015–16 Norwich C 0 0
2015–16 *Burton Alb* 2 0 **2 0**
2015–16 *Doncaster R* 9 0 **9 0**
2016–17 Norwich C 0 0
2016–17 *Hamilton A* 17 0 **17 0**
2017–18 Norwich C 0 0
2017–18 *Plymouth Arg* 26 0 **26 0**
2018–19 Bolton W 18 0
2019–20 Bolton W 33 0 **51 0**
2020–21 Sunderland 6 0 **6 0**
2021–22 Crystal Palace 0 0
2022–23 Crystal Palace 0 0
2022–23 *St Johnstone* 34 0 **34 0**
2023–24 Crystal Palace 1 0
2024–25 Crystal Palace 0 0 **1 0**

MITCHELL, Tyrick (D) 169 3
H: 5 9 W: 10 03 b.Brent 1-9-99
Internationals: England Full caps.
From Brentford.
2019–20 Crystal Palace 4 0
2020–21 Crystal Palace 19 1
2021–22 Crystal Palace 36 0
2022–23 Crystal Palace 36 0
2023–24 Crystal Palace 37 2
2024–25 Crystal Palace 37 0 **169 3**

MOULDEN, Louie (G) 12 0
H: 6 3 W: 13 01 b.Bolton 6-1-02
Internationals: England U16, U17, U18.
From Liverpool, Manchester C.
2021–22 Wolverhampton W 0 0
2022–23 Wolverhampton W 0 0
2023–24 Wolverhampton W 0 0
2023–24 *Northampton T* 12 0 **12 0**
2024–25 Crystal Palace 0 0

MUNOZ, Daniel (D) 283 27
H: 5 11 W: 11 11 b.Amalfi 25-5-96
Internationals: Colombia Full caps.
2017 Rionegro Aguilas 30 0
2018 Rionegro Aguilas 32 3
2019 Rionegro Aguilas 19 0 **81 3**
2019 Atletico Nacional 21 7
2020 Atletico Nacional 6 0 **27 7**
2020–21 Genk 40 0
2021–22 Genk 29 0
2022–23 Genk 36 8
2023–24 Genk 17 5 **122 13**
2023–24 Crystal Palace 16 0
2024–25 Crystal Palace 37 4 **53 4**

NASCIMENTO, Adler (F) 1 0
H: 6 0 b. 25-11-04
2020–21 Peterborough U 1 0 **1 0**
2021–22 Crystal Palace 0 0
2022–23 Crystal Palace 0 0
2023–24 Crystal Palace 0 0
2024–25 Crystal Palace 0 0

NKETIAH, Eddie (F) 162 25
H: 5 9 W: 11 00 b.Lewisham 30-5-99
Internationals: England U18, U19, U20, U21, Full caps.
From Chelsea.
2017–18 Arsenal 3 0
2018–19 Arsenal 5 1
2019–20 Arsenal 13 2
2019–20 *Leeds U* 17 3 **17 3**
2020–21 Arsenal 17 2
2021–22 Arsenal 21 5
2022–23 Arsenal 30 4
2023–24 Arsenal 27 5 **116 19**
2024–25 Crystal Palace 29 3 **29 3**

OZOH, David (M) 20 1
H: 6 2 W: 10 10 b.Valencia 6-5-05
Internationals: England U18.
2022–23 Crystal Palace 1 0
2023–24 Crystal Palace 9 0
2024–25 Crystal Palace 0 0 **10 0**
2024–25 *Derby Co* 10 1 **10 1**

PLANGE, Luke (F) 94 10
H: 5 10 W: 11 11 b.Kingston upon Thames 4-11-02
Internationals: England U20.
From Arsenal.
2021–22 Crystal Palace 0 0
2021–22 *Derby Co* 26 4 **26 4**
2022–23 Crystal Palace 0 0
2022–23 *RWD Molenbeek* 13 2 **13 2**
2022–23 *Lincoln C* 18 0 **18 0**
2023–24 Crystal Palace 0 0
2023–24 *Carlisle U* 22 2 **22 2**
2023–24 *HJK* 11 2 **11 2**
2024–25 Crystal Palace 0 0
2024–25 *Motherwell* 4 0 **4 0**

RAK-SAKYI, Jesurun (M) 85 22
H: 5 10 W: 10 03 b.Southwark 5-10-02
Internationals: England U20, U21.
2020–21 Crystal Palace 0 0
2021–22 Crystal Palace 2 0
2022–23 Crystal Palace 0 0
2022–23 *Charlton Ath* 43 15 **43 15**
2023–24 Crystal Palace 6 0
2024–25 Crystal Palace 0 0 **8 0**
2024–25 *Sheffield U* 34 7 **34 7**

RAYMOND, Jadan (M) 5 0
H: 5 11 W: 8 09 b.London 15-10-03
Internationals: England U16, U17. Wales U19, U21.
2020–21 Crystal Palace 0 0
2021–22 Crystal Palace 0 0
2022–23 Crystal Palace 0 0
2023–24 Crystal Palace 0 0
2024–25 Crystal Palace 0 0
2024–25 *Queen's Park* 5 0 **5 0**

REID, Dylan (M) 8 0
b.Kilbirnie 1-3-05
2020–21 St Mirren 1 0
2021–22 St Mirren 3 0
2021–22 *Queen's Park* 2 0 **2 0**
2022–23 St Mirren 2 0 **6 0**
2023–24 Crystal Palace 0 0
2024–25 Crystal Palace 0 0

RIAD, Chadi (D) 64 2
H: 6 1　W: 12 04　b.Palma de Mallorca 17-7-03
Internationals: Morocco U17, U20, U23, Full caps.

Season	Club				
2020–21	Sabadell	1	0	1	0
2021–22	Barcelona Atletic	35	2	35	2
2022–23	Barcelona	1	0		
2023–24	Barcelona	0	0	1	0
2023–24	*Real Betis*	26	0	26	0
2024–25	Crystal Palace	1	0	1	0

RICHARDS, Chris (D) 94 3
H: 6 2　W: 12 06　b.Birrmingham, Alabama 28-3-00
Internationals: USA U20, U23, Full caps.
From FC Dallas.

Season	Club				
2019–20	Bayern Munich	1	0		
2020–21	Bayern Munich	3	0		
2020–21	*TSG 1899 Hoffenheim*	11	0		
2021–22	Bayern Munich	1	0	5	0
2021–22	*TSG 1899 Hoffenheim*	19	1	30	1
2022–23	Crystal Palace	9	0		
2023–24	Crystal Palace	26	1		
2024–25	Crystal Palace	24	1	59	2

RODNEY, Kaden (M) 0 0
H: 6 2　W: 10 08　b. 7-10-04
Internationals: England U18.

Season	Club				
2022–23	Crystal Palace	0	0		
2023–24	Crystal Palace	0	0		
2024–25	Crystal Palace	0	0		

SARR, Ismaila (F) 279 62
H: 6 1　W: 12 00　b.Saint-Louis 25-2-98
Internationals: Senegal U23, Full caps.

Season	Club				
2016–17	Metz	31	5	31	5
2017–18	Rennes	24	5		
2018–19	Rennes	35	8	59	13
2019–20	Watford	28	5		
2020–21	Watford	39	13		
2021–22	Watford	22	5		
2022–23	Watford	39	10	128	33
2023–24	Marseille	23	3	23	3
2024–25	Crystal Palace	38	8	38	8

SCHLUPP, Jeffrey (F) 368 57
H: 5 10　W: 11 05　b.Hamburg 23-12-92
Internationals: Ghana Full caps.

Season	Club				
2010–11	Leicester C	0	0		
2010–11	*Brentford*	9	6	9	6
2011–12	Leicester C	21	2		
2012–13	Leicester C	19	3		
2013–14	Leicester C	26	1		
2014–15	Leicester C	32	3		
2015–16	Leicester C	24	1		
2016–17	Leicester C	4	0	126	10
2016–17	Crystal Palace	15	0		
2017–18	Crystal Palace	24	0		
2018–19	Crystal Palace	30	4		
2019–20	Crystal Palace	17	3		
2020–21	Crystal Palace	27	2		
2021–22	Crystal Palace	32	4		
2022–23	Crystal Palace	34	3		
2023–24	Crystal Palace	29	2		
2024–25	Crystal Palace	12	0	220	18
2024–25	*Celtic*	13	1	13	1

UMEH, Franco (F) 2 0
H: 6 1　W: 11 07　b. 26-1-05
Internationals: Republic of Ireland U17, U18, U19, U21.

Season	Club				
2022	Cork C	2	0	2	0
2022–23	Crystal Palace	0	0		
2023–24	Crystal Palace	0	0		
2024–25	Crystal Palace	0	0		

UMOLU, Jemiah (F) 9 0
b. 28-10-05

Season	Club				
2024–25	Crystal Palace	0	0		
2024–25	*Port Vale*	9	0	9	0

WARD, Joel (D) 441 12
H: 6 2　W: 13 00　b.Emsworth 29-10-89

Season	Club				
2008–09	Portsmouth	0	0		
2008–09	*Bournemouth*	21	1	21	1
2009–10	Portsmouth	3	0		
2010–11	Portsmouth	42	3		
2011–12	Portsmouth	44	3	89	6
2012–13	Crystal Palace	25	0		
2013–14	Crystal Palace	36	0		
2014–15	Crystal Palace	37	1		
2015–16	Crystal Palace	30	2		
2016–17	Crystal Palace	38	0		
2017–18	Crystal Palace	19	0		
2018–19	Crystal Palace	7	1		
2019–20	Crystal Palace	29	0		
2020–21	Crystal Palace	26	0		
2021–22	Crystal Palace	28	0		
2022–23	Crystal Palace	28	1		
2023–24	Crystal Palace	26	0		
2024–25	Crystal Palace	2	0	331	5

WELLS-MORRISON, Jack (M) 0 0
H: 5 11　W: 11 07　b.Wandsworth 18-2-04
Internationals: England U18.

Season	Club				
2021–22	Crystal Palace	0	0		
2022–23	Crystal Palace	0	0		
2023–24	Crystal Palace	0	0		
2024–25	Crystal Palace	0	0		

WHARTON, Adam (M) 80 4
H: 6 0　W: 12 00　b.Blackburn 2-6-04
Internationals: England U19, U20, U21, Full caps.

Season	Club				
2021–22	Blackburn R	0	0		
2022–23	Blackburn R	18	2		
2023–24	Blackburn R	26	2	44	4
2023–24	Crystal Palace	16	0		
2024–25	Crystal Palace	20	0	36	0

WHITWORTH, Joseph (G) 48 0
H: 5 10　W: 11 00　b.Sutton 29-2-04
Internationals: England U16, U18.
From AFC Wimbledon.

Season	Club				
2022–23	Crystal Palace	2	0		
2023–24	Crystal Palace	0	0		
2024–25	Crystal Palace	0	0	2	0
2024–25	*Exeter C*	46	0	46	0

Players retained or with offer of contract
Akinwale, Victor Tolulope Oluwatosin; Browne, Luke; Brownlie, Rylan Neal; Cardines, Rio Solomon; Dashi, Matteo; Farquhar, Craig John; Gibbard, Joseph Finbarr; Grante, Jake Frederico; Izquierdo, Jackson; Jemide, Eyimofe Uyighosa John; King, George Callum Michael; Mustapha, Hindolo Thomas Eric; Ola-Adebomi, Ademola Oladipupo; Ouedraogo, Abdul Aziz; Walker-Smith, Charlie George; Williams, Sebastian Harry Christopher.

Scholars
Adams-Collman, Kai Reece; Angibeaud Montjen, David Alun; Benamar, Dean; Casey, Benjamin Omena; Danaher, Euan Maurice; Derry, Jesse Shaun; Henry, Zack; Hill, Marcus Edward James; Judd, Jasper; Kyremeh, Jerome Osei; Mason, Jack Freddie George; Muwama, Joshua-Rhys Ferdinand; Oduro, Stuart Agyemang; Okoli, Chukwunonyelum Uchenna; Somade, Oreoluwatomiwa Sean; Whitworth, Harry Anthony; Whyte, Tyler Shae.

DERBY CO (32)

ADAMS, Ebou (M) 185 16
H: 5 11　W: 12 00　b.Greenwich 15-1-96
Internationals: Gambia Full caps.
From Dartford.

Season	Club				
2017–18	Norwich C	0	0		
2017–18	*Shrewsbury T*	5	0	5	0

From Ebbsfleet U.

Season	Club				
2019–20	Forest Green R	34	4		
2020–21	Forest Green R	37	2		
2021–22	Forest Green R	37	3		
2022–23	Forest Green R	0	0	108	9
2023–24	Cardiff C	0	0		
2023–24	Cardiff C	11	0	11	0
2023–24	*Derby Co*	17	1		
2024–25	Derby Co	44	6	61	7

AGBAWODIKEIZU, Charles (F) 0 0
H: 6 0　W: 11 11　b. 31-12-07

Season	Club			
2024–25	Derby Co	0	0	

ALLEN, Cruz (M) 0 0
H: 6 0　b. 25-2-07
Internationals: Wales U16, U17, U18, U19.

Season	Club			
2023–24	Derby Co	0	0	
2024–25	Derby Co	0	0	

BARDELL, Max (D) 0 0
H: 5 11　b.Huddersfield 14-11-02
From Manchester C.

Season	Club			
2020–21	Derby Co	0	0	
2021–22	Derby Co	0	0	
2022–23	Derby Co	0	0	
2023–24	Derby Co	0	0	
2024–25	Derby Co	0	0	

BARKHUIZEN, Tom (F) 427 71
H: 5 9　W: 11 00　b.Blackpool 4-7-93

Season	Club				
2011–12	Blackpool	0	0		
2011–12	*Hereford U*	38	11	38	11
2012–13	Blackpool	0	0		
2012–13	*Fleetwood T*	13	1	13	1
2013–14	Blackpool	14	1		
2014–15	Blackpool	7	0	21	1
2014–15	*Morecambe*	5	0		
2015–16	Morecambe	40	10		
2016–17	Morecambe	14	5	59	15
2016–17	Preston NE	17	6		
2017–18	Preston NE	46	8		
2018–19	Preston NE	34	6		
2019–20	Preston NE	44	9		
2020–21	Preston NE	45	4		
2021–22	Preston NE	13	0	199	33
2022–23	Derby Co	41	4		
2023–24	Derby Co	37	6		
2024–25	Derby Co	19	0	97	10

BLACKETT-TAYLOR, Corey (F) 160 22
H: 5 7　W: 11 11　b.Erdington 23-9-97
Internationals: England U17.

Season	Club				
2015–16	Aston Villa	0	0		
2016–17	Aston Villa	1	0		
2017–18	Aston Villa	0	0		
2018–19	Aston Villa	0	0	1	0
2018–19	*Walsall*	10	0	10	0
2019–20	Tranmere R	24	2		
2020–21	Tranmere R	20	1	44	3
2021–22	Charlton Ath	27	2		
2022–23	Charlton Ath	29	8		
2023–24	Charlton Ath	25	8	81	18
2023–24	Derby Co	12	0		
2024–25	Derby Co	12	1	24	1

BRADLEY, Sonny (D) 467 25
H: 6 0　W: 11 05　b.Kingston upon Hull 13-9-91

Season	Club				
2011–12	Hull C	2	0		
2011–12	*Aldershot T*	14	0		
2012–13	Hull C	0	0	2	0
2012–13	*Aldershot T*	42	1	56	1
2013–14	Portsmouth	33	2	33	2
2014–15	Crawley T	26	1		
2015–16	Crawley T	46	1	72	2
2016–17	Plymouth Arg	44	7		
2017–18	Plymouth Arg	40	4	84	11
2018–19	Luton T	45	0		
2019–20	Luton T	40	3		
2020–21	Luton T	37	0		
2021–22	Luton T	22	2		
2022–23	Luton T	19	0	163	5
2023–24	Derby Co	33	3		
2024–25	Derby Co	7	0	40	3
2024–25	*Wycombe W*	17	1	17	1

BROWN, Dajaune (F) 17 1
b.Nottingham 16-10-05

Season	Club				
2022–23	Derby Co	0	0		
2023–24	Derby Co	2	0		
2024–25	Derby Co	15	1	17	1

CLARKE, Matthew (M) 324 13
H: 5 11　W: 11 00　b.Ipswich 22-9-96

Season	Club				
2013–14	Ipswich T	0	0		
2014–15	Ipswich T	4	0		
2015–16	Ipswich T	0	0	4	0
2015–16	*Portsmouth*	29	1		
2016–17	Portsmouth	33	1		
2017–18	Portsmouth	42	2		
2018–19	Portsmouth	46	3	150	7
2019–20	Brighton & HA	0	0		
2019–20	*Derby Co*	35	1		
2020–21	Brighton & HA	0	0		
2020–21	*Derby Co*	42	0		
2021–22	Brighton & HA	0	0		
2021–22	*WBA*	33	1	33	1
2022–23	Brighton & HA	6	0		
2023–24	Middlesbrough	6	0		
2023–24	Middlesbrough	24	1		
2024–25	Middlesbrough	14	2	44	3
2024–25	Derby Co	16	1	93	2

COX, Daniel (D) 0 0
H: 6 0　W: 11 03　b. 30-1-06
Internationals: Wales U16, U17, U19.

Season	Club			
2023–24	Derby Co	0	0	
2024–25	Derby Co	0	0	

DAVIDSON, Jaydan (F) 0 0
H: 5 10　W: 10 01　b.Derby 22-8-06

Season	Club			
2023–24	Derby Co	0	0	
2024–25	Derby Co	0	0	

EAMES, Owen (M) 0 0
b.Swadlincote --

Season	Club			
2024–25	Derby Co	0	0	

ELDER, Callum (D) 263 2
H: 5 11　W: 10 08　b.Sydney 27-1-95
Internationals: Australia U20, Full caps.

Season	Club				
2013–14	Leicester C	0	0		
2014–15	Leicester C	0	0		
2014–15	*Mansfield T*	21	0	21	0
2015–16	Leicester C	0	0		
2015–16	*Peterborough U*	18	1	18	1
2016–17	Leicester C	0	0		
2016–17	*Brentford*	6	0	6	0
2016–17	*Barnsley*	5	0	5	0
2017–18	Leicester C	0	0		
2017–18	*Wigan Ath*	27	0	27	0
2018–19	Leicester C	0	0		
2018–19	*Ipswich T*	4	0		
2019–20	Ipswich T	0	0	4	0
2019–20	Hull C	30	0		
2020–21	Hull C	44	1		
2021–22	Hull C	28	0		
2022–23	Hull C	29	0	131	1
2023–24	Derby Co	22	0		
2024–25	Derby Co	29	0	51	0

FAPETU, Adebayo (M) 0 0
b.Greenwich 18-1-05
2023–24 Derby Co 0 0
2024–25 Derby Co 0 0

FORNAH, Tyrese (M) 159 3
H: 5 11 W: 12 04 b.Camden 11-9-99
Internationals: Sierra Leone Full caps.
From Brighton & HA.
2019–20 Nottingham F 0 0
2019–20 *Casa Pia* 5 0 **5 0**
2020–21 Nottingham F 0 0
2020–21 *Plymouth Arg* 39 0 **39 0**
2021–22 Nottingham F 1 0
2021–22 *Shrewsbury T* 19 0 **19 0**
2022–23 Nottingham F 0 0 **1 0**
2022–23 *Reading* 35 2 **35 2**
2023–24 Derby Co 19 0
2024–25 Derby Co 1 0 **20 0**
2024–25 *Salford C* 40 1 **40 1**

FORSYTH, Craig (D) 456 28
H: 6 2 W: 13 01 b.Carnoustie 24-2-89
Internationals: Scotland Full caps.
2006–07 Dundee 1 0
2007–08 Dundee 0 0
2007–08 *Montrose* 9 0 **9 0**
2008–09 Dundee 1 0
2008–09 *Arbroath* 26 2 **26 2**
2009–10 Dundee 24 2
2010–11 Dundee 33 8 **59 10**
2011–12 Watford 20 3
2012–13 Watford 2 0 **22 3**
2012–13 *Bradford C* 7 0 **7 0**
2012–13 *Derby Co* 10 0
2013–14 Derby Co 46 2
2014–15 Derby Co 44 1
2015–16 Derby Co 12 0
2016–17 Derby Co 3 1
2017–18 Derby Co 31 0
2018–19 Derby Co 13 0
2019–20 Derby Co 22 0
2020–21 Derby Co 20 0
2021–22 Derby Co 26 3
2022–23 Derby Co 41 0
2023–24 Derby Co 26 3
2024–25 Derby Co 39 3 **333 13**

GOUDMIJN, Kenzo (M) 135 7
H: 5 8 W: 9 02 b.Hoorn 18-12-01
Internationals: Netherlands U16, U17, U18, U19.
2017–18 AZ Alkmaar 0 0
2018–19 AZ Alkmaar 1 0
2019–20 AZ Alkmaar 1 0
2020–21 AZ Alkmaar 3 0
2021–22 AZ Alkmaar 0 0
2021–22 *Sparta Rotterdam* 11 0 **11 0**
2021–22 *Excelsior* 18 1
2022–23 AZ Alkmaar 0 0
2022–23 *Excelsior* 34 4
2023–24 AZ Alkmaar 8 0 **13 0**
2023–24 *Excelsior* 18 0 **70 5**
2024–25 Derby Co 41 2 **41 2**

HAWKINS, Harry (M) 0 0
b. 27-3-06
2022–23 Derby Co 0 0
2023–24 Derby Co 0 0
2024–25 Derby Co 0 0

JACKSON, Kayden (F) 283 44
H: 5 11 W: 11 07 b.Bradford 22-2-94
Internationals: England C.
2013–14 Swindon T 0 0
2014–15 Swindon T 0 0
From Oxford C, Tamworth, Wrexham.
2016–17 Barnsley 0 0
2016–17 *Grimsby T* 20 1 **20 1**
2017–18 Accrington S 44 16
2018–19 Accrington S 1 0 **45 16**
2018–19 Ipswich T 36 3
2019–20 Ipswich T 32 11
2020–21 Ipswich T 25 1
2021–22 Ipswich T 12 3
2022–23 Ipswich T 38 3
2023–24 Ipswich T 29 3 **172 24**
2024–25 Derby Co 46 3 **46 3**

LANGAS, Sondre (M) 109 2
H: 6 2 W: 13 01 b.Namsos 2-2-01
Internationals: Norway Full caps.
2017 Namsos 1 0
2018 Namsos 4 0
2019 Namsos 0 0 **5 0**
2020 Ranheim 2 0
2020 Ranheim 7 0
2021 *Stjordals-Blink* 3 0 **3 0**
2022 Ranheim 27 0
2023 Ranheim 11 0 **47 0**
2023 Viking 10 1
2024 Viking 30 1 **40 2**
2024–25 Derby Co 14 0 **14 0**

LUTHRA, Rohan (G) 1 0
H: 6 5 W: 12 06 b.Hounslow 6-5-02
2021–22 Cardiff C 0 0
2022–23 Cardiff C 1 0
2023–24 Cardiff C 0 0 **1 0**
2024–25 Derby Co 0 0

MENDEZ-LAING, Nathaniel (M) 432 61
H: 5 10 W: 11 12 b.Birmingham 15-4-92
Internationals: England U16, U17. Guatemala Full caps.
2009–10 Wolverhampton W 0 0
2010–11 Wolverhampton W 0 0
2010–11 *Peterborough U* 33 5
2011–12 Wolverhampton W 0 0
2011–12 *Sheffield U* 8 1 **8 1**
2012–13 Peterborough U 21 3
2012–13 *Portsmouth* 8 0 **8 0**
2013–14 Peterborough U 16 1
2013–14 *Shrewsbury T* 6 0 **6 0**
2014–15 Peterborough U 14 0 **84 9**
2014–15 *Cambridge U* 11 1 **11 1**
2015–16 Rochdale 33 7
2016–17 Rochdale 39 8 **72 15**
2017–18 Cardiff C 38 6
2018–19 Cardiff C 20 4
2019–20 Cardiff C 27 3
2020–21 Cardiff C 0 0 **85 13**
2020–21 Middlesbrough 9 1 **9 1**
2021–22 Sheffield Wed 18 2 **18 2**
2022–23 Derby Co 44 7
2023–24 Derby Co 46 9
2024–25 Derby Co 41 3 **131 19**

NELSON, Curtis (D) 517 22
H: 6 0 W: 11 09 b.Newcastle-under-Lyme 21-5-93
Internationals: England U18.
From Stoke C.
2010–11 Plymouth Arg 35 0
2011–12 Plymouth Arg 17 0
2012–13 Plymouth Arg 27 3
2013–14 Plymouth Arg 44 1
2014–15 Plymouth Arg 42 1
2015–16 Plymouth Arg 46 3 **211 8**
2016–17 Oxford U 33 2
2017–18 Oxford U 20 1
2018–19 Oxford U 46 4 **99 7**
2019–20 Cardiff C 33 1
2020–21 Cardiff C 44 1
2021–22 Cardiff C 30 0
2022–23 Cardiff C 9 0 **116 2**
2022–23 Blackpool 18 1 **18 1**
2023–24 Derby Co 46 2
2024–25 Derby Co 27 2 **73 4**

NYAMBE, Ryan (D) 250 0
H: 6 0 W: 12 00 b.Katima Mulilo 4-12-97
Internationals: Namibia Full caps.
2014–15 Blackburn R 0 0
2015–16 Blackburn R 0 0
2016–17 Blackburn R 25 0
2017–18 Blackburn R 29 0
2018–19 Blackburn R 29 0
2019–20 Blackburn R 31 0
2020–21 Blackburn R 38 0
2021–22 Blackburn R 31 0 **183 0**
2022–23 Wigan Ath 31 0 **31 0**
2023–24 Derby Co 19 0
2024–25 Derby Co 17 0 **36 0**

OSAYANDE, Adisa (D) 0 0
b. 8-10-06
2023–24 Derby Co 0 0
2024–25 Derby Co 0 0

OSBORN, Ben (M) 352 20
H: 5 9 W: 11 11 b.Derby 5-8-94
Internationals: England U18, U19, U20.
2011–12 Nottingham F 0 0
2012–13 Nottingham F 0 0
2013–14 Nottingham F 8 0
2014–15 Nottingham F 37 3
2015–16 Nottingham F 36 3
2016–17 Nottingham F 46 4
2017–18 Nottingham F 46 4
2018–19 Nottingham F 39 1 **212 15**
2019–20 Sheffield U 13 0
2020–21 Sheffield U 24 1
2021–22 Sheffield U 34 3
2022–23 Sheffield U 20 1
2023–24 Sheffield U 24 0 **115 5**
2024–25 Derby Co 25 0 **25 0**

OSONG, Johnson (F) 0 0
b. 21-9-06
2024–25 Derby Co 0 0

PIETERS, Erik (D) 464 6
H: 6 0 W: 13 01 b.Tiel 7-8-88
Internationals: Netherlands U17, U19, U21, Full caps.
2006–07 Utrecht 20 0
2007–08 Utrecht 31 2 **51 2**
2008–09 PSV Eindhoven 17 0
2009–10 PSV Eindhoven 27 0
2010–11 PSV Eindhoven 31 0
2011–12 PSV Eindhoven 16 0
2012–13 PSV Eindhoven 2 0 **93 0**
2013–14 Stoke C 36 1
2014–15 Stoke C 31 0
2015–16 Stoke C 35 0
2016–17 Stoke C 36 0
2017–18 Stoke C 31 0
2018–19 Stoke C 21 2 **190 3**
2018–19 *Amiens* 15 1 **15 1**
2019–20 Burnley 24 0
2020–21 Burnley 20 0
2021–22 Burnley 12 0 **56 0**
2022–23 WBA 36 0
2023–24 WBA 22 0 **58 0**
2024–25 Luton T 0 0
2024–25 Derby Co 1 0 **1 0**

ROBINSON, Darren (M) 1 0
H: 6 2 b.Portadown 29-12-04
Internationals: Northern Ireland U18, U19, U21.
From Dungannon Swifts.
2021–22 Derby Co 1 0
2022–23 Derby Co 0 0
2023–24 Derby Co 0 0
2024–25 Derby Co 0 0 **1 0**

ROBINSON, Keilen (D) 0 0
H: 6 2 W: 11 09 b.Leicester 10-2-05
Internationals: England U19.
2023–24 Derby Co 0 0
2024–25 Derby Co 0 0

ROOFE, Kemar (M) 262 85
H: 5 10 W: 11 03 b.Walsall 6-1-93
Internationals: Jamaica Full caps.
2011–12 WBA 0 0
2012–13 WBA 0 0
2012–13 *Northampton T* 6 0 **6 0**
2013–14 WBA 0 0
2013–14 *Cheltenham T* 9 1 **9 1**
2014–15 WBA 0 0
2014–15 *Colchester U* 2 0 **2 0**
2014–15 *Oxford U* 16 6
2015–16 Oxford U 40 18 **56 24**
2016–17 Leeds U 42 3
2017–18 Leeds U 36 11
2018–19 Leeds U 32 14 **110 28**
2019–20 Anderlecht 13 6 **13 6**
2020–21 Rangers 24 14
2021–22 Rangers 21 10
2022–23 Rangers 3 1
2023–24 Rangers 15 1 **63 26**
2024–25 Derby Co 3 0 **3 0**

ROONEY, Jake (D) 12 0
H: 6 2 W: 12 04 b.Liverpool 22-8-03
From Burnley.
2022–23 Derby Co 9 0
2023–24 Derby Co 3 0
2024–25 Derby Co 0 0 **12 0**

SALVESEN, Lars-Jorgen (F) 235 79
H: 5 9 W: 11 00 b.Kristiansand 19-2-96
Internationals: Norway U19.
2013 Vigor 19 15 **19 15**
2014 Start 3 1
2015 Start 22 2
2016 Start 26 4
2017 Start 1 0
2018 Start 4 0 **56 7**
2018 Ullensaker/Kisa 12 8 **12 8**
2019 Sarpsborg 13 2 **13 2**
2019 Stromsgodset 13 7
2020 Stromsgodset 30 10
2021 Stromsgodset 0 0
2022 Stromsgodset 15 5 **58 22**
2022 Bodo/Glimt 13 2 **13 2**
2023 Viking 29 10
2024 Viking 27 12 **56 22**
2024–25 Derby Co 8 1 **8 1**

THOMPSON, Liam (M) 88 1
H: 5 8 W: 10 10 b.Nottingham 29-4-02
2020–21 Derby Co 0 0
2021–22 Derby Co 23 0
2022–23 Derby Co 13 0
2023–24 Derby Co 24 1
2024–25 Derby Co 28 0 **88 1**

TURLEY, Freddie (M) 0 0
H: 6 1 W: 11 11 b.Bray 3-7-06
Internationals: Republic of Ireland U16, U17, U18, U19.
2024–25 Derby Co 0 0

VICKERS, Josh (G) 129 0
H: 6 0 W: 11 05 b.Billericay 1-12-95
From Arsenal.
2015–16 Swansea C 0 0
2016–17 Swansea C 0 0
2016–17 *Barnet* 23 0 **23 0**
2017–18 Lincoln C 17 0
2018–19 Lincoln C 18 0
2019–20 Lincoln C 35 0 **70 0**

2020–21	Rotherham U	0	0		
2021–22	Rotherham U	20	0		
2022–23	Rotherham U	3	0	**23**	**0**
2023–24	Derby Co	7	0		
2024–25	Derby Co	6	0	**13**	**0**

WARD, Joe (M) **231** **20**
H: 5 6 W: 10 10 b.Chelmsford 9-4-95
Internationals: England C.
From Chelmsford C.

2015–16	Brighton & HA	0	0		
2016–17	Brighton & HA	0	0		
2017–18	Peterborough U	17	0		
2018–19	Peterborough U	43	4		
2019–20	Peterborough U	28	3		
2020–21	Peterborough U	37	5		
2021–22	Peterborough U	38	0		
2022–23	Peterborough U	40	6	**203**	**18**
2023–24	Derby Co	21	2		
2024–25	Derby Co	7	0	**28**	**2**

WASHINGTON, Conor (F) **353** **77**
H: 5 10 W: 11 09 b.Chatham 18-5-92
Internationals: Northern Ireland Full caps.
From St Ives T.

2013–14	Newport Co	24	4	**24**	**4**
2013–14	Peterborough U	17	4		
2014–15	Peterborough U	40	13		
2015–16	Peterborough U	25	10	**82**	**27**
2015–16	QPR	15	0		
2016–17	QPR	40	7		
2017–18	QPR	33	6		
2018–19	QPR	4	0	**92**	**13**
2018–19	Sheffield U	15	0	**15**	**0**
2019–20	Hearts	15	3	**15**	**3**
2020–21	Charlton Ath	36	11		
2021–22	Charlton Ath	35	11	**71**	**22**
2022–23	Rotherham U	35	5	**35**	**5**
2023–24	Derby Co	19	3		
2024–25	Derby Co	0	0	**19**	**3**

WHEELDON, Lennon (F) **1** **0**
H: 6 2 W: 11 05 b.Nottingham 16-2-06
Internationals: England U19.

2023–24	Derby Co	0	0		
2024–25	Derby Co	1	0	**1**	**0**

WILSON, Kane (D) **212** **10**
H: 5 10 W: 11 03 b.Birmingham 11-3-00
Internationals: England U16, U17.

2016–17	WBA	0	0		
2017–18	WBA	0	0		
2017–18	*Exeter C*	19	1		
2018–19	WBA	0	0		
2018–19	*Walsall*	14	0	**14**	**0**
2018–19	*Exeter C*	17	0	**36**	**1**
2019–20	WBA	0	0		
2019–20	*Tranmere R*	13	0	**13**	**0**
2020–21	Forest Green R	25	1		
2021–22	Forest Green R	45	3	**70**	**4**
2022–23	Bristol C	5	0	**5**	**0**
2023–24	Derby Co	41	3		
2024–25	Derby Co	33	2	**74**	**5**

ZETTERSTROM, Jacob (G) **171** **0**
H: 6 6 W: 12 13 b.Stockholm 11-7-98
Internationals: Sweden Full caps.

2015	Lidingo	3	0		
2016	Lidingo	5	0		
2017	Lidingo	4	0		
2018	Lidingo	25	0		
2019	Djurgarden	0	0		
2019	*Lidingo*	7	0	**44**	**0**
2020	Djurgarden	0	0		
2021	Djurgarden	19	0		
2022	Djurgarden	28	0		
2023	Djurgarden	23	0		
2024	Djurgarden	17	0	**87**	**0**
2024–25	Derby Co	40	0	**40**	**0**

Players retained or with offer of contract
Evans, Harry Jack; Gill, Tristan Louie Miles; Gough, Billy James; McAndrew, Niall Patrick; Perry, Jack Darren; Richards, Jerome Sean.

Scholars
Agbawodikiezu, Charles Chuckwuebuka; Agustien, Demiane Hesus; Banks, Luke Marcus; Canoville, Rio Joseph; Connell-Webster, Braidy Aaron; Corry, Sean Niall; Doyle, Anthony Junior; Eames, Owen Thomas; Friars, Alfie Kevin; Gordon, Isaac Samuel; Gordon, Khace Sheene; Green, Israel Henry; Hodges, Dantel Dayan; Mintus, Marley Harry; Oguntolu, Justin Femi; Osayande, Adisa Kweli; Osong, Johnson Shum; Price, Harley Leslie; Rees, Harvey William; Tola, Marsel; Ward, James Stewart Keith.

DONCASTER R (33)

ANDERSON, Thomas (D) **294** **12**
H: 6 4 W: 13 01 b.Burnley 2-9-93

2012–13	Burnley	0	0		
2013–14	Burnley	0	0		
2014–15	Burnley	0	0		
2014–15	*Carlisle U*	8	0	**8**	**0**
2015–16	Burnley	0	0		
2015–16	*Chesterfield*	18	0		
2016–17	Burnley	0	0		
2016–17	*Chesterfield*	35	2	**53**	**2**
2017–18	Burnley	0	0		
2017–18	*Port Vale*	20	0	**20**	**0**
2017–18	*Doncaster R*	7	2		
2018–19	Doncaster R	23	1		
2019–20	Doncaster R	32	1		
2020–21	Doncaster R	44	2		
2021–22	Doncaster R	19	1		
2022–23	Doncaster R	25	1		
2023–24	Doncaster R	34	1		
2024–25	Doncaster R	29	1	**213**	**10**

BAILEY, Owen (M) **92** **7**
H: 5 11 W: 11 11 b.Newcastle 22-1-99

2023–24	Doncaster R	46	2		
2024–25	Doncaster R	46	5	**92**	**7**

BROADBENT, George (M) **92** **2**
H: 5 10 W: 12 06 b.Ashton-under-Lyne 30-9-00

2020–21	Sheffield U	0	0		
2020–21	*Beerschot*	2	0	**2**	**0**
2021–22	Sheffield U	0	0		
2021–22	*Rochdale*	21	1	**21**	**1**
2022–23	Sheffield U	0	0		
2023–24	Doncaster R	31	0		
2024–25	Doncaster R	38	1	**69**	**1**

CLIFTON, Harry (M) **236** **20**
H: 5 8 W: 10 01 b.Grimsby 12-6-98
Internationals: Wales U21.

2016–17	Grimsby T	0	0		
2017–18	Grimsby T	10	0		
2018–19	Grimsby T	39	2		
2019–20	Grimsby T	25	0		
2020–21	Grimsby T	35	2		

From Grimsby T.

2022–23	Grimsby T	44	7		
2023–24	Grimsby T	42	3	**195**	**14**
2024–25	Doncaster R	41	6	**41**	**6**

CLOSE, Ben (M) **215** **19**
H: 5 9 W: 11 11 b.Portsmouth 8-8-96

2013–14	Portsmouth	0	0		
2014–15	Portsmouth	6	0		
2015–16	Portsmouth	7	0		
2016–17	Portsmouth	0	0		
2017–18	Portsmouth	40	2		
2018–19	Portsmouth	34	8		
2019–20	Portsmouth	29	3		
2020–21	Portsmouth	22	1		
2021–22	Portsmouth	0	0	**138**	**14**
2021–22	Doncaster R	14	0		
2022–23	Doncaster R	36	2		
2023–24	Doncaster R	20	3		
2024–25	Doncaster R	7	0	**77**	**5**

DEGRUCHY, Jack (M) **3** **0**
H: 5 10 W: 11 05 b.Knaresborough 13-8-03
From York C.

2022–23	Doncaster R	2	0		
2023–24	Doncaster R	1	0		
2024–25	Doncaster R	0	0	**3**	**0**

EMMANUEL, Josh (D) **167** **0**
H: 5 11 W: 11 00 b.London 18-8-97
From West Ham U.

2015–16	Ipswich T	4	0		
2015–16	*Crawley T*	2	0	**2**	**0**
2016–17	Ipswich T	15	0		
2017–18	Ipswich T	0	0		
2017–18	*Rotherham U*	31	0	**31**	**0**
2018–19	Ipswich T	4	0		
2018–19	*Shrewsbury T*	14	0	**14**	**0**
2019–20	Ipswich T	0	0	**23**	**0**
2019–20	Bolton W	27	0	**27**	**0**
2020–21	Hull C	28	0		
2021–22	Hull C	6	0	**34**	**0**
2022–23	Grimsby T	17	0	**17**	**0**
2023–24	Carlisle U	14	0	**14**	**0**
2024–25	Doncaster R	5	0	**5**	**0**

Transferred to FC Halifax T, March 2025.

FAULKNER, Bobby (D) **21** **2**
H: 5 11 W: 11 00 b.Doncaster 5-8-04

2021–22	Doncaster R	0	0		
2022–23	Doncaster R	19	2		
2023–24	Doncaster R	2	0		
2024–25	Doncaster R	0	0	**21**	**2**

FLINT, Will (M) **2** **0**
H: 6 0 W: 11 05 b.Sutton 29-4-06

2022–23	Doncaster R	0	0		
2023–24	Doncaster R	2	0		
2024–25	Doncaster R	0	0	**2**	**0**

GIBSON, Jordan (F) **230** **32**
H: 5 10 W: 12 08 b.Birmingham 26-2-98
From Rangers.

2017–18	Bradford C	5	1		
2018–19	Bradford C	11	0		
2018–19	*Stevenage*	6	1	**6**	**1**
2019–20	Bradford C	6	0	**22**	**1**
2020	St Patrick's Ath	14	2	**14**	**2**
2021	Sligo R	22	7	**22**	**7**
2021–22	Carlisle U	39	6		
2022–23	Carlisle U	45	2		
2023–24	Carlisle U	40	7	**124**	**15**
2024–25	Doncaster R	42	6	**42**	**6**

GOODMAN, Jack (F) **14** **0**
H: 5 8 W: 10 01 b.Nottingham 21-3-05

2021–22	Doncaster R	0	0		
2022–23	Doncaster R	7	0		
2023–24	Doncaster R	7	0		
2024–25	Doncaster R	0	0	**14**	**0**

HURST, Kyle (M) **97** **11**
H: 5 10 W: 11 05 b.Milton Keynes 20-1-02

2020–21	Birmingham C	0	0		
2021–22	Birmingham C	0	0		
2022–23	Doncaster R	45	6		
2023–24	Doncaster R	21	2		
2024–25	Doncaster R	21	3	**87**	**11**
2024–25	*Queen's Park*	10	0	**10**	**0**

IMARIAGBE, Kenneth (D) **0** **0**
b. 22-6-07

2024–25	Doncaster R	0	0		

IRONSIDE, Joe (F) **262** **65**
H: 6 0 W: 11 11 b.Middlesbrough 16-10-93
Internationals: England C.

2012–13	Sheffield U	12	0		
2013–14	Sheffield U	4	0		
2014–15	Sheffield U	0	0	**16**	**0**
2014–15	*Hartlepool U*	4	1	**4**	**1**

From Alfreton T, Nuneaton T, Kidderminister H.

2019–20	Macclesfield T	33	6	**33**	**6**
2020–21	Cambridge U	44	14		
2021–22	Cambridge U	38	14		
2022–23	Cambridge U	43	6	**125**	**34**
2023–24	Doncaster R	45	20		
2024–25	Doncaster R	39	4	**84**	**24**

JONES, Louis (G) **51** **0**
H: 6 1 W: 11 09 b.Doncaster 12-10-98

2015–16	Doncaster R	0	0		
2016–17	Doncaster R	0	0		
2017–18	Doncaster R	0	0		
2018–19	Doncaster R	0	0		
2019–20	Doncaster R	0	0		
2020–21	Doncaster R	13	0		
2021–22	Doncaster R	10	0		
2022–23	Doncaster R	2	0		
2023–24	Doncaster R	20	0		
2024	*Waterford*	6	0	**6**	**0**
2024–25	Doncaster R	0	0	**45**	**0**

Transferred to Dagenham & Red, February 2025.

KULEYA, Tavonga (F) **8** **0**
H: 6 0 W: 12 06 b.Bradford 15-6-04

2021–22	Doncaster R	0	0		
2022–23	Doncaster R	3	0		
2023–24	Doncaster R	5	0		
2024–25	Doncaster R	0	0	**8**	**0**

LAWLOR, Ian (G) **144** **0**
H: 6 4 W: 12 08 b.Dublin 27-10-94
Internationals: Republic of Ireland U17, U19, U21.

2011–12	Manchester C	0	0		
2012–13	Manchester C	0	0		
2013–14	Manchester C	0	0		
2014–15	Manchester C	0	0		
2015–16	Manchester C	0	0		
2015–16	*Barnet*	5	0	**5**	**0**
2015–16	*Bury*	12	0	**12**	**0**
2016–17	Doncaster R	19	0		
2017–18	Doncaster R	34	0		
2018–19	Doncaster R	10	0		
2019–20	Doncaster R	7	0		
2019–20	*Scunthorpe U*	4	0	**4**	**0**
2020–21	Doncaster R	0	0		
2020–21	*Oldham Ath*	30	0	**30**	**0**
2021–22	Dundee	8	0		
2022–23	Dundee	5	0	**13**	**0**
2023–24	Doncaster R	10	0		
2024–25	Doncaster R	0	0	**80**	**0**

MAXWELL, James (D) **135** **12**
H: 5 10 W: 11 09 b.Crewe 9-12-01

2019–20	Rangers	0	0		
2020–21	Rangers	0	0		
2020–21	*Queen of the South*	26	3	**26**	**3**
2021–22	Rangers	0	0		
2021–22	*Ayr U*	34	5	**34**	**5**
2022–23	Doncaster R	29	2		
2023–24	Doncaster R	22	2		
2024–25	Doncaster R	24	0	**75**	**4**

McGRATH, Jay (D) 65 1
H: 6 3　W: 11 11　b.Doncaster 15-4-03
From Mickleover.
2020–21	Coventry C	0	0
2021–22	Coventry C	0	0
2022–23	Coventry C	0	0
2023	St Patrick's Ath	27	1	27	1
2023–24	Doncaster R	5	0
2024–25	Doncaster R	33	0	38	0

MOLYNEUX, Luke (M) 176 36
H: 5 11　W: 11 09　b.Bishop Auckland 29-3-98
2017–18	Sunderland	1	0
2018–19	Sunderland	2	0	3	0
From Hartlepool U.			
2021–22	Hartlepool U	43	8	43	8
2022–23	Doncaster R	40	3
2023–24	Doncaster R	45	9
2024–25	Doncaster R	45	16	130	28

NIXON, Thomas (D) 34 1
H: 6 1　W: 13 01　b.Trentham 25-11-02
From Stoke C.
2021–22	Hull C	0	0
2022–23	Hull C	0	0
2023–24	Hull C	0	0
2023–24	*Doncaster R*	25	1
2024–25	Doncaster R	9	0	34	1

OLOWU, Joseph Olugbenga (D) 120 8
H: 6 0　W: 11 11　b.Ibadan 27-11-99
2018–19	Arsenal	0	0
2019–20	Arsenal	0	0
2020–21	Arsenal	0	0
2021–22	Doncaster R	35	4
2022–23	Doncaster R	17	1
2023–24	Doncaster R	37	0
2024–25	Doncaster R	31	3	120	8

ORAM, Jake (G) 0 0
b.Rotherham 22-8-06
2022–23	Doncaster R	0	0
2023–24	Doncaster R	0	0
2024–25	Doncaster R	0	0

SBARRA, Joe (M) 76 2
H: 5 10　W: 11 00　b.Lichfield 21-12-98
Internationals: England C.
2016–17	Burton Alb	1	0
2017–18	Burton Alb	17	0
2018–19	Burton Alb	9	0
2019–20	Burton Alb	22	1	49	1
From Solihull Moors.			
2024–25	Doncaster R	27	1	27	1

SENIOR, Jack (D) 54 0
H: 5 8　W: 9 12　b.Halifax 1-3-97
2015–16	Huddersfield T	0	0
2016–17	Luton T	10	0
2017–18	Luton T	0	0
2018–19	Luton T	0	0	10	0
From Halifax T.			
2023–24	Doncaster R	23	0
2024–25	Doncaster R	21	0	44	0

SHARP, Billy (F) 690 264
H: 5 9　W: 11 00　b.Sheffield 5-2-86
2004–05	Sheffield U	0	0
2004–05	*Rushden & D*	16	9	16	9
2005–06	Scunthorpe U	37	23
2006–07	Scunthorpe U	45	30	82	53
2007–08	Sheffield U	29	4
2008–09	Sheffield U	22	4
2009–10	Sheffield U	0	0
2009–10	*Doncaster R*	33	15
2010–11	Doncaster R	29	15
2011–12	Doncaster R	20	10
2011–12	Southampton	15	9
2012–13	Southampton	2	0
2012–13	*Nottingham F*	39	10	39	10
2013–14	Southampton	0	0	17	9
2013–14	*Reading*	10	2	10	2
2013–14	*Doncaster R*	16	4
2014–15	Leeds U	33	5	33	5
2015–16	Sheffield U	44	21
2016–17	Sheffield U	46	30
2017–18	Sheffield U	34	13
2018–19	Sheffield U	40	23
2019–20	Sheffield U	25	3
2020–21	Sheffield U	16	3
2021–22	Sheffield U	39	14
2022–23	Sheffield U	38	2	335	117
2023	LA Galaxy	6	6	6	6
2023–24	Hull C	11	0	11	0
2024–25	Doncaster R	43	9	141	53

STERRY, Jamie (D) 159 6
H: 5 11　W: 11 00　b.Newcastle upon Tyne 21-11-95
2014–15	Newcastle U	0	0
2015–16	Newcastle U	1	0
2016–17	Newcastle U	2	0
2016–17	*Coventry C*	16	0	16	0
2017–18	Newcastle U	0	0
2017–18	*Crewe Alex*	9	0

2018–19	Newcastle U	0	0
2018–19	*Crewe Alex*	1	0	10	0
2019–20	Newcastle U	0	0	3	0
From South Shields, Hartlepool U.			
2021–22	Hartlepool U	37	2
2022–23	Hartlepool U	26	2	63	4
2023–24	Doncaster R	26	0
2024–25	Doncaster R	41	2	67	2

STRAUGHAN-BROWN, Sam (M) 1 0
H: 5 9　W: 10 10　b.Retford 24-9-06
2023–24	Doncaster R	1	0
2024–25	Doncaster R	0	0	1	0

STRAUGHAN-BROWN, Sam (M) 0 0
b. 24-9-06
2024–25	Doncaster R	0	0

WESTBROOKE, Zain (M) 133 7
H: 5 11　W: 10 03　b.Chertsey 28-10-96
From Chelsea.
2016–17	Brentford	1	0
2017–18	Brentford	0	0	1	0
2017–18	Coventry C	0	0
2018–19	Coventry C	7	0
2019–20	Coventry C	25	4	32	4
2020–21	Bristol R	42	2
2021–22	Bristol R	3	0
2021–22	*Stevenage*	12	0	12	0
2022–23	Bristol R	1	0	46	2
2022–23	Doncaster R	8	0
2023–24	Doncaster R	27	1
2024–25	Doncaster R	7	0	42	1

WILLIAMS, Kasper (D) 0 0
2024–25	Doncaster R	0	0

WOOD, Richard (D) 593 37
H: 6 3　W: 12 13　b.Ossett 5-7-85
2002–03	Sheffield Wed	3	1
2003–04	Sheffield Wed	12	0
2004–05	Sheffield Wed	34	1
2005–06	Sheffield Wed	30	1
2006–07	Sheffield Wed	12	0
2007–08	Sheffield Wed	27	2
2008–09	Sheffield Wed	42	0
2009–10	Sheffield Wed	11	2	171	7
2009–10	Coventry C	24	3
2010–11	Coventry C	40	1
2011–12	Coventry C	17	1
2012–13	Coventry C	36	3	117	8
2013–14	Charlton Ath	21	0	21	0
2014–15	Rotherham U	6	0
2014–15	*Crawley T*	10	3	10	3
2015–16	Rotherham U	13	0
2015–16	*Fleetwood T*	6	0	6	0
2015–16	*Chesterfield*	5	0	5	0
2016–17	Rotherham U	29	3
2017–18	Rotherham U	36	4
2018–19	Rotherham U	26	2
2019–20	Rotherham U	23	3
2020–21	Rotherham U	30	2
2021–22	Rotherham U	39	1
2022–23	Rotherham U	28	4	230	19
2022–23	Doncaster R	0	0
2023–24	Doncaster R	25	0
2024–25	Doncaster R	8	0	33	0

Scholars
Bacon, Jacob Adam; Bryant, Jacob Samuel; Campbell-Ryce, Jaiden Jamal Reece; Cashmore, Aaron Andrew Oberholzer; Corbett, Dylan John; Gardham, Harry Joe; Glaves, Harry Robert; Imariagbe, Kenneth Osasenaga; Middleton, Franklin Alan; Murray, Rhomani Junior Noel; Musgrave-Dore, Deshaun Josiah; Parkin, Tyler Shaun; Piekarski, Oliver; Straughan-Brown, Samuel Ellis; Thompson, Charles Robert; Tomlinson, Jamie; Williams, Kasper.

EVERTON (34)

ALCARAZ, Carlos (M) 119 15
H: 6 1　W: 12 11　b.La plata 30-11-02
Internationals: Argentina U23.
2019–20	Racing Club	1	0
2021	Racing Club	18	1
2022	Racing Club	19	3	38	4
2022–23	Southampton	18	4
2023–24	Southampton	23	3
2023–24	*Juventus*	10	0	10	0
2024–25	Southampton	1	0	42	7
2024–25	Flamengo	14	2	14	2
On loan Flamengo.			
2024–25	Everton	15	2	15	2

ARMSTRONG, Harrison (M) 18 1
H: 6 2　W: 11 05　b.Liverpool 19-7-07
Internationals: England U18.
2024–25	Everton	3	0	3	0
2024–25	*Derby Co*	15	1	15	1

BARKER, Owen (M) 0 0
H: 5 8　W: 9 11　b.Bolton 23-2-05
2024–25	Everton	0	0

BATES, Callum (M) 0 0
H: 5 11　W: 12 04　b. 28-9-05
2024–25	Everton	0	0

BEGOVIC, Asmir (G) 393 1
H: 6 6　W: 13 01　b.Trebinje 20-6-87
Internationals: Canada U20. Bosnia & Herzogovina Full caps.
2005–06	Portsmouth	0	0
2005–06	*La Louviere*	2	0	2	0
2006–07	Portsmouth	0	0
2006–07	*Macclesfield T*	3	0	3	0
2007–08	Portsmouth	0	0
2007–08	*Bournemouth*	8	0
2007–08	*Yeovil T*	2	0
2008–09	Portsmouth	2	0
2008–09	*Yeovil T*	14	0	16	0
2009–10	Portsmouth	9	0	11	0
2009–10	*Ipswich T*	6	0	6	0
2009–10	Stoke C	4	0
2010–11	Stoke C	28	0
2011–12	Stoke C	23	0
2012–13	Stoke C	38	0
2013–14	Stoke C	32	1
2014–15	Stoke C	35	0	160	1
2015–16	Chelsea	17	0
2016–17	Chelsea	2	0	19	0
2017–18	Bournemouth	38	0
2018–19	Bournemouth	24	0
2019–20	Bournemouth	0	0
2019–20	*Qarabag*	10	0	10	0
2019–20	*AC Milan*	2	0	2	0
2020–21	Bournemouth	45	0	115	0
2021–22	Everton	3	0
2022–23	Everton	1	0
2023–24	QPR	45	0	45	0
2024–25	Everton	0	0	4	0

BETO, Norberto (F) 200 66
H: 6 4　W: 13 12　b.Lisboa 31-1-98
Internationals: Guineau-Bissau Full caps.
From Uniao Tires.
2018–19	Olimpico Montijo	34	21	34	21
2019–20	Portimonense	11	0
2020–21	Portimonense	30	11
2021–22	Portimonense	3	2	44	13
2021–22	*Udinese*	28	11
2022–23	Udinese	33	10
2023–24	Udinese	1	0	62	21
2023–24	Everton	30	3
2024–25	Everton	30	8	60	11

BRANTHWAITE, Jarrad (D) 115 6
H: 6 5　W: 10 08　b.Carlisle 27-6-02
Internationals: England U20, U21, Full caps.
2018–19	Carlisle U	0	0
2019–20	Carlisle U	9	0	9	0
2019–20	Everton	4	0
2020–21	Everton	0	0
2020–21	*Blackburn R*	10	0	10	0
2021–22	Everton	6	1
2022–23	Everton	0	0
2022–23	*PSV Eindhoven*	21	2	21	2
2023–24	Everton	35	3
2024–25	Everton	30	0	75	4

BUTTERFIELD, Luke (M) 0 0
H: 5 9　W: 11 03　b. 29-9-03
Internationals: Scotland U16, U19.
2020–21	Everton	0	0
2021–22	Everton	0	0
2022–23	Everton	0	0
2023–24	Everton	0	0
2024–25	Everton	0	0

CALVERT-LEWIN, Dominic (F) 270 62
H: 5 9　W: 10 01　b.Sheffield 16-3-97
Internationals: England U20, U21, Full caps.
2013–14	Sheffield U	0	0
2014–15	Sheffield U	2	0
2015–16	Sheffield U	9	0
2015–16	*Northampton T*	20	5	20	5
2016–17	Sheffield U	0	0	11	0
2016–17	Everton	11	1
2017–18	Everton	32	4
2018–19	Everton	35	6
2019–20	Everton	36	13
2020–21	Everton	33	16
2021–22	Everton	17	5
2022–23	Everton	17	2
2023–24	Everton	32	7
2024–25	Everton	26	3	239	57

CAMPBELL, Elijah (D) 38 1
b.Manchester 4-8-04
Internationals: England U18.
2021–22	Everton	0	0
2022–23	Everton	0	0
2023–24	Everton	0	0
2023–24	*Fleetwood T*	12	0	12	0
2024–25	Everton	0	0
2024–25	*Ross Co*	26	1	26	1

CHERMITI, Youssef (F) 38 3
H: 6 4 W: 13 03 b.Santa Maria 24-5-04
Internationals: Portugal U16, U18, U19, U20, U21.

2021–22	Sporting Lisbon	0	0		
2022–23	Sporting Lisbon	16	3	16	3
2023–24	Everton	18	0		
2024–25	Everton	4	0	22	0

CLARKE, Justin (F) 0 0
H: 5 9 W: 10 08 b.Atlanta --

2023–24	AFC Wimbledon	0	0		
2024–25	AFC Wimbledon	0	0		
2024–25	Everton	0	0		

COLEMAN, Seamus (D) 434 24
H: 6 4 W: 10 08 b.Donegal 11-10-88
Internationals: Republic of Ireland U21, U23, Full caps.

2006	Sligo R	4	0		
2007	Sligo R	26	0		
2008	Sligo R	26	1	56	1
2008–09	Everton	0	0		
2009–10	Everton	3	0		
2009–10	Blackpool	9	1	9	1
2010–11	Everton	34	4		
2011–12	Everton	18	0		
2012–13	Everton	26	0		
2013–14	Everton	36	6		
2014–15	Everton	35	3		
2015–16	Everton	28	1		
2016–17	Everton	26	4		
2017–18	Everton	12	0		
2018–19	Everton	29	2		
2019–20	Everton	27	0		
2020–21	Everton	25	0		
2021–22	Everton	30	1		
2022–23	Everton	23	1		
2023–24	Everton	12	0		
2024–25	Everton	5	0	369	22

CRELLIN, Billy (G) 50 0
H: 6 1 W: 9 06 b.Blackpool 30-1-00
Internationals: England U17, U18, U19, U20.

2017–18	Fleetwood T	0	0		
2018–19	Fleetwood T	0	0		
2019–20	Fleetwood T	5	0		
2020–21	Fleetwood T	0	0		
2020–21	Bolton W	11	0	11	0
2021–22	Fleetwood T	0	0	5	0
2022–23	Everton	0	0		
2023–24	Everton	0	0		
2024–25	Everton	0	0		
2024–25	Accrington S	34	0	34	0

DIXON, Roman (D) 1 0
H: 5 9 W: 10 03 b.Stafford 26-12-04
Internationals: England U16, U20.

| 2024–25 | Everton | 1 | 0 | 1 | 0 |

DOUCOURE, Abdoulaye (M) 368 48
H: 6 0 W: 12 00 b.Meulan-en-Yvelines 1-1-93
Internationals: France U17, U18, U19, U20, U21, Mali Full caps.

2012–13	Rennes	4	1		
2013–14	Rennes	20	6		
2014–15	Rennes	35	3		
2015–16	Rennes	16	2	75	12
2015–16	Watford	0	0		
2015–16	Granada	15	0	15	0
2016–17	Watford	20	1		
2017–18	Watford	37	7		
2018–19	Watford	35	5		
2019–20	Watford	37	4	129	17
2020–21	Everton	29	2		
2021–22	Everton	30	2		
2022–23	Everton	25	5		
2023–24	Everton	32	7		
2024–25	Everton	33	3	149	19

EBERE, Coby (M) 0 0
H: 6 2 b. 17-9-05

| 2024–25 | Everton | 0 | 0 | | |

GANA, Idrissa (M) 437 18
H: 5 9 W: 11 05 b.Dakar 26-9-89
Internationals: Senegal Full caps.

2010–11	Lille	11	0		
2011–12	Lille	25	0		
2012–13	Lille	29	0		
2013–14	Lille	37	1		
2014–15	Lille	32	4	134	5
2015–16	Aston Villa	35	0	35	0
2016–17	Everton	33	1		
2017–18	Everton	33	2		
2018–19	Everton	33	0		
2019–20	Paris Saint-Germain	20	1		
2020–21	Paris Saint-Germain	28	2		
2021–22	Paris Saint-Germain	26	3	74	6
2022–23	Everton	33	0		
2023–24	Everton	25	4		
2024–25	Everton	37	3	194	7

GARNER, James (M) 157 9
H: 5 10 W: 11 11 b.Birkenhead 13-3-01
Internationals: England U17, U18, U19, U20, U21.

2018–19	Manchester U	1	0		
2019–20	Manchester U	1	0		
2020–21	Manchester U	0	0		
2020–21	Watford	20	0	20	0
2020–21	Nottingham F	20	4		
2021–22	Manchester U	0	0	2	0
2021–22	Nottingham F	41	4	61	8
2022–23	Everton	16	0		
2023–24	Everton	37	1		
2024–25	Everton	21	0	74	1

HEATH, Isaac (M) 0 0
H: 5 9 W: 8 09 b. 28-10-04

| 2024–25 | Everton | 0 | 0 | | |

HOLGATE, Mason (D) 207 6
H: 5 11 W: 11 11 b.Doncaster 22-10-96
Internationals: England U20, U21. Jamaica Full caps.

2014–15	Barnsley	20	1	20	1
2015–16	Everton	0	0		
2016–17	Everton	18	0		
2017–18	Everton	15	0		
2018–19	Everton	5	0		
2018–19	WBA	19	1		
2019–20	Everton	27	0		
2020–21	Everton	28	1		
2021–22	Everton	25	2		
2022–23	Everton	8	0		
2023–24	Everton	0	0		
2023–24	Southampton	5	0	5	0
2023–24	Sheffield U	10	0	10	0
2024–25	Everton	1	0	127	3
2024–25	WBA	26	1	45	2

IROEGBUNAM, Tim (M) 62 2
H: 6 0 W: 12 06 b.West Bromwich 30-6-03
Internationals: England U19, U20.

2020–21	WBA	0	0		
2021–22	Aston Villa	3	0		
2022–23	Aston Villa	0	0		
2022–23	QPR	32	2	32	2
2023–24	Aston Villa	9	0	12	0
2024–25	Everton	18	0	18	0

KEANE, Michael (D) 339 26
H: 6 3 W: 12 13 b.Stockport 11-1-93
Internationals: Republic of Ireland U17, U19. England U19, U20, U21, Full caps.

2011–12	Manchester U	0	0		
2012–13	Manchester U	0	0		
2012–13	Leicester C	22	2	22	2
2013–14	Manchester U	0	0		
2013–14	Derby Co	7	0	7	0
2013–14	Blackburn R	13	3	13	3
2014–15	Manchester U	1	0	1	0
2014–15	Burnley	9	0		
2015–16	Burnley	44	5		
2016–17	Burnley	35	2	100	7
2017–18	Everton	30	0		
2018–19	Everton	33	1		
2019–20	Everton	31	2		
2020–21	Everton	35	3		
2021–22	Everton	32	3		
2022–23	Everton	12	1		
2023–24	Everton	0	0		
2024–25	Everton	14	3	196	14

LEBAN, Zan-Luk (G) 0 0
H: 6 2 W: 11 11 b. 15-12-02
Internationals: Slovenia U16, U17, U21.
From Escola.

2020–21	Everton	0	0		
2021–22	Everton	0	0		
2022–23	Everton	0	0		
2023–24	Everton	0	0		
2024–25	Everton	0	0		

LINDSTROM, Jesper (M) 161 25
H: 6 0 W: 9 13 b.Taastrup 29-2-00
Internationals: Denmark U19, U21, Full caps.

2018–19	Brondby	1	0		
2019–20	Brondby	28	3		
2020–21	Brondby	29	10	57	13
2021–22	Eintracht Frankfurt	29	5		
2022–23	Eintracht Frankfurt	27	7		
2023–24	Eintracht Frankfurt	1	0	57	12
2023–24	Napoli	22	0		
2024–25	Napoli	0	0	22	0

On loan from Napoli.

| 2024–25 | Everton | 25 | 0 | 25 | 0 |

MANGALA, Orel (M) 205 8
H: 5 11 W: 12 08 b.Brussels 18-3-98
Internationals: Belgium U16, U17, U18, U19, U21, Full caps.

2017–18	VfB Stuttgart	20	0		
2018–19	VfB Stuttgart	0	0		
2018–19	Hamburger SV	29	0	29	0
2019–20	VfB Stuttgart	29	1		
2020–21	VfB Stuttgart	24	1		
2021–22	VfB Stuttgart	28	1	101	3
2022–23	Nottingham F	27	1		
2023–24	Nottingham F	20	1	47	2
2023–24	Lyon	8	2		
2024–25	Lyon	1	0	9	2

On loan from Lyon.

| 2024–25 | Everton | 19 | 1 | 19 | 1 |

MAUPAY, Neal (F) 354 92
H: 5 7 W: 10 12 b.Versailles 14-8-96
Internationals: France U16, U17, U19, U21.

2012–13	Nice	15	3		
2013–14	Nice	16	2		
2014–15	Nice	13	1	44	6
2015–16	Saint-Etienne	15	1		
2016–17	Saint-Etienne	0	0	15	1
2016–17	Brest	28	11	28	11
2017–18	Brentford	42	12		
2018–19	Brentford	43	25		
2019–20	Brighton & HA	37	10		
2020–21	Brighton & HA	33	8		
2021–22	Brighton & HA	32	8	102	26
2022–23	Everton	27	1		
2023–24	Everton	2	0		
2023–24	Brentford	29	6	114	43
2024–25	Everton	0	0	29	1
2024–25	Marseille	22	4	22	4

McALLISTER, Sean (M) 8 2
H: 5 10 W: 11 07 b.Randalstown 1-1-03
Internationals: Northern Ireland U19.
From Dungannon Swifts.

2022–23	Everton	0	0		
2023–24	Everton	0	0		
2024–25	Inverness CT	8	2	8	2
2024–25	Everton	0	0		

Transferred to Marine, February 2025.

McNEIL, Dwight (M) 226 21
H: 6 0 W: 11 00 b.Rochdale 22-11-99
Internationals: England U20, U21.
From Manchester U.

2017–18	Burnley	1	0		
2018–19	Burnley	21	3		
2019–20	Burnley	38	2		
2020–21	Burnley	36	2		
2021–22	Burnley	38	0	134	7
2022–23	Everton	36	7		
2023–24	Everton	35	3		
2024–25	Everton	21	4	92	14

METCALFE, Jenson (M) 28 1
H: 6 0 W: 11 03 b.Wigan 6-9-04

2023–24	Everton	0	0		
2024–25	Everton	0	0		
2024–25	Chesterfield	28	1	28	1

MOONAN, Bradley (D) 0 0
H: 6 0 W: 11 07 b.Wigan 2-4-06

| 2024–25 | Everton | 0 | 0 | | |

MYKOLENKO, Vitaliy (D) 198 9
H: 5 10 W: 11 03 b.Cherkasy 29-5-99
Internationals: Ukraine U17, U18, U19, U21, Full caps.

2017–18	Dynamo Kyiv	5	0		
2018–19	Dynamo Kyiv	23	0		
2019–20	Dynamo Kyiv	23	3		
2020–21	Dynamo Kyiv	22	2		
2021–22	Dynamo Kyiv	15	0	88	5
2021–22	Everton	13	1		
2022–23	Everton	34	0		
2023–24	Everton	28	2		
2024–25	Everton	35	1	110	4

NDIAYE, Iliman-Cheikh (M) 140 33
H: 5 11 W: 9 08 b.Rouen 6-3-00
Internationals: Senegal Full caps.
From Boreham Wood.

2019–20	Sheffield U	0	0		
2020–21	Sheffield U	1	0		
2021–22	Sheffield U	30	7		
2022–23	Sheffield U	46	14	77	21
2023–24	Marseille	30	3	30	3
2024–25	Everton	33	9	33	9

O'BRIEN, Jake (D) 105 9
H: 6 6 W: 13 03 b.Cork 15-5-01
Internationals: Republic of Ireland U21, Full caps.

2019	Cork C	1	0		
2020	Cork C	8	0		
2021	Cork C	0	0	9	0
2021–22	Crystal Palace	0	0		
2021–22	Swindon T	19	0	19	0
2022–23	Crystal Palace	0	0		
2022–23	RWD Molenbeek	30	3	30	3
2023–24	Lyon	27	4	27	4
2024–25	Everton	20	2	20	2

OKORONKWO, Francis (F) 22 3
H: 6 0 W: 11 05 b.Blyth 18-9-04

2022–23	Everton	0	0		
2023–24	Everton	0	0		
2024–25	Salford C	22	3	22	3

ONYANGO, Tyler (M) 30 0
H: 6 3 W: 11 11 b.Luton 4-3-03
Internationals: England U17.
2019–20 Everton 0 0
2020–21 Everton 0 0
2021–22 Everton 3 0
2022–23 Everton 0 0
2022–23 *Burton Alb* 16 0 **16 0**
2022–23 *Forest Green R* 3 0 **3 0**
2023–24 Everton 1 0
2024–25 Everton 0 0 **4 0**
2024–25 *Stockport Co* 7 0 **7 0**

PATTERSON, Nathan (D) 62 0
H: 6 0 W: 11 05 b.Glasgow 16-10-01
Internationals: Scotland U17, U18, U19, U21, Full caps.
2019–20 Rangers 0 0
2020–21 Rangers 7 0
2021–22 Rangers 6 0 **13 0**
2021–22 Everton 0 0
2022–23 Everton 19 0
2023–24 Everton 20 0
2024–25 Everton 10 0 **49 0**

PICKFORD, Jordan (G) 411 0
H: 6 1 W: 12 02 b.Washington 7-3-94
Internationals: England U16, U17, U18, U19, U20, U21, Full caps.
2010–11 Sunderland 0 0
2011–12 Sunderland 0 0
2012–13 Sunderland 0 0
2013–14 Sunderland 0 0
2013–14 *Burton Alb* 12 0 **12 0**
2013–14 *Carlisle U* 18 0 **18 0**
2014–15 Sunderland 0 0
2014–15 *Bradford C* 33 0 **33 0**
2015–16 Sunderland 2 0
2015–16 *Preston NE* 24 0 **24 0**
2016–17 Sunderland 29 0 **31 0**
2017–18 Everton 38 0
2018–19 Everton 38 0
2019–20 Everton 38 0
2020–21 Everton 31 0
2021–22 Everton 35 0
2022–23 Everton 37 0
2023–24 Everton 38 0
2024–25 Everton 38 0 **293 0**

SHERIF, Martin (F) 0 0
H: 6 2 W: 11 11 b. 10-6-06
Internationals: Netherlands U17.
2024–25 Everton 0 0

TARKOWSKI, James (D) 449 19
H: 6 2 W: 12 11 b.Manchester 19-11-92
Internationals: England Full caps.
2010–11 Oldham Ath 9 0
2011–12 Oldham Ath 16 1
2012–13 Oldham Ath 21 2
2013–14 Oldham Ath 26 2 **72 5**
2013–14 Brentford 13 2
2014–15 Brentford 34 1
2015–16 Brentford 23 1 **70 4**
2015–16 Burnley 4 0
2016–17 Burnley 19 0
2017–18 Burnley 31 0
2018–19 Burnley 35 3
2019–20 Burnley 38 2
2020–21 Burnley 36 1
2021–22 Burnley 35 1 **198 7**
2022–23 Everton 38 1
2023–24 Everton 38 1
2024–25 Everton 33 1 **109 3**

TYRER, Harry (G) 38 0
H: 6 4 W: 13 12 b.Crosby 6-12-01
2020–21 Everton 0 0
2021–22 Everton 0 0
2022–23 Everton 0 0
2023–24 Everton 0 0
2024–25 Everton 0 0
2024–25 *Blackpool* 38 0 **38 0**

VIRGINIA, Joao (G) 21 0
H: 6 3 W: 13 01 b.Faro 10-10-99
Internationals: Portugal U16, U17, U18, U19, U20, U21.
From Benfica, Arsenal.
2018–19 Everton 0 0
2019–20 *Reading* 2 0 **2 0**
2019–20 Everton 0 0
2020–21 Everton 1 0
2021–22 Everton 0 0
2021–22 *Sporting Lisbon* 1 0 **1 0**
2022–23 Everton 0 0
2022–23 *Cambuur* 17 0 **17 0**
2023–24 Everton 0 0
2024–25 Everton 0 0 **1 0**

WELCH, Reece (D) 19 0
H: 6 6 W: 12 04 b.Huddersfield 19-9-03
Internationals: England U16, U17, U19, U20.
2020–21 Everton 0 0
2021–22 Everton 0 0
2022–23 Everton 0 0
2023–24 Everton 0 0
2023–24 *Forest Green R* 17 0 **17 0**
2024–25 Everton 0 0
2024–25 *Deinze* 2 0 **2 0**

YOUNG, Ashley (M) 607 71
H: 5 9 W: 10 03 b.Stevenage 9-7-85
Internationals: England U21, Full caps.
2002–03 Watford 0 0
2003–04 Watford 5 3
2004–05 Watford 34 0
2005–06 Watford 39 13
2006–07 Watford 20 3 **98 19**
2006–07 Aston Villa 13 2
2007–08 Aston Villa 37 9
2008–09 Aston Villa 36 7
2009–10 Aston Villa 37 5
2010–11 Aston Villa 34 7
2011–12 Manchester U 25 6
2012–13 Manchester U 19 0
2013–14 Manchester U 20 2
2014–15 Manchester U 26 2
2015–16 Manchester U 18 1
2016–17 Manchester U 12 0
2017–18 Manchester U 30 2
2018–19 Manchester U 30 2
2019–20 Manchester U 12 0 **192 15**
2019–20 Internazionale 18 4
2020–21 Internazionale 26 1 **44 5**
2021–22 Aston Villa 24 0
2022–23 Aston Villa 29 1 **210 31**
2023–24 Everton 31 0
2024–25 Everton 32 1 **63 1**

Players retained or with offer of contract
Barnsley, Fraser Paul; Beaumont-Clark, Jacob Adam; Benjamin, Omari Kai; Boakye, Kingsford Yiadom; Catesby, Joel William; Graham, Braiden David Jay; Lukjanciks, Douglass; Morgan, George Charlie; Samuels-Smith, Odin Darren; Tambadou, Francis Gomez; Tamen, William Nkwawu.

Scholars
Akarakiri, Ademide Oreoluwa; Clarke, Jaykar Justin Donte; Finney, George; Foster, Harvey John; Freedman, Freddie Ray; Gardner, Luis John; Gospel-Eze, Goodness Chiemerie; Hacker Davis, Luca Isaac; Lambert, Rocco Marlo; Loney, Ceiran; Matos, Melvin Wiafe Akenten; Poland, Louis Thomas; Stewart, Charlie David; Thomas, Aled Osian; Van Schoor, Joshua Mark; Wren, Kean Adam.

EXETER C (35)

AITCHISON, Jack (F) 212 20
H: 5 11 W: 11 00 b.Fauldhouse 5-3-00
Internationals: Scotland U16, U17, U19.
2015–16 Celtic 1 1
2016–17 Celtic 2 0
2017–18 Celtic 0 0
2018–19 Celtic 0 0
2018–19 *Dumbarton* 4 0 **4 0**
2018–19 *Alloa Ath* 10 1 **10 1**
2019–20 Celtic 0 0 **3 1**
2019–20 *Forest Green R* 28 5
2020–21 Barnsley 0 0
2020–21 *Stevenage* 26 1 **26 1**
2021–22 Barnsley 0 0
2021–22 *Forest Green R* 46 5 **74 10**
2022–23 Barnsley 20 3 **20 3**
2022–23 Motherwell 10 0 **10 0**
2023–24 Exeter C 37 4
2024–25 Exeter C 28 0 **65 4**

BEARDMORE, Mitch (F) 1 0
H: 5 9 W: 11 03 b.Yeovil 7-6-04
From Yeovil T.
2022–23 Exeter C 0 0
2023–24 Exeter C 1 0
2024–25 Exeter C 0 0 **1 0**

BILLINGTON, Gabe (M) 0 0
H: 5 10 W: 10 06 b.Taunton 17-12-04
2023–24 Exeter C 0 0
2024–25 Exeter C 0 0

BIRCH, George (M) 0 0
b. 9-6-07
2024–25 Exeter C 0 0

BIRD, Jay (F) 49 6
H: 6 1 W: 11 00 b.Hartlepool 13-9-00
2017–18 Milton Keynes D 0 0
2018–19 Milton Keynes D 0 0
2019–20 Milton Keynes D 0 0
2020–21 Milton Keynes D 2 0
2021–22 Milton Keynes D 0 0 **2 0**
From Dagenham & Red.
2023–24 Arbroath 33 6 **33 6**
2024–25 Exeter C 14 0 **14 0**

BORGES, Pedro (M) 9 0
H: 6 1 W: 12 00 b. 23-7-05
From SC Coimbroes, Boavista, Bessa.
2022–23 Exeter C 5 0
2023–24 Exeter C 3 0
2024–25 Exeter C 1 0 **9 0**

CARAYOL, Mustapha (M) 306 36
H: 5 10 W: 11 09 b.Gambia 10-6-89
Internationals: Gambia Full caps.
2007–08 Milton Keynes D 0 0
From Torquay U.
2009–10 Torquay U 20 6 **20 6**
2010–11 Lincoln C 33 3 **33 3**
2011–12 Bristol R 30 4
2012–13 Bristol R 0 0 **30 4**
2012–13 Middlesbrough 18 3
2013–14 Middlesbrough 32 8
2014–15 Middlesbrough 0 0
2014–15 *Brighton & HA* 5 0 **5 0**
2015–16 Middlesbrough 0 0 **50 11**
2015–16 *Huddersfield T* 15 3 **15 3**
2015–16 *Leeds U* 12 1 **12 1**
2016–17 Nottingham F 19 1
2017–18 Nottingham F 15 1 **34 2**
2017–18 Ipswich T 8 1 **8 1**
2018–19 Apollon Limassol 10 2 **10 2**
2019–20 Adana Demirspor 8 1 **8 1**
2021–22 Gillingham 22 1 **22 1**
2022–23 Burton Alb 23 0
2023–24 Burton Alb 30 1 **53 1**
2024–25 Exeter C 6 0 **6 0**
Transferred to Wealdstone, March 2025.

CAYLESS, Louie (D) 0 0
2024–25 Exeter C 0 0

COLE, Reece (M) 114 15
H: 5 10 W: 10 03 b.Hillingdon 17-2-98
2015–16 Brentford 0 0
2016–17 Brentford 1 0
2017–18 Brentford 0 0
2017–18 *Newport Co* 4 1 **4 1**
2018–19 Brentford 0 0
2018–19 *Yeovil T* 1 0 **1 0**
2018–19 *Macclesfield T* 18 1 **18 1**
2019–20 Brentford 0 0 **1 0**
2019–20 *Partick Thistle* 19 2 **19 2**
2020–21 QPR 0 0
2021–22 Dunfermline Ath 10 1 **10 1**
From Hayes & Yeading.
2023–24 Exeter C 39 7
2024–25 Exeter C 22 3 **61 10**

COX, Sonny (F) 67 7
H: 5 10 W: 12 06 b.Exeter 11-10-04
2020–21 Exeter C 0 0
2021–22 Exeter C 0 0
2022–23 Exeter C 12 1
2023–24 Exeter C 32 5
2024–25 Exeter C 23 1 **67 7**

CUMMINS, Charlie (M) 0 0
H: 6 2 W: 12 13 b.Blarney 13-6-05
2024–25 Exeter C 0 0

CUTLER, Theo (F) 0 0
b.Dorchester 3-7-07
2023–24 Exeter C 0 0
2024–25 Exeter C 0 0

DEAN, Tom (M) 3 0
b.Exeter 30-11-05
2023–24 Exeter C 0 0
2024–25 Exeter C 3 0 **3 0**

DIABATE, Cheick (D) 81 3
H: 6 4 W: 13 10 b.Southwark 19-6-01
2019–20 Exeter C 0 0
2020–21 Exeter C 0 0
2021–22 Exeter C 18 2
2022–23 Exeter C 20 1
2023–24 Exeter C 28 0
2024–25 Exeter C 4 0 **70 3**
2024–25 *Bradford C* 11 0 **11 0**

EDGECOMBE, Max (D) 0 0
H: 5 9 W: 11 00 b.Taunton 10-10-05
2023–24 Exeter C 0 0
2024–25 Exeter C 0 0

FITZWATER, Jack (D) 157 10
H: 6 2 W: 11 00 b.Solihull 23-9-97
2015–16 WBA 0 0
2015–16 *Chesterfield* 1 0 **1 0**
2016–17 WBA 0 0
2017–18 WBA 0 0
2017–18 *Forest Green R* 14 1 **14 1**
2017–18 *Walsall* 15 3
2018–19 WBA 0 0
2018–19 *Walsall* 21 0 **36 3**
2019–20 WBA 0 0
2020–21 Livingston 20 1
2021–22 Livingston 38 3
2022–23 Livingston 28 1 **86 5**
2023–24 Exeter C 4 0
2024–25 Exeter C 16 1 **20 1**

FRANCIS, Edward (D) — 63 3
H: 6 0 W: 11 11 b.Stockport 11-9-91
Internationals: England U16, U17, U18, U19, C.

Season	Club	Apps	Gls	Tot A	Tot G
2017–18	Manchester C	0	0		
2018–19	Manchester C	0	0		
2018–19	*Almere C*	1	0	1	0
2019–20	Wolverhampton W	0	0		
2019–20	*Grasshopper*	0	0		
2020–21	Wolverhampton W	0	0		
2020–21	Harrogate T	20	1	20	1

From Notts Co, Gateshead.

| 2024–25 | Exeter C | 42 | 2 | 42 | 2 |

HARPER, Vincent (D) — 53 2
H: 5 10 W: 11 00 b.Bristol 22-9-00
Internationals: England C.

| 2023–24 | Exeter C | 31 | 1 | | |
| 2024–25 | Exeter C | 22 | 1 | 53 | 2 |

JAMES, Edward (M) — 1 0
H: 6 1 W: 12 00 b.Exeter 23-12-04
Internationals: Wales U21.

2022–23	Exeter C	1	0		
2023–24	Exeter C	0	0		
2024–25	Exeter C	0	0	1	0

JONES, Patrick (F) — 32 1
H: 5 11 W: 14 11 b.Stockport 9-6-03
Internationals: Wales U17, U21.
From Wrexham.

2020–21	Huddersfield T	2	0		
2021–22	Huddersfield T	6	1		
2022–23	Huddersfield T	6	1		
2023–24	Huddersfield T	7	0		
2024–25	Huddersfield T	0	0	15	1
2024–25	Exeter C	17	0	17	0

LEE, Harry (G) — 1 0
H: 6 0 W: 11 11 b.Torbay 20-12-05

2021–22	Exeter C	0	0		
2022–23	Exeter C	1	0		
2023–24	Exeter C	0	0		
2024–25	Exeter C	0	0	1	0

MACDONALD, Angus (D) — 205 3
H: 6 0 W: 11 00 b.Winchester 15-10-92
Internationals: England U16, U17, C.

2011–12	Reading	0	0		
2011–12	*Torquay U*	2	0		
2012–13	Reading	0	0		
2012–13	*AFC Wimbledon*	4	0	4	0
2012–13	*Torquay U*	14	0	16	0

From Salisbury C, Torquay U.

2016–17	Barnsley	39	1		
2017–18	Barnsley	11	0	50	1
2017–18	Hull C	12	0		
2018–19	Hull C	1	0		
2019–20	Hull C	5	0	18	0
2020–21	Rotherham U	39	1		
2021–22	Rotherham U	7	0	46	1
2022–23	Swindon T	16	0	16	0
2022–23	Aberdeen	15	0		
2023–24	Aberdeen	20	0		
2024–25	Aberdeen	5	0	40	0
2024–25	Exeter C	15	1	15	1

MACDONALD, Shaun (G) — 0 0
H: 6 1 W: 12 00 b.Newcastle upon Tyne 20-10-96
From Gateshead, Blyth Spartans, Torquay U.

2022–23	Cheltenham T	0	0		
2023–24	Exeter C	0	0		
2024–25	Exeter C	0	0		

MAGENNIS, Josh (F) — 541 93
H: 6 2 W: 14 07 b.Bangor 15-8-90
Internationals: Northern Ireland U17, U19, U21, Full caps.

2009–10	Cardiff C	9	0	9	0
2009–10	*Grimsby T*	2	0	2	0
2010–11	Aberdeen	29	3		
2011–12	Aberdeen	23	1		
2012–13	Aberdeen	35	5		
2013–14	Aberdeen	18	1	105	10
2013–14	*St Mirren*	13	0	13	0
2014–15	Kilmarnock	38	8		
2015–16	Kilmarnock	34	10	72	18
2016–17	Charlton Ath	39	10		
2017–18	Charlton Ath	42	10	81	20
2018–19	Bolton W	42	4		
2019–20	Bolton W	0	0	42	4
2019–20	Hull C	29	4		
2020–21	Hull C	40	18		
2021–22	Hull C	19	2	88	24
2021–22	Wigan Ath	17	3		
2022–23	Wigan Ath	36	1		
2023–24	Wigan Ath	36	7	89	11
2024–25	Exeter C	40	6	40	6

McDONALD, Kevin (M) — 520 39
H: 6 2 W: 13 00 b.Carnoustie 4-11-88
Internationals: Scotland U19, U21, Full caps.

2005–06	Dundee	26	3		
2006–07	Dundee	30	2		
2007–08	Dundee	34	9	90	14
2008–09	Burnley	25	1		
2009–10	Burnley	26	1		
2010–11	Burnley	0	0	51	2
2010–11	*Scunthorpe U*	5	1	5	1
2010–11	*Notts Co*	11	0	11	0
2011–12	Sheffield U	31	3		
2012–13	Sheffield U	45	1		
2013–14	Sheffield U	1	1	77	5
2013–14	Wolverhampton W	41	5		
2014–15	Wolverhampton W	46	0		
2015–16	Wolverhampton W	33	3	120	8
2016–17	Fulham	43	3		
2017–18	Fulham	42	3		
2018–19	Fulham	15	0		
2019–20	Fulham	16	0		
2020–21	Fulham	0	0	116	6
2021–22	Dundee U	9	0		
2022–23	Dundee U	0	0	9	0
2022–23	Exeter C	11	3		
2023–24	Bradford C	19	0	19	0
2024–25	Exeter C	11	0	22	3

McMILLAN, Jack (D) — 198 8
H: 6 0 W: 12 02 b.Livingston 18-12-97

2016–17	Motherwell	14	0		
2017–18	Motherwell	0	0	14	0
2017–18	Livingston	13	1		
2018–19	Livingston	7	1		
2018–19	*Partick Thistle*	13	0		
2019–20	Livingston	20	0		
2020–21	Livingston	8	0		
2021–22	Livingston	16	1	64	3
2022–23	Partick Thistle	36	1		
2023–24	Partick Thistle	28	2	77	3
2024–25	Exeter C	43	2	43	2

MITCHELL, Demetri (M) — 137 10
H: 5 9 W: 11 11 b.Manchester 11-1-97
Internationals: England U16, U17, U18, U20.

2016–17	Manchester U	1	0		
2017–18	Manchester U	0	0		
2017–18	*Hearts*	9	0		
2018–19	Manchester U	0	0		
2018–19	*Hearts*	20	0	29	0
2019–20	Manchester U	0	0	1	0
2020–21	Blackpool	32	1		
2021–22	Blackpool	13	0	45	1
2021–22	Hibernian	6	1		
2022–23	Hibernian	3	0	9	1
2022–23	Exeter C	16	2		
2023–24	Exeter C	14	2		
2023–24	Exeter C	23	4	53	8

NISKANEN, Ilmari (F) — 330 31
H: 5 10 W: 12 04 b.Kiuruvesi 27-10-97
Internationals: Finland U19, U21, Full caps.
From PK-37.

2013	KuPS	1	0		
2013	*PK-37*	22	9		
2014	KuPS	4	1		
2014	*Ku-Fu-98*	7	0		
2014	*PK-37*	1	0	23	9
2015	KuPS	20	1		
2016	KuPS	24	0		
2017	KuPS	32	1		
2017	*Ku-Fu-98*	1	0	8	0
2018	KuPS	33	4		
2019	KuPS	26	5		
2020	KuPS	13	6	153	18
2020–21	Ingolstadt 04	20	0		
2021–22	Ingolstadt 04	0	0	20	0
2021–22	Dundee U	33	1		
2022–23	Dundee U	30	1		
2023–24	Dundee U	0	0	53	2
2023–24	Exeter C	33	0		
2024–25	Exeter C	40	2	73	2

OAKES, Liam (D) — 1 0
b. 10-1-07

| 2023–24 | Exeter C | 0 | 0 | | |
| 2024–25 | Exeter C | 1 | 0 | 1 | 0 |

OHANAKA, Santino (M) — 0 0
H: 5 9 b.London 3-4-07

| 2023–24 | Exeter C | 0 | 0 | | |
| 2024–25 | Exeter C | 0 | 0 | | |

OLUWABORI, Andrew (F) — 6 1
b.30-9-01

| 2021–22 | Peterborough U | 0 | 0 | | |
| 2022–23 | Peterborough U | 0 | 0 | | |

From FC Halifax T.

| 2024–25 | Exeter C | 6 | 1 | 6 | 1 |

PERKINS, David (D) — 474 17
H: 5 7 W: 12 00 b.Heysham 21-6-82
Internationals: England C.

2006–07	Rochdale	18	0		
2007–08	Rochdale	40	4		
2008–09	Colchester U	38	5		
2009–10	Colchester U	5	1		
2009–10	*Chesterfield*	13	1	13	1
2009–10	*Stockport Co*	22	0	22	0
2010–11	Colchester U	36	1	79	7
2011–12	Barnsley	33	1		
2012–13	Barnsley	35	1		
2013–14	Barnsley	23	0	91	2
2013–14	Blackpool	20	0		
2014–15	Blackpool	45	0	65	0
2015–16	Wigan Ath	45	0		
2016–17	Wigan Ath	27	0		
2017–18	Wigan Ath	13	1	85	1
2018–19	Rochdale	17	0	75	4
2018–19	Tranmere R	17	2		
2019–20	Tranmere R	27	0	44	2

From AFC Fylde, Bamber Bridge.

| 2023–24 | Exeter C | 0 | 0 | | |
| 2024–25 | Exeter C | 0 | 0 | | |

PHILLIPS, Frankie (G) — 0 0

| 2024–25 | Exeter C | 0 | 0 | | |

PURRINGTON, Ben (D) — 258 8
H: 6 0 W: 11 07 b.Exeter 5-5-96

2013–14	Plymouth Arg	12	0		
2014–15	Plymouth Arg	8	0		
2015–16	Plymouth Arg	13	0		
2016–17	Plymouth Arg	19	0	52	0
2016–17	Rotherham U	10	0		
2017–18	Rotherham U	10	0		
2018–19	Rotherham U	0	0	20	0
2018–19	*AFC Wimbledon*	26	0	26	0
2018–19	*Charlton Ath*	18	0		
2019–20	Charlton Ath	31	2		
2020–21	Charlton Ath	28	2		
2021–22	Charlton Ath	27	3	104	7
2022–23	Ross Co	11	0		
2023–24	Ross Co	12	0	23	0
2023–24	Exeter C	12	1		
2024–25	Exeter C	21	0	33	1

RICHARDS, Amani (F) — 6 1
H: 5 9 W: 10 03 b.16-11-04
Internationals: England U16.

| 2024–25 | Exeter C | 6 | 1 | 6 | 1 |

RICHARDS, Jake (M) — 19 1
H: 5 9 W: 10 03 b. 8-8-07

| 2023–24 | Exeter C | 6 | 0 | | |
| 2024–25 | Exeter C | 13 | 1 | 19 | 1 |

SWEENEY, Pierce (D) — 344 19
H: 5 10 W: 12 08 b.Dublin 11-9-94
Internationals: Republic of Ireland U17, U19, U21.

2012	Bray W	12	0	12	0
2012–13	Reading	0	0		
2013–14	Reading	0	0		
2014–15	Reading	0	0		
2015–16	Reading	0	0		
2016–17	Exeter C	29	0		
2017–18	Exeter C	40	8		
2018–19	Exeter C	43	4		
2019–20	Exeter C	36	3		
2020–21	Exeter C	38	3		
2021–22	Exeter C	43	0		
2022–23	Exeter C	43	2		
2023–24	Exeter C	42	0		
2024–25	Exeter C	18	0	332	19

TURNS, Ed (D) — 54 3
H: 6 1 W: 12 00 b.Brighton 18-10-02
Internationals: Wales U21.

2021–22	Brighton & HA	0	0		
2022–23	Brighton & HA	0	0		
2022–23	*Leyton Orient*	16	2		
2023–24	Brighton & HA	0	0		
2023–24	*Leyton Orient*	13	0	29	2
2023–24	*Crewe Alex*	12	1	12	1
2024–25	Brighton & HA	0	0		
2024–25	Exeter C	13	0	13	0

WATTS, Caleb (M) — 67 7
H: 5 8 W: 11 07 b.Essex 16-1-02
Internationals: Australia U17, U23.
From QPR.

2020–21	Southampton	3	0		
2021–22	Southampton	0	0		
2021–22	*Crawley T*	1	0	1	0
2022–23	Southampton	0	0	3	0
2022–23	*Morecambe*	23	2	23	2
2023–24	Exeter C	9	1		
2024–25	Exeter C	31	4	40	5

WILDSCHUT, Yanic (F) — 381 38
H: 6 2 W: 13 08 b.Amsterdam 1-11-91
Internationals: Netherlands U21. Suriname Full caps.

2010–11	Zwolle	33	3	33	3
2011–12	VVV Venlo	29	7		
2012–13	VVV Venlo	32	1	61	8
2013–14	Heerenveen	18	2		
2013–14	*Den Haag*	7	0	7	0
2014–15	Heerenveen	4	0	22	2
2014–15	Middlesbrough	11	2		
2015–16	Middlesbrough	1	0	12	2
2015–16	Wigan Ath	34	7		
2016–17	Wigan Ath	25	4	59	11
2016–17	Norwich C	9	1		
2017–18	Norwich C	16	1		
2017–18	*Cardiff C*	10	0	10	0
2018–19	Norwich C	0	0	25	2

2018–19	Bolton W	16	2	**16** **2**
2019–20	Maccabi Haifa	32	5	
2020–21	Maccabi Haifa	22	1	**54** **6**
2021–22	CSKA Sofia	28	0	**28** **0**
2022–23	Oxford U	23	1	**23** **1**
2023–24	Exeter C	31	1	
2024–25	Exeter C	0	0	**31** **1**

WILSON, Kieran (F) **0** **0**

2024–25	Exeter C	0	0

WOODS, Ryan (M) **428** **6**
H: 5 8   W: 13 01   b.Norton Canes 13-12-93

2012–13	Shrewsbury T	2	0	
2013–14	Shrewsbury T	41	1	
2014–15	Shrewsbury T	43	0	
2015–16	Shrewsbury T	5	0	**91** **1**
2015–16	Brentford	41	2	
2016–17	Brentford	42	0	
2017–18	Brentford	39	1	
2018–19	Brentford	0	0	**122** **3**
2018–19	Stoke C	27	0	
2019–20	Stoke C	8	0	
2019–20	Millwall	18	0	
2020–21	Stoke C	0	0	**35** **0**
2020–21	Millwall	41	0	**59** **0**
2021–22	Birmingham C	30	0	
2022–23	Birmingham C	2	0	**32** **0**
2022–23	Hull C	26	0	
2023–24	Hull C	0	0	**26** **0**
2023–24	Bristol R	12	0	**12** **0**
2023–24	Exeter C	14	0	
2024–25	Exeter C	37	2	**51** **2**

YFEKO, Johnly (D) **12** **0**
H: 6 3   W: 12 08   b.Newham 23-6-03
From Southampton, Leicester C.

2022–23	Rangers	0	0
2023–24	Rangers	0	0
2024–25	Rangers	0	0

On loan from Rangers.

2024–25	Exeter C	12	0	**12** **0**

Scholars
Anthony, Jack Harvey; Birch, George Edward; Bown, Aidan Andrew Dupain; Cartwright, Liam Robert; Cavendish, Jacca Francis; Cooper, Kye Kaden John; Crees, Harry Kian; Cutler, Theo Charles; Graham, Callum Phillip; Hodgetts, Luke Robert; Horn, Jude; Layer, Daniel Harry Gareth; Oakes, Liam Andrew; Ohanaka, Santino Elijah Ramario; Richards, Jake Thomas; Shanahan, Dylan Joseph; Wilson, Kieran.

FLEETWOOD T (36)

BAGGLEY, Barry (M) **62** **9**
H: 5 9   W: 10 01   b.Belfast 11-2-02
Internationals: Northern Ireland U17, U19, U21.

2018–19	Fleetwood T	3	0	
2019–20	Fleetwood T	0	0	
2020–21	Fleetwood T	2	0	
2021–22	Fleetwood T	7	1	
2022–23	Fleetwood T	0	0	
2023	Waterford	33	2	
2023–24	Fleetwood T	0	0	
2024	Waterford	17	6	**50** **8**
2024–25	Fleetwood T	0	0	**12** **1**

Transferred to St Patrick's Ath, December 2024.

BELLIZIA, Oliver (D) **0** **0**

2024–25	Fleetwood T	0	0

BOLTON, James (D) **178** **9**
H: 5 11   W: 11 11   b.Stone 13-8-94
Internationals: England C.
From Macclesfield T, Halifax T, Gateshead.

2017–18	Shrewsbury T	33	1	
2018–19	Shrewsbury T	31	1	**64** **2**
2019–20	Portsmouth	23	1	
2020–21	Portsmouth	13	1	**36** **2**
2021–22	Plymouth Arg	13	0	
2022–23	Plymouth Arg	6	1	**19** **1**
2023–24	St Mirren	21	0	**21** **0**
2024–25	Fleetwood T	38	4	**38** **4**

BONDS, Elliott (M) **136** **5**
H: 5 10   W: 10 06   b.Brent 23-3-00
Internationals: Guyana Full caps.
From Dagenham & Red.

2019–20	Hull C	0	0	
2020–21	Hull C	0	0	
2020–21	Cheltenham T	5	0	
2021–22	Cheltenham T	23	1	
2022–23	Cheltenham T	37	2	
2023–24	Cheltenham T	38	2	**103** **5**
2024–25	Fleetwood T	33	0	**33** **0**

BROOM, Ryan (M) **254** **23**
H: 5 10   W: 12 08   b.Newport 4-9-96

2015–16	Bristol R	1	0	
2016–17	Bristol R	5	0	
2017–18	Bristol R	3	0	**9** **0**
2018–19	Cheltenham T	39	2	
2019–20	Cheltenham T	34	8	
2020–21	Peterborough U	15	1	
2020–21	Burton Alb	11	2	**11** **2**
2021–22	Peterborough U	0	0	
2021–22	Plymouth Arg	43	4	**43** **4**
2022–23	Peterborough U	0	0	**15** **1**
2022–23	Cheltenham T	40	2	**113** **12**
2023–24	Fleetwood T	36	2	
2024–25	Fleetwood T	27	2	**63** **4**

CIRINO, Rafaele (D) **0** **0**
Internationals: Montserrat Full caps.

2024–25	Fleetwood T	0	0

COUGHLAN, Ronan (F) **176** **71**
H: 5 10   W: 11 11   b.Limerick 2-10-95
From Huddersfield T.

2018	Bray W	21	4	**21** **4**
2018	Cork C	4	1	**4** **1**
2019	Sligo R	27	8	
2020	Sligo R	18	6	**45** **14**
2021	St Patrick's Ath	28	7	
2022	St Patrick's Ath	10	0	**38** **7**
2023	Waterford	32	35	**32** **35**
2023–24	Fleetwood T	13	2	
2024–25	Fleetwood T	23	8	**36** **10**

CROSS-ADAIR, Finlay (F) **10** **1**
b. 11-1-05

2022–23	Preston NE	4	0	
2023–24	Preston NE	0	0	**4** **0**
2023–24	Annan Ath	5	1	**5** **1**
2024–25	Fleetwood T	1	0	**1** **0**

DEVONPORT, Owen (M) **24** **1**
b.Burnley 9-10-04

2023–24	Accrington S	0	0	
2023–24	Fleetwood T	0	0	
2024–25	Fleetwood T	24	1	**24** **1**

DOLAN, Callum (M) **15** **0**
H: 5 11   W: 10 10   b.Manchester 29-9-00

2019–20	Oldham Ath	0	0

From Radcliffe, Matlock T, Warrington Rylands.

2022–23	Fleetwood T	4	0	
2023–24	Fleetwood T	11	0	
2024–25	Fleetwood T	0	0	**15** **0**

DONAGHY, Tom (G) **0** **0**
H: 6 3   W: 13 10   b.Leeds 18-4-03
From Bradford C.

2021–22	Fleetwood T	0	0
2022–23	Fleetwood T	0	0
2023	Waterford	0	0
2023–24	Fleetwood T	0	0
2024–25	Fleetwood T	0	0

GRAYDON, Ryan (M) **165** **22**
H: 6 2   W: 12 00   b.Dublin 11-4-99
Internationals: Republic of Ireland U19.

2018	Bohemians	1	0	
2019	Bohemians	12	0	**13** **0**
2020	Bray W	18	2	
2021	Bray W	19	3	**37** **5**
2022	Longford T	18	2	**18** **2**
2022	Derry C	13	2	
2023	Derry C	23	2	**36** **4**
2023–24	Fleetwood T	27	2	
2024–25	Fleetwood T	34	9	**61** **11**

HARRINGTON, David (G) **21** **0**
H: 6 0   W: 11 03   b.Cork 1-7-00
From Cobh Ramblers, Cork C.

2022–23	Fleetwood T	0	0	
2023–24	Fleetwood T	1	0	
2024–25	Fleetwood T	20	0	**21** **0**

HELM, Mark (M) **100** **15**
H: 5 8   W: 9 08   b.Warrington 21-10-01
From Manchester U.

2021–22	Burnley	0	0	
2022–23	Burnley	0	0	
2022–23	Burton Alb	19	3	
2023–24	Burton Alb	37	5	**56** **8**
2024–25	Fleetwood T	44	7	**44** **7**

HEWITSON, Luke (G) **0** **0**
H: 6 2   b.Newcastle 15-10-04

2024–25	Fleetwood T	0	0

HOLGATE, Harrison (D) **60** **1**
H: 6 1   W: 11 00   b.Leeds 5-10-00

2018–19	Fleetwood T	0	0	
2019–20	Fleetwood T	0	0	
2020–21	Fleetwood T	18	0	
2021–22	Fleetwood T	6	0	
2022–23	Fleetwood T	19	1	
2023–24	Fleetwood T	12	0	
2024–25	Fleetwood T	5	0	**60** **1**

HUGHES, Kayden (D) **8** **2**
b. 28-11-05

2024–25	Fleetwood T	8	2	**8** **2**

HUNT, MacKenzie (M) **39** **1**
H: 5 8   W: 9 13   b.Liverpool 14-11-01
Internationals: United Arab Emirates Full caps.

2020–21	Everton	0	0	
2021–22	Everton	0	0	
2022–23	Everton	0	0	
2023–24	Everton	0	0	
2024–25	Fleetwood T	39	1	**39** **1**

JOHNSON, Will (D) **2** **0**
b. 6-6-05

2022–23	Fleetwood T	0	0	
2023–24	Fleetwood T	0	0	
2024–25	Fleetwood T	2	0	**2** **0**

LANE, Mikey (F) **1** **0**

2022–23	Fleetwood T	0	0	
2023–24	Fleetwood T	0	0	
2024–25	Fleetwood T	1	0	**1** **0**

LITTLER, Zack (M) **0** **0**
b. 19-5-05

2024–25	Fleetwood T	0	0

LONERGAN, Tom (F) **82** **16**
H: 6 0   W: 12 02   b.Dublin 2-1-04
Internationals: Republic of Ireland U16, U18, U19, U21.

2021	St Patrick's Ath	0	0	
2022	UCD	19	6	**19** **6**
2023	St Patrick's Ath	31	4	**31** **4**
2023–24	Fleetwood T	9	1	
2024–25	Fleetwood T	6	0	**15** **1**
2025	Waterford	17	5	**17** **5**

LYNCH, Jay (G) **168** **0**
H: 6 0   W: 12 13   b.Salford 31-3-93

2012–13	Bolton W	0	0	
2013–14	Bolton W	0	0	
2014–15	Accrington S	2	0	**2** **0**

From Salford C, AFC Fylde.

2019–20	Rochdale	8	0	
2020–21	Rochdale	17	0	
2021–22	Rochdale	25	0	**50** **0**
2022–23	Fleetwood T	45	0	
2023–24	Fleetwood T	44	0	
2024–25	Fleetwood T	27	0	**116** **0**

MANSFIELD, Ronan (F) **0** **0**

2023	Waterford	0	0
2024–25	Fleetwood T	0	0

MAYOR, Danny (M) **500** **40**
H: 6 0   W: 12 00   b.Leyland 18-10-90

2008–09	Preston NE	0	0	
2008–09	Tranmere R	3	0	**3** **0**
2009–10	Preston NE	7	0	
2010–11	Preston NE	21	0	
2011–12	Preston NE	36	2	
2012–13	Preston NE	0	0	**64** **2**
2012–13	Sheffield Wed	8	0	
2012–13	Southend U	5	0	**5** **0**
2013–14	Sheffield Wed	0	0	**8** **0**
2013–14	Bury	39	5	
2014–15	Bury	44	8	
2015–16	Bury	44	5	
2016–17	Bury	21	3	
2017–18	Bury	20	1	
2018–19	Bury	39	8	**207** **30**
2019–20	Plymouth Arg	34	1	
2020–21	Plymouth Arg	44	1	
2021–22	Plymouth Arg	33	3	
2022–23	Plymouth Arg	30	1	**141** **6**
2023–24	Fleetwood T	33	0	
2024–25	Fleetwood T	39	2	**72** **2**

McLEAN, Crispin (D) **0** **0**

2024–25	Fleetwood T	0	0

McMULLAN, Stephen (G) **45** **0**
H: 6 1   W: 12 04   b.Dundalk 31-12-04
Internationals: Republic of Ireland U18. Northern Ireland U18, U19, U20, U21.

2020–21	Warrenpoint T	0	0	
2021–22	Warrenpoint T	10	0	**10** **0**
2022–23	Fleetwood T	1	0	
2023–24	Fleetwood T	2	0	
2024	Caernarfon T	13	0	**13** **0**
2024–25	Fleetwood T	0	0	**3** **0**
2025	Waterford	19	0	**19** **0**

MEDLEY, Zechariah (D) **85** **5**
H: 6 5   W: 14 02   b.London 7-7-00
Internationals: England U16.

2018–19	Arsenal	0	0	
2019–20	Arsenal	0	0	
2020–21	Arsenal	0	0	
2020–21	Gillingham	12	0	**12** **0**
2020–21	Kilmarnock	8	1	**8** **1**
2021–22	Oostende	18	1	
2022–23	Oostende	15	1	
2023–24	Oostende	25	1	**58** **3**
2024–25	Fleetwood T	7	1	**7** **1**

MORRISON, George (M) 7 0
b. 24-10-05
Internationals: Scotland U18, U19.
2022–23	Fleetwood T	0	0	
2023–24	Fleetwood T	0	0	
2024–25	Fleetwood T	7	0	7 0

NEAL, Harrison (M) 113 1
H: 5 11 W: 10 10 b.Doncaster 12-5-01
2021–22	Sheffield U	0	0	
2022–23	Sheffield U	0	0	
2022–23	Barrow	45	0	45 0
2023–24	Stevenage	0	0	
2023–24	Stevenage	5	0	5 0
2023–24	Carlisle U	21	0	
2024–25	Carlisle U	21	1	42 1
2024–25	Fleetwood T	21	0	21 0

ODUBEKO, Ademipo (F) 49 5
H: 5 11 b.Tallaght 21-10-02
Internationals: Republic of Ireland U16, U17, U21.
From Manchester U.
2020–21	West Ham U	0	0	
2021–22	West Ham U	0	0	
2021–22	Huddersfield T	6	0	6 0
2021–22	Doncaster R	16	2	16 2
2022–23	West Ham U	0	0	
2022–23	*Port Vale*	22	3	22 3
2023–24	Maritimo	0	0	
2024–25	Fleetwood T	5	0	5 0

Transferred to Shelbourne, December 2024.

PATTERSON, Phoenix (F) 137 27
H: 5 10 W: 11 00 b.High Wycombe 1-9-00
Internationals: Scotland U19.
2018–19	Tottenham H	0	0	
2019–20	Tottenham H	0	0	
2021	Waterford	15	4	
2022	Waterford	31	17	46 21
2022–23	Fleetwood T	18	1	
2023–24	Fleetwood T	34	2	
2024–25	Fleetwood T	39	3	91 6

POTTER, Finley (D) 29 0
H: 6 0 W: 11 00 b.Sheffield 14-3-04
Internationals: England U18.
From Sheffield U.
2023–24	Fleetwood T	1	0	
2024–25	Fleetwood T	28	0	29 0

ROBERTS, Liam (D) 1 0
2024–25	Fleetwood T	0	0	
2025	*Waterford*	1	0	1 0

ROONEY, Shaun (D) 266 25
H: 6 3 W: 13 05 b.Bellshill 26-7-96
2013–14	Queen's Park	8	0	
2014–15	Queen's Park	24	4	32 4
2015–16	Dunfermline Ath	11	1	11 1
From York C.				
2017–18	Queen of the South	24	0	24 0
2018–19	Inverness CT	31	5	
2019–20	Inverness CT	25	3	56 8
2020–21	St Johnstone	27	2	
2021–22	St Johnstone	23	1	50 3
2022–23	Fleetwood T	39	6	
2023–24	Fleetwood T	29	1	
2024–25	St Mirren	6	0	6 0
2024–25	Fleetwood T	19	2	87 9

SARPENG-WIREDU, Brendan (M) 172 8
H: 6 3 W: 11 00 b.London 7-11-99
2018–19	Charlton Ath	0	0	
2019–20	Charlton Ath	0	0	
2019–20	Colchester U	7	0	
2020–21	Charlton Ath	0	0	
2020–21	Colchester U	20	1	
2021–22	Colchester U	38	1	65 2
2022–23	Fleetwood T	37	1	
2023–24	Fleetwood T	36	3	
2024–25	Fleetwood T	34	2	107 6

SMITH, Pele (M) 1 0
b. 21-2-09
2024–25	Fleetwood T	1	0	1 0

VIRTUE, Matthew (M) 168 19
H: 5 9 W: 11 00 b.Epsom 2-5-97
2017–18	Liverpool	0	0	
2017–18	Notts Co	13	0	13 0
2018–19	Blackpool	13	3	
2019–20	Blackpool	24	2	
2020–21	Blackpool	16	2	
2021–22	Blackpool	3	0	
2022–23	Blackpool	3	0	
2022–23	Lincoln C	30	3	30 3
2023–24	Blackpool	25	0	84 7
2024–25	Fleetwood T	41	9	41 9

WILKES, Reece (D) 0 0
Internationals: England U16.
2024–25	Fleetwood T	0	0	

Players retained or with offer of contract
Oliver, Toby Adam.

Scholars
Animasaun, David Oluwasemilore O; Bellizia, Oliver Ernest-James; Cirino, Raffaele Alexander; Currie, Harvey John; Doherty, Jack Pearse; Doherty, Jake Joseph Steven; Eccles, Joshua Joseph; Elmore, Harry Alexander; Graham, Cameron James; Haughey, Conor Joseph; Lane, Michael Eric David; McLean, Crispin Robert; Ruocco, Alessio Dantae; Slater, Adham; Stansfield, Jensen Roger; Taylor, Lucas Russell William; Thompson, Leo Christopher; Wilkinson, Rylee.

FULHAM (37)

AMISSAH, Samuel (D) 0 0
H: 6 0 W: 11 05 b. 7-3-07
Internationals: England U17, U18.
2023–24	Fulham	0	0	
2024–25	Fulham	0	0	

ANDERSEN, Joachim (D) 274 9
H: 6 2 W: 14 02 b.Frederiksberg 31-5-96
Internationals: Denmark U16, U17, U19, U20, U21, Full caps.
2014–15	FC Twente	7	1	
2015–16	FC Twente	18	1	
2016–17	FC Twente	22	2	
2017–18	FC Twente	2	0	49 4
2017–18	Sampdoria	7	0	
2018–19	Sampdoria	32	0	39 0
2019–20	Lyon	18	1	
2020–21	Lyon	3	0	21 1
2020–21	*Fulham*	31	1	
2021–22	Crystal Palace	34	0	
2022–23	Crystal Palace	32	1	
2023–24	Crystal Palace	38	2	
2024–25	Crystal Palace	1	0	105 3
2024–25	Fulham	29	0	60 1

ARAUJO, Harvey (D) 20 0
H: 6 0 W: 11 03 b. 7-11-04
Internationals: England U16, U18.
2024–25	Fulham	0	0	
2024–25	*Chesterfield*	20	0	20 0

ASHBY-HAMMOND, Luca (G) 19 0
H: 6 0 W: 11 11 b.Kingston upon Thames 25-3-01
Internationals: England U16, U17, U18, U19, U20.
2018–19	Fulham	0	0	
2019–20	Fulham	0	0	
2020–21	Fulham	0	0	
2021–22	Fulham	0	0	
2022–23	Fulham	0	0	
2023–24	Fulham	0	0	
2023–24	*Crawley T*	7	0	7 0
2023–24	*Notts Co*	11	0	11 0
2024–25	Fulham	0	0	
2024–25	*Gillingham*	1	0	1 0

BASSEY, Calvin (D) 126 3
H: 6 1 W: 12 00 b.Aosta 31-12-99
Internationals: Nigeria Full caps.
2017–18	Leicester C	0	0	
2018–19	Leicester C	0	0	
2019–20	Leicester C	0	0	
2020–21	Rangers	8	0	
2021–22	Rangers	29	0	37 0
2022–23	Ajax	25	1	25 1
2023–24	Fulham	29	1	
2024–25	Fulham	35	1	64 2

BENDA, Steven (G) 60 0
H: 6 4 W: 13 01 b.Stuttgart 1-1-98
From Aalen, Heidenheim, TSV 1860.
2018–19	Swansea C	0	0	
2019–20	Swansea C	0	0	
2019–20	*Swindon T*	24	0	24 0
2020–21	Swansea C	1	0	
2021–22	Swansea C	5	0	
2021–22	*Peterborough U*	9	0	9 0
2022–23	Swansea C	21	0	27 0
2023–24	Fulham	0	0	
2024–25	Fulham	0	0	

BERGE, Sander (M) 282 18
H: 6 5 W: 15 02 b.Baerum 14-2-98
Internationals: Norway U16, U17, U18, U19, U21, Full caps.
2013	Asker	1	0	
2014	Asker	7	0	8 0
2015	Valerenga	11	0	
2016	Valerenga	25	0	36 0
2016–17	Genk	9	0	
2017–18	Genk	13	0	
2018–19	Genk	28	0	
2019–20	Sheffield U	23	4	73 4
2020–21	Sheffield U	15	1	
2021–22	Sheffield U	31	5	
2022–23	Sheffield U	37	6	97 13

CAIRNEY, Tom (M) 462 53
H: 6 0 W: 11 05 b.Nottingham 20-1-91
Internationals: Scotland U19, U21, Full caps.
From Leeds U.
2009–10	Hull C	11	1	
2010–11	Hull C	22	1	
2011–12	Hull C	27	0	
2012–13	Hull C	10	0	
2013–14	Hull C	0	0	70 2
2013–14	Blackburn R	37	5	
2014–15	Blackburn R	39	3	76 8
2015–16	Fulham	39	8	
2016–17	Fulham	45	12	
2017–18	Fulham	34	5	
2018–19	Fulham	31	1	
2019–20	Fulham	39	8	
2020–21	Fulham	10	1	
2021–22	Fulham	26	3	
2022–23	Fulham	33	2	
2023–24	Fulham	34	1	
2024–25	Fulham	25	2	316 43

CASTAGNE, Timothy (D) 304 12
H: 6 1 W: 12 08 b.Arlon 5-12-95
Internationals: Belgium U18, U19, U21, Full caps.
2013–14	Genk	0	0	
2014–15	Genk	27	1	
2015–16	Genk	21	0	
2016–17	Genk	32	0	80 1
2017–18	Atalanta	20	0	
2018–19	Atalanta	28	4	
2019–20	Atalanta	27	1	
2020–21	Atalanta	0	0	75 5
2020–21	Leicester C	27	2	
2021–22	Leicester C	27	1	
2022–23	Leicester C	37	2	91 5
2023–24	Fulham	34	1	
2024–25	Fulham	24	0	58 1

CUENCA, Jorge (D) 119 7
H: 6 2 W: 11 11 b.Madrid 17-11-99
Internationals: Spain U19, U21.
2016–17	Alcorcon	5	0	5 0
2017–18	Barcelona	0	0	
2018–19	Barcelona	0	0	
2019–20	Barcelona	0	0	
2020–21	Barcelona	0	0	
2020–21	Almeira	35	3	35 3
2021–22	Villarreal	0	0	
2021–22	Getafe	32	1	32 1
2022–23	Villarreal	10	0	
2023–24	Villarreal	29	3	39 3
2024–25	Villarreal	8	0	8 0

DE FOUGEROLLES, Luc (D) 0 0
H: 5 11 W: 11 05 b.London 12-10-05
Internationals: Canada Full caps.
2023–24	Fulham	0	0	
2024–25	Fulham	0	0	

DIBLEY-DIAS, Matthew (M) 2 0
H: 5 7 W: 10 03 b.Lower Hutt 29-10-03
2022–23	Fulham	0	0	
2023–24	Fulham	0	0	
2024–25	Fulham	0	0	
2024–25	*Northampton T*	2	0	2 0

DIOP, Issa (D) 237 12
H: 6 4 W: 13 03 b.Toulouse 9-1-97
Internationals: France U16, U17, U18, U19, U20, U21.
2015–16	Toulouse	21	1	
2016–17	Toulouse	30	2	
2017–18	Toulouse	26	2	77 5
2018–19	West Ham U	33	1	
2019–20	West Ham U	32	3	
2020–21	West Ham U	18	2	
2021–22	West Ham U	13	0	96 6
2022–23	Fulham	25	1	
2023–24	Fulham	18	0	
2024–25	Fulham	21	0	64 1

GODO, Martial (F) 36 4
H: 5 7 W: 9 08 b.Greenwich 14-3-03
Internationals: England U20. Ivory Coast U23.
From Dartford.
2022–23	Fulham	0	0	
2022–23	Fulham	0	0	
2023–24	*Wigan Ath*	34	4	34 4
2024–25	Fulham	2	0	2 0

HARRIS, Luke (M) 54 7
H: 5 10 W: 9 13 b.Jersey 3-4-05
Internationals: Wales U17, U18, U19, U21.
2022–23	Fulham	3	0	
2023–24	Fulham	1	0	
2023–24	*Exeter C*	21	4	21 4
2024–25	Fulham	0	0	4 0
2024–25	*Birmingham C*	29	3	29 3

IWOBI, Alex (M) 291 31
H: 5 11 W: 11 12 b.Lagos 3-5-96
Internationals: England U16, U17, U18. Nigeria Full caps.

2012–13	Arsenal	0	0		
2013–14	Arsenal	0	0		
2014–15	Arsenal	0	0		
2015–16	Arsenal	13	2		
2016–17	Arsenal	26	3		
2017–18	Arsenal	26	3		
2018–19	Arsenal	35	3		
2019–20	Arsenal	0	0	**100**	**11**
2019–20	Everton	25	1		
2020–21	Everton	30	1		
2021–22	Everton	28	2		
2022–23	Everton	38	2		
2023–24	Everton	2	0	**123**	**6**
2023–24	Fulham	30	5		
2024–25	Fulham	38	9	**68**	**14**

JIMENEZ, Raul (F) 373 107
H: 6 2 W: 12 04 b.Tepeji 5-5-91
Internationals: Mexico U23, Full caps.

2011–12	Club America	15	2		
2012–13	Club America	29	11		
2013–14	Club America	27	12		
2014–15	Club America	4	4	**75**	**29**
2014–15	Atletico Madrid	21	1	**21**	**1**
2015–16	Benfica	28	5		
2016–17	Benfica	19	7		
2017–18	Benfica	33	6		
2018–19	Benfica	0	0	**80**	**18**
2018–19	*Wolverhampton W*	38	13		
2019–20	Wolverhampton W	38	17		
2020–21	Wolverhampton W	10	4		
2021–22	Wolverhampton W	34	6		
2022–23	Wolverhampton W	15	0	**135**	**40**
2023–24	Fulham	24	7		
2024–25	Fulham	38	12	**62**	**19**

KING, Joshua (M) 8 0
H: 5 8 W: 10 06 b. 3-1-07
Internationals: England U16, U17, U18, U19.

2023–24	Fulham	0	0		
2024–25	Fulham	8	0	**8**	**0**

LENO, Bernd (G) 446 0
H: 6 3 W: 12 06 b.Bietigheim-Bissingen 4-3-92
Internationals: Germany, U17, U18, U19, U21, Full caps.
From Stuttgart.

2011–12	Bayer Leverkusen	33	0		
2012–13	Bayer Leverkusen	32	0		
2013–14	Bayer Leverkusen	34	0		
2014–15	Bayer Leverkusen	34	0		
2015–16	Bayer Leverkusen	33	0		
2016–17	Bayer Leverkusen	34	0		
2017–18	Bayer Leverkusen	33	0	**233**	**0**
2018–19	Arsenal	32	0		
2019–20	Arsenal	30	0		
2020–21	Arsenal	35	0		
2021–22	Arsenal	4	0	**101**	**0**
2022–23	Fulham	36	0		
2023–24	Fulham	38	0		
2024–25	Fulham	38	0	**112**	**0**

LUKIC, Sasa (M) 299 25
H: 6 0 W: 12 02 b.Sabac 13-8-96
Internationals: Serbia U17, U21, Full caps.

2013–14	Partizan Belgrade	0	0		
2013–14	*Teleoptik*	23	3		
2014–15	Partizan Belgrade	2	0		
2014–15	*Teleoptik*	16	6	**39**	**9**
2015–16	Partizan Belgrade	25	2	**27**	**2**
2016–17	Torino	14	0		
2017–18	Torino	0	0		
2017–18	*Levante*	16	0	**16**	**0**
2018–19	Torino	24	2		
2019–20	Torino	30	1		
2020–21	Torino	32	3		
2021–22	Torino	35	5		
2022–23	Torino	16	2	**151**	**13**
2022–23	Fulham	12	0		
2023–24	Fulham	24	1		
2024–25	Fulham	30	0	**66**	**1**

PEREIRA, Andreas (M) 263 25
H: 5 10 W: 10 06 b.Duffel 1-1-96
Internationals: Belgium U16, U17. Brazil U20, U23, Full caps.
From PSV Eindhoven.

2014–15	Manchester U	1	0		
2015–16	Manchester U	4	0		
2016–17	Manchester U	0	0		
2016–17	*Granada*	35	5	**35**	**5**
2017–18	Manchester U	0	0		
2017–18	*Valencia*	23	1	**23**	**1**
2018–19	Manchester U	15	1		
2019–20	Manchester U	25	1		
2020–21	Manchester U	0	0		
2020–21	*Lazio*	26	1	**26**	**1**
2021–22	Manchester U	0	0	**45**	**2**
2022	*Flamengo*	31	7	**31**	**7**
2022–23	Fulham	33	4		
2023–24	Fulham	37	3		
2024–25	Fulham	33	2	**103**	**9**

REED, Harrison (M) 260 7
H: 5 11 W: 11 09 b.Worthing 27-1-95
Internationals: England U19, U20.

2011–12	Southampton	0	0		
2012–13	Southampton	0	0		
2013–14	Southampton	4	0		
2014–15	Southampton	9	0		
2015–16	Southampton	1	0		
2016–17	Southampton	3	0		
2017–18	Southampton	0	0		
2017–18	*Norwich C*	39	1	**39**	**1**
2018–19	Southampton	0	0		
2018–19	*Blackburn R*	33	3	**33**	**3**
2019–20	Southampton	0	0	**17**	**0**
2019–20	*Fulham*	25	0		
2020–21	Fulham	31	0		
2021–22	Fulham	39	0		
2022–23	Fulham	37	3		
2023–24	Fulham	27	0		
2024–25	Fulham	12	0	**171**	**3**

ROBINSON, Antonee (D) 266 3
H: 6 0 W: 11 07 b.Milton Keynes 8-8-97
Internationals: USA U18, Full caps.

2015–16	Everton	0	0		
2016–17	Everton	0	0		
2017–18	Everton	0	0		
2017–18	*Bolton W*	30	0	**30**	**0**
2018–19	Everton	0	0		
2018–19	*Wigan Ath*	26	0		
2019–20	Wigan Ath	38	1	**64**	**1**
2020–21	Fulham	28	0		
2021–22	Fulham	36	2		
2022–23	Fulham	35	0		
2023–24	Fulham	37	0		
2024–25	Fulham	36	0	**172**	**2**

RODRIGO MUNIZ, Carvalho (F) 118 28
H: 5 10 W: 12 08 b.Sao Domingos de Prata 4-5-01

2020	Flamengo	4	0		
2020	*Coritiba*	6	1	**6**	**1**
2021	Flamengo	9	3	**13**	**3**
2021–22	Fulham	25	5		
2022–23	Fulham	0	0		
2022–23	*Middlesbrough*	17	2	**17**	**2**
2023–24	Fulham	26	9		
2024–25	Fulham	31	8	**82**	**22**

SANDERSON, Oliver (F) 41 6
H: 6 0 W: 12 06 b.Chichester 30-12-03

2023–24	Fulham	0	0		
2023–24	*Sutton U*	20	4	**20**	**4**
2024–25	Fulham	0	0		
2024–25	*Bradford C*	13	2	**13**	**2**
2024–25	*Harrogate T*	8	0	**8**	**0**

SEKULARAC, Kristian (M) 0 0
H: 6 1 W: 10 08 b.London 7-12-03
Internationals: Switzerland U16, U19, U21.
From Servette, Juventus.

2022–23	Fulham	0	0		
2023–24	Fulham	0	0		
2024–25	Fulham	0	0		

Transferred to Fehervar, February 2025.

SESSEGNON, Ryan (M) 183 30
H: 5 10 W: 11 02 b.Roehampton 18-5-00
Internationals: England U16, U17, U19, U21.

2016–17	Fulham	25	5		
2017–18	Fulham	46	15		
2018–19	Fulham	35	2		
2019–20	Fulham	0	0		
2019–20	Tottenham H	6	0		
2020–21	Tottenham H	0	0		
2020–21	*TSG 1899 Hoffenheim*	23	2	**23**	**2**
2021–22	Tottenham H	15	0		
2022–23	Tottenham H	17	2		
2023–24	Tottenham H	0	0	**38**	**2**
2024–25	Fulham	16	4	**122**	**26**

SMITH ROWE, Emile (M) 136 20
H: 6 0 W: 11 07 b.Croydon 28-7-00
Internationals: England U16, U17, U18, U19, U20, U21, Full caps.

2017–18	Arsenal	0	0		
2018–19	Arsenal	0	0		
2018–19	*RB Leipzig*	3	0	**3**	**0**
2019–20	Arsenal	2	0		
2019–20	*Huddersfield T*	19	2	**19**	**2**
2020–21	Arsenal	20	2		
2021–22	Arsenal	33	10		
2022–23	Arsenal	12	0		
2023–24	Arsenal	13	0	**80**	**12**
2024–25	Fulham	34	6	**34**	**6**

TANTON, Devan (M) 8 0
H: 5 9 W: 11 03 b.Texas 3-1-04
Internationals: USA U17. Colombia U20, U23, Full caps.

2022–23	Fulham	0	0		
2023–24	Fulham	0	0		
2024–25	Fulham	0	0		
2024–25	*Chesterfield*	8	0	**8**	**0**

TETE, Kenny (D) 193 5
H: 5 9 W: 11 00 b.Amsterdam 9-10-95
Internationals: Netherlands U17, U19, U20, U21, Full caps.

2013–14	Ajax	0	0		
2014–15	Ajax	5	0		
2015–16	Ajax	21	0		
2016–17	Ajax	5	0	**31**	**0**
2017–18	Lyon	22	1		
2018–19	Lyon	13	0		
2019–20	Lyon	18	0		
2020–21	Lyon	0	0	**53**	**1**
2020–21	Fulham	22	0		
2021–22	Fulham	20	2		
2022–23	Fulham	31	1		
2023–24	Fulham	14	1		
2024–25	Fulham	22	0	**109**	**4**

TRAORE, Adama (F) 294 19
H: 5 10 W: 12 00 b.L'Hospitalet de Llobregat 25-1-96
Internationals: Spain U16, U17, U19, U21, Full caps.

2013–14	Barcelona	1	0		
2014–15	Barcelona	0	0		
2015–16	Aston Villa	10	0		
2016–17	Aston Villa	1	0	**11**	**0**
2016–17	Middlesbrough	27	0		
2017–18	Middlesbrough	34	5	**61**	**5**
2018–19	Wolverhampton W	29	1		
2019–20	Wolverhampton W	37	4		
2020–21	Wolverhampton W	37	2		
2021–22	Wolverhampton W	20	1		
2021–22	*Barcelona*	11	0	**12**	**0**
2022–23	Wolverhampton W	34	2	**157**	**10**
2023–24	Fulham	17	2		
2024–25	Fulham	36	2	**53**	**4**

VINICIUS, Carlos (F) 190 62
H: 6 3 W: 13 08 b.Rio 22-3-95

2016	Caldense	0	0		
2017	Caldense	0	0		
2017	Gremio Anapolis	2	0	**2**	**0**
2017–18	*Real*	37	19	**37**	**19**
2018–19	Napoli	0	0		
2018–19	*Rio Ave*	14	8	**14**	**8**
2018–19	*Monaco*	16	2	**16**	**2**
2019–20	Benfica	32	18		
2020–21	Benfica	1	0		
2020–21	*Tottenham H*	9	1	**9**	**1**
2021–22	Benfica	1	0		
2021–22	*PSV Eindhoven*	23	6		
2022–23	Benfica	0	0	**34**	**18**
2022–23	*PSV Eindhoven*	1	0	**24**	**6**
2022–23	Fulham	28	5		
2023–24	Fulham	13	2		
2023–24	*Galatasaray*	10	1	**10**	**1**
2024–25	Fulham	3	0	**44**	**7**

WILLIAN, da Silva (M) 527 70
H: 5 9 W: 11 11 b.Ribeirao 9-8-88
Internationals: Brazil U20, Full caps.

2006	Corinthians	5	0		
2007	Corinthians	15	2		
2007–08	Shakhtar Donetsk	20	0		
2008–09	Shakhtar Donetsk	29	5		
2009–10	Shakhtar Donetsk	22	5		
2010–11	Shakhtar Donetsk	28	3		
2011–12	Shakhtar Donetsk	27	5		
2012–13	Shakhtar Donetsk	14	2	**140**	**20**
2012–13	Anzhi Makhachkala	7	1		
2013–14	Anzhi Makhachkala	4	0	**11**	**1**
2013–14	Chelsea	25	4		
2014–15	Chelsea	36	2		
2015–16	Chelsea	35	5		
2016–17	Chelsea	34	8		
2017–18	Chelsea	36	6		
2018–19	Chelsea	32	3		
2019–20	Chelsea	36	9	**234**	**37**
2020–21	Arsenal	25	1	**25**	**1**
2021	Corinthians	9	0		
2022	Corinthians	14	0	**43**	**2**
2022–23	Fulham	27	5		
2023–24	Fulham	31	4		
2024–25	Olympiacos	6	0	**6**	**0**
2024–25	Fulham	10	0	**68**	**9**

WILSON, Harry (M) 258 58
H: 5 8 W: 11 00 b.Wrexham 22-3-97
Internationals: Wales U17, U19, U21, Full caps.

2015–16	Liverpool	0	0		
2015–16	*Crewe Alex*	7	0	**7**	**0**
2016–17	Liverpool	0	0		
2017–18	Liverpool	0	0		
2017–18	*Hull C*	13	7	**13**	**7**
2018–19	Liverpool	0	0		
2018–19	*Derby Co*	40	15	**40**	**15**
2019–20	Liverpool	0	0		
2019–20	*Bournemouth*	31	7	**31**	**7**
2020–21	Liverpool	0	0		
2020–21	*Cardiff C*	37	7	**37**	**7**

2021–22	Fulham	41	10		
2022–23	Fulham	29	2		
2023–24	Fulham	35	4		
2024–25	Fulham	25	6	130	22

Players retained or with offer of contract
Allen, Michael Thomas; Borto, Alexander Paul; Chingwaro, Seth Tinashe; Esenga, Jonathan Batotele Alenge; Gofford, Oliver Ronald; Gordon, Lemar Mark; Kaiser, Dino; Loupalo-Bi, Aaron Bradley; McNally, Alfie Shane; Moniz De Jesus, Bradley Jose; Nsasi, Eddy; Nwoko Junior, Chibuzo Udo; Olyott, Thomas James Ward; Osmand, Callum James; Pajaziti, Adrion; Quashie, Jayden Louie; Slade, Bradley Gregory; Underwood, Marco Jenson; Walters, Joseph Edward; Works, Terrell Lawreece Isaiah.

Scholars
Cliff, Callum James; Cooke, Logan Thomas Michael; Dair, Brodie; Faux, Alexander Charles; Hall, Marcell Levin; Khan, Ruban Hamilton; Mayer, Oliver James; Platel, Harley William; Schutter, Quinn Ashton; Wahid, Farhaan Ali; White, Alfie William Philip; Wingate, Tom Henry; Zepa, MacAulay Adams.

GILLINGHAM (38)

ANDREWS, Josh (F)   63   9
H: 6 5   W: 12 08   b.Solihull 16-10-01

2020–21	Birmingham C	0	0		
2020–21	*Harrogate T*	3	0	3	0
2021–22	Birmingham C	0	0		
2021–22	*Rochdale*	17	3	17	3
2022–23	Birmingham C	0	0		
2022–23	*Doncaster R*	4	0	4	0
2023–24	Birmingham C	0	0		
2023–24	*Accrington S*	20	5	20	5
2023–24	Gillingham	7	1		
2024–25	Gillingham	12	0	19	1

BAYLISS, Joshua (F)   0   0
H: 6 0   W: 11 11   b. 1-1-06

2024–25	Gillingham	0	0		

CLARK, Max (D)   242   9
H: 5 11   W: 11 07   b.Kingston-upon-Hull 19-1-96
Internationals: England U16, U17.

2015–16	Hull C	0	0		
2015–16	*Cambridge U*	9	0		
2016–17	Hull C	0	0		
2016–17	*Cambridge U*	27	1	36	1
2017–18	Hull C	27	0		
2018–19	Vitesse	23	1		
2019–20	Vitesse	23	1		
2020–21	Vitesse	0	0	46	2
2020–21	Hull C	0	0	27	0
2021–22	Fleetwood T	10	0	10	0
2021–22	Rochdale	23	1	23	1
2022–23	Stevenage	38	1	38	1
2023–24	Gillingham	22	1		
2024–25	Gillingham	40	3	62	4

CLARKE, Jayden (M)   68   7
H: 5 9   W: 12 04   b.Islington 8-5-01
From Hendon, Dulwich Hamlet.

2022–23	Gillingham	3	0		
2023–24	Gillingham	32	0		
2024–25	Gillingham	33	7	68	7

COLEMAN, Ethan (M)   90   1
H: 6 0   W: 12 06   b.Reading 28-1-00
From Brackley T, King's Lynn T.

2021–22	Leyton Orient	15	1	15	1
2022–23	Gillingham	11	0		
2023–24	Gillingham	43	0		
2024–25	Gillingham	21	0	75	0

DACK, Bradley (M)   353   83
H: 5 9   W: 11 03   b.Greenwich 31-12-93

2012–13	Gillingham	16	1		
2013–14	Gillingham	28	3		
2014–15	Gillingham	42	9		
2015–16	Gillingham	40	13		
2016–17	Gillingham	34	5		
2017–18	Blackburn R	42	18		
2018–19	Blackburn R	42	15		
2019–20	Blackburn R	22	9		
2020–21	Blackburn R	16	3		
2021–22	Blackburn R	9	1		
2022–23	Blackburn R	27	4	158	50
2023–24	Sunderland	16	1	16	1
2024–25	Gillingham	19	1	179	32

DIENG, Timothee (M)   371   40
H: 5 11   W: 12 00   b.Grenoble 9-4-92

2011–12	Brest	0	0		
2012–13	Brest	2	0		
2013–14	Brest	4	0	6	0
2014–15	Oldham Ath	22	0		
2015–16	Oldham Ath	38	1	60	1

2016–17	Bradford C	39	3		
2017–18	Bradford C	26	2	65	5
2018–19	Southend U	43	3		
2019–20	Southend U	21	2		
2020–21	Southend U	36	3	100	8
2021–22	Exeter C	42	12		
2022–23	Exeter C	17	3	59	15
2022–23	Gillingham	21	2		
2023–24	Gillingham	32	5		
2024–25	Gillingham	13	3	66	10
2024–25	*Cheltenham T*	15	1	15	1

EHMER, Max (D)   490   15
H: 6 2   W: 11 00   b.Frankfurt 3-2-92

2009–10	QPR	0	0		
2010–11	QPR	0	0		
2010–11	*Yeovil T*	27	0		
2011–12	QPR	0	0		
2011–12	*Yeovil T*	24	0	51	0
2011–12	*Preston NE*	9	0	9	0
2012–13	QPR	0	0		
2012–13	*Stevenage*	6	1	6	1
2013–14	QPR	1	0		
2013–14	*Carlisle U*	12	1	12	1
2014–15	QPR	0	0	1	0
2014–15	*Gillingham*	27	1		
2015–16	Gillingham	30	0		
2016–17	Gillingham	45	6		
2017–18	Gillingham	42	2		
2018–19	Gillingham	40	1		
2019–20	Gillingham	35	1		
2020–21	Bristol R	28	1	28	1
2021–22	Gillingham	45	0		
2022–23	Gillingham	45	1		
2023–24	Gillingham	39	0		
2024–25	Gillingham	35	0	383	12

GALE, Sam (M)   23   0
H: 5 11   W: 11 07   b. 1-10-04

2021–22	Gillingham	1	0		
2022–23	Gillingham	0	0		
2023–24	Gillingham	0	0		
2024–25	Gillingham	22	0	23	0

GBODE, Joseph (M)   43   3
H: 5 11   W: 11 03   b.Southwark 8-4-05

2021–22	Gillingham	2	0		
2022–23	Gillingham	4	0		
2023–24	Gillingham	3	0		
2024–25	Gillingham	34	3	43	3

GILES, Alex (D)   0   0
H: 5 9   W: 12 00   b. 29-1-05

2023–24	Gillingham	0	0		
2024–25	Gillingham	0	0		

HAWKINS, Oliver (F)   249   41
H: 6 2   W: 11 00   b.Ealing 8-4-92
From North Greenford U, Hillingdon Bor, Northwood, Hemel Hempstead T.

2015–16	Dagenham & Red	18	1	18	1
	From Dagenham & Red.				
2017–18	Portsmouth	31	7		
2018–19	Portsmouth	39	7		
2019–20	Portsmouth	7	0	77	14
2020–21	Ipswich T	20	1		
2021–22	Ipswich T	0	0	20	1
2021–22	Mansfield T	41	7		
2022–23	Mansfield T	22	3	63	10
2022–23	Gillingham	22	3		
2023–24	Gillingham	24	4		
2024–25	Gillingham	25	0	71	7

HOLTAM, Taite (G)   2   0
H: 6 3   W: 13 10   b. 14-2-05

2022–23	Gillingham	0	0		
2023–24	Gillingham	0	0		
2024–25	Gillingham	2	0	2	0

HUTTON, Remeao (D)   205   2
H: 5 9   W: 11 05   b.Walsall 28-9-98
From Hednesford T.

2017–18	Birmingham C	0	0		
2018–19	Birmingham C	0	0		
2019–20	Birmingham C	0	0		
2020–21	Birmingham C	0	0		
2020–21	*Stevenage*	26	0	26	0
2021–22	Barrow	44	0	44	0
2022–23	Swindon T	44	0		
2023–24	Swindon T	27	1	71	1
2023–24	Gillingham	20	0		
2024–25	Gillingham	44	1	64	1

KHUMBENI, Nelson (M)   47   2
H: 5 7   W: 10 08   b.Lilongwe 14-10-02

2018–19	Norwich C	0	0		
2019–20	Norwich C	0	0		
2020–21	Norwich C	0	0		
2021–22	Norwich C	0	0		
2022–23	Bolton W	0	0		
2023–24	Bolton W	0	0		
2023–24	*Morecambe*	19	1	19	1
2024–25	Bolton W	0	0		
2024–25	*Accrington S*	18	1	18	1
2024–25	Gillingham	10	0	10	0

LITTLE, Armani (M)   111   6
H: 5 8   W: 9 13   b.Portsmouth 5-4-97
Internationals: England C.
From Southampton.

2018–19	Oxford U	1	0	1	0
	From Torquay U.				
2022–23	Forest Green R	21	0	21	0
2022–23	AFC Wimbledon	18	0		
2023–24	AFC Wimbledon	38	4	56	4
2024–25	Gillingham	33	2	33	2

MASTERSON, Conor (D)   141   10
H: 6 1   W: 11 11   b.Dublin 8-9-98
Internationals: Republic of Ireland U16, U17, U18, U19, U21.

2015–16	Liverpool	0	0		
2016–17	Liverpool	0	0		
2017–18	Liverpool	0	0		
2018–19	Liverpool	0	0		
2019–20	QPR	12	1		
2020–21	QPR	4	0		
2020–21	*Swindon T*	5	0	5	0
2021–22	QPR	0	0		
2021–22	*Cambridge U*	16	0	16	0
2021–22	*Gillingham*	18	0		
2022–23	QPR	1	0	17	1
2022–23	Gillingham	20	2		
2023–24	Gillingham	41	6		
2024–25	Gillingham	24	1	103	9

McKENZIE, Robbie (D)   195   12
H: 6 0   W: 11 09   b.Kingston upon Hull 25-9-98

2017–18	Hull C	0	0		
2018–19	Hull C	18	0		
2019–20	Hull C	8	0	26	0
2020–21	Gillingham	33	1		
2021–22	Gillingham	38	3		
2022–23	Gillingham	34	1		
2023–24	Gillingham	25	1		
2024–25	Gillingham	39	6	169	12

MORRIS, Glenn (G)   535   0
H: 6 0   W: 11 00   b.Woolwich 20-12-83

2001–02	Leyton Orient	2	0		
2002–03	Leyton Orient	23	0		
2003–04	Leyton Orient	27	0		
2004–05	Leyton Orient	12	0		
2005–06	Leyton Orient	4	0		
2006–07	Leyton Orient	3	0		
2007–08	Leyton Orient	16	0		
2008–09	Leyton Orient	26	0		
2009–10	Leyton Orient	11	0	124	0
2010–11	Southend U	33	0		
2011–12	Southend U	24	0		
2012–13	Southend U	0	0	57	0
2012–13	Aldershot T	2	0	2	0
	From Woking, Eastleigh.				
2014–15	Gillingham	10	0		
2015–16	Gillingham	0	0		
2016–17	Crawley T	39	0		
2017–18	Crawley T	44	0		
2018–19	Crawley T	46	0		
2019–20	Crawley T	37	0		
2020–21	Crawley T	45	0		
2021–22	Crawley T	46	0		
2022–23	Crawley T	0	0	257	0
2023–24	*Gillingham*	40	0		
2023–24	Gillingham	9	0		
2024–25	Gillingham	36	0	95	0

NADESAN, Ashley (F)   236   41
H: 6 2   W: 11 11   b.Redhill 9-9-94

2015–16	Fleetwood T	0	0		
2016–17	Fleetwood T	0	0		
2017–18	Fleetwood T	1	0		
2017–18	Carlisle U	15	4		
2018–19	Fleetwood T	20	1	21	1
2018–19	*Carlisle U*	25	8	40	12
2019–20	Crawley T	25	5		
2020–21	Crawley T	40	5		
2021–22	Crawley T	39	9		
2022–23	Crawley T	42	7	146	26
2023–24	Gillingham	29	2		
2024–25	Gillingham	0	0	29	2

NEVITT, Elliott (F)   162   31
H: 6 0   W: 12 08   b.Liverpool 30-10-96

2021–22	Tranmere R	40	7		
2022–23	Tranmere R	22	4	62	11
2022–23	Crewe Alex	21	0		
2023–24	Crewe Alex	43	16	64	16
2024–25	Gillingham	36	4	36	4

NOLAN, Jack (M)   107   18
H: 5 11   W: 11 05   b.Portsmouth 25-5-01
Internationals: England U17.

2018–19	Reading	0	0		
2019–20	Walsall	4	0		
2020–21	Walsall	9	0	13	0
2021–22	Accrington S	5	0		
2022–23	Accrington S	13	0		
2023–24	Accrington S	45	17	63	17
2024–25	Gillingham	31	1	31	1

OGIE, Shadrach (D) 117 1
H: 6 1 W: 11 07 b.Limerick 26-8-01
Internationals: Republic of Ireland U18, U19.
From Hornchurch.
2019–20	Leyton Orient	0	0	
2020–21	Leyton Orient	0	0	
2021–22	Leyton Orient	34	0	
2022–23	Leyton Orient	10	0	44 0
2023–24	Gillingham	39	1	
2024–25	Gillingham	34	0	73 1

ROWE, Aaron (M) 81 4
H: 5 10 W: 10 12 b.Hackney 7-9-00
From Leyton Orient.
2018–19	Huddersfield T	2	0	
2019–20	Huddersfield T	1	0	
2020–21	Huddersfield T	20	1	
2021–22	Huddersfield T	1	0	
2022–23	Huddersfield T	1	0	
2022–23	Stockport Co	2	0	2 0
2023–24	Huddersfield T	0	0	25 1
2023–24	Crewe Alex	38	2	38 2
2024–25	Gillingham	16	1	16 1

SARGENT, Stan (F) 0 0
2024–25	Gillingham	0	0

SKIPPER, Stanley (M) 0 0
H: 5 11 b.Havering 29-9-05
2023–24	Gillingham	0	0
2024–25	Gillingham	0	0

THEODORE, Damien (F) 0 0
2024–25	Gillingham	0	0

TURNER, Jake (G) 76 0
H: 6 0 W: 12 13 b.Wilmslow 25-2-99
Internationals: England U18, U19.
2016–17	Bolton W	0	0	
2017–18	Bolton W	0	0	
2018–19	Bolton W	0	0	
2019–20	Newcastle U	0	0	
2020–21	Newcastle U	0	0	
2020–21	Morecambe	14	0	14 0
2021–22	Newcastle U	0	0	
2021–22	Colchester U	9	0	9 0
2022–23	Gillingham	7	0	
2023–24	Gillingham	37	0	
2024–25	Gillingham	9	0	53 0

WALDOCK, Harry (M) 0 0
2024–25	Gillingham	0	0

WEBSTER, Harry (D) 2 0
H: 6 0 b. 8-9-06
2024–25	Gillingham	2	0	2 0

WILLIAMS, Euan (M) 10 0
H: 5 9 W: 11 05 b. 15-1-03
Internationals: England U16. Northern Ireland U19, U21.
2021–22	Charlton Ath	0	0	
2022–23	Charlton Ath	0	0	
2023–24	Charlton Ath	0	0	
2024–25	Gillingham	0	0	10 0

WILLIAMS, Jon (M) 332 21
H: 5 6 W: 9 06 b.Tunbridge Wells 9-10-93
Internationals: Wales U17, U19, U21, Full caps.
2010–11	Crystal Palace	0	0	
2011–12	Crystal Palace	14	0	
2012–13	Crystal Palace	29	0	
2013–14	Crystal Palace	9	0	
2013–14	Ipswich T	13	1	
2014–15	Crystal Palace	2	0	
2014–15	Ipswich T	7	1	
2015–16	Crystal Palace	1	0	
2015–16	Nottingham F	10	0	10 0
2015–16	Milton Keynes D	13	0	13 0
2016–17	Crystal Palace	0	0	
2016–17	Ipswich T	8	0	28 2
2017–18	Crystal Palace	0	0	
2017–18	Sunderland	12	1	12 1
2018–19	Crystal Palace	0	0	55 0
2018–19	Charlton Ath	16	0	
2019–20	Charlton Ath	26	0	
2020–21	Charlton Ath	18	2	60 2
2020–21	Cardiff C	9	0	9 0
2021–22	Swindon T	40	5	
2022–23	Swindon T	37	10	77 15
2023–24	Gillingham	42	0	
2024–25	Gillingham	26	1	68 1

WYLLIE, Marcus (F) 12 0
H: 5 10 W: 11 09 b. 16-7-99
2024–25	Gillingham	12	0	12 0

Scholars
Beszant, Cruz Paul; Bridle, Harry Nicholas; Broadbent, Zack Mark; Clark, Benjamin; Dayal, Louie; De Wilde, William David; Dobbs, Logan Keagan; Heasman, James Wing; Hegarty, Fletcher Jeremy; Kot, Kacper; Luxton, Michael George; Orpwood, Josef Jason Anthony; Sargent, Stanley George; Sullivan, Carter; Waldock, Harry Lee; Walker, Jonah John; White, Ben Robert; Whitelock, Zachery Grant.

GRIMSBY T (39)

AINLEY, Callum (M) 275 17
H: 5 8 W: 10 01 b.Swindon 2-11-97
2015–16	Crewe Alex	16	1	
2016–17	Crewe Alex	27	1	
2017–18	Crewe Alex	45	4	
2018–19	Crewe Alex	43	6	
2019–20	Crewe Alex	25	2	
2020–21	Crewe Alex	22	1	
2021–22	Crewe Alex	31	0	
2022–23	Crewe Alex	33	2	242 17
2023–24	Grimsby T	7	0	
2024–25	Grimsby T	26	0	33 0

AUTON, Sebastian (G) 1 0
H: 6 1 W: 12 11 b. 7-11-06
2023–24	Grimsby T	0	0	
2024–25	Grimsby T	1	0	1 0

BROWN, Henry (M) 1 0
2024–25	Grimsby T	1	0	1 0

BURNS, Darragh (M) 105 13
H: 5 9 W: 9 11 b.Stamullen, Meath 6-8-02
Internationals: Northern Ireland U17, U19. Republic of Ireland U17, U20, U21.
From St Kevin's Boys.
2019	St Patrick's Ath	0	0	
2020	St Patrick's Ath	0	0	
2021	St Patrick's Ath	26	4	
2022	St Patrick's Ath	22	4	54 4
2022–23	Milton Keynes D	14	0	
2023–24	Milton Keynes D	0	0	
2024	Shamrock R	28	5	28 5
2024–25	Milton Keynes D	0	0	14 0
2024–25	Grimsby T	9	0	9 0

CARSON, Matty (M) 19 0
H: 6 1 W: 11 11 b.Chester 17-10-02
From Liverpool, Burnley.
2021–22	Accrington S	0	0	
2022–23	Accrington S	0	0	
2023–24	Reading	10	0	10 0
2024–25	Grimsby T	9	0	9 0

CASS, Lewis (D) 85 2
H: 6 1 W: 11 09 b.North Shields 27-2-00
2018–19	Newcastle U	0	0	
2019–20	Newcastle U	0	0	
2020–21	Newcastle U	0	0	
2021–22	Newcastle U	0	0	
2021–22	Port Vale	19	0	
2022–23	Port Vale	19	0	
2023–24	Port Vale	12	0	50 0
2023–24	Stockport Co	9	1	9 1
2024–25	Grimsby T	26	1	26 1

CLEMENTS, Charlie (F) 0 0
2024–25	Grimsby T	0	0

CRIBB, Harvey (M) 8 0
H: 5 8 W: 10 08 b. 21-1-06
2021–22	Scunthorpe U	8	0	8 0
2024–25	Grimsby T	0	0	

EASTWOOD, Jake (G) 61 0
H: 6 3 W: 11 00 b.Sheffield 3-10-96
2017–18	Chesterfield	4	0	4 0
2017–18	Sheffield U	1	0	
2018–19	Sheffield U	0	0	
2019–20	Sheffield U	0	0	
2019–20	Scunthorpe U	11	0	11 0
2020–21	Sheffield U	0	0	
2020–21	Kilmarnock	1	0	1 0
2020–21	Grimsby T	7	0	
2021–22	Sheffield U	0	0	
2021–22	Portsmouth	0	0	
2021–22	Rochdale	2	0	
2022–23	Sheffield U	0	0	1 0
2022–23	Ross Co	0	0	
2023–24	Rochdale	7	0	9 0
2023–24	Sheffield U	22	0	
2024–25	Grimsby T	6	0	35 0

GARDNER, Cameron (M) 13 0
H: 6 0 W: 11 00 b.Newcastle upon Tyne 22-11-05
2023–24	Grimsby T	2	0	
2024–25	Grimsby T	11	0	13 0

GREEN, Kieran (M) 103 9
H: 5 9 W: 12 08 b.Stockton-on-Tees 30-6-97
2014–15	Hartlepool U	1	0	
2015–16	Hartlepool U	0	0	
2016–17	Hartlepool U	1	0	2 0
From Gateshead, Blyth Spartans, York C, FC Halifax T.
2022–23	Grimsby T	31	0	
2023–24	Grimsby T	31	2	
2024–25	Grimsby T	39	7	101 9

HUME, Denver (D) 149 3
H: 5 10 W: 11 03 b.Ashington 11-8-98
2017–18	Sunderland	1	0
2018–19	Sunderland	8	0
2019–20	Sunderland	32	1
2020–21	Sunderland	23	1
2021–22	Sunderland	4	0	68 2
2021–22	Portsmouth	9	0	
2022–23	Portsmouth	11	0	
2023–24	Portsmouth	0	0	20 0
2023–24	Grimsby T	16	1	
2024–25	Grimsby T	45	0	61 1

KHOURI, Evan (M) 68 3
H: 5 10 W: 11 07 b.London 21-1-03
From West Ham U.
2019–20	Grimsby T	0	0	
2020–21	Grimsby T	6	0	
From Grimsby T.
2022–23	Grimsby T	11	0	
2023–24	Grimsby T	5	0	
2024–25	Grimsby T	46	3	68 3

McEACHRAN, George (M) 104 3
H: 5 8 W: 10 03 b.Oxford 30-8-00
Internationals: England U16, U17, U18, U19.
2018–19	Chelsea	0	0	
2019–20	Chelsea	0	0	
2019–20	Cambuur	2	0	2 0
2020–21	Chelsea	0	0	
2020–21	Maastricht	3	0	3 0
2021–22	Chelsea	0	0	
2022–23	Swindon T	16	0	
2023–24	Swindon T	39	1	55 1
2024–25	Grimsby T	44	2	44 2

McJANNETT, Cameron (D) 168 11
H: 5 11 W: 10 08 b.Milton Keynes 6-9-98
From Luton T.
2019–20	Derry C	0	0	
2020	Derry C	9	0	
2021	Derry C	33	5	
2022	Derry C	34	2	
2023	Derry C	30	2	
2024	Derry C	21	0	127 9
2024–25	Grimsby T	41	2	41 2

PYKE, Rekeil (F) 148 8
H: 6 2 W: 10 03 b.Leeds 1-9-97
2016–17	Huddersfield T	0	0	
2016–17	Colchester U	12	0	12 0
2017–18	Huddersfield T	0	0	
2017–18	Port Vale	7	0	7 0
2018–19	Huddersfield T	0	0	
2018–19	Rochdale	6	0	
2019–20	Huddersfield T	1	0	1 0
2019–20	Rochdale	13	1	19 1
2020–21	Shrewsbury T	12	0	
2021–22	Shrewsbury T	16	0	
2021–22	Scunthorpe U	10	0	10 0
2022–23	Shrewsbury T	37	3	65 3
2023–24	Grimsby T	27	4	
2024–25	Grimsby T	7	0	34 4

RODGERS, Harvey (D) 213 10
H: 6 2 W: 12 06 b.York 20-10-96
2016–17	Hull C	0	0	
2016–17	Accrington S	19	1	
2017–18	Fleetwood T	0	0	
2017–18	Accrington S	5	0	
2018–19	Accrington S	5	0	
2019–20	Accrington S	6	0	
2020–21	Accrington S	28	0	
2021–22	Accrington S	22	0	
2022–23	Accrington S	41	4	127 5
2023–24	Grimsby T	42	1	
2024–25	Grimsby T	44	0	86 5

ROSE, Danny (F) 427 95
H: 5 8 W: 8 05 b.Barnsley 10-12-93
2010–11	Barnsley	1	0	
2011–12	Barnsley	4	0	
2012–13	Barnsley	8	1	
2013–14	Barnsley	6	3	
2013–14	Bury	6	3	
2014–15	Barnsley	1	0	17 1
2014–15	Bury	35	10	
2015–16	Bury	28	5	69 18
2016–17	Mansfield T	37	9	
2017–18	Mansfield T	39	14	
2018–19	Mansfield T	34	4	
2019–20	Mansfield T	31	11	
2020–21	Mansfield T	0	0	141 38
2020–21	Northampton T	39	4	
2021–22	Northampton T	36	1	75 5
2022–23	Stevenage	43	6	43 6
2023–24	Grimsby T	37	13	
2024–25	Grimsby T	45	14	82 27

STORR, Callum (D) 0 0
b.Sutton on Sea 23-12-08
2024–25	Grimsby T	0	0

SVANTHORSSON, Jason (F) 166 43
H: 5 10 W: 11 11 b.Mosfellsbær 31-12-99
Internationals: Iceland Full caps.
2019	Afturelding	22	5	
2020	Afturelding	19	8	41 13
2021	Breidablik	20	6	
2022	Breidablik	27	11	
2023	Breidablik	22	4	

2024 Breidablik 13 5 **82 26**
2024–25 Grimsby T 43 4 **43 4**

THARME, Doug (D) 74 2
H: 6 0 W: 12 04 b.Birkenhead 17-8-99
From Wrexham, Curzon Ashton, Connah's Quay Nomads, Southport.
2022–23 Blackpool 0 0
2022–23 *Accrington S* 31 0 **31 0**
2023–24 Blackpool 0 0
2023–24 Grimsby T 15 1
2024–25 Grimsby T 28 1 **43 2**

THOMPSON, Curtis (M) 271 7
H: 5 10 W: 12 01 b.Nottingham 2-9-93
From Lincoln C.
2011–12 Notts Co 0 0
2012–13 Notts Co 2 0
2013–14 Notts Co 11 0
2014–15 Notts Co 31 0
2015–16 Notts Co 26 2
2016–17 Notts Co 13 0
2017–18 Notts Co 0 0 **83 2**
2017–18 *Wycombe W* 7 0
2018–19 Wycombe W 39 1
2019–20 Wycombe W 21 0
2020–21 Wycombe W 33 0
2021–22 Wycombe W 28 2
2022–23 Wycombe W 6 0 **134 3**
2023–24 Cheltenham T 19 0 **19 0**
2023–24 Grimsby T 16 2
2024–25 Grimsby T 19 0 **35 2**

TURI, Geza David (M) 4 0
b. 6-10-01
2024–25 Grimsby T 4 0 **4 0**

VERNAM, Charles (F) 201 26
H: 5 7 W: 11 09 b.Lincoln 8-10-96
From Scunthorpe U.
2013–14 Derby Co 0 0
2014–15 Derby Co 0 0
2015–16 Derby Co 0 0
2016 *Vestmannaeyjar* 9 1 **9 1**
2016–17 Derby Co 0 0
2016–17 *Coventry C* 4 0 **4 0**
2017–18 Derby Co 0 0
2017–18 *Grimsby T* 9 1
2018–19 Grimsby T 35 3
2019–20 Grimsby T 27 7
2020–21 Burton Alb 14 2 **14 2**
2020–21 Bradford C 21 2
2021–22 Bradford C 28 8 **49 10**
2022–23 Lincoln C 20 0 **20 0**
2023–24 Grimsby T 17 0
2024–25 Grimsby T 17 2 **105 13**

WARREN, Tyrell (D) 93 4
H: 5 11 W: 11 11 b.Manchester 5-10-98
2016–17 Manchester U 0 0
2017–18 Manchester U 0 0
2018–19 Manchester U 0 0
2019–20 Salford C 0 0
From Boston U, FC Halifax T.
2022–23 Barrow 45 2
2023–24 Barrow 16 2 **61 4**
2024–25 Grimsby T 32 0 **32 0**

WILSON, Donovan (F) 137 17
H: 5 11 W: 11 00 b.Yate 14-3-97
2014–15 Wolverhampton W 0 0
2015–16 Wolverhampton W 0 0
2016–17 Wolverhampton W 1 0
2017–18 Wolverhampton W 0 0
2017–18 *Port Vale* 8 1 **8 1**
2018–19 Wolverhampton W 0 0 **1 0**
2018–19 *Exeter C* 10 0 **10 0**
2019–20 Macclesfield T 5 0 **5 0**
From Bath C.
2021–22 Sutton U 38 4
2022–23 Sutton U 36 3 **74 7**
2023–24 Grimsby T 27 8
2024–25 Grimsby T 12 1 **39 9**

WRIGHT, Jordan (G) 54 0
H: 6 3 W: 11 11 b.Stoke-on-Trent 27-2-99
2015–16 Nottingham F 0 0
2016–17 Nottingham F 0 0
2017–18 Nottingham F 0 0
2018–19 Nottingham F 0 0
2019–20 Nottingham F 0 0
2020–21 Nottingham F 0 0
2020–21 *Alloa Ath* 0 0
2021–22 Lincoln C 13 0
2022–23 Lincoln C 6 0
2023–24 Lincoln C 1 0 **20 0**
2024–25 Grimsby T 34 0 **34 0**

Scholars
Auton, Sebastian James; Axcell, Finley Reuben; Blankley, Jaxon Thomas; Brown, Henry Oscar; Carrick, Charlie Thomas; Clements, Charlie James; Collins, Jack Michael; Foster, Corey Mark Jonathon; Foy, Alfie James; Giles, Grayson William; Graham, Alexander Allenby; Hatton, Charlie Brian; Hawley, Kian Harrison; Jalloh, Mamudu; Midwinter, Carlo Finlay; Onoh, Fortune Ndubisi; Rennardson, Thomas David; Rogers, Hayden George; Shipstone, Harry John; Smith, Elliot Alfie Dolan; Storr, Callum Harvey Dawson.

HARROGATE T (40)

ASARE, Zico (D) 26 1
H: 5 9 W: 12 06 b.London 11-4-01
Internationals: England U16, C.
2024–25 Harrogate T 26 1 **26 1**

BARNES, Lucas (D) 1 0
b. 17-5-07
2024–25 Harrogate T 1 0 **1 0**

BELSHAW, James (G) 199 0
H: 6 3 W: 13 01 b.Nottingham 12-10-90
2020–21 Harrogate T 38 0
2021–22 Harrogate T 0 0
2021–22 Bristol R 42 0
2022–23 Bristol R 38 0
2023–24 Bristol R 0 0 **80 0**
2023–24 *Forest Green R* 10 0 **10 0**
2023–24 Harrogate T 26 0
2024–25 Harrogate T 45 0 **109 0**

BRAY, Jack (F) 1 0
b. 23-2-07
2024–25 Harrogate T 1 0 **1 0**

BURRELL, Warren (D) 177 4
H: 5 10 W: 12 00 b.Sheffield 3-6-90
2020–21 Harrogate T 43 0
2021–22 Harrogate T 45 2
2022–23 Harrogate T 34 1
2023–24 Harrogate T 28 1
2024–25 Harrogate T 27 0 **177 4**

CORNELIUS, Dean (M) 120 5
H: 5 11 W: 11 09 b.Bellshill 11-4-01
2018–19 Motherwell 1 0
2019–20 Motherwell 0 0
2020–21 Motherwell 1 0
2021–22 Motherwell 12 2
2022–23 Motherwell 32 0 **46 2**
2023–24 Harrogate T 39 2
2024–25 Harrogate T 35 1 **74 3**

CURSONS, Tom (F) 16 2
b.Chertsey 8-12-01
2024–25 Harrogate T 16 2 **16 2**

DALY, James (F) 98 7
H: 5 10 W: 11 05 b.Brighton 12-1-00
2017–18 Crystal Palace 0 0
2018–19 Crystal Palace 0 0
2019–20 Crystal Palace 0 0
2019–20 Bristol R 3 0
2020–21 Bristol R 28 3 **31 3**
2021–22 Stevenage 15 0 **15 0**
From Woking.
2023–24 Harrogate T 14 1
2024–25 Harrogate T 38 3 **52 4**

DALY, Matty (M) 129 18
H: 5 9 W: 11 11 b.Stockport 10-3-01
Internationals: England U17, U18.
2018–19 Huddersfield T 2 0
2019–20 Huddersfield T 4 1
2020–21 Huddersfield T 5 0
2021–22 Huddersfield T 0 0
2021–22 *Hartlepool U* 19 2 **19 2**
2021–22 *Bradford C* 9 1 **9 1**
2022–23 Huddersfield T 0 0 **11 1**
2022–23 *Harrogate T* 35 7
2023–24 Harrogate T 40 6
2024–25 Harrogate T 15 1 **90 14**

DOOLEY, Stephen (M) 250 17
H: 5 11 W: 12 08 b.Portstewart 19-10-91
2014 Derry C 14 1
2015 Derry C 15 2 **29 3**
2016 Cork C 26 5
2017 Cork C 27 4 **53 9**
2018–19 Rochdale 22 0
2019–20 Rochdale 22 3
2020–21 Rochdale 31 1
2021–22 Rochdale 38 0 **113 4**
2022–23 Harrogate T 7 0
2023–24 Harrogate T 25 0
2024–25 Harrogate T 23 1 **55 1**

DUKE-McKENNA, Stephen (M) 61 3
H: 5 9 W: 11 00 b.Liverpool 17-8-00
Internationals: Guyana Full caps.
2017–18 Everton 0 0
2018–19 Bolton W 0 0
2019–20 QPR 0 0
2020–21 QPR 1 0
2021–22 QPR 0 0
2022–23 QPR 0 0
2022–23 *Leyton Orient* 10 0 **10 0**
2023–24 QPR 5 0 **6 0**
2023–24 *Sutton U* 16 2 **16 2**
2024–25 Harrogate T 18 1 **18 1**
2024–25 *St Johnstone* 11 0 **11 0**

ETHERINGTON, Marcus (D) 0 0
b. 11-9-06
2024–25 Harrogate T 0 0

FALKINGHAM, Joshua (M) 335 31
H: 5 6 W: 10 06 b.Leeds 25-8-90
2009–10 St Johnstone 1 0 **1 0**
2010–11 Arbroath 35 9
2011–12 Arbroath 35 8 **70 17**
2012–13 Dunfermline Ath 30 3
2013–14 Dunfermline Ath 30 5
2014–15 Dunfermline Ath 32 3
2015–16 Dunfermline Ath 28 3 **120 14**
From Darlington.
2020–21 Harrogate T 43 0
2021–22 Harrogate T 34 0
2022–23 Harrogate T 35 0
2023–24 Harrogate T 24 0
2024–25 Harrogate T 8 0 **144 0**

FOLARIN, Sam (M) 82 9
H: 5 9 W: 10 08 b.Lambeth 23-9-00
From Tooting & Mitcham U.
2020–21 Middlesbrough 2 0
2021–22 Middlesbrough 0 0 **2 0**
2021–22 *Queen of the South* 7 0 **7 0**
2022–23 Harrogate T 27 4
2023–24 Harrogate T 27 3
2024–25 Harrogate T 19 2 **73 9**
Transferred to Hartlepool U, January 2025.

FOULDS, Matthew (D) 120 4
H: 6 0 W: 11 09 b.Bradford 1-2-98
2015–16 Bury 0 0
2015–16 Everton 0 0
2016–17 Everton 0 0
2017–18 Everon 0 0
2018–19 Everton 0 0
2019–20 Everton 0 0
2020–21 Como 1907 3 0 **3 0**
2020–21 Bradford C 3 0
2021–22 Bradford C 23 2
2022–23 Bradford C 18 0 **44 2**
2022–23 *Harrogate T* 21 0
2023–24 Harrogate T 37 2
2024–25 Harrogate T 15 0 **73 2**

FOX, Ben (M) 105 6
H: 5 11 W: 12 00 b.Burton upon Trent 1-2-98
2016–17 Burton Alb 1 0
2017–18 Burton Alb 0 0
2018–19 Burton Alb 27 1
2019–20 Burton Alb 0 0
2020–21 Burton Alb 9 0 **37 1**
From Grimsby T.
2022–23 Northampton T 22 4
2023–24 Northampton T 19 0
2024–25 Northampton T 13 0 **54 4**
2024–25 Harrogate T 14 1 **14 1**

GIBSON, Liam (D) 156 1
H: 6 1 W: 12 08 b.Stanley 25-4-97
2015–16 Newcastle U 0 0
2016–17 Newcastle U 0 0
2017–18 Newcastle U 0 0
2018–19 Newcastle U 0 0
2018–19 *Accrington S* 5 0 **5 0**
2019–20 Newcastle U 0 0
2019–20 *Grimsby T* 17 0 **17 0**
2020–21 Morecambe 23 0
2021–22 Morecambe 29 1
2022–23 Morecambe 44 0 **96 1**
2023–24 Harrogate T 29 0
2024–25 Harrogate T 9 0 **38 0**

HILL, Thomas (M) 6 0
H: 6 1 W: 11 11 b.Formby 13-10-02
Internationals: Wales U21.
2019–20 Liverpool 0 0
2020–21 Liverpool 0 0
2021–22 Liverpool 0 0
2022–23 Liverpool 0 0
2023–24 Liverpool 0 0
2024–25 Liverpool 0 0
2024–25 Harrogate T 6 0 **6 0**

MARCH, Josh (F) 165 28
H: 5 9 W: 13 03 b.Stourbridge 18-3-97
2019–20 Forest Green R 10 2
2020–21 Forest Green R 4 0
2020–21 *Harrogate T* 14 5
2021–22 Forest Green R 35 5
2022–23 Forest Green R 26 4 **75 11**
2022–23 Stevenage 9 2
2023–24 Stevenage 4 0 **13 2**
2023–24 Harrogate T 29 1
2024–25 Harrogate T 34 9 **77 15**

McLARIN, Jack (M) 0 0
b. 14-12-06
2024–25 Harrogate T 0 0

MOORBY, James (D) 0 0
H: 5 11 W: 11 00 b. 2-2-06
2024–25 Harrogate T 0 0

MORRIS, Bryn (M) 240 17
H: 6 0 W: 11 03 b.Hartlepool 25-4-96
Internationals: England U16, U17, U18, U19, U20.
2012–13 Middlesbrough 1 0
2013–14 Middlesbrough 1 0
2014–15 Middlesbrough 0 0
2014–15 *Burton Alb* 5 0
2015–16 Middlesbrough 0 0
2015–16 *Coventry C* 6 0 6 0
2015–16 *York C* 3 0 3 0
2015–16 *Walsall* 1 0 1 0
2016–17 Middlesbrough 0 0 2 0
2016–17 *Shrewsbury T* 13 0
2017–18 Shrewsbury T 18 0
2018–19 Shrewsbury T 0 0 31 0
2018–19 *Wycombe W* 19 3 19 3
2018–19 Portsmouth 7 1
2019–20 Portsmouth 9 0
2020–21 Portsmouth 9 0 16 1
2020–21 *Northampton T* 22 0 22 0
2021–22 Burton Alb 7 0 12 0
2021–22 *Hartlepool U* 10 1 10 1
2022–23 Grimsby T 31 2 31 2
2023–24 Newport Co 46 7
2024–25 Newport Co 19 3 65 10
2024–25 Harrogate T 22 0 22 0

MULDOON, Jack (F) 205 44
H: 5 10 W: 10 12 b.Scunthorpe 19-5-89
2014–15 Rochdale 1 0
From Brigg T, Sheffield, Glapwell, Alfreton T, Stocksbridge Park Steels, Brigg T, North Ferriby U, Worksop T.
2020–21 Harrogate T 42 15
2021–22 Harrogate T 42 12
2022–23 Harrogate T 42 4
2023–24 Harrogate T 37 11
2024–25 Harrogate T 39 2 202 44

MUSKWE, Admiral (F) 63 6
H: 6 0 W: 11 03 b.Harare 21-8-98
Internationals: England U17. Zimbabwe Full caps.
2019–20 Leicester C 0 0
2019–20 *Swindon T* 5 0 5 0
2020–21 Leicester C 0 0
2020–21 *Wycombe W* 17 3
2021–22 Leicester C 0 0
2021–22 *Wycombe W* 0 0 17 3
2021–22 Luton T 20 0
2022–23 Luton T 2 0
2022–23 *Fleetwood T* 12 3 12 3
2023–24 Luton T 0 0 22 0
2023–24 *Exeter C* 6 0 6 0
2024–25 Harrogate T 1 0 1 0
Transferred to IFK Mariehamn, January 2025.

NTO, Eno (M) 2 0
H: 5 11 b.Derby 18-9-02
2024–25 Harrogate T 2 0 2 0

O'CONNOR, Anthony (D) 489 27
H: 6 2 W: 11 11 b.Cork 25-10-92
Internationals: Republic of Ireland U17, U19, U21.
2010–11 Blackburn R 0 0
2011–12 Blackburn R 0 0
2012–13 Blackburn R 0 0
2012–13 *Burton Alb* 46 0
2013–14 Blackburn R 0 0
2013–14 *Torquay U* 31 0 31 0
2014–15 Plymouth Arg 40 3 40 3
2015–16 Burton Alb 21 1 67 1
2016–17 Aberdeen 32 3
2017–18 Aberdeen 38 2 70 5
2018–19 Bradford C 42 6
2019–20 Bradford C 36 0
2020–21 Bradford C 45 2 123 8
2021–22 Morecambe 40 2
2022–23 Morecambe 10 1 50 3
2022–23 Harrogate T 20 2
2023–24 Harrogate T 43 4
2024–25 Harrogate T 45 1 108 0

OXLEY, Mark (G) 341 1
H: 6 3 W: 11 07 b.Sheffield 2-6-90
Internationals: England U18.
2007–08 Rotherham U 0 0
2008–09 Hull C 0 0
2009–10 Hull C 0 0
2009–10 *Grimsby T* 3 0 3 0
2010–11 Hull C 0 0
2011–12 Hull C 0 0
2012–13 Hull C 1 0
2012–13 *Burton Alb* 3 0 3 0
2013–14 Hull C 0 0
2013–14 *Oldham Ath* 36 0 36 0
2014–15 Hull C 0 0 1 0
2014–15 *Hibernian* 35 1

2015–16 Hibernian 34 0 69 1
2016–17 Southend U 20 0
2017–18 Southend U 46 0
2018–19 Southend U 25 0
2019–20 Southend U 19 0
2020–21 Southend U 41 0 151 0
2021–22 Harrogate T 41 0
2022–23 Harrogate T 19 0
2023–24 Harrogate T 16 0
2024–25 Harrogate T 2 0 78 0

ROBINSON, Oli (F) 0 0
b. 4-1-07
2024–25 Harrogate T 0 0

SIMS, Toby (D) 66 3
H: 6 1 W: 12 11 b.Worksop 15-10-97
From Mickleover Sports, Greenville, South Carolina U, Pittsburgh Riverhounds.
2022–23 Harrogate T 17 1
2023–24 Harrogate T 9 0
2024–25 Harrogate T 40 2 66 3

SUTTON, Levi (M) 224 7
H: 5 11 W: 11 09 b.Scunthorpe 24-3-96
2014–15 Scunthorpe U 0 0
2015–16 Scunthorpe U 1 0
2016–17 Scunthorpe U 8 0
2017–18 Scunthorpe U 15 0
2018–19 Scunthorpe U 18 1
2019–20 Scunthorpe U 16 0 58 1
2019–20 Bradford C 0 0
2020–21 Bradford C 34 2
2021–22 Bradford C 32 2
2022–23 Bradford C 17 0 83 4
2022–23 Harrogate T 17 1
2023–24 Harrogate T 39 1
2024–25 Harrogate T 27 0 83 2

TAYLOR, Ellis (M) 40 7
H: 6 0 W: 11 05 b.Hartlepool 14-4-03
2021–22 Sunderland 0 0
2022–23 Sunderland 0 0
2022–23 *Hartlepool U* 4 0 4 0
2023–24 Sunderland 0 0
2024–25 Harrogate T 36 7 36 7

THOMSON, George (M) 166 28
H: 5 9 W: 11 00 b.Melton Mowbray 19-5-92
2020–21 Harrogate T 46 3
2021–22 Harrogate T 46 5
2022–23 Harrogate T 30 4
2023–24 Harrogate T 43 16
2024–25 Harrogate T 1 0 166 28

WILSON, Robbie (M) 0 0
b. 10-5-07
2024–25 Harrogate T 0 0

Scholars
Barnes, Lucas Robert; Bray, Jack Owen; Etherington, Marcus James; Hindle, Harry Mark; McClarin, Jack Thomas; Obarotimi, Jayden Olufemi Ireoluwa; Pow, Adam James; Robinson, Oliver James; Shepherd, Frankie Dawson; Wilson, Robert Alexander.

HUDDERSFIELD T (41)

ASHIA, Cameron (M) 0 0
H: 5 9 b.London 8-10-06
2024–25 Huddersfield T 0 0

AYINA, Loick (D) 26 0
H: 6 0 W: 11 11 b.Brazzaville 20-4-03
From Sarcelles.
2020–21 Huddersfield T 0 0
2021–22 Huddersfield T 0 0
2022–23 Huddersfield T 0 0
2022–23 *Dundee U* 12 0 12 0
2023–24 Huddersfield T 2 0
2023–24 *Ross Co* 12 0 12 0
2024–25 Huddersfield T 0 0 2 0

BALKER, Radinio (D) 127 7
H: 6 3 W: 12 13 b.Amsterdam 3-9-98
2017–18 Almere C 1 0
2018–19 Almere C 19 0
2019–20 Almere C 22 1
2020–21 Almere C 15 2 56 3
2021–22 Groningen 0 0
2022–23 Groningen 31 1
2023–24 Groningen 19 3 50 4
2023–24 Huddersfield T 7 0
2024–25 Huddersfield T 14 0 21 0

CHAPMAN, Jacob (G) 27 0
H: 6 1 W: 12 08 b.Wahroonga 22-10-00
Internationals: Australia U23.
2019–20 Huddersfield T 0 0
2020–21 Huddersfield T 0 0
2021–22 Huddersfield T 0 0
2022–23 Huddersfield T 0 0
2022–23 *Salford C* 2 0 2 0
2023–24 Huddersfield T 0 0
2024–25 Huddersfield T 23 0 25 0

CHARLES, Dion (F) 221 72
H: 5 10 W: 10 08 b.Preston 7-10-95
Internationals: Northern Ireland U21, Full caps.
2013–14 Blackpool 0 0
From AFC Fylde.
2016–17 Fleetwood T 0 0
From Southport.
2019–20 Accrington S 33 8
2020–21 Accrington S 42 19
2021–22 Accrington S 6 0 81 27
2021–22 Bolton W 23 8
2022–23 Bolton W 42 16
2023–24 Bolton W 33 14
2024–25 Bolton W 24 7 122 45
2024–25 Huddersfield T 18 0 18 0

DALEY, Luke (D) 0 0
H: 5 11 b. 30-12-02
2023–24 Huddersfield T 0 0
2024–25 Huddersfield T 0 0

ECCLESTON, Neo (D) 20 1
H: 5 10 W: 11 09 b.London 11-8-03
2023–24 Huddersfield T 0 0
2024–25 Huddersfield T 3 0 3 0
2024–25 *Barrow* 17 1 17 1

EVANS, Antony (M) 201 25
H: 6 1 W: 10 10 b.Fazakerley 23-9-98
Internationals: England U19.
2016–17 Everton 0 0
2016–17 *Morecambe* 14 2 14 2
2017–18 Everton 0 0
2018–19 Everton 0 0
2018–19 *Blackpool* 12 0 12 0
2019–20 Paderborn 6 0
2020–21 Paderborn 0 0 6 0
2020–21 *Crewe Alex* 14 0 14 0
2021–22 Bristol R 35 10
2022–23 Bristol R 43 5
2023–24 Bristol R 43 6 121 21
2024–25 Huddersfield T 34 2 34 2

FALLS, Conor (F) 1 0
H: 6 0 W: 12 00 b.Cookstown 2-1-04
Internationals: Northern Ireland U16, U18, U19, U21.
From Glentoran.
2023–24 Huddersfield T 0 0
2024–25 Huddersfield T 1 0 1 0

HARRATT, Kian (F) 66 6
H: 5 10 W: 10 01 b.Pontefract 21-6-02
From Barnsley, Leeds U.
2019–20 Huddersfield T 1 0
2020–21 Huddersfield T 0 0
2021–22 Huddersfield T 0 0
2021–22 *Port Vale* 19 3 19 3
2022–23 Huddersfield T 4 1
2022–23 *Bradford C* 5 0 5 0
2023–24 Huddersfield T 15 1
2024–25 Huddersfield T 2 0 22 2
2024–25 *Fleetwood T* 20 1 20 1

HEALEY, Rhys (M) 225 89
H: 5 8 W: 10 10 b.Manchester 6-12-94
2011–12 Connah's Quay Nomads 10 3
2012–13 Connah's Quay Nomads 19 12 29 15
2012–13 Cardiff C 0 0
2013–14 Cardiff C 1 0
2014–15 Cardiff C 0 0
2014–15 *Colchester U* 21 4 21 4
2015–16 Cardiff C 1 0
2015–16 *Dundee* 7 1 7 1
2016–17 Cardiff C 7 1
2016–17 *Newport Co* 17 6 17 6
2017–18 Cardiff C 3 0
2018–19 Cardiff C 3 0 14 1
2018–19 *Milton Keynes D* 18 8
2019–20 Milton Keynes D 19 11 37 19
2020–21 Toulouse 33 15
2021–22 Toulouse 32 20
2022–23 Toulouse 4 2 69 37
2023–24 Watford 11 2 11 2
2023–24 Huddersfield T 11 3
2024–25 Huddersfield T 9 1 20 4

HIGH, Scott (M) 88 1
H: 5 10 W: 10 03 b.Dewsbury 15-2-01
Internationals: Scotland U21.
2019–20 Huddersfield T 1 0
2020–21 Huddersfield T 14 0
2020–21 *Shrewsbury T* 12 0 12 0
2021–22 Huddersfield T 23 0
2022–23 Huddersfield T 9 0
2022–23 *Rotherham U* 13 0 13 0
2023–24 Huddersfield T 0 0
2023–24 *Ross Co* 2 0 2 0
2023–24 *Dundalk* 14 1 14 1
2024–25 Huddersfield T 0 0 47 0

HOGG, Jonathan (M) 488 6
H: 5 10 W: 11 08 b.Middlesbrough 6-12-88
2007–08 Aston Villa 0 0
2008–09 Aston Villa 0 0

2009–10 Aston Villa 0 0
2009–10 *Darlington* 5 1 **5 1**
2010–11 Aston Villa 5 0
2010–11 *Portsmouth* 19 0 **19 0**
2011–12 Aston Villa 0 0 **5 0**
2011–12 Watford 40 0
2012–13 Watford 38 0 **78 0**
2013–14 Huddersfield T 34 0
2014–15 Huddersfield T 26 0
2015–16 Huddersfield T 22 0
2016–17 Huddersfield T 37 1
2017–18 Huddersfield T 30 0
2018–19 Huddersfield T 29 0
2019–20 Huddersfield T 37 0
2020–21 Huddersfield T 37 1
2021–22 Huddersfield T 31 2
2022–23 Huddersfield T 30 0
2023–24 Huddersfield T 34 0
2024–25 Huddersfield T 34 1 **381 5**

HUDLIN, Kyle (F)   54 6
H: 6 9   W: 13 05   b.Birmingham 15-6-00
From Solihull Moors.
2022–23 Huddersfield T 0 0
2022–23 *AFC Wimbledon* 13 0 **13 0**
2023–24 Huddersfield T 9 0
2023–24 *Burton Alb* 5 0 **5 0**
2024–25 Huddersfield T 0 0 **9 0**
2024–25 *Newport Co* 27 6 **27 6**

HURL, Francis (G)   0 0
b. 30-9-05
2024–25 Huddersfield T 0 0

IORPENDA, Tom (M)   7 0
H: 5 10   W: 10 03   b. 6-4-05
2023–24 Huddersfield T 2 0
2024–25 Huddersfield T 5 0 **7 0**

KANE, Herbie (M)   213 21
H: 5 9   W: 10 08   b.Bristol 23-11-98
Internationals: England U16, U17, U18.
From Bristol C.
2018–19 Liverpool 0 0
2018–19 *Doncaster R* 38 4 **38 4**
2019–20 Liverpool 0 0
2019–20 *Hull C* 7 2 **7 2**
2020–21 Barnsley 24 0
2021–22 Barnsley 0 0
2021–22 *Oxford U* 35 0 **35 0**
2022–23 Barnsley 40 3
2023–24 Barnsley 41 9 **105 12**
2024–25 Huddersfield T 28 3 **28 3**

KASUMU, David (M)   165 5
H: 5 11   W: 11 00   b.Lambeth 5-10-99
2015–16 Milton Keynes D 0 0
2016–17 Milton Keynes D 0 0
2017–18 Milton Keynes D 1 0
2018–19 Milton Keynes D 0 0
2019–20 Milton Keynes D 21 1
2020–21 Milton Keynes D 24 0
2021–22 Milton Keynes D 23 0 **69 1**
2022–23 Huddersfield T 33 0
2023–24 Huddersfield T 31 1
2024–25 Huddersfield T 32 3 **96 4**

KOROMA, Josh (F)   202 38
H: 5 10   W: 10 06   b.Southwark 8-11-98
Internationals: England C. Sierra Leone Full caps.
2015–16 Leyton Orient 3 0
2016–17 Leyton Orient 22 3 **25 3**
From Leyton Orient.
2019–20 Huddersfield T 7 0
2019–20 *Rotherham U* 5 0 **5 0**
2020–21 Huddersfield T 20 8
2021–22 Huddersfield T 34 4
2022–23 Huddersfield T 19 4
2022–23 *Portsmouth* 16 2 **16 2**
2023–24 Huddersfield T 39 6
2024–25 Huddersfield T 37 11 **156 33**

LADAPO, Freddie (F)   296 78
H: 6 0   W: 12 06   b.Romford 1-2-93
2011–12 Colchester U 0 0
2012–13 Colchester U 4 0
2013–14 Colchester U 2 0 **6 0**
From Margate.
2015–16 Crystal Palace 0 0
2016–17 Crystal Palace 0 0
2016–17 *Oldham Ath* 17 2 **17 2**
2016–17 *Shrewsbury T* 15 4 **15 4**
2017–18 Crystal Palace 1 0 **1 0**
2017–18 *Southend U* 6 0
2017–18 *Plymouth Arg* 45 18 **45 18**
2018–19 *Rotherham U* 31 14
2019–20 Rotherham U 42 9
2020–21 Rotherham U 31 11 **104 34**
2022–23 Ipswich T 46 17
2023–24 Ipswich T 17 2 **63 19**
2023–24 *Charlton Ath* 14 1 **14 1**
2024–25 Huddersfield T 21 0 **21 0**

LEES, Tom (D)   598 22
H: 6 0   W: 11 07   b.Warwick 28-11-90
Internationals: England U21.
2008–09 Leeds U 0 0
2009–10 Leeds U 0 0
2009–10 *Accrington S* 39 0 **39 0**
2010–11 Leeds U 0 0
2010–11 *Bury* 45 4 **45 4**
2011–12 Leeds U 42 2
2012–13 Leeds U 40 1
2013–14 Leeds U 41 0 **123 3**
2014–15 Sheffield Wed 44 0
2015–16 Sheffield Wed 34 3
2016–17 Sheffield Wed 35 1
2017–18 Sheffield Wed 29 1
2018–19 Sheffield Wed 42 2
2019–20 Sheffield Wed 27 2
2020–21 Sheffield Wed 38 1 **249 10**
2021–22 Huddersfield T 40 3
2022–23 Huddersfield T 42 2
2023–24 Huddersfield T 31 0
2024–25 Huddersfield T 29 0 **142 5**

MAXWELL, Chris (G)   308 0
H: 6 1   W: 11 07   b.St Asaph 30-7-90
Internationals: Wales U17, U19, U21, U23.
From Wrexham.
2012–13 Fleetwood T 0 0
2013–14 Fleetwood T 18 0
2014–15 Fleetwood T 46 0
2015–16 Fleetwood T 46 0 **110 0**
2016–17 Preston NE 38 0
2017–18 Preston NE 30 0
2018–19 Preston NE 8 0
2018–19 *Charlton Ath* 0 0
2019–20 Preston NE 0 0 **76 0**
2019–20 *Hibernian* 12 0 **12 0**
2019–20 Blackpool 9 0
2020–21 Blackpool 43 0
2021–22 Blackpool 21 0
2022–23 Blackpool 28 0 **101 0**
2023–24 Huddersfield T 9 0
2024–25 Huddersfield T 0 0 **9 0**

MILLER, Mickel (F)   163 12
H: 5 10   W: 11 00   b.Croydon 2-12-95
From Carshalton Ath.
2017–18 Hamilton A 6 0
2018–19 Hamilton A 31 5
2019–20 Hamilton A 21 3 **58 8**
2020–21 Rotherham U 9 0
2020–21 *Northampton T* 12 0 **12 0**
2021–22 Rotherham U 23 3 **32 3**
2022–23 Plymouth Arg 9 0
2023–24 Plymouth Arg 34 1 **43 1**
2024–25 Huddersfield T 18 0 **18 0**

MRISHO, Omari (D)   0 0
b. 29-9-05
2024–25 Huddersfield T 0 0

NICHOLLS, Lee (G)   341 0
H: 6 3   W: 13 05   b.Huyton 5-10-92
Internationals: England U19.
2009–10 Wigan Ath 0 0
2010–11 Wigan Ath 0 0
2010–11 *Hartlepool U* 0 0
2010–11 *Shrewsbury T* 0 0
2010–11 *Sheffield Wed* 0 0
2011–12 Wigan Ath 0 0
2011–12 *Accrington S* 9 0 **9 0**
2012–13 Wigan Ath 0 0
2012–13 *Northampton T* 46 0 **46 0**
2013–14 Wigan Ath 6 0
2014–15 Wigan Ath 1 0
2015–16 Wigan Ath 2 0 **9 0**
2015–16 *Bristol R* 15 0 **15 0**
2016–17 Milton Keynes D 8 0
2017–18 Milton Keynes D 41 0
2018–19 Milton Keynes D 40 0
2019–20 Milton Keynes D 35 0
2020–21 Milton Keynes D 7 0 **131 0**
2021–22 Huddersfield T 43 0
2022–23 Huddersfield T 28 0
2023–24 Huddersfield T 37 0
2024–25 Huddersfield T 23 0 **131 0**

PEARSON, Matthew (D)   366 37
H: 6 3   W: 11 05   b.Keighley 3-8-93
Internationals: England U18, C.
2011–12 Blackburn R 0 0
2012–13 Rochdale 9 0
2013–14 Rochdale 0 0 **9 0**
From FC Halifax T.
2015–16 Accrington S 46 3
2016–17 Accrington S 43 8 **89 11**
2017–18 Barnsley 17 0 **17 0**
2018–19 Luton T 46 6
2019–20 Luton T 42 2
2020–21 Luton T 40 2 **128 10**
2021–22 Huddersfield T 37 3
2022–23 Huddersfield T 18 5
2023–24 Huddersfield T 39 3
2024–25 Huddersfield T 29 5 **123 16**

PHILLIPS, Kieran (F)   103 25
H: 6 1   W: 12 08   b.Huddersfield 18-2-00
From Everton.
2020–21 Huddersfield T 10 0
2021–22 Huddersfield T 0 0
2021–22 *Walsall* 26 4 **26 4**
2021–22 *Exeter C* 11 2 **11 2**
2022–23 Huddersfield T 0 0
2022–23 *Morecambe* 20 7 **20 7**
2023–24 Huddersfield T 0 0
2023–24 *Shrewsbury T* 8 0 **8 0**
2023–24 *Sacramento Republic* 28 12 **28 12**
2024–25 Huddersfield T 0 0 **10 0**

RADULOVIC, Bojan (F)   107 29
H: 6 4   W: 12 08   b.Lleida 1-1-99
Internationals: Serbia U19.
From Lleida.
2017–18 Brighton & HA 0 0
2018–19 Brighton & HA 0 0
2019–20 Brighton & HA 0 0
2020 AIK 3 0
2021 AIK 26 3
2022 AIK 0 0 **29 3**
2022 HJK 15 5
2023 HJK 24 18 **39 23**
2023–24 Huddersfield T 11 1
2024–25 Huddersfield T 17 1 **28 2**
2024–25 *Fortuna Sittard* 11 1 **11 1**

ROOSKEN, Ruben (D)   129 4
H: 6 0   W: 11 00   b.Emmen 2-3-00
2019–20 Emmen 3 0 **3 0**
2020–21 TOP Oss 29 0 **29 0**
2021–22 Heracles 7 0
2022–23 Heracles 37 1
2023–24 Heracles 23 0
2024–25 Heracles 16 1 **83 2**
2024–25 Huddersfield T 14 2 **14 2**

RUFFELS, Joshua (D)   332 24
H: 5 10   W: 11 11   b.Oxford 23-10-93
2011–12 Coventry C 1 0
2012–13 Coventry C 0 0 **1 0**
2013–14 Oxford U 29 1
2014–15 Oxford U 33 0
2015–16 Oxford U 16 0
2016–17 Oxford U 20 2
2017–18 Oxford U 38 5
2018–19 Oxford U 44 4
2019–20 Oxford U 35 3
2020–21 Oxford U 42 6 **257 21**
2021–22 Huddersfield T 8 0
2022–23 Huddersfield T 33 3
2023–24 Huddersfield T 11 0
2024–25 Huddersfield T 22 0 **74 3**

SOLOMON, Eko (D)   3 0
H: 6 1   b. 30-5-06
2024–25 Huddersfield T 0 0
2024–25 *Harrogate T* 3 0 **3 0**

SORENSON, Lasse (M)   179 8
H: 6 1   W: 12 04   b.Vejen 21-10-99
Internationals: Denmark U16, U17, U18, U19, U20.
From Esbjerg.
2017–18 Stoke C 1 0
2018–19 Stoke C 1 0
2019–20 Stoke C 6 0
2020–21 Stoke C 0 0 **8 0**
2020–21 *Milton Keynes D* 24 0 **24 0**
2021–22 Lincoln C 30 1
2022–23 Lincoln C 41 3
2023–24 Lincoln C 44 4 **115 8**
2024–25 Huddersfield T 32 0 **32 0**

SPENCER, Brodie (D)   75 3
H: 6 0   W: 11 11   b.Belfast 6-5-04
Internationals: Northern Ireland U16, U19, Full caps.
From Cliftonville.
2022–23 Huddersfield T 4 0
2023–24 Huddersfield T 20 0
2023–24 *Motherwell* 18 0 **18 0**
2024–25 Huddersfield T 33 3 **57 3**

STONE, Michael (M)   0 0
H: 5 10   W: 11 03   b. 29-5-04
2023–24 Huddersfield T 0 0
2024–25 Huddersfield T 0 0

TAYLOR, Joseph (F)   89 23
H: 6 0   b.Peterborough 18-11-02
Internationals: Wales U21.
From King's Lynn T.
2021–22 Peterborough U 4 0
2022–23 Peterborough U 8 0 **12 0**
2022–23 Luton T 5 0
2023–24 Luton T 0 0
2023–24 *Colchester U* 25 11 **25 11**
2023–24 *Lincoln C* 19 10 **19 10**
2024–25 Luton T 13 0 **18 0**
2024–25 Huddersfield T 15 2 **15 2**

THOMAS, Peter (F)   0 0
b.Gorton 20-8-04
2019–20 Rochdale 0 0
2020–21 Rochdale 0 0
2021–22 Rochdale 0 0
2022–23 Rochdale 0 0
From Hyde U.
2024–25 Huddersfield T 0 0

TURTON, Oliver (D)   399 7
H: 5 11 W: 11 11 b.Manchester 6-12-92
2010–11 Crewe Alex 1 0
2011–12 Crewe Alex 2 0
2012–13 Crewe Alex 20 0
2013–14 Crewe Alex 12 1
2014–15 Crewe Alex 44 1
2015–16 Crewe Alex 46 1
2016–17 Crewe Alex 45 1 170 4
2017–18 Blackpool 41 1
2018–19 Blackpool 32 1
2019–20 Blackpool 30 0
2020–21 Blackpool 37 0 140 2
2021–22 Huddersfield T 40 0
2022–23 Huddersfield T 18 0
2023–24 Huddersfield T 3 0
2024–25 Huddersfield T 28 1 89 1

VOST, Daniel (M)   0 0
H: 6 1 b.17-3-06
2024–25 Huddersfield T 0 0

WARD, Danny (F)   438 78
H: 5 11 W: 13 11 b.Bradford 9-12-90
From Leeds U.
2008–09 Bolton W 0 0
2009–10 Bolton W 2 0
2009–10 Swindon T 28 7 28 7
2010–11 Bolton W 0 0 2 0
2010–11 Coventry C 5 0 5 0
2010–11 Huddersfield T 7 3
2011–12 Huddersfield T 39 4
2012–13 Huddersfield T 28 2
2013–14 Huddersfield T 38 10
2014–15 Huddersfield T 12 0
2014–15 Rotherham U 16 3
2015–16 Rotherham U 34 4
2016–17 Rotherham U 41 10 91 17
2017–18 Cardiff C 18 4
2018–19 Cardiff C 14 1
2019–20 Cardiff C 28 7 60 12
2020–21 Huddersfield T 19 1
2021–22 Huddersfield T 40 14
2022–23 Huddersfield T 36 5
2023–24 Huddersfield T 20 3
2024–25 Huddersfield T 13 0 252 42

WILES, Ben (M)   247 23
H: 5 9 W: 10 06 b.Rotherham 17-4-99
2017–18 Rotherham U 0 0
2018–19 Rotherham U 20 0
2019–20 Rotherham U 33 3
2020–21 Rotherham U 44 2
2021–22 Rotherham U 46 8
2022–23 Rotherham U 27 2
2023–24 Rotherham U 2 0 172 15
2023–24 Huddersfield T 30 0
2024–25 Huddersfield T 45 8 75 8

Players retained or with offer of contract
Gilmore, Brodie; Knowles, Charlie James; Neil, Marlie James; O'Reilly, Aaron Christopher.

Scholars
Bennett, Hugo Radley; Bowker, Zac Joseph; Calland, Oliver Ben; Fikri, Mohammed Mubarak; Gregory, Anthony; Mebrahtu, Milkyas Gezae; Nicholson, Joe John Nathaniel; Ohonba Idemudia, Nicolasomoregie; Schofield, Luke; Shelton, Gabriano Jabez; Smith-Sway, Jay; Walpole, Alexander Guy.

HULL C (42)

ALZATE, Steve (M)   156 9
H: 5 10 W: 10 03 b.Camden Town 1-9-98
Internationals: Colombia Full caps.
2016–17 Leyton Orient 12 1 12 1
2017–18 Brighton & HA 22 2 22 2
2018–19 Swindon T 2 0
2019–20 Brighton & HA 19 0
2020–21 Brighton & HA 15 1
2021–22 Brighton & HA 9 0
2022–23 Standard Liege 27 3
2023–24 Brighton & HA 0 0 43 1
2023–24 Standard Liege 24 2 51 5
2024–25 Hull C 28 0 28 0

AMRABAT, Nordin (F)   514 86
H: 5 10 W: 12 02 b.Naarden 31-3-87
Internationals: Netherlands U21. Morocco Full caps.
2006–07 Omniworld 36 14 36 14

2007–08 VVV Venlo 33 10 33 10
2008–09 PSV Eindhoven 25 5
2009–10 PSV Eindhoven 25 3
2010–11 PSV Eindhoven 6 1 56 9
2010–11 Kayserispor 14 1
2011–12 Kayserispor 25 5 39 6
2012–13 Galatasaray 30 1
2013–14 Galatasaray 4 0
2013–14 *Malaga* 15 2
2014–15 Galatasaray 0 0 34 1
2014–15 *Malaga* 31 6
2015–16 *Malaga* 13 0 59 8
2016–17 Watford 12 0
2016–17 Watford 29 0
2017–18 Watford 3 0 44 0
2017–18 *Leganes* 30 2 30 2
2018–19 Al-Nassr 26 5
2019–20 Al-Nassr 29 4
2020–21 Al-Nassr 25 6 80 15
2021–22 AEK Athens 29 6
2022–23 AEK Athens 31 8
2023–24 AEK Athens 27 6
2024–25 AEK Athens 6 1 93 21
2024–25 Hull C 10 0 10 0

ASHBEE, Stanley (D)   0 0
b. 28-11-06
Internationals: Republic of Ireland U16, U17, U18, U19.
2023–24 Hull C 0 0
2024–25 Hull C 0 0

BEDIA, Chris (F)   255 53
b.Abidjan 5-3-96
Internationals: Ivory Coast U20.
2013–14 Tours 0 0
2014–15 Tours 9 1
2015–16 Tours 11 4 20 5
2016–17 Charleroi 35 5
2017–18 Charleroi 31 1
2018–19 Charleroi 2 0
2018–19 *Zulte Waregem* 16 0 16 0
2019–20 Charleroi 3 0
2019–20 *Troyes* 22 3 22 3
2020–21 Charleroi 9 1 80 7
2020–21 *Sochaux* 35 9 35 9
2021–22 Servette 14 3
2022–23 Servette 23 12
2023–24 Servette 17 10 54 25
2023–24 Union Berlin 7 1
2024–25 Union Berlin 0 0 7 1
On loan from Union Berlin.
2024–25 Hull C 21 3 21 3

BELLOUMI, Mohamed (M)   71 12
H: 6 0 W: 10 06 ' b.Mascara 1-6-02
Internationals: Algeria U20.
2020–21 Oran 28 3 28 3
2021–22 Farense 0 0
2022–23 Farense 1 0
2023–24 Farense 32 7 33 7
2024–25 Hull C 10 2 10 2

BROWN, Pharrell (M)   1 0
H: 5 11 b.Manchester 31-8-05
From Manchester U.
2022–23 Fleetwood T 1 0
2023–24 Fleetwood T 0 0
2024–25 Hull C 0 0

BURSTOW, Mason (F)   69 5
H: 6 2 W: 13 05 b.Plumstead 4-8-03
Internationals: England U20.
2021–22 Charlton Ath 16 2 16 2
2021–22 Chelsea 0 0
2022–23 Chelsea 0 0
2023–24 Chelsea 2 0 2 0
2023–24 *Sunderland* 20 1 20 1
2024–25 Hull C 31 2 31 2

CARTWRIGHT, Harvey (G)   28 0
H: 6 4 W: 12 13 b.Grimsby 9-5-02
Internationals: England U18, U20.
2020–21 Hull C 1 0
2021–22 Hull C 2 0
2022–23 Hull C 0 0
2022–23 *Peterborough U* 0 0
2022–23 *Wycombe W* 1 0 1 0
2023–24 Hull C 0 0
2023–24 *Grimsby T* 25 0 25 0
2024–25 Hull C 0 0

COYLE, Lewie (D)   308 4
H: 5 8 W: 10 08 b.Hull 15-10-95
2015–16 Leeds U 11 0
2016–17 Leeds U 4 0
2017–18 Leeds U 0 0
2017–18 *Fleetwood T* 42 0
2018–19 Leeds U 0 0 15 0
2018–19 *Fleetwood T* 41 0
2019–20 Fleetwood T 34 1
2020–21 Fleetwood T 0 0 117 1
2020–21 Hull C 28 0
2021–22 Hull C 23 1
2022–23 Hull C 41 0

2023–24 Hull C 40 1
2024–25 Hull C 44 1 176 3

COYLE, Rocco (M)   0 0
H: 5 11 W: 12 02 b.Hull 20-8-06
2023–24 Hull C 0 0
2024–25 Hull C 0 0

CROOKS, Matt (M)   357 62
H: 6 0 W: 11 05 b.Leeds 20-1-94
2011–12 Huddersfield T 0 0
2012–13 Huddersfield T 0 0
2013–14 Huddersfield T 0 0
2014–15 Huddersfield T 1 0 1 0
2014–15 *Hartlepool U* 3 0 3 0
2015–16 Accrington S 16 0
2015–16 Accrington S 32 6 48 6
2016–17 Rangers 2 0 2 0
2016–17 Scunthorpe U 12 3 12 3
2017–18 Northampton T 30 4
2018–19 Northampton T 21 5 51 9
2018–19 Rotherham U 16 3
2019–20 Rotherham U 33 9
2020–21 Rotherham U 40 6 89 18
2021–22 Middlesbrough 40 10
2022–23 Middlesbrough 37 7
2023–24 Middlesbrough 25 3 102 20
2024 Real Salt Lake 31 3 31 3
On loan from Real Salt Lake.
2024–25 Hull C 18 3 18 3

DRAMEH, Cody (D)   99 1
H: 5 9 W: 10 12 b.Lambeth 8-12-01
Internationals: England U18, U20, U21.
From Fulham.
2020–21 Leeds U 0 0
2021–22 Leeds U 3 0
2021–22 *Cardiff C* 22 0 22 0
2022–23 Leeds U 1 0
2022–23 *Luton T* 16 0 16 0
2023–24 Leeds U 1 0 5 0
2023–24 *Birmingham C* 28 0 28 0
2024–25 Hull C 28 1 28 1

EGAN, John (D)   393 24
H: 6 1 W: 11 05 b.Cork 20-10-92
Internationals: Republic of Ireland U17, U19, U21, Full caps.
2009–10 Sunderland 0 0
2010–11 Sunderland 0 0
2011–12 Sunderland 0 0
2011–12 *Crystal Palace* 1 0 1 0
2011–12 *Sheffield U* 1 0
2012–13 Sunderland 0 0
2012–13 *Bradford C* 4 0 4 0
2013–14 Sunderland 0 0
2013–14 *Southend U* 13 1 13 1
2014–15 Gillingham 45 4
2015–16 Gillingham 36 6 81 10
2016–17 Brentford 34 4
2017–18 Brentford 33 2 67 6
2018–19 Sheffield U 44 1
2019–20 Sheffield U 36 2
2020–21 Sheffield U 31 0
2021–22 Sheffield U 46 2
2022–23 Sheffield U 45 2
2023–24 Sheffield U 6 0 209 7
2024–25 Burnley 7 0 7 0
2024–25 Hull C 11 0 11 0

ESTUPINAN, Oscar (F)   210 68
H: 6 0 W: 12 00 b.Cali 29-12-96
Internationals: Colombia Full caps.
2014 Once Caldas 0 0
2015 Once Caldas 10 1
2016 Once Caldas 34 13
2017 Once Caldas 14 4 58 18
2017–18 Vitoria de Guimaraes 10 1
2018–19 Vitoria de Guimaraes 4 0
2019 *Barcelona SC* 9 5 9 5
2019–20 Vitoria de Guimaraes 0 0
2019–20 *Denizlispor* 28 7 28 7
2020–21 Vitoria de Guimaraes 23 8
2021–22 Vitoria de Guimaraes 28 15 65 24
2022–23 Hull C 35 13
2023–24 Hull C 4 0
2023–24 *Metz* 6 0 6 0
2023–24 *Bahia* 3 0 3 0
2024–25 Hull C 2 1 41 14
Transferred to Juarez, August 2024.

FLEMING, Brandon (D)   80 0
H: 5 9 W: 10 03 b.Dewsbury 3-12-99
2017–18 Hull C 4 0
2018–19 Hull C 4 0
2019–20 Hull C 4 0
2019–20 *Bolton W* 10 0 10 0
2020–21 Hull C 3 0
2021–22 Hull C 16 0
2022–23 Hull C 4 0
2022–23 *Oxford U* 14 0 14 0
2023–24 Hull C 0 0
2023–24 *Shrewsbury T* 8 0 8 0
2024–25 Hull C 0 0 31 0
2024–25 *Doncaster R* 17 0 17 0

FURLONG, James (D) 38 0
H: 5 10 W: 11 03 b.Dublin 7-6-02
Internationals: Republic of Ireland U16, U17, U18, U21.

2020–21	Brighton & HA	0	0		
2021–22	Brighton & HA	0	0		
2022–23	Brighton & HA	0	0		
2022–23	*Motherwell*	16	0	**16**	**0**
2023–24	Hull C	0	0		
2024–25	Hull C	0	0		
2024–25	*AFC Wimbledon*	22	0	**22**	**0**

GILES, Ryan (M) 195 3
H: 5 10 W: 11 00 b.Telford 26-1-00
Internationals: England U20.

2018–19	Wolverhampton W	0	0		
2019–20	Wolverhampton W	0	0		
2019–20	*Shrewsbury T*	19	1	**19**	**1**
2019–20	*Coventry C*	1	0		
2020–21	Wolverhampton W	0	0		
2020–21	*Coventry C*	19	0	**20**	**0**
2020–21	*Rotherham U*	23	2	**23**	**2**
2021–22	Wolverhampton W	0	0		
2021–22	*Cardiff C*	21	0	**21**	**0**
2021–22	*Blackburn R*	11	0	**11**	**0**
2022–23	Wolverhampton W	0	0		
2022–23	*Middlesbrough*	45	0		
2023–24	Luton T	11	0	**11**	**0**
2023–24	*Hull C*	17	0		
2024–25	Hull C	16	0	**33**	**0**
2024–25	*Middlesbrough*	12	0	**57**	**0**

HUGHES, Charlie (D) 91 6
H: 6 1 W: 12 08 b.Wigan 16-10-03
Internationals: England U20.
From Liverpool.

2021–22	Wigan Ath	0	0		
2022–23	Wigan Ath	20	1		
2023–24	Wigan Ath	43	4		
2024–25	Wigan Ath	1	0	**64**	**5**
2024–25	Hull C	27	1	**27**	**1**

JACOB, Matty (D) 22 1
H: 5 11 W: 12 06 b.Barnsley 3-6-01

2020–21	Hull C	0	0		
2021–22	Hull C	0	0		
2022–23	Hull C	0	0		
2023–24	Hull C	14	0		
2024–25	Hull C	8	1	**22**	**1**

JOAO PEDRO, Galvao (M) 405 109
H: 5 7 W: 10 08 b.Ipatinga 9-3-92
Internationals: Brazil U17. Italy Full caps.

2010	Atletico Mineiro	11	0	**11**	**0**
2010–11	Palermo	1	0		
2010–11	*Vitoria de Guimaraes*	6	0	**6**	**0**
2011–12	Palermo	0	0	**1**	**0**
2011–12	*Penarol*	15	6	**15**	**6**
2012–13	Santos	10	0	**10**	**0**
2013–14	Estoril	24	8		
2014–15	Estoril	3	1	**27**	**9**
2014–15	Cagliari	29	5		
2015–16	Cagliari	38	13		
2016–17	Cagliari	22	7		
2017–18	Cagliari	22	5		
2018–19	Cagliari	34	7		
2019–20	Cagliari	36	18		
2020–21	Cagliari	37	16		
2021–22	Cagliari	37	13	**255**	**84**
2022–23	Fenerbahce	20	4		
2023	*Gremio*	14	0		
2023–24	Fenerbahce	0	0		
2024	*Gremio*	11	0	**25**	**0**
2024–25	Fenerbahce	0	0	**20**	**4**
2024–25	Hull C	35	6	**35**	**6**

JONES, Alfie (D) 224 5
H: 6 0 W: 11 00 b.Bristol 7-10-97

2018–19	Southampton	0	0		
2018–19	*St Mirren*	14	1	**14**	**1**
2019–20	Southampton	0	0		
2019–20	*Gillingham*	30	2	**30**	**2**
2020–21	Hull C	31	0		
2021–22	Hull C	23	1		
2022–23	Hull C	40	0		
2023–24	Hull C	45	1		
2024–25	Hull C	41	0	**180**	**2**

JONES, Callum (M) 75 3
H: 5 9 W: 12 00 b.Birkenhead 5-4-01
Internationals: Wales U18.
From The New Saints, Owestry T, Bury.

2019–20	Hull C	0	0		
2020–21	Hull C	1	0		
2021–22	Hull C	2	0		
2021–22	*Morecambe*	11	1		
2022–23	Hull C	1	0		
2023–24	Hull C	0	0		
2023–24	*Forest Green R*	26	1	**26**	**1**
2024–25	Hull C	0	0	**4**	**0**
2024–25	*Morecambe*	34	1	**45**	**2**

JOSEPH, Kyle (F) 154 27
H: 6 1 W: 11 11 b.Barnet 10-9-01
Internationals: Scotland U18, U19, U21.

2020–21	Wigan Ath	18	5		
2021–22	Wigan Ath	0	0	**18**	**5**
2021–22	*Cheltenham T*	19	4	**19**	**4**
2021–22	Swansea C	10	0		
2022–23	Swansea C	0	0	**10**	**0**
2022–23	*Oxford U*	37	9	**37**	**9**
2023–24	Blackpool	30	1		
2024–25	Blackpool	24	8	**54**	**9**
2024–25	Hull C	16	0	**16**	**0**

KAMARA, Abu (D) 87 13
H: 6 0 W: 12 11 b.London 21-7-03
Internationals: England U20.

2021–22	Norwich C	0	0		
2022–23	Norwich C	3	0		
2023–24	Norwich C	0	0		
2023–24	*Portsmouth*	46	8	**46**	**8**
2024–25	Norwich C	2	0	**5**	**0**
2024–25	Hull C	36	5	**36**	**5**

LINCOLN, dos Santos (M) 200 13
H: 5 10 W: 10 03 b.Porto Alegre 7-11-98
Internationals: Brazil U17.

2015	Gremio	2	0		
2016	Gremio	10	0		
2017	Gremio	8	0		
2017	*Caykur Rizesport*	18	3	**18**	**3**
2018	Gremio	1	0	**21**	**0**
2018	*America Mineiro*	3	0	**3**	**0**
2019–20	Santa Clara	30	1		
2020–21	Santa Clara	30	1		
2021–22	Santa Clara	32	5	**92**	**7**
2022–23	Fenerbahce	21	0		
2023–24	Fenerbahce	0	0		
2023–24	*Red Bull Bragantino*	28	3	**28**	**3**
2024–25	Fenerbahce	0	0	**21**	**0**
2024–25	*Bragantino*	6	0	**6**	**0**

On loan from Fenerbahce.

2024–25	Hull C	11	0	**11**	**0**

LO-TUTALA, Thimothee (G) 26 0
H: 6 1 W: 14 09 b.Paris 13-2-03
Internationals: France U19, U20.
From Tottenham H.

2022–23	Hull C	0	0		
2022–23	*Stevenage*	7	0	**7**	**0**
2023–24	Hull C	0	0		
2023–24	*Doncaster R*	18	0	**18**	**0**
2024–25	Hull C	0	0		
2024–25	*Crawley T*	1	0	**1**	**0**

MATAZO, Eliot (M) 76 4
H: 5 9 W: 11 05 b.Woluwe-Saint-Lambert 15-2-02
Internationals: Belgium U16, U18, U21.

2020–21	Monaco	10	1		
2021–22	Monaco	18	0		
2022–23	Monaco	23	1		
2023–24	Monaco	6	0		
2023–24	*Royal Antwerp*	10	1	**10**	**1**
2024–25	Monaco	3	0	**60**	**2**
2024–25	Hull C	6	1	**6**	**1**

McLOUGHLIN, Sean (D) 198 6
H: 6 3 W: 12 04 b.Cork 13-11-96
Internationals: Republic of Ireland U21.

2017	Cork C	1	0		
2018	Cork C	27	3		
2019	Cork C	20	2	**48**	**5**
2019–20	Hull C	7	0		
2019–20	*St Mirren*	21	1	**21**	**1**
2020–21	Hull C	3	0		
2021–22	Hull C	32	0		
2022–23	Hull C	27	0		
2023–24	Hull C	23	0		
2024–25	Hull C	37	0	**129**	**0**

MEHLEM, Marvin (M) 224 23
b.Karlruhe 11-9-97
Internationals: Germany U16, U17, U18, U19.

2015–16	Karlsruher	3	0		
2016–17	Karlsruher	8	0	**11**	**0**
2017–18	Darmstadt 98	21	2		
2018–19	Darmstadt 98	30	5		
2019–20	Darmstadt 98	26	1		
2020–21	Darmstadt 98	32	5		
2021–22	Darmstadt 98	20	0		
2022–23	Darmstadt 98	32	3		
2023–24	Darmstadt 98	20	3	**181**	**19**
2024–25	Hull C	16	0	**16**	**0**
2024–25	*Paderborn*	16	4	**16**	**4**

MILLAR, Liam (F) 163 17
H: 6 1 W: 11 11 b.Toronto 27-9-99
Internationals: Canada U20, U23, Full caps.

2018–19	Liverpool	0	0		
2018–19	*Kilmarnock*	13	1		
2019–20	Liverpool	0	0		
2019–20	*Kilmarnock*	20	1	**33**	**2**
2020–21	Liverpool	0	0		
2020–21	*Charlton Ath*	27	2	**27**	**2**
2021–22	FC Basel	31	7		
2022–23	FC Basel	26	0		
2023–24	FC Basel	0	0	**57**	**7**
2023–24	*Preston NE*	35	5	**35**	**5**
2024–25	Hull C	11	1	**11**	**1**

MYERS, Zane (D) 0 0
b. 11-8-05

2024–25	Hull C	0	0		

OMUR, Abdulkadir (M) 217 22
H: 5 6 W: 9 11 b.Trabzon 25-6-99
Internationals: Turkey U17, U19, U21, Full caps.

2015–16	Trabzonspor	0	0		
2016–17	Trabzonspor	2	0		
2017–18	Trabzonspor	29	3		
2018–19	Trabzonspor	29	5		
2019–20	Trabzonspor	14	3		
2020–21	Trabzonspor	23	2		
2021–22	Trabzonspor	33	7		
2022–23	Trabzonspor	29	2		
2023–24	Trabzonspor	16	0	**175**	**22**
2023–24	Hull C	16	0		
2024–25	Hull C	20	0	**36**	**0**
2024–25	*Rizespor*	6	0	**6**	**0**

PALMER, Kasey (M) 228 21
H: 5 9 W: 10 10 b.Lewisham 9-11-96
Internationals: England U17, U18, U20, U21. Jamaica Full caps.
From Charlton Ath.

2015–16	Chelsea	0	0		
2016–17	Chelsea	0	0		
2016–17	*Huddersfield T*	24	4		
2017–18	Chelsea	0	0		
2017–18	*Huddersfield T*	4	0	**28**	**4**
2017–18	*Derby Co*	15	2	**15**	**2**
2018–19	Chelsea	0	0		
2018–19	*Blackburn R*	14	1	**14**	**1**
2018–19	*Bristol C*	15	2		
2019–20	Bristol C	25	1		
2020–21	Bristol C	23	2		
2020–21	*Swansea C*	12	1	**12**	**1**
2021–22	Bristol C	6	1	**69**	**6**
2022–23	Coventry C	29	3		
2023–24	Coventry C	32	2		
2024–25	Coventry C	3	1	**64**	**6**
2024–25	Hull C	26	1	**26**	**1**

PANDUR, Ivor (G) 116 0
H: 6 2 W: 12 00 b.Rijeka 25-3-00
Internationals: Croatia U17, U18, U19, U20, U21.

2019–20	Rijeka	18	0		
2020–21	Rijeka	2	0	**20**	**0**
2020–21	Verona	4	0		
2021–22	Verona	3	0		
2022–23	Verona	0	0	**7**	**0**
2022–23	*Fortuna Sittard*	29	0		
2023–24	Fortuna Sittard	16	0	**45**	**0**
2023–24	Hull C	0	0		
2024–25	Hull C	44	0	**44**	**0**

PUERTA, Gustavo (M) 71 4
H: 5 7 W: 11 07 b.La Victoria 23-7-03
Internationals: Colombia U20.

2021	Bogata	11	0		
2022	Bogata	23	3	**34**	**3**
2022–23	Bayer Leverkusen	0	0		
2022–23	*1. FC Nurnberg*	0	0		
2023–24	Bayer Leverkusen	7	0	**7**	**0**

On loan from Bayer Leverkusen.

2024–25	Hull C	30	1	**30**	**1**

RACIOPPI, Anthony (G) 64 0
H: 6 1 W: 12 08 b.Geneva 31-12-98
Internationals: Switzerland U20, U21.

2016–17	Lyon	0	0		
2017–18	Lyon	0	0		
2018–19	Lyon	0	0		
2019–20	Lyon	0	0		
2020–21	Dijon	21	0		
2021–22	Dijon	2	0	**23**	**0**
2021–22	Young Boys	5	0		
2022–23	Young Boys	19	0		
2023–24	Young Boys	16	0	**40**	**0**
2024–25	Hull C	0	0		
2024–25	*Cologne*	1	0	**1**	**0**

SELLARS-FLEMING, Tyrell (M) 6 0
b.Lincoln 31-5-05
From Scunthorpe U.

2023–24	Hull C	2	0		
2024–25	Hull C	4	0	**6**	**0**

SERI, Jean (M) 337 20
H: 5 5 W: 10 08 b.Grand-Bereby 19-7-91
Internationals: Ivory Coast U23, Full caps.

2013–14	Pacos de Ferreira	21	1		
2014–15	Pacos de Ferreira	33	1	**54**	**2**
2015–16	Nice	38	3		
2016–17	Nice	34	7		
2017–18	Nice	31	2	**103**	**12**
2018–19	Fulham	32	1		
2019–20	Fulham	0	0		
2019–20	*Galatasaray*	27	2	**27**	**2**
2020–21	Fulham	0	0		
2020–21	*Bordeaux*	12	0	**12**	**0**
2021–22	Fulham	33	1	**65**	**2**
2022–23	Hull C	37	1		

| 2023–24 | Hull C | 39 | 1 | | |
| 2024–25 | Hull C | 0 | 0 | 76 | 2 |

Transferred to Al-Orobah, August 2024.

SIMONS, Xavier (M) 60 3
H: 6 0 W: 12 06 b.Hammersmith 20-2-03
Internationals: England U16, U17, U19, U20.

2020–21	Chelsea	0	0		
2021–22	Chelsea	0	0		
2022–23	Hull C	12	0		
2023–24	Hull C	2	0		
2023–24	*Fleetwood T*	12	1	12	1
2024–25	Hull C	20	2	34	2
2024–25	*Wycombe W*	14	0	14	0

SINIK, Dogukan (F) 174 10
H: 5 9 W: 11 03 b.Antalya 21-1-99
Internationals: Turkey U16, U18, U19, U21, Full caps.

2014–15	Antalyaspor	1	0		
2015–16	Antalyaspor	1	0		
2016–17	Antalyaspor	1	0		
2017–18	Antalyaspor	0	0		
2017–18	*Kemerspor 2003*	30	2	30	2
2018–19	Antalyaspor	33	0		
2019–20	Antalyaspor	21	0		
2020–21	Antalyaspor	21	1		
2021–22	Antalyaspor	32	3		
2022–23	Antalyaspor	12	3	122	7
2022–23	Hull C	12	0		
2023–24	Hull C	1	0		
2023–24	*Hatayspor*	9	1	9	1
2024–25	Hull C	0	0	13	0

SLATER, Regan (M) 217 11
H: 5 8 W: 10 03 b.Sheffield 11-9-99

2016–17	Sheffield U	0	0		
2017–18	Sheffield U	1	0		
2018–19	Sheffield U	0	0		
2018–19	*Carlisle U*	35	2	35	2
2019–20	Sheffield U	0	0		
2019–20	*Scunthorpe U*	12	0	12	0
2020–21	Sheffield U	0	0		
2020–21	*Hull C*	27	1		
2021–22	Sheffield U	0	0	1	0
2021–22	Hull C	16	0		
2022–23	Hull C	44	5		
2023–24	Hull C	38	2		
2024–25	Hull C	44	1	169	9

SMITH, Andy (D) 62 1
b.Banbury 11-9-01

2019–20	Hull C	0	0		
2020–21	Hull C	0	0		
2021–22	Hull C	0	0		
2021–22	*Salford C*	0	0		
2022–23	Hull C	0	0		
2022–23	*Grimsby T*	37	1	37	1
2023–24	Hull C	0	0		
2023–24	*Cheltenham T*	12	0	12	0
2024–25	Hull C	0	0	1	0
2024–25	*Gillingham*	12	0	12	0

TINSDALE, Nathan (M) 0 0
H: 5 10 W: 10 06 b. 20-12-04

| 2023–24 | Hull C | 0 | 0 | | |
| 2024–25 | Hull C | 0 | 0 | | |

VAUGHAN, Harry (M) 56 1
H: 5 9 W: 10 08 b.Trafford 6-4-04
Internationals: Republic of Ireland U19, U21.

2020–21	Oldham Ath	6	0		
2021–22	Oldham Ath	23	1	29	1
2022–23	Hull C	5	0		
2023–24	Hull C	8	0		
2023–24	*Bristol R*	11	0	11	0
2024–25	Hull C	3	0	16	0

ZAMBRANO, Oscar (M) 58 3
H: 5 9 W: 10 10 b.Santo Domingo 24-4-04
Internationals: Ecuador U20.

2022	LDU Quito	13	1		
2023	LDU Quito	24	0		
2024	LDU Quito	13	1	50	2

On loan from LDU Quito.

| 2024–25 | Hull C | 8 | 1 | 8 | 1 |

Players retained or with offer of contract
Alzate, Steven; Cartwright, Harvey Jay; Devine, Edward James; Howard, Archie George; McCarthy, Cathal; Parker, Hugh William; Revill, Harry Charles; Shehu, Aidon; Wadsworth, Noah John Michael; Yam, Callum.

Scholars
Alfie, Perry; Batty, Joseph William; Carter, Ramell Lee McKenzie; Cole, Cayden Peter Maxwell; Dawson, Lucas Anthony; Durkan, Aidan James; Gray, Cameron Samuel; Gruszkowski, Oskar; Hewitt, Stanley Vaughan; Hopper, Jake Michael Anthony; Jagielka, Zac Alexander; Leach, Charlie Anthony; Leech, Rory James; Maskell, Alfie; Okike, Calvin Lorenzo Chikezie; Okot Ocaya, Joshua Aaron Mbabazi; Silk, Reuben David Michael; Topley, Jack Cole.

IPSWICH T (43)

AL-HAMADI, Ali (F) 91 29
H: 6 2 W: 12 00 b.Maysan Governorate 1-3-02
Internationals: Iraq U23, Full caps.
From Tranmere R.

2020–21	Swansea C	0	0		
2021–22	Wycombe W	0	0		
2022–23	Wycombe W	9	0	9	0
2022–23	AFC Wimbledon	19	10		
2023–24	AFC Wimbledon	23	13	42	23
2023–24	Ipswich T	14	4		
2024–25	Ipswich T	11	0	25	4
2024–25	Stoke C	15	2	15	2

AYINDE, Leon (M) 0 0
b. 5-9-04

| 2023–24 | Ipswich T | 0 | 0 | | |
| 2024–25 | Ipswich T | 0 | 0 | | |

BAGGOTT, Elkan (D) 54 3
H: 6 4 W: 13 08 b.Bangkok 23-10-02
Internationals: Indonesia U19, Full caps.

2020–21	Ipswich T	0	0		
2021–22	Ipswich T	2	0		
2022–23	Ipswich T	0	0		
2022–23	*Gillingham*	19	2	19	2
2022–23	*Cheltenham T*	1	0	1	0
2023–24	Ipswich T	0	0		
2023–24	*Bristol R*	14	1	14	1
2024–25	Ipswich T	0	0	2	0
2024–25	*Blackpool*	18	0	18	0

BONIFACE, Somto (D) 0 0
H: 5 11 W: 11 00 b.London 11-3-06
Internationals: England U16, U17, U18.

| 2024–25 | Ipswich T | 0 | 0 | | |

BROADHEAD, Nathan (F) 137 40
H: 5 10 W: 11 07 b.Bangor 5-4-98
Internationals: Wales U17, U19, U20, U21, Full caps.

2017–18	Everton	0	0		
2018–19	Everton	0	0		
2019–20	Everton	0	0		
2019–20	*Burton Alb*	19	2	19	2
2020–21	Everton	1	0		
2021–22	Everton	0	0		
2021–22	*Sunderland*	20	10	20	10
2022–23	Everton	0	0	1	0
2022–23	*Wigan Ath*	22	5	22	5
2022–23	Ipswich T	19	8		
2023–24	Ipswich T	38	13		
2024–25	Ipswich T	18	2	75	23

BUABO, Gerard (M) 1 0
H: 6 1 W: 12 06 b.Redbridge 24-5-05

2022–23	Ipswich T	0	0		
2023–24	Ipswich T	1	0		
2024–25	Ipswich T	0	0	1	0

BURGESS, Cameron (D) 291 13
H: 6 4 W: 12 11 b.Aberdeen 21-10-95
Internationals: Scotland U18, U19. Australia U20, U23, Full caps.

2014–15	Fulham	4	0		
2014–15	*Ross Co*	0	0		
2015–16	Fulham	0	0		
2016–17	Fulham	0	0	4	0
2016–17	*Oldham Ath*	23	1	23	1
2016–17	*Bury*	18	0	18	0
2017–18	Scunthorpe U	25	2		
2018–19	Scunthorpe U	36	1		
2019–20	Scunthorpe U	0	0	61	3
2019–20	*Salford C*	29	2	29	2
2020–21	Accrington S	44	3		
2021–22	Accrington S	1	0	45	3
2021–22	Ipswich T	21	0		
2022–23	Ipswich T	33	2		
2023–24	Ipswich T	39	2		
2024–25	Ipswich T	18	0	111	4

BURNS, Wes (F) 369 55
H: 5 8 W: 10 10 b.Cardiff 23-11-94
Internationals: Wales U21, Full caps.

2012–13	Bristol C	6	0		
2013–14	Bristol C	20	1		
2014–15	Bristol C	3	1		
2014–15	*Oxford U*	9	1	9	1
2014–15	*Cheltenham T*	14	4	14	4
2015–16	Bristol C	14	1	43	3
2015–16	*Fleetwood T*	14	5		
2016–17	*Fleetwood T*	10	0		
2016–17	*Aberdeen*	13	0	13	0
2017–18	Fleetwood T	28	2		
2018–19	Fleetwood T	39	7		
2019–20	Fleetwood T	34	2		
2020–21	Fleetwood T	33	5	158	21
2021–22	Ipswich T	37	12		
2022–23	Ipswich T	42	8		
2023–24	Ipswich T	35	6		
2024–25	Ipswich T	18	0	132	26

CAJUSTE, Jens (M) 167 8
H: 6 2 W: 12 02 b.Gothenburg 10-8-99
Internationals: Sweden U21, Full caps.

2016	Orgryte	3	0		
2017	Orgryte	3	0		
2018	Orgryte	8	0	14	0
2018–19	Midtjylland	2	0		
2019–20	Midtjylland	24	1		
2020–21	Midtjylland	27	1		
2021–22	Midtjylland	5	0	58	2
2021–22	Reims	8	2		
2022–23	Reims	31	3	39	5
2023–24	Napoli	26	0		
2024–25	Napoli	0	0	26	0

On loan from Napoli.

| 2024–25 | Ipswich T | 30 | 1 | 30 | 1 |

CHAPLIN, Conor (M) 363 94
H: 5 10 W: 10 12 b.Worthing 16-2-97

2014–15	Portsmouth	9	1		
2015–16	Portsmouth	30	8		
2016–17	Portsmouth	39	8		
2017–18	Portsmouth	26	5	104	22
2018–19	Coventry C	31	8	31	8
2019–20	Barnsley	44	11		
2020–21	Barnsley	34	4	78	15
2021–22	Ipswich T	39	9		
2022–23	Ipswich T	45	26		
2023–24	Ipswich T	44	13		
2024–25	Ipswich T	22	1	150	49

CLARKE, Harrison (D) 142 8
H: 5 10 W: 11 03 b.Ipswich 2-3-01
Internationals: England U17.

2019–20	Arsenal	0	0		
2020–21	Arsenal	0	0		
2020–21	*Oldham Ath*	32	1	32	1
2021–22	Arsenal	0	0		
2021–22	*Ross Co*	17	3	17	3
2021–22	*Hibernian*	7	1	7	1
2022–23	Arsenal	0	0		
2022–23	*Stoke C*	18	2	18	2
2022–23	Ipswich T	20	0		
2023–24	Ipswich T	35	1		
2024–25	Ipswich T	7	0	62	1
2024–25	*Sheffield U*	6	0	6	0

CLARKE, Jack (F) 179 28
H: 5 11 W: 11 00 b.York 23-11-00
Internationals: England U20.

2017–18	Leeds U	0	0		
2018–19	Leeds U	22	2		
2019–20	Tottenham H	0	0		
2019–20	*Leeds U*	1	0	23	2
2020–21	QPR	6	0	6	0
2020–21	Tottenham H	0	0		
2020–21	*Stoke C*	14	0	14	0
2021–22	Tottenham H	0	0		
2021–22	Sunderland	17	1		
2022–23	Sunderland	45	9		
2023–24	Sunderland	40	15		
2024–25	Sunderland	2	1	104	26
2024–25	Ipswich T	32	0	32	0

DAVIS, Leif (D) 140 6
H: 5 5 W: 10 08 b.Newcastle upon Tyne 12-1-00
From Morecambe.

2018–19	Leeds U	4	0		
2019–20	Leeds U	3	0		
2020–21	Leeds U	2	0		
2021–22	Leeds U	0	0	9	0
2021–22	*Bournemouth*	12	0	12	0
2022–23	Ipswich T	43	3		
2023–24	Ipswich T	43	2		
2024–25	Ipswich T	33	1	119	6

DELAP, Liam (F) 107 24
H: 6 1 W: 11 05 b.Winchester 8-2-03
Internationals: England U16, U17, U18, U19, U20, U21.
From Derby Co.

2020–21	Manchester C	1	0		
2021–22	Manchester C	1	0		
2022–23	Manchester C	0	0		
2022–23	*Stoke C*	22	3	22	3
2022–23	*Preston NE*	15	1	15	1
2023–24	Manchester C	0	0	2	0
2023–24	*Hull C*	31	8	31	8
2024–25	Ipswich T	37	12	37	12

EDMUNDSON, Sam (D) 168 10
H: 6 3 W: 12 06 b.Timperley 15-8-97

2015–16	Oldham Ath	2	0		
2016–17	Oldham Ath	3	0		
2017–18	Oldham Ath	15	1		
2018–19	Oldham Ath	45	2	65	3
2019–20	Rangers	7	1		
2020–21	Rangers	1	0	8	1
2021–22	*Derby Co*	10	1	10	1
2021–22	Ipswich T	32	2		
2022–23	Ipswich T	18	2		
2023–24	Ipswich T	10	0		
2024–25	*Middlesbrough*	24	1	24	1

GODFREY, Ben (D) 204 6
H: 6 0 W: 11 09 b.York 15-1-98
Internationals: England U20, U21, Full caps.

2014–15	York C	0 0	
2015–16	York C	12 1	12 1
2015–16	Norwich C	0 0	
2016–17	Norwich C	2 0	
2017–18	Norwich C	0 0	
2017–18	*Shrewsbury T*	40 1	
2018–19	Norwich C	31 4	
2019–20	Norwich C	30 0	
2019–20	*Shrewsbury T*	0 0	40 1
2020–21	Norwich C	3 0	66 4
2020–21	Everton	31 0	
2021–22	Everton	23 0	
2022–23	Everton	13 0	
2023–24	Everton	15 0	82 0
2024–25	Atalanta	1 0	1 0

On loan from Atalanta.

2024–25	Ipswich T	3 0	3 0

GREAVES, Jacob (D) 226 7
H: 6 1 W: 11 00 b.Cottingham 12-9-00

2019–20	Hull C	0 0	
2019–20	*Cheltenham T*	29 0	29 0
2020–21	Hull C	39 0	
2021–22	Hull C	46 0	
2022–23	Hull C	44 4	
2023–24	Hull C	43 2	172 6
2024–25	Ipswich T	25 1	25 1

HARNESS, Marcus (M) 331 43
H: 6 0 W: 11 00 b.Coventry 1-8-94

2013–14	Burton Alb	3 0	
2014–15	Burton Alb	8 0	
2015–16	Burton Alb	5 0	
2016–17	Burton Alb	10 0	
2017–18	Burton Alb	0 0	
2017–18	*Port Vale*	35 1	35 1
2018–19	Burton Alb	32 5	68 5
2019–20	Portsmouth	25 5	
2020–21	Portsmouth	46 7	
2021–22	Portsmouth	40 11	111 23
2022–23	Portsmouth	40 6	
2023–24	Ipswich T	34 4	
2024–25	Ipswich T	2 0	76 10
2024–25	Derby Co	41 4	41 4

HIRST, George (F) 178 32
H: 6 3 W: 11 00 b.Sheffield 15-2-99
Internationals: England U17, U18, U19, U20. Scotland Full caps.

2016–17	Sheffield Wed	1 0	
2017–18	Sheffield Wed	0 0	1 0
2018–19	*Oh Leuven*	22 3	22 3
2019–20	Leicester C	2 0	
2020–21	Leicester C	0 0	
2020–21	*Rotherham U*	31 0	31 0
2021–22	Leicester C	0 0	
2021–22	*Portsmouth*	40 13	40 13
2022–23	Leicester C	0 0	2 0
2022–23	*Blackburn R*	9 0	9 0
2022–23	*Ipswich T*	21 6	
2023–24	Ipswich T	26 7	
2024–25	Ipswich T	26 3	73 16

HUMPHREYS, Cameron (M) 64 9
H: 5 10 W: 11 00 b.Colchester 30-10-03

2021–22	Ipswich T	1 0	
2022–23	Ipswich T	17 2	
2023–24	Ipswich T	3 0	
2024–25	Ipswich T	0 0	22 2
2024–25	*Wycombe W*	42 7	42 7

HUTCHINSON, Omari (M) 76 13
H: 5 9 W: 10 03 b.Redhill 30-10-03
Internationals: England U17, U19. Jamaica Full caps.

2021–22	Arsenal	0 0	
2022–23	Chelsea	1 0	
2023–24	Chelsea	0 0	1 0
2023–24	*Ipswich T*	44 10	
2024–25	Ipswich T	31 3	75 13

JOHNSON, Ben (D) 92 3
H: 5 9 W: 10 08 b.Waltham Forest 24-1-00
Internationals: England U21.

2017–18	West Ham U	0 0	
2018–19	West Ham U	1 0	
2019–20	West Ham U	3 0	
2020–21	West Ham U	14 1	
2021–22	West Ham U	20 1	
2022–23	West Ham U	17 0	
2023–24	West Ham U	14 0	69 2
2024–25	Ipswich T	23 1	23 1

LUONGO, Massimo (F) 372 62
H: 5 9 W: 12 00 b.Sydney 25-9-92
Internationals: Australia U20, Full caps.

2010–11	Tottenham H	0 0	
2011–12	Tottenham H	0 0	
2012–13	Tottenham H	0 0	
2012–13	*Ipswich T*	9 0	
2012–13	*Swindon T*	7 1	
2013–14	Swindon T	44 6	
2014–15	Swindon T	34 6	85 13

2015–16	QPR	30 0	
2016–17	QPR	35 1	
2017–18	QPR	39 6	
2018–19	QPR	41 3	145 10
2019–20	Sheffield Wed	27 3	
2020–21	Sheffield Wed	12 0	
2021–22	Sheffield Wed	25 1	64 4
2022–23	Middlesbrough	0 0	
2022–23	*Ipswich T*	15 2	
2023–24	Ipswich T	43 3	
2024–25	Ipswich T	11 0	78 5

MORSY, Sam (M) 526 31
H: 5 9 W: 12 06 b.Wolverhampton 10-9-91
Internationals: Egypt Full caps.

2009–10	Port Vale	1 0	
2010–11	Port Vale	16 1	
2011–12	Port Vale	26 1	
2012–13	Port Vale	28 2	71 4
2013–14	Chesterfield	34 1	
2014–15	Chesterfield	39 2	
2015–16	Chesterfield	26 4	99 7
2015–16	Wigan Ath	16 1	
2016–17	Wigan Ath	15 1	
2016–17	*Barnsley*	14 0	14 0
2017–18	Wigan Ath	41 0	
2018–19	Wigan Ath	40 1	
2019–20	Wigan Ath	43 3	155 8
2020–21	Middlesbrough	31 1	
2021–22	Middlesbrough	3 0	34 1
2021–22	Ipswich T	34 3	
2022–23	Ipswich T	44 4	
2023–24	Ipswich T	42 3	
2024–25	Ipswich T	33 1	153 11

MURIC, Arijanet (G) 121 0
H: 6 6 W: 12 11 b.Zurich 7-11-98
Internationals: Montenegro U21. Kosovo Full caps.

2017–18	Manchester C	0 0	
2018–19	Manchester C	0 0	
2018–19	*NAC Breda*	1 0	1 0
2019–20	Manchester C	0 0	
2019–20	*Nottingham F*	4 0	4 0
2020–21	Manchester C	0 0	
2020–21	*Girona*	2 0	2 0
2020–21	*Willem II*	14 0	14 0
2021–22	Manchester C	0 0	
2021–22	*Adana Demirspor*	31 0	31 0
2022–23	Burnley	41 0	
2023–24	Burnley	10 0	51 0
2024–25	Ipswich T	18 0	18 0

NWABUEZE, Jesse (F) 0 0
H: 6 0 W: 12 00 b.27-9-03

2024–25	Ipswich T	0 0	

O'SHEA, Dara (D) 193 11
H: 6 1 W: 10 03 b.Dublin 4-3-99
Internationals: Republic of Ireland U18, U19, U21, Full caps.

2018–19	WBA	0 0	
2018–19	*Exeter C*	27 0	27 0
2019–20	WBA	17 3	
2020–21	WBA	28 0	
2021–22	WBA	14 2	
2022–23	WBA	37 2	96 7
2023–24	Burnley	33 3	
2024–25	Burnley	2 1	35 4
2024–25	Ipswich T	35 0	35 0

OGBENE, Chiedozie (M) 219 27
H: 5 11 W: 11 11 b.Lagos 1-5-97
Internationals: Republic of Ireland Full caps.

2015	Cork C	1 0	
2016	Cork C	8 3	9 3
2017	Limerick	24 8	32 8
2017–18	Brentford	2 0	
2018–19	Brentford	4 0	6 0
2018–19	*Exeter C*	14 0	14 0
2019–20	Rotherham U	25 1	
2020–21	Rotherham U	11 0	
2021–22	Rotherham U	45 3	
2022–23	Rotherham U	39 8	120 12
2023–24	Luton T	30 4	
2024–25	Luton T	3 0	33 4
2024–25	Ipswich T	5 0	5 0

OUDNIE-MORGAN, Rio (M) 0 0
H: 5 10 b.Welwyn Garden City 6-12-05
Internationals: Northern Ireland U17, U19.

2024–25	Ipswich T	0 0	

PALMER, Alex (G) 199 0
H: 6 3 W: 11 05 b.Kidderminster 10-8-96
Internationals: England U16.

2014–15	WBA	0 0	
2015–16	WBA	0 0	
2016–17	WBA	0 0	
2017–18	WBA	0 0	
2018–19	WBA	0 0	
2018–19	*Oldham Ath*	1 0	1 0
2018–19	*Notts Co*	1 0	1 0
2019–20	WBA	0 0	
2019–20	*Plymouth Arg*	37 0	37 0
2020–21	WBA	0 0	

2020–21	*Lincoln C*	46 0	46 0
2021–22	WBA	0 0	
2021–22	*Luton T*	2 0	2 0
2022–23	WBA	23 0	
2023–24	WBA	46 0	
2024–25	WBA	30 0	99 0
2024–25	Ipswich T	13 0	13 0

PHILOGENE-BIDACE, Jayden (M) 104 19
H: 5 9 W: 10 01 b.Hammersmith 18-5-02
Internationals: England U19, U20, U21.

2020–21	Aston Villa	1 0	
2021–22	Aston Villa	1 0	
2021–22	*Stoke C*	11 1	11 1
2022–23	Aston Villa	0 0	
2022–23	*Cardiff C*	37 4	37 4
2023–24	Aston Villa	1 0	
2023–24	*Hull C*	32 12	32 12
2024–25	Aston Villa	11 0	14 0
2024–25	Ipswich T	10 2	10 2

SLICKER, Cieran (G) 0 0
H: 6 3 W: 12 13 b.Oldham 15-9-02
Internationals: Scotland U17, U18, U21, Full caps.

2020–21	Manchester C	0 0	
2021–22	Manchester C	0 0	
2022–23	Manchester C	0 0	
2022–23	*Rochdale*	0 0	
2023–24	Ipswich T	0 0	
2024–25	Ipswich T	0 0	

SZMODICS, Sammie (M) 333 97
H: 5 6 W: 10 01 b.Colchester 24-9-95
Internationals: Republic of Ireland Full caps.

2013–14	Colchester U	7 0	
2014–15	Colchester U	31 4	
2015–16	Colchester U	5 0	
2016–17	Colchester U	19 5	
2017–18	Colchester U	37 12	
2018–19	Colchester U	43 14	142 35
2019–20	*Bristol C*	3 0	3 0
2019–20	Peterborough U	10 4	
2020–21	Peterborough U	42 15	
2021–22	Peterborough U	36 6	
2022–23	Peterborough U	1 0	89 25
2022–23	Blackburn R	34 5	
2023–24	Blackburn R	44 27	
2024–25	Blackburn R	1 1	79 33
2024–25	Ipswich T	20 4	20 4

TAYLOR, Jack (D) 242 22
H: 6 1 W: 11 00 b.Hammersmith 23-6-98
Internationals: Republic of Ireland U21, Full caps.

2016–17	Barnet	14 0	
2017–18	Barnet	38 2	52 2

From Barnet.

2019–20	Peterborough U	11 2	
2020–21	Peterborough U	36 4	
2021–22	Peterborough U	34 3	
2022–23	Peterborough U	44 8	125 17
2023–24	Ipswich T	33 2	
2024–25	Ipswich T	32 1	65 3

TAYLOR, Tom (F) 0 0

2024–25	Ipswich T	0 0	

TOWNSEND, Conor (D) 330 9
H: 5 4 W: 9 11 b.Hessle 4-3-93

2011–12	Hull C	0 0	
2012–13	Hull C	0 0	
2012–13	*Chesterfield*	20 1	20 1
2013–14	Hull C	0 0	
2013–14	*Carlisle U*	12 0	12 0
2014–15	Hull C	0 0	
2014–15	*Dundee U*	17 0	17 0
2014–15	*Scunthorpe U*	6 0	
2015–16	Hull C	0 0	
2015–16	Scunthorpe U	20 1	
2016–17	Scunthorpe U	24 0	
2017–18	Scunthorpe U	30 4	80 5
2018–19	WBA	12 0	
2019–20	WBA	27 0	
2020–21	WBA	25 0	
2021–22	WBA	43 0	
2022–23	WBA	46 3	
2023–24	WBA	42 0	195 3
2024–25	Ipswich T	6 0	6 0

TUANZEBE, Axel (D) 103 0
H: 6 0 W: 11 11 b.Bunia 14-11-97
Internationals: England U19, U20, U21. DR Congo Full caps.

2015–16	Manchester U	0 0	
2016–17	Manchester U	4 0	
2017–18	Manchester U	1 0	
2017–18	*Aston Villa*	5 0	
2018–19	Manchester U	0 0	
2018–19	*Aston Villa*	25 0	
2019–20	Manchester U	5 0	
2020–21	Manchester U	9 0	
2021–22	Manchester U	0 0	
2021–22	*Aston Villa*	9 0	39 0
2021–22	*Napoli*	1 0	1 0
2022–23	Manchester U	0 0	19 0

2022–23 *Stoke C* 4 0 **4 0**
2023–24 Ipswich T 18 0
2024–25 Ipswich T 22 0 **40 0**

WALTON, Christian (G) 244 0
H: 6 0 W: 11 11 b.Wadebridge 9-11-95
Internationals: England U19, U20, U21.
2011–12 Plymouth Arg 0 0
2012–13 Plymouth Arg 0 0
2013–14 Brighton & HA 0 0
2014–15 Brighton & HA 3 0
2015–16 Brighton & HA 0 0
2015–16 *Bury* 4 0 **4 0**
2015–16 *Plymouth Arg* 4 0 **4 0**
2016–17 Brighton & HA 0 0
2016–17 *Luton T* 27 0 **27 0**
2016–17 *Southend U* 7 0 **7 0**
2017–18 Brighton & HA 0 0
2017–18 *Wigan Ath* 31 0
2018–19 Brighton & HA 0 0
2018–19 *Wigan Ath* 34 0 **65 0**
2019–20 Brighton & HA 0 0
2019–20 *Blackburn R* 46 0 **46 0**
2020–21 Brighton & HA 0 0 **3 0**
2021–22 *Ipswich T* 34 0
2022–23 Ipswich T 46 0
2023–24 Ipswich T 1 0
2024–25 Ipswich T 7 0 **88 0**

WOOLFENDEN, Luke (D) 219 7
H: 6 4 W: 11 00 b.Ipswich 21-10-98
2017–18 Ipswich T 2 0
2018–19 Ipswich T 1 0
2018–19 *Swindon T* 32 2 **32 2**
2019–20 Ipswich T 31 1
2020–21 Ipswich T 25 1
2021–22 Ipswich T 31 0
2022–23 Ipswich T 41 2
2023–24 Ipswich T 41 1
2024–25 Ipswich T 15 0 **187 5**

Players retained or with offer of contract
Babb, Daniel Elijah; Barbrook, Finley Frank; Boatswain, Ashley Frank; Boswell, Ashton Luke; Carr, Ryan George; Compton, Matthew Charles; Elliott, Leon Levi; Eze, Nelson Chudi; Gray, Henry Merson Leonard; Mazionis, Jokubas; Mendel, Tudor Olorunninbe; Onuchukwu, Abube Calvin; Pitts, Joshua Nathaniel; Turner, Steven Jack; Valentine, Nico Andre; Williamson, Woody Scott.

Scholars
Adebayo, Afikunoluwa Emmanuel (Offer Contract); Brouwers, Stevy Joshua; Chukwu-Nsofor, Jackson; Eldred, Sidney Christopher; Fletcher, William Mark; Heard, Fraser William (Offer Contract); Lewis, Joshua James (Offer Contract); Longwe, Usisya Tyrese; Mauge, James Carlton (Offer Contract); McCann, Darragh Francis; Nicolaou, Shakil; O'Sullivan, Lenny John; Sains, Bobby Barrie; Unadike, William Chika.

LEEDS U (44)

AARONSON, Brenden (M) 206 28
H: 5 10 W: 10 06 b.Medford 22-10-00
Internationals: USA U23, Full caps.
2017 Philadelphia Union 0 0
2018 Philadelphia Union 0 0
2019 Philadelphia Union 28 3
2020 Philadelphia Union 20 4 **48 7**
2020–21 Red Bull Salzburg 20 5
2021–22 Red Bull Salzburg 26 4 **46 9**
2022–23 Leeds U 36 1
2023–24 Leeds U 0 0
2023–24 *Union Berlin* 30 2 **30 2**
2024–25 Leeds U 46 9 **82 10**

AMPADU, Ethan (M) 173 1
H: 6 0 W: 11 05 b.Exeter 14-9-00
Internationals: England U16, Wales U17, U19, Full caps.
2016–17 Exeter C 8 0 **8 0**
2017–18 Chelsea 1 0
2018–19 Chelsea 0 0
2019–20 Chelsea 0 0
2019–20 *RB Leipzig* 3 0 **3 0**
2020–21 Chelsea 0 0
2020–21 *Sheffield U* 25 0 **25 0**
2021–22 Chelsea 0 0
2021–22 *Venezia* 29 0 **29 0**
2022–23 Chelsea 0 0 **1 0**
2022–23 *Spezia* 32 1 **32 1**
2023–24 Leeds U 46 0
2024–25 Leeds U 29 0 **75 0**

BAMFORD, Patrick (F) 356 111
H: 6 1 W: 11 03 b.Newark 5-9-93
Internationals: Republic of Ireland U18. England U18, U19, U21, Full caps.
2010–11 Nottingham F 0 0
2011–12 Nottingham F 2 0 **2 0**
2011–12 Chelsea 0 0
2012–13 Chelsea 0 0
2012–13 *Milton Keynes D* 14 4
2013–14 Chelsea 0 0
2013–14 *Milton Keynes D* 23 14 **37 18**
2013–14 *Derby Co* 21 8 **21 8**
2014–15 Chelsea 0 0
2014–15 *Middlesbrough* 38 17
2015–16 Chelsea 0 0
2015–16 *Crystal Palace* 6 0 **6 0**
2015–16 *Norwich C* 7 0 **7 0**
2016–17 Chelsea 0 0
2016–17 *Burnley* 6 0 **6 0**
2016–17 *Middlesbrough* 8 1
2017–18 Middlesbrough 39 11 **85 29**
2018–19 Leeds U 22 9
2019–20 Leeds U 45 16
2020–21 Leeds U 38 17
2021–22 Leeds U 9 2
2022–23 Leeds U 28 4
2023–24 Leeds U 33 8
2024–25 Leeds U 17 0 **192 56**

BOGLE, Jayden (D) 209 19
H: 5 10 W: 10 12 b.Reading 27-7-00
Internationals: England U20.
2017–18 Derby Co 0 0
2018–19 Derby Co 40 2
2019–20 Derby Co 37 1 **77 3**
2020–21 Sheffield U 16 2
2021–22 Sheffield U 18 3
2022–23 Sheffield U 20 2
2023–24 Sheffield U 34 3 **88 10**
2024–25 Leeds U 44 6 **44 6**

BYRAM, Samuel (D) 279 13
H: 5 11 W: 11 05 b.Thurrock 16-9-93
2012–13 Leeds U 44 3
2013–14 Leeds U 25 0
2014–15 Leeds U 39 3
2015–16 Leeds U 22 3
2015–16 West Ham U 4 0
2016–17 West Ham U 18 0
2017–18 West Ham U 5 0
2018–19 West Ham U 0 0 **27 0**
2018–19 *Nottingham F* 6 0 **6 0**
2019–20 Norwich C 17 0
2020–21 Norwich C 0 0
2021–22 Norwich C 15 0
2022–23 Norwich C 15 1 **47 1**
2023–24 Leeds U 33 2
2024–25 Leeds U 36 1 **199 12**

CAIRNS, Alex (G) 279 0
H: 6 0 W: 11 05 b.Doncaster 4-1-93
2011–12 Leeds U 1 0
2012–13 Leeds U 0 0
2013–14 Leeds U 0 0
2014–15 Leeds U 0 0
2015–16 Chesterfield 0 0
2015–16 Rotherham U 0 0
2016–17 Fleetwood T 30 0
2017–18 Fleetwood T 38 0
2018–19 Fleetwood T 46 0
2019–20 Fleetwood T 25 0
2020–21 Fleetwood T 28 0
2021–22 Fleetwood T 42 0
2022–23 Fleetwood T 0 0 **209 0**
2022–23 *Hartlepool U* 0 0
2022–23 *Salford C* 23 0
2023–24 Salford C 46 0 **69 0**
2024–25 Leeds U 0 0 **1 0**

CHAMBERS, Sam (M) 1 0
H: 5 9 W: 10 10 b. 18-8-07
Internationals: Scotland U16, U17.
2024–25 Leeds U 1 0 **1 0**

CHRISTY, Harry (G) 0 0
H: 6 2 b.Harrogate 19-10-03
2023–24 Leeds U 0 0
2024–25 Leeds U 0 0

COOK, Robert (G) 0 0
H: 6 2 W: 11 11 b. 27-1-07
2023–24 Perth Glory 0 0
2024–25 Perth Glory 0 0
2024–25 Leeds U 0 0

CREW, Charlie (M) 14 0
H: 6 1 b.Cardiff 15-6-06
Internationals: Wales U16, U17, U19, U21, Full caps.
2023–24 Leeds U 0 0
2024–25 Leeds U 1 0 **1 0**
2024–25 *Doncaster R* 13 0 **13 0**

DARLOW, Karl (G) 222 0
H: 6 1 W: 12 06 b.Northampton 8-10-90
Internationals: Wales Full caps.
2009–10 Nottingham F 0 0
2010–11 Nottingham F 1 0
2011–12 Nottingham F 0 0
2012–13 Nottingham F 20 0
2012–13 *Walsall* 9 0 **9 0**
2013–14 Nottingham F 43 0
2014–15 Newcastle U 0 0
2014–15 *Nottingham F* 42 0 **106 0**
2015–16 Newcastle U 9 0
2016–17 Newcastle U 34 0
2017–18 Newcastle U 10 0
2018–19 Newcastle U 0 0
2019–20 Newcastle U 0 0
2020–21 Newcastle U 25 0
2021–22 Newcastle U 8 0
2022–23 Newcastle U 0 0 **86 0**
2022–23 *Hull C* 12 0 **12 0**
2023–24 Leeds U 2 0
2024–25 Leeds U 7 0 **9 0**

DEBAYO, James (D) 1 0
H: 6 2 W: 11 03 b.London 11-7-05
Internationals: England U17, U18.
From Watford.
2022–23 Leeds U 0 0
2023–24 Leeds U 0 0
2024–25 Leeds U 1 0 **1 0**

FERNANDEZ, Mateo (F) 62 4
H: 5 11 W: 11 11 b.Santander 19-10-03
Internationals: England U20. Spain U21.
From Espanyol.
2022–23 Leeds U 3 0
2023–24 Leeds U 20 1
2024–25 Leeds U 39 3 **62 4**

FIRPO, Junior (D) 163 12
H: 6 0 W: 12 04 b.Santo Domingo 22-8-96
Internationals: Dominican Republic Full caps. Spain U21.
2014–15 Real Betis 0 0
2015–16 Real Betis 0 0
2016–17 Real Betis 0 0
2017–18 Real Betis 14 2
2018–19 Real Betis 24 3 **38 5**
2019–20 Barcelona 17 1
2020–21 Barcelona 7 1 **24 2**
2021–22 Leeds U 24 0
2022–23 Leeds U 19 1
2023–24 Leeds U 26 0
2024–25 Leeds U 32 4 **101 5**

GELHARDT, Joe (F) 104 11
H: 5 10 W: 11 03 b.Liverpool 4-5-02
Internationals: England U16, U17, U18, U20.
2018–19 Wigan Ath 1 0
2019–20 Wigan Ath 18 1 **19 1**
2020–21 Leeds U 0 0
2021–22 Leeds U 20 2
2022–23 Leeds U 15 0
2022–23 *Sunderland* 18 3 **18 3**
2023–24 Leeds U 10 0
2024–25 Leeds U 2 0 **47 2**
2024–25 *Hull C* 20 5 **20 5**

GNONTO, Wilfried (F) 168 28
H: 5 7 W: 10 03 b.Verbania 5-11-03
Internationals: Italy U16, U17, U18, U19, U21, Full caps.
2020–21 Zurich 26 1
2021–22 Zurich 33 8
2022–23 Zurich 6 0 **65 9**
2022–23 Leeds U 24 2
2023–24 Leeds U 36 8
2024–25 Leeds U 43 9 **103 19**

GRAY, Harry (F) 1 0
b. 8-10-08
Internationals: England U16, U17.
2024–25 Leeds U 1 0 **1 0**

GREENWOOD, Sam (F) 101 11
H: 5 11 W: 10 01 b.Sunderland 26-1-02
Internationals: England U16, U17, U18, U19, U20, U21.
2019–20 Arsenal 0 0
2020–21 Leeds U 0 0
2021–22 Leeds U 7 0
2022–23 Leeds U 18 1
2023–24 Leeds U 1 0
2023–24 *Middlesbrough* 37 5 **37 5**
2024–25 Leeds U 0 0 **26 1**
2024–25 *Preston NE* 38 5 **38 5**

GRUEV, Ilia (M) 111 1
H: 6 1 W: 11 05 b.Sofia 6-5-00
Internationals: Bulgaria U17, U18, U19, U21, Full caps.
2019–20 Werder Bremen 0 0
2020–21 Werder Bremen 1 0
2021–22 Werder Bremen 26 1
2022–23 Werder Bremen 31 0
2023–24 Werder Bremen 1 0 **59 1**
2023–24 Leeds U 29 0
2024–25 Leeds U 23 0 **52 0**

GUILAVOGUI, Josuha (M) 353 16
H: 6 2 W: 12 04 b.Ollioules 19-9-90
Internationals: France U21, Full caps.
2009–10 Saint-Etienne 2 0
2010–11 Saint-Etienne 22 1
2011–12 Saint-Etienne 32 2
2012–13 Saint-Etienne 38 3

2013–14	Saint-Etienne	9	0	103	6
2013–14	Atletico Madrid	1	0		
2014–15	Atletico Madrid	0	0		
2014–15	VfL Wolfsburg	27	1		
2015–16	Atletico Madrid	0	0	1	0
2015–16	VfL Wolfsburg	30	2		
2016–17	VfL Wolfsburg	19	0		
2017–18	VfL Wolfsburg	29	3		
2018–19	VfL Wolfsburg	19	2		
2019–20	VfL Wolfsburg	20	0		
2020–21	VfL Wolfsburg	15	0		
2021–22	VfL Wolfsburg	15	0		
2021–22	*Bordeaux*	15	1	15	1
2022–23	VfL Wolfsburg	23	1	207	9
2023–24	Mainz 05	11	0		
2024–25	Leeds U	16	0	16	0

GYABI, Darko (M) 55 1
H: 6 5 W: 12 08 b.London 18-2-04
Internationals: England U16, U18, U19, U20, U21.

2020–21	Manchester C	0	0		
2021–22	Manchester C	0	0		
2022–23	Leeds U	1	0		
2023–24	Leeds U	1	0		
2023–24	*Plymouth Arg*	10	0		
2024–25	Leeds U	0	0	2	0
2024–25	*Plymouth Arg*	43	1	53	1

HARRISON, Jack (M) 312 49
H: 5 9 W: 11 03 b.Stoke-on-Trent 20-11-96
Internationals: England U21.

2016	New York City	21	4		
2017	New York City	34	10	55	14
2017–18	Manchester C	0	0		
2017–18	Middlesbrough	4	0	4	0
2018–19	Manchester C	0	0		
2018–19	*Leeds U*	37	4		
2019–20	Manchester C	0	0		
2019–20	*Leeds U*	46	6		
2020–21	Manchester C	0	0		
2020–21	*Leeds U*	36	8		
2021–22	Leeds U	35	8		
2022–23	Leeds U	36	5		
2023–24	*Everton*	29	3		
2024–25	Leeds U	0	0	190	31
2024–25	*Everton*	34	1	63	4

JAMES, Daniel (M) 215 41
H: 5 11 W: 12 00 b.Kingston upon Hull 10-11-97
Internationals: Wales U17, U19, U20, U21, Full caps.
Full Hull C.

2015–16	Swansea C	0	0		
2016–17	Swansea C	0	0		
2017–18	Swansea C	0	0		
2017–18	*Shrewsbury T*	0	0		
2018–19	Swansea C	33	4	33	4
2019–20	Manchester U	33	3		
2020–21	Manchester U	15	3		
2021–22	Manchester U	2	0	50	6
2021–22	Leeds U	32	4		
2022–23	Leeds U	4	0		
2022–23	*Fulham*	20	2	20	2
2023–24	Leeds U	40	13		
2024–25	Leeds U	36	12	112	29

MESLIER, Illan (G) 228 0
H: 6 6 W: 11 09 b.Lorient 2-3-00
Internationals: France U18, U19, U20, U21.

2016–17	Lorient	0	0		
2017–18	Lorient	0	0		
2018–19	Lorient	28	0		
2019–20	Lorient	0	0	28	0
2019–20	*Leeds U*	10	0		
2020–21	Leeds U	35	0		
2021–22	Leeds U	38	0		
2022–23	Leeds U	34	0		
2023–24	Leeds U	44	0		
2024–25	Leeds U	39	0	200	0

MOORE, Kris (D) 0 0
H: 6 1 W: 11 05 b.Leeds 13-11-03

2021–22	Leeds U	0	0		
2022–23	Leeds U	0	0		
2023–24	Leeds U	0	0		
2024–25	Leeds U	0	0		

MULLEN, Jeremiah (D) 3 0
H: 5 10 b.Leeds 17-6-04
Internationals: Scotland U19, U21.
From Liverpool.

2022–23	Leeds U	0	0		
2023–24	Leeds U	0	0		
2023–24	*Inverness CT*	3	0	3	0
2024–25	Leeds U	0	0		

Transferred to Dunfermline Ath, February 2025.

PERKINS, Sonny (M) 35 4
H: 5 10 W: 11 11 b.Waltham Forest 10-2-04
Internationals: England U16, U18, U19.

2021–22	West Ham U	1	0	1	0

2022–23	Leeds U	0	0		
2023–24	Leeds U	1	0		
2023–24	*Oxford U*	3	0	3	0
2024–25	Leeds U	0	0	1	0
2024–25	*Leyton Orient*	30	4	30	4

PIROE, Joel (F) 208 76
H: 6 1 W: 11 09 b.Wijchen, Netherlands 2-8-99
Internationals: Netherlands U16, U18, U19, U20.

2016–17	PSV Eindhoven	0	0		
2017–18	PSV Eindhoven	0	0		
2018–19	PSV Eindhoven	0	0		
2019–20	PSV Eindhoven	0	0		
2019–20	*Sparta Rotterdam*	18	2	18	2
2020–21	PSV Eindhoven	11	1	11	1
2021–22	Swansea C	45	22		
2022–23	Swansea C	43	19		
2023–24	Swansea C	3	0	91	41
2023–24	*Leeds U*	42	13		
2024–25	Leeds U	46	19	88	32

RAMAZANI, Largie (F) 146 24
H: 5 6 W: 9 06 b.Berchem-Sainte-Agathe 27-2-01
Internationals: Belgium U17, U18, U19, U21. From Charlton Ath.

2019–20	Manchester U	0	0		
2020–21	Almeria	25	4		
2021–22	Almeria	30	8		
2022–23	Almeria	33	3		
2023–24	Almeria	29	3		
2024–25	Almeria	0	0	117	18
2024–25	Leeds U	29	6	29	6

RODON, Joe (D) 184 2
H: 6 4 W: 12 08 b.Swansea 22-10-97
Internationals: Wales U20, U21, Full caps.

2015–16	Swansea C	0	0		
2016–17	Swansea C	0	0		
2017–18	Swansea C	0	0		
2017–18	*Cheltenham T*	12	0	12	0
2018–19	Swansea C	27	0		
2019–20	Swansea C	21	0		
2020–21	Swansea C	4	0	52	0
2020–21	Tottenham H	12	0		
2021–22	Tottenham H	3	0		
2022–23	Tottenham H	0	0		
2022–23	*Rennes*	16	1	16	1
2023–24	Tottenham H	0	0	15	0
2023–24	*Leeds U*	43	0		
2024–25	Leeds U	46	1	89	1

SCHMIDT, Isaac (M) 118 6
H: 5 8 W: 11 00 b.Lausanne 7-12-99
Internationals: Switzerland U21, Full caps.

2019–20	Lausanne-Sport	7	0		
2020–21	Lausanne-Sport	7	0	14	0
2021–22	St Gallen	25	1		
2022–23	St Gallen	34	2		
2023–24	St Gallen	34	2		
2024–25	St Gallen	4	1	92	6
2024–25	Leeds U	12	0	12	0

STRUIJK, Pascal (D) 148 12
H: 6 3 W: 12 06 b.Deurne 11-8-99
Internationals: Netherlands U17.
From Ajax.

2017–18	Leeds U	0	0		
2018–19	Leeds U	0	0		
2019–20	Leeds U	5	0		
2020–21	Leeds U	27	1		
2021–22	Leeds U	29	1		
2022–23	Leeds U	29	2		
2023–24	Leeds U	23	3		
2024–25	Leeds U	35	5	148	12

TANAKA, Ao (M) 206 22
H: 5 11 W: 11 09 b.Miyamae-ku 10-9-98
Internationals: Japan U23, Full caps.

2018	Kawasaki Frontale	4	1		
2019	Kawasaki Frontale	24	1		
2020	Kawasaki Frontale	31	5		
2021	Kawasaki Frontale	20	1	79	8
2021–22	*Fortuna Dusseldorf*	29	1		
2022–23	*Fortuna Dusseldorf*	22	1		
2023–24	*Fortuna Dusseldorf*	30	7		
2024–25	*Fortuna Dusseldorf*	3	0	84	9
2024–25	Leeds U	43	5	43	5

WOBER, Maximilian (D) 183 10
H: 6 2 W: 12 13 b.Vienna 4-2-98
Internationals: Austria U16, U17, U18, U19, Full caps.

2015–16	Rapid Vienna	0	0		
2016–17	Rapid Vienna	11	0		
2017–18	Rapid Vienna	5	1	16	1
2017–18	Ajax	22	1		
2018–19	Ajax	8	0	30	1
2018–19	*Sevilla*	7	0	7	0
2019–20	Red Bull Salzburg	24	0		
2020–21	Red Bull Salzburg	20	0		
2021–22	Red Bull Salzburg	22	4		
2022–23	Red Bull Salzburg	15	1	81	5
2022–23	Leeds U	16	0		
2023–24	Leeds U	0	0		
2023–24	*Borussia M'gladbach*	25	2	25	2
2024–25	Leeds U	8	1	24	1

Players retained or with offer of contract
Chadwick, Rhys Alexander; Cresswell, Alfie Wesley; Douglas, Connor Lee; Kristensen, Rasmus Nissen; Lopata-White, Reuben; Mahady, Rory Alexander; McDonald, Joshua William; Ombang, Darryl Merveil; Pinheiro Monteiro, Diogo; Pirie, Lewis.

Scholars
Baird, Alexander James; Billett, Joseph Derek; Bird, Coban Rocket; Brockie, Devon; Brown, Lleyton William; Dudley, Louie Reuben; Firth, William Jamie; Grainger, Owen John; Hamilton, Joshua Thomas; Kenyon, George Patrick; Lane, Freddie Daniel; Matykiewicz, Luke; Morris, Jack Lewis; Pickles, Oliver Craig; Render, Jacob Davis; Vincent, Harvey Jake; Wamba Simo, Elton.

LEICESTER C (45)

ALUKO, Olabade (D) 1 0
b. 30-11-06

2024–25	Leicester C	1	0	1	0

ALVES, Will (M) 15 1
H: 6 4 W: 13 01 b.Leicester 3-2-05
Internationals: England U17, U18, U20.

2021–22	Leicester C	0	0		
2022–23	Leicester C	0	0		
2023–24	Leicester C	0	0		
2024–25	Leicester C	1	0	1	0
2024–25	*Cardiff C*	14	1	14	1

AYEW, Jordan (F) 485 75
H: 6 0 W: 12 11 b.Marseille 11-9-91
Internationals: Ghana U20, Full caps.

2009–10	Marseille	4	1		
2010–11	Marseille	22	2		
2011–12	Marseille	34	3		
2012–13	Marseille	35	7		
2013–14	Marseille	16	1	111	14
2013–14	*Sochaux*	17	5	17	5
2014–15	*Lorient*	31	12	31	12
2015–16	Aston Villa	30	7		
2016–17	Aston Villa	21	2	51	9
2016–17	Swansea C	14	1		
2017–18	Swansea C	36	7		
2018–19	Swansea C	0	0	50	8
2018–19	*Crystal Palace*	20	1		
2019–20	Crystal Palace	37	9		
2020–21	Crystal Palace	33	1		
2021–22	Crystal Palace	31	3		
2022–23	Crystal Palace	38	4		
2023–24	Crystal Palace	35	4		
2024–25	Crystal Palace	1	0	195	22
2024–25	Leicester C	30	5	30	5

BRAYBROOKE, Sammy (M) 7 0
H: 5 10 W: 10 03 b.Leicester 12-3-04
Internationals: England U18, U19, U20.

2021–22	Leicester C	0	0		
2022–23	Leicester C	0	0		
2023–24	Leicester C	0	0		
2024–25	Leicester C	0	0		
2024–25	*Dundee*	7	0	7	0

BRIGGS, Logan (M) 0 0
b.Northampton 7-2-05
Internationals: Wales U21.

2023–24	Leicester C	0	0		
2024–25	Leicester C	0	0		

CARTWRIGHT, Henry (M) 0 0
H: 5 10 W: 10 08 b. 11-12-04

2024–25	Leicester C	0	0		

CHOUDHURY, Hamza (M) 169 1
H: 5 10 W: 10 01 b.Loughborough 1-10-97
Internationals: England U21. Bangladesh Full caps.

2015–16	Leicester C	0	0		
2015–16	*Burton Alb*	13	0		
2016–17	Leicester C	0	0		
2016–17	*Burton Alb*	13	0	26	0
2017–18	Leicester C	8	0		
2018–19	Leicester C	9	0		
2019–20	Leicester C	20	1		
2020–21	Leicester C	10	0		
2021–22	Leicester C	6	0		
2022–23	Leicester C	0	0		
2022–23	*Watford*	36	0	36	0
2023–24	Leicester C	34	0		
2024–25	Leicester C	4	0	91	1
2024–25	*Sheffield U*	16	0	16	0

COADY, Conor (D) 416 16
H: 6 1 W: 11 11 b.Liverpool 25-2-93
Internationals: England U16, U17, U18, U19, U20, Full caps.

2010–11	Liverpool	0	0		

2011–12 Liverpool 0 0
2012–13 Liverpool 1 0
2013–14 Liverpool 0 0 **1 0**
2013–14 *Sheffield U* 39 5 **39 5**
2014–15 Huddersfield T 45 3 **45 3**
2015–16 Wolverhampton W 37 0
2016–17 Wolverhampton W 40 0
2017–18 Wolverhampton W 45 1
2018–19 Wolverhampton W 38 0
2019–20 Wolverhampton W 38 0
2020–21 Wolverhampton W 37 1
2021–22 Wolverhampton W 38 4
2022–23 Wolverhampton W 0 0 **273 6**
2022–23 *Everton* 24 1 **24 1**
2023–24 Leicester C 12 0
2024–25 Leicester C 22 1 **34 1**

COULIBALY, Woyo (D) 125 1
H: 6 2 W: 12 02 b.Gonesse 26-5-99
Internationals: Mali Full caps.
2019–20 Le Havre 11 0
2020–21 Le Havre 26 0
2021–22 Le Havre 2 0 **39 0**
2021–22 *Parma* 22 0
2022–23 Parma 20 1
2023–24 Parma 26 0
2024–25 Parma 14 0 **82 1**
2024–25 Leicester C 4 0 **4 0**

COVER, Brandon (M) 27 2
H: 6 2 W: 12 00 b.Colchester 25-9-03
Internationals: Jamaica U23, Full caps.
2023–24 Leicester C 0 0
2024–25 Leicester C 0 0
2024–25 *Port Vale* 19 2 **19 2**
2024–25 *Fleetwood T* 8 0 **8 0**

DAKA, Patson (F) 205 77
H: 6 0 W: 11 03 b.Kafue 9-10-98
Internationals: Zambia U17, U20, Full caps.
2016–17 Kafue Celtic 0 0
2016–17 *Liefering* 9 2
2017–18 Red Bull Salzburg 8 0
2017–18 *Liefering* 18 4 **27 6**
2018–19 Red Bull Salzburg 15 3
2019–20 Red Bull Salzburg 31 24
2020–21 Red Bull Salzburg 28 27 **82 54**
2021–22 Leicester C 23 5
2022–23 Leicester C 30 4
2023–24 Leicester C 20 7
2024–25 Leicester C 23 1 **96 17**

DECORDOVA-REID, Bobby (M) 411 64
H: 5 7 W: 10 10 b.Bristol 2-2-93
Internationals: Jamaica Full caps.
2010–11 Bristol C 1 0
2011–12 Bristol C 0 0
2011–12 *Cheltenham T* 1 0 **1 0**
2012–13 Bristol C 4 1
2012–13 *Oldham Ath* 7 0 **7 0**
2013–14 Bristol C 24 1
2014–15 Bristol C 2 0
2014–15 *Plymouth Arg* 33 3 **33 3**
2015–16 Bristol C 28 2
2016–17 Bristol C 30 3
2017–18 Bristol C 46 19 **135 26**
2018–19 Cardiff C 27 5
2019–20 Cardiff C 1 0 **28 5**
2019–20 Fulham 41 6
2020–21 Fulham 33 5
2021–22 Fulham 41 8
2022–23 Fulham 36 4
2023–24 Fulham 33 6 **184 29**
2024–25 Leicester C 23 1 **23 1**

EL KHANNOUS, Bilal (M) 110 6
H: 5 11 W: 11 00 b.Strombeek 10-5-04
Internationals: Belgium U16, U18. Morocco U20, U23, Full caps.
2021–22 Genk 1 0
2022–23 Genk 39 1
2023–24 Genk 37 3
2024–25 Genk 1 0 **78 4**
2024–25 Leicester C 32 2 **32 2**

EVANS, Jake (F) 4 0
b. 21-8-08
Internationals: England U16.
2024–25 Leicester C 4 0 **4 0**

FAES, Wout (D) 261 10
H: 6 2 W: 13 03 b.Mol 3-4-98
Internationals: Belgium U17, U19, U21, Full caps.
2015–16 Anderlecht 0 0
2016–17 Anderlecht 0 0
2016–17 *Heerenveen* 7 0 **7 0**
2017–18 Anderlecht 0 0
2017–18 *Excelsior* 19 0 **19 0**
2018–19 Oostende 26 1
2019–20 Oostende 28 0 **54 1**
2020–21 Reims 33 1
2021–22 Reims 37 4
2022–23 Reims 3 0 **73 5**
2022–23 Leicester C 31 1
2023–24 Leicester C 43 2
2024–25 Leicester C 34 1 **108 4**

FATAWU, Issahaku (D) 91 32
H: 5 10 W: 11 07 b.Tamale 8-3-04
Internationals: Ghana U17, U20, U23, Full caps.
2019–20 Steadfast 13 8
2020–21 Steadfast 14 12
2021–22 Steadfast 0 0 **27 20**
2021–22 *Dreams* 7 6 **7 6**
2022–23 Sporting Lisbon 6 0
2023–24 Sporting Lisbon 0 0 **6 0**
2023–24 *Leicester C* 40 6
2024–25 Leicester C 11 0 **51 6**

GOLDING, Michael (M) 1 0
H: 5 11 W: 9 13 b.Kingston upon Thames 23-5-06
Internationals: England U16, U17, U18, U19.
2022–23 Chelsea 0 0
2023–24 Chelsea 0 0
2024–25 Leicester C 1 0 **1 0**

HERMANSEN, Mads (G) 127 0
H: 6 2 W: 12 11 b.Odense 11-7-00
Internationals: Denmark U16, U17, U18, U19, U21.
2020–21 Brondby 0 0
2021–22 Brondby 29 0
2022–23 Brondby 27 0 **56 0**
2023–24 Leicester C 44 0
2024–25 Leicester C 27 0 **71 0**

IVERSEN, Daniel (G) 180 0
H: 6 5 W: 12 08 b.Gording 19-7-97
Internationals: Denmark U16, U17, U18, U19, U20, U21.
2014–15 Esbjerg 0 0
2015–16 Esbjerg 0 0
2015–16 Leicester C 0 0
2016–17 Leicester C 0 0
2017–18 Leicester C 0 0
2018–19 Leicester C 0 0
2018–19 *Oldham Ath* 42 0 **42 0**
2019–20 Leicester C 0 0
2019–20 *Rotherham U* 34 0 **34 0**
2020–21 Leicester C 0 0
2020–21 *OH Leuven* 5 0 **5 0**
2020–21 *Preston NE* 23 0
2021–22 Leicester C 0 0
2021–22 *Preston NE* 46 0 **69 0**
2022–23 Leicester C 12 0
2023–24 Leicester C 0 0
2023–24 *Stoke C* 18 0 **18 0**
2024–25 Leicester C 0 0 **12 0**

JUSTIN, James (D) 228 12
H: 6 0 W: 11 03 b.Luton 23-2-98
Internationals: England U20, U21, Full caps.
2015–16 Luton T 1 0
2016–17 Luton T 29 1
2017–18 Luton T 17 2
2018–19 Luton T 43 3 **90 6**
2019–20 Leicester C 13 0
2020–21 Leicester C 23 2
2021–22 Leicester C 13 0
2022–23 Leicester C 14 0
2023–24 Leicester C 39 2
2024–25 Leicester C 36 2 **138 6**

KRISTIANSEN, Victor (D) 125 1
H: 5 11 W: 11 07 b.Copenhagen 16-12-02
Internationals: Denmark U16, U17, U18, U21, Full caps.
2020–21 Copenhagen 15 0
2021–22 Copenhagen 21 0
2022–23 Copenhagen 15 1 **51 1**
2022–23 Leicester C 12 0
2023–24 Leicester C 0 0
2023–24 *Bologna* 32 0 **32 0**
2024–25 Leicester C 30 0 **42 0**

MARCAL-MADIVADUA, Wanya (M) 15 2
H: 5 11 W: 11 05 b.Leicester 19-10-02
Internationals: Portugal U20.
2021–22 Leicester C 0 0
2022–23 Leicester C 0 0
2023–24 Leicester C 3 1
2024–25 Leicester C 0 0 **3 1**
2024–25 *De Graafschap* 12 1 **12 1**

MAVIDIDI, Stephy (F) 219 44
H: 6 0 W: 11 03 b.Derby 31-5-98
Internationals: England U17, U18, U19, U20.
2016–17 Arsenal 0 0
2016–17 *Charlton Ath* 5 0
2017–18 Arsenal 0 0
2017–18 *Preston NE* 10 0 **10 0**
2017–18 *Charlton Ath* 12 2 **17 2**
2018–19 Juventus 1 0
2019–20 Juventus 0 0 **1 0**
2019–20 *Dijon* 24 5 **24 5**
2020–21 Montpellier 35 9
2021–22 Montpellier 30 8
2022–23 Montpellier 26 4 **91 21**
2023–24 Leicester C 46 12
2024–25 Leicester C 30 4 **76 16**

McATEER, Kasey (M) 69 8
H: 5 10 W: 10 12 b.Northampton 22-11-01
Internationals: Republic of Ireland Full caps.
2021–22 Leicester C 1 0
2021–22 *Forest Green R* 9 0 **9 0**
2022–23 Leicester C 0 0
2022–23 *AFC Wimbledon* 18 1 **18 1**
2023–24 Leicester C 23 6
2024–25 Leicester C 18 1 **42 7**

MONGA, Jeremy (F) 7 0
H: 5 3 W: 8 09 b. 10-7-09
Internationals: England U16.
2024–25 Leicester C 7 0 **7 0**

NDIDI, Onyinye (M) 315 15
H: 6 2 W: 12 08 b.Lagos 16-12-96
Internationals: Nigeria U20, Full caps.
2014–15 Genk 6 0
2015–16 Genk 38 4
2016–17 Genk 19 0 **63 4**
2016–17 Leicester C 17 2
2017–18 Leicester C 33 0
2018–19 Leicester C 38 2
2019–20 Leicester C 32 2
2020–21 Leicester C 26 1
2021–22 Leicester C 19 0
2022–23 Leicester C 27 0
2023–24 Leicester C 32 4
2024–25 Leicester C 28 0 **252 11**

NELSON, Ben (D) 47 2
H: 5 11 W: 13 10 b.Northampton 18-3-04
Internationals: Scotland U16. England U18, U19, U20.
2020–21 Leicester C 0 0
2021–22 Leicester C 0 0
2022–23 Leicester C 0 0
2022–23 *Rochdale* 10 0 **10 0**
2022–23 *Doncaster R* 15 0 **15 0**
2023–24 Leicester C 5 1
2024–25 Leicester C 0 0 **5 1**
2024–25 *Oxford U* 17 1 **17 1**

OKOLI, Caleb (D) 113 2
H: 6 3 W: 10 12 b.Vicenza 13-7-01
Internationals: Italy U19, U20, U21.
2020–21 Atalanta 0 0
2020–21 *SPAL* 16 1 **16 1**
2021–22 Atalanta 0 0
2021–22 *Cremonese* 27 0 **27 0**
2022–23 Atalanta 17 0
2023–24 Atalanta 0 0 **17 0**
2023–24 *Frosinone* 34 0 **34 0**
2024–25 Leicester C 19 1 **19 1**

POPOV, Chris (M) 11 0
H: 6 2 W: 12 04 b. 26-10-04
Internationals: Wales U18, U19, U21.
2024–25 Leicester C 0 0
2024–25 *Barrow* 11 0 **11 0**

RAIKHY, Arjan (M) 1 0
H: 6 0 W: 11 07 b.Wolverhampton 25-8-03
2020–21 Aston Villa 0 0
2021–22 Aston Villa 0 0
2022–23 Aston Villa 0 0
2023–24 Leicester C 1 0
2024–25 Leicester C 0 0 **1 0**

RICARDO PEREIRA, Domingos (D) 277 16
H: 5 9 W: 11 00 b.Lisbon 6-10-93
Internationals: Portugal U19, U20, U21, Full caps.
2011–12 Vitoria de Guimaraes 3 0
2012–13 Vitoria de Guimaraes 27 0 **30 0**
2013–14 Porto 14 2
2014–15 Porto 5 0
2015–16 Porto 0 0
2015–16 *Nice* 26 0
2016–17 Porto 0 0
2016–17 *Nice* 24 2 **50 2**
2017–18 Porto 27 2 **46 4**
2018–19 Leicester C 35 2
2019–20 Leicester C 28 3
2020–21 Leicester C 15 0
2021–22 Leicester C 14 1
2022–23 Leicester C 10 1
2023–24 Leicester C 39 3
2024–25 Leicester C 10 0 **151 10**

SKIPP, Oliver (M) 146 2
H: 5 9 W: 11 00 b.Hatfield 16-9-00
Internationals: England U16, U17, U18, U21.
2018–19 Tottenham H 8 0
2019–20 Tottenham H 7 0
2020–21 Tottenham H 0 0
2020–21 *Norwich C* 45 1 **45 1**
2021–22 Tottenham H 18 0
2022–23 Tottenham H 23 1
2023–24 Tottenham H 21 0 **77 1**
2024–25 Leicester C 24 0 **24 0**

SOUMARE, Boubakary (M) — 188 1
H: 6 2 W: 11 00 b.Noisy-le-Sec 27-2-99
Internationals: France U16, U17, U18, U19, U20, U21.

Season	Club				
2016–17	Paris Saint-Germain	0	0		
2017–18	Lille	14	0		
2018–19	Lille	18	1		
2019–20	Lille	20	0		
2020–21	Lille	32	0	84	1
2021–22	Leicester C	19	0		
2022–23	Leicester C	26	0		
2023–24	Leicester C	0	0		
2023–24	Sevilla	28	0	28	0
2024–25	Leicester C	31	0	76	0

SOUTAR, Harry (D) — 157 6
H: 6 6 W: 12 08 b.Aberdeen 22-10-98
Internationals: Scotland U17, U19. Australia U23, Full caps.

Season	Club				
2015–16	Dundee U	2	1		
2016–17	Dundee U	0	0	2	1
2016–17	Stoke C	0	0		
2017–18	Stoke C	0	0		
2017–18	Ross Co	13	0	13	0
2018–19	Stoke C	0	0		
2018–19	Fleetwood T	11	1		
2019–20	Stoke C	0	0		
2019–20	Fleetwood T	34	3	45	4
2020–21	Stoke C	38	1		
2021–22	Stoke C	16	0		
2022–23	Stoke C	7	0	61	1
2022–23	Leicester C	12	0		
2023–24	Leicester C	3	0		
2024–25	Leicester C	0	0	15	0
2024–25	Sheffield U	21	0	21	0

STOLARCZYK, Jakub (G) — 40 0
H: 6 4 W: 12 11 b.Checiny 19-12-00
Internationals: Poland U18, U19, U21.

Season	Club				
2020–21	Leicester C	0	0		
2021–22	Leicester C	0	0		
2021–22	Dunfermline Ath	11	0	11	0
2022–23	Leicester C	0	0		
2022–23	Fleetwood T	0	0		
2022–23	Hartlepool U	17	0	17	0
2023–24	Leicester C	2	0		
2024–25	Leicester C	10	0	12	0

THOMAS, Luke (D) — 94 1
H: 5 11 W: 11 00 b.Leicester 10-6-01
Internationals: England U18, U19, U20, U21.

Season	Club				
2019–20	Leicester C	3	0		
2020–21	Leicester C	14	1		
2021–22	Leicester C	22	0		
2022–23	Leicester C	17	0		
2023–24	Leicester C	0	0		
2023–24	Sheffield U	12	0	12	0
2023–24	Middlesbrough	12	0	12	0
2024–25	Leicester C	14	0	70	1

THOMAS, Silko (M) — 24 0
H: 5 10 W: 11 07 b.London 25-6-04
Internationals: England U18.

Season	Club				
2023–24	Leicester C	0	0		
2024–25	Leicester C	0	0		
2024–25	Wigan Ath	24	0	24	0

VARDY, Jamie (F) — 440 183
H: 5 10 W: 12 00 b.Sheffield 11-1-87
Internationals: England Full caps.
From Stocksbridge Park Steels, FC Halifax T, Fleetwood T.

Season	Club				
2012–13	Leicester C	26	4		
2013–14	Leicester C	37	16		
2014–15	Leicester C	34	5		
2015–16	Leicester C	36	24		
2016–17	Leicester C	35	13		
2017–18	Leicester C	37	20		
2018–19	Leicester C	34	18		
2019–20	Leicester C	35	23		
2020–21	Leicester C	34	15		
2021–22	Leicester C	25	15		
2022–23	Leicester C	37	3		
2023–24	Leicester C	35	18		
2024–25	Leicester C	35	9	440	183

VESTERGAARD, Jannik (D) — 327 20
H: 6 6 W: 15 02 b.Copenhagen 3-8-92
Internationals: Denmark U18, U19, U20, U21, Full caps.

Season	Club				
2010–11	TSG 1899 Hoffenheim	1	0		
2011–12	TSG 1899 Hoffenheim	23	2		
2012–13	TSG 1899 Hoffenheim	26	0		
2013–14	TSG 1899 Hoffenheim	25	1		
2014–15	TSG 1899 Hoffenheim	6	1	71	4
2014–15	Werder Bremen	15	1		
2015–16	Werder Bremen	33	2	48	3
2016–17	Borussia M'gladbach	34	4		
2017–18	Borussia M'gladbach	32	3	66	7
2018–19	Southampton	23	0		
2019–20	Southampton	19	1		
2020–21	Southampton	30	3	72	4
2021–22	Leicester C	10	0		
2022–23	Leicester C	23	0		
2023–24	Leicester C	42	2		
2024–25	Leicester C	18	0	70	2

WARD, Danny (G) — 100 0
H: 5 11 W: 13 12 b.Wrexham 22-6-93
Internationals: Wales U17, U19, U21, Full caps.
From Wrexham.

Season	Club				
2011–12	Liverpool	0	0		
2012–13	Liverpool	0	0		
2013–14	Liverpool	0	0		
2014–15	Liverpool	0	0		
2014–15	Morecambe	5	0	5	0
2015–16	Liverpool	2	0		
2015–16	Aberdeen	21	0	21	0
2016–17	Liverpool	0	0		
2016–17	Huddersfield T	43	0	43	0
2017–18	Liverpool	0	0	2	0
2018–19	Leicester C	0	0		
2019–20	Leicester C	0	0		
2020–21	Leicester C	0	0		
2021–22	Leicester C	1	0		
2022–23	Leicester C	26	0		
2023–24	Leicester C	0	0		
2024–25	Leicester C	2	0	29	0

WILSON-BROWN, Thomas (D) — 0 0
H: 6 4 b. 5-10-04

Season	Club		
2024–25	Leicester C	0	0
2024–25	Kilmarnock	0	0

WINKS, Harry (M) — 215 1
H: 5 10 W: 10 03 b.Hemel Hempstead 2-2-96
Internationals: England U17, U18, U19, U20, U21, Full caps.

Season	Club				
2013–14	Tottenham H	0	0		
2014–15	Tottenham H	0	0		
2015–16	Tottenham H	0	0		
2016–17	Tottenham H	21	1		
2017–18	Tottenham H	16	0		
2018–19	Tottenham H	26	1		
2019–20	Tottenham H	31	0		
2020–21	Tottenham H	15	0		
2021–22	Tottenham H	19	0		
2022–23	Tottenham H	0	0	128	2
2022–23	Sampdoria	20	0	20	0
2023–24	Leicester C	45	2		
2024–25	Leicester C	22	0	67	2

Players retained or with offer of contract
Ali, Mirsad Mohamed; Amartey, Rahman Amarteye Addico; Bausor, Stevie Ethan; French, Harry George; Gray, Kevon Olando; Joseph, Jayden Kyle; King, Joshua David; Lindsay, Jahmari Samuel; Louis-Marie Richards, Amani Tye; Neale, Tommy; Onanaye, Toby Oluwatobi; Opoku Onyina, Nathaniel; Pennant, Kian Darnell Leroy.

Scholars
Adedeji, Maxwell Henry Oliver; Akolbire, Bless; Corden, Joseph John; Daniels, William Robert; Diallo, Alpha; Donnelly, Ryan Martin; Donohue, Jake Phillip James; Evans, Jake Benjamin; Fisken, Alfie Graham; Hutchinson, Lorenz William Lucas; Khela, Reiss; Kosiorek, Bartosz; Lawrence, William James; Omobolaji, Olaoluwa Andre Onobote; Otchere, Kirsten Fiifi Yamoah; Page, Louis Donald; Sutherington, Harry.

LEYTON ORIENT (46)

ABDULAI, Azeem (M) — 45 5
H: 6 0 W: 11 11 b.Glasgow 9-12-02
Internationals: Scotland U21.
From Leicester C.

Season	Club				
2021–22	Swansea C	0	0		
2022–23	Swansea C	0	0		
2023–24	Swansea C	7	0		
2024–25	Swansea C	17	1	24	1
2024–25	Leyton Orient	21	4	21	4

AGYEI, Daniel (F) — 225 45
H: 6 0 W: 12 02 b.Dansoman 1-6-97

Season	Club				
2014–15	AFC Wimbledon	0	0		
2015–16	Burnley	0	0		
2016–17	Burnley	3	0		
2016–17	Coventry C	16	4	16	4
2017–18	Burnley	0	0		
2017–18	Walsall	18	4	18	4
2017–18	Blackpool	9	0	9	0
2018–19	Burnley	0	0		
2019–20	Burnley	0	0	3	0
2019–20	Oxford U	13	3		
2020–21	Oxford U	39	5		
2021–22	Oxford U	14	0	66	8
2021–22	Crewe Alex	9	1		
2022–23	Crewe Alex	46	16	55	17
2023–24	Leyton Orient	17	5		
2024–25	Leyton Orient	41	7	58	12

ARCHIBALD, Theo (M) — 167 20
H: 5 11 W: 9 06 b.Glasgow 5-3-98
Internationals: Scotland U16, U19, U21.

Season	Club				
2016–17	Celtic	0	0		
2016–17	Albion R	14	0	14	0
2017–18	Brentford	2	0		
2018–19	Brentford	0	0	2	0
2018–19	Forest Green R	14	1	14	1
2018–19	Brentford	0	0		
2019–20	Macclesfield T	28	4	28	4
2020–21	Lincoln C	7	0		
2021–22	Lincoln C	0	0	7	0
2021–22	Leyton Orient	38	8		
2022–23	Leyton Orient	35	5		
2023–24	Leyton Orient	29	2		
2024–25	Leyton Orient	0	0	102	15

AVGOUSTIDIS, Thomas (M) — 0 0
H: 5 10 b.Thessaloniki 10-10-05

Season	Club		
2024–25	Leyton Orient	0	0

BALL, Dominic (D) — 245 4
H: 6 0 W: 12 06 b.Welwyn Garden City 2-8-95
Internationals: Northern Ireland U16, U17, U19, U21. England U19, U20.

Season	Club				
2013–14	Tottenham H	0	0		
2014–15	Tottenham H	0	0		
2014–15	Cambridge U	11	0	11	0
2015–16	Tottenham H	0	0		
2015–16	Rangers	21	0	21	0
2016–17	Rotherham U	13	0		
2016–17	Peterborough U	6	1	6	1
2017–18	Rotherham U	0	0		
2017–18	Aberdeen	16	0		
2018–19	Rotherham U	0	0	13	0
2018–19	Aberdeen	31	0	47	0
2019–20	QPR	31	1		
2020–21	QPR	39	1		
2021–22	QPR	20	1	90	3
2022–23	Ipswich T	16	0		
2023–24	Ipswich T	10	0	26	0
2024–25	Leyton Orient	31	0	31	0

BECKLES, Omar (D) — 333 24
H: 6 3 W: 12 04 b.Kettering 25-10-91
Internationals: Grenada Full caps.
From Jerez Industrial, Boreham Wood, Kettering T, Billericay T, Histon, St Albans C, Aldershot T.

Season	Club				
2016–17	Accrington S	41	2		
2017–18	Accrington S	2	1	43	3
2017–18	Shrewsbury T	33	3		
2018–19	Shrewsbury T	36	1		
2019–20	Shrewsbury T	28	3	97	7
2020–21	Crewe Alex	41	1	41	1
2021–22	Leyton Orient	44	5		
2022–23	Leyton Orient	41	3		
2023–24	Leyton Orient	35	2		
2024–25	Leyton Orient	32	3	152	13

BROWN, Jordan (D) — 133 7
H: 5 11 W: 11 00 b.Stoke-on-Trent 21-6-01

Season	Club				
2019–20	Derby Co	1	0		
2020–21	Derby Co	0	0		
2021–22	Derby Co	0	0	1	0
2021–22	Leyton Orient	11	1		
2022–23	Leyton Orient	34	1		
2023–24	Leyton Orient	43	3		
2024–25	Leyton Orient	44	2	132	7

BULLAS, Hayden (M) — 0 0
H: 5 10 W: 11 09 b. 31-5-06

Season	Club		
2024–25	Leyton Orient	0	0

BYRNE, Rhys (G) — 0 0
H: 5 11 W: 11 09 b.Redbridge 24-8-02

Season	Club		
2021–22	Leyton Orient	0	0
2022–23	Leyton Orient	0	0
2023–24	Leyton Orient	0	0
2024–25	Leyton Orient	0	0

CARTER, Dan (D) — 0 0

Season	Club		
2024–25	Leyton Orient	0	0

CHINEDU, Phillip (D) — 0 0
b. 5-10-06

Season	Club		
2023–24	Leyton Orient	0	0
2024–25	Leyton Orient	0	0

CLARE, Sean (M) — 267 17
H: 6 3 W: 12 06 b.Sheffield 18-9-96

Season	Club				
2015–16	Sheffield Wed	0	0		
2015–16	Bury	4	0	4	0
2016–17	Sheffield Wed	0	0		
2016–17	Accrington S	8	1	8	1
2017–18	Sheffield Wed	5	1	5	1
2017–18	Gillingham	21	1	21	1
2018–19	Hearts	28	3		
2019–20	Hearts	26	4	54	7
2020–21	Oxford U	17	0	17	0
2020–21	Burton Alb	20	1	20	1
2021–22	Charlton Ath	36	1		
2022–23	Charlton Ath	40	1	76	2
2023–24	Wigan Ath	33	1	33	1
2024–25	Leyton Orient	29	3	29	3

COOPER, Brandon (D) 112 1
H: 6 1   W: 11 09   b.Bridgend 14-1-00
Internationals: Wales U21.

2018–19	Swansea C	0	0	
2019–20	Swansea C	0	0	
2020–21	Swansea C	1	0	
2020–21	Newport Co	19	1	19 1
2021–22	Swansea C	4	0	
2021–22	Swindon T	8	0	8 0
2022–23	Swansea C	0	0	
2022–23	Forest Green R	21	0	21 0
2023–24	Swansea C	0	0	5 0
2023–24	Leyton Orient	29	0	
2024–25	Leyton Orient	30	0	59 0

EDMONDS-GREEN, Rarmani (D) 134 7
H: 5 11   W: 11 07   b.Peckham 14-1-99

2019–20	Huddersfield T	0	0	
2019–20	Swindon T	9	1	9 1
2020–21	Huddersfield T	24	2	
2021–22	Huddersfield T	0	0	
2021–22	Rotherham U	28	3	28 3
2022–23	Huddersfield T	11	0	
2022–23	Wigan Ath	4	0	4 0
2023–24	Huddersfield T	14	0	51 2
2023–24	Charlton Ath	14	0	
2024–25	Charlton Ath	11	1	25 1
2024–25	Leyton Orient	17	0	17 0

GALBRAITH, Ethan (M) 143 15
H: 5 9   W: 10 08   b.Belfast 11-5-01
Internationals: Northern Ireland U17, U19, U21, Full caps.
From Linfield.

2019–20	Manchester U	0	0	
2020–21	Manchester U	0	0	
2021–22	Manchester U	0	0	
2021–22	Doncaster R	33	1	33 1
2022–23	Manchester U	0	0	
2022–23	Salford C	32	4	32 4
2023–24	Leyton Orient	39	4	
2024–25	Leyton Orient	39	6	78 10

GRAHAM, Jordan (M) 163 14
H: 6 0   W: 10 10   b.Coventry 5-3-95
Internationals: England U16, U17.

2011–12	Aston Villa	0	0	
2012–13	Aston Villa	0	0	
2013–14	Aston Villa	0	0	
2013–14	Ipswich T	2	0	
2013–14	Bradford C	1	0	1 0
2014–15	Wolverhampton W	0	0	
2015–16	Wolverhampton W	11	1	
2015–16	Oxford U	5	0	
2016–17	Wolverhampton W	2	0	
2017–18	Wolverhampton W	1	0	
2017–18	Fulham	3	0	3 0
2018–19	Wolverhampton W	0	0	
2018–19	Ipswich T	4	0	6 0
2018–19	Oxford U	16	1	21 1
2019–20	Wolverhampton W	0	0	14 1
2019–20	Gillingham	7	0	
2020–21	Gillingham	39	12	46 12
2021–22	Birmingham C	24	0	
2022–23	Birmingham C	25	0	49 0
2023–24	Leyton Orient	15	0	
2024–25	Leyton Orient	8	0	23 0

HAMBURY, Zack (M) 0 0
2024–25	Leyton Orient	0	0	

HAPPE, Daniel (D) 166 6
H: 6 6   W: 14 00   b.Tower Hamlets 28-9-98
Internationals: England C.
From Leyton Orient.

2016–17	Leyton Orient	2	0	
2019–20	Leyton Orient	32	1	
2020–21	Leyton Orient	40	3	
2021–22	Leyton Orient	12	0	
2022–23	Leyton Orient	25	0	
2023–24	Leyton Orient	30	0	
2024–25	Leyton Orient	25	2	166 6

HOWES, Sam (G) 4 0
H: 6 3   W: 13 05   b.London 10-11-97
Internationals: England U16, U17, U18, U19, C.

2015–16	West Ham U	0	0	
2016–17	West Ham U	0	0	
2017–18	Watford	0	0	
2018–19	Watford	0	0	

From Woking, Dorking W, Horsham, Wealdstone.

2023–24	Leyton Orient	4	0	
2024–25	Leyton Orient	0	0	4 0

JAIYESIMI, Diallang (M) 188 17
H: 5 11   W: 11 05   b.Southwark 18-3-99
From Dulwich Hamlet.

2017–18	Norwich C	0	0	
2017–18	Grimsby T	30	0	30 0
2018–19	Norwich C	0	0	
2018–19	Yeovil T	9	2	9 2
2019–20	Norwich C	0	0	
2019–20	Swindon T	21	5	
2020–21	Swindon T	18	4	39 9

JAMES, Tom (D) 236 19
H: 5 11   W: 11 00   b.Cardiff 15-4-96
Internationals: Wales U19.

2013–14	Cardiff C	1	0	
2014–15	Cardiff C	0	0	
2015–16	Cardiff C	0	0	
2016–17	Cardiff C	0	0	1 0
2016–17	Yeovil T	2	0	
2017–18	Yeovil T	38	0	
2018–19	Yeovil T	38	6	78 6
2019–20	Hibernian	6	0	
2020–21	Hibernian	0	0	6 0
2020–21	Wigan Ath	20	3	20 3
2021–22	Salford C	4	0	4 0
2021–22	Leyton Orient	21	4	
2022–23	Leyton Orient	41	4	
2023–24	Leyton Orient	43	0	
2024–25	Leyton Orient	22	2	127 10

LAMB, Teddie (M) 0 0
2024–25	Leyton Orient	0	0	

MOHAMUD, Abdi (M) 0 0
2023–24	Leyton Orient	0	0	
2024–25	Leyton Orient	0	0	

MONCUR, George (M) 332 53
H: 5 9   W: 9 13   b.Swindon 18-8-93
Internationals: England U18.

2010–11	West Ham U	0	0	
2011–12	West Ham U	0	0	
2011–12	AFC Wimbledon	20	2	20 2
2012–13	West Ham U	0	0	
2013–14	West Ham U	0	0	
2013–14	Partick Thistle	2	1	2 1
2014–15	Colchester U	41	8	
2015–16	Colchester U	45	12	86 20
2016–17	Peterborough U	13	2	13 2
2016–17	Barnsley	12	2	
2017–18	Barnsley	34	2	
2018–19	Barnsley	21	1	67 5
2018–19	Luton T	14	6	
2019–20	Luton T	17	1	
2020–21	Luton T	21	3	
2021–22	Luton T	0	0	52 10
2021–22	Hull C	14	0	14 0
2022–23	Leyton Orient	43	9	
2023–24	Leyton Orient	35	4	
2024–25	Leyton Orient	0	0	78 13

Transferred to Ebbsfleet U, March 2025.

O'NEILL, Oliver (M) 62 8
H: 6 1   W: 11 07   b.Hammersmith 8-1-03
Internationals: Republic of Ireland U17, U19, U21.

2021–22	Fulham	0	0	
2022–23	Fulham	0	0	
2022–23	Derry C	19	1	19 1
2023–24	Fulham	0	0	
2023–24	Leyton Orient	17	5	
2024–25	Leyton Orient	26	2	43 7

OBIERO, Zech (M) 17 0
H: 5 7   W: 10 08   b.Redbridge 18-1-05
Internationals: Kenya U20.

2021–22	Leyton Orient	1	0	
2022–23	Leyton Orient	0	0	
2023–24	Leyton Orient	6	0	
2024–25	Leyton Orient	10	0	17 0

PEGRUM, Charlie (M) 4 0
H: 5 7   W: 10 08   b.Havering 11-10-04

2023–24	Leyton Orient	4	0	
2024–25	Leyton Orient	0	0	4 0

PHILLIPS, Noah (G) 0 0
H: 6 3   W: 11 00   b.Havering 7-12-04

2021–22	Leyton Orient	0	0	
2022–23	Leyton Orient	0	0	
2023–24	Leyton Orient	0	0	
2024–25	Leyton Orient	0	0	

PIGOTT, Joe (F) 355 74
H: 6 2   W: 9 06   b.London 24-11-93

2012–13	Charlton Ath	0	0	
2013–14	Charlton Ath	11	0	
2013–14	Gillingham	7	1	7 1
2014–15	Charlton Ath	1	0	
2014–15	Newport Co	10	3	10 3
2014–15	Southend U	20	6	
2015–16	Charlton Ath	0	0	12 0
2015–16	Southend U	23	3	43 9
2015–16	Luton T	15	4	15 4
2016–17	Cambridge U	10	0	10 0

From Maidstone U.

2017–18	AFC Wimbledon	18	5	
2018–19	AFC Wimbledon	40	15	
2019–20	AFC Wimbledon	34	7	
2020–21	AFC Wimbledon	45	20	
2021–22	AFC Wimbledon	0	0	
2021–22	Ipswich T	22	2	
2022–23	Ipswich T	0	0	22 2
2022–23	Portsmouth	35	4	35 4
2023–24	Leyton Orient	36	2	
2024–25	Leyton Orient	0	0	36 2
2024–25	AFC Wimbledon	28	2	165 49

PRATLEY, Darren (M) 647 50
H: 6 1   W: 11 00   b.Barking 22-4-85

2001–02	Fulham	0	0	
2002–03	Fulham	0	0	
2003–04	Fulham	1	0	
2004–05	Fulham	0	0	
2004–05	Brentford	14	1	
2005–06	Fulham	0	0	1 0
2005–06	Brentford	32	4	46 5
2006–07	Swansea C	28	1	
2007–08	Swansea C	42	5	
2008–09	Swansea C	37	4	
2009–10	Swansea C	36	7	
2010–11	Swansea C	34	9	177 26
2011–12	Bolton W	25	1	
2012–13	Bolton W	31	2	
2013–14	Bolton W	20	2	
2014–15	Bolton W	22	4	
2015–16	Bolton W	36	1	
2016–17	Bolton W	12	0	
2017–18	Bolton W	32	2	178 12
2018–19	Charlton Ath	28	2	
2019–20	Charlton Ath	36	2	
2020–21	Charlton Ath	39	1	103 5
2021–22	Leyton Orient	39	1	
2022–23	Leyton Orient	39	1	
2023–24	Leyton Orient	33	0	
2024–25	Leyton Orient	31	0	142 2

SIMPSON, Jack (D) 71 0
H: 5 10   W: 13 01   b.Wandsworth 8-1-97
Internationals: England U21.

2015–16	Bournemouth	0	0	
2016–17	Bournemouth	0	0	
2017–18	Bournemouth	1	0	
2018–19	Bournemouth	6	0	
2019–20	Bournemouth	4	0	
2020–21	Bournemouth	9	0	20 0
2020–21	Rangers	5	0	
2021–22	Rangers	4	0	9 0
2022–23	Cardiff C	19	0	
2023–24	Cardiff C	1	0	20 0
2023–24	Leyton Orient	5	0	
2024–25	Leyton Orient	17	0	22 0

SMITH-KOUASSI, Reon (F) 0 0
H: 5 11   W: 11 11   b. 1-1-06

2021–22	Leyton Orient	0	0	
2022–23	Leyton Orient	0	0	
2023–24	Leyton Orient	0	0	
2024–25	Leyton Orient	0	0	

STERLING, Aaron (F) 0 0
2024–25	Leyton Orient	0	0	

SWEENEY, Jayden (D) 60 1
H: 5 10   W: 10 10   b.Camden 4-12-01

2019–20	Leyton Orient	1	0	
2020–21	Leyton Orient	5	0	
2021–22	Leyton Orient	22	0	
2023–24	Leyton Orient	13	0	
2024–25	Leyton Orient	19	1	60 1

WARRINGTON, Lewis (M) 82 2
H: 6 0   W: 9 06   b.Birkenhead 10-10-02

2020–21	Everton	0	0	
2021–22	Tranmere R	17	1	17 1
2022–23	Everton	0	0	
2022–23	Fleetwood T	38	0	38 0
2023–24	Everton	1	0	1 0
2023–24	Plymouth Arg	2	0	2 0
2024–25	Leyton Orient	8	0	8 0
2024–25	Salford C	16	1	16 1

WELCH, Makai (M) 0 0
b. 4-10-05
Internationals: Jamaica U20.

2023–24	Leyton Orient	0	0	
2024–25	Leyton Orient	0	0	

WELLENS, Alfie (M) 0 0
2024–25	Leyton Orient	0	0	

WILLIAMS, Randell (M) 199 19
H: 6 3   W: 12 00   b.Lambeth 30-12-96
From Tower Hamlets.

2016–17	Crystal Palace	0	0	
2017–18	Watford	0	0	
2017–18	Wycombe W	6	1	
2018–19	Watford	0	0	
2018–19	Wycombe W	20	2	26 3
2019–20	Exeter C	10	0	
2019–20	Exeter C	37	5	
2020–21	Exeter C	29	4	76 9
2021–22	Hull C	13	0	
2022–23	Hull C	7	0	20 0
2022–23	Bolton W	15	1	
2023–24	Bolton W	32	3	

2024–25 Bolton W	16	1	63	5
2024–25 Leyton Orient	14	2	14	2

Players retained or with offer of contract
Perkins, Sonny Tufail.

Scholars
Anderson, Charlie Jay; Archibald, Aaron David Emanuel; Asumu Nzang, Claudio; Avgoustidis, Thomas; Bello, Tajuddin Adebiyi Osuolale A; Bullas, Hayden Anthony John; Carter, Daniel Edward; Chinedu, Philip Chukwuemeka; Hajdini, Anduan; Hambury, Zachary Daniel; Jhuti, Reece Singh; Knight, Preston James; Mohamud, Abdirahman Hasan; Norman, Freddie George; Northwood, Luke; Oji, Uko Kalu Ifeatu Olisa; Okafor, Izuchukwu Christopher D S; O'Keefe, Zak Daniel; Pike, Ethan Kenneth; Smith-Kouassi, Reon; Sterling, Aaron Lewis; Welch, Makai Jaydan William Bond; Wellens, Alfie Lee; Wright, Eddie Emmanuel.

LINCOLN C (47)

ALLAN, Isaac (G) — 0 0

2022–23 Lincoln C	0	0
2023–24 Lincoln C	0	0
2024–25 Lincoln C	0	0

BAYLISS, Tom (M) — 187 21
H: 6 0 W: 12 04 b.Leicester 6-4-99
Internationals: England U19.

2017–18 Coventry C	24	5		
2018–19 Coventry C	38	3		
2019–20 Coventry C	0	0	62	8
2019–20 Preston NE	1	0		
2020–21 Preston NE	11	1		
2021–22 Preston NE	0	0	12	1
2021–22 Wigan Ath	8	0	8	0
2022–23 Shrewsbury T	36	6		
2023–24 Shrewsbury T	35	3	71	9
2024–25 Lincoln C	34	3	34	3

BENN, Jay (D) — 20 0
H: 5 10 W: 11 07 b.Brighouse 22-8-01
From FC Halifax T.

2022–23 Lincoln C	0	0		
2023 *Bohemians*	8	0	8	0
2023–24 Lincoln C	0	0		
2024–25 Lincoln C	0	0		
2024–25 *Bradford C*	12	0	12	0

BRADSHAW, Zak (D) — 45 0
H: 6 2 W: 11 00 b.Hatfield 22-9-03

2021–22 Ipswich T	0	0		
2022–23 Ipswich T	0	0		
2023–24 Ipswich T	0	0		
2023–24 Lincoln C	0	0		
2024 *Dundalk*	18	0	18	0
2024–25 Lincoln C	0	0		
2024–25 *Tranmere R*	27	0	27	0

CLUCAS, Sam (M) — 405 49
H: 5 10 W: 11 09 b.Lincoln 25-9-90
Internationals: England C.

2009–10 Lincoln C	0	0		
2010–11 *Jerez Industrial*	20	0	20	0
2011–12 Hereford U	17	0	17	0
From Hereford U.				
2013–14 Mansfield T	38	8		
2014–15 Mansfield T	5	0	43	8
2014–15 Chesterfield	41	9	41	9
2015–16 Hull C	44	6		
2016–17 Hull C	37	3		
2017–18 Hull C	3	0	84	9
2017–18 Swansea C	29	3	29	3
2018–19 Stoke C	26	3		
2019–20 Stoke C	44	11		
2020–21 Stoke C	24	2		
2021–22 Stoke C	25	2		
2022–23 Stoke C	12	0	131	18
2023–24 Rotherham U	32	1	32	1
2024–25 Lincoln C	8	1	8	1

COLLINS, James S (F) — 615 203
H: 6 2 W: 13 08 b.Coventry 1-12-90
Internationals: Republic of Ireland U19, U21, Full caps.

2008–09 Aston Villa	0	0		
2009–10 Aston Villa	0	0		
2009–10 *Darlington*	7	2	7	2
2010–11 Aston Villa	0	0		
2010–11 *Burton Alb*	10	4	10	4
2010–11 Shrewsbury T	24	8		
2011–12 Shrewsbury T	42	14		
2012–13 Swindon T	45	15	45	15
2013–14 Hibernian	36	6	36	6
2014–15 Shrewsbury T	45	15		
2015–16 Shrewsbury T	23	5	134	42
2015–16 *Northampton T*	21	8	21	8
2016–17 Crawley T	45	20	45	20
2017–18 Luton T	42	19		
2018–19 Luton T	44	25		

2019–20 Luton T	46	14		
2020–21 Luton T	42	10	174	68
2021–22 Cardiff C	26	3	26	3
2022–23 Derby Co	42	11		
2023–24 Derby Co	38	14		
2024–25 Derby Co	17	0	97	25
2024–25 Lincoln C	20	10	20	10

DARIKWA, Tendayi (D) — 386 18
H: 6 0 W: 12 02 b.Nottingham 13-12-91
Internationals: Zimbabwe Full caps.

2010–11 Chesterfield	0	0		
2011–12 Chesterfield	2	0		
2012–13 Chesterfield	36	5		
2013–14 Chesterfield	41	3		
2014–15 Chesterfield	46	1	125	9
2015–16 Burnley	21	1		
2016–17 Burnley	0	0	21	1
2017–18 Nottingham F	30	0		
2018–19 Nottingham F	28	0		
2019–20 Nottingham F	0	0		
2020–21 Nottingham F	0	0	58	0
2020–21 Wigan Ath	26	0		
2021–22 Wigan Ath	43	2		
2022–23 Wigan Ath	37	0	106	2
2023–24 *Apollon Limassol*	32	1	32	1
2024–25 Lincoln C	44	5	44	5

DRAPER, Freddie (F) — 103 24
H: 5 10 W: 13 03 b.Oxford 28-7-04

2020–21 Lincoln C	0	0		
2021–22 Lincoln C	8	0		
2022–23 Lincoln C	0	0		
2023 *Drogheda U*	21	8	21	8
2023–24 Lincoln C	15	2		
2023–24 *Walsall*	21	10	21	10
2024–25 Lincoln C	38	4	61	6

ERHAHON, Ethan (M) — 188 5
H: 5 10 W: 10 12 b.Glasgow 9-5-01
Internationals: Scotland U17, U18, U19, U21.

2017–18 St Mirren	1	0		
2018–19 St Mirren	20	0		
2019–20 St Mirren	0	0		
2019–20 *Barnsley*	0	0		
2020–21 St Mirren	31	2		
2021–22 St Mirren	23	1		
2022–23 St Mirren	20	0	95	3
2022–23 Lincoln C	19	0		
2023–24 Lincoln C	43	2		
2024–25 Lincoln C	31	0	93	2

GALLAGHER, Oisin (M) — 19 1
H: 6 2 W: 12 06 b.Derry 2-12-04
Internationals: Republic of Ireland U19.
From Derry C.

2021–22 Lincoln C	0	0		
2022–23 Lincoln C	0	0		
2023–24 Lincoln C	1	0		
2024 *Drogheda U*	18	1	18	1
2024–25 Lincoln C	0	0	1	0

HACKETT-FAIRCHILD, Recco (F) — 159 19
H: 6 3 W: 11 00 b.Redbridge 30-6-98
Internationals: Saint Lucia Full caps.
From Norwich C.

2017–18 Charlton Ath	5	0		
2018–19 Charlton Ath	7	0	12	0
2019–20 Portsmouth	0	0		
2020–21 Portsmouth	0	0		
2020–21 *Southend U*	25	1	25	1
2021–22 Portsmouth	27	4		
2022–23 Portsmouth	33	3	60	7
2023–24 Lincoln C	29	7		
2024–25 Lincoln C	33	4	62	11

HAMER, Tom (D) — 235 16
H: 6 2 W: 12 08 b.Bolton 16-11-99

2017–18 Oldham Ath	7	1		
2018–19 Oldham Ath	28	2		
2019–20 Oldham Ath	37	3		
2020–21 Oldham Ath	12	0	84	6
2020–21 Burton Alb	21	3		
2021–22 Burton Alb	45	1		
2022–23 Burton Alb	35	3		
2023–24 Burton Alb	27	1	128	3
2024–25 Lincoln C	23	2	23	2

HAMILTON, Ethan (M) — 212 18
H: 6 2 W: 11 11 b.Edinburgh 18-10-98
Internationals: Scotland U16, U19.

2017–18 Manchester U	0	0		
2018–19 Manchester U	0	0		
2018–19 Rochdale	14	4	14	4
2019–20 Manchester U	0	0		
2019–20 *Southend U*	14	0	14	0
2019–20 *Bolton W*	12	1	12	1
2020–21 Peterborough U	34	0		
2021–22 Peterborough U	2	0	36	0
2021–22 Accrington S	41	6		
2022–23 Accrington S	33	4	74	10
2023–24 Lincoln C	30	3		
2024–25 Lincoln C	32	0	62	3

HOUSE, Ben (F) — 111 21
H: 6 0 W: 11 09 b.Guildford 5-7-99
Internationals: Scotland U20, U21.

2018–19 Reading	0	0		
2018–19 *Swindon T*	6	0	6	0
2019–20 Reading	0	0		
From Eastleigh.				
2021–22 Lincoln C	6	1		
2022–23 Lincoln C	38	12		
2023–24 Lincoln C	20	2		
2024–25 Lincoln C	41	6	105	21

JACKSON, Adam (D) — 224 12
H: 6 2 W: 12 04 b.Darlington 18-5-94
Internationals: England U16, U17, U18, U19.

2011–12 Middlesbrough	0	0		
2012–13 Middlesbrough	0	0		
2013–14 Middlesbrough	0	0		
2014–15 Middlesbrough	0	0		
2015–16 Middlesbrough	0	0		
2015–16 *Coventry C*	0	0		
2015–16 *Hartlepool U*	29	3	29	3
2016–17 Barnsley	10	0		
2017–18 Barnsley	22	1		
2018–19 Barnsley	6	0	38	1
2019–20 Hibernian	14	3	14	3
2020–21 Lincoln C	28	1		
2021–22 Lincoln C	25	0		
2022–23 Lincoln C	29	1		
2023–24 Lincoln C	34	1		
2024–25 Lincoln C	27	2	143	5

JEACOCK, Zach (G) — 16 0
H: 6 2 W: 12 02 b.Birmingham 8-5-01
Internationals: England U19.

2020–21 Birmingham C	2	0		
2021–22 Birmingham C	2	0		
2021–22 *Salford C*	1	0	1	0
2022–23 Birmingham C	0	0		
2023–24 Birmingham C	0	0	4	0
2024–25 Birmingham C	11	0	11	0

JEFFERIES, Dom (M) — 90 5
H: 5 10 W: 12 04 b.Newport 22-5-02

2019–20 Newport Co	0	0		
From Salisbury.				
2021–22 Brentford	0	0		
2022–23 Gillingham	34	1		
2023–24 Gillingham	22	1	56	2
2024–25 Lincoln C	34	3	34	3

KAMARA, MJ (M) — 0 0
H: 6 1 W: 12 04 b. 14-2-06

2024–25 Lincoln C	0	0

MAKAMA, Jovon (F) — 79 9
H: 6 0 W: 14 00 b.Nottingham 1-2-04

2021–22 Lincoln C	0	0		
2022–23 Lincoln C	8	0		
2023–24 Lincoln C	33	2		
2024–25 Lincoln C	38	7	79	9

McGRANDLES, Conor (M) — 302 16
H: 6 0 W: 10 00 b.Falkirk 24-9-95

2012–13 Falkirk	26	2		
2013–14 Falkirk	36	5		
2014–15 Falkirk	3	0		
2014–15 Norwich C	1	0		
2015–16 Norwich C	0	0		
2015–16 *Falkirk*	5	0	70	7
2016–17 Norwich C	0	0	1	0
2017–18 Milton Keynes D	19	0		
2018–19 Milton Keynes D	25	1		
2019–20 Milton Keynes D	31	1	75	2
2021–22 Lincoln C	39	4		
2021–22 Lincoln C	39	2		
2022–23 Charlton Ath	9	0		
2022–23 *Cambridge U*	19	0	19	0
2023–24 Charlton Ath	3	1	12	1
2023–24 *Lincoln C*	5	0		
2024–25 Lincoln C	42	0	125	6

McKIERNAN, JJ (M) — 60 8
H: 6 0 W: 11 09 b.Southampton 18-1-02
Internationals: Northern Ireland U21.

2018–19 Watford	0	0		
2019–20 Watford	0	0		
2020–21 Watford	0	0		
2021–22 Watford	0	0		
2022 *Bohemians*	1	0	1	0
2022–23 Watford	0	0		
2023–24 Morecambe	28	7	28	7
2024–25 Lincoln C	12	0	12	0
2024–25 *Burton Alb*	19	1	19	1

MONTSMA, Lewis (D) — 129 9
H: 6 3 W: 12 13 b.Amsterdam 25-4-98

2017–18 Dordrecht	23	1		
2018–19 Dordrecht	23	0	46	1
2020–21 Lincoln C	40	6		
2021–22 Lincoln C	19	1		
2023–24 Lincoln C	8	0		
2024–25 Lincoln C	16	1	83	8

MOYLAN, Jack (M) 129 35
H: 6 1 W: 10 03 b.Killbarrack, North
Dublin 1-9-01
2019	Bohemians	0	0	
2020	Bohemians	2	0	
2021	Bohemians	4	0	6 0
2021	Wexford	14	7	14 7
2022	Shelbourne	27	7	
2023	Shelbourne	36	15	63 22
2023–24	Lincoln C	18	4	
2024–25	Lincoln C	28	2	46 6

O'CONNOR, Paudie (D) 250 13
H: 6 3 W: 12 02 b.Limerick 14-7-97
From Limerick.
2017–18	Leeds U	4	0	
2018–19	Leeds U	0	0	4 0
2018–19	Blackpool	10	0	10 0
2019–20	Bradford C	9	0	
2020-21	Bradford C	42	2	
2021–22	Bradford C	45	3	115 7
2022-23	Lincoln C	44	1	
2023–24	Lincoln C	38	2	
2024–25	Lincoln C	39	3	121 6

OKEWOYE, Gbolahan (M) 0 0
2023–24	Lincoln C	0	0
2024–25	Lincoln C	0	0

OKORO, Zane (F) 2 0
b.Norwalk 24-9-07
2023–24	Lincoln C	0	0	
2024–25	Lincoln C	2	0	2 0

OLIVER, Denny (M) 0 0
2024–25	Lincoln C	0	0

PARDINGTON, James (G) 4 0
H: 6 5 W: 11 03 b.Walsall 20-7-00
From Rushall.
2018–19	Wolverhampton W	0	0	
2019–20	Wolverhampton W	0	0	
2020–21	Wolverhampton W	0	0	
2020–21	Mansfield T	2	0	2 0
2021–22	Wolverhampton W	0	0	
2022-23	Grimsby T	0	0	
2022-23	Larne	1	0	1 0
2023–24	Cheltenham T	1	0	1 0
2024–25	Lincoln C	0	0	

PARKS, Charlie (D) 0 0
2023–24	Lincoln C	0	0
2024–25	Lincoln C	0	0

RING, Erik (M) 103 9
H: 6 1 W: 11 11 b.Sodertalje 24-4-02
Internationals: Sweden U21.
2020	AIK	10	0	
2021	AIK	17	0	
2022	AIK	17	0	
2023	AIK	0	0	
2023	Helsingborg	29	6	29 6
2024	AIK	6	0	50 0
2024–25	Lincoln C	24	3	24 3

ROUGHAN, Sean (D) 138 3
H: 6 0 W: 11 07 b.Dublin 14-3-03
Internationals: Republic of Ireland U17, U19,
U21.
2020–21	Lincoln C	6	0	
2021–22	Lincoln C	0	0	
2022	Drogheda U	15	0	15 0
2022-23	Lincoln C	32	1	
2023–24	Lincoln C	39	1	
2024–25	Lincoln C	46	1	123 3

SMITH, Alistair (M) 159 22
H: 5 10 W: 10 08 b.Beverley 19-5-99
2018–19	Mansfield T	0	0	
2019–20	Mansfield T	5	0	
2020–21	Mansfield T	1	0	6 0
2021–22	Sutton U	33	8	
2022-23	Sutton U	35	5	68 13
2023–24	Colchester U	15	2	15 2
2024–25	Lincoln C	0	0	25 1
2024–25	AFC Wimbledon	45	6	45 6

STREET, Rob (F) 106 20
H: 6 2 W: 11 00 b.Oxford 26-9-01
2020–21	Crystal Palace	0	0	
2021–22	Crystal Palace	0	0	
2021–22	Newport Co	18	2	18 2
2022-23	Crystal Palace	0	0	
2022-23	Shrewsbury T	38	4	38 4
2023–24	Cheltenham T	22	2	22 2
2024–25	Lincoln C	6	0	6 0
2024–25	Doncaster R	22	12	22 12

WALKER, Tyler (F) 227 58
H: 5 10 W: 9 13 b.Nottingham 17-10-96
Internationals: England U20.
2013–14	Nottingham F	0	0	
2014–15	Nottingham F	7	1	
2015–16	Nottingham F	14	0	
2015–16	Burton Alb	6	1	6 1
2016–17	Nottingham F	0	0	

2016–17	Stevenage	8	3	8 3
2016–17	Port Vale	6	2	6 2
2017–18	Nottingham F	12	3	
2017–18	Bolton W	5	0	5 0
2018–19	Nottingham F	0	0	
2018–19	Mansfield T	44	22	44 22
2019–20	Lincoln C	29	14	
2019–20	Nottingham F	7	1	40 5
2021–22	Coventry C	31	7	
2021–22	Coventry C	19	2	
2021–22	Portsmouth	15	1	15 1
2022–23	Coventry C	18	1	68 10
2023–24	Lincoln C	6	0	
2024–25	Lincoln C	0	0	35 14

WICKENS, George (G) 49 0
H: 6 0 W: 10 01 b.Petersfield 8-11-01
Internationals: England U16, U18.
2020–21	Fulham	0	0
2021–22	Fulham	0	0
2022–23	Fulham	0	0
2023–24	Fulham	0	0
2023–24	Ross Co	13	0	13 0
2024–25	Lincoln C	36	0	36 0

Scholars
Aldridge, Orin Lewis; Allan, Isaac; Blant,
Joshua Benjamin; Carlisle, Charlie James;
Fombad, Kelly Musaga; Ford, Carter Samuel;
McLean, Resharne Josiah; Okewoye,
Gbolahan Olarewaju; Okoro, Zane Kola;
Oliver, Denny; Parks, Charles Kenneth;
Simmons, Noah Christopher Francis;
Vanderpuye, Daniel Tei; Vasiloiu, Nicolae-
Mario; Wifa, Dakara Deebari Arinze.

LIVERPOOL (48)

ALEXANDER-ARNOLD, Trent (D) 259 18
H: 5 9 W: 10 12 · b.Liverpool 7-10-98
Internationals: England U16, U17, U18, U19,
U21, Full caps.
2016–17	Liverpool	7	0	
2017–18	Liverpool	19	1	
2018–19	Liverpool	29	1	
2019–20	Liverpool	38	4	
2020–21	Liverpool	36	2	
2021–22	Liverpool	32	2	
2022–23	Liverpool	37	2	
2023–24	Liverpool	28	3	
2024–25	Liverpool	33	3	259 18

ALISSON, Ramses (G) 310 1
H: 6 4 W: 14 05 b.Novo Hamburgo 2-10-92
Internationals: Brazil U17, U21, Full caps.
2013	Internacional	6	0	
2014	Internacional	11	0	
2015	Internacional	26	0	
2016	Internacional	1	0	44 0
2016–17	Roma	0	0	
2017–18	Roma	37	0	37 0
2018–19	Liverpool	38	0	
2019–20	Liverpool	29	0	
2020–21	Liverpool	33	1	
2021–22	Liverpool	36	0	
2022–23	Liverpool	37	0	
2023–24	Liverpool	28	0	
2024–25	Liverpool	28	0	229 1

BAJCETIC, Stefan (D) 38 2
H: 6 3 W: 13 03 b.Saint-Etienne 23-12-01
Internationals: Spain U18, U21.
From Celta Vigo.
2022–23	Liverpool	11	1	
2023–24	Liverpool	1	0	
2024–25	Liverpool	0	0	12 1
2024–25	Red Bull Salzburg	12	0	12 0
2024–25	Las Palmas	14	1	14 1

BALAGIZI, James (M) 22 2
H: 6 2 b.Manchester 20-9-03
Internationals: England U16, U17, U18, U19,
U20.
2021–22	Liverpool	0	0	
2022–23	Liverpool	0	0	
2022–23	Crawley T	14	2	14 2
2023–24	Liverpool	0	0	
2023–24	Wigan Ath	3	0	3 0
2023–24	Kilmarnock	5	0	5 0

BECK, Owen (D) 55 3
H: 5 10 W: 10 03 b.Wrexham 9-8-02
Internationals: Wales U17, U21.
2020–21	Liverpool	0	0	
2022–23	Liverpool	0	0	
2022–23	Famalicao	0	0	
2022–23	Bolton W	5	0	5 0
2023–24	Liverpool	1	0	
2023–24	Dundee	25	2	25 2
2024–25	Liverpool	0	0	1 0
2024–25	Blackburn R	24	1	24 1

BRADLEY, Conor (M) 71 6
H: 5 11 W: 11 03 b.Tyrone 9-7-03
Internationals: Northern Ireland U16, U17,
Full caps.
From Dungannon Swifts.
2020–21	Liverpool	0	0	
2021–22	Liverpool	0	0	
2022–23	Liverpool	0	0	
2022–23	Bolton W	41	5	41 5
2023–24	Liverpool	11	1	
2024–25	Liverpool	19	0	30 1

CHAMBERS, Luke (D) 30 2
H: 5 11 W: 13 10 b.Preston 24-7-04
Internationals: England U16, U18, U19, U20.
2022–23	Liverpool	0	0	
2022–23	Kilmarnock	0	0	
2023–24	Liverpool	0	0	
2023–24	Wigan Ath	18	1	
2024–25	Liverpool	0	0	
2024–25	Wigan Ath	12	1	30 2

CHIESA, Federico (F) 241 47
H: 5 9 W: 11 00 b.Genoa 25-10-97
Internationals: Italy U19, U20, U21, Full caps.
2016–17	Fiorentina	27	3	
2017–18	Fiorentina	36	6	
2018–19	Fiorentina	37	6	
2019–20	Fiorentina	34	10	
2020–21	Fiorentina	3	1	
2020–21	Juventus	30	8	
2021–22	Fiorentina	0	0	137 26
2021–22	Juventus	14	2	
2022–23	Juventus	21	2	
2023–24	Juventus	33	9	98 21
2024–25	Liverpool	6	0	6 0

CORNESS, Dominic (M) 6 0
Internationals: England U20.
2023–24	Liverpool	0	0	
2024–25	Liverpool	0	0	
2024–25	Gillingham	6	0	6 0

DANNS, Jayden (F) 3 0
H: 6 0 W: 10 08 b.Liverpool 16-1-06
Internationals: England U16, U18.
2023–24	Liverpool	2	0	
2024–25	Liverpool	1	0	3 0
2024–25	Sunderland	0	0	

DAVIES, Harvey (G) 27 0
H: 6 3 W: 12 02 b.Liverpool 3-9-03
Internationals: England U19, U20.
2020–21	Liverpool	0	0	
2021–22	Liverpool	0	0	
2022–23	Liverpool	0	0	
2023–24	Liverpool	0	0	
2023–24	Crewe Alex	27	0	27 0
2024–25	Liverpool	0	0	

DIAZ, Luis (F) 281 63
H: 5 11 W: 10 03 b.Barrancas 13-1-97
Internationals: Colombia U20, Full caps.
2016	Barranquilla	19	2	
2017	Barranquilla	15	1	34 3
2017	Junior	12	0	
2018	Junior	38	13	
2019	Junior	17	2	67 15
2019–20	Porto	29	6	
2020–21	Porto	30	6	
2021–22	Porto	18	4	77 16
2021–22	Liverpool	13	4	
2022–23	Liverpool	17	4	
2023–24	Liverpool	37	8	
2024–25	Liverpool	36	13	103 29

DOAK, Ben (M) 29 3
H: 5 8 W: 10 10 b.Dalry 11-11-05
Internationals: Scotland U16, U17, U21, Full
caps.
2021–22	Celtic	2	0	2 0
2022–23	Liverpool	2	0	
2023–24	Liverpool	1	0	
2024–25	Liverpool	0	0	3 0
2024–25	Middlesbrough	24	3	24 3

ELLIOTT, Harvey (M) 135 12
H: 5 7 W: 10 08 b.Chertsey 4-4-03
Internationals: England U16, U17, U21.
2018–19	Fulham	2	0	2 0
2019–20	Liverpool	0	0	
2020–21	Liverpool	0	0	
2020–21	Blackburn R	41	7	41 7
2021–22	Liverpool	6	0	
2022–23	Liverpool	32	1	
2023–24	Liverpool	34	3	
2024–25	Liverpool	18	1	92 5

ENDO, Wataru (M) 428 44
H: 5 10 W: 11 11 b.Yokohama 9-2-93
Internationals: Japan U19, U23, Full caps.
2010	Shonan Bellmare	6	1	
2011	Shonan Bellmare	34	1	
2012	Shonan Bellmare	32	7	
2013	Shonan Bellmare	17	3	
2014	Shonan Bellmare	38	7	
2015	Shonan Bellmare	31	4	158 23

2016	Urawa Red Dragons	27	0		
2017	Urawa Red Dragons	30	3		
2018	Urawa Red Dragons	16	2	73	5
2018–19	Sint-Truidense	26	2		
2019–20	Sint-Truidense	2	0	28	2
2019–20	*VfB Stuttgart*	21	1		
2020–21	VfB Stuttgart	33	3		
2021–22	VfB Stuttgart	33	4		
2022–23	VfB Stuttgart	33	5		
2023–24	VfB Stuttgart	0	0	120	13
2023–24	Liverpool	29	1		
2024–25	Liverpool	20	0	49	1

GAKPO, Cody (M)   197 61
H: 5 10   W: 10 01   b.Eindhoven 7-5-99
Internationals: Netherlands U18, U19, U20, U21, Full caps.

2016–17	PSV Eindhoven	5	0		
2017–18	PSV Eindhoven	1	0		
2018–19	PSV Eindhoven	16	1		
2019–20	PSV Eindhoven	25	7		
2020–21	PSV Eindhoven	23	7		
2021–22	PSV Eindhoven	27	12		
2022–23	PSV Eindhoven	14	9	106	36
2022–23	Liverpool	21	7		
2023–24	Liverpool	35	8		
2024–25	Liverpool	35	10	91	25

GOMEZ, Joseph (D)   170 0
H: 6 2   W: 14 00   b.Catford 23-5-97
Internationals: England U16, U17, U19, U21, Full caps.

2014–15	Charlton Ath	21	0	21	0
2015–16	Liverpool	5	0		
2016–17	Liverpool	0	0		
2017–18	Liverpool	23	0		
2018–19	Liverpool	16	0		
2019–20	Liverpool	28	0		
2020–21	Liverpool	7	0		
2021–22	Liverpool	8	0		
2022–23	Liverpool	21	0		
2023–24	Liverpool	32	0		
2024–25	Liverpool	9	0	149	0

GORDON, Kaide (F)   18 1
H: 5 8   W: 9 08   b.Burton-upon-Trent 5-10-04
Internationals: England U16, U18, U20.

2020–21	Derby Co	1	0	1	0
2020–21	Liverpool	0	0		
2021–22	Liverpool	1	0		
2022–23	Liverpool	0	0		
2023–24	Liverpool	1	0		
2024–25	Liverpool	0	0	2	0
2024–25	*Norwich C*	10	1	10	1
2024–25	Portsmouth	5	0	5	0

GRAVENBERCH, Ryan (M)   160 8
H: 5 10   W: 11 09   b.Amsterdam 16-5-02
Internationals: Netherlands U16, U17, U19, U21, Full caps.

2018–19	Ajax	1	0		
2019–20	Ajax	9	2		
2020–21	Ajax	32	3		
2021–22	Ajax	30	2	72	7
2022–23	Bayern Munich	24	0		
2023–24	Bayern Munich	1	0	25	0
2023–24	Liverpool	26	1		
2024–25	Liverpool	37	0	63	1

JAROS, Vitezslav (G)   26 0
H: 6 0   W: 10 12   b.Pribram 23-7-01
Internationals: Czech Republic U16, U18, U21, Full caps.
From Slavia Prague.

2020–21	Liverpool	0	0		
2021–22	Liverpool	0	0		
2022–23	Liverpool	0	0		
2022–23	*Stockport Co*	11	0	11	0
2023–24	Liverpool	0	0		
2023–24	*Sturm Graz*	14	0	14	0
2024–25	Liverpool	1	0	1	0

JONES, Curtis (M)   119 10
H: 6 1   W: 11 11   b.Liverpool 30-1-01
Internationals: England U16, U17, U18, U19, U21, Full caps.

2017–18	Liverpool	0	0		
2018–19	Liverpool	0	0		
2019–20	Liverpool	6	1		
2020–21	Liverpool	24	1		
2021–22	Liverpool	15	1		
2022–23	Liverpool	18	3		
2023–24	Liverpool	23	1		
2024–25	Liverpool	33	3	119	10

JOTA, Diogo (F)   302 102
H: 5 10   W: 11 00   b.Massarelos 4-12-96
Internationals: Portugal U19, U21, U23, Full caps.

2014–15	Pacos de Ferreira	10	2		
2015–16	Pacos de Ferreira	31	12	41	14
2016–17	Atletico Madrid	0	0		
2016–17	*Porto*	27	8	27	8
2017–18	Atletico Madrid	0	0		
2017–18	*Wolverhampton W*	44	17		

2018–19	Wolverhampton W	33	9		
2019–20	Wolverhampton W	34	7	111	33
2020–21	Liverpool	19	9		
2021–22	Liverpool	35	15		
2022–23	Liverpool	22	7		
2023–24	Liverpool	21	10		
2024–25	Liverpool	26	6	123	47

KELLEHER, Caoimhin (G)   25 0
H: 5 11   W: 11 03   b.Cork 23-11-98
Internationals: Republic of Ireland U17, U19, U21, Full caps.

2018–19	Liverpool	0	0		
2019–20	Liverpool	0	0		
2020–21	Liverpool	2	0		
2021–22	Liverpool	2	0		
2022–23	Liverpool	1	0		
2023–24	Liverpool	10	0		
2024–25	Liverpool	10	0	25	0

KONATE, Ibrahima (D)   160 4
H: 6 4   W: 13 03   b.Paris 25-5-99
Internationals: France U16, U17, U19, U20, U21, Full caps.

2016–17	Sochaux	12	1	12	1
2017–18	RB Leipzig	16	0		
2018–19	RB Leipzig	28	1		
2019–20	RB Leipzig	8	0		
2020–21	RB Leipzig	14	1	66	2
2021–22	Liverpool	11	0		
2022–23	Liverpool	18	0		
2023–24	Liverpool	20	0		
2024–25	Liverpool	31	1	82	1

KONE-DOHERTY, Trent (F)   0 0
H: 5 9   W: 10 03   b.Derry 30-6-06
Internationals: Republic of Ireland U16, U17, U19.

| 2024–25 | Liverpool | 0 | 0 | | |

KOUMAS, Lewis (F)   43 3
H: 6 0   W: 10 10   b.Chester 19-9-05
Internationals: Wales U19, U21, Full caps.

2023–24	Liverpool	0	0		
2024–25	Liverpool	0	0		
2024–25	*Stoke C*	43	3	43	3

MABAYA, Isaac (M)   0 0
H: 6 1   W: 11 11   b.Preston 22-9-04
Internationals: England U16, U17, U18, U19.

2021–22	Liverpool	0	0		
2022–23	Liverpool	0	0		
2023–24	Liverpool	0	0		
2024–25	Liverpool	0	0		

MAC ALLISTER, Alexis (M)   245 37
H: 5 9   W: 11 05   b.La Pampa 24-12-98
Internationals: Argentina U23, Full caps.

2016–17	Argentinos Juniors	23	3		
2017–18	Argentinos Juniors	24	2		
2018–19	Argentinos Juniors	19	5	66	10
2019–20	*Boca Juniors*	9	0		
2019–20	Brighton & HA	13	1	13	1
2020–21	Brighton & HA	21	1		
2021–22	Brighton & HA	33	5		
2022–23	Brighton & HA	35	10	98	16
2023–24	Liverpool	33	5		
2024–25	Liverpool	35	5	68	10

MAMARDASHVILI, Giorgi (G)   184 0
H: 6 6   W: 13 08   b.Tbilisi 29-9-00
Internationals: Georgia U17, U21, Full caps.

2018	Dinamo Tbilisi	0	0		
2019	Dinamo Tbilisi	0	0		
2019	*Rustavi*	28	0	28	0
2020	Dinamo Tbilisi	0	0		
2020	*Locomotive Tbilisi*	11	0		
2021	Dinamo Tbilisi	0	0		
2021	*Locomotive Tbilisi*	18	0	29	0
2021–22	Valencia	18	0		
2022–23	Valencia	38	0		
2023–24	Valencia	37	0		
2024–25	Valencia	0	0		
2024–25	*Valencia*	34	0	127	0

MARCELO (G)   4 0
H: 5 11   W: 12 04   b.Niteroi 20-12-02
Internationals: Brazil U17.
From Fluminense.

2020–21	Liverpool	0	0		
2021–22	Liverpool	0	0		
2022–23	Liverpool	0	0		
2023–24	Liverpool	0	0		
2024	*St Patrick's Ath*	4	0	4	0
2024–25	Liverpool	0	0		
2024–25	*Livingston*	0	0		

Transferred to Fluminense, January 2025.

McCONNELL, James (M)   3 0
H: 5 11   W: 11 05   b.Newcastle upon Tyne 13-9-04
Internationals: England U20.

| 2023–24 | Liverpool | 3 | 0 | | |
| 2024–25 | Liverpool | 0 | 0 | 3 | 0 |

MORRISON, Kieran (M)   0 0
H: 5 11   W: 10 03   b. 9-11-06
Internationals: Northern Ireland U17, U19.

| 2024–25 | Liverpool | 0 | 0 | | |

MORTON, Tyler (M)   81 3
H: 5 10   W: 11 11   b.Wirral 31-10-02
Internationals: England U20, U21.

2020–21	Liverpool	0	0		
2021–22	Liverpool	2	0		
2022–23	Liverpool	0	0		
2022–23	*Blackburn R*	40	0	40	0
2023–24	Liverpool	0	0		
2023–24	*Hull C*	39	3	39	3
2024–25	Liverpool	0	0	2	0

MROZEK, Fabian (G)   5 0
b.Wroclaw 28-9-03

2023–24	Liverpool	0	0		
2023–24	*Brommapojkarna*	5	0	5	0
2024–25	Liverpool	0	0		

NALLO, Amara (D)   0 0
H: 6 1   W: 11 05   b.Enfield 18-11-06
Internationals: England U18, U19.

| 2023–24 | Liverpool | 0 | 0 | | |
| 2024–25 | Liverpool | 0 | 0 | | |

NGUMOHA, Rio (F)   0 0
H: 5 7   W: 11 11   b. 29-8-08
Internationals: England U16, U17.

| 2024–25 | Liverpool | 0 | 0 | | |

NORRIS, James (D)   36 0
H: 5 8   W: 9 06   b.Liverpool 4-4-03
Internationals: England U16, U17, U18, U19.

2019–20	Liverpool	0	0		
2020–21	Liverpool	0	0		
2021–22	Liverpool	0	0		
2022–23	Liverpool	0	0		
2023–24	Liverpool	0	0		
2023–24	*Tranmere R*	16	0	16	0
2024–25	Liverpool	0	0		
2024–25	*Shelbourne*	20	0	20	0

NUNEZ, Darwin (F)   196 77
H: 6 2   W: 12 11   b.Artigas 24-6-99
Internationals: Uruguay U20, Full caps.

2017	Penarol	1	0		
2018	Penarol	10	1		
2019	Penarol	3	3	14	4
2019–20	Almeria	30	16	30	16
2020–21	Benfica	29	6		
2021–22	Benfica	28	26	57	32
2022–23	Liverpool	29	9		
2023–24	Liverpool	36	11		
2024–25	Liverpool	30	5	95	25

NYONI, Treymaurice (M)   0 0
H: 5 11   W: 11 11   b.Leicester 30-6-07
Internationals: England U16, U17, U18, U19, U20.

| 2023–24 | Liverpool | 0 | 0 | | |
| 2024–25 | Liverpool | 0 | 0 | | |

PHILLIPS, Nathaniel (D)   111 3
H: 6 3   W: 11 07   b.Bolton 21-3-97

2019–20	Liverpool	0	0		
2019–20	*VfB Stuttgart*	19	0	19	0
2020–21	Liverpool	17	1		
2021–22	Liverpool	0	0		
2021–22	*Bournemouth*	17	0	17	0
2022–23	Liverpool	2	0		
2023–24	Liverpool	0	0		
2023–24	*Celtic*	6	0	6	0
2023–24	*Cardiff C*	18	1	18	1
2024–25	Liverpool	0	0	19	1
2024–25	*Derby Co*	32	1	32	1

QUANSAH, Jarell (D)   46 2
H: 6 3   W: 12 08   b.Warrington 29-1-03
Internationals: England U16, U17, U18, U19, U20, U21.

2020–21	Liverpool	0	0		
2021–22	Liverpool	0	0		
2022–23	Liverpool	0	0		
2022–23	*Bristol R*	16	0	16	0
2023–24	Liverpool	17	2		
2024–25	Liverpool	13	0	30	2

RAMSAY, Calvin (D)   49 1
H: 5 10   W: 9 13   b.Aberdeen 31-7-03
Internationals: Scotland U16, U17, U21, Full caps.

2019–20	Aberdeen	0	0		
2020–21	Aberdeen	4	0		
2021–22	Aberdeen	24	1	28	1
2022–23	Liverpool	0	0		
2023–24	Liverpool	0	0		
2023–24	*Preston NE*	2	0	2	0
2023–24	*Bolton W*	3	0	3	0
2024–25	*Wigan Ath*	8	0	8	0
2024–25	*Kilmarnock*	8	0	8	0

ROBERTSON, Andrew (D) 420 18
H: 5 10 W: 10 00 b.Glasgow 11-3-94
Internationals: Scotland U21, Full caps.
2012–13 Queen's Park 34 2 34 2
2013–14 Dundee U 36 3 36 3
2014–15 Hull C 24 0
2015–16 Hull C 42 2
2016–17 Hull C 33 1 99 3
2017–18 Liverpool 22 1
2018–19 Liverpool 36 0
2019–20 Liverpool 36 2
2020–21 Liverpool 38 1
2021–22 Liverpool 29 3
2022–23 Liverpool 34 0
2023–24 Liverpool 23 3
2024–25 Liverpool 33 0 251 10

SALAH, Mohamed (F) 467 241
H: 5 9 W: 11 05 b.Basion 15-6-92
Internationals: Egypt U20, U23, Full caps.
2009–10 Al-Mokawloon 3 0
2010–11 Al-Mokawloon 20 4
2011–12 Al-Mokawloon 15 7 38 11
2012–13 FC Basel 29 5
2013–14 FC Basel 18 4 47 9
2013–14 Chelsea 10 2
2014–15 Chelsea 3 0
2014–15 *Fiorentina* 16 6 16 6
2015–16 Chelsea 0 0 13 2
2015–16 *Roma* 34 14
2016–17 Roma 31 15 65 29
2017–18 Liverpool 36 32
2018–19 Liverpool 38 22
2019–20 Liverpool 34 19
2020–21 Liverpool 37 22
2021–22 Liverpool 35 23
2022–23 Liverpool 38 19
2023–24 Liverpool 32 18
2024–25 Liverpool 38 29 288 184

SCANLON, Calum (D) 4 1
H: 5 7 W: 9 06 b.Birmingham 14-2-05
Internationals: England U17, U18, U19, U20.
2023–24 Liverpool 0 0
2024–25 Liverpool 0 0
2024–25 *Millwall* 4 1 4 1

STEPHENSON, Luca (M) 61 3
b. 17-9-03
2023–24 Liverpool 0 0
2023–24 *Barrow* 30 0 30 0
2024–25 Liverpool 0 0
2024–25 *Dundee U* 31 3 31 3

SZOBOSZLAI, Dominik (M) 229 53
H: 6 2 W: 11 09 b.Szekesfehervar 25-10-00
Internationals: Hungary U17, U19, U21, Full caps.
2017–18 Red Bull Salzburg 1 0
2017–18 *Liefering* 33 10
2018–19 Red Bull Salzburg 16 3
2018–19 *Liefering* 9 6 42 16
2019–20 Red Bull Salzburg 27 9
2020–21 Red Bull Salzburg 12 4 56 16
2020–21 RB Leipzig 0 0
2021–22 RB Leipzig 31 6
2022–23 RB Leipzig 31 6 62 12
2023–24 Liverpool 33 3
2024–25 Liverpool 36 6 69 9

TSIMIKAS, Konstantinos (D) 121 2
H: 5 10 W: 11 00 b.Thessaloniki 12-5-96
Internationals: Greece U19, U21, Full caps.
2015–16 Olympiacos 3 0
2016–17 Olympiacos 1 0
2016–17 *Esbjerg* 9 2 9 2
2017–18 Olympiacos 0 0
2017–18 *Willem II* 0 0
2018–19 Olympiacos 15 0
2019–20 Olympiacos 27 0
2020–21 Olympiacos 0 0 46 0
2020–21 Liverpool 2 0
2021–22 Liverpool 13 0
2022–23 Liverpool 20 0
2023–24 Liverpool 13 0
2024–25 Liverpool 18 0 66 0

VAN DIJK, Virgil (D) 439 41
H: 6 4 W: 14 07 b.Breda 8-7-91
Internationals: Netherlands U19, U21, Full caps.
From Willem II.
2010–11 Groningen 5 2
2011–12 Groningen 23 3
2012–13 Groningen 34 2 62 7
2013–14 Celtic 36 5
2014–15 Celtic 35 4
2015–16 Celtic 5 0 76 9
2015–16 Southampton 34 3
2016–17 Southampton 21 1
2017–18 Southampton 12 0 67 4
2017–18 Liverpool 14 0
2018–19 Liverpool 38 4
2019–20 Liverpool 38 5
2020–21 Liverpool 5 1
2021–22 Liverpool 34 3
2022–23 Liverpool 32 3
2023–24 Liverpool 36 2
2024–25 Liverpool 37 3 234 21

WILLIAMS, Rhys (D) 64 1
H: 6 5 W: 11 05 b.Preston 3-2-01
Internationals: England U18, U19, U21.
2019–20 Liverpool 0 0
2020–21 Liverpool 9 0
2021–22 Liverpool 0 0
2021–22 *Swansea C* 5 0 5 0
2022–23 Liverpool 0 0
2022–23 *Blackpool* 17 0 17 0
2023–24 Liverpool 0 0
2023–24 *Aberdeen* 0 0
2023–24 *Port Vale* 0 0
2024–25 Liverpool 0 0 9 0
2024–25 *Morecambe* 33 1 33 1

YOUNG, Ranel (F) 0 0
H: 5 9 W: 10 03 b.Huddersfield 26-12-05
2024–25 Liverpool 0 0

Players retained or with offer of contract
Ayman, Alvin; Cannonier, Oakley William; Davidson, Josh John James; Ewing, Clae Louis Adrian; Figueroa Norales, Keyrol Alexis; Hall-MacDonald, Bailey Graham; Kelly, Kyle Damian; Laffey, Michael Mark Paul; Lucky Omoruyi, Wellity; McLoughlin Miles, Terence James; Misciur, Kornel Artur; Mrozek, Fabian; Onanuga, Daniel Folami Jesusemilore; Pilling, Tommy James; Pinnington, Carter William; Pitt, Lucas Rafael Philip Jose; Sonni Lambie, Joshua Junior; Stephenson, Luca; Trueman, Ben.

Scholars
Ahmed, Kareem; Airoboma, Emmanuel Ehigie; Bernard, Dwayne Junior; Bradshaw, Joseph Daniel; Cisse, Prince Kobe; Cowley, Ryan Robert; Esdaille, DJ; Evans O'Connor, Oliver James; Lonmeni Dekam, Scofield Dupierrot; Martin, Tyler Emmanuel Alexander; Ngumoha, Chima Rio; Upton, Joseph James.

LUTON T (49)

AASGAARD, Thelo (M) 157 25
H: 5 7 W: 9 02 b.Liverpool 2-5-02
Internationals: Norway U16, U20, U21, Full caps.
2020–21 Wigan Ath 33 3
2021–22 Wigan Ath 5 1
2022–23 Wigan Ath 41 3
2023–24 Wigan Ath 35 8
2024–25 Wigan Ath 26 8 140 23
2024–25 Luton T 17 2 17 2

ADEBAYO, Elijah (F) 255 68
H: 6 4 W: 14 00 b.Brent 7-1-98
2017–18 Fulham 0 0
2017–18 *Cheltenham T* 7 2 7 2
2018–19 Fulham 0 0
2018–19 *Swindon T* 25 5 25 5
2018–19 *Stevenage* 2 0 2 0
2019–20 Walsall 30 8
2020–21 Walsall 25 10 55 18
2020–21 Luton T 18 5
2021–22 Luton T 40 16
2022–23 Luton T 42 7
2023–24 Luton T 27 10
2024–25 Luton T 39 5 166 43

ALLI, Millenic (F) 51 17
H: 5 9 W: 12 04 b.Dublin 6-2-00
From South Shields, Ashton U, Stockport Co, FC Halifax T.
2023–24 Exeter C 10 4
2024–25 Exeter C 25 9 35 13
2024–25 Luton T 16 4 16 4

ANDERSEN, Mads (D) 225 11
H: 6 5 W: 12 13 b.Albertslund 27-12-97
Internationals: Denmark U19.
2016–17 Brondby 0 0
2016–17 *Koge* 25 2 25 2
2017–18 Horsens 8 1
2018–19 Horsens 20 3 28 4
2019–20 Barnsley 38 0
2020–21 Barnsley 46 1
2021–22 Barnsley 28 1
2022–23 Barnsley 44 2 156 4
2023–24 Luton T 8 1
2024–25 Luton T 8 0 16 1

BAPTISTE, Shandon (M) 110 4
H: 5 11 W: 10 08 b.Grenada 8-4-98
Internationals: Grenada Full caps.
2017–18 Oxford U 0 0
2018–19 Oxford U 9 0
2019–20 Oxford U 17 1 26 1
2019–20 Brentford 12 0
2020–21 Brentford 1 0
2021–22 Brentford 22 1
2022–23 Brentford 23 0
2023–24 Brentford 10 1 68 2
2024–25 Luton T 16 1 16 1

BELL, Amari (D) 360 11
H: 5 11 W: 12 00 b.Burton-upon-Trent 5-5-94
Internationals: Jamaica Full caps.
2012–13 Birmingham C 0 0
2013–14 Birmingham C 1 0
2014–15 Birmingham C 0 0 1 0
2014–15 *Swindon T* 10 0 10 0
2014–15 *Gillingham* 7 0 7 0
2015–16 Fleetwood T 44 0
2016–17 Fleetwood T 44 2
2017–18 Fleetwood T 27 4 115 6
2017–18 Blackburn R 12 0
2018–19 Blackburn R 38 3
2019–20 Blackburn R 21 0
2020–21 Blackburn R 19 0 90 3
2021–22 Luton T 41 1
2022–23 Luton T 44 1
2023–24 Luton T 21 0
2024–25 Luton T 31 0 137 2

BENAGR, Benedict (D) 0 0
b. 17-9-07
2024–25 Luton T 0 0

BROWN, Jacob (F) 260 43
H: 5 10 W: 9 11 b.Halifax 10-4-98
Internationals: Scotland Full caps.
From Guiseley.
2014–15 Barnsley 0 0
2015–16 Barnsley 0 0
2016–17 Barnsley 2 0
2017–18 Barnsley 0 0
2017–18 *Chesterfield* 13 0 13 0
2018–19 Barnsley 32 8
2019–20 Barnsley 40 3 74 11
2020–21 Stoke C 41 5
2021–22 Stoke C 45 13
2022–23 Stoke C 38 7
2023–24 Stoke C 1 1 125 26
2023–24 Luton T 19 2
2024–25 Luton T 29 4 48 6

BURKE, Reece (D) 264 10
H: 6 2 W: 12 11 b.Newham 2-9-96
Internationals: England U18, U19, U20.
2013–14 West Ham U 0 0
2014–15 West Ham U 5 0
2015–16 West Ham U 0 0
2015–16 *Bradford C* 34 2 34 2
2016–17 West Ham U 0 0
2016–17 *Wigan Ath* 10 1 10 1
2017–18 West Ham U 0 0 5 0
2017–18 *Bolton W* 25 1 25 1
2018–19 Hull C 34 0
2019–20 Hull C 36 0
2020–21 Hull C 34 4 104 4
2021–22 Luton T 27 0
2022–23 Luton T 20 2
2023–24 Luton T 22 0
2024–25 Luton T 17 0 86 2

CAMPBELL, Allan (M) 234 21
H: 5 8 W: 10 08 b.Glasgow 4-7-98
Internationals: Scotland U21, Full caps.
2015–16 Motherwell 0 0
2016–17 Motherwell 7 1
2017–18 Motherwell 29 2
2018–19 Motherwell 35 2
2019–20 Motherwell 30 5
2020–21 Motherwell 34 4 135 14
2021–22 Luton T 33 4
2022–23 Luton T 42 3
2023–24 Luton T 0 0
2023–24 *Millwall* 12 0 12 0
2024–25 Luton T 0 0 75 7
2024–25 *Charlton Ath* 12 0 12 0

CHIGOZIE, Christian (D) 0 0
H: 6 1 W: 11 09 b. 1-3-07
2023–24 Luton T 0 0
2024–25 Luton T 0 0

CHONG, Tahith (F) 149 11
H: 6 1 W: 11 00 b.Willemstad 4-12-99
Internationals: Netherlands U16, U17, U19, U20, U21.
From Feyenoord.
2018–19 Manchester U 2 0
2019–20 Manchester U 3 0
2020–21 Manchester U 0 0
2020–21 *Werder Bremen* 13 0 13 0
2020–21 *Club Brugge* 10 0 10 0
2021–22 Manchester U 0 0 5 0
2021–22 *Birmingham C* 20 1
2022–23 Birmingham C 38 4 58 5
2023–24 Luton T 33 4
2024–25 Luton T 30 2 63 6

CLARK, Jordan (M) 378 37
H: 6 0 W: 11 07 b.Barnsley 22-9-93
2010–11 Barnsley 4 0

2011–12 Barnsley 2 0
2012–13 Barnsley 0 0
2012–13 *Chesterfield* 2 0 **2 0**
2013–14 Barnsley 0 0 **6 0**
2013–14 *Scunthorpe U* 1 0 **1 0**
2014–15 Shrewsbury T 27 3
2015–16 Shrewsbury T 20 2 **47 5**
2016–17 Accrington S 42 1
2017–18 Accrington S 43 8
2018–19 Accrington S 43 5
2019–20 Accrington S 34 6 **162 20**
2020–21 Luton T 34 1
2021–22 Luton T 25 2
2022–23 Luton T 38 2
2023–24 Luton T 23 1
2024–25 Luton T 40 6 **160 12**

DABO, Lamine (M) **32 0**
H: 6 1 W: 12 02 b.Kandiounkou 30-1-04
2024 AIK 20 0 **20 0**
2024–25 Luton T 12 0 **12 0**

DOUGHTY, Alfie (M) **147 9**
H: 6 0 W: 10 10 b.Poplar 21-12-99
2018–19 Charlton Ath 1 0
2019–20 Charlton Ath 29 2
2020–21 Charlton Ath 7 1 **36 3**
2020–21 Stoke C 0 0
2021–22 Stoke C 11 0 **11 0**
2021–22 *Cardiff C* 9 1 **9 1**
2022–23 Luton T 28 2
2023–24 Luton T 37 2
2024–25 Luton T 26 1 **91 5**

FRANCIS-CLARKE, Aidan (D) **0 0**
b. 8-11-03
2021–22 Luton T 0 0
2022–23 Luton T 0 0
2023–24 Luton T 0 0
2024–25 Luton T 0 0
Transferred to Braintree T, February 2025.

HARRIS, Taylan (F) **0 0**
H: 5 11 W: 11 07 b. 30-10-05
2023–24 Reading 0 0
2023–24 Luton T 0 0
2024–25 Luton T 0 0

HASHIOKA, Daiki (D) **187 4**
b.Urawa 17-5-99
Internationals: Japan U23, Full caps.
2017 Urawa Red Diamonds 0 0
2018 Urawa Red Diamonds 25 1
2019 Urawa Red Diamonds 18 2
2020 Urawa Red Diamonds 31 1 **74 4**
2020–21 Sint-Truidense 6 0
2021–22 Sint-Truidense 30 0
2022–23 Sint-Truidense 32 0
2023–24 Sint-Truidense 18 0 **86 0**
2023–24 Luton T 10 0
2024–25 Luton T 17 0 **27 0**

HOLMES, Thomas (D) **156 2**
H: 6 0 W: 12 13 b.Ealing 3-12-00
2017–18 Reading 1 0
2018–19 Reading 0 0
2019–20 Reading 0 0
2019–20 *KSV Roeselare* 11 0 **11 0**
2020–21 Reading 39 0
2021–22 Reading 32 1
2022–23 Reading 40 0
2023–24 Reading 0 0
2023–24 *Reading* 13 0 **125 1**
2024–25 Luton T 18 1 **18 1**
2024–25 *Dender* 2 0 **2 0**

HORLICK, Jameson (G) **0 0**
b. 12-8-03
2021–22 Luton T 0 0
2022–23 Luton T 0 0
2024–25 Luton T 0 0

JOHNSON, Joseph (D) **12 0**
H: 5 8 W: 9 13 b.London 9-2-06
Internationals: England U17, U18, U19.
2022–23 Luton T 2 0
2023–24 Luton T 2 0
2024–25 Luton T 8 0 **12 0**

JONES, Isaiah (M) **160 15**
H: 5 11 W: 10 10 b.Lambeth 26-6-99
Internationals: Guyana Full caps.
From Tooting & Mitcham U.
2019–20 Middlesbrough 0 0
2019–20 *St Johnstone* 0 0
2020–21 Middlesbrough 0 0
2020–21 *Queen of the South* 11 1 **11 1**
2021–22 Middlesbrough 42 1
2022–23 Middlesbrough 34 3
2023–24 Middlesbrough 35 8
2024–25 Middlesbrough 21 0 **132 12**
2024–25 Luton T 17 2 **17 2**

KAMINSKI, Thomas (G) **438 0**
H: 6 2 W: 11 00 b.Dendermonde 23-10-92
Internationals: Belgium U16, U17, U19, U21, Full caps.
2008–09 Beerschot 2 0

2009–10 Beerschot 4 0
2010–11 Beerschot 30 0
2011–12 Beerschot 2 0 **38 0**
2011–12 OH Leuven 25 0 **25 0**
2012–13 Anderlecht 1 0
2013–14 Anderlecht 10 0
2014–15 Anderlecht 2 0
2014–15 *Anorthosis Famagusta* 30 0 **30 0**
2015–16 Anderlecht 0 0 **13 0**
2015–16 *FC Copenhagen* 2 0 **2 0**
2016–17 Kortrijk 32 0
2017–18 Kortrijk 34 0
2018–19 Kortrijk 18 0 **84 0**
2018–19 Gent 19 0
2019–20 Gent 29 0
2020–21 Gent 0 0 **48 0**
2020–21 Blackburn R 43 0
2021–22 Blackburn R 44 0
2022–23 Blackburn R 28 0 **115 0**
2023–24 Luton T 38 0
2024–25 Luton T 45 0 **83 0**

KRAUSS, Tom (M) **148 10**
b.Leipzig 22-6-01
Internationals: Germany U16, U17, U18, U19, U20, U21.
2019–20 RB Leipzig 1 0
2020–21 RB Leipzig 0 0
2020–21 *1. FC Nurnberg* 31 2
2021–22 RB Leipzig 0 0
2021–22 *1. FC Nurnberg* 32 3 **63 5**
2022–23 *Schalke 04* 32 2 **32 2**
2023–24 Mainz 05 29 1
2024–25 Mainz 05 0 0 **29 1**
On loan from Mainz 05.
2024–25 Luton T 23 2 **23 2**

KRUL, Tim (G) **372 0**
H: 6 4 W: 13 00 b.Den Haag 3-4-88
Internationals: Netherlands U16, U17, U19, U20, U21, Full caps.
From ADO Den Haag.
2005–06 Newcastle U 0 0
2006–07 Newcastle U 0 0
2007–08 *Falkirk* 22 0 **22 0**
2007–08 Newcastle U 0 0
2008–09 Newcastle U 0 0
2008–09 *Carlisle U* 9 0 **9 0**
2009–10 Newcastle U 3 0
2010–11 Newcastle U 21 0
2011–12 Newcastle U 38 0
2012–13 Newcastle U 24 0
2013–14 Newcastle U 36 0
2014–15 Newcastle U 30 0
2015–16 Newcastle U 8 0
2016–17 Newcastle U 0 0
2016–17 *Ajax* 0 0
2016–17 *AZ Alkmaar* 18 0 **18 0**
2017–18 Newcastle U 0 0 **160 0**
2017–18 *Brighton & HA* 0 0
2018–19 Norwich C 46 0
2019–20 Norwich C 36 0
2020–21 Norwich C 36 0
2021–22 Norwich C 29 0
2022–23 Norwich C 16 0
2022–23 Norwich C 0 0 **163 0**
2023–24 Luton T 0 0
2024–25 Luton T 0 0 **102 0**

LOCKYER, Tom (D) **356 11**
H: 6 0 W: 11 05 b.Bristol 30-12-94
Internationals: Wales U21, Full caps.
2012–13 Bristol R 4 0
2013–14 Bristol R 41 1
From Bristol R.
2015–16 Bristol R 43 0
2016–17 Bristol R 46 0
2017–18 Bristol R 37 1
2018–19 Bristol R 40 3 **211 5**
2019–20 Charlton Ath 43 1 **43 1**
2020–21 Luton T 20 0
2021–22 Luton T 29 1
2022–23 Luton T 39 3
2023–24 Luton T 14 1
2024–25 Luton T 0 0 **102 5**

LUKER, Jayden (M) **22 3**
H: 5 9 W: 11 03 b.Southwark 30-4-05
2022–23 Luton T 0 0
2023–24 Luton T 0 0
2024–25 Luton T 0 0
2024–25 *Grimsby T* 22 3 **22 3**

MAKOSSO, Christ (D) **49 1**
H: 6 4 W: 13 05 b.Brazzaville 9-5-04
Internationals: DR Congo Full caps.
2019–20 Ajax Moungali 0 0
2020–21 Ajax Moungali 0 0
2021–22 CARA Brazzaville 0 0
2022–23 CARA Brazzaville 0 0
2022–23 Sochaux 5 0
2023–24 Sochaux 8 0 **13 0**
2023–24 RWD Molenbeek 10 0

2024–25 RWD Molenbeek 13 1 **23 1**
2024–25 Luton T 13 0 **13 0**

MARTINS, Dominic (D) **0 0**
H: 5 10 W: 11 00 b.London 13-10-05
2023–24 Luton T 0 0
2024–25 Luton T 0 0

McGUINNESS, Mark (D) **167 10**
H: 6 4 W: 11 00 b.Slough 5-1-01
Internationals: Republic of Ireland U19, U21, Full caps.
2019–20 Arsenal 0 0
2020–21 Arsenal 0 0
2021–22 *Ipswich T* 24 1 **24 1**
2021–22 Cardiff C 34 3
2022–23 Cardiff C 19 0
2022–23 *Sheffield Wed* 17 1 **17 1**
2023–24 Cardiff C 30 2
2024–25 Cardiff C 0 0 **83 5**
2024–25 Luton T 43 3 **43 3**

MENGI, Teden (D) **68 2**
H: 6 0 W: 12 04 b.Manchester 30-4-02
Internationals: England U16, U17, U18, U20, U21.
2019–20 Manchester U 0 0
2020–21 Manchester U 0 0
2021–22 *Derby Co* 9 0
2021–22 *Derby Co* 0 0 **9 0**
2021–22 Manchester U 0 0
2021–22 *Birmingham C* 9 0 **9 0**
2022–23 Manchester U 0 0
2023–24 Luton T 30 1
2024–25 Luton T 20 1 **50 2**

MORRIS, Carlton (F) **321 75**
H: 6 1 W: 13 05 b.Cambridge 16-12-95
Internationals: England U19.
2014–15 Norwich C 1 0
2014–15 *Oxford U* 7 0
2014–15 *York C* 8 0 **8 0**
2015–16 Norwich C 0 0
2015–16 *Hamilton A* 32 8 **32 8**
2016–17 Norwich C 0 0
2016–17 *Rotherham U* 8 0
2017–18 Norwich C 0 0
2017–18 *Shrewsbury T* 42 6 **42 6**
2018–19 Norwich C 0 0
2019–20 Norwich C 0 0
2019–20 *Rotherham U* 21 3 **29 3**
2019–20 *Milton Keynes D* 10 2
2020–21 Norwich C 0 0 **1 0**
2020–21 *Milton Keynes D* 18 3 **28 5**
2020–21 Barnsley 23 7
2021–22 Barnsley 28 7 **51 14**
2022–23 Luton T 44 20
2023–24 Luton T 38 11
2024–25 Luton T 41 8 **123 39**

MOSES, Victor (M) **392 45**
H: 5 10 W: 11 07 b.Lagos 12-12-90
Internationals: England U16, U17, U19, U21. Nigeria Full caps.
2007–08 Crystal Palace 13 3
2008–09 Crystal Palace 27 2
2009–10 Crystal Palace 18 6 **58 11**
2009–10 Wigan Ath 14 1
2010–11 Wigan Ath 21 1
2011–12 Wigan Ath 38 6
2012–13 Wigan Ath 1 0 **74 8**
2012–13 Chelsea 23 1
2013–14 Chelsea 0 0
2013–14 *Liverpool* 19 1 **19 1**
2014–15 Chelsea 0 0
2014–15 *Stoke C* 19 3 **19 3**
2015–16 Chelsea 0 0
2015–16 *West Ham U* 21 1 **21 1**
2016–17 Chelsea 34 3
2017–18 Chelsea 28 3
2018–19 Chelsea 2 0
2018–19 *Fenerbahce* 14 4 **14 4**
2019–20 Chelsea 0 0
2019–20 *Internazionale* 12 0 **12 0**
2020–21 Chelsea 0 0 **87 7**
2020–21 Spartak Moscow 19 4
2021–22 Spartak Moscow 25 2
2022–23 Spartak Moscow 10 2
2023–24 Spartak Moscow 16 1 **70 9**
2024–25 Luton T 18 1 **18 1**

NAKAMBA, Marvelous (M) **231 2**
H: 5 10 W: 11 03 b.Hwange 19-1-94
Internationals: Zimbabwe U20, Full caps.
2012–13 Nancy 0 0
2013–14 Nancy 2 0 **2 0**
2014–15 Vitesse 30 1
2015–16 Vitesse 30 1
2016–17 Vitesse 31 1 **67 2**
2017–18 Club Brugge 35 0
2018–19 Club Brugge 18 0 **53 0**
2019–20 Aston Villa 29 0
2020–21 Aston Villa 13 0
2021–22 Aston Villa 16 0
2022–23 Aston Villa 0 0 **58 0**

2022–23	Luton T	17	0	
2023–24	Luton T	13	0	
2024–25	Luton T	21	0	51 0

NELSON, Zack (M)   23 0
H: 6 0 W: 11 09 b.London 24-9-04
Internationals: England U20.

2022–23	Luton T	0	0	
2023–24	Luton T	2	0	
2024–25	Luton T	21	0	23 0

NORDAS, Lasse (F)   114 26
H: 6 4 W: 12 08 b.Lillestrom 10-2-02
Internationals: Norway U19, U20, U21.

2020	Strommen	26	11	26 11
2021	Bodo/Glimt	11	2	
2022	Bodo/Glimt	1	0	
2022	Tromso	14	2	
2023	Bodo/Glimt	10	0	22 2
2023	Tromso	14	2	
2024	Tromso	28	9	56 13
2024–25	Luton T	10	0	10 0

PEPPLE, Aribim (F)   64 12
H: 6 0 W: 13 01 b.Kettering 25-12-02

2019	Cavalry	7	0	
2020	Cavalry	6	0	
2021	Cavalry	1	0	
2022	Cavalry	7	6	20 6
2022–23	Luton T	0	0	
2022–23	*Grimsby T*	11	0	11 0
2023–24	Luton T	0	0	
2023–24	*Inverness CT*	13	1	13 1
2024–25	Luton T	0	0	
2024–25	*Chesterfield*	20	5	20 5

PHILLIPS, Joshua (M)   1 0
b.London 17-8-05

2024–25	Luton T	1	0	1 0

PIESOLD, Axel (M)   0 0
H: 5 10 W: 11 05 b.Haringey 31-3-05
From Tottenham H.

2022–23	Luton T	0	0	
2023–24	Luton T	0	0	
2024–25	Luton T	0	0	

PINNINGTON, Jacob (D)   0 0
b. 27-11-04

2024–25	Luton T	0	0	

RUDDOCK, Pelly (M)   360 22
H: 5 9 W: 9 13 b.Hendon 17-7-93
Internationals: DR Congo Full caps.

2011–12	West Ham U	0	0	
2012–13	West Ham U	0	0	
2013–14	West Ham U	0	0	
2014–15	Luton T	16	1	
2015–16	Luton T	21	2	
2016–17	Luton T	42	2	
2017–18	Luton T	28	2	
2018–19	Luton T	46	5	
2019–20	Luton T	44	3	
2020–21	Luton T	44	2	
2021–22	Luton T	34	1	
2022–23	Luton T	30	3	
2023–24	Luton T	27	0	
2024–25	Luton T	10	0	342 21
2024–25	*Rotherham U*	18	1	18 1

SHEA, James (G)   188 0
H: 5 11 W: 12 00 b.Islington 16-6-91

2009–10	Arsenal	0	0	
2010–11	Arsenal	0	0	
2011–12	Arsenal	0	0	
2011–12	*Dagenham & Red*	1	0	1 0
2012–13	Arsenal	0	0	
2013–14	Arsenal	0	0	
2014–15	AFC Wimbledon	38	0	
2015–16	AFC Wimbledon	21	0	
2016–17	AFC Wimbledon	36	0	95 0
2017–18	Luton T	8	0	
2018–19	Luton T	41	0	
2019–20	Luton T	13	0	
2020–21	Luton T	7	0	
2021–22	Luton T	19	0	
2022–23	Luton T	1	0	
2023–24	Luton T	1	0	
2024–25	Luton T	2	0	92 0

TOWNSEND, Andros (M)   381 35
H: 5 11 W: 12 02 b.Chingford 16-7-91
Internationals: England U16, U17, U19, U21, Full caps.

2008–09	Tottenham H	0	0	
2008–09	*Yeovil T*	10	1	10 1
2009–10	Tottenham H	0	0	
2009–10	*Leyton Orient*	22	2	22 2
2009–10	*Milton Keynes D*	9	2	9 2
2010–11	Tottenham H	0	0	
2010–11	*Ipswich T*	13	1	13 1
2010–11	*Watford*	3	0	3 0
2010–11	*Millwall*	11	2	11 2
2011–12	Tottenham H	0	0	
2011–12	*Leeds U*	6	1	6 1
2011–12	*Birmingham C*	15	0	15 0
2012–13	Tottenham H	5	0	

2012–13	*QPR*	12	2	12 2
2013–14	Tottenham H	25	1	
2014–15	Tottenham H	17	2	
2015–16	Tottenham H	3	0	50 3
2015–16	Newcastle U	13	4	13 4
2016–17	Crystal Palace	36	3	
2017–18	Crystal Palace	36	2	
2018–19	Crystal Palace	38	6	
2019–20	Crystal Palace	24	1	
2020–21	Crystal Palace	34	1	
2021–22	Crystal Palace	0	0	168 13
2021–22	Everton	21	3	
2022–23	Everton	0	0	21 3
2023–24	Luton T	27	1	
2024–25	Luton T	1	0	28 1

Transferred to Antalyaspor, September 2024.

WALSH, Liam (M)   123 6
H: 5 10 W: 10 06 b.Huyton 15-9-97
Internationals: England U16, U18.

2015–16	Everton	0	0	
2015–16	*Yeovil T*	15	1	15 1
2016–17	Everton	0	0	
2017–18	Everton	0	0	
2017–18	*Birmingham C*	3	0	3 0
2017–18	Bristol C	6	0	
2018–19	Bristol C	9	0	
2019–20	Bristol C	0	0	
2019–20	*Coventry C*	26	3	26 3
2020–21	Bristol C	3	0	18 0
2021–22	Swansea C	5	0	
2021–22	*Hull C*	3	0	3 0
2022–23	Swansea C	7	0	
2023–24	Swansea C	20	2	32 2
2024–25	Luton T	26	0	26 0

WALTERS, Reuell (D)   14 0
H: 6 0 W: 10 03 b.London 16-12-04
Internationals: England U18, U19, U20.

2022–23	Arsenal	0	0	
2023–24	Arsenal	0	0	
2024–25	Luton T	14	0	14 0

WOODROW, Cauley (F)   317 66
H: 6 0 W: 12 04 b.Hemel Hempstead 2-12-94
Internationals: England U17, U20, U21.
From Luton T.

2011–12	Fulham	0	0	
2012–13	Fulham	0	0	
2013–14	Fulham	6	1	
2013–14	*Southend U*	19	2	19 2
2014–15	Fulham	29	3	
2015–16	Fulham	14	4	
2016–17	Fulham	5	0	
2016–17	*Burton Alb*	14	5	14 5
2017–18	Fulham	0	0	54 8
2017–18	*Bristol C*	14	2	14 2
2018–19	Barnsley	31	16	
2019–20	Barnsley	40	14	
2020–21	Barnsley	42	12	
2021–22	Barnsley	28	4	141 46
2022–23	Luton T	27	2	
2023–24	Luton T	24	1	
2024–25	Luton T	15	0	66 3
2024–25	*Blackburn R*	9	0	9 0

Players retained or with offer of contract
Blackledge, Henry; Coyne, Liam Brian; Fanne Dabo, Mouhamed Lamine; Iwhiwhu, Jordan Ogheneserue; Kayibanda, Claude Smith; Lorentzen-Jones, Jack; Lynch, Oliver David James; Paternoster, Vladimir; Walton, Jack James.

Scholars
Anderson, Sam; Asamoah Junior, Lloyd Kofi; Booth, Charlie John; Emery, Charlie Michael; Fox, Harry Joe Edward; Giwa, Tyrell Bwalya Addo; Harvey, Isaiah Andrew; Hincapie Alfonso, Samuel; Hockey, Cai Vernon; Ioannides, Zacharias; Odegah, Anthony Jamie Habib; Pipa, Oliver; Roberts-Edema, Kyron Oguti Sebert; Sampson, Enoch Kwame Anson; Shepherd, Archie Patrick; Stitt, Dylan; Takawira, Matthew Kudakwashe; Thomas, Lucas Anthony; Trustram, Charlie Joseph Gordon; Xavier-Jones, Tate Hugh.

MANCHESTER C (50)

AKANJI, Manuel (D)   281 12
H: 6 2 W: 13 05 b.Wiesendangen 19-7-95
Internationals: Switzerland U20, U21, Full caps.

2013–14	Winterthur	2	0	
2014–15	Winterthur	33	1	35 1
2015–16	FC Basel	8	0	
2016–17	FC Basel	15	4	
2017–18	FC Basel	19	1	42 5
2017–18	Borussia Dortmund	11	0	
2018–19	Borussia Dortmund	25	1	
2019–20	Borussia Dortmund	29	0	
2020–21	Borussia Dortmund	28	2	
2021–22	Borussia Dortmund	26	1	119 4
2022–23	Manchester C	29	0	
2023–24	Manchester C	30	2	
2024–25	Manchester C	26	0	85 2

AKE, Nathan (D)   240 18
H: 5 11 W: 11 11 b.Den Haag 18-2-95
Internationals: Netherlands U15, U16, U17, U19, U21, Full caps.
From Feyenoord.

2012–13	Chelsea	3	0	
2013–14	Chelsea	1	0	
2014–15	Chelsea	1	0	
2014–15	*Reading*	5	0	5 0
2015–16	Chelsea	0	0	
2015–16	*Watford*	24	1	24 1
2016–17	Chelsea	2	0	7 0
2016–17	Bournemouth	10	3	
2017–18	Bournemouth	38	2	
2018–19	Bournemouth	38	4	
2019–20	Bournemouth	29	2	115 11
2020–21	Manchester C	10	1	
2021–22	Manchester C	14	2	
2022–23	Manchester C	26	1	
2023–24	Manchester C	29	2	
2024–25	Manchester C	10	0	89 6

ALFA-RUPRECHT, Farid (M)   0 0
H: 5 9 W: 10 03 b.Hamburg 28-3-06
Internationals: Germany U16, U17, U18.

2024–25	Manchester C	0	0	

ALLEYNE, Max (D)   0 0
H: 6 1 W: 11 03 b.Bristol 21-7-05
Internationals: England U17, U18, U19, U20.

2023–24	Manchester C	0	0	
2024–25	Manchester C	0	0	

BAH, Juma (D)   22 0
H: 6 5 W: 12 13 b.Freetown 11-4-06
Internationals: Sierra Leone Full caps.

2024–25	Real Valladolid	12	0	12 0
2024–25	Manchester C	0	0	
2024–25	*Lens*	10	0	10 0

BERNARDO SILVA, Mota (M)   368 67
H: 5 8 W: 9 11 b.Lisbon 10-8-94
Internationals: Portugal U19, U21, Full caps.

2013–14	Benfica	1	0	1 0
2014–15	Monaco	32	9	
2015–16	Monaco	32	7	
2016–17	Monaco	37	8	101 24
2017–18	Manchester C	35	6	
2018–19	Manchester C	36	7	
2019–20	Manchester C	34	6	
2020–21	Manchester C	26	2	
2021–22	Manchester C	35	8	
2022–23	Manchester C	34	4	
2023–24	Manchester C	33	6	
2024–25	Manchester C	33	4	266 43

BOBB, Oscar (M)   17 1
H: 5 9 W: 11 07 b.Oslo 12-7-03
Internationals: Norway U16, U17, U18, U19, U21, Full caps.
From Valerenga.

2020–21	Manchester C	0	0	
2021–22	Manchester C	0	0	
2022–23	Manchester C	0	0	
2023–24	Manchester C	14	1	
2024–25	Manchester C	3	0	17 1

BRAITHWAITE, Kaden (D)   0 0
H: 5 11 W: 12 04 b.Bolton 2-2-08
Internationals: England U16, U17.

2024–25	Manchester C	0	0	

BRECKIN, Kian (M)   15 0
H: 5 10 W: 11 05 b.Manchester 10-12-03

2023–24	Manchester C	0	0	
2023–24	*Wycombe W*	2	0	2 0
2024–25	Manchester C	0	0	
2024–25	*Crewe Alex*	13	0	13 0

BRITS, Spike (G)   0 0
H: 6 3 W: 10 03 b.Wimbledon 24-6-07
Internationals: England U16, U17, U18.

2024–25	Manchester C	0	0	

BURNS, Finley (D)   49 0
H: 6 1 W: 11 03 b.Southwark 17-6-03
Internationals: England U16, U17, U18.

2020–21	Manchester C	0	0	
2021–22	Manchester C	0	0	
2021–22	*Swansea C*	3	0	3 0
2022–23	Manchester C	0	0	
2023–24	*Stevenage*	37	0	37 0
2024–25	Manchester C	0	0	
2024–25	*Hull C*	9	0	9 0

CARSON, Scott (G)   469 0
H: 6 0 W: 13 07 b.Whitehaven 3-9-85
Internationals: England U18, U21, B, Full caps.

2002–03	Leeds U	0	0	
2003–04	Leeds U	3	0	
2004–05	Leeds U	0	0	3 0

2004–05	Liverpool	4	0		
2005–06	Liverpool	0	0		
2005–06	*Sheffield Wed*	9	0	**9**	**0**
2006–07	Liverpool	0	0		
2006–07	*Charlton Ath*	36	0	**36**	**0**
2007–08	Liverpool	0	0	**4**	**0**
2007–08	*Aston Villa*	35	0	**35**	**0**
2008–09	WBA	35	0		
2009–10	WBA	43	0		
2010–11	WBA	32	0	**110**	**0**
2011–12	Bursaspor	34	0		
2012–13	Bursaspor	29	0	**63**	**0**
2013–14	Wigan Ath	16	0		
2014–15	Wigan Ath	34	0	**50**	**0**
2015–16	Derby Co	36	0		
2016–17	Derby Co	46	0		
2017–18	Derby Co	46	0		
2018–19	Derby Co	30	0		
2019–20	Derby Co	0	0		
2019–20	*Manchester C*	0	0		
2020–21	Derby Co	0	0		
2020–21	*Manchester C*	1	0		
2021–22	Derby Co	0	0	**158**	**0**
2021–22	Manchester C	0	0		
2022–23	Manchester C	0	0		
2023–24	Manchester C	0	0		
2024–25	Manchester C	0	0	**1**	**0**

COUTO, Yan (D) 133 5
H: 5 6 b.Curitiba 3-6-02
Internationals: Brazil U17, Full caps.

2020	Coritiba	2	0	**2**	**0**
2020–21	Manchester C	0	0		
2020–21	*Girona*	23	2		
2021–22	Manchester C	0	0		
2021–22	*Braga*	28	1	**28**	**1**
2022–23	Manchester C	0	0		
2022–23	*Girona*	25	1		
2023–24	Manchester C	0	0		
2023–24	*Girona*	34	1	**82**	**4**
2024–25	Manchester C	0	0		
2024–25	*Borussia Dortmund*	21	0	**21**	**0**

DE BRUYNE, Kevin (M) 470 111
H: 5 11 W: 10 10 b.Ghent 28-6-91
Internationals: Belgium U18, U19, U21, Full caps.

2008–09	Genk	2	0		
2009–10	Genk	35	3		
2010–11	Genk	32	5		
2011–12	Genk	28	8	**97**	**16**
2011–12	Chelsea	0	0		
2012–13	Chelsea	0	0		
2012–13	*Werder Bremen*	33	10	**33**	**10**
2013–14	Chelsea	3	0	**3**	**0**
2013–14	VfL Wolfsburg	16	3		
2014–15	VfL Wolfsburg	34	10		
2015–16	VfL Wolfsburg	2	0	**52**	**13**
2015–16	Manchester C	25	7		
2016–17	Manchester C	36	6		
2017–18	Manchester C	37	8		
2018–19	Manchester C	19	2		
2019–20	Manchester C	35	13		
2020–21	Manchester C	25	6		
2021–22	Manchester C	30	15		
2022–23	Manchester C	32	7		
2023–24	Manchester C	18	4		
2024–25	Manchester C	28	4	**285**	**72**

DIAS, Ruben (D) 233 11
H: 6 1 W: 11 00 b.Amadora 14-5-97
Internationals: Portugal U16, U17, U19, U20, U21, Full caps.

2015–16	Benfica	0	0		
2016–17	Benfica	0	0		
2017–18	Benfica	24	3		
2018–19	Benfica	32	3		
2019–20	Benfica	33	2		
2020–21	Benfica	0	0	**89**	**8**
2020–21	Manchester C	32	1		
2021–22	Manchester C	29	2		
2022–23	Manchester C	26	0		
2023–24	Manchester C	30	0		
2024–25	Manchester C	27	0	**144**	**3**

DICKSON, Will (F) 7 0
b. 25-11-04

2024–25	Manchester C	0	0		
2024–25	*Motherwell*	7	0	**7**	**0**

DOKU, Jeremy (M) 167 21
H: 5 7 W: 10 06 b.Borgerhout 27-5-02
Internationals: Belgium U16, U17, U21, Full caps.

2018–19	Anderlecht	6	0		
2019–20	Anderlecht	21	3		
2020–21	Anderlecht	7	2	**34**	**5**
2020–21	Rennes	30	2		
2021–22	Rennes	14	1		
2022–23	Rennes	29	6		
2023–24	Rennes	2	1	**75**	**10**
2023–24	Manchester C	29	3		
2024–25	Manchester C	29	3	**58**	**6**

DOYLE, Callum (D) 134 2
H: 6 1 W: 11 05 b.Manchester 3-10-03
Internationals: England U18, U19, U20, U21.

2021–22	Manchester C	0	0		
2021–22	*Sunderland*	36	1	**36**	**1**
2022–23	Manchester C	0	0		
2022–23	*Coventry C*	41	0	**41**	**0**
2023–24	Manchester C	0	0		
2023–24	*Leicester C*	17	0	**17**	**0**
2024–25	Manchester C	0	0		
2024–25	*Norwich C*	40	1	**40**	**1**

ECHEVERRI, Claudio (M) 36 3
H: 5 7 W: 9 13 b.Resistencia 2-1-06
Internationals: Argentina U17, U20, U23, Ful caps.

2023	River Plate	5	0		
2023–24	Manchester C	0	0		
2024	*River Plate*	30	3	**35**	**3**
2024–25	Manchester C	1	0	**1**	**0**

EDERSON, de Moraes (G) 379 0
H: 6 2 W: 13 08 b.Osasco 17-8-93
Internationals: Brazil U23, Full caps.

2011–12	Ribeirao	29	0	**29**	**0**
2012–13	Rio Ave	2	0		
2013–14	Rio Ave	18	0		
2014–15	Rio Ave	17	0	**37**	**0**
2015–16	Benfica	10	0		
2016–17	Benfica	27	0	**37**	**0**
2017–18	Manchester C	36	0		
2018–19	Manchester C	38	0		
2019–20	Manchester C	35	0		
2020–21	Manchester C	36	0		
2021–22	Manchester C	37	0		
2022–23	Manchester C	35	0		
2023–24	Manchester C	33	0		
2024–25	Manchester C	26	0	**276**	**0**

FODEN, Phil (M) 192 61
H: 5 7 W: 11 00 b.Stockport 28-5-00
Internationals: England U16, U17, U18, U19, U21, Full caps.

2016–17	Manchester C	0	0		
2017–18	Manchester C	5	0		
2018–19	Manchester C	13	1		
2019–20	Manchester C	23	5		
2020–21	Manchester C	28	9		
2021–22	Manchester C	28	9		
2022–23	Manchester C	32	11		
2023–24	Manchester C	35	19		
2024–25	Manchester C	28	7	**192**	**61**

GALVEZ, Tomaz (D) 18 0
H: 5 9 b.London 28-2-05
Internationals: Finland U17, U18, U19, U21, Full caps.

2024–25	Manchester C	0	0		
2024–25	*LASK*	3	0	**3**	**0**
2024–25	*Cambuur*	15	0	**15**	**0**

GONZALEZ, Nico (M) 106 11
H: 6 2 W: 13 08 b.La Coruna 3-1-02
Internationals: Spain U17, U20.

2019–20	Barcelona	0	0		
2020–21	Barcelona	0	0		
2021–22	Barcelona	27	2		
2022–23	Barcelona	0	0	**27**	**2**
2022–23	*Valencia*	26	1	**26**	**1**
2023–24	Porto	25	2		
2024–25	Porto	17	5	**42**	**7**
2024–25	Manchester C	11	1	**11**	**1**

GREALISH, Jack (M) 316 46
H: 5 9 W: 10 10 b.Birmingham 10-9-95
Internationals: Republic of Ireland U17, U18, U21. England U21, Full caps.

2012–13	Aston Villa	0	0		
2013–14	Aston Villa	1	0		
2013–14	*Notts Co*	37	5	**37**	**5**
2014–15	Aston Villa	17	0		
2015–16	Aston Villa	16	1		
2016–17	Aston Villa	31	5		
2017–18	Aston Villa	27	3		
2018–19	Aston Villa	31	6		
2019–20	Aston Villa	36	8		
2020–21	Aston Villa	26	6	**185**	**29**
2021–22	Manchester C	26	3		
2022–23	Manchester C	28	5		
2023–24	Manchester C	20	3		
2024–25	Manchester C	20	1	**94**	**12**

GUNDOGAN, Ilkay (M) 410 66
H: 5 11 W: 11 00 b.Gelsenkirchen 24-10-90
Internationals: Germany U18, U19, U20, U21, Full caps.

2008–09	Bochum	0	0		
2008–09	Nuremburg	1	0		
2009–10	Nuremburg	22	1		
2010–11	Nuremburg	25	5	**48**	**6**
2011–12	Borussia Dortmund	28	3		
2012–13	Borussia Dortmund	28	3		
2013–14	Borussia Dortmund	1	0		
2014–15	Borussia Dortmund	23	3		
2015–16	Borussia Dortmund	25	1	**105**	**10**
2016–17	Manchester C	10	3		
2017–18	Manchester C	30	4		
2018–19	Manchester C	31	6		
2019–20	Manchester C	31	2		
2020–21	Manchester C	28	13		
2021–22	Manchester C	27	8		
2022–23	Manchester C	31	8		
2023–24	Barcelona	36	5	**36**	**5**
2024–25	Manchester C	33	1	**221**	**45**

GVARDIOL, Josko (D) 160 15
H: 6 1 W: 12 08 b.Zagreb 23-1-02
Internationals: Croatia U16, U17, U19, U21, Full caps.

2019–20	Dinamo Zagreb	11	1		
2020–21	Dinamo Zagreb	25	2	**36**	**3**
2021–22	RB Leipzig	29	2		
2022–23	RB Leipzig	30	1	**59**	**3**
2023–24	Manchester C	28	4		
2024–25	Manchester C	37	5	**65**	**9**

HAALAND, Erling Braut (F) 235 178
H: 6 4 W: 13 10 b.Leeds 21-7-00
Internationals: Norway U16, U17, U18, U19, U20, U21, Full caps.

2015	Bryne	0	0		
2016	Bryne	16	0	**16**	**0**
2017	Molde	14	2		
2018	Molde	25	12	**39**	**14**
2018–19	Red Bull Salzburg	2	1		
2019–20	Red Bull Salzburg	14	16	**16**	**17**
2019–20	Borussia Dortmund	15	13		
2020–21	Borussia Dortmund	28	27		
2021–22	Borussia Dortmund	24	22	**67**	**62**
2022–23	Manchester C	35	36		
2023–24	Manchester C	31	27		
2024–25	Manchester C	31	22	**97**	**85**

HUDSON, Max (G) 0 0
H: 5 11 W: 11 03 b. 20-9-07
Internationals: Wales U17, U18.

2024–25	Manchester C	0	0		

KABORE, Issa (D) 121 1
H: 5 11 W: 11 05 b.Ouagadougou 12-5-01
Internationals: Burkina Faso U20, Full caps.

2019–20	Mechelen	5	0		
2019–20	Manchester C	0	0		
2020–21	Manchester C	0	0		
2020–21	*Mechelen*	27	0	**32**	**0**
2021–22	Manchester C	0	0		
2021–22	*Troyes*	31	0	**31**	**0**
2022–23	Manchester C	0	0		
2022–23	*Marseille*	22	1	**22**	**1**
2023–24	Manchester C	0	0		
2023–24	*Luton T*	24	0	**24**	**0**
2024–25	Manchester C	0	0		
2024–25	*Benfica*	3	0	**3**	**0**
2024–25	*Werder Bremen*	9	0	**9**	**0**

KATONGO, Jadel (D) 47 1
H: 6 0 b.Manchester 14-9-04
Internationals: England U16, U18, U20.

2023–24	Manchester C	0	0		
2023–24	*Peterborough U*	30	1		
2024–25	Manchester C	0	0		
2024–25	*Peterborough U*	17	0	**47**	**1**

KAYKY, Chagas (F) 43 3
H: 5 9 W: 10 10 b.Rio de Janeiro 11-6-03
Internationals: Brazil U16.

2021	Fluminense	11	0	**11**	**0**
2021–22	Manchester C	1	0		
2022–23	Manchester C	0	0		
2022–23	*Pacos de Ferreira*	8	0	**8**	**0**
2023	*Bahia*	10	2		
2023–24	Manchester C	0	0		
2024–25	Manchester C	0	0	**1**	**0**
2024–25	*Sparta Rotterdam*	6	0	**6**	**0**
2024–25	*Bahia*	7	1	**17**	**3**

KHUSANOV, Abduqodir (D) 65 4
H: 6 1 W: 13 03 b.Tashkent 29-2-04
Internationals: Uzbekistan U17, U19, U20, U23, Full caps.

2022	Energetik-BGU	27	3		
2023	Energetik-BGU	8	1	**35**	**4**
2023–24	Lens	11	0		
2024–25	Lens	13	0	**24**	**0**
2024–25	Manchester C	6	0	**6**	**0**

KOVACIC, Mateo (M) 399 23
H: 5 11 W: 11 07 b.Linz 6-5-94
Internationals: Croatia U17, U19, U21, Full caps.

2010–11	Dinamo Zagreb	7	1		
2011–12	Dinamo Zagreb	25	4		
2012–13	Dinamo Zagreb	11	1	**43**	**6**
2012–13	Internazionale	13	0		
2013–14	Internazionale	32	0		
2014–15	Internazionale	35	5	**80**	**5**
2015–16	Real Madrid	25	0		
2016–17	Real Madrid	27	1		
2017–18	Real Madrid	21	0		
2018–19	Real Madrid	0	0	**73**	**1**
2018–19	*Chelsea*	32	0		
2019–20	Chelsea	31	1		
2020–21	Chelsea	27	0		

2021–22 Chelsea 25 2
2022–23 Chelsea 27 1 **142 4**
2023–24 Manchester C 30 1
2024–25 Manchester C 31 6 **61 7**

LEWIS, Rico (D) 58 3
H: 5 7 W: 11 00 b.Manchester 21-11-04
Internationals: England U16, U18, U19, U21, Full caps.
2022–23 Manchester C 14 0
2023–24 Manchester C 16 2
2024–25 Manchester C 28 1 **58 3**

MARMOUSH, Omar (F) 161 51
H: 6 0 W: 11 09 b.Kairo 7-2-99
Internationals: Egypt U20, U23, Full caps.
2015–16 Wadi Degla 1 0
2016–17 Wadi Degla 15 2 **16 2**
2017–18 VfL Wolfsburg 0 0
2018–19 VfL Wolfsburg 0 0
2019–20 VfL Wolfsburg 5 0
2020–21 VfL Wolfsburg 1 0
2020–21 *St Pauli* 21 7 **21 7**
2021–22 VfL Wolfsburg 2 0
2021–22 *VfB Stuttgart* 21 3 **21 3**
2022–23 VfL Wolfsburg 33 5 **41 5**
2023–24 Eintracht Frankfurt 29 12
2024–25 Eintracht Frankfurt 17 15 **46 27**
2024–25 Manchester C 16 7 **16 7**

MATHEUS LUIZ, Nunes (M) 161 9
H: 6 0 W: 11 11 b.Rio de Janeiro 27-8-98
Internationals: Portugal Full caps.
2018–19 Estoril 6 0 **6 0**
2019–20 Sporting Lisbon 10 0
2020–21 Sporting Lisbon 31 3
2021–22 Sporting Lisbon 33 3
2022–23 Sporting Lisbon 2 1 **76 7**
2022–23 Wolverhampton W 34 1
2023–24 Wolverhampton W 2 0 **36 1**
2023–24 Manchester C 17 0
2024–25 Manchester C 26 1 **43 1**

MBETE-TABU, Luke (D) 50 3
H: 6 1 W: 12 00 b.Westminster 18-9-03
Internationals: England U16, U19, U20, U21.
2020–21 Manchester C 0 0
2021–22 Manchester C 0 0
2022–23 Manchester C 0 0
2022–23 *Huddersfield T* 6 0 **6 0**
2022–23 *Bolton W* 8 1 **8 1**
2023–24 Manchester C 0 0
2023–24 *Den Bosch* 23 2 **23 2**
2024–25 Manchester C 0 0
2024–25 *Northampton T* 13 0 **13 0**

McATEE, James (M) 85 15
H: 5 11 W: 11 05 b.Salford 18-10-02
Internationals: England U18, U20, U21.
2020–21 Manchester C 0 0
2021–22 Manchester C 2 0
2022–23 Manchester C 0 0
2022–23 *Sheffield U* 37 9
2023–24 Manchester C 1 0
2023–24 *Sheffield U* 30 3 **67 12**
2024–25 Manchester C 15 3 **18 3**

McFARLANE, Christian (D) 8 0
H: 6 0 W: 9 13 b.Basildon 25-1-07
Internationals: USA U16. England U16, U17, U18.
2022 New York City 0 0
2023 New York City 0 0
2024 New York City 8 0 **8 0**
2024–25 Manchester C 0 0

MUBAMA, Divin (F) 9 0
H: 6 0 W: 11 00 b.Newham 25-10-04
Internationals: England U16, U18, U19, U20.
2022–23 West Ham U 3 0
2023–24 West Ham U 5 0 **8 0**
2024–25 Manchester C 1 0 **1 0**

NDALA, Joel (F) 0 0
b.Mancheser 31-5-06
Internationals: England U16, U17, U18, U19.
2022–23 Manchester C 0 0
2023–24 Manchester C 0 0
2024–25 Manchester C 0 0
2024–25 *Nottingham F* 0 0

NFONKEU, Brooklyn (F) 0 0
b.Leeds 1-7-07
2024–25 Manchester C 0 0
2024–25 *Leeds U* 0 0

O'REILLY, Nico (M) 9 2
H: 6 4 W: 9 13 b.Manchester 21-3-05
Internationals: England U16, U17, U18, U20.
2022–23 Manchester C 0 0
2023–24 Manchester C 0 0
2024–25 Manchester C 9 2 **9 2**

ORTEGA, Stefan (G) 191 0
H: 6 1 W: 12 13 b.Calden 6-11-92
2017–18 Arminia Bielefeld 34 0
2018–19 Arminia Bielefeld 31 0
2019–20 Arminia Bielefeld 34 0
2020–21 Arminia Bielefeld 34 0
2021–22 Arminia Bielefeld 33 0 **166 0**
2022–23 Manchester C 3 0
2023–24 Manchester C 9 0
2024–25 Manchester C 13 0 **25 0**

PERRONE, Maximo (M) 71 2
H: 5 10 W: 10 01 b.Buenos Aires 7-1-03
Internationals: Argentina U16, U20.
2022 Velez Sarsfield 15 2 **15 2**
2022–23 Manchester C 1 0
2023–24 Manchester C 0 0
2023–24 *Las Palmas* 29 0 **29 0**
2024–25 Manchester C 0 0 **1 0**
2024–25 *Como* 26 0 **26 0**

PHILLIPS, Kalvin (M) 257 13
H: 5 10 W: 11 05 b.Leeds 2-12-95
Internationals: England Full caps.
2014–15 Leeds U 2 1
2015–16 Leeds U 10 0
2016–17 Leeds U 33 1
2017–18 Leeds U 41 7
2018–19 Leeds U 42 1
2019–20 Leeds U 37 2
2020–21 Leeds U 29 1
2021–22 Leeds U 20 0 **214 13**
2022–23 Manchester C 12 0
2023–24 Manchester C 4 0
2023–24 *West Ham U* 8 0 **8 0**
2024–25 Manchester C 0 0 **16 0**
2024–25 *Ipswich T* 19 0 **19 0**

RODRI, Rodrigo Hernandez (M) 272 26
H: 6 3 W: 12 13 b.Madrid 22-6-96
Internationals: Spain U16, U19, U21, Full caps.
2014–15 Villarreal 0 0
2015–16 Villarreal 3 0
2016–17 Villarreal 23 0
2017–18 Villarreal 37 1 **63 1**
2018–19 Atletico Madrid 34 3 **34 3**
2019–20 Manchester C 35 3
2020–21 Manchester C 34 2
2021–22 Manchester C 33 7
2022–23 Manchester C 36 2
2023–24 Manchester C 34 8
2024–25 Manchester C 3 0 **175 22**

SAVIO, de Oliveira (F) 92 11
H: 5 9 W: 11 07 b.Sao Mateus 10-4-04
Internationals: Brazil U17, U20, Full caps.
2020 Atletico Mineiro 8 0
2021 Atletico Mineiro 4 0
2022 Atletico Mineiro 8 1 **20 1**
2022–23 Troyes 0 0
2022–23 *PSV Eindhoven* 6 0 **6 0**
2023–24 Troyes 0 0
2023–24 *Girona* 37 9 **37 9**
2024–25 Manchester C 29 1 **29 1**

SIMPSON-PUSEY, Jahmai (D) 2 0
H: 6 2 W: 11 00 b.Manchester 4-11-05
Internationals: England U18.
2024–25 Manchester C 2 0 **2 0**

STONES, John (D) 272 11
H: 6 2 W: 11 00 b.Barnsley 28-5-94
Internationals: England U19, U20, U21, Full caps.
2010–11 Barnsley 0 0
2011–12 Barnsley 2 0
2012–13 Barnsley 22 0 **24 0**
2012–13 Everton 0 0
2013–14 Everton 21 0
2014–15 Everton 23 1
2015–16 Everton 33 0 **77 1**
2016–17 Manchester C 27 0
2017–18 Manchester C 18 0
2018–19 Manchester C 24 0
2019–20 Manchester C 16 0
2020–21 Manchester C 22 4
2021–22 Manchester C 14 1
2022–23 Manchester C 23 2
2023–24 Manchester C 16 1
2024–25 Manchester C 11 2 **171 10**

SUSOHO, Mahamadou (M) 15 1
H: 5 9 b.Granollers 20-1-05
Internationals: England U16. Spain U17, U18.
2023–24 Manchester C 0 0
2024–25 Manchester C 0 0
2024–25 *Peterborough U* 15 1 **15 1**

VITOR REIS, de Oliveira (D) 19 1
H: 6 1 W: 10 08 b.San Jose dos Campos 12-1-06
Internationals: Brazil U16, U17.
2024 Palmeiras 18 1 **18 1**
2024–25 Manchester C 1 0 **1 0**

WALKER, Kyle (D) 478 8
H: 5 10 W: 11 07 b.Sheffield 28-5-90
Internationals: England U19, U21, Full caps.
2008–09 Sheffield U 2 0
2008–09 *Northampton T* 9 0 **9 0**
2009–10 Tottenham H 2 0
2009–10 *Sheffield U* 26 0 **28 0**
2010–11 Tottenham H 1 0
2010–11 *QPR* 20 0 **20 0**
2010–11 *Aston Villa* 15 1 **15 1**
2011–12 Tottenham H 37 2
2012–13 Tottenham H 36 0
2013–14 Tottenham H 26 1
2014–15 Tottenham H 15 0
2015–16 Tottenham H 33 1
2016–17 Tottenham H 33 0 **183 4**
2017–18 Manchester C 32 0
2018–19 Manchester C 33 1
2019–20 Manchester C 29 1
2020–21 Manchester C 24 1
2021–22 Manchester C 20 0
2022–23 Manchester C 27 0
2023–24 Manchester C 32 0
2024–25 Manchester C 15 0 **212 3**
2024–25 *AC Milan* 11 0 **11 0**

WILSON-ESBRAND, Josh (D) 40 1
H: 5 9 W: 11 05 b.Hackney 26-12-02
Internationals: England U16, U18, U20, U21.
From West Ham U.
2020–21 Manchester C 0 0
2021–22 Manchester C 0 0
2022–23 Manchester C 0 0
2022–23 *Coventry C* 14 0 **14 0**
2023–24 Manchester C 0 0
2023–24 *Reims* 9 1 **9 1**
2023–24 *Cardiff C* 11 0 **11 0**
2024–25 Manchester C 0 0
2024–25 *Stoke C* 6 0 **6 0**

WRIGHT, Jacob (M) 15 0
H: 5 10 W: 10 03 b.Manchester 21-9-05
Internationals: England U16, U17, U18, U19, U20.
2023–24 Manchester C 0 0
2024–25 Manchester C 0 0
2024–25 *Norwich C* 15 0 **15 0**

Players retained or with offer of contract
Alcala, Alejandro; Carrington, Ezra Sheridan; Da Silva Chagas, Kayky; Dada-Mascoll, Isaiah Jelani Oladele Adedeji; Fapetu, Oluwafemi David Adetayo; Fletcher, Luca George Murphy; Grant, True Blakeley; Gray, Charlie George; Henderson-Hall, Matthew James; Heskey, Jaden Emile Tyrone; Lawrence, Emilio Alford Anthony; Muir, Ashton Lee; Mukasa, Divine Tayon Mahogany; Naylor, Sebastian Jacob; Noble, Kian Lee; Oboavwoduo, Justin Oke; Okeke, Michael Chinonso; Parker, Harrison Percival; Samuel, Lakyle; Smith, Isaac James; Thomas, Rhys Lloyd; Warhurst, Matthew Ethan; Wint, Jack Thomas Charles.

Scholars
Braithwaite, Kaden Elliot; Courtman, Charlie; Drake, Leke; Dunbar-McDonald, Christian Ky-Andre; Heskey, Reigan William Stephen; Hudson, Max; Lienou, Jayden Patipe; McAidoo, Ryan Kelly; Mfuni, Stephen-Nevin Mutanda; Midwood, Kylan Jo-Aiden Ian; Miles, Harrison Frank; Samba, Tyrone Prosper William; Tevenan, Oliver Louis; Whatmuff, Oliver Jackson.

MANCHESTER U (51)

ALJOFREE, Sonny (D) 25 3
H: 6 1 W: 11 00 b.Plymouth 19-12-04
2022–23 Manchester U 0 0
2023–24 Manchester U 0 0
2024–25 Manchester U 0 0
2024–25 *Accrington S* 25 3 **25 3**

AMASS, Harry (D) 5 0
H: 5 11 W: 11 05 b.London 16-5-07
Internationals: England U16, U17, U18.
2022–23 Watford 0 0
2023–24 Manchester U 0 0
2024–25 Manchester U 5 0 **5 0**

ANTONY, dos Santos (F) 168 32
H: 5 9 W: 9 13 b.Sao Paulo 24-2-00
Internationals: Brazil U23, Full caps.
2018 Sao Paulo 3 0
2019 Sao Paulo 29 4
2020 Sao Paulo 0 0 **32 4**
2020–21 Ajax 32 9
2021–22 Ajax 23 8
2022–23 Ajax 2 1 **57 18**
2022–23 Manchester U 25 4
2023–24 Manchester U 29 1
2024–25 Manchester U 8 0 **62 5**
2024–25 *Real Betis* 17 5 **17 5**

BAYINDIR, Altay (G) 148 0
H: 6 6 W: 14 00 b.Osmangazi 14-4-98
Internationals: Turkey U17, U19, U20, U21, Full caps.
2015–16 Ankaragucu 2 0

2016–17 Ankaragucu 1 0
2017–18 Ankaragucu 8 0
2018–19 Ankaragucu 17 0 **28 0**
2019–20 Fenerbahce 32 0
2020–21 Fenerbahce 33 0
2021–22 Fenerbahce 24 0
2022–23 Fenerbahce 26 0
2023–24 Fenerbahce 1 0 **116 0**
2023–24 Manchester U 0 0
2024–25 Manchester U 4 0 **4 0**

BENNETT, Rhys (D) **36 1**
H: 6 2 b.Manchester 30-10-03
2022–23 Manchester U 0 0
2023–24 Manchester U 0 0
2023–24 Stockport Co 1 0 **1 0**
2024–25 Manchester U 0 0
2024–25 Fleetwood T 35 1 **35 1**

BRUNO FERNANDES, Miguel (M) **420 120**
H: 5 8 W: 9 08 b.Maia 8-9-94
Internationals: Portugal U19, U20, U21, U23, Full caps.
2012–13 Novara 23 4 **23 4**
2013–14 Udinese 24 4
2014–15 Udinese 31 3
2015–16 Udinese 31 3 **86 10**
2016–17 Sampdoria 33 5 **33 5**
2017–18 Sporting Lisbon 33 11
2018–19 Sporting Lisbon 33 20
2019–20 Sporting Lisbon 17 8 **83 39**
2019–20 Manchester U 14 8
2020–21 Manchester U 37 18
2021–22 Manchester U 36 10
2022–23 Manchester U 37 8
2023–24 Manchester U 35 10
2024–25 Manchester U 36 8 **195 62**

CASEMIRO, Carlos (M) **388 39**
H: 6 0 W: 12 08 b.Sao Jose dos Campos 23-2-92
Internationals: Brazil U17, U20, Full caps.
2010 Sao Paulo 18 2
2011 Sao Paulo 21 4
2012 Sao Paulo 22 0 **61 6**
2012–13 Real Madrid 1 0
2013–14 Real Madrid 12 0
2014–15 Porto 28 3 **28 3**
2015–16 Real Madrid 23 1
2016–17 Real Madrid 25 4
2017–18 Real Madrid 30 5
2018–19 Real Madrid 29 3
2019–20 Real Madrid 35 4
2020–21 Real Madrid 34 6
2021–22 Real Madrid 32 1
2022–23 Real Madrid 1 0 **222 24**
2022–23 Manchester U 28 4
2023–24 Manchester U 25 1
2024–25 Manchester U 24 1 **77 6**

COLLYER, Toby (M) **6 0**
H: 5 11 W: 10 03 b.Worthing 3-1-04
Internationals: England U16, U17.
2020–21 Brighton & HA 0 0
2021–22 Manchester U 0 0
2022–23 Manchester U 0 0
2023–24 Manchester U 0 0
2024–25 Manchester U 6 0 **6 0**

DALOT, Diogo (D) **166 4**
H: 6 0 W: 11 11 b.Braga 18-3-99
Internationals: Portugal U16, U17, U19, U20, U21, Full caps.
2016–17 Porto 0 0
2017–18 Porto 6 0 **6 0**
2018–19 Manchester U 16 0
2019–20 Manchester U 4 0
2020–21 Manchester U 0 0
2020–21 AC Milan 21 1 **21 1**
2021–22 Manchester U 24 0
2022–23 Manchester U 26 1
2023–24 Manchester U 36 2
2024–25 Manchester U 33 0 **139 3**

DE LIGT, Matthijs (D) **246 23**
H: 6 2 W: 12 08 b.Leiderdorp 12-8-99
Internationals: Netherlands U16, U17, U19, Full caps.
2016–17 Ajax 11 2
2017–18 Ajax 33 3
2018–19 Ajax 33 3 **77 8**
2019–20 Juventus 29 4
2020–21 Juventus 27 1
2021–22 Juventus 31 3 **87 8**
2022–23 Bayern Munich 31 3
2023–24 Bayern Munich 22 2 **53 5**
2024–25 Manchester U 29 2 **29 2**

DIALLO, Amad (F) **88 26**
H: 5 9 W: 11 00 b.Abidjan 11-7-02
Internationals: Ivory Coast U23, Full caps.
2019–20 Atalanta 3 1
2020–21 Atalanta 0 0 **3 1**
2020–21 Manchester U 3 0
2021–22 Manchester U 0 0

2021–22 *Rangers* 10 3 **10 3**
2022–23 Manchester U 0 0
2022–23 *Sunderland* 37 13 **37 13**
2023–24 Manchester U 9 1
2024–25 Manchester U 26 8 **38 9**

DORGU, Patrick (D) **65 5**
H: 6 2 W: 11 11 b.Copenhagen 26-10-04
Internationals: Denmark U18, U19, U20, U21, Full caps.
2023–24 Lecce 32 2
2024–25 Lecce 21 3 **53 5**
2024–25 Manchester U 12 0 **12 0**

ENNIS, Ethan (M) **15 0**
2024–25 Manchester U 0 0
2024–25 *Doncaster R* 15 0 **15 0**

ERIKSEN, Christian (M) **466 84**
H: 6 0 W: 11 03 b.Middelfart 14-2-92
Internationals: Denmark U17, U18, U19, U21, Full caps.
2009–10 Ajax 15 0
2010–11 Ajax 28 6
2011–12 Ajax 33 7
2012–13 Ajax 33 10
2013–14 Ajax 4 2 **113 25**
2013–14 Tottenham H 25 7
2014–15 Tottenham H 38 10
2015–16 Tottenham H 35 6
2016–17 Tottenham H 36 8
2017–18 Tottenham H 37 10
2018–19 Tottenham H 35 8
2019–20 Tottenham H 20 2 **226 51**
2019–20 Internazionale 17 1
2020–21 Internazionale 26 3 **43 4**
2021–22 Brentford 11 1 **11 1**
2022–23 Manchester U 28 1
2023–24 Manchester U 22 1
2024–25 Manchester U 23 1 **73 3**

EVANS, Jonny (D) **415 17**
H: 6 2 W: 12 02 b.Belfast 3-1-88
Internationals: Northern Ireland U16, U17, U21, Full caps.
2004–05 Manchester U 0 0
2005–06 Manchester U 0 0
2006–07 Manchester U 0 0
2006–07 Antwerp 11 2 **11 2**
2006–07 *Sunderland* 18 1
2007–08 *Sunderland* 15 0 **33 1**
2007–08 Manchester U 0 0
2008–09 Manchester U 17 0
2009–10 Manchester U 18 0
2010–11 Manchester U 13 0
2011–12 Manchester U 29 1
2012–13 Manchester U 23 3
2013–14 Manchester U 17 0
2014–15 Manchester U 14 0
2015–16 WBA 30 1
2016–17 WBA 31 2
2017–18 WBA 28 2 **89 5**
2018–19 Leicester C 24 1
2019–20 Leicester C 38 1
2020–21 Leicester C 28 2
2021–22 Leicester C 18 1
2022–23 Leicester C 13 0 **121 5**
2023–24 Manchester U 23 0
2024–25 Manchester U 7 0 **161 0**

FITZGERALD, Jayce (M) **0 0**
b. 9-5-07
Internationals: England U16, U17.
2024–25 Manchester U 0 0

FLETCHER, Jack (M) **0 0**
H: 5 11 W: 12 04 b.Manchester 19-3-07
Internationals: Scotland U16. England U16, U17, U18.
2024–25 Manchester U 0 0

FREDRICSON, Tyler (D) **2 0**
H: 6 1 W: 11 00 b. 23-2-05
Internationals: England U17, U18.
2022–23 Manchester U 0 0
2023–24 Manchester U 0 0
2024–25 Manchester U 2 0 **2 0**

GARNACHO, Alejandro (F) **93 16**
H: 5 11 W: 11 07 b.Madrid 1-7-04
Internationals: Spain U18. Argentina U20, Full caps.
2021–22 Manchester U 2 0
2022–23 Manchester U 19 3
2023–24 Manchester U 36 7
2024–25 Manchester U 36 6 **93 16**

GORE, Daniel (M) **5 0**
H: 5 7 W: 9 11 b.Manchester 26-9-04
Internationals: England U16, U18, U20.
From Burnley.
2022–23 Manchester U 0 0
2023–24 Manchester U 1 0
2023–24 *Port Vale* 1 0 **1 0**
2024–25 Manchester U 0 0
2024–25 *Rotherham U* 3 0 **3 0**

GRACZYK, Hubert (G) **0 0**
H: 6 4 W: 13 05 b.Skwierzyna 28-2-03
Internationals: England U16, U17, U18.
2020–21 Arsenal 0 0
2021–22 Arsenal 0 0
2022–23 Arsenal 0 0
2023–24 Arsenal 0 0
2024–25 Manchester U 0 0

HARRISON, Elyh (G) **0 0**
H: 6 1 W: 11 11 b. 19-2-06
Internationals: England U18, U19, U20.
2024–25 Manchester U 0 0

HEATON, Tom (G) **343 0**
H: 6 2 W: 13 06 b.Chester 15-4-86
Internationals: England U16, U17, U18, U19, U21, Full caps.
2003–04 Manchester U 0 0
2004–05 Manchester U 0 0
2005–06 Manchester U 0 0
2005–06 *Swindon T* 14 0 **14 0**
2006–07 Manchester U 0 0
2007–08 Manchester U 0 0
2008–09 Manchester U 0 0
2008–09 *Cardiff C* 21 0
2009–10 Manchester U 0 0
2009–10 *Rochdale* 12 0 **12 0**
2009–10 *Wycombe W* 16 0 **16 0**
2010–11 Cardiff C 27 0
2011–12 Cardiff C 2 0 **50 0**
2012–13 Bristol C 43 0 **43 0**
2013–14 Burnley 46 0
2014–15 Burnley 38 0
2015–16 Burnley 46 0
2016–17 Burnley 35 0
2017–18 Burnley 4 0
2018–19 Burnley 19 0 **188 0**
2019–20 Aston Villa 20 0
2020–21 Aston Villa 0 0 **20 0**
2021–22 Manchester U 0 0
2022–23 Manchester U 0 0
2023–24 Manchester U 0 0
2024–25 Manchester U 0 0

HEAVEN, Ayden (F) **4 0**
H: 6 2 W: 12 02 b.London 22-9-06
Internationals: England U18, U19.
2023–24 Arsenal 0 0
2024–25 Arsenal 0 0
2024–25 Manchester U 4 0 **4 0**

HOJLUND, Rasmus (F) **131 32**
H: 6 3 W: 13 08 b.Copenhagen 4-2-03
Internationals: Denmark U16, U17, U19, U21, Full caps.
2020–21 Copenhagen 4 0
2021–22 Copenhagen 15 0 **19 0**
2021–22 Sturm Graz 13 6
2022–23 Sturm Graz 5 3 **18 9**
2022–23 Atalanta 32 9 **32 9**
2023–24 Manchester U 30 10
2024–25 Manchester U 32 4 **62 14**

HUGILL, Joe (F) **48 6**
H: 6 2 W: 11 05 b.Durham 19-10-03
From Sunderland.
2020–21 Manchester U 0 0
2021–22 Manchester U 0 0
2022–23 Manchester U 0 0
2023–24 Manchester U 0 0
2023–24 *Burton Alb* 18 1 **18 1**
2024–25 Manchester U 0 0
2024–25 *Wigan Ath* 13 3 **13 3**
2024–25 *Carlisle U* 17 2 **17 2**

JACKSON, Louis (D) **0 0**
H: 5 9 W: 10 03 b.Oldham 18-9-05
Internationals: England U16. Scotland U17, U18, U19.
2023–24 Manchester U 0 0
2024–25 Manchester U 0 0
2024–25 *Tranmere R* 0 0

KAMASON, Jaydan (D) **0 0**
H: 5 9 W: 10 10 b. 8-12-06
Internationals: England U16.
2024–25 Manchester U 0 0

KONE, Sekou (D) **0 0**
H: 5 9 W: 10 03 b. 3-2-06
Internationals: Mali U17.
2024–25 Manchester U 0 0

KUKONKI, Godwill (D) **0 0**
H: 6 5 W: 11 05 b.Stoke-on-Trent 6-2-08
Internationals: England U17.
2024–25 Manchester U 0 0

LINDELOF, Victor (D) **292 6**
H: 6 2 W: 12 11 b.Vasteras 17-7-94
Internationals: Sweden U17, U19, U21, Full caps.
2009 Vasteras 1 0
2010 Vasteras 9 0
2011 Vasteras 27 0
2012 Vasteras 13 0 **50 0**
2012–13 Benfica

2013–14 Benfica 1 0
2014–15 Benfica 0 0
2015–16 Benfica 15 1
2016–17 Benfica 32 1 **48 2**
2017–18 Manchester U 17 0
2018–19 Manchester U 30 1
2019–20 Manchester U 35 1
2020–21 Manchester U 29 1
2021–22 Manchester U 28 0
2022–23 Manchester U 20 0
2023–24 Manchester U 19 1
2024–25 Manchester U 16 0 **194 4**

MAGUIRE, Harry (D) 440 24
H: 6 4 W: 15 10 b.Sheffield 5-3-93
Internationals: England U21, Full caps.
2010–11 Sheffield U 5 0
2011–12 Sheffield U 44 1
2012–13 Sheffield U 44 3
2013–14 Sheffield U 41 5 **134 9**
2014–15 Hull C 3 0
2014–15 *Wigan Ath* 16 1 **16 1**
2015–16 Hull C 22 0
2016–17 Hull C 29 2 **54 2**
2017–18 Leicester C 38 2
2018–19 Leicester C 31 3
2019–20 Leicester C 0 0 **69 5**
2019–20 Manchester U 38 1
2020–21 Manchester U 34 2
2021–22 Manchester U 30 1
2022–23 Manchester U 16 0
2023–24 Manchester U 22 2
2024–25 Manchester U 27 1 **167 7**

MAINOO, Kobbie (M) 50 3
H: 5 9 W: 12 08 b.Stockport 19-4-05
Internationals: England U17, U18, U19, Full caps.
2022–23 Manchester U 1 0
2023–24 Manchester U 24 3
2024–25 Manchester U 25 0 **50 3**

MALACIA, Tyrell (D) 131 4
H: 5 7 W: 10 08 b.Rotterdam 17-8-99
Internationals: Netherlands U16, U17, U18, U20, U21, Full caps.
2017–18 Feyenoord 11 0
2018–19 Feyenoord 17 3
2019–20 Feyenoord 12 0
2020–21 Feyenoord 26 0
2021–22 Feyenoord 32 1 **98 4**
2022–23 Manchester U 22 0
2023–24 Manchester U 0 0
2024–25 Manchester U 3 0 **25 0**
2024–25 *PSV Eindhoven* 8 0 **8 0**

MANTATO, Bendito (F) 0 0
H: 5 10 W: 11 05 b.Manchester 25-1-08
Internationals: England U16, U17.
2024–25 Manchester U 0 0

MARTINEZ, Lisandro (D) 179 12
H: 5 10 W: 12 02 b.Gualehuay 18-1-98
Internationals: Argentina U20, U23, Full caps.
2016–17 Newell's Old Boys 1 0
2017–18 Newell's Old Boys 0 0 **1 0**
2017–18 *Defensa y Justicia* 21 1
2018–19 Defensa y Justicia 25 2 **46 3**
2019–20 Ajax 24 2
2020–21 Ajax 26 3
2021–22 Ajax 24 1 **74 6**
2022–23 Manchester U 27 1
2023–24 Manchester U 11 0
2024–25 Manchester U 20 2 **58 3**

MATHER, Sam (M) 2 0
b. 3-9-04
Internationals: England U16, U18, U19.
2020–21 Manchester U 0 0
2021–22 Manchester U 0 0
2022–23 Manchester U 0 0
2023–24 Manchester U 0 0
2024–25 Manchester U 0 0
2024–25 *Tranmere R* 2 0 **2 0**

MAZRAOUI, Noussair (D) 168 7
H: 5 10 W: 9 13 b.Leiderdorp 14-11-97
Internationals: Morocco U20, U23, Full caps.
2016–17 Ajax 0 0
2017–18 Ajax 8 0
2018–19 Ajax 28 1
2019–20 Ajax 13 0
2020–21 Ajax 19 0
2021–22 Ajax 25 5 **93 6**
2022–23 Bayern Munich 19 1
2023–24 Bayern Munich 19 0 **38 1**
2024–25 Manchester U 37 0 **37 0**

McTOMINAY, Scott (M) 178 19
H: 6 4 W: 10 08 b.Lancaster 8-12-96
Internationals: Scotland Full caps.
2016–17 Manchester U 2 0
2017–18 Manchester U 13 0
2018–19 Manchester U 16 2
2019–20 Manchester U 27 4
2020–21 Manchester U 32 4
2021–22 Manchester U 30 1
2022–23 Manchester U 24 1
2023–24 Manchester U 32 7
2024–25 Manchester U 2 0 **178 19**
Transferred to Napoli, August 2024.

MEE, Dermot (G) 0 0
H: 6 0 W: 11 05 b.Birmingham 20-11-02
Internationals: Northern Ireland U17, U19, U21.
2023–24 Manchester U 0 0
2024–25 Manchester U 0 0

MOORHOUSE, Jack (M) 0 0
H: 6 0 W: 11 00 b. 29-11-05
Internationals: Republic of Ireland U21.
2024–25 Manchester U 0 0

MOUNT, Mason (M) 224 46
H: 5 10 W: 11 00 b.Portsmouth 10-1-99
Internationals: England U16, U17, U18, U19, U21, Full caps.
2017–18 Chelsea 0 0
2017–18 *Vitesse* 29 9 **29 9**
2018–19 Chelsea 0 0
2018–19 *Derby Co* 35 8 **35 8**
2019–20 Chelsea 37 7
2020–21 Chelsea 36 6
2021–22 Chelsea 32 11
2022–23 Chelsea 24 3 **129 27**
2023–24 Manchester U 14 1
2024–25 Manchester U 17 1 **31 2**

MURDOCK, William (G) 0 0
b. 26-5-07
Internationals: Northern Ireland U16, U17.
2024–25 Manchester U 0 0

OBI-MARTIN, Chidozie (F) 7 0
H: 6 2 W: 10 10 b.Glostrup 29-11-07
Internationals: England U16. Denmark U16, U17, U18, U20, U21.
2024–25 Manchester U 7 0 **7 0**

OGUNNEYE, Habeeb (D) 0 0
H: 5 10 W: 10 01 b.London 12-11-05
Internationals: England U17.
2023–24 Manchester U 0 0
2024–25 Manchester U 0 0

ONANA, Andre (G) 244 0
H: 6 3 W: 12 13 b.Nkol Ngok 2-4-96
Internationals: Cameroon Full caps.
From Barcelona.
2014–15 Ajax 0 0
2015–16 Ajax 0 0
2016–17 Ajax 32 0
2017–18 Ajax 33 0
2018–19 Ajax 33 0
2019–20 Ajax 24 0
2020–21 Ajax 20 0
2021–22 Ajax 6 0 **148 0**
2022–23 Internazionale 24 0 **24 0**
2023–24 Manchester U 38 0
2024–25 Manchester U 34 0 **72 0**

PELLISTRI, Facundo (M) 91 3
H: 5 9 W: 10 12 b.Montevideo 20-12-01
Internationals: Uruguay U16, Full caps.
2019 Penarol 18 1
2020 Penarol 12 0
2020–21 Penarol 0 0 **30 1**
2020–21 Manchester U 0 0
2020–21 *Alaves* 12 0
2021–22 Manchester U 0 0
2021–22 *Alaves* 21 0 **33 0**
2022–23 Manchester U 4 0
2023–24 Manchester U 9 0
2023–24 *Granada* 15 2 **15 2**
2024–25 Manchester U 0 0 **13 0**

RASHFORD, Marcus (F) 297 89
H: 6 1 W: 11 00 b.Manchester 31-10-97
Internationals: England U16, U18, U20, U21, Full caps.
2015–16 Manchester U 11 5
2016–17 Manchester U 32 5
2017–18 Manchester U 35 7
2018–19 Manchester U 33 10
2019–20 Manchester U 31 17
2020–21 Manchester U 37 11
2021–22 Manchester U 25 4
2022–23 Manchester U 35 17
2023–24 Manchester U 33 7
2024–25 Manchester U 15 4 **287 87**
2024–25 *Aston Villa* 10 2 **10 2**

SANCHO, Jadon (M) 207 52
H: 5 10 W: 11 07 b.Camberwell 25-3-00
Internationals: England U16, U17, U19, Full caps.
2016–17 Manchester C 0 0
2017–18 Borussia Dortmund 12 1
2018–19 Borussia Dortmund 34 12
2019–20 Borussia Dortmund 32 17
2020–21 Borussia Dortmund 26 8
2021–22 Manchester U 29 3
2022–23 Manchester U 26 6
2023–24 Manchester U 3 0
2023–24 *Borussia Dortmund* 14 2 **118 40**
2024–25 Manchester U 0 0 **58 9**
2024–25 *Chelsea* 31 3 **31 3**

SCANLON, James (M) 0 0
H: 5 9 W: 11 00 b. 28-9-06
Internationals: Gibraltar U17, U21, Full caps.
2024–25 Manchester U 0 0

SHAW, Luke (D) 258 3
H: 6 1 W: 11 11 b.Kingston 12-7-95
Internationals: England U16, U17, U21, Full caps.
2011–12 Southampton 0 0
2012–13 Southampton 25 0
2013–14 Southampton 35 0 **60 0**
2014–15 Manchester U 16 0
2015–16 Manchester U 5 0
2016–17 Manchester U 11 0
2017–18 Manchester U 11 0
2018–19 Manchester U 29 1
2019–20 Manchester U 24 0
2020–21 Manchester U 32 1
2021–22 Manchester U 20 0
2022–23 Manchester U 31 1
2023–24 Manchester U 12 0
2024–25 Manchester U 7 0 **198 3**

UGARTE, Manuel (M) 183 4
H: 6 0 W: 11 05 b.Montevideo 11-4-01
Internationals: Uruguay U20, U23, Full caps.
2016 Fenix 1 0
2017 Fenix 0 0
2018 Fenix 1 0
2019 Fenix 35 1
2020 Fenix 16 1 **53 2**
2020–21 Famalicao 20 1
2021–22 Famalicao 0 0 **20 1**
2021–22 Sporting Lisbon 25 0
2022–23 Sporting Lisbon 31 0 **56 0**
2023–24 Paris Saint-Germain 25 0 **25 0**
2024–25 Manchester U 29 1 **29 1**

VÕTEK, Radek (G) 44 0
H: 6 6 b.Vsetin 24-10-03
Internationals: Czech Republic U17, U20.
2020–21 Manchester U 0 0
2022–23 Manchester U 0 0
2023–24 Manchester U 0 0
2023–24 *Accrington S* 18 0 **18 0**
2024–25 Manchester U 0 0
2024–25 *BW Linz* 26 0 **26 0**

WHEATLEY, Ethan (F) 7 0
H: 6 2 W: 12 11 b.Stockport 20-1-06
Internationals: England U17, U18, U19.
2023–24 Manchester U 3 0
2024–25 Manchester U 0 0 **3 0**
2024–25 *Walsall* 4 0 **4 0**

WILLIAMS, Ethan (F) 17 2
H: 6 0 W: 12 02 b.Manchester 14-11-05
2024–25 Manchester U 0 0
2024–25 *Cheltenham T* 17 2 **17 2**

YORO, Leny (D) 67 2
H: 6 3 W: 11 07 b.Saint-Maurice 13-11-05
Internationals: France U17, U18, U19, U21, U23.
2021–22 Lille 1 0
2022–23 Lille 13 0
2023–24 Lille 32 2 **46 2**
2024–25 Manchester U 21 0 **21 0**

ZIRKZEE, Joshua (F) 139 36
H: 6 4 W: 13 03 b.Schiedam 22-5-01
Internationals: Netherlands U16, U17, U18, U19, U21, Full caps.
2018–19 Bayern Munich 0 0
2019–20 Bayern Munich 9 4
2020–21 Bayern Munich 3 0
2020–21 *Parma* 4 0 **4 0**
2021–22 Bayern Munich 0 0 **12 4**
2021–22 *Anderlecht* 38 16 **38 16**
2022–23 Bologna 19 2
2023–24 Bologna 34 11 **53 13**
2024–25 Manchester U 32 3 **32 3**

Players retained or with offer of contract
Aigbomian Musa, Victor Osezele; Baumann, Zachary Joseph; Biancheri, Gabriele Cataldo; Devaney, Jacob Patrick John; Ibragimov, Amir; Lacey, Shea; Lusale, Samuel Malama; McAllister, Finley Joseph; Missin, Ashton Brett; Rowe, Thomas; Sharpe, Malachi Israel; Thwaites, Jim Alec Joseph.

Scholars
Armer, Daniel James; Bailey, James Alexander Mo; Byrne-Hughes, Cameron Samuel; Heath, Frederick Henry; Kukonki, Godwill; Mantato, Bendito Boanova; Mills, Albert Frederick; Munro, Reece Stafford; Overy, James Harrison; Plunkett, Dante Jeevan Jamal.

MANSFIELD T (52)

ABDULLAH, McKeal (F) 1 0
H: 5 9 b. 24-7-05
Internationals: Pakistan Full caps.
2022–23	Mansfield T	0	0		
2023–24	Mansfield T	1	0		
2024–25	Mansfield T	0	0	**1**	**0**

AKINS, Lucas (F) 623 109
H: 5 11 W: 12 06 b. Huddersfield 25-2-89
Internationals: Grenada Full caps.
2006–07	Huddersfield T	2	0		
2007–08	Huddersfield T	3	0	**5**	**0**
2008–09	Hamilton A	11	0		
2008–09	Partick Thistle	9	1	**9**	**1**
2009–10	Hamilton A	0	0	**11**	**0**
2010–11	Tranmere R	33	2		
2011–12	Tranmere R	44	5	**77**	**7**
2012–13	Stevenage	46	10		
2013–14	Stevenage	31	3	**77**	**13**
2014–15	Burton Alb	35	9		
2015–16	Burton Alb	44	12		
2016–17	Burton Alb	38	5		
2017–18	Burton Alb	42	5		
2018–19	Burton Alb	46	13		
2019–20	Burton Alb	35	9		
2020–21	Burton Alb	45	9		
2021–22	Burton Alb	23	3	**307**	**65**
2021–22	Mansfield T	19	1		
2022–23	Mansfield T	39	8		
2023–24	Mansfield T	45	12		
2024–25	Mansfield T	34	2	**137**	**23**

ANDERSON, Taylor (M) 4 0
H: 5 10 W: 11 07 b. Nottingham 5-11-04
2022–23	Mansfield T	3	0		
2023–24	Mansfield T	1	0		
2024–25	Mansfield T	0	0	**4**	**0**

BACCUS, Keanu (M) 209 13
H: 5 10 W: 9 13 b. Durban 7-6-98
Internationals: Australia U20, U23, Full caps.
2016–17	Western Sydney W	3	0		
2017–18	Western Sydney W	14	0		
2018–19	Western Sydney W	24	3		
2019–20	Western Sydney W	20	1		
2020–21	Western Sydney W	25	1		
2021–22	Western Sydney W	20	1	**106**	**6**
2022–23	St Mirren	33	2		
2023–24	St Mirren	31	1	**64**	**3**
2024–25	Mansfield T	39	4	**39**	**4**

BLAKE-TRACY, Frazer (D) 121 3
H: 6 0 W: 10 01 b. Dereham 10-9-95
From Dereham T, Lowestoft, King's Lynn T.
2019–20	Peterborough U	14	0		
2020–21	Peterborough U	9	0	**23**	**0**
2021–22	Burton Alb	7	0	**7**	**0**
2022–23	Swindon T	34	1		
2023–24	Swindon T	39	2	**73**	**3**
2024–25	Mansfield T	18	0	**18**	**0**

BOATENG, Hiram (M) 302 16
H: 5 7 W: 11 00 b. Wandsworth 8-1-96
2012–13	Crystal Palace	0	0		
2013–14	Crystal Palace	0	0		
2013–14	Crawley T	1	0	**1**	**0**
2014–15	Crystal Palace	0	0		
2015–16	Crystal Palace	1	0		
2015–16	Plymouth Arg	24	1	**24**	**1**
2016–17	Crystal Palace	0	0		
2016–17	Bristol R	9	0	**9**	**0**
2016–17	Northampton T	16	0	**16**	**0**
2017–18	Exeter C	38	1		
2018–19	Exeter C	27	1	**65**	**2**
2019–20	Milton Keynes D	20	0		
2020–21	Milton Keynes D	0	0		
2020–21	Cambridge U	25	0	**25**	**0**
2021–22	Milton Keynes D	29	3	**49**	**3**
2022–23	Mansfield T	37	3		
2023–24	Mansfield T	34	5		
2024–25	Mansfield T	41	2	**112**	**10**

BOWERY, Jordan (F) 515 72
H: 6 1 W: 12 00 b. Nottingham 2-7-91
Internationals: Saint Kitts and Nevis Full caps.
2008–09	Chesterfield	3	0		
2009–10	Chesterfield	10	0		
2010–11	Chesterfield	40	8		
2011–12	Chesterfield	3	1	**83**	**10**
2012–13	Chesterfield	10	0		
2012–13	Aston Villa	9	0	**19**	**0**
2013–14	Aston Villa	0	0		
2013–14	Doncaster R	3	0	**3**	**0**
2014–15	Rotherham U	33	5		
2015–16	Rotherham U	7	0	**40**	**5**
2015–16	Bradford C	3	0	**3**	**0**
2015–16	Oxford U	17	7	**17**	**7**
2016–17	Leyton Orient	17	1	**17**	**1**
2016–17	Crewe Alex	19	2		
2017–18	Crewe Alex	45	12		
2018–19	Crewe Alex	44	8	**108**	**22**
2019–20	Milton Keynes D	16	2	**16**	**2**

CARGILL, Baily (D) 250 12
H: 6 2 W: 13 10 b. Winchester 5-7-95
Internationals: England U20.
2012–13	Bournemouth	0	0		
2013–14	Bournemouth	0	0		
2013–14	Torquay U	5	0	**5**	**0**
2014–15	Bournemouth	0	0		
2015–16	Bournemouth	0	0		
2015–16	Coventry C	5	1	**5**	**1**
2016–17	Bournemouth	1	0		
2016–17	Gillingham	9	1	**9**	**1**
2017–18	Bournemouth	0	0	**1**	**0**
2017–18	Fleetwood T	11	0	**11**	**0**
2017–18	Partick Thistle	16	0	**16**	**0**
2018–19	Milton Keynes D	29	0		
2019–20	Milton Keynes D	12	0		
2020–21	Milton Keynes D	11	1	**52**	**1**
2020–21	Forest Green R	23	2		
2021–22	Forest Green R	36	0		
2022–23	Forest Green R	22	1	**81**	**3**
2023–24	Mansfield T	36	5		
2024–25	Mansfield T	34	1	**70**	**6**

CARTER, Charlie (M) 0 0
H: 5 9 W: 9 08 b. 16-11-04
| 2023–24 | Mansfield T | 0 | 0 | | |
| 2024–25 | Mansfield T | 0 | 0 | | |

CHAMBERS, Jayden (M) 0 0
b. 20-5-08
| 2024–25 | Mansfield T | 0 | 0 | | |

COOPER, George (D) 11 1
H: 6 2 W: 13 01 b. 25-10-02
2022–23	Mansfield T	0	0		
2023–24	Mansfield T	2	0		
2024–25	Mansfield T	0	0	**2**	**0**
2025	Drogheda U	9	1	**9**	**1**

DWYER, Dom (F) 254 90
H: 5 9 W: 12 11 b. 30-7-90
Internationals: USA Full caps.
2012	Sporting Kansas C	1	0		
2013	Sporting Kansas C	16	2		
2014	Sporting Kansas C	33	22		
2015	Sporting Kansas C	30	12		
2016	Sporting Kansas C	33	16		
2017	Sporting Kansas C	15	5	**128**	**57**
2017	Orlando C	12	4		
2018	Orlando C	26	7		
2019	Orlando C	27	7		
2020	Orlando C	2	0	**67**	**24**
2021	Toronto	14	0	**14**	**0**
2022	Atlanta U	22	4	**22**	**4**
2024	Oakland Roots	14	1	**14**	**1**
2024–25	Mansfield T	9	4	**9**	**4**

EVANS, Will (M) 293 81
H: 6 1 W: 12 13 b. Llangedwyn 11-8-00
Internationals: Wales C.
From Hereford U, Eastleigh, Aldershot T, Chesterfield.
2016–17	Cardiff Met Uni	28	5		
2017–18	Cardiff Met Uni	27	2		
2018–19	Cardiff Met Uni	29	6		
2019–20	Cardiff Met Uni	23	7	**107**	**20**
2020–21	Bala T	31	13		
2021–22	Bala T	24	11	**55**	**24**
2022–23	Newport Co	45	2		
2023–24	Newport Co	46	21	**91**	**23**
2024–25	Mansfield T	40	14	**40**	**14**

FLANAGAN, Finn (M) 0 0
H: 6 2 W: 12 02 b. Nottingham 4-5-05
| 2023–24 | Mansfield T | 0 | 0 | | |
| 2024–25 | Mansfield T | 0 | 0 | | |

FLINDERS, Scott (G) 492 1
H: 6 4 W: 13 10 b. Rotherham 12-6-86
Internationals: England U20.
2004–05	Barnsley	11	0		
2005–06	Barnsley	3	0	**14**	**0**
2006–07	Crystal Palace	8	0		
2006–07	Gillingham	9	0	**9**	**0**
2006–07	Brighton & HA	12	0	**12**	**0**
2007–08	Crystal Palace	0	0		
2007–08	Yeovil T	9	0	**9**	**0**
2008–09	Crystal Palace	0	0	**8**	**0**
2009–10	Hartlepool U	46	0		
2010–11	Hartlepool U	26	1		
2011–12	Hartlepool U	45	0		
2012–13	Hartlepool U	46	0		
2013–14	Hartlepool U	43	0		
2014–15	Hartlepool U	46	0	**252**	**1**
2015–16	York C	43	0	**43**	**0**
From Macclesfield T.
2017–18	Cheltenham T	41	0		
2018–19	Cheltenham T	46	0		
2019–20	Cheltenham T	25	0		
2020–21	Cheltenham T	2	0		

2021–22	Cheltenham T	19	0	**133**	**0**
2022–23	Mansfield T	4	0		
2023–24	Mansfield T	0	0		
2024–25	Mansfield T	8	0	**12**	**0**

FLINT, Aiden (D) 511 55
H: 6 6 W: 12 00 b. Pinxton 11-7-89
Internationals: England C.
From Alfreton T.
2010–11	Swindon T	3	0		
2011–12	Swindon T	32	2		
2012–13	Swindon T	29	2	**64**	**4**
2013–14	Bristol C	34	3		
2014–15	Bristol C	46	14		
2015–16	Bristol C	44	6		
2016–17	Bristol C	39	8	**209**	**36**
2017–18	Bristol C	39	3	**39**	**1**
2018–19	Middlesbrough	39	1		
2019–20	Cardiff C	24	2		
2020–21	Cardiff C	23	1		
2020–21	Sheffield Wed	4	0		
2021–22	Cardiff C	38	6	**86**	**10**
2022–23	Stoke C	9	0	**9**	**0**
2022–23	Sheffield Wed	18	1	**22**	**1**
2023–24	Mansfield T	46	2		
2024–25	Mansfield T	36	1	**82**	**3**

GALE, James (F) 37 4
H: 6 4 W: 12 04 b. Nottingham 20-12-01
From Long Eaton U.
2021–22	Mansfield T	3	0		
2022–23	Mansfield T	14	3		
2023–24	Mansfield T	20	1		
2024–25	Mansfield T	0	0	**37**	**4**

GREGORY, Lee (F) 368 111
H: 6 2 W: 12 08 b. Sheffield 26-8-88
2014–15	Millwall	39	9		
2015–16	Millwall	41	18		
2016–17	Millwall	37	17		
2017–18	Millwall	43	10		
2018–19	Millwall	44	10	**204**	**64**
2019–20	Stoke C	40	6		
2020–21	Derby Co	11	3	**11**	**3**
2021–22	Sheffield Wed	36	16		
2022–23	Sheffield Wed	38	10		
2023–24	Sheffield Wed	13	1	**87**	**27**
2024–25	Mansfield T	20	10	**20**	**10**

HEWITT, Elliott (D) 390 13
H: 5 11 W: 11 11 b. Rhyl 30-5-94
Internationals: Wales U17, U21.
2010–11	Macclesfield T	1	0		
2011–12	Macclesfield T	21	0	**22**	**0**
2012–13	Ipswich T	7	0		
2013–14	Ipswich T	4	0		
2013–14	Gillingham	20	0	**20**	**0**
2014–15	Ipswich T	3	0	**14**	**0**
2014–15	Colchester U	21	1	**21**	**1**
2015–16	Notts Co	38	0		
2016–17	Notts Co	29	2		
2017–18	Notts Co	43	4		
2018–19	Notts Co	25	2	**135**	**8**
2019–20	Grimsby T	20	0		
2020–21	Grimsby T	37	1	**57**	**1**
2020–21	Mansfield T	0	0		
2021–22	Mansfield T	43	1		
2022–23	Mansfield T	40	1		
2023–24	Mansfield T	4	0		
2024–25	Mansfield T	34	0	**121**	**3**

KILGOUR, Alfie (D) 132 8
H: 5 10 W: 11 11 b. Bath 18-5-98
2015–16	Bristol R	0	0		
2016–17	Bristol R	0	0		
2017–18	Bristol R	0	0		
2018–19	Bristol R	4	0		
2019–20	Bristol R	33	2		
2020–21	Bristol R	35	1		
2021–22	Bristol R	11	1		
2022–23	Bristol R	8	0	**91**	**4**
2022–23	Mansfield T	21	4		
2023–24	Mansfield T	3	0		
2024–25	Mansfield T	17	0	**41**	**4**

KOKKINOS, Ronnie (D) 1 0
H: 5 4 W: 8 07 b. Nottingham 18-3-06
| 2024–25 | Mansfield T | 1 | 0 | **1** | **0** |

KRUSZYNSKI, Jakub (M) 0 0
| 2023–24 | Mansfield T | 0 | 0 | | |
| 2024–25 | Mansfield T | 0 | 0 | | |

LEWIS, Aaron (D) 175 9
H: 6 0 W: 13 05 b. Swansea 26-6-98
Internationals: Wales U17, U19, U20, U21.
2018–19	Swansea C	0	0		
2018–19	Doncaster R	7	0	**7**	**0**
2019–20	Lincoln C	2	1		
2020–21	Lincoln C	0	0	**2**	**1**
2020–21	Newport Co	20	1		
2021–22	Newport Co	27	1		
2022–23	Newport Co	39	1	**86**	**3**
2023–24	Mansfield T	38	2		
2024–25	Mansfield T	42	2	**80**	**4**

MACDONALD, Calum (D) 125 3
H: 5 11 W: 9 06 b.Nottingham 18-12-97
Internationals: Scotland U21.

2016–17	Derby Co	0	0	
2017–18	Derby Co	0	0	
2018–19	Derby Co	0	0	
2019–20	Derby Co	0	0	
2019–20	Blackpool	12	0	
2020–21	Blackpool	0	0	12 0
2020–21	Tranmere R	39	1	
2021–22	Tranmere R	34	1	73 2
2022–23	Stockport Co	10	0	10 0
2022–23	Bristol R	4	0	4 0
2023–24	Mansfield T	20	0	
2024–25	Mansfield T	6	1	26 1

MARIS, George (F) 316 43
H: 5 11 W: 11 11 b.Sheffield 6-3-96

2014–15	Barnsley	2	0	
2015–16	Barnsley	1	0	3 0
2016–17	Cambridge U	23	4	
2017–18	Cambridge U	40	10	
2018–19	Cambridge U	39	5	
2019–20	Cambridge U	30	1	132 20
2020–21	Mansfield T	40	1	
2021–22	Mansfield T	37	3	
2022–23	Mansfield T	34	4	
2023–24	Mansfield T	43	11	
2024–25	Mansfield T	27	4	181 23

MASON, Owen (G) 19 0
H: 6 6 W: 13 08 b. 24-3-04
Internationals: Republic of Ireland U18, U19.

2021–22	Mansfield T	0	0	
2022–23	Mansfield T	0	0	
2023–24	Mansfield T	0	0	
2024	Wexford	18	0	18 0
2024–25	Mansfield T	1	0	1 0

McLAUGHLIN, Stephen (M) 461 50
H: 5 9 W: 12 02 b.Donegal 14-6-90

2009	Finn Harps	16	1	
2010	Finn Harps	32	1	48 2
2011	Derry C	33	3	
2012	Derry C	24	10	57 13
2012–13	Nottingham F	0	0	
2013–14	Nottingham F	3	0	
2013–14	Bristol C	5	0	5 0
2014–15	Nottingham F	6	0	9 0
2014–15	Notts Co	13	0	13 0
2014–15	Southend U	6	1	
2015–16	Southend U	17	1	
2016–17	Southend U	34	7	
2017–18	Southend U	45	6	
2018–19	Southend U	30	1	
2019–20	Southend U	27	4	
2020–21	Southend U	0	0	159 20
2020–21	Mansfield T	36	4	
2021–22	Mansfield T	43	7	
2022–23	Mansfield T	25	1	
2023–24	Mansfield T	25	1	
2024–25	Mansfield T	41	2	170 15

NICHOLS, Tom (F) 439 82
H: 5 10 W: 10 10 b.Wellington 1-9-93

2010–11	Exeter C	1	0	
2011–12	Exeter C	7	1	
2012–13	Exeter C	3	0	
2013–14	Exeter C	28	6	
2014–15	Exeter C	36	15	
2015–16	Exeter C	23	10	98 32
2015–16	Peterborough U	7	1	
2016–17	Peterborough U	43	10	50 11
2017–18	Bristol R	39	1	
2018–19	Bristol R	36	1	
2019–20	Bristol R	19	2	94 4
2019–20	Cheltenham T	5	0	5 0
2020–21	Crawley T	43	11	
2021–22	Crawley T	39	10	
2022–23	Crawley T	19	2	101 23
2022–23	Gillingham	23	6	
2023–24	Gillingham	25	1	48 7
2023–24	Mansfield T	18	3	
2024–25	Mansfield T	5	0	23 3
2024–25	Swindon T	20	2	20 2

NUNEZ, Anthony (G) 0 0
H: 6 1 W: 12 04 b. 14-10-05

2024–25	Mansfield T	0	0

OATES, Rhys (F) 189 36
H: 6 0 W: 11 09 b.Pontefract 4-12-94

2012–13	Barnsley	0	0	
2013–14	Barnsley	0	0	
2014–15	Barnsley	9	0	9 0
2015–16	Hartlepool U	38	2	
2016–17	Hartlepool U	26	3	64 5
From Hartlepool U.				
2018–19	Morecambe	31	6	
2019–20	Morecambe	5	0	36 6
From Hartlepool U.				
2021–22	Mansfield T	38	9	
2022–23	Mansfield T	24	4	
2023–24	Mansfield T	14	2	
2024–25	Mansfield T	4	0	80 15

OSHILAJA, Adedeji (D) 351 18
H: 5 11 W: 11 11 b.Bermondsey 16-7-93

2012–13	Cardiff C	0	0	
2013–14	Cardiff C	0	0	
2013–14	Newport Co	8	0	8 0
2013–14	Sheffield Wed	2	0	2 0
2014–15	Cardiff C	0	0	
2014–15	AFC Wimbledon	23	1	
2015–16	Cardiff C	0	0	
2015–16	Gillingham	22	3	
2016–17	Cardiff C	0	0	
2016–17	Gillingham	33	2	55 5
2017–18	AFC Wimbledon	42	2	
2018–19	AFC Wimbledon	25	1	90 4
2019–20	Charlton Ath	25	0	
2020–21	Charlton Ath	17	1	42 1
2021–22	Burton Alb	30	0	
2022–23	Burton Alb	42	3	
2023–24	Burton Alb	43	2	115 5
2024–25	Mansfield T	39	3	39 3

PYM, Christy (G) 382 0
H: 6 0 W: 11 09 b.Exeter 24-4-95
Internationals: England U20.

2012–13	Exeter C	0	0	
2013–14	Exeter C	9	0	
2014–15	Exeter C	25	0	
2015–16	Exeter C	0	0	
2016–17	Exeter C	28	0	
2017–18	Exeter C	46	0	
2018–19	Exeter C	43	0	151 0
2019–20	Peterborough U	35	0	
2020–21	Peterborough U	40	0	
2021–22	Peterborough U	7	0	
2021–22	Stevenage	23	0	23 0
2022–23	Peterborough U	0	0	82 0
2022–23	Mansfield T	42	0	
2023–24	Mansfield T	46	0	
2024–25	Mansfield T	38	0	126 0

QUINN, Ben (M) 1 0
H: 5 8 W: 10 08 b.Dublin 11-11-04
Internationals: Republic of Ireland U16, U18, U21.

2022–23	Celtic	0	0	
2023–24	Celtic	0	0	
2024–25	Mansfield T	1	0	1 0

QUINN, Stephen (M) 611 37
H: 5 6 W: 9 06 b.Dublin 4-4-86
Internationals: Republic of Ireland U21, Full caps.

2004	St Patrick's Ath	1	0	
2005	St Patrick's Ath	0	0	1 0
2005–06	Sheffield U	0	0	
2005–06	Milton Keynes D	15	0	15 0
2005–06	Rotherham U	16	0	16 0
2006–07	Sheffield U	15	2	
2007–08	Sheffield U	19	2	
2008–09	Sheffield U	43	7	
2009–10	Sheffield U	44	4	
2010–11	Sheffield U	37	1	
2011–12	Sheffield U	45	4	
2012–13	Sheffield U	3	0	206 20
2012–13	Hull C	42	3	
2013–14	Hull C	15	0	
2014–15	Hull C	28	1	85 4
2015–16	Reading	27	1	
2016–17	Reading	7	0	
2017–18	Reading	0	0	34 1
2018–19	Burton Alb	42	1	
2019–20	Burton Alb	29	0	
2020–21	Burton Alb	22	1	93 2
2020–21	Mansfield T	23	2	
2021–22	Mansfield T	36	1	
2022–23	Mansfield T	40	2	
2023–24	Mansfield T	32	4	
2024–25	Mansfield T	30	1	161 10

REED, Louis (M) 300 11
H: 5 8 W: 9 06 b.Sheffield 25-7-97
Internationals: England U18, U19, U20.

2013–14	Sheffield U	1	0	
2014–15	Sheffield U	19	0	
2015–16	Sheffield U	19	0	
2016–17	Sheffield U	0	0	
2017–18	Sheffield U	0	0	39 0
2017–18	Chesterfield	42	4	42 4
2018–19	Peterborough U	28	1	
2019–20	Peterborough U	24	1	
2020–21	Peterborough U	17	0	69 2
2021–22	Swindon T	39	2	
2022–23	Swindon T	20	1	59 3
2022–23	Mansfield T	5	0	
2023–24	Mansfield T	45	2	
2024–25	Mansfield T	41	0	91 2

TAYLOR, Ollie (M) 0 0
H: 5 9 W: 10 01 b. 30-9-06

2023–24	Mansfield T	0	0
2024–25	Mansfield T	0	0

WARNABY, Lewis (M) 0 0
b. 10-4-06

2024–25	Mansfield T	0	0

WAUCHOPE, Darien (D) 0 0
H: 5 11 W: 10 10 b. 8-12-04

2022–23	Mansfield T	0	0
2023–24	Mansfield T	0	0
2024–25	Mansfield T	0	0

WILLIAMS, George B (D) 294 6
H: 5 9 W: 11 00 b.Hillingdon 14-4-93

2011–12	Milton Keynes D	2	0	
From Worcester C.				
2014–15	Barnsley	4	0	
2015–16	Barnsley	19	1	23 1
2016–17	Milton Keynes D	33	2	
2017–18	Milton Keynes D	43	1	
2018–19	Milton Keynes D	30	0	
2019–20	Milton Keynes D	28	1	
2020–21	Milton Keynes D	8	0	144 4
2020–21	Bristol R	26	0	26 0
2021–22	Cambridge U	40	1	
2022–23	Cambridge U	29	0	69 1
2023–24	Mansfield T	21	0	
2024–25	Mansfield T	11	0	32 0

Players retained or with offer of contract
Bonser, Louis Harrison.

Scholars
Burgess-Allen, George Robert; Cappin, Joshua Thomas; Chambers-Morgan, Jayden Romeo; Cheetham, Charlie James; Ellis, Lucas James; Harrad, Tyler; Hartmann, Elliot Jacob; Johnson, Callum Lewis; Leech, Harrison James; Maher, Cormac Michael; Monington, Oliver; Murray, Toure Andre; Oldershaw, MacE Kid; Organ, Daniel Jack; Peets, Emeer Shannon Warren; Scott, Harvey Elliott; Scott, Morgan Harry Alan; Spink, Louis Dale; Stubbs, Jacob William; Taylor, Oliver Robert; Whitman-Brown, Chae; Woolf, Lincoln Jack Leslie.

MIDDLESBROUGH (53)

AYLING, Luke (D) 542 17
H: 6 0 W: 11 05 b.Lambeth 25-8-91

2009–10	Arsenal	0	0	
2009–10	Yeovil T	4	0	
2010–11	Yeovil T	37	0	
2011–12	Yeovil T	44	0	
2012–13	Yeovil T	39	0	
2013–14	Yeovil T	42	2	166 2
2014–15	Bristol C	46	4	
2015–16	Bristol C	33	0	
2016–17	Bristol C	1	0	80 4
2016–17	Leeds U	42	0	
2017–18	Leeds U	27	0	
2018–19	Leeds U	38	2	
2019–20	Leeds U	37	4	
2020–21	Leeds U	38	0	
2021–22	Leeds U	26	2	
2022–23	Leeds U	29	2	
2023–24	Leeds U	14	1	251 11
2023–24	Middlesbrough	19	0	
2024–25	Middlesbrough	26	0	45 0

AZAZ, Finn (M) 204 39
H: 6 1 W: 11 00 b.Westminster 7-9-00
Internationals: Republic of Ireland U21, Full caps.

2020–21	WBA	0	0	
2020–21	Cheltenham T	37	1	37 1
2021–22	Aston Villa	0	0	
2021–22	Newport Co	42	7	42 7
2022–23	Aston Villa	0	0	
2022–23	Plymouth Arg	34	8	
2023–24	Aston Villa	0	0	
2023–24	Plymouth Arg	26	7	60 15
2023–24	Middlesbrough	20	4	
2024–25	Middlesbrough	45	12	65 16

BANGURA, Alex (D) 120 7
H: 6 0 W: 10 10 b.Mokomre 13-7-99
Internationals: Sierra Leone Full caps.
From Feyenoord.

2018–19	Cambuur	13	0	
2019–20	Cambuur	10	1	
2020–21	Cambuur	24	0	
2021–22	Cambuur	27	3	
2022–23	Cambuur	29	1	
2023–24	Cambuur	3	0	106 5
2023–24	Middlesbrough	14	2	
2024–25	Middlesbrough	0	0	14 2

BARLASER, Daniel (M) 242 18
H: 6 0 W: 9 11 b.Gateshead 18-1-97
Internationals: Turkey U16, U17. England U18.

2015–16	Newcastle U	0	0	
2016–17	Newcastle U	0	0	
2017–18	Newcastle U	0	0	
2017–18	Crewe Alex	4	0	4 0
2018–19	Newcastle U	0	0	
2018–19	Accrington S	39	1	39 1
2019–20	Newcastle U	0	0	

2019–20 *Rotherham U* 27 2
2020–21 Rotherham U 33 3
2021–22 Rotherham U 44 9
2022–23 Rotherham U 28 2 **132 16**
2022–23 Middlesbrough 11 0
2023–24 Middlesbrough 33 0
2024–25 Middlesbrough 23 1 **67 1**

BORGES, Neto (D) 181 5
H: 6 1 W: 13 03 b.Saubara 13-9-96
2017 Itabaiana 5 0 **5 0**
2018 Hammarby 26 0 **26 0**
2018–19 Genk 1 0
2019–20 Genk 5 0
2020 *Vasco da Gama* 19 0 **19 0**
2020–21 Genk 0 0 **6 0**
2020–21 *Tondela* 29 1 **29 1**
2021–22 Clermont 0 0
2022–23 Clermont 33 3
2023–24 Clermont 28 0 **61 3**
2024–25 Middlesbrough 35 1 **35 1**

BRYNN, Solomon (G) 110 0
H: 6 0 W: 11 09 b.Middlesbrough 30-10-00
2019–20 Middlesbrough 0 0
2020–21 Middlesbrough 0 0
2021–22 Middlesbrough 0 0
2021–22 *Queen of the South* 16 0 **16 0**
2022–23 Middlesbrough 0 0
2022–23 *Swindon T* 46 0 **46 0**
2023–24 Middlesbrough 0 0
2023–24 *Leyton Orient* 42 0 **42 0**
2024–25 Middlesbrough 6 0 **6 0**

BURGZORG, Delano (M) 185 28
H: 6 1 W: 12 00 b.Amsterdam 7-11-98
2016–17 De Graafschap 0 0
2017–18 De Graafschap 6 0
2018–19 De Graafschap 26 5 **32 5**
2019–20 Spezia 8 0 **8 0**
2019–20 *Heracles* 5 1
2020–21 Heracles 32 5
2021–22 Heracles 17 4 **54 10**
2021–22 *Mainz 05* 3 1
2022–23 Mainz 05 13 0
2023–24 Mainz 05 0 0 **16 1**
2023–24 *Huddersfield T* 33 7 **33 7**
2024–25 Middlesbrough 42 5 **42 5**

CARTWRIGHT, Finley (M) 0 0
H: 6 1 W: 12 08 b.Redcar 28-2-07
Internationals: England U16, U17.
2023–24 Middlesbrough 0 0
2024–25 Middlesbrough 0 0

COBURN, Josh (F) 101 25
H: 6 3 W: 11 09 b.Bedale 6-12-02
2020–21 Middlesbrough 4 1
2021–22 Middlesbrough 18 4
2022–23 Middlesbrough 1 0
2022–23 *Bristol R* 35 10 **35 10**
2023–24 Middlesbrough 21 5
2024–25 Middlesbrough 2 0 **46 10**
2024–25 *Millwall* 20 5 **20 5**

CONNOR, Shea (G) 0 0
b.Stockton-on-Tees 30-10-05
2023–24 Middlesbrough 0 0
2024–25 Middlesbrough 0 0

CONWAY, Tommy (F) 118 33
H: 6 1 W: 11 11 b.Taunton 6-8-02
Internationals: Scotland U21, Full caps.
2020–21 Bristol C 5 1
2021–22 Bristol C 4 0
2022–23 Bristol C 34 9
2023–24 Bristol C 39 10 **82 20**
2024–25 Middlesbrough 36 13 **36 13**

DEDE, Josh (M) 0 0
H: 5 10 W: 10 01 b.Glasgow 4-1-06
Internationals: Scotland U16, U17, U19.
2024–25 Celtic 0 0
2024–25 Middlesbrough 0 0

DIENG, Timothy (G) 227 1
H: 6 4 W: 14 02 b.Zurich 23-11-94
Internationals: Senegal Full caps.
2010–11 Red Star Zurich 0 0
2011–12 Grasshopper 0 0
2012–13 Grasshopper 0 0
2012–13 *Grenchen* 3 0 **3 0**
2013–14 Grasshopper 0 0
2014–15 Grasshopper 0 0
2015–16 MSV Duisburg 0 0
2016–17 QPR 0 0
2017–18 QPR 0 0
2018–19 QPR 0 0
2018–19 *Stevenage* 13 0 **13 0**
2018–19 *Dundee* 16 0 **16 0**
2019–20 QPR 0 0
2019–20 *Doncaster R* 27 0 **27 0**
2020–21 QPR 42 0
2021–22 QPR 28 0
2022–23 QPR 46 1 **116 1**
2023–24 Middlesbrough 35 0
2024–25 Middlesbrough 17 0 **52 0**

DIJKSTEEL, Anfernee (D) 193 3
H: 6 0 W: 11 05 b.Amsterdam 27-10-96
Internationals: Netherlands U20. Suriname Full caps.
2016–17 Charlton Ath 0 0
2017–18 Charlton Ath 10 0
2018–19 Charlton Ath 30 1
2019–20 Charlton Ath 1 0 **41 1**
2019–20 Middlesbrough 16 0
2020–21 Middlesbrough 29 0
2021–22 Middlesbrough 34 0
2022–23 Middlesbrough 20 0
2023–24 Middlesbrough 20 0
2024–25 Middlesbrough 33 2 **152 2**

ENGEL, Lukas (F) 228 27
b. 14-12-98
From Kastrup Boldklub.
2017–18 Fremad Amager 11 0
2018–19 Fremad Amager 32 9
2019–20 Fremad Amager 30 5
2020–21 Fremad Amager 16 4 **89 18**
2020–21 Vejle 17 2
2021–22 Vejle 17 2 **34 4**
2021–22 *Silkeborg* 15 2
2022–23 Silkeborg 25 1
2023–24 Silkeborg 3 0 **43 3**
2023–24 Middlesbrough 35 2
2024–25 Middlesbrough 9 0 **44 2**
2025 *Cincinnati* 18 0 **18 0**

FINCH, Sonny (F) 10 1
H: 5 10 W: 11 00 b.Sunderland 5-8-05
Internationals: England U17, U18.
2022–23 Middlesbrough 3 0
2023–24 Middlesbrough 1 0
2024–25 Middlesbrough 0 0 **4 0**
2024–25 *Milton Keynes D* 6 1 **6 1**

FORSS, Marcus (F) 166 38
H: 6 0 W: 11 07 b.Turku 18-6-99
Internationals: Finland U17, U18, U19, U21, Full caps.
From WBA.
2018–19 Brentford 6 1
2019–20 Brentford 2 0
2019–20 *AFC Wimbledon* 18 11 **18 11**
2020–21 Brentford 39 7
2021–22 Brentford 7 0 **54 8**
2021–22 *Hull C* 11 1 **11 1**
2022–23 Middlesbrough 38 10
2023–24 Middlesbrough 21 7
2024–25 Middlesbrough 24 1 **83 18**

FRY, Dael (D) 244 2
H: 6 4 W: 11 05 b.Middlesbrough 30-8-97
Internationals: England U17, U18, U19, U20, U21.
2015–16 Middlesbrough 7 0
2016–17 Middlesbrough 0 0
2016–17 *Rotherham U* 10 0 **10 0**
2017–18 Middlesbrough 13 0
2018–19 Middlesbrough 34 0
2019–20 Middlesbrough 36 0
2020–21 Middlesbrough 32 1
2021–22 Middlesbrough 33 1
2022–23 Middlesbrough 30 0
2023–24 Middlesbrough 28 0
2024–25 Middlesbrough 21 0 **234 2**

GILBERT, Alex (F) 39 2
H: 6 0 b.Birmingham 28-12-01
Internationals: Republic of Ireland U19, U21.
From WBA.
2020–21 Brentford 0 0
2021–22 Brentford 0 0
2021–22 *Swindon T* 8 0 **8 0**
2022–23 Brentford 0 0
2023–24 Middlesbrough 12 1
2024–25 Middlesbrough 7 1 **19 2**
2024–25 *Charlton Ath* 12 0 **12 0**

GLOVER, Tom (G) 100 0
H: 6 3 W: 14 02 b.Sydney 24-11-97
Internationals: Australia U20, U23.
2015–16 Tottenham H 0 0
2016–17 Tottenham H 0 0
2017–18 Tottenham H 0 0
2017–18 *Central Coast Mariners* 4 0 **4 0**
2018–19 Tottenham H 0 0
2019 *Helsingborg* 0 0
2019–20 Melbourne C 15 0
2020–21 Melbourne C 27 0
2021–22 Melbourne C 27 0
2022–23 Melbourne C 8 0 **77 0**
2023–24 Middlesbrough 12 0
2024–25 Middlesbrough 7 0 **19 0**

GREENUP, Isaac (M) 0 0
2024–25 Middlesbrough 0 0

HACKNEY, Hayden (M) 127 9
H: 5 10 W: 11 00 b.Redcar 26-6-02
Internationals: Scotland U21. England U21.
2019–20 Middlesbrough 0 0
2020–21 Middlesbrough 1 0
2021–22 Middlesbrough 0 0
2021–22 *Scunthorpe U* 28 0 **28 0**
2022–23 Middlesbrough 34 3
2023–24 Middlesbrough 21 1
2024–25 Middlesbrough 43 5 **99 9**

HAMILTON, Micah (M) 18 0
H: 5 10 b.Manchester 13-11-03
Internationals: England U16, U20.
2023–24 Manchester C 0 0
2024–25 Middlesbrough 13 0 **13 0**
2024–25 *Stockport Co* 5 0 **5 0**

HEMMING, Zachary (G) 73 0
H: 6 2 W: 12 08 b.Bishop Auckland 7-3-00
2020–21 Middlesbrough 0 0
2021–22 Middlesbrough 0 0
2021–22 *Kilmarnock* 36 0
2022–23 Middlesbrough 0 0
2022–23 *Kilmarnock* 10 0 **46 0**
2024–25 Middlesbrough 0 0
2024–25 *Leyton Orient* 10 0 **10 0**
2024–25 *St Mirren* 17 0 **17 0**

HOPPE, Matthew (F) 51 9
H: 6 3 W: 12 08 b.Yorba Linda 13-3-01
Internationals: USA Full caps.
From Barcelona.
2019–20 Schalke 04 0 0
2020–21 Schalke 04 22 6
2021–22 Schalke 04 1 0 **23 6**
2021–22 Mallorca 5 0 **5 0**
2022–23 Middlesbrough 6 0
2022–23 *Hibernian* 9 1 **9 1**
2023–24 Middlesbrough 0 0
2023–24 *San Jose Earthquakes* 8 2 **8 2**
2024–25 Middlesbrough 0 0 **6 0**

HOWSON, Jonathan (M) 680 54
H: 5 11 W: 12 01 b.Morley 21-5-88
Internationals: England U21.
2006–07 Leeds U 9 1
2007–08 Leeds U 26 3
2008–09 Leeds U 40 4
2009–10 Leeds U 45 4
2010–11 Leeds U 46 10
2011–12 Leeds U 19 1 **185 23**
2011–12 Norwich C 11 1
2012–13 Norwich C 30 2
2013–14 Norwich C 27 2
2014–15 Norwich C 34 8
2015–16 Norwich C 36 3
2016–17 Norwich C 38 6 **176 22**
2017–18 Middlesbrough 43 3
2018–19 Middlesbrough 46 1
2019–20 Middlesbrough 41 0
2020–21 Middlesbrough 41 1
2021–22 Middlesbrough 45 1
2022–23 Middlesbrough 44 0
2023–24 Middlesbrough 38 2
2024–25 Middlesbrough 21 1 **319 9**

HUNT, Harley (D) 3 0
H: 6 4 W: 11 11 b. 21-3-07
2023–24 Swindon T 3 0 **3 0**
2024–25 Middlesbrough 0 0

IHEANACHO, Kelechi (F) 243 48
H: 6 2 W: 13 08 b.Imo 3-10-96
Internationals: Nigeria U17, U20, Full caps.
2014–15 Manchester C 0 0
2015–16 Manchester C 26 8
2016–17 Manchester C 20 4 **46 12**
2017–18 Leicester C 21 3
2018–19 Leicester C 30 1
2019–20 Leicester C 20 5
2020–21 Leicester C 25 12
2021–22 Leicester C 26 4
2022–23 Leicester C 28 5
2023–24 Leicester C 23 5 **173 35**
2024–25 Sevilla 9 0 **9 0**
On loan from Sevilla.
2024–25 Middlesbrough 15 1 **15 1**

LATTE LATH, Emmanuel (F) 201 57
H: 5 11 W: 11 11 b.Anoumalo Marcory 2-1-99
Internationals: Ivory Coast Full caps.
2016–17 Atalanta 0 0
2017–18 Atalanta 0 0
2017–18 *Pescara* 0 0
2018–19 Atalanta 0 0
2018–19 *Pistoiese* 18 2 **18 2**
2018–19 *Carrarese* 17 0 **17 0**
2019–20 Atalanta 0 0
2019–20 *Imolese* 19 2 **19 2**
2019–20 *Pianese* 5 0 **5 0**
2020–21 Atalanta 0 0
2020–21 *Pro Patria* 34 9 **34 9**
2021–22 Atalanta 0 0
2021–22 *SPAL* 18 3 **18 3**
2022–23 Atalanta 0 0
2022–23 *St Gallen* 31 14 **31 14**
2023–24 Middlesbrough 30 16
2024–25 Middlesbrough 29 11 **59 27**
Transferred to Atlanta U, February 2025.

LENIHAN, Darragh (M) 299 11
H: 5 10 W: 12 00 b.Dublin 16-3-94
Internationals: Republic of Ireland U17, U19, U21, Full caps.
2011–12 Blackburn R 0 0
2012–13 Blackburn R 0 0
2013–14 Blackburn R 0 0
2014–15 Blackburn R 3 0
2014–15 *Burton Alb* 17 1 17 1
2015–16 Blackburn R 23 0
2016–17 Blackburn R 40 0
2017–18 Blackburn R 14 1
2018–19 Blackburn R 34 2
2019–20 Blackburn R 37 3
2020–21 Blackburn R 41 0
2021–22 Blackburn R 41 3 233 9
2022–23 Middlesbrough 41 0
2023–24 Middlesbrough 8 1
2024–25 Middlesbrough 0 0 49 1

LENNON, Charlie (M) 1 0
b.Spennymoor 9-4-06
Internationals: England U16, U17.
2023–24 Middlesbrough 1 0
2024–25 Middlesbrough 0 0 1 0

McCABE, Law (M) 3 0
b. 12-6-06
Internationals: England U18.
2023–24 Middlesbrough 3 0
2024–25 Middlesbrough 0 0 3 0

McCORMICK, George (D) 1 0
b.Middlesbrough 27-1-05
2024–25 Middlesbrough 1 0 1 0

McGREE, Riley (M) 200 39
H: 5 10 W: 11 05 b.Gawler 2-11-98
Internationals: Australia U17, U23, Full caps.
2015–16 Adelaide U 1 0
2016–17 Adelaide U 16 1
2017–18 Club Brugge 0 0
2017–18 *Newcastle Jets* 12 5 12 5
2018–19 Club Brugge 0 0
2018–19 *Melbourne C* 27 7 27 7
2019–20 Adelaide U 23 10 40 11
2020–21 Charlotte 0 0
2020–21 Birmingham C 15 1
2021–22 Charlotte 0 0
2021–22 *Birmingham C* 13 2 28 3
2021–22 Middlesbrough 11 2
2022–23 Middlesbrough 43 6
2023–24 Middlesbrough 22 4
2024–25 Middlesbrough 17 1 93 13

MORRIS, Aidan (M) 118 6
H: 5 8 W: 9 08 b.Fort Lauderdale,Florida 16-11-01
Internationals: USA U18, U20, U23, Full caps.
2020 Columbus Crew 10 0
2021 Columbus Crew 0 0
2022 Columbus Crew 27 0
2023 Columbus Crew 30 4
2024 Columbus Crew 16 2 83 6
2024–25 Middlesbrough 35 0 35 0

NKRUMAH, Daniel (M) 3 0
b.Redbridge 5-11-03
2021–22 Leyton Orient 3 0
2022–23 Leyton Orient 0 0 3 0
2023–24 Middlesbrough 0 0
2023–24 *Dagenham & Red* 0 0
2024–25 Middlesbrough 0 0

PALMER, Anton (M) 0 0
b. 27-11-08
Internationals: England U17.
2024–25 Middlesbrough 0 0

PALMER, Bailey (M) 0 0
H: 5 10 W: 9 11 b. 27-11-08
Internationals: England U17.
2024–25 Middlesbrough 0 0

SILVERA, Samuel (M) 144 14
H: 5 10 b.London 25-10-00
Internationals: Australia U23, Full caps.
From Western Sydney W.
2019–20 Central Coast Mariners 21 1
2020–21 Pacos de Ferreira 0 0
2020–21 *Casa Pia* 4 0 4 0
2021–22 Pacos de Ferreira 0 0
2021–22 *Sanjoanense* 11 1 11 1
2022–23 Central Coast Mariners 26 6 47 7
2023–24 Middlesbrough 37 4
2024–25 Middlesbrough 0 0 37 4
2024–25 *Portsmouth* 11 0 11 0
2024–25 *Blackpool* 15 1 15 1

SIMPSON, Nathan (D) 1 0
b. 24-2-04
2024–25 Middlesbrough 1 0 1 0

SMITH, Tommy (D) 321 7
H: 6 1 W: 13 02 b.Warrington 14-4-92
2012–13 Huddersfield T 0 0

2013–14 Huddersfield T 24 0
2014–15 Huddersfield T 41 0
2015–16 Huddersfield T 36 0
2016–17 Huddersfield T 42 4
2017–18 Huddersfield T 24 0
2018–19 Huddersfield T 15 0 182 4
2019–20 Stoke C 30 0
2020–21 Stoke C 35 2
2021–22 Stoke C 32 1 97 3
2022–23 Middlesbrough 36 0
2023–24 Middlesbrough 6 0
2024–25 Middlesbrough 0 0 42 0

STOTT, Jack (M) 0 0
b.Middlesbrough 6-12-03
2022–23 Middlesbrough 0 0
2023–24 Middlesbrough 0 0
2024–25 Middlesbrough 0 0

VAN DEN BERG, Rav (D) 89 1
H: 6 3 W: 11 11 b.Zwolle 7-7-04
Internationals: Netherlands U16, U18, U19, U20, U21.
2020–21 PEC Zwolle 1 0
2021–22 PEC Zwolle 10 0
2022–23 PEC Zwolle 17 0 28 0
2023–24 Middlesbrough 34 1
2024–25 Middlesbrough 27 0 61 1

WHITTAKER, Morgan (F) 185 39
H: 6 0 W: 10 12 b.Derby 7-1-01
Internationals: England U16, U17, U18, U19, U20.
2019–20 Derby Co 16 1
2020–21 Derby Co 9 0 25 1
2020–21 Swansea C 12 1
2021–22 Swansea C 6 0
2021–22 *Lincoln C* 20 5 20 5
2022–23 *Swansea C* 15 1 33 2
2022–23 Plymouth Arg 25 9
2023–24 Plymouth Arg 46 19
2024–25 Plymouth Arg 20 3 91 31
2024–25 Middlesbrough 16 0 16 0

WILLIS, Pharrell (F) 6 1
H: 6 1 W: 10 10 b.London 23-2-03
2022–23 Middlesbrough 1 0
2023–24 Middlesbrough 0 0
2024–25 Middlesbrough 0 0 1 0
2024–25 *Queen of the South* 5 1 5 1

WILSON, James (D) 1 0
b. 11-3-07
2023–24 Middlesbrough 1 0
2024–25 Middlesbrough 0 0 1 0

WOOLSTON, Luke (M) 0 0
H: 6 0 W: 11 11 b.Hartlepool 30-11-04
2022–23 Middlesbrough 0 0
2023–24 Middlesbrough 0 0
2024–25 Middlesbrough 0 0

Players retained or with offer of contract
Bakre, Hazeem Ademola; Coulson, Frankie Jake; Edmundson, Samuel George Alan; Fisher, Nathan Joseph; Howells, Max Isaak; James, Daniel Michael Sisihu; Johnson, Brayden Nana Yaw; Patterson Powell, Rio Dior Kayden; Sykes, Cain; Weller-Ayling, Luke David.

Scholars
Acheampong, Prince Kofi; Dore, Addis Sekou; Elliott, Felix Rufus; Greenup, Isaac James; Guarro Bevin, Leandro; Hamelberg, Eric Albert Baptista; Harrison, Lucas Christopher; Lloyd, Oliver Anthony Robert; Martin, Oliver Allan; McPartland, Will John Greg; Muwana, Noah Etienne Nzuzi; Myers-Smith, Alfie; Nino, Collins Theo; O'Gorman, Finley Harry; Okine, William Kodjo; Parker, Leon Kai; Roberts, Joseph Stephen; Samuels, Oliver; Scott, Ethan; Smith, Tyler; Tawiah, Judah-Jeremiah Nii Adjetey; Williams, Logan Joseph; Woodhouse, McCartney James.

MILLWALL (54)

AZEEZ, Femi (F) 115 12
H: 5 11 W: 10 12 b.Westminster 5-6-01
From Wealdstone.
2020–21 Reading 1 0
2021–22 Reading 13 2
2022–23 Reading 20 0
2023–24 Reading 46 8
2024–25 Reading 1 0 81 10
2024–25 Millwall 34 2 34 2

BAKER, Frankie (F) 0 0
b. 29-11-05
2024–25 Millwall 0 0

BANGURA-WILLIAMS, Raees (F) 10 0
b.London 2-7-04
Internationals: England U20.
2024–25 Millwall 10 0 10 0

BOAITEY, Benicio (F) 15 0
H: 5 5 W: 9 06 b.Hammersmith 9-1-04
Internationals: England U16, U20.
2023–24 Brighton & HA 5 0
2024–25 Brighton & HA 0 0 5 0
2024–25 *Port Vale* 10 0 10 0
2024–25 Millwall 0 0

BRYAN, Joe (D) 383 22
H: 5 7 W: 11 05 b.Bristol 17-9-93
2011–12 Bristol C 1 0
2012–13 Bristol C 13 0
2012–13 *Plymouth Arg* 11 0 10 1
2013–14 Bristol C 21 2
2014–15 Bristol C 41 6
2015–16 Bristol C 39 2
2016–17 Bristol C 44 1
2017–18 Bristol C 43 5
2018–19 Fulham 1 0 203 16
2018–19 Fulham 28 0
2019–20 Fulham 43 1
2020–21 Fulham 16 1
2021–22 Fulham 15 0
2022–23 Fulham 0 0 102 2
2022–23 *Nice* 6 0
2023–24 Millwall 23 2
2024–25 Millwall 39 1 62 3

CONNOLLY, Aaron (F) 128 19
H: 5 8 W: 12 02 b.Galway 28-1-00
Internationals: Republic of Ireland U17, U19, U21, Full caps.
2017–18 Brighton & HA 0 0
2018–19 Brighton & HA 0 0
2018–19 *Luton T* 2 0 2 0
2019–20 Brighton & HA 24 3
2020–21 Brighton & HA 17 2
2021–22 Brighton & HA 4 0
2021–22 *Middlesbrough* 19 2 19 2
2022–23 Brighton & HA 0 0 45 5
2022–23 *Venezia* 5 0 5 0
2022–23 *Hull C* 5 2
2023–24 Hull C 28 8 33 10
2024–25 *Sunderland* 10 1 10 1
2024–25 Millwall 14 1 14 1

COOPER, Jake (D) 397 32
H: 6 4 W: 13 05 b.Bracknell 3-2-95
Internationals: England U18, U19, U20.
2013–14 Reading 0 0
2014–15 Reading 15 2
2015–16 Reading 24 2
2016–17 Reading 3 0 42 4
2016–17 Millwall 15 2
2017–18 Millwall 38 4
2018–19 Millwall 46 6
2019–20 Millwall 46 3
2020–21 Millwall 41 1
2021–22 Millwall 42 4
2022–23 Millwall 46 3
2023–24 Millwall 44 2
2024–25 Millwall 36 3 355 28

CRAMA, Tristan (D) 69 3
H: 6 4 W: 13 01 b.Beziers 8-11-01
From Beziers.
2020–21 Brentford 0 0
2021–22 Brentford 0 0
2022–23 Brentford 0 0
2023–24 Brentford 0 0
2023–24 *Bristol R* 27 0 27 0
2024–25 Brentford 0 0
2024–25 *Exeter C* 22 3 22 3
2024–25 Millwall 20 0 20 0

CUNDLE, Luke (M) 92 9
H: 5 7 W: 10 08 b.Warrington 26-4-02
2019–20 Wolverhampton W 0 0
2020–21 Wolverhampton W 0 0
2021–22 Wolverhampton W 4 0
2022–23 Wolverhampton W 0 0
2022–23 *Swansea C* 32 3 32 3
2023–24 Wolverhampton W 0 0
2023–24 *Plymouth Arg* 24 3 24 3
2023–24 *Stoke C* 16 2 16 2
2024–25 Wolverhampton W 0 0 4 0
2024–25 Millwall 16 1 16 1

DE NORRE, Casper (D) 248 13
H: 5 9 W: 11 11 b.Hasselt 7-2-97
Internationals: Belgium U17, U21.
2015–16 Sint-Truidense 2 0
2016–17 Sint-Truidense 1 0
2017–18 Sint-Truidense 36 0
2018–19 Sint-Truidense 19 2 57 2
2018–19 Genk 11 0
2019–20 Genk 13 0 24 0
2020–21 OH Leuven 23 1
2021–22 OH Leuven 32 2
2022–23 OH Leuven 34 4 89 7
2023–24 Millwall 32 1
2024–25 Millwall 46 3 78 4

DRAKE, Ben (D) 0 0
b.Doncaster 6-1-05
2024–25 Millwall 0 0

EMAKHU, Aidomo (D)   **81 3**
H: 5 11 W: 12 13 b.Clondalkin 26-10-03
Internationals: Republic of Ireland U19, U21.

2020	Shamrock R	0	0		
2021	Shamrock R	12	1		
2022	Shamrock R	22	1	34	2
2022–23	Millwall	1	0		
2023–24	Millwall	21	1		
2024–25	Millwall	25	0	47	1

EVANS, George (G)   **4 0**
H: 6 0 W: 12 00 b. 16-5-05

2024–25	Millwall	4	0	4	0

EVANS, Ollie (F)   **0 0**

2024–25	Millwall	0	0		

FLEMMING, Zian (M)   **238 73**
H: 6 4 W: 13 03 b.Amsterdam 1-8-98

2017–18	Ajax	0	0		
2018–19	PEC Zwolle	25	2		
2019–20	PEC Zwolle	4	0	29	2
2019–20	NEC Nijmegen	24	13	24	13
2020–21	Fortuna Sittard	33	12		
2021–22	Fortuna Sittard	28	12	61	24
2022–23	Millwall	43	15		
2023–24	Millwall	46	7		
2024–25	Millwall	0	0	89	22
2024–25	Burnley	35	12	35	12

GRANT, Kamarl (D)   **40 2**
H: 6 2 W: 13 01 b. 26-1-03

2023–24	Millwall	0	0		
2024–25	Millwall	0	0		
2024–25	Bromley	40	2	40	2

HARDING, Wes (D)   **207 4**
H: 5 11 W: 12 06 b.Leicester 20-10-96
Internationals: Jamaica Full caps.

2017–18	Birmingham C	9	0		
2018–19	Birmingham C	27	0		
2019–20	Birmingham C	15	0	51	0
2020–21	Rotherham U	46	0		
2021–22	Rotherham U	38	0		
2022–23	Rotherham U	43	1	127	1
2023–24	Millwall	24	3		
2024–25	Millwall	5	0	29	3

HONEYMAN, George (M)   **311 25**
H: 5 8 W: 11 05 b.Prudhoe 8-9-94

2014–15	Sunderland	0	0		
2015–16	Sunderland	1	0		
2016–17	Sunderland	5	0		
2017–18	Sunderland	42	6		
2018–19	Sunderland	35	6		
2019–20	Sunderland	0	0	83	12
2019–20	Hull C	42	1		
2020–21	Hull C	42	4		
2021–22	Hull C	35	5	119	10
2022–23	Millwall	38	1		
2023–24	Millwall	31	0		
2024–25	Millwall	40	2	109	3

HUTCHINSON, Shaun (D)   **398 22**
H: 6 1 W: 12 04 b.Newcastle upon Tyne 23-11-90

2008–09	Motherwell	1	0		
2009–10	Motherwell	5	3		
2010–11	Motherwell	19	1		
2011–12	Motherwell	30	1		
2012–13	Motherwell	31	1		
2013–14	Motherwell	35	1	121	7
2014–15	Fulham	25	2		
2015–16	Fulham	9	0	34	2
2016–17	Millwall	16	2		
2017–18	Millwall	46	2		
2018–19	Millwall	26	1		
2019–20	Millwall	36	6		
2020–21	Millwall	39	1		
2021–22	Millwall	29	0		
2022–23	Millwall	33	0		
2023–24	Millwall	14	1		
2024–25	Millwall	9	0	243	13

IVANOVIC, Mihailo (F)   **76 22**
H: 6 2 W: 12 06 b.Novi Sad 29-11-04
Internationals: Serbia U17, U18, U21, Full caps.

2021–22	Vojvodina	1	0		
2022–23	Vojvodina	0	0		
2022–23	Sampdoria	1	0	1	0
2023–24	Vojvodina	32	9		
2024–25	Vojvodina	5	1	38	10
2024–25	Millwall	37	12	37	12

JENSEN, Lukas (G)   **130 0**
H: 6 6 W: 14 02 b.Helsingor 18-3-99

2017–18	Helsingor	1	0		
2018–19	Helsingor	0	0	1	0
2018–19	HIK	6	0	6	0
2019–20	Burnley	0	0		
2020–21	Burnley	0	0		
2020–21	Bolton W	0	0		
2020–21	Kordrengir	7	0	7	0
2021–22	Burnley	0	0		
2021–22	Carlisle U	1	0	1	0
2022–23	Burnley	0	0		
2022–23	Accrington S	29	0	29	0
2023–24	Lincoln C	45	0	45	0
2024–25	Millwall	41	0	41	0

KELLY, Daniel (M)   **6 1**
H: 5 11 W: 10 03 b. 3-10-05
Internationals: Scotland U18, U19.

2023–24	Celtic	4	1	4	1
2024–25	Millwall	2	0	2	0

KENDALL, Sheldon (F)   **0 0**
b. 31-12-07

2024–25	Millwall	0	0		

LANGSTAFF, Macaulay (F)   **80 29**
H: 5 10 W: 12 02 b.Stockton 3-2-97

2023–24	Notts Co	46	28	46	28
2024–25	Millwall	34	1	34	1

LAWSON, Sha'mar (M)   **0 0**
b. 14-6-03

2023–24	Ajax	0	0		
2024–25	Millwall	0	0		

LEAHY, Tom (F)   **1 0**
b. 31-3-04

2023–24	Millwall	0	0		
2024–25	Millwall	1	0	1	0

LEONARD, Ryan (D)   **429 24**
H: 5 9 W: 12 13 b.Plympton 24-5-92

2009–10	Plymouth Arg	1	0		
2010–11	Plymouth Arg	0	0	1	0
2011–12	Southend U	17	1		
2012–13	Southend U	22	2		
2013–14	Southend U	43	5		
2014–15	Southend U	41	3		
2015–16	Southend U	37	2		
2016–17	Southend U	43	3		
2017–18	Southend U	25	4	228	20
2017–18	Sheffield U	13	0		
2018–19	Sheffield U	3	0	16	0
2018–19	Millwall	37	2		
2019–20	Millwall	17	1		
2020–21	Millwall	26	1		
2021–22	Millwall	19	0		
2022–23	Millwall	17	0		
2023–24	Millwall	35	0		
2024–25	Millwall	33	0	184	4

LOVELACE, Zak (F)   **8 0**
H: 5 11 W: 11 11 b.Wandsworth 23-1-06
Internationals: England U17.

2021–22	Millwall	5	0		
2022–23	Rangers	2	0		
2023–24	Rangers	2	0		
2024–25	Rangers	0	0	3	0
2024–25	Millwall	0	0	5	0

MASSEY, Alfie (M)   **0 0**
H: 6 0 W: 10 01 b.London 18-1-06

2024–25	Millwall	0	0		

MATTHEWS, Ajay (F)   **2 0**
H: 6 0 W: 11 11 b.Middlesbrough 11-6-06
Internationals: England U17, U18.

2023–24	Middlesbrough	2	0		
2024–25	Middlesbrough	0	0	2	0

MAYOR, Adam (F)   **78 6**
H: 5 7 W: 10 03 b.Liverpool 10-4-04

2022–23	Morecambe	34	3		
2023–24	Morecambe	23	3	57	6
2023–24	Millwall	4	0		
2024–25	Millwall	0	0	4	0
2024–25	Bromley	17	0	17	0

McNAMARA, Danny (D)   **184 3**
H: 5 9 W: 11 05 b.Sidcup 27-12-98
Internationals: Republic of Ireland U21.

2018–19	Millwall	0	0		
2019–20	Millwall	0	0		
2019–20	Newport Co	21	0	21	0
2020–21	Millwall	16	0		
2020–21	St Johnstone	22	1	22	1
2021–22	Millwall	37	2		
2022–23	Millwall	42	0		
2023–24	Millwall	33	0		
2024–25	Millwall	13	0	141	2

MITCHELL, Billy (M)   **155 1**
H: 5 10 W: 11 11 b.Orpington 7-4-01

2018–19	Millwall	1	0		
2019–20	Millwall	0	0		
2020–21	Millwall	16	1		
2021–22	Millwall	42	0		
2022–23	Millwall	36	0		
2023–24	Millwall	34	0		
2024–25	Millwall	19	0	155	1

NEGHLI, Camiel (M)   **105 26**
H: 5 10 W: 11 05 b.Ede 6-11-01
Internationals: Algeria U20, U23.

2020–21	De Graafschap	8	1		
2021–22	De Graafschap	14	3		
2022–23	De Graafschap	32	11	54	15
2023–24	Sparta Rotterdam	27	5		
2024–25	Sparta Rotterdam	20	5	47	10
2024–25	Millwall	4	1	4	1

NISBET, Kevin (F)   **254 102**
H: 5 11 W: 12 02 b.Glasgow 8-3-97
Internationals: Scotland Full caps.

2014–15	Partick Thistle	0	0		
2014–15	East Stirlingshire	11	6	11	6
2015–16	Partick Thistle	8	0		
2016–17	Partick Thistle	3	0		
2016–17	Ayr U	20	2	20	2
2017–18	Partick Thistle	6	0	17	0
2017–18	Dumbarton	9	0	9	0
2018–19	Raith R	34	29	34	29
2019–20	Dumfermline Ath	25	18	25	18
2020–21	Hibernian	33	14		
2021–22	Hibernian	26	5		
2022–23	Hibernian	19	12	78	31
2023–24	Millwall	27	5		
2024–25	Millwall	1	0	28	5
2024–25	Aberdeen	32	11	32	11

PRZEWOZNY, Jakub (G)   **0 0**
b. 19-1-07

2024–25	Millwall	0	0		

ROBERTS, Liam (G)   **221 0**
H: 6 0 W: 12 13 b.Walsall 24-11-94

2012–13	Walsall	0	0		
2013–14	Walsall	0	0		
2014–15	Walsall	0	0		
2015–16	Walsall	1	0		
2016–17	Walsall	0	0		
2017–18	Walsall	24	0		
2018–19	Walsall	42	0		
2019–20	Walsall	32	0		
2020–21	Walsall	32	0		
2021–22	Walsall	0	0	131	0
2021–22	Northampton T	46	0	46	0
2022–23	Middlesbrough	4	0		
2023–24	Middlesbrough	0	0	4	0
2023–24	Barnsley	38	0	38	0
2024–25	Millwall	2	0	2	0

SAVILLE, George (M)   **437 38**
H: 5 9 W: 11 07 b.Camberley 1-6-93
Internationals: Northern Ireland Full caps.

2010–11	Chelsea	0	0		
2011–12	Chelsea	0	0		
2012–13	Chelsea	0	0		
2012–13	Millwall	3	0		
2013–14	Chelsea	0	0		
2013–14	Brentford	40	3	40	3
2014–15	Wolverhampton W	7	0		
2014–15	Bristol C	7	1	7	1
2015–16	Wolverhampton W	19	5		
2015–16	Millwall	12	0		
2016–17	Wolverhampton W	24	1	50	6
2017–18	Millwall	44	10		
2018–19	Millwall	4	0		
2018–19	Middlesbrough	34	4		
2019–20	Middlesbrough	37	1		
2020–21	Middlesbrough	42	6	113	11
2021–22	Millwall	37	2		
2022–23	Millwall	42	2		
2023–24	Millwall	40	2		
2024–25	Millwall	45	1	227	17

SMITH, Kyle (D)   **0 0**
H: 5 10 W: 11 05 b. 7-6-04

2024–25	Millwall	0	0		

TANGANGA, Japhet (D)   **85 4**
H: 6 0 W: 11 07 b.Hackney 31-3-99
Internationals: England U16, U17, U18, U19, U20, U21.

2019–20	Tottenham H	6	0		
2020–21	Tottenham H	6	0		
2021–22	Tottenham H	11	0		
2022–23	Tottenham H	4	0		
2023–24	Tottenham H	0	0	27	0
2023–24	Augsburg	0	0		
2024–25	Millwall	18	2		
2024–25	Millwall	40	2	58	4

WALKER, George (M)   **0 0**
H: 5 9 b. 24-9-03

2023–24	Millwall	0	0		
2024–25	Millwall	0	0		

WALLACE, Murray (D)   **416 21**
H: 5 9 W: 11 11 b.Glasgow 10-1-93
Internationals: Scotland U20, U21.

2010–11	Falkirk	0	0		
2011–12	Falkirk	19	2		
2011–12	Huddersfield T	0	0		
2011–12	Falkirk	15	2	34	4
2012–13	Huddersfield T	6	1		
2013–14	Huddersfield T	17	0		
2014–15	Huddersfield T	26	2		
2015–16	Huddersfield T	2	0	51	3
2015–16	Scunthorpe U	33	2		
2016–17	Scunthorpe U	46	2		
2017–18	Scunthorpe U	45	1	124	5
2018–19	Millwall	21	2		
2019–20	Millwall	43	0		
2020–21	Millwall	23	1		

2021–22	Millwall	42	4	
2022–23	Millwall	37	0	
2023–24	Millwall	30	2	
2024–25	Millwall	11	0	207 9

WATMORE, Duncan (F)   248   38
H: 5 9   W: 11 05   b.Cheadle Hulme 8-3-94
Internationals: England U20, U21.
From Altrincham.

2013–14	Sunderland	0	0	
2013–14	*Hibernian*	9	1	9 1
2014–15	Sunderland	0	0	
2015–16	Sunderland	23	3	
2016–17	Sunderland	14	0	
2017–18	Sunderland	6	0	
2018–19	Sunderland	11	1	
2019–20	Sunderland	17	1	71 5
2020–21	Middlesbrough	30	9	
2021–22	Middlesbrough	41	7	
2022–23	Middlesbrough	21	5	92 21
2022–23	Millwall	16	3	
2023–24	Millwall	34	3	
2024–25	Millwall	26	5	76 11

Players retained or with offer of contract
Celestine-Charles, Jaiden Oscar Jermel; Clark Evans, George David; Dyer, Jet Max; Howland, Jack Thomas; Lamptey, Rafiq Yaw Nii Lantei.

Scholars
Abdulazeez, Abdulahi Olalekan Oladimeji; Ashburn, Luke Alfred George; Beaumont, George Hedley; Dixon, Kane Bobby Douglas; Forbes, Dean Jeremiah Kyle; Kirby, Archie James; Lindner, Caspar Raymond Jackson; Mansor, Elias; O'Boyle, Elidon; Taylor, Harry Dwain; Tektas, Jayden Marc Jem; Thomas-Smith, Jaydon Darnell; Tsugita Vieira, Sacha Natsuki; Whitby, Oliver Daniel; Whiteman, Harvey Max; Wright, William David.

MILTON KEYNES D (55)

ANKER, Joel (M)   0   0
H: 5 6   W: 9 13   b. 11-10-04

2023–24	Milton Keynes D	0	0
2024–25	Milton Keynes D	0	0

BRAMMELD, Michael (D)   0   0
H: 6 0   b.Bekfast 4-6-07
Internationals: Northern Ireland U21.

2024–25	Milton Keynes D	0	0

CROWLEY, Daniel (M)   286   32
H: 5 9   W: 10 10   b.Coventry 3-8-97
Internationals: Republic of Ireland U16, U17. England U16, U17, U19.
From Aston Villa.

2015–16	Arsenal	0	0	
2015–16	*Barnsley*	11	0	11 0
2016–17	Arsenal	0	0	
2016–17	*Oxford U*	6	2	6 2
2016–17	*Go Ahead Eagles*	16	2	16 2
2017–18	Willem II	10	0	
2018–19	Willem II	34	5	
2019–20	Birmingham C	38	1	
2020–21	Birmingham C	3	0	41 1
2020–21	*Hull C*	22	0	22 0
2021–22	*Cheltenham T*	12	0	12 0
2021–22	Willem II	14	0	
2022–23	Willem II	17	1	75 6
2022–23	*Morecambe*	21	2	21 2
2023–24	Notts Co	46	15	
2024–25	Notts Co	18	4	64 19
2024–25	Milton Keynes D	18	0	18 0

GILBEY, Alex (M)   406   52
H: 6 0   W: 11 07   b.Dagenham 9-12-94

2011–12	Colchester U	0	0	
2012–13	Colchester U	3	0	
2013–14	Colchester U	36	1	
2014–15	Colchester U	34	1	
2015–16	Colchester U	37	5	110 7
2016–17	Wigan Ath	15	2	
2017–18	Wigan Ath	2	0	17 2
2017–18	Milton Keynes D	23	3	
2018–19	Milton Keynes D	39	3	
2019–20	Milton Keynes D	30	5	
2020–21	Charlton Ath	23	3	
2021–22	Charlton Ath	37	2	
2022–23	Charlton Ath	0	0	60 5
2022–23	*Stevenage*	39	3	39 3
2023–24	Milton Keynes D	46	13	
2024–25	Milton Keynes D	42	11	180 35

HARNESS, Nathan (G)   2   0
H: 6 1   W: 10 10   b. 19-1-00
From Stevenage, Dunstable.

2019–20	Charlton Ath	0	0	
2020–21	Charlton Ath	0	0	
2021–22	Charlton Ath	1	0	
2022–23	Charlton Ath	0	0	1 0
2023–24	Milton Keynes D	1	0	
2024–25	Milton Keynes D	0	0	1 0

HARRISON, Ellis (F)   348   72
H: 5 11   W: 12 06   b.Newport 1-2-94
Internationals: Wales U21.

2010–11	Bristol R	1	0	
2011–12	Bristol R	0	0	
2012–13	Bristol R	13	3	
2013–14	Bristol R	25	1	
2014–15	Bristol R	0	0	
2015–16	Bristol R	30	7	
2015–16	*Hartlepool U*	2	0	2 0
2016–17	Bristol R	37	8	
2017–18	Bristol R	44	12	150 31
2018–19	Ipswich T	16	1	16 1
2019–20	Portsmouth	28	5	
2020–21	Portsmouth	25	4	
2021–22	Portsmouth	11	0	64 9
2021–22	Fleetwood T	18	6	
2022–23	Fleetwood T	2	0	20 6
2023–24	Port Vale	33	11	
2023–24	Port Vale	1	0	34 11
2023–24	Milton Keynes D	31	8	
2024–25	Milton Keynes D	19	3	50 11
2024–25	*Walsall*	12	3	12 3

HENDRY, Callum (F)   204   48
H: 6 0   W: 11 00   b.Lytham St Annes 8-12-97

2016–17	Blackburn R	0	0	
2017–18	St Johnstone	5	0	
2018–19	St Johnstone	12	2	
2018–19	*Brechin C*	12	1	12 1
2019–20	St Johnstone	20	7	
2020–21	St Johnstone	16	0	
2020–21	*Aberdeen*	12	2	12 2
2021–22	St Johnstone	19	8	72 17
2021–22	*Kilmarnock*	13	4	13 4
2022–23	Salford C	39	12	
2023–24	Salford C	27	9	66 21
2023–24	Milton Keynes D	29	3	29 3

HOGAN, Scott (F)   325   93
H: 5 11   W: 10 01   b.Salford 13-4-92
Internationals: Republic of Ireland Full caps.

2009–10	Rochdale	0	0	

From FC Halifax T, Stocksbridge PS, Ashton U, Hyde U.

2013–14	Rochdale	33	17	33 17
2014–15	Brentford	1	0	
2015–16	Brentford	7	7	
2016–17	Brentford	25	14	33 21
2016–17	Aston Villa	13	1	
2017–18	Aston Villa	37	6	
2018–19	Aston Villa	6	0	
2018–19	*Sheffield U*	8	2	8 2
2019–20	Aston Villa	0	0	
2019–20	*Stoke C*	13	3	13 3
2019–20	*Birmingham C*	17	7	
2020–21	Aston Villa	0	0	56 7
2020–21	Birmingham C	33	7	
2021–22	Birmingham C	36	10	
2022–23	Birmingham C	37	10	
2023–24	Birmingham C	26	1	149 35
2024–25	Milton Keynes D	33	8	33 8

KELLY, Liam (M)   249   18
H: 5 10   W: 11 09   b.Basingstoke 22-11-95
Internationals: Republic of Ireland U19, U21.

2014–15	Reading	0	0	
2015–16	Reading	0	0	
2016–17	Reading	28	1	
2017–18	Reading	34	5	
2018–19	Reading	20	1	82 7
2019–20	Feyenoord	1	0	
2019–20	*Oxford U*	3	0	
2020–21	Feyenoord	0	0	1 0
2021–22	Oxford U	26	0	29 0
2021–22	*Rochdale*	30	5	
2022–23	Rochdale	33	1	63 6
2023–24	Crawley T	37	4	37 4
2024–25	Milton Keynes D	37	1	37 1

LEKO, Jonathan (F)   170   14
H: 6 0   W: 11 11   b.Kinshasa 24-4-99
Internationals: England U16, U17, U18, U19, U20.

2015–16	WBA	5	0	
2016–17	WBA	9	0	
2017–18	*Bristol C*	11	0	11 0
2017–18	WBA	0	0	
2018–19	WBA	2	0	
2019–20	WBA	0	0	16 0
2019–20	*Charlton Ath*	21	5	
2020–21	Birmingham C	34	0	
2021–22	Birmingham C	4	0	
2021–22	*Charlton Ath*	25	2	46 7
2022–23	Birmingham C	8	0	46 0
2022–23	Milton Keynes D	18	4	
2023–24	Milton Keynes D	23	3	
2023–24	*Burton Alb*	1	0	
2024–25	Milton Keynes D	9	0	50 7

LEMONHEIGH-EVANS, Connor (F)   89   12
H: 5 10   W: 11 07   b.Swansea 24-1-97
Internationals: Wales U16, U17, U18, U21.

2013–14	Bristol C	0	0	
2014–15	Bristol C	0	0	
2015–16	Bristol C	0	0	
2016–17	Bristol C	0	0	
2017–18	Bristol C	0	0	
2018–19	Bristol C	0	0	
2019–20	Bristol C	0	0	

From Torquay U.

2022–23	Stockport Co	19	3	
2023–24	Stockport Co	22	6	41 9
2023–24	*AFC Wimbledon*	14	1	14 1
2024–25	Milton Keynes D	34	2	34 2

LEWINGTON, Dean (D)   820   22
H: 5 11   W: 11 00   b.Kingston 18-5-84

2002–03	Wimbledon	1	0	
2003–04	Wimbledon	28	1	29 1
2004–05	Milton Keynes D	43	2	
2005–06	Milton Keynes D	44	1	
2006–07	Milton Keynes D	45	1	
2007–08	Milton Keynes D	45	0	
2008–09	Milton Keynes D	40	2	
2009–10	Milton Keynes D	42	1	
2010–11	Milton Keynes D	42	3	
2011–12	Milton Keynes D	46	3	
2012–13	Milton Keynes D	38	1	
2013–14	Milton Keynes D	43	1	
2014–15	Milton Keynes D	41	3	
2015–16	Milton Keynes D	46	1	
2016–17	Milton Keynes D	36	1	
2017–18	Milton Keynes D	22	0	
2018–19	Milton Keynes D	46	1	
2019–20	Milton Keynes D	33	0	
2020–21	Milton Keynes D	43	0	
2021–22	Milton Keynes D	44	0	
2022–23	Milton Keynes D	26	0	
2023–24	Milton Keynes D	20	0	
2024–25	Milton Keynes D	6	0	791 21

LEWIS-BURGESS, Keon (M)   0   0
H: 6 3   W: 10 12   b. 28-5-07

2023–24	Milton Keynes D	0	0
2024–25	Milton Keynes D	0	0

MACGILLIVRAY, Craig (G)   241   0
H: 6 2   W: 12 04   b.Harrogate 12-1-93
From Stalybridge Celtic, Harrogate T.

2014–15	Walsall	2	0	
2015–16	Walsall	5	0	
2016–17	Walsall	5	0	12 0
2017–18	Shrewsbury T	8	0	8 0
2018–19	Portsmouth	46	0	
2019–20	Portsmouth	20	0	
2020–21	Portsmouth	46	0	
2021–22	Portsmouth	0	0	112 0
2021–22	Charlton Ath	43	0	
2022–23	Charlton Ath	4	0	47 0
2022–23	*Burton Alb*	19	0	19 0
2023–24	Milton Keynes D	24	0	
2023–24	*Stevenage*	11	0	11 0
2024–25	Milton Keynes D	8	0	32 0

MAGUIRE, Laurence (D)   93   4
H: 5 10   W: 11 00   b.Sheffield 8-2-97
Internationals: England C.

2013–14	Chesterfield	0	0	
2014–15	Chesterfield	0	0	
2015–16	Chesterfield	0	0	
2016–17	Chesterfield	11	0	
2017–18	Chesterfield	18	0	29 0

From Chesterfield.

2023–24	Crawley T	34	3	34 3
2024–25	Milton Keynes D	30	1	30 1

MEDWYNTER, Chase (F)   0   0
H: 5 7   W: 8 09   b. 23-11-06

2023–24	Milton Keynes D	0	0
2024–25	Milton Keynes D	0	0

NEMANE, Aaron (M)   128   11
H: 5 9   W: 9 11   b.Amiens, France 26-9-97
From Amiens.

2017–18	Manchester C	0	0	
2017–18	*Rangers*	5	0	5 0
2017–18	*Go Ahead Eagles*	17	2	17 2
2018–19	Manchester C	0	0	
2018–19	*Tubize*	22	1	22 1

From Torquay U, Notts Co.

2023–24	Notts Co	44	8	44 8
2024–25	Milton Keynes D	40	0	40 0

OFFORD, Josh (M)   194   5
H: 5 7   W: 10 06   b.Chichester 19-11-99

2017–18	Crewe Alex	0	0	
2018–19	Crewe Alex	0	0	
2019–20	Crewe Alex	9	0	
2020–21	Crewe Alex	28	0	
2021–22	Crewe Alex	40	0	
2022–23	Crewe Alex	40	0	
2023–24	Crewe Alex	31	1	152 2
2024–25	Milton Keynes D	42	3	42 3

PRITCHARD, Joe (M)   120   17
H: 5 8   W: 10 06   b.Watford 10-9-96
From Tottenham H.
2018–19 Bolton W   4   0   4   0
2019–20 Accrington S   30   2
2020–21 Accrington S   28   7
2021–22 Accrington S   10   0
2022–23 Accrington S   18   2
2023–24 Accrington S   26   6   112   17
2024–25 Milton Keynes D   4   0   4   0
Transferred to Oldham Ath, February 2025.

SANDERS, Jack (D)   79   5
H: 6 4   W: 13 01   b.Bolton 18-3-99
2019–20 Wigan Ath   0   0
2020–21 Wigan Ath   0   0
2021–22 Kilmarnock   14   1
2022–23 Kilmarnock   4   0
2022–23 Cove Rangers   12   1   12   1
2023–24 Kilmarnock   0   0   18   1
2023–24 Ayr U   14   1   14   1
2024–25 St Johnstone   22   1   22   1
2024–25 Milton Keynes D   13   1   13   1

SANDFORD, Ronnie (G)   0   0
H: 6 0   W: 11 07   b.24-2-05
2021–22 Milton Keynes D   0   0
2022–23 Milton Keynes D   0   0
2023–24 Milton Keynes D   0   0
2024–25 Milton Keynes D   0   0

SCHOLTZ, Phoenix (D)   2   0
H: 5 10   W: 11 09   b.7-11-05
Internationals: Northern Ireland U18, U19.
2023–24 Milton Keynes D   2   0
2024–25 Milton Keynes D   0   0   2   0

SHERRING, Sam (D)   107   2
H: 6 2   W: 12 04   b.Dorchester 8-5-00
2020–21 Bournemouth   0   0
2021–22 Bournemouth   0   0
2021–22 Accrington S   10   0   10   0
2021–22 Cambridge U   14   0   14   0
2022–23 Northampton T   36   2
2023–24 Northampton T   37   0   73   2
2024–25 Milton Keynes D   10   0   10   0

SILVER, Rian (M)   0   0
b.7-11-07
2023–24 Milton Keynes D   0   0
2024–25 Milton Keynes D   0   0

SINCLAIR-LINTON, Kobe (F)   0   0
b.Milton Keynes 26-11-06
2024–25 Milton Keynes D   0   0

SINGH-HURDITT, Damerai (M)   0   0
2024–25 Milton Keynes D   0   0

STACEY, Sebastian (G)   0   0
b.19-5-06
2022–23 Milton Keynes D   0   0
2023–24 Milton Keynes D   0   0
2024–25 Milton Keynes D   0   0

STIRLAND, Charlie (D)   0   0
H: 6 0   b.1-10-05
2023–24 Milton Keynes D   0   0
2024–25 Milton Keynes D   0   0

THOMPSON, Nathan (D)   392   8
H: 5 7   W: 11 03   b.Chester 9-11-90
2009–10 Swindon T   0   0
2010–11 Swindon T   3   0
2011–12 Swindon T   5   0
2012–13 Swindon T   26   0
2013–14 Swindon T   41   1
2014–15 Swindon T   35   0
2015–16 Swindon T   23   1
2016–17 Swindon T   34   2   167   4
2017–18 Portsmouth   36   0
2018–19 Portsmouth   31   0   67   0
2019–20 Peterborough U   15   0
2020–21 Peterborough U   39   2
2021–22 Peterborough U   27   1
2022–23 Peterborough U   34   1   115   4
2023–24 Stevenage   26   0
2024–25 Stevenage   15   0   41   0
2024–25 Milton Keynes D   2   0   2   0

THOMPSON-SOMMERS, Kane (M)   23   2
H: 5 10   W: 11 09   b.London 1-12-00
From Tottenham H.
2020–21 Birmingham C   0   0
From Hereford, FC Halifax T.
2024–25 Milton Keynes D   23   2   23   2

TOMLINSON, Joseph (M)   102   13
H: 5 9   W: 11 00   b.9-6-00
From Brighton & HA, Hungerford T,
Eastleigh.
2021–22 Peterborough U   5   0
2021–22 Swindon T   10   1
2022–23 Peterborough U   2   0
2022–23 Swindon T   7   1
2023–24 Peterborough U   2   0   9   0
2023–24 Swindon T   0   0   17   2
2024–25 Milton Keynes D   36   7
2024–25 Milton Keynes D   40   4   76   11

TRIPP, Callum (M)   8   0
H: 6 5   b.Milton Keynes 28-8-06
Internationals: Wales U21.
2021–22 Milton Keynes D   0   0
2022–23 Milton Keynes D   0   0
2023–24 Milton Keynes D   1   0
2024–25 Milton Keynes D   7   0   8   0

TROSO, Simone (M)   0   0
2024–25 Milton Keynes D   0   0

TRUEMAN, Connal (G)   56   0
H: 6 1   W: 11 10   b.Birmingham 26-3-96
2014–15 Birmingham C   0   0
2014–15 Oldham Ath   0   0
2015–16 Birmingham C   0   0
2016–17 Birmingham C   0   0
2017–18 Birmingham C   0   0
2018–19 Birmingham C   2   0
2019–20 Birmingham C   10   0
2020–21 Birmingham C   1   0
2020–21 AFC Wimbledon   19   0   19   0
2020–21 Swindon T   4   0   4   0
2021–22 Oxford U   2   0   2   0
2021–22 Birmingham C   1   0   14   0
2022–23 Millwall   0   0
2023–24 Millwall   0   0
2024–25 Millwall   0   0
2024–25 Crawley T   4   0   4   0
2024–25 Milton Keynes D   13   0   13   0

TUCKER, Jack (D)   189   4
H: 6 4   W: 13 05   b.Canterbury 13-11-99
2017–18 Gillingham   1   0
2018–19 Gillingham   0   0
2019–20 Gillingham   28   0
2020–21 Gillingham   43   1
2021–22 Gillingham   44   2   116   3
2022–23 Milton Keynes D   38   1
2023–24 Milton Keynes D   16   0
2024–25 Milton Keynes D   9   0   63   1
2024–25 Colchester U   10   0   10   0

WALLER, Charlie (M)   8   0
H: 6 4   W: 13 05   b.Kettering 11-3-00
2023–24 Milton Keynes D   0   0
2024–25 Milton Keynes D   8   0   8   0

WILLIAMS, Jay (D)   79   2
H: 6 2   W: 11 11   b.Northampton 4-10-00
2018–19 Northampton T   10   0
2019–20 Northampton T   0   0   10   0
2020–21 Harrogate T   7   1   7   1
From Banbury T, Brackley T.
2023–24 Crawley T   40   1
2024–25 Crawley T   12   0   52   1
2024–25 Milton Keynes D   10   0   10   0

WOOD, Albert (D)   0   0
H: 5 10   W: 11 07   b.15-6-06
2023–24 Milton Keynes D   0   0
2024–25 Milton Keynes D   0   0

Scholars
Bedford, Jesse Beau; Boyce, Hayden Jack;
Clark-Anderson, Joshua Remiah; Clarridge-
Ansell, Alexander Colin; Guzynski, Marcel
Valentino; Kelly, Ryan James; Lewis-Burgess,
Keon Nico; Medwynter, Chase Karalis; Nash,
Ben William Paul; Olaleye, Isaac Abayomi
Oluwakorede; Pickering, Corvell Amarru;
Sandford, Lewis Anthony; Silver, Rian
Thomas; Sinclair-Linton, Kobe Jae; Singh-
Hurditt, Damerai Markel; Troso, Simone;
Walker, Ronnie Graham; Ward Brammeld,
Michael Kyle; White, Zachary Thomas.

MORECAMBE (56)

ANGOL, Lee (F)   236   47
H: 5 10   W: 11 05   b.Carshalton 4-8-94
2012–13 Wycombe W   3   0
2013–14 Wycombe W   0   0   3   0
2014–15 Luton T   0   0
2015–16 Peterborough U   33   11
2016–17 Peterborough U   13   1   46   12
2017–18 Mansfield T   29   9   29   9
2018–19 Lincoln C   2   0   2   0
2018–19 Shrewsbury T   17   3   17   3
2019–20 Leyton Orient   26   4
2020–21 Leyton Orient   12   1   38   5
2021–22 Bradford C   18   6
2022–23 Bradford C   14   0   32   6
2022–23 Sutton U   17   3
2023–24 Sutton U   26   2   43   5
2024–25 Morecambe   26   7   26   7

BURGOYNE, Harry (G)   76   0
H: 6 4   W: 13 05   b.Ludlow 28-12-96
2015–16 Wolverhampton W   0   0
2016–17 Barnet   2   0   2   0
2016–17 Wolverhampton W   6   0
2017–18 Wolverhampton W   1   0
2018–19 Falkirk   15   0   15   0
2019–20 Wolverhampton W   0   0   7   0
2019–20 Shrewsbury T   0   0
2020–21 Shrewsbury T   18   0
2021–22 Shrewsbury T   0   0
2022–23 Shrewsbury T   2   0
2023–24 Shrewsbury T   4   0   24   0
2024–25 Morecambe   28   0   28   0

COOKE, Callum (F)   214   17
H: 5 8   W: 11 05   b.Peterlee 21-2-97
Internationals: England U16, U17, U18.
2016–17 Middlesbrough   0   0
2016–17 Crewe Alex   18   4   18   4
2017–18 Middlesbrough   0   0
2017–18 Blackpool   30   2   30   2
2018–19 Peterborough U   13   1
2019–20 Peterborough U   0   0   13   1
2019–20 Bradford C   25   0
2020–21 Bradford C   34   3
2021–22 Bradford C   42   2   101   5
2022–23 Hartlepool U   34   4   34   4
From Hartlepool U.
2024–25 Morecambe   18   1   18   1

DAVIDSON, Mani (M)   0   0
2022–23 Morecambe   0   0
2023–24 Morecambe   0   0
2024–25 Morecambe   0   0

DOBSON, Lennon (M)   1   0
H: 5 6   b.20-5-06
2023–24 Morecambe   0   0
2024–25 Morecambe   1   0   1   0

EDWARDS, Gwion (M)   342   46
H: 5 9   W: 12 00   b.Carmarthen 1-3-93
Internationals: Wales U19, U21.
2011–12 Swansea C   0   0
2012–13 Swansea C   0   0
2012–13 St Johnstone   6   0
2013–14 Swansea C   0   0
2013–14 St Johnstone   13   0   19   0
2013–14 Crawley T   6   2
2014–15 Crawley T   37   4
2015–16 Crawley T   42   8   85   14
2016–17 Peterborough U   33   7
2017–18 Peterborough U   26   4   59   11
2018–19 Ipswich T   33   6
2019–20 Ipswich T   27   2
2020–21 Ipswich T   36   6   96   14
2021–22 Wigan Ath   30   1
2022–23 Wigan Ath   2   0   32   1
2022–23 Ross Co   5   0   5   0
2023–24 Morecambe   21   3
2024–25 Morecambe   25   3   46   6

FAIRCLOUGH, Adam (M)   7   1
H: 5 5   W: b.3-5-07
2023–24 Morecambe   2   1
2024–25 Morecambe   5   0   7   1

FODEN, Daniel (D)   0   0
b.21-7-05
2022–23 Morecambe   0   0
2023–24 Morecambe   0   0
2024–25 Morecambe   0   0

FOX, Saul (F)   1   0
H: 6 2   W: 13 01   b.Liverpool 27-7-06
2023–24 Morecambe   1   0
2024–25 Morecambe   0   0

HARRACK, Kayden (D)   15   0
H: 6 3   W: 13 08   b.London 5-11-03
Internationals: Grenada Full caps.
2023–24 QPR   0   0
2023–24 Morecambe   7   0
2024–25 Morecambe   8   0   15   0
Transferred to Dagenham & Red, December 2024.

HENDRIE, Luke (D)   246   5
H: 6 2   W: 10 01   b.Leeds 27-8-94
Internationals: England U16, U17.
2012–13 Manchester U   0   0
2013–14 Derby Co   0   0
2014–15 Derby Co   0   0
2015–16 Burnley   0   0
2015–16 Hartlepool U   3   0
2015–16 York C   18   0   18   0
2016–17 Burnley   0   0
2016–17 Kilmarnock   32   0   32   0
2017–18 Burnley   0   0
2017–18 Bradford C   13   0
2017–18 Shrewsbury T   10   0   10   0
2018–19 Grimsby T   41   2
2019–20 Grimsby T   32   1
2020–21 Grimsby T   38   2   111   5
2021–22 Hartlepool U   7   0   10   0
2021–22 Bradford C   16   0
2022–23 Bradford C   2   0
2023–24 Bradford C   0   0   31   0
2024–25 Morecambe   34   0   34   0

HOPE, Hallam (F)   303   52
H: 5 10   W: 12 00   b.Manchester 17-3-94
Internationals: England U16, U17, U18, U19.
Barbados Full caps.
2010–11 Everton   0   0

2011–12 Everton	0	0		
2012–13 Everton	0	0		
2013–14 Everton	0	0		
2013–14 *Northampton T*	3	1	3	1
2013–14 *Bury*	8	5		
2014–15 Everton	0	0		
2014–15 *Sheffield Wed*	4	0	4	0
2014–15 Bury	19	0		
2015–16 Bury	6	0		
2015–16 Carlisle U	21	4		
2016–17 Bury	33	3	66	8
2017–18 Carlisle U	41	9		
2018–19 Carlisle U	40	14		
2019–20 Carlisle U	23	2	125	29
2019–20 Swindon T	5	2		
2020–21 Swindon T	32	5	37	7
2021–22 Oldham Ath	39	5	39	5
From Oldham Ath.				
2024–25 Morecambe	29	2	29	2

LEWIS, Adam (D) 129 5
H: 5 9 W: 9 13 b.Liverpool 8-11-99
Internationals: England U16, U17, U19, U20.

2019–20 Liverpool	0	0		
2020–21 Liverpool	0	0		
2020–21 *Amiens*	9	0	9	0
2020–21 *Plymouth Arg*	20	1	20	1
2021–22 Liverpool	0	0		
2021–22 *Livingston*	9	0	9	0
2022–23 Liverpool	0	0		
2022–23 *Newport Co*	21	1		
2023–24 *Newport Co*	0	0		
2023–24 *Newport Co*	26	2	47	3
2024–25 Morecambe	44	1	44	1

LEWIS, Paul (M) 230 23
H: 6 1 W: 11 00 b.Liverpool 17-12-94
Internationals: England C.
From Macclesfield T.

2016–17 Cambridge U	13	0		
2017–18 Cambridge U	12	1		
2018–19 Cambridge U	23	4		
2019–20 Cambridge U	36	4	84	9
2020–21 Tranmere R	40	6		
2021–22 Tranmere R	0	0		
2021–22 *Northampton T*	39	6	39	6
2022–23 Tranmere R	24	2		
2023–24 Tranmere R	14	0	78	8
2024–25 Morecambe	29	0	29	0

MACADAM, Harvey (M) 79 3
H: 6 3 W: 13 03 b.Burnley 9-1-02
From Ashton U.

2021–22 Fleetwood T	10	1		
2022–23 Fleetwood T	25	1		
2023–24 Fleetwood T	2	0	37	2
2024 *Waterford*	13	0	13	0
2024–25 Morecambe	29	1	29	1

MERCER, Nathan (M) 0 0
2023–24 Morecambe	0	0		
2024–25 Morecambe	0	0		

MILLEN, Ross (D) 252 13
H: 5 8 W: 10 00 b.Glasgow 28-9-94

2012–13 Dunfermline Ath	11	0		
2013–14 Dunfermline Ath	22	1		
2014–15 Dunfermline Ath	27	2	60	3
2015–16 Livingston	9	0	9	0
2015–16 Clyde	15	0	15	0
2016–17 Queen's Park	27	7		
2017–18 Queen's Park	25	1	52	8
2018–19 Kilmarnock	4	1		
2019–20 Kilmarnock	4	0		
2020–21 Kilmarnock	19	0	27	1
2021–22 Scunthorpe U	20	0	20	0
2022–23 Raith R	33	0		
2023–24 Raith R	19	1	52	1
2024–25 Morecambe	17	0	17	0

MOORE, Stuart (G) 59 0
H: 6 2 W: 11 05 b.Sandown 8-9-94

2013–14 Reading	0	0		
2014–15 Reading	0	0		
2015–16 Reading	0	0		
2015–16 *Peterborough U*	4	0	4	0
2016–17 Reading	0	0		
2016–17 *Luton T*	8	0	8	0
2017–18 Swindon T	10	0	10	0
2018–19 Milton Keynes D	6	0		
2019–20 Milton Keynes D	0	0	6	0
2020–21 Blackpool	1	0		
2021–22 Blackpool	1	0		
2022–23 Blackpool	0	0	2	0
2022–23 *Doncaster R*	2	0	2	0
2023–24 Morecambe	12	0		
2024–25 Morecambe	15	0	27	0

RAY, George (D) 270 10
H: 5 10 W: 11 03 b.Warrington 13-10-93
Internationals: Wales U21.

2011–12 Crewe Alex	0	0		
2012–13 Crewe Alex	4	0		
2013–14 Crewe Alex	9	0		
2014–15 Crewe Alex	35	2		
2015–16 Crewe Alex	22	0		

2016–17 Crewe Alex	23	1		
2017–18 Crewe Alex	12	0		
2018–19 Crewe Alex	32	2	137	5
2019–20 Tranmere R	15	0		
2020–21 Tranmere R	11	1	26	1
2021–22 Exeter C	19	1	19	1
2021–22 *Leyton Orient*	9	0	9	0
2022–23 Barrow	36	0		
2023–24 Barrow	41	3	77	3
2024–25 Morecambe	2	0	2	0

SCALES, Alfie (F) 0 0
b. 30-11-06

2024–25 Morecambe	0	0	

SCHOFIELD, Ryan (G) 58 0
H: 5 11 W: 11 00 b.Huddersfield 11-12-99
Internationals: England U18, U19, U20.

2018–19 Huddersfield T	0	0		
2018–19 *Notts Co*	17	0	17	0
2019–20 Huddersfield T	1	0		
2019–20 *Livingston*	1	0	1	0
2020–21 Huddersfield T	30	0		
2021–22 Huddersfield T	2	0		
2022–23 Huddersfield T	0	0	33	0
2022–23 *Hibernian*	0	0		
2022–23 *Crawley T*	2	0	2	0
2023–24 Portsmouth	0	0		
2024–25 Morecambe	5	0	5	0

SLEW, Jordan (F) 230 21
H: 6 3 W: 12 11 b.Sheffield 7-9-92
Internationals: England U19.

2010–11 Sheffield U	7	2		
2011–12 Sheffield U	4	1	11	3
2011–12 Blackburn R	1	0		
2011–12 *Stevenage*	9	0	9	0
2012–13 Blackburn R	0	0		
2012–13 *Oldham Ath*	3	0	3	0
2012–13 *Rotherham U*	7	0	7	0
2013–14 Blackburn R	0	0		
2013–14 *Ross Co*	20	1	20	1
2014–15 Blackburn R	0	0	0	1
2014–15 *Port Vale*	9	2	9	2
2014–15 Cambridge U	13	1		
2015–16 Cambridge U	10	0	23	1
2015–16 Chesterfield	7	0	7	0
2016–17 Plymouth Arg	32	4	32	4
2017–18 Rochdale	5	0	5	0
From Boston U.				
2019–20 Morecambe	11	0		
2020–21 Morecambe	17	1		
From FC Halifax T.				
2023–24 Morecambe	44	8		
2024–25 Morecambe	31	1	103	10

SNOWBALL, Nathan (D) 0 0
2024–25 Morecambe	0	0	

SONGO'O, Yann (D) 346 18
H: 6 0 W: 12 02 b.Yaounde 17-11-91
Internationals: Cameroon U20.
From Real Zaragoza.

2011–12 Sabadell	6	0	6	0
2013 Sporting Kansas C	0	0		
2013 *Orlando C*	12	1	12	1
2013–14 Blackburn R	0	0		
2013–14 *Ross Co*	17	3	17	3
2014–15 Blackburn R	0	0		
2016–17 Plymouth Arg	46	2		
2017–18 Plymouth Arg	33	0		
2018–19 Plymouth Arg	42	0	121	2
2019–20 Scunthorpe U	16	0	16	0
2020–21 Morecambe	38	6		
2021–22 Bradford C	41	3		
2022–23 Bradford C	14	0	55	3
2022–23 Walsall	5	0	5	0
2023–24 Morecambe	40	0		
2024–25 Morecambe	36	3	114	9

STOTT, Jamie (D) 61 3
H: 6 2 W: 12 06 b.Failsworth 22-12-97

2016–17 Oldham Ath	4	0		
2017–18 Oldham Ath	1	0		
2018–19 Oldham Ath	3	0		
2019–20 Oldham Ath	9	0	16	0
From Stockport Co.				
2024–25 Morecambe	45	3	45	3

TAYLOR, Max (D) 61 5
H: 6 4 W: 12 02 b.Manchester 10-1-00

2019–20 Manchester U	0	0		
2020–21 Manchester U	0	0		
2021–22 Rochdale	22	3		
2022–23 Rochdale	19	1	41	4
From Rochdale.				
2024–25 Morecambe	20	1	20	1

TOLLITT, Ben (M) 60 7
H: 6 0 W: 11 11 b.Liverpool 30-11-94

2015–16 Portsmouth	12	1		
2016–17 Portsmouth	0	0	12	1
2018–19 Tranmere R	4	0	4	0
2019–20 Blackpool	0	0		
2019–20 Macclesfield T	5	0	5	0
From AFC Fylde, Oldham Ath.				
2024–25 Morecambe	39	6	39	6

TUTONDA, David (D) 225 6
H: 5 11 W: 11 00 b.Kinshasa 11-10-95

2014–15 Cardiff C	0	0		
2014–15 *Newport Co*	12	2	12	2
2015–16 Cardiff C	0	0		
2015–16 *York C*	12	0	12	0
2016–17 Cardiff C	0	0		
2016–17 Barnet	7	1		
2017–18 Barnet	41	0	48	1
From Barnet.				
2020–21 Bristol R	20	0	20	0
2021–22 Gillingham	29	0		
2022–23 Gillingham	25	1	54	1
2023–24 Morecambe	37	2		
2024–25 Morecambe	42	0	79	2

WHAITE, Billy (F) 1 0
b. 19-1-08
2024–25 Morecambe	1	0	1	0

WHITE, Tom (M) 144 0
H: 5 11 W: 10 00 b.Newcastle upon Tyne 9-5-97
Internationals: England C.
From Gateshead.

2020–21 Blackburn R	0	0		
2020–21 *Bolton W*	9	0	9	0
2021–22 Barrow	27	0		
2022–23 Barrow	43	0		
2023–24 Barrow	31	0	101	0
2024–25 Morecambe	34	0	34	0

Scholars
Ascroft, Harry John; Byron, Ellis Neil; Cox, Alfie John Joseph; Crane, Jack; Dobson, Lennon Liam; Evans, Andrew James; Fairclough, Adam Anthony; Goodyear, Corey Daniel; Gordon, Freddie; Holden, Max Lee; Illingworth, Harley Wayne; Lynchey, Joe Thomas; Mercer, Nathan Mark; Pooke, Matthew Christopher; Scales, Alfie Marlow; Snowball, Nathan Kristian; Sowerby, Joseph Harry; Stewart-Cooney, Callum John; Vilchez, Elijah Alexander; Whaite, Billy David; Wright, Oscar John.

NEWCASTLE U (57)

ALMIRON, Miguel (M) 322 53
H: 5 10 W: 11 00 b.Asuncion 10-2-94
Internationals: Paraguay U17, U20, Full caps.

2013 Cerro Porteno	6	1		
2014 Cerro Porteno	14	0		
2015 Cerro Porteno	19	5	39	6
2015 Lanus	10	0		
2016 Lanus	25	3	35	3
2017 Atalanta	30	9		
2018 Atalanta	32	12	62	21
2018–19 Newcastle U	10	0		
2019–20 Newcastle U	36	4		
2020–21 Newcastle U	34	4		
2021–22 Newcastle U	30	1		
2022–23 Newcastle U	34	11		
2023–24 Newcastle U	33	3		
2024–25 Newcastle U	9	0	186	23
Transferred to Atlanta U, January 2025.				

ASHBY, Harrison (D) 43 1
H: 5 10 W: 11 05 b.Milton Keynes 14-11-01
Internationals: Scotland U17, U19, U21.

2020–21 West Ham U	0	0		
2021–22 West Ham U	1	0		
2022–23 West Ham U	0	0	1	0
2022–23 Newcastle U	0	0		
2023–24 *Swansea C*	13	1	13	1
2024–25 Newcastle U	0	0		
2024–25 *QPR*	29	0	29	0

BARNES, Harvey (M) 270 69
H: 5 9 W: 10 06 b.Burnley 8-12-97
Internationals: England U18, U20, U21, Full caps.

2016–17 Leicester C	0	0		
2016–17 *Milton Keynes D*	21	6	21	6
2017–18 Leicester C	3	0		
2017–18 *Barnsley*	23	5	23	5
2018–19 Leicester C	16	1		
2018–19 *WBA*	26	9	26	9
2019–20 Leicester C	36	6		
2020–21 Leicester C	25	9		
2021–22 Leicester C	32	6		
2022–23 Leicester C	34	13	146	35
2023–24 Newcastle U	21	5		
2024–25 Newcastle U	33	9	54	14

BOTMAN, Sven (D) 149 7
H: 6 5 W: 12 11 b.Badhoevedorp 12-1-00
Internationals: Netherlands U16, U18, U19, U20, U21.

2018–19 Ajax	0	0		
2019–20 Ajax	0	0		
2019–20 *Heerenveen*	26	2	26	2
2020–21 Lille	37	0		

2021–22	Lille	25	3	62 3
2022–23	Newcastle U	36	0	
2023–24	Newcastle U	17	2	
2024–25	Newcastle U	8	0	61 0

BRUNO GUIMARAES, Moura (M)   241 27
H: 6 0   W: 11 09   b.Rio 16-11-97
Internationals: Brazil U23, Full caps.

2017	Athletico Paranaense	4	0	
2018	Athletico Paranaense	32	1	
2019	Athletico Paranaense	25	2	61 3
2019–20	Lyon	3	0	
2020–21	Lyon	33	3	
2021–22	Lyon	20	0	56 3
2021–22	Newcastle U	17	5	
2022–23	Newcastle U	32	4	
2023–24	Newcastle U	37	7	
2024–25	Newcastle U	38	5	124 21

BURN, Dan (D)   422 15
H: 6 6   W: 13 10   b.Blyth 1-5-92
Internationals: England Full caps.

2009–10	Darlington	4	0	4 0
2010–11	Fulham	0	0	
2011–12	Fulham	0	0	
2012–13	Fulham	0	0	
2012–13	*Yeovil T*	34	2	34 2
2013–14	Fulham	9	0	
2013–14	*Birmingham C*	24	0	24 0
2014–15	Fulham	20	1	
2015–16	Fulham	32	0	61 1
2016–17	Wigan Ath	42	1	
2017–18	Wigan Ath	45	5	
2018–19	Brighton & HA	0	0	
2018–19	*Wigan Ath*	14	0	101 6
2019–20	Brighton & HA	34	0	
2020–21	Brighton & HA	27	1	
2021–22	Brighton & HA	13	1	74 2
2021–22	Newcastle U	16	0	
2022–23	Newcastle U	38	1	
2023–24	Newcastle U	33	2	
2024–25	Newcastle U	37	1	124 4

DUBRAVKA, Martin (G)   365 0
H: 6 3   W: 13 01   b.Zilina 15-1-89
Internationals: Slovakia U19, U21, Full caps.

2008–09	Zilina	1	0	
2009–10	Zilina	26	0	
2010–11	Zilina	24	0	
2011–12	Zilina	8	0	
2012–13	Zilina	26	0	
2013–14	Zilina	13	0	98 0
2013–14	Esbjerg	15	0	
2014–15	Esbjerg	33	0	
2015–16	Esbjerg	18	0	66 0
2016–17	Slovan Liberec	28	0	28 0
2017–18	Sparta Prague	11	0	11 0
2017–18	*Newcastle U*	12	0	
2018–19	Newcastle U	38	0	
2019–20	Newcastle U	38	0	
2020–21	Newcastle U	13	0	
2021–22	Newcastle U	26	0	
2022–23	Newcastle U	2	0	
2022–23	*Manchester U*	0	0	
2023–24	Newcastle U	23	0	
2024–25	Newcastle U	10	0	162 0

GILLESPIE, Mark (G)   241 0
H: 6 1   W: 13 08   b.Newcastle upon Tyne 27-3-92
From Newcastle U.

2009–10	Carlisle U	1	0	
2010–11	Carlisle U	0	0	
2011–12	Carlisle U	0	0	
2012–13	Carlisle U	35	0	
2013–14	Carlisle U	15	0	
2014–15	Carlisle U	19	0	
2015–16	Carlisle U	45	0	
2016–17	Carlisle U	46	0	161 0
2017–18	Walsall	23	0	23 0
2018–19	Motherwell	27	0	
2019–20	Motherwell	30	0	57 0
2020–21	Newcastle U	0	0	
2021–22	Newcastle U	0	0	
2022–23	Newcastle U	0	0	
2023–24	Newcastle U	0	0	
2024–25	Newcastle U	0	0	

GORDON, Anthony (M)   161 25
H: 5 9   W: 11 00   b.Liverpool 24-2-01
Internationals: England U18, U19, U20, U21, Full caps.

2017–18	Everton	0	0	
2018–19	Everton	0	0	
2019–20	Everton	11	0	
2020–21	Everton	3	0	
2020–21	*Preston NE*	11	0	11 0
2021–22	Everton	35	4	
2022–23	Everton	16	3	65 7
2022–23	Newcastle U	16	1	
2023–24	Newcastle U	35	11	
2024–25	Newcastle U	34	6	85 18

HALL, Lewis (M)   54 1
H: 5 10   W: 11 07   b.Slough 8-9-04
Internationals: England U16, U18, U19, U20, U21, Full caps.

2021–22	Chelsea	0	0	
2022–23	Chelsea	9	0	
2023–24	Chelsea	0	0	9 0
2023–24	*Newcastle U*	18	1	
2024–25	Newcastle U	27	0	45 1

HARPER, Fraser (M)   0 0
H: 5 10   b. 2-10-06

2024–25	Newcastle U	0	0	

HARRIS, Aidan (G)   0 0
H: 6 1   W: 11 11   b.Sunderland 16-12-06

2023–24	Newcastle U	0	0	
2024–25	Newcastle U	0	0	

HARRISON, Adam (G)   0 0
H: 6 2   W: 12 04   b.Newcastle 20-10-06

2023–24	Newcastle U	0	0	
2024–25	Newcastle U	0	0	

HARRISON, Alfie (M)   0 0
H: 5 9   W: 10 03   b.Manchester 28-11-05
From Manchester C.

2023–24	Newcastle U	0	0	
2024–25	Newcastle U	0	0	

HAYDEN, Isaac (D)   228 7
H: 6 2   W: 12 06   b.Chelmsford 22-3-95
Internationals: England U16, U17, U18, U19, U20, U21. Jamaica Full caps.

2011–12	Arsenal	0	0	
2012–13	Arsenal	0	0	
2013–14	Arsenal	0	0	
2014–15	Arsenal	0	0	
2015–16	Arsenal	0	0	
2015–16	*Hull C*	18	1	18 1
2016–17	Newcastle U	33	2	
2017–18	Newcastle U	26	1	
2018–19	Newcastle U	25	1	
2019–20	Newcastle U	29	1	
2020–21	Newcastle U	24	0	
2021–22	Newcastle U	14	1	
2022–23	Newcastle U	0	0	
2022–23	*Norwich C*	14	0	14 0
2023–24	Newcastle U	0	0	
2023–24	*Standard Liege*	11	0	11 0
2023–24	*QPR*	17	0	17 0
2024–25	Newcastle U	0	0	151 6
2024–25	*Portsmouth*	17	0	17 0

HERNES, Travis (M)   14 0
H: 5 9   W: 11 09   b.Heradsbygda 4-11-05
Internationals: Norway U17, U19, U20.

2022–23	Shrewsbury T	0	0	
2023–24	Shrewsbury T	2	0	2 0
2023–24	Newcastle U	0	0	
2024–25	Newcastle U	0	0	
2024–25	*AaB*	12	0	12 0

HUNTLEY, James (M)   0 0
H: 5 11   W: 11 00   b.Ashington 2-3-04

2023–24	Newcastle U	0	0	
2024–25	Newcastle U	0	0	

ISAK, Alexander (F)   236 110
H: 6 4   W: 11 00   b.Soina, Stockholm 21-9-99
Internationals: Sweden U17, U19, U21, Full caps.

2016	AIK	24	10	24 10
2016–17	Borussia Dortmund	0	0	
2017–18	Borussia Dortmund	5	0	
2018–19	Borussia Dortmund	0	0	5 0
2018–19	*Willem II*	16	13	16 13
2019–20	Real Sociedad	37	9	
2020–21	Real Sociedad	34	17	
2021–22	Real Sociedad	32	6	
2022–23	Real Sociedad	2	1	105 33
2022–23	Newcastle U	22	10	
2023–24	Newcastle U	30	21	
2024–25	Newcastle U	34	23	86 54

JOELINTON, de Lira (F)   286 47
H: 6 1   W: 12 11   b.Alianca 14-8-96
Internationals: Brazil U17, Full caps.

2014	Sport Recife	7	2	
2015	Sport Recife	5	1	12 3
2015–16	TSG 1899 Hoffenheim	1	0	
2016–17	TSG 1899 Hoffenheim	0	0	
2016–17	*Rapid Vienna*	33	8	
2017–18	TSG 1899 Hoffenheim	0	0	
2017–18	*Rapid Vienna*	27	7	60 15
2018–19	TSG 1899 Hoffenheim	29	7	29 7
2019–20	Newcastle U	38	2	
2020–21	Newcastle U	31	4	
2021–22	Newcastle U	35	4	
2022–23	Newcastle U	32	6	
2023–24	Newcastle U	20	2	
2024–25	Newcastle U	24	4	185 22

KELLY, Lloyd (D)   196 4
H: 5 10   W: 11 00   b.Bristol 1-10-98
Internationals: England U20, U21.

2016–17	Bristol C	0	0	
2017–18	Bristol C	11	1	
2018–19	Bristol C	32	1	43 2
2019–20	Bournemouth	8	0	
2020–21	Bournemouth	36	1	
2021–22	Bournemouth	41	1	
2022–23	Bournemouth	23	0	
2023–24	Bournemouth	23	0	131 2
2024–25	Newcastle U	10	0	10 0
2024–25	*Juventus*	12	0	12 0

KRAFTH, Emil (D)   260 5
H: 6 0   W: 12 02   b.Ljungby 2-8-94
Internationals: Sweden U17, U19, U21, Full caps.
From Lagans.

2011	Osters	24	0	24 0
2012	Helsingborg	9	0	
2013	Helsingborg	27	1	
2014	Helsingborg	28	1	
2015	Helsingborg	12	1	76 3
2015–16	Bologna	4	0	
2016–17	Bologna	26	0	
2017–18	Bologna	12	0	42 0
2018–19	Amiens	35	1	35 1
2019–20	Newcastle U	17	0	
2020–21	Newcastle U	16	1	
2021–22	Newcastle U	20	0	
2022–23	Newcastle U	1	0	
2023–24	Newcastle U	17	0	
2024–25	Newcastle U	12	0	83 1

KUOL, Garang (F)   23 2
H: 5 9   W: 10 10   b.Khartoum 15-9-04
Internationals: Australia U20, U23, Full caps.

2022–23	Central Coast Mariners	0	0	
2022–23	Newcastle U	0	0	
2022–23	*Hearts*	8	1	8 1
2023–24	Newcastle U	0	0	
2023–24	*Volendam*	15	1	15 1
2024–25	Newcastle U	0	0	

LASCELLES, Jamaal (D)   283 17
H: 6 2   W: 13 01   b.Derby 11-11-93
Internationals: England U18, U19, U20, U21.

2010–11	Nottingham F	0	0	
2011–12	Nottingham F	1	0	
2011–12	*Stevenage*	7	1	7 1
2012–13	Nottingham F	2	0	
2013–14	Nottingham F	29	2	
2014–15	Nottingham F	0	0	
2014–15	Nottingham F	26	1	58 3
2015–16	Newcastle U	18	2	
2016–17	Newcastle U	43	3	
2017–18	Newcastle U	33	3	
2018–19	Newcastle U	32	0	
2019–20	Newcastle U	24	1	
2020–21	Newcastle U	19	2	
2021–22	Newcastle U	26	1	
2022–23	Newcastle U	7	0	
2023–24	Newcastle U	16	1	
2024–25	Newcastle U	0	0	218 13

LEWIS, Jamal (D)   165 1
H: 5 10   W: 11 00   b.Luton 25-1-98
Internationals: Northern Ireland U19, U21, Full caps.

2017–18	Norwich C	22	0	
2018–19	Norwich C	42	0	
2019–20	Norwich C	28	1	
2020–21	Norwich C	0	0	92 1
2021–22	Newcastle U	24	0	
2021–22	Newcastle U	5	0	
2022–23	Newcastle U	2	0	
2023–24	Newcastle U	0	0	
2023–24	*Watford*	36	0	36 0
2024–25	Newcastle U	0	0	31 0
2024–25	*Sao Paulo*	6	0	6 0

LIVRAMENTO, Valentino (D)   93 2
H: 5 8   W: 11 03   b.Croydon 12-11-02
Internationals: England U16, U17, U18, U19, U21, Full caps.

2020–21	Chelsea	0	0	
2021–22	Chelsea	0	0	
2021–22	Scunthorpe U	0	0	
2021–22	Southampton	28	1	
2022–23	Southampton	2	0	30 1
2023–24	Southampton	26	1	
2024–25	Newcastle U	37	0	63 1

LONGSTAFF, Sean (M)   245 24
H: 5 11   W: 10 03   b.North Shields 30-10-97

2016–17	Newcastle U	0	0	
2016–17	Kilmarnock	16	3	
2016–17	Kilmarnock	16	3	32 6
2017–18	Newcastle U	0	0	
2017–18	*Blackpool*	42	8	42 8
2018–19	Newcastle U	9	1	
2019–20	Newcastle U	23	1	
2020–21	Newcastle U	22	0	
2021–22	Newcastle U	24	1	
2022–23	Newcastle U	33	1	
2023–24	Newcastle U	35	6	
2024–25	Newcastle U	25	0	171 10

McARTHUR, Charlie (D) — 11 0
b. 12-5-05
Internationals: Scotland U17, U19, U21.

Season	Club	A	G	A	G
2021–22	Kilmarnock	1	0	1	0
2022–23	Newcastle U	0	0		
2023–24	Newcastle U	0	0		
2024–25	Newcastle U	0	0		
2024–25	Carlisle U	10	0	10	0

MILEY, Lewis (M) — 32 2
H: 6 1 W: 10 03 b.Stanley 1-5-05
Internationals: England U17, U19, U20, U21.

2022–23	Newcastle U	1	0		
2023–24	Newcastle U	17	1		
2024–25	Newcastle U	14	1	32	2

MURPHY, Alex (D) — 46 4
H: 5 8 W: 11 03 b.Annaghdown 25-6-04
Internationals: Republic of Ireland U18, U19, U21.

2021	Galway U	11	0		
2022	Galway U	20	2	31	2
2022–23	Newcastle U	0	0		
2023–24	Newcastle U	2	0		
2024–25	Newcastle U	0	0	2	0
2024–25	Bolton W	13	2	13	2

MURPHY, Jacob (M) — 350 55
H: 5 9 W: 11 03 b.Wembley 24-2-95
Internationals: England U18, U19, U20, U21.

2013–14	Norwich C	0	0		
2013–14	Swindon T	6	0	6	0
2013–14	Southend U	7	1	7	1
2014–15	Norwich C	0	0		
2014–15	Blackpool	9	2	9	2
2014–15	Scunthorpe U	3	0	3	0
2014–15	Colchester U	11	4	11	4
2015–16	Norwich C	0	0		
2015–16	Coventry C	40	9	40	9
2016–17	Norwich C	37	9	37	9
2017–18	Newcastle U	25	1		
2018–19	Newcastle U	9	0		
2018–19	WBA	13	2	13	2
2019–20	Newcastle U	0	0		
2019–20	Sheffield Wed	39	9	39	9
2020–21	Newcastle U	26	2		
2021–22	Newcastle U	33	1		
2022–23	Newcastle U	36	4		
2023–24	Newcastle U	21	3		
2024–25	Newcastle U	35	8	185	19

NEAVE, Sean (F) — 0 0
H: 6 0 b.Newcastle 27-5-07
Internationals: England U17, U18.

2024–25	Newcastle U	0	0		

OSULA, William (F) — 58 3
H: 5 11 W: 12 11 b.Denmark 4-8-03
Internationals: Denmark U19, U21.

2020–21	Sheffield U	0	0		
2021–22	Sheffield U	5	0		
2022–23	Sheffield U	2	0		
2022–23	Derby Co	16	2	16	2
2023–24	Sheffield U	21	0	28	0
2024–25	Newcastle U	14	1	14	1

PARKINSON, Ben (F) — 1 0
H: 6 0 W: 10 06 b.Newcastle 10-3-05

2023–24	Newcastle U	1	0		
2024–25	Newcastle U	0	0	1	0

PIVAS, Miodrag (D) — 45 1
b.Novi Sad 17-5-05
Internationals: Serbia U17.

2021–22	Grodig	15	0		
2022–23	Grodig	0	0	15	0
2023–24	Jedinstov	25	1	25	1
2023–24	Newcastle U	0	0		
2024–25	Willem II	5	0	5	0

POPE, Nick (G) — 298 0
H: 6 6 W: 12 00 b.Cambridge 19-4-92
Internationals: England Full caps.
From Bury T.

2011–12	Charlton Ath	0	0		
2012–13	Charlton Ath	1	0		
2013–14	Charlton Ath	0	0		
2013–14	York C	22	0	22	0
2014–15	Charlton Ath	8	0		
2014–15	Bury	22	0	22	0
2015–16	Charlton Ath	24	0	33	0
2016–17	Burnley	0	0		
2017–18	Burnley	35	0		
2018–19	Burnley	9	0		
2019–20	Burnley	38	0		
2020–21	Burnley	32	0		
2021–22	Burnley	36	0	141	0
2022–23	Newcastle U	37	0		
2023–24	Newcastle U	15	0		
2024–25	Newcastle U	28	0	80	0

RUDDY, John (G) — 506 0
H: 6 4 W: 15 04 b.St Ives 24-10-86
Internationals: England Full caps.

2003–04	Cambridge U	1	0		
2004–05	Cambridge U	38	0	39	0
2005–06	Everton	1	0		
2005–06	Walsall	5	0	5	0
2005–06	Rushden & D	3	0	3	0
2005–06	Chester C	4	0	4	0
2006–07	Everton	0	0		
2006–07	Stockport Co	11	0		
2006–07	Wrexham	5	0	5	0
2006–07	Bristol C	1	0	1	0
2007–08	Everton	0	0		
2007–08	Stockport Co	12	0	23	0
2008–09	Everton	0	0		
2008–09	Crewe Alex	19	0	19	0
2009–10	Everton	0	0	1	0
2009–10	Motherwell	34	0	34	0
2010–11	Norwich C	45	0		
2011–12	Norwich C .	37	0		
2012–13	Norwich C	15	0		
2013–14	Norwich C	38	0		
2014–15	Norwich C	46	0		
2015–16	Norwich C	27	0		
2016–17	Norwich C	27	0	235	0
2017–18	Wolverhampton W	45	0		
2018–19	Wolverhampton W	1	0		
2019–20	Wolverhampton W	0	0		
2020–21	Wolverhampton W	2	0		
2021–22	Wolverhampton W	2	0	50	0
2022–23	Birmingham C	43	0		
2023–24	Birmingham C	44	0	87	0
2024–25	Newcastle U	0	0		

SANUSI, Trevan (F) — 0 0
H: 5 10 W: 9 06 b. 25-4-07
Internationals: England U16, U17, U18.

2022–23	Birmingham C	0	0		
2023–24	Newcastle U	0	0		
2024–25	Newcastle U	0	0		

SCHAR, Fabian (D) — 379 35
H: 6 2 W: 13 05 b.Wil 20-12-91
Internationals: Switzerland U20, U21, U23, Full caps.

2009–10	FC Wil	2	0		
2010–11	FC Wil	24	4		
2011–12	FC Wil	30	1	56	5
2012–13	FC Basel	21	4		
2013–14	FC Basel	22	4		
2014–15	FC Basel	30	1	73	9
2015–16	TSG 1899 Hoffenheim	24	1		
2016–17	TSG 1899 Hoffenheim	6	0	30	1
2017–18	Deportivo La Coruna	25	2	25	2
2018–19	Newcastle U	24	4		
2019–20	Newcastle U	22	2		
2020–21	Newcastle U	18	1		
2021–22	Newcastle U	25	2		
2022–23	Newcastle U	36	1		
2023–24	Newcastle U	36	4		
2024–25	Newcastle U	34	4	195	18

SHAHAR, Leo (D) — 0 0
b. 18-3-07
Internationals: England U17, U18.

2024–25	Newcastle U	0	0		

TARGETT, Matt (D) — 182 4
H: 6 0 W: 11 00 b.Eastleigh 18-9-95
Internationals: Scotland U19, England U19, U20, U21.

2013–14	Southampton	0	0		
2014–15	Southampton	6	0		
2015–16	Southampton	14	0		
2016–17	Southampton	5	0		
2017–18	Southampton	2	0		
2017–18	Fulham	18	1	18	1
2018–19	Southampton	16	1	43	1
2019–20	Aston Villa	28	1		
2020–21	Aston Villa	38	0		
2021–22	Aston Villa	17	1	83	2
2021–22	Newcastle U	16	0		
2022–23	Newcastle U	17	0		
2023–24	Newcastle U	3	0		
2024–25	Newcastle U	2	0	38	0

THOMPSON, Max (G) — 33 0
H: 6 2 W: 12 04 b. 1-8-04
Internationals: England U18.

2023–24	Newcastle U	0	0		
2023–24	Northampton T	15	0	15	0
2024–25	Newcastle U	0	0		
2024–25	Chesterfield	18	0	18	0

TONALI, Sandro (M) — 227 18
H: 5 11 W: 12 06 b.Lodi 8-5-00
Internationals: Italy U19, U21, Full caps.

2017–18	Brescia	19	2		
2018–19	Brescia	34	3		
2019–20	Brescia	35	1		
2020–21	AC Milan	0	0	88	6
2020–21	AC Milan	25	0		
2021–22	AC Milan	36	5		
2022–23	AC Milan	34	2	95	7
2023–24	Newcastle U	8	1		
2024–25	Newcastle U	36	4	44	5

TRIPPIER, Keiran (D) — 446 12
H: 5 10 W: 11 02 b.Bury 19-9-90
Internationals: England U18, U19, U20, U21, Full caps.

2007–08	Manchester C	0	0		
2008–09	Manchester C	0	0		
2009–10	Manchester C	0	0		
2009–10	Barnsley	3	0		
2010–11	Manchester C	0	0		
2010–11	Barnsley	39	2	42	2
2011–12	Manchester C	0	0		
2011–12	Burnley	46	3		
2012–13	Burnley	45	0		
2013–14	Burnley	41	1		
2014–15	Burnley	38	0	170	4
2015–16	Tottenham H	6	1		
2016–17	Tottenham H	12	0		
2017–18	Tottenham H	24	0		
2018–19	Tottenham H	27	1	69	2
2019–20	Atletico Madrid	25	0		
2020–21	Atletico Madrid	28	0		
2021–22	Atletico Madrid	15	0	68	0
2021–22	Newcastle U	6	2		
2022–23	Newcastle U	38	1		
2023–24	Newcastle U	28	1		
2024–25	Newcastle U	25	0	97	4

VLACHODIMOS, Odisseas (G) — 206 0
H: 6 3 W: 12 02 b.Stuttgart 26-4-94
Internationals: Germany U16, U17, U18, U19, U20, U21. Greece Full caps.

2011–12	VfB Stuttgart	0	0		
2012–13	VfB Stuttgart	0	0		
2013–14	VfB Stuttgart	0	0		
2014–15	VfB Stuttgart	0	0		
2015–16	VfB Stuttgart	3	0	3	0
2015–16	Panathinaikos	1	0		
2016–17	Panathinaikos	21	0		
2017–18	Panathinaikos	25	0	47	0
2018–19	Benfica	34	0		
2019–20	Benfica	33	0		
2020–21	Benfica	18	0		
2021–22	Benfica	32	0		
2022–23	Benfica	34	0		
2023–24	Benfica	0	0	151	0
2023–24	Nottingham F	5	0	5	0
2024–25	Newcastle U	0	0		

WHITE, Joe (M) — 89 9
H: 6 1 W: 11 00 b.Carlisle 1-10-02
Internationals: England U18.

2020–21	Newcastle U	0	0		
2021–22	Newcastle U	0	0		
2021–22	Hartlepool U	15	0	15	0
2022–23	Newcastle U	0	0		
2022–23	Exeter C	16	0	16	0
2023–24	Newcastle U	4	0		
2023–24	Crewe Alex	20	3	20	3
2024–25	Newcastle U	0	0	4	0
2024–25	Milton Keynes D	34	6	34	6

WILLOCK, Joe (M) — 159 15
H: 5 10 W: 11 09 b.Waltham Forest 20-8-99
Internationals: England U16, U19, U20, U21.

2017–18	Arsenal	2	0		
2018–19	Arsenal	2	0		
2019–20	Arsenal	29	1		
2020–21	Arsenal	7	0	40	1
2020–21	Newcastle U	14	8		
2021–22	Newcastle U	29	2		
2022–23	Newcastle U	35	3		
2023–24	Newcastle U	9	1		
2024–25	Newcastle U	32	0	119	14

WILSON, Callum (F) — 333 130
H: 5 11 W: 10 06 b.Coventry 27-2-92
Internationals: England U21, Full caps.

2009–10	Coventry C	0	0		
2010–11	Coventry C	1	0		
2011–12	Coventry C	0	0		
2012–13	Coventry C	11	1		
2013–14	Coventry C	37	21	49	22
2014–15	Bournemouth	45	20		
2015–16	Bournemouth	13	5		
2016–17	Bournemouth	20	6		
2017–18	Bournemouth	28	8		
2018–19	Bournemouth	30	14		
2019–20	Bournemouth	35	8		
2020–21	Bournemouth	0	0	171	61
2020–21	Newcastle U	26	12		
2021–22	Newcastle U	18	8		
2022–23	Newcastle U	31	18		
2023–24	Newcastle U	20	9		
2024–25	Newcastle U	18	0	113	47

Players retained or with offer of contract
Bailey, Scott Harris; Charlton, Dylan Harry; Emerson, Johnny William; Finneran, Rory James; Fitzgerald, Kyle Wesley; Heffernan, Cathal Sean; Munda, Anthony Junior; Palmer, Darren Joseph Zabid; Sidibeh, Muhamadou; Taylor, James David; Yildiz, Baran.

Scholars
Anderson, Will Robert; Bloomer, Guy Thomas; Brayson, Joe; Bryant, Thomas Jon; Cogdon, Jude Anthony; Craggs, Luke Steven; Durrant, Jake Thomas; Epia, Aaron Ovie; Johnson, Henry William; Jones, Tyler Stuart; Lucas Kayden; O'Donovan, Alexander John; Rodrigues Ferreira, Matheos; Taylor, Matthew David; Tika-Lemba, Ezra Gabriel Mekhi; Waddani, Mohammed; Watts, Logan Mathew; Wooster, Kacey Robert Mikie.

NEWPORT CO (58)

ALEXANDER-WALKER, Moses (F) 1 0
b. 27-7-07

2024–25	Newport Co	1	0	1	0

ANTWI, Cameron (M) 40 1
H: 5 10 W: 9 13 b.Sutton 7-10-01
From Fulham.

2020–21	Blackpool	0	0		
2021–22	Blackpool	0	0		
2022–23	Cardiff C	0	0		
2023–24	Cardiff C	0	0		
2024–25	Newport Co	40	1	40	1

BABAH, Armani (D) 0 0

2024–25	Newport Co	0	0		

BAKER, Matthew (D) 91 4
H: 6 0 W: 11 07 b.Kent 6-2-03
Internationals: Wales U16, U17, U19, U21.
From Gillingham.

2022–23	Stoke C	0	0		
2022–23	*Newport Co*	18	0		
2023–24	Stoke C	0	0		
2023–24	*Newport Co*	32	0		
2024–25	Newport Co	41	4	91	4

BAKER-RICHARDSON, Courtney (F) 151 32
H: 6 1 W: 11 07 b.Coventry 5-12-95

2013–14	Coventry C	0	0		
2014–15	Coventry C	0	0		

From Tamworth, Nuneaton T, Redditch U, Kettering T, Leamington.

2017–18	Swansea C	0	0		
2018–19	Swansea C	17	3		
2019–20	Swansea C	0	0	17	3
2019–20	*Accrington S*	2	0	2	0
2020–21	Barrow	0	0		
2021–22	Newport Co	31	8		
2022–23	Crewe Alex	29	8		
2023–24	Crewe Alex	36	9	65	17
2024–25	Newport Co	36	4	67	12

BONY, Geoffroy (F) 6 0
H: 5 10 W: 11 09 b. 24-12-04

2024–25	Newport Co	6	0	6	0

BRENNAN, Ciaran (D) 55 0
H: 6 2 W: 12 04 b.Kilkenny 5-5-00
Internationals: Republic of Ireland U18, U19.
From Waterford.

2019–20	Sheffield Wed	0	0		
2020–21	Sheffield Wed	0	0		
2021–22	Sheffield Wed	11	0		
2022–23	Sheffield Wed	0	0		
2022–23	*Swindon T*	17	0	17	0
2023–24	Sheffield Wed	0	0	11	0
2024–25	Newport Co	27	0	27	0

CARNEY, Jacob (G) 30 0
H: 6 2 W: 11 11 b.Rotherham 21-4-01

2016–17	Manchester U	0	0		
2017–18	Manchester U	0	0		
2018–19	Manchester U	0	0		
2019–20	Manchester U	0	0		
2020–21	Manchester U	0	0		
2020–21	*Portadown*	26	0	26	0
2021–22	Sunderland	0	0		
2022–23	Sunderland	0	0		
2023–24	Castellon	1	0	1	0
2024–25	Newport Co	3	0	3	0

CLARKE, James (D) 277 9
H: 6 0 W: 13 03 b.Aylesbury 17-11-89
From Watford, Oxford U, Oxford C, Salisbury C, Woking.

2015–16	Bristol R	37	0		
2016–17	Bristol R	22	0		
2017–18	Bristol R	11	0		
2018–19	Bristol R	42	2	112	2
2019–20	Walsall	27	3		
2020–21	Walsall	31	2	58	5
2021–22	Newport Co	35	1		
2022–23	Newport Co	23	0		
2023–24	Newport Co	25	0		
2024–25	Newport Co	24	1	107	2

DAVIES, Thomas (D) 19 4
b.Cardiff 11-11-03
Internationals: Wales U18, U19, U21.

2021–22	Cardiff C	0	0		
2022–23	Cardiff C	0	0		
2022–23	*Pontypridd U*	9	4	9	4
2023–24	Cardiff C	0	0		
2023–24	*Kilmarnock*	6	0	6	0
2024–25	Cardiff C	0	0		
2024–25	Newport Co	4	0	4	0

DRISCOLL-GLENNON, Anthony (D) 112 3
H: 5 11 W: 11 05 b.Bootle 26-11-99
From Liverpool.

2018–19	Burnley	0	0		
2019–20	Burnley	0	0		
2019–20	*Grimsby T*	12	1		
2020–21	Burnley	0	0		
2021–22	Burnley	0	0		
2021–22	*Barrow*	15	0	15	0
2022–23	Grimsby T	31	2		
2023–24	Grimsby T	15	0	58	3
2024–25	Newport Co	39	0	39	0

EVANS, Morgan (M) 0 0
H: 5 10 W: 11 03 b. 22-12-06

2023–24	Newport Co	0	0		
2024–25	Newport Co	0	0		

GREAVES, Oliver (M) 16 2
H: 5 9 W: 11 00 b.Sheffield 2-11-99

2024–25	Newport Co	16	2	16	2

HOPKINS, Bailey (G) 0 0
b. 4-2-07

2024–25	Newport Co	0	0		

JAMESON, Kyle (D) 88 3
H: 6 0 W: 12 06 b.Urmston 11-9-98
From Chelsea.

2017–18	WBA	0	0		

From AFC Fylde.

2020–21	Oldham Ath	25	2		
2021–22	Oldham Ath	11	0	36	2
2022–23	Tranmere R	10	0	10	0
2023–24	Newport Co	18	1		
2024–25	Newport Co	24	0	42	1

JEPHCOTT, Luke (F) 174 40
H: 5 10 W: 11 11 b.Truro 26-1-00
Internationals: Wales U19, U21.

2018–19	Plymouth Arg	9	0		
2019–20	Plymouth Arg	14	7		
2020–21	Plymouth Arg	41	16		
2021–22	Plymouth Arg	40	10		
2022–23	Plymouth Arg	2	0	106	33
2022–23	*Swindon T*	32	7	32	7
2023–24	St Johnstone	8	0	8	0
2023–24	Newport Co	16	0		
2024–25	Newport Co	12	0	28	0

KAMWA, Bobby (F) 85 13
H: 6 0 W: 12 08 b.Yaounde 18-3-00

2022–23	Burton Alb	17	2		
2023–24	Burton Alb	25	2	42	4
2024–25	Newport Co	43	9	43	9

KARGBO, Hamzad (F) 2 0
H: 6 6 W: 13 01 b. 20-1-02

2020–21	QPR	0	0		
2021–22	QPR	0	0		
2022–23	QPR	0	0		
2023–24	QPR	0	0		
2024–25	Newport Co	2	0	2	0

LONERGAN, Riley (M) 0 0
b.Newport 23-12-06

2024–25	Newport Co	0	0		

MARTIN, Josh (M) 87 7
H: 5 9 W: 11 00 b.Luton 9-9-01
From Arsenal.

2019–20	Norwich C	5	0		
2020–21	Norwich C	9	1		
2021–22	Norwich C	0	0		
2021–22	*Milton Keynes D*	5	0	5	0
2021–22	*Doncaster R*	20	4	20	4
2022–23	Norwich C	0	0	14	1
2022–23	*Barnsley*	17	1	17	1
2023–24	Portsmouth	8	0	8	0
2024–25	Notts Co	8	1	8	1
2024–25	Newport Co	15	0	15	0

McLOUGHLIN, Shane (D) 195 10
H: 5 9 W: 11 00 b.Castleisland 1-3-97
Internationals: Republic of Ireland U16, U18.

2014–15	Ipswich T	0	0		
2015–16	Ipswich T	0	0		
2016–17	Ipswich T	0	0		
2017–18	Ipswich T	1	0		
2018–19	Ipswich T	0	0	1	0
2018–19	AFC Wimbledon	10	1		
2019–20	AFC Wimbledon	23	1		
2020–21	AFC Wimbledon	38	1		
2021–22	AFC Wimbledon	0	0	71	3
2021–22	Morecambe	36	1		
2022–23	Morecambe	7	0	43	1
2022–23	Salford C	10	0	10	0
2023–24	Newport Co	34	3		
2024–25	Newport Co	36	3	70	6

NEEDHAM, Fraser (G) 0 0
b. 1-1-07

2023–24	Newport Co	0	0		
2024–25	Newport Co	0	0		

NORRIS, Jack (F) 4 0
b.Newport 9-11-06

2023–24	Newport Co	3	0		
2024–25	Newport Co	0	0	3	0
2025	*Briton Ferry*	1	0	1	0

PAGE, Harrison (D) 0 0
b. 20-2-06

2022–23	Newport Co	0	0		
2023–24	Newport Co	0	0		
2024–25	Newport Co	0	0		

PATTEN, Keenan (M) 61 9
b.Cardiff 7-4-01
Internationals: Wales U17, U19.

2019–20	Penybont	12	1	12	1
2020–21	Cardiff C	0	0		
2021–22	Cardiff C	0	0		

From AFC Fylde.

2023–24	Barry Town U	21	1		
2024–25	Barry Town U	22	7	43	8
2024–25	Newport Co	6	0	6	0

RAI, Kiban (F) 21 0
H: 5 8 W: 10 10 b.Brecon 28-5-05

2022–23	Newport Co	4	0		
2023–24	Newport Co	13	0		
2024–25	Newport Co	4	0	21	0

SANCA, Nelson (D) 16 0
H: 6 1 W: 12 04 b.Lisbon 10-10-06

2023–24	Newport Co	3	0		
2024–25	Newport Co	1	0	4	0
2024–25	*Briton Ferry*	12	0	12	0

SEBERRY, Josh (D) 9 0
H: 6 4 W: 13 05 b.London 9-1-05

2023–24	Newport Co	9	0		
2024–25	Newport Co	0	0	9	0

SPELLMAN, Michael (M) 31 2
H: 6 0 W: 10 12 b.Durham 21-9-02

2022–23	Sunderland	0	0		
2023–24	Sunderland	0	0		
2024–25	Newport Co	31	2	31	2

THOMAS, Joe (M) 23 1
H: 6 4 W: 12 06 b. 12-3-02

2024–25	Newport Co	23	1	23	1

TOWNSEND, Nick (G) 185 0
H: 5 11 W: 14 05 b.Solihull 1-11-94
Internationals: Antigua and Barbuda Full caps.

2012–13	Birmingham C	0	0		
2013–14	Birmingham C	0	0		
2014–15	Birmingham C	0	0		
2015–16	Barnsley	8	0		
2016–17	Barnsley	0	0		
2017–18	Barnsley	8	0	16	0
2018–19	Newport Co	3	0		
2019–20	Newport Co	5	0		
2020–21	Newport Co	38	0		
2021–22	Newport Co	19	0		
2022–23	Newport Co	18	0		
2023–24	Newport Co	43	0		
2024–25	Newport Co	43	0	169	0

WARNER, Jaden (D) 17 0
H: 6 4 b.Hillingdon 28-10-02

2020–21	Norwich C	0	0		
2021–22	Norwich C	0	0		
2022–23	Norwich C	0	0		
2023–24	Norwich C	2	0		
2023–24	*Notts Co*	10	0	10	0
2024–25	Norwich C	0	0	2	0
2024–25	Newport Co	5	0	5	0

WEBB, Lewis (G) 42 0
H: 6 1 W: 11 05 b.Newport 12-9-01
Internationals: Wales U19, U20, U21.

2020–21	Swansea C	0	0		
2021–22	Swansea C	0	0		
2022	*Shelbourne*	7	0	7	0
2022–23	Swansea C	0	0		
2022–23	*Aberystwyth T*	15	0	15	0
2023–24	Swansea C	0	0		
2023–24	*Caernarfon T*	20	0	20	0
2024–25	Newport Co	0	0		

WHITMORE, Kai (M) 99 8
H: 5 10 W: 11 09 b. 17-2-01

2021–22	Penybont	12	0		
2022–23	Penybont	32	2	44	2
2023–24	Haverfordwest Co	27	4	27	4
2024–25	Newport Co	28	2	28	2

WILDIG, Aaron (M) 368 35
H: 5 9 W: 11 07 b.Hereford 15-4-92
Internationals: Wales U16.

2009–10	Cardiff C	11	1		
2010–11	Cardiff C	2	0		
2010–11	*Hamilton A*	3	0	3	0
2011–12	Cardiff C	0	0	13	1
2011–12	*Shrewsbury T*	12	2		
2012–13	Shrewsbury T	21	1		
2013–14	Shrewsbury T	30	2		
2014–15	Shrewsbury T	1	0	64	5
2014–15	*Morecambe*	9	1		

2015–16 Morecambe	32	2		
2016–17 Morecambe	28	2		
2017–18 Morecambe	31	1		
2018–19 Morecambe	26	1		
2019–20 Morecambe	28	3		
2020–21 Morecambe	37	8		
2021–22 Morecambe	22	2	213	20
2022–23 Newport Co	29	3		
2023–24 Newport Co	31	2		
2024–25 Newport Co	15	4	75	9

WOOD, Nathan (F) 155 29
H: 6 1 W: 11 00 b. 23-4-97
Internationals: Wales C.
From Undy Ath.

2019–20 Penybont	23	1		
2020–21 Penybont	31	4		
2021–22 Penybont	28	9		
2022–23 Penybont	32	11		
2023–24 Newport Co	12	0		
2023–24 *Cork C*	13	0	13	0
2024–25 Newport Co	1	0	13	0
2024–25 *Penybont*	15	4	129	29

YOUNG, Alfie (F) 0 0
b. 28-11-05

2023–24 Newport Co	0	0		
2024–25 Newport Co	0	0		

Players retained or with offer of contract
Balde Sanca, Nelson Diogo.

Scholars
Alexander-Walker, Moses Harrison; Babah,
Amani Imona Emmanuel; Bahumaid, Jaden
Clive Hussien; Bony, Bolou Ange Orphee;
Davison, Adam Lee; Egan, Cameron Lewis;
Evans, Corey Enrico; Evans, Morgan Howell
John; Hopkins, Bailey; Jones, George Yang;
Lloyd, Tomos Marc; Lonergan, Riley George;
McKenzie, Myles Matthew; Needham, Fraser
James; Osborne, Jed Beaujean; Pugh,
Harrison John; Rowsell, Declan; Watkins,
Samuel Tomos Martin.

NORTHAMPTON T (59)

BALDWIN, Jack (D) 376 17
H: 6 1 W: 11 00 b.Barking 30-6-93

2011–12 Hartlepool U	17	0		
2012–13 Hartlepool U	32	2		
2013–14 Hartlepool U	28	2	77	4
2013–14 Peterborough U	11	0		
2014–15 Peterborough U	11	0		
2015–16 Peterborough U	18	1		
2016–17 Peterborough U	27	1		
2017–18 Peterborough U	33	2	100	4
2018–19 Sunderland	34	3		
2019–20 Sunderland	0	0	34	3
2019–20 Salford C	13	1	13	1
2020–21 Bristol R	38	1		
2021–22 Bristol R	3	0	41	1
2021–22 Ross Co	30	2		
2022–23 Ross Co	29	1		
2023–24 Ross Co	30	0	89	3
2024–25 Northampton T	22	1	22	1

BROUGH, Patrick (D) 243 8
H: 6 3 W: 11 09 b.Carlisle 20-2-96

2013–14 Carlisle U	3	0		
2014–15 Carlisle U	29	0		
2015–16 Carlisle U	7	0		
2016–17 Carlisle U	1	0	40	0
2017–18 Morecambe	20	0	20	0
2018–19 Falkirk	16	0	16	0
From Barrow.				
2020–21 Barrow	43	6		
2021–22 Barrow	41	0		
2022–23 Barrow	41	0	125	6
2023–24 Northampton T	37	2		
2024–25 Northampton T	5	0	42	2

BURGE, Lee (G) 277 0
H: 5 11 W: 11 00 b.Hereford 9-1-93

2011–12 Coventry C	0	0		
2012–13 Coventry C	0	0		
2013–14 Coventry C	0	0		
2014–15 Coventry C	18	0		
2015–16 Coventry C	9	0		
2016–17 Coventry C	33	0		
2017–18 Coventry C	40	0		
2018–19 Coventry C	40	0	140	0
2019–20 Sunderland	5	0		
2020–21 Sunderland	41	0		
2021–22 Sunderland	3	0	49	0
2022–23 Northampton T	38	0		
2023–24 Northampton T	20	0		
2024–25 Northampton T	30	0	88	0

CARROLL, Charlie (D) 0 0
2024–25 Northampton T 0 0

CHOUCHANE, Samy (M) 22 0
H: 5 11 W: 9 08 b.Paris 5-9-03
Internationals: Tunisia U20.

2023–24 Brighton & HA	0	0		
2024–25 Northampton T	22	0	22	0

DADGE, James (G) 1 0
H: 6 2 W: 12 06 b.Northampton 18-10-04

2022–23 Northampton T	0	0		
2023–24 Northampton T	0	0		
2024–25 Northampton T	1	0	1	0

DOBSON, Neo (F) 4 0
H: 6 3 W: 13 10 b.Northampton 6-12-06

2023–24 Northampton T	0	0		
2024–25 Northampton T	4	0	4	0

DYCHE, Max (D) 45 1
b.Northampton 22-2-03

2020–21 Northampton T	2	0		
2021–22 Northampton T	1	0		
2022–23 Northampton T	18	1		
2023–24 Northampton T	4	0		
2024–25 Northampton T	20	0	45	1

EAVES, Tom (F) 389 83
H: 6 3 W: 13 08 b.Liverpool 14-1-92

2009–10 Oldham Ath	15	0		
2010–11 Bolton W	0	0		
2010–11 *Oldham Ath*	0	0	15	0
2011–12 Bolton W	0	0		
2012–13 Bolton W	3	0		
2012–13 *Bristol R*	16	7	16	7
2012–13 *Shrewsbury T*	10	6		
2013–14 Bolton W	0	0		
2013–14 *Rotherham U*	8	0		
2013–14 *Shrewsbury T*	25	2	35	8
2014–15 Bolton W	1	0		
2014–15 *Yeovil T*	5	0		
2014–15 *Bury*	9	1	9	1
2015–16 Bolton W	0	0	4	0
2016–17 Yeovil T	40	4	45	4
2017–18 Gillingham	41	17		
2018–19 Gillingham	43	21	84	38
2019–20 Hull C	40	5		
2020–21 Hull C	26	4		
2021–22 Hull C	31	5	97	14
2022–23 Rotherham U	20	0		
2023–24 Rotherham U	33	6	61	6
2024–25 Northampton T	23	5	23	5

EYOMA, Timothy (D) 137 5
H: 6 0 W: 11 11 b.Hackney 29-1-00
Internationals: England U16, U17, U18, U19.

2018–19 Tottenham H	0	0		
2019–20 Tottenham H	0	0		
2019–20 *Lincoln C*	0	0		
2020–21 Tottenham H	0	0		
2020–21 *Lincoln C*	39	1		
2021–22 Lincoln C	23	1		
2022–23 Lincoln C	25	0		
2023–24 Lincoln C	26	3	113	5
2024–25 Northampton T	24	0	24	0

FINDLAY, Freddie (F) 0 0
2024–25 Northampton T 0 0

FOSU, Tarique (M) 253 38
H: 5 11 W: 11 11 b.Wandsworth 5-11-95
Internationals: England U18. Ghana Full
caps.

2013–14 Reading	0	0		
2014–15 Reading	1	0		
2015–16 Reading	0	0		
2015–16 *Fleetwood T*	6	1	6	1
2015–16 *Accrington S*	8	3	8	3
2016–17 Reading	0	0	1	0
2016–17 *Colchester U*	33	5	33	5
2017–18 Charlton Ath	30	9		
2018–19 Charlton Ath	27	2	57	11
2019–20 Oxford U	25	8	25	8
2019–20 Brentford	10	1		
2020–21 Brentford	39	4		
2021–22 Brentford	1	0		
2022–23 Brentford	0	0	50	5
2022–23 *Stoke C*	20	0	20	0
2022–23 *Rotherham U*	19	1	19	1
2024–25 Northampton T	34	4	34	4

GUESS, Harry (D) 0 0
2024–25 Northampton T 0 0

GUINNESS-WALKER, Nesta (D) 159 6
H: 5 9 W: 11 05 b.Hounslow 30-11-99
From Metropolitan Police.

2019–20 AFC Wimbledon	23	1		
2020–21 AFC Wimbledon	31	1		
2021–22 AFC Wimbledon	28	1	82	3
2022–23 Reading	28	0		
2023–24 Reading	8	0	36	0
2023–24 *Stevenage*	14	0	14	0
2024–25 Northampton T	27	1	27	1

GUTHRIE, Jon (D) 419 30
H: 6 1 W: 11 00 b.Devizes 1-2-93

2011–12 Crewe Alex	25	0		
2012–13 Crewe Alex	23	0		
2013–14 Crewe Alex	23	0		
2014–15 Crewe Alex	25	0		
2015–16 Crewe Alex	39	1		
2016–17 Crewe Alex	33	0	122	1
2017–18 Walsall	46	1		
2018–19 Walsall	42	2	88	3

2019–20 Livingston	28	6		
2020–21 Livingston	36	5	64	11
2021–22 Northampton T	44	8		
2022–23 Northampton T	41	2		
2023–24 Northampton T	36	4		
2024–25 Northampton T	24	1	145	15

HART, Jamari (M) 0 0
b. 18-1-06

2023–24 Northampton T	0	0		
2024–25 Northampton T	0	0		

HONDERMARCK, William (M) 93 2
H: 6 1 W: 11 09 b.Orleans 21-11-00
Internationals: DR Congo Full caps.
From Drogheda U.

2020–21 Norwich C	0	0		
2020–21 *Harrogate T*	3	0	3	0
2021–22 Barnsley	9	0		
2022–23 Barnsley	2	0	11	0
2022–23 Northampton T	17	1		
2023–24 Northampton T	29	1		
2024–25 Northampton T	33	0	79	2

HOSKINS, Sam (F) 424 92
H: 5 8 W: 10 07 b.Dorchester 4-2-93

2011–12 Southampton	0	0		
2011–12 *Preston NE*	0	0		
2011–12 *Rotherham U*	8	2	8	2
2012–13 Southampton	0	0		
2012–13 *Stevenage*	14	1	14	1
2013–14 *Yeovil T*	19	0		
2014–15 *Yeovil T*	12	1	31	1
2015–16 Northampton T	34	6		
2016–17 Northampton T	25	3		
2017–18 Northampton T	27	2		
2018–19 Northampton T	42	5		
2019–20 Northampton T	37	8		
2020–21 Northampton T	46	7		
2021–22 Northampton T	44	13		
2022–23 Northampton T	41	22		
2023–24 Northampton T	38	15		
2024–25 Northampton T	37	7	371	88

IRELAND, Matthew (D) 0 0
b.Northampton 30-10-06

2023–24 Northampton T	0	0		
2024–25 Northampton T	0	0		

JENKINS, Leo (D) 0 0
H: 6 1 b. 19-10-06

2023–24 Northampton T	0	0		
2024–25 Northampton T	0	0		

KOIKI, Ali (D) 105 1
H: 6 2 W: 12 11 b.Chelsea 22-8-99

2018–19 Burnley	0	0		
2018–19 *Swindon T*	15	0	15	0
2019–20 Burnley	0	0		
2020–21 Burnley	0	0		
2020–21 *Bristol R*	10	0	10	0
2021–22 Northampton T	42	0		
2022–23 Northampton T	22	0		
2023–24 Northampton T	11	1		
2024–25 Northampton T	5	0	80	1

LICORISH MULLINGS, Kiantay (M) 1 0
b.Kettering 3-12-06
2024–25 Northampton T 1 0 1 0

LINTOTT, Harvey (D) 68 1
H: 6 2 W: 12 06 b.Canterbury 20-2-03

2020–21 Gillingham	1	0		
2021–22 Gillingham	6	0	6	0
2022–23 Northampton T	33	1		
2023–24 Northampton T	16	0		
2024–25 Northampton T	1	0	50	1
2024–25 *Sligo R*	12	0	12	0

MAGLIORE, Tyler (D) 67 3
H: 6 1 W: 11 07 b.Bradford 21-12-98

2018–19 Blackburn R	2	0		
2019–20 Blackburn R	0	0		
2019–20 *Rochdale*	2	0	2	0
2020–21 Blackburn R	0	0		
2020–21 *Motherwell*	10	0	10	0
2021–22 Blackburn R	4	0	6	0
2021–22 *Northampton T*	10	0		
2022–23 Northampton T	18	2		
2023–24 Northampton T	0	0		
2024–25 Northampton T	21	1	49	3

McCARRON, Liam (M) 35 1
H: 5 9 W: 9 08 b.Preston 7-3-01
Internationals: Scotland U19.

2018–19 Carlisle U	16	0	16	0
2019–20 Leeds U	0	0		
2020–21 Leeds U	0	0		
2021–22 Leeds U	1	0	1	0
2022–23 Stoke C	0	0		
2022–23 *Port Vale*	2	0	2	0
2023–24 Stoke C	0	0		
2024–25 Northampton T	16	1	16	1

McGEEHAN, Cameron (M) 299 63
H: 5 11 W: 11 03 b.Kingston upon Thames 6-4-95
Internationals: Northern Ireland U17, U19, U21, Full caps.

2013–14	Norwich C	0	0		
2014–15	Norwich C	0	0		
2014–15	*Luton T*	15	3		
2014–15	*Cambridge U*	4	3	**4**	**3**
2015–16	Luton T	41	12		
2016–17	Luton T	24	10	**80**	**25**
2017–18	Barnsley	9	1		
2017–18	*Scunthorpe U*	13	0	**13**	**0**
2018–19	Barnsley	39	6		
2019–20	Barnsley	13	2	**61**	**9**
2019–20	*Portsmouth*	12	0	**12**	**0**
2020–21	Oostende	20	3		
2021–22	Oostende	13	0		
2022–23	Oostende	19	4	**52**	**7**
2023–24	Colchester U	37	9	**37**	**9**
2024–25	Northampton T	40	10	**40**	**10**

McGOWAN, Aaron (D) 299 7
H: 5 9 W: 11 07 b.Liverpool 24-7-97

2012–13	Morecambe	1	0		
2013–14	Morecambe	2	0		
2014–15	Morecambe	8	1		
2015–16	Morecambe	21	0		
2016–17	Morecambe	30	0		
2017–18	Morecambe	40	0	**102**	**1**
2018–19	Hamilton A	35	2		
2019–20	Hamilton A	22	1	**57**	**3**
2020–21	Kilmarnock	18	0	**18**	**0**
2021–22	Northampton T	42	2		
2022–23	Northampton T	17	0		
2023–24	Northampton T	28	0		
2024–25	Northampton T	35	1	**122**	**3**

OBIAGWU, Fran (F) 2 0
b. 4-7-08

2024–25	Northampton T	2	0	**2**	**0**

ODIMAYO, Akinwale (D) 158 0
H: 6 0 W: 11 11 b.Camden 28-11-99

2019–20	Reading	0	0		
2020	*Waterford*	4	0	**4**	**0**
2020–21	Swindon T	30	0		
2021–22	Swindon T	35	0	**65**	**0**
2022–23	Northampton T	19	0		
2023–24	Northampton T	29	0		
2024–25	Northampton T	41	0	**89**	**0**

PINNOCK, Mitch (M) 273 34
H: 5 10 W: 10 12 b.Gravesend 12-12-94
Internationals: England C.

2012–13	Southend U	2	0		
2013–14	Southend U	0	0	**2**	**0**

From Bromley, Maidstone U, Dover Ath, Kingstonian, Dover Ath.

2018–19	AFC Wimbledon	34	3		
2019–20	AFC Wimbledon	25	3	**59**	**6**
2020–21	Kilmarnock	30	4	**30**	**4**
2021–22	Northampton T	46	9		
2022–23	Northampton T	45	6		
2023–24	Northampton T	45	7		
2024–25	Northampton T	46	2	**182**	**24**

RAYFIELD, Josh (D) 0 0
b.Kent 25-5-07

2024–25	Northampton T	0	0		

SHAW, Liam (M) 94 5
H: 5 10 W: 10 03 b.Sheffield 12-3-01

2018–19	Sheffield Wed	0	0		
2019–20	Sheffield Wed	2	0		
2020–21	Sheffield Wed	19	1	**21**	**1**
2022–23	Celtic	0	0		
2022–23	Morecambe	34	2	**34**	**2**
2023–24	Celtic	0	0		
2023–24	*Wigan Ath*	20	0	**20**	**0**
2024–25	Fleetwood T	11	0	**11**	**0**
2024–25	Northampton T	8	2	**8**	**2**

SOWERBY, Jack (M) 242 9
H: 5 9 W: 12 04 b.Preston 23-3-95

2014–15	Fleetwood T	0	0		
2015–16	Fleetwood T	8	0		
2016–17	Fleetwood T	8	1		
2017–18	Fleetwood T	22	2		
2018–19	Fleetwood T	15	0		
2018–19	*Carlisle U*	25	4	**25**	**4**
2019–20	Fleetwood T	24	0		
2020–21	Fleetwood T	0	0	**77**	**3**
2020–21	Northampton T	28	0		
2021–22	Northampton T	34	1		
2022–23	Northampton T	38	1		
2023–24	Northampton T	30	0		
2024–25	Northampton T	10	0	**140**	**2**

TOMLINSON, Joshua (D) 0 0
H: 6 1 W: 11 11 b.Kettering 1-12-05

2021–22	Northampton T	0	0		
2022–23	Northampton T	0	0		
2023–24	Northampton T	0	0		
2024–25	Northampton T	0	0		

TZANEV, Nikola (G) 121 0
H: 6 5 W: 14 02 b.Wellington 23-12-96
Internationals: New Zealand U20, Full caps.
From Brentford.

2016–17	AFC Wimbledon	0	0		
2017–18	AFC Wimbledon	0	0		
2018–19	AFC Wimbledon	0	0		
2019–20	AFC Wimbledon	2	0		
2020–21	AFC Wimbledon	15	0		
2021–22	AFC Wimbledon	46	0		
2022–23	AFC Wimbledon	39	0		
2023–24	AFC Wimbledon	2	0	**104**	**0**
2024–25	Northampton T	17	0	**17**	**0**

WAGHORN, Martyn (F) 466 112
H: 5 10 W: 13 01 b.South Shields 23-1-90
Internationals: England U19, U21.

2007–08	Sunderland	3	0		
2008–09	Sunderland	1	0		
2008–09	*Charlton Ath*	7	1	**7**	**1**
2009–10	Sunderland	0	0		
2009–10	*Leicester C*	43	12		
2010–11	Sunderland	2	0	**6**	**0**
2010–11	Leicester C	30	4		
2011–12	Leicester C	4	1		
2011–12	*Hull C*	5	1	**5**	**1**
2012–13	Leicester C	24	3		
2013–14	Leicester C	2	0	**103**	**20**
2013–14	*Millwall*	14	3	**14**	**3**
2013–14	Wigan Ath	15	5		
2014–15	Wigan Ath	23	3	**38**	**8**
2015–16	Rangers	25	20		
2016–17	Rangers	32	7	**57**	**27**
2017–18	Ipswich T	44	16	**44**	**16**
2018–19	Derby Co	36	9		
2019–20	Derby Co	43	12		
2020–21	Derby Co	32	5		
2021–22	Derby Co	0	0		
2021–22	Coventry C	27	1		
2022–23	Coventry C	11	1	**38**	**2**
2022–23	*Huddersfield T*	13	1	**13**	**1**
2023–24	Derby Co	24	7	**135**	**33**
2024–25	Northampton T	6	0	**6**	**0**

WILLIS, Jordan (D) 280 6
H: 5 11 W: 11 00 b.Coventry 24-8-94
Internationals: England U18, U19.

2011–12	Coventry C	3	0		
2012–13	Coventry C	1	0		
2013–14	Coventry C	28	0		
2014–15	Coventry C	34	0		
2015–16	Coventry C	4	0		
2016–17	Coventry C	36	3		
2017–18	Coventry C	35	0		
2018–19	Coventry C	38	1	**179**	**4**
2019–20	Sunderland	35	2		
2020–21	Sunderland	15	0		
2021–22	Sunderland	0	0	**50**	**2**
2022–23	Wycombe W	9	0	**9**	**0**
2023–24	Northampton T	27	0		
2024–25	Northampton T	15	0	**42**	**0**

WILSON, James (F) 218 39
H: 6 0 W: 12 04 b.Biddulph 1-12-95
Internationals: England U16, U19, U20, U21.

2013–14	Manchester U	1	2		
2014–15	Manchester U	13	1		
2015–16	Manchester U	1	0		
2015–16	*Brighton & HA*	25	5	**25**	**5**
2016–17	Manchester U	0	0		
2016–17	*Derby Co*	4	0	**4**	**0**
2017–18	Manchester U	0	0		
2017–18	*Sheffield U*	8	1	**8**	**1**
2018–19	Manchester U	0	0	**15**	**3**
2018–19	*Aberdeen*	24	4		
2019–20	Aberdeen	11	0	**35**	**4**
2019–20	Salford C	5	2		
2020–21	Salford C	24	7	**29**	**9**
2021–22	Port Vale	41	9		
2022–23	Port Vale	25	4		
2023–24	Port Vale	27	4	**93**	**17**
2024–25	Northampton T	9	0	**9**	**0**

WYATT, Ruben (M) 0 0
H: 6 0 W: 11 00 b.Northampton 22-2-06

2022–23	Northampton T	0	0		
2023–24	Northampton T	0	0		
2024–25	Northampton T	0	0		

Scholars
Barnett, Joziah Anthony; Baxter, Jozef Alec Mark; Carroll, Charlie William; Daldy, George Ryland; Dobson, Neo Isaiah; Evans, Oliver Luke; Findlay, Freddie Joseph; Guess, Harry James; Ireland, Matthew John; Jenkins, Leo Robert; Jevterevs, Aleksandr; Licorish-Mullings, Kiantay Tyrese; Murray, Archie Jacob; Obiagwu, Francesco Obiajulu; Okunnu, Jason Oluwadurotimi; Rayfield, Josh William; Ronald, William David; Smith, Elliot George Jack; Wyatt, Reuben David Ziggy.

NORWICH C (60)

ABOH, Kenneth (F) 6 0
H: 5 9 W: 11 03 b. 9-11-04

2023–24	Norwich C	1	0		
2024–25	Norwich C	0	0	**1**	**0**
2024–25	*Stevenage*	3	0	**3**	**0**
2024–25	*Colchester U*	2	0	**2**	**0**

ANSEN, Caleb (G) 0 0
b. 18-9-05

2023–24	Norwich C	0	0		
2024–25	Norwich C	0	0		

BARDEN, Daniel (G) 14 0
H: 6 5 W: 12 13 b.Camden 2-1-01
Internationals: Wales U16, U19, U21.
From Arsenal.

2020–21	Norwich C	2	0		
2021–22	Norwich C	0	0		
2021–22	*Livingston*	0	0		
2022–23	Norwich C	0	0		
2022–23	*Livingston*	0	0		
2023–24	Norwich C	0	0		
2024–25	Norwich C	0	0	**2**	**0**
2024–25	*Swindon T*	12	0	**12**	**0**

BARNES, Ashley (F) 501 106
H: 6 1 W: 12 02 b.Bath 30-10-89
Internationals: Austria U20.
From Paulton R.

2006–07	Plymouth Arg	0	0		
2007–08	Plymouth Arg	0	0		
2008–09	Plymouth Arg	15	1		
2009–10	Plymouth Arg	7	1	**22**	**2**
2009–10	*Torquay U*	6	0	**6**	**0**
2009–10	*Brighton & HA*	8	4		
2010–11	Brighton & HA	42	18		
2011–12	Brighton & HA	43	11		
2012–13	Brighton & HA	34	8		
2013–14	Brighton & HA	22	5	**149**	**46**
2013–14	Burnley	21	3		
2014–15	Burnley	35	5		
2015–16	Burnley	8	0		
2016–17	Burnley	28	6		
2017–18	Burnley	36	9		
2018–19	Burnley	37	12		
2019–20	Burnley	19	6		
2020–21	Burnley	22	3		
2021–22	Burnley	23	1		
2022–23	Burnley	39	6		
2023–24	Norwich C	35	6		
2024–25	Norwich C	8	0	**43**	**6**
2024–25	*Burnley*	13	1	**281**	**52**

BRIDGE, Aidan (M) 0 0
H: 5 11 W: 11 00 b. 21-3-05

2023–24	Middlesbrough	0	0		
2024–25	Middlesbrough	0	0		
2024–25	Norwich C	0	0		

CHRISENE, Benjamin (M) 56 1
H: 6 0 W: 12 08 b.Exeter 12-1-04
Internationals: England U16, U17, U19, U20, U21.

2019–20	Exeter C	1	0	**1**	**0**
2020–21	Aston Villa	0	0		
2021–22	Aston Villa	0	0		
2022–23	Aston Villa	0	0		
2022–23	*Kilmarnock*	13	0	**13**	**0**
2023–24	Aston Villa	0	0		
2023–24	*Blackburn R*	16	0	**16**	**0**
2024–25	Norwich C	26	1	**26**	**1**

CORDOBA, Jose (D) 138 1
H: 6 1 W: 12 11 b.Panama City 3-6-01
Internationals: Panama U20, Full caps.

2018–19		4	0		
2019–20		8	0	**12**	**0**
2020–21	Etar Veliko Tarnova	10	0		
2021–22	Etar Veliko Tarnova	8	0	**18**	**0**
2021–22	*Levski Sofia*	20	0		
2022–23	Levski Sofia	25	0		
2023–24	Levski Sofia	29	0	**74**	**0**
2024–25	Norwich C	34	1	**34**	**1**

CRNAC, Ante (F) 122 27
H: 6 3 W: 13 01 b.Sisak 17-12-03
Internationals: Croatia U16, U17, U19, U20, U21.

2020–21	Dinamo Zagreb	0	0		
2021–22	Dinamo Zagreb	0	0		
2021–22	Slaven Belupo	12	2		
2022–23	Slaven Belupo	35	6		
2023–24	Slaven Belupo	6	3	**53**	**11**
2023–24	Rakow Czestochowa	26	8		
2024–25	Rakow Czestochowa	5	1	**31**	**9**
2024–25	Norwich C	38	7	**38**	**7**

DJEDJE, Uriah (M) 0 0
H: 6 2 W: 11 11 b.London 16-3-06

2024–25	Norwich C	0	0		

DOMERACKI, Alan (M) 0 0
H: 5 10 W: 10 08 b. 23-10-06

2024–25	Dundee U	0	0		
2024–25	Norwich C	0	0		

DUFFY, Shane (D) **368 25**
H: 6 4 W: 12 00 b.Derry 1-1-92
Internationals: Northern Ireland U16, U17, U19, U21, B. Republic of Ireland U19, U21, Full caps.

2008–09	Everton	0	0		
2009–10	Everton	0	0		
2010–11	Everton	0	0		
2010–11	*Burnley*	1	0	**1**	**0**
2011–12	Everton	4	0		
2011–12	*Scunthorpe U*	18	2	**18**	**2**
2012–13	Everton	1	0		
2013–14	Everton	0	0		
2013–14	*Yeovil T*	37	1	**37**	**1**
2014–15	Everton	0	0	**5**	**0**
2014–15	Blackburn R	19	1		
2015–16	Blackburn R	41	4		
2016–17	Blackburn R	3	0	**63**	**5**
2016–17	Brighton & HA	31	2		
2017–18	Brighton & HA	37	0		
2018–19	Brighton & HA	35	5		
2019–20	Brighton & HA	19	1		
2020–21	Brighton & HA	0	0		
2020–21	*Celtic*	18	3	**18**	**3**
2021–22	Brighton & HA	18	1		
2022–23	Brighton & HA	0	0	**140**	**9**
2022–23	*Fulham*	5	0	**5**	**0**
2023–24	Norwich C	36	1		
2024–25	Norwich C	45	4	**81**	**5**

FASSNACHT, Christian (M) **324 95**
H: 6 1 W: 11 09 b.Zurich 11-11-93
Internationals: Switzerland Full caps.

2014–15	Tuggen	17	10	**17**	**10**
2014–15	Winterthur	13	2		
2015–16	Winterthur	34	9	**47**	**11**
2016–17	Thun	35	10	**35**	**10**
2017–18	Young Boys	34	11		
2018–19	Young Boys	35	11		
2019–20	Young Boys	30	7		
2020–21	Young Boys	36	10		
2021–22	Young Boys	18	11		
2022–23	Young Boys	29	8	**182**	**58**
2023–24	Norwich C	40	6		
2024–25	Norwich C	3	0	**43**	**6**

Transferred to Young Boys, December 2024.

FISHER, Kellen (M) **47 0**
H: 6 0 W: 11 07 b.Sidcup 5-5-04
Internationals: England U20.

2023–24	Norwich C	9	0		
2024–25	Norwich C	38	0	**47**	**0**

FORSON, Amankwah (F) **118 12**
H: 5 8 W: 10 03 b. 31-12-02
Internationals: Ghana Full caps.

2019–20	WAFA	10	1		
2020–21	WAFA	6	0	**16**	**1**
2020–21	*Liefering*	10	3		
2021–22	Red Bull Salzburg	1	0		
2021–22	*Liefering*	19	3	**29**	**6**
2022–23	Red Bull Salzburg	12	0		
2022–23	*Rheindorf Altach*	17	1	**17**	**1**
2023–24	Red Bull Salzburg	22	2	**35**	**2**
2024–25	Norwich C	21	2	**21**	**2**

FORSYTH, Gabriel (M) **7 0**
H: 6 0 W: 12 06 b.Glasgow 4-8-06
Internationals: Scotland U16, U17, U19.

2022–23	Hamilton A	2	0	**2**	**0**
2023–24	Norwich C	0	0		
2024–25	Norwich C	5	0	**5**	**0**

GEE, Billy (M) **0 0**
H: 5 10 W: 11 00 b.Tooting 30-7-05
Internationals: England U16, U17, U19.

2021–22	Chelsea	0	0		
2022–23	Chelsea	0	0		
2023–24	Chelsea	0	0		
2024–25	Norwich C	0	0		

GIBBS, Liam (M) **66 1**
H: 5 10 W: 9 06 b.Bury St Edmunds 16-12-02

2019–20	Ipswich T	0	0		
2020–21	Ipswich T	1	0	**1**	**0**
2021–22	Norwich C	0	0		
2022–23	Norwich C	34	1		
2023–24	Norwich C	22	0		
2024–25	Norwich C	9	0	**65**	**1**

GUNN, Angus (G) **197 0**
H: 6 5 W: 12 02 b.Norwich 22-1-96
Internationals: England U16, U17, U18, U19, U20, U21. Scotland full caps.

2013–14	Manchester C	0	0		
2014–15	Manchester C	0	0		
2015–16	Manchester C	0	0		
2016–17	Manchester C	0	0		
2017–18	Manchester C	0	0		
2017–18	*Norwich C*	46	0		
2018–19	Southampton	12	0		
2019–20	Southampton	10	0		
2020–21	Southampton	0	0	**22**	**0**
2020–21	*Stoke C*	15	0	**15**	**0**
2021–22	Norwich C	9	0		
2022–23	Norwich C	30	0		
2023–24	Norwich C	40	0		
2024–25	Norwich C	35	0	**160**	**0**

GWANZURA, Takundzwa (D) **0 0**
From Everton.

2024–25	Blackpool	0	0		
2024–25	Norwich C	0	0		

HERNANDEZ, Onel (M) **309 21**
H: 5 8 W: 10 12 b.Moron 1-2-93
Internationals: Germany U18. Cuba Full caps.

2010–11	Arminia Bielefeld	10	0		
2011–12	Arminia Bielefeld	18	0	**28**	**0**
2012–13	Werder Bremen	0	0		
2013–14	Werder Bremen	0	0		
2013–14	VfL Wolfsburg	0	0		
2014–15	VfL Wolfsburg	0	0		
2015–16	VfL Wolfsburg	0	0		
2016–17	Eintracht Brauschweig	34	5		
2017–18	Eintracht Brauschweig	17	1	**51**	**6**
2017–18	Norwich C	12	0		
2018–19	Norwich C	40	8		
2019–20	Norwich C	26	1		
2020–21	Norwich C	21	0		
2021–22	Norwich C	0	0		
2021–22	*Middlesbrough*	17	1	**17**	**1**
2021–22	*Birmingham C*	22	3	**22**	**3**
2022–23	Norwich C	39	2		
2023–24	Norwich C	30	0		
2024–25	Norwich C	23	0	**191**	**11**

HILLS, Bradley (D) **60 4**
H: 6 2 b.Great Yarmouth 10-3-04
Internationals: England U20.

2022–23	Norwich C	0	0		
2023–24	Norwich C	0	0		
2023–24	*Accrington S*	41	3	**41**	**3**
2024–25	Norwich C	3	0	**3**	**0**
2024–25	*Stockport Co*	16	1	**16**	**1**

IDAH, Adam (F) **115 20**
H: 6 3 W: 13 01 b.Cork 11-2-01
Internationals: Republic of Ireland U16, U17, U18, U19, U21, Full caps.

2019–20	Norwich C	12	0		
2020–21	Norwich C	17	3		
2021–22	Norwich C	17	1		
2022–23	Norwich C	25	2		
2023–24	Norwich C	28	6		
2023–24	*Celtic*	15	8	**15**	**8**
2024–25	Norwich C	1	0	**100**	**12**

Transferred to Celtic, August 2024.

JONES, Dylan (F) **0 0**

2024–25	Norwich C	0	0		

JURASEK, Matej (F) **98 15**
H: 5 11 W: 11 07 b.Karvina 30-8-03
Internationals: Czech Republic U16, U17, U19, U20, U21, Full caps.

2020–21	Slavia Prague	2	0		
2020–21	*Vlasim*	13	1		
2021–22	Slavia Prague	0	0		
2021–22	*Karvina*	7	0	**7**	**0**
2021–22	*Vlasim*	14	2	**27**	**3**
2022–23	Slavia Prague	21	6		
2023–24	Slavia Prague	25	5		
2024–25	Slavia Prague	14	1	**62**	**12**
2024–25	Norwich C	2	0	**2**	**0**

LIMA, Pedro (M) **0 0**
b.Brasilia 27-3-03
Internationals: Brazil U20.

2023–24	Norwich C	0	0		
2024–25	Norwich C	0	0		

LONG, George (G) **277 0**
H: 6 4 W: 14 11 b.Sheffield 5-11-93
Internationals: England U18, U20.

2010–11	Sheffield U	1	0		
2011–12	Sheffield U	2	0		
2012–13	Sheffield U	36	0		
2013–14	Sheffield U	27	0		
2014–15	Sheffield U	0	0		
2014–15	*Oxford U*	10	0	**10**	**0**
2014–15	*Motherwell*	13	0	**13**	**0**
2015–16	Sheffield U	31	0		
2016–17	Sheffield U	3	0		
2017–18	Sheffield U	0	0	**100**	**0**
2017–18	*AFC Wimbledon*	45	0	**45**	**0**
2018–19	Hull C	4	0		
2019–20	Hull C	45	0		
2020–21	Hull C	8	0	**57**	**0**
2021–22	Millwall	0	0		
2022–23	Millwall	36	0	**36**	**0**
2023–24	Norwich C	7	0		
2024–25	Norwich C	9	0	**16**	**0**

MAHOVO, Lucien (D) **9 0**
H: 6 0 W: 11 11 b. 7-6-05

2023–24	Notts Co	1	0	**1**	**0**
2024–25	Norwich C	8	0	**8**	**0**

MAIR, Archie (G) **22 0**
H: 6 6 W: 12 08 b.Turriff 10-2-01
Internationals: Scotland U17, U18, U19, U21.
From Aberdeen.

2019–20	Norwich C	0	0		
2020–21	Norwich C	0	0		
2021–22	Norwich C	0	0		
2021–22	*Lincoln C*	0	0		
2022–23	Norwich C	0	0		
2023–24	Norwich C	0	0		
2023–24	*Morecambe*	21	0	**21**	**0**
2024–25	Norwich C	0	0		
2024–25	*Motherwell*	1	0	**1**	**0**

MARCONDES, Emiliano (M) **279 55**
H: 6 0 W: 11 11 b.Hvidovre 9-3-95
Internationals: Denmark U17, U18, U19, U20, U21.

2012–13	Nordsjaelland	3	0		
2013–14	Nordsjaelland	11	1		
2014–15	Nordsjaelland	24	5		
2015–16	Nordsjaelland	30	2		
2016–17	Nordsjaelland	25	12		
2017–18	Nordsjaelland	19	17		
2017–18	Brentford	12	0		
2018–19	Brentford	13	0		
2019–20	Brentford	25	2		
2019–20	*Midtjylland*	12	2	**12**	**2**
2020–21	Brentford	31	1		
2021–22	Brentford	0	0	**81**	**3**
2021–22	Bournemouth	17	2		
2022–23	Bournemouth	1	0		
2022–23	*Nordsjaelland*	8	3	**120**	**40**
2023–24	Bournemouth	0	0	**18**	**2**
2023–24	*Hibernian*	15	3	**15**	**3**
2024–25	Norwich C	33	5	**33**	**5**

McCONVILLE, Ruairi (D) **8 0**
H: 6 4 W: 12 08 b.Belfast 1-5-05
Internationals: Northern Ireland U16, U17, U19, U21, Full caps.

2024–25	Brighton & HA	0	0		
2024–25	Norwich C	8	0	**8**	**0**

McLEAN, Kenny (M) **518 48**
H: 6 0 W: 11 00 b.Rutherglen 8-1-92
Internationals: Scotland U19, U21, Full caps.

2009–10	St Mirren	0	0		
2009–10	*Arbroath*	20	1	**20**	**1**
2010–11	St Mirren	19	0		
2011–12	St Mirren	28	4		
2012–13	St Mirren	29	3		
2013–14	St Mirren	30	6		
2014–15	St Mirren	25	7	**131**	**20**
2014–15	Aberdeen	13	0		
2015–16	Aberdeen	38	6		
2016–17	Aberdeen	38	4		
2017–18	Aberdeen	22	3		
2017–18	Norwich C	0	0		
2017–18	*Aberdeen*	15	5	**126**	**18**
2018–19	Norwich C	20	3		
2019–20	Norwich C	37	1		
2020–21	Norwich C	38	2		
2021–22	Norwich C	31	1		
2022–23	Norwich C	35	1		
2023–24	Norwich C	46	1		
2024–25	Norwich C	34	0	**241**	**9**

MUNDLE-SMITH, Errol (F) **0 0**
H: 6 2 W: 11 09 b.London 19-3-06

2024–25	Norwich C	0	0		

MYLES, Elliot (M) **3 0**
H: 5 10 W: 11 03 b. 20-1-07
Internationals: England U17. Wales U16, U17, U18, U19.

2024–25	Norwich C	3	0	**3**	**0**

NUNEZ, Marcelino (M) **169 19**
H: 5 8 W: 11 07 b.Recoleta 1-3-00
Internationals: Chile Full caps.

2020	Universidad Catolica	20	2		
2021	Universidad Catolica	28	6		
2022	Universidad Catolica	16	0	**64**	**8**
2022–23	Norwich C	37	3		
2023–24	Norwich C	36	2		
2024–25	Norwich C	32	6	**105**	**11**

RENECKE, Waylon (D) **0 0**
H: 6 0 W: 11 00 b.Peterborough 12-5-06
Internationals: England U17. South Africa U17.

2023–24	Norwich C	0	0		
2024–25	Norwich C	0	0		

Transferred to Copenhagen, September 2024.

REYES, Vicente (G) **40 0**
H: 6 4 W: 12 08 b.Charleston 19-11-03
Internationals: Chile U17, U20, U23.

2023–24	Norwich C	0	0		
2023–24	*Forest Green R*	16	0	**16**	**0**
2024–25	Norwich C	4	0	**4**	**0**
2024–25	*Cambridge U*	20	0	**20**	**0**

ROWE, Jonathan (F)   76 15
H: 5 8   W: 10 08   b.Westminster 30-4-03
Internationals: England U21.
2020–21 Norwich C   0   0
2021–22 Norwich C   13   0
2022–23 Norwich C   3   0
2023–24 Norwich C   32   12
2024–25 Norwich C   0   0   48 12
2024–25 *Marseille*   28   3   28 3

SAINZ, Borja (F)   178 38
H: 5 9   W: 11 11   b.Leioa 1-2-01
Internationals: Spain U19.
From Athletic Bilbao.
2018–19 Alaves   0   0
2019–20 Alaves   19   1
2020–21 Alaves   21   1   40 2
2021–22 Real Zaragoza   32   3   32 3
2022–23 Giresunspor   32   9   32 9
2023–24 Norwich C   33   6
2024–25 Norwich C   41   18   74 24

SARGENT, Josh (F)   196 59
H: 6 1   W: 12 06   b.Missouri 20-2-00
Internationals: USA U17, U20, U23, Full caps.
From Saint Louis.
2018–19 Werder Bremen   10   2
2019–20 Werder Bremen   28   4
2020–21 Werder Bremen   32   5
2021–22 Werder Bremen   2   2   72 13
2021–22 Norwich C   26   2
2023–24 Norwich C   40   13
2023–24 Norwich C   26   16
2024–25 Norwich C   32   15   124 46

SCHWARTAU, Oscar (F)   76 5
H: 6 1   W: 12 08   b.Sengelose 17-5-06
Internationals: Denmark U16, U17, U18, U19, U20.
2022–23 Brondby   18   4
2023–24 Brondby   14   0
2024–25 Brondby   4   0   36 4
2024–25 Norwich C   40   1   40 1

SHIPLEY, Lewis (D)   34 2
H: 6 0   W: 11 11   b.Cambridge 29-11-03
2020–21 Norwich C   0   0
2021–22 Norwich C   0   0
2022–23 Norwich C   0   0
2023–24 Norwich C   0   ,0
2023–24 *Accrington S*   26   2   26 2
2024–25 Norwich C   0   0
2024–25 *Cheltenham T*   8   0   8 0

SORENSEN, Jacob (M)   203 8
H: 5 9   W: 11 07   b.Esbjerg 3-3-98
Internationals: Denmark U18, U20, U21.
2016–17 Esbjerg   8   0
2017–18 Esbjerg   29   1
2018–19 Esbjerg   36   3
2019–20 Esbjerg   29   1   102 5
2020–21 Norwich C   30   1
2021–22 Norwich C   19   1
2023–24 Norwich C   13   1
2024–25 Norwich C   27   0   101 3

SPRINGETT, Tony (F)   37 1
H: 5 9   W: 11 00   b.London 22-9-02
Internationals: Republic of Ireland U18, U21.
2021–22 Norwich C   3   0
2022–23 Norwich C   1   0
2022–23 *Derby Co*   10   0   10 0
2023–24 Norwich C   10   0
2023–24 *Northampton T*   13   1   13 1
2024–25 Norwich C   0   0   14 0

STACEY, Jack (M)   308 11
H: 6 4   W: 13 05   b.Bracknell 6-4-96
2014–15 Reading   6   0
2015–16 Reading   0   0
2015–16 *Barnet*   2   0   2 0
2015–16 *Carlisle U*   9   2   9 2
2016–17 Reading   0   0   6 0
2016–17 *Exeter C*   34   0   34 0
2017–18 Luton T   41   1
2018–19 Luton T   45   4   86 5
2019–20 Bournemouth   19   0
2020–21 Bournemouth   30   1
2021–22 Bournemouth   25   0
2022–23 Bournemouth   10   0   84 1
2023–24 Norwich C   46   1
2024–25 Norwich C   41   2   87 3

TOMKINSON, Jonathan (D)   44 0
H: 6 3   W: 11 00   b.Plano 11-4-02
Internationals: USA U17, U23.
2020–21 Norwich C   0   0
2021–22 Norwich C   0   0
2022–23 Norwich C   1   0
2022–23 *Stevenage*   7   0   7 0
2023–24 Norwich C   0   0
2023–24 *Bradford C*   23   0   23 0
2024–25 Norwich C   0   0   1 0
2024–25 *Ross Co*   13   0   13 0

WELCH, Finley (M)   1 0
H: 5 8   W: 10 12   b. 3-10-04
2023–24 Norwich C   1   0
2024–25 Norwich C   0   0   1 0

Players retained or with offer of contract
Adegboyega, Emmanuel Oluwanifemi; Adelusi, Theodore Olakitan Ademide; Ben Slimane, Anis; Bracking Makonese, Miles Munyaradzi; Brooke, Harry Roy Leslie; Chilvers, Toby James; Corke, Finlay John Patrick; Daley, Damari Anthony; Forbes, Brandon Alexander; Mundle, Rio York; Okwumo, Chinaza Harmony; Owen, Jaiden Myles; Ozcan, Vatan Oguz; Roberts, Alexander James; Rowland, Sonny William; Sealey, Kaleel La'Sean Reo; Williams, Tyler James; Wilson, Charles Robert.

Scholars
Binnie, Ethan Alexander; Bullen, Henry James; Keita, Gabriel Ofosu; Madu, Ubachukwu Victor Oluebube; Northover, Foden William; Ofori-Manteaw, Lloyd Junior; Okpiabhele, Emmanuel Oserhiemen; Oligbo, Finlay Nicholas; Ruddy, Jack Peter; Sclare, Zachariah Marvin; Simbai, Kingston Paris; Valencia Gomez, Hugo.

NOTTINGHAM F (61)

ABBOTT, Zach (D)   0 0
H: 5 11   W: 11 00   b. 13-5-06
Internationals: England U16, U17, U18, U19.
2022–23 Nottingham F   0   0
2023–24 Nottingham F   0   0
2024–25 Nottingham F   0   0

AINA, Ola (D)   237 7
H: 5 9   W: 10 03   b.London 8-10-96
Internationals: England U16, U17, U18, U19, U20. Nigeria Full caps.
2015–16 Chelsea   0   0
2016–17 Chelsea   3   0
2017–18 Chelsea   0   0
2017–18 *Hull C*   44   0   44 0
2018–19 Chelsea   0   0   3 0
2018–19 Torino   30   1
2019–20 Torino   32   0
2020–21 Torino   0   0
2020–21 *Fulham*   31   2   31 2
2021–22 Torino   21   0
2022–23 Torino   19   1   102 2
2023–24 Nottingham F   22   1
2024–25 Nottingham F   35   2   57 3

ANDERSON, Elliot (M)   102 9
H: 5 9   W: 9 13   b.Whitley Bay 6-11-02
Internationals: Scotland U16, U17, U18, U21. England U21.
2020–21 Newcastle U   1   0
2021–22 Newcastle U   0   0
2021–22 *Bristol R*   21   7   21 7
2022–23 Newcastle U   22   0
2023–24 Newcastle U   21   0   44 0
2024–25 Nottingham F   37   2   37 2

AWONIYI, Taiwo (F)   220 55
H: 5 10   W: 11 07   b.Ilorin 12-8-97
Internationals: Nigeria U17, U20, U23, Full caps.
2015–16 Liverpool   0   0
2015–16 *Frankfurt*   13   1   13 1
2016–17 Liverpool   0   0
2016–17 *NEC Nijmegen*   18   2   18 2
2017–18 Liverpool   0   0
2017–18 *Mouscron*   27   7
2018–19 Liverpool   0   0
2018–19 *Gent*   16   0   16 0
2018–19 *Mouscron*   9   7   36 14
2019–20 Liverpool   0   0
2019–20 *Mainz 05*   12   1   12 1
2020–21 Liverpool   0   0
2020–21 *Union Berlin*   21   5
2021–22 *Union Berlin*   31   15   52 20
2022–23 Nottingham F   27   10
2023–24 Nottingham F   20   6
2024–25 Nottingham F   26   1   73 17

BINDON, Tyler (D)   84 4
H: 6 2   W: 13 03   b.Auckland 27-1-05
Internationals: USA U19. New Zealand Full caps.
2023–24 Reading   40   2
2024–25 Nottingham F   0   0
2024–25 *Reading*   44   2   84 4

BOLY, Willy (D)   288 15
H: 6 1   W: 12 11   b.Melun 3-2-91
Internationals: France U16, U17, U19. Ivory Coast Full caps.
2010–11 Auxerre   8   1
2011–12 Auxerre   33   1
2012–13 Auxerre   25   1
2013–14 Auxerre   30   1
2014–15 Auxerre   1   0   97 3
2014–15 Braga   0   0
2015–16 Braga   22   2
2016–17 Braga   3   0   25 2
2016–17 Porto   4   0
2017–18 Porto   0   0   4 0
2017–18 Wolverhampton W   36   3
2018–19 Wolverhampton W   36   4
2019–20 Wolverhampton W   22   0
2020–21 Wolverhampton W   21   1
2021–22 Wolverhampton W   10   0
2022–23 Wolverhampton W   0   0   125 8
2022–23 Nottingham F   11   0
2023–24 Nottingham F   20   2
2024–25 Nottingham F   6   0   37 2

BONAVENTURE, Emmanuel (F)   201 41
H: 5 9   W: 10 08   b.Yola, Nigeria 15-11-97
Internationals: Nigeria U23, Full caps.
2016–17 Zorya Luhansk   22   6   22 6
2017–18 Club Brugge   30   7
2018–19 Club Brugge   26   7
2019–20 Club Brugge   9   0
2020–21 Club Brugge   20   5   85 19
2020–21 *Cologne*   9   0   9 0
2021–22 Watford   33   10
2022–23 Watford   2   0
2022–23 Nottingham F   19   2
2023–24 Nottingham F   0   0
2023–24 *Istanbul Basaksehir*   8   0   8 0
2023–24 *Watford*   17   4   52 14
2024–25 Nottingham F   0   0   19 2
2024–25 *Blackburn R*   6   0   6 0

BOWLER, Josh (M)   156 17
H: 5 9   W: 11 00   b.Chertsey 5-3-99
2016–17 QPR   1   0   1 0
2017–18 Everton   0   0
2018–19 Everton   0   0
2019–20 Everton   0   0
2019–20 *Hull C*   28   1   28 1
2021–22 Blackpool   42   7
2022–23 Nottingham F   0   0
2022–23 *Olympiacos*   4   0   4 0
2022–23 *Blackpool*   25   4   67 11
2023–24 *Cardiff C*   38   5   38 5
2024–25 Nottingham F   0   0
2024–25 *Preston NE*   10   0   10 0
2024–25 *Luton T*   8   0   8 0

CARLOS MIGUEL, Pereira (G)   10 0
H: 6 8   W: 11 05   b.Cardoso Moreira 9-10-98
2020 Santa Cruz   0   0
2021 Boa Esporte   0   0
2021 Corinthians   2   0
2022 Corinthians   2   0
2023 Corinthians   0   0
2024 Corinthians   6   0   10 0
2024–25 Nottingham F   0   0

CARMO, David (D)   92 1
b. 19-7-99
Internationals: Portugal U19, U20. Angola Full caps.
2018–19 Braga   0   0
2019–20 Braga   18   0
2020–21 Braga   12   0
2021–22 Braga   12   0   42 0
2022–23 Porto   9   0
2023–24 Porto   7   0   16 0
2023–24 Olympiacos   11   0
2024–25 Olympiacos   23   1   34 1

DANILO, dos Santos (M)   124 8
H: 5 9   W: 11 02   b.Salvador 29-4-01
2020 Palmeiras   18   0
2021 Palmeiras   22   2
2022 Palmeiras   34   1   74 3
2022–23 Nottingham F   13   3
2023–24 Nottingham F   29   2
2024–25 Nottingham F   8   0   50 5

DOMINGUEZ, Nicolas (M)   238 15
H: 5 10   W: 11 07   b.Haedo 28-6-98
Internationals: Argentina Full caps.
2016–17 Velez Sarsfield   12   1
2017–18 Velez Sarsfield   24   0
2018–19 Velez Sarsfield   25   3
2019–20 Velez Sarsfield   14   5   75 9
2019–20 Bologna   16   0
2020–21 Bologna   28   1
2021–22 Bologna   28   0
2022–23 Bologna   31   3   103 4
2023–24 Nottingham F   26   2
2024–25 Nottingham F   34   0   60 2

DONNELLY, Aaron (D)   58 1
H: 6 1   W: 11 07   b.Magherafelt 8-6-03
Internationals: Northern Ireland U17, U21, Full caps.
From Dungannon Swifts.
2022–23 Nottingham F   0   0
2022–23 *Port Vale*   20   1   20 1

2023–24 Nottingham F   0   0
2023–24 *Dundee*   21   0   21   0
2024–25 Nottingham F   0   0
2024–25 *Colchester U*   17   0   17   0
Transferred to Dundee, January 2025.

ELANGA, Anthony (F)   113 14
H: 5 10   W: 10 03   b.Malmo 27-4-02
Internationals: Sweden U17, U19, U21, Full caps.
2020–21 Manchester U   2   1
2021–22 Manchester U   21   2
2022–23 Manchester U   16   0   39   3
2023–24 Nottingham F   36   5
2024–25 Nottingham F   38   6   74 11

ESAPA, Detlef (F)   8   0
H: 5 11   W: 11 11   b. 21-9-04
2022–23 Nottingham F   0   0
2023–24 Nottingham F   0   0
2024–25 *Rotherham U*   6   0   6   0
2024–25 *Cambridge U*   2   0   2   0

FLETCHER, Kristian (F)   12   1
b.Bowie 6-8-05
Internationals: USA U19.
2022   DC United   2   1
2023   DC United   10   0
2023–24 DC United   0   0
On loan from DC United.
2023–24 *Swansea C*   0   0
2024   DC United   0   0   12   1
On loan from DC United.
2024–25 Nottingham F   0   0

GARDNER, Joseph (F)   11   1
b.Nottingham 6-6-05
Internationals: Republic of Ireland U21.
2023–24 Nottingham F   0   0
2024–25 Nottingham F   0   0
2024–25 *Lincoln C*   11   1   11   1

GIBBS-WHITE, Morgan (M)   214 30
H: 5 10   W: 11 07   b.Stafford 27-1-00
Internationals: England U16, U17, U18, U19, U21, Full caps.
2016–17 Wolverhampton W   7   0
2017–18 Wolverhampton W   13   0
2018–19 Wolverhampton W   26   0
2019–20 Wolverhampton W   7   0
2020–21 Wolverhampton W   11   1
2020–21 *Swansea C*   5   1   5   1
2021–22 Wolverhampton W   2   0
2021–22 *Sheffield U*   35 11   35 11
2022–23 Wolverhampton W   2   0   68   1
2022–23 Nottingham F   35   5
2023–24 Nottingham F   34   5
2024–25 Nottingham F   34   7   106 17

HENNESSEY, Wayne (G)   295   0
H: 6 6   W: 14 02   b.Bangor 24-1-87
Internationals: Wales U17, U19, U21, Full caps.
2004–05 Wolverhampton W   0   0
2005–06 Wolverhampton W   0   0
2006–07 Wolverhampton W   0   0
2006–07 *Bristol C*   0   0
2006–07 *Stockport Co*   15   0   15   0
2007–08 Wolverhampton W   46   0
2008–09 Wolverhampton W   35   0
2009–10 Wolverhampton W   13   0
2010–11 Wolverhampton W   24   0
2011–12 Wolverhampton W   34   0
2012–13 Wolverhampton W   0   0
2013–14 Wolverhampton W   0   0   152   0
2013–14 *Yeovil T*   12   0   12   0
2013–14 Crystal Palace   1   0
2014–15 Crystal Palace   3   0
2015–16 Crystal Palace   29   0
2016–17 Crystal Palace   29   0
2017–18 Crystal Palace   27   0
2018–19 Crystal Palace   18   0
2019–20 Crystal Palace   3   0
2020–21 Crystal Palace   0   0
2021–22 Crystal Palace   0   0   110   0
2021–22 *Burnley*   2   0   2   0
2022–23 Nottingham F   4   0
2023–24 Nottingham F   0   0
2024–25 Nottingham F   0   0   4   0

HUDSON-ODOI, Callum (M)   146 17
H: 6 0   W: 11 11   b.Wandsworth 7-11-00
Internationals: England U16, U17, U18, U19, Full caps.
2017–18 Chelsea   2   0
2018–19 Chelsea   10   0
2019–20 Chelsea   22   1
2020–21 Chelsea   23   2
2021–22 Chelsea   15   1
2022–23 Chelsea   0   0   72   4
2022–23 *Bayer Leverkusen*   14   0   14   0
2023–24 Nottingham F   29   8
2024–25 Nottingham F   31   5   60 13

JOTA SILVA, Pedro (D)   214 61
H: 5 10   W: 12 02   b.Meires 1-8-99
Internationals: Portugal Full caps.
2016–17 Sousense
2017–18 Pacos de Ferreira   0   0
2018–19 Sousense   34 16   35 16
2019–20 Espinho   25 14   25 14
2020–21 Leixoes   10   2   10   2
2020–21 Casa Pia   17   2
2021–22 Casa Pia   33 11   50 13
2022–23 Vitoria de Guimaraes   30   2
2023–24 Vitoria de Guimaraes   33 11   63 13
2024–25 Nottingham F   31   3   31   3

McDONNELL, Jamie (M)   32   1
H: 6 0   W: 12 04   b. 16-2-04
Internationals: Northern Ireland U16, U17, U18, U19, U21.
From Glentoran.
2020–21 Nottingham F   0   0
2021–22 Nottingham F   0   0
2022–23 Nottingham F   0   0
2023–24 Nottingham F   0   0
2024–25 Nottingham F   0   0
2024–25 *Colchester U*   32   1   32   1

MIGHTEN, Alex (F)   85   5
H: 5 7   W: 11 00   b.Nottingham 11-4-02
Internationals: England U16, U17, U18, U20.
2019–20 Nottingham F   8   0
2020–21 Nottingham F   24   3
2021–22 Nottingham F   23   1
2022–23 Nottingham F   1   0
2022–23 *Sheffield Wed*   9   1   9   1
2023–24 Nottingham F   0   0
2023–24 *Kortrijk*   10   0   10   0
2023–24 *Port Vale*   10   0   10   0
2024–25 Nottingham F   0   0   56   4

MILENKOVIC, Nikola (D)   302 22
H: 6 5   W: 14 02   b.Belgrade 12-10-97
Internationals: Serbia U21, Full caps.
2015–16 Partizan Belgrade   4   1
2015–16 *Teleoptik*   13   0   13   0
2016–17 Partizan Belgrade   32   2   36   3
2017–18 Fiorentina   16   0
2018–19 Fiorentina   34   3
2019–20 Fiorentina   37   5
2020–21 Fiorentina   34   3
2021–22 Fiorentina   34   1
2022–23 Fiorentina   27   2
2023–24 Fiorentina   34   0   216 14
2024–25 Nottingham F   37   5   37   5

MORATO, Felipe (D)   73   1
H: 6 4   W: 13 12   b.Francisco Morato 30-6-01
2019–20 Benfica   0   0
2020–21 Benfica   2   0
2021–22 Benfica   14   0
2022–23 Benfica   9   1
2023–24 Benfica   21   0
2024–25 Benfica   1   0   47   1
2024–25 Nottingham F   26   0   26   0

MOREIRA, Eric (F)   3   0
H: 6 1   W: 11 07   b.Hamburg 3-5-06
Internationals: Germany U16, U17.
2023–24 *St Pauli*   1   0   1   0
2024–25 Nottingham F   2   0   2   0

MURILLO, dos Santos (D)   81   2
H: 6 0   W: 11 11   b.Sao Paulo 4-7-02
Internationals: Brazil Full caps.
2023   Corinthians   13   0   13   0
2023–24 Nottingham F   32   0
2024–25 Nottingham F   36   2   68   2

NORKETT, Manni (F)   5   1
H: 5 11   W: 11 11   b.Nottingham 30-10-04
2021–22 Manchester U   0   0
2022–23 Manchester U   0   0
2023–24 Nottingham F   0   0
2024–25 Nottingham F   0   0
2024–25 *Cheltenham T*   5   1   5   1

O'BRIEN, Lewis (M)   242 15
H: 5 8   W: 9 13   b.Colchester 14-10-98
2017–18 Huddersfield T   0   0
2018–19 Huddersfield T   0   0
2018–19 *Bradford C*   40   4   40   4
2019–20 Huddersfield T   38   2
2020–21 Huddersfield T   43   3   123   8
2021–22 Huddersfield T   43   3
2022–23 Nottingham F   13   1
2023   DC United   14   1   14   1
2023–24 Nottingham F   0   0
2023–24 *Middlesbrough*   23   0   23   0
2024   Los Angeles   13   0   13   0
2024–25 Nottingham F   0   0   13   1
2024–25 *Swansea C*   16   1   16   1

OMOBAMIDELE, Andrew (D)   71   2
H: 6 2   W: 11 11   b.Dublin 23-6-02
Internationals: Republic of Ireland U17, U19, U21, Full caps.
2019–20 Norwich C   0   0

2020–21 Norwich C   9   0
2021–22 Norwich C   5   1
2022–23 Norwich C   34   1
2023–24 Norwich C   2   0   50   2
2023–24 Nottingham F   11   0
2024–25 Nottingham F   0   0   11   0
2024–25 *Strasbourg*   10   0   10   0

PERRY, Benjamin (M)   17   0
H: 6 0   b. 11-10-04
2023–24 Nottingham F   0   0
2024–25 Nottingham F   0   0
2024–25 *Northampton T*   17   0   17   0

RICHARDS, Omar (D)   140   2
H: 6 1   W: 10 12   b.London 15-2-98
Internationals: England U21.
2017–18 Reading   13   2
2018–19 Reading   10   0
2019–20 Reading   28   0
2020–21 Reading   41   0   92   2
2021–22 Bayern Munich   12   0   12   0
2022–23 Nottingham F   0   0
2023–24 Nottingham F   0   0
2023–24 *Olympiacos*   10   0   10   0
2024–25 Nottingham F   0   0
2024–25 *Rio Ave*   26   0   26   0

SANGARE, Ibrahim (M)   199 11
H: 6 3   W: 12 02   b.Abidjan 2-12-97
Internationals: Ivory Coast U20, U23, Full caps.
From Denguele.
2016–17 Toulouse   5   0
2017–18 Toulouse   20   1
2018–19 Toulouse   28   1
2019–20 Toulouse   25   0
2020–21 Toulouse   2   0   80   2
2020–21 PSV Eindhoven   29   1
2021–22 PSV Eindhoven   29   3
2022–23 PSV Eindhoven   29   5
2023–24 PSV Eindhoven   2   0   89   9
2023–24 Nottingham F   17   0
2024–25 Nottingham F   13   0   30   0

SELS, Matz (G)   360   0
H: 6 2   W: 11 11   b.Lint 26-2-92
Internationals: Belgium U17, U18, U19, U21, Full caps.
2010–11 Lierse   1   0
2011–12 Lierse   0   0
2012–13 Lierse   30   0
2013–14 Lierse   0   0   31   0
2013–14 Gent   9   0
2014–15 Gent   30   0
2015–16 Gent   30   0   69   0
2016–17 Newcastle U   9   0
2017–18 Newcastle U   0   0   9   0
2017–18 *Anderlecht*   32   0   32   0
2018–19 Strasbourg   37   0
2019–20 Strasbourg   27   0
2020–21 Strasbourg   6   0
2021–22 Strasbourg   37   0
2022–23 Strasbourg   38   0
2023–24 Strasbourg   20   0   165   0
2023–24 Nottingham F   16   0
2024–25 Nottingham F   38   0   54   0

SOSA, Ramon (M)   159 27
H: 5 10   W: 11 09   b.Maracana 31-8-99
Internationals: Paraguay Full caps.
2020   River Plate   29   4   29   4
2021   Olimpia   24   2   24   2
2022   Gimasia La Plata   39   6   39   6
2023   Talleres   32   8
2024   Talleres   16   6   48 14
2024–25 Nottingham F   19   1   19   1

TAYLOR, Dale (F)   105 21
H: 6 1   W: 11 03   b.Belfast 12-12-03
Internationals: Northern Ireland U17, U21, Full caps.
From Linfield.
2020–21 Nottingham F   0   0
2021–22 Nottingham F   0   0
2022–23 Nottingham F   0   0
2022–23 *Burton Alb*   20   5   20   5
2023–24 Nottingham F   0   0
2023–24 *Wycombe W*   42   5   42   5
2024–25 Nottingham F   0   0
2024–25 *Wigan Ath*   43 11   43 11

TOFFOLO, Harry (D)   287 17
H: 6 0   W: 11 03   b.Welwyn Garden City 19-8-95
Internationals: England U18, U19, U20.
2014–15 Norwich C   0   0
2014–15 *Swindon T*   28   1   28   1
2015–16 Norwich C   0   0
2015–16 *Rotherham U*   7   0   7   0
2015–16 *Peterborough U*   7   0   7   0
2016–17 Norwich C   0   0
2016–17 *Scunthorpe U*   22   2   22   2
2017–18 Norwich C   0   0
2017–18 *Doncaster R*   13   0   13   0
2017–18 Millwall   0   0
2018–19 Lincoln C   46   3

2019–20	Lincoln C	26	1	72	4
2019–20	Huddersfield T	19	1		
2020–21	Huddersfield T	31	2		
2021–22	Huddersfield T	42	6	92	9
2022–23	Nottingham F	19	0		
2023–24	Nottingham F	23	1		
2024–25	Nottingham F	4	0	46	1

TURNER, Matt (G)   153 0
H: 6 3 W: 12 06 b.Park Ridge, New Jersey 24-6-94
Internationals: USA Full caps.

2016	*New England Revolution*	0	0		
2016	*Richmond Kickers*	7	0		
2017	*New England Revolution*	0	0		
2017	*Richmond Kickers*	20	0	27	0
2018	*New England Revolution*	27	0		
2019	*New England Revolution*	21	0		
2020	*New England Revolution*	27	0		
2021	*New England Revolution*	29	0		
2022	*New England Revolution*	5	0	109	0
2022–23	Arsenal	0	0		
2023–24	Nottingham F	17	0		
2024–25	Nottingham F	0	0	17	0
2024–25	*Crystal Palace*	0	0		

WILLIAMS, Neco (D)   119 4
H: 5 10 W: 9 06 b.Wrexham 13-4-01
Internationals: Wales U19, Full caps.

2019–20	Liverpool	6	0		
2020–21	Liverpool	6	0		
2021–22	Liverpool	1	0	13	0
2021–22	Fulham	14	2	14	2
2022–23	Nottingham F	31	1		
2023–24	Nottingham F	26	0		
2024–25	Nottingham F	35	1	92	2

WOOD, Chris (F)   515 175
H: 6 3 W: 14 12 b.Auckland 7-12-91
Internationals: New Zealand U17, U23, Full caps.
From Waikato.

2008–09	WBA	2	0		
2009–10	WBA	18	1		
2010–11	WBA	1	0		
2010–11	*Barnsley*	7	0	7	0
2010–11	*Brighton & HA*	29	8	29	8
2011–12	WBA	0	0		
2011–12	*Birmingham C*	23	9	23	9
2011–12	*Bristol C*	19	3	19	3
2012–13	WBA	0	0	21	1
2012–13	*Millwall*	19	11	19	11
2012–13	Leicester C	20	9		
2013–14	Leicester C	26	4		
2014–15	Leicester C	7	1	53	14
2014–15	*Ipswich T*	8	0	8	0
2015–16	Leeds U	36	13		
2016–17	Leeds U	44	27		
2017–18	Leeds U	3	1	83	41
2017–18	Burnley	24	10		
2018–19	Burnley	38	10		
2019–20	Burnley	32	14		
2020–21	Burnley	33	12		
2021–22	Burnley	17	3	144	49
2021–22	Newcastle U	17	2		
2022–23	Newcastle U	18	2	35	4
2022–23	*Nottingham F*	7	1		
2023–24	Nottingham F	31	14		
2024–25	Nottingham F	36	20	74	35

YATES, Ryan (M)   269 22
H: 6 3 W: 12 02 b.Nottingham 21-11-97

2016–17	Nottingham F	0	0		
2016–17	*Shrewsbury T*	12	0	12	0
2017–18	Nottingham F	0	0		
2017–18	*Notts Co*	25	3	25	3
2017–18	*Scunthorpe U*	16	2	16	2
2018–19	Nottingham F	16	1		
2019–20	Nottingham F	27	3		
2020–21	Nottingham F	34	2		
2021–22	Nottingham F	43	8		
2022–23	Nottingham F	26	0		
2023–24	Nottingham F	35	1		
2024–25	Nottingham F	35	2	216	17

Players retained or with offer of contract
Anisjko, Danny Brian Ambato; Berry, Adam Evan; Blake, Zyan Julius; Bott, Aaron Charlie; Bradshaw, Alfie William; Broomes, Ethan Thomas; Cahill, Shae Lou Tim; Daly, Cormac; Davies, Isaac Tiger; Hammond, Benjamin George; Hanks, Justin Thomas; McAdam, Kyle James; Modupe, David Dennis Ayodeji; Murray-Jones, George David; Newton, Jamie Christopher; Ngatang Djamna, Frank Evans; Powell, Jayden Anthony; Powell, Joshua Alan; Sinclair, James; Smith, Fuad Ayorinde; Stamenic, Marko Seufatu Nikola; Thompson, Jack Ethan; Whitehall, Archie Harry Thomas.

Scholars
Boulter, Evan James; Brandy, Taeneal Riquelme; Carrion Whiteley, Jonathan; Clarke Kristian Takura; Hamilton, Scott Joseph; Sanneh, Buba; Smith, Zac Alan; Thompson, Will Iain; Willows, Jordan Scott; Willows, Keehan Martyn.

NOTTS CO (62)

ADIEFEH, Daniel (M)   0 0

2024–25	Notts Co	0	0

AUSTIN, Sam (F)   68 5
H: 6 0 W: 11 00 b.Stourbridge 19-12-96

2014–15	Burton Alb	1	0		
2015–16	Burton Alb	0	0	1	0

From Kidderminster H, Notts Co.

2023–24	Notts Co	44	4		
2024–25	Notts Co	23	1	67	5

AVES, Archie (D)   0 0

2024–25	Notts Co	0	0

BASS, Alex (G)   123 0
H: 6 2 W: 11 00 b.Southampton 1-4-98

2014–15	Portsmouth	0	0		
2015–16	Portsmouth	0	0		
2016–17	Portsmouth	0	0		
2017–18	Portsmouth	1	0		
2018–19	Portsmouth	0	0		
2019–20	Portsmouth	15	0		
2020–21	Portsmouth	0	0		
2020–21	*Southend U*	1	0	1	0
2021–22	Portsmouth	2	0	18	0
2021–22	*Bradford C*	21	0	21	0
2022–23	Sunderland	0	0		
2023–24	Sunderland	0	0		
2023–24	*AFC Wimbledon*	44	0	44	0
2024–25	Notts Co	39	0	39	0

BEDEAU, Jacob (D)   200 4
H: 6 0 W: 12 04 b.Waltham Forest 24-12-99
Internationals: Grenada Full caps.

2016–17	Bury	7	0	7	0
2017–18	Aston Villa	0	0		
2018–19	Aston Villa	0	0		
2019–20	Scunthorpe U	11	1		
2020–21	Scunthorpe U	34	1	45	2
2021–22	Burnley	0	0		
2021–22	*Morecambe*	22	0		
2022–23	Morecambe	39	0		
2023–24	Morecambe	43	2	104	2
2024–25	Notts Co	44	0	44	0

CAMERON, Kyle (D)   107 3
H: 6 3 W: 12 00 b.Hexham 15-1-97
Internationals: England U16. Scotland U17, U19, U21.

2015–16	Newcastle U	0	0		
2015–16	*York C*	18	1	18	1
2016–17	Newcastle U	0	0		
2016–17	*Newport Co*	6	0	6	0
2017–18	Newcastle U	0	0		
2017–18	*Queen of the South*	8	0	8	0

From Torquay U, Notts Co.

2023–24	Notts Co	43	1		
2024–25	Notts Co	0	0	43	1
2024–25	*St Johnstone*	15	0	15	0
2024–25	*Barrow*	17	1	17	1

CHICKSEN, Adam (D)   215 3
H: 5 8 W: 11 09 b.Milton Keynes 27-9-91
Internationals: Zimbabwe Full caps.

2008–09	Milton Keynes D	1	0		
2009–10	Milton Keynes D	6	0		
2010–11	Milton Keynes D	14	0		
2011–12	Milton Keynes D	20	0		
2011–12	*Leyton Orient*	3	0		
2012–13	Milton Keynes D	32	2		
2013–14	Milton Keynes D	0	0	73	2
2013–14	Brighton & HA	1	0		
2014–15	Brighton & HA	5	0		
2014–15	*Gillingham*	3	0		
2014–15	*Fleetwood T*	13	0	13	0
2015–16	Brighton & HA	1	0	7	0
2015–16	*Leyton Orient*	6	0	9	0
2015–16	*Gillingham*	6	0	9	0
2016–17	Charlton Ath	21	1	21	1
2017–18	Bradford C	18	0		
2018–19	Bradford C	28	0	46	0
2019–20	Bolton W	16	0	16	0

From Notts Co.

2023–24	Notts Co	19	0		
2024–25	Notts Co	2	0	21	0

CISSE, Cassius (M)   0 0
b.6-3-06

2024–25	Notts Co	0	0

CISSE, Madou (M)   3 0
H: 5 7 W: 10 06 b.21-4-05

2023–24	Notts Co	1	0		
2024–25	Notts Co	2	0	3	0

COONEY, Kieran (D)   0 0
H: 5 10 b.Birmingham 20-1-05
Internationals: Saint Kitts and Nevis Full caps.

2024–25	Notts Co	0	0

CUNDY, Robbie (D)   81 3
H: 6 2 W: 12 13 b.Oxford 30-5-97

2014–15	Oxford U	0	0		
2015–16	Oxford U	0	0		
2016–17	Oxford U	0	0		

From Gloucester C.

2019–20	Bristol C	0	0		
2020–21	Bristol C	0	0		
2020–21	*Cambridge U*	17	0	17	0
2020–21	*Gillingham*	18	1	18	1
2021–22	Bristol C	14	0	14	0
2022–23	Barnsley	25	2		
2023–24	Barnsley	0	0	25	2
2024–25	Notts Co	7	0	7	0

DENMAN, Zac (D)   0 0

2024–25	Notts Co	0	0

EDWARDS, Curtis (M)   176 20
H: 6 0 W: 11 00 b.Middlesbrough 12-1-94

2011–12	Middlesbrough	0	0		

From Middlesbrough, Darlington, Thornaby, Spennymoor T, Ytterhogdals.

2016	Ostersund	12	3		
2017	Ostersund	24	3		
2018	Ostersund	28	7		
2019	Ostersund	12	1	76	14
2020	Djurgarden	25	3		
2021	Djurgarden	7	0	32	3
2022	Stabaek	27	1		
2023	Stabaek	25	2	52	3
2024–25	Notts Co	16	0	16	0

EMMANUEL, Daniel (F)   0 0

2024–25	Notts Co	0	0

FEARON, Ashaiah (D)   0 0
H: 5 6 b.14-2-04

2023–24	Notts Co	0	0
2024–25	Notts Co	0	0

GILL, Charlie (F)   0 0
H: 5 9 W: 11 03 b.15-9-05

2023–24	Notts Co	0	0
2024–25	Notts Co	0	0

GORDON, Kellan (D)   183 8
H: 5 10 W: 12 00 b.Burton 25-12-97
From Stoke C.

2017–18	Derby Co	0	0		
2017–18	*Swindon T*	26	3	26	3
2018–19	Derby Co	0	0		
2018–19	*Lincoln C*	6	2		
2019–20	Lincoln C	0	0	6	2
2019–20	*Mansfield T*	18	1		
2020–21	Mansfield T	32	0		
2021–22	Mansfield T	7	0		
2022–23	Mansfield T	16	1	73	2
2022–23	Crawley T	15	0		
2023–24	Crawley T	33	1	48	1
2024–25	Notts Co	30	0	30	0

GRANT, Conor (M)   137 11
H: 6 1 W: 11 00 b.Dublin 23-7-01
Internationals: Republic of Ireland U17, U19, U21.
From Shamrock R.

2019–20	Sheffield Wed	0	0		
2020–21	Sheffield Wed	0	0		
2020–21	*Rochdale*	20	1		
2021–22	Sheffield Wed	0	0		
2021–22	*Rochdale*	33	4	53	5
2022–23	Milton Keynes D	29	1		
2023–24	Milton Keynes D	11	0	40	1
2023–24	*Barnsley*	12	1	12	1
2024–25	Notts Co	32	4	32	4

HINCHY, Jack (M)   37 1
H: 5 11 W: 11 00 b.Swindon 30-1-03
From Stockport Co.

2022–23	Brighton & HA	0	0		
2023–24	Brighton & HA	0	0		
2023–24	*Shrewsbury T*	12	0	12	0
2024–25	Notts Co	25	1	25	1

JARVIS, William (F)   67 13
H: 6 1 W: 14 09 b.York 17-12-02

2021–22	Hull C	1	0		
2022–23	Hull C	2	0		
2023	*Shelbourne*	12	3		
2024	*Shelbourne*	25	8	37	11
2024–25	Hull C	6	0	9	0
2024–25	Notts Co	21	2	21	2

JATTA, Alassana (F)   161 52
H: 6 4 W: 11 11 b.Sukuta 12-1-99
Internationals: Gambia Full caps.

2019–20	Viborg	24	7		
2019–20	*Paide*	17	13	17	13
2020–21	Viborg	11	2		
2021–22	Viborg	26	3		
2022–23	Viborg	21	2		
2023–24	Viborg	13	1	95	15
2023–24	Notts Co	10	5		
2024–25	Notts Co	39	19	49	24

JONES, Jodi (M)   **179 22**
H: 5 10 W: 11 07 b.Bow 22-10-97
Internationals: Malta Full caps.
2014–15 Dagenham & Red 8 1
2015–16 Dagenham & Red 27 3 35 4
2015–16 Coventry C 6 0
2016–17 Coventry C 34 1
2017–18 Coventry C 19 5
2018–19 Coventry C 8 1
2019–20 Coventry C 0 0
2020–21 Coventry C 0 0
2021–22 Coventry C 9 0 76 7
2022–23 Oxford U 5 0 5 0
2023–24 Notts Co 43 6
2024–25 Notts Co 20 5 63 11

MACARI, Lewis (D)   **87 2**
H: 6 0 W: 12 13 b.8-2-02
Internationals: Scotland U18, U19.
2020–21 Stoke C 0 0
2021–22 Stoke C 0 0
2022 *Dundalk* 34 1 34 1
2022–23 Stoke C 0 0
2023–24 Notts Co 22 1
2024–25 Notts Co 31 0 53 1

McDONALD, Rod (D)   **239 6**
H: 6 3 W: 12 13 b.Liverpool 11-4-92
2009–10 Stoke C 0 0
2010–11 Oldham Ath 0 0
From Colwyn Bay, Hereford U, AFC Telford U.
2015–16 Northampton T 23 3
2016–17 Northampton T 7 0 30 3
2016–17 Coventry C 0 0
2017–18 Coventry C 37 0 37 0
2018–19 AFC Wimbledon 23 0
2019–20 AFC Wimbledon 15 0 38 0
2020–21 Carlisle U 29 0
2021–22 Carlisle U 31 1 60 1
2022–23 Crewe Alex 33 2 33 2
2023–24 Harrogate T 23 0 23 0
2024–25 Notts Co 18 0 18 0

McGOLDRICK, David (F)   **576 163**
H: 6 0 W: 11 09 b.Nottingham 29-11-87
Internationals: Republic of Ireland Full caps.
2003–04 Notts Co 4 0
2004–05 Notts Co 0 0
2005–06 Southampton 1 0
2005–06 *Notts Co* 6 0
2006–07 Southampton 9 0
2006–07 Bournemouth 12 6 12 6
2007–08 Southampton 8 0
2007–08 Port Vale 17 2 17 2
2008–09 Southampton 46 12 64 12
2009–10 Nottingham F 33 3
2010–11 Nottingham F 21 5
2011–12 Nottingham F 9 0
2011–12 *Sheffield Wed* 4 1 4 1
2012–13 Nottingham F 0 0 63 8
2012–13 *Coventry C* 22 16 22 16
2012–13 Ipswich T 13 4
2013–14 Ipswich T 31 14
2014–15 Ipswich T 26 7
2015–16 Ipswich T 24 4
2016–17 Ipswich T 30 5
2017–18 Ipswich T 22 6 146 40
2018–19 Sheffield U 45 15
2019–20 Sheffield U 28 2
2020–21 Sheffield U 35 8
2021–22 Sheffield U 19 2 127 27
2022–23 Derby Co 39 22 39 22
2023–24 Notts Co 37 12
2024–25 Notts Co 35 17 82 29

MORIAS, Junior (F)   **143 19**
H: 5 8 W: 10 10 b.Kingston 4-7-95
2012–13 Wycombe W 19 0
2013–14 Wycombe W 9 0
2014–15 Wycombe W 0 0 28 0
From Boreham Wood, Whitehawk, St Albans C.
2016–17 Peterborough U 20 4
2017–18 Peterborough U 25 6 45 10
2018–19 Northampton T 19 6
2019–20 Northampton T 2 0 21 6
2019–20 St Mirren 26 2
2020–21 St Mirren 14 0 40 2
From King's Lynn T, Dagenham & Red, Notts Co.
2023–24 Notts Co 9 1
2024–25 Notts Co 0 0 9 1

MUIR, Kameron (M)   **0 0**
b.23-8-09
2024–25 Notts Co 0 0

NESS, Lucas (D)   **36 0**
H: 6 3 W: 12 08 b.Kingston upon Thames 7-2-02
From Metropolitan Police.
2021–22 Charlton Ath 0 0
2022–23 Charlton Ath 15 0

2023–24 Charlton Ath 14 0 29 0
2024–25 Notts Co 7 0 7 0

NYIRENDA, Themba (M)   **0 0**
b.16-7-07
2024–25 Notts Co 0 0

PALMER, Matthew (M)   **286 8**
H: 5 10 W: 12 06 b.Derby 1-8-93
Internationals: England C.
2012–13 Burton Alb 2 0
2013–14 Burton Alb 40 0
2014–15 Burton Alb 33 4
2015–16 Burton Alb 14 0
2015–16 *Oldham Ath* 14 1 14 1
2016–17 Burton Alb 36 1
2017–18 Burton Alb 11 1 136 6
2017–18 Rotherham U 14 0
2018–19 Rotherham U 10 0
2019–20 Rotherham U 0 0 24 0
2019–20 *Bradford C* 18 0 18 0
2019–20 Swindon U 1 0
2020–21 Swindon T 24 1 25 1
2020–21 *Wigan Ath* 10 0 10 0
From Notts Co.
2023–24 Notts Co 16 0
2024–25 Notts Co 43 0 59 0

PEROTT, Milai (D)   **0 0**
b.12-4-04
2024–25 Notts Co 0 0

PLATT, Matt (D)   **171 8**
H: 6 0 W: 10 08 b.Knowsley 3-10-97
2016–17 Blackburn R 0 0
2017–18 Blackburn R 0 0
2018–19 Blackburn R 0 0
2018–19 *Accrington S* 0 0
2019–20 Blackburn R 0 0
2020–21 Barrow 24 2
2021–22 Barrow 28 2 52 4
2022–23 Bradford C 39 0
2023–24 Bradford C 35 2 74 2
2024–25 Notts Co 45 2 45 2

REYNOLDS, Ryley (F)   **0 0**
H: 5 11 b.Birmingham 30-8-05
2024–25 Notts Co 0 0

ROBERTSON, Scott (M)   **99 2**
H: 5 8 W: 12 02 b.Dundee 27-7-01
2019–20 Celtic 0 0
2019–20 Celtic 0 0
2020–21 Celtic 0 0
2020–21 Gillingham 15 0 15 0
2020–21 Doncaster R 15 0
2021–22 Doncaster R 0 0 15 0
2021–22 Celtic 0 0
2021–22 Crewe Alex 20 1 20 1
2022–23 Fleetwood T 12 0
2023–24 Fleetwood T 13 0 25 0
2023–24 Notts Co 17 0
2024–25 Notts Co 7 1 24 1

SANDERSON, James (D)   **2 0**
H: 5 9 W: 11 00 b.30-11-06
2023–24 Notts Co 2 0
2024–25 Notts Co 0 0 2 0

SLOCOMBE, Sam (G)   **219 0**
H: 6 0 W: 11 11 b.Scunthorpe 5-6-88
2008–09 Scunthorpe U 0 0
2009–10 Scunthorpe U 1 0
2010–11 Scunthorpe U 2 0
2011–12 Scunthorpe U 28 0
2012–13 Scunthorpe U 29 0
2013–14 Scunthorpe U 46 0
2014–15 Scunthorpe U 9 0 115 0
2015–16 Oxford U 23 0 23 0
2016–17 Blackpool 34 0 34 0
2017–18 Bristol R 23 0
2018–19 Bristol R 2 0 25 0
2018–19 Lincoln C 0 0
From Notts Co.
2023–24 Notts Co 14 0
2024–25 Notts Co 8 0 22 0

STONE, Aiden (G)   **86 0**
H: 6 1 W: 11 11 b.Stafford 20-7-99
Internationals: England U18.
2018–19 Burnley 0 0
2019–20 Mansfield T 3 0
2020–21 Mansfield T 22 0 25 0
2021–22 Port Vale 18 0
2022–23 Port Vale 20 0 38 0
2023–24 Notts Co 23 0
2024–25 Notts Co 23 0 23 0
Transferred to Yeovil T, February 2025.

TRAORE, Mai (D)   **155 51**
H: 6 1 b.Conakry 24-11-99
2018 Vasalund 24 11
2019 Vasalund 18 2
2020 Vasalund 29 23
2021 Vasalund 10 5 81 41
2021 Viking 10 0
2022 Viking 23 4
2023 Viking 0 0 33 4

2023 *OH Leuven* 1 0 1 0
2023 *Tromso* 15 4 15 4
2024 *Fredrikstad* 13 2 13 2
2024–25 Notts Co 12 0 12 0

TSAROULLA, Nicholas (D)   **153 11**
H: 5 10 W: 11 00 b.Bristol 29-3-99
Internationals: Cyprus U21.
2020–21 Crawley T 17 0
2021–22 Crawley T 27 3
2022–23 Crawley T 28 2
2023–24 Crawley T 43 4 115 9
2024–25 Notts Co 38 2 38 2

WHITAKER, Charlie (M)   **20 4**
b.16-9-03
2020–21 Everton 0 0
2021–22 Everton 0 0
2022–23 Everton 0 0
2023–24 Everton 0 0
2024–25 Notts Co 20 4 20 4

Players retained or with offer of contract
Devereux, Frankie John; Foxe, Carter Alexander; Robinson, Theo Henry Felix.

Scholars
Baker, Mylo William; Bickley, Owen Jack; Cisse, Cassius Clay; Denman, Zac Alfie Scott; Emmanuel, Daniel Tosin; Gill, Charlie; Goodwin, Alfie Paul; Hazard, Harrison Stuart; Hipkiss, Stanley George; Martin, Ellis George; Nyirenda, Themba Precious; Reaney, Elias Scott; Rice, Alfie Robert Adebowale; Rowe, Adam William; Saleh, Sudais Suleiman; Smart, Isaac Thomas; Szczesny, Nikodem Mikolaj.

OXFORD U (63)

BENNETT, Joe (D)   **377 8**
H: 5 10 W: 11 09 b.Rochdale 28-3-90
Internationals: England U19, U20, U21.
2008–09 Middlesbrough 1 0
2009–10 Middlesbrough 12 0
2010–11 Middlesbrough 31 0
2011–12 Middlesbrough 41 1
2012–13 Middlesbrough 0 0 85 1
2012–13 Aston Villa 25 0
2013–14 Aston Villa 5 0
2014–15 Aston Villa 0 0
2014–15 Brighton & HA 41 1 41 1
2015–16 Aston Villa 0 0
2015–16 Bournemouth 0 0
2015–16 Sheffield Wed 3 0 3 0
2016–17 Aston Villa 0 0 30 0
2016–17 Cardiff C 24 3
2017–18 Cardiff C 38 1
2018–19 Cardiff C 30 0
2019–20 Cardiff C 44 0
2020–21 Cardiff C 28 1 164 5
2021–22 Wigan Ath 11 1
2022–23 Wigan Ath 15 0 26 1
2023–24 Oxford U 16 0
2024–25 Oxford U 12 0 28 0

BRADSHAW, Tom (F)   **449 112**
H: 5 10 W: 11 03 b.Shrewsbury 27-7-92
Internationals: Wales U19, U21, Full caps.
From Aberystwyth T.
2009–10 Shrewsbury T 6 3
2010–11 Shrewsbury T 26 6
2011–12 Shrewsbury T 8 1
2012–13 Shrewsbury T 21 0
2013–14 Shrewsbury T 28 7 89 17
2014–15 Walsall 29 17
2015–16 Walsall 41 17 70 34
2016–17 Barnsley 42 8
2017–18 Barnsley 39 9
2018–19 Barnsley 4 1 85 18
2018–19 *Millwall* 10 0
2019–20 Millwall 45 8
2020–21 Millwall 29 4
2021–22 Millwall 24 9
2022–23 Millwall 41 17
2023–24 Millwall 34 4
2024–25 Millwall 11 1 194 43
2024–25 Oxford U 11 0 11 0

BRANNAGAN, Cameron (M)   **291 47**
H: 5 11 W: 11 03 b.Manchester 9-5-96
Internationals: England U18, U20.
2013–14 Liverpool 0 0
2014–15 Liverpool 0 0
2015–16 Liverpool 3 0
2016–17 Liverpool 0 0
2016–17 *Fleetwood T* 13 0 13 0
2017–18 Liverpool 0 0 3 0
2017–18 Oxford U 12 0
2018–19 Oxford U 41 3
2019–20 Oxford U 30 5
2020–21 Oxford U 31 1
2021–22 Oxford U 41 14
2022–23 Oxford U 44 9

2023–24	Oxford U	43	12	
2024–25	Oxford U	33	3	**275 47**

BROWN, Ciaran (D) **191 13**
H: 6 1 W: 12 00 b.Hillingdon 14-1-98
Internationals: Northern Ireland U21, Full caps.
From Bedfont Sports, Wealdstone.

2018–19	Cardiff C	0	0	
2018–19	Livingston	6	0	
2019–20	Livingston	0	0	
2019–20	Livingston	9	0	
2020–21	Cardiff C	12	0	
2020–21	Livingston	16	1	**31 1**
2021–22	Oxford U	5	0	**17 0**
2021–22	Oxford U	13	1	
2022–23	Oxford U	44	2	
2023–24	Oxford U	45	5	
2024–25	Oxford U	41	4	**143 12**

BURTON, Kasway (F) **0 0**

2023–24	Oxford U	0	0	
2024–25	Oxford U	0	0	

CUMMING, Jamie (G) **195 0**
H: 6 1 W: 12 06 b.Winchester 4-9-99
Internationals: England U17, U19.

2018–19	Chelsea	0	0	
2019–20	Chelsea	0	0	
2020–21	Stevenage	41	0	**41 0**
2021–22	Chelsea	0	0	
2021–22	Gillingham	22	0	**22 0**
2021–22	Milton Keynes D	21	0	
2022–23	Chelsea	0	0	
2022–23	Milton Keynes D	46	0	**67 0**
2023–24	Chelsea	0	0	
2023–24	Oxford U	20	0	
2024–25	Oxford U	45	0	**65 0**

CURRIE, Jack (D) **116 2**
H: 5 9 W: 10 08 b.Kingston upon Thames 16-12-01

2020–21	AFC Wimbledon	0	0	
2021–22	AFC Wimbledon	0	0	
2022–23	AFC Wimbledon	41	1	
2023–24	AFC Wimbledon	39	1	**80 2**
2024–25	Oxford U	0	0	
2024–25	Leyton Orient	36	0	**36 0**

DALE, Owen (F) **216 20**
H: 5 9 W: 10 03 b.Warrington 1-11-98

2016–17	Crewe Alex	0	0	
2017–18	Crewe Alex	4	0	
2018–19	Crewe Alex	16	1	
2019–20	Crewe Alex	27	0	
2020–21	Crewe Alex	43	11	
2021–22	Crewe Alex	2	0	**92 12**
2021–22	Blackpool	15	2	
2022–23	Blackpool	0	0	
2022–23	Portsmouth	43	2	**43 2**
2023–24	Blackpool	23	2	**38 4**
2023–24	Oxford U	15	1	
2024–25	Oxford U	11	0	**26 1**
2024–25	Wigan Ath	17	1	**17 1**

DEMBELE, Siriki (M) **255 40**
H: 5 7 W: 10 08 b.Ivory Coast 7-9-96
From Dundee U, Ayr U.

2017–18	Grimsby T	36	4	**36 4**
2018–19	Peterborough U	38	5	
2019–20	Peterborough U	25	5	
2020–21	Peterborough U	42	11	
2021–22	Peterborough U	24	5	**129 26**
2021–22	Bournemouth	13	2	
2022–23	Bournemouth	6	0	**19 2**
2022–23	Auxerre	12	0	**12 0**
2023–24	Birmingham C	33	6	
2024–25	Birmingham C	1	0	**34 6**
2024–25	Oxford U	25	2	**25 2**

EASTWOOD, Simon (G) **290 0**
H: 6 2 W: 14 02 b.Luton 26-6-89
Internationals: England U18, U19.

2005–06	Huddersfield T	0	0	
2006–07	Huddersfield T	0	0	
2007–08	Huddersfield T	0	0	
2008–09	Huddersfield T	1	0	
2009–10	Huddersfield T	0	0	**1 0**
2009–10	Bradford C	22	0	**22 0**
2010–11	Oxford U	0	0	
From FC Halifax T.				
2012–13	Portsmouth	27	0	**27 0**
2013–14	Blackburn R	7	0	
2014–15	Blackburn R	6	0	
2015–16	Blackburn R	0	0	**13 0**
2016–17	Oxford U	46	0	
2017–18	Oxford U	46	0	
2018–19	Oxford U	34	0	
2019–20	Oxford U	29	0	
2020–21	Oxford U	13	0	
2021–22	Oxford U	14	0	
2022–23	Oxford U	43	0	
2023–24	Oxford U	2	0	
2024–25	Oxford U	0	0	**227 0**

EL MIZOUNI, Idris (M) **145 6**
H: 6 1 W: 11 09 b.Paris 26-9-00
Internationals: Tunisia U23, Tunisia Full caps.

2018–19	Ipswich T	4	0	
2019–20	Ipswich T	3	0	
2019–20	Cambridge U	7	1	
2020–21	Ipswich T	0	0	
2020–21	Cambridge U	11	0	**18 1**
2020–21	Grimsby T	6	0	**6 0**
2021–22	Ipswich T	5	0	
2022–23	Ipswich T	41	3	
2023–24	Ipswich T	0	0	**12 0**
2023–24	Leyton Orient	40	1	**81 4**
2024–25	Oxford U	28	1	**28 1**

FERDINAN, Marselino (M) **38 8**
H: 5 10 W: 10 08 b.Jakarta 9-9-04
Internationals: Indonesia U16, U20, U20, Full caps.

2021–22	Persebaya Surabaya	23	4	
2022–23	Persebaya Surabaya	7	3	**30 7**
2022–23	Deinze	4	1	
2023–24	Deinze	3	0	**7 1**
2024–25	Oxford U	1	0	**1 0**

FRANKLIN, George (M) **0 0**
b.9-9-04

2023–24	Oxford U	0	0	
2024–25	Oxford U	0	0	

GOLDING, James (D) **3 0**
b.Sutton 10-8-04
Internationals: Republic of Ireland U19.

2021–22	Oxford U	1	0	
2022–23	Oxford U	2	0	
2023–24	Oxford U	0	0	
2024–25	Oxford U	0	0	**3 0**

GOODRHAM, Tyler (M) **117 14**
H: 5 7 W: 9 06 b.High Wycombe 7-8-03

2019–20	Oxford U	0	0	
2020–21	Oxford U	0	0	
2021–22	Oxford U	0	0	
2022–23	Oxford U	36	3	
2023–24	Oxford U	40	8	
2024–25	Oxford U	41	3	**117 14**

GOODWIN, William (F) **55 8**
H: 6 1 b.Tarporley 7-5-02
From FC Chester.

2020–21	Stoke C	0	0	
2021–22	Stoke C	0	0	
2021–22	Hartlepool U	10	1	**10 1**
2022–23	Cheltenham T	12	0	
2023–24	Cheltenham T	16	6	**28 6**
2023–24	Oxford U	8	1	
2024–25	Oxford U	3	0	**11 1**
2024–25	Wigan Ath	6	0	**6 0**

GRIFFITHS, Louis (F) **0 0**
H: 5 9 W: 10 10 b. 3-9-07
Internationals: Wales U16, U17, U18.

2023–24	Oxford U	0	0	
2024–25	Oxford U	0	0	

HARRIS, Mark (F) **198 32**
H: 6 0 W: 11 11 b.Swansea 29-12-98
Internationals: Wales U17, U19, U20, U21, Wales Full caps.

2016–17	Cardiff C	2	0	
2017–18	Cardiff C	0	0	
2018–19	Cardiff C	0	0	
2018–19	Newport Co	16	2	**16 2**
2018–19	Port Vale	6	0	**6 0**
2019–20	Cardiff C	0	0	
2020–21	Cardiff C	16	3	
2021–22	Cardiff C	34	3	
2022–23	Cardiff C	35	3	**87 9**
2023–24	Oxford U	43	15	
2024–25	Oxford U	46	6	**89 21**

HELIK, Michal (D) **328 34**
H: 6 3 W: 12 08 b.Chorzow 9-9-95
Internationals: Poland Full caps.

2013–14	Ruch Chorzow	8	0	
2014–15	Ruch Chorzow	18	1	
2015–16	Ruch Chorzow	0	0	
2016–17	Ruch Chorzow	20	0	**46 1**
2017–18	Cracovia	32	8	
2018–19	Cracovia	32	0	
2019–20	Cracovia	23	1	
2020–21	Cracovia	0	0	**87 9**
2020–21	Barnsley	43	5	
2021–22	Barnsley	38	1	
2022–23	Barnsley	0	0	**81 6**
2022–23	Huddersfield T	36	2	
2023–24	Huddersfield T	41	9	
2024–25	Huddersfield T	17	2	**94 13**
2024–25	Oxford U	20	5	**20 5**

INGRAM, Matt (G) **258 0**
H: 6 3 W: 12 13 b.Croydon 18-12-93

2011–12	Wycombe W	0	0	
2012–13	Wycombe W	8	0	
2013–14	Wycombe W	46	0	
2014–15	Wycombe W	46	0	

2015–16	Wycombe W	24	0	
2015–16	QPR	4	0	
2016–17	QPR	0	0	
2017–18	Northampton T	20	0	**20 0**
2017–18	QPR	2	0	
2018–19	Wycombe W	1	0	**125 0**
2018–19	QPR	4	0	**10 0**
2019–20	Hull C	1	0	
2020–21	Hull C	38	0	
2021–22	Hull C	29	0	
2021–22	Luton T	2	0	**2 0**
2022–23	Hull C	22	0	
2023–24	Hull C	10	0	**100 0**
2024–25	Oxford U	1	0	**1 0**

KIOSO, Peter (D) **145 11**
H: 6 0 W: 11 00 b.Swords 15-8-99
Internationals: DR Congo Full caps.
From Milton Keynes D, Dunstable T, Hartlepool U.

2019–20	Luton T	1	0	
2020–21	Bolton W	13	3	**13 3**
2020–21	Luton T	0	0	
2020–21	Northampton T	21	3	**21 3**
2021–22	Luton T	16	0	**17 0**
2021–22	Milton Keynes D	18	4	**18 4**
2022–23	Rotherham U	10	0	
2023–24	Rotherham U	12	0	**22 0**
2023–24	Peterborough U	24	1	**24 1**
2024–25	Oxford U	30	0	**30 0**

LEIGH, Greg (D) **288 20**
H: 5 11 W: 11 07 b.Manchester 30-9-94
Internationals: England U19. Jamaica Full caps.

2013–14	Manchester C	0	0	
2014–15	Manchester C	0	0	
2014–15	Crewe Alex	38	1	**38 1**
2015–16	Bradford C	6	1	**6 1**
2016–17	Bury	45	1	
2017–18	Bury	41	1	**86 2**
2018–19	NAC Breda	16	1	
2019–20	NAC Breda	0	0	**16 1**
2019–20	Aberdeen	18	1	
2020–21	Aberdeen	8	0	**26 1**
2021–22	Morecambe	36	2	**36 2**
2022–23	Ipswich T	14	0	
2023–24	Ipswich T	1	0	**15 0**
2024–25	Oxford U	34	6	**65 12**

LONG, Sam (D) **218 14**
H: 5 11 W: 11 11 b.Oxford 16-1-95

2012–13	Oxford U	3	0	
2013–14	Oxford U	0	0	
2014–15	Oxford U	10	1	
2015–16	Oxford U	1	0	
2016–17	Oxford U	3	0	
2017–18	Oxford U	0	0	
2018–19	Oxford U	18	0	
2019–20	Oxford U	16	1	
2020–21	Oxford U	36	6	
2021–22	Oxford U	36	1	
2022–23	Oxford U	43	3	
2023–24	Oxford U	27	1	
2024–25	Oxford U	24	1	**218 14**

MARRIOTT, Monty (G) **0 0**
b. 24-8-06

2023–24	Oxford U	0	0	
2024–25	Oxford U	0	0	

McEACHRAN, Josh (D) **309 1**
H: 5 10 W: 10 03 b.Oxford 1-3-93
Internationals: England U16, U17, U19, U20, U21.

2010–11	Chelsea	9	0	
2011–12	Chelsea	2	0	
2011–12	Swansea C	4	0	**4 0**
2012–13	Chelsea	0	0	
2012–13	Middlesbrough	38	0	**38 0**
2013–14	Chelsea	0	0	
2013–14	Watford	7	0	**7 0**
2013–14	Wigan Ath	8	0	**8 0**
2014–15	Chelsea	0	0	**11 0**
2014–15	Vitesse	19	0	**19 0**
2015–16	Brentford	14	0	
2016–17	Brentford	27	0	
2017–18	Brentford	25	0	
2018–19	Brentford	24	1	**90 1**
2019–20	Birmingham C	8	0	
2020–21	Birmingham C	0	0	**8 0**
2021–22	Milton Keynes D	14	0	
2021–22	Milton Keynes D	35	0	
2022–23	Milton Keynes D	39	0	**88 0**
2023–24	Oxford U	24	0	
2024–25	Oxford U	12	0	**36 0**

McINTYRE, Richard (D) **0 0**
H: 6 0 b. 16-7-06

2023–24	Oxford U	0	0	
2024–25	Oxford U	0	0	

MILLS, Stanley (F) 32 2
H: 5 11 W: 11 00 b.Harrogate 25-10-03
From Leeds U.

Season	Club				
2022–23	Everton	0	0		
2023–24	Everton	0	0		
2023–24	Oxford U	21	1		
2024–25	Everton	0	0		
2024–25	Oxford U	11	1	32	2

MOORE, Elliott (D) 251 17
H: 6 5 W: 12 04 b.Leicester 16-3-97
Internationals: England U18, U20, U21.

2016–17	Leicester C	0	0		
2017–18	Leicester C	0	0		
2017–18	*OH Leuven*	24	2		
2018–19	Leicester C	0	0		
2018–19	*OH Leuven*	28	5	52	7
2019–20	Oxford U	20	1		
2020–21	Oxford U	46	5		
2021–22	Oxford U	31	1		
2022–23	Oxford U	37	1		
2023–24	Oxford U	39	1		
2024–25	Oxford U	26	1	199	10

NEGRU, Stephan (D) 51 1
H: 6 1 W: 11 09 b.Floresti 24-7-02

2022	*Shelbourne*	6	1	6	1
2022–23	Oxford U	2	0		
2023–24	Oxford U	13	0		
2024–25	Oxford U	0	0	15	0
2024–25	Salford C	30	0	30	0

O'DONKOR, Gatlin (F) 79 6
H: 5 10 W: 10 01 b.Reading 14-10-04

2021–22	Oxford U	0	0		
2022–23	Oxford U	29	2		
2023–24	Oxford U	20	0		
2024–25	Oxford U	1	0	51	2
2024–25	Bristol R	28	4	28	4

PHILLIPS, Matthew (M) 534 67
H: 6 0 W: 11 11 b.Aylesbury 13-3-91
Internationals: England U19, U20. Scotland Full caps.

2007–08	Wycombe W	2	0		
2008–09	Wycombe W	37	3		
2009–10	Wycombe W	36	5		
2010–11	Wycombe W	3	0	78	8
2010–11	Blackpool	27	1		
2011–12	Blackpool	33	7		
2011–12	*Sheffield U*	6	5	6	5
2012–13	Blackpool	34	4		
2013–14	Blackpool	0	0	94	12
2013–14	QPR	23	1		
2014–15	QPR	25	3		
2015–16	QPR	44	8	90	14
2016–17	WBA	27	4		
2017–18	WBA	30	2		
2018–19	WBA	30	5		
2019–20	WBA	39	7		
2020–21	WBA	33	2		
2021–22	WBA	28	3		
2022–23	WBA	26	3	238	28
2024–25	Oxford U	0	0	28	0

PLACHETA, Przemyslaw (M) 172 21
H: 5 10 W: 11 05 b.Lowicz 23-9-98
Internationals: Poland U18, U19, U20, U21, Full caps.

2017–18	Sonnenhof Grossaspach	2	0	2	0
2017–18	*Pogon Siedice*	11	2	11	2
2018–19	*Podbeskidzie*	23	6	23	6
2019–20	*Slask Wroclaw*	35	8	35	8
2020–21	Norwich C	26	1		
2021–22	Norwich C	12	0		
2022–23	Norwich C	0	0		
2022–23	*Birmingham C*	5	1	5	1
2023–24	Norwich C	16	0	54	1
2023–24	Swansea C	10	0	10	0
2024–25	Oxford U	32	3	32	3

RODRIGUES, Ruben (F) 133 29
H: 5 11 W: 12 04 b.Oliveira de Azemeis 2-8-96

2018–19	Den Bosch	6	0		
2018–19	*De Treffers*	17	4	17	4
2019–20	*Den Bosch*	27	12	33	12
From Notts Co.					
2023–24	Oxford U	44	9		
2024–25	Oxford U	39	4	83	13

ROMENY, Ole (F) 168 26
H: 6 1 W: 12 11 b.Nijmegen 20-6-00
Internationals: Netherlands U18, U19, U20. Indonesia Full caps.

2017–18	NEC	4	0		
2018–19	NEC	23	1		
2019–20	NEC	27	8		
2020–21	NEC	5	0		
2020–21	*Willem II*	11	0	11	0
2021–22	NEC	10	0	69	9
2021–22	Emmen	12	2		
2022–23	Emmen	33	11	45	13
2023–24	Utrecht	16	1		
2024–25	Utrecht	13	2	29	3
2024–25	Oxford U	14	1	14	1

SIBLEY, Louie (M) 179 16
H: 5 11 W: 11 09 b.Birmingham 1-9-01
Internationals: England U17, U18, U19, U20.

2019–20	Derby Co	11	5		
2020–21	Derby Co	30	1		
2021–22	Derby Co	26	1		
2022–23	Derby Co	42	3		
2023–24	Derby Co	38	3	147	13
2024–25	Oxford U	11	1	11	1
2024–25	*Rotherham U*	21	2	21	2

SNOWDEN, Leo (F) 0 0
b. 3-6-08

2023–24	Oxford U	0	0		
2024–25	Oxford U	0	0		

TER AVEST, Hidde (D) 239 6
H: 6 0 W: 11 09 b.Wierden 20-5-97
Internationals: Netherlands U16, U17, U18, U19, U20, U21.

2014–15	FC Twente	10	0		
2015–16	FC Twente	29	1		
2016–17	FC Twente	31	1		
2017–18	FC Twente	22	0	92	2
2018–19	Udinese	13	0		
2019–20	Udinese	20	0		
2020–21	Udinese	6	0	39	0
2020–21	Utrecht	18	2		
2021–22	Utrecht	26	1		
2022–23	Utrecht	20	0		
2023–24	Utrecht	23	0	87	3
2024–25	Oxford U	21	1	21	1

THORNILEY, Jordan (D) 141 1
H: 5 11 W: 10 01 b.Warrington 24-11-96
From Everton.

2016–17	Sheffield Wed	0	0		
2017–18	Sheffield Wed	11	0		
2017–18	*Accrington S*	14	0	14	0
2018–19	Sheffield Wed	20	0		
2019–20	Sheffield Wed	0	0	31	0
2019–20	Blackpool	2	0		
2020–21	Blackpool	19	0		
2021–22	Oxford U	21	0		
2021–22	Blackpool	14	0		
2022–23	Blackpool	30	1	65	1
2023–24	Oxford U	8	0		
2024–25	Oxford U	2	0	31	0

TOOK OXLEY, Zaide (M) 0 0
b.Oxford 4-5-06

2023–24	Oxford U	0	0		
2024–25	Oxford U	0	0		

VAULKS, Will (D) 459 37
H: 5 11 W: 11 11 b.Birkenhead 13-9-93
Internationals: Wales Full caps.

2012–13	Tranmere R	1	0		
2012–13	Falkirk	6	0		
2013–14	Falkirk	33	1		
2014–15	Falkirk	34	3		
2015–16	Falkirk	35	6	108	10
2016–17	Rotherham U	40	1		
2017–18	Rotherham U	44	5		
2018–19	Rotherham U	41	7	125	13
2019–20	Cardiff C	27	4		
2020–21	Cardiff C	42	5		
2021–22	Cardiff C	36	2	105	11
2022–23	Sheffield Wed	43	2		
2023–24	Sheffield Wed	34	0	77	2
2024–25	Oxford U	44	1	44	1

WOLTMAN, Max (F) 13 0
H: 5 11 W: 10 08 b.Wirral 20-8-03

2020–21	Liverpool	0	0		
2021–22	Liverpool	0	0		
2022–23	Liverpool	0	0		
2022–23	*Doncaster R*	13	0	13	0
2023–24	Oxford U	0	0		
2024–25	Oxford U	0	0		

Players retained or with offer of contract
Elliott-Wheeler, Aidan Jamie; Findlay, Stuart John; Johnson, Joshua Emmanuel; Knightbridge, Jacob Christopher.

Scholars
Abolade, Mubarak Olamiposi; Bangurah, Ibrahim Sidic; Blackmore, Jameson Beau; Bradney, Harrison Joseph; Burton, Kasway Ramone; Cramond, Charlie; Doyle, Calum Andrew Scott; Holton, Joshua Samuel; Lacey, Aaron Joseph; Lee, Jack James; Marriott, Monty James; Missanga, Mohamedy Hamis; Mole, Harrison George; Patel, Ajac; Snowden, Leo Thomas; Took-Oxley, Zaide Noah; Travin, Denis.

PETERBOROUGH U (64)

ADEBISI, Rio (D) 118 7
H: 5 9 W: 11 07 b.Croydon 27-9-00

2019–20	Crewe Alex	2	0		
2020–21	Crewe Alex	15	0		
2021–22	Crewe Alex	22	0		
2022–23	Crewe Alex	32	3		
2023–24	Crewe Alex	46	4	117	7
2024–25	Peterborough U	1	0	1	0

ADUBOFOUR-POKU, Kwame (M) 183 32
H: 5 10 W: 10 08 b.Croydon 11-8-01
Internationals: Ghana Full caps.
From Cray W, Worthing.

2019–20	Colchester U	29	5		
2020–21	Colchester U	33	0		
2021–22	Colchester U	0	0	62	5
2021–22	Peterborough U	20	0		
2022–23	Peterborough U	37	4		
2023–24	Peterborough U	37	11		
2024–25	Peterborough U	27	12	121	27

AJIBOYE, David (F) 135 17
H: 5 7 W: 11 00 b.Bromley 28-9-98

2021–22	Sutton U	43	8		
2022–23	Sutton U	4	0		
2022–23	Peterborough U	41	3	64	12
2023–24	Peterborough U	40	3		
2024–25	Peterborough U	6	0	50	3
2024–25	*Newport Co*	21	2	21	2

ANDREWS, Joe (M) 1 0
b.Trowbridge 14-2-06
Internationals: Wales U17, U18.

2024–25	Peterborough U	1	0	1	0

BEECH, Max (M) 0 0
b. 19-11-06

2023–24	Peterborough U	0	0		
2024–25	Peterborough U	0	0		

BILOKAPIC, Nicholas (G) 54 0
H: 6 5 W: 13 05 b.Australia 8-9-02
Internationals: Australia U17, U23.
From Sydney U.

2020–21	Huddersfield T	0	0		
2021–22	Huddersfield T	0	0		
2021–22	*Hartlepool U*	2	0	2	0
2022–23	Huddersfield T	6	0	6	0
2023–24	Peterborough U	28	0		
2024–25	Peterborough U	18	0	46	0

BLACKMORE, Will (G) 7 0
H: 6 1 W: 11 11 b.Worthing 1-10-01

2020–21	Peterborough U	1	0		
2021–22	Peterborough U	3	0		
2022–23	Peterborough U	3	0		
2023–24	Peterborough U	0	0		
2024–25	Peterborough U	3	0	7	0

CHANGUNDA, Andre (F) 1 0
b. 13-6-07

2024–25	Peterborough U	1	0	1	0

COLLINS, Archie (M) 275 14
H: 5 9 W: 9 13 b.Taunton 31-8-99

2016–17	Exeter C	0	0		
2017–18	Exeter C	0	0		
2018–19	Exeter C	26	1		
2019–20	Exeter C	36	1		
2020–21	Exeter C	46	4		
2021–22	Exeter C	38	0		
2022–23	Exeter C	45	4	191	10
2023–24	Peterborough U	44	3		
2024–25	Peterborough U	40	1	84	4

CONN-CLARKE, Chris (F) 43 2
H: 5 9 W: 10 03 b.Belfast 22-11-01
Internationals: Northern Ireland U17, U19, U21.

2017–18	Glentoran	1	0	1	0
2018–19	Burnley	0	0		
2019–20	Burnley	0	0		
2020–21	Burnley	0	0		
2021–22	Fleetwood T	4	0		
2022–23	Fleetwood T	0	0	4	0
2023	*Waterford*	15	1	15	1
From Altrincham.					
2024–25	Peterborough U	23	1	23	1

DAVIES, Joe (F) 0 0
b. 30-9-06

2023–24	Peterborough U	0	0		
2024–25	Peterborough U	0	0		

DE HAVILLAND, Ryan (M) 49 3
H: 5 10 W: 11 05 b.London 15-6-01
Internationals: England C.

2023–24	Peterborough U	22	1		
2024–25	Peterborough U	27	2	49	3

DORNELLY, James (D) 30 1
H: 5 9 W: 10 03 b.14-4-05
Internationals: England U20.

2023–24	Peterborough U	3	0		
2024–25	Peterborough U	27	1	30	1

EDUN, Tayo (M) 130 5
H: 5 9 W: 9 13 b.Islington 14-5-98
Internationals: England U17, U18, U19, U20.

2016–17	Fulham	0	0		
2017–18	Fulham	2	0		
2018–19	Fulham	0	0		
2019–20	*Ipswich T*	6	1	6	1
2019–20	Fulham	0	0	2	0
2019–20	Lincoln C	6	0		

2020–21 Lincoln C 41 1
2021–22 Lincoln C 4 1 **51 2**
2021–22 Blackburn R 20 0
2022–23 Blackburn R 8 0 **28 0**
2023–24 Charlton Ath 26 0
2024–25 Charlton Ath 0 0 **26 0**
2024–25 Peterborough U 17 2 **17 2**

FERNANDEZ, Emmanuel (D) 38 5
H: 6 4 W: 11 11 b. 20-11-01
From Gillingham, Ramsgate.
2021–22 Peterborough U 1 0
2022–23 Peterborough U 0 0
2023–24 Peterborough U 7 0
2024–25 Peterborough U 30 5 **38 5**

FREEMAN, Noah (D) 0 0
H: 6 0 b. 17-6-07
2023–24 Peterborough U 0 0
2024–25 Peterborough U 0 0

GILBERT, Luke (D) 0 0
b. 28-12-06
2023–24 Peterborough U 0 0
2024–25 Peterborough U 0 0

HAYES, Cian (F) 102 5
H: 5 7 W: 11 07 b.Preston 29-6-03
Internationals: Republic of Ireland U19.
2019–20 Fleetwood T 0 0
2020–21 Fleetwood T 0 0
2021–22 Fleetwood T 24 1
2022–23 Fleetwood T 34 1
2023–24 Fleetwood T 10 0 **68 2**
2024–25 Peterborough U 34 3 **34 3**

HOLLEY, George (M) 0 0
2023–24 Peterborough U 0 0
2024–25 Peterborough U 0 0

IHIONVIEN, Brad (F) 43 4
H: 6 3 W: 11 11 b.Greenwich 1-1-04
2021–22 Colchester U 1 0
2022–23 Colchester U 0 0
2023–24 Colchester U 29 4
2024–25 Colchester U 2 0 **32 4**
2024–25 Peterborough U 11 0 **11 0**

JADE-JONES, Ricky (M) 159 25
H: 6 0 W: 10 12 b.Peterborough 24-6-01
2019–20 Peterborough U 11 0
2020–21 Peterborough U 15 1
2021–22 Peterborough U 18 0
2022–23 Peterborough U 26 3
2023–24 Peterborough U 43 10
2024–25 Peterborough U 46 11 **159 25**

JOHNSTON, Carl (M) 112 3
H: 5 9 W: 10 01 b.Belfast 29-5-02
Internationals: Northern Ireland U17, U19, U21.
From Linfield.
2019–20 Fleetwood T 0 0
2020–21 Fleetwood T 0 0
2021–22 Fleetwood T 17 0
2022–23 Fleetwood T 23 1
2023–24 Fleetwood T 33 1
2024–25 Fleetwood T 19 1 **92 3**
2024–25 Peterborough U 20 0 **20 0**

KAMARA, David (F) 0 0
H: 6 0 b.London 9-9-05
2024–25 Peterborough U 0 0

KYPRIANOU, Hector (M) 179 14
H: 6 2 W: 12 04 b.Enfield 27-5-01
Internationals: Cyprus U19, U21, Full caps.
2019–20 Leyton Orient 6 0
2020–21 Leyton Orient 22 0
2021–22 Leyton Orient 38 0 **66 0**
2022–23 Peterborough U 37 3
2023–24 Peterborough U 42 8
2024–25 Peterborough U 34 3 **113 14**

LINDGREN, Gustav (F) 76 27
b. 16-8-01
2022 Sollentuna 19 10 **19 10**
2023 Degerfors 16 3
2024 Degerfors 28 13 **44 16**
2024–25 Peterborough U 13 1 **13 1**

MENDONCA, Lucca (D) 0 0
b. 2-10-07
2024–25 Peterborough U 0 0

MILLS, Harley (D) 12 0
H: 5 11 b.Northamptonshire 13-11-05
2023–24 Peterborough U 1 0
2024–25 Peterborough U 11 0 **12 0**

MOTHERSILLE, Malik (M) 67 15
H: 6 2 W: 10 08 b.Croyden 23-10-03
Internationals: Jamaica Full caps.
2023–24 Peterborough U 22 3
2024–25 Peterborough U 45 12 **67 15**

NEVETT, George (D) 17 0
H: 6 1 W: 12 04 b. 14-2-06
Internationals: Wales U19.
2022–23 Rochdale 1 0 **1 0**
From Rochdale.
2024–25 Peterborough U 16 0 **16 0**

O'BRIEN-BRADY, Donay (M) 20 1
H: 5 9 b.London 15-1-04
2023–24 Peterborough U 0 0
2024–25 Peterborough U 20 1 **20 1**

ODOH, Abraham (M) 159 18
H: 5 6 W: 8 11 b.Lambeth 25-6-00
From Tooting & Mitcham U.
2019–20 Charlton Ath 0 0
2020–21 Rochdale 2 0
2021–22 Rochdale 32 3
2022–23 Rochdale 45 1 **79 4**
2023–24 Harrogate T 42 9 **42 9**
2024–25 Peterborough U 38 5 **38 5**

ROSE, Oliver (D) 1 0
b. 2-1-05
2024–25 Peterborough U 1 0 **1 0**

SHOFOWOKE, Bolu (F) 1 0
b. 15-10-08
2024–25 Peterborough U 1 0 **1 0**

SPARKES, Jack (M) 187 6
H: 5 9 W: 9 13 b.Exeter 29-9-00
2017–18 Exeter C 3 0
2018–19 Exeter C 0 0
2019–20 Exeter C 17 0
2020–21 Exeter C 42 3
2021–22 Exeter C 21 2
2022–23 Exeter C 35 1 **118 6**
2023–24 Portsmouth 38 0 **38 0**
2024–25 Peterborough U 21 0 **21 0**
2024–25 *Chesterfield* 10 0 **10 0**

STEER, Jed (G) 158 0
H: 6 2 W: 12 08 b.Norwich 23-9-92
Internationals: England U16, U17, U19.
2009–10 Norwich C 0 0
2010–11 Norwich C 0 0
2011–12 Norwich C 0 0
2011–12 *Yeovil T* 12 0
2012–13 Cambridge U 0 0
2012–13 Norwich C 0 0
2013–14 Aston Villa 0 0
2014–15 Aston Villa 1 0
2014–15 *Doncaster R* 13 0 **13 0**
2014–15 *Yeovil T* 12 0 **24 0**
2015–16 Aston Villa 0 0
2015–16 *Huddersfield T* 38 0 **38 0**
2016–17 Aston Villa 0 0
2017–18 Aston Villa 0 0
2018–19 Aston Villa 16 0
2018–19 *Charlton Ath* 19 0 **19 0**
2019–20 Aston Villa 1 0
2020–21 Aston Villa 0 0
2021–22 Aston Villa 1 0
2021–22 *Luton T* 3 0 **3 0**
2022–23 Aston Villa 0 0 **19 0**
2023–24 Peterborough U 17 0
2024–25 Peterborough U 25 0 **42 0**

TSHIMANGA, Kabongo (F) 69 11
H: 5 11 W: 12 04 b.Kinshasa 31-5-96
Internationals: England C.
2014–15 Milton Keynes D 0 0
2015–16 Milton Keynes D 0 0
2016–17 Milton Keynes D 6 0 **6 0**
2016–17 *Yeovil T* 0 0
From Boston U, Oxford C, Boreham Wood, Chesterfield.
2022–23 Peterborough U 8 0
2023–24 Peterborough U 2 0
2023–24 *Fleetwood T* 14 0 **14 0**
2024–25 Peterborough U 0 0 **10 0**
2024–25 *Swindon T* 39 11 **39 11**

UNWIN, Tom (D) 0 0
b.Cambridge 4-1-00
2023–24 Peterborough U 0 0
2024–25 Peterborough U 0 0

WAKELING, Jacob (F) 75 9
H: 5 10 W: 12 00 b.Redditch 15-9-01
2021–22 Leicester C 0 0
2021–22 *Barrow* 4 0 **4 0**
2022–23 Swindon T 45 8
2023–24 Swindon T 2 0 **47 8**
2023–24 Peterborough U 8 0
2024–25 Peterborough U 0 0 **8 0**
2024–25 *Gillingham* 16 1 **16 1**

WALLIN, Oscar (D) 90 1
H: 6 3 b.Sundsvall 9-7-01
2021 Hudiksvalls 27 1 **27 1**
2022 Degerfors 0 0
2023 Degerfors 13 0
2024 Degerfors 16 0 **29 0**
2024–25 Peterborough U 34 0 **34 0**

YOUNG, Tyler (M) 0 0
H: 5 10 b. 4-6-06
2024–25 Peterborough U 0 0

Players retained or with offer of contract
Aderoju, Oluwalopemiwa; Fox, Edward Arthur Chang; Smith, Bastian.

Scholars
Aboim Poyart De Mendonca, Lucca; Aikins, Nathan Jordan; Beech, Max; Changunda, Andre Tony; Claxton, Fabian Oliver; Davies, Joseph Gabriel; Fitzpatrick, Rylie Angus; Freeman, Noah Clarke; Gbajumo, Davon Nana Kwabena Abdul; Gilbert, Luke Harry; Holley, George Joseph; Kovaci, Milan; McWilliams-Marcano, Benjamin Gilbert; Sakalas, Ignas; Sykut, Patryk Oleksandr; Unwin, Thomas Ben; Westcott, Ben.

PLYMOUTH ARG (65)

AL HAJJ, Rami (M) 124 7
H: 5 11 W: 11 11 b.Beirut 17-9-01
Internationals: Sweden U19, U21.
2019–20 Heerenveen 5 0
2020–21 Heerenveen 23 0
2021–22 Heerenveen 21 1
2022–23 Heerenveen 18 0 **67 1**
2023–24 OB 29 3 **29 3**
2024–25 Plymouth Arg 28 3 **28 3**

BAIDOO, Michael (M) 173 33
H: 5 9 W: 11 05 b.Accra 14-5-99
Internationals: Ghana U20, Full caps.
2017–18 Midtjylland 1 0
2018–19 Midtjylland 0 0 **1 0**
2018–19 *Fredericia* 16 0 **16 0**
2019 Jerv 13 2
2020 Jerv 27 4 **40 6**
2021 Sandnes Ulf 29 4 **29 4**
2022 Elfsborg 21 8
2023 Elfsborg 28 5
2024 Elfsborg 27 10 **76 23**
2024–25 Plymouth Arg 11 0 **11 0**

BAKER, Zak (G) 0 0
H: 6 2 W: 12 08 b. 27-1-06
2021–22 Plymouth Arg 0 0
2022–23 Plymouth Arg 0 0
2023–24 Plymouth Arg 0 0
2024–25 Plymouth Arg 0 0

BOATENG, Malachi (M) 93 2
H: 6 0 W: 8 11 b.London 5-7-02
2020–21 Crystal Palace 0 0
2021–22 Crystal Palace 0 0
2022–23 Crystal Palace 0 0
2022–23 *Queen's Park* 34 2 **34 2**
2023–24 Crystal Palace 0 0
2023–24 *Dundee* 32 0 **32 0**
2024–25 Hearts 20 0 **20 0**
2024–25 Plymouth Arg 7 0 **7 0**

BUNDU, Mustapha (M) 229 37
b.Freetown 27-2-97
Internationals: Sierre Leone Full caps.
From Newquay, Hereford.
2016–17 AGF 9 1
2017–18 AGF 28 4
2018–19 AGF 27 4
2019–20 AGF 27 8
2020–21 Anderlecht 9 0
2020–21 *Copenhagen* 14 1 **14 1**
2021–22 Anderlecht 1 0
2021–22 *AGF* 22 3 **113 20**
2022–23 Anderlecht 0 0 **10 0**
2022–23 *Andorra* 28 3 **28 3**
2023–24 Plymouth Arg 27 3
2024–25 Plymouth Arg 37 10 **64 13**

EARLEY, Saxon (M) 31 2
H: 5 9 W: 11 00 b.Norwich 11-10-02
2022–23 Norwich C 0 0
2022–23 *Stevenage* 21 0 **21 0**
2022–23 Plymouth Arg 9 2
2023–24 Plymouth Arg 1 0
2023–24 *Wycombe W* 0 0
2024–25 Plymouth Arg 0 0 **10 2**
2024–25 *Lincoln C* 0 0

EDWARDS, Joe (D) 467 40
H: 5 8 W: 11 07 b.Gloucester 31-10-90
2009–10 Bristol C 0 0
2010–11 Bristol C 2 0
2011–12 Bristol C 2 0
2011–12 *Yeovil T* 4 1
2012–13 Bristol C 0 0 **4 0**
2012–13 Yeovil T 35 2
2013–14 Yeovil T 46 1
2014–15 Yeovil T 34 0 **119 4**
2015–16 Colchester U 42 2 **42 2**
2016–17 Walsall 43 3
2017–18 Walsall 30 7
2018–19 Walsall 20 2 **93 12**
2019–20 Plymouth Arg 34 3
2020–21 Plymouth Arg 40 7
2021–22 Plymouth Arg 41 5
2022–23 Plymouth Arg 42 3
2023–24 Plymouth Arg 35 3
2024–25 Plymouth Arg 17 1 **209 22**

FINN, Tegan (F) 4 0
b. 17-3-08
2024–25 Plymouth Arg 4 0 **4 0**

GALLOWAY, Brendon (D) 111 2
H: 6 2 W: 13 10 b.Harare, Zimbabwe 17-3-96
Internationals: England U17, U18, U19, U21. Zimbabwe Full caps.

2011–12	Milton Keynes D	1	0	
2012–13	Milton Keynes D	1	0	
2013–14	Milton Keynes D	8	0	10 0
2014–15	Everton	2	0	
2015–16	Everton	15	0	
2016–17	Everton	0	0	
2016–17	WBA	3	0	3 0
2017–18	Everton	0	0	
2017–18	Sunderland	7	0	7 0
2018–19	Everton	0	0	17 0
2019–20	Luton T	3	0	
2020–21	Luton T	0	0	3 0
2021–22	Plymouth Arg	14	2	
2022–23	Plymouth Arg	18	0	
2023–24	Plymouth Arg	26	0	
2024–25	Plymouth Arg	13	0	71 2

GRAY, Andre (F) 336 97
H: 5 10 W: 13 01 b.Wolverhampton 26-6-91
Internationals: England C. Jamaica Full caps.

2009–10	Shrewsbury T	4	0	4 0

From Hinckley U, Luton T.

2014–15	Brentford	45	16	
2015–16	Brentford	2	2	47 18
2015–16	Burnley	41	23	
2016–17	Burnley	32	9	73 32
2017–18	Watford	31	5	
2018–19	Watford	29	7	
2019–20	Watford	23	2	
2020–21	Watford	30	5	
2021–22	Watford	0	0	113 19
2021–22	QPR	28	10	28 10
2022–23	Aris	32	8	32 8
2023–24	Al Riyadh	26	7	26 7
2024–25	Plymouth Arg	13	3	13 3

Transferred to Fatih Karagumruk, January 2025.

GRIMSHAW, Daniel (G) 122 0
H: 6 1 W: 12 02 b.Manchester 16-1-98

2018–19	Manchester C	0	0	
2019–20	Manchester C	0	0	
2020–21	Manchester C	0	0	
2020–21	Lommel	10	0	10 0
2021–22	Blackpool	26	0	
2022–23	Blackpool	18	0	
2023–24	Blackpool	45	0	
2024–25	Blackpool	2	0	91 0
2024–25	Plymouth Arg	21	0	21 0

HARDIE, Ryan (F) 315 95
H: 5 10 W: 9 11 b.Stranraer 17-3-97
Internationals: Scotland U16, U17, U19, U20, U21.

2014–15	Rangers	5	2	
2015–16	Rangers	1	0	
2015–16	Raith R	10	6	
2016–17	Rangers	0	0	
2016–17	St Mirren	16	3	16 3
2016–17	Raith R	18	6	28 12
2017–18	Rangers	7	0	
2017–18	Livingston	16	8	
2018–19	Rangers	0	0	13 2
2018–19	Livingston	21	7	37 15
2019–20	Blackpool	7	0	7 0
2019–20	Plymouth Arg	13	7	
2020–21	Plymouth Arg	43	5	
2021–22	Plymouth Arg	37	16	
2022–23	Plymouth Arg	44	13	
2023–24	Plymouth Arg	40	12	
2024–25	Plymouth Arg	37	10	214 63

HATCH, Joseph (F) 1 0
b.Bristol 7-9-06
Internationals: Wales U16, U17

2024–25	Plymouth Arg	1	0	1 0

HAZARD, Conor (G) 114 0
H: 6 6 W: 12 02 b.Belfast 5-3-98
Internationals: Northern Ireland U16, U17, U19, U21, Full caps.
From Cliftonville.

2017–18	Celtic	0	0	
2017–18	Falkirk	11	0	11 0
2018–19	Celtic	0	0	
2018–19	Partick Thistle	11	0	11 0
2019–20	Celtic	0	0	
2019–20	Dundee	11	0	11 0
2020–21	Celtic	5	0	
2021–22	Celtic	0	0	5 0
2022	HJK	24	0	24 0
2023–24	Plymouth Arg	27	0	
2024–25	Plymouth Arg	25	0	52 0

HOLMAN, Daniel (G) 0 0
b.23-11-06

2024–25	Plymouth Arg	0	0	

HOUGHTON, Jordan (M) 339 8
H: 6 2 W: 12 13 b.Chertsey 9-11-95
Internationals: England U16, U17, U20.

2015–16	Chelsea	0	0	
2015–16	Gillingham	11	1	11 1
2015–16	Plymouth Arg	10	1	
2016–17	Chelsea	0	0	
2016–17	Doncaster R	32	1	
2017–18	Chelsea	0	0	
2017–18	Doncaster R	37	0	69 1
2018–19	Milton Keynes D	44	2	
2019–20	Milton Keynes D	30	2	
2020–21	Milton Keynes D	19	0	93 4
2021–22	Plymouth Arg	42	1	
2022–23	Plymouth Arg	44	0	
2023–24	Plymouth Arg	40	0	
2024–25	Plymouth Arg	30	0	166 2

ISSAKA, Frederick (F) 25 1
H: 5 10 b.Truro 28-7-05
Internationals: England U16. Wales U17, U19.

2021–22	Plymouth Arg	0	0	
2022–23	Plymouth Arg	1	0	
2023–24	Plymouth Arg	5	0	
2024–25	Plymouth Arg	19	1	25 1

JENKINS-DAVIES, Will (M) 3 0
H: 5 11 W: 11 11 b.Torquay 22-10-04
Internationals: Wales U18.

2021–22	Plymouth Arg	1	0	
2022–23	Plymouth Arg	2	0	
2023–24	Plymouth Arg	0	0	
2024–25	Plymouth Arg	0	0	3 0

KATIC, Nikola (D) 241 14
H: 6 4 W: 12 08 b.Ljubuski 10-10-96
Internationals: Croatia U21, Full caps. Bosnia & Herzegovina Full caps.

2014–15	Neretvanac Opuzen	14	2	
2015–16	Neretvanac Opuzen	15	0	29 2
2015–16	Slaven Belupo	1	0	
2016–17	Slaven Belupo	29	1	
2017–18	Slaven Belupo	35	0	65 1
2018–19	Rangers	18	1	
2019–20	Rangers	19	2	
2020–21	Rangers	0	0	
2021–22	Rangers	0	0	37 3
2021–22	Hajuk Split	21	0	21 0
2022–23	FC Zurich	22	1	
2023–24	FC Zurich	34	4	
2024–25	FC Zurich	18	2	74 7

On loan from FC Zurich.

2024–25	Plymouth Arg	15	1	15 1

MATTHEWS, Jack (D) 0 0
b.13-5-06

2023–24	Plymouth Arg	0	0	
2024–25	Plymouth Arg	0	0	

MUMBA, Bali (D) 147 9
H: 5 6 W: 9 08 b.South Shields 8-10-01
Internationals: England U16, U17, U18, U19.

2017–18	Sunderland	1	0	
2018–19	Sunderland	4	0	
2019–20	Sunderland	0	0	5 0
2020–21	Norwich C	4	0	
2021–22	Norwich C	1	0	
2021–22	Peterborough U	10	0	10 0
2022–23	Norwich C	0	0	5 0
2022–23	Plymouth Arg	41	6	
2023–24	Plymouth Arg	43	3	
2024–25	Plymouth Arg	43	0	127 9

OGBETA, Nathaniel (D) 105 6
b.Salford 28-4-01
Internationals: England U16, U17, U18, U20.

2018–19	Manchester C	0	0	
2019–20	Manchester C	0	0	
2020–21	Shrewsbury T	25	2	
2021–22	Shrewsbury T	26	0	51 2
2021–22	Swansea C	2	0	
2022–23	Swansea C	0	0	
2022–23	Peterborough U	20	1	20 1
2023–24	Swansea C	0	0	2 0
2023–24	Bolton W	15	2	15 2
2024–25	Plymouth Arg	17	1	17 1

PALSSON, Victor (M) 397 20
H: 6 1 W: 9 13 b.Reykjavik 30-4-91
Internationals: Iceland U17, U19, U21, Full caps.

2010–11	Liverpool	0	0	
2010–11	Dagenham & Red	2	0	2 0
2010–11	Hibernian	16	1	
2011–12	Hibernian	15	0	31 1
2012	New York Red Bulls	16	0	16 0
2012–13	NEC Nijmegen	27	2	
2013–14	NEC Nijmegen	22	2	50 4
2014	Helsingborg	12	2	
2015	Helsingborg	21	1	33 3
2015–16	Esbjerg	5	1	
2016–17	Esbjerg	30	2	35 3
2017–18	FC Zurich	33	1	
2018–19	FC Zurich	14	0	47 1
2018–19	Darmstadt 98	15	0	
2019–20	Darmstadt 98	31	3	
2020–21	Darmstadt 98	21	3	67 6
2021–22	Schalke 04	28	0	28 0
2022	DC United	10	0	
2023	DC United	18	0	28 0
2023–24	Eupen	35	2	35 2
2024–25	Plymouth Arg	25	0	25 0

PLEGUEZUELO, Julio (D) 165 4
H: 5 9 W: 11 00 b.Palma de Mallorca 26-1-97
Internationals: Spain U17, U18.

2016–17	Arsenal	0	0	
2016–17	Mallorca	15	0	15 0
2017–18	Arsenal	0	0	
2018	Gimnastic	10	0	10 0
2018–19	Arsenal	0	0	
2019–20	FC Twente	19	0	
2020–21	FC Twente	19	1	
2021–22	FC Twente	23	0	
2022–23	FC Twente	23	2	84 3
2023–24	Plymouth Arg	32	0	
2024–25	Plymouth Arg	24	1	56 1

PUCHACZ, Tymoteusz (D) 184 9
H: 5 11 W: 11 09 b.Sulechow 23-1-99
Internationals: Poland U16, U17, U18, U19, U20, U21, Full caps.

2015–16	Lech Poznan	0	0	
2016–17	Lech Poznan	1	0	
2017–18	Lech Poznan	0	0	
2017–18	Zaglebie Sosnowiec	15	0	
2018–19	Lech Poznan	0	0	
2018–19	Zaglebie Sosnowiec	2	0	17 0
2018–19	Katowice	4	4	4 4
2019–20	Lech Poznan	35	3	
2020–21	Lech Poznan	27	1	63 4
2021–22	Union Berlin	9	0	
2021–22	Trabzonspor	9	0	9 0
2022–23	Union Berlin	3	0	
2022–23	Panathinaikos	13	0	13 0
2023–24	Union Berlin	0	0	1 0
2023–24	Kaiserslautern	31	1	31 1
2024–25	Holstein Kiel	10	0	10 0

On loan from Holstein Kiel.

2024–25	Plymouth Arg	15	0	15 0

RANDELL, Adam (M) 145 8
H: 5 9 W: 10 03 b.Plymouth 1-10-00

2018–19	Plymouth Arg	0	0	
2019–20	Plymouth Arg	4	0	
2020–21	Plymouth Arg	0	0	
2021–22	Plymouth Arg	24	1	
2022–23	Plymouth Arg	33	3	
2023–24	Plymouth Arg	45	3	
2024–25	Plymouth Arg	39	1	145 8

ROBERTS, Caleb (M) 6 0
b.Ivybridge 24-10-04

2021–22	Plymouth Arg	0	0	
2022–23	Plymouth Arg	1	0	
2023–24	Plymouth Arg	0	0	
2024–25	Plymouth Arg	5	0	6 0

SORINOLA, Matthew (D) 114 5
H: 5 8 W: 10 03 b.Lambeth 19-2-01
From Fulham.

2019–20	Milton Keynes D	0	0	
2020–21	Milton Keynes D	34	1	34 1
2021–22	Union SG	14	1	
2022–23	Union SG	0	0	
2022–23	Swansea C	29	2	29 2
2023–24	Union SG	0	0	14 1
2023–24	Plymouth Arg	12	1	
2024–25	Plymouth Arg	25	0	37 1

SZUCS, Kornel (D) 128 1
H: 5 9 W: 10 03 b.Miskolc 24-9-01
Internationals: Hungary U17, U18, U19, Full caps.

2018–19	Diosgyor	1	0	
2019–20	Diosgyor	5	0	
2019–20	Kazincbarcika	4	0	
2020–21	Diosgyor	15	0	
2020–21	Kazincbarcika	1	1	16 1
2021–22	Diosgyor	23	0	
2022–23	Diosgyor	3	0	47 0
2023–24	Kecskemet	28	0	
2024–25	Kecskemet	1	0	29 0
2024–25	Plymouth Arg	36	0	36 0

TALOVEROV, Maksym (D) 131 3
H: 6 5 W: 13 03 b.Donetsk 28-6-00
Internationals: Ukraine U21, U23, Full caps.

2016–17	Olimpik Donetsk	0	0	
2017–18	Olimpik Donetsk	0	0	
2018–19	Olimpik Donetsk	0	0	
2019–20	Dynamo Ceske	7	0	
2020–21	Dynamo Ceske	26	1	
2021–22	Dynamo Ceske	14	0	47 1
2021–22	Slavia Prague	11	0	
2022–23	Slavia Prague	0	0	
2022–23	Slovan Liberec	13	1	13 1
2022–23	LASK	12	0	
2023–24	Slavia Prague	0	0	11 0
2023–24	LASK	25	0	
2024–25	LASK	12	0	49 0
2024–25	Plymouth Arg	11	1	11 1

TIJANI, Muhamed (F)   135   22
b. 26-7-00
Internationals: Nigeria U20.
2019–20 Banik Ostrava   0   0
2019–20 *Trinec*   10   0
2019–20 *MFK Karvina*   5   0   5   0
2020–21 Banik Ostrava   11   1
2020–21 *Trinec*   8   0   18   0
2021–22 Banik Ostrava   21   3
2021–22 *Zaborsko*   32   11   32   11
2022–23 Banik Ostrava   21   3   53   7
2023–24 Slavia Prague   14   2
2024–25 Slavia Prague   0   0   14   2
On loan from Slavia Prague.
2024–25 Plymouth Arg   13   2   13   2

WAINE, Ben (F)   140   22
H: 5 10   W: 11 11   b.Wellington 11-6-01
Internationals: New Zealand U20, U23, Full caps.
2017–18 Wellington Phoenix   0   0
2018–19 Wellington Phoenix   3   0
2019–20 Wellington Phoenix   15   1
2020–21 Wellington Phoenix   22   7
2021–22 Wellington Phoenix   25   6
2022–23 Wellington Phoenix   8   3   73   17
2022–23 Plymouth Arg   9   1
2023–24 Plymouth Arg   32   2
2024–25 Plymouth Arg   1   0   42   3
2024–25 *Mansfield T*   25   2   25   2

WRIGHT, Callum (M)   136   18
H: 6 0   W: 11 05   b.Liverpool 2-5-00
2020–21 Leicester C   0   0
2020–21 *Cheltenham T*   16   4
2021–22 Leicester C   0   0
2021–22 *Cheltenham T*   34   9   50   13
2022–23 Blackpool   10   0   10   0
2022–23 Plymouth Arg   20   4
2023–24 Plymouth Arg   21   0
2024–25 Plymouth Arg   35   1   76   5

Scholars
Burch, Kian Brian; Davy, Malachi Kane; Dean, Oscar William; Flew, Tegan-Lee; Fisher, Cole Louis; Flower, Jack Cameron; Flowers, Lewis Les; Haley, Toby Iain; Hatch, Joseph Colin; Holman, Daniel Thomas; Ireland, Jensen Lee; Lord, Sam Michael; Poole, Fletcher David; Shield, Harry Charles; Sneap, Harley James; Sullivan, Joel; Thomas, Lewis Richard.

PORT VALE (66)

AGNERO, Karl (M)   0   0
2023–24 Port Vale   0   0
2024–25 Port Vale   0   0

AMOS, Ben (G)   319   0
H: 6 1   W: 14 02   b.Macclesfield 10-4-90
Internationals: England U16, U17, U18, U19, U20, U21.
2007–08 Manchester U   0   0
2008–09 Manchester U   0   0
2009–10 Manchester U   0   0
2009–10 *Peterborough U*   1   0   1   0
2010 *Molde*   8   0   8   0
2010–11 Manchester U   0   0
2010–11 *Oldham Ath*   16   0   16   0
2011–12 Manchester U   1   0
2012–13 Manchester U   0   0
2012–13 *Hull C*   17   0   17   0
2013–14 Manchester U   0   0
2013–14 *Carlisle U*   9   0   9   0
2014–15 Manchester U   1   0   1   0
2014–15 *Bolton W*   9   0
2015–16 Bolton W   40   0
2016–17 Bolton W   0   0
2016–17 *Cardiff C*   16   0   16   0
2017–18 Bolton W   0   0
2017–18 *Charlton Ath*   46   0
2018–19 Bolton W   0   0   49   0
2018–19 *Millwall*   12   0   12   0
2019–20 Charlton Ath   0   0
2020–21 Charlton Ath   46   0   92   0
2021–22 Wigan Ath   46   0
2022–23 Wigan Ath   29   0
2023–24 Wigan Ath   0   0   75   0
2024–25 Port Vale   23   0   23   0

BRAZIER, Liam (M)   0   0
b.Stockton Brook --
2023–24 Port Vale   0   0
2024–25 Port Vale   0   0

BUAH, Andrew (D)   1   0
H: 6 2   W: 10 12   b.Manchester 4-5-06
2023–24 Port Vale   1   0
2024–25 Port Vale   0   0   1   0

BYERS, George (M)   178   19
H: 5 11   W: 11 07   b.Ilford 29-5-96
Internationals: Scotland U16, U17.
2014–15 Watford   0   0
2015–16 Watford   0   0   1   0
2016–17 Swansea C   0   0
2017–18 Swansea C   14   0
2018–19 Swansea C   21   2
2019–20 Swansea C   35   2
2020–21 Swansea C   0   0   56   4
2020–21 *Portsmouth*   14   0   14   0
2021–22 Sheffield Wed   22   6
2022–23 Sheffield Wed   24   6
2023–24 Sheffield Wed   22   1   68   13
2023–24 *Blackpool*   16   0   16   0
2024–25 Port Vale   23   2   23   2

CHISLETT, Ethan (M)   168   26
H: 5 10   W: 10 10   b.Durban 11-8-98
From Metropolitan Police, Aldershot T.
2020–21 AFC Wimbledon   27   2
2021–22 AFC Wimbledon   44   9   100   13
2022–23 AFC Wimbledon   43   9
2023–24 Port Vale   45   9
2024–25 Port Vale   25   4   68   13

CLARK, Mitchell (D)   153   3
H: 5 10   W: 10 10   b.Nuneaton 13-3-99
Internationals: Wales U17, U19.
2017–18 Aston Villa   0   0
2018–19 Aston Villa   0   0
2018–19 *Port Vale*   40   0
2019–20 Leicester C   0   0
2019–20 *Port Vale*   4   0
2020–21 Leicester C   0   0
2020–21 *Port Vale*   11   1
2021–22 Accrington S   25   1
2022–23 Accrington S   40   0   65   1
2023–24 Port Vale   13   0
2024–25 Port Vale   20   1   88   2

COUSINS, Logan (M)   0   0
2023–24 Port Vale   0   0
2024–25 Port Vale   0   0

CROASDALE, Ryan (M)   125   7
H: 5 9   W: 10 12   b.Lancaster 26-9-94
Internationals: England C.
2013–14 Preston NE   0   0
2014–15 Sheffield Wed   0   0
2015–16 Sheffield Wed   0   0
From Kidderminster H, AFC Fylde, Stockport Co.
2022–23 Stockport Co   44   1
2023–24 Stockport Co   36   2   80   3
2024–25 Port Vale   45   4   45   4

CURTIS, Ronan (F)   333   70
H: 6 0   W: 12 02   b.Derry 29-3-96
Internationals: Republic of Ireland U21, Full caps.
2015 Derry C   13   1
2016 Derry C   24   4
2017 Derry C   32   8
2018 Derry C   22   5   91   18
2018–19 Portsmouth   41   11
2019–20 Portsmouth   33   11
2020–21 Portsmouth   42   10
2021–22 Portsmouth   43   8
2022–23 Portsmouth   25   2   184   42
2023–24 *AFC Wimbledon*   16   5   16   5
2024–25 Port Vale   42   5   42   5

DAVIES, Arron (G)   0   0
b. 27-11-05
2024–25 Port Vale   0   0

DEBRAH, Jesse (F)   66   2
H: 6 0   W: 11 07   b.Croydon 11-1-00
Internationals: England C.
2018–19 Millwall   0   0
2019–20 Millwall   0   0
From Dulwich Hamlet, FC Halifax T.
2023–24 Port Vale   31   0
2024–25 Port Vale   35   2   66   2

DIPEPA, Baylee (F)   25   3
H: 6 0   W: 12 02   b.Blythe Bridge 12-1-07
Internationals: England U17, U18.
2023–24 Port Vale   22   3
2024–25 Port Vale   3   0   25   3

EDWARDS, Diamond (M)   1   0
H: 5 8   W: 10 06   b.Reading 18-9-03
From Reading.
2022–23 Southampton   0   0
2023–24 Southampton   0   0
2024–25 Port Vale   1   0   1   0

FRANCIS, Louis (D)   0   0
b. 30-6-07
2024–25 Port Vale   0   0

GARRITY, Ben (M)   174   29
H: 6 0   W: 11 09   b.Liverpool 21-2-97
From Warrington T.
2019–20 Blackpool   0   0
2020–21 Blackpool   0   0
2020–21 *Oldham Ath*   29   2   29   2
2021–22 Blackpool   43   12
2022–23 Blackpool   34   1
2023–24 Port Vale   39   9
2024–25 Port Vale   29   5   145   27

HALL, Connor (D)   210   6
H: 6 4   W: 14 07   b.Huntingdon 23-5-93
2020–21 Harrogate T   41   1
2021–22 Harrogate T   20   0   61   1
2021–22 Port Vale   24   2
2022–23 Port Vale   20   1
2022–23 *Colchester U*   21   2
2023–24 *Colchester U*   40   0   61   2
2024–25 Port Vale   44   0   88   3

HARPER, Rekeem (M)   144   3
H: 6 0   W: 10 01   b.Birmingham 8-3-00
Internationals: England U17, U19.
2016–17 WBA   0   0
2017–18 WBA   1   0
2017–18 *Blackburn R*   4   0   4   0
2018–19 WBA   16   1
2019–20 WBA   10   0
2020–21 WBA   2   0
2020–21 *Birmingham C*   18   0   18   0
2021–22 WBA   0   0   29   1
2021–22 *Ipswich T*   13   0
2021–22 *Crewe Alex*   15   0   15   0
2022–23 *Ipswich T*   0   0   13   0
2022–23 *Exeter C*   20   1   20   1
2023–24 Burton Alb   27   0
2024–25 Burton Alb   0   0   27   0
2024–25 Port Vale   18   1   18   1

HART, Sam (D)   174   3
H: 5 11   W: 11 05   b.Bolton 10-9-96
2016–17 Liverpool   0   0
2016–17 *Port Vale*   11   1
2017–18 *Port Vale*   10   0
2017–18 Blackburn R   3   0
2017–18 *Rochdale*   3   0
2018–19 Blackburn R   0   0
2018–19 *Rochdale*   11   0   14   0
2018–19 *Southend U*   18   0
2019–20 Blackburn R   0   0   3   0
2019–20 *Shrewsbury T*   4   0   4   0
2020–21 Southend U   21   0   39   0
2022–23 Sutton U   20   0
2023–24 Sutton U   30   0   50   0
2024–25 Port Vale   22   1   33   2

HEADLEY, Jaheim (D)   75   7
H: 5 9   W: 11 00   b.London 24-9-01
2020–21 Huddersfield T   0   0
2021–22 Huddersfield T   0   0
2022–23 Huddersfield T   11   1
2022–23 *Harrogate T*   20   2   20   2
2023–24 Huddersfield T   29   1
2024–25 Huddersfield T   7   0   47   2
2024–25 Port Vale   8   3   8   3

HENEGHAN, Ben (D)   245   8
H: 6 3   W: 12 06   b.Manchester 19-9-93
Internationals: England C.
From Everton, Stoke C, Chester.
2016–17 Motherwell   37   0
2017–18 Motherwell   4   1   41   1
2017–18 Sheffield U   0   0
2018–19 Sheffield U   0   0
2018–19 *Blackpool*   42   1
2019–20 Sheffield U   0   0
2019–20 *Blackpool*   26   2   68   3
2020–21 AFC Wimbledon   23   2
2021–22 AFC Wimbledon   41   2   64   4
2022–23 Sheffield Wed   10   0   10   0
2023–24 Fleetwood T   37   0   37   0
2024–25 Port Vale   25   0   25   0

JOHN, Kyle (D)   28   0
H: 5 9   W: 10 10   b.Chester 13-2-01
2020–21 Everton   0   0
2022–23 Everton   0   0
2023–24 Everton   0   0
2024–25 Port Vale   28   0   28   0

JONES, Dan (D)   125   1
H: 6 0   W: 12 06   b.Bishop Auckland 14-12-94
Internationals: England C.
2013–14 Hartlepool U   1   0
2014–15 Hartlepool U   25   0
2015–16 Hartlepool U   11   0   37   0
2016–17 *Grimsby T*   3   0   3   0
From Barrow.
2019–20 Salford C   3   0
2020–21 Salford C   0   0   3   0
2020–21 *Harrogate T*   21   1   21   1
2021–22 Port Vale   22   0
2022–23 Port Vale   25   0
2023–24 Port Vale   14   0
2024–25 Port Vale   0   0   61   0

LOMAX, Ben (D)   3   0
H: 6 1   W: 12 02   b.Warrington 26-10-05
2023–24 Port Vale   3   0
2024–25 Port Vale   0   0   3   0

LOWE, Jason (M)   409   5
H: 5 10   W: 12 08   b.Wigan 2-9-91
Internationals: England U20, U21.
2009–10 Blackburn R   0   0
2010–11 Blackburn R   1   0

2010–11	Oldham Ath	7	2	7	2
2011–12	Blackburn R	32	0		
2012–13	Blackburn R	36	0		
2013–14	Blackburn R	39	1		
2014–15	Blackburn R	12	0		
2015–16	Blackburn R	10	0		
2016–17	Blackburn R	43	0	173	1
2017–18	WBA	0	0		
2017–18	Birmingham C	9	0	9	0
2018–19	Bolton W	35	0		
2019–20	Bolton W	29	0	64	0
2019–20	Salford C	0	0		
2020–21	Salford C	45	0		
2021–22	Salford C	45	2		
2022–23	Salford C	26	0	116	2
2023–24	Port Vale	29	0		
2024–25	Port Vale	11	0	40	0

OJO, Funso (M)   403   9
H: 5 10   W: 11 03   b.Antwerp 28-8-91
Internationals: Belgium U16, U17, U20, U21.

2008–09	PSV Eindhoven	1	0		
2009–10	PSV Eindhoven	3	0		
2010–11	PSV Eindhoven	2	0		
2010–11	VVV Venlo	8	0	8	0
2011–12	PSV Eindhoven	5	0	11	0
2012–13	Beerschot	24	1	24	1
2013–14	Antwerp	8	0	8	0
2013–14	Dordrecht	13	0		
2014–15	Dordrecht	19	0	32	0
2015–16	Willem II	32	0		
2016–17	Willem II	28	0	60	0
2017–18	Scunthorpe U	41	2		
2018–19	Scunthorpe U	39	1	80	3
2019–20	Aberdeen	16	0		
2020–21	Aberdeen	11	0		
2020–21	Wigan Ath	23	0	23	0
2021–22	Aberdeen	30	1	57	1
2022–23	Port Vale	28	2		
2023–24	Port Vale	40	2		
2024–25	Port Vale	1	0	69	4
2024–25	Shrewsbury T	31	0		

PATON, Ruari (F)   158   49
H: 5 10   W: 10 03   b.Dublin 9-8-00
Internationals: Republic of Ireland U16.

2020–21	Stranraer	21	6	21	6
2021–22	Queen of the South	34	3		
2022–23	Queen of the South	36	22	70	25
2023–24	Queen's Park	36	17	36	17
2024–25	Port Vale	19	1	19	1
2024–25	Dundee U	12	0	12	0

PLANT, James (M)   33   2
H: 5 9   W: 11 00   b.Werrington 3-11-04

2022–23	Port Vale	6	2		
2023–24	Port Vale	26	0		
2024–25	Port Vale	1	0	33	2

SANG, Tom (M)   106   0
H: 6 2   W: 12 06   b.Liverpool 29-6-99
From Bolton W, Manchester U.

2019–20	Cardiff C	0	0		
2020–21	Cardiff C	9	0		
2020–21	Cheltenham T	10	0	10	0
2021–22	Cardiff C	3	0		
2021–22	St Johnstone	9	0	9	0
2022–23	Cardiff C	9	0	21	0
2023–24	Port Vale	38	0		
2024–25	Port Vale	28	0	66	0

SHORROCK, Jack (M)   30   3
H: 5 10   W: 11 07   b.Stockport 28-4-07

2022–23	Port Vale	1	0		
2023–24	Port Vale	12	1		
2024–25	Port Vale	17	2	30	3

SILVA PEVIDE, Joao (M)   0   0
H: 6 0   W: 9 13

2022–23	Port Vale	0	0		
2023–24	Port Vale	0	0		
2024–25	Port Vale	0	0		

SMITH, Nathan (D)   369   21
H: 6 0   W: 11 05   b.Madeley 3-4-96

2013–14	Port Vale	0	0		
2014–15	Port Vale	0	0		
2015–16	Port Vale	0	0		
2016–17	Port Vale	46	4		
2017–18	Port Vale	46	1		
2018–19	Port Vale	44	0		
2019–20	Port Vale	34	5		
2020–21	Port Vale	44	4		
2021–22	Port Vale	45	3		
2022–23	Port Vale	42	0		
2023–24	Port Vale	24	0	369	21

STOCKLEY, Jayden (F)   429   117
H: 6 2   W: 12 06   b.Poole 10-10-93

2009–10	Bournemouth	2	0		
2010–11	Bournemouth	4	0		
2011–12	Bournemouth	10	0		
2011–12	Accrington S	9	3	9	3
2012–13	Bournemouth	0	0		
2013–14	Bournemouth	0	0		
2013–14	Leyton Orient	8	1	8	1
2013–14	Torquay U	19	1	19	1
2014–15	Bournemouth	0	0		
2014–15	Cambridge U	3	2	3	2
2014–15	Luton T	13	3	13	3
2015–16	Bournemouth	0	0		
2015–16	Portsmouth	9	2	9	2
2015–16	Exeter C	22	10		
2016–17	Aberdeen	27	5	27	5
2017–18	Exeter C	41	19		
2018–19	Exeter C	25	16	88	45
2018–19	Preston NE	17	4		
2019–20	Preston NE	32	4		
2020–21	Preston NE	16	1	65	9
2020–21	Charlton Ath	22	8		
2021–22	Charlton Ath	33	13		
2022–23	Charlton Ath	24	2	79	23
2022–23	Fleetwood T	18	3		
2023–24	Fleetwood T	37	9	55	12
2024–25	Port Vale	38	11	38	11

TOLAJ, Lorent (F)   54   14
H: 5 9   W: 11 11   b.Aigle 23-10-01
Internationals: Switzerland U17, U18, U19.
From Sion.

2020–21	Brighton & HA	0	0		
2021–22	Brighton & HA	0	0		
2021–22	Cambridge U	4	0	4	0
2022–23	Brighton & HA	0	0		
2022–23	Salford C	11	0	11	0
2022–23	Dundee	2	0	2	0

From Aldershot T.

2024–25	Port Vale	37	14	37	14

WALTERS, Rhys (D)   24   0
H: 5 9   W: 11 07   b.Wolverhampton 18-11-05

2022–23	Port Vale	0	0		
2023–24	Port Vale	11	0		
2024–25	Port Vale	13	0	24	0

WYNNE, Deklan (D)   0   0
H: 5 10   W: 11 11   b.Johnsnesburg 20-3-96
Internationals: New Zealand U20, U23, Full caps.

2023–24	Port Vale	0	0		
2024–25	Port Vale	0	0		

Scholars
Agnero, Karl Gabriel Lohouess; Barker, George Jamieson; Blight, Dougie Anthony; Brazier, Liam Mathew; Bussell, Charlie William; Cousins, Logan Patrick; Francis, Louis John; Hunter, Joseph Anthony; Jenkins, Georgie Aroon; Lake, Edward John; Malbon, Clayton Tyler; Moseley, Keaton Blane; Orisakwe Nwoko, Miracle; Sadiq, Zayn; Silva Pevide, Joao Gabriel; Trapasso-Tully, Alessandro Daniel; Wara, Tomasi Jerahmeel Gregory; Williams, Joseph Edward.

PORTSMOUTH (67)

ANI, Michael (M)   0   0

2024–25	Portsmouth	0	0		

ARCHER, Jordan (G)   201   0
H: 6 1   W: 12 08   b.Walthamstow 12-4-93
Internationals: Scotland U19, U20, U21, Full caps.

2011–12	Tottenham H	0	0		
2012–13	Tottenham H	0	0		
2012–13	Wycombe W	27	0	27	0
2013–14	Tottenham H	0	0		
2014–15	Tottenham H	0	0		
2014–15	Northampton T	13	0	13	0
2014–15	Millwall	0	0		
2015–16	Millwall	39	0		
2016–17	Millwall	36	0		
2017–18	Millwall	45	0		
2018–19	Millwall	24	0	144	0
2019–20	Oxford U	6	0	6	0
2019–20	Fulham	0	0		
2020–21	Fulham	0	0		
2020–21	Motherwell	4	0	4	0
2020–21	Middlesbrough	5	0	5	0
2021–22	QPR	0	0		
2022–23	QPR	0	0		
2024–25	QPR	0	0		
2024–25	Portsmouth	2	0	2	0

BISHOP, Colby (M)   235   84
H: 5 11   W: 11 05   b.Nottingham 14-11-94

2013–14	Notts Co	0	0		
2014–15	Notts Co	3	0		
2015–16	Notts Co	1	0	4	0

From Worcester C, Boston U, Leamington.

2019–20	Accrington S	27	10		
2020–21	Accrington S	41	10		
2021–22	Accrington S	41	12	109	32
2022–23	Portsmouth	46	20		
2023–24	Portsmouth	44	21		
2024–25	Portsmouth	32	11	122	52

BLAIR, Harvey (F)   0   0
H: 5 10   W: 11 00   b.Huddersfield 14-9-03

2020–21	Liverpool	0	0		
2021–22	Liverpool	0	0		
2022–23	Liverpool	0	0		
2023–24	Liverpool	0	0		
2024–25	Portsmouth	12	1	12	1

BOWAT, Ibane (D)   47   1
H: 6 3   W: 13 01   b.Kingston upon Thames 15-9-02
Internationals: Scotland U21.

2022–23	Fulham	0	0		
2022–23	Den Bosch	16	0	16	0
2023–24	Fulham	0	0		
2023–24	TSV Hartberg	31	1	31	1
2024–25	Portsmouth	0	0		

BRAMALL, Cohen (D)   201   5
H: 5 9   W: 11 03   b.Crewe 2-4-96
From Hednesford T.

2017–18	Arsenal	0	0		
2017–18	Birmingham C	5	0	5	0
2018–19	Arsenal	0	0		
2019–20	Colchester U	24	1		
2020–21	Colchester U	23	0	47	1
2020–21	Lincoln C	17	0		
2021–22	Lincoln C	29	2	46	2
2022–23	Rotherham U	39	1		
2023–24	Rotherham U	36	1		
2024–25	Rotherham U	16	0	91	2
2024–25	Portsmouth	12	0	12	0

CLOUT, Harry (M)   0   0

2024–25	Portsmouth	0	0		

DEVLIN, Terry (M)   132   5
b.Cookstown 6-11-03
Internationals: Northern Ireland U21, Full caps.

2019–20	Dungannon Swifts	8	0		
2020–21	Dungannon Swifts	11	0		
2021–22	Dungannon Swifts	21	0		
2022–23	Dungannon Swifts	4	0	44	0
2022–23	Glentoran	35	4	35	4
2023–24	Portsmouth	19	1		
2024–25	Portsmouth	34	0	53	1

DOZZELL, Andre (M)   218   7
H: 5 10   W: 10 01   b.Ipswich 2-5-99
Internationals: England U16, U17, U18, U19, U20.

2015–16	Ipswich T	2	1		
2016–17	Ipswich T	6	0		
2017–18	Ipswich T	1	0		
2018–19	Ipswich T	19	1		
2019–20	Ipswich T	10	0		
2020–21	Ipswich T	43	0	81	2
2021–22	QPR	27	0		
2022–23	QPR	36	0		
2023–24	QPR	25	2	88	2
2023–24	Birmingham C	10	1	10	1
2024–25	Portsmouth	39	2	39	2

FARRELL, Jacob (D)   80   5
b. 19-11-02
Internationals: Australia U23.

2020	Central Coast Mariners	0	0		
2021	Valentine	4	0	4	0
2021–22	Central Coast Mariners	25	1		
2022–23	Central Coast Mariners	25	1		
2023–24	Central Coast Mariners	25	2	75	5
2024–25	Portsmouth	1	0	1	0

FOLARIN, Sam (F)   36   4
b. 23-8-00
From Tooting & Mitcham U.

2019–20	Middlesbrough	0	0		
2020–21	Middlesbrough	2	0		
2021–22	Middlesbrough	0	0	2	0
2021–22	Queen of the South	7	0	7	0
2022–23	Harrogate T	27	4	27	4
2023–24	Portsmouth	0	0		
2024–25	Portsmouth	0	0		

KAMARA, Abdoulaye (M)   5   0
b.Conakry 6-11-04

2021–22	Borussia Dortmund	0	0		
2022–23	Borussia Dortmund	0	0		
2023–24	Borussia Dortmund	0	0		
2024–25	Portsmouth	5	0	5	0

KILLIP, Ben (G)   105   0
H: 6 2   W: 11 09   b.Isleworth 24-11-95
Internationals: England C.
From Norwich C.

2017–18	Grimsby T	7	0	7	0

From Braintree T, Hartlepool U.

2021–22	Hartlepool U	42	0		
2022–23	Hartlepool U	29	0	71	0
2023–24	Barnsley	8	0		
2024–25	Barnsley	17	0	25	0
2024–25	Portsmouth	2	0	2	0

LANE, Paddy (F)   136   20
H: 5 9   W: 10 03   b.Halifax 18-2-01
Internationals: Northern Ireland U21, Full caps.
From Hyde U.

2021–22	Fleetwood T	37	5		
2022–23	Fleetwood T	20	1	57	6
2023–24	Fleetwood T	15	1		
2023–24	Portsmouth	42	12		
2024–25	Portsmouth	22	1	79	14

LANG, Callum (F) 273 70
H: 5 11 W: 11 00 b.Liverpool 8-9-98
2016–17 Wigan Ath 0 0
2017–18 Wigan Ath 0 0
2017–18 Morecambe 30 10 30 10
2018–19 Wigan Ath 0 0
2018–19 Oldham Ath 42 13 42 13
2019–20 Wigan Ath 1 0
2019–20 Shrewsbury T 16 3 16 3
2020–21 Wigan Ath 23 9
2020–21 Motherwell 17 3 17 3
2021–22 Wigan Ath 42 15
2022–23 Wigan Ath 35 1
2023–24 Wigan Ath 23 2 124 27
2023–24 Portsmouth 12 4
2024–25 Portsmouth 32 10 44 14

LOWERY, Tom (M) 194 15
H: 5 6 W: 11 11 b.Holmes Chapel 31-12-97
2016–17 Crewe Alex 7 0
2017–18 Crewe Alex 31 0
2018–19 Crewe Alex 15 1
2019–20 Crewe Alex 29 5
2020–21 Crewe Alex 37 3
2021–22 Crewe Alex 32 4
2022–23 Portsmouth 17 0
2023–24 Portsmouth 9 0
2024–25 Portsmouth 0 0 26 0
2024–25 Crewe Alex 17 2 168 15

MATTHEWS, Hayden (D) 35 0
b. 19-6-04
Internationals: Australia Full caps.
2022–23 Sydney 0 0
2023–24 Sydney 17 0
2024–25 Sydney 12 0 29 0
2024–25 Portsmouth 6 0 6 0

McINTYRE, Tom (D) 128 6
H: 6 1 W: 11 07 b.Reading 6-11-98
Internationals: Scotland U17, U20, U21.
2018–19 Reading 2 0
2019–20 Reading 10 0
2020–21 Reading 26 2
2021–22 Reading 19 2
2022–23 Reading 38 2
2023–24 Reading 10 0 105 6
2023–24 Portsmouth 1 0
2024–25 Portsmouth 12 0 13 0
2024–25 Charlton Ath 10 0 10 0

MORRELL, Joe (M) 170 4
H: 5 3 W: 11 05 b.Ipswich 3-1-97
Internationals: Wales U17, U19, U21, Full caps.
2013–14 Bristol C 0 0
2014–15 Bristol C 0 0
2015–16 Bristol C 0 0
2016–17 Bristol C 0 0
2017–18 Bristol C 0 0
2017–18 Cheltenham T 38 3 38 3
2018–19 Bristol C 1 0
2019–20 Bristol C 0 0 1 0
2019–20 Lincoln C 29 0 29 0
2020–21 Luton T 10 0 10 0
2021–22 Portsmouth 36 0
2022–23 Portsmouth 29 1
2023–24 Portsmouth 27 0
2024–25 Portsmouth 0 0 92 1

MURPHY, Josh (F) 330 40
H: 5 8 W: 10 08 b.Wembley 24-2-95
Internationals: England U18, U19, U20.
2012–13 Norwich C 0 0
2013–14 Norwich C 9 0
2014–15 Norwich C 13 1
2014–15 Wigan Ath 5 0 5 0
2015–16 Norwich C 0 0
2015–16 Milton Keynes D 42 5 42 5
2016–17 Norwich C 27 4
2017–18 Norwich C 41 7 90 12
2018–19 Cardiff C 29 3
2019–20 Cardiff C 27 5
2020–21 Cardiff C 32 2
2021–22 Cardiff C 0 0 88 10
2021–22 Preston NE 12 0 12 0
2022–23 Oxford U 23 0
2023–24 Oxford U 28 6 51 6
2024–25 Portsmouth 42 7 42 7

OGILVIE, Connor (D) 331 22
H: 6 0 W: 12 08 b.Harlow 14-2-96
Internationals: England U16, U17.
2013–14 Tottenham H 0 0
2014–15 Tottenham H 0 0
2015–16 Tottenham H 0 0
2015–16 Stevenage 21 1
2016–17 Tottenham H 0 0
2016–17 Stevenage 18 0 39 1
2017–18 Tottenham H 0 0
2017–18 Gillingham 37 1
2018–19 Tottenham H 0 0
2018–19 Gillingham 31 0
2019–20 Gillingham 33 4
2021–22 Gillingham 45 4 146 9
2021–22 Portsmouth 34 1
2022–23 Portsmouth 43 5
2023–24 Portsmouth 24 2
2024–25 Portsmouth 45 4 146 12

PACK, Marlon (M) 605 39
H: 6 0 W: 11 09 b.Portsmouth 25-3-91
2008–09 Portsmouth 0 0
2009–10 Portsmouth 0 0
2009–10 Wycombe W 8 0 8 0
2009–10 Dagenham & Red 17 1 17 1
2010–11 Portsmouth 1 0
2010–11 Cheltenham T 38 2
2011–12 Cheltenham T 43 5
2012–13 Cheltenham T 43 7
2013–14 Cheltenham T 0 0 124 14
2013–14 Bristol C 43 0
2014–15 Bristol C 34 3
2015–16 Bristol C 45 1
2016–17 Bristol C 33 2
2017–18 Bristol C 42 3
2018–19 Bristol C 46 2
2019–20 Bristol C 1 0 244 11
2019–20 Cardiff C 37 2
2020–21 Cardiff C 39 2
2021–22 Cardiff C 24 1 100 5
2022–23 Portsmouth 32 5
2023–24 Portsmouth 38 3
2024–25 Portsmouth 41 0 112 8

POOLE, Regan (D) 248 8
H: 5 11 W: 11 00 b.Cardiff 18-6-98
Internationals: Wales U17, U19, U20, U21, Full caps.
2014–15 Newport Co 11 0
2015–16 Newport Co 4 0
2015–16 Manchester U 0 0
2016–17 Manchester U 0 0
2017–18 Manchester U 0 0
2017–18 Northampton T 22 0 22 0
2018–19 Manchester U 0 0
2018–19 Newport Co 20 0 35 0
2019–20 Milton Keynes D 19 0
2020–21 Milton Keynes D 20 1 39 1
2020–21 Lincoln C 22 0
2021–22 Lincoln C 44 1
2022–23 Lincoln C 45 2 111 3
2023–24 Lincoln C 14 3
2024–25 Portsmouth 27 1 41 4

QUARM, Brian (D) 0 0
b. 9-12-05
2022–23 Portsmouth 0 0
2023–24 Portsmouth 0 0
2024–25 Portsmouth 0 0

RITCHIE, Matt (M) 523 96
H: 5 8 W: 11 02 b.Gosport 10-9-89
Internationals: Scotland Full caps.
2008–09 Portsmouth 0 0
2008–09 Dagenham & Red 37 11 37 11
2009–10 Portsmouth 2 0
2009–10 Notts Co 16 3 16 3
2009–10 Swindon T 4 0
2010–11 Portsmouth 5 0
2010–11 Swindon T 36 7
2011–12 Swindon T 43 9
2012–13 Swindon T 27 9 107 26
2012–13 Bournemouth 17 3
2013–14 Bournemouth 30 9
2014–15 Bournemouth 46 15
2015–16 Bournemouth 37 4 130 31
2016–17 Newcastle U 42 12
2017–18 Newcastle U 35 3
2018–19 Newcastle U 36 2
2019–20 Newcastle U 18 2
2020–21 Newcastle U 18 0
2021–22 Newcastle U 18 0
2022–23 Newcastle U 7 0
2023–24 Newcastle U 13 1 187 20
2024–25 Portsmouth 39 5 46 5

SAYDEE, Christian (F) 120 12
H: 5 11 W: 11 03 b.Hillingdon 10-5-02
2019–20 Bournemouth 0 0
2020–21 Bournemouth 0 0
2021–22 Bournemouth 2 0
2021–22 Burton Alb 18 0 18 0
2022–23 Bournemouth 0 0 2 0
2022–23 Shrewsbury T 35 7 35 7
2023–24 Portsmouth 36 2
2024–25 Portsmouth 29 3 65 5

SCHMID, Nicolas (G) 217 0
b.Linz 22-2-97
2015–16 FC Juniors 17 0
2016–17 FC Juniors 18 0
2017–18 FC Juniors 16 0 51 0
2018–19 Blau-Weiss Linz 1 0
2019–20 Blau-Weiss Linz 11 0
2020–21 Blau-Weiss Linz 28 0
2021–22 Blau-Weiss Linz 29 0
2022–23 Blau-Weiss Linz 29 0
2023–24 Blau-Weiss Linz 31 0
2024–25 Blau-Weiss Linz 2 0 131 0
2024–25 Portsmouth 35 0 35 0

SCULLY, Anthony (M) 111 26
H: 5 7 W: 10 06 b.Watford 19-4-99
Internationals: Republic of Ireland U16, U17, U18, U19, U21.
2018–19 West Ham U 0 0
2019–20 Lincoln C 5 2
2019–20 Lincoln C 40 11
2021–22 Lincoln C 35 11
2022–23 Lincoln C 5 1 85 25
2022–23 Wigan Ath 5 0 5 0
2023–24 Portsmouth 6 0
2024–25 Portsmouth 0 0 6 0
2024–25 Colchester U 15 1 15 1

SHAUGHNESSY, Conor (D) 171 10
H: 6 3 W: 11 09 b.Galway 30-6-96
Internationals: Republic of Ireland U17, U18, U19, U21, Full caps.
From Reading.
2017–18 Leeds U 9 0
2018–19 Leeds U 0 0
2018–19 Hearts 10 0 10 0
2019–20 Leeds U 0 0
2019–20 Mansfield T 15 0 15 0
2020–21 Burton Alb 8 0
2020–21 Leeds U 0 0 9 0
2020–21 Rochdale 18 1 18 1
2021–22 Burton Alb 38 3
2022–23 Burton Alb 19 1 65 4
2023–24 Portsmouth 45 4
2024–25 Portsmouth 9 1 54 5

SINGERR, Olutayo (F) 0 0
2024–25 Portsmouth 0 0

SMITH, Bastian (G) 0 0
b. 23-10-05
2022–23 Portsmouth 0 0
2023–24 Portsmouth 0 0
2024–25 Portsmouth 0 0

SORENSEN, Elias (F) 122 45
H: 6 2 W: 12 02 b.Sjunkeby 18-9-99
Internationals: Denmark U17, U19, U21.
From HB Køge.
2018–19 Newcastle U 0 0
2018–19 Blackpool 1 0 1 0
2019–20 Newcastle U 0 0
2019–20 Carlisle U 8 0 8 0
2020–21 Newcastle U 0 0
2020–21 Almere C 23 5 23 5
2021–22 Esbjerg 26 7
2022–23 Esbjerg 20 7
2023–24 Esbjerg 30 24
2024–25 Esbjerg 2 1 78 39
2024–25 Portsmouth 12 1 12 1
Transferred to Valerenga, January 2025.

STEWARD, Toby (G) 4 0
H: 6 4 b. 12-2-05
2021–22 Portsmouth 0 0
2022–23 Portsmouth 0 0
2023–24 Portsmouth 0 0
2024–25 Portsmouth 0 0
2024–25 Crawley T 4 0 4 0

SWANN, Reuben (M) 0 0
2024–25 Portsmouth 0 0

SWANSON, Zak (D) 57 2
H: 6 2 W: 12 02 b.Cambridge 28-9-00
2019–20 Arsenal 0 0
2020–21 Arsenal 0 0
2021–22 Arsenal 0 0
2022–23 Portsmouth 15 1
2023–24 Portsmouth 12 0
2024–25 Portsmouth 30 1 57 2

TOWLER, Ryley (M) 59 4
H: 6 1 W: 11 03 b.Bristol 6-5-01
2020–21 Bristol C 3 0
2021–22 Bristol C 1 0
2022–23 Bristol C 0 0 4 0
2022–23 AFC Wimbledon 17 1 17 1
2023–24 Portsmouth 20 2
2023–24 Portsmouth 6 0
2024–25 Portsmouth 12 1 38 3

WADDINGHAM, Thomas (F) 39 12
H: 6 1 W: b.Cairns 5-4-05
Internationals: Australia U20, U23.
2022–23 Brisbane Roar 0 0
2023–24 Brisbane Roar 3 0
2024–25 Brisbane Roar 11 4 34 11
2024–25 Portsmouth 5 1 5 1

WHYTE, Gavin (F) 299 56
H: 5 7 W: 10 08 b.Belfast 31-1-96
Internationals: Northern Ireland U21, Full caps.
2013–14 Crusaders 1 0
2014–15 Crusaders 34 9
2015–16 Crusaders 27 3
2016–17 Crusaders 34 10
2017–18 Crusaders 36 21 132 43
2018–19 Oxford U 36 7
2019–20 Cardiff C 24 0
2020–21 Cardiff C 7 0

2020–21	Hull C	20	4	**20 4**
2021–22	Cardiff C	0	0	
2021–22	Oxford U	37	1	**73 8**
2022–23	Cardiff C	14	1	**45 1**
2023–24	Portsmouth	29	0	
2024–25	Portsmouth	0	0	**29 0**

Transferred to Derry C, January 2025.

WILLIAMS, Jordan (D)   **201 6**
H: 5 10 W: 11 11 b.Huddersfield 22-10-99
Internationals: England U17, U18.

2017–18	Huddersfield T	0	0	
2017–18	Bury	9	0	**9 0**
2018–19	Barnsley	11	0	
2019–20	Barnsley	30	0	
2020–21	Barnsley	21	0	
2021–22	Barnsley	21	0	
2022–23	Barnsley	43	5	
2023–24	Barnsley	46	1	**172 6**
2024–25	Portsmouth	20	0	**20 0**

YENGI, Kusini (F)   **85 19**
b.Adelaide 15-1-96
Internationals: Australia U23, Full caps.

2019–20	Adelaide U	3	0	
2020–21	Adelaide U	16	4	
2021–22	Adelaide U	8	2	**27 6**
2022–23	Western Sydney W	18	4	**18 4**
2023–24	Portsmouth	26	9	
2024–25	Portsmouth	14	0	**40 9**

Players retained or with offer of contract
Ogilvie, Connor Stuart.

Scholars
Agu, Chinedu Fred Ayomide; Ani, Michael Obinna; Buckland, Reggie Eli; Chioma, Nathaniel Ugochukwu; Clout, Harry Thomas; Glover, Oscar Benjamin; Howard, Cody Richard; Keteku, Jayden David; Martin, Ciaran Anthony; May, Connor Philip Donald; McDermott, Conal Ciaran; Mullins, Beau William; Osifo, Jermaine Uyiosa Orleans; Singerr, Olutayo Joseph Kai; Staight, Luke Arthur Richard.

PRESTON NE (68)

BAUER, Patrick (D)   **264 17**
H: 6 4 W: 13 08 b.Backnang 28-10-92
Internationals: Germany U17, U18, U20.

2010–11	VfB Stuttgart	0	0	
2011–12	VfB Stuttgart	0	0	
2012–13	VfB Stuttgart	0	0	
2013–14	Maritimo	16	0	
2014–15	Maritimo	29	2	**45 2**
2015–16	Charlton Ath	19	1	
2016–17	Charlton Ath	36	4	
2017–18	Charlton Ath	34	3	
2018–19	Charlton Ath	35	0	**124 8**
2019–20	Preston NE	41	3	
2020–21	Preston NE	12	1	
2021–22	Preston NE	34	3	
2022–23	Preston NE	6	0	
2023–24	Preston NE	1	0	
2024–25	Preston NE	1	0	**95 7**

BEST, Kian (D)   **14 0**
b. 27-8-05
Internationals: England U19.

2023–24	Preston NE	12	0	
2024–25	Preston NE	1	0	**13 0**
2025	Bohemians	1	0	**1 0**

BRADY, Robert (F)   **355 22**
H: 5 9 W: 10 12 b.Dublin 14-1-92
Internationals: Republic of Ireland Youth, U21, Full caps.

2008–09	Manchester U	0	0	
2009–10	Manchester U	0	0	
2010–11	Manchester U	0	0	
2011–12	Manchester U	0	0	
2011–12	Hull C	39	3	
2012–13	Manchester U	0	0	
2012–13	Hull C	32	4	
2013–14	Hull C	16	3	
2014–15	Hull C	27	0	**114 10**
2015–16	Norwich C	36	3	
2016–17	Norwich C	23	4	**59 7**
2016–17	Burnley	14	1	
2017–18	Burnley	15	1	
2018–19	Burnley	16	0	
2019–20	Burnley	17	1	
2020–21	Burnley	19	1	**81 4**
2021–22	Bournemouth	6	0	**6 0**
2022–23	Preston NE	34	0	
2023–24	Preston NE	32	1	
2024–25	Preston NE	29	0	**95 1**

CARROLL, Theo (M)   **1 0**
b. 26-6-07

2024–25	Preston NE	1	0	**1 0**

CORNELL, David (G)   **188 0**
H: 6 2 W: 12 07 b.Waunarlwydd 28-3-91
Internationals: Wales U17, U19, U20.

2009–10	Swansea C	0	0	

2010–11	Swansea C	0	0	
2011–12	Swansea C	0	0	
2011–12	Hereford U	25	0	**25 0**
2012–13	Swansea C	0	0	
2013–14	Swansea C	0	0	
2013–14	St Mirren	5	0	**5 0**
2014–15	Swansea C	0	0	
2014–15	Portsmouth	0	0	
2015–16	Oldham Ath	14	0	**14 0**
2016–17	Northampton T	6	0	
2017–18	Northampton T	6	0	
2018–19	Northampton T	46	0	
2019–20	Northampton T	34	0	**92 0**
2020–21	Ipswich T	10	0	**10 0**
2021–22	Peterborough U	30	0	**30 0**
2022–23	Preston NE	0	0	
2023–24	Preston NE	2	0	
2024–25	Preston NE	10	0	**12 0**

EVANS, Ched (F)   **361 105**
H: 6 0 W: 12 00 b.Rhyl 28-12-88
Internationals: Wales U21, Full caps.
From Chester.

2006–07	Manchester C	0	0	
2007–08	Manchester C	0	0	
2007–08	Norwich C	28	10	**28 10**
2008–09	Manchester C	16	1	**16 1**
2009–10	Sheffield U	33	4	
2010–11	Sheffield U	34	9	
2011–12	Sheffield U	36	29	
2016–17	Chesterfield	25	5	**25 5**
2017–18	Sheffield U	9	0	
2018–19	Sheffield U	0	0	**112 42**
2018–19	Fleetwood T	39	17	
2019–20	Fleetwood T	28	9	
2020–21	Fleetwood T	17	5	**84 31**
2020–21	Preston NE	21	5	
2021–22	Preston NE	23	2	
2022–23	Preston NE	26	9	
2023–24	Preston NE	18	0	
2024–25	Preston NE	8	0	**96 16**

FELIPE, Rodriguez-Gentile (F)   **0 0**
b.Vinhedo 4-10-06

2023–24	Preston NE	0	0	
2024–25	Preston NE	0	0	

FROKJAER-JENSEN, Mads (M)   **183 21**
b.Copenhagen 29-7-99
Internationals: Denmark U21.

2018–19	OB	4	0	
2019–20	OB	25	2	
2020–21	OB	19	0	
2021–22	OB	28	6	
2022–23	OB	28	8	**104 16**
2023–24	Preston NE	41	3	
2024–25	Preston NE	38	2	**79 5**

GIBSON, Lewis (D)   **136 3**
H: 6 1 W: 11 07 b.Durham 19-7-00
Internationals: England U17, U18, U20.
From Newcastle U.

2019–20	Everton	0	0	
2019–20	Fleetwood T	9	0	**9 0**
2020–21	Everton	0	0	
2020–21	Reading	13	0	**13 0**
2021–22	Everton	0	0	
2021–22	Sheffield Wed	5	0	**5 0**
2022–23	Everton	0	0	
2022–23	Bristol R	31	1	**31 1**
2023–24	Plymouth Arg	41	0	
2024–25	Plymouth Arg	18	1	**59 1**
2024–25	Preston NE	19	1	**19 1**

HOLMES, Duane (M)   **330 30**
H: 5 8 W: 10 03 b.Wakefield 6-11-94
Internationals: USA Full caps.

2012–13	Huddersfield T	0	0	
2013–14	Huddersfield T	16	0	
2013–14	Yeovil T	5	0	**5 0**
2014–15	Huddersfield T	0	0	
2014–15	Bury	6	0	**6 0**
2015–16	Huddersfield T	6	1	
2016–17	Scunthorpe U	32	5	
2017–18	Scunthorpe U	45	7	
2018–19	Scunthorpe U	19	2	**78 10**
2019–20	Derby Co	25	2	
2020–21	Derby Co	33	2	
2020–21	Derby Co	14	1	**72 5**
2020–21	Huddersfield T	19	2	
2021–22	Huddersfield T	37	5	
2022–23	Huddersfield T	27	2	**105 10**
2023–24	Preston NE	35	4	
2024–25	Preston NE	29	1	**64 5**

Transferred to Houston D, March 2025.

HUGHES, Andrew (D)   **392 13**
H: 6 0 W: 11 11 b.Cardiff 5-6-92
Internationals: Wales C, U18, U23.

2013–14	Newport Co	26	2	
2014–15	Newport Co	16	1	
2015–16	Newport Co	25	0	**67 3**
2016–17	Peterborough U	39	1	
2017–18	Peterborough U	43	2	**82 3**
2018–19	Preston NE	29	0	
2019–20	Preston NE	28	0	
2020–21	Preston NE	34	0	

2021–22	Preston NE	40	1	
2022–23	Preston NE	30	2	
2023–24	Preston NE	39	1	
2024–25	Preston NE	40	0	**243 7**

JAKOBSEN, Emil (F)   **238 54**
H: 6 3 W: 13 01 b.Hobro 24-6-98
Internationals: Denmark U16, U17, U19, U20, U21.

2017–18	Derby Co	0	0	
2017–18	VVV Venlo	3	0	**3 0**
2018–19	Randers	30	4	
2019–20	Randers	33	9	
2020–21	Randers	0	0	**63 13**
2020–21	Randers	38	2	
2021–22	Randers	44	16	
2022–23	Randers	24	5	
2023–24	Randers	21	6	
2024–25	Preston NE	45	12	**172 41**

KAMARA, Kaedyn (M)   **0 0**
H: 5 10 W: 11 09 b.Liverpool 29-11-05
From Burnley.

2022–23	Preston NE	0	0	
2023–24	Preston NE	0	0	
2024–25	Preston NE	0	0	

KEANE, Will (F)   **289 75**
H: 6 2 W: 11 05 b.Stockport 11-1-93
Internationals: England U16, U17, U19, U20, U21. Republic of Ireland Full caps.

2009–10	Manchester U	0	0	
2010–11	Manchester U	0	0	
2011–12	Manchester U	1	0	
2012–13	Manchester U	0	0	
2013–14	Manchester U	0	0	
2013–14	Wigan Ath	4	0	
2013–14	QPR	10	0	**10 0**
2014–15	Manchester U	0	0	
2014–15	Sheffield Wed	13	3	**13 3**
2015–16	Manchester U	1	0	
2015–16	Preston NE	20	1	
2016–17	Manchester U	0	0	**2 0**
2016–17	Hull C	5	0	
2017–18	Hull C	9	1	
2018–19	Hull C	8	0	**22 1**
2018–19	Ipswich T	11	3	
2019–20	Ipswich T	23	3	**34 6**
2020–21	Wigan Ath	32	10	
2021–22	Wigan Ath	44	26	
2022–23	Wigan Ath	43	12	**123 48**
2023–24	Preston NE	38	13	
2024–25	Preston NE	3	0	**85 17**

LEDSON, Ryan (M)   **284 8**
H: 5 9 W: 10 12 b.Liverpool 19-8-97
Internationals: England U16, U17, U18, U19, U21.

2013–14	Everton	0	0	
2014–15	Everton	0	0	
2015–16	Everton	0	0	
2015–16	Cambridge U	27	0	**27 0**
2016–17	Oxford U	22	1	
2017–18	Oxford U	44	3	**66 4**
2018–19	Preston NE	24	0	
2019–20	Preston NE	13	0	
2020–21	Preston NE	36	2	
2021–22	Preston NE	25	0	
2022–23	Preston NE	40	1	
2023–24	Preston NE	27	0	
2024–25	Preston NE	26	1	**191 4**

LINDSAY, Liam (D)   **336 17**
H: 6 4 W: 12 06 b.Paisley 12-10-95

2012–13	Partick Thistle	1	0	
2013–14	Alloa Ath	10	0	**10 0**
2013–14	Partick Thistle	1	0	
2014–15	Partick Thistle	1	0	
2014–15	Airdrieonians	13	1	**13 1**
2015–16	Partick Thistle	25	1	
2016–17	Partick Thistle	36	6	**64 7**
2017–18	Barnsley	42	1	
2018–19	Barnsley	41	1	**83 2**
2019–20	Stoke C	20	1	
2020–21	Stoke C	0	0	**20 1**
2020–21	Preston NE	13	2	
2021–22	Preston NE	15	0	
2022–23	Preston NE	37	0	
2023–24	Preston NE	46	3	
2024–25	Preston NE	35	1	**146 6**

MAWENE, Noah (M)   **22 0**
H: 6 1 W: 11 09 b.Preston 1-2-05

2022–23	Preston NE	0	0	
2023–24	Preston NE	7	0	
2024–25	Preston NE	0	0	**8 0**
2024–25	Newport Co	14	0	**14 0**

MAWENE, Theo (M)   **1 0**
b. 12-7-07

2023–24	Preston NE	1	0	
2024–25	Preston NE	0	0	**1 0**

McCANN, Alistair (M)   **203 9**
H: 5 9 W: 10 01 b.Edinburgh 4-12-99
Internationals: Northern Ireland U21, Full caps.

2016–17	St Johnstone	0	0	
2017–18	St Johnstone	3	0	

Season	Club	A	G	TA	TG
2018–19	St Johnstone	1	0		
2018–19	*Stranraer*	13	1	13	1
2019–20	St Johnstone	29	4		
2020–21	St Johnstone	34	2		
2021–22	St Johnstone	4	0	71	6
2021–22	Preston NE	28	1		
2022–23	Preston NE	31	0		
2023–24	Preston NE	31	0		
2024–25	Preston NE	29	1	119	2

McGHEE, Cole (D) 0 0
| 2024–25 | Preston NE | 0 | 0 | | |

NELSON, Kitt (M) 18 4
b. 12-1-05
2023–24	Preston NE	0	0		
2024–25	Preston NE	0	0		
2025	*Cork C*	18	4	18	4

OKKELS, Jeppe (F) 217 34
b. 27-7-99
Internationals: Denmark U16, U17, U18, U19, U20, U21.
2015–16	Silkeborg	1	0		
2016–17	Silkeborg	7	0		
2017–18	Silkeborg	21	0		
2018–19	Silkeborg	31	6		
2019–20	Silkeborg	29	3	89	9
2020	Elfsborg	11	3		
2021	Elfsborg	30	8		
2022	Elfsborg	29	2		
2023	Elfsborg	30	11	100	24
2023–24	*Utrecht*	5	0	5	0
2024–25	Preston NE	7	0	7	0
2024–25	*Aberdeen*	16	1	16	1

OSMAJIC, Milutin (M) 207 50
b. 25-7-99
Internationals: Montenegro U21, Full caps.
2017–18	Sutjeska	13	2		
2018–19	Sutjeska	23	2		
2019–20	Sutjeska	12	1		
2020–21	Sutjeska	34	13	82	18
2021–22	Cadiz	10	0		
2021–22	*Bandirmaspor*	13	7	13	7
2022–23	Cadiz	0	0		
2022–23	*Vizela*	31	8	31	8
2023–24	Cadiz	1	0	11	0
2023–24	Preston NE	36	8		
2024–25	Preston NE	34	9	70	17

PASIEK, Kacper (D) 0 0
b. 8-10-05
| 2024–25 | Preston NE | 0 | 0 | | |

POTTS, Brad (M) 467 54
H: 6 2 W: 12 11 b.Hexham 3-7-94
Internationals: England U19.
2012–13	Carlisle U	27	0		
2013–14	Carlisle U	37	2		
2014–15	Carlisle U	39	7	103	9
2015–16	Blackpool	45	6		
2016–17	Blackpool	42	10	87	16
2017–18	Barnsley	37	3		
2018–19	Barnsley	22	6	59	9
2018–19	Preston NE	10	2		
2019–20	Preston NE	32	2		
2020–21	Preston NE	42	5		
2021–22	Preston NE	35	1		
2022–23	Preston NE	39	4		
2023–24	Preston NE	31	2		
2024–25	Preston NE	29	4	218	20

PRADIC, James (G) 0 0
b. 2-7-05
Internationals: Wales U16, U17, U18.
From Charlton Ath.
2022–23	Preston NE	0	0		
2023–24	Preston NE	0	0		
2024–25	Preston NE	0	0		

SEARY, Joshua (D) 4 0
b.Liverpool 10-9-04
Internationals: Republic of Ireland U19.
| 2023–24 | Preston NE | 4 | 0 | | |
| 2024–25 | Preston NE | 0 | 0 | 4 | 0 |

STEWART, Layton (F) 31 4
H: 5 11 W: 10 06 b.Liverpool 2-9-02
Internationals: England U18.
2019–20	Liverpool	0	0		
2020–21	Liverpool	0	0		
2021–22	Liverpool	0	0		
2022–23	Liverpool	0	0		
2023–24	Preston NE	16	0		
2024–25	Preston NE	0	0	16	0
2024–25	*Thun*	15	4	15	4

STOREY, Jordan (D) 237 0
H: 6 2 W: 11 11 b.Yeovil 2-9-97
2016–17	Exeter C	0	0		
2017–18	Exeter C	13	2	13	2
2018–19	Preston NE	28	1		
2019–20	Preston NE	10	0		
2020–21	Preston NE	30	1		
2021–22	Preston NE	17	0		
2021–22	*Sheffield Wed*	19	2	19	2
2022–23	Preston NE	44	2		

| 2023–24 | Preston NE | 41 | 0 | | |
| 2024–25 | Preston NE | 35 | 1 | 205 | 5 |

STOWELL, Li-Bau (G) 0 0
| 2024–25 | Preston NE | 0 | 0 | | |

TARRY, Troy (D) 0 0
| 2024–25 | Preston NE | 0 | 0 | | |

TAYLOR, Kian (M) 0 0
b. 15-2-05
| 2023–24 | Preston NE | 0 | 0 | | |
| 2024–25 | Preston NE | 0 | 0 | | |

THORDARSON, Stefan (M) 220 37
H: 6 2 W: 12 02 b.Akranes 16-10-98
Internationals: Iceland U21, Full caps.
2016	IA	3	0		
2017	IA	16	2		
2018	IA	22	10		
2019	IA	20	1		
2020	IA	17	8	78	21
2020–21	Silkeborg	20	1		
2021–22	Silkeborg	28	2		
2022–23	Silkeborg	27	1		
2023–24	Silkeborg	28	9	103	13
2024–25	Preston NE	39	3	39	3

WHATMOUGH, Jack (D) 242 6
H: 6 0 W: 10 06 b.Gosport 19-8-96
Internationals: England U18, U19.
2012–13	Portsmouth	0	0		
2013–14	Portsmouth	12	0		
2014–15	Portsmouth	22	0		
2015–16	Portsmouth	2	0		
2016–17	Portsmouth	10	1		
2017–18	Portsmouth	14	0		
2018–19	Portsmouth	26	0		
2019–20	Portsmouth	1	0		
2020–21	Portsmouth	34	2	121	3
2021–22	Wigan Ath	46	2		
2022–23	Wigan Ath	37	1	83	3
2023–24	Preston NE	22	0		
2024–25	Preston NE	16	0	38	0

WHITEMAN, Ben (M) 332 37
H: 6 1 W: 10 10 b.Rochdale 17-6-96
2014–15	Sheffield U	0	0		
2015–16	Sheffield U	6	0		
2016–17	Sheffield U	2	0	8	0
2016–17	*Mansfield T*	23	7	23	7
2017–18	Doncaster R	42	6		
2018–19	Doncaster R	40	3		
2019–20	Doncaster R	33	5		
2020–21	Doncaster R	18	5	133	19
2020–21	Preston NE	23	1		
2021–22	Preston NE	44	4		
2022–23	Preston NE	36	3		
2023–24	Preston NE	30	3		
2024–25	Preston NE	35	0	168	11

WOODMAN, Freddie (G) 249 0
H: 6 1 W: 10 12 b.Croydon 4-3-97
Internationals: England U16, U17, U18, U19, U20, U21.
From Crystal Palace.
2014–15	Newcastle U	0	0		
2014–15	*Hartlepool U*	0	0		
2015–16	Newcastle U	0	0		
2015–16	*Crawley T*	11	0	11	0
2016–17	Newcastle U	0	0		
2016–17	*Kilmarnock*	14	0	14	0
2017–18	Newcastle U	0	0		
2017–18	*Aberdeen*	5	0	5	0
2018–19	Newcastle U	0	0		
2019–20	Newcastle U	0	0		
2019–20	*Swansea C*	43	0		
2020–21	Newcastle U	0	0		
2020–21	*Swansea C*	45	0	88	0
2021–22	Newcastle U	4	0		
2021–22	*Bournemouth*	0	0		
2022–23	Preston NE	46	0		
2023–24	Preston NE	44	0		
2024–25	Preston NE	37	0	127	0

Players retained or with offer of contract
Wilson, Max Riley.

Scholars
Blake, Joseph Ellis; Brindle, Jonathan James; Carroll, Theo Jon; Critchley, Peter Anthony Frederick; Davis, Thomas Stephen; Fitton, Benjamin James; Forwood, Charlie; Gairns, Dylan John; Garrigan, Ayden James; Haji, Muhammad Raiyaan; Ifezue, Somtochukwu Chikelu; Kamara, Kaedyn Kabbar; Lam, Isaac Daniel Gar Lai; Lescott, Clayton Patrick; Mawene, Theodore Beaumont; McGhee, Cole James; Muir, Joshua Jack; Nolan, Edward Anthony; Pasiek, Kacper Nikodem; Robinson, Ben Alexander; Stowell, Li-Bau Kenny; Stringfellow, Harry; Tarry, Troy Junior.

QPR (69)

ANDERSEN, Lucas (M) 345 48
H: 6 1 W: 11 05 b.Aalborg 13-9-94
Internationals: Denmark U16, U17, U18, U19, U21, Full caps.
Season	Club	A	G	TA	TG
2010–11	AaB	11	0		
2011–12	AaB	22	1		
2012–13	AaB	7	2		
2013–14	Ajax	1	0		
2013–14	Ajax	9	0		
2014–15	Ajax	27	2		
2015–16	Ajax	0	0	37	2
2015–16	*Willem II*	30	6	30	6
2016–17	Grasshopper	33	6		
2017–18	Grasshopper	32	4		
2018–19	Grasshopper	4	0	69	10
2018–19	AaB	23	10		
2019–20	AaB	27	10		
2020–21	AaB	18	1		
2021–22	AaB	7	0		
2022–23	AaB	31	1		
2023–24	AaB	14	2	160	27
2023–24	QPR	16	1		
2024–25	QPR	33	2	49	3

AORAHA, Alexander (M) 0 0
H: 5 10 W: 10 01 b.London 17-1-03
Internationals: Iraq U20, U23, Full caps.
2022–23	QPR	0	0		
2023–24	QPR	0	0		
2024–25	QPR	0	0		

BENNIE, Daniel (F) 37 1
b. 13-4-06
2022–23	Perth Glory	0	0		
2023–24	Perth Glory	25	1	25	1
2024–25	QPR	12	0	12	0

CELAR, Zan (F) 164 47
H: 6 1 W: 12 13 b.Kranj 14-3-99
Internationals: Australia U17, U20.
2015–16	Maribor	1	0		
2016–17	Maribor	0	0		
2017–18	Maribor	0	0	1	0
2018–19	Roma	0	0		
2018–19	Roma	1	0		
2019–20	Roma	0	0		
2019–20	*Cittadella*	10	1	10	1
2019–20	*Cremonese*	11	2		
2020–21	Roma	0	0	1	0
2020–21	*Cremonese*	27	2	38	4
2021–22	Lugano	29	10		
2022–23	Lugano	30	16		
2023–24	Lugano	36	14	95	40
2024–25	QPR	19	2	19	2

CHAIR, Ilias (M) 263 42
H: 5 2 W: 8 09 b.Antwerp 30-10-97
Internationals: Morocco U20, U23, Full caps.
2015–16	Lierse	2	0		
2016–17	Lierse	0	0	2	0
2017–18	QPR	4	1		
2018–19	QPR	4	0		
2018–19	*Stevenage*	16	6	16	6
2019–20	QPR	41	4		
2020–21	QPR	45	8		
2021–22	QPR	39	9		
2022–23	QPR	40	5		
2023–24	QPR	44	7		
2024–25	QPR	28	2	245	36

CLARKE-SALTER, Jake (D) 170 4
H: 6 2 W: 11 00 b.Carshalton 22-9-97
Internationals: England U18, U19, U20, U21.
2015–16	Chelsea	1	0		
2016–17	Chelsea	0	0		
2016–17	*Bristol R*	12	1	12	1
2017–18	Chelsea	0	0		
2017–18	*Sunderland*	11	0	11	0
2018–19	Chelsea	0	0		
2018–19	*Vitesse*	28	1	28	1
2019–20	Chelsea	0	0		
2019–20	*Birmingham C*	19	1		
2020–21	Chelsea	0	0		
2020–21	*Birmingham C*	10	0	29	1
2021–22	Chelsea	0	0	1	0
2021–22	*Coventry C*	29	0	29	0
2022–23	QPR	16	0		
2023–24	QPR	33	1		
2024–25	QPR	11	0	60	1

COLBACK, Jack (M) 431 24
H: 5 10 W: 11 13 b.Killingworth 24-10-89
Internationals: England U20.
2007–08	Sunderland	0	0		
2008–09	Sunderland	0	0		
2009–10	Sunderland	1	0		
2009–10	*Ipswich T*	37	4		
2010–11	Sunderland	11	0		
2010–11	*Ipswich T*	13	0	50	4
2011–12	Sunderland	35	1		
2012–13	Sunderland	35	0		
2013–14	Sunderland	33	3	115	4
2014–15	Newcastle U	35	4		
2015–16	Newcastle U	29	1		

2016–17 Newcastle U 29 0
2017–18 Newcastle U 0 0
2017–18 *Nottingham F* 16 1
2018–19 Newcastle U 0 0
2018–19 *Nottingham F* 38 3
2019–20 Newcastle U 0 0 **93 5**
2020–21 Nottingham F 17 0
2021–22 Nottingham F 38 3
2022–23 Nottingham F 11 0 **120 7**
2023–24 QPR 29 3
2024–25 QPR 24 1 **53 4**

COOK, Steve (D) 452 23
H: 6 1 W: 12 13 b.Hastings 19-4-91
2008–09 Brighton & HA 2 0
2009–10 Brighton & HA 0 0
2010–11 Brighton & HA 0 0
2011–12 Brighton & HA 1 0 **3 0**
2011–12 Bournemouth 26 0
2012–13 Bournemouth 33 1
2013–14 Bournemouth 38 3
2014–15 Bournemouth 46 5
2015–16 Bournemouth 36 4
2016–17 Bournemouth 38 2
2017–18 Bournemouth 34 2
2018–19 Bournemouth 31 1
2019–20 Bournemouth 29 1
2020–21 Bournemouth 42 0
2021–22 Bournemouth 3 0 **356 19**
2021–22 Nottingham F 14 0
2022–23 Nottingham F 12 0 **26 0**
2023–24 QPR 36 2
2024–25 QPR 31 2 **67 4**

DEMBELE, Karamoko (M) 86 12
H: 5 3 W: 8 09 b.Lambeth 22-2-03
Internationals: Scotland U16, U17. England U17, U18, U19.
2018–19 Celtic 1 0
2019–20 Celtic 1 0
2020–21 Celtic 5 1
2021–22 Celtic 1 0 **8 1**
2022–23 Brest 15 0
2023–24 Brest 1 0
2023–24 *Blackpool* 39 8 **39 8**
2024–25 Brest 0 0 **16 0**
On loan from Brest.
2024–25 QPR 23 3 **23 3**

DIXON-BONNER, Elijah (M) 33 0
H: 5 8 W: 9 11 b.Harlow 1-1-01
Internationals: England U16, U17.
2019–20 Liverpool 0 0
2020–21 Liverpool 0 0
2021–22 Liverpool 0 0
2022–23 QPR 1 0
2023–24 QPR 24 0
2024–25 QPR 3 0 **28 0**
2024–25 *Vasteras* 5 0 **5 0**

DUNNE, Jimmy (D) 208 16
H: 6 1 W: 11 05 b.Drogheda 19-10-97
Internationals: Republic of Ireland U21, Full caps.
From Manchester U.
2017–18 Burnley 0 0
2017–18 *Accrington S* 20 0 **20 0**
2018–19 Burnley 0 0
2018–19 *Hearts* 12 2 **12 2**
2018–19 *Sunderland* 12 1 **12 1**
2019–20 Burnley 0 0
2019–20 *Fleetwood T* 9 1 **9 1**
2020–21 Burnley 3 1 **3 1**
2021–22 QPR 38 3
2022–23 QPR 40 2
2023–24 QPR 29 1
2024–25 QPR 45 5 **152 11**

ESQUERDINHA, Joao Henrique (D) 6 0
b. 28-2-06
Internationals: Brazil U17.
2023–24 Fluminense 1 0
2024–25 Fluminense 5 0 **6 0**
2024–25 QPR 0 0
2024–25 QPR 0 0

FIELD, Sam (M) 223 12
H: 5 10 W: 11 07 b.Stourbridge 8-5-98
Internationals: England U18, U19, U20.
2015–16 WBA 1 0
2016–17 WBA 8 0
2017–18 WBA 10 1
2018–19 WBA 12 1
2019–20 WBA 0 0
2019–20 *Charlton Ath* 17 0
2020–21 Charlton Ath 0 0 **17 0**
2020–21 WBA 3 0 **34 2**
2020–21 *QPR* 19 1
2021–22 QPR 29 0
2022–23 QPR 46 2
2023–24 QPR 43 4
2024–25 QPR 35 3 **172 10**

FOX, Morgan (D) 316 7
H: 6 1 W: 12 04 b.Chelmsford 21-9-93
Internationals: Wales U21.
2012–13 Charlton Ath 0 0
2013–14 Charlton Ath 6 0
2013–14 *Notts Co* 7 1 **7 1**
2014–15 Charlton Ath 31 0
2015–16 Charlton Ath 42 1
2016–17 Charlton Ath 24 0 **103 1**
2016–17 Sheffield Wed 10 1
2017–18 Sheffield Wed 28 0
2018–19 Sheffield Wed 25 0
2019–20 Sheffield Wed 27 2 **90 3**
2020–21 Stoke C 20 0
2021–22 Stoke C 10 0
2022–23 Stoke C 40 0 **70 0**
2023–24 QPR 20 1
2024–25 QPR 26 1 **46 2**

FREY, Michael (F) 344 102
b.Munsingen 19-7-94
Internationals: Switzerland U17, U19, U20, U21.
2011–12 Young Boys 2 1
2012–13 Young Boys 31 4
2013–14 Young Boys 33 9
2014–15 Young Boys 7 3
2014–15 Lille 15 2
2015–16 Lille 0 0 **15 2**
2015–16 *Luzern* 16 4 **16 4**
2016–17 Young Boys 29 8 **102 25**
2017–18 Zurich 31 12
2018–19 Zurich 3 0 **34 12**
2018–19 Fenerbahce 14 3
2019–20 Fenerbahce 0 0
2019–20 *1. FC Nurnberg* 29 4 **29 4**
2020–21 Fenerbahce 1 0 **15 3**
2020–21 *Beveren* 27 12 **27 12**
2021–22 Antwerp 39 24
2022–23 Antwerp 14 7 **53 31**
2022–23 *Shalke 04* 15 0 **15 0**
2023–24 QPR 9 1
2024–25 QPR 29 8 **38 9**

FRIEL, Rocco (D) 0 0
b. 14-10-06
Internationals: Scotland U17.
2024–25 QPR 0 0

HEVERTTON, Santos (D) 53 0
b.Sao Mateus 1-2-01
2020–21 Sporting Lisbon 0 0
2021–22 Sporting Lisbon 0 0
2022–23 Estrela da Amadora 12 0
2023–24 Estrela da Amadora 29 0 **41 0**
2024–25 QPR 6 0 **6 0**
2024–25 *Vitoria de Guimaraes* 6 0 **6 0**

KELMAN, Charlie (F) 180 39
H: 5 11 W: 11 00 b.Basildon 2-11-01
Internationals: USA U18, U20.
2018–19 Southend U 10 1
2019–20 Southend U 18 5
2020–21 Southend U 3 0 **31 6**
2020–21 QPR 11 0
2021–22 QPR 1 0
2021–22 *Gillingham* 23 2 **23 2**
2022–23 QPR 0 0
2022–23 *Leyton Orient* 43 7
2023–24 QPR 11 0
2023–24 *Wigan Ath* 14 3 **14 3**
2024–25 QPR 0 0 **23 0**
2024–25 *Leyton Orient* 46 21 **89 28**

KOLLI, Rayan (M) 30 4
b.London 10-2-05
Internationals: Algeria U20.
2023–24 QPR 10 0
2024–25 QPR 20 4 **30 4**

LLOYD, Alfie (F) 27 2
b. 30-4-03
2020–21 QPR 0 0
2021–22 QPR 0 0
2022–23 QPR 0 0
2023–24 QPR 0 0
2024–25 QPR 27 2 **27 2**

MADSEN, Nicolas (M) 161 19
H: 6 4 b.Odense 17-3-00
Internationals: Denmark U17, U18, U19, U21.
2019–20 Midtjylland 9 0
2020–21 Midtjylland 17 0
2021–22 Midtjylland 4 0 **30 0**
2021–22 *Heerenveen* 26 0 **26 0**
2022–23 Westerlo 36 2
2023–24 Westerlo 34 13
2024–25 Westerlo 4 1 **74 16**
2024–25 QPR 31 3 **31 3**

MORGAN, Kieran (M) 30 1
b. 17-3-06
2024–25 QPR 30 1 **30 1**

MORRISON, Liam (M) 49 1
b.Saltcoats 7-4-03
Internationals: Scotland U16, U17, U19, U21.
From Celtic.
2021–22 Bayern Munich 0 0
2022–23 Bayern Munich 0 0
2023–24 Bayern Munich 0 0
2023–24 *Wigan Ath* 30 1 **30 1**
2024–25 QPR 19 0 **19 0**

MURPHY, Harry (M) 0 0
b. 21-1-04
2024–25 QPR 0 0

NARDI, Paul (G) 298 0
H: 6 1 W: 12 02 b.Vesoul 18-5-94
Internationals: France U17, U18, U19, U20, U21.
2010–11 Nancy 0 0
2011–12 Nancy 0 0
2012–13 Nancy 0 0
2013–14 Nancy 33 0
2014–15 Nancy 29 0 **62 0**
2015–16 Monaco 2 0
2016–17 Monaco 0 0
2016–17 *Rennes* 0 0
2016–17 Cercle Brugge 14 0
2017–18 Monaco 0 0
2017–18 *Cercle Brugge* 29 0
2018–19 Monaco 0 0 **2 0**
2018–19 *Cercle Brugge* 38 0 **81 0**
2019–20 Lorient 28 0
2020–21 Lorient 23 0
2021–22 Lorient 22 0 **73 0**
2022–23 Gent 30 0
2023–24 Gent 5 0 **35 0**
2024–25 QPR 45 0 **45 0**

PAAL, Kenneth (D) 228 9
H: 5 9 W: 11 00 b.Arnhem 24-6-97
Internationals: Netherlands U17. Suriname Full caps.
2014–15 PSV Eindhoven 0 0
2015–16 PSV Eindhoven 0 0
2016–17 PSV Eindhoven 0 0
2017–18 PSV Eindhoven 5 0
2018–19 PSV Eindhoven 0 0 **5 0**
2018–19 *PEC Zwolle* 29 0
2019–20 PEC Zwolle 19 3
2020–21 PEC Zwolle 27 0
2021–22 PEC Zwolle 25 0 **100 3**
2022–23 QPR 40 1
2023–24 QPR 44 4
2024–25 QPR 39 1 **123 6**

PEDDER, Rafferty (M) 0 0
b.Maidstone 6-4-02
From Tottenham H.
2023–24 QPR 0 0
2024–25 QPR 0 0

PETRIE, Kieran (F) 0 0
b. 16-12-04
2024–25 QPR 0 0

SAITO, Koki (F) 181 27
b. 10-8-01
Internationals: Japan U16, U17, U18, U19, U20, U21, U23.
2018 Yokohama 2 0
2019 Yokohama 29 6
2020 Yokohama 32 3 **63 9**
2020–21 Lommel 9 0
2021–22 Lommel 20 5
2022–23 Lommel 0 0
2022–23 *Sparta Rotterdam* 30 7
2023–24 Lommel 0 0
2023–24 *Sparta Rotterdam* 20 3 **50 10**
2024–25 Lommel 0 0 **29 5**
On loan from Lommel.
2024–25 QPR 39 3 **39 3**

SALAMON, Matteo (G) 0 0
b.Porto Seguro 18-2-04
2023–24 QPR 0 0
2024–25 QPR 0 0

SHEPPERD, Nathan (G) 69 0
b.Tonypandy 10-9-00
Internationals: Wales U21.
2020–21 Brentford 0 0
2022 Dundalk 33 0
2023 Dundalk 36 0 **69 0**
2023–24 Wycombe W 0 0
2024–25 QPR 0 0

SMYTH, Paul (F) 237 27
H: 5 10 W: 11 07 b.Belfast 10-9-97
Internationals: Northern Ireland U19, U21, Full caps.
2017–18 Linfield 0 0
2017–18 QPR 13 2
2018–19 QPR 3 0
2018–19 *Accrington S* 15 3
2019–20 QPR 0 0
2019–20 *Wycombe W* 19 1 **19 1**
2020–21 QPR 3 0
2020–21 *Charlton Ath* 14 1 **14 1**
2020–21 *Accrington S* 21 3 **36 6**
2021–22 Leyton Orient 24 3
2022–23 Leyton Orient 38 10 **62 13**
2023–24 QPR 44 3
2024–25 QPR 43 1 **106 6**

SUTTON, Emmerson (M) 2 0
b.London 28-12-06
2024–25 QPR 2 0 **2 0**

TALLA, Lorent (M)   0   0
b. 1-1-05
Internationals: Albania U19. Kosovo U19.

2023–24	QPR	0	0
2024–25	QPR	0	0

TUCK, Alfie (M)   0   0
b. 9-5-06
Internationals: Wales U17, U19.

2024–25	QPR	0	0

VALE, Harvey (M)   41   2
H: 5 11 W: 11 07 b.Hayards Heath 11-9-03
Internationals: England U16, U17, U19, U20.

2020–21	Chelsea	0	0	
2021–22	Chelsea	0	0	
2022–23	*Hull C*	2	0	2 0
2023–24	Chelsea	0	0	
2023–24	*Bristol R*	39	2	39 2
2024–25	Chelsea	0	0	
2024–25	QPR	0	0	

VARANE, Jonathan (M)   85   0
b. 9-9-01

2020–21	Lens	0	0	
2021–22	Lens	1	0	1 0
2021–22	*Rodez*	6	0	6 0
2022–23	Sporting Gijon	17	0	
2023–24	Sporting Gijon	22	0	39 0
2024–25	QPR	39	0	39 0

WALSH, Joe (G)   10   0
H: 6 4 W: 11 11 b.Gillingham 1-4-02

2019–20	Gillingham	0	0	
2020–21	Gillingham	1	0	1 0
2020–21	QPR	0	0	
2021–22	QPR	0	0	
2022–23	QPR	0	0	
2023–24	QPR	0	0	
2023–24	*Accrington S*	7	0	7 0
2024–25	QPR	1	0	2 0

Players retained or with offer of contract
Cooper, Murphy Joseph; Halliday, Joel Stuart Mark; Larkeche, Ziyad; Leahy, Jake; McDowell, Jack; O'Brien, Archie Joseph; Putman, Jaiden Ellis; Richards, Taylor Jerome; Shelly Dillon, Cian; Vaughan, Rohan Ellis.

Scholars
Adjetey-Brew, Cory Ugene Michael; Balogun, Isaiah Ajibayo Abdul-Gafar; Clark, Conor Crispin; Coomes, Jake Thomas; Cuthbert, Gabriel Kalel Hamilton; Hamid, Hassan Ali Faheem; Hassan, Ridwanullahi Oladeji Ayinde; Hayati, Kooshan; Jones, La'Trell MacKenzie; Keita-Turay, Kemoko Alpha; Kennedy, Rico Nathaniel Kyan; Loades, Callum James; Manufor, Samuel George Ikenna; McCann, Noah Albert Peter; Neill, Fraser George Drew; Neziri, Enis; Radojevic, Luka; Recber, Mehmet Burak; Sanyaolu, Philip Olanrewaju Tobiloba; Skeete, Mason Martin; Strachan, Lorenzo Wade; Tarbotton, Teddy.

READING (70)

ABREFA, Kelvin (D)   49   0
H: 6 2 W: 12 00 b.Wenchi 9-12-03
Internationals: Ghana U20.

2021–22	Reading	3	0	
2022–23	Reading	8	0	
2023–24	Reading	11	0	
2024–25	Reading	27	0	49 0

AHMED, Ashqar (D)   5   0
H: 5 7 W: 10 10 b. 31-8-07

2023–24	Reading	0	0	
2024–25	Reading	5	0	5 0

AKANDE, Adrian (F)   15   0
H: 5 9 W: 10 10 b. 22-10-03

2024–25	Reading	15	0	15 0

ANDRESSON, Jokull (G)   76   0
H: 6 4 W: 12 13 b.Mosfellsbaer 25-8-01
Internationals: Iceland U17, U19, U21, Full caps.
From Afturelding.

2019–20	Reading	0	0	
2020–21	Reading	0	0	
2020–21	*Morecambe*	2	0	
2020–21	*Exeter C*	29	0	
2021–22	Reading	0	0	
2021–22	*Morecambe*	13	0	15 0
2022–23	Reading	0	0	
2022–23	*Exeter C*	1	0	30 0
2022–23	*Stevenage*	3	0	3 0
2023–24	Reading	0	0	
2023–24	*Carlisle U*	6	0	6 0
2024–25	Reading	0	0	
2024–25	*Afturelding*	22	0	22 0

BAROUGH, Joe (D)   0   0
b. 3-4-06

2024–25	Reading	0	0

BEACROFT, Boyd (F)   0   0
b. 22-11-05

2024–25	Reading	0	0

BORGNIS, Jacob (D)   0   0
b. 5-5-03

2024–25	Reading	0	0

BOYCE-CLARKE, Coniah (G)   2   0
H: 6 0 W: 13 08 b.Reading 1-3-03
Internationals: England U16, U17. Jamaica U20, Full caps.

2019–20	Reading	0	0	
2020–21	Reading	0	0	
2021–22	Reading	0	0	
2022–23	Reading	1	0	
2023–24	Reading	0	0	
2024–25	Reading	1	0	2 0

BUTTON, David (G)   359   0
H: 6 3 W: 11 00 b.Stevenage 27-2-89
Internationals: England U16, U17, U19, U20.

2005–06	Tottenham H	0	0	
2006–07	Tottenham H	0	0	
2007–08	*Rochdale*	0	0	
2007–08	Tottenham H	0	0	
2008–09	Tottenham H	0	0	
2008–09	*Bournemouth*	4	0	4 0
2008–09	*Luton T*	1	0	
2008–09	*Dagenham & Red*	3	0	3 0
2009–10	Tottenham H	0	0	
2009–10	*Crewe Alex*	10	0	10 0
2009–10	*Shrewsbury T*	26	0	26 0
2010–11	Tottenham H	0	0	
2010–11	*Plymouth Arg*	30	0	30 0
2011–12	Tottenham H	0	0	
2011–12	*Leyton Orient*	1	0	1 0
2011–12	*Doncaster R*	7	0	7 0
2011–12	*Barnsley*	9	0	9 0
2012–13	Tottenham H	0	0	
2012–13	*Charlton Ath*	5	0	5 0
2013–14	Brentford	42	0	
2014–15	Brentford	46	0	
2015–16	Brentford	46	0	134 0
2016–17	Fulham	40	0	
2017–18	Fulham	20	0	60 0
2018–19	Brighton & HA	4	0	
2019–20	Brighton & HA	0	0	
2020–21	Brighton & HA	0	0	4 0
2020–21	WBA	1	0	
2021–22	WBA	10	0	
2022–23	WBA	13	0	24 0
2023–24	Reading	37	0	
2024–25	Reading	5	0	42 0

CAMARA, Mamadi (F)   51   3
H: 5 9 W: 10 08 b.Guinea-Bissau 31-12-03
Internationals: Guinea-Bissau Full caps.

2020–21	Reading	1	0	
2021–22	Reading	6	0	
2022–23	Reading	5	0	
2023–24	Reading	6	0	
2024–25	Reading	33	3	51 3

CARROLL, Tommy (M)   267   4
H: 5 10 W: 10 00 b.Watford 28-5-92
Internationals: England U19, U21.

2010–11	Tottenham H	0	0	
2010–11	*Leyton Orient*	12	0	12 0
2011–12	Tottenham H	0	0	
2011–12	*Derby Co*	12	1	12 1
2012–13	Tottenham H	7	0	
2013–14	Tottenham H	0	0	
2013–14	*QPR*	26	0	
2014–15	Tottenham H	0	0	
2014–15	*Swansea C*	13	0	
2015–16	Tottenham H	19	1	
2016–17	Tottenham H	1	0	27 1
2016–17	*Swansea C*	17	1	
2017–18	Swansea C	37	0	
2018–19	Swansea C	12	0	
2018–19	*Aston Villa*	2	0	2 0
2019–20	Swansea C	8	0	87 1
2020–21	QPR	22	0	
2021–22	QPR	0	0	48 0
2021–22	*Ipswich T*	14	0	14 0
2023–24	*Exeter C*	42	1	42 1
2024–25	*Milton Keynes D*	14	0	14 0
2024–25	Reading	9	0	9 0

CASTRO, Joel (G)   99   0
H: 6 2 W: 12 13 b.Le Locle 28-6-96
Internationals: Switzerland U16, U17. Portugal U17, U18, U19, U20, U21.

2015–16	Manchester U	0	0	
2015–16	*Rochdale*	6	0	6 0
2016–17	Manchester U	1	0	
2016–17	*Belenenses*	8	0	8 0
2017–18	Manchester U	0	0	
2018–19	Manchester U	0	0	
2018–19	*Vitoria Setubal*	9	0	9 0
2018–19	*Kortrijk*	0	0	
2019–20	Manchester U	0	0	
2019–20	*Hearts*	20	0	20 0

CLARKE, John (D)   3   0
H: 5 9 W: 11 05 b.Annfield Plain 24-4-04
Internationals: Republic of Ireland U19.
From Port Vale.

2022–23	Reading	3	0	
2023–24	Reading	0	0	
2024–25	Reading	0	0	3 0

CRAIG, Michael (M)   60   2
H: 6 0 W: 11 09 b.Barnet 16-4-03
Internationals: Scotland U16, U17, U19, U21.

2020–21	Tottenham H	0	0	
2021–22	Tottenham H	0	0	
2022–23	Reading	2	0	
2023–24	Reading	28	0	
2024–25	Reading	30	2	60 2

DEAN, Harlee (D)   453   16
H: 6 3 W: 11 11 b.Basingstoke 26-7-91

2008–09	Dagenham & Red	0	0	
2009–10	Dagenham & Red	1	0	1 0
2010–11	Southampton	0	0	
2011–12	Southampton	0	0	
2011–12	Brentford	26	1	
2012–13	Brentford	44	3	
2013–14	Brentford	32	0	
2014–15	Brentford	35	1	
2015–16	Brentford	42	0	
2016–17	Brentford	42	3	
2017–18	Brentford	3	0	224 8
2017–18	Birmingham C	34	1	
2018–19	Birmingham C	44	1	
2019–20	Birmingham C	39	1	
2020–21	Birmingham C	43	4	
2021–22	Birmingham C	15	0	
2021–22	*Sheffield Wed*	7	0	7 0
2022–23	Birmingham C	16	1	191 8
2023–24	Reading	11	0	
2024–25	Reading	19	0	30 0

DORSETT, Jeriel (D)   85   2
H: 5 10 W: 10 01 b.Enfield 4-5-02
Internationals: England U17, U18. Montserrat Full caps.

2019–20	Reading	0	0	
2020–21	Reading	0	0	
2021–22	Reading	0	0	
2021–22	*Rochdale*	37	0	37 0
2022–23	Reading	0	0	
2022–23	*Kilmarnock*	11	1	11 1
2023–24	Reading	23	1	
2024–25	Reading	14	0	37 1

DUAH, Phillip (F)   0   0
H: 6 3 b. 13-11-06

2024–25	Reading	0	0

EHIBHATIONHAM, Kelvin (F)   81   10
H: 6 3 W: 12 13 b.Benin City 23-4-03

2021–22	Reading	0	0	
2022–23	Reading	8	1	
2023–24	Reading	40	5	
2024–25	Reading	33	4	81 10

ELLIOTT, Ben (M)   56   2
H: 5 10 W: 10 03 b.London 5-11-02
Internationals: England U16. Cameroon Full caps.

2023–24	Reading	0	0	
2024–25	Reading	19	2	56 2

GARCIA, Andre (M)   38   0
H: 5 6 W: 9 11 b. 8-3-08
Internationals: England U18.

2024–25	Reading	38	0	38 0

HARRISON, Sam (D)   0   0
b. 24-10-06

2024–25	Reading	0	0

HOLZMAN, Louie (D)   9   0
H: 5 10 W: 12 00 b.Windsor 16-11-03

2021–22	Reading	0	0	
2022–23	Reading	0	0	
2023	*Bohemians*	0	0	
2023–24	Reading	0	0	
2024–25	Reading	9	0	9 0

KANU, Abrham (D)   10   0
H: 6 1 W: 12 00 b. 3-7-05
Internationals: Sierra Leone U20.

2024–25	Reading	10	0	10 0

KNIBBS, Harvey (F)   209   43
H: 6 2 W: 11 03 b.Bristol 26-4-99

2017–18	Aston Villa	0	0	
2018–19	Aston Villa	0	0	
2019–20	Cambridge U	24	7	
2020–21	Cambridge U	23	2	
2021–22	Cambridge U	34	4	
2022–23	Cambridge U	40	5	121 18
2023–24	Reading	45	11	
2024–25	Reading	43	14	88 25

NORCOTT, Tom (G) 0 0
H: 6 1 W: 11 00 b. 3-1-05
2023–24 Reading 0 0
2024–25 Reading 0 0

OKINE-PETERS, Jeremiah (D) 0 0
2024–25 Reading 0 0

OSHO, Emmanuel (D) 1 0
H: 6 0 W: 10 10 b. 26-9-06
2024–25 Reading 1 0 1 0

RHONE, Harrison (G) 0 0
H: 6 5 b. 25-3-06
2024–25 Reading 0 0

ROWLEY, Matthew (G) 0 0
H: 6 0 b. 30-7-04
2024–25 Reading 0 0

RUSHESHA, Tivonge (D) 22 0
H: 5 11 W: 11 11 b.Zimbabwe 24-7-02
Internationals: Wales U17.
2019–20 Swansea C 0 0
2020–21 Swansea C 0 0
2021–22 Swansea C 0 0
2022–23 Swansea C 0 0
2023–24 Reading 4 0
2024–25 Reading 18 0 22 0

RYAN, John (D) 0 0
H: 5 11 W: 11 00 b.County Limerick 21-1-04
Internationals: Republic of Ireland U16, U18, U19.
2023–24 Reading 0 0
2024–25 Reading 0 0

SACKEY, Tyler (M) 0 0
H: 5 10 W: 11 05 b. 2-9-06
2024–25 Reading 0 0

SAINT-LOUIS, T'Shay (F) 0 0
2024–25 Reading 0 0

SALIF, Amadou (D) 109 2
H: 5 11 W: 11 11 b. 5-1-02
Internationals: Senegal U23.
2020–21 Metz 0 0
2021–22 Metz 12 0 12 0
2022–23 Reading 26 1
2023–24 Reading 37 0
2024–25 Reading 34 1 97 2

SAVAGE, Charlie (M) 100 9
H: 6 0 W: 11 05 b.Leicester 2-5-03
Internationals: Wales U17, U18, U19, U21, Full caps.
2020–21 Manchester U 0 0
2021–22 Manchester U 0 0
2022–23 Manchester U 0 0
2022–23 Forest Green R 15 1 15 1
2023–24 Reading 40 3
2024–25 Reading 45 5 85 8

SENGA-NGOYI, Jack (G) 12 0
H: 6 1 b. 27-1-04
2021–22 Reading 0 0
2022–23 Reading 1 0
2023–24 Reading 0 0
2023–24 Ayr U 11 0 11 0
2024–25 Reading 0 0 1 0

SPENCER, Shay (M) 1 0
b. 9-11-03
2024–25 Reading 1 0 1 0

STICKLAND, Michael (D) 6 0
H: 6 3 W: 11 07 b. 9-11-03
2021–22 Reading 1 0
2022–23 Reading 0 0
2023–24 Reading 0 0
2024–25 Reading 5 0 6 0

TUMA, Basil (D) 6 0
H: 5 10 W: 11 00 b. 24-4-05
Internationals: Malta U19, U21, Full caps.
2022–23 Reading 0 0
2023–24 Reading 2 0
2024–25 Reading 4 0 6 0

WAREHAM, Jayden (F) 49 5
H: 5 10 W: 11 07 b.Ascot 13-5-03
2022–23 Chelsea 0 0
2022–23 Leyton Orient 5 0 5 0
2023–24 Reading 7 0
2024–25 Reading 37 5 44 5

WELLENS, Charlie (M) 0 0
H: 5 9 W: 9 08 b.Salford 5-12-02
2023–24 Reading 0 0
2024–25 Reading 0 0

WING, Lewis (M) 283 47
H: 5 9 W: 11 00 b.Newton Aycliffe 23-5-95
From Tow Law T, Seaham Red Star, Darlington 1883, Newton Aycliffe, Seaham Red Star, Shildon.
2017–18 Middlesbrough 0 0
2017–18 Yeovil T 20 3 20 3
2018–19 Middlesbrough 28 3
2019–20 Middlesbrough 40 7
2020–21 Middlesbrough 12 2
2020–21 Rotherham U 20 2 20 2
2021–22 Middlesbrough 0 0 80 12
2021–22 Sheffield Wed 18 0 18 0
2021–22 Wycombe W 13 2
2022–23 Wycombe W 44 9 57 11
2023–24 Reading 42 0
2024–25 Reading 46 9 88 19

YIADOM, Andy (M) 365 14
H: 5 11 W: 11 11 b.Camden 9-12-91
Internationals: England C. Ghana Full caps.
From Hayes & Yeading U, Braintree T.
2011–12 Barnet 7 1
2012–13 Barnet 39 3
From Barnet.
2015–16 Barnet 40 6 86 10
2016–17 Barnsley 32 0
2017–18 Barnsley 32 0 64 0
2018–19 Reading 45 1
2019–20 Reading 24 1
2020–21 Reading 21 1
2021–22 Reading 38 1
2022–23 Reading 41 0
2023–24 Reading 32 0
2024–25 Reading 14 0 215 4

Players retained or with offer of contract
Coke-Miles-Smith, Kiyan David Slevin; Jones, Jerae Ashford; Mbengue, Amadou Salif.

Scholars
Ahmed, Ashqar Zamil; Booth, George Thomas; Bossman, Dennis Amenama; Covus, Ainsley Javan; Dove, Anthony Benjamin; Duah, Philip Kwadwo Owusu; Fuller-Thompson, Kallum Anthony Trae; Garcia, Andre Jacob; George, Verrell Ron; Harrison, Samuel Reece; Howard, Luke James; Irish, Harley Richard; Neptune, Jacob Benjamin; Nour, Aaron Augustine; Omoregie, Larry Osatohanmwen; Pullinger, Matthew John; Sharlott, James Reese; Source, Kai William; St. Louis, T'Shay Luke; Welland, Joshua Daniel; Zie, Ryan Emmanuel.

ROTHERHAM U (71)

AYRES, Josh (M) 0 0
H: 6 3 W: 12 13 b. 24-11-05
2023–24 Rotherham U 0 0
2024–25 Rotherham U 0 0

BASSETT, Louis (G) 0 0
2024–25 Rotherham U 0 0

CLARKE, James (M) 0 0
2024–25 Rotherham U 0 0

CLARKE, Lewis (D) 0 0
2024–25 Rotherham U 0 0

CLARKE-HARRIS, Jonson (F) 426 138
H: 6 0 W: 11 03 b.Leicester 21-7-94
Internationals: Jamaica Full caps.
2010–11 Coventry C 0 0
2011–12 Coventry C 0 0
2012–13 Peterborough U 0 0
2012–13 Southend U 3 0 3 0
2012–13 Bury 12 4 12 4
2013–14 Oldham Ath 40 6
2014–15 Oldham Ath 5 1 45 7
2014–15 Rotherham U 15 3
2014–15 Milton Keynes D 5 0 5 0
2014–15 Doncaster R 9 1 9 1
2015–16 Rotherham U 35 6
2016–17 Rotherham U 7 0
2017–18 Rotherham U 14 0
2017–18 Coventry C 17 3
2018–19 Coventry C 27 5 44 8
2018–19 Bristol R 26 13
2019–20 Bristol R 26 13 42 24
2020–21 Peterborough U 45 31
2021–22 Peterborough U 41 12
2022–23 Peterborough U 46 26
2023–24 Peterborough U 34 9 166 78
2024–25 Rotherham U 29 7 100 16

DAWSON, Cameron (G) 167 0
H: 6 0 W: 10 12 b.Sheffield 7-7-95
Internationals: England U18, U19.
2013–14 Sheffield Wed 0 0
2013–14 Plymouth Arg 0 0
2014–15 Sheffield Wed 0 0
2015–16 Sheffield Wed 0 0
2016–17 Sheffield Wed 0 0
2016–17 Wycombe W 1 0 1 0
2017–18 Sheffield Wed 3 0
2017–18 Chesterfield 2 0 2 0
2018–19 Sheffield Wed 26 0
2019–20 Sheffield Wed 24 0
2020–21 Sheffield Wed 8 0
2021–22 Sheffield Wed 0 0
2021–22 Exeter C 45 0 45 0
2022–23 Sheffield Wed 0 0
2023–24 Sheffield Wed 18 0 105 0
2024–25 Rotherham U 14 0 14 0

DOUGLAS, Hamish (M) 2 0
b. 4-6-05
2022–23 Rotherham U 0 0
2023–24 Rotherham U 0 0
2024–25 Rotherham U 2 0 2 0

DUNCAN, Harrison (M) 0 0
2024–25 Rotherham U 0 0

GARDNER, Dean (M) 0 0
2024–25 Rotherham U 0 0

GREEN, Andre (F) 149 14
H: 5 11 W: 11 03 b.Solihull 2-5-98
Internationals: England U16, U17, U18, U19, U20.
2014–15 Aston Villa 0 0
2015–16 Aston Villa 2 0
2016–17 Aston Villa 15 0
2017–18 Aston Villa 5 1
2018–19 Aston Villa 18 1
2018–19 Portsmouth 6 1 6 1
2019–20 Aston Villa 0 0 40 2
2019–20 Preston NE 4 0 4 0
2019–20 Charlton Ath 13 2 13 2
2020–21 Sheffield Wed 11 0
2021–22 Sheffield Wed 2 0 13 0
2021–22 Slovan Bratislava 5 0
2022–23 Slovan Bratislava 25 6 51 6
2023–24 Rotherham U 9 0
2024–25 Rotherham U 13 3 22 3

HATTON, Ben (M) 3 0
H: 5 10 W: 11 00 b. 1-11-05
2023–24 Rotherham U 3 0
2024–25 Rotherham U 0 0 3 0

HOLMES, Jack (M) 28 0
H: 5 9 W: 10 12 b. 19-9-01
2024–25 Rotherham U 28 0 28 0

HUGILL, Jordan (F) 377 71
H: 6 0 W: 10 01 b.Middlesbrough 4-6-92
From Seaham Red Star, Consett, Whitby T.
2013–14 Port Vale 4 0 20 4
2014–15 Preston NE 3 0
2014–15 Tranmere R 6 1 6 1
2014–15 Hartlepool U 8 4 8 4
2015–16 Preston NE 29 3
2016–17 Preston NE 44 12
2017–18 Preston NE 27 8 103 23
2017–18 West Ham U 3 0
2018–19 West Ham U 0 0
2018–19 Middlesbrough 37 6 37 6
2019–20 West Ham U 0 0 3 0
2019–20 QPR 39 13
2020–21 QPR 0 0 39 13
2020–21 Norwich C 31 4
2021–22 Norwich C 0 0
2021–22 WBA 20 1 20 1
2021–22 Cardiff C 18 4 18 4
2022–23 Norwich C 7 0 38 4
2022–23 Rotherham U 18 5
2023–24 Rotherham U 39 5
2024–25 Rotherham U 28 1 85 11

HULL, Jake (D) 7 0
H: 6 6 W: 14 11 b.Sheffield 22-10-01
2020–21 Rotherham U 0 0
2021–22 Rotherham U 0 0
2021–22 Hartlepool U 7 0 7 0
2022–23 Rotherham U 0 0
2023–24 Rotherham U 0 0
2024–25 Rotherham U 0 0

HUMPHREYS, Cameron (D) 161 2
H: 6 2 W: 12 08 b.Manchester 22-7-98
Internationals: England U16, U17, U18, U19.
2015–16 Manchester C 0 0
2016–17 Manchester C 0 0
2017–18 Manchester C 0 0
2018–19 Zulte-Waregem 3 0
2019–20 Excelsior 3 0 3 0
2020–21 Zulte-Waregem 26 0
2021–22 Zulte-Waregem 26 0 55 0
2022–23 Rotherham U 38 0
2023–24 Rotherham U 25 0
2024–25 Rotherham U 40 2 103 2

JAMES, Reece (D) 252 13
H: 5 6 W: 11 03 b.Bacup 7-11-93
2012–13 Manchester U 0 0
2013–14 Manchester U 0 0
2013–14 Carlisle U 1 0 1 0
2014–15 Rotherham U 7 0
2014–15 Huddersfield T 6 1 6 1
2015–16 Wigan Ath 26 1
2016–17 Wigan Ath 0 0
2017–18 Wigan Ath 22 0 48 1
2018–19 Sunderland 27 0 27 0
2019–20 Doncaster R 27 2
2020–21 Doncaster R 43 7 70 9
2021–22 Blackpool 17 0
2022–23 Blackpool 0 0 17 0
2022–23 Sheffield Wed 0 0
2023–24 Sheffield Wed 8 0 33 0
2024–25 Rotherham U 43 2 50 2

JULES, Zak (D) **207** **8**
H: 6 3 W: 11 05 b.Islington 2-7-97
Internationals: Scotland U17, U18, U19, U20, U21.

2016–17	Reading	0	0		
2016–17	*Motherwell*	10	1	**10**	**1**
2017–18	Shrewsbury T	0	0		
2017–18	*Chesterfield*	6	0	**6**	**0**
2017–18	*Port Vale*	2	0	**2**	**0**
2018–19	Macclesfield T	14	0	**14**	**0**
2019–20	Walsall	17	0		
2020–21	Walsall	17	1	**34**	**1**
2020–21	Milton Keynes D	20	1		
2021–22	Milton Keynes D	7	0		
2021–22	*Fleetwood T*	20	0	**20**	**0**
2022–23	Milton Keynes D	32	1	**59**	**2**
2023–24	Exeter C	40	2	**40**	**2**
2024–25	Rotherham U	22	2	**22**	**2**

KAYODE, Joshua (F) **89** **12**
H: 6 3 W: 11 11 b.Lagos 4-5-00
Internationals: Republic of Ireland U21.

2017–18	Rotherham U	0	0		
2018–19	Rotherham U	0	0		
2019–20	Rotherham U	0	0		
2019–20	*Carlisle U*	5	3		
2020–21	Rotherham U	0	0		
2020–21	*Carlisle U*	34	8		
2021–22	Rotherham U	20	1		
2021–22	*Carlisle U*	0	0		
2022–23	Rotherham U	0	0		
2022–23	*Milton Keynes D*	6	0	**6**	**0**
2023–24	Rotherham U	4	0		
2023–24	*Carlisle U*	3	0	**42**	**11**
2024–25	Rotherham U	12	0	**36**	**1**
2024–25	*Shrewsbury T*	5	0	**5**	**0**

KELLY, Liam (M) **393** **30**
H: 6 2 W: 13 12 b.Milton Keynes 10-2-90
Internationals: Scotland U18, U21, Full caps.

2009–10	Kilmarnock	15	1		
2010–11	Kilmarnock	32	7		
2011–12	Kilmarnock	34	1		
2012–13	Kilmarnock	19	6	**100**	**15**
2012–13	Bristol C	19	0		
2013–14	Bristol C	2	0	**21**	**0**
2014–15	Oldham Ath	37	1		
2015–16	Oldham Ath	41	6	**78**	**7**
2016–17	Leyton Orient	21	4	**21**	**4**
2017–18	Coventry C	33	1		
2018–19	Coventry C	30	0		
2019–20	Coventry C	27	0		
2020–21	Coventry C	23	2		
2021–22	Coventry C	16	0		
2022–23	Coventry C	10	0		
2023–24	Coventry C	16	0	**155**	**3**
2024–25	Rotherham U	18	1	**18**	**1**

MACDONALD, Alex (F) **451** **35**
H: 5 7 W: 11 05 b.Warrington 14-4-90
Internationals: Scotland U19, U21.

2007–08	Burnley	2	0		
2008–09	Burnley	3	0		
2009–10	Burnley	0	0		
2009–10	*Falkirk*	11	0	**11**	**0**
2010–11	Burnley	0	0		
2010–11	*Inverness CT*	10	1	**10**	**1**
2011–12	Burnley	5	0		
2011–12	*Plymouth Arg*	18	4		
2012–13	Burnley	1	0	**11**	**0**
2012–13	*Plymouth Arg*	16	1	**34**	**5**
2012–13	*Burton Alb*	15	1		
2013–14	Burton Alb	35	0		
2014–15	Burton Alb	21	6	**71**	**7**
2014–15	Oxford U	15	3		
2015–16	Oxford U	40	5		
2016–17	Oxford U	22	1	**77**	**9**
2016–17	Mansfield T	18	1		
2017–18	Mansfield T	41	3		
2018–19	Mansfield T	21	1		
2019–20	Mansfield T	29	1	**109**	**6**
2020–21	Gillingham	37	1		
2021–22	Gillingham	7	1		
2022–23	Gillingham	43	2	**87**	**4**
2023–24	Stevenage	26	2	**26**	**2**
2024–25	Rotherham U	15	1	**15**	**1**

McCART, Jamie (D) **212** **4**
H: 6 2 W: 13 08 b.Bellshill 20-6-97
Internationals: Scotland U19, U21.

2016–17	Celtic	0	0		
2016–17	*Inverness CT*	11	0		
2017–18	Celtic	0	0		
2017–18	*St Mirren*	3	0	**3**	**0**
2017–18	*Alloa Ath*	13	1	**13**	**1**
2018–19	Inverness CT	26	1		
2019–20	Inverness CT	19	1	**56**	**2**
2019–20	St Johnstone	8	0		
2020–21	St Johnstone	37	0		
2021–22	St Johnstone	37	1	**82**	**1**
2022–23	Rotherham U	7	0		
2022–23	*Leyton Orient*	8	0	**8**	**0**
2023–24	Rotherham U	1	0		
2023–24	*Barnsley*	26	0	**26**	**0**
2024–25	Rotherham U	16	0	**24**	**0**

Transferred to Hearts, January 2025.

McGUCKIN, Ciaran (M) **11** **0**
H: 6 2 W: 12 04 b.Leeds 30-12-03
Internationals: Northern Ireland U16, U17, U19, U21.

2021–22	Rotherham U	0	0		
2022–23	Rotherham U	0	0		
2023–24	Rotherham U	3	0		
2024	*Dundalk*	5	0	**5**	**0**
2024–25	Rotherham U	3	0	**6**	**0**

McWILLIAMS, Shaun (M) **224** **6**
H: 5 11 W: 10 12 b.Northampton 14-8-98

2014–15	Northampton T	0	0		
2015–16	Northampton T	0	0		
2016–17	Northampton T	5	0		
2017–18	Northampton T	19	0		
2018–19	Northampton T	25	0		
2019–20	Northampton T	17	1		
2020–21	Northampton T	32	0		
2021–22	Northampton T	36	0		
2022–23	Northampton T	30	3		
2023–24	Northampton T	36	2	**200**	**6**
2024–25	Rotherham U	24	0	**24**	**0**

NOMBE, Sam (F) **202** **42**
H: 5 11 W: 11 00 b.Croydon 22-10-98

2016–17	Milton Keynes D	0	0		
2017–18	Milton Keynes D	6	0		
2018–19	Milton Keynes D	0	0		
2019–20	Milton Keynes D	21	2		
2020–21	Milton Keynes D	4	0	**31**	**2**
2020–21	*Luton T*	11	0	**11**	**0**
2021–22	Exeter C	28	8		
2022–23	Exeter C	43	15		
2023–24	Exeter C	5	0	**76**	**23**
2023–24	Rotherham U	41	3		
2024–25	Rotherham U	43	14	**84**	**17**

ODOFIN, Hakeem (D) **186** **16**
H: 6 3 W: 12 11 b.Barnet 13-4-98

2015–16	Barnet	1	0	**1**	**0**
2016–17	Wolverhampton W	0	0		
2017–18	Wolverhampton W	0	0		
2018–19	Northampton T	12	0	**12**	**0**
2018–19	Livingston	13	0		
2019–20	Livingston	7	0	**20**	**0**
2020–21	Hamilton A	37	3	**37**	**3**
2021–22	Rotherham U	11	0		
2022–23	Rotherham U	23	4		
2023–24	Rotherham U	38	4		
2024–25	Rotherham U	44	5	**116**	**13**

PHILLIPS, Dillon (M) **161** **0**
H: 6 2 W: 11 11 b.Hornchurch 11-6-95

2012–13	Charlton Ath	0	0		
2013–14	Charlton Ath	0	0		
2014–15	Charlton Ath	0	0		
2015–16	Charlton Ath	0	0		
2016–17	Charlton Ath	8	0		
2017–18	Charlton Ath	0	0		
2018–19	Charlton Ath	27	0		
2019–20	Charlton Ath	46	0	**81**	**0**
2020–21	Cardiff C	16	0		
2021–22	Cardiff C	17	0		
2022–23	Cardiff C	0	0	**33**	**0**
2022–23	*Oostende*	12	0	**12**	**0**
2023–24	Rotherham U	2	0		
2024–25	Rotherham U	33	0	**35**	**0**

POWELL, Joe (M) **219** **22**
H: 5 10 W: 10 10 b.Newham 30-10-98

2018–19	West Ham U	0	0		
2018–19	*Northampton T*	10	2	**10**	**2**
2019–20	West Ham U	0	0		
2019–20	Burton Alb	10	3		
2020–21	Burton Alb	39	6		
2021–22	Burton Alb	34	3		
2022–23	Burton Alb	36	2		
2023–24	Burton Alb	44	5	**163**	**19**
2024–25	Rotherham U	46	1	**46**	**1**

RAFFERTY, Joe (D) **379** **5**
H: 5 11 W: 11 11 b.Liverpool 6-10-93
Internationals: Republic of Ireland U18, U19.
From Liverpool.

2012–13	Rochdale	21	0		
2013–14	Rochdale	31	0		
2014–15	Rochdale	31	1		
2015–16	Rochdale	31	1		
2016–17	Rochdale	40	0		
2017–18	Rochdale	33	1		
2018–19	Rochdale	27	0	**214**	**3**
2018–19	Preston NE	6	0		
2019–20	Preston NE	29	1		
2020–21	Preston NE	22	0		
2021–22	Preston NE	5	0	**62**	**1**
2022–23	Portsmouth	25	0		
2023–24	Portsmouth	39	0	**64**	**0**
2024–25	Rotherham U	39	1	**39**	**1**

RAGGETT, Sean (D) **241** **17**
H: 6 5 W: 12 04 b.Gillingham 17-4-93
Internationals: England C.
From Dover Ath.

2017–18	Lincoln C	25	2	**25**	**2**
2017–18	Norwich C	2	0		
2018–19	Norwich C	0	0		
2018–19	*Rotherham U*	7	1		
2019–20	Norwich C	0	0	**2**	**0**
2019–20	*Portsmouth*	26	2		
2020–21	Portsmouth	45	3		
2021–22	Portsmouth	45	6		
2022–23	Portsmouth	44	1		
2023–24	Portsmouth	38	1	**198**	**13**
2024–25	Rotherham U	9	1	**16**	**2**

RICHARDSON, Kane (M) **0** **0**
b. 30-5-07

2024–25	Rotherham U	0	0		

TIEHI, Christ (M) **117** **3**
H: 5 10 W: 12 04 b.Paris 16-6-98
Internationals: Ivory Coast U20.

2015–16	Le Havre	0	0		
2016–17	Le Havre	0	0		
2017–18	Le Havre	0	0		
2018–19	Le Havre	0	0		

From Woking, Tonbridge Angels.

2020–21	Opava	19	0		
2021–22	Opava	6	1	**25**	**1**
2021–22	Slovan Liberec	22	0		
2022–23	Slovan Liberec	0	0	**22**	**0**
2022–23	*Wigan Ath*	19	0	**19**	**0**
2023–24	Rotherham U	35	2		
2024–25	Rotherham U	16	0	**51**	**2**

Transferred to Diosgyor, January 2025.

WILSON, Reece (F) **0** **0**

2024–25	Rotherham U	0	0		

Scholars
Bassett, Louis-Jon; Blow, Hayden James; Clarke, James Anthony; Duncan, Harrison Anthony; Gardner, Dean Josef; Giwa, Oluwagbenga George Kamal; Gordon, Owain Craig; Hazell, Cairo Omari; Hibbard, Zac John George; Lee, Cohen Steven; Lewens, Micah Jude McKoy; Niewiem, Oskar; Paisley, McKenzie J; Renshaw, Thomas Alan; Richardson, Kane David Rudge; Scothern, Benjamin Andrew; Tchekwa, Harry Sylvan; Truswell, Maximilian Oscar; Wilson, Reece Shaun.

SALFORD C (72)

ADELAKUN, Hakeeb (F) **283** **46**
H: 6 3 W: 11 11 b.Hackney 11-6-96

2012–13	Scunthorpe U	2	0		
2013–14	Scunthorpe U	28	2		
2014–15	Scunthorpe U	32	6		
2015–16	Scunthorpe U	21	2		
2016–17	Scunthorpe U	17	2		
2017–18	Scunthorpe U	39	4	**139**	**16**
2018–19	Bristol C	5	0		
2019–20	Bristol C	0	0		
2019–20	*Rotherham U*	9	0	**9**	**0**
2020–21	Bristol C	2	0	**7**	**0**
2020–21	*Hull C*	14	3	**14**	**3**
2021–22	Lincoln C	23	2		
2022–23	Lincoln C	2	0		
2022–23	*Gillingham*	21	0	**21**	**0**
2023–24	Lincoln C	19	3	**44**	**5**
2023–24	*Doncaster R*	19	9	**19**	**9**
2024–25	Salford C	30	13	**30**	**13**

ASHLEY, Ossama (M) **69** **1**
H: 5 11 W: 12 13 b.Greenwich 11-12-00

2017–18	AFC Wimbledon	0	0		
2018–19	AFC Wimbledon	0	0		
2019–20	AFC Wimbledon	0	0		
2020–21	West Ham U	0	0		
2021–22	West Ham U	0	0		
2022–23	Colchester U	28	0	**28**	**0**
2023–24	Salford C	8	0		
2024–25	Salford C	33	1	**41**	**1**

AUSTERFIELD, Joshua (M) **82** **2**
H: 5 10 W: 9 00 b.Leeds 2-11-01

2019–20	Huddersfield T	0	0		
2020–21	Huddersfield T	0	0		
2021–22	Huddersfield T	0	0		
2021–22	*Harrogate T*	9	0		
2022–23	Huddersfield T	0	0		
2022–23	*Harrogate T*	17	0	**26**	**0**
2022–23	*Morecambe*	14	0	**14**	**0**
2023–24	Huddersfield T	3	0	**3**	**0**
2023–24	*Crewe Alex*	18	2	**18**	**2**
2024–25	Salford C	21	0	**21**	**0**

BAIRSTOW, Alfie (D) **0** **0**

2024–25	Salford C	0	0		

BERKOE, Kevin (D) **26** **1**
H: 5 10 W: 10 03 b.Redbridge 5-7-01
From Wolverhampton W.

2019–20	Oxford U	0	0		
2020–21	Salford C	0	0		
2021–22	Salford C	0	0		
2022–23	Salford C	4	0		
2023–24	Salford C	7	1		
2024–25	Salford C	15	0	**26**	**1**

BUTT, Ruben (F) **0** **0**

2024–25	Salford C	0	0		

CARR, James (G)   0   0
H: 6 6   b.Wythenshawe 21-2-06
2024–25   Salford C   0   0

CHESTER, James (D)   424   23
H: 5 10   W: 11 11   b.Warrington 23-1-89
Internationals: Wales Full caps.
2007–08   Manchester U   0   0
2008–09   Manchester U   0   0
2008–09   Peterborough U   5   0   5   0
2009–10   Manchester U   0   0
2009–10   Plymouth Arg   3   0   3   0
2010–11   Manchester U   0   0
2010–11   Carlisle U   18   2   18   2
2010–11   Hull C   21   1
2011–12   Hull C   44   2
2012–13   Hull C   44   1
2013–14   Hull C   24   1
2014–15   Hull C   23   2   156   7
2015–16   WBA   13   0   13   0
2016–17   Aston Villa   45   3
2017–18   Aston Villa   46   4
2018–19   Aston Villa   28   5
2019–20   Aston Villa   0   0   119   12
2019–20   Stoke C   16   0
2020–21   Stoke C   32   0
2021–22   Stoke C   17   0   65   0
2022–23   Derby Co   7   0   7   0
2023–24   Barrow   38   2   38   2
2024–25   Salford C   0   0

CHESTERS, Daniel (F)   35   0
H: 5 10   W: 10 03   b.Hitchin 4-4-02
2020–21   West Ham U   0   0
2021–22   West Ham U   1   0
2021–22   Colchester U   14   0   14   0
2023–24   West Ham U   0   0   1   0
2023–24   Salford C   13   0
2024–25   Salford C   7   0   20   0

CLEARY, Robbie (F)   24   2
H: 6 0   W: 12 06   b.Burlington 15-5-03
2021   Forge   5   0   5   0
2021   Sigma   1   0
2022   Sigma   18   2   19   2
2024–25   Salford C   0   0

COLLINS, Ben (M)   0   0
2023–24   Salford C   0   0
2024–25   Salford C   0   0

CURRAN-NICHOLLS, Jai (D)   1   0
b. 30-7-04
2024–25   Salford C   1   0   1   0

DA COSTA, Sandro (F)   2   0
H: 5 7   W: 10 06   b. 14-12-03
2023–24   Salford C   2   0
2024–25   Salford C   0   0   2   0

DACKERS, Marcus (M)   51   1
H: 6 7   W: 14 09   b.Manchester 9-1-03
Internationals: Wales U16, U17.
From Manchester C.
2018–19   Brighton & HA   0   0
2019–20   Brighton & HA   0   0
2020–21   Brighton & HA   0   0
2021–22   Salford C   1   0
2022–23   Salford C   5   0
2023–24   Salford C   6   0
2024–25   Salford C   3   0   15   0
2024–25   Morecambe   36   1   36   1

DAVIES, Jezreel (M)   1   0
H: 6 0   W: 11 07   b.London 10-7-04
2023–24   Salford C   1   0
2024–25   Salford C   0   0   1   0

EDWARDS, Thomas (D)   144   1
H: 5 9   W: 12 00   b.Stafford 22-1-99
Internationals: England U20.
2016–17   Stoke C   0   0
2017–18   Stoke C   6   0
2018–19   Stoke C   27   1
2019–20   Stoke C   13   0
2020–21   Stoke C   0   0
2020–21   Fleetwood T   11   0   11   0
2021   New York Red Bulls   28   0
2021–22   Stoke C   0   0
2022   New York Red Bulls   17   0   45   0
2022–23   Stoke C   0   0
2022–23   Barnsley   10   0   10   0
2023–24   Stoke C   0   0   46   1
2023–24   Huddersfield T   13   0   13   0
2024–25   Salford C   19   0   19   0

GARBUTT, Luke (D)   274   23
H: 5 10   W: 11 07   b.Harrogate 21-5-93
Internationals: England U16, U17, U18, U19, U20, U21.
From Leeds U.
2010–11   Everton   0   0
2011–12   Everton   0   0
2011–12   Cheltenham T   34   2   34   2
2012–13   Everton   0   0
2013–14   Everton   1   0
2013–14   Colchester U   19   2   19   2
2014–15   Everton   4   0

2015–16   Everton   0   0
2015–16   Fulham   25   1   25   1
2016–17   Everton   0   0
2016–17   Wigan Ath   8   0   8   0
2017–18   Everton   0   0
2018–19   Everton   0   0
2018–19   Oxford U   25   4   25   4
2019–20   Everton   0   0   5   0
2019–20   Ipswich T   28   5   28   5
2020–21   Blackpool   31   4
2021–22   Blackpool   17   0
2022–23   Blackpool   8   0   56   4
2023–24   Salford C   33   2
2024–25   Salford C   41   3   74   5

HAMMAN, Jacob (M)   0   0
b.Northwich --
2023–24   Salford C   0   0
2024–25   Salford C   0   0

HENDERSON, Alfie (M)   0   0
H: 5 6   W: 9 13   b. 23-11-04
2022–23   Salford C   0   0
2023–24   Salford C   0   0
2024–25   Salford C   0   0

HEYS, Marshall (M)   0   0
2024–25   Salford C   0   0

HUMBLES, Liam (M)   11   1
b. 5-12-03
2022–23   Salford C   0   0
2023–24   Salford C   10   1
2024–25   Salford C   1   0   11   1

JONES, Jamie (G)   377   0
H: 6 3   W: 14 05   b.Kirkby 18-2-89
2007–08   Everton   0   0
2008–09   Leyton Orient   20   0
2009–10   Leyton Orient   36   0
2010–11   Leyton Orient   35   0
2011–12   Leyton Orient   6   0
2012–13   Leyton Orient   26   0
2013–14   Leyton Orient   28   0   151   0
2014–15   Preston NE   17   0
2014–15   Coventry C   4   0   4   0
2014–15   Rochdale   13   0   13   0
2015–16   Preston NE   0   0   17   0
2015–16   Colchester U   17   0   17   0
2015–16   Stevenage   17   0
2016–17   Stevenage   36   0   53   0
2017–18   Wigan Ath   15   0
2018–19   Wigan Ath   12   0
2019–20   Wigan Ath   7   0
2020–21   Wigan Ath   45   0
2021–22   Wigan Ath   17   0
2022–23   Wigan Ath   17   0   96   0
2023–24   Middlesbrough   0   0
2024–25   Salford C   26   0   26   0

LARA, Jacob (F)   0   0
H: 6 2   W: 13 01   b. 1-10-04
2023–24   Salford C   0   0
2024–25   Salford C   0   0

LONGELO, Rosaire (M)   100   6
H: 6 0   W: 11 05   b.Kinshasa 20-10-99
From West Ham U.
2020–21   Newcastle U   0   0
2021–22   Accrington S   12   1
2022–23   Accrington S   34   2
2023–24   Accrington S   22   2   68   5
2024–25   Swindon T   16   1   16   1
2024–25   Salford C   16   0   16   0

LUAMBA, Junior (F)   48   4
H: 6 2   W: 11 09   b. 27-4-03
2020–21   Oldham Ath   2   0
2021–22   Oldham Ath   15   2   17   2
From Oldham Ath.
2023–24   Salford C   21   1
2024–25   Salford C   10   1   31   2

LUND, Matthew (M)   406   67
H: 6 0   W: 12 00   b.Manchester 21-11-90
Internationals: Northern Ireland U21, Full caps.
From Crewe Alex.
2009–10   Stoke C   0   0
2010–11   Stoke C   0   0
2010–11   Hereford U   2   0   2   0
2011–12   Stoke C   0   0
2011–12   Oldham Ath   3   0   3   0
2011–12   Bristol R   13   2
2012–13   Bristol R   18   2   31   4
2012–13   Southend U   12   1   12   1
2013–14   Rochdale   40   8
2014–15   Rochdale   14   2
2015–16   Rochdale   29   1
2016–17   Rochdale   29   9
2017–18   Burton Alb   12   1   12   1
2017–18   Bradford C   10   2   10   2
2018–19   Scunthorpe U   22   2
2019–20   Scunthorpe U   22   4   44   6
2019–20   Rochdale   5   1
2020–21   Rochdale   33   11   149   32
2021–22   Salford C   40   7
2022–23   Salford C   28   7

2023–24   Salford C   38   3
2024–25   Salford C   37   4   143   21

MALCOLM, Kyrell (M)   4   0
b.Manchester 12-6-07
2023–24   Salford C   2   0
2024–25   Salford C   2   0   4   0

McALENY, Conor (F)   288   63
H: 5 10   W: 12 05   b.Liverpool 12-8-92
2009–10   Everton   0   0
2010–11   Everton   2   0
2011–12   Everton   2   0
2011–12   Scunthorpe U   3   0   3   0
2012–13   Everton   0   0
2013–14   Everton   0   0
2013–14   Brentford   4   0   4   0
2014–15   Everton   0   0
2014–15   Cardiff C   8   2   8   2
2015–16   Everton   0   0
2015–16   Charlton Ath   8   0   8   0
2015–16   Wigan Ath   13   4   13   4
2016–17   Everton   0   0
2016–17   Oxford U   18   10   18   10
2017–18   Fleetwood T   29   5
2018–19   Fleetwood T   14   0
2018–19   Kilmarnock   11   3   11   3
2019–20   Fleetwood T   12   2   55   7
2019–20   Shrewsbury T   5   0   5   0
2020–21   Oldham Ath   40   17
2021–22   Oldham Ath   0   0   40   17
2022–23   Salford C   24   2
2022–23   Salford C   32   11
2023–24   Salford C   38   6
2024–25   Salford C   27   1   121   20

MNOGA, Haji (D)   48   1
H: 6 1   W: 12 04   b.Portsmouth 16-4-02
Internationals: England U17. Tanzania Full caps.
2018–19   Portsmouth   0   0
2019–20   Portsmouth   0   0
2020–21   Portsmouth   5   0
2021–22   Portsmouth   0   0
2022–23   Portsmouth   0   0
2022–23   Gillingham   4   0   4   0
2023–24   Portsmouth   0   0   5   0
2024–25   Salford C   39   1   39   1

MORTON, Callum (F)   116   17
H: 5 10   W: 10 03   b.Torquay 19-1-00
From Yeovil T.
2019–20   WBA   0   0
2019–20   Northampton T   9   5
2020–21   WBA   0   0
2020–21   Lincoln C   17   2   17   2
2021–22   WBA   0   0
2021–22   Fleetwood T   18   4
2021–22   Peterborough U   7   0   7   0
2022–23   Fleetwood T   20   2   38   6
2022–23   Salford C   14   0
2023–24   Salford C   13   0
2023–24   Forest Green R   11   3   11   3
2024–25   Salford C   0   0   27   0
2024–25   Northampton T   7   1   16   6

N'MAI, Kelly (M)   35   3
b.Netherlands 1-5-04
2021–22   Salford C   7   0
2022–23   Salford C   0   0
2023–24   Salford C   28   3
2024–25   Salford C   0   0   35   3

N'MAI, Kelly (M)   67   12
H: 5 6   W: 9 13   b. 1-5-04
2021–22   Salford C   7   0
2022–23   Salford C   0   0
2023–24   Salford C   28   3
2024–25   Salford C   32   9   67   12

O'GARA, Harry (M)   0   0
2023–24   Salford C   0   0
2024–25   Salford C   0   0

OLOPADE, Tosin (D)   1   0
H: 5 10   W: 11 03   b. 14-12-04
2023–24   Salford C   0   0
2024–25   Salford C   1   0   1   0

PADOVANI, Bruno (M)   0   0
2024–25   Salford C   0   0

SHEPHARD, Liam (D)   266   13
H: 5 10   W: 10 08   b.Rhondda 22-11-94
Internationals: Wales U21.
2013–14   Swansea C   0   0
2014–15   Swansea C   0   0
2014–15   Yeovil T   20   0
2015–16   Swansea C   0   0
2015–16   Yeovil T   6   0
2016–17   Swansea C   0   0
2016–17   Yeovil T   38   1   64   1
2017–18   Peterborough U   24   0   24   0
2018–19   Forest Green R   39   5
2019–20   Forest Green R   19   1   58   6
2021–22   Newport Co   42   2
2021–22   Salford C   0   0   42   2
2021–22   Salford C   35   3
2022–23   Salford C   9   0

2023–24 Salford C 12 0
2024–25 Salford C 22 1 **78 4**

STOCKTON, Cole (F) 359 93
H: 6 1 W: 11 11 b.Huyton 13-3-94
2011–12 Tranmere R 1 0
2012–13 Tranmere R 31 3
2013–14 Tranmere R 21 2
2014–15 Tranmere R 22 4
2015–16 Tranmere R 0 0
2015–16 *Morecambe* 7 2
2016–17 Tranmere R 0 0
2016–17 *Morecambe* 19 5
2017–18 Hearts 12 0 **12 0**
2017–18 Carlisle U 12 1 **12 1**
2018–19 Tranmere R 16 1 **91 10**
2019–20 Morecambe 30 5
2020–21 Morecambe 40 13
2021–22 Morecambe 44 23
2022–23 Morecambe 39 11 **179 59**
2023–24 Burton Alb 10 0 **10 0**
2023–24 *Barrow* 17 7 **17 7**
2024–25 Salford C 38 16 **38 16**

TAYLOR, Jon (M) 407 59
H: 5 6 W: 12 02 b.Liverpool 23-12-89
2009–10 Shrewsbury T 2 0
2010–11 Shrewsbury T 20 6
2011–12 Shrewsbury T 33 0
2012–13 Shrewsbury T 37 7
2013–14 Shrewsbury T 41 9 **133 22**
2014–15 Peterborough U 24 3
2015–16 Peterborough U 44 11 **68 14**
2016–17 Rotherham U 42 4
2017–18 Rotherham U 25 4
2018–19 Rotherham U 41 4
2019–20 Rotherham U 0 0 **108 12**
2019–20 Doncaster R 28 6
2020–21 Doncaster R 25 4
2021–22 Doncaster R 3 0
2022–23 Doncaster R 11 0
2023–24 Doncaster R 3 0 **70 10**
2024–25 Salford C 28 1 **28 1**

TILT, Curtis (D) 264 15
H: 6 4 W: 11 11 b.Walsall 4-8-91
Internationals: Jamaica Full caps.
From Halesowen T, Hednesford T, AFC Telford U, Wrexham.
2017–18 Blackpool 42 1
2018–19 Blackpool 37 4
2019–20 Blackpool 20 0 **99 5**
2019–20 Rotherham U 1 0
2020–21 Rotherham U 0 0 **1 0**
2020–21 *Wigan Ath* 36 3
2021–22 Wigan Ath 20 2
2022–23 Wigan Ath 26 1 **82 6**
2023–24 Salford C 45 3
2024–25 Salford C 37 1 **82 4**

WATSON, Ryan (M) 285 34
H: 6 1 W: 11 07 b.Crewe 7-7-93
2011–12 Wigan Ath 0 0
2012–13 Wigan Ath 0 0
2012–13 *Accrington S* 0 0
2013–14 Leicester C 0 0
2014–15 Leicester C 0 0
2014–15 *Northampton T* 5 0
2015–16 Leicester C 0 0
2015–16 *Northampton T* 11 0
2016–17 Barnet 19 1
2017–18 Barnet 28 1 **47 2**
2018–19 Milton Keynes D 22 0 **22 0**
2019–20 Northampton T 25 5
2020–21 Northampton T 39 8
2021–22 Northampton T 0 0 **80 13**
2021–22 Tranmere R 16 1 **16 1**
2021–22 Salford C 23 4
2022–23 Salford C 34 7
2023–24 Salford C 45 7
2024–25 Salford C 18 0 **120 18**

WOODBURN, Ben (F) 153 8
H: 5 9 W: 11 05 b.Nottingham 16-11-99
Internationals: Wales U16, U17, U19, Full caps.
2016–17 Liverpool 5 0
2017–18 Liverpool 1 0
2018–19 Liverpool 0 0
2018–19 *Sheffield U* 7 0 **7 0**
2019–20 Liverpool 0 0
2019–20 *Oxford U* 11 1 **11 1**
2020–21 Liverpool 0 0
2020–21 *Blackpool* 10 0 **10 0**
2021–22 Liverpool 0 0 **6 0**
2021–22 *Hearts* 28 3 **28 3**
2022–23 Preston NE 38 1
2023–24 Preston NE 20 0 **58 1**
2024–25 Salford C 33 3 **33 3**

WRIGHT, Will (D) 2 0
H: 6 3 b.Preston --
2024–25 Salford C 2 0 **2 0**

Scholars
Bairstow, Alfie; Butt, Ruben; Carroll, Riley Anthony; Clifford, Thomas Ferguson; Diop Diouf, Khadim; Dodd, Jake Alan; Kane, Joel; Midgley, Billy Patrick; Mundy, Bradley John; Nnadede, Alexander Emenike; O'Gara, Harry Finn; Padovani Ascenio, Bruno; Ramplin, Jacob James; Showman, Harry Max; Simmons, Luke Paul; Wright, James John; Wright, William Stephen.

SHEFFIELD U (73)

AHMEDHODZIC, Anel (D) 193 15
H: 6 3 W: 12 00 b.Malmo 26-3-99
Internationals: Sweden U16, U17, U18, U19, U21, Full caps. Bosnia-Herzegovina Full caps.
From Malmo.
2016–17 Nottingham F 1 0
2018–19 Nottingham F 0 0 **1 0**
2019 Malmo 1 0
2019–20 *Hobro IK* 19 1 **19 1**
2020 Malmo 29 2
2021 Malmo 25 1 **55 3**
2021–22 *Bordeaux* 15 0 **15 0**
2022–23 Sheffield U 34 6
2023–24 Sheffield U 31 2
2024–25 Sheffield U 38 3 **103 11**

ARBLASTER, Oliver (M) 48 4
H: 5 11 W: 10 03 b.Sheffield 5-5-04
Internationals: England U18, U20.
2020–21 Sheffield U 0 0
2021–22 Sheffield U 0 0
2022–23 Sheffield U 4 0
2023–24 Sheffield U 12 0
2023–24 *Port Vale* 20 2 **20 2**
2024–25 Sheffield U 12 2 **28 2**

ASTON, Sam (M) 0 0
b. 6-5-06
2024–25 Sheffield U 0 0

BAPTISTE, Jamal (M) 4 0
H: 6 1 W: 11 11 b.Redbridge 11-11-03
Internationals: England U16, U17, U19.
2020–21 West Ham U 0 0
2021–22 West Ham U 0 0
2022–23 West Ham U 0 0
2023–24 Manchester C 0 0
2023–24 *Lommel* 3 0 **3 0**
2024–25 Sheffield U 1 0 **1 0**

BEN SLIMANE, Anis (M) 173 13
H: 6 2 W: 13 03 b.Copenhagen 16-5-01
Internationals: Denmark U19. Tunisia U20, Full caps.
2017–18 AB 2 0
2018–19 AB 16 2 **18 2**
2019–20 Brondby 16 1
2020–21 Brondby 27 3
2021–22 Brondby 31 2
2022–23 Brondby 30 3 **104 9**
2023–24 Sheffield U 15 0
2024–25 Sheffield U 3 0 **18 0**
2024–25 *Norwich C* 33 2 **33 2**

BLACKER, Billy (F) 1 0
b. 25-5-06
2023–24 Sheffield U 0 0
2024–25 Sheffield U 1 0 **1 0**

BOYES, Harry (M) 57 0
b.Barnsley 2-11-01
From Manchester C.
2020–21 Sheffield U 0 0
2021–22 Sheffield U 0 0
2022–23 Sheffield U 0 0
2022–23 *Forest Green R* 12 0 **12 0**
2022–23 *Lincoln C* 18 0 **18 0**
2023–24 Sheffield U 0 0
2023–24 *Wycombe W* 22 0 **22 0**
2023–24 *Fleetwood T* 5 0 **5 0**
2024–25 Sheffield U 0 0

BREWSTER, Rhian (F) 126 18
H: 5 9 W: 11 11 b.Chadwell Heath 1-4-00
Internationals: England U16, U17, U18, U21
From Chelsea.
2016–17 Liverpool 0 0
2017–18 Liverpool 0 0
2018–19 Liverpool 0 0
2019–20 Liverpool 0 0
2019–20 *Swansea C* 20 10 **20 10**
2020–21 Sheffield U 27 0
2021–22 Sheffield U 14 3
2022–23 Sheffield U 16 1
2023–24 Sheffield U 13 0
2024–25 Sheffield U 36 4 **106 8**

BROOKS, Andre (M) 43 3
H: 5 11 W: 11 00 b.Sheffield 20-8-03
2020–21 Sheffield U 0 0
2021–22 Sheffield U 0 0
2022–23 Sheffield U 1 0
2023–24 Sheffield U 20 0
2024–25 Sheffield U 22 3 **43 3**

BURROWS, Harrison (M) 191 19
H: 5 11 W: 10 10 b.Peterborough 12-1-02
2017–18 Peterborough U 0 0
2018–19 Peterborough U 0 0
2019–20 Peterborough U 4 0
2020–21 Peterborough U 21 1
2021–22 Peterborough U 37 3
2022–23 Peterborough U 41 4
2023–24 Peterborough U 45 6 **148 14**
2024–25 Sheffield U 43 5 **43 5**

BUYABU, Jili (M) 1 0
H: 5 7 b.Enfield 9-8-01
2022–23 Sheffield U 1 0
2023–24 Sheffield U 0 0
2023–24 *Motherwell* 0 0
2024–25 Sheffield U 0 0 **1 0**

CACERES, Jefferson (F) 57 11
b.Lima 22-8-02
Internationals: Peru U23.
2020 Melgar 0 0
2021 Melgar 8 0
2022 Melgar 4 0
2023 Melgar 0 0
2023 *Binacional* 21 3 **21 3**
2024 Melgar 24 8 **36 8**
2024–25 Sheffield U 0 0

CAMPBELL, Tyrese (F) 194 46
H: 6 0 W: 11 11 b.Cheadle Hulme 28-12-99
Internationals: England U17, U20.
From Manchester C.
2017–18 Stoke C 4 0
2018–19 Stoke C 3 0
2018–19 *Shrewsbury T* 15 5 **15 5**
2019–20 Stoke C 33 9
2020–21 Stoke C 16 6
2021–22 Stoke C 26 4
2022–23 Stoke C 41 9
2023–24 Stoke C 23 3 **146 31**
2024–25 Sheffield U 33 10 **33 10**

CANNON, Thomas (F) 73 20
H: 5 11 W: 10 03 b.Aintree 28-12-02
Internationals: Republic of Ireland U19, U20, U21, Full caps.
2022–23 Everton 2 0
2022–23 *Preston NE* 20 8 **20 8**
2023–24 Everton 1 0 **3 0**
2023–24 Leicester C 13 2
2024–25 Leicester C 0 0 **13 2**
2024–25 *Stoke C* 22 9 **22 9**
2024–25 Sheffield U 15 1 **15 1**

COLECHIN, Sam (D) 0 0
2024–25 Sheffield U 0 0

COOPER, Michael (G) 185 0
H: 6 1 W: 10 03 b.Exeter 8-10-99
2017–18 Plymouth Arg 1 0
2018–19 Plymouth Arg 1 0
2019–20 Plymouth Arg 0 0
2020–21 Plymouth Arg 46 0
2021–22 Plymouth Arg 46 0
2022–23 Plymouth Arg 29 0
2023–24 Plymouth Arg 19 0 **142 0**
2024–25 Sheffield U 43 0 **43 0**

COULIBALY, Ismaila (M) 80 11
H: 6 0 W: 10 10 b.Mali 25-12-00
Internationals: Mali U20, Full caps.
2019 Sarpsborg 08 13 0
2020 Sarpsborg 08 14 4 **27 4**
2020–21 Sheffield U 0 0
2020–21 *Beerschot* 22 5
2021–22 Sheffield U 0 0
2021–22 *Beerschot* 20 0 **42 5**
2022–23 Sheffield U 1 0
2023–24 Sheffield U 0 0
2023–24 *AIK* 10 2 **10 2**
2024–25 Sheffield U 0 0 **1 0**
Transferred to LASK, January 2025.

CURTIS, Sam (D) 84 3
H: 6 1 b.Navan Navan 1-12-05
Internationals: Republic of Ireland U17, U18, U19, U21.
2021 St Patrick's Ath 1 0
2022 St Patrick's Ath 18 0
2023 St Patrick's Ath 34 3 **53 3**
2023–24 Sheffield U 1 0
2024–25 Sheffield U 0 0 **1 0**
2024–25 *Peterborough U* 17 0 **17 0**
2024–25 *St Johnstone* 13 0 **13 0**

DAVIES, Adam (G) 227 0
H: 6 1 W: 11 11 b.Rinteln 17-7-92
Internationals: Wales Full caps.
2009–10 Everton 0 0
2010–11 Everton 0 0
2011–12 Everton 0 0
2012–13 Sheffield Wed 0 0
2013–14 Sheffield Wed 0 0
2014–15 Barnsley 23 0
2015–16 Barnsley 38 0
2016–17 Barnsley 46 0
2017–18 Barnsley 35 0
2018–19 Barnsley 42 0 **184 0**
2019–20 Stoke C 4 0
2020–21 Stoke C 17 0
2021–22 Stoke C 12 0 **33 0**
2021–22 Sheffield U 0 0

2022–23	Sheffield U	7	0		
2023–24	Sheffield U	0	0		
2024–25	Sheffield U	3	0	**10**	**0**

DAVIES, Tom (M) **177 7**
H: 5 11 W: 11 00 b.Liverpool 30-6-98
Internationals: England U16, U17, U18, U19, U21.

2015–16	Everton	2	0		
2016–17	Everton	24	2		
2017–18	Everton	33	2		
2018–19	Everton	16	0		
2019–20	Everton	30	1		
2020–21	Everton	25	0		
2021–22	Everton	6	1		
2022–23	Everton	19	0	**155**	**6**
2023–24	Sheffield U	9	0		
2024–25	Sheffield U	13	1	**22**	**1**

EASTON, Evan (D) **0 0**
b. 14-1-05

2023–24	Sheffield U	0	0		
2024–25	Sheffield U	0	0		

FAXON, Luke (G) **0 0**
b.Sheffield 15-2-05

2024–25	Sheffield U	0	0		

FRECKLETON, Miguel (D) **28 1**
H: 6 4 W: 12 08 b.Bristol 8-9-02

2024–25	Sheffield U	0	0		
2024–25	*Swindon T*	28	1	**28**	**1**

GRBIC, Ivo (G) **142 0**
H: 6 5 W: 13 01 b.Split 18-1-96
Internationals: Croatia U16, U17, U18, U19, U21, Full caps.

2013–14	Hajduk Split	0	0		
2014–15	Hajduk Split	3	0		
2015–16	Hajduk Split	4	0		
2016–17	Hajduk Split	0	0		
2017–18	Hajduk Split	0	0	**7**	**0**
2018–19	Lokomativa Zagreb	36	0	**36**	**0**
2019–20	Lokomativa Zagreb	35	0	**35**	**0**
2020–21	Atletico Madrid	0	0		
2021–22	Atletico Madrid	0	0		
2021–22	*Lille*	21	0	**21**	**0**
2022–23	Atletico Madrid	12	0		
2023–24	Atletico Madrid	0	0	**12**	**0**
2023–24	Sheffield U	9	0		
2024–25	Sheffield U	0	0	**9**	**0**
2024–25	*Rizespor*	22	0	**22**	**0**

HACKFORD, Antwoine (F) **33 4**
H: 6 1 b.Sheffield 20-3-04
Internationals: England U16.

2020–21	Sheffield U	1	0		
2021–22	Sheffield U	0	0		
2022–23	Sheffield U	0	0		
2023–24	Sheffield U	2	0		
2023–24	*Burton Alb*	6	0	**6**	**0**
2024–25	Sheffield U	0	0	**3**	**0**
2024–25	*Port Vale*	24	4	**24**	**4**

HAMER, Gustavo (M) **284 37**
H: 5 7 W: 9 08 b.Itajai 24-6-97
Internationals: Netherlands U18, U20.

2016–17	Feyenoord	2	0		
2017–18	Feyenoord	0	0	**2**	**0**
2017–18	*Dordrecht*	34	3	**34**	**3**
2018–19	PEC Zwolle	23	0		
2019–20	PEC Zwolle	25	4	**48**	**4**
2020–21	Coventry C	42	5		
2021–22	Coventry C	39	3		
2022–23	Coventry C	41	9		
2023–24	Coventry C	1	0	**123**	**17**
2023–24	Sheffield U	36	4		
2024–25	Sheffield U	41	9	**77**	**13**

HAMPSON, Owen (M) **2 0**
b. 17-11-04
Internationals: Wales U19, U21.

2023–24	Sheffield U	0	0		
2024–25	Sheffield U	0	0		
2024–25	*Dunfermline Ath*	2	0	**2**	**0**

MARSH, Louie (F) **22 2**
H: 6 1 W: 10 03 b.Sheffield 16-10-03
Internationals: England U20.

2022–23	Sheffield U	0	0		
2023–24	Sheffield U	0	0		
2023–24	*Doncaster R*	6	0	**6**	**0**
2024–25	Sheffield U	0	0		
2024–25	*Fleetwood T*	16	2	**16**	**2**

McCALLUM, Sam (D) **174 8**
H: 5 10 W: 10 10 b.Canterbury 2-9-00
From Herne Bay.

2018–19	Coventry C	7	0		
2019–20	Norwich C	0	0		
2019–20	*Coventry C*	26	2		
2020–21	Norwich C	0	0		
2020–21	*Coventry C*	41	1	**74**	**3**
2021–22	Norwich C	0	0		
2021–22	*QPR*	17	2	**17**	**2**
2022–23	Norwich C	23	0		
2023–24	Norwich C	27	1	**50**	**1**
2024–25	Sheffield U	33	2	**33**	**2**

MOORE, Kieffer (F) **327 97**
H: 6 5 W: 13 01 b.Torquay 8-8-92
Internationals: England C. Wales Full caps.
From Truro C, Dorchester T.

2013–14	Yeovil T	20	4		
2014–15	Yeovil T	30	3	**50**	**7**
2015	Viking	9	0	**9**	**0**
From Forest Green R.					
2016–17	Ipswich T	11	0		
2017–18	Ipswich T	0	0		
2017–18	*Rotherham U*	22	13	**22**	**13**
2017–18	Barnsley	20	4		
2018–19	Barnsley	31	17		
2019–20	Barnsley	0	0	**51**	**21**
2019–20	Wigan Ath	36	10	**36**	**10**
2020–21	Cardiff C	42	20		
2021–22	Cardiff C	22	5	**64**	**25**
2021–22	Bournemouth	4	4		
2022–23	Bournemouth	27	4		
2023–24	Bournemouth	8	1	**39**	**9**
2023–24	*Ipswich T*	18	7	**29**	**7**
2024–25	Sheffield U	27	5	**27**	**5**

NORRINGTON-DAVIES, Rhys (D) **121 2**
H: 5 11 W: 10 10 b.Riyadh 22-4-99
Internationals: Wales U19, U21, Full caps.

2017–18	Sheffield U	0	0		
2018–19	Sheffield U	0	0		
2019–20	Sheffield U	0	0		
2019–20	*Rochdale*	27	1	**27**	**1**
2020–21	Sheffield U	0	0		
2020–21	*Luton T*	18	0	**18**	**0**
2020–21	*Stoke C*	20	1	**20**	**1**
2021–22	Sheffield U	22	0		
2022–23	Sheffield U	15	0		
2023–24	Sheffield U	5	0		
2024–25	Sheffield U	14	0	**56**	**0**

NWACHUKWU, Christian (M) **26 4**
b. 27-12-05

2023–24	Botev Plovdiv	8	1		
2024–25	Botev Plovdiv	18	3	**26**	**4**
2024–25	Sheffield U	0	0		

O'HARE, Callum (M) **226 22**
H: 5 8 W: 10 03 b.Solihull 1-5-98
Internationals: England U20.

2016–17	Aston Villa	0	0		
2017–18	Aston Villa	4	0		
2018–19	Aston Villa	0	0		
2018–19	*Carlisle U*	16	3	**16**	**3**
2019–20	Aston Villa	0	0	**4**	**0**
2019–20	*Coventry C*	29	3		
2020–21	Coventry C	46	3		
2021–22	Coventry C	45	5		
2022–23	Coventry C	11	0		
2023–24	Coventry C	31	6	**162**	**17**
2024–25	Sheffield U	44	2	**44**	**2**

ONE, Ryan (F) **30 1**
b.Coatbridge 26-6-06
Internationals: Scotland U17, U19, U21.

2022–23	Hamilton A	17	0	**17**	**0**
2023–24	Sheffield U	1	0		
2024–25	Sheffield U	12	1	**13**	**1**

PECK, Sydie (F) **43 0**
b.Enfield 13-9-04
Internationals: England U17, U20.

2023–24	Sheffield U	1	0		
2024–25	Sheffield U	42	0	**43**	**0**

ROBINSON, Jack (D) **312 11**
H: 5 11 W: 10 08 b.Warrington 1-9-93
Internationals: England U16, U17, U18, U19, U21.

2009–10	Liverpool	1	0		
2010–11	Liverpool	2	0		
2011–12	Liverpool	0	0		
2012–13	Liverpool	0	0		
2012–13	*Wolverhampton W*	11	0	**11**	**0**
2013–14	Liverpool	0	0	**3**	**0**
2013–14	*Blackpool*	34	0	**34**	**0**
2014–15	QPR	0	0		
2014–15	*Huddersfield T*	30	0	**30**	**0**
2015–16	QPR	1	0		
2016–17	QPR	7	0		
2017–18	QPR	31	2	**39**	**2**
2018–19	Nottingham F	38	2		
2019–20	Nottingham F	18	0	**56**	**2**
2019–20	Sheffield U	6	0		
2020–21	Sheffield U	11	0		
2021–22	Sheffield U	27	3		
2022–23	Sheffield U	27	3		
2023–24	Sheffield U	34	1		
2024–25	Sheffield U	34	0	**139**	**7**

SACHDEV, Sai (D) **2 0**
H: 5 11 W: 11 11 b.Leicester 23-10-04
Internationals: England U17, U18, U19.

2022–23	Sheffield U	1	0		
2023–24	Sheffield U	0	0		
2024–25	Sheffield U	1	0	**2**	**0**

SASNAUSKAS, Dovydas (D) **0 0**
H: 6 1 W: 11 11 b. 16-2-07
Internationals: Lithuania U16, U17.

2023–24	Sheffield U	0	0		
2024–25	Sheffield U	0	0		

SERIKI, Femi (F) **67 0**
H: 6 0 b.Manchester 28-4-02

2018–19	Bury	0	0		
2019–20	Sheffield U	0	0		
2020–21	Sheffield U	1	0		
2021–22	Sheffield U	1	0		
2021–22	*Beerschot*	1	0	**1**	**0**
2022–23	*Rochdale*	29	0	**29**	**0**
2022–23	Sheffield U	0	0		
2023–24	Sheffield U	0	0		
2023–24	*Rotherham U*	10	0	**10**	**0**
2024–25	Sheffield U	25	0	**27**	**0**

SHACKLETON, Jamie (M) **127 2**
H: 5 6 W: 10 01 b.Leeds 8-10-99
Internationals: England U20.

2018–19	Leeds U	19	0		
2019–20	Leeds U	22	2		
2020–21	Leeds U	13	0		
2021–22	Leeds U	14	0		
2022–23	Leeds U	0	0		
2022–23	*Millwall*	36	0	**36**	**0**
2023–24	Leeds U	11	0	**79**	**2**
2024–25	Sheffield U	12	0	**12**	**0**

TRUSTY, Auston (D) **190 7**
H: 6 4 W: 12 13 b.Media 12-8-98
Internationals: USA U17, U19, U20, U23, Full caps.

2016	Philadelphia Union	0	0		
2017	Philadelphia Union	0	0		
2018	Philadelphia Union	34	1		
2019	Philadelphia Union	22	1	**56**	**2**
2020	Colorado Rapids	8	0		
2021	Colorado Rapids	33	1		
2022	Colorado Rapids	16	0	**57**	**1**
2022–23	Arsenal	0	0		
2022–23	*Birmingham C*	44	4	**44**	**4**
2023–24	Sheffield U	32	0		
2024–25	Sheffield U	1	0	**33**	**0**

Transferred to Celtic, August 2024.

VINICIUS SOUZA, Costa (M) **151 4**
b.Rio de Janeiro 17-6-99
Internationals: Brazil U20.

2019	Flamengo	1	0		
2020	Flamengo	0	0	**1**	**0**
2020–21	Lommel	18	0		
2021–22	Lommel	0	0		
2021–22	*Mechelen*	27	2	**27**	**2**
2022–23	Lommel	0	0	**18**	**0**
2022–23	*Espanyol*	34	1	**34**	**1**
2023–24	Sheffield U	36	1		
2024–25	Sheffield U	35	0	**71**	**1**

Players retained or with offer of contract
Atherton, Alfie Jake; Beattie, Jevan; Francis, Marshall Emmanuel; Patterson, Lennon Alex; Prunty, Jayden Ramell; Tahir, Zain Ashan; Tinsdale, Jay Dillan; Waldron, Jack William.

Scholars
Abraha, Siem Eyob; Christie-Crainie, Archie John Gordon; Colechin, Samuel Gary; Coubrough, Arlo Hughie; Giggs, Zach Joseph; Gordon, Franklyn James; Grainger, Benjamin Anthony; Hewitson, Coby Anthony Mark; Hough, Alfie David; Howard, Theo Charles; Jones, Frankie; Kiwomya, Noah Malachi; Long, Jaye Terrence Nicholas; Makhalira, Jaydon Maziko; McLachlan, Riley Adam; Okyere, Seth Okyere Boah; Reid, Aaron John; Sidibe, Lamine; Stylianou Blaize, Jackson; Tawodzera, Dylan Kudzaishe; Venners, Alfie Richard Paul.

SHEFFIELD WED (74)

ARMSTRONG, Stuart (M) **433 63**
H: 6 0 W: 10 10 b.Inverness 30-3-92
Internationals: Scotland U19, U21, Full caps.

2010–11	Dundee U	12	0		
2011–12	Dundee U	23	1		
2012–13	Dundee U	36	3		
2013–14	Dundee U	36	8		
2014–15	Dundee U	20	6	**127**	**18**
2014–15	Celtic	15	1		
2015–16	Celtic	25	4		
2016–17	Celtic	31	15		
2017–18	Celtic	27	3	**98**	**23**
2018–19	Southampton	29	3		
2019–20	Southampton	30	5		
2020–21	Southampton	33	4		
2021–22	Southampton	25	2		
2022–23	Southampton	32	2		
2023–24	Southampton	42	5	**191**	**21**
2024	Vancouver Whitecaps	6	1	**6**	**1**
2024–25	Sheffield Wed	11	0	**11**	**0**

BANNAN, Barry (M) **546 37**
H: 5 7 W: 9 08 b.Glasgow 1-12-89
Internationals: Scotland U21, Full caps.

2008–09	Aston Villa	0	0		
2008–09	*Derby Co*	10	1	**10**	**1**
2009–10	Aston Villa	0	0		
2009–10	*Blackpool*	20	1	**20**	**1**
2010–11	Aston Villa	12	0		
2010–11	*Leeds U*	7	0	**7**	**0**
2011–12	Aston Villa	28	1		
2012–13	Aston Villa	24	0		
2013–14	Aston Villa	0	0	**64**	**1**
2013–14	Crystal Palace	15	1		
2014–15	Crystal Palace	7	0		
2014–15	*Bolton W*	16	0	**16**	**0**
2015–16	Crystal Palace	0	0	**22**	**1**
2015–16	Sheffield Wed	35	2		
2016–17	Sheffield Wed	43	1		
2017–18	Sheffield Wed	29	0		
2018–19	Sheffield Wed	41	5		
2019–20	Sheffield Wed	44	2		
2020–21	Sheffield Wed	46	2		
2021–22	Sheffield Wed	45	9		
2022–23	Sheffield Wed	41	7		
2023–24	Sheffield Wed	42	1		
2024–25	Sheffield Wed	41	4	**407**	**33**

BARRETT, Killian (G) **0 0**
b. 15-4-04

2024–25	Sheffield Wed	0	0		

BERNARD, Di'shon (D) **125 4**
H: 6 2 W: 12 11 b.London 14-10-00
Internationals: Jamaica Full caps.
From Chelsea.

2019–20	Manchester U	0	0		
2020–21	Manchester U	0	0		
2020–21	*Salford C*	30	2	**30**	**2**
2021–22	Manchester U	0	0		
2021–22	*Hull C*	26	0	**26**	**0**
2022–23	Manchester U	0	0		
2022–23	*Portsmouth*	10	0	**10**	**0**
2023–24	Sheffield Wed	32	0		
2024–25	Sheffield Wed	27	2	**59**	**2**

CADAMARTERI, Bailey-Tye (F) **46 9**
H: 6 0 W: 12 00 b.Leeds 9-5-05
Internationals: England U19, U20.

2022–23	Sheffield Wed	0	0		
2023–24	Sheffield Wed	23	4		
2024–25	Sheffield Wed	0	0	**23**	**4**
2024–25	*Lincoln C*	23	5	**23**	**5**

CHALOBAH, Nathaniel (D) **264 12**
H: 6 1 W: 11 11 b.Sierra Leone 12-12-94
Internationals: England U16, U17, U19, U20, U21, Full caps.

2010–11	Chelsea	0	0		
2011–12	Chelsea	0	0		
2012–13	Chelsea	0	0		
2012–13	*Watford*	38	5		
2013–14	Chelsea	0	0		
2013–14	*Nottingham F*	12	2	**12**	**2**
2013–14	*Middlesbrough*	19	1	**19**	**1**
2014–15	Chelsea	0	0		
2014–15	*Burnley*	4	0	**4**	**0**
2014–15	*Reading*	15	1	**15**	**1**
2015–16	Chelsea	0	0		
2015–16	*Napoli*	5	0	**5**	**0**
2016–17	Chelsea	10	0	**10**	**0**
2017–18	Watford	6	0		
2018–19	Watford	9	0		
2019–20	Watford	22	0		
2020–21	Watford	38	3		
2021–22	Watford	0	0	**113**	**8**
2021–22	Fulham	20	0		
2022–23	Fulham	4	0	**24**	**0**
2022–23	WBA	13	0		
2023–24	WBA	33	0	**46**	**0**
2024–25	Sheffield Wed	16	0	**16**	**0**

CHARLES, Pierce (G) **8 0**
b.Manchester 21-7-05
Internationals: Northern Ireland U17, U19, U21, Full caps.
From Manchester C.

2022–23	Sheffield Wed	0	0		
2023–24	Sheffield Wed	0	0		
2024–25	Sheffield Wed	8	0	**8**	**0**

CISSOKO, Ibrahim (M) **59 7**
b.Nijmegen 26-3-03
Internationals: Netherlands U21.

2021–22	NEC	4	1		
2022–23	NEC	26	2	**30**	**3**
2023–24	Toulouse	11	1		
2024–25	Toulouse	0	0	**11**	**1**
2024–25	*Plymouth Arg*	13	3	**13**	**3**

On loan from Toulouse.

2024–25	Sheffield Wed	5	0	**5**	**0**

DIABY, Bambo (D) **139 6**
H: 6 2 W: 12 11 b.Mataro 17-12-97

2015–16	Cornelia	1	0	**1**	**0**
2016–17	Sampdoria	0	0		
2016–17	*Mantova*	7	0	**7**	**0**
2017–18	Sampdoria	0	0		
2017–18	*Peralada*	34	4	**34**	**4**
2017–18	*Girona*	0	0		
2018–19	Lokeren	18	1	**18**	**1**
2019–20	Barnsley	21	1	**21**	**1**
2021–22	Preston NE	7	0		
2022–23	Preston NE	17	0	**24**	**0**
2023–24	Sheffield Wed	34	0		
2024–25	Sheffield Wed	0	0	**34**	**0**

Transferred to Elche, August 2024.

FAMEWO, Akin (D) **150 2**
H: 6 2 W: 10 06 b.Lewisham 9-11-98

2016–17	Luton T	3	0		
2017–18	Luton T	3	0		
2018–19	Luton T	0	0	**6**	**0**
2018–19	*Grimsby T*	10	0	**10**	**0**
2018–19	Norwich C	0	0		
2019–20	Norwich C	1	0		
2019–20	*St Mirren*	9	0	**9**	**0**
2020–21	Norwich C	0	0		
2020–21	*Charlton Ath*	22	0		
2021–22	Norwich C	0	0	**1**	**0**
2021–22	*Charlton Ath*	37	1	**59**	**1**
2022–23	Sheffield Wed	17	1		
2023–24	Sheffield Wed	35	0		
2024–25	Sheffield Wed	13	0	**65**	**1**

FUSIRE, Sean (M) **14 0**
b.Sheffield 31-5-05
Internationals: Zimbabwe Full caps.

2022–23	Sheffield Wed	0	0		
2023–24	Sheffield Wed	0	0		
2024–25	Sheffield Wed	0	0		
2024–25	*Carlisle U*	14	0	**14**	**0**

GASSAMA, Djeidi (M) **98 12**
b.Nieleba Haouisse 10-9-03
Internationals: France U20.
From Brest.

2021–22	Paris Saint-Germain	1	0		
2022–23	Paris Saint-Germain	0	0	**1**	**0**
2022–23	*Eupen*	19	2	**19**	**2**
2023–24	Sheffield Wed	35	3		
2024–25	Sheffield Wed	43	7	**78**	**10**

HALL, Jack (G) **0 0**
b.Worksop 10-10-04
Internationals: England U18.

2023–24	Sheffield Wed	0	0		
2024–25	Sheffield Wed	0	0		

HAMER, Ben (G) **311 0**
H: 6 4 W: 12 04 b.Chard 20-11-87

2006–07	Reading	0	0		
2007–08	Reading	0	0		
2007–08	*Brentford*	20	0		
2008–09	Reading	0	0		
2008–09	*Brentford*	45	0		
2009–10	Reading	0	0		
2010–11	Reading	0	0		
2010–11	*Brentford*	10	0	**75**	**0**
2010–11	*Exeter C*	18	0	**18**	**0**
2011–12	Charlton Ath	41	0		
2012–13	Charlton Ath	41	0		
2013–14	Charlton Ath	32	0	**114**	**0**
2014–15	Leicester C	8	0		
2015–16	Leicester C	0	0		
2015–16	*Bristol C*	4	0	**4**	**0**
2016–17	Leicester C	0	0		
2017–18	Leicester C	4	0	**12**	**0**
2018–19	Huddersfield T	7	0		
2019–20	*Derby Co*	25	0	**25**	**0**
2020–21	Huddersfield T	15	0	**22**	**0**
2020–21	Swansea C	0	0		
2021–22	Swansea C	21	0	**21**	**0**
2022–23	Watford	1	0		
2023–24	Watford	19	0	**20**	**0**
2024–25	Sheffield Wed	0	0		

HATSUSE, Ryo (D) **200 2**
b.Kishiwada 10-7-97
Internationals: Japan U20.

2016	Gamba Osaka	5	0		
2017	Gamba Osaka	19	0		
2018	Gamba Osaka	10	0	**34**	**0**
2019	Vissel Kobe	17	0		
2019	*Avispa Fukuoka*	9	0	**9**	**0**
2020	Vissel Kobe	16	0		
2021	Vissel Kobe	33	0		
2022	Vissel Kobe	17	1		
2023	Vissel Kobe	33	1		
2024	Vissel Kobe	35	0	**151**	**2**
2024–25	Sheffield Wed	6	0	**6**	**0**

IHIEKWE, Michael (D) **302 15**
H: 6 1 W: 12 09 b.Liverpool 20-11-92
Internationals: England C.

2011–12	Wolverhampton W	0	0		
2012–13	Wolverhampton W	0	0		
2013–14	Wolverhampton W	0	0		
2013–14	*Cheltenham T*	13	0	**13**	**0**
2014–15	Tranmere R	38	1	**38**	**1**

From Tranmere R.

2017–18	Rotherham U	31	1		
2018–19	Rotherham U	15	2		
2018–19	*Accrington S*	20	1	**20**	**1**
2019–20	Rotherham U	33	2		
2020–21	Rotherham U	42	2		
2021–22	Rotherham U	42	3	**163**	**10**
2022–23	Sheffield Wed	20	0		
2023–24	Sheffield Wed	26	1		
2024–25	Sheffield Wed	22	2	**68**	**3**

INGELSSON, Svante (M) **207 8**
H: 6 2 W: 13 01 b.Kalmar 14-6-98
Internationals: Sweden U17, U19, U21.

2015	Kalmar	4	0		
2016	Kalmar	11	0		
2017	Kalmar	11	1		
2017–18	Udinese	7	1		
2018–19	Udinese	3	0		
2019–20	Udinese	0	0		
2019–20	*Pescara*	4	0	**4**	**0**
2019–20	*Kalmar*	18	2	**44**	**3**
2020–21	Udinese	0	0	**10**	**1**
2020–21	*Paderborn*	32	0	**32**	**0**
2021–22	Hansa Rostock	28	1		
2022–23	Hansa Rostock	24	1		
2023–24	Hansa Rostock	30	1	**82**	**3**
2024–25	Sheffield Wed	35	1	**35**	**1**

IORFA, Dominic (D) **278 7**
H: 6 2 W: 12 04 b.Southend-on-Sea 24-6-95
Internationals: England U18, U20, U21.

2013–14	Wolverhampton W	0	0		
2013–14	*Shrewsbury T*	7	0	**7**	**0**
2014–15	Wolverhampton W	20	0		
2015–16	Wolverhampton W	42	0		
2016–17	Wolverhampton W	22	0		
2017–18	Wolverhampton W	0	0		
2017–18	*Ipswich T*	23	1	**23**	**1**
2018–19	Wolverhampton W	0	0	**84**	**0**
2018–19	Sheffield Wed	12	3		
2019–20	Sheffield Wed	41	2		
2020–21	Sheffield Wed	10	0		
2021–22	Sheffield Wed	19	0		
2022–23	Sheffield Wed	32	0		
2023–24	Sheffield Wed	28	0		
2024–25	Sheffield Wed	22	1	**164**	**6**

JOHNSON, Marvin (F) **352 23**
H: 5 10 W: 11 09 b.Birmingham 1-12-90
From Solihull Moors, Kidderminster H.

2014–15	Motherwell	11	0		
2015–16	Motherwell	38	5		
2016–17	Motherwell	4	1	**53**	**6**
2016–17	Oxford U	39	3		
2017–18	Oxford U	2	0	**41**	**3**
2017–18	Middlesbrough	17	1		
2018–19	Middlesbrough	0	0		
2018–19	*Sheffield U*	11	0	**11**	**0**
2019–20	Middlesbrough	38	1		
2020–21	Middlesbrough	42	3	**97**	**5**
2021–22	Sheffield Wed	39	2		
2022–23	Sheffield Wed	41	3		
2023–24	Sheffield Wed	29	4		
2024–25	Sheffield Wed	41	0	**150**	**9**

KOBACKI, Olaf (M) **94 20**
b. 10-7-01
Internationals: Poland U16, U17, U18, U20.

2021–22	Atalanta	0	0		
2021–22	*Arka Gdynia*	26	6		
2022–23	Arka Gdynia	0	0		
2022–23	*Miedz Legnica*	24	1	**24**	**1**
2023–24	Arka Gdynia	32	13	**58**	**19**
2024–25	Sheffield Wed	12	0	**12**	**0**

LOWE, Jamal (F) **323 67**
H: 6 0 W: 12 06 b.Harrow 21-7-94
Internationals: England C. Jamaica Full caps.

2012–13	Barnet	8	0	**8**	**0**

From St Albans C, Hemel Hempstead T, Hampton & Richmond.

2016–17	Portsmouth	14	4		
2017–18	Portsmouth	44	6		
2018–19	Portsmouth	45	15		
2019–20	Portsmouth	0	0	**103**	**25**
2019–20	Wigan Ath	46	6	**46**	**6**
2020–21	Swansea C	46	14		
2021–22	Swansea C	5	0		
2021–22	Bournemouth	34	7		
2022–23	Bournemouth	2	0		
2022–23	*QPR*	20	3	**20**	**3**
2023–24	Bournemouth	0	0	**36**	**7**
2023–24	*Swansea C*	35	9	**86**	**23**
2024–25	Sheffield Wed	24	3	**24**	**3**

LOWE, Max (D) **184 4**
H: 5 9 W: 11 09 b.Birmingham 11-5-97
Internationals: England U16, U17, U18, U20.

2013–14	Derby Co	0	0		
2014–15	Derby Co	0	0		
2015–16	Derby Co	0	0		
2016–17	Derby Co	9	0		
2017–18	Derby Co	0	0		
2017–18	*Shrewsbury T*	12	0	**12**	**0**
2018–19	Derby Co	3	0		
2018–19	*Aberdeen*	33	2	**33**	**2**
2019–20	Derby Co	29	0	**41**	**0**
2020–21	Sheffield U	8	0		
2021–22	Sheffield U	0	0		
2021–22	*Nottingham F*	20	1	**20**	**1**
2022–23	Sheffield U	26	1		

2023–24 Sheffield U 10 0 **44 1**
2024–25 Sheffield Wed 34 0 **34 0**

MALTBY, Mackenzie (D) **0 0**
b.Chesterfield 4-12-04
2023–24 Sheffield Wed 0 0
2024–25 Sheffield Wed 0 0

McNEILL, Charlie (F) **27 3**
H: 5 11 b.Droylsden 9-9-03
Internationals: England U16.
2022–23 Manchester U 0 0
2022–23 Newport Co 20 2 **20 2**
2023–24 Manchester U 0 0
2023–24 Stevenage 3 1 **3 1**
2024–25 Sheffield Wed 4 0 **4 0**

MUSABA, Anthony (F) **183 25**
b. 6-12-00
Internationals: Netherlands U21.
2018–19 NEC 3 0 **3 0**
2019–20 NEC 25 7
2020–21 Monaco 0 0
2020–21 Cercle Brugge 29 6 **29 6**
2021–22 Monaco 0 0
2021–22 Heerenveen 31 1 **31 1**
2022–23 Monaco 0 0
2022–23 Metz 7 0 **7 0**
2022–23 NEC 16 1 **41 8**
2023–24 Sheffield Wed 43 7
2024–25 Sheffield Wed 29 3 **72 10**

ONUKWULI, Favour (F) **0 0**
b. 1-1-06
2024–25 Sheffield Wed 0 0

OTEGBAYO, Gabriel (D) **11 1**
H: 6 4 b.Cork 25-4-04
Internationals: Republic of Ireland U21.
2024–25 Sheffield Wed 11 1 **11 1**

PALMER, Liam (M) **448 10**
H: 6 2 W: 12 11 b.Worksop 19-9-91
Internationals: Scotland U19, U21, Full caps.
2010–11 Sheffield Wed 9 0
2011–12 Sheffield Wed 14 1
2012–13 Sheffield Wed 0 0
2012–13 Tranmere R 43 0 **43 0**
2013–14 Sheffield Wed 39 0
2014–15 Sheffield Wed 35 0
2015–16 Sheffield Wed 15 0
2016–17 Sheffield Wed 21 0
2017–18 Sheffield Wed 25 0
2018–19 Sheffield Wed 35 0
2019–20 Sheffield Wed 33 0
2020–21 Sheffield Wed 39 1
2021–22 Sheffield Wed 39 1
2022–23 Sheffield Wed 44 5
2023–24 Sheffield Wed 34 2
2024–25 Sheffield Wed 23 0 **405 10**

PATERSON, Callum (D) **392 77**
H: 6 2 W: 12 00 b.London 13-10-94
Internationals: Scotland U18, U21, Full caps.
2012–13 Hearts 22 3
2013–14 Hearts 37 11
2014–15 Hearts 29 6
2015–16 Hearts 29 5
2016–17 Hearts 20 8 **137 33**
2017–18 Cardiff C 32 10
2018–19 Cardiff C 27 4
2019–20 Cardiff C 36 5 **95 19**
2020–21 Sheffield Wed 43 8
2021–22 Sheffield Wed 40 6
2022–23 Sheffield Wed 25 5
2023–24 Sheffield Wed 25 0
2024–25 Sheffield Wed 27 6 **160 25**

PHUTHI, Joey (D) **1 0**
b. 2-1-05
Internationals: Zimbabwe Full caps.
2023–24 Sheffield Wed 1 0
2024–25 Sheffield Wed 0 0 **1 0**

REED, Samuel (D) **0 0**
b. 27-3-01
2023–24 Sheffield Wed 0 0
2024–25 Sheffield Wed 0 0

SHIPSTON, Rio (M) **21 0**
b.Sheffield 7-11-04
2022–23 Sheffield Wed 3 0
2023–24 Sheffield Wed 0 0
2024–25 Sheffield Wed 0 0 **3 0**
2025 Cork C 18 0 **18 0**

SIQUEIRA, Guilherme (D) **0 0**
H: 5 11 b. 6-12-04
2023–24 Sheffield Wed 0 0
2024–25 Sheffield Wed 0 0

SMITH, Michael (F) **517 131**
H: 6 4 W: 11 03 b.Wallsend 17-10-91
2009–10 Darlington 7 1
2010–11 Darlington 29 5 **36 6**
2011–12 Charlton Ath 0 0
2011–12 Accrington S 6 3 **6 3**
2012–13 Charlton Ath 0 0
2012–13 Colchester U 8 1 **8 1**
2013–14 Charlton Ath 0 0

2013–14 AFC Wimbledon 23 9 **23 9**
2013–14 Swindon T 20 8
2014–15 Swindon T 40 13
2015–16 Swindon T 5 0 **65 21**
2015–16 Barnsley 13 0 **13 0**
2015–16 Portsmouth 16 4
2016–17 Portsmouth 18 3 **34 7**
2016–17 Northampton T 14 2
2017–18 Northampton T 0 0 **14 2**
2017–18 Bury 19 1 **19 1**
2017–18 Rotherham U 20 6
2018–19 Rotherham U 45 8
2019–20 Rotherham U 34 9
2020–21 Rotherham U 44 10
2021–22 Rotherham U 45 19 **188 52**
2022–23 Sheffield Wed 39 17
2023–24 Sheffield Wed 31 4
2024–25 Sheffield Wed 41 8 **111 29**

UGBO, Ike (F) **234 54**
H: 5 11 W: 11 07 b.Lewisham 21-9-98
Internationals: England U17, U20. Canada Full caps.
2017–18 Chelsea 0 0
2017–18 Barnsley 16 1 **16 1**
2017–18 Milton Keynes D 15 2 **15 2**
2018–19 Chelsea 0 0
2018–19 Scunthorpe U 15 1 **15 1**
2019–20 Chelsea 0 0
2019–20 Roda 28 13 **28 13**
2020–21 Chelsea 0 0
2020–21 Cercle Brugge 32 16 **32 16**
2021–22 Genk 18 3 **18 3**
2021–22 Troyes 14 5
2022–23 Troyes 24 2
2023–24 Troyes 0 0 **38 7**
2023–24 Cardiff C 20 4 **20 4**
2024–25 Sheffield Wed 34 0 **52 7**

VALENTIN, Pol (D) **232 3**
b.Avinyonet de PuigventÛs 21-2-97
From Gimnastic.
2014–15 Figueres 12 0 **12 0**
2015–16 Pobla Mafumet 0 0
2016–17 Pobla Mafumet 21 1
2017–18 Pobla Mafumet 25 0 **46 1**
2017–18 Gimnastic 1 0
2018–19 Gimnastic 10 0
2019–20 Gimnastic 16 1 **27 1**
2019–20 Valencia 0 0
2020–21 Fuenlabrada 12 0
2021–22 Fuenlabrada 32 0 **55 0**
2022–23 Sporting Gijon 22 0 **22 0**
2023–24 Sheffield Wed 36 0
2024–25 Sheffield Wed 34 1 **70 1**

VALERY, Yann (D) **154 5**
H: 5 11 W: 11 00 b.Champigny-sur-Marne 22-2-99
Internationals: France U17, U18. Tunisia Full caps.
From Rennes.
2018–19 Southampton 23 2
2019–20 Southampton 11 0
2020–21 Southampton 3 0
2020–21 Birmingham C 7 0 **7 0**
2021–22 Southampton 5 0
2022–23 Southampton 1 0 **43 2**
2022–23 Angers 30 0
2023–24 Angers 35 0 **65 0**
2024–25 Sheffield Wed 39 3 **39 3**

WILKS, Mallik (F) **241 55**
H: 5 11 W: 11 03 b.Leeds 15-12-98
2016–17 Leeds U 0 0
2017–18 Leeds U 0 0
2017–18 Accrington S 19 3 **19 3**
2017–18 Grimsby T 6 0 **6 0**
2018–19 Leeds U 0 0
2018–19 Doncaster R 46 14 **46 14**
2019–20 Barnsley 15 1 **15 1**
2019–20 Hull C 18 5
2020–21 Hull C 44 19
2021–22 Hull C 20 3
2022–23 Hull C 1 0 **83 27**
2022–23 Sheffield Wed 16 1
2023–24 Sheffield Wed 15 0
2024–25 Sheffield Wed 0 0 **31 1**
2024–25 Rotherham U 41 9 **41 9**

WINDASS, Josh (M) **346 89**
H: 5 9 W: 10 10 b.Hull 9-1-94
From Huddersfield T, Harrogate Railway Ath.
2013–14 Accrington S 10 0
2014–15 Accrington S 35 6
2015–16 Accrington S 30 15 **75 21**
2016–17 Rangers 21 0
2017–18 Rangers 33 13
2018–19 Rangers 1 0 **55 13**
2018–19 Wigan Ath 39 5
2019–20 Sheffield Wed 9 3
2019–20 Wigan Ath 15 4 **54 9**
2020–21 Sheffield Wed 41 9
2021–22 Sheffield Wed 9 4

2022–23 Sheffield Wed 34 11
2023–24 Sheffield Wed 25 6
2024–25 Sheffield Wed 44 13 **162 46**

Players retained or with offer of contract
Brown, George William; Kamwa, Donald Junior; Moses, Devlan Geo; Phillips, Jack James; Thornton, Jarvis Harry; Vilela De Carvalho, Bruno Henrique.

Scholars
Clayton, Liam Mark; Emery, Joseph Alfred; Hatfield, Kailen Thomas; Hobbs, Charlie Dennis; Hunt, Finley James; Jessop, Jacob William; Kakay, Sutura; Lihe, Harris Immanuel; Mbaya, Voldi Lembo; Pinhal Da Costa, Daniel Carlos; Remy-Dee, Caiden Ellis; Shaw, Ari-Jae; Sopala, Aodhan Mark; Stretch, Logan Scott; Swales, Jack Alexander; Weaver, Ernie Luke; Weston, Dominic David.

SHREWSBURY T (75)

BENNING, Malvind (D) **417 16**
H: 5 10 W: 12 02 b.Sandwell 2-11-93
2012–13 Walsall 10 0
2013–14 Walsall 16 2
2014–15 Walsall 20 0 **46 2**
2014–15 York C 9 0 **9 0**
2015–16 Mansfield T 31 4
2016–17 Mansfield T 45 1
2017–18 Mansfield T 28 1
2018–19 Mansfield T 45 3
2019–20 Mansfield T 33 0
2020–21 Mansfield T 32 0 **214 9**
2021–22 Port Vale 26 1
2022–23 Port Vale 39 1 **65 2**
2023–24 Shrewsbury T 39 0
2024–25 Shrewsbury T 44 3 **83 3**

BIGGINS, Harrison (M) **212 18**
H: 5 9 W: 12 06 b.Sheffield 15-3-96
From Stocksbridge Park Steels.
2017–18 Fleetwood T 7 0
2018–19 Fleetwood T 23 1
2019–20 Fleetwood T 10 0
2020–21 Fleetwood T 10 0
2020–21 Barrow 22 2 **22 2**
2021–22 Fleetwood T 32 5 **82 6**
2022–23 Doncaster R 36 5
2023–24 Doncaster R ,38 5 **74 10**
2024–25 Shrewsbury T 17 0 **17 0**
2024–25 Carlisle U 17 0 **17 0**

BLACKMAN, Jamal (G) **199 0**
H: 6 6 W: 14 09 b.Croydon 27-10-93
Internationals: England U16, U17, U19.
2011–12 Chelsea 0 0
2012–13 Chelsea 0 0
2013–14 Chelsea 0 0
2014–15 Chelsea 0 0
2014–15 Middlesbrough 0 0
2015–16 Chelsea 0 0
2015–16 Ostersund 12 0 **12 0**
2016–17 Chelsea 0 0
2016–17 Wycombe W 42 0 **42 0**
2017–18 Sheffield U 31 0 **31 0**
2018–19 Chelsea 0 0
2018–19 Leeds U 0 0
2019–20 Chelsea 0 0
2019–20 Vitesse 0 0
2019–20 Bristol R 10 0 **10 0**
2020–21 Chelsea 0 0
2020–21 Rotherham U 26 0 **26 0**
2021 Los Angeles 8 0 **8 0**
2021–22 Huddersfield T 1 0 **1 0**
2022–23 Exeter C 38 0 **38 0**
2023–24 Burton Alb 4 0 **4 0**
2024–25 Shrewsbury T 27 0 **27 0**

CAIRNS, Karsten (M) **0 0**
2024–25 Shrewsbury T 0 0

COLLINS, Jude (M) **0 0**
b.Leicester 16-10-05
2022–23 Shrewsbury T 0 0
2023–24 Shrewsbury T 0 0
2024–25 Shrewsbury T 0 0

DINANGA, Ricardo (F) **8 1**
H: 5 9 W: 12 06 b.Cork 6-12-01
2019 Cork C 5 0
2020 Cork C 6 1 **7 1**
2021–22 Coventry C 0 0
2022–23 Coventry C 0 0
From Telford U.
2024–25 Shrewsbury T 1 0 **1 0**

ENGLAND, Isaac (M) **2 0**
b. 29-4-08
2024–25 Shrewsbury T 2 0 **2 0**

FEENEY, Morgan (D) **141 5**
H: 6 3 W: 12 02 b.Bootle 8-2-98
Internationals: England U17, U18, U19.
2017–18 Everton 0 0

2018–19 Everton 0 0
2019–20 Everton 0 0
2019–20 *Tranmere R* 1 0 **1 0**
2020–21 Sunderland 0 0
2020–21 Carlisle U 0 0
2021–22 Carlisle U 35 1
2022–23 Carlisle U 31 3 **66 4**
2023–24 Shrewsbury T 38 0
2024–25 Shrewsbury T 36 1 **74 1**

GAPE, Dominic (M) **200 4**
H: 5 11 W: 11 00 b.Southampton 9-9-94
2012–13 Southampton 0 0
2013–14 Southampton 0 0
2014–15 Southampton 1 0
2015–16 Southampton 0 0
2016–17 Southampton 0 0 **1 0**
2016–17 Wycombe W 32 1
2017–18 Wycombe W 35 1
2018–19 Wycombe W 43 1
2019–20 Wycombe W 28 0
2020–21 Wycombe W 14 0
2021–22 Wycombe W 10 0
2022–23 Wycombe W 15 1 **177 4**
2023–24 Sutton U 4 0 **4 0**
2023–24 Northampton T 2 0 **2 0**
2024–25 Shrewsbury T 16 0 **16 0**

GILLIEAD, Alex (F) **375 20**
H: 6 0 W: 11 00 b.Shotley Bridge 11-2-96
Internationals: England U16, U17, U18, U20.
2014–15 Newcastle U 0 0
2015–16 Newcastle U 0 0
2015–16 *Carlisle U* 35 5 **35 5**
2016–17 Newcastle U 0 0
2016–17 *Luton T* 18 1 **18 1**
2016–17 *Bradford C* 9 0
2017–18 Newcastle U 0 0
2017–18 *Bradford C* 42 1
2018–19 Shrewsbury T 27 1
2019–20 Scunthorpe U 35 6
2020–21 Scunthorpe U 44 1 **79 7**
2021–22 Bradford C 43 1
2022–23 Bradford C 42 1
2023–24 Bradford C 38 3 **174 6**
2024–25 Shrewsbury T 42 0 **69 1**

GODWIN, Isaac (D) **0 0**
2023–24 Shrewsbury T 0 0
2024–25 Shrewsbury T 0 0

HOOLE, Luca (D) **128 4**
H: 5 10 W: 10 01 b.Newport 2-6-02
Internationals: Wales U19, U20, U21.
2019–20 Bristol R 0 0
2020–21 Bristol R 0 0
2021–22 Bristol R 29 1
2022–23 Bristol R 37 2
2023–24 Bristol R 23 0 **89 3**
2024–25 Shrewsbury T 39 1 **39 1**

LLOYD, George (F) **183 18**
H: 5 8 W: 9 13 b.Gloucester 11-2-00
2017–18 Cheltenham T 7 2
2018–19 Cheltenham T 7 1
2019–20 Cheltenham T 13 0
2020–21 Cheltenham T 32 2
2021–22 Port Vale 7 0 **7 0**
2021–22 Cheltenham T 12 1
2022–23 Cheltenham T 13 0
2022–23 *Grimsby T* 21 5 **21 5**
2023–24 Cheltenham T 27 2 **111 8**
2024–25 Shrewsbury T 44 5 **44 5**

LOUGHRAN, Jack (M) **2 0**
H: 5 10 W: 11 11 b. 9-11-06
2023–24 Shrewsbury T 1 0
2024–25 Shrewsbury T 1 0 **2 0**

MARQUIS, John (F) **496 144**
H: 6 1 W: 11 03 b.Lewisham 16-5-92
2009–10 Millwall 1 0
2010–11 Millwall 11 4
2011–12 Millwall 17 1
2012–13 Millwall 10 0
2013–14 Millwall 2 0
2013–14 *Portsmouth* 5 1
2013–14 *Torquay U* 5 3 **5 3**
2013–14 *Northampton T* 14 2
2014–15 Millwall 1 0
2014–15 *Cheltenham T* 13 1 **13 1**
2014–15 *Gillingham* 21 8 **21 8**
2015–16 Millwall 10 0 **52 5**
2015–16 *Leyton Orient* 13 0 **13 0**
2015–16 *Northampton T* 15 6 **29 8**
2016–17 Doncaster R 45 26
2017–18 Doncaster R 45 14
2018–19 Doncaster R 44 21 **134 61**
2019–20 Portsmouth 33 8
2020–21 Portsmouth 41 16
2021–22 Portsmouth 19 4 **98 29**
2021–22 Lincoln C 20 5
2022–23 Lincoln C 0 0 **20 5**
2022–23 Bristol R 36 9
2023–24 Bristol R 35 4 **71 13**
2024–25 Shrewsbury T 40 11 **40 11**

MORRIS, Cammron (F) **0 0**
2023–24 Shrewsbury T 0 0
2024–25 Shrewsbury T 0 0

MORRIS, Joe (M) **0 0**
Internationals: Wales U16.
2024–25 Shrewsbury T 0 0

NSIALA, Aristote (D) **305 8**
H: 6 4 W: 13 01 b.Kinshasa 25-3-92
Internationals: DR Congo Full caps.
2009–10 Everton 0 0
2010–11 Everton 0 0
2010–11 *Macclesfield T* 10 0 **10 0**
2011–12 Everton 0 0
2011–12 *Accrington S* 19 0
2012–13 Accrington S 17 0
2013–14 Accrington S 0 0 **36 0**
From Southport, Grimsby T.
2016–17 Hartlepool U 21 1 **21 1**
2016–17 Shrewsbury T 21 1
2017–18 Shrewsbury T 44 3
2018–19 Ipswich T 22 1
2019–20 Ipswich T 3 0
2019–20 *Bolton W* 12 0 **12 0**
2020–21 Ipswich T 27 0
2021–22 Ipswich T 11 0 **63 1**
2021–22 Fleetwood T 20 0
2022–23 Fleetwood T 35 0
2023–24 Fleetwood T 12 0 **67 0**
2023–24 Burton Alb 11 1 **11 1**
2024–25 Shrewsbury T 20 1 **85 5**

NURSE, George (D) **104 2**
H: 5 11 W: 12 04 b.Bristol 30-4-99
2019–20 Bristol C 0 0
2019–20 *Newport Co* 17 1 **17 1**
2020–21 Bristol C 0 0
2020–21 *Walsall* 10 1 **10 1**
2021–22 Shrewsbury T 45 0
2022–23 Shrewsbury T 10 0
2023–24 Shrewsbury T 0 0
2024–25 Shrewsbury T 22 0 **77 0**

PERRY, Taylor (M) **120 8**
H: 5 11 W: 12 06 b.Stourbridge 15-8-01
2019–20 Wolverhampton W 0 0
2020–21 Wolverhampton W 0 0
2021–22 Wolverhampton W 0 0
2021–22 *Cheltenham T* 10 1
2022–23 Wolverhampton W 0 0
2022–23 *Cheltenham T* 34 2 **44 3**
2023–24 Shrewsbury T 42 2
2024–25 Shrewsbury T 34 3 **76 5**

PIERRE, Aaron (D) **333 27**
H: 6 1 W: 13 12 b.Southall 17-2-93
Internationals: Grenada Full caps.
2011–12 Brentford 0 0
2012–13 Brentford 0 0
2013–14 Brentford 0 0
2013–14 *Wycombe W* 8 1
2014–15 Wycombe W 42 4
2015–16 Wycombe W 40 2
2016–17 Wycombe W 39 2 **129 9**
2017–18 Northampton T 19 0
2018–19 Northampton T 41 6 **60 6**
2019–20 Shrewsbury T 30 3
2020–21 Shrewsbury T 26 4
2021–22 Shrewsbury T 25 0
2022–23 Sutton U 2 0 **2 0**
2022–23 AFC Wimbledon 11 1 **11 1**
2023–24 Shrewsbury T 17 1
2024–25 Shrewsbury T 33 3 **131 11**

ROSSITER, Jordan (M) **123 3**
H: 5 10 W: 10 10 b.Liverpool 24-3-97
Internationals: England U16, U17, U18, U19.
2013–14 Liverpool 0 0
2014–15 Liverpool 0 0
2015–16 Liverpool 1 0 **1 0**
2016–17 Rangers 4 0
2017–18 Rangers 2 1
2018–19 Rangers 4 0
2018–19 *Bury* 16 1 **16 1**
2019–20 Rangers 0 0 **10 1**
2019–20 *Fleetwood T* 15 0
2020–21 Fleetwood T 35 1
2021–22 Fleetwood T 10 0 **60 1**
2022–23 Bristol R 17 0
2023–24 Bristol R 4 0 **21 0**
2024–25 Shrewsbury T 15 0 **15 0**

SAVIN, Toby (G) **114 0**
H: 6 4 W: 13 03 b.Ormskirk 4-5-01
2017–18 Accrington S 0 0
2018–19 Accrington S 0 0
2019–20 Accrington S 0 0
2020–21 Accrington S 31 0
2021–22 Accrington S 33 0
2022–23 Accrington S 18 0
2022–23 *Stevenage* 4 0 **4 0**
2023–24 Accrington S 9 0 **91 0**
2024–25 Shrewsbury T 19 0 **19 0**

SHIPLEY, Jordan (M) **244 28**
H: 6 0 W: 11 07 b.Leamington Spa 26-9-97
Internationals: Republic of Ireland U21.
2016–17 Coventry C 1 0
2017–18 Coventry C 30 4
2018–19 Coventry C 33 3
2019–20 Coventry C 31 5
2020–21 Coventry C 27 3
2021–22 Coventry C 11 1 **133 16**
2022–23 Shrewsbury T 45 4
2023–24 Shrewsbury T 33 6
2024–25 Shrewsbury T 33 2 **111 12**

STEWART, Callum (F) **15 0**
b. 14-12-01
2024–25 Shrewsbury T 15 0 **15 0**

WATTS, Harvey (M) **1 0**
b. 17-6-06
2022–23 Shrewsbury T 0 0
2023–24 Shrewsbury T 1 0
2024–25 Shrewsbury T 0 0 **1 0**

WHEELER, David (M) **373 56**
H: 5 11 W: 12 00 b.Brighton 4-10-90
From Brighton & HA.
2013–14 Exeter C 35 3
2014–15 Exeter C 45 7
2015–16 Exeter C 31 6
2016–17 Exeter C 38 17
2017–18 Exeter C 2 0 **151 33**
2017–18 QPR 9 1
2018–19 QPR 0 0 **9 1**
2018–19 *Portsmouth* 11 0 **11 0**
2018–19 *Milton Keynes D* 19 4 **19 4**
2019–20 Wycombe W 31 3
2020–21 Wycombe W 38 3
2021–22 Wycombe W 30 2
2022–23 Wycombe W 37 7
2023–24 Wycombe W 32 3
2024–25 Wycombe W 5 0 **173 18**
2024–25 Shrewsbury T 10 0 **10 0**

WHITNEY, Luca (F) **1 0**
b. 27-10-06
2023–24 Shrewsbury T 1 0
2024–25 Shrewsbury T 0 0 **1 0**

WINCHESTER, Carl (M) **440 29**
H: 5 10 W: 11 09 b.Belfast 12-4-93
Internationals: Northern Ireland U16, U17, U18, U19, U21, Full caps.
From Linfield.
2010–11 Oldham Ath 6 1
2011–12 Oldham Ath 12 0
2012–13 Oldham Ath 9 0
2013–14 Oldham Ath 12 1
2014–15 Oldham Ath 41 4
2015–16 Oldham Ath 31 1
2016–17 Oldham Ath 9 1 **120 8**
2016–17 Cheltenham T 20 1
2017–18 Cheltenham T 44 5 **64 6**
2018–19 Forest Green R 45 3
2019–20 Forest Green R 35 5
2020–21 Forest Green R 18 2 **98 10**
2020–21 Sunderland 20 1
2021–22 Sunderland 40 3
2022–23 Sunderland 0 0 **60 4**
2022–23 *Shrewsbury T* 39 0
2023–24 Shrewsbury T 44 0
2024–25 Shrewsbury T 15 1 **98 1**
Transferred to Derry C, January 2025.

YOUNG, Joe (G) **0 0**
H: 6 1 W: 12 13 b.Telford 22-9-02
Internationals: England U17.
2024–25 Shrewsbury T 0 0

Players retained or with offer of contract
Idowu, Roland; Mata, Max Andrew.

Scholars
Byrne, Shayne Oliver; Cairns, Karsten Charles Karner; Falding, Reuben Boyd Erickson; Godwin, Isaac Joseph; Hardeman, William Andrew; Hughes, Leon Mark; Lewis, Haydn Arthur; Loughran, Jack Daniel; Male, John Junior Alfred; Manseya, Arnold Adiwa-Bawa; McKenzie, Jeval Maurice Thompson; Morris, Joe Robert; Nyamwanza, Simbarashe Joel; Prior, Zac David; Snook, Jay Douglas; Starkey-Jones, Findlay James; Valentine, Jayden Andrew; Whitney, Luca Jack.

SOUTHAMPTON (76)

AKACHUKWU, Romeo (M) **28 3**
H: 5 10 W: 11 09 b. 28-7-06
Internationals: Republic of Ireland U16, U17, U19.
2022 Waterford 2 0
2023 Waterford 19 3
2024 Waterford 7 0 **28 3**
2024–25 Southampton 0 0

AMO-AMEYAW, Samuel (F)   15   2
H: 5 9   W: 9 08   b.London 18-7-06
Internationals: England U16, U17, U18, U19.
From Tottenham H.
2022–23 Southampton   1   0
2023–24 Southampton   3   0
2024–25 Southampton   2   0   6   0
2024–25 Strasbourg   9   2   9   2

ARCHER, Cameron (F)   114   24
H: 6 1   W: 11 03   b.Walsall 21-7-01
Internationals: England U20, U21.
2019–20 Aston Villa   0   0
2020–21 Aston Villa   0   0
2021–22 Aston Villa   3   0
2021–22 Preston NE   20   7   20   7
2022–23 Aston Villa   6   0
2022–23 Middlesbrough   20   11   20   11
2023–24 Aston Villa   1   0
2023–24 Sheffield U   29   4   29   4
2024–25 Aston Villa   0   0   10   0
2024–25 Southampton   35   2   35   2

ARIBO, Joe (M)   261   41
H: 6 0   W: 12 00   b.Camberwell 21-7-96
Internationals: Nigeria Full caps.
From Staines T.
2015–16 Charlton Ath   0   0
2016–17 Charlton Ath   19   0
2017–18 Charlton Ath   26   5
2018–19 Charlton Ath   36   9   81   14
2019–20 Rangers   27   3
2020–21 Rangers   31   7
2021–22 Rangers   34   8   92   18
2022–23 Southampton   21   2
2023–24 Southampton   35   4
2024–25 Southampton   32   3   88   0

ARMITAGE, Will (D)   0   0
H: 5 9   W: 10 06   b. 7-3-05
2021–22 Cheltenham T   0   0
2021–22 Southampton   0   0
2022–23 Southampton   0   0
2023–24 Southampton   0   0
2024–25 Southampton   0   0

ARMSTRONG, Adam (F)   397   115
H: 5 8   W: 10 12   b.Newcastle upon Tyne 10-2-97
Internationals: England U16, U17, U18, U19, U20, U21.
2013–14 Newcastle U   4   0
2014–15 Newcastle U   11   0
2015–16 Newcastle U   0   0
2015–16 Coventry C   40   20   40   20
2016–17 Newcastle U   2   0
2016–17 Barnsley   34   6   34   6
2017–18 Newcastle U   0   0   17   0
2017–18 Bolton W   20   1   20   1
2017–18 Blackburn R   21   9
2018–19 Blackburn R   44   5
2019–20 Blackburn R   46   16
2020–21 Blackburn R   40   28   151   58
2021–22 Southampton   23   2
2022–23 Southampton   30   2
2023–24 Southampton   46   21
2024–25 Southampton   20   2   119   27
2024–25 WBA   16   3   16   3

AWE, Zach (D)   21   1
H: 6 4   W: 11 11   b.London 9-1-04
Internationals: England U16.
2021–22 Arsenal   0   0
2022–23 Arsenal   0   0
2023–24 Southampton   0   0
2024–25 Southampton   0   0
2024–25 Accrington S   21   1   21   1

BALLARD, Dominic (F)   47   6
H: 5 10   W: 11 09   b.Guildford 1-4-05
Internationals: England U17, U18, U19, U20.
2022–23 Southampton   2   0
2023–24 Southampton   0   0
2023–24 Reading   10   3   10   3
2024–25 Southampton   0   0   2   0
2024–25 Blackpool   18   1   18   1
2024–25 Cambridge U   17   2   17   2

BAZUNU, Gavin (G)   154   0
H: 6 0   W: 12 06   b.Dublin 20-2-02
Internationals: Republic of Ireland U17, U21, Full caps.
From Shamrock R.
2019–20 Manchester C   0   0
2020–21 Manchester C   0   0
2020–21 Rochdale   29   0   29   0
2021–22 Manchester C   0   0
2021–22 Portsmouth   44   0   44   0
2022–23 Southampton   32   0
2023–24 Southampton   41   0
2024–25 Southampton   0   0   73   0
2024–25 Standard Liege   8   0   8   0

BEDNAREK, Jan (D)   274   12
H: 6 2   W: 12 02   b.Slupca 12-4-96
Internationals: Poland U16, U17, U18, U19, U20, U21, Full caps.
2013–14 Lech Poznan   2   0

2014–15 Lech Poznan   2   0
2015–16 Lech Poznan   0   0
2015–16 Gornik Leczna   17   0   17   0
2016–17 Lech Poznan   27   1   31   1
2017–18 Southampton   5   1
2018–19 Southampton   25   0
2019–20 Southampton   34   1
2020–21 Southampton   36   1
2021–22 Southampton   31   4
2022–23 Southampton   20   0
2022–23 Aston Villa   3   0   3   0
2023–24 Southampton   42   2
2024–25 Southampton   30   2   223   11

BRAGG, Cameron (M)   6   0
H: 5 10   W: 10 12   b. 10-4-05
Internationals: Scotland U21.
2023–24 Southampton   0   0
2024–25 Southampton   0   0
2024–25 Crawley T   6   0   6   0

BREE, James (D)   258   2
H: 5 10   W: 11 09   b.Wakefield 11-12-97
2013–14 Barnsley   1   0
2014–15 Barnsley   11   0
2015–16 Barnsley   19   0
2016–17 Barnsley   19   0   50   0
2016–17 Aston Villa   7   0
2017–18 Aston Villa   6   0
2018–19 Aston Villa   8   0
2018–19 Ipswich T   14   0   14   0
2019–20 Aston Villa   0   0   21   0
2019–20 Luton T   39   0
2020–21 Luton T   24   1
2021–22 Luton T   42   1
2021–22 Luton T   27   0   132   2
2022–23 Southampton   5   0
2023–24 Southampton   19   0
2024–25 Southampton   17   0   41   0

BRERETON, Ben (F)   268   63
H: 6 1   W: 11 11   b.Stoke-on-Trent 18-4-99
Internationals: England U19, U20. Chile Full caps.
From Stoke C.
2016–17 Nottingham F   18   3
2017–18 Nottingham F   35   5   53   8
2018–19 Blackburn R   25   1
2019–20 Blackburn R   15   1
2020–21 Blackburn R   40   7
2021–22 Blackburn R   37   22
2022–23 Blackburn R   43   14   160   45
2023–24 Villarreal   14   0   14   0
2023–24 Sheffield U   14   6
2024–25 Southampton   10   0   10   0
2024–25 Sheffield U   17   4   31   10

CHARLES, Shea (M)   76   1
H: 5 11   W: 11 03   b.Manchester 5-11-03
Internationals: Northern Ireland U16, U19, U21, Full caps.
2022–23 Manchester C   1   0   1   0
2023–24 Southampton   32   0
2024–25 Southampton   0   0   32   0
2024–25 Sheffield Wed   43   1   43   1

DIBLING, Tyler (M)   34   2
H: 5 10   W: 11 05   b.Exeter 12-3-06
Internationals: England U16, U17, U18, U19, U21.
2021–22 Southampton   0   0
2022–23 Southampton   0   0
2023–24 Southampton   1   0
2024–25 Southampton   33   2   34   2

DOWNES, Flynn (M)   220   7
H: 5 8   W: 11 00   b.Brentwood 21-1-99
Internationals: England U19, U20.
2016–17 Ipswich T   0   0
2017–18 Ipswich T   10   0
2017–18 Luton T   10   0   10   0
2018–19 Ipswich T   29   1
2019–20 Ipswich T   29   2
2020–21 Ipswich T   24   0   92   3
2021–22 Swansea C   37   1   37   1
2022–23 West Ham U   12   0
2023–24 West Ham U   0   0   21   0
2023–24 Southampton   33   2
2024–25 Southampton   27   1   60   3

EDOZIE, Samuel (F)   74   9
H: 5 11   b.Lewisham 28-1-03
Internationals: England U18, U19, U20.
From Millwall.
2020–21 Manchester C   0   0
2021–22 Manchester C   0   0
2022–23 Southampton   17   0
2023–24 Southampton   32   6
2024–25 Southampton   2   0   51   6
2024–25 Anderlecht   23   3   23   3

EDWARDS, Ronnie (D)   143   3
H: 5 11   W: 12 00   b.Harlow 28-3-03
Internationals: England U18, U19, U20, U21.
From Barnet.
2020–21 Peterborough U   2   0
2021–22 Peterborough U   34   0
2022–23 Peterborough U   40   0
2023–24 Peterborough U   45   1   121   1

2024–25 Southampton   1   0   1   0
2024–25 QPR   21   2   21   2

FERNANDES, Mateus (M)   41   2
H: 5 10   W: 11 09   b.Olhao 10-7-04
Internationals: Portugal U18, U19, U20, U21.
2021–22 Sporting Lisbon   0   0
2022–23 Sporting Lisbon   3   0
2023–24 Sporting Lisbon   1   0
2024–25 Sporting Lisbon   1   0   5   0
2024–25 Southampton   36   2   36   2

FRASER, Ryan (M)   322   32
H: 5 4   W: 11 00   b.Aberdeen 24-2-94
Internationals: Scotland U19, U21, Full caps.
2010–11 Aberdeen   2   0
2011–12 Aberdeen   3   0
2012–13 Aberdeen   16   0   21   0
2012–13 Bournemouth   5   0
2013–14 Bournemouth   37   3
2014–15 Bournemouth   21   1
2015–16 Bournemouth   0   0
2015–16 Ipswich T   18   4   18   4
2016–17 Bournemouth   28   3
2017–18 Bournemouth   26   5
2018–19 Bournemouth   38   7
2019–20 Bournemouth   28   1   183   20
2020–21 Newcastle U   18   0
2021–22 Newcastle U   27   2
2022–23 Newcastle U   8   0
2023–24 Newcastle U   0   0   53   2
2023–24 Southampton   39   6
2024–25 Southampton   8   0   47   6

GRONBAEK, Albert (M)   149   29
H: 5 9   W: 10 03   b.Risskov 23-5-01
Internationals: Denmark U18, U19, U21, Full caps.
2019–20 AGF   8   0
2020–21 AGF   31   5
2021–22 AGF   31   3
2022 Bodo/Glimt   12   2
2022–23 AGF   4   0   74   8
2023 Bodo/Glimt   28   9
2024 Bodo/Glimt   15   8   55   19
On loan from Rennes.
2024–25 Southampton   4   0   4   0

HARWOOD-BELLIS, Taylor (D)   163   4
H: 6 1   W: 11 05   b.Stockport 30-1-02
Internationals: England U16, U17, U19, U20, U21, Full caps.
2019–20 Manchester C   0   0
2020–21 Manchester C   0   0
2020–21 Blackburn R   19   0   19   0
2021–22 Manchester C   0   0
2021–22 Anderlecht   16   0   16   0
2021–22 Stoke C   22   0   22   0
2022–23 Manchester C   0   0
2022–23 Burnley   32   1   32   1
2023–24 Southampton   40   2
2024–25 Southampton   34   1   74   3

KAYI SANDA, Joachim (D)   20   0
H: 6 1   W: 12 08   b.Antony 29-11-06
Internationals: France U16, U17, U18.
2022–23 Valenciennes   0   0
2023–24 Valenciennes   20   0   20   0
2024–25 Southampton   0   0

KOTCHAP, Armel (D)   98   1
H: 6 3   W: 13 10   b.Paris 11-12-01
Internationals: Germany U18, U20, U21, Full caps.
2018–19 VfL Bochum   4   0
2019–20 VfL Bochum   12   0
2020–21 VfL Bochum   28   1
2021–22 VfL Bochum   22   0   66   1
2022–23 Southampton   24   0
2023–24 Southampton   0   0
2023–24 PSV Eindhoven   4   0   4   0
2024–25 Southampton   4   0   28   0

LALLANA, Adam (M)   475   69
H: 5 10   W: 11 06   b.St Albans 10-5-88
Internationals: England U18, U19, U21, Full caps.
2005–06 Southampton   0   0
2006–07 Southampton   1   0
2007–08 Southampton   5   1
2007–08 Bournemouth   3   0   3   0
2008–09 Southampton   40   1
2009–10 Southampton   44   15
2010–11 Southampton   36   8
2011–12 Southampton   41   11
2012–13 Southampton   30   3
2013–14 Southampton   38   9
2014–15 Liverpool   27   5
2015–16 Liverpool   30   4
2016–17 Liverpool   31   8
2017–18 Liverpool   13   0
2018–19 Liverpool   13   0
2019–20 Liverpool   15   1   128   18
2020–21 Brighton & HA   30   1
2021–22 Brighton & HA   24   0
2022–23 Brighton & HA   16   2

2023–24 Brighton & HA 25 0 95 3
2024–25 Southampton 14 0 249 48

LARIOS, Juan (D) 5 0
H: 5 7 W: 10 10 b.Tomares 12-1-04
Internationals: Spain U18, U19.
From Sevilla, Barcelona, Manchester C.
2022–23 Southampton 5 0
2023–24 Southampton 0 0
2024–25 Southampton 0 0 **5 0**

LAWRENCE, Nico (D) 26 0
H: 6 0 W: 12 02 b. 22-11-03
2022–23 Southampton 0 0
2023–24 Southampton 0 0
2023–24 *Colchester U* 4 0 **4 0**
2024–25 Southampton 0 0
2024–25 *Milton Keynes D* 22 0 **22 0**

LUMLEY, Joe (G) 206 0
H: 6 3 W: 11 07 b.Harlow 15-2-95
2013–14 QPR 0 0
2014–15 QPR 0 0
2014–15 *Accrington S* 5 0 **5 0**
2014–15 *Morecambe* 0 0
2015–16 QPR 1 0
2015–16 *Stevenage* 0 0
2016–17 QPR 0 0
2016–17 *Bristol R* 19 0 **19 0**
2017–18 QPR 2 0
2017–18 *Blackpool* 17 0 **17 0**
2018–19 QPR 42 0
2019–20 QPR 27 0
2020–21 QPR 5 0 **77 0**
2020–21 *Gillingham* 2 0 **2 0**
2020–21 *Doncaster R* 8 0 **8 0**
2021–22 Middlesbrough 34 0
2022–23 Middlesbrough 0 0 **34 0**
2022–23 *Reading* 41 0 **41 0**
2023–24 Southampton 0 0
2024–25 Southampton 3 0 **3 0**

MANNING, Ryan (M) 311 31
H: 5 8 W: 10 06 b.Galway 14-6-96
Internationals: Republic of Ireland U17, U19, U21, Full caps.
2013 Mervue U 26 9 **26 9**
2014 Galway U 21 4 **21 4**
2014–15 QPR 0 0
2015–16 QPR 0 0
2016–17 QPR 18 1
2017–18 QPR 19 2
2018–19 QPR 9 0
2018–19 *Rotherham U* 18 4 **18 4**
2019–20 QPR 41 4
2020–21 QPR 0 0 **87 7**
2020–21 Swansea C 17 0
2021–22 Swansea C 38 2
2022–23 Swansea C 43 5 **98 7**
2023–24 Southampton 37 0
2024–25 Southampton 24 0 **61 0**

McCARTHY, Alex (G) 281 0
H: 6 4 W: 12 07 b.Guildford 3-12-89
Internationals: England U21, Full caps.
2008–09 Reading 0 0
2008–09 *Aldershot T* 4 0 **4 0**
2009–10 Reading 0 0
2009–10 *Yeovil T* 44 0 **44 0**
2010–11 Reading 13 0
2010–11 *Brentford* 3 0 **3 0**
2011–12 Reading 0 0
2011–12 *Leeds U* 6 0 **6 0**
2011–12 *Ipswich T* 10 0 **10 0**
2012–13 Reading 13 0
2013–14 Reading 44 0 **70 0**
2014–15 QPR 3 0 **3 0**
2015–16 Crystal Palace 7 0 **7 0**
2016–17 Southampton 0 0
2017–18 Southampton 18 0
2018–19 Southampton 25 0
2019–20 Southampton 28 0
2020–21 Southampton 30 0
2021–22 Southampton 17 0
2022–23 Southampton 6 0
2023–24 Southampton 5 0
2024–25 Southampton 5 0 **134 0**

MOORE, Jayden (D) 0 0
H: 6 4 W: 10 10 b. 12-12-06
2024–25 Southampton 0 0

O'BRIEN-WHITMARSH, Joseph (M) 36 7
H: 5 8 W: 11 07 b.Cork 11-5-05
Internationals: Republic of Ireland U18, U19, U21.
2021 Cork C 0 0
2022 Cork C 0 0
2023 Cork C 23 4 **23 4**
2023–24 Southampton 0 0
2024–25 Southampton 0 0
2024–25 *Accrington S* 13 3 **13 3**

ONUACHU, Ebere Paul (F) 319 155
H: 6 7 W: 13 03 b.Owerri 28-5-94
Internationals: Nigeria Full caps.
2012–13 Midtjylland 1 0
2013–14 Midtjylland 11 0
2014–15 Midtjylland 10 1
2014–15 *Vejle* 13 5 **13 5**
2015–16 Midtjylland 25 6
2016–17 Midtjylland 36 18
2017–18 Midtjylland 22 10
2018–19 Midtjylland 30 17 **135 52**
2019–20 Genk 22 9
2020–21 Genk 38 33
2021–22 Genk 35 21
2022–23 Genk 19 16 **114 79**
2022–23 Southampton 11 0
2023–24 Southampton 0 0
2023–24 *Trabzonspor* 21 15 **21 15**
2024–25 Southampton 25 4 **36 4**

RAMSDALE, Aaron (G) 224 0
H: 6 2 W: 12 02 b.Stoke-on-Trent 14-5-98
Internationals: England U18, U19, U20, U21, Full caps.
2015–16 Sheffield U 0 0
2016–17 Sheffield U 0 0
2016–17 Bournemouth 0 0
2017–18 Bournemouth 0 0
2017–18 *Chesterfield* 19 0 **19 0**
2018–19 Bournemouth 0 0
2018–19 *AFC Wimbledon* 20 0 **20 0**
2019–20 Bournemouth 37 0 **37 0**
2020–21 Sheffield U 38 0
2021–22 Sheffield U 2 0 **40 0**
2021–22 Arsenal 34 0
2022–23 Arsenal 38 0
2023–24 Arsenal 6 0
2024–25 Arsenal 0 0 **78 0**
2024–25 Southampton 30 0 **30 0**

ROBINSON, Jay (D) 4 0
H: 5 9 W: 10 03 b. 15-3-07
Internationals: England U17, U18.
2024–25 Southampton 4 0 **4 0**

SANDA, Joachim (D) 33 0
H: 6 1 W: 12 00 b.Antony 29-11-06
Internationals: France U16, U17, U18.
2022–23 Valenciennes 0 0
2023–24 Valenciennes 20 0
2024–25 Valenciennes 11 0 **31 0**
2024–25 Southampton 2 0 **2 0**

SMALLBONE, William (M) 120 10
H: 5 8 W: 9 08 b.Basingstoke 21-2-00
Internationals: Republic of Ireland U18, U19, U21, Full caps.
2016–17 Southampton 0 0
2017–18 Southampton 0 0
2018–19 Southampton 0 0
2019–20 Southampton 9 0
2020–21 Southampton 3 0
2021–22 Southampton 4 0
2022–23 Southampton 0 0
2022–23 *Stoke C* 43 3 **43 3**
2023–24 Southampton 43 6
2024–25 Southampton 18 1 **77 7**

STEPHENS, Jack (D) 248 6
H: 6 1 W: 11 11 b.Torpoint 27-1-94
Internationals: England U18, U19, U20, U21.
2010–11 Plymouth Arg 5 0 **5 0**
2010–11 Southampton 0 0
2011–12 Southampton 0 0
2012–13 Southampton 0 0
2013–14 Southampton 0 0
2013–14 *Swindon T* 10 0
2014–15 Southampton 0 0
2014–15 *Swindon T* 37 1 **47 1**
2015–16 Southampton 0 0
2015–16 *Middlesbrough* 1 0 **1 0**
2015–16 *Coventry C* 16 0 **16 0**
2016–17 Southampton 17 0
2017–18 Southampton 22 2
2018–19 Southampton 24 1
2019–20 Southampton 28 1
2020–21 Southampton 18 0
2021–22 Southampton 11 0
2022–23 Southampton 2 0
2022–23 *Bournemouth* 15 0 **15 0**
2023–24 Southampton 23 0
2024–25 Southampton 19 1 **164 5**

STEWART, Ross C (F) 183 69
H: 6 2 W: 13 05 b.Irvine 1-9-96
Internationals: Scotland Full caps.
2016–17 Albion R 25 12 **25 12**
2017–18 St Mirren 9 0
2017–18 *Alloa Ath* 19 7 **19 7**
2018–19 St Mirren 1 0 **10 0**
2018–19 Ross Co 23 6
2019–20 Ross Co 21 7
2020–21 Ross Co 0 0 **44 13**
2020–21 Sunderland 11 2
2021–22 Sunderland 46 24
2022–23 Sunderland 13 10
2023–24 Sunderland 0 0 **70 36**
2023–24 Southampton 3 0
2024–25 Southampton 12 1 **15 1**

SUGAWARA, Yukinari (D) 178 13
H: 5 10 W: 10 10 b.Toyokawa 28-6-00
Internationals: Japan U17, U20, U23, Full caps.
2018 Nagoya Grampus 13 0
2019 Nagoya Grampus 0 0 **13 0**
2019–20 *AZ Alkmaar* 16 2
2020–21 AZ Alkmaar 25 2
2021–22 AZ Alkmaar 33 1
2022–23 AZ Alkmaar 31 3
2023–24 AZ Alkmaar 30 4 **135 12**
2024–25 Southampton 30 1 **30 1**

SULEMANA, Kamaldeen (F) 131 21
H: 5 9 W: 10 08 b.Techiman 15-2-02
Internationals: Ghana Full caps.
2019–20 Nordsjaelland 13 4
2020–21 Nordsjaelland 29 10 **42 14**
2021–22 Rennes 20 4 **20 4**
2022–23 Southampton 18 2
2023–24 Southampton 25 0
2024–25 Southampton 26 1 **69 3**

TAKAOKA, Rento (F) 0 0
H: 5 5 W: 9 11 b.Miyazaki 12-3-07
Internationals: Japan U17, U18.
2024–25 Southampton 0 0

TAYLOR, Charlie (D) 341 4
H: 6 1 W: 11 00 b.York 18-9-93
Internationals: England U19.
2011–12 Leeds U 2 0
2011–12 *Bradford C* 3 0 **3 0**
2012–13 Leeds U 0 0
2012–13 *York C* 4 0 **4 0**
2012–13 *Inverness CT* 7 0 **7 0**
2013–14 Leeds U 0 0
2013–14 *Fleetwood T* 32 0 **32 0**
2014–15 Leeds U 23 2
2015–16 Leeds U 39 1
2016–17 Leeds U 29 0 **93 3**
2017–18 Burnley 11 0
2018–19 Burnley 38 0
2019–20 Burnley 24 0
2020–21 Burnley 29 0
2021–22 Burnley 31 0
2022–23 Burnley 33 0
2023–24 Burnley 28 1 **194 1**
2024–25 Southampton 8 0 **8 0**

WALKER-PETERS, Kyle (F) 191 4
H: 5 8 W: 9 13 b.Edmonton 13-4-97
Internationals: England U18, U19, U20, U21, Full caps.
2015–16 Tottenham H 0 0
2016–17 Tottenham H 0 0
2017–18 Tottenham H 3 0
2018–19 Tottenham H 6 0
2019–20 Tottenham H 3 0 **12 0**
2019–20 *Southampton* 10 0
2020–21 Southampton 30 0
2021–22 Southampton 32 1
2022–23 Southampton 31 1
2023–24 Southampton 43 2
2024–25 Southampton 33 0 **179 4**

WELINGTON, Santos (D) 97 0
H: 5 9 W: 11 07 b.Sao Paulo 19-2-01
Internationals: Brazil U23.
2020 Sao Paulo 1 0
2021 Sao Paulo 16 0
2022 Sao Paulo 32 0
2023 Sao Paulo 16 0
2024 Sao Paulo 22 0 **87 0**
2024–25 Southampton 10 0 **10 0**

WOOD-GORDON, Nathan (D) 95 1
H: 6 2 W: 11 05 b.Middlesbrough 31-5-02
Internationals: England U16, U17, U18, U20, U21.
From Stockton T.
2018–19 Middlesbrough 0 0
2019–20 Middlesbrough 1 0
2020–21 Middlesbrough 4 0
2020–21 *Crewe Alex* 12 0 **12 0**
2021–22 Middlesbrough 0 0 **5 0**
2021–22 *Hibernian* 1 0 **1 0**
2022–23 Swansea C 40 0
2023–24 Swansea C 26 1 **66 1**
2024–25 Southampton 11 0 **11 0**

Players retained or with offer of contract
Boot, Nathanael Joshua Asiimwe; Davis, Sonnie Kelvin; Dipepa, Baylee Jack; Dobson-Ventura, Tommy Eric; Ehibhatiomhan, Princewill Omonefe; Fry, Max Joseph; Jeffries, Josh David; Matsuki, Kuryu; Merry, William George; Mohamed, Adli Hatim Othman Husain; Myers, Brook Cameron Reeco; Ofuyaekpone-Shombe, Khiani Hrukti Toju; Oyekunle Adetokunbo, Adewale; Reeves, Benjamin Neil; Santos da Silva, Juan; Sesay, Jonathan Moses Momoh; Tabares, Samuel Ethan; Traore, Daouda; Udoh, Victor; Williams, Barnaby Joe; Wright, Oliver.

Scholars
Adjei-Afriyie, Hansel; Daley, Aston Robert; Frederick, Cameron Joseph; Gathercole, Harry John; Goremusandu, Tinotenda Blessing; McMullan, Korban James; Moody, Dylan Lewis; Newman, Oliver Jacob; Okunola, Abdulhalim Olarewaju; Rohart-Brown, Thierry David; Sillah Dibaga, Sufianu; Umeh, Leo Chidiebere.

STEVENAGE (77)

APPERE, Louis (F) 176 23

H: 6 1 W: 12 13 b.Perth 26-3-99

2017–18	Dundee U	0	0		
2018–19	Dundee U	0	0		
2019–20	Dundee U	26	4		
2020–21	Dundee U	22	1		
2021–22	Dundee U	13	1	**61**	**6**
2021–22	Northampton T	18	3		
2022–23	Northampton T	43	8		
2023–24	Northampton T	37	6	**98**	**17**
2024–25	Stevenage	17	0	**17**	**0**

ASHBY-HAMMOND, Taye (G) 66 0

H: 6 3 W: 13 10 b.Richmond 21-3-99

Internationals: England U16, U17.

2021–22	Fulham	0	0		
2022–23	Fulham	0	0		
2022–23	*Stevenage*	26	0		
2023–24	Stevenage	31	0		
2024–25	Stevenage	9	0	**66**	**0**

BATES, Ellis (D) 1 0

b. 8-6-07

2024–25	Stevenage	1	0	**1**	**0**

BROWN, Lenny (F) 0 0

b. 3-7-08

2024–25	Stevenage	0	0

BUTLER, Dan (D) 372 11

H: 5 9 W: 11 11 b.Cowes 26-8-94

2012–13	Portsmouth	17	0		
2013–14	Portsmouth	1	0		
2014–15	Portsmouth	30	0		
2015–16	Portsmouth	0	0	**48**	**0**
2016–17	Newport Co	40	3		
2017–18	Newport Co	44	1		
2018–19	Newport Co	45	3	**129**	**7**
2019–20	Peterborough U	29	2		
2020–21	Peterborough U	42	1		
2021–22	Peterborough U	22	0		
2022–23	Peterborough U	27	0	**120**	**3**
2023–24	Stevenage	43	1		
2024–25	Stevenage	32	0	**75**	**1**

COCHRANE, Owen (D) 1 0

H: 5 11 W: 12 06 b.Huntingdon 3-9-04

2021–22	Stevenage	1	0		
2022–23	Stevenage	0	0		
2023–24	Stevenage	0	0		
2024–25	Stevenage	0	0	**1**	**0**

COOPER, Murphy (G) 62 0

b.Reading 27-12-01

2021–22	QPR	2	0		
2022–23	QPR	0	0		
2023–24	QPR	0	0	**2**	**0**
2023–24	*Swindon T*	23	0	**23**	**0**
2024–25	Stevenage	37	0	**37**	**0**

DOHERTY, Ryan (M) 0 0

b. 26-8-08

2024–25	Stevenage	0	0

EDWARDS, Kyle (M) 130 7

H: 5 8 W: 10 01 b.Dudley 17-2-98

Internationals: England U16, U17, U20.

2015–16	WBA	0	0		
2016–17	WBA	0	0		
2017–18	WBA	0	0		
2017–18	*Exeter C*	23	0	**23**	**0**
2018–19	WBA	6	1		
2019–20	WBA	26	2		
2020–21	WBA	5	0	**37**	**3**
2021–22	Ipswich T	18	0		
2022–23	Ipswich T	32	3		
2023–24	Ipswich T	0	0	**50**	**3**
2023–24	Oxford U	5	1		
2024–25	Oxford U	7	0	**12**	**1**
2024–25	Stevenage	8	0	**8**	**0**

ENGLAND, Riley (M) 0 0

2024–25	Stevenage	0	0

EVANS, Makise (F) 2 0

H: 6 0 W: 11 07 b. 20-8-06

2022–23	Stevenage	2	0		
2023–24	Stevenage	0	0		
2024–25	Stevenage	0	0	**2**	**0**

FORSTER-CASKEY, Jake (M) 271 24

H: 5 10 W: 10 01 b.Southend 25-4-94

Internationals: England U16, U17, U18, U20, U21.

2009–10	Brighton & HA	1	0		
2010–11	Brighton & HA	0	0		
2011–12	Brighton & HA	4	1		
2012–13	Brighton & HA	3	0		
2012–13	*Oxford U*	16	3	**16**	**3**
2013–14	Brighton & HA	28	3		
2014–15	Brighton & HA	29	1		
2015–16	Brighton & HA	2	0	**67**	**5**
2015–16	*Milton Keynes D*	20	1	**20**	**1**
2016–17	Charlton Ath	15	2		
2016–17	*Rotherham U*	6	0	**6**	**0**
2017–18	Charlton Ath	41	5		
2018–19	Charlton Ath	1	0		
2019–20	Charlton Ath	11	0		
2020–21	Charlton Ath	34	6		
2021–22	Charlton Ath	4	0		
2022–23	Charlton Ath	3	0	**109**	**13**
2022–23	Stevenage	20	0		
2023–24	Stevenage	30	2		
2024–25	Stevenage	3	0	**53**	**2**

FREEMAN, Nick (M) 233 10

H: 5 11 W: 12 04 b.Stevenage 7-11-95

From Histon, Hemel Hempstead T, Biggleswade T.

2016–17	Wycombe W	14	0		
2017–18	Wycombe W	27	3		
2018–19	Wycombe W	27	0		
2019–20	Wycombe W	26	2		
2020–21	Wycombe W	7	0		
2020–21	*Leyton Orient*	15	0	**15**	**0**
2021–22	Wycombe W	3	0		
2022–23	Wycombe W	43	2	**147**	**7**
2023–24	Stevenage	42	3		
2024–25	Stevenage	29	0	**71**	**3**

FREESTONE, Lewis (D) 139 1

H: 5 9 W: 10 01 b.King's Lynn 26-10-99

2016–17	Peterborough U	4	0		
2017–18	Peterborough U	4	0		
2018–19	Peterborough U	0	0	**8**	**0**
2019–20	Brighton & HA	0	0		
2020–21	Cheltenham T	14	0		
2021–22	Cheltenham T	28	1		
2022–23	Cheltenham T	29	0		
2023–24	Cheltenham T	34	0	**105**	**1**
2024–25	Stevenage	26	0	**26**	**0**

GOODE, Charlie (D) 169 8

H: 6 5 W: 11 11 b.Watford 3-8-95

Internationals: England C.

From Hadley, AFC Hayes, Hendon.

2015–16	Scunthorpe U	10	1		
2016–17	Scunthorpe U	20	0		
2017–18	Scunthorpe U	13	1		
2018–19	Scunthorpe U	21	3	**64**	**5**
2018–19	*Northampton T*	17	0		
2019–20	Northampton T	36	3	**53**	**3**
2020–21	Brentford	8	0		
2021–22	Brentford	6	0		
2021–22	*Sheffield U*	2	0	**2**	**0**
2022–23	Brentford	0	0		
2022–23	*Blackpool*	2	0	**2**	**0**
2023–24	Brentford	0	0	**14**	**0**
2023–24	*Wigan Ath*	13	0	**13**	**0**
2024–25	Stevenage	21	0	**21**	**0**

HENRY, Louie (D) 0 0

H: 5 9 b. 11-2-07

2024–25	Stevenage	0	0

HICKS, David (F) 0 0

2023–24	Stevenage	0	0
2024–25	Stevenage	0	0

KEMP, Daniel (M) 169 42

H: 5 3 W: 9 13 b.Sidcup 11-1-99

Internationals: England U19, U20.

From Chelsea.

2016–17	West Ham U	0	0		
2017–18	West Ham U	0	0		
2018–19	West Ham U	0	0		
2019–20	West Ham U	0	0		
2019–20	*Stevenage*	6	1		
2020–21	West Ham U	0	0		
2020–21	*Blackpool*	8	0	**8**	**0**
2020–21	Leyton Orient	24	5		
2021–22	Leyton Orient	19	0	**43**	**5**
2021–22	Milton Keynes D	5	0		
2022–23	Milton Keynes D	5	0		
2022–23	*Hartlepool U*	16	9	**16**	**9**
2023–24	Milton Keynes D	21	3	**31**	**3**
2023–24	*Swindon T*	25	14	**25**	**14**
2024–25	Stevenage	40	10	**46**	**11**

LIST, Elliott (M) 256 35

H: 5 10 W: 11 05 b.Camberwell 12-5-97

From Crystal Palace.

2015–16	Gillingham	6	0		
2016–17	Gillingham	15	0		
2017–18	Gillingham	23	2		
2018–19	Gillingham	37	5		
2019–20	Gillingham	4	0	**85**	**7**
2019–20	Stevenage	21	2		
2020–21	Stevenage	44	9		
2021–22	Stevenage	37	9		
2022–23	Stevenage	1	0		
2023–24	Stevenage	29	4		
2024–25	Stevenage	39	4	**171**	**28**

MITCHELL, Rylee (G) 0 0

H: 6 5 W: 13 01 b. 14-12-05

2022–23	Stevenage	0	0
2023–24	Stevenage	0	0
2024–25	Stevenage	0	0

PHILLIPS, Daniel (M) 124 0

H: 5 9 W: 11 00 b.Enfield 18-1-01

Internationals: Trindad & Tobago Full caps.

2019–20	Watford	0	0		
2020–21	Watford	2	0		
2021–22	Watford	0	0	**2**	**0**
2021–22	*Gillingham*	24	0	**24**	**0**
2022–23	St Johnstone	23	0		
2023–24	St Johnstone	33	0	**56**	**0**
2024–25	Stevenage	42	0	**42**	**0**

PIERGIANNI, Carl (D) 236 22

H: 6 1 W: 13 05 b.Peterborough 3-5-92

2010–11	Peterborough U	1	0	**1**	**0**

From Stockport Co, Corby T, Boston U, South Melbourne.

2019–20	Salford C	13	0	**13**	**0**
2019–20	*Oldham Ath*	11	0		
2020–21	Oldham Ath	38	5		
2021–22	Oldham Ath	40	3	**89**	**8**
2022–23	Stevenage	46	7		
2023–24	Stevenage	43	4		
2024–25	Stevenage	44	3	**133**	**14**

PRESSLEY, Aaron (F) 91 14

H: 6 2 W: 11 11 b.Edinburgh 7-11-01

Internationals: Scotland U17.

From Hearts.

2019–20	Aston Villa	0	0		
2020–21	Aston Villa	0	0		
2020–21	Brentford	2	0		
2021–22	Brentford	0	0		
2021–22	*AFC Wimbledon*	21	2	**21**	**2**
2022–23	Brentford	0	0	**2**	**0**
2022–23	*Accrington S*	22	6	**22**	**6**
2023–24	Stevenage	21	2		
2024–25	Stevenage	4	0	**25**	**2**
2024–25	*Barrow*	21	4	**21**	**4**

REID, Jamie (F) 229 52

H: 5 11 W: 11 09 b.Torquay 15-7-94

Internationals: Northern Ireland U21, Full caps.

2012–13	Exeter C	4	2		
2013–14	Exeter C	6	0		
2014–15	Exeter C	0	0		
2015–16	Exeter C	13	1		
2016–17	Exeter C	0	0	**23**	**3**

From Torquay U.

2020–21	Mansfield T	39	6	**39**	**6**
2021–22	Stevenage	38	7		
2022–23	Stevenage	45	10		
2023–24	Stevenage	42	18		
2024–25	Stevenage	42	8	**167**	**43**

ROBERTS, Jordan (M) 265 33

H: 5 11 W: 12 13 b.Watford 5-1-94

Internationals: England C.

2011–12	Aldershot T	4	0		
2012–13	Aldershot T	5	0	**9**	**0**

From Havant & Waterlooville, Bishops Stortford, Aldershot T.

2015–16	Inverness CT	9	2	**9**	**2**
2016–17	Crawley T	23	3		
2017–18	Crawley T	35	6	**58**	**9**
2018–19	Ipswich T	12	0		
2018–19	*Lincoln C*	5	0	**5**	**0**
2019–20	Ipswich T	1	0	**13**	**0**
2019–20	*Gillingham*	10	2	**10**	**2**
2020–21	Hearts	6	0		
2020–21	*Motherwell*	7	1		
2021–22	Hearts	0	0	**6**	**0**
2021–22	*Motherwell*	11	0		
2021–22	Motherwell	7	0	**25**	**1**
2022–23	Stevenage	42	10		
2023–24	Stevenage	46	5		
2024–25	Stevenage	42	4	**130**	**19**

SIMPSON, Tyreece (F) 117 14

H: 6 1 W: 11 07 b.Ipswich 7-2-02

Internationals: Saint Kitts and Nevis Full caps.

2019–20	Ipswich T	3	0		
2020–21	Ipswich T	1	0		
2021–22	Ipswich T	0	0	**4**	**0**
2021–22	*Swindon T*	25	9	**25**	**9**
2022–23	Huddersfield T	9	0		
2023–24	Huddersfield T	0	0	**9**	**0**
2023–24	*Northampton T*	40	3	**40**	**3**
2024–25	Stevenage	19	0	**19**	**0**
2024–25	*Colchester U*	20	2	**20**	**2**

SMITH, Harrison (F) 1 0

b. 20-1-05

2022–23	Stevenage	0	0		
2023–24	Stevenage	1	0		
2024–25	Stevenage	0	0	**1**	**0**

Transferred to St Albans C, January 2025.

SMITH, Kane (D) 47 1

H: 5 9 W: 11 07 b.Luton 7-2-96

From Biggleswade U, Hitchin T, Boreham Wood.

2022–23 Stevenage 22 1
2023–24 Stevenage 11 0
2024–25 Stevenage 14 0 **47 1**

SWEENEY, Dan (M) 170 7
H: 6 3 W: 12 04 b.Kingston upon Thames 25-4-94
Internationals: England C.
From AFC Wimbledon, Kingstonian, Dulwich Hamlet, Maidstone U.
2016–17 Barnet 4 0
2017–18 Barnet 21 0 **25 0**
From Barnet.
2020–21 Forest Green R 21 0
2021–22 Forest Green R 36 1 **57 1**
2022–23 Stevenage 44 4
2023–24 Stevenage 23 1
2024–25 Stevenage 21 1 **88 6**

THOMPSON, Ben (M) 282 21
H: 5 11 W: 12 04 b.Sidcup 3-10-95
2014–15 Millwall 0 0
2015–16 Millwall 28 1
2016–17 Millwall 38 0
2017–18 Millwall 3 0
2018–19 Millwall 0 0
2018–19 *Portsmouth* 23 2 **23 2**
2018–19 Millwall 13 4
2019–20 Millwall 28 1
2020–21 Millwall 30 3
2021–22 Millwall 2 0 **142 9**
2021–22 Gillingham 17 1 **17 1**
2022–23 Peterborough U 26 1 **26 1**
2023–24 Stevenage 31 2
2024–25 Stevenage 1 0 **32 2**
2024–25 *Bromley* 42 6 **42 6**

THOMPSON, Louis (M) 268 12
H: 5 11 W: 11 11 b.Bristol 19-12-94
Internationals: Wales U19, U21.
2012–13 Swindon T 4 0
2013–14 Swindon T 28 2
2014–15 Norwich C 0 0
2014–15 *Swindon T* 32 2
2015–16 Norwich C 0 0
2015–16 *Swindon T* 28 2 **92 6**
2016–17 Norwich C 3 0
2017–18 Norwich C 0 0
2018–19 Norwich C 6 0
2019–20 Norwich C 0 0
2019–20 *Shrewsbury T* 10 0 **10 0**
2019–20 *Milton Keynes D* 9 0
2020–21 Norwich C 0 0 **9 0**
2020–21 *Milton Keynes D* 17 0 **26 0**
2021–22 Portsmouth 32 1
2022–23 Portsmouth 17 1 **49 2**
2023–24 Stevenage 42 2
2024–25 Stevenage 40 2 **82 4**

THORNETT, Alfie (D) 0 0
2024–25 Stevenage 0 0

WHITE, Harvey (M) 89 3
H: 5 6 W: 9 06 b.Maidstone 19-9-01
Internationals: England U18, U20.
2019–20 Tottenham H 0 0
2020–21 Tottenham H 0 0
2020–21 *Portsmouth* 21 1 **21 1**
2021–22 Tottenham H 0 0
2022–23 Tottenham H 1 0 **1 0**
2022–23 *Derby Co* 15 0 **15 0**
2023–24 Stevenage 11 0
2024–25 Stevenage 41 2 **52 2**

WILDIN, Luther (D) 235 7
H: 5 10 W: 11 11 b.Leicester 3-12-97
Internationals: Antigua and Barbuda U20, Full caps.
2015–16 Notts Co 0 0
2016–17 Notts Co 0 0
From Nuneaton T.
2018–19 Stevenage 39 1
2019–20 Stevenage 21 1
2020–21 Stevenage 39 2
2021–22 Stevenage 40 0
2022–23 Stevenage 36 1
2023–24 Stevenage 31 2
2024–25 Stevenage 29 0 **235 7**

WOODFORD, Max (G) 0 0
b. 5-5-08
2023–24 Stevenage 0 0
2024–25 Stevenage 0 0

YOUNG, Jake (F) 133 31
H: 6 1 W: 12 02 b.Huddersfield 22-7-01
2020–21 Forest Green R 29 6
2021–22 Forest Green R 22 3 **51 9**
2021–22 Bradford C 0 0
2022–23 Bradford C 7 2
2022–23 *Barrow* 17 0 **17 0**
2023–24 Bradford C 4 0
2023–24 *Swindon T* 25 16 **25 16**
2024–25 Bradford C 0 0 **11 2**
2024–25 Stevenage 29 4 **29 4**

Scholars
Bates, Ellis Alfie; Brown, Lenny Jude; Buckmaster, Michael Edward; Doherty, Ryan Sean; England, Riley Mitchell; Evans, Makise Flavius; Henry, Louie; Howell, Zack George David; Impey, Frankie Albert; Mutanga, Tatenda Milton; Norris, Frank Robert; O'Keefe, Albie Jay; Reeve, Oliver David Thomas; Salik, Fahmeed; Thornett, Alfie Michael; Woodford, Max.

STOCKPORT CO (78)

ADDAI, Corey (G) 104 0
H: 6 4 W: 11 05 b.Hackney 10-10-97
2015–16 Coventry C 0 0
2016–17 Coventry C 0 0
2017–18 Coventry C 0 0
2018–19 Coventry C 0 0
2019–20 Coventry C 0 0
2020–21 Barnsley 0 0
2021–22 Esbjerg 4 0 **4 0**
2022–23 Crawley T 32 0
2023–24 Crawley T 39 0 **71 0**
2024–25 Stockport Co 29 0 **29 0**

ANDRESSON, Benony (F) 62 34
H: 5 11 b. 3-8-05
Internationals: Iceland U17, U19, U21.
2023 KR 25 9
2024 KR 26 21 **51 30**
2024–25 Stockport Co 11 4 **11 4**

BAILEY, Odin (M) 160 13
H: 5 9 W: 11 00 b.Birmingham 8-12-99
Internationals: England U16.
2017–18 Birmingham C 0 0
2018–19 Birmingham C 0 0
2019–20 Birmingham C 6 1
2019–20 *Forest Green R* 5 1
2020–21 Birmingham C 0 0
2020–21 *Forest Green R* 34 4 **39 5**
2021–22 Birmingham C 0 0
2021–22 *Livingston* 31 3 **31 3**
2022–23 Birmingham C 0 0 **6 1**
2022–23 Salford C 16 0 **16 0**
2023–24 Stockport Co 38 2
2024–25 Stockport Co 30 2 **68 4**

BATE, Lewis (M) 83 3
H: 5 7 W: 9 13 b.Sidcup 29-10-02
Internationals: England U17, U18, U20.
2019–20 Chelsea 0 0
2020–21 Chelsea 0 0
2021–22 Leeds U 3 0
2022–23 Leeds U 0 0
2022–23 *Oxford U* 28 1 **28 1**
2023–24 Leeds U 0 0 **3 0**
2023–24 *Milton Keynes D* 20 0 **20 0**
2024–25 Stockport Co 32 2 **32 2**

CAMPS, Callum (M) 364 46
H: 5 11 W: 11 11 b.Stockport 30-11-95
Internationals: Northern Ireland U18, U21.
2012–13 Rochdale 2 0
2013–14 Rochdale 0 0
2014–15 Rochdale 12 1
2015–16 Rochdale 32 5
2016–17 Rochdale 44 8
2017–18 Rochdale 42 2
2018–19 Rochdale 41 3
2019–20 Rochdale 28 6 **201 25**
2020–21 Fleetwood T 42 9
2021–22 Fleetwood T 31 3 **73 12**
2022–23 Stockport Co 34 4
2023–24 Stockport Co 29 4
2024–25 Stockport Co 27 1 **90 9**

CINA, Bruno (F) 0 0
2024–25 Stockport Co 0 0

COLLAR, Will (M) 122 23
H: 5 10 W: 12 00 b.Horsham 14-7-97
2018–19 Brighton & HA 0 0
2019–20 Hamilton A 16 1
2020–21 Hamilton A 6 0 **22 1**
From Stockport Co.
2022–23 Stockport Co 40 10
2023–24 Stockport Co 20 4
2024–25 Stockport Co 40 8 **100 22**

CONNOLLY, Callum (D) 283 17
H: 6 1 W: 11 00 b.Liverpool 23-9-97
Internationals: England U17, U18, U19, U20, U21.
2015–16 Everton 1 0
2015–16 *Barnsley* 3 0 **3 0**
2016–17 Everton 0 0
2016–17 *Wigan Ath* 17 2
2017–18 Everton 0 0
2017–18 *Ipswich T* 34 4 **34 4**
2018–19 Everton 0 0
2018–19 *Wigan Ath* 17 1 **34 3**
2018–19 *Bolton W* 16 2 **16 2**
2019–20 Everton 0 0
2019–20 *Lincoln C* 11 0 **11 0**
2019–20 *Fleetwood T* 13 2
2020–21 Everton 0 0 **1 0**
2020–21 *Fleetwood T* 40 2 **53 4**
2021–22 Blackpool 31 2
2022–23 Blackpool 41 1
2023–24 Blackpool 21 0 **93 3**
2024–25 Stockport Co 38 1 **38 1**

DIAMOND, Jack (F) 147 25
H: 5 9 W: 9 08 b.Gateshead 12-1-00
2018–19 Sunderland 0 0
2019–20 Sunderland 0 0
2020–21 Sunderland 24 1
2021–22 Sunderland 3 0
2021–22 *Harrogate T* 39 13 **39 13**
2022–23 Sunderland 1 0
2022–23 *Lincoln C* 31 6 **31 6**
2023–24 Sunderland 0 0 **28 1**
2023–24 *Carlisle U* 16 0 **16 0**
2024–25 Stockport Co 33 5 **33 5**

FARRAR, Ellis (D) 0 0
H: 6 0 b. 9-9-03
From Guiseley.
2023–24 Stockport Co 0 0
2024–25 Stockport Co 0 0

FEVRIER, Jayden (D) 81 7
H: 5 8 W: 11 03 b.Waltham Forest 14-4-03
From West Ham U.
2022–23 Colchester U 12 0
2023–24 Colchester U 44 4 **56 4**
2024–25 Stockport Co 25 3 **25 3**

FIORINI, Lewis (M) 104 12
H: 5 10 W: 11 07 b.Manchester 17-5-02
Internationals: Scotland U16, U17, U19, U21.
2020–21 Manchester C 0 0
2020–21 *NAC Breda* 32 5 **32 5**
2021–22 Manchester C 0 0
2021–22 *Lincoln C* 39 6 **39 6**
2022–23 Manchester C 0 0
2022–23 *Blackpool* 13 1 **13 1**
2023–24 Manchester C 0 0
2023–24 *Charlton Ath* 5 0 **5 0**
2024–25 Stockport Co 11 0 **11 0**
2024–25 *Dundee U* 4 0 **4 0**

FLIGG, Kingston (M) 0 0
H: 5 10 b.Manchester 8-10-05
2023–24 Stockport Co 0 0
2024–25 Stockport Co 0 0

GARDNER, Che (M) 1 0
H: 5 9 W: 10 10
2024–25 Stockport Co 1 0 **1 0**

GARDNER, Saul (M) 0 0
b. 17-3-08
2024–25 Stockport Co 0 0

HILLARY, Joe (D) 0 0
2023–24 Stockport Co 0 0
2024–25 Stockport Co 0 0

HINCHLIFFE, Ben (G) 103 0
H: 5 10 W: 11 07 b.Preston 9-10-88
2006–07 Preston NE 0 0
2006–07 *Tranmere R* 2 0 **2 0**
2007–08 Derby Co 0 0
From Bamber Bridge, Northwich Vic, AFC Fylde, Stockport Co.
2022–23 Stockport Co 36 0
2023–24 Stockport Co 46 0
2024–25 Stockport Co 19 0 **101 0**

HORSFALL, Fraser (D) 217 18
H: 6 3 W: 12 13 b.Huddersfield 12-11-96
Internationals: England C.
2015–16 Huddersfield T 0 0
2016–17 Huddersfield T 0 0
2017–18 Huddersfield T 0 0
From Kidderminster H.
2019–20 Macclesfield T 26 0 **26 0**
2020–21 Northampton T 40 3
2021–22 Northampton T 45 9 **85 12**
2022–23 Stockport Co 32 2
2023–24 Stockport Co 45 2
2024–25 Stockport Co 29 2 **106 6**

HUGHES, Sam (D) 141 7
H: 5 10 W: 11 00 b.West Kirby 15-4-97
From Chester.
2017–18 Leicester C 0 0
2018–19 Leicester C 0 0
2019–20 Leicester C 0 0
2019–20 *Salford C* 8 0 **8 0**
2020–21 Leicester C 0 0
2020–21 *Burton Alb* 14 2
2021–22 Leicester C 0 0
2021–22 Burton Alb 21 1
2022–23 Burton Alb 42 3
2023–24 Burton Alb 29 0 **106 6**
2024–25 Stockport Co 8 0 **8 0**
2024–25 *Peterborough U* 19 1 **19 1**

JOHNSON, Cody (M) 4 0
H: 5 9 W: 11 07 b.Oldham 3-10-04
2022–23 Stockport Co 0 0
2023–24 Stockport Co 4 0
2024–25 Stockport Co 0 0 **4 0**

JOHNSON, Harry (M) 0 0
H: 5 9 W: 11 07 b. 16-4-07
2023–24 Stockport Co 0 0
2024–25 Stockport Co 0 0

KENNY, Jack (M)   0   0
2022–23 Stockport Co   0   0
2023–24 Stockport Co   0   0
2024–25 Stockport Co   0   0

KNOYLE, Kyle (D)   282   7
H: 5 10   W: 9 13   b.Newham 24-9-96
Internationals: England U18.
2015–16 West Ham U   0   0
2015–16 *Dundee U*   9   0   9   0
2016–17 West Ham U   0   0
2016–17 *Wigan Ath*   1   0   1   0
2017–18 Swindon T   18   0
2018–19 Swindon T   42   0   60   0
2019–20 Cambridge U   26   1
2020–21 Cambridge U   46   2
2021–22 Cambridge U   0   0   72   3
2021–22 Doncaster R   45   1
2022–23 Doncaster R   25   1   70   2
2022–23 Stockport Co   23   2
2023–24 Stockport Co   24   0
2024–25 Stockport Co   23   0   70   2

LAWLESS WILLIAMS, John (D)   0   0
b. 2-10-07
2024–25 Stockport Co   0   0

LEWIS, Jake (M)   0   0
2024–25 Stockport Co   0   0

MAPENGU, Nathaniel (D)   0   0
b. 9-9-07
2024–25 Stockport Co   0   0

MEE, Ashton (M)   2   0
b. 2-5-06
2022–23 Stockport Co   1   0
2023–24 Stockport Co   1   0
2024–25 Stockport Co   0   0   2   0

METCALFE, Max (G)   0   0
H: 6 6   W: 13 08   b. 28-1-03
Internationals: Scotland U16, U19.
2024–25 Stockport Co   0   0

MINGI, Jade (M)   56   1
H: 5 8   W: 10 08   b.Hackney 22-10-00
From West Ham U.
2020–21 Charlton Ath   1   0
2021–22 Portsmouth   3   0
2022–23 Portsmouth   17   0   20   0
2023–24 Colchester U   25   1   25   1
2024–25 Stockport Co   11   0   11   0

MOXON, Owen (D)   237   22
H: 6 1   b.Carlisle 17-1-98
2015–16 Queen of the South   1   0
2016–17 Queen of the South   5   0   6   0
2017–18 Annan Ath   32   1
2018–19 Annan Ath   32   4
2019–20 Annan Ath   18   1
2020–21 Annan Ath   34   6
2022–23 Annan Ath   45   6   116   12
2023–24 Carlisle U   26   3   71   9
2023–24 Portsmouth   15   1
2024–25 Portsmouth   12   0   27   1
2024–25 Stockport Co   17   0   17   0

NORWOOD, Oliver (M)   541   31
H: 5 11   W: 12 00   b.Burnley 12-4-91
Internationals: England U16, U17. Northern
Ireland U19, U21, B, Full caps.
2009–10 Manchester U   0   0
2010–11 Manchester U   0   0
2010–11 *Carlisle U*   6   0   6   0
2011–12 Manchester U   0   0
2011–12 *Scunthorpe U*   15   1   15   1
2011–12 *Coventry C*   18   2   18   2
2012–13 Huddersfield T   39   3
2013–14 Huddersfield T   40   5
2014–15 Huddersfield T   1   0   80   8
2014–15 Reading   38   1
2015–16 Reading   43   3   81   4
2016–17 Brighton & HA   33   0
2017–18 Brighton & HA   0   0   33   0
2017–18 *Fulham*   36   5   36   5
2018–19 Sheffield U   43   3
2019–20 Sheffield U   38   1
2020–21 Sheffield U   32   0
2021–22 Sheffield U   44   1
2022–23 Sheffield U   46   2
2023–24 Sheffield U   27   1   230   8
2024–25 Stockport Co   42   3   42   3

OKEKE, Jid (D)   0   0
b.Ahaus 11-11-04
2023–24 Stockport Co   0   0
2024–25 Stockport Co   0   0

OLAOFE, Isaac (F)   134   39
H: 5 10   W: 12 13   b.Lewisham 21-11-99
2019–20 Millwall   0   0
2020–21 Millwall   0   0
2020–21 *St Johnstone*   2   0   2   0
2021–22 Millwall   0   0
2021–22 *Sutton U*   27   8   27   8
2022–23 Millwall   0   0   2   0
2022–23 Millwall   18   2

2023–24 Stockport Co   43   20
2024–25 Stockport Co   42   9   103   31

POWELL, Nick (F)   337   81
H: 6 0   W: 10 06   b.Crewe 23-3-94
Internationals: England U16, U17, U18, U19,
U21.
2010–11 Crewe Alex   17   0
2011–12 Crewe Alex   38   14   55   14
2012–13 Manchester U   2   1
2013–14 Manchester U   0   0
2013–14 *Wigan Ath*   31   7
2014–15 Manchester U   0   0
2014–15 *Leicester C*   3   0   3   0
2015–16 Manchester U   1   0   3   1
2015–16 *Hull C*   3   0   3   0
2016–17 Wigan Ath   21   6
2017–18 Wigan Ath   39   15
2018–19 Wigan Ath   32   8   123   36
2019–20 Stoke C   29   5
2020–21 Stoke C   39   12
2021–22 Stoke C   18   6
2022–23 Stoke C   25   4   111   27
2023–24 Stockport Co   32   3
2024–25 Stockport Co   7   0   39   3

PYE, Ethan (D)   77   2
H: 6 0   W: 12 11   b.Manchester 7-11-02
From Rochdale.
2022–23 Stockport Co   0   0
2023–24 Stockport Co   35   1
2024–25 Stockport Co   42   1   77   2

REDSHAW, Freddie (M)   0   0
2024–25 Stockport Co   0   0

RYDEL, Ryan (D)   61   3
H: 5 11   W: 11 11   b.Oldham 9-2-01
2018–19 Fleetwood T   5   0
2019–20 Fleetwood T   0   0
2020–21 Fleetwood T   7   0   12   0
From Stockport Co.
2022–23 Stockport Co   26   2
2023–24 Stockport Co   6   1
2024–25 Stockport Co   17   0   49   3

SOUTHAM, Macauley (M)   49   2
H: 5 9   W: 10 12   b.Cardiff 2-2-96
2014–15 Cardiff C   1   0
2015–16 Cardiff C   0   0
From Barry T.
2018–19 Fleetwood T   1   0
2019–20 Fleetwood T   1   0   2   0
From Stockport Co.
2022–23 Stockport Co   9   0
2023–24 Stockport Co   21   0
2024–25 Stockport Co   17   2   47   2

TOURAY, Ibou (D)   228   6
H: 5 10   W: 10 10   b.Liverpool 24-12-94
Internationals: Gambia Full caps.
2013–14 Everton   0   0
2014–15 Everton   0   0
From Rhyl, Chester.
2019–20 Salford C   35   4
2020–21 Salford C   46   1
2021–22 Salford C   27   0
2022–23 Salford C   45   0   153   5
2023–24 Stockport Co   32   1
2024–25 Stockport Co   43   0   75   1

WATSON, Rhys (M)   0   0
b. 19-8-07
Internationals: Wales U18.
2024–25 Stockport Co   0   0

WILLIAMS, Lee (M)   0   0
H: 6 2   b. 2-4-07

WOGAN, Andrew (G)   37   0
H: 6 2   b.Ardee, Louth 1-12-05
Internationals: Republic of Ireland U19, U21.
2023   Drogheda U   18   0
2024   Drogheda U   19   0   37   0
2024–25 Stockport Co   0   0

WOOTTON, Kyle (M)   210   47
H: 6 2   W: 12 04   b.Kidderminster 11-10-96
2014–15 Scunthorpe U   12   1
2015–16 Scunthorpe U   20   3
2016–17 Scunthorpe U   2   1
2016–17 *Cheltenham T*   16   2   16   2
2017–18 Stevenage   8   1   8   1
2017–18 Scunthorpe U   1   0
2018–19 Scunthorpe U   26   6
2019–20 Scunthorpe U   5   0   66   11
From Notts Co.
2022–23 Stockport Co   42   14
2023–24 Stockport Co   32   8
2024–25 Stockport Co   46   11   120   33

Players retained or with offer of contract
Allen, Arian; Mann, Ethan Geoffrey John;
O'Shea, Cian Michael.

Scholars
Berry, Leo Joseph; Cina, Bruno; Davis,
Archie Oliver; Dialundama, Michee; Fowles,
Joshua James; Gardner, Saul Joseph;
Johnson, Harry; Kouam, Marcus; Lewis, Jake

Thomas; Mapengu, Nathaniel; Mavrantziotis-
Bove, Kane Lee; Okoligan Okoligan, Desire
Chima; Redshaw, Freddie Thomas; Watson,
Rhys Dean; Williams, Lee Oliver Grant;
Williams-Lawless, John Leon.

STOKE C (79)

ANDERSON, Freddie (D)   17   1
b. 13-10-06
2024–25 Stoke C   0   0
2025   *Cork C*   17   1   17   1

ANDRE VIDIGAL, Filipe (F)   203   35
H: 5 9   W: 10 08   b.Elvas 17-8-98
Internationals: Portugal U18, U19, U20, U21.
Angola Full caps.
2016–17 Academica   6   0   6   0
2017–18 Fortuna Sittard   29   10
2018–19 Fortuna Sittard   10   2
2018–19 *APOEL*   9   1
2019–20 Fortuna Sittard   0   0
2019–20 *APOEL*   13   1   22   2
2020–21 Fortuna Sittard   0   0   39   12
2020–21 *Estoril*   32   6   32   6
2021–22 Maritimo   33   1
2022–23 Maritimo   32   8   65   9
2023–24 Stoke C   29   6
2024–25 Stoke C   10   0   39   6

BADLEY-MORGAN, Luke (D)   13   0
H: 6 2   W: 11 03   b.London 15-4-03
Internationals: England U17. Jamaica U20.
2020–21 Chelsea   0   0
2021–22 Chelsea   0   0
2022–23 Stoke C   0   0
2023–24 Stoke C   0   0
2024–25 Stoke C   0   0
2024–25 *Airdrieonians*   13   0   13   0

BAE, Jun-Ho (M)   109   8
b.Daegu 21-8-03
Internationals: South Korea U20, U23, Full
caps.
From Pyeongtaek Jinwee.
2022   Daejeon Hana Citizen   8   1
2023   Daejeon Hana Citizen   18   2   26   3
2023–24 Stoke C   38   2
2024–25 Stoke C   45   3   83   5

BAKER, Lewis (M)   281   46
H: 6 1   W: 11 00   b.Luton 25-4-95
Internationals: England U17, U19, U20, U21.
2012–13 Chelsea   0   0
2013–14 Chelsea   0   0
2014–15 Chelsea   0   0
2014–15 *Sheffield Wed*   4   0   4   0
2014–15 *Milton Keynes D*   12   3   12   3
2015–16 Chelsea   0   0
2015–16 *Vitesse*   31   5
2016–17 Chelsea   0   0
2016–17 *Vitesse*   33   10   64   15
2017–18 Chelsea   0   0
2017–18 *Middlesbrough*   12   1   12   1
2018–19 Chelsea   0   0
2018–19 *Leeds U*   11   0   11   0
2018–19 *Reading*   19   1   19   1
2019–20 Chelsea   0   0
2019–20 *Fortuna Dusseldorf*   8   0   8   0
2020–21 Chelsea   0   0
2020–21 *Trabzonspor*   34   2   34   2
2021–22 Chelsea   0   0
2021–22 Stoke C   21   8
2022–23 Stoke C   44   7
2023–24 Stoke C   20   2
2024–25 Stoke C   19   6   104   23
2024–25 *Blackburn R*   13   1   13   1

BOCAT, Eric Junior (D)   122   3
b. 16-7-99
2017–18 Dijon   0   0
2018–19 Brest   0   0
2019–20 Lille   0   0
2020–21 Mouscron   8   0
2021–22 Mouscron   25   1   33   1
2022–23 Sint-Truiden   22   0
2023–24 Sint-Truiden   37   2   59   2
2024–25 Stoke C   30   0   30   0

BONHAM, Jack (G)   216   0
H: 6 4   W: 14 13   b.Stevenage 14-9-93
Internationals: Republic of Ireland U17.
2010–11 Watford   0   0
2011–12 Watford   0   0
2012–13 Watford   1   0   1   0
2013–14 Brentford   0   0
2014–15 Brentford   0   0
2015–16 Brentford   0   0
2016–17 Brentford   1   0
2017–18 Brentford   0   0
2017–18 *Carlisle U*   42   0   42   0
2018–19 Brentford   0   0   2   0
2018–19 *Bristol R*   40   0   40   0
2019–20 Gillingham   35   0
2020–21 Gillingham   44   0   79   0
2021–22 Stoke C   15   0

2022–23 Stoke C 23 0
2023–24 Stoke C 14 0
2024–25 Stoke C 0 0 **52 0**

BURGER, Wouter (M) 171 10
H: 6 3 W: 11 07 b.Zuid-Beijerland 16-2-01
Internationals: Netherlands U16, U17, U18, U19, U21.
2018–19 Feyenoord 1 0
2019–20 Feyenoord 6 0
2019–20 *Excelsior* 7 0 **7 0**
2020–21 Feyenoord 1 0
2020–21 *Sparta Rotterdam* 18 2 **18 2**
2021–22 Feyenoord 1 0 **9 0**
2021–22 FC Basel 26 0
2022–23 FC Basel 30 4
2023–24 FC Basel 3 0 **59 4**
2023–24 Stoke C 39 3
2024–25 Stoke C 39 1 **78 4**

CHIBUEZE, Chinonso (F) 0 0
b. 28-1-06
2024–25 Stoke C 0 0

CURLEY, Ruben (M) 0 0
b. 5-9-05
2024–25 Manchester U 0 0
2024–25 Stoke C 0 0

DIXON, Jaden (D) 2 0
b. 7-2-07
Internationals: England U17, U18.
2023–24 Stoke C 0 0
2024–25 Stoke C 2 0 **2 0**

ENNIS, Niall (F) 179 36
H: 5 11 W: 12 00 b.Wolverhampton 20-5-99
Internationals: England U17, U18, U19.
2017–18 Wolverhampton W 0 0
2017–18 *Shrewsbury T* 1 0 **1 0**
2018–19 Wolverhampton W 0 0
2019–20 Wolverhampton W 0 0
2019–20 *Doncaster R* 29 6 **29 6**
2020–21 Wolverhampton W 0 0
2020–21 *Burton Alb* 9 0 **9 0**
2020–21 Plymouth Arg 24 6
2021–22 Plymouth Arg 25 4
2022–23 Plymouth Arg 38 12 **87 22**
2023–24 Blackburn R 11 0 **11 0**
2023–24 Stoke C 14 1
2024–25 Stoke C 9 0 **23 1**
2024–25 *Blackpool* 19 7 **19 7**

ETEBO, Peter (M) 172 10
H: 5 8 W: 11 00 b.Warri, Nigeria 9-11-95
Internationals: Nigeria U23, Full caps.
From Warri Wolves.
2015–16 Feirense 4 1
2016–17 Feirense 23 2
2017–18 Feirense 18 4 **45 7**
2017–18 *Las Palmas* 14 0 **14 0**
2018–19 Stoke C 34 2
2019–20 Stoke C 11 0
2019–20 *Getafe* 10 1 **10 1**
2020–21 Stoke C 0 0
2020–21 *Galatasaray* 24 0 **24 0**
2021–22 Stoke C 0 0
2021–22 *Watford* 9 0 **9 0**
2022–23 Stoke C 0 0
2022–23 *Aris* 25 0 **25 0**
2023–24 Stoke C 0 0
2024–25 Stoke C 0 0 **45 2**

FAWUNMI, Favour (F) 0 0
b.London 26-4-06
2024–25 Stoke C 0 0

FIELDING, Frank (G) 326 0
H: 6 1 W: 12 00 b.Blackburn 4-4-88
Internationals: England U19, U21.
2006–07 Blackburn R 0 0
2007–08 Blackburn R 0 0
2007–08 *Wycombe W* 36 0 **36 0**
2008–09 Blackburn R 0 0
2008–09 *Northampton T* 12 0 **12 0**
2008–09 *Rochdale* 23 0
2009–10 Blackburn R 0 0
2009–10 *Rochdale* 18 0 **41 0**
2009–10 *Leeds U* 0 0
2010–11 Blackburn R 0 0
2010–11 *Derby Co* 16 0
2011–12 Derby Co 44 0
2012–13 Derby Co 16 0 **76 0**
2013–14 Bristol C 16 0
2014–15 Bristol C 46 0
2015–16 Bristol C 21 0
2016–17 Bristol C 27 0
2017–18 Bristol C 43 0
2018–19 Bristol C 5 0 **158 0**
2019–20 Millwall 1 0
2020–21 Millwall 0 0 **1 0**
2021–22 Stoke C 0 0
2021–22 *Salford C* 2 0 **2 0**
2022–23 Stoke C 0 0
2023–24 Stoke C 0 0
2024–25 Stoke C 0 0

GALLAGHER, Sam (F) 309 55
H: 6 4 W: 11 11 b.Crediton 15-9-95
Internationals: Scotland U19. England U19, U20.
From Plymouth Arg.
2013–14 Southampton 18 1
2014–15 Southampton 0 0
2015–16 Southampton 0 0
2015–16 *Milton Keynes D* 13 0 **13 0**
2016–17 Southampton 0 0
2016–17 *Blackburn R* 43 11
2017–18 Southampton 0 0
2017–18 *Birmingham C* 33 6 **33 6**
2018–19 Southampton 4 0 **22 1**
2019–20 Blackburn R 42 6
2020–21 Blackburn R 39 8
2021–22 Blackburn R 37 9
2022–23 Blackburn R 34 8
2023–24 Blackburn R 24 3 **219 45**
2024–25 Stoke C 22 3 **22 3**

GIANI, Laurence (D) 0 0
b. 11-3-08
Internationals: Italy U17.
2024–25 Stoke C 0 0

GIBSON, Ben (D) 364 9
H: 6 1 W: 12 04 b.Nunthorpe 15-1-93
Internationals: England U17, U18, U20, U21.
2010–11 Middlesbrough 1 0
2011–12 Middlesbrough 0 0
2011–12 *Plymouth Arg* 13 0 **13 0**
2012–13 Middlesbrough 1 0
2012–13 *Tranmere R* 28 1 **28 1**
2013–14 Middlesbrough 31 1
2014–15 Middlesbrough 36 0
2015–16 Middlesbrough 33 1
2016–17 Middlesbrough 38 1
2017–18 Middlesbrough 45 1 **185 4**
2018–19 Burnley 1 1
2019–20 Burnley 0 0
2020–21 Burnley 0 0 **1 1**
2020–21 *Norwich C* 27 0
2021–22 Norwich C 28 0
2022–23 Norwich C 23 0
2023–24 Norwich C 35 0 **113 0**
2024–25 Stoke C 24 3 **24 3**

GOOCH, Lynden (M) 271 23
H: 5 8 W: 10 12 b.Santa Cruz, California 24-12-95
Internationals: Republic of Ireland U18. USA U20, Full caps.
2015–16 Sunderland 0 0
2015–16 *Doncaster R* 10 0 **10 0**
2016–17 Sunderland 11 0
2017–18 Sunderland 24 1
2018–19 Sunderland 39 5
2019–20 Sunderland 30 10
2020–21 Sunderland 38 4
2021–22 Sunderland 38 0
2022–23 Sunderland 30 1
2023–24 Sunderland 2 0 **212 21**
2023–24 Stoke C 29 2
2024–25 Stoke C 20 0 **49 2**

GRIFFIN, Jake (D) 0 0
b. 30-12-05
Internationals: Republic of Ireland U19.
2024–25 Stoke C 0 0

GRIFFITHS, Jack (M) 0 0
b. 31-7-05
Internationals: England U17.
2024–25 Stoke C 0 0

JEFFERS, Keke (F) 0 0
H: 6 1 b. 18-2-05
2024–25 Stoke C 0 0

JOHANSSON, Viktor (G) 181 0
H: 6 1 W: 11 05 b.Stockholm 14-9-98
Internationals: Sweden U17, U19, U21, Full caps.
From Hammarby.
2017–18 Aston Villa 0 0
2018–19 Leicester C 0 0
2019–20 Leicester C 0 0
2020–21 Rotherham U 21 0
2021–22 Rotherham U 26 0
2022–23 Rotherham U 43 0
2023–24 Rotherham U 45 0 **135 0**
2024–25 Stoke C 46 0 **46 0**

JOHNSON, Daniel (M) 361 58
H: 5 9 W: 10 08 b.Kingston, Jamaica 8-10-92
Internationals: Jamaica Full caps.
2010–11 Aston Villa 0 0
2011–12 Aston Villa 0 0
2012–13 Aston Villa 0 0
2012–13 *Yeovil T* 5 0 **5 0**
2013–14 Aston Villa 0 0
2014–15 Aston Villa 0 0
2014–15 *Chesterfield* 11 0 **11 0**
2014–15 *Oldham Ath* 6 3 **6 3**
2014–15 Preston NE 20 8
2015–16 Preston NE 43 8
2016–17 Preston NE 40 4
2017–18 Preston NE 33 3
2018–19 Preston NE 35 6
2019–20 Preston NE 33 12
2020–21 Preston NE 33 4
2021–22 Preston NE 41 7
2022–23 Preston NE 34 1 **312 53**
2023–24 Stoke C 26 2
2024–25 Stoke C 1 0 **27 2**
Transferred to Fatih Karagumruk, September 2024.

JOJIC, Nikola (M) 58 10
b.Cacak 15-9-03
Internationals: Serbia U19, U21.
2020–21 Mladost Lucani 0 0
2021–22 Mladost Lucani 5 2
2022–23 Mladost Lucani 37 7
2023–24 Stoke C 1 0
2024–25 Stoke C 0 0 **1 0**
2024–25 *Mladost Lucani* 12 1 **54 10**
2024–25 *Gorica* 3 0 **3 0**

LAWAL, Bosun (M) 49 6
H: 6 3 b. 30-5-03
Internationals: Republic of Ireland U17, U19, U21.
2023–24 Celtic 0 0
2023–24 *Fleetwood T* 42 6 **42 6**
2024–25 Stoke C 7 0 **7 0**

LIPSIUC, Darius (M) 0 0
b. 16-9-05
Internationals: Republic of Ireland U18, U19, U21.
From St Patrick's Ath.
2023–24 Stoke C 0 0
2024–25 Stoke C 0 0
2024–25 *Walsall* 0 0

LOWE, Nathan (F) 46 17
H: 6 4 W: 12 08 b.Harlow 18-9-05
Internationals: England U19.
2022–23 Stoke C 1 0
2023–24 Stoke C 13 1
2024–25 Stoke C 10 1 **24 2**
2024–25 *Walsall* 22 15 **22 15**

MANHOEF, Million (M) 125 24
b. 3-1-02
Internationals: Netherlands U16, U17, U21.
2020–21 Vitesse 11 0
2021–22 Vitesse 15 2
2022–23 Vitesse 33 9
2023–24 Vitesse 18 4 **77 15**
2023–24 Stoke C 14 4
2024–25 Stoke C 34 5 **48 9**

MMAEE, Ryan (F) 162 49
b.Geraardsbergen 1-10-97
Internationals: Belgium U19, U21. Morocco Full caps.
2014–15 Standard Liege 1 0
2015–16 Standard Liege 5 0
2016–17 Standard Liege 7 1
2017–18 Standard Liege 0 0
2017–18 *Waasland-Beveren* 18 1 **18 1**
2018–19 Standard Liege 0 0 **13 1**
2018–19 *AGF* 9 0 **9 0**
2019–20 AEL Limassol 20 5
2020–21 AEL Limassol 30 14 **50 19**
2021–22 Ferencvaros 21 13
2022–23 Ferencvaros 24 12 **45 25**
2023–24 Stoke C 24 3
2024–25 Stoke C 3 0 **27 3**
2024–25 *Rapid Vienna* 0 0

MORRIS, Scott (G) 58 1
b. 24-2-01
Internationals: New Zealand U23.
2019–20 Tasman U 0 0
2020–21 Hawke's Bay U 13 0 **13 0**
2021–22 Christchurch U 24 1
2022–23 Christchurch U 21 0 **45 1**
2023–24 Stoke C 0 0
2024–25 Stoke C 0 0

PEARSON, Ben (M) 305 4
H: 5 9 W: 11 03 b.Oldham 4-1-95
Internationals: England U16, U17, U18, U19, U21, Full caps.
2013–14 Manchester U 0 0
2014–15 Manchester U 0 0
2014–15 *Barnsley* 22 1
2015–16 Manchester U 0 0
2015–16 *Barnsley* 23 1 **45 2**
2015–16 Preston NE 15 0
2016–17 Preston NE 31 1
2017–18 Preston NE 35 0
2018–19 Preston NE 30 0
2019–20 Preston NE 38 1
2020–21 Preston NE 9 0 **158 2**
2020–21 Bournemouth 16 0
2021–22 Bournemouth 23 0
2022–23 Bournemouth 7 0 **46 0**
2022–23 *Stoke C* 14 0
2023–24 Stoke C 29 0
2024–25 Stoke C 13 0 **56 0**

ROSE, Michael (D)   256   10
H: 5 11   W: 11 00   b.Aberdeen 11-10-95

2015–16	Aberdeen	1	0	1 0
2015–16	Forfar Ath	7	0	7 0
2016–17	Ayr U	20	1	
2017–18	Ayr U	34	2	
2018–19	Ayr U	34	2	88 5
2019–20	Coventry C	31	2	
2020–21	Coventry C	17	0	
2021–22	Coventry C	29	2	
2022–23	Coventry C	24	0	101 4
2023–24	Stoke C	37	1	
2024–25	Stoke C	22	0	59 1

SEKO, Tatsuki (M)   157   4
b.Adachi 22-12-97

2020	Yokohama	33	2	
2021	Yokohama	33	1	66 3
2022	Kawasaki Frontale	13	0	
2023	Kawasaki Frontale	28	1	
2024	Kawasaki Frontale	25	0	66 1
2024–25	Stoke C	25	0	25 0

SIDIBE, Souleymane (M)   12   0
b.Paris 10-2-07
Internationals: England U17, U18.

2023–24	Stoke C	4	0	
2024–25	Stoke C	8	0	12 0

SMITH, Will (M)   0   0
b. 30-11-05

2024–25	Stoke C	0	0	

STEVENS, Enda (D)   453   11
H: 6 0   W: 12 04   b.Dublin 9-7-90
Internationals: Republic of Ireland U21, Full caps.

2008	UCD	2	0	2 0
2009	St Patrick's Ath	30	0	30 0
2010	Shamrock R	18	0	
2011	Shamrock R	28	0	46 0
2011–12	Aston Villa	0	0	
2012–13	Aston Villa	7	0	
2013–14	Notts Co	2	0	2 0
2013–14	Doncaster R	13	0	
2014–15	Aston Villa	0	0	7 0
2014–15	Northampton T	4	1	4 1
2014–15	Doncaster R	28	1	41 1
2015–16	Portsmouth	45	0	
2016–17	Portsmouth	45	1	90 1
2016–17	Sheffield U	0	0	
2017–18	Sheffield U	45	1	
2018–19	Sheffield U	45	4	
2019–20	Sheffield U	38	2	
2020–21	Sheffield U	30	0	
2021–22	Sheffield U	22	1	
2022–23	Sheffield U	12	0	192 8
2023–24	Stoke C	21	0	
2024–25	Stoke C	18	0	39 0

TCHAMADEU, Junior (D)   138   7
b.Redbridge 22-12-03
Internationals: Cameroon Full caps.

2020–21	Colchester U	11	0	
2021–22	Colchester U	26	1	
2022–23	Colchester U	41	5	
2023–24	Colchester U	4	0	82 6
2023–24	Stoke C	15	0	
2024–25	Stoke C	41	1	56 1

TEZGEL, Emre (F)   30   3
H: 6 0   b.Burton-upon-Trent 19-9-05
Internationals: England U16, U17, U20.

2021–22	Stoke C	2	0	
2022–23	Stoke C	3	0	
2023–24	Stoke C	0	0	
2023–24	Milton Keynes D	15	3	15 3
2024–25	Stoke C	12	0	15 0

THOMPSON, Jordan (M)   261   9
H: 5 9   W: 10 03   b.Belfast 3-1-97
Internationals: Northern Ireland U17, U19, U21, Full caps.
From Manchester U.

2015–16	Rangers	2	0	
2015–16	Airdrieonians	7	1	7 1
2016–17	Rangers	0	0	
2016–17	Raith R	29	1	29 1
2017–18	Rangers	0	0	2 0
2017–18	Livingston	11	0	11 0
2018–19	Blackpool	38	3	
2019–20	Blackpool	18	1	56 4
2019–20	Stoke C	15	0	
2020–21	Stoke C	34	1	
2021–22	Stoke C	18	0	
2022–23	Stoke C	34	0	
2023–24	Stoke C	32	2	
2024–25	Stoke C	23	0	156 3

WILLOX, Kieron (M)   0   0
b.Inverness 18-4-06

2024–25	Stoke C	0	0	

WILMOT, Ben (D)   201   11
H: 6 2   W: 12 08   b.Stevenage 4-11-99
Internationals: England U19, U20, U21.

2016–17	Stevenage	0	0	
2017–18	Stevenage	10	0	10 0

2018–19	Watford	2	0	
2018–19	Udinese	5	0	5 0
2019–20	Watford	0	0	
2019–20	Swansea C	21	2	21 2
2020–21	Watford	25	1	27 1
2021–22	Stoke C	35	1	
2022–23	Stoke C	39	3	
2023–24	Stoke C	25	1	
2024–25	Stoke C	39	3	138 8

Players retained or with offer of contract
Bickerton, Joshua Paul; Cooper, Noah Kailen; Gromek, Wiktor Artur; Kelly, Gabriel Francis; Liu, Ryan James Jun Wen; Matondo, Japhet Mpadi; Mears, Jaden Jamil; Oppong, Francis; Otegbayo, Raphael Pijus; Simkin, Tommy James; Walker, Adriel Donald Thomas.

Scholars
Agina, Sydney Cesc Jean; Bailey, Lewis Gregory; Brammer, Ruben Harry; Day, Connor Matthew; Enabulele, Oghosaiwi Rafael; Enright, Luke James; Fearn, Elliot; Festus Eyaife, Daniel; Giani, Laurence Adam; Hines-Leacock, Kobie Jay; Kelly, Jackson Cole; Maskall, Joshua Flynn; McNally, Tommy Lee; Nzau, Pedro Jonas; Ogbebor, Jayden Chukwudi Nosakhare; Phillips, Sanchez Amore; Powell, Owen Johny; Togo, Ian Edmond; Tortoishell, Jensen Paul; Walker, Lewis Daniel; Watson, Adam David; Zeitzen, Michael Andrew.

SUNDERLAND (80)

ABDUL SAMED, Salis (M)   113   2
H: 5 11   W: 9 08   b.Accra 26-3-00
Internationals: Ghana Full caps.

2019–20	Clermont	6	0	
2020–21	Clermont	6	0	
2021–22	Clermont	31	1	43 1
2022–23	Lens	33	1	
2023–24	Lens	27	0	
2024–25	Lens	0	0	60 1
On loan from Lens.				
2024–25	Sunderland	10	0	10 0

ALEKSIC, Milan (M)   33   2
b. 30-8-05
Internationals: Serbia U18, U19, U21.

2023–24	Radnicki 1923	25	2	25 2
2024–25	Sunderland	8	0	8 0

ALESE, Ajibola (D)   52   1
H: 6 4   W: 12 04   b.Islington 17-1-01
Internationals: England U16, U17, U18, U19, U20.

2019–20	West Ham U	0	0	
2019–20	Accrington S	10	0	10 0
2020–21	West Ham U	0	0	
2020–21	Cambridge U	2	0	2 0
2021–22	West Ham U	0	0	
2022–23	Sunderland	20	1	
2023–24	Sunderland	8	0	
2024–25	Sunderland	12	0	40 1

ANDERSON, Joseph (M)   30   0
H: 6 2   b.Stalybridge 6-2-01
From Everton.

2022–23	Sunderland	4	0	
2023–24	Sunderland	0	0	
2023–24	Shrewsbury T	24	0	24 0
2024–25	Sunderland	2	0	6 0

AOUCHICHE, Adil (M)   131   5
H: 5 11   W: 11 05   b.Le Blanc-Mesnil 15-7-02
Internationals: France U16, U17, U18, U20.

2019–20	Paris Saint-Germain	1	0	1 0
2020–21	Saint-Etienne	34	2	
2021–22	Saint-Etienne	35	0	
2022–23	Saint-Etienne	2	0	71 2
2022–23	Lorient	11	0	11 0
2023–24	Sunderland	28	2	
2024–25	Sunderland	8	0	36 2
2024–25	Portsmouth	12	1	12 1

BA, Abdullah (M)   99   6
H: 5 11   W: 10 10   b.Saint-Aubin-les-Elbeuf 31-7-03
Internationals: France U16, U17, U19, U20.

2020–21	Le Havre	3	1	
2021–22	Le Havre	18	0	
2022–23	Le Havre	5	0	26 1
2022–23	Sunderland	27	1	
2023–24	Sunderland	39	3	
2024–25	Sunderland	0	0	66 4
2024–25	Dunkerque	7	1	7 1

BAINBRIDGE, Oliver (D)   6   0
H: 6 2   W: 11 07   b. 13-6-05

2023–24	Sunderland	0	0	
2024–25	Sunderland	0	0	
2024–25	Kilmarnock	6	0	6 0

BALLARD, Daniel (D)   139   8
H: 6 2   W: 13 05   b.Stevenage 22-9-99
Internationals: Northern Ireland U18, U21, Full caps.

2019–20	Arsenal	0	0	
2019–20	Swindon T	1	0	1 0
2020–21	Arsenal	0	0	
2020–21	Blackpool	25	2	25 2
2021–22	Arsenal	0	0	
2021–22	Millwall	31	1	31 1
2022–23	Sunderland	19	0	
2023–24	Sunderland	43	3	
2024–25	Sunderland	20	2	82 5

BELLINGHAM, Jobe (M)   109   11
H: 5 10   W: 11 09   b.Stourbridge 23-9-05
Internationals: England U16, U17, U18, U19, U20, U21.

2021–22	Birmingham C	2	0	
2022–23	Birmingham C	22	0	24 0
2023–24	Sunderland	45	7	
2024–25	Sunderland	40	4	85 11

BENNETTE, Jewison (M)   49   2
H: 5 9   W: 10 10   b.Heredia 15-6-04
Internationals: Costa Rica U20, Full caps.

2021–22	Herediano	31	1	31 1
2022–23	Sunderland	15	1	
2023–24	Sunderland	0	0	
2023–24	Aris	2	0	2 0
2024–25	Sunderland	0	0	16 1
Transferred to LNZ Cherkasy, March 2025.

BISHOP, Nathan (G)   94   0
H: 6 1   W: 11 05   b.Hillingdon 15-10-99
Internationals: England U20.

2016–17	Southend U	0	0	
2017–18	Southend U	1	0	
2018–19	Southend U	18	0	
2019–20	Southend U	12	0	31 0
2019–20	Manchester U	0	0	
2020–21	Manchester U	0	0	
2021–22	Manchester U	0	0	
2021–22	Mansfield T	46	0	46 0
2022–23	Manchester U	0	0	
2023–24	Sunderland	1	0	
2024–25	Sunderland	0	0	1 0
2024–25	Wycombe W	2	0	2 0
2024–25	Cambridge U	14	0	14 0

BROWNE, Alan (M)   396   44
H: 5 11   W: 11 03   b.Cork 15-4-95
Internationals: Republic of Ireland U19, U21, Full caps.

2013	Cork C	0	0	
2013–14	Preston NE	8	1	
2014–15	Preston NE	20	3	
2015–16	Preston NE	36	3	
2016–17	Preston NE	31	0	
2017–18	Preston NE	44	7	
2018–19	Preston NE	38	12	
2019–20	Preston NE	43	4	
2020–21	Preston NE	38	4	
2021–22	Preston NE	39	4	
2022–23	Preston NE	36	1	
2023–24	Preston NE	41	4	374 43
2024–25	Sunderland	22	1	22 1

CIRKIN, Dennis (D)   106   8
H: 5 11   W: 11 05   b.Dublin 6-4-02
Internationals: England U16, U17, U18, U20.

2019–20	Tottenham H	0	0	
2020–21	Tottenham H	0	0	
2021–22	Tottenham H	0	0	
2021–22	Sunderland	34	0	
2022–23	Sunderland	28	5	
2023–24	Sunderland	8	0	
2024–25	Sunderland	36	3	106 8

CROMPTON, Ben (D)   0   0
b. 17-12-03

2023–24	Sunderland	0	0	
2024–25	Sunderland	0	0	

EKWAH, Pierre (D)   83   6
H: 6 2   W: 12 11   b.Massy 15-1-02
Internationals: France U16, U20.
From Nantes.

2020–21	Chelsea	0	0	
2021–22	West Ham U	0	0	
2022–23	West Ham U	0	0	
2022–23	Sunderland	14	0	
2023–24	Sunderland	40	5	
2024–25	Sunderland	0	0	54 5
2024–25	Saint-Etienne	29	1	29 1

HJELDE, Leo (D)   53   1
H: 6 2   b.Nottingham 26-8-03
Internationals: Norway U16, U17, U18, U19, U21.
From Rosenborg.

2020–21	Celtic	0	0	
2020–21	Ross Co	11	1	11 1
2021–22	Leeds U	2	0	
2022–23	Leeds U	0	0	
2022–23	Rotherham U	13	0	13 0
2023–24	Leeds U	1	0	3 0

| 2023–24 Sunderland | 11 | 0 | | |
| 2024–25 Sunderland | 15 | 0 | 26 | 0 |

HUGGINS, Niall (D)   23 1
H: 5 8 W: 11 00 b.York 18-12-00
Internationals: Wales U21.

2020–21 Leeds U	1	0	1	0
2021–22 Sunderland	2	0		
2022–23 Sunderland	1	0		
2023–24 Sunderland	19	1		
2024–25 Sunderland	0	0	22	1

HUME, Trai (D)   176 13
H: 5 11 W: 11 00 b.Ballymena 18-3-02
Internationals: Northern Ireland U17, U19, U21, Full caps.

2018–19 Linfield	2	0		
2019–20 Linfield	2	0		
2020–21 Linfield	1	0		
2020–21 *Ballymena U*	34	5	34	5
2021–22 Linfield	17	3	21	3
2021–22 Sunderland	3	0		
2022–23 Sunderland	28	1		
2023–24 Sunderland	46	1		
2024–25 Sunderland	44	3	121	5

ISIDOR, Wilson (F)   143 47
H: 5 11 b.Rennes 27-8-00
Internationals: France U17, U18, U19, U20.

2017–18 Rennes	1	0		
2018–19 Monaco	1	0		
2019–20 Monaco	4	0		
2019–20 *Laval*	14	1	14	1
2020–21 Monaco	0	0	5	0
2020–21 *Bastia-Borgo*	29	15	29	15
2021–22 Lokomotiv Moscow	11	7		
2022–23 Lokomotiv Moscow	20	8		
2023–24 Lokomotiv Moscow	4	1	35	16
2023–24 *Zenit St Petersburg*	14	2		
2024–25 *Zenit St Petersburg*	3	1	17	3
2024–25 Sunderland	43	12	43	12

JOHNSON, Zak (D)   26 0
H: 6 2 b.Sunderland 30-7-04
Internationals: England U18.

2021–22 Sunderland	0	0		
2022–23 Sunderland	0	0		
2023–24 Sunderland	0	0		
2024 *Dundalk*	16	0	16	0
2024–25 Sunderland	0	0		
2024–25 *Notts Co*	10	0	10	0

JONES, Harrison (M)   4 0
b.Sunderland 13-2-05

| 2023–24 Sunderland | 0 | 0 | | |
| 2024–25 Sunderland | 4 | 0 | 4 | 0 |

KELLY, Caden (D)   0 0
b.Buncrana 20-11-03

2021–22 Sunderland	0	0		
2022–23 Sunderland	0	0		
2023–24 Sunderland	0	0		
2024–25 Sunderland	0	0		

LAVERY, Thomas (D)   0 0
H: 6 3 b. 19-12-05

| 2023–24 Sunderland | 0 | 0 | | |
| 2024–25 Sunderland | 0 | 0 | | |

LE FEE, Enzo (M)   181 8
b.Lorient 3-2-00
Internationals: France U20, U21, U23.

2017–18 Lorient	0	0		
2018–19 Lorient	2	0		
2019–20 Lorient	26	0		
2020–21 Lorient	36	0		
2021–22 Lorient	36	2		
2022–23 Lorient	35	5	135	7
2023–24 Rennes	25	0	25	0
2024–25 Roma	6	0	6	0

On loan from Roma.

| 2024–25 Sunderland | 15 | 1 | 15 | 1 |

LENZ, Elias (M)   0 0
b.1-9-05

| 2024–25 Sunderland | 0 | 0 | | |

MATETE, Jay (M)   129 8
H: 5 8 W: 9 08 b.Lambeth 11-2-01
From Reading.

2019–20 Fleetwood T	0	0		
2020–21 Fleetwood T	7	0		
2020–21 *Grimsby T*	20	3	20	3
2021–22 Fleetwood T	20	1	27	1
2021–22 Sunderland	14	0		
2022–23 Sunderland	8	0		
2022–23 *Plymouth Arg*	19	1	19	1
2023–24 Sunderland	0	0		
2023–24 *Oxford U*	6	0	6	0
2024–25 Sunderland	0	0	22	0
2024–25 *Bolton W*	35	3	35	3

MAYENDA, Eliezer (F)   62 9
b.Zaragoza 8-5-05
Internationals: Spain U17, U21.

2021–22 Sochaux	0	0		
2022–23 Sochaux	15	1	15	1
2023–24 Sunderland	8	0		
2023–24 *Hibernian*	2	0	2	0
2024–25 Sunderland	37	8	45	8

MIDDLEMAS, Ben (M)   0 0
b.Ashington 13-12-04

2021–22 Sunderland	0	0		
2022–23 Sunderland	0	0		
2024–25 Sunderland	0	0		

MOORE, Simon (G)   203 0
H: 6 3 W: 13 01 b.Sandown 19-5-90
Internationals: Isle of Wight Full caps.

2009–10 Brentford	1	0		
2010–11 Brentford	10	0		
2011–12 Brentford	10	0		
2012–13 Brentford	43	0	64	0
2013–14 Cardiff C	0	0		
2013–14 *Bristol C*	11	0	11	0
2014–15 Cardiff C	10	0		
2015–16 Cardiff C	7	0	17	0
2016–17 Sheffield U	43	0		
2017–18 Sheffield U	18	0		
2018–19 Sheffield U	0	0		
2019–20 Sheffield U	2	0	63	0
2021–22 Coventry C	41	0		
2022–23 Coventry C	3	0		
2023–24 Coventry C	0	0	44	0
2024–25 Sunderland	4	0	4	0

MUNDLE, Romaine (M)   39 6
H: 5 8 W: 10 10 b.London 24-4-03

2020–21 Tottenham H	0	0		
2021–22 Tottenham H	0	0		
2022–23 Tottenham H	0	0		
2023–24 Standard Liege	6	0	6	0
2023–24 Sunderland	11	1		
2024–25 Sunderland	22	5	33	6

NEIL, Daniel (M)   172 11
H: 5 10 W: 9 11 b.South Shields 30-11-01
Internationals: England U20.

2018–19 Sunderland	0	0		
2019–20 Sunderland	0	0		
2020–21 Sunderland	2	0		
2021–22 Sunderland	39	3		
2022–23 Sunderland	45	2		
2023–24 Sunderland	42	4		
2024–25 Sunderland	44	2	172	11

NNA NOUKEU, Blondy (G)   0 0
H: 6 0 W: 11 00 b.Douala, Cameroon 17-9-01

2019–20 Stoke C	0	0		
2020–21 Stoke C	0	0		
2021–22 Stoke C	0	0		
2021–22 *Crawley T*	0	0		
2022–23 Stoke C	0	0		
2023–24 Stoke C	0	0		
2024–25 Sunderland	0	0		

O'NIEN, Luke (M)   367 36
H: 5 9 W: 11 09 b.Hemel Hempstead 21-11-94

2013–14 Watford	1	0		
2014–15 Watford	0	0	1	0
2015–16 Wycombe W	35	5		
2016–17 Wycombe W	31	3		
2017–18 Wycombe W	35	7	101	15
2018–19 Sunderland	37	5		
2019–20 Sunderland	35	4		
2020–21 Sunderland	38	2		
2021–22 Sunderland	26	3		
2022–23 Sunderland	41	2		
2023–24 Sunderland	43	2		
2024–25 Sunderland	45	3	265	21

OGUNSUYI, Trey (F)   0 0
b. 26-11-06
Internationals: Belgium U18, U19.

| 2024–25 Sunderland | 0 | 0 | | |

PATTERSON, Anthony (G)   153 0
H: 6 2 W: 12 02 b.North Shields 10-5-00
Internationals: England U21.

2018–19 Sunderland	0	0		
2019–20 Sunderland	0	0		
2020–21 Sunderland	0	0		
2021–22 Sunderland	20	0		
2022–23 Sunderland	46	0		
2023–24 Sunderland	45	0		
2024–25 Sunderland	42	0	153	0

PEMBELE, Timothee (D)   65 3
b.Beaumont-sur-Oise 9-9-01
Internationals: France U16, U17, U18, U20, U23.

2020–21 Paris Saint-Germain	6	1		
2021–22 Paris Saint-Germain	0	0		
2021–22 *Bordeaux*	26	1	26	1
2022–23 Paris Saint-Germain	5	0	11	1
2023–24 Sunderland	8	0		
2024–25 Sunderland	0	0	8	0
2024–25 *Le Havre*	20	1	20	1

POVEDA-OCAMPO, Ian (M)   75 3
H: 5 5 W: 9 08 b.Southwark 9-2-00
Internationals: England U16, U17, U18, U19, U20. Colombia Full caps.
From Chelsea, Arsenal, Barcelona, Brentford.

| 2018–19 Manchester C | 0 | 0 | | |
| 2019–20 Manchester C | 0 | 0 | | |

2019–20 Leeds U	4	0		
2020–21 Leeds U	14	0		
2021–22 Leeds U	0	0		
2021–22 *Blackburn R*	10	1	10	1
2022–23 Leeds U	0	0		
2022–23 *Blackpool*	24	2	24	2
2023–24 Leeds U	7	0	25	0
2023–24 *Sheffield Wed*	10	0	10	0
2024–25 Sunderland	6	0	6	0

RIGG, Chris (M)   63 6
b.Hebburn 18-6-07
Internationals: England U16, U17, U18, U19.

2022–23 Sunderland	0	0		
2023–24 Sunderland	21	2		
2024–25 Sunderland	42	4	63	6

ROBERTS, Patrick (M)   265 25
H: 5 6 W: 10 06 b.Kingston upon Thames 5-2-97
Internationals: England U16, U17, U18, U19, U20.

2013–14 Fulham	2	0		
2014–15 Fulham	17	0	19	0
2015–16 Manchester C	1	0		
2015–16 *Celtic*	11	6		
2016–17 Manchester C	0	0		
2016–17 *Celtic*	32	9		
2017–18 Manchester C	0	0		
2017–18 *Celtic*	12	0	55	15
2018–19 Manchester C	0	0		
2018–19 *Girona*	19	0	19	0
2019–20 Manchester C	0	0		
2019–20 *Norwich C*	3	0	3	0
2019–20 *Middlesbrough*	10	1		
2020–21 Manchester C	0	0		
2020–21 *Middlesbrough*	9	0	19	1
2020–21 *Derby Co*	15	1	15	1
2021–22 Manchester C	0	0	1	0
2021–22 *Troyes*	1	0	1	0
2021–22 Sunderland	14	1		
2022–23 Sunderland	42	5		
2023–24 Sunderland	32	0		
2024–25 Sunderland	45	2	133	8

RUSYN, Nazarii (F)   132 29
H: 5 10 W: 10 10 b.Novoyavorivsk 25-10-98
Internationals: Ukraine U17, U18, U19, U21.
From Lviv.

2017–18 Dynamo Kyiv	1	0		
2018–19 Dynamo Kyiv	19	5		
2019–20 Dynamo Kyiv	12	2		
2019–20 *Zorya Luhansk*	14	5		
2020–21 Dynamo Kyiv	1	0		
2020–21 *Legia Warsaw*	0	0		
2021–22 Dynamo Kyiv	0	0	33	7
2021–22 *Dnipro-1*	8	1	8	1
2022–23 Zorya Luhansk	30	13		
2023–24 Zorya Luhansk	2	1	46	19
2023–24 Sunderland	21	2		
2024–25 Sunderland	8	0	29	2
2024–25 *Hajduk Split*	16	0	16	0

SEELT, Jenson (D)   19 0
b.Ede 23-5-03

2020–21 PSV Eindhoven	0	0		
2021–22 PSV Eindhoven	1	0		
2022–23 PSV Eindhoven	0	0	1	0
2023–24 Sunderland	17	0		
2024–25 Sunderland	1	0	18	0

SEMEDO, Luis (F)   23 0
b.Lisbon 11-8-03
Internationals: Portugal U19, U20.

| 2023–24 Sunderland | 23 | 0 | | |
| 2024–25 Sunderland | 0 | 0 | 23 | 0 |

TRIANTIS, Nectarios (D)   75 3
H: 6 3 W: 12 04 b.Sydney 11-5-03
Internationals: Australia U20, U23.

2021–22 Western Sydney W	1	0	1	0
2022–23 *Central Coast Mariners*	25	0	25	0
2023–24 Sunderland	2	0		
2023–24 *Hibernian*	12	0		
2024–25 Sunderland	1	0	3	0
2024–25 *Hibernian*	34	3	46	3

TUTIEROV, Tymur (F)   0 0
H: 6 0 b.Bakhchysaray 11-6-05
Internationals: Ukraine U19.

| 2024–25 Sunderland | 0 | 0 | | |

WATSON, Tom (F)   22 2
b.8-4-06
Internationals: England U17, U18, U19.

2022–23 Sunderland	1	0		
2023–24 Sunderland	1	0		
2024–25 Sunderland	20	2	22	2

YOUNG, Matt (G)   20 0
H: 6 3 W: 13 01 b.24-11-06
Internationals: England U18, U19, U20.

2023–24 Sunderland	0	0		
2024–25 Sunderland	0	0		
2024–25 *Salford C*	20	0	20	0

Players retained or with offer of contract
Abdullahi, Ahmed; Bell, Luke Anthony; Burke, Marshall Aaron; Cameron, Daniel

Robert; Richardson, Adam Lee; Walsh, Rhys David; Waters, Jake Robert.

Scholars
Bell, George Brian; Chungh, Aaron Singh; Dinsdale, Charles Richard; Geragusian, Finn Casper Adam; Hester, Bayley; Holcroft, Finlay; Hunt, Liam; Jones, Jaydon Mark; Kindon, Ben Anthony; Lightfoot, Archie Jay Stephen; Metcalf, Benjamin Laurence; Neild, Joseph Matthew; Neill, Marcus Edward; Parker, Daniel James; Scott, Felix; Struk, Ivan; Whittaker, Jack Thomas.

SWANSEA C (81)

ABBEY, Nelson (D) 25 0
H: 6 2 b. 28-8-03
Internationals: England U17, U20.

2020–21	Reading	0	0	
2021–22	Reading	0	0	
2022–23	Reading	3	0	
2023–24	Reading	22	0	25 0
2024–25	Olympiacos	0	0	

On loan from Olympiacos.
| 2024–25 | Swansea C | 0 | 0 | |

ALLEN, Joe (M) 499 33
H: 5 7 W: 9 11 b.Carmarthen 14-3-90
Internationals: Wales U17, U19, U21, Full caps. Great Britain.

2006–07	Swansea C	1	0	
2007–08	Swansea C	6	0	
2008–09	Swansea C	23	1	
2009–10	Swansea C	21	0	
2010–11	Swansea C	40	2	
2011–12	Swansea C	36	4	
2012–13	Swansea C	0	0	
2012–13	Liverpool	27	0	
2013–14	Liverpool	24	1	
2014–15	Liverpool	21	1	
2015–16	Liverpool	19	2	91 4
2016–17	Stoke C	36	6	
2017–18	Stoke C	36	2	
2018–19	Stoke C	46	6	
2019–20	Stoke C	35	4	
2020–21	Stoke C	18	0	
2021–22	Stoke C	41	3	212 18
2022–23	Swansea C	25	1	
2023–24	Swansea C	19	2	
2024–25	Swansea C	25	1	196 11

BIANCHINI, Florian (F) 132 13
b.Reims 25-6-01
Internationals: France U19.

2018–19	Amiens	0	0	
2019–20	Amiens	0	0	
2020–21	Amiens	16	0	
2021–22	Amiens	0	0	
2021–22	Avranches	31	3	31 3
2022–23	Amiens	3	0	19 0
2022–23	Chateauroux	17	2	17 2
2023–24	Bastia	28	5	
2024–25	Bastia	1	0	29 5
2024–25	Swansea C	36	3	36 3

BROOME, Nathan (G) 7 0
b.Manchester 3-1-02
Internationals: England U17, U18.
From Manchester C, Stoke C.

2021–22	AFC Wimbledon	0	0	
2022–23	AFC Wimbledon	7	0	
2023–24	AFC Wimbledon	0	0	7 0
2023–24	Swansea C	0	0	
2024–25	Swansea C	0	0	
2024–25	Port Vale	0	0	

CABANGO, Ben (D) 211 10
H: 6 3 W: 11 11 b.Cardiff 30-5-00
Internationals: Wales U17, U19, U21, Full caps.

2018–19	Swansea C	0	0	
2019–20	Swansea C	21	1	
2020–21	Swansea C	30	4	
2021–22	Swansea C	37	1	
2022–23	Swansea C	43	2	
2023–24	Swansea C	35	0	
2024–25	Swansea C	45	2	211 10

CHRISTIE, Cyrus (D) 424 12
H: 6 2 W: 12 04 b.Coventry 30-9-92
Internationals: Republic of Ireland Full caps.

2011–12	Coventry C	37	0	
2012–13	Coventry C	31	2	
2013–14	Coventry C	34	0	102 2
2014–15	Derby Co	38	0	
2015–16	Derby Co	42	1	
2016–17	Derby Co	27	1	
2017–18	Derby Co	0	0	107 2
2017–18	Middlesbrough	25	1	25 1
2017–18	Fulham	5	0	
2018–19	Fulham	28	0	
2019–20	Fulham	24	1	
2020–21	Nottingham F	44	0	44 0
2021–22	Fulham	0	0	57 1

CONGREVE, Cameron (M) 55 5
H: 5 11 W: 11 00 b.Blaenau 24-1-04
Internationals: Wales U18, U19, U21.

2021–22	Swansea C	5	0	
2022–23	Swansea C	10	0	
2023–24	Swansea C	0	0	
2024–25	Swansea C	0	0	15 0
2024–25	Bromley	40	5	40 5

COOPER, Oliver (M) 139 8
H: 5 9 W: 10 10 b.Derby 14-12-99
Internationals: Wales U19, U21, Full caps.

2020–21	Swansea C	3	0	
2021–22	Swansea C	0	0	
2021–22	Newport Co	33	1	33 1
2022–23	Swansea C	41	5	
2023–24	Swansea C	34	1	
2024–25	Swansea C	28	1	106 7

COTTERILL, Joel (M) 50 4
H: 6 0 W: 11 00 b. 10-10-04
Internationals: Wales U16, U18, U19, U21.

2021–22	Swansea C	0	0	
2022–23	Swansea C	0	0	
2023–24	Swansea C	0	0	
2023–24	Stockport Co	9	1	9 1
2024–25	Swansea C	0	0	
2024–25	Swindon T	41	3	41 3

CULLEN, Liam (F) 167 29
H: 5 8 W: 10 06 b.Kilgetty 23-4-99
Internationals: Wales U16, U17, U19, U20, U21, Full caps.

2018–19	Swansea C	0	0	
2019–20	Swansea C	6	1	
2020–21	Swansea C	13	1	
2021–22	Swansea C	12	0	
2021–22	Lincoln C	20	1	20 1
2022–23	Swansea C	29	8	
2023–24	Swansea C	45	7	
2024–25	Swansea C	42	11	147 28

DARLING, Harry (D) 227 21
H: 5 11 W: 11 11 b.Cambridge 8-8-99

2016–17	Cambridge U	0	0	
2017–18	Cambridge U	3	0	
2018–19	Cambridge U	12	0	
2019–20	Cambridge U	24	2	
2020–21	Cambridge U	16	0	55 2
2020–21	Milton Keynes D	23	0	
2021–22	Milton Keynes D	47	7	64 7
2022–23	Swansea C	31	4	
2023–24	Swansea C	38	3	
2024–25	Swansea C	39	5	108 12

EOM, Ji-Sung (F) 145 23
H: 5 9 b.Gimje-si 9-5-02
Internationals: South Korea U17, U23, Full caps.

2021	Gwangju	37	4	
2022	Gwangju	28	9	
2023	Gwangju	28	5	
2024	Gwangju	15	2	108 20
2024–25	Swansea C	37	3	37 3

EVANS, Cameron James (D) 63 4
H: 6 0 W: 12 04 b.Swansea 23-2-01
Internationals: Wales U16, U17, U19, U20.

2019–20	Swansea C	0	0	
2020–21	Swansea C	0	0	
2021	Waterford	30	0	30 0
2021	Sligo R	2	0	2 0

From Taunton T.
| 2024–25 | Newport Co | 31 | 4 | 31 4 |

FISHER, Andy (G) 118 0
H: 6 0 W: 13 01 b.Wigan 12-2-98

2016–17	Blackburn R	0	0	
2017–18	Blackburn R	0	0	
2018–19	Blackburn R	0	0	
2019–20	Blackburn R	0	0	
2019–20	Northampton T	0	0	
2019–20	Milton Keynes D	0	0	
2020–21	Blackburn R	0	0	
2020–21	Milton Keynes D	39	0	
2021–22	Milton Keynes D	23	0	62 0
2021–22	Swansea C	20	0	
2022–23	Swansea C	26	0	
2023–24	Swansea C	0	0	
2024–25	Swansea C	0	0	46 0
2024–25	St Johnstone	10	0	10 0

FULTON, Jay (M) 274 14
H: 5 10 W: 10 10 b.Bolton 4-4-94
Internationals: Scotland U18, U19, U21.
From Falkirk.

2013–14	Swansea C	2	0	
2014–15	Swansea C	2	0	
2015–16	Swansea C	2	0	
2015–16	Oldham Ath	11	0	11 0
2016–17	Swansea C	11	0	
2017–18	Swansea C	2	0	
2017–18	Wigan Ath	5	1	5 1
2018–19	Swansea C	33	2	

2019–20	Swansea C	36	3	
2020–21	Swansea C	40	3	
2021–22	Swansea C	18	0	
2022–23	Swansea C	38	3	
2023–24	Swansea C	43	1	
2024–25	Swansea C	31	1	258 13

GINNELLY, Josh (M) 139 26
H: 5 8 W: 10 03 b.Coventry 24-3-97

2013–14	Shrewsbury T	0	0	
2014–15	Shrewsbury T	3	0	3 0
2015–16	Burnley	0	0	
2016–17	Burnley	0	0	
2016–17	Walsall	9	0	
2017–18	Burnley	0	0	
2017–18	Lincoln C	15	2	15 2
2018–19	Walsall	21	2	30 2
2018–19	Preston NE	5	0	
2019–20	Preston NE	1	0	
2019–20	Bristol V	9	1	9 1
2020–21	Preston NE	0	0	6 0
2020–21	Hearts	6	3	
2021–22	Hearts	31	5	
2022–23	Hearts	30	12	67 20
2023–24	Swansea C	6	1	
2024–25	Swansea C	3	0	9 1

GONCALO FRANCO, Baptista (M) 158 8
b.Porto 17-11-00
Internationals: Portugal U20.

2019–20	Leixoes	6	0	6 0
2020–21	Moreirense	26	1	
2021–22	Moreirense	23	0	
2022–23	Moreirense	30	3	
2023–24	Moreirense	33	2	112 6
2024–25	Swansea C	40	2	40 2

GOVEA, Aimar (F) 5 0
H: 5 5 b.Madrid 8-6-06
Internationals: Ecuador U17.

2023–24	Swansea C	5	0	
2024–25	Swansea C	0	0	5 0

JEANES, Zac (D) 0 0
b. 18-11-05
| 2024–25 | Swansea C | 0 | 0 | |

KEY, Josh (M) 203 10
H: 5 10 W: 10 12 b.Torquay 19-11-99

2017–18	Exeter C	0	0	
2018–19	Exeter C	0	0	
2019–20	Exeter C	0	0	
2020–21	Exeter C	43	1	
2021–22	Exeter C	44	2	
2022–23	Exeter C	42	4	129 7
2023–24	Swansea C	29	2	
2024–25	Swansea C	45	1	74 3

KUKHAREVYCH, Mykola (F) 86 16
H: 6 4 W: 12 06 b.Udrytsk, Rivne Oblast 1-7-01
Internationals: Ukraine U21, U23.

2019–20	Rukh Vynnyky	6	2	
2020–21	Rukh Vynnyky	18	2	24 4
2021–22	Troyes	2	0	
2021–22	OH Leuven	6	0	
2022–23	Troyes	0	0	2 0
2022–23	OH Leuven	4	0	10 0
2022–23	Hibernian	15	5	
2023–24	Swansea C	10	1	
2024–25	Swansea C	0	0	10 1
2024–25	Hibernian	25	6	40 11

LISSAH, Filip (D) 0 0
b. 8-12-04

2023–24	Swansea C	0	0	
2024–25	Swansea C	0	0	

LLOYD, Ben (M) 2 0
H: 5 9 b.Swansea 14-3-05
Internationals: Wales U16, U17, U18, U19, U21.

2021–22	Swansea C	0	0	
2022–23	Swansea C	0	0	
2023–24	Swansea C	0	0	
2024–25	Swansea C	2	0	2 0

MARGETSON, Kit (G) 0 0
Internationals: Wales U16, U17, U19.
| 2024–25 | Swansea C | 0 | 0 | |

McLAUGHLIN, Jon (G) 398 0
H: 6 2 W: 13 00 b.Edinburgh 9-9-87
Internationals: Scotland Full caps.

2008–09	Bradford C	1	0	
2009–10	Bradford C	7	0	
2010–11	Bradford C	25	0	
2011–12	Bradford C	23	0	
2012–13	Bradford C	23	0	
2013–14	Bradford C	46	0	125 0
2014–15	Burton Alb	45	0	
2015–16	Burton Alb	45	0	
2016–17	Burton Alb	43	0	133 0
2017–18	Hearts	33	0	33 0
2018–19	Sunderland	46	0	
2019–20	Sunderland	32	0	78 0
2020–21	Rangers	11	0	
2021–22	Rangers	8	0	
2022–23	Rangers	10	0	

2023–24	Rangers	0	0	**29**	**0**
2024–25	Swansea C	0	0		

NAUGHTON, Kyle (D) **481** **11**
H: 5 11 W: 11 07 b.Sheffield 11-11-88
Internationals: England U21.

2006–07	Sheffield U	0	0		
2007–08	*Gretna*	18	0	**18**	**0**
2007–08	Sheffield U	0	0		
2008–09	Sheffield U	40	1		
2009–10	Sheffield U	0	0	**40**	**1**
2009–10	Tottenham H	1	0		
2009–10	*Middlesbrough*	15	0	**15**	**0**
2010–11	Tottenham H	0	0		
2010–11	*Leicester C*	34	5	**34**	**5**
2011–12	Tottenham H	0	0		
2011–12	*Norwich C*	32	0	**32**	**0**
2012–13	Tottenham H	14	0		
2013–14	Tottenham H	22	0		
2014–15	Tottenham H	5	0	**42**	**0**
2014–15	Swansea C	10	0		
2015–16	Swansea C	27	0		
2016–17	Swansea C	31	1		
2017–18	Swansea C	34	0		
2018–19	Swansea C	35	1		
2019–20	Swansea C	32	3		
2020–21	Swansea C	30	0		
2021–22	Swansea C	38	0		
2022–23	Swansea C	25	0		
2023–24	Swansea C	15	0		
2024–25	Swansea C	23	0	**300**	**5**

PARKER, Arthur (D) **0** **0**
b. 3-5-06

2024–25	Swansea C	0	0		

PARKER, Sam (D) **9** **0**
b.Cardiff 7-7-06
Internationals: Wales U17, U19, U21.

2023–24	Swansea C	2	0		
2024–25	Swansea C	7	0	**9**	**0**

PEDERSEN, Kristian (D) **302** **14**
H: 6 2 W: 13 01 b.Ringsted 4-8-94
Internationals: Denmark U21, Full caps.

2014–15	HB Koge	28	1		
2015–16	HB Koge	30	1	**58**	**2**
2016–17	Union Berlin	29	0		
2017–18	Union Berlin	32	1	**61**	**1**
2018–19	Birmingham C	39	1		
2019–20	Birmingham C	44	4		
2020–21	Birmingham C	35	2		
2021–22	Birmingham C	37	2	**155**	**9**
2022–23	Cologne	6	0	**6**	**0**
2023–24	Swansea C	4	0		
2023–24	*Sheffield Wed*	4	0	**4**	**0**
2024–25	Swansea C	0	0	**4**	**0**
2024–25	*Queen of the South*	14	2	**14**	**2**

RONALD, Martins (F) **120** **11**
b.Corumba 14-6-01

2019	Corumbaense	1	0	**1**	**0**
2020	Atletico Goianiense	0	0		
2021	Atletico Goianiense	0	0		
2021	*Gremio Anapolis*	0	0		
2022	Gremio Anapolis	0	0		
2022	*Guarani*	9	0	**9**	**0**
2022–23	Gremio Anapolis	0	0		
2022–23	*Estrela da Amadora*	29	5		
2023–24	Gremio Anapolis	0	0		
2023–24	*Estrela da Amadora*	17	1	**46**	**6**
2023–24	Swansea C	18	3		
2024–25	Swansea C	46	2	**64**	**5**

SMITH, Liam (D) **20** **2**
H: 5 9 W: 10 01 b.Kilmarnock 28-10-03
Internationals: Scotland U16, U17, U19, U21.
From Kilmarnock, Manchester C.

2022–23	Swansea C	0	0		
2023–24	Swansea C	0	0		
2024–25	Swansea C	0	0		
2024–25	*Partick Thistle*	6	0	**6**	**0**
2024–25	*Queen of the South*	14	2	**14**	**2**

THOMAS, Joshua (F) **17** **1**
H: 5 8 W: 10 03 b.Bridgend 24-9-02
Internationals: Wales U16, U17, U19, U20, U21.

2020–21	Swansea C	0	0		
2021–22	Swansea C	0	0		
2022–23	Swansea C	0	0		
2023–24	Swansea C	0	0		
2023–24	*Port Vale*	11	0	**11**	**0**
2024–25	Swansea C	1	0	**1**	**0**
2024–25	*Bromley*	3	0	**3**	**0**
2025	*Drogheda U*	2	1	**2**	**1**

TJOE-A-ON, Nathan (D) **54** **1**
b.Rotterdam 22-12-01
Internationals: Indonesia U23, Full caps.

2019–20	Excelsior	0	0		
2020–21	Excelsior	10	0		
2021–22	Excelsior	10	0		
2022–23	Excelsior	29	1	**49**	**1**
2023–24	Swansea C	0	0		
2023–24	*Heerenveen*	4	0	**4**	**0**
2024–25	Swansea C	1	0	**1**	**0**

TYMON, Josh (D) **211** **4**
H: 5 10 W: 11 09 b.Kingston-upon-Hull 22-5-99
Internationals: England U17, U18, U19, U20.

2015–16	Hull C	0	0		
2016–17	Hull C	5	0	**5**	**0**
2017–18	Stoke C	3	0		
2017–18	*Milton Keynes D*	9	0	**9**	**0**
2018–19	Stoke C	1	0		
2019–20	Stoke C	2	0		
2019–20	*Famalicao*	5	0	**5**	**0**
2020–21	Stoke C	26	0		
2021–22	Stoke C	44	1		
2022–23	Stoke C	28	1		
2023–24	Stoke C	2	0	**106**	**2**
2023–24	Swansea C	41	0		
2024–25	Swansea C	45	2	**86**	**2**

VIGOUROUX, Lawrence (G) **308** **0**
H: 6 4 W: 12 00 b.Camden 19-11-93
Internationals: Chile U20.

2012–13	Tottenham H	0	0		
2013–14	Tottenham H	0	0		
2014–15	Liverpool	0	0		
2015–16	Liverpool	0	0		
2015–16	*Swindon T*	33	0		
2016–17	Swindon T	43	0		
2017–18	Swindon T	14	0		
2018–19	Swindon T	29	0	**119**	**0**
2019–20	Leyton Orient	6	0		
2020–21	Leyton Orient	46	0		
2021–22	Leyton Orient	46	0		
2022–23	Leyton Orient	45	0	**143**	**0**
2023–24	Burnley	0	0		
2024–25	Swansea C	46	0	**46**	**0**

VIPOTNIK, Zan (F) **147** **47**
H: 6 1 W: 12 08 b.Celje 18-3-02
Internationals: Slovenia U16, U17, U18, U19, U21, Full caps.

2020–21	Maribor	0	0		
2020–21	*Gorica*	17	1	**17**	**1**
2021–22	Maribor	9	0		
2021–22	*Triglav Kranj*	12	9	**12**	**9**
2022–23	Maribor	30	20	**39**	**20**
2023–24	Bordeaux	37	10	**37**	**10**
2024–25	Swansea C	42	7	**42**	**7**

WATTS, Daniel (M) **0** **0**
b. 16-12-05
Internationals: Wales U17, U18, U19, U21.

2024–25	Swansea C	0	0		

WATTS, Evan (G) **10** **0**
Internationals: Wales U16, U21.

2024–25	Swansea C	0	0		
2024–25	*Galway U*	10	0	**10**	**0**

WIDELL, Melker (F) **96** **13**
b.Billeberga 19-4-02
Internationals: Sweden U17, U21, Full caps.

2022	Malmo	0	0		
2022	*BK Olympic*	27	3	**27**	**3**
2022–23	Landskrona	14	1	**14**	**1**
2023–24	AaB	28	6		
2024–25	Swansea C	0	0		
2024–25	*AaB*	27	3	**55**	**9**

WILSON, Kyrell (F) **0** **0**
b.Eastbourne 1-12-04

2023–24	Swansea C	0	0		
2024–25	Swansea C	0	0		

YATES, Jerry (F) **310** **81**
H: 5 9 W: 10 10 b.Doncaster 10-11-96

2014–15	Rotherham U	1	0		
2015–16	Rotherham U	0	0		
2016–17	Rotherham U	21	1		
2017–18	Rotherham U	17	1		
2018–19	Carlisle U	23	6	**23**	**6**
2018–19	Rotherham U	7	0		
2019–20	Rotherham U	1	0	**47**	**2**
2019–20	*Swindon T*	31	13	**31**	**13**
2020–21	Blackpool	44	20		
2021–22	Blackpool	39	8		
2022–23	Blackpool	41	14	**124**	**42**
2023–24	Swansea C	43	8		
2024–25	Swansea C	0	0	**43**	**8**
2024–25	*Derby Co*	42	10	**42**	**10**

Players retained or with offer of contract
Bates, Mitchell David Brinley; Cook, Jacob Benjamin; Dabrowski, Sebastian; Fanning, Jack William; Griffith, Yori; Jones, Iestyn David; Nzingo, Glory; Woodward, Thomas Charles.

Scholars
Bates, Morgan Trevor; Clarke, Billy Oscar; Deacon, Callum James; Dudding, Isaac James; Higgins, Aidan Michael; Higginson, Kiel Scott; Ifans, Caio Sion; Jones, Callum David; Ojetoro Amachree, Abdulwahab Iyanda; Perry, Harlan Emrys; Pescatore, Joshua Mario Brian; Phillips, Benjamin Ioan Thomas; Popham, Brogan John; Rees-Siso, Ramon; Robinson, Milo Carter; Seager, Samuel Michael; Searle, Thomas Christopher; Williams, Osian Tomos.

SWINDON T (82)

ALSTON, George (F) **1** **0**
b.Chester 21-11-06

2023–24	Swindon T	0	0		
2024–25	Swindon T	1	0	**1**	**0**

AMEEN, Botan (F) **14** **1**
H: 5 10 W: 10 10 b.London 24-4-07
Internationals: Iraq U20.

2024–25	Swindon T	14	1	**14**	**1**

BROWN, Jaxon (D) **4** **0**
b.Grays 27-7-06

2022–23	Swindon T	0	0		
2023–24	Swindon T	1	0		
2024–25	Swindon T	3	0	**4**	**0**

BUTTERWORTH, Daniel (F) **121** **13**
H: 5 11 W: 10 12 b.Manchester 14-9-94
From Manchester U.

2017–18	Blackburn R	0	0		
2018–19	Blackburn R	1	0		
2019–20	Blackburn R	0	0		
2020–21	Blackburn R	1	0		
2021–22	Blackburn R	11	0		
2021–22	*Fleetwood T*	12	1	**12**	**1**
2022–23	Blackburn R	0	0	**13**	**0**
2022–23	*Port Vale*	31	3	**31**	**3**
2023–24	Carlisle U	28	4		
2024–25	Carlisle U	3	0	**31**	**4**
2024–25	Swindon T	34	5	**34**	**5**

BYCROFT, Jack (G) **40** **0**
H: 6 0 W: 11 03 b.Salisbury 21-9-01
Internationals: England U19.

2020–21	Southampton	0	0		
2021–22	Southampton	0	0		
2022–23	Southampton	0	0		
2023–24	Southampton	0	0		
2023–24	Swindon T	19	0		
2024–25	Swindon T	21	0	**40**	**0**

CAIN, Jake (M) **84** **3**
H: 5 9 W: 9 04 b.Wigan 2-9-01

2019–20	Liverpool	0	0		
2020–21	Liverpool	0	0		
2021–22	Liverpool	0	0		
2021–22	*Newport Co*	25	0	**25**	**0**
2022–23	Liverpool	0	0		
2022–23	*Swindon T*	16	1		
2023–24	Swindon T	24	2		
2024–25	Swindon T	19	0	**59**	**3**

CHARD, Harry (D) **0** **0**

2024–25	Swindon T	0	0		

CLARKE, Ollie (M) **373** **35**
H: 5 11 W: 11 11 b.Bristol 29-6-92

2009–10	Bristol R	0	0		
2010–11	Bristol R	1	0		
2011–12	Bristol R	0	0		
2012–13	Bristol R	5	0		
2013–14	Bristol R	32	2		
From Bristol R.					
2015–16	Bristol R	33	2		
2016–17	Bristol R	30	4		
2017–18	Bristol R	40	1		
2018–19	Bristol R	40	6		
2019–20	Bristol R	27	1	**208**	**16**
2019–20	Mansfield T	0	0		
2020–21	Mansfield T	33	3		
2021–22	Mansfield T	26	4		
2022–23	Mansfield T	37	5		
2023–24	Mansfield T	39	3	**135**	**15**
2024–25	Swindon T	30	4	**30**	**4**

COX, George (M) **162** **10**
H: 5 10 W: 11 00 b.Worthing 14-1-98

2018–19	Brighton & HA	0	0		
2018–19	*Northampton T*	5	0	**5**	**0**
2019–20	Brighton & HA	0	0		
2019–20	*Fortuna Sittard*	21	1		
2020–21	Fortuna Sittard	33	5		
2021–22	Fortuna Sittard	27	2		
2022–23	Fortuna Sittard	27	0	**108**	**8**
2023–24	Volendam	23	0	**23**	**0**
2024–25	Swindon T	26	2	**26**	**2**

DELANEY, Ryan (D) **230** **15**
H: 6 0 W: 11 05 b.Wexford 6-9-96
Internationals: Republic of Ireland U21.
From Wexford.

2016–17	Burton Alb	0	0		
2017	*Cork C*	30	6	**30**	**6**
2017–18	Rochdale	18	2		
2018–19	Rochdale	30	1		
2019–20	*AFC Wimbledon*	14	1	**14**	**1**
2019–20	Rochdale	0	0	**48**	**3**
2019–20	Bolton W	4	1		
2020–21	Bolton W	20	1	**24**	**2**
2021–22	Morecambe	13	0		
2021–22	*Scunthorpe U*	18	0	**18**	**0**
2022–23	Morecambe	32	1	**45**	**1**
2023–24	Newport Co	30	1	**30**	**1**
2024–25	Swindon T	21	1	**21**	**1**

DRINAN, Aaron (F)   157 24
H: 6 0 W: 11 07 b.Cork 6-5-98
Internationals: Republic of Ireland U21.
From Cork C.

2017	Waterford	5	1	5 1
2017–18	Ipswich T	0	0	
2018–19	Ipswich T	0	0	
2019–20	Ipswich T	0	0	
2020–21	Ipswich T	22	1	22 1
2021–22	Leyton Orient	40	13	
2022–23	Leyton Orient	33	2	
2023–24	Leyton Orient	12	0	85 15
2023–24	Swindon T	17	4	
2024–25	Swindon T	28	3	45 7

DWORZAK, Anton (M)   5 0
H: 5 3 b.3-3-05

2021–22	Swindon T	0	0
2022–23	Swindon T	1	0
2023–24	Swindon T	4	0
2024–25	Swindon T	0	0	5 0

EVANS, Redman (G)   1 0
H: 6 5 W: 13 01 b. 1-10-05

2023–24	Swindon T	1	0
2024–25	Swindon T	0	0	1 0

FOX, Harvey (D)   0 0
H: 5 9 W: 10 06 b.Swindon 24-9-04

2021–22	Swindon T	0	0
2022–23	Swindon T	0	0
2023–24	Swindon T	0	0
2024–25	Swindon T	0	0

FOYE, Owen (F)   1 0
2024–25	Swindon T	1	0	1 0

GLATZEL, Paul (F)   75 14
H: 5 9 W: 10 08 b.Liverpool 20-2-01
Internationals: England U16. Germany U18.

2021–22	Liverpool	0	0	
2021–22	Tranmere R	16	4	
2022–23	Liverpool	0	0	
2022–23	Tranmere R	1	0	17 4
2023–24	Liverpool	0	0	
2023–24	Swindon T	19	7	
2024–25	Swindon T	39	3	58 10

GONZALEZ, Dani (M)   0 0
b. 23-5-07

2024–25	Swindon T	0	0

HALL, Grant (D)   235 10
H: 5 9 W: 11 03 b.Brighton 29-10-91
From Lewes.

2009–10	Brighton & HA	0	0	
2010–11	Brighton & HA	0	0	
2011–12	Brighton & HA	1	0	1 0
2012–13	Tottenham H	0	0	
2013–14	Tottenham H	0	0	
2013–14	*Swindon T*	27	0	
2014–15	Tottenham H	0	0	
2014–15	*Birmingham C*	7	0	7 0
2014–15	*Blackpool*	12	1	12 1
2015–16	QPR	39	1	
2016–17	QPR	34	0	
2017–18	QPR	4	0	
2018–19	QPR	12	0	
2019–20	QPR	30	5	119 6
2020–21	Middlesbrough	19	2	
2021–22	Middlesbrough	8	0	
2022–23	Middlesbrough	0	0	27 2
2022–23	*Rotherham U*	20	0	
2023–24	Rotherham U	8	1	28 1
2024–25	Swindon T	14	0	41 0

HART, Sonny (M)   2 0
H: 5 11 W: 12 00 b. 8-5-06

2022–23	Swindon T	0	0
2023–24	Swindon T	1	0
2024–25	Swindon T	1	0	2 0

JOHNSON, Pharrell (D)   1 0
H: 6 1 b. 19-5-04
From Nottingham F.

2023–24	Swindon T	1	0
2024–25	Swindon T	0	0	1 0

KANU, Abu (M)   2 0
H: 5 10 W: 11 05 b. 14-6-06

2022–23	Swindon T	2	0
2023–24	Swindon T	0	0
2024–25	Swindon T	0	0	2 0

KEYES, Josh (M)   0 0
b. 26-4-06

2022–23	Swindon T	0	0
2023–24	Swindon T	0	0
2024–25	Swindon T	0	0

KHAN, Saidou (M)   76 2
H: 6 2 W: 12 00 b.Sanchaba 5-12-95
Internationals: Gambia Full caps.
From Tooting & Mitcham U, Dulwich
Hamlet, Kingstonian, Chipstead, Tooting &
Mitcham U, Maidstone U, Chesterfield.

2022–23	Swindon T	35	1	
2023–24	Swindon T	31	1	
2024–25	Swindon T	0	0	66 2
2024–25	*Tranmere R*	10	0	10 0

KILKENNY, Gavin (M)   84 2
H: 5 8 W: 10 01 b.Dublin 1-2-00
Internationals: Republic of Ireland U17, U19,
U21.

2019–20	Bournemouth	0	0	
2020–21	Bournemouth	1	0	
2021–22	Bournemouth	14	0	
2022–23	Bournemouth	0	0	
2022–23	Stoke C	3	0	3 0
2022–23	*Charlton Ath*	8	0	8 0
2023–24	Bournemouth	0	0	
2023–24	*Fleetwood T*	16	1	16 1
2024–25	Bournemouth	0	0	15 0
2024–25	Swindon T	42	1	42 1

KING, Jeff (M)   9 0
H: 5 9 W: 12 08 b.Transferred to York C,
November 2024. 19-12-95
From Droylsden.

2017–18	Bolton W	1	0	1 0
2018–19	St Mirren	0	0	
From FC Halifax T, Chesterfield.				
2024–25	Swindon T	8	0	8 0

KIRKMAN, Billy (D)   57 1
b.Blackburn 26-2-04

2022–23	The New Saints	5	0	
2022–23	*Aberystwyth T*	12	0	
2023–24	The New Saints	0	0	5 0
2023–24	*Aberystwyth T*	26	1	38 1
2024–25	Swindon T	14	0	14 0

LARKINS, Kian (M)   0 0
2023–24	Swindon T	0	0
2024–25	Swindon T	0	0

McCORMICK, Antony (F)   0 0
b. 30-4-07

2024–25	Swindon T	0	0

McGREGOR, Joel (M)   24 1
H: 5 7 W: 9 11 b. 24-3-06

2023–24	Swindon T	5	0	
2024–25	Swindon T	19	1	24 1

McGURK, Sean (M)   17 2
H: 5 7 W: 10 01 b.Liverpool 15-3-03

2023–24	Leeds U	0	0	
2023–24	Swindon T	9	2	
2024–25	Swindon T	8	0	17 2

MILNE, Archie (F)   0 0
H: 5 9 b. 11-11-05

2023–24	Swindon T	0	0
2024–25	Swindon T	0	0

MINTURN, Harrison (M)   36 0
H: 6 2 W: 12 06 b.Swindon 26-12-03

2021–22	Swindon T	0	0	
2022–23	Swindon T	8	0	
2023–24	Swindon T	20	0	
2024–25	Swindon T	8	0	36 0

MITCHELL, Dylan (M)   2 0
H: 5 7 W: 10 08 b.Birmingham 1-10-05

2024–25	Swindon T	2	0	2 0

MYERS, Lucas (G)   0 0
2024–25	Swindon T	0	0

OBODO, Miles (F)   4 0
H: 5 9 b.London 24-9-06

2023–24	Swindon T	4	0
2024–25	Swindon T	0	0	4 0

OFOBORH, Nnamdi (F)   73 2
H: 5 9 W: 12 02 b.Southwark 7-11-99
Internationals: Nigeria U20.

2018–19	Bournemouth	0	0	
2019–20	Bournemouth	0	0	
2019–20	*Wycombe W*	18	0	
2020–21	Bournemouth	3	0	3 0
2020–21	*Wycombe W*	8	0	26 0
2021–22	Rangers	0	0	
2022–23	Rangers	0	0	
2023–24	Swindon T	7	0	
2024–25	Swindon T	37	2	44 2

RIPLEY, Connor (G)   276 0
H: 6 3 W: 15 02 b.Middlesbrough 13-2-93
Internationals: England U19, U20.

2010–11	Middlesbrough	0	0	
2011–12	Middlesbrough	0	0	
2011–12	*Oxford U*	1	0	1 0
2012–13	Middlesbrough	0	0	
2013–14	Middlesbrough	0	0	
2013–14	*Bradford C*	0	0	
2014	*Ostersund*	14	0	14 0
2014–15	Middlesbrough	0	0	
2015–16	Middlesbrough	0	0	
2015–16	*Motherwell*	36	0	36 0
2016–17	Middlesbrough	0	0	
2016–17	*Oldham Ath*	46	0	46 0
2017–18	Middlesbrough	0	0	
2017–18	*Burton Alb*	2	0	2 0
2017–18	*Bury*	15	0	15 0
2018–19	Middlesbrough	0	0	2 0
2018–19	*Accrington S*	21	0	21 0
2019–20	Preston NE	2	0	
2020–21	Preston NE	1	0	

2021–22	Preston NE	0	0	3 0
2021–22	*Salford C*	7	0	7 0
2022–23	Morecambe	46	0	46 0
2023–24	Port Vale	46	0	
2024–25	Port Vale	23	0	69 0
2024–25	Swindon T	14	0	14 0

SMITH, Harry (F)   227 57
H: 6 5 W: 13 01 b.Chatham 18-5-95
From Sittingbourne, Folkestone Invicta.

2016–17	Millwall	9	1	
2017–18	Millwall	0	0	9 1
2017–18	*Swindon T*	14	2	
2018–19	Macclesfield T	39	8	39 8
2019–20	Northampton T	19	4	
2020–21	Motherwell	0	0	
2020–21	Northampton T	16	3	
2021–22	Northampton T	0	0	35 7
2021–22	Leyton Orient	41	13	
2022–23	Leyton Orient	8	0	49 13
2022–23	*Exeter C*	5	0	5 0
2023–24	Sutton U	37	11	37 11
2024–25	Swindon T	39	15	53 17

SOBOWALE, Oluwatunmise (D)   155 5
H: 5 11 W: 10 10 b.Waterford 19-3-99

2016	Waterford	4	0	
2017	Waterford	1	0	
2017–18	Hercules	0	0	
2018	Finn Harps	7	1	7 1
2020	Waterford	13	0	
2021	Waterford	11	0	
2021	*Athlone T*	10	0	10 0
2022	Waterford	24	3	
2023	Waterford	19	1	72 4
2023–24	Shrewsbury T	29	0	29 0
2024–25	Swindon T	37	0	37 0

UWAKWE, Tariq (M)   67 2
H: 6 0 W: 10 01 b.Islington 19-11-99
Internationals: England U19, U20.

2020–21	Chelsea	0	0	
2020–21	*Accrington S*	15	1	15 1
2021–22	Crewe Alex	8	0	
2022–23	Crewe Alex	36	1	44 1
2023–24	Swindon T	8	0	
2024–25	Swindon T	0	0	8 0

WRIGHT, Will (D)   125 12
H: 6 3 W: 13 01 b.Luton 12-6-97
From Biggleswade U, Hitchin T, Colchester
U, Dagenham & Red.

2022–23	Gillingham	34	1	34 1
2023–24	Crawley T	45	4	45 4
2024–25	Swindon T	46	7	46 7

Scholars
Alston, George Henry; Ameen, Botan; Betts,
Charlie Andrew Laurence; Britchford-
Stanley, Conor Lewis; Chard, Harry Lee;
Foye, Owen Curtis; Gonzalez Birchall, Daniel
Frutos; Gray, Harrison Steven; Hutt, Liam
Anthony; Larkins, Kian James; McCormick,
Antony Robert; Myers, Lucas Garry David;
Obodo, Miles Szymon Odafe; Owiti, Joseph
Godston; Robinson, Anton Joshua; Terry,
Joshua Lewis; Tombs, Finlay Benjamin.

TOTTENHAM H (83)

ABBOTT, George (M)   41 5
H: 5 9 W: 12 02 b.London 16-8-05
Internationals: England U18.

2022–23	Tottenham H	1	0	
2023–24	Tottenham H	0	0	
2024–25	Tottenham H	0	0	1 0
2024–25	*Notts Co*	40	5	40 5

AJAYI, Damola (F)   0 0
H: 5 8 W: 10 10 b.London 27-12-05

2024–25	Tottenham H	0	0

ASHCROFT, Tyrell (D)   4 0
b. 7-7-04

2021–22	Reading	4	0	4 0
2022–23	Tottenham H	0	0	
2023–24	Tottenham H	0	0	
2024–25	Tottenham H	0	0	

AUSTIN, Brandon (G)   16 0
H: 6 2 W: 12 13 b.Hemel Hempstead
8-1-99
Internationals: USA U18.

2019–20	Tottenham H	0	0	
2019–20	*Viborg*	14	0	14 0
2020–21	Tottenham H	0	0	
2021	*Orlando C*	1	0	1 0
2021–22	Tottenham H	0	0	
2022–23	Tottenham H	0	0	
2023–24	Tottenham H	0	0	
2024–25	Tottenham H	1	0	1 0

BENTANCUR, Rodrigo (M)   268 11
H: 6 2 W: 11 07 b.Nueva Helvecia 25-6-97
Internationals: Uruguay U20, Full caps.

2015	Boca Juniors	18	0	
2016	Boca Juniors	11	1	
2016–17	Boca Juniors	22	0	51 1

2017–18	Juventus	20	0		
2018–19	Juventus	31	2		
2019–20	Juventus	30	0		
2020–21	Juventus	33	0		
2021–22	Juventus	19	0	**133**	**2**
2021–22	Tottenham H	17	0		
2022–23	Tottenham H	18	5		
2023–24	Tottenham H	23	1		
2024–25	Tottenham H	26	2	**84**	**8**

BERGVALL, Lucas (M) 64 3
H: 6 1 W: 11 09 b.Stockholm 2-2-06
Internationals: Sweden U17, U19, U21, Full caps.

2021	Brommapojkarna	1	0		
2022	Brommapojkarna	11	1	**12**	**1**
2023	Djurgarden	25	2	**25**	**2**
2023–24	Tottenham H	0	0		
2024–25	Tottenham H	27	0	**27**	**0**

BISSOUMA, Yves (M) 238 8
H: 5 9 W: 12 04 b.Issia 30-8-96
Internationals: Mali Full caps.
From Real Bamako.

2016–17	Lille	23	1		
2017–18	Lille	24	2	**47**	**3**
2018–19	Brighton & HA	28	0		
2019–20	Brighton & HA	22	1		
2020–21	Brighton & HA	36	1		
2021–22	Brighton & HA	26	1	**112**	**3**
2022–23	Tottenham H	23	0		
2023–24	Tottenham H	28	0		
2024–25	Tottenham H	28	2	**79**	**2**

CASSANOVA, Dante (M) 0 0
H: 5 10 W: 10 06 b.London 21-6-04

2024–25	Tottenham H	0	0		

CRAIG, Matthew (M) 38 2
H: 6 0 W: 11 00 b.London 16-3-03
Internationals: Scotland U16, U19, U21.

2021–22	Tottenham H	0	0		
2022–23	Tottenham H	1	0		
2023–24	Tottenham H	0	0		
2023–24	*Doncaster R*	18	1	**18**	**1**
2024–25	Tottenham H	0	0	**1**	**0**
2024–25	*Barnsley*	14	0	**14**	**0**
2024–25	*Mansfield T*	5	1	**5**	**1**

DANSO, Kevin (D) 201 9
H: 6 3 W: 11 11 b.Dachau 3-9-93
Internationals: Austria U16, U17, U18, U19, U21, Full caps.

2015–16	Augsburg	0	0		
2016–17	Augsburg	7	0		
2017–18	Augsburg	16	2		
2018–19	Augsburg	18	1		
2019–20	Augsburg	0	0		
2019–20	*Southampton*	6	0	**6**	**0**
2020–21	Augsburg	0	0	**41**	**3**
2020–21	*Fortuna Dusseldorf*	32	2	**32**	**2**
2021–22	Lens	33	2		
2022–23	Lens	37	1		
2023–24	Lens	30	1		
2024–25	Lens	12	0	**112**	**4**

On loan from Lens.

2024–25	Tottenham H	10	0	**10**	**0**

DAVIES, Ben (D) 313 10
H: 5 7 W: 12 00 b.Neath 24-4-93
Internationals: Wales U19, Full caps.

2011–12	Swansea C	0	0		
2012–13	Swansea C	37	1		
2013–14	Swansea C	34	2	**71**	**3**
2014–15	Tottenham H	14	0		
2015–16	Tottenham H	17	0		
2016–17	Tottenham H	23	1		
2017–18	Tottenham H	29	2		
2018–19	Tottenham H	27	0		
2019–20	Tottenham H	18	0		
2020–21	Tottenham H	20	0		
2021–22	Tottenham H	29	1		
2022–23	Tottenham H	31	2		
2023–24	Tottenham H	17	1		
2024–25	Tottenham H	17	0	**242**	**7**

DEVINE, Alfie (M) 65 8
H: 5 10 W: 11 11 b.Warrington 1-8-04
Internationals: England U16, U19, U20.
From Wigan Ath.

2020–21	Tottenham H	0	0		
2021–22	Tottenham H	0	0		
2022–23	Tottenham H	0	0		
2023–24	Tottenham H	0	0		
2023–24	*Port Vale*	20	2	**20**	**2**
2023–24	*Plymouth Arg*	15	0	**15**	**0**
2024–25	Tottenham H	0	0		
2024–25	*Westerlo*	30	6	**30**	**6**

DONLEY, Jamie (F) 42 8
H: 6 0 W: 11 00 b.Antrim 3-1-05
Internationals: England U16, U17, U18, U19. Northern Ireland U19, Full caps.

2023–24	Tottenham H	3	0		
2024–25	Tottenham H	0	0	**3**	**0**
2024–25	*Leyton Orient*	39	8	**39**	**8**

DORRINGTON, Alfie (D) 13 1
H: 6 4 W: 12 04 b.Enfield 20-4-05
Internationals: England U17, U18, U19.

2023–24	Tottenham H	0	0		
2024–25	Tottenham H	1	0	**1**	**0**
2024–25	*Aberdeen*	12	1	**12**	**1**

DRAGUSIN, Radu (D) 103 6
H: 6 3 W: 13 05 b.Bukarest 3-2-02
Internationals: Romania U17, U19, U21, Full caps.
From Regal Sport Bucuresti.

2019–20	Juventus	0	0		
2020–21	Juventus	1	0		
2021–22	Juventus	0	0		
2021–22	*Sampdoria*	13	0	**13**	**0**
2021–22	*Salernitana*	7	0	**7**	**0**
2022–23	Juventus	0	0	**1**	**0**
2022–23	*Genoa*	38	4		
2023–24	Genoa	19	2	**57**	**6**
2023–24	Tottenham H	9	0		
2024–25	Tottenham H	16	0	**25**	**0**

EMERSON, Junior (D) 181 9
H: 6 0 W: 11 00 b.Sao Paulo 14-1-99
Internationals: Brazil U20, U23, Full caps.

2016	Ponte Preta	0	0		
2017	Ponte Preta	3	0		
2018	Ponte Preta	0	0	**3**	**0**
2018	Atletico Mineiro	23	1	**23**	**1**
2018–19	Barcelona	0	0		
2018–19	*Real Betis*	6	0		
2019–20	Barcelona	0	0		
2019–20	*Real Betis*	33	3		
2020–21	Barcelona	0	0		
2020–21	*Real Betis*	34	1	**73**	**4**
2021–22	Barcelona	3	0	**3**	**0**
2021–22	Tottenham H	31	1		
2022–23	Tottenham H	26	2		
2023–24	Tottenham H	22	1		
2024–25	Tottenham H	0	0	**79**	**4**

FORSTER, Fraser (G) 371 0
H: 6 7 W: 14 09 b.Hexham 17-3-88
Internationals: England Full caps.

2007–08	Newcastle U	0	0		
2008–09	Newcastle U	0	0		
2008–09	*Stockport Co*	6	0	**6**	**0**
2009–10	Newcastle U	0	0		
2009–10	*Bristol R*	4	0	**4**	**0**
2009–10	*Norwich C*	38	0	**38**	**0**
2010–11	Newcastle U	0	0		
2010–11	*Celtic*	36	0		
2011–12	Newcastle U	0	0		
2011–12	*Celtic*	33	0		
2012–13	Celtic	34	0		
2013–14	Celtic	37	0		
2014–15	Southampton	30	0		
2015–16	Southampton	18	0		
2016–17	Southampton	38	0		
2017–18	Southampton	20	0		
2018–19	Southampton	1	0		
2019–20	Southampton	0	0		
2019–20	*Celtic*	28	0	**168**	**0**
2020–21	Southampton	8	0		
2021–22	Southampton	19	0	**134**	**0**
2022–23	Tottenham H	14	0		
2023–24	Tottenham H	0	0		
2024–25	Tottenham H	7	0	**21**	**0**

FURNELL-GILL, Luca (D) 0 0
b. 29-12-06

2023–24	Liverpool	0	0		
2024–25	Liverpool	0	0		
2024–25	Tottenham H	0	0		

GIL SALVATIERRA, Bryan (M) 131 11
H: 5 9 W: 9 06 b.Barbate 11-2-01
Internationals: Spain U16, U17, U18, U19, U21, U23, Full caps.

2018–19	Sevilla	11	1		
2019–20	Sevilla	2	0		
2019–20	*Leganes*	12	1	**12**	**1**
2020–21	Sevilla	1	0		
2020–21	*Eibar*	28	4	**28**	**4**
2021–22	Tottenham H	9	0		
2021–22	*Valencia*	11	0	**11**	**0**
2022–23	Tottenham H	4	0		
2022–23	*Sevilla*	17	2	**31**	**3**
2023–24	Tottenham H	11	0		
2024–25	Tottenham H	0	0	**24**	**0**
2024–25	*Girona*	25	3	**25**	**3**

GRAY, Archie (F) 72 0
H: 6 0 W: 11 09 b.Durham 12-3-06
Internationals: England U16, U17, U19, U20, U21.

2021–22	Leeds U	0	0		
2022–23	Leeds U	0	0		
2023–24	Leeds U	44	0	**44**	**0**
2024–25	Tottenham H	28	0	**28**	**0**

HARDY, Malachi (D) 0 0
H: 6 2 W: 12 04 b.Watford 10-3-08
Internationals: England U16, U17.

2024–25	Tottenham H	0	0		

HOJBJERG, Pierre (M) 340 16
H: 6 1 W: 12 11 b.Copenhagen 5-8-95
Internationals: Denmark U16, U17, U19, U21, Full caps.
From Brondby.

2012–13	Bayern Munich	2	0		
2013–14	Bayern Munich	7	0		
2014–15	Bayern Munich	8	0		
2014–15	*Augsburg*	16	2	**16**	**2**
2015–16	Bayern Munich	0	0	**17**	**0**
2015–16	*Schalke 04*	23	0	**23**	**0**
2016–17	Southampton	22	0		
2017–18	Southampton	23	0		
2018–19	Southampton	31	4		
2019–20	Southampton	33	0	**109**	**4**
2020–21	Tottenham H	38	2		
2021–22	Tottenham H	36	2		
2022–23	Tottenham H	35	4		
2023–24	Tottenham H	36	0		
2024–25	Tottenham H	0	0	**145**	**8**
2024–25	*Marseille*	30	2	**30**	**2**

JOHNSON, Brennan (M) 196 50
H: 5 10 W: 11 07 b.Nottingham 23-5-01
Internationals: England U16, U17. Wales U19, U21, Full caps.

2019–20	Nottingham F	4	0		
2020–21	Nottingham F	0	0		
2020–21	*Lincoln C*	40	10	**40**	**10**
2021–22	Nottingham F	46	16		
2022–23	Nottingham F	38	8		
2023–24	Nottingham F	3	0	**91**	**24**
2023–24	Tottenham H	32	5		
2024–25	Tottenham H	33	11	**65**	**16**

KEELEY, Josh (G) 37 0
H: 6 1 W: 12 06 b.Dunboyne 17-5-03
Internationals: Republic of Ireland U18, U21.

2020	St Patrick's Ath	0	0		
2021	St Patrick's Ath	1	0		
2022	St Patrick's Ath	0	0	**1**	**0**
2022–23	Tottenham H	0	0		
2023–24	Tottenham H	0	0		
2024–25	Tottenham H	0	0		
2024–25	*Leyton Orient*	36	0	**36**	**0**

KING, Maeson (D) 0 0
H: 5 9 W: 10 03 b.Basildon 9-9-05

2024–25	Tottenham H	0	0		

KINSKY, Antonin (G) 92 0
H: 6 3 W: 12 08 b. 13-3-03
Internationals: Czech Republic U16, U17, U19, U20, U21.

2019–20	Dukla Prague	1	0		
2020–21	Dukla Prague	5	0	**6**	**0**
2021–22	Slavia Prague	0	0		
2021–22	*Vyskov*	13	0		
2022–23	Slavia Prague	0	0		
2022–23	*Vyskov*	30	0	**43**	**0**
2023–24	Slavia Prague	0	0		
2023–24	*Pardubice*	18	0	**18**	**0**
2024–25	Slavia Prague	19	0	**19**	**0**
2024–25	Tottenham H	6	0	**6**	**0**

KULUSEVSKI, Dejan (F) 210 37
H: 6 1 W: 11 11 b.Stockholm 25-4-00
Internationals: Macedonia U17. Sweden U17, U19, U21, Full caps.

2018–19	Atalanta	3	0		
2019–20	Atalanta	0	0	**3**	**0**
2019–20	*Parma*	17	4		
2019–20	Juventus	0	0		
2019–20	*Parma*	19	6	**36**	**10**
2020–21	Juventus	35	4		
2021–22	Juventus	20	1	**55**	**5**
2021–22	*Tottenham H*	18	5		
2022–23	Tottenham H	30	2		
2023–24	Tottenham H	36	8		
2024–25	Tottenham H	32	7	**116**	**22**

KYEREMATEN, Rio (M) 0 0
H: 5 9 W: 10 10 b.London 9-6-05
Internationals: England U17, U18.

2024–25	Tottenham H	0	0		

LANKSHEAR, Will (F) 14 0
H: 6 2 W: 12 08 b.Welwyn Garden City 20-4-05
Internationals: England U19, U20.

2022–23	Tottenham H	0	0		
2023–24	Tottenham H	0	0		
2024–25	Tottenham H	3	0	**3**	**0**
2024–25	*WBA*	11	0	**11**	**0**

MADDISON, James (M) 318 78
H: 5 9 W: 11 07 b.Coventry 23-11-96
Internationals: England U21, Full caps.

2013–14	Coventry C	0	0		
2014–15	Coventry C	12	2		
2015–16	Norwich C	0	0		
2015–16	*Coventry C*	23	3	**35**	**5**
2016–17	Norwich C	3	1		
2016–17	*Aberdeen*	14	2	**14**	**2**
2017–18	Norwich C	44	14	**47**	**15**
2018–19	Leicester C	36	7		
2019–20	Leicester C	31	6		
2020–21	Leicester C	31	8		

2021–22	Leicester C	35	12		
2022–23	Leicester C	30	10	**163**	**43**
2023–24	Tottenham H	28	4		
2024–25	Tottenham H	31	9	**59**	**13**

MOORE, Mikey (M) **12** **0**
H: 5 11 W: 11 11 b.London 11-8-07
Internationals: England U16, U17, U19.

2023–24	Tottenham H	2	0		
2024–25	Tottenham H	10	0	**12**	**0**

ODOBERT, Wilson (F) **78** **9**
H: 6 0 W: 11 11 b.Meaux 28-11-04
Internationals: France U16, U18, U19, U20, U21, U23.

2022–23	Troyes	32	4	**32**	**4**
2023–24	Burnley	29	3		
2024–25	Burnley	1	1	**30**	**4**
2024–25	Tottenham H	16	1	**16**	**1**

OLUSESI, Callum (M) **0** **0**
H: 5 9 W: 10 03 b.London 11-3-07
Internationals: England U16, U17, U18.

2024–25	Tottenham H	0	0		

PHILLIPS, Ashley (D) **61** **0**
H: 6 4 W: 12 00 b.Salford 26-6-05
Internationals: Wales U16. England U17, U18, U19, U20.

2021–22	Blackburn R	0	0		
2022–23	Blackburn R	8	0	**8**	**0**
2023–24	Tottenham H	0	0		
2023–24	*Plymouth Arg*	18	0	**18**	**0**
2024–25	Tottenham H	0	0		
2024–25	*Stoke C*	35	0	**35**	**0**

PORRO, Pedro (D) **205** **23**
H: 5 9 W: 11 03 b.Don Benito 13-9-99
Internationals: Spain U21, Full caps.

2017–18	Peralada	5	3	**5**	**3**
2017–18	Girona	5	3		
2018–19	Girona	32	0	**37**	**3**
2019–20	Manchester C	0	0		
2019–20	*Real Valladolid*	13	0	**13**	**0**
2020–21	Manchester C	0	0		
2020–21	*Sporting Lisbon*	30	3		
2021–22	Manchester C	0	0		
2021–22	*Sporting Lisbon*	23	4		
2022–23	Sporting Lisbon	14	2	**67**	**9**
2022–23	*Tottenham H*	15	3		
2023–24	Tottenham H	35	3		
2024–25	Tottenham H	33	2	**83**	**8**

REGUILON, Sergio (D) **176** **12**
H: 5 11 W: 10 08 b.Madrid 16-12-96
Internationals: Spain U21, Full caps.

2015–16	Real Madrid	0	0		
2015–16	*Logrones*	9	0		
2016–17	Real Madrid	0	0		
2016–17	*Logrones*	30	8	**39**	**8**
2017–18	Real Madrid	0	0		
2018–19	Real Madrid	14	0		
2019–20	Real Madrid	0	0	**14**	**0**
2019–20	*Sevilla*	31	2		
2020–21	Sevilla	0	0	**31**	**2**
2020–21	Tottenham H	27	0		
2021–22	Tottenham H	25	2		
2022–23	Tottenham H	0	0		
2022–23	*Atletico Madrid*	11	0	**11**	**0**
2023–24	Tottenham H	0	0		
2023–24	*Manchester U*	9	0	**9**	**0**
2023–24	*Brentford*	16	0	**16**	**0**
2024–25	Tottenham H	4	0	**56**	**2**

RICHARLISON, de Andrade (F) **309** **82**
H: 5 10 W: 11 03 b.Nova Venecia 10-5-97
Internationals: Brazil U20, Full caps.

2015	America Mineiro	24	9	**24**	**9**
2016	Fluminense	28	4		
2017	Fluminense	14	5	**42**	**9**
2017–18	Watford	38	5	**38**	**5**
2018–19	Everton	35	13		
2019–20	Everton	36	13		
2020–21	Everton	34	7		
2021–22	Everton	30	10	**135**	**43**
2022–23	Tottenham H	27	1		
2023–24	Tottenham H	28	11		
2024–25	Tottenham H	15	4	**70**	**16**

ROMERO, Cristian (D) **204** **12**
H: 6 1 W: 12 06 b.Cordoba 27-4-98
Internationals: Argentina U20, Full caps.

2016–17	Belgrano	13	0		
2017–18	Belgrano	3	0	**16**	**0**
2018–19	Genoa	27	2		
2019–20	Juventus	0	0		
2019–20	*Genoa*	30	1	**57**	**3**
2020–21	Juventus	0	0		
2020–21	*Atalanta*	31	2		
2021–22	Atalanta	0	0	**31**	**2**
2021–22	*Tottenham H*	22	1		
2022–23	Tottenham H	27	0		
2023–24	Tottenham H	33	5		
2024–25	Tottenham H	18	1	**100**	**7**

SARR, Pape (M) **136** **10**
H: 5 11 W: 12 00 b.Thiaroye 14-9-02
Internationals: Senegal U17, Full caps.

2020–21	Metz	22	3		
2021–22	Metz	3	0		
2021–22	Tottenham H	0	0		
2021–22	*Metz*	30	1	**55**	**4**
2022–23	Tottenham H	11	0		
2023–24	Tottenham H	34	3		
2024–25	Tottenham H	36	3	**81**	**6**

SCARLETT, Dane (F) **75** **8**
H: 6 1 W: 12 00 b.Hillingdon 24-3-04
Internationals: England U16, U19, U20, U21.

2020–21	Tottenham H	1	0		
2021–22	Tottenham H	1	0		
2022–23	Tottenham H	0	0		
2022–23	*Portsmouth*	34	4	**34**	**4**
2023–24	Tottenham H	4	0		
2023–24	*Ipswich T*	12	0	**12**	**0**
2024–25	Tottenham H	3	0	**9**	**0**
2024–25	*Oxford U*	20	4	**20**	**4**

SOLANKE, Dominic (F) **272** **89**
H: 6 1 W: 11 11 b.Reading 14-9-97
Internationals: England U16, U17, U18, U19, U20, U21, Full caps.

2014–15	Chelsea	0	0		
2015–16	Chelsea	0	0		
2015–16	*Vitesse*	25	7	**25**	**7**
2016–17	Chelsea	0	0		
2017–18	Liverpool	21	1		
2018–19	Liverpool	0	0	**21**	**1**
2018–19	Bournemouth	10	0		
2019–20	Bournemouth	32	3		
2020–21	Bournemouth	40	15		
2021–22	Bournemouth	46	29		
2022–23	Bournemouth	33	6		
2023–24	Bournemouth	38	19	**199**	**72**
2024–25	Tottenham H	27	9	**27**	**9**

SOLOMON, Manor (F) **201** **38**
H: 5 7 W: 9 13 b.Saba 24-7-99
Internationals: Israel U16, U17, U18, U19, U21, Full caps.

2016–17	Maccabi Petah Tikva	23	2		
2017–18	Maccabi Petah Tikva	33	4		
2018–19	Maccabi Petah Tikva	12	2	**68**	**8**
2018–19	Shakhtar Donetsk	11	0		
2019–20	Shakhtar Donetsk	20	3		
2020–21	Shakhtar Donetsk	23	9		
2021–22	Shakhtar Donetsk	16	4		
2022–23	Shakhtar Donetsk	0	0	**70**	**16**
2022–23	*Fulham*	19	4	**19**	**4**
2023–24	Tottenham H	5	0		
2024–25	Tottenham H	0	0	**5**	**0**
2024–25	*Leeds U*	39	10	**39**	**10**

SON, Heung-Min (F) **468** **168**
H: 6 0 W: 12 00 b.Chuncheon 8-7-92
Internationals: South Korea U17, U23, Full caps.

2010–11	Hamburger SV	13	3		
2011–12	Hamburger SV	27	5		
2012–13	Hamburger SV	33	12	**73**	**20**
2013–14	Bayer Leverkusen	31	10		
2014–15	Bayer Leverkusen	30	11		
2015–16	Bayer Leverkusen	1	0	**62**	**21**
2015–16	Tottenham H	28	4		
2016–17	Tottenham H	34	14		
2017–18	Tottenham H	37	12		
2018–19	Tottenham H	31	12		
2019–20	Tottenham H	30	11		
2020–21	Tottenham H	37	17		
2021–22	Tottenham H	35	23		
2022–23	Tottenham H	36	10		
2023–24	Tottenham H	35	17		
2024–25	Tottenham H	30	7	**333**	**127**

SPENCE, Djed (D) **162** **5**
H: 6 0 W: 11 03 b.London 9-8-00
Internationals: England U21.
From Fulham.

2018–19	Middlesbrough	0	0		
2019–20	Middlesbrough	22	1		
2020–21	Middlesbrough	38	1		
2021–22	Middlesbrough	3	0	**63**	**2**
2021–22	*Nottingham F*	39	2	**39**	**2**
2022–23	Tottenham H	4	0		
2022–23	*Rennes*	8	0	**8**	**0**
2023–24	Tottenham H	0	0		
2023–24	*Leeds U*	7	0	**7**	**0**
2023–24	*Genoa*	16	0	**16**	**0**
2024–25	Tottenham H	25	1	**29**	**1**

TEL, Mathys (F) **80** **14**
H: 6 0 W: 12 02 b.Sarcelles 27-4-05
Internationals: France U17, U18, U19, U21.

2021–22	Rennes	7	0	**7**	**0**
2022–23	Bayern Munich	22	5		
2023–24	Bayern Munich	30	7		
2024–25	Bayern Munich	8	0	**60**	**12**

On loan from Bayern Munich.

2024–25	Tottenham H	13	2	**13**	**2**

UDOGIE, Iyenoma (D) **127** **10**
H: 6 2 W: 11 07 b.Verona 28-11-02
Internationals: Italy U16, U17, U18, U19, U21, Full caps.

2020–21	Verona	6	0		
2021–22	Verona	0	0	**6**	**0**
2021–22	*Udinese*	35	5		
2022–23	Tottenham H	0	0		
2022–23	*Udinese*	33	3	**68**	**8**
2023–24	Tottenham H	28	2		
2024–25	Tottenham H	25	0	**53**	**2**

VAN DE VEN, Mickey (D) **123** **6**
H: 6 4 W: 14 00 b.Wormer 19-4-01
Internationals: Netherlands U21, Full caps.

2019–20	Volendam	19	0		
2020–21	Volendam	26	2	**45**	**2**
2021–22	VfL Wolfsburg	5	0		
2022–23	VfL Wolfsburg	33	1	**38**	**1**
2023–24	Tottenham H	27	3		
2024–25	Tottenham H	13	0	**40**	**3**

VELIZ, Alejo (F) **94** **19**
H: 6 1 W: 12 02 b.Bernardo de Irigoyen 19-9-03
Internationals: Argentina U20.

2021	Rosario Central	4	0		
2022	Rosario Central	26	6		
2023	Rosario Central	23	11	**53**	**17**
2023–24	Tottenham H	8	1		
2023–24	*Sevilla*	6	0	**6**	**0**
2024–25	Tottenham H	0	0	**8**	**1**
2024–25	*Espanyol*	27	1	**27**	**1**

VICARIO, Guglielmo (G) **277** **0**
H: 6 4 W: 13 01 b.Udine 7-10-96
Internationals: Italy Full caps.

2013–14	Udinese	0	0		
2014–15	Udinese	0	0		
2014–15	*Fontanafredda*	30	0	**30**	**0**
2015–16	Venezia	36	0		
2016–17	Venezia	2	0		
2017–18	Venezia	7	0		
2018–19	Venezia	32	0		
2019–20	Venezia	0	0	**77**	**0**
2019–20	*Perugia*	35	0	**35**	**0**
2020–21	Cagliari	4	0		
2021–22	Cagliari	0	0	**4**	**0**
2021–22	*Empoli*	38	0		
2022–23	Empoli	31	0	**69**	**0**
2023–24	Tottenham H	38	0		
2024–25	Tottenham H	24	0	**62**	**0**

WERNER, Timo (F) **344** **114**
H: 5 11 W: 11 11 b.Stuttgart 6-3-96
Internationals: Germany U16, U17, U18, U19, U21, Full caps.

2013–14	VfB Stuttgart	30	4		
2014–15	VfB Stuttgart	32	3		
2015–16	VfB Stuttgart	33	6		
2016–17	VfB Stuttgart	31	21		
2017–18	VfB Stuttgart	32	13		
2018–19	VfB Stuttgart	30	16		
2019–20	VfB Stuttgart	34	28	**222**	**91**
2020–21	Chelsea	35	6		
2021–22	Chelsea	21	4	**56**	**10**
2022–23	RB Leipzig	27	9		
2023–24	RB Leipzig	8	2		
2023–24	*Tottenham H*	13	2		
2024–25	RB Leipzig	0	0	**35**	**11**

On loan from RB Leipzig.

2024–25	Tottenham H	18	0	**31**	**2**

WHITEMAN, Alfie (G) **38** **0**
H: 6 2 W: 13 03 b.London 2-10-98
Internationals: England U16, U17, U18, U19.

2016–17	Tottenham H	0	0		
2017–18	Tottenham H	0	0		
2018–19	Tottenham H	0	0		
2019–20	Tottenham H	0	0		
2020–21	Tottenham H	0	0		
2021	*Degerfors*	13	0		
2021–22	Tottenham H	0	0		
2022	*Degerfors*	4	0		
2022–23	Tottenham H	0	0		
2023	*Degerfors*	21	0	**38**	**0**
2023–24	Tottenham H	0	0		
2024–25	Tottenham H	0	0		

WILLIAMS-BARNET, Luca (M) **0** **0**
H: 5 9 W: 10 03 b.Luton 2-10-08
Internationals: England U16, U17.

2024–25	Tottenham H	0	0		

YANG, Min-Hyeok (M) **52** **14**
H: 5 8 W: 9 08 b. 16-4-06
Internationals: South Korea U17, Full caps.

2024	Gangwon	38	12	**38**	**12**
2024–25	Tottenham H	0	0		
2024–25	*QPR*	14	2	**14**	**2**

Players retained or with offer of contract
Adewole, Miracle Adetonmiwa Jimoh; Akhamrich, Yusuf; Archer, Samual Cyril; Arganese-McDermott, Pele; Baptiste, Archie; Batty, Daniel Jake; Beggs, Jamel Jordan Fred; Black, Leo Amarri John-Baptiste; Bloedorn, Carey Brian; Byrne, Harry Luke; Egan-Riley, Roman Jay; Elliott-Parris, Reiss Dennis; Feeney, George James; Gunter Luca Jackson; Hall, Tye Fitz; Hall, Tyrese Shaun; Irow, Oliver; James, Herbie George; Lehane Ellis Anthony Mark; Logan, Calum Reece; Maguire, Aaron Joseph; Moncur, Ronny Alan; Rowswell, James Patrick Lynch;

Russell-Denny, Reiss-Alexander; Thompson, Tynan Torres.

Scholars
Bangura, Samal Junior; Myrtaj, Leon; Thompson, Dylan Warren Edward; Upson, Elijah Richard.

TRANMERE R (84)

DAVIES, Tom (D) **254 8**
H: 5 11 W: 11 00 b.Warrington 18-4-92
From FC United of Manchester.
2014–15 Fleetwood T 0 0
2015–16 Accrington S 32 1 **32 1**
2016–17 Portsmouth 12 0
2017–18 Portsmouth 0 0 **12 0**
2017–18 Coventry C 21 0
2018–19 Coventry C 23 0 **44 0**
2019–20 Bristol R 19 1
2020–21 Bristol R 0 0 **19 1**
2020–21 *Barrow* 12 1 **12 1**
2021–22 Tranmere R 36 1
2022–23 Tranmere R 28 0
2023–24 Tranmere R 37 3
2024–25 Tranmere R 34 1 **135 5**

DAVISON, Joshua (F) **170 31**
H: 5 11 W: 12 06 b.Enfield 16-9-99
From Peterborough U, Enfield T.
2019–20 Charlton Ath 9 1
2020–21 Charlton Ath 0 0
2020–21 *Forest Green R* 20 3 **20 3**
2021–22 Charlton Ath 15 2 **24 3**
2021–22 *Swindon T* 21 9 **21 9**
2022–23 AFC Wimbledon 37 9
2023–24 AFC Wimbledon 36 4 **73 13**
2024–25 Tranmere R 32 3 **32 3**

DENNIS, Kristian (F) **264 68**
H: 5 11 W: 11 00 b.Macclesfield 12-3-90
2007–08 Macclesfield T 1 0
2008–09 Macclesfield T 3 1
2009–10 Macclesfield T 0 0 **4 1**
From Woodley Sports, Mossley, Curzon Ashton, Stockport Co.
2015–16 Chesterfield 0 0
2016–17 Chesterfield 35 8
2017–18 Chesterfield 43 19 **78 27**
2018–19 Notts Co 24 3 **24 3**
2018–19 *Grimsby T* 13 1 **13 1**
From Notts Co.
2020–21 St Mirren 17 3 **17 3**
2021–22 Carlisle U 17 2
2022–23 Carlisle U 44 20 **61 22**
2023–24 Tranmere R 30 2
2024–25 Tranmere R 37 9 **67 11**

DRYSDALE, Declan (D) **71 1**
H: 6 1 W: 10 12 b.Birkenhead 14-11-99
2018–19 Tranmere R 0 0
2018–19 Coventry C 0 0
2019–20 Coventry C 1 0
2020–21 Coventry C 0 0
2020–21 *Gillingham* 10 0 **10 0**
2020–21 *Cambridge U* 13 1 **13 1**
2021–22 Coventry C 0 0 **1 0**
2021–22 *Ross Co* 5 0 **5 0**
2022–23 Newport Co 22 0
2023–24 Newport Co 12 0 **34 0**
2024–25 Tranmere R 8 0 **8 0**

EGAN, Reuben (G) **0 0**
H: 6 4 W: 13 10 b.Ferbane 27-7-05
2024–25 Tranmere R 0 0

FINLEY, Sam (M) **234 13**
H: 5 7 W: 10 10 b.Liverpool 4-8-92
From Southport, Warrington T, The New Saints, AFC Fylde.
2018–19 Accrington S 37 1
2019–20 Accrington S 31 2 **68 3**
2020–21 Fleetwood T 29 3 **29 3**
2021–22 Bristol R 36 5
2022–23 Bristol R 38 0
2023–24 Bristol R 30 0 **104 5**
2024–25 Tranmere R 33 2 **33 2**

HAWKES, Josh (M) **141 24**
H: 6 0 W: 12 08 b.Stockton-on-Tees 28-1-99
2016–17 Hartlepool U 2 0 **2 0**
From Hartlepool U.
2020–21 Sunderland 0 0
2021–22 Sunderland 1 0 **1 0**
2021–22 Tranmere R 35 6
2022–23 Tranmere R 44 10
2023–24 Tranmere R 36 6
2024–25 Tranmere R 23 2 **138 24**

HENDRY, Regan (M) **205 17**
H: 5 10 W: 11 07 b.Edinburgh 21-1-98
Internationals: Scotland U16, U17.
2017–18 Celtic 0 0
2017–18 *Raith R* 11 0
2018–19 Celtic 0 0
2018–19 *Raith R* 4 0
2019–20 Raith R 22 1
2020–21 Raith R 25 3
2021–22 Raith R 0 0 **62 4**
2021–22 Forest Green R 31 3
2022–23 Forest Green R 22 1 **53 4**
2022–23 *Tranmere R* 19 1
2023–24 Tranmere R 45 5
2024–25 Tranmere R 26 3 **90 9**

JENNINGS, Connor (F) **203 32**
H: 6 0 W: 11 05 b.Manchester 21-1-91
Internationals: England C.
2011–12 Scunthorpe U 4 0
2012–13 Scunthorpe U 12 0
2013–14 Scunthorpe U 0 0 **16 0**
From Wrexham.
2018–19 Tranmere R 45 8
2019–20 Tranmere R 29 4
From Stockport Co.
2022–23 Stockport Co 7 0 **7 0**
2022–23 Hartlepool U 18 4 **18 4**
2023–24 Tranmere R 44 12
2024–25 Tranmere R 44 4 **162 28**

McGEE, Luke (G) **279 0**
H: 6 2 W: 12 08 b.Edgware 2-9-95
Internationals: England U17.
2014–15 Tottenham H 0 0
2015–16 Tottenham H 0 0
2016–17 Tottenham H 0 0
2016–17 *Peterborough U* 39 0 **39 0**
2017–18 Portsmouth 44 0
2018–19 Portsmouth 0 0
2019–20 Portsmouth 0 0 **44 0**
2019–20 *Bradford C* 4 0 **4 0**
2020–21 Forest Green R 33 0
2021–22 Forest Green R 46 0
2022–23 Forest Green R 22 0 **101 0**
2022–23 *Derby Co* 0 0
2023–24 Tranmere R 45 0
2024–25 Tranmere R 46 0 **91 0**

MERRIE, Christopher (M) **116 0**
H: 5 11 W: 11 05 b.Liverpool 2-11-98
From Everton.
2017–18 Wigan Ath 0 0
2018–19 Wigan Ath 0 0
2019–20 Wigan Ath 0 0
2020–21 Wigan Ath 26 0
2021–22 Wigan Ath 0 0 **26 0**
2021–22 Tranmere R 15 0
2022–23 Tranmere R 31 0
2023–24 Tranmere R 12 0
2024–25 Tranmere R 32 0 **90 0**

MORRIS, Kieron (M) **360 41**
H: 5 10 W: 11 03 b.Hereford 3-6-94
2012–13 Walsall 0 0
2013–14 Walsall 2 0
2014–15 Walsall 14 2
2015–16 Walsall 33 3
2016–17 Walsall 35 5
2017–18 Walsall 42 3
2018–19 Walsall 17 2 **143 15**
2018–19 *Tranmere R* 14 1
2019–20 Tranmere R 34 2
2020–21 Tranmere R 42 5
2021–22 Tranmere R 37 5
2022–23 Tranmere R 23 3
2023–24 Tranmere R 39 9
2024–25 Tranmere R 28 1 **217 26**

MURPHY, Joe (G) **576 0**
H: 6 2 W: 12 08 b.Dublin 21-8-81
Internationals: Republic of Ireland U21, Full caps.
1999–2000 Tranmere R 21 0
2000–01 Tranmere R 20 0
2001–02 Tranmere R 22 0
2002–03 WBA 2 0
2003–04 WBA 3 0
2004–05 WBA 0 0 **5 0**
2004–05 *Walsall* 25 0
2005–06 Sunderland 0 0
2005–06 *Walsall* 14 0 **39 0**
2006–07 Scunthorpe U 45 0
2007–08 Scunthorpe U 45 0
2008–09 Scunthorpe U 42 0
2009–10 Scunthorpe U 40 0
2010–11 Scunthorpe U 29 0 **201 0**
2011–12 Coventry C 46 0
2012–13 Coventry C 45 0
2013–14 Coventry C 46 0 **137 0**
2014–15 Huddersfield T 2 0
2014–15 *Chesterfield* 0 0
2015–16 Huddersfield T 7 0
2016–17 Huddersfield T 0 0 **9 0**
2016–17 *Bury* 16 0
2017–18 Bury 17 0
2018–19 Bury 46 0 **79 0**
2019–20 Shrewsbury T 4 0 **4 0**
2020–21 Tranmere R 13 0
2021–22 Tranmere R 17 0
2022–23 Tranmere R 7 0
2023–24 Tranmere R 2 0
2024–25 Tranmere R 0 0 **102 0**

NORMAN, Cameron (D) **242 9**
H: 6 2 W: 11 09 b.Norwich 12-10-95
From Norwich C, Concord Rangers, Needham Market, King's Lynn T.
2018–19 Oxford U 7 0 **7 0**
2018–19 Walsall 9 0
2019–20 Walsall 18 0
2020–21 Walsall 35 0 **62 0**
2021–22 Newport Co 46 1
2022–23 Newport Co 46 5 **92 6**
2023–24 Milton Keynes D 40 0 **40 0**
2024–25 Tranmere R 41 3 **41 3**

NORRIS, Luke (F) **394 95**
H: 6 0 W: 13 03 b.Stevenage 3-6-93
2011–12 Brentford 1 0
2012–13 Brentford 0 0
2013–14 Brentford 1 0 **2 0**
2013–14 *Northampton T* 10 4 **10 4**
2013–14 *Dagenham & Red* 19 4 **19 4**
2014–15 Gillingham 37 6
2015–16 Gillingham 33 8 **70 14**
2016–17 Swindon T 39 4
2017–18 Swindon T 35 13 **74 17**
2018–19 Colchester U 34 7
2019–20 Colchester U 32 9
2020–21 Colchester U 17 4 **83 20**
2020–21 Stevenage 23 7
2021–22 Stevenage 43 14
2022–23 Stevenage 38 10 **104 31**
2023–24 Tranmere R 19 4
2024–25 Tranmere R 13 1 **32 5**

O'CONNOR, Lee (D) **189 0**
H: 5 9 W: 11 11 b.Waterford 28-7-00
Internationals: Republic of Ireland U17, U19, U21, Full caps.
From Waterford.
2019–20 Manchester U 0 0
2019–20 Celtic 0 0
2019–20 *Partick Thistle* 4 0 **4 0**
2020–21 Celtic 0 0
2020–21 *Tranmere R* 33 0
2021–22 Celtic 0 0
2021–22 *Tranmere R* 31 0
2022–23 Tranmere R 39 0
2023–24 Tranmere R 40 0
2024–25 Tranmere R 42 0 **185 0**

PATRICK, Omari (F) **200 37**
H: 6 1 W: 12 08 b.Slough 24-5-96
From Kidderminster H.
2018–19 Bradford C 1 0
2018–19 *Yeovil T* 9 1 **9 1**
2019–20 Bradford C 2 0 **3 0**
2019–20 Carlisle U 7 2
2020–21 Carlisle U 37 5
2021–22 Burton Alb 7 0 **7 0**
2021–22 Carlisle U 24 9
2022–23 Carlisle U 32 4 **100 20**
2023–24 Sutton U 35 5 **35 5**
2024–25 Tranmere R 46 11 **46 11**

SAUNDERS, Harvey (F) **154 12**
H: 5 11 W: 11 05 b.Wolverhampton 20-7-97
From Darlington Railway Ath, Bishop Auckland, Durham C, Darlington.
2018–19 Fleetwood T 0 0
2019–20 Fleetwood T 6 0
2020–21 Fleetwood T 21 3 **27 3**
2021–22 Bristol R 21 2
2022–23 Bristol R 12 0 **33 2**
2022–23 Tranmere R 19 3
2023–24 Tranmere R 38 3
2024–25 Tranmere R 37 1 **94 7**

SOLOMON, Sol (F) **14 2**
H: 5 11 W: 11 11 b. 17-3-01
Internationals: Jersey Full caps.
2024–25 Tranmere R 14 2 **14 2**

TAYLOR, Samuel (F) **35 3**
H: 5 10 W: 11 09 b. 23-12-03
2022–23 Tranmere R 4 1
2023–24 Tranmere R 20 2
2024–25 Tranmere R 11 0 **35 3**

TURNBULL, Jordan (D) **396 16**
H: 6 1 W: 11 05 b.Trowbridge 30-10-94
Internationals: England U19, U20.
2014–15 Southampton 0 0
2014–15 *Swindon T* 44 1
2015–16 Southampton 0 0
2015–16 *Swindon T* 42 0 **86 1**
2016–17 Coventry C 36 0
2017–18 Coventry C 0 0 **36 0**
2017–18 *Partick Thistle* 0 0
2017–18 Northampton T 14 0
2018–19 Northampton T 31 0
2019–20 Northampton T 31 5 **76 5**
2020–21 Salford C 42 1
2021–22 Salford C 37 3 **79 4**
2022–23 Tranmere R 39 3
2023–24 Tranmere R 36 2
2024–25 Tranmere R 44 1 **119 6**

WALKER, Brad (M) 248 13
H: 6 1 W: 12 08 b.Billingham 25-4-95
2012–13 Hartlepool U 0 0
2013–14 Hartlepool U 1 0
2014–15 Hartlepool U 28 5
2015–16 Hartlepool U 23 1
2016–17 Hartlepool U 20 1 107 10
2017–18 Crewe Alex 27 1
2018–19 Crewe Alex 1 0 28 1
2019–20 Shrewsbury T 15 0
2020–21 Shrewsbury T 23 1 38 1
2021–22 Port Vale 28 1
2022–23 Port Vale 7 0 35 1
2022–23 Tranmere R 4 0
2023–24 Tranmere R 28 0
2024–25 Tranmere R 8 0 40 0

WILLIAMS, Josh (M) 53 5
H: 5 10 W: 11 09 b. 13-7-04
Internationals: Wales C.
2021–22 Connah's Quay Nomads 3 0
2022–23 Connah's Quay Nomads 20 1
2023–24 Connah's Quay Nomads 28 4 51 5
2024–25 Tranmere R 2 0 2 0

WOOD, Connor (D) 214 2
H: 5 10 W: 12 04 b.Harlow 17-7-96
From Soham Town Rangers, Chesham U.
2016–17 Leicester C 0 0
2017–18 Leicester C 0 0
2018–19 Bradford C 22 1
2019–20 Bradford C 35 0
2020–21 Bradford C 46 1 103 2
2021–22 Leyton Orient 32 0
2022–23 Leyton Orient 0 0 32 0
2022–23 Colchester U 16 0 16 0
2023–24 Walsall 29 0
2024–25 Tranmere R 34 0 63 0

WALSALL (85)

ADOMAH, Albert (F) 682 93
H: 6 0 W: 11 09 b.Lambeth 13-12-87
Internationals: Ghana Full caps.
From Harrow Bor.
2007–08 Barnet 22 5
2008–09 Barnet 45 9
2009–10 Barnet 45 5 112 19
2010–11 Bristol C 46 5
2011–12 Bristol C 45 5
2012–13 Bristol C 40 7 131 17
2013–14 Middlesbrough 42 12
2014–15 Middlesbrough 43 5
2015–16 Middlesbrough 43 6
2016–17 Middlesbrough 2 0 130 23
2016–17 Aston Villa 38 3
2017–18 Aston Villa 39 14
2018–19 Aston Villa 36 4 113 21
2019–20 Nottingham F 24 2 24 2
2019–20 *Cardiff C* 9 0 9 0
2020–21 QPR 34 2
2021–22 QPR 33 2
2022–23 QPR 38 2
2023–24 QPR 16 0 121 6
2024–25 Walsall 42 5 42 5

AHUI, Elicha (D) 54 3
H: 6 0 W: 11 11 b.Nottingham 28-12-03
2020–21 Lincoln C 0 0
2021–22 Lincoln C 0 0
2022–23 Lincoln C 0 0
2023 *Drogheda U* 20 1
2023–24 Lincoln C 0 0
2023–24 *Ayr U* 12 0 12 0
2024 *Drogheda U* 14 1
2024–25 Walsall 0 0
2025 *Drogheda U* 8 1 42 3

ALLEN, Taylor (M) 109 14
H: 5 10 W: 11 05 b.Walsall 16-6-00
From Romulus, Nuneaton Bor.
2019–20 Forest Green R 5 1
2020–21 Forest Green R 5 0
2021–22 Forest Green R 4 0 14 1
2022–23 Walsall 22 0
2023–24 Walsall 28 3
2024–25 Walsall 45 10 95 13

AMANTCHI, Levi (F) 32 3
H: 6 4 W: 13 11 b.Lewisham 26-11-00
From Chesterfield, Workington, Darlington, Blyth Spartans, Redditch U, Potters Bar T, Braintree T, Brackley T, Maidstone U.
2024–25 Bromley 14 0 14 0
2024–25 Walsall 18 3 18 3

BARRETT, Connor (D) 43 0
H: 6 0 W: 12 13 b.Leicester 1-3-02
2024–25 Walsall 43 0 43 0

BARRETT, George (G) 0 0
H: 6 1 W: 12 08 b.Puerto Limon 17-8-02
2022–23 Walsall 0 0
2023–24 Walsall 0 0
2024–25 Walsall 0 0

BENNETT, Cayden (D) 0 0
b. 9-9-06
Internationals: Saint Kitts & Nevis Full caps.
2023–24 Walsall 0 0
2024–25 Walsall 0 0

BROWNE, Rico (D) 0 0
H: 6 2 W: 12 04 b.Manchester 28-12-03
Internationals: St Kitts & Nevis U17.
2023–24 Birmingham C 0 0
2024–25 Walsall 0 0

COMLEY, Brandon (M) 223 4
H: 5 11 W: 11 05 b.Islington 18-11-95
Internationals: Montserrat Full caps.
2014–15 QPR 1 0
2015–16 QPR 0 0
2015–16 *Carlisle U* 12 0 12 0
2016–17 QPR 1 0 2 0
2016–17 Grimsby T 33 0
2017–18 Grimsby T 0 0 33 0
2017–18 Colchester U 38 1
2018–19 Colchester U 13 0
2019–20 Colchester U 24 1 75 2
2020–21 Bolton W 0 0
2021–22 Bolton W 0 0 10 0
2022–23 Walsall 40 1
2023–24 Walsall 33 1
2024–25 Walsall 18 0 91 2

DANIELS, Donervon (D) 265 11
H: 6 1 W: 14 05 b.Montserrat 24-11-93
Internationals: Montserrat Full caps.
2011–12 WBA 0 0
2012–13 WBA 0 0
2012–13 *Tranmere R* 13 1 13 1
2013–14 WBA 0 0
2013–14 *Gillingham* 3 1 3 1
2014–15 WBA 0 0
2014–15 *Blackpool* 19 1
2014–15 *Aberdeen* 9 0 9 0
2015–16 Wigan Ath 42 3
2016–17 Wigan Ath 1 0
2017–18 Wigan Ath 1 0 44 3
2017–18 *Rochdale* 15 0 15 0
2018–19 Blackpool 24 0 43 1
2019–20 Luton T 3 1 3 1
2019–20 *Doncaster R* 10 0 10 0
2020–21 Crewe Alex 15 0
2021–22 Crewe Alex 11 0 26 0
2021–22 Walsall 18 1
2022–23 Walsall 39 2
2023–24 Walsall 35 1
2024–25 Walsall 7 0 99 4

EARING, Jack (M) 94 9
H: 6 0 W: 12 08 b.Bury 21-1-99
2016–17 Bolton W 0 0
2017–18 Bolton W 0 0
2018–19 Bolton W 1 0 1 0
From FC Halifax T.
2021–22 Walsall 45 4
2022–23 Walsall 11 0
2023–24 Walsall 17 3
2024–25 Walsall 20 2 93 9

FARQUHARSON, Priestley (D) 75 5
H: 6 3 W: 13 01 b.Halifax 15-3-97
2020–21 Connah's Quay Nomads 0 0
2020–21 Newport Co 13 0
2021–22 Newport Co 10 0
2022–23 Newport Co 31 4 54 4
2023–24 Walsall 18 1
2024–25 Walsall 3 0 21 1

GORDON, Josh (F) 227 44
H: 5 10 W: 11 00 b.Stoke-on-Trent 19-1-95
From Stafford Rangers.
2017–18 Leicester C 0 0
2018–19 Walsall 37 7
2019–20 Walsall 34 9
2020–21 Walsall 36 5
2021–22 Barrow 36 6
2022–23 Barrow 37 15 73 21
2023–24 Burton Alb 18 0 18 0
2023–24 Walsall 21 1
2024–25 Walsall 8 1 136 23

GORDON, Liam (D) 141 6
H: 6 0 W: 12 00 b.Croyden 15-5-99
Internationals: Guyana Full caps.
From Dagenham & Red.
2020–21 Bolton W 10 0
2021–22 Bolton W 13 0 23 0
2022–23 Walsall 30 1
2023–24 Walsall 44 2
2024–25 Walsall 44 3 118 6

HORNBY, Sam (G) 67 0
H: 6 2 W: 11 11 b.Sutton Coldfield 14-2-95
From Hednesford T, Redditch U.
2015–16 Burton Alb 0 0
2016–17 Burton Alb 0 0
2017–18 Port Vale 11 0
2018–19 Port Vale 0 0 11 0
2019–20 Bradford C 0 0
2020–21 Bradford C 18 0
2021–22 Bradford C 6 0 24 0

2021–22 Colchester U 8 0
2022–23 Colchester U 13 0
2023–24 Colchester U 5 0 26 0
2024–25 Walsall 6 0 6 0

JAMES-TAYLOR, Douglas (F) 73 11
H: 6 1 b.Camden 18-11-01
From Salford C.
2022–23 Stoke C 0 0
2022–23 Stoke C 0 0
2022–23 *Walsall* 22 1
2023–24 Walsall 26 2
2024 *Drogheda U* 14 6
2024–25 Walsall 0 0 48 3
2025 *Drogheda* 11 2 25 8

JELLIS, Jamie (M) 45 5
H: 5 9 W: 11 00 b.Aylesbury 12-1-01
2023–24 Walsall 2 0
2024–25 Walsall 43 5 45 5

JOHNSON, Danny (F) 196 57
H: 5 10 W: 12 13 b.Middlesbrough 28-2-93
From Harrogate T, Billingham Synthonia, Guisborough T.
2014–15 Cardiff C 0 0
2014–15 *Tranmere R* 4 0 4 0
2014–15 *Stevenage* 4 0 4 0
From Gateshead.
2018–19 Motherwell 22 6 22 6
2019–20 Dundee 19 5 19 5
2019–20 Leyton Orient 6 2
2020–21 Leyton Orient 42 17
2021–22 Leyton Orient 0 0 48 19
2021–22 Mansfield T 22 4
2022–23 Mansfield T 8 1 30 5
2022–23 *Walsall* 22 12
2023–24 Walsall 23 5
2024–25 Walsall 24 5 69 22

KILROY, Jenson (G) 0 0
H: 6 2
2024–25 Walsall 0 0

LAKIN, Charlie (M) 151 16
H: 6 0 W: 12 00 b.Solihull 8-5-99
2017–18 Birmingham C 0 0
2018–19 Birmingham C 0 0
2019–20 Birmingham C 0 0
2019–20 *Stevenage* 20 2 20 2
2020–21 Birmingham C 0 0
2020–21 *Ross Co* 19 3 19 3
2021–22 Birmingham C 0 0 10 0
2021–22 Burton Alb 27 1
2022–23 Burton Alb 3 0
2022–23 *Doncaster R* 10 0 10 0
2023–24 Burton Alb 0 0 29 1
2023–24 *AFC Wimbledon* 6 0 6 0
2023–24 *Sutton U* 21 8 21 8
2024–25 Walsall 36 2 36 2

LEYDON, Jaiy (F) 0 0
H: 5 11
2023–24 Walsall 0 0
2024–25 Walsall 0 0

MAHER, Ronan (M) 15 0
H: 5 7 W: 10 06 b.Birmingham 30-12-04
Internationals: Republic of Ireland U19, U21.
2022–23 Walsall 10 0
2023–24 Walsall 3 0
2024–25 Walsall 2 0 15 0

MATT, Jamille (F) 409 102
H: 6 1 W: 11 11 b.Walsall 20-10-89
From Sutton Coldfield T, Kidderminster H.
2012–13 Fleetwood T 14 3
2013–14 Fleetwood T 25 8
2014–15 Fleetwood T 0 0
2015–16 Fleetwood T 17 3 56 14
2015–16 *Stevenage* 8 1 8 1
2015–16 *Plymouth Arg* 11 5 11 5
2016–17 Blackpool 32 3
2017–18 Blackpool 0 0 32 3
2017–18 Grimsby T 34 4 34 4
2018–19 Newport Co 43 14
2019–20 Newport Co 33 6 76 20
2020–21 Forest Green R 36 16
2021–22 Forest Green R 46 19
2022–23 Forest Green R 16 1 98 36
2022–23 Walsall 13 2
2023–24 Walsall 38 5
2024–25 Walsall 43 12 94 19

McENTEE, Oisin (D) 89 5
H: 6 4 W: 12 04 b.New York 5-1-01
Internationals: Republic of Ireland U17, U18, U19, U21.
2020–21 Newcastle U 0 0
2021–22 Newcastle U 0 0
2021–22 *Greenock Morton* 25 1 25 1
2022–23 Walsall 13 0
2023–24 Walsall 20 4
2024–25 Walsall 31 0 64 4

OKAGBUE, David (D) 74 3
H: 6 0 W: 12 04 b. 5-10-03
Internationals: Republic of Ireland U19, U21.
From St Kevin's Boys.
2022–23 Stoke C 0 0

Season	Club				
2023–24	Stoke C	0	0		
2023–24	*Walsall*	30	1		
2024–25	Walsall	44	2	74	3

SIMKIN, Tommy (G)   42   0
H: 6 3 W: 12 13 b.Walsall 8-12-04
Internationals: England U18, U20.

Season	Club				
2022–23	Stoke C	0	0		
2023–24	Stoke C	1	0	1	0
2023–24	*Forest Green R*	1	0	1	0
2024–25	Walsall	40	0	40	0

STIRK, Ryan (M)   115   6
H: 5 10 W: 11 11 b.Birmingham 25-9-00
Internationals: Wales U17, U19, U21.

Season	Club				
2019–20	Birmingham C	0	0		
2020–21	Birmingham C	2	0		
2021–22	Birmingham C	0	0		
2021–22	*Mansfield T*	31	2	31	2
2022–23	Birmingham C	1	0	3	0
2023–24	Walsall	37	3		
2024–25	Walsall	44	1	81	4

THOMAS, Dylan (M)   0   0
H: 5 10 W: 11 07 b.10-12-06

Season	Club				
2023–24	Walsall	0	0		
2024–25	Walsall	0	0		

WEIR, Evan (D)   121   9
H: 6 1 W: 13 03 b.Ratoath 16-4-02

Season	Club				
2020	UCD	16	0		
2021	UCD	21	0	37	0
2022	Drogheda U	27	4		
2023	Drogheda U	24	1		
2024	Drogheda U	19	4	70	9
2024–25	Walsall	14	0	14	0

WILLIAMS, Harry (D)   44   3
H: 6 5 W: 12 00 b. 15-8-02

Season	Club				
2023–24	Walsall	14	0		
2024–25	Walsall	30	3	44	3

WRAGG, Charlie (F)   0   0
H: 5 9

Season	Club				
2023–24	Walsall	0	0		
2024–25	Walsall	0	0		

Players retained or with offer of contract
Taylor, Douglas Edward James.

Scholars
Barber, Harrison Simon; Beckford, Cailen Nathan; Bennett, Cayden Joshua; Etheridge, William Jacob; Kilroy, Jenson Michael; Leydon, Jaiy Anthony; Makavore, Paul Nyakeh; Oben, McLloyd Ayuk; Owen, Thomas Nigel; Pawlowski, Jakub Krzysztof; Preece, Jackson Daniel; Roberts, Marley John Craig; Straw, Stanley Thomas; Teesdale, Finley Richard; Webb, Louie Keith; Wilkes, Kobe Louis; Wragg, Charles Josiah.

WATFORD (86)

ABANKWAH, James (D)   49   0
b.Dublin 16-1-04
Internationals: Republic of Ireland U16, U18, U19, U21.

Season	Club				
2021	St Patrick's Ath	9	0		
2021–22	Udinese	0	0		
2022	*St Patrick's Ath*	11	0	20	0
2022–23	Udinese	2	0		
2023–24	*Charlton Ath*	2	0	2	0
2024–25	Udinese	6	0	8	0
	On loan from Udinese.				
2024–25	Watford	19	0	19	0

ADU-POKU, Michael (F)   2   0
H: 5 9 W: 10 08 b.Hackney 22-9-05

Season	Club				
2022–23	Watford	1	0		
2023–24	Watford	0	0		
2024–25	Watford	1	0	2	0

AKOMEAH, Travis (D)   0   0
b. 1-6-06
Internationals: England U17, U18.

Season	Club				
2024–25	Watford	0	0		

ANDREWS, Ryan (D)   84   6
b.Watford 26-8-04
Internationals: England U20.

Season	Club				
2022–23	Watford	6	0		
2023–24	Watford	40	3		
2024–25	Watford	38	3	84	6

BAAH, Kwadwo (F)   91   9
H: 6 0 W: 11 11 b.Horb am Neckar 27-1-03
Internationals: England U18. Germany U19.

Season	Club				
2019–20	Rochdale	7	0		
2020–21	Rochdale	30	3		
2021–22	Rochdale	0	0	37	3
2021–22	Watford	0	0		
2022–23	Watford	0	0		
2022–23	*Fortuna Dusseldorf*	7	0	7	0
2023–24	Watford	0	0		
2023–24	*Burton Alb*	20	2	20	2
2024–25	Watford	27	4	27	4

BACHMANN, Daniel (G)   163   0
H: 6 3 W: 12 11 b.Vienna 9-7-94
Internationals: Austria U16, U17, U18, U19, U21, Full caps.

Season	Club				
2011–12	Stoke C	0	0		
2012–13	Stoke C	0	0		
2013–14	Stoke C	0	0		
2014–15	Stoke C	0	0		
2015–16	Stoke C	0	0		
2015–16	*Ross Co*	1	0	1	0
2015–16	*Bury*	8	0	8	0
2016–17	Stoke C	0	0		
2017–18	Watford	0	0		
2018–19	Watford	0	0		
2018–19	*Kilmarnock*	25	0	25	0
2019–20	Watford	0	0		
2020–21	Watford	23	0		
2021–22	Watford	12	0		
2022–23	Watford	45	0		
2023–24	Watford	27	0		
2024–25	Watford	22	0	129	0

BAYO, Vakoun (F)   209   60
H: 6 0 W: 11 05 b.Daloa 10-1-97
Internationals: Ivory Coast U23, Full caps.

Season	Club				
2015–16	Etoile du Sahel	2	0		
2016–17	Etoile du Sahel	9	0	11	0
2017–18	DAC Dunajska Streda	9	4		
2018–19	DAC Dunajska Streda	16	10	25	14
2018–19	Celtic	1	0		
2019–20	Celtic	8	2		
2020–21	Celtic	0	0	9	2
2020–21	*Toulouse*	31	10	31	10
2021–22	Gent	3	0	3	0
2021–22	Charleroi	16	11		
2022–23	Watford	24	4		
2022–23	*Charleroi*	10	3	26	14
2023–24	Watford	39	6		
2024–25	Udinese	0	0		
	On loan from Udinese.				
2024–25	Watford	41	10	104	20

BOND, Jonathan (G)   189   0
H: 6 3 W: 13 03 b.Hemel Hempstead 19-5-93
Internationals: Wales U17, U19. England U20, U21.

Season	Club				
2010–11	Watford	0	0		
2011–12	Watford	1	0		
2011–12	*Dagenham & Red*	5	0	5	0
2011–12	*Bury*	6	0	6	0
2012–13	Watford	8	0		
2013–14	Watford	10	0		
2014–15	Watford	3	0		
2015–16	Reading	14	0		
2016–17	Reading	0	0		
2016–17	*Gillingham*	7	0	7	0
2017–18	Reading	0	0	14	0
2017–18	*Peterborough U*	37	0	37	0
2018–19	WBA	0	0		
2019–20	WBA	0	0		
2020–21	WBA	0	0		
2021	LA Galaxy	31	0		
2022	LA Galaxy	34	0		
2023	LA Galaxy	24	0	89	0
2024–25	Watford	9	0	31	0
	Transferred to Houston TX, April 2025.				

CHAKVETADZE, Giorgi (M)   199   16
H: 6 0 W: 12 04 b.Tbilisi 29-8-99
Internationals: Georgia U16, U18, U19, U21, Full caps.

Season	Club				
2016	Dinamo Tbilisi	5	0		
2017	Dinamo Tbilisi	24	5	29	5
2017–18	Gent	19	1		
2018–19	Gent	23	5		
2019–20	Gent	9	0		
2020–21	Gent	3	0		
2021–22	Gent	8	0		
2021–22	*Hamburger SV*	10	1	10	1
2022–23	Gent	0	0	62	6
2022–23	*Slovan Bratislava*	25	1	25	1
2023–24	Watford	34	1		
2024–25	Watford	39	2	73	3

COYNE, Aidan (D)   5   0
b. 16-11-03

Season	Club				
2020–21	Perth Glory	0	0		
2021–22	Perth Glory	5	0	5	0
2022–23	Watford	0	0		
2023–24	Watford	0	0		
2024–25	Watford	0	0		

DELE-BASHIRU, Ayotomiwa (M)   108   10
H: 6 0 W: 10 10 b.Manchester 17-9-99
Internationals: England U16. Nigeria U20, U23.

Season	Club				
2017–18	Manchester C	0	0		
2018–19	Manchester C	0	0		
2019–20	Watford	0	0		
2020–21	Watford	2	0		
2021–22	Watford	0	0		
2021–22	*Reading*	38	4	38	4
2022–23	Watford	6	0		
2023–24	Watford	35	2		
2024–25	Watford	27	4	70	6

DOUMBIA, Mamadou (F)   19   2
b.Bamako 18-2-06
Internationals: Mali U17, Full caps.

Season	Club				
2024–25	Watford	19	2	19	2

DWOMOH, Pierre (M)   58   1
b.Ghent 21-6-04
Internationals: Belgium U17, U18, U20, U21.

Season	Club				
2020–21	Genk	2	0	2	0
2021–22	Antwerp	9	0		
2022–23	Antwerp	0	0		
2022–23	Braga	0	0		
2022–23	*Oostende*	8	0	8	0
2023–24	Antwerp	9	0	9	0
2023–24	*RWD Molenbeek*	30	1	30	1
2024–25	Watford	9	0	9	0

EAMES, Albert (D)   1   0
b. 20-9-05

Season	Club				
2023–24	Watford	1	0		
2024–25	Watford	0	0	1	0

EBOSELE, Festy (D)   104   3
H: 5 11 W: 10 01 b.Wexford 2-8-02
Internationals: Republic of Ireland U16, U17, U19, U21, Full caps.
From Bray W.

Season	Club				
2020–21	Derby Co	3	0		
2021–22	Derby Co	35	2	38	2
2022–23	Udinese	17	0		
2023–24	Udinese	31	0		
2024–25	Udinese	0	0	48	0
	On loan from Udinese.				
2024–25	Watford	18	1	18	1
	Transferred to Basaksehir, January 2025.				

INCE, Tom (M)   478   99
H: 5 10 W: 10 06 b.Stockport 30-1-92
Internationals: England U17, U19, U21.

Season	Club				
2009–10	Liverpool	0	0		
2010–11	Liverpool	0	0		
2010–11	*Notts Co*	6	2	6	2
2011–12	Blackpool	33	6		
2012–13	Blackpool	44	18		
2013–14	Blackpool	23	7	100	31
2013–14	*Crystal Palace*	8	1	8	1
2014–15	*Hull C*	7	0	7	0
2014–15	*Nottingham F*	6	0	6	0
2014–15	Derby Co	18	11		
2015–16	Derby Co	42	12		
2016–17	Derby Co	45	14	105	37
2017–18	Huddersfield T	33	2	33	2
2018–19	Stoke C	38	6		
2019–20	Stoke C	38	3		
2020–21	Stoke C	7	0		
2020–21	*Luton T*	7	0	7	0
2021–22	Stoke C	11	3	94	12
2021–22	Reading	15	2		
2022–23	Reading	38	9	53	11
2023–24	Watford	27	2		
2024–25	Watford	32	1	59	3

KAYEMBE, Edo (M)   186   17
H: 6 0 W: 12 02 b.Kananga 3-6-98
Internationals: DR Congo U23, Full caps.

Season	Club				
2017–18	Anderlecht	1	0		
2018–19	Anderlecht	12	0		
2019–20	Anderlecht	18	0		
2020–21	Anderlecht	2	0	33	0
2020–21	Eupen	23	0		
2021–22	Eupen	17	4	40	4
2021–22	Watford	13	0		
2022–23	Watford	21	0		
2023–24	Watford	35	5		
2024–25	Watford	44	8	113	13

KAYKY ALMEIDA, da Silva (D)   0   0
H: 6 1 b. 1-5-05
Internationals: Brazil U20.

Season	Club				
2024	Fluminense	0	0		
2024–25	Watford	0	0		
	Transferred to Fluminense, January 2025.				

KEBEN, Kevin (D)   25   0
b.Bertoua 26-1-04
Internationals: Cameroon U23.

Season	Club				
2020–21	Toulouse	0	0		
2021–22	Toulouse	0	0		
2022–23	Toulouse	11	0		
2023–24	Toulouse	8	0	19	0
2024–25	Watford	6	0	6	0

LAROUCI, Yasser (D)   92   1
H: 5 9 W: 10 10 b.El Oued 1-1-01
Internationals: France U21. Algeria Full caps.
From Le Havre.

Season	Club				
2019–20	Liverpool	0	0		
2020–21	Liverpool	0	0		
2021–22	Troyes	12	0		
2022–23	Troyes	30	1		
2023–24	Troyes	0	0		
2023–24	*Sheffield U*	11	0	11	0
2024–25	Troyes	0	0	42	1
	On loan from Troyes.				
2024–25	Watford	39	0	39	0

LIVERMORE, Jake (M) 445 22
H: 5 11 W: 12 00 b.Enfield 14-11-89
Internationals: England Full caps.

2006–07	Tottenham H	0	0		
2007–08	Tottenham H	0	0		
2007–08	*Milton Keynes D*	5	0	**5**	**0**
2008–09	Tottenham H	0	0		
2008–09	*Crewe Alex*	0	0		
2009–10	Tottenham H	1	0		
2009–10	*Derby Co*	16	1	**16**	**1**
2009–10	*Peterborough U*	9	1	**9**	**1**
2010–11	Tottenham H	0	0		
2010–11	*Ipswich T*	12	0	**12**	**0**
2010–11	*Leeds U*	5	0	**5**	**0**
2011–12	Tottenham H	24	0		
2012–13	Tottenham H	11	0		
2013–14	Tottenham H	0	0	**36**	**0**
2013–14	*Hull C*	36	3		
2014–15	Hull C	35	1		
2015–16	Hull C	34	4		
2016–17	Hull C	21	1	**126**	**9**
2016–17	WBA	16	0		
2017–18	WBA	34	2		
2018–19	WBA	39	2		
2019–20	WBA	45	3		
2020–21	WBA	18	0		
2021–22	WBA	37	0		
2022–23	WBA	17	1	**206**	**8**
2023–24	Watford	30	3		
2024–25	Watford	0	0	**30**	**3**

LOUZA, Imran (M) 161 18
H: 5 10 W: 10 03 b.Nantes 1-5-99
Internationals: France U20, U21. Morocco U20, Full caps.

2017–18	Nantes	0	0		
2018–19	Nantes	1	0		
2019–20	Nantes	24	2		
2020–21	Nantes	33	7	**58**	**9**
2021–22	Watford	20	0		
2022–23	Watford	21	5		
2023–24	Watford	15	1		
2023–24	*Lorient*	14	1	**14**	**1**
2024–25	Watford	33	2	**89**	**8**

MARRIOTT, Alfie (G) 0 0
b.Watford 26-3-04

2024–25	Watford	0	0		

MASSIAH-EDWARDS, Zavier (M) 5 0
b. 16-1-07

2023–24	Watford	1	0		
2024–25	Watford	4	0	**5**	**0**

MORRIS, James (D) 42 0
H: 5 10 b.Portsmouth 23-11-01
From Southampton.

2021–22	Watford	0	0		
2022–23	Watford	12	0		
2023–24	Watford	12	0		
2024–25	Watford	18	0	**42**	**0**

MOULTON, Jai-Dea (M) 0 0
b. 29-1-08

2024–25	Watford	0	0		

NABIZADA, Amin (F) 1 0
b.London 21-6-07
Internationals: England U18.

2023–24	Watford	0	0		
2024–25	Watford	1	0	**1**	**0**

NGAKIA, Jeremy (D) 103 1
H: 6 0 W: 11 03 b.Deptford 7-9-00

2019–20	West Ham U	5	0	**5**	**0**
2020–21	Watford	25	0		
2021–22	Watford	16	0		
2022–23	Watford	14	0		
2023–24	Watford	14	0		
2024–25	Watford	29	1	**98**	**1**

OGBONNA, Angelo (D) 420 9
H: 6 3 W: 13 08 b.Cassino 23-5-88
Internationals: Italy U21, Full caps.

2006–07	Torino	4	0		
2007–08	Torino	0	0		
2007–08	*Crotone*	22	0	**22**	**0**
2008–09	Torino	19	0		
2009–10	Torino	31	1		
2010–11	Torino	35	0		
2011–12	Torino	39	0		
2012–13	Torino	22	0	**150**	**1**
2013–14	Juventus	16	0		
2014–15	Juventus	25	0	**41**	**0**
2015–16	West Ham U	28	0		
2016–17	West Ham U	20	0		
2017–18	West Ham U	32	1		
2018–19	West Ham U	24	1		
2019–20	West Ham U	31	2		
2020–21	West Ham U	28	3		
2021–22	West Ham U	11	1		
2022–23	West Ham U	16	0		
2023–24	West Ham U	11	0	**201**	**8**
2024–25	Watford	6	0	**6**	**0**

POLLOCK, Matthew (D) 161 8
H: 6 3 W: 12 08 b.Redhill 28-9-01

2018–19	Grimsby T	2	0		
2019–20	Grimsby T	19	0		
2020–21	Grimsby T	25	3	**46**	**3**
2021–22	Watford	0	0		
2021–22	*Cheltenham T*	34	1	**34**	**1**
2022–23	Watford	3	0		
2022–23	*Aberdeen*	15	2	**15**	**2**
2023–24	Watford	18	0		
2024–25	Watford	45	2	**66**	**2**

PORTEOUS, Ryan (M) 209 19
H: 6 1 W: 10 10 b.Dalkeith 1-3-99
Internationals: Scotland U19, U20, U21, Full caps.

2016–17	Hibernian	0	0		
2016–17	*FC Edinburgh*	23	3	**23**	**3**
2017–18	Hibernian	6	1		
2018–19	Hibernian	16	3		
2019–20	Hibernian	14	1		
2020–21	Hibernian	34	1		
2021–22	Hibernian	29	2		
2022–23	Hibernian	0	0	**99**	**8**
2022–23	Watford	17	2		
2023–24	Watford	37	3		
2024–25	Watford	22	2	**76**	**7**
2024–25	*Preston NE*	11	1	**11**	**1**

RAJOVIC, Mileta (F) 122 38
H: 6 4 b. 17-7-99
From B.93.

2018–19	HB Koge	1	0	**1**	**0**
2019–20	Roskilde	18	6		
2020–21	Roskilde	0	0	**18**	**6**
2021–22	Naestved IF	15	9	**15**	**9**
2023	Kalmar	20	7	**20**	**7**
2023–24	Watford	41	10		
2024–25	Watford	3	1	**44**	**11**
2024–25	*Brondby*	24	5	**24**	**5**

RAMIREZ-ESPAIN, Leo (M) 0 0
b. 2-10-06

2023–24	Watford	0	0		
2024–25	Watford	0	0		

ROBERTS, Myles (G) 19 0
H: 6 1 W: 12 04 b.Reading 9-12-01
From Reading.

2020–21	Watford	0	0		
2021–22	Watford	0	0		
2022–23	Watford	0	0		
2023–24	Watford	0	0		
2024–25	Watford	0	0		
2024–25	*Partick Thistle*	19	0	**19**	**0**
2024–25	*Bristol R*	0	0		

SANGHRAJKA, Amar (M) 0 0
b. 23-10-06

2024–25	Watford	0	0		

SELVIK, Egil (G) 166 0
b. 30-7-97
Internationals: Norway U19, Full caps.

2017	Sandnes Ulf	3	0		
2018	Sandnes Ulf	0	0	**3**	**0**
2018	*Nest-Sotra*	29	0	**29**	**0**
2019	Odd	0	0		
2020	Odd	1	0	**1**	**0**
2021	Haugesund	29	0		
2022	Haugesund	30	0		
2023	Haugesund	29	0		
2024	Haugesund	29	0	**117**	**0**
2024–25	Watford	16	0	**16**	**0**

SEMA, Ken (M) 331 36
H: 5 11 W: 11 03 b.Norrkoping 30-9-93
Internationals: Sweden U23, Full caps.

2013	IFK Norrkoping	0	0		
2013	*IF Sylvia*	22	4	**22**	**4**
2014	Ljungskile	30	7		
2015	Ljungskile	30	4	**60**	**11**
2016	Ostersund	23	4		
2017	Ostersund	24	4		
2018	Ostersund	11	0	**58**	**8**
2018–19	Watford	17	1		
2019–20	Watford	0	0		
2019–20	*Udinese*	32	2	**32**	**2**
2020–21	Watford	41	5		
2021–22	Watford	18	0		
2022–23	Watford	40	4		
2023–24	Watford	29	1		
2024–25	Watford	14	0	**159**	**11**

Transferred to Pafos, January 2025.

SIERRALTA, Francisco (D) 155 5
H: 6 4 W: 13 01 b.Las Condes 6-5-97
Internationals: Chile U20, Full caps.

2015–16	Universidad Catolica	2	1		
2016–17	Universidad Catolica	0	0	**2**	**1**
2016–17	Palestino	17	1	**17**	**1**
2017–18	Udinese	0	0		
2017–18	*Parma*	10	0		
2018–19	Udinese	0	0		
2018–19	*Parma*	6	0	**16**	**0**
2019–20	Udinese	0	0		
2019–20	*Empoli*	11	1		
2020–21	Empoli	0	0	**11**	**1**
2020–21	Udinese	0	0		
2020–21	Watford	26	1		
2021–22	Watford	5	0		
2022–23	Watford	18	1		
2023–24	Watford	27	0		
2024–25	Watford	33	0	**109**	**2**

SISSOKO, Moussa (M) 583 44
H: 6 2 W: 13 01 b.Le Blanc Mesnil 16-8-89
Internationals: France U16, U17, U18, U19, U21, Full caps.

2007–08	Toulouse	30	1		
2008–09	Toulouse	35	4		
2009–10	Toulouse	37	7		
2010–11	Toulouse	36	5		
2011–12	Toulouse	35	2		
2012–13	Toulouse	19	1	**192**	**20**
2012–13	Newcastle U	12	3		
2013–14	Newcastle U	35	3		
2014–15	Newcastle U	34	4		
2015–16	Newcastle U	37	1	**118**	**11**
2016–17	Tottenham H	25	0		
2017–18	Tottenham H	33	1		
2018–19	Tottenham H	29	0		
2019–20	Tottenham H	29	2		
2020–21	Tottenham H	25	0		
2021–22	Tottenham H	0	0	**141**	**3**
2021–22	Watford	36	2		
2022–23	Nantes	30	2		
2023–24	Nantes	26	0	**56**	**2**
2024–25	Watford	40	6	**76**	**8**

TIKVIC, Antonio (D) 21 0
b.Hamburg 21-4-04
Internationals: Croatia U18, U19, U21.

2021–22	Turkgucu Munchen	5	0	**5**	**0**
2022–23	Bayern Munich	0	0		
2023–24	Bayern Munich	0	0		
2023–24	Udinese	1	0	**1**	**0**
2024–25	Watford	0	0		
2024–25	*Grazer*	15	0	**15**	**0**

VATA, Rocco (M) 38 3
H: 6 0 b.Glasgow 18-4-05
Internationals: Republic of Ireland U17, U18, U19, U21, Full caps.

2021–22	Celtic	0	0		
2022–23	Celtic	4	0		
2023–24	Celtic	1	0	**5**	**0**
2024–25	Watford	33	3	**33**	**3**

Players retained or with offer of contract
Adeyemo, Emmanuel Oluwatobi; Browne, Roraigh Woodthorpe; Cabezas Hurtado, Jorge Leguin; Clarridge, James Andrew; Fonseca Ferreira, Joao Diogo; Grieves, Jack Alexander; Kamga, Ian Gaston; Keyes, Joshua Brendan; Lawson, Jonathan Ayoola; MacAulay, Jonathan Ludvig; Mullins, Joshua George Jack; Okosun, Nickson Ebigualor; Ortelli, Gabriel George.

Scholars
Akinyimika, Oluwatobi Mikel; Assiedou, Bently Emmanuel; Barrett, Hayden Cameron; Bolding, Charlie Harrison; Bowlin, Amani Baraka Solomon; Braverman, Zack David; Burton, Aaron Ernest; Cowie, Tony James Luciano; Galajevs, Marat; Georgiou, Thomas Joe; Morris, Samuel Anthony; Moulton, Jai-Dea Stephen Angel; Norville, Jael Orlando Glenovan; Notley, Tyler Romeo; Odiase, Kashopefoluwa Orlando; Riza, Josh Phillip; Sala, Joel; Sanghrajka, Amar Nur; Scriven, Jonny Day; Shevchenko, Kristian Michael; Smith Daley, Kymani Jahiem; Smith, Max James; Stephenson, Oliver Michael; Thrussell, Sebastian Beau; Vancea, Raul Mihai.

WBA (87)

AHEARNE-GRANT, Karlan (F) 332 83
H: 6 0 W: 11 00 b.Greenwich 19-12-97
Internationals: England U17, U18, U19.

2014–15	Charlton Ath	5	0		
2015–16	Charlton Ath	17	1		
2015–16	*Cambridge U*	3	0	**3**	**0**
2016–17	Charlton Ath	8	0		
2017–18	Charlton Ath	22	1		
2017–18	*Crawley T*	15	9	**15**	**9**
2018–19	Charlton Ath	28	14	**80**	**16**
2018–19	Huddersfield T	13	4		
2019–20	Huddersfield T	43	19	**56**	**23**
2020–21	WBA	21	1		
2021–22	WBA	44	18		
2022–23	WBA	31	3		
2023–24	WBA	0	0		
2023–24	*Cardiff C*	39	6	**39**	**6**
2024–25	WBA	43	7	**139**	**29**

AJAYI, Semi (D) 286 24
H: 6 4 W: 13 01 b.Crayford 9-11-93
Internationals: Nigeria U20, Full caps.

2012–13	Charlton Ath	0	0		
2013–14	Charlton Ath	0	0		
2014–15	Arsenal	0	0		
2014–15	*Cardiff C*	0	0		
2015–16	Cardiff C	0	0		
2015–16	*AFC Wimbledon*	5	0	**5**	**0**

2015–16	*Crewe Alex*	13	0	**13**	**0**
2016–17	*Cardiff C*	0	0		
2016–17	*Rotherham U*	17	1		
2017–18	*Rotherham U*	35	4		
2018–19	*Rotherham U*	46	7	**98**	**12**
2019–20	WBA	43	5		
2020–21	WBA	33	2		
2021–22	WBA	31	1		
2022–23	WBA	22	2		
2023–24	WBA	26	2		
2024–25	WBA	15	0	**170**	**12**

AMIHERE, Idrissa (D)   **0 0**
b.Brescia 8-1-08
Internationals: Italy U17.
| 2024–25 | WBA | 0 | 0 | | |

BANY, Tammer (F)   **41 5**
b. 19-10-03
2023–24	B 93	14	3	**14**	**3**
2023–24	Randers	8	0		
2024–25	Randers	15	2	**23**	**2**
2024–25	WBA	4	0	**4**	**0**

BARTLEY, Kyle (D)   **357 24**
H: 6 4 W: 14 11 b.Stockport 22-5-91
Internationals: England U16, U17.
2008–09	Arsenal	0	0		
2009–10	Arsenal	0	0		
2009–10	*Sheffield U*	14	0		
2010–11	Arsenal	0	0		
2010–11	*Sheffield U*	21	0	**35**	**0**
2010–11	*Rangers*	5	1		
2011–12	Arsenal	0	0		
2011–12	*Rangers*	19	0	**24**	**1**
2012–13	Arsenal	0	0		
2012–13	Swansea C	2	0		
2013–14	Swansea C	2	0		
2013–14	*Birmingham C*	17	3	**17**	**3**
2014–15	Swansea C	7	0		
2015–16	Swansea C	5	0		
2016–17	Swansea C	0	0		
2016–17	*Leeds U*	45	6	**45**	**6**
2017–18	Swansea C	5	0	**21**	**0**
2018–19	WBA	28	1		
2019–20	WBA	38	2		
2020–21	WBA	30	3		
2021–22	WBA	39	2		
2022–23	WBA	13	2		
2023–24	WBA	36	4		
2024–25	WBA	31	0	**215**	**14**

BOSTOCK, Oliver (M)   **0 0**
b.London 20-2-07
Internationals: Wales U16, U17, U19.
| 2024–25 | WBA | 0 | 0 | | |

CANN, Ted (G)   **0 0**
H: 6 2 W: 12 00 b.Stockport 27-12-00
From Liverpool.
2021–22	WBA	0	0		
2022–23	WBA	0	0		
2023–24	WBA	0	0		
2024–25	WBA	0	0		

CLEARY, Reyes (F)   **5 0**
H: 6 1 W: 11 11 b.Birmingham 13-4-04
Internationals: England U19.
2021–22	WBA	0	0		
2022–23	WBA	2	0		
2023–24	WBA	0	0		
2024–25	WBA	0	0	**2**	**0**
2024–25	*Walsall*	3	0	**3**	**0**

COLE, Devante (F)   **314 77**
H: 6 1 W: 11 07 b.Alderley Edge 10-5-95
Internationals: England U16, U17, U18, U19.
2013–14	Manchester C	0	0		
2014–15	Manchester C	0	0		
2014–15	*Barnsley*	19	5		
2014–15	*Milton Keynes D*	15	3	**15**	**3**
2015–16	Bradford C	19	5	**19**	**5**
2015–16	Fleetwood T	14	2		
2016–17	Fleetwood T	35	5		
2017–18	Fleetwood T	28	10	**77**	**17**
2017–18	Wigan Ath	6	0		
2018–19	Wigan Ath	0	0	**6**	**0**
2018–19	*Burton Alb*	13	2	**13**	**2**
2019–20	*Motherwell*	0	0		
2019–20	Doncaster R	9	0	**9**	**0**
2020–21	Motherwell	27	11	**27**	**11**
2021–22	Barnsley	24	1		
2022–23	Barnsley	45	15		
2023–24	Barnsley	46	18	**134**	**39**
2024–25	WBA	14	0	**14**	**0**

DEEMING, Cole (M)   **0 0**
b.Sutton Coldfield 19-1-07
| 2024–25 | WBA | 0 | 0 | | |

DIAKITE, Ousmane (M)   **109 5**
H: 6 2 b. 25-7-00
Internationals: Mali U17, U20.
2018–19	Red Bull Salzburg	0	0		
2018–19	*Liefering*	19	1	**19**	**1**
2019–20	Red Bull Salzburg	0	0		
2019–20	*Rheindorf Altach*	9	0	**9**	**0**
2020–21	Red Bull Salzburg	0	0		
2021–22	Red Bull Salzburg	0	0		

2021–22	St Gallen	13	2	**13**	**2**
2022–23	TSV Hartberg	15	0		
2023–24	TSV Hartberg	31	2	**46**	**2**
2024–25	WBA	22	0	**22**	**0**

DIANGANA, Grady (F)   **209 26**
H: 5 11 W: 11 07 b.Lubumbashi 19-4-98
Internationals: England U20, U21. DR Congo
Full caps.
2016–17	West Ham U	0	0		
2017–18	West Ham U	0	0		
2018–19	West Ham U	17	0		
2019–20	West Ham U	0	0	**17**	**0**
2019–20	*WBA*	30	8		
2020–21	WBA	20	1		
2021–22	WBA	41	2		
2022–23	WBA	31	4		
2023–24	WBA	36	7		
2024–25	WBA	34	4	**192**	**26**

DIKE, Daryl (F)   **95 36**
H: 6 2 W: 15 10 b.Edmond 3-6-00
Internationals: United States Full caps.
From OKC Energy.
2020	Orlando C	17	8		
2020–21	*Barnsley*	19	9	**19**	**9**
2021	Orlando C	19	11	**36**	**19**
2021–22	WBA	2	0		
2022–23	WBA	23	7		
2023–24	WBA	4	0		
2024–25	WBA	11	1	**40**	**8**

DIOMANDE, Muhamed (D)   **0 0**
b.Assisi 16-2-06
| 2024–25 | WBA | 0 | 0 | | |

FELLOWS, Tom (F)   **120 8**
H: 6 0 b.Solihull 25-7-03
Internationals: England U20, U21.
2021–22	WBA	4	0		
2022–23	WBA	0	0		
2022–23	*Crawley T*	38	0	**38**	**0**
2023–24	WBA	33	4		
2024–25	WBA	45	4	**82**	**8**

FRABOTTA, Gianluca (D)   **80 3**
b.Roma 27-6-99
Internationals: Italy U18, U19, U20, U21.
2017–18	Juventus	0	0		
2018–19	Juventus	0	0		
2018–19	*Renate*	12	0	**12**	**0**
2019–20	Juventus	1	0		
2020–21	Juventus	15	0		
2021–22	Juventus	0	0		
2021–22	*Hellas Verona*	2	0	**2**	**0**
2022–23	Juventus	0	0		
2022–23	*Frosinone*	22	0	**22**	**0**
2023–24	Juventus	0	0	**16**	**0**
2023–24	*Bari*	7	0	**7**	**0**
2023–24	*Cosenza*	15	3	**15**	**3**
2024–25	WBA	6	0	**6**	**0**

FURLONG, Darnell (D)   **354 14**
H: 5 11 W: 12 00 b.Luton 31-10-95
2014–15	QPR	3	0		
2015–16	QPR	0	0		
2015–16	*Northampton T*	10	0	**10**	**0**
2015–16	*Cambridge U*	21	0	**21**	**0**
2016–17	QPR	14	0		
2016–17	*Swindon T*	24	2	**24**	**2**
2017–18	QPR	22	0		
2018–19	QPR	25	1	**64**	**1**
2019–20	WBA	31	2		
2020–21	WBA	35	1		
2021–22	WBA	41	0		
2022–23	WBA	40	2		
2023–24	WBA	46	5		
2024–25	WBA	42	1	**235**	**11**

GRIFFITHS, Joshua (G)   **143 0**
H: 6 1 W: 11 03 b.Hereford 5-9-01
Internationals: England U18, U21.
2020–21	WBA	0	0		
2020–21	*Cheltenham T*	44	0	**44**	**0**
2021–22	WBA	0	0		
2021–22	*Lincoln C*	33	0	**33**	**0**
2022–23	WBA	10	0		
2022–23	*Portsmouth*	22	0	**22**	**0**
2023–24	WBA	0	0		
2024–25	WBA	6	0	**16**	**0**
2024–25	*Bristol C*	28	0	**28**	**0**

HALL, Reece (D)   **0 0**
b.Birmingham 25-9-03
| 2023–24 | WBA | 0 | 0 | | |
| 2024–25 | WBA | 0 | 0 | | |

HEARD, Fenton (M)   **0 0**
b.Birmingham 1-10-04
| 2023–24 | WBA | 0 | 0 | | |
| 2024–25 | WBA | 0 | 0 | | |

HEGGEM, Torbjorn (D)   **194 5**
b. 12-1-99
Internationals: Norway Full caps.
2018	Rosenborg	0	0		
2019	Rosenborg	0	0		
2019	*Ranheim*	18	0		
2020	Rosenborg	0	0		
2020	*Ranheim*	30	1	**48**	**1**

2021	Sandnes Ulf	30	0		
2022	Sandnes Ulf	31	1	**61**	**1**
2023	Brommapojkarna	28	1		
2024	Brommapojkarna	12	1	**40**	**2**
2024–25	WBA	45	1	**45**	**1**

HIGGINS, Akeel (M)   **0 0**
b.Birmingham 24-7-05
| 2023–24 | WBA | 0 | 0 | | |
| 2024–25 | WBA | 0 | 0 | | |

JOHNSTON, Michael (F)   **135 18**
H: 5 9 W: 10 03 b.Glasgow 19-4-99
Internationals: Scotland U19, U21. Republic
of Ireland Full caps.
2016–17	Celtic	1	0		
2017–18	Celtic	3	0		
2018–19	Celtic	14	5		
2019–20	Celtic	11	2		
2020–21	Celtic	10	0		
2021–22	Celtic	12	0		
2022–23	Celtic	0	0		
2022–23	*Vitoria de Guimaraes*	25	1	**25**	**1**
2023–24	Celtic	0	0		
2023–24	*WBA*	18	7		
2024–25	Celtic	1	0	**52**	**7**
2024–25	*WBA*	40	3	**58**	**10**

LOVE, Layton (F)   **0 0**
b.Dudley 28-9-04
| 2023–24 | WBA | 0 | 0 | | |
| 2024–25 | WBA | 0 | 0 | | |

MAJA, Josh (F)   **194 58**
H: 5 11 W: 11 09 b.Lewisham 27-12-98
Internationals: Nigeria Full caps.
From Fulham.
2016–17	Sunderland	0	0		
2017–18	Sunderland	17	1		
2018–19	Sunderland	24	15	**41**	**16**
2018–19	Bordeaux	7	1		
2019–20	Bordeaux	21	6		
2020–21	Bordeaux	17	2		
2020–21	*Fulham*	15	3	**15**	**3**
2021–22	Bordeaux	2	0		
2022–23	*Stoke C*	15	1	**15**	**1**
2022–23	Bordeaux	38	16	**85**	**25**
2023–24	WBA	12	1		
2024–25	WBA	26	12	**38**	**13**

MALCOLM, Jovan (F)   **18 0**
H: 5 11 W: 10 06 b. 10-12-02
2021–22	WBA	0	0		
2021–22	*Accrington S*	10	0	**10**	**0**
2022–23	WBA	1	0		
2023–24	*Cheltenham T*	7	0	**7**	**0**
2024–25	WBA	0	0	**1**	**0**

McNAIR, Paddy (D)   **247 19**
H: 6 0 W: 11 05 b.Ballyclare 27-4-95
Internationals: Northern Ireland U16, U17,
U19, U21, Full caps.
2011–12	Manchester U	0	0		
2012–13	Manchester U	0	0		
2013–14	Manchester U	0	0		
2014–15	Manchester U	16	0		
2015–16	Manchester U	8	0	**24**	**0**
2016–17	Sunderland	9	0		
2017–18	Sunderland	16	5	**25**	**5**
2018–19	Middlesbrough	16	0		
2019–20	Middlesbrough	41	6		
2020–21	Middlesbrough	46	2		
2021–22	Middlesbrough	42	5		
2022–23	Middlesbrough	30	1		
2023–24	Middlesbrough	21	0	**196**	**14**
2024	San Diego	0	0		
On loan from San Diego.
2024–25	WBA	2	0	**2**	**0**

MFUAMBA, Kevin (M)   **0 0**
b.Birmingham 25-8-06
Internationals: England U17.
| 2023–24 | WBA | 0 | 0 | | |
| 2024–25 | WBA | 0 | 0 | | |

MOHAMMED, Jamal (D)   **0 0**
b. 4-4-06
| 2024–25 | WBA | 0 | 0 | | |

MOLUMBY, Jayson (M)   **187 10**
H: 5 10 W: 11 07 b.Waterford 6-8-99
Internationals: Republic of Ireland U16, U17,
U19, U21, Full caps.
2017–18	Brighton & HA	0	0		
2018–19	Brighton & HA	0	0		
2019–20	Brighton & HA	0	0		
2019–20	*Millwall*	36	1	**36**	**1**
2020–21	Brighton & HA	1	0		
2020–21	*Preston NE*	15	0	**15**	**0**
2021–22	Brighton & HA	0	0	**1**	**0**
2021–22	*WBA*	31	1		
2022–23	WBA	43	4		
2023–24	WBA	24	0		
2024–25	WBA	37	4	**135**	**9**

MOWATT, Alex (D)   **441 47**
H: 5 10 W: 11 03 b.Doncaster 13-2-95
Internationals: England U19, U20.
| 2013–14 | Leeds U | 29 | 1 | | |

2014–15 Leeds U 38 9
2015–16 Leeds U 34 2
2016–17 Leeds U 15 0 **116 12**
2016–17 Barnsley 11 1
2017–18 Barnsley 1 0
2017–18 *Oxford U* 30 2 **30 2**
2018–19 Barnsley 46 8
2019–20 Barnsley 44 3
2020–21 Barnsley 44 8
2021–22 Barnsley 0 0 **146 20**
2021–22 WBA 34 4
2022–23 WBA 1 0
2022–23 *Middlesbrough* 28 0 **28 0**
2023–24 WBA 43 2
2024–25 WBA 43 7 **121 13**

NELSON, Deago (D) 0 0
b. 5-12-05
2024–25 WBA 0 0

PARKER, Michael (D) 0 0
b. 18-12-04
2023–24 Shrewsbury T 0 0
2024–25 WBA 0 0

PRICE, Isaac (M) 76 2
b. 26-9-03
Internationals: Northern Ireland U16, U17, U19, U21, Full caps.
2020–21 Everton 0 0
2021–22 Everton 1 0
2022–23 Everton 1 0 **2 0**
2023–24 Standard Liege 37 1
2024–25 Standard Liege 22 0 **59 1**
2024–25 WBA 15 1 **15 1**

RACIC, Uros (M) 229 11
H: 6 4 W: 12 11 b.Kraljevo 17-3-98
Internationals: Serbia U18, U19, U21, Full caps.
2015–16 Beograd 0 0
2015–16 Red Star Belgrade 1 0
2016–17 Red Star Belgrade 8 0
2017–18 Red Star Belgrade 22 3 **31 3**
2018–19 Valencia 0 0
2018–19 *Tenerife* 16 1 **16 1**
2019–20 Valencia 0 0
2019–20 *Famalicao* 33 3 **33 3**
2020–21 Valencia 31 1
2021–22 Valencia 28 0
2022–23 Valencia 0 0 **59 1**
2022–23 *Braga* 25 1 **25 1**
2023–24 Sassuolo 22 1
2024–25 Sassuolo 22 1 **44 2**
On loan from Sassuolo.
2024–25 WBA 21 0 **21 0**

RICHARDS, Matthew (M) 0 0
b. 7-10-04
2024–25 WBA 0 0

SHAW, Josh (D) 0 0
H: 6 0 b.Manchester 5-10-03
2023–24 WBA 0 0
2024–25 WBA 0 0

STYLES, Callum (M) 244 16
H: 5 6 W: 9 06 b.Bury 28-3-00
Internationals: Hungary Full caps.
From Burnley.
2015–16 Bury 1 0
2016–17 Bury 13 0
2017–18 Bury 11 0
2018–19 Bury 16 0 **41 0**
2018–19 Barnsley 7 0
2019–20 Barnsley 17 1
2020–21 Barnsley 42 4
2021–22 Barnsley 43 3
2022–23 Barnsley 6 1
2022–23 *Millwall* 22 1 **22 1**
2023–24 Barnsley 20 3 **135 12**
2023–24 *Sunderland* 12 0 **12 0**
2024–25 WBA 34 3 **34 3**

SULE, Eseosa (F) 0 0
b.Glasgow 1-4-06
2024–25 WBA 0 0

SWIFT, John (M) 354 58
H: 6 0 W: 11 07 b.Portsmouth 23-6-95
Internationals: England U16, U17, U18, U19, U20, U21.
2013–14 Chelsea 1 0
2014–15 Chelsea 0 0
2014–15 *Rotherham U* 3 0 **3 0**
2014–15 *Swindon T* 18 2 **18 2**
2015–16 Chelsea 0 0 **1 0**
2015–16 *Brentford* 27 7 **27 7**
2016–17 Reading 36 8
2017–18 Reading 24 2
2018–19 Reading 34 3
2019–20 Reading 41 6
2020–21 Reading 14 1
2021–22 Reading 38 11 **187 31**
2022–23 WBA 45 6
2023–24 WBA 37 9
2024–25 WBA 36 3 **118 18**

TAYLOR, Caleb (D) 92 5
H: 5 6 W: 8 09 b.Burnley 14-1-03
2020–21 WBA 0 0
2021–22 WBA 1 0
2022–23 WBA 0 0
2022–23 *Cheltenham T* 45 2 **45 2**
2023–24 WBA 3 0
2023–24 *Bolton W* 7 0 **7 0**
2024–25 WBA 0 0 **4 0**
2024–25 *Wycombe W* 36 3 **36 3**

WALLACE, Jed (M) 484 82
H: 5 10 W: 10 12 b.Reading 15-12-93
Internationals: England U19.
2011–12 Portsmouth 0 0
2012–13 Portsmouth 22 6
2013–14 Portsmouth 44 7
2014–15 Portsmouth 44 14 **110 27**
2015–16 Wolverhampton W 9 0
2015–16 *Millwall* 12 1
2016–17 Wolverhampton W 9 0 **18 0**
2016–17 *Millwall* 16 3
2017–18 Millwall 43 6
2018–19 Millwall 42 5
2019–20 Millwall 43 10
2020–21 Millwall 45 11
2021–22 Millwall 38 6 **239 42**
2022–23 WBA 46 6
2023–24 WBA 42 6
2024–25 WBA 29 1 **117 13**

WHITWELL, Harry (M) 1 0
b.Oxford 16-11-05
Internationals: England U16, U17, U18.
2023–24 WBA 0 0
2024–25 WBA 1 0 **1 0**

WILDSMITH, Joe (G) 165 0
H: 6 0 W: 10 03 b.Sheffield 28-12-95
Internationals: England U20.
2013–14 Sheffield Wed 0 0
2014–15 Sheffield Wed 0 0
2014–15 *Barnsley* 2 0 **2 0**
2015–16 Sheffield Wed 9 0
2016–17 Sheffield Wed 1 0
2017–18 Sheffield Wed 26 0
2018–19 Sheffield Wed 0 0
2019–20 Sheffield Wed 9 0
2020–21 Sheffield Wed 19 0
2021–22 Sheffield Wed 3 0 **67 0**
2022–23 Derby Co 46 0
2023–24 Derby Co 40 0 **86 0**
2024–25 WBA 10 0 **10 0**

Players retained or with offer of contract
Bani Odeh, Tamer Jehad Abdallah; Cisse, Ben Foumba; Crowther, Matthew William; Dupont, Noah Charles Evenor; Humphries, Evan Alfie; Iddrisa, Dauda Amihere; McDonald, Miller; Parmar, Rio; Wallis, Joseph; Williams, Alexander David.

Scholars
Abudu, Abdulhakeem Oluwatobiloba; Beedie, Sam Alec; Blackshields, Charlie Brian; Brady, Louis James; Cherchi, Francesco; Chimeziri, Nnaemeka Daniel; Colesby, Ryan Stuart; Francis-Caesar, Jaiden Desean; German-Ranger, Donte Javani; Letlat, Adam; Mandey, Souleyman; Maughan, Alfie James; Morrish, Rhys Elliot; Okorodudu, Adam; Onyemachi, Divine Chidiebube; Sears, Corey Lucius; Wilkes, Liam Kyle.

WEST HAM U (88)

AGUERD, Nayef (D) 231 17
H: 6 2 W: 12 00 b.Kenitra 30-3-96
Internationals: Morocco U23, Full caps.
2014–15 FAS Rabat 12 1
2015–16 FAS Rabat 22 2
2016–17 FAS Rabat 24 2
2017–18 FAS Rabat 23 0 **81 5**
2018–19 Dijon 13 3
2019–20 Dijon 11 1 **24 4**
2020–21 Rennes 35 3
2021–22 Rennes 31 2 **66 5**
2022–23 West Ham U 18 2
2023–24 West Ham U 21 1
2024–25 West Ham U 0 0 **39 3**
2024–25 *Real Sociedad* 21 0 **21 0**

ALVAREZ, Edson (D) 227 13
H: 6 3 W: 11 07 b.Tlalnepantla de Baz 24-10-97
Internationals: Mexico U18, U20, Full caps.
2016–17 Club America 15 1
2017–18 Club America 25 0
2018–19 Club America 30 1 **70 2**
2019–20 Ajax 12 0
2020–21 Ajax 24 2
2021–22 Ajax 31 5
2022–23 Ajax 31 3 **98 10**
2023–24 West Ham U 31 1
2024–25 West Ham U 28 0 **59 1**

ANTONIO, Michael (F) 476 109
H: 5 11 W: 12 11 b.Wandsworth 28-3-90
Internationals: Jamaica Full caps.
From Tooting & Mitcham U.
2008–09 Reading 0 0
2008–09 *Cheltenham T* 9 0 **9 0**
2009–10 Reading 1 0
2009–10 *Southampton* 28 3 **28 3**
2010–11 Reading 21 1
2011–12 Reading 6 0
2011–12 *Colchester U* 15 4 **15 4**
2011–12 *Sheffield Wed* 14 5
2012–13 Reading 0 0 **28 1**
2012–13 Sheffield Wed 37 8
2013–14 Sheffield Wed 27 4 **78 17**
2014–15 Nottingham F 46 14
2015–16 Nottingham F 4 2 **50 16**
2015–16 West Ham U 26 8
2016–17 West Ham U 29 9
2017–18 West Ham U 21 3
2018–19 West Ham U 33 6
2019–20 West Ham U 24 10
2020–21 West Ham U 26 10
2021–22 West Ham U 36 10
2022–23 West Ham U 33 5
2023–24 West Ham U 26 6
2024–25 West Ham U 14 1 **268 68**

AREOLA, Alphonse (G) 280 0
H: 6 5 W: 13 05 b.Paris 27-2-93
Internationals: France U16, U17, U18, U19, U20, U21, Full caps.
2012–13 Paris Saint-Germain 2 0
2013–14 Paris Saint-Germain 0 0
2013–14 *Lens* 35 0 **35 0**
2014–15 Paris Saint-Germain 0 0
2014–15 *Bastia* 35 0 **35 0**
2015–16 Paris Saint-Germain 0 0
2015–16 *Villarreal* 32 0 **32 0**
2016–17 Paris Saint-Germain 15 0
2017–18 Paris Saint-Germain 34 0
2018–19 Paris Saint-Germain 21 0
2019–20 Paris Saint-Germain 3 0
2019–20 *Real Madrid* 4 0 **4 0**
2020–21 Paris Saint-Germain 0 0
2020–21 *Fulham* 36 0 **36 0**
2021–22 Paris Saint-Germain 0 0 **75 0**
2021–22 *West Ham U* 1 0
2022–23 West Ham U 5 0
2023–24 West Ham U 31 0
2024–25 West Ham U 26 0 **63 0**

BOWEN, Jarrod (F) 317 108
H: 5 9 W: 11 00 b.Leominster 20-12-96
Internationals: England Full caps.
2014–15 Hull C 0 0
2015–16 Hull C 0 0
2016–17 Hull C 7 0
2017–18 Hull C 42 14
2018–19 Hull C 46 22
2019–20 Hull C 29 16 **124 52**
2019–20 West Ham U 13 1
2020–21 West Ham U 38 8
2021–22 West Ham U 36 12
2022–23 West Ham U 38 6
2023–24 West Ham U 34 16
2024–25 West Ham U 34 13 **193 56**

CASEY, Kaelan (D) 2 0
H: 6 1 W: 11 00 b.London 28-10-04
Internationals: England U20.
2022–23 West Ham U 0 0
2023–24 West Ham U 1 0
2024–25 West Ham U 1 0 **2 0**

CLAYTON, Regan (D) 0 0
H: 5 9 W: 10 03 b.Havering 11-11-04
2022–23 West Ham U 0 0
2023–24 West Ham U 0 0
2024–25 West Ham U 0 0

CORNET, Maxwel (F) 263 44
H: 5 10 W: 10 12 b.Bregbo 27-9-96
Internationals: France U16, U17, U18, U19, U20, U21. Ivory Coast Full caps.
2012–13 Metz 9 1
2013–14 Metz 14 0
2014–15 Metz 0 0 **23 1**
2014–15 Lyon 4 0
2015–16 Lyon 31 8
2016–17 Lyon 33 6
2017–18 Lyon 30 4
2018–19 Lyon 27 7
2019–20 Lyon 22 4
2020–21 Lyon 36 2
2021–22 Lyon 1 0 **184 31**
2021–22 Burnley 26 9 **26 9**
2022–23 West Ham U 14 0
2023–24 West Ham U 7 1
2024–25 West Ham U 0 0 **21 1**
2024–25 *Southampton* 2 0 **2 0**
2024–25 *Genoa* 7 2 **7 2**

COUFAL, Vladimir (D) 352 10
H: 5 9 W: 11 00 b.Ludgerovice 22-8-92
Internationals: Czech Republic U21, Full caps.

2010-11	Hlucin	14	0		
2011-12	Hlucin	0	0	14	0
2011-12	Opava	13	1	13	1
2012-13	Slovan Liberec	10	0		
2013-14	Slovan Liberec	21	0		
2014-15	Slovan Liberec	13	0		
2015-16	Slovan Liberec	27	1		
2016-17	Slovan Liberec	17	0		
2017-18	Slovan Liberec	30	2	118	3
2018-19	Slavia Prague	28	3		
2019-20	Slavia Prague	32	3		
2020-21	Slavia Prague	0	0	60	6
2020-21	West Ham U	34	0		
2021-22	West Ham U	28	0		
2022-23	West Ham U	27	0		
2023-24	West Ham U	36	0		
2024-25	West Ham U	22	0	147	0

CRESSWELL, Aaron (D) 514 21
H: 5 7 W: 10 06 b.Liverpool 15-12-89
Internationals: England Full caps.

2008-09	Tranmere R	13	1		
2009-10	Tranmere R	14	0		
2010-11	Tranmere R	43	4	70	5
2011-12	Ipswich T	44	1		
2012-13	Ipswich T	46	3		
2013-14	Ipswich T	42	2	132	6
2014-15	West Ham U	38	2		
2015-16	West Ham U	37	2		
2016-17	West Ham U	26	0		
2017-18	West Ham U	36	1		
2018-19	West Ham U	20	0		
2019-20	West Ham U	31	3		
2020-21	West Ham U	36	0		
2021-22	West Ham U	31	2		
2022-23	West Ham U	28	0		
2023-24	West Ham U	11	0		
2024-25	West Ham U	18	0	312	10

DOLAGHAN, Brad (F) 0 0
b. 30-12-04

| 2024-25 | West Ham U | 0 | 0 | | |

EARTHY, George (M) 40 4
H: 5 11 W: 11 00 b.London 5-9-04
Internationals: England U16, U20, U21.

2023-24	West Ham U	3	1		
2024-25	West Ham U	0	0	3	1
2024-25	Bristol C	37	3	37	3

EMERSON, dos Santos (D) 212 7
H: 5 9 W: 9 13 b.Santos 13-3-94
Internationals: Brazil U17. Italy Full caps.

2011	Santos	0	0		
2012	Santos	1	0		
2013	Santos	14	1		
2014	Santos	3	0	18	1
2014-15	Palermo	9	0	9	0
2015-16	Roma	8	1		
2016-17	Roma	25	0		
2017-18	Roma	1	0	34	1
2017-18	Chelsea	5	0		
2018-19	Chelsea	10	0		
2019-20	Chelsea	15	0		
2020-21	Chelsea	2	0		
2021-22	Chelsea	1	0	33	0
2021-22	Lyon	29	1	29	1
2022-23	West Ham U	22	1		
2023-24	West Ham U	36	1		
2024-25	West Ham U	31	2	89	4

FABIANSKI, Lukasz (G) 429 0
H: 6 3 W: 13 01 b.Costrzyn nad Odra 18-4-85
Internationals: Poland U21, Full caps.

2004-05	Lech Poznan	0	0		
2005-06	Legia Warsaw	30	. 0		
2006-07	Legia Warsaw	23	0	53	0
2007-08	Arsenal	3	0		
2008-09	Arsenal	6	0		
2009-10	Arsenal	4	0		
2010-11	Arsenal	14	0		
2011-12	Arsenal	0	0		
2012-13	Arsenal	4	0		
2013-14	Arsenal	1	0	32	0
2014-15	Swansea C	37	0		
2015-16	Swansea C	37	0		
2016-17	Swansea C	37	0		
2017-18	Swansea C	38	0	149	0
2018-19	West Ham U	38	0		
2019-20	West Ham U	25	0		
2020-21	West Ham U	35	0		
2021-22	West Ham U	37	0		
2022-23	West Ham U	36	0		
2023-24	West Ham U	10	0		
2024-25	West Ham U	14	0	195	0

FODERINGHAM, Wesley (G) 378 0
H: 6 1 W: 11 11 b.Hammersmith 14-1-91
Internationals: England U16, U17, U19.

2009-10	Fulham	0	0		
2010-11	Crystal Palace	0	0		
2011-12	Crystal Palace	0	0		
2011-12	Swindon T	33	0		
2012-13	Swindon T	46	0		
2013-14	Swindon T	41	0		
2014-15	Swindon T	44	0	164	0
2015-16	Rangers	36	0		
2016-17	Rangers	37	0		
2017-18	Rangers	33	0		
2018-19	Rangers	4	0		
2019-20	Rangers	2	0	112	0
2020-21	Sheffield U	0	0		
2021-22	Sheffield U	32	0		
2022-23	Sheffield U	40	0		
2023-24	Sheffield U	30	0	102	0
2024-25	West Ham U	0	0		

FORBES, Michael (D) 7 0
H: 6 2 W: 12 00 b.Ardboe 29-4-04
Internationals: Northern Ireland U16, U18, U19, U21, Full caps.
From Dungannon Swifts.

2022-23	West Ham U	0	0		
2023-24	West Ham U	0	0		
2024-25	West Ham U	0	0		
2024-25	Bristol R	7	0	7	0
2024-25	Colchester U	0	0		

FULLKRUG, Niclas (F) 310 106
H: 6 2 W: 12 06 b.Hannover 9-2-93
Internationals: Germany U18, U19, U20, Full caps.

2011-12	Werder Bremen	11	1		
2012-13	Werder Bremen	12	1		
2013-14	Werder Bremen	0	0		
2013-14	Greuther Furth	21	6	21	6
2014-15	1. FC Nurnberg	24	3		
2015-16	1. FC Nurnberg	30	14	54	17
2016-17	Hannover 96	27	5		
2017-18	Hannover 96	34	14		
2018-19	Hannover 96	14	2	75	21
2019-20	Werder Bremen	8	4		
2020-21	Werder Bremen	19	6		
2021-22	Werder Bremen	33	19		
2022-23	Werder Bremen	28	16		
2023-24	Werder Bremen	2	0	113	47
2023-24	Borussia Dortmund	29	12	29	12
2024-25	West Ham U	18	3	18	3

HEGYI, Krisztian (G) 28 0
H: 6 4 W: 11 09 b.Budapest 24-9-02
Internationals: Hungary U16, U17, U18, U21.

2020-21	West Ham U	0	0		
2021-22	West Ham U	0	0		
2022-23	West Ham U	0	0		
2023-24	Stevenage	4	0	4	0
2023-24	Den Bosch	17	0	17	0
2024-25	West Ham U	0	0		
2024-25	Motherwell	0	0		
2024-25	Debrecen	7	0	7	0

INGS, Danny (F) 354 106
H: 5 10 W: 11 07 b.Winchester 16-3-92
Internationals: England U21, Full caps.

2009-10	Bournemouth	0	0		
2010-11	Bournemouth	26	7		
2011-12	Bournemouth	1	0	27	7
2011-12	Burnley	15	3		
2012-13	Burnley	32	3		
2013-14	Burnley	40	21		
2014-15	Burnley	35	11	122	38
2015-16	Liverpool	6	2		
2016-17	Liverpool	0	0		
2017-18	Liverpool	8	1		
2018-19	Liverpool	0	0	14	3
2018-19	Southampton	24	7		
2019-20	Southampton	38	22		
2020-21	Southampton	29	12	91	41
2021-22	Aston Villa	30	7		
2022-23	Aston Villa	18	6	48	13
2022-23	West Ham U	17	2		
2023-24	West Ham U	20	1		
2024-25	West Ham U	15	1	52	4

IRVING, Andrew (M) 175 18
H: 6 3 W: 12 08 b.Edinburgh 13-5-00
Internationals: Scotland U17, U19, U21, Full caps.

2016-17	Hearts	0	0		
2017-18	Hearts	4	0		
2017-18	Berwick Rangers	18	2	18	2
2018-19	Hearts	1	0		
2018-19	Falkirk	19	0	19	0
2019-20	Hearts	17	0		
2020-21	Hearts	24	2	46	2
2021-22	Turkgucu Munchen	23	1	23	1
2022-23	Austria Klagenfurt	31	4		
2023-24	Austria Klagenfurt	28	9	59	13
2024-25	Hearts	10	0	10	0

KELLY, Patrick (M) 53 2
H: 6 0 W: 12 02 b.Portstewart 2-10-04
Internationals: Northern Ireland U18, U19, U21.

2021-22	Coleraine	23	0	23	0
2022-23	West Ham U	0	0		
2023-24	West Ham U	0	0		
2024-25	West Ham U	0	0		
2024-25	Doncaster R	30	2	30	2

KILMAN, Max (D) 165 3
H: 6 4 W: 12 06 b.Chelsea 23-5-97
From Welling U, Maidenhead U.

2018-19	Wolverhampton W	1	0		
2019-20	Wolverhampton W	3	0		
2020-21	Wolverhampton W	18	0		
2021-22	Wolverhampton W	30	1		
2022-23	Wolverhampton W	37	0		
2023-24	Wolverhampton W	38	2	127	3
2024-25	West Ham U	38	0	38	0

KODUA, Gideon (F) 30 2
H: 5 10 W: 11 07 b.Newham 2-10-04

2023-24	West Ham U	0	0		
2023-24	Wycombe W	10	0		
2024-25	West Ham U	0	0		
2024-25	Wycombe W	20	2	30	2

KUDUS, Mohammed (M) 181 44
H: 5 10 W: 11 00 b.Accra 2-8-00
Internationals: Ghana U17, U20, Full caps.
From Right to Dream Academy.

2018-19	Nordsjaelland	26	3		
2019-20	Nordsjaelland	25	11	51	14
2020-21	Ajax	17	4		
2021-22	Ajax	16	1		
2022-23	Ajax	30	11		
2023-24	Ajax	2	1	65	17
2023-24	West Ham U	33	8		
2024-25	West Ham U	32	5	65	13

LAING, Levi (M) 6 0
H: 6 2 W: 11 07 b.London 12-4-03
Internationals: England U16.
From Arsenal.

2022-23	West Ham U	0	0		
2023-24	West Ham U	0	0		
2024-25	West Ham U	0	0		
2024-25	Cheltenham T	6	0	6	0

Transferred to Aldershot T, March 2025.

LUCAS PAQUETA, de Lima (M) 245 42
H: 5 11 W: 11 05 b.Rio de Janeiro 27-8-97
Internationals: Brazil U20, Full caps.

2016	Flamengo	0	0		
2017	Flamengo	17	1		
2018	Flamengo	32	10	49	11
2018-19	AC Milan	13	1		
2019-20	AC Milan	24	0	37	1
2020-21	Lyon	30	9		
2021-22	Lyon	35	9		
2022-23	Lyon	2	0	67	18
2022-23	West Ham U	28	4		
2023-24	West Ham U	31	4		
2024-25	West Ham U	33	4	92	12

LUIS GUILHERME, dos Santos (F) 36 0
H: 5 9 W: 11 00 b.Aracaju 9-2-06
Internationals: Brazil U17, U20.

2023	Palmeiras	19	0		
2024	Palmeiras	5	0	24	0
2024-25	West Ham U	12	0	12	0

LUIZAO, Gustavo Oliveira (D) 18 1
H: 6 2 W: 11 05 b.Sao Paulo 8-3-02

2022-23	Sao Paulo	14	1	14	1
2022-23	West Ham U	0	0		
2023-24	West Ham U	0	0		
2024-25	West Ham U	0	0		
2024-25	Pogon Szczecin	4	0	4	0

MARSHALL, Callum (F) 46 9
H: 5 9 W: 13 01 b.Glengormley 28-11-04
Internationals: Northern Ireland Full caps.
From Linfield.

2022-23	West Ham U	0	0		
2023-24	West Ham U	0	0		
2023-24	WBA	3	0	3	0
2024-25	West Ham U	0	0		
2024-25	Huddersfield T	43	9	43	9

MAVROPANOS, Konstantinos (D) 166 10
H: 6 4 W: 12 08 b.Athens 11-12-97
Internationals: Greece U21, Full caps.

2016-17	PAS Giannina	2	0		
2017-18	PAS Giannina	14	3	16	3
2017-18	Arsenal	3	0		
2018-19	Arsenal	4	0		
2019-20	Arsenal	0	0		
2019-20	1. FC Nurnberg	11	0	11	0
2019-20	VfB Stuttgart	0	0		
2020-21	Arsenal	0	0		
2020-21	VfB Stuttgart	21	0		
2021-22	Arsenal	0	0	7	0
2021-22	VfB Stuttgart	31	4		
2022-23	VfB Stuttgart	28	2	80	6
2023-24	West Ham U	19	1		
2024-25	West Ham U	33	0	52	1

MAYERS, Ezra (D) 0 0
H: 6 0 b. 16-1-07

| 2024-25 | West Ham U | 0 | 0 | | |

ORFORD, Lewis (M) 2 0
H: 6 1 W: 11 05 b.Havering 18-2-06
Internationals: England U16, U18, U20.

| 2022-23 | West Ham U | 0 | 0 | | |

2023–24 West Ham U 0 0
2024–25 West Ham U 2 0 **2 0**

POTTS, Freddie (M) 73 3
H: 5 11 W: 11 00 b.Romford 12-9-03
2021–22 West Ham U 0 0
2022–23 West Ham U 0 0
2023–24 West Ham U 0 0
2023–24 *Wycombe W* 36 2 **36 2**
2024–25 West Ham U 0 0
2024–25 *Portsmouth* 37 1 **37 1**

RODRIGUEZ, Guido (M) 335 24
H: 6 1 W: 12 04 b.Caseros 12-4-94
Internationals: Argentina Full caps.
2014 River Plate 7 0
2015 River Plate 9 1
2016 River Plate 0 0 **16 1**
2016 *Defensa y Justicia* 15 0 **15 0**
2016–17 Tijuana 39 5 **39 5**
2017–18 America 37 1
2018–19 America 44 8
2019–20 America 22 3 **103 12**
2019–20 Real Betis 14 1
2020–21 Real Betis 35 1
2021–22 Real Betis 32 1
2022–23 Real Betis 34 1
2023–24 Real Betis 24 2 **139 6**
2024–25 West Ham U 23 0 **23 0**

SCARLES, Oliver (M) 15 0
H: 5 11 W: 11 11 b.Bromley 12-12-05
Internationals: England U16, U17, U18, U20.
2022–23 West Ham U 0 0
2023–24 West Ham U 0 0
2024–25 West Ham U 15 0 **15 0**

SOLER, Carlos (M) 263 37
H: 6 0 W: 11 05 b.Valencia 2-1-97
Internationals: Spain U19, U21, U23, Full caps.
2014–15 Valencia 0 0
2015–16 Valencia 0 0
2016–17 Valencia 23 3
2017–18 Valencia 33 1
2018–19 Valencia 31 2
2019–20 Valencia 28 2
2020–21 Valencia 32 11
2021–22 Valencia 32 11
2022–23 Valencia 3 1 **182 31**
2022–23 Paris Saint-Germain 26 3
2023–24 Paris Saint-Germain 24 2
2024–25 Paris Saint-Germain 0 0 **50 5**
On loan from Paris Saint-Germain.
2024–25 West Ham U 31 1 **31 1**

SOUCEK, Tomas (M) 334 67
H: 6 4 W: 13 08 b.Havlickuv Brod 27-2-95
Internationals: Czech Republic U19, U20, U21, Full caps.
2014–15 Slavia Prague 0 0
2014–15 *Viktoria Zizkov* 14 0 **14 0**
2015–16 Slavia Prague 29 7
2016–17 Slavia Prague 7 0
2016–17 *Slovan Liberec* 12 0 **12 0**
2017–18 Slavia Prague 27 3
2018–19 Slavia Prague 34 13
2019–20 Slavia Prague 17 8 **114 31**
2019–20 *West Ham U* 13 3
2020–21 West Ham U 38 10
2021–22 West Ham U 35 5
2022–23 West Ham U 36 2
2023–24 West Ham U 37 7
2024–25 West Ham U 35 9 **194 36**

SUMMERVILLE, Crysencio (M) 135 31
H: 5 9 W: 9 08 b.Rotterdam 30-10-01
Internationals: Netherlands U16, U17, U18, U19, U21.
2018–19 Feyenoord 0 0
2018–19 *Dordrecht* 18 5 **18 5**
2019–20 Feyenoord 0 0
2019–20 *ADO Den Haag* 21 2 **21 2**
2020–21 Leeds U 0 0
2021–22 Leeds U 6 0
2022–23 Leeds U 28 4
2023–24 Leeds U 43 19
2024–25 Leeds U 0 0 **77 23**
2024–25 West Ham U 19 1 **19 1**

SWYER, Kamarai (M) 6 0
H: 6 0 W: 10 06 b.Redbridge 4-12-02
2020–21 West Ham U 0 0
2021–22 West Ham U 0 0
2022–23 West Ham U 0 0
2023–24 West Ham U 0 0
2023–24 *Crawley T* 6 0 **6 0**
2024–25 West Ham U 0 0

TODIBO, Jean-Clair (D) 164 3
H: 6 2 W: 12 11 b.Cayenne 30-12-99
Internationals: France U21, Full caps.
2016–17 Toulouse 0 0
2017–18 Toulouse 0 0
2018–19 Toulouse 10 1 **10 1**
2018–19 Barcelona 2 0
2019–20 Barcelona 2 0
2019–20 *Schalke 04* 8 0 **8 0**
2020–21 Barcelona 0 0 **4 0**
2020–21 *Benfica* 0 0
2020–21 *Nice* 15 1
2021–22 Nice 36 1
2022–23 Nice 34 0
2023–24 Nice 30 0
2024–25 Nice 0 0 **115 2**
On loan from Nice.
2024–25 West Ham U 27 0 **27 0**

WAN BISSAKA, Aaron (D) 208 4
H: 6 0 W: 11 05 b.Croyden 26-11-97
Internationals: DR Congo U20. England U20, U21.
2016–17 Crystal Palace 0 0
2017–18 Crystal Palace 7 0
2018–19 Crystal Palace 35 0 **42 0**
2019–20 Manchester U 35 0
2020–21 Manchester U 34 2
2021–22 Manchester U 20 0
2022–23 Manchester U 19 0
2023–24 Manchester U 22 0 **130 2**
2024–25 West Ham U 36 2 **36 2**

WARD-PROWSE, James (M) 405 57
H: 5 8 W: 10 06 b.Portsmouth 1-11-94
Internationals: England U17, U19, U20, U21, Full caps.
2011–12 Southampton 0 0
2012–13 Southampton 15 0
2013–14 Southampton 34 0
2014–15 Southampton 25 1
2015–16 Southampton 33 2
2016–17 Southampton 30 4
2017–18 Southampton 30 3
2018–19 Southampton 26 7
2019–20 Southampton 38 5
2020–21 Southampton 38 8
2021–22 Southampton 36 10
2022–23 Southampton 38 9
2023–24 Southampton 1 0 **344 49**
2023–24 West Ham U 37 7
2024–25 West Ham U 15 1 **52 8**
2024–25 *Nottingham F* 9 0 **9 0**

ZOUMA, Kurt (D) 328 19
H: 6 2 W: 13 05 b.Lyon 27-10-94
Internationals: France U16, U17, U19, U20, U21, Full caps.
2010–11 Saint-Etienne 0 0
2011–12 Saint-Etienne 20 1
2012–13 Saint-Etienne 18 2
2013–14 Chelsea 0 0
2013–14 *Saint-Etienne* 24 0 **62 3**
2014–15 Chelsea 15 0
2015–16 Chelsea 23 1
2016–17 Chelsea 9 0
2017–18 Chelsea 0 0
2017–18 *Stoke C* 34 1 **34 1**
2018–19 Chelsea 0 0
2018–19 *Everton* 32 2 **32 2**
2019–20 Chelsea 28 0
2020–21 Chelsea 24 5
2021–22 Chelsea 0 0 **99 6**
2021–22 West Ham U 24 1
2022–23 West Ham U 25 2
2023–24 West Ham U 33 3
2024–25 West Ham U 0 0 **82 6**
2024–25 *Al Orobah* 19 1 **19 1**

Players retained or with offer of contract
Adiele, Chukwuemeka Fortune; Ajala, Joshua Oluwaseun Oladimeji; Akpata, Tyron Onyedikachi; Awesu, Olanrewaju Mubarak; Battrum, Ryan Lewis Denis; Briggs, Joshua Joseph; Brown, Luis George; Caliste, Gabriel Paul Russie; Chigwada, David; Fearon, Preston Royston; Golambeckis, Airidas; Herrick, Finlay Jacob; Kamara, Aaron Affieu; Kante, Mohamadou; Kelly, Patrick John; Landers, Josh Finlay; Medine, Jethro Claude; Moore, Sean Ryan; Oyebade, Rayan Oladayo; Rigge, Daniel Arron; Robinson, Carl Junior; Terry, Mason James.

Scholars
Balogun, Majid; Beckford, Lewis Wayne; Dike, Andre Obinna; Hargan, Riley Mason Christopher; Hooper, Finley; Nwosu, Chinazaekpere Samuel; Sowunmi, Elisha; Unwin, Jonathan Brian Haile.

WIGAN ATH (89)

ADAMS, Joe (M) 22 2
H: 5 9 W: 9 11 b.Bolton 3-6-04
2022–23 Wigan Ath 0 0
2023–24 Wigan Ath 0 0
2023–24 *Morecambe* 21 2 **21 2**
2024–25 Wigan Ath 0 0
2024–25 *Bradford C* 1 0 **1 0**

ADEEKO, Badajide (M) 73 1
H: 5 9 W: 11 00 b.Ballybane 3-4-03
Internationals: Republic of Ireland U19, U21.
2021–22 Wigan Ath 0 0
2022–23 Wigan Ath 0 0
2023–24 Wigan Ath 42 0
2024–25 Wigan Ath 31 1 **73 1**

AIMSON, Will (D) 267 12
H: 6 1 W: 13 05 b.Christchurch 1-1-94
From Eastleigh.
2013–14 Hull C 0 0
2014–15 Hull C 0 0
2014–15 *Tranmere R* 2 0 **2 0**
2015–16 Hull C 0 0
2015–16 Blackpool 15 0
2016–17 Blackpool 18 0
2017–18 Blackpool 17 0 **50 0**
2018–19 Bury 37 4 **37 4**
2019–20 Plymouth Arg 5 2
2020–21 Plymouth Arg 40 0 **45 2**
2021–22 Bolton W 25 1
2022–23 Bolton W 11 0 **36 1**
2022–23 *Exeter C* 18 0
2023–24 Exeter C 36 5 **54 5**
2024–25 Wigan Ath 43 0 **43 0**

ASAMOAH, Maleace (F) 45 7
H: 6 0 W: 11 07 b.Oxford 15-11-02
From Cheshunt.
2021–22 Kalamata 0 0
2021–22 *Olympiacos Volos* 3 0 **3 0**
2022–23 Kalamata 1 0 **1 0**
From New Salamis.
2023–24 Fleetwood T 8 0 **8 0**
2023–24 *Waterford* 17 6 **17 6**
2024–25 Wigan Ath 16 1 **16 1**

CARRAGHER, James (D) 47 2
H: 6 4 W: 13 10 b.Liverpool 11-11-02
Internationals: Malta Full caps.
From Liverpool.
2021–22 Wigan Ath 0 0
2022–23 Wigan Ath 0 0
2023–24 Wigan Ath 0 0
2023–24 *Inverness CT* 14 0 **14 0**
2024–25 Wigan Ath 33 2 **33 2**

DARCY, Ronan (F) 169 13
H: 5 9 W: 9 06 b.Ormskirk 4-11-00
2018–19 Bolton W 1 0
2019–20 Bolton W 19 1
2020–21 Bolton W 8 0
2021 *Sogndal* 8 0 **8 0**
2021–22 Bolton W 1 0 **29 1**
2021–22 *Queen's Park* 10 1 **10 1**
2022–23 Swindon T 43 4 **43 4**
2023–24 Crawley T 45 5
2024–25 Crawley T 21 1 **66 6**
2024–25 Wigan Ath 13 1 **13 1**

FRANCOIS, Tyrese (M) 34 1
H: 5 6 W: 8 11 b.Campbelltown 16-7-00
Internationals: Australia U23.
2019–20 Fulham 0 0
2020–21 Fulham 1 0
2021–22 Fulham 2 0
2022–23 Fulham 1 0
2022–23 *Gorica* 10 1 **10 1**
2023–24 Fulham 0 0 **4 0**
2023–24 *Vejle* 15 0 **15 0**
2024–25 Wigan Ath 5 0 **5 0**

HUNGBO, Joseph (M) 100 10
H: 5 8 W: 11 05 b.Lambeth 15-1-00
2018–19 Crystal Palace 0 0
2019–20 Watford 0 0
2020–21 Watford 5 0
2021–22 Watford 0 0
2021–22 *Ross Co* 33 7 **33 7**
2022–23 Watford 7 0 **12 0**
2022–23 *Huddersfield T* 14 3 **14 3**
2023–24 Nuremberg 17 0
2024–25 Nuremberg 0 0 **17 0**
2024–25 *Rotherham U* 13 0 **13 0**
2024–25 Wigan Ath 11 0 **11 0**

KERR, Jason (D) 298 23
H: 5 11 W: 11 00 b.Edinburgh 6-2-97
Internationals: Scotland U21.
2015–16 St Johnstone 0 0
2015–16 *East Fife* 34 3
2016–17 St Johnstone 0 0
2016–17 *East Fife* 33 8 **67 11**
2017–18 St Johnstone 15 1
2017–18 *Queen of the South* 18 4 **18 4**
2018–19 St Johnstone 37 2
2019–20 St Johnstone 29 1
2020–21 St Johnstone 31 1
2021–22 St Johnstone 3 0 **115 5**
2021–22 Wigan Ath 24 1
2022–23 Wigan Ath 16 0
2023–24 Wigan Ath 14 1
2024–25 Wigan Ath 44 1 **98 3**

LONERGAN, Andrew (G) 353 1
H: 6 4 W: 13 10 b.Preston 19-10-83
Internationals: Republic of Ireland U16. England U16, U17, U18, U19, U20.
2000–01 Preston NE 1 0
2001–02 Preston NE 0 0
2002–03 Preston NE 0 0
2002–03 *Darlington* 2 0 **2 0**
2003–04 Preston NE 8 0

2004–05	Preston NE	23	1		
2005–06	Preston NE	0	0		
2005–06	Wycombe W	2	0	2	0
2006–07	Preston NE	13	0		
2006–07	Swindon T	1	0	1	0
2007–08	Preston NE	43	0		
2008–09	Preston NE	46	0		
2009–10	Preston NE	45	0		
2010–11	Preston NE	29	0	208	0
2011–12	Leeds U	35	0		
2012–13	Bolton W	5	0		
2013–14	Bolton W	17	0		
2014–15	Bolton W	29	0	51	0
2015–16	Fulham	29	0	29	0
2016–17	Wolverhampton W	11	0		
2017–18	Wolverhampton W	0	0	11	0
2017–18	Leeds U	7	0	42	0
2018–19	Middlesbrough	0	0		
2018–19	Rochdale	7	0	7	0
2019–20	Liverpool	0	0		
2020–21	Stoke C	0	0		
2020–21	WBA	0	0		
2021–22	Everton	0	0		
2022–23	Everton	0	0		
2023–24	Everton	0	0		
2024–25	Wigan Ath	0	0		

McHUGH, Harry (F) 29 1
H: 5 10 W: 11 11 b.Liverpool 14-10-02
From Everton.

2020–21	Wigan Ath	1	0		
2021–22	Wigan Ath	0	0		
2022–23	Wigan Ath	0	0		
2023–24	Wigan Ath	2	0		
2023–24	Ayr U	12	1	12	1
2024–25	Wigan Ath	14	0	17	0

McMANAMAN, Callum (F) 303 27
H: 5 9 W: 11 07 b.Huyton 25-4-91
Internationals: England U20.

2008–09	Wigan Ath	1	0		
2009–10	Wigan Ath	0	0		
2010–11	Wigan Ath	3	0		
2011–12	Wigan Ath	2	0		
2011–12	Blackpool	14	2	14	2
2012–13	Wigan Ath	20	2		
2013–14	Wigan Ath	30	3		
2014–15	Wigan Ath	23	5		
2014–15	WBA	8	0		
2015–16	WBA	12	0		
2016–17	WBA	0	0	20	0
2017–18	Sheffield Wed	11	0	11	0
2017–18	Sunderland	24	1	24	1
2018–19	Wigan Ath	22	1		
2019–20	Luton T	23	4	23	4
2020–21	Melbourne Victory	18	4	18	4
2021–22	Tranmere R	29	2	29	2
2023–24	Wigan Ath	37	2		
2024–25	Wigan Ath	26	1	164	14

MELLISH, Jon (D) 234 28
H: 6 2 W: 11 07 b.South Shields 19-9-97
Internationals: England C.
From Gateshead.

2019–20	Carlisle U	15	0		
2020–21	Carlisle U	44	11		
2021–22	Carlisle U	42	3		
2022–23	Carlisle U	43	6		
2023–24	Carlisle U	46	5		
2024–25	Carlisle U	23	2	213	27
2024–25	Wigan Ath	21	1	21	1

MILLER, K'Marni (D) 2 0
H: 5 10 W: 10 10 b.Huddersfield 9-11-05

2024–25	Wigan Ath	2	0	2	0

PAYNE, Kai (M) 2 0
H: 5 10 W: 11 09 b. 26-11-04

2023–24	Wigan Ath	2	0		
2024–25	Wigan Ath	2	0	2	0

RANKINE, Dion (M) 53 2
H: 5 5 W: 9 13 b.Barnet 15-10-02

2020–21	Chelsea	0	0		
2021–22	Chelsea	0	0		
2022–23	Chelsea	0	0		
2023–24	Chelsea	0	0		
2023–24	Exeter C	33	1	33	1
2024–25	Wigan Ath	20	1	20	1

REILLY, Jack (G) 0 0
H: 5 11 W: 11 05 b. 9-2-04

2023–24	Wigan Ath	0	0		
2024–25	Wigan Ath	0	0		

ROBINSON, Josh (D) 0 0
H: 5 11 W: 12 08 b.London 20-12-04
Internationals: England U18.

2023–24	Arsenal	0	0		
2024–25	Arsenal	0	0		
2024–25	Wigan Ath	0	0		

ROBINSON, Luke (D) 66 1
H: 5 9 W: 11 05 b.Berkinhead 19-11-01
Internationals: Scotland U18, U19.
From Wrexham.

2020–21	Wigan Ath	25	0		
2021–22	Wigan Ath	1	0		
2022–23	Wigan Ath	0	0		
2022–23	Tranmere R	2	0	2	0
2023–24	Wigan Ath	1	0		
2023–24	St Johnstone	14	0	14	0
2024–25	Wigan Ath	23	1	50	1

SESSEGNON, Steven (D) 112 1
H: 5 8 W: 10 06 b.Roehampton 18-5-00
Internationals: England U16, U17, U18, U19, U20, U21.

2017–18	Fulham	0	0		
2018–19	Fulham	14	0		
2019–20	Fulham	14	0		
2020–21	Fulham	0	0		
2020–21	Bristol C	16	0	16	0
2021–22	Fulham	0	0		
2021–22	Plymouth Arg	10	0	10	0
2022–23	Fulham	0	0		
2022–23	Charlton Ath	33	1	33	1
2023–24	Wigan Ath	26	0		
2024–25	Wigan Ath	13	0	39	0

SIBBICK, Toby (D) 177 1
H: 6 0 W: 10 12 b.Isleworth 23-5-99
Internationals: Uganda Full caps.

2016–17	AFC Wimbledon	2	0		
2017–18	AFC Wimbledon	1	0		
2018–19	AFC Wimbledon	23	0	26	0
2019–20	Barnsley	18	0		
2019–20	Hearts	2	0		
2020–21	Barnsley	21	0		
2020–21	Oostende	0	0		
2021–22	Barnsley	12	1	51	1
2021–22	Hearts	14	0		
2022–23	Hearts	32	0		
2023–24	Hearts	21	0	69	0
2024–25	Wigan Ath	31	0	31	0

SMITH, Jonny (M) 184 25
H: 5 10 W: 10 01 b.Liverpool 28-7-97
From Wrexham.

2019–20	Bristol C	0	0		
2019–20	Oldham Ath	28	9	28	9
2020–21	Burton Alb	16	2		
2020–21	Swindon T	16	1	16	1
2021–22	Burton Alb	29	4		
2022–23	Burton Alb	32	3	77	9
2023–24	Wigan Ath	27	3		
2024–25	Wigan Ath	36	3	63	6

SMITH, Matthew (M) 122 4
H: 5 9 W: 11 00 b.Harlow 5-10-00

2019–20	Arsenal	0	0		
2020–21	Swindon T	24	2	24	2
2020–21	Arsenal	0	0		
2020–21	Charlton Ath	8	0	8	0
2021–22	Arsenal	0	0		
2021–22	Doncaster R	43	0	43	0
2022–23	Arsenal	0	0		
2023–24	Wigan Ath	28	1		
2024–25	Wigan Ath	19	1	47	2

SMITH, Scott (M) 71 1
H: 5 10 W: 11 09 b.Wigan 7-2-01
Internationals: Wales U19.

2020–21	Wigan Ath	0	0		
2021–22	Wigan Ath	0	0		
2022–23	Wigan Ath	2	0		
2023–24	Wigan Ath	31	1		
2024–25	Wigan Ath	38	0	71	1

STONES, Josh (F) 15 0
H: 5 11 W: 12 08 b.Bradford 12-11-03
From Bradford C, Guiseley.

2022–23	Wigan Ath	0	0		
2022–23	Ross Co	6	0	6	0
2023–24	Wigan Ath	6	0		
2024–25	Wigan Ath	3	0	9	0

Transferred to York C, January 2025.

SZE, Chris (M) 32 2
H: 6 1 W: 12 11 b. 9-12-03

2021–22	Wigan Ath	0	0		
2022–23	Wigan Ath	1	0		
2023–24	Wigan Ath	19	1		
2024–25	Wigan Ath	12	1	32	2

TICKLE, Sam (G) 93 0
H: 5 11 W: 11 07 b.Warrington 31-3-02
Internationals: England U21.

2020–21	Wigan Ath	0	0		
2021–22	Wigan Ath	0	0		
2022–23	Wigan Ath	1	0		
2023–24	Wigan Ath	46	0		
2024–25	Wigan Ath	46	0	93	0

WATSON, Tom (G) 0 0
H: 6 2 W: 12 02 b. 27-8-04

2022–23	Wigan Ath	0	0		
2023–24	Wigan Ath	0	0		
2024–25	Wigan Ath	0	0		

WEIR, Jensen (M) 119 12
H: 6 0 W: 11 09 b.Warrington 31-1-02
Internationals: Scotland U16, U17. England U17, U18, U20.

2017–18	Wigan Ath	0	0		
2018–19	Wigan Ath	1	0		
2019–20	Wigan Ath	0	0		
2020–21	Brighton & HA	0	0		
2021–22	Brighton & HA	0	0		
2021–22	Cambridge U	15	1	15	1
2022–23	Brighton & HA	0	0		
2022–23	Morecambe	43	10	43	10
2023–24	Brighton & HA	0	0		
2023–24	Blackpool	10	0	10	0
2023–24	Port Vale	17	1	17	1
2024–25	Brighton & HA	0	0		
2024–25	Wigan Ath	33	0	34	0

Players retained or with offer of contract
Bettoni, Harrison Lee; Brenan, Tobias Toumai Moses; Chapman, Llyton Levi; Corran, Matthew Nicholas; Costello, Thomas Anthony; Graham, Leo James David; Igiehon, Elijah Omoruyi; Rogers, Jack; Spinelli, Matteo David.

Scholars
Bolland, Samuel Michael; Cavanagh, John-Paul Francis; Clifford, Alastair John; Edwards, Christy John; Edwards, Zachariah Elliot; Fairhurst, Oliver Christopher; Flight, Liam Patrick; Goulding, Mason Jak; Greenhalgh, Reece Lucus; Hagan, Lucas Mark; Harris, Oscar Thomas; Hughes, Alex Joseph; Jones, Callum; Knott, James Jack; McKee, Charley; Rimmer, Harrison Lewis; Simms, Cole Leslie; Spaven, Jake Michael; Spelman, Sebastian Joseph; Taylor, Rohan James; Wilson, Lewis Paul Patrick Austin.

WOLVERHAMPTON W (90)

AGBADOU, Emmanuel (D) 165 9
H: 6 4 W: 13 08 b.Abidjan 17-6-97
Internationals: Ivory Coast Full caps.

2019–20	Monastir	18	1	18	1
2020–21	Eupen	23	1		
2021–22	Eupen	33	5	56	6
2022–23	Reims	29	0		
2023–24	Reims	32	1		
2024–25	Reims	14	0	75	1
2024–25	Wolverhampton W	16	1	16	1

AIT NOURI, Rayan (D) 158 9
H: 5 10 W: 11 00 b.Montreuil 6-6-01
Internationals: France U18, U21. Algeria Full caps.

2018–19	Angers	3	0		
2019–20	Angers	17	0		
2020–21	Angers	3	0	23	0
2020–21	Wolverhampton W	21	1		
2021–22	Wolverhampton W	23	1		
2022–23	Wolverhampton W	21	1		
2023–24	Wolverhampton W	33	2		
2024–25	Wolverhampton W	37	4	135	9

ANDRE TRINDADE, Neto (M) 146 2
H: 5 9 W: 12 02 b.Ibirataia 16-7-01
Internationals: Brazil Full caps.

2020	Fluminense	10	0		
2021	Fluminense	26	1		
2022	Fluminense	34	1		
2023	Fluminense	31	0		
2024	Fluminense	12	0	113	2
2024–25	Wolverhampton W	33	0	33	0

ASHWORTH, Finlay (M) 0 0
b. 18-9-05
Internationals: Wales U17.

2024–25	Wolverhampton W	0	0		
2024–25	Port Vale	0	0		

BALLARD-MATTHEWS, Emilio (F) 0 0
b. 30-11-07
Internationals: England U16.

2023–24	Wolverhampton W	0	0		
2024–25	Wolverhampton W	0	0		

BARNETT, Ty (F) 0 0
H: 5 9 W: 10 06 b.Birmingham 19-7-05

2023–24	Wolverhampton W	0	0		
2024–25	Wolverhampton W	0	0		

BELLEGARDE, Jeanricner (M) 241 16
H: 5 8 W: 11 00 b.Colombes 27-6-98
Internationals: France U19, U20, U21.

2015–16	Lens	0	0		
2016–17	Lens	9	0		
2017–18	Lens	25	1		
2018–19	Lens	21	4	55	5
2019–20	Strasbourg	24	0		
2020–21	Strasbourg	36	1		
2021–22	Strasbourg	36	2		
2022–23	Strasbourg	30	2		
2023–24	Strasbourg	3	2	129	7
2023–24	Wolverhampton W	22	2		
2024–25	Wolverhampton W	35	2	57	4

BENTLEY, Daniel (G) 410 0
H: 6 2 W: 11 05 b.Basildon 13-7-93

2011–12	Southend U	1	0		
2012–13	Southend U	9	0		
2013–14	Southend U	46	0		
2014–15	Southend U	42	0		
2015–16	Southend U	43	0	141	0
2016–17	Brentford	45	0		
2017–18	Brentford	45	0		

2018–19 Brentford 33 0 **123** **0**
2019–20 Bristol C 43 0
2020–21 Bristol C 43 0
2021–22 Bristol C 38 0
2022–23 Bristol C 13 0 **137** **0**
2022–23 Wolverhampton W 2 0
2023–24 Wolverhampton W 5 0
2024–25 Wolverhampton W 2 0 **9** **0**

BUENO, Hugo (D) 63 0
H: 5 11 W: 11 07 b.Vigo 18-9-02
Internationals: Spain U18, U21.
2020–21 Wolverhampton W 0 0
2021–22 Wolverhampton W 0 0
2022–23 Wolverhampton W 21 0
2023–24 Wolverhampton W 22 0
2024–25 Wolverhampton W 0 0 **43** **0**
2024–25 *Feyenoord* 20 0 **20** **0**

BUENO, Santiago (D) 143 3
H: 6 3 W: 11 03 b.Montevideo 9-11-98
Internationals: Uruguay U17, U20, U23, Full caps.
2017–18 Barcelona 0 0
2018–19 Barcelona 0 0
2019–20 Girona 1 0
2020–21 Girona 36 2
2021–22 Girona 31 1
2022–23 Girona 34 0 **102** **3**
2023–24 Wolverhampton W 12 0
2024–25 Wolverhampton W 29 0 **41** **0**

CAMPBELL, Chem (M) 82 10
H: 5 11 W: 11 05 b.Birmingham 30-12-02
Internationals: Wales U17.
2019–20 Wolverhampton W 0 0
2020–21 Wolverhampton W 0 0
2021–22 Wolverhampton W 1 0
2022–23 Wolverhampton W 5 0
2022–23 *Wycombe W* 17 3
2023–24 Wolverhampton W 0 0
2023–24 *Charlton Ath* 12 2 **12** **2**
2023–24 *Wycombe W* 8 0 **25** **3**
2024–25 Wolverhampton W 0 0 **6** **0**
2024–25 *Reading* 39 5 **39** **5**

CHIQUINHO, Oliveira (F) 83 9
H: 5 10 W: 14 05 b.Cascais 5-2-00
Internationals: Portugal U20, U21.
From Sporting Lisbon.
2019–20 Estoril 8 1
2020–21 Estoril 13 0
2021–22 Estoril 15 3 **36** **4**
2021–22 Wolverhampton W 8 0
2022–23 Wolverhampton W 0 0
2023–24 Wolverhampton W 0 0
2023–24 *Stoke C* 3 0 **3** **0**
2023–24 *Famalicao* 27 5 **27** **5**
2024–25 Wolverhampton W 1 0 **9** **0**
2024–25 *Mallorca* 8 0 **8** **0**

CHIREWA, Tawanda (M) 26 0
H: 5 11 W: 11 05 b.Chelmsford 11-10-03
Internationals: Zimbabwe Full caps.
2019–20 Ipswich T 0 0
2020–21 Ipswich T 0 0
2021–22 Ipswich T 0 0
2022–23 Ipswich T 0 0
2023–24 Wolverhampton W 8 0
2024–25 Wolverhampton W 0 0 **8** **0**
2024–25 *Derby Co* 5 0 **5** **0**
2024–25 *Huddersfield T* 13 0 **13** **0**

CHIWOME, Leon (F) 3 0
H: 6 1 W: 11 11 b.Brighton 10-1-06
Internationals: England U17, U18.
2023–24 Wolverhampton W 3 0
2024–25 Wolverhampton W 0 0 **3** **0**

DANIEL PODENCE, Castelo (F) 199 33
H: 5 5 W: 9 02 b.Oeiras 21-10-95
Internationals: Portugal U16, U18, U19, U20, U21, Full caps
2012–13 Sporting Lisbon 0 0
2013–14 Sporting Lisbon 0 0
2014–15 Sporting Lisbon 0 0
2015–16 Sporting Lisbon 0 0
2016–17 Sporting Lisbon 13 0
2016–17 *Moreirense* 14 4 **14** **4**
2017–18 Sporting Lisbon 12 0 **25** **0**
2018–19 Olympiacos 27 5
2019–20 Olympiacos 15 3
2019–20 Wolverhampton W 9 1
2020–21 Wolverhampton W 24 3
2021–22 Wolverhampton W 26 2
2022–23 Wolverhampton W 32 6
2023–24 Wolverhampton W 0 0
2023–24 *Olympiacos* 25 9 **67** **17**
2024–25 Wolverhampton W 2 0 **93** **12**
Transferred to Al-Shabab, September 2024.

DAWSON, Craig (D) 447 46
H: 6 2 W: 13 05 b.Rochdale 6-5-90
Internationals: England U21. Great Britain.
2008–09 Rochdale 0 0
2009–10 Rochdale 42 9
2010–11 WBA 0 0
2010–11 *Rochdale* 45 10 **87** **19**
2011–12 WBA 8 0
2012–13 WBA 1 0
2012–13 *Bolton W* 16 4 **16** **4**
2013–14 WBA 12 0
2014–15 WBA 29 2
2015–16 WBA 38 4
2016–17 WBA 37 4
2017–18 WBA 28 2
2018–19 WBA 41 2 **194** **14**
2019–20 Watford 29 2
2020–21 Watford 0 0 **29** **2**
2020–21 *West Ham U* 22 3
2021–22 West Ham U 34 2
2022–23 West Ham U 8 0 **64** **5**
2022–23 Wolverhampton W 17 1
2023–24 Wolverhampton W 25 1
2024–25 Wolverhampton W 15 0 **57** **2**

DJIGA, Nasser (D) 76 3
H: 6 4 W: 13 03 b.Bobo-Dioulasso 15-11-02
Internationals: Burkina Faso U20, Full caps.
2021–22 Basel 6 0
2022–23 Basel 1 0
2022–23 *Nimes* 21 0 **21** **0**
2023–24 Basel 4 0 **11** **0**
2023–24 Red Star Belgrade 22 1
2024–25 Red Star Belgrade 17 2 **39** **3**
2024–25 Wolverhampton W 5 0 **5** **0**

DOHERTY, Matthew (D) 396 29
H: 6 0 W: 14 01 b.Dublin 16-1-92
Internationals: Republic of Ireland U19, U21, Full caps.
2010–11 Wolverhampton W 0 0
2011–12 Wolverhampton W 1 0
2011–12 *Hibernian* 13 2 **13** **2**
2012–13 Wolverhampton W 13 1
2012–13 *Bury* 17 1 **17** **1**
2013–14 Wolverhampton W 18 1
2014–15 Wolverhampton W 33 0
2015–16 Wolverhampton W 34 2
2016–17 Wolverhampton W 42 4
2017–18 Wolverhampton W 45 4
2018–19 Wolverhampton W 38 4
2019–20 Wolverhampton W 36 4
2020–21 Tottenham H 17 0
2021–22 Tottenham H 15 2
2022–23 Tottenham H 12 1 **44** **3**
2022–23 Atletico Madrid 2 0 **2** **0**
2023–24 Wolverhampton W 30 1
2024–25 Wolverhampton W 30 2 **320** **23**

DOYLE, Tommy (M) 103 5
H: 5 10 W: 11 05 b.Manchester 17-10-01
Internationals: England U16, U17, U18, U19, U20, U21.
2019–20 Manchester C 1 0
2020–21 Manchester C 0 0
2021–22 Manchester C 0 0
2021–22 *Hamburger SV* 0 0
2021–22 *Cardiff C* 19 2 **19** **2**
2022–23 Manchester C 0 0
2022–23 *Sheffield U* 33 3 **33** **3**
2023–24 Manchester C 0 0 **1** **0**
2023–24 *Wolverhampton W* 26 0
2024–25 Wolverhampton W 24 0 **50** **0**

EDOZIE, Tom (F) 0 0
H: 5 10 W: 10 10 b. 18-5-06
2024–25 Wolverhampton W 0 0

FORBS, Carlos (F) 32 2
H: 5 7 W: 10 03 b.Sintra 19-3-04
Internationals: Portugal U16, U18, U19, U21.
2020–21 Manchester C 0 0
2021–22 Manchester C 0 0
2022–23 Manchester C 0 0
2023–24 Ajax 21 2
2024–25 Ajax 1 0 **22** **2**
On loan from Ajax.
2024–25 Wolverhampton W 10 0 **10** **0**

FRASER, Nathan (F) 11 0
H: 6 2 W: 12 13 b.Wolverhampton 22-2-05
Internationals: Republic of Ireland U19.
2022–23 Wolverhampton W 0 0
2023–24 Wolverhampton W 7 0
2024–25 Wolverhampton W 0 0 **7** **0**
2024–25 *Zulte-Waregem* 4 0 **4** **0**

GOMES, Rodrigo (M) 86 10
H: 5 9 W: 10 03 b.Povoa de Varzim 7-7-03
Internationals: Portugal U16, U17, U18, U19, U20, U21.
2020–21 Braga 4 0
2021–22 Braga 12 0
2022–23 Braga 15 1
2023–24 Braga 0 0 **31** **1**
2023–24 *Estoril* 30 7 **30** **7**
2024–25 Wolverhampton W 25 2 **25** **2**

GOMES, Tote (D) 140 5
H: 6 2 W: 11 05 b.Bissau 16-1-99
Internationals: Portugal U20, Full caps.
2018–19 Estoril 3 0
2019–20 Estoril 0 0 **3** **0**
2020–21 Wolverhampton W 0 0
2020–21 *Grasshopper* 34 2 **34** **2**
2021–22 Wolverhampton W 4 0
2021–22 *Grasshopper* 16 1 **16** **1**
2022–23 Wolverhampton W 17 1
2023–24 Wolverhampton W 35 1
2024–25 Wolverhampton W 31 0 **87** **2**

GONCALO GUEDES, Manuel (F) 273 40
H: 5 10 W: 10 01 b.Benavente 29-11-96
Internationals: Portugal U16, U17, U18, U19, U20, U21, U23, Full caps.
2013–14 Benfica 0 0
2014–15 Benfica 5 0
2015–16 Benfica 18 3
2016–17 Benfica 16 2
2016–17 Paris Saint-Germain 7 0
2017–18 Paris Saint-Germain 1 0 **8** **0**
2017–18 *Valencia* 33 5
2018–19 Valencia 25 5
2019–20 Valencia 21 2
2020–21 Valencia 31 5
2021–22 Valencia 36 11 **146** **28**
2022–23 Wolverhampton W 13 1
2022–23 *Benfica* 12 1
2023–24 Wolverhampton W 0 0
2023–24 *Benfica* 9 0 **60** **6**
2023–24 *Villarreal* 17 3 **17** **3**
2024–25 Wolverhampton W 29 2 **42** **3**

GONZALEZ, Enso (F) 33 3
H: 5 7 W: 10 12 b.Asuncion 20-1-05
Internationals: Paraguay U23.
2022 Libertad 9 0
2023 Libertad 23 3 **32** **3**
2023–24 Wolverhampton W 1 0
2024–25 Wolverhampton W 0 0 **1** **0**

GRIFFITHS, Harvey (M) 1 0
H: 6 3 W: 12 04 b.Oldham 22-9-03
2022–23 Wolverhampton W 0 0
2023–24 Wolverhampton W 0 0
2023–24 *Walsall* 1 0 **1** **0**
2024–25 Wolverhampton W 0 0

HODGE, Joseph (M) 41 2
H: 5 8 W: 9 02 b.Manchester 14-9-02
Internationals: England U16, U17. Republic of Ireland U16, U17, U19, U21.
2020–21 Manchester C 0 0
2021–22 Wolverhampton W 0 0
2022–23 Wolverhampton W 6 0
2023–24 Wolverhampton W 0 0
2023–24 *QPR* 8 1 **8** **1**
2024–25 Wolverhampton W 0 0 **6** **0**
2024–25 *Huddersfield T* 27 1 **27** **1**

HOEVER, Ki-Jana (D) 110 9
H: 5 11 W: 10 03 b.Amsterdam 18-1-02
Internationals: Netherlands U16, U17, U18, U21.
From Ajax.
2018–19 Liverpool 0 0
2019–20 Liverpool 0 0
2020–21 Wolverhampton W 12 0
2021–22 Wolverhampton W 8 0
2022–23 Wolverhampton W 0 0
2022–23 *PSV Eindhoven* 5 0 **5** **0**
2022–23 *Stoke C* 15 4
2023–24 Wolverhampton W 0 0
2023–24 *Stoke C* 40 4 **55** **8**
2024–25 Wolverhampton W 0 0 **20** **0**
2024–25 *Auxerre* 30 1 **30** **1**

HOLMAN, Fletcher (F) 0 0
H: 6 0 W: 12 04 b. 12-10-04
2023–24 Wolverhampton W 0 0
2024–25 Wolverhampton W 0 0

HUBNER, Justin (D) 3 0
H: 6 2 W: 11 11 b.Den Bosch 14-9-03
Internationals: Netherlands U20. Indonesia U20, U23, Full caps.
From Den Bosch.
2022–23 Wolverhampton W 0 0
2023–24 Wolverhampton W 0 0
2023–24 *Cerezo Osaka* 3 0 **3** **0**
2024–25 Wolverhampton W 0 0

HWANG, Hee-Chan (F) 264 65
H: 5 10 W: 12 02 b.Chuncheon 26-1-96
Internationals: South Korea U17, U20, U23, Full caps.
2014–15 Red Bull Salzburg 0 0
2014–15 *Liefering* 13 2
2015–16 Red Bull Salzburg 13 0
2015–16 *Liefering* 18 11 **31** **13**
2016–17 Red Bull Salzburg 26 12
2017–18 Red Bull Salzburg 20 5
2018–19 Red Bull Salzburg 0 0
2018–19 *Hamburger SV* 20 2 **20** **2**
2019–20 Red Bull Salzburg 27 11 **86** **28**
2020–21 RB Leipzig 18 0
2021–22 RB Leipzig 2 0 **20** **0**
2021–22 *Wolverhampton W* 30 5
2022–23 Wolverhampton W 27 3
2023–24 Wolverhampton W 29 12
2024–25 Wolverhampton W 21 2 **107** **22**

JOAO GOMES, da Silva (M) 140 6
H: 5 10 W: 11 09 b.Rio de Janeiro 12-2-01
Internationals: Brazil Full caps.

2020	Flamengo	11	0		
2021	Flamengo	19	0		
2022	Flamengo	29	0		
2022–23	Flamengo	0	0	**59**	**0**
2022–23	Wolverhampton W	11	1		
2023–24	Wolverhampton W	34	2		
2024–25	Wolverhampton W	36	3	**81**	**6**

JOHNSTONE, Samuel (G) 341 0
H: 6 3 W: 13 05 b.Preston 25-3-93
Internationals: England U16, U17, U19, U20, Full caps.

2009–10	Manchester U	0	0		
2010–11	Manchester U	0	0		
2011–12	Manchester U	0	0		
2011–12	*Oldham Ath*	0	0		
2011–12	*Scunthorpe U*	12	0	**12**	**0**
2012–13	Manchester U	0	0		
2012–13	*Walsall*	7	0	**7**	**0**
2013–14	Manchester U	0	0		
2013–14	*Yeovil T*	1	0	**1**	**0**
2013–14	*Doncaster R*	18	0		
2014–15	Manchester U	0	0		
2014–15	*Doncaster R*	10	0	**28**	**0**
2014–15	*Preston NE*	22	0		
2015–16	Manchester U	0	0		
2015–16	*Preston NE*	4	0	**26**	**0**
2016–17	Manchester U	0	0		
2016–17	*Aston Villa*	21	0		
2017–18	Manchester U	0	0		
2017–18	*Aston Villa*	45	0	**66**	**0**
2018–19	WBA	46	0		
2019–20	WBA	46	0		
2020–21	WBA	37	0		
2021–22	WBA	36	0	**165**	**0**
2022–23	Crystal Palace	9	0		
2023–24	Crystal Palace	20	0	**29**	**0**
2024–25	Wolverhampton W	7	0	**7**	**0**

JOSE SA, Pedro (G) 251 0
H: 6 4 W: 13 03 b.Braga 17-1-93
Internationals: Portugal U20, U21, U23, Full caps.

2012–13	Maritimo	0	0		
2013–14	Maritimo	8	0		
2014–15	Maritimo	3	0		
2015–16	Maritimo	5	0	**16**	**0**
2015–16	Porto	0	0		
2016–17	Porto	1	0		
2017–18	Porto	14	0	**15**	**0**
2018–19	Olympiacos	21	0		
2019–20	Olympiacos	33	0		
2020–21	Olympiacos	29	0	**83**	**0**
2021–22	Wolverhampton W	37	0		
2022–23	Wolverhampton W	36	0		
2023–24	Wolverhampton W	35	0		
2024–25	Wolverhampton W	29	0	**137**	**0**

KALAJDZIC, Sasa (F) 107 36
H: 6 7 W: 12 00 b.Vienna 7-7-97
Internationals: Austria U21, Full caps.

2016–17	Admira Wacker	0	0		
2017–18	Admira Wacker	18	3		
2018–19	Admira Wacker	15	8	**33**	**11**
2019–20	VfB Stuttgart	6	1		
2020–21	VfB Stuttgart	33	16		
2021–22	VfB Stuttgart	15	6		
2022–23	VfB Stuttgart	3	0	**57**	**23**
2022–23	Wolverhampton W	1	0		
2023–24	Wolverhampton W	11	2		
2023–24	*Eintracht Frankfurt*	5	0	**5**	**0**
2024–25	Wolverhampton W	0	0	**12**	**2**

KETO-DIYAWA, Aaron (D) 0 0
H: 5 8 W: 10 08 b. 11-9-03

2023–24	Wolverhampton W	0	0		
2024–25	Wolverhampton W	0	0		

KING, Tom (G) 147 1
H: 6 1 W: 12 08 b.Plymouth 9-3-95
Internationals: England U17. Wales Full caps.

2011–12	Crystal Palace	0	0		
2012–13	Crystal Palace	0	0		
2013–14	Crystal Palace	0	0		
2014–15	Millwall	0	0		
2015–16	Millwall	0	0		
2016–17	Millwall	11	0		
2017–18	Millwall	0	0		
2017–18	*Stevenage*	18	0	**18**	**0**
2018–19	Millwall	0	0	**11**	**0**
2018–19	*AFC Wimbledon*	12	0	**12**	**0**
2019–20	Newport Co	31	0		
2020–21	Newport Co	9	1		
2021–22	Newport Co	0	0	**40**	**1**
2021–22	Salford C	36	0		
2022–23	Salford C	21	0	**57**	**0**
2022–23	Northampton T	8	0	**8**	**0**
2023–24	Wolverhampton W	0	0		
2024–25	Wolverhampton W	1	0	**1**	**0**

LARSEN, Jorgen (F) 219 61
H: 6 4 W: 12 06 b.Halden 6-2-00
Internationals: Norway U16, U17, U18, U19, U20, U21, Full caps.

2017	Sarpsborg 08	3	0		
2018	Sarpsborg 08	6	0		
2019	Sarpsborg 08	23	4		
2020	Sarpsborg 08	16	2	**48**	**6**
2020–21	Groningen	31	9		
2021–22	Groningen	32	14		
2022–23	Groningen	4	1	**67**	**24**
2022–23	Celta Vigo	32	4		
2023–24	Celta Vigo	37	13		
2024–25	Celta Vigo	0	0	**69**	**17**

On loan from Celta Vigo.

2024–25	Wolverhampton W	35	14	**35**	**14**

LEMBIKISA, Dexter (D) 55 3
H: 5 11 W: 10 10 b.Lambeth 4-11-03
Internationals: Jamaica Full caps.

2021–22	Wolverhampton W	0	0		
2022–23	Wolverhampton W	1	0		
2023–24	Wolverhampton W	0	0		
2023–24	*Rotherham U*	25	1	**25**	**1**
2023–24	*Hearts*	14	2	**14**	**2**
2024–25	Wolverhampton W	0	0	**1**	**0**
2024–25	*Yverdon-Sport*	3	0	**3**	**0**
2024–25	*Barnsley*	12	0	**12**	**0**

LEMINA, Mario (M) 295 15
H: 6 0 W: 12 00 b.Libreville 1-9-93
Internationals: France U20, U21. Gabon Full caps.

2012–13	Lorient	10	0		
2013–14	Lorient	4	0	**14**	**0**
2013–14	Marseille	14	0		
2014–15	Marseille	23	2		
2015–16	Marseille	4	0	**41**	**2**
2015–16	Juventus	10	2		
2016–17	Juventus	19	1	**29**	**3**
2017–18	Southampton	25	1		
2018–19	Southampton	21	1		
2019–20	Southampton	0	0		
2019–20	*Galatasaray*	20	0	**20**	**0**
2020–21	Southampton	0	0	**46**	**2**
2020–21	*Fulham*	28	1	**28**	**1**
2021–22	Nice	32	2		
2022–23	Nice	14	0	**46**	**2**
2022–23	Wolverhampton W	19	0		
2023–24	Wolverhampton W	35	4		
2024–25	Wolverhampton W	17	1	**71**	**5**

Transferred to Galatasaray, February 2025.

LOCHHEAD, Sebastian (D) 0 0
H: 5 11 W: 12 04

2023–24	Dundee	0	0		
2024–25	Dundee	0	0		
2024–25	Wolverhampton W	0	0		

LONWIJK, Nigel (D) 90 4
H: 6 2 W: 9 13 b.Goirle 27-10-02
Internationals: Netherlands U16.
From PSV Eindhoven.

2020–21	Wolverhampton W	0	0		
2021–22	Wolverhampton W	0	0		
2021–22	*Fortuna Sittard*	22	1	**22**	**1**
2022–23	Wolverhampton W	0	0		
2022–23	*Plymouth Arg*	35	0	**35**	**0**
2023–24	Wolverhampton W	0	0		
2023–24	*Grasshopper*	1	0	**1**	**0**
2023–24	*Wycombe W*	11	2	**11**	**2**
2024–25	Wolverhampton W	0	0		
2024–25	*Huddersfield T*	21	1	**21**	**1**

MANE, Mateus (F) 1 0
H: 5 11 W: 11 00 b. 16-7-07
Internationals: England U18.

2024–25	Wolverhampton W	1	0	**1**	**0**

MATHEUS CUNHA, Santos (F) 225 59
H: 6 0 W: 12 00 b.Joao Pessoa 27-5-99
Internationals: Brazil U23, Full caps.

2017–18	Sion	29	10	**29**	**10**
2018–19	RB Leipzig	25	2		
2019–20	RB Leipzig	10	0	**35**	**2**
2019–20	Hertha Berlin	11	5		
2020–21	Hertha Berlin	27	7		
2021–22	Hertha Berlin	1	0	**39**	**12**
2021–22	Atletico Madrid	29	6		
2022–23	Atletico Madrid	11	0	**40**	**6**
2022–23	Wolverhampton W	17	2		
2023–24	Wolverhampton W	32	12		
2024–25	Wolverhampton W	33	15	**82**	**29**

MEUPIYOU, Bastien (D) 1 0
H: 6 3 W: 12 08 b.Paris 19-3-06
Internationals: France U16, U17, U18.

2022–23	Nantes	0	0		
2023–24	Nantes	1	0	**1**	**0**
2024–25	Wolverhampton W	0	0		

MOSQUERA, Yerson (D) 80 7
H: 6 2 W: 13 03 b.Apartado 2-5-01
Internationals: Colombia U18, U20, Full caps.

2020	Atletico Nacional	4	1		
2021	Atletico Nacional	12	0	**16**	**1**
2021–22	Wolverhampton W	0	0		
2022–23	Wolverhampton W	0	0		
2023	*Cincinnati*	17	2		
2023–24	Wolverhampton W	0	0		
2023–24	*Cincinnati*	30	3	**47**	**5**
2023–24	*Villarreal*	12	1	**12**	**1**
2024–25	Wolverhampton W	5	0	**5**	**0**

MUNETSI, Marshall (M) 216 25
H: 6 2 W: 13 01 b. 22-6-96
Internationals: Zimbabwe Full caps.

2016–17	Baroka	26	2	**26**	**2**
2017–18	Orlando Pirates	12	0		
2018–19	Orlando Pirates	16	0	**28**	**0**
2019–20	Reims	17	0		
2020–21	Reims	27	1		
2021–22	Reims	24	5		
2022–23	Reims	34	7		
2023–24	Reims	27	4		
2024–25	Reims	19	4	**148**	**21**
2024–25	Wolverhampton W	14	2	**14**	**2**

NELSON SEMEDO, Cabral (D) 345 10
H: 5 10 W: 10 08 b.Lisbon 16-11-93
Internationals: Portugal U23, Full caps.

2011–12	Sintrense	26	5	**26**	**5**
2012–13	Benfica	0	0		
2012–13	*Fatima*	29	0	**29**	**0**
2013–14	Benfica	0	0		
2014–15	Benfica	0	0		
2015–16	Benfica	12	1		
2016–17	Benfica	31	1	**43**	**2**
2017–18	Barcelona	24	0		
2018–19	Barcelona	26	1		
2019–20	Barcelona	32	1		
2020–21	Barcelona	0	0	**82**	**2**
2020–21	Wolverhampton W	34	1		
2021–22	Wolverhampton W	25	0		
2022–23	Wolverhampton W	36	0		
2023–24	Wolverhampton W	36	0		
2024–25	Wolverhampton W	34	0	**165**	**1**

OJINNAKA, Temple (M) 0 0
H: 6 0 W: 11 00 b.Venezia 30-3-05

2023–24	Wolverhampton W	0	0		
2024–25	Wolverhampton W	0	0		

OKODUWA, Wesley (M) 0 0
H: 5 9 W: 10 08 b.New York 12-5-08
Internationals: England U16, U17, U18.

2023–24	Wolverhampton W	0	0		
2024–25	Wolverhampton W	0	0		

OLAGUNJU, Saheed (D) 0 0
H: 6 0 W: 11 03 b.London 7-1-07
Internationals: England U18.

2024–25	Wolverhampton W	0	0		

PEDRO LIMA, Cardoso (D) 11 0
H: 5 9 W: 11 11 b.Cabedelo 1-7-06
Internationals: Brazil U17, U20.

2024	Sport Recife	8	0	**8**	**0**
2024–25	Wolverhampton W	3	0	**3**	**0**

POND, Alfie (D) 7 0
H: 6 1 W: 13 08 b.Exeter 17-2-04

2020–21	Exeter C	0	0		
2021–22	Exeter C	0	0		
2022–23	Wolverhampton W	0	0		
2023–24	Wolverhampton W	0	0		
2023–24	*Stockport Co*	6	0	**6**	**0**
2024–25	Wolverhampton W	1	0	**1**	**0**

RAWLINGS, Luke (D) 0 0
H: 5 10 W: 11 00 b.Tokyo 1-1-08
Internationals: England U16, U17.

2024–25	Wolverhampton W	0	0		

SARABIA, Pablo (M) 391 70
H: 5 9 W: 11 05 b.Madrid 11-5-92
Internationals: Spain U16, U17, U18, U19, U21, Full caps.

2009–10	Real Madrid	0	0		
2010–11	Real Madrid	0	0		
2011–12	Getafe	19	0		
2012–13	Getafe	13	0		
2013–14	Getafe	33	1		
2014–15	Getafe	35	2		
2015–16	Getafe	31	7	**131**	**10**
2016–17	Sevilla	34	8		
2017–18	Sevilla	34	6		
2018–19	Sevilla	33	12	**101**	**26**
2019–20	Paris Saint-Germain	21	4		
2020–21	Paris Saint-Germain	27	6		
2021–22	Paris Saint-Germain	2	1		
2021–22	*Sporting Lisbon*	29	15	**29**	**15**
2022–23	Paris Saint-Germain	14	0	**64**	**11**
2022–23	Wolverhampton W	13	1		
2023–24	Wolverhampton W	30	4		
2024–25	Wolverhampton W	23	3	**66**	**8**

SILVA, Fabio (F) 150 30
H: 6 1 W: 11 11 b.Porto 19-7-02
Internationals: Portugal U16, U17, U19, U21, Full caps.

2019–20	Porto	12	1	**12**	**1**
2020–21	Wolverhampton W	32	4		
2021–22	Wolverhampton W	22	0		
2022–23	Wolverhampton W	0	0		
2022–23	*Anderlecht*	20	7	**20**	**7**
2022–23	*PSV Eindhoven*	14	4	**14**	**4**
2023–24	Wolverhampton W	8	0		

2023–24 Rangers	18	4	18	4
2024–25 Wolverhampton W	0	0	62	4
2024–25 Las Palmas	24	10	24	10

STORER, James (G) 0 0
b.Buxton 5-11-01
Internationals: Republic of Ireland U19.

2021–22 Wolverhampton W	0	0
2022–23 Wolverhampton W	0	0
2023–24 Wolverhampton W	0	0
2024–25 Wolverhampton W	0	0

SUTHERLAND, Ethan (M) 17 2
Internationals: Scotland U19.

2023–24 St Mirren	0	0		
2023–24 Alloa Ath	16	2	16	2
2024–25 St Mirren	1	0	1	0
2024–25 Wolverhampton W	0	0		

TRAORE, Boubacar (M) 67 2
H: 6 0 W: 10 08 b.Bamako 20-8-01
Internationals: Mali U20, U23, Full caps.

2019–20 Metz	0	0		
2020–21 Metz	2	1		
2021–22 Metz	27	1		
2022–23 Metz	3	0	32	2
2022–23 Wolverhampton W	10	0		
2023–24 Wolverhampton W	24	0		
2024–25 Wolverhampton W	1	0	35	0

WHITTINGHAM, Matthew (M) 0 0
H: 6 0 W: 11 05 b.St Helens 21-10-04
From Manchester C.

2023–24 Wolverhampton W	0	0
2024–25 Wolverhampton W	0	0

Players retained or with offer of contract
Lopes, Leo; Benjamin, Lewys James; Bowen, Reiss Jaya; Carson, Hayden Jack; Enguru Mangue, Daniel Esen, Halis Joshua; Gracey, Joshua Daniel; Kaleta, Marvin Marvellous; McLeod, Conor William; Nasta, Arthur John Michael; Nolan-Ruddock, Max Ethan; O'Donnell, Luke Francis; Reynolds, Fabian Howard; Voice, Caden John Brian; White, Alfie Thomas.

Scholars
Ballard-Matthews, Emilio Les; Bradbury, Makenzie Jack; Bula Dami Mane, Mateus; Dayman, Myles Jayden Alfie; Gidaree, Joshua Connor Valerie; Hardy, George Henry; In Min Kyu; Marwa, Bjorn Fabian; Okoduwa, Wesley Eboselume; Osifo, David Etinosa; Salmon, Fabian Leo; Wilcox, Jake William Edward.

WREXHAM (91)

ADAM, Josh (M) 0 0
H: 5 10 W: 10 08 b.Glasgow 3-2-04
Internationals: Scotland U16, U19, U21.

2024–25 Wrexham	0	0

ASHFIELD, Harry (M) 0 0
H: 5 10 W: 11 09 b.Wrexham 23-3-06

2023–24 Wrexham	0	0
2024–25 Wrexham	0	0

BARNETT, Ryan (M) 80 4
H: 5 11 W: 11 00 b.Shrewsbury 23-9-99

2016–17 Shrewsbury T	0	0		
2017–18 Shrewsbury T	0	0		
2018–19 Shrewsbury T	1	0		
2019–20 Shrewsbury T	0	0		
2020–21 Shrewsbury T	7	0	8	0

From Solihull Moors.

2023–24 Wrexham	32	2		
2024–25 Wrexham	40	2	72	4

BICKERSTAFF, Jake (F) 17 3
H: 6 2 W: 12 08 b.Liverpool 11-9-01

2023–24 Accrington S	10	1	10	1
2024–25 Wrexham	0	0	7	2

BOLTON, Luke (F) 154 7
H: 5 9 W: 11 05 b.Manchester 7-10-99
Internationals: England U20.

2018–19 Manchester C	0	0		
2018–19 Wycombe W	10	0	10	0
2019–20 Manchester C	0	0		
2019–20 Luton T	24	0	24	0
2020–21 Manchester C	0	0		
2020–21 Dundee U	24	1	24	1
2021–22 Salford C	15	0		
2022–23 Salford C	44	6		
2023–24 Salford C	20	0	79	6
2023–24 Wrexham	17	0		
2024–25 Wrexham	0	0	17	0

BOYLE, William (D) 231 26
H: 6 2 W: 11 00 b.Garforth 1-9-95

2014–15 Huddersfield T	1	0		
2015–16 Huddersfield T	0	0		
2015–16 York C	12	0	12	0
2016–17 Huddersfield T	0	0		
2016–17 Kilmarnock	11	0	11	0
2016–17 Cheltenham T	21	2		
2017–18 Cheltenham T	34	5		
2018–19 Cheltenham T	38	4		
2019–20 Cheltenham T	13	2		
2020–21 Cheltenham T	29	6		
2021–22 Cheltenham T	31	4	166	23
2022–23 Huddersfield T	16	0	18	0
2023–24 Wrexham	24	3		
2024–25 Wrexham	0	0	24	3

BRUNT, Lewis (M) 58 2
H: 6 2 W: 11 03 b.Burton-upon-Trent 6-11-00

2019–20 Aston Villa	0	0		
2020–21 Aston Villa	0	0		
2021–22 Leicester C	1	0		
2022–23 Leicester C	1	0		
2023–24 Leicester C	0	0	2	0
2023–24 Mansfield T	34	2	34	2
2024–25 Wrexham	22	0	22	0

BURTON, Callum (G) 60 0
H: 6 2 W: 12 00 b.Newport, Shropshire 15-8-96
Internationals: England U16, U17, U18.

2013–14 Shrewsbury T	0	0		
2014–15 Shrewsbury T	0	0		
2015–16 Shrewsbury T	1	0		
2016–17 Shrewsbury T	0	0	1	0
2017–18 Hull C	0	0		
2018–19 Cambridge U	0	0		
2019–20 Cambridge U	10	0		
2020–21 Cambridge U	27	0	37	0
2021–22 Plymouth Arg	0	0		
2022–23 Plymouth Arg	18	0		
2023–24 Plymouth Arg	0	0	18	0
2024–25 Wrexham	4	0	4	0

CANNON, Andy (M) 238 16
H: 5 9 W: 11 09 b.Ashton-under-Lyne 14-3-96

2014–15 Rochdale	18	0		
2015–16 Rochdale	25	0		
2016–17 Rochdale	25	2		
2017–18 Rochdale	21	2		
2018–19 Rochdale	12	0	101	4
2018–19 Portsmouth	2	0		
2019–20 Portsmouth	18	1		
2020–21 Portsmouth	43	2	63	3
2021–22 Hull C	10	1		
2022–23 Hull C	5	0	15	1
2023–24 Wrexham	35	6		
2024–25 Wrexham	24	2	59	8

CLEWORTH, Max (D) 66 8
H: 6 3 W: 11 09 b.Chester 9-8-02

2023–24 Wrexham	24	1		
2024–25 Wrexham	42	7	66	8

DALBY, Sam (F) 85 17
H: 6 3 W: 12 04 b.Leytonstone 17-1-00

2016–17 Leyton Orient	16	1		
2017–18 Leyton Orient	0	0	16	1
2018–19 Leeds U	0	0		
2018–19 Morecambe	2	0	2	0
2019–20 Watford	0	0		
2020–21 Watford	0	0		

From Southend U.

2023–24 Wrexham	31	1		
2024–25 Wrexham	1	0	32	1
2024–25 Dundee U	35	15	35	15

DAVIES, Jordan (D) 43 6
H: 5 6 W: 10 03 b.Wrexham 18-8-98
Internationals: Wales U17, U19.

2019–20 Brighton & HA	0	0		

From Wrexham.

2023–24 Wrexham	25	2		
2024–25 Wrexham	0	0	25	2
2024–25 Grimsby T	18	4	18	4

DOBSON, George (M) 312 8
H: 6 1 W: 11 07 b.Harold Wood 15-11-97
From Arsenal.

2015–16 West Ham U	0	0		
2016–17 West Ham U	0	0		
2016–17 Walsall	21	1		
2017–18 Sparta Rotterdam	5	0	5	0
2017–18 Walsall	21	1		
2018–19 Walsall	39	0	81	2
2019–20 Sunderland	29	0		
2020–21 Sunderland	5	0	34	0
2020–21 AFC Wimbledon	24	1	24	1
2021–22 Charlton Ath	38	1		
2022–23 Charlton Ath	45	1		
2023–24 Charlton Ath	43	2	126	4
2024–25 Wrexham	42	1	42	1

EDWARDS, Callum (D) 10 1
H: 5 11 W: 11 11 b.Liverpool 22-6-06

2023–24 Wrexham	0	0		
2024–25 Wrexham	0	0		
2024–25 Bala T	10	1	10	1

EVANS, George (M) 233 10
H: 6 0 W: 12 00 b.Cheadle 13-12-94
Internationals: England U16, U17, U19.

2012–13 Manchester C	0	0		
2013–14 Manchester C	0	0		
2013–14 Crewe Alex	23	1	23	1
2014–15 Manchester C	0	0		
2014–15 Scunthorpe U	16	1	16	1
2015–16 Manchester C	0	0		
2015–16 Walsall	12	3	12	3
2015–16 Reading	6	0		
2016–17 Reading	35	2		
2017–18 Reading	18	1	59	3
2018–19 Derby Co	11	0		
2019–20 Derby Co	17	0		
2020–21 Derby Co	6	0	34	0
2020–21 Millwall	19	1		
2021–22 Millwall	23	1		
2022–23 Millwall	11	0		
2023–24 Millwall	2	0	55	2
2023–24 Wrexham	27	0		
2024–25 Wrexham	7	0	34	0

FAAL, Mo (F) 54 13
H: 6 5 W: 14 00 b.Hackney 1-7-97

2021–22 WBA	0	0		
2022–23 WBA	1	0		
2023–24 WBA	0	0		
2023–24 Doncaster R	25	7	25	7
2023–24 Walsall	20	6	20	6
2024–25 WBA	0	0		
2024–25 Wrexham	8	0	8	0

FLETCHER, Steven (F) 660 171
H: 6 1 W: 12 00 b.Shrewsbury 26-3-87
Internationals: Scotland U20, U21, B, Full caps.

2003–04 Hibernian	5	0		
2004–05 Hibernian	20	5		
2005–06 Hibernian	34	8		
2006–07 Hibernian	31	6		
2007–08 Hibernian	32	13		
2008–09 Hibernian	34	11	156	43
2009–10 Burnley	35	8	35	8
2010–11 Wolverhampton W	29	10		
2011–12 Wolverhampton W	32	12	61	22
2012–13 Sunderland	28	11		
2013–14 Sunderland	20	3		
2014–15 Sunderland	30	5		
2015–16 Sunderland	16	4	94	23
2015–16 Marseille	12	2	12	2
2016–17 Sheffield Wed	38	10		
2017–18 Sheffield Wed	19	2		
2018–19 Sheffield Wed	40	11		
2019–20 Sheffield Wed	27	13	124	36
2020–21 Stoke C	37	9		
2021–22 Stoke C	35	3	72	12
2022–23 Dundee U	33	9	33	9
2023–24 Wrexham	33	8		
2024–25 Wrexham	40	8	73	16

FOSTER, Bradley (G) 0 0
H: 6 4 b.5-10-01
From Stoke C.

2020–21 Derby Co	0	0
2021–22 Derby Co	0	0
2022–23 Derby Co	0	0
2022–23 WBA	0	0
2023–24 WBA	0	0
2024–25 Wrexham	0	0

HALL, Liam (G) 0 0
H: 6 3 W: 13 01 b.Dewsbury 18-12-04

2023–24 Wrexham	0	0
2024–25 Wrexham	0	0

HOWARD, Mark (G) 306 0
H: 6 0 W: 12 00 b.Southwark 21-9-86

2005–06 Arsenal	0	0		
2005–06 Falkirk	8	0	8	0
2006–07 Cardiff C	0	0		
2006–07 Swansea C	0	0		
2007–08 St Mirren	10	0		
2008–09 St Mirren	33	0		
2009–10 St Mirren	2	0	45	0
2010–11 Aberdeen	9	0	9	0
2011–12 Blackpool	4	0		
2011–12 Sheffield U	0	0		
2012–13 Sheffield U	11	0		
2013–14 Sheffield U	19	0		
2014–15 Sheffield U	35	0		
2015–16 Sheffield U	15	0	80	0
2016–17 Bolton W	27	0		
2017–18 Bolton W	8	0	35	0
2018–19 Blackpool	32	0		
2019–20 Salford C	3	0	3	0
2019–20 Blackpool	4	0	40	0
2020–21 Scunthorpe U	34	0	34	0
2021–22 Carlisle U	35	0	35	0

From Wrexham.

2023–24 Wrexham	7	0		
2024–25 Wrexham	10	0	17	0

JAMES, Aaron (D) 1 0
H: 5 10 W: 11 07 b.Chester 30-6-05

2023–24 Wrexham	1	0		
2024–25 Wrexham	0	0	1	0

JAMES, Matthew (M) 321 16
H: 5 10 W: 11 08 b.Bacup 22-7-91
Internationals: England U16, U17, U19, U20.

2007–08 Manchester U	0	0
2008–09 Manchester U	0	0
2009–10 Manchester U	0	0

2009–10	*Preston NE*	18	2		
2010–11	Manchester U	0	0		
2010–11	*Preston NE*	10	0	**28**	**2**
2011–12	Manchester U	0	0		
2012–13	Leicester C	24	3		
2013–14	Leicester C	35	1		
2014–15	Leicester C	27	0		
2015–16	Leicester C	0	0		
2016–17	Leicester C	1	0		
2016–17	*Barnsley*	18	1		
2017–18	Leicester C	13	0		
2018–19	Leicester C	0	0		
2019–20	Leicester C	1	0		
2020–21	Leicester C	0	0	**101**	**4**
2020–21	*Barnsley*	15	0	**33**	**1**
2020–21	*Coventry C*	23	3	**23**	**3**
2021–22	Bristol C	33	1		
2022–23	Bristol C	34	0		
2023–24	Bristol C	37	3	**104**	**4**
2024–25	Wrexham	32	2	**32**	**2**

LEE, Elliot (F) 271 63
H: 5 11 W: 11 05 b.Durham 16-12-94

2011–12	West Ham U	0	0		
2012–13	West Ham U	0	0		
2013–14	West Ham U	1	0		
2013–14	*Colchester U*	4	1		
2014–15	West Ham U	1	0		
2014–15	*Southend U*	0	0		
2014–15	*Luton T*	11	3		
2015–16	West Ham U	0	0	**2**	**0**
2015–16	*Blackpool*	4	0	**4**	**0**
2015–16	*Colchester U*	15	2	**19**	**3**
2016–17	Barnsley	6	0	**6**	**0**
2017–18	Luton T	32	10		
2018–19	Luton T	38	12		
2019–20	Luton T	11	1		
2020–21	Luton T	12	1		
2020–21	*Oxford U*	18	6	**18**	**6**
2021–22	Luton T	0	0	**104**	**27**
2021–22	*Charlton Ath*	34	3	**34**	**3**
From Wrexham.					
2023–24	Wrexham	46	16		
2024–25	Wrexham	38	8	**84**	**24**

LONGMAN, Ryan (M) 179 19
H: 5 11 W: 11 07 b.Redhill 6-11-00

2019–20	Brighton & HA	0	0		
2020–21	Brighton & HA	0	0		
2020–21	*AFC Wimbledon*	44	8	**44**	**8**
2021–22	Hull C	35	4		
2022–23	Hull C	37	2		
2023–24	Hull C	0	0		
2023–24	*Millwall*	35	3	**35**	**3**
2024–25	Hull C	9	1	**81**	**7**
2024–25	Wrexham	19	1	**19**	**1**

MARRIOTT, Jack (F) 351 93
H: 5 8 W: 11 03 b.Beverley 9-9-94

2012–13	Ipswich T	1	0		
2013–14	Ipswich T	1	0		
2013–14	*Gillingham*	1	0	**1**	**0**
2014–15	Ipswich T	0	0	**2**	**0**
2014–15	*Carlisle U*	4	0	**4**	**0**
2014–15	*Colchester U*	5	1	**5**	**1**
2015–16	Luton T	40	14		
2016–17	Luton T	39	8	**79**	**22**
2017–18	Peterborough U	44	27		
2018–19	Derby Co	33	7		
2019–20	Derby Co	32	2		
2020–21	Derby Co	4	1	**69**	**10**
2020–21	*Sheffield Wed*	12	0	**12**	**0**
2021–22	Peterborough U	28	9		
2022–23	Peterborough U	21	4	**93**	**40**
2022–23	Fleetwood T	19	8		
2023–24	Fleetwood T	24	5	**43**	**13**
2023–24	Wrexham	17	1		
2024–25	Wrexham	26	6	**43**	**7**

McCLEAN, James (M) 569 67
H: 5 11 W: 11 00 b.Derry 22-4-89
Internationals: Northern Ireland U21. Republic of Ireland Full caps.

2008	Derry C	1	0		
2009	Derry C	26	1		
2010	Derry C	30	8		
2011	Derry C	21	7	**78**	**16**
2011–12	Sunderland	23	5		
2012–13	Sunderland	36	2		
2013–14	Sunderland	0	0	**59**	**7**
2013–14	Wigan Ath	37	3		
2014–15	Wigan Ath	36	6		
2015–16	WBA	35	2		
2016–17	WBA	34	1		
2017–18	WBA	30	1	**99**	**4**
2018–19	Stoke C	42	3		
2019–20	Stoke C	36	7		
2020–21	Stoke C	24	2	**102**	**12**
2021–22	Wigan Ath	33	9		
2022–23	Wigan Ath	46	3	**152**	**21**
2023–24	Wrexham	37	3		
2024–25	Wrexham	42	4	**79**	**7**

McNICHOLAS, Luke (G) 62 0
H: 6 4 b.Ballycarra 1-1-00
Internationals: Republic of Ireland U19.

2019	Sligo R	2	0		
2020	Sligo R	0	0		
2021	Sligo R	2	0		
2021	*Finn Harps*	0	0		
2021–22	*Cliftonville*	24	0	**24**	**0**
2022	Sligo R	8	0		
2023	Sligo R	26	0	**38**	**0**
From Wrexham.					
2023–24	Wrexham	0	0		
2024–25	Wrexham	0	0		

MENDY, Jacob (M) 35 2
H: 5 11 W: 10 08 b.Faji Kunda 27-12-96
Internationals: Gambia Full caps.

2023–24	Wrexham	31	2		
2024–25	Wrexham	4	0	**35**	**2**

MULLIN, Paul (F) 320 100
H: 5 10 W: 11 02 b.Liverpool 6-11-94

2013–14	Huddersfield T	0	0		
2014–15	Morecambe	42	8		
2015–16	Morecambe	40	9		
2016–17	Morecambe	40	8	**122**	**25**
2017–18	Swindon T	40	6	**40**	**6**
2018–19	Tranmere R	22	5		
2019–20	Tranmere R	20	3	**42**	**8**
2019–20	*Cambridge U*	6	2		
2020–21	Cambridge U	46	32	**52**	**34**
From Wrexham.					
2023–24	Wrexham	38	24		
2024–25	Wrexham	26	3	**64**	**27**

O'CONNELL, Eoghan (D) 279 7
H: 6 2 W: 12 08 b.Cork 13-8-95
Internationals: Republic of Ireland U19, U21.

2013–14	Celtic	1	0		
2014–15	Celtic	3	0		
2015–16	Celtic	1	0		
2015–16	*Oldham Ath*	2	0	**2**	**0**
2016	*Cork C*	7	1	**7**	**1**
2016–17	Celtic	2	0	**7**	**0**
2016–17	*Walsall*	17	1	**17**	**1**
2017–18	Bury	12	0		
2018–19	Bury	31	2	**43**	**2**
2019–20	Rochdale	31	0		
2020–21	Rochdale	39	1		
2021–22	Rochdale	45	1	**115**	**2**
2022–23	Charlton Ath	19	1	**19**	**1**
2023–24	Wrexham	30	0		
2024–25	Wrexham	39	0	**69**	**0**

O'CONNOR, Thomas (M) 145 6
H: 5 11 W: 11 00 b.Kilkenny 21-4-99
Internationals: Republic of Ireland U19, U21.

2019–20	Southampton	0	0		
2019–20	*Gillingham*	28	1		
2020–21	Southampton	0	0		
2020–21	*Gillingham*	34	0	**62**	**1**
2021–22	Burton Alb	18	5	**18**	**5**
From Wrexham.					
2023–24	Wrexham	34	0		
2024–25	Wrexham	31	0	**65**	**0**

OKONKWO, Arthur (G) 107 0
H: 6 5 W: 13 05 b.Camden 9-9-01
Internationals: England U16, U17, U18.

2019–20	Arsenal	0	0		
2020–21	Arsenal	0	0		
2021–22	Arsenal	0	0		
2022–23	Arsenal	0	0		
2022–23	*Crewe Alex*	23	0	**23**	**0**
2022–23	*Sturm Graz*	15	0	**15**	**0**
2023–24	Arsenal	0	0		
2023–24	*Wrexham*	36	0		
2024–25	Wrexham	33	0	**69**	**0**

PALMER, Oliver (F) 356 75
H: 6 5 W: 12 02 b.Epsom 21-1-92
From Woking, Havant & Waterlooville.

2013–14	Mansfield T	38	4		
2014–15	Mansfield T	16	1	**54**	**5**
2015–16	Leyton Orient	45	7		
2016–17	Leyton Orient	20	5	**65**	**12**
2016–17	*Luton T*	17	3	**17**	**3**
2017–18	Lincoln C	45	8	**45**	**8**
2018–19	Crawley T	40	14		
2019–20	Crawley T	28	13		
2020–21	Crawley T	0	0	**68**	**27**
2020–21	AFC Wimbledon	23	5		
2021–22	AFC Wimbledon	18	5	**41**	**10**
From Wrexham.					
2023–24	Wrexham	39	7		
2024–25	Wrexham	27	3	**66**	**10**

RAINBIRD, James (F) 6 0
b.Chelmsford 1-9-05

2024–25	Wrexham	0	0		
2024–25	*Newtown*	6	0	**6**	**0**

RATHBONE, Oliver (M) 315 27
H: 5 7 W: 10 06 b.Blackburn 10-10-96
From Manchester U.

2016–17	Rochdale	27	2		
2017–18	Rochdale	33	1		
2018–19	Rochdale	28	4		
2019–20	Rochdale	24	2		
2020–21	Rochdale	40	3	**152**	**12**
2021–22	Rotherham U	42	2		
2022–23	Rotherham U	38	4		
2023–24	Rotherham U	42	1	**122**	**7**
2024–25	Wrexham	41	8	**41**	**8**

REVAN, Sebastian (D) 55 1
H: 5 11 W: 10 12 b.West Bromwich 14-7-03

2022–23	Aston Villa	0	0		
2023–24	Aston Villa	0	0		
2023–24	*Rotherham U*	36	1	**36**	**1**
2024–25	Wrexham	19	0	**19**	**0**

RODRIGUEZ, Jay (F) 490 117
H: 6 1 W: 13 03 b.Burnley 29-7-89
Internationals: England U21, Full caps.

2007–08	Burnley	1	0		
2007–08	*Stirling Alb*	11	3	**11**	**3**
2008–09	Burnley	25	2		
2009–10	Burnley	0	0		
2009–10	*Barnsley*	6	1	**6**	**1**
2010–11	Burnley	42	14		
2011–12	Burnley	37	15		
2012–13	Southampton	35	6		
2013–14	Southampton	33	15		
2014–15	Southampton	0	0		
2015–16	Southampton	12	0		
2016–17	Southampton	24	5	**104**	**26**
2017–18	WBA	37	7		
2018–19	WBA	45	22	**82**	**29**
2019–20	Burnley	36	8		
2020–21	Burnley	31	1		
2021–22	Burnley	29	2		
2022–23	Burnley	28	10		
2023–24	Burnley	21	2		
2024–25	Burnley	20	2	**270**	**56**
2024–25	Wrexham	17	2	**17**	**2**

SCARR, Dan (D) 216 11
H: 6 2 W: 12 08 b.Bromsgrove 24-12-94
From Reddich U, Stourbridge.

2017–18	Birmingham C	0	0		
2017–18	*Wycombe W*	22	1	**22**	**1**
2018–19	Birmingham C	0	0		
2018–19	Walsall	17	1		
2019–20	Walsall	33	0		
2020–21	Walsall	35	4	**85**	**5**
2021–22	Plymouth Arg	35	2		
2022–23	Plymouth Arg	32	2		
2023–24	Plymouth Arg	28	1	**95**	**5**
2024–25	Wrexham	14	0	**14**	**0**

SMITH, Sam (F) 248 73
H: 6 1 W: 11 07 b.Manchester 8-3-98

2017–18	Reading	8	1		
2018–19	Reading	0	0		
2018–19	*Oxford U*	15	0	**15**	**0**
2018–19	*Shrewsbury T*	3	0	**3**	**0**
2019–20	Reading	0	0		
2019–20	*Cambridge U*	28	7		
2020–21	Reading	0	0		
2020–21	*Tranmere R*	5	0	**5**	**0**
2020–21	*Cheltenham T*	21	4	**21**	**4**
2021–22	Cambridge U	46	15		
2022–23	Cambridge U	45	13	**119**	**35**
2023–24	Reading	34	15		
2024–25	Reading	25	11	**67**	**27**
2024–25	Wrexham	18	7	**18**	**7**

WATERS, Billy (M) 200 31
H: 5 9 W: 11 07 b.Epsom 15-10-94
Internationals: England C.

2012–13	Crewe Alex	0	0		
2013–14	Crewe Alex	9	0		
2014–15	Crewe Alex	16	2	**25**	**2**
2016–17	Cheltenham T	46	12		
2017–18	Northampton T	17	0		
2017–18	*Cambridge U*	18	2	**18**	**2**
2018–19	Northampton T	15	2		
2018–19	*Cheltenham T*	18	4	**64**	**16**
2019–20	Northampton T	7	0	**39**	**2**
2019–20	*Newport Co*	6	0	**6**	**0**
From Torquay U, FC Halifax T.					
2022–23	Barrow	34	9	**34**	**9**
2023–24	Wrexham	3	0		
2023–24	*Doncaster R*	11	0	**11**	**0**
2024–25	Wrexham	0	0	**3**	**0**

Transferred to Oldham Ath, January 2025.

Scholars
Almeida, Daymeon Leandro Alves; Bedford, Casey Owen; Chesworth, Samuel David; Clayton, Tommy Stuart Neil; Connolly, Anthony; Cruise, George Anthony; Edwards, Dafydd Vaughan; Hazeldine, Keane Mason Carter; Jones, Elliott George Johnson; Kelly, Thomas Christopher; Lussey, Alfie Neil; McTweed, Oliver Jack Wilson; Moore, Alexander James; Nawaz, Umar; Nicholas, Reagan Partick James; Owen, Bryn Dafydd; Owen, Rio Lloyd; Purvis, Max Denis; Rees, Joe Gavin; Roberts, Hari Annwyl; Slosarczyk, Nikolas Jan.

WYCOMBE W (92)

BACK, Finley (D) **44** **0**
H: 6 2 W: 11 05 b.Leicester 25-9-02

2021–22	Nottingham F	3	0		
2022–23	Nottingham F	0	0		
2022–23	*Carlisle U*	18	0		
2023–24	Nottingham F	0	0		
2023–24	*Carlisle U*	21	0	**39**	**0**
2024–25	Nottingham F	0	0	**3**	**0**
2024–25	Wycombe W	2	0	**2**	**0**

BAKINSON, Tyreeq (M) **183** **12**
H: 6 1 W: 11 00 b.Camden 8-1-98

2015–16	Luton T	1	0		
2016–17	Luton T	0	0		
2017–18	Luton T	0	0	**1**	**0**
2017–18	Bristol C	0	0		
2018–19	Bristol C	0	0		
2018–19	*Newport Co*	30	1	**30**	**1**
2019–20	Bristol C	0	0		
2019–20	*Plymouth Arg*	14	2	**14**	**2**
2020–21	Bristol C	34	4		
2021–22	Bristol C	13	1	**47**	**5**
2021–22	*Ipswich T*	17	2	**17**	**2**
2022–23	Sheffield Wed	26	1		
2023–24	Sheffield Wed	8	0	**34**	**1**
2023–24	*Charlton Ath*	15	1	**15**	**1**
2024–25	Wycombe W	25	0	**25**	**0**

BARTOLO, Jaiden (F) **2** **0**
H: 6 0 W: 11 11 b.Slough 10-2-06
Internationals: Gibraltar U16, U17, U19, U21, Full caps.

2024–25	Wycombe W	2	0	**2**	**0**

BERRY, James (F) **26** **7**
H: 6 0 W: 11 03 b.Wigan 10-2-00
From Liverpool.

2017–18	Wigan Ath	0	0		
2018–19	Wigan Ath	0	0		
2019–20	Hull C	1	0		
2020–21	Hull C	0	0	**1**	**0**

From Altrincham, Macclesfield, Chesterfield.

2024–25	Chesterfield	22	7	**22**	**7**
2024–25	Wycombe W	3	0	**3**	**0**

BUTCHER, Matt (M) **219** **14**
H: 6 2 W: 12 13 b.Portsmouth 14-5-97
From Poole T.

2015–16	Bournemouth	0	0		
2016–17	Bournemouth	0	0		
2016–17	*Yeovil T*	34	2	**34**	**2**
2017–18	Bournemouth	0	0		
2018–19	Bournemouth	0	0		
2019–20	Bournemouth	0	0		
2019–20	*St Johnstone*	6	0	**6**	**0**
2020–21	Accrington S	42	2		
2021–22	Accrington S	33	4	**75**	**6**
2022–23	Plymouth Arg	40	3		
2023–24	Plymouth Arg	15	0	**55**	**3**
2023–24	Wycombe W	18	3		
2024–25	Wycombe W	13	0	**31**	**3**
2024–25	*Bristol R*	18	0	**18**	**0**

CLARK, Taylor (M) **0** **0**
H: 5 9 W: 10 10 b. 17-5-05

2023–24	Wycombe W	0	0		
2024–25	Wycombe W	0	0		

DOTSE, Jahiem (M) **0** **0**
H: 5 8 W: 11 05

2024–25	Wycombe W	0	0		

GEORGE, Shamal (G) **116** **0**
H: 6 3 W: 11 11 b.Birkenhead 6-1-98

2017–18	Liverpool	0	0		
2017–18	*Carlisle U*	4	0	**4**	**0**
2018–19	Liverpool	0	0		
2018–19	*Tranmere R*	0	0		
2019–20	Liverpool	0	0		
2020–21	Colchester U	15	0		
2021–22	Colchester U	30	0	**45**	**0**
2022–23	Livingston	32	0		
2023–24	Livingston	32	0		
2024–25	Livingston	3	0	**67**	**0**
2024–25	Wycombe W	0	0		

GRIMMER, Jack (D) **322** **7**
H: 6 0 W: 12 13 b.Aberdeen 25-1-94
Internationals: Scotland U16, U17, U18, U19, U21.

2009–10	Aberdeen	2	0		
2010–11	Aberdeen	2	0		
2011–12	Aberdeen	0	0	**4**	**0**
2011–12	Fulham	0	0		
2012–13	Fulham	0	0		
2013–14	Fulham	0	0		
2013–14	*Port Vale*	13	1	**13**	**1**
2014–15	Fulham	13	0		
2014–15	*Shrewsbury T*	6	0		
2015–16	Fulham	0	0		
2015–16	*Shrewsbury T*	21	1		
2016–17	Fulham	0	0	**13**	**0**
2016–17	*Shrewsbury T*	24	0	**51**	**1**
2017–18	Coventry C	42	1		
2018–19	Coventry C	11	0	**53**	**1**
2019–20	Wycombe W	18	0		
2020–21	Wycombe W	40	0		
2021–22	Wycombe W	26	2		
2022–23	Wycombe W	40	0		
2023–24	Wycombe W	27	2		
2024–25	Wycombe W	37	0	**188**	**4**

HAGELSKJAER, Anders (D) **200** **5**
H: 6 4 b.Herning 16-2-97
Internationals: Denmark U18.

2016–17	Skive	13	0		
2017–18	Skive	29	0	**42**	**0**
2018–19	Silkeborg	31	1		
2019–20	Silkeborg	24	2		
2020–21	Silkeborg	19	0	**74**	**3**
2021–22	AaB	29	1		
2022	*Sarpsborg*	10	0	**10**	**0**
2022–23	AaB	3	1	**32**	**2**
2023	Molde	21	0		
2024	Molde	19	0	**40**	**0**
2024–25	Wycombe W	2	0	**2**	**0**

HANLAN, Brandon (F) **256** **35**
H: 6 0 W: 11 07 b.Chelsea 31-5-97

2016–17	Charlton Ath	9	0		
2017–18	*Colchester U*	18	2	**18**	**2**
2017–18	Charlton Ath	0	0	**9**	**0**
2018–19	Gillingham	39	9		
2019–20	Gillingham	35	4	**74**	**13**
2020–21	Bristol R	44	7		
2021–22	Bristol R	1	0	**45**	**7**
2021–22	Wycombe W	36	6		
2022–23	Wycombe W	34	3		
2023–24	Wycombe W	16	2		
2024–25	Wycombe W	8	0	**94**	**11**
2024–25	*Stevenage*	16	2	**16**	**2**

HARTRIDGE, Alex (D) **155** **1**
H: 6 1 W: 13 03 b.Torquay 9-3-99

2017–18	Exeter C	0	0		
2018–19	Exeter C	3	0		
2019–20	Exeter C	0	0		
2020–21	Exeter C	29	0		
2021–22	Exeter C	28	0		
2022–23	Exeter C	43	0		
2023–24	Exeter C	28	0		
2024–25	Wycombe W	6	0	**6**	**0**
2024–25	*Exeter C*	18	1	**149**	**1**

HARVIE, Daniel (D) **272** **15**
H: 5 7 W: 9 11 b.Drumchapel 14-7-98
Internationals: Scotland U16, U17, U19, U21.

2015–16	Aberdeen	2	0		
2016–17	Aberdeen	0	0		
2016–17	*Dumbarton*	34	3	**34**	**3**
2017–18	Aberdeen	2	0	**4**	**0**
2018–19	Ayr U	33	0		
2019–20	Ayr U	27	1	**60**	**1**
2020–21	Milton Keynes D	31	3		
2021–22	Milton Keynes D	41	1		
2022–23	Milton Keynes D	34	3		
2023–24	Milton Keynes D	38	3	**144**	**10**
2024–25	Wycombe W	30	1	**30**	**1**

KONE, Richard (F) **58** **21**
H: 6 1 W: 12 02 b.Abidjan, Ivory Coast 13-7-04

2023–24	Wycombe W	17	3		
2024–25	Wycombe W	41	18	**58**	**21**

LEAHY, Luke (M) **458** **56**
H: 5 10 W: 11 07 b.Coventry 19-11-92
From Rugby T.

2012–13	Falkirk	8	1		
2013–14	Falkirk	19	1		
2014–15	Falkirk	33	3		
2015–16	Falkirk	36	3		
2016–17	Falkirk	31	3	**127**	**11**
2017–18	Walsall	46	2		
2018–19	Walsall	44	3	**90**	**5**
2019–20	Bristol R	32	0		
2020–21	Bristol R	38	8	**70**	**8**
2021–22	Shrewsbury T	42	8		
2022–23	Shrewsbury T	46	9	**88**	**17**
2023–24	Wycombe W	44	11		
2024–25	Wycombe W	39	4	**83**	**15**

LOW, Joseph (D) **88** **9**
H: 6 5 W: 12 06 b.Filton 20-2-02
Internationals: Wales U17, U19, U21, Full caps.

2020–21	Bristol C	0	0		
2021–22	Bristol C	0	0		
2022–23	Bristol C	1	0	**1**	**0**
2022–23	*Walsall*	15	1	**15**	**1**
2023–24	Wycombe W	34	4		
2024–25	Wycombe W	38	4	**72**	**8**

LOWRY, Alexander (M) **30** **1**
b.Uddingston 23-6-03
Internationals: Scotland U16, U19, U21.

2019–20	Rangers	0	0		
2020–21	Rangers	0	0		
2021–22	Rangers	4	1		
2022–23	Rangers	5	0		
2023–24	Rangers	0	0		
2023–24	*Hearts*	12	0	**12**	**0**
2024–25	Rangers	0	0	**9**	**1**
2024–25	Wycombe W	9	0	**9**	**0**

LUBULA, Beryly (F) **133** **24**
H: 5 10 W: 12 00 b.DR Congo 8-1-98

2017–18	Birmingham C	1	0		
2018–19	Birmingham C	3	0	**4**	**0**
2019–20	Crawley T	34	12	**34**	**12**
2020–21	Blackpool	12	0		
2021–22	Blackpool	0	0		
2021–22	*Northampton T*	14	0	**14**	**0**
2022–23	Blackpool	0	0	**12**	**0**
2022–23	*Colchester U*	8	1	**8**	**1**
2023–24	Burton Alb	20	5	**20**	**5**
2023–24	Wycombe W	14	2		
2024–25	Wycombe W	27	4	**41**	**6**

MATTON, Jack (D) **0** **0**
H: 6 5

2024–25	Wycombe W	0	0		

McCARTHY, Jason (D) **261** **14**
H: 6 1 W: 12 08 b.Southampton 7-11-95

2013–14	Southampton	0	0		
2014–15	Southampton	1	0		
2015–16	Southampton	0	0		
2015–16	*Wycombe W*	35	2		
2016–17	Southampton	0	0	**1**	**0**
2016–17	*Walsall*	46	5	**46**	**5**
2017–18	Barnsley	21	0	**21**	**0**
2018–19	Wycombe W	44	2		
2019–20	Millwall	2	0	**2**	**0**
2019–20	*Wycombe W*	9	1		
2020–21	Wycombe W	24	2		
2021–22	Wycombe W	31	1		
2022–23	Wycombe W	36	1		
2023–24	Wycombe W	10	0		
2024–25	Wycombe W	2	0	**191**	**9**

McCLEARY, Garath (M) **549** **68**
H: 6 2 W: 12 00 b.Oxford 15-5-87
Internationals: Jamaica Full caps.
From Oxford C, Slough T, Bromley.

2007–08	Nottingham F	8	1		
2008–09	Nottingham F	39	1		
2009–10	Nottingham F	24	0		
2010–11	Nottingham F	18	2		
2011–12	Nottingham F	22	9	**111**	**13**
2011–12	Reading	0	0		
2012–13	Reading	31	3		
2013–14	Reading	42	5		
2014–15	Reading	26	1		
2015–16	Reading	34	4		
2016–17	Reading	41	9		
2017–18	Reading	18	0		
2018–19	Reading	31	0		
2019–20	Reading	19	1	**242**	**23**
2020–21	Wycombe W	32	4		
2021–22	Wycombe W	42	11		
2022–23	Wycombe W	39	7		
2023–24	Wycombe W	40	6		
2024–25	Wycombe W	43	4	**196**	**32**

NORRIS, Will (G) **181** **0**
H: 6 5 W: 11 09 b.Watford 12-8-93
From Hatfield T, Royston T.

2014–15	Cambridge U	3	0		
2015–16	Cambridge U	21	0		
2016–17	Cambridge U	45	0	**69**	**0**
2017–18	Wolverhampton W	1	0		
2018–19	Wolverhampton W	1	0		
2019–20	Wolverhampton W	0	0	**2**	**0**
2019–20	*Ipswich T*	15	0	**15**	**0**
2020–21	Burnley	2	0		
2021–22	Burnley	0	0		
2022–23	Burnley	0	0	**2**	**0**
2022–23	*Peterborough U*	22	0	**22**	**0**
2023–24	Portsmouth	46	0		
2024–25	Portsmouth	8	0	**54**	**0**
2024–25	Wycombe W	17	0	**17**	**0**

ONYEDINMA, Fred (M) **331** **38**
H: 6 1 W: 11 00 b.Lagos 24-11-96

2013–14	Millwall	4	0		
2014–15	Millwall	2	0		
2014–15	*Wycombe W*	25	8		
2015–16	Millwall	34	4		
2016–17	Millwall	42	3		
2017–18	Millwall	37	1		
2018–19	Millwall	1	0	**120**	**8**
2018–19	*Wycombe W*	21	4		
2019–20	Wycombe W	13	4		
2020–21	Wycombe W	43	3		
2021–22	Luton T	29	3		
2022–23	Luton T	17	0		
2023–24	Luton T	8	0	**54**	**3**
2023–24	*Rotherham U*	16	2	**16**	**2**
2024–25	Wycombe W	39	6	**141**	**25**

PATTENDEN, Jasper (M) **24** **0**
H: 5 8 W: 10 03 b.Rustington 15-4-02
From Brighton & HA, Worthing.

2022–23	Wycombe W	3	0		
2023–24	Wycombe W	8	0		
2024–25	Wycombe W	13	0	**24**	**0**

PEART, Brody (F) **0** **0**
H: 5 9 W: 11 00 b. 26-8-05

2024–25	Wycombe W	0	0		

RAVIZZOLI, Franco (G)   42   0
H: 6 3   b.Mar el Plata 9-7-97
From Eastbourne Bor.

2021–22 Milton Keynes D	1	0		
2022–23 Milton Keynes D	0	0	1	0
2023–24 Wycombe W	14	0		
2024–25 Wycombe W	27	0	41	0

REACH, Adam (M)   427   39
H: 6 1   W: 11 07   b.Gateshead 3-2-93
Internationals: England U19, U20.

2010–11 Middlesbrough	1	1		
2011–12 Middlesbrough	1	0		
2012–13 Middlesbrough	16	2		
2013–14 Middlesbrough	2	0		
2013–14 *Shrewsbury T*	22	3	22	3
2013–14 *Bradford C*	18	3	18	3
2014–15 Middlesbrough	39	2		
2015–16 Middlesbrough	4	1		
2015–16 *Preston NE*	35	4	35	4
2016–17 Middlesbrough	0	0	63	6
2016–17 Sheffield Wed	39	3		
2017–18 Sheffield Wed	46	4		
2018–19 Sheffield Wed	42	8		
2019–20 Sheffield Wed	37	1		
2020–21 Sheffield Wed	44	5	208	21
2021–22 WBA	34	2		
2022–23 WBA	18	0		
2023–24 WBA	17	0	69	2
2024–25 Wycombe W	12	0	12	0

SADLIER, Kieran (M)   285   59
H: 5 10   W: 10 06   b.Haywards Heath 14-9-94
Internationals: Republic of Ireland U17, U19, U21.

2013–14 West Ham U	0	0		
2014–15 St Mirren	11	1	11	1
2015–16 Peterborough U	0	0		
2015–16 *FC Halifax T*	0	0		
2016 Sligo R	29	8		
2017 Sligo R	20	7	49	15
2017 Cork C	13	2		
2018 Cork C	35	16	48	18
2018–19 Doncaster R	14	3		
2019–20 Doncaster R	33	11	47	14
2020–21 Rotherham U	15	1		
2021–22 Rotherham U	12	1	27	2
2021–22 Bolton W	18	4		
2022–23 Bolton W	19	1	37	5
2022–23 *Leyton Orient*	19	0	19	0
2023–24 Wycombe W	37	3		
2024–25 Wycombe W	10	1	47	4

SCOWEN, Josh (M)   476   21
H: 5 10   W: 11 09   b.Cheshunt 28-3-93

2010–11 Wycombe W	2	0		
2011–12 Wycombe W	0	0		
2012–13 Wycombe W	34	1		
2013–14 Wycombe W	37	1		
2014–15 Wycombe W	18	1		
2014–15 Barnsley	21	4		
2015–16 Barnsley	34	4		
2016–17 Barnsley	41	2	96	10

2017–18 QPR	42	1		
2018–19 QPR	35	2		
2019–20 QPR	18	0	95	3
2019–20 Sunderland	4	0		
2020–21 Sunderland	43	1	47	1
2021–22 Wycombe W	37	1		
2022–23 Wycombe W	35	2		
2023–24 Wycombe W	37	1		
2024–25 Wycombe W	38	0	238	7

SHALA, Laurence (G)   0   0
H: 6 3   b.London 11-9-04
Internationals: Kosova U16, U19.

2023–24 Wycombe W	0	0
2024–25 Wycombe W	0	0

SKURA, Declan (D)   8   0
H: 6 2   W: 12 08   b.Kingston upon Thames 9-4-02

2023–24 Wycombe W	0	0		
2024–25 Wycombe W	8	0	8	0

TAFAZOLLI, Ryan (D)   343   25
H: 6 5   W: 14 09   b.Sutton Bonington 28-9-91

2010–11 Southampton	0	0		
From Concorde Rangers, Cambridge C.				
2014–15 Mansfield T	24	2		
2014–15 Mansfield T	36	1		
2015–16 Mansfield T	44	5	104	8
2016–17 Peterborough U	31	3		
2017–18 Peterborough U	33	1		
2018–19 Peterborough U	37	1	101	5
2019–20 Hull C	15	2	15	2
2020–21 Wycombe W	20	2		
2021–22 Wycombe W	33	4		
2022–23 Wycombe W	25	2		
2023–24 Wycombe W	32	1		
2024–25 Wycombe W	1	0	111	9
2024–25 Lee Man	12	1	12	1

UDOH, Daniel (F)   211   39
H: 6 0   W: 13 01   b.Lagos 30-8-96
Internationals: Nigeria U17.
From Worcester C, North Greenwood U, Grays Ath, Hoddesdon T, Ilkeston.

2015–16 Crewe Alex	6	0		
2016–17 Crewe Alex	9	0	15	0
From AFC Telford U.				
2019–20 Shrewsbury T	25	4		
2020–21 Shrewsbury T	39	4		
2021–22 Shrewsbury T	46	13		
2022–23 Shrewsbury T	5	0		
2023–24 Shrewsbury T	40	10	155	31
2024–25 Wycombe W	41	8	41	8

VOKES, Sam (F)   576   122
H: 6 1   W: 14 02   b.Lymington 21-10-89
Internationals: Wales U21, Full caps.

2006–07 Bournemouth	13	4		
2007–08 Bournemouth	41	12	54	16
2008–09 Wolverhampton W	36	6		
2009–10 Wolverhampton W	5	0		
2009–10 Leeds U	8	1	8	1
2010–11 Wolverhampton W	2	0		
2010–11 Bristol C	1	0	1	0

2010–11 Sheffield U	6	1	6	1
2010–11 Norwich C	4	1	4	1
2011–12 Wolverhampton W	4	0		
2011–12 Burnley	9	2		
2011–12 *Brighton & HA*	14	3	14	3
2012–13 Wolverhampton W	0	0	47	6
2012–13 Burnley	46	4		
2013–14 Burnley	39	20		
2014–15 Burnley	15	0		
2015–16 Burnley	43	15		
2016–17 Burnley	37	10		
2017–18 Burnley	30	4		
2018–19 Burnley	20	3	239	58
2018–19 Stoke C	12	3		
2019–20 Stoke C	36	5		
2020–21 Stoke C	30	0	78	8
2021–22 Wycombe W	43	16		
2022–23 Wycombe W	35	6		
2023–24 Wycombe W	40	4		
2024–25 Wycombe W	7	2	125	28

WARD, Christie (M)   3   0
H: 5 10   W: 10 06   b.Wareham 9-11-03

2022–23 Wycombe W	3	0		
2023–24 Wycombe W	0	0		
2024–25 Wycombe W	0	0	3	0

WESTERGAARD, Magnus (M)   156   14
H: 6 2   b.Frederiksberg 27-5-98

2017–18 Lyngby	1	0		
2018–19 Lyngby	14	1		
2019–20 Lyngby	19	0		
2020–21 Lyngby	0	0		
2020–21 Hvidovre	22	4	22	4
2021–22 Lyngby	26	4		
2022–23 Lyngby	15	0	75	5
2023–24 Viborg	16	1		
2023–24 Viborg	23	2		
2024–25 Viborg	15	2	54	5
2024–25 Wycombe W	5	0	5	0

WOODHOUSE, Luca (F)   0   0
H: 6 0   b.25-7-04
From Tonbridge Angels.

2022–23 Wycombe W	0	0
2023–24 Wycombe W	0	0
2024–25 Wycombe W	0	0

YOUNG, Jack (M)   25   0
H: 5 7   W: 10 01   b.Newcastle upon Tyne 21-10-00

2019–20 Newcastle U	0	0		
2020–21 Newcastle U	0	0		
2020–21 Tranmere R	5	0	5	0
2021–22 Wycombe W	2	0		
2022–23 Wycombe W	1	0		
2023–24 Wycombe W	0	0		
2024–25 Ayr U	17	0	17	0
2024–25 Wycombe W	0	0	3	0

Players retained or with offer of contract
Berry-McNally, James Jon; Cole, Ryan Mark; Gurpinar, Koray Metin; Pettitt, John Nicholas; Swaby, Christian Thomas.

ENGLISH LEAGUE PLAYERS – INDEX

CUPS AND UPS AND DOWNS DIARY 2024–25

JULY 2024
14 Copa America Final: Argentina 1 Colombia 0 *(aet)*. 25 UEFA Under-19 Championship Final: Spain 2 France 0.

AUGUST 2024
10 The FA Community Shield: Manchester C 1 Manchester U 1 *(Mancheser C won 7-6 on penalties)*.
14 European Super Cup: Real Madrid 2 Atalanta 0.

NOVEMBER 2024
23 Copa Sudamericana Final: Racing 3 Cruzeiro 1. 30 Copa Libertadores Final: Atletico Mineiro 1 Botafogo 3.

DECEMBER 2024
7 MLS Cup Final: LA Galaxy 2 New York Red Bulls 1.
15 Premier Sports Scottish League Cup Final: Celtic 3 Rangers 3 *(aet; Celtic won 5-4 on penalties)*.

FEBRUARY 2025
28 Nathaniel MG Welsh League Cup Final: The New Saints 1 Aberystwyth T 0.

MARCH 2025
9 BetMcLean Northern Irish League Cup Final: Cliftonville 1 Glentoran 0 *(aet)*.
15 Subway Women's League Cup Final: Chelsea 2 Manchester C 1.
17 Boodles Independent Schools FA Cup Final: Bradfield 2 Shrewsbury 0.
22 Ebbsfleet U relegated from National League. Dumbarton relegated from Scottish League One to Scottish League Two.
30 SPFL Trust Trophy Final: Queen's Park 0 Livingston 5.

APRIL 2025
6 Southampton relegated from Premier League to EFL Championship.
8 Birmingham C promoted from EFL League One to EFL Championship.
12 Birmingham C champions of EFL League One and promoted to EFL Championship. Arbroath champions of Scottish League One and promoted to Scottish Championship.
13 Vertu EFL Trophy Final: Peterborough U 2 Birmingham C 0.
18 Shrewsbury T relegated from EFL League One to EFL League Two. AFC Fylde relegated from National League.
19 Hamilton A relegated from Scottish Championship to Scottish League One. Dragon Signs FAW Trophy Final: Port Talbot T 2 Penygraig U 1.
20 Leicester C relegated from Premier League to EFL Championship.
21 Leeds U and Burnley promoted from EFL Championship to Premier League. Morecambe relegated from EFL Two to National League.
26 Liverpool champions of Premier League. Celtic champions of Scottish Premiership and qualify for UEFA Champions League play-off round. Ipswich T relegated from Premier League to EFL Championship. Cardiff C relegated from EFL Championship to EFL League One. Wrexham promoted from EFL League One to EFL Championship. Doncaster R and Port Vale promoted from EFL League Two to EFL League One. Cambridge U relegated from EFL League One to EFL League Two. Carlisle U relegated from EFL League Two to National League. Peterhead champions of Scottish League Two and promoted to Scottish League One. Barnet champions of National League and promoted to EFL League Two.
27 Crystal Palace relegated from Women's Super League. 28 UEFA Youth League Final: Barcelona 4 Trabzonspor 1.
29 Bristol R and Crawley T relegated from EFL League One to EFL League Two.
30 Chelsea champions of Women's Super League.

MAY 2025
2 Falkirk champions of Scottish Championship and promoted to Scottish Premiership.
3 Leeds U champions of EFL Championship; Burnley runners-up of EFL Championship. Sheffield U, Sunderland, Bristol C and Coventry C confirmed in EFL Championship play-offs. Luton T and Plymouth Arg relegated from EFL Championship to EFL League One. Bradford C promoted from EFL League One to EFL League Two. Stockport Co, Charlton Ath, Wycombe W and Leyton Orient confirmed in EFL League One play-offs. Doncaster R champions of EFL League Two. Walsall, AFC Wimbledon, Notts Co and Chesterfield confirmed in EFL League Two play-offs.
4 London City Lionesses champions of Women's Championship and promoted to Women's Super League. JD Welsh FA Cup Final: The New Saints 2 Connah's Quay Nomads 1. FA Sunday Cup Final: Highgate Alb 3 North Solihull 0.
5 Maidenhead U and Dagenham & Red relegated from National League. FA Youth Cup Final: Aston Villa 3 Manchester C 1. Clearer Water Northern Irish FA Cup Final: Dungannon Swifts 1 Cliftonville 1 *(Dungannon Swifts won 4-3 on penalties)*. William Hill Scottish League Pyramid play-off final first leg: East Kilbride 4 Bonnyrigg Rose 1.
11 The Isuzu FA Trophy Final: Aldershot 3 Spennymoor T 0. The Isuzu FA Vase Final: AFC Whyteleafe 1 Whistable T 2 *(aet)*.
13 William Hill Scottish League One play-off final first leg: East Fife 3 Annan Ath 2.
14 William Hill Scottish Championship play-off final first leg: Cove Rangers 1 Airdrieonians 2.
16 William Hill Scottish League One play-off final second leg: Annan Ath 1 East Fife 1 *(East Fife won 4-3 on aggregate and promoted from William Hill League Two to William Hill Scottish League One)*.
17 Emirates FA Cup Final: Crystal Palace 1 Manchester C 0 *(Crystal Palace qualify for UEFA Europa League)*. Rangers qualify to UEFA Champions League second qualifying round. Hibernian qualify to UEFA Europa League play-off round. Dundee U qualify to UEFA Europa League second qualifying round. Aberdeen qualify for UEFA Conference League second qualifying round. William Hill Scottish Championship play-off final second leg: Airdrieonians 0 Cove Rangers 0 *(Airdrieonians won 2-1 on aggregate and remain in William Hill Scottish Championship)*. William Hill Scottish League Pyramid play-off final second leg: Bonnyrigg Rose 3 East Kilbride 3 *(East Kilbride won 7-4 on aggregate and promoted from Lowland League to William Hill Scottish League Two; Bonnyrigg Rose relegated from William Hill Scottish League Two to Lowland League)*.
18 The Adobe Women's FA Cup Final: Chelsea 3 Manchester U 0.
21 UEFA Europa League Final: Tottenham H 1 Manchester U 0.
22 William Hill Scottish Premiership play-off final first leg: Livingston 1 Ross Co 1.
24 Scottish Gas Scottish Cup Final: Aberdeen 1 Celtic 1 *(aet; Aberdeen won 4-3 on penalties)*. UEFA Women's Champions League Final: Arsenal 1 Barcelona 0. EFL Championship play-off final: Sheffield U 1 Sunderland 2 *(Sunderland promoted from EFL Championship to Premier League)*.
25 EFL League One play-off final: Charlton Ath 1 Leyton Orient 0 *(Charlton Ath promoted from EFL League One to EFL Championship)*.
26 EFL League Two play-off final: AFC Wimbledon 1 Walsall 0 *(AFC Wimbledon promoted from EFL League Two to EFL League One)*. William Hill Scottish Premiership play-off final second leg: Ross Co 2 Livingston 4 *(Livingston won 5-3 on aggregate and promoted to William Hill Scottish Premiership; Ross Co relegated to Scottish Championship)*.
28 UEFA Europa Conference League Final: Chelsea 4 Real Betis 1.
31 UEFA Champions League Final: Paris Saint-Germain 5 Internazionale 0.

JUNE 2025
1 National League play-off final: Oldham Ath 3 Southend U 2 *(aet; Oldham Ath promoted from National League to EFL League Two)*. UEFA U17 Championship Final: France 0 Portugal 3.

JULY 2025
13 FIFA Club World Cup Final 2025: Chelsea 3 Paris Saint-Germain 0.

MANAGERS – IN AND OUT 2024–25

AUGUST 2024
12 Ryan Lowe leaves Preston NE by mutual consent.
20 Paul Heckingbottom appointed manager of Preston NE.
21 Neil Critchley sacked as manager of Blackpool. First-team coach Richard Keogh takes temporary charge.
31 Paul Simpson sacked as manager of Carlisle U. Academy coaches Mark Birch, Steven Rudd and Jamie Devitt take temporary charge.

SEPTEMBER 2024
3   Steve Bruce appointed manager of Blackpool.
17 Steven Schumacher sacked as manager of Stoke C. First-team coach Alex Morris and Under-21 coach Ryan Shawcross take temporary charge.
18 Narcis Pelach appointed manager of Stoke C.
19 Mike Williamson leaves as manager of Milton Keynes D to take over as manager of Carlisle U.
22 Erol Bulut sacked as manager of Cardiff C. Assistant manager Omer Riza takes temporary charge.
25 Scott Lindsey leaves as manager of Crawley T to take over as manager of Milton Keynes D. Ben Gladwin takes temporary charge of Crawley T.

OCTOBER 2024
1   Rob Elliot appointed manager of Crawley T.
23 Mark Robinson sacked as manager of Burton Alb. Assistant manager Tom Hounsell takes temporary charge.
25 Mark Kennedy sacked as manager of Swindon T. First-team coaches Marcus Bignot, Steve Mildenhall and Gavin Gunning take temporary charge.
25 Ian Holloway appointed manager of Swindon T.
28 Erik ten Hag sacked as manager of Manchester U. Assistant manager Ruud van Nistelrooy takes temporary charge.

NOVEMBER 2024
3   Paul Hurst sacked as manager of Shrewsbury T. First-team coach Sean Parrish takes temporary charge.
7   Mark Robins sacked as manager of Coventry C. First-team coach Rhys Carr takes temporary charge.
11 Ruben Amorim appointed manager of Manchester U.
13 Gareth Ainsworth appointed manager of Shrewsbury T.
24 Steve Cooper sacked as manager of Leicester C. First-team coach Ben Dawson takes temporary charge.
27 Tim Walter sacked as manager of Hull C. First-team coach Andy Dawson takes temporary charge.
28 Frank Lampard appointed manager of Coventry C.
29 Ruud van Nistelrooy appointed manager of Leicester C.

DECEMBER 2024
5   Omer Riza appointed manager of Cardiff C until the end of the season having been in temporary charge.
5   Jon Brady resigns as manager of Northampton T. Assistant manager Ian Sampson takes temporary charge.
6   Ruben Selles leaves as manager of Reading to take over as manager of Hull C.
6   Noel Hunt appointed manager of Reading.
15 Gary O'Neil sacked as manager of Wolverhampton W.
15 Russell Martin sacked as manager of Southampton. Under-21 manager Simon Rusk takes temporary charge.
15 Neil Harris leaves as manager of Millwall. Assistant manager Dave Livermore takes temporary charge.
15 Des Buckingham sacked as manager of Oxford U.
16 Matt Taylor sacked as manager of Bristol R. First-team coach Lee Cattermole takes temporary charge.
17 Gary Bowyer appointed manager of Burton Alb.
19 Vitor Pereira appointed manager of Wolverhampton W.
20 Gary Rowett appointed manager of Oxford U.
21 Ivan Juric appointed manager of Southampton.
22 Charlie Adam sacked as manager of Fleetwood T.
23 Kevin Nolan appointed manager of Northampton T.
24 Pete Wild appointed manager of Fleetwood T.
25 Carlos Coberan leaves as manager of WBA to take charge at Valencia. Coaches Christ Brunt, Damia Abella and Boaz Myhill take temporary charge.
27 Naric Pelach sacked as manager of Stoke C. Under-21 coach Ryan Shawcross takes temporary charge.
26 Inigo Calderon appointed manager of Bristol R.
30 Alex Neil appointed manager of Millwall.
31 Wayne Rooney leaves as manager of Plymouth Arg by mutual consent. First-team coach Kevin Nancekivell and club captain Joe Edwards take temporary charge.

JANUARY 2025
1   Mark Robins appointed manager of Stoke C.
5   Mark Bonner sacked as manager of Gillingham.
5   John Coleman appointed manager of Gillingham.
8   Julien Lopetegui sacked as manager of West Ham U.
8   Graham Potter appointed manager of West Ham U.
9   Sean Dyche sacked as manager of Everton. Club captain Seamus Coleman and professional development coach Leighton Baines take temporary charge.
9   Rob Edwards leaves as manager of Luton T by mutual consent. Assistants Richie Kyle and Paul Trollope take temporary charge.
10 Miron Muslic appointed manager of Plymouth Arg.

11 David Moyes appointed manager of Everton.
14 Matt Bloomfield leaves as manager of Wycombe W to become manager of Luton T. Sam Grace, Harry Hudson, Matty Dye and Jerome John take temporary charge of Wycombe W.
17 Tony Mowbray appointed manager of WBA.
18 Stephen Clemence sacked as manager of Barrow.
20 Andy Whing appointed manager of Barrow.
22 Ian Evatt leaves as manager of Bolton W by mutual consent. Academy coaches Julian Darby, Andy Taylor and Andrew Tutte take temporary charge.
30 Steven Schumacher appointed manager of Bolton W.

FEBRUARY 2025
2 Mike Dodds appointed manager of Wycombe W.
3 Mike Williamson sacked as manager of Carlisle U.
7 Mark Hughes appointed manager of Carlisle U.
13 John Eustace leaves as manager of Blackburn R and is appointed manager of Derby Co. First-team coach David Lowe takes temporary charge of Blackburn R.
16 Garry Monk sacked as manager of Cambridge U.
17 Luke Williams sacked as manager of Swansea C. Assistant Alan Sheehan takes temporary charge.
19 Neil Harris appointed manager of Cambridge U.
25 Valerien Ismael appointed manager of Blackburn R.
26 Nigel Adkins leaves as manager of Tranmere R by mutual consent. First-team coach Andy Crosby takes temporary charge.

MARCH 2025
2 Scott Lindsey sacked as manager of Milton Keynes D. First-team coach Ben Gladwin takes temporary charge.
2 Shaun Maloney sacked as manager of Wigan Ath. First-team coach Glenn Whelan takes temporary charge.
9 Michael Duff sacked as manager of Huddersfield T. Academy manager Jon Worthington takes temporary charge.
12 Darrell Clarke sacked as manager of Barnsley. Assistant coach Conor Hourihane takes temporary charge.
12 Ryan Lowe appointed manager of Wigan Ath.
20 Rob Elliot sacked as manager of Crawley T. Assistant manager Louis Storey takes temporary charge.
21 Scott Lindsey appointed manager of Crawley T.
25 Gareth Ainsworth leaves as manager of Shrewsbury T and is appointed manager of Gillingham.
26 Michael Appleton appointed manager of Shrewsbury T.
30 Steve Evans sacked as manager of Rotherham U. Former coach Matt Hamshaw takes temporary charge.

APRIL 2025
7 Ivan Juric sacked as manager of Southampton. Simon Rusk takes temporary charge.
15 Matt Hamshaw appointed manager of Rotherham U after being in temporary charge.
15 Paul Warne appointed manager of Milton Keynes D.
18 Omer Riza sacked as manager of Cardiff C. Aaron Ramsey takes temporary charge.
18 Conor Hourihane appointed manager of Barnsley after being in temporary charge.
21 Tony Mowbray sacked as manager of WBA. James Morrison takes temporary charge.
22 Johannes Hoff Thorup sacked as manager of Norwich C. First-team coach Jack Wilshire takes temporary charge.
24 Nelson Jardim leaves as manager of Newport Co by mutual consent. Dafydd Williams takes charge for the remainder of the season.

MAY 2025
4 Inigo Calderon sacked as manager of Bristol R.
6 Darrell Clarke appointed manager of Bristol R.
6 Tom Cleverley sacked as manager of Watford.
13 Paulo Pezzolano appointed manager of Watford.
14 Andy Crosby appointed manager of Tranmere R after being in temporary charge.
15 Ruben Selles sacked as manager of Hull C.
28 Lee Grant appointed manager of Huddersfield T.
31 Miron Muslic leaves as manager of Plymouth Arg to take up the manager's job at Schalke.

JUNE 2025
2 Ryan Mason appointed manager of WBA.
3 Liam Manning leaves as manager of Bristol C to become manager of Norwich C.
4 Michael Carrick sacked as manager of Middlesbrough.
6 Ange Postecoglou sacked as manager of Tottenham H.
11 Sergej Jakirovic appointed manager of Hull C.
12 Thomas Frank leaves as manager of Brentford and is appointed manager of Tottenham H.
13 Tom Cleverley appointed manager of Plymouth Arg.
16 Brian Barry-Murphy appointed manager of Cardiff C.
22 Martin Paterson appointed manager of Notts Co.
24 Rob Edwards appointed manager of Middlesbrough.
24 Marti Cifuentes leaves as manager of QPR.
25 Julien Stephan appointed manager of QPR.
27 Keith Andrews appointed manager of Brentford.
27 Ruud van Nistelrooy leaves as manager of Leicester C by mutual consent.

JULY 2025
15 Marti Cifuentes appointed manager of Leicester C.

ENGLISH LEAGUE HONOURS 1888–2025

**Won or placed on goal average (ratio), goal difference or most goals scored. ‡Not promoted after play-offs.
No official competition during 1915–19 and 1939–46, regional leagues operated.*

FOOTBALL LEAGUE (1888–89 to 1891–92) – TIER 1

MAXIMUM POINTS: a 44; b 52.

1	1888–89a	Preston NE	40	Aston Villa	29	Wolverhampton W	28
1	1889–90a	Preston NE	33	Everton	31	Blackburn R	27
1	1890–91a	Everton	29	Preston NE	27	Notts Co	26
1	1891–92b	Sunderland	42	Preston NE	37	Bolton W	36

DIVISION 1 (1892–93 to 1991–92)

MAXIMUM POINTS: c 60; d 68; e 76; f 84; g 126; h 120; k 114.

1	1892–93c	Sunderland	48	Preston NE	37	Everton	36
1	1893–94c	Aston Villa	44	Sunderland	38	Derby Co	36
1	1894–95c	Sunderland	47	Everton	42	Aston Villa	39
1	1895–96c	Aston Villa	45	Derby Co	41	Everton	39
1	1896–97c	Aston Villa	47	Sheffield U*	36	Derby Co	36
1	1897–98c	Sheffield U	42	Sunderland	37	Wolverhampton W*	35
1	1898–99d	Aston Villa	45	Liverpool	43	Burnley	39
1	1899–1900d	Aston Villa	50	Sheffield U	48	Sunderland	41
1	1900–01d	Liverpool	45	Sunderland	43	Notts Co	40
1	1901–02d	Sunderland	44	Everton	41	Newcastle U	37
1	1902–03d	The Wednesday	42	Aston Villa*	41	Sunderland	41
1	1903–04d	The Wednesday	47	Manchester C	44	Everton	43
1	1904–05d	Newcastle U	48	Everton	47	Manchester C	46
1	1905–06e	Liverpool	51	Preston NE	47	The Wednesday	44
1	1906–07e	Newcastle U	51	Bristol C	48	Everton*	45
1	1907–08e	Manchester U	52	Aston Villa*	43	Manchester C	43
1	1908–09e	Newcastle U	53	Everton	46	Sunderland	44
1	1909–10e	Aston Villa	53	Liverpool	48	Blackburn R*	45
1	1910–11e	Manchester U	52	Aston Villa	51	Sunderland*	45
1	1911–12e	Blackburn R	49	Everton	46	Newcastle U	44
1	1912–13e	Sunderland	54	Aston Villa	50	The Wednesday	49
1	1913–14e	Blackburn R	51	Aston Villa	44	Middlesbrough*	43
1	1914–15e	Everton	46	Oldham Ath	45	Blackburn R*	43
1	1919–20f	WBA	60	Burnley	51	Chelsea	49
1	1920–21f	Burnley	59	Manchester C	54	Bolton W	52
1	1921–22f	Liverpool	57	Tottenham H	51	Burnley	49
1	1922–23f	Liverpool	60	Sunderland	54	Huddersfield T	53
1	1923–24f	Huddersfield T*	57	Cardiff C	57	Sunderland	53
1	1924–25f	Huddersfield T	58	WBA	56	Bolton W	55
1	1925–26f	Huddersfield T	57	Arsenal	52	Sunderland	48
1	1926–27f	Newcastle U	56	Huddersfield T	51	Sunderland	49
1	1927–28f	Everton	53	Huddersfield T	51	Leicester C	48
1	1928–29f	The Wednesday	52	Leicester C	51	Aston Villa	50
1	1929–30f	Sheffield Wed	60	Derby Co	50	Manchester C*	47
1	1930–31f	Arsenal	66	Aston Villa	59	Sheffield Wed	52
1	1931–32f	Everton	56	Arsenal	54	Sheffield Wed	50
1	1932–33f	Arsenal	58	Aston Villa	54	Sheffield Wed	51
1	1933–34f	Arsenal	59	Huddersfield T	56	Tottenham H	49
1	1934–35f	Arsenal	58	Sunderland	54	Sheffield Wed	49
1	1935–36f	Sunderland	56	Derby Co*	48	Huddersfield T	48
1	1936–37f	Manchester C	57	Charlton Ath	54	Arsenal	52
1	1937–38f	Arsenal	52	Wolverhampton W	51	Preston NE	49
1	1938–39f	Everton	59	Wolverhampton W	55	Charlton Ath	50
1	1946–47f	Liverpool	57	Manchester U*	56	Wolverhampton W	56
1	1947–48f	Arsenal	59	Manchester U*	52	Burnley	52
1	1948–49f	Portsmouth	58	Manchester U*	53	Derby Co	53
1	1949–50f	Portsmouth*	53	Wolverhampton W	53	Sunderland	52
1	1950–51f	Tottenham H	60	Manchester U	56	Blackpool	50
1	1951–52f	Manchester U	57	Tottenham H*	53	Arsenal	53
1	1952–53f	Arsenal*	54	Preston NE	54	Wolverhampton W	51
1	1953–54f	Wolverhampton W	57	WBA	53	Huddersfield T	51
1	1954–55f	Chelsea	52	Wolverhampton W*	48	Portsmouth*	48
1	1955–56f	Manchester U	60	Blackpool*	49	Wolverhampton W	49
1	1956–57f	Manchester U	64	Tottenham H*	56	Preston NE	56
1	1957–58f	Wolverhampton W	64	Preston NE	59	Tottenham H	51
1	1958–59f	Wolverhampton W	61	Manchester U	55	Arsenal*	50
1	1959–60f	Burnley	55	Wolverhampton W	54	Tottenham H	53
1	1960–61f	Tottenham H	66	Sheffield Wed	58	Wolverhampton W	57
1	1961–62f	Ipswich T	56	Burnley	53	Tottenham H	52
1	1962–63f	Everton	61	Tottenham H	55	Burnley	54
1	1963–64f	Liverpool	57	Manchester U	53	Everton	52
1	1964–65f	Manchester U*	61	Leeds U	61	Chelsea	56
1	1965–66f	Liverpool	61	Leeds U*	55	Burnley	55
1	1966–67f	Manchester U	60	Nottingham F*	56	Tottenham H	56
1	1967–68f	Manchester C	58	Manchester U	56	Liverpool	55
1	1968–69f	Leeds U	67	Liverpool	61	Everton	57
1	1969–70f	Everton	66	Leeds U	57	Chelsea	55
1	1970–71f	Arsenal	65	Leeds U	64	Tottenham H*	52
1	1971–72f	Derby Co	58	Leeds U*	57	Liverpool*	57
1	1972–73f	Liverpool	60	Arsenal	57	Leeds U	53
1	1973–74f	Leeds U	62	Liverpool	57	Derby Co	48

1	1974–75f	Derby Co	53	Liverpool*	51	Ipswich T	51
1	1975–76f	Liverpool	60	QPR	59	Manchester U	56
1	1976–77f	Liverpool	57	Manchester C	56	Ipswich T	52
1	1977–78f	Nottingham F	64	Liverpool	57	Everton	55
1	1978–79f	Liverpool	68	Nottingham F	60	WBA	59
1	1979–80f	Liverpool	60	Manchester U	58	Ipswich T	53
1	1980–81f	Aston Villa	60	Ipswich T	56	Arsenal	53
1	1981–82g	Liverpool	87	Ipswich T	83	Manchester U	78
1	1982–83g	Liverpool	82	Watford	71	Manchester U	70
1	1983–84g	Liverpool	80	Southampton	77	Nottingham F*	74
1	1984–85g	Everton	90	Liverpool*	77	Tottenham H	77
1	1985–86g	Liverpool	88	Everton	86	West Ham U	84
1	1986–87g	Everton	86	Liverpool	77	Tottenham H	71
1	1987–88h	Liverpool	90	Manchester U	81	Nottingham F	73
1	1988–89k	Arsenal*	76	Liverpool	76	Nottingham F	64
1	1989–90k	Liverpool	79	Aston Villa	70	Tottenham H	63
1	1990–91k	Arsenal[1]	83	Liverpool	76	Crystal Palace	69
1	1991–92g	Leeds U	82	Manchester U	78	Sheffield Wed	75

[1] *Arsenal deducted 2pts due to player misconduct in match on 20/10/1990 v Manchester U at Old Trafford.*

PREMIER LEAGUE (1992–93 to 2024–25)

MAXIMUM POINTS: a 126; b 114.

1	1992–93a	Manchester U	84	Aston Villa	74	Norwich C	72
1	1993–94a	Manchester U	92	Blackburn R	84	Newcastle U	77
1	1994–95a	Blackburn R	89	Manchester U	88	Nottingham F	77
1	1995–96b	Manchester U	82	Newcastle U	78	Liverpool	71
1	1996–97b	Manchester U	75	Newcastle U*	68	Arsenal*	68
1	1997–98b	Arsenal	78	Manchester U	77	Liverpool	65
1	1998–99b	Manchester U	79	Arsenal	78	Chelsea	75
1	1999–2000b	Manchester U	91	Arsenal	73	Leeds U	69
1	2000–01b	Manchester U	80	Arsenal	70	Liverpool	69
1	2001–02b	Arsenal	87	Liverpool	80	Manchester U	77
1	2002–03b	Manchester U	83	Arsenal	78	Newcastle U	69
1	2003–04b	Arsenal	90	Chelsea	79	Manchester U	75
1	2004–05b	Chelsea	95	Arsenal	83	Manchester U	77
1	2005–06b	Chelsea	91	Manchester U	83	Liverpool	82
1	2006–07b	Manchester U	89	Chelsea	83	Liverpool*	68
1	2007–08b	Manchester U	87	Chelsea	85	Arsenal	83
1	2008–09b	Manchester U	90	Liverpool	86	Chelsea	83
1	2009–10b	Chelsea	86	Manchester U	85	Arsenal	75
1	2010–11b	Manchester U	80	Chelsea*	71	Manchester C	71
1	2011–12b	Manchester C*	89	Manchester U	89	Arsenal	70
1	2012–13b	Manchester U	89	Manchester C	78	Chelsea	75
1	2013–14b	Manchester C	86	Liverpool	84	Chelsea	82
1	2014–15b	Chelsea	87	Manchester C	79	Arsenal	75
1	2015–16b	Leicester C	81	Arsenal	71	Tottenham H	70
1	2016–17b	Chelsea	93	Tottenham H	86	Manchester C	78
1	2017–18b	Manchester C	100	Manchester U	81	Tottenham H	77
1	2018–19b	Manchester C	98	Liverpool	97	Chelsea	72
1	2019–20b	Liverpool	99	Manchester C	81	Mancheser U*	66
1	2020–21b	Manchester C	86	Manchester U	74	Liverpool	69
1	2021–22b	Manchester C	93	Liverpool	92	Chelsea	74
1	2022–23b	Manchester C	89	Arsenal	84	Manchester U	75
1	2023–24b	Manchester C	91	Arsenal	89	Liverpool	82
1	2024–25b	Liverpool	84	Arsenal	74	Manchester C	71

DIVISION 2 (1892–93 to 1991–92) – TIER 2

MAXIMUM POINTS: a 44; b 56; c 60; d 68; e 76; f 84; g 126; h 132; k 138.

2	1892–93a	Small Heath	36	Sheffield U	35	Darwen	30
2	1893–94b	Liverpool	50	Small Heath	42	Notts Co	39
2	1894–95c	Bury	48	Notts Co	39	Newton Heath*	38
2	1895–96c	Liverpool*	46	Manchester C	46	Grimsby T*	42
2	1896–97c	Notts Co	42	Newton Heath	39	Grimsby T	38
2	1897–98c	Burnley	48	Newcastle U	45	Manchester C	39
2	1898–99d	Manchester C	52	Glossop NE	46	Leicester Fosse	45
2	1899–1900d	The Wednesday	54	Bolton W	52	Small Heath	46
2	1900–01d	Grimsby T	49	Small Heath	48	Burnley	44
2	1901–02d	WBA	55	Middlesbrough	51	Preston NE*	42
2	1902–03d	Manchester C	54	Small Heath	51	Woolwich Arsenal	48
2	1903–04d	Preston NE	50	Woolwich Arsenal	49	Manchester U	48
2	1904–05d	Liverpool	58	Bolton W	56	Manchester U	53
2	1905–06e	Bristol C	66	Manchester U	62	Chelsea	53
2	1906–07e	Nottingham F	60	Chelsea	57	Leicester Fosse	48
2	1907–08e	Bradford C	54	Leicester Fosse	52	Oldham Ath	50
2	1908–09e	Bolton W	52	Tottenham H*	51	WBA	51
2	1909–10e	Manchester C	54	Oldham Ath*	53	Hull C*	53
2	1910–11e	WBA	53	Bolton W	51	Chelsea	49
2	1911–12e	Derby Co*	54	Chelsea	54	Burnley	52
2	1912–13e	Preston NE	53	Burnley	50	Birmingham	46
2	1913–14e	Notts Co	53	Bradford PA*	49	Woolwich Arsenal	49
2	1914–15e	Derby Co	53	Preston NE	50	Barnsley	47
2	1919–20f	Tottenham H	70	Huddersfield T	64	Birmingham	56
2	1920–21f	Birmingham*	58	Cardiff C	58	Bristol C	51
2	1921–22f	Nottingham F	56	Stoke*	52	Barnsley	52
2	1922–23f	Notts Co	53	West Ham U*	51	Leicester C	51
2	1923–24f	Leeds U	54	Bury*	51	Derby Co	51

2	1924–25f	Leicester C	59	Manchester U	57	Derby Co	55
2	1925–26f	The Wednesday	60	Derby Co	57	Chelsea	52
2	1926–27f	Middlesbrough	62	Portsmouth*	54	Manchester C	54
2	1927–28f	Manchester C	59	Leeds U	57	Chelsea	54
2	1928–29f	Middlesbrough	55	Grimsby T	53	Bradford PA*	48
2	1929–30f	Blackpool	58	Chelsea	55	Oldham Ath	53
2	1930–31f	Everton	61	WBA	54	Tottenham H	51
2	1931–32f	Wolverhampton W	56	Leeds U	54	Stoke C	52
2	1932–33f	Stoke C	56	Tottenham H	55	Fulham	50
2	1933–34f	Grimsby T	59	Preston NE	52	Bolton W*	51
2	1934–35f	Brentford	61	Bolton W*	56	West Ham U	56
2	1935–36f	Manchester U	56	Charlton Ath	55	Sheffield U*	52
2	1936–37f	Leicester C	56	Blackpool	55	Bury	52
2	1937–38f	Aston Villa	57	Manchester U*	53	Sheffield U	53
2	1938–39f	Blackburn R	55	Sheffield U	54	Sheffield Wed	53
2	1946–47f	Manchester C	62	Burnley	58	Birmingham C	55
2	1947–48f	Birmingham C	59	Newcastle U	56	Southampton	52
2	1948–49f	Fulham	57	WBA	56	Southampton	52
2	1949–50f	Tottenham H	61	Sheffield Wed*	52	Sheffield U*	52
2	1950–51f	Preston NE	57	Manchester C	52	Cardiff C	50
2	1951–52f	Sheffield Wed	53	Cardiff C*	51	Birmingham C	51
2	1952–53f	Sheffield U	60	Huddersfield T	58	Luton T	52
2	1953–54f	Leicester C*	56	Everton	56	Blackburn R	55
2	1954–55f	Birmingham C*	54	Luton T*	54	Rotherham U	54
2	1955–56f	Sheffield Wed	55	Leeds U	52	Liverpool*	48
2	1956–57f	Leicester C	61	Nottingham F	54	Liverpool	53
2	1957–58f	West Ham U	57	Blackburn R	56	Charlton Ath	55
2	1958–59f	Sheffield Wed	62	Fulham	60	Sheffield U*	53
2	1959–60f	Aston Villa	59	Cardiff C	58	Liverpool*	50
2	1960–61f	Ipswich T	59	Sheffield U	58	Liverpool	52
2	1961–62f	Liverpool	62	Leyton Orient	54	Sunderland	53
2	1962–63f	Stoke C	53	Chelsea*	52	Sunderland	52
2	1963–64f	Leeds U	63	Sunderland	61	Preston NE	56
2	1964–65f	Newcastle U	57	Northampton T	56	Bolton W	50
2	1965–66f	Manchester C	59	Southampton	54	Coventry C	53
2	1966–67f	Coventry C	59	Wolverhampton W	58	Carlisle U	52
2	1967–68f	Ipswich T	59	QPR*	58	Blackpool	58
2	1968–69f	Derby Co	63	Crystal Palace	56	Charlton Ath	50
2	1969–70f	Huddersfield T	60	Blackpool	53	Leicester C	51
2	1970–71f	Leicester C	59	Sheffield U	56	Cardiff C*	53
2	1971–72f	Norwich C	57	Birmingham C	56	Millwall	55
2	1972–73f	Burnley	62	QPR	61	Aston Villa	50
2	1973–74f	Middlesbrough	65	Luton T	50	Carlisle U	49
2	1974–75f	Manchester U	61	Aston Villa	58	Norwich C	53
2	1975–76f	Sunderland	56	Bristol C*	53	WBA	53
2	1976–77f	Wolverhampton W	57	Chelsea	55	Nottingham F	52
2	1977–78f	Bolton W	58	Southampton	57	Tottenham H*	56
2	1978–79f	Crystal Palace	57	Brighton & HA*	56	Stoke C	56
2	1979–80f	Leicester C	55	Sunderland	54	Birmingham C*	53
2	1980–81f	West Ham U	66	Notts Co	53	Swansea C*	50
2	1981–82g	Luton T	88	Watford	80	Norwich C	71
2	1982–83g	QPR	85	Wolverhampton W	75	Leicester C	70
2	1983–84g	Chelsea*	88	Sheffield Wed	88	Newcastle U	80
2	1984–85g	Oxford U	84	Birmingham C	82	Manchester C*	74
2	1985–86g	Norwich C	84	Charlton Ath	77	Wimbledon	76
2	1986–87g	Derby Co	84	Portsmouth	78	Oldham Ath‡	75
2	1987–88h	Millwall	82	Aston Villa*	78	Middlesbrough	78
2	1988–89k	Chelsea	99	Manchester C	82	Crystal Palace	81
2	1989–90k	Leeds U*	85	Sheffield U	85	Newcastle U‡	80
2	1990–91k	Oldham Ath	88	West Ham U	87	Sheffield Wed	82
2	1991–92k	Ipswich T	84	Middlesbrough	80	Derby Co	78

FIRST DIVISION (1992–93 to 2003–04)

MAXIMUM POINTS: 138

2	1992–93	Newcastle U	96	West Ham U*	88	Portsmouth‡	88
2	1993–94	Crystal Palace	90	Nottingham F	83	Millwall‡	74
2	1994–95	Middlesbrough	82	Reading‡	79	Bolton W	77
2	1995–96	Sunderland	83	Derby Co	79	Crystal Palace‡	75
2	1996–97	Bolton W	98	Barnsley	80	Wolverhampton W‡	76
2	1997–98	Nottingham F	94	Middlesbrough	91	Sunderland‡	90
2	1998–99	Sunderland	105	Bradford C	87	Ipswich T‡	86
2	1999–2000	Charlton Ath	91	Manchester C	89	Ipswich T	87
2	2000–01	Fulham	101	Blackburn R	91	Bolton W	87
2	2001–02	Manchester C	99	WBA	89	Wolverhampton W‡	86
2	2002–03	Portsmouth	98	Leicester C	92	Sheffield U‡	80
2	2003–04	Norwich C	94	WBA	86	Sunderland‡	79

FOOTBALL LEAGUE CHAMPIONSHIP (2004–05 to 2024–25)

MAXIMUM POINTS: 138

2	2004–05	Sunderland	94	Wigan Ath	87	Ipswich T‡	85
2	2005–06	Reading	106	Sheffield U	90	Watford	81
2	2006–07	Sunderland	88	Birmingham C	86	Derby Co	84
2	2007–08	WBA	81	Stoke C	79	Hull C	75
2	2008–09	Wolverhampton W	90	Birmingham C	83	Sheffield U‡	80
2	2009–10	Newcastle U	102	WBA	91	Nottingham F‡	79
2	2010–11	QPR	88	Norwich C	84	Swansea C*	80

2	2011–12	Reading	89	Southampton	88	West Ham U	86
2	2012–13	Cardiff C	87	Hull C	79	Watford‡	77
2	2013–14	Leicester C	102	Burnley	93	Derby Co‡	85
2	2014–15	Bournemouth	90	Watford	89	Norwich C	86
2	2015–16	Burnley	93	Middlesbrough*	89	Brighton & HA‡	89
2	2016–17	Newcastle U	94	Brighton & HA	93	Reading‡	85
2	2017–18	Wolverhampton W	99	Cardiff C	90	Fulham	88
2	2018–19	Norwich C	94	Sheffield U	89	Leeds U‡	83
2	2019–20	Leeds U	93	WBA	83	Brentford*‡	81
2	2020–21	Norwich C	97	Watford	91	Brentford	87
2	2021–22	Fulham	90	Bournemouth	88	Huddersfield T‡	82
2	2022–23	Burnley	101	Sheffield U	91	Luton T	80
2	2023–24	Leicester C	97	Ipswich T	96	Leeds U‡	87
2	2024–25	Leeds U*	100	Burnley	100	Sheffield U‡	90

DIVISION 3 (1920–1921) – TIER 3

MAXIMUM POINTS: *a* 84.

3	1920–21*a*	Crystal Palace	59	Southampton	54	QPR	53

DIVISION 3—SOUTH (1921–22 to 1957–58)

MAXIMUM POINTS: *a* 84; *b* 92.

3	1921–22*a*	Southampton*	61	Plymouth Arg	61	Portsmouth	53
3	1922–23*a*	Bristol C	59	Plymouth Arg*	53	Swansea T	53
3	1923–24*a*	Portsmouth	59	Plymouth Arg	55	Millwall	54
3	1924–25*a*	Swansea T	57	Plymouth Arg	56	Bristol C	53
3	1925–26*a*	Reading	57	Plymouth Arg	56	Millwall	53
3	1926–27*a*	Bristol C	62	Plymouth Arg	60	Millwall	56
3	1927–28*a*	Millwall	65	Northampton T	55	Plymouth Arg	53
3	1928–29*a*	Charlton Ath*	54	Crystal Palace	54	Northampton T*	52
3	1929–30*a*	Plymouth Arg	68	Brentford	61	QPR	51
3	1930–31*a*	Notts Co	59	Crystal Palace	51	Brentford	50
3	1931–32*a*	Fulham	57	Reading	55	Southend U	53
3	1932–33*a*	Brentford	62	Exeter C	58	Norwich C	57
3	1933–34*a*	Norwich C	61	Coventry C*	54	Reading*	54
3	1934–35*a*	Charlton Ath	61	Reading	53	Coventry C	51
3	1935–36*a*	Coventry C	57	Luton T	56	Reading	54
3	1936–37*a*	Luton T	58	Notts Co	56	Brighton & HA	53
3	1937–38*a*	Millwall	56	Bristol C	55	QPR*	53
3	1938–39*a*	Newport Co	55	Crystal Palace	52	Brighton & HA	49
3	1946–47*a*	Cardiff C	66	QPR	57	Bristol C	51
3	1947–48*a*	QPR	61	Bournemouth	57	Walsall	51
3	1948–49*a*	Swansea T	62	Reading	55	Bournemouth	52
3	1949–50*a*	Notts Co	58	Northampton T*	51	Southend U	51
3	1950–51*b*	Nottingham F	70	Norwich C	64	Reading*	57
3	1951–52*b*	Plymouth Arg	66	Reading*	61	Norwich C	61
3	1952–53*b*	Bristol R	64	Millwall*	62	Northampton T	62
3	1953–54*b*	Ipswich T	64	Brighton & HA	61	Bristol C	56
3	1954–55*b*	Bristol C	70	Leyton Orient	61	Southampton	59
3	1955–56*b*	Leyton Orient	66	Brighton & HA	65	Ipswich T	64
3	1956–57*b*	Ipswich T*	59	Torquay U	59	Colchester U	58
3	1957–58*b*	Brighton & HA	60	Brentford*	58	Plymouth Arg	58

DIVISION 3—NORTH (1921–22 to 1957–58)

MAXIMUM POINTS: *a* 76; *b* 84; *c* 80; *d* 92.

3	1921–22*a*	Stockport Co	56	Darlington*	50	Grimsby T	50
3	1922–23*a*	Nelson	51	Bradford PA	47	Walsall	46
3	1923–24*b*	Wolverhampton W	63	Rochdale	62	Chesterfield	54
3	1924–25*b*	Darlington	58	Nelson*	53	New Brighton	53
3	1925–26*b*	Grimsby T	61	Bradford PA	60	Rochdale	59
3	1926–27*b*	Stoke C	63	Rochdale	58	Bradford PA	55
3	1927–28*b*	Bradford PA	63	Lincoln C	55	Stockport Co	54
3	1928–29*b*	Bradford C	63	Stockport Co	62	Wrexham	52
3	1929–30*b*	Port Vale	67	Stockport Co	63	Darlington*	50
3	1930–31*b*	Chesterfield	58	Lincoln C	57	Wrexham*	54
3	1931–32*c*	Lincoln C*	57	Gateshead	57	Chester	50
3	1932–33*b*	Hull C	59	Wrexham	57	Stockport Co	54
3	1933–34*b*	Barnsley	62	Chesterfield	61	Stockport Co	59
3	1934–35*b*	Doncaster R	57	Halifax T	55	Chester	54
3	1935–36*b*	Chesterfield	60	Chester*	55	Tranmere R	55
3	1936–37*b*	Stockport Co	60	Lincoln C	57	Chester	53
3	1937–38*b*	Tranmere R	56	Doncaster R	54	Hull C	53
3	1938–39*b*	Barnsley	67	Doncaster R	56	Bradford C	52
3	1946–47*b*	Doncaster R	72	Rotherham U	64	Chester	56
3	1947–48*b*	Lincoln C	60	Rotherham U	59	Wrexham	50
3	1948–49*b*	Hull C	65	Rotherham U	62	Doncaster R	50
3	1949–50*b*	Doncaster R	55	Gateshead	53	Rochdale*	51
3	1950–51*d*	Rotherham U	71	Mansfield T	64	Carlisle U	62
3	1951–52*d*	Lincoln C	69	Grimsby T	66	Stockport Co	59
3	1952–53*d*	Oldham Ath	59	Port Vale	58	Wrexham	56
3	1953–54*d*	Port Vale	69	Barnsley	58	Scunthorpe U	57
3	1954–55*d*	Barnsley	65	Accrington S	61	Scunthorpe U*	58
3	1955–56*d*	Grimsby T	68	Derby Co	63	Accrington S	59
3	1956–57*d*	Derby Co	63	Hartlepools U	59	Accrington S*	58
3	1957–58*d*	Scunthorpe U	66	Accrington S	59	Bradford C	57

DIVISION 3 (1958–59 to 1991–92)

MAXIMUM POINTS: 92; 138 FROM 1981–82.

	Season						
3	1958–59	Plymouth Arg	62	Hull C	61	Brentford*	57
3	1959–60	Southampton	61	Norwich C	59	Shrewsbury T*	52
3	1960–61	Bury	68	Walsall	62	QPR	60
3	1961–62	Portsmouth	65	Grimsby T	62	Bournemouth*	59
3	1962–63	Northampton T	62	Swindon T	58	Port Vale	54
3	1963–64	Coventry C*	60	Crystal Palace	60	Watford	58
3	1964–65	Carlisle U	60	Bristol C*	59	Mansfield T	59
3	1965–66	Hull C	69	Millwall	65	QPR	57
3	1966–67	QPR	67	Middlesbrough	55	Watford	54
3	1967–68	Oxford U	57	Bury	56	Shrewsbury T	55
3	1968–69	Watford*	64	Swindon T	64	Luton T	61
3	1969–70	Orient	62	Luton T	60	Bristol R	56
3	1970–71	Preston NE	61	Fulham	60	Halifax T	56
3	1971–72	Aston Villa	70	Brighton & HA	65	Bournemouth*	62
3	1972–73	Bolton W	61	Notts Co	57	Blackburn R	55
3	1973–74	Oldham Ath	62	Bristol R*	61	York C	61
3	1974–75	Blackburn R	60	Plymouth Arg	59	Charlton Ath	55
3	1975–76	Hereford U	63	Cardiff C	57	Millwall	56
3	1976–77	Mansfield T	64	Brighton & HA	61	Crystal Palace*	59
3	1977–78	Wrexham	61	Cambridge U	58	Preston NE*	56
3	1978–79	Shrewsbury T	61	Watford*	60	Swansea C	60
3	1979–80	Grimsby T	62	Blackburn R	59	Sheffield Wed	58
3	1980–81	Rotherham U	61	Barnsley	59	Charlton Ath	59
3	1981–82	Burnley*	80	Carlisle U	80	Fulham	78
3	1982–83	Portsmouth	91	Cardiff C	86	Huddersfield T	82
3	1983–84	Oxford U	95	Wimbledon	87	Sheffield U*	83
3	1984–85	Bradford C	94	Millwall	90	Hull C	87
3	1985–86	Reading	94	Plymouth Arg	87	Derby Co	84
3	1986–87	Bournemouth	97	Middlesbrough	94	Swindon T	87
3	1987–88	Sunderland	93	Brighton & HA	84	Walsall	82
3	1988–89	Wolverhampton W	92	Sheffield U*	84	Port Vale	84
3	1989–90	Bristol R	93	Bristol C	91	Notts Co	87
3	1990–91	Cambridge U	86	Southend U	85	Grimsby T*	83
3	1991–92	Brentford	82	Birmingham C	81	Huddersfield T‡	78

SECOND DIVISION (1992–93 to 2003–04)

MAXIMUM POINTS: 138

	Season						
3	1992–93	Stoke C	93	Bolton W	90	Port Vale‡	89
3	1993–94	Reading	89	Port Vale	88	Plymouth Arg*‡	85
3	1994–95	Birmingham C	89	Brentford‡	85	Crewe Alex‡	83
3	1995–96	Swindon T	92	Oxford U	83	Blackpool‡	82
3	1996–97	Bury	84	Stockport Co	82	Luton T‡	78
3	1997–98	Watford	88	Bristol C	85	Grimsby T	72
3	1998–99	Fulham	101	Walsall	87	Manchester C	82
3	1999–2000	Preston NE	95	Burnley	88	Gillingham	85
3	2000–01	Millwall	93	Rotherham U	91	Reading‡	86
3	2001–02	Brighton & HA	90	Reading	84	Brentford*‡	83
3	2002–03	Wigan Ath	100	Crewe Alex	86	Bristol C*‡	83
3	2003–04	Plymouth Arg	90	QPR	83	Bristol C‡	82

FOOTBALL LEAGUE ONE (2004–05 to 2024–25)

MAXIMUM POINTS: 138

	Season						
3	2004–05	Luton T	98	Hull C	86	Tranmere R‡	79
3	2005–06	Southend U	82	Colchester U	79	Brentford‡	76
3	2006–07	Scunthorpe U	91	Bristol C	85	Blackpool	83
3	2007–08	Swansea C	92	Nottingham F	82	Doncaster R*	80
3	2008–09	Leicester C	96	Peterborough U	89	Milton Keynes D‡	87
3	2009–10	Norwich C	95	Leeds U	86	Millwall	85
3	2010–11	Brighton & HA	95	Southampton	92	Huddersfield T‡	87
3	2011–12	Charlton Ath	101	Sheffield Wed	93	Sheffield U‡	90
3	2012–13	Doncaster R	84	Bournemouth	83	Brentford‡	79
3	2013–14	Wolverhampton W	103	Brentford	94	Leyton Orient‡	86
3	2014–15	Bristol C	99	Milton Keynes D	91	Preston NE	89
3	2015–16	Wigan Ath	87	Burton Alb	85	Walsall‡	84
3	2016–17	Sheffield U	100	Bolton W	86	Scunthorpe U*‡	82
3	2017–18	Wigan Ath	98	Blackburn R	96	Shrewsbury T‡	87
3	2018–19	Luton T	94	Barnsley	91	Charlton Ath*	88
3	2019–20²	Coventry C	67	Rotherham U	62	Wycombe W	59
3	2020–21	Hull C	89	Peterborough U	87	Blackpool	80
3	2021–22	Wigan Ath	92	Rotherham U	90	Milton Keynes D‡	89
3	2022–23	Plymouth Arg	101	Ipswich T	98	Sheffield Wed	96
3	2023–24	Portsmouth	97	Derby Co	92	Bolton W‡	87
3	2024–25	Birmingham C	111	Wrexham	92	Stockport Co‡	87

² *Season curtailed due to COVID-19 pandemic. League positions decided on points-per-game basis.*

DIVISION 4 (1958–59 to 1991–92) – TIER 4

MAXIMUM POINTS: 92; 138 FROM 1981–82.

	Season								
4	1958–59	Port Vale	64	Coventry C*	60	York C	60	Shrewsbury T	58
4	1959–60	Walsall	65	Notts Co*	60	Torquay U	60	Watford	57
4	1960–61	Peterborough U	66	Crystal Palace	64	Northampton T*	60	Bradford PA	60
4	1961–62³	Millwall	56	Colchester U	55	Wrexham	53	Carlisle U	52
4	1962–63	Brentford	62	Oldham Ath*	59	Crewe Alex	59	Mansfield T*	57
4	1963–64	Gillingham*	60	Carlisle U	60	Workington	59	Exeter C	58
4	1964–65	Brighton & HA	63	Millwall*	62	York C	62	Oxford U	61

4	1965–66	Doncaster R*	59	Darlington	59	Torquay U	58	Colchester U*	56
4	1966–67	Stockport Co	64	Southport*	59	Barrow	59	Tranmere R	58
4	1967–68	Luton T	66	Barnsley	61	Hartlepools U	60	Crewe Alex	58
4	1968–69	Doncaster R	59	Halifax T	57	Rochdale*	56	Bradford C	56
4	1969–70	Chesterfield	64	Wrexham	61	Swansea C	60	Port Vale	59
4	1970–71	Notts Co	69	Bournemouth	60	Oldham Ath	59	York C	56
4	1971–72	Grimsby T	63	Southend U	60	Brentford	59	Scunthorpe U	57
4	1972–73	Southport	62	Hereford U	58	Cambridge U	57	Aldershot*	56
4	1973–74	Peterborough U	65	Gillingham	62	Colchester U	60	Bury	59
4	1974–75	Mansfield T	68	Shrewsbury T	62	Rotherham U	59	Chester*	57
4	1975–76	Lincoln C	74	Northampton T	68	Reading	60	Tranmere R	58
4	1976–77	Cambridge U	65	Exeter C	62	Colchester U*	59	Bradford C	59
4	1977–78	Watford	71	Southend U	60	Swansea C*	56	Brentford	56
4	1978–79	Reading	65	Grimsby T*	61	Wimbledon*	61	Barnsley	61
4	1979–80	Huddersfield T	66	Walsall	64	Newport Co	61	Portsmouth*	60
4	1980–81	Southend U	67	Lincoln C	65	Doncaster R	56	Wimbledon	55
4	1981–82	Sheffield U	96	Bradford C*	91	Wigan Ath	91	Bournemouth	88
4	1982–83	Wimbledon	98	Hull C	90	Port Vale	88	Scunthorpe U	83
4	1983–84	York C	101	Doncaster R	85	Reading*	82	Bristol C	82
4	1984–85	Chesterfield	91	Blackpool	86	Darlington	85	Bury	84
4	1985–86	Swindon T	102	Chester C	84	Mansfield T	81	Port Vale	79
4	1986–87	Northampton T	99	Preston NE	90	Southend U	80	Wolverhampton W‡	79
4	1987–88	Wolverhampton W	90	Cardiff C	85	Bolton W	78	Scunthorpe U*‡	77
4	1988–89	Rotherham U	82	Tranmere R	80	Crewe Alex	78	Scunthorpe U*‡	77
4	1989–90	Exeter C	89	Grimsby T	79	Southend U	75	Stockport Co‡	74
4	1990–91	Darlington	83	Stockport Co*	82	Hartlepool U	82	Peterborough U	80
4	1991–92[4]	Burnley	83	Rotherham U*	77	Mansfield T	77	Blackpool	76

[3] *Maximum points: 88 owing to Accrington Stanley's resignation.*
[4] *Maximum points: 126 owing to Aldershot being expelled (and only 23 teams started the competition).*

THIRD DIVISION (1992–93 to 2003–04)

MAXIMUM POINTS: *a* 126; *b* 138.

4	1992–93*a*	Cardiff C	83	Wrexham	80	Barnet	79	York C	75
4	1993–94*a*	Shrewsbury T	79	Chester C	74	Crewe Alex	73	Wycombe W	70
4	1994–95*a*	Carlisle U	91	Walsall	83	Chesterfield	81	Bury‡	80
4	1995–96*b*	Preston NE	86	Gillingham	83	Bury	79	Plymouth Arg*	78
4	1996–97*b*	Wigan Ath*	87	Fulham	87	Carlisle U	84	Northampton T	72
4	1997–98*b*	Notts Co	99	Macclesfield T	82	Lincoln C	75	Colchester U*	74
4	1998–99*b*	Brentford	85	Cambridge U	81	Cardiff C	80	Scunthorpe U	74
4	1999–2000*b*	Swansea C	85	Rotherham U	84	Northampton T	82	Darlington‡	79
4	2000–01*b*	Brighton & HA	92	Cardiff C	82	Chesterfield[5]	80	Hartlepool U‡	77
4	2001–02*b*	Plymouth Arg	102	Luton T	97	Mansfield T	79	Cheltenham T*	78
4	2002–03*b*	Rushden & D	87	Hartlepool U	85	Wrexham	84	Bournemouth	74
4	2003–04*b*	Doncaster R	92	Hull C	88	Torquay U*	81	Huddersfield T	81

[5] *Chesterfield deducted 9pts for irregularities.*

FOOTBALL LEAGUE TWO (2004–05 to 2024–25)

MAXIMUM POINTS: 138

4	2004–05	Yeovil T	83	Scunthorpe U*	80	Swansea C	80	Southend U	78
4	2005–06	Carlisle U	86	Northampton T	83	Leyton Orient	81	Grimsby T‡	78
4	2006–07	Walsall	89	Hartlepool U	88	Swindon T	85	Milton Keynes D‡	84
4	2007–08	Milton Keynes D	97	Peterborough U	92	Hereford U	88	Stockport Co	82
4	2008–09	Brentford	85	Exeter C	79	Wycombe W*	78	Bury‡	78
4	2009–10	Notts Co	93	Bournemouth	83	Rochdale	82	Morecambe*‡	73
4	2010–11	Chesterfield	86	Bury	81	Wycombe W	80	Shrewsbury T	79
4	2011–12	Swindon T	93	Shrewsbury T	88	Crawley T	84	Southend U‡	83
4	2012–13	Gillingham	83	Rotherham U	79	Port Vale	78	Burton Alb	76
4	2013–14	Chesterfield	84	Scunthorpe U*	81	Rochdale	81	Fleetwood T	76
4	2014–15	Burton Alb	94	Shrewsbury T	89	Bury	85	Wycombe W*‡	84
4	2015–16	Northampton T	99	Oxford U	86	Bristol R*	85	Accrington S‡	85
4	2016–17	Portsmouth*	87	Plymouth Arg	87	Doncaster R	85	Luton T‡	77
4	2017–18	Accrington S	93	Luton T	88	Wycombe W	84	Exeter C‡	80
4	2018–19	Lincoln C	85	Bury*	79	Milton Keynes D	79	Mansfield T‡	76
4	2019–20[6]	Swindon T	69	Crewe Alex	69	Plymouth Arg	68	Cheltenham T‡	64
4	2020–21	Cheltenham T	82	Cambridge U	80	Bolton W	79	Morecambe	78
4	2021–22	Forest Green R*	84	Exeter C	84	Bristol R*	80	Northampton T‡	80
4	2022–23	Leyton Orient	91	Stevenage	85	Northampton T	83	Stockport Co‡	79
4	2023–24	Stockport Co	92	Wrexham	88	Mansfield T	86	Milton Keynes D‡	78
4	2024–25	Doncaster R	84	Port Vale	80	Bradford C	78	Walsall‡	77

[6] *Season curtailed due to COVID-19 pandemic. League positions decided on points-per-game basis.*

LEAGUE TITLE WINS

DIVISION 1 (1888–89 to 1991–92) – TIER 1
Liverpool 18, Arsenal 10, Everton 9, Aston Villa 7, Manchester U 7, Sunderland 6, Newcastle U 4, Sheffield Wed 4 (3 as The Wednesday), Huddersfield T 3, Leeds U 3, Wolverhampton W 3, Blackburn R 2, Burnley 2, Derby Co 2, Manchester C 2, Portsmouth 2, Preston NE 2, Tottenham H 2, Chelsea 1, Ipswich T 1, Nottingham F 1, Sheffield U 1, WBA 1.

PREMIER LEAGUE (1992–93 to 2024–25) – TIER 1
Manchester U 13, Manchester C 8, Chelsea 5, Arsenal 3, Liverpool 2, Blackburn R 1, Leicester C 1.

DIVISION 2 (1892–93 TO 1991–92) – TIER 2
Leicester C 6, Manchester C 6, Sheffield Wed 5 (1 as The Wednesday), Birmingham C 4 (1 as Small Heath), Derby Co 4, Liverpool 4, Ipswich T 3, Leeds U 3, Middlesbrough 3, Notts Co 3, Preston NE 3, Aston Villa 2, Bolton W 2, Burnley 2, Chelsea 2, Grimsby T 2, Manchester U 2, Norwich C 2, Nottingham F 2, Stoke C 2, Tottenham H 2, WBA 2, West Ham U 2, Wolverhampton W 2, Blackburn R 1, Blackpool 1, Bradford C 1, Brentford 1, Bristol C 1, Bury 1, Coventry C 1, Crystal Palace 1, Everton 1, Fulham 1, Huddersfield T 1, Luton T 1, Millwall 1, Newcastle U 1, Oldham Ath 1, Oxford U 1, QPR 1, Sheffield U 1, Sunderland 1.

FIRST DIVISION (1992–93 to 2003–04) – TIER 2
Sunderland 1, Bolton W 1, Charlton Ath 1, Crystal Palace 1, Fulham 1, Manchester C 1, Middlesbrough 1, Newcastle U 1, Norwich C 1, Nottingham F 1, Portsmouth 1.

FOOTBALL LEAGUE CHAMPIONSHIP (2004–05 to 2024–25) – TIER 2
Burnley 2, Leeds U 2, Leicester C 2, Newcastle U 2, Norwich C 2, Reading 2, Sunderland 2, Wolverhampton W 2, Bournemouth 1, Cardiff C 1, Fulham 1, QPR 1, WBA 1.

DIVISION 3—SOUTH (1920–21 to 1957–58) – TIER 3
Bristol C 3, Charlton Ath 2, Ipswich T 2, Millwall 2, Notts Co 2, Plymouth Arg 2, Swansea T 2, Brentford 1, Brighton & HA 1, Bristol R 1, Cardiff C 1, Coventry C 1, Crystal Palace 1, Fulham 1, Leyton Orient 1, Luton T 1, Newport Co 1, Norwich C 1, Nottingham F 1, Portsmouth 1, QPR 1, Reading 1, Southampton 1.

DIVISION 3—NORTH (1921–22 to 1957–58) – TIER 3
Barnsley 3, Doncaster R 3, Lincoln C 3, Chesterfield 2, Grimsby T 2, Hull C 2, Port Vale 2, Stockport Co 2, Bradford C 1, Bradford PA 1, Darlington 1, Derby Co 1, Nelson 1, Oldham Ath 1, Rotherham U 1, Scunthorpe U 1, Stoke C 1, Tranmere R 1, Wolverhampton W 1.

DIVISION 3 (1958–59 to 1991–92) – TIER 3
Oxford U 2, Portsmouth 2, Aston Villa 1, Blackburn R 1, Bolton W 1, Bournemouth 1, Bradford C 1, Brentford 1, Bristol R 1, Burnley 1, Bury 1, Cambridge U 1, Carlisle U 1, Coventry C 1, Grimsby T 1, Hereford U 1, Hull C 1, Mansfield T 1, Northampton T 1, Oldham Ath 1, Orient 1, Plymouth Arg 1, Preston NE 1, QPR 1, Reading 1, Rotherham U 1, Shrewsbury T 1, Southampton 1, Sunderland 1, Watford 1, Wolverhampton W 1, Wrexham 1.

SECOND DIVISION (1992–93 to 2003–04) – TIER 3
Birmingham C 1, Brighton & HA 1, Bury 1, Fulham 1, Millwall 1, Plymouth Arg 1, Preston NE 1, Reading 1, Stoke C 1, Swindon T 1, Watford 1, Wigan Ath 1.

FOOTBALL LEAGUE ONE (2004–05 to 2024–25) – TIER 3
Luton T 2, Wigan Ath 2, Birmingham C 1, Brighton & HA 1, Bristol C 1, Charlton Ath 1, Coventry C 1, Doncaster R 1, Hull C 1, Leicester C 1, Norwich C 1, Plymouth Arg 1, Portsmouth 1, Scunthorpe U 1, Sheffield U 1, Southend U 1, Swansea C 1, Wigan Ath 1, Wolverhampton W 1.

DIVISION 4 (1958–59 to 1991–92) – TIER 4
Chesterfield 2, Doncaster R 2, Peterborough U 2, Brentford 1, Brighton & HA 1, Burnley 1, Cambridge U 1, Darlington 1, Exeter C 1, Gillingham 1, Grimsby T 1, Huddersfield T 1, Lincoln C 1, Luton T 1, Mansfield T 1, Millwall 1, Northampton T 1, Notts Co 1, Port Vale 1, Reading 1, Rotherham U 1, Sheffield U 1, Southend U 1, Southport 1, Stockport Co 1, Swindon T 1, Walsall 1, Watford 1, Wimbledon 1, Wolverhampton W 1, York C 1.

THIRD DIVISION (1992–93 to 2003–04) – TIER 4
Brentford 1, Brighton & HA 1, Cardiff C 1, Carlisle U 1, Doncaster R 1, Notts Co 1, Plymouth Arg 1, Preston NE 1, Rushden & D 1, Shrewsbury T 1, Swansea C 1, Wigan Ath 1.

FOOTBALL LEAGUE TWO (2004–05 to 2024–25) – TIER 4
Chesterfield 2, Swindon T 2, Accrington S 1, Brentford 1, Burton Alb 1, Carlisle U 1, Cheltenham T 1, Doncaster R 1, Forest Green R 1, Gillingham 1, Leyton Orient 1, Lincoln C 1, Milton Keynes D 1, Northampton T 1, Notts Co 1, Portsmouth 1, Stockport Co 1, Walsall 1, Yeovil T 1.

PROMOTED AFTER PLAY-OFFS

1986–87	Charlton Ath to Division 1; Swindon T to Division 2; Aldershot to Division 3
1987–88	Middlesbrough to Division 1; Walsall to Division 2; Swansea C to Division 3
1988–89	Crystal Palace to Division 1; Port Vale to Division 2; Leyton Orient to Division 3
1989–90	Sunderland to Division 1; Notts Co to Division 2; Cambridge U to Division 3
1990–91	Notts Co to Division 1; Tranmere R to Division 2; Torquay U to Division 3
1991–92	Blackburn R to Premier League; Peterborough U to First Division; Blackpool to Second Division
1992–93	Swindon T to Premier League; WBA to First Division; York C to Second Division
1993–94	Leicester C to Premier League; Burnley to First Division; Wycombe W to Second Division
1994–95	Bolton W to Premier League; Huddersfield T to First Division; Wycombe W to Second Division
1995–96	Leicester C to Premier League; Bradford C to First Division; Plymouth Arg to Second Division
1996–97	Crystal Palace to Premier League; Crewe Alex to First Division; Northampton T to Second Division
1997–98	Charlton Ath to Premier League; Grimsby T to First Division; Colchester U to Second Division
1998–99	Watford to Premier League; Manchester C to First Division; Scunthorpe U to Second Division
1999–2000	Ipswich to Premier League; Gillingham to First Division; Peterborough U to Second Division
2000–01	Bolton W to Premier league; Walsall to First Division; Blackpool to Second Division
2001–02	Birmingham C to Premier League; Stoke C to First Division; Cheltenham T to Second Division
2002–03	Wolverhampton W to Premier League; Cardiff C to First Division; Bournemouth to Second Division
2003–04	Crystal Palace to Premier League; Brighton & HA to First Division; Huddersfield T to Second Division
2004–05	West Ham U to Premier League; Sheffield Wed to Championship; Southend U to Football League One
2005–06	Watford to Premier League; Barnsley to Championship; Cheltenham T to Football League One
2006–07	Derby Co to Premier League; Blackpool to Championship; Bristol R to Football League One
2007–08	Hull C to Premier League; Doncaster R to Championship; Stockport Co to Football League One
2008–09	Burnley to Premier League; Scunthorpe U to Championship; Gillingham to Football League One
2009–10	Blackpool to Premier League; Millwall to Championship; Dagenham & Red to Football League One
2010–11	Swansea C to Premier League; Peterborough U to Championship; Stevenage to Football League One
2011–12	West Ham U to Premier League; Huddersfield T to Championship; Crewe Alex to Football League One
2012–13	Crystal Palace to Premier League; Yeovil T to Championship; Bradford C to Football League One
2013–14	QPR to Premier League; Rotherham U to Championship; Fleetwood T to Football League One
2014–15	Norwich C to Premier League; Preston NE to Championship; Southend U to Football League One
2015–16	Hull C to Premier League; Barnsley to Championship; AFC Wimbledon to Football League One
2016–17	Huddersfield T to Premier League; Millwall to Championship; Blackpool to Football League One
2017–18	Fulham to Premier League; Rotherham U to Championship; Coventry C to Football League One
2018–19	Aston Villa to Premier League; Charlton Ath to Championship; Tranmere R to Football League One
2019–20	Fulham to Premier League; Wycombe W to Championship; Northampton T to Football League One
2020–21	Brentford to Premier League; Blackpool to Championship; Morecambe to Football League One
2021–22	Nottingham F to Premier League; Sunderland to Championship; Port Vale to Football League One
2022–23	Luton T to Premier League; Sheffield Wed to Championship; Carlisle U to Football League One
2023–24	Southampton to Premier League; Oxford U to Championship; Crawley T to Football League One
2024–25	Sunderland to Premier League; Charlton Ath to Championship; AFC Wimbledon to Football League One

RELEGATED CLUBS

1891–92 League extended. Newton Heath, Sheffield Wed and Nottingham F admitted. *Second Division formed* including Darwen.
1892–93 In Test matches, Sheffield U and Darwen won promotion in place of Notts Co and Accrington S.
1893–94 In Tests, Liverpool and Small Heath won promotion. Newton Heath and Darwen relegated.
1894–95 After Tests, Bury promoted, Liverpool relegated.
1895–96 After Tests, Liverpool promoted, Small Heath relegated.
1896–97 After Tests, Notts Co promoted, Burnley relegated.
1897–98 Test system abolished after success of Stoke C and Burnley. League extended. Blackburn R and Newcastle U elected to First Division. *Automatic promotion and relegation introduced.*

DIVISION 1 TO DIVISION 2 (1898–99 to 1991–92)

1898–99 Bolton W and The Wednesday
1899–1900 Burnley and Glossop NE
1900–01 Preston NE and WBA
1901–02 Small Heath and Manchester C
1902–03 Grimsby T and Bolton W
1903–04 Liverpool and WBA
1904–05 League extended. Bury and Notts Co, two bottom clubs in First Division, re-elected.
1905–06 Nottingham F and Wolverhampton W
1906–07 Derby Co and Stoke C
1907–08 Bolton W and Birmingham C
1908–09 Manchester C and Leicester Fosse
1909–10 Bolton W and Chelsea
1910–11 Bristol C and Nottingham F
1911–12 Preston NE and Bury
1912–13 Notts Co and Woolwich Arsenal
1913–14 Preston NE and Derby Co
1914–15 Tottenham H and Chelsea*
1919–20 Notts Co and The Wednesday
1920–21 Derby Co and Bradford PA
1921–22 Bradford C and Manchester U
1922–23 Stoke C and Oldham Ath
1923–24 Chelsea and Middlesbrough
1924–25 Preston NE and Nottingham F
1925–26 Manchester C and Notts Co
1926–27 Leeds U and WBA
1927–28 Tottenham H and Middlesbrough
1928–29 Bury and Cardiff C
1929–30 Burnley and Everton
1930–31 Leeds U and Manchester U
1931–32 Grimsby T and West Ham U
1932–33 Bolton W and Blackpool
1933–34 Newcastle U and Sheffield U
1934–35 Leicester C and Tottenham H
1935–36 Aston Villa and Blackburn R
1936–37 Manchester U and Sheffield Wed
1937–38 Manchester C and WBA
1938–39 Birmingham C and Leicester C
1946–47 Brentford and Leeds U
1947–48 Blackburn R and Grimsby T
1948–49 Preston NE and Sheffield U
1949–50 Manchester C and Birmingham C
1950–51 Sheffield Wed and Everton
1951–52 Huddersfield T and Fulham

1952–53 Stoke C and Derby Co
1953–54 Middlesbrough and Liverpool
1954–55 Leicester C and Sheffield Wed
1955–56 Huddersfield T and Sheffield U
1956–57 Charlton Ath and Cardiff C
1957–58 Sheffield Wed and Sunderland
1958–59 Portsmouth and Aston Villa
1959–60 Luton T and Leeds U
1960–61 Preston NE and Newcastle U
1961–62 Chelsea and Cardiff C
1962–63 Manchester C and Leyton Orient
1963–64 Bolton W and Ipswich T
1964–65 Wolverhampton W and Birmingham C
1965–66 Northampton T and Blackburn R
1966–67 Aston Villa and Blackpool
1967–68 Fulham and Sheffield U
1968–69 Leicester C and QPR
1969–70 Sunderland and Sheffield Wed
1970–71 Burnley and Blackpool
1971–72 Huddersfield T and Nottingham F
1972–73 Crystal Palace and WBA
1973–74 Southampton, Manchester U, Norwich C
1974–75 Luton T, Chelsea, Carlisle U
1975–76 Wolverhampton W, Burnley, Sheffield U
1976–77 Sunderland, Stoke C, Tottenham H
1977–78 West Ham U, Newcastle U, Leicester C
1978–79 QPR, Birmingham C, Chelsea
1979–80 Bristol C, Derby Co, Bolton W
1980–81 Norwich C, Leicester C, Crystal Palace
1981–82 Leeds U, Wolverhampton W, Middlesbrough
1982–83 Manchester C, Swansea C, Brighton & HA
1983–84 Birmingham C, Notts Co, Wolverhampton W
1984–85 Norwich C, Sunderland, Stoke C
1985–86 Ipswich T, Birmingham C, WBA
1986–87 Leicester C, Manchester C, Aston Villa
1987–88 Chelsea**, Portsmouth, Watford, Oxford U
1988–89 Middlesbrough, West Ham U, Newcastle U
1989–90 Sheffield Wed, Charlton Ath, Millwall
1990–91 Sunderland and Derby Co
1991–92 Luton T, Notts Co, West Ham U
**Relegated after play-offs.*
**Subsequently re-elected to Division 1 when League was extended after the War.*

PREMIER LEAGUE TO DIVISION 1 (1992–93 to 2003–04)

1992–93 Crystal Palace, Middlesbrough, Nottingham F
1993–94 Sheffield U, Oldham Ath, Swindon T
1994–95 Crystal Palace, Norwich C, Leicester C, Ipswich T
1995–96 Manchester C, QPR, Bolton W
1996–97 Sunderland, Middlesbrough, Nottingham F
1997–98 Bolton W, Barnsley, Crystal Palace

1998–99 Charlton Ath, Blackburn R, Nottingham F
1999–2000 Wimbledon, Sheffield Wed, Watford
2000–01 Manchester C, Coventry C, Bradford C
2001–02 Ipswich T, Derby Co, Leicester C
2002–03 West Ham U, WBA, Sunderland
2003–04 Leicester C, Leeds U, Wolverhampton W

PREMIER LEAGUE TO CHAMPIONSHIP (2004–05 to 2024–25)

2004–05 Crystal Palace, Norwich C, Southampton
2005–06 Birmingham C, WBA, Sunderland
2006–07 Sheffield U, Charlton Ath, Watford
2007–08 Reading, Birmingham C, Derby Co
2008–09 Newcastle U, Middlesbrough, WBA
2009–10 Burnley, Hull C, Portsmouth
2010–11 Birmingham C, Blackpool, West Ham U
2011–12 Bolton W, Blackburn R, Wolverhampton W
2012–13 Wigan Ath, Reading, QPR
2013–14 Norwich C, Fulham, Cardiff C
2014–15 Hull C, Burnley, QPR

2015–16 Newcastle U, Norwich C, Aston Villa
2016–17 Hull C, Middlesbrough, Sunderland
2017–18 Swansea C, Stoke C, WBA
2018–19 Cardiff C, Fulham, Huddersfield T
2019–20 Bournemouth, Watford, Norwich C
2020–21 Fulham, WBA, Sheffield U
2021–22 Burnley, Watford, Norwich C
2022–23 Leicester C, Leeds U, Southampton
2023–24 Luton T, Burnley, Sheffield U
2024–25 Leicester C, Ipswich T, Southampton

DIVISION 2 TO DIVISION 3 (1920–21 to 1991–92)

1920–21 Stockport Co
1921–22 Bradford PA and Bristol C
1922–23 Rotherham Co and Wolverhampton W
1923–24 Nelson and Bristol C
1924–25 Crystal Palace and Coventry C
1925–26 Stoke C and Stockport Co
1926–27 Darlington and Bradford C
1927–28 Fulham and South Shields
1928–29 Port Vale and Clapton Orient
1929–30 Hull C and Notts Co
1930–31 Reading and Cardiff C
1931–32 Barnsley and Bristol C
1932–33 Chesterfield and Charlton Ath
1933–34 Millwall and Lincoln C
1934–35 Oldham Ath and Notts Co
1935–36 Port Vale and Hull C
1936–37 Doncaster R and Bradford C
1937–38 Barnsley and Stockport Co
1938–39 Norwich C and Tranmere R
1946–47 Swansea T and Newport Co
1947–48 Doncaster R and Millwall
1948–49 Nottingham F and Lincoln C
1949–50 Plymouth Arg and Bradford PA
1950–51 Grimsby T and Chesterfield
1951–52 Coventry C and QPR
1952–53 Southampton and Barnsley
1953–54 Brentford and Oldham Ath
1954–55 Ipswich T and Derby Co
1955–56 Plymouth Arg and Hull C
1956–57 Port Vale and Bury
1957–58 Doncaster R and Notts Co
1958–59 Barnsley and Grimsby T
1959–60 Bristol C and Hull C

1960–61 Lincoln C and Portsmouth
1961–62 Brighton & HA and Bristol R
1962–63 Walsall and Luton T
1963–64 Grimsby T and Scunthorpe U
1964–65 Swindon T and Swansea T
1965–66 Middlesbrough and Leyton Orient
1966–67 Northampton T and Bury
1967–68 Plymouth Arg and Rotherham U
1968–69 Fulham and Bury
1969–70 Preston NE and Aston Villa
1970–71 Blackburn R and Bolton W
1971–72 Charlton Ath and Watford
1972–73 Huddersfield T and Brighton & HA
1973–74 Crystal Palace, Preston NE, Swindon T
1974–75 Millwall, Cardiff C, Sheffield Wed
1975–76 Oxford U, York C, Portsmouth
1976–77 Carlisle U, Plymouth Arg, Hereford U
1977–78 Blackpool, Mansfield T, Hull C
1978–79 Sheffield U, Millwall, Blackburn R
1979–80 Fulham, Burnley, Charlton Ath
1980–81 Preston NE, Bristol C, Bristol R
1981–82 Cardiff C, Wrexham, Orient
1982–83 Rotherham U, Burnley, Bolton W
1983–84 Derby Co, Swansea C, Cambridge U
1984–85 Notts Co, Cardiff C, Wolverhampton W
1985–86 Carlisle U, Middlesbrough, Fulham
1986–87 Sunderland**, Grimsby T, Brighton & HA
1987–88 Huddersfield T, Reading, Sheffield U**
1988–89 Shrewsbury T, Birmingham C, Walsall
1989–90 Bournemouth, Bradford C, Stoke C
1990–91 WBA and Hull C
1991–92 Plymouth Arg, Brighton & HA, Port Vale

FIRST DIVISION TO SECOND DIVISION (1992–93 to 2003–04)

1992–93 Brentford, Cambridge U, Bristol R
1993–94 Birmingham C, Oxford U, Peterborough U
1994–95 Swindon T, Burnley, Bristol C, Notts Co
1995–96 Millwall, Watford, Luton T
1996–97 Grimsby T, Oldham Ath, Southend U
1997–98 Manchester C, Stoke C, Reading

1998–99 Bury, Oxford U, Bristol C
1999–2000 Walsall, Port Vale, Swindon T
2000–01 Huddersfield T, QPR, Tranmere R
2001–02 Crewe Alex, Barnsley, Stockport Co
2002–03 Sheffield Wed, Brighton & HA, Grimsby T
2003–04 Walsall, Bradford C, Wimbledon

FOOTBALL LEAGUE CHAMPIONSHIP TO FOOTBALL LEAGUE ONE (2004–05 to 2024–25)

2004–05 Gillingham, Nottingham F, Rotherham U
2005–06 Crewe Alex, Millwall, Brighton & HA
2006–07 Southend U, Luton T, Leeds U
2007–08 Leicester C, Scunthorpe U, Colchester U
2008–09 Norwich C, Southampton, Charlton Ath
2009–10 Sheffield Wed, Plymouth Arg, Peterborough U
2010–11 Preston NE, Sheffield U, Scunthorpe U
2011–12 Portsmouth, Coventry C, Doncaster R
2012–13 Peterborough U, Wolverhampton W, Bristol C
2013–14 Doncaster R, Barnsley, Yeovil T
2014–15 Millwall, Wigan Ath, Blackpool

2015–16 Charlton Ath, Milton Keynes D, Bolton W
2016–17 Blackburn R, Wigan Ath, Rotherham U
2017–18 Barnsley, Burton Alb, Sunderland
2018–19 Rotherham U, Bolton W, Ipswich T
2019–20 Charlton Ath, Wigan Ath, Hull C
2020–21 Wycombe W, Rotherham U, Sheffield Wed
2021–22 Peterborough U, Derby Co, Barnsley
2022–23 Reading, Blackpool, Wigan Ath
2023–24 Birmingham C, Huddersfield T, Rotherham U
2024–25 Luton T, Plymouth Arg, Cardiff C

DIVISION 3 TO DIVISION 4 (1958–59 to 1991–92)

1958–59 Stockport Co, Doncaster R, Notts Co, Rochdale
1959–60 York C, Mansfield T, Wrexham, Accrington S
1960–61 Tranmere R, Bradford C, Colchester U, Chesterfield
1961–62 Torquay U, Lincoln C, Brentford, Newport Co
1962–63 Bradford PA, Brighton & HA, Carlisle U, Halifax T
1963–64 Millwall, Crewe Alex, Wrexham, Notts Co
1964–65 Luton T, Port Vale, Colchester U, Barnsley
1965–66 Southend U, Exeter C, Brentford, York C
1966–67 Swansea T, Darlington, Doncaster R, Workington
1967–68 Grimsby T, Colchester U, Scunthorpe U, Peterborough U (demoted)
1968–69 Northampton T, Hartlepool, Crewe Alex, Oldham Ath
1969–70 Bournemouth, Southport, Barrow, Stockport Co
1970–71 Reading, Bury, Doncaster R, Gillingham
1971–72 Mansfield T, Barnsley, Torquay U, Bradford C
1972–73 Rotherham U, Brentford, Swansea C, Scunthorpe U
1973–74 Cambridge U, Shrewsbury T, Southport, Rochdale
1974–75 Bournemouth, Tranmere R, Watford, Huddersfield T

1975–76 Aldershot, Colchester U, Southend U, Halifax T
1976–77 Reading, Northampton T, Grimsby T, York C
1977–78 Port Vale, Bradford C, Hereford U, Portsmouth
1978–79 Peterborough U, Walsall, Tranmere R, Lincoln C
1979–80 Bury, Southend U, Mansfield T, Wimbledon
1980–81 Sheffield U, Colchester U, Blackpool, Hull C
1981–82 Wimbledon, Swindon T, Bristol C, Chester
1982–83 Reading, Wrexham, Doncaster R, Chesterfield
1983–84 Scunthorpe U, Southend U, Port Vale, Exeter C
1984–85 Burnley, Orient, Preston NE, Cambridge U
1985–86 Lincoln C, Cardiff C, Wolverhampton W, Swansea C
1986–87 Bolton W**, Carlisle U, Darlington, Newport Co
1987–88 Rotherham U**, Grimsby T, York C, Doncaster R
1988–89 Southend U, Chesterfield, Gillingham, Aldershot
1989–90 Cardiff C, Northampton T, Blackpool, Walsall
1990–91 Crewe Alex, Rotherham U, Mansfield T
1991–92 Bury, Shrewsbury T, Torquay U, Darlington

** *Relegated after play-offs.*

SECOND DIVISION TO THIRD DIVISION (1992–93 to 2003–04)

1992–93 Preston NE, Mansfield T, Wigan Ath, Chester C
1993–94 Fulham, Exeter C, Hartlepool U, Barnet
1994–95 Cambridge U, Plymouth Arg, Cardiff C, Chester C, Leyton Orient
1995–96 Carlisle U, Swansea C, Brighton & HA, Hull C
1996–97 Peterborough U, Shrewsbury T, Rotherham U, Notts Co
1997–98 Brentford, Plymouth Arg, Carlisle U, Southend U

1998–99 York C, Northampton T, Lincoln C, Macclesfield T
1999–2000 Cardiff C, Blackpool, Scunthorpe U, Chesterfield
2000–01 Bristol R, Luton T, Swansea C, Oxford U
2001–02 Bournemouth, Bury, Wrexham, Cambridge U
2002–03 Cheltenham T, Huddersfield T, Mansfield T, Northampton T
2003–04 Grimsby T, Rushden & D, Notts Co, Wycombe W

FOOTBALL LEAGUE ONE TO FOOTBALL LEAGUE TWO (2004–05 to 2024–25)

2004–05 Torquay U, Wrexham, Peterborough U, Stockport Co
2005–06 Hartlepool U, Milton Keynes D, Swindon T, Walsall
2006–07 Chesterfield, Bradford C, Rotherham U, Brentford
2007–08 Bournemouth, Gillingham, Port Vale, Luton T
2008–09 Northampton T, Crewe Alex, Cheltenham T, Hereford U
2009–10 Gillingham, Wycombe W, Southend U, Stockport Co
2010–11 Dagenham & Red, Bristol R, Plymouth Arg, Swindon T
2011–12 Wycombe W, Chesterfield, Exeter C, Rochdale
2012–13 Scunthorpe U, Bury, Hartlepool U, Portsmouth
2013–14 Tranmere R, Carlisle U, Shrewsbury T, Stevenage

2014–15 Notts Co, Crawley T, Leyton Orient, Yeovil T
2015–16 Doncaster R, Blackpool, Colchester U, Crewe Alex
2016–17 Port Vale, Swindon T, Coventry C, Chesterfield
2017–18 Oldham Ath, Northampton T, Milton Keynes D, Bury
2018–19 Plymouth Arg, Walsall, Scunthorpe U, Bradford C
2019–20 Tranmere R, Southend U, Bolton W
2020–21 Rochdale, Northampton T, Swindon T, Bristol R
2021–22 Gillingham, Doncaster R, AFC Wimbledon, Crewe Alex
2022–23 Milton Keynes D, Morecambe, Accrington S, Forest Green R
2023–24 Cheltenham T, Fleetwood T, Port Vale, Carlisle U
2024–25 Crawley T, Bristol R, Cambridge U, Shrewsbury T

LEAGUE STATUS FROM 1986–87

RELEGATED FROM LEAGUE

1986–87 Lincoln C	1987–88 Newport Co
1988–89 Darlington	1989–90 Colchester U
1990–91 —	1991–92 —
1992–93 Halifax T	1993–94 —
1994–95 —	1995–96 —
1996–97 Hereford U	1997–98 Doncaster R
1998–99 Scarborough	1999–2000 Chester C
2000–01 Barnet	2001–02 Halifax T

2002–03 Shrewsbury T, Exeter C
2003–04 Carlisle U, York C
2004–05 Kidderminster H, Cambridge U
2005–06 Oxford U, Rushden & D
2006–07 Boston U, Torquay U
2007–08 Mansfield T, Wrexham
2008–09 Chester C, Luton T
2009–10 Grimsby T, Darlington
2010–11 Lincoln C, Stockport Co
2011–12 Hereford U, Macclesfield T
2012–13 Barnet, Aldershot
2013–14 Bristol R, Torquay U
2014–15 Cheltenham T, Tranmere R
2015–16 Dagenham & Red, York C
2016–17 Hartlepool U, Leyton Orient
2017–18 Barnet, Chesterfield
2018–19 Notts Co, Yeovil T
2019–20 Macclesfield T
2020–21 Southend U, Grimsby T
2021–22 Oldham Ath, Scunthorpe U
2022–23 Hartlepool U, Rochdale
2023–24 Sutton U, Forest Green R
2024–25 Carlisle U, Morecambe

PROMOTED TO LEAGUE

1986–87 Scarborough	1987–88 Lincoln C
1988–89 Maidstone U	1989–90 Darlington
1990–91 Barnet	1991–92 Colchester U
1992–93 Wycombe W	1993–94 —
1994–95 —	1995–96 —
1996–97 Macclesfield T	1997–98 Halifax T
1998–99 Cheltenham T	1999–2000 Kidderminster H
2000–01 Rushden & D	2001–02 Boston U

2002–03 Yeovil T, Doncaster R
2003–04 Chester C, Shrewsbury T
2004–05 Barnet, Carlisle U
2005–06 Accrington S, Hereford U
2006–07 Dagenham & Red, Morecambe
2007–08 Aldershot T, Exeter C
2008–09 Burton Alb, Torquay U
2009–10 Stevenage B, Oxford U
2010–11 Crawley T, AFC Wimbledon
2011–12 Fleetwood T, York C
2012–13 Mansfield T, Newport Co
2013–14 Luton T, Cambridge U
2014–15 Barnet, Bristol R
2015–16 Cheltenham T, Grimsby T
2016–17 Lincoln C, Forest Green R
2017–18 Macclesfield T, Tranmere R
2018–19 Leyton Orient, Salford C
2019–20 Barrow, Harrogate T
2020–21 Sutton U, Hartlepool U
2021–22 Stockport Co, Grimsby T
2022–23 Wrexham, Notts Co
2023–24 Chesterfield, Bromley
2024–25 Barnet, Oldham Ath

APPLICATIONS FOR RE-ELECTION

FOURTH DIVISION

Eleven: Hartlepool U (7 as Hartlepools U).
Seven: Crewe Alex.
Six: Barrow (lost League place to Hereford U 1972), Halifax T, Rochdale, Southport (lost League place to Wigan Ath 1978), York C.
Five: Chester C, Darlington, Lincoln C, Stockport Co, Workington (lost League place to Wimbledon 1977).
Four: Bradford PA (lost League place to Cambridge U 1970), Newport Co, Northampton T.
Three: Doncaster R, Hereford U.
Two: Bradford C, Exeter C, Oldham Ath, Scunthorpe U, Torquay U.
One: Aldershot, Colchester U, Gateshead (lost League place to Peterborough U 1960), Grimsby T, Swansea C, Tranmere R, Wrexham, Blackpool, Cambridge U, Preston NE.

THIRD DIVISIONS NORTH & SOUTH

Seven: Walsall.
Six: Exeter C, Halifax T, Newport Co.
Five: Accrington S, Barrow, Gillingham, New Brighton, Southport.
Four: Rochdale, Norwich C.
Three: Crystal Palace, Crewe Alex, Darlington, Hartlepool U, Merthyr T, Swindon T.
Two: Aberdare Ath, Aldershot, Ashington, Bournemouth, Brentford, Chester, Colchester U, Durham C, Millwall, Nelson, QPR, Rotherham U, Southend U, Tranmere R, Watford, Workington.
One: Bradford C, Bradford PA, Brighton & HA, Bristol R, Cardiff C, Carlisle U, Charlton Ath, Gateshead, Grimsby T, Mansfield T, Shrewsbury T, Torquay U, York C.

Accrington S resigned and Oxford U were elected 1962. Port Vale forced to re-apply following expulsion in 1968. Aldershot expelled March 1992. Maidstone U resigned August 1992.

ENGLISH LEAGUE ATTENDANCES 2024–25

PREMIER LEAGUE ATTENDANCES

	Average Gate			Season 2024–25	
	2023–24	*2024–25*	*+/–%*	*Highest*	*Lowest*
Arsenal	60,236	60,251	+0.02	60,383	60,067
Aston Villa	41,921	41,854	–0.16	42,743	37,890
Bournemouth	11,114	11,214	+0.89	11,248	11,129
Brentford	17,082	17,094	+0.07	17,215	16,955
Brighton & HA	31,543	31,472	–0.22	31,715	30,893
Chelsea	39,576	39,620	+0.11	39,894	39,092
Crystal Palace	24,932	25,063	+0.52	25,185	24,564
Everton	39,042	39,170	+0.33	39,376	38,742
Fulham	24,301	26,826	+10.39	27,770	24,931
Ipswich T	28,845	29,742	+3.11	30,017	29,180
Leicester C	31,238	31,448	+0.67	32,057	29,766
Liverpool	55,809	60,330	+8.10	60,420	60,107
Manchester C	53,120	52,575	–1.03	53,282	51,764
Manchester U	73,534	73,747	+0.29	73,839	73,297
Newcastle U	52,153	52,187	+0.07	52,252	51,975
Nottingham F	29,386	30,059	+2.29	30,263	29,040
Southampton	29,373	30,865	+5.08	31,289	28,946
Tottenham H	61,459	61,127	–0.54	61,645	59,314
West Ham U	62,429	62,464	+0.06	62,476	62,435
Wolverhampton W	31,046	30,660	–1.24	31,518	26,685

TOTAL ATTENDANCES:	15,347,584 (380 games)
	Average 40,388 (+4.76%)
HIGHEST:	73,839 Manchester U v Aston Villa
LOWEST:	11,129 Bournemouth v Crystal Palace
HIGHEST AVERAGE:	73,747 Manchester U
LOWEST AVERAGE:	11,214 Bournemouth

SKY BET ENGLISH FOOTBALL LEAGUE CHAMPIONSHIP ATTENDANCES

	Average Gate			Season 2024–25	
	2023–24	*2024–25*	*+/–%*	*Highest*	*Lowest*
Blackburn R	15,583	16,161	+3.71	25,909	12,819
Bristol C	22,813	22,283	–2.32	25,915	18,457
Burnley	21,153	19,876	–6.03	21,486	18,187
Cardiff C	21,213	19,344	–8.81	26,536	15,006
Coventry C	25,468	27,812	+9.21	31,452	24,583
Derby Co	27,278	29,018	+6.38	32,471	25,141
Hull C	21,980	21,323	–2.99	24,463	18,694
Leeds U	35,989	36,134	+0.40	36,804	34,401
Luton T	11,278	11,555	+2.46	11,965	10,537
Middlesbrough	26,905	25,416	–5.53	32,147	22,177
Millwall	16,540	15,490	–6.35	18,385	12,041
Norwich C	26,077	26,316	+0.91	26,838	25,498
Oxford U	9,021	11,367	+26.00	11,567	10,213
Plymouth Arg	16,507	16,537	+0.18	17,005	15,305
Portsmouth	18,953	20,263	+6.91	20,451	19,388
Preston NE	16,720	16,505	–1.29	20,945	12,838
QPR	16,718	15,856	–5.16	17,457	13,407
Sheffield U	29,962	28,087	–6.26	31,127	25,070
Sheffield Wed	26,762	26,636	–0.47	33,827	22,452
Stoke C	22,742	22,804	+0.27	29,163	19,679
Sunderland	41,028	40,423	–1.47	44,009	35,421
Swansea C	16,574	15,503	–6.47	20,174	12,869
Watford	18,876	19,379	+2.66	20,696	16,397
WBA	24,057	25,057	+4.16	25,951	23,305

TOTAL ATTENDANCES:	12,170,350 (552 games)
	Average 22,048 (–4.36%)
HIGHEST:	44,009 Sunderland v Hull C
LOWEST:	10,213 Oxford U v Hull C
HIGHEST AVERAGE:	40,423 Sunderland
LOWEST AVERAGE:	11,367 Oxford U

SKY BET ENGLISH FOOTBALL LEAGUE ONE ATTENDANCES

	Average Gate			Season 2024–25	
	2023–24	*2024–25*	*+/–%*	*Highest*	*Lowest*
Barnsley	12,680	12,211	–3.69	15,600	9,857
Birmingham C	21,180	26,717	+26.14	34,393	22,456
Blackpool	10,667	9,619	–9.83	12,567	7,873
Bolton W	21,022	21,325	+1.44	25,957	18,477
Bristol R	8,190	7,880	–3.78	9,508	6,342
Burton Alb	3,419	3,254	–4.84	5,027	1,749
Cambridge U	6,679	6,597	–1.23	7,414	5,085
Charlton Ath	13,481	15,255	+13.16	24,692	11,149
Crawley T	3,557	4,393	+23.51	5,530	3,220
Exeter C	6,800	6,513	–4.22	8,192	5,022
Huddersfield T	19,418	18,817	–3.10	21,657	17,036
Leyton Orient	8,116	7,687	–5.28	8,942	3,069
Lincoln C	8,424	9,004	+6.88	10,347	7,253
Mansfield T	7,426	7,769	+4.62	8,592	6,836
Northampton T	6,842	6,629	–3.12	7,947	5,559
Peterborough U	9,077	9,151	+0.81	12,370	5,913
Reading	13,115	12,535	–4.42	21,481	7,955
Rotherham U	10,674	9,330	–12.59	11,235	7,798
Shrewsbury T	6,361	6,207	–2.42	8,789	4,956
Stevenage	4,836	4,008	–17.13	5,704	2,767
Stockport Co	9,331	9,600	+2.89	10,554	8,128
Wigan Ath	10,442	9,946	–4.75	15,445	7,419
Wrexham	11,210	12,781	+14.02	13,341	10,670
Wycombe W	4,980	5,362	+7.66	9,333	3,456

TOTAL ATTENDANCES: 5,579,580 (552 games)
Average 10,108 (+4.11%)
HIGHEST: 34,393 Birmingham C v Rotherham U
LOWEST: 1,749 Burton Alb v Charlton Ath
HIGHEST AVERAGE: 26,717 Birmingham C
LOWEST AVERAGE: 3,254 Burton Alb

SKY BET ENGLISH FOOTBALL LEAGUE TWO ATTENDANCES

	Average Gate			Season 2024–25	
	2023–24	*2024–25*	*+/–%*	*Highest*	*Lowest*
Accrington S	2,706	2,539	–+6.17	4,572	1,503
AFC Wimbledon	7,893	8,008	+1.46	8,664	6,519
Barrow	3,804	3,381	–+11.12	4,665	2,783
Bradford C	17,004	17,766	+4.48	24,033	14,547
Bromley	2,637	3,111	+17.97	4,102	2,057
Carlisle U	8,000	7,425	–+7.18	12,305	5,594
Cheltenham T	4,609	4,198	–+8.91	5,561	2,976
Chesterfield	7,893	8,440	+6.93	10,032	7,192
Colchester U	4,177	4,998	+19.65	7,623	3,401
Crewe Alex	5,090	5,382	+5.75	9,288	3,881
Doncaster R	7,090	8,014	+13.03	12,574	5,632
Fleetwood T	3,430	2,950	–+14.00	4,025	2,106
Gillingham	6,226	6,268	+0.67	7,667	5,262
Grimsby T	6,354	6,067	–+4.51	8,369	3,874
Harrogate T	2,660	2,948	+10.82	4,136	1,694
Milton Keynes D	6,855	6,833	–+0.33	10,244	2,427
Morecambe	4,002	3,410	–+14.79	4,901	2,488
Newport Co	4,336	4,356	+0.46	5,465	3,465
Notts Co	10,905	10,202	–+6.44	15,427	4,610
Port Vale	6,600	7,617	+15.41	13,661	4,533
Salford C	3,000	2,849	–+5.04	3,737	1,838
Swindon T	8,483	7,229	–+14.78	9,503	5,819
Tranmere R	6,263	6,403	+2.24	9,496	4,968
Walsall	5,618	6,334	+12.76	9,203	4,237

TOTAL ATTENDANCES: 3,374,721 (552 games)
Average 6,114 (–1.98%)
HIGHEST: 24,033 Bradford C v Fleetwood T
LOWEST: 1,503 Accrington S v Newport Co
HIGHEST AVERAGE: 17,766 Bradford C
LOWEST AVERAGE: 2,539 Accrington S

LEAGUE ATTENDANCES SINCE 1946–47

Season	Matches	Total	Div. 1	Div. 2	Div. 3 (S)	Div. 3 (N)
1946–47	1848	35,604,606	15,005,316	11,071,572	5,664,004	3,863,714
1947–48	1848	40,259,130	16,732,341	12,286,350	6,653,610	4,586,829
1948–49	1848	41,271,414	17,914,667	11,353,237	6,998,429	5,005,081
1949–50	1848	40,517,865	17,278,625	11,694,158	7,104,155	4,440,927
1950–51	2028	39,584,967	16,679,454	10,780,580	7,367,884	4,757,109
1951–52	2028	39,015,866	16,110,322	11,066,189	6,958,927	4,880,428
1952–53	2028	37,149,966	16,050,278	9,686,654	6,704,299	4,708,735
1953–54	2028	36,174,590	16,154,915	9,510,053	6,311,508	4,198,114
1954–55	2028	34,133,103	15,087,221	8,988,794	5,996,017	4,051,071
1955–56	2028	33,150,809	14,108,961	9,080,002	5,692,479	4,269,367
1956–57	2028	32,744,405	13,803,037	8,718,162	5,622,189	4,601,017
1957–58	2028	33,562,208	14,468,652	8,663,712	6,097,183	4,332,661

Season	Matches	Total	Div. 1	Div. 2	Div. 3	Div. 4
1958–59	2028	33,610,985	14,727,691	8,641,997	5,946,600	4,276,697
1959–60	2028	32,538,611	14,391,227	8,399,627	5,739,707	4,008,050
1960–61	2028	28,619,754	12,926,948	7,033,936	4,784,256	3,874,614
1961–62	2015	27,979,902	12,061,194	7,453,089	5,199,106	3,266,513
1962–63	2028	28,885,852	12,490,239	7,792,770	5,341,362	3,261,481
1963–64	2028	28,535,022	12,486,626	7,594,158	5,419,157	3,035,081
1964–65	2028	27,641,168	12,708,752	6,984,104	4,436,245	3,512,067
1965–66	2028	27,206,980	12,480,644	6,914,757	4,779,150	3,032,429
1966–67	2028	28,902,596	14,242,957	7,253,819	4,421,172	2,984,648
1967–68	2028	30,107,298	15,289,410	7,450,410	4,013,087	3,354,391
1968–69	2028	29,382,172	14,584,851	7,382,390	4,339,656	3,075,275
1969–70	2028	29,600,972	14,868,754	7,581,728	4,223,761	2,926,729
1970–71	2028	28,194,146	13,954,337	7,098,265	4,377,213	2,764,331
1971–72	2028	28,700,729	14,484,603	6,769,308	4,697,392	2,749,426
1972–73	2028	25,448,642	13,998,154	5,631,730	3,737,252	2,081,506
1973–74	2027	24,982,203	13,070,991	6,326,108	3,421,624	2,163,480
1974–75	2028	25,577,977	12,613,178	6,955,970	4,086,145	1,992,684
1975–76	2028	24,896,053	13,089,861	5,798,405	3,948,449	2,059,338
1976–77	2028	26,182,800	13,647,585	6,250,597	4,152,218	2,132,400
1977–78	2028	25,392,872	13,255,677	6,474,763	3,332,042	2,330,390
1978–79	2028	24,540,627	12,704,549	6,153,223	3,374,558	2,308,297
1979–80	2028	24,623,975	12,163,002	6,112,025	3,999,328	2,349,620
1980–81	2028	21,907,569	11,392,894	5,175,442	3,637,854	1,701,379
1981–82	2028	20,006,961	10,420,793	4,750,463	2,836,915	1,998,790
1982–83	2028	18,766,158	9,295,613	4,974,937	2,943,568	1,552,040
1983–84	2028	18,358,631	8,711,448	5,359,757	2,729,942	1,557,484
1984–85	2028	17,849,835	9,761,404	4,030,823	2,667,008	1,390,600
1985–86	2028	16,488,577	9,037,854	3,551,968	2,490,481	1,408,274
1986–87	2028	17,379,218	9,144,676	4,168,131	2,350,970	1,715,441
1987–88	2030	17,959,732	8,094,571	5,341,599	2,751,275	1,772,287
1988–89	2036	18,464,192	7,809,993	5,887,805	3,035,327	1,791,067
1989–90	2036	19,445,442	7,883,039	6,867,674	2,803,551	1,891,178
1990–91	2036	19,508,202	8,618,709	6,285,068	2,835,759	1,768,666
1991–92	2064*	20,487,273	9,989,160	5,809,787	2,993,352	1,694,974

Season	Matches	Total	Premier	Div. 1	Div. 2	Div. 3
1992–93	2028	20,657,327	9,759,809	5,874,017	3,483,073	1,540,428
1993–94	2028	21,683,381	10,644,551	6,487,104	2,972,702	1,579,024
1994–95	2028	21,856,020	11,213,168	6,044,293	3,037,752	1,560,807
1995–96	2036	21,844,416	10,469,107	6,566,349	2,843,652	1,965,308
1996–97	2036	22,783,163	10,804,762	6,931,539	3,195,223	1,851,639
1997–98	2036	24,692,608	11,092,106	8,330,018	3,503,264	1,767,220
1998–99	2036	25,435,542	11,620,326	7,543,369	4,169,697	2,102,150
1999–2000	2036	25,341,090	11,668,497	7,810,208	3,700,433	2,161,952
2000–01	2036	26,030,167	12,472,094	7,909,512	3,488,166	2,160,395
2001–02	2036	27,756,977	13,043,118	8,352,128	3,963,153	2,398,578
2002–03	2036	28,343,386	13,468,965	8,521,017	3,892,469	2,460,935
2003–04	2036	29,197,510	13,303,136	8,772,780	4,146,495	2,975,099

Season	Matches	Total	Premier	Championship	League One	League Two
2004–05	2036	29,245,870	12,878,791	9,612,761	4,270,674	2,483,644
2005–06	2036	29,089,084	12,871,643	9,719,204	4,183,011	2,315,226
2006–07	2036	29,541,949	13,058,115	10,057,813	4,135,599	2,290,422
2007–08	2036	29,914,212	13,708,875	9,397,036	4,412,023	2,396,278
2008–09	2036	29,881,966	13,527,815	9,877,552	4,171,834	2,304,765
2009–10	2036	30,057,892	12,977,251	9,909,882	5,043,099	2,127,660
2010–11	2036	29,459,105	13,406,990	9,595,236	4,150,547	2,306,332
2011–12	2036	29,454,401	13,148,465	9,784,100	4,091,897	2,429,939
2012–13	2036	29,225,443	13,653,958	9,662,232	3,485,290	2,423,963
2013–14	2036	29,629,309	13,930,810	9,168,922	4,126,701	2,402,876
2014–15	2036	30,052,575	13,746,753	9,838,940	3,884,414	2,582,468
2015–16	2036	30,207,923	13,852,291	9,705,865	3,955,385	2,694,382
2016–17	2036	31,727,248	13,612,316	11,106,918	4,385,178	2,622,836
2017–18	2036	32,656,695	14,560,349	11,313,826	4,303,525	2,478,995
2018–19	2035†	32,911,714	14,515,181	11,119,775	4,811,797	2,464,961
2019–20	1572‡	25,151,300	11,323,981	8,265,475	3,501,237	2,060,607
2020–21		Due to the COVID-19 pandemic, the majority of matches were played behind closed doors.				
2021–22	2036	32,528,271	15,037,940	9,268,320	5,523,493	2,698,518
2022–23	2036	34,762,759	15,287,024	10,418,221	5,857,456	3,200,058
2023–24	2036	36,178,201	15,450,440	12,725,488	5,359,482	3,442,791
2024–25	2036	36,472,235	15,347,584	12,170,350	5,579,580	3,374,721

*Figures include matches played by Aldershot. †The Championship match between Bolton W v Brentford on 7 May 2019 was not played. ‡Premier League and Championship games behind closed doors from 17 June 2020. League 1 and 2 curtailed from 9 June 2020. Football League official total for their three divisions in 2001–02 was 14,716,162.

LEAGUE CUP FINALS 1961–2025

*Played as a two-leg final until 1966. All subsequent finals played at Wembley except between 2001 and 2007 (inclusive) which were played at Millennium Stadium, Cardiff. *After extra time.*

FOOTBALL LEAGUE CUP

1961	Rotherham U v Aston Villa	2-0
	Aston Villa v Rotherham U	3-0*
	Aston Villa won 3-2 on aggregate.	
1962	Rochdale v Norwich C	0-3
	Norwich C v Rochdale	1-0
	Norwich C won 4-0 on aggregate.	
1963	Birmingham C v Aston Villa	3-1
	Aston Villa v Birmingham C	0-0
	Birmingham C won 3-1 on aggregate.	
1964	Stoke C v Leicester C	1-1
	Leicester C v Stoke C	3-2
	Leicester C won 4-3 on aggregate.	
1965	Chelsea v Leicester C	3-2
	Leicester C v Chelsea	0-0
	Chelsea won 3-2 on aggregate.	
1966	West Ham U v WBA	2-1
	WBA v West Ham U	4-1
	WBA won 5-3 on aggregate.	
1967	QPR v WBA	3-2
1968	Leeds U v Arsenal	1-0
1969	Swindon T v Arsenal	3-1*
1970	Manchester C v WBA	2-1*
1971	Tottenham H v Aston Villa	2-0
1972	Stoke C v Chelsea	2-1
1973	Tottenham H v Norwich C	1-0
1974	Wolverhampton W v Manchester C	2-1
1975	Aston Villa v Norwich C	1-0
1976	Manchester C v Newcastle U	2-1
1977	Aston Villa v Everton	0-0
Replay	Aston Villa v Everton	1-1*
	(at Hillsborough)	
Replay	Aston Villa v Everton	3-2*
	(at Old Trafford)	
1978	Nottingham F v Liverpool	0-0*
Replay	Nottingham F v Liverpool	1-0
	(at Old Trafford)	
1979	Nottingham F v Southampton	3-2
1980	Wolverhampton W v Nottingham F	1-0
1981	Liverpool v West Ham U	1-1*
Replay	Liverpool v West Ham U	2-1
	(at Villa Park)	

MILK CUP

1982	Liverpool v Tottenham H	3-1*
1983	Liverpool v Manchester U	2-1*
1984	Liverpool v Everton	0-0*
Replay	Liverpool v Everton	1-0
	(at Maine Road)	
1985	Norwich C v Sunderland	1-0
1986	Oxford U v QPR	3-0

LITTLEWOODS CUP

1987	Arsenal v Liverpool	2-1
1988	Luton T v Arsenal	3-2
1989	Nottingham F v Luton T	3-1
1990	Nottingham F v Oldham Ath	1-0

RUMBELOWS LEAGUE CUP

1991	Sheffield Wed v Manchester U	1-0
1992	Manchester U v Nottingham F	1-0

COCA-COLA CUP

1993	Arsenal v Sheffield Wed	2-1
1994	Aston Villa v Manchester U	3-1
1995	Liverpool v Bolton W	2-1
1996	Aston Villa v Leeds U	3-0
1997	Leicester C v Middlesbrough	1-1*
Replay	Leicester C v Middlesbrough	1-0*
	(at Hillsborough)	
1998	Chelsea v Middlesbrough	2-0*

WORTHINGTON CUP

1999	Tottenham H v Leicester C	1-0
2000	Leicester C v Tranmere R	2-1
2001	Liverpool v Birmingham C	1-1*
	Liverpool won 5-4 on penalties.	
2002	Blackburn R v Tottenham H	2-1
2003	Liverpool v Manchester U	2-0

CARLING CUP

2004	Middlesbrough v Bolton W	2-1
2005	Chelsea v Liverpool	3-2*
2006	Manchester U v Wigan Ath	4-0
2007	Chelsea v Arsenal	2-1
2008	Tottenham H v Chelsea	2-1*
2009	Manchester U v Tottenham H	0-0*
	Manchester U won 4-1 on penalties.	
2010	Manchester U v Aston Villa	2-1
2011	Birmingham C v Arsenal	2-1
2012	Liverpool v Cardiff C	2-2*
	Liverpool won 3-2 on penalties.	

CAPITAL ONE CUP

2013	Swansea C v Bradford C	5-0
2014	Manchester C v Sunderland	3-1
2015	Chelsea v Tottenham H	2-0
2016	Manchester C v Liverpool	1-1*
	Manchester C won 3-1 on penalties.	

EFL CUP

2017	Manchester U v Southampton	3-2

CARABAO CUP

2018	Manchester C v Arsenal	3-0
2019	Manchester C v Chelsea	0-0*
	Manchester C won 4-3 on penalties.	
2020	Manchester C v Aston Villa	2-1
2021	Manchester C v Tottenham H	1-0
2022	Liverpool v Chelsea	0-0*
	Liverpool won 11-10 on penalties.	
2023	Manchester U v Newcastle U	2-0
2024	Liverpool v Chelsea	1-0*
2025	Newcastle U v Liverpool	2-1

LEAGUE CUP WINS
Liverpool 10, Manchester C 8, Manchester U 6, Aston Villa 5, Chelsea 5, Nottingham F 4, Tottenham H 4, Leicester C 3, Arsenal 2, Birmingham C 2, Norwich C 2, Wolverhampton W 2, Blackburn R 1, Leeds U 1, Luton T 1, Middlesbrough 1, Newcastle U 1, Oxford U 1, QPR 1, Sheffield Wed 1, Stoke C 1, Swansea C 1, Swindon T 1, WBA 1.

APPEARANCES IN FINALS
Liverpool 15, Chelsea 10, Manchester U 10, Aston Villa 9, Manchester C 9, Tottenham H 9, Arsenal 8, Nottingham F 6, Leicester C 5, Norwich C 4, Birmingham C 3, Middlesbrough 3, Newcastle U 3, WBA 3, Bolton W 2, Everton 2, Leeds U 2, Luton T 2, QPR 2, Sheffield Wed 2, Southampton 2, Stoke C 2, Sunderland 2, West Ham U 2, Wolverhampton W 2, Blackburn R 1, Bradford C 1, Cardiff C 1, Oldham Ath 1, Oxford U 1, Rochdale 1, Rotherham U 1, Swansea C 1, Swindon T 1, Tranmere R 1, Wigan Ath 1.

APPEARANCES IN SEMI-FINALS
Liverpool 20, Tottenham H 18, Arsenal 17, Manchester U 17, Chelsea 16, Aston Villa 15, Manchester C 13, West Ham U 9, Nottingham F 7, Blackburn R 6, Leicester C 6, Middlesbrough 6, Birmingham C 5, Everton 5, Leeds U 5, Norwich C 5, Bolton W 4, Burnley 4, Crystal Palace 4, Ipswich T 4, Sheffield Wed 4, Southampton 4, Sunderland 4, WBA 4, Bristol C 3, Newcastle U 3, QPR 3, Stoke C 3, Swindon T 3, Wolverhampton W 3, Cardiff C 2, Coventry C 2, Derby Co 2, Luton T 2, Oxford U 2, Plymouth Arg 2, Sheffield U 2, Tranmere R 2, Watford 2, Wimbledon 2, Blackpool 1, Bradford C 1, Brentford 1, Burton Alb 1, Bury 1, Carlisle U 1, Chester C 1, Fulham 1, Huddersfield T 1, Hull C 1, Oldham Ath 1, Peterborough U 1, Rochdale 1, Rotherham U 1, Shrewsbury T 1, Stockport Co 1, Swansea C 1, Walsall 1, Wigan Ath 1, Wycombe W 1.

CARABAO CUP 2024–25

■ *Denotes player sent off.*

FIRST ROUND NORTH

Tuesday, 13 August 2024

Barrow (1) 3 *(Garner 1, Acquah 70, Jackson 76)*
Port Vale (1) 2 *(Paton 26, Sang 66)*   1711

Barrow: (4231) Farman; Feely (Eccleston 62), Vassell, Canavan, Jackson; Gotts (Telford 71), Campbell; Mahoney (Newby 71), Spence, Kouyate (Worrall 88); Garner (Acquah 62).
Port Vale: (3421) Amos; Lomax, Debrah, John; Plant, Lowe, Ojo, Shorrock (Croasdale 84); Baker-Boaitey (Tolaj 46), Dipepa (Buah 77); Paton (Sang 62).

Bolton W (0) 1 *(Thomason 68)*
Mansfield T (0) 1 *(Keillor-Dunn 83)*   4131

Bolton W: (3421) Southwood; Forino-Joseph (Dacres-Cogley 74), Santos (Toal 46), Johnston; Osei-Tutu, Morley (Thomason 63), Matete, Williams; Arfield (Collins 63), McAtee (Charles 62); Adeboyejo.
Mansfield T: (4231) Pym; Williams (Hewitt 79), Flint (Bowery 46), McLaughlin (Oshilaja 46), MacDonald; Lewis, Boateng; Swan, Nichols, Quinn B (Keillor-Dunn 63); Evans (Gregory 63).
Bolton W won 5-4 on penalties.

Burton Alb (0) 0
Blackpool (0) 4 *(Finnigan 69, Pennington 76, 81, Evans 90)*   1522

Burton Alb: (3421) Crocombe; Vancooten, Sweeney■, Armer; Akoto, Watt, Chauke, Williams; Whitfield (Cooper-Love 68), Kalinauskas (Bodin 77); Bennett (Burrell 63).
Blackpool: (352) O'Donnell; Pennington, Baggott (Casey 65), Husband; Apter, Embleton (Finnigan 63), Carey, Norburn (Evans 64), Ashworth (Coulson 84); Beesley (Joseph 64), Fletcher.

Carlisle U (0) 0
Stoke C (0) 2 *(Anderson 48, Tezgel 79)*   4441

Carlisle U: (532) Lewis; Davies (Williams 60), Hayden, Thomas, Mellish, Ellis; Vela, Barclay (Lavelle 83), Neal; Wyke (Butterworth 73), Adu-Adjei (Armstrong 61).
Stoke C: (433) Fielding; Dixon, Wilmot, Anderson, Johnson; Sidibe (Laurent 78), Burger (Thompson 66), Baker; Manhoef (Gooch 66), Ennis (Tezgel 78), Koumas (Bocat 78).

Derby Co (1) 2 *(Thompson 38, Jackson 68)*
Chesterfield (1) 1 *(Faal 29)*   8538

Derby Co: (4231) Vickers; Nyambe, Cashin (Nelson 60), Bradley, Forsyth; Ozoh, Thompson; Wilson (Mendez-Laing 60), Goudmijn (Osborn 60), Barkhuizen (Jackson 60); Brown (Collins 69).
Chesterfield: (4231) Boot; Tanton (Daley-Campbell 46), Naylor (Grimes 68), Dunkley, Gordon; Banks (Akinola 74), Oldaker; Dobra, Hobson, Berry-McNally (Drummond 65); Quigley (Jacobs 74).

Fleetwood T (2) 2 *(Graydon 12, Coughlan 33)*
WBA (1) 1 *(Faal 8)*   2611

Fleetwood T: (352) Lynch; Wiredu, Holgate, Medley; Broom, Virtue, Bonds (Helm 57), Mayor, Patterson; Graydon (Johnston 66), Coughlan (Lonergan 66).
WBA: (4231) Wildsmith; Hall, Taylor, McNair (Nelson 61), Frabotta (Deeming 62); Whitwell (Amihere 78), Diakite; Cole (Cleary 72), Heard, Dobbin (Sule 72); Faal.

Grimsby T (1) 1 *(Wilson 36)*
Bradford C (0) 1 *(Cook 76)*   3082

Grimsby T: (4231) Eastwood; Warren (Cass 87), Rodgers, McJannet, Khouri; McEachran, Davies; Barrington (Ainley 77), Green, Vernam; Wilson (Gardner 72).

Bradford C: (3511) Walker S; Baldwin, Byrne, Shepherd; Halliday, Walker J (Sarcevic 66), Smallwood, Oduor, Richards (Pointon 66); Kavanagh (Young 66); Oliver (Cook 45).
Grimsby T won 9-8 on penalties.

Huddersfield T (3) 3 *(Headley 1, Marshall 38, Ward 43)*
Morecambe (0) 0   5111

Huddersfield T: (352) Maxwell; Pearson, Helik (Turton 46), Spencer; Sorensen (Hogg 61), Iorpenda (Wiles 61), Kane, Kasumu, Headley; Marshall (Harratt 71), Ward (Koroma 71).
Morecambe: (541) Burgoyne, Millen, Taylor, Songo'o (Jones 59), Stott (Tutonda 73), Lewis A; Tollitt (Macadam 59), Harrack■, White (Hendrie 76), Slew; Angol (Edwards 58).

Lincoln C (0) 1 *(Makama 85 (pen))*
Harrogate T (0) 2 *(Folarin 49, Daly J 61)*   3507

Lincoln C: (3142) Jeacock; Montsma (Makama 79), O'Connor (Jackson 46), Hamer; Erhahon (Bayliss 46); Benn, McKiernan (House 66), Moylan, Jefferies (Duffy 65); Street, Draper.
Harrogate T: (343) Belshaw; Sims, O'Connor, Foulds; Asare, Burrell, Sutton, Taylor; Folarin (Muldoon 79), Daly M, Daly J.

Preston NE (1) 2 *(Ledson 37, Frokjaer-Jensen 70)*
Sunderland (0) 0   7231

Preston NE: (3142) Woodman; Storey, Lindsay, Hughes; Whiteman (Holmes 69); Potts, Ledson, Frokjaer-Jensen (Kesler-Hayden 74), Brady (Greenwood 57); Keane (Thordarson 69), Jakobsen (Osmajic 69).
Sunderland: (451) Moore; Johnson, Triantis, Hjelde, Anderson; Ba (Bennette 81), Rigg (Jones 70), Ekwah, Aouchiche (Watson 81), Mundle; Rusyn (Semedo 81).

Rotherham U (0) 2 *(Nombe 55, Odofin 86)*
Crewe Alex (0) 1 *(Holicek 50)*   2182

Rotherham U: (442) Dawson; MacDonald, Raggett, McCart, James; McWilliams (Odofin 65), Tiehi (Esapa Osong 81), Kelly, Powell; Nombe, Clarke-Harris.
Crewe Alex: (352) Marschall; Connolly, Knight-Lebel, Williams; Cooney, Lunt (Sanders 68), Breckin (Tabiner 56), Holicek, Conway (Demetriou 79); Lankester (Hemmings 56), Tracey (Roberts 56).

Salford C (0) 0
Doncaster R (1) 2 *(Sharp 21, Molyneux 90)*   1328

Salford C: (4231) Young; Edwards, Chester, Tilt (Negru 46), Garbutt (McAleny 65); Davies, Lund; Luamba (Malcolm 66), Woodburn (N'Mai 66), Chesters (Stockton 75); Dackers.
Doncaster R: (4231) Sharman-Lowe; Nixon, Olowu, McGrath, Senior; Westbrooke (Bailey 61), Kelly (Broadbent 70); Clifton, Yeboah (Molyneux 71), Sbarra (Gibson 70); Sharp (Ironside 77).

Sheffield U (1) 4 *(Trusty 35, Brunt 57 (og), Marsh 69, Ben Slimane 85)*
Wrexham (1) 2 *(Boyle 29, Revan 90)*   11,446

Sheffield U: (4411) Grbic; Seriki (Gilchrist 21), Souttar, Trusty, Boyes (Norrington-Davies 70); Hampson (Brooks 80), Peck, Coulibaly, Ben Slimane; Marsh (Hamer 70); Brewster (One 70).
Wrexham: (352) Burton; Brunt, Scarr, Boyle; Bolton (Barnett 79), Jones, Evans (Dobson 70), McClean (Marriott 62), Revan; Rathbone (Lee 62), Dalby (Fletcher 62).

Shrewsbury T (0) 3 *(Kayode 68, Shipley 71, 84)*
Notts Co (2) 3 *(Grant 4, Austin 23, Jatta 89)*   2914

Shrewsbury T: (4231) Savin; Hoole, Nsiala, Feeney M, Benning; Winchester, Rossiter; O'Reilly (Bloxham 86), Biggins, Shipley; Kayode (Lloyd 73).

Notts Co: (3421) Slocombe; Cundy (Cisse 87), Macari, Bedeau; Jones (Crowley 64), Edwards, Hinchy (Scott 64), Chicksen (Platt 64); Austin, Grant (Jatta 74); McGoldrick.
Shrewsbury T won 4-3 on penalties.

Stockport Co (0) 1 *(Mapengu 67)*
Blackburn R (4) 6 *(Szmodics 8, 25, Weimann 22, Ohashi 31, Gueye 72, Vale 88)*   5790
Stockport Co: (343) Hinchliffe; Mapengu (Lawless Williams 82), Hughes (Camps 39), Touray; Okeke, Onyango, Bailey, Redshaw (Cina 46); Gardner, Williams (Watson 46), Fevrier (Lewis 83).
Blackburn R: (442) Pears; Brittain (Duru 46), Carter (McFadzean 46), Batth, Pickering; Weimann (Gueye 63), Buckley, Tronstad (Travis 63), Sigurdsson; Szmodics (Vale 63), Ohashi.

Tranmere R (2) 3 *(Saunders 3, Williams 45, Patrick 71)*
Accrington S (0) 0   2288
Tranmere R: (442) Murphy; Norman, Walker, Bradshaw, Wood; Solomon, Williams (O'Connor 86), Hendry (Norris 85), Patrick (Merrie 77); Saunders (Davison 61), Dennis (Jennings 61).
Accrington S: (4231) Kelly; O'Brien, Rawson, Awe, Quirk; Coyle (Woods B 81), Martin; Whalley (Knowles 85), Henderson (Woods J 46), Costelloe (Walton 22); Mooney (Hunter 46).

Wigan Ath (1) 1 *(Aasgaard 35 (pen))*
Barnsley (0) 1 *(Pines 48)*   1990
Wigan Ath: (4231) Tickle; Ramsay (McHugh 72), Carragher, Aimson, Chambers; Adeeko, Smith M (Smith S 61); Rankine (Thomas 61), Sze (Jones 46), Aasgaard; Hugill (Stones 61).
Barnsley: (532) Slonina; Cotter, Durand de Gevigney, Pines (Lopata 56), Earl, Gent (Lofthouse 57); Russell, Craig (Connell 57), Yoganathan (Phillips 46); Marsh, Cosgrove (Watters 57).
Barnsley won 4-2 on penalties.

Wednesday, 14 August 2024

Hull C (1) 1 *(Mehlem 9)*
Sheffield Wed (2) 2 *(McNeill 1, 10)*   9281
Hull C: (433) Racioppi; Slater, Jones (Seri 46), McLoughlin, Giles; Omur (Simons 63), Burns (Smith 70), Mehlem (Coyle L 63); Jarvis, Sellars-Fleming, Millar (Estupinan 64).
Sheffield Wed: (4231) Charles P; Valentin, Ihiekwe, Diaby (Otegbayo 79), Johnson; Palmer, Fusire; Paterson (Ugbo 79), McNeill (Cadamarteri 57), Kobacki (Gassama 67); Smith (Bannan 79).

Leeds U (0) 0
Middlesbrough (0) 3 *(Dijksteel 50, Burgzorg 60, Coburn 67)*   35,150
Leeds U: (4231) Darlow; Byram (Gruev 64), Rodon, Wober (Struijk 63), Firpo (Bogle 64); Ampadu, Rothwell; Gelhardt (Gnonto 63), Piroe, Aaronson (Rutter 63); Bamford.
Middlesbrough: (4231) Brynn; Dijksteel, Howson (Ayling 56), Clarke, Engel (McCormick 70); Barlaser, Morris; Jones (Hamilton 81), Gilbert, Burgzorg (Azaz 70); Coburn (Latte Lath 81).

FIRST ROUND SOUTH
Tuesday, 13 August 2024
Bristol C (0) 0
Coventry C (0) 1 *(Simms 65)*   10,940
Bristol C: (4231) Bajic; Tanner, Vyner, Naismith, Roberts; Gardner-Hickman, Knight (Williams 46); Sykes (Mehmeti 68), Wells (Stokes 69), Bell (Cornick 44); Mayulu (Armstrong 80).
Coventry C: (4231) Wilson; Latibeaudiere, Thomas (van Ewijk 46), Kitching, Dasilva; Eccles (Rudoni 62), Overgaard (Allen 62); Tavares (Sakamoto 63), Palmer, Wright (Simms 62); Thomas-Asante.

Bromley (1) 1 *(Amantchi 19)*
AFC Wimbledon (1) 2 *(Kelly 24, Pigott 61)*   3677
Bromley: (3142) Long; Sowunmi, Reynolds, Grant; Leigh (Charles 76); Paul-Lavely, Arthurs, Congreve (Olomola 76), Topalloj (Odutayo 76); Dinanga, Amantchi (Cheek 76).
AFC Wimbledon: (352) Goodman; Lewis, Ogundere, Johnson; Biler (Neufville 86), Maycock, Reeves, Hippolyte (Smith 86), Tilley (Furlong 90); Pigott (Stevens 75), Kelly (Bugiel 75).

Cambridge U (0) 1 *(Digby 57)*
QPR (2) 2 *(Frey 13, Smyth 36)*   4529
Cambridge U: (3421) Stevens; O'Riordan (Okedina 66), Morrison, Ibsen Rossi; Bennett, Digby, Brophy (Smith 66), Andrew; Kachunga (KaiKai 46), Barton (Kaunda 88); Njoku (Lavery 46).
QPR: (4231) Walsh; Dunne, Morrison, Clarke-Salter, Paal; Varane (Hevertton 65), Dixon-Bonner; Smyth (Dykes 65), Andersen (Field 46), Lloyd (Bennie 80); Frey (Celar 80).

Cardiff C (0) 2 *(McGuinness 68, Colwill R 90)*
Bristol R (0) 0   5718
Cardiff C: (4231) Alnwick; Kpakio, McGuinness (Walcott 76), Bagan, Giles; Rinomhota, King; Conte (Evans 76), Robertson (Tanner 59), Colwill R; Kanga (Reindorf 59).
Bristol R: (4141) Griffiths; Senior, Taylor, Forbes, Mola (Akono Bilongo 61); Garrett; Thomas, Lindsay (Conteh 77), McCormick (Sotiriou 77), Sinclair (Anthony 62); Omochere (Shaw 61).

Charlton Ath (0) 0
Birmingham C (1) 1 *(Khela 32)*   5899
Charlton Ath: (352) Mannion; Edmonds-Green (Mitchell Z 66), Jones, Gillesphey; Watson (Ramsay 76), Coventry, Berry (Docherty 66), Anderson (Edun 66), Small; Kanu, Campbell T (Aneke 66).
Birmingham C: (4231) Allsop; Laird (Sampsted 69), Klarer, Sanderson■, Khela (Cochrane 58); Roberts (Paik 58), Leonard; Anderson, Harris, Hansson (Bielik 79); Jutkiewicz (May 57).

Colchester U (1) 2 *(Hopper 3, Payne 55 (pen))*
Reading (0) 2 *(Savage 65, Wing 73)*   3123
Colchester U: (3142) Macey; Hunt, Kelleher, Iandolo (Terry 62); Woodyard; Egbo, Payne (Oni 78), Bishop (Read 46), Edwards O; Hopper (Gordon 62), Tovide (Ihionvien 46).
Reading: (433) Boyce-Clarke; Osho (Camara 46), Dean, Kanu (Bindon 34); Abrefa (Mbengue 75); Knibbs (Elliott 72), Wing, Savage; Garcia, Wareham, Akande (Ehibhatiomhan 46).
Colchester U won 4-3 on penalties.

Crawley T (1) 4 *(Adeyemo 34, Roles 56, 88, Khaleel 89)*
Swindon T (0) 2 *(Ofoborh 60, Smith 66)*   2396
Crawley T: (343) Wollacott; Mullarkey, Mukena, Flint; Khaleel, Bragg (Barker 66), Anderson (Darcy 67), Kelly (Quitirna 46); Camara (Papadopoulos 46), Adeyemo, Roles (Malone 90).
Swindon T: (532) Bycroft; King, Sobowale, Wright, Freckleton (Minturn 71), Longelo (Hall 61); Ofoborh (Clarke 61), Cotterill (Mitchell 71), Cain; Drinan (Smith 61), Glatzel.

Leyton Orient (2) 4 *(Agyei 1, Jaiyesimi 45, Cooper 51, Kelman 74)*
Newport Co (0) 1 *(Clarke 61)*   2141
Leyton Orient: (4141) Hemming; Clare (Brown 60), Cooper, James, Sweeney; Warrington (Beckles 67); Perkins, Galbraith (O'Neill 46), Obiero, Jaiyesimi (Pratley 75); Agyei (Kelman 59).
Newport Co: (4231) Carney; McLoughlin, Baker, Jameson (Clarke 59), Driscoll-Glennon; Brennan (Antwi 70), Whitmore; Wood (Kamwa 59), Wildig, Rai (Baker-Richardson 70); Jephcott (Evans C 89).

Northampton T (0) 0
Wycombe W (2) 2 *(Udoh 9, Mbete-Tabu 45 (og))*   2012
Northampton T: (4231) Tzanev; Odimayo (McCarron 62), Magloire (Guthrie 46), Baldwin, Mbete-Tabu; McGeehan, Fox (Hondermarck 50); Pinnock, Fosu (Hoskins 62), Wilson; Morton (Dibley-Dias 62).
Wycombe W: (352) Bishop; Low, Tafazolli (Grimmer 86), Hartridge◼; Pattenden, Leahy, Bakinson (Scowen 58), Butcher, Harvie (McCarthy 86); Kone (McCleary 70), Udoh (Vokes 86).

Norwich C (2) 4 *(Kamara 26, Hernandez 35, 60, Sainz 48)*
Stevenage (2) 3 *(Goode 28, Appere 45, Hills 88 (og))*
13,054
Norwich C: (4231) Long; Stacey, Warner (Doyle 61), Hills, Fisher (Duffy 82); Nunez, McLean (Myles 81); Kamara, Forson (Gibbs 61), Sainz (Forsyth 69); Hernandez.
Stevenage: (4141) Cooper; Smith, Goode (Sweeney 46), Piergianni, Butler (Freestone 61); Thompson N; Kemp (Simpson 70), Freeman (Phillips 59), White, Roberts (Thompson B 70); Appere.

Oxford U (2) 2 *(Goodrham 20, Phillips 41)*
Peterborough U (0) 0   3693
Oxford U: (4141) Ingram; Kioso, Long (Moore 61), Thorniley, Leigh; McEachran (Vaulks 87); Phillips (Ebiowei 46), Sibley, El Mizouni, Goodrham (Brannagan 61); Rodrigues (O'Donkor 61).
Peterborough U: (4231) Bilokapic; Curtis (Ajiboye 68), Fernandez, Wallin (Crichlow-Noble 82), Sparkes; O'Brien-Brady, Collins; Hayes, Randall (Conn-Clarke 67), Odoh; Jones (Mothersille 67).

Portsmouth (0) 0
Millwall (1) 1 *(Esse 13)*   13,913
Portsmouth: (4231) Norris; Swanson, Williams (Dozzell 64), Towler, Ogilvie; Stevenson, Devlin; Whyte (Ritchie 64), Lowery (Sorensen 66), Silvera (Lane 76); Saydee (Lang 76).
Millwall: (4231) Roberts; McNamara, Harding, Cooper, Bryan (Leonard 65); De Norre (Hutchinson 83), Massey (Saville 65); Emakhu (Watmore 74), Honeyman, Esse; Langstaff (Bradshaw 64).

Swansea C (1) 3 *(Ronald 24, Cullen 70, Abdulai 90)*
Gillingham (0) 1 *(Hawkins 87)*   6019
Swansea C: (4231) Vigouroux; Naughton (Key 67), Cabango, Pedersen, Tjoe-A-On (Tymon 67); Fulton, Grimes; Abdulai, Cooper (Goncalo Franco 73); Ronald (Eom 72); Vipotnik (Cullen 67).
Gillingham: (4231) Morris; Giles, Ehmer, Ogie, Clark (Hawkins 46); McKenzie, Williams E◼; Nolan (Rowe 46), Williams J (Lapslie 60), Clarke (Wakeling 78); Gbode (Wyllie 66).

Walsall (0) 1 *(Jellis 90)*
Exeter C (1) 1 *(Alli 40)*   2352
Walsall: (352) Simkin; Okagbue, Williams, Allen; Barrett (Matt 59), Maher (Jellis 73), Stirk, Lakin (Earing 59), Weir (Gordon L 59); Adomah (McEntee 79), Gordon J.
Exeter C: (3421) Whitworth; Sweeney (Fitzwater 69), Diabate, Purrington; Watts (Harper 46), McMillan, Oakes (Aitchison 56), Niskanen; Cole (Crama 83), Borges (Magennis 69); Alli.
Walsall won 4-3 on penalties.

Watford (2) 5 *(Pollock 24, Ince 45, 67, 74, Baah 64)*
Milton Keynes D (0) 0   6885
Watford: (3421) Bond; Pollock, Sierralta (Tikvic 76), Morris; Andrews, Ince, Dele-Bashiru (Ramirez-Espain 76), Sema (Larouci 61); Louza, Vata (Baah 62); Rajovic (Doumbia 62).
Milton Keynes D: (3421) Harness; Sherring (Nemane 70), Tripp, Lewington; Tomlinson, Williams M, Carroll, Pritchard (Tucker 46); Hendry (Gilbey 46), Leigh (Wearne 46); Harrison (Singh-Hurditt 88).

Wednesday, 14 August 2024
Plymouth Arg (0) 3 *(Waine 62, Hardie 81, Bundu 84)*
Cheltenham T (0) 0   12,058
Plymouth Arg: (4231) Hazard; Edwards, Szucs, Pleguezuelo, Mumba; Randell, Gyabi (Forshaw 79); Issaka (Whittaker 68), Wright (Bundu 68), Waine (Cissoko 68); Hardie (Sorinola 82).
Cheltenham T: (4231) Day; Payne, Laing, Bakare, Haynes (Willcox 71); Pett (Young 58), Sohna (Miller 68); Thomas (Jude-Boyd 58), Archer, Dulson; Taylor (Colwill 59).

SECOND ROUND NORTH
Tuesday, 27 August 2024
Barnsley (0) 1 *(Watters 52)*
Sheffield U (0) 0   10,739
Barnsley: (4312) Slonina; Durand de Gevigney, Pines, Roberts, Earl; Cotter (O'Keeffe 71), Connell, Yoganathan (Russell 73); Phillips; Marsh (Lofthouse 79), Watters.
Sheffield U: (4411) Davies A; Sachdev, Ahmedhodzic, Norrington-Davies (Trusty 62), McCallum (Burrows 73); Rak-Sakyi (Campbell 62), Peck, Coulibaly, Hampson (Brooks 62); Marsh; Brewster (Hamer 73).

Barrow (0) 0
Derby Co (0) 0   3003
Barrow: (4231) Farman; Eccleston, Vassell, Canavan, Jackson; Campbell (Gotts 78), Foley (Dallas 86); Newby, Telford (Spence 66), Kouyate (Worrall 86); Garner (Acquah 66).
Derby Co: (4231) Zetterstrom; Ward (Nyambe 72), Nelson, Bradley, Forsyth; Goudmijn (Ozoh 46), Adams; Chirewa (Mendez-Laing 46), Thompson (Brown 61), Barkhuizen (Jackson 46); Collins.
Barrow won 3-2 on penalties.

Blackburn R (1) 1 *(Gueye 21 (pen))*
Blackpool (0) 2 *(Beesley 72, Coulson 77)*   9418
Blackburn R: (4231) Pears; Duru, Carter, Batth (Hyam 66), Pickering (McFadzean 66); Rankin-Costello, Buckley; Weimann (Hedges 66), Vale (Dolan 65), Sigurdsson; Gueye (Ohashi 65).
Blackpool: (442) O'Donnell; Lawrence-Gabriel (Coulson 69), Pennington, Casey (Husband 26), Ashworth; Apter, Finnigan (Evans 26), Norburn (Ballard 69), Embleton; Beesley, Joseph (Fletcher 68).

Everton (0) 3 *(McNeil 53, Ndiaye 74, Beto 83)*
Doncaster R (0) 0   37,245
Everton: (4231) Pickford; Coleman (Young 67), Keane, O'Brien, Mykolenko; Iroegbunam (Armstrong 85), Garner (Gueye 67); Lindstrom (Harrison 67), Ndiaye (Dixon 78); McNeil; Beto.
Doncaster R: (4141) Lawlor; Nixon (Sterry 56), Olowu, McGrath, Senior (Sharp 75); Kelly (Broadbent 64); Molyneux, Bailey, Westbrooke (Sbarra 46), Gibson (Hurst 46); Ironside.

Fleetwood T (2) 2 *(Graydon 16, 29)*
Rotherham U (1) 1 *(McCart 2)*   1744
Fleetwood T: (3142) Lynch; Wiredu, Holgate, Hughes; Bonds; Johnston, Virtue, Mayor (Broom 75), Hunt; Helm (Patterson 74), Graydon (Lonergan 45 (Odubeko 88)).
Rotherham U: (4231) Dawson; MacDonald, Humphreys, McCart, Bramall (James 46); Odofin, Powell (Kelly 62); Holmes (McWilliams 46), Wilks (Esapa Osong 87), Hungbo (Nombe 46); Clarke-Harris.

Grimsby T (1) 1 *(McJannett 18)*
Sheffield Wed (0) 5 *(Ugbo 53, Lowe J 54, Paterson 72, 81, Valentin 90)*   6364
Grimsby T: (4141) Eastwood; Warren, Rodgers, McJannet, Hume (Gardner 73); McEachran, Svanthorsson (Ainley 67), Green (Barrington 60), Khouri, Vernam (Carson 73); Rose (Wilson 67).
Sheffield Wed: (442) Charles P; Palmer, Ihiekwe, Famewo (Bernard 78), Johnson; Paterson, Chalobah (Bannan 62), Fusire (Valentin 46), Kobacki; McNeill (Lowe J 46), Ugbo (Windass 62).

Harrogate T (0) 0
Preston NE (4) 5 *(Greenwood 14, 37 (pen),*
Osmajic 39, 45, 83) 2570
Harrogate T: (3412) Belshaw; Sims, O'Connor (Dooley 59), Foulds; Asare, Burrell (Cornelius 58), Sutton (Gibson 59), Taylor; Daly M (Duke-Mckenna 59); March, Daly J (Muldoon 59).
Preston NE: (442) Woodman; Potts (Kesler-Hayden 60), Whatmough, Lindsay (Storey 60), Hughes (Best 60); Holmes, Ledson, Thordarson (Frokjaer-Jensen 73), Okkels; Greenwood (McCann 73), Osmajic.

Leicester C (1) 4 *(Ayew 38, Mavididi 51 (pen), Ndidi 71,*
Winks 90)
Tranmere R (0) 0 13,011
Leicester C: (433) Ward; Ricardo Pereira, Faes (Coady 72), Okoli, Thomas; Skipp (Choudhury 63), Winks, Ndidi (Alves 72); McAteer (Fatawu 83), Ayew (Popov 73), Mavididi.
Tranmere R: (442) Murphy; Norman, Davies, Walker (Wood 62), Turnbull; Jennings, O'Connor (Williams 75), Merrie, Patrick (Solomon 75); Saunders (Dennis 62), Davison (Bradshaw 62).

Middlesbrough (0) 0
Stoke C (1) 5 *(Tezgel 14, Mmaee 57, Koumas 60,*
Manhoef 65, 69) 17,408
Middlesbrough: (4231) Brynn; Ayling (Dijksteel 46), Hunt, Clarke, McCormick (Engel 46); Barlaser, McCabe (Morris 78); Finch (Jones 63), Gilbert, Hamilton (Conway 63); Coburn.
Stoke C: (4231) Johansson; Tchamadeu, Phillips (Smith 76), Dixon, Bocat; Burger, Sidibe; Koumas (Manhoef 62), Moran (Bae 70), Tezgel (Gooch 63); Mmaee (Ennis 62).

Shrewsbury T (0) 0
Bolton W (0) 2 *(Osei-Tutu 52, Charles 65)* 3220
Shrewsbury T: (4231) Savin; Hoole, Feeney M, Pierre, Benning (Nurse 83); Winchester (Biggins 56), Perry; Bloxham (O'Reilly 77), Castledine (Shipley 82), Sagoe Junior; Marquis (Lloyd 77).
Bolton W: (3421) Southwood; Forino-Joseph, Santos, Johnston; Dacres-Cogley, Thomason (Sharples 90), Matete (Sheehan 72), Osei-Tutu (Schon 72); Arfield (McAtee 59), Dempsey; Charles (Collins 72).

Walsall (0) 3 *(Lowe 63, 70, Helik 77 (og))*
Huddersfield T (1) 2 *(Koroma 16, Ruffels 53)* 3378
Walsall: (352) Hornby; Okagbue, Williams, Weir; Barrett (Gordon J 61), Maher (Jellis 61), Stirk (Lakin 60), Earing (Allen 73), Gordon L; Adomah, Lowe.
Huddersfield T: (352) Maxwell; Pearson■, Turton, Ruffels; Sorensen (Helik 46), Evans (Jones 85), Hogg, Wiles (Iorpenda 67), Headley; Marshall (Ward 46), Koroma (Harratt 67).

Wednesday, 28 August 2024
Nottingham F (0) 1 *(Jota Silva 50)*
Newcastle U (1) 1 *(Willock 1)* 23,083
Nottingham F: (3412) Carlos Miguel; Boly, Omobamidele, Abbott (Milenkovic 60); Moreira (Williams 68), Anderson (Elanga 79), Dominguez, Alex; Jota Silva (Sangare 61); Awoniyi, Sosa (Hudson-Odoi 69).
Newcastle U: (433) Pope; Trippier (Livramento 62), Krafth, Burn, Hall; Tonali (Longstaff 62), Joelinton, Willock (Guimaraes 15); Almiron (Gordon 61), Isak, Barnes.
Newcastle U won 4-3 on penalties.

Wolverhampton W (1) 2 *(Goncalo Guedes 38, 54)*
Burnley (0) 0 19,236
Wolverhampton W: (4231) Bentley; Pedro Lima, Bueno, Dawson (Gomes T 62), Ait Nouri (Doherty 62); Traore (Lemina 45), Doyle; Sarabia (Hwang 62), Daniel Podence, Oliveira; Goncalo Guedes (Bellegarde 75).
Burnley: (4411) Hladky; Egan-Riley (Lucas Pires 46), McNally, Worrall (Hugill 79), Humphreys; Hountondji, Brownhill (Roberts 46), Massengo, Sambo; Mejbri (McDermott 46); Rodriguez (Foster 58).

SECOND ROUND SOUTH
Tuesday, 27 August 2024
Birmingham C (0) 0
Fulham (2) 2 *(Jimenez 10 (pen), Stansfield 14)* 11,949
Birmingham C: (4231) Allsop; Laird (Sampsted 73), Klarer, Bielik, Cochrane; Paik (Jutkiewicz 82), Leonard; Anderson (Yokoyama 62), Willumsson, Hansson (Miyoshi 62); May (Roberts 61).
Fulham: (4231) Benda; Castagne, Andersen, Cuenca, Sessegnon; Berge (King 65), Reed (Smith Rowe 87); Wilson (Traore 87), Cairney (Lukic 78), Stansfield (Iwobi 78); Jimenez.

Brighton & HA (1) 4 *(Adingra 31, Sarmiento 48,*
Webster 84, O'Mahony 86)
Crawley T (0) 0 19,175
Brighton & HA: (4231) Verbruggen; Lamptey (Offiah 80), Webster, Igor, Samuels (Estupinan 71); O'Riley (O'Mahony 9), Baleba; Sarmiento (Weir 79), Ayari, Adingra, Enciso (Peupion 72).
Crawley T: (3421) Wollacott; Mullarkey, Mukena, Flint; Williams (Barker 59), Anderson (Camara 59), Bragg, Kelly (Khaleel 85); Quitirna, Darcy (Roles■ 76); Hepburn-Murphy (Adeyemo 58).

Coventry C (0) 1 *(Thomas-Asante 57)*
Oxford U (0) 0 11,808
Coventry C: (4231) Wilson; Latibeaudiere (van Ewijk 63), Thomas, Kitching, Dasilva; Allen (Sheaf 73), Eccles (Overgaard 63); Mason-Clark, Palmer (Rudoni 90), Thomas-Asante; Bassette (Sakamoto 63).
Oxford U: (4141) Ingram; Kioso, Long, Brown, Leigh; McEachran (Vaulks 61); Dale (Goodrham 61), Sibley, Brannagan (El Mizouni 61), Ebiowei (Rodrigues 77); Scarlett (Harris 83).

Crystal Palace (1) 4 *(Kamada 2, Mateta 57, 68, Sarr 84)*
Norwich C (0) 0 12,503
Crystal Palace: (3421) Henderson; Clyne, Guehi, Riad (Richards 10); Munoz (Ward 79), Hughes (Wharton 70), Doucoure (Lerma 70), Mitchell; Kamada (Sarr 70), Eze; Mateta.
Norwich C: (4231) Long; Fisher, Hanley, Cordoba, Chrisene (Doyle 58); Nunez (Stacey 83), Gibbs; Forsyth (Schwartau 58), Forson (McLean 13), Hernandez, Crnac (Sainz 83).

Millwall (0) 0
Leyton Orient (1) 1 *(Agyei 14)* 5875
Millwall: (4231) Roberts; McNamara, Hutchinson, Wallace, Bryan (Bradshaw 64); Kelly (De Norre 46), Saville, Azeez (Watmore 73), Honeyman (Esse 46); Emakhu (Leonard 64); Langstaff.
Leyton Orient: (4141) Hemming; James, Beckles, Cooper, Sweeney; Warrington; Agyei (Donley 81), Pratley (Brown 82), Obiero (Galbraith 82), Jaiyesimi (O'Neill 77); Perkins (Kelman 77).

QPR (1) 1 *(Hevertton 11)*
Luton T (1) 1 *(Nelson 16)* 7132
QPR: (4231) Walsh; Dunne (Lloyd 59), Cook (Clarke-Salter 46), Morrison, Paal; Colback (Madsen 71), Varane; Hevertton, Dixon-Bonner (Dembele 71), Saito (Smyth 59); Celar.
Luton T: (3421) Kaminski; Walters, Burke (Holmes 46), Bell (Andersen 46); Nelson, Nakamba (Walsh 46), Clark (Baptiste 63), Doughty; Morris (Woodrow 75), Chong; Adebayo.
QPR won 4-1 on penalties.

Watford (1) 2 *(Rajovic 17, 72)*
Plymouth Arg (0) 0 8319
Watford: (3421) Bond; Porteous, Sierralta (Tkvic 65), Morris; Andrews, Louza (Kayembe 24), Dele-Bashiru (Ramirez-Espain 75), Sema; Ince, Baah (Vata 64); Rajovic (Doumbia 75).
Plymouth Arg: (3421) Grimshaw; Pleguezuelo, Szucs, Galloway (Gibson 46); Sorinola (Hardie 65), Houghton (Randell 74), Gyabi (Davies 86), Ogbeta; Wright, Bundu (Cissoko 74); Obafemi.

Wednesday, 28 August 2024

AFC Wimbledon (1) 2 *(Bugiel 40, Stevens 56)*
Ipswich T (1) 2 *(Al Hamadi 3, Chaplin 86)*   7934
AFC Wimbledon: (352) Goodman; Ogundere, Lewis,
Johnson; Biler, Maycock, Reeves, Ball (Smith 71), Tilley
(Furlong 90); Bugiel (Pigott 72), Stevens.
Ipswich T: (4231) Walton; Johnson, O'Shea, Burgess,
Townsend; Phillips (Luongo 66), Cajuste (Taylor J 66);
Ogbene (Harness 46), Chaplin, Clarke J (Hutchinson 78);
Al Hamadi (Delap 78).
AFC Wimbledon won 4-2 on penalties.

Cardiff C (1) 3 *(Colwill R 21, Edwards 48 (og),
Robertson 57)*
Southampton (2) 5 *(Fernandes 10, Amo-Ameyaw 30,
Archer 55, 90, Bree 90)*   7225
Cardiff C: (4231) Alnwick; Kpakio (Jefferies 78), Goutas,
Walcott, Bagan; Rinomhota, Gbadehan (Robertson 46);
Conte, Colwill R (Twose 63), Ashford; Reindorf.
Southampton: (433) Lumley; Bree, Edwards (Akachukwu
86), Wood-Gordon, Taylor; Downes (Lallana 90),
Ugochukwu (Lallana 64), Fernandes (Bella-Kotchap 64);
Amo-Ameyaw (O'Brien-Whitmarsh 90), Archer, Edozie.

Colchester U (0) 0
Brentford (1) 1 *(Lewis-Potter 45)*   6716
Colchester U: (3142) Macey; Hunt (Egbo 46), Goodliffe,
Donnelly; Woodyard (Payne 46); Anderson (Edwards O
62), Oni (Tovide 66), Read, Iandolo (Gordon 46);
Hopper, Ihionvien.
Brentford: (4231) Valdimarsson; Trevitt, van den Berg,
Mee, Janelt (Collins 74); Yarmolyuk, Onyeka (Konak
89); Damsgaard (Jensen 73), Carvalho (Peart-Harris 84),
Lewis-Potter; Schade (Wissa 73).

Swansea C (0) 0
Wycombe W (1) 1 *(Kone 40)*   6000
Swansea C: (4231) Vigouroux; Naughton (Cullen 73),
Pedersen, Abbey (Cabango 58), Tjoe-A-On (Tymon 58);
Fulton (Allen 73), Grimes; Bianchini, Eom (Ronald 58),
Abdulai; Vipotnik.
Wycombe W: (4231) Ravizzoli; Pattenden, Low, Skura,
Hartridge; Bakinson, Butcher; Kodua (McCleary 58),
Scowen (Humphreys 58), Sadlier (Harvie 58); Kone
(Udoh 58).

West Ham U (0) 0
Bournemouth (0) 0   47,381
West Ham U: (4141) Fabianski; Coufal, Todibo
(Mavropanos 46), Kilman, Wan-Bissaka; Alvarez
(Rodriguez 60); Bowen, Soucek, Ward-Prowse (Lucas
Paqueta 60); Summerville (Emerson Palmieri 74);
Fullkrug (Kudus 74).
Bournemouth: (4231) Neto; Hill, Huijsen, Senesi, Smith;
Scott (Cook 79), Christie; Ouattara (Araujo 87),
Tavernier (Kluivert 68), Sinisterra (Semenyo 46);
Jebbison (Evanilson 46).

THIRD ROUND

Tuesday, 17 September 2024

Blackpool (0) 0
Sheffield Wed (1) 1 *(Bernard 34)*   5429
Blackpool: (352) O'Donnell; Pennington, Casey,
Ashworth; Coulson (Lawrence-Gabriel 62), Embleton
(Apter 73), Morgan (Finnigan 73), Carey, Thompson
(Hamilton 62); Rhodes, Beesley (Joseph 74).
Sheffield Wed: (442) Charles P; Valentin, Otegbayo
(Famewo 58), Bernard, Lowe M; Paterson, Ingelsson
(Bannan 76), Fusire (Palmer 76), Musaba (Gassama 46);
Lowe J (McNeill 69), Smith.

Brentford (3) 3 *(Carvalho 17, Damsgaard 26, Norgaard 45)*
Leyton Orient (1) 1 *(Cooper 11)*   13,634
Brentford: (433) Valdimarsson; Roerslev, van den Berg
(Kim 77), Mee, Meghoma (Yogane 84); Trevitt (Mbeumo
76), Norgaard (Konak 63), Yarmolyuk; Carvalho,
Schade, Damsgaard (Lewis-Potter 76).
Leyton Orient: (4141) Keeley; James, Cooper, Simpson■,
Sweeney; Warrington, Jaiyesimi (Galbraith 53), Ball
(Pratley 71), Donley (Agyei 72), Obiero (Beckles 72);
Perkins (Kelman 54).

Everton (1) 1 *(Doucoure 20)*
Southampton (1) 1 *(Harwood-Bellis 32)*   33,842
Everton: (4231) Virginia; Dixon, Keane, O'Brien,
McNeil; Mangala, Armstrong (Harrison 62); Lindstrom,
Doucoure (Iroegbunam 79), Ndiaye; Beto (Young 62).
Southampton: (4231) McCarthy; Bree, Harwood-Bellis,
Wood-Gordon, Taylor; Ugochukwu (Downes 62),
Lallana (Fernandes 46); Cornet (Dibling 63), Aribo,
Fraser (Brereton Diaz 63); Armstrong (Stewart 79).
Southampton won 6-5 on penalties.

Manchester U (3) 7 *(Rashford 16, 57, Antony 35 (pen),
Garnacho 45, 49, Eriksen 81, 85)*
Barnsley (0) 0   72,063
Manchester U: (4231) Bayindir; Dalot (Mazraoui 63),
Maguire, Evans (de Ligt 78), Collyer; Casemiro, Ugarte
(Fernandes 62); Antony, Eriksen, Garnacho (Diallo 84);
Rashford (Zirkzee 63).
Barnsley: (532) Slonina; Cotter (Lofthouse 63), Durand
de Gevigney, Roberts (McCarthy 46), Earl, O'Keeffe;
Phillips, Connell, Yoganathan (Craig 46); Watters
(Cosgrove 56), Jalo (Humphrys 46).

Preston NE (1) 1 *(Ledson 35)*
Fulham (0) 1 *(Nelson 61)*   5530
Preston NE: (442) Woodman; Storey, Bauer (Hughes 61),
Lindsay, Kesler-Hayden; Bowler (Okkels 83),
Thordarson (McCann 68), Ledson, Holmes (Whiteman
82); Frokjaer-Jensen (Greenwood 68), Osmajic.
Fulham: (4231) Benda; Castagne, Diop, Cuenca,
Sessegnon; Reed (Smith Rowe 77), Berge; Wilson (Iwobi
77), Cairney (Godo 85), Nelson (Jimenez 86); Rodrigo
Muniz (Lukic 90).
Preston NE won 16-15 on penalties.

QPR (0) 1 *(Field 53)*
Crystal Palace (1) 2 *(Nketiah 16, Eze 64)*   13,945
QPR: (4231) Walsh; Ashby (Lloyd 68), Cook, Field, Paal;
Varane, Dixon-Bonner (Dembele 46); Smyth (Andersen
81), Madsen (Dunne 81), Saito (Hevertton 68); Celar.
Crystal Palace: (3421) Henderson; Lacroix, Guehi,
Richards; Munoz, Lerma, Kamada (Schlupp 90),
Mitchell; Nketiah (Sarr 65), Eze; Mateta (Hughes 74).

Stoke C (0) 1 *(Rose 54)*
Fleetwood T (0) 1 *(Bennett 90)*   8927
Stoke C: (4231) Johansson; Dixon, Phillips (Wilmot 41),
Rose, Stevens (Bocat 46); Sidibe, Thompson; Manhoef
(Tezgel 63), Moran (Burger 63), Bae (Cannon 63);
Koumas (Lipsiuc 89).
Fleetwood T: (3142) Lynch; Wiredu, Bolton, Holgate
(Hughes 7 (Bennett 70)); Bonds, Johnston (Broom 59),
Virtue, Mayor (Lonergan 72), Patterson; Helm
(Odubeko 70), Coughlan (Graydon 59).
Stoke C won 2-1 on penalties.

Wednesday, 18 September 2024

Brighton & HA (2) 3 *(Baleba 14, Adingra 31, Kadioglu 85)*
Wolverhampton W (1) 2 *(Goncalo Guedes 44, Doyle 90)*
          16,018
Brighton & HA: (442) Steele; Hinshelwood, Webster,
Igor, Estupinan; Minteh (Kadioglu 82), Baleba (Wieffer
63), Moder (Ayari 71), Adingra; Ferguson (Welbeck 63),
Enciso (Lamptey 82).
Wolverhampton W: (4231) Jose Sa; Pedro Lima (Nelson
Semedo 64), Bueno, Pond, Doherty; Doyle, Joao Gomes
(Lemina 64); Sarabia (Forbs 64), Hwang (Cunha 71),
Gomes R; Goncalo Guedes (Larsen 82).

Coventry C (0) 1 *(Thomas-Asante 63)*
Tottenham H (0) 2 *(Spence 88, Johnson 90)*   24,616
Coventry C: (4231) Wilson; van Ewijk, Thomas, Binks,
Bidwell; Eccles (Sheaf 71), Allen; Thomas-Asante,
Rudoni (Overgaard 78), Wright (Mason-Clark 71);
Bassette (Simms 70).
Tottenham H: (433) Forster; Gray, Dragusin, Davies,
Udogie (Spence 46); Sarr, Bentancur, Bergvall
(Maddison 62); Odobert (Johnson 18), Solanke (Son 62),
Werner (Kulusevski 74).

Tuesday, 24 September 2024

Chelsea (3) 5 *(Nkunku 8, 15, 75, Farman 28 (og), Pedro Neto 48)*

Barrow (0) 0   38,868

Chelsea: (4231) Jorgensen; Gusto (Chilwell 46), Disasi (Acheampong 63), Badiashile, Veiga; Casadei, Dewsbury-Hall; Pedro Neto (George 63), Joao Felix (Chukwuemeka 76), Mudryk; Nkunku (Guiu 76).
Barrow: (532) Farman; Feely (Eccleston 46), Vassell, Stokes (Worrall 86), Jackson, Newby (Kouyate 65); Spence, Campbell, Foley; Garner (Tiensia 65), Acquah (Telford 46).

Manchester C (2) 2 *(Doku 5, Matheus Luiz 38)*

Watford (0) 1 *(Ince 86)*   40,584

Manchester C: (3241) Ortega; Walker, Braithwaite (Gvardiol 76), Lewis; O'Reilly (Wright 73), Doku (Savio 46); McAtee, Matheus Luiz, Grealish; Foden.
Watford: (532) Bond; Ebosele (Pollock 75), Porteous, Ogbonna, Morris, Larouci (Dele-Bashiru 61); Ince, Louza (Dwomoh 83), Sema; Baah (Vata 76), Bayo (Chakvetadze 61).

Walsall (0) 0

Leicester C (0) 0   8010

Walsall: (352) Simkin; Okagbue, Williams, Weir; Barrett, Maher (Allen 71), Stirk, Lakin (Jellis 66), Gordon L; Lowe (Matt 75), Adomah (Johnson 75).
Leicester C: (4231) Ward; Ricardo Pereira, Coady, Okoli, Thomas; Soumare, Choudhury (Skipp 80); Fatawu, Buonanotte (El Khannous 79), De Cordova-Reid (McAteer 80); Edouard (Ayew 69).
Leicester C won 3-0 on penalties.

Wycombe W (0) 1 *(Kone 90)*

Aston Villa (0) 2 *(Buendia 55, Duran 85 (pen))*   8158

Wycombe W: (4141) Ravizzoli; Pattenden, Low, Skura, Hartridge; Bakinson; Wheeler (Onyedinma 63), Scowen (Humphreys 64), Butcher (Leahy 75), Sadlier (McCleary 63); Lubala (Kone 63).
Aston Villa: (4231) Gauci; Nedeljkovic, Bogarde, Swinkels, Maatsen (Patterson 90); Onana (Borland 62), Barkley; Bailey (Ramsey 62), Buendia (Jimoh 90), Young (Broggio 86); Duran.

Wednesday, 25 September 2024

Arsenal (2) 5 *(Rice 16, Nwaneri 37, 49, Sterling 64, Havertz 77)*

Bolton W (0) 1 *(Collins 53)*   59,056

Arsenal: (433) Porter; Nichols, Kiwior, Calafiori (Kacurri 70), Lewis-Skelly (Gabriel 62); Nwaneri, Jorginho, Rice (Havertz 62); Saka (Martinelli 71), Gabriel Jesus, Sterling (Kabia 81).
Bolton W: (352) Southwood; Forino-Joseph (Johnston 71), Santos, Toal; Dacres-Cogley, Arfield (Thomason 69), Sheehan, Dempsey (Matete 69), Williams; McAtee (Adeboyejo 78), Collins (Charles 79).

Liverpool (1) 5 *(Jota 25, 49, Salah 74, Gakpo 90, 90)*

West Ham U (1) 1 *(Quansah 21 (og))*   60,044

Liverpool: (4231) Kelleher; Bradley, Quansah, Gomez, Tsimikas (Robertson 82); Endo (Morton 82), Jones; Chiesa (Salah 59), Jota (Mac Allister 59), Gakpo; Nunez.
West Ham U: (4231) Fabianski; Coufal, Todibo, Kilman, Cresswell; Alvarez■, Soucek (Lucas Paqueta 59); Bowen (Kudus 78), Soler (Irving 78), Summerville; Ings (Antonio 60).

Tuesday, 1 October 2024

Newcastle U (1) 1 *(Schar 45 (pen))*

AFC Wimbledon (0) 0   51,739

Newcastle U: (433) Dubravka (Vlachodimos 46); Livramento, Krafth (Hall 62), Schar (Burn 90), Kelly; Joelinton (Gordon 62), Longstaff, Willock; Almiron, Osula, Barnes (Guimaraes 46).
AFC Wimbledon: (352) Goodman; Harbottle, Lewis, Ogundere; Biler (Neufville 62), Maycock (Kelly 90), Ball, Hippolyte (Smith 90), Tilley (Furlong 89); Pigott (Stevens 62), Bugiel.

FOURTH ROUND

Tuesday, 29 October 2024

Brentford (1) 1 *(Schade 11)*

Sheffield Wed (0) 1 *(Gassama 57)*   16,701

Brentford: (4231) Flekken; van den Berg, Collins, Mee, Meghoma (Roerslev 70); Jensen (Damsgaard 66), Janelt; Mbeumo, Carvalho (Wissa 66), Lewis-Potter; Schade.
Sheffield Wed: (3421) Charles P; Iorfa (Bernard 60), Otegbayo, Lowe M; Paterson, Fusire (Palmer 59), Ingelsson, Johnson; Musaba (Windass 69), Gassama (Smith 69); Ugbo (Lowe J 68).
Brentford won 5-4 on penalties.

Southampton (2) 3 *(Harwood-Bellis 19, Armstrong 35 (pen), Bree 88)*

Stoke C (1) 2 *(Phillips 45, Cannon 54)*   16,092

Southampton: (433) Ramsdale; Sugawara, Harwood-Bellis, Bednarek (Sulemana 81), Bree; Aribo, Ugochukwu, Fernandes (Brereton Diaz 68); Armstrong (Amo-Ameyaw 81), Archer (Onuachu 67), Fraser (Cornet 77).
Stoke C: (541) Bonham; Tchamadeu, Phillips, Rose, Dixon, Bocat (Burger 84); Andre Vidigal (Manhoef 72), Thompson, Seko, Sidibe (Moran 71); Cannon (Koumas 60).

Wednesday, 30 October 2024

Aston Villa (1) 1 *(Duran 23)*

Crystal Palace (1) 2 *(Eze 8, Kamada 64)*   34,851

Aston Villa: (4231) Gauci; Nedeljkovic, Diego Carlos, Mings, Maatsen; McGinn (Bogarde 79), Kamara; Bailey (Young 78), Buendia (Jimoh 78), Philogene-Bidace; Duran.
Crystal Palace: (3421) Turner; Chalobah, Lacroix, Guehi; Munoz, Wharton, Schlupp 27 (Clyne 88)), Hughes, Mitchell; Nketiah (Sarr 88), Eze (Kamada 18); Mateta.

Brighton & HA (0) 2 *(Adingra 81, Lamptey 90)*

Liverpool (0) 3 *(Gakpo 46, 63, Diaz 85)*   28,441

Brighton & HA: (4231) Steele; Lamptey, van Hecke (Veltman 68), Igor, Kadioglu (Estupinan 46); Moder (Hinshelwood 68), Wieffer; Gruda (Mitoma 75), Enciso (Welbeck 76), Adingra; Ferguson.
Liverpool: (442) Jaros; Bradley, Quansah (Konate 90), Gomez, Robertson; Diaz, Morton (Mac Allister 64), Endo (Nyoni 64); Gakpo (Salah 71); Szoboszlai (Nunez 71), Jones.

Manchester U (4) 5 *(Casemiro 15, 39, Garnacho 28, Fernandes 36, 59)*

Leicester C (2) 2 *(El Khannous 33, Coady 45)*   73,470

Manchester U: (4231) Bayindir; Dalot, de Ligt (Evans 72), Lindelof, Martinez (Mazraoui 62); Ugarte, Casemiro; Rashford (Diallo 63), Fernandes, Garnacho (Hojlund 73); Zirkzee (Wheatley 85).
Leicester C: (4231) Ward; Justin, Okoli (Vestergaard 71), Coady, Thomas; Skipp, Soumare; De Cordova-Reid (Buonanotte 72), El Khannous (Alves 72), McAteer (Mavididi 72); Ayew (Edouard 72).

Newcastle U (2) 2 *(Isak 23, Disasi 26 (og))*

Chelsea (0) 0   51,934

Newcastle U: (433) Pope; Krafth, Schar, Kelly, Hall (Burn 72); Longstaff, Tonali (Miley 90), Joelinton; Gordon (Livramento 72), Isak (Osula 63), Willock (Guimaraes 63).
Chelsea: (4231) Jorgensen; Disasi, Adarabioyo, Badiashile, Cucurella; Veiga, Fernandez; Dewsbury-Hall (Madueke 72), Joao Felix, Mudryk; Nkunku.

Preston NE (0) 0

Arsenal (2) 3 *(Gabriel Jesus 24, Nwaneri 33, Havertz 57)*
                                                    21,811

Preston NE: (4231) Woodman; Kesler-Hayden (Potts 60), Whatmough, Lindsay (Storey 77), Hughes (Best 68); Thordarson, Ledson; Bowler (Frokjaer-Jensen 59), Holmes, Okkels; Greenwood (Jakobsen 60).
Arsenal: (433) Setford; Timber (Partey 46), Saliba, Kiwior, Zinchenko (Lewis-Skelly 62); Nwaneri (Heaven 80), Jorginho, Merino (Havertz 46); Sterling, Gabriel Jesus, Martinelli (Saka 62).

Tottenham H (2) 2 *(Werner 5, Sarr 25)*

Manchester C (1) 1 *(Matheus Luiz 45)*   60,797

Tottenham H: (433) Vicario; Gray, Romero (Davies 52), Dragusin, van de Ven (Udogie 14); Kulusevski, Bentancur, Sarr (Bissouma 46); Johnson (Moore 68), Solanke, Werner (Richarlison 69).
Manchester C: (4141) Ortega; Lewis, Stones, Dias (Gvardiol 46), Ake (Simpson-Pusey 74); Gundogan (Kovacic 46); Savio (Wright 63), O'Reilly, McAtee, Matheus Luiz; Foden (Silva 58).

QUARTER-FINALS

Wednesday, 18 December 2024

Arsenal (0) 3 *(Gabriel Jesus 54, 73, 81)*

Crystal Palace (1) 2 *(Mateta 4, Nketiah 85)*   59,298

Arsenal: (433) Raya; Partey (Saliba 46), Timber, Kiwior (Gabriel 87), Tierney (Lewis-Skelly 69); Nwaneri (Odegaard 46), Jorginho, Merino; Sterling (Saka 70), Gabriel Jesus, Trossard.
Crystal Palace: (3421) Henderson; Chalobah, Lacroix, Guehi; Kporha (Clyne 46), Hughes (Devenny 80), Lerma, Mitchell (Schlupp 86); Sarr, Eze (Kamada 59); Mateta (Nketiah 59).

Newcastle U (2) 3 *(Tonali 9, 43, Schar 69)*

Brentford (0) 1 *(Wissa 90)*   51,765

Newcastle U: (433) Dubravka; Livramento, Schar, Burn, Hall (Trippier 77); Guimaraes, Tonali, Joelinton (Willock 46); Murphy J (Barnes 65), Isak (Osula 77), Gordon (Almiron 77).
Brentford: (3421) Flekken; Collins, Pinnock (Roerslev 14), Mee; Ajer, Yarmolyuk, Janelt (Damsgaard 62), Lewis-Potter (Meghoma 74); Schade (Maghoma 74), Carvalho (Mbeumo 61); Wissa.

Southampton (0) 1 *(Archer 59)*

Liverpool (2) 2 *(Nunez 23, Elliott 32)*   26,503

Southampton: (541) McCarthy; Bree (Sugawara 61), Harwood-Bellis, Bednarek (Brereton Diaz 84), Wood-Gordon, Manning; Dibling, Downes (Sulemana 73), Aribo (Lallana 84), Fernandes; Archer (Onuachu 73).
Liverpool: (433) Kelleher; Alexander-Arnold (Chiesa 46), Quansah, Endo, Gomez (Tsimikas 46); Mac Allister (McConnell 63), Morton, Nyoni (Danns 86); Elliott, Nunez, Gakpo (Jota 63).

Thursday, 19 December 2024

Tottenham H (1) 4 *(Solanke 15, 54, Kulusevski 46, Son 88)*

Manchester U (0) 3 *(Zirkzee 63, Diallo 70, Evans 90)*   57,409

Tottenham H: (4231) Forster; Porro, Dragusin, Gray, Spence (Reguilon 90); Sarr, Bissouma; Kulusevski, Maddison (Bergvall 79); Son; Solanke (Johnson 90).
Manchester U: (3421) Bayindir; Yoro, Lindelof (Evans 45), Martinez; Mazraoui, Eriksen (Mainoo 56), Ugarte (Garnacho 70), Dalot; Antony (Diallo 55), Fernandes; Hojlund (Zirkzee 56).

SEMI-FINALS FIRST LEG

Tuesday, 7 January 2025

Arsenal (0) 0

Newcastle U (1) 2 *(Isak 37, Gordon 51)*   59,125

Arsenal: (433) Raya; Timber, Saliba, Gabriel, Lewis-Skelly (Zinchenko 78); Odegaard, Partey (Jorginho 59), Rice; Trossard (Gabriel Jesus 59), Havertz, Martinelli.
Newcastle U: (433) Dubravka; Livramento, Botman, Burn, Hall; Willock (Longstaff 65), Tonali, Joelinton; Murphy J (Kelly 65), Isak (Barnes 65), Gordon (Almiron 76).

Wednesday, 8 January 2025

Tottenham H (0) 1 *(Bergvall 86)*

Liverpool (0) 0   59,037

Tottenham H: (433) Kinsky; Porro, Dragusin, Gray, Spence; Bissouma, Bentancur (Johnson 15), Bergvall; Kulusevski, Solanke, Son (Werner 72).
Liverpool: (4231) Alisson; Bradley (Alexander-Arnold 60), Quansah (Endo 30), van Dijk, Tsimikas; Gravenberch, Mac Allister (Konate 80); Salah, Jones, Gakpo (Diaz 60); Jota (Nunez 60).

SEMI-FINALS SECOND LEG

Wednesday, 5 February 2025

Newcastle U (1) 2 *(Murphy J 19, Gordon 52)*

Arsenal (0) 0   52,173

Newcastle U: (541) Dubravka; Trippier, Schar, Botman (Krafth 80), Burn, Hall; Murphy J (Willock 80), Guimaraes (Miley 90), Tonali (Longstaff 87), Gordon; Isak (Wilson 87).
Arsenal: (433) Raya; Timber (Calafiori 78), Saliba, Gabriel, Lewis-Skelly; Odegaard (Sterling 61), Partey (Jorginho 78), Rice; Martinelli (Nwaneri 37), Havertz, Trossard (Merino 61).
Newcastle U won 4-0 on aggregate.

Thursday, 6 February 2025

Liverpool (1) 4 *(Gakpo 34, Salah 51 (pen), Szoboszlai 75, van Dijk 80)*

Tottenham H (0) 0   60,395

Liverpool: (4231) Kelleher; Bradley, Konate, van Dijk (Quansah 87), Robertson; Gravenberch, Jones (Mac Allister 72); Salah (Elliott 82), Szoboszlai, Gakpo (Diaz 82); Nunez (Jota 72).
Tottenham H: (433) Kinsky; Gray, Danso, Davies (Moore 82), Spence; Bissouma (Porro 57), Bentancur, Sarr (Bergvall 57); Kulusevski, Richarlison (Tel 45), Son.
Liverpool won 4-1 on aggregate.

CARABAO CUP FINAL 2024–25

Sunday, 16 March 2025

(at Wembley Stadium, attendance 88,513)

Liverpool (0) 1   Newcastle U (1) 2

Liverpool: (4231) Kelleher; Quansah, Konate (Jones 57), van Dijk, Robertson; Gravenberch (Chiesa 74), Mac Allister (Gakpo 67); Salah, Szoboszlai, Diaz (Elliott 74); Jota (Nunez 57).
Scorer: Chiesa 90.

Newcastle U: (433) Pope; Trippier, Schar, Burn, Livramento; Guimaraes, Tonali, Joelinton; Murphy J (Krafth 90), Isak (Wilson 81), Barnes (Willock 81).
Scorers: Burn 45, Isak 52.

Referee: John Brooks.

LEAGUE CUP ATTENDANCES 1960–2025

Season	Attendances	Games	Average	Season	Attendances	Games	Average
1960–61	1,204,580	112	10,755	1999–2000	1,354,233	153	8,851
1961–62	1,030,534	104	9,909	2000–01	1,501,304	154	9,749
1962–63	1,029,893	102	10,097	2001–02	1,076,390	93	11,574
1963–64	945,265	104	9,089	2002–03	1,242,478	92	13,505
1964–65	962,802	98	9,825	2003–04	1,267,729	93	13,631
1965–66	1,205,876	106	11,376	2004–05	1,313,693	93	14,216
1966–67	1,394,553	118	11,818	2005–06	1,072,362	93	11,531
1967–68	1,671,326	110	15,194	2006–07	1,098,403	93	11,811
1968–69	2,064,647	118	17,497	2007–08	1,332,841	94	14,179
1969–70	2,299,819	122	18,851	2008–09	1,329,753	93	14,298
1970–71	2,035,315	116	17,546	2009–10	1,376,405	93	14,800
1971–72	2,397,154	123	19,489	2010–11	1,197,917	93	12,881
1972–73	1,935,474	120	16,129	2011–12	1,209,684	93	13,007
1973–74	1,722,629	132	13,050	2012–13	1,210,031	93	13,011
1974–75	1,901,094	127	14,969	2013–14	1,362,360	93	14,649
1975–76	1,841,735	140	13,155	2014–15	1,274,413	93	13,690
1976–77	2,236,636	147	15,215	2015–16	1,430,554	93	15,382
1977–78	2,038,295	148	13,772	2016–17	1,462,722	93	15,728
1978–79	1,825,643	139	13,134	2017–18	1,454,912	93	15,644
1979–80	2,322,866	169	13,745	2018–19	1,275,575	93	13,716
1980–81	2,051,576	161	12,743	2019–20	1,337,845	92	14,542
1981–82	1,880,682	161	11,681	2020–21	Due to the COVID-19 pandemic all games		
1982–83	1,679,756	160	10,498		played behind closed doors until the final.		
1983–84	1,900,491	168	11,312	2021–22	1,415,787	92	15,389
1984–85	1,876,429	167	11,236	2022–23	1,555,364	93	16,724
1985–86	1,579,916	163	9,693	2023–24	1,510,604	93	16,243
1986–87	1,531,498	157	9,755	2024–25	1,793,877	93	19,289
1987–88	1,539,253	158	9,742				
1988–89	1,552,780	162	9,585				
1989–90	1,836,916	168	10,934				
1990–91	1,675,496	159	10,538				
1991–92	1,622,337	164	9,892				
1992–93	1,558,031	161	9,677				
1993–94	1,744,120	163	10,700				
1994–95	1,530,478	157	9,748				
1995–96	1,776,060	162	10,963				
1996–97	1,529,321	163	9,382				
1997–98	1,484,297	153	9,701				
1998–99	1,555,856	153	10,169				

CARABAO CUP 2024–25

Round	Aggregate	Games	Average
One	212,663	35	6,076
Two	302,436	25	12,097
Three	460,463	16	28,779
Four	304,097	8	38,012
Quarter-finals	194,975	4	48,744
Semi-finals	230,730	4	57,683
Final	88,513	1	88,513
Total	1,793,877	93	19,289

A historic victory: Newcastle United celebrate with the trophy after winning the Carabao Cup final against Liverpool at Wembley. (Charlotte Wilson/Offside/Offside via Getty Images)

FOOTBALL LEAGUE TROPHY
FINALS 1984–2025

The 1984 final was played at Boothferry Park, Hull. All subsequent finals played at Wembley except between 2001 and 2007 (inclusive) which were played at Millennium Stadium, Cardiff.

ASSOCIATE MEMBERS' CUP

1984	Bournemouth v Hull C	2-1

FREIGHT ROVER TROPHY

1985	Wigan Ath v Brentford	3-1
1986	Bristol C v Bolton W	3-0
1987	Mansfield T v Bristol C	1-1*
	Mansfield T won 5-4 on penalties.	

SHERPA VANS TROPHY

1988	Wolverhampton W v Burnley	2-0
1989	Bolton W v Torquay U	4-1

LEYLAND DAF CUP

1990	Tranmere R v Bristol R	2-1
1991	Birmingham C v Tranmere R	3-2

AUTOGLASS TROPHY

1992	Stoke C v Stockport Co	1-0
1993	Port Vale v Stockport Co	2-1
1994	Swansea C v Huddersfield T	1-1*
	Swansea C won 3-1 on penalties.	

AUTO WINDSCREENS SHIELD

1995	Birmingham C v Carlisle U	1-0*
1996	Rotherham U v Shrewsbury T	2-1
1997	Carlisle U v Colchester U	0-0*
	Carlisle U won 4-3 on penalties.	
1998	Grimsby T v Bournemouth	2-1
1999	Wigan Ath v Millwall	1-0
2000	Stoke C v Bristol C	2-1

LDV VANS TROPHY

2001	Port Vale v Brentford	2-1
2002	Blackpool v Cambridge U	4-1
2003	Bristol C v Carlisle U	2-0
2004	Blackpool v Southend U	2-0
2005	Wrexham v Southend U	2-0*

FOOTBALL LEAGUE TROPHY

2006	Swansea C v Carlisle U	2-1

JOHNSTONE'S PAINT TROPHY

2007	Doncaster R v Bristol R	3-2*
2008	Milton Keynes D v Grimsby T	2-0
2009	Luton T v Scunthorpe U	3-2*
2010	Southampton v Carlisle U	4-1
2011	Carlisle U v Brentford	1-0
2012	Chesterfield v Swindon T	2-0
2013	Crewe Alex v Southend U	2-0
2014	Peterborough U v Chesterfield	3-1
2015	Bristol C v Walsall	2-0
2016	Barnsley v Oxford U	3-2

EFL CHECKATRADE TROPHY

2017	Coventry C v Oxford U	2-1
2018	Lincoln C v Shrewsbury T	1-0
2019	Portsmouth v Sunderland	2-2*
	Portsmouth won 5-4 on penalties.	

PAPA JOHN'S EFL TROPHY

2020†	Salford C v Portsmouth	0-0*
	Salford C won 4-2 on penalties.	
2021	Sunderland v Tranmere R	1-0
2022	Rotherham U v Sutton U	4-2*
2023	Bolton W v Plymouth Arg	4-0

BRISTOL STREET MOTORS TROPHY

2024	Peterborough U v Wycombe W	2-1

VERTU TROPHY

2025‡	Peterborough U v Birmingham C	2-0

After extra time. †Due to the COVID-19 pandemic, the final due to be played on Sunday 5 April 2020 was postponed and played on Saturday 13 March 2021. ‡Competition known as the Vertu Trophy from the end of the group stage.

FOOTBALL LEAGUE TROPHY WINS
Bristol C 3, Peterborough U 3, Birmingham C 2, Blackpool 2, Bolton W 2, Carlisle U 2, Port Vale 2, Rotherham U 2, Stoke C 2, Swansea C 2, Wigan Ath 2, Barnsley 1, Bournemouth 1, Chesterfield 1, Coventry C 1, Crewe Alex 1, Doncaster R 1, Grimsby T 1, Lincoln C 1, Luton T 1, Mansfield T 1, Milton Keynes D 1, Portsmouth 1, Salford C 1, Southampton 1, Sunderland 1, Tranmere R 1, Wolverhampton W 1, Wrexham 1.

APPEARANCES IN FINALS
Carlisle U 6, Bristol C 5, Birmingham C 3, Bolton W 3, Brentford 3, Peterborough U 3, Southend U 3, Tranmere R 3, Blackpool 2, Bournemouth 2, Bristol R 2, Chesterfield 2, Grimsby T 2, Oxford U 2, Port Vale 2, Portsmouth 2, Rotherham U 2, Shrewsbury T 2, Stockport Co 2, Stoke C 2, Sunderland 2, Swansea C 2, Wigan Ath 2, Barnsley 1, Burnley 1, Cambridge U 1, Colchester U 1, Coventry C 1, Crewe Alex 1, Doncaster R 1, Huddersfield T 1, Hull C 1, Lincoln C 1, Luton T 1, Mansfield T 1, Millwall 1, Milton Keynes D 1, Plymouth Arg 1, Salford C 1, Scunthorpe U 1, Southampton 1, Sutton U 1, Swindon T 1, Torquay U 1, Walsall 1, Wolverhampton W 1, Wrexham 1, Wycombe W 1.

EFL TROPHY ATTENDANCES 2024–25

Round	Aggregate	Games	Average
Group Stage	169,328	96	1,764
Two	22,276	16	1,392
Three	16,753	8	2,094
Quarter-finals	16,063	4	4,016
Semi-finals	36,324	2	18,162
Final	71,722	1	71,722
Total	332,466	127	2,618

VERTU TROPHY 2024–25

■ *Denotes player sent off.*
Competition known as the Bristol Street Motors Trophy during the group stage. In the group stage drawn matches were decided on a penalty shoot-out. Two points were awarded to the team that won on penalties (PW). The team that lost on penalties were awarded one point (PL).

NORTHERN SECTION GROUP A
Tranmere R v Everton U21 — 1-3
Accrington S v Stockport Co — 1-4
Stockport Co v Everton U21 — 4-1
Tranmere R v Accrington S — 2-1
Accrington S v Everton U21 — 2-1
Stockport Co v Tranmere R — 0-2

North Group A	P	W	PW	PL	L	F	A	GD	Pts
Stockport Co	3	2	0	0	1	8	4	4	6
Tranmere R	3	2	0	0	1	5	4	1	6
Everton U21	3	1	0	0	2	5	7	-2	3
Accrington S	3	1	0	0	2	4	7	-3	3

NORTHERN SECTION GROUP B
Salford C v Port Vale — 0-2
Port Vale v Wolverhampton W U21 — 2-2
  Port Vale won 5-4 on penalties.
Wrexham v Salford C — 2-1
Wrexham v Wolverhampton W U21 — 3-0
Port Vale v Wrexham — 1-1
  Port Vale won 3-1 on penalties.
Salford C v Wolverhampton W U21 — 3-2

North Group B	P	W	PW	PL	L	F	A	GD	Pts
Wrexham	3	2	0	1	0	6	2	4	7
Port Vale	3	1	2	0	0	5	3	2	7
Salford C	3	1	0	0	2	4	6	-2	3
Wolverhampton W U21	3	0	0	1	2	4	8	-4	1

NORTHERN SECTION GROUP C
Carlisle U v Nottingham F U21 — 1-2
Wigan Ath v Morecambe — 1-2
Carlisle U v Wigan Ath — 0-2
Morecambe v Nottingham F U21 — 4-2
Morecambe v Carlisle U — 1-2
Wigan Ath v Nottingham F U21 — 0-0
  Wigan Ath won 3-0 on penalties.

North Group C	P	W	PW	PL	L	F	A	GD	Pts
Morecambe	3	2	0	0	1	7	5	2	6
Wigan Ath	3	1	1	0	1	3	2	1	5
Nottingham F U21	3	1	0	1	1	4	5	-1	4
Carlisle U	3	1	0	0	2	3	5	-2	3

NORTHERN SECTION GROUP D
Fleetwood T v Aston Villa U21 — 2-3
Barrow v Bolton W — 2-3
Fleetwood T v Barrow — 3-0
Bolton W v Aston Villa U21 — 1-1
  Aston Villa U21 won 4-1 on penalties.
Barrow v Aston Villa U21 — 3-0
Bolton W v Fleetwood T — 2-1

North Group D	P	W	PW	PL	L	F	A	GD	Pts
Bolton W	3	2	0	1	0	6	4	2	7
Aston Villa U21	3	1	1	0	1	4	6	-2	5
Fleetwood T	3	1	0	0	2	6	5	1	3
Barrow	3	1	0	0	2	5	6	-1	3

NORTHERN SECTION GROUP E
Crewe Alex v Liverpool U21 — 5-1
Blackpool v Crewe Alex — 4-1
Harrogate T v Liverpool U21 — 1-1
  Harrogate T won 4-2 on penalties.
Crewe Alex v Harrogate T — 1-0
Blackpool v Liverpool U21 — 0-0
  Liverpool U21 won 8-7 on penalties.
Harrogate T v Blackpool — 2-2
  Blackpool won 5-4 on penalties.

North Group E	P	W	PW	PL	L	F	A	GD	Pts
Blackpool	3	1	1	1	0	6	3	3	6
Crewe Alex	3	2	0	0	1	7	5	2	6
Liverpool U21	3	0	1	1	1	2	6	-4	3
Harrogate T	3	0	1	1	1	3	4	-1	3

NORTHERN SECTION GROUP F
Barnsley v Manchester U U21 — 2-3
Doncaster R v Huddersfield T — 2-1
Doncaster R v Manchester U U21 — 3-3
  Manchester U U21 won 5-3 on penalties.
Huddersfield T v Barnsley — 2-0
Barnsley v Doncaster R — 1-3
Huddersfield T v Manchester U U21 — 4-1

North Group F	P	W	PW	PL	L	F	A	GD	Pts
Doncaster R	3	2	0	1	0	8	5	3	7
Huddersfield T	3	2	0	0	1	7	3	4	6
Manchester U U21	3	1	1	0	1	7	9	-2	5
Barnsley	3	0	0	0	3	3	8	-5	0

NORTHERN SECTION GROUP G
Chesterfield v Manchester C U21 — 1-1
  Chesterfield won 4-2 on penalties.
Lincoln C v Chesterfield — 0-1
Grimsby T v Lincoln C — 1-2
Grimsby T v Manchester C U21 — 1-1
  Manchester C U21 won 5-4 on penalties.
Chesterfield v Grimsby T — 3-2
Lincoln C v Manchester C U21 — 5-0

North Group G	P	W	PW	PL	L	F	A	GD	Pts
Chesterfield	3	2	1	0	0	5	3	2	8
Lincoln C	3	2	0	0	1	7	2	5	6
Manchester C U21	3	0	1	1	1	2	7	-5	3
Grimsby T	3	0	0	1	2	4	6	-2	1

NORTHERN SECTION GROUP H
Rotherham U v Mansfield T — 2-0
Bradford C v Newcastle U U21 — 2-2
  Newcastle U U21 won 4-3 on penalties.
Mansfield T v Bradford C — 0-3
Rotherham U v Newcastle U U21 — 3-1
Mansfield T v Newcastle U U21 — 3-0
Bradford C v Rotherham U — 0-1

North Group H	P	W	PW	PL	L	F	A	GD	Pts
Rotherham U	3	3	0	0	0	6	1	5	9
Bradford C	3	1	0	1	1	5	3	2	4
Mansfield T	3	1	0	0	2	3	5	-2	3
Newcastle U U21	3	0	1	0	2	3	8	-5	2

SOUTHERN SECTION GROUP A
Shrewsbury T v Fulham U21 — 1-2
Birmingham C v Walsall — 1-1
  Walsall won 4-3 on penalties.
Walsall v Fulham U21 — 1-0
Shrewsbury T v Birmingham C — 0-4
Birmingham C v Fulham U21 — 7-1
Walsall v Shrewsbury T — 3-0

South Group A	P	W	PW	PL	L	F	A	GD	Pts
Walsall	3	2	1	0	0	5	1	4	8
Birmingham C	3	2	0	1	0	12	2	10	7
Fulham U21	3	1	0	0	2	3	9	-6	3
Shrewsbury T	3	0	0	0	3	1	9	-8	0

SOUTHERN SECTION GROUP B
AFC Wimbledon v Wycombe W — 1-0
Crawley T v Brighton & HA U21 — 2-2
  Crawley T won 4-3 on penalties.
Wycombe W v Brighton & HA U21 — 5-3
Crawley T v AFC Wimbledon — 3-4
AFC Wimbledon v Brighton & HA U21 — 0-3
Wycombe W v Crawley T — 2-1

South Group B	P	W	PW	PL	L	F	A	GD	Pts
Wycombe W	3	2	0	0	1	7	5	2	6
AFC Wimbledon	3	2	0	0	1	5	6	-1	6
Brighton & HA U21	3	1	0	1	1	8	7	1	4
Crawley T	3	0	1	0	2	6	8	-2	2

SOUTHERN SECTION GROUP C
Bromley v Cambridge U — 3-3
  Bromley won 5-4 on penalties.
Cambridge U v Charlton Ath — 1-2
Bromley v Chelsea U21 — 2-3
Charlton Ath v Chelsea U21 — 3-0
Cambridge U v Chelsea U21 — 1-0
Charlton Ath v Bromley — 1-0

South Group C

	P	W	PW	PL	L	F	A	GD	Pts
Charlton Ath	3	3	0	0	0	6	1	5	9
Cambridge U	3	1	0	1	1	5	5	0	4
Chelsea U21	3	1	0	0	2	3	6	–3	3
Bromley	3	0	1	0	2	5	7	–2	2

SOUTHERN SECTION GROUP D

Stevenage v Crystal Palace U21	1-0
Gillingham v Peterborough U	1-2
Gillingham v Crystal Palace U21	1-3
Peterborough U v Stevenage	2-0
Peterborough U v Crystal Palace U21	4-1
Stevenage v Gillingham	1-1

Gillingham won 5-4 on penalties.

South Group D

	P	W	PW	PL	L	F	A	GD	Pts
Peterborough U	3	3	0	0	0	8	2	6	9
Stevenage	3	1	0	1	1	2	3	–1	4
Crystal Palace U21	3	1	0	0	2	4	6	–2	3
Gillingham	3	0	1	0	2	3	6	–3	2

SOUTHERN SECTION GROUP E

Leyton Orient v Arsenal U21	1-2
Colchester U v Milton Keynes D	2-1
Leyton Orient v Colchester U	1-1

Leyton Orient won 4-2 on penalties.

Milton Keynes D v Arsenal U21	2-2

Milton Keynes D won 3-1 on penalties.

Milton Keynes D v Leyton Orient	1-3
Colchester U v Arsenal U21	3-0

South Group E

	P	W	PW	PL	L	F	A	GD	Pts
Colchester U	3	2	0	1	0	6	2	4	7
Leyton Orient	3	1	1	0	1	5	4	1	5
Arsenal U21	3	1	0	1	1	4	6	–2	4
Milton Keynes D	3	0	1	0	2	4	7	–3	2

SOUTHERN SECTION GROUP F

Burton Albion v Leicester C U21	3-1
Burton Albion v Notts Co	1-2
Notts Co v Northampton T	0-2
Northampton T v Leicester C U21	3-0
Northampton T v Burton Albion	2-5
Notts Co v Leicester C U21	1-0

South Group F

	P	W	PW	PL	L	F	A	GD	Pts
Burton Alb	3	2	0	0	1	9	5	4	6
Northampton T	3	2	0	0	1	7	5	2	6
Notts Co	3	2	0	0	1	3	1	2	6
Leicester C U21	3	0	0	0	3	1	7	–6	0

SOUTHERN SECTION GROUP G

Bristol R v Tottenham H U21	3-3

Tottenham H U21 won 6-5 on penalties.

Exeter C v Swindon T	2-1
Exeter C v Tottenham H U21	2-0
Swindon T v Bristol R	4-0
Bristol R v Exeter C	2-3
Swindon T v Tottenham H U21	2-1

South Group G

	P	W	PW	PL	L	F	A	GD	Pts
Exeter C	3	3	0	0	0	7	3	4	9
Swindon T	3	2	0	0	1	7	3	4	6
Tottenham H U21	3	0	1	0	2	4	7	–3	2
Bristol R	3	0	0	1	2	5	10	–5	1

SOUTHERN SECTION GROUP H

Reading v West Ham U U21	3-1
Newport Co v Cheltenham T	1-2
Newport Co v West Ham U U21	1-0
Cheltenham T v West Ham U U21	3-1
Cheltenham T v Reading	1-0
Reading v Newport Co	3-0

South Group H

	P	W	PW	PL	L	F	A	GD	Pts
Cheltenham T	3	3	0	0	0	6	2	4	9
Reading	3	2	0	0	1	6	2	4	6
Newport Co	3	1	0	0	2	2	5	–3	3
West Ham U U21	3	0	0	0	3	2	7	–5	0

NORTHERN SECTION SECOND ROUND

Tuesday, 10 December 2024

Bolton W (1) 3 *(Lolos 40, Collins 83, 88)*

Huddersfield T (0) 1 *(Dacres-Cogley 90 (og))*   1802

Bolton W: (3412) Southwood; Jones, Santos (Johnston 70), Forrester; Williams (Dacres-Cogley 78), Matete, Thomason (McAtee 70), Osei-Tutu (Schon 57); Lolos, Charles, Adeboyejo (Collins 77).

Huddersfield T: (3412) Chapman; Pearson (Sorensen 66), Helik, Lonwijk; Spencer, Kasumu, Iorpenda, Ruffels (Headley 66); Ward (Ladapo 66); Radulovic, Koroma (Wiles 80).
Referee: Scott Jackson.

Chesterfield (1) 3 *(Dobra 3, Berry-McNally 78 (pen), Markanday 87)*

Wigan Ath (1) 2 *(McManaman 19, Hugill 90)*   1583

Chesterfield: (4141) Boot; Jessop (Gordon 65), Grimes, Araujo, Horton (Cook 79); Oldaker; Mandeville (Colclough 66), Hobson, Dobra (Markanday 46), Berry-McNally; Drummond (Grigg 79).

Wigan Ath: (4231) Watson; Ramsay (Payne 70), Carragher, Sibbick, Robinson L (Dummett 46); Adeeko, Smith M (Smith S 63); McManaman (Smith J 58), Sze (Aasgaard 58), Olakigbe; Hugill.
Referee: Greg Rollason.

Doncaster R (0) 0

Port Vale (0) 1 *(Harper 90)*   1396

Doncaster R: (4231) Lawlor; Emmanuel, Anderson, McGrath, Fleming; Close (Westbrooke 75), Kelly (Bailey 67); Sbarra (Hurst 75), Clifton (Molyneux 66), Gibson; Ironside (Sharp 67).

Port Vale: (343) Amos; Smith, Heneghan, Grant; Clark (Hart 84), Byers (Harper 46), Lowe, Shorrock (John 78); Edwards (Richards 61), Tolaj, Paton (Hackford 60).
Referee: Paul Marsden.

Morecambe (0) 0

Lincoln C (1) 1 *(Cadamarteri 19)*   496

Morecambe: (4231) Moore; Millen, Williams, Taylor, Tutonda; Harrack (White 64), Jones; Tollitt (Brown 76), Macadam (Lewis P 64), Slew (Lewis A 76); Hope.

Lincoln C: (3241) Pardington; Gallagher, Darikwa, Roughan; Jefferies (Bayliss 74), Hamilton; Ring, Draper (Walker 67), McKiernan (Erhahon 42), Duffy (Hackett 68); Cadamarteri (Street 74).
Referee: Michael Barlow.

Rotherham U (1) 3 *(Clarke-Harris 24 (pen), Jules 48, Odofin 90)*

Tranmere R (0) 2 *(Dennis 85, Patrick 90)*   1093

Rotherham U: (433) Dawson; Rafferty, Odofin, Jules, James; McWilliams (McCart 81), Tiehi, Powell (Hungbo 81); Wilks (Holmes 74), Clarke-Harris (Hugill 60), Green (Nombe 46).

Tranmere R: (4231) O'Connor, Drysdale, Turnbull, Bradshaw; Finley (Solomon 90), Merrie; Taylor (Wood 57), Jennings (Morris 90), Saunders (Dennis 66); Davison (Patrick 66).
Referee: Scott Tallis.

Stockport Co (2) 2 *(Norwood 26, Bailey 33)*

Bradford C (2) 3 *(Kavanagh 13, 63, Cook 15)*   1433

Stockport Co: (3421) Addai; Hughes, Horsfall, Rydel; Diamond, Mingi (Mellon 46), Norwood (Connolly 70), Adaramola (Bate 76); Fiorini, Bailey; Olaofe.

Bradford C: (3421) Doyle; Byrne, Shepherd, Kelly (Baldwin 62); Halliday, Pattison, Evans (Smallwood 62), Richards; Kavanagh, Pointon; Cook.
Referee: Aaron Bannister.

Wrexham (0) 1 *(James A 79)*

Crewe Alex (0) 0   3119

Wrexham: (352) Foster; James A, Scarr, O'Connor; Forde (Palmer 78), Jones (Cannon 32), Dobson, Adam (Mullin 65), Mendy (Revan 78); Faal, Bodvarsson (Lee 64).

Crewe Alex: (532) Marschall; Billington, Connolly, Knight-Lebel, Williams (Cooney 63), Finney (Tabiner 62); Breckin (Dancey 84), Powell, Lunt; Thibaut (Holicek 63), Roberts (Sanders 84).
Referee: Martin Woods.

Tuesday, 17 December 2024

Blackpool (0) 1 *(Embleton 46)*

Aston Villa U21 (0) 1 *(Jimoh 78)* 1055

Blackpool: (442) O'Donnell; Lawrence-Gabriel, Sassi, Ashworth, Thompson (Ballard 80); Embleton (Richardson 85), Finnigan (Morgan 80), Norburn, Coulson; Rhodes, Bondo (Fletcher 71).
Aston Villa U21: (4231) Zych; Rowe, Smith, Swinkels, Patterson; Alcock, Borland; Pierre (Lynch 65), Jimoh (Taylor 90), Broggio (Hemmings 65); Burrowes (Cotcher 73).
Aston Villa U21 won 18-17 on penalties.
Referee: John Mulligan.

SOUTHERN SECTION SECOND ROUND

Tuesday, 10 December 2024

Burton Alb (0) 0

Stevenage (1) 4 *(Freestone 6, Simpson 54, Aboh 78, White 83)* 329

Burton Alb: (4231) Isted; Akoto (Armer 21), Bannon, Sraha, Williams; Bran (Taroi 46), Webster (Gilligan 46); Hazlehurst (Cooper-Love 68), Orsi-Dadomo, Bodin (Larsson 69); Whitfield.
Stevenage: (4321) Ashby-Hammond; Smith, James-Wildin (Thompson N 46), Freestone, Butler (Piergianni 46); Freeman, King, Phillips (White 46); Young (Aboh 10), Roberts; Simpson (Pressley 66).
Referee: Richard Eley.

Charlton Ath (0) 0

Leyton Orient (0) 2 *(Agyei 90, Kelman 90)* 1336

Charlton Ath: (4312) Maynard-Brewer; Laqeretabua, Edmonds-Green, Potts (Gillesphey 79), Small; Dixon (Campbell T 59), Docherty (Campbell A 73), Edun; Berry (Taylor 73); Leaburn, Godden (Kanu 73).
Leyton Orient: (4231) Hemming; Galbraith, Cooper, Simpson, Currie; Pratley (Brown 76), Obiero; Perkins (Agyei 76), Donley, Jaiyesimi (O'Neill 77); Kelman.
Referee: Stephen Parkinson.

Cheltenham T (0) 2 *(Taylor 54, Jude-Boyd 57)*

Cambridge U (1) 1 *(Stokes 45 (pen))* 847

Cheltenham T: (4231) Day; Bakare, Stubbs, Bradbury, Jude-Boyd (Thomas 73); Kinsella, Pett; Payne, Archer, Dulson; Taylor (Bowman 81).
Cambridge U: (4141) Stevens; Okedina, O'Riordan, Watts, Andrew; Ibsen Rossi; Njoku (Barton 77), Stokes (Bennett 46), Brophy (Holmes 77), Longelo (Kaunda 46); Loft.
Referee: Dale Baines.

Colchester U (2) 2 *(Taylor 6, 33)*

AFC Wimbledon (0) 0 1139

Colchester U: (4231) Macey; Hunt, Flanagan, Donnelly, Iandolo (Egbo 46); McDonnell, Bishop (Read 46); Thorn, Payne, Edwards O (Gordon 66); Taylor (Sandah 84).
AFC Wimbledon: (3421) Ward; Harbottle (Johnson 46), O'Toole, Ogundere; Biler (Neufville 68), Sawyers (Hutchinson 46), Williams, Furlong (Tilley 68); Stevens (Bugiel 68), Kelly; Pigott.
Referee: Oliver Mackey.

Exeter C (1) 1 *(Sweeney 32)*

Birmingham C (1) 2 *(Harris 22, Anderson 78)* 1987

Exeter C: (3412) MacDonald; Sweeney, Fitzwater, Purrington; Harper (Niskanen 79), Richards J (Doyle 83), McDonald (Mitchell 78), McMillan; Aitchison (Cole 46); Bird (Magennis 61), Alli.
Birmingham C: (4231) Peacock-Farrell; Laird (Bielik 80), Sanderson, Davies, Buchanan (Paik 60); Gardner-Hickman, Leonard; Anderson, Harris, Yokoyama; Jutkiewicz (May 60).
Referee: Sam Mulhall.

Walsall (0) 0 *(Johnson 90)*

Reading (1) 1 *(Sackey 72)* 1501

Walsall: (352) Hornby; McEntee, Daniels, Weir; Browne (Barrett 77), Hall (Lowe 61), Lakin (Cleary 78), Earing, Allen (Gordon L 60); Johnson, Adomah.

Reading: (433) Button■; Ahmed■, Dean, Holzman, Garcia (Kanu 81); Sackey, Craig (Senga-Ngoyi 56), Savage (Wellens 46); Osho, Wareham, Camara (Norcott 59).
Walsall won 4-2 on penalties.
Referee: Steven Copeland.

Wycombe W (0) 1 *(Lubala 90)*

Swindon T (1) 2 *(Kirkman 5, Tshimanga 68)* 611

Wycombe W: (4231) Bishop; McCarthy, Skura, Tafazolli, Woodhouse (Morley 70); Bakinson (Wheeler 46), Butcher; McCleary (Lubala 60), Leahy, Udoh (Humphreys 70); Hanlan (Clark 79).
Swindon T: (4231) Barden; McGregor (Cox 76), Delaney, Kirkman, Sobowale; Ofoborh (Kilkenny 64), Cain (Wright 64); Longelo■, Cotterill (McGurk 76), Butterworth; Tshimanga (Glatzel 81).
Referee: Farai Hallam.

Tuesday, 17 December 2024

Peterborough U (0) 3 *(Jones 48, De Havilland 52, Odoh 65)*

Northampton T (0) 0 2549

Peterborough U: (4231) Blackmore; Dornelly (Katongo 54), Fernandez, Nevett, Mills (Sparkes 67); Collins (Kyprianou 46), De Havilland; Hayes (Kamara 66), Randall, Odoh; Mothersille (Jones 46).
Northampton T: (4231) Tzanev; McGowan (Willis 66), Tomlinson, Eyoma■, Lintott (Licorish Mullings 46); Chouchane, Hondermarck; Hoskins (Findlay 72), Fox (Pinnock 46), McCarron; Eaves (Dobson 81).
Referee: James Oldham.

NORTHERN SECTION THIRD ROUND

Tuesday, 14 January 2025

Aston Villa U21 (1) 1 *(Pierre 24)*

Bradford C (3) 3 *(Kavanagh 9, Shepherd 15, Johnson 26)* 1079

Aston Villa U21: (4231) Zych; Rowe, Katsukunya, Swinkels, Patterson; Alcock (Barnes 83), Borland; Pierre (Cotcher 79), Taylor (Young 60), Hemmings (Pavey 78); Burrowes.
Bradford C: (3421) Walker S; Johnson (Baldwin 46), Shepherd, Kelly; Halliday, Smallwood, Pattison (Sarcevic 46), Richards (Walker J 67); Oduor, Pointon (Wright 88); Kavanagh (Oliver 66).
Referee: Ross Joyce.

Chesterfield (0) 0

Rotherham U (0) 0 3517

Chesterfield: (4141) Boot; Sheckelford (Donacien 73), Naylor, Grimes, Horton; Oldaker; Hobson (Banks 73), Mandeville (Akinola 85), Dobra, Colclough (Drummond 59); Pepple (Cook 85).
Rotherham U: (41212) Dawson; Rafferty, Odofin, Jules, James, Kelly (Humphreys 76); Holmes (McWilliams 78), Bramall (Hatton 80); Green (Powell 77); Hugill (Nombe 77), Clarke-Harris.
Rotherham U won 4-3 on penalties.
Referee: Scott Oldham.

Lincoln C (0) 0

Bolton W (1) 1 *(Collins 21)* 2252

Lincoln C: (3142) Jeacock; Jackson, O'Connor, Roughan; Erhahon; Darikwa (Jefferies 70), Hamilton (Bayliss 71), Moylan, Hackett (Duffy 71); Makama (House 71), Draper (Cadamarteri 79).
Bolton W: (3412) Southwood; Jones, Santos, Johnston; Dacres-Cogley, Matete, Thomason, Osei-Tutu (Schon 80); Lolos; Collins (McAtee 73), Adeboyejo (Mendes Gomes 73).
Referee: Thomas Parsons.

Tuesday, 4 February 2025

Port Vale (1) 1 *(Curtis 1)*

Wrexham (1) 4 *(Cannon 31, Ashfield 48, Lee 63, Faal 82)* 1621

Port Vale: (3412) Broome; Debrah, Heneghan, Hart; Clark (Sang 11), Lowe, Walters (Croasdale 79), Shorrock (Tolaj 79); Richards (Harper 55); Curtis, Hackford.
Wrexham: (352) Okonkwo; Cleworth (Brunt 85), Scarr, O'Connor; Longman (Mendy 72), Cannon (Dobson 72), Evans, Lee, Revan; Ashfield (Palmer 60), Faal.
Referee: Darren Drysdale.

SOUTHERN SECTION THIRD ROUND

Tuesday, 14 January 2025

Cheltenham T (1) 2 *(Pett 3, Miller 90)*

Colchester U (1) 1 *(Taylor 45)*   1084

Cheltenham T: (4231) Day; Jude-Boyd (Power 85), Bennett, Stubbs, Bradbury (Adedokun 16); Kinsella, Young; Thomas, Pett (Miller 46), Archer; Hay.
Colchester U: (4231) Macey; Egbo, Kelleher, Flanagan, Iandolo (Terry 46); McDonnell, Bishop (Read 81); Anderson (Thorn 78), Payne, Edwards O (Gordon 78); Taylor (Hopper 66).
Referee: David Rock.

Peterborough U (3) 4 *(Lindgren 7, 31,*
Mothersille 15 (pen), 74)

Walsall (1) 2 *(Johnson 30, Gordon J 90)*   2133

Peterborough U: (4231) Bilokapic; Katongo, Wallin (Nevett 64), Fernandez, Mills; Kyprianou (De Havilland 68), Collins (O'Brien-Brady 75); Odoh (Jones 64), Conn-Clarke, Mothersille; Lindgren (Ihionvien 64).
Walsall: (532) Hornby; Browne (Gordon J 72), Okagbue, Daniels (Jellis 24), Allen (Gordon L 63), Weir; McEntee (Barrett 63), Comley, Lakin; Adomah, Johnson (Matt 72).
Referee: Scott Simpson.

Swindon T (0) 1 *(Smith 76)*

Birmingham C (0) 2 *(Yokoyama 49, Smith 89 (og))*   3509

Swindon T: (4312) Bycroft; Sobowale, McCormick, Wright, Kirkman (Chard 46); Cotterill, Kilkenny (Ofoborh 72), Butterworth (Ameen 72); Cain; Drinan (Smith 62), Tshimanga (Glatzel 62).
Birmingham C: (4231) Peacock-Farrell; Laird, Sampsted, Davies, Cochrane; Gardner-Hickman, Leonard; Harris (Jutkiewicz 70), Dykes, Yokoyama; May (Wright 73).
Referee: Ed Duckworth.

Tuesday, 21 January 2025

Leyton Orient (0) 0

Stevenage (1) 1 *(Cooper 25 (og))*   1558

Leyton Orient: (4231) Keeley; James (Currie 63), Cooper, Simpson (Beckles 81), Sweeney; Brown, Clare; Perkins, Galbraith (Donley 46), Obiero (Kelman 73); Jaiyesimi (Pratley 73).
Stevenage: (4231) Ashby-Hammond; Smith (James-Wildin 83), Sweeney, Goode, Freestone; Thompson L (Phillips 70), White (King 70); Young, Kemp (Roberts 70), Freeman; Appere (Reid 83).
Referee: Carl Brook.

QUARTER-FINALS

Tuesday, 4 February 2025

Rotherham U (0) 0

Bradford C (0) 1 *(Smallwood 58 (pen))*   3073

Rotherham U: (41212) Dawson; Rafferty, Raggett, Jules, James; Humphreys; Odofin, Powell (Ayres 77); Sibley; Hugill, Green (Holmes 62).
Bradford C: (3421) Walker S; Byrne, Huntington, Crichlow-Noble; Halliday, Pattison (Sarcevic 46), Smallwood, Wright (Shepherd 70); Oduor (Walker J 46), Pointon (Johnson 90); Kavanagh (Baldwin 86).
Referee: Adam Herczeg.

Stevenage (0) 0

Birmingham C (0) 1 *(Stansfield 83)*   2812

Stevenage: (4231) Ashby-Hammond; Freeman, Sweeney, Piergianni, Freestone; Thompson L, White (Phillips 75); Roberts (Reid 75), Kemp, List (Doherty 87); Young (Appere 75).
Birmingham C: (4231) Peacock-Farrell; Bielik, Klarer, Hanley (Laird 70), Cochrane; Dowell, Leonard; Wright (Stansfield 70), Jutkiewicz (Iwata 57), Harris (Anderson 57); May (Dykes 80).
Referee: Declan Bourne.

Wednesday, 5 February 2025

Peterborough U (1) 3 *(Kyprianou 24, Odoh 52, Jones 69)*

Cheltenham T (2) 2 *(Thomas 34, Miller 45)*   2587

Peterborough U: (343) Steer; Wallin, Fernandez, Nevett (Dornelly 46); Kyprianou, Collins, O'Brien-Brady (Mothersille 46); Hayes (Mills 46); Odoh (Ihionvien 89), Lindgren, Conn-Clarke (Jones 46).
Cheltenham T: (4231) Day; Jude-Boyd, Stubbs (Bakare 74), Bradbury, Adedokun (Power 69); Young, Kinsella (Dieng 73); Thomas, Backwell (Taylor 54), Archer; Miller (Hay 54).
Referee: Scott Oldham.

Tuesday, 11 February 2025

Wrexham (0) 1 *(Cannon 70)*

Bolton W (0) 0   7591

Wrexham: (352) Okonkwo; Brunt, Scarr, O'Connor; Longman (Barnett 63), Cannon (Cleworth 87), Evans, Lee (Rathbone 63), Revan; Marriott (Smith 63), Faal (Rodriguez 63).
Bolton W: (3421) Baxter; Toal, Forrester (Andreucci 83), Johnston; Jones, Thomason, Sheehan, Dacres-Cogley; Matete (Collins 57), Lolos (McAtee 57); Adeboyejo (Osei-Tutu 71).
Referee: Ross Joyce.

SEMI-FINALS

Tuesday, 18 February 2025

Birmingham C (1) 2 *(Stansfield 45, Dykes 88)*

Bradford C (0) 1 *(Pointon 52)*   27,066

Birmingham C: (4231) Allsop; Gardner-Hickman (Laird 60), Klarer, Davies, Cochrane; Paik, Iwata; Dowell (Dykes 80), Willumsson (Hanley 90), Wright (Anderson 60); Stansfield (May 59).
Bradford C: (3421) Walker S; Baldwin, Shepherd, Crichlow-Noble; Halliday (Johnson 90), Pattison, Smallwood, Wright; Sarcevic, Pointon; Walker J (Ibbitson 90).
Referee: Scott Oldham.

Wednesday, 26 February 2025

Wrexham (2) 2 *(Faal 34, Dobson 38)*

Peterborough U (0) 2 *(Mothersille 72, Ihionvien 90)*   9258

Wrexham: (532) Okonkwo; Barnett, Cleworth, Scarr, Brunt, Mendy; Dobson (Lee 66), Evans (O'Connell 85), Ashfield (Rathbone 77); Marriott (Mullin 66), Faal (Fletcher 66).
Peterborough U: (4231) Steer; Dornelly, Wallin, Fernandez, Mills; Kyprianou, Collins (Susoho 46); Odoh (De Havilland 90), Mothersille, Hayes; Jones (Ihionvien 46).
Peterborough U won 4-2 on penalties.
Referee: Lewis Smith.

VERTU EFL TROPHY FINAL 2024–25

Sunday, 13 April 2025

(at Wembley Stadium, attendance 71,722)

Birmingham C (0) 0   **Peterborough U (2) 2**

Birmingham C: (4231) Allsop; Laird (Gardner-Hickman 64), Klarer, Davies (Jutkiewicz 86), Cochrane; Iwata, Paik (Leonard 72); Dowell, Willumsson (May 46), Anderson, Stansfield.

Peterborough U: (4231) Steer; Dornelly, Wallin, Fernandez (Katongo 90), Mills; Kyprianou, Collins; Poku, Mothersille (Susoho 75), Odoh; Jones (Lindgren 86).
Scorers: Mills 15, Kyprianou 45.

Referee: Ben Speedie.

FA CUP ATTENDANCES 1969–2025

	1st Round	2nd Round	3rd Round	4th Round	5th Round	6th Round	Semi-finals & Final	Total	No. of matches	Average per match
1969–70	345,229	195,102	925,930	651,374	319,893	198,537	390,700	3,026,765	170	17,805
1970–71	329,687	230,942	956,683	757,852	360,687	304,937	279,644	3,220,432	162	19,879
1971–72	277,726	236,127	986,094	711,399	486,378	230,292	248,546	3,158,562	160	19,741
1972–73	259,432	169,114	938,741	735,825	357,386	241,934	226,543	2,928,975	160	18,306
1973–74	214,236	125,295	840,142	747,909	346,012	233,307	273,051	2,779,952	167	16,646
1974–75	283,956	170,466	914,994	646,434	393,323	268,361	291,369	2,968,903	172	17,261
1975–76	255,533	178,099	867,880	573,843	471,925	206,851	205,810	2,759,941	161	17,142
1976–77	379,230	192,159	942,523	631,265	373,330	205,379	258,216	2,982,102	174	17,139
1977–78	258,248	178,930	881,406	540,164	400,751	137,059	198,020	2,594,578	160	16,216
1978–79	243,773	185,343	880,345	537,748	243,683	263,213	249,897	2,604,002	166	15,687
1979–80	267,121	204,759	804,701	507,725	364,039	157,530	355,541	2,661,416	163	16,328
1980–81	246,824	194,502	832,578	534,402	320,530	288,714	339,250	2,756,800	169	16,312
1981–82	236,220	127,300	513,185	356,987	203,334	124,308	279,621	1,840,955	160	11,506
1982–83	191,312	150,046	670,503	452,688	260,069	193,845	291,162	2,209,625	154	14,348
1983–84	192,276	151,647	625,965	417,298	181,832	185,382	187,000	1,941,400	166	11,695
1984–85	174,604	137,078	616,229	320,772	269,232	148,690	242,754	1,909,359	157	12,162
1985–86	171,142	130,034	486,838	495,526	311,833	184,262	192,316	1,971,951	168	11,738
1986–87	209,290	146,761	593,520	349,342	263,550	119,396	195,533	1,877,400	165	11,378
1987–88	204,411	104,561	720,121	443,133	281,461	119,313	177,585	2,050,585	155	13,229
1988–89	212,775	121,326	690,199	421,255	206,781	176,629	167,353	1,966,318	164	12,173
1989–90	209,542	133,483	683,047	412,483	351,423	123,065	277,420	2,190,463	170	12,885
1990–91	194,195	121,450	594,592	530,279	276,112	124,826	196,434	2,038,518	162	12,583
1991–92	231,940	117,078	586,014	372,576	270,537	155,603	201,592	1,935,340	160	12,095
1992–93	241,968	174,702	612,494	377,211	198,379	149,675	293,241	2,047,670	161	12,718
1993–94	190,683	118,031	691,064	430,234	172,196	134,705	228,233	1,965,146	159	12,359
1994–95	219,511	125,629	640,017	438,596	257,650	159,787	174,059	2,015,249	161	12,517
1995–96	185,538	115,669	748,997	391,218	274,055	174,142	156,500	2,046,199	167	12,252
1996–97	209,521	122,324	651,139	402,293	199,873	67,035	191,813	1,843,998	151	12,211
1997–98	204,803	130,261	629,127	455,557	341,290	192,651	172,007	2,125,696	165	12,883
1998–99	191,954	132,341	609,486	431,613	359,398	181,005	202,150	2,107,947	155	13,599
1999–2000	181,485	127,728	514,030	374,795	182,511	105,443	214,921	1,700,913	158	10,765
2000–01	171,689	122,061	577,204	398,241	256,899	100,663	177,778	1,804,535	151	11,951
2001–02	198,369	119,781	566,284	330,434	249,190	173,757	171,278	1,809,093	148	12,224
2002–03	189,905	104,103	577,494	404,599	242,483	156,244	175,498	1,850,326	150	12,336
2003–04	162,738	117,967	624,732	347,964	292,521	156,780	167,401	1,870,103	149	12,551
2004–05	161,197	98,702	602,152	477,472	339,082	127,914	193,233	1,999,752	146	13,697
2005–06	188,876	107,456	654,570	388,339	286,225	163,449	177,723	1,966,638	160	12,291
2006–07	168,884	113,924	708,628	478,924	340,612	230,064	177,810	2,218,846	158	14,043
2007–08	175,195	99,528	704,300	356,404	276,903	142,780	256,210	2,011,320	152	13,232
2008–09	161,526	96,923	631,070	529,585	297,364	149,566	264,635	2,131,669	163	13,078
2009–10	147,078	100,476	613,113	335,426	288,604	144,918	254,806	1,884,421	151	12,480
2010–11	169,259	101,291	637,202	390,524	284,311	164,092	250,256	1,996,935	150	13,313
2011–12	155,858	92,267	640,700	391,214	250,666	194,971	262,064	1,987,740	151	13,164
2012–13	135,642	115,965	645,676	373,892	288,509	221,216	234,210	2,015,110	156	12,917
2013–14	144,709	75,903	668,242	346,706	254,084	156,630	243,350	1,889,624	149	12,682
2014–15	156,621	111,434	609,368	515,229	208,908	233,341	258,780	2,093,681	153	13,684
2015–16	134,914	94,855	755,187	397,217	235,433	227,262	253,793	2,098,661	149	14,085
2016–17	147,448	97,784	685,467	409,084	212,842	163,620	261,552	1,977,797	156	12,678
2017–18	125,978	87,075	712,036	371,650	210,328	140,641	245,730	1,893,438	149	12,708
2018–19	146,449	92,928	655,501	402,836	146,476	86,028	237,467	1,767,685	150	11,785
2019–20*	160,471	91,200	697,152	489,571	233,190			1,671,584	149	11,219
2020–21	Due to the COVID-19 pandemic most games were played behind closed doors.									
2021–22	199,848	86,847	596,352	482,808	223,647	115,014	234,928	1,939,444	137	14,157
2022–23	158,621	100,289	672,723	444,622	225,850	180,428	234,227	2,016,760	144	14,005
2023–24	174,824	102,144	825,216	564,241	221,783	195,268	249,388	2,332,864	150	15,552
2024–25	161,556	84,665	724,362	381,848	288,615	89,304	239,440	1,969,790	123	16,015

*Due to the COVID-19 pandemic, the 6th Round, Semi-finals and Final were played behind closed doors.

FA CUP FINALS 1872–2025

VENUES

1872 and 1874–92	Kennington Oval		1895–1914	Crystal Palace
1873	Lillie Bridge, Fulham		1915	Old Trafford
1893	Fallowfield, Manchester		1920–22	Stamford Bridge
1894	Goodison Park		2001–06	Millennium Stadium, Cardiff
1923–2000	Wembley Stadium (old)		2007 to date	Wembley Stadium (new)

THE FA CUP

1872	Wanderers v Royal Engineers	1-0
1873	Wanderers v Oxford University	2-0
1874	Oxford University v Royal Engineers	2-0
1875	Royal Engineers v Old Etonians	1-1*
Replay	Royal Engineers v Old Etonians	2-0
1876	Wanderers v Old Etonians	1-1*
Replay	Wanderers v Old Etonians	3-0
1877	Wanderers v Oxford University	2-1*
1878	Wanderers v Royal Engineers	3-1

Wanderers won the cup outright, but it was restored to the Football Association.

1879	Old Etonians v Clapham R	1-0
1880	Clapham R v Oxford University	1-0
1881	Old Carthusians v Old Etonians	3-0
1882	Old Etonians v Blackburn R	1-0
1883	Blackburn Olympic v Old Etonians	2-1*
1884	Blackburn R v Queen's Park, Glasgow	2-1
1885	Blackburn R v Queen's Park, Glasgow	2-0
1886	Blackburn R v WBA	0-0
Replay	Blackburn R v WBA	2-0
	(at Racecourse Ground, Derby Co)	

A special trophy was awarded to Blackburn R for third consecutive win.

1887	Aston Villa v WBA	2-0
1888	WBA v Preston NE	2-1
1889	Preston NE v Wolverhampton W	3-0
1890	Blackburn R v The Wednesday	6-1
1891	Blackburn R v Notts Co	3-1
1892	WBA v Aston Villa	3-0
1893	Wolverhampton W v Everton	1-0
1894	Notts Co v Bolton W	4-1
1895	Aston Villa v WBA	1-0

FA Cup was stolen from a shop window in Birmingham and never found.

1896	The Wednesday v Wolverhampton W	2-1
1897	Aston Villa v Everton	3-2
1898	Nottingham F v Derby Co	3-1
1899	Sheffield U v Derby Co	4-1
1900	Bury v Southampton	4-0
1901	Tottenham H v Sheffield U	2-2
Replay	Tottenham H v Sheffield U	3-1
	(at Burnden Park, Bolton W)	
1902	Sheffield U v Southampton	1-1
Replay	Sheffield U v Southampton	2-1
1903	Bury v Derby Co	6-0
1904	Manchester C v Bolton W	1-0
1905	Aston Villa v Newcastle U	2-0
1906	Everton v Newcastle U	1-0
1907	The Wednesday v Everton	2-1
1908	Wolverhampton W v Newcastle U	3-1
1909	Manchester U v Bristol C	1-0
1910	Newcastle U v Barnsley	1-1
Replay	Newcastle U v Barnsley	2-0
	(at Goodison Park, Everton)	
1911	Bradford C v Newcastle U	0-0
Replay	Bradford C v Newcastle U	1-0
	(at Old Trafford, Manchester U)	

Trophy was given to Lord Kinnaird – he made nine FA Cup Final appearances – for services to football.

1912	Barnsley v WBA	0-0
Replay	Barnsley v WBA	1-0
	(at Bramall Lane, Sheffield U)	

1913	Aston Villa v Sunderland	1-0
1914	Burnley v Liverpool	1-0
1915	Sheffield U v Chelsea	3-0
1920	Aston Villa v Huddersfield T	1-0*
1921	Tottenham H v Wolverhampton W	1-0
1922	Huddersfield T v Preston NE	1-0
1923	Bolton W v West Ham U	2-0
1924	Newcastle U v Aston Villa	2-0
1925	Sheffield U v Cardiff C	1-0
1926	Bolton W v Manchester C	1-0
1927	Cardiff C v Arsenal	1-0
1928	Blackburn R v Huddersfield T	3-1
1929	Bolton W v Portsmouth	2-0
1930	Arsenal v Huddersfield T	2-0
1931	WBA v Birmingham	2-1
1932	Newcastle U v Arsenal	2-1
1933	Everton v Manchester C	3-0
1934	Manchester C v Portsmouth	2-1
1935	Sheffield Wed v WBA	4-2
1936	Arsenal v Sheffield U	1-0
1937	Sunderland v Preston NE	3-1
1938	Preston NE v Huddersfield T	1-0*
1939	Portsmouth v Wolverhampton W	4-1
1946	Derby Co v Charlton Ath	4-1*
1947	Charlton Ath v Burnley	1-0*
1948	Manchester U v Blackpool	4-2
1949	Wolverhampton W v Leicester C	3-1
1950	Arsenal v Liverpool	2-0
1951	Newcastle U v Blackpool	2-0
1952	Newcastle U v Arsenal	1-0
1953	Blackpool v Bolton W	4-3
1954	WBA v Preston NE	3-2
1955	Newcastle U v Manchester C	3-1
1956	Manchester C v Birmingham C	3-1
1957	Aston Villa v Manchester U	2-1
1958	Bolton W v Manchester U	2-0
1959	Nottingham F v Luton T	2-1
1960	Wolverhampton W v Blackburn R	3-0
1961	Tottenham H v Leicester C	2-0
1962	Tottenham H v Burnley	3-1
1963	Manchester U v Leicester C	3-1
1964	West Ham U v Preston NE	3-2
1965	Liverpool v Leeds U	2-1*
1966	Everton v Sheffield Wed	3-2
1967	Tottenham H v Chelsea	2-1
1968	WBA v Everton	1-0*
1969	Manchester C v Leicester C	1-0
1970	Chelsea v Leeds U	2-2*
Replay	Chelsea v Leeds U	2-1
	(at Old Trafford, Manchester U)	
1971	Arsenal v Liverpool	2-1*
1972	Leeds U v Arsenal	1-0
1973	Sunderland v Leeds U	1-0
1974	Liverpool v Newcastle U	3-0
1975	West Ham U v Fulham	2-0
1976	Southampton v Manchester U	1-0
1977	Manchester U v Liverpool	2-1
1978	Ipswich T v Arsenal	1-0
1979	Arsenal v Manchester U	3-2
1980	West Ham U v Arsenal	1-0
1981	Tottenham H v Manchester C	1-1*
Replay	Tottenham H v Manchester C	3-2

1982	Tottenham H v QPR	1-1*
Replay	Tottenham H v QPR	1-0
1983	Manchester U v Brighton & HA	2-2*
Replay	Manchester U v Brighton & HA	4-0
1984	Everton v Watford	2-0
1985	Manchester U v Everton	1-0*
1986	Liverpool v Everton	3-1
1987	Coventry C v Tottenham H	3-2*
1988	Wimbledon v Liverpool	1-0
1989	Liverpool v Everton	3-2*
1990	Manchester U v Crystal Palace	3-3*
Replay	Manchester U v Crystal Palace	1-0
1991	Tottenham H v Nottingham F	2-1*
1992	Liverpool v Sunderland	2-0
1993	Arsenal v Sheffield Wed	1-1*
Replay	Arsenal v Sheffield Wed	2-1*
1994	Manchester U v Chelsea	4-0

THE FA CUP SPONSORED BY LITTLEWOODS POOLS

1995	Everton v Manchester U	1-0
1996	Manchester U v Liverpool	1-0
1997	Chelsea v Middlesbrough	2-0
1998	Arsenal v Newcastle U	2-0

THE AXA-SPONSORED FA CUP

1999	Manchester U v Newcastle U	2-0
2000	Chelsea v Aston Villa	1-0
2001	Liverpool v Arsenal	2-1
2002	Arsenal v Chelsea	2-0

THE FA CUP

2003	Arsenal v Southampton	1-0
2004	Manchester U v Millwall	3-0

2005	Arsenal v Manchester U	0-0*
	Arsenal won 5-4 on penalties.	
2006	Liverpool v West Ham U	3-3*
	Liverpool won 3-1 on penalties.	

THE FA CUP SPONSORED BY E.ON

2007	Chelsea v Manchester U	1-0*
2008	Portsmouth v Cardiff C	1-0
2009	Chelsea v Everton	2-1
2010	Chelsea v Portsmouth	1-0
2011	Manchester C v Stoke C	1-0

THE FA CUP WITH BUDWEISER

2012	Chelsea v Liverpool	2-1
2013	Wigan Ath v Manchester C	1-0
2014	Arsenal v Hull C	3-2*

THE FA CUP

2015	Arsenal v Aston Villa	4-0

THE EMIRATES FA CUP

2016	Manchester U v Crystal Palace	2-1*
2017	Arsenal v Chelsea	2-1
2018	Chelsea v Manchester U	1-0
2019	Manchester C v Watford	6-0
2020	Arsenal v Chelsea	2-1
2021	Leicester C v Chelsea	1-0
2022	Liverpool v Chelsea	0-0*
	Liverpool won 6-5 on penalties.	
2023	Manchester C v Manchester U	2-1
2024	Manchester U v Manchester C	2-1
2025	Crystal Palace v Manchester C	1-0

After extra time.

FA CUP WINS

Arsenal 14, Manchester U 13, Chelsea 8, Liverpool 8, Tottenham H 8, Aston Villa 7, Manchester C 7, Blackburn R 6, Newcastle U 6, Everton 5, The Wanderers 5, WBA 5, Bolton W 4, Sheffield U 4, Wolverhampton W 4, Sheffield Wed 3 (2 as The Wednesday), West Ham U 3, Bury 2, Nottingham F 2, Old Etonians 2, Portsmouth 2, Preston NE 2, Sunderland 2, Barnsley 1, Blackburn Olympic 1, Bradford C 1, Burnley 1, Cardiff C 1, Charlton Ath 1, Clapham R 1, Coventry C 1, Crystal Palace 1, Derby Co 1, Huddersfield T 1, Ipswich T 1, Leeds U 1, Leicester C 1, Notts Co 1, Old Carthusians 1, Oxford University 1, Royal Engineers 1, Southampton 1, Wigan Ath 1, Wimbledon 1.

APPEARANCES IN FINALS

Manchester U 22, Arsenal 21, Chelsea 16, Liverpool 15, Manchester C 14, Everton 13, Newcastle U 13, Aston Villa 11, WBA 10, Tottenham H 9, Blackburn R 8, Wolverhampton W 8, Bolton W 7, Preston NE 7, Old Etonians 6, Sheffield U 6, Sheffield Wed 6, Huddersfield T 5, Leicester C 5, Portsmouth 5, *The Wanderers 5, West Ham U 5, Derby Co 4, Leeds U 4, Oxford University 4, Royal Engineers 4, Southampton 4, Sunderland 4, Blackpool 3, Burnley 3, Cardiff C 3, Crystal Palace 3, Nottingham F 3, Barnsley 2, Birmingham C 2, *Bury 2, Charlton Ath 2, Clapham R 2, Notts Co 2, Queen's Park (Glasgow) 2, Watford 2, *Blackburn Olympic 1, *Bradford C 1, Brighton & HA 1, Bristol C 1, *Coventry C 1, Fulham 1, Hull C 1, *Ipswich T 1, Luton T 1, Middlesbrough 1, Millwall 1, *Old Carthusians 1, QPR 1, Stoke C 1, *Wigan Ath 1, *Wimbledon 1.
* *Denotes undefeated in final.*

APPEARANCES IN SEMI-FINALS

Manchester U 32, Arsenal 30, Chelsea 27, Everton 26, Liverpool 25, Aston Villa 22, Tottenham H 21, Manchester C 20, WBA 20, Blackburn R 18, Newcastle U 17, Sheffield Wed 16, Sheffield U 15, Wolverhampton W 15, Bolton W 14, Derby Co 13, Nottingham F 13, Southampton 13, Sunderland 12, Preston NE 10, Birmingham C 9, Burnley 8, Leeds U 8, Leicester C 8, Huddersfield T 7, Portsmouth 7, West Ham U 7, Watford 7, Crystal Palace (professional club) 6, Fulham 6, Old Etonians 6, Oxford University 6, Millwall 5, Notts Co 5, The Wanderers 5, Cardiff C 4, Luton T 4, Queen's Park (Glasgow) 4, Royal Engineers 4, Stoke C 4, Barnsley 3, Blackpool 3, Brighton & HA 3, Clapham R 3, Ipswich T 3, Middlesbrough 3, Norwich C 3, Old Carthusians 3, The Swifts 3, Blackburn Olympic 2, Bristol C 2, Bury 2, Charlton Ath 2, Coventry C 2, Grimsby T 2, Hull C 2, Reading 2, Swansea T 2, Swindon T 2, Wigan Ath 2, Wimbledon 2, Bradford C 1, Cambridge University 1, Chesterfield 1, Crewe Alex 1, Crystal Palace (amateur club) 1, Darwen 1, Derby Junction 1, Glasgow Rangers 1, Marlow 1, Old Harrovians 1, Orient 1, Plymouth Arg 1, Port Vale 1, QPR 1, Shropshire W 1, Wycombe W 1, York C 1.

THE EMIRATES FA CUP 2024–25

PRELIMINARY AND QUALIFYING ROUNDS

*After extra time.

EXTRA PRELIMINARY ROUND

Crook T v Marske U	4-1
Consett v Redcar Ath	2-3
West Auckland T v Bishop Auckland	0-2
Newcastle Benfield v Knaresborough T	3-0
Garforth T v Northallerton T	2-0
Kendal T v Guisborough T	2-2
Replay: Guisborough T v Kendal T	1-2
Whickham v Carlisle T	1-0
Boro Rangers v West Allotment Celtic	3-0
Shildon v Ashington	2-4
Beverley T v Whitley Bay	2-3
Heaton Stannington v Easington Colliery	2-0
Birtley T v Bridlington T	3-2
Tow Law T v Blyth T	2-3
North Shields v Newcastle Blue Star	1-2
Tadcaster Alb v Seaham Red Star	3-0
Penrith v Pickering T	3-0
Colne v Mossley	0-4
Longridge T v Cheadle T	2-0
Sheffield v Nantwich T	2-1
Ossett U v Widnes	0-1
Vauxhall Motors v Eccleshill U	1-1
Replay: Eccleshill U v Vauxhall Motors	3-2
AFC Liverpool v Abbey Hey	2-1
Wythenshawe T v Chadderton	7-1
Whitchurch Alport v Irlam	3-0
Thackley v Frickley Ath	2-0
Stocksbridge Park Steels v Prestwich Heys	2-1
West Didsbury & Chorlton v Burscough	3-2
Penistone Church v Charnock Richard	1-2
Ramsbottom U v Stalybridge Celtic	1-3
Barnoldswick T v Brighouse T	0-0
Replay: Brighouse T v Barnoldswick T	2-2*
2-2 at the end of normal time; Barnoldswick T	
won 5-3 on penalties.	
Liversedge v Silsden	0-2
Albion Sports v Trafford	1-2
Campion v Parkgate	1-0
Padiham v Golcar U	1-1
Replay: Golcar U v Padiham	1-0
Wythenshawe v Pilkington	0-0
Replay: Pilkington v Wythenshawe	3-1
Northwich Vic v Squires Gate	3-2
Handsworth v South Liverpool	2-2
Replay: South Liverpool v Handsworth	2-0
Congleton T v Bury	2-4
Hallam v Lower Breck	2-1
Stockport T v 1874 Northwich	1-2
Litherland Remyca v Glossop North End	1-3
Emley v FC St Helens	1-0
Brocton v Tividale	3-2
Wolverhampton Casuals v Rugby T	0-3
Lutterworth T v Studley	3-2
Coventry Sphinx v Ashby Ivanhoe	0-1
OJM Black Country v Chasetown	1-2
Rugby Bor v Darlaston T	0-4
Kidsgrove Ath v Pershore T	2-0
AFC Wulfrunians v Atherstone T	1-2
Sporting Khalsa v Coventry U	3-0
Sutton Coldfield T v Romulus	2-0
Hinckley v Highgate U	3-1
Westfields v Daventry T	1-0
Worcester Raiders v Stourport Swifts	2-0
Racing Club Warwick v Hednesford T	1-4
Stone Old Alleynians v Bedworth U	2-1
Hanley T v Boldmere St Michaels	1-1
Replay: Boldmere St Michaels v Hanley T	0-0*
Hanley T won 4-2 on penalties.	
Worcester C v Walsall Wood	0-0
Replay: Worcester C v Walsall Wood	1-0
The replay at Walsall Wood on 6 August 2024 was	
abandoned after 50 minutes with the score 0-0 and	
ordered to be replayed at Worcester C.	

Uttoxeter T v Heanor T	2-3
Shifnal T v Belper U	3-0
Malvern T v Hereford Pegasus	2-1
Sporting Club Inkberrow v Dudley T	0-3
Evesham U v Newcastle T	1-1
Replay: Newcastle T v Evesham U	3-2
Coleshill T v Eastwood Community	0-0
Replay: Eastwood Community v Coleshill T	1-3*
1-1 at the end of normal time.	
Gresley R v Lichfield C	4-2
Corby T v AFC Rushden & Diamonds	1-1
Replay: AFC Rushden & Diamonds v Corby T	1-1*
AFC Rushden & Diamonds won 2-1 on penalties.	
Grimsby Bor v GNG Oadby T	3-0
Leicester Nirvana v Northampton ON Chenecks	0-6
Rossington Main v AFC Mansfield	0-3
Shirebrook T v Deeping Rangers	1-2
Bourne T v Aylestone Park	0-1
Yaxley v Godmanchester R	2-1
Barton T v Newark T	5-2
Lincoln U v Goole	2-3
Melton T v Harrowby U	2-0
Shepshed Dynamo v Winterton Rangers	0-3
Sherwood Colliery v Grantham T	1-1
Replay: Grantham T v Sherwood Colliery	4-0
Kimberley MW v Cleethorpes T	0-7
Skegness T v Newark & Sherwood U	1-3
Wellingborough T v Sleaford T	1-1
Replay: Sleaford T v Wellingborough T	2-2*
Wellingborough T won 5-4 on penalties.	
Bugbrooke St Michaels v Loughborough Students	0-2
Northampton Sileby Rangers v Boston T	1-1
Replay: Boston T v Northampton Sileby Rangers	1-0
Hucknall T v Bottesford T	2-3
Dereham T v Wisbech T	1-1
Replay: Wisbech T v Dereham T	0-1
Ely C v Mulbarton W	1-1
Replay: Mulbarton W v Ely C	2-1*
1-1 at the end of normal time.	
Sheringham v Woodbridge T	2-1
Cambridge C v Lakenheath	5-1
Harleston T v Heacham	4-0
Great Yarmouth T v Kirkley & Pakefield	2-0
Wroxham v Walsham Le Willows	1-1
Replay: Walsham Le Willows v Wroxham	0-2
Thetford T v Ipswich W	0-0
Replay: Ipswich W v Thetford T	1-0
Stowmarket T v Histon	2-1
Cornard U v Fakenham T	3-0
Newmarket T v March T U	3-1
Gorleston v Hadleigh U	2-0
Long Melford v Downham T	1-4
Soham Town Rangers v Mildenhall T	4-1
Great Wakering R v Redbridge	2-2
Replay: Redbridge v Great Wakering R	1-0
Newport Pagnell T v Ilford	3-3
Replay: Newport Pagnell T v Ilford	
The replay at Ilford on 7 August 2024 which ended in a	
0-3 victory to Newport Pagnell T was ordered	
to be replayed at Newport Pagnell T due to an	
administrative error.	
Stansted v Biggleswade	0-0
Replay: Biggleswade v Stansted	2-1
Leverstock Green v Baldock T	3-1
Eynesbury R v Romford	2-2
Replay: Romford v Eynesbury R	3-2
Tring Ath v Barking	1-1
Replay: Barking v Tring Ath	1-0
Biggleswade U v Frenford	2-2
Replay: Frenford v Biggleswade U	2-4*
1-1 at the end of normal time.	
Milton Keynes Irish v Welwyn Garden City	2-0
Witham T v Hertford T	2-1
London Lions v Arlesey T	4-0
Colney Heath v Takeley	1-2

Cockfosters v Kings Langley	1-1
Replay: Kings Langley v Cockfosters	1-0
Sawbridgeworth T v FC Romania	0-5
Real Bedford v St Neots T	2-3
West Essex v Enfield	0-1
Little Oakley v Dunstable T	3-1
Basildon U v Hadley	2-1
Shefford T & Campton v Brantham Ath	0-2
FC Clacton v Leighton T	0-6
Kempston R v Brightlingsea Regent	2-4
Potton U v White Ensign	1-3
Barton R v Saffron Walden T	1-1
Replay: Saffron Walden T v Barton R	2-1
Heybridge Swifts v Wormley R	2-1
Benfleet v Woodford T	3-1
Grays Ath v Hullbridge Sports	5-1
Edgware & Kingsbury v Crawley Green	2-2
Replay: Crawley Green v Edgware & Kingsbury	1-1*
Edgware & Kingsbury won 5-4 on penalties.	
Stanway R v Maldon & Tiptree	0-0
Replay: Maldon & Tiptree v Stanway R	1-2
Tilbury v Buckhurst Hill	4-1
Harpenden T v Halstead T	3-1
Portishead T v Easington Sports	0-1
Tuffley R v Kidlington	0-3
Malmesbury Vic v Slimbridge	1-3
Reading C v Ardley U	3-2
Lydney T v Thornbury T	5-1
Burnham v Corsham T	3-3
Replay: Corsham T v Burnham	2-0
Brislington v Wallingford & Crowmarsh	0-2
Flackwell Heath v Aylesbury Vale Dynamos	0-1
Binfield v Wokingham & Emmbrook	3-1
Longlevens v Winslow U	1-1
Replay: Winslow U v Longlevens	1-3*
1-1 at the end of normal time.	
Cinderford T v Nailsea & Tickenham	1-2
Virginia Water v Brimscombe & Thrupp	4-2
Ascot U v Milton U	1-0
Thame U v Aylesbury U	3-0
Oldland Abbotonians v Amersham T	2-4
Highworth T v Bishop's Cleeve	0-1
Roman Glass St George v North Leigh	2-0
Fairford T v Cirencester T	7-0
Hartpury University v Risborough Rangers	2-0
Yate T v Holyport	2-0
Berks Co v Clevedon T	1-4
Royal Wootton Bassett T v Mangotsfield U	2-1
British Airways v Loxwood	0-0
Replay: Loxwood v British Airways	3-1
Horsham YMCA v Newhaven	5-1
Larkfield & New Hythe v Kennington	2-1
Rayners Lane v Broadfields U	3-1
Littlehampton T v Tooting & Mitcham U	1-0
Cobham v Uxbridge	3-4
Chipstead v Athletic Newham	0-2
Peacehaven & Telscombe v Shoreham	0-2
Hanworth Villa v Knaphill	4-0
Deal T v Roffey	4-0
Epsom & Ewell v Phoenix Sports	0-0
Replay: Phoenix Sports v Epsom & Ewell	1-3
Saltdean U v AFC Varndeanians	3-2
North Greenford U v Corinthian Casuals	1-1
Replay: Corinthian Casuals v North Greenford U	0-1*
0-0 at the end of normal time.	
Steyning T Community v Hilltop	4-0
Merstham v Wick	7-0
Wembley v Bedfont Sports Club	0-2
Abbey Rangers v Hythe T	2-2
Replay: Hythe T v Abbey Rangers	2-3
Punjab U v Snodland T	2-0
Hassocks v Haywards Heath T	2-3
Broadbridge Heath v Horley T	2-1
Badshot Lea v Stansfeld	5-0
Sevenoaks T v Whitstable T	2-1
Fisher v Redhill	2-5
Tunbridge Wells v Farnham T	1-3
Balham v Midhurst & Easebourne	3-1
Holmesdale v Crawley Down Gatwick	0-1
Lordswood v Erith & Belvedere	1-0
Eastbourne T v Little Common	2-0

Ashford U v Egham T	3-0
Bexhill U v Faversham T	0-1
Northwood v Ashford T (Middlesex)	0-2
Spelthorne Sports v Burgess Hill T	0-1
Camberley T v Lydd T	2-1
Sheerwater v Rusthall	1-1
Replay: Rusthall v Sheerwater	4-1
Beckenham T v Harefield U	1-3
Lingfield v Hollands & Blair	1-0
AFC Croydon Ath v Guildford C	3-1
South Park (Reigate) v Sutton Common R	3-1
Corinthian v AFC Whyteleafe	2-0
Sutton Ath v Sandhurst T	1-2
Erith T v Pagham	6-2
Glebe v East Grinstead T	0-2
Metropolitan Police v VCD Ath	1-3
Eastbourne U v Sporting Bengal U	4-0
Crowborough Ath v Bearsted	1-1
Replay: Bearsted v Crowborough Ath	1-2*
1-1 at the end of normal time.	
Tadley Calleva v Millbrook (Hampshire)	2-3
Fareham T v Sherborne T	1-1
Replay: Sherborne T v Fareham T	2-0
AFC Portchester v United Services Portsmouth	5-1
Melksham T v Welton R	3-0
Thatcham T v Christchurch	3-1
Bournemouth v Shaftesbury	0-4
Portland U v Hamworthy Recreation	0-2
Baffins Milton R v Petersfield T	5-0
Hamble Club v Westbury U	0-0
Replay: Westbury U v Hamble Club	1-0
Alton v Fleet T	1-1
Replay: Fleet T v Alton	4-1
Andover New Street v Hythe & Dibden	4-2
Laverstock & Ford v Cowes Sports	1-1
Replay: Cowes Sports v Laverstock & Ford	1-3
Bemerton Heath Harlequins v Brockenhurst	1-1
Replay: Brockenhurst v Bemerton Heath Harlequins	0-1
Hartley Wintney v Downton	3-0
Shepton Mallet v Horndean	1-0
Moneyfields v AFC Stoneham	1-2
Paulton R v Bashley	2-1
Wincanton T v Blackfield & Langley	2-1
Falmouth T v Torpoint Ath	5-0
Exmouth T v Street	1-0
Ilfracombe T v Tavistock	0-2
St Blazey v Ivybridge T	1-3
Barnstaple T v Helston Ath	3-3
Replay: Helston Ath v Barnstaple T	0-2
Brixham v Saltash U	2-0
Willand R v AFC St Austell	2-0
Wellington v Buckland Ath	1-0
Bideford v Bridgwater U	1-0

PRELIMINARY ROUND

Garforth T v Heaton Stannington	1-1
Replay: Heaton Stannington v Garforth T	2-3*
2-2 at the end of normal time.	
Newcastle Blue Star v North Ferriby	1-1
Replay: North Ferriby v Newcastle Blue Star	2-4*
2-2 at the end of normal time.	
Newton Aycliffe v Whitley Bay	3-0
Boro Rangers v Tadcaster Alb	0-1
Blyth T v Birtley T	0-2
Whickham v Dunston UTS	1-1
Replay: Dunston UTS v Whickham	3-0
Kendal T v Newcastle Benfield	1-2
Pontefract Collieries v Redcar Ath	3-0
Penrith v Crook T	2-3
Ashington v Bishop Auckland	1-1
Replay: Bishop Auckland v Ashington	1-2*
1-1 at the end of normal time.	
Longridge T v 1874 Northwich	1-3
Stalybridge Celtic v Widnes	0-1
Runcorn Linnets v Wythenshawe T	2-2
Replay: Wythenshawe T v Runcorn Linnets	3-1
Campion v AFC Liverpool	1-0
Trafford v Emley	0-3
South Liverpool v Witton Alb	1-1
Replay: Witton Alb v South Liverpool	2-1
Silsden v Atherton Collieries	2-0
Hallam v Charnock Richard	2-0

Barnoldswick T v Northwich Vic	1-1
Replay: Northwich Vic v Barnoldswick T	2-4
Clitheroe v Sheffield	2-2
Replay: Sheffield v Clitheroe	3-2
Avro v Bury	1-2
Bootle v City of Liverpool	1-3
Bradford (Park Avenue) v Stocksbridge Park Steels	2-3
Mossley v Eccleshill U	0-0
Replay: Eccleshill U v Mossley	1-3
Golcar U v Thackley	0-1
Glossop North End v West Didsbury & Chorlton	1-2
Whitchurch Alport v Pilkington	3-1
Atherstone T v Kidsgrove Ath	0-6
Rugby T v Stone Old Alleynians	3-0
Hanley T v Stafford Rangers	0-1
Brocton v Coleshill T	0-1
Worcester Raiders v Hednesford T	0-1
Westfields v Newcastle T	1-1
Replay: Newcastle T v Westfields	2-0
Heanor T v Hinckley LR	3-2
Worcester C v Dudley T	1-2
Belper T v Lutterworth T	3-1
Shifnal T v Sutton Coldfield T	1-0
Chasetown v Ashby Ivanhoe	0-1
Hinckley v Malvern T	2-5
Gresley R v Sporting Khalsa	1-1
Replay: Sporting Khalsa v Gresley R	2-0*
0-0 at the end of normal time.	
Darlaston T v Lye T	3-0
AFC Mansfield v Carlton T	1-3
Aylestone Park v Wellingborough T	0-2
Yaxley v Grantham T	1-3
Newark & Sherwood U v AFC Rushden & Diamonds	2-0
Long Eaton U v Boston T	3-2
Cleethorpes T v Quorn	4-0
Bottesford T v Winterton Rangers	3-0
Northampton ON Chenecks v Barton T	2-3
Grimsby Borough v Anstey Nomads	0-5
Goole v Melton T	2-3
Deeping Rangers v Loughborough Students	2-2
Replay: Loughborough Students v Deeping Rangers	4-0
Mulbarton W v Gorleston	1-3
Bury T v Felixstowe & Walton U	2-2
Replay: Felixstowe & Walton U v Bury T	4-0
Stowmarket T v Cornard U	1-5
Soham Town Rangers v Harleston T	2-2
Replay: Harleston T v Soham Town Rangers	4-0
Wroxham v Newmarket T	1-3
Downham T v Ipswich W	1-3
Great Yarmouth T v Cambridge C	2-1
Dereham T v Sheringham	1-3
Tilbury v Stanway R	3-1
White Ensign v Brantham Ath	1-3
St Neots T v Edgware & Kingsbury	3-0
Concord Rangers v Milton Keynes Irish	1-3
Benfleet v Haringey Bor	1-5
Newport Pagnell T v AFC Dunstable	0-1
Leighton T v Waltham Abbey	2-3
Biggleswade U v Enfield	1-2
Biggleswade v London Lions	3-1
Leverstock Green v Heybridge Swifts	1-1
Replay: Heybridge Swifts v Leverstock Green	1-1*
Leverstock Green won 4-3 on penalties.	
Stotfold v Takeley	1-0
Grays Ath v Witham T	1-4
Walthamstow v Saffron Walden T	3-2
Ware v Brentwood T	0-1
Redbridge v Barking	0-1
Harpenden T v FC Romania	1-0
Little Oakley v Berkhamsted	1-4
Basildon U v Kings Langley	1-0
Brightlingsea Regent v Romford	4-0
Royal Wootton Bassett T v Didcot T	0-2
Thame U v Beaconsfield T	5-0
Aylesbury Vale Dynamos v Corsham T	3-2
Cribbs v Roman Glass St George	2-0
Amersham T v Clevedon T	4-1
Wallingford & Crowmarsh v Slimbridge	3-0
Reading C v Nailsea & Tickenham	1-1
Replay: Nailsea & Tickenham v Reading C	1-0
Kidlington v Yate T	0-4

Virginia Water v Ascot U	2-1
Fairford T v Hartpury University	1-5
Longlevens v Binfield	1-9
Bishop's Cleeve v Lydney T	4-0
Easington Sports v Bristol Manor Farm	3-1
Sevenoaks T v Leatherhead	0-2
Steyning T Community v Crawley Down Gatwick	3-1
Ashford T (Middlesex) v Uxbridge	1-1
Replay: Uxbridge v Ashford T (Middlesex)	1-2
Crowborough Ath v South Park (Reigate)	0-1
Harrow Bor v Ashford U	1-1
Replay: Ashford U v Harrow Bor	3-1
Ramsgate v Southall	5-0
Horsham YMCA v Broadbridge Heath	1-3
North Greenford U v Sheppey U	0-3
AFC Croydon Ath v VCD Ath	4-0
Herne Bay v Rayners Lane	2-2
Replay: Rayners Lane v Herne Bay	1-2
Corinthian v Camberley T	3-1
Kingstonian v Eastbourne U	3-2
Margate v Loxwood	4-0
Epsom & Ewell v Hayes & Yeading U	1-3
Harefield U v Sandhurst T	3-0
Lordswood v Shoreham	3-1
Merstham v Erith T	2-1
Saltdean U v Three Bridges	0-0
Replay: Three Bridges v Saltdean U	3-1
Haywards Heath T v Deal T	2-0
Hanworth Villa v Abbey Rangers	4-1
Larkfield & New Hythe v Lingfield	3-1
Littlehampton T v Faversham T	2-3
Farnham T v Sittingbourne	2-4
Bedfont Sports Club v Raynes Park Vale	2-3
Badshot Lea v Balham	4-1
Lancing v Athletic Newham	2-4
Burgess Hill T v Eastbourne T	2-1
Rusthall v Punjab U	1-2
East Grinstead T v Redhill	1-3
Thatcham T v Andover New Street	1-2
Hartley Wintney v Larkhall Ath	0-2
Wincanton T v Fleet T	2-2
Replay: Fleet T v Wincanton T	4-1
Baffins Milton R v Shepton Mallet	2-1
Bemerton Heath Harlequins v Laverstock & Ford	1-3
Hamworthy Recreation v Paulton R	1-2
Shaftesbury v Melksham T	0-0
Replay: Melksham T v Shaftesbury	4-1
Westfield v Sherborne T	3-1
AFC Stoneham v Millbrook (Hampshire)	1-1
Replay: Millbrook (Hampshire) v AFC Stoneham	1-3
The replay on 20 August 2024 was abandoned due	
to floodlight failure after 45 mins with the score 0-1.	
Westbury U v AFC Portchester	1-0
Barnstaple T v Falmouth T	4-1
Mousehole v Willand R	2-2
Replay: Willand R v Mousehole	1-0
Exmouth T v Brixham	0-2
Ivybridge T v Tavistock	0-1
Bideford v Wellington	1-1
Replay: Wellington v Bideford	0-2

FIRST ROUND QUALIFYING

Garforth T v Bury	0-2
Crook T v Ashington	2-1
Guiseley v Ashton U	3-0
Morpeth T v Emley	1-0
West Didsbury & Chorlton v Silsden	4-2
Warrington Rylands v Thackley	4-0
Campion v Blyth Spartans	1-1
Replay: Blyth Spartans v Campion	3-1*
1-1 at the end of normal time.	
Bamber Bridge v Newton Aycliffe	1-1
Replay: Newton Aycliffe v Bamber Bridge	1-1*
Newton Aycliffe won 5-3 on penalties.	
Lancaster C v Barnoldswick T	0-0
Replay: Barnoldswick T v Lancaster C	1-0*
0-0 at the end of normal time.	
Tadcaster Alb v Macclesfield	0-3
1874 Northwich v Stocksbridge Park Steels	3-2
Workington v Hebburn T	0-1
FC United of Manchester v Hyde U	3-3
Replay: Hyde U v FC United of Manchester	1-0

Mossley v Whitby T   2-2
Replay: Whitby T v Mossley   3-3*
  2-2 at the end of normal time; Mossley won 4-3 on penalties.
Witton Alb v City of Liverpool   3-2
Newcastle Benfield v Prescot Cables   2-1
Newcastle Blue Star v Hallam   2-3
Whitchurch Alport v Wythenshawe T   1-1
Replay: Wythenshawe T v Whitchurch Alport   2-1
Birtley T v Dunston UTS   1-5
Stockton T v Widnes   1-0
Sheffield v Pontefract Collieries   5-0
Newcastle T v Long Eaton U   2-1
Belper T v Bromsgrove Sporting   2-2
Replay: Bromsgrove Sporting v Belper T   2-1
Spalding U v Matlock T   0-0
Replay: Matlock T v Spalding U   0-1*
  0-0 at the end of normal time.
Gainsborough Trinity v AFC Telford U   2-1
Basford U v Sporting Khalsa   6-1
Barton T v Rugby T   0-1
Anstey Nomads v Alvechurch   3-1
Melton T v Hednesford T   1-6
Heanor T v Ilkeston T   0-1
Barwell v Kidsgrove Ath   3-0
Dudley T v Stourbridge   0-5
Bottesford T v Loughborough Students   1-0
Harborough T v Darlaston T   0-0
Replay: Darlaston T v Harborough T   2-3
Carlton T v Stamford   1-0
Mickleover v Coleshill T   5-0
Stratford T v Worksop T   2-3
Leek T v Ashby Ivanhoe   2-0
Malvern T v Cleethorpes T   0-1
Wellingborough T v Shifnal T   0-2
Grantham T v Newark & Sherwood U   1-0
Kettering T v Stafford Rangers   2-1
Redditch U v Halesowen T   3-1
Gorleston v Walthamstow   1-0
Tilbury v Brantham Ath   2-2
Replay: Brantham Ath v Tilbury   1-2
Lowestoft T v Potters Bar T   6-2
Leiston v Waltham Abbey   4-1
Basildon U v Biggleswade   0-1
Hitchin T v Berkhamsted   0-2
AFC Dunstable v AFC Sudbury   1-0
Bishop's Stortford v Cornard U   5-0
Hashtag U v Stotfold   2-0
Harleston T v Biggleswade T   1-1
Replay: Biggleswade T v Harleston T   3-1
St Neots T v Barking   2-2
Replay: Barking v St Neots T   3-2*
  2-2 at the end of normal time.
Billericay v Bowers & Pitsea   1-2
Royston T v Bedford T   1-1
Replay: Bedford T v Royston T   0-3
Harpenden T v St Ives T   0-0
Replay: St Ives T v Harpenden T   5-2
Enfield v Brentwood T   0-5
Great Yarmouth T v Cheshunt   1-2
Felixstowe & Walton U v Leverstock Green   5-1
Brightlingsea Regent v Haringey Bor   1-1
Replay: Haringey Bor v Brightlingsea Regent   2-1
Newmarket T v Ipswich W   1-1
Replay: Ipswich W v Newmarket T   0-1
Canvey Island v Milton Keynes Irish   2-1
Witham T v Sheringham   1-0
Burgess Hill T v AFC Croydon Ath   2-1
Harefield U v Lewes   1-1
Replay: Lewes v Harefield U   0-0*
  Harefield U won 4-2 on penalties.
Kingstonian v Chichester C   1-4
Dulwich Hamlet v Leatherhead   2-2
Replay: Leatherhead v Dulwich Hamlet   1-0
Thame v Wingate & Finchley   0-4
Ashford U v Three Bridges   6-1
Ashford T (Middlesex) v Herne Bay   0-2
Horsham v Virginia Water   4-0
Bracknell T v South Park (Reigate)   0-1
Athletic Newham v Amersham T   3-3
Replay: Amersham T v Athletic Newham   1-0

Aylesbury Vale Dynamos v Bognor Regis T   0-3
Hanworth Villa v Walton & Hersham   3-3
Replay: Walton & Hersham v Hanworth Villa   4-2
Sheppey U v Hanwell T   1-1
Replay: Hanwell T v Sheppey U   6-0
Hendon v Whitehawk   3-0
Dartford v Marlow   6-2
Larkfield & New Hythe v Cray W   1-1
Replay: Cray W v Larkfield & New Hythe   8-0
Steyning T Community v Merstham   1-2
Margate v Hayes & Yeading U   0-0
Replay: Hayes & Yeading U v Margate   1-3
Lordswood v Binfield   3-1
Badshot Lea v Cray Valley (PM)   1-3
Hastings U v Redhill   3-1
Sittingbourne v Dover Ath   2-2
Replay: Dover Ath v Sittingbourne   0-1
Ramsgate v Folkestone Invicta   3-1
Carshalton Ath v Haywards Heath T   3-1
Punjab U v Corinthian   0-1
Broadbridge Heath v Faversham T   0-0
Replay: Faversham T v Broadbridge Heath   1-3
Westfield v Chatham T   0-2
Chertsey v Raynes Park Vale   3-2
Willand R v Brixham   1-0
Hartpury University v Nailsea & Tickenham   0-2
Havant & Waterlooville v Wallingford & Crowmarsh   3-0
Easington Sports v Frome T   1-1
Replay: Frome T v Easington Sports   2-1
Plymouth Parkway v Baffins Milton R   4-1
Gloucester C v Paulton R   2-0
Tiverton T v Wimborne T   0-3
Basingstoke T v Sholing   1-3
Fleet T v AFC Stoneham   2-4
Gosport Bor v Andover New Street   4-0
Barnstaple T v Larkhall Ath   1-2
Hungerford T v Yate T   1-0
Bideford v Melksham T   0-1
Banbury U v Dorchester T   2-0
Taunton T v Didcot T   3-0
Westbury U v AFC Totton   3-1
Tavistock v Winchester C   0-1
Merthyr T v Cribbs   3-2
Bishop's Cleeve v Laverstock & Ford   1-1
Replay: Laverstock & Ford v Bishop's Cleeve   1-2
Swindon Supermarine v Poole T   1-1
Replay: Poole T v Swindon Supermarine   2-0

SECOND ROUND QUALIFYING

Dunston UTS v Scarborough Ath   1-1
Replay: Scarborough Ath v Dunston UTS   5-2
Crook T v Witton Alb   1-2
Southport v Hyde U   2-1
Mossley v Chorley   0-3
Stockton T v Marine   3-2
Newcastle Benfield v Wythenshawe T   0-1
Guiseley v 1874 Northwich   3-0
Newton Aycliffe v Warrington Rylands   1-1
Replay: Warrington Rylands v Newton Aycliffe   3-1
Chester v Hebburn T   3-0
Farsley Celtic v Hallam   3-1
Curzon Ashton v Barnoldswick T   6-0
Warrington T v Radcliffe   1-2
Blyth Spartans v Bury   0-3
Spennymoor T v Morpeth T   3-1
Macclesfield v South Shields   5-0
West Didsbury & Chorlton v Darlington   1-2
Newcastle T v Scunthorpe U   1-1
Replay: Scunthorpe U v Newcastle T   5-0
Gainsborough Trinity v Grantham T   2-1
Hereford v Ilkeston T   1-1
Replay: Ilkeston T v Hereford   0-1
Kidderminster H v Leek T   2-1
Kettering T v Cleethorpes T   1-0
Mickleover v Anstey Nomads   0-1
Harborough T v Stourbridge   4-2
Spalding U v Alfreton T   0-0
Replay: Alfreton T v Spalding U   1-1*
  0-0 at the end of normal time; Alfreton T won 4-3 on penalties.
Shifnal T v Redditch U   1-1
Replay: Redditch U v Shifnal T   0-1

Bromsgrove Sporting v Bottesford T	2-0
Buxton v Barwell	2-2
Replay: Barwell v Buxton	1-2
Rushall Olympic v Sheffield	5-0
Leamington v Carlton T	1-0
Rugby T v Hednesford T	2-2
Replay: Hednesford T v Rugby T	4-1
Worksop T v Basford U	6-3
Needham Market v St Albans C	0-3
Lowestoft T v Newmarket T	5-2
Hemel Hempstead T v Bishop's Stortford	0-1
King's Lynn T v Cheshunt	1-0
Canvey Island v Felixstowe & Walton U	2-0
St Ives T v Berkhamsted	5-0
Bowers & Pitsea v Biggleswade T˜	1-2
Tilbury v Chelmsford C	0-2
Haringey Bor v Witham T	1-1
Replay: Witham T v Haringey Bor	1-1*
Haringey Bor won 4-3 on penalties.	
Gorleston v Barking	2-2
Replay: Barking v Gorleston	0-1
Hornchurch v Hashtag U	2-1
Enfield T v Peterborough Sports	0-1
Aveley v Royston T	1-2
Biggleswade v AFC Dunstable	2-1
Brentwood T v Leiston	2-2
Replay: Leiston v Brentwood T	3-1
Ashford U v Corinthian	3-0
Ramsgate v Broadbridge Heath	1-0
Burgess Hill T v Amersham T	2-3
Hanwell T v Chertsey T	0-2
Welling U v Chatham T	0-1
Eastbourne Bor v Boreham Wood	0-1
Carshalton Ath v South Park (Reigate)	1-0
Hastings U v Harefield U	1-0
Lordswood v Sittingbourne	0-1
Tonbridge Angels v Merstham	2-1
Chichester C v Slough T	2-2
Replay: Slough T v Chichester C	2-1
Maidstone U v Hampton & Richmond Bor	2-1
Dartford v Leatherhead	2-0
Worthing v Havant & Waterlooville	3-2
Horsham v Dorking W	1-0
Bognor Regis T v Margate	0-4
Cray Valley (PM) v Chesham U	0-2
Walton & Hersham v Farnborough	2-1
Cray W v Wingate & Finchley	1-1
Replay: Wingate & Finchley v Cray W	0-1
Herne Bay v Hendon	3-0
Poole T v Taunton T	2-3
Frome T v Larkhall Ath	0-1
Wimborne T v Weston-super-Mare	0-2
AFC Stoneham v Salisbury	1-7
Nailsea & Tickenham v Chippenham T	1-6
Truro C v Brackley T	0-2
Oxford C v Willand R	6-0
Bath C v Merthyr T	2-1
Sholing v Weymouth	1-4
Bishop's Cleeve v Torquay U	3-0
Winchester C v Hungerford T	1-1
Replay: Hungerford T v Winchester C	0-1
Plymouth Parkway v Westbury U	4-3
Melksham H v Banbury U	1-1
Replay: Banbury U v Melksham T	2-3
Gosport Bor v Gloucester C	2-2
Replay: Gloucester C v Gosport Bor	0-2

THIRD ROUND QUALIFYING

Guiseley v Scunthorpe U	1-0
Stockton T v Chester	1-1
Replay: Chester v Stockton T	1-0
Radcliffe v Bury	2-3
Southport v Curzon Ashton	0-1
Wythenshawe T v Farsley Celtic	0-1
Darlington v Gainsborough Trinity	1-2
Warrington Rylands v Scarborough Ath	0-2
Spennymoor T v Chorley	1-0
Macclesfield v Witton Alb	6-1
Buxton v Kidderminster H	1-1
Replay: Kidderminster H v Buxton	2-0
Leiston v Hornchurch	1-1

Replay: Hornchurch v Leiston	1-3*
1-1 at the end of normal time.	
Haringey Bor v Lowestoft T	3-3
Replay: Lowestoft T v Haringey Bor	3-1
Shifnal T v Hednesford T	0-0
Replay: Hednesford T v Shifnal T	1-0
Harborough T v Leamington	1-0
Biggleswade T v Alfreton T	0-6
Royston T v Peterborough Sports	0-0
Replay: Peterborough Sports v Royston T	1-0
Biggleswade v Canvey Island	1-0
St Ives T v Kettering T	0-3
Rushall Olympic v Anstey Nomads	2-1
Chelmsford C v Bromsgrove Sporting	2-1
Gorleston v St Albans C	4-2
Bishop's Stortford v Hereford	3-2
Worksop T v King's Lynn T	1-1
Replay: King's Lynn T v Worksop T	0-0*
King's Lynn T won 4-3 on penalties.	
Salisbury v Bath C	1-2
Cray W v Hastings U	3-0
Chertsey T v Ashford U	3-2
Worthing v Dartford	3-1
Winchester C v Weymouth	2-2
Replay: Weymouth v Winchester C	3-0
Margate v Horsham	1-1
Replay: Horsham v Margate	2-0
Tonbridge Angels v Walton & Hersham	2-1
Taunton T v Amersham T	2-1
Sittingbourne v Plymouth Parkway	0-3
Chatham T v Slough T	0-3
Bishop's Cleeve v Chesham U	0-0
Replay: Chesham U v Bishop's Cleeve	4-0
Brackley T v Ramsgate	4-1
Herne Bay v Maidstone U	0-1
Oxford C v Gosport Bor	2-3
Carshalton Ath v Melksham T	3-2
Boreham Wood v Larkhall Ath	2-1
Chippenham T v Weston-super-Mare	1-1
Replay: Weston-super-Mare v Chippenham T	1-0

FOURTH ROUND QUALIFYING

Rushall Olympic v Peterborough Sports	1-1
Replay: Peterborough Sports v Rushall Olympic	0-0*
Rushall Olympic won 5-4 on penalties.	
Tamworth v Macclesfield	4-2
Oldham Ath v FC Halifax T	4-2
Hartlepool U v Brackley T	1-1
Replay: Brackley T v Hartlepool U	3-1
Farsley Celtic v Kettering T	1-2
Altrincham v Solihull Moors	1-1
Replay: Solihull Moors v Altrincham	2-2*
Solihull Moors won 3-1 on penalties.	
AFC Fylde v Rochdale	1-4
Scarborough Ath v Chester	3-1
Biggleswade v York C	1-3
Harborough T v Bury	1-0
Curzon Ashton v King's Lynn T	1-0
Gainsborough Trinity v Boston U	2-2
Replay: Boston U v Gainsborough Trinity	0-4
Hednesford T v Gateshead	1-1
Replay: Gateshead v Hednesford T	1-3
Alfreton T v Spennymoor T	1-0
Kidderminster H v Guiseley	0-1
Taunton T v Maidenhead U	1-1
Replay: Maidenhead U v Taunton T	3-0
Horsham v Gorleston	1-0
Aldershot T v Bath C	2-1
Eastleigh v Southend U	0-1
Chertsey T v Sutton U	1-3
Boreham Wood v Carshalton Ath	4-0
Lowestoft T v Weston-super-Mare	1-3
Wealdstone v Gosport Bor	4-1
Leiston v Dagenham & Red	1-5
Barnet v Chelmsford C	4-0
Chesham U v Yeovil T	1-0
Cray W v Tonbridge Angels	0-1
Woking v Slough T	2-1
Forest Green R v Weymouth	2-0
Maidstone U v Ebbsfleet U	3-0
Plymouth Parkway v Worthing	0-4
Braintree T v Bishop's Stortford	1-0

THE EMIRATES FA CUP 2024–25

COMPETITION PROPER

■ *Denotes player sent off.*

FIRST ROUND
Friday, 1 November 2024

Notts Co (1) 5 *(Platt 16, Jatta 48, 62, Brown 85 (pen), 90)*
Alfreton T (1) 1 *(Waldock 14)* 6658
Notts Co: (343) Bass; Ness (Cundy 81), Bedeau, Platt (McDonald 68); Abbott, Palmer, Hinchy, Gordon; Brown (Muir 90), Jatta (Reynolds 81), Martin (Cisse 68).
Alfreton T: (433) Willis; Clackstone, Hunt, Wiley (Anson 82), Newall; Cantrill, Lund (Perritt 68), Waldock; Whitehouse (Fewster 76), Day, Abbey (Salmon 68).
Referee: Scott Simpson.

Tamworth (1) 1 *(Maxwell 44 (og))*
Huddersfield T (0) 0 3533
Tamworth: (4411) Singh; Browne, Cullinane-Liburd, Hollis, Fairlamb; Finn (Enoru 76), Tonks, Milnes (Wallace 83), McLinchey; Tshikuna (Fletcher 90); Creaney.
Huddersfield T: (3142) Maxwell; Lees, Lonwijk, Pearson, Kasumu; Turton, Iorpenda (Kane 66), Wiles, Headley (Miller 66); Radulovic (Ladapo 84), Ward (Marshall 46).
Referee: Ben Speedie.

Saturday, 2 November 2024

Barrow (0) 0
Doncaster R (0) 1 *(Kelly 83)* 2605
Barrow: (4231) Stanway; Eccleston, Vassell, Canavan, Jackson; Foley (Popov 78), Campbell; Mahoney (Kirk 63), Gotts, Kouyate (Newby 56); Garner (Telford 78).
Doncaster R: (3421) Sharman-Lowe; McGrath, Olowu, Senior (Kelly 46); Sterry (Clifton 25), Bailey, Broadbent, Maxwell (Fleming 52); Molyneux, Hurst (Gibson 76); Sharp (Ironside 76).
Referee: Dale Baines.

Brackley T (0) 0
Braintree T (0) 0 1121
Brackley T: (4312) Maxted; Lyttle, Dean (Craig 15), Lilly, Carline; Lowe, Bates, Byrne; Roberts (O'Sullivan 119); Hall (Pollock 60 (Abbey 72)), Newton.
Braintree T: (4231) Lucas Covolan; Annesley (Powell 94), Langston, Terry, Clampin (Fyfield 83); Vennings, Robinson; Francis, Wilkinson (Blackwell 46), Cooper (Lisbie 73); Effiong (Akinde 68).
aet; Brackley T won 5-4 on penalties.
Referee: Stuart Morland.

Bradford C (0) 3 *(Oliver 50, Maghoma 65 (og), Kavanagh 68)*
Aldershot T (1) 1 *(Barham 32)* 4737
Bradford C: (352) Walker S; Halliday, Byrne, Shepherd; Benn (Diabate 72), Evans (Walker J 72), Smallwood, Kavanagh, Richards; Oliver (Cook 72), Sanderson (Pointon 73).
Aldershot T: (532) Dewhurst; Jones A, Menayese, Maghoma, Ellison, Scott (Henry 79); Frost (Jones R 84), Widdrington (Tetek 79), Hargreaves (Barham Mullins 87), Barrett (Ghandour 79).
Referee: Craig Hicks.

Bristol R (1) 3 *(Lindsay 42, Taylor 95, Ward G 120)*
Weston-super-Mare (0) 1 *(Bastin 64)* 6898
Bristol R: (4231) Griffiths; Hunt (Forbes 65), Taylor, Moore, Mola; Lindsay (Ward G 78), Sinclair (McCormick 79); Sotiriou (Thomas 73), Martin (Akono Bilongo 79).
Weston-super-Mare: (451) Harris; Thomas, Avery, Lewis (Chamberlain 38 (Bak 109)), Kirkman (Rose 106); Coulson, Kadji, Pope, Dodd, Bastin (McCootie 65); Reid.
aet.
Referee: Ollie Yates.

Burton Alb (0) 1 *(Kalinauskas 69)*
Scarborough Ath (0) 0 3066
Burton Alb: (3412) Isted; Akoto (Godwin-Malife 54), Sweeney, Vancooten; Whitfield, Watt, Bran (Kalinauskas 54); Webster; Cooper-Love, Donovan (Orsi-Dadomo 65).
Scarborough Ath: (3511) Whitley; Maltby, Thornton, Gooda (Glynn 78); Weledji, Purver (Wilson 85), Wiles (Mulhern 78), Colville (Green 71), Brown; Tear; Bennett (Maloney 78).
Referee: Simon Mather.

Carlisle U (0) 0
Wigan Ath (0) 2 *(Smith S 105, Smith J 120)* 4532
Carlisle U: (541) Breeze; Burey (Ellis 59), Thomas (Barclay 111), Lavelle, Hayden (Robinson 75), Mellish; Sadi, Neal, Robson■, Charters (Harper 75); Adu-Adjei (Armstrong 59).
Wigan Ath: (4141) Tickle; Sessegnon (Ramsay 46), Kerr, Sibbick, Robinson L (Smith S 57); Smith M; Francois, Rankine (Smith J 46), Aasgaard, Olakigbe (Thomas 46); Taylor (Hugill 75).
aet.
Referee: Martin Woods.

Chesterfield (1) 3 *(Grigg 6, 49, Dobra 65)*
Horsham (0) 1 *(Dickson 85)* 4887
Chesterfield: (4231) Thompson; Tanton (Mandeville 57), Naylor, Araujo, Gordon; Metcalfe, Oldaker (Fleck 72); Jacobs, Dobra (Banks 72), Berry-McNally (Colclough 57); Grigg (Madden 57).
Horsham: (433) Carey; Philpott, Strange, Barker (Ogunwamide 62), Sparks; Hammond, Hester-Cook (Daly 71), Brivio; Meekums (Ajakaiye 62), Fenelon (Dickson 54), Harding (Rodrigues 71).
Referee: Martin Coy.

Crewe Alex (0) 0
Dagenham & Red (0) 1 *(Pereira 73 (pen))* 3123
Crewe Alex: (532) Marschall; Billington, Knight-Lebel, Demetriou, Connolly, Conway (Holicek 61); Lunt, Sanders (Williams 61), Tabiner (Breckin 63); Tracey (Bogle 61), Thibaut (Long 81).
Dagenham & Red: (4231) Justham; Rutherford, Eastman, Crichlow-Noble, Woodhouse; Phipps, N'Guessan; Pereira, Morias, Hill; Umerah (Vincent 86).
Referee: John Mulligan.

Exeter C (1) 5 *(Magennis 13, 76 (pen), 85 (pen), Bird 90, Doyle 90)*
Barnet (1) 3 *(Glover 39, Brunt 59, Kabamba 78)* 4244
Exeter C: (3412) Whitworth; Sweeney, Crama, Purrington (Mitchell 73); McMillan, Cole (Francis 63), Woods (Fitzwater 90), Niskanen; Aitchison (Doyle 63); Alli (Bird 73), Magennis.
Barnet: (343) Hayes; Rye (Collinge 46), Oluwo, Kenlock; Kanu, Hobson, Hartigan, Coker (Grimwood 90); Brunt (Cropper 86), Kabamba, Glover (Okimo 90).
Referee: Lee Swabey.

Gillingham (0) 0
Blackpool (1) 2 *(Carey 38, 90)* 4403
Gillingham: (4231) Morris; Hutton, Ehmer, Masterson (Wyllie 79), Ogie; Williams E, Little; Nolan (Andrews 90), Dieng (Gbode 70), Clarke; Wakeling.
Blackpool: (442) O'Donnell; Offiah, Lawrence-Gabriel, Casey, Coulson; Finnigan (Onomah 90), Evans, Carey, Embleton (Pennington 84); Joseph (Beesley 70), Ballard (Rhodes 70).
Referee: Carl Brook.

Grimsby T (0) 0
Wealdstone (0) 1 *(Reid 90)*   3174
Grimsby T: (442) Wright; Cass (Luker 90), Rodgers, McJannet, Hume; Khouri, McEachran (Ainley 72), Green (Barrington 64), Svanthorsson (Warren 64); Obikwu (Gardner 72), Rose.
Wealdstone: (442) Howes; Cook, Mariappa, Mundle-Smith, Boldewijn (Obiero 85); Cesay, Scott (Wells-Morrison 46), Georgiou, Kretzschmar (Adarkwa 69); Ashford, Reid.
Referee: James Westgate.

Hednesford T (2) 4 *(Duku 4, Holness 21, McHale 49, 95)*
Gainsborough Trinity (0) 4 *(Howe 65, 77, Lancaster 90, Clarke 109)*   3866
Hednesford T: (442) Rose; Roberts, Endall (Rowe 91), Johnson, Taylor; Trickett-Smith (Gwilt 89), Maye (Spence 66), Holness, Bearne; McHale (Sparkes 106), Duku (Stevenson 72).
Gainsborough Trinity: (433) Wharton; Simpson (Tuntulawana 46), Lancaster, Cogill, Jackson (McLoughlin 119); Preston, Conway (Johnson 46), Helliwell; Clarke, Howe (Hornshaw 106), Butroid (Stacey 46).
aet; Gainsborough Trinity won 5-4 on penalties.
Referee: Jason Richardson.

Maidenhead U (0) 1 *(McCoulsky 64)*
Crawley T (0) 2 *(Mullarkey 90, Showunmi 116)*   1814
Maidenhead U: (4141) Ross; Welch-Hayes, De Havilland, Lokko, Latty-Fairweather; Golding (Cochrane 91); Smith (Sho-Silva 117), Pettit, Ferguson, Barratt (Carvalho 58); McCoulsky (Abrahams 91).
Crawley T: (343) Wollacott (Sheik 72); Tanimu (Ibrahim 71), Mukena, Mullarkey; Hepburn-Murphy, Camara (Swan 71), Bragg (Forster 82), Kelly (Adeyemo 60); Roles, Showunmi, Holohan (Anderson 115).
aet.
Referee: Stephen Parkinson.

Newport Co (2) 2 *(Driscoll-Glennon 5, Whitmore 7)*
Peterborough U (1) 4 *(Odoh 27, Randall 71, Jones 89, 90)*
                                                  2941
Newport Co: (352) Townsend; Baker, Brennan, Jameson; Evans C, Whitmore (Jephcott 74), Miley, Evans K, Driscoll-Glennon; Hudlin, Baker-Richardson (Kamwa 65).
Peterborough U: (4231) Bilokapic; Dornelly, Fernandez, Nevett, Sparkes; Collins, De Havilland (O'Brien-Brady 86); Odoh, Randall, Poku; Mothersille (Jones 63).
Referee: Stephen Martin.

Northampton T (1) 1 *(Johnson 28 (og))*
Kettering T (0) 2 *(Millar 66, Ranger 92)*   7104
Northampton T: (4231) Tzanev; Odimayo (Eyoma 91), Baldwin, Guthrie, Guinness-Walker (Magloire 71); Fox, Chouchane (Sowerby 71); Pinnock, McGeehan, Fosu (Waghorn 83); McCarron (Hondermarck 71).
Kettering T: (4411) Jezeph; Hart, White, Johnson, Powell; Wilson (York 89), Thanoj (Stohrer 79), Kelly-Evans, Andrade (Hooper 61); Williams (Millar 62); Ranger (Sordell 97).
aet.
Referee: Elliot Bell.

Port Vale (1) 1 *(Curtis 31)*
Barnsley (1) 3 *(Roberts 17, Keillor-Dunn 64, Phillips 82 (pen))*   5128
Port Vale: (343) Ripley; Debrah, Hall, Heneghan; Cover, Lowe, Sang, Grant (Shorrock 62); Baker-Boaitey (Richards 62), Paton (Stockley 71), Curtis (Hackford 71).
Barnsley: (3412) Killip; Durand de Gevigney, Earl, Roberts; O'Keeffe, Russell, Connell, Gent; Keillor-Dunn; Humphrys, Watters (Phillips 58).
Referee: Charles Breakspear.

Reading (0) 2 *(Bindon 48, Odubeko 86 (og))*
Fleetwood T (0) 0   3685
Reading: (433) Button; Ahmed (Craig 78), Holzman, Bindon (Mbengue 63), Rushesha; Elliott, Spencer (Knibbs 78), Savage; Camara (Akande 63), Wareham, Campbell (Tuma 85).
Fleetwood T: (3142) Harrington; Bonds, Potter, Hughes; Virtue (Shaw 75); Johnston (Broom 76), Helm (Lonergan 76), Mayor, Patterson; Coughlan (Odubeko 75), Graydon (Harratt 75).
Referee: Paul Howard.

Rochdale (1) 3 *(Beckwith 24, Webster 52 (og), Henderson 80)*
Bromley (2) 4 *(Whitely 1, 90, Cheek 3, Amantchi 90)* 2329
Rochdale: (343) Robson; Gordon, Hogan (Senior 90), Beckwith; Allarakhia, East, Burger (Barlow 90), Buyabu; McBride (Ferguson 86), Mitchell, Dennis (Henderson 55).
Bromley: (343) Smith; Sowunmi (Reynolds 68), Webster (Amantchi 86), Odutayo; Imray■, Thompson (Leigh 81), Arthurs (Congreve 69); Grant; Cheek, Whitely, Dennis (Olomola 81).
Referee: Aaron Bannister.

Rotherham U (1) 1 *(Wilks 37)*
Cheltenham T (2) 3 *(Colwill 36, 45, Archer 58)* 2770
Rotherham U: (433) Dawson; Rafferty (MacDonald 70), Humphreys, Jules, Bramall; Odofin, Tiehi (Nombe 46), Powell (Kelly 69); Holmes (Hungbo 70), Hugill, Wilks (Hatton 73).
Cheltenham T: (4231) Day; Payne, Stubbs, Bennett, Bradbury; Kinsella, Young; Thomas (Jude-Boyd 69), Colwill (Pett 87), Archer; Miller (Taylor 87).
Referee: Adam Herczeg.

Rushall Olympic (0) 0
Accrington S (0) 2 *(Woods J 73, Walton 82)* 1311
Rushall Olympic: (4231) White; McDonald (Charles 85), Cameron, Fairnie, McAlinden (Rees 85); McGlinchey, Mantom (King 85); Heard (McDonagh 61), Martin, Pennant (Arlott-John 72); Benbow■.
Accrington S: (3412) Crellin; Aljofree, Rawson, Awe; Love, Coyle, Khumbeni (Hunter 87), Batty; Whalley (Conneely 87); Costelloe (Woods J 43), Walton (Knowles 90).
Referee: Steven Copeland.

Salford C (2) 2 *(Lund 5, 42)*
Shrewsbury T (1) 1 *(Marquis 15)*   2374
Salford C: (3412) Young; Austerfield (Heys 90), Tilt, Mnoga; Garbutt, Ashley (Fornah 69), N'Mai, Shephard; Lund; Malcolm (Okoronkwo 69), Kouassi.
Shrewsbury T: (343) Savin; Hoole (Bloxham 63), Feeney J, Benning; Winchester, Ojo, O'Reilly (Castledine 63), Sagoe Junior (Gilliead 46); Marquis, Lloyd (Shipley 80), Nsiala.
Referee: Leigh Doughty.

Solihull Moors (0) 3 *(Clarke 49, Stevens 88 (pen), Wilkinson 90)*
Maidstone U (0) 0   1682
Solihull Moors: (442) Walker; Oakley, Clarke, Whitmore, Howell (Newton 69); Gale (Stevenson 80), Osborne, Bowen, Stevens (Tipton 90); Adu-Poku, Wilkinson.
Maidstone U: (4231) Andre Jr; Fowler, Eweka, Greenidge, Brookes (Lodovica 78); Corne, Trusty (Gurung 87); Seaman, Fonkeu (Bentley 62), Papadopoulos (Krasniqi 78); Blair.
Referee: Richie Watkins.

Southend U (1) 3 *(Bridge 45 (pen), Coker 52, Gillesphey 90 (og))*
Charlton Ath (2) 4 *(Leaburn 9, Mitchell Z 40, Godden 66, Ahadme 120)*   8875
Southend U: (352) Andeng-Ndi; Taylor, Crowther, Ralph; Scott-Morriss, Coker (Moncur 78), Morton (Miley 68), Husin (Appiah-Forson 100), Bridge; Bonne (Waldron 90), Ralph (Walker 67).
Charlton Ath: (4222) Mannion; Mitchell Z, Mitchell A, Gillesphey, Edwards; Coventry (Small 55), Taylor (Docherty 89); Berry (Anderson 89), Campbell A (Ahadme 117); Godden, Leaburn (Hylton 83).
aet. Referee: Darren Drysdale.

Stevenage (0) 1 *(Reid 53)*
Guiseley (0) 1 *(Longbottom 83)*   2224
Stevenage: (41212) Cooper; Freeman, Smith, Freestone, Butler; King (List 104); Roberts, White; Kemp; Reid, Pressley (Young 60).
Guiseley: (4231) Cracknell; Brown, Lawlor, Mbeka, Ridehalgh; Moke (Bentley 120), Ekpolo; Lufudu (Ible 109), Johnson (Ackroyd 99), Longbottom; Farrell (Emmett 33).
aet; Stevenage won 5-4 on penalties.
Referee: Oliver Mackey.

Stockport Co (0) 2 *(Horsfall 64, Wootton 97)*
Forest Green R (0) 1 *(Doidge 82)*   4624
Stockport Co: (3412) Hinchliffe; Onyango (Wootton 76), Hughes, Horsfall; Diamond (Touray 77), Norwood (Southam-Hales 67), Fevrier, Adaramola (Rydel 67); Bailey; Mellon (Bate 32), Olaofe.
Forest Green R: (433) Searle; Long (Jenks 116), Tozer (Cardwell 70), Moore-Taylor, Robson; McCann, Bunker, May; McAllister (Omotoye 120), Quigley (Doidge 81), Knowles (Lavinier 119).
aet. Referee: Scott Tallis.

Swindon T (0) 2 *(McGregor 83, Tshimanga 106)*
Colchester U (0) 1 *(Anderson 64)*   4855
Swindon T: (3412) Bycroft, Sobowale (McGregor 82), Minturn, Wright; Tshimanga, Clarke (Cotterill 72), Kilkenny (Butterworth 72), Cox; Freckleton (Ofoborh 46); Smith, Drinan (McGurk 72).
Colchester U: (4231) Macey; Hunt (Sandah 113), Read, Donnelly, Iandolo; Payne, McDonnell (Woodyard 65); Anderson (Egbo 78), Flanagan, Gordon (Scully 78); Taylor (Hopper 69).
aet. Referee: Scott Jackson.

Tonbridge Angels (0) 1 *(Shields 90)*
Harborough T (1) 4 *(Malone 41, Stephens 60, 72, Forbes 87)*   3132
Tonbridge Angels: (3421) Rowley; Nelson, Fielding, Bakrin (Dabre 73); Lema (Hinds 46), Maloney (Wagstaff 66), Hanson, Vincent; Adigun (Robinson 46), Shields; Leighton.
Harborough T: (3412) Taylor; Williams, Malone, Morris; Cooper, Robinson (Forbes 74), Kennedy (Mulligan 90), Walsh; Stephens (Daire 81); O'Sullivan (Tonga 90), Starkie (Sandhu 90).
Referee: Ross Martin.

Tranmere R (1) 1 *(Jennings 9)*
Oldham Ath (1) 2 *(Norwood 39, Uchegbulam 61)*   6464
Tranmere R: (442) McGee; Norman, Davies, Turnbull, Wood (Hawkes 90); Morris (Dennis 90), Finley, Hendry, Patrick; Jennings, Norris (Saunders 62).
Oldham Ath: (343) Hudson; Ogle, Raglan, Clucas (Uchegbulam 58); Caprice, Payne, Conlon, Kitching; Lundstram (Hammond 87), Norwood (Fondop-Talom 88), Drummond (Khan 76).
Referee: Declan Bourne.

Walsall (0) 2 *(Gordon L 59, Jellis 90)*
Bolton W (0) 1 *(Sheehan 55)*   6684
Walsall: (352) Simkin; Okagbue, Williams (Daniels 78), Allen; Barrett, Jellis, Stirk (Lakin 30), Earing (Hall 79), Gordon L; Lowe, Adomah (Matt 86).
Bolton W: (532) Southwood; Williams, Dacres-Cogley, Forrester, Johnston, Schon; Sheehan, Arfield (McAtee 68), Matete; Lolos (Collins 68), Charles (Adeboyejo 75).
Referee: Ruebyn Ricardo.

Woking (0) 0
Cambridge U (0) 1 *(Brophy 73)*   3105
Woking: (451) Jaaskelainen; Kelly-Evans (Stretton 84), Odusina, Dyche, Chicksen; Moss, Andrews, Beautyman, Akinola (Gorman 78), Lewis (Conte 22 (Ward 84)); Moore (Kendall 84).
Cambridge U: (343) Reyes; Okedina (Andrew 46), Morrison, Gibbons; Bennett, Digby (Cousins 83), Smith, Brophy; Kachunga (Watts 83), N'Lundulu (Njoku 87), KaiKai.
Referee: Jamie O'Connor.

Worthing (0) 0
Morecambe (0) 2 *(Slew 7, Williams 88)*   3110
Worthing: (3421) Haigh; Cook, Young (Black 82), Beard; Colbran, Rea (Smith 86), Wadham, Wheeler; Spong, Willard (Babalola 74); Cashman.
Morecambe: (4231) Moore; Hendrie, Williams, Stott, Lewis A; White (Harrack 81), Jones; Tollitt (Millen 90), Macadam (Lewis P 70), Slew (Edwards 70); Dackers (Hope 70).
Referee: Sam Mulhall.

Wycombe W (2) 3 *(Leahy 14 (pen), 57, Kodua 21)*
York C (1) 2 *(Sinclair 31, Felix 90)*   2765
Wycombe W: (442) George; Scowen (Humphreys 54), Hartridge, Butcher, Leahy; Bakinson, Kodua (Wheeler 67), Kone (Udoh 54), Skura; Lubala (Hanlan 82), Pattenden (McCarthy 82).
York C: (442) Male; Fallowfield, Howe, Sinclair, Hunt; Pearce, Nathaniel-George (Crookes 72), Aguiar (Armstrong 72); Felix; Walcott, Thomas (Akinyemi 60).
Referee: Tom Reeves.

Sunday, 3 November 2024

Boreham Wood (0) 2 *(Marsh 69, O'Connell 85)*
Leyton Orient (1) 2 *(Perkins 12, Agyei 49)*   2101
Boreham Wood: (3412) Ashmore; Agbontohoma, Bush, Ilesanmi; Richardson (Hare 115), Whelan, Payne (O'Connell 40), Sousa (Clayden 110); Marsh (Sagaf 80); Appiah, Ndlovu (Dixon 80).
Leyton Orient: (4231) Keeley; Cooper (Brown 66), Beckles, Simpson (Happe 87), Sweeney■; Ball (Pratley 109), Galbraith; Perkins (Jaiyesimi 72), Donley (Obiero 65), O'Neill; Agyei (Kelman 72).
aet; Leyton Orient won 3-1 on penalties.
Referee: James Durkin.

Curzon Ashton (0) 0
Mansfield T (2) 4 *(Akins 16 (pen), Quinn S 30, Waine 73, Quinn B 86)*   2553
Curzon Ashton: (4231) Jones; Richards, Poscha■, Matthews, Hayhurst; Sinclair (Tetlow 90), Barton; Buckley-Rickett (Worrall 63), Afuye (Lacey 63), Mols (Mahon 63); Spencer (Sobowale 78).
Mansfield T: (352) Pym; Flint, Kilgour, Oshilaja; Quinn S (McLaughlin 74), Hewitt (Bowery 46), Reed (Quinn B 70), Maris (Lewis 46), Blake-Tracy; Evans (Waine 61), Akins.
Referee: Thomas Parsons.

Harrogate T (1) 1 *(Muldoon 24)*
Wrexham (0) 0   3893
Harrogate T: (4411) Belshaw; Asare, O'Connor, Moon, Foulds; Taylor, Cornelius, Dooley, Duke-Mckenna (Daly J 69); March (Folarin 69); Muldoon (Sutton 86).
Wrexham: (532) Okonkwo; Barnett, Cleworth, O'Connell, O'Connor (Faal 75), Revan (McClean 59); Cannon, Dobson, Rathbone (Lee 59); Mullin, Palmer (Bodvarsson 59).
Referee: Ed Duckworth.

Milton Keynes D (0) 0
AFC Wimbledon (1) 2 *(Stevens 44, Bugiel 51)*   10,419
Milton Keynes D: (343) MacGillivray; Sherring, Offord, Lewington; Nemane, Lemonheigh-Evans■, Thompson-Sommers (Williams M 85), Tomlinson (Harrison 57); Leigh (Wearne 58), Hogan (Hendry 85), Gilbey.
AFC Wimbledon: (352) Goodman; Lewis, Ball (Harbottle 54), Johnson; Neufville, Maycock, Smith, Hippolyte, Tilley; Stevens (Kelly 88), Bugiel (Pigott 87).
Referee: Matthew Corlett.

Sutton U (0) 0
Birmingham C (1) 1 *(Willumsson 34)*   4804
Sutton U: (4321) Sims; Coley, French, Kirk, Sivi (Rush 75); Barbrook, Odelusi, Waller; Harris, Vaz (De Silva 61); Davies (Nadesan 50).
Birmingham C: (4231) Allsop; Laird (Sampsted 79), Klarer, Davies, Cochrane; Iwata, Paik; Willumsson, Harris (May 66), Anderson (Yokoyama 66); Stansfield (Jutkiewicz 79).
Referee: Ben Atkinson.

Monday, 4 November 2024

Chesham U (0) 0

Lincoln C (1) 4 *(Moylan 44, Makama 49, McGrandles 65, Adebiyi 87 (og))* 3963

Chesham U: (343) Goode; Stevens (Brown 80), Cawley, Adebiyi; Rolfe (Jones 61), Lodge, Gallimore (Upward 79), Lafleur; Weiss, Minhas (Grant 80), Esan (Rowe 61).
Lincoln C: (3142) Wickens; Darikwa, O'Connor, Roughan; McGrandles (Hamilton 69); Ring, McKiernan, Moylan (Earley 80), Hackett (Jefferies 76); Draper (Okoro 80), Makama (Cadamarteri 69).
Referee: Alex Chilowicz.

SECOND ROUND

Friday, 29 November 2024

Harrogate T (0) 1 *(Cornelius 57)*

Gainsborough Trinity (0) 0 4010

Harrogate T: (442) Belshaw; Sims, O'Connor, Moon, Asare; Duke-Mckenna, Dooley (Falkingham 54), Cornelius, Daly J; March (Folarin 76), Muldoon (Burrell 86).
Gainsborough Trinity: (442) Wharton; Tuntulawana (Simpson 82), Lancaster, Cogill, Jackson; Preston, Johnson, Helliwell, Stacey (Butroid 72); Clarke, Howe.
Referee: Farai Hallam.

Saturday, 30 November 2024

Accrington S (1) 2 *(Walton 17, 90)*

Swindon T (1) 2 *(Hall 45, Cotterill 70)* 1534

Accrington S: (3412) Crellin; Aljofree, Love, Awe; O'Brien (Hunter 78), Coyle (Conneely 90), Khumbeni, Woods B; Costelloe (Popoola 98); Walton (Knowles 111), Woods J (Henderson 78).
Swindon T: (343) Bycroft; Wright, Hall (Minturn 91), Delaney (McGregor 91); Sobowale, Tshimanga (Cotterill 45), Kilkenny, Cox (Longelo 91); Drinan, Smith (Glatzel 96), Butterworth■.
aet; Accrington S won 4-1 on penalties.
Referee: Geoff Eltringham.

AFC Wimbledon (1) 1 *(Stevens 45)*

Dagenham & Red (1) 2 *(Morias 35, Rees 79)* 5907

AFC Wimbledon: (352) Goodman; Harbottle (Kelly 87), Ball (Pigott 78), Johnson; Neufville, Tilley, Smith, Ogundere, Furlong (Biler 76); Stevens, Bugiel.
Dagenham & Red: (4231) Justham; Rutherford, Kalambayi, Crichlow-Noble, Woodhouse; Phipps (Hessenthaler 67), N'Guessan; Pereira (Rendall 90), Morias (Rees 67), Hill; Umerah.
Referee: Craig Hicks.

Barnsley (0) 0

Bristol R (0) 0 4801

Barnsley: (352) Killip; Durand de Gevigney, Roberts, Earl; O'Keeffe (Lofthouse 80), Phillips, Nwakali (Russell 67), Connell, Gent (Cotter 85); Humphrys (Cosgrove 91), Keillor-Dunn (Jalo 68).
Bristol R: (4231) Griffiths; Senior (Wilson 46), Moore, Forbes, Mola; Lindsay (Ward G 66), Conteh (Sinclair 116); Forde, McCormick, Hutchinson (Sotiriou 60); O'Donkor (Martin 60).
aet; Bristol R won 4-3 on penalties.
Referee: Scott Oldham.

Cambridge U (0) 1 *(Njoku 77)*

Wigan Ath (0) 2 *(Aasgaard 85, Smith J 119)* 3830

Cambridge U: (442) Bennett, Ibsen Rossi (Longelo 106), Watts, Andrew; KaiKai (Smith 36), Brophy, Cousins (Morrison 46), Kachunga; N'Lundulu (Njoku 74), Loft (Lavery 46).
Wigan Ath: (4141) Tickle; Sibbick, Kerr, Aimson, Sessegnon (Robinson L 73); Smith S (Smith M 73), Rankine (Smith J 56), Adeeko (McManaman 81), Aasgaard, Thomas (Asamoah 56); Taylor.
aet. Referee: Zac Kennard-Kettle.

Crawley T (2) 3 *(Roles 10, Showunmi 13, Kelly 82)*

Lincoln C (2) 4 *(O'Connor 19, Makama 39, Ring 47, Moylan 48)* 2831

Crawley T: (3421) Beach; Mullarkey, Mukena, Barker; Adeyemo (Khaleel 80), Ibrahim, Tanimu (Anderson 46), Kelly; John-Jules (Holohan 46), Roles; Showunmi (Fish 70).

Lincoln C: (3142) Wickens; Darikwa, O'Connor (Jackson 79), Roughan; Erhahon; Ring (Jefferies 84), Moylan (McKiernan 79), Montsma, Hamilton; Draper (Cadamarteri 70), Makama (Hackett 71).
Referee: Sunny Gill.

Exeter C (1) 2 *(Crama 45, Magennis 69)*

Chesterfield (0) 0 4782

Exeter C: (3412) Whitworth; McMillan (McDonald 83), Crama, Francis; Sweeney, Richards J (Doyle 70), Woods, Niskanen (Harper 78); Aitchison (Cox 82); Alli, Magennis (Bird 78).
Chesterfield: (433) Thompson; Sheckelford (Jessop 72), Grimes, Williams, Horton (Gordon 72); Oldaker, Naylor (Banks 46), Jacobs (Dobra 34); Colclough, Grigg, Berry-McNally (Mandeville 66).
Referee: Jacob Miles.

Leyton Orient (0) 2 *(Keeley 90, Agyei 120)*

Oldham Ath (0) 1 *(Monthe 47)* 6078

Leyton Orient: (4231) Keeley; Ball, Simpson, Cooper (Beckles 59), James; Pratley (Brown 83), Jaiyesimi (Perkins 59); Galbraith (Sweeney 46), Agyei, O'Neill; Kelman (Donley 72).
Oldham Ath: (352) Hudson; Ogle, Raglan, Monthe; Kitching, Gardner (Kay 81), Lundstram (Khan 86 (Uchegbulam 105)), Conlon, Caprice (Garner 105); Norwood, Fondop-Talom (Drummond 90).
aet. Referee: Alan Young.

Morecambe (0) 1 *(Slew 81)*

Bradford C (0) 0 3101

Morecambe: (4231) Burgoyne; Hendrie, Williams, Stott, Lewis A; Songo'o, White; Tollitt, Macadam (Lewis P 85), Slew; Hope (Dackers 55).
Bradford C: (352) Walker S; Byrne■, Huntington, Shepherd; Benn, Walker J (Pattison 71), Smallwood (Oliver 87), Pointon (Oduor 71), Halliday (Richards 87); Sanderson (Kavanagh 71), Cook.
Referee: Sebastian Stockbridge.

Peterborough U (1) 4 *(Jones 10, 73, Randall 77, Odoh 87)*

Notts Co (2) 3 *(Scott 13, Platt 16, Abbott 90)* 6310

Peterborough U: (4231) Bilokapic; Katongo (Sparkes 71), Fernandez (Nevett 46), Wallin, Curtis; De Havilland, Collins; Poku (Conn-Clarke 46), Mothersille (Odoh 71), Randall (Hayes 90); Jones.
Notts Co: (3421) Bass; Macari (Ness 65), Platt, Bedeau; Tsaroulla (Austin 65), Hinchy (McDonald 75), Palmer, Gordon; Abbott, Jatta (Brown 66); Scott (Martin 65).
Referee: Ruebyn Ricardo.

Salford C (2) 2 *(Okoronkwo 20, Stockton 22 (pen))*

Cheltenham T (0) 0 1968

Salford C: (442) Young; Edwards (Shephard 75), Austerfield (Ashley 65), Tilt, Garbutt; Okoronkwo (Berkoe 87), Lund, Fornah (McAleny 64), N'Mai; Taylor, Stockton (Kouassi 64).
Cheltenham T: (4231) Day; Payne (Jude-Boyd 46), Stubbs, Bennett, Bradbury; Kinsella (Bowman 79), Young; Thomas (Taylor 46), Colwill, Archer (Norkett 83); Miller (Dulson 63).
Referee: Martin Coy.

Stevenage (0) 0

Mansfield T (0) 1 *(McLaughlin 48)* 2464

Stevenage: (4231) Cooper; James-Wildin (Smith 74), Thompson N, Piergianni, Butler; Thompson L (Freeman 83), White (King 74); Roberts, Kemp, Young (Aboh 74); List (Simpson 74).
Mansfield T: (532) Pym; Quinn B (Evans 61), Bowery, Kilgour, Cargill, McLaughlin; Baccus (Boateng 53), Reed, Quinn S (Maris 86); Akins, Waine (Williams 61).
Referee: Tom Reeves.

Stockport Co (2) 3 *(Collar 15, Wootton 18, Olaofe 86)*

Brackley T (0) 1 *(Connolly 55 (og))* 5637

Stockport Co: (3412) Addai; Connolly, Horsfall, Pye; Southam-Hales (Adaramola 72), Camps, Norwood (Fiorini 72), Touray; Bailey; Wootton (Olaofe 46), Collar (Fevrier 46).
Brackley T: (3412) Maxted; Lyttle, Dean, Carline; Lowe, Bates, Byrne, Craig; O'Sullivan (Abbey 87); Donawa (Calder 77), Hall.
Referee: Simon Mather.

Walsall (0) 0
Charlton Ath (2) 4 *(Ahadme 16, 85, Godden 28,*
Campbell T 90)   6161
Walsall: (352) Simkin; McEntee, Williams, Allen; Barrett,
Lakin (Hall 69), Comley (Stirk 45), Jellis (Earing 19),
Gordon L; Lowe (Johnson 69), Adomah (Matt 46).
Charlton Ath: (4312) Maynard-Brewer; Edmonds-Green,
Mitchell A, Gillesphey, Edwards; Taylor, Coventry
(Campbell A 88), Berry (Campbell T 63); Godden (Small
63); Ahadme (Hylton 88), Anderson (Laqeretabua 90).
Referee: Ollie Yates.

Wealdstone (0) 0
Wycombe W (1) 2 *(Lubala 29, Kone 84)*   3534
Wealdstone: (532) Adams; Boldewijn (Thorpe 63), Cook,
Mariappa, Mundle-Smith, Georgiou; Cesay, Wells-
Morrison (Grant 71), Ashford; Reid, Kretzschmar
(Obiero 83).
Wycombe W: (4231) George; Grimmer, Skura, Tafazolli,
Hartridge; Bakinson (Leahy 74), Butcher; Wheeler
(Onyedinma 65), Udoh (Morley 87), Lubala (McCleary
65); Hanlan (Kone 74).
Referee: Alex Chilowicz.

Sunday, 1 December 2024
Blackpool (0) 1 *(Rhodes 55)*
Birmingham C (2) 2 *(Dykes 6, Jutkiewicz 24)*   4835
Blackpool: (442) Tyrer; Offiah (Lawrence-Gabriel 68),
Pennington, Casey, Husband; Apter, Finnigan (Onomah
46), Norburn, Embleton (Fletcher 46); Joseph (Rhodes
46 (Morgan 81)), Ballard (Thompson 46).
Birmingham C: (3421) Peacock-Farrell; Gardner-Hickman,
Sanderson, Bielik, Laird, Leonard, Khela (Paik 59), Harris;
Yokoyama (Anderson 59), Dykes; Jutkiewicz (May 59).
Referee: Tom Nield.

Burton Alb (0) 1 *(Bennett 92)*
Tamworth (0) 1 *(Maher 94)*   4393
Burton Alb: (4231) Crocombe; Godwin-Malife,
Vancooten, Sweeney, Armer (Williams 80); Watt,
Chauke (Bennett 80), Kalinauskas (Gilligan 91), Cooper-
Love (Whitfield 54), Bodin (Larsson 74); Orsi-Dadomo.
Tamworth: (4411) Singh; Crompton, Cullinane-Liburd,
Hollis, Fairlamb; Maher (Enoru 114), Morrison, Tonks
(Milnes 84), Williams (McLinchey 90); Tshikuna
(Fletcher 74); Creaney (Wreh 114).
aet; Tamworth won 4-3 on penalties.
Referee: Thomas Kirk.

Kettering T (1) 1 *(Williams 30)*
Doncaster R (0) 2 *(Sharp 75, 105)*   2803
Kettering T: (4231) Alexander; Hart, White, Johnson,
Powell; Stohrer, Thanoj (Millar 59); York (Fifield 107),
Williams (Andrade 107), Wilson (Hooper 84); Ranger
(Sordell 83).
Doncaster R: (4231) Sharman-Lowe; Sterry (Emmanuel
46), Olowu, Anderson, Senior; Kelly (Ironside 46),
Bailey; Molyneux (Clifton 119), Sbarra (Hurst 60),
Gibson (Broadbent 46); Sharp.
aet. Referee: Ben Speedie.

Reading (1) 5 *(Camara 20, Savage 59, Akande 65,*
Campbell 93, 96)
Harborough T (2) 3 *(Robinson 18, O'Sullivan 21,*
Tonga 86)   7916
Reading: (433) Button; Ahmed, Holzman, Kanu■, Garcia;
Elliott (Savage 46), Wing (Campbell 60), Tuma (Dorsett
73); Akande (Dean 76), Wareham, Camara (Craig 46).
Harborough T: (343) Taylor; Williams, Malone, Morris;
Cooper (Forbes 73), Sandro (Carta 46), Robinson
(Sandhu 73), Walsh; O'Sullivan (Tonga 66), Stephens
(Rose 66), Starkie.
aet. Referee: Declan Bourne.

Solihull Moors (1) 1 *(Wilkinson 12)*
Bromley (1) 2 *(Sowunmi 15, Imray 61)*   1770
Solihull Moors: (4231) Walker; Oakley, Morrison, Whit-
more, Howell (Newton 79); Tipton (Stevenson 77), Bowen
(Warburton 86); Adu-Poku, Bostock, Gale; Wilkinson.
Bromley: (532) Smith; Imray (Jenkinson 82), Sowunmi,
Webster, Grant, Odutayo; Arthurs, Thompson, Whitely
(Congreve 82); Cheek (Amantchi 88), Olomola (Dennis
82).
Referee: Matthew Russell.

THIRD ROUND
Thursday, 9 January 2025
Everton (1) 2 *(Beto 42, Ndiaye 90 (pen))*
Peterborough U (0) 0   38,895
Everton: (343) Virginia; O'Brien, Keane, Branthwaite;
Patterson (Young 73), Gueye, Mangala (Doucoure 89),
Mykolenko; Armstrong (Harrison 68), Beto (Broja 68
(Lindstrom 90)), Ndiaye.
Peterborough U: (3511) Bilokapic; Katongo, Fernandez,
Nevett (Wallin 46); Dornelly (Odoh 76), Kyprianou (De
Havilland 65), Collins, O'Brien-Brady (Mothersille 88),
Hayes; Conn-Clarke; Jones (Lindgren 46).
Referee: Matthew Bramall.

Fulham (1) 4 *(Rodrigo Muniz 26, Jimenez 49 (pen),*
Andersen 65, Castagne 85)
Watford (1) 1 *(Vata 33)*   15,981
Fulham: (4231) Benda; Castagne, Andersen (Diop 66),
Cuenca, Sessegnon; Andreas Pereira, Lukic (Reed 77);
Traore, Smith Rowe (King 66), Iwobi (Godo 66);
Rodrigo Muniz (Jimenez 46).
Watford: (541) Bond; Andrews, Porteous, Ogbonna, Tikvic,
Larouci; Ince (Baah 67), Dwomoh (Louza 31), Kayembe,
Vata (Chakvetadze 67); Doumbia (Nabizada 89).
Referee: Thomas Donohue.

Sheffield U (0) 0
Cardiff C (1) 1 *(Ashford 19)*   6126
Sheffield U: (4231) Davies A; Gilchrist (Colechin 89),
Baptiste, Norrington-Davies (Robinson 57), McCallum;
Burrows, Blacker; Brooks, Marsh (Hampson 81),
Brewster; One.
Cardiff C: (532) Horvath; Kpakio (Davies T 46), Fish,
Daland, Bagan, Tanner; Ng (Rinomhota 76), Colwill R
(Robertson 63), Ralls; Etete (Pearce 46), Ashford (Siopis
76).
Referee: Adam Herczeg.

Friday, 10 January 2025
Aston Villa (0) 2 *(Onana 71, Rogers 76)*
West Ham U (1) 1 *(Lucas Paqueta 9)*   40,989
Aston Villa: (4231) Olsen; Cash (Nedeljkovic 72), Konsa,
Mings, Maatsen; Kamara (Buendia 72), Barkley (Onana
23); Bailey (Ramsey 72), Tielemans, Rogers; Watkins.
West Ham U: (4231) Fabianski; Wan-Bissaka,
Mavropanos (Luis Guilherme 85), Kilman, Scarles
(Cresswell 77); Soucek, Alvarez (Soler 85); Summerville
(Coufal 46), Kudus, Lucas Paqueta; Fullkrug (Ings 15).
Referee: Tim Robinson.

Wycombe W (2) 2 *(Hanlan 17, Bradley 27)*
Portsmouth (0) 0   5240
Wycombe W: (4231) George (Bishop 7); Kodua, Skura,
Bradley, Harvie; Butcher, Bakinson (Scowen 75);
McCleary (Onyedinma 75), Leahy, Lubala (Wheeler 87);
Hanlan (Kone 75).
Portsmouth: (4231) Archer (Schmid 46); Devlin,
McIntyre, Atkinson (Towler 46), Williams (Swanson 62);
Potts (Dozzell 46), Kamara; Ritchie, Moxon, Lane (Clout
76); Saydee.
Referee: Tom Reeves.

Saturday, 11 January 2025
Birmingham C (1) 2 *(Yokoyama 1, Dykes 77)*
Lincoln C (0) 1 *(Makama 90 (pen))*   17,032
Birmingham C: (442) Peacock-Farrell; Gardner-
Hickman, Klarer, Sampsted (Chang 72), Cochrane;
Yokoyama (Willumsson 72), Leonard, Harris (Betteka
86), Wright (Laird 61); Dykes, Jutkiewicz (Paik 72).
Lincoln C: (532) Jeacock; Darikwa (Hackett 68),
Montsma, O'Connor, Erhahon, Roughan; McGrandles
(Hamilton 81), Moylan (Bayliss 68), Jefferies (Ring 85);
Makama, Cadamarteri (Draper 68).
Referee: Martin Coy.

Bournemouth (3) 5 *(Kluivert 27, Ouattara 34, 44,*
Semenyo 47, Jebbison 90)
WBA (1) 1 *(Taylor 14)*   10,916
Bournemouth: (4231) Arrizabalaga; Aarons (Semenyo
46), Zabarnyi, Huijsen, Soler; Hill, Adams (Kinsey-
Wellings 89); Brooks (Kerkez 77), Winterburn, Kluivert
(Jebbison 90); Ouattara (Rees-Dottin 89).

WBA: (442) Wildsmith; Furlong, Holgate, Taylor, Styles; Fellows (Wallace 63), Racic (Molumby 54), Mowatt (Diakite 54), Swift (Johnston 63); Diangana, Ahearne-Grant (Cole 77).
Referee: John Busby.

Brentford (0) 0

Plymouth Arg (0) 1 *(Whittaker 82)*   16,790
Brentford: (442) Valdimarsson; Roerslev, Kim, van den Berg (Collins 71), Henry (Lewis-Potter 63); Yarmolyuk (Mbeumo 63), Maghoma (Wissa 71), Jensen, Damsgaard; Schade, Carvalho.
Plymouth Arg: (343) Hazard; Pleguezuelo, Palsson, Galloway (Puchacz 81); Sorinola, Randell (Gyabi 81), Roberts, Mumba; Whittaker, Baidoo (Bundu 60), Wright (Ogbeta 90).
Referee: Ben Toner.

Bristol C (1) 1 *(Twine 45)*

Wolverhampton W (2) 2 *(Ait Nouri 10, Gomes R 21)*   23,485
Bristol C: (343) O'Leary; Tanner, Vyner, McNally; McCrorie, Knight (Bird 65), McGuane (Earthy 69), Roberts; Twine, Mayulu (Wells 77), Mehmeti (Hirakawa 64).
Wolverhampton W: (343) Johnstone; Doherty, Bueno, Agbadou; Gomes R (Pedro Lima 89), Andre Trindade, Joao Gomes, Ait Nouri (Pond 90); Goncalo Guedes (Bellegarde 76), Larsen, Hwang (Sarabia 75).
Referee: Robert Jones.

Chelsea (1) 5 *(Adarabioyo 39, 70, Nkunku 50, Joao Felix 75, 77)*

Morecambe (0) 0   38,998
Chelsea: (4141) Jorgensen; James (Gusto 46), Adarabioyo, Disasi, Veiga; Lavia (Cucurella 46); Pedro Neto (Sancho 46), Nkunku, Joao Felix, George; Guiu.
Morecambe: (451) Burgoyne; Hendrie, Williams, Stott, Tutonda; Tollitt (Macadam 68), Songo'o (Taylor 81), Jones (Hope 81), White, Edwards (Lewis A 68); Dackers (Slew 53).
Referee: Andrew Kitchen.

Coventry C (1) 1 *(Kitching 26)*

Sheffield W (0) 1 *(Musaba 90)*   20,906
Coventry C: (352) Dovin; Thomas, Kitching, Binks (Sakamoto 96); van Ewijk, Allen (Borges Rodrigues 105), Rudoni, Overgaard, Dasilva (Bidwell 79); Thomas-Asante (Eccles 96), Simms (Bassette 88).
Sheffield W: (433) Charles P; Valery, Otegbayo (Ihiekwe 46), Bernard, Lowe M; Chalobah (Windass 46), Charles S, Ingelsson (Kobacki 76); Musaba, Ugbo (Lowe J 58), Gassama (Bannan 67).
aet; Coventry C won 4-3 on penalties.
Referee: Thomas Kirk.

Exeter C (2) 3 *(Mitchell 22, 40, Harper 64)*

Oxford U (1) 1 *(Phillips 14)*   6149
Exeter C: (3421) Whitworth; Fitzwater, Crama, Yfeko (Francis 46); McMillan, Richards J (McDonald 86), Woods, Harper; Watts (Aitchison 67), Mitchell (Jones 75); Magennis (Alli 67).
Oxford U: (4231) Ingram; ter Avest (Kioso 70), Long, Thorniley, Leigh; El Mizouni (Matos 64), McEachran (Goodrham 64); Phillips (Placheta 70), Dembele (Ferdinan 89), Sibley; Scarlett.
Referee: Scott Oldham.

Leeds U (0) 1 *(Ramazani 59)*

Harrogate T (0) 0   35,584
Leeds U: (4231) Darlow; Schmidt, Guilavogui, Struijk (Rodon 65), Byram (Firpo 77); Ampadu, Rothwell (Tanaka 65); Gnonto (Gruev 90), Solomon (James 78), Ramazani; Fernandez.
Harrogate T: (442) Belshaw; Sims (Asare 83), O'Connor, Moon, Burrell; Cornelius (Taylor 72), Sutton (Dooley 77), Morris, Daly (Duke-Mckenna 83); Muldoon (Folarin 71), March.
Referee: James Bell.

Leicester C (3) 6 *(Justin 8, 63, Mavididi 35, Buonanotte 38, Vardy 51 (pen), Faes 90)*

QPR (2) 2 *(Varane 18, Kolli 45)*   28,242
Leicester C: (4231) Stolarczyk; Justin, Coady, Faes, Kristiansen; Soumare, Winks (Skipp 60); Buonanotte (De Cordova-Reid 81), El Khannous (Ayew 60), Mavididi (McAteer 66); Vardy (Daka 60).
QPR: (4231) Walsh; Ashby, Edwards, Clarke-Salter, Paal (Colback 72); Varane, Field (Morgan 70); Saito (Frey 81), Madsen, Chair (Smyth 70); Kolli (Lloyd 72).
Referee: David Webb.

Liverpool (2) 4 *(Jota 29, Alexander-Arnold 45, Danns 76, Chiesa 90)*

Accrington S (0) 0   60,261
Liverpool: (433) Kelleher; Alexander-Arnold (Bradley 60), Quansah, Endo (Nyoni 79), Tsimikas; Jota, Morton (McConnell 60), Szoboszlai (Chiesa 46); Elliott, Nunez, Ngumoha (Danns 72).
Accrington S: (4312) Crellin; Love, Rawson, Awe, Woods B; Woods J (O'Brien 63), Khumbeni (Coyle 46); Martin (Conneely 63); Hunter (Henderson 46); Walton (Mooney 78), Whalley.
Referee: Lewis Smith.

Manchester C (3) 8 *(Doku 8, 69 (pen), Mubama 20, O'Reilly 43, Grealish 49 (pen), McAtee 62, 72, 81)*

Salford C (0) 0   52,056
Manchester C: (3421) Ederson; Simpson-Pusey, Ake (Akanji 46), O'Reilly; Matheus Luiz, McAtee, Gundogan, Grealish; Savio (Foden 55), Doku (Kovacic 74); Mubama.
Salford C: (3142) Young; Shephard, Tilt, Garbutt; Ashley (Watson 58); Mnoga (Taylor 58), Lund (McAleny 70), Fornah, Berkoe; Kouassi (Stockton 70), Adelakun (Wright 87).
Referee: Josh Smith.

Middlesbrough (0) 0

Blackburn R (0) 1 *(Weimann 70)*   16,794
Middlesbrough: (4231) Glover; Dijksteel, Edmundson, Clarke, Engel; Barlaser, McCabe (Hackney 76); Hamilton (Forss 65), Gilbert, McGree (Latte Lath 76); Burgzorg.
Blackburn R: (4231) Toth; Brittain, Hyam, Batth, Beck; Buckley, Tronstad; Weimann (O'Grady-Macken 90), Cantwell (Dolan 81), Rankin-Costello; Leonard (Gueye 81).
Referee: Dean Whitestone.

Norwich C (0) 0

Brighton & HA (2) 4 *(Rutter 37, 45, Enciso 59, March 74)*   24,738
Norwich C: (433) Long; Stacey, Cordoba, Doyle (Hills 46), Chrisene (Duffy 79); Forson (Fisher 46), McLean, Nunez (Hernandez 61); Schwartau, Crnac (Sargent 79), Dobbin.
Brighton & HA: (4231) Steele; Veltman (Moder 78), van Hecke, Webster (McConville 71), Estupinan; Baleba, Ayari; Minteh (March 71), Enciso (Welbeck 63), Mitoma; Rutter (Gruda 63).
Referee: Simon Hooper.

Nottingham F (1) 2 *(Yates 40, Sosa 68)*

Luton T (0) 0   29,445
Nottingham F: (343) Carlos Miguel; Boly, Morato, Toffolo; Moreira, Yates (Dominguez 74), Ward-Prowse (Danilo 85), Alex; Jota Silva (Elanga 74), Awoniyi (Wood 74), Sosa (Hudson-Odoi 74).
Luton T: (4231) Kaminski; Walters, McGuinness, Holmes, Bell; Walsh, Nakamba; Jones (Adebayo 69), Dabo (Clark 49), Nelson (Brown 57); Morris.
Referee: Darren England.

Reading (0) 0 *(Wing 71)*

Burnley (0) 3 *(Foster 71, Flemming 100, 109)*   7039
Reading: (433) Button; Rushesha (Ahmed 107), Dean (Holzman 76), Bindon, Kanu; Savage, Wing (Senga-Ngoyi 113), Knibbs; Abrefa (Osho 76), Smith, Wareham (Sackey 91).
Burnley: (4231) Hladky; Sonne (Humphreys 87), Worrall, Egan (Ekdal 72), Lucas Pires; Bauress, McDermott (Laurent 106); Koleosho (Ndayishimiye 87), Barnes (Flemming 94), Foster; Rodriguez.
aet. Referee: Andy Davies.

Sunderland (0) 1 *(Aleksic 64)*

Stoke C (1) 2 *(Cannon 4 (pen), Ennis 112)*   15,774

Sunderland: (4231) Moore; Hume, O'Nien, Hjelde (Rusyn 106), Alese (Johnson 59); Neil, Jones (Abdul Samed 79); Mayenda (Ogunsuyi 111), Rigg (Aleksic 60), Aouchiche; Connolly.
Stoke C: (4231) Johansson; Tchamadeu, Phillips, Wilmot, Stevens (Gooch 60); Seko (Sidibe 60), Burger (Tezgel 95); Moran, Baker, Koumas (Bae 75); Cannon (Ennis 76).
aet. Referee: Elliot Bell.

Sunday, 12 January 2025

Arsenal (0) 1 *(Gabriel 63)*

Manchester U (0) 1 *(Fernandes 52)*   60,109

Arsenal: (433) Raya; Timber (Partey 100), Saliba, Gabriel, Lewis-Skelly (Trossard 91); Odegaard, Jorginho (Tierney 113), Merino (Rice 73); Gabriel Jesus (Sterling 40), Havertz, Martinelli.
Manchester U: (3421) Bayindir; de Ligt, Maguire (Yoro 104), Martinez; Mazraoui, Ugarte (Malacia 91), Mainoo (Collyer 81), Dalot■; Garnacho (Diallo 80), Fernandes; Hojlund (Zirkzee 81).
aet; Manchester U won 5-3 on penalties.
Referee: Andrew Madley.

Crystal Palace (1) 1 *(Eze 4)*

Stockport Co (0) 0   21,014

Crystal Palace: (3421) Turner; Guehi, Richards, Riad; Munoz, Lerma, Kamada, Clyne (Schlupp 77); Sarr (Devenny 64), Eze; Nketiah.
Stockport Co: (352) Addai; Knoyle (Mingi 84), Connolly, Pye; Southam-Hales, Collar, Camps, Bailey (Norwood 62), Touray (Rydel 77); Wootton (Diamond 76), Olaofe (Andresson 77).
Referee: Stuart Attwell.

Hull C (0) 1 *(Puerta 80)*

Doncaster R (0) 1 *(Molyneux 51)*   10,032

Hull C: (4231) Rushworth; Drameh, Burns (Jones 46), McLoughlin, Giles (Coyle L 61); Slater, Alzate (Simons 46); Kamara, Puerta, Vaughan (Burstow 61); Joao Pedro.
Doncaster R: (4231) Sharman-Lowe; Sterry, Olowu, McGrath, Maxwell; Bailey (Gibson 120), Broadbent (Close 91); Molyneux, Street (Ennis 84), Sbarra (Clifton 62); Sharp (Ironside 71).
aet; Doncaster R won 5-4 on penalties.
Referee: Sunny Gill.

Ipswich T (3) 3 *(Phillips 18, Clarke J 24, Taylor J 37)*

Bristol R (0) 0   27,678

Ipswich T: (4231) Muric (Slicker 81); Godfrey (Clarke H 73), Woolfenden, Burgess, Townsend; Phillips, Luongo; Burns (Johnson 46), Taylor J (Broadhead 73), Clarke J; Al Hamadi (Hirst 73).
Bristol R: (4231) Griffiths; Moore, Wilson, Taylor (Senior 86), Sousa; Sawyers (Lindsay 74), Ward G; Forde (Thomas 68), Sotiriou (Hutchinson 74), Sinclair; Martin (O'Donkor 68).
Referee: Oliver Langford.

Newcastle U (1) 3 *(Miley 16, Gordon 49 (pen), Osula 61)*

Bromley (1) 1 *(Congreve 8)*   52,088

Newcastle U: (433) Dubravka; Trippier, Schar, Kelly, Targett (Hall 69); Miley, Longstaff, Joelinton (Guimaraes 46); Almiron (Tonali 84), Osula (Sanusi 69), Barnes (Gordon 46).
Bromley: (3421) Smith; Sowunmi, Reynolds (Webster 82), Elerewe; Imray, Arthurs (Leigh 83), Thompson (Charles 65), Odutayo; Congreve (Passley 77), Whitely; Cheek (Amantchi 78).
Referee: Will Finnie.

Southampton (2) 3 *(Sulemana 20, Dibling 35, 65)*

Swansea C (0) 0   12,120

Southampton: (3412) Ramsdale; Bree, Bednarek (Wood-Gordon 73), Harwood-Bellis; Walker-Peters, Ugochukwu (Smallbone 68), Aribo (Lallana 86), Manning; Fernandes; Dibling (Archer 67), Sulemana (Armstrong 67).
Swansea C: (4231) McLaughlin; Key, Christie (Cullen 66), Naughton, Tymon; Goncalo Franco (Allen 66), Grimes (Fulton 66); Ronald (Abdulai 79), Peart-Harris, Eom (Ginnelly 79); Bianchini.
Referee: Tony Harrington.

Tamworth (0) 0

Tottenham H (0) 3 *(Tshikuna 101 (og), Kulusevski 107, Johnson 118)*   3720

Tamworth: (4231) Singh; Crompton, Cullinane-Liburd, Hollis, Cockerill-Mollett (Sundire 68); Milnes (Fletcher 81), Morrison; McLinchey, Tonks (Tshikuna 85), Enoru (Williams 81); Creaney (Wreh 85).
Tottenham H: (433) Kinsky; Porro, Dragusin (Spence 91), Gray, Reguilon; Sarr (Bergvall 68), Bissouma, Maddison (Kulusevski 91); Johnson, Werner (Son 91), Moore (Solanke 68).
aet. Referee: Peter Bankes.

Monday, 13 January 2025

Millwall (1) 3 *(Ivanovic 30, De Norre 70, Bangura-Williams 85)*

Dagenham & Red (0) 0   5625

Millwall: (4231) Jensen; Leonard, Tanganga, Cooper, Bryan; Mitchell, De Norre (Massey 83); Azeez (Saville 63), Honeyman, Mayor (Bangura-Williams 75); Ivanovic (Kendall 84).
Dagenham & Red: (4141) Justham; Rendall (Eastman 75), Phipps, Kalambayi, Rutherford; N'Guessan (Morias 76); Remy (Pereira 55), Hessenthaler, Rees, Hill; Stephenson (Umerah 55).
Referee: Robert Madley.

Tuesday, 14 January 2025

Leyton Orient (1) 1 *(Kelman 20)*

Derby Co (1) 1 *(Brown 24)*   8279

Leyton Orient: (4231) Keeley; Clare■, Simpson (Cooper 100), Beckles, Currie; Pratley (Brown 62), Jaiyesimi (James 71); Perkins (Obiero 101), Donley, Galbraith (Sweeney 82); Kelman.
Derby Co: (4231) Zetterstrom; Wilson, Nelson, Phillips (Elder 46), Forsyth; Goudmijn, Thompson (Adams 46); Brown (Jackson 68), Harness, Mendez-Laing (Collins 75); Blackett-Taylor (Barkhuizen 68).
aet; Leyton Orient won 6-5 on penalties.
Referee: Ben Speedie.

Mansfield T (0) 0

Wigan Ath (0) 2 *(Aasgaard 48, 54)*   4523

Mansfield T: (352) Pym; Bowery, Kilgour, Cargill (Blake-Tracy 80); Hewitt, Craig (Reed 67), Boateng (Baccus 68), Quinn S (Maris 68), McLaughlin; Gregory (Evans 68), Akins.
Wigan Ath: (4231) Tickle; Robinson L, Aimson, Kerr, Sibbick; Smith S, Weir (McHugh 88); Olakigbe (Carragher 74), Aasgaard, Smith J (Thomas 68); Taylor (Goodwin 74).
Referee: Alex Chilowicz.

Preston NE (1) 2 *(Osmajic 32, 47)*

Charlton Ath (1) 1 *(Berry 40)*   7734

Preston NE: (3142) Woodman; Storey, Gibson, Hughes; Whiteman; Bowler (Kesler-Hayden 60), Thordarson (Greenwood 61), Frokjaer-Jensen (McCann 60), Holmes (Lindsay 81); Osmajic, Keane (Jakobsen 77).
Charlton Ath: (4231) Mannion; Mitchell A (Mitchell Z 74), Jones, Gillesphey, Edwards (Aneke 81); Coventry, Docherty (Godden 82); Campbell T, Berry (Anderson 74), Small; Ahadme (Leaburn 56).
Referee: Ruebyn Ricardo.

FOURTH ROUND

Friday, 7 February 2025

Manchester U (0) 2 *(Zirkzee 68, Maguire 90)*

Leicester C (1) 1 *(De Cordova-Reid 42)*   73,693

Manchester U: (343) Onana; Yoro, Maguire, Mazraoui; Dorgu (Garnacho 46), Ugarte (Casemiro 90), Fernandes, Dalot; Diallo, Hojlund, Mainoo (Zirkzee 64).
Leicester C: (4231) Hermansen; Justin, Faes, Okoli, Thomas (Coulibaly 58); Ndidi (Winks 58), Soumare; De Cordova-Reid (McAteer 73), El Khannous, Ayew; Daka (Buonanotte 81).
Referee: Michael Salisbury.

Saturday, 8 February 2025

Birmingham C (2) 2 *(Laird 1, Iwata 40)*
Newcastle U (2) 3 *(Willock 21, 82, Wilson 26)*　　27,914
Birmingham C: (4231) Peacock-Farrell; Laird, Klarer, Davies, Cochrane; Iwata (Hanley 84), Leonard (Willumsson 62); Wright (Bielik 77), Dowell, Anderson (May 76); Stansfield (Dykes 77).
Newcastle U: (433) Pope; Livramento, Krafth, Burn (Schar 55), Targett; Longstaff, Guimaraes (Tonali 46), Miley; Osula (Isak 90), Wilson (Murphy J 55), Willock.
Referee: Matthew Donohue.

Brighton & HA (1) 2 *(Rutter 12, Mitoma 57)*
Chelsea (1) 1 *(Verbruggen 5 (og))*　　23,279
Brighton & HA: (4231) Verbruggen; Veltman, van Hecke, Dunk (Webster 46), Lamptey; Baleba (Ayari 75), Hinshelwood (Gomez 68); Minteh, Rutter (Joao Pedro 75), Mitoma; Welbeck (O'Riley 89).
Chelsea: (4231) Sanchez; Gusto, Adarabioyo, Chalobah, Cucurella; Caicedo, Dewsbury-Hall (Fernandez 58); Pedro Neto (Madueke 74), Palmer, Sancho (George 74); Nkunku.
Referee: Jarred Gillett.

Coventry C (1) 1 *(Latibeaudiere 8)*
Ipswich T (3) 4 *(Hirst 2 (pen), Clarke J 28, 37, Philogene-Bidace 63)*　　30,055
Coventry C: (541) Dovin; Latibeaudiere (Burroughs 88), Thomas, Binks, Kitching, Dasilva; Sakamoto, Allen (Borges Rodrigues 75), Eccles, Rudoni (Overgaard 62); Thomas-Asante (Bassette 62).
Ipswich T: (4231) Palmer; Godfrey, Woolfenden, Burgess, Townsend; Phillips (Luongo 68), Clarke J (Cajuste 79); Philogene-Bidace (Johnson 79), Szmodics (Broadhead 35), Clarke J; Hirst (Delap 79).
Referee: Ben Toner.

Everton (0) 0
Bournemouth (2) 2 *(Semenyo 23 (pen), Jebbison 43)*　　38,909
Everton: (4231) Pickford; O'Brien, Tarkowski, Branthwaite, Young; Gueye (Keane 84), Garner (Iroegbunam 74); Lindstrom (Harrison 65), Doucoure (Alcaraz 65), Ndiaye; Beto.
Bournemouth: (4231) Arrizabalaga; Cook, Zabarnyi, Huijsen, Kerkez; Christie (Silcott-Duberry 90), Adams; Tavernier (Brooks 78), Winterburn (Kluivert 64), Semenyo; Jebbison (Ouattara 78).
Referee: John Brooks.

Leeds U (0) 0
Millwall (1) 2 *(Azeez 30, 55)*　　34,923
Leeds U: (4231) Darlow; Schmidt, Ampadu (Debayo 83), Struijk, Byram (Firpo 69); Guilavogui (Tanaka 69), Rothwell; Chambers (Solomon 69), Gnonto (Piroe 80), Ramazani; Fernandez.
Millwall: (4231) Roberts; Harding, Tanganga, Cooper, Bryan; Mitchell (Wintle 74), De Norre; Neghli (Bangura-Williams 69), Cundle (Kelly 81), Azeez (Honeyman 74); Ivanovic (Watmore 69).
Referee: Gavin Ward.

Leyton Orient (1) 1 *(Ortega 16 (og))*
Manchester C (0) 2 *(Khusanov 56, De Bruyne 79)*　　8749
Leyton Orient: (4231) Keeley; James, Simpson, Happe, Currie; Galbraith (Obiero 86), Brown (Ball 85); Perkins (Cooper 65), Donley (Agyei 85), Jaiyesimi (Pratley 54); Kelman.
Manchester C: (4231) Ortega; Lewis, Vitor Reis (Khusanov 46), Dias (Stones 46), O'Reilly (De Bruyne 72); Gonzalez (Silva 22), Gundogan; Savio, McAtee (Foden 72), Grealish; Marmoush.
Referee: Darren Bond.

Preston NE (0) 0
Wycombe W (0) 0　　10,444
Preston NE: (352) Woodman; Whatmough (Kesler-Hayden 66), Lindsay, Gibson (Hughes 73); Potts, Holmes (Evans 96), McCann, Thordarson (Ledson 66), Meghoma (Frokjaer-Jensen 66); Greenwood, Osmajic.

Wycombe W: (4231) Norris; Skura, Low, Bradley, Harvie (Reach 64); Bakinson, Leahy (Scowen 65); McCleary (Udoh 83), Lowry (Westergaard 64), Onyedinma (Kodua 78); Lubala.
aet; Preston NE won 4-2 on penalties.
Referee: Ben Speedie.

Southampton (0) 0
Burnley (0) 1 *(Edwards 77)*　　15,253
Southampton: (3412) McCarthy; Bree, Bednarek, Welington; Walker-Peters, Ugochukwu (Smallbone 82), Aribo, Manning; Fernandes (Archer 86); Dibling (Onuachu 67), Sulemana (Gronbaek 86).
Burnley: (541) Hladky; Sonne, Egan-Riley (Esteve 58), Worrall, Humphreys, Lucas Pires; Benson (Edwards 59), Shelvey (Bauress 59), Mejbri, Sarmiento (Redmond 83); Barnes.
Referee: Will Finnie.

Stoke C (1) 3 *(Koumas 42, 46, Baker 57 (pen))*
Cardiff C (2) 3 *(Colwill R 8, 68, Salech 19)*　　12,641
Stoke C: (4231) Bonham; Tchamadeu, Rose, Gibson, Wilson-Esbrand (Stevens 87); Baker (Pearson 73), Burger; Andre Vidigal (Fawunmi 74), Bae (Lawal 87), Koumas (Seko 91); Tezgel.
Cardiff C: (4231) Horvath; Rinomhota, Fish, Bagan, Giles (Daland 46 (Chambers 57)); Ramsey (O'Dowda 63), Mannsverk (Ralls 63); El Ghazi (Alves 82), Colwill R, Willock; Salech.
aet; Cardiff C won 4-2 on penalties.
Referee: Thomas Kirk.

Wigan Ath (0) 0 *(Smith J 50)*
Fulham (1) 2 *(Rodrigo Muniz 23, 55)*　　12,281
Wigan Ath: (4231) Tickle; Sibbick, Carragher, Kerr, Robinson L (McHugh 75); Adeeko (Darcy 61), Smith S; Smith J (McManaman 70), Weir, Asamoah (Dale 61); Taylor (Goodwin 71).
Fulham: (4231) Benda; Castagne, Diop, Cuenca, Sessegnon; Cairney (Berge 85), Reed; King (Smith Rowe 86), Andreas Pereira (Traore 75), Godo (Iwobi 75); Rodrigo Muniz (Vinicius 90).
Referee: David Webb.

Sunday, 9 February 2025

Aston Villa (1) 2 *(Ramsey 1, Rogers 64)*
Tottenham H (0) 1 *(Tel 90)*　　40,773
Aston Villa: (4231) Martinez; Garcia, Konsa (Bogarde 27), Kamara, Digne (Maatsen 81); McGinn, Tielemans; Bailey (Asensio 66), Rogers, Ramsey; Malen (Rashford 66).
Tottenham H: (4231) Kinsky; Porro, Danso, Gray, Spence; Bergvall, Bentancur (Sarr 72); Moore (Bissouma 46), Kulusevski, Tel; Son.
Referee: Anthony Taylor.

Blackburn R (0) 0
Wolverhampton W (2) 2 *(Joao Gomes 33, Cunha 34)*　　15,141
Blackburn R: (4231) Toth; Rankin-Costello, Hyam, Batth, Yuri Ribeiro; Buckley, Forshaw (Hedges 84); Cozier-Duberry (Dolan 57), Cantwell (Gueye 57), Kargbo (Weimann 67); Dennis (Woodrow 66).
Wolverhampton W: (3421) Johnstone; Bueno (Doherty 46), Agbadou, Gomes T; Nelson Semedo (Ait Nouri 83), Bellegarde (Andre Trindade 66), Joao Gomes, Gomes R; Goncalo Guedes (Munetsi 66), Cunha; Hwang (Sarabia 46).
Referee: Lewis Smith.

Plymouth Arg (0) 1 *(Hardie 53 (pen))*
Liverpool (0) 0　　16,724
Plymouth Arg: (3421) Hazard; Taloverov, Katic, Pleguezuelo (Palsson 67); Sorinola, Randell (Boateng 72), Gyabi, Puchacz; Hardie (Obafemi 81), Wright; Bundu (Tijani 72).
Liverpool: (433) Kelleher; McConnell, Quansah, Gomez (Mabaya 11; Nunez 58)), Tsimikas; Elliott, Endo, Nyoni (Kone-Doherty 76); Chiesa, Jota, Diaz.
Referee: Sam Barrott.

Monday, 10 February 2025

Doncaster R (0) 0

Crystal Palace (1) 2 *(Munoz 31, Devenny 55)*   12,739

Doncaster R: (442) Sharman-Lowe; Sterry (Nixon 80), Olowu, Anderson, Maxwell; Molyneux, Bailey, Broadbent (Kelly 70), Ennis (Senior 46); Street (Gibson 46), Sharp (Ironside 62).

Crystal Palace: (3421) Turner; Richards, Lacroix, Guehi; Munoz (Kporha 90), Wharton (Lerma 62), Hughes, Mitchell (Chilwell 46); Devenny (Esse 62), Kamada (Franca 90); Mateta.

Referee: Farai Hallam.

Tuesday, 11 February 2025

Exeter C (1) 2 *(Magennis 5, 50)*

Nottingham F (2) 2 *(Sosa 15, Awoniyi 37)*   8330

Exeter C: (541) Whitworth; Niskanen, McMillan (Bird 90), MacDonald, Turns[■], Harper (Jones 83); Mitchell (Yogane 74), Francis (Woods 83), Trevitt (Watts 71), Richards J (Cole 83); Magennis.

Nottingham F: (4231) Carlos Miguel (Sels 59); Moreira, Boly, Toffolo, Alex (Williams 91); Yates (Anderson 71), Sangare (Gibbs-White 72); Jota Silva, Danilo (Dominguez 59), Sosa; Awoniyi (Wood 90).

aet; Nottingham F won 4-2 on penalties.

Referee: Andrew Kitchen.

FIFTH ROUND

Friday, 28 February 2025

Aston Villa (0) 2 *(Asensio 68, 80)*

Cardiff C (0) 0   40,175

Aston Villa: (4231) Martinez; Garcia, Konsa, Bogarde, Maatsen (Digne 83); McGinn, Tielemans; Bailey, Asensio (Ramsey 82), Rashford (Rogers 82); Watkins (Jimoh 82).

Cardiff C: (3421) Horvath; Lawlor (Davies I 81), Goutas, Fish; Ng, Ramsey (Robertson 65), Colwill R, Giles (Bagan 64); El Ghazi, Willock (Ashford 81); Robinson (Salech 46).

Referee: Peter Bankes.

Saturday, 1 March 2025

Bournemouth (1) 1 *(Evanilson 30)*

Wolverhampton W (0) 1 *(Cunha 60)*   11,021

Bournemouth: (4231) Arrizabalaga; Cook, Hill, Huijsen, Kerkez; Scott (Sinisterra 84), Adams, Semenyo (Jebbison 106), Brooks (Kluivert 67), Tavernier; Evanilson (Ouattara 67).

Wolverhampton W: (3421) Johnstone; Djiga (Traore 86), Bueno, Gomes T; Nelson Semedo (Doherty 72), Joao Gomes (Andre Trindade 72), Bellegarde (Pond 91), Ait Nouri; Sarabia (Munetsi 72), Cunha[■]; Larsen.

aet; Bournemouth won 5-4 on penalties.

Referee: Chris Kavanagh.

Crystal Palace (2) 3 *(Tanganga 33 (og), Munoz 40, Nketiah 81)*

Millwall (1) 1 *(Harding 45)*   21,263

Crystal Palace: (3421) Turner; Richards, Lacroix, Guehi; Munoz (Clyne 90), Hughes (Wharton 65), Lerma (Devenny 65), Chilwell; Sarr (Esse 65), Eze (Franca 85); Mateta (Nketiah 15).

Millwall: (4231) Roberts[■]; Harding, Tanganga, Cooper, Bryan; De Norre (Honeyman 66), Mitchell (Saville 66); Neghli (Bangura-Williams 33), Cundle (Jensen 13), Azeez (Emakhu 85); Coburn (Ivanovic 66).

Referee: Michael Oliver.

Manchester C (1) 3 *(O'Reilly 45, 76, De Bruyne 90)*

Plymouth Arg (1) 1 *(Taloverov 38)*   50,044

Manchester C: (4141) Ortega; Lewis, Vitor Reis, Ake (Dias 46), O'Reilly; Gundogan; Silva, McAtee (Haaland 59), De Bruyne, Grealish; Foden (Gonzalez 83).

Plymouth Arg: (541) Hazard; Sorinola (Szucs 80), Taloverov, Katic, Pleguezuelo, Ogbeta (Puchacz 71); Wright, Boateng, Gyabi (Houghton 64), Mumba (Al Hajj 64); Bundu (Baidoo 64).

Referee: Craig Pawson.

Preston NE (2) 3 *(Brady 31, Osmajic 44, Keane 73)*

Burnley (0) 0   17,761

Preston NE: (532) Woodman; Potts, Kesler-Hayden, Lindsay, Gibson, Brady (Hughes 71); Ledson (Greenwood 84), Thordarson, McCann; Osmajic (Evans 84), Keane (Jakobsen 77).

Burnley: (4231) Hladky; Sonne, Worrall, Esteve, Lucas Pires; Shelvey (Laurent 58), Brownhill; Benson (Barnes 58), Sarmiento (Banel 68), Koleosho (Flemming 58); Foster (Edwards 67).

Referee: John Brooks.

Sunday, 2 March 2025

Manchester U (0) 1 *(Fernandes 71)*

Fulham (1) 1 *(Bassey 45)*   67,614

Manchester U: (3421) Onana; de Ligt, Maguire (Heaven 91), Yoro (Lindelof 53); Mazraoui, Ugarte (Garnacho 53), Fernandes, Dalot; Zirkzee, Eriksen (Casemiro 68); Hojlund (Obi 68).

Fulham: (4231) Leno; Castagne, Andersen, Bassey, Robinson; Lukic (Reed 101), Berge; Traore (Smith Rowe 53), Andreas Pereira (Willian 90), Iwobi (Sessegnon 107); Rodrigo Muniz (Jimenez 90).

aet; Fulham won 4-3 on penalties.

Referee: Stuart Attwell.

Newcastle U (1) 1 *(Isak 22 (pen))*

Brighton & HA (1) 2 *(Minteh 44, Welbeck 114)*   51,566

Newcastle U: (433) Dubravka; Trippier (Targett 69), Schar, Burn, Livramento; Miley (Guimaraes 56), Tonali, Joelinton (Willock 56); Barnes (Murphy J 57), Isak (Wilson 86), Gordon[■].

Brighton & HA: (4231) Verbruggen; Lamptey[■], van Hecke, Webster, Estupinan (Wieffer 80); Baleba (Gomez 69), Hinshelwood; Minteh (Gruda 69), Rutter (Welbeck 80), Mitoma (March 90); Joao Pedro.

aet.

Referee: Anthony Taylor.

Monday, 3 March 2025

Nottingham F (0) 1 *(Yates 68)*

Ipswich T (0) 1 *(Hirst 53)*   29,171

Nottingham F: (4231) Sels; Aina, Morato, Murillo, Alex (Williams 82); Yates, Sangare (Gibbs-White 60); Hudson-Odoi, Danilo (Anderson 59), Elanga (Jota Silva 111); Awoniyi (Wood 82).

Ipswich T: (4231) Palmer; Tuanzebe (O'Shea 46), Woolfenden, Burgess (Greaves 46), Townsend; Morsy, Luongo (Cajuste 67); Johnson, Taylor J, Broadhead (Clarke J 67); Hirst (Delap 90).

aet; Nottingham F won 5-4 on penalties.

Referee: Tony Harrington.

QUARTER-FINALS

Saturday, 29 March 2025

Brighton & HA (0) 0

Nottingham F (0) 0   29,930

Brighton & HA: (4231) Verbruggen; Hinshelwood, van Hecke, Webster (Dunk 91), Estupinan; Baleba, Ayari (Gomez 80); Minteh, Rutter (Gruda 75), Mitoma (Adingra 72); Welbeck (Joao Pedro 72).

Nottingham F: (4231) Sels; Aina, Milenkovic, Murillo, Williams; Yates, Anderson; Dominguez (Jota Silva 96), Gibbs-White (Morato 120), Danilo (Hudson-Odoi 61); Awoniyi (Elanga 61).

aet; Nottingham F won 4-3 on penalties.

Referee: Peter Bankes.

Fulham (0) 0

Crystal Palace (2) 3 *(Eze 34, Sarr 38, Nketiah 75)*   26,222

Fulham: (4231) Leno; Castagne, Andersen, Bassey, Robinson (Sessegnon 71); Berge, Lukic (Traore 63); Iwobi (Cairney 82), Andreas Pereira (Smith Rowe 63), Willian (Jimenez 71); Rodrigo Muniz.

Crystal Palace: (3421) Henderson; Richards, Lacroix, Guehi; Munoz (Clyne 87), Wharton (Kamada 70), Lerma, Mitchell; Sarr (Devenny 87), Eze (Franca 90); Mateta (Nketiah 70).

Referee: Darren England.

Sunday, 30 March 2025

Bournemouth (1) 1 *(Evanilson 21)*

Manchester C (0) 2 *(Haaland 49, Marmoush 63)* 10,954

Bournemouth: (4231) Arrizabalaga; Cook, Zabarnyi, Senesi (Jebbison 85), Soler (Hill 57); Christie (Smith 73), Adams; Brooks (Ouattara 57), Kluivert, Semenyo; Evanilson (Scott 73).
Manchester C: (433) Ederson; Matheus Luiz, Khusanov (O'Reilly 46), Dias, Gvardiol; Silva, Kovacic (Gonzalez 83), Gundogan (McAtee 83); Foden (Grealish 69), Haaland (Marmoush 61), De Bruyne.
Referee: Stuart Attwell.

Preston NE (0) 0

Aston Villa (0) 3 *(Rashford 58, 63 (pen), Ramsey 71)*
22,198

Preston NE: (352) Cornell; Storey, Gibson, Hughes; Brady, Thordarson (Mawene 83), Whiteman, Frokjaer-Jensen (Carroll 83), Meghoma (Lindsay 77); Jakobsen (Evans 77), Keane (Osmajic 64).
Aston Villa: (4231) Martinez; Cash (Garcia 81), Konsa, Mings, Digne; Kamara, Tielemans (McGinn 73); Rogers (Malen 73), Asensio (Onana 73), Ramsey; Rashford (Watkins 81).
Referee: Chris Kavanagh.

SEMI-FINALS (at Wembley Stadium)

Saturday, 26 April 2025

Crystal Palace (1) 3 *(Eze 31, Sarr 58, 90)*

Aston Villa (0) 0 82,301

Crystal Palace: (3421) Henderson; Richards, Lacroix, Guehi; Munoz, Wharton (Hughes 88), Kamada, Mitchell (Chilwell 84); Sarr, Eze (Lerma 88); Mateta (Nketiah 79).
Aston Villa: (4231) Martinez; Cash, Konsa, Torres, Digne (Maatsen 60); Kamara (Barkley 70), Tielemans; Rogers (Malen 79), Asensio (Ramsey 69), McGinn (Bailey 60); Watkins.
Referee: Anthony Taylor.

Sunday, 27 April 2025

Nottingham F (0) 0

Manchester C (1) 2 *(Lewis 2, Gvardiol 51)* 72,976

Nottingham F: (442) Sels; Abbott (Sosa 82), Milenkovic, Murillo, Toffolo; Gibbs-White, Dominguez (Jota Silva 82), Danilo (Elanga 46), Anderson (Sangare 71); Wood (Awoniyi 71), Hudson-Odoi.
Manchester C: (4222) Ortega; Matheus Luiz, Dias, Gvardiol, O'Reilly; Silva, Kovacic (Gonzalez 89); Lewis, Grealish (Gundogan 71); Savio (Foden 81), Marmoush (Doku 81).
Referee: Michael Oliver.

THE EMIRATES FA CUP FINAL 2024–25

Saturday, 17 May 2025

(at Wembley Stadium, attendance 84,163)

Crystal Palace (1) 1   **Manchester C (0) 0**

Crystal Palace: (3421) Henderson; Richards, Lacroix, Guehi (Lerma 61); Munoz, Wharton (Hughes 87), Kamada, Mitchell; Sarr, Eze; Mateta (Nketiah 78).
Scorer: Eze 16.

Manchester C: (4231) Ortega; Akanji, Dias, Gvardiol, O'Reilly; De Bruyne, Silva (Gundogan 88); Savio (Foden 76), Marmoush (Echeverri 76), Doku; Haaland.

Referee: Stuart Attwell.

Crystal Palace joined the history books too; celebrating after Eberechi Eze scored what proved to be the only goal of the Emirates FA Cup final against Manchester City at Wembley.
(Ed Sykes/Sportsphoto/Allstar via Getty Images)

NATIONAL LEAGUE 2024–25

NATIONAL LEAGUE TABLE 2024–25

(P) *promoted into division at end of 2023–24 season.*   (R) *Relegated into division at end of 2023–24 season.*

				Home				Away					Total						
		P	W	D	L	F	A	W	D	L	F	A	W	D	L	F	A	GD	Pts
1	Barnet	46	18	5	0	58	15	13	5	5	39	23	31	9	6	97	38	59	102
2	York C	46	16	4	3	57	20	5	5	38	22		9	9	8	95	42	53	96
3	Forest Green R (R)	46	15	7	1	38	17	7	10	6	31	25	22	17	7	69	42	27	83
4	Rochdale	46	13	4	6	43	21	8	7	8	26	23	21	11	14	69	44	25	74
5	Oldham Ath¶	46	11	6	6	35	23	8	10	5	29	25	19	16	11	64	48	16	73
6	FC Halifax T	46	9	5	9	22	24	10	8	5	28	22	19	13	14	50	46	4	70
7	Southend U	46	10	7	6	33	24	7	10	6	26	24	17	17	12	59	48	11	68
8	Gateshead	46	11	4	8	37	31	8	6	9	39	37	19	10	17	76	68	8	67
9	Altrincham	46	9	8	6	34	21	8	5	10	34	41	17	13	16	68	62	6	64
10	Tamworth (P)	46	10	8	5	40	28	7	5	11	25	44	17	13	16	65	72	–7	64
11	Hartlepool U	46	8	11	4	29	23	6	7	10	30	39	14	18	14	59	62	–3	60
12	Sutton U (R)	46	7	8	8	28	30	8	8	3	31	34	15	15	16	59	64	–5	60
13	Eastleigh	46	9	9	5	35	27	5	8	10	23	34	14	17	15	58	61	–3	59
14	Solihull Moors	46	8	5	10	34	40	8	5	10	27	27	16	10	20	61	67	–6	58
15	Woking	46	10	8	5	27	22	3	11	9	25	37	13	19	14	52	59	–7	58
16	Aldershot T	46	9	9	5	42	35	5	6	12	27	48	14	15	17	69	83	–14	57
17	Braintree T (P)	46	10	5	8	21	18	5	6	12	30	41	15	11	20	51	59	–8	56
18	Yeovil T (P)	46	7	7	9	25	27	8	4	11	26	33	15	11	20	51	60	–9	56
19	Boston U (P)	46	7	7	9	28	31	8	3	12	26	36	15	10	21	54	67	–13	55
20	Wealdstone	46	9	6	8	31	34	4	8	11	25	42	13	14	19	56	76	–20	53
21	Dagenham & Red	46	9	6	8	44	35	3	10	10	17	27	12	16	18	61	62	–1	52
22	Maidenhead U	46	7	7	9	32	36	7	3	13	25	39	14	10	22	57	75	–18	52
23	AFC Fylde	46	8	4	11	35	39	3	3	17	15	46	11	7	28	50	85	–35	40
24	Ebbsfleet U	46	3	7	13	18	41	0	6	17	20	57	3	13	30	38	98	–60	22

¶*Oldham Ath promoted via play-offs.*

NATIONAL LEAGUE PLAY-OFFS 2024–25

NATIONAL LEAGUE PLAY-OFF ELIMINATORS
Wednesday, 14 May 2025
Oldham Ath (3) 4 *(Garner 3, Kitching 10, Fondop-Talom 12, Pritchard 54)*
FC Halifax T (0) 0   10,865
Oldham Ath: (532) Hudson; Pritchard (Lundstram 88), Kitching, Ogle, Raglan, Monthe (Sutton 77); Yoganathan (Conlon 56), Evans (Rossiter 67), Pett; Fondop-Talom, Garner (Norwood 57).
FC Halifax T: (3421) Johnson; Jenkins (Alimi-Adetoro 16), Senior, Hoti; Emmanuel, Galvin, Cooke, Pugh (Emmerson 16); Thomas (High 64), Tarima (Nkrumah 57); Capello.
Referee: Aaron Bannister.

Thursday, 15 May 2025
Rochdale (2) 3 *(Rodney 8, 56 (pen), Bird 28)*
Southend U (1) 4 *(Ralph 22, Hopper 74, Chambers-Parillon 80, Kendall 101)*   5560
Rochdale: (343) Barrett; Beckwith (Buyabu 106), Ebanks-Landell (Ayinde 106), Gordon; Adebayo-Rowling, Allarakhia (Hogan 64), East (Weston 109), Gilmour; Bird (Mitchell 79), Rodney, Barlow (Henderson 71).
Southend U: (4132) Hayes; Scott-Morriss, Ralph, Taylor, Goodliffe; Husin (Gubbins 115); Appiah-Forson, Coker (Miley 90), Bridge (Chambers-Parillon 60); Walker (Bonne 60), Hopper (Kendall 98).
aet. Referee: Andrew Humphries.

NATIONAL LEAGUE PLAY-OFF SEMI-FINALS
Tuesday, 20 May 2025
York C (0) 0
Oldham Ath (1) 3 *(Garner 23, Yoganathan 49, Pritchard 51)*   8153
York C: (4231) Male; Walcott, John, Hunt (Batty 76), Howe; Felix, Sinclair (Luamba 59); Richardson (Armstrong 60), Akinyemi (Stones 60), Nathaniel-George (John-Lewis 82); Pearce.
Oldham Ath: (352) Hudson; Monthe, Raglan, Ogle; Pritchard, Kitching, Yoganathan (Conlon 77), Pett, Evans (Rossiter 85); Fondop-Talom, Garner (Norwood 80).
Referee: Zac Kennard-Kettle.

Wednesday, 21 May 2025
Forest Green R (0) 2 *(Inniss 62, Osadebe 94)*
Southend U (0) 2 *(Goodliffe 54, Bridge 116)*   3937
Forest Green R: (433) Cann; Long, Robson, Inniss, Moore-Taylor; May (Bunker 118), Sercombe, McCann; Quigley (Cardwell 90), McAllister (Knowles 113), Garrick (Osadebe 90).
Southend U: (4132) Hayes; Scott-Morriss, Ralph, Taylor, Goodliffe; Husin (Bridge 82); Appiah-Forson, Coker (Miley 67), Chambers-Parillon (Walker 95); Kendall (Bonne 60), Hopper (Gubbins 106).
aet; Southend U won 4-2 on penalties.
Referee: David Rock.

NATIONAL LEAGUE PLAY-OFF FINAL
Wembley Stadium, Sunday, 1 June 2025
Oldham Ath (0) 3 *(Garner 48 (pen), Norwood 110, Harratt 112)*
Southend U (1) 2 *(Monthe 5 (og), Chambers-Parillon 91)*   52,115
Oldham Ath: (352) Hudson; Monthe, Raglan, Ogle; Pritchard (Uchegbulam 67 (Rossiter 114)), Kitching (Hobson 98), Evans (Harratt 101), Pett, Yoganathan (Conlon 84); Garner (Norwood 75), Fondop-Talom.
Southend U: (352) Hayes; Ralph, Goodliffe, Taylor; Scott-Morriss, Bridge (Chambers-Parillon 64), Appiah-Forson (Gubbins 114), Miley (Coker 77), Husin; Kendall (Bonne 64), Hopper (Walker 90).
aet.
Referee: Elliot Bell.

NATIONAL LEAGUE ATTENDANCES BY CLUB 2024–25

	Aggregate 2024–25	Average 2024–25	Highest Attendance 2024–25
Southend U	168,805	7,339	9,677 v Wealdstone
York C	139,167	6,051	7,918 v Oldham Ath
Oldham Ath	134,779	5,860	8,611 v Rochdale
Hartlepool U	83,182	3,617	4,502 v Oldham Ath
Yeovil T	73,934	3,215	4,355 v Eastleigh
Sutton U	60,479	2,630	3,769 v Southend U
Rochdale	58,677	2,551	5,880 v Oldham Ath
Aldershot T	56,014	2,435	5,412 v Woking
Woking	53,587	2,330	4,701 v Aldershot T
Barnet	53,222	2,314	4,990 v Aldershot T
Eastleigh	51,378	2,234	3,212 v Hartlepool U
Boston U	48,896	2,126	3,865 v Wealdstone
Altrincham	47,967	2,086	3,561 v Oldham Ath
Forest Green R	42,201	1,835	3,002 v Yeovil T
FC Halifax T	40,104	1,744	3,961 v York C
Dagenham & Red	39,437	1,715	3,599 v Southend U
Wealdstone	36,780	1,599	2,843 v FC Halifax T
Ebbsfleet U	33,402	1,452	3,125 v Southend U
Gateshead	32,565	1,416	4,108 v Southend U
Maidenhead U	32,331	1,406	3,017 v Boston U
Solihull Moors	30,162	1,311	3,273 v Dagenham & Red
AFC Fylde	30,159	1,311	2,612 v Oldham Ath
Tamworth	30,030	1,306	1,933 v Oldham Ath
Braintree T	26,388	1,147	3,285 v Southend U

NATIONAL LEAGUE LEADING GOALSCORERS 2024–25

Player (Club)	League	FA Cup	FA Trophy	NL Cup	Play-offs	Total
Ollie Pearce (York C)	31	2	0	0	0	33
Regan Linney (Altrincham)	23	1	1	0	0	25
Daniel Creaney (Tamworth)	19	1	0	0	0	20
Will Davies (Sutton U)	18	0	2	0	0	20
Mike Fondop-Talum (Oldham Ath)	17	2	0	0	1	20
Nicolas Haughton (AFC Fylde)	19	0	1	0	0	20
Alex Reid (Wealdstone)	16	4	0	0	0	20
On loan from Oldham Ath.						
Devante Rodney (Rochdale)	17	0	1	0	2	20
Callum Stead (Barnet)	18	2	0	0	0	20
Kairo Mitchell (Rochdale)	14	3	2	0	0	19
Joshua Barrett (Aldershot T)	16	0	1	1	0	18
Emmanuel Dieseruvwe (Hartlepool U)	17	1	0	0	0	18
Josh Rees (Dagenham & Red)	15	2	0	1	0	18
James Henry (Aldershot T)	13	0	2	2	0	17
Kyrell Lisbie (Braintree T)	13	0	1	3	0	17
Shaun McCoulsky (Maidenhead U)	15	1	0	1	0	17
Gus Scott-Morris (Southend U)	17	0	0	0	0	17
Luke Hannant (Gateshead)	15	0	0	1	0	16
Jacob Hazel (Boston U)	13	1	1	1	0	16
Christian Doidge (Forest Green R)	12	2	0	1	0	15
Alex Newby (Altrincham)	15	0	0	0	0	15
Conor Wilkinson (Solihull Moors)	13	2	0	0	0	15
Owen Oseni (Gateshead)	13	1	0	0	0	14
Tyrese Shade (Eastleigh)	14	0	0	0	0	14
Jack Stevens (Solihull Moors)	13	1	0	0	0	14
Mark Shelton (Barnet)	12	0	0	0	0	12

NATIONAL LEAGUE NORTH LEADING GOALSCORERS 2024–25 (League only)

Player (Team)	Goals	Player (Team)	Goals
Ashley Hemmings (Kidderminster H)	30	Danny Whitehall (Scunthorpe U)	14
Paul Blackett (South Shields)	22	Mark Ellis (Chorley)	13
Callum Roberts (Scunthorpe U)	20	Matt Lowe (Brackley T)	13
Tom Peers (Chester)	19	Amari Morgan-Smith (Kidderminster H)	13
Connor Hall (Brackley T)	18	Mike Calveley (Chorley)	12
Glen Taylor (Spennymoor T)	18	Danny Lloyd-McGoldrick (Southport)	12
Michael Gyasi (Peterborough Sports)	15	Qamaruddine Kohyar (Kidderminster H)	12
Charlie Katon (Chester)	14	Lewis Salmon (Alfreton T)	12
Callum Stewart (Leamington)	14	James Spencer (Curzon Ashton)	12

NATIONAL LEAGUE SOUTH LEADING GOALSCORERS 2024–25 (League only)

Player (Team)	Goals	Player (Team)	Goals
Tyler Harvey (Truro C)	27	Sam Youngs (Enfield T)	17
George Alexander (Eastbourne Bor)	24	Danny Cashman (Worthing)	16
Kwesi Appiah (Boreham Wood)	24	Jaze Kabia (Truro C)	16
Cody Cooke (Torquay U)	20	Slavi Spasov (Slough T)	15
Luke Coulson (Weston-super-Mare)	20	Charlie Carter (Dorking W)	14
Alfie Rutherford (Dorking W)	20	Liam Nash (Worthing)	14
Aaron Blair (Maidstone U)	19	*Includes 7 goals for Hornchurch*	
Matt Rush (Boreham Wood)	18		
Includes 3 goals for Maidstone U			

NATIONAL LEAGUE NORTH 2024–25

NATIONAL LEAGUE NORTH TABLE 2024–25

(P) *promoted into division at end of 2023–24 season.*   (R) *Relegated into division at end of 2023–24 season.*

			Home					Away					Total						
		P	W	D	L	F	A	W	D	L	F	A	W	D	L	F	A	GD	Pts
1	Brackley T	46	15	1	7	37	17	14	4	5	38	25	29	5	12	75	42	33	92
2	Scunthorpe U¶	46	15	7	1	49	14	11	5	7	27	16	26	12	8	76	30	46	90
3	Kidderminster H (R)	46	15	3	5	44	13	12	5	6	42	24	27	8	11	86	37	49	89
4	Chester	46	14	7	2	36	13	11	5	7	37	32	25	12	9	73	45	28	87
5	Chorley	46	15	6	2	48	18	7	7	9	28	31	22	13	11	76	49	27	79
6	King's Lynn T	46	11	6	6	28	23	12	4	7	24	22	23	10	13	52	45	7	79
7	Buxton	46	13	2	8	36	25	11	3	9	40	27	24	5	17	76	52	24	77
8	Curzon Ashton	46	9	6	8	25	18	13	5	5	34	23	22	11	13	59	41	18	77
9	Spennymoor T	46	12	8	3	42	19	9	5	9	34	31	21	13	12	76	50	26	76
10	Hereford	46	12	5	6	38	24	10	5	8	30	27	22	10	14	68	51	17	76
11	Darlington	46	11	9	3	37	25	7	6	10	24	29	18	15	13	61	54	7	69
12	Peterborough Sports	46	10	5	8	29	21	7	7	9	26	36	17	12	17	55	57	–2	63
13	Scarborough Ath	46	10	5	8	34	26	6	8	9	30	32	16	13	17	64	58	6	61
14	Alfreton T	46	8	7	8	30	31	7	7	9	24	28	15	14	17	54	59	–5	59
15	Marine (P)	46	9	6	8	30	27	7	4	12	15	30	16	10	20	45	57	–12	58
16	Leamington (P)	46	12	5	6	38	26	3	5	15	14	30	15	10	21	52	56	–4	55
17	South Shields	46	10	4	9	33	27	6	2	15	27	46	16	6	24	60	73	–13	54
18	Southport	46	8	8	7	27	27	5	6	12	16	31	13	14	19	43	58	–15	53
19	Oxford C (R)	46	7	7	9	32	39	6	7	10	26	35	13	14	19	58	74	–16	53
20	Radcliffe (P)	46	8	3	12	36	43	5	9	9	20	32	13	12	21	56	75	–19	51
21	Needham Market (P)	46	5	4	14	22	31	5	5	13	22	45	10	9	27	44	76	–32	39
22	Rushall Olympic	46	6	5	12	25	38	3	3	17	17	60	9	8	29	42	98	–56	35
23	Warrington T	46	5	5	13	18	30	1	8	14	16	40	6	13	27	34	70	–36	31
24	Farsley Celtic	46	1	3	19	13	58	6	2	15	22	55	7	5	34	35	113	–78	26

¶*Scunthorpe U promoted via play-offs.*

NATIONAL LEAGUE NORTH PLAY-OFFS 2024–25

NATIONAL LEAGUE NORTH PLAY-OFF ELIMINATORS
Tuesday, 29 April 2025

Chorley (0) 1 *(Ellis 84)*

King's Lynn T (0) 0   2665

Chorley: Urwin; Henley, Ellis, Wilson, Blakeman, Calveley, Horbury, Clarke (Whitehouse 71), Senior, Carr, Hall.
Kings Lynn T: Jones; Sass (Crane 90), McFadden, Coulson (Barnes 90), Wilson, Crowe, Johnson, Taylor (Williams 90), IImami, Warburton, Omotayo.
Referee: Declan Brown.

Wednesday, 30 April 2025

Chester (1) 2 *(Murray 2, Burke 108)*

Buxton (1) 1 *(Elliott 18)*   4066

Chester: Storer; Roberts, Bainbridge, Woodthorpe, Leak, Burke, Weeks, Peers (Mottley-Henry 62), Murray (Rawlinson 116), Willoughby (O'Kane 57), Woods (Mooney 76).
Buxton: Grant; Lusala (Trueman 69 (Viggers 112)), Faulkner, Burton, Mann, Elliott (Martin 106), Kirby (De Girolamo 112), Ewing, Coleman (Sault 86), Brennan, Johnston (Popoola 81).
aet. Referee: Kavan Hurn.

NATIONAL LEAGUE NORTH PLAY-OFF SEMI-FINALS
Saturday, 3 May 2025

Scunthorpe U (3) 4 *(Whitehall 5, 22, Roberts 36, Ubaezuonu 66)*

Chorley (1) 2 *(Hall 7, 78)*   6365

Scunthorpe U: Fitzsimons; Evans, Kelly, Kouogun (Boyce 42), Denton (Scales 73), Starbuck, Clunan, Beestin (Brogan 90), Rowley, Whitehall (Fadera 82), Roberts (Ubaezuonu 44).
Chorley: Unwin; Ellis, Henley, Blakeman (Nolan 90), Wilson (Leckie 90), Senior (Touray 76), Calveley, Clarke (Whitehouse 61), Horbury, Hall, Carr (Lalkovic 90).
Referee: Dean Watson.

Sunday, 4 May 2025

Kidderminster H (1) 1 *(Morrison 19)*

Chester (1) 2 *(Mottley-Henry 35, Weeks 82)*   4647

Kidderminster H: Dibble; Morrison, Richards, Devine (Davis 55), McNally, Kandola (Beresford 90), Worrall (Obadeyi 86), Hemmings, Kouhyar (Reynolds 81), Brown, Morgan-Smith.
Chester: Storer; Roberts, Bainbridge, Woodthorpe, Leak, Burke, Weeks, Mottley-Henry (O'Kane 86), Murray, Willoughby (Mooney 70), Woods.
Referee: Jonathan Maskrey.

NATIONAL LEAGUE NORTH PLAY-OFF FINAL
Saturday, 17 May 2025

Scunthorpe U (1) 2 *(Whitehall 20, Ubaezuonu 105)*

Chester (0) 1 *(Woods 62 (pen))*   9860

Scunthorpe U: Fitzsimons; Evans, Kelly, Kouogun, Denton (Scales 84), Starbuck, Clunan, Beestin (Boyce 106), Rowley (Brogan 106), Whitehall (Fadera 96), Ubaezuonu (Fishburn 120).
Chester: Storer; Roberts (Willoughby 106), Bainbridge, Woodthorpe, Leak, Burke, Weeks, Mottley-Henry (Mooney 90), Peers, Murray (O'Kane 87), Woods.
aet.
Referee: Issac Searle.

NATIONAL LEAGUE SOUTH 2024–25

NATIONAL LEAGUE SOUTH TABLE 2024–25

(P) *promoted into division at end of 2023–24 season.*   (R) *Relegated into division at end of 2023–24 season.*

			Home					Away					Total					
		P	W	D	L	F	A	W	D	L	F	A	W	D	L	F	A	GD	Pts
1	Truro C	46	14	5	4	40	21	12	6	5	35	21	26	11	9	75	42	33	89
2	Torquay U	46	14	7	2	39	18	11	7	5	34	24	25	14	7	73	42	31	89
3	Eastbourne Bor	46	14	9	0	44	18	11	4	8	26	25	25	13	8	70	43	27	88
4	Worthing	46	14	6	3	41	22	12	4	7	37	36	26	10	10	78	58	20	88
5	Boreham Wood (R)¶	46	15	4	4	48	15	11	4	8	38	33	26	8	12	86	48	38	86
6	Dorking W (R)	46	12	7	4	42	28	12	7	4	47	26	24	14	8	89	54	35	86
7	Maidstone U	46	11	7	5	37	21	10	9	4	33	17	21	16	9	70	38	32	79
8	Weston-super-Mare	46	8	9	6	36	29	13	3	7	31	25	21	12	13	67	54	13	75
9	Hornchurch (P)	46	10	6	7	26	24	7	8	8	33	30	17	14	15	59	54	5	65
10	Farnborough	46	13	3	7	36	25	5	6	12	33	43	18	9	19	69	68	1	63
11	Chelmsford C	46	9	8	6	34	27	7	6	10	40	35	16	14	16	74	62	12	62
12	Hemel Hempstead	46	10	7	6	48	44	7	4	12	16	31	17	11	18	64	75	−11	62
13	Chesham U (P)	46	10	3	10	36	38	6	8	9	25	34	16	11	19	61	72	−11	59
14	Chippenham T	46	7	4	12	23	33	10	4	9	34	36	17	8	21	57	69	−12	59
15	Bath C	46	9	6	8	23	21	6	6	11	24	27	15	12	19	47	48	−1	57
16	Slough T	46	10	8	5	38	27	5	4	14	32	48	15	12	19	70	75	−5	57
17	Tonbridge Angels	46	11	3	9	29	28	4	9	10	22	33	15	12	19	51	61	−10	57
18	Hampton & Richmond Bor	46	8	4	11	35	40	6	5	12	25	34	14	9	23	60	74	−14	51
19	Enfield T (P)	46	7	4	12	24	47	6	5	12	25	41	13	9	24	49	88	−39	48
20	Salisbury (P)	46	7	5	11	26	30	3	11	9	30	39	10	16	20	56	69	−13	46
21	St Albans C	46	7	8	8	27	28	2	10	11	20	36	9	18	19	47	64	−17	45
22	Welling U	46	7	5	11	25	33	3	3	17	22	58	10	8	28	47	91	−44	38
23	Weymouth	46	4	8	11	31	41	2	7	14	12	36	6	15	25	43	77	−34	33
24	Aveley	46	5	6	12	26	35	3	2	18	19	46	8	8	30	45	81	−36	32

¶*Boreham Wood promoted via play-offs.*

NATIONAL LEAGUE SOUTH PLAY-OFFS 2024–25

■ *Denotes player sent off.*

NATIONAL LEAGUE SOUTH PLAY-OFF ELIMINATORS
Tuesday, 29 April 2025

Boreham Wood (1) 4 *(Sousa 16, Abdulmalik 83, Coxe 89, Ilesanmi 90)*

Dorking W (0) 3 *(Reynolds 53 (og), Prior 60, Bush 81 (og))* 1648

Boreham Wood: Ashmore; Reynolds, Ilesanmi, Coxe, Yarney (Bush 74), O'Connell (Appiah 76), Sousa, Whelan, Abdulmalik (Sagaf 90), Clayden (Dixon 64), Rush.
Dorking W: Foulkes; Craig, Norville-Williams, Camp, McManus (Briggs 53), Gallagher, Carter, Muitt■, Prior, Rutherford (Murphy 64 (Milsom 71)), Taylor.
Referee: Niall Smith.

Wednesday, 30 April 2025

Worthing (0) 0

Maidstone U (1) 2 *(Brookes 15 (pen), 90 (pen))* 2983

Worthing: Haig; Partington (Willard 64), Rea, Cook, Packham (Black 86), Colbran, Wheeler, Spong (Cashman 90), Martin, Faal, Babalola (Nash 61).
Maidstone U: Andre; Greenidge, Fowler, Seaman (Kyprianou 82), Brookes, Higgs (Gurung 86), Eweka, Trusty, Berkeley-Agyepong (Court 74), Leahy (Coulthirst 86), Blair (Wanjau-Smith 90).
Referee: Adam Merchant.

NATIONAL LEAGUE SOUTH PLAY-OFF SEMI-FINALS
Saturday, 3 May 2025

Torquay U (0) 0

Boreham Wood (0) 1 *(Rush 59)* 5721

Torquay U: Hamon; Threlkeld (Mussa 65), Foulston, Thomas (Palmer 86), Dyer, Dreyer, Jay (Moxey 89), Young, Hasani (Ash 83), Hayfield (Jenkins-Davies 62), Cooke.

Boreham Wood: Ashmore; Reynolds, Ilesanmi, Coxe (Bush 89), Yarney, O'Connell, Sousa, Whelan, Abdulmalik (Dixon 74), Clayden (Benton 63), Rush (Appiah 83).
Referee: Phillip Eddie.

Sunday, 4 May 2025

Eastbourne Bor (0) 1 *(Pavey 63)*

Maidstone U (1) 2 *(Berkeley-Agyepong 42, Blair 90)* 3194

Eastbourne Bor: Wright; Barry, Woollard Innocent, Kensdale, Gbadebo (Davis 46), Carter, Clarke J (Green 90), Clarke C, Adigun (Klass 76), Pavey (Alexander 80), Bamba (Ligendza 76).
Maidstone U: Andre; Greenidge, Fowler, Seaman■, Brookes, Higgs (Kyprianou 90), Eweka, Gurung (Come 84), Court (Brown 90), Berkeley-Agyepong, Blair.
Referee: Matthew Scholes.

NATIONAL LEAGUE SOUTH PLAY-OFF FINAL
Saturday, 17 May 2025

Boreham Wood (0) 1 *(Clayden 47)*

Maidstone U (0) 0 3500

Boreham Wood: Ashmore; Reynolds, Ilesanmi, Yarney (Bush 64), Richardson, O'Connell, Whelan, Abdulmalik (Payne 81), Benton (Marsh 84), Clayden (Appiah 72), Rush.
Maidstone U: Andre; Greenidge (Kyprianou 90), Fowler, Brookes, Higgs (Coulthirst 77), Eweka, Gurung (Willis 68), Court (Krasniqi 68), Berkeley-Agyepong, Leahy (Corne 55), Blair.
Referee: Gareth Thomas.

NATIONAL LEAGUE CUP 2024–25

GROUP A

Woking v Brighton & HA U21	2-2
Brighton & HA U21 won 4-3 on penalties.	
Maidenhead U v Fulham U21	2-0
Aldershot T v Derby Co U21	3-0
Aldershot T v Brighton & HA U21	2-3
Wealdstone v Fulham U21	0-2
Woking v Southampton U21	4-4
Woking won 3-0 on penalties.	
Maidenhead U v Derby Co U21	3-3
Maidenhead U won 7-6 on penalties.	
Wealdstone v Southampton U21	3-1
Aldershot T v Southampton U21	2-1
Wealdstone v Derby Co U21	2-0
Woking v Fulham U21	2-3
Maidenhead U v Brighton & HA U21	2-1
Woking v Derby Co U21	2-0
Aldershot T v Fulham U21	2-1
Wealdstone v Brighton & HA U21	0-1
Maidenhead U v Southampton U21	0-6

Group A Table	P	W	PW	PL	L	F	A	GD	Pts
Aldershot T	4	3	0	0	1	9	5	4	9
Brighton & HA U21	4	2	1	0	1	7	6	1	8
Maidenhead U	4	2	1	0	1	7	10	–3	8
Wealdstone	4	2	0	0	2	5	4	1	6
Woking	4	1	1	1	1	10	9	1	6
Fulham U21	4	2	0	0	2	6	6	0	6
Southampton U21	4	1	0	1	2	12	9	3	4
Derby Co U21	4	0	0	1	3	3	10	–7	1

GROUP B

Oldham Ath v Stoke C U21	2-1
Altrincham v Blackburn R U21	3-3
Altrincham won 6-5 on penalties.	
Forest Green R v Manchester U U21	2-3
Rochdale v Blackburn R U21	4-1
Forest Green R v Stoke C U21	0-4
Oldham Ath v Wolverhampton W U21	2-2
Wolverhampton W U21 won 4-2 on penalties.	
Altrincham v Manchester U U21	0-4
Rochdale v Manchester U U21	0-1
Altrincham v Stoke C U21	4-1
Oldham Ath v Blackburn R U21	3-2
Forest Green R v Wolverhampton W U21	0-2
Forest Green R v Blackburn R U21	4-2
Rochdale v Stoke C U21	2-0
Altrincham v Wolverhampton W U21	2-1
Oldham Ath v Manchester U U21	0-5
Rochdale v Wolverhampton W U21	2-2
Wolverhampton W U21 won 4-1 on penalties.	

Group B Table	P	W	PW	PL	L	F	A	GD	Pts
Manchester U U21	4	4	0	0	0	13	2	11	12
Altrincham	4	2	1	0	1	9	9	0	8
Rochdale	4	2	0	1	1	8	4	4	7
Wolverhampton W U21	4	1	2	0	1	7	6	1	7
Oldham Ath	4	2	0	1	1	7	10	–3	7
Stoke C U21	4	1	0	0	3	6	8	–2	3
Forest Green R	4	1	0	0	3	6	11	–5	3
Blackburn R U21	4	0	0	1	3	8	14	–6	1

GROUP C

FC Halifax T v Newcastle U U21	1-2
Boston U v Leeds U U21	3-4
Gateshead v Middlesbrough U21	1-0
Boston U v Sunderland U21	1-0
Tamworth v Newcastle U U21	1-1
Newcastle U U21 won 6-5 on penalties.	
Gateshead v Leeds U U21	1-2
FC Halifax T v Middlesbrough U21	1-4
Tamworth v Sunderland U21	1-5
Boston U v Newcastle U U21	3-2
FC Halifax T v Leeds U U21	2-2
Leeds U U21 won 5-3 on penalties.	
Gateshead v Sunderland U21	2-2
Gateshead won 5-4 on penalties.	
Boston U v Middlesbrough U21	1-1
Boston U won 5-4 on penalties.	
Gateshead v Newcastle U U21	2-4
Tamworth v Leeds U U21	2-1
FC Halifax T v Sunderland U21	2-1
Tamworth v Middlesbrough U21	0-2

Group C Table	P	W	PW	PL	L	F	A	GD	Pts
Newcastle U U21	4	2	1	0	1	9	7	2	8
Leeds U U21	4	2	1	0	1	9	8	1	8
Boston U	4	2	1	0	1	8	7	1	8
Middlesbrough U21	4	2	0	1	1	7	3	4	7
Gateshead	4	1	1	0	2	6	8	–2	5
Sunderland U21	4	1	0	1	2	8	6	2	4
FC Halifax T	4	1	0	1	2	6	9	–3	4
Tamworth	4	1	0	1	2	4	9	–5	4

GROUP D

Ebbsfleet U v WBA U21	2-2
Ebbsfleet U won 5-4 on penalties.	
Dagenham & Red v Tottenham H U21	5-5
Tottenham H U21 won 5-3 on penalties.	
Ebbsfleet U v Tottenham H U21	1-1
Tottenham H U21 won 4-3 on penalties.	
Braintree T v West Ham U U21	4-2
Dagenham & Red v WBA U21	2-1
Braintree T v WBA U21	3-2
Dagenham & Red v Nottingham F U21	1-3
Sutton U v Tottenham H U21	3-0
Braintree T v Nottingham F U21	1-0
Sutton U v West Ham U U21	0-2
Ebbsfleet U v West Ham U U21	1-2
Ebbsfleet U v Nottingham F U21	1-1
Nottingham F U21 won 2-1 on penalties.	
Sutton U v WBA U21	2-2
Sutton U won 3-1 on penalties.	
Dagenham & Red v West Ham U U21	2-0
Braintree T v Tottenham H U21	3-1
Sutton U v Nottingham F U21	3-2

Group D Table	P	W	PW	PL	L	F	A	GD	Pts
Braintree T	4	4	0	0	0	11	5	6	12
Sutton U	4	2	1	0	1	8	6	2	8
Dagenham & Red	4	2	0	1	1	8	9	–1	7
West Ham U U21	4	2	0	0	2	6	5	1	6
Ebbsfleet U	4	0	2	1	1	4	5	–1	5
Nottingham F U21	4	1	0	1	2	6	6	0	4
Tottenham H U21	4	0	2	0	2	7	12	–5	4
WBA U21	4	0	0	2	2	5	7	–2	2

QUARTER-FINALS

Sutton U v Manchester U U21	3-0
Altrincham v Newcastle U U21	3-3
Atrincham won 3-2 on penalties.	
Aldershot T v Leeds U U21	1-3
Braintree T v Brighton & HA U21	2-1

SEMI-FINALS

Altrincham v Leeds U U21	1-2
Braintree T v Sutton U	0-0
Sutton U won 5-4 on penalties.	

NATIONAL LEAGUE CUP FINAL 2024–25

VBS Community Stadium, Sutton,
Tuesday, 29 April 2025

Sutton U (0) 1 *(Simper 77)*

Leeds U U21 (1) 2 *(Monteiro 25, Gray 56)*   3062

Sutton U: (4231) Sims; Jackson (French 61), Muller, Ransom, Topallaj; Wadham, Odelusi, Nadesan, Simper, Boateng (De Silva 46); Davies.

Leeds U U21: (343) Mahady; Debayo, Diogo Monteiro, Moore; Douglas, Cresswell, Chadwick, Ferguson (Richards 85); Vincent (Snowdon 76), Gray (Nfonkeu 90), McDonald (Pickles 26).

Referee: Sam Mulhall.

AFC FYLDE

Ground: Mill Farm Sports Village, Coronation Way, Wesham, Lancashire PR4 3JZ. *Tel:* (01772) 682 593.
Website: afcfylde.co.uk *Email:* see website. *Year Formed:* 1988.
Record Attendance: 3,858 v Chorley, National League North, 26 December 2016. *Nickname:* 'The Coasters'.
Manager: Craig Mahon. *Colours:* White shirts with blue and red trim, white shorts, white socks.

AFC FYLDE – NATIONAL LEAGUE 2024–25 LEAGUE RECORD

Match No.	Date	Venue	Opponents	Result	H/T Score	Lg Pos.	Goalscorers	Attendance
1	Aug 10	H	Solihull Moors	W 3-2	1-2	5	Haughton 3 [10, 57, 83]	1090
2	17	A	Eastleigh	L 2-4	2-1	15	Haughton 2 (1 pen) [20 (p), 27]	1820
3	20	A	Oldham Ath	D 1-1	1-0	16	Riley [36]	5682
4	24	H	Maidenhead U	D 0-0	0-0	17		1005
5	26	A	Wealdstone	L 0-1	0-1	18		1325
6	Sept 7	H	Yeovil T	L 3-4	2-0	20	Haughton 2 [3, 35], Roberts [84]	1305
7	10	A	Forest Green R	L 0-3	0-1	22		1249
8	14	A	York C	L 0-3	0-0	23		5038
9	17	H	Southend U	W 2-1	1-0	19	Ustabasi [45], Haughton [90]	1088
10	21	H	Woking	D 1-1	0-0	20	Haughton [49]	1108
11	24	H	Tamworth	L 1-2	0-0	20	Haughton (pen) [66]	942
12	28	A	Barnet	L 0-2	0-0	22		2432
13	Oct 5	H	Aldershot T	W 5-2	3-2	21	Haughton [26], Jolley 2 [31, 66], Massey 2 [38, 54]	1147
14	19	A	Dagenham & Red	L 0-4	0-1	21		1312
15	23	A	Boston U	W 2-1	0-1	20	Whelan [53], Long [58]	1529
16	26	H	Altrincham	L 0-5	0-3	20		1392
17	Nov 9	H	Gateshead	W 3-0	1-0	18	Roberts [31], Massey [77], Haughton [81]	1287
18	16	A	Braintree T	L 0-1	0-0	21		900
19	26	A	Hartlepool U	L 0-2	0-0	22		2934
20	30	A	Sutton U	L 0-2	0-0	22		2050
21	Dec 10	H	Ebbsfleet U	W 2-0	0-0	19	Jolley [56], Ustabasi [71]	963
22	14	H	Eastleigh	D 2-2	1-0	18	Jolley [45], Ormerod [90]	985
23	21	A	Solihull Moors	L 1-4	1-2	20	Jolley [12]	1080
24	26	H	Rochdale	L 1-3	1-1	22	Massey [5]	2292
25	Jan 18	A	Maidenhead U	L 1-4	0-2	22	McFayden [60]	1017
26	25	H	Wealdstone	W 2-0	0-0	22	Boatswain [67], Haughton [81]	1082
27	28	A	Southend U	L 0-2	0-1	22		5638
28	Feb 1	H	Oldham Ath	L 1-2	0-0	22	Whelan [49]	2612
29	4	A	FC Halifax T	W 2-1	1-1	20	Roberts [23], Haughton (pen) [55]	1203
30	15	H	Dagenham & Red	D 1-1	0-1	22	Hugill [70]	1077
31	18	H	Boston U	L 1-2	1-2	22	Haughton (pen) [42]	1050
32	22	A	Altrincham	W 2-1	2-1	22	Massey [7], Haughton [26]	2034
33	Mar 1	A	Gateshead	D 1-1	0-1	21	Davis [64]	1458
34	4	H	Hartlepool U	W 2-1	2-1	20	Massey [12], Jolley [19]	924
35	8	H	Braintree T	L 0-2	0-1	20		1014
36	15	H	Ebbsfleet U	L 0-1	0-0	22		1215
37	18	H	Sutton U	L 1-2	1-0	23	Mitchell [15]	943
38	22	H	Forest Green R	W 3-0	1-0	21	Hugill [25], Davis [63], Haughton [71]	1444
39	29	A	Yeovil T	L 0-1	0-0	22		2734
40	Apr 1	A	Aldershot T	L 0-2	0-1	22		1460
41	5	H	York C	L 1-3	0-1	23	Haughton [79]	1977
42	12	A	Woking	L 0-1	0-0	23		1976
43	18	H	FC Halifax T	L 0-1	0-1	23		1733
44	21	A	Rochdale	D 0-0	0-0	23		2957
45	26	A	Tamworth	L 3-4	3-2	23	Haughton [30], Jolley [36], McFayden [45]	1100
46	May 5	H	Barnet	L 0-3	0-2	23		1699

Final League Position: 23

GOALSCORERS

League (50): Haughton 19 (4 pens), Jolley 7, Massey 6, Roberts 3, Davis 2, Hugill 2, McFayden 2, Ustabasi 2, Whelan 2, Boatswain 1, Long 1, Mitchell 1, Ormerod 1, Riley 1.
FA Cup (1): Roberts 1.
FA Trophy (2): Haughton 1, Jolley 1.

Richardson 6	Obi 14 + 8	Long 15 + 3	Mitchell 39 + 1	Whelan 43 + 2	Hosannah 18 + 7	Evans 28 + 4	Haughton 42 + 3	Ustabasi 23 + 10	Jolley 26 + 13	Ormerod 11 + 22	Riley 30 + 10	Gamble 6 + 4	Brennan 1 + 4	McFayden 23 + 8	O'Kane 6 + 14	Zanzala 4 + 8	Winterbottom 41	Davis 25 + 1	Massey 25 + 13	Roberts 23 + 6	Bardell 21 + 4	Hugill 20 + 6	Sassi 4 + 2	Stokes 5 + 1	Boatswain 7 + 11	Adom — + 6	Match No.
1	2¹	3	4	5⁵	6	7²	8	9³	10⁴	11	12	13	14	15	16												1
1	2	3	4	5	6³	9	8¹	10	12	11²	7			14	13												2
		4	5	6	12	8	9	11¹	10¹	15	7²		2³	14		13	1	3									3
		6	13	4²	3	7⁴	8	11¹	10³	14	5	16	9⁵	15	12		1	2									4
	3	7²	6³	9	12	5	8⁴	11	15	10⁵	13	2		4¹	14		1	16									5
	3	4⁵	5	6	8	9	10²	12	7⁴	14				15	11³		1	2¹	13	16							6
15	3²	4	5	6			8	10¹	14	16	7			12	9⁵		1	2⁵	11⁴	13							7
	3	4	5	6			8⁴	9²	13	14	7³		15	12	11¹		1	2	10								8
15	3	10	2	4	5	7²	9	14	11⁴	8¹	12	13					1		6³								9
	3	10	2	4	5	7	9⁴	14	11¹	8³	13	12					1		6								10
		9	2	3	4	7	12	8¹	11²	13	5			10⁴	14		1		6³	15							11
13	3⁴	9	2	4	10⁵	6	8²	11¹	7³	5				16	15		1		12	14							12
1		3	10	2⁵	4	5¹	8	11³	13	9	6	14	12					7									13
13		3	9	2		6¹	12	8³	14	7⁴	5	4		11²	15			10									14
1			4	8	3	5	7	12			6			9				2	11¹	10							15
1			4¹	8	3⁴	5	12	7²	15	13	6⁵	16		9	14			2	11³	10							16
	2		8	3	4²	5¹	6	7	11⁴		13		16	14	10³	1		12	9⁵	15							17
	2		8	3	4	5	6	7	11¹	10							1	12	9⁴								18
	2	3		4²	5	7	9	11¹	8				13	10		1		6	12								19
11	2	6	3		4¹	5	13	12	10²				7	9		1		8									20
	2		8	3	5	6²	7	11¹	12			13				1		9	4	10							21
	2		8	3	5	6	7	11²	12							1		13	9	4	10¹						22
	2		8	3	5¹	6²	7³	11	14	12						1		13	9	4	10						23
	4		5	3	12		8³		13	11⁴	14		2	15		1		9²	10	6¹	7						24
			8¹	4	7	12	9	11³	10²	15				3			1		14	6	2⁴			5	13		25
	2		8	15	7¹				10²	4³	14	12		3			1		9	13	6⁴			5	11		26
	4		8⁴	12	15	9	7	11¹	6				3	16		1		13	10⁵	2²	14		5³				27
	4		9	5		9	7	13	12				3			1		11	10	2²	6¹						28
			9	5	2²		8³	10	14	6			3			1	4	11¹	7	13	12						29
12				5³			8¹	9	14		6		3			1	4	11	7²	2	10	13					30
				5			8	11¹			6		3			1	4	9	7²	2	10	13	12				31
			8	6	10				7³		6		3			1	4	9²	13	7	14			11¹	12		32
			8	4	11			12			6		3			1	5	7	9¹	2	13			10²			33
			8	5	9		11¹			6			3			1	4	10³	13	2	7²	14	12				34
16			6⁴	5	3				9	14	7³		8	14			4	11⁵	10²	2	13	12	15				35
16			8¹	5	3⁵				9³		13	6			14		4	7	11	2⁴	12	15			10²		36
			8	5	13	12				11¹	9			3			1	4	10⁴	7³		6	2²		14	15	37
14			8	5		12		11²		9³				3			1	2	10¹	7⁴	4	6			13	15	38
			8	5	13	9	12				6³			3			1	4	11²	10¹	2	7			14		39
			6	5	15	3²	11	7⁵	16	12	14						1	4	9¹	10⁴		8³	2		13		40
			8	5	15	13	11	12	7²	16	6⁴			3			1	4	9¹	2³	10⁵	14					41
14			6	5	3¹	10	12	7³	8			15					1	4	13	2	9²	11⁴					42
			5	4	3¹	9	7⁴	14	16	12				8⁵			1	11	10²	2³	6	13			15		43
13			8		10²			14	15		7¹	9		3			1	5	12	2	6			3⁴	11³		44
			4			7⁴	8²	10	15	9	14	12		3			1	5¹	16	2	6³	13			11¹		45
15					12	9¹	10	14	11³	13	6⁵		8			1	5	16	2	7	4²	3⁴					46

FA Cup
Fourth Qualifying   Rochdale   (h)   1-4

FA Trophy
Third Round   Kidderminster H   (h)   2-2
(Kidderminster H won 3-0 on penalties)

ALDERSHOT TOWN

Ground: The EBB Stadium at the Recreation Ground, High Street, Aldershot, Hampshire GU11 1TW.
Tel: (01252) 320 211.   *Website:* www.theshots.co.uk   *Email:* admin@theshots.co.uk   *Year Formed:* 1926
(Reformed 1992).   *Record Attendance:* 19,138 v Carlisle U, FA Cup 4th rd (replay), 28 January 1970.
Nickname: 'The Shots'.   *Manager:* Tommy Widdrington.   *Colours:* Red and blue striped shirts with red sleeves and
blue trim, red shorts with blue trim, red socks with blue trim.

ALDERSHOT TOWN – NATIONAL LEAGUE 2024–25 LEAGUE RECORD

Match No.	Date	Venue	Opponents	Result		H/T Score	Lg Pos.	Goalscorers	Attendance
1	Aug 10	H	Forest Green R	D	3-3	2-1	10	Ghandour 2 [7, 11], Henry [80]	2564
2	17	A	FC Halifax T	W	1-0	1-0	8	Barrett [3]	1642
3	20	A	Braintree T	L	1-2	1-0	13	Jones R [45]	1227
4	24	H	Oldham Ath	W	4-1	1-0	7	Henry 2 [38, 58], Frost [67], Widdrington (pen) [90]	2407
5	26	A	Tamworth	L	2-3	1-1	11	Barham [32], Henry [90]	1563
6	31	H	Maidenhead U	W	4-3	1-1	7	Henry [3], Scott [57], Corbett [62], Ghandour [72]	2408
7	Sept 7	H	Rochdale	L	0-2	0-2	8		2565
8	10	A	Ebbsfleet U	D	0-0	0-0	10		1175
9	14	A	Boston U	D	1-1	1-0	14	Barrett [29]	1949
10	21	H	York C	D	0-0	0-0	14		2567
11	24	H	Barnet	L	0-1	0-1	17		1915
12	28	A	Yeovil T	D	1-1	1-0	15	Barrett [7]	3408
13	Oct 5	A	AFC Fylde	L	2-5	2-3	17	Barrett [40], Henry [45]	1147
14	19	H	Eastleigh	W	2-1	0-0	16	Barham [70], Jones R [79]	3037
15	23	H	Southend U	D	0-0	0-0	16		2557
16	26	A	Hartlepool U	L	0-2	0-1	17		3356
17	Nov 9	H	Wealdstone	L	0-2	0-1	17		3156
18	16	A	Gateshead	D	2-2	1-2	18	Barrett [10], Barham [56]	1332
19	23	H	Altrincham	W	2-1	2-0	17	Henry 2 [26, 30]	1532
20	26	A	Dagenham & Red	L	2-3	0-0	17	Tetek [83], Barham [90]	1210
21	Dec 10	A	Solihull Moors	L	1-2	0-1	17	Barham [56]	740
22	14	H	FC Halifax T	L	3-4	2-2	17	Akpan [46], Henry [79], Barham [90]	2047
23	21	A	Forest Green R	D	1-1	1-0	19	Jones R [44]	2116
24	26	H	Woking	D	2-2	1-1	18	Frost [28], Barrett [67]	5412
25	Jan 1	A	Sutton U	D	1-1	0-1	18	Hargreaves [90]	3013
26	14	A	Braintree T	D	2-2	2-2	18	Henry [16], Barrett [24]	1437
27	18	A	Oldham Ath	W	3-1	2-1	18	Barrett 3 [44, 45, 51]	5960
28	25	H	Tamworth	D	2-2	0-0	18	Barham [53], Woodhouse [80]	2323
29	Feb 15	A	Eastleigh	L	0-2	0-2	19		2794
30	18	A	Southend U	L	1-2	0-0	20	Hargreaves [78]	6632
31	22	H	Hartlepool U	W	3-2	0-1	20	Ferguson (og) [60], Hargreaves [67], Barrett [90]	2203
32	25	H	Solihull Moors	W	3-1	3-0	17	Hargreaves [2], Jones A [16], Jones R [37]	1603
33	Mar 4	H	Dagenham & Red	D	0-0	0-0	18		1657
34	8	H	Gateshead	W	3-1	1-1	18	Barrett [5], Jones R [58], Barham [81]	2188
35	15	A	Altrincham	W	2-1	0-0	16	Hargreaves [65], Mullins [88]	2015
36	18	A	Maidenhead U	W	1-0	0-0	14	Frost [54]	1386
37	22	H	Ebbsfleet U	D	3-3	2-3	16	Jones R [14], Barrett [19], Frost (pen) [67]	2685
38	25	A	Wealdstone	W	3-1	0-1	13	Henry 2 [63, 67], Barrett [73]	1331
39	29	A	Rochdale	L	0-4	0-2	15		2270
40	Apr 1	H	AFC Fylde	W	2-0	1-0	12	Henry [40], Barrett [90]	1460
41	8	H	Boston U	L	1-2	1-0	14	Frost [45]	1738
42	12	A	York C	L	2-7	2-4	15	Barham [21], Thomas [45]	5872
43	18	A	Sutton U	D	1-1	0-1	16	Barrett [56]	3464
44	21	A	Woking	L	0-3	0-3	17		4701
45	26	A	Barnet	L	0-4	0-2	18		4990
46	May 5	H	Yeovil T	W	2-1	1-0	16	Barham [39], Frost [49]	3089

Final League Position: 16

GOALSCORERS

League (69): Barrett 16, Henry 13, Barham 10, Jones R 6, Hargreaves 5, Ghandour 3, Akpan 1, Corbett 1, Jones A 1, Mullins 1, Scott 1, Tetek 1, Thomas 1, Widdrington 1 (1 pen), Woodhouse 1, own goal 1.
FA Cup (3): Akpan 1, Barham 1, Mullins 1.
FA Trophy (21): Corbett 4, Jones 3, Barham 3, Barret 2, Henry 2 (1 pen), Stuttle 2, Armitage 1, Ellison 1, Frost 1, Maghoma 1, Mullins 1.

Dewhurst 43	Harfield 6	Hargreaves 39 + 4	Jenkins 6 + 4	Jones R 29 + 11	Maghoma 21 + 2	Widdrington 31 + 5	Frost 29 + 8	Barrett 33 + 5	Corbett 11 + 23	Ghandour 15 + 5	Henry 25 + 15	Barham 30 + 14	Tetek 13 + 9	Byrd 15 + 2	Mullins 5 + 27	Akpan 16 + 1	Vaughan — + 2	Menayese 10 + 2	Scott 20 + 3	Jones A 30 + 2	Bray 1 + 5	Krusnell 1 + 1	Ellison 18 + 4	van Stappershoef 3	Maja-Awesu 1 + 8	Stuttle 1 + 5	Armitage 20	Woodhouse 20	Dolaghan — + 3	Uwakwe — + 3	Anderson 7 + 2	Laing 4	Thomas 3 + 5	Match No.
1	2	3	4	5	6	7^2	8	9^3	10^1	11	12	13	14																					1
1		5	3	6	4	7	8	10^3	9^1	11^2	12	13				2	14																	2
1		6	3	5	4	7	8	10^1	9^2	11	12	13				2																		3
1		4^3	3	5^2	6	7	8^5	11^4	10	9^1	13	14				2		15	12	16														4
1		5	16		6		13^5	14	10	15	9^3	2^1	4	11^2	8^4	3		7	12															5
1	2	4	14	3		7^2		11^3	10^4	9^1	12	13				16			5	6	8^5		15											6
1	2	6	14	3		7		13	9^1	10	11^2	12							4	5	8^3													7
1		3	5		4	7	10^3	14	11^1	12	13	9^2				2				6	8													8
1		3	15	5	4	7	10^1	13	12	9^3	11^5	14				2	16		8^4	6^2														9
1	3^2	7	13	2	6		10^5	14	11	9^4	15	4		8^1		12		16	5^5															10
1		7	11	2	3		14	10^5	12	9^5	8^3	4	13			5			6^4															11
1		6	11^4	2		12	9	14	10^5	5^3		7^1	3	16		4	15	13					8^2											12
1		6	7^1	2	5	15	10^2	16	11^3	9^5	14	3		8		12		13	4^4	1														13
1		7	12		6	14	10^2	11^3	9^4	13	5	15		8		2		4^1	3															14
1		7	11^4		6	2^2	13	10^1	12	14	9^3	5		8		3		15	4															15
1		7	15			10^3	9^1	16	11^4	6^2	12	5^5		8		2		4	3				14	13										16
1	8^1	9	2	7	5	11^3		13	14	10^2	3	12						6^4		4^4														17
1	12	7	2	6^1	13	11^3		14	5^4	10	8^2	15	9	3		4																		18
1		6	7		5	13	11^1	15	9^4	10^3	12	14		8		2	3		4^2															19
1		7^2	8^1	2	6^4	5	11^3	14	10	13	12	9		3		4																		20
1		6	7		5^2		14	13	10	8	3	11^3	9			2^1							4	1			12							21
1		6	3^2	7	12		14	11^1		5	10	8^4	15	9^1		2							4	1			13							22
1		7		8	6	13	2^1		12	5^2	10	9^3		11		3							4				14							23
1	7^3	6		3	13	8	12	14	10^2	11^3	9^1			2		5							4											24
1	14	6		3	7	9^4	10^1	13	11^3	8	12^5	16		2		5							4^2		15									25
1	13	9^1	4	8	12	10	14	7^4	11	6^3	15	2^2		3												5								26
1		7		6^3	9	11^1		8	12	14	13			3		2										10^2	4	5						27
1		7		6	9	11		8^1	10^2		12			3		2										13	4	5						28
1		7	16	14	6^1	9	11^3	12		8^2	10			15		3^4	2^5										4	5	13					29
1		6	15	12	7	8	10^3	11^4		9	14			2^2		5^1										4	3	13					30
1		7	4^4	10^1	13	6	9^2			11				12		2	5		15	14			3^3	8										31
1	7^2		10	4	6	9^4	15	11^3		14				2^1		5							12				3	8	13					32
1		8	9^3	3^2	7^1	6	11			10				13		5			12								4	2	14					33
1		7	14	9	8^5	6	11^4	15		10^1	13			5		3^2		12								4	2	16					34
1		6		9^1	8	11^2		14	10^4	12				2	15	5		13	4	3			7^3											35
1		8	15	14		11	12	10^3	9^4		7^5			5	16	3^2		6^1	4	2			13											36
1		7	11	13	6	9	14		12	10^2				5					4	2			8^3	3^1										37
1		8	10	13	6	9^5	15	12	11^1	14				5					4	2			7^3	3^2										38
1		8	6	13		10^4	11^3	16		5				14					4	2			7^2	3^1	12									39
1	15	12		8^2	14		6^3		9^4	13		11		5^1		3			2				7	4	10									40
1	8		5	6		9^1			13									10^2	3	12			4	2	7			11						41
1	8^4	9^1	7^3	6^2	11^5	15	13	10		5									3				4	2^4	16	14	12							42
1		7	8	11		6^1	9^2	10	13					3					5				4	2			12							43
1		7^5		6^1	14	11^3	13	12	8	16				5^2		3		15	4	2			9^4	10										44
1		7^3	6	11^2	15	9	10^5	8	16					5^4	14	3		12	4^1	2							13							45
1		7^2	8^5	6	9^4	15	10^3	11^1	12	14				5	16	3			4	2							13							46

FA Cup
Fourth Qualifying	Bath C	(h)	2-1
First Round	Bradford C	(a)	1-3

FA Trophy
Third Round	Wealdstone	(h)	3-1
Fourth Round	Chertsey T	(h)	8-0
Fifth Round	Boreham Wood	(h)	2-0
Quarter-Finals	Sittingbourne	(a)	3-0
Semi-Finals	Woking	(h)	2-1
Final	Spennymoor T	(Wembley)	3-0

ALTRINCHAM

Ground: J. Davidson Stadium, Moss Lane, Altrincham WA15 8AP.   *Tel:* (0161) 928 1045.
Website: www.altrinchamfc.com   *Email:* hello@altyfc.com   *Year Formed:* 1891 (renamed Altrincham 1903).
Record Attendance: 10,275 Altrincham Boys v Sunderland Boys, ESFA Shield, 28 February 1925 at Moss Lane; 35,175
v Everton, FA Cup 3rd rd replay, 7 January 1975 at Old Trafford.   *Nickname:* 'The Robins'.   *Manager:* Phil Parkinson.
Colours: Red and white striped shirts with red sleeves, black shorts with white trim, white socks with red trim.

ALTRINCHAM – NATIONAL LEAGUE 2024–25 LEAGUE RECORD

Match No.	Date	Venue	Opponents	Result	H/T Score	Lg Pos.	Goalscorers	Atten-dance
1	Aug 10	H	Woking	W 1-0	1-0	8	Golden [27]	1548
2	17	A	Sutton U	L 0-5	0-4	16		2456
3	20	A	Maidenhead U	W 1-0	1-0	9	Jones J [36]	1027
4	24	H	Eastleigh	L 0-1	0-0	11		1601
5	26	A	Forest Green R	L 1-2	0-1	16	Wilson [83]	1982
6	31	H	Oldham Ath	D 1-1	0-1	15	Linney [68]	3561
7	Sept 7	H	Ebbsfleet U	W 4-0	2-0	11	Linney [9], Newby [10], Jones E [46], Reddin [87]	2024
8	10	A	Barnet	L 1-2	1-1	16	Amaluzor [14]	1207
9	14	A	Yeovil T	D 0-0	0-0	16		2838
10	21	H	Boston U	D 2-2	0-0	17	Newby [66], Linney [67]	2031
11	24	H	Dagenham & Red	W 2-1	1-1	11	Linney [1], Crawford [71]	1236
12	28	A	Tamworth	W 2-1	0-0	9	Newby [61], Amaluzor [78]	1358
13	Oct 5	A	Braintree T	L 0-2	0-1	11		726
14	19	H	Gateshead	D 2-2	1-2	14	Crawford (pen) [20], Newby [86]	1881
15	23	H	Hartlepool U	D 1-1	1-1	13	Banks [29]	1463
16	26	A	AFC Fylde	W 5-0	3-0	9	Linney 3 [5, 10, 41], Newby [54], Osborne [80]	1392
17	Nov 9	A	Solihull Moors	D 3-3	0-2	10	Linney 2 [72, 82], Kosylo [90]	1059
18	16	H	Southend U	W 2-0	2-0	10	Nuttall [9], Newby [42]	2536
19	23	A	Aldershot T	L 1-2	0-2	10	Bickerstaff [90]	1532
20	26	H	York C	W 3-0	3-0	7	Linney 2 [20, 36], Kosylo [40]	2006
21	Dec 10	A	Wealdstone	D 3-3	2-2	8	Crawford [34], Linney 2 (1 pen) [42, 54 (p)]	1005
22	14	H	Sutton U	W 1-0	1-0	6	Linney [10]	1820
23	21	A	Woking	L 1-2	0-0	9	Newby [71]	1848
24	26	H	FC Halifax T	D 0-0	0-0	9		3312
25	Jan 14	H	Maidenhead U	W 4-0	4-0	9	Newby 3 [7, 26, 45], Linney (pen) [33]	1608
26	18	A	Eastleigh	W 2-1	1-1	6	Newby [6], Crawford [71]	1931
27	25	H	Forest Green R	D 1-1	1-0	7	Nuttall [11]	2089
28	Feb 8	H	Braintree T	W 3-1	2-0	7	Newby [8], Linney (pen) [30], Nuttall [74]	1674
29	11	A	Oldham Ath	D 2-2	1-0	7	Newby [41], Linney [46]	5491
30	15	A	Gateshead	W 1-0	1-0	7	Taylor [14]	1114
31	18	A	Hartlepool U	W 2-1	0-0	6	Linney [87], Weaver [90]	3302
32	22	H	AFC Fylde	L 1-2	1-2	7	Banks [16]	2034
33	Mar 4	A	York C	W 2-1	1-0	7	Stones (og) [25], Amaluzor [75]	6365
34	8	A	Southend U	L 1-2	0-2	7	Linney [59]	7776
35	11	A	Rochdale	L 0-3	0-0	8		2053
36	15	H	Aldershot T	L 1-2	0-0	8	Newby [73]	2015
37	18	H	Wealdstone	L 0-1	0-0	8		1435
38	22	H	Barnet	L 0-1	0-1	9		3071
39	25	A	Solihull Moors	D 1-1	1-0	8	Linney [17]	1336
40	29	A	Ebbsfleet U	D 2-2	1-1	9	Linney (pen) [17], Amaluzor [75]	1173
41	Apr 5	H	Yeovil T	W 2-1	1-1	8	Golden [30], Baines [88]	1851
42	12	A	Boston U	L 0-1	0-1	8		2320
43	18	H	Rochdale	L 1-2	0-1	9	Marriott [58]	3464
44	21	A	FC Halifax T	W 3-0	1-0	9	Bickerstaff [10], Linney 2 (1 pen) [65 (p), 73]	1896
45	26	A	Dagenham & Red	L 1-6	0-4	9	Nuttall [90]	2002
46	May 5	H	Tamworth	D 1-1	0-1	9	Newby [48]	2371

Final League Position: 9

GOALSCORERS

League (68): Linney 23 (5 pens), Newby 15, Amaluzor 4, Crawford 4 (1 pen), Nuttall 4, Banks 2, Bickerstaff 2, Golden 2, Kosylo 2, Baines 1, Jones E 1, Jones J 1, Marriott 1, Osborne 1, Reddin 1, Taylor 1, Weaver 1, Wilson 1, own goal 1.
FA Cup (3): Crawford 1, Linney 1 (1 pen), Olson 1.
FA Trophy (4): Crawford 2, Linney 1, Nuttall 1.

Ross 27	Banks 41 + 3	Jones E 10 + 4	Baines 36 + 1	Cooper 15 + 9	Osborne 35 + 7	Newby 42 + 2	Haygarth 4 + 2	Crawford 39 + 2	Nuttall 13 + 13	Amaluzor 25 + 4	Golden 38 + 3	Wilson 15 + 14	Linney 36 + 6	Reddin 9 + 25	Jones J 21 + 6	Weaver 3 + 17	Kosylo 13 + 12	Bickerstaff 12 + 14	Humbles 6 + 2	Thompson — + 1	Crankshaw 3 + 4	Teale 1	Olson 20	Randle 1 + 1	Marriott 12 + 6	Pasiek 4 + 3	Fallon — + 1	Taylor 3 + 2	Ansen 11 + 1	Griffiths — + 2	Penney — + 3	Lainton 7	Dolan 4 + 2	Match No.
1	2	3^4	4	5	6	7^1	8^3	9	10^4	11^2	12	13	14	15																				1
1	2		3	4^1	10^4	9	7^2	6	11^3	8^5	5	14	13	15	12	16																		2
1	2		3	4	6	7^2	8^1	9^4	10	11^3	5	13	12	14	15																			3
1	2		3	4	6	7	8^1	9	10	11^2	5	12	13																					4
1	2		3^1	4	6^2	7	8^5	15	10	11^4	5	12	13	9^3	14		16																	5
1	15		3	5^3	12	6^1	14	9	10	4	8	2	7^4	13	11^2																			6
1	2	4^1	5		6	7^3	8^4	9	10^2	15	14	3	13	11^5	12	16																		7
1	2^5		5	14	6	7^4	8^1	10	11^2	16	4	3	13	15	12		9^3																	8
1	2		5		6	7^1	8^2	11	12	14	4	3	13	9^3	10																			9
1	3		5		6	7	8^1	9	11^2		4	2	12	10	13																			10
1	3		5		6^2	7	8	9	12	10^3	4	2	11^1	13	14																			11
1	3		5^1	14	6^4	7	8	9^5	12	10^2	4	2	11^1	13	15																			12
1	3		5	14	6	7^2	8^4	9		10^3	4^1	2	11	15	13	12																		13
1	15	3	4	14	6^3	7^4	8	9^1	10		5	2	11^2	13		12																		14
1	3		5		6	7	8	9			4	2	11	10																				15
1	3^4	15	5	14	6^2	7^1	8	9	12	10	4	2	11^3	13																				16
1		3	5	14	6^1	7^5	8	9^3	10^2	16	4	2	11^4	13		12		15																17
	3		5		6^2	7^1	8^1	9	10		4	2	11^3	13		12	14	15				1												18
1	3		5		6^3	7	8	9^8	10^1		4	2	11^2	13		12	14																	19
1	3	15	5		6^4	7^2	8	9	10^1	14	4^5	2	11^3	13	16	12																		20
1	2		4	14	15	6		10				3	13	7^3	16	12	11^1	9^5					5^2		8^4									21
1	2		4		7^1	10^3		8				3	6	11^2	13	14	9^4	15					5		12									22
1	2		4		11^1	7		8				3	6^3	10	12	14	9^2						5		13									23
1	2	13	5		10^3	11		6				3	8^2	9^1		14	7^8						4		12									24
1			5		9	7^1		8	12			2		11^3	14		13	15		10^2			4	6^4	3									25
1	2^4		5	15	8	9		6				3	10^2	11	14	12	7^1				13		4^3											26
1	2		5	13	6	9^4		8				3	11^1	10^2	12	14	15				7^3		4											27
1^2	2		5	6	9^1	8		11	10^4			3^3		15		7	13^8						4			12	14							28
	2		5	13	6	9^3		8				3	7^1	10^2		12	11						4			14			1					29
	2		5		6	10^1		8	15	14		3		12	7^2		11^3						4			9^4			1				13	30
	2	15			6			8	11			3	7^3	10^4	16		4						14			5^1	9^2		1	13	12^5			31
	2		5		6			8	15			3^1	7^4	10		12	4						13			9^3	14	11^2	1					32
	2		5	4	8	7			9			3	10^3	11^2		12							13		6^1			14	1					33
	2		5	4	8^1	10^4			9			3	7^2			12	11	15					13		6^3			14	1					34
13			5	4	10	9			12			2	7^4				11						14		6^2	3^1		8^3	1					35
	2	4	5	13	6	10			12	14		3	9^3		7^4		11	15							5^1			8^2	1					36
	2		5	4	8	7						3^2	10^1	9^3		12	11						13		6			14	1					37
	2	3^1	5	4					9	14				10	7^2		11	15					13		6^4		12	8^3	1					38
	2		5	4	10			8	9			3	7^8	11^2		12	11						13		6		12		1					39
	2		5		10^1	7		8				3		11^4		12	9^3	15					4		6^2			14				1	13	40
	2		5	13	6	7		8				3		11		12	10^1						4		9^2							1		41
	2		5		6^5	10		8		14		3^4		11	16	12	9^2	13					13		4^1						15	1	7^3	42
	2		5	13	10			8^3		14		3		11		12	9^4						4		6^2						15	1	7^1	43
	2		4		6	9^4		7		14		3		10		12	11^1	15					8^2		5^3							1	13	44
	2		4^1		6	9		7		15		3^3		10	16	12	11^5						13		5					14	8^2	1^4		45
	2		5		6	9^2		8				3		10		12	11^1						13		4							1	7	46

FA Cup

Fourth Qualifying	Solihull Moors	(h)	1-1
Replay	Solihull Moors	(a)	2-2

(aet; Solihull Moors won 3-1 on penalties)

FA Trophy

Third Round	Macclesfield	(h)	0-0
(Altrincham won 4-2 on penalties)			
Fourth Round	Barnet	(h)	3-1
Fifth Round	Eastleigh	(h)	1-0
Quarter-Finals	Rochdale	(a)	0-2

BARNET

Ground: The Hive Stadium, Camrose Avenue, Edgware, London HA8 6AG. *Tel:* (020) 8381 3800.
Website: www.barnetfc.com *Email:* justtellus@thehivelondon.com *Year Formed:* 1888.
Record Attendance: 11,026 v Wycombe Wanderers, FA Amateur Cup 4th rd, 2 February 1952 (at Underhill);
6,215 v Brentford, FA Cup 4th rd, 28 January 2019 (at The Hive Stadium). *Nickname:* 'The Bees'.
Manager: Dean Brennan. *Colours:* Amber shirts with black trim, black shorts, black socks.

BARNET – NATIONAL LEAGUE 2024–25 LEAGUE RECORD

Match No.	Date	Venue	Opponents	Result	H/T Score	Lg Pos.	Goalscorers	Attendance
1	Aug 10	A	FC Halifax T	L	1-2	0-0	17	Coker [55]	1634
2	17	A	Ebbsfleet U	W	2-1	1-0	12	Stead 2 [43, 70]	1636
3	20	H	Forest Green R	W	1-0	0-0	7	Brunt [90]	1710
4	24	H	Southend U	W	2-1	1-0	3	Chapman [31], Shelton (pen) [70]	2932
5	26	A	Maidenhead U	L	1-3	1-2	5	Stead [45]	1426
6	31	H	Tamworth	W	7-0	3-0	3	Brunt 3 (1 pen) [7, 33, 49 (p)], Glover [27], Shelton [60], Stead [62], Chapman [76]	1372
7	Sept 7	A	Gateshead	L	0-2	0-1	6		1461
8	10	A	Altrincham	W	2-1	1-1	6	Chapman [27], Browne [90]	1207
9	14	H	Braintree T	W	3-1	2-1	3	Shelton [4], Stead [16], Langston (og) [83]	1507
10	21	A	Wealdstone	W	3-0	0-0	1	Shelton (pen) [61], Stead [66], Kabamba [90]	2590
11	24	H	Aldershot T	W	1-0	1-0	1	Kabamba [26]	1915
12	28	H	AFC Fylde	W	2-0	0-0	1	Kabamba [57], Stead [90]	2432
13	Oct 5	H	Boston U	W	3-1	0-1	1	Stead [57], Tavares [70], Kabamba [86]	2006
14	19	A	Solihull Moors	L	3-4	1-2	1	Kabamba 2 [12, 90], Brunt [90]	1822
15	22	A	York C	L	1-3	1-1	3	Hobson [37]	6041
16	26	H	Rochdale	W	2-1	2-0	3	Kabamba [6], Coker [41]	2137
17	Nov 9	H	Oldham Ath	D	0-0	0-0	3		2230
18	16	A	Dagenham & Red	W	4-3	1-2	3	Kanu [4], Kabamba 2 (2 pens) [65, 68], Browne [77]	2428
19	23	H	Woking	W	2-0	1-0	1	Browne [19], Hobson [52]	1500
20	27	A	Yeovil T	W	2-1	1-0	1	Glover [10], Collinge [81]	2722
21	30	A	Hartlepool U	D	0-0	0-0	2		3604
22	Dec 14	H	Ebbsfleet U	W	4-1	4-0	1	Kabamba [10], Shelton [18], Browne [27], Glover [32]	1583
23	21	H	FC Halifax T	D	1-1	1-1	2	Shelton [24]	1854
24	26	H	Sutton U	D	3-3	2-1	2	Glover 2 [30, 90], Oluwo [42]	2430
25	Jan 1	A	Eastleigh	D	1-1	0-1	3	Stead [71]	2188
26	14	A	Forest Green R	D	0-0	0-0	3		1492
27	18	A	Southend U	W	3-0	2-0	2	Collinge 2 [24, 74], Shelton [33]	6955
28	25	H	Maidenhead U	W	3-0	1-0	1	Stead [27], Shelton [47], Kanu [70]	1630
29	28	H	Hartlepool U	W	2-0	0-0	1	Glover [51], Ndlovu [63]	1289
30	Feb 1	A	Tamworth	W	1-0	1-0	1	Stead [36]	1438
31	8	A	Boston U	D	0-0	0-0	1		1973
32	15	H	Solihull Moors	W	3-1	1-0	1	Telford [28], Ndlovu 2 [76, 90]	1732
33	18	H	York C	W	3-1	1-0	1	Oluwo [16], Ndlovu [51], Hartigan [57]	4050
34	22	A	Rochdale	W	4-0	2-0	1	Stead [5], Browne [41], Telford [50], Glover [85]	2316
35	Mar 1	A	Oldham Ath	W	3-0	0-0	1	Brunt [50], Stead [51], Oluwo [84]	6098
36	4	A	Yeovil T	W	5-0	3-0	1	Glover [17], Stead [37], Hartigan [44], Chapman (pen) [82], Telford (pen) [86]	1596
37	8	H	Dagenham & Red	W	1-0	0-0	1	Ndlovu [90]	3655
38	15	A	Woking	W	1-0	1-0	1	Browne [27]	3281
39	22	H	Altrincham	W	1-0	1-0	1	Browne [44]	3071
40	29	H	Gateshead	W	3-1	2-0	1	Kenlock [10], Stead 2 [40, 90]	2641
41	Apr 5	A	Braintree T	L	1-2	1-1	1	Stead [36]	1726
42	12	H	Wealdstone	D	1-1	1-0	1	Oluwo [31]	3674
43	18	H	Eastleigh	D	1-1	1-1	1	Collinge [44]	3065
44	21	A	Sutton U	W	3-1	1-1	1	Shelton 2 (1 pen) [7, 53 (p)], Oluwo [81]	3557
45	26	H	Aldershot T	W	4-0	2-0	1	Shelton 2 (2 pens) [7, 20], Stead 2 [51, 55]	4990
46	May 5	A	AFC Fylde	W	3-0	2-0	1	Oluwo [12], Shelton (pen) [39], Ndlovu [60]	1699

Final League Position: 1

GOALSCORERS

League (97): Stead 19, Shelton 13 (6 pens), Kabamba 10 (2 pens), Glover 8, Browne 7, Brunt 6 (1 pen), Ndlovu 6, Oluwo 6, Chapman 4 (1 pen), Collinge 4, Telford 3 (1 pen), Coker 2, Hartigan 2, Hobson 2, Kanu 2, Kenlock 1, Tavares 1, own goal 1.
FA Cup (7): Brunt 2, Glover 2, Stead 2, Kabamba 1.
FA Trophy (3): Browne 1, Brunt 1, Kabamba 1.

Hayes 25	Coker 20+11	Collinge 26+3	Clifford 6+15	Oluwo 33+3	Kenlock 42	Brunt 31+13	Hartigan 46	Kabamba 13+5	Stead 37+7	Kanu 29+9	Kizzi 6+6	Chapman 9+13	Wilkinson —+4	Francis —+5	Tavares 34+4	Okimo —+11	Hall-Johnson 3+2	Shelton 27+6	Nartey —+2	Glover 41+1	Rye 3	Cropper 1+28	Grimwood 7+11	Browne 16+13	Hobson 10+3	Evans 18	Ndlovu 17+3	Telford 3+12	Savin 2	Bellagambi 1	Match No.
1	2	3¹	4⁴	5	6	7³	8	9	10	11²	12	13	14	15																	1
1	2	14	6³	5	4⁴	8⁵	7	9¹	10	11		3²	15	16	12	13															2
1	2³		3²	4	6	8	9		10	11	7	12			5¹			13	14												3
1					3	6³	7	9	10⁴	4	11¹			14	2	15	5	8²	12	13											4
1	2²			4¹	7	8		10	11⁴	5	14		16	3	13	15	9³	12⁵	6												5
1			14	4	8	9	10²	15	5	11	13	16			3⁴		6³	12		7¹	2⁵										6
1			2	3⁴	7¹	8		10²	13	4	11	14			12	5³	9		6		15										7
1			2	5	7	8	10			14	11¹				15	9⁴		6	4³	12	3²	13									8
1	2⁴		5	3	9	8		11²		12	7³							6	10		14	4¹ 13 15									9
1	2¹		5	3	9²	8	13	12	16		7⁵				4			6	10³		15		11⁴ 14								10
1	13		4	2⁴	9	8	11	14	7¹	12				3	15			6³	5⁵		16		10²								11
1	14		4	2	9⁴	8	12	10	11²		7⁵				3	16		6¹	5³		15		13								12
1	2²		5	3	7⁴	6	11	8	12					4	14			9¹		13 15		10³									13
1	2⁵		5	3	14	7	11	8¹ 13	12	6				4⁴		16		9³		15		10²									14
1		14	4	2	7	6	9		10¹	13					5³			8²		12	3		11								15
1	2¹	14	13	5	3			8	10	12⁵	15				7²			9		6⁴	4³ 16		11								16
1	2²	3³		5	4	7¹	6	9	14	10								8			13	12	11								17
1	2¹	3		5	4	7⁴	6	9	12	10³				15				8²		14	13	11									18
1	2²	13	15	5	7	12	3	11	9¹	8					4⁴			14		6³ 10											19
1	2		5	6	13	3	9¹	10²	7³						4		14	11			12 8										20
1	5²	6¹		4	2	13	8	12							3		7	10		14		9 11³									21
1	12	2	15	5	3	8¹	7³ 11	13	14						4⁴		6	9²	16		10⁵										22
1		2		5	3	8	7 11	12	13						4		6	9¹		10²											23
1	6³	5		4	2	8¹	9	12 11	13						3²		7	10		14											24
1	5³	2	3⁴	6	4	7²	9 13	11							8¹		14	10		15	12										25
			6		5¹	3	14	7		9 10²					4		8	2		13	12				1	11³						26
	15	4				3² 13	10		7⁴ 2						5		9	6		14 12	8³			1	11¹							27
	13	4 14				2	7⁴ 8		10 5¹						3²		9	6		15 12				1	11³							28
	13	4				2	7³ 8		9 11¹						3		6	5		14	12			1	10²						29
	13	4				2	10¹ 8		11 5						3		7	6²			12			1	9						30
		4⁴	12		2	10⁴ 8			11 5¹						3		7	6³		13 15				1	9² 14						31
	16		12	4⁴	2	10² 8			11 5⁵						3		7³	6		14 15				1	13	9¹					32
		13	2	4	14	9	7	6	8						5²		12	3⁰ 10⁴							11¹ 15		1		33
	15			8	4	14	9		5⁵ 6			16			2¹			7		13	3⁴ 11¹³			10² 12		1			34
		3	14 12		4	7² 8			6⁴ 5¹			15			2		11	9⁵		16				10³ 13		1			35
	6	3	14		4	7⁴ 8			11 5¹			12			2⁵			9⁹		15 16				10² 13		1			36
	6³	3	15		4	7⁵ 8			11 5¹			12			2			9²		16		13		14 10⁴		1			37
		3	7⁴		4	14 8			10¹ 5						2			9		13 12	6²			11³ 15		1			38
		4	7⁴		2	12 8			10 5²		13		15					6		14	3¹ 11³			9		1			39
		4	15	3⁴	2	7² 8			10 5¹		12			14			6		16 11⁵				9³ 13		1			40
	13	4	12	3⁴	2	7⁴ 8			10			11³			5²		15	6		16ᴮ 14				9¹		1			41
	3⁵	6		5	4⁴	13 9			7¹			14			16 12			8		2³		10		11¹² 15		1			42
		2		3	10⁵ 8			11 5¹	13						4		7	6³		9				12 14		1			43
	6³	4	14	2			8		10¹				12 3			7¹		5		13		11⁴			9² 15		1			44
	6²	4	15	2		12 8			10¹			13		3		7³		5		14		11⁵			9⁴ 16		1			45
	12		13	8		14 6³			9 2¹						5 16			7⁴		3		4 10²			11⁵ 15			1	46

FA Cup

Fourth Qualifying   Chelmsford C   (h)   4-0
First Round   Exeter C   (a)   3-5

FA Trophy

Third Round   Aveley   (h)   2-0
Fourth Round   Altrincham   (a)   1-3

BOSTON UNITED

Ground: The Jakemans Community Stadium, Pilgrim Way, Wyberton, Boston, Lincolnshire PE21 7NE.
Tel: (01205) 364 406.   *Website:* www.bostonunited.co.uk   *Email:* admin@bufc.co.uk   *Year Formed:* 1933.
Record Attendance: 11,000 v Derby Co, FA Cup 3rd rd replay, 9 January 1974.   *Nickname:* 'The Pilgrims'.
Manager: Graham Coughlan.
Colours: Amber and black striped shirts with black trim, black shorts, black socks.

BOSTON UNITED – NATIONAL LEAGUE 2024–25 LEAGUE RECORD

Match No.	Date	Venue	Opponents	Result		H/T Score	Lg Pos.	Goalscorers	Attendance
1	Aug 10	H	Rochdale	L	0-3	0-2	22		2578
2	17	H	Forest Green R	L	0-4	0-3	24		1830
3	20	A	Southend U	L	0-2	0-1	24		6924
4	24	H	Tamworth	D	1-1	1-0	23	Rowe [41]	1620
5	26	A	York C	W	2-0	0-0	23	Hazel [69], Ward [87]	5893
6	31	H	Yeovil T	L	1-3	1-2	23	Osborne [14]	1956
7	Sept 7	A	Sutton U	W	3-0	1-0	19	Hazel 2 [23, 74], Mills [68]	2758
8	10	H	Hartlepool U	L	1-2	1-0	19	Hazel [4]	1925
9	14	H	Aldershot T	D	1-1	0-1	18	Hazel [73]	1949
10	21	A	Altrincham	D	2-2	0-0	19	Ward [78], Green, C [84]	2031
11	24	A	Gateshead	L	0-2	0-2	21		1431
12	28	H	Maidenhead U	L	1-2	1-1	21	Mills [8]	1865
13	Oct 5	A	Barnet	L	1-3	1-0	22	Ward [6]	2006
14	19	H	FC Halifax T	L	0-1	0-1	22		1720
15	23	H	AFC Fylde	L	1-2	1-0	23	Aderoju [45]	1529
16	26	A	Eastleigh	D	1-1	1-0	23	Osborne [10]	1942
17	Nov 9	H	Dagenham & Red	D	1-1	1-1	23	Rowe [39]	2039
18	16	A	Woking	L	0-1	0-1	23		2394
19	23	H	Braintree T	W	3-1	2-0	23	Green, C [1], Hazel [43], Maguire [57]	1688
20	26	A	Oldham Ath	L	0-4	0-2	23		5013
21	30	A	Ebbsfleet U	D	0-0	0-0	23		1563
22	Dec 14	A	Forest Green R	L	0-1	0-1	23		1796
23	26	H	Solihull Moors	L	0-1	0-1	23		2364
24	Jan 11	H	Ebbsfleet U	D	2-2	1-1	23	Marriott [39], Osborne [67]	1909
25	18	A	Tamworth	L	0-3	0-2	23		1479
26	25	H	York C	W	3-1	1-1	23	Teale [28], Knowles [67], Hazel [86]	2362
27	Feb 8	H	Barnet	D	0-0	0-0	23		1973
28	15	A	FC Halifax T	L	0-1	0-0	23		1668
29	18	A	AFC Fylde	W	2-1	2-1	23	Hazel 2 [14, 25]	1050
30	22	H	Eastleigh	L	1-2	0-1	23	Teale [90]	1832
31	Mar 1	A	Dagenham & Red	W	3-1	1-1	23	Hazel [22], Rowe [82], Marriott [90]	1791
32	4	H	Oldham Ath	D	0-0	0-0	23		1695
33	8	H	Woking	D	2-2	0-1	23	Rowe 2 [66, 90]	1787
34	11	A	Yeovil T	W	3-0	2-0	23	Knowles [38], Hazel [42], Mills [63]	2138
35	15	A	Braintree T	W	1-0	1-0	23	Ward [16]	1077
36	18	H	Rochdale	W	3-2	2-0	21	Hazel [25], Mills [28], Knowles [69]	1974
37	22	A	Hartlepool U	L	1-4	1-2	23	Hazel [20]	4242
38	25	H	Southend U	W	3-0	0-0	21	Maguire [50], Knowles [57], Mills [79]	2387
39	29	H	Sutton U	W	2-1	1-1	20	Rowe [23], Gale [90]	2302
40	Apr 1	A	Wealdstone	L	0-1	0-1	21		1405
41	8	A	Aldershot T	W	2-1	0-1	20	Gale [72], Rowe [90]	1738
42	12	H	Altrincham	W	1-0	1-0	19	Maguire [26]	2320
43	18	A	Wealdstone	W	2-0	2-0	19	Maguire 2 [2, 17]	3865
44	21	A	Solihull Moors	L	2-3	2-1	19	Mills [2], Teale [37]	1393
45	26	H	Gateshead	W	2-1	2-1	17	Ward [10], Gale [35]	3401
46	May 5	A	Maidenhead U	L	0-3	0-1	19		3017

Final League Position: 19

GOALSCORERS

League (54): Hazel 13, Rowe 7, Mills 6, Maguire 5, Ward 5, Knowles 4, Gale 3, Osborne 3, Teale 3, Green, C 2, Marriott 2, Aderoju 1.
FA Cup (2): Aderoju 1, Hazel 1.
FA Trophy (6): Rowe 2, Hazel 1, Marriott 1, Osborne 1, Weston 1.

Gregory 31	Green C 42 + 1	Roberts 6 + 1	Rowe 43 + 3	Mills 39	Bostwick 17	Richards 38 + 3	Maguire 30 + 7	Mooney 6 + 7	Weston 14 + 11	Aderoju 8 + 14	Hazel 37 + 8	Woods 11 + 8	Osborne 11 + 8	Ward 18 + 26	Hill 40 + 5	Marriott 1 + 28	Leak 10 + 7	Craven — + 1	Stone 13	Coates 3 + 9	Welch 2	Chadwick 2 + 1	Wheeldon 2 + 1	Reed 3 + 1	Teale 23	Adshead 2 + 1	Donaghy 2	Gallagher 4	Knowles 17 + 1	Gale 3 + 17	Nicholson 17 + 2	Scott 2 + 1	Green O 1 + 5	Sloggett 6 + 3	Wadsworth 2 + 1	Alonzi — + 1	Match No.
1	2	3	4	5	6	7^4	8^2	9^1	10^5	11^3	12	13	14	15	16																						1
1	2	3	4	5	6^3	8	14	9^1	10^2	11^5	12	7^4	16		13	15																					2
1	3	2	4	5		8	13	11^5	12	10^2	9^4	7^1		15	16	14	6^5																				3
1		2	4		5	6	7	10^1	12		9	13	11^2		8		3																				4
1	4^1	14	12	3	2^4	6	7		10^6	16	9^2	5	11^3	15	8		13																				5
1	2		3	4	5^4	7^4	8^3	14	10^6	13	9	6^1	11^2	16	12		15																				6
1	2		4	3	5^4	7	15	10^3	14	9^1	6	11^2	13		8		12																				7
1	2	3	4	5		7^3	14	10^2	12	9	6^4	11^1	15		8		13																				8
1	12	2^3	3	4	5		7	10^1	13	14	9		11^2	6^4	8	15																					9
1^*		4		5	3	2^1	6	7		11^3	14	9^5	10^4	12	8^2	15	16	13																			10
	4		5	3	2^2	6^3	7^1	12	10	11^4	9		14	8	13	15			1																		11
	4		5	3	2	6	7^2	10^3	11^1	13	9		12	8	14				1																		12
	3		4	2		6	7	15	10^4	13	9^1		12	8^3	11^2	14	5		1																		13
	4		12	3	2	6	14		13	9	10^2	11	7						1	5^3	8^1																14
	14			2	6	12		11	13	9^4	10^3	7	15		4				1	5^2	8^1																15
	3		4	2		6	12		11^1	13	14	7^3	8	9	10^2				1	5																	16
	4		5	2	6	3	7^2	14	13	10^4	12	8^3	9	15					1			11^1															17
	4		5^4	2	6	3	7	15	14	10^3	12	8^2	9^1	16					1			11^5															18
	4		5	3	2	6	8^1		12	10	7^2	14	9		13				1				11^3														19
	4		7	3^1	2^4	6	8		15	10^3		11^2	9		5				1				14	12													20
	2		3			6	7^3		12	10^4	14	15	8		4				1				13	11^2	9^1	5											21
	2		3			6	7^4		11	14	15	12	8^3	13	4				1					9^1	5	10^2											22
	2		5			8^4	9^5		11^1	10^2	13		14	12	7^4	16	4		1					6^3	3	15											23
	3		2			7^2		11^4		10	15	13	9^3	8	12	4									14			6^1	1	5							24
	3		2			6^4		7^3		11^1	16	13	12	9^5	15	4									5				1	8	10^2	14					25
1	3		2	4	13	6^5		15		10^1	11^3			16	9									12				5	8^1	10^2	11^3					26
1	3		2	4	12				10^1	13	6^3			7^5	9	16									5				8^2	11^4	14					27
1	3^1		2	4	8				14	11	6^2			7^4	10	15									5				9^3	13	12					28
1	6^1		2	4	8				15	11^2	12			7^3	10										14				9^4	13	3					29
1	6^2		2	4	8^4	12		13		11	10^5			7^3	15	14									5				9^1	16	3					30
1	6		2	4	8	9^1			11^3				14	7	13										5				10^2	12	3					31
1	6		2	5	8	7^2			9^3			12	10	13											4				11^1	14	3					32
1	6		2	5	8	7^2			9^1			12	10	14											4				11^3	13	3					33
1	6		2	5	8^1		14		9^5	7^2		12	10	15					13										11^3		3	4^4	16				34
1	6		2	5	8		13		9^2			7	10	14											4				11^3	12	3					35
1	9		7	4	5		13		10^1			6	8												2				11^2	12	3					36
1	9^3		7	4	5	13			10^4			6	8	15					12						2				11^1	14	3^2					37
1	9		7	4	5	6^2			10^3			13	8^4	15											2				11^1		3		14	12		38
1	9		2	5	6	7^3			10^4			13	8^1	15											4				11^2	12	3			14		39
1	9^2		2	5	6^4	7^1			10			13	8^5	16											4				11^3	12	3			14	15	40
1	8		2	5		7	11^2		9^1			13	10^3												4					12	3	14		6		41
1	6		5	3		7	10^1		9^3			12	11^2												4					13	2	14	8			42
1	6		5	3		7	10^1		9^3			13	11^2												4					12	2	14	8			43
1		8	4		6		14		11^4			12	10	15											2				13	9^2	5			7	3^3	44
1	3	8	4		6				11^1			9^2	10												2					12	5	13	7			45
1		3^1	2	5	15							9	16						13										11^4	10^3	12	4	8^5	6	7^2	14	46

FA Cup

| Fourth Qualifying | Gainsborough Trinity | (a) | 2-2 |
| *Replay* | Gainsborough Trinity | (h) | 0-4 |

FA Trophy

Third Round	Alvechurch	(h)	1-0
Fourth Round	Gateshead	(a)	3-1
Fifth Round	Spennymoor T	(a)	2-2

(Spennymoor T won 3-1 on penalties)

BRAINTREE TOWN

Ground: The Rare Breed Meat Co Stadium, off Clockhouse Way, Braintree, Essex CM7 3DE.   *Tel:* (01376) 345 617.
Website: www.braintreetownfc.org.uk   *Email:* info@braintreetownfc.org.uk   *Year Formed:* 1898.
Record Attendance: 2,029 v Cambridge U, Blue Square Premier League, 1 January 2012.
Nickname: 'The Iron'.   *Manager:* Steve Pitt.   *Colours:* Orange shirts with white trim, blue shorts, orange socks.

BRAINTREE TOWN – NATIONAL LEAGUE 2024–25 LEAGUE RECORD

Match No.	Date	Venue	Opponents	Result		H/T Score	Lg Pos.	Goalscorers	Attendance
1	Aug 10	A	Oldham Ath	L	0-3	0-2	22		5552
2	17	A	Yeovil T	L	0-1	0-0	22		1128
3	20	H	Aldershot T	W	2-1	0-1	19	Kyrell Lisbie 2 [75, 89]	1227
4	24	A	Solihull Moors	D	1-1	1-0	19	Kyrell Lisbie [6]	1037
5	26	H	Ebbsfleet U	D	0-0	0-0	20		1313
6	31	A	Hartlepool U	D	0-0	0-0	18		3516
7	Sept 7	H	Woking	D	0-0	0-0	18		1129
8	10	A	York C	L	1-2	1-2	18	Terry [4]	4494
9	14	A	Barnet	L	1-3	1-2	20	Akinde [1]	1507
10	21	H	Tamworth	L	0-1	0-0	21		970
11	24	H	FC Halifax T	W	1-0	0-0	19	Effiong (pen) [90]	849
12	28	A	Rochdale	L	0-1	0-1	20		2609
13	Oct 5	H	Altrincham	W	2-0	1-0	20	Francis [17], Akinde (pen) [90]	726
14	19	A	Forest Green R	L	1-2	1-1	20	Wilkinson [10]	1997
15	23	A	Wealdstone	L	2-3	2-1	21	Annesley [13], Powell [16]	1163
16	26	H	Sutton U	L	0-1	0-0	21		917
17	Nov 9	A	Eastleigh	W	2-1	0-1	20	Blackwell [53], McCallum (og) [81]	1942
18	16	H	AFC Fylde	W	1-0	0-0	19	Effiong [59]	900
19	23	A	Boston U	L	1-3	0-2	20	Francis [71]	1688
20	26	H	Maidenhead U	L	1-3	0-2	20	Kyrell Lisbie [66]	777
21	30	H	Gateshead	D	2-2	2-2	19	Francis [4], Annesley [14]	703
22	Dec 14	A	Yeovil T	L	1-3	1-1	21	Akinde [15]	2767
23	21	H	Oldham Ath	L	0-2	0-1	21		1046
24	26	A	Dagenham & Red	W	4-2	2-1	20	Kyrell Lisbie 2 [20, 58], Cooper 2 [24, 49]	1842
25	Jan 1	H	Southend U	L	0-1	0-1	20		3285
26	14	A	Aldershot T	D	2-2	2-2	19	Kyrell Lisbie [2], Akinde [40]	1437
27	18	A	Solihull Moors	W	1-0	1-0	19	Robinson [17]	807
28	25	A	Ebbsfleet U	W	1-0	1-0	19	Akinde (pen) [36]	1385
29	Feb 1	H	Hartlepool U	D	1-1	0-0	18	Francis [71]	869
30	8	A	Altrincham	L	1-3	0-2	17	Cooper [82]	1674
31	15	H	Forest Green R	W	2-0	2-0	18	Kyrell Lisbie [10], Blackwell [32]	860
32	19	H	Wealdstone	L	1-2	1-0	18	Robinson [6]	888
33	22	A	Sutton U	D	1-1	0-0	19	Akinde [57]	2508
34	Mar 1	H	Eastleigh	W	1-0	1-0	17	Marshall [3]	910
35	4	A	Maidenhead U	D	3-3	2-1	17	Robinson [4], Kyrell Lisbie [24], Francis [77]	748
36	8	A	AFC Fylde	W	2-0	1-0	16	Francis [36], Kyrell Lisbie [61]	1014
37	15	H	Boston U	L	0-1	0-1	17		1077
38	18	A	Gateshead	W	3-1	0-1	17	Cooper [57], Akinde (pen) [71], Kyreece Lisbie [74]	625
39	22	H	York C	W	2-1	1-1	15	Akinde [25], Francis [66]	1137
40	29	H	Woking	L	1-2	0-1	17	Francis-Clarke [70]	2102
41	Apr 5	H	Barnet	W	2-1	1-1	16	Kyrell Lisbie [41], Akinde (pen) [90]	1726
42	12	A	Tamworth	L	2-4	2-3	18	Francis [7], Akinde (pen) [25]	1007
43	18	H	Southend U	D	0-0	0-0	18		9614
44	21	H	Dagenham & Red	D	0-0	0-0	18		1717
45	26	A	FC Halifax T	L	0-1	0-0	19		1631
46	May 5	H	Rochdale	W	2-0	1-0	17	Kyrell Lisbie 2 [45, 56]	1427

Final League Position: 17

GOALSCORERS

League (51): Kyrell Lisbie 13, Akinde 10 (5 pens), Francis 8, Cooper 4, Robinson 3, Annesley 2, Blackwell 2, Effiong 2 (1 pen), Francis-Clarke 1, Kyreece Lisbie 1, Marshall 1, Powell 1, Terry 1, Wilkinson 1, own goal 1.
FA Cup (1): Effiong 1.
FA Trophy (1): Lisbie 1.

Knightbridge 2	Clampin 33 + 2	Langston 42	Annesley 42	Vennings 31 + 2	Blackwell 24 + 18	Marshall-Miranda 8	Effiong 15 + 6	Akinde 28 + 12	Robinson 38 + 5	Grimwood 7	Cooper 26 + 17	Powell 7 + 9	Lisbie Kyrell 30 + 10	Fyfield 13 + 11	Lambe — + 6	Lucas Covolan 23	Terry 19	Ward C — + 2	Lock — + 5	Marshall 19 + 4	Wilkinson 7	Francis 26 + 3	Davidson-Phipps 3 + 4	Balogun — + 3	Brothers — + 1	Hinds 1 + 2	Gray 20	Pinnington 14 + 6	Francis-Clarke 18 + 2	Judge 4 + 9	Okunowo — + 6	Lisbie Kyreece 5	MacLorg 1	Amartey — + 1	McPherson — + 1	Match No.
1	2	3	4^1	5	6^3	7^4	8	9^2	10	11	12	13	14	15																						1
1	5	4^3	2	6^4	15	7	10	13	8	3	9^1	11^2	12			14																				2
	3	4	5	6	15	9	10^3	14	7^4	2	8^2	11^1	12		13	1																				3
	5	2	4^1	6	15	8^5	12	10^4	7	3	9^3	14	11^2	16	13	1																				4
	5	2	4^1	6	16	8	10^5	13	7^3	3	9^2	14	11^4	15	12	1																				5
	5^5	2	3	13	9^3	6^2	11^4	10	7^1	4	15	14	8	12	16	1																				6
	2					7	9^3	6	13	10^2		4	8^4	12	11^1	3				1	5	14	15													7
		5	4	6	10^5	9^1	13	11^3	15		7^2	12	8^4	3			1			2	14	16														8
		4	3	8	10^4		6^3	11	12		13	7		2^2	14		1			5	15	9^1														9
	4^2	3	7			13	11^5	12			15		6^1	14	2		1			5	16	8^3	9	10^4												10
	4	3	7			13	12	6			14	11^2	9^1	2			1			5		8^3	10													11
	4	3	7		13			6^2	14	11^4	12	2					1			5^3	15	8	9^1	10												12
	4	3	7	14		11^1	12	6				2					1			5	8^2	9^3	10	13												13
12	4	3	7	8^4		11^3	14	6			2						1			5^2	9^1	10	13													14
4^5		3	8	16		13	15	6^1		13	7^4	2					1			5	9^2	10^3	14	12												15
3^3	4	2^1	8	15		11	13	6		7^4	12	14					1			5	9^2	10														16
3	4	2	8	9		11		6^1		7^2	13						1			5		10	12		13											17
2	4		7	8		9	12			10^1	11^2						1			5	3	6		13												18
3	4	2	8	9^2		10	13	15		7^4	14						1			5	11^1	12	6^3													19
3	4	2		11		10	12	6^2		7^1	14						1			5	8	9	13													20
2	4	6^3	7	8^4		10^1	14	12		11^*			13	15			1			5	9^2	3														21
3	4	2	8	10^1		9	6			7	12	11^2					1			5	13															22
3^2	4	2	9			10	6^1	8		12	14						1			5	11					7^3										23
	4	3	7	12		11	6	8		10^2							1	2		5^1	9					13										24
3^1	4	5	8	12		11^3	9	6		10^2							1	2			7	13				14										25
3	4	5	6	12		11	9	8^2		10^1											7					1	2	13								26
3	4	5	6	12		11	8	10^1													9^2					1	7	2								27
2^4	5	6^2	4	11^3		10	8	14		9^1	13										7					1	12	3	15							28
4^3	5	3	7^2			9	8	12		11^1											6					1	2	10	14							29
4^2		5	3	13		9	8	12		11^3	12										6					1	2^1	10	14							30
	4	7	10^1			9	8	12		11^2	3										6					1	2	5		13						31
13		4	7^*	10^2		9	8	12		11^1	3										6					1	2	5			7					32
3	4	5		12		9	8	13		11^1					6						10					1	7^2	2								33
3^*	4	5		7^1		9	8	13		11^2					6						10					1	12	2								34
	4	5	12	7^1		11^*	8	13		10^2					8						9					1	2^3	3		14						35
3	4	5	6^4	7^2			8^3	12		10^1					9						11					1	15	2	13	14						36
3	4	5		7		8	9	13							6^2						11					1		2	12		10^1					37
3	4		12			11	8	9		10^1					6^3											1	2	5	13	14	7^2					38
3	4		13			11	8	9^2		10^1					6	12										1	2	5		14	7^3					39
3	4	6		15		11		9^1		10^3					8^4	12											2^2	5	13	14	7	1				40
3	4	5		12		11	6	9^1		10^2					8											1	2		13		7					41
3	4	5		13		11	6	9^2		10					6^3	7										1	2^1	12	14							42
3	4	5^3		7		11^2	6	13		10	14				8											1	12	2	9^1							43
3	4	5		11			6	9		10	12															1	7^1	2	8							44
3	5	6		10			9			7		11	4^1													1	12	2	8							45
3^2	4	6		10			9			7		11^3	5													1	12	2	8^1					13	14	46

FA Cup

Fourth Qualifying Bishop's Stortford (h) 1-0
First Round Brackley T (a) 0-0
(Brackley T won 5-4 on penalties)

FA Trophy

Third Round Forest Green R (h) 1-1
(Forest Green R won 5-3 on penalties)

DAGENHAM & REDBRIDGE

Ground: Chigwell Construction Stadium, Victoria Road, Dagenham, Essex RM10 7XL.
Tel: (020) 8592 1549.   *Website:* www.daggers.co.uk   *Email:* info@daggers.co.uk   *Year Formed:* 1992.
Record Attendance: 5,949 v Ipswich T, FA Cup 3rd rd, 5 January 2002.   *Nickname:* 'The Daggers'.
Manager: Lee Bradbury.   *Colours:* Red shirts with blue horizontal stripes and white trim, blue shorts, blue socks.

DAGENHAM & REDBRIDGE – NATIONAL LEAGUE 2024–25 LEAGUE RECORD

Match No.	Date	Venue	Opponents	Result	H/T Score	Lg Pos.	Goalscorers	Attendance
1	Aug 10	H	Wealdstone	W 2-1	0-0	6	Rees [55], Pereira [81]	1523
2	17	A	Rochdale	D 1-1	0-0	9	Pereira [52]	2631
3	20	A	Woking	L 0-1	0-0	14		2103
4	23	H	FC Halifax T	D 1-1	1-0	11	Rees [26]	1481
5	26	A	Southend U	D 2-2	1-1	14	Grego-Cox (pen) [29], Rees [74]	8495
6	31	H	York C	L 0-2	0-0	17		1543
7	Sept 7	A	Maidenhead U	D 1-1	0-1	17	Umerah [61]	1412
8	10	H	Sutton U	W 3-0	1-0	14	Rees [14], Pereira 2 (1 pen) [49 (p), 89]	1374
9	14	H	Gateshead	W 7-1	2-1	9	Pereira 2 (1 pen) [4, 70 (p)], Rees 2 [16, 90], Morias 2 [64, 72], Umerah [76]	1549
10	21	A	Hartlepool U	W 1-0	1-0	8	Umerah [7]	3507
11	24	A	Altrincham	L 1-2	1-1	8	Pereira (pen) [40]	1236
12	28	H	Solihull Moors	D 1-1	0-0	10	Phipps [49]	1384
13	Oct 5	A	Yeovil T	L 0-1	0-0	13		2998
14	19	H	AFC Fylde	W 4-0	1-0	10	N'Guessan [42], Long (og) [51], Morias [76], Stephenson [89]	1312
15	22	A	Eastleigh	D 2-2	2-1	10	Umerah [19], Morias [40]	1258
16	26	A	Oldham Ath	L 0-1	0-1	13		5651
17	Nov 9	A	Boston U	D 1-1	1-1	12	Stephenson [27]	2039
18	16	H	Barnet	L 3-4	2-1	13	Umerah [1], Crichlow-Noble [34], Hill [48]	2428
19	23	A	Tamworth	L 1-2	1-0	15	Phipps [31]	807
20	26	H	Aldershot T	W 3-2	0-0	13	Pereira (pen) [52], Woodhouse [58], Morias [77]	1210
21	Dec 14	H	Rochdale	W 1-0	0-0	14	Morias [79]	1569
22	21	A	Wealdstone	L 0-3	0-2	15		1404
23	26	A	Braintree T	L 2-4	1-2	16	Pereira (pen) [43], Hill [90]	1842
24	Jan 1	A	Ebbsfleet U	W 2-0	0-0	15	Remy [56], Hessenthaler [65]	1395
25	8	A	Forest Green R	D 1-1	0-0	15	Rees [90]	1038
26	25	H	Southend U	L 0-2	0-1	16		3599
27	Feb 1	A	York C	L 1-2	0-1	16	Umerah [51]	5331
28	4	H	Forest Green R	L 0-2	0-1	16		1266
29	8	H	Yeovil T	D 1-1	1-1	16	Rees [5]	1703
30	11	H	Woking	L 1-2	0-1	17	Rees [46]	1335
31	15	A	AFC Fylde	D 1-1	1-0	17	Khaleel [37]	1077
32	19	A	Eastleigh	L 0-3	0-2	17		1865
33	22	H	Oldham Ath	D 2-2	1-0	17	Loupalo-Bi [45], Hill (pen) [67]	1573
34	Mar 1	H	Boston U	L 1-3	1-1	19	Rees [3]	1791
35	4	A	Aldershot T	D 0-0	0-0	19		1657
36	8	A	Barnet	L 0-1	0-0	19		3655
37	15	H	Tamworth	L 1-3	1-1	20	Hill [22]	2435
38	18	A	FC Halifax T	W 1-0	1-0	19	Rees [44]	1243
39	22	H	Sutton U	D 1-1	0-0	20	Umerah [64]	2648
40	29	H	Maidenhead U	W 1-0	0-0	19	Rees [54]	1809
41	Apr 5	A	Gateshead	L 1-2	0-2	20	Shelvey (og) [61]	1371
42	12	H	Hartlepool U	D 1-1	0-1	21	Phipps [87]	1704
43	18	H	Ebbsfleet U	W 1-0	0-0	21	Umerah (pen) [87]	1747
44	21	A	Braintree T	D 0-0	0-0	21		1717
45	26	H	Altrincham	W 6-1	4-0	20	Rees 3 [6, 22, 73], Phipps [25], Pereira (pen) [45], Olson (og) [84]	2002
46	May 5	A	Solihull Moors	D 1-1	1-0	21	Rutherford [32]	3273

Final League Position: 21

GOALSCORERS

League (61): Rees 15, Pereira 10 (6 pens), Umerah 8 (1 pen), Morias 6, Hill 4 (1 pen), Phipps 4, Stephenson 2, Crichlow-Noble 1, Grego-Cox 1 (1 pen), Hessenthaler 1, Khaleel 1, Loupalo-Bi 1, N'Guessan 1, Remy 1, Rutherford 1, Woodhouse 1, own goals 3.
FA Cup (8): Rees 2, Umerah 2, Hill 1, Morias 1, Pereira 1 (1 pen), Remy 1.
FA Trophy (0).

Justham 28	Eastman 25 + 1	N'Guessan 33 + 7	Kalambayi 39 + 1	Vincent 11 + 8	Hessenthaler 32 + 2	Pereira 29 + 6	Rees 38 + 3	Rendall 19 + 15	Grego-Cox 6 + 10	Morias 19	Hill 32 + 7	Ling 8 + 5	Remy 12 + 11	Phipps 28 + 6	Umerah 30 + 7	Lawless —+ 8	Stephenson 4 + 10	Rutherford 30 + 10	Woodhouse 7 + 7	Akinola 2 + 3	Vigrass —+ 6	Crichlow-Noble 10	Bakre —+ 3	Harrack 9 + 3	Adigun —+ 1	Parsons —+ 2	Francis 10 + 2	Loupalo-Bi 12 + 8	Khaleel 3 + 7	Clayton 7 + 4	Harvey 4 + 1	Jones 7	Hector 2	Wylie 3 + 7	Turner 7	Match No.
1	2	3	4	5⁴	6	7³	8	9	10¹	11²	12	13	14	15																						1
1	3	2	4	12	7	10²	9	8	11³				6¹	5⁴	14	13	15																			2
1	4	10	2	5³	3	8	6²	9¹		11	7⁴		12	14	13			15																		3
1	3	4	2	5	6¹	7	8	10	14	11³	9²		12	13																						4
1	3	9	2	15	6⁴	8	5²	10⁵	11¹	4	7³	12	13	14	16																					5
1	2	3²	5³	15	6⁵	7	9	10¹	11	4	8⁴	13	14	16	12																					6
1	2	3²	5	7	8	12	14	11¹	4⁵	6	10³	16	13	15	9⁴																					7
1	2	3²	4	5¹	7⁴	8	9	13	11	6	10³	14	12	15																						8
1	2	7¹	3	4	8⁵	10	5³	14	9⁴	12	16	6	11²	15	13																					9
1	2		4	8¹	11	6	12	9²	14	3	13		5³																							10
1		12	4	8	11²	7	9⁴	6	13	2³	3	10	14	15	5¹																					11
1	9³	3	4¹	12	10	7	11²	6⁴	13	15	2	8	5	14																						12
1	12	2	3¹	6²	9	7				10			8	11	13	5			4																	13
1	2	9	3	13	7³	12	8	6⁵	10¹				16	11²	14	5		15	4⁴																	14
1	2	9	13	7¹	12	8	6²	10	3	11	14	5³		4																						15
1	8	3¹	12	7⁸	9	6²	10	2	11⁴	13	5³	14	15	4																						16
1	2	7	12	8	10	9	6¹	11²	5	4	13	3																								17
1	2	8²	13	12	14	10	9	7	6	11³	5	4¹	3																							18
1	2	8⁴	16	9	7³	13	6⁵	10	3²	11	14	5¹	12	15	4⁸																					19
1	2¹	7	3	4	8²	13	5	10	9	6	11	12																								20
1	7	2	6	11	5	9¹	10	12	8	4	3																									21
1	7	2	6¹	11	9³	5⁴	12	13	10	8	4²	15	3	14																					22
1	15	4	7³	11	9	12	5	14	10	2¹	8	6⁴	3²	13																					23
1	5²	2	7	11³	4	6⁵	3	10⁴	9	8¹	14	15	12	13	16																					24
1	5	2	7⁵	9	4	13	6⁴	3¹	10²	8	11³	12	15	14	16																					25
1	13	14	5³	8⁴	7²	9	2	15	10⁵	16	4	11	3					6¹	12																	26
1	4	6	5	9	12	8	2	15	10³	7	11¹		2	8	3²	14																				27
1	4	10³	5	12	8	2	15	9⁶	7	11²	3¹	6⁴	14	13	16																					28
	4	5	6	8	2	12	9	7	11²	13	10³	14	3¹	1																						29
	4	5	6	13	8	2¹	9	7²	10³	12	11	14	3	1																						30
	5	8	4	6	12	14	13	7⁴	11	3	9¹	15	10³	2²	1																					31
	4	8³	5	6¹	7⁴	12	10	13	15	2	14	11	9²	3	1																					32
	4	3	8	9²	10	6	7¹	12		2	5	11	13	1																						33
	4	6¹	8	14	9	2	10	7²	12	3⁴	15	5	11³	13	1																					34
	4²	8	6	7	9	13	10	11¹	2	5	12	3	1																							35
	16	6	8	7²	9	12	10⁴	14	2	4	13	15	3¹	1	5³																					36
	7	6²	9	8	12	14	2	4⁸	11¹	10³	3	1	5	13																						37
	7	2	8	9	13	6	3	10¹	14	5	4²	11³	1	12																						38
	7	2	8	9	6	3	10¹	14	5	4	12	13	1³	11²																						39
	8	2	7	9	6²	3	10	5	4	12	13	11¹	1																								40
	7¹	2	5³	9	8	3	11	13	6	4⁴	14	15	10²	1																						41
	8¹	2³	7	12	9	13	6	3	10	5	4²	11⁴	15	14	1																					42
	15	4	7³	2¹	9	16	6	14	3	11⁴	13	5	8²	10⁵	12	1																				43
	4	7	9⁴	8	14	6¹	13	3	10	15	5	2²	11³	12	1																					44
	13	3	7	8²	9⁴	12	6¹	5	11⁵	15	4	2	10³	16	14	1																				45
	4²	7	9	8	13	12	6¹	3	11	5	2³	10	14	1																						46

FA Cup

Fourth Qualifying	Leiston	(a)	5-1
First Round	Crewe Alex	(a)	1-0
Second Round	AFC Wimbledon	(a)	2-1
Third Round	Millwall	(a)	0-3

FA Trophy

Third Round	Chertsey T	(a)	0-1

EASTLEIGH

Ground: The Silverlake Stadium, Ten Acres, Stoneham Lane, Eastleigh, Hampshire SO50 9HT.   *Tel:* (02380) 613 361.
Website: www.eastleighfc.com   *Email:* admin@eastleighfc.com   *Year Formed:* 1946.
Record Attendance: 5,075 v Newport Co, FA Cup 3rd rd, 16 January 2024.   *Nickname:* 'Spitfires'.
Manager: Kelvin Davies.   *Colours:* Blue checkered shirts with white trim, blue shorts with white trim, blue socks.

EASTLEIGH – NATIONAL LEAGUE 2024–25 LEAGUE RECORD

Match No.	Date	Venue	Opponents	Result	H/T Score	Lg Pos.	Goalscorers	Attendance
1	Aug 10	A	Maidenhead U	W 2-0	2-0	4	De Havilland (og) 34, Vokins 39	1379
2	17	H	AFC Fylde	W 4-2	1-2	2	Taylor 35, McCallum 2 (1 pen) 48 (p), 76, Maguire 70	1820
3	20	H	Solihull Moors	W 2-1	2-0	1	Taylor 3, McCallum 10	2565
4	24	A	Altrincham	W 1-0	0-0	1	Maguire (pen) 71	1601
5	26	H	Sutton U	D 1-1	1-1	1	McCallum 37	2378
6	31	A	Gateshead	L 1-2	0-1	2	Quigley 63	1302
7	Sept 7	H	Tamworth	W 1-0	1-0	2	McCallum 6	2158
8	10	A	Southend U	L 0-2	0-2	5		6359
9	14	A	FC Halifax T	L 1-3	0-2	6	Brindley 82	1242
10	21	H	Rochdale	W 4-2	2-1	4	McCallum 2 (1 pen) 22, 77 (p), Francillette 35, Maguire 60	1836
11	24	H	Woking	D 2-2	1-1	7	Shade 18, Maguire 80	1968
12	28	A	York C	D 0-0	0-0	7		5671
13	Oct 5	H	Forest Green R	L 1-3	1-0	7	Maguire 37	2355
14	19	A	Aldershot T	L 1-2	0-0	9	Francillette 49	3037
15	22	A	Dagenham & Red	D 2-2	1-2	9	Maher 10, McCallum 90	1258
16	26	H	Boston U	D 1-1	0-1	11	Maguire (pen) 90	1942
17	Nov 9	H	Braintree T	L 1-2	1-0	11	Shade 25	1942
18	16	A	Hartlepool U	D 0-0	0-0	12		3655
19	23	H	Wealdstone	D 1-1	1-0	11	Boutin 7	2020
20	27	A	Ebbsfleet U	W 1-0	0-0	10	Quigley 61	1023
21	Dec 14	A	AFC Fylde	D 2-2	0-1	13	Shade 2 55, 78	985
22	21	H	Maidenhead U	W 1-0	1-0	12	Francillette 16	2000
23	26	H	Yeovil T	D 2-2	0-0	11	Humphries 80, Brindley 90	4355
24	Jan 1	H	Barnet	D 1-1	1-0	12	Shade 16	2188
25	7	H	Oldham Ath	D 2-2	1-0	11	Francillette 32, Brindley 69	1846
26	14	A	Solihull Moors	W 1-0	1-0	10	Shade 10	751
27	18	A	Altrincham	L 1-2	1-1	11	Francillette 27	1931
28	25	A	Sutton U	L 0-1	0-0	11		2526
29	Feb 8	A	Forest Green R	L 1-2	0-0	14	Taylor (pen) 69	1634
30	15	H	Aldershot T	W 2-0	2-0	13	Semenyo 30, Shade 45	2794
31	19	H	Dagenham & Red	W 3-0	2-0	10	Shade 9, Maher 13, Francillette 67	1865
32	22	A	Boston U	W 2-1	1-0	8	Taylor 38, Shade 77	1832
33	25	H	Gateshead	D 1-1	0-0	8	Taylor (pen) 90	1588
34	Mar 1	A	Braintree T	L 0-1	0-1	8		910
35	4	H	Ebbsfleet U	W 2-0	1-0	8	Maher 18, Taylor 64	2090
36	8	H	Hartlepool U	D 1-1	1-1	9	Shade 42	3212
37	11	A	Oldham Ath	L 0-2	0-1	10		4769
38	15	A	Wealdstone	D 3-3	3-0	10	Francillette 2 2, 35, Shade 40	1293
39	22	H	Southend U	L 1-2	0-2	11	Shade 55	3148
40	29	A	Tamworth	L 0-0	0-0	11		1383
41	Apr 5	H	FC Halifax T	D 1-1	0-0	12	Maguire (pen) 60	2161
42	12	A	Rochdale	L 0-4	0-2	14		1762
43	18	A	Barnet	D 1-1	1-1	14	McCallum 36	3065
44	21	H	Yeovil T	W 1-0	1-0	12	Maguire 30	2657
45	26	A	Woking	D 2-2	1-1	11	Shade 2 14, 60	2711
46	May 5	H	York C	L 0-2	0-2	13		2914

Final League Position: 13

GOALSCORERS

League (58): Shade 14, McCallum 9 (2 pens), Francillette 8, Maguire 8 (3 pens), Taylor 6 (2 pens), Brindley 3, Maher 3, Quigley 2, Boutin 1, Humphries 1, Semenyo 1, Vokins 1, own goal 1.
FA Cup (0).
FA Trophy (6): McCallum 2, Brindley 1, Maguire 1 (1 pen), Quigley 1, Stepie-Iwumene 1.

McDonnell 46	Brindley 33 + 4	Vokins 20 + 4	Humphries 26 + 11	Francillette 43	Panter 11 + 11	Taylor 40 + 2	Shade 41 + 2	Nwabuokei 3 + 1	McCallum 26 + 9	Quigley 17 + 6	Sotona — + 1	Semenyo 7 + 17	Maguire 24 + 18	Waruih 37 + 6	Maher 35 + 1	Fernandez 23 + 10	Hodson 12 + 18	Boutin 26 + 8	McDonald — + 6	Gape 7 + 3	Ryan — + 5	Underhill 2 + 10	Stepien-Iwumene — + 1	Uchegbulam 4 + 3	Pyke 2	Close 16	Tshikuna 5 + 2	Match No.
1	2^3	3^4	4	5	6	7	8^2	9	10	11^1	12^5	13	14	15	16													1
1	2^3	3^4	4	5^4	15	7^2	8^1	9	10	11		14	12			6	13											2
1	2	3	4^3		6	7	8^1	9	10^2	11		13	12	14		5												3
1		2^3	3	4	12	7	8^2		11			5^1	10	9	6	13	14											4
1		2	3	4	14	7	13		9	10^2		5^3	11	8	6^1	12												5
1		2^2	3	4		7	8		11	12^3		5^1	10	9	6	13	14											6
1	2	3^2	4	5	14	7	8		11			10^3	9^1	6	13	12												7
1	2	3^2	4	5^3	14	7	8		11			10^1	9	6	13	12												8
1	2^5	3^1	14		5	7	8	12	11			16	10^3	9^4	6	4^2	15	13										9
1	3	4	8^2	6	14	7	5^1		11			10^3	9	2	13	12												10
1	3	4	7^2	5	6	8	11^1		10	9		2	13	12														11
1	2	3^1	8^3	4	14	6	9		11			13	10^2	5	7	12												12
1	3	4^1	5		6	7	10	11^2	9	8		2				13	12											13
1	13	3	5^3	6	7^2	10	11	14	9^4	8	2	4				15	12											14
1	3^4	15	5	6	13	12	10	9^1	11	2	4^4	7^2	8^3	14														15
1	14	3^1	5	13	7	9	10^8	15	12	11	2^4	4^3	6	8^2														16
1	12	3	13	5^1	6	8	11	10^2	9	2	4^3	14	7^4	15														17
1	3^1	8	14	5	6	10	12	9	11	2	4^2	7^3	13															18
1	3	4^2	5	6	7^1	11^3	10	9	2	8	12	14	13															19
1	13	6^2	3	4	5	7^1	9^3	10	15	8	2	14	11	12^4														20
1	5^4	3	4	9	11^2	10	13	12	8^1	2	14	7	6^3	15														21
1	5	3	4	9	11	12	10^3	13	8	2	14	7^1	6^2															22
1	8	4	3	6^1	11	12	9^2	10	2	13	5	7	8^1															23
1	2^2	6	5	7	11	10	12	9	4	13	3	8^1																24
1	2	6	5	7	11	10	9	4	12	3	8^1																	25
1	2	6	5	7	11	10^1	12	9	4	13	8^2	3																26
1	2	6^1	5	7	11^8	13	10	9	4	8	3^2	12																27
1	2	6	5	8	13	10	9	4	3^1	14	12	7^3	11^2															28
1	2	15	5	7	14	9^4	12^5	8	3	6	4^1	13	16	10^2	11^3													29
1	2^5	16	5	7^3	11^4	13	9	15	8	3	6	14	12	4^2	10^1													30
1	14	5	12^5	11^3	10^4	2^6	15	9	4	6	7	3	16	8^1														31
1	12	5	15	7^1	11^1	10	9	4	6	2	3^3	14	13	8^2														32
1	6^3	3	7	11	12	14	5	4	13	10	2	9^1	8^2															33
1	5^1	4	14	7	11	10^6	13	8^4	2	3^2	15	6^3	16	12	9													34
1	5^2	8	7	10	14	11^1	13	2	3	12	6	4	9^3															35
1	5	8^3	4	15	7^4	10	14	11^5	3^1	2	12	13	6^2	16	9													36
1	5	3	10	11^3	14	4^1	2^2	9	7	6	13	8	12^8															37
1	2	7^2	5	14	10^6	11^4	13	12	16	15	6	4	3	9^3	8^1													38
1	2^4	5	4	7	11	10^1	13	14	12	9^3	6	15	3	8^2														39
1	2^3	5	4	7	11	12	10^8	13	9	6^1	14	3	8^2															40
1	5^2	3	2	8^1	11	7	13	4	12	6	9	10																41
1	12	3	2^5	7	10	13	11	4	5^1	6	14	9^2	8															42
1	16	13	3	2	7^5	10	11^1	15	14	12	4	5^2	6^3	9	8^4													43
1	14	12	3	2	10	13	5^1	11^2	7	4	15	6^4	8	9^3														44
1	2	3^2	15	5	8	11	9^4	12	10	6	4^3	14	7^1	13														45
1	7^1	3	12	4	5	6^3	10	15	13	11^2	8	2^4	14	9														46

FA Cup

Fourth Qualifying   Southend U   (h)   0-1

FA Trophy

Third Round	Hanwell T	(a)	2-1
Fourth Round	Basford U	(a)	4-1
Fifth Round	Altrincham	(a)	0-1

EBBSFLEET UNITED

Ground: The Kuflink Stadium, Stonebridge Road, Northfleet, Kent DA11 9GN. *Tel:* (01474) 533 796.
Website: ebbsfleetunited.co.uk *Email:* info@eufc.co.uk *Year Formed:* 1946 (as Gravesend & Northfleet); 2007
(renamed Ebbsfleet United). *Record Attendance:* 12,032 v Sunderland, FA Cup 4th rd, 12 February 1963.
Nickname: 'The Fleet'. *Manager:* Josh Wright. *Colours:* Red shirts with white trim, white shorts with red trim, red
socks.

EBBSFLEET UNITED – NATIONAL LEAGUE 2024–25 LEAGUE RECORD

Match No.	Date	Venue	Opponents	Result	H/T Score	Lg Pos.	Goalscorers	Attendance
1	Aug 10	A	Gateshead	L 1-5	0-3	24	Poleon [90]	1242
2	17	H	Barnet	L 1-2	0-1	23	Poleon (pen) [90]	1636
3	20	A	Yeovil T	L 2-3	0-2	23	Page [64], Samuel [67]	3295
4	24	H	Woking	L 0-3	0-1	24		1575
5	26	A	Braintree T	D 0-0	0-0	24		1313
6	31	H	FC Halifax T	L 0-1	0-1	24		1379
7	Sept 7	A	Altrincham	L 0-4	0-2	24		2024
8	10	H	Aldershot T	D 0-0	0-0	24		1175
9	14	H	Hartlepool U	W 1-0	1-0	24	Bingham [40]	1424
10	21	A	Sutton U	L 2-3	0-1	24	Poleon [56], Domi [67]	3131
11	24	A	Maidenhead U	L 1-2	0-1	24	Wright [90]	1412
12	28	H	Oldham Ath	L 1-2	0-0	24	Poleon (pen) [81]	1589
13	Oct 5	H	Rochdale	D 2-2	0-2	24	Chapman [64], Bingham (pen) [67]	1452
14	19	A	York C	L 0-4	0-1	24		5716
15	22	A	Forest Green R	L 1-3	0-1	24	Fonguck [71]	1311
16	26	H	Wealdstone	D 2-2	0-0	24	Cosgrave [86], Kwame Thomas [90]	1498
17	Nov 9	A	Tamworth	D 1-1	1-0	24	Cosgrave [28]	1141
18	16	H	Solihull Moors	L 0-6	0-0	24		1664
19	27	H	Eastleigh	L 0-1	0-0	24		1023
20	30	H	Boston U	D 0-0	0-0	24		1563
21	Dec 10	A	AFC Fylde	L 0-2	0-0	24		963
22	14	A	Barnet	L 1-4	0-4	24	Poleon [83]	1583
23	21	H	Gateshead	L 1-4	0-2	24	Cordner [85]	1275
24	26	A	Southend U	L 0-4	0-2	24		8406
25	Jan 1	H	Dagenham & Red	L 0-2	0-0	24		1395
26	11	A	Boston U	D 2-2	1-1	24	Cosgrave [22], Moncur [84]	1909
27	14	H	Yeovil T	D 1-1	0-1	24	Cosgrave [56]	1125
28	18	A	Woking	D 1-1	0-0	24	Akinola (og) [74]	2048
29	25	H	Braintree T	L 0-1	0-1	24		1385
30	Feb 1	A	FC Halifax T	L 0-2	0-1	24		1465
31	8	A	Rochdale	D 0-0	0-0	24		2134
32	15	H	York C	L 0-2	0-0	24		1745
33	18	H	Forest Green R	D 0-0	0-0	24		1057
34	22	A	Wealdstone	L 2-4	2-2	24	Domi [17], Stewart [33]	1401
35	Mar 1	H	Tamworth	L 2-3	1-3	24	Moncur [27], Hollis (og) [73]	1322
36	4	A	Eastleigh	L 0-2	0-1	24		2090
37	8	A	Solihull Moors	L 1-2	1-1	24	Kwame Thomas (pen) [45]	848
38	15	H	AFC Fylde	W 1-0	0-0	24	Lankshear [48]	1215
39	22	A	Aldershot T	D 3-3	3-2	24	Domi [16], Moncur [27], Cosgrave [30]	2685
40	29	H	Altrincham	D 2-2	1-1	24	Cosgrave [32], Olagunju [68]	1173
41	Apr 5	A	Hartlepool U	L 2-3	0-1	24	Manktelow [51], Cosgrave [73]	4156
42	12	H	Sutton U	W 4-1	1-0	24	Carr [45], Olagunju [51], Cosgrave 2 [68, 77]	1295
43	18	A	Dagenham & Red	L 0-1	0-0	24		1747
44	21	H	Southend U	L 0-4	0-1	24		3125
45	26	H	Maidenhead U	L 0-2	0-0	24		1312
46	May 5	A	Oldham Ath	L 0-2	0-1	24		7493

Final League Position: 24

GOALSCORERS

League (38): Cosgrave 9, Poleon 5 (2 pens), Domi 3, Moncur 3, Bingham 2 (1 pen), Olagunju 2, Kwame Thomas 2 (1 pen), Carr 1, Chapman 1, Cordner 1, Fonguck 1, Lankshear 1, Manktelow 1, Page 1, Samuel 1, Stewart 1, Wright 1, own goals 2.
FA Cup (0).
FA Trophy (3): Cosgrave 1, Harriott 1, Kane 1.

Cousins 43	O'Neill 21 + 1	Page 15 + 1	Cordner 15 + 1	Bolger 16	John 7 + 3	Passley 9 + 2	Wright 19 + 1	Kellermann 11 + 1	Edser 33 + 4	Chapman 31 + 7	Poleon 14 + 13	Samuel 8 + 7	Dallison 28 + 2	Thomas Kwame 13 + 15	Lucas Covolan 1	Fonguck 9 + 7	Phillips 4 + 1	Tanner 7 + 9	Domi 24 + 12	Candle 3 + 7	Tanga 6 + 12	Ondo — + 1	Randall 3 + 4	Carr 6 + 4	Bingham 11 + 12	Olagunju 24	Lawson 2 + 4	Anthony — + 1	Kane 10 + 1	Goddard 1	Wakely 1 + 3	Souare 5 + 3	Stewart 18 + 1	Cosgrave 27 + 5	Davies 4 + 2	Manktelow 7 + 19	Berry 1	Aoraha 11 + 5	Harriott 4 + 6	Thomas Kymani — + 1	Moncur 21	Lankshear 13 + 1	Odokonyero — + 1	Match No.
1	2^5	3	4^2	5^4	6^3	7	8^1	9	10	11	12	13	14	15	16																													1
1	2	3	4^5	16	7^1	8^3	13	9	12	10	11^4	15	6	14		5^2																												2
1	5	8^5	6	2^2	7	15	4	13	12	3	11^4	9^3				10^1	14	16																									3
1	2^4	3	4	12	9^2	7	8	11^3	10	6			14	5^3		15	13																										4
1	2	3	6	7^2	13	12	11^3	5	8^1	4		14	10	9																													5
1	2^5	3	6	7^4	13	15	10	5	8^3	4^2	16	14	11^1	9	12																												6
1	15	2^1	5	6^5	13	8	9	10	4	16	14	3^4		12					7^2	11^3																							7
1	2^1	3	15		7^3	8	9	11	6		12		14	4^4					13	10^2	5																						8
1	2	14	6	9	10	5	7^3		3^2	12	13		8^1	11	4																												9
1	3	14	6^2	4	12	2	8^3	7^1	9	15	11^4	10	5	13																													10
1	6	3	11	2	8	7^2	4	12	13	10	5	9^1																															11
1	6^3	3	5	_	7	9	2	10^2	13	8	12	14	15	4^4	11^1																												12
1	4	6	7^1	10^3	3	9^4	5	11^2	8	14	13	12	2	15																													13
1	5	6	10^1	16	14	11^3	8^2	7^4	9	13	15	3^6	2	4	12																												14
1	4^2	6	9^4	5	10	3	15	13	7	14	12	8^3	2	11^1																													15
1	6	5	10^1	4	12	8^3	13	9^4	15	7^2	14	2	3	11																													16
1	5	6	7^2	8^1	4	10	12	9■	2	13	3	11																															17
1	5	6^1	7	8^3	4	10^2	13	14^4	9	2	15	3	11	12■																													18
1	2^4	5	6	7	4	14	12	8^2	9^3	10	13	3	11^1	15																													19
1	2	5^4	8	7^3	15	16	14	11^5	9	6^2	4	12	3	10^1	13																												20
1	4	5^3	6	10^4	16	14	15	2	3	11^1	8	12	1	7^5	9^2	13																											21
1	6^2	5	8	13	4	10^3	14	15	3	2	12	11^5	16	9^4	7^1																												22
1	2^5	6^4	3	10	3	16	5	11^3	15	9^2	13	12	8	14	7^1																												23
1	4	5^4	3	6^1	10^5	2	14	16	15	8^2	12	11^3	13	7	9																												24
1	5^3	3	6	9	15	8	13	10^1	4	2	11^2	7^4	12	14																													25
1	4^1	8^4	13	3	11^2	6	14	5	2	7	15	12	10^3	9																													26
1	4^5	8^1	10	14	3	7^3	16	5■	2^4	13	11	12	15	6	9^2																												27
1	2	9	7	12	5	11^1	3	4	10	13	6^2	8																															28
1	2	9	3^1	15	5	11	14	4	5	8^2	10	13	6^3	7^4	12																												29
1	2^1	8^3	11^2	3	10	13	14	5	4	15	6^4	7	9	12																													30
1	6	9^4	8	12	5	13	11	2	10^1	7^3																																	31
1	b	7^3	8^3	12	14	5	13	1	11	16	4^1	2	10^2	15	9^4	3																											32
1	6	7^1	8	14	5	11^2	13	10^3	4	2	12	9	3																														33
1	6	7^2	8^5	12	14	5	15	10^1	13	4■	2	11^3	16	9^4	3																												34
1	6^1	7^2	8	15	10^3	4	13	3^4	16	2	11^5	14	9	5																													35
1	14	3^4	6	2	9	7^3	11^1	4	12	5^2		15	6	13																								8^5	10					36
1	3^4	6	9■	7	11^3	5^2	12	14	16	4	10^1	15	13																									8^5	2					37
1	6	4^4	8	12	7	14	2	13	5	11^2	15	9^1	10^3	3																													38
1	6	9	7^3	8	3	14	13	2^4	15	5	12	11^2	4	10^1																													39
1	4	7	8	6	15	5^4	12	13	14	3	2^2	9^1	10	11^3																													40
1	4	7	13	8	6	5	3	9	2	10^2	12	11^1																															41
1	2^2	6	9	7	3	8	4	11	5	12	13	10^1																															42
1	6	9■	7^1	3	12	8	4	11	2^2	13	14	10^3	5																														43
1	6	8	3	12	7	4	9	2	10^2	13	11^1	5																															44
1	4^2	7	9	6	10^3	12	5^1	3	11	14	13	8	2																														45
	4	7	6	5	12	10	3	1	9^1	2	11	8																															46

FA Cup
Fourth Qualifying   Maidstone U   (a)   0-3

FA Trophy
Third Round   Sutton U   (a)   3-3
(Sutton U won 4-2 on penalties)

FC HALIFAX TOWN

Ground: The Shay Stadium, Halifax, West Yorkshire HX1 2YT (satnav HX1 2YS). *Tel:* (01422) 341 222.
Website: www.fchalifaxtown.com *Email:* tonyallan@fchalifaxtown.com *Year Formed:* 1911 (Reformed 2008).
Record Attendance: 36,885 v Tottenham H, FA Cup 5th rd, 14 February 1953 (as Halifax T); 8042 v Bradford C, FA Cup
1st rd, 9 November 2014 (as FC Halifax T). *Nickname:* 'The Shaymen'. *Manager:* Adam Lakeland.
Colours: Blue patterned shirts, blue shorts with white and blue trim, blue socks with white trim.

FC HALIFAX TOWN – NATIONAL LEAGUE 2024–25 LEAGUE RECORD

Match No.	Date	Venue	Opponents	Result		H/T Score	Lg Pos.	Goalscorers	Attendance
1	Aug 10	H	Barnet	W	2-1	0-0	6	Cooke [49], Alimi-Adetoro [59]	1634
2	17	H	Aldershot T	L	0-1	0-1	13		1642
3	20	H	Gateshead	D	1-1	0-0	15	Senior [48]	1379
4	23	A	Dagenham & Red	D	1-1	0-1	12	Oluwabori [83]	1481
5	26	A	Solihull Moors	L	0-1	0-1	17		1554
6	31	A	Ebbsfleet U	W	1-0	1-0	14	Capello [2]	1379
7	Sept 7	A	Hartlepool U	D	0-0	0-0	14		4012
8	10	H	Oldham Ath	D	1-1	0-0	15	Senior [62]	3146
9	14	H	Eastleigh	W	3-1	2-0	10	Waters [27], Smith [45], Alimi-Adetoro [61]	1242
10	21	A	Maidenhead U	W	1-0	0-0	9	Hoti [69]	1121
11	24	A	Braintree T	L	0-1	0-0	10		849
12	28	H	Wealdstone	D	2-2	0-1	11	Hoti (pen) [52], Pugh [90]	1442
13	Oct 5	H	Tamworth	W	3-2	0-2	8	Waters [62], Cooke [74], High [87]	1480
14	19	A	Boston U	W	1-0	1-0	7	Oluwabori [1]	1720
15	22	A	Rochdale	L	1-2	0-1	7	Waters [76]	2926
16	26	H	York C	L	1-2	1-0	10	Cooke [14]	3961
17	Nov 9	H	Woking	W	1-0	1-0	8	Capello [14]	1546
18	16	A	Yeovil T	W	1-0	0-0	7	Hoti [57]	3829
19	27	A	Forest Green R	D	1-1	0-0	8	Oluwabori [86]	1205
20	30	H	Southend U	L	0-2	0-1	10		1766
21	Dec 10	H	Sutton U	D	0-0	0-0	11		1006
22	14	A	Aldershot T	W	4-3	2-0	8	Waters [18], Oluwabori [33], Cooke [84], Emmerson [89]	2047
23	21	A	Barnet	D	1-1	1-1	8	Waters [11]	1854
24	26	A	Altrincham	D	0-0	0-0	8		3312
25	Jan 14	A	Gateshead	W	3-1	2-0	8	Bray [16], Oluwabori [45], Wright [66]	685
26	25	A	Solihull Moors	W	2-0	1-0	8	Oluwabori [12], Bray [55]	1316
27	Feb 1	H	Ebbsfleet U	W	2-0	1-0	6	Thomas [12], Cooke [69]	1465
28	4	H	AFC Fylde	L	1-2	1-1	6	Cooke (pen) [39]	1203
29	8	A	Tamworth	W	2-1	1-0	6	Emmerson [8], High [79]	1074
30	11	A	Southend U	L	1-3	0-0	6	Thomas [84]	6250
31	15	H	Boston U	W	1-0	0-0	6	Cooke [61]	1668
32	19	H	Rochdale	D	0-0	0-0	7		2682
33	22	A	York C	D	2-2	2-1	6	Senior [2], Pugh [3]	6926
34	Mar 4	H	Forest Green R	W	2-1	1-0	6	Emmerson [11], Hoti [69]	1143
35	8	H	Yeovil T	W	1-0	1-0	6	Capello [13]	1688
36	15	H	Sutton U	W	3-0	2-0	6	Emmerson [1], Senior [21], Hoti [56]	2292
37	18	H	Dagenham & Red	L	0-1	0-1	5		1243
38	22	A	Oldham Ath	L	0-2	0-1	5		7256
39	25	A	Woking	D	0-0	0-0	5		1809
40	29	H	Hartlepool U	L	0-1	0-1	5		2202
41	Apr 5	A	Eastleigh	D	1-1	0-0	6	Galvin [89]	2161
42	12	H	Maidenhead U	L	0-2	0-0	7		1485
43	18	A	AFC Fylde	W	1-0	1-0	6	Galvin [28]	1733
44	21	A	Altrincham	L	0-3	0-1	6		1896
45	26	H	Braintree T	W	1-0	0-0	6	Senior [83]	1631
46	May 5	A	Wealdstone	L	1-3	0-3	6	Thomas [56]	2843

Final League Position: 6

GOALSCORERS

League (50): Cooke 7 (1 pen), Oluwabori 6, Hoti 5 (1 pen), Senior 5, Waters 5, Emmerson 4, Capello 3, Thomas 3,
Alimi-Adetoro 2, Bray 2, Galvin 2, High 2, Pugh 2, Smith 1, Wright 1.
FA Cup (2): Cummings 1, Waters 1.
FA Trophy (2): Cooke 2.
National League Play-offs (0).

Johnson 38	Senior 46	Smith 33	Evans 33+3	Alimi-Adetoro 29+7	Jenkins 22+7	Oluwabori 17+10	Cooke 33+11	Pugh 18+21	Capello 30+8	George 13+6	Bray 12+24	Emmerson 12+21	Cosgrave —+5	Arthur 7+2	Hoti 31+6	Sinfield —+1	Wright 9+13	Galvin 28+9	High 20+1	Waters 18	Cummings 12+1	Thomas 13+7	Suttcliffe 5+4	Leigh 3+4	Emmanuel 10+2	Ford —+1	Savin 8	Eze 1+5	Tarima 1+6	Nkrumah 4+2	Match No.
1	2	3	4	5	6¹	7⁴	8	9	10³	11²	12	13	14	15																	1
1	2	3	4	5	6⁴	7	8	9¹	10²	11³		13	15	14	12		13														2
1	2	3	4	5	6²	7³	8	9	10	11¹		14	12		13																3
1	2	3	4	5	6²	7	8	9¹	10³	11⁴		13	15	14	12																4
1	2	3	4	5			8	9³	10	11²	6¹	13	12		7		14														5
1	2	3	4	5			8³	9⁸	15	10²	11¹	6⁴	13		7		12	14													6
1	2	3	4	5			8⁴		9³	10¹	15	14		7	13		12	6	11²												7
1	2	3	4	5			8³	13		9	10¹	15		7²	12		14	6	11⁴												8
1	2	3	4	5			13	8	15	9²	10³	16		7⁴	14		12	6¹	11⁵												9
1	3	2	7	4²			15	11	16	8⁴	10¹	5⁵	13	14	6		9³	12													10
1	4	3			8		12	9		13	14		11		6²	5	7³	10¹	2												11
1	4	3			9²	14	13	12		8³			11		6	5¹	7	10	2												12
1	4	3	12		10¹	14	8⁴		15	13		8	12	13	7³		6	5²	9	11	2										13
1	4	3	7	14	10¹	9²		8⁸	12			13			5		6³	11	2												14
1	4	3	8		10	9	12			13					6		5	7¹	11	2²											15
1	4	3	8	12		13	10¹	15	9³	14					6		5²	7	11⁴	2											16
1	4	3		5²	7¹	14	11	6	8³	13	12			10				9	2												17
1	4	3	13	5⁴	7²	14	11	6	8³	12	15			10¹				9	2												18
1	4	3	12	5²	7⁴	14	11³	6	8¹	13	15	16		10⁵				9	2												19
1	4	3¹	6	13	8³	12	11		5	7	14	15		10²				9	2⁴												20
1	4	3	6		7²	8	11	12	5¹					10	13	14		9³	2												21
1	3	2	7	5	8⁴	11¹	10	13	4³		15			6	14	12		9²													22
1	3	2	7	5	8¹	11³	10	15	4²		16			6⁴	14	13	12	9⁹													23
1	2	4	6	5¹		13	11⁴	15	10²		14			8³	12	3	7	9													24
1	2	4	6	5	15	10⁴		13	14	12	8¹	9²		11³	3	7															25
1	2	4	5¹	6	10⁵	12	14	15		8²	11³			9⁴	3	7		13													26
1	2	4	9⁵	5	15	16	12	13	14		8¹	11²		7³	3	6		10⁴													27
1	2	4	8	5³	15		10	6¹	9⁴		12	14		13	3	7		11²													28
1	5	4	6	12	16		9	15	7⁵		10²	11³		13	2	8⁴	3¹	14													29
1	2	4	6	5		11	14	10²		9¹	12			7³	3	8		13													30
1	2	4	6		13		9		10¹		11		5	12	3	8		7²													31
1	2	4	6	5		9⁷	12	10¹		11		13		7³	3	8		14													32
1	2	4²	6	5	11⁴	7⁵	12		16	14	15	9¹		13	3	8		10³													33
1	4		6⁴	12	8		13	16	10³		15	11		5	7²	2¹	3		9⁵	14											34
1	4		6		8²		12	16	10⁴		15	9⁹		5	7³		3	11	2¹	13	14										35
1	4		6		8	15	14	9³		16	7		5	10⁵		3⁴		11²	2¹	13	12										36
1	4		6	12	8³		14	10¹		13	7²		5	9		3		11		2											37
1⁵	4		6	10	8³⁷		7	15		16	13		5²	9		3		11¹	14	2⁴	12										38
	4		6	13		9	5		7³	12		8		3		10¹	11²	2		1	14										39
	4		5		11³	6²	12	10¹		9			3		13	7⁵	8⁴	2		1	15	14	16								40
	4		5¹	6		14	8¹	10		11		9²		3		7³		2		1	13	12	15								41
	4		5	8¹	7²	6⁴	10³		16	13		9		3		14	15	2		1		12	11⁵								42
1	4		6	12	8³		14	10¹		13	7²		6³			8		10⁵	14	12	5	1	16	15	11⁴						43
	3		8³		5	6⁵	11¹	12	15					2		9⁴	16	7⁷	4	1	13	14	10²								44
	4	16	8³		5	15	12	9¹	13	3²	7		6			10¹		2		1		14	11⁵								45
	2		6	11	15	7	16	10²	9³		13		14			12	3⁵	4¹	1	8⁴	5										46

FA Cup
Fourth Qualifying Oldham Ath (a) 2-4

FA Trophy
Third Round Basford U (a) 2-2
(Basford U won 6-5 on penalties)

National League Play-offs
Quarter-Finals Oldham Ath (a) 0-4

FOREST GREEN ROVERS

Ground: The New Lawn Stadium, Another Way, Nailsworth, Gloucestershire GL6 0FG. *Tel:* (0333) 123 1889.
Website: www.fgr.co.uk *Email:* reception@fgr.co.uk *Year Formed:* 1889.
Record Attendance: 4,836 v Derby Co, FA Cup 3rd rd, 3 January 2009. *Nicknames:* 'Rovers', 'The Green', 'FGR',
'The Little Club on the Hill', 'Green Army', 'The Green Devils'. *Manager:* Robbie Savage. *Colours:* Green and
black patterned shirts with black trim, green shorts with black patterned trim, green socks with black trim.

FOREST GREEN ROVERS – NATIONAL LEAGUE 2024–25 LEAGUE RECORD

Match No.	Date	Venue	Opponents	Result	H/T Score	Lg Pos.	Goalscorers	Atten- dance
1	Aug 10	A	Aldershot T	D 3-3	1-2	10	Inniss [22], McAllister [48], Doidge [57]	2564
2	17	A	Boston U	W 4-0	3-0	5	Doidge 2 [3, 56], Sercombe 2 [21, 42]	1830
3	20	A	Barnet	L 0-1	0-0	11		1710
4	24	A	Rochdale	D 0-0	0-0	12		2261
5	26	H	Altrincham	W 2-1	1-0	6	Doidge [20], McCann [90]	1982
6	31	A	Sutton U	W 2-1	1-0	5	Doidge [30], McCann [90]	2607
7	Sept 7	A	Solihull Moors	W 1-0	0-0	4	Jenks [48]	1515
8	10	H	AFC Fylde	W 3-0	1-0	3	McCann [35], Robson [89], Bunker [90]	1249
9	14	H	Wealdstone	D 2-2	2-1	2	Doidge [2], May [6]	2165
10	21	A	Gateshead	W 2-0	1-0	2	Sercombe [6], Doidge [90]	1112
11	24	A	Oldham Ath	L 0-1	0-1	3		5034
12	28	H	Hartlepool U	W 1-0	0-0	3	McCann [71]	1764
13	Oct 5	A	Eastleigh	W 3-1	0-1	2	Cardwell [47], Knowles [57], McCann [69]	2355
14	19	H	Braintree T	W 2-1	1-1	2	Cardwell [35], McAllister [87]	1997
15	22	H	Ebbsfleet U	W 3-1	1-0	1	McAllister [7], Robson [47], Knowles [52]	1311
16	26	A	Woking	D 1-1	1-0	2	McAllister [42]	2280
17	Nov 9	A	Maidenhead U	W 4-1	2-0	2	Bunker [20], McCann [35], Moore-Taylor [69], Jenks [80]	1246
18	16	H	York C	W 2-0	0-0	1	Bunker [64], McAllister [83]	2697
19	23	A	Southend U	D 2-2	1-0	2	Bunker [40], Doidge [73]	6725
20	27	H	FC Halifax T	D 1-1	0-0	2	McAllister [63]	1205
21	Dec 14	H	Boston U	W 1-0	1-0	3	Bunker [36]	1796
22	21	H	Aldershot T	D 1-1	0-1	3	McCann [46]	2116
23	26	A	Tamworth	D 1-1	1-0	3	McAllister [38]	1721
24	Jan 1	H	Yeovil T	W 2-1	0-1	2	McAllister (pen) [76], Inniss [90]	3002
25	8	H	Dagenham & Red	D 1-1	0-0	2	Inniss [90]	1038
26	14	H	Barnet	D 0-0	0-0	1		1492
27	18	A	Rochdale	W 1-0	0-0	1	Sercombe [71]	1771
28	25	A	Altrincham	D 1-1	0-1	2	Doidge [90]	2089
29	Feb 4	A	Dagenham & Red	W 2-0	1-0	2	McAllister [22], McCann [72]	1266
30	8	H	Eastleigh	W 2-1	0-0	2	McDonnell (og) [64], Robson [90]	1634
31	15	A	Braintree T	L 0-2	0-2	3		860
32	18	A	Ebbsfleet U	D 0-0	0-0	3		1057
33	22	H	Woking	D 1-1	0-0	3	Garrick [72]	1728
34	Mar 1	H	Maidenhead U	W 2-0	1-0	3	Osadebe [11], Cardwell [72]	1800
35	4	A	FC Halifax T	L 1-2	0-1	3	McAllister [62]	1143
36	8	A	York C	D 1-1	0-0	3	Cardwell [54]	6810
37	11	H	Sutton U	W 2-1	2-0	3	McCann [29], Doidge [36]	1275
38	15	H	Southend U	D 2-2	2-1	3	Inniss [21], Garrick [30]	2251
39	22	A	AFC Fylde	L 0-3	0-1	3		1444
40	29	H	Solihull Moors	W 1-0	1-0	3	May [30]	1568
41	Apr 5	A	Wealdstone	L 1-2	1-1	3	Garrick [19]	1441
42	12	H	Gateshead	L 2-3	0-2	3	Shelvey (og) [87], Doidge [90]	1776
43	18	A	Yeovil T	D 1-1	0-1	3	Inniss [90]	4092
44	21	H	Tamworth	W 3-0	3-0	3	Garrick [29], McCann [31], Robson [41]	1783
45	26	H	Oldham Ath	W 1-0	1-0	3	McCann [45]	2801
46	May 5	A	Hartlepool U	D 1-1	0-1	3	Doidge [89]	4176

Final League Position: 3

GOALSCORERS

League (69): Doidge 12, McCann 11, McAllister 10 (1 pen), Bunker 5, Inniss 5, Cardwell 4, Garrick 4, Robson 4, Sercombe 4, Jenks 2, Knowles 2, May 2, Moore-Taylor 1, Osadebe 1, own goals 2.
FA Cup (3): Doidge 2, Sercombe 1.
FA Trophy (3): Quigley 2, May 1.
National League Play-offs (2): Inniss 1, Osadebe 1.

Ward 28	Bunker 16 + 19	Tozer 21 + 8	Inniss 39 + 2	Robson 46	Long 32 + 5	McCann 35 + 3	Osadebe 24 + 17	May 46	McAllister 39 + 5	Doidge 21 + 20	Knowles 28 + 12	Sercombe 31 + 4	Jenks 8 + 11	Omotoye — + 4	Lavinier — + 6	Moore-Taylor 19 + 4	Cardwell 15 + 22	Quigley 11 + 26	Garrick 12 + 9	McCormick 1 + 4	Harries 13 + 1	Mrozek 11	Fleming 3 + 7	Cann 6	Searle 1	Match No.
1	2^3	3	4	5	6	7	8^4	9^2	10	11^1	12	13	14	15												1
1	12	3	4	5^1	2	13	6	8^2	9	10^5	11^4	7^3	14	16	15											2
1	8	3	4	5	2^8	12	6	9	10^1	11^2	13	7^3	14													3
1		2	3	4		5	12	7	10	11	9^1	6	8													4
1	15	2	3	4	12	6	5^1	8		10	11^4	7^2	9^3	14		13										5
1		3	5	4	2	6	13	8	12	10^2	11^3	7^1	9^4			15	14									6
1	16	3	4	5	2	6	14	8^4	12	11^3	10^1	7^5	9^2			15		13								7
1	15	4	3	2^1	5	8	14	7	12	10^5	11^2	6^3	9^4			16	13									8
1	13	3		2	5	7^3	14	6	11	10^1	9^4	8^2				4	12	15								9
1	12	2		5	4^1	8	14	7	10^3	13	11^4	6^2			16	3	9^6	15								10
1		2		4		8	7	6	10	14	11^2	12	5^1			3	13	9^3								11
1	5^3	2	13	4		8	14	7	10^5	9^1	11^2	6^4			15	3	12	16								12
1	15	16	2	4^1		8	5	7^4	10	13	11^3	6^2		14		3	9^6	12								13
1		15	2	4	14	8	5	7	10^2	12	11^1	6^3				3	9^4	13								14
1	13	16	2	5^1	4	8	10^5	7	11^2	9^3	12	6^4				3	15	14								15
1	12	2^8	5	4	10	7^3	6	8	11^1	9^2			13			3		14								16
1	8	2		5^2	4^3	7^1		6	10	16	11^4		13	15	14	3	12	9^6								17
1	8	2		5	4	7		6	10^3	13	11^1	12				3	13	9^2								18
1	10^3	2^4	12	5	4		9		6	7	14	8^2		13		3	11^1	15								19
1	10^3		2	5	4	9	13	6	7	11^2	8^1					3	12	14								20
1	10		2	5	4	9		6	7	11^1	8^2		13			3	12									21
1	8^3		2	7	6	4	13	10	11	14	12			3^2		5	9^1									22
1	7^4	14	4	6	8		12	9	11^3	15	2^1	3				5	13	10^2								23
1		4	3	2^1		9	8	7	11^2	10^3	6					5	12	13	14							24
1	12	4	3	2		9^1	8	7	14	10^2	6					5		11^3	13							25
1	11	12	4	3	2		14	8	7^1		9^2	6				5^4	10^3	13	15							26
1	7	5	4	3	2		14	8	11^2	10^3		6					13	9^1	12							27
1	15	4	5	2^4		7^1	9	11	14	6^2	8					10^3	13	12		3						28
	14		4	3	2	8^4	12		6	11^5		9^1	7^3			10^2	16	13	15		5	1				29
	12		4	3	2	8^4	15		6	11^1	14	9^3	7^5			10^2	13	16			5	1				30
	14		4	3	2^4	9	12	8^5	7^2	15	11^1	6				10^3	13		16		5	1				31
		4	3		9	2	6	7^4	11^2			8^3				14	13	15	12		5	1	10^1			32
	14		4	3		9	2	6	7							13	11^3	12		8^1	5	1	10^2			33
	10	4	3^2	14	9	2^1	6	7^4	13							15	12	11^5	8^3		5	1	16			34
	2^3	4	3		9^2	7	6	10^4	13			14				12	11^1	8			5	1	15			35
	5	4	3		9	2	6	7^3			13	8				11^1	12	10^2				1	14			36
	12	5^2	4	3	15	9^4	2	6	11^1	7^3	8					13	14	10^5				1	16			37
	13	5	4	3		9^4	2	6	16	15	8^5		13			11^1	14	7^3	12			1	10^2			38
	12	5	4	3	15	9^4	2^1	6	5	13	16	8^3				14	11^2	7^5	10			1				39
	8		4	3	2		9^1	6	7^4	11^3	12					13	15	10^2			5		14	1		40
	8	15	4	3	2^1		9^6	6	7	11^4	14	13				12	16	10^3			5^2			1		41
	5	4	3	2^1	16	9^2	6	7^5	12	15	13		8			11^3	14	10^4						1		42
	5^1	4	3^4	2	6	7^3	8	10	9^5	14			12			11^2	15	13						1		43
	12	4	3^2	2	6^4		8	9	16	13	7^1					14	11^3	10^5			5		15	1		44
	12	4	3	2	9	15	6	7^4		13		8^5	16			14	11^3	10^1			5^2			1		45
	12	4^4	3	2^5		9^2	16	6	15	14	7^3	8	10			5	11^1	13							1	46

FA Cup

Fourth Qualifying	Weymouth	(h)	2-0	
First Round	Stockport Co	(a)	1-2	
(aet; 1-1 at end of normal time)				

FA Trophy

Third Round	Braintree T	(a)	1-1
(Forest Green R won 5-3 on penalties)			
Fourth Round	Chorley	(h)	2-0
Fifth Round	Oxford C	(a)	0-1

National League Play-offs

Semi-Finals	Southend U	(h)	2-2
(aet; Southend U won 4-2 on penalties)			

GATESHEAD

Ground: Gateshead International Stadium, Neilson Road, Gateshead, Tyne and Wear NE10 0EF. *Tel:* (0191) 477 1983. *Website:* www.gateshead-fc.com *Email:* info@gateshead-fc.com *Year Formed:* as South Shields 1889 (as Gateshead 1930, Reformed 1977). *Record Attendance:* 20,752 v Lincoln C, Division 3N (at Redheugh Park), 25 September 1937; 11,750 v Newcastle U, Friendly, 28 October 2009 (at International Stadium). *Nicknames:* 'The Tynesiders', 'The Heed'. *Manager:* Alun Armstrong. *Colours:* White shirts with black sleeves and thin black stripes, black shorts with white trim, black socks with white trim.

GATESHEAD – NATIONAL LEAGUE 2024–25 LEAGUE RECORD

Match No.	Date	Venue	Opponents	Result	H/T Score	Lg Pos.	Goalscorers	Attendance
1	Aug 10	H	Ebbsfleet U	W 5-1	3-0	1	Whelan [11], Oseni [33], Olley 3 [45, 48, 59]	1242
2	17	A	Woking	W 2-0	1-0	1	Richardson [44], Beck [79]	2099
3	20	A	FC Halifax T	D 1-1	0-0	2	Oseni [46]	1379
4	24	H	Yeovil T	W 3-1	2-1	2	Thomas (og) [14], Haunstrup [21], Hannant (pen) [90]	1096
5	26	A	Oldham Ath	D 1-1	1-0	2	Newton [10]	5583
6	31	H	Eastleigh	W 2-1	1-0	1	Oseni [45], Storey [90]	1302
7	Sept 7	A	Barnet	W 2-0	1-0	1	Whelan [6], Adom [50]	1461
8	14	A	Dagenham & Red	L 1-7	1-2	5	Kalambayi (og) [31]	1549
9	21	H	Forest Green R	L 0-2	0-1	7		1112
10	24	A	Boston U	W 2-0	2-0	5	Radcliffe [16], Oseni [34]	1431
11	28	A	Southend U	W 3-1	1-1	5	Butterfield [12], Hannant (pen) [53], Radcliffe [70]	6837
12	Oct 5	H	Wealdstone	W 1-0	0-0	4	Malcolm [73]	1147
13	8	A	Tamworth	L 1-2	0-1	4	Whelan [90]	815
14	19	A	Altrincham	D 2-2	2-1	4	Butterfield [32], Oseni [40]	1881
15	23	A	Sutton U	W 1-0	0-0	4	Hannant (pen) [53]	2100
16	26	H	Solihull Moors	W 1-0	0-0	4	Oseni [90]	1001
17	Nov 9	A	AFC Fylde	L 0-3	0-1	4		1287
18	16	H	Aldershot T	D 2-2	2-1	5	Oseni [19], Whelan [34]	1332
19	23	A	Maidenhead U	W 5-0	2-0	4	Butterfield 2 [19, 65], Massey (og) [45], Booty [52], Whelan [59]	847
20	26	H	Rochdale	L 0-1	0-0	5		712
21	30	A	Braintree T	D 2-2	2-2	4	Oseni [7], Grayson [19]	703
22	Dec 14	H	Woking	W 4-0	3-0	4	Hannant 2 (2 pens) [6, 29], Newton [15], Oseni [48]	845
23	21	A	Ebbsfleet U	W 4-1	2-0	4	Whelan [20], Hannant (pen) [40], Oseni 2 [57, 63]	1275
24	26	H	Hartlepool U	W 4-3	2-1	4	Newton 2 [18, 60], Worman [33], Oseni [86]	2152
25	Jan 1	A	York C	L 0-1	0-1	4		7554
26	14	A	FC Halifax T	L 1-3	0-2	4	Hannant (pen) [50]	685
27	17	H	Yeovil T	D 0-0	0-0	4		2919
28	25	H	Oldham Ath	D 1-1	0-1	4	Hannant [63]	1694
29	Feb 8	A	Wealdstone	W 4-0	2-0	5	Hannant 2 (2 pens) [32, 45], Gunter (og) [69], Malcolm [90]	1323
30	15	H	Altrincham	L 0-1	0-1	5		1114
31	18	H	Sutton U	W 4-3	2-1	4	Roles 2 [16, 80], Malcolm [35], Hannant [74]	668
32	22	H	Solihull Moors	W 3-1	1-0	4	Malcolm [4], Hannant 2 (2 pens) [59, 85]	903
33	25	A	Eastleigh	D 1-1	0-0	4	Sellars-Fleming [84]	1588
34	Mar 1	H	AFC Fylde	D 1-1	1-0	4	Booty [25]	1458
35	4	A	Rochdale	L 0-1	0-0	4		1540
36	8	A	Aldershot T	L 1-3	1-1	4	Roles [2]	2188
37	15	H	Maidenhead U	L 0-2	0-1	6		1811
38	18	H	Braintree T	L 1-3	1-0	6	Jones [35]	625
39	22	H	Tamworth	L 0-2	0-0	6		1184
40	29	A	Barnet	L 1-3	0-2	7	Malcolm [82]	2641
41	Apr 5	H	Dagenham & Red	W 2-1	2-0	6	Akinola [19], Robson [37]	1371
42	12	A	Forest Green R	W 3-2	2-0	5	Malcolm 2 [1, 44], Humbles [62]	1776
43	18	H	York C	L 1-3	1-1	7	Hannant [11]	3014
44	21	A	Hartlepool U	L 2-3	0-2	7	Malcolm [48], Bramwell [90]	4160
45	26	A	Boston U	L 1-2	1-2	8	Hannant [16]	3401
46	May 5	H	Southend U	D 0-0	0-0	8		4108

Final League Position: 8

GOALSCORERS

League (76): Hannant 15 (11 pens), Oseni 12, Malcolm 8, Whelan 6, Butterfield 4, Newton 4, Olley 3, Roles 3, Booty 2, Radcliffe 2, Adom 1, Akinola 1, Beck 1, Bramwell 1, Grayson 1, Haunstrup 1, Humbles 1, Jones 1, Richardson 1, Robson 1, Sellars-Fleming 1, Storey 1, Worman 1, own goals 4.
FA Cup (2): Newton 1, Oseni 1.
FA Trophy (9): Thompson 2, Booty 1, Lowery 1, Lynne 1, Malcolm 1, McGowan 1, Newton 1, Worman 1.

Brooks 24	Tinkler 29 + 1	Richardson 14 + 1	Grayson 11 + 2	Hannant 44	Newton 20 + 14	Booty 43	Whelan 23 + 1	Bond 1 + 1	Butterfield 18 + 1	Olley 2	Bartley 6 + 3	Oseni 21 + 3	Allan 6 + 6	Bramwell 3 + 2	Adom 7 + 15	McGowan 10 + 5	Beck 3 + 12	Worman 29 + 15	Storey 9 + 1	Nouble 3 + 4	Leroy-Belehouan 16 + 9	Haunstrup 7 + 2	Thompson — + 5	Colkett 5 + 13	Moss 3	Radcliffe 17 + 2	Robson 3	Carr — + 1	Malcolm 21 + 16	Jones 18 + 5	Johnson — + 4	Home — + 2	Mason 11	Akinola 6	Williams J 9 + 1	Milmore — + 1	Humbles 15 + 6	Flower 3 + 1	Sheal 2 + 4	Tripp 5	Shelvey 7	Horton 15 + 2	Roles 11 + 1	Sellars-Fleming 6 + 9	Match No.
1	2	3	4	5	6⁵		8¹	9⁴	10³	11²	12	13	14	15	16																														1
1	2⁴	4		5	6³	7	8	9	10¹	11²	16	14		15	13			3		12⁵																									2
1		4			6	7²	8¹	11³	12	10	9⁴	14	5	15	12	10	9	3	16	4¹			2	13	15																				3
1		2		5	13	7	8⁵	10²	11³	6⁴	14	15	12	9	3	16	4¹																												4
1	2	4		5	7⁴	6	13	15	16	10	9⁵	11¹	12	14	3²	8³																												5
1	3	4²	5	13	6	7³	9⁴	11¹	10⁴	14	15	8	2	12																															6
3²			5³	14	6	7	9¹	11	10⁵	13	8⁴	2	4	12	1	15	16																												7
1	3		4	15	10	7²	9⁴	11	13	8¹	14	6³	2	5⁵	16	12																												8
1	3		4	10¹	6	8²	14	11³	7⁵	12	9	16	2⁴	15	5	13																												9
1	3		4	14	7	8³	6⁵	11¹	12	10²	16	13	2	9⁴	5	15																												10
1	3¹		4	8	6	7⁵	9²	11³	10⁴	12	16	13	2	5	14	15																												11
1	3		7	9⁴	6	8³	5¹	11⁵	10²	14	16	15	12	4	13	2																												12
3⁵			8	15	7	9	5³	16	10¹	14	13	12	6⁴	1	4	11²	2																												13
1			8	10²	7	9	5¹	11⁴	14	15	13	3	6³	4	12	2																												14
1			8	11	7	9	5¹	12	6²	13	3	14⁴	4	10³	2	15																												15
1	3		8	12	7	9	5²	11	10	6¹	14	4	13	2																														16
3			7	9²	6	10	5¹	11	12	8	1	4	13	2																														17
3			9	6	10	5²	11	8³	7	12	2¹	4	14	1	13																														18
3	7³	13	6	10⁴	5	11¹	15	8	4²	2	14	1	9³	16																															19
3	13	4	12	5	7	10¹	6²	8	14	2³	1	9																																	20
2	3¹	6	12	5	8	11²	10³	7	13	4	1	9																																	21
14		2²	6	10	5	8	11³	7¹	3	13	4	12	15	1	9⁴																														22
		2	6¹	10	5²	8	11⁴	15	7³	3	14	4	12	1	9	13																												23
		2	5	11	7	8	10	6²	4¹	3	13	1	9	12																															24
		2²	6	11³	9	14	12	8	3	13	4	10	15	1	5⁴	7¹																												25
3	14	6		8	10	4	9²	11³	2¹	1	5	7	12	13																															26
3	2²	6	15	8	10	4	12	13	14	1	5¹	7	9⁴	11³																															27
3	6	7	5	10¹	11	12	2	1	8	9	4																																		28
3	6	7	14	10	11¹	15	12	2	1	13	9⁴	4	1	5²	8³																														29
3¹	5	7	13	10	11²	9	2	4	1	6	8	12																																	30
4	2	6	12	14	7³	10	5	13	8	12³	3	9	11¹																																	31
4	8	6	1	10⁵	14	12	7⁵	5⁴	13	15	7	3	9¹	11²																															32
1	5	2	8	14	12	7	4	13	10	6³	3	9¹	11²																																	33
1	3	5	8	4	10¹	2	11	12	6	7	9																																		34
1	3²	5	4	11³	10	12	14	9	2	8	13	6	7¹																																	35
1	5	7	4⁴	11³	13	14	9²	2	3	10²	6	8	12																																	36
1	10	12	2	7²	4	13	11	3	8	6	5¹	9																																		37
1	5	12	3	10³	4²	14	11	2	13	6	8	9¹																																		38
1	10	12	5	3	6¹	9	4	11	7	2	8²	13																																		39
1	3	2⁴	5	10²	7	4	9¹	15	8³	11	12	6	13	14																															40
3	4	12	6	9⁵	7	15	16	2²	10¹	11³	14	8⁴	5	1	13																															41
4	2¹	7	11⁴	8	13	14	3²	6³	9⁵	16	10	5	1	12	15																															42
1	4	2	5	11⁴	9	15	13	14	3³	10¹	7²	8	6	12																															43
1	3	2³	5	10²	9	4	15	12	14	11	13	7¹	8⁴	6																															44
4	2	5	12	9	3	13	10	11	7²	8¹	1	6²	14																																45
3³	2	9	11²	8	4⁵	16	6¹	14	12	10	7	5⁴	1	13	15																															46

FA Cup
Fourth Qualifying	Hednesford T	(a)	1-1
Replay	Hednesford T	(h)	1-3

FA Trophy
Third Round	Farsley Celtic	(h)	8-1
Fourth Round	Boston U	(h)	1-3

HARTLEPOOL UNITED

Ground: The Prestige Group Stadium, Clarence Road, Hartlepool TS24 8BZ.   *Tel:* (01429) 272 584.
Website: www.hartlepoolunited.co.uk   *Email:* enquiries@hartlepoolunited.co.uk   *Year Formed:* 1908.
Record Attendance: 17,426 v Manchester U, FA Cup 3rd rd, 5 January 1957.
Nicknames: 'The Pool'; 'Monkey Hangers'.   *Manager:* Simon Grayson.
Colours: Blue and white striped shirts with blue trim, blue shorts with white trim, blue socks with white trim.

HARTLEPOOL UNITED – NATIONAL LEAGUE 2024–25 LEAGUE RECORD

Match No.	Date	Venue	Opponents	Result		H/T Score	Lg Pos.	Goalscorers	Attendance
1	Aug 10	A	Yeovil T	W	1-0	0-0	8	Hunter [65]	3646
2	17	H	Southend U	D	0-0	0-0	10		4452
3	20	A	Tamworth	W	1-0	0-0	6	Grey [82]	1293
4	24	H	Wealdstone	D	1-1	0-1	6	Dieseruvwe [90]	3614
5	26	A	Woking	L	2-3	2-0	10	Grey 2 [3, 9]	2646
6	31	H	Braintree T	D	0-0	0-0	10		3516
7	Sept 7	H	FC Halifax T	D	0-0	0-0	10		4012
8	10	A	Boston U	W	2-1	0-1	7	Mancini [53], Dieseruvwe [61]	1925
9	14	A	Ebbsfleet U	L	0-1	0-1	11		1424
10	21	H	Dagenham & Red	L	0-1	0-1	15		3507
11	24	H	Rochdale	L	0-3	0-1	18		4012
12	28	A	Forest Green R	L	0-1	0-0	18		1764
13	Oct 5	H	Sutton U	W	4-3	0-2	15	Charman [55], Dieseruvwe 3 [57, 71, 85]	3408
14	19	A	Maidenhead U	D	1-1	0-1	17	Campbell [68]	1305
15	23	A	Altrincham	D	1-1	1-1	17	Sheron [5]	1463
16	26	H	Aldershot T	W	2-0	1-0	15	Dieseruvwe 2 [5, 54]	3356
17	Nov 9	A	York C	L	3-5	0-2	16	Ferguson [50], Charman [87], Dieseruvwe [90]	7654
18	16	H	Eastleigh	D	0-0	0-0	14		3655
19	23	H	Solihull Moors	W	4-3	2-1	13	Campbell [17], Grey 2 [39, 60], Dieseruvwe [65]	972
20	26	H	AFC Fylde	W	2-0	0-0	12	Parkes [70], Madine [88]	2934
21	30	H	Barnet	D	0-0	0-0	11		3604
22	Dec 14	A	Southend U	D	0-0	0-0	12		6877
23	21	W	Yeovil T	W	2-0	0-0	11	Dieseruvwe (pen) [64], Madine [83]	3420
24	26	A	Gateshead	L	3-4	1-2	13	Grey [34], Madine 2 [84, 90]	2152
25	Jan 1	H	Oldham Ath	W	2-1	1-1	9	Waterfall [39], Mancini [53]	4502
26	18	A	Wealdstone	D	1-1	1-0	13	Madine [21]	1467
27	25	H	Woking	D	1-1	0-0	12	Charman [67]	3612
28	28	A	Barnet	L	0-2	0-0	13		1289
29	Feb 1	A	Braintree T	D	1-1	0-0	12	Miley [90]	869
30	8	A	Sutton U	W	2-1	0-0	10	Madine [76], Taylor (og) [86]	2321
31	11	H	Tamworth	D	2-2	1-2	9	Cleary [15], Dieseruvwe [60]	3177
32	15	H	Maidenhead U	D	0-0	0-0	9		3631
33	18	H	Altrincham	L	1-2	0-0	10	Featherstone [90]	3302
34	22	A	Aldershot T	L	2-3	1-0	12	Frost (og) [20], Dieseruvwe [80]	2203
35	Mar 1	H	York C	L	0-1	0-1	12		775
36	4	A	AFC Fylde	L	1-2	1-2	14	Ferguson [4]	924
37	8	A	Eastleigh	D	1-1	1-1	15	Cleary [30]	3212
38	15	H	Solihull Moors	D	1-1	0-0	14	Parkes [54]	3959
39	22	H	Boston U	W	4-1	2-1	13	Madine [4], Dieseruvwe [24], Cleary [67], Miley [87]	4242
40	29	A	FC Halifax T	W	1-0	1-0	12	Cleary [41]	2202
41	Apr 5	H	Ebbsfleet U	W	3-2	1-0	11	Cleary [29], Dieseruvwe [54], Folarin [90]	4156
42	12	A	Dagenham & Red	D	1-1	1-0	11	Dieseruvwe [17]	1704
43	18	A	Oldham Ath	L	1-2	1-1	11	Dieseruvwe [39]	6717
44	21	H	Gateshead	W	3-2	2-0	11	Charman [25], Cleary [43], Dieseruvwe [72]	4160
45	26	A	Rochdale	L	1-5	1-3	12	Featherstone [11]	3550
46	May 5	H	Forest Green R	D	1-1	1-0	11	Ferguson [37]	4176

Final League Position: 11

GOALSCORERS

League (59): Dieseruvwe 17 (1 pen), Madine 7, Cleary 6, Grey 6, Charman 4, Ferguson 3, Campbell 2, Featherstone 2, Mancini 2, Miley 2, Parkes 2, Folarin 1, Hunter 1, Sheron 1, Waterfall 1, own goals 2.
FA Cup (2): Campbell 1, Dieseruvwe 1 (1 pen).
FA Trophy (1): Madine 1

Dixon 6	Dodds 17+6	Waterfall 25+2	Parkes 41	Ferguson 42+3	Sheron 44	Hunter 21+9	Campbell 26+12	Charman 26+14	Grey 33+6	Dieseruuwe 41+5	Sass-Davies 20+4	Mancini 7+18	Onariase —+4	Stephenson 12+5	Freeman 5+2	Featherstone 29+15	Robinson D 2+4	Sloggett 8+10	Smith 30+1	Madine 17+12	Mathurin 3+6	Asiimwe 4+1	Young 10	LuaLua 2+5	Bondswell —+1	Cleary 18+2	Folarin 2+14	Miley 13+3	Robinson J 2+1	Darcy —+1	Foreman —+1	Match No.
1	2²	3¹	4	5	6	7	8⁴	9³	10	11	12	13	14	15																		1
1		3⁴	4	6	5	7	8¹	9	10	11²	13	12⁴	15	2	14																	2
1			4	5	8	7	9¹		10²	11	3	12	13	2		6																3
1	3		4	5	6	7¹	9⁴		10	11		8³		2²	13	12	14	15														4
1		4⁵	5	8	7¹	9¹		10⁴	11	3	16	12	15	2³	6²	13	14															5
1¹	3⁴	4	5	6		10³		9⁵	11²	13	14		16	2⁴	7	8	12	15														6
		4	5	8³	15	16	12	10²	11⁴	3	9¹			2	6⁵	7	1	14	13													7
		5	6	4	7		13	10	11³	3	12			2⁴	14	8²	1	15	9¹													8
12		4	5	6⁴	7³	15	13	10	11	3	8			2¹	14		1	9²														9
	5		2	3⁴	7²		8	11¹	10	4⁴	14			6	16	15	1	13	12	9³												10
	8	2	3		7³	15	4⁴	11	10		13			6¹	16	12	1	9²	14	5⁵												11
	5	2	3	4	7³		10	11¹	13	12		15		16	8⁵	6²		9⁴	14	1												12
	5	2		3	7		10³	11¹	12	13	4	14		15	8⁴	6⁵		9²	16	1												13
	5	2	3	4	8		12	13	9³	11		4		6		7¹		10²		1												14
	5	2		3	8		7²	12	9	11	4	13		6				10¹		1												15
	5	2	3	8			7²	12	9³	11	4	13		6			14	10¹		1												16
	5	2	3	8			7¹	9	10²	11	4	12		6³		14		13		1												17
	5¹	2	3	4	8	12	7²	9	10¹	11				6					1	13												18
		2	3	4	8	5²	7	9	10¹	11	14			6		12³			1	13												19
		2	3	4	5	8	7	9¹	10³	11²		13		6			14		1	12												20
		2	3	4	5	8	7	9²	10¹	11		13		6					1	12												21
	13	2	3	4	5	8	7	9¹	10²	11		12		6			1															22
	14	2	3	4	5	8	7¹	9³	12	11		10²		6			1	13														23
	14	4	3	2	5¹	7		10²	8	11		9³		6			1	13		12												24
	2	4	5	3	8	13		10¹	9		7³			6		14	1	11²		12												25
	2	4	5	3	6	12		9		11				8		13	1	10²		7¹												26
	2	4	5	3	6¹	14	10²	7		11				8		1	9³				12	13										27
	2		3	5	4¹	7³	12	10		8	6			14		9²	1	15			11⁴	13										28
	14		3	5	4	2³		10	8¹	9				7²		1	11				6	13	12									29
	2	5		3	4	7⁴	10	12		6				8¹		14	1	11³			9²	13	15									30
	4¹	3³		2	4	7	12	9	5	11				8²		1	10				6	13										31
		3		2	4	9³	5¹	11				13		8		14	1	10			6	12	7²									32
		3		2	4	9¹	15	13	11					5⁴		14	8	1	12		6	10²	7³									33
		3	8	12	5	4	9⁴	11	13	15						14		1	10¹		6³	16	7⁵	2²								34
		3	8	12	7	4	16	5	10⁴	13				9⁵				1	11¹		6	14	15	2³								35
15		3	5	2	6⁹	14	9	11³	12	4		8²					1	10¹		13	7⁴	16										36
6²		5	3	2	9		11	7	4	12	13			1							10	8¹										37
		3	2	7	9³	12	11¹	10	4	13	5⁴		14		1		15				6	8²										38
		3	2	7		13	14	11	4	9¹	5	12		1	10³						6²	8										39
		3	2	7	15	13	9³	11	4	5	12		1	10⁴							6¹	14	8²									40
	13	3²	2	7⁵	16	14	11¹	9	4	5³	12		1	10⁴							6	15	8									41
		3	2	7		13	9³	10	4	5⁴	12		1	11²							6¹	14	8									42
	12	3³	2	7		13	5⁴	9	10	4	14		1	11²							6	15	8¹									43
		2	9	12	13	5	11³	10⁴	3²	4	8		1				15				6¹	7		14								44
		3	2	9	12	14	5⁵	11⁴	10	4²	8		1				15				6¹	13	7³		16							45
		3	2	9	4	14	12	11¹	10	5	8		1								6³	13	7²									46

FA Cup

Fourth Qualifying	Brackley T	(h)	1-1	
Replay	Brackley T	(a)	1-3	

FA Trophy

Third Round	Tamworth	(h)	1-1
(Tamworth won 3-0 on penalties)			

MAIDENHEAD UNITED

Ground: York Road, Maidenhead, Berkshire SL6 1SF. *Tel:* (01628) 636 314.
Website: www.maidenheadunitedfc.org *Email:* social@maidenheadunitedfc.org *Year Formed:* 1870.
Record Attendance: 7,989 v Southall, FA Amateur Cup quarter-final, 7 March 1936. *Nickname:* 'The Magpies'.
Manager: Alan Devonshire. *Colours:* Black and white striped shirts with red trim, black shorts, red socks.

MAIDENHEAD UNITED – NATIONAL LEAGUE 2024–25 LEAGUE RECORD

Match No.	Date	Venue	Opponents	Result	H/T Score	Lg Pos.	Goalscorers	Atten- dance
1	Aug 10	H	Eastleigh	L	0-2	0-2	21		1379
2	17	A	Solihull Moors	L	1-2	0-0	20	McCoulsky [57]	1037
3	20	H	Altrincham	L	0-1	0-1	22		1027
4	24	A	AFC Fylde	D	0-0	0-0	22		1005
5	26	H	Barnet	W	3-1	2-1	21	Smith 2 [14, 53], Abrahams [40]	1426
6	31	A	Aldershot T	L	3-4	1-1	22	Abrahams 2 [11, 60], Lokko [78]	2408
7	Sept 7	H	Dagenham & Red	D	1-1	1-0	21	Golding [44]	1412
8	10	A	Rochdale	L	1-3	0-2	20	Ajose [61]	2313
9	14	A	Tamworth	L	1-3	0-1	22	Sho-Silva [90]	1050
10	21	H	FC Halifax T	L	0-1	0-0	23		1121
11	24	H	Ebbsfleet U	W	2-1	1-0	22	Abrahams [40], McCoulsky (pen) [56]	1412
12	28	A	Boston U	W	2-1	1-1	19	McCoulsky [19], Smith [70]	1865
13	Oct 5	A	Southend U	W	2-0	1-0	18	Lokko 2 [13, 68]	6774
14	19	H	Hartlepool U	D	1-1	1-0	19	Barratt (pen) [31]	1305
15	22	H	Oldham Ath	D	2-2	2-1	18	Golding [14], Monthe (og) [37]	1223
16	26	A	Yeovil T	L	1-3	1-1	19	Lokko [26]	3333
17	Nov 9	H	Forest Green R	L	1-4	0-2	21	De Havilland [66]	1246
18	16	A	Sutton U	L	0-1	0-1	22		2905
19	23	H	Gateshead	L	0-5	0-2	22		847
20	26	A	Braintree T	W	3-1	2-0	21	McCoulsky [1], Abrahams [9], Barratt (pen) [74]	777
21	30	A	York C	L	2-6	1-4	21	McCoulsky [37], Barratt (pen) [67]	5442
22	Dec 14	H	Solihull Moors	D	1-1	0-0	22	Smith [69]	1094
23	21	A	Eastleigh	L	0-1	0-1	22		2000
24	26	H	Wealdstone	W	3-1	1-0	21	McCoulsky 2 [25, 52], Smith [81]	1725
25	Jan 1	A	Woking	L	1-3	1-1	21	Abrahams [39]	1848
26	14	A	Altrincham	L	0-4	0-4	21		1608
27	18	H	AFC Fylde	W	4-1	2-0	20	Abrahams 2 [33, 75], McCoulsky [36], Latty-Fairweather [53]	1017
28	25	A	Barnet	L	0-3	0-1	20		1630
29	Feb 8	H	Southend U	W	1-0	0-0	20	De Havilland [56]	1978
30	15	A	Hartlepool U	D	0-0	0-0	20		3631
31	18	A	Oldham Ath	W	1-0	0-0	19	McCoulsky [64]	5181
32	22	H	Yeovil T	L	0-2	0-1	21		1330
33	25	H	York C	L	1-3	0-1	21	Abrahams [63]	1075
34	Mar 1	A	Forest Green R	L	0-2	0-1	22		1800
35	4	H	Braintree T	D	3-3	1-2	22	Smith [43], McCoulsky [67], Abrahams (pen) [72]	748
36	8	H	Sutton U	L	0-1	0-1	22		1292
37	15	A	Gateshead	W	2-0	1-0	19	Onariase [15], McCoulsky [84]	1811
38	18	H	Aldershot T	L	0-1	0-0	22		1386
39	22	H	Rochdale	D	1-1	0-1	22	Kiernan [50]	2261
40	29	A	Dagenham & Red	L	0-1	0-0	23		1809
41	Apr 5	H	Tamworth	W	3-1	1-0	22	McCoulsky [23], Kiernan [52], Johnson J [89]	1034
42	12	A	FC Halifax T	W	2-0	0-0	22	Barratt [86], McCoulsky [88]	1485
43	18	H	Woking	D	2-2	1-0	22	Kiernan [25], Welch-Hayes [60]	1976
44	21	A	Wealdstone	D	1-1	1-1	22	Kiernan [4]	1975
45	26	A	Ebbsfleet U	W	2-0	1-0	22	McCoulsky [50], Kiernan [59]	1312
46	May 5	H	Boston U	W	3-0	1-0	22	McCoulsky 2 (1 pen) [32, 66 (p)], Abrahams [90]	3017

Final League Position: 22

GOALSCORERS

League (57): McCoulsky 16 (2 pens), Abrahams 11 (1 pen), Smith 6, Kiernan 5, Barratt 4 (3 pens), Lokko 4, De Havilland 2, Golding 2, Ajose 1, Johnson J 1, Latty-Fairweather 1, Onariase 1, Sho-Silva 1, Welch-Hayes 1, own goal 1.
FA Cup (5): Barratt 1, Carvalho 1, McCoulsky 1, Sho-Silva 1, Smith 1.
FA Trophy (1): Ajose 1.

Ross 40	Bell 2 + 3	Dyce 6 + 5	De Havilland 38	Lokko 26 + 1	Carvalho 1 + 12	Ferguson 35 + 1	Mitchell-Lawson 11	Pettit 46	Smith 40 + 3	Abrahams 32 + 9	McCoulsky 36 + 8	Keetch 2 + 10	Johnson J 11 + 11	Ajose 4 + 12	Massey 13 + 8	Latty-Fairweather 31 + 3	Cochrane 22 + 11	Welch-Hayes 28 + 3	Golding 7	Barratt 13 + 19	Sho-Silva 1 + 17	Uwakwe — + 1	Ferdinand 16 + 2	Clerima 11 + 2	Onariase 19 + 1	Coyne — + 2	Korboa 2 + 3	Stewart — + 2	Kiernan 7 + 2	Wreh — + 3	Howes 6	Match No.
1	2	3	4	5	6^2	7^4	8^3	9^1	10	11	12	13	14	15																		1
1	2	5		3	12	8	7^2	6^1	9	13	11	14	10^3		4																	2
1				2	13	6	11	8	9	10^3	12		7^1	14	5	3^2	4															3
1				2		6	11^1	8	9		10		7		12	3	5	4														4
1				2	15	6	10^3	8	9^4	11^1	13	14	7^2		12	5	3	4														5
1				2	13	6	10^4	8^3	9	11	15	12	7^1		4	5	3^2	14														6
1		3		5			11	8	9		10^2	13	7^1		6	4			2	12												7
1	2		3	14				8	10^4	11^1	12	15	7^3		4	5	6			9^2					13							8
1				2	15		8	6^1		11^4	10	13	7		12	3^2	4	5	14	9^3												9
1			3	2		6		8	9	11^1	10		7^3		12		5^2	4		13					14							10
1			3	2		6		8	9^1	11	10		7^2			5		4		12		13										11
1			3	2		6		8	9	11	10		7			5		4		12												12
1			3	2		6		8	9	11^1	10		7^2			5		4		12					13							13
1			3	2		6		8	10	11					12	5		4	9^1	7												14
1			3	2		6		8	10	11		13				5^2		4	9^1	7		12										15
1			3^4	2	14	6		8^1	10	11^2	12				16	5	15	4^3	9	7^5					13							16
1			3	2	12			9	10	11^3		13	7^1			5^4	14	4	15	8^2			6									17
1			3	2				8	9	11	10	13				5	6^2	4^1		7		12										18
1		2^4	4		16	6		8^1	9	11	10^4	15	14		12	5^2				7^3			13^5									19
1	12		3	14		6		8^3	9^4	11	10	15	7			5^2		4	2						13							20
1	12	3	4	14		6		8^3	9^2	11^3	10	13	7			5			2^4													21
1	13		2			6		8^3	9^1	11^2	10^1		14		12	5^4		4		7						3	15					22
1	13		2	14	15	6		8^2	9^3	11	10^4	16			12	5^5		4		7						3^1						23
1	13		2^5	5		6		8	9	11	10^1		7^3			3		4					14		12							24
1		3^2	4	5		6^1		8	9	11	10		7		12		2^4						13									25
1		3	4	5		6		8	9^3	11^2	10^1	13			15		2			12								7^4	14			26
1	13		4			6		8	9^1	11	10^4		7		15	3^3	2^2						14		5			12				27
1	13		4			6^2		8	9	11	10^1		7^3			3	2^4						14		5		15	12				28
1			4			6		8	9	11	10^3	13	7^1		12	3^2	2	5					14									29
1			4			6		8	9^3	11^2	10^4	13	7		12	3^1	2	5	15				14									30
1			4			6		8	9^1	11	10^4		7^2		12	3	2	5	15				14		13							31
1						6		8	9^3	11	10^5	13	7^2		16	3^4	2	4^1	15				14		5			12				32
1						6		8	9	11	10		7			3	2	4					14		5							33
1			4			6		8	9	11^1		13				3	2	5		10^3			14		12			7^2				34
1			4^4			6		8	9^1	11	10	13	7^3		12	3^2	2	5	15				14									35
1			4			6^1		8^3	9	11	10				12	3	2	5					14		13				7^2			36
1			4			6			9	11^1	10^4	13	7		12	3^5	2	5		15			14		8^2							37
1			4			6		8	9^4	11	10^4				12	3^2	2^1	5		13			14		7^3				15			38
1			4			6		8	9	11^1		13	7^1			3	2	5		10^3			14						12			39
1			4			6		8	9	11^1	10		7			3	2^2	5											12	13		40
			4			6		8^3		11^1	10^4				12	3		14		13	15				9	2	5		7^2		1	41
			4			6^4			9	11^3	10^1				12	3^2		14		15	13		16		8	2	5		7^5		1	42
			4			6^1			9^2	11	10	13			12	3	2			15			14		8		5^3		7^4		1	43
			4^3		15	6^5		8		11	10	13			12	3^2	2	5			16		14		9^1				7^4		1	44
						6^1		8^2		11^4	10	13			15	3	2	4		12					9		5		7^3	14	1	45
			4^1			6		8^3		11	10^2	13			15	3	2			12	16		14		9^4		5		7^5		1	46

FA Cup

Fourth Qualifying	Taunton T		(a)	1-1
Replay	Taunton T		(h)	3-0
First Round	Crawley T		(h)	1-2

(aet; 1-1 at end of normal time)

FA Trophy

Third Round	Slough T	(a)	1-2

OLDHAM ATHLETIC

Ground: Boundary Park, Furtherwood Road, Oldham, Lancashire OL1 2PA. *Tel:* (0161) 624 4972.
Website: www.oldhamathletic.co.uk *Email:* contact@oldhamathletic.co.uk *Year Formed:* 1895.
Record Attendance: 47,671 v Sheffield Wed, FA Cup 4th rd, 25 January 1930.
Nicknames: 'The Latics', 'The Blues', 'The Owls'. *Manager:* Micky Mellon.
Colours: Blue shirts with white side panels and blue and orange trim, blue shorts with orange trim, white socks.

OLDHAM ATHLETIC – NATIONAL LEAGUE 2024–25 LEAGUE RECORD

Match No.	Date	Venue	Opponents	Result		H/T Score	Lg Pos.	Goalscorers	Attendance
1	Aug 10	H	Braintree T	W	3-0	2-0	2	Uchegbulam [8], Charsley [29], Fondop-Talom [59]	5552
2	17	A	Wealdstone	W	1-0	0-0	3	Charsley [85]	1825
3	20	A	AFC Fylde	D	1-1	0-1	4	Monthe [60]	5682
4	24	A	Aldershot T	L	1-4	0-1	8	Ogle [60]	2407
5	26	H	Gateshead	D	1-1	0-1	8	Monthe [55]	5583
6	31	A	Altrincham	D	1-1	1-0	9	Norwood [23]	3561
7	Sept 7	A	Southend U	D	1-1	0-1	9	Fondop-Talom [76]	5622
8	10	A	FC Halifax T	D	1-1	0-0	11	Kitching [47]	3146
9	14	A	Woking	W	3-1	1-0	7	Lundstram [12], Akinola (og) [49], Fondop-Talom [76]	2373
10	21	H	Yeovil T	W	1-0	0-0	6	Fondop-Talom [81]	511
11	24	H	Forest Green R	W	1-0	1-0	6	Fondop-Talom [9]	5034
12	28	A	Ebbsfleet U	W	2-1	0-0	6	Kitching [48], Khan [85]	1589
13	Oct 5	H	Solihull Moors	L	2-3	0-0	6	Kitching [76], Lundstram [90]	7030
14	19	A	Sutton U	W	3-1	1-0	5	Fondop-Talom [18], Raglan [52], Norwood [90]	3329
15	22	A	Maidenhead U	D	2-2	1-2	6	Monthe [44], Raglan [80]	1223
16	26	H	Dagenham & Red	W	1-0	1-0	5	Fondop-Talom [20]	5651
17	Nov 9	A	Barnet	D	0-0	0-0	5		2230
18	16	H	Tamworth	W	4-0	3-0	4	Norwood 3 (1 pen) [15, 37 (p), 45], Kay [73]	6345
19	26	A	Boston U	W	4-0	2-0	4	Lundstram [8], Norwood [19], Stones [67], Fondop-Talom (pen) [87]	5013
20	Dec 14	A	Wealdstone	W	3-2	1-2	5	Stones 2 [43, 46], Fondop-Talom [80]	5544
21	21	A	Braintree T	W	2-0	1-0	5	Stones [15], Norwood [50]	1046
22	Jan 1	A	Hartlepool U	L	1-2	1-1	5	Lundstram [20]	4502
23	7	A	Eastleigh	D	2-2	0-1	5	Raglan [62], Fondop-Talom [65]	1846
24	18	H	Aldershot T	L	1-3	1-2	5	Monthe [41]	5960
25	21	H	York C	L	0-2	0-2	5		8234
26	25	A	Gateshead	D	1-1	1-0	5	Fondop-Talom [31]	1694
27	Feb 1	A	AFC Fylde	W	2-1	0-0	5	Fondop-Talom 2 [62, 90]	2612
28	4	A	Rochdale	W	1-0	1-0	4	Fondop-Talom [17]	5880
29	8	A	Solihull Moors	W	1-0	1-0	4	Waters [45]	1686
30	11	H	Altrincham	D	2-2	0-1	4	Norwood [57], Lundstram [81]	5491
31	15	H	Sutton U	D	0-0	0-0	4		5738
32	18	H	Maidenhead U	L	0-1	0-0	4		5181
33	22	A	Dagenham & Red	D	2-2	0-1	5	Fondop-Talom [48], Pritchard [90]	1573
34	Mar 1	H	Barnet	L	0-3	0-0	5		6098
35	4	A	Boston U	D	0-0	0-0	5		1695
36	8	A	Tamworth	D	1-1	1-1	5	Pritchard (pen) [36]	1933
37	11	A	Eastleigh	W	2-0	1-0	4	Waters [8], Caprice [73]	4769
38	15	H	Rochdale	D	1-1	0-1	4	Yoganathan [85]	8611
39	22	H	FC Halifax T	W	2-0	1-0	4	Harratt [28], Fondop-Talom [90]	7256
40	29	A	Southend U	L	0-1	0-1	4		8395
41	Apr 8	H	Woking	L	1-2	1-0	4	Harratt [3]	5664
42	12	A	Yeovil T	L	1-2	0-1	4	Caprice [90]	3373
43	18	H	Hartlepool U	W	2-1	1-1	4	Raglan [41], Fondop-Talom [63]	6717
44	21	A	York C	D	1-1	0-1	4	Raglan [70]	7918
45	26	A	Forest Green R	L	0-1	0-1	5		2801
46	May 5	H	Ebbsfleet U	W	2-0	1-0	5	Garner 2 (1 pen) [36 (p), 86]	7493

Final League Position: 5

GOALSCORERS

League (64): Fondop-Talom 17 (1 pen), Norwood 8 (1 pen), Lundstram 5, Raglan 5, Monthe 4, Stones 4, Kitching 3, Caprice 2, Charsley 2, Garner 2 (1 pen), Harratt 2, Pritchard 2 (1 pen), Waters 2, Kay 1, Khan 1, Ogle 1, Uchegbulam 1, Yoganathan 1, own goal 1.
FA Cup (7): Fondop-Talum 2, Lundstram 1, Monthe 1, Norwood 1, Uchegbulam 1, own goal 1.
FA Trophy (0).
National League Play-offs (10): Garner 3, Pritchard 2, Fondop-Talum 1, Harratt 1, Kitching 1, Norwood 1, Yoganathan 1.

Hudson 35	Ogle 34+2	Hobson 19+2	Monthe 27	Charsley 7+4	Fondop-Talom 32+13	Conlon 29+1	Raglan 40+1	Uchegbulam 12+15	Gardner 10+11	Hammond 6+2	Kitching 35+5	Lundstram 28+9	Caprice 32+8	Reid 2+3	Kay 5+16	Norwood 14+11	Dolan 3+3	Khan 2+5	Garner 5+9	Drummond 4+3	Sutton 13+2	Payne 4	Stretton —+1	Clucas 6+1	Stones 5+1	Taylor —+1	Evans 2+4	Rossiter 18+3	Waters 9+4	Pett 19+2	Leake 15+1	Worthington 5+4	Yoganathan 6+8	Pritchard 6+8	Dennis 1	Donaghy 10	Harratt 6+3	Match No.
1	2³	3	4	5	6²	7	8	9⁴	10¹	11	12	13	14	15																								1
1	2⁴	3	4	6	10	7	5	11³	8¹	9³	15	14	12			13																						2
1	12	2	3	6	10		4	11³	9	13	14	7	5²			8¹																						3
1	2	3	5	6²	10⁴	8	4	11³	15	12		7	14	13	9¹																							4
1	2¹	3	4	6	12	8	5	10	9²			7	14			11³	13																					5
1	2	4	5	6	13	8	3	10²	9³		12	7				11¹	14																					6
1	2	3⁴	5	6⁵	13	8	4	9³	12		15	7²	14			11	10¹	16																				7
1	2		3		10¹	8	4	13	9		6	7³	5			14	11²	12⁴																				8
1	2		3		11²	8	4	13	9¹	10	6	7	5³			12			14																			9
1	6		4		11	7	3	12			9³	5	8	2¹		10²	13		14																			10
1	5	6¹	3		11	10	2	14			4	8				7²	9³	12	13																			11
1	3	4	2		11²	6			13	14		7	8	5¹			12		10	9³																			12
1	5		3	15	11	8⁴	2	12	14			4	10	7³			9²	6¹	13																			13
1	7		3		9¹	5⁴	2		16		6	10³	13			14	12				11²	4⁵	8	15														14
1	7		3		9	5	2				6	10⁴	12			14	13				11³	4¹	8															15
1	4		3		9	6¹	2	14	15		7	10³	5⁴			12⁴			13		11²		8															16
1	4		3			6	2	15			7	10⁵	5			14	9⁴				11³		8²		12	13												17
1	3		2		12	7²		16	14		8¹	9⁵	6			13	10³				15	4			5	11⁴												18
1	4		3		13	7¹	2		15		8	9³	6			12	10⁴				14				5	11²												19
1	3		2	14	12	7					8	9⁶	6⁴			13	10¹				15		4		5	11²												20
1	3		2	14	12	7⁴			13		8	9³	6				10³				15		4		5	11²												21
1	4		2		12			3			7	6	9³	5¹			14	10							8	11²	13											22
1	4		2		11			3			7	6	9⁵	5	12	13				10²					8													23
1	4		2	13	11			3	14		6	12	5⁴	10³	7¹															8²	9	15						24
1	4		2		12			3			6²	11	5¹	10⁵	13	7⁴														9	14	8	15					25
1	4		2		10			3				9²	5⁴		12			14			15									8	11³	7	6¹	13				26
1	3	4¹			11			6				7²	9		14															8	10⁵	5	2	13	12				27
1	4				10			3			6	9¹	5		14															8²	11³	7	2	12		13		28
1	4³				11			3			6	15	5								12									7⁴	10¹	8	2	9²	13	14		29
					11			3			6²	14	5		15	12					4								7³	10¹	13	2	9⁵	8⁴	16	1	30
					11			3			6	9³	5			13					4								7¹	10²	8	2	14		12	1	31
					10			3			6	13	5		8¹	12					4								7²		9	2			11	1	32
	14				10			3			6³	15	5		13						4²								12	11⁴	9	2	7¹		8	1	33
					10						8¹	5	6																	7	12	9	2			11	1	34
4	3				10	8²	5	9³																						12	13	6	3	11¹	14	7	1	35
2³	4				10	5	9	13			3		14			12													8	6			11¹	7²		1	36
4					10¹	7⁴	5				8		2			15													6	11²	9³	3		14	12	1 13	37
4⁴	12				10³	7¹	5	14			8		2			15													6	11²	9⁵	3	16			1 13	38
	4				13	7³	5	14	12		9		2¹			10												15	8³		6⁵		14		1 11²	39
	4				12	7²	5	13	9⁴		3		2			10¹					16							15	8³		6⁵		11¹		40
1	4				10	9⁴	5	7			3	8									12								6³	13		2²	14	15	11¹	41
1	4				14	8	5	12			3		2			10³													6²		7	9¹	13		11	42
1	5				10	9³	4				3	12	2			14					7							13		8			6¹		11²	43
1	5				9	12	8		10		3	2²									4							6³	14		7	11¹	13		44
1	15				11²	6⁴	4	10		9³	3									13	2⁵							16		8		7¹	12		14	45
1	5				12	14	4	15		3¹	16					10⁵					2							13	9³	8²		6	7		11⁴	46

FA Cup

Fourth Qualifying	FC Halifax T	(h)	4-2
First Round	Tranmere R	(a)	2-1
Second Round	Leyton Orient	(a)	1-2

FA Trophy

Third Round	Stockton T	(a)	0-2

National League Play-offs

Quarter-Finals	FC Halifax T	(h)	4-0
Semi-Finals	York C	(a)	3-0
Final	Southend U	(Wembley)	3-2

ROCHDALE

Ground: Crown Oil Arena, Sandy Lane, Rochdale, Lancashire OL11 5DR.   *Tel:* (01706) 644 648.
Website: www.rochdaleafc.co.uk   *Email:* office@rochdaleafc.co.uk   *Year Formed:* 1907.
Record Attendance: 24,231 v Notts Co, FA Cup 2nd rd, 10 December 1949.   *Nickname:* 'The Dale'.
Manager: Jimmy McNulty.
Colours: Blue and black patterned shirts with blue and white trim, black shorts with blue trim, blue socks.

ROCHDALE – NATIONAL LEAGUE 2024–25 LEAGUE RECORD

Match No.	Date	Venue	Opponents	Result	H/T Score	Lg Pos.	Goalscorers	Attendance
1	Aug 10	A	Boston U	W 3-0	2-0	2	Rodney 2 [14, 40], Henderson [90]	2578
2	17	H	Dagenham & Red	D 1-1	0-0	6	Allarakhia [76]	2631
3	20	A	York C	L 0-1	0-1	12		5362
4	24	H	Forest Green R	D 0-0	0-0	13		2261
5	26	A	Yeovil T	W 1-0	0-0	7	McBride [90]	3686
6	31	H	Woking	W 3-0	1-0	4	Mitchell 2 [5, 87], Henry [60]	2315
7	Sept 7	A	Aldershot T	W 2-0	2-0	3	Mitchell [13], Rodney [27]	2565
8	10	H	Maidenhead U	W 3-1	2-0	2	East [18], Mitchell 2 [41, 47]	2313
9	14	H	Solihull Moors	L 1-2	0-1	4	Mitchell [85]	2614
10	21	A	Eastleigh	L 2-4	1-2	5	Mitchell [6], Rodney [70]	1836
11	24	H	Hartlepool U	W 3-0	1-0	4	McBride [45], Mitchell [58], Rodney [79]	4012
12	28	H	Braintree T	W 1-0	1-0	4	Mitchell [7]	2609
13	Oct 5	A	Ebbsfleet U	D 2-2	2-0	5	Allarakhia [36], McBride [45]	1452
14	19	H	Southend U	L 0-1	0-1	6		2806
15	22	H	FC Halifax T	W 2-1	1-0	4	Gordon [40], McBride [81]	2926
16	26	A	Barnet	L 1-2	0-2	6	Henderson [70]	2137
17	Nov 9	H	Sutton U	W 2-1	1-1	6	East [22], Rodney [90]	2602
18	16	A	Wealdstone	L 0-2	0-0	6		1922
19	26	A	Gateshead	W 1-0	0-0	6	Tinkler (og) [55]	712
20	Dec 14	A	Dagenham & Red	L 0-1	0-0	9		1569
21	17	H	Tamworth	W 3-0	0-0	6	Gilmour [73], Gordon [80], Rodney [87]	1705
22	26	A	AFC Fylde	W 3-1	1-1	6	Mitchell 2 [18, 64], Gilmour [56]	2292
23	Jan 18	A	Forest Green R	L 0-1	0-0	8		1771
24	25	H	Yeovil T	W 4-0	0-0	6	Rodney [49], Mitchell (pen) [57], Ayinde [64], Burger [90]	2463
25	Feb 4	A	Oldham Ath	L 0-1	0-1	7		5880
26	8	H	Ebbsfleet U	D 0-0	0-0	8		2134
27	15	A	Southend U	D 1-1	1-0	8	Rodney [21]	6908
28	19	A	FC Halifax T	D 0-0	0-0	9		2682
29	22	H	Barnet	L 0-4	0-2	10		2316
30	25	A	Tamworth	D 1-1	0-1	10	Mitchell [90]	805
31	Mar 4	H	Gateshead	W 1-0	0-0	9	Allarakhia [82]	1540
32	8	H	Wealdstone	W 4-1	1-0	8	Adebayo-Rowling [9], Henderson [54], Allarakhia [58], Barlow [83]	2289
33	11	H	Altrincham	W 3-0	0-0	7	Barlow [64], Bird [67], Mitchell [82]	2053
34	15	A	Oldham Ath	D 1-1	1-0	7	Bird [5]	8611
35	18	H	Boston U	L 2-3	0-2	7	Henderson [80], Bird [88]	1974
36	22	H	Maidenhead U	D 1-1	1-0	7	Henderson [16]	2261
37	25	H	York C	L 0-4	0-1	7		2707
38	29	H	Aldershot T	W 4-0	2-0	6	Beckwith [15], Rodney 2 [36, 54], Henderson [56]	2270
39	Apr 1	A	Woking	D 1-1	1-0	6	Rodney [27]	1853
40	8	A	Sutton U	L 0-1	0-0	7		2087
41	12	A	Eastleigh	W 4-0	2-0	6	Rodney 2 [11, 75], Fernandez (og) [18], Henderson [63]	1762
42	18	A	Altrincham	W 2-1	1-0	5	Beckwith [20], Rodney [89]	3464
43	21	H	AFC Fylde	D 0-0	0-0	5		2957
44	26	H	Hartlepool U	W 5-1	3-1	4	Rodney 2 (1 pen) [5 (p), 52], Henderson [19], Ayinde [23], Bird [86]	3550
45	29	A	Solihull Moors	W 1-0	0-0	4	Henderson [53]	838
46	May 5	A	Braintree T	L 0-2	0-1	4		1427

Final League Position: 4

GOALSCORERS

League (69): Rodney 17 (1 pen), Mitchell 14 (1 pen), Henderson 9, Allarakhia 4, Bird 4, McBride 4, Ayinde 2, Barlow 2, Beckwith 2, East 2, Gilmour 2, Gordon 2, Adebayo-Rowling 1, Burger 1, Henry 1, own goals 2.
FA Cup (7): Mitchell 3, Barlow 1, Beckwith 1, Henderson 1, own goal 1.
FA Trophy (8): Mitchell 2, Adebayo-Rowling 1, Allarkhia 1, Barlow 1 (pen), Bird 1, Dennis 1, Rodney 1.
National League Play-offs (3): Rodney 2 (1 pen), Bird 1.

McNicholas 9	Gordon 38	Ebanks-Landell 11 + 5	Adebayo-Rowling 36 + 3	Henry 8 + 6	Allarakhia 34 + 8	Gilmour 34 + 3	Mitchell 35 + 9	McBride 19 + 12	Beckwith 43 + 2	Rodney 28 + 7	Burger 13 + 12	East 36 + 1	Armstrong 2 + 10	Henderson 9 + 32	Alfa — + 3	Senior 1 + 5	Ferguson 6 + 9	Barlow 18 + 8	Robson 8	Sassi 4	Ayinde 11 + 16	Westley — + 3	Hogan 26 + 3	Buyabu 16 + 6	Dennis 1 + 3	Okeke 6 + 2	Waller 20	Penney — + 1	Weston 1 + 7	Kingdon 9 + 7	Bird 6 + 3	Adu-Poku 4 + 3	Kelly — + 1	Barrett 9	Edwards 5 + 1	Match No.
1	2	3	4^4	5^2	6^1	7	8	9^5	10	11^3	12	13	14	15	16																					1
1	2	4	3	5^2	6	13	7^1	12	8	11	10^3	9		14																						2
1	5	3	4	15	11^2	6	9	7^3	12	10	13	2^4	8^1				14																			3
1	2	3	4^4	12		6	7^2	8	9	10	11^3	13	5	14		15																				4
1	2	3^2	13	6		7	8^5	14	11	16	10^3	5		4^1	15		9^4	12																		5
1	2		3^5	6	7^4		8^2	9	10	11^3	14		5	12	13	15		4	16																	6
	2		4	15	6^5	7	8	12	10	11^2	9^3	5^1	13				16		1		3^4	14														7
	2		4^2	6^1	7^5	12	8	10^4	11		15	5	14		13		16		1		3	9^3														8
	2		3	14	6	7^2	8		10	11^3	12	5		15					1		4	9^1	13^4													9
	2		5^1		8^4	7^2	9	13	3	10	11^3	6		15		12			1		4^5	16	14													10
1	3		5		8^3	7^4	9^5	11^1	4	10^2	12	6	13	14			2				15	16														11
1	3		5		7^4		9	11^3	4	10^1	8^2	6	13	12			2				14		15													12
	3		5	15	10^2		9	11^1	4		8	6	12	14			2^3			1	7^4		13													13
	3			7^1	6		9	12	4^4		11	5	14	13		15		10^2	1		2		8^3													14
	3			6			10	11^3	4		8	5	13	9^1			12	14	1		2		7^2													15
	3			12	6		9	10^3	4		8^1	5		13		14	11^2	1			2		7													16
1	4		3^4	7^2	9			10^5	8	13	14	6		12			16				2		5^1	11^3	15											17
	3		5	7^2	10^5	12		11^4	4		9^1	6		15			13				2	14	16	8^3	1											18
	3		5			7	9^2	11^1	4^8	10^3		6		14							2	8		13	1	12										19
	3		5		14	7	9		4	10^1	11^2	6		13							2	8^3	12		1											20
	3^5		13		7^4	6	9		4	10^2	16	5^1					14	8^3			15		2		12	11	1									21
	4		2			6	10^1		7	11^2	16	8^4		13			15	9^3			12		3			5^5	1		14							22
	4			12	8^3	9	13	2	10		7							11^2			14		3	6^1		5	1									23
	4		5			8	9^1	13	2	10^2	14	7^3		12							11^4		3	15		6^5	1		16							24
	4		5^2		14	8	9	12	2	10^3		7		15							11^1		3	13		6^4	1									25
	4		5		6	8	9^2	10^1	2	13	11^3	7		14							12		3				1									26
	4		5		6^1	8	9		2	10^3		7		14							13		3	11^2			1		12							27
	4		5		6^4	8	9^1	11^2	2	12		7		14			13				10^3		3	15			1									28
	4^3		5		10^1	8	9	14	2	11^5		7^4		13			12				3		6^2			1		15	16							29
	4		6^2		12	7	15		2	13		8		9			10				11^4		3^3	5^1			1		14							30
			5^3		14	8	9^1	10^4	2			7		15			12				11^2		3	6			1		4	13						31
	16		8		6^3	7	14	12	2			15	5	10^5			9^2						3^4	13			1		4	11^1						32
			4		11^4	7^2	13	10^3	6			5	14				8^5				12		2	15			1		16	3	9^1					33
	13		4		11^3	7	10		6		5		12				8^2				14		2				1		3	9^1						34
			5^3		11	8	14	15	3^4			6^2	12				7						4	9^1			1		13	10	2					35
			4		10^1	8	11		2	14		6	7^3				9^2				13		5				1		3		12					36
			2			8	11^3	7^1	3			6	13				12				10		5^9		1^2		4			14					37
	4^2	16	2		9	6	13	15	3^5	10^1	8		11^3				7						5^4				12		14		1					38
	4	3			5	7	9	10^2		11^1		12					13						6				8	2			1					39
	2	12	7		13	6	9		5	11^4		14					10				15		4^4					3^2			1	8			40
	4	3	5		6^3	7	12		2	11^2		9				13	10^4											15	14		16	1	8^5			41
	4	3	5		6^5	7	13		2	11^3		15	9^2			16	10											12	14			1	8^4			42
	4		6^3		13	7	9^1		2	11		12				3	10	14											5		1	8^2			43
	4	3	5		6^4	7	14		2^3	11^2		9^5				16	8	10^1										13	15		1	12			44
	4	15	13		10^2	7	11	16	14			12				3^4	8				5^3		6^5				2	9^1		1					45
	3			13		15		2^5	11^3		7^1	10^2				16					12	6					14	4	9^4	5	1	8				46

FA Cup

Fourth Qualifying	AFC Fylde		(a)	4-1
First Round	Bromley		(h)	3-4

National League Play-offs

Quarter-Finals	Southend U		(h)	3-4
(aet)				

FA Trophy

Third Round	Leamington		(a)	2-0
Fourth Round	Stockton T		(h)	0-0
(Rochdale won 4-3 on penalties)				
Fifth Round	Worthing		(a)	2-1
Quarter-Finals	Altrincham		(h)	2-0
Semi-Finals	Spennymoor T		(h)	2-2
(Spennymoor T won 5-4 on penalties)				

SOLIHULL MOORS

Ground: Damson Park, Damson Parkway, Solihull, West Midlands B91 2PP (satnav B92 9EJ).
Tel: (0121) 705 6770. *Website:* www.solihullmoorsfc.co.uk *Email:* see website. *Year Formed:* 2007.
Record Attendance: 4,026 v Chesterfield, National League Play-off semi-final, 29 May 2022.
Nickname: 'Moors'. *Head Coach:* Matt Taylor.
Colours: Yellow shirts with blue trim, blue shorts with yellow trim, blue socks with yellow trim.

SOLIHULL MOORS – NATIONAL LEAGUE 2024–25 LEAGUE RECORD

Match No.	Date	Venue	Opponents	Result	H/T Score	Lg Pos.	Goalscorers	Atten-dance
1	Aug 10	A	AFC Fylde	L	2-3	2-1	16	Evans (og) [28], Stevens [39]	1090
2	17	H	Maidenhead U	W	2-1	0-0	11	Warburton [46], Campbell [55]	1037
3	20	A	Eastleigh	L	1-2	0-2	17	Stevenson [90]	2565
4	24	H	Braintree T	D	1-1	0-1	18	Stevenson [81]	1037
5	26	A	FC Halifax T	W	1-0	1-0	12	Tunnicliffe [30]	1554
6	31	H	Wealdstone	D	1-1	1-0	13	Gale [42]	948
7	Sept 7	H	Forest Green R	L	0-1	0-0	15		1515
8	10	A	Yeovil T	W	1-0	1-0	12	Wilkinson [11]	2849
9	14	A	Rochdale	W	2-1	1-0	8	Wilkinson 2 [26, 59]	2614
10	21	H	Southend U	L	2-4	1-2	11	Bowen [41], Stevens (pen) [67]	1390
11	24	H	York C	L	0-3	0-1	15		1515
12	28	A	Dagenham & Red	D	1-1	0-0	14	Stevens [67]	1384
13	Oct 5	A	Oldham Ath	W	3-2	0-0	12	Stevens [51], Gale [81], Oakley [90]	7030
14	19	A	Barnet	W	4-3	2-1	10	Stevens [36], Stevenson [38], Bowen [55], Gale [75]	1822
15	23	H	Woking	W	2-1	1-1	7	Stevens 2 (1 pen) [43 (p), 82]	1064
16	26	A	Gateshead	L	0-1	0-0	8		1001
17	Nov 9	H	Altrincham	D	3-3	2-0	9	Whitmore [27], Bowen [40], Stevens [79]	1059
18	16	A	Ebbsfleet U	W	6-0	0-0	9	Stewart (og) [48], Adu-Poku [51], Wilkinson 3 [57, 60, 73], Bowen [90]	1664
19	23	H	Hartlepool U	L	3-4	1-2	8	Wilkinson [35], Warburton [51], Stevenson [59]	972
20	26	A	Sutton U	L	0-1	0-1	9		1821
21	Dec 10	H	Aldershot T	W	2-1	1-0	9	Wilkinson [10], Stevens [89]	740
22	14	A	Maidenhead U	D	1-1	0-0	10	Whitmore [90]	1094
23	21	H	AFC Fylde	W	4-1	2-1	7	Wilkinson 2 [10, 77], Stevens 2 (1 pen) [31, 53 (p)]	1080
24	26	A	Boston U	W	1-0	1-0	7	Osborne [17]	2364
25	31	H	Tamworth	W	2-0	1-0	6	Wilkinson 2 [20, 59]	2797
26	Jan 14	H	Eastleigh	L	0-1	0-1	6		751
27	18	A	Braintree T	L	0-1	0-1	7		807
28	25	H	FC Halifax T	L	0-2	0-1	9		1316
29	Feb 1	A	Wealdstone	D	1-1	1-1	9	Whitmore [45]	1418
30	8	H	Oldham Ath	L	0-1	0-1	9		1686
31	15	A	Barnet	L	1-3	0-1	11	Holman [46]	1732
32	19	A	Woking	L	0-1	0-1	12		1526
33	22	H	Gateshead	L	1-3	0-1	14	Holman [90]	903
34	25	A	Aldershot T	L	1-3	0-3	14	Holman [76]	1603
35	Mar 4	A	Sutton U	D	1-1	1-1	15	Stevens [18]	683
36	8	H	Ebbsfleet U	W	2-1	1-1	13	Duku 2 [43, 85]	848
37	15	A	Hartlepool U	D	1-1	0-0	12	Duku [76]	3959
38	22	H	Yeovil T	L	0-3	0-1	17		1495
39	25	A	Altrincham	D	1-1	0-1	16	Dodoo (pen) [52]	1336
40	29	A	Forest Green R	L	0-1	0-1	16		1568
41	Apr 12	A	Southend U	W	1-0	1-0	17	Thorpe [10]	8668
42	18	A	Tamworth	W	2-1	0-1	15	Wilkinson [50], Whitmore [87]	1850
43	21	H	Boston U	W	3-2	1-2	13	Osborne [7], Campbell (pen) [72], Clarke [90]	1393
44	26	A	York C	L	0-2	0-1	14		6249
45	29	H	Rochdale	L	0-1	0-0	14		838
46	May 5	H	Dagenham & Red	D	1-1	0-1	14	Duku [75]	3273

Final League Position: 14

GOALSCORERS

League (61): Wilkinson 13, Stevens 12 (3 pens), Bowen 4, Duku 4, Stevenson 4, Whitmore 4, Gale 3, Holman 3, Campbell 2 (1 pen), Osborne 2, Warburton 2, Adu-Poku 1, Clarke 1, Dodoo 1 (1 pen), Oakley 1, Thorpe 1, Tunnicliffe 1, own goals 2.
FA Cup (7): Wilkinson 2, Clarke 1, Ladabie 1, Osborne 1, Stevens 1 (1 pen), Stevenson 1.
FA Trophy (1): Ryley 1.

Walker 27	Clarke 40+1	Newton 36+4	Tipton 27+12	Whitmore 43+1	Bostock 28+12	Labadie 4+15	Stevens 25+2	Campbell 6+3	Gale 6+9	Warburton 10+9	Bowen 29+3	Pinnington 2+7	Holmes —+3	Tunnicliffe 21+2	Wilkinson 25+5	Osborne 37+2	Ryley —+6	Stevenson 15+26	Howell —+2	Oakley 27+2	Adu-Poku 11	Morrison 5+6	Barrett 9	Holman 9+11	Bruck —+3	Fish —+1	Wells-Morrison 14+1	Wright 10	Sutherland 2+3	Whyte-Hall 4+8	Akinola 2	Hall-Johnson 6+1	Cundy 8	Duku 6+3	Dodoo 6+1	Thorpe 6	Match No.
1	2	3	4[2]	5	6	7[8]	8	9	10[1]	11[3]	12	13	14																								1
1	2	4	7	3				8	10[3]	5[2]	11[1]	9[4]	15	6	12	13	14																				2
1	2	3	4[4]	6			8[2]	9	10[1]	11[3]	12	14			5	13	7			15																	3
1	2[1]	3	12	4	13					11	10	9	7[2]		5	8[3]	6			14																	4
1	14[8]	2	4[3]	3	7	13	11		10[1]	9[4]	8	15			5	12	6[2]																				5
1		2	4	3	8[1]				11	10	7	13			5	9[2]	6			12																	6
1		2	4	3	8					11	9[2]	6[1]			5	10	7	13		12																	7
1		5	10	4	7	12				11	6	2[1]			8	9[2]	3			13																	8
1	2	3	5	4	8	13			10[2]		7				6	11[1]	9	14		12[3]																	9
1	4	8	5[2]	3	6[1]				12			9	13		2	10	7			11																	10
1	11	4[1]	5[3]	3[4]	6				12			9	13		2	8[2]	7	15	10	14																	11
1	3	4	5		6	14	9[4]	12			8	13			2	10[3]	7[1]	15	11[2]																		12
1	3	4	5		2[1]	14	9		13		8				7	10[2]	6		11[3]	12																	13
1	3	4	13	2	6[2]	15	9[4]		12		8			14	7	10		5[1]	11[3]																		14
1	3	4	13	2	6[1]				12	8					7	10		5[2]	11																		15
1	3	4[4]	13	2		14	8[2]		12						7	10[3]	6	11[1]	15	5	9																16
1	4	7		2	12						5		13		8	10	6[2]		3[1]	9	11																17
1	4[8]	7	13	2	16		5[1]		15	14	8				10[4]	6[5]		3[2]	9	11[3]	12																18
1		4	13	2					12	7[1]	9[2]				10	6		8	5	11	3																19
1		4	14	2	6				13	12	9[2]				11	7		8[3]	5	10	3																20
	3	4	13	2	6[2]	9			14	8					11[1]	7		12	5[1]	10[3]	15	1															21
	3[2]	4		2	6[1]	9			13	8					11	7		12	5	10		1															22
	3	4	12	2	6	9[1]			13	8[2]					11	7		14	5	10[4]	15	1															23
	5	2	13	3	7[1]	9			12[3]	8					11	6		4	10[2]	14	1																24
	2	3	6	4	9[4]	14	10	15		8					11[2]	7[3]		12	5[1]	13	1																25
	4	3	2[2]	5	8[3]	10			14	9[1]					11	6		13	7		1	12															26
	4	3	12	5	8[2]	10			9[1]	7[3]					6			13	2	1	11	14															27
	3	2	5	4	14	10			13	8[2]					6[1]	9		7	12	1	11[3]																28
	6	3[2]	9	4			8			13				14	10	7[1]		15	2[4]		5	1	11[3]	12													29
1	2	13	7		5	14	10			6[4]					9[3]	12		3[1]	4		11[2]	15	8														30
	6	3	7	4	8[2]				9						12			2[1]	5		11		10	1	13												31
	6	8	4	13					7[4]					5		12	10[1]	2			11[2]	15	3	1		9[3]	14										32
	6	3	11	4[1]	12				5	14					9[2]		2			13		8	1		10	7[3]											33
	4		6[1]	13	7[2]		9			5	10[8]				14	2		12			3	1	15	11[4]	8[3]												34
	8	14	9	4	6[2]	10									15			2[4]		11[1]		12	1	7[3]							3	5	13			35
	8	3[3]	9	5	16	10[2]									13			12[9]	7		14		6[4]	1	15						2[1]	4	11			36
	7	3	8	5	12	6[2]								14				10			13				1	11[3]	15			2[4]	4	9[1]				37
	8[2]	3[1]	9[3]	4	12	16								15		5[4]		13		7			11[5]	1				14			2	6	10			38
	3		12	5	14	9[1]									6[3]			13		7[4]		8	1	15			2[2]	4	11	10						39
	3		8	5	13					16	14				9[1]			12			15		6	1		2[3]	4[5]	11[4]	10	7[2]							40
1	3	14		5	7				4	10[3]	9[4]				15			2[1]		13			6			12				11	8[2]					41
1	3	12	2[2]	5	7[5]	16	13		4	10[4]	9[3]				15			14				6				11	8[1]									42
1	2	3		5	14	16	12		4	9[2]	6[1]				7[5]			13			8		15				11[4]	10[3]								43
1	2	3[6]		5	6	14	10[4]		4	11[3]	12				13			8			15		16				9[4]	7[1]								44
1	8			5	6[2]	16	10[4]		4	11	13				7			3			14		2[1]	15			12[5]	9[3]								45
1	7			5	6[1]	15	10		4	8	14				12			3			13	9[4]	2[3]	11[2]												46

FA Cup

Fourth Qualifying	Altrincham	(a)	1-1
Replay	Altrincham	(h)	2-2
(aet; Solihull Moors won 3-1 on penalties)			
First Round	Maidstone U	(h)	3-0
Second Round	Bromley	(h)	1-2

FA Trophy

Third Round	Radcliffe	(h)	1-2

SOUTHEND UNITED

Ground: Roots Hall Stadium, Victoria Avenue, Southend-on-Sea, Essex SS2 6NQ.   *Tel:* (01702) 304 050.
Website: www.southendunited.co.uk   *Email:* info@southend-united.co.uk   *Year Formed:* 1906.
Record Attendance: 31,033 v Liverpool, FA Cup 3rd rd, 10 January 1979 (at Roots Hall).   *Nickname:* 'The Shrimpers'.
Manager: Kevin Maher.
Colours: Navy blue shirts with thin yellow stripes and yellow trim, navy blue shorts, white socks with navy blue trim.

SOUTHEND UNITED – NATIONAL LEAGUE 2024–25 LEAGUE RECORD

Match No.	Date	Venue	Opponents	Result	H/T Score	Lg Pos.	Goalscorers	Attendance
1	Aug 10	H	York C	D	1-1	1-0	12	Scott-Morriss [16]	7962
2	17	A	Hartlepool U	D	0-0	0-0	17		4452
3	20	H	Boston U	W	2-0	1-0	10	Cardwell [2], Scott-Morriss [52]	6924
4	24	A	Barnet	L	1-2	0-1	14	Scott-Morriss [64]	2932
5	26	H	Dagenham & Red	D	2-2	1-1	13	Coker [5], Scott-Morriss [90]	8495
6	Sept 7	A	Oldham Ath	D	1-1	1-0	13	Scott-Morriss [34]	5622
7	10	H	Eastleigh	W	2-0	2-0	13	Ralph [24], Bridge (pen) [45]	6359
8	14	H	Sutton U	L	1-3	1-1	17	Scott-Morriss [12]	7179
9	17	A	AFC Fylde	L	1-2	0-1	17	Scott-Morriss [57]	1088
10	21	A	Solihull Moors	W	4-2	2-1	13	Appiah-Forson [19], Pepple 2 [27, 69], Scott-Morriss [56]	1390
11	24	A	Wealdstone	D	1-1	0-0	13	Walker [90]	1847
12	28	H	Gateshead	L	1-3	1-1	15	Scott-Morriss [32]	6837
13	Oct 5	H	Maidenhead U	L	0-2	0-1	16		6774
14	19	A	Rochdale	W	1-0	1-0	15	Walker [45]	2806
15	23	A	Aldershot T	D	0-0	0-0	15		2557
16	26	H	Tamworth	W	2-0	2-0	14	Pepple [11], Coker [16]	6710
17	Nov 9	H	Yeovil T	L	0-1	0-0	15		6911
18	16	A	Altrincham	L	0-2	0-2	16		2536
19	23	H	Forest Green R	D	2-2	0-1	16	Ralph [63], Coker [77]	6725
20	26	A	Woking	D	0-0	0-0	16		2424
21	30	A	FC Halifax T	W	2-0	1-0	14	Pepple [35], Crowther [61]	1766
22	Dec 14	H	Hartlepool U	D	0-0	0-0	15		6877
23	21	A	York C	L	0-3	0-0	16		6446
24	26	H	Ebbsfleet U	W	4-0	2-0	14	Coker [7], Pepple 2 [45, 52], Scott-Morriss [56]	8406
25	Jan 1	A	Braintree T	W	1-0	1-0	14	Pepple [20]	3285
26	18	H	Barnet	L	0-3	0-2	14		6955
27	25	A	Dagenham & Red	W	2-0	1-0	14	Bonne [45], Scott-Morriss [59]	3599
28	28	H	AFC Fylde	W	2-0	1-0	11	Walker [44], Obi (og) [66]	5638
29	Feb 8	A	Maidenhead U	L	0-1	0-0	12		1978
30	11	H	FC Halifax T	W	3-1	0-0	11	Scott-Morriss [54], Hopper [58], Kendall [86]	6250
31	15	A	Rochdale	D	1-1	0-1	10	Hogan [84]	6908
32	18	H	Aldershot T	W	2-1	0-0	8	Husin [52], Scott-Morriss [71]	6632
33	22	A	Tamworth	D	1-1	0-1	9	Scott-Morriss [53]	1631
34	Mar 1	A	Yeovil T	D	2-2	1-2	9	Kendall [1], Golding [90]	3508
35	4	A	Woking	D	2-2	1-1	10	Golding [34], Scott-Morriss [64]	6133
36	8	H	Altrincham	W	2-1	2-0	10	Golding [14], Bonne [38]	7776
37	15	A	Forest Green R	D	2-2	1-2	9	Bonne [26], Scott-Morriss [75]	2251
38	22	A	Eastleigh	W	2-1	2-0	9	Hopper [1], Scott-Morriss [45]	3148
39	25	A	Boston U	L	0-3	0-0	9		2387
40	29	H	Oldham Ath	W	1-0	1-0	8	Appiah-Forson [10]	8395
41	Apr 5	A	Sutton U	D	1-1	1-0	9	Goodliffe [32]	3769
42	12	H	Solihull Moors	L	0-1	0-1	9		8668
43	18	H	Braintree T	D	0-0	0-0	8		9614
44	21	A	Ebbsfleet U	W	4-0	1-0	8	Kendall [15], Coker [63], Bonne [76], Walker [90]	3125
45	26	H	Wealdstone	W	3-0	1-0	7	Goodliffe [8], Kendall [64], Bonne [90]	9677
46	May 5	A	Gateshead	D	0-0	0-0	7		4108

Final League Position: 7

GOALSCORERS

League (59): Scott-Morriss 17, Pepple 7, Bonne 5, Coker 5, Kendall 4, Walker 4, Golding 3, Appiah-Forson 2, Goodliffe 2, Hopper 2, Ralph 2, Bridge 1 (1 pen), Cardwell 1, Crowther 1, Husin 1, own goals 2.
FA Cup (4): Bridge 1 (1 pen), Coker 1, Pepple 1, own goal 1.
FA Trophy (6): Pepple 3, Appiah-Forson 1, Miley 1, Walker 1.
National League Play-offs (8): Chambers-Parillon 2, Hopper 1, Bridge 1, Goodliffe 1, Kendall 1, Ralph 1, own goal 1

Andeng-Ndi 23+1	Scott-Morriss 44	Ralph 39+1	Kensdale 3	Gubbins 14+10	Taylor 45	Bridge 31+11	Miley 12+13	Coker 24+8	Cardwell 5	Walker 20+15	Morton 32+11	Waldron 2+9	Wood —+10	Crowther 20+1	Husin 36+7	Moncur 12+2	Wind 2+11	Pepple 17+2	Appiah-Forson 15+21	Bonne 20+20	Foran 1+1	Jeacock 3	Kendall 13+9	Golding 13+1	Harness 2+1	Goodliffe 14+5	Hopper 15+4	Hayes 18	Chambers-Parillon 11+7	Match No.
1	2	3	4	5^4	6	7^1	8	9^2	10	11^3	12	13	14	15																1
1	2	3	4	5^2	6	12	7	9^4	10	11^1	8^3	14	15		13															2
1	2^1	3	4	14	7	5^2	8	9	10^4	13	11				6^3	12	15													3
1	2	3			5	6	8	9^1	10	13	11^2	14		4	7^3	12														4
1	2	5		14	4	6	7^2	8^1	11	13				12	3^3	10	9													5
1	2	3			5	6	7^2			10				13	4	8	9^1	14	11^3	12										6
1	2	3			5	6	7^3			10				14	4	8	9^1	11^2	13	12										7
1	2	3			5^2	6	7			10^3				14	4	8	9	11^1	13	12										8
1	4	2		6^2	3	11				7^1					5	9	8	12	13	10										9
1	4	2		12	3	8^1				13				14	6	9	7^2	11^3	5	10										10
1	4	2		14	3^2	8^4				13	12				6	9	7^3	15	11^1	5	10									11
1	2			5		8					12			7^2	14	4	9	10^3	13	3	11	6^1								12
1	7	2		15	3	5				11	12			4^2	6	9^4	14	8^1	10^3	13										13
1		6		4	2	14				10^2	9^1	5		3	7	8	11^3	12	13											14
1	4	2		6	3	12		9^2		10^3	7			5	8	11^1	14	13												15
	5	3		15	4	7^5	14	9^3		12	2			6	8^1	16	11^2	13	10^4			1								16
12	8	2			3	6^2	13	9^4		10^3	5^5			4	7^1	15	11	16	14			$1^■$								17
9	2	3			6	8^3		10^4	15	14	4	7^1	5^2	11	13	12						1								18
1	5	3			4	7^1	8^2	9		10	2	13		6	14	11^3			12											19
1	4	2			3	14	$7^■$	8^2		10^1	6			5	12	11^3	13	9												20
1	4	2			3	7^4	8^5			10^1	6	13		5^{14}	9^2	16	11^3	15	12											21
1		2			3	7	15	12		10^3	6			4^8	9^4	5	11^1	13					14							22
1	4	2		14	3	7	8	9^1		10^5	6^3			5^{13}	11^4	15	12						16							23
1	5	3		14	4	6^4	7^1	9		13	16			2^5	11^2	15	12						10^3	8						24
1	2	5		14	4	9^4	8	7		12^5	15			3^3	11^2	16	13						10^4	6						25
	2	5		3^2	4	12	8^1	7		11^3	14	16		9^4	15	13							10^5	6	1					26
1^3	2	3			4	8^1	$7^■$			11		7^2		16	14	13	9^5						10^4	5	12	15				27
	2^5	3			4	8^1		15		11^2	6	16		14	13	9^5						10^4	5	1	12	15			28
	2^5	3			4	8^1		15		11^2	6			7^3	14	13	9^4					10	5	1	16	12			29
	2	8			4		10^3			11^1	6^2			7		14	13					15	5	3	9^4	1	12		30
	2	3			4	8^3	14			11^2	6			7^3		14	12					15	9^2	1	15				31
	2	3			4	9^4	12	10^2		6				7		11^3	14	5	15	13^1	8^1								32
	2	3			4		12	6^2	14	7				10^1	13	8	5	9	1	11^3									33
	2				6	3	7^3	13	9	12	14			11	4	5	10^2	1	8^1											34
	2				6	3^4	7	9	15	13				8	10^3	5	12	1	14											35
	2			3^2	4	15	6	14		13	12			8	11^4	7^3	5	10	1	9^1										36
	2	3			4	14	13	6^1		8^4				7	10	12	5	15^{11^2}	1	9^3										37
	2			3	4	13	12	14	6^2	8				7^3	10^4	5	15	11	1	9^1										38
	2			3	4	14	13	6^1		8^2				7	10	12	5	11^3	1	9										39
	2	13		8^2	5	15	12	14	6^1	9				3^4	10	4	11	1	7^3											40
	2	3			4	14	13	12	6^3	8				7^4	10	5	11^2	1	9^1											41
	2^1	3			4	13	12	15	6^2	8				7^5	10	16	5	11^3	1	9^4										42
	2	3			4	12	16	7^3	10^1	6^4				8^2	15	11^5	14	5	13	1	9									43
	2^2	4			6	3^1	14	9		12				8^4	15	7	13	10^1	5	11^5	1	16								44
	2	4^4	16		6	3^1	14	9^3		12				8	7	13	11^1	5	10^2	1	15									45
	6	4			2	8^2	14	9^3		12				3	7	13	11^4	5	10^1	1	15									46

FA Cup

Fourth Qualifying	Eastleigh	(a)	1-0
First Round	Charlton Ath	(h)	3-4

(aet; 3-3 at the end of normal time)

FA Trophy

Third Round	Brentwood T	(a)	5-3
Fourth Round	Southport	(h)	1-0
Fifth Round	Sittingbourne	(h)	0-1

National League Play-offs

Quarter-Finals	Rochdale	(a)	4-3
(aet)			
Semi-Finals	Forest Green R	(a)	2-2
(aet; Southend U won 4-2 on penalties)			
Final	Oldham Ath	(Wembley)	2-3

SUTTON UNITED

Ground: VBS Community Stadium, Gander Green Lane, Sutton, Surrey SM1 2EY.   *Tel:* (0208) 644 4440.
Website: www.suttonunited.net   *Email:* see website.   *Year Formed:* 1898.
Record Attendance: 14,000 v Leeds U, FA Cup 4th rd, 24 January 1970.   *Nicknames:* 'The U's', 'The Amber and Chocolates', 'The Yellows'.   *Manager:* Steve Morison.
Colours: Amber shirts with chocolate trim, amber shorts with chocolate trim, amber socks with chocolate trim.

SUTTON UNITED – NATIONAL LEAGUE 2024–25 LEAGUE RECORD

Match No.	Date	Venue	Opponents	Result		H/T Score	Lg Pos.	Goalscorers	Attendance
1	Aug 10	A	Tamworth	D	1-1	0-0	12	Coley [90]	1676
2	17	H	Altrincham	W	5-0	4-0	4	Coley [30], Harris [32], Davies [39], Odelusi (pen) [44], Nadesan [84]	2456
3	20	A	Wealdstone	W	1-0	1-0	3	Waller [11]	1566
4	24	H	York C	D	2-2	0-0	4	Davies [49], Coley [72]	2624
5	26	A	Eastleigh	D	1-1	1-1	3	Vaz [13]	2378
6	31	H	Forest Green R	L	1-2	0-1	8	Sivi [86]	2607
7	Sept 7	A	Boston U	L	0-3	0-1	13		2758
8	10	A	Dagenham & Red	L	0-3	0-1	17		1374
9	14	A	Southend U	W	3-1	1-1	15	Coley [45], Gubbins (og) [51], Nadesan [75]	7179
10	21	H	Ebbsfleet U	W	3-2	1-0	10	Davies [7], Harris [51], Nadesan [77]	3131
11	24	H	Yeovil T	D	0-0	0-0	9		2246
12	28	A	Woking	W	2-1	2-0	8	Simper [13], Sivi [17]	2076
13	Oct 5	A	Hartlepool U	L	3-4	2-0	9	Harris [6], Nadesan [24], Simper [83]	3408
14	19	H	Oldham Ath	L	1-3	0-1	13	Davies [47]	3329
15	23	L	Gateshead	L	0-1	0-0	14		2100
16	26	H	Braintree T	W	1-0	0-0	12	Davies [47]	917
17	Nov 9	A	Rochdale	L	1-2	1-1	13	Vaz [29]	2602
18	16	H	Maidenhead U	W	1-0	1-0	11	Barbrook [30]	2905
19	26	H	Solihull Moors	W	1-0	1-0	14	Wadham [14]	1821
20	30	H	AFC Fylde	W	2-0	0-0	7	Nadesan [68], Davies [71]	2050
21	Dec 10	A	FC Halifax T	D	0-0	0-0	7		1006
22	14	A	Altrincham	L	0-1	0-1	11		1820
23	21	H	Tamworth	L	1-2	1-0	13	Davies [9]	2478
24	26	A	Barnet	D	3-3	1-2	12	Nadesan [21], Davies [69], Topalloj [72]	2430
25	Jan 1	H	Aldershot T	D	1-1	1-0	13	Nadesan [23]	3013
26	15	H	Wealdstone	D	2-2	1-1	13	Simper [44], Davies [47]	1983
27	18	A	York C	W	2-1	2-0	10	Davies 2 [15, 24]	6369
28	25	H	Eastleigh	W	1-0	0-0	10	Davies (pen) [60]	2526
29	Feb 8	H	Hartlepool U	L	1-2	0-0	11	Davies [46]	2321
30	15	A	Oldham Ath	D	0-0	0-0	12		5738
31	18	A	Gateshead	L	3-4	1-2	12	Davies [45], Kirk [49], Simper [57]	668
32	22	H	Braintree T	D	1-1	0-0	13	Coley [54]	2508
33	Mar 4	A	Solihull Moors	D	1-1	1-1	13	Vaz [7]	683
34	8	A	Maidenhead U	W	1-0	1-0	12	De Silva [30]	1292
35	11	A	Forest Green R	L	1-2	0-2	12	Davies [57]	1275
36	15	H	FC Halifax T	L	0-3	0-2	13		2292
37	18	A	AFC Fylde	W	2-1	0-1	12	Barbrook [86], Davies (pen) [88]	943
38	22	H	Dagenham & Red	D	1-1	0-0	12	Davies [90]	2648
39	29	A	Boston U	L	1-2	1-1	14	Davies [29]	2302
40	Apr 5	H	Southend U	D	1-1	0-1	14	Nadesan [90]	3769
41	8	H	Rochdale	W	1-0	0-0	12	Gordon (og) [87]	2087
42	12	A	Ebbsfleet U	L	1-4	0-1	12	Simper [52]	1295
43	18	H	Aldershot T	D	1-1	1-0	12	Simper [31]	3464
44	21	A	Barnet	L	1-3	1-1	14	Odelusi (pen) [33]	3557
45	26	A	Yeovil T	W	2-1	0-1	13	Odelusi [50], Simper [61]	3566
46	May 5	H	Woking	D	1-1	0-1	12	Wadham [64]	3270

Final League Position: 12

GOALSCORERS

League (59): Davies 18 (2 pens), Nadesan 8, Simper 7, Coley 5, Harris 3, Odelusi 3 (2 pens), Vaz 3, Barbrook 2, Sivi 2, Wadham 2, De Silva 1, Kirk 1, Topalloj 1, Waller 1, own goals 2.
FA Cup (3): Coley 1, Rush 1, own goal 1.
FA Trophy (5): Davies 2, Barbrook 1, Boateng 1, Odelusi 1 (1 pen).

Arnold 14	Jackson 21+3	French 39+2	Muller 21+5	Vaz 23+6	Odelusi 20+14	Simper 39+1	Harris 14+2	De Silva 11+10	Davies 40+4	Boateng 11+16	Coley 22+11	Nadesan 28+15	Sivi 10+10	Wadham 19+6	Rush 1+6	Ransom 13+8	Waller 20+1	Barbrook 34+1	Okoli 6+3	Eccleston 1	Kirk 9+2	Sims 31	Agbaje 1	Topalloi 25	Kerbey —+1	Evans 1	Taylor 12+1	Woodyard 11+1	Sandat 2+9	Robinson 1	Adom 6+1	Tume —+2	Fennelow —+1	Match No.
1	2	3	4	5	6¹	7	8	9³	10	11²	12	13	14																					1
1	2	3⁵	4	5	7²	6	8	10⁴	9¹	11³	13	14	12	15	16																			2
1		2	4		12	6	8	14	13	9¹	11¹	10²		15		3	5	7³																3
1	2	3	4			8	7		11	10²	13	12	9¹	14			5	6³																4
1	2	3	4²	5¹	13	14	12	8⁴	10	16	7⁵	9³	11	15		6																		5
1	2	3	4¹		9	7			10	11²	13	8	12				5	6																6
1	4	2	3	5¹		9	7		11		12	10²	13				6	8																7
1	2	3	4²	5³		8	13		10	11⁴	9		12	15			6	7¹	14															8
1	2²	12			13	7		6	11	8³	9¹	14		15		10	4	5⁴	3															9
1			12	13		8	11		10	7¹	6	14				2	4	9³	3	5²														10
1		3			9³	8¹	7	6	10	12	11²	14				2	5	13	4															11
1		3			13	8		6	11	7²	12	9				2	5	10¹	4															12
1	2	3¹			9	7	13		11	8²	6						5	10	4		12													13
1	2	12			9²	7	14		11	8¹	6⁴	13		15			5³	10	4		3													14
	2				9²	7		6	13	11	3	8¹	12				5	10	4			1												15
	2				10	7		8²	11¹	12	3	6³	9			13	5	14	4			1												16
	2	12	11³			7		10¹		9		14				6	13	5	8		3	1		4²										17
	2	12				7		9	13	6²	10	4¹	11				5	8			3	1												18
	2	3				7		13		9	6¹	10	11			12	5²	8				1		4										19
	2	3				7		13		9	14	6²	10¹			4³	11	12	8			1		5										20
6²	2	3				7				10¹	12	9	13				11	5	8			1		4										21
	2	3			13			5		9	12	10	6¹			11²	4	8				1		7										22
		3				7¹		11		9	13	6	10			12²	2	5	8			1		4										23
4²		3	2			7				12	10	14	11³			9¹	6	8	13			1		5										24
4		3				8		5¹		9		10	11			6		12			7	1²		2	13									25
	2	5				6		11¹	9		8²	10					7					1		3		1	4	12	13					26
16	2	13	5¹			11		15	9²	12	7³	10⁵					6					1		3			4	8⁶	14					27
	2		5	13	11	10¹		9		7²							6				14	1		3			4	8³	12					28
	4	3¹	6	11		10³		9		13							7				8	1		5			12	14	2²					29
7⁴	15	3	12	6		10²	9		13			11¹					4				1	5		2	8³			14						30
	6	3	9³	10		2	11		13	12		7					5¹				1	4			8⁷			14						31
	7	3¹		10		12	11		9²	8³	14						5				6	1		4⁴			2	13						32
	2	4	3		6	10	11		7¹	12	9						8					1		5										33
	2	4	3	7	6¹	10²	11		9³	13	12	14					8					1		5			10¹							34
	2	4	3	9²	6	13⁴	15		14	12		7³					8					1		5			10¹							35
	2	4¹	13	9⁴	10		11	15		14	12	7³					6					1		3			5	8²						36
	2	4	10¹	14	9		11		13	12	7³						8					1		3			5	6²						37
	2²	4³	12	15	9		11		14	10¹	7					13	8					1		3			5	6⁴						38
	13	4	2	14	9		11		7		12						8					1		3			5¹	6²			10³			39
7	2⁴	15	3²		11		9		13	12	14					4	6					1		3			5	8¹			10³			40
	2	4	14	12	6		11²		9		7					5						1		3			8¹				10³	13		41
5		4	6¹	12	8		11²		10		7³	9				3						1		2								14	13	42
	2	4	13	6	8		12		7²	11		9¹				5						1		3			14				10³			43
2³	4⁴	5	6	9	13		10²	14	11¹	8	12											1		3				15	7⁴					44
2¹	4	15	13	9	14		11	10²	12	8						5						1		3				6³	7⁴					45
15	4⁴	13	3²	9	2¹		11	14	7	10						5						1		6				8³	12					46

FA Cup

Fourth Qualifying	Chertsey T	(a)	3-1
First Round	Birmingham C	(h)	0-1

FA Trophy

Third Round	Ebbsfleet U	(h)	3-3
(Sutton U won 4-2 on penalties)			
Fourth Round	Tamworth	(h)	1-1
Fifth Round	Kidderminster H	(a)	1-0
Quarter-Finals	Spennymoor T	(h)	0-2

TAMWORTH

Ground: The Lamb Ground, Kettlebrook Road, Tamworth, Staffordshire B77 1AA.   *Tel:* (01827) 65798.
Website: www.tamworthfootballclub.com   *Email:* office@thelambs.co.uk   *Year Formed:* 1933.
Record Attendance: 4,920 v Atherstone T, Birmingham Combination, 3 April 1948.   *Nickname:* 'The Lambs'.
Manager: Andy Peaks.   *Colours:* Red and black patterned shirts, black shorts, red socks with black trim.

TAMWORTH – NATIONAL LEAGUE 2024–25 LEAGUE RECORD

Match No.	Date	Venue	Opponents	Result	H/T Score	Lg Pos.	Goalscorers	Attendance
1	Aug 10	H	Sutton U	D	1-1	0-0	12	Tshikuna [84]	1676
2	17	A	York C	L	0-2	0-0	18		4684
3	20	A	Hartlepool U	L	0-1	0-0	20		1293
4	24	A	Boston U	D	1-1	0-1	20	Wreh [90]	1620
5	26	H	Aldershot T	W	3-2	1-1	19	Cullinane-Liburd [8], Wreh [50], Tshikuna [55]	1563
6	31	A	Barnet	L	0-7	0-3	21		1372
7	Sept 7	A	Eastleigh	L	0-1	0-1	23		2158
8	14	H	Maidenhead U	W	3-1	1-0	19	Wreh [45], Acquaye [54], Tshikuna [79]	1050
9	21	A	Braintree T	W	1-0	0-0	18	Tonks [90]	970
10	24	A	AFC Fylde	W	2-1	0-0	16	McGlinchey [47], Creaney [90]	942
11	28	H	Altrincham	L	1-2	0-0	17	Creaney [90]	1358
12	Oct 5	A	FC Halifax T	L	2-3	2-0	19	Hollis [4], Creaney [32]	1480
13	8	H	Gateshead	W	2-1	1-0	14	Tshikuna [24], Creaney [73]	815
14	19	H	Woking	W	3-2	2-0	12	Tshikuna [9], McGlinchey [42], Creaney [90]	1233
15	22	H	Yeovil T	D	0-0	0-0	12		1068
16	26	A	Southend U	L	0-2	0-2	16		6710
17	Nov 9	H	Ebbsfleet U	D	1-1	0-1	14	Williams [79]	1141
18	16	A	Oldham Ath	L	0-4	0-3	15		6345
19	23	A	Dagenham & Red	W	2-1	0-1	14	Creaney 2 [56, 76]	807
20	Dec 14	H	York C	D	1-1	0-1	16	Cullinane-Liburd [90]	1739
21	17	A	Rochdale	L	0-3	0-0	16		1705
22	21	A	Sutton U	W	2-1	0-1	14	McGlinchey 2 [47, 66]	2478
23	26	H	Forest Green R	D	1-1	0-1	15	Creaney [90]	1721
24	31	A	Solihull Moors	L	0-2	0-1	15		2797
25	Jan 18	H	Boston U	W	3-0	2-0	15	McGlinchey 2 [17, 36], Milnes [66]	1479
26	25	A	Aldershot T	D	2-2	0-0	15	Creaney 2 [49, 68]	2323
27	Feb 1	H	Barnet	L	0-1	0-1	15		1438
28	4	A	Wealdstone	W	1-0	0-0	15	Enoru [73]	1013
29	8	H	FC Halifax T	L	1-2	0-1	15	Tshikuna (pen) [90]	1074
30	11	A	Hartlepool U	D	2-2	2-1	15	Ponticelli [44], Enoru [45]	3177
31	15	A	Woking	D	1-1	0-0	15	Finn [88]	2092
32	18	A	Yeovil T	L	1-2	1-0	15	Maher [26]	2649
33	22	H	Southend U	D	1-1	1-0	15	Digie [9]	1631
34	25	H	Rochdale	D	1-1	1-0	15	Waller (og) [43]	805
35	Mar 1	A	Ebbsfleet U	W	3-2	3-1	13	Creaney 2 [38, 40], Lankshear (og) [43]	1322
36	4	H	Wealdstone	W	4-1	0-0	11	Tshikuna 2 (1 pen) [51, 54 (p)], Creaney [71], Fletcher [90]	866
37	8	H	Oldham Ath	D	1-1	1-1	11	Creaney [42]	1933
38	15	A	Dagenham & Red	W	3-1	1-1	11	Creaney (pen) [45], Maher [48], Hollis [65]	2435
39	22	A	Gateshead	W	2-0	0-0	10	Creaney [60], McGlinchey [78]	1184
40	29	A	Eastleigh	W	2-0	0-0	10	Hollis [53], McGlinchey [60]	1383
41	Apr 5	H	Maidenhead U	L	1-3	0-1	10	Milnes (pen) [77]	1034
42	12	H	Braintree T	W	4-2	3-2	10	Enoru [17], Ponticelli [20], McGlinchey [45], Creaney [90]	1007
43	18	H	Solihull Moors	L	1-2	1-0	10	McGlinchey [25]	1850
44	21	A	Forest Green R	L	0-3	0-3	10		1783
45	26	H	AFC Fylde	W	4-3	2-3	10	Creaney 2 [9, 78], Digie [45], Finn [90]	1100
46	May 5	A	Altrincham	D	1-1	1-0	10	Crompton [14]	2371

Final League Position: 10

GOALSCORERS

League (65): Creaney 19 (1 pen), McGlinchey 10, Tshikuna 8 (2 pens), Enoru 3, Hollis 3, Wreh 3, Cullinane-Liburd 2, Digie 2, Finn 2, Maher 2, Milnes 2 (1 pen), Ponticelli 2, Acquaye 1, Crompton 1, Fletcher 1, Tonks 1, Williams 1, own goals 2.
FA Cup (6): Tshikuna 2, Creaney 1, Maher 1, McGlinchey 1, own goal 1.
FA Trophy (1): Wreh 1.

Singh 45	Willets 5 + 1	Hollis 46	Cullinane-Liburd 22 + 4	Fletcher 12 + 15	Finn 13 + 16	Fairlamb 25 + 2	Morrison 32 + 2	Acquaye 9 + 3	Tshikuna 24 + 4	Creaney 31 + 11	Okafor 1 + 13	Enoru 18 + 20	McClinchey 35 + 7	Tonks 26 + 16	Curley 9 + 7	Wreh 10 + 7	Milnes 23 + 5	Lissimore — + 5	Moore — + 1	Sundire 17 + 12	Williams 4 + 16	Digie 27 + 2	Browne 4	Wallace 3 + 3	Powell 2	Cockerill-Mollett 20	Crompton 22 + 3	Maher 10 + 3	Ponticelli 9 + 10	Raikhy 1 + 6	Waldron — + 7	Edge — + 1	Hitchman — + 1	Phillips 1	Match No.
1	2	3	4	5	6¹	7	8	9	10	11²	12	13																							1
1	4	2	3²	5	6⁴	7	8	9⁵	10¹	11¹	13	12	14	15	16																				2
1	2	4	3	5³	6²	7	8	9	10¹	11⁴	12	13		15		14																			3
1	13	4	3	5⁵		7	8	9	10⁴	16	11¹	14	12			2³	15	6²																	4
1	4	2	3	9⁴	7	6	12		10	15		5³	8¹	11²	13	14																			5
1	2³	4	3	6¹	7	8	13	10	16	15	9²	5⁴	11⁵	14	12																				6
1	2	4		5	6³	10	9⁴	13		15	8¹	14	11	7²	12				3																7
1	2	3		5	6	8²	9⁵	12	15	14	10⁴	13	11¹	7³						4	16														8
1	2	4			3	10	8³	9²	14	7	13	11⁴	6¹	12						5	15														9
1	2				3	10	8²	12	15	7	14	11³	6²	13⁴						5⁴	9	4													10
1	2	12			3	10	15	8¹	13	16	7	14	11³	6²						5⁴	9⁵	4													11
1	2	5	13	3	9²	8⁴	11	10³		16	7⁵	12	14	15	6¹							4													12
1	2	4	7¹	3	9	8²	11	10³	13	14	12	6⁴													5	15									13
1	2	4	13	8⁴	3	11³	10	15	14	9²	6	12									16			5⁵	7¹										14
1	2	4	12	8³	3	11²	10	15	13	9	6	14⁵									16			5⁴	7¹										15
1	2	4	14		3	11¹	10³	12	9⁴	8	6²	15	7⁵							13				5	16										16
1	2	5	12		3	11	10	9³	6⁴	15	7²									14	4		13	8¹											17
1	2	4	8⁴		6	14	11³	10¹	13	16	15									12	3		7	9⁵	5²										18
1	2	4	6		3	9³	11¹	10			14	13	15		12					7²				5	8										19
1	2	4	15		3	11	10	13	8²	6⁴	12	7³			9¹									5	14										20
1	2	4¹	7²	14	3	11	10	9³	8	6¹			13	12										5											21
1	2	7		9		12	11³	8	10¹	6	14	13	3							4²	5														22
1	3	7³		8⁴		14	10¹	9²	13	11	6⁵	16	15	4						2	5	12													23
1	4		12	7		13	9	8¹	5⁵	10²	6	14	16	3						2⁴	11³	15													24
1	5	4	13	14		9	11⁴	12	10⁵	7	8²	6³	16							3¹	2	15													25
1	5	4	12	14		9	11	10³	7	8¹	6²	13								3	2														26
1	5	4¹	8¹	12		9	13	11	10²	7³	15	6⁴								3	2⁴	14													27
1	5		8	14		9	12	11³	10¹	7	2²	6⁴	13	4						3		15													28
1	5	6⁵	16	11³		12		9²	7¹	15	2	8⁴	4							3		13	10	14											29
1	5	6²	11	16		9⁴	8	13	2	7⁵	15	4								3³	12	14	10¹												30
1	8		15	6²		11¹	13	5⁵	12	14	3			4						2		7³	10⁴	15											31
1	5		16	11		13	14	9¹	12	3	6²			8⁵						2		7³	10⁴	15											32
1	5		10¹	7		8⁴	11	12	14	2	15	13								3	9³	6²													33
1	5		7²	6		10	11³	12	13	8⁴		14								3	2	9¹	15												34
1	5	13	14		11	15	7²	9⁴		6	12			4						3	2	10³		8¹											35
1	5	13	15		9	11	14	7⁵	8¹	6²	12			4						3	2⁴	10³		16											36
1	5	14	15	16	12	9⁵	11	13	7³	8	6¹			4						3	2⁴	10²													37
1	5		16	9	11²	12	7³	8⁶	6¹	4				3					2	10⁴	15	13	14												38
1	5	9²	11¹	10⁵	7	8⁴		12	6³	13	4			3					2	15	16	14													39
1	5	9²	11³	10⁵	7	8¹	12	14	6	4	3			2⁴	13	16	15																		40
1	5	11	14	7²	9	13	8	6⁵	15	4	3	2¹	10⁴	12																						41
1	5	13	15	12	11	10³	7⁵	8	2²	6	16	4	3¹	14	9⁴																				42
1	5	12	16	3	11⁴	10	7¹	8	2³	6⁵	15	4	14	9⁵	13																				43
1	5	13	12	7¹	3	11	10	8⁴	2³	6	15	4⁶	9²	14	16																				44
1	5	16	15	14	3	11	10³	7¹	6⁵	8	12	4	2²	9⁴	13																				45
	5	13	7²	3	11	10³	6¹	8	12	4	2	9	14	1																					46

FA Cup

Fourth Qualifying	Macclesfield	(h)	4-2
First Round	Huddersfield T	(h)	1-0
Second Round	Burton Alb	(a)	1-1

(aet; 0-0 at end of normal time, Tamworth won 4-3 on penalties)

Third Round	Tottenham H	(h)	0-3

(aet.)

FA Trophy

Third Round	Hartlepool U	(a)	1-1

(Tamworth won 3-0 on penalties)

Fourth Round	Sutton U	(a)	0-1

WEALDSTONE

Ground: Grosvenor Vale, Ruislip, Middlesex HA4 6JQ.   *Tel:* (01895) 637 487.   *Website:* www.wealdstone-fc.com
Email: see website.   *Year Formed:* 1899.   *Record Attendance:* 13,504 v Leytonstone, FA Amateur Cup, 4th rd replay,
5 March 1949 (at Lower Mead); 3,534 v Wycombe W, FA Cup 2nd rd, 30 November 2024 (at Grosvenor Vale).
Nicknames: 'The Stones', 'The Royals'.   *Manager:* Sam Cox.   *Colours:* Royal blue shirts with white trim, white shorts,
white socks with royal blue trim.

WEALDSTONE – NATIONAL LEAGUE 2024–25 LEAGUE RECORD

Match No.	Date	Venue	Opponents	Result	H/T Score	Lg Pos.	Goalscorers	Attendance
1	Aug 10	A	Dagenham & Red	L	1-2	0-0	17	Ashford [71]	1523
2	17	H	Oldham Ath	L	0-1	0-0	19		1825
3	20	H	Sutton U	L	0-1	0-1	21		1566
4	24	A	Hartlepool U	D	1-1	1-0	21	Obiero [39]	3614
5	26	H	AFC Fylde	W	1-0	1-0	22	Sandat [19]	1325
6	31	A	Solihull Moors	D	1-1	0-1	20	Boldewijn [56]	948
7	Sept 7	H	York C	L	0-2	0-1	22		1904
8	10	A	Woking	L	0-1	0-1	21		2125
9	14	A	Forest Green R	D	2-2	1-2	21	McFarlane 2 [43, 88]	2165
10	21	H	Barnet	L	0-3	0-0	22		2590
11	24	H	Southend U	D	1-1	0-0	23	McFarlane [90]	1847
12	28	A	FC Halifax T	D	2-2	1-0	23	Ashford (pen) [35], Obiero [60]	1442
13	Oct 5	A	Gateshead	L	0-1	0-0	23		1147
14	19	H	Yeovil T	L	0-3	0-1	23		1510
15	23	H	Braintree T	W	3-2	1-2	22	Ashford 2 [10, 67], Reid [54]	1163
16	26	A	Ebbsfleet U	D	2-2	0-0	22	Ashford [57], Reid [70]	1498
17	Nov 9	A	Aldershot T	W	2-0	1-0	22	Reid (pen) [45], Kretzschmar [90]	3156
18	16	H	Rochdale	W	2-0	0-0	20	Kretzschmar [46], Cesay [67]	1922
19	23	A	Eastleigh	D	1-1	0-1	19	Ashford [65]	2020
20	Dec 10	H	Altrincham	D	3-3	2-2	20	Cesay [20], Reid 2 [45, 74]	1005
21	14	A	Oldham Ath	L	2-3	2-1	20	Obiero [3], Kretzschmar [29]	5544
22	21	H	Dagenham & Red	W	3-0	2-0	18	Ashford [23], Kalambayi (og) [29], Reid (pen) [69]	1404
23	26	A	Maidenhead U	L	1-3	0-1	19	Reid [49]	1725
24	Jan 15	A	Sutton U	D	2-2	1-1	19	Grant [34], Cesay [68]	1983
25	18	H	Hartlepool U	D	1-1	0-1	21	Boldewijn [86]	1467
26	25	A	AFC Fylde	L	0-2	0-0	21		1082
27	Feb 1	H	Solihull Moors	D	1-1	1-1	20	Reid [4]	1418
28	4	H	Tamworth	L	0-1	0-0	21		1013
29	8	H	Gateshead	L	0-4	0-2	22		1323
30	15	A	Yeovil T	W	2-1	1-1	21	Boldewijn [15], Grant [54]	3179
31	19	A	Braintree T	W	2-1	0-1	20	Gray (og) [72], Grant [77]	888
32	22	H	Ebbsfleet U	W	4-2	2-2	18	Reid 2 (1 pen) [26 (pl), 79], Sohna 2 [45, 69]	1401
33	Mar 4	A	Tamworth	L	1-4	0-0	21	Georgiou [90]	866
34	8	A	Rochdale	L	1-4	0-1	21	Cook [75]	2289
35	15	H	Eastleigh	D	3-3	0-3	21	Walker [69], Reid 2 (1 pen) [76 (pl), 87]	1293
36	18	A	Altrincham	W	1-0	0-0	20	Reid [47]	1435
37	22	H	Woking	W	1-0	0-0	18	Cesay [90]	1809
38	25	H	Aldershot T	L	1-3	1-0	19	Hutchinson [8]	1331
39	29	A	York C	L	0-3	0-1	21		6206
40	Apr 1	H	Boston U	W	1-0	1-0	19	Reid [20]	1405
41	5	H	Forest Green R	W	2-1	1-1	18	Reid 2 (1 pen) [45 (pl), 82]	1441
42	12	A	Barnet	D	1-1	0-1	20	Sohna [80]	3674
43	18	A	Boston U	L	0-2	0-2	20		3865
44	21	H	Maidenhead U	D	1-1	1-1	20	Cesay [39]	1975
45	26	A	Southend U	L	0-3	0-1	21		9677
46	May 5	H	FC Halifax T	W	3-1	3-0	20	Cook [4], Cesay [17], Carayol [25]	2843

Final League Position: 20

GOALSCORERS

League (56): Reid 16 (5 pens), Ashford 7 (1 pen), Cesay 6, Boldewijn 3, Grant 3, Kretzschmar 3, McFarlane 3, Obiero 3, Sohna 3, Cook 2, Carayol 1, Georgiou 1, Hutchinson 1, Sandat 1, Walker 1, own goals 2.
FA Cup (5): Reid 4 (1 pen), Kretzschmar 1.
FA Trophy (1): Cesay 1.

Matthews 9	Cook 35 + 1	Mariappa 33 + 4	Cesay 33 + 4	Dyer 21 + 11	Georgiou 26 + 8	Traore 3 + 4	Ashford 20 + 8	Obiero 21 + 14	Boldewijn 41 + 4	Sandal 6 + 8	Hutchinson 15 + 14	Kretzschmar 35 + 4	Miller — + 3	Woodman 9 + 3	Clarke — + 2	Scott 5 + 9	Mason 4 + 3	Dreher 2 + 1	Walker 7 + 1	McFarlane 6 + 2	Wells-Morrison 15 + 2	Barrett 9	Adams 2 + 2	Omole — + 3	Thorpe 4 + 6	Howes 8	Brown — + 1	Mundle-Smith 15 + 2	Reid 30	Eastmond 8 + 4	Adarkwa — + 2	Grant 17 + 7	Steward 6	Sekyere — + 4	Clark 1 + 1	Baptiste 7	Gunter 14	McAvoy 13 + 3	Sohna 13 + 5	Randall 8 + 3	Carayol 5 + 7	Match No.
1	2	3	4	5	6^1	7^3	8^2	9^4	10	11	12	13	14	15																												1
1	2	3	5^2	7^1	6		15	14	9	11	10	8^3				4^4	12	13■																								2
1	2	3	5^2	6^4	13	7^1		9	10	8	11	12	15	14		4^3																										3
1	2	4	3^2	7	6^1	15	10	11	12	14	8^4					9^3	5	13																								4
1	3	2	4	13	14	7^3	9	5	11^1	10	8^4	15				12		6^2																								5
1	2	3	4	6	7^5	16	15	11^1	9	8^2	10^4					5^3	14	12	13																							6
1	2	3	5^2		16	15	10^5	11	8	13	9^4		14	6^3	12^7	4■																										7
1	2	3		7			8^3	9	11^2	12	6	14		13		10	5^1	4																								8
1^4	2	3	5	7^5		13	10^2	16	15	9^3				6^1		11	8	4	12	14																						9
4^1	2	7^3	5^2	13	10^4	9		12			15					11	8	3	6	1	14																					10
3	2^4	12	13				5^2	10	9	14	15					8^3		11	7		6^1	1	4																			11
	2^8	13	5	15		6^4	10^3	9		14						16	12		11^5	8	3^2		7^1	1	4■																	12
3			5	13		9^2	10	6	14	12						4		11^1	8	2		7^3	1																			13
	3	5^4	6^5	14	16	11^3	7^1	15		9^2						8	2		12	1	4	10	13																			14
	3	14	7^3	13	6^2	11		12		15	9^1					8	2		1	4	10	5^4																				15
	3	13	7	12	6	11^3	15	14		9^5						8^2	16	2^1	1	4	10	5^4																				16
	3	2	7	15	6	11^4	9		5^2	4^3						8	12	13	1^1		10		14																			17
	3	2	7		6	11^1	15	5		9^2						8		1	14	4	10^3		12^4	13																		18
	4	2	8^2		7		11		3^1			6					9		1	13	5	10		12																			19
	3	2	8		5		11		6			7					9			4^1	10			12	1																	20
	4	2	8		5^2		10	11	6	14		7^3					9		13		12			3^1	1																	21
	3	2	8	14	5		11^2	13	6	15		7^4					9^3			4	10^1	12■			1																	22
	5^3	4	8		2		11	13	9^1			6^2	14				7			3	10	12■			1																	23
	2	4	6		3		11^1	10	7			9								5			8	1	12																	24
	2	12	6		5		11	10	7			9								3			8^2	1	13	4^1																25
	4	5	8^1		6		7		2			3								10	9		11^2		13	12	1															26
	4		6		3		11^3	13	7			14								5	10	8^2	12		7			1		2^1	9											27
	3		5		6		10^1	12	4			$9^■$								2	11		7				1			8												28
	4	5	10^3	14	3^2		13	8	12											11	6^1		7				1		2	9												29
	4		13	3			10^1	8^2	12	7										11	6		5				1		2	9												30
	4		8^2	3		13	10^4	15	9^1	7^3										11	6		5				1				2^4	8	16									31
13	4		12	3^1		15	11^2	14	7^3	10										9	6^5		5				1			8												32
	4	5		12	13	14	9^3	11	2^2	6										10	$7^■$		3				1				8^1										33
	3	13		7	6^3		10^2	15	5^4			9					14			11			2^1				1		4	8	12											34
	2	4^5		13		16	9^4	10	12	7								15		11			3				1		5^2	8^1	6^3	14										35
	5	12	16	9		15		7		2^1	8^2					10^3				11			4^4				1		13	6	3^5	14										36
	4	14	8			15		7		2	6^1					16	11^5			10			5^4				1		12	9^2	3^3	13										37
4^5	12	6^3	3^2			2		7^1	9^4	2	13	11^2					15			11				16			1		5			12	39									38
4		8	6^3	3			7^1	9	2	13	11^2						11			10							1		5				12	39								39
	8	6				7		9	2		11						10			1				5			3	4														40
	12	6	8	13^4		2		9	4		10						11			14			1				5^5	15	7^1	3^3												41
	3	7	6^3			12^5	4	2	8^1	5							11^2		16			10				15		1					13	9^4	14							42
	3	7	6			11^3	4	2^2	8^1	5^4										10			14				1				15	13	9^2	12	43						
	14	7	8^1			10		12	13	5										11			3				1			4	6^3	2^2	9								44
	4	2				13	11	12	8	5^2							14			10			7				1			6	9^2		3^1	45						
	4	5	7	9^1		12	11	6^2	8											10	13		3				1				14		2^3	46						

FA Cup

Fourth Qualifying	Gosport Bor	(h)	4-1
First Round	Grimsby T	(a)	1-0
Second Round	Wycombe W	(h)	0-2

FA Trophy

Third Round	Aldershot T	(a)	1-3

WOKING

Ground: The Laithwaite Community Stadium, Kingfield, Woking, Surrey GU22 9AA. *Tel:* (01483) 722 470.
Website: www.wokingfc.co.uk   *Email:* see website   *Year Formed:* 1887.   *Record Attendance:* 7,020 v Finchley,
FA Amateur Cup 4th rd, 22 February 1958.   *Nicknames:* 'The Cardinals', 'The Cards'.
Manager: Neal Ardley.   *Colours:* Red and white halved shirts with black and white trim, black shorts with white trim,
black socks with white trim.

WOKING – NATIONAL LEAGUE 2024–25 LEAGUE RECORD

Match No.	Date	Venue	Opponents	Result		H/T Score	Lg Pos.	Goalscorers	Attendance
1	Aug 10	A	Altrincham	L	0-1	0-1	19		1548
2	17	H	Gateshead	L	0-2	0-1	21		2099
3	20	H	Dagenham & Red	W	1-0	0-0	18	Kendall [80]	2103
4	24	A	Ebbsfleet U	W	3-0	1-0	9	Dyche [34], Kendall [78], Ward [90]	1575
5	26	H	Hartlepool U	W	3-2	0-2	4	Ward [68], Akinola [79], Beautyman [90]	2646
6	31	A	Rochdale	L	0-3	0-1	12		2315
7	Sept 7	A	Braintree T	D	0-0	0-0	12		1129
8	10	H	Wealdstone	W	1-0	1-0	8	Harries (pen) [31]	2125
9	14	H	Oldham Ath	L	1-3	0-1	13	Kendall [75]	2373
10	21	A	AFC Fylde	D	1-1	0-0	12	Walker [64]	1108
11	24	A	Eastleigh	D	2-2	1-1	12	Walker [39], Wynter [57]	1968
12	28	H	Sutton U	L	1-2	0-2	13	Leahy [74]	2076
13	Oct 5	H	York C	D	1-1	0-0	14	Moss [55]	2361
14	19	A	Tamworth	L	2-3	0-2	18	Dyche [47], Gorman [90]	1233
15	23	A	Solihull Moors	L	1-2	1-1	19	Beautyman [8]	1064
16	26	H	Forest Green R	D	1-1	0-1	18	Moss [52]	2280
17	Nov 9	A	FC Halifax T	L	0-1	0-1	19		1546
18	16	H	Boston U	W	1-0	1-0	17	Ward [38]	2394
19	23	A	Barnet	L	0-2	0-1	18		1500
20	26	H	Southend U	D	0-0	0-0	18		2424
21	30	H	Yeovil T	L	0-2	0-1	18		2911
22	Dec 14	A	Gateshead	L	0-4	0-3	19		845
23	21	H	Altrincham	W	2-1	0-0	17	Effiong [57], Anderson [82]	1848
24	26	A	Aldershot T	D	2-2	1-1	17	Beautyman (pen) [14], Vincent [50]	5412
25	Jan 1	H	Maidenhead U	W	3-1	1-1	17	Effiong 2 [4, 90], Beautyman (pen) [66]	1848
26	11	A	Yeovil T	D	1-1	0-1	17	O'Brien [74]	3188
27	18	A	Ebbsfleet U	D	1-1	0-0	17	Beautyman (pen) [64]	2048
28	25	A	Hartlepool U	D	1-1	0-0	17	Ferguson (og) [54]	3612
29	Feb 8	A	York C	L	0-3	0-1	18		5484
30	11	A	Dagenham & Red	W	2-1	1-0	16	Morias 2 [16, 52]	1335
31	15	H	Tamworth	D	1-1	0-0	16	Effiong (pen) [78]	2092
32	19	H	Solihull Moors	W	1-0	1-0	16	Ward [18]	1526
33	22	A	Forest Green R	D	1-1	0-0	16	Beautyman [69]	1728
34	Mar 4	A	Southend U	D	2-2	1-1	16	Okoli [5], Beautyman [68]	6133
35	8	A	Boston U	D	2-2	1-0	17	Beautyman [23], Effiong [76]	1787
36	15	H	Barnet	L	0-1	0-1	18		3281
37	22	A	Wealdstone	L	0-1	0-0	19		1809
38	25	H	FC Halifax T	D	0-0	0-0	18		1809
39	29	H	Braintree T	W	2-1	1-0	18	Beautyman (pen) [24], Akinola [48]	2102
40	Apr 1	H	Rochdale	D	1-1	0-1	18	Beautyman (pen) [87]	1853
41	8	A	Oldham Ath	W	2-1	0-1	17	Kelly-Evans [49], Walker [58]	5664
42	12	H	AFC Fylde	W	1-0	0-0	16	Gorman [76]	1976
43	18	H	Maidenhead U	D	2-2	0-1	16	Walker [62], O'Brien [66]	1976
44	21	H	Aldershot T	W	3-0	3-0	15	Hinds 2 [3, 18], Moss [13]	4701
45	26	H	Eastleigh	D	2-2	1-1	15	O'Brien [42], Andrews [86]	2711
46	May 5	A	Sutton U	D	1-1	1-0	15	Walker [6]	3270

Final League Position: 15

GOALSCORERS
League (52): Beautyman 10 (5 pens), Effiong 5 (1 pen), Walker 5, Ward 4, Kendall 3, Moss 3, O'Brien 3, Akinola 2, Dyche 2, Gorman 2, Hinds 2, Morias 2, Anderson 1, Andrews 1, Harries 1 (1 pen), Kelly-Evans 1, Leahy 1, Okoli 1, Vincent 1, Wynter 1, own goal 1.
FA Cup (2): Beautyman 2.
FA Trophy (13): Walker 4, Effiong 2, Leahy 2, Anderson 1, Beautyman 1, Lewis 1, O'Brien 1, Ward 1.

Jaaskelainen 43	Moss 25+2	Harries 24	Odusina 16+5	Kelly-Evans 25+4	Dyche 21	Gorman 32+4	Andrews 37+6	Lewis 10+8	Kendall 8+9	Moore 7+3	Beautyman 29+6	Anderson 13+13	Jones 8+3	Akinola 37+3	Ward 19+15	Walker 17+21	Smith —+1	Wynter 7+3	Conte 6+2	Leahy 4+9	Chicksen 25+1	Webber 3	Stretton 4+2	Judge 2+3	Vincent 8+5	Effiong 18+5	Ince —+1	O'Brien 7+2	Mazionis 6	Hinds 13+2	Okoli 16+1	Morias 3+4	Lawson 3+3	Ashford 7+1	Osude 2+6	Sayers 1	Match No.
1	2	3	4	5^1	6	7^8	8^3	9	10	11^2	12	13	14																								1
1	2	4	3^4	7^8	5		9^3		11^1		10	8^2	6	12	13	14	15																				2
1	2	4	3		5	8^1	9		12			10^3	14	6	7	13	11^2																				3
1	2	3	4^5		5	9	8^1	12	13	11^4	10^3	15	6^2	7	14				16																		4
1	2	4			5	8	9	12^5	14	16	10^3	15	6^4	7	13	11^2		3^1																			5
1	2	3	4^1	6^3	5^2	9	8			13	11^4	10	15		7	12	14																				6
1	2	5			6	8	9	11^1				3	7^2	13				4	10	12																	7
1	2	3		4	7		13			12	10^3	5	6	9^1	14	8	11^2																				8
1	2	3		4	7	12	14	15	8	13	5^4	6	10^2					9^3	11^1																		9
1	4	2		15	3	7	9		11^2		10^3	6^4		8^1	13	12			5	14																	10
1	5	2		7	4	6	8		11^2			13	10^1		3	9	12																				11
1	7	2		4	5	8		11^1	14		9^2	6	13	10^3				3^4	12	15																	12
1	7	4	3		8	12	13		10^3		6	14	11^1	5	9^2	2																					13
	8^3	3			5	6	9	7^2	11^1		10	15	13	12	4^4	14	2	1																			14
1	9^3	4		3	5	10	7	11^2	6^4	15	8^1	14	12	13	2																						15
1	9	4^1	16	3^4	5	14	10	7	13	11^3	6	8^2	12	15		2^5																					16
1	8		4	3^1	5	7	9	10^3	6^4	12	13	14	2	11^2	15																						17
1	5^1	3	12^4	14	4	6	9	15	7	8	13	11^2	11^2	10^3																							18
1	3	4^5	7	5	6^3	15	16	8^4	9	12	13	10^2	11^1	14																							19
1	4	3^4	5	15	10	11^3	8^1	13	7	9	14	2	12	6^2																							20
1	4^4	3	5	12	10^2	7	6^1	8^3	9	13	14	2	11^1	15																							21
1	3	5	12^2	7	13	8	9	14	2	6^1	4^3	11																									22
1	4	3	8	13	12	7	6^1	5	10	2	9^2	11																									23
1	3	5	6	13	8	9	4	10^1	2	12	7^2	11																									24
1	5	2	6	12	10	9^3	4	7	13	3	8^1	11^2	14																								25
1	5	2^2	6	7	10	9^3	4	13	12	3	8^1	11	14																								26
1			6	9^2	8	5	7	10^3	2^1	3	13	11	14	4	12																						27
1	12		6	13	9	10^1	7	3	8^2	11	4	2	5^8																								28
1	4		6	8^2	3	14	9	12	7^3	11^1	10	5	2	13																							29
1		4	6	9	12	10^1	14	9	12	13	7^1	5	2	4	8^3																						30
1		4	6	9	12	10^1	7	11	3	13	7^1	8^2	4																								31
1	15		8	9	14	13	5	7^3	12	3	6^1	11^4	2	4	10^2																						32
1	4	2^1	8	14	10^2	9	6	7^3	11^4	3	13	5	15^8	16	12^6																						33
1 14	4^2	2^1	8	10	12	9	6	3	11	7^3	5	13																									34
1 12		2	8	6	10	9	7^1	5	3	11	4																										35
1 7		2	8^2	6	10^1	9	14	5	13	3^3	11	4	12																								36
1 7^2	14	2	8	9^1	10	6^3	5	12	3	11	4	13																									37
1 9		2	8	10	13	6	5	12	7	4	3^1	11^2																									38
1 2	5		7	9	6	12	10	3	4	13	11^2	8^1																									39
1	5	7	12	9	6^1	4	14	15	10	3	8^4	11^3	13	2^2																							40
1	5	2	6^4	8	9^1	16	14	11^2	15	13	7^5	3	4	10^3	12																						41
1	5	2	6	9	8	10^2	11	7^1	3	4	13	12																									42
1	5	3	6	9	13	8^1	10	11	7	2	4	12^2																									43
1	2^5	14	6^3	8	12	5	15	11	3^2	13	9^1	7	4	10^4	16																						44
	4	8	3^2	6	7^3	11	1	13	9^1	2	5	14	10	12																							45
	2	12	8	5	7^1	11	1	13	14	3	4	6^2	10^3	9																							46

FA Cup

Fourth Qualifying	Slough T	(h)	2-1
First Round	Cambridge U	(h)	0-1

FA Trophy

Third Round	Havant & Waterlooville	(h)	3-3
(Woking won 4-2 on penalties)			
Fourth Round	Radcliffe	(h)	4-0
Fifth Round	Gainsborough Trinity	(a)	3-0
Quarter-Finals	Oxford C	(a)	2-2
(Woking won 2-1 on penalties)			
Semi-Finals	Aldershot T	(a)	1-2

YEOVIL TOWN

Ground: Huish Park Stadium, Lufton Way, Yeovil, Somerset BA22 8YF.   *Tel:* (01935) 423 662.
Website: www.ytfc.net   *Email:* see website.   *Year Formed:* 1895.   *Record Attendance:* 16,318 v Sunderland, FA Cup
4th rd, 29 January 1949 (at Huish); 9,527 v Leeds U, FL 1, 25 April 2008 (at Huish Park).   *Nickname:* 'The Glovers'.
Manager: Mark Cooper.   *Colours:* Green patterned shirts with dark green patterned stripes, white shorts with green
trim, green socks with white trim.

YEOVIL TOWN – NATIONAL LEAGUE 2024–25 LEAGUE RECORD

Match No.	Date	Venue	Opponents	Result	H/T Score	Lg Pos.	Goalscorers	Attendance
1	Aug 10	H	Hartlepool U	L 0-1	0-0	19		3646
2	17	A	Braintree T	W 1-0	0-0	14	Williams [60]	1128
3	20	H	Ebbsfleet U	W 3-2	2-0	7	McGavin [25], Smith [40], Greenslade [81]	3295
4	24	A	Gateshead	L 1-3	1-2	10	Jarvis [29]	1096
5	26	H	Rochdale	L 0-1	0-0	15		3686
6	31	A	Boston U	W 3-1	2-1	11	McGavin 2 [7, 37], Young [75]	1956
7	Sept 7	A	AFC Fylde	W 4-3	0-2	7	Pearson [65], Jarvis [69], Lo-Everton [79], Bernard [87]	1305
8	10	H	Solihull Moors	L 0-1	0-1	9		2849
9	14	H	Altrincham	D 0-0	0-0	12		2838
10	21	A	Oldham Ath	L 0-1	0-0	16		511
11	24	A	Sutton U	D 0-0	0-0	14		2246
12	28	H	Aldershot T	D 1-1	0-1	12	McGuckin [57]	3408
13	Oct 5	H	Dagenham & Red	W 1-0	0-0	10	McGuckin [55]	2998
14	19	A	Wealdstone	W 3-0	1-0	8	McGavin [26], Jarvis [52], McGuckin [58]	1510
15	22	A	Tamworth	D 0-0	0-0	8		1068
16	26	H	Maidenhead U	W 3-1	1-1	7	Jarvis 2 [10, 52], Cooper [63]	3333
17	Nov 9	A	Southend U	W 1-0	0-0	7	Plant [65]	6911
18	16	H	FC Halifax T	L 0-1	0-0	8		3829
19	23	A	York C	L 0-4	0-2	9		5642
20	27	H	Barnet	L 1-2	0-1	13	Plant [73]	2722
21	30	A	Woking	W 2-0	1-0	8	McGavin [31], Cousin-Dawson [79]	2911
22	Dec 14	H	Braintree T	W 3-1	1-1	7	Jarvis [27], James [62], McGavin [90]	2767
23	21	A	Hartlepool U	L 1-2	0-0	10	Shaw [80]	3420
24	26	H	Eastleigh	D 2-2	0-0	10	McGurk [47], Williams [89]	4355
25	Jan 1	A	Forest Green R	L 1-2	1-0	11	Shaw [38]	3002
26	11	H	Woking	D 1-1	1-0	9	Jarvis [45]	3188
27	14	A	Ebbsfleet U	D 1-1	1-0	11	McGurk [38]	1125
28	17	H	Gateshead	D 0-0	0-0	11		2919
29	25	A	Rochdale	L 0-4	0-0	13		2463
30	Feb 8	A	Dagenham & Red	D 1-1	1-1	13	McGavin [39]	1703
31	15	H	Wealdstone	L 1-2	1-1	14	Cousin-Dawson [45]	3179
32	18	H	Tamworth	W 2-1	0-1	13	Cooper [49], Nouble [59]	2649
33	22	A	Maidenhead U	W 2-0	1-0	11	De Havilland (og) [38], Greenslade [83]	1330
34	Mar 1	H	Southend U	D 2-2	2-1	11	Wilson [13], Nouble [18]	3508
35	4	A	Barnet	L 0-5	0-3	12		1596
36	8	A	FC Halifax T	L 0-1	0-1	14		1688
37	11	H	Boston U	L 0-3	0-2	14		2138
38	15	H	York C	L 0-1	0-0	15		2862
39	22	A	Solihull Moors	W 3-0	1-0	14	Sims [28], McGuckin [50], Whittle [56]	1495
40	29	H	AFC Fylde	W 1-0	0-0	13	Greenslade [90]	2734
41	Apr 5	A	Altrincham	L 1-2	1-1	15	Terry [32]	1851
42	12	H	Oldham Ath	W 2-1	1-0	13	Lo-Everton 2 [10, 49]	3373
43	18	H	Forest Green R	D 1-1	1-0	13	Lo-Everton [24]	4092
44	21	A	Eastleigh	L 0-1	0-1	16		2657
45	26	H	Sutton U	L 1-2	1-0	16	McGuckin [30]	3566
46	May 5	A	Aldershot T	L 1-2	0-1	18	Bernard [60]	3089

Final League Position: 18

GOALSCORERS

League (51): Jarvis 7, McGavin 7, McGuckin 5, Lo-Everton 4, Greenslade 3, Bernard 2, Cooper 2, Cousin-Dawson 2,
McGurk 2, Nouble 2, Plant 2, Shaw 2, Williams 2, James 1, Pearson 1, Sims 1, Smith 1, Terry 1, Whittle 1, Wilson 1,
Young 1, own goal 1.
FA Cup (0).
FA Trophy (1): Jarvis 1.

Wright 29	Whittle 33+1	Williams 25+3	Smith 22+5	Wannell 31+2	Worthington 16+5	Jarvis 24+3	McGavin 35+4	Morgan 5+6	Nouble 25+11	Young 6+8	Greenslade 7+20	Thomas 1+4	Lo-Everton 19+10	Pearson 5+7	Sims 17+20	Cooper 36+5	Araoye 2+3	Cousin-Dawson 28+9	Bernard 24+7	McGuckin 20+6	Plant 12+1	Shaw 10+6	Borges 6+2	James 2	McGurk 7+3	Maddox 2+3	Twamley 1+8	Wilson 10+5	Stone 17	McLean 2+5	Lavinier 4+4	Terry 10	Clarke —+1	Ferguson 4	Khan 4+1	Koerner —+1	Kite 5+2	Match No.
1	2	3	4[1]	5	6	7	8[4]	9[2]	10[3]	11	12	13	14	15																								1
1	2[5]	3	4	5	6	7[3]	8[1]		9	10[4]	11[2]	16	12	13	14	15																						2
1	2[5]	3	5	4		7	8[2]	9[1]	10				16	14	15	6[3]		11[4]	12	13																		3
1		3	5[5]	4		7	8[2]	9[4]	13	12	11[3]				2	14	6	10[1]	15	16																		4
1	2[3]	5[2]	6	14		7	8	10	9[1]	13	15		12	11[5]	3[4]	4	16																					5
1			4	6[8]	7		8[2]	9	10	13	14[4]	15	12	11[1]	5	3[3]	2																					6
1	5		4			7	8	9[3]	10	13			14	12	11[2]	3	6[1]	2																				7
1	3	13	4[3]	7	8	9	10[2]		11	12				15	6[1]	14	5		2[4]																			8
1	2	3	4[4]		6	8	9	13	12	14		10[2]	7[3]	11[1]	5	15																						9
1	3	5	2[3]	4	8	11[2]	13		7	15		10[1]	9[4]		6	12	14																					10
1	2[4]	4		3	13	11[3]	9		7	8[1]			15	12		6		14	5	10[2]																		11
1	2[4]	4		3	14	13	9[2]	11	7	8[3]				15		6			5	10[1]	12																	12
1		4	2[3]	3	14		9	10[2]	7	8[4]					15	6	13		12	11[1]	5																	13
1	13	4		2	3[2]	11[4]	8[1]	10[5]	12	15			14			7		16	5	9[3]	6																	14
1	3[8]		2		7[1]	11[2]	8	10[3]	14	12[4]						6		15	4	9	5	13																15
1	2[4]		3			11[3]	9	15	8				14		13	12	7	5	4		6[1]	10[2]																16
1	2		3				13	12	8				11[3]	14	9[1]		7	4			6	10[2]	5															17
1	2	13	3[8]			11	8		7[1]					9[2]		12		4			6	10	5															18
1	3	8	7[4]			11[3]	9		16				14		15	13	2[2]		4[4]	12[8]	6	10[5]	5[1]															19
1	2	3	6			10[1]	7[3]	15	9				13			14	5				8[4]	12	11[2]	4														20
1	2	3				14	11[2]	8[3]	13	7[4]			15			12	6		4		5	10[1]	9															21
1	4[1]	2	3			7[2]	10	11	15	12						16	6	13	14				9[3]	8[4]	5[5]													22
1	3	7[1]	2			8[3]	11	9	10							12	6	5	4[2]				13	14														23
1	3	13	4			6	11	9	12							5[2]	7	2					10[1]	14	8[3]													24
1	3	13	2			5	9	8								6[2]	7	12	4				10[8]		11[1]													25
1		12	2			10	8		5[3]				14			11	7	3	4	9[1]				6[2]	13													26
1		4		2		11[2]	7[1]		13	15						12	8	3	5	10				6[3]		9[4]	14											27
1	9			4	3[2]		7[4]	15								11[3]	8	5	2	10				14		6[1]	13	12										28
1	3[2]	13		5			7	14								12	6[5]	4	2[1]	10		16			9[4]	8[3]	15	11										29
	3	4	2	5			6	9								12			13	8[1]	7[3]					14	10[2]		11	1								30
	3			4			6	15		14				7[2]			5	2[3]	11[1]	8	12					10[4]		13	9	1								31
	3		2	5			8	9	13		6[1]		14	7			4			12	11[2]					10[3]	1			1								32
	3		2	5			8[1]	9	12	6			13	7			5	4	11[1]							10[2]				1								33
	3		2				8	9	12	6			13	7			5	4	11[1]							10[2]				1								34
	3		2[3]				8	9	10[1]	6[4]			12	7			5	4				13		14	11[2]	1	15											35
	3						6	11					9[4]	15	8		5	14	12					13[5]	16	10[2]	1	7[3]	2[1]	4								36
	6						8[2]		14	9			12	5			4		11[1]					10		1	7[3]	2	3	13								37
	3[4]						6[3]	11					15	9			10[2]	8			5	2	12				14	1	13	7[1]		4						38
	3												12	6			8[1]	6			5	4	10[4]				15		1	13		2		7	11[3]	14		39
	3[4]												13	6			11[2]	7			8	2[3]	10					1	12	15	5		4	9[1]			14	40
	3[1]		14										15	9			7[5]	8[3]			6	2	11[2]					1	13	16	5		4	10[4]			12	41
	3	12	2[3]	6									13	10[2]			7[1]				4	8	11[4]					14	1		15	5					9	42
	3	4[2]											7				10[1]	12			6	2	11[4]					15	1		13	5			14		8[3]	43
		4	2[3]										11[2]	3			13	14			6		12					15	8	1	10[1]	5			9[8]		7[4]	44
	3[2]	4		12		13							7[1]	9			14	10			8	2[5]	11[3]					16	15	1			5				6[4]	45
	6		4	16	5					12	15			8				9			14	2[3]	10[2]					10[5]	13	1			3[1]				7[4]	46

FA Cup   Fourth Qualifying   Chesham U   (a)   0-1

FA Trophy   Third Round   Weymouth   (h)   1-2

YORK CITY

Ground: LNER Community Stadium, Kathryn Av, Monks Cross Dr, Huntington, York YO32 9AF. *Tel:* (01904) 624 447.
Website: www.yorkcityfootballclub.co.uk *Email:* enquiries@yorkcityfootballclub.co.uk *Year Formed:* 1922. *Record Attendance:* 28,123 v Huddersfield T, FA Cup 6th rd, 5 March 1938 (at Bootham Crescent); 8,153 v Oldham Ath, National League play-off semi-final, 20 May 2025 (at LNER Community Stadium). *Nickname:* 'Minstermen'. *Manager:* Adam Hinshelwood. *Colours:* Red shirts with white pinstripe and navy blue and white trim, navy blue shorts, white socks.

YORK CITY – NATIONAL LEAGUE 2024–25 LEAGUE RECORD

Match No.	Date	Venue	Opponents	Result	H/T Score	Lg Pos.	Goalscorers	Attendance
1	Aug 10	A	Southend U	D	1-1	0-1	12	John-Lewis [84]	7962
2	17	H	Tamworth	W	2-0	0-0	7	Pearce (pen) [54], Chadwick [56]	4684
3	20	H	Rochdale	W	1-0	1-0	5	Aguiar [4]	5362
4	24	A	Sutton U	D	2-2	0-0	5	Armstrong [47], John-Lewis [85]	2624
5	26	H	Boston U	L	0-2	0-0	9		5893
6	31	A	Dagenham & Red	W	2-0	0-0	6	John-Lewis [80], Pearce [90]	1543
7	Sept 7	A	Wealdstone	W	2-0	1-0	5	Nathaniel-George [12], Pearce [52]	1904
8	10	H	Braintree T	W	2-1	2-1	4	Aguiar [17], Nathaniel-George [42]	4494
9	14	H	AFC Fylde	W	3-0	0-0	1	Armstrong [50], John-Lewis [70], Harriott [90]	5038
10	21	A	Aldershot T	D	0-0	0-0	3		2567
11	24	A	Solihull Moors	W	3-0	1-0	2	Nathaniel-George [42], Sinclair 2 [81, 84]	1515
12	28	H	Eastleigh	D	0-0	0-0	2		5671
13	Oct 5	A	Woking	D	1-1	1-0	3	John-Lewis (pen) [82]	2361
14	19	H	Ebbsfleet U	W	4-0	1-0	3	Pearce 2 [41, 86], Sinclair [73], Thomas [90]	5716
15	22	H	Barnet	W	3-1	1-1	2	Armstrong [45], Hunt [74], Pearce [76]	6041
16	26	A	FC Halifax T	W	2-1	0-1	1	Walcott [90], Pearce [90]	3961
17	Nov 9	H	Hartlepool U	W	5-3	2-0	1	Pearce 2 (1 pen) [18, 90 (p)], Hunt [43], Nathaniel-George [67], Akinyemi [85]	7654
18	16	A	Forest Green R	L	0-2	0-0	2		2697
19	23	H	Yeovil T	W	4-0	2-0	1	Pearce 3 [11, 63, 71], Sinclair [45]	5642
20	26	A	Altrincham	L	0-3	0-3	2		2006
21	30	H	Maidenhead U	W	6-2	4-1	1	Pearce 2 (1 pen) [15, 25 (p)], Sinclair [28], Nathaniel-George [32], Crookes [71], Thomas [84]	5442
22	Dec 14	A	Tamworth	D	1-1	1-0	2	Pearce [17]	1739
23	21	H	Southend U	W	3-0	0-0	1	Akinyemi [64], Howe [68], Ajiboye [76]	6446
24	Jan 1	H	Gateshead	W	1-0	1-0	1	Armstrong [22]	7554
25	18	H	Sutton U	L	1-2	0-2	3	Akinyemi [83]	6369
26	21	A	Oldham Ath	W	2-0	2-0	2	Walcott [24], Pearce [38]	8234
27	25	A	Boston U	L	1-3	1-1	3	Sinclair [7]	2362
28	Feb 1	H	Dagenham & Red	W	2-1	1-0	2	Sinclair [43], Hunt (pen) [90]	5331
29	8	H	Woking	W	3-0	1-0	3	Stones 3 [5, 72, 80]	5484
30	15	A	Ebbsfleet U	W	2-0	0-0	2	Pearce 2 (1 pen) [65 (p), 76]	1745
31	18	A	Barnet	L	1-3	0-1	2	Walcott [90]	4050
32	22	H	FC Halifax T	D	2-2	1-2	2	Pearce (pen) [15], Howe [90]	6926
33	25	A	Maidenhead U	W	3-1	1-0	2	Pearce 2 [42, 90], Stones [90]	1075
34	Mar 1	A	Hartlepool U	W	1-0	1-0	2	Pearce [40]	775
35	4	A	Altrincham	L	1-2	0-1	2	Hunt [49]	6365
36	8	H	Forest Green R	D	1-1	0-0	2	Richardson [48]	6810
37	15	A	Yeovil T	W	1-0	0-0	2	Pearce (pen) [56]	2862
38	22	A	Braintree T	L	1-2	1-1	2	Stones [35]	1137
39	25	A	Rochdale	W	4-0	1-0	2	Pearce 2 [23, 69], Richardson [62], Fallowfield [75]	2707
40	29	H	Wealdstone	W	3-0	1-0	2	Walcott [45], Stones [64], Pearce (pen) [67]	6206
41	Apr 5	A	AFC Fylde	W	3-1	1-0	2	Pearce (pen) [45], Felix [74], Walcott [78]	1977
42	12	H	Aldershot T	W	7-2	4-2	2	Pearce 3 [3, 45, 84], Richardson 2 [9, 17], Stones [70], Howe [75]	5872
43	18	A	Gateshead	W	3-1	1-1	2	Nathaniel-George [36], Luamba [74], Walcott [85]	3014
44	21	H	Oldham Ath	D	1-1	0-0	2	Felix [31]	7918
45	26	H	Solihull Moors	W	2-0	1-0	2	John [3], Akinyemi [90]	6249
46	May 5	A	Eastleigh	W	2-0	2-0	2	Pearce [16], John [21]	2914

Final League Position: 2

GOALSCORERS

League (95): Pearce 31 (8 pens), Sinclair 7, Stones 7, Nathaniel-George 6, Walcott 6, John-Lewis 5 (1 pen), Akinyemi 4, Armstrong 4, Hunt 4 (1 pen), Richardson 4, Howe 3, Aguiar 2, Felix 2, John 2, Thomas 2, Ajiboye 1, Chadwick 1, Crookes 1, Fallowfield 1, Harriott 1, Luamba 1.
FA Cup (5): Pearce 2, Akinyemi 1, Felix 1, Sinclair 1.
FA Trophy (3): Ajiboye 1, Aguiar 1, Sinclair 1.
National League Play-offs (0).

Male 41	Howe 46	John 27 + 5	Felix 45 + 1	Fallowfield 19 + 8	Hunt 42 + 3	Armstrong 30 + 9	Batty 32 + 9	Chadwick 8 + 12	Akinyemi 11 + 14	Pearce 44 + 1	Aguiar 18 + 12	Sinclair 32 + 13	John-Lewis — + 33	Nathaniel-George 24 + 12	McLaughlin — + 6	O'Connor 2 + 2	Watson 5 + 2	Fagan-Walcott 2 + 1	Harriott 2 + 4	Walcott 36	Fadera — + 5	Thomas 2 + 7	Ajiboye 5 + 2	Crookes 7 + 6	King 3 + 7	Stones 8 + 13	Grumley — + 1	Richardson 10 + 4	Luamba 5 + 12	Match No.
1	2	3	4	5	6	7^3	8		9^2	10^4	11^1	12	13	14	15															1
1	3	4	2	5	7^1	15	8	9	11^4	10^3	6^2	12	13	14																2
1	3	4^1	5	2	8^4	15	10	7	14	11^5	6^3	9^2	12			16	13													3
	3	13	4	5	6^3	8^4	9	12	11^5	10	15	14	16	7^2		2^1	1													4
1	5	4	3	2	7^4	15	8	9^1	14	11	10^1	6^3	12	13																5
1	2	3	4	5^2	7^3	9	10	15	11^1	16	13	6^5	12	8^4	14															6
	3	4	5	7^1	9	10	14	11^4	6^2	13	8^5	15				2^3	1	12	16											7
1	4	5	2	13	8	10	7^1	11	6^3	14	12	9^2				3														8
1	2	3	5	7	9^4	15	13	11^1	10^5	6^2	12	8^1	16	4	14															9
	2	13	4	3	7^2	10	12	11^4	8^1	9^3	15	6^5	16				1			5	14									10
1	2	4	5	3	13	11^4	9^1	6^2	10^5	15	12	14		7^3						8	16									11
1	2	6	5	3^5	12	10^2	13	9^4	4	11^1	16	8^3								15	7									12
1	2	15	8	3^3	9^4	13	4	7	11^2	10^5	12	14								6^1	5	16								13
1	2	4	7	3	8	5^1	6^3	11	9^2	10^4	14									13	15	12								14
1	2	3	4	13	9	10^2	8	7^1	11^4	12	15									6^3	5	14								15
1	2	6	3^4	7	9^1	4	13	11	14	8^2	12									5		15	10^3							16
1	2	3	4	13	8	6^3	14	11	9^1	10^5	15									5^4	16	7^2		12						17
1	2	3^3	4	10	13	7^1	6^4	11	15	14	8^2									5					9	12				18
1	2	3	15	7	10^3	16	12	11^2	8^1	9^5	14									5^4	13	6	4							19
	2	4	3	8	12	11	9^1	13	6^2								1			5	10^3	7	14							20
1	2	6^4	7^1	11^5	5	13	9	14	8^3	10^2										4	16	12	3		15					21
1	2	6	13	7	11^2	5	12	9	3^1	8	10^3									4	14									22
1	2	3	8	10^3	6^4	12	11^2	4	9^5	14	7^1									5	16	13	15							23
1	5	2	15	6	9	8^1	10^4	11	3^2	13	14	12								4		7^3								24
1	4^4	12	2	6	9^3	8^2	10	7	3^5	14	15	13								5					16	11^1				25
1	4	11	2	6	9^1	8^3	13	7^2	14	3^5	15	10^4								5					12	16				26
1^1	5	3^9	2	8	14	15	7^2	9	6^4	10	16	13		12						4					11^3					27
1	5	3	2^5	6	9^3	8	11	10^2	7^1											4					12	13		14		28
1	5	3	2^5	6	9^4	8	12	10^3	14	7^1										4				16	11^2			15	13	29
1	5	3^2	2	14	6	9^4	8	11	10^1	12	7^2									4					13			15		30
1	5	3	2	6	9	8^1	11	10^2	13	7^3										4					12			14		31
1	5	3	6	2^3	8^2	14	15	11	10^1	16	13									4					12	9^4	7^5			32
	5	6	8^1	2	11	7	10	12									1			4					3	9				33
1	5	6	14	7^2	15	3^9	16	11	9^3	10^1	13									4					2	8^4		12		34
1	5	3	2	6	8^3	7^2	9	11^1	12											4					13	10		14		35
1	4	12	3	8^2	16	6	11	14	15	10^1										5				2^3	13			9^4	7^5	36
1	4	2^2	9	14	6^5	5	16	11	12	15										3				13	10^1			7^3	8^4	37
1	5	2	12	8^1	6^2	15	11	16	9^5	13	14									4				3^4	10			7^3		38
1	5	3	7^1	2	6	8^4	16	12	9^2	11^3	14									4					15	10^5		13		39
1	5	7	2	6^4	8^1	16	15	13	9	11^3										4				3^2	12	10^5		14		40
1	3	2^4	7	5	8^2	6^1	15	9	16	11^3										4					14	13		12	10^6	41
1	3	2^1	7	6	8^5	13	9	5^4	16	11										4^3					14	12		10^2	15	42
1	5	3^9	8	6^4	9^{15}	11	2^2	16	10											4					13	12		7^3	14	43
1	5	2	6	9^2	8^1	11	14	15	10^4											4					3	13		12	7^3	44
1	4	3	8^4	6	13	15	11	10^3	16	9^1										2^5					5	12		7^2	14	45
1^1	4	3	8	6	14	12	11^4	10^2	9	13										2^5					5	16		7^3	15	46

FA Cup

Fourth Qualifying	Biggleswade	(a)	3-1
First Round	Wycombe W	(a)	2-3

FA Trophy

Third Round	Darlington	(h)	3-1
Fourth Round	Gainsborough Trinity	(a)	0-1

National League Play-offs

Semi-Finals	Southend U	(h)	0-3

SCOTTISH LEAGUE TABLES 2024–25

(P) *Promoted into division at end of 2023–24 season.*   (R) *Relegated into division at end of 2023–24 season.*

WILLIAM HILL PREMIERSHIP 2024–25

			Home				Away					Total						
		P	W	D	L	F	A	W	D	L	F	A	W	D	L	F	A	GD	Pts
1	Celtic[1]	38	16	2	1	62	9	13	3	3	50	17	29	5	4	112	26	86	92
2	Rangers[2]	38	14	2	3	44	12	8	7	4	36	29	22	9	7	80	41	39	75
3	Hibernian[3]	38	10	6	3	39	23	5	7	7	23	27	15	13	10	62	50	12	58
4	Dundee U (P)[4]	38	8	3	8	23	27	7	5	7	22	27	15	8	15	45	54	–9	53
5	Aberdeen[5]	38	10	4	5	31	26	5	4	10	17	35	15	8	15	48	61	–13	53
6	St Mirren	38	8	5	7	30	27	6	3	9	23	32	14	8	16	53	59	–6	50
7	Hearts	38	9	3	7	28	21	6	4	9	24	26	15	7	16	52	47	5	52
8	Motherwell	38	8	5	5	27	27	6	2	12	19	36	14	7	17	46	63	–17	49
9	Kilmarnock	38	9	5	5	27	20	9	3	13	18	44	18	8	18	45	64	–19	44
10	Dundee	38	5	5	9	34	39	6	3	10	23	38	11	8	19	57	77	–20	41
11	Ross Co®	38	5	6	8	22	28	4	4	11	15	37	9	10	19	37	65	–28	37
12	St Johnstone	38	6	2	11	19	30	3	3	13	19	38	9	5	24	38	68	–30	32

Top 6 split after 33 games, teams in the bottom 6 cannot pass teams in the top 6 after the split. [1]*Celtic qualify for UEFA Champions League play-off round.* [2]*Rangers qualify for UEFA Champions League second qualifying round.* [3]*Hibernian qualify for UEFA Europa League play-off round.* [4]*Dundee U qualify for UEFA Conference League second qualifying round.* [5]*Aberdeen qualify for UEFA Europa League second qualifying round.* ®*Ross Co relegated after Premiership play-offs: Ross Co v Livingston (3-5 on aggregate).*

WILLIAM HILL PREMIERSHIP LEADING GOALSCORERS 2024–25 (LEAGUE ONLY)

Player (Club)	Goals	Player (Club)	Goals
Cyril Dessers (Rangers)	18	Luke McCowan (Celtic)	8
Daizen Maeda (Celtic)	16	*Includes 2 goals for Dundee.*	
Simon Murray (Dundee)	16	Callum McGregor (Celtic)	8
Martin Boyle (Hibernian)	15	Toyosi Olusanya (St Mirren)	8
Sam Dalby (Dundee U)	15	Lawrence Shankland (Hearts)	8
Adam Idah (Celtic)	13	Mikael Mandron (St Mirren)	7
Nikolas Kuhn (Celtic)	13	Kieran Bowie (Hibernian)	6
Vaclav Cerny (Rangers)	12	Nicky Clark (St Johnstone)	6
On loan from VfL Wolfsburg.		Dwight Gayle (Hibernian)	6
Ronan Hale (Ross Co)	12	Pape Habib Gueye (Aberdeen)	6
Hamza Igamane (Rangers)	12	Elton Kabangu (Hearts)	6
Bruce Anderson (Kilmarnock)	11	*On loan from Union Saint-Gilloise.*	
Kevin Nisbet (Aberdeen)	11	Mykola Kukharevych (Hibernian)	6
On loan from Millwall.		Benjamin Mbunga-Kimpioka (St Johnstone)	6
Kyogo Furuhashi (Celtic)	10	Tawanda Maswanhise (Motherwell)	6
Reo Hatate (Celtic)	10	Callum Slattery (Motherwell)	6
Lyall Cameron (Dundee)	9	Tom Sparrow (Motherwell)	6
Arne Engels (Celtic)	9	Scott Tiffoney (Dundee)	6
Mackenzie Kirk (St Johnstone)	8	Jordan White (Ross Co)	6

WILLIAM HILL CHAMPIONSHIP 2024–25

			Home					Away					Total						
		P	W	D	L	F	A	W	D	L	F	A	W	D	L	F	A	GD	Pts
1	Falkirk (P)	36	13	3	2	40	13	9	4	5	32	20	22	7	7	72	33	39	73
2	Livingston¶ (R)	36	12	4	2	31	9	8	6	4	24	18	20	10	6	55	27	28	70
3	Ayr U	36	11	5	2	39	17	7	4	7	18	22	18	9	9	57	39	18	63
4	Partick Thistle	36	8	8	2	26	16	7	2	9	17	22	15	10	11	43	38	5	55
5	Raith R	36	10	4	4	25	17	5	4	9	22	26	15	8	13	47	43	4	53
6	Greenock Morton	36	8	5	5	25	18	4	7	7	17	30	12	12	12	42	48	–6	48
7	Dunfermline Ath	36	7	6	5	20	16	2	2	14	8	27	9	8	19	28	43	–15	35
8	Queen's Park	36	5	2	11	16	31	4	6	8	20	24	9	8	19	36	55	–19	35
9	Airdrieonians‡	36	6	3	9	17	28	1	5	12	17	34	7	8	21	34	62	–28	29
10	Hamilton A* (P)	36	6	3	9	18	30	4	3	11	20	34	10	6	20	38	64	–26	21

Hamilton A deducted 15 points for breaking multiple SPFL rules. ¶*Livingston promoted after Premiership play-offs.* ‡*Airdrieonians not relegated after Championship play-offs.*

WILLIAM HILL CHAMPIONSHIP LEADING GOALSCORERS 2024–25 (LEAGUE ONLY)

Player (Club)	Goals	Player (Club)	Goals
Brian Graham (Partick Thistle)	15	Logan Chalmers (Partick Thistle)	7
Dylan Easton (Raith R)	13	Jay Henderson (Ayr U)	7
Robbie Muirhead (Livingston)	13	Christopher Mochrie (Airdrieonians)	7
George Oakley (Ayr U)	13	Liam Henderson (Falkirk)	6
Christopher Kane (Dunfermline Ath)	11	Stephen Kelly (Livingston)	6
Oliver Shaw (Hamilton A)	11	Curtis Main (Ayr U)	6
Calvin Miller (Falkirk)	10	*Includes 2 goals in Premiership for Dundee.*	
Scott Arfield (Falkirk)	9	Finlay Pollock (Raith R)	6
Zak Rudden (Queen's Park)	9	*On loan from Hearts.*	
Ben Wilson (Airdrieonians)	8	Scott Robinson (Hamilton A)	6
Ethan Ross (Falkirk)	8	*Includes 3 goals for Partick Thistle.*	
Brad Spencer (Falkirk)	8	Jack Turner (Queen's Park)	6

WILLIAM HILL LEAGUE ONE 2024–25

		Home					Away					Total						
		P	W	D	L	F	A	W	D	L	F	A	W	D	L	F	A	GD	Pts
1	Arbroath (R)	36	11	4	3	28	14	8	3	7	30	28	19	7	10	58	42	16	64
2	Cove Rangers‡	36	7	6	5	24	24	9	3	6	38	20	16	9	11	62	44	18	57
3	Queen of the South	36	13	2	3	32	21	3	5	10	14	20	16	7	13	46	41	5	55
4	Stenhousemuir (P)	36	9	4	5	28	22	6	4	8	20	23	15	8	13	48	45	3	53
5	Alloa Ath	36	7	4	7	26	23	6	8	4	29	24	13	12	11	55	47	8	51
6	Kelty Hearts	36	6	4	8	18	28	5	7	6	22	18	11	11	14	40	46	–6	44
7	Inverness CT* (R)	36	7	7	4	20	16	9	3	6	25	22	16	10	10	45	38	7	43
8	Montrose	36	4	7	7	22	28	5	6	7	18	21	9	13	14	40	49	–9	40
9	Annan Ath®	36	6	4	8	22	30	4	2	12	19	38	10	6	20	41	68	–27	36
10	Dumbarton* (P)	36	4	5	9	25	35	4	2	8	26	31	8	11	17	51	66	–15	20

Inverness CT and Dumbarton deducted 15 points for entering administration. ‡Cove Rangers not promoted after Championship play-offs. ®Annan Ath relegated after League One play-offs.

WILLIAM HILL LEAGUE ONE LEADING GOALSCORERS 2024–25 (LEAGUE ONLY)

Player (Club)	Goals
Jordan Allan (Queen of the South)	13
On loan from Falkirk. Includes 8 goals in League Two for Clyde (also on loan from Falkirk).	
Ross Cunningham (Kelty Hearts)	13
Mitchell Megginson (Cove Rangers)	13
Adam Emslie (Cove Rangers)	12
Keith Bray (Inverness CT)	10
Adam Brooks (Queen of the South)	10
Tommy Muir (Annan Ath)	10
Luke Rankin (Alloa Ath)	10
Owen Stirton (Montrose)	10
On loan from Dundee U. Includes 1 league goal in Premiership for Dundee U.	
Scott Williamson (Kelty Hearts)	10
On loan from Queen's Park. Includes 3 goals in League Two for Clyde.	
Blair Alston (Stenhousemuir)	9
Luke Donnelly (Alloa Ath)	9
Corey O'Donnell (Stenhousemuir)	9
Michael Ruth (Dumbarton)	9

Player (Club)	Goals
Alfie Bayidge (Inverness CT)	8
On loan from Aberdeen. Includes 2 goals in Championship for Ayr U (also on loan from Aberdeen).	
Ryan Dow (Arbroath)	8
Findlay Marshall (Cove Rangers)	8
On loan from Aberdeen.	
Carlo Pignatiello (Dumbarton)	8
Fraser Fyvie (Cove Rangers)	7
Kane Hester (Montrose)	7
Includes 2 goals in League Two for Elgin C.	
Blair Lyons (Montrose)	7
Gavin Reilly (Arbroath)	7
Connor Sammon (Alloa Ath)	7
Andrew Winter (Arbroath)	7
On loan from Livingston. Includes 1 goal in Championship for Livingston.	
James Hilton (Dumbarton)	6
Steven Scoughall (Alloa Ath)	6
Fraser Taylor (Arbroath)	6
On loan from St Mirren.	
Matt Yates (Stenhousemuir)	6

WILLIAM HILL LEAGUE TWO 2024–25

		Home					Away					Total						
		P	W	D	L	F	A	W	D	L	F	A	W	D	L	F	A	GD	Pts
1	Peterhead	36	13	3	2	33	16	6	6	6	19	25	19	9	8	52	40	12	66
2	East Fife¶	36	13	3	2	42	14	7	2	9	23	23	20	5	11	65	37	28	65
3	Edinburgh C (R)	36	10	2	6	32	22	7	3	8	22	25	17	5	14	54	47	7	56
4	Elgin C	36	11	2	5	35	21	5	5	8	13	20	16	7	13	48	41	7	55
5	The Spartans	36	10	3	5	25	16	5	4	9	23	31	15	7	14	48	47	1	52
6	Stirling Alb (R)	36	9	1	8	27	29	5	5	8	23	28	14	6	16	50	57	–7	48
7	Clyde	36	8	6	4	28	18	3	4	11	21	36	11	10	15	49	54	–5	43
8	Stranraer	36	5	6	7	17	17	6	1	11	17	25	11	7	18	34	42	–8	40
9	Forfar Ath	36	3	8	7	13	20	5	4	9	16	22	8	12	16	29	42	–13	36
10	Bonnyrigg Rose*®	36	8	3	7	24	21	4	3	11	16	41	12	6	18	40	62	–22	36

Bonnyrigg Rose deducted 6 points for breaching SPFL rules. ¶East Fife promoted after League One play-offs. ®Bonnyrigg Rose relegated to Lowland League after Pyramid play-offs. East Kilbride promoted from Lowland League to William Hill League Two for 2025–26 season.

WILLIAM HILL LEAGUE TWO LEADING GOALSCORERS 2024–25 (LEAGUE ONLY)

Player (Club)	Goals
Allan Trouten (East Fife)	22
Connor Young (Edinburgh C)	18
Jordan Allan (Clyde)	13
On loan from Falkirk. Includes 5 goals in League One for Queen of the South (also on loan from Falkirk).	
Nathan Austin (East Fife)	13
Blair Henderson (The Spartans)	13
Cameron Ross (Bonnyrigg Rose)	11
Cameron Russell (The Spartans)	10
Kieran Shanks (Peterhead)	10
Adam Brown (Stirling Alb)	9
Russell Dingwall (Edinburgh C)	9
Inness Lawson (Edinburgh C)	9
Martin Rennie (Clyde)	9
Mark Russell (Stranraer)	9
Ouzy See (Edinburgh C)	8
Russell McLean (Forfar Ath)	7

Player (Club)	Goals
Max Barry (Peterhead)	6
Oliver Colloty (Peterhead)	6
Dylan Gavin (Elgin C)	6
Dajon Golding (Elgin C)	6
Joshua Kerr (Stirling Alb)	6
Neil Martyniuk (Bonnyrigg Rose)	6
Ryan Shanley (Stirling Alb)	6
James Stokes (Edinburgh C)	6
Dale Carrick (Stirling Alb)	5
Jamie Dishington (The Spartans)	5
Mark Gallagher (Elgin C)	5
Max Guthrie (Stranraer)	5
On loan from Ayr U.	
Adam Laaref (East Fife)	5
Robbie Leitch (Clyde)	5
Jack Murray (Elgin C)	5
Liam Scullion (Clyde)	5

ABERDEEN

Year Formed: 1903. *Ground & Address:* Pittodrie Stadium, Pittodrie St, Aberdeen AB24 5QH.
Telephone: 01224 650 400. *Fax:* 01224 644 173. *E-mail:* contact@afc.co.uk *Website:* afc.co.uk
Ground Capacity: 20,866 (all seated). *Size of Pitch:* 105m × 66m.
Chairman: Dave Cormack. *Chief Executive:* Alan Burrows.
Managers: Jimmy Thelin. *Assistant Managers:* Peter Leven and Christer Persson.
Club Nicknames: 'The Dons'; 'The Reds'; 'The Dandies'.
Record Attendance: 45,061 v Hearts, Scottish Cup 4th rd, 13 March 1954.
Record Transfer Fee received: £6,500,000 from Girona for Bojan Miovski (August 2024).
Record Transfer Fee paid: £1,000,000 to Oldham Ath for Paul Bernard (September 1995).
Record Victory: 13-0 v Peterhead, Scottish Cup 3rd rd, 10 February 1923.
Record Defeat: 0-9 v Celtic, Premier League, 6 November 2010.
Most Capped Player: Alex McLeish, 77 (Scotland).
Most League Appearances: 556: Willie Miller, 1973-90.
Most League Goals in Season (Individual): 38: Benny Yorston, Division I, 1929-30.
Most Goals Overall (Individual): 199: Joe Harper, 1969-72; 1976-81.

Honours
League Champions: Division I 1954-55; Premier Division 1979-80, 1983-84, 1984-85.
Runners-up: Premiership 2014-15, 2015-16, 2016-17, 2017-18; Division I 1910-11, 1936-37, 1955-56, 1970-71, 1971-72;
Premier Division 1977-78, 1980-81, 1981-82, 1988-89, 1989-90, 1990-91, 1992-93, 1993-94.

ABERDEEN – WILLIAM HILL PREMIERSHIP 2024–25 LEAGUE RECORD

Match No.	Date		Venue	Opponents	Result		H/T Score	Lg Pos.	Goalscorers	Atten- dance
1	Aug	5	A	St Johnstone	W	2-1	1-0	3	Devlin [22], McGrath [62]	9203
2		11	H	St Mirren	W	3-1	1-1	2	Gueye [39], McGrath [54], Besuijen [81]	17,057
3		25	H	Kilmarnock	W	2-0	1-0	2	Gueye 2 [23, 65]	16,146
4		31	A	Ross Co	W	1-0	0-0	1	Nisbet [90]	5480
5	Sept	14	H	Motherwell	W	2-1	0-0	2	Gueye 2 [27, 80]	17,155
6		28	A	Dundee	W	2-1	2-1	2	Nisbet [15], Keskinen [32]	9030
7	Oct	6	H	Hearts	W	3-2	1-1	2	Keskinen [2], Devlin [65], Palaversa [88]	19,175
8		19	A	Celtic	D	2-2	0-2	2	Sokler [50], Shinnie [60]	58,890
9		26	H	Dundee U	W	1-0	0-0	1	Ambrose [84]	19,274
10		30	H	Rangers	W	2-1	1-0	2	Devlin [31], Morris [74]	19,274
11	Nov	9	H	Dundee	W	4-1	0-0	1	Palaversa [52], Keskinen [57], Besuijen [72], Nisbet [90]	19,274
12		23	A	St Mirren	L	1-2	0-1	2	McGrath [50]	7533
13		26	A	Hibernian	D	3-3	0-1	2	McGrath [55], Devlin [76], Sokler [90]	15,845
14	Dec	1	A	Hearts	D	1-1	1-0	2	Clarkson [37]	18,810
15		4	H	Celtic	L	0-1	0-0	2		18,043
16		7	H	St Johnstone	D	1-1	0-1	2	Clarkson [56]	15,880
17		21	H	Hibernian	L	1-3	1-2	3	Keskinen [14]	18,375
18		26	A	Kilmarnock	L	0-4	0-1	3		6846
19		29	A	Dundee U	L	0-1	0-0	3		13,581
20	Jan	2	H	Ross Co	L	1-2	1-1	4	Nisbet [45]	17,007
21		5	A	Motherwell	L	0-2	0-2	4		5308
22		12	H	Hearts	D	0-0	0-0	4		17,000
23		15	A	Rangers	L	0-3	0-1	4		45,887
24		25	H	St Mirren	L	0-3	0-2	4		15,829
25	Feb	1	A	Hibernian	L	0-2	0-1	4		16,533
26		15	A	Dundee	W	2-1	1-0	3	Nisbet [29], Keskinen [52]	7632
27		22	H	Kilmarnock	W	1-0	0-0	3	Dabbagh [90]	16,993
28		25	A	Celtic	L	1-5	0-3	3	Morris [90]	58,756
29	Mar	2	H	Dundee U	D	2-2	0-2	4	Nisbet 2 [75, 90]	17,862
30		15	A	St Johnstone	D	0-0	0-0	4		7733
31		29	H	Motherwell	W	4-1	2-1	4	Dorrington [13], Clarkson [37], Nisbet 2 [77, 90]	19,274
32	Apr	5	A	Ross Co	W	1-0	1-0	4	Morris [33]	5194
33		13	H	Rangers	D	2-2	2-0	5	Clarkson [31], Gueye [44]	18,863
34		26	H	Hibernian	W	1-0	0-0	4	Nisbet [80]	17,396
35	May	3	A	St Mirren	L	0-1	0-0	4		7587
36		11	A	Rangers	L	0-4	0-0	4		50,343
37		14	H	Celtic	L	1-5	1-2	4	Nisbet [42]	17,089
38		17	A	Dundee U	L	1-2	1-0	5	Okkels [15]	11,490

Final League Position: 5

Scottish Cup Winners: 1947, 1970, 1982, 1983, 1984, 1986, 1990, 2025; *Runners-up:* 1937, 1953, 1954, 1959, 1967, 1978, 1993, 2000, 2017.
League Cup Winners: 1955-56, 1976-77, 1985-86, 1989-90, 1995-96, 2013-14; *Runners-up:* 1946-47, 1978-79, 1979-80, 1987-88, 1988-89, 1992-93, 1999-2000, 2016-17, 2018-19, 2023-24.
Drybrough Cup Winners: 1971, 1980.

European: *European Cup:* 12 matches (1980-81, 1984-85, 1985-86); *Cup Winners' Cup:* 39 matches (1967-68, 1970-71, 1978-79, 1982-83 winners, 1983-84 semi-finals, 1986-87, 1990-91, 1993-94); *UEFA Cup:* 56 matches (*Fairs Cup:* 1968-69. *UEFA Cup:* 1971-72, 1972-73, 1973-74, 1977-78, 1979-80, 1981-82, 1987-88, 1988-89, 1989-90, 1991-92, 1994-95, 1996-97, 2000-01, 2002-03, 2007-08). *Europa League:* 37 matches (2009-10, 2014-15, 2015-16, 2016-17, 2017-18, 2018-19, 2019-20, 2020-21, 2023-24). *UEFA Europa Conference League*: 12 matches (2021-22, 2023-24).

Club colours: All: Red with white trim.

Goalscorers: *League (48):* Nisbet 11, Gueye 6, Keskinen 5, Clarkson 4, Devlin 4, McGrath 4, Morris 3, Besuijen 2, Palaversa 2, Sokler 2, Ambrose 1, Dabbagh 1, Dorrington 1, Okkels 1, Shinnie 1.
Scottish Cup (13): Dabbagh 3, Lopes 2, Nisbet 2, Gueye 1, Jensen 1, Morris 1, Shinnie 1, own goals 2.
Premier Sports Scottish League Cup (20): Sokler 5, Clarkson 3, Shinnie 2, Ambrose 1, Devlin 1, Gueye 1, Keskinen 1, MacKenzie 1, McGarry 1, McGrath 1, Morris 1, Nisbet 1, Rubezic 1.
SPFL Trust Trophy (0).

Mitov D 24	Devlin N 26+5	Rubezic S 20	Molloy G 19	MacKenzie J 23+2	Shinnie G 31+5	Nilsen S 26	Morris S 11+27	Sokler E 12+9	McGrath J 21+4	Miovski B 1+1	Gueye P 15+5	Ambrose P 1+14	Besuijen V —+11	Jensen R —+1	Keskinen T 32+1	Nisbet K 22+10	Palaversa A 20+10	Milne J 1+8	Clarkson L 22+12	Lopes L 8+11	MacDonald A 4+1	McGarry J 5+2	Doohan R 14+1	Polvara D 1+10	Tobers K 10	Okkels J 12+4	Dorrington A 8+4	Jensen A 13+2	Knoester M 13	Dabbagh O 3+10	Boyd F —+2	Match No.
1	2	3	4	5	6	7	8²	9¹	10	11	12	13																				1
1	2	3	4	5	7	6³	8²	11⁴	10	14	9¹	13	12	15																		2
1	2	3	4	5	6	7⁵	15	11²	10⁴	9³	14	12			8¹	13	16															3
1	2⁵	3	4	5	6	7	14	11²	10¹	9⁴	15	13			8³	12	16															4
1	2	3	4	5		7	12	13	10⁴	9⁵	16	15			8¹	11³	6²	14														5
1	2	3	4	5	6	7	14	10¹	13	15					8⁴	11²	12		9³													6
1	2	3	4	5	6	7	14	13	10⁴		12				8³	11¹	15		9²													7
1	2	3	4	5⁵	6	7⁴	14	13	10		12				8³	11¹	15	16	9²													8
1	2	3	4	5	13	7	12	11³	10⁵	9⁴	16	15			8¹		6²	14														9
1	2	3	4	5	6	7³	12	11⁴	10¹	9⁵	15	13			8²	14	16															10
1	2⁴	3	4	5		7	12	11³	10⁵		15	14	16		8¹	13	6		9²													11
1	2	3	4	5	6	7³	8⁴	11²	10⁵	16	15	12	14			13			9¹													12
1	2⁴	3	4	5	6	7	13	14	10³	9	12				8²	11¹	15															13
1¹	2		4		13	7	8⁵	11⁴	10		12				16		6²	14	15	3	5³											14
	2	3	4		6	7	12	13	9⁴		14				10³	11¹			15	8²	5⁵	1	16									15
12		3	4		6	7³	8²	10				16			15	11⁵	14	2⁴	9	13	5¹	1										16
	2⁴	3	4	5	7³	6⁵	14	11²	8		12				10	16			9⁵	15		1	13									17
1	2	3		5	7⁴	6¹	13		9		11³				10²	15	12		14	8	4											18
1	2	3	4³	5		7	15	11¹	10⁴		8²				9⁵	13	14			16												19
	2		4	5⁴	7	13	11¹	9²	15		8				12		6³		10⁵	3	14	1	16									20
	2	3⁴		5⁴	8	7	14		16						9³	10²	6⁵		12	11	4¹	15	1	13								21
	2		6	4	15		13								8	11¹	7		9²	12	5		1		14	3³	10⁴					22
	2		6	4	14										8³	11¹	7²		9	12	5⁴	1	16			3	10⁵	13	15			23
	2	4¹		7	6²	15		11⁵							8	14	13		9³	16		1				3	10⁴	12	5			24
	2³			13	7	16									11⁴	14	8¹		12	6³	9	15	1			3	10²	4	5			25
13				5²	14	7	12					9⁶			8²	11	6⁴		16			1				3	10¹	2	4	15		26
1	12²			5¹	13	6	16					9³			8	11	7⁴		15			3				3	10⁵	2	4	14		27
				5	7	6⁴	12					13			8	9²			15			1				3³	10¹ 14	2	4	11⁵	16	28
1				5²	13	7	16					9⁶			8	11	6⁴		15			3¹				3	10³ 12	2	4	14		29
1				5¹	6	8²	15					14			10⁴	9	7		13							12	3	2	4	11³		30
1				5	13	12	9¹					8²	11		6	14	7						1			10⁴	3³	2	4	15		31
1				5	8¹	13	9²					10³	11		6		7						1			12	3	2	4	14		32
14				5	8¹	12	9²					10³	11		6⁴		7						1			13	3	2	4	15		33
1				5	8¹	13	9²					10⁴	11		6³		7		15							12	3	2	4	16		34
1	2			5	8	12	15					9³	11		6⁴		7¹		13							10²	3⁵	4	14	16		35
1	2³			5	16	9	13					8	12		15	7	6⁵									3⁴	10² 14	4	11¹			36
1	16			13	5²	8⁴	14					9	10⁵		11³	6	12		7							3⁸	2	4¹	15			37
1				5	14	8⁴	9²					15	12		11⁵	7³	6		13							3	10¹	2	4	16		38

AIRDRIEONIANS

Year Formed: 2002. *Ground & Address:* Excelsior Stadium, New Broomfield, Craigneuk Avenue, Airdrie ML6 8QZ.
Telephone: (Stadium) 01236 622 000. *Fax:* 01236 622 001.
E-mail: enquiries@airdriefc.com *Website:* airdriefc.com
Ground Capacity: 10,101 (all seated). *Size of Pitch:* 105m × 67m.
Chairman: Paul Hetherington.
Managing Director: Scott Russell.
Manager: Rhys McCabe. *Assistant Manager:* Aaron Taylor-Sinclair.
Club Nickname: 'The Diamonds'.
Record Attendance: 9,044 v Rangers, League 1, 23 August 2013.
Record Victory: 11-0 v Gala Fairydean, Scottish Cup 3rd rd, 19 November 2011.
Record Defeat: 0-7 v Partick Thistle, First Division, 20 October 2012.
Most Capped Player: Aaron Taylor-Sinclair, 9 (Antigua & Barbuda).
Most League Appearances: 195: Jamie Bain, 2009-16.
Most League Goals in Season (Individual): 23: Andy Ryan, 2016-17.
Most Goals Overall (Individual): 69: Calum Gallagher, 2019-24.

AIRDRIEONIANS – WILLIAM HILL CHAMPIONSHIP 2024–25 LEAGUE RECORD

Match No.	Date		Venue	Opponents	Result		H/T Score	Lg Pos.	Goalscorers	Atten- dance
1	Aug	3	H	Raith R	W	1-0	0-0	5	MacDonald 75	1462
2		9	A	Ayr U	L	0-5	0-2	4		2716
3		24	H	Queen's Park	L	0-2	0-2	8		1499
4		31	A	Hamilton A	D	2-2	0-0	7	Reid 80, Aiken 87	1525
5	Sept	14	H	Falkirk	L	0-2	0-0	8		2973
6		21	A	Greenock Morton	L	0-2	0-1	10		1871
7		28	A	Livingston	L	1-2	1-1	10	Reid 31	1532
8	Oct	5	H	Dunfermline Ath	D	1-1	0-1	10	Hancock 67	1807
9		19	A	Partick Thistle	L	1-2	1-1	10	Frizzell 39	3609
10		26	H	Ayr U	L	0-1	0-0	10		1747
11		29	A	Raith R	L	0-1	0-1	10		3258
12	Nov	2	H	Hamilton A	L	0-4	0-2	10		1501
13		9	A	Falkirk	L	0-2	0-1	10		6008
14		16	A	Dunfermline Ath	L	0-1	0-0	10		4583
15	Dec	7	H	Queen's Park	L	0-2	0-2	10		1076
16		14	A	Greenock Morton	D	2-2	1-2	10	Wilson B 2 (1 pen) 35 (p), 79	1200
17		17	H	Livingston	L	0-3	0-1	10		1433
18		21	H	Partick Thistle	L	0-2	0-2	10		1970
19		28	A	Hamilton A	L	2-3	2-2	10	Mochrie 19, Gallagher 45	1476
20	Jan	14	A	Livingston	L	1-2	1-1	10	Mochrie 13	1051
21		25	H	Dunfermline Ath	W	3-0	2-0	10	McGrattan 14, Mochrie 45, Wilson B 57	1865
22	Feb	1	H	Queen's Park	W	2-1	1-0	10	Wilson B 2 (2 pens) 45, 65	1486
23		15	A	Greenock Morton	D	2-2	1-1	10	Wilson B 6, Diack 68	1752
24		22	A	Partick Thistle	D	1-1	0-1	10	Wilson B 54	3599
25		25	H	Raith R	W	1-0	0-0	10	McGrattan 78	1583
26	Mar	1	A	Ayr U	L	1-4	0-3	10	Wilson B (pen) 59	2537
27		4	H	Falkirk	L	0-3	0-2	10		3069
28		8	H	Hamilton A	W	2-1	0-0	10	Frizzell 64, Gallagher 85	1584
29		15	A	Livingston	D	3-3	2-1	10	McMaster 22, Wilson B 31, McStravick 85	1580
30		22	A	Falkirk	L	0-2	0-0	10		6287
31	Apr	2	A	Queen's Park	W	5-0	3-0	10	Hancock 2 11, 43, Diack 2 23, 57, Mochrie 70	1034
32		5	H	Partick Thistle	W	2-1	0-0	10	Mochrie 2 48, 90	2249
33		12	A	Raith R	D	1-1	1-1	10	Mochrie 19	3898
34		19	H	Greenock Morton	L	0-1	0-1	9		1706
35		26	A	Dunfermline Ath	D	0-0	0-0	9		5504
36	May	2	H	Ayr U	L	0-1	0-1	9		1637

Final League Position: 9

Honours
League Champions: Second Division 2003-04.
Runners-up: Second Division 2007-08; League One 2020-21, 2021–22.
Promoted via play-offs: 2022-23 (to Championship).
League Challenge Cup Winners: 2008-09, 2023-24; *Runners-up:* 2003-04.

Club colours: Shirt: White with red diamond. Shorts: Red with white trim. Socks: Red.

Goalscorers: *League (34):* Wilson B 9 (4 pens), Mochrie 7, Diack 3, Hancock 3, Frizzell 2, Gallagher 2, McGrattan 2, Reid 2, Aiken 1, MacDonald 1, McMaster 1, McStravick 1.
Scottish Cup (6): Gallagher 1, McGrattan 1, McGregor 1, Mochrie 1, Watson 1, Wilson B 1.
Premier Sports Scottish League Cup (16): Wilson B 6 (1 pen), McGregor 3, Agyemang 2, Armstrong 2, Frizzell 1, Hancock 1, McGrattan 1.
SPFL Trust Trophy (4): Frizzell 1, Gallagher 1, McGregor 1, Mochrie 1.
Championship Play-offs (7): McGrattan 2, Bannon 1, MacDonald 1, Mochrie 1, Strapp 1, Wilson B 1.

Johnson M 11	MacDonald D 27	McCabe R 9	Wilson A 10	Hancock M 17+3	Armstrong R 18+12	McMaster D 19+2	McGrattan L 24+6	Frizzell A 34+1	Agyemang T 5+7	Wilson B 26+6	McGregor L 11+18	Aiken M 6+7	Watson C 18+3	Gallagher G 26+10	Mochrie C 18+15	Bruce C 4+5	Reid A 5+9	Graham S 24+2	Badley-Morgan L 13	Cooper C 3+10	Taylor-Sinclair A —+1	Wright K 16	Duffy F 6+4	White J —+1	Williams C —+2	Williams D —+2	Strapp L 10+3	Diack R 6+9	McStravick L 9+5	Bannon A 12	Melrose C 9	Match No.
1	2	3⁴	4	5	6	7	8²	9³	10¹	11	12⁵	13	14	15	16																	1
1	2		4	5	6⁵	7	8³	12	14	11		10²	3¹	15	9⁴	13	16															2
1	2			5²	6²		8¹	9	10	11		14		7⁴	13	15	12	3	4													3
1	2			5	6¹		8³	9	10	11		13		7²	12		14	3	4													4
1	2			5	13			8	9	11	12	14		7²	6³		10¹	3	4													5
1	2		15	6⁸			10		11¹	8³	13	3	7	9²	5⁴	12	4		14													6
1	2¹			5			12	9			11²	6	3	7	13	8	10³	4	14													7
1	2			5	14		9²	10		12	13	8	3	7³			11¹	4	6													8
1				6³			8⁴	10	14	11²	12	2	3	7	9¹		4	5	13													9
1	2⁴			6			10	12	11²	14	8	3	7¹	13			4	5	9	15												10
1				6²			8	12	11	9	2¹	3	14	13	10		4	5	7³													11
			15		7	8	6¹	10³	11		2	12	9⁴	5²		3	4	14		1	13											12
			10		6³	9	14	12	8²		2	5	13			3	4	11¹		1	7											13
	2¹				7³	9		10	11²	12	4	6	14			3	5	13		1												14
			9		7¹	8		11	10²		2	6	12			3	4	13		1	5											15
			9		7²	8		11	10¹		2	6	12			3	4	13		1	5											16
			8		9	6⁸	12	10³		5	7¹	11⁴		4	3²	13		1	2	14	15	16										17
	4²			9	6¹	7	8	13	15	10³		2	12	11⁴		3		14		1	5											18
	2³	4		5	7	8	10		11	13	12	14	6¹	9²		3				1												19
	2	4²		8	16	7	13	9		10⁵	15		3	6⁴	11³		12			1							5¹	14				20
	2				14	7	8⁴	10		11¹	16		3	6³	9⁵		4			1	12						5²	13	15			21
	2				7	8⁴	10⁵			9³	15		3	6	13	16	4		14	1	12						5¹	11²				22
	2			5⁸	8	7	16	10⁵		11⁴			6²	9¹		15	3		1					14	12	13		4				23
	2			5¹	6²	7	8³	10		11⁵	16			12	9⁴		15	3		1				13		14		4				24
	2	3		14	7	12	10			11⁴			6³	9¹		15				1				5	13	8²		4				25
	2			14	7³	8¹	9			11	12		6⁴		15	13	3			1				5⁵	10²	16		4				26
	2	3		12	7	15	8			11⁴	14		6	10³	13			3		1				5	16	9⁴		4				27
	2	6¹	3	16		12	7⁵	9		10⁴				13	14	11²								5	15	8³		4	1			28
	2		3	16		6	7⁵	8		10²	14			9	13	11¹								5⁴	12³	15		4	1			29
	2¹	7³	3	5	14	6	8⁴	9		11				10⁵	16	12²					13				15			4	1			30
	2	3⁴	5	14	6³	7	9			13		15	8¹	12											10²	11		4	1			31
	2	7¹	3	5	12	8	6	9		13				14	11³											10²		4	1			32
	2	3⁴	5	13	7	6¹	8			16	12			14	10⁵		15								11²	9³		4	1			33
	2	3		5		8		9		6²	12			7¹	11			3							14	13	10	4³	1			34
	2			5	6	7³		8		12	14			13	10			3							4	11²	9¹		1			35
	7¹			9⁴	12	15		16	8		2	6³			3									5	13	14	4	10⁵	11²⁷	1		36

ALLOA ATHLETIC

Year Formed: 1878. *Ground & Address:* Indodrill Stadium, Recreation Park, Clackmannan Rd, Alloa FK10 1RY.
Telephone: 01259 722 695. *Fax:* 01259 210 886. *E-mail:* fcadmin@alloaathletic.co.uk *Website:* alloaathletic.co.uk
Ground Capacity: 3,100 (seated: 905). *Size of Pitch:* 102m × 69m.
Chairman: Andrew Allan. *Vice-Chairman:* Martin Ross.
Manager: Andy Graham. *First-Team Coaches:* Niall Marshall and Graeme Holmes.
Club Nicknames: 'The Wasps'; 'The Hornet'.
Previous Grounds: West End Public Park: Gabberston Park; Bellevue Park.
Record Attendance: 15,467 v Celtic, Scottish Cup 5th rd, 5 February 1955.
Record Transfer Fee received: £100,000 from Bristol R for Martin Cameron (July 2000); £100,000 from Celtic for Greig Spence (August 2009).
Record Transfer Fee paid: £26,000 to Stenhousemuir for Ross Hamilton (July 2000).
Record Victory: 9-0 v Selkirk, Scottish Cup 1st rd, 28 November 2005.
Record Defeat: 0-10 v Dundee, Division II, 8 March 1947; v Third Lanark, League Cup, 8 August 1953.
Most Capped Player: Jock Hepburn, 1, Scotland.
Most League Appearances: 413: Kevin Cawley 2011-15; 2016-25.
Most League Goals in Season (Individual): 49: 'Wee' Willie Crilley, Division II, 1921-22.
Most Goals Overall (Individual): 91: Willie Irvine, 1996-2001.

ALLOA ATHLETIC – WILLIAM HILL LEAGUE ONE 2024–25 LEAGUE RECORD

Match No.	Date		Venue	Opponents	Result	H/T Score	Lg Pos.	Goalscorers	Atten- dance
1	Aug	3	H	Queen of the South	D 0-0	0-0	7		767
2		10	A	Dumbarton	D 3-3	2-2	6	Donnelly [10], Cawley [27], Taggart [84]	505
3		17	H	Stenhousemuir	W 1-0	0-0	4	Sammon [69]	709
4		24	A	Annan Ath	W 1-0	1-0	2	Scougall [12]	494
5		31	A	Arbroath	D 0-0	0-0	3		1143
6	Sept	14	H	Inverness CT	D 2-2	0-1	1	Sammon [70], Donnelly [73]	778
7		21	H	Kelty Hearts	W 1-0	0-0	1	Sammon [70]	676
8		28	A	Montrose	D 2-2	1-1	2	Neill [22], Rankin [90]	630
9	Oct	5	H	Cove Rangers	L 0-2	0-2	3		652
10		19	A	Stenhousemuir	W 1-0	0-0	1	Rankin [78]	408
11		26	A	Arbroath	L 0-1	0-1	3		701
12	Nov	2	A	Annan Ath	W 5-0	3-0	2	O'Donnell [13], Rankin [23], Donnelly 2 [45, 55], Sammon [90]	533
13		9	A	Queen of the South	D 1-1	0-0	1	Rankin [53]	853
14		16	A	Inverness CT	L 0-1	0-0	3		1578
15	Dec	3	H	Dumbarton	D 2-2	1-1	3	Donnelly [3], Waters [76]	426
16		7	A	Kelty Hearts	W 2-0	1-0	2	Donnelly [39], Taggart (pen) [90]	385
17		14	H	Montrose	L 1-2	0-0	3	Thomson [70]	597
18		21	A	Cove Rangers	L 0-2	0-1	4		323
19		28	H	Stenhousemuir	L 1-3	0-1	5	Sammon [75]	806
20	Jan	4	A	Arbroath	W 3-1	2-1	5	Scougall [21], Rankin [40], McKay [56]	1340
21		11	H	Queen of the South	D 1-1	0-1	4	Taggart (pen) [90]	732
22		25	H	Inverness CT	L 1-2	0-1	6	O'Donnell [46]	741
23	Feb	1	A	Dumbarton	D 1-1	0-1	6	Gentles [50]	582
24		8	A	Montrose	D 2-2	0-1	6	O'Donnell [53], Buchanan [65]	502
25		15	H	Kelty Hearts	W 2-0	2-0	4	Flatman (og) [11], Buchanan [33]	604
26		22	A	Annan Ath	W 4-3	0-1	4	Thomson [54], Graham [78], Gentles [82], Neill [90]	278
27	Mar	1	H	Cove Rangers	W 2-1	0-1	4	Donnelly [75], Scougall [84]	622
28		8	A	Arbroath	L 2-3	0-1	4	Rankin [73], Scougall [76]	805
29		15	A	Queen of the South	L 2-3	1-2	4	Rankin 2 [38, 69]	934
30		22	A	Inverness CT	D 1-1	0-1	4	Taggart [52]	1655
31		29	H	Dumbarton	L 2-3	1-0	5	Donnelly [22], Sammon [86]	594
32	Apr	4	A	Stenhousemuir	W 4-1	1-0	5	Donnelly [44], Scougall 2 [60, 90], Gentles [73]	612
33		12	H	Annan Ath	W 1-0	0-0	5	MacKenzie [51]	514
34		19	A	Cove Rangers	D 1-1	0-1	5	MacKenzie [65]	484
35		26	H	Montrose	W 2-1	0-1	4	Sammon [71], Rankin [84]	662
36	May	3	A	Kelty Hearts	L 1-2	1-2	5	Rankin [44]	854

Final League Position: 5

Honours
League Champions: Division II 1921-22; Third Division 1997-98, 2011-12.
Runners-up: Division II 1938-39; Second Division 1976-77, 1981-82, 1984-85, 1988-89, 1999-2000, 2001-02, 2009-10, 2012-13; League One 2016-17.
Promoted via play-offs: 2012-13 (to First Division); 2017-18 (to Championship).
League Challenge Cup Winners: 1999-2000; *Runners-up:* 2001-02, 2014-15.

Club colours: Shirt: Gold and black hoops. Shorts: Black. Socks: Black with gold trim.

Goalscorers: *League (55):* Rankin 10, Donnelly 9, Sammon 7, Scougall 6, Taggart 4 (2 pens), Gentles 3, O'Donnell 3, Buchanan 2, MacKenzie 2, Neill 2, Thomson 2, Cawley 1, Graham 1, McKay 1, Waters 1, own goal 1.
Scottish Cup (2): Donnelly 1, Scougall 1.
Premier Sports Scottish League Cup (7): Rankin 3, Cawley 1, Neill 1, Sammon 1, Taggart 1 (1 pen).
SPFL Trust Trophy (4): Cawley 2, Donnelly 1, Taggart 1 (1 pen).

Morrison P 36	Thomson K 17+4	Taggart S 35	McKay D 24+3	Waters C 17	Roberts K 17	Hetherington S 13+2	Buchanan S 27+9	Cawley K 12+8	Scougall S 29+3	Rankin L 21+7	Nevans S —+3	Donnelly L 28+4	O'Donnell C 25+9	Virtanen M 13+9	Sammon C 8+24	Neill M 29+3	McDonnell T 4+8	Devine D 3+3	Honeyman S 4+7	Mullen S 4+7	Bruin L —+1	Dewar C 12+2	Gentles J 13+1	Graham A —+1	MacKenzie M 7+3	Match No.
1	2	3	4	5	6²	7	8³	9¹	10	11	12	13	14													1
1	2	4	3	5		7	10¹	8		11		9	13	6²	12											2
1	2¹	4	3	5	6	7	8	10²	14			9¹	13	11	12											3
1		2	3	5	7³	9	6	10²	8¹			12	13	14	11	4										4
1	14	2	3	5		7	8⁴	10³	9²	15	12	13	6¹	11		4										5
1	5	2	3			7	8	10¹	13	11		9	6²	12		4										6
1	5	2	3			7	8	10¹	9²	11	6	13	12			4										7
1	5	2	3			8	6	9²	7	13	10¹			11	4	12										8
1	15	2	3⁴	5		6	8³	10¹	7	11		9⁴		16	14	4²	13	12⁵								9
1		2	3	5		6	8	10¹	7	11³		14	9²	13		4	12									10
1	2	3	4	5⁴		7	8⁴	10¹	9³	11		13	6⁴	15	12	14⁴										11
1	5	2	3			8²	14	7⁴	11¹	16		9⁵	10³	6	13	4			12	15						12
1	2	3	5			14	8¹	7³	11⁴			9	10²	6	15	4	13	12								13
1	2	3	5			12	8²	13	7³	11		9	10⁴	6¹	15	4	14									14
1	2	3	5			7⁴	12	10²	6¹	11³		9	8	16	4³	13	15									15
1	13	2	3	5²		8	12	11³	9¹	7		6	14	4	10											16
1	5	2	3			8¹	13	11	9	6²		14	4	10³	12	7										17
1	5	2	3			8²	13	11	9	7	6	12	4	10¹												18
1	5¹	2	4			13	12	11	9	6	7	14	3	10³	8²											19
1	2	5	3			7¹	15	14	6³	11⁴	9	8	12	10²	4	13										20
1	2²	5	3³			13	12	7	10	9	8	6¹	11	4						14						21
1	2	5				13	8	11¹	9	7²	6	10³	4	14							3	12				22
1	2	5		8²		12	6	15	10³	9	13	4	14	7¹							3	11⁴				23
1		2	5	7²		6	8	12	10¹	9	4		13								3	11				24
1	2⁴		5	8		6	9²	13	10	12	4		7¹								3	11				25
1	2	5²	8			6	9³	14	7	12	4		10¹								3	11	13			26
1	2²	5	7			6⁴	8³	13	9	14¹	11¹	4		15							3	10	12			27
1	3	2²	8³	5¹		7	12	11	6	4		14									13	10	9			28
1	2	3	5⁴	7³		12	6	11	9²	8	15	4¹	13								10	14				29
1	2	3²	5¹	6		14	15	7⁵	11	9⁴	8	16			4	10³	13			12				5		30
1	2	13	6			12	7	11¹	9	8³	14		4²							3	10			5		31
1	2	13	7			8	6	11¹	10²	12	4		3	9	9³						5					32
1	13	2	15			6	8⁴	7	12	11²	10¹	14	4							3	9³			5		33
1	3			8		2¹	7		10²	9	13	12	4							5	11	6				34
1	2		7¹	8		6	10⁴	11²	14	15	13	4³		12							3	9		5		35
1	2	6³	5			7	10	9¹	14	12	13	3²								4	11	8				36

ANNAN ATHLETIC

Year Formed: 1942. *Ground & Address:* Galabank, North Street, Annan DG12 5DQ.
Telephone: 01461 204 108. *E-mail:* exec@annanathleticfc.com *Website:* annanathleticfc.com
Ground capacity: 2,517 (seated: 500). *Size of Pitch:* 100m × 62m.
Chairman: Russell Brown. *Vice-Chairman:* Stephen Bryson.
Secretary: Alan Irving.
Manager: Wullie Gibson.
Assistant Manager: Steven Bell.
Club Nicknames: 'Galabankies'; 'Black and Golds'.
Previous Ground: Mafeking Park.
Record attendance: 2,517, v Rangers, Third Division, 15 September 2012.
Record Victory: 6-0 v Elgin C, Third Division, 7 March 2009; 6-0 v Berwick Rangers, League Two, 6 April 2019; 6-0 v Dumbarton, League Two play-off semi-finals, 9 May 2023.
Record Defeat: 1-8 v Inverness CT, Scottish Cup 3rd rd, 24 January 1998.
Most League Appearances: 270: Aidan Smith, 2016-25.
Most League Goals in Season (Individual): 23: Tommy Goss, 2022-23.
Most Goals Overall (Individual): 78: Aidan Smith, 2016-25.

ANNAN ATHLETIC – WILLIAM HILL LEAGUE ONE 2024–25 LEAGUE RECORD

Match No.	Date	Venue	Opponents	Result	H/T Score	Lg Pos.	Goalscorers	Attendance
1	Aug 3	A	Cove Rangers	W 3-1	0-0	1	Kilsby [56], Todd [80], Zaid [90]	452
2	10	H	Inverness CT	W 1-0	0-0	1	Goss (pen) [50]	386
3	17	A	Queen of the South	L 0-2	0-1	3		2214
4	24	H	Alloa Ath	L 0-1	0-1	5		494
5	31	A	Stenhousemuir	L 1-5	1-2	7	Smith A (pen) [36]	607
6	Sept 14	H	Dumbarton	D 1-1	0-1	8	McGowan [90]	375
7	21	A	Arbroath	L 0-2	0-0	8		1193
8	28	A	Kelty Hearts	L 0-3	0-2	9		369
9	Oct 5	H	Montrose	W 1-0	1-0	8	Breen [27]	324
10	19	A	Inverness CT	L 0-1	0-1	8		1501
11	26	H	Queen of the South	W 1-0	0-0	8	Smith A [57]	1005
12	Nov 2	A	Alloa Ath	L 0-5	0-3	8		533
13	9	H	Stenhousemuir	D 1-1	1-1	8	Todd [30]	365
14	16	H	Kelty Hearts	L 0-2	0-2	9		394
15	23	A	Montrose	L 1-2	1-1	9	Smith A [45]	367
16	Dec 7	H	Cove Rangers	D 1-1	0-1	8	Muir T [70]	315
17	14	A	Dumbarton	W 5-1	2-1	8	Smith P [34], Gibson (pen) [38], Breen [51], Smith A [66], Muir T [76]	506
18	21	H	Arbroath	L 0-4	0-3	8		478
19	28	A	Queen of the South	D 1-1	0-1	8	Gibson (pen) [87]	2702
20	Jan 4	A	Stenhousemuir	D 1-1	0-0	8	Muir T [59]	502
21	18	H	Inverness CT	L 0-3	0-1	8		438
22	25	H	Montrose	D 2-2	0-2	8	Muir T 2 [71, 89]	233
23	Feb 1	A	Kelty Hearts	W 3-1	0-1	8	Muir T 2 [50, 59], Brown [68]	395
24	8	H	Dumbarton	W 2-1	0-0	7	Smith P [47], Gibson (pen) [77]	428
25	15	A	Cove Rangers	L 1-3	1-2	8	Scully (og) [15]	331
26	22	H	Alloa Ath	L 3-4	1-0	8	Gibson (pen) [27], Brown 2 [74, 90]	278
27	Mar 1	A	Arbroath	L 0-3	0-1	8		1180
28	8	A	Stenhousemuir	L 0-2	0-1	9		454
29	15	A	Inverness CT	W 1-0	1-0	9	Smith P [3]	1703
30	22	A	Montrose	L 1-3	1-3	9	Muir T [14]	657
31	29	H	Kelty Hearts	W 2-1	0-1	9	Kilsby [75], Ross [80]	393
32	Apr 5	H	Queen of the South	L 0-2	0-0	9		1353
33	12	A	Alloa Ath	L 0-1	0-0	9		514
34	19	H	Arbroath	W 5-1	2-1	9	Dixon [31], Muir T 2 [40, 61], Ross 2 [72, 79]	604
35	26	A	Dumbarton	L 1-3	0-1	9	Goss [60]	581
36	May 3	H	Cove Rangers	L 2-4	0-2	9	Smith P [50], Smith A [84]	415

Final League Position: 9

Honours
Promoted via play-offs: 2022-23 (to League One).
League Two Runners-up: 2013-14.
League Challenge Cup: Semi-finals: 2009-10, 2011-12.

Club colours: Shirt: Gold with black trim. Shorts: Black. Socks: Gold with black tops.

Goalscorers: *League (41):* Muir T 10, Smith A 5 (1 pen), Gibson 4 (4 pens), Smith P 4, Brown 3, Ross 3, Breen 2, Goss 2 (1 pen), Kilsby 2, Todd 2, Dixon 1, McGowan 1, Zaid 1, own goal 1.
Scottish Cup (0).
Premier Sports Scottish League Cup (7): Goss 3, Dixon 1, McGowan 1, Smith P 1, Todd 1.
SPFL Trust Trophy (6): Smith A 2, Dixon 1, Gibson 1 (1 pen), Maxwell 1, Wood 1.
League One Play-offs (8): Muir T 3, Goss 2, Kilsby 1, Smith A 1, own goal 1.

Smith J 35	Gibson W 34	Muir T 31 + 1	Kilsby M 26 + 3	Muir R 15 + 4	Smith P 24	McGowan P 34 + 1	Todd J 30 + 3	Zaid M 7 + 6	Goss T 7 + 2	Smith A 29 + 1	Dixon J 24 + 5	Quitongo R 3 + 6	Quigg A — + 4	Barnes C 2 + 4	Fleming K 9 + 8	Stevenson J 6 + 8	Wood H 3 + 2	Ross L 16 + 10	Lennon G 4 + 3	Maxwell C 10 + 3	Breen R 17	Hooper S 12 + 4	Carmichael D 1 + 6	Bisland L 7 + 3	Brown A 6 + 6	Strachan M 1 + 1	Watson P 2	Bell S — + 1	Fleming G 1	Match No.
1	2	3	4	5^2	6	7^1	8	9	10	11^3	12	13	14																	1
1	5	3^1	4	2		7	6	9^2	10^4	11	8^3	12			13	14	15													2
1	2	3	4				8	7	11^2	10	9	13	5				6^1	12												3
1	5	3	4	2		7			10	11		9			12	8^1	6													4
1	7^3	3	4	5		6^4	9^2	14	10	13					2^1			8	11	12	15									5
1	8	3	4	15			6	7	13	11	9^1				2^2		14	5^4	10^3	12										6
1		3	4	2			7	8	6^1	11	9		13				14	12	10^3	5^2										7
1	6	3^4		2			7			11	10		13		9^3	14	8^1	5^2	12	4										8
1	2		4				6^1	5	13	11	10	8	9^2				7			12	3									9
1	2	3^1					6	7	9^3	11	5^2	12	14		8	10		13		4										10
1	5	3^1	14	2^3			8^2	6		11	9	13			7	10				4	12									11
1		3	4	2^1			7	10	11		8		13		6^2	9				5	12									12
1	6	3		12		9^2	7	10	13	11					8		5^1			4	2									13
1	7	3^2	13			8^3	9	6	14	11					10^1	12	5			4	2									14
1	2	3	5	12		7^2	6	10	13	11	8			14				9^1		4^3										15
1		3	11	5	2		7	6	10	8^2	12				9^1			13		4										16
1		3^3	11	5^1	2		7^2	8	6	10	9		14			12		13		4										17
1		3	11	5^2	2^1		9^3	6	8	10	7^4	12	14	15				13		4										18
1	4	3					7	8		10	9				11	2					6	5								19
1	4	3					7^1	8	10^2	9	11		2					13	12		6	5								20
1		3	11		2¹		8^2	9	6^3						7			12		13	5		14							21
1		3	11	*			7	8	6						9	5^1		14		10		2^2	4	12^3	13					22
1	5	10					6	7^2	12	11	8^3				14			13			3	4			2	9^1				23
1	5	10					7	8	6	11					9			12				4	3		2^1					24
1	5	11	12				7	6	9^3	10					8^2			14			15	4^4	3		2^1	13				25
1	5	11	4				8	7	13	10					9^1			6					3		2^2	12				26
1	5	11	4				8	7^1	12	10					9^2			6					3		2	13				27
1		3	4^1	12			8	7	9	10								6		5			5							28
1		3	4				8	7^3	9	10								12		5		2		13	11^1		6^2	14		29
1	2	10^3	5				9	7	6	11								13		8^2		3		14	12		4^1			30
1	2	6	4				7	9	3	10	12							5		8^2			13		11^1					31
1		3	10	4^3			7	6	2	11^1	8^4							5		9^2			14	13	15	12				32
1	6	11	5				8^2	7	3		13							10		9^3			4	14	2^1	12				33
1	4	11	5		2^2		8	7^1	6	10								12		9^3			3	13	14					34
1	4	11	5		2		7	6	12	10								8		9^1			3^4							35
	13		4		5^4		8^2	14	3^1	12	15	9			11			6^3				2	10	7					1	36

ARBROATH

Year Formed: 1878. *Ground & Address:* Gayfield Park, Arbroath DD11 1QB.
Telephone: 01241 872 157. *Fax:* 01241 431 125. *E-mail:* office@arbroathfc.co.uk *Website:* arbroathfc.co.uk
Ground Capacity: 6,600 (seated: 861). *Size of Pitch:* 105m × 65m.
Chairman: Brian Cargill. *Chief Executive:* Paul Reid.
Co-Player Managers: Colin Hamilton and David Gold. *Assistant Manager:* Jimmy Boyle.
Club Nickname: 'The Red Lichties'.
Previous Ground: Lesser Gayfield.
Record Attendance: 13,510 v Rangers, Scottish Cup 3rd rd, 23 February 1952.
Record Transfer Fee received: £120,000 from Dundee for Paul Tosh (August 1993).
Record Transfer Fee paid: £20,000 to Montrose for Douglas Robb (1981).
Record Victory: 36-0 v Bon Accord, Scottish Cup 1st rd, 12 September 1885.
Record Defeat: 0-8 v Kilmarnock, Division II, 3 January 1949; 1-9 v Celtic, League Cup 3rd rd, 25 August 1993.
Most Capped Player: Ned Doig, 2 (5), Scotland.
Most League Appearances: 445: Tom Cargill, 1966-81.
Most League Goals in Season (Individual): 45: Dave Easson, Division II, 1958-59.
Most Goals Overall (Individual): 120: Jimmy Jack, 1966-71.

ARBROATH – WILLIAM HILL LEAGUE ONE 2024–25 LEAGUE RECORD

Match No.	Date	Venue	Opponents	Result		H/T Score	Lg Pos.	Goalscorers	Atten- dance
1	Aug 3	A	Stenhousemuir	L	1-2	0-0	9	Coulson 90	738
2	10	H	Montrose	D	0-0	0-0	8		2040
3	17	H	Kelty Hearts	L	0-3	0-0	10		1023
4	24	A	Dumbarton	D	2-2	1-0	9	Stewart 5, Dow 50	688
5	31	H	Alloa Ath	D	0-0	0-0	10		1143
6	Sept 14	A	Queen of the South	L	1-2	1-1	10	Dow 10	996
7	21	H	Annan Ath	W	2-0	0-0	10	Dow 73, Reilly 79	1193
8	28	A	Cove Rangers	W	4-2	2-2	7	Stewart 31, Murray 38, Spalding 47, Wilkie 73	645
9	Oct 5	H	Inverness CT	W	1-0	0-0	6	Reilly 67	1381
10	19	H	Dumbarton	L	1-3	1-1	7	O'Brien 11	1159
11	26	A	Alloa Ath	W	1-0	1-0	6	Gallagher 43	701
12	Nov 2	H	Stenhousemuir	W	1-0	1-0	3	Taylor 12	1141
13	9	A	Montrose	D	1-1	0-1	4	Dow 80	1565
14	16	H	Cove Rangers	W	2-1	2-1	2	Stewart 18, Murray 32	1278
15	Dec 7	A	Queen of the South	W	2-1	0-0	3	Murray 76, Gallagher 90	709
16	14	A	Inverness CT	W	2-0	0-0	1	Smith 52, Reilly 90	1531
17	17	A	Kelty Hearts	L	2-3	1-1	1	Reilly 42, Murray 57	523
18	21	A	Annan Ath	W	4-0	3-0	1	Taylor 12, Reilly 2 (1 pen) 22, 49 (p), Murray 43	478
19	28	H	Montrose	W	3-0	1-0	1	Spalding 21, O'Brien 65, Taylor 84	2714
20	Jan 4	H	Alloa Ath	L	1-3	1-2	1	Reilly 13	1340
21	Feb 1	A	Cove Rangers	L	1-2	1-0	3	Winter 7	758
22	8	H	Inverness CT	W	3-0	2-0	2	Steele 26, Winter (pen) 42, Dow 70	1500
23	15	A	Queen of the South	W	3-0	3-0	1	Stewart 13, Taylor 22, Douglas (og) 26	1203
24	22	A	Stenhousemuir	L	0-2	0-0	3		705
25	25	H	Kelty Hearts	W	2-1	1-0	1	Stewart 3, Winter 80	628
26	Mar 1	H	Annan Ath	W	3-0	1-0	1	Taylor 40, Winter 74, Gallagher 87	1180
27	4	A	Dumbarton	W	2-1	1-1	1	Winter 15, Dow 47	355
28	8	A	Alloa Ath	W	3-2	1-0	1	Dow 20, Muirhead 47, Gallagher 89	805
29	15	H	Dumbarton	D	1-1	1-0	1	Stanton 11	1434
30	22	A	Kelty Hearts	D	1-1	1-0	1	Watson 17	754
31	29	H	Cove Rangers	W	1-0	1-0	1	Muirhead 8	1422
32	Apr 5	A	Montrose	W	1-0	1-0	1	Flynn 45	1792
33	12	H	Stenhousemuir	W	4-0	1-0	1	Stanton 2 45, 52, Taylor 48, Winter 60	2205
34	19	A	Annan Ath	L	1-5	1-2	1	King 17	604
35	26	A	Inverness CT	L	0-3	0-2	1		2329
36	May 3	H	Queen of the South	D	1-1	0-1	1	Dow 75	2314

Final League Position: 1

Honours
League Champions: League One 2018-19, 2024-25. Third Division 2010-11; League Two 2016-17.
Runners-up: Championship 2021-22; Division II 1934-35, 1958-59, 1967-68, 1971-72; Second Division 2000-01; Third Division 1997-98, 2006-07.
Promoted via play-offs: 2007-08 (to Second Division).
Scottish Cup: Semi-finals 1947, Quarter-finals 1993.

Club colours: All: Maroon with white trim.

Goalscorers: *League (58):* Dow 8, Reilly 7 (1 pen), Taylor 6, Winter 6 (1 pen), Murray 5, Stewart 5, Gallagher 4, Stanton 3, Muirhead 2, O'Brien 2, Spalding 2, Coulson 1, Flynn 1, King 1, Smith 1, Steele 1, Watson 1, Wilkie 1, own goal 1.
Scottish Cup (0).
Premier Sports Scottish League Cup (1): Reilly 1.
SPFL Trust Trophy (3): Callaghan 1, O'Brien 1 (1 pen), Stewart 1.

McAdams A 35	Bisland L 6+3	Watson K 24+4	O'Brien T 26+4	Wilkie J 36	Murray I 13+16	Callaghan L 4+6	Slater C 2+12	Stewart S 33+1	Reilly G 14+7	Gallagher C 8+19	Coulson Q 6+7	Stowe M —+3	Steele A 8+5	Richardson J —+4	Gold D 10+8	Dow R 26+5	Sinclair B 4+1	Flynn R 25+3	Taylor F 27+1	Smith D 11	Stanton S 15+1	Winter A 15+1	McKechnie K 1+7	King B 2+5	Penman C 13	Thomson J —+2	Muirhead A 11+1	McConnell J 1	Match No.
1	2²	3⁴	4	5	6³	7	8	9¹	10	11	12	13	14	15															1
1		3	4	5	9²	7	8¹	12	2	11	10	6³	14		13														2
1	15	3	4	5	9²	7³		13	2	11	10¹	6	14		12	8⁴													3
1		4	3	5	10¹	7		8	9	11	13	6²		2³	14	12													4
1		3	4	5				8	6	11	13		9		12	10²	2	7¹											5
1	13	3	4	5	15		12	6¹	8	11	14	10³				9	2²	7⁴											6
1	2⁵	3	4	5	9²	16	15	7³	6	12	11¹	13			14	10		8⁴											7
1	2	4¹		5	10³	15	13	6⁵	8	11⁴		14			16	9²	3	7	12										8
1	5	3⁹		8	14	15	13			10³		12			6⁵	11⁴	4¹	7	9		2								9
1	2⁴		4	5	14		12		8	11	13	15			6¹	9³	3	7	10²										10
1		4	3		8		12	6²	5	13	10¹				9	7	11	2											11
1		3	4	5			12	9¹	6	13	11²				14	10	8	7³	2										12
1		3	4	5¹	12		13	7¹	6			9			10	8	11	2											13
1	2	3	4²	5	12		15	7⁵	6¹	14	11³				16	9	13	8	10⁴										14
1		4	12	5²	13		15	9³	8	11⁴	14				2¹	10	6	7	3										15
1		3	4	5	6¹		13	12	9	14	10³				11	7	8²	2											16
1	13	3²	4	5	10			6¹	8	11	14				12	7³	9	2											17
1		4	5		6⁴	15	12	13	8¹	11⁵	16	14			2³	10	7²	9	3										18
1		4	5	13	8⁴	14	12	7³		11²	13	15			2	10	6¹	9	3										19
1		4	5	13	14		7²	8	11	12					2	10	6	9	3										20
1		4		5	7¹		14	2					3		13	10³		6²	8⁴	9	11	12	15						21
1		3	4¹		8	15		6⁵	9⁴				2		16	12		10³		7	11²·14	13	5						22
1		4		5	16		6¹	9²					3		12	8⁶		11³		7	10⁴·15	14	2·13						23
1		4		5	13		6²	9	14				3⁴			8¹		11³		7	10·15	12	2						24
1		4		5			6¹	8	13				14		12	10		9²		7	11			2³	3				25
1		4	15	5	16			8⁶	12						6²·10⁴		13	9¹		7	11·14		2	3³					26
1	15	3²		5			8	14				4		6¹·10⁴		12	9²		7	11		2·16	13					27
1		4		5	14		6¹	8⁵	15			13			10⁴				7	11		2²·16	3						28
1		4		5	10²		14	8	13	12				6³	9		7	11		2¹	3								29
1		4	14	5			12	8					2	7¹		6²·10³		9	11	13			3						30
1	13	4		5			8						12		7·10	9	11³·14	6¹	2²	3									31
1	15	4³	5	12			8	14	13			6¹		7·10⁴	9	11	2²	3											32
1	13	4	5	12		15	8	16				10²	6	9³	7	11·15	14	2⁴	3¹										33
1	3	16		5	9³		10⁴·12	11		2⁵			13	6		14·15	8²·7¹		4	1									34
1		4		5	13		8·12					10²	6	9	7	11	2¹	3											35
1		4⁹	5		14	8·12	13					10	7³·9	6	11¹	2²	3												36

AYR UNITED

Year Formed: 1910. *Ground & Address:* Somerset Park, Tryfield Place, Ayr KA8 9NB.
Telephone: 01292 263 435. *Fax:* 01292 281 314. *E-mail:* info@ayrunitedfc.co.uk *Website:* ayrunitedfc.co.uk
Ground Capacity: 10,185 (seated: 1,597). *Size of Pitch:* 101m × 66m.
Chairman: David Smith. *Vice-Chairman:* Fraser MacIntyre.
Head Coach: Scott Brown. *Assistant Head Coach:* Steven Whittaker.
Club Nickname: 'The Honest Men'.
Record Attendance: 25,225 v Rangers, Division I, 13 September 1969.
Record Transfer Fee received: £300,000 from Liverpool for Steve Nicol (October 1981).
Record Transfer Fee paid: £90,000 to Stranraer for Mark Campbell (March 1999).
Record Victory: 11-1 v Dumbarton, League Cup, 13 August 1952.
Record Defeat: 0-9 in Division I v Rangers (1929); v Hearts (1931); B Division v Third Lanark (1954).
Most Capped Player: Frankie Musonda, 9, Zambia.
Most League Appearances: 459: John Murphy, 1963-78.
Most League League and Cup Goals in Season (Individual): 66: Jimmy Smith, 1927-28.
Most League and Cup Goals Overall (Individual): 213: Peter Price, 1955-61.

AYR UNITED – WILLIAM HILL CHAMPIONSHIP 2024–25 LEAGUE RECORD

Match No.	Date	Venue	Opponents	Result	H/T Score	Lg Pos.	Goalscorers	Atten-dance
1	Aug 3	A	Hamilton A	W 2-0	1-0	1	Stanger [18], Dowds [72]	1468
2	9	H	Airdrieonians	W 5-0	2-0	1	Henderson 2 [7, 49], Oakley [24], Dowds 2 (1 pen) [56, 77 (p)]	2716
3	17	H	Hamilton A	W 3-2	1-2	1	Murphy [8], Rus [51], Oakley [66]	2846
4	24	H	Raith R	W 2-0	1-0	1	Dowds (pen) [40], Walker [90]	2928
5	31	A	Dunfermline Ath	D 1-1	1-1	1	Watret [22]	4921
6	Sept 14	H	Partick Thistle	D 1-1	1-0	2	Dowds (pen) [25]	3118
7	21	A	Queen's Park	L 1-1	0-1	1	Dempsey [57]	1635
8	28	H	Greenock Morton	W 1-0	0-0	1	Henderson (pen) [66]	2846
9	Oct 5	A	Falkirk	L 0-2	0-1	1		6753
10	19	H	Livingston	L 1-2	1-2	3	McLennan [42]	2470
11	26	A	Airdrieonians	W 1-0	0-0	3	Watret [70]	1747
12	Nov 1	A	Raith R	L 0-2	0-2	3		3427
13	8	A	Greenock Morton	D 1-1	0-1	3	Oakley [50]	1697
14	16	H	Queen's Park	W 3-2	2-0	3	Henderson (pen) [31], McKenzie [39], Oakley [76]	2012
15	23	H	Dunfermline Ath	W 1-0	0-0	3	Henderson [67]	1701
16	Dec 7	A	Partick Thistle	L 0-1	0-0	3		3521
17	14	H	Falkirk	W 5-2	3-2	3	McLennan [34], Dempsey [38], McMann [40], Bavidge 2 [60, 70]	3039
18	21	A	Livingston	W 1-0	1-0	3	Oakley [41]	1521
19	28	H	Greenock Morton	D 0-0	0-0	3		2974
20	Jan 4	H	Raith R	W 3-0	3-0	2	Oakley 3 [2, 12, 25]	2733
21	14	A	Dunfermline Ath	W 2-0	0-0	2	Henderson [61], Oakley [71]	4634
22	25	H	Partick Thistle	W 2-1	2-0	2	Oakley 2 [19, 36]	3175
23	Feb 1	A	Hamilton A	W 2-0	0-0	1	McKenzie [80], Stanger [84]	2561
24	15	A	Falkirk	D 2-2	2-1	2	Henderson (pen) [14], Oakley [38]	7419
25	22	H	Livingston	L 1-2	0-1	3	Rus [73]	3063
26	Mar 1	H	Airdrieonians	W 4-1	3-0	3	Oakley [6], Stanger [36], Main 2 [39, 78]	2537
27	4	A	Queen's Park	W 3-2	0-0	2	Rus [66], Dempsey [76], Main [79]	1557
28	8	A	Greenock Morton	L 1-2	1-0	2	Main [8]	2235
29	15	A	Partick Thistle	L 0-2	0-2	3		4289
30	22	H	Hamilton A	D 1-1	0-0	2	Walker [90]	2587
31	29	H	Dunfermline Ath	W 3-0	1-0	2	McLennan [43], Murphy [68], Walker [90]	3253
32	Apr 5	A	Raith R	L 0-1	0-0	3		3919
33	11	H	Falkirk	D 1-1	0-1	3	Walker [90]	4471
34	18	A	Livingston	L 0-5	0-3	3		1606
35	26	H	Queen's Park	D 2-2	1-2	3	Murphy [16], McKenzie [54]	2122
36	May 2	A	Airdrieonians	W 1-0	1-0	3	Dempsey [44]	1637

Final League Position: 3

Honours
League Champions: Division II 1911-12, 1912-13, 1927-28, 1936-37, 1958-59, 1965-66; Second Division 1987-88, 1996-97; League One 2017-18.
Runners-up: Division II 1910-11, 1955-56, 1968-69; Second Division 2008-09; League One 2015-16; Championship: 2022-23.
Promoted via play-offs: 2008-09 (to First Division); 2010-11 (to First Division); 2015-16 (to Championship).
Scottish Cup: Semi-finals 2002.
League Cup: Runners-up: 2001-02.
League Challenge Cup Runners-up: 1990-91, 1991-92.

Club colours: Shirt: White with black trim. Shorts: Black with white trim. Socks: Black and white hoops.

Goalscorers: *League (57):* Oakley 13, Henderson 7 (3 pens), Dowds 5 (3 pens), Dempsey 4, Main 4, Walker 4, McKenzie 3, McLennan 3, Murphy 3, Rus 3, Stanger 3, Bavidge 2, Watret 2, McMann 1.
Scottish Cup (10): Henderson 3 (1 pen), Agbaire 1, Devlin 1, Hastie 1, McKenzie 1, Murphy 1, Oakley 1, Watret 1.
Premier Sports Scottish League Cup (9): Henderson 3, Dowds 2, Hastie 1, Musonda 1, Oakley 1, Rus 1.
SPFL Trust Trophy (7): Dowds 2 (1 pen), Henderson 1, Murphy 1, Oakley 1, Rus 1, Walker 1.
Premiership Play-offs (1): Murphy 1.

Stone H 15	Reading P 26 + 2	Stanger G 35 + 1	McMann S 29 + 2	Musonda F 11 + 5	Hastie J 7 + 18	Dempsey B 34	Rus M 19 + 10	Henderson J 32 + 3	Oakley G 32 + 4	Dowds A 6	McKenzie M 10 + 20	Murphy J 14 + 11	Syla R 2 + 7	McAllister N 20 + 5	Walker E 3 + 16	Tomlinson S — + 1	Watret D 16 + 8	Devlin M 10	Bavidge A 3 + 11	Howley R 3 + 7	McIntyre J 1	Russell L 11	Hislop J — + 3	McLennan C 25 + 1	Craig D — + 1	McKinnon C 7 + 5	Agbaire L 9 + 3	Main C 7 + 5	Mutch R 1	Clarke J 8	Match No.
1	2	3	4	5^5	6^1	7	8^3	9^2	10	11^4	12	13	14	15	16																1
1	5	3	4	2	12	7^5	8^4	6^2	10^3	11	14	9^1	15	13	16																2
1	5	3	4	2^2	13	7	8^4	6	10	11^3	14	9^1	15		12																3
1	5	3	4		12	7	8^4	6^2	10^3	11	15	9^1	14	13			2														4
1	5	3		16		7	8^4	9^3	11	10^9		6^2		12	15		2	4^1	13	14											5
	5	3		15	7		6^4	10	11^2	9	13^3		6^2		12	15		2	12	8^1	1										6
	5	3	15	9^1	7		6	10^3		14		12	4^1	13	2^4		11^5	8^2		1	16										7
	3		5	14	7	9^3	6	10^2		13		8	4^1	11^1		2	12			1											8
	5	3	8^3	15	7	9	6^4	12		13		16	4^1	11^2		2^5		10^1	14		1										9
	5	3	12	2		7	8^2	6^1	10		9	14		4^1			13			1		11									10
	4	5	3	14	7	8^2	6^1	11^3		9^4	12	15			2		13			1		10									11
5^5	3	4	16		7	13	12	11^2		9^4	14	8^1		15		2	10^3			1		6									12
	3	4	5		7	9^2	6	11	12			2^3			13		14	8^1		1		10									13
8	2	4		14	6	7^1	9^3	10	5					3		12				1	13	11^2									14
8	2	4	15		6	7^3	9^4	10		5^1	13			12	3	14				1		11^2									15
8	2	4	7^1		6	9^3	10			14	13			5^2	3^4	15	12			1		11									16
8	4	2	15	7		9^4	10^3			6^5	12			5^2	3^1	13	14			1		11	16								17
1	9	2	4		7		10^2	11^3	12	8^1		5			3	14	13					6									18
1	9^2	2	4		7	13	10	11	12	8^3		5^1			3	14						6									19
1	2^2	4	4		14	7	10	11^4	13	8^9		5^3		15	3		12					16	6^1								20
1	9	2	4	15	7^5		10^2	11^4	12	13		5^3		14	3							6^1		8	16						21
1	9	2	4		7		10^3	11^2	14	8^1		5^4			3							6		12		13					22
1	9^4	2	4	15	7	13	10^2	11	14	8^1				5^3								6		8^3	3	14					23
1	9	2	4		7	13	10^1	11^2		5	12											6		8^3	3	12	1				24
	9	2	4		13	7	14	11^2	10			5^1										6		8^3	3	12	1				25
	3	5	14	15	7	9^3	6^5	10^4	16			2^2	13									8^1		12	4	11		1			26
	2	9		13	7	8^4	10^2	11	14			4	15	5^1										6^3	3	12		1			27
	3	5		13	7	9^1	6^2	10	12			2^3	14									8		4	11	1					28
9	2	4^4	14		6	8^1	13	10	5^2			16		15								7		12	3^3	11^5		1			29
	3	5	2^1		7	13	6	10^4		15		14	12									9^3		8^2	4	11		1			30
16	4	5		9^4	7	13	6^1	14	12	10^2		3	15	2								8^9			11^3	1					31
1	4	5		9^4	7	13	6^2	15	12	10^3		3	14	2^1								8			11	1					32
1	5	3	4		6^3	7	9^1	14	11^4	16	12		2	15^4								8^2		13	10^5	1					33
1	5^2	3	4		13		15	8	11	7	10^3		2		12							9^4		6^1	14	1					34
16	12	4	2^2	9	7	8		13	11^2	10		3^5	14	5^1								6^4		15		1					35
4^3	3^5	15		8	6^4	12^2	9	10^2				16	11	5								14		7^1	2	13		1			36

BONNYRIGG ROSE

Year Formed: 1881. *Ground & Address:* New Dundas Park, Bonnyrigg, Midlothian EH19 3AE.
Telephone: 0131 663 7702. *Email:* via website. *Website:* bonnyriggrosefc.co.uk
Ground Capacity: 2,640 (seats). *Size of Pitch:* 96m × 60 m.
Chairman: Ian Durie. *Vice-chair:* Grant Fitzsimmons.
Manager: Jonathan Stewart. *Assistant Manager:* Ross Gray.
Club Nicknames: 'Rose'; 'Rosey Posey'.
Record Attendance: 2,400 v Hibernian, League Cup 1st rd Group D, 17 July 2022.
Record Victory: 14-0 v Burntisland Shipyard, Scottish Cup Intermediate Round, 3 September 2016. 5-2 v Bo'ness U,
Scottish FA Cup 1st rd, 1 January 2021.
Record Defeat: 8-1 v Hibernian, Scottish Cup 4th rd, 21 January 2017.
Most League Appearances: 99: Callum Connolly, 2022-25.
Most League Goals in Season (Individual): 13: Neil Martyniuk, 2023-24.
Most Goals Overall (Individual): 28: Neil Martyniuk, 2022-25.

BONNYRIGG ROSE – WILLIAM HILL LEAGUE TWO 2024–25 LEAGUE RECORD

Match No.	Date	Venue	Opponents		Result	H/T Score	Lg Pos.	Goalscorers	Attendance
1	Aug 3	H	Peterhead	L	0-1	0-0	9		543
2	10	A	The Spartans	L	0-2	0-0	10		616
3	17	A	Edinburgh C	D	2-2	1-1	10	Young [16], Martyniuk [78]	309
4	24	H	Clyde	W	2-1	0-1	7	Barrett [52], Mailer [61]	655
5	31	H	Stranraer	W	2-0	2-0	5	Young [24], Connolly [43]	607
6	Sept 14	A	Elgin C	L	1-2	0-0	6	Higginbotham [70]	688
7	21	H	Stirling Alb	W	2-0	1-0	4	McKinley (og) [18], Barrett [79]	718
8	28	H	Forfar Ath	L	0-1	0-0	5		572
9	Oct 5	A	East Fife	L	0-5	0-2	6		792
10	19	H	Edinburgh C	W	2-0	0-0	5	Ross [67], Connolly [83]	683
11	Nov 2	A	Clyde	D	2-2	1-1	5	Ross 2 [1,87]	705
12	9	H	Elgin C	W	2-0	1-0	5	Mailer [15], Ferrie [69]	756
13	16	A	Stranraer	W	2-1	1-1	7	Ross [11], McGachie [90]	644
14	30	H	East Fife	D	1-1	1-0	7	Currie [8]	568
15	Dec 3	H	Stirling Alb	W	2-1	0-0	5	Lorimer [53], Ross [61]	446
16	14	A	Forfar Ath	L	1-5	0-2	7	Ross [76]	503
17	21	A	Peterhead	L	0-2	0-0	7		584
18	Jan 4	A	Edinburgh C	L	0-2	0-1	9		356
19	21	H	The Spartans	D	2-2	1-1	8	Martyniuk (pen) [4], Barrett [56]	628
20	25	A	Stirling Alb	L	0-3	0-3	9		642
21	28	H	Stranraer	W	3-1	2-0	8	Barrett [33], Martyniuk (pen) [36], Ross [53]	526
22	Feb 1	H	Clyde	W	2-1	2-0	7	Ross [8], Martyniuk (pen) [30]	659
23	4	A	Elgin C	L	0-3	0-1	7		610
24	8	H	Peterhead	L	3-4	2-3	8	Ferrie [14], Ross [41], Currie [47]	469
25	15	A	East Fife	D	1-1	1-0	9	Ross [45]	644
26	22	H	Forfar Ath	L	0-2	0-0	9		680
27	Mar 1	A	The Spartans	L	1-3	0-1	9	Aiken [79]	701
28	8	H	Edinburgh C	L	0-1	0-0	10		698
29	15	H	Stirling Alb	D	1-1	0-1	9	Watson [66]	662
30	22	A	Clyde	L	1-3	0-1	10	Martyniuk (pen) [63]	757
31	29	H	Elgin C	L	0-1	0-0	10		476
32	Apr 5	A	Peterhead	L	0-5	0-2	10		653
33	12	H	East Fife	L	0-2	0-0	10		705
34	19	A	Forfar Ath	W	2-0	1-0	10	Martyniuk (pen) [29], Ross [68]	903
35	26	H	The Spartans	W	2-1	0-0	10	Aiken [75], Arnott [90]	816
36	May 3	A	Stranraer	W	1-0	0-0	10	Arnott [70]	852

Final League Position: 10

Honours
Scottish Cup: 5th rd, 2023-24.
Promoted via play-offs: 2021-22 (to League Two).

Club colours: Shirts: Red and white hoops with red sleeves. Shorts: Red with white trim. Socks: Red.

Goalscorers: *League (40):* Ross 11, Martyniuk 6 (5 pens), Barrett 4, Aiken 2, Arnott 2, Connolly 2, Currie 2, Ferrie 2, Mailer 2, Young 2, Higginbotham 1, Lorimer 1, McGachie 1, Watson 1, own goal 1.
Scottish Cup (1): Ross 1.
Premier Sports Scottish League Cup (3): Barrett 1, Osadolor 1, Rodden 1.
SPFL Trust Trophy (1): own goal 1.
League Two Play-offs (1): Arnott 1.

Ritchie T 12+1	Mailer A 31	Young K 30	Martyniuk N 32	Somerville K 21+4	Scarborough B 6+7	Murphy S 26+2	Currie L 31+3	Barrett B 25+2	Arnott A 18+14	Higginbotham K 15+3	Watson D 3+6	McGachie K 8+20	Wardell O —+2	Lorimer L 4+8	Ross C 32+1	Connolly C 21+11	Haspell C 1	McRoberts L —+2	Ferrie M 15+12	Allen G 1+1	Gardiner C —+1	Martin P 9	Andrews M 4	Hepburn C 1	Lennon G 12+4	Anderson M 1	Porteous R 11+3	Smutek K 1	Stenhouse L —+4	Watson B 6+8	McNeil A 9	Aiken M 10	Hogg C —+2	Match No.
1	2^4	3	4	5	6^1	7	8	9^3	10	11^2	12	13	14																					1
1		4	3	5	13	7	6	10^1	8	9^3	12	14		2^2	11																			2
1		3^1	4	5	9^2	6^1	7	10	12	11	13			2^3	8	14																		3
1	5	3	4	2			8	9	7	10	12				11^1	6																		4
1	2	3	4		5	12	6	9	7^2	10^3	13			14	11^1	8																		5
1	2	3		5		7		11^3	8^2	10		9^1	13	14	12	6	4																	6
1	3	4		5		6^2	7	10	2	9		8^1		14	12	11	13																	7
1	2	4^3	3		5		8	11	6^2	7^5	9^1	16		15	10^4	12			14	13														8
1	2			5	6	9	8^2	7^3	13	14		12	10^1	3^4		11	4^4	15																9
	2	3	4	5		6^1	7	8	14	10^3		9^2			11	12			13			1												10
12	2	3	4	5		6	7	10^3	13	14		15			11^4	8^1			9^2			1^1												11
1	2	3	4	5		6		10^1	12	9^2					11	7			8	13														12
1	2	3^1	4	5	14	6	13	10^3	12	9^4		15		16	11	7^2			8^5															13
1	2	3	4	5^2	12		7		8^1	9^3		14		13	11	6			10															14
	2	3	4	5	15	8	6		9^3	12		10^1			7^2	11^4			14						1									15
	2	3	4^5	5^1	16	8	7	15	9^2	10^3		13			6^1	11	12		14							1								16
	$3■$		4	2	15	6^2	7^3	5^4	12	13					10^1	14	9		8						11					1				17
	4	3	2^1	16		7	13	5^5	12	11^2		15	14		10	8^3			6						1		9^4							18
	3	4	2	12		6	10^1	8		13					11^3	7			14						5	1	9^2							19
	3^4	4	2^1		6	14	10^2	8		9^5					11	7^3			15			1			16		13	5	12					20
	2	3	4		6	7	10	12		14					11^3	13			8^1			1			5		9^2							21
	2	3	4		6	7	10	14		13					11^3	12			8^2			1			5		9^1							22
	2	3	4		6^1	7	10^4	13		16					11^5	12			8^3			1			5		9^2		15	14				23
	2	3	4		6^4	7	10	12		14					11^3	13			8^1				1		5^5		9^2		16	15				24
	2	3^1	4	12	6	7	10								11	9			8^2						5					13	1			25
	2^5	3^2	4	13	7	8	10			14					11	6^3			12						5^4		9^1		16	15	1			26
	2^3		4	3		8^2	9^1	6		14					10	12			13						5				11	1	7		27
	2	3	4		7	12		$11■$							$10■$	13			8^2						5				9^1	1	6		28
	2	3	4	13		6	10^1			14					8				12						5		11^2		7	1	9		29
	2	3	4	9		7^3		13		12									11^2						5		10^1		6	1	8	14	30
	2^2	3	4			7		13		12					10	8			5^1						11				9	1	6		31
	2^5	3	5	15		8^4	7^3	13		12					6	4			16						14		11^1		9^2	1	10		32
	2	3		5^2		8	6^1	7							10	4			12								$11■$		13	1	9^2	14	33
	2		4	5		8	6	7		10^1					11	3				$1■$									12		9		34
	2^1		4	5^4		8^3	6	7		10^2					11	3		14				1			12		13		15		9		35
	2^2		4	5		8^3	6	7		11^1					10	3						1			13		12		14		9		36

CELTIC

Year Formed: 1888. *Ground & Address:* Celtic Park, Glasgow G40 3RE.
Telephone: 0871 226 1888. *Fax:* 0141 551 8106. *E-mail:* customerservices@celticfc.co.uk *Website:* celticfc.com
Ground Capacity: 60,832 (all seated). *Size of Pitch:* 105m × 68m.
Chairman: Peter Lawwell. *Chief Executive:* Michael Nicholson.
Manager: Brendan Rodgers. *Assistant Manager:* John Kennedy.
Club Nicknames: 'The Bhoys'; 'The Hoops'; 'The Celts'.
Record Attendance: 92,000 v Rangers, Division I, 1 January 1938.
Record Transfer Fee received: £25,000,000 from Arsenal for Kieran Tierney (August 2019); £25,000,000 from Al-Ittihad
for Jota (July 2023); £25,000,000 for Matt O'Riley from Brighton & HA (August 2024).
Record Transfer Fee paid: £11,000,000 to Augsburg for Arne Engels (August 2024).
Record Victory: 11-0 Dundee, Division I, 26 October 1895. *Record Defeat:* 0-8 v Motherwell, Division I, 30 April 1937.
Most Capped Player: Pat Bonner, 80, Republic of Ireland.
Most League Appearances: 486: Billy McNeill, 1957-75. 583: Alec McNair, 1904-25 (includes 134 matches during WW1
seasons).
Most League Goals in Season (Individual): 50: James McGrory, Division I, 1935-36.
Most League Goals Overall (Individual): 397: James McGrory, 1922-39.

Honours
League Champions: (55 times) Division I 1892-93, 1893-94, 1895-96, 1897-98, 1904-05, 1905-06, 1906-07, 1907-08, 1908-09,
1909-10, 1913-14, 1914-15, 1915-16, 1916-17, 1918-19, 1921-22, 1925-26, 1935-36, 1937-38, 1953-54, 1965-66, 1966-67,
1967-68, 1968-69, 1969-70, 1970-71, 1971-72, 1972-73, 1973-74; Premier Division 1976-77, 1978-79, 1980-81, 1981-82,
1985-86, 1987-88, 1997-98, 2000-01, 2001-02, 2003-04, 2005-06, 2006-07, 2007-08, 2011-12, 2012-13; Premiership 2013-14,
2014-15, 2015-16, 2016-17, 2017-18, 2018-19, 2019-20, 2021-22, 2022-23, 2023-24, 2024-25. *Runners-up:* 32 times.
Scottish Cup Winners: (42 times) 1892, 1899, 1900, 1904, 1907, 1908, 1911, 1912, 1914, 1923, 1925, 1927, 1931, 1933, 1937,
1951, 1954, 1965, 1967, 1969, 1971, 1972, 1974, 1975, 1977, 1980, 1985, 1988, 1989, 1995, 2001, 2004, 2005, 2007, 2011, 2013,
2017, 2018, 2019, 2020, 2023, 2024. *Runners-up:* 19 times.

CELTIC – WILLIAM HILL PREMIERSHIP 2024-25 LEAGUE RECORD

Match No.	Date	Venue	Opponents	Result	H/T Score	Lg Pos.	Goalscorers	Attendance
1	Aug 4	H	Kilmarnock	W 4-0	2-0	1	Hatate [17], Scales [40], Kuhn [59], Ralston [90]	58,712
2	11	A	Hibernian	W 2-0	2-0	1	Kuhn [3], McGregor [19]	17,918
3	25	A	St Mirren	W 3-0	2-0	1	McGregor [3], Hatate [33], Johnston A [71]	6940
4	Sept 1	H	Rangers	W 3-0	2-0	1	Maeda [17], Furuhashi [40], McGregor [75]	59,612
5	14	H	Hearts	W 2-0	0-0	1	Engels (pen) [52], McCowan [89]	58,872
6	28	A	St Johnstone	W 6-0	3-0	1	Furuhashi 2 [35, 45], Bernardo [43], McGregor [54], Maeda [72], Idah [83]	7036
7	Oct 6	A	Ross Co	W 2-1	0-1	1	Johnston, A [76], Kuhn [88]	6372
8	19	H	Aberdeen	D 2-2	2-0	1	Hatate [24], Furuhashi [27]	58,890
9	27	A	Motherwell	W 3-0	1-0	1	McCowan [27], Johnston A [56], Idah [88]	8692
10	30	H	Dundee	W 2-0	0-0	1	Johnston A [60], Engels (pen) [67]	58,751
11	Nov 10	A	Kilmarnock	W 2-0	1-0	1	McGregor [45], Kuhn [71]	8657
12	23	A	Hearts	W 4-1	0-0	1	Furuhashi [55], Kuhn [60], Idah 2 (1 pen) [78, 90 (p)]	17,894
13	30	H	Ross Co	W 5-0	5-0	1	Scales [10], McCowan [27], Bernardo [35], McGregor [36], Idah [40]	58,436
14	Dec 4	A	Aberdeen	W 1-0	0-0	1	Hatate [78]	18,043
15	7	H	Hibernian	W 3-0	1-0	1	Engels [6], Newell (og) [54], Furuhashi [84]	58,641
16	22	A	Dundee U	D 0-0	0-0	1		13,662
17	26	H	Motherwell	W 4-0	1-0	1	Engels (pen) [45], Maeda [57], Kuhn [74], Hatate [81]	58,687
18	29	H	St Johnstone	W 4-0	1-0	1	Kuhn [30], Furuhashi 2 [59, 64], Maeda [73]	58,645
19	Jan 2	A	Rangers	L 0-3	0-1	1		51,065
20	5	H	St Mirren	W 3-0	2-0	1	Kuhn 2 [33, 68], Trusty [43]	58,838
21	8	H	Dundee U	W 2-0	1-0	1	Maeda [23], Hatate [83]	58,460
22	11	A	Ross Co	W 4-1	1-0	1	Furuhashi 2 [40, 81], Engels (pen) [90], McCowan [90]	6254
23	14	A	Dundee	D 3-3	1-1	1	McCowan [5], Yang [53], Engels (pen) [90]	8816
24	Feb 2	A	Motherwell	W 3-1	2-1	1	Maeda [1], Idah [29], Jota [90]	8293
25	5	H	Dundee	W 6-0	2-0	1	Engels 2 (1 pen) [18 (p), 71], Idah [45], Maeda 2 [55, 59], Kuhn [81]	58,541
26	15	H	Dundee U	W 3-0	2-0	1	McGregor [23], Jota [35], Idah [84]	58,989
27	22	H	Hibernian	L 1-2	0-2	1	Maeda [68]	18,357
28	25	H	Aberdeen	W 5-1	3-0	1	Maeda 2 [24, 90], Jota [30], McGregor [45], Yang [72]	58,756
29	Mar 1	A	St Mirren	W 5-2	2-1	1	Schlupp [28], Engels (pen) [45], Yang 2 [68, 90], Maeda [88]	7127
30	16	A	Rangers	L 2-3	0-2	1	Maeda [49], Hatate [74]	58,913
31	29	H	Hearts	W 3-0	3-0	1	Maeda 2 [17, 41], Jota [24]	59,062
32	Apr 6	A	St Johnstone	L 0-1	0-1	1		8795
33	12	H	Kilmarnock	W 5-1	4-1	1	Hatate 2 [9, 24], Maeda [11], Carter-Vickers [21], Ralston [90]	58,712
34	26	A	Dundee U	W 5-0	3-0	1	Strain (og) [30], Kuhn 2 [38, 45], Idah 2 [47, 58]	13,568
35	May 4	A	Rangers	D 1-1	0-1	1	Idah [57]	49,883
36	10	H	Hibernian	W 3-1	2-1	1	Kuhn [41], Idah [45], Hatate [58]	58,972
37	14	A	Aberdeen	W 5-1	2-1	1	Nawrocki [31], Yang [45], McCowan [48], Kenny [54], Idah [90]	17,089
38	17	H	St Mirren	D 1-1	0-0	1	Forrest [90]	58,889

Final League Position: 1

League Cup Winners: (22 times) 1956-57, 1957-58, 1965-66, 1966-67, 1967-68, 1968-69, 1969-70, 1974-75, 1982-83, 1997-98, 1999-2000, 2000-01, 2005-06, 2008-09, 2014-15, 2016-17, 2017-18, 2018-19, 2019-20, 2021-22, 2022-23, 2024-25. *Runners-up:* 15 times.

European: *European Cup/Champions League:* 238 matches (1966-67 winners, 1967-68, 1968-69, 1969-70 runners-up, 1970-71, 1971-72, 1972-73, 1973-74 semi-finals, 1974-75, 1977-78, 1979-80, 1981-82, 1982-83, 1986-87, 1988-89, 1998-99, 2001-02, 2002-03, 2003-04, 2004-05, 2005-06, 2006-07, 2007-08, 2008-09, 2009-10, 2010-11, 2012-13, 2013-14, 2014-15, 2015-16, 2016-17, 2017-18, 2018-19, 2019-20, 2020-21, 2021-22, 2022-23, 2023-24, 2024-25). *Cup Winners' Cup:* 38 matches (1963-64 semi-finals, 1965-66 semi-finals, 1975-76, 1980-81, 1984-85, 1985-86, 1989-90, 1995-96). *UEFA Cup:* 75 matches (*Fairs Cup:* 1962-63, 1964-65. *UEFA Cup:* 1976-77, 1983-84, 1987-88, 1991-92, 1992-93, 1993-94, 1996-97, 1997-98, 1998-99, 1999-2000, 2000-01, 2001-02, 2002-03 runners-up, 2003-04 quarter-finals). *Europa League:* 70 matches (2009-10, 2010-11, 2011-12, 2014-15, 2015-16, 2017-18, 2018-19, 2019-20, 2020-21, 2021-22). *UEFA Europa Conference League:* 2 matches (2021-22).

Club colours: Shirt: Green and white hoops. Shorts: White with black trim. Socks: White with dark green tops.

Goalscorers: *League (112):* Maeda 16, Idah 13 (1 pen), Kuhn 13, Furuhashi 10, Hatate 10, Engels 9 (7 pens), McGregor 8, McCowan 6, Yang 5, Johnston A 4, Jota 4, Bernardo 2, Ralston 2, Scales 2, Carter-Vickers 1, Forrest 1, Kenny 1, Nawrocki 1, Schlupp 1, Trusty 1, own goals 2.
Scottish Cup (15): Maeda 7, Idah 2, McGregor 2, Jota 1, McCowan 1, Yang 1, own goal 1.
Premier Sports Scottish League Cup (17): Maeda 6, Kuhn 5, Idah 2, Bernardo 1, Carter-Vickers 1, Furuhashi 1, Taylor 1.
SPFL Trust Trophy (0).
Champions League (15): Maeda 4, Idah 3, Kuhn 3, Engels 1 (1 pen), Furuhashi 1, Hatate 1, Scales 1, own goal 1.

Schmeichel K 32	Johnston A 30+2	Carter-Vickers C 29+1	Scales L 21+5	Taylor G 24+4	O'Riley M 2	McGregor C 34+1	Hatate R 27+10	Kuhn N 24+8	Furuhashi K 15+7	Forrest J 8+15	Ralston A 8+8	Palma L 1+7	Yang H 9+14	Holm O —+3	Maeda D 30+4	Johnston M —+1	Bernardo P 13+15	Idah A 19+16	Turley F —+1	Engels A 25+9	McCowan L 13+20	Trusty A 22	Valle A 7+4	Welsh S 1	Kenny J 1+7	Jota J 7+4	Schlupp J 7+6	Bonnar J —+1	Nawrocki M 3	Sinisalo V 6	McArdle S —+2	Match No.
1	2¹	3	4	5	6	7	8⁴	9²	10	11³	12	13	14	15																		1
1	2⁵	3	4	5	6	7	8³	9⁴	10²	11¹	16			15	17	12	13⁶	14														2
1	2	3	4	5³		7	8⁵	13	12		9²	15			14	11	6⁴	10¹	16													3
1	2	3	4	5		7	8³	9²	10⁴	13					11		6¹	14		12	15											4
1	2	3	4	5		7	8¹	9²	10³	13		15			11⁵		12	14		6⁴	16											5
1	2		4	5¹		7⁵	13	9⁴	10²	14					11		8	15		6³	16	3	12									6
1	2		4			7	8²	9	14	15					11⁴		12	10¹		6³	13	3	5									7
1	2		4			7	8¹	9	10³	13					11²		12	14		6⁴	15	3	5									8
1	2	13	4			8	12	10⁴	9¹		16			7	14	15	6³	3	5²														9
1	13	3⁵	16	5		12		10	15	2¹	11³	9⁴			14	7²		8		6	4											10
1	2³		4	5		7	8⁵	9⁴	13	15	14				11	12	10¹			6²	16	3										11
1	2³	3		5		7	8	9⁵	10⁴	13	14			15	11²		12	16		6¹												12
1	2³	3	4	16		7²	15		9	13	12				11¹		8	10		14	6⁴	5⁵										13
1	2	3		12		7	8⁵	9	10²	15					11⁴		6³	13		16	14	4	5¹									14
1	2		4	5		7	15	9¹	14	12				13	11²		16	10³		8⁴	6⁵	3										15
1			4	5		7	6³		10		2	13	9²		11⁴		14	12		15	8¹				3							16
1		3	4	5⁵		7	12	13	14	2			9³		11		8²	10¹		6⁴	15		16									17
1	2⁴	3	4			12	8⁵	9³	10²	15			11		14		7	13		6¹	16		5									18
1	2	3	4	5¹		7	8⁴	9	10³	11					6²		13	15		14	12											19
1	2	3		5		7	12	9²	14	15	13			11³		10⁴	8		6¹	4											20
1	2	3		5		7	12		13				14	9²	11		15	10¹		8⁴	6³	4										21
1	2	3	14			6	9¹		7				10				11²			8	13	4	5³		12							22
1	2	3		5⁵		6	12	13	7		16			10⁴	9¹	11²		14		8³	4	15										23
1		3	15	5⁴		7	8⁵	9¹		2			14		11		16	10³		13	6²	4			12							24
1	2	3		5³		7²	8⁵	12						9	13		10⁴	6		16		4			14	11¹	15					25
1		3		14		7	8⁵	9			2		9³		13		10⁵			12	6	4			16	11¹	5⁴					26
1	2	3		5³		7	12	9					11		10¹		8	6²		4						13	14					27
1	2	3	16			7	8²	9¹			12		10		13		6⁴	14		4					11³	5⁵	15					28
1	2	3	12			7⁴	8	9³			15		11⁵		10²		6	14		4¹					16	13	5					29
1	2	3				8	9		13				10		12		7	6		11²	5	4										30
	2	3				7¹	8⁴	9³	15				14		10²		12	13		6	16					11⁵	5	4	1			31
	2	3		12		7	8	9¹	16				13		10³		14			6¹	15	4				11⁵	5²		1			32
	2⁴	3	4	5³		7	8	12					9²	15	11⁵			10¹		6	16					13	14		1			33
	2	3	4	5⁴		7	8⁵	9	14						10		13	12		6²	16					11¹	15		1			34
		3	4	5³		7	8						9¹	2	12		11	13		10⁴	6²					15	14		1			35
1			4	5		7²	8³	9¹		12	2			11	13		10⁴			6⁵	15	3	14								16	36
	12					7²	13	15		6	2¹		9⁴		8	14				10⁵	4		11³		5		3	1	16			37
1	2	3	4	5		7		9¹		12			13		11⁴		8³	10²		6⁹	14					15	16					38

CLYDE

Year Formed: 1877. *Ground & Address:* New Douglas Park, Cadzow Avenue, Hamilton ML3 0FT (groundshare with Hamilton A for 2023-24).
Telephone: 01236 341 711. *Fax:* 01236 733 490. *E-mail:* info@clydefc.co.uk *Website:* clydefc.co.uk
Ground Capacity: 6,078 (all seated). *Size of Pitch:* 105m × 68m.
Chairman: Allan Maitland. *Company Secretary:* Bryan MacPherson.
Manager: Darren Young. *Assistant Manager:* Neil Scally.
Club Nickname: 'The Bully Wee'.
Previous Grounds: Barrowfield Park 1877-98; Shawfield Stadium 1898-1986; Firhill Stadium 1986-91; Douglas Park 1991-94; Broadwood Stadium 1994-2022.
Record Attendance: 52,000 v Rangers, Division I, 21 November 1908.
Record Transfer Fee received: £200,000 from Blackburn R for Gordon Greer (May 2001).
Record Transfer Fee paid: £14,000 to Sunderland for Harry Hood (1966).
Record Victory: 11-1 v Cowdenbeath, Division II, 6 October 1951.
Record Defeat: 0-11 v Dumbarton, Scottish Cup 4th rd, 22 November, 1879; v Rangers, Scottish Cup 4th rd, 13 November 1880.
Most Capped Player: Tommy Ring, 12, Scotland.
Most League Appearances: 420: Brian Ahern, 1971-81; 1983-87.
Most League Goals in Season (Individual): 32: Bill Boyd, 1932-33.
Most League Goals Overall (Individual): 124: Tommy Ring, 1950-60.

CLYDE – WILLIAM HILL LEAGUE TWO 2024–25 LEAGUE RECORD

Match No.	Date	Venue	Opponents	Result	H/T Score	Lg Pos.	Goalscorers	Attendance
1	Aug 3	A	Forfar Ath	D	0-0	0-0	6		711
2	10	H	Stranraer	W	1-0	0-0	4	Grant [63]	656
3	17	H	Stirling Alb	L	0-2	0-1	6		709
4	24	A	Bonnyrigg Rose	L	1-2	1-0	8	Scullion L [9]	655
5	31	A	East Fife	L	1-5	1-3	8	Redfern (pen) [42]	704
6	Sept 14	H	Edinburgh C	D	1-1	0-0	9	Allan (pen) [90]	612
7	21	H	Elgin C	D	0-0	0-0	7		617
8	28	A	Peterhead	D	2-2	0-1	8	Dunachie (pen) [59], Allan [81]	595
9	Oct 5	H	The Spartans	D	1-1	0-1	9	Rennie [62]	612
10	19	A	Stirling Alb	L	1-3	1-1	10	Leitch [32]	769
11	Nov 2	H	Bonnyrigg Rose	D	2-2	1-1	10	Allan [24], Redfern [90]	705
12	9	A	Edinburgh C	L	0-1	0-0	9		228
13	16	H	East Fife	W	3-1	1-0	9	Allan 2 [21, 50], Scullion L [80]	738
14	Dec 7	H	Peterhead	W	3-2	2-1	8	Leitch [34], Scullion L 2 [38, 90]	595
15	14	A	The Spartans	L	2-3	1-2	9	Hamilton [42], Allan [75]	471
16	17	A	Elgin C	L	2-4	0-3	9	Rennie [52], Leitch [63]	603
17	21	H	Forfar Ath	W	2-0	1-0	8	Allan [2], Rennie [70]	419
18	28	A	Stranraer	D	1-1	1-0	7	Allan [37]	728
19	Jan 4	H	Stirling Alb	W	2-0	1-0	7	Leitch [42], Scullion L [53]	810
20	11	A	East Fife	L	0-3	0-0	7		767
21	17	H	Edinburgh C	L	0-2	0-1	7		766
22	25	H	Elgin C	D	0-0	0-0	7		566
23	Feb 1	A	Bonnyrigg Rose	L	1-2	0-2	9	Rennie [79]	659
24	8	H	Stranraer	W	2-0	0-0	7	Rennie [49], Williamson [84]	754
25	15	A	Peterhead	D	2-2	1-1	8	Murdoch [38], Williamson [79]	641
26	22	H	The Spartans	L	0-2	0-1	8		598
27	Mar 1	A	Forfar Ath	W	1-0	0-0	8	Howie [52]	610
28	8	H	East Fife	L	1-2	0-1	8	Rennie (pen) [55]	765
29	15	A	Elgin C	L	0-2	0-2	8		611
30	22	H	Bonnyrigg Rose	W	3-1	1-0	8	Rennie [14], Williamson [76], Hynes [90]	757
31	29	A	Stranraer	W	2-1	0-0	8	Rennie 2 [83, 90]	515
32	Apr 5	A	Edinburgh C	L	1-2	0-1	8	Connell [70]	324
33	12	H	Forfar Ath	D	1-1	1-1	8	Dunachie [17]	711
34	19	A	The Spartans	L	0-2	0-0	8		451
35	26	A	Stirling Alb	W	4-1	2-0	8	Redfern [19], Connell [39], Sutherland [61], Bradley [84]	830
36	May 3	H	Peterhead	W	6-1	3-1	7	Redfern [9], Hynes [30], Dunachie [45], Bradley [47], Leitch [83], Docherty [90]	788

Final League Position: 7

Honours
League Champions: Division II 1904-05, 1951-52, 1956-57, 1961-62, 1972-73; Second Division 1977-78, 1981-82, 1992-93, 1999-2000.
Runners-up: Division II 1903-04, 1905-06, 1925-26, 1963-64; First Division 2002-03, 2003-04; League Two 2018-19.
Promoted via play-offs: 2018-19 (to League Two).
Scottish Cup Winners: 1939, 1955, 1958; *Runners-up:* 1910, 1912, 1949.
League Cup: Semi-finals 1956, 1957, 1968.
League Challenge Cup Runners-up: 2006-07.

Club colours: Shirt: White with red trim. Shorts: Black. Socks: Red.

Goalscorers: *League (49):* Rennie 9 (1 pen), Allan 8 (1 pen), Leitch 5, Scullion L 5, Redfern 4 (1 pen), Dunachie 3 (1 pen), Williamson 3, Bradley 2, Connell 2, Hynes 2, Docherty 1, Grant 1, Hamilton 1, Howie 1, Murdoch 1, Sutherland 1.
Scottish Cup (1): Allan 1.
Premier Sports Scottish League Cup (9): Dunachie 3, Connell 1, Connelly 1, Hamilton 1, Redfern 1, Rennie 1, own goal 1.
SPFL Trust Trophy (2): Dunachie 1 (1 pen), Leitch 1.

Kinnear B 6	Hamilton L 28	Howie C 25+5	McKay P 15	Robson T 30	Murdoch A 30+3	Grant R 23+2	Scullion L 21+5	Rennie M 22+8	Allan J 16+3	Redfern M 12+12	Dunachie L 20+12	Connelly L 3+4	Houston J 13+3	Leitch R 17+11	Connell K 10+14	Hynes D 7+6	Docherty D 6+16	Lyon D 10+4	Lyon R 13+5	Hemfrey R 23	Cuddihy B 11+4	McGinn C 1	Kennedy J 7	Hannah C 5+5	Sutherland T 12+2	Williamson S 6+5	Scullion C —+2	Bradley J 4+3	Nevans S —+1	Match No.
1	2	3	4	5^1	6^4	7	8	9^6	10^2	11^1	12	13	14	15	16															1
1	4	16	3	5^5	6	7	8^4	15	10^2	11^3	12	13	2	9^1	14															2
1	2^1	16	3	4	5	6	7	8^2	9	10^3	13	14		15	11^4	12														3
1	2	3	4	5	6	7^3	10^4	12	13	14	11	8^1		15	9^2															4
1	2	4	3	5^5	8	7^2	11	14	12	9^1	13				10^3			6^4	15	16										5
1	3	12	4^1	9	8			13	14	10	6^5	2^2	11^4	5	15	16	7^3													6
	3	4		5^4		7		9	8^5	11^2	6^3	12	13	14	10^1	15	16	2		1										7
	4	3	9^5	7	8^2	6^3	14	16	12	10^4	11^1	2	15	13	5					1										8
	4	3	9^4	7			15	12	10^3	6^1	14	2	11	8^2	5					1	13									9
	4^4	15	8	6		14	13	11	10	12	2	9^2	7	5^1						1	3^3									10
	3	4	8	5^4	16	12	6^5	10^2	11	14	15	2	9^1	13						1	7^1									11
	3	4	8^1	5		12	7^4	15	11	9^1	10^2	2	6	13	14					1										12
	3	4	8^2	5		12	7^4	6	11^3	10^5	9^1	14	2	13	16	15				1										13
	3^1	4	5	8		7	6	11^2	10	14	12	2	9^3	13						1										14
	2^1	4	5	8^7		7	6	10^3	11	12	3	9	13							1	14									15
	4	2^1	5	8			6	10	11	13	3	9	7^2							1	12									16
	4		5			7^3	8	9	11	10^2	13	3	2	6^1	14					1	12									17
	4		5	8		7	6	10	11	12		9^1								1	2	3								18
	3	9	6^3	5^2				10^1	11	12	8	2	7	14	13					4	1									19
	3	13	5	9		8^3	6	12	4	2	10^1	11^2	14							1	7									20
	3	12	5	7		8	9^2	4	2	11^1	13									1	6				10					21
	3	4	5	8		6	11	14	10^2	2^3	13	12								1	7					9^1				22
	3	4	5^4	8		6	13	2	14	15	12									1	7			9^1	10^3	11^2				23
	4^1	3	5	7		8	6	10^3	12	14	9									1	2					11^2	13			24
	4	3	5	7		8	6^1	10	13	2										1	9					11^2	12			25
	4^3	3	5	7		8	12	10^6	13	16	14	2								1	9^1					11^2	6^8	15		26
	4^1	3	5	7		8	10	12	11^3	9	14	2^4								1					15	13	6^2			27
	4^1	3	5	9		6	7^5	12	8^4	16	2^3	10								1					13	11^2		14	15	28
		3	5^4	9	6^1	7	4	10^5	15	8^2	12	2								1	14				11^3	13	16			29
		3	5	6	9^4	4	11^1	16	13	8^3	7^5	2								1	14				10^2	12	15			30
		4	5^1	6	9	3				12	13	8^7	7	2						1	14				10	11^1				31
		3	5	6		8^1	14	4	12	15	13	9^4	7^2	2						1				10		11^3				32
		3	5	6		10	4			9^2	2	13	7							1					11	12		8^1		33
		3	5^1	6		10	4			9	2	13	7							1				12		11		8^2		34
		3		6		10	4	12	9	2^1	13	7^3	14							1				5		11^1		8		35
		3		6	14	10^3	4	13	9^2	2^1	15	7^4	12							1				5		11	16	8^5		36

COVE RANGERS

Year Formed: 1922. *Ground & Address:* Balmoral Stadium, Wellington Circle, Altens, Aberdeen AB12 3JG.
Telephone: 01224 392 111. *Fax:* 01224 392 858. *E-mail:* info@coverangersfc.com *Website:* coverangersfc.com
Ground Capacity: 3,023 (2,012 seated). *Size of Pitch:* 105yd × 68yd.
Chairman: Keith Moorhouse. *Vice-Chairman:* Graeme Reid. *Secretary:* Duncan Little.
Manager: Paul Hartley. *Coach:* Gary Hake.
Club Nickname: 'Wee Rangers'; 'Toonsers'.
Previous Grounds: Allan Park.
Record Attendance: 2,100 v Deveronvale, 2009, Highland League; 1,914 v Berwick Rangers, League Two play-offs, 11 May 2019.
Record Transfer Fee received: £25,000 from Liverpool for Scott Paterson (March 1992).
Record Victory: 7-0 v Dunipace, Scottish Cup 3rd rd, 26 November 2022.
Record Defeat: 0-7 v Ross County, League Cup Group rd, 30 July 2016.
Most League Appearances: 198: Connor Scully, 2019-25.
Most League Goals in Season (Individual): 24: Mitch Megginson, 2019-20.
Most Goals Overall (Individual): 116: Mitch Megginson, 2016-25.

COVE RANGERS – WILLIAM HILL LEAGUE ONE 2024–25 LEAGUE RECORD

Match No.	Date	Venue	Opponents	Result	H/T Score	Lg Pos.	Goalscorers	Attendance
1	Aug 3	H	Annan Ath	L 1-3	0-0	10	Marshall [86]	452
2	10	A	Queen of the South	L 1-2	0-0	10	Emslie [62]	1126
3	17	H	Dumbarton	D 1-1	0-0	9	Emslie [64]	462
4	24	A	Stenhousemuir	L 2-3	1-1	10	Marshall [33], McGrath [90]	561
5	31	H	Montrose	W 1-0	0-0	9	Megginson [49]	479
6	Sept14	A	Kelty Hearts	W 3-1	1-0	7	Megginson [41], Yule [86], Marshall [90]	377
7	21	A	Inverness CT	D 1-1	1-0	7	Emslie [21]	1505
8	28	H	Arbroath	L 2-4	2-2	8	Yule [39], Parker [42]	645
9	Oct 5	A	Alloa Ath	W 2-0	2-0	7	Scully [16], Fyvie [24]	652
10	19	H	Queen of the South	W 2-0	1-0	4	Fyvie [35], Megginson [62]	519
11	26	A	Montrose	W 2-0	0-0	1	Doyle [48], Megginson [86]	691
12	Nov 2	A	Dumbarton	W 3-0	0-0	1	Durnan (og) [50], Megginson [55], Emslie [89]	568
13	9	H	Inverness CT	L 1-2	1-1	2	Megginson [10]	551
14	16	A	Arbroath	L 1-2	1-2	5	Megginson [5]	1278
15	Dec 3	H	Stenhousemuir	L 0-3	0-2	6		176
16	7	A	Annan Ath	D 1-1	1-0	5	Glass [24]	315
17	14	H	Kelty Hearts	D 0-0	0-0	6		443
18	21	H	Alloa Ath	W 2-0	1-0	5	Darge [22], Gaffney [88]	323
19	28	A	Inverness CT	W 4-1	2-1	4	Glass [5], Megginson [18], Darge [49], Emslie [90]	1974
20	Jan 4	A	Queen of the South	L 0-1	0-1	4		915
21	25	A	Stenhousemuir	W 4-0	3-0	4	Glass [29], Megginson [31], Marshall [38], Fyvie [84]	336
22	Feb 1	H	Arbroath	W 2-1	0-1	2	Megginson [80], Harrington [85]	758
23	11	H	Montrose	D 1-1	0-0	3	Marshall [90]	452
24	15	A	Annan Ath	W 3-1	2-1	2	Breen (og) [8], Marshall 2 [28, 78]	331
25	22	H	Dumbarton	W 2-1	1-1	1	Megginson (pen) [45], Fyvie [87]	353
26	Mar 1	A	Alloa Ath	L 1-2	1-0	3	Emslie [7]	622
27	8	H	Queen of the South	W 3-1	2-1	3	Yule [28], Emslie 2 [36, 62]	411
28	11	A	Kelty Hearts	W 4-0	1-0	2	Megginson [11], Fyvie 2 [46, 71], Emslie [73]	339
29	15	A	Montrose	D 2-2	0-0	2	Harrington [88], Coulson [90]	735
30	22	H	Stenhousemuir	D 0-0	0-0	2		533
31	29	A	Arbroath	L 0-1	0-1	2		1422
32	Apr 5	H	Inverness CT	L 0-3	0-2	2		454
33	12	A	Dumbarton	W 3-1	2-0	2	Lobban 2 [28, 81], Fyvie [34]	531
34	19	H	Alloa Ath	D 1-1	1-0	2	O'Donnell (og) [45]	484
35	26	H	Kelty Hearts	D 2-2	2-0	2	Emslie [30], Megginson (pen) [37]	389
36	May 3	A	Annan Ath	W 4-2	2-0	2	Marshall [10], Coulson [35], Emslie 2 [67, 73]	415

Final League Position: 2

Honours
League Champions: League One: 2021-22; League Two 2019-20. *Runners-up:* League One: 2024-25.
Scottish Highland League Champions: 2000-01, 2007-08, 2008-09, 2012-13, 2015-16, 2017-18, 2018-19.
Promoted via play-offs: 2018-19.
Scottish Cup: 5th rd, 2023-24, 2024-25.

Club colours: All: Royal blue with white trim.

Goalscorers: *League (62):* Megginson 13 (2 pens), Emslie 12, Marshall 8, Fyvie 7, Glass 3, Yule 3, Coulson 2, Darge 2, Harrington 2, Lobban 2, Doyle 1, Gaffney 1, McGrath 1, Parker 1, Scully 1, own goals 3.
Scottish Cup (4): Emslie 1, Gaffney 1, Glass 1 (1 pen), McGrath 1.
Premier Sports Scottish League Cup (3): Doyle 1, Gaffney 1, Scully 1.
SPFL Trust Trophy (2): Gaffney 1, Megginson 1.
Championship Play-offs (3): Megginson 1 (1 pen), Yule 1, own goal 1.

Suman N 24	Murray F 3+1	Gillingham W 21+1	Doyle M 36	Yule B 25+3	Fyvie F 25+3	Darge A 31+1	Scully C 32+2	Harrington R 36	Glass D 19+6	Gaffney M 4+21	Emslie A 30+4	Marshall F 22+9	Megginson M 26+1	McGrath G 7+12	Parker L 15+5	McAllister R 3+5	Demus B 12+1	Lobban D 22+5	Coulson Q 3+7	Match No.
1	2^1	3	4	5^3	6	7	8	9	10	11^2	12	13	14^8							1
1		3	4			2	9	5	10	12	6	8		11^1						2
1		3	4	6	12	2	8	5	10^2	13	9	7			11^1					3
1	4^2	3			7	2	10	5		9	12	8^1	6^2	11	13	14				4
1		3	2	6	8	7	9	5	10^1		12		11^2	13	4					5
1		3	2	6	8	7	9^2	5	10^1		13	12	11		4					6
1^1		3	2	6		7	8	5^2	14	9	10	11^3			4	13	12			7
	3	2	8	12	6	7	5^1		10^3	9^2	11	13		4	14		1			8
	4	2	8	9	7	6	5		12	10^1	11				3		1			9
	3	2	7	10	8	9	5			6^1	11				4		1	12		10
	3	2	7	10^2	8	9	5			6^1	13	11			4		1	12		11
	4	3	7	10	8	9	5			6	12	11					1	2^1		12
	3	2	8	11		5	4	12	14	9	7^2	10^3			13		1		6^1	13
12	3	2	6			5^1	4	9^3	15	10	8^1	11	14		13		1		7^2	14
3	4	2			7	5	11^2	14	9	8	10^3	13			6^1		1		12	15
1		4	3		6	9	5	8^2	13	10	12			11^1		7		2		16
1		4	3		7	2	6	5	9^2	15	10^3	13	11^4	14		8^1		12		17
1		4	3		7	6	8	5	9^2	12	11	13				10^1		2		18
1			3			7	4	9	5	8	12	11	6			10^1		2		19
1			3	12	7	4	9^2	5	8	14	11^3	6^1	10	13				2		20
1			3	13	7	4	8	5	9^1	14	11^3	6^2	10^4	15				2	12	21
1		4		12	6	3	8	5	9^2	13	11	7^1	10					2		22
1		4	7	11^4	3	8^3	5	9^2	12		6	10^1	14	15				2	13	23
1			3	7		4	9	5	8	13		6	10^2	12				2	11^1	24
1			3	7	13	6	9^3	5	12	11	8^2	10^4	15	4^1				2	14	25
1			3	8		4	9^2	5	12	6	7	11	13					2	10^1	26
1		4	6	9^1	3	7	5	13	10	8	11^2				12		1	2		27
	3	9	8^3		6	5	12	10	7^2	11^1	14	4					1	2	13	28
	3		9	12	7^3	5	6^2	10	8^1	11	14	4					1	2	13	29
1			3	7	11^2	4	6	5	13	9	8^1	10						2	12	30
1			3	8	9	6^3	7^1	5	13	10^2	12	11^8	14	4				2		31
1			3	6	9	4	7^2	5	12	11	10	8^1						2	13	32
1		3	2	8	10	7	12	5	11^1	9					4			6		33
1		3	2	6	9^3	7	13	5	12	8	14	11			4			10^2		34
1		3	4	7	10	5^1		8	12	9				11	2			6		35
	3	14	2		8		5	7	10^3	13	6	11^1	4				1	12	9^2	36

DUMBARTON

Year Formed: 1872. *Ground:* Dumbarton Football Stadium, Castle Road, Dumbarton G82 1JJ.
Telephone/Fax: 01389 762 569. *E-mail:* office@dumbartonfc.com *Website:* dumbartonfootballclub.co.uk
Ground Capacity: total: 2,025 (all seated). *Size of Pitch:* 98m × 67m.
Owner: Mario Lapointe.
Manager: Stevie Farrell. *Assistant Manager:* Frank McKeown.
Club Nicknames: 'The Sons'; 'Sons of the Rock'.
Previous Grounds: Broadmeadow; Ropework Lane; Townend Ground; Boghead Park; Cliftonhill Stadium.
Record Attendance: 18,000 v Raith R, Scottish Cup Quarter-Final, 2 March 1957.
Record Transfer Fee received: £300,000 from Sunderland for Neill Collins (July 2004).
Record Transfer Fee paid: £50,000 to Stirling Alb for Charlie Gibson (1989).
Record Victory: 13-1 v Kirkintilloch Central, Scottish Cup 1st rd, 1 September 1888.
Record Defeat: 1-11 v Albion R, Division II, 30 January 1926: v Ayr U, League Cup, 13 August 1952.
Most Capped Player: James McAulay, 9, Scotland.
Most League Appearances: 298: Andy Jardine, 1957-67.
Most Goals in Season (Individual): 38: Kenny Wilson, Division II, 1971-72. *(League and Cup):* 46 Hughie Gallacher, 1955-56.
Most Goals Overall (Individual): 202: Hughie Gallacher, 1954-62

DUMBARTON – WILLIAM HILL LEAGUE ONE 2024–25 LEAGUE RECORD

Match No.	Date	Venue	Opponents	Result	H/T Score	Lg Pos.	Goalscorers	Attendance
1	Aug 3	A	Inverness CT	D 1-1	0-1	3	Pignatiello [59]	1439
2	10	H	Alloa Ath	D 3-3	1-2	5	Ruth 2 [5, 76], Hilton [64]	505
3	17	H	Cove Rangers	D 1-1	0-0	5	Durnan [90]	462
4	24	H	Arbroath	D 2-2	0-1	7	Ruth [74], Shiels [79]	688
5	31	H	Kelty Hearts	D 2-2	1-1	8	Durnan 2 [43, 89]	471
6	Sept14	A	Annan Ath	D 1-1	1-0	9	Hilton [9]	375
7	21	H	Montrose	L 0-1	0-1	9		628
8	28	A	Queen of the South	L 0-2	0-1	10		1146
9	Oct 5	H	Stenhousemuir	L 1-3	1-2	10	Pignatiello [42]	620
10	19	H	Arbroath	W 3-1	1-1	9	Pignatiello [18], Smith (og) [47], Gray [90]	1159
11	26	H	Inverness CT	W 3-1	1-1	9	Hilton 2 [14, 72], Blair [63]	872
12	Nov 2	A	Cove Rangers	L 0-3	0-0	9		568
13	9	A	Kelty Hearts	L 0-2	0-0	9		507
14	16	H	Queen of the South	W 2-1	0-0	8	Ruth [73], Wallace (pen) [90]	708
15	Dec 3	A	Alloa Ath	D 2-2	1-1	10	Wallace 2 (1 pen) [15, 58 (p)]	426
16	7	A	Stenhousemuir	L 0-4	0-2	10		436
17	14	H	Annan Ath	L 1-5	1-2	10	Niang [45]	506
18	21	A	Montrose	W 2-1	1-0	10	Gray 2 [25, 76]	541
19	28	H	Kelty Hearts	W 2-0	0-0	10	Orsi 2 [70, 89]	695
20	Jan 4	A	Inverness CT	L 0-2	0-1	10		1894
21	25	A	Queen of the South	L 1-3	1-1	10	Durnan [28]	1027
22	Feb 1	H	Alloa Ath	D 1-1	1-0	10	Hilton [2]	582
23	8	A	Annan Ath	L 1-2	0-0	10	Mumbongo [64]	428
24	15	H	Montrose	L 2-3	2-2	10	Ruth (pen) [19], Pignatiello [37]	533
25	22	A	Cove Rangers	L 1-2	1-1	10	Pignatiello [5]	353
26	Mar 1	H	Stenhousemuir	L 1-3	0-3	10	Pignatiello [54]	540
27	4	A	Arbroath	L 1-2	1-1	10	Ruth [4]	355
28	8	A	Inverness CT	L 0-1	0-0	10		757
29	15	A	Arbroath	D 1-1	0-1	10	Ruth [86]	1434
30	22	H	Queen of the South	D 0-0	0-0	10		688
31	29	A	Alloa Ath	W 3-2	0-1	10	Ruth (pen) [69], Morrison (og) [79], Durnan [90]	594
32	Apr 5	H	Kelty Hearts	W 6-0	3-0	10	Mumbongo [18], Orsi [25], Pignatiello [34], Ruth [50], Shiels [78], McGuffie [80]	317
33	12	H	Cove Rangers	L 1-3	0-2	10	Webster [49]	531
34	19	A	Montrose	D 2-2	1-1	10	Pignatiello [41], Wallace (pen) [63]	1087
35	26	H	Annan Ath	W 3-1	1-0	10	Blair [35], Wallace [77], Hilton [79]	581
36	May 3	A	Stenhousemuir	L 1-2	0-1	10	Shiels [53]	764

Final League Position: 10

Honours
League Champions: Division I 1890-91 (shared with Rangers), 1891-92; Division II 1910-11, 1971-72; Second Division 1991-92; Third Division 2008-09.
Runners-up: First Division 1983-84; Division II 1907-08; Second Division 1994-95; Third Division 2001-02; League Two 2022-23.
Promoted via play-offs: 2011-12 (Second Division), 2023-24 (to League One).
Scottish Cup Winners: 1883; *Runners-up:* 1881, 1882, 1887, 1891, 1897.
League Challenge Cup: Runners-up: 2017-18.

Club colours: Shirt: White with black and yellow horizontal hoop. Shorts: White. Socks: White.

Goalscorers: *League (51):* Ruth 9 (2 pens), Pignatiello 8, Hilton 6, Durnan 5, Wallace 5 (3 pens), Gray 3, Orsi 3, Shiels 3, Blair 2, Mumbongo 2, McGuffie 1, Niang 1, Webster 1, own goals 2.
Scottish Cup (4): Hilton 1, McGuffie 1, Niang 1, Ruth 1.
Premier Sports Scottish League Cup (4): Hilton 2 (1 pen), Gray 1, Orsi 1.
SPFL Trust Trophy (4): McGuffie 2, Ruth 1, Wilson 1.

Long B 18	Lynas A 10+6	Durnan M 30+1	Miller M 20+1	Shiels M 21+4	Niang M 32+2	Orsi K 21+10	Hilton J 22+8	Gray F 26+9	Wallace T 10+18	Ruth M 25+6	Pignatiello C 29+2	Mumbongo J 5+27	Clark C 23+3	Blair R 18+6	McGuffie C 23+10	Wilson D 11+11	Smallwood L 2+1	Brown E 14	O'Neil P 4+3	Nicol M —+1	Webster K 15	Sliwinski M 9	Young G 5	Gilfedder A —+2	Kelly S 3	Queen Z —+1	Match No.
1	2	3	4	5	6^4	7^2	8^3	9	10^1	11^4	12	13	14	15													1
1		3	4	5		6	10^1	7	13	11		2	12			8	9^2										2
1	12	3	4	5	8	11	7^2	6^1	13	10		2			9												3
1		3	4	5	6		9^1	7	10			2	12	13	11^3	14											4
1		3	4^2	8	6	13	9^1	7	10			2	12	5^3	11	14											5
1^8	14	3	4	8	6		9^1	7	10^3			2	13	5	11^2		12										6
1		3		6	8	13	11^1	7	14	10	5	12	2^3		9^2		4										7
1		3^8		11^3	7		9	12	6	14	10^4	2	13	5		8^2	15	4									8
1^1	2^2		3^3	8	7	13	15	9		10	6	14	5^4		11^4		4	12									9
1		3	2	11^1	8		9^2	13	12	10^3	6	14		5		7		4									10
1		3	2	11^1	8	16	9^2	12	13	10^6	6^4	14		5	15	7^3		4									11
1		3	2	11^5	8^1	6^3	9^4	13	14	10		12	16	5^2	15	7		4									12
1		3	2^2		7	10	9	12		11^3	8	13	5	14	6^1			4									13
1		3			7	8	9^1	6	13	11	2	12	5		10^2			4									14
1		3			6		9^2	7	8	11^1	2	12	5	14	10^3	13		4									15
1^8	13	3		12	6	8		7^4	9^3		2^2	11^4	5		10^1	14		4	15								16
	12		2^1	4	7	8		6	9^2		11	5^3	14	10	13			3	1								17
		3		8	7	11		6	12		2		5	9		10^1		4	1								18
1	3			10	6	11^4		2	14	5	7^2	12	8^1			4					13						19
1^1	3^3	14		10^6	6	11	13	9^4		2	15	5	7	16	8^2			4	12								20
		3	14		7	10	6^1	9		13	5^2	12	4	8	11				1			2^3					21
		3			7	11	6^1	9		12	5	13	4	8^2	10				1			2					22
		3			7	11^2	6^3	9	14	12	5	13	4	8^1	10							2	1				23
	15	3	4		7^4	10^2	9^1	12	13	11^5	6	16	5		8	14						2^3	1				24
	4	3			7	12		10	13	11^3	9^2	14	5		8	6^1						2	1				25
	14	3	5		6^4	13		9	15	11	8	12	4^3	7^1	10							2^2	1				26
	2	3	4	13	7^5	9^3	12	15	8^2	10^1	6	11		16	14						1	5^4					27
	3	4	6	5	13		14	10		12	9	11^1		7^2	8^3							2	1				28
	3^5	4	6^2		7	12		8^1	10^4	15	11		9^3	16	5		13	14				2	1				29
	3				6^5	10^1	15	14	9^3	11		13	4	8^2	7^4	12						2	1	5	16		30
	4	3			15	10^2	9	13	11^1	8	12		14	7^4	6^3	1						2		5			31
	3	4		15	8^1	10^2	14		9^4	12	7	11^3	5^5	6	13		1					2			16		32
	4	3	13		6^2	14	10^3	8	15	11^5	12		16	9	7^4							2	1	5^1			33
	3	4^1		7	16	11^2	8^5	14	10^1	13	9^4		5	6	12	15						2				1	34
	3		4	6	10^2	13	8^5	15	11^3		14		7	12	9^4							2		5^1	1	16	35
	3		4	6^1	14	8^2	15	10^3	11^4		13	9	7	5	12							2			1		36

DUNDEE

Year Formed: 1893. *Ground & Address:* Scot Foam Stadium at Dens Park, Sandeman St, Dundee DD3 7JY.
Telephone: 01382 889 966. *Fax:* 01382 832 284. *E-mail:* reception@dundeefc.co.uk *Website:* dundeefc.co.uk
Ground Capacity: 11,850 (all seated). *Size of Pitch:* 101m × 66m.
Chairman: Tim Keyes. *Managing Director:* John Nelms. *Technical Director:* Gordon Strachan.
Head Coach: Steven Pressley. *First-Team Coach:* Scott Paterson.
Club Nicknames: 'The Dark Blues'; 'The Dee'.
Previous Grounds: West Craigie Park 1893; Carolina Port 1893-98.
Record Attendance: 43,024 v Rangers, Scottish Cup 2nd rd, 7 February 1953.
Record Transfer Fee received: £1,500,000 from Celtic for Jack Hendry (January 2018); £1,500,000 from Celtic for Robert Douglas (October 2000).
Record Transfer Fee paid: £600,000 to Sol de América (Paraguay) for Fabian Caballero (July 2000).
Record Victory: 10-0 Division II v Alloa Ath, 9 March 1947 and v Dunfermline Ath, 22 March 1947.
Record Defeat: 0-11 v Celtic, Division I, 26 October 1895.
Most Capped Player: Alex Hamilton, 24, Scotland.
Most League Appearances: 400: Barry Smith, 1995-2006.
Most League Goals in Season (Individual): 32: Alan Gilzean, 1963-64.
Most Goals Overall (Individual): 169: Alan Gilzean 1960-64.

DUNDEE – WILLIAM HILL PREMIERSHIP 2024–25 LEAGUE RECORD

Match No.	Date	Venue	Opponents	Result	H/T Score	Lg Pos.	Goalscorers	Attendance
1	Aug 4	A	Dundee U	D 2-2	1-2	3	Palmer-Houlden [18], McCowan (pen) [79]	12,616
2	10	H	Hearts	W 3-1	3-0	1	Tiffoney [23], Taylor (og) [45], McCowan (pen) [45]	7266
3	24	A	Hibernian	D 2-2	1-1	4	Tiffoney [9], Murray [88]	15,710
4	31	H	St Mirren	D 2-2	1-2	5	Main [30], Larkeche [54]	5779
5	Sept 14	A	Ross Co	L 0-2	0-2	6		4068
6	28	H	Aberdeen	L 1-2	1-2	8	Murray (pen) [45]	9030
7	Oct 5	H	Kilmarnock	L 2-3	1-0	8	Larkeche [24], Adewumi [81]	5316
8	19	A	Motherwell	W 1-0	1-0	6	Cameron [39]	5084
9	26	H	St Johnstone	L 1-2	1-0	8	Murray [12]	6548
10	30	A	Celtic	L 0-2	0-0	10		58,751
11	Nov 3	H	Kilmarnock	W 3-2	1-2	6	Palmer-Houlden [41], McGhee [56], Larkeche [90]	5014
12	9	A	Aberdeen	L 1-4	0-0	7	Murray [70]	19,274
13	23	H	Hibernian	W 4-1	3-1	7	McGhee [26], Triantis (og) [31], Palmer-Houlden [45], Main [90]	5310
14	30	A	Kilmarnock	D 1-1	0-0	7	Cameron [71]	5454
15	Dec 4	H	Motherwell	W 4-1	1-1	5	Adewumi [14], Tiffoney [60], Cameron 2 [63, 67]	5381
16	7	A	Hearts	L 0-2	0-2	6		18,737
17	21	H	Rangers	L 0-1	0-0	7		47,208
18	26	H	Ross Co	L 0-3	0-1	9		5207
19	29	A	St Mirren	W 2-1	1-1	8	Murray 2 [29, 66]	6798
20	Jan 2	H	Dundee U	L 1-2	0-0	9	Murray (pen) [61]	11,585
21	5	A	St Johnstone	W 3-1	3-0	8	Murray [3], Palmer-Houlden [10], Cameron [22]	5246
22	9	H	Rangers	D 1-1	1-1	7	Adewumi [6]	8606
23	14	H	Celtic	D 3-3	1-1	7	Adewumi [41], Carter-Vickers (og) [54], Donnelly [78]	8816
24	Feb 1	H	Hearts	L 0-6	0-2	10		7458
25	5	A	Celtic	L 0-6	0-2	10		58,541
26	15	A	Aberdeen	L 1-2	0-1	11	Palmer-Houlden [54]	7632
27	22	A	Ross Co	L 1-3	1-1	11	Murray [4]	4075
28	26	A	Motherwell	L 1-2	0-1	11	Murray [79]	4258
29	Mar 1	H	St Johnstone	D 1-1	1-1	11	Murray [43]	7681
30	16	A	Dundee U	W 4-2	3-1	11	McGhee 2 [17, 39], Tiffoney [23], Murray (pen) [90]	13,000
31	29	H	Rangers	L 3-4	2-1	11	Murray [2], Shaughnessy [19], Tiffoney [62]	8710
32	Apr 5	H	St Mirren	W 2-0	1-0	11	Murray 2 [2, 63]	6580
33	13	A	Hibernian	L 0-4	0-1	11		17,926
34	26	A	Hearts	W 1-0	1-0	10	Murray [38]	18,085
35	May 3	H	Motherwell	L 1-2	1-0	10	Portales [31]	5692
36	10	A	Kilmarnock	L 2-3	0-1	10	Cameron 2 [76, 90]	5669
37	14	H	Ross Co	D 1-1	0-0	10	Tiffoney [55]	5905
38	18	A	St Johnstone	W 2-0	1-0	10	Cameron 2 (1 pen) [28, 90 (p)]	7170

Final League Position: 10

Honours
League Champions: Division I 1961-62; First Division 1978-79, 1991-92, 1997-98; Championship 2013-14, 2022-23; Division II 1946-47, 1947-48.
Runners-up: Division I 1902-03, 1906-07, 1908-09, 1948-49; First Division 1980-81, 2007-08, 2009-10, 2011-12; Championship: 2020-21.
Promoted via play-offs: 2020-21 (to Premiership).
Scottish Cup Winners: 1910; *Runners-up:* 1925, 1952, 1964, 2003.
League Cup Winners: 1951-52, 1952-53, 1973-74; *Runners-up:* 1967-68, 1980-81, 1995-96.
League Challenge Cup Winners: 1990-91, 2009-10; *Runners-up:* 1994-95.

European: *European Cup:* 8 matches (1962-63 semi-finals). *Cup Winners' Cup:* 2 matches: (1964-65).
UEFA Cup: 22 matches: (*Fairs Cup:* 1967-68 semi-finals. *UEFA Cup:* 1971-72, 1973-74, 1974-75, 2003-04).

Club colours: Shirt: Navy blue white trim. Shorts: White. Socks: White with navy blue tops.

Goalscorers: *League (57):* Murray 16 (3 pens), Cameron 9 (1 pen), Tiffoney 6, Palmer-Houlden 5, Adewumi 4, McGhee 4, Larkeche 3, Main 2, McCowan 2 (2 pens), Donnelly 1, Portales 1, Shaughnessy 1, own goals 3.
Scottish Cup (6): Cameron 2, Adewumi 1, Murray 1, Robertson C 1, Shaughnessy 1.
Premier Sports Scottish League Cup (24): Murray 5, Main 4, Palmer-Houlden 4, Cameron 3, Portales 3, Astley 1, Ingram 1, McCowan 1 (1 pen), McGhee 1, Tiffoney 1.
SPFL Trust Trophy (2): Mohammed 1, Sweenie-Rowe 1.

McCracken J 16	Portales J 23 + 1	McGhee J 20 + 3	Graham L 3	Ingram E 12 + 12	Cameron L 32 + 1	Sylla M 31 + 2	McCowan L 3	Larkeche Z 25 + 2	Murray S 36 + 2	Palmer-Houlden S 18 + 15	Tiffoney S 21 + 14	Main C 4 + 10	Mulligan J 29 + 5	Koumetio B 14 + 5	Robertson F 15 + 14	Braybrooke S 2 + 5	Adewumi O 20 + 8	Robertson C 21	Fraser S 1 + 4	Vetro J — + 5	Astley R 24 + 2	Carson T 22	Kelly S — + 3	Garza C 5 + 4	Donnelly A 10 + 1	Samuels 11 + 2	Shaughnessy J 10 + 1	Reilly C — + 6	Match No.
1	2	3	4	5¹	6³	7	8	9	10	11¹²	12	13	14																1
1	3	4		2	6	7	8	5¹	10³	9	11²	13		12	14														2
1	3	2		13	6	7	8	5¹	10	9¹	11²	12		4	14														3
1	3	2		12	8	6		5	11	14	9³	10	13	4¹		7²													4
1	3	13		2¹	8	7		5⁵	10	9²	11⁴	14	6³	4	16	15	12												5
1	3			2⁵	9	8¹		6⁹	11²		10	13	12	5		7⁴	14	4	15	16									6
1	2			5⁴	6	7ª		9	11²	13	8³	10¹		4			14	3	12		15								7
1	3			5	6¹			9	11³	14	12	10		3	7		4	8²		2	1								8
				5³	6⁵	7¹		9⁴	11	15	13	10²	16		3	8	12	14	4		2	1							9
1	4			2	8²	9		6	11¹	12			7		10	13		5			3								10
1	3	13		5²	6¹	7		8	11	9	14		12	15		10³	4⁴			2									11
1		2¹		12	8	6		5³	10⁴	9	13	15	7⁵	14	16		11²	4		3									12
2	7			13	9	6³		11	10		15	5²	3	8⁴	14		4¹			2	1								13
1	3	6		12	8	7¹		11	10		5²	4	9		13			2											14
1	3	6		9	7			11²	12	8¹	5	4³	13	10⁴			15	2	14										15
1	3	6		12	9	7		13	11³	14	5⁴	4	8¹	10²			15	2											16
4	6			9	8		12	11²	10¹		7	5	2		13	3	1												17
4²	6¹			15	9	8		10⁴	16	7³	14	2	5	13	11⁵		3	1	12										18
	3²			13	6	7		11	10	14	5	4¹	8	9³		2	1	12											19
			4	7	6		11	10²	12	13	5	8¹	9	3	2	1													20
			4	12	6	7	11¹	9⁸	8	14	5	10²	3	2	1	13													21
1				8	6		11¹	12	9²	5		14	10	3	13	2	1	7³	4										22
				8	13	6	11¹	12	14	5		10²	9	3		2	1	7³	4										23
				9	6	14	11⁴	12	15	5		13	10³	3		2	1	7²	4	8¹									24
3	13			8²	6		12	11⁴	15	14	5		10	9³		2	1	7¹	4										25
1	2	6		10³	7²		8⁴	11	12	9¹	5		13	14	3			15	4										26
1	3¹	6		9⁴	13		8	11	10³	15	5		7	14	4²		2		12										27
1	2			8	7		5³	10		9²	6		14	11			3¹			4		12	13						28
	2			11	7¹		5	10		13	6²		12	9³			1			8	4		3	14					29
	2			8	7		5	10		11	6		12	9¹			1			4	3								30
	2			8	7		5	10²		11	6		8¹	9			1			12	4		3	13					31
	2	14		7			5	10³	12	11	6		13	8			9¹	4²		1			3						32
	2³	14		7			5¹	10	13	11²	6		8	9⁴	4					1			12	3	15				33
6⁴		14	9				5²11	7¹10		8	12		4	15		2³	1			13	3								34
7²				8			5	10	12	9	6			11¹	4	13			2³	1			3	14					35
	7			8			5	10	9²11¹		6		13	12			2	1			4		3						36
	7			8⁴14			5	10	9²12		6	13		11¹	4		2	1		15			3²						37
	7			8			5	10²9¹11		6		12		4		2	1						3	13					38

DUNDEE UNITED

Year Formed: 1909 (1923). *Ground & Address:* Tannadice Park, Tannadice St, Dundee DD3 7JW.
Telephone: 01382 833 166. *Fax:* 01382 889 398. *E-mail:* admin@dundeeunited.co.uk *Website:* dundeeunitedfc.co.uk
Ground Capacity: 14,223 (all seated). *Size of Pitch:* 100m × 66m.
Chairman: Mark Ogren. *Chief Executive Officer:* Luigi Capuano.
Manager: Jim Goodwin. *Assistant Manager:* Lee Sharp.
Club Nicknames: 'The Terrors'; 'The Arabs'.
Previous Name: Dundee Hibernian (up to 1923).
Record Attendance: 28,000 v Barcelona, Fairs Cup, 16 November 1966.
Record Transfer Fee received: £4,000,000 from Rangers for Duncan Ferguson (July 1993).
Record Transfer Fee paid: £750,000 to Coventry C for Steven Pressley (July 1995).
Record Victory: 14-0 v Nithsdale Wanderers, Scottish Cup 1st rd, 17 January 1931.
Record Defeat: 1-12 v Motherwell, Division II, 23 January 1954.
Most Capped Player: Maurice Malpas, 55, Scotland.
Most League Appearances: 618: Maurice Malpas, 1980-2000.
Most Appearances in European Matches: 76: Dave Narey (record for Scottish player at the time).
Most League Goals in Season (Individual): 40: John Coyle, Division II, 1955-56.
Most Goals Overall (Individual): 199: Peter McKay, 1947-54.

DUNDEE UNITED – WILLIAM HILL PREMIERSHIP 2024–25 LEAGUE RECORD

Match No.	Date	Venue	Opponents		Result	H/T Score	Lg Pos.	Goalscorers	Attendance
1	Aug 4	H	Dundee	D	2-2	2-1	3	Trapanovski [13], Thomson [23]	12,616
2	10	A	Ross Co	D	1-1	0-0	6	Babunski [48]	4169
3	24	H	St Johnstone	W	2-0	0-0	5	Stephenson [54], Sanders (og) [88]	7806
4	Sept 1	A	Hearts	W	1-0	0-0	3	Graham [76]	18,648
5	15	H	Rangers	L	0-1	0-1	4		14,268
6	28	A	Kilmarnock	D	3-3	1-0	5	Moult [21], Sibbald [79], Graham (pen) [90]	6257
7	Oct 5	A	St Mirren	W	1-0	0-0	5	Adegboyega [75]	7166
8	19	H	Hibernian	W	3-2	1-1	4	Dalby [20], Stephenson [90], Ubochioma [90]	10,870
9	26	A	Aberdeen	L	0-1	0-0	4		19,274
10	30	H	Motherwell	L	1-2	1-1	5	Dalby [36]	8415
11	Nov 3	A	Hibernian	D	1-1	0-1	4	Dalby (pen) [90]	15,454
12	9	H	Ross Co	W	3-0	0-0	4	Stephenson [57], Dalby [68], Stirton [90]	8349
13	23	A	Rangers	D	1-1	1-0	4	Dalby [36]	47,714
14	30	H	St Mirren	W	2-0	0-0	4	Holt K (pen) [79], Adegboyega [90]	8868
15	Dec 7	H	Kilmarnock	D	1-1	0-0	4	Dalby [79]	8402
16	14	A	Motherwell	L	3-4	1-3	5	Dalby 2 (1 pen) [7 (p), 54], Moult [87]	4473
17	22	H	Celtic	D	0-0	0-0	5		13,662
18	26	A	St Johnstone	W	2-1	0-1	4	Middleton [51], Dalby [60]	7306
19	29	H	Aberdeen	W	1-0	0-0	4	Holt K [90]	13,581
20	Jan 2	A	Dundee	W	2-1	0-0	3	Sevelj [65], Dalby [88]	11,585
21	5	A	Hearts	L	0-1	0-0	3		10,214
22	8	A	Celtic	L	0-2	0-1	3		58,460
23	11	A	St Mirren	W	1-0	0-0	3	Moult [88]	7440
24	26	H	Rangers	L	1-3	1-1	3	Dalby [19]	13,653
25	Feb 1	A	Kilmarnock	L	0-1	0-0	3		5661
26	15	A	Celtic	L	0-3	0-2	4		58,989
27	22	H	Motherwell	W	1-0	1-0	4	Dalby [31]	9044
28	26	H	Hibernian	L	1-3	1-1	5	Graham [6]	10,674
29	Mar 2	A	Aberdeen	D	2-2	2-0	5	Sevelj [20], Dalby [45]	17,862
30	16	H	Dundee	L	2-4	1-3	5	Middleton [31], Trapanosvki [49]	13,000
31	30	A	Ross Co	W	1-0	0-0	5	Graham [74]	4088
32	Apr 6	A	Hearts	W	1-0	0-0	5	Dalby [67]	18,888
33	12	H	St Johnstone	W	1-0	1-0	4	Adegboyega [25]	10,160
34	26	H	Celtic	L	0-5	0-3	5		13,568
35	May 3	A	Hibernian	L	1-3	0-2	5	Trapanosvki [50]	18,399
36	10	H	St Mirren	L	0-2	0-1	5		9821
37	14	A	Rangers	L	1-3	1-1	5	Cleall-Harding [20]	49,361
38	17	H	Aberdeen	W	2-1	0-1	4	Gallagher [56], Dalby (pen) [63]	11,490

Final League Position: 4

Honours
League Champions: Premier Division 1982-83; Championship 2019-20, 2023-24; Division II 1924-25, 1928-29.
Runners-up: Division II 1930-31, 1959-60; First Division 1995-96; Championship 2018-19.
Scottish Cup Winners: 1994, 2010; *Runners-up:* 1974, 1981, 1985, 1987, 1988, 1991, 2005, 2014.
League Cup Winners: 1979-80, 1980-81; *Runners-up:* 1981-82, 1984-85, 1997-98, 2007-08, 2014-15.
League Challenge Cup Winners: 2016-17; *Runners-up:* 1995-96.

European: *European Cup:* 8 matches (1983-84, semi-finals). *Cup Winners' Cup:* 10 matches (1974-75, 1988-89, 1994-95). *UEFA Cup:* 86 matches (*Fairs Cup:* 1966-67, 1969-70, 1970-71. *UEFA Cup:* 1975-76, 1977-78, 1978-79, 1979-80, 1980-81, 1981-82, 1982-83, 1984-85, 1985-86, 1986-87 runners-up, 1987-88, 1989-90, 1990-91, 1993-94, 1997-98, 2005-06). *Europa League:* 6 matches (2010-2011, 2011-12, 2012-13). *UEFA Europa Conference League:* 2 matches (2022-23).

Club colours: Shirt: Tangerine with black trim. Shorts: Black with tangerine trim. Socks: Tangerine with black tops.

Goalscorers: *League (45):* Dalby 15 (3 pens), Graham 4 (1 pen), Adegboyega 3, Moult 3, Stephenson 3, Trapanosvki 3, Holt K 2 (1 pen), Middleton 2, Sevelj 2, Babunski 1, Cleall-Harding 1, Gallagher 1, Sibbald 1, Stirton 1, Thomson 1, Ubochioma 1, own goal 1.
Scottish Cup (0).
Premier Sports Scottish League Cup (12): Trapanosvki 3, Babunski 2, Holt K 2 (2 pens), Moult 2, Forbes 1, Gallagher 1, Graham 1.
SPFL Trust Trophy (3): O'Donnell 1, Stirton 1, Zekou 1.

Walton J 36	Graham R 13+2	Gallagher D 34	Holt K 22+1	Sevelj V 32+3	Sibbald C 12+4	Babunski D 18+6	Ferry W 35	Thomson M 5+9	Trapanosvki K 16+13	van der Sande J 9+23	Fotheringham K 7+9	Odada R 3+10	Moult L 4+15	Adegboyega E 29+2	Ubochioma M —+2	Stephenson L 28+3	Docherty R 14+8	Dalby S 32+3	Middleton G 23+6	Strain R 26+3	Stirton O —+1	Paton R 5+7	Fiorini L —+4	Campbell A 9+4	Cleall-Harding S 4	Richards D 2	Match No
1	2	3	4	5¹	6	7	8	9²	10³	11	12	13	14														1
1		3	4	5	6	7²	8	9	10³	11¹	12	13	14	2													2
1	4	3	6			7	9²	8	11¹	10			12	2		5	13										3
1	4	3	6¹	12		7	9³	8	10⁴	11²			15	2		5	13	14									4
1	4	3	6¹	13		7	9³	8	10	11⁴			15	2		5	12	14									5
1	4	3³		13		7	9²	8	15	12	16	11⁵		2		5	6⁴	10¹	14								6
1	4²	3	13		6		8	9	10¹				14	2		5³	7	11	12								7
1		3	4		6	7	8	9¹	12	13				2²	14	5		10	11³								8
1		3	4		6	7⁴	8		12	9¹	14		13	2²		11³	10	15									9
1		3	4		6	7³	8	15	9²	12	14			2		5⁴		10	11¹	13							10
1	3¹	4	6⁴			7	8		12²	15	14	13		2		9		10	11	5²							11
1		3	4		6	7³	11	13	8²	14	12			2		9¹		10⁴		5	15						12
1		3	4		8	11¹	5	13	12	6²	14					7		10³	9	2							13
1		3	4		6	7¹	8		12			13	14	2		9		10²	11³	5							14
1		3	4		7	8¹	9	14				13		2		12	11²	6³	10	5							15
1	3²	4	7			8¹		13	12	14				2		11		6³	10	9	5						16
1		3	4		8	5	10¹	13	12	6	15			2		7³	14	11⁴	9²	5							17
1	16	3⁴	4			7³	8	12	14	9¹	6²			3		6	12	11	8	2³							18
1			4	7			9¹	5	10²	14	13			3		6	12	11	8	2³							19
1	12		4	7			5		10¹	13		14		3		9	6³	11	8²	2							20
1	3⁴	4	7⁵			8	11²	14	12	16	6¹			2		9³	13	10	15	5							21
1	4	3	8¹			5	15	10³	11⁴	6	7²			13		12	14	9									22
1		3	4	7			8		13			12		2		9²	6	11	10¹	5							23
1		3	4	8			5		12	14	6¹			13		7³		10	9⁴	2		11²	15				24
1		3	4	6			8		14					13	2⁴	9²		10	15	5		11¹	12	7³			25
1	4	3	7⁴	16			12		8¹				14	2⁵		5	6²	10	15		13	9					26
1	4	3	8				9		13					2		12	7¹	10		5	11²	14	6³				27
1	4	3	7	13	15	9³		12						2		6²		10		5	11²	14	8⁴				28
1	4	3¹	7	8³			9²	14	13				12			5		11	6	2			10				29
1	4⁴	3⁶	7⁶	12		5	9³	17	15	13	16		8¹			10	6	2		14		11²					30
1	4		3	8¹		5	10²		12			9³	6	11	7	2		13		14							31
1		3		15	14	9	12	16	11³	4		6⁴	7	10⁵	13	5						8¹	2²				32
1		3		12	15	8	10¹		13	4		6⁴	7	11³	9²	5		14					2				33
1			4	10	14	5		13	12			3		7¹	11³	9	2		6²	8							34
1	3		4	7	9²	8		12	11¹				2³			6	10	13	5		14						35
1	3		4	7³		8		9¹					13	2		6²	10	11	5		12	14					36
	4		8⁴		13	5		12	14	6				7²	11³	9¹	2		15			10		3	1		37
	4		7			9¹	5	8²					13			6	11	10³	2		12	14		3	1		38

DUNFERMLINE ATHLETIC

Year Formed: 1885. *Ground & Address:* KDM Group East End Park, Halbeath Road, Dunfermline KY12 7RB.
Telephone: 01383 724 295. *Fax:* 01383 745 959. *E-mail:* enquiries@dafc.co.uk
Website: dafc.co.uk
Ground Capacity: 11,380 (all seated). *Size of Pitch:* 105m × 65m.
Chairman and CEO: David Cook.
Manager: Neil Lennon. *Assistant Managers:* Kevin McDonald and Iain Brunskill.
Club Nickname: 'The Pars'.
Record Attendance: 27,816 v Celtic, Division I, 30 April 1968.
Record Transfer Fee received: £650,000 from Celtic for Jackie McNamara (October 1995).
Record Transfer Fee paid: £540,000 to Bordeaux for Istvan Kozma (September 1989).
Record Victory: 11-2 v Stenhousemuir, Division II, 27 September 1930.
Record Defeat: 1-13 v St. Bernard's, Scottish Cup 1st rd, 15 September 1883.
Most Capped Player: Colin Miller 16 (61), Canada.
Most League Appearances: 497: Norrie McCathie, 1981-96.
Most League Goals in Season (Individual): 53: Bobby Skinner, Division II, 1925-26.
Most Goals Overall (Individual): 212: Charles Dickson, 1954-64.

DUNFERMLINE ATHLETIC – WILLIAM HILL CHAMPIONSHIP 2024–25 LEAGUE RECORD

Match No.	Date	Venue	Opponents	Result		H/T Score	Lg Pos.	Goalscorers	Atten- dance
1	Aug 3	A	Livingston	L	0-2	0-0	9		1917
2	10	H	Falkirk	L	0-2	0-1	10		7595
3	24	A	Hamilton A	L	0-1	0-1	10		2022
4	31	H	Ayr U	D	1-1	1-1	10	Otoo [15]	4921
5	Sept 13	H	Raith R	W	2-0	0-0	7	Otoo [52], Wotherspoon [80]	6993
6	21	A	Partick Thistle	L	0-1	0-0	8		4301
7	28	H	Queen's Park	L	1-2	0-1	9	Cooper [78]	4494
8	Oct 5	A	Airdrieonians	D	1-1	1-0	9	Kane (pen) [28]	1807
9	19	H	Greenock Morton	D	0-0	0-0	9		4645
10	26	A	Falkirk	L	1-2	0-1	9	McCann [72]	7321
11	29	H	Livingston	W	3-0	1-0	9	Kane 2 [7, 71], Benedictus [56]	4810
12	Nov 2	H	Partick Thistle	L	0-1	0-0	9		5162
13	9	A	Queen's Park	L	1-2	0-1	9	Todd [61]	1331
14	16	H	Airdrieonians	W	1-0	0-0	9	McCann [61]	4583
15	23	A	Ayr U	L	0-1	0-0	9		1701
16	Dec 7	H	Hamilton A	W	3-2	0-0	6	Todd [56], Cooper [83], Comrie [88]	4286
17	14	A	Raith R	L	0-2	0-1	9		5542
18	21	A	Greenock Morton	L	0-2	0-1	9		1722
19	27	H	Falkirk	D	3-3	1-1	9	Kane (pen) [25], Todd (pen) [63], Benedictus [90]	8558
20	Jan 4	A	Partick Thistle	W	4-1	3-1	9	McCann [4], Comrie [35], Kane [45], Cooper [82]	3938
21	14	H	Ayr U	L	0-2	0-0	9		4634
22	25	A	Airdrieonians	L	0-3	0-2	9		1865
23	Feb 1	H	Raith R	W	3-1	0-1	8	Kane 3 (2 pens) [51 (p), 65, 76 (p)]	6812
24	15	A	Livingston	D	0-0	0-0	9		1798
25	22	H	Queen's Park	D	0-0	0-0	8		4527
26	25	A	Hamilton A	L	0-1	0-0	9		1098
27	Mar 1	H	Greenock Morton	W	2-1	0-1	9	Kane 2 [60, 79]	4620
28	8	A	Falkirk	L	0-1	0-1	9		7106
29	14	A	Raith R	L	0-2	0-1	9		5586
30	29	A	Ayr U	L	0-3	0-1	9		3253
31	Apr 2	H	Livingston	W	1-0	1-0	8	Otoo [45]	4890
32	5	H	Hamilton A	L	0-1	0-1	9		7636
33	12	A	Queen's Park	W	1-0	0-0	8	Kane [69]	1705
34	19	H	Partick Thistle	D	0-0	0-0	7		5688
35	26	H	Airdrieonians	D	0-0	0-0	7		5504
36	May 2	A	Greenock Morton	L	0-2	0-2	7		2849

Final League Position: 7

Honours
League Champions: First Division 1988-89, 1995-96, 2010-11; Division II 1925-26; Second Division 1985-86; League One 2015-16, 2022-23.
Runners-up: First Division 1986-87, 1993-94, 1994-95, 1999-2000; Division II 1912-13, 1933-34, 1954-55, 1957-58, 1972-73; Second Division 1978-79; League One 2013-14.
Scottish Cup Winners: 1961, 1968; *Runners-up:* 1965, 2004, 2007.
League Cup Runners-up: 1949-50, 1991-92, 2005-06.
League Challenge Cup Runners-up: 2007-08.

European: *Cup Winners' Cup:* 14 matches (1961-62, 1968-69 semi-finals). *UEFA Cup:* 32 matches (*Fairs Cup:* 1962-63, 1964-65, 1965-66, 1966-67, 1969-70. *UEFA Cup:* 2004-05, 2007-08).

Club colours: Shirt: White with black pinstripes. Shorts: White. Socks: White with black tops.

Goalscorers: *League (28):* Kane 11 (4 pens), Cooper 3, McCann 3, Otoo 3, Todd 3 (1 pen), Benedictus 2, Comrie 2, Wotherspoon 1.
Scottish Cup (5): Hamilton 1, McCann 1, Mebude 1, Otoo 1, Todd 1.
Premier Sports Scottish League Cup (4): Sutherland T 2, McCann 1, Ritchie-Hosler 1.
SPFL Trust Trophy (5): McCann 2, Comrie 1, Kane 1, Todd 1.

Mehmet D 6+1	Comrie A 32	Fisher S 3+2	Benedictus K 30	Ngwenya K 23+3	Hamilton C 25+7	Ritchie-Hosler K 20+6	Wotherspoon D 15+12	Otoo E 34+2	Sutherland T 2+10	McCann L 29+1	Breen R —+1	Chalmers J 10+10	Wighton C 4+9	Kane C 24+4	O'Halloran M 1+4	Young S 9+2	Cooper J 4+20	Oluwayemi T 30	Fogarty T 17+2	Tod A —+2	Todd M 17+7	Clay C 13+5	Mebude D 5+9	Young C 4+4	Stevens A 7+3	Yeboah E 7+7	Mullen J 13	Oakley-Boothe T 7+2	Taylor-Clarke O —+2	Raymond A 4+1	Hampson O —+2	Wanyama V 1+3	Match No.
1	2	3³	4	5¹	6	7	8	9	10³	11	12	13	14																				1
1	5³	3	2		4	6	7²	8	14	9			10	11¹	12	13																	2
1	5	3¹	2³	4²		7	6⁶	8	9	15			10	14	16	11⁴	12	13															3
	5		2¹	3	8	9	13	4		10⁴				14	11³	12	7²	1	6	15													4
	5		5²	6	8¹	9	7		10			13	14	11³		3	12	1	4														5
1	2	13		5	6	8⁵	9¹	7		10³		15	11⁴		3	16	4²																6
1	2	12		6³	15	9¹	5		10	13	16	11	3⁴	14		4	8²	7⁵															7
1	5		3	8	14	4	15		7	10¹	11³		13		2	9²	6⁴	12															8
2		5	4	6³	13	8⁴	15	11⁵		7	11³	10		4	14	1	9²	8¹															9
2		5	4	6³	13	8⁴	15	11⁵	16	10¹			3	14	1		9²	7	12														10
2	3⁵	5	7²		9	13		14	10³		4	16	1	15		12	8	6¹															11
2	4	5⁸	7⁴	12	9	14	16	11¹	17	10²		3	15	1		13	8³	6⁵															12
2	4	5	13	8	9³	6	15	10	14				1	3²	12	7¹	11⁴															13
2	3	8	6	5³	13	4		10²	7	11¹		14	1	9	12																		14
2	3	9	12	5	15	4	13	8⁴	10²			7³	6¹	11	1																		15
2	3	4	7¹	5	8⁴	10²	11	12	6	14	1	9³	15	13																			16
2	3	8		5	13	4	14	10	6¹	7	12	1	9²	11³																			17
2	4	5¹	6⁴	8	9⁸	7		11³	14	10²	1	3	12	15	13																		18
2	4	5	6	13	7	15	11⁴	9²	10¹	1	3	8³	14	12																			19
2	4	5	6¹	8⁵	16	7³	10	13	11²	15	1	3	9⁴	12	14																		20
2	4	5¹	8⁴	6	9	14	11	15	10³	13	1	3	7²	12																			21
2	4	12	6	7³	16	8⁴	11	5¹	15	10⁵	14	1	3	9²	13																		22
2	3	5	6	12	9³	7	8	11²	1	4	14	10¹	13																				23
2	4	5	12	8	9	7²	14	15	1	11¹	6⁴	10³	3	13																			24
	3	5	2	10	7	12	13	1	14	11¹	8³	9	4	6²																			25
	4	5	2	9¹	7	10	1	12	8	11	3	6²	13																				26
2	3¹	13		7	8	12	14	1	15	11¹	9⁴	10³	4	6²	5																		27
2	3	12	7³	8	11	1	13	10²	9	4	6	14	5¹																				28
2	4	6	8³	5	10¹	11	1	13	9²	12	3	7	14																				29
5	3	6³	8	11⁴	4	10	15	1	9¹	12	2	7²	13	14¹																			30
5	3	12	8	11	6	10³	1	2	9²	7¹	13	14	4	8³																			31
5	3	13	7	11	14	1	4	9²	6	12	10¹	2	8³																				32
5	3	14	12	7	10³	11⁵	13	1	4	9⁴	6²	15	2	8¹	16																		33
5⁵	3	7	16	13	8	11¹	9⁵	15	1	4	10²	6⁴	12	2	14																		34
	3	8⁴	12	5¹	15	7	10	14	1	4	11²	6¹	16	9³	2	13																	35
13	3	9¹	5⁵	8	4	10⁴	11³	1²	12	14	15	2	6	16	7																		36

EAST FIFE

Year Formed: 1903. *Ground & Address:* MGM Timber Bayview Stadium, Harbour View, Methil, Fife KY8 3RW.
Telephone: 01333 426 323. *Fax:* 01333 426 376. *E-mail:* office@eastfifefc.info. *Website:* eastfifefc.info
Ground Capacity: 1,992. *Size of Pitch:* 105m × 65m.
Chairman: Jim Stevenson. *Vice-Chairman:* John Donaldson.
Manager: Dick Campbell. *Assistant Manager:* Ian Campbell.
Club Nickname: 'The Fifers'.
Previous Ground: Bayview Park.
Record Attendance: 22,515 v Raith Rovers, Division I, 2 January 1950 (Bayview Park); 4,700 v Rangers, League One, 26 October 2013 (Bayview Stadium).
Record Transfer Fee received: £150,000 from Hull C for Paul Hunter (March 1990).
Record Transfer Fee paid: £70,000 to Kilmarnock for John Sludden (July 1991).
Record Victory: 13-2 v Edinburgh C, Division II, 11 December 1937.
Record Defeat: 0-9 v Hearts, Division I, 5 October 1957.
Most Capped Player: George Aitken, 5 (8), Scotland.
Most League Appearances: 517: David Clarke, 1968-86.
Most League Goals in Season (Individual): 41: Jock Wood, Division II; 1926-27 and Henry Morris, Division II, 1947-48.
Most Goals Overall (Individual): 225: Phil Weir, 1922-35.

EAST FIFE – WILLIAM HILL LEAGUE TWO 2024–25 LEAGUE RECORD

Match No.	Date	Venue	Opponents	Result	H/T Score	Lg Pos.	Goalscorers	Atten-dance
1	Aug 3	A	Elgin C	L 2-4	0-2	10	Munro [71], McManus [76]	703
2	10	H	Edinburgh C	W 2-0	0-0	5	Newton [68], Trouten [73]	571
3	17	H	Forfar Ath	W 2-1	1-0	4	Austin [43], Trouten (pen) [79]	645
4	24	A	Stirling Alb	W 4-0	2-0	2	Austin 3 [40, 52, 84], Peggie [43]	794
5	31	H	Clyde	W 5-1	3-1	2	Austin 2 [13, 45], Trouten 2 (1 pen) [21 (p), 77], Laaref [80]	704
6	Sept 14	A	Stranraer	L 1-2	0-1	2	Trouten [71]	413
7	21	H	Peterhead	W 2-0	2-0	2	Trouten [7], Murdoch [44]	628
8	28	A	The Spartans	W 1-0	0-0	1	Austin [62]	589
9	Oct 5	H	Bonnyrigg Rose	W 5-0	2-0	1	Trouten 3 (1 pen) [14 (p), 38, 76], Ritchie (og) [86], Tod [90]	792
10	19	A	Forfar Ath	D 0-0	0-0	1		655
11	Nov 2	H	Stirling Alb	D 1-1	1-1	1	Munro [42]	728
12	9	H	Stranraer	L 1-2	0-1	2	Munro [49]	639
13	16	A	Clyde	L 1-3	0-1	3	Healy [90]	738
14	30	A	Bonnyrigg Rose	D 1-1	0-1	2	Norey [75]	568
15	Dec 7	H	Elgin C	W 2-1	1-1	1	Peggie [14], Norey [90]	564
16	14	A	Peterhead	L 0-1	0-1	1		651
17	21	H	The Spartans	W 5-1	2-0	2	Trouten 2 (1 pen) [27 (p), 36], McManus [52], Shepherd [67], Millar [90]	597
18	Jan 4	H	Forfar Ath	W 1-0	0-0	1	Trouten (pen) [67]	785
19	8	A	Edinburgh C	W 4-2	0-1	1	Shepherd [50], Trouten 2 [51, 87], Healy [81]	318
20	11	H	Clyde	W 3-0	0-0	1	Norey [50], Trouten [55], Laaref [89]	767
21	18	A	Stranraer	W 2-0	2-0	1	Healy [15], Trouten [25]	518
22	25	H	Edinburgh C	W 4-1	0-0	1	Austin [80], Laaref [87], Peggie [90], Trouten (pen) [90]	615
23	Feb 1	A	Elgin C	L 0-1	0-1	1		1001
24	8	A	The Spartans	W 1-0	0-0	1	Trouten (pen) [77]	630
25	15	H	Bonnyrigg Rose	D 1-1	0-1	1	Trouten (pen) [85]	644
26	22	H	Peterhead	D 0-0	0-0	1		1106
27	Mar 1	A	Stirling Alb	L 0-1	0-0	1		865
28	8	A	Clyde	W 2-1	1-0	1	Jones [2], Trouten [56]	765
29	15	H	Stranraer	L 0-3	0-0	1		914
30	22	A	Edinburgh C	L 2-5	0-2	2	Trouten (pen) [61], Laaref [90]	395
31	29	H	The Spartans	W 4-2	0-2	2	Trouten [50], McKenna [53], Austin 2 [84, 88]	674
32	Apr 5	A	Forfar Ath	L 0-1	0-1	2		744
33	12	A	Bonnyrigg Rose	W 2-0	0-0	2	Austin [53], Laaref [90]	705
34	19	H	Stirling Alb	W 2-0	2-0	2	Austin 2 [9, 29]	962
35	26	A	Peterhead	L 0-1	0-1	2		1979
36	May 3	H	Elgin C	W 2-0	1-0	2	Jones [8], Nicol [90]	776

Final League Position: 2

Honours
League Champions: Division II 1947-48; Third Division 2007-08; League Two 2015-16.
Runners-up: Division II 1929-30, 1970-71; Second Division 1983-84, 1995-96; Third Division 2002-03; League Two 2024-25.
Promoted via play-offs: 2024-25 (to League One).
Scottish Cup Winners: 1938; *Runners-up:* 1927, 1950.
League Cup Winners: 1947-48, 1949-50, 1953-54.

Club colours: Shirt: Gold and black stripes with gold sleeves. Shorts: White. Socks: Black.

Goalscorers: *League (65):* Trouten 22 (9 pens), Austin 13, Laaref 5, Healy 3, Munro 3, Norey 3, Peggie 3, Jones 2, McManus 2, Shepherd 2, McKenna 1, Millar 1, Murdoch 1, Newton 1, Nicol 1, Tod 1, own goal 1.
Scottish Cup (0).
Premier Sports Scottish League Cup (8): Trouten 4 (1 pen), Austin 2, Newton 1, Shepherd 1.
SPFL Trust Trophy (2): Austin 1, Shepherd 1.
League One Play-offs (7): Laaref 2, Munro 2, Trouten 2, McKenna 1.

McFarlane L 31	Murdoch S 22 + 1	Munro A 36	Easton B 26	Peggie R 31 + 3	Healy J 21 + 14	Millar K 35	Norey J 24 + 7	Newton L 14 + 3	Trouten A 31 + 2	Austin N 23 + 3	Shepherd S 17 + 16	Docherty S 2 + 12	Laaref A 5 + 26	McManus C 30 + 4	Slattery P 3 + 15	Walker G 9 + 3	Fleming A 5	Tod A 5	Winn M — + 3	Jones R 4 + 12	Higginbotham K 5 + 10	McKenna M 13	Bah M 4 + 1	Nicol G — + 2	Match No.
1	2^3	3	4	5^3	6^1	7^5	8^4	9	10	11	12	13	14	15	16										1
1		4	3	9	12	6	8	5^1	7^2	11	10^3		14	2	13										2
1	12	4	3	5^3	13	7	6	9	8	11^4	10^2		14	2^1	15										3
1	2^1	4	3	9	10^4	7^2	6^5	5	8^3	11	16	12	15	14	13										4
1	2^1	4	3	5^4	10^2	7^3	6	9	8	11	15		13	12	14										5
1*		3	4	9	6^1	8		5^2	10	11^4	13	14	12	7	15	2^3									6
	2	4			15	7	8^1	5	9^5	11^4	14	12	16	6	13	3^3	1	10^2							7
	4^1	3		10^2	13	7	12	5^3	9	11	16		15	6	14	2^4	1	8^5							8
		3		10^3	7			5	9	11	14		12^4	13	6	4^2	2^1	1	8		15				9
		3		5	12		7		9	11	10^2		13		6	4^1	2	1	8						10
1	2	3	4	5^3		14	8	12	11	10^4	13		15	7			6^2		9^1						11
1	2	3		5	10^1	6	9	14	11^2	8	12			7		4^3	13								12
1		4	3	5	12	6	9		11	8^1	10^3			7^2	13	2				14					13
1	5	4		10^2	8	6	7		9	11	13		3	12		2^1									14
1	2^4	3	4	10		8	6	12	9	11^3	15		13	7^2	5^1	14									15
1		3	4	9	5^2	6^3		7	11	10^4	2^1	14		8	13				12	15					16
1		3	4	9^3	5^1	6	8^2		10	11	13	14		7	12	2									17
1	2	3	4	5	10^1	6	8^3		9	11^2	13			7	14					12					18
1	2	3	4	5	10^3	7	6		9	8^2	12			14					13	11^1					19
1	2	4	3	5	10^2	6	8^3		9	11^1	13			7	14					12					20
1	2	4	3	5	10^3	7	8^1		9	11^2	13			6						14	12				21
1	2	4	3	5	10^2	6^4	8^1		9	12	11^3			14	7					15	13				22
1	2	3	4	5^4	13	6^3	14		8	12	11^2	16		7^5						15	10^1	9			23
1		4	3	5	10	2	8^2		9	11^1	12			7							13	6			24
1		4	3	5^2	10^1		7	13	9	11	12				2					14	8^9	6			25
1		4	3	5^2	10^1	6		2^2	15	9^5	11^1			14	12	7				16	13	8			26
		4	3^5	16	13	6		2^3	5	9	11^1			12	7^4					14	10^2	8	15		27
1	2	4			11^3	14		7	12	5	9			13	8^1						10^2	6	3		28
1	2	4			11^3	8^1	13		5	9^4	12	16		14	6^5						10^2	15	7	3	29
7^5		3	4	13	12	6^3	5	8^9	9	10^4				14			1			15	16	11	2^1		30
1	2^1	4	3	13	10^6	6	8^2	5^3	9^4	11	15	16		14							12	7			31
1		3	4	5^4	9^3	6	13		16	11	10^2			14	7^5	12					2^1	8		15	32
1	2^3	3	4	5	10^1	6			9	11^2	12			7							13	14	8		33
1	2	3	4	5	12	6			9	11^3	14			10^1	7							13	8^2		34
1		3	4	5	14	6^2		2^3	9	11^4	15			10^1	7						13	12	8		35
1		4		5	13	2	8^4		14	10^3	12			6^2	7						11^1	9	3	15	36

EDINBURGH CITY

Year formed: 1928 (disbanded 1955, reformed from Postal United in 1986; name changed to FC Edinburgh in June 2022; named reverted in June 2023).
Ground & Address: Meadowbank Stadium, London Road, Edinburgh EH7 6AE.
Telephone: 0131 210 0478. *E-mail:* hello@edinburghcityfc.com *Website:* edinburghcityfc.com
Ground Capacity: 1,500 (seated 500). *Size of Pitch:* 96m × 66m.
Director: John Dickson.
Manager: Michael McIndoe. *Assistant Manager:* Kirk Crichton.
Previous name: Postal United, FC Edinburgh.
Club Nickname: 'The Citizens'.
Previous Grounds: City Park 1928-55; Fernieside 1986-95; Meadowbank Stadium 1996-2017; Ainslie Park 2018-22.
Record victory: 6-0 v Airdrieonians, League One, 3 September 2022.
Record defeat: 1-11 v Rangers, Scottish Cup, 19 January 1929.
Most League Appearances: 150: Ouzy See, 2016-17 and 2020-25.
Most League Goals in Season (Individual): 30: Blair Henderson, League Two, 2018-19.
Most Goals Overall (Individual): 56: Blair Henderson, 2018-21.

EDINBURGH CITY – WILLIAM HILL LEAGUE TWO 2024–25 LEAGUE RECORD

Match No.	Date	Venue	Opponents	Result		H/T Score	Lg Pos.	Goalscorers	Atten- dance
1	Aug 3	H	Stirling Alb	L	1-2	0-0	8	Young [67]	243
2	10	A	East Fife	L	0-2	0-0	9		571
3	17	H	Bonnyrigg Rose	D	2-2	1-1	9	Stokes [42], Young [65]	309
4	24	A	Forfar Ath	W	3-0	2-0	6	Lawson 2 [11, 60], Young [18]	524
5	31	H	Peterhead	L	0-4	0-4	7		249
6	Sept 14	A	Clyde	D	1-1	0-0	8	Young [64]	612
7	28	A	Elgin C	D	3-3	1-0	9	Young 2 [36, 90]; Lawson [72]	726
8	Oct 5	H	Stranraer	L	1-2	0-1	10	Mitchell [68]	306
9	12	H	The Spartans	W	2-0	0-0	7	Young 2 (1 pen) [55 (p), 90]	476
10	19	A	Bonnyrigg Rose	L	0-2	0-0	7		683
11	Nov 2	H	Forfar Ath	W	2-0	1-0	6	Robertson [20], Young [86]	251
12	9	H	Clyde	W	1-0	0-0	6	Young [73]	228
13	16	A	Peterhead	W	3-2	2-1	5	Young 3 (1 pen) [22 (p), 44, 84]	694
14	Dec 7	A	Stirling Alb	W	3-0	2-0	4	Young [35], Wells [39], See [79]	531
15	14	A	Stranraer	D	0-0	0-0	4		381
16	21	H	Elgin C	W	1-0	0-0	4	Stokes [51]	239
17	28	A	The Spartans	L	0-1	0-0	4		743
18	Jan 4	H	Bonnyrigg Rose	W	2-0	1-0	4	Young (pen) [8], See [89]	356
19	8	H	East Fife	L	2-4	1-0	4	Young 2 [34, 80]	318
20	11	H	Peterhead	L	0-1	0-1	4		226
21	17	A	Clyde	W	2-0	1-0	4	McArthur [45], Young [51]	766
22	25	A	East Fife	L	1-4	0-0	4	Stokes [58]	615
23	Feb 1	H	Stirling Alb	W	4-3	2-1	4	Lawson 2 [12, 88], Zaid [42], See [61]	237
24	8	A	Forfar Ath	W	1-0	1-0	4	Robertson [34]	484
25	15	H	The Spartans	W	5-0	2-0	4	Lawson 2 [9, 75], See 2 [14, 71], McArthur [89]	338
26	22	A	Elgin C	W	2-1	1-1	3	See [40], Stokes [74]	826
27	Mar 1	H	Stranraer	L	0-1	0-0	3		228
28	8	A	Bonnyrigg Rose	W	1-0	0-0	3	Stokes [90]	698
29	15	A	Peterhead	L	0-2	0-0	3		823
30	22	H	East Fife	W	5-2	2-0	3	Jarvis 2 (1 pen) [5 (p), 55], Lawson [38], Daramola [56], Zaid [77]	395
31	29	A	Stirling Alb	L	1-2	0-1	3	Stokes [47]	634
32	Apr 5	A	Clyde	W	2-1	1-0	3	See 2 [15, 49]	324
33	12	H	Elgin C	W	2-0	1-0	3	Zaid [34], Lawson [65]	326
34	19	A	Stranraer	L	0-2	0-1	3		603
35	26	H	Forfar Ath	D	0-0	0-0	3		289
36	May 3	A	The Spartans	L	1-3	0-1	3	Hamilton [85]	549

Final League Position: 3

Honours

League Champions: Scottish Lowland League Champions: 2014-15, 2015-16. *Runners-up:* League Two 2019-20, 2020-21. *Promoted via play-offs:* 2021-22 (to League One); 2015-16 (to League Two). *League Challenge Cup:* Semi-finals 2018-19.

Club colours: Shirt: White with black trim. Shorts: Black with white trim. Socks: White with black trim.

Goalscorers: *League (54):* Young 18 (3 pens), Lawson 9, See 8, Stokes 6, Zaid 3, Jarvis 2 (1 pen), McArthur 2, Robertson 2, Daramola 1, Hamilton 1, Mitchell 1, Wells 1.
Scottish Cup (2): Lawson 1, Young 1 (1 pen).
Premier Sports Scottish League Cup (1): Lawson 1.
SPFL Trust Trophy (0).
League One Play-offs (1): Zaid 1.

Weir M 36	Robertson J 28 + 3	Gormley S 19 + 12	Lynch E 26 + 4	Mitchell O 34	Scally S 2 + 16	Jones S 29 + 5	Lawson J 33	Stokes J 35	Young C 21	Hamilton R 4 + 21	McKinstray K 2 + 6	Rennie J 2 + 7	Walker R — + 1	Pitt C 1 + 9	Mair S — + 2	McArthur L 27 + 1	Grigor J 29 + 1	Jarvis J 25 + 4	See O 14 + 11	Wells D 12 + 4	Zaid M 14 + 3	Daramola T 3 + 12	Beveridge D — + 1	Match No.
1	2	3	4	5	6¹	7	8	9	10	11	12													1
1	2	4	3	5¹	12	7	9²	6⁴	10	11³	8¹	13	14	15	16									2
1	2	5	4	9	6¹		8	10³	11	7²		14	13	12		3								3
1	2	13	4²	9³	14	7	8	10	11⁴	12				6¹	15	3	5							4
1	2	16	4	9³	14	6	8²	7	10	13	12			11¹	15	3	5⁴							5
1	2²	9	4	10³	12	6	8	7	11³	14						3	5	13						6
1	2	8¹	4²	10	6	9	7	11		13						3	5	12						7
1	2	8	4	10²	13	6	9	7	11							3	5¹	12						8
1	2	8¹	4	9³	14	7	11²	6⁴	10	13				15		3	5	12						9
1	2	3	4		6		11	10	9	7¹	12					5	8							10
1	2	3	10²	12	6	9	8¹	11⁴		15	14	13				4	5	7³						11
1	2	3		9³	14	7	10	6²	11	13						4	5	8¹	12					12
1	2⁴	3	15	10³	6	9²	8	11	13							4	5	7¹	14	12				13
1	2	3	5	13	6	10²	7⁴	11³	16	14				15		4	8¹	12	9⁵					14
1		4	3	5	6		7	11	12							2	8¹	10	9					15
1		4	2	9¹	14	6	11	10	15					3¹		12	5	8¹	13	7²				16
1		4	2	9¹	14	6	7	10	11	13						3	5³	8²	12					17
1	14	4	2	9¹	6	10²	7⁵	11⁴	16	15						3	5	8¹	12	13				18
1	2	4	3	9²	6	7¹	10⁴	11	15							5	8³	12	14	13				19
1	2	4	3⁸	9⁴	6	7¹	11³	10	15							5	8²	12	14	13				20
1	2		5		6	9²	11¹	10³	13							3	4	7	14	8	12			21
1	12	3⁸	8¹		6	11²	9⁴	13								2	4	7³	10	14	5	15		22
1	2	5			6¹	9³	11	14								4	3	8	10²	12	7	13		23
1	2	5		9			11									4	3	8	10	6	7			24
1	2	13	5	16	12	9	11⁴	14	15							3	4²	8⁵	10	6³	7¹			25
1	2	14	15	5³	13	9	11⁴									3	4	6	10¹	8	7²	12		26
1	2	13	14	5	16	6²	7	10¹	15							3⁴	4	8	11³	9⁵	12			27
1	2	14	15	5		6²	7¹	10								3	4³	8	11⁴	12	9⁸	13		28
1	2⁸	12	3	5¹	14	7³	9	10	15							4	8⁴	11	6²	13				29
1	15	2	5³	12	7²	10	16	14								3⁹	4	8	13	6¹	9	11⁴		30
1	15	14	2	5	13	7³	10									3	4²	8	12	6⁴	9	11¹		31
1	2	12	4	5	6		8	10								3		11	7¹	9				32
1	2	14	4	5³	13		8²	11								3	15	6⁴	10	7¹	9	12		33
1⁴	2	8	4	5	12	7		11	13							3²		10³	6¹		9	15		34
1	2		4	5		7	8¹	11								3		6	10		9	12		35
1	2	12	4		13	6	7⁴	11³	16							3¹	5	8²	10		9⁵	14		36

ELGIN CITY

Year Formed: 1893. *Ground and Address:* Borough Briggs, Borough Briggs Road, Elgin IV30 1AP.
Telephone: 01343 551 114. *Fax:* 01343 547 921. *E-mail:* elgincityfc@btconnect.com *Website:* elgincity.net
Ground Capacity: 4,520 (seated: 478). *Size of pitch:* 102m × 68m.
Chairman: Alan Murray. *Vice-Chairwoman:* Isla Benzie.
Manager: Allan Hale. *First-Team Coach:* Stefan Laird.
Previous name: Elgin City United 1900-03.
Club Nicknames: 'City'; 'The Black & Whites'.
Previous Grounds: Association Park 1893-95; Milnfield Park 1895-1909; Station Park 1909-19; Cooper Park 1919-21.
Record Attendance: 12,608 v Arbroath, Scottish Cup 3rd rd, 17 February 1968.
Record Transfer Fee received: £32,000 from Dundee for Michael Teasdale (January 1994).
Record Transfer Fee paid: £10,000 to Fraserburgh for Russell McBride (July 2001).
Record Victory: 8-1 v Hawick Royal Albert United, Scottish Cup 3rd rd, 26 November 2016.
Record Defeat: 1-14 v Hearts, Scottish Cup, 4 February 1939.
Most League Appearances: 474: Brian Cameron, 2008-25.
Most League Goals in Season (Individual): 21: Craig Gunn, 2015-16.
Most Goals Overall (Individual): 128: Craig Gunn, 2009-17.

ELGIN CITY – WILLIAM HILL LEAGUE TWO 2024–25 LEAGUE RECORD

Match No.	Date	Venue	Opponents	Result	H/T Score	Lg Pos.	Goalscorers	Attendance
1	Aug 3	H	East Fife	W 4-2	2-0	1	Girvan [38], Murray [41], Dingwall [49], Sargent [85]	703
2	10	A	Stirling Alb	W 1-0	1-0	1	Gallagher [21]	671
3	24	A	Stranraer	D 1-1	0-0	3	Murray [82]	477
4	31	A	Forfar Ath	D 1-1	0-0	4	Booth [51]	548
5	Sept 14	H	Bonnyrigg Rose	W 2-1	0-0	3	McDonald [88], Dingwall [90]	688
6	17	H	The Spartans	D 1-1	0-0	3	Murray [75]	439
7	21	A	Clyde	D 0-0	0-0	3		617
8	28	H	Edinburgh C	D 3-3	0-1	3	Dingwall 2 [48, 60], Cairns [89]	726
9	Oct 5	A	Peterhead	W 1-0	1-0	2	Dolzanski [42]	751
10	19	A	The Spartans	W 3-1	1-1	2	Girvan [12], McDonald [71], Gavin [89]	364
11	Nov 2	H	Stranraer	W 1-0	1-0	2	Murray [2]	757
12	9	A	Bonnyrigg Rose	L 0-2	0-1	3		756
13	16	H	Forfar Ath	W 2-1	1-1	1	Golding [12], Gallagher [73]	651
14	Dec 7	A	East Fife	L 1-2	1-1	2	Gallagher [27]	564
15	14	H	Stirling Alb	L 2-4	1-3	3	Dingwall (pen) [32], Golding [74]	873
16	17	H	Clyde	W 4-2	3-0	1	Gavin 3 [11, 37, 84], Golding [33]	603
17	21	A	Edinburgh C	L 0-1	0-0	3		239
18	28	H	Peterhead	W 2-0	1-0	1	Hyde [24], Gavin [61]	1356
19	Jan 11	A	Forfar Ath	D 1-1	0-0	3	Dingwall [76]	622
20	25	A	Clyde	D 0-0	0-0	3		566
21	Feb 1	H	East Fife	W 1-0	1-0	3	Girvan [10]	1001
22	4	H	Bonnyrigg Rose	W 3-0	1-0	3	Hester 2 [22, 79], Dolzanski [56]	610
23	8	A	Stirling Alb	L 1-3	0-2	3	Draper [70]	632
24	15	A	Stranraer	L 0-1	0-0	3		442
25	22	H	Edinburgh C	L 1-2	1-1	4	Draper [27]	826
26	Mar 1	A	Peterhead	L 0-2	0-1	4		1028
27	8	A	Forfar Ath	L 0-1	0-0	4		733
28	11	H	The Spartans	L 0-2	0-1	4		456
29	15	H	Clyde	W 2-0	2-0	4	Gallagher [10], Dingwall [45]	611
30	22	A	The Spartans	W 2-1	2-0	4	Golding [36], MacIver [43]	576
31	29	A	Bonnyrigg Rose	W 1-0	0-0	4	Golding [72]	476
32	Apr 5	H	Stirling Alb	L 0-2	0-1	4		816
33	12	A	Edinburgh C	L 0-2	0-1	4		326
34	19	H	Peterhead	W 4-0	3-0	4	Murray [12], Dingwall [17], Sargent [20], Gavin [84]	901
35	26	H	Stranraer	W 3-0	2-0	4	Dingwall [35], Golding [41], Gallagher [83]	904
36	May 3	A	East Fife	L 0-2	0-1	4		776

Final League Position: 4

Honours
League Runners-up: League Two 2015-16.
Scottish Cup: Quarter-finals 1968.
Highland League Champions: winners 15 times.

Club colours: Shirt: Black and white stripes. Shorts: Black with white trim. Socks: Black with thin white hoops.

Goalscorers: *League (48):* Dingwall 9 (1 pen), Gavin 6, Golding 6, Gallagher 5, Murray 5, Girvan 3, Dolzanski 2, Draper 2, Hester 2, McDonald 2, Sargent 2, Booth 1, Cairns 1, Hyde 1, MacIver 1.
Scottish Cup (4): Sargent 2, Gavin 1, Murray 1.
Premier Sports Scottish League Cup (3): Dangana 1, Golding 1 (1 pen), Murray 1.
SPFL Trust Trophy (3): Cameron 1, Dingwall 1 (1 pen), Gavin 1.
League One Play-offs (4): Sargent 2, McDonald 1, Murray 1.

McHale T 10	Cameron B 26+5	Dolzanski J 23+2	Murray J 26+1	Girvan K 32+2	Hyde L 23+9	Gallagher M 33+1	Booth L 26	Dingwall R 34	Golding D 30+5	Gavin D 18+9	Sargent R 19+17	Dangana M —+1	Cairns O 14+15	Draper R 11+6	MacLeman R —+6	McDonald O 4+24	Glavin A 26	Lesley K 13+11	Fraser D —+4	MacDonald L 1+3	Haspell C 1	Allen F —+1	Hester K 7+2	MacIver J 10+3	Fleming K 6+5	MacEwan R 1+2	MacIver J 1	Cooper M 1+1	Match No.
1	2	3	4	5^3	6^1	7	8	9	10	11^2	12	13	14																1
1		3^1	4	5	6^2	7	8	9	10^3	11	12		14	2	13														2
1		2	4	5^3	6	7^1	8	9	10^2	11^1	13		12	3	14	15													3
1	14	2	4	5^1	6	7^4	8	9^2	11	10^5	13		12	3^1	16	15													4
	14	3^1	4	5	6^4	7^3	8	11		9^2	10^5	12		2	16	15	1	13											5
	6	3	4	5^3	15	7^4	8	9	10^2	14	11^1			2	13		1	12											6
	6^3	3^4	4	5	14	7	8	9^4	13	10^2	11^1			2		15	1	12											7
	2		4	5^3	6^1	7	8	11	12	10^4	13		14	3^4		15	1	9^2											8
	7	3	4	2			8	5	6	11	10^1	9^2	12				1	13											9
	6	2^2	3	5^4		7	4	9	11^3	10	8^1	12	14	15			1	13											10
	6		4	3		7	5		9^5	13	11	12		2		10^1	1	8^2											11
	6		4	3	13	7^4	5		10^5	11^3	12			2	16	9^1	1	8^2	14	15									12
	6		4	3	13	7	5	9	8	11^1	10^2			2			1	12											13
	2		4	3^2	7	6^1	5	9	11	13	10	12	14				1	8^3											14
	2		3		6^3	7^2	5	9	11^5	13	10^1	12	14				1	8^4	15	16	4								15
	6		4	3	7		5^4	9	8^2	11^3	12		14	2		10^1	1	13	15										16
	6		4^1	3	7		5	9		11	10	12		2		8^2	1	13											17
	6		4	3	7		5	9^1		11	10	12		2		8^2	1	13											18
	6		4	3	7		5	9^3		11^1	10	12	14	2		8^2	1	13											19
1	6		4	3	7		5	9		12	10^1			2		8^2		13					11						20
1	6		4	3	7		5	9		11	10^1	12		2		8^2		13					11						21
1	6^4		4	3	7		5	9		11^5	10^1		14	2^2	16	8^3		13	15										22
1	9		4	3	13	7^4	5	8	6^1	11	10^3	12	14	2^2					15										23
1	9^2		4	3^1		7	5	8	10^3	11^4		12	14	2^5	16			13		15					6				24
	14		4	3		7	5^4	9	6^1	11	10^3	12		2		8^2	1	13	15										25
	9^3		4	3		7^4	5	8	6^2	11	10^1	12	14	2			1	13	15										26
			4	3		7^2	5^1	9	6^4	11^5	10^3		14	2^4	16	8	1	13	15										27
	9^1		4	3		7				11	10	12		2^2		8	1	13					5		6				28
	9		4	3		7^5				11^3	10^1	12	14	2	16	8	1	13	15				5^4		6^2				29
	9^4		4	3		7				11	10^2	12	14	2^5	16	8	1	13	15				5^1		6^1				30
	9		4	3	13	7^5	5		6	11^2		12	14	2		8^1	1								10				31
	9^4		4	3^1	13	7^2	5^3		6^3	11	10	12	14	2	16	8	1		15										32
			4	3		7^4	5	9	6^3	11	10^2	12	14	2		8^1	1	13	15										33
			4	3		7^2	5	9	6^4	11^3	10^1	12	14	2		8	1	13	15										34
			4	3		7^2	5	9	6	11^3	10^1	12	14	2^5	16	8^4	1	13	15										35
1			4	3	13	7	5	9^1	10	11^5	12^4		14	2^2	16	8^3			15					6					36

FALKIRK

Year Formed: 1876. *Ground & Address:* The Falkirk Stadium, 4 Stadium Way, Falkirk FK2 9EE.
Telephone: 01324 624 121. *Fax:* 01324 612 418. *Email:* post@falkirkfc.co.uk *Website:* falkirkfc.co.uk
Ground Capacity: 8,750 (all seated). *Size of Pitch:* 105m × 68m.
Owner: Falkirk Supporters Society. *CEO:* Jamie Swinney.
Manager: John McGlynn. *Assistant Manager:* Paul Smith.
Club Nickname: 'The Bairns'.
Previous Grounds: Randyford 1876-81; Blinkbonny Grounds 1881-83; Brockville Park 1883-2003.
Record Attendance: 23,100 v Celtic, Scottish Cup 3rd rd, 21 February 1953.
Record Transfer Fee received: £945,000 from Norwich C for Conor McGrandles (August 2014).
Record Transfer Fee paid: £225,000 to Chelsea for Kevin McAllister (August 1991).
Record Victory: 11-1 v Tillicoultry, Scottish Cup 1st rd, 7 Sep 1889.
Record Defeat: 1-11 v Airdrieonians, Division I, 28 April 1951.
Most Capped Player: Alex Parker, 14 (15), Scotland.
Most League Appearances: 451: Tom Ferguson, 1919-32.
Most League Goals in Season (Individual): 43: Evelyn Morrison, Division I, 1928-29.
Most Goals Overall (Individual): 154: Kenneth Dawson, 1934-51.

FALKIRK – WILLIAM HILL CHAMPIONSHIP 2024–25 LEAGUE RECORD

Match No.	Date	Venue	Opponents	Result	H/T Score	Lg Pos.	Goalscorers	Attendance
1	Aug 2	H	Queen's Park	W 2-1	1-0	1	Miller [33], Mackie [48]	5505
2	10	A	Dunfermline Ath	W 2-0	1-0	2	MacIver [6], Morrison (pen) [87]	7595
3	24	H	Partick Thistle	W 2-1	0-0	2	Henderson [58], Spencer [83]	6502
4	31	A	Greenock Morton	W 3-2	2-2	2	Spencer (pen) [30], Tait [42], Agyeman [75]	2961
5	Sept 14	A	Airdrieonians	W 2-0	0-0	1	Tait [72], Mackie [79]	2973
6	28	H	Raith R	L 0-1	0-1	2		5030
7	Oct 5	H	Ayr U	W 2-0	1-0	2	Ross 2 [8, 51]	6753
8	8	H	Livingston	D 0-0	0-0	1		5715
9	12	A	Partick Thistle	D 1-1	0-0	1	Ross [59]	4762
10	18	A	Hamilton A	W 3-1	3-0	1	Maguire (og) [5], Miller [29], Spencer [34]	1753
11	26	H	Dunfermline Ath	W 2-1	1-0	1	Hamilton (og) [24], Miller [57]	7321
12	Nov 2	H	Greenock Morton	W 6-0	2-0	1	Adams [16], Ross [37], Spencer 2 (1 pen) [46 ipi, 82], Oliver [52], Miller [54]	5708
13	9	H	Airdrieonians	W 2-0	1-0	1	Adams [33], Miller [59]	6008
14	16	A	Livingston	L 0-1	0-1	1		3745
15	22	A	Queen's Park	W 1-0	1-0	1	Nesbitt [26]	2071
16	Dec 7	H	Raith R	W 3-0	1-0	1	Agyeman 2 [5, 57], Montagu (og) [66]	6248
17	14	A	Ayr U	L 2-5	2-3	1	MacIver [2], Agyeman [36]	3039
18	21	H	Hamilton A	W 1-0	0-0	1	Morrison [80]	5532
19	27	A	Dunfermline Ath	D 3-3	1-1	1	Morrison [24], Nesbitt [54], Henderson [87]	8558
20	Jan 11	A	Queen's Park	D 0-0	0-0	1		5745
21	25	A	Raith R	W 2-0	1-0	1	Henderson [6], MacIver [60]	4495
22	31	H	Livingston	L 1-2	0-2	1	Spencer (pen) [55]	6381
23	Feb 8	H	Partick Thistle	W 5-2	3-2	1	Arfield 3 (1 pen) [1, 40, 60 (p)], Oliver [35], McCann [76]	6471
24	15	H	Ayr U	D 2-2	1-2	1	Henderson [45], Arfield [62]	7419
25	21	A	Greenock Morton	W 2-0	2-0	1	Arfield [19], Ross [27]	2194
26	Mar 1	A	Hamilton A	D 2-2	1-2	1	Henderson [21], Agyeman [90]	2291
27	4	A	Airdrieonians	W 3-0	2-0	1	Wilson (og) [9], Spencer [39], Stewart [77]	3069
28	8	H	Dunfermline Ath	W 1-0	1-0	1	Spencer [6]	7106
29	15	A	Queen's Park	W 4-0	1-0	1	Henderson [43], Oliver [51], Miller [59], Lang [72]	2685
30	22	H	Airdrieonians	W 2-0	0-0	1	Miller [61], Arfield (pen) [90]	6287
31	25	A	Livingston	L 0-1	0-0	1		3827
32	Apr 5	H	Greenock Morton	W 5-0	3-0	1	Arfield 2 [4, 44], Miller [17], Ross [54], Stewart [79]	6128
33	11	A	Ayr U	D 1-1	1-0	1	Mackie [44]	4471
34	19	H	Raith R	L 1-3	1-0	1	Miller [17]	7539
35	25	A	Partick Thistle	L 1-2	1-1	1	Arfield [39]	4997
36	May 2	H	Hamilton A	W 3-1	1-1	1	Ross 2 [33, 59], Miller [71]	7633

Final League Position: 1

Honours
League Champions: Division II 1935-36, 1969-70, 1974-75; First Division 1990-91, 1993-94, 2002-03, 2004-05; Championship 2024-25; Second Division 1979-80; League One 2023-24.
Runners-up: Division I 1907-08, 1909-10; First Division 1985-86, 1988-89, 1997-98, 1998-99; Division II 1904-05, 1951-52, 1960-61; Championship: 2015-16, 2016-17; League One 2019-20, 2022-23.
Scottish Cup Winners: 1913, 1957; *Runners-up:* 1997, 2009, 2015.
League Cup Runners-up: 1947-48.
League Challenge Cup Winners: 1993-94, 1997-98, 2004-05, 2011-12.

European: *Europa League:* 2 matches (2009-10).

Club colours: Shirts: Navy blue with red and white vertical stripe. Shorts: White with navy blue and red trim. Socks: Red with navy blue and white trim.

Goalscorers: *League (72):* Miller 10, Arfield 9 (2 pens), Ross 8, Spencer 8 (3 pens), Henderson 6, Agyeman 5, MacIver 3, Mackie 3, Morrison 3 (1 pen), Oliver 3, Adams 2, Nesbitt 2, Stewart 2, Tait 2, Lang 1, McCann 1, own goals 4.
Scottish Cup (4): Morrison 2, Agyeman 1, Miller 1.
Premier Sports Scottish League Cup (15): MacIver 4, Nesbitt 2, Tait 2, Henderson 1, Mackie 1, Morrison 1 (1 pen), Ross 1, Shanley 1, Yeats 1, own goal 1.
SPFL Trust Trophy (1): Miller 1.

Hogarth N 36	Adams K 36	Henderson L 35	Donaldson C 19+1	Mackie S 19+1	Spencer B 36	Tait D 28+5	Morrison C 4+8	Oliver G 22+11	Miller C 34+2	MacIver R 13+7	Ross E 30+6	McKenna M 1+16	Agyeman A 8+23	Yeats F 1+26	Nesbitt A 15+16	Shanley R —+8	Graham L 20+3	McCann L 12+3	Brophy E 1+3	Stewart B 5+11	Lang T 8+3	Arfield S 12+1	O'Connor D —+1	Thomson M 1+8	Match No.
1	2	3	4⁴	5	6	7	8³	9¹	10²	11	12	13	14	15											1
1	2	3	4	5	6	7	8	9²	10¹	11³	12		14	13⁴	15										2
1	2	3	4	5	6	7⁴	12	9²	8³	11⁵	10¹	14	13	16	15										3
1	2	4	3	5	6	7³		9¹	8²	11⁴	10	12	13	14	15										4
1	2	4	3	5	6	7³		9¹	10²	11	12	13	8	14											5
1	2	4	5⁴		7	8	16	14	11⁵	10³	9²	6¹	13	12			3	15							6
1	2	4	5⁵		6	7⁴	11¹	8⁵	10³	16	15	14	9	13			3	12							7
1	2	3			6	7⁴	13	11³	8¹	10²	12	15	9	14			4	5							8
1	2	3			6	7⁴		11³	8²	10¹	13	12	15	9	14		4	5							9
1	2	4			6	7⁴		11³	8	10¹	14	12	13	9²	15		3	5							10
1	2	4			6	7²		11³	8⁴	13	10¹	15	14	12	9		3	5							11
1	2	4			6	7⁵	14	11³	8²	12	10²	16	13	15	9⁴		3	5							12
1	2	4			6	7⁵	14	11¹	8³	12	10²	16	13	15	9⁴		3	5							13
1	2	4			6	7¹	14	16	8⁴	11⁵	10³	13	15	12	9²		3	5							14
1	2	4	16		6	7³		11²	8¹	12	10⁵	15	13	14	9⁴		3								15
1	2	4	5		6	14		11¹	9³	12	10²	15	8	13	7⁴		3								16
1	2	4	12	5	6	13	15	9¹	11³	10²	8	14	7⁴				3								17
1	2	4			6	12	13	9²	11	8	14	10³	7¹				3	5							18
1	2	4	5		6	9⁴	8¹	16	12	11⁵	10²	15	13	14	7³		3								19
1	2	3	4		6	7⁵	8²	14	10¹	12	16	13	9³					5		11⁴	15				20
1	5	3	4		7	6⁴	14	8	11³	9¹	10²	15	12				13			2					21
1	5	2	4		7	6	14	8³	10¹	9	13	12					11²			3					22
1	5	3	2⁴		6	7²	11⁵	10	9	13	15						4¹	12				16	8⁵	14	23
1	5	3	2⁴		6	7⁵		11¹	10³	8²	14	16	15				2	12				9⁴		13	24
1	2	3		5	6	7³	16	8²	10¹	13	14	15					4	11⁴				9⁵		12	25
1	2	4	3¹		6	7³	15	8	10²	14	13	12					5	11⁵				9⁴		16	26
1	2	7⁵			6	11²	10	13	8³	16	12						4⁴	14				3		9¹	27
1	2	7⁴	3	5	6	13	8⁵	10³	16	14	12						11¹	4				9²		15	28
1	2	7	3⁶	5	6	12	8²	10³	15	14	16						11¹	4				9⁴		13	29
1	2	7⁴	3	5	6	12	11²	8⁵	10¹	15	9³						13	14				4		16	30
1	2	7³	3		6	14	8⁵	11²	15	10²	13		5				16	12				4		9⁴	31
1	2	4	3³	5	6	7	11¹	8⁵	15	10⁴	13						14	16	12			9²			32
1	2	4	3⁴	5	7	6	11¹	8	10³	14	12		15				13					9²			33
1	2	4	3¹	5⁴	6	7⁵	11³	8	14	10⁴	16		15				12					9²		13	34
1	2	4			6	7¹	16	8	11³	10⁴	15	12	5⁵				14	3				9²		13	35
1	2	3⁶		5	6	7	11¹	8⁴	10²	13	14		4				12	16				9³		15	36

FORFAR ATHLETIC

Year Formed: 1885. *Ground & Address:* The Alpha Projects Stadium @ Station Park, Carseview Road, Forfar DD8 3BT.
Telephone: 01307 463 576. *Fax:* 01307 466 956. *E-mail:* info@forfarathletic.co.uk *Website:* forfarathletic.co.uk
Ground Capacity: 6,777 (seated: 739). *Size of Pitch:* 103m × 64m.
Chairman: Scott Murdie. *Vice Chair:* Paul Stephen.
Manager: Jim Weir. *Assistant Manager:* Gavin Price.
Club Nicknames: 'The Loons'; 'The Sky Blues'.
Record Attendance: 10,780 v Rangers, Scottish Cup 2nd rd, 2 February 1970.
Record Transfer Fee received: £65,000 from Dunfermline Ath for David Bingham (September 1995).
Record Transfer Fee paid: £50,000 to Airdrieonians for Ian McPhee (1991).
Record Victory: 14-1 v Lindertis, Scottish Cup 1st rd, 1 September 1888.
Record Defeat: 2-12 v King's Park, Division II, 2 January 1930.
Most League Appearances: 463: Ian McPhee, 1978-88 and 1991-98.
Most League Goals in Season (Individual): 46: Dave Kilgour, Division II, 1929-30.
Most Goals Overall: 125: John Clark, 1978-91.

FORFAR ATHLETIC – WILLIAM HILL LEAGUE TWO 2024–25 LEAGUE RECORD

Match No.	Date	Venue	Opponents	Result		H/T Score	Lg Pos.	Goalscorers	Attendance
1	Aug 3	H	Clyde	D	0-0	0-0	6		711
2	10	A	Peterhead	L	1-2	0-1	8	Mylchreest [76]	525
3	17	A	East Fife	L	1-2	0-1	7	Munro (og) [50]	645
4	24	H	Edinburgh C	L	0-3	0-2	10		524
5	31	H	Elgin C	D	1-1	0-0	10	Morrison [60]	548
6	Sept 14	A	The Spartans	L	0-1	0-0	10		398
7	21	H	Stranraer	W	2-1	1-1	10	Cannon [43], Malcolm [66]	469
8	28	A	Bonnyrigg Rose	W	1-0	0-0	7	Cannon [54]	572
9	Oct 5	A	Stirling Alb	L	1-2	1-2	8	Rodden (pen) [15]	686
10	19	H	East Fife	D	0-0	0-0	9		655
11	Nov 2	A	Edinburgh C	L	0-2	0-1	9		251
12	9	H	The Spartans	L	0-3	0-2	10		427
13	16	A	Elgin C	L	1-2	1-1	10	McLean [27]	651
14	Dec 14	H	Bonnyrigg Rose	W	5-1	2-0	10	Skelly [6], Allan M [21], McLean 3 [62, 65, 81]	503
15	17	H	Peterhead	D	1-1	0-1	10	Cannon [78]	522
16	21	A	Clyde	L	0-2	0-1	10		419
17	28	H	Stirling Alb	D	2-2	1-0	10	Rodden [40], McLean [74]	759
18	Jan 4	A	East Fife	L	0-1	0-0	10		785
19	11	H	Elgin C	D	1-1	0-0	10	Logan [83]	622
20	25	H	Stranraer	L	0-1	0-0	10		535
21	Feb 1	A	Peterhead	D	2-2	0-2	10	McLean [49], Byrne [84]	662
22	8	H	Edinburgh C	L	0-1	0-1	10		484
23	15	A	Stirling Alb	L	1-3	1-1	10	McLean [33]	596
24	22	A	Bonnyrigg Rose	W	2-0	1-0	10	McAllister [29], Somerville (og) [81]	680
25	25	A	The Spartans	D	1-1	1-0	10	McAllister [38]	289
26	Mar 1	H	Clyde	L	0-1	0-0	10		610
27	4	A	Stranraer	W	2-1	0-1	10	Slater [75], Rodden (pen) [90]	482
28	8	A	Elgin C	W	1-0	0-0	9	Rodden [79]	733
29	15	H	The Spartans	L	0-2	0-0	10		604
30	22	A	Stranraer	W	1-0	0-0	9	Ferguson [51]	496
31	29	H	Peterhead	D	0-0	0-0	9		668
32	Apr 5	H	East Fife	W	1-0	0-0	9	McAllister [9]	744
33	12	A	Clyde	D	1-1	1-1	9	McAllister [26]	711
34	19	H	Bonnyrigg Rose	L	0-2	0-1	9		903
35	26	A	Edinburgh C	D	0-0	0-0	9		289
36	May 3	H	Stirling Alb	D	0-0	0-0	9		995

Final League Position: 9

Honours
League Champions: Second Division 1983-84; Third Division 1994-95; C Division 1948-49.
Runners-up: League One 2018-19; Third Division 1996-97, 2009-10; League Two 2016-17, 2021-22.
Promoted via play-offs: 2009-10 (to Second Division); 2016-17 (to League One).
Scottish Cup: Semi-finals 1982.
League Cup: Semi-finals 1977-78.
League Challenge Cup: Semi-finals 2004-05.

Club colours: Shirt: Sky blue with white trim. Shorts: White. Socks: Sky blue.

Goalscorers: *League (29):* McLean 7, McAllister 4, Rodden 4 (2 pens), Cannon 3, Allan M 1, Byrne 1, Ferguson 1, Logan 1, Malcolm 1, Morrison 1, Mylchreest 1, Skelly 1, Slater 1, own goals 2.
Scottish Cup (4): McLean 3, Cocks 1.
Premier Sports Scottish League Cup (3): Malcolm 1, McLean 1, Whatley 1.
SPFL Trust Trophy (1): Reekie 1.

McCallum M 36	Taylor M 13+6	Hutchinson A 13+2	Morrison S 33	Allan M 35+1	Robson F 24+6	Whatley M 14+7	MacLean R 13+10	Malcolm B 18+5	Cannon N 22+10	McLean R 16+12	Inglis K 13+15	Cocks A 4+5	Reekie S 2+2	Skelly J 18+10	Mylchreest J 1+4	Klimionek B 2+4	Rodden B 21+7	Mohammed R —+2	Allan F 2+7	Logan C 4+1	Logan C 23	Slater C 17	Sweenie-Rowe M 7	Byrne D 1+6	McAllister R 14+2	Young S 5+3	Lemon M 7	Denholm D 8	Ferguson A 10+1	Match No.
1	2	3	4	5	6	7^1	8	9	10^2	11	12	13																		1
1		4	3	5	7	14	11	8	6		12		9^1	2	10^2	13^3														2
1	6	5	4	2	9	8	7^2		11	12				10^1	13	14	3^3													3
1	6^4		4	3	8	12	7	9^3	11	13	15			10^1	2^2	14	5													4
1	5	2	4	3	8	7	9^1		10	11^3	6^2	12		13					14											5
1	5		3	4	8	2		9	6^2		7	13		11^1			10		12											6
1	5		3	4	8	2^3	12	9	6	15	7^4	14		11^1			10^2	13												7
1	5		3	4	8	2	10	9	6^1	13	7^2			12			11													8
1	5		3	4	8	2^4	10^3	9^5	6	14	7^1	13		16			11^2				12	15								9
1	5		3	4	8	14	10^3	15	6		7^4	12		13			11^2			9^1	2									10
1	5		3	4	8			9	6^3	14	7^1	13		10^1		12	9^2				2									11
1			3	4	7	2^5		6	13	16	8^1	11^2		15	10^4	12	9^3			14	5									12
1	5		3	4	7			8	6^3	11^3	13	15		10^1	12		9^2			14	2									13
1			4	3	8	6	12	5	10	11^3	13			7^2		14	9^1				2									14
1			3	4	8	7	12	5	6	11				10^2			9^1			13	2									15
1	12		3	4	7	6^4	13	5^1	8	11	15			9^3			10^2		14		2									16
1	9^1	4	3	5	8	7			11	13				10			6^2		12		2									17
1	12	4	3	5	8	7^3		14	9	11	13			10^2			6^1				2									18
1	12	4	3	5	6	8^3		14	9	10^2	13			11							2	7^1								19
1			3	4	8^4	14	9^2	15	6	11	7^3			10^1			13		12		2	5								20
1	14	4^3	2	3	6		11^1	7^2	15	10												5	8	9^4	12	13				21
1	15		4	3	6^1	12	10^4	8^2	14	11											2	7	5	13	9^5					22
1	15		4	16	6^3		13		8	10^1	14			11^2							2	7	5^5	12	9^4	3				23
1			8	3				12	11			9^1					14				2	6		13	7^2	4	5	10^3		24
1	14		5	3				7	4^3		8^1						13				2	11		12	6^2	10	9			25
1	8^4		5	3				7^1	4^3	13	15						16				2	11		14	6^2	10^5	9		12	26
1	12	5	3	15								13		14							2	11		4^3	7^1	10^9	9^8	8	6^4	27
1	4^4	2	3	13			7^2			14				10^3			11^4				5	6		12	15		8^1	9		28
1	4^2	5	3	6^4	14	12			15					10^1			11				2	7^3		9	13			8		29
1		4	3	14	15	12		13	8^3					10^2			11				2	7^4	5	6^1				9		30
1		4	3	14		15		12	10			13					11^2				2	7	5^1	6^4			8	9		31
1		3	5			13		14	12			10					11				2	8		6^3	4	7^2	9			32
1		4^4	3			13		14	12	15				10^1			11				2	7		6^3	16	5	9^2	8^5		33
1	4		3	15				13	12	14				10^2			11^3				2	7		6		5	9^1	8^4		34
1	4		3	14				10^3	13	14	7			12			11^1				2	8	5	6^2				9		35
1	4		3	14	10			13	11^1	9^3							12				2	6		8^2			5	7		36

GREENOCK MORTON

Year Formed: 1874. *Ground & Address:* Cappielow Park, Sinclair St, Greenock PA15 2TU.
Telephone: 01475 723 571. *Fax:* 01475 781 084. *E-mail:* admin@gmfc.net *Website:* gmfc.net
Ground Capacity: 11,612 (seated: 6,062). *Size of Pitch:* 100m × 65m.
Chairman: John Laird.
Manager: Dougie Imrie. *Assistant Manager:* Andy Millen.
Club Nickname: 'The Ton'.
Previous Grounds: Grant Street 1874; Garvel Park 1875; Cappielow Park 1879; Ladyburn Park 1882; Cappielow Park 1883.
Record Attendance: 23,500 v Celtic, 29 April 1922; (40,000 v Rangers 25 April 1949 at Love Street, Paisley).
Record Transfer Fee received: £500,000 from Leeds U for Derek Lilley (March 1997).
Record Transfer Fee paid: £250,000 to MyPa (Finland) for Janne Lindberg and Marko Rajamäki (November 1994).
Record Victory: 11-0 v Carfin Shamrock, Scottish Cup 4th rd, 13 November 1886.
Record Defeat: 1-10 v Port Glasgow Ath, Division II, 5 May, 1894 and v St Bernards, Division II, 14 October 1933.
Most Capped Player: Jimmy Cowan, 25, Scotland.
Most League Appearances: 534: Derek Collins, 1987-98, 2001-05.
Most League Goals in Season (Individual): 58: Allan McGraw, Division II, 1963-64.
Most Goals Overall (Individual): 136: Andy Ritchie, 1976-83.

GREENOCK MORTON – WILLIAM HILL CHAMPIONSHIP 2024–25 LEAGUE RECORD

Match No.	Date	Venue	Opponents	Result	H/T Score	Lg Pos.	Goalscorers	Attendance
1	Aug 3	A	Partick Thistle	D 0-0	0-0	6		4148
2	10	H	Hamilton A	D 0-0	0-0	6		1866
3	24	A	Livingston	D 1-1	0-0	6	Moffat (pen) [71]	1512
4	31	H	Falkirk	L 2-3	2-2	8	Boyes [19], Baird [26]	2961
5	Sept 14	A	Queen's Park	L 0-1	0-1	9		883
6	21	H	Airdrieonians	W 2-0	1-0	6	Delaney [41], Ballantyne [87]	1871
7	28	A	Ayr U	L 0-1	0-0	8		2846
8	Oct 5	H	Raith R	W 2-0	0-0	5	Stuparevic [49], Garrity [54]	2976
9	19	A	Dunfermline Ath	D 0-0	0-0	6		4645
10	26	A	Hamilton A	L 0-3	0-0	7		1071
11	29	H	Queen's Park	L 0-1	0-1	8		1741
12	Nov 2	A	Falkirk	L 0-6	0-2	8		5708
13	8	H	Ayr U	D 1-1	1-0	8	Wilson [37]	1697
14	16	A	Raith R	W 3-2	2-0	8	Stuparevic 2 [6, 25], Garrity [90]	3508
15	Dec 7	H	Livingston	D 0-0	0-0	9		1664
16	14	A	Airdrieonians	D 2-2	2-1	8	Blues [30], Davies [43]	1200
17	21	H	Dunfermline Ath	W 2-0	1-0	7	Boyes [22], Blues [47]	1722
18	28	A	Ayr U	D 0-0	0-0	8		2974
19	31	H	Partick Thistle	W 2-1	0-0	7	Stuparevic [54], Blues [90]	2340
20	Jan 25	A	Queen's Park	W 2-1	0-1	6	Reynolds [67], Garrity [76]	1398
21	Feb 1	A	Partick Thistle	D 2-2	1-0	6	Shaw [45], Stuparevic [69]	3966
22	15	H	Airdrieonians	D 2-2	1-1	7	Shaw [25], Baird [69]	1752
23	18	H	Hamilton A	W 2-0	1-0	5	Adeloye [28], Lyall [79]	1541
24	21	H	Falkirk	L 0-2	0-2	5		2194
25	25	A	Livingston	L 2-3	1-3	6	Lyall [28], McGinn [90]	1050
26	Mar 1	A	Dunfermline Ath	L 1-2	1-0	7	Moffat [33]	4620
27	8	H	Ayr U	W 2-1	0-1	5	Blues [56], Davies [77]	2235
28	15	A	Hamilton A	W 2-0	0-0	5	Keay [86], Crawford [90]	1055
29	22	H	Queen's Park	W 2-1	1-0	5	Moffat [20], Garrity [64]	2044
30	25	H	Raith R	D 3-3	1-2	6	Shaw [31], Blues [63], Adeloye [75]	1750
31	29	H	Partick Thistle	L 0-1	0-0	6		2570
32	Apr 5	A	Falkirk	L 0-5	0-3	6		6128
33	12	H	Livingston	L 1-2	1-2	6	Crawford [44]	1737
34	19	A	Airdrieonians	W 1-0	1-0	6	Adeloye [34]	1706
35	26	A	Raith R	D 1-1	1-1	6	Gillespie (pen) [28]	4033
36	May 2	H	Dunfermline Ath	W 2-0	2-0	6	Moffat [3], Gillespie (pen) [7]	2849

Final League Position: 6

Honours
League Champions: First Division 1977-78, 1983-84, 1986-87; Division II 1949-50, 1963-64, 1966-67; Second Division 1994-95, 2006-07; League One 2014–15; Third Division 2002-03.
Runners-up: Division 1 1916-17; First Division 2012-13; Second Division 2005-06; Division II 1899-1900, 1928-29, 1936-37.
Scottish Cup Winners: 1922; *Runners-up:* 1948.
League Cup Runners-up: 1963-64.
League Challenge Cup Runners-up: 1992-93.

European: *UEFA Cup:* 2 matches (*Fairs Cup:* 1968-69).

Club colours: Shirt: Blue and white hoops. Shorts: White with blue trim. Socks: Blue.

Goalscorers: *League (42):* Blues 5, Stuparevic 5, Garrity 4, Moffat 4 (1 pen), Adeloye 3, Shaw 3, Baird 2, Boyes 2, Crawford 2, Davies 2, Gillespie 2 (2 pens), Lyall 2, Ballantyne 1, Delaney 1, Keay 1, McGinn 1, Reynolds 1, Wilson 1.
Scottish Cup (0).
Premier Sports Scottish League Cup (3): Ballantyne 1, Garrity 1, Moffat 1.
SPFL Trust Trophy (3): Garrity 1, Samuels 1, Stuparevic 1 (1 pen).

Mullen R 23+1	Ballantyne C 28	Broadfoot K 10+1	Boyes M 30+1	Delaney Z 35	Wilson J 18+4	Garrity M 16+15	Crawford A 20+5	Lyall A 35+1	Moffat O 26+8	Emmanuel-Thomas J 5	Blues C 26+10	Davies J 8+26	Gillespie G 12+16	Reynolds L 5+17	King A 3+7	Baird J 33+2	Woods G 6	McGinn N 7+13	Stuparevic F 15+1	O'Boy L —+2	Budinauckas L 4	Samuels A —+5	Shaw N 20+2	Adeloye T 7+3	Corr D 1+6	Keay C —+6	Murdoch S 3	Match No.
1	2	3	4	5	6	7^5	8^2	9^1	10^3	11^4	12	13	14	15	16													1
1	2		4	5	6	11^4	7^3	8^2	9^5	10^1	14	12	15	13	16	3												2
	2		4	5	6	10^1	8^3	7	9^4	11^2	14	12		13	15	3		1										3
	2		4	5	6^5	11^4	7^1	8	9^3	10^2	12		15	13	16	3	1	14										4
1	2	3	4	5			8^3	9	10^5	11^1	13	12	7^2	14	15	16			6^4									5
1	2	3	4^1	5	7		8	6	10^4		14	13		11^2	15	12		9^3										6
1	2	3		5	7^3		8	6	10^2		14	13		11^1		4		9	12									7
1	2		4	5	6^2	12	7^1	8^3	9		13		15	14		3		11	10^6									8
		3		5	12	10^1		6	8		7^2	13	14		2^4	4	1	9^3	11	15								9
		4		5	6	10^1		9^2	8		7	15	14		2^3	3		13	11^4	1	12							10
		4		5	6^1	10^2		7^4	8^3		2^1	15	12			3		9	11	14	1	13						11
	4^1	13	5			10^3		6	8		2	12	7	14		3		9^2	11^4	1	15							12
	4	5		7		10^1		9	8^3		2	15	6^2		12	3		14	11^4	1		13						13
1		4	5	6	14			9	8^3		2	12	7		10^2	3			11^1			13						14
	2		4	5	7	14		9^3	10^2		6	11		13		3	1	12				8^1						15
1	2		4	5	7^3	12		9	13		6	10				3		14	11^2			8^1						16
1	2^5		4	5	6			9^2	12		7	10^4	16	13		3		14	11^3			15	8^1					17
1	2		4	5	6			9^3	10		7^1	8	12			3		14	11^2			13						18
1	2		4	5	7	13	12	9^3	8^1		6	10^4		14		3		15	11^2									19
1	2		4	5	6	12	14	9			7^3	10^1	15	13		3			11^2				8^4					20
1	2	15	4	5	7^1	13	12	9^4			6	10^2		14		3		16	11^3				8^5					21
1	2		4	5		10^1		9	14		6	15	7^2	12		3			11^4				8^3	13				22
1	2		4	5		9^4	15	8	14		7	12		13		3			10^1				6^3	11^2				23
1	2^4		4	5		9^2	13	7^5	12		6^3	10	14	11^1		3		16					8		15			24
1	2		4	5		12	7	9^4	10^1		6^3	13	14	11^2		3			15				8					25
1	2^3		4^5	5		12	7	9^4	10^4		6	13	14	11^1		3			15				8^2	16				26
1	5		4	8			14	7^4	9	10^3	6^1	12	13			3			11^2					2^4	15			27
1	2		4	5		12	7	9^4	10^3		8	13	6^1			3			11^2				$8^{?}$	14				28
1	2		4	5		12	7	9^3	10^2		8	14	6^1	15		3			11^4	13								29
1	2		4	5		10^1	6^5	8^1	9^2		14	12	13			3			7	11^4	16	15						30
1	2		4	5		14	6	9^2	12		10	13	7^1			3			8^3	11								31
	2		4	5^2		12	6	9^3	10^1		13	15	7^4	16		3	1		8^5	11	14							32
	2		4	5		13	7	9^2	10^2		6	16	14			3	1^1		8^5	11^4		15						33
12	2		4^1	5		16	10^4	7	13	15	6	12	9^3			3			8^2	11	14						1	34
	3		5	14		10^2	8^5	7^4	13	9	12	2	16			4			6^3	11^1		15					1	35
	4^4		5	13		10^5	9	6^3	11^1		7	12	2			3			8^2	15	16	14					1	36

HAMILTON ACADEMICAL

Year Formed: 1874. *Ground:* Broadwood Stadium, Cumbernauld G68 9NE.
Telephone: 01698 368 650. *Fax:* 01698 285 422. *E-mail:* enquiries@acciesfc.co.uk *Website:* hamiltonacciesfc.co.uk
Ground Capacity: 6,078 (all seated). *Size of Pitch:* 105m × 68m.
Owner and CEO: Seref Zengin. *Chairman:* John Brown.
Head Coach: John Rankin. *Assistant Head Coach:* Darian MacKinnon.
Club Nickname: 'The Accies'.
Previous Grounds: Bent Farm; South Avenue; South Haugh; Douglas Park; Cliftonhill Stadium; Firhill Stadium; New Douglas Park.
Record Attendance: 28,690 v Hearts, Scottish Cup 3rd rd, 3 March 1937 (at Douglas Park); 5,895 v Rangers, 28 February 2009 (at New Douglas Park).
Record Transfer Fee received: £1,200,000 (rising to £3,200,000) from Wigan Ath for James McCarthy (July 2009).
Record Transfer Fee paid: £180,000 to Sigma Olomouc for Tomas Cerny (July 2009).
Record Victory: 10-2 v Greenock Morton, Scottish Championship, 3 May 2014; 10-2 v Cowdenbeath, Division 1, 15 October 1932.
Record Defeat: 1-11 v Hibernian, Division I, 6 November 1965.
Most Capped Player: Colin Miller, 29 (61), Canada, 1988-94.
Most League Appearances: 452: Rikki Ferguson, 1974-88.
Most League Goals in Season (Individual): 35: David Wilson, Division I; 1936-37.
Most Goals Overall (Individual): 246: David Wilson, 1928-39.

HAMILTON ACADEMICAL – WILLIAM HILL CHAMPIONSHIP 2024–25 LEAGUE RECORD

Match No.	Date		Venue	Opponents	Result		H/T Score	Lg Pos.	Goalscorers	Atten- dance
1	Aug	3	H	Ayr U	L	0-2	0-1	9		1468
2		10	A	Greenock Morton	D	0-0	0-0	9		1866
3		17	A	Ayr U	L	2-3	2-1	9	Shaw [27], Barjonas [38]	2846
4		24	H	Dunfermline Ath	W	1-0	1-0	5	Tumilty [26]	2022
5		31	H	Airdrieonians	D	2-2	0-0	4	Shaw 2 [47, 77]	1525
6	Sept	14	A	Livingston	L	0-3	0-0	6		1241
7		21	A	Raith R	D	3-3	1-2	7	O'Hara (pen) [2], Smith [79], Shaw [90]	3322
8		28	H	Partick Thistle	W	1-0	0-0	5	Kilday [56]	1677
9	Oct	5	A	Queen's Park	L	0-1	0-0	7		1259
10		18	H	Falkirk	L	1-3	0-3	7	Henderson [47]	1753
11		26	H	Greenock Morton	W	3-0	0-0	6	Shaw 3 [77, 81, 84]	1071
12	Nov	2	A	Airdrieonians	W	4-0	2-0	6	Smith [3], Graham (og) [9], O'Hara [54], McGowan [82]	1501
13		9	H	Livingston	L	1-3	1-1	6	O'Hara [42]	1033
14		16	A	Partick Thistle	L	1-5	1-2	7	O'Hara [45]	3845
15	Dec	7	A	Dunfermline Ath	L	2-3	0-0	7	McGinty [74], Shaw (pen) [90]	4286
16		14	H	Queen's Park	W	2-1	2-1	6	Bradley 2 [3, 37]	1076
17		21	A	Falkirk	L	0-1	0-0	8		5532
18		28	H	Airdrieonians	W	3-2	2-2	7	Shaw 2 [14, 90], McKinstry [38]	1476
19	Jan	10	A	Partick Thistle	L	1-2	0-0	8	Tumilty [61]	1122
20		25	A	Livingston	L	0-3	0-2	8		1078
21		28	H	Raith R	L	0-3	0-3	8		1005
22	Feb	1	H	Ayr U	L	0-2	0-0	9		2561
23		15	A	Queen's Park	W	2-1	2-0	8	Robinson [5], Lamie [13]	1147
24		18	A	Greenock Morton	L	0-2	0-1	8		1541
25		22	A	Raith R	L	0-2	0-1	9		3344
26		25	H	Dunfermline Ath	W	1-0	0-0	8	McKinstry [63]	1098
27	Mar	1	H	Falkirk	D	2-2	2-1	8	Tumilty [36], McKinstry [44]	2291
28		8	A	Airdrieonians	L	1-2	0-0	8	McGinty [83]	1584
29		15	A	Greenock Morton	L	0-2	0-0	8		1055
30		22	A	Ayr U	D	1-1	0-0	8	Shaw [65]	2587
31		29	H	Raith R	L	0-3	0-1	8		1007
32	Apr	5	H	Dunfermline Ath	W	1-0	1-0	8	Tumilty [41]	7636
33		12	A	Partick Thistle	W	2-1	2-0	7	Todorov [15], Robinson [17]	3421
34		19	H	Queen's Park	D	0-0	0-0	10		1102
35		26	H	Livingston	L	0-3	0-2	10		1155
36	May	2	A	Falkirk	L	1-3	1-1	10	Robinson [5]	7633

Final League Position: 10

Honours
League Champions: Division II 1903-04; First Division 1985-86, 1987-88, 2007-08; Third Division 2000-01.
Runners-up: Division II 1952-53, 1964-65; Second Division 1996-97, 2003-04; Championship 2013-14; League One 2023-24.
Promoted via play-offs: 2013-14 (to Premiership), 2023-24 (to Championship).
Scottish Cup Runners-up: 1911, 1935. *League Cup:* Semi-finalists three times.
League Challenge Cup Winners: 1991-92, 1992-93, 2022-23; *Runners-up:* 2005-06, 2011-12.

Club colours: Shirt: Red and white hoops. Shorts: Red. Socks: Red.

Goalscorers: *League (38):* Shaw 11 (1 pen), O'Hara 4 (1 pen), Tumilty 4, McKinstry 3, Robinson 3, Bradley 2, McGinty 2, Smith 2, Barjonas 1, Henderson 1, Kilday 1, Lamie 1, McGowan 1, Todorov 1, own goal 1.
Scottish Cup (5): Shaw 3, Hendrie 1, McGinty 1.
Premier Sports Scottish League Cup (5): Bradley 1, Henderson 1, MacDonald 1, McGinty 1, Shaw 1.
SPFL Trust Trophy (4): O'Hara 2, MacDonald 1, Shaw 1.

Albinson C 17	Tumilty R 27 + 4	Kilday L 7 + 4	McGinty S 34 + 1	Hendrie S 21 + 5	MacDonald K 22 + 3	Barjonas J 19 + 13	Martin S 20	O'Hara K 19 + 15	Shaw O 33 + 2	Bradley S 21 + 11	Maguire B 28 + 2	Todorov N 9 + 23	Henderson E 10 + 22	Newbury C — + 2	O'Connor D — + 4	Williamson B 4 + 8	Longridge J 13 + 10	Murray C — + 1	Smith C 22 + 3	Olufunwa O 1 + 2	Lyness D 19	McKinstry S 7 + 12	McGowan D 12 + 2	Lamie R 7 + 3	Robinson S 14	Gallacher T 4 + 2	Telfer C 6 + 3	Match No.
1	2	3^1	4	5	6	7^3	8^8		9^6	10^2	11^4	12	13	14	15	16												1
1	2		4	5^3	6	7^4			9	11	8^2	3	10^1	12		14	13		15									2
1	2	14	4	5^1	6	7^4	8^3	9	11			3^2	15	10^5		16	13	12										3
1	2		4	5	6	9^3	7^1	10	11^2			3	13	12		8	14											4
1	2		4	5	3		8^1	7^4	10^3	11	12	6	14	9^2			13		15									5
1	2	3^4	4				8^1	7	9	11^5	16	6^2	14	13	12	5	10^3		15									6
	2^9	14	4		6^1	13	7	10	11	15	16	12	8^2			5	9^4	3^5			1							7
			4	3	7	6	8	11^2	12	2	13	10^1	14			5	9^3				1							8
	15	3	4		7^1	6	8	11	13	2^4	9^2	12				5	10^3				1							9
	14	3	4	13	6^3		8	11	10	15	2^1	9	12			5^2	7^4				1							10
1	2	3	4	5		14	7	10^3	11^4	12	15	8^1	6^2	9^5		13	16											11
1	2	3^1	4	5^3		14	8	9	10^4	11^5	16	7^2	13	6		15	12											12
1	2^3	3		5	9	7	10	14	11	6^1	8	13	12			4^2												13
1	2		4	5^2	6	7^3	11^4	10^1	16	15	9^5	13	14			8	12	3										14
1	2	3		5	6^2	7	8^4	9^3	10	15	14	13	12			4	11^1											15
1	2	3		5	16	7	8	15	10	9	6^1	14	13			4^2	12	11^4										16
1	2		4	5	13	6	8^1	14	10^3	7	3	15	12			9^4	11^2											17
1	2		4	5	6	7^1	13	11^4	8^1	3	14	12	15			9	10^2											18
1	2	3		5		7	8^2	13	10	6	14	12				4^3	9	11^1										19
1	5	3	8	9^1	6	7^3	11	13	2^2	14	12	10^4	15			4												20
1	13		8	12	6^1	7	14	10^3	5	2	15	9^2	11^5			16	3	4^4										21
	14		3		9^5	7		11^4	12	5^2	8	10^1	16			4^2			6		1	15	2	13				22
			3	13	6^5	16	14	11^4	5^3	2	10^1		15			8					1	12	4	7	9^2			23
			3	8	5^5	14	13	11	12	6	10^1		16			12	7^4				1	2^2	4		9^3	15		24
	15		3		9	6		11	7^2	2	16	14	12			10^5					1	13	4^1	5^4	8^3			25
	2		4	15	6	7^1	13	11	8^2	3	14	12									1	10^3	9^4	5^5	16			26
	2		4	12	7	15	11^3	6^5	3	14	13	8^4									1	9^2	10	5^1	16			27
	2		4		6		8	12	11^3	3	14	13				5	7				1	10^2	9^1					28
	2		4		6^1		8^2	11^3	14	3	15	13				5	7				1	12	9	10^4				29
	2		4	12	13		8^1	10	11^2	6		5									1	3	9	7				30
	2		4	13			8^2	10^1	11	6^2	14	5							15		1	12	3^4	9	7			31
			3	5^5	7	16	13	11^2	8^2	4	10^4	12									1	2	15	9	6^1			32
	15		3	5^1	7	13	14	10^4	8	4	11^3	12									1	2	16	9^2	6^6			33
			3	5^1	12	7	14	16	10	8^4	4	11^2	15								1	13	2	9^3	6^5			34
			4^1	5	7^4	6	14	16	10	8^3	11^2	13	15								1	2	3	9^5	12			35
			4^5	5	6		8^1	14	10^5	9	12	11^2	13						15		1	2	3	7^4	16			36

HEART OF MIDLOTHIAN

Year Formed: 1874. *Ground & Address:* Tynecastle Stadium, McLeod Street, Edinburgh EH11 2NL.
Telephone: 0333 043 1874. *Fax:* 0131 200 7222. *E-mail:* supporterservices@homplc.co.uk *Website:* heartsfc.co.uk
Ground Capacity: 20,099. *Size of Pitch:* 100m × 64m.
Chairwoman: Ann Budge. *Chief Executive:* Andrew McKinlay.
Head Coach: Derek McInnes. *Assistant Head Coaches:* Paul Sheerin and Alan Archibald.
Club Nicknames: 'Hearts'; 'Jam Tarts'; 'Jambos'.
Previous Grounds: The Meadows 1874; Powderhall 1878; Old Tynecastle 1881; Tynecastle Park 1886.
Record Attendance: 53,396 v Rangers, Scottish Cup 3rd rd, 13 February 1932 (57,857 v Barcelona, 28 July 2007 at Murrayfield).
Record Transfer Fee received: £9,000,000 from Sunderland for Craig Gordon (August 2008).
Record Transfer Fee paid: £850,000 to Genk for Mirsad Beslija (January 2006).
Record Victory: 15-0 v King's Park, Scottish Cup 2nd rd, 13 February 1937 (21-0 v Anchor, EFA Cup, 30 October 1880).
Record Defeat: 1-8 v Vale of Leven, Scottish Cup 3rd rd, 1883; 0-7 v Celtic, Scottish Cup 4th rd, 1 December 2013.
Most Capped Player: Craig Gordon, 43, Scotland.
Most League Appearances: 515: Gary Mackay, 1980-97.
Most League Goals in Season (Individual): 44: Barney Battles, 1930-31.
Most Goals Overall (Individual): 214: John Robertson, 1983-98.

HEART OF MIDLOTHIAN – WILLIAM HILL PREMIERSHIP 2024–25 LEAGUE RECORD

Match No.	Date	Venue	Opponents	Result	H/T Score	Lg Pos.	Goalscorers	Atten- dance
1	Aug 3	H	Rangers	D	0-0	0-0	1		18,478
2	10	A	Dundee	L	1-3	0-3	9	Kent [61]	7266
3	25	A	Motherwell	L	1-3	0-1	10	Oda [65]	6895
4	Sept 1	H	Dundee U	L	0-1	0-0	11		18,648
5	14	A	Celtic	L	0-2	0-0	12		58,872
6	21	H	St Mirren	L	1-2	1-2	12	Halkett [18]	7341
7	28	H	Ross Co	D	1-1	0-1	12	Shankland [90]	18,399
8	Oct 6	A	Aberdeen	L	2-3	1-1	12	Kent [36], Spittal [63]	19,175
9	19	H	St Mirren	W	4-0	1-0	11	Vargas [15], Oyegoke [47], Wilson [86], Spittal [90]	18,757
10	27	A	Hibernian	D	1-1	0-0	11	Wilson [86]	20,011
11	30	H	Kilmarnock	L	1-2	1-0	12	Forrest [44]	18,402
12	Nov 2	A	St Johnstone	W	2-1	1-0	11	Clark (og) [23], Vargas [76]	5917
13	10	A	Rangers	L	0-1	0-1	11		48,254
14	23	H	Celtic	L	1-4	0-0	11	Drammeh [82]	17,894
15	Dec 1	H	Aberdeen	D	1-1	0-1	12	Devlin (og) [62]	18,810
16	7	H	Dundee	W	2-0	2-0	11	Shankland 2 [21, 31]	18,737
17	15	A	Kilmarnock	L	0-1	0-1	12		5474
18	22	H	St Johnstone	W	2-1	1-0	11	Penrice [16], Spittal [58]	18,676
19	26	A	Hibernian	L	1-2	1-1	11	Bushiri (og) [45]	18,726
20	29	A	Ross Co	D	2-2	1-0	11	Wilson 2 [2, 48]	4994
21	Jan 2	H	Motherwell	W	1-0	1-0	11	Drammeh [7]	18,715
22	5	A	Dundee U	W	1-0	0-0	11	Penrice [73]	10,214
23	12	A	Aberdeen	D	0-0	0-0	11		17,000
24	25	H	Kilmarnock	W	3-2	1-0	9	Kabangu [7], McCart [58], Grant [61]	18,677
25	Feb 1	A	Dundee	W	6-0	2-0	7	Shankland [15], Spittal [17], Kabangu 2 [51, 77], Drammeh [67], Vargas [90]	7458
26	16	H	Rangers	L	1-3	0-1	9	Steinwender [49]	18,356
27	23	A	St Johnstone	W	2-1	1-0	7	Kabangu 2 [36, 57]	5577
28	26	H	St Mirren	W	3-1	0-1	6	Wilson [56], Nieuwenhof [63], Vargas [90]	18,770
29	Mar 2	A	Hibernian	L	1-2	1-1	7	Grant [9]	19,873
30	15	H	Ross Co	W	2-0	1-0	6	Kabangu [26], Grant [89]	18,648
31	29	A	Celtic	L	0-3	0-3	6		59,062
32	Apr 6	H	Dundee U	L	0-1	0-0	7		18,888
33	12	A	Motherwell	D	0-0	0-0	7		7481
34	26	H	Dundee	L	0-1	0-1	7		18,085
35	May 3	W	Ross Co	W	3-1	1-0	7	Shankland 2 [40, 58], Forrest [82]	4181
36	10	H	Motherwell	W	3-0	1-0	7	Shankland 2 [30, 60], Forrest [62]	18,496
37	14	H	St Johnstone	W	2-1	2-0	7	Douglas (og) [17], Forrest [31]	18,021
38	18	A	Kilmarnock	W	1-0	0-0	7	Kingsley [89]	6601

Final League Position: 7

Honours
League Champions: Division I 1894-95, 1896-97, 1957-58, 1959-60; First Division 1979-80; Championship 2014-15, 2020-21.
Runners-up: Division I 1893-94, 1898-99, 1903-04, 1905-06, 1914-15, 1937-38, 1953-54, 1956-57, 1958-59, 1964-65; Premier Division 1985-86, 1987-88, 1991-92, 2005-06; First Division 1977-78, 1982-83.
Scottish Cup Winners: 1891, 1896, 1901, 1906, 1956, 1998, 2006, 2012; *Runners-up:* 1903, 1907, 1968, 1976, 1986, 1996, 2019, 2020, 2022.
League Cup Winners: 1954-55, 1958-59, 1959-60, 1962-63; *Runners-up:* 1961-62, 1996-97, 2012-13.

European: *European Cup:* 8 matches (1958-59, 1960-61, 2006-07). *Cup Winners' Cup:* 10 matches (1976-77, 1996-97, 1998-99). *UEFA Cup:* 46 matches (*Fairs Cup:* 1961-62, 1963-64, 1965-66. *UEFA Cup:* 1984-85, 1986-87, 1988-89, 1990-91, 1992-93, 1993-94, 2000-01, 2003-04, 2004-05, 2006-07). *Europa League:* 16 matches (2010-11, 2011-12, 2012-13, 2016-17, 2022-23, 2024-25). *UEFA Europa Conference League:* 16 matches (2022-23, 2023-24, 2024-25).

Club colours: Shirt: Maroon. Shorts: White. Socks: Maroon.

Goalscorers: *League (52):* Shankland 8, Kabangu 6, Wilson 5, Forrest 4, Spittal 4, Vargas 4, Drammeh 3, Grant 3, Kent 2, Penrice 2, Halkett 1, Kingsley 1, McCart 1, Nieuwenhof 1, Oda 1, Oyegoke 1, Steinwender 1, own goals 4.
Scottish Cup (9): Kabangu 2, Kartum 2, Dhanda 1, Nieuwenhof 1, Shankland 1, own goals 2.
Premier Sports Scottish League Cup (0).
SPFL Trust Trophy (1): Ross 1.
Europa League (0).
UEFA Conference League (6): Spittal 2, Dhanda 1, Forrest 1, Wilson 1, own goal 1.

Clark Z 3	Taylor F 6 7 + 1	Kent F 18	Rowles K 20	Penrice J 32 + 1	Devlin C 22 + 7	Grant J 21 + 10	Dhanda Y 8 + 17	Shankland L 29 + 3	McKay B 2 + 6	Vargas K 14 + 16	Spittal B 29 + 6	Forrest A 12 + 19	Oyegoke D 14 + 5	Oda Y 1 + 4	Boateng M 14 + 6	Boyce L 3 + 7	Gordon C 33	Kingsley S 8 + 1	Salazar A 1	Halkett C 13 + 4	Baningime B 25 + 3	Drammeh M 11 + 11	Forrester A 19 + 6	Wilson J 15 + 9	McCart J 10 + 1	Kabangu E 11 + 3	Neilson L 3 + 2	Steinwender M 8 + 1	Kartum S 5 + 7	Nieuwenhof C 2 + 10	Milne H 3	Fulton R 2 + 1	Match No.
1	2⁴	3	4	5	6	7³	8¹	9	10²	11⁵	12	13	14	15	16																		1
1	5	3	4	8	6⁴	7³	14	11		9²	10⁵	15			2¹	13	12	16															2
	5³	3	4		14		9²	11	15	13	7⁴	10¹		12	6	16		1	2	8⁶													3
	4			5⁴	15	6⁴	13	10	12	11²	8¹	16	14	9⁵	7		1	2		3													4
5		4	9⁴	13	8²	14	10⁵		11¹	15	16			6		1	2		3	7³	12												5
2¹			5⁵		9⁴	14	11		8¹	10³	16	12	13	7	15	1	4		3	6													6
	3	4		6¹		9⁵	14	11	13	8²	12	10⁵	15		16	1	5			7		2⁴											7
	3	4	12		8⁴	10⁴	11		7³	9	15	2²		6		1	5¹			14		13											8
	3	4	5	14		6⁵	10¹	16	11⁴	9	12	2²		7	1					8³		13	15										9
	3	4	5	7⁴	13	6²	11	14	10¹	9	12	2⁵		8³		1						16	15										10
	3	4	5	7⁴	13	16	11	15	10²	9³	6⁵	12		8		1						2¹	14										11
	3	4	5	13	14	10¹	11³		12	9	8	2		7²		1				6													12
	3	4	5	8³		12	10		11	9	6²	2		7¹		1				13	14												13
	3	4	5	6³	13	14	10		12	11⁴	9²	2		8¹		1				7	15												14
	3²	4		6	15		11		14	9	10³	2			1	5¹		12	7	8⁴	13												15
		4	5	6	14		9		13	10³	12	2		7		1			3		8²		11¹										16
		4	5	6	13	12			8⁴	9³	10¹	2⁵		7²	14	1			3		11	16	15										17
		4	5	7			11³		13	9²	12	3		8	14	1				6¹	2	10											18
		4	5	6		12	9		14	10¹		2		13	15	1			3⁴	7²	8³		11										19
		4	5		6²				13	10	12	3		14	9	1			15	7	8¹	2⁴	11³										20
		4	5	6	7³	15			12	10	14			9¹		1			3	13	8⁴	2	11²										21
		4	5	6	7³				14	10	12			13	9²	1			3		8¹	2	11⁴	15									22
			5	6	9	13			14	10³	15	2⁴			1				3	7²	8¹	16	11⁵	4	12								23
			5	8	6⁴	14	13			9²				16		1			3¹	7	15	2	11³	4	10⁵	3⁶							24
			5	8		15	11³		13	9²	12					1				7	6¹	2	14	4	10⁴	3⁵	16						25
			5		7²		9	15	8¹							1				6	16	2	10⁴	4	11⁵	14	3³	12	13				26
	12		5		6²		9⁵		8³	16						1				7	14	2¹	10⁴	4	11		3	13	15				27
	2		5		13		9		14	12						1				6	15		10³	4	11⁴		3	7²	8¹				28
	2		5		7¹		9		14	8⁴						1				6³	15		10²	4	11		3	12	13				29
			5		12		9³			8¹	14					1				6	15	2	10	4		11	4	3	7²	13			30
			8	6⁴	15		9³		14	16						1				7²		5	10¹		11⁵	3	2	13	12	4			31
			5	12	9³		13			8²						1				6⁴	15	2	10⁸	4	11		3	7¹	14				32
			5	13	9		12			8	14					1				16	6³	10¹	2		4	11⁴		3⁵	7²	15			33
	3		5	7	9	15		14	10⁴	16						1			12		6²	13	2		4¹	11⁵		8³					34
	3		5		6	13	10		9³	8¹	11³					1				4	7		2	14					12				35
	3		5	6	8²	12	10³		9¹		11⁴					1				4	7⁵		2	13		16			14	15		1	36
	3			6	8³	11²	10			9¹						1				4	7		2	12					14	13	5	1	37
1¹	3			6		11⁸	10⁴			9⁵					4					13	7		2	15		16			14	8³	5²	12	38

HIBERNIAN

Year Formed: 1875. *Ground & Address:* Easter Road Stadium, 12 Albion Place, Edinburgh EH7 5QG.
Telephone: 0131 661 2159. *Fax:* 0131 659 6488. *E-mail:* club@hibernianfc.co.uk *Website:* hibernianfc.co.uk
Ground Capacity: 20,421 (all seated). *Size of Pitch:* 105m × 68m.
Chairman: Ian Gordon.
Head Coach: David Gray. *Assistant Head Coaches:* Eddie May and Liam Craig.
Club Nickname: 'Hibs'; 'Hibees'.
Previous Grounds: Meadows 1875-78; Powderhall 1878-79; Mayfield 1879-80; First Easter Road 1880-92; Second Easter Road 1892.
Record Attendance: 65,860 v Hearts, Division I, 2 January 1950.
Record Transfer Fee received: £4,400,000 from Celtic for Scott Brown (July 2007).
Record Transfer Fee paid: £700,000 to LDU Quito for Ulises de la Cruz (2001).
Record Victory: 15-1 v Pebbles Rovers, Scottish Cup 2nd rd, 11 February 1961.
Record Defeat: 0-10 v Rangers, Division I, 24 December 1898.
Most Capped Player: Lawrie Reilly, 38, Scotland.
Most League Appearances: 481: Lewis Stevenson, 2007-24.
Most League Goals in Season (Individual): 42: Joe Baker, 1959-60.
Most Goals Overall (Individual): 303: Gordon Smith, 1941-1959.

HIBERNIAN – WILLIAM HILL PREMIERSHIP 2024–25 LEAGUE RECORD

Match No.	Date	Venue	Opponents	Result	H/T Score	Lg Pos.	Goalscorers	Attendance
1	Aug 4	A	St Mirren	L	0-3	0-0	9		6171
2	11	H	Celtic	L	0-2	0-2	11		17,918
3	24	H	Dundee	D	2-2	1-1	11	Boyle [45], Bowie [72]	15,710
4	Sept 1	A	Kilmarnock	D	1-1	0-0	9	Newell [50]	7763
5	14	H	St Johnstone	W	2-0	1-0	8	Kukharevych [45], Boyle [72]	15,448
6	29	A	Rangers	L	0-1	0-1	9		48,217
7	Oct 5	H	Motherwell	L	1-2	0-0	10	Hoilett [59]	15,892
8	19	A	Dundee U	L	2-3	1-1	12	O'Hora [43], Gayle [72]	10,870
9	27	H	Hearts	D	1-1	0-0	12	Kukharevych [65]	20,011
10	30	A	Ross Co	D	0-0	0-0	11		3468
11	Nov 3	H	Dundee U	D	1-1	1-0	12	Miller [28]	15,454
12	9	H	St Mirren	L	1-2	0-2	12	Cadden N (pen) [90]	15,594
13	23	A	Dundee	L	1-4	1-3	12	Cadden N [2]	5310
14	26	H	Aberdeen	D	3-3	1-0	12	Newell [40], Bushiri [90], Cadden N [90]	15,845
15	30	A	Motherwell	W	3-0	2-0	11	Hoilett [26], Kukharevych [38], Campbell [81]	5212
16	Dec 7	A	Celtic	L	0-3	0-1	12		58,641
17	14	H	Ross Co	W	3-1	1-1	8	Gayle [45], Youan (pen) [73], Campbell [90]	14,885
18	21	A	Aberdeen	W	3-1	2-1	8	Youan [18], Cadden N [35], Boyle [49]	18,375
19	26	A	Hearts	W	2-1	1-1	7	Rowles (og) [9], Gayle [78]	18,726
20	29	H	Kilmarnock	W	1-0	1-0	7	Triantis [25]	19,265
21	Jan 2	A	St Johnstone	D	1-1	0-1	7	Gayle [79]	6287
22	5	H	Rangers	D	3-3	1-2	7	Boyle 2 (1 pen) [32, 61 (p)], Bushiri [83]	17,539
23	11	H	Motherwell	W	3-1	2-0	6	Boyle 2 (1 pen) [27, 81 (p)], Triantis [30]	15,829
24	25	A	Ross Co	D	1-1	1-0	6	Levitt [42]	4003
25	Feb 1	H	Aberdeen	W	2-0	1-0	5	Triantis [24], Cadden N [48]	16,533
26	16	A	St Mirren	D	0-0	0-0	5		7468
27	22	H	Celtic	W	2-1	2-0	5	Campbell 2 [2, 45]	18,357
28	26	A	Dundee U	W	3-1	1-1	4	Kukharevych [18], Bowie [90], Hoilett [90]	10,674
29	Mar 2	H	Hearts	W	2-1	1-1	3	Boyle [6], Iredale [74]	19,873
30	15	A	Kilmarnock	D	1-1	1-0	3	Boyle [25]	6703
31	29	H	St Johnstone	W	3-0	2-0	3	Hoilett [18], Boyle [29], Bowie (pen) [90]	17,002
32	Apr 5	A	Rangers	W	2-0	1-0	3	Levitt [8], Boyle [69]	50,922
33	13	H	Dundee	W	4-0	1-0	3	Bushiri [26], Bowie 2 [68, 84], Gayle [78]	17,926
34	26	A	Aberdeen	L	0-1	0-0	3		17,396
35	May 3	H	Dundee U	W	3-1	2-0	3	Boyle [3], Kukharevych [14], Gayle [87]	18,399
36	10	A	Celtic	L	1-3	1-2	3	Boyle [25]	58,972
37	14	A	St Mirren	D	2-2	2-1	3	Boyle [3], Kukharevych [10]	7671
38	17	H	Rangers	D	2-2	1-1	3	Bowie [16], Boyle [66]	18,793

Final League Position: 3

Honours
League Champions: Division I 1902-03, 1947-48, 1950-51, 1951-52; First Division 1980-81, 1998-99; Championship 2016-17; Division II 1893-94, 1894-95, 1932-33.
Runners-up: Division I 1896-97, 1946-47, 1949-50, 1952-53, 1973-74, 1974-75; Championship 2014-15.
Scottish Cup Winners: 1887, 1902, 2016; *Runners-up:* 1896, 1914, 1923, 1924, 1947, 1958, 1972, 1979, 2001, 2012, 2013, 2021.
League Cup Winners: 1972-73, 1991-92, 2006-07; *Runners-up:* 1950-51, 1968-69, 1974-75, 1985-86, 1993-94, 2003-04, 2015-16, 2021-22. *Drybrough Cup Winners:* 1972-73, 1973-74.

European: *European Cup:* 6 matches (1955-56 semi-finals). *Cup Winners' Cup:* 6 matches (1972-73). *UEFA Cup:* 64 matches (*Fairs Cup:* 1960-61 semi-finals, 1961-62, 1962-63, 1965-66, 1967-68, 1968-69, 1970-71. *UEFA Cup:* 1973-74, 1974-75, 1976-77, 1978-79, 1989-90, 1992-93, 2001-02, 2005-06). *Europa League:* 10 matches (2010-11, 2013-14, 2018-19). *UEFA Europa Conference League:* 10 matches (2021-22, 2023-24).

Club colours: Shirt: Green with white sleeves. Shorts: Green. Socks: Green with white tops.

Goalscorers: *League (62):* Boyle 15 (2 pens), Bowie 6 (1 pen), Gayle 6, Kukharevych 6, Cadden N 5 (1 pen), Campbell 4, Hoilett 4, Bushiri 3, Triantis 3, Levitt 2, Newell 2, Youan 2 (1 pen), Iredale 1, Miller 1, O'Hora 1, own goal 1.
Scottish Cup (4): Boyle 2, Bushiri 1, Molotnikov 1.
Premier Sports Scottish League Cup (15): Boyle 3, Vente 3, Miller 2, Molotnikov 2, Ekpiteta 1, Kukharevych 1, Levitt 1, Moriah-Welsh 1, O'Hora 1.
SPFL Trust Trophy (3): McMurdo 2, McAllister 1.

Bursik J 13	Miller L 22 + 10	Ekpiteta M 12 + 1	O'Hora W 30 + 2	Obita J 22 + 13	Moriah-Welsh N 4 + 13	Newell J 16	Boyle M 29 + 7	Campbell J 19 + 14	Molotnikov R 6 + 5	Vente D 1 + 1	Cadden C 27 + 5	Kukharevych M 20 + 5	Amos L — + 1	Levitt D 12 + 7	Bowie K 5 + 13	Kwon H 12 + 9	Cadden N 20 + 9	Bushiri R 26 + 2	Triantis N 34	Youan T 11 + 2	Hoilett D 19 + 9	McKirdy H — + 6	Gayle D 7 + 21	Iredale J 25 + 3	Doyle-Hayes J — + 1	Smith J 25	Manneh A 1 + 3	Match No.
1	2	3	4	5	6³	7	8	9	10¹	11²	12	13	14															1
1	2	3	4	5	15	7	8	6¹	10³	14	12	11²		9⁴	13													2
1	2²	3	4	5	15	7	8	14	9⁴	12	11⁵	13				6¹	10³	16										3
1	2	3	4	5		8	9²	11¹			13	10³		14	6	12		7											4
1	16	3	4	5			13	14	9²		2⁴	11⁵				6	10³	7	8¹	12	15								5
1	2	3	4	5	16		10³				6	11¹	15	7⁴		8⁵	13	9²	14	12								6
1	2	3	4	5	14		9¹	12			8⁴	11²	15		7	6⁸		10³	15	13								7
1	2¹	3	4	5		7⁸	12	16	9³		8²	11⁴	15		6		10⁵			14	13							8
1	2	3	4	5	13		8				12			6		7	10²	9³		11¹	14							9
1	2	3	4	5		8²	6⁴	14			11			12	15	7		9³	10¹	13								10
1	2¹	3	4	5		8²	9³	13			10⁸			6	14	7	15	11⁴		12								11
1		3	4²	5		8	9⁵				2		14			6³	13	12	7¹	10	11⁴	16	15					12
1	13		3	5⁸	6⁴	14	9	15			2²	11³	16			8¹	4	7⁵	10					12				13
	5	2		7	15	14	10¹				13	8					3	6²	11		9³		12	4⁴		1		14
16	2		7³	14	13		5⁵	10¹			15	8			3		6	11⁴	9²		12		4			1		15
2⁵		3	6	9³	13	12	16	11¹				10²		4	8	7⁴	15		14	5					1			16
	2⁴	12	7	14	13		5				15	8	3	6	11	9¹			10³	4²					1			17
12	2³	14	7²	10	9		5³	13			8	3	6	11								4		1				18
14	2³	15	7²	10	9		5	13			8⁴	3	6	11¹					12	4				1				19
2	13		7¹	10	9		5				12	8	3	6	11³				14	4²				1				20
2¹	13		10	9⁶	16		5	14			7²	8	3	6	11⁴	15			12	4³				1				21
3	12		10	7	2		9¹				6	4	8	11		5			4	1								22
14	2	12	16	10	9⁶		5⁴	7³			13	8¹	3	6	15				11²	4				1				23
2	13	12		10	9		5	7²			14	8¹	3	6	11³					4				1				24
14	2	16		10⁴	9		5³	7²			12	13	8⁵	3	6	15			11¹	4				1				25
15	2	13	16	10	9		5⁴	12			7³	8⁵	3	6					11¹	4²			1			14		26
5	14	2	13	6²	10⁴	9		12			11¹	8	3³	7	15					4				1				27
5	2	14	6	10²	9⁴		11³	13			8¹	3	7	15					12	4				1				28
12	2¹	16	7³	10⁵	9		5	14			11²	8⁴	3	6	15				13	4				1				29
2	8	13	10⁴	14			5	15			7²	11¹		3	6	9³			12	4				1				30
2	8	10²	15				5	11¹			7³	12		3	6	9⁴			13	4				1			14	31
2	16	8	15	10³	13		5⁵	11¹			6⁴	12		3	7	9²			14	4				1				32
2		8	15	10³	13		5⁵	11¹			7⁴	12	16	3	6	9²			14	4				1				33
	2	9		10	8		5⁴	14			6²	11¹	13	3	7	15			12	4³				1				34
15	2	8⁵		9³	12		5⁴	10²			7	13	16	3	6	11¹			14	4				1				35
	3	6		10¹	9⁴		2	11²			7⁵	12	13	4	8	14		15	5³			1	16					36
2	16	8²		9⁴	14		5⁵	10¹			7	12	13	3	6	11³			15	4				1				37
	2	16	13	9	14		5	15			10¹	8		3	6⁴	11³			12	4⁵				1	7²			38

INVERNESS CALEDONIAN THISTLE

Year Formed: 1994. *Ground & Address:* Caledonian Stadium, Stadium Road, Inverness IV1 1FF.
Telephone: 01463 222 880. *Fax:* 01463 227 479. *E-mail:* admin@ictfc.co.uk *Website:* ictfc.com
Ground Capacity: 7,780 (all seated). *Size of Pitch:* 105m × 68m.
Chairman (acting): Alan Savage. *Chief Executive:* Charlie Christie.
Head Coach: Scott Kellacher. *Assistant Head Coach:* Billy McKay.
Club Nicknames: 'Caley Thistle'; 'Caley Jags'; 'ICT'.
Record Attendance: 7,753 v Rangers, SPL, 20 January 2008.
Record Transfer Fee received: £500,000 from Celtic for Ryan Christie (September 2015).
Record Transfer Fee paid: £65,000 to Ross Co for John Rankin (July 2006).
Record Victory: 8-1 v Annan Ath, Scottish Cup 3rd rd, 24 January 1998; 7-0 v Ayr U, First Division, 24 April 2010; 7-0 v Arbroath, League Cup Northern Section Group C, 30 July 2016.
Record Defeats: 0-6 v Airdrieonians, First Division, 21 Sep 2000; 0-6 v Celtic, League Cup 3rd rd, 22 Sep 2010; 0-6 v Celtic, Scottish Premiership, 27 April 2014; 0-6 v Celtic, Scottish Cup 5th rd, 11 February 2017.
Most Capped Player: Richard Hastings, 38 (59), Canada.
Most League Appearances: 490: Ross Tokely, 1995-2012.
Most League Goals in Season: 27: Iain Stewart, 1996-97.
Most Goals Overall (Individual): 111: Billy McKay, 2011-15, 2017, 2021-24.

INVERNESS CALEDONIAN THISTLE – WILLIAM HILL LEAGUE ONE 2024–25 LEAGUE RECORD

Match No.	Date	Venue	Opponents	Result		H/T Score	Lg Pos.	Goalscorers	Attendance
1	Aug 3	H	Dumbarton	D	1-1	1-0	3	Devine [44]	1439
2	10	A	Annan Ath	L	0-1	0-0	9		386
3	17	H	Montrose	D	1-1	0-1	8	Mackinnon [63]	1902
4	24	A	Kelty Hearts	D	0-0	0-0	8		692
5	31	H	Queen of the South	W	1-0	1-0	6	McKay [19]	1703
6	Sept14	A	Alloa Ath	D	2-2	1-0	6	Devine [7], Macleod [67]	778
7	21	H	Cove Rangers	D	1-1	0-1	6	Nolan [51]	1505
8	28	H	Stenhousemuir	D	0-0	0-0	6		1601
9	Oct 5	A	Arbroath	L	0-1	0-0	9		1381
10	19	H	Annan Ath	W	1-0	1-0	10	Devine [21]	1501
11	26	A	Dumbarton	L	1-3	1-1	10	Davidson [28]	872
12	Nov 2	H	Kelty Hearts	D	1-1	1-1	10	Longstaff [4]	1502
13	9	A	Cove Rangers	W	2-1	1-1	10	Mackinnon [39], Bray [67]	551
14	16	H	Alloa Ath	W	1-0	0-0	10	Gilmour [70]	1578
15	Dec 7	A	Montrose	W	3-2	0-2	9	Longstaff [64], Allan 2 [88, 90]	502
16	14	H	Arbroath	L	0-2	0-0	9		1531
17	21	A	Stenhousemuir	W	1-0	0-0	9	Gilmour [86]	719
18	28	H	Cove Rangers	L	1-4	1-2	9	Savage [37]	1974
19	Jan 4	H	Dumbarton	W	2-0	1-0	9	Bavidge [15], Gilmour [68]	1894
20	18	A	Annan Ath	W	3-0	1-0	9	Bavidge [40], Bray [49], McKay (pen) [87]	438
21	21	A	Queen of the South	L	2-3	1-1	9	Bavidge [10], Bray [74]	775
22	25	A	Alloa Ath	W	2-1	1-0	9	Bray [21], Stewart [79]	741
23	Feb 1	H	Queen of the South	W	1-0	1-0	9	Bavidge [36]	1726
24	8	A	Arbroath	L	0-3	0-2	9		1500
25	22	A	Kelty Hearts	W	1-0	0-0	9	Bavidge [73]	641
26	Mar 1	H	Montrose	D	1-1	0-1	9	Bray [80]	1653
27	8	H	Dumbarton	W	1-0	0-0	8	Bavidge [90]	757
28	11	A	Stenhousemuir	W	4-1	2-1	7	Brennan [3], Gilmour [17], Bray [47], Allan [51]	1482
29	15	H	Annan Ath	L	0-1	0-1	8		1703
30	22	H	Alloa Ath	D	1-1	1-0	8	Stewart [8]	1655
31	29	A	Queen of the South	L	1-4	1-1	8	Stewart [24]	1006
32	Apr 5	A	Cove Rangers	W	3-0	2-0	8	Bray 3 [13, 36, 72]	454
33	12	H	Kelty Hearts	L	0-2	0-0	8		1812
34	19	A	Stenhousemuir	D	1-1	0-0	8	McKay [56]	764
35	26	H	Arbroath	W	3-0	2-0	7	Bray [9], Allan (pen) [24], McKay [47]	2329
36	May 3	A	Montrose	W	2-0	1-0	7	Allan [45], McKay [61]	1018

Final League Position: 7

Honours
League Champions: First Division 2003-04, 2009-10; Third Division 1996-97.
Runners-up: Championship 2019-20; Second Division 1998-99.
Scottish Cup Winners: 2015; *Runners-up:* 2023.
League Cup Runners-up: 2013-14.
League Challenge Cup Winners: 2003-04, 2017-18; *Runners-up:* 1999-2000, 2009-10.

European: *Europa League:* 4 matches (2015-16).

Club colours: Shirt: Blue and red vertical stripes with black detail and sleeves. Shorts: Blue. Socks: Blue.

Goalscorers: *League (45):* Bray 10, Bavidge 6, Allan 5 (1 pen), McKay 5 (1 pen), Gilmour 4, Devine 3, Stewart 3, Longstaff 2, Mackinnon 2, Brennan 1, Davidson 1, Macleod 1, Nolan 1, Savage 1.
Scottish Cup (0).
Premier Sports Scottish League Cup (3): Bray 1, Brooks 1, Longstaff 1.
SPFL Trust Trophy (5): Brooks 2, Allan 1, Gilmour 1, Mackinnon 1.

Newman J 2	Davidson J 14	Devine D 35	Savage R 35	Duffy F 5	Bray K 27 + 5	Mackinnon A 34	Gilmour C 32	Longstaff L 22 + 3	Brooks A 5 + 4	McKay B 33 + 3	Macleod C 7 + 15	Thompson R 4 + 18	Ferguson C — + 7	Duffy W 8	Strachan M 8 + 5	Dibaga M 30	Allan P 29 + 3	Nolan J 24 + 6	Ewan C 3 + 3	MacKay C — + 4	Reilly C 1	Cairns E — + 17	Gardiner B — + 5	Bavidge A 10	Stewart A 14 + 4	Brennan B 10 + 1	Rice A 1	Rebillas S — + 1	Gill M 3	Keogh S — + 2	Nixon S — + 1	Match No.
1	2	3	4	5	6³	7¹	8	9	10²	11	12	13	14																			1
1	2	3	4	5⁴	13	7³	8	9	11¹	10²	12	16	14	6⁹	15																	2
	6⁵	4	3	5¹	10	7	8	9³	14	11⁴	13	16	15	2²	12	1																3
	6	4	3	5	10	8	7	12	11³	9²	14			2¹		1	13															4
	10	4	3	5³		9	6	8⁴	11	12					2²	1	7¹	13	14	15												5
	8	3	10	12	5	6	2³	4¹	9			14	7			1	11²	13														6
	2	4	5	13	10	7	8	11²	9⁴	6³	15		3¹			1	14	12														7
	7	3	4	8	9	6	12	11¹	10²				2			1	13	5														8
	2	3	4	8	9	6	13	11³	12		14					1	7¹	5				10²										9
	9	3	4	7	10		6²	11³	12	14	13	2¹				1	8	5⁴	15													10
	2		4	7²	8³	10	11	12	9¹		14					1	6	5	3	13												11
	8	3	5	6²	7	9		11	12							1	10	2	4¹			13										12
	2	3	4	8	9	6	10	11¹								1	7	5				12										13
	2¹	3	4	9	6	10	11³	13	8²		12					1	7	5				14										14
	3	4		12	9	6	10	11	8¹		5²					1	7	2				13										15
	3	4		12	9²	6	10	11	8⁴		5¹					1	7	2				13										16
	4	3		9	7	6	11	10¹		5						1	8	2				12										17
	3	4		9	7	6	11	10	13	5¹						1	8	2²				12										18
	3	4		2	6²	7	11¹	10								1	8	6	5			14		9³	12							19
	4	3		9	8¹	7	11²	10³	13	14						1	6	5				15		2⁴	12							20
	3	2		9	6	7	10¹	13	14							1	8³	4				12		5	11²							21
	3	4		2	8²	7	10¹									1	6	5				12		11	9							22
	3	4		2	8²	7	12									1	6	5				13		10	9¹							23
	3	4		2	8²	7	11	12⁴	13	14						1	6³	5				15		10	9¹							24
	3	4		2	8	7	11	10¹								1	6					12		9	5							25
	3	4		2	8²	7	9¹	10								1	6	12				14		11	5³	13						26
	3	4		9	8	7	10³	13	14							1	6²	5						11	12	2						27
	3	4		10	8³	7	12	9	14							1	6²	5						11¹	13	2						28
	3	4		9	8	7	10	13								1	6	5⁵				12		11¹		2						29
	3	4⁸		9	8	7	11²	13								6	5¹	12						10	2			1				30
	4			9	8⁴	7	11²	14	13	12	1	6³	5¹	3			15	10	2													31
	4	3		10³	9²	7	11¹	13	14	5	1	6	15				12	8⁴	2													32
	4	3		9	8²	7	11	13	14	5	1¹	6³				15	10⁴	2	12													33
	4	3		9	8¹	7	12	11		5		6	13				10²	2		1												34
	3	4		9⁴		7	13	10³	8	5¹	6⁵	12				16	15	11²	2					1		14						35
	4⁸	3		9¹		7	12	11²	8	14	6⁵	5					13	10³	2					1		16	15					36

KELTY HEARTS

Year Formed: 1975. *Ground & Address:* New Central Park, Bath Street, Kelty KY4 0AG.
Email: enquiries@keltyhearts.co.uk *Website:* keltyhearts.co.uk
Ground Capacity: 2,181 (353 seated). *Size of Pitch:* 100m × 60m.
Chairman: George McTrustey. *Vice-Chairman:* Stuart Mill.
Managing Director: Stefan Winiarski.
Manager: Thomas O'Ware. *Assistant Manager:* Michael Paton.
Club Nicknames: 'Maroon Machine'; 'Hearts'.
Record Attendance: 2,300 v Rangers, Friendly, 7 October 2012.
Record Victory: 6-1 v Albion R, League Two, 11 December 2021.
Record Defeat: 6-1 v Airdrieonians, League One, 11 March 2023; 6-0 v Queen's Park, League Cup Group stage, 27 July 2024; 6-0 v Dumbarton, League One, 5 April 2025.
Most Capped Player: Kieran Mgwenya, 1, Malawi.
Most League Appearances: 107: Michael Tidser, 2020-25.
Most League Goals in Season (Individual): 17: Nathan Austin, 2021-22.
Most Goals Overall (Individual): 29: Nathan Austin, 2019-23.

KELTY HEARTS – WILLIAM HILL LEAGUE ONE 2024–25 LEAGUE RECORD

Match No.	Date	Venue	Opponents	Result	H/T Score	Lg Pos.	Goalscorers	Attendance
1	Aug 3	A	Montrose	D 1-1	0-0	3	Cunningham 68	516
2	10	H	Stenhousemuir	W 2-0	1-0	2	Allan S 1, Cunningham 56	385
3	17	A	Arbroath	W 3-0	0-0	1	Allan S 70, Williamson 76, Cunningham 79	1023
4	24	H	Inverness CT	D 0-0	0-0	1		692
5	31	A	Dumbarton	D 2-2	1-1	1	McCarvel 10, Johnston 59	471
6	Sept 14	A	Cove Rangers	L 1-3	0-1	3	Cunningham 64	377
7	21	A	Alloa Ath	L 0-1	0-0	5		676
8	28	H	Annan Ath	W 3-0	2-0	4	Mercer 12, Moore 27, Williamson 69	369
9	Oct 5	A	Queen of the South	W 5-1	3-0	1	Cunningham 2 (1 pen) 26, 35 (p), Williamson 2 41, 70, Cleall-Harding 63	1306
10	19	H	Montrose	L 0-2	0-0	3		500
11	26	H	Stenhousemuir	L 1-2	0-1	5	Cunningham 76	546
12	Nov 2	A	Inverness CT	D 1-1	1-1	6	Cunningham 14	1502
13	9	H	Dumbarton	W 2-0	0-0	3	Cunningham 52, Williamson 65	507
14	16	A	Annan Ath	W 2-0	2-0	1	Williamson 26, Allan C 27	394
15	Dec 7	H	Alloa Ath	L 0-2	0-1	4		385
16	14	A	Cove Rangers	D 0-0	0-0	4		443
17	17	H	Arbroath	W 3-2	1-1	3	MacIntyre 2 45, 53, Williamson 73	523
18	21	H	Queen of the South	W 2-0	0-0	2	Cunningham 2 (1 pen) 64, 87 (p)	434
19	28	A	Dumbarton	L 0-2	0-0	3		695
20	Jan 4	A	Montrose	D 0-0	0-0	3		609
21	11	H	Stenhousemuir	D 0-0	0-0	3		439
22	Feb 1	H	Annan Ath	L 1-3	1-0	5	McLeish 7	395
23	15	A	Alloa Ath	L 0-2	0-2	6		604
24	22	H	Inverness CT	L 0-1	0-0	6		641
25	25	A	Arbroath	L 1-2	0-1	6	Cunningham 75	628
26	Mar 1	A	Queen of the South	W 1-0	1-0	6	Moore 45	923
27	8	H	Montrose	D 0-0	0-0	5		520
28	11	H	Cove Rangers	L 0-4	0-1	5		339
29	15	A	Stenhousemuir	D 0-0	0-0	6		575
30	22	H	Arbroath	D 1-1	0-1	6	Flatman 90	754
31	29	A	Annan Ath	L 1-2	1-0	7	Brown 25	393
32	Apr 5	H	Dumbarton	L 0-6	0-3	7		317
33	12	A	Inverness CT	W 2-0	0-0	6	McCarvel 79, Cole 87	1812
34	19	H	Queen of the South	L 1-3	1-1	7	MacIntyre 3	590
35	26	A	Cove Rangers	D 2-2	0-2	6	Johnston 61, Cunningham 68	389
36	May 3	H	Alloa Ath	W 2-1	2-1	6	Johnston 23, Cole 26	854

Final League Position: 6

Honours
League Champions: League Two 2021-22. *Promoted via play-offs:* 2020-21. (to League Two).

Club colours: Shirts: Maroon with white trim. Shorts: White. Socks: Maroon with white trim.

Goalscorers: *League (40):* Cunningham 13 (2 pens), Williamson 7, Johnston 3, MacIntyre 3, Allan S 2, Cole 2, McCarvel 2, Moore 2, Allan C 1, Brown 1, Cleall-Harding 1, Flatman 1, McLeish 1, Mercer 1.
Scottish Cup (2): Cunningham 1 (1 pen), Flatman 1.
Premier Sports Scottish League Cup (2): Flatman 1, Williamson 1.
SPFL Trust Trophy (4): Johnston 3, Williamson 1.

Adams R 34	Mercer S 22+2	Flatman C 24+7	O'Ware T 34	Paterson B 36	Tidser M 10	Allan S 8+10	Moore L 23+3	Cunningham R 30+2	Johnston C 32+4	Williamson S 14+7	Owens B 9+13	Cole B 4+13	McCarvel L 16+9	Thomas M 7+18	Miller M —+3	Owens L —+1	Cleall-Harding S 15	Allan C 21+1	Bryce R —+3	MacIntyre J 22+3	Strachan M —+1	McLeish L 6+5	McClure B 10+3	Lyon J 2+6	Broadfoot K 8	Watson J 2	Brown L 5	Adamson R 2	Fellows C —+2	Match No.
1	2^1	3	4	5	6	7	8	9	10	11	12																			1
1	2	3	4	5	6^1	8	7^2	9	10	11	12	13																		2
1	2	3	4	5	6	7^2	8^1	9^3	11	10^4	13		12	14	15															3
1	2	3	4^2	5	6^1	8		9	10	11	12						7	13												4
1	2	3	4	5		8^1	12	9	10	11^4	6^2		7^1	15	14	13														5
1	2		4	5	6^2		9	8	10	11	12		7^1		13			3	6											6
1	2^2		4	5			12	9^3	8	11^1	7	14	10	13				3	6											7
1	2^3	3	5	6^2			9^4	8	10	11^1	13	12		14			4	7	15											8
1	2^1	15	3	5	6^3			8^2	10^4	11	16	13		12			4^5	7	14	9										9
1	2^3	3^4	5				8	9	11	12	10^2	13	14				4	7	6^1											10
1	2^1	3	5				8^3	11	9	10^2	14	15	6^4	12			4	7	13											11
1	2^3	14	3	5	9^6		8^1	11^4	10	12	15		6^2	13			4	7		16										12
1	2^1	13	3	5	7^3		12	6	9	10^4	14	15	11^2				4	8												13
1	2^1	12	3	5			11^3	8	9	10^4	7^2		14	15			4	6		13										14
1		3^2	4	5	14	11^1	7	9	10^4		15	13	12				2	6		8^3										15
1			4	5	7^1		11^2	10	9^3	13	12	14			2		3	6		8										16
1	15	14	4	5		12	11^2	10	10^3	9^5	13	7^1	16		2^4		3	6		8										17
1	7	2	3	5		13	11^2	9	10^1	12							4	6		8										18
1	6^2	12	4	5		13^4	10^4	9	11	14		15		2^1			3	7		8^3										19
1	2^2	13	4	5			11	6	12	14	8	10^1		14			3	7		9^3										20
1	2	3	4	5^3			11	6	12	13	8	10^1		14				7		9^2										21
1		3	4	5	14	9		7^3		6^1		13	2					8		10^2		11	12							22
1	2	3	4	5	13	10		7^1		14			9^2					8		11		6^3	12							23
1	2	3		5		10		13					12	14				9		8^3		11^2	6	7^1	4					24
1		3	4	5		10	12	13					14					9		7^2		11^3	6	8^1		2				25
1	14		4	3	9		5^2	7	10					12				8^1		13		11^3	6		2					26
1			4	2	8			7	10				12	9						5		11^1	6		3					27
1			4	2	9	13		10	11^5				6^3	12				14		16		7^4	15	3	8^1	5^2				28
1			4	2	7			10	11^2				6^1					9		13		8	12	3		5				29
		4	3	9		12		10^1	11				8^2					6		13^7		7		2		5	1			30
1	2	3	8		14			9^2	10				11^1	13				5		12		7	4		6^3					31
1		2	3	5		14		8^4	11				10^9	13				6^2		12		9	4		7^1					32
1	2^4	3	4	5		8^3	9^1		11^5		7^2	13	10	14				6				12	15					16		33
1	2	3	4	5		8^2	11^1	12	10		6	13	9					7^3					14							34
1		4	3	5		8^2	2^1	9	11			13	10	7			12	6												35
	3	4	5^4				6^3	9	14	10	11^2	2		7^1				8				12	13						1	15	36

KILMARNOCK

Year Formed: 1869. *Ground & Address:* Rugby Park, Rugby Road, Kilmarnock KA1 2DP.
Telephone: 01563 545 300. *Fax:* 01563 522 181. *E-mail:* info@kilmarnockfc.co.uk *Website:* kilmarnockfc.co.uk
Ground Capacity: 18,128 (all seated). *Size of Pitch:* 102m × 67m.
Chairman: Billy Bowie.
Manager: Stuart Kettlewell. *Assistant Manager:* Stephen Frail.
Club Nickname: 'Killie'.
Previous Grounds: Rugby Park (Dundonald Road); The Grange; Holm Quarry; Rugby Park 1899.
Record Attendance: 35,995 v Rangers, Scottish Cup Quarter-final, 10 March 1962.
Record Transfer Fee received: £2,200,000 from Celtic for Greg Taylor (August 2019).
Record Transfer Fee paid: £340,000 to St Johnstone for Paul Wright (1995).
Record Victory: 11-1 v Paisley Academical, Scottish Cup 1st rd, 18 January 1930.
Record Defeat: 1-9 v Celtic, Division I, 13 August 1938.
Most Capped Player: Joe Nibloe, 11, Scotland.
Most League Appearances: 481: Alan Robertson, 1972-88.
Most League Goals in Season (Individual): 34: Harry 'Peerie' Cunningham 1927-28; Andy Kerr 1960-61.
Most Goals Overall (Individual): 148: Willy Culley, 1912-23.

KILMARNOCK – WILLIAM HILL PREMIERSHIP 2024–25 LEAGUE RECORD

Match No.	Date	Venue	Opponents	Result	H/T Score	Lg Pos.	Goalscorers	Atten- dance
1	Aug 4	A	Celtic	L	0-4	0-2	10		58,712
2	11	H	St Johnstone	L	0-3	0-2	12		4843
3	25	A	Aberdeen	L	0-2	0-1	12		16,146
4	Sept 1	H	Hibernian	D	1-1	0-0	12	Anderson (pen) 90	7763
5	14	A	St Mirren	D	2-2	1-2	11	Watkins 11, Ayunga (og) 70	6957
6	28	H	Dundee U	D	3-3	0-1	11	Watson 2 47, 57, Watkins 64	6257
7	Oct 5	A	Dundee	W	3-2	0-1	9	Kennedy 2 86, 90, Anderson 88	5316
8	20	H	Rangers	W	1-0	0-0	7	Watkins 87	8924
9	26	H	Ross Co	L	1-2	1-0	9	Ndaba 39	3419
10	30	A	Hearts	W	2-1	0-1	6	Kennedy 58, Vassell 63	18,402
11	Nov 3	A	Dundee	L	2-3	2-1	8	Anderson 24, Kennedy 40	5014
12	10	H	Celtic	L	0-2	0-1	8		8657
13	23	A	St Johnstone	L	0-1	0-0	10		1872
14	30	H	Dundee	D	1-1	0-0	10	Wales 80	5454
15	Dec 4	A	Rangers	L	0-6	0-1	10		44,188
16	7	A	Dundee U	D	1-1	0-0	10	Anderson (pen) 90	8402
17	15	H	Hearts	W	1-0	1-0	8	Anderson (pen) 18	5474
18	20	A	Motherwell	D	1-1	0-1	8	Polworth 74	4966
19	26	H	Aberdeen	W	4-0	1-0	8	Vassell 18, Watson 59, Cameron 87, Anderson 90	6846
20	29	A	Hibernian	L	0-1	0-1	9		19,265
21	Jan 2	H	St Mirren	W	2-0	1-0	8	Anderson 2 (1 pen) 8, 65 (p)	6603
22	5	A	Ross Co	L	0-1	0-0	10		5426
23	8	H	Motherwell	D	0-0	0-0	9		4601
24	25	A	Hearts	L	2-3	0-1	11	Wales 50, Murray 67	18,677
25	Feb 1	H	Dundee U	W	1-0	0-0	9	Watkins 72	5661
26	15	H	St Johnstone	W	3-1	1-0	6	Polworth 9, Murray 56, Wales 60	5479
27	22	A	Aberdeen	L	0-1	0-0	8		16,993
28	26	H	Rangers	L	2-4	2-1	10	Wright 11, Lyons 14	8751
29	Mar 1	A	Ross Co	L	0-1	0-1	10		3385
30	15	A	Hibernian	D	1-1	0-1	10	Murray 90	6703
31	29	A	St Mirren	L	1-5	0-2	10	Anderson (pen) 88	7542
32	Apr 5	H	Motherwell	W	2-0	1-0	9	Murray 22, Wright 53	5671
33	12	A	Celtic	L	1-5	1-4	9	Armstrong 29	58,712
34	26	H	Ross Co	W	2-0	1-0	9	Anderson 36, Donnelly 69	5425
35	May 3	A	St Johnstone	W	2-0	1-0	9	Watson 12, Armstrong (pen) 53	5191
36	10	H	Dundee	W	3-2	1-0	9	Armstrong (pen) 31, Anderson 77, Deas 90	5669
37	14	A	Motherwell	L	0-3	0-0	9		4941
38	18	H	Hearts	L	0-1	0-0	9		6601

Final League Position: 9

Honours
League Champions: Division I 1964-65; Championship 2021-22; Division II 1897-98, 1898-99.
Runners-up: Division I 1959-60, 1960-61, 1962-63, 1963-64; First Division 1975-76, 1978-79, 1981-82, 1992-93; Division II 1953-54, 1973-74; Second Division 1989-90.
Scottish Cup Winners: 1920, 1929, 1997; *Runners-up:* 1898, 1932, 1938, 1957, 1960.
League Cup Winners: 2011-12; *Runners-up:* 1952-53, 1960-61, 1962-63, 2000-01, 2006-07.

European: *European Cup:* 4 matches (1965-66). *Cup Winners' Cup:* 4 matches (1997-98). *UEFA Cup:* 32 matches (*Fairs Cup:* 1964-65, 1966-67 semi-finals, 1969-70, 1970-71. *UEFA Cup:* 1998-99, 1999-2000, 2001-02). *UEFA Conference League:* 2 matches (2024-25).

Club colours: Shirt: Blue with white stripes. Shorts: White. Socks: White.

Goalscorers: *League (45):* Anderson 11 (5 pens), Kennedy 4, Murray 4, Watkins 4, Watson 4, Armstrong 3 (2 pens), Wales 3, Polworth 2, Vassell 2, Wright 2, Cameron 1, Deas 1, Donnelly 1, Lyons 1, Ndaba 1, own goal 1.
Scottish Cup (1): Wales 1.
Premier Sports Scottish League Cup (0).
SPFL Trust Trophy (2): Cooper 1, own goal 1.
Europa League (1): Watson 1.
UEFA Conference League (4): Vassell 1, Wales 1, Watkins 1, own goal 1.

McCrorie R 21	Lyons B 31	Mayo B +1	Findlay S 16 +1	Bainbridge O 2 +4	Watson D 23 +12	Donnelly L 16 +9	Polworth L 16 +10	Murray F 26 +7	Vassell K 21 +2	Kennedy M 13 +6	Armstrong D 26 +7	McKenzie R 2 +17	Cameron I 2 +19	Wales B 17 +11	Mackay-Steven G 1 +9	Wright J 26 +2	Deas R 25 +7	Watkins M 22 +9	O'Hara K 17 +2	Burroughs J 3 +9	Anderson B 15 +15	Ndaba B 15 +1	Magennis K 5 +7	Ramsay C 1 +7	Burke C — +2	Match No.
1	2	3	4	5	6	7^4	8^1	9^5	10^3	11^2	12	13	14	15	16											1
1	7	12	3		6			9^5	11^2	13		5^4	8^1	10^3	16	15	2^4	4	14							2
2^4	3		4^6	17	9^1	6	15			10^3	7^2	13	14			5^4	11^5	1	8	12	16					3
	2		4		7^3	8	15	10^4	9^1	6^2	13	12	14			3	14	11	1	2	5^3					4
			4		7	8	12	10^2	9^1	6		13				3^4	14	11	1	2	5^3					5
8	3		4^1	15	13	14	7^4	16	11	9^1	6					12	10^5	1	2^2		5					6
1	6	2^4			9^2	7^1			11^5	8	5^3	12		16	14	3	10		15	13	4					7
1	7	2	4		14	8^3		10^1	9^4	6^2	15		13			3	11^5		16	12	5					8
1	7	2	4^1		13	8^4		10^2	9^4	6^3					12	3	11		14	15	5					9
1	7	3		15	8		16	10^3	9^5	6^4	13	14				2^1	4	11^2	12		5					10
1	7	2	4^1		6^4			10	8	5^2	15	14				12	3		13	11^3	9					11
1	6	2			8^4	7^5		13	10^1	9^3		15	12		16	3	5	11^2		14	4					12
1	6	3			9^1	7^4		12	11^4		5^3	16	15		13	2^5	4	10^2		14	8					13
1	6	3				13	8^3	11^4		12		15	14	5^1	2	4	10		9^2	7						14
1	6	2		8^2	9^5		16	13	11^3		5^4	14		15		3^1	4	10		12		7				15
1^1	9	2			6^3	8	10^5		5^2			13	14		3	4^4	15	12		11	7	16				16
12^1	9	2			12	13^3	7	6			16	15	8		5	3^4	10^4	14		11^3	4					17
5	3				6^3		7^4	8	11		13	15		12		2	10^1	1		9^2	4	14				18
1	2	3		16	7	15	8^1	9^5	11^2		6^4		12	10^3		4				14	5	13				19
1	2	4			7^5		8^3	9	10^4	6^4		13	11^2			3^1	12		16	15	5	14				20
1	7	2			15	13	8^2	6	10^1			14	9^3			3	4			11^4	5	12				21
1	2	4			7^8	8^3	9		6^4		10^1	13	15	3		12^2			11	5	14					22
1	5	2				7	9^2		13			10		3		4	11		12	14	8^3	6^1				23
	2				13	14	6^3	8		12			10			3	4^4	11	1	15	9	7^2	5^1			24
7^1	3				6^5	15	12	9		5^3			10			2	13	11^4	1	14	4	8^2	16			25
2	4				12	14	7^4	11^5		15			16	9^2		3	5	10^3	1	13	8	6^1				26
2^3	3				13	7^2	8	6^4		15	14		16	11^1		4	5	10^5	1	12	9					27
	7	3			14	12	13	9		6^1			15	11		2	4^4	10^3	1		5	8^2				28
2	3				6^2		7^3	9^1		15	12		16	14		4	5	10^5	1	11	8	13^4				29
1	6^5	3			12		13	8		11^4	5^2		16	9		2	4^1	10^3		14	7		15			30
1	2^1	3	15		12	7	8^3	6		9^4		16		13		4	14	11^5		10	5^2					31
8^4	2^1	4^5			13	14		10^3		16	6	7^2		9		3	15		1	11	5		12			32
	7	2	4		8^4	9		10^3		14	6^1			11^2		3	13	12	1		5		15			33
	2	4			8	7		10^3			6^2	14	15	9^4		3	12	1		11^1	5		13			34
	2	4			8^5	7	16	9^4	14		6^2	12		11^1		3	13	1		10^3	5		15			35
	2	4			7^4	8^2	14	9	12		6	13		10^1		3	15	1		11^3	5					36
	2	4			7		8	14	9^5	11^2		6^4	13^3			3^4	12	1		10^1	5		15	16		37
1	2^3	3	4^1		7	8	14	9	10^5		6^4			11^2	16		13			12	5		15			38

LIVINGSTON

Year Formed: 1974. *Ground:* Home of the Set Fare Arena, Alderstone Road, Livingston EH54 7DN.
Telephone: 01506 417 000. *Fax:* 01506 429 948. *E-mail:* lfcreception@livingstonfc.co.uk *Website:* livingstonfc.co.uk
Ground Capacity: 9,865 (all seated). *Size of Pitch:* 98m × 69m.
Chairman: Calvin Ford. *Chief Executive:* Dave Black.
Manager: David Martindale. *Assistant Manager:* Neil Hastings.
Club Nickname: 'Livi', 'Livi Lions'.
Previous Ground: Meadowbank Stadium (as Meadowbank Thistle).
Record Attendance: 10,024 v Celtic, Premier League, 18 August 2001.
Record Transfer Fee received: £2,000,000 from QPR for Lyndon Dykes (August 2020).
Record Transfer Fee paid: £225,000 to Queen of the South for Lyndon Dykes (January 2019).
Record Victory: 8-0 v Stranraer, League Cup, 1st rd, 31 July 2012.
Record Defeat: 0-8 v Hamilton A. Division II, 14 December 1974.
Most League Appearances: 446: Walter Boyd, 1979-89.
Most League Goals in Season (Individual): 22: Leigh Griffiths, 2008-09; Iain Russell, 2010-11; Liam Buchanan, 2016-17.
Most Goals Overall (Individual): 64: David Roseburgh, 1986-93.

LIVINGSTON – WILLIAM HILL CHAMPIONSHIP 2024–25 LEAGUE RECORD

Match No.	Date	Venue	Opponents	Result	H/T Score	Lg Pos.	Goalscorers	Attendance
1	Aug 3	H	Dunfermline Ath	W 2-0	0-0	1	Pitman [49], Kelly [71]	1917
2	9	A	Queen's Park	D 1-1	0-1	2	Clarke [60]	881
3	24	H	Greenock Morton	D 1-1	0-0	3	Pitman [54]	1512
4	31	A	Raith R	W 1-0	0-0	3	Brandon [90]	3517
5	Sept 14	H	Hamilton A	W 3-0	0-0	3	Pitman [56], Muirhead 2 [81, 87]	1241
6	28	H	Airdrieonians	W 2-1	1-1	3	Kelly [29], Shinnie [90]	1532
7	Oct 5	A	Partick Thistle	D 0-0	0-0	3		3668
8	8	A	Falkirk	D 0-0	0-0	3		5715
9	19	A	Ayr U	W 2-1	2-1	2	Muirhead [8], Pitman [38]	2470
10	26	H	Raith R	W 2-1	0-1	2	Wilson [75], Nottingham [90]	1750
11	29	A	Dunfermline Ath	L 0-3	0-1	2		4810
12	Nov 2	H	Queen's Park	D 1-1	0-0	2	May [50]	1138
13	9	A	Hamilton A	W 3-1	1-1	2	May [40], Smith [50], Winter [90]	1033
14	16	H	Falkirk	W 1-0	1-0	2	Yengi [41]	3745
15	Dec 7	A	Greenock Morton	D 0-0	0-0	2		1664
16	13	H	Partick Thistle	W 2-0	1-0	2	Yengi [7], Muirhead [69]	1544
17	17	A	Airdrieonians	W 3-0	1-0	2	May 2 [35, 67], Clarke [56]	1433
18	21	H	Ayr U	L 0-1	0-1	2		1521
19	28	H	Raith R	L 1-2	0-2	2	May (pen) [65]	3955
20	Jan 4	A	Queen's Park	L 0-2	0-1	3		1266
21	14	H	Airdrieonians	W 2-1	1-1	3	Strapp (og) [5], Fraser [59]	1051
22	25	H	Hamilton A	W 3-0	2-0	3	Muirhead [3], Montano [16], Smith [90]	1078
23	31	A	Falkirk	W 2-1	2-0	2	Muirhead (pen) [13], McAlear [45]	6381
24	Feb 15	H	Dunfermline Ath	D 0-0	0-0	3		1798
25	22	A	Ayr U	W 2-1	1-0	2	Wilson [33], Muirhead [90]	3063
26	25	H	Greenock Morton	W 3-2	3-1	2	Yengi [29], Wilson [35], Shinnie [37]	1050
27	28	A	Partick Thistle	D 1-1	0-1	2	Muirhead [78]	2946
28	Mar 5	H	Raith R	D 0-0	0-0	3		1331
29	15	A	Airdrieonians	D 3-3	1-2	2	Muirhead [25], Wilson [67], Kelly [76]	1580
30	25	H	Falkirk	W 1-0	0-0	2	Shinnie [88]	3827
31	Apr 2	A	Dunfermline Ath	L 0-1	0-1	3		4890
32	5	A	Queen's Park	W 3-0	3-0	2	Smith [14], Muirhead [17], Kelly [40]	1396
33	12	A	Greenock Morton	W 2-1	2-1	2	Montano [17], Pitman [23]	1737
34	18	H	Ayr U	W 5-0	3-0	2	Kelly 2 [6, 45], Muirhead (pen) [33], Montano [79], McAlear [90]	1606
35	26	A	Hamilton A	W 3-0	2-0	2	Muirhead 2 (1 pen) [27 (p), 36], Yengi [52]	1155
36	May 2	H	Partick Thistle	L 0-1	0-1	2		4500

Final League Position: 2

Honours
League Champions: First Division 2000-01; Second Division 1986-87, 1998-99, 2010-11; League One 2016-17; Third Division 1995-96, 2009-10.
Runners-up: Second Division 1982-83; First Division 1987-88; Championship 2017-18, 2024-25.
Promoted via play-offs: 2017-18, 2024-25 (to Premiership).
Scottish Cup: Semi-finals 2001, 2004.
League Cup Winners: 2003-04. *Runners-up:* 2020-21. *Semi-finals:* 1984-85.
League Challenge Cup Winners: 2014-15, 2024-25; *Runners-up:* 2000-01.

European: *UEFA Cup:* 4 matches (2002-03).

Club colours: All: Yellow with black trim.

Goalscorers: *League (55):* Muirhead 13 (3 pens), Kelly 6, May 5 (1 pen), Pitman 5, Wilson 4, Yengi 4, Montano 3, Shinnie 3, Smith 3, Clarke 2, McAlear 2, Brandon 1, Fraser 1, Nottingham 1, Winter 1, own goal 1.
Scottish Cup (8): Yengi 3, McAlear 1, McGowan 1, Montano 1, Muirhead 1 (1 pen), Shinnie 1.
Premier Sports Scottish League Cup (5): Muirhead 2, Sole 2, own goal 1.
SPFL Trust Trophy (13): May 4, Muirhead 2, Yengi 2, Brandon 1, McAlear 1, Pitman 1, Shinnie 1, Smith 1.
Premiership Play-offs (9): Wilson 3, Brandon 1, May 1, Muirhead 1, Pitman 1, Smith 1, Yengi 1.

George S 3	Finlayson D 21 + 13	McGowan R 36	Nottingham M 22 + 4	Clarke M 18 + 2	Brandon J 34	Pitman S 31 + 4	Kelly S 26 + 6	Sole L 3 + 9	Yengi T 19 + 9	Shinnie A 10 + 21	Smith L 13 + 13	McAlear R 9 + 15	Lawal S — + 2	Muirhead R 27 + 6	Green O — + 1	May S 27 + 6	Prior J 33	Montano C 17 + 8	Winter A — + 16	Carson D — + 1	Wilson D 19 + 2	Korhoa R — + 1	Fraser R 13 + 3	Culbert S — + 1	Tait M 15	Ubochioma M — + 4	Match No.
1	2	3	4	5	6[3]	7	8	9[1]	10	11[2]	12	13	14														1
1	2[3]	3	4	5	7	6	8	12	10	11[2]		13		9[1]	14												2
1	2	3	4	5	7[3]	6	8	12	11[2]	9[1]		13	14	10													3
	2[3]	3	4	5[2]	7	6	8		9	11[1]			14	12		10	1	13									4
	2[5]	3	4	5[1]	7	6	8	13		11[1]	9[3]			14		10[4]	1	12	15	16							5
	2	3	4	5	7	6	8	14	9[3]	11[1]				10[2]			1	12									6
	2	3	4	5[1]	7	6	8[4]16	13	9[3]	14	11[2]			10[5]			1	12	15								7
	2	3	4		8[3]	7	9	6[1]	15	12	14			10[4]		11[2]	1	5	13								8
	2[2]	3	4	12	7	6	8		11[3]14		9[4]			10		1	5[1]	15		13							9
	3[2]	2	5	7	6[4]	8	12	9[1]	15	13	10			1		14	4[8]										10
	2[1]	3	4	5	6	8	9[3]10[2]		13	16		15	7[5]		11[4]	1	12	14								11
	3	12	5	2	6	8	13	11[4]	7[3]16	14			9[2]		10[5]	1		15		4[1]							12
13	3	4	5	2	6[1]	8	15	11	7[2]	9[4]12			10[3]		1		14										13
2	4	3	5	7	6	8[1]		9	14	11[2]12			10[3]		1		13										14
2[3]	4	3	5	7	6	14		11	13	12	8		9[1]		10[2]	1											15
2	4	3	5[1]	7[5]	6	13		11	16	9[2]	8[1]		12		10[4]	1	14	15									16
2	4	3	5[2]	7[1]	6[5]12			11	15	14	8[4]		9		10[3]	1	13	16									17
2	4	3	5[4]	7[3]	6[5]13	12	11					9[2]	8[1]		14	10	1	15	16								18
2[2]	4	3	5[5]		8	6		11[1]14	12	7[3]			9[4]		10	1	16	15	13								19
13	3	2[3]	5[2]	7	8	6			9[1]				12		10	1	11[4]	15		4		14				20
12	3			2	6	8[1]			7[4]		14		9		10[3]	1	11[2]	13		4		5	15				21
12	3			2	6				14	15	8[2]		9[2]		10[4]	1	11[1]			4		5		7[3]	13		22
12	3	2		7				13	14			6	9[2]		10[3]	1	11			4		5[1]	8				23
2	3			7	12			13			15	8[2]	9[3]		10[4]	1	11[1]			4		5	6	14			24
13	3	2		7	5			11	12			6			10[1]	1	9			4			8[2]				25
2	3		14	7[2]	6[5]15			11	10	12	13		9[3]			1				4		5[1]	8[4]16				26
12	3	2		7[5]	6	16		11[2]14		15			9		10[4]	1	5[3]			4		13	8[1]				27
14	3			2[3]	6[4]	8		12		13	15		9		10[1]	1	11			4		5[2]	7				28
14	3			2[2]	13	8		11[1]	10[4]	15	6[3]		9		12	1	5[5]			4		16	7				29
2[3]	3			7	14	8		12	15	13			9[4]		10[2]	1	11[1]			4		5	6				30
2	3	12		7[4]	13	8		11	15				9		10[1]	1	14			4		5[3]	6[2]				31
16	3			2[5]	6	8[4]		12	14	9[3]			10[1]		13	1	11[2]			4		5	7	15			32
5	4	14			6	8		12		9[2]			10[3]		13	1	11[1]			3		2	7				33
13	3			2[2]	6[3]	8		12	15	9[5]16			10[1]		14	1	11[4]			4		5	7				34
16	3[5]15			2[4]	6[3]	8		12	13	9			10[2]		14	1	11			4		5[1]	7				35
14	3			2[4]	6[2]	8		12	13	9			10[3]		15	1	11[1]			4		5	7				36

MONTROSE

Year Formed: 1879. *Ground & Address:* Links Park, Wellington St, Montrose DD10 8QD.
Telephone: 01674 673 200. *Fax:* 01674 677 311. *E-mail:* office@montrosefc.co.uk *Website:* montrosefc.co.uk
Ground Capacity: total: 4,936, (seated: 1,338). *Size of Pitch:* 100m × 64m.
Chairman: John Crawford. *Chief Executive:* Peter Stuart.
Manager: Stewart Petrie. *Assistant Manager:* Ross Campbell.
Club Nickname: 'The Gable Endies'.
Previous Ground: First Links Park.
Record Attendance: 8,983 v Dundee, Scottish Cup 3rd rd, 17 March 1973.
Record Transfer Fee received: £60,000 from Hibernian for Gary Murray (December 1980).
Record Transfer Fee paid: £17,500 to Airdrieonians for Jim Smith (February 1992).
Record Victory: 12-0 v Vale of Leithen, Scottish Cup 2nd rd, 4 January 1975.
Record Defeat: 0-13 v Aberdeen, Division C, 17 March 1951.
Most Capped Player: Alexander Keillor, 2 (6), Scotland.
Most League Appearances: 432: David Larter, 1987-98.
Most League Goals in Season (Individual): 28: Brian Third, Division II, 1972-73.
Most Goals Overall (Individual): 126: Bobby Livingstone, 1967-79.

MONTROSE – WILLIAM HILL LEAGUE ONE 2024–25 LEAGUE RECORD

Match No.	Date		Venue	Opponents	Result	H/T Score	Lg Pos.	Goalscorers	Attendance
1	Aug	3	H	Kelty Hearts	D 1-1	0-0	3	Brown [59]	516
2		10	A	Arbroath	D 0-0	0-0	7		2040
3		17	A	Inverness CT	D 1-1	1-0	6	Hester [20]	1902
4		24	H	Queen of the South	W 1-0	1-0	4	Brown [21]	377
5		31	A	Cove Rangers	L 0-1	0-0	5		479
6	Sept	14	H	Stenhousemuir	W 3-0	2-0	4	Hester [9], Williamson [30], Quinn [90]	371
7		21	A	Dumbarton	W 1-0	1-0	2	Hester [6]	628
8		28	H	Alloa Ath	D 2-2	1-1	3	Shrive [3], Hester [58]	630
9	Oct	5	A	Annan Ath	L 0-1	0-1	5		324
10		19	A	Kelty Hearts	W 2-0	0-0	2	Machado [68], MacIver-Redwood [74]	500
11		26	H	Cove Rangers	L 0-2	0-0	4		691
12	Nov	2	A	Queen of the South	L 0-1	0-1	7		945
13		9	H	Arbroath	D 1-1	1-0	7	Watson [4]	1565
14		16	A	Stenhousemuir	L 0-1	0-0	7		561
15		23	H	Annan Ath	W 2-1	1-1	6	Webster [35], MacIver-Redwood [60]	367
16	Dec	7	H	Inverness CT	L 2-3	2-0	6	Webster [27], Lyons [38]	502
17		14	A	Alloa Ath	W 2-1	0-0	5	Lyons [67], Hester [89]	597
18		21	A	Dumbarton	L 1-2	0-1	6	Mackenzie [80]	541
19		28	A	Arbroath	L 0-3	0-1	6		2714
20	Jan	4	H	Kelty Hearts	D 0-0	0-0	7		609
21		25	A	Annan Ath	D 2-2	2-0	7	Stirton [9], Lyons [19]	233
22	Feb	1	H	Stenhousemuir	L 0-3	0-1	7		531
23		8	A	Alloa Ath	D 2-2	1-0	8	Stirton 2 (1 pen) [17, 86 (p)]	502
24		11	A	Cove Rangers	D 1-1	0-0	7	Stirton [46]	452
25		15	A	Dumbarton	W 3-2	2-2	7	Stirton 2 (1 pen) [13 (p), 24], Quinn [68]	533
26		22	H	Queen of the South	L 0-3	0-1	7		573
27	Mar	1	A	Inverness CT	D 1-1	1-0	7	Sandilands [34]	1653
28		8	H	Kelty Hearts	D 0-0	0-0	7		520
29		15	H	Cove Rangers	D 2-2	0-0	7	Lyons [52], Wighton [78]	735
30		22	H	Annan Ath	W 3-1	3-1	7	Lyons 2 [16, 20], Brown [43]	657
31		29	A	Stenhousemuir	W 3-2	3-0	6	Sandilands 2 [25, 45], Stirton [28]	486
32	Apr	5	H	Arbroath	L 0-1	0-1	6		1792
33		12	A	Queen of the South	L 1-2	0-1	7	Lyons [80]	978
34		19	H	Dumbarton	D 2-2	1-1	6	Stirton [21], Quinn [84]	1087
35		26	A	Alloa Ath	L 1-2	1-0	8	Stirton [26]	662
36	May	3	H	Inverness CT	L 0-2	0-1	8		1018

Final League Position: 8

Honours
League Champions: Second Division 1984-85; League Two 2017-18.
Runners-up: Second Division 1990-91; Third Division 1994-95.
Scottish Cup: Quarter-finals 1973, 1976.
League Cup: Semi-finals 1975-76.
League Challenge Cup: Semi-finals 1992-93, 1996-97.

Club colours: Shirt: Royal blue with white detail and sleeves. Shorts: Royal blue. Socks: White.

Goalscorers: *League (40):* Stirton 9 (2 pens), Lyons 7, Hester 5, Brown 3, Quinn 3, Sandilands 3, MacIver-Redwood 2, Webster 2, Machado 1, Mackenzie 1, Shrive 1, Watson 1, Wighton 1, Williamson 1.
Scottish Cup (5): Lyons 3, Hester 2 (1 pen).
Premier Sports Scottish League Cup (6): Brown 1, Hermiston 1, Lyons 1, MacIver-Redwood 1, Shrive 1, Smith 1.
SPFL Trust Trophy (0).

Gill C 35	Williamson R 12+2	Dillon S 25+6	Steeves A 24+4	Hannah C 7+9	Gardyne M 28+2	Masson T 26+4	Brown C 17+13	Shrive A 8+12	MacIver-Redwood B 11+17	Hester K 14+5	Machado M 20+7	Smith C 4+6	Quinn A 25+2	Emslie O —+1	Mackenzie B 14+5	Bertie K 9+13	Webster G 14+12	Watson P 3+22	Balfour A —+3	Waddell K 8+3	Sandilands C 16+1	Freeman K 16	Stirton O 14	Martin A 1+3	Pollard L 1+3	Wighton C 10+2	Matthews R 1	Match No.
1	2	3	4	5	6	7[1]	8	9[1]	10	11[2]	12	13	14															1
1	5	3	4	8[1]	6[4]	7[4]	9[3]	14	11[5]	10[2]	13	12	15	2	16													2
1	5	3[4]	4	8[1]		7[2]	9	13	11[3]	14	10[4]	6[5]	16	2	12	15												3
1	5		4	9[1]	12	7[1]	6	14	11[2]	13	10	8[3]	2	3	15													4
1	2	13	4	9[2]	8	7[5]	5	15	11[3]	14	10	6[1]	3[4]		12	16												5
1	2	5[3]	15	6	8	7[4]	12	11[1]	10[5]	9[2]	16		3		4	13	14											6
1	5[1]	2[3]	15	6	8	9[2]	14	13	10[5]	11[4]	7	12	4	3	16													7
1	2	12	14	5[3]	6	7		9[5]	10[4]	13	11[2]	8[1]	3		4	15	16											8
1	2	3	5	16	7		13	8[1]	10[4]	11[2]	6[3]	12	4		15		9[5]	14										9
1	2	3	5[5]	16	6	7[4]	9[3]	15	11[2]	13	10	12	4		8[1]	14												10
1	2	3	5	6	7[4]	9[6]	16	11	12	10[3]	8[2]	4[1]	13	14	15													11
1	4	5[4]	3[2]	6[8]	2[8]	14	15	9[5]	10	8[3]	11	12	7[1]	13	16													12
1	3	5	14		13	6	9	10[4]	15	8[3]	11[1]	12	4		7[8]	2[2]												13
1	3	5	13		7	8	9[2]	11	10[3]	14	12	6[4]	4		2[1]		15											14
1	2	5		8	7[5]	12	15	9[3]	10[4]	11[1]	13	3	4		6[2]	14	16											15
1	2	12[4]	16	7	6[2]	14	15	10[4]	13	11[3]	9	3	4[1]	5	8[5]													16
1	3		13	8	7[3]		12	11	10[2]	9	6[4]	4	5[1]	2	14	15												17
1	3		14	6[5]	7	16	13	11[4]	10[1]	9	8[2]	4[8]	12	5[3]	2	15												18
1	3	5[4]		6[1]	7	10[3]	8[2]	11	13	9	12	4	15	2	14													19
1				7[2]	14		11	10[1]	12	6		3	4	5	9	13				8[3]								20
1	3	14		6[2]	11	12		7	2[3]	4[1]	9		13							8	5	10						21
1	3	12		9	7[4]	13	8[2]	11		4	5[1]	10[3]	14		6[5]	2					15	16						22
1	4	5		7[1]	16		10	14		6[5]	3[2]		12	13	15				9[3]	2	11					8[4]		23
1		5		13	4	4	10[4]	15		6[2]	3		12	8				9	2	11[3]						7[1]		24
1	12	5		6	7[3]	15	11[4]			3			14	13				4[1]	6	8	2	10				9[2]		25
1		5		6[4]	16		11	15		7[3]	3		13	14	12			4[2]	8	2[1]	10					9[5]		26
1	13	5		7	14	11[4]				3			12	15				4[3]	8	2	10	6[1]				9[2]		27
1	4	5		6	7[2]	14	11			3[5]			12	15	16			8[4]	2[1]	10	13					9[3]		28
1	14	5		6	7[3]		11[1]			3			13	12				4[2]	8	2	10					9		29
1	3	4		6	7	8[1]	11[3]	12	15				5[4]	13	14			9[6]	2				16	10[2]				30
1	4	5[1]		6	8	11				3		12						7	2	10	9							31
1	4[4]			6[5]	12	8[3]		11	15				3			13	16	5[2]	7	2	10	14			9[1]			32
1	15	2		7[3]	8[8]	9	11	13					3[5]			12		14	4[1]	6	5[2]	10[4]		16				33
1		4		6	10[3]		7	14		8[2]	12		5[1]	13	15			3	9	2	11[4]							34
1	12	2		8		9	11[2]	14					3		16	6[9]	15	4[1]	7[3]	5	10[4]				13			35
	3[4]	12		7[1]	14	16				8		4[2]		2	6	10[3]		13	5	11		9[9]	15			1		36

MOTHERWELL

Year Formed: 1886. *Ground & Address:* Fir Park Stadium, Motherwell ML1 2QN.
Telephone: 01698 333 333. *Fax:* 01698 338 001. *E-mail:* mfcenquiries@motherwellfc.co.uk *Website:* motherwellfc.co.uk
Ground Capacity: 13,742 (all seated). *Size of Pitch:* 105m × 65m.
Chairman: Kyrk Macmillan. *Chief Executive:* Brian Caldwell.
Manager: Jens Berthel Askou. *Assistant Manager:* Max Rogers.
Club Nicknames: 'The Well'; 'The Steelmen'.
Previous Grounds: The Meadows; Dalziel Park.
Record Attendance: 35,632 v Rangers, Scottish Cup 4th rd replay, 12 March 1952.
Record Transfer Fee received: £3,000,000 (rising to £3,250,000) from Celtic for David Turnbull (August 2020).
Record Transfer Fee paid: £500,000 to Everton for John Spencer (January 1999).
Record Victory: 12-1 v Dundee U, Division II, 23 January 1954.
Record Defeat: 0-8 v Aberdeen, Premier Division, 26 March 1979.
Most Capped Player: Stephen Craigan, 54, Northern Ireland.
Most League Appearances: 626: Bobby Ferrier, 1918-37.
Most League Goals in Season (Individual): 52: Willie McFadyen, Division I, 1931-32.
Most Goals Overall (Individual): 283: Hugh Ferguson, 1916-25.

MOTHERWELL – WILLIAM HILL PREMIERSHIP 2024–25 LEAGUE RECORD

Match No.	Date		Venue	Opponents		Result	H/T Score	Lg Pos.	Goalscorers	Attendance
1	Aug	3	H	Ross Co	D	0-0	0-0	1		4353
2		10	A	Rangers	L	1-2	1-2	8	Propper (og) [17]	48,529
3		25	H	Hearts	W	3-1	1-0	6	McGinn [24], O'Donnell [59], Sparrow [81]	6895
4		31	A	St Johnstone	W	2-1	1-0	4	Casey [11], Ebiye [90]	3629
5	Sept	14	A	Aberdeen	L	1-2	0-1	5	Ebiye [88]	17,155
6		28	H	St Mirren	W	2-1	2-1	4	Miller 2 (1 pen) [19 (p), 44]	5214
7	Oct	5	A	Hibernian	W	2-1	0-0	4	Stamatelopoulos [56], Halliday [79]	15,892
8		19	H	Dundee	L	0-1	0-1	5		5084
9		27	H	Celtic	L	0-3	0-1	5		8692
10		30	A	Dundee U	W	2-1	1-1	4	Maswanhise 2 [23, 74]	8415
11	Nov	9	H	St Johnstone	W	2-1	2-0	5	Maswanhise [20], Sparrow [34]	4306
12		23	A	Ross Co	L	1-2	0-0	5	Robinson [83]	3410
13		30	H	Hibernian	L	0-3	0-2	5		5212
14	Dec	4	A	Dundee	L	1-4	1-1	6	Stamatelopoulos [19]	5381
15		7	A	St Mirren	W	1-0	0-0	5	Watt [90]	6111
16		14	H	Dundee U	W	4-3	3-1	4	Stamatelopoulos 2 [1, 40], Halliday [33], Sparrow [67]	4473
17		20	A	Kilmarnock	D	1-1	1-0	4	Gordon [17]	4966
18		26	A	Celtic	L	0-4	0-1	6		58,687
19		29	H	Rangers	D	2-2	2-0	6	Stamatelopoulos [16], Maswanhise [35]	8728
20	Jan	2	A	Hearts	L	0-1	0-1	6		18,715
21		5	H	Aberdeen	W	2-0	2-0	5	Wilson [34], Maswanhise [45]	5308
22		8	A	Kilmarnock	D	0-0	0-0	5		4601
23		11	A	Hibernian	L	1-3	0-2	5	Slattery [76]	15,829
24		25	A	St Johnstone	L	1-2	1-0	5	Halliday (pen) [4]	3892
25	Feb	2	H	Celtic	L	1-3	1-2	6	Armstrong [23]	8293
26		15	A	Ross Co	L	0-3	0-1	7		3973
27		22	A	Dundee U	L	0-1	0-1	9		9044
28		26	H	Dundee	W	2-1	1-0	8	Casey 2 [12, 84]	4258
29	Mar	1	A	Rangers	W	2-1	2-0	6	Armstrong [9], Sparrow [30]	50,056
30		15	H	St Mirren	D	2-2	1-2	7	Slattery 2 [35, 71]	6121
31		29	A	Aberdeen	L	1-4	1-2	8	Slattery [5]	19,274
32	Apr	5	A	Kilmarnock	L	0-2	0-1	8		5671
33		12	H	Hearts	D	0-0	0-0	8		7481
34		26	H	St Johnstone	W	3-2	2-1	7	Slattery [39], Sprangler (og) [40], Sparrow [48]	4412
35	May	3	A	Dundee	W	2-1	0-1	7	Sparrow [59], Maswanhise [90]	5692
36		10	A	Hearts	L	0-3	0-1	8		18,496
37		14	H	Kilmarnock	W	3-0	0-0	8	Armstrong 2 [77, 86], Slattery [83]	4941
38		18	A	Ross Co	D	1-1	0-1	8	Ebiye [83]	4170

Final League Position: 8

Honours
League Champions: Division I 1931-32;. First Division 1981-82, 1984-85; Division II 1953-54, 1968-69.
Runners-up: Premier Division 1994-95, 2012-13; Premiership 2013-14; Division I 1926-27, 1929-30, 1932-33, 1933-34; Division II 1894-95, 1902-03.
Scottish Cup: 1952, 1991; *Runners-up:* 1931, 1933, 1939, 1951, 2011, 2018.
League Cup Winners: 1950-51; *Runners-up:* 1954-55, 2004-05, 2017-18.

European: *Champions League:* 2 matches (2012-13). *Cup Winners' Cup:* 2 matches (1991-92). *UEFA Cup:* 8 matches (1994-95, 1995-96, 2008-09). *Europa League:* 21 matches (2009-10, 2010-11, 2012-13, 2013-14, 2014-15, 2020-21). *UEFA Europa Conference League:* 2 matches (2022-23).

Club colours: Shirt: Amber with broad maroon hoop. Shorts: Maroon. Socks: Amber with maroon tops.

Goalscorers: *League (46):* Maswanhise 6, Slattery 6, Sparrow 6, Stamatelopoulos 5, Armstrong 4, Casey 3, Ebiye 3, Halliday 3 (1 pen), Miller 2 (1 pen), Gordon 1, McGinn 1, O'Donnell 1, Robinson 1, Watt 1, Wilson 1, own goals 2.
Scottish Cup (0).
Premier Sports Scottish League Cup (11): Ebiye 2, Miller 2 (2 pens), Balmer 1, Blaney 1, Casey 1, Halliday 1, O'Donnell 1, Robinson 1, Stuparevic 1.
SPFL Trust Trophy (0).

Oxborough A 25	Casey D 31+2	Gordon L 27	Blaney S 10+1	O'Donnell S 26+3	Zdravkovski D 13+12	Halliday A 35+3	Wilson E 24+7	Miller L 32	Robinson Z 7+5	Ebiye M 3+24	Stamatelopoulos A 13+3	Callachan R —+1	McGinn P 7+3	Wells D —+1	Seddon S 11+3	Sparrow T 21+11	Maswanhise T 17+13	Watt T 15+13	Vale J 2+4	Kaleta M 13+8	Tavares J 2+7	Balmer K 16+4	Koutroumbis J 4+4	Paton H 11+10	Nicholson S 2+7	Slattery C 12+3	Andrews K 5+6	Mair A 1	Balcombe E 12	Thompson D 11+4	Armstrong L 8+6	Plange L 1+3	Dickson W 1+6	Match No.
1	2	3	4³	5	6	7	8	9²	10¹	11⁴	12	13	14	15																				1
1	5	4		2	8³	9	10		7	12	14	11¹			3	6²	13																	2
1	4	3		5	6	7¹	8	9		11²			2		13	14	10³	12																3
1	4	3		5	6⁴	7³	8	9	11¹	15			2		14	10²	12	13																4
1	4	3		5³	6¹	7⁵	8	9	11²	16			2		10⁴	14	12	13	15															5
1	4⁸	3		5²	6⁵	7³	8	9	11⁴	10¹	13		2		16		15	14	12															6
1	3			5⁴	6¹	8⁹	9	7	11²	13	10³		2		12	16	4		15															7
1	4⁴	3		5⁵	7	8⁹	9	6	10¹	12	11²				15	13		16	14	2														8
1	15	3⁸		2	7¹	6²	9	8	12	16	11³				10⁵	13	14		5⁴	4														9
1	4		12	2¹		14	7	6	13		10⁹		8		9²	11⁴			5⁵	16	3	15												10
1	2				12	8⁹	7	14	15	11¹			4		6¹	10³	13		5		3		15											11
1	2	6			11¹	8	7	14	15	10³			4⁷		9⁴	13			5⁵	16	3	12												12
1	2	3			6⁴	7²	8⁵	9	12	14	10¹		16		11	13			5		4³	15												13
1	4	3			12	8	7		13	11³			9		15	10⁴		14	5¹	2		6²												14
1	2	3	4		6⁴	7¹	9		13	11¹²	8				10		15	11⁵	5³		8¹	16												15
1	2	3	4		14	6²	12	7	15	11⁵			9¹		14	15	11⁴	5³	8¹	16		7³												16
1	2⁸	3	4		13	8³	12	5		16	10⁶		9¹		14	15	11⁴	6			7³													17
1	2		4	16		13	8	7		12			9¹		10⁵	11²		5⁴	15	3		6³	14											18
1	3	4	5		14	8³	6	9²		16	10¹		13		11	12		2⁵			7⁴	15												19
1	2	3	4¹	5	12	6⁴	8		13				9²		10⁵	11	16	15			7³	14												20
1	4	3			6²	7	8		11¹				15		14	9³	10⁵	12	5		2⁴		13	16										21
1	4	3¹		16	6	7⁴	8		15				12		13	9³	11	10²	5³		2				14									22
	12			4	5		7²	9³		15			3¹		8⁴	14	10⁵	11⁸	13		2			16	6	1			1	12	14			23
	3	4	2	13	6²			5¹	9	11			8⁵			15	7⁴	10³		16			1	12	14									24
	4	5	3	15	8⁴	13		7	11³				2¹			12	9²			1	6⁵	10	14	16										25
	3		2		7¹	12	8		5³	14	11				4		15	6⁴		1	9²	10	13											26
	4	3	2		6⁵	8⁴	7	12		9¹	11³		5			16		13		1	14	10²	15											27
	4	3	2	13	7¹	8²	15		5	12			16		14	11³	6⁵		1	9	10⁴													28
	4	3		12	6²	16	11⁴		13	5			15		2	14		10³	7	1	8⁹	9¹												29
	4	3³		2	15	6⁴	10		16	5			12		14	13	9⁵	7²		1	8	11¹												30
	4	3¹		2		6	7			5⁴	15	13			12	10³	9		8	11¹²		14												31
	4			2		6	9			5	14		12		3⁴	15			10⁴	7¹	8	11¹²	13											32
	4			3		7²	6			5⁴	11⁶	10³			15	2¹	12	17		9⁵	13		1	8	14	16								33
	4			3	13	7²		8	14	6		11³			2	9¹	10⁴	15	1	5	12													34
1	4			3		7	14	8		13	6²	12	11⁴		2⁸	9¹	10³			5	15													35
1	4			3	15	6⁵	12	7		5	2	8¹	11²		9⁴	16			10³	13	14													36
1	2			3	15	7²	8	6⁵		13	4		5³		10²	11¹			9⁴		14	12	16											37
	3			6³	7⁵	5¹	9		15	4		13	16		2		8	14	1	12	11⁴	10²												38

PARTICK THISTLE

Year Formed: 1876. *Ground & Address:* Wyre Stadium at Firhill, 80 Firhill Rd, Glasgow G20 7AL.
Telephone: 0141 579 1971. *Fax:* 0141 945 1525. *E-mail:* mail@ptfc.co.uk *Website:* ptfc.co.uk
Ground Capacity: 10,102 (all seated). *Size of Pitch:* 105m × 68m.
Chairman: Richard Beastall. *General Manager:* Levi Gill.
Manager: Brian Graham. *Assistant Manager:* Mark Wilson.
Club Nickname: 'The Jags'.
Previous Grounds: Overnewton Park; Jordanvale Park; Muirpark; Inchview; Meadowside Park.
Record Attendance: 49,838 v Rangers, Division I, 18 February 1922. *Ground Record:* 54,728, Scotland v Ireland, 25 February 1928.
Record Transfer Fee received: £350,000 from Barnsley for Liam Lindsay (June 2017); £350,000 from Norwich C for Aidan Fitzpatrick (July 2019).
Record Transfer Fee paid: £85,000 to Celtic for Andy Murdoch (February 1991).
Record Victory: 16-0 v Royal Albert, Scottish Cup 1st rd, 17 January 1931.
Record Defeat: 0-10 v Queen's Park, Scottish Cup 5th rd, 3 December 1881.
Most Capped Player: Alan Rough, 51 (53), Scotland.
Most League Appearances: 410: Alan Rough, 1969-82.
Most League Goals in Season (Individual): 41: Alex Hair, Division I, 1926-27.
Most Goals Overall (Individual): 229: Willie Sharp, 1939-57.

PARTICK THISTLE – WILLIAM HILL CHAMPIONSHIP 2024–25 LEAGUE RECORD

Match No.	Date	Venue	Opponents	Result	H/T Score	Lg Pos.	Goalscorers	Attendance
1	Aug 3	H	Greenock Morton	D	0-0	0-0	6		4148
2	10	A	Raith R	L	0-1	0-1	8		4002
3	24	A	Falkirk	L	1-2	0-0	9	Ablade [76]	6502
4	31	H	Queen's Park	W	3-0	1-0	5	Milne [11], Fitzpatrick [72], Mackenzie [89]	4034
5	Sept 14	A	Ayr U	D	1-1	0-1	5	Milne [74]	3118
6	21	H	Dunfermline Ath	W	1-0	0-0	4	Fitzpatrick [88]	4301
7	28	A	Hamilton A	L	0-1	0-0	6		1677
8	Oct 5	H	Livingston	D	0-0	0-0	6		3668
9	12	H	Falkirk	D	1-1	0-0	5	Graham [61]	4762
10	19	H	Airdrieonians	W	2-1	1-1	5	Graham 2 [5, 72]	3609
11	26	A	Queen's Park	W	1-0	1-0	4	Chalmers [14]	2779
12	Nov 2	A	Dunfermline Ath	W	1-0	0-0	4	Robinson [57]	5162
13	9	H	Raith R	D	1-1	1-0	5	Graham [6]	4348
14	16	H	Hamilton A	W	5-1	2-1	4	Robinson 2 [5, 20], Graham 2 [49, 66], Chalmers [64]	3845
15	Dec 7	H	Ayr U	W	1-0	0-0	4	Turner (pen) [82]	3521
16	13	A	Livingston	L	0-2	0-1	4		1544
17	21	A	Airdrieonians	W	2-0	2-0	4	Graham [37], O'Reilly [43]	1970
18	28	H	Queen's Park	W	2-1	1-1	4	Graham 2 [7, 47]	4350
19	31	A	Greenock Morton	L	1-2	0-0	4	Fitzpatrick [61]	2340
20	Jan 4	H	Dunfermline Ath	L	1-4	1-3	4	Chalmers [6]	3938
21	10	A	Hamilton A	W	2-1	1-0	4	Graham [75], Stanway [82]	1122
22	25	A	Ayr U	L	1-2	0-2	4	Milne [87]	3175
23	Feb 1	H	Greenock Morton	D	2-2	0-1	4	O'Reilly [61], Chalmers [90]	3966
24	8	A	Falkirk	L	2-5	2-3	4	Chalmers [10], Graham [24]	6471
25	15	A	Raith R	L	0-3	0-2	4		3749
26	22	H	Airdrieonians	D	1-1	1-0	4	Graham [17]	3599
27	28	H	Livingston	D	1-1	1-0	4	Graham [25]	2946
28	Mar 11	A	Queen's Park	W	2-0	1-0	4	Chalmers [5], Jakubiak [90]	1758
29	15	H	Ayr U	W	2-0	2-0	4	Chalmers [19], McBeth [27]	4289
30	21	H	Raith R	D	0-0	0-0	4		3213
31	29	A	Greenock Morton	W	1-0	0-0	4	O'Reilly [74]	2570
32	Apr 5	A	Airdrieonians	L	1-2	0-0	4	Stanway [83]	2249
33	12	H	Hamilton A	L	1-2	0-2	4	Graham [90]	3421
34	19	A	Dunfermline Ath	D	0-0	0-0	4		5688
35	25	H	Falkirk	W	2-1	1-1	4	Graham [6], Ablade [90]	4997
36	May 2	A	Livingston	W	1-0	1-0	4	Tait (og) [39]	4500

Final League Position: 4

Honours
League Champions: First Division 1975-76, 2001-02, 2012-13; League One: 2020-21; Division II 1896-97, 1899-1900, 1970-71; Second Division 2000-01.
Runners-up: First Division 1991-92, 2008-09; Division II 1901-02.
Promoted via play-offs: 2005-06 (to First Division).
Scottish Cup Winners: 1921; *Runners-up:* 1930.
League Cup Winners: 1971-72; *Runners-up:* 1953-54, 1956-57, 1958-59.
League Challenge Cup Runners-up: 2012-13.

European: *Fairs Cup:* 4 matches (1963-64). *UEFA Cup:* 2 matches (1972-73). *Intertoto Cup:* 4 matches (1995-96).

Club colours: Shirt: Red and yellow broad stripes and black sleeves. Shorts: Black with red and yellow trim. Socks: Red with black tops.

Goalscorers: *League (43):* Graham 15, Chalmers 7, Fitzpatrick 3, Milne 3, O'Reilly 3, Robinson 3, Ablade 2, Stanway 2, Jakubiak 1, Mackenzie 1, McBeth 1, Turner 1 (1 pen), own goal 1.
Scottish Cup (2): Crawford 1, own goal 1.
Premier Sports Scottish League Cup (11): Graham 3, Turner 2, Diack 1, Fitzpatrick 1, Milne 1, Muirhead 1, Robinson 1, Williams 1.
SPFL Trust Trophy (1): Graham 1.
Premiership Play-offs (2): Graham 2.

Roberts M 19	Williams O 3+1	McBeth L 24+11	O'Reilly D 36	Milne H 17	Crawford R 28+6	Turner K 30+6	Chalmers L 28+5	Robinson S 17+1	Fitzpatrick A 24+11	Graham B 33	Bannigan S 25+4	Mackenzie Z —+10	Diack R 2+7	Ashcroft L 30+3	Stanway B 7+12	Nilsson C 3	Ablade T 5+20	Sayers C 5+2	Lyon J 1	Smith L —+6	Muirhead A 3+6	Megwa K 23+3	Lawless S 1+12	Mitchell D 9	Martin S 4+1	Reid J 7+2	Budinauckas L 8	Falconer M —+1	Kelly S 3+2	Jakubiak A 1+4	Rooney L —+1	Match No.
1	2	3	4	5	6^1	7	8^2	9	10	11	12	13																				1
1	2^3	4	3	5	6^2	7	8^1	9^4	10	11				15	12	13^1	14															2
1	2	6	4	5			9	14	10^4				13	11^1	3^3	8^6	7^2	12	15													3
1	15	3	4	5		7	8^3		10^4	11^2	6	12		14	2^5	13	9^1	16														4
1		3	4	9	7^3	6	13	12	10	14	15			8^4	5^1	11^2	2															5
1		2	4	9	7	6^1	13	8	10	14	12			11^2	3^3	5																6
1		3^2	4	8	7	6^3	13	9	11	14	12			10^1	2	5																7
1		7	4	5	8^2	6^1	12	9	11	14	10^1			3	13	2																8
1		6^2	4	5	8^1	7^4	13	11^3	9	10	12	14		3^5	15	16	2															9
1		15	4	5	13	6^3	8^2	9^4	10	11	7			3^1	14	12	2															10
1		12	4	5	13	6^2	8	9^1	10^4	11^3	7			14	3	15	2															11
1		14	4	5	7^4	10^1	8	9	11^3	6^2	3			15	12	13	2															12
1			4	5	6^2	10^1	8	9	12	11	7			3	13	2																13
1		14	4	5	6^3	2^9	8^2	9	10^4	11	7^1			3	16	15	12	13														14
1		6^4	4	5^1	9	2	8^3	11	10	7	14			3	12	13																15
1		15	4	7^1	2	6^2	10	9^3	11	8	3			13	5^4	14	12														16
1		12	4	7^1	2	6^4	10	9^2	11^3	8	14			3	15	5	13															17
1		13	4	7^2	2	8^3	9	10^4	11	6	3			15	5^1	12	14															18
1		13	4	6^1	2	8^3	9^2	10	11	7	3			14	5	12																19
		12	4	13	6	8^4	9^5	10^3	11	7	3			14	5^1	16									2^2	15	1					20
			4	5	8^1	6	9^3	11	12	10	7			3	13										2^2	14	1					21
		2	4	8	6^1	5^2	9^3	11^4	12	10	7			3^5	15	16	13	14									1					22
		14	4	5	15	6^2	8	9^1	10^{11}	7	3^4			13	2	12											1					23
			4	5	12	13	11	14	10^8	6	15			3^5	8^5		9^4				16	2^2				1			7^1			24
			4	5	13	8^5	9	11^3	7^4	15	3			14	10		16				2^2					1			6^1	12		25
		13	4	9^6	10^2	7	14	11^4	6^1	3	8^3			15	2		12		5			1	16									26
		2	4	9^1	14	11	13	10	7^2	3	12			5			6^3	8	1													27
		2	4	9^2	12	10	13	11^4	7	3	5			6^1			8^3	1							14	15						28
		2	4	9^1	6	10^4	12	11^2	7	15	3			5			8^3	1							14	13				12		29
		2	4	9	6	10^4	12	10	7	15	3		14	5^3	11^1		7	13	8	1									12			30
		2^2	4	6^2	13	9^4	12	10	7	14	3			15	5		8					5			11^1		1					31
		2	4	9^4	6^1	10	13	11^3	7^5	3	12			16	5		14				8^2				15		1					32
		2	4	9^2	7	11	8		10	3	6^1			14	5^2		12					1				13						33
		2	8	9	12		7		10	3	6^1			13	5		11^2				1				4							34
		2	8	6	12	9		10^1	11^3	7	3			14	15		5				1		13^4			4^2						35
		2	8	6^2	7		11^3		10	13	3			9	14		5				12	1				4^1						36

PETERHEAD

Year Formed: 1891. *Ground and Address:* Balmoor Stadium, Balmoor Terrace, Peterhead AB42 1EQ.
Telephone: 01779 478 256. *Fax:* 01779 490 682. *E-mail:* office@peterheadfc.co.uk *Website:* peterheadfc.co.uk
Ground Capacity: 3,150 (seated: 1,000). *Size of Pitch:* 101m × 64m.
Chairman: Rodger Morrison. *Vice-Chairman:* Les Hill.
Player/Co-Managers: Jordon Brown and Ryan Strachan.
Club Nickname: 'Blue Toon'.
Previous Ground: Recreation Park.
Record Attendance: 8,643 v Raith R, Scottish Cup 4th rd replay, 25 February 1987 (Recreation Park); 4,855 v Rangers, Third Division, 19 January 2013 (at Balmoor).
Record Victory: 9-0 v Colville Park, Scottish Cup 2nd rd, 14 October 2017.
Record Defeat: 0-13 v Aberdeen, Scottish Cup 3rd rd, 10 February 1923.
Most League Appearances: 347: Rory McAllister, 2008, 2011-19, 2023-25.
Most League Goals in Season (Individual): 32: Rory McAllister, 2013-14.
Most Goals Overall (Individual): 210: Rory McAllister, 2008, 2011-19, 2023-25.

PETERHEAD – WILLIAM HILL LEAGUE TWO 2024–25 LEAGUE RECORD

Match No.	Date	Venue	Opponents	Result		H/T Score	Lg Pos.	Goalscorers	Attendance
1	Aug 3	A	Bonnyrigg Rose	W	1-0	0-0	3	Armour [90]	543
2	10	H	Forfar Ath	W	2-1	1-0	2	McAllister [26], Sebastian Ross [90]	525
3	17	H	Stranraer	W	1-0	1-0	1	Sebastian Ross [29]	502
4	24	A	The Spartans	D	0-0	0-0	1		420
5	31	A	Edinburgh C	W	4-0	4-0	1	McAllister [12], Pawlett [18], Barry [37], Strachan R [43]	249
6	Sept 14	H	Stirling Alb	W	2-1	1-0	1	McGeachie (og) [18], McAllister [86]	566
7	21	A	East Fife	L	0-2	0-2	1		628
8	28	A	Clyde	D	2-2	1-0	2	Strachan R [42], Barry [70]	595
9	Oct 5	H	Elgin C	L	0-1	0-1	3		751
10	19	A	Stranraer	D	0-0	0-0	3		469
11	Nov 2	H	The Spartans	W	2-1	1-1	3	Jack Brown [17], Barry (pen) [71]	609
12	9	A	Stirling Alb	W	3-2	1-2	1	Jason Brown [43], Smith [69], McAllister (pen) [77]	663
13	16	H	Edinburgh C	L	2-3	1-2	2	Forrest (pen) [42], Sebastian Ross [56]	694
14	Dec 7	A	Clyde	L	2-3	1-2	3	McCarthy [43], Jack Brown [82]	595
15	14	H	East Fife	W	1-0	1-0	2	Shanks [9]	651
16	17	H	Forfar Ath	D	1-1	1-0	2	Shanks [45]	522
17	21	H	Bonnyrigg Rose	W	2-0	0-0	1	Pawlett [64], Shanks [71]	584
18	28	A	Elgin C	L	0-2	0-1	2		1356
19	Jan 11	A	Edinburgh C	W	1-0	1-0	2	Shanks [22]	226
20	14	H	Stranraer	W	1-0	0-0	2	Jason Brown [59]	483
21	18	H	Stirling Alb	W	3-2	2-1	2	Barry [10], Shanks 2 [26, 75]	662
22	25	A	The Spartans	L	0-1	0-0	2		398
23	Feb 1	H	Forfar Ath	D	2-2	2-0	2	Shanks 2 (1 pen) [3, 23 (p)]	662
24	8	A	Bonnyrigg Rose	W	4-3	3-2	2	Colloty [17], Shanks [24], Barry [26], Smith [88]	469
25	15	H	Clyde	D	2-2	1-1	2	Smith [42], Jason Brown [71]	641
26	22	A	East Fife	D	0-0	0-0	2		1106
27	Mar 1	H	Elgin C	W	2-0	1-0	2	McCarthy [45], Shanks [53]	1028
28	8	A	Stranraer	D	0-0	0-0	2		447
29	15	A	Edinburgh C	W	2-0	0-0	2	Barry [55], Colloty [75]	823
30	22	A	Stirling Alb	W	2-1	1-1	1	Gaston (og) [4], Strachan D [86]	755
31	29	A	Forfar Ath	D	0-0	0-0	1		668
32	Apr 5	H	Bonnyrigg Rose	W	5-0	2-0	1	Colloty 3 [19, 26, 47], Forrest [61], Carnwath [90]	653
33	12	H	The Spartans	W	1-0	1-0	1	Smith [19]	690
34	19	A	Elgin C	L	0-4	0-3	1		901
35	26	H	East Fife	W	1-0	1-0	1	Pawlett [29]	1979
36	May 3	A	Clyde	L	1-6	1-3	1	Colloty [31]	788

Final League Position: 1

Honours
League Champions: League Two 2013-14, 2018-19, 2024-25.
Runners up: Third Division 2004-05, 2012-13; League Two 2017-18, 2023-24.
Scottish Cup: Quarter-finals 2001.
League Challenge Cup: Runners up: 2015-16.

Club colours: Shirt: Royal blue with navy blue detail. Shorts: Royal blue. Socks: Royal blue.

Goalscorers: *League (52):* Shanks 10 (1 pen), Barry 6 (1 pen), Colloty 6, McAllister 4 (1 pen), Smith 4, Jason Brown 3, Pawlett 3, Sebastian Ross 3, Jack Brown 2, Forrest 2 (1 pen), McCarthy 2, Strachan R 2, Armour 1, Carnwath 1, Strachan D 1, own goals 2.
Scottish Cup (8): Jason Brown 2, Barry 1, Dunne 1, McCarthy 1, Pawlett 1, Sebastian Ross 1, Smith 1.
Premier Sports Scottish League Cup (5): Jason Brown 2, Armour 1, Barry 1, Goldie 1.
SPFL Trust Trophy (2): Barry 1, Smith 1.

McKenzie S 24	Goldie C 19 + 4	Ross Scott 21 + 2	Armstrong J 4 + 1	Dunne C 32 + 2	Forrest D 34 + 2	Brown Jack 16 + 20	Pawlett P 24 + 4	McCarthy A 27 + 1	Barry M 34 + 2	McAllister R 7 + 19	Armour B 1 + 12	Ross Sebastian 19 + 14	Smith C 23 + 5	Strachan D 22 + 7	Brown Jason 30 + 2	Strachan R 5 + 1	Ward R — + 5	Duthie C — + 5	Brown Jordon 1 + 3	Shanks K 18 + 6	Oluyemi B 12	Wilson D 13 + 2	Colloty O 6 + 11	Walker J 3 + 4	Carnwath A 1 + 9	*Match No.*
1	2^{4}	3	4	5	6	7^{2}	8	9^{3}	10	11^{1}	12	13	14	15												1
1		4	5^{4}	10	6	15	9^{3}	8	7^{2}	11^{1}	12	14	13	2	3											2
1		4^{1}		5	7^{2}	13	9	6	8^{4}	15		10^{3}	11	2	3	12	14									3
1				5	6	12	8^{2}	7^{1}	9	13	14	11^{3}	10	2	3	4										4
1		13		5	6	12	7^{2}		11^{3}	10^{4}		8^{5}	9	2^{1}	3	4	14	15	16							5
1				5	6	7^{1}	9		8^{3}	12	14	10^{2}	11	2	3	4	13									6
1	14	4		5	6	7^{3}	9		8	11^{2}	12	10^{1}		2^{4}	3		13		15							7
1	13		14	5	6	8	9^{3}		7^{4}		12	10^{2}	11	2	3	4^{1}	15									8
1	2		5^{1}	10	6^{4}	14	9		7^{2}	11	15	13	8	12	3	4^{3}										9
1	3	4		5^{3}	6	7^{1}	9^{4}	14	10^{2}	15		13	11	2	8					12						10
1	2	4		5	6	10^{1}	9	7^{2}	8^{3}			12	11		3			14		13						11
1	2	4		5	6	10^{1}	9^{2}	7	8^{3}	14	15	12	11^{4}		3					13						12
1	2	4		5	7^{3}	12	9	6	8	14		10^{1}	11^{2}		3					13						13
1	2	4^{3}		5	7^{1}	12	9	6	8	13		10		14	3					11^{2}						14
	3			5	7	12	9^{1}	6	8^{2}	15	14	10^{3}		2				13		11^{4}	1	4				15
	3			5	7	8	9^{3}	6■	12		13	10^{2}		2	14					11^{1}	1	4				16
	3			5	7	6^{1}	8^{5}		9^{4}	12	14	11^{2}	13	2				15	16	10^{3}	1	4				17
	3			5■	7^{4}	6	8^{1}		9	14	12	11^{2}		2	13			15		10^{3}	1	4				18
	4	14			7^{2}	6	9	8	10^{3}	13				5	3					11^{1}	1	2	12			19
	3			5	7^{1}	10	9^{2}	6^{4}	8	15				13	2					11^{3}	1	4	14	12		20
	5			10	7	8^{2}		6^{5}	9^{3}	14			16	2^{1}	3					11^{4}	1	4	13	12	15	21
	2^{3}			5	7	11^{2}	6^{1}	8	9	16		13	12	14	3					10^{4}	1	4^{5}	15			22
	2			10^{2}	14	7^{1}		6	8^{3}			15	9^{4}	12	3					11	1	4	13	5		23
		3		15	6^{3}	14		8	9^{2}	13		12	7	2	4					11	1		10^{1}	5^{4}		24
	2	4		5	7^{2}	12	16	6^{4}	10^{1}	14		13	8^{5}	15	3					11	1		9^{3}			25
1		4		5	8^{2}	13	7^{4}	6	9^{1}			12	10	2	3					11^{3}			14		15	26
1		4		5	7	13	9^{1}	6^{2}	8^{4}			12	10	2	3					11^{3}			14		15	27
1	5^{4}	4			7^{3}	13		6^{2}	8	12		9^{1}	10	2	3					11■				14	15	28
1		3^{4}		5	7	13		6^{2}	8^{3}	11^{1}		10	9	2	4							14	12		15	29
1	12	3^{1}		5	7	16		6^{4}	8^{5}	14		10^{2}	9	2	4					11^{3}			13		15	30
1		3		5	7	12		6^{2}	8			10^{1}	9^{3}	2	4					11■			13	14		31
1		3		5	7^{5}	15	16	6^{2}	8	13		10	9^{3}	2^{1}	4							12	11^{4}		14	32
1		3		5	7	14	12	6^{3}	8			10^{2}	9		4							2	11^{1}		13	33
1	15	3^{4}		5	7	12	14	6^{5}	8			10^{3}	9^{2}		4					13		2^{1}	11		16	34
1		3		5	8	14	6	10^{1}	9^{3}			12	7		4					11^{2}		2	13			35
	4		2	16	12	6			13	11^{4}	9^{3}	14							8^{1}	15	1	3	10^{2}	5^{5}	7	36

QUEEN OF THE SOUTH

Year Formed: 1919. *Ground & Address:* Palmerston Park, Terregles Street, Dumfries DG2 9BA.
Telephone: 01387 254 853. *Fax:* 01387 240 470. *E-mail:* admin@qosfc.com *Website:* qosfc.com
Ground Capacity: 8,690 (seated: 3,377) *Size of Pitch:* 102m × 66m.
Chairman: Billy Hewitson. *Vice-Chairman:* Craig Paterson.
Manager: Peter Murphy. *Assistant Manager:* Colin McMenamin.
Club Nickname: 'The Doonhamers', 'Queens'.
Record Attendance: 26,552 v Hearts, Scottish Cup 3rd rd, 23 February 1952.
Record Transfer Fee received: £250,000 from Southend U for Andy Thomson (July 1994).
Record Transfer Fee paid: £30,000 to Alloa Ath for Jim Butter (1995).
Record Victory: 11-1 v Stranraer, Scottish Cup 1st rd, 16 January 1932.
Record Defeat: 2-10 v Dundee, Division I, 1 December 1962.
Most Capped Player: Billy Houliston, 3, Scotland.
Most League Appearances: 731: Allan Ball, 1963-82.
Most League Goals in Season (Individual): 37: Jimmy Gray, Division II, 1927-28.
Most Goals in Season: 43: Stephen Dobbie, 2018-19.
Most Goals Overall (Individual): 251: Jim Patterson, 1949-63.

QUEEN OF THE SOUTH – WILLIAM HILL LEAGUE ONE 2024–25 LEAGUE RECORD

Match No.	Date	Venue	Opponents	Result		H/T Score	Lg Pos.	Goalscorers	Atten- dance
1	Aug 3	A	Alloa Ath	D	0-0	0-0	7		767
2	10	H	Cove Rangers	W	2-1	0-0	3	McKechnie [69], Hewitt [71]	1126
3	17	H	Annan Ath	W	2-0	1-0	2	Douglas [11], McKechnie [81]	2214
4	24	A	Montrose	L	0-1	0-1	3		377
5	31	A	Inverness CT	L	0-1	0-1	4		1703
6	Sept 14	H	Arbroath	W	2-1	1-1	2	McKechnie [6], Lyon [48]	996
7	21	A	Stenhousemuir	D	0-0	0-0	3		583
8	28	H	Dumbarton	W	2-0	1-0	1	O'Donnell [14], Hewitt [50]	1146
9	Oct 5	H	Kelty Hearts	L	1-5	0-3	4	Hewitt [58]	1306
10	19	A	Cove Rangers	L	0-2	0-1	6		519
11	26	A	Annan Ath	L	0-1	0-0	7		1005
12	Nov 2	H	Montrose	W	1-0	1-0	5	Willis [17]	945
13	9	H	Alloa Ath	D	1-1	0-0	6	Walker [59]	853
14	16	A	Dumbarton	L	1-2	0-0	6	Doherty [83]	708
15	Dec 7	A	Arbroath	L	1-2	0-0	7	Douglas [72]	709
16	14	H	Stenhousemuir	W	2-1	1-0	7	Lyon [12], Brooks [59]	906
17	21	A	Kelty Hearts	L	0-2	0-0	7		434
18	28	H	Annan Ath	D	1-1	1-0	7	Brooks [17]	2702
19	Jan 4	H	Cove Rangers	W	1-0	1-0	6	Hewitt [23]	915
20	11	A	Alloa Ath	D	1-1	1-0	6	Luissint [4]	732
21	21	H	Inverness CT	W	3-2	1-1	5	Brooks 2 [12, 53], Allan [79]	775
22	25	H	Dumbarton	W	3-1	1-1	3	Brooks 2 [3, 54], Dickenson [66]	1027
23	Feb 1	A	Inverness CT	L	0-1	0-1	4		1726
24	8	A	Stenhousemuir	L	1-2	0-2	4	Dickenson [90]	630
25	15	A	Arbroath	L	0-3	0-3	5		1203
26	22	A	Montrose	W	3-0	1-0	5	Brooks (pen) [20], Cochrane [80], Bryden (pen) [85]	573
27	Mar 1	H	Kelty Hearts	L	0-1	0-1	5		923
28	8	A	Cove Rangers	L	1-3	1-2	6	Lyon [7]	411
29	15	A	Alloa Ath	W	3-2	2-1	5	O'Donnell [11], Smith [24], Kennedy [50]	934
30	22	A	Dumbarton	D	0-0	0-0	5		688
31	29	H	Inverness CT	W	4-1	1-1	4	Hannah [29], Allan [57], Brooks 2 [68, 89]	1006
32	Apr 5	A	Annan Ath	W	2-0	0-0	4	Smith [57], Allan [72]	1353
33	12	H	Montrose	W	2-1	1-0	4	Brooks [6], Allan [61]	978
34	19	A	Kelty Hearts	W	3-1	1-1	3	Luissint [28], Allan [63], Kennedy [69]	590
35	26	H	Stenhousemuir	W	2-0	0-0	3	Bryden [59], Cochrane (pen) [63]	2242
36	May 3	A	Arbroath	D	1-1	1-0	3	Lyon [43]	2314

Final League Position: 3

Honours
League Champions: Division II 1950-51; Second Division 2001-02, 2012-13.
Runners-up: Division II 1932-33, 1961-62, 1974-75; Second Division 1980-81, 1985-86; Division Three 1924-25.
Scottish Cup Runners-up: 2007-08.
League Cup: semi-finals 1950-51, 1960-61.
League Challenge Cup Winners: 2002-03, 2012-13; *Runners-up:* 1997-98, 2010-11, 2021-22.

European: *UEFA Cup:* 2 matches (2008-09).

Club colours: Shirt: Royal blue with white trim. Shorts: White with royal blue trim. Socks: Royal blue.

Goalscorers: *League (46):* Brooks 10 (1 pen), Allan 5, Hewitt 4, Lyon 4, McKechnie 3, Bryden 2 (1 pen), Cochrane 2 (1 pen), Dickenson 2, Douglas 2, Kennedy 2, Luissint 2, O'Donnell 2, Smith 2, Doherty 1, Hannah 1, Walker 1, Willis 1.
Scottish Cup (2): Dickenson 1, Doherty 1.
Premier Sports Scottish League Cup (5): Dickenson 1, Lyon 1, McIntosh 1, McKechnie 1, Walker 1.
SPFL Trust Trophy (0).
Championship Play-offs (1): Kennedy 1.

Stewart R 36	Hewitt M 27	Douglas M 29	Brydon J 16+6	Macintyre O 30+5	Johnstone B 2+3	Ross E 2	Walker J 7+14	Kennedy K 20+4	McKechnie K 11+2	Doherty K 15+8	Craik Z —+1	Cochrane H 25+4	Hannah J 29+2	McIntosh L 8+7	Dickenson B 19+3	Strachan M —+1	O'Donnell L 12+12	Bryden F 1+16	Lyon R 32	Willis P 2+3	Church D —+1	Brooks A 21+2	Allan J 11+5	Charters T 9+3	Smith L 12+2	Thomson J —+3	Johnson M —+1	Match No.
1	2	3	4	5	6	7	8[1]	9[2]	10	11	12	13																1
1	4	3	2	9	7	6	5[1]	13	8[3]	10	11[2]	12	14															2
1	4	3	2	9	15	7	5[3]	8[1]	10	11[2]		6[4]	12	13	14													3
1	4	3	2	9			7[1]	5[2]	8[3]	10	11[4]	6[4]	16	13	12		14[5]	15										4
1	2[1]	3		5	12		9[2]	13	10[5]	8	14	4	11	6					7									5
1	2	3		12	14		9[1]	10	6	13		4	11[2]	5			7[3]		8									6
1	2	3		5			9	6[2]		12		4	10	11[1]			8		7	13								7
1	2	3	14	5			12	13	10	8[2]		6[1]	4[3]	11			7		9									8
1	2	3[1]	13	5			8[2]	12	10[3]	6[1]	14	4	11[4]				7		9	15								9
1	2	3		5	15		12	10[3]	8[4]	13		6[1]	4	11[2]			7		9	14								10
1	2	4	3[3]	9	15	6	12	7[2]	5	11[1]		8[4]	13	10			14											11
1	3	7	2	5			12	8				6[2]	4	13			10	14	9[3]	11[1]								12
1	5	3	2[4]	8	15		9[3]	12				6	4	13			10[1]	14	7	11[2]								13
1	5	3	2	8[1]			14	11[3]	10[2]	9		6	4	12			7					13						14
1	5	2	3[1]	9	16		14	15	12	7[3]		4	10[2]	13			6[5]	8				11[4]						15
1	2	3		9	12		5	7				4	13	10			6[1]		8			11[2]						16
1	2	3		9			5	7				4	12	10[2]			6[1]	13	8			11						17
1	2	3	4[3]	12			8	6	14	5		10[2]	7[1]	13			9					11						18
1	2	3		9			6	5				7[1]	4	10			12		8			11						19
1	2	3	13	9			6	5[2]				7	4	11					8[1]			10	12					20
1	2	3		12			5	7				6[1]	8	4			10		9			11[2]	13					21
1	5	3	14	4			6	9[2]				2	10				7[1]	13	8			11[3]	12					22
1	6	2	14[8]	3			9[2]					5	4[3]	10			15		8			11[4]	7[1]	12	13			23
1	4	3		5	12		13	7[2]				2		14	15		6					11[4]	10[1]	8[9]	9			24
1	3[3]	2		9[2]	8[1]		10[4]	7				4		14			6					11	12	13	5	15		25
1		2		12			15	10[1]	7			3[4]	4	13	14		6					11[3]	9	8	5[2]			26
1		2	13				15	5[2]	7[1]			3	4	12	14		6					11	10[3]	9[4]	8			27
1		2[1]	4				7	13	5[2]			3			11[3]		14		6			10	12	9	8			28
1		2					7	12	8[1]			14	4				6		3			11[3]	10	5[2]	9	13		29
1		2						8	6			7	4				12		3			11	10[1]	5	9			30
1		2					7	14	6[1]			8	4	12			13	3				10	11[2]	5	9[3]			31
1	3	2	13		15			6[4]	8[2]				4				12	14	7			10	11[1]	5	9[3]			32
1	3	2	13		14			6[3]	8				4				12		7			10[2]	11	5[1]	9			33
1[4]	2	3					8	14	6[3]			7			4		12	13	5			10[1]	11[2]	9	15			34
1	2	3	13				7[2]	15	6				8[3]		4		14	12	5			10	11[1]	9[4]				35
1	2[1]	3	4				8[3]	7	9[5]			16			10[2]		6	11	5[4]			15		13	14	12		36

QUEEN'S PARK

Year Formed: 1867. *Ground & Address:* City Stadium, Mount Florida, Glasgow G42 9BA.
Telephone: 0141 632 1275. *Fax:* 0141 636 1612. *E-mail:* generalenquiries@queensparkfc.co.uk *Website:* queensparkfc.co.uk
Ground Capacity: 990 (all seated). *Size of Pitch:* 105m × 68m.
President: Graham Shields.
Head Coach: Sean Crighton. *Assistant Head Coach:* Jim Duffy.
Club Nickname: 'The Spiders'.
Previous Grounds: 1st Hampden (Recreation Ground); (Titwood Park was used as an interim measure between 1st &
2nd Hampdens); 2nd Hampden (Cathkin); 3rd Hampden, Hampden Park; Falkirk Stadium (2020-21); Firhill (2021-22);
Ochilview (2022-23). *Record Attendance:* 95,772 v Rangers, Scottish Cup 1st rd, 18 January 1930.
Record for Ground: 149,547 Scotland v England, 1937.
Record Transfer Fee received: £300,000 from Bournemouth for Callan McKenna (Feb 2024).
Record Transfer Fee paid: £40,000 to Inverness Caledonian Thistle for Nikola Ujdur (Jul 2024).
Record Victory: 16-0 v St Peter's, Scottish Cup 1st rd, 12 September 1885.
Record Defeat: 0-9 v Motherwell, Division I, 26 April 1930.
Most Capped Player: Walter Arnott, 14, Scotland.
Most League Appearances: 532: Ross Caven, 1982-2002.
Most League Goals in Season (Individual): 30: William Martin, Division I, 1937-38.
Most Goals Overall (Individual): 163: James B. McAlpine, 1919-33.

QUEEN'S PARK – WILLIAM HILL CHAMPIONSHIP 2024–25 LEAGUE RECORD

Match No.	Date		Venue	Opponents	Result		H/T Score	Lg Pos.	Goalscorers	Atten- dance
1	Aug	2	A	Falkirk	L	1-2	0-1	1	Thomas [46]	5505
2		9	H	Livingston	D	1-1	1-0	7	Rudden [36]	881
3		24	A	Airdrieonians	W	2-0	2-0	4	Turner [2], Rudden [24]	1499
4		31	A	Partick Thistle	L	0-3	0-1	6		4034
5	Sept	14	H	Greenock Morton	W	1-0	1-0	4	Thomas [44]	883
6		21	H	Ayr U	D	1-1	1-0	5	Kerr [35]	1635
7		28	A	Dunfermline Ath	W	2-1	1-0	4	Rudden [15], Welsh [61]	4494
8	Oct	5	H	Hamilton A	W	1-0	0-0	4	Turner [62]	1259
9		19	A	Raith R	D	1-1	0-1	4	McLeish [62]	3396
10		26	H	Partick Thistle	L	0-1	0-1	5		2779
11		29	A	Greenock Morton	W	1-0	1-0	4	Rudden [25]	1741
12	Nov	2	A	Livingston	D	1-1	0-0	5	Drozd [59]	1138
13		9	H	Dunfermline Ath	W	2-1	1-0	4	Duncan [31], Turner [72]	1331
14		16	A	Ayr U	L	2-3	0-2	5	Hinds [81], Turner [83]	2012
15		22	H	Falkirk	L	0-1	0-1	5		2071
16	Dec	7	H	Airdrieonians	W	2-0	2-0	5	Thomas [14], Longridge [21]	1076
17		14	H	Hamilton A	L	1-2	1-2	5	Rudden (pen) [16]	1076
18		20	H	Raith R	L	1-2	0-1	5	Duncan [74]	1141
19		28	A	Partick Thistle	L	1-2	1-1	5	Thomas [26]	4350
20	Jan	4	H	Livingston	W	2-0	1-0	5	Turner [38], Muirhead (og) [52]	1266
21		11	A	Falkirk	D	0-0	0-0	5		5745
22		25	H	Greenock Morton	L	1-2	1-0	5	Rudden [23]	1398
23	Feb	1	A	Airdrieonians	L	1-2	0-1	5	Scott J [59]	1486
24		15	H	Hamilton A	L	1-2	0-2	6	Welsh [60]	1147
25		22	A	Dunfermline Ath	D	0-0	0-0	7		4527
26	Mar	1	A	Raith R	W	4-0	1-0	5	Rudden [29], Devine [49], Montgomery [51], Ujdur [72]	3600
27		4	H	Ayr U	L	2-3	0-0	5	Turner [49], Rudden [54]	1557
28		11	H	Partick Thistle	L	0-2	0-1	7		1758
29		15	H	Falkirk	L	0-4	0-1	7		2685
30		22	A	Greenock Morton	L	1-2	0-1	7	Rudden [69]	2044
31	Apr	2	H	Airdrieonians	L	0-5	0-3	7		1034
32		5	A	Livingston	L	0-3	0-3	7		1396
33		12	H	Dunfermline Ath	L	0-1	0-0	9		1705
34		19	A	Hamilton A	D	0-0	0-0	8		1102
35		26	A	Ayr U	D	2-2	2-1	8	Drozd [22], MacGregor [31]	2122
36	May	2	H	Raith R	L	1-5	0-2	8	Drozd [50]	2609

Final League Position: 8

Honours
League Champions: Division II 1922-23; B Division 1955-56; Second Division 1980-81; Third Division 1999-2000; League Two: 2020-21.
Runners-up: Third Division 2011-12; League Two 2014-15.
Promoted via play-offs: 2021-22 (to Championship); 2015-16 (to League One); 2006-07 (to Second Division).
Scottish Cup Winners: 1874, 1875, 1876, 1880, 1881, 1882, 1884, 1886, 1890, 1893; *Runners-up:* 1892, 1900.
League Challenge Cup Runners-up: 2024-25.
FA Cup Runners-up: 1884, 1885.
FA Charity Shield: 1899 (shared with Aston Villa).

Club colours: Shirt: Black and white hoops with black sleeves. Shorts: Black with white trim. Socks: Black with white hooped tops.

Goalscorers: *League (36):* Rudden 9 (1 pen), Turner 6, Thomas 4, Drozd 3, Duncan 2, Welsh 2, Devine 1, Hinds 1, Kerr 1, Longridge 1, MacGregor 1, McLeish 1, Montgomery 1, Scott J 1, Ujdur 1, own goal 1.
Scottish Cup (7): Rudden 2, Drozd 1, Longridge 1, MacGregor 1, McLeish 1, Scott J 1.
Premier Sports Scottish League Cup (16): MacGregor 5, Turner 3, Thomas 2, Mauchin 1, McLeish 1, Rudden 1, Scott J 1, Welsh 1, own goal 1.
SPFL Trust Trophy (14): Rudden 3, Duncan 2, Evans 2, Turner 2, McLeish 1, Thomas 1, Ujdur 1, own goals 2.

Ferrie C 34	Thomson J 11 + 2	Ujdur N 11	Kerr C 15	Longridge L 21 + 13	Turner J 29 + 5	Welsh S 32	MacGregor R 18 + 6	Scott J 12 + 6	Rudden Z 32 + 2	Thomas D 15	Mauchin 27 + 9	Hinds J 11 + 13	McLeish L 3 + 16	Murray D 18	Fieldson H 12 + 3	Duncan R 24 + 7	Wills J 1 + 1	McDonnell T — +1	Tizzard W 28	Hickey-Fugaccia R 2 + 18	MacKenzie M — +1	Evans R 2 + 8	Drozd S 10 + 14	Scott T 3 + 3	Devine A 12 + 1	Montgomery A 11 + 1	Hurst K 6 + 4	Raymond J 2 + 3	King L 8 + 1	Jackson B 9 + 1	McGinlay A 6	Savoury G — + 2	Sliwinski M 1	Smith J — + 1	Fox C — + 1	Match No.
1	2	3	4	5^1	6^2	7	8	9^2	10	11	12	13	14																							1
1			4	5	6^2	7	8	9	10^1	11	2	13	12	3																						2
1▪	2		14	6^3	7	8	9	11^1	10^4		13	12	3	4	5^2	15																				3
1		3	15	7^3	8^1	9	6	11	10		12	13	4	5^4	2^2	1	14																			4
1		3	2	13	6	7	8^3	9	10^1	11			14	12	4	5^2																				5
1			2	13	7^4	6	9	5^3	11			8^2	16		4	15	10^1						3^5	12	14											6
1			5	12	8	7	6		10^3	11^2	13		14	2	4	9^1			3																	7
1			2	12	8	7	6		10^3	11^2	13		14	4	5	9^1			3																	8
1	13		2	6^3		8	7		10^2					11^1	3	5	9		4					12	14											9
1			2^4	8^2	9^1	6	7		11			15	14	13	4	5	10^3		3					12												10
1	13		2	12	7^3	8	6^4	15	11				10^1	4	5	9^2			3					14												11
1	7^3		2	13	14	6	10▪	11					4	5	12				3	8^1				9^2												12
1	7^1		2	13	12	6		16	11^4				14	15	4	5	10^2		3	8^3				9^5												13
1	7		2^3		14	6		12			9^4	15	13	11^5	4	5^1	10^2		3	16▪				8												14
1	7		2	15	9^5	6^3	13	5^2	11^4	8			14	4	12			3					10^1	16											15
1	6		2	8^4	9^2	7	13	11^3	10^5			16	15	4	12	5			3^1					14												16
1	7		2	8^4	9^5	6	13	12^2	11	10				3	4	5^1			14					15												17
1	6		10	8	7^1	13	5^2	11^4	9	2^2			15	4		12			3^5	14	16															18
1	6		10^1	8	7		5^2	11	9^4	2	12			4		13			3^3	15				14												19
1	7	3	10	8^3	6			12	11^4	9^2	2▪			15		5^1	13		4	14																20
1	6^1	4	2	8	7			5	11^3	9^2		14				10			3	12				13												21
1		3		6	9	7		5	11			2^1	12	13		10^3			4	14				8^2												22
1		3		6^3	9	7		5	11				13			10^1			4			12	8^2	14	2▪											23
1		3		6	8^4	7			11			2^1	14			10			4			15	12				5^3	9^2	13							24
1		3		6	8	7			11^2				14			10^4			4			12	13	15			2	5^3	9^1							25
1		3		13	9^2	7^5			11^4	6						10^1			4			15	8^1		2	5	12	16	14							26
1				8^3	6	7			11		13					9			3	15			12			5^4	14	10^2	2^1	4						27
1				7^3	6			12	10							8			4	14		11^2	15			5			13	9^1	2^4	3				28
1				8	7^3	9^1			11			14				12			3	15		13	2	5^1	10^2				6	4						29
1				8	6^2	7^5	9^4		11							10^1			4^3	15	16	12	2	5	14				3	13						30
1				7	6		9^5		11	13						12						15	14^4		2	5	10^2	16		4	3^1	8^6				31
1				7	8^3			13	11							12					14			10^1	2	5			9^2	4	3	6				32
1				6^3	9	7			12										3	13		15		14	5	10^2			2^4	4	8^1					33
1				15	13	6	7^5	12								10^3			4	14		11^1	8^4	2	5				3	9^2	16					34
1				12	14	6	7^5	13								10^1			4	16		11^2	8^4	2	5				3	9^3	15					35
1				10		7													4	13		11	8^3	2^1	5	14			6^4	3	9^2		1	12	15	36

RAITH ROVERS

Year Formed: 1883. *Ground & Address:* Stark's Park, Pratt St, Kirkcaldy KY1 1SA.
Telephone: 01592 263 514. *Fax:* 01592 642 833. *E-mail:* info@raithrovers.net *Website:* raithrovers.net
Ground Capacity: 8,867 (all seated). *Size of Pitch:* 103m × 64m.
Chairman (Interim): Colin Smart. *Director of Football:* Allan Halliday.
Manager: Barry Robson. *Assistant Manager:* Colin Cameron.
Club Nickname: 'Rovers'.
Previous Grounds: Robbie's Park.
Record Attendance: 31,306 v Hearts, Scottish Cup 2nd rd, 7 February 1953.
Record Transfer Fee received: £900,000 from Bolton W for Steve McAnespie (September 1995).
Record Transfer Fee paid: £225,000 to Airdrieonians for Paul Harvey (July 1996).
Record Victory: 10-1 v Coldstream, Scottish Cup 2nd rd, 13 February 1954.
Record Defeat: 2-11 v Morton, Division II, 18 March 1936; 0-10 v Aberdeen, Division I, 13 October 1962.
Most Capped Player: David Morris, 6, Scotland.
Most League Appearances: 430: Willie McNaught, 1946-51.
Most League Goals in Season (Individual): 38: Norman Haywood, Division II, 1937-38.
Most League Goals Overall (Individual): 154: Gordon Dalziel, 1987-94.

RAITH ROVERS – WILLIAM HILL CHAMPIONSHIP 2024–25 LEAGUE RECORD

Match No.	Date	Venue	Opponents	Result		H/T Score	Lg Pos.	Goalscorers	Attendance
1	Aug 3	A	Airdrieonians	L	0-1	0-0	8		1462
2	10	H	Partick Thistle	W	1-0	1-0	4	Easton (pen) [27]	4002
3	24	A	Ayr U	L	0-2	0-1	7		2928
4	31	H	Livingston	L	0-1	0-0	9		3517
5	Sept 13	A	Dunfermline Ath	L	0-2	0-0	10		6993
6	21	H	Hamilton A	D	3-3	2-1	9	Stevenson [15], Pollock [36], Easton [54]	3322
7	28	H	Falkirk	W	1-0	1-0	7	Hamilton (pen) [11]	5030
8	Oct 5	A	Greenock Morton	L	0-2	0-0	8		2976
9	19	A	Queen's Park	D	1-1	0-0	8	Hamilton (pen) [39]	3396
10	26	A	Livingston	L	1-2	1-0	8	Hamilton [21]	1750
11	29	H	Airdrieonians	W	1-0	1-0	7	Brown [20]	3258
12	Nov 1	H	Ayr U	W	2-0	2-0	6	Jamieson 2 [19, 43]	3427
13	9	A	Partick Thistle	D	1-1	0-1	7	Easton [68]	4348
14	16	H	Greenock Morton	L	2-3	0-2	6	Delaney (og) [59], Easton (pen) [81]	3508
15	Dec 7	A	Falkirk	L	0-3	0-1	8		6248
16	14	H	Dunfermline Ath	W	2-0	1-0	7	Easton [42], Adedoyin [74]	5542
17	20	A	Queen's Park	W	2-1	1-0	6	Jamieson (pen) [41], Connolly [69]	1141
18	28	H	Livingston	W	2-1	2-0	6	Easton [7], Connolly [28]	3955
19	Jan 4	A	Ayr U	L	0-3	0-3	6		2733
20	25	H	Falkirk	L	0-2	0-1	7		4495
21	28	A	Hamilton A	W	3-0	3-0	6	Pollock [3], Gullan [7], Marsh [31]	1005
22	Feb 1	A	Dunfermline Ath	L	1-3	1-0	7	Easton (pen) [43]	6812
23	15	H	Partick Thistle	W	3-0	2-0	5	Pollock 2 [8, 26], Easton (pen) [62]	3749
24	22	H	Hamilton A	W	2-0	1-0	5	Easton (pen) [30], Pollock [64]	3344
25	25	A	Airdrieonians	L	0-1	0-0	5		1583
26	Mar 1	H	Queen's Park	L	0-4	0-1	6		3600
27	5	A	Livingston	D	0-0	0-0	5		1331
28	14	H	Dunfermline Ath	W	2-0	1-0	5	Pollock [22], Hanlon [56]	5586
29	21	A	Partick Thistle	D	0-0	0-0	5		3213
30	25	A	Greenock Morton	D	3-3	2-1	6	Gullan 2 [11, 20], Connolly [90]	1750
31	29	A	Hamilton A	W	3-0	1-0	5	Easton [43], Fordyce [65], Mullin [75]	1007
32	Apr 5	H	Ayr U	W	1-0	0-0	5	Easton [62]	3919
33	12	H	Airdrieonians	D	1-1	1-1	5	Gullan [41]	3898
34	19	A	Falkirk	W	3-1	0-1	5	Marsh [88], Hanlon [90], Easton (pen) [90]	7539
35	26	H	Greenock Morton	D	1-1	1-1	5	Mullin [38]	4033
36	May 2	A	Queen's Park	W	5-1	2-0	5	Fordyce [41], Vaughan 2 (1 pen) [45 ipl, 59], Easton (pen) [74], Marsh [85]	2609

Final League Position: 5

Honours
League Champions: First Division 1992-93, 1994-95; League One 2019-20; Second Division 2002-03, 2008-09; Division II 1907-08, 1909-10 (shared with Leith Ath), 1937-38, 1948-49.
Runners-up: Division II 1908-09, 1926-27, 1966-67. Second Division 1975-76, 1977-78, 1986-87; League One 2017-18; Championship 2023-24.
Scottish Cup Runners-up: 1913.
League Cup Winners: 1994-95; *Runners-up:* 1948-49.
League Challenge Cup Winners: 2013-14, 2021-22; *Runners-up:* 2022-23.

European: *UEFA Cup:* 6 matches (1995-96).

Club colours: Shirt: Navy with white trim. Shorts: Navy. Socks: White.

Goalscorers: *League (47):* Easton 13 (7 pens), Pollock 6, Gullan 4, Connolly 3, Hamilton 3 (2 pens), Jamieson 3 (1 pen), Marsh 3, Fordyce 2, Hanlon 2, Mullin 2, Vaughan 2 (1 pen), Adedoyin 1, Brown 1, Stevenson 1, own goal 1.
Scottish Cup (6): Easton 3 (2 pens), Gibson 1, Hamilton 1, Stanton 1.
Premier Sports Scottish League Cup (7): Connolly 3, Hamilton 1, Murray 1, Smith 1, own goal 1.
SPFL Trust Trophy (2): Easton 1, Smith 1.

Dabrowski M 22	Matthews R 29 + 2	Murray E 17 + 1	Fordyce C 17 + 2	Stevenson L 34 + 2	Stanton S 7 + 1	Byrne S 18 + 5	Connolly A 8 + 16	Vaughan L 7 + 7	Easton D 34 + 1	Smith C 6 + 5	Dick L 19 + 5	Gibson L 5 + 12	Mullin J 18 + 10	Hamilton J 10 + 3	Montagu K 1 + 12	Hanlon P 33	Jamieson L 11 + 6	Freeman K 7	Pollock F 18 + 5	Dabo F 7 + 2	Brown S 20 + 2	Adedoyin K —+ 8	Doherty J 17 + 1	Marsh A 1 + 14	Gullan J 16 + 1	Rae J 14	Match No.
1	2	3	4^1	5	6	7	8^2	9^4	10^3	11	12	13	14	15													1
1	2	3		5	7	6	12		10^2	11	4	8^1	9			13											2
1	2	3		7		6^a	12		9^1	11	5	10^2	8				4	13									3
1	6	2^1		9			12	13	7^3	10	4	8	5	14		3	11^2										4
1	6	2^a		9		7	12	8	11^1		4	13	5^3	14		3	10^2										5
1	8			5		7	9^1	11^1	6^a	13	4		15	10^3		3	14	2	12								6
1	7	3		5	6		8^3	9^5			12	13	11^4			4	14	2^2	10^1	15	16						7
1	6^5	3	15	5		7^1	8^3	9		16	11					4	14	2^2	10^4	13	12						8
1				4	5	12	7^2	14	9^a	13		11				3	8^3		10^1	2	6						9
1				4	12	9^3	7			13	5^a		14	11^4		3	8^1		10^2	2	6	15					10
1	13	3		5	9^1	7^2	10^5			12		14	15	11^3		4	16		8^4	2	6						11
1		2		8	7^2	13	9		11^1	4	12		3	10^3		14	5	6									12
1	14	2^1		8	6^3	9			4	13	11^2		3	10^4		12	5	7	15								13
1	14	5^4		7	10	4	12	15	11^1	3		9^3	8^2	2	6	13											14
1	7	4		13	9^4		8	5	10^3	14	11^5		3	16		2^2	6^1	15									15
1	6	4		5	7	8^4	9^2	14	13	11^1	15	3	10^3		2						12						16
1	6	4		5	7	8^3	13	12	10^1	9^2	3	11^4	2	14	15							12					17
1	7	3	13	9	8^3	6^1	10^2	5	15	4	11^4	2	14	12													18
1	4	3	9	7	8^4	6	10	5^3	15	14	11^1	2^2	13	12													19
1	7	2^2	9		13	10	4	14	3	8^3	6		5	11^1	12												20
1	7		9^4	13	10^3	4	14	5	15	3	8^1	6	2	12	11^2												21
1	7	5		13	9	4	8^1	3	10^2	6	2	12	11														22
	6		8	10^1	4	14	5	12	3	9^3	7	2	13	11^2	1												23
	6		8	15	14	10^1	4	5	12	3	9^2	7^4	2	13	11^3	1											24
	6		8	14	10^1	4	5^3	13	3	9^2	7	2	12	11	1												25
	6^3		8^1	15	14	11	4	12	5	3	9^4	7	2	13	10^2	1											26
	6	3^4	2	8^2		14	10	13	15	12	4	9^3	7^1	5	11	1											27
	7	3	2	8		12	9^1	5	4	10	6	13	11^2	1													28
	7	3	2	8		12	9^3	5	14	4	10^1	6	13	11	1												29
	7	3^4	2	8		12	9^1	10	5	4	6	13	11	1													30
	7	3		8	13	14	12	9^3	5	4	10^4	6^2	2	15	11^1	1											31
	7	3		8	12	11^2	5	13	4	9^1	6	2	10	1													32
	7	3		8	12	9^1	11	13	5^2	4	6	2	14	10^3	1												33
	7	3	8^3	13	12	9	11	5^2	4	6^1	2	14	10	1													34
	6	3	8	7^3	12	9^1	11	5	14	4	2	13	10^2	1													35
	6	3	8	7	12	9	11	5^1	4	2	13	10^2	1														36

RANGERS

Year Formed: 1873. *Ground & Address:* Ibrox Stadium, 150 Edmiston Drive, Glasgow G51 2XD.
Telephone: 0871 702 1972. *Fax:* 0870 600 1978. *Website:* rangers.co.uk
Ground Capacity: 51,082 (all seated). *Size of Pitch:* 105m × 68m.
Chairman: Andrew Cavenagh. *Chief Executive:* Patrick Stewart. *Manager:* Russell Martin. *Assistant Manager:* Matt Gill.
Club Nickname: 'The Gers'; 'The Teddy Bears'.
Previous Grounds: Flesher's Haugh, Burnbank, Kinning Park, Old Ibrox.
Record Attendance: 118,567 v Celtic, Division I, 2 January 1939.
Record Transfer Fee received: £19,600,000 from Ajax for Calvin Bassey (July 2022).
Record Transfer Fee paid: £12,000,000 to Chelsea for Tore Andre Flo (November 2000).
Record Victory: 13-0 v Possilpark, Scottish Cup 1st rd, 6 October 1877; v Uddingston, Scottish Cup 3rd rd, 10 November 1877; v Kelvinside Athletic, Scottish Cup 2nd rd, 28 September 1889.
Record Defeat: 1-7 v Celtic, League Cup Final, 19 October 1957; 1-7 v Liverpool, Champions League Group A, 12 October 2022. *Most Capped Player:* Ally McCoist, 61, Scotland. *Most League Appearances:* 498: John Greig, 1962-78; 513: Sandy Archibald, 1917-34 (includes 34 matches during WW1 seasons).
Most League Goals in Season (Individual): 44: Sam English, Division I, 1931-32.
Most Goals Overall (Individual): 355: Ally McCoist; 1985-98.

Honours
League Champions: (55 times) Division I 1890-91 (shared with Dumbarton), 1898-99, 1899-1900, 1900-01, 1901-02, 1910-11, 1911-12, 1912-13, 1917-18, 1919-20, 1920-21, 1922-23, 1923-24, 1924-25, 1926-27, 1927-28, 1928-29, 1929-30, 1930-31, 1932-33, 1933-34, 1934-35, 1936-37, 1938-39, 1946-47, 1948-49, 1949-50, 1952-53, 1955-56, 1956-57, 1958-59, 1960-61, 1962-63, 1963-64, 1974-75. Premier Division: 1975-76, 1977-78, 1986-87, 1988-89, 1989-90, 1990-91, 1991-92, 1992-93, 1993-94, 1994-95, 1995-96, 1996-97, 1998-99, 1999-2000, 2002-03, 2004-05, 2008-09, 2009-10, 2010-11; Premiership: 2020-21. *Runners-up, tier 1:* 36 times. Championship 2015-16. League One 2013-14. Third Division 2012-13.
Scottish Cup Winners: (34 times) 1894, 1897, 1898, 1903, 1928, 1930, 1932, 1934, 1935, 1936, 1948, 1949, 1950, 1953, 1960, 1962, 1963, 1964, 1966, 1973, 1976, 1978, 1979, 1981, 1992, 1993, 1996, 1999, 2000, 2002, 2003, 2008, 2009, 2022; *Runners-up:* 19 times.

RANGERS – WILLIAM HILL PREMIERSHIP 2024–25 LEAGUE RECORD

Match No.	Date		Venue	Opponents	Result		H/T Score	Lg Pos.	Goalscorers	Attendance
1	Aug	3	A	Hearts	D	0-0	0-0	1		18,478
2		10	H	Motherwell	W	2-1	2-1	2	Dessers [13], Cerny [24]	48,529
3		24	H	Ross Co	W	6-0	2-0	1	Dessers 2 [18, 58], Matondo 2 [45, 69], Lawrence [65], Danilo [90]	48,832
4	Sept	1	A	Celtic	L	0-3	0-2	4		59,612
5		15	A	Dundee U	W	1-0	1-0	3	Lawrence [7]	14,268
6		29	H	Hibernian	W	1-0	1-0	3	Lawrence [34]	48,217
7	Oct	6	H	St Johnstone	W	2-0	1-0	3	Cerny 2 [34, 58]	44,744
8		20	A	Kilmarnock	L	0-1	0-0	3		8924
9		27	H	St Mirren	W	2-1	1-1	3	Diomande [13], Cerny [69]	48,859
10		30	A	Aberdeen	L	1-2	0-1	3	Bajrami [63]	19,274
11	Nov	10	H	Hearts	W	1-0	1-0	3	Dessers [6]	48,254
12		23	A	Dundee U	D	1-1	0-1	3	Cerny [66]	47,714
13	Dec	1	A	St Johnstone	W	1-0	0-0	3	Holt (og) [63]	7446
14		4	H	Kilmarnock	W	6-0	1-0	3	Tavernier [37], Danilo [53], Igamane [55], Cerny [61], Dessers 2 [69, 77]	44,188
15		8	A	Ross Co	W	3-0	2-0	3	Igamane [6], Danilo [37], Tavernier [86]	6011
16		21	H	Dundee	W	1-0	0-0	2	Cerny [46]	47,208
17		26	A	St Mirren	L	1-2	0-1	2	Danilo [61]	7175
18		29	A	Motherwell	D	2-2	0-2	2	Igamane 2 [50, 68]	8728
19	Jan	2	H	Celtic	W	3-0	1-0	2	Hagi [7], Propper [66], Danilo [81]	51,065
20		5	A	Hibernian	D	3-3	2-1	2	Igamane 3 [4, 19, 74]	17,539
21		9	A	Dundee	D	1-1	1-1	2	Cerny [34]	8606
22		12	H	St Johnstone	W	3-1	3-0	2	Igamane [16], Cerny [20], Diomande [25]	45,818
23		15	H	Aberdeen	W	3-0	1-0	2	Igamane [13], Balogun [90], Dessers [90]	45,887
24		26	A	Dundee U	W	3-1	1-1	2	Diomande [37], Propper [49], Dessers [86]	13,653
25	Feb	2	H	Ross Co	W	4-0	3-0	2	Hagi 2 [18, 25], Souttar [35], Tavernier (pen) [79]	46,973
26		16	A	Hearts	W	3-1	1-0	2	McCart (2 ogs) [20, 73], Cerny [61]	18,356
27		22	H	St Mirren	L	0-2	0-0	2		49,994
28		26	A	Kilmarnock	W	4-2	1-2	2	Cerny [35], Dessers 2 [53, 62], Bajrami [85]	8751
29	Mar	1	H	Motherwell	L	1-2	0-2	2	Dessers [54]	50,056
30		16	A	Celtic	W	3-2	2-0	2	Raskin [4], Diomande [37], Igamane [88]	58,913
31		29	A	Dundee	W	4-3	1-2	2	Shaughnessy (og) [43], Tavernier [75], Lawrence [81], Dessers [90]	8710
32	Apr	5	H	Hibernian	L	0-2	0-1	2		50,922
33		13	A	Aberdeen	D	2-2	0-2	2	Igamane [49], Hagi [90]	18,863
34		26	A	St Mirren	D	2-2	1-1	2	Dessers [42], Raskin [52]	7019
35	May	4	H	Celtic	D	1-1	1-0	2	Dessers [44]	49,883
36		11	H	Aberdeen	W	4-0	0-0	2	Cerny [55], Dessers [61], Igamane [70], Jefte [90]	50,343
37		14	H	Dundee U	W	3-1	1-1	2	Dessers (1 pen) [25, 73 (p)], Raskin [75]	49,361
38		17	A	Hibernian	D	2-2	1-1	2	Dessers [2], Raskin [50]	18,793

Final League Position: 2

League Cup Winners: (28 times) 1946-47, 1948-49, 1960-61, 1961-62, 1963-64, 1964-65, 1970-71, 1975-76, 1977-78, 1978-79, 1981-82, 1983-84, 1984-85, 1986-87, 1987-88, 1988-89, 1990-91, 1992-93, 1993-94, 1996-97, 1998-99, 2001-02, 2002-03, 2004-05, 2007-08, 2009-10, 2010-11, 2023-24; *Runners-up:* 10 times. *League Challenge Cup Winners:* 2015-16; *Runners-up:* 2013-14.

European: *European Cup/Champions League:* 179 matches (1956-57, 1957-58, 1959-60 semi-finals, 1961-62, 1963-64, 1964-65, 1975-76, 1976-77, 1978-79, 1987-88, 1989-90, 1990-91, 1991-92, 1992-93 final pool, 1993-94, 1994-95, 1995-96, 1996-97, 1997-98, 1999-2000, 2000-01, 2001-02, 2003-04, 2004-05, 2005-06, 2007-08, 2008-09, 2009-10, 2010-11, 2011-12, 2021-22, 2022-23, 2023-24, 2024-25). *Cup Winners' Cup:* 54 matches (1960-61 runners-up, 1962-63, 1966-67 runners-up, 1969-70, 1971-72 winners, 1973-74, 1977-78, 1979-80, 1981-82, 1983-84).
UEFA Cup: 88 matches (*Fairs Cup:* 1967-68, 1968-69 semi-finals, 1970-71. *UEFA Cup:* 1982-83, 1984-85, 1985-86, 1986-87, 1988-89, 1997-98, 1998-99, 1999-2000, 2000-01, 2001-02, 2002-03, 2004-05, 2006-07, 2007-08 runners-up). *Europa League:* 68 matches (2010-11, 2011-12, 2017-18, 2019-20, 2020-21, 2021-22 runners-up, 2023-24, 2024-25).

Club colours: Shirt: Royal blue. Shorts: White. Socks: Black with red tops.

Goalscorers: *League (80):* Dessers 18 (1 pen), Cerny 12, Igamane 12, Danilo 5, Diomande 4, Hagi 4, Lawrence 4, Raskin 4, Tavernier 4 (1 pen), Bajrami 2, Matondo 2, Propper 2, Balogun 1, Jefte 1, Souttar 1, own goals 4.
Scottish Cup (5): Dessers 3, McCausland 1, Nsiala-Makengo 1. *Premier Sports Scottish League Cup (10):* Dessers 4, Bajrami 2, Danilo 1, Diomande 1, McCausland 1, Tavernier 1 (1 pen). *SPFL Trust Trophy (16):* Curtis 3, Lowry 2, Adamson 1, Allan 1, Burnside 1, Danilo 1, Eadie 1, Gentles 1, McKinnon 1, Nsio 1, Stevens 1, own goals 2.
Champions League (1): Dessers 1. *Europa League (19):* Cerny 6, Igamane 4, Dessers 3, Lawrence 2, Bajrami 1, Diomande 1, McCausland 1, Raskin 1.

Butland J 28	Tavernier J 30+3	Souttar J 24	Davies B 1	Yilmaz R 11+6	Diomande M 32+4	Barron C 23+5	Wright S 2	Lawrence T 8+10	Cortes O 4+6	Dessers C 24+11	Matondo R 2+4	Cerny V 30+3	Balogun L 13+7	Dowell K 2+10	Propper R 22+5	Sterling D 11+9	McCausland R 4+9	Jefte V 30+3	Danilo P 8+15	Fraser R —+2	Igamane H 23+10	Raskin N 29+4	Bajrami N 15+13	Kasanwirjo N 3+6	Hagi I 16+8	Kelly L 10	King L 10	Nsiala-Makengo C 10+1	Lovelace Z —+1	Nsio P —+1	Rice B 1+6	Fernandes R 1+2	Curtis F 1+2	Match No.
1	2	3		4[2]	5	6	7[4]	8[3]	9	10[1]	11	12	13	14	15																			1
1	2	3		5	7[5]	6	10[3]	9[1]		11	14	8[2]	15	16		4[4]	12	13																2
1	2	3		12	7	9[2]	11[3]	10[4]	8[5]	4[1]	14		6	15	5	13	16																	3
1	2	3		8[2]	7	13		10	11[1]	9[3]	16	4[4]	6[5]	12	5			14	15															4
1	2	3		6[4]	7	8	11[1]	10[2]	9[3]	4	14	5	13	15	12																			5
1	2	3		6	9[5]	14	8[4]	13	4	15	10[1]	5	11[3]	7	9[5]	15	13[9]																	6
1	2	3		6[1]	14	11[3]	8[4]	4	16	10[2]	5	14	7	9[5]	15	13																		7
1	2	3		6	7[1]	9[4]	11[3]	8[5]	12	16	4[2]	5	14	13	10	15																		8
1	13			9	6[3]	12	8[4]	3	4[2]	14	15	5	11[1]	7	10	2																		9
1	2	3		6	9[2]	11[4]	4	12	8[1]	13	15	7	10[3]	5	14																			10
1	2[2]	3		9	6[1]	11[3]	8[4]	4	16	12	15	5	14	7	10[5]	13																		11
1				14	9[1]	6	11[2]	8	4	2	5[3]	12	15	7	10[4]	13																		12
1	2	3		13	15	6	8[6]	12	16	4[1]	5[3]	14	11[4]	7	10[2]	9																		13
1	2	3		16	9	15	13	8[3]	4	14	5[4]	11[1]	10[2]	6[5]	12	7																		14
1	2	3		15	8[4]	14	7[1]	4	16	13	5	11[2]	10[3]	6	12	9																		15
	2			14	6	15	9[2]		4	3	13	5	10[1]	11[4]	7	12	8[3]	1																16
1	2			15	6	7[3]	16	8	3[1]	12	4	5[4]	13	11[5]	14	9[2]	10																	17
1	2			5	8[4]			9[3]	10[1]	14	13	7[2]	4	3	11	12	6	15																18
	2	6		13	14	16	8	4	3	5[3]	12	15	11[4]	7[3]	9[1]	10[2]	1																	19
	2	6		15	12		8[4]		4	3[3]	5	13	11	7	9[2]	10[1]	1	14																20
	2[3]	7	6[2]	15		12	8[4]		3	14	5	13	11	9	10[1]	1		4																21
	2[5]	7		12	13	8[2]		15	3	14	5	9[4]	11[1]	6	10[3]	1	16	4																22
	14	2	6		15	8	13	3[2]	5	9[1]	11[4]	7	12	10[3]	1	4																		23
1	2			6[9]	9			3		5		11	7	10[2]	8[1]		4	12	13															24
1	2	3[2]		6[1]	14	11	8	13	5	9[4]	7	15	10[3]	4[5]	12	16																		25
1	2[3]	3[2]		6	9[1]	12	8	13	5	11	7	10[4]	4	14	15																			26
1	2			6[2]	13	11	8	3	5	12	9[1]	7	14	10[3]	4																			27
1	2			12	6	13	11	8[4]	3	15	5	9[2]	7	14	10[3]	4[1]																		28
1	3			2[5]	8[4]	12	10	6	14	4[3]	16	5	15	11[2]	7	13	9[1]																	29
1	5	3		8	9[2]	6[4]	16	11	10[5]	4[1]	12	2[3]		15	7	13	14																	30
1	5	3		8[3]	9[5]	6[2]	16	11	4[1]	2	14	15	10[7]	7	12	13																		31
1	2	4		9[2]	6	11[4]	8	3	5	13	10[3]	7	12	14		15																		32
	12			14	7	11[2]	16	3	5[8]	13	9[3]	10	6[4]	15	1	4	2[1]	8[6]																33
	5	2		9	13	10[1]	12	3	8	11	6	14	1	4[3]	7[2]																			34
	2	3		6[4]	7	11	9[2]	4	5	15	12	8	10[1]	13[3]	1	14																		35
	2	3		9[2]	6	16	11[5]	8	4[3]	5	15	12	7[4]	10[1]	14	1	13																	36
1	2	3		9[1]	6[5]	13	15	11	8[3]	4	5[2]	14	10[4]	7	12	16																		37
1	2	3		6[2]	7	13	14	10	9[4]	4[1]	12	11	8[3]	5	15																			38

ROSS COUNTY

Year Formed: 1929. *Ground & Address:* The Global Energy Stadium, Victoria Park, Dingwall IV15 9QZ.
Telephone: 01349 860 860. *Fax:* 01349 866 277. *E-mail:* info@rosscountyfootballclub.co.uk
Website: rosscountyfootballclub.co.uk
Ground Capacity: 6,634 (all seated). *Size of Ground:* 105 × 68m.
Chairman: Roy MacGregor. *Chief Executive:* Steven Ferguson.
Manager: Don Cowie. *Assistant Manager:* Carl Tremarco.
Club Nickname: 'The Staggies'.
Record Attendance: 6,590 v Rangers, Premiership, 13 November 2016; 6,590 v Celtic, Premiership, 18 November 2017.
Record Transfer Fee received: £500,000 from Burton Albion for Liam Boyce (June 2017).
Record Transfer Fee paid: £100,000 to Inverness CT for Ross Draper (August 2017).
Record Victory: 11-0 v St Cuthbert Wanderers, Scottish Cup 1st rd, 11 December 1993.
Record Defeat: 0-7 v Kilmarnock, Scottish Cup 3rd rd, 17 February 1962.
Most League Appearances: 353: Michael Gardyne, 2006-07, 2008-12, 2014-21.
Most League Goals in Season: 24: Andrew Barrowman, 2007-08.
Most League Goals (Overall): 48: Liam Boyce, 2014-17; Michael Gardyne, 2006-07, 2008-12, 2014-21.

ROSS COUNTY – WILLIAM HILL PREMIERSHIP 2024–25 LEAGUE RECORD

Match No.	Date	Venue	Opponents	Result		H/T Score	Lg Pos.	Goalscorers	Attendance
1	Aug 3	A	Motherwell	D	0-0	0-0	1		4353
2	10	H	Dundee U	D	1-1	0-0	7	Hale [90]	4169
3	24	A	Rangers	L	0-6	0-2	8		48,832
4	31	H	Aberdeen	L	0-1	0-0	9		5480
5	Sept 14	H	Dundee	W	2-0	2-0	9	Wright [6], White (pen) [45]	4068
6	21	H	St Johnstone	D	3-3	1-1	8	Hale [19], Samuel [87], Wright [90]	3063
7	28	A	Hearts	D	1-1	0-1	7	Hale [35]	18,399
8	Oct 6	H	Celtic	L	1-2	1-0	7	Hale (pen) [43]	6372
9	19	A	St Johnstone	L	0-3	0-2	9		3688
10	26	H	Kilmarnock	W	2-1	0-1	7	White [61], Wright (og) [82]	3419
11	30	H	Hibernian	D	0-0	0-0	8		3468
12	Nov 2	A	St Mirren	D	0-0	0-0	8		6142
13	9	A	Dundee U	L	0-3	0-0	9		8349
14	23	H	Motherwell	W	2-1	0-0	8	Hale [47], Nisbet [54]	3410
15	30	A	Celtic	L	0-5	0-5	8		58,436
16	Dec 8	H	Rangers	L	0-3	0-2	8		6011
17	14	A	Hibernian	L	1-3	1-1	9	Campbell [2]	14,885
18	21	H	St Mirren	L	1-2	0-1	10	Efete [46]	3271
19	26	A	Dundee	W	3-0	1-0	10	Chilvers [23], Nisbet [70], White (pen) [78]	5207
20	29	H	Hearts	D	2-2	0-1	10	Nisbet [90], White [90]	4994
21	Jan 2	A	Aberdeen	W	2-1	1-1	10	Wright [24], Chilvers [60]	17,007
22	5	A	Kilmarnock	W	1-0	0-0	9	Harmon [86]	5426
23	11	H	Celtic	L	1-4	0-1	10	White (pen) [60]	6254
24	25	H	Hibernian	D	1-1	0-1	10	Hale (pen) [87]	4003
25	Feb 2	A	Rangers	L	0-4	0-3	11		46,973
26	15	A	Motherwell	W	3-0	1-0	10	Hale 2 [32, 59], Randall [89]	3973
27	22	H	Dundee	W	3-1	1-1	7	Phillips [18], Wright [47], Chilvers [49]	4075
28	26	A	St Johnstone	L	0-1	0-0	9		3576
29	Mar 1	H	Kilmarnock	W	1-0	0-0	8	Phillips [35]	3385
30	15	A	Hearts	L	0-2	0-1	9		18,648
31	30	H	Dundee U	L	0-1	0-0	9		4088
32	Apr 5	H	Aberdeen	L	0-1	0-1	10		5194
33	12	A	St Mirren	L	2-3	1-1	10	Hale [22], White [63]	6318
34	26	A	Kilmarnock	L	0-2	0-1	11		5425
35	May 3	H	Hearts	L	1-3	1-1	11	Hale [26]	4181
36	10	A	St Johnstone	L	1-2	1-1	11	Samuel [41]	4355
37	14	A	Dundee	D	1-1	0-0	11	Hale (pen) [90]	5905
38	18	H	Motherwell	D	1-1	1-0	11	Hale [29]	4170

Final League Position: 11

Honours
League Champions: First Division 2011-12; Championship 2018-19; Second Division 2007-08; Third Division 1998-99.
Scottish Cup Runners-up: 2010.
League Cup Winners: 2015-16.
League Challenge Cup Winners: 2006-07, 2010-11, 2018-19; *Runners-up:* 2004-05, 2008-09.

Club colours: Shirt: Navy blue with red trim. Shorts: White. Socks: Red.

Goalscorers: *League (37):* Hale 12 (3 pens), White 6 (3 pens), Wright 4, Chilvers 3, Nisbet 3, Phillips 2, Samuel 2, Campbell 1, Efete 1, Harmon 1, Randall 1, own goal 1.
Scottish Cup (2): Hale 1, White 1.
Premier Sports Scottish League Cup (10): White 4, Hale 3, Brophy 1, Brown 1, Harmon 1.
Premiership Play-offs (3): Hale 2 (1 pen), Nisbet 1.

Laidlaw R 15	Wright A 38	Nightingale W 6	Leak R 14 + 2	Brown J 18 + 9	Loturi V 2 + 9	Randall C 37	Grieves J 8 + 14	Harmon G 21 + 2	White J 20 + 18	Hale R 28 + 8	Denholm A 8 + 7	Samuel A 7 + 15	Efete M 12 + 8	Chilvers N 25 + 5	Allardice S 6 + 11	Brophy E 3 + 8	Robesten G 2 + 10	Nisbet J 26 + 10	Reid Josh 2 + 4	Lopata K 30	Campbell E 25 + 3	Telfer C 1 + 6	Hamilton J 3 + 1	Amissah J 20	Kenneh N 14 + 1	Phillips K 9 + 7	Tomkinson J 11 + 2	Ashworth Z 7 + 3	MacLeod A — + 2	Smith D — + 6	Match No.
1	2	3	4	5^3	6	7	8^1	9	10^4	11^2	12	13	14	15																	1
1	3	4		16		7	9^5	5	14	11	6^2	13		2^4	12	8^3	10^1	15													2
1	3	4		12	8^4	7	6^1	5^5	10^5	11	9^2	14		2^3	13	15		16	17												3
1	3		5	2	13	8	16	6	12	11^4	7^2		14					10^1		9^5	4^3	15									4
1	2		12	5	14	7	15	9^1	10	11^4	13			8^2				6^3		3	4										5
1	2		4	5^1		7	7^2	15	10^3	11	13	16	12	8^4	14			6		3^5	9										6
1	2		4	13	12		6^5	15	10^4	11^2		14	5^3	9^1				7		3	8	16									7
1	2		4	15	13		6	14	12	11^2	10^1	16		5^4	9^3			7^5		3	8										8
1	2		4	13		6		15	10	14			5^2		7^5	11^1		8^3	12	3^4	9^4	16									9
1	2		4^1	5		7			10	11^4	6^2	12	13	9^5	14	15		16	8^3	3											10
1	2		4	5	16		7		10^3	11^1	6^2	14		9^4	15	13		12		3	8										11
1	2		5			6^3	11^2		10	13	12		15	9^1	14			7	8^4	3	4										12
1	2		4^3	5		6^2			11	10^5	9^1	15		14	13	12		7^4		3	8	16									13
1	2		4^1	5		6	16	8^3	10	11^4	14	15	13	9^5				7		3^2	12										14
1^1	2		3	5^3	15		8	10^2	11^5		16	13	9^4	14	15			7		4	6	12									15
	2			13		6	16	8^4	12	10^3		11		5^2	9^1	3^5	14		7	15			1								16
	2		12	5	13	6		9	14	15		11^3		10	7^2			8^4		3	4^1		1								17
	2			4				8^3	10	11	12		5	9	7^1	14		6^2	13	3			1								18
	2	4			8	7^2	9	13	11^3	6^1		5	10^4		14			12		3		15		1							19
	2	4^1	13		7^4	6^2	9	12	11^3			5	8	14	15	10		3				1									20
	2	4^2	5		7		12	11	15			9^1	10	14				8^4	3		13	1	6^3								21
	2		5	13	4	6^1	9	11	12			10^3				8^2		3		14	1	7									22
	2		5	16	7^5	14	9	12	11^2			6	15			10^4		3^1	4		1	8^1	13								23
	2	5^4	6				10^1	14				11		9	7^2		4		1	12	3	8^3	13	15							24
7	2	12	5		14				10^4	13		9^5	6^2	3	4		1	8^1	11^3	2	15	16									25
5			7	16	9^3	12	11^3		8^4			14	15	3	4		1	6^5	10^1	2	13										26
5			7	15	9^3	13	11^1		8^4			12	14	3	4		1	6	10^1	2	16										27
5			7	15	9^2	12	11^2		8^3			13	14	3^4	4		1	6	10^1	2	16										28
5			6		10			14	9^3		13	7^4	3	4		1	12	11^1	2	8^2	15										29
5			6	14	9^2	12	13	15	10^2		16	8	3^4	4		1	7^1	11^3	2												30
5	16		6	12	8^3	14	13	11^4	9^1		15	7^5	3	4		1		10^2	2												31
2	5^2		6	10^1		11	13				12	14	3^4	9		1	7^3	8	4			15									32
2	5^3		6		10	11^2	12		15		9^1		3	4		1	7^4	13		8	14										33
6			7		10	11		13	12		5^3		14	3^1	4		1	8^2	15	2	9^4										34
2	5^1		6	15	8^4	9^2	11		10^5	13		16	12				1	7^3	14	3	4										35
2	4		7		10^3	12	11	9					6				1		3^2	14		8^1		5^1	13						36
2	4		6			13	11	10	5^3			15	9^2	3^1	8^4		1	7	14	12											37
2	3		6		13	14	11^3	10^4	5^1			9		4			1	7^2	15	16	8^5		12								38

ST JOHNSTONE

Year Formed: 1884. *Ground & Address:* McDiarmid Park, Crieff Road, Perth PH1 2SJ.
Telephone: 01738 459 090. *Fax:* 01738 625 771. *E-mail:* enquiries@perthsaints.co.uk *Website:* perthstjohnstonefc.co.uk
Ground Capacity: 10,673 (all seated). *Size of Pitch:* 105m × 68m.
Chair/Owner: Adam Webb. *CEO/Vice-chair:* Francis Smith.
Head Coach: Simo Valakari. *Assistant Head Coach:* Andy Kirk.
Club Nickname: 'Saints'.
Previous Grounds: Recreation Grounds; Muirton Park.
Record Attendance: 29,972 v Dundee, Scottish Cup 2nd rd, 10 February 1951 (Muirton Park): 10,545 v Dundee, Premier Division, 23 May 1999 (McDiarmid Park).
Record Transfer Fee received: £1,750,000 from Blackburn R for Callum Davidson (March 1998).
Record Transfer Fee paid: £400,000 to Dundee for Billy Dodds (January 1994).
Record Victory: 9-0 v Albion R, League Cup, 9 March 1946.
Record Defeat: 1-10 v Third Lanark, Scottish Cup 1st rd, 24 January 1903.
Most Capped Player: Nick Dasovic, 26, Canada.
Most League Appearances: 378: Liam Craig, 2007-13, 2015-22.
Most League Goals in Season (Individual): 36: Jimmy Benson, Division II, 1931-32.
Most Goals Overall (Individual): 140: John Brogan, 1977-83.

ST JOHNSTONE – WILLIAM HILL PREMIERSHIP 2024–25 LEAGUE RECORD

Match No.	Date	Venue	Opponents	Result	H/T Score	Lg Pos.	Goalscorers	Attendance
1	Aug 5	H	Aberdeen	L 1-2	0-1	10	Molloy (og) 88	9203
2	11	A	Kilmarnock	W 3-0	2-0	5	Sidibeh 2 3, 33, Mbunga-Kimpioka (pen) 81	4843
3	24	A	Dundee U	L 0-2	0-0	7		7806
4	31	H	Motherwell	L 1-2	0-1	8	Mbunga-Kimpioka 64	3629
5	Sept 14	A	Hibernian	L 0-2	0-1	10		15,448
6	21	A	Ross Co	D 3-3	1-1	10	Wright 44, Clark 2 60, 84	3063
7	28	H	Celtic	L 0-6	0-3	10		7036
8	Oct 6	A	Rangers	L 0-2	0-1	11		44,744
9	19	H	Ross Co	W 3-0	2-0	8	Mbunga-Kimpioka 2 16, 45, Kirk 90	3688
10	26	A	Dundee	W 2-1	0-1	6	Carey 64, Clark 90	6548
11	30	A	St Mirren	L 1-3	1-1	9	Mbunga-Kimpioka 8	6042
12	Nov 2	H	Hearts	L 1-2	0-1	9	Clark (pen) 66	5917
13	9	A	Motherwell	L 1-2	0-2	10	Clark (pen) 58	4306
14	23	H	Kilmarnock	W 1-0	0-0	9	Kirk 53	1872
15	Dec 1	H	Rangers	L 0-1	0-0	9		7446
16	7	A	Aberdeen	D 1-1	1-0	9	Kirk 25	15,880
17	14	H	St Mirren	L 2-3	0-1	10	Kirk 52, Mbunga-Kimpioka 81	4001
18	22	A	Hearts	L 1-2	0-1	12	Carey (pen) 53	18,676
19	26	A	Dundee U	L 1-2	1-0	12	Kirk 44	7306
20	29	A	Celtic	L 0-4	0-1	12		58,645
21	Jan 2	H	Hibernian	D 1-1	1-0	12	Clark (pen) 45	6287
22	5	H	Dundee	L 1-3	0-3	12	McPake 67	5246
23	12	A	Rangers	L 1-3	0-3	12	Sanders 54	45,818
24	25	H	Motherwell	W 2-1	0-1	12	Steven 86, Mikulic 88	3892
25	Feb 1	A	St Mirren	W 1-0	0-0	12	Mikulic 71	6298
26	15	A	Kilmarnock	L 1-3	0-1	12	Carey 90	5479
27	23	H	Hearts	L 1-2	0-1	12	Sidibeh 53	5577
28	26	H	Ross Co	W 1-0	0-0	12	Kirk 66	3576
29	Mar 1	A	Dundee	D 1-1	1-1	12	Kirk 40	7681
30	15	H	Aberdeen	D 0-0	0-0	12		7733
31	29	A	Hibernian	L 0-3	0-2	12		17,002
32	Apr 6	H	Celtic	W 1-0	1-0	12	Balodis 4	8795
33	12	A	Dundee U	L 0-1	0-1	12		10,160
34	26	A	Motherwell	L 2-3	1-2	12	Kirk 6, Watt 66	4412
35	May 3	H	Kilmarnock	L 0-2	0-1	12		5191
36	10	A	Ross Co	W 2-1	1-1	12	Balodis 31, Watt 60	4355
37	14	A	Hearts	L 1-2	0-2	12	Carey 74	18,021
38	18	H	Dundee	L 0-2	0-1	12		7170

Final League Position: 12

Honours
League Champions: First Division 1982-83, 1989-90, 1996-97, 2008-09; Division II 1923-24, 1959-60, 1962-63.
Runners-up: Division II 1931-32; First Division 2005-06, 2006-07; Second Division 1987-88.
Scottish Cup Winners: 2014, 2021.
League Cup Winners: 2020-21; *Runners-up:* 1969-70, 1998-99.
League Challenge Cup Winners: 2007-08; *Runners-up:* 1996-97.

European: *UEFA Cup:* 10 matches (1971-72, 1999-2000). *Europa League:* 16 matches (2012-13, 2013-14, 2014-15, 2015-16, 2017-18, 2021-22). *UEFA Europa Conference League:* 2 matches (2021-22).

Club colours: Shirt: Blue with gold trim. Shorts: White. Socks: Blue with white tops.

Goalscorers: *League (38):* Kirk 8, Clark 6 (3 pens), Mbunga-Kimpioka 6 (1 pen), Carey 4 (1 pen), Sidibeh 3, Balodis 2, Mikulic 2, Watt 2, McPake 1, Sanders 1, Steven 1, Wright 1, own goal 1.
Scottish Cup (3): Carey 1, Kirk 1, Sidibeh 1.
Premier Sports Scottish League Cup (11): Mbunga-Kimpioka 5, Sidibeh 2, Cameron 1, Carey 1 (1 pen), Kirk 1, Sanders 1.
SPFL Trust Trophy (3): Essel 1, Kirk 1, Smith C 1.

Rae J 13 + 1	Neilson L 13 + 4	McClelland S 1	Cameron K 13 + 2	Raymond A 16 + 1	Wright D 31	MacPherson C 3 + 4	Essel A 9 + 6	Smith M 16 + 4	Mbunga-Kimpioka B 19 + 7	Sanders J 21 + 1	Carey G 15 + 19	Kirk M 24 + 11	Clark N 18 + 11	McPake J 5 + 8	Sinclair R 11	Holt J 26 + 2	Sprangler S 30 + 3	Keltjens D 1 + 6	Franczak F 4 + 4	Douglas B 13 + 3	Mikulic B 13 + 1	Kucheriavyi M 2 + 2	Fisher A 14	Steven T 5 + 9	Curtis S 13	Griffith V 9 + 2	Watt E 6 + 2	Balodis D 13	Svedberg J 4 + 1	Duke-Mckenna S 8 + 3	Mitchell Z 6 + 2	Ikpeazu U 2 + 2	Hamill C — + 1	Match No.
1	2	3^1	4	5	6	7^3	8^2	9	10	11^4	12	13	14	15																				1
1	2		4	9^1	5	6^2	7	8^4	10^3	11		3	12	13	14	15																		2
1	7		4	5	2	13	8^1	6	11^4	10		3	9^2			12																		3
	2		4	9	5	7^2	6^1	8		11		3^4	14	13	10^3	1	12																	4
	3		4	9	5^2		2	8	$11^•$			12	10^1	13		1	6	7																5
	2		4	9^1	5	15	8^2					3	13	10^3	11	14	1	6	7^4	12														6
	2		4^1	9^3	5	13	12	8				3	6	11^4	10^2	15	1	7	14															7
	5		6^4	2^2	13	3^5	8	12	10	4	15	7^3	11			9^1	14	16																8
	4		5	2	13	6^3	10^1	11		3	14	12	9		1	8	7^2																	9
	4	12	5^2	2		7^1	10^3	11		3	13	14	9		1	6	8																	10
	4	5^1	2			6^2	10	11^3		3	14	13	9		1	8	7		12															11
12		4	2			13	10^3	11		3	6	14	9^2		1	8	7		5															12
1	13		4	12	2		8^2	10^3	14	3	6	15	11^4			9^1	7		5^5	16														13
1	13	15	5	2		14		12	11	3		6^1	10^4	9^2		8	7			4^3														14
1	13		5	2		12		14	11^4	3		6^1	10	9^2	15	8^5	7^3			4	16													15
1	2	4		5			6^1	12	11	3	13	9^2	10			8	7																	16
1	$.2^1$			5			6	11	10	3		8	9			7		12			4													17
1			5^1	6		2^3	14	10	9	3	12	11				8^2	7	13			4													18
1		4		6		15	14	12	11^1	2	8	10	13			9^3	7^4	5^2			3													19
1	14	3	9			6^3	8	13	12	2^5	15	11^1	10^2			16	7^4		5		4													20
1			5	2			13	11^{12}	10	3			9			$8^•$	7	12	6^1		4													21
1			5^2	2		12	7^1	11	10^3	3	8		9	14			6				4	13												22
				8		2^1		10^3		3	15	11	9^2	14			6		5^4	13	4	7	1	12										23
				2			12			9	11^4	13				7^2	3		15	8^3	4	6^1	1	14	5	10								24
				8			12			9^1	11^2			1	6	2			4	3			13	5	10	7								25
				8			16			15	11^5					6			4^3	3		1	13	5^2	10^1	7^4	2	9	12	14				26
				8			11^4			9	13					6			4	3		1	15	5^3		7^1	2	10^2	12	14				27
				4^1			11^3			13	9	14				7	6		12			1		5			2	10^2	8	3				28
				8			10^3			13	9^1	14				7^2	6		4			1		5			2	12	11	3				29
				8			10^1	13		14	9^2					6	7		4^4			1	15	5	12		2		11^3	3				30
				8^3				12		15	11^2	16				7	6		4^4			1	13	5^1	9		2	10^5	14	3				31
				5^4			11^3	12		6^1	10^5	15				7	13					1	14	2	8		3		9	4				32
				11			13			9	10	16	15			6^3	12			4		1	14	5^2	7^4		2		8^5	3^1				33
				11^1			14			7	9		10			6^3	4					1	8	2		12	3		5^2		13			34
				12						5		9^1	13	10^3			2	14	4			1	8		7^2	6	3				11			35
				10						12			11²			6^2	2		4			1	8	5	13	7	3					9^1		36
										13	10^3		11			7^4	12	14	4			1	5	2^2	6^1	8	3		9		15			37
				11						12	9		10	1		7^2	4		2				5		8	13^3	3		6^1			14	38

ST MIRREN

Year Formed: 1877. *Ground & Address:* SMiSA Stadium, St Mirren Park, Greenhill Road, Paisley PA3 1RU.
Telephone: 0141 889 2558. *Fax:* 0141 848 6444. *E-mail:* info@stmirren.com *Website:* stmirren.com
Ground Capacity: 7,937 (all seated). *Size of Pitch:* 105m × 68m.
Chairman: John Needham. *Chief Operating Officer:* Keith Lasley.
Manager: Stephen Robinson. *Assistant Manager:* Brian Kerr.
Club Nickname: 'The Buddies'.
Previous Grounds: Shortroods 1877-79, Thistle Park Greenhill 1879-83, Westmarch 1883-94, Love Street 1894-2009.
Record Attendance: 47,438 v Celtic, League Cup, 20 August 1949.
Record Transfer Fee received: £850,000 from Rangers for Ian Ferguson (February 1988).
Record Transfer Fee paid: £400,000 to Bayer Uerdingen for Thomas Stickroth (March 1990).
Record Victory: 15-0 v Glasgow University, Scottish Cup 1st rd, 30 January 1960.
Record Defeat: 0-9 v Rangers, Division I, 4 December 1897.
Most Capped Player: Godmundur Torfason, 29, Iceland.
Most League Appearances: 403: Hugh Murray, 1997-2012.
Most League Goals in Season (Individual): 45: Dunky Walker, Division I, 1921-22.
Most League Goals Overall (Individual): 222: David McCrae, 1923-34.

ST MIRREN – WILLIAM HILL PREMIERSHIP 2024–25 LEAGUE RECORD

Match No.	Date	Venue	Opponents	Result	H/T Score	Lg Pos.	Goalscorers	Attendance
1	Aug 4	H	Hibernian	W 3-0	0-0	2	Idowu [48], Smyth 2 [78, 80]	6171
2	11	A	Aberdeen	L 1-3	1-1	6	Olusanya [45]	17,057
3	25	H	Celtic	L 0-3	0-2	8		6940
4	31	H	Dundee	D 2-2	2-1	7	Olusanya [26], Mandron [36]	5779
5	Sept 14	A	Kilmarnock	D 2-2	2-1	7	Olusanya [7], O'Hara (pen) [41]	6957
6	21	H	Hearts	W 2-1	2-1	5	Taylor (og) [8], Olusanya [34]	7341
7	28	A	Motherwell	L 1-2	1-2	6	Phillips [9]	5214
8	Oct 5	H	Dundee U	L 0-1	0-0	6		7166
9	19	A	Hearts	L 0-4	0-1	7		18,757
10	27	A	Rangers	L 1-2	1-1	10	Gogic [26]	48,859
11	30	H	St Johnstone	W 3-1	1-1	7	Tanser [30], O'Hara [57], Ayunga [90]	6042
12	Nov 2	H	Ross Co	D 0-0	0-0	6		6142
13	9	A	Hibernian	W 2-1	2-0	6	McMenamin 2 [16, 31]	15,594
14	23	H	Aberdeen	W 2-1	1-0	6	Olusanya [20], Taylor R [83]	7533
15	30	A	Dundee U	L 0-2	0-0	6		8868
16	Dec 7	H	Motherwell	L 0-1	0-0	7		6111
17	14	A	St Johnstone	W 3-2	1-0	6	Phillips [10], Mooney [88], Idowu (pen) [90]	4001
18	21	A	Ross Co	W 2-1	1-0	6	Iacovitti [27], Smyth [89]	3271
19	26	H	Rangers	W 2-1	1-0	5	Smyth (pen) [30], Boyd-Munce [90]	7175
20	29	H	Dundee	L 1-2	1-1	5	Olusanya [40]	6798
21	Jan 2	A	Kilmarnock	L 0-2	0-1	5		6603
22	5	A	Celtic	L 0-3	0-2	6		58,838
23	11	H	Dundee U	L 0-1	0-0	7		7440
24	25	A	Aberdeen	W 3-0	2-0	7	Olusanya [7], Mandron 2 [36, 78]	15,829
25	Feb 1	H	St Johnstone	L 0-1	0-0	8		6298
26	16	H	Hibernian	D 0-0	0-0	6		7468
27	22	A	Rangers	W 2-0	0-0	6	Mandron [51], Olusanya [70]	49,994
28	26	A	Hearts	L 1-3	1-0	7	Mandron [37]	18,770
29	Mar 1	H	Celtic	L 2-5	1-2	9	John [33], Phillips [48]	7127
30	15	A	Motherwell	D 2-2	2-1	8	Boyd-Munce [23], Phillips [33]	6121
31	29	H	Kilmarnock	W 5-1	2-0	7	Boyd-Munce 2 [6, 58], Idowu (pen) [9], O'Hara [65], John [69]	7542
32	Apr 5	A	Dundee	L 0-2	0-1	7		6580
33	12	H	Ross Co	W 3-2	1-0	6	Boyd-Munce [36], Ayunga [50], Idowu [86]	6318
34	26	H	Rangers	D 2-2	1-1	6	O'Hara [44], McMenamin [73]	7019
35	May 3	H	Aberdeen	W 1-0	0-0	6	Mandron [60]	7587
36	10	A	Dundee U	W 2-0	1-0	6	Mandron [31], Ayunga [66]	9821
37	14	H	Hibernian	D 2-2	1-2	6	Taylor R [45], McMenamin [64]	7671
38	17	A	Celtic	D 1-1	0-0	6	Ayunga [51]	58,889

Final League Position: 6

Honours
League Champions: First Division 1976-77, 1999-2000, 2005-06; Division II 1967-68; Championship 2017-18.
Runners-up: First Division 2004-05; Division II 1935-36.
Scottish Cup Winners: 1926, 1959, 1987; *Runners-up:* 1908, 1934, 1962.
League Cup Winners: 2012-13; *Runners-up:* 1955-56, 2009-10.
League Challenge Cup Winners: 2005-06; *Runners-up:* 2016-17.
B&Q Cup Runners-up: 1993-94. *Anglo-Scottish Cup:* 1979-80.

European: *Cup Winners' Cup:* 4 matches (1987-88). *UEFA Cup:* 10 matches (1980-81, 1983-84, 1985-86).
UEFA Conference League: 4 matches (2024-25).

Club colours: Shirt: Black and white stripes. Shorts: Black. Socks: Black with white and amber tops.

Goalscorers: *League (53):* Olusanya 8, Mandron 7, Boyd-Munce 5, Ayunga 4, Idowu 4 (2 pens), McMenamin 4, O'Hara 4 (1 pen), Phillips 4, Smyth 4 (1 pen), John 2, Taylor R 2, Gogic 1, Iacovitti 1, Mooney 1, Tanser 1, own goal 1.
Scottish Cup (4): Olusanya 2, Boyd-Munce 1, Mandron 1.
Premier Sports Scottish League Cup (0).
SPFL Trust Trophy (0).
UEFA Conference League (6): Iacovitti 2, Olusanya 2, O'Hara 1, Rooney 1.

Balcombe E 21	Fraser M 38	Gogic A 35 + 1	Taylor R 32 + 2	Rooney S 6	Adeniran D 2 + 4	Boyd-Munce C 22 + 8	Idowu R 13 + 18	Tanser S 19 + 10	Olusanya J 14 + 14	Ayunga J 14 + 14	Brown J 3 + 4	Scott J 4 + 9	Mandron M 18 + 16	Smyth O 6 + 13	Iacovitti A 8 + 6	Bwomono E 15 + 10	Phillips K 35	O'Hara M 30 + 2	Sutherland E — + 1	van Veen K 2 + 3	Kiltie G 14 + 15	Dunne C 4	Mooney E — + 7	McMenamin C 5 + 6	John D 15 + 3	Kenny L — + 2	Penman C 1 + 3	Oseni O — + 10	Hemming Z 17	Alebiosu R 13	Match No.
1	2	3	4^5	5	6^4	7	8	9^1	10^2	11^3	12	13	14	15	16																1
1	2	3	*	5^5	6	7	8^1	9^2	11^4	15	13	10^3	14	12	4	16															2
1	2	8^1	4	5		12		10^4	11^2	9			13	14	3	6^3	7	15													3
1	2	3	4^1	5^5	14	7^4	13	9^3	10^4	17	15		11			12	16	6^2	8												4
1	2	3	4^3	6	16	5^5	8^4	11^2	12	9	13	10^1	14		7	15															5
1	2	3	4	5		7^5	16	12	10^2	9^1	13	11^3	15		6^4	8	14														6
1	2	3	4			7^3	15	8^1	10^4		12	14	11^2		5^1	6	8^5		13	16											7
1	2	3	5			7^5	9^1		11		12	15	16		14	6	8^3	10^2	13	4^4											8
1	2	3		13		15	5	7^3		16	6^2		12	8^1	9	11^4	10^5	4	14												9
1	2	3				14	13	8	10		9^1	15		5^3	6	7^4		11^2	4		12										10
1	2	3	12					14	13	8	10^2	15		9^3	5^3	6		11^4	4^1	13											11
1	2	3	4			16	14	8	10^4	13		9^1	15		5^2	6^5	7		11^3		12										12
1	2	3	4					8	10^1	12		13	14		5	6	7		11^3		9^2										13
1	2	3	4			14		8	10^2	13		12			5	6	7		11^3		9^1										14
1	2^1	3*	4			15	8^4	10^2	13			12			5	6	7		11^3		9^1	14									15
1	2	3^1	4			12	8	10^2	14			13			5^3	6	7		11^1		9										16
1	2	4^1				14	8^2	15			11^3		3	5	6	7		10^5		16	9^4	13	12								17
1	2	12	4		14	15	9^1	8^4		13			10^2	6^3	3	5	7		11^4												18
1	2	3	4			14	9	11^5	13		7	12		5^1	6		10^2			8^4	15										19
1	2	3				15	9^1		11^2	12		13	7^4	4	5^5	6		10^3		14	8		16								20
1	5	2^4	4			9^2	8	11^5	10^3		13		7^1	3	14	6	12		16					15							21
	2	3	4			7^4	15	9^5	11^3	14			12		5	6	8^1		10^2				16		13	1					22
	2		3			13	11^1	8	12				10^4		4^5	6^3	7		9^2		15				14	16	1				23
	2	4	3			7^3		9	11^5				10^4	14	12	6	8^2		13		15				5^1	16	1				24
	2	3	4			7^4		9	10^5		12	11^1	14		5^3	6	8^2		13		16					15	1				25
	2	3	4			7^4			10^2	13		11^5	15	12	6	8^3		14							9	16	1		5^1		26
	2	3	4			7^2	16	14	10^3	11		13		12	6^4	8		15						9^5			1		5^1		27
	2	3	4^4			7	15	13	10^2	11		12		6^3	8		14		9								1		5^1		28
	2	3	4			7^4	15		10^2		12	11^1		6^3	8		13		9						14		1		5		29
	2	3	12			7^1	15^5	16	10^1	11^{13}			13	4^2	6^4	8		14						9^6		17	1		5		30
	2^5	3	4			7^2	10^3	16	11			13		6^1	8		12		9^4	15					14		1		5		31
	2	3	4			7	10	12	13	11^3		14		6^4	8		15		9								1		5^2		32
	2	3	4			7	14	15	10^1	11^1		12	16	6	8^3		13		9^5								1		5^2		33
	2	3	4			7^2	13	14	10^1		11^4			6	8		12		9^3		15						1		5		34
	2	3	4			13	12		11^1		14	10	7^2	6	8^3			9									1		5		35
	2	3	4^2			7	8^3	12	11		10	13	6		14		9										1		5		36
	2	3	4			7^3	8^4	12	11^2		10		6	14	15		13	9^1									1		5		37
	2	3	4			7^1	12	14	11^2		15	10^4	16	6	8		13		9^3								1		5^5		38

STENHOUSEMUIR

Year Formed: 1884. *Ground & Address:* Ochilview Park, Gladstone Rd, Stenhousemuir FK5 4QL.
Telephone: 01324 562 992. *Fax:* 01324 562 980. *E-mail:* info@stenhousemuirfc.com *Website:* stenhousemuirfc.com
Ground Capacity: 3,746 (seated: 626). *Size of Pitch:* 101m × 66m.
Chairman: Dan Wharton.
Manager: Gary Naysmith. *Assistant Manager:* Brown Ferguson.
Club Nickname: 'The Warriors'.
Previous Grounds: Tryst Ground 1884-86; Goschen Park 1886-90.
Record Attendance: 12,500 v East Fife, Scottish Cup quarter-final, 11 March 1950.
Record Transfer Fee received: £70,000 from St Johnstone for Euan Donaldson (May 1995).
Record Transfer Fee paid: £20,000 to Livingston for Ian Little (June 1995); £20,000 to East Fife for Paul Hunter
(September 1995).
Record Victory: 9-2 v Dundee U, Division II, 16 April 1937.
Record Defeat: 2-11 v Dunfermline Ath, Division II, 27 September 1930.
Most League Appearances: 434: Jimmy Richardson, 1957-73.
Most League Goals in Season (Individual): 32: Robert Taylor, Division II, 1925-26.
Most Goals Overall (Individual): 58: Mark McGuigan, 2017-21.

STENHOUSEMUIR – WILLIAM HILL LEAGUE ONE 2024–25 LEAGUE RECORD

Match No.	Date	Venue	Opponents	Result	H/T Score	Lg Pos.	Goalscorers	Attendance
1	Aug 3	H	Arbroath	W 2-1	0-0	2	Taylor [50], Banner [54]	738
2	10	A	Kelty Hearts	L 0-2	0-1	4		385
3	17	A	Alloa Ath	L 0-1	0-0	7		709
4	24	H	Cove Rangers	W 3-2	1-1	6	O'Donnell [45], Andersen [48], Wedderburn [58]	561
5	31	A	Annan Ath	W 5-1	2-1	2	Bilham [12], Andersen [31], Alston 3 (1 pen) [57, 61, 64 (p)]	607
6	Sept 14	A	Montrose	L 0-3	0-2	5		371
7	21	H	Queen of the South	D 0-0	0-0	4		583
8	28	A	Inverness CT	D 0-0	0-0	5		1601
9	Oct 5	A	Dumbarton	W 3-1	2-1	2	Alston (pen) [11], Aitken M 2 [35, 80]	620
10	19	H	Alloa Ath	L 0-1	0-0	5		408
11	26	H	Kelty Hearts	W 2-1	1-0	2	O'Reilly [15], Buchanan [47]	546
12	Nov 2	A	Arbroath	L 0-1	0-1	4		1141
13	9	A	Annan Ath	D 1-1	1-1	5	Yates [8]	365
14	16	H	Montrose	W 1-0	0-0	4	Yates [82]	561
15	Dec 3	A	Cove Rangers	W 3-0	2-0	1	Aitken M [25], Tomlinson [31], O'Donnell [90]	176
16	7	H	Dumbarton	W 4-0	2-0	1	Yates 3 (2 pens) [8, 73 (p), 88 (p)], Steele [25]	436
17	14	A	Queen of the South	L 1-2	0-1	2	O'Donnell [64]	906
18	21	H	Inverness CT	L 0-1	0-0	3		719
19	28	A	Alloa Ath	W 3-1	1-0	2	Steele [34], Andersen [59], O'Donnell [80]	806
20	Jan 4	H	Annan Ath	D 1-1	0-0	2	Buchanan [48]	502
21	11	A	Kelty Hearts	D 0-0	0-0	2		439
22	25	H	Cove Rangers	L 0-4	0-3	2		336
23	Feb 1	A	Montrose	W 3-0	1-0	1	Alston (pen) [19], Taylor [69], O'Donnell [90]	531
24	8	H	Queen of the South	W 2-1	2-0	1	Alston [12], O'Donnell [28]	630
25	22	H	Arbroath	W 2-0	0-0	2	Alston [77], Taylor [90]	705
26	Mar 1	A	Dumbarton	W 3-1	3-0	2	O'Donnell 3 [22, 31, 40]	540
27	8	A	Annan Ath	W 2-0	1-0	2	Buchanan [37], O'Reilly [80]	454
28	11	A	Inverness CT	L 1-4	1-2	3	O'Reilly [10]	1482
29	15	H	Kelty Hearts	D 0-0	0-0	3		575
30	22	A	Cove Rangers	D 0-0	0-0	3		533
31	29	H	Montrose	L 2-3	0-3	3	Alston [66], Aitken M [87]	486
32	Apr 5	H	Alloa Ath	L 1-4	0-1	3	Yates [76]	612
33	12	A	Arbroath	L 0-4	0-1	3		2205
34	19	H	Inverness CT	D 1-1	0-0	4	Gilmour (og) [90]	764
35	26	A	Queen of the South	L 0-2	0-0	5		2242
36	May 3	H	Dumbarton	W 2-1	1-0	4	Aitken M [9], Alston [60]	764

Final League Position: 4

Honours
League Champions: League Two 2023-24. *League Runners-up:* Third Division 1998-99.
Promoted via play-offs: 2008-09 (to Second Division); 2017-18 (to League One).
Scottish Cup: Semi-finals 1902-03. Quarter-finals 1948-49, 1949-50, 1994-95.
League Cup: Quarter-finals 1947-48, 1960-61, 1975-76.
League Challenge Cup Winners: 1995-96.

Club colours: Shirt: Maroon with blue vertical stripes. Shorts: Maroon with blue side stripes. Socks: Maroon.

Goalscorers: *League (48):* Alston 9 (3 pens), O'Donnell 9, Yates 6 (2 pens), Aitken M 5, Andersen 3, Buchanan 3, O'Reilly 3, Taylor 3, Steele 2, Banner 1, Bilham 1, Tomlinson 1, Wedderburn 1, own goal 1.
Scottish Cup (5): O'Reilly 3, Aitken M 1, Steele 1.
Premier Sports Scottish League Cup (5): Andersen 2, Taylor 2, Aitken M 1.
SPFL Trust Trophy (2): Alston 2 (1 pen).
Championship Play-offs (2): Aitken M 1 (1 pen), Yates 1.

Jamieson D 36	Meechan R 36	Buchanan G 35	Banner K 14+11	Bilham K 32+3	Berry J 8+11	Andersen M 36	Taylor R 17+6	O'Reilly E 29+4	Yates M 23+12	Jacobs K 7+16	Brown A —+4	Aitken M 20+6	Wedderburn N 21+11	Ewen K 12+8	O'Donnell C 13+18	Allan F 1+3	Alston B 18+10	Steele A 9+2	Tomlinson S 5+15	Cameron E —+8	McGill S 10+3	Black B 1	Fisher S 11	McLuckie B 2+7	Match No.
1	2	3	4	5	6[5]	7	8[4]	9[1]	10[3]	11[2]	12	13	14	15	16										1
1	2	4	3	5	6[1]	7	8[2]	9[1]	11[5]	10[3]	15		13	12	14	16									2
1	2	4	3	5		9	10[1]	6[5]	16	8[4]	12	11[2]	7[3]		13	15	14								3
1	2	4	3	5	13	6[5]	8[3]	10[1]	15	12	16	14	7		11[4]		9[2]								4
1	2	3	4	5[5]	14	7[4]	8	10[3]	13	12		11[2]	6	16			15	9[1]							5
1	2	3	4	5[3]	15	7[4]	8		14	16		11	6[5]	13			10[2]	9[1]	12						6
1	2	3	14	15	16	7	8[4]	10[2]		6[1]		11	12	5			9[5]	4[3]	13						7
1	6	3	2	4	8	9		14	10[3]			11	7[1]	5[2]			12		13						8
1	5	4		3	6[2]	7		8[1]	10[3]			11[4]	13	2	15		9		12	14					9
1	2	4		3	6[3]	7		10[1]	8[4]			11[2]	13	5	12		9		14	15					10
1	2	4		3	6	8		10[1]	9[2]			11	7	5					12	13					11
1	2	4	15	3[4]	9[2]	6		10	8			11[1]	7[3]	5	12				13	14					12
1	2	4		3	14	6		9[3]	8			11[1]	7	5[2]	12			13	10						13
1	2	3	15	5	13	6		9[2]	8[4]	14		11[1]	7		12			4	10[3]						14
1	2	4	13	3	12	6	14	9[1]	8[5]			11[4]	7[3]	15			5	10[2]	16						15
1	2	3[5]	14	5[3]	15	7	12	10	9			11[2]	6[4]	13			4	8[1]	16						16
1	2	3[4]	15	5	12	9	14	10[1]	8			11[3]	7[5]	13	16		4	6[2]							17
1	2		3	5	8	7	13	10[1]	6[2]			9[3]	11	12	4			14							18
1	2	3	6	5[2]	12	8		14	10[1]	13		7	11[4]		9[3]	4		15							19
1	2	3		5		8	14	6	10[3]	12		7[1]	11		9[2]	4	13								20
1	5	2	3[3]	9	12	8		6	10	14		7[2]	11[1]			4	13								21
1	2	3	4[1]	5		6	10[5]		8	16		7[2]	12	15	13		14				9[3]	11[4]			22
1	5	3	16	4		6	10[4]	8[2]	13	12		14	2[5]	11	9[3]		15		7[1]						23
1	5	3	16	4		6	10[1]	8[4]	13	15		14	2[5]	11	9[2]		12		7[3]						24
1	2	3		5		6	10	8	12					11	9[1]				7	4					25
1	2	3		5		6	10[2]	8[4]	13	12				11[5]	9[3]				7[1]	4	14				26
1	2	3		5		7	10[2]	6[4]	12			15	16	11[3]	8[1]		14		9[5]	4	13				27
1	2	3		5[1]		7[5]		9[3]	10	16		11[2]	15	12	13		14		8[4]	4	6				28
1	2	3	13	5		6	8[5]	9[2]	14	12			7[1]	15	11		10[4]		16	4[3]					29
1	2	3		5		6	8[2]	9[4]	14	12		15		11[4]	10[3]		16		7[1]	4	13				30
1	2[3]	3	12	5		7[4]	9[2]	13	10	16		11		15	14		8[5]		4[1]	6					31
1	2[5]	4	3	5[4]		7[3]	12	6	10	9[2]		11[1]	15	14	8		13			16				32
1	2	3		5[5]		9[4]	6	7	12	14		13	15	16	10[1]		11[2]		8[3]	4					33
1	2	3	5[1]		7		13	11[4]	8[3]			10[5]	6[2]	9	16		15			14	4	12			34
1	2	3	5	16		7		11[4]	8[1]			10[2]	6[3]	9[5]	14		12	15			4	13			35
1	2	3	14	12[8]		7		9[5]	11[2]			10	6[3]	5	15		8[4]	16			4[1]	13			36

STIRLING ALBION

Year Formed: 1945. *Ground & Address:* Forthbank Stadium, Springkerse, Stirling FK7 7UJ.
Telephone: 01786 450 399. *Fax:* 01786 448 592. *E-mail:* office@stirlingalbionfc.co.uk *Website:* stirlingalbionfc.co.uk
Ground Capacity: 3,808 (seated: 2,508). *Size of Pitch:* 101m × 68m.
Chair: Alasdair Dunn.
Manager: Alan Maybury. *Assistant Manager:* Tony McMinn.
Club Nickname: 'The Binos'.
Previous Ground: Annfield 1945-92.
Record Attendance: 26,400 v Celtic, Scottish Cup 4th rd, 14 March 1959 (Annfield); 3,808 v Aberdeen, Scottish Cup 4th rd, 15 February 1996 (Forthbank).
Record Transfer Fee received: £90,000 from Motherwell for Stephen Nicholas (March 1999).
Record Transfer Fee paid: £25,000 to Falkirk for Craig Taggart (August 1994).
Record Victory: 20-0 v Selkirk, Scottish Cup 1st rd, 8 December 1984.
Record Defeat: 0-9 v Dundee U, Division I, 30 December 1967; 0-9 v Ross Co, Scottish Cup 5th rd, 6 February 2010.
Most League Appearances: 504: Matt McPhee, 1967-81.
Most League Goals in Season (Individual): 27: Joe Hughes, Division II, 1969-70.
Most Goals Overall (Individual): 129: Billy Steele, 1971-83.

STIRLING ALBION – WILLIAM HILL LEAGUE TWO 2024–25 LEAGUE RECORD

Match No.	Date	Venue	Opponents	Result	H/T Score	Lg Pos.	Goalscorers	Attendance
1	Aug 3	A	Edinburgh C	W 2-1	0-0	2	Kerr [86], Carrick [90]	243
2	10	H	Elgin C	L 0-1	0-1	6		671
3	17	A	Clyde	W 2-0	1-0	3	Howie (og) [11], McKinley [84]	709
4	24	H	East Fife	L 0-4	0-2	4		794
5	31	H	The Spartans	W 1-0	1-0	3	Davidson [19]	658
6	Sept 14	A	Peterhead	L 1-2	0-1	4	Brown [50]	566
7	21	H	Bonnyrigg Rose	L 0-2	0-1	6		718
8	28	A	Stranraer	W 2-0	1-0	4	Sula [44], Brown [88]	435
9	Oct 5	H	Forfar Ath	W 2-1	2-1	4	Sula [29], Waugh [34]	686
10	19	H	Clyde	W 3-1	1-1	4	Kerr [14], Hilson [65], Carrick [75]	769
11	Nov 2	A	East Fife	D 1-1	1-1	4	Sula [16]	728
12	9	H	Peterhead	L 2-3	2-1	4	Brown [24], Kerr [35]	663
13	16	A	The Spartans	L 0-3	0-0	4		501
14	Dec 3	A	Bonnyrigg Rose	L 1-2	0-0	4	Brown [90]	446
15	7	H	Edinburgh C	L 0-3	0-2	5		531
16	14	A	Elgin C	W 4-2	3-1	5	Brown 2 [38, 44], Haspell (og) [43], Carrick [57]	873
17	21	H	Stranraer	D 1-1	0-0	5	Kerr [90]	764
18	28	A	Forfar Ath	D 2-2	0-1	5	Roy [46], Kerr [60]	759
19	Jan 4	A	Clyde	L 0-2	0-1	5		810
20	18	A	Peterhead	L 2-3	1-2	5	Brown [23], Crane [49]	662
21	25	H	Bonnyrigg Rose	W 3-0	3-0	5	Graham [2], McNab [39], Brown [45]	642
22	Feb 1	A	Edinburgh C	L 3-4	1-2	5	Kerr [17], Graham 2 [48, 51]	237
23	4	H	The Spartans	L 1-3	0-2	6	Carrick [85]	444
24	8	H	Elgin C	W 3-1	2-0	5	Hilson [29], Harkness [32], Brown [64]	632
25	15	A	Forfar Ath	W 3-1	1-1	5	Harkness [43], McNab [47], Shanley [63]	596
26	22	A	Stranraer	L 0-3	0-2	5		449
27	Mar 1	H	East Fife	W 1-0	0-0	6	Hilson [58]	865
28	8	A	The Spartans	D 0-0	0-0	6		421
29	15	A	Bonnyrigg Rose	D 1-1	1-0	6	Lennon (og) [35]	662
30	22	H	Peterhead	L 1-2	1-1	6	Shanley [2]	755
31	29	H	Edinburgh C	W 2-1	1-0	6	Graham [45], Shanley [64]	634
32	Apr 5	A	Elgin C	W 2-0	1-0	6	Carrick [45], Knox [59]	816
33	12	H	Stranraer	W 3-1	0-1	5	McGeachie [52], Shanley 2 [58, 90]	667
34	19	A	East Fife	L 0-2	0-2	6		962
35	26	H	Clyde	L 1-4	0-2	6	Shanley [70]	830
36	May 3	A	Forfar Ath	D 0-0	0-0	6		995

Final League Position: 6

Honours
League Champions: Division II 1952-53, 1957-58, 1960-61, 1964-65; Second Division 1976-77, 1990-91, 1995-96, 2009-10; Division C 1946-47; League Two 2022-23.
Runners-up: Division II 1948-49, 1950-51; Second Division 2006-07; Third Division 2003-04.
Promoted via play-offs: 2006-07 (to First Division); 2013-14 (to League One).
League Cup: Semi-finals 1961-62.
League Challenge Cup: Semi-finals 1995-96, 1999-2000.

Club colours: Shirt: Red with white sleeves. Shorts: Red. Socks: Red.

Goalscorers: *League (50):* Brown 9, Kerr 6, Shanley 6, Carrick 5, Graham 4, Hilson 3, Sula 3, Harkness 2, McNab 2, Crane 1, Davidson 1, Knox 1, McGeachie 1, McKinley 1, Roy 1, Waugh 1, own goals 3.
Scottish Cup (9): Brown 2, Carrick 2, Kerr 2, Crane 1, Hilson 1, Weir 1.
Premier Sports Scottish League Cup (2): McKinley 1, Roy 1.
SPFL Trust Trophy (0).

Gaston D 36	McGeachie R 33	Sula E 19 + 2	Kerr J 30 + 2	Dall B 9 + 2	Howe H 1 + 2	Waugh R 29 + 6	Ewen H 1	Crane C 25 + 1	Carrick D 22 + 12	Roy A 7 + 9	Weir A 5 + 6	McKinley C 3 + 10	Knox C 13 + 15	Wright H 7 + 8	Hilson D 15 + 8	Featherstone S — + 1	Davidson R 6 + 8	Milne L — + 5	Harkness J 25	Brown A 22 + 2	Ferguson A 7	Graham J 13 + 9	McNab R 15 + 1	Shanley R 18	Grant 16	Deveney E 1 + 7	Constable S 8 + 5	Carse M 10 + 4	Boyle S — + 1	McKinstray K — + 1	Match No.
1	2	3	4	5¹	6¹	7	8²	9	10	11	12	13	14																		1
1	5	2	3	4³		6		7	12	11		8¹	10²	14	9⁴	13	15														2
1	3	4	8	5	12	6³		7	10	11		2¹	13	14	9²																3
1	4	3	7	5		8¹		9¹	10	11		2³	12	13	6²				14	15											4
1	4	3	7⁵			13		5	10	11⁴	12		15	16	6³		8²		14	2¹	9										5
1	4	3⁸	8	5	12			11	10²	14	15	7¹	13	2³	9		6⁴														6
1	4	3	5			7³		10	13	11¹	14		8	12	2²		9		6												7
1	4	3	6	5		11²			14	9¹		13		8			2		10	7³	12										8
1	4	3	6	5⁴		8³			11¹	14	13	9²		15			2		10⁴	7	12										9
1	4	3	8			7¹		5	10³		14		13	12			15		2	9⁴	6	11²									10
1	3	4	6			8		5	10³	14		12			11²		13		2¹	9	7										11
1	4	3	7			6⁴		5¹	11³	15	2⁴	13		14	8²		12			10	9										12
1	2³	4	3	5		6⁴			10	13		15	14	12	8²		2		11	9¹											13
1	4	3	6	12		15		5¹	11³	14		13	8⁴	9			7⁵		2²	10		16									14
1	3	4¹	7	12		6⁴		5³	11	15		13	9³	14	16		2		10	8²											15
1	2	4	3			8³		9¹	10	13		7	11²	12			5		6	14											16
1	3	4				6¹		7	11	13	2²		9	10³	12		5		8	14											17
1	3	4				6²		5	9¹	11			7		10		13		2	8	12										18
1	2	4	6			13		3		9³				12	8¹				5	10		14	7²	11							19
1	2	3				7¹		9³	13			15							14	5	6	11²	8⁴	10		4	12				20
1	2	3				7⁴		8²	12			15	14						5	10³		11¹	6	9		4	13				21
1	2	3				7⁴		8¹	14						16				5	10⁶		11³	6	9	4²	12	13	15			22
1	4	15	3⁴			12		8	14						16				5³	11		9¹	6²	10⁵	2	13	7				23
1	4	3				7		8	12				13						9¹	5		11		6	10³		2				24
1	4¹	12	3			7⁵		8	15					9²					5³	11		6	10	2	16	13	14				25
1	4¹	3				7⁴		14				15		9	2				8	11³		6	10	2	13	5²	12				26
1	2	3				8		9	13			14	10³				5¹			7		11²	4		12	6					27
1	2	3				8		12				9	10¹				5			7²		11	4		13	6					28
1	2¹					8		10				9					5			12		3	11	4	7	6					29
1	2		6			12		11³				8²	13				5			9¹		3	10	4	7	14					30
1	2		6			9		13				12					5²			10¹		8	11	4³	14	3	7				31
1	2		8			9		10²				5					12			6		11	4¹		3	7	13				32
1	3	13	8			9		12				5					10			6¹		11	4		2	7					33
1	2	13	6			8		10³				5²	12	14			9			11		4	3		7¹						34
1	2	6¹	7⁴			10		5²	15			9⁵	14				8³		13	11		4	12	3	16						35
1	4	3	15			13		12	16			14	6	9³	10¹		5			11⁵		8²	2	7⁴							36

STRANRAER

Year Formed: 1870. *Ground & Address:* Stair Park, London Rd, Stranraer DG9 8BS.
Telephone/Fax: 01776 703 271. *E-mail:* secretary@stranraerfc.org *Website:* stranraerfc.org
Ground Capacity: 4,178 (seated: 1,830). *Size of Pitch:* 103m × 64m.
Chairman: Iain Dougan.
Manager: Chris Aitken. *Assistant Manager:* Stephen Aitken.
Club Nicknames: 'The Blues'; 'The Clayholers', 'The Trotters'.
Previous Grounds: Rephad, Sandmill, Recreation Ground, Trotting track.
Record Attendance: 6,500 v Rangers, Scottish Cup 1st rd, 24 January 1948.
Record Transfer Fee received: £90,000 from Ayr U for Mark Campbell (1999).
Record Transfer Fee paid: £35,000 to St Johnstone for Michael Moore (March 2005).
Record Victory: 9-0 v St Cuthbert Wanderers, Scottish Cup 2nd rd, 23 October 2010; 9-0 v Wigtown & Bladnoch, Scottish Cup 2nd rd, 22 October 2011.
Record Defeat: 1-11 v Queen of the South, Scottish Cup 1st rd, 16 January 1932.
Most League Appearances: 321: Scott Robertson, 2013-18; 2019-25.
Most League Goals in Season (Individual): 27: Derek Frye, 1977-78.
Most Goals Overall (Individual): 136: Jim Campbell, 1965-75.

STRANRAER – WILLIAM HILL LEAGUE TWO 2024–25 LEAGUE RECORD

Match No.	Date	Venue	Opponents	Result		H/T Score	Lg Pos.	Goalscorers	Attendance
1	Aug 3	H	The Spartans	D	2-2	2-0	4	Lang [20], Dunlop [26]	470
2	10	A	Clyde	L	0-1	0-0	7		656
3	17	A	Peterhead	L	0-1	0-1	7		502
4	24	H	Elgin C	D	1-1	0-0	9	Robertson [87]	477
5	31	A	Bonnyrigg Rose	L	0-2	0-2	9		607
6	Sept 14	H	East Fife	W	2-1	1-0	7	Russell 2 [24, 75]	413
7	21	A	Forfar Ath	L	1-2	1-1	9	Guthrie [22]	469
8	28	H	Stirling Alb	L	0-2	0-1	10		435
9	Oct 5	A	Edinburgh C	W	2-1	1-0	7	Russell [10], Guthrie [90]	306
10	19	H	Peterhead	D	0-0	0-0	8		469
11	Nov 2	A	Elgin C	L	0-1	0-1	8		757
12	9	A	East Fife	W	2-1	1-0	8	Guthrie [26], Grant [81]	639
13	16	H	Bonnyrigg Rose	L	1-2	1-1	8	Robertson [45]	644
14	Dec 10	A	The Spartans	W	3-1	2-1	8	Dunlop [34], Russell 2 (1 pen) [40, 90 (p)]	306
15	14	H	Edinburgh C	D	0-0	0-0	8		381
16	21	A	Stirling Alb	D	1-1	0-0	9	Russell [88]	764
17	28	H	Clyde	D	1-1	0-1	8	Russell (pen) [72]	728
18	Jan 14	A	Peterhead	L	0-1	0-0	8		483
19	18	H	East Fife	L	0-2	0-2	9		518
20	25	A	Forfar Ath	W	1-0	0-0	8	Gallagher [51]	535
21	28	A	Bonnyrigg Rose	L	1-3	0-2	9	Russell [58]	526
22	Feb 1	H	The Spartans	W	2-0	1-0	8	Docherty [24], Edgar [90]	455
23	8	A	Clyde	L	0-2	0-0	9		754
24	15	H	Elgin C	W	1-0	0-0	7	Grant [67]	442
25	22	H	Stirling Alb	W	3-0	2-0	7	McKnight [43], Dunlop [45], Foster [90]	449
26	Mar 1	A	Edinburgh C	W	1-0	0-0	7	Ross [49]	228
27	4	H	Forfar Ath	L	1-2	1-0	7	Edgar [20]	482
28	8	H	Peterhead	D	0-0	0-0	7		447
29	15	A	East Fife	W	3-0	0-0	7	Hawkshaw (pen) [62], Lang 2 [64, 84]	914
30	22	H	Forfar Ath	L	0-1	0-0	7		496
31	29	H	Clyde	L	1-2	0-0	7	Russell (pen) [80]	515
32	Apr 5	A	The Spartans	L	1-2	0-1	7	Guthrie [59]	352
33	12	A	Stirling Alb	L	1-3	1-0	7	Dunlop [42]	667
34	19	H	Edinburgh C	W	2-0	1-0	7	Guthrie [43], Lang [49]	603
35	26	A	Elgin C	L	0-3	0-2	7		904
36	May 3	H	Bonnyrigg Rose	L	0-1	0-0	8		852

Final League Position: 8

Honours
League Champions: Second Division 1993-94, 1997-98; Third Division 2003-04.
Runners-up: Second Division 2004-05; Third Division 2007-08; League One 2014-15.
Promoted via play-offs: 2011-12 (to Second Division).
Scottish Cup: Quarter-finals 2003.
League Cup: Quarter-finals 1968-69.
League Challenge Cup Winners: 1996-97. Semi-finals: 2000-01, 2014-15.

Club colours: Shirt: Blue with white trim. Shorts: White. Socks: Blue with thin white hoops.

Goalscorers: *League (34):* Russell 9 (3 pens), Guthrie 5, Dunlop 4, Lang 4, Edgar 2, Grant 2, Robertson 2, Docherty 1, Foster 1, Gallagher 1, Hawkshaw 1 (1 pen), McKnight 1, Ross 1.
Scottish Cup (4): Edgar 2, Dunlop 1, Lang 1.
Premier Sports Scottish League Cup (4): Lang 2, Dunlop 1, Edgar 1.
SPFL Trust Trophy (3): Dunlop 1, Ross 1, Russell 1.

Pazikas J 9	McIntosh S 9+3	Cummins A 14+2	Ross C 36	Ecrepont F 26+5	Dunlop E 27+6	Brindley T 18+8	Russell M 28+1	Lang D 14+11	McKnight K 16+8	Foster R 10+10	Edgar R 15+17	McQueen C 6+1	Hawkshaw D 18+5	Gallagher G 20+1	Woods P 1+4	Robertson S 23+7	Broun H 1	Hughes B 1	Guthrie M 14+14	Adam M —+2	Reid L 23+2	Mutch R 6	Gibson J 1	Kane S 8	Quigg A 13+6	Lane J 11	Byrne D —+2	Docherty S 10+1	Mitchell H —+2	Wilde A —+2	Hilferty A —+2	Ellis J —+1	Match No.
1	2	3	4	5	6	7	8	9²	10	11¹	12	13																					1
1	2³	3	4		6	7	8	12	10²	11¹	13	14	5	9																			2
1		4	3	2	8	7⁴	9³	11²	6¹		12	5	10	13	14	15																	3
	2	4	3	5	8³	7¹	10	13	12		11²	14		9⁴	6	15	1																4
1	2²	4	3	5	8⁴		10	14		15	12		9³	6		13			7	11¹													5
1		4	3	5	10	6	7		13		14	2¹		9²	8	12			11³														6
1	12	3	4	5	7	2	10³	13		14			8²	6	9¹				11														7
1	2⁴	4	3	14	10³	5	9¹			12	7		8¹	7		11	13																8
1	5³	2	3		10²	9	6					13	8¹	7	14	12			11		4												9
	5⁴	2	3	9	15		6	10³			14	8²	13	7		12			11¹		4	1											10
	5²	3	2	9	14		6	11⁴			10¹	13	8³	7⁵		15			12	16	4	1											11
		13	2	5³	15	16	9	10			14	12	8³	7		6¹			11⁴		4	1											12
		15	3	6⁵	14	16	7	10⁴			13¹	12	4	9³	8	2¹			11²		5	1											13
		3	4	14	9⁴	5	11	10³	13			6	12	8²	7	2¹			15				1										14
		3		7		5	10	11³	12	13		8	4	9¹	6	2²			14			1											15
		3	14	9	5³	11	10¹	8³	13		6	4⁴		7	2	12			15	1													16
1		3	15	9⁴	5	10		8¹	12	14	6	4²	7		2	11³	13																17
		3	9		5¹	10		8³	11²	14	6		7		2	13	4		1	12													18
15	4	3	5²		13	9	12³		10	14	6		8		2	11¹			1	7⁴													19
12	2¹	3	5		7	9		10²	11³		8	6				4			14	1	13												20
2¹		3	5		9	6		10²	12	15	7		11³		4				8⁴	1	14	13											21
		3		9²	5	6	13	11¹	10³	12	7	8				4			14	1	2												22
		3		9³	5	6¹	11²	10	12	7	8			13		4			14	1	2												23
		3	5	10⁴		14	12	13	11²	7³	8¹	6		15		4			9	1	2												24
		3	5	10		9¹	12	11³	7²	14	6	13		15		4			8	1	2												25
		3	5	10		14	9	12	11²	7⁴	13		6³	15		4			8¹	1	2												26
		3	5	9		14	6	12	11³	8	10²	13	15	4⁴		7	1		2¹														27
		3	5	10		12	8	15	11¹	7³	13	6²	14	4	1	9⁴			2														28
		3	5²	10²	14	7	6	15	11¹	12	8	2⁴	13	4	1	9																	29
		3	5	16	12	13	10⁴	8³	15	11²	6⁵	9	2¹	14	4	1	7																30
		3	5	9	15	11¹	12	7²	10³	14	6¹	8			4	1	13			2⁴													31
		4	13	9	5²		11³	2	10¹	14	6⁴	15	8	12	3	1	7																32
		4	5	9		8	13	12	10²		7¹	2	11	3	1	14			6³														33
		3	9	13	14	6⁴	11⁵	8¹		16	12	2³	10²	4		7	1		5	15													34
		3	9	5	8	6	11¹	12	10³			2		4		7²	1							13	14								35
		3	5	9³	13	6		2⁵	11¹			7²	10⁴	4		8	1							12	14	16	15						36

THE SPARTANS

Year Formed: 1951.
Ground & Address: The Vanloq Community Stadium, Ainslie Park, 94 Pilton Drive, Edinburgh EH5 2HF.
Telephone: 0131 552 7854. *E-mail:* info@spartansfc.com *Website:* spartansfc.com
Ground Capacity: 3,612 (504 seated).
Chairman: Craig Graham.
Secretary: Findlay Murray.
Manager: Dougie Samuel.
Assistant Manager: Darren Cameron.
Previous Grounds: Canal Field, City Park.
Record Attendance: 3,346 v St. Mirren, Scottish Cup 4th rd, 5 February 2006.
Record Victory: 6-0 v Fort William, Scottish Cup 1st rd, 29 September 2007.
Record Defeat: 1-7 v Stranraer, Challenge Cup 2nd rd, 16 August 2016.
Most League Appearances: 77: Blair Henderson, 2023-25.
Most League Goals in Season (Individual): 23: Blair Henderson, 2023-24.
Most Goals Overall (Individual): 43: Blair Henderson, 2023-25.

THE SPARTANS – WILLIAM HILL LEAGUE TWO 2024–25 LEAGUE RECORD

Match No.	Date	Venue	Opponents	Result	H/T Score	Lg Pos.	Goalscorers	Attendance
1	Aug 3	A	Stranraer	D	2-2	0-2	4	Watson P 2 [50, 74]	470
2	10	H	Bonnyrigg Rose	W	2-0	0-0	3	Henderson 2 [59, 86]	616
3	24	H	Peterhead	D	0-0	0-0	5		420
4	31	A	Stirling Alb	L	0-1	0-1	6		658
5	Sept 14	H	Forfar Ath	W	1-0	0-0	5	Watson K [90]	398
6	17	A	Elgin C	D	1-1	0-0	4	Ritchie [74]	439
7	28	H	East Fife	L	0-1	0-0	6		589
8	Oct 5	A	Clyde	D	1-1	1-0	5	Stowe [34]	612
9	12	H	Edinburgh C	L	0-2	0-0	5		476
10	19	H	Elgin C	L	1-3	1-1	6	Henderson (pen) [36]	364
11	Nov 2	A	Peterhead	L	1-2	1-1	7	Whyte [22]	609
12	9	A	Forfar Ath	W	3-0	2-0	7	Russell [31], Walls [36], Henderson (pen) [90]	427
13	16	H	Stirling Alb	W	3-0	0-0	6	Henderson [55], Russell 2 [62, 89]	501
14	Dec 10	H	Stranraer	L	1-3	1-2	7	Henderson [18]	306
15	14	H	Clyde	W	3-2	2-1	6	Watson P [7], Russell 2 [20, 59]	471
16	21	A	East Fife	L	1-5	0-2	6	Stowe [57]	597
17	28	H	Edinburgh C	W	1-0	0-0	6	Henderson (pen) [68]	743
18	Jan 21	A	Bonnyrigg Rose	D	2-2	1-1	6	Russell [39], Henderson (pen) [73]	628
19	25	H	Peterhead	W	1-0	0-0	6	Stowe [59]	398
20	Feb 1	A	Stranraer	L	0-2	0-1	6		455
21	4	A	Stirling Alb	W	3-1	2-0	5	Henderson 2 [33, 50], Dishington [37]	444
22	8	H	East Fife	L	0-1	0-0	6		630
23	15	A	Edinburgh C	L	0-5	0-2	6		338
24	22	A	Clyde	W	2-0	1-0	6	Ritchie [45], Sonkur [56]	598
25	25	H	Forfar Ath	D	1-1	0-1	5	Russell [55]	289
26	Mar 1	H	Bonnyrigg Rose	W	3-1	1-0	5	Booth [18], Dishington [54], Stowe [88]	701
27	8	H	Stirling Alb	D	0-0	0-0	5		421
28	11	A	Elgin C	W	2-0	1-0	5	Henderson [40], Sonkur [73]	456
29	15	A	Forfar Ath	W	2-0	0-0	5	Ritchie [46], Ferguson (og) [74]	604
30	22	H	Elgin C	L	1-2	0-2	5	Dishington [51]	576
31	29	A	East Fife	L	2-4	2-0	5	Dishington [17], Henderson (pen) [45]	674
32	Apr 5	H	Stranraer	W	2-1	1-0	5	Walls [35], Russell [80]	352
33	12	H	Peterhead	L	0-1	0-1	6		690
34	19	H	Clyde	W	2-0	0-0	5	Russell [58], Dishington [81]	451
35	26	A	Bonnyrigg Rose	L	1-2	0-0	5	Henderson [86]	816
36	May 3	H	Edinburgh C	W	3-1	1-0	5	Walls [17], Russell [52], Dall [69]	549

Final League Position: 5

Honours: *League Cup:* Quarter finals (2024-25). *Promoted via play-offs:* 2022-23 (to League Two).

Club colours: Shirt: White with red trim. Shorts: Red. Socks: White.

Goalscorers: *League (48):* Henderson 13 (5 pens), Russell 10, Dishington 5, Stowe 4, Ritchie 3, Walls 3, Watson P 3, Sonkur 2, Booth 1, Dall 1, Watson K 1, Whyte 1, own goal 1.
Scottish Cup (1): Walls 1.
Premier Sports Scottish League Cup (8): Henderson 3 (1 pen), Russell 3, Dishington 1, own goal 1.
SPFL Trust Trophy (0).

Carswell B 35	Watson K 23+5	Sonkur A 32	Watson P 13	Booth C 23+1	Hunter L 19+14	Craigen J 34+2	Dishington J 24+9	Whyte B 33	Russell C 31+1	Henderson B 28+7	Walls B 17+16	Heraghty J 1	Denholm D 4+5	Whitaker R 2+8	Wylie A 1+4	Stowe M 11+18	Waugh K 25+4	Ritchie H 9+7	Scott A 13+4	Cunningham J 1+1	Chisholm H —+1	Laing J 3+3	Morgan L 6+11	Preston A 4+8	Dall B 4+3	Match No.
1	2	3	4	5	6	7	8¹	9	10	11	12															1
	4	3		5	7¹	6	2	8	11³	10	13	1	9²	12	14											2
1	2¹	3	4	5	7	6²	8	9	10	11	13			12												3
1	2⁴	3	4	5	7¹	6	8³	9²	10	11	12		15	13		14										4
1	14	3	2	5	7²	6³	10⁴	9		11	13			12		8¹	4	15								5
1	2	3	4	14	7¹	6	12	10	11⁴	9⁶						5³	8²	16	13	15						6
1	12	3	2		15	7	8³	6	11	9²						5⁴	14	13	4	10¹						7
1		3	2	5	6	7		11	9¹	14	13					8²	4	10³	12							8
1	12	3		5²	7	6	2	14	11³	9						8¹	4⁸	10	13							9
1		3	4	5	7²	9⁴	2	8	11¹	10	12		14	15		6³	13									10
1	2³	3	4	5⁵	13	8⁴	7	10	11	12	16			15	14	9¹	6²									11
1	2²	3	4	5	12	8	14	10	11	9					7³	13	6¹									12
1	2	3	4	5	13	6⁴	12	8	11	10³	9²					14	15	7¹								13
1	3³	2		5	14	13	7¹	8	11	10	9²					12	4⁸	6								14
1	4¹	3		5	7		2	9	10	11	14				13	8²	6³	12								15
1	5³	3		6⁴			2	9	10	11	12		14	13		8²	7¹	4	15							16
1	5⁴	3			6		9	11	10¹	8	12					2	13	4	7²							17
1		3				6	12	9	11	10						8²	5¹	4	7				2	13		18
1	15	3		6	9¹		12	5	11	14						8¹	10³	4	7²				2	13		19
1	12	3		5	6⁴	9¹	15	7	10	11						8²	14	4					2³	13		20
1	2³	3		5	9	7⁴	6⁵	10¹	11	16				15	14	8²	4		13				12	14		21
1	7⁵	3		5⁴			9²	12	8	11	10			13	14	4	15	6¹					16	2³		22
1	2	3		5	16	7	6²	9¹	11	10¹	8³					14	4⁵	12					13	15		23
1	2	3		5	14	7³	12	9	11	15	13					6¹	4	8²					10⁴			24
1	2	3		5	14	6³	13	7	10	11²						8¹	4						9			25
1	2⁴	3		5⁵	16	6	8	7	11²	13	12			15		4	10³						9¹	14		26
1	2	3		5¹	16	6⁵	8²	7	11⁴	14	15			13		4	10						9³	12		27
1	5	3		12	6	13	7⁴	8²	11							10³	4	14	15			16	9¹	2⁵		28
1	2¹	3		13	8³	6	5	10		14						15	4	9⁴	7				11²	12		29
1		3		6²	7	9	5	11	10	13						14	4		8¹					2³	12	30
1		4		6⁵	7²	8	5	10	11¹	14					16	9³	3					15	13	2⁴	12	31
1	2¹	3		14	7³	9	8	11	10	6²						13	4						12	14	5	32
1	2³	3			7	9	8	11	12	6²						10¹	4						13	14	5	33
1	2	3		12	7	9	8	11	10	6²							4						13		5¹	34
1	7	3		6³	8	2	5¹	11	10	9²						13	4						14	12		35
1	2⁵	3		7	8	5³		11⁴	15	6¹	10²					14	4					16	13	12	9	36

SCOTTISH LEAGUE ATTENDANCES 2024–25

WILLIAM HILL PREMIERSHIP ATTENDANCES

	Average Gate			Season 2024–25	
	2023–24	*2024–25*	*+/–%*	*Highest*	*Lowest*
Aberdeen	16,055	17,735	+10.46	19,274	15,829
Celtic	58,827	58,809	–0.03	59,612	58,436
Dundee	6,965	7,027	+0.89	11,585	5,014
Dundee U	8,408	10,972	+30.49	14,268	7,806
Hearts	18,406	18,536	+0.71	18,888	17,894
Hibernian	16,808	17,172	+2.17	20,011	14,885
Kilmarnock	6,523	6,358	–2.53	8,924	4,601
Motherwell	5,829	5,706	–2.11	8,728	3,973
Rangers	49,141	48,255	–1.80	51,065	44,188
Ross Co	4,427	4,372	–1.23	6,372	3,063
St Johnstone	4,547	5,680	+24.92	9,203	1,872
St Mirren	6,646	6,942	+4.46	7,671	6,042

WILLIAM HILL CHAMPIONSHIP ATTENDANCES

	Average Gate			Season 2024–25	
	2023–24	*2024–25*	*+/–%*	*Highest*	*Lowest*
Airdrieonians	1,916	1,797	–6.19	3,069	1,200
Ayr U	2,114	2,811	+32.97	4,471	1,701
Dunfermline Ath	5,444	5,575	+2.41	8,558	4,286
Falkirk	4,750	6,445	+35.67	7,633	5,505
Greenock Morton	2,083	2,084	+0.06	2,976	1,541
Hamilton A	1,293	1,417	+9.52	2,561	1,005
Livingston	3,582	1,863	–47.99	4,500	1,050
Partick Thistle	3,517	3,942	+12.09	4,997	2,946
Queen's Park	1,839	1,568	–14.75	2,779	881
Raith R	4,191	3,977	–5.12	5,586	3,258

WILLIAM HILL LEAGUE ONE ATTENDANCES

	Average Gate			Season 2024–25	
	2023–24	*2024–25*	*+/–%*	*Highest*	*Lowest*
Alloa Ath	769	662	–13.90	806	426
Annan Ath	599	485	–19.05	1,353	233
Arbroath	2,027	1,434	–29.28	2,714	628
Cove Rangers	583	456	–21.66	758	176
Dumbarton	533	602	+12.92	872	355
Inverness CT	2,289	1,694	–25.98	2,329	1,439
Kelty Hearts	547	501	–8.32	854	317
Montrose	729	726	–0.42	1,792	367
Queen of the South	1,143	1,233	+7.88	2,702	775
Stenhousemuir	631	585	–7.26	764	336

WILLIAM HILL LEAGUE TWO ATTENDANCES

	Average Gate			Season 2024–25	
	2023–24	*2024–25*	*+/–%*	*Highest*	*Lowest*
Bonnyrigg Rose	733	619	–15.48	816	446
Clyde	650	677	+4.17	810	419
East Fife	560	728	+30.04	1,106	564
Edinburgh C	447	297	–33.66	476	226
Elgin C	661	759	+14.81	1,356	439
Forfar Ath	566	627	+10.76	995	427
Peterhead	695	728	+4.65	1,979	483
Stirling Alb	1,091	684	–37.25	865	444
Stranraer	395	515	+30.50	852	381
The Spartans	536	488	–9.10	743	289

SCOTTISH LEAGUE HONOURS 1890–2025

=Until 1921–22 season teams were equal if level on points, unless a play-off took place. §Not promoted after play-offs.
*Won or placed on goal average (ratio), goal difference or most goals scored (goal average from 1921–22 until 1971–72
when it was replaced by goal difference). No official competition during 1939–46; regional leagues operated.

DIVISION 1 (1890–91 to 1974–75) – TIER 1

Tier	Season	Max Pts	First	Pts	Second	Pts	Third	Pts
1	1890–91	36	Dumbarton=	29	Rangers=	29	Celtic	21
	Dumbarton and Rangers held title jointly after indecisive play-off ended 2-2. Celtic deducted 4 points for fielding an ineligible player.							
1	1891–92	44	Dumbarton	37	Celtic	35	Hearts	34
1	1892–93	36	Celtic	29	Rangers	28	St Mirren	20
1	1893–94	36	Celtic	29	Hearts	26	St Bernard's	23
1	1894–95	36	Hearts	31	Celtic	26	Rangers	22
1	1895–96	36	Celtic	30	Rangers	26	Hibernian	24
1	1896–97	36	Hearts	28	Hibernian	26	Rangers	25
1	1897–98	36	Celtic	33	Rangers	29	Hibernian	22
1	1898–99	36	Rangers	36	Hearts	26	Celtic	24
1	1899–1900	36	Rangers	32	Celtic	25	Hibernian	24
1	1900–01	40	Rangers	35	Celtic	29	Hibernian	25
1	1901–02	36	Rangers	28	Celtic	26	Hearts	22
1	1902–03	44	Hibernian	37	Dundee	31	Rangers	29
1	1903–04	52	Third Lanark	43	Hearts	39	Celtic / Rangers=	38
1	1904–05	52	Celtic=	41	Rangers=	41	Third Lanark	35
	Celtic won title after beating Rangers 2-1 in play-off.							
1	1905–06	60	Celtic	49	Hearts	43	Airdrieonians	38
1	1906–07	68	Celtic	55	Dundee	48	Rangers	45
1	1907–08	68	Celtic	55	Falkirk	51	Rangers	50
1	1908–09	68	Celtic	51	Dundee	50	Clyde	48
1	1909–10	68	Celtic	54	Falkirk	52	Rangers	46
1	1910–11	68	Rangers	52	Aberdeen	48	Falkirk	44
1	1911–12	68	Rangers	51	Celtic	45	Clyde	42
1	1912–13	68	Rangers	53	Celtic	49	Hearts / Airdrieonians=	41
1	1913–14	76	Celtic	65	Rangers	59	Hearts / Morton=	54
1	1914–15	76	Celtic	65	Hearts	61	Rangers	50
1	1915–16	76	Celtic	67	Rangers	56	Morton	51
1	1916–17	76	Celtic	64	Morton	54	Rangers	53
1	1917–18	68	Rangers	56	Celtic	55	Kilmarnock / Morton=	43
1	1918–19	68	Celtic	58	Rangers	57	Morton	47
1	1919–20	84	Rangers	71	Celtic	68	Motherwell	57
1	1920–21	84	Rangers	76	Celtic	66	Hearts	50
1	1921–22	84	Celtic	67	Rangers	66	Raith R	51
1	1922–23	76	Rangers	55	Airdrieonians	50	Celtic	46
1	1923–24	76	Rangers	59	Airdrieonians	50	Celtic	46
1	1924–25	76	Rangers	60	Airdrieonians	57	Hibernian	52
1	1925–26	76	Celtic	58	Airdrieonians*	50	Hearts	50
1	1926–27	76	Rangers	56	Motherwell	51	Celtic	49
1	1927–28	76	Rangers	60	Celtic*	55	Motherwell	55
1	1928–29	76	Rangers	67	Celtic	51	Motherwell	50
1	1929–30	76	Rangers	60	Motherwell	55	Aberdeen	53
1	1930–31	76	Rangers	60	Celtic	58	Motherwell	56
1	1931–32	76	Motherwell	66	Rangers	61	Celtic	48
1	1932–33	76	Rangers	62	Motherwell	59	Hearts	50
1	1933–34	76	Rangers	66	Motherwell	62	Celtic	47
1	1934–35	76	Rangers	55	Celtic	52	Hearts	50
1	1935–36	76	Celtic	66	Rangers*	61	Aberdeen	61
1	1936–37	76	Rangers	61	Aberdeen	54	Celtic	52
1	1937–38	76	Celtic	61	Hearts	58	Rangers	49
1	1938–39	76	Rangers	59	Celtic	48	Aberdeen	46
1	1946–47	60	Rangers	46	Hibernian	44	Aberdeen	39
1	1947–48	60	Hibernian	48	Rangers	46	Partick Thistle	36
1	1948–49	60	Rangers	46	Dundee	45	Hibernian	39
1	1949–50	60	Rangers	50	Hibernian	49	Hearts	43
1	1950–51	60	Hibernian	48	Rangers*	38	Dundee	38
1	1951–52	60	Hibernian	45	Rangers	41	East Fife	37
1	1952–53	60	Rangers*	43	Hibernian	43	East Fife	39
1	1953–54	60	Celtic	43	Hearts	38	Partick Thistle	35
1	1954–55	60	Aberdeen	49	Celtic	46	Rangers	41
1	1955–56	68	Rangers	52	Aberdeen	46	Hearts*	45
1	1956–57	68	Rangers	55	Hearts	53	Kilmarnock	42
1	1957–58	68	Hearts	62	Rangers	49	Celtic	46

1	1958–59	68	Rangers	50	Hearts	48	Motherwell	44
1	1959–60	68	Hearts	54	Kilmarnock	50	Rangers*	42
1	1960–61	68	Rangers	51	Kilmarnock	50	Third Lanark	42
1	1961–62	68	Dundee	54	Rangers	51	Celtic	46
1	1962–63	68	Rangers	57	Kilmarnock	48	Partick Thistle	46
1	1963–64	68	Rangers	55	Kilmarnock	49	Celtic*	47
1	1964–65	68	Kilmarnock*	50	Hearts	50	Dunfermline Ath	49
1	1965–66	68	Celtic	57	Rangers	55	Kilmarnock	45
1	1966–67	68	Celtic	58	Rangers	55	Clyde	46
1	1967–68	68	Celtic	63	Rangers	61	Hibernian	45
1	1968–69	68	Celtic	54	Rangers	49	Dunfermline Ath	45
1	1969–70	68	Celtic	57	Rangers	45	Hibernian	44
1	1970–71	68	Celtic	56	Aberdeen	54	St Johnstone	44
1	1971–72	68	Celtic	60	Aberdeen	50	Rangers	44
1	1972–73	68	Celtic	57	Rangers	56	Hibernian	45
1	1973–74	68	Celtic	53	Hibernian	49	Rangers	48
1	1974–75	68	Rangers	56	Hibernian	49	Celtic*	45

PREMIER DIVISION (1975–76 to 1997–98)

1	1975–76	72	Rangers	54	Celtic	48	Hibernian	43
1	1976–77	72	Celtic	55	Rangers	46	Aberdeen	43
1	1977–78	72	Rangers	55	Aberdeen	53	Dundee U	40
1	1978–79	72	Celtic	48	Rangers	45	Dundee U	44
1	1979–80	72	Aberdeen	48	Celtic	47	St Mirren	42
1	1980–81	72	Celtic	56	Aberdeen	49	Rangers*	44
1	1981–82	72	Celtic	55	Aberdeen	53	Rangers	43
1	1982–83	72	Dundee U	56	Celtic*	55	Aberdeen	55
1	1983–84	72	Aberdeen	57	Celtic	50	Dundee U	47
1	1984–85	72	Aberdeen	59	Celtic	52	Dundee U	47
1	1985–86	72	Celtic*	50	Hearts	50	Dundee U	47
1	1986–87	88	Rangers	69	Celtic	63	Dundee U	60
1	1987–88	88	Celtic	72	Hearts	62	Rangers	60
1	1988–89	72	Rangers	56	Aberdeen	50	Celtic	46
1	1989–90	72	Rangers	51	Aberdeen*	44	Hearts	44
1	1990–91	72	Rangers	55	Aberdeen	53	Celtic*	41
1	1991–92	88	Rangers	72	Hearts	63	Celtic	62
1	1992–93	88	Rangers	73	Aberdeen	64	Celtic	60
1	1993–94	88	Rangers	58	Aberdeen	55	Motherwell	54
1	1994–95	108	Rangers	69	Motherwell	54	Hibernian	53
1	1995–96	108	Rangers	87	Celtic	83	Aberdeen*	55
1	1996–97	108	Rangers	80	Celtic	75	Dundee U	60
1	1997–98	108	Celtic	74	Rangers	72	Hearts	67

PREMIER LEAGUE (1998–99 to 2012–13)

1	1998–99	108	Rangers	77	Celtic	71	St Johnstone	57
1	1999–2000	108	Rangers	90	Celtic	69	Hearts	54
1	2000–01	114	Celtic	97	Rangers	82	Hibernian	66
1	2001–02	114	Celtic	103	Rangers	85	Livingston	58
1	2002–03	114	Rangers*	97	Celtic	97	Hearts	63
1	2003–04	114	Celtic	98	Rangers	81	Hearts	68
1	2004–05	114	Rangers	93	Celtic	92	Hibernian*	61
1	2005–06	114	Celtic	91	Hearts	74	Rangers	73
1	2006–07	114	Celtic	84	Rangers	72	Aberdeen	65
1	2007–08	114	Celtic	89	Rangers	86	Motherwell	60
1	2008–09	114	Rangers	86	Celtic	82	Hearts	59
1	2009–10	114	Rangers	87	Celtic	81	Dundee U	63
1	2010–11	114	Rangers	93	Celtic	92	Hearts	63
1	2011–12	114	Celtic	93	Rangers	73	Motherwell	62

Rangers deducted 10 points for entering administration.

1	2012–13	114	Celtic	79	Motherwell	63	St Johnstone	56

SPFL SCOTTISH PREMIERSHIP (2013–14 to 2024–25)

1	2013–14	114	Celtic	99	Motherwell	70	Aberdeen	68
1	2014–15	114	Celtic	92	Aberdeen	75	Inverness CT	65
1	2015–16	114	Celtic	86	Aberdeen	71	Hearts	65
1	2016–17	114	Celtic	106	Aberdeen	76	Rangers	67
1	2017–18	114	Celtic	82	Aberdeen	73	Rangers	70
1	2018–19	114	Celtic	87	Rangers	78	Kilmarnock*	67
1	2019–20	114	Celtic	80	Rangers	67	Motherwell	46

The 2019–20 season was curtailed due to the COVID-19 pandemic and positions awarded on a points-per-game basis.

1	2020–21	114	Rangers	102	Celtic	77	Hibernian	63
1	2021–22	114	Celtic	93	Rangers	89	Hearts	61
1	2022–23	114	Celtic	99	Rangers	92	Aberdeen	57
1	2023–24	114	Celtic	93	Rangers	85	Hearts	64
1	2024–25	114	Celtic	92	Rangers	75	Hibernian	58

DIVISION 2 (1893–93 to 1974–75) – TIER 2

Tier	Season	Max Pts	First	Pts	Second	Pts	Third	Pts
2	1893–94	36	Hibernian	29	Cowlairs	27	Clyde	24
2	1894–95	36	Hibernian	30	Motherwell	22	Port Glasgow Ath	20
2	1895–96	36	Abercorn	27	Leith Ath	23	Renton / Kilmarnock=	21
2	1896–97	36	Partick Thistle	31	Leith Ath	27	Airdrieonians / Kilmarnock=	21
2	1897–98	36	Kilmarnock	29	Port Glasgow Ath	25	Morton	22
2	1898–99	36	Kilmarnock	32	Leith Ath	27	Port Glasgow Ath	25
2	1899–1900	36	Partick Thistle	29	Morton	28	Port Glasgow Ath	20
2	1900–01	36	St Bernard's	26	Airdrieonians	23	Abercorn	21
2	1901–02	44	Port Glasgow Ath	32	Partick Thistle	30	Motherwell	26
2	1902–03	44	Airdrieonians	35	Motherwell	28	Ayr U / Leith Ath=	27
2	1903–04	44	Hamilton A	37	Clyde	29	Ayr U	28
2	1904–05	44	Clyde	32	Falkirk	28	Hamilton A	27
2	1905–06	44	Leith Ath	34	Clyde	31	Albion R	27
2	1906–07	44	St Bernard's	32	Vale of Leven=	27	Arthurlie=	27
2	1907–08	44	Raith R	30	Dumbarton=	27	Ayr U=	27

Dumbarton deducted 2 points for registration irregularities.

Tier	Season	Max Pts	First	Pts	Second	Pts	Third	Pts
2	1908–09	44	Abercorn	31	Raith R=	28	Vale of Leven=	28
2	1909–10	44	Leith Ath=	33	Raith R=	33	St Bernard's	27

Leith Ath and Raith R held title jointly, no play-off game played.

Tier	Season	Max Pts	First	Pts	Second	Pts	Third	Pts
2	1910–11	44	Dumbarton	31	Ayr U	27	Albion R	25
2	1911–12	44	Ayr U	35	Abercorn	30	Dumbarton	27
2	1912–13	52	Ayr U	34	Dunfermline Ath	33	East Stirlingshire	32
2	1913–14	44	Cowdenbeath	31	Albion R	27	Dunfermline Ath / Dundee Hibernian=	26
2	1914–15	52	Cowdenbeath=	37	St Bernard's=	37	Leith Ath=	37

Cowdenbeath won title after a round robin tournament between the three tied clubs.

Tier	Season	Max Pts	First	Pts	Second	Pts	Third	Pts
2	1921–22	76	Alloa Ath	60	Cowdenbeath	47	Armadale	45
2	1922–23	76	Queen's Park	57	Clydebank	50	St Johnstone	48

Clydebank and St Johnstone both deducted 2 points for fielding an ineligible player.

Tier	Season	Max Pts	First	Pts	Second	Pts	Third	Pts
2	1923–24	76	St Johnstone	56	Cowdenbeath	55	Bathgate	44
2	1924–25	76	Dundee U	50	Clydebank	48	Clyde	47
2	1925–26	76	Dunfermline Ath	59	Clyde	53	Ayr U	52
2	1926–27	76	Bo'ness	56	Raith R	49	Clydebank	45
2	1927–28	76	Ayr U	54	Third Lanark	45	King's Park	44
2	1928–29	72	Dundee U	51	Morton	50	Arbroath	47
2	1929–30	76	Leith Ath*	57	East Fife	57	Albion R	54
2	1930–31	76	Third Lanark	61	Dundee U	50	Dunfermline Ath	47
2	1931–32	76	East Stirlingshire*	55	St Johnstone	55	Raith R*	46
2	1932–33	68	Hibernian	54	Queen of the South	49	Dunfermline Ath	47

Armadale and Bo'ness were expelled for failing to meet match guarantees. Their records were expunged.

Tier	Season	Max Pts	First	Pts	Second	Pts	Third	Pts
2	1933–34	68	Albion R	45	Dunfermline Ath*	44	Arbroath	44
2	1934–35	68	Third Lanark	52	Arbroath	50	St Bernard's	47
2	1935–36	68	Falkirk	59	St Mirren	52	Morton	48
2	1936–37	68	Ayr U	54	Morton	51	St Bernard's	48
2	1937–38	68	Raith R	59	Albion R	48	Airdrieonians	47
2	1938–39	68	Cowdenbeath	60	Alloa Ath*	48	East Fife	48
2	1946–47	52	Dundee	45	Airdrieonians	42	East Fife	31
2	1947–48	60	East Fife	53	Albion R	42	Hamilton A	40
2	1948–49	60	Raith R*	42	Stirling Alb	42	Airdrieonians*	41
2	1949–50	60	Morton	47	Airdrieonians	44	Dunfermline Ath*	36
2	1950–51	60	Queen of the South*	45	Stirling Alb	45	Ayr U*	36
2	1951–52	60	Clyde	44	Falkirk	43	Ayr U	39
2	1952–53	60	Stirling Alb	44	Hamilton A	43	Queen's Park	37
2	1953–54	60	Motherwell	45	Kilmarnock	42	Third Lanark*	36
2	1954–55	60	Airdrieonians	46	Dunfermline Ath	42	Hamilton A	39
2	1955–56	72	Queen's Park	54	Ayr U	51	St Johnstone	49
2	1956–57	72	Clyde	64	Third Lanark	51	Cowdenbeath	45
2	1957–58	72	Stirling Alb	55	Dunfermline Ath	53	Arbroath	47
2	1958–59	72	Ayr U	60	Arbroath	51	Stenhousemuir	46
2	1959–60	72	St Johnstone	53	Dundee U	50	Queen of the South	49
2	1960–61	72	Stirling Alb	55	Falkirk	54	Stenhousemuir	50
2	1961–62	72	Clyde	54	Queen of the South	53	Morton	44
2	1962–63	72	St Johnstone	55	East Stirlingshire	49	Morton	48
2	1963–64	72	Morton	67	Clyde	53	Arbroath	46
2	1964–65	72	Stirling Alb	59	Hamilton A	50	Queen of the South	45
2	1965–66	72	Ayr U	53	Airdrieonians	50	Queen of the South	47
2	1966–67	76	Morton	69	Raith R	58	Arbroath	57
2	1967–68	72	St Mirren	62	Arbroath	53	East Fife	49
2	1968–69	72	Motherwell	64	Ayr U	53	East Fife*	48
2	1969–70	72	Falkirk	56	Cowdenbeath	55	Queen of the South	50

2	1970–71	72	Partick Thistle	56	East Fife	51	Arbroath	46
2	1971–72	72	Dumbarton*	52	Arbroath	52	Stirling Alb*	50
2	1972–73	72	Clyde	56	Dunfermline Ath	52	Raith R*	47
2	1973–74	72	Airdrieonians	60	Kilmarnock	58	Hamilton A	55
2	1974–75	76	Falkirk	54	Queen of the South*	53	Montrose	53

Elected to First Division: 1894 Clyde; 1895 Hibernian; 1896 Abercorn; 1897 Partick Thistle; 1899 Kilmarnock; 1900 Morton and Partick Thistle; 1902 Port Glasgow and Partick Thistle; 1903 Airdrieonians and Motherwell; 1905 Falkirk and Aberdeen; 1906 Clyde and Hamilton A; 1910 Raith R; 1913 Ayr U and Dumbarton.

FIRST DIVISION (1975–76 to 2012–13)

2	1975–76	52	Partick Thistle	41	Kilmarnock	35	Montrose	30
2	1976–77	78	St Mirren	62	Clydebank	58	Dundee	51
2	1977–78	78	Morton*	58	Hearts	58	Dundee	57
2	1978–79	78	Dundee	55	Kilmarnock*	54	Clydebank	54
2	1979–80	78	Hearts	53	Airdrieonians	51	Ayr U*	44
2	1980–81	78	Hibernian	57	Dundee	52	St Johnstone	51
2	1981–82	78	Motherwell	61	Kilmarnock	51	Hearts	50
2	1982–83	78	St Johnstone	55	Hearts	54	Clydebank	50
2	1983–84	78	Morton	54	Dumbarton	51	Partick Thistle	46
2	1984–85	78	Motherwell	50	Clydebank	48	Falkirk	45
2	1985–86	78	Hamilton A	56	Falkirk	45	Kilmarnock*	44
2	1986–87	88	Morton	57	Dunfermline Ath	56	Dumbarton	53
2	1987–88	88	Hamilton A	56	Meadowbank Thistle	52	Clydebank	49
2	1988–89	78	Dunfermline Ath	54	Falkirk	52	Clydebank	48
2	1989–90	78	St Johnstone	58	Airdrieonians	54	Clydebank	44
2	1990–91	78	Falkirk	54	Airdrieonians	53	Dundee	52
2	1991–92	88	Dundee	58	Partick Thistle*	57	Hamilton A	57
2	1992–93	88	Raith R	65	Kilmarnock	54	Dunfermline Ath	52
2	1993–94	88	Falkirk	66	Dunfermline Ath	65	Airdrieonians	54
2	1994–95	108	Raith R	69	Dunfermline Ath*	68	Dundee	68
2	1995–96	108	Dunfermline Ath	71	Dundee U*	67	Greenock Morton	67
2	1996–97	108	St Johnstone	80	Airdrieonians	60	Dundee*	58
2	1997–98	108	Dundee	70	Falkirk	65	Raith R*	60
2	1998–99	108	Hibernian	89	Falkirk	66	Ayr U	62
2	1999–2000	108	St Mirren	76	Dunfermline Ath	71	Falkirk	68
2	2000–01	108	Livingston	76	Ayr U	69	Falkirk	56
2	2001–02	108	Partick Thistle	66	Airdrieonians	56	Ayr U*	52
2	2002–03	108	Falkirk	81	Clyde	72	St Johnstone	67
2	2003–04	108	Inverness CT	70	Clyde	69	St Johnstone	57
2	2004–05	108	Falkirk	75	St Mirren*	60	Clyde	60
2	2005–06	108	St Mirren	76	St Johnstone	66	Hamilton A	59
2	2006–07	108	Gretna	66	St Johnstone	65	Dundee*	53
2	2007–08	108	Hamilton A	76	Dundee	69	St Johnstone	58
2	2008–09	108	St Johnstone	65	Partick Thistle	55	Dunfermline Ath	51
2	2009–10	108	Inverness CT	73	Dundee	61	Dunfermline Ath	58
2	2010–11	108	Dunfermline Ath	70	Raith R	60	Falkirk	58
2	2011–12	108	Ross Co	79	Dundee	55	Falkirk	52
2	2012–13	108	Partick Thistle	78	Greenock Morton	67	Falkirk	53

SPFL SCOTTISH CHAMPIONSHIP (2013–14 to 2024–25)

2	2013–14	108	Dundee	69	Hamilton A	67	Falkirk§	66
2	2014–15	108	Hearts	91	Hibernian§	70	Rangers§	67
2	2015–16	108	Rangers	81	Falkirk*§	70	Hibernian§	70
2	2016–17	108	Hibernian	71	Falkirk§	60	Dundee U§	57
2	2017–18	108	St Mirren	74	Livingston	62	Dundee U§	61
2	2018–19	108	Ross Co	71	Dundee U§	65	Inverness CT§	56
2	2019–20	41	Dundee U	59	Inverness CT	45	Dundee	41

The 2019–20 season was curtailed due to the COVID-19 pandemic and positions awarded on a points-per-game basis.

2	2020–21	81	Hearts	57	Dundee	45	Raith R§	43
2	2021–22	108	Kilmarnock	67	Arbroath§	65	Inverness CT§	59
2	2022–23	108	Dundee	63	Ayr U*§	58	Queen's Park*§	58
2	2023–24	108	Dundee U	75	Raith R§	69	Partick Thistle§	55
2	2024–25	108	Falkirk	73	Livingston	70	Ayr U§	63

SECOND DIVISION (1975–76 to 2012–13) – TIER 3

Tier	Season	Max Pts	First	Pts	Second	Pts	Third	Pts
3	1975–76	52	Clydebank*	40	Raith R	40	Alloa Ath	35
3	1976–77	78	Stirling Alb	55	Alloa Ath	51	Dunfermline Ath	50
3	1977–78	78	Clyde*	53	Raith R	53	Dunfermline Ath*	48
3	1978–79	78	Berwick Rangers	54	Dunfermline Ath	52	Falkirk	50
3	1979–80	78	Falkirk	50	East Stirlingshire	49	Forfar Ath	46
3	1980–81	78	Queen's Park	50	Queen of the South	46	Cowdenbeath	45
3	1981–82	78	Clyde	59	Alloa Ath*	50	Arbroath	50
3	1982–83	78	Brechin C	55	Meadowbank Thistle	54	Arbroath	49
3	1983–84	78	Forfar Ath	63	East Fife	47	Berwick Rangers	43
3	1984–85	78	Montrose	53	Alloa Ath	50	Dunfermline Ath	49
3	1985–86	78	Dunfermline Ath	57	Queen of the South	55	Meadowbank Thistle	49
3	1986–87	78	Meadowbank Thistle	55	Raith R*	52	Stirling Alb*	52

3	1987–88	78	Ayr U	61	St Johnstone	59	Queen's Park	51
3	1988–89	78	Albion R	50	Alloa Ath	45	Brechin C	43
3	1989–90	78	Brechin C	49	Kilmarnock	48	Stirling Alb	47
3	1990–91	78	Stirling Alb	54	Montrose	46	Cowdenbeath	45
3	1991–92	78	Dumbarton	52	Cowdenbeath	51	Alloa Ath	50
3	1992–93	78	Clyde	54	Brechin C*	53	Stranraer	53
3	1993–94	78	Stranraer	56	Berwick Rangers	48	Stenhousemuir*	47
3	1994–95	108	Greenock Morton	64	Dumbarton	60	Stirling Alb	58
3	1995–96	108	Stirling Alb	81	East Fife	67	Berwick Rangers	60
3	1996–97	108	Ayr U	77	Hamilton A	74	Livingston	64
3	1997–98	108	Stranraer	61	Clydebank	60	Livingston	59
3	1998–99	108	Livingston	77	Inverness CT	72	Clyde	53
3	1999–2000	108	Clyde	65	Alloa Ath	64	Ross Co	62
3	2000–01	108	Partick Thistle	75	Arbroath	58	Berwick Rangers*	54
3	2001–02	108	Queen of the South	67	Alloa Ath	59	Forfar Ath	53
3	2002–03	108	Raith R	59	Brechin C	55	Airdrie U	54
3	2003–04	108	Airdrie U	70	Hamilton A	62	Dumbarton	60
3	2004–05	108	Brechin C	72	Stranraer	63	Greenock Morton	62
3	2005–06	108	Gretna	88	Greenock Morton§	70	Peterhead*§	57
3	2006–07	108	Greenock Morton	77	Stirling Alb	69	Raith R§	62
3	2007–08	108	Ross Co	73	Airdrie U	66	Raith R§	60
3	2008–09	108	Raith R	76	Ayr U	74	Brechin C§	62
3	2009–10	108	Stirling Alb*	65	Alloa Ath§	65	Cowdenbeath	59
3	2010–11	108	Livingston	82	Ayr U*	59	Forfar Ath§	59
3	2011–12	108	Cowdenbeath	71	Arbroath§	63	Dumbarton	58
3	2012–13	108	Queen of the South	92	Alloa Ath	67	Brechin C§	61

SPFL SCOTTISH LEAGUE ONE (2013–14 to 2024–25)

3	2013–14	108	Rangers	102	Dunfermline Ath§	63	Stranraer§	51
3	2014–15	108	Greenock Morton	69	Stranraer§	67	Forfar Ath	66
3	2015–16	108	Dunfermline Ath	79	Ayr U	61	Peterhead§	59
3	2016–17	108	Livingston	81	Alloa Ath§	62	Airdrieonians§	52
3	2017–18	108	Ayr U	76	Raith R§	75	Alloa Ath	60
3	2018–19	108	Arbroath	70	Forfar Ath§	63	Raith R§	60
3	2019–20	108	Raith R	53	Falkirk	52	Airdrieonians	48

The 2019–20 season was curtailed due to the COVID-19 pandemic and positions awarded on a points-per-game basis.

3	2020–21	66	Partick Thistle	40	Airdrieonians§	38	Cove Rangers§	36
3	2021–22	108	Cove Rangers	79	Airdrieonians§	72	Montrose§	59
3	2022–23	108	Dunfermline Ath	81	Falkirk§	67	Airdrieonians	60
3	2023–24	108	Falkirk	90	Hamilton A	74	Alloa Ath§	56
3	2024–25	108	Arbroath	64	Cove Rangers§	57	Queen of the South§	55

THIRD DIVISION (1994–95 to 2012–13) – TIER 4

Tier	Season	Max Pts	First	Pts	Second	Pts	Third	Pts
4	1994–95	108	Forfar Ath	80	Montrose	67	Ross Co	60
4	1995–96	108	Livingston	72	Brechin C	63	Inverness CT	57
4	1996–97	108	Inverness CT	76	Forfar Ath*	67	Ross Co	67
4	1997–98	108	Alloa Ath	76	Arbroath	68	Ross Co	67
4	1998–99	108	Ross Co	77	Stenhousemuir	64	Brechin C	59
4	1999–2000	108	Queen's Park	69	Berwick Rangers	66	Forfar Ath	61
4	2000–01	108	Hamilton A*	76	Cowdenbeath	76	Brechin C	72
4	2001–02	108	Brechin C	73	Dumbarton	61	Albion R	59
4	2002–03	108	Greenock Morton	72	East Fife	71	Albion R	70
4	2003–04	108	Stranraer	79	Stirling Alb	77	Gretna	68
4	2004–05	108	Gretna	98	Peterhead	78	Cowdenbeath	51
4	2005–06	108	Cowdenbeath*	76	Berwick Rangers§	76	Stenhousemuir§	73
4	2006–07	108	Berwick Rangers	75	Arbroath§	70	Queen's Park	68
4	2007–08	108	East Fife	88	Stranraer	65	Montrose§	59
4	2008–09	108	Dumbarton	67	Cowdenbeath	63	East Stirlingshire§	61
4	2009–10	108	Livingston	78	Forfar Ath	63	East Stirlingshire§	61
4	2010–11	108	Arbroath	66	Albion R	61	Queen's Park*§	59
4	2011–12	108	Alloa Ath	77	Queen's Park§	63	Stranraer	58
4	2012–13	108	Rangers	83	Peterhead§	59	Queen's Park§	56

SPFL SCOTTISH LEAGUE TWO (2013–14 to 2024–25)

4	2013–14	108	Peterhead	76	Annan Ath§	63	Stirling Alb	57
4	2014–15	108	Albion R	71	Queen's Park§	61	Arbroath§	56
4	2015–16	108	East Fife	62	Elgin C§	59	Clyde§	57
4	2016–17	108	Arbroath	66	Forfar Ath	64	Annan Ath§	58
4	2017–18	108	Montrose	77	Peterhead§	76	Stirling Alb§	55
4	2018–19	108	Peterhead	79	Clyde	74	Edinburgh C§	67
4	2019–20	108	Cove Rangers	68	Edinburgh C	55	Elgin C	43

The 2019–20 season was curtailed due to the COVID-19 pandemic and positions awarded on a points-per-game basis.

4	2020–21	66	Queen's Park	54	Edinburgh C*§	38	Elgin C*§	38
4	2021–22	108	Kelty Hearts	81	Forfar Ath	60	Annan Ath§	59
4	2022–23	108	Stirling Alb	73	Dumbarton§	62	Annan Ath	51
4	2023–24	108	Stenhousemuir	68	Peterhead	60	The Spartans§	58
2	2024–25	108	Peterhead	66	East Fife	65	Edinburgh C§	56

RELEGATED CLUBS

RELEGATED FROM DIVISION I (1921–22 to 1973–74)

1921–22 *Dumbarton, Queen's Park, Clydebank	1951–52 Morton, Stirling Alb
1922–23 Albion R, Alloa Ath	1952–53 Motherwell, Third Lanark
1923–24 Clyde, Clydebank	1953–54 Airdrieonians, Hamilton A
1924–25 Ayr U, Third Lanark	1954–55 *No clubs relegated as league extended to 18 teams*
1925–26 Raith R, Clydebank	1955–56 Clyde, Stirling Alb
1926–27 Morton, Dundee U	1956–57 Dunfermline Ath, Ayr U
1927–28 Bo'ness, Dunfermline Ath	1957–58 East Fife, Queen's Park
1928–29 Third Lanark, Raith R	1958–59 Falkirk, Queen of the South
1929–30 Dundee U, St Johnstone	1959–60 Stirling Alb, Arbroath
1930–31 Hibernian, East Fife	1960–61 Clyde, Ayr U
1931–32 Dundee U, Leith Ath	1961–62 St Johnstone, Stirling Alb
1932–33 Morton, East Stirlingshire	1962–63 Clyde, Raith R
1933–34 Third Lanark, Cowdenbeath	1963–64 Queen of the South, East Stirlingshire
1934–35 St Mirren, Falkirk	1964–65 Airdrieonians, Third Lanark
1935–36 Airdrieonians, Ayr U	1965–66 Morton, Hamilton A
1936–37 Dunfermline Ath, Albion R	1966–67 St Mirren, Ayr U
1937–38 Dundee, Morton	1967–68 Motherwell, Stirling Alb
1938–39 Queen's Park, Raith R	1968–69 Falkirk, Arbroath
1946–47 Kilmarnock, Hamilton A	1969–70 Raith R, Partick Thistle
1947–48 Airdrieonians, Queen's Park	1970–71 St Mirren, Cowdenbeath
1948–49 Morton, Albion R	1971–72 Clyde, Dunfermline Ath
1949–50 Queen of the South, Stirling Alb	1972–73 Kilmarnock, Airdrieonians
1950–51 Clyde, Falkirk	1973–74 East Fife, Falkirk

Season 1921–22 – only 1 club promoted, 3 clubs relegated.

RELEGATED FROM PREMIER DIVISION (1974–75 to 1997–98)

1974–75 *No relegation due to League reorganisation*	1986–87 Clydebank, Hamilton A
1975–76 Dundee, St Johnstone	1987–88 Falkirk, Dunfermline Ath, Morton
1976–77 Hearts, Kilmarnock	1988–89 Hamilton A
1977–78 Ayr U, Clydebank	1989–90 Dundee
1978–79 Hearts, Motherwell	1990–91 *No clubs relegated*
1979–80 Dundee, Hibernian	1991–92 St Mirren, Dunfermline Ath
1980–81 Kilmarnock, Hearts	1992–93 Falkirk, Airdrieonians
1981–82 Partick Thistle, Airdrieonians	1993–94 St Johnstone, Raith R, Dundee
1982–83 Morton, Kilmarnock	1994–95 Dundee U
1983–84 St Johnstone, Motherwell	1995–96 Partick Thistle, Falkirk
1984–85 Dumbarton, Morton	1996–97 Raith R
1985–86 *No relegation due to League reorganisation*	1997–98 Hibernian

RELEGATED FROM PREMIER LEAGUE (1998–99 to 2012–13)

1998–99 Dunfermline Ath	2006–07 Dunfermline Ath
1999–2000 *No relegation due to League reorganisation*	2007–08 Gretna
2000–01 St Mirren	2008–09 Inverness CT
2001–02 St Johnstone	2009–10 Falkirk
2002–03 *No clubs relegated*	2010–11 Hamilton A
2003–04 Partick Thistle	2011–12 Dunfermline Ath, Rangers (demoted to Third Division)
2004–05 Dundee	
2005–06 Livingston	2012–13 Dundee

RELEGATED FROM SPFL SCOTTISH PREMIERSHIP (2013–14 to 2024–25)

2013–14 Hibernian, Hearts	2019–20 Hearts
2014–15 St Mirren	2020–21 Hamilton A, Kilmarnock
2015–16 Dundee U	2021–22 Dundee
2016–17 Inverness CT	2022–23 Dundee U
2017–18 Ross Co, Partick Thistle	2023–24 Livingston
2018–19 Dundee	2024–25 Ross Co, St Johnstone

RELEGATED FROM FIRST DIVISION (1975–76 to 2012–13)

1975–76 Dunfermline Ath, Clyde	1988–89 Kilmarnock, Queen of the South
1976–77 Raith R, Falkirk	1989–90 Albion R, Alloa Ath
1977–78 Alloa Ath, East Fife	1990–91 Clyde, Brechin C
1978–79 Montrose, Queen of the South	1991–92 Montrose, Forfar Ath
1979–80 Arbroath, Clyde	1992–93 Meadowbank Thistle, Cowdenbeath
1980–81 Stirling Alb, Berwick Rangers	1993–94 Dumbarton, Stirling Alb, Clyde, Morton, Brechin C
1981–82 East Stirlingshire, Queen of the South	1994–95 Ayr U, Stranraer
1982–83 Dunfermline Ath, Queen's Park	1995–96 Hamilton A, Dumbarton
1983–84 Raith R, Alloa Ath	1996–97 Clydebank, East Fife
1984–85 Meadowbank Thistle, St Johnstone	1997–98 Partick Thistle, Stirling Alb
1985–86 Ayr U, Alloa Ath	1998–99 Hamilton A, Stranraer
1986–87 Brechin C, Montrose	1999–2000 Clydebank
1987–88 East Fife, Dumbarton	

2000–01 Greenock Morton, Alloa Ath	2007–08 Stirling Alb
2001–02 Raith R	2008–09 Livingston *(for breaching rules)*, Clyde
2002–03 Alloa Ath, Arbroath	2009–10 Airdrie U, Ayr U
2003–04 Ayr U, Brechin C	2010–11 Cowdenbeath, Stirling Alb
2004–05 Partick Thistle, Raith R	2011–12 Ayr U, Queen of the South
2005–06 Stranraer, Brechin C	2012–13 Dunfermline Ath, Airdrie U
2006–07 Airdrie U, Ross Co	

RELEGATED FROM SPFL SCOTTISH CHAMPIONSHIP (2013–14 to 2024–25)

2013–14 Greenock Morton	2019–20 Partick Thistle
2014–15 Cowdenbeath	2020–21 Alloa Ath
2015–16 Livingston, Alloa Ath	2021–22 Dunfermline Ath, Queen of the South
2016–17 Raith R, Ayr U	2022–23 Hamilton A, Cove Rangers
2017–18 Brechin C, Dumbarton	2023–24 Inverness CT, Arbroath
2018–19 Falkirk	2024–25 Hamilton A

RELEGATED FROM SECOND DIVISION (1993–94 to 2012–13)

1993–94 Alloa Ath, Forfar Ath, East Stirlingshire, Montrose, Queen's Park, Arbroath, Albion R, Cowdenbeath
    (all relegated to new third division for 1994–95 season)

1994–95 Meadowbank Thistle, Brechin C	2004–05 Arbroath, Berwick Rangers
1995–96 Forfar Ath, Montrose	2005–06 Dumbarton
1996–97 Dumbarton, Berwick Rangers	2006–07 Stranraer, Forfar Ath
1997–98 Stenhousemuir, Brechin C	2007–08 Cowdenbeath, Berwick Rangers
1998–99 East Fife, Forfar Ath	2008–09 Queen's Park, Stranraer
1999–2000 Hamilton A *(after being deducted 15 points)*	2009–10 Arbroath, Clyde
2000–01 Queen's Park, Stirling Alb	2010–11 Alloa Ath, Peterhead
2001–02 Greenock Morton	2011–12 Stirling Alb
2002–03 Stranraer, Cowdenbeath	2012–13 Albion R
2003–04 East Fife, Stenhousemuir	

RELEGATED FROM SPFL SCOTTISH LEAGUE ONE (2013–14 to 2024–25)

2013–14 East Fife, Arbroath	2019–20 Stranraer
2014–15 Stirling Alb	2020–21 Forfar Ath
2015–16 Cowdenbeath, Forfar Ath	2021–22 Dumbarton, East Fife
2016–17 Peterhead, Stenhousemuir	2022–23 Clyde, Peterhead
2017–18 Albion R, Queen's Park	2023–24 Stirling Alb, Edinburgh C
2018–19 Stenhousemuir, Brechin C	2024–25 Dumbarton, Annan Ath

RELEGATED FROM SPFL SCOTTISH LEAGUE TWO (2015–16 to 2024–25)

2015–16 East Stirlingshire (replaced by Edinburgh C)	2020–21 Brechin C (replaced by Kelty Hearts)
2016–17 None	2021–22 Cowdenbeath (replaced by Bonnyrigg Rose Ath)
2017–18 None	2022–23 Albion R (replaced by The Spartans)
2018–19 Berwick Rangers (replaced by Cove Rangers)	2023–24 None
2019–20 None	2024–25 Bonnyrigg Rose (replaced by East Kilbride)

SCOTTISH LEAGUE CHAMPIONSHIP WINS

Celtic 55, Rangers 55, Aberdeen 4, Hearts 4, Hibernian 4, Dumbarton 2, Dundee 1, Dundee U 1, Kilmarnock 1, Motherwell 1, Third Lanark 1.

The totals for Rangers and Dumbarton each include the shared championship of 1890–91.

Since the formation of the Scottish Football League in 1890, there have been periodic reorganisations of the leagues to allow for expansion, improve competition and commercial aspects of the game. The table below lists the league names by tier and chronology. This table can be used to assist when studying the records.

Tier	Division		Tier	Division	
1	Scottish League Division I	1890–1939	3	Scottish League Division III	1923–1926
	Scottish League Division A	1946–1956		Scottish League Division C	1946–1949
	Scottish League Division I	1956–1975		Second Division	1975–2013
	Premier Division	1975–1998		SPFL League One	2013–
	Scottish Premier League	1998–2013			
	SPFL Premiership	2013–	4	Third Division	1994–2013
				SPFL League Two	2013–
2	Scottish League Division II	1893–1939			
	Scottish League Division B	1946–1956			
	Scottish League Division II	1956–1975			
	First Division	1975–2013			
	SPFL Championship	2013–			

In 2013–14 the SPFL introduced play-offs to determine a second promotion/relegation place for the Premiership, Championship and League One.
    The team finishing second bottom of the Premiership plays two legs against the team from the Championship that won the eliminator games played between the teams finishing second, third and fourth.
    For both the Championship and League One, the team finishing second bottom joins the teams from second, third and fourth places of the lower league in a play-off series of two-legged semi-finals and finals.
    In 2014–15 a play-off was introduced for promotion/relegation from League Two. The team finishing bottom of League Two plays two legs against the victors of the eliminator games between the winners of the Highland and Lowland leagues.

SCOTTISH LEAGUE PLAY-OFFS 2024–25

■ *Denotes player sent off.*

PREMIERSHIP QUARTER-FINAL FIRST LEG
Tuesday, 6 May 2025
Partick Thistle (0) 0
Ayr U (0) 1 *(Murphy 55)*   5250
Partick Thistle: (4231) Mitchell; Megwa, McBeth, Ashcroft, O'Reilly; Bannigan, Turner; Lawless, Crawford (Ablade 61), Fitzpatrick (Stanway 84); Graham.
Ayr U: (343) Clarke; McAllister (Watret 10), Agbaire, McMann; McKenzie, Dempsey, Rus (Walker 71), Reading; McLennan, Oakley (Main 77), Murphy (Henderson 76).
Referee: David Dickinson.

PREMIERSHIP QUARTER-FINAL SECOND LEG
Friday, 9 May 2025
Ayr U (0) 0
Partick Thistle (1) 2 *(Graham 6, 88)*   5308
Ayr U: (3421) Clarke; Watret (Walker 90), Agbaire, McMann; McKenzie (Main 56), Dempsey, Rus (Henderson 56), Reading; McLennan, Murphy; Oakley.
Partick Thistle: (352) Mitchell; Megwa, Ashcroft, McBeth; Turner (Mackenzie 40), Crawford, Bannigan, Stanway (Jakubiak 83), Low; Fitzpatrick, Graham.
Partick Thistle won 2-1 on aggregate.
Referee: Nick Walsh.

PREMIERSHIP SEMI-FINAL FIRST LEG
Tuesday, 13 May 2025
Partick Thistle (0) 0
Livingston (1) 2 *(Pitman 39, Wilson 52)*   5470
Partick Thistle: (3412) Mitchell; McBeth (Jakubiak 46), Ashcroft (Mackenzie 88), O'Reilly; Megwa, Crawford, Bannigan (Stanway 66), Low; Chalmers; Graham, Fitzpatrick (Lawless 65).
Livingston: (433) Prior; Brandon (Finlayson 66), McGowan, Wilson, Fraser; Pitman, Tait, Kelly; Smith (Yengi 63), Muirhead (May 62), Montano (Shinnie 79).
Referee: Don Robertson.

PREMIERSHIP SEMI-FINAL SECOND LEG
Friday, 16 May 2025
Livingston (1) 2 *(Brandon 40, May 67)*
Partick Thistle (0) 0   3432
Livingston: (433) Prior; Brandon (Finlayson 46), McGowan, Wilson, Fraser; Pitman (McAlear 71), Tait, Kelly; Smith (May 59), Muirhead (Shinnie 46), Montano (Yengi 90).
Partick Thistle: (4231) Mitchell; Megwa, McBeth, O'Reilly, Bannigan (Dolan 84); Crawford, Stanway (Mackenzie 72); Lawless, Chalmers, Fitzpatrick (Jakubiak 65); Graham.
Livingston won 4-0 on aggregate.
Referee: Kevin Clancy.

PREMIERSHIP FINAL FIRST LEG
Thursday, 22 May 2025
Livingston (1) 1 *(Wilson 45)*
Ross Co (0) 1 *(Hale 90 (pen))*   2643
Livingston: (433) Prior; Brandon, McGowan, Wilson, Fraser; Pitman, Tait (Finlayson 61), Kelly; Smith, Muirhead (May 74), Montano (Yengi 82).
Ross Co: (3412) Amissah; Wright, Nightingale, Campbell; Efete (Smith 70), Kenneh, Randall, Ashworth (Harmon 70); Nisbet; Samuel (White 60), Hale.
Referee: John Beaton.

PREMIERSHIP FINAL SECOND LEG
Monday, 26 May 2025
Ross Co (2) 2 *(Nisbet 7, Hale 24)*
Livingston (1) 4 *(Smith 39, Wilson 57, Muirhead 61, Yengi 90)*   4138
Ross Co: (3412) Amissah; Wright, Nightingale (Phillips 81), Campbell; Efete (Samuel 67), Kenneh, Randall, Harmon (Ashworth 54); Nisbet; White, Hale.
Livingston: (433) Prior; Finlayson, McGowan, Wilson, Fraser; Pitman, Brandon, Kelly (Tait 85); Smith (Nottingham 85), Muirhead (May 77), Montano (Yengi 72).
Livingston won 5-3 on aggregate.
Referee: Nick Walsh.

CHAMPIONSHIP SEMI-FINALS FIRST LEG
Tuesday, 6 May 2025
Queen of the South (0) 0
Cove R (0) 0   1784
Queen of the South: (3421) Stewart; Hannah, Hewitt (Charters 66), Douglas; Macintyre, Lyon, Cochrane (O'Donnell 86), Smith; Kennedy, Allan (Bryden 66); Brooks (Luissint 79).
Cove R: (442) Suman; Doyle, Gillingham, Darge, Harrington; Lobban, Marshall, Yule, Emslie; Fyvie (Glass 43), Megginson.
Referee: Ryan Lee.

Stenhousemuir (0) 1 *(Aitken M 89 (pen))*
Airdrieonians (2) 3 *(McGrattan 21, 29, Mochrie 51)* 1458
Stenhousemuir: (4231) Jamieson D; Ewen, Buchanan, Banner, Meechan; Andersen, Wedderburn (Yates 76); McLuckie (Tomlinson 63), Alston (O'Donnell 63), O'Reilly; Aitken M.
Airdrieonians: (433) Melrose; MacDonald, Bannon, Strapp, Hancock (Graham 14); McGrattan (Gallagher 67), McMaster, Frizzell; McStravick (Armstrong 67), Mochrie (Diack 71), Wilson B (McGregor 71).
Referee: Grant Irvine.

CHAMPIONSHIP SEMI-FINALS SECOND LEG
Saturday, 10 May 2025
Airdrieonians (1) 2 *(Bannon 38, Wilson B 52)*
Stenhousemuir (0) 1 *(Yates 58)*   1350
Airdrieonians: (41212) Melrose; MacDonald, Bannon, Graham, Strapp (Duffy 86); McMaster; McGrattan (Diack 57), McStravick (Armstrong 57); Frizzell (McGregor 57); Mochrie (Gallagher 56), Wilson B.
Stenhousemuir: (4231) Jamieson D; Ewen, Buchanan, Banner, Meechan; Andersen, Wedderburn (Alston 67); Yates (Tomlinson 75), O'Donnell, O'Reilly (McLuckie 82); Aitken M.
Airdrieonians won 5-2 on aggregate.
Referee: Matthew MacDermid.

Cove Rangers (1) 2 *(Megginson 8 (pen), Yule 47)*
Queen of the South (0) 1 *(Kennedy 77)*   1065
Cove Rangers: (4411) Suman; Lobban, Doyle, Gillingham, Harrington; Marshall (Parker 76), Darge, Yule, Emslie; Glass (Fyvie 69); Megginson (Scully 56).
Queen of the South: (3421) Stewart; Hannah, Hewitt, Douglas (Luissint 49); Macintyre, Lyon, Cochrane (Bryden 63), Smith; Kennedy, Allan; Brooks.
Cove Rangers won 2-1 on aggregate.
Referee: Calum Scott.

CHAMPIONSHIP FINAL FIRST LEG
Wednesday, 14 May 2025
Cove Rangers (1) 1 *(McGrattan 35 (og))*
Airdrieonians (1) 2 *(MacDonald 16, Strapp 63)* 811
Cove Rangers: (4411) Suman; Lobban, Gillingham, Doyle, Harrington; Yule, Darge, Glass, Marshall (Scully 75); Fyvie; Megginson (Gaffney 82).

Airdrieonians: (4231) Melrose; MacDonald, Graham, Bannon, Strapp; McMaster, Frizzell; McGrattan (Gallagher 61), Mochrie (McGregor 79), McStravick (Armstrong 61); Wilson B (Diack 78).
Referee: Lloyd Wilson.

CHAMPIONSHIP FINAL SECOND LEG
Saturday, 17 May 2025
Airdrieonians (0) 0
Cove Rangers (0) 0   1904
Airdrieonians: (41212) Melrose; MacDonald, Bannon, Wilson A, Strapp; McMaster; Armstrong, McGrattan (Gallagher 64); Frizzell; Mochrie (McStravick 59), Wilson B.
Cove Rangers: (433) Suman; Darge, Gillingham (Gaffney 80), Doyle, Harrington (Parker 84); Marshall (Megginson 70), Fyvie, Yule; Emslie, Glass (McGrath 80), Lobban.
Airdrieonians won 2-1 on aggregate.
Referee: Ross Hardie.

LEAGUE ONE SEMI-FINALS FIRST LEG
Tuesday, 6 May 2025
Edinburgh C (0) 1 *(Zaid 76)*
East Fife (0) 0   723
Edinburgh C: (4132) Weir; Robertson, McArthur, Lynch, Mitchell; Jarvis; Jones, Lawson, Zaid; Stokes, See.
East Fife: (442) McFarlane; Millar, Munro, Easton, Peggie; Norey (Laaref 61), McManus, McKenna, Higginbotham (Healy 81); Trouten, Austin (Shepherd 79).
Referee: Graham Grainger.

Elgin C (2) 2 *(Sargent 22, Murray 45)*
Annan Ath (4) 4 *(Goss 17, Kilsby 23, Muir T 26, 36)* 1104
Elgin C: (4231) Glavin; Girvan (Gavin 34), Dolzanski, Murray; Cairns; Gallagher, Cameron, MacIver, Dingwall, Golding (McDonald 71); Sargent (Hester 84).
Annan Ath: (4231) Smith J; Muir T, Hooper, Gibson, Kilsby; Todd, McGowan; Ross, Smith A, Smith P; Goss (Carmichael 37).
Referee: Duncan Nicolson.

LEAGUE ONE SEMI-FINALS SECOND LEG
Saturday, 10 May 2025
Annan Ath (1) 1 *(Muir T 1)*
Elgin C (1) 2 *(Sargent 22, McDonald 59)*   671
Annan Ath: (352) Smith J; Todd, Hooper, Gibson; Ross, McGowan, Maxwell (Carmichael 48), Smith P (Bisland 71), Dixon; Smith A, Muir T.
Elgin C: (451) Glavin; Gavin (Golding 57), Dolzanski, Murray, Cairns; MacIver, Gallagher, Dingwall, Cameron, McDonald (Hester 78); Sargent.
Annan Ath won 5-4 on aggregate.
Referee: Euan Anderson.

East Fife (1) 3 *(Laaref 26, McKenna 55, Trouten 58)*
Edinburgh C (0) 0   1070
East Fife: (4231) McFarlane; Bah (Nicol 75), Munro, Easton, Peggie; Millar, McManus (Norey 46); McKenna, Trouten (Higginbotham 72), Laaref (Healy 72); Austin (Shepherd 67).
Edinburgh C: (4132) Weir; Robertson, McArthur (Hamilton 75), Lynch, Mitchell (Daramola 60); Jones; Jarvis, Lawson, Zaid (Grigor 75); Stokes, See.
East Fife won 3-1 on aggregate.
Referee: Lloyd Wilson.

LEAGUE ONE FINAL FIRST LEG
Tuesday, 13 May 2025
East Fife (2) 3 *(Trouten 5, Munro 33, 80)*
Annan Ath (1) 2 *(McKenna 43 (og), Smith A 49)*   1327
East Fife: (4231) McFarlane; Bah, Munro, Easton, Peggie; Millar (Jones 67), McManus; McKenna, Trouten (Shepherd 90), Laaref (Healy 67); Austin (Norey 68).
Annan Ath: (343) Smith J; Todd, Hooper■, Kilsby; Muir R (Bisland■ 83), McGowan, Smith P (Strachan 37), Smith A; Ross, Dixon (Maxwell 83), Muir T.
Referee: Ross Hardie.

LEAGUE ONE FINAL SECOND LEG
Friday, 16 May 2025
Annan Ath (1) 1 *(Goss 6)*
East Fife (1) 1 *(Laaref 37)*   1304
Annan Ath: (442) Smith J; Muir R (Carmichael 62), Todd, Muir T, Kilsby (Maxwell 79); Ross, McGowan, Smith P, Dixon (Brown 62); Goss, Smith A.
East Fife: (433) McFarlane; Bah, Munro, Easton, Peggie (Murdoch 73); McKenna, Millar (Norey 80), McManus; Trouten (Shepherd 73), Austin (Jones 63), Laaref (Healy 63).
East Fife won 4-3 on aggregate.
Referee: Colin Steven.

LEAGUE TWO FINAL FIRST LEG
Saturday, 10 May 2025
East Kilbride (1) 3 *(Elliott 2, 52, McGregor 72)*
Bonnyrigg Rose (1) 1 *(Arnott 16)*   685
East Kilbride: (4141) Truesdale; Fagan, McGregor, Hamilton, Mimnaugh; Spence; Robertson, Leitch, Balde, Flanagan; Elliott.
Bonnyrigg Rose: (41212) Martin; Mailer, Connolly, Martyniuk, Somerville; Currie; Arnott, Murphy (Lennon 90); Aiken (Ferrie 59); McGachie (Porteous 50), Ross.
Referee: Dan McFarlane.

LEAGUE TWO FINAL SECOND LEG
Saturday, 17 May 2025
Bonnyrigg Rose (0) 0
East Kilbride (0) 0   2170
Bonnyrigg Rose: (4222) Martin; Mailer (Lennon 57), Young, Martyniuk, Somerville (Ferrie 77); Murphy (Porteous 67), Currie; Connolly, Arnott; Ross, McGachie.
East Kilbride: (4141) Truesdale; Fagan, McGregor, Hamilton, Mimnaugh; Spence; Robertson, Leitch, Balde, Flanagan; Elliott.
East Kilbride won 3-1 on aggregate.
Referee: Euan Anderson.

PREMIER SPORTS SCOTTISH LEAGUE CUP 2024–25

■ *Denotes player sent off.*
PW = Drawn match won on penalties (2 pts).
PL = Drawn match lost on penalties (1 pt).
* Qualified for Second Round as best runners-up.*

GROUP STAGE

GROUP A
Dumbarton v East Kilbride	1-1
East Kilbride won 4-2 on penalties.	
Queen of the South v Aberdeen	0-3
Airdrieonians v East Kilbride	8-0
Queen of the South v Dumbarton	2-0
Dumbarton v Airdrieonians	3-4
East Kilbride v Aberdeen	0-4
Aberdeen v Airdrieonians	2-1
East Kilbride v Queen of the South	1-3
Aberdeen v Dumbarton	6-0
Airdrieonians v Queen of the South	2-0

Group A Table	P	W	PW	PL	L	F	A	GD	Pts
Aberdeen	4	4	0	0	0	15	1	14	12
Airdrieonians	4	3	0	0	1	15	5	10	9
Queen of the South	4	2	0	0	2	5	6	–1	6
East Kilbride	4	0	1	0	3	2	16	–14	2
Dumbarton	4	0	0	1	3	4	13	–9	1

GROUP B
Falkirk v Dundee U	2-0
Stenhousemuir v Buckie Thistle	4-0
Ayr U v Falkirk	1-0
Dundee U v Stenhousemuir	3-0
Buckie Thistle v Falkirk	1-5
Dundee U v Ayr U	2-1
Stenhousemuir v Ayr U	1-4
Buckie Thistle v Dundee U	2-5
Ayr U v Buckie Thistle	3-2
Falkirk v Stenhousemuir	4-0

Group B Table	P	W	PW	PL	L	F	A	GD	Pts
Falkirk	4	3	0	0	1	11	2	9	9
Dundee U	4	3	0	0	1	10	5	5	9
Ayr U	4	3	0	0	1	9	5	4	9
Stenhousemuir	4	1	0	0	3	5	11	–6	3
Buckie Thistle	4	0	0	0	4	5	17	–12	0

GROUP C
Elgin C v Hibernian	0-5
Peterhead v Queen's Park	0-5
Elgin C v Kelty Hearts	1-1
Elgin C won 5-4 on penalties.	
Hibernian v Queen's Park	5-1
Kelty Hearts v Hibernian	1-0
Peterhead v Elgin C	4-2
Kelty Hearts v Peterhead	0-1
Queen's Park v Elgin C	4-0
Hibernian v Peterhead	4-0
Queen's Park v Kelty Hearts	6-0

Group C Table	P	W	PW	PL	L	F	A	GD	Pts
Hibernian	4	3	0	0	1	14	2	12	9
Queen's Park	4	3	0	0	1	16	5	11	9
Peterhead	4	2	0	0	2	5	11	–6	6
Kelty Hearts	4	1	0	1	2	2	8	–6	4
Elgin C	4	0	1	0	3	3	14	–11	2

GROUP D
Annan Ath v Inverness CT	1-0
Bonnyrigg Rose v Dundee	1-7
Annan Ath v Bonnyrigg Rose	2-2
Bonnyrigg Rose won 7-6 on penalties.	
Arbroath v Dundee	0-2
Arbroath v Annan Ath	0-3
Inverness CT v Bonnyrigg Rose	3-0
Dundee v Annan Ath	3-1
Inverness CT v Arbroath	0-0
Arbroath won 5-3 on penalties.	
Bonnyrigg Rose v Arbroath	0-1
Dundee v Inverness CT	6-0

Group D Table	P	W	PW	PL	L	F	A	GD	Pts
Dundee	4	4	0	0	0	18	2	16	12
Annan Ath	4	2	0	1	1	7	5	2	7
Arbroath	4	1	1	0	2	1	5	–4	5
Inverness CT	4	1	0	1	2	3	7	–4	4
Bonnyrigg Rose	4	0	1	0	3	3	13	–10	2

GROUP E
Forfar Ath v Livingston	0-2
The Spartans v Dunfermline Ath	0-3
Cove Rangers v The Spartans	0-5
Dunfermline Ath v Forfar Ath	0-2
Forfar v Cove Rangers	1-1
Forfar Ath won 3-1 on penalties.	
Forfar Ath were later awarded a 3-0 win over Cove Rangers, who fielded an ineligible player.	
Livingston v Dunfermline Ath	1-0
Cove Rangers v Livingston	0-2
The Spartans v Forfar Ath	1-0
Dunfermline Ath v Cove Rangers	1-2
Livingston v The Spartans	0-1

Group E Table	P	W	PW	PL	L	F	A	GD	Pts
The Spartans	4	3	0	0	1	7	3	4	9
Livingston	4	3	0	0	1	5	1	4	9
Forfar Ath	4	2	0	0	2	5	3	2	6
Dunfermline Ath	4	1	0	0	3	4	5	–1	3
Cove Rangers	4	1	0	0	3	2	11	–9	3

GROUP F
Brechin C v St Johnstone	1-2
East Fife v Greenock Morton	3-0
Alloa Ath v East Fife	0-0
Alloa Ath won 5-3 on penalties.	
Greenock Morton v Brechin C	1-0
Brechin C v Alloa Ath	1-3
St Johnstone v Greenock Morton	2-0
Alloa Ath v St Johnstone	3-2
East Fife v Brechin C	4-0
Greenock Morton v Alloa Ath	2-1
St Johnstone v East Fife	5■1

Group F Table	P	W	PW	PL	L	F	A	GD	Pts
St Johnstone	4	3	0	0	1	11	5	6	9
Alloa Ath	4	2	1	0	1	7	5	2	8
East Fife	4	2	0	1	1	8	5	3	7
Greenock Morton	4	2	0	0	2	3	6	–3	6
Brechin C	4	0	0	0	4	2	10	–8	0

GROUP G
Motherwell v Edinburgh C	3-0
Partick Thistle v Montrose	3-2
Montrose v Motherwell	1-1
Motherwell won 5-4 on penalties.	
Edinburgh C v Clyde	0-5
Clyde v Motherwell	1-3
Edinburgh C v Partick Thistle	0-6
Montrose v Edinburgh C	2-1
Partick Thistle v Clyde	2-3
Clyde v Montrose	0-1
Motherwell v Partick Thistle	0-0
Partick Thistle won 3-1 on penalties.	

Group G Table	P	W	PW	PL	L	F	A	GD	Pts
Motherwell	4	2	1	1	0	7	2	5	9
Partick Thistle	4	2	1	0	1	11	5	6	8
Montrose	4	2	0	1	1	6	5	1	7
Clyde	4	2	0	0	2	9	6	3	6
Edinburgh C	4	0	0	0	4	1	16	–15	0

GROUP H
Stirling Alb v Raith R	0-3
Stranraer v Ross Co	1-3
Hamilton A v Stirling Alb	0-0
Stirling Alb won 4-2 on penalties.	
Raith R v Stranraer	2-1
Ross Co v Raith R	2-1
Stranraer v Hamilton A	0-3
Hamilton A v Ross Co	1-2
Stirling Alb v Stranraer	2-2
Stirling Alb won 4-2 on penalties.	
Raith R v Hamilton A	1-1
Raith R won 5-3 on penalties.	
Ross Co v Stirling Alb	3-0

Group H Table	P	W	PW	PL	L	F	A	GD	Pts
Ross Co	4	4	0	0	0	10	3	7	12
Raith R	4	2	1	0	1	7	4	3	8
Hamilton A	4	1	0	2	1	5	3	2	5
Stirling Alb	4	0	2	0	2	2	8	–6	4
Stranraer	4	0	0	1	3	4	10	–6	1

KNOCKOUT STAGE

SECOND ROUND

Saturday, 17 August 2024

Aberdeen (0) 1 *(Keskinen 90)*

Queen's Park (0) 0   8939

Aberdeen: (4231) Mitov; Devlin, Milne, Molloy, MacKenzie (McGarry 78); Nilsen, Shinnie; Morris (Keskinen 57), Sokler (Ambrose 79), McGrath; Gueye (Besuijen 46).
Queen's Park: (352) Ferrie; Thomson (Hinds 63), Ujdur (Fieldson 63), Kerr; Longridge (MacGregor 63), Turner (McLeish 90), Welsh, Murray, Scott J (MacKenzie 74); Thomas, Rudden.

Dundee (2) 6 *(Palmer-Houlden 12, McGhee 40, Tiffoney 61, Portales 74, Main 86, Cameron 90)*

Airdrieonians (0) 1 *(Frizzell 76)*   3327

Dundee: (433) Carson; Ingram, Portales, McGhee, Larkeche; Cameron, Sylla (Astley 74), McCowan; Palmer-Houlden (Robertson F 54), Murray (Main 69), Tiffoney.
Airdrieonians: (4231) Wright; MacDonald■, McCabe (Armstrong 46), Hancock, Bruce; Gallagher, McMaster (Mochrie 46); Agyemang (Cooper 70), Aiken (McGrattan 46), Frizzell; Wilson B (Reid 70).

Falkirk (0) 2 *(Ross 53, Tait 81)*

Hearts (0) 0   6653

Falkirk: (4231) Hogarth; Adams, Henderson, Donaldson, Mackie; Spencer, Tait; Ross (Yeats 75), Oliver (Agyeman 66), Miller; MacIver (Shanley■ 88).
Hearts: (4132) Gordon; Taylor (Grant 81), Halkett, Kingsley, Penrice; Boateng; Oda (Devlin 64), Dhanda (Forrest 56), Spittal (McKay 64); Vargas, Boyce (Shankland 56).

Rangers (0) 2 *(Dessers 61, McCausland 90)*

St Johnstone (0) 0   23,261

Rangers: (4231) Butland; Tavernier, Souttar, Propper (Davies 45), Jefte; Sterling, Dowell (Barron 62); Cerny (McCausland 82), Diomande, Matondo (Fraser 82); Danilo (Dessers 46).
St Johnstone: (352) Rae; Neilson, Sanders, Cameron; Wright, MacPherson (Kirk 75), Carey, Smith M (Clark 83), Raymond; Sidibeh, Mbunga-Kimpioka.

The Spartans (0) 1 *(Henderson 46)*

Ross Co (0) 0   712

The Spartans: (451) Heraghty; Watson K, Sonkur, Watson P, Booth; Dishington (Whittaker 86), Craigen, Hunter, Whyte; Russell; Henderson.
Ross Co: (442) Laidlaw; Brown, Leak (Grieves 81), Nightingale, Harmon; Chilvers (Samuel 58), Loturi (Telfer 81), Randall, Denholm (Robesten 70); White (Brophy 70), Hale.

Sunday, 18 August 2024

Celtic (2) 3 *(Maeda 4, 15, Kuhn 56)*

Hibernian (1) 1 *(Kukharevych 34)*   47,370

Celtic: (433) Schmeichel; Johnston A, Carter-Vickers, Scales, Taylor; O'Riley, McGregor, Hatate (Bernardo 82); Kuhn (Palma 81), Maeda (Yang 72), Forrest (Idah 60).
Hibernian: (532) Bursik; Miller, Bushiri, Ekpiteta (Cadden C 63), O'Hora, Obita; Moriah-Welsh (Cadden N 46), Campbell, Newell (Amos 90); Boyle (Molotnikov 77), Kukharevych (Bowie 63).

Dundee U (1) 1 *(Graham 34)*

St Mirren (0) 0   4285

Dundee U: (343) Walton; Adegboyega, Graham, Gallagher; Stephenson, Sibbald, Holt K, Ferry; Babunski (Docherty 78), van der Sande (Moult 67), Trapanovski (Middleton 86).
St Mirren: (352) Balcombe; Fraser (Sutherland 82), Gogic, Iacovitti; Rooney, Idowu (Scott 60), Smyth, Taylor F (Taylor R 57), Tanser (Brown 60); Olusanya, Mandron (Ayunga 60).

Motherwell (0) 1 *(Ebiye 96)*

Kilmarnock (0) 0   4371

Motherwell: (3421) Oxborough; McGinn, Gordon, Casey (Watt 58); O'Donnell, Zdravkovski (Maswanhise 58), Halliday (Sparrow 74), Seddon (Ebiye 74); Miller (Balmer 120), Wilson; Robinson (Kaleta 74).
Kilmarnock: (3412) O'Hara; Wright (Bainbridge 58), Findlay■, Deas; Mackay-Steven (Lyons 58), Watson, Polworth (Mayo 58), McKenzie (Wales 91); Murray (Donnelly 90); Watkins (Kennedy 58), Anderson (Vassell 58).   *aet.*

QUARTER-FINALS

Friday, 20 September 2024

Motherwell (1) 2 *(Robinson 45, Miller 90 (pen))*

Dundee U (0) 1 *(Moult 83)*   8327

Motherwell: (343) Oxborough; McGinn, Gordon, Casey; O'Donnell (Kaleta 51), Zdravkovski, Halliday (Sparrow 79), Wilson; Miller, Robinson (Stamatelopoulos 82), Maswanhise.
Dundee U: (3421) Walton; Adegboyega (Ubochioma 82), Gallagher, Graham; Stephenson, Docherty, Sibbald, Ferry; Babunski (Middleton 73), Trapanovski (Dalby 58); van der Sande (Moult 59).

Saturday, 21 September 2024

Aberdeen (2) 4 *(Gueye 14, Nisbet 44, Clarkson 46, Sokler 72)*

The Spartans (0) 0   11,615

Aberdeen: (4231) Mitov; Devlin (Milne 75), Rubezic, Molloy (MacDonald 76), MacKenzie; Palaversa, Nilsen (Shinnie 55); Gueye (Keskinen 46), Clarkson, McGrath; Nisbet (Sokler 66).
The Spartans: (4231) Carswell; Watson P (Watson K 68), Sonkur, Waugh, Booth (Denholm 73); Craigen, Hunter; Dishington (Walls 61), Whyte, Russell (Stowe 60); Henderson (Ritchie 61).

Rangers (1) 3 *(Dessers 18, 66, Tavernier 50 (pen))*

Dundee (0) 0   33,665

Rangers: (4231) Butland; Tavernier (Kasanwirjo 81), Souttar, Propper, Jefte; Barron, Sterling (Diomande 46); Cerny (McCausland 68), Lawrence, Bajrami (Cortes 73); Dessers (Igamane 68).
Dundee: (433) Carson; McGhee (Ingram 77), Koumetio, Portales, Larkeche; Braybrooke (Mulligan 69), Sylla, Cameron; Adewumi (Palmer-Houlden 46), Murray (Main 77), Tiffoney (Vetro 77).

Sunday, 22 September 2024

Celtic (1) 5 *(Bernardo 21, Idah 70, 72, Kuhn 81, 84)*

Falkirk (2) 2 *(MacIver 11, Yeats 45)*   42,960

Celtic: (433) Schmeichel; Ralston, Welsh (Nawrocki 85), Trusty, Valle (Taylor 61); Bernardo, McGregor, Hatate (Engels 60); Forrest (Kuhn 61), Idah, Palma (Yang 60).
Falkirk: (433) Hogarth; Adams, Donaldson, Henderson, Mackie; Spencer, Yeats (McKenna■ 67), Tait; Agyeman (Ross 75), MacIver (Oliver 55), Miller.

SEMI-FINALS

Saturday, 2 November 2024

Celtic (3) 6 *(Carter-Vickers 29, Furuhashi 32, Maeda 40, 49, 85, Kuhn 59)*

Aberdeen (0) 0   47,544

Celtic: (433) Schmeichel; Johnston A, Carter-Vickers (Scales 64), Trusty, Valle (Taylor 63); Engels (Bernardo 63), McGregor, Hatate; Kuhn (Forrest 72), Maeda, Furuhashi (Idah 69).
Aberdeen: (4231) Mitov; Devlin, Rubezic, Molloy, MacKenzie; Shinnie, Nilsen (Ambrose 70); Keskinen (Palaversa 46), McGrath (Besuijen 82), Lopes (Morris 46); Sokler (Clarkson 70).

Sunday, 3 November 2024

Motherwell (1) 1 *(Halliday 25)*

Rangers (0) 2 *(Dessers 49, Bajrami 81)*   37,077

Motherwell: (352) Oxborough; Casey, Gordon, Balmer; Kaleta (Blaney 75), Halliday, Miller, Wilson, Seddon (Sparrow 56); Stamatelopoulos (Tavares 63), Maswanhise (Robinson 63).
Rangers: (4231) Butland; Tavernier (Sterling 67), Souttar, Balogun (Kasanwirjo 78), Jefte; Barron, Raskin; Cerny, Lawrence (Diomande 36), Bajrami; Dessers (Danilo 67).

PREMIER SPORTS SCOTTISH LEAGUE CUP FINAL 2024–25

Sunday, 15 December 2024 (at Hampden Park, attendance 49,420)

Celtic (0) 3   Rangers (1) 3

Celtic: (433) Schmeichel; Johnston A (Ralston 70), Carter-Vickers, Trusty (Scales 46), Taylor (Valle 91); Bernardo (Engels 71), McGregor, Hatate; Kuhn (Forrest 106), Furuhashi (Idah 76), Maeda.
Scorers: Taylor 56, Maeda 60, Kuhn 87.

Rangers: (4231) Butland; Tavernier, Balogun (Sterling 67), Propper, Jefte (Yilmaz 61); Diomande (Barron 106), Raskin; Cerny (Dowell 106), Bajrami (Danilo 86), Hagi; Igamane (Dessers 101).
Scorers: Bajrami 41, Diomande 75, Danilo 88.

aet; Celtic won 5-4 on penalties. Referee: John Beaton.

SCOTTISH LEAGUE CUP FINALS 1946–2025

SCOTTISH LEAGUE CUP

1946–47	Rangers v Aberdeen	4-0
1947–48	East Fife v Falkirk	0-0*
Replay	East Fife v Falkirk	4-1
1948–49	Rangers v Raith R	2-0
1949–50	East Fife v Dunfermline Ath	3-0
1950–51	Motherwell v Hibernian	3-0
1951–52	Dundee v Rangers	3-2
1952–53	Dundee v Kilmarnock	2-0
1953–54	East Fife v Partick Thistle	3-2
1954–55	Hearts v Motherwell	4-2
1955–56	Aberdeen v St Mirren	2-1
1956–57	Celtic v Partick Thistle	0-0*
Replay	Celtic v Partick Thistle	3-0
1957–58	Celtic v Rangers	7-1
1958–59	Hearts v Partick Thistle	5-1
1959–60	Hearts v Third Lanark	2-1
1960–61	Rangers v Kilmarnock	2-0
1961–62	Rangers v Hearts	1-1*
Replay	Rangers v Hearts	3-1
1962–63	Hearts v Kilmarnock	1-0
1963–64	Rangers v Morton	5-0
1964–65	Rangers v Celtic	2-1
1965–66	Celtic v Rangers	2-1
1966–67	Celtic v Rangers	1-0
1967–68	Celtic v Dundee	5-3
1968–69	Celtic v Hibernian	6-2
1969–70	Celtic v St Johnstone	1-0
1970–71	Rangers v Celtic	1-0
1971–72	Partick Thistle v Celtic	4-1
1972–73	Hibernian v Celtic	2-1
1973–74	Dundee v Celtic	1-0
1974–75	Celtic v Hibernian	6-3
1975–76	Rangers v Celtic	1-0
1976–77	Aberdeen v Celtic	2-1*
1977–78	Rangers v Celtic	2-1*
1978–79	Rangers v Aberdeen	2-1

BELL'S LEAGUE CUP

1979–80	Dundee U v Aberdeen	0-0*
Replay	Dundee U v Aberdeen	3-0
1980–81	Dundee U v Dundee	3-0

SCOTTISH LEAGUE CUP

1981–82	Rangers v Dundee U	2-1
1982–83	Celtic v Rangers	2-1
1983–84	Rangers v Celtic	3-2*

SKOL CUP

1984–85	Rangers v Dundee U	1-0
1985–86	Aberdeen v Hibernian	3-0
1986–87	Rangers v Celtic	2-1
1987–88	Rangers v Aberdeen	3-3*
	Rangers won 5-3 on penalties.	
1988–89	Rangers v Aberdeen	3-2
1989–90	Aberdeen v Rangers	2-1*
1990–91	Rangers v Celtic	2-1*
1991–92	Hibernian v Dunfermline Ath	2-0
1992–93	Rangers v Aberdeen	2-1*

SCOTTISH LEAGUE CUP

1993–94	Rangers v Hibernian	2-1

COCA-COLA CUP

1994–95	Raith R v Celtic	2-2*
	Raith R won 6-5 on penalties.	
1995–96	Aberdeen v Dundee	2-0
1996–97	Rangers v Hearts	4-3
1997–98	Celtic v Dundee U	3-0

SCOTTISH LEAGUE CUP

1998–99	Rangers v St Johnstone	2-1

CIS INSURANCE CUP

1999–2000	Celtic v Aberdeen	2-0
2000–01	Celtic v Kilmarnock	3-0
2001–02	Rangers v Ayr U	4-0
2002–03	Rangers v Celtic	2-1
2003–04	Livingston v Hibernian	2-0
2004–05	Rangers v Motherwell	5-1
2005–06	Celtic v Dunfermline Ath	3-0
2006–07	Hibernian v Kilmarnock	5-1
2007–08	Rangers v Dundee U	2-2*
	Rangers won 3-2 on penalties.	

CO-OPERATIVE INSURANCE CUP

2008–09	Celtic v Rangers	2-0*
2009–10	Rangers v St Mirren	1-0
2010–11	Rangers v Celtic	2-1*

SCOTTISH COMMUNITIES LEAGUE CUP

2011–12	Kilmarnock v Celtic	1-0
2012–13	St Mirren v Hearts	3-2
2013–14	Aberdeen v Inverness CT	0-0*
	Aberdeen won 4-2 on penalties.	

SCOTTISH LEAGUE CUP PRESENTED BY QTS

2014–15	Celtic v Dundee U	2-0
2015–16	Ross Co v Hibernian	2-1

BETFRED SCOTTISH LEAGUE CUP

2016–17	Celtic v Aberdeen	3-0
2017–18	Celtic v Motherwell	2-0
2018–19	Celtic v Aberdeen	1-0
2019–20	Celtic v Rangers	1-0
2020–21	St Johnstone v Livingston	1-0

PREMIER SPORTS SCOTTISH LEAGUE CUP

2021–22	Celtic v Hibernian	2-1

VIAPLAY SCOTTISH LEAGUE CUP

2022–23	Celtic v Rangerrs	2-1
2023–24	Rangers v Aberdeen	1-0

PREMIER SPORTS SCOTTISH LEAGUE CUP

2024–25	Celtic v Rangers	3-3*
	Celtic won 5-4 on penalties.	

*After extra time.

SCOTTISH LEAGUE CUP WINS

Rangers 28, Celtic 22, Aberdeen 6, Hearts 4, Dundee 3, East Fife 3, Hibernian 3, Dundee U 2, Kilmarnock 1, Livingston 1, Motherwell 1, Partick Thistle 1, Raith R 1, Ross Co 1, St Johnstone 1, St Mirren 1.

APPEARANCES IN FINALS

Rangers 38, Celtic 37, Aberdeen 16, Hibernian 11, Dundee U 7, Hearts 7, Dundee 6, Kilmarnock 6, Motherwell 4, Partick Thistle 4, Dunfermline Ath 3, East Fife 3, St Johnstone 3, St Mirren 3, Livingston 2, Raith R 2, Ayr U 1, Falkirk 1, Inverness CT 1, Morton 1, Ross Co 1, Third Lanark 1.

SPFL TRUST TROPHY 2024–25

ᵇ *Denotes player sent off.*

FIRST ROUND – NORTH

Tuesday, 30 July 2024

Fraserburgh (0) 1 *(Butcher 73)*

Hearts U21 (1) 1 *(Ross 29)* 211

Fraserburgh: (442) Inglis; Garden (Hay 86), Beagrie, Simpson, Hawkins (West 69); Bolton (Sopel 69), Buchan, Young, Wood; Barbour S (Butcher 69), Watt (McKay 87).
Hearts U21: (442) MacDonald; Forrester, Smutek, Smith, Lister; Plank, Gillies (Crookson 79), McLuckie (Stevenson 54), Duncan (Osbourne 61); Ross, Sandilands.
Fraserburgh won 5-4 on penalties.

Banks o' Dee (1) 1 *(Philipson 33)*

Aberdeen U21 (0) 0 460

Banks o' Dee: (4411) Hoban; Davidson, Cooney, Reynolds (Kelly 53), Emmett (Selbie 74); Alexander, Vigurs (Milne 64), Lewecki (Gilmour 53), Antoniazzi; Philipson; MacLeod (Stark 74).
Aberdeen U21: (4411) Vitols; Wilson, Carroll, McKenzie, Akindileni; Stewart, Lobban, Marshall, Emslie; Boyd (Mackie 61); Bavidge (Clark 61).

Dundee U21 (2) 2 *(Mohammed 14, Sweenie-Rowe 19)*

Formatine U (0) 0 145

Dundee U21: (352) Sharp; Lorimer, Lochhead, Davies-Browne; Leiper, Richardson, Mitchell, Clark, Sweenie-Rowe; Mohammed, Corrigan (Hunter 89).
Formatine U: (442) Middleton; Norris, Crawford, McLean, Smith (Alberts 70); Mykyta, Youngson (Lawrence 70), Rodger, Combe (Adams 70); Lisle (Cambell 59), Wade (Spink 70).

Buckie Thistle (0) 1 *(Peters 54)*

Dundee U U21 (1) 3 *(Stirton 18, Cameron 81, O'Donnell 88)* 640

Buckie Thistle: (4231) Ridgers; McCabe, Fyffe, McKay (McHardy 63), Wood (Ramsay 63); Pugh, Robertson (Goodall 63); Keir (Harvey 85), MacIver (Fraser 77), MacAskill; Peters.
Dundee U U21: (442) Adams; Constable, Harding, Dewar, Simpson; Mwangi, Domeracki (Beattie 79), O'Donnell, Borland (Cameron 64); Watt, Stirton.

Wednesday, 31 July 2024

St Johnstone U21 (0) 2 *(Essel 50, Smith C 90)*

Brechin C (1) 1 *(Robertson 28)* 259

St Johnstone U21: (3421) Hepburn; Klimionek, Essel (McCrystal 88), Parker; Franczak, Smith C, Sprangler, Bright; Cocks, Steven (Mylchreest 75); Kirk.
Brechin C: (4231) Wilson; Ferguson, Martin**ᵇ**, Spark, Cruickshank; Patrick, Moreland (Henry 76); Scott, Logan (McDonald 88), Tosh (Loudon 63); Robertson (McLeod 76).

FIRST ROUND – SOUTH

Tuesday, 30 July 2024

Berwick Rangers (1) 2 *(McNamara 34, Devers 50)*

St Mirren (3) 3 *(Sutherland 4, Mooney 7, McCormick 12)* 288

Berwick Rangers: (442) Antell; McGinley, Robinson, McCormack, Fellows; Devers, Barr, Nelson, Collins; Buchanan, Laidlaw (McNamara 29).
St Mirren: (352) Kelly; Kenny, Foster, Lennon; Penman, Taylor F, Hunter, Turner, Sutherland; Mooney, McCormick (Farquhar 77).
Match awarded as a 3-0 win for Berwick Rangers as St Mirren U21 fielded an ineligible player.

Cowdenbeath (1) 4 *(McLean 11, 74, McDonald 72, Kerr 90)*

Kilmarnock U21 (2) 2 *(McLean 37 (og), Cooper 41)* 171

Cowdenbeath: (4321) Blair; Dunsmore, McLean, Denham, Kerr; Whyte, McNab, McLaughlin (Jordan 68); Docherty, McDonald; Healy (Sutherland 63).
Kilmarnock U21: (4231) Glavin; Mackle, Ellis, Brown, Bowie; Brannan, Traynor (Duruh 83 (Burgues 88)); Leslie, Marchant (Burke 75), Cooper; Craik (Allan 83).

East Kilbride (2) 3 *(Elliott 5, Robertson 22, Leitch 61)*

Celtic U21 (0) 0 330

East Kilbride: (4321) Wilson; Ferguson D, Fagan, Lockie, Livingstone; Biggar (Thomson 77), Spence, Leitch (Balde 64); Robertson (Daramola 64), Stirling; Elliott (Samspm 64).
Celtic U21: (4321) Morrison; Bonetig (Kyle 73), Robertson, Agbaire, Frame; Kelly (Haddow 83), Ure, Bonnar; Hatton, Dobbie; Cummings (Isiguzo 64).

Hibernian U21 (1) 3 *(McAllister 21, McMurdo 72, 79)*

Albion R (1) 3 *(McMahon 18, Home 53, Paton 90)* 140

Hibernian: (4231) Owens; Whittaker, McGrath, Gillie, Calder; Megwa, McAllister; McMurdo, McDonald (Davidson 77), Cleland; Landers.
Albion R: (4231) Connelly; McCaw, Fernie, Home, Lavery; Duncan, McMahon; Brown (McMillan 63), Kirkpatrick, Kennedy (Paton 78); Bright Prince.
Albion R won 4-2 on penalties.

Motherwell U21 (0) 0

East Stirlingshire (0) 0 338

Motherwell U21: (3421) McConnell; Ross M, McGinn (Tominay 64), Flatman; Kaleta (Marshall 64), Sparrow (Williamson 64), Booth, McDermott; Ross L (Lawson 18), Wells (Nelson 64)); Ferrie.
East Stirlingshire: (4411) Ecrepont; Curtis, Campbell, Pyper, Brown; Murray (Flynn 71), Liddell, Gomis, O'Neill; Penker (Reilly 61); Spence.
East Stirlingshire won 8-7 on penalties.

Rangers U21 (3) 3 *(Nsio 24, Stevens 32, Curtis 43)*

Bo'ness U 1) 1 *(Malcolm 1)* 266

Rangers U21: (4231) Munn; Devine, Allan (Allen 83), Webster, Harkness (Eadie 70); Robertson (McClure 83), Nsio; Stevens, Lowry (Hutton 70), Curtis (Burnside 70); Gentles.
Bo'ness: (532) Campbell; Stevenson, Hawkins, Travis, Duffy, Macaulay; Henderson (Kennedy 74), Gemmell (Grant 53), Porteous; Malcolm (Johnston 46), Mitchell (Stenhouse 13 (Irving 74)).

SECOND ROUND – NORTH

Tuesday, 13 August 2024

Dundee U U21 (0) 0

Dundee U21 (0) 0) 681

Dundee U U21: (442) Adams; Borland, Dewar, Harding, Gilligan; Ubochioma (Beattie 67), Odada (Mwangi 67), O'Donnell, Forbes; Cameron (Welsh 69), Stirton.
Dundee U21: (352) Sharp; Graham, Lochhead, Lorimer; Allan, Clark, Mitchell, Richardson, Sweenie-Rowe; Mohammed (Scott 81), Corrigan (Leiper 59).
Dundee U U21 won 3-1 on penalties.

East Fife (0) 2 *(Austin 49, Shepherd 51)*

St Johnstone U21 (0) 1 *(Kirk 9)* 296

East Fife: (442) Fleming; Docherty (Easton 56), Murdoch, Munro, Peggie (Newton 63); Healy, McManus (Norey 64), Slattery (Millar 64), Laaref; Shepherd, Austin (Trouten 72).
St Johnstone U21: (3421) Hepburn (Thomson 46); Klimionek, Essel, Parker; Franzak, McCrystal, Clark (Dair 64), Bright; Steven, Cocks; Kirk.

Elgin C (0) 2 *(Dingwall 56 (pen), Gavin 65)*

Banks o' Dee (1) 1 *(Antoniazzi 22)*   370

Elgin C: (3421) McHale; Dilzanski, Draper, Murray; Girvan (Cairns 60), Cameron (Hyde 46), Gallagher, Booth; Dingwall (MacLeman 85), Sargent (Gavin 46); Golding (McDonald 85).
Banks o' Dee: (4231) Hoban; Kelly, Reynolds, Cooney, Selbie; Winton (Gilmour 46), Vigurs (Davidson 75); Antoniazzi (McLeod 66), Philipson, Alexander (Lewecki 66); Milne (Stark 75).

Fraserburgh (0) 2 *(Barbour S 76, Wood 86)*

Forfar Ath (1) 1 *(Reekie 19)*   254

Fraserburgh: (4231) Barbour J; Garden (Wood 74), Hay, Simpson, Hawkins (Watt 74); Buchan, Young; Butcher (West 74), Bolton, Sopel (McKay 90); Barbour S.
Forfar Ath: (4321) McCallum; Reekie, Morrison, Allan M, Malcolm (Franczak 69); Inglis, Whatley, Robson; MacLean, Cannon; Skelly.

SECOND ROUND – SOUTH

Tuesday, 13 August 2024

Albion R (1) 3 *(Reid 22, Kennedy 65, 68)*

Cowdenbeath (0) 4 *(Fernie 58 (og), Sutherland 64, Docherty 83 (pen), McLean 88)*   158

Albion R: (4231) Connelly; Fernie, Reid, Home, Lavery; Kirk, McMahon; Kennedy, MacKintosh (McCaw 80), Paton (Bright Prince 65); Duthie (Brown 55).
Cowdenbeath: (4321) Blair; Dunsmore, McLean, Denham, Newman (Kerr 71); Whyte, McNab, Burke (McPherson 63 (Jordon 90)); Docherty, Walker (Sutherland 64); Healy.

Dumbarton (4) 4 *(McGuffie 7, 31, Ruth 23, Wilson 37)*

Berwick Rangers (0) 0   240

Dumbarton: (4231) O'Neil; Lynas (Pignatiello 65), Miller (Shields 61), Clark, Young; Blair, Niang (Gray 46); McGuffie (Orsi 46), Wilson, Wallace; Ruth (Grivas 46).
Berwick Rangers: (442) Antell; McGinley, Robinson, McCormack (Devers 66), Fellows (Armstrong 78); Nelson, Barr, Stevenson, McNamara; Buchanan (Collins 63), Laidlaw (Ashraf 78).

Stranraer (1) 2 *(Russell 32, Ross 57)*

Bonnyrigg Rose (0) 1 *(Ross 84 (og))*   341

Stranraer: (3142) Pazikas; Ross, Cummins, McQueen; Brindley (Gallagher 71); Russell (Ecrepont 82), Hawkshaw (McIntosh 82), Dunlop, Grant (Hughes 82); Lang (McKnight 71), Edgar.
Bonnyrigg Rose: (4411) Ritchie; Somerville, Mailer, Martyniuk, Scarborough (Young 46[■]); Arnott, Wardell (Higginbotham 46), Watson (Currie 46); Connolly; Ross; McGachie (Barrett 46).

Wednesday, 14 August 2024

Clyde (1) 2 *(Dunachie 43 (pen), Leitch 85)*

Rangers U21 (0) 3 *(Lowry 59, 90, Burnside 69)*   607

Clyde: (451) Kennedy; Hynes, Howie, McKay, Lyon R; Redfern (Leitch 73), Docherty, Connell (Rennie 70), Scullion L (Houston 70 (Robson 79)), Connelly; Dunachie (Allan 73).
Rangers: (4231) Munn; Devine, King (Adams 76), Nsiala, Hutton; Rice, Nsio (Webster 82); Curtis, Adamson (Burnside 60[■]), Lowry; Gentles (Lovelace 60).

East Stirlingshire (1) 2 *(Spence 18, Penker 55)*

East Kilbride (1) 2 *(Elliott 43, Spence 47)*   170

East Stirlingshire: (442) Cantley; Brown, Campbell, Pyper, Coutts; Curtis, Gomis, Hynd, O'Neill (Murray 79); Penker, Spence.
East Kilbride: (4321) Wilson; Ferguson D, Fagan (McDonald 46), McGregor, Lockie; Biggar (Boyd 75), Spence, Balde; Stirling, Daramola[■]; Elliott (Robertson 46).
East Kilbride won 3-1 on penalties.

THIRD ROUND

Tuesday, 3 September 2024

Hamilton A (2) 4 *(O'Hara 4, 49, MacDonald 7, Shaw 89)*

Dundee U U21 (0) 0   308

Hamilton A: (4312) Lyness; Eadie (Barjonas 46), Newbury, McGinty, Longridge; MacDonald, Martin (Maguire 46), Henderson (Bradley 60); O'Hara (Shaw 76); Todorov, Morgan (Tumilty 65).
Dundee U U21: (442) Adams; Shields, Dewar (Holt 35), Cleall-Harding (Simpson F 77), Simpson O; Mwangi, Borland, Domeracki, Welsh; Stirton, Beattie.

Saturday, 7 September 2024

Arbroath (2) 3 *(O'Brien 23 (pen), Stewart 29, Callaghan 82)*

Montrose (0) 0   1051

Arbroath: (4411) McAdams; Sinclair (Bisland 86), Watson, O'Brien, Wilkie; Stewart, Flynn (Slater 72), Spalding, Coulson (Gallagher 72); Dow; Reilly (Callaghan 80).
Montrose: (352) Matthews; Williamson, Quinn, Smith; Brown, Bertie (Hannah 81), Shrive (Machado 65), Gardyne, Steeves (Lyons 65); Hester (Balfour 86), MacIver-Redwood (Watson 86).

Cowdenbeath (0) 0

Greenock Morton (0) 1 *(Garrity 62)*   379

Cowdenbeath: (352) Lynch; Hill (Denham 60), McLean, Jordan; Dunsmore (Kerr 80), Whyte, Burke[■], Swanson (Sutherland 48), Newman (Haston 80); McNab, Docherty (Walker 80).
Greenock Morton: (4231) Mullen; Blues, Ballantyne, Boyes, Delaney[■]; Lyall, King; Crawford, Moffat (Emmanuel-Thomas 82), Garrity (Davies 72); McGinn.

East Fife (0) 0

Dunfermline Ath (0) 2 *(Comrie 53, McCann 58)*   1264

East Fife: (4411) Fleming; McManus, Munro, Easton, Newton; Healy (Shepherd 63), Norey (Walker 64), Millar, Laaref (Peggie 64); Trouten; Austin (Slattery 83).
Dunfermline Ath: (352) Oluwayemi; Fisher, Young, Otoo; Comrie, Chalmers, Hamilton, Cooper (Wotherspoon 64), Ritchie-Hosler (Tod 83); Kane (Wighton 64), McCann (Sutherland T 77).

East Kilbride (1) 3 *(Livingstone 3, Leitch 87, Boyd 90)*

Cove Rangers (1) 2 *(Megginson 14, Gaffney 84)*   253

East Kilbride: (4231) Connelly; Ferguson D, McGregor (Fagan 65), Hamilton, Lockie; Spence, Balde; Stirling (Flanagan 65), Leitch, Livingstone (Boyd 77); Robertson.
Cove Rangers: (442) Demus; Darge, Doyle, Gillingham, Harrington; Yule, Glass, Fyvie, Scully; Megginson (Ochmanski 76), McGrath (Gaffney 66).

Inverness CT (2) 3 *(Brooks 29, 38, Mackinnon 60)*

Stirling Alb (0) 0   774

Inverness CT: (442) Dibaga; Duffy, Devine (Strachan 63), Ewan, Savage; Nolan (Thompson 61), Davidson (Keogh 74), Macleod, Mackinnon (Ferguson 73); McKay (MacKay 61), Brooks.
Stirling Alb: (442) Gaston; Weir (Milne 46), Sula, McGeachie, Crane (Dall 66); Waugh (Howe 80), Davidson (Knox 66), Kerr, Brown; Roy, McKinley.

Kelty Hearts (2) 3 *(Johnston 32, 40, Williamson 58)*

Elgin C (0) 1 *(Cameron 84)*   268

Kelty Hearts: (433) Russell; Mercer, Flatman (Thomas 37), O'Ware, Paterson; Cunningham, Owens B (Miller 54), Moore (Bryce 46); McCarvel, Williamson (Tidser 68), Johnston.
Elgin C: (352) Ross; Draper, Dolzanski, Murray; Cairns, Dingwall (Allen 77), Cameron, Hyde (Gavin 68), Booth (MacLeman 68); McDonald (Gallagher 68), Sargent (Golding 81).

Partick Thistle (1) 1 *(Graham 14)*

Alloa Ath (0) 3 *(Cawley 65, 76, Taggart 90 (pen))*   1969

Partick Thistle: (4231) Roberts; Nilsson, McBeth, Sayers, Milne; Turner (Diack 84), Bannigan (Stanway 84); Chalmers (Ablade 70), Lyon (Mackenzie 56), Fitzpatrick; Graham.

Alloa Ath: (4231) Ogayi; Taggart, McKay, Neill, Waters; Virtanen, Hetherington; Buchanan, Donnelly (Nevans 89), Cawley (Thomson 89); Sammon (O'Donnell 62).

Peterhead (0) 1 *(Barry 66)*
Dumbarton (0) 0 586
Peterhead: (4231) Oluyemi; Goldie, Jason Brown, Scott Ross, Armstrong (Dunne 68); Jack Brown, Forrest; Barry (Armour 80), Pawlett, Ward (Sebastian Ross 68); Smith.
Dumbarton: (433) O'Neil; Lynas (Pignatiello 75), Clark, Miller, Young; Blair, Gray (Hilton 64), Wilson (Shields 85); Orsi (McGuffie 75), Mumbongo (Ruth 64), Wallace.

Queen of the South (0) 0
Airdrieonians (1) 3 *(Frizzell 8, Mochrie 64, McGregor 71)*
957
Queen of the South: (3511) Hogarth; Hannah, Douglas, Macintyre (McKechnie 72); Willis (Luissint 68), Cochrane, Lyon (Kennedy 68), Johnstone, Dickenson; Walker (Doherty 57); McIntosh.
Airdrieonians: (442) Wright; MacDonald, Graham, Badley-Morgan, Bruce; Mochrie (McGrattan 79), Gallagher (Armstrong 65), Frizzell (Cooper 73), Agyemang (Aiken 79); Reid (McGregor 65), Wilson B.

Stenhousemuir (0) 1 *(Alston 84 (pen))*
Falkirk (0) 1 *(Miller 89)* 2426
Stenhousemuir: (442) Jamieson D; Meechan, Buchanan, Banner, Bilham; Andersen, Jacobs (Steele 70), Wedderburn (Alston 59), Berry (Taylor 59); Aitken M, Yates (O'Reilly 59).
Falkirk: (4231) Hogarth; Adams, Donaldson, Henderson■, McCann (Mackie 71); Yeats, Tait; Agyeman, McKenna (Oliver 63), Ross (Miller 63); Shanley (MacIver 63).
Stenhousemuir won 5-4 on penalties.

Stranraer (1) 1 *(Dunlop 29)*
Annan Ath (3) 5 *(Smith A 7, 90, Gibson 38 (pen), Wood 42, Dixon 61)* 469
Stranraer: (4231) Pazikas; McIntosh (McKnight 66), Ross, Cummins, Ecrepont; Gallagher, Dunlop (Adam 84), Grant, Hawkshaw (Woods 74), Russell (Edgar 74); Guthrie (Lang 74).
Annan Ath: (4231) Smith J; Barnes, Muir T (Maxwell 75), Kilsby, Muir R (Quigg 75); Gibson, McGowan (Stevenson 67); Wood, Todd (Quitongo 83), Dixon (Fleming 67); Smith A.

The Spartans (0) 0
Livingston (0) 2 *(May 65, Smith 81)* 681
The Spartans: (451) Meek; Watson K, Sonkur, Waugh (Watson P 46), Booth (Russell 59); Stowe (Craigen 59), Walls (Scott 79), Hunter (Lamont 80), Whyte, Denholm; Henderson.
Livingston: (433) Prior; Brandon (Finlayson 80), Nottingham, McGowan, Montano (Clarke 80); Pitman (Green 72), McAlear, Kelly; Smith, May (Winter 80), Sole (Lawal 63).

Sunday, 8 September 2024
Ayr U (0) 3 *(Dowds 49 (pen), 69, Oakley 70)*
Raith R (2) 2 *(Smith 11, Easton 15)* 1750
Ayr U: (442) Stone; Watret, Stanger, McAllister, Reading; Henderson (Walker 87), Dempsey, Rus (Hastie 82), Howley (McKenzie 63); Dowds, Oakley.
Raith R: (352) Dabrowski; Matthews, Hanlon, Dick; Gibson (Freeman 64), Mullin (Vaughan 75), Byrne, Easton (Stanton 64), Stevenson; Jamieson (Connolly 82), Smith.

Queen's Park (0) 1 *(Turner 59)*
Edinburgh C (0) 0 597
Queen's Park: (352) Wills; Kerr, Ujdur, Fieldson; Longridge, (Hickey-Fugaccia 70), MacGregor, Turner, Duncan (Hinds 53), Scott J; Thomas, McLeish (McDonnell 82).
Edinburgh C: (4132) Weir; Robertson, McArthur, Lynch, Grigor (Rennie 70); Jones; Gormley, Stokes, Mitchell (McKinstray 14); Young, Lawson (Scally 79).

Tuesday, 17 September 2024
Rangers U21 (2) 5 *(Allan 16, West 23 (og), Eadie 49, Adamson 61, Gentles 80)*
Fraserburgh (0) 0 381
Rangers U21: (4231) Munn; Allan, Grant, Nsiala-Makengo, Fraser (Hutton 77); Rice (Robertson 30), Adamson (McClure 77); Stevens, Lowry, Curtis (McCallion 78); Eadie (Gentles 62).
Fraserburgh: (4411) Barbour J; Bolton, Simpson, Hay (Strachan 66); West; Wood, Young (Garden 75), Hawkins, Sopel (Watt 65); Butcher (McKay 74); Barbour S (Laird 65).

FOURTH ROUND
Friday, 11 October 2024
Alloa Ath (1) 1 *(Donnelly 16)*
Arbroath (0) 0 480
Alloa Ath: (4231) Ogayi; Thomson, Taggart, McKay, Waters; Hetherington, Scougall (Virtanen 78); Cawley (Nevans 90), Donnelly, Buchanan; Rankin (Sammon 71).
Arbroath: (4231) McAdams; Bisland, Watson, Sinclair, Wilkie; Callaghan (Dow 71), Slater (O'Brien 86); Murray (Stewart 71), Gold (Flynn 78), Coulson; Reilly.

Annan Ath (0) 1 *(Maxwell 85)*
Queen's Park (2) 4 *(McLeish 16, Duncan 28, Rudden 63, Ujdur 76)* 423
Annan Ath: (451) Smith J; Gibson, Kilsby, Breen, Quitongo (Barnes 76); Todd, Fleming (Zaid 60), McGowan (Maxwell 76), Dixon (Quigg 67), Stevenson (Muir R 67); Smith A.
Queen's Park: (442) Wills; Mauchin, Ujdur, Tizzard, Fieldson; Longridge, Welsh (Collie 80), Duncan (Hinds 66), Hickey-Fugaccia (Scott T 66); Rudden (Drozd 73), McLeish (Evans 80).

Hamilton A (0) 0
Greenock Morton (1) 1 *(Stuparevic 17 (pen))* 711
Hamilton A: (4231) Lyness; Tumilty (Olufunwa 69), Maguire (McGowan 68), McGinty, Longridge; Barjonas, Williamson; Bradley (O'Connor 75), O'Hara, Henderson; Todorov (Shaw 53).
Greenock Morton: (4132) Woods; Ballantyne, Baird, Broadfoot, King; Blues (O'Boy 83), Moffat, Lyall (Gillespie 73), Garrity (Wilson 73); McGinn (Davies 64), Stuparevic (Samuels 64).

Saturday, 12 October 2024
Airdrieonians (0) 1 *(Gallagher 86)*
East Kilbride (1) 1 *(McGregor 39)* 703
Airdrieonians: (343) Wright; Watson, Graham, Badley-Morgan (Cooper 56); MacDonald, Gallagher, Aiken, Bruce (Taylor-Sinclair 90); Armstrong (Mochrie 63), Wilson B, Frizzell (McGrattan 63).
East Kilbride: (4231) Connelly; Fagan, McGregor, Hamilton, Ferguson D; Mimnaugh, Spence; Robertson, Leitch, Balde; Elliott.
East Kilbride won 6-5 on penalties.

Ayr U (1) 2 *(Murphy 34, Walker 53)*
Peterhead (0) 1 *(Smith 62)* 1698
Ayr U: (442) Stone; Syla (Walker 46), Stanger, McAllister, Reading; Henderson, Dempsey, Howley (McKenzie 10), Murphy (Rus 72); Oakley, McLennan (Hastie 72).
Peterhead: (4141) Oluyemi; Strachan D, Goldie, Scott Ross, Dunne; Forrest (Barry 46); Jack Brown, Pawlett (McAllister 86), Wilson (Jordon Brown 86), Sebastian Ross (Smith 62); Armour (Shanks 61).

Dunfermline Ath (2) 2 *(Kane 23, Todd 32)*
Kelty Hearts (1) 1 *(Johnston 15)* 1821
Dunfermline Ath: (343) Mehmet; Young, Hamilton, Otoo; Comrie, Clay (Wotherspoon 67), Chalmers, Ritchie-Hosler; Mebude (Todd 13), Wighton, Kane.
Kelty Hearts: (4132) Adamson; O'Ware, Flatman, Paterson; MacIntyre; Owens B (Thomas 70), Cunningham, Cole; Johnston, Williamson (Bryce 85).

Livingston (2) 2 *(May 17, Pitman 28)*
Inverness CT (2) 2 *(Allan 10, Gilmour 30)*   943
Livingston: (433) Pitaluga; Finlayson, McGowan, Nottingham, Clarke (Yengi 84); Kelly, Pitman, Lawal (Montano 72); Smith (Sole 55), May (Winter 71), Shinnie.
Inverness CT: (451) Newman; Bray (Thompson 84), Duffy, Savage, Nolan (Strachan 63); Longstaff, Allan (Macleod 63), Davidson, Gilmour, Mackinnon; McKay.
Livingston won 5-4 on penalties.

Tuesday, 22 October 2024

Rangers U21 (2) 4 *(Curtis 19, 60, Danilo 41, O'Reilly 90 (og))*
Stenhousemuir (0) 1 *(Alston 66)*   525
Rangers U21: (4231) Munn; Hutton, Webster (Grant 73), King, Nsiala-Makengo; Rice (Robertson 73), Nsio; Lovelace (Stevens 46), Hagi, Curtis (McClure 90); Danilo (Gentles 61).
Stenhousemuir: (4231) Jamieson; Meechan, Buchanan, Bilham, Ewen; Andersen (Berry 61), Wedderburn; Tomlinson, Alston (Cameron 73), Yates (O'Reilly 73); Aitken (O'Donnell 62).

QUARTER-FINALS

Tuesday, 12 November 2024

Dunfermline Ath (1) 1 *(McCann 37)*
Alloa Ath (0) 0   1400
Dunfermline Ath: (4231) Oluwayemi; Comrie, Benedictus, Otoo, Ngwenya; Hamilton, Chalmers; Ritchie-Hosler (Fisher 79), Todd (Cooper 68), McCann (Sutherland T 79); Mebude (Wighton 67).
Alloa Ath: (4231) Ogayi; Taggart, McKay, Neill, Thomson; Virtanen (Hetherington 62), Scougall; Buchanan (Cawley 62), Donnelly, O'Donnell (Honeyman 77); Rankin (Sammon 77).

East Kilbride (2) 3 *(Robertson 1, Balde 12, Elliott 67)*
Ayr U (0) 2 *(Henderson 58, Rus 64)*   605
East Kilbride: (433) Connelly; Fagan, McGregor, Spence, Ferguson D; Mimnaugh (Lockie 62), Leitch, McShane (Ferguson S 72); Robertson, Elliott, Balde.
Ayr U: (4411) Stone; McAllister, Stanger, McMann, Reading; Henderson, Dempsey (Howley 71), McKenzie (Hastie 78), Rus (Hislop 89); McLennan; Oakley.

Livingston (1) 2 *(McAlear 41, May 87)*
Greenock Morton (0) 1 *(Samuels 90)*   858
Livingston: (433) Pitaluga; Finlayson, Nottingham, McGowan, Clarke (Lawal 56); McAlear, Green (Shinnie 57), Kelly; Sole (Smith 57), Winter (May 78), Muirhead (Yengi 64).
Greenock Morton: (4231) Mullen; Blues, Baird, Broadfoot, Boyes; King (Gillespie 70), Wilson; Garrity (McGinn 46), Lyall (Shaw 62), Moffat (Samuels 71); Stuparevic (Davies 62).

Tuesday, 3 December 2024

Queen's Park (0) 3 *(Thomas 47, Turner 55, Webster 68 (og))*
Rangers U21 (1) 1 *(McKinnon 26)*   692
Queen's Park: (4411) Wills; Mauchin, Tizzard, Murray, Scott J; Hickey-Fugaccia (Hinds 60), Welsh, Turner (Longridge 84), MacGregor (Duncan 61); Thomas (Thompson 85); Rudden (McLeish 71).
Rangers U21: (4231) Munn; Hutton, Webster, Nsiala-Makengo■, Fraser; McKinnon, Rice; Stevens (Gentles 69), Nsio (Burnside 61), Curtis; Eadie (Grant 38).

SEMI-FINALS

Tuesday, 28 January 2025

Queen's Park (2) 6 *(Rudden 1, 97, Duncan 22, Evans 92, 109, Connelly 97 (og))*
East Kilbride (2) 2 *(Leitch 31, Ferguson D 44)*   758
Queen's Park: (4231) Wills; Longridge, Jackson (Ujdur 113), Tizzard, Scott J (Hinds 99); Turner, Welsh (Carrick 73); Hickey-Fugaccia (Scott T 73), Drozd (Evans 76), Duncan; Rudden (Thompson 106).
East Kilbride: (3511) Connelly; Fagan (Ferguson S 96), Hamilton, Ferguson D; Flanagan, Leitch, Spence, McShane (Balde 64), MacDonald (Mimnaugh 96); Robertson (Main 106); Elliott.
aet.

Wednesday, 5 February 2025

Dunfermline Ath (0) 0
Livingston (1) 2 *(Muirhead 41, Yengi 89)*   2072
Dunfermline Ath: (4231) Oluwayemi; Comrie, Mullen, Benedictus, Ngwenya; Hamilton (O'Halloran 69), Otoo; Ritchie-Hosler (Wotherspoon 69), Taylor-Clarke (Kane 55), McCann; Yeboah.
Livingston: (433) Prior; Nottingham (Finlayson 57), McGowan, Wilson, Clarke; McAlear (Shinnie 70), Brandon, Tait; Muirhead, May (Smith 77), Montano (Yengi 57).

SPFL TRUST TROPHY FINAL 2024–25

Sunday, 30 March 2025

Queen's Park (0) 0   Livingston (2) 5

(at Falkirk Stadium, attendance 4079)

Queen's Park: (4231) Ferrie; Mauchin, Tizzard (Carrick 31 (Duncan 45)), Jackson, Montgomery; Longridge (Hickey-Fugaccia 56), Welsh; Drozd (Evans 56), MacGregor, Hurst (Turner 56); Rudden.

Livingston: (433) Prior; Brandon, McGowan, Wilson, Montano (Clarke 62); Kelly, Pitman, Tait (McAlear 62); Muirhead (Smith 76), May (Shinnie 75), Yengi (Finlayson 83).
Scorers: Muirhead 26, May 45, Yengi 50, Shinnie 82, Brandon 90.

Referee: Calum Scott.

SCOTTISH CUP FINALS 1874–2025

SCOTTISH CUP

1874	Queen's Park v Clydesdale	2-0
1875	Queen's Park v Renton	3-0
1876	Queen's Park v Third Lanark	1-1
Replay	Queen's Park v Third Lanark	2-0
1877	Vale of Leven v Rangers	1-1
Replay	Vale of Leven v Rangers	1-1
2nd Replay	Vale of Leven v Rangers	3-2
1878	Vale of Leven v Third Lanark	1-0
1879	Vale of Leven v Rangers	1-1
	Vale of Leven awarded cup, Rangers failing to appear for replay.	
1880	Queen's Park v Thornliebank	3-0
1881	Queen's Park v Dumbarton	2-1
Replay	Queen's Park v Dumbarton	3-1
	After Dumbarton protested the first game.	
1882	Queen's Park v Dumbarton	2-2
Replay	Queen's Park v Dumbarton	4-1
1883	Dumbarton v Vale of Leven	2-2
Replay	Dumbarton v Vale of Leven	2-1
1884	Queen's Park v Vale of Leven	
	Queen's Park awarded cup, Vale of Leven failing to appear.	
1885	Renton v Vale of Leven	0-0
Replay	Renton v Vale of Leven	3-1
1886	Queen's Park v Renton	3-1
1887	Hibernian v Dumbarton	2-1
1888	Renton v Cambuslang	6-1
1889	Third Lanark v Celtic	3-0
Replay	Third Lanark v Celtic	2-1
	Replay by order of Scottish FA because of playing conditions in first match.	
1890	Queen's Park v Vale of Leven	1-1
Replay	Queen's Park v Vale of Leven	2-1
1891	Hearts v Dumbarton	1-0
1892	Celtic v Queen's Park	1-0
Replay	Celtic v Queen's Park	5-1
	After mutually protested first match.	
1893	Queen's Park v Celtic	0-1
Replay	Queen's Park v Celtic	2-1
	Replay by order of Scottish FA because of playing conditions in first match.	
1894	Rangers v Celtic	3-1
1895	St Bernard's v Renton	2-1
1896	Hearts v Hibernian	3-1
1897	Rangers v Dumbarton	5-1
1898	Rangers v Kilmarnock	2-0
1899	Celtic v Rangers	2-0
1900	Celtic v Queen's Park	4-3
1901	Hearts v Celtic	4-3
1902	Hibernian v Celtic	1-0
1903	Rangers v Hearts	1-1
Replay	Rangers v Hearts	0-0
2nd Replay	Rangers v Hearts	2-0
1904	Celtic v Rangers	3-2
1905	Third Lanark v Rangers	0-0
Replay	Third Lanark v Rangers	3-1
1906	Hearts v Third Lanark	1-0
1907	Celtic v Hearts	3-0
1908	Celtic v St Mirren	5-1
1909	Celtic v Rangers	2-2
Replay	Celtic v Rangers	1-1
	Owing to riot, the cup was withheld.	
1910	Dundee v Clyde	2-2
Replay	Dundee v Clyde	0-0*
2nd Replay	Dundee v Clyde	2-1
1911	Celtic v Hamilton A	0-0
Replay	Celtic v Hamilton A	2-0
1912	Celtic v Clyde	2-0
1913	Falkirk v Raith R	2-0
1914	Celtic v Hibernian	0-0
Replay	Celtic v Hibernian	4-1
1920	Kilmarnock v Albion R	3-2
1921	Partick Thistle v Rangers	1-0
1922	Morton v Rangers	1-0

1923	Celtic v Hibernian	1-0
1924	Airdrieonians v Hibernian	2-0
1925	Celtic v Dundee	2-1
1926	St Mirren v Celtic	2-0
1927	Celtic v East Fife	3-1
1928	Rangers v Celtic	4-0
1929	Kilmarnock v Rangers	2-0
1930	Rangers v Partick Thistle	0-0
Replay	Rangers v Partick Thistle	2-1
1931	Celtic v Motherwell	2-2
Replay	Celtic v Motherwell	4-2
1932	Rangers v Kilmarnock	1-1
Replay	Rangers v Kilmarnock	3-0
1933	Celtic v Motherwell	1-0
1934	Rangers v St Mirren	5-0
1935	Rangers v Hamilton A	2-1
1936	Rangers v Third Lanark	1-0
1937	Celtic v Aberdeen	2-1
1938	East Fife v Kilmarnock	1-1
Replay	East Fife v Kilmarnock	4-2*
1939	Clyde v Motherwell	4-0
1947	Aberdeen v Hibernian	2-1
1948	Rangers v Morton	1-1*
Replay	Rangers v Morton	1-0*
1949	Rangers v Clyde	4-1
1950	Rangers v East Fife	3-0
1951	Celtic v Motherwell	1-0
1952	Motherwell v Dundee	4-0
1953	Rangers v Aberdeen	1-1
Replay	Rangers v Aberdeen	1-0
1954	Celtic v Aberdeen	2-1
1955	Clyde v Celtic	1-1
Replay	Clyde v Celtic	1-0
1956	Hearts v Celtic	3-1
1957	Falkirk v Kilmarnock	1-1
Replay	Falkirk v Kilmarnock	2-1*
1958	Clyde v Hibernian	1-0
1959	St Mirren v Aberdeen	3-1
1960	Rangers v Kilmarnock	2-0
1961	Dunfermline Ath v Celtic	0-0
Replay	Dunfermline Ath v Celtic	2-0
1962	Rangers v St Mirren	2-0
1963	Rangers v Celtic	1-1
Replay	Rangers v Celtic	3-0
1964	Rangers v Dundee	3-1
1965	Celtic v Dunfermline Ath	3-2
1966	Rangers v Celtic	0-0
Replay	Rangers v Celtic	1-0
1967	Celtic v Aberdeen	2-0
1968	Dunfermline Ath v Hearts	3-1
1969	Celtic v Rangers	4-0
1970	Aberdeen v Celtic	3-1
1971	Celtic v Rangers	1-1
Replay	Celtic v Rangers	2-1
1972	Celtic v Hibernian	6-1
1973	Rangers v Celtic	3-2
1974	Celtic v Dundee U	3-0
1975	Celtic v Airdrieonians	3-1
1976	Rangers v Hearts	3-1
1977	Celtic v Rangers	1-0
1978	Rangers v Aberdeen	2-1
1979	Rangers v Hibernian	0-0
Replay	Rangers v Hibernian	0-0*
2nd Replay	Rangers v Hibernian	3-2*
1980	Celtic v Rangers	1-0*
1981	Rangers v Dundee U	0-0*
Replay	Rangers v Dundee U	4-1
1982	Aberdeen v Rangers	4-1*
1983	Aberdeen v Rangers	1-0*
1984	Aberdeen v Celtic	2-1*
1985	Celtic v Dundee U	2-1
1986	Aberdeen v Hearts	3-0
1987	St Mirren v Dundee U	1-0*
1988	Celtic v Dundee U	2-1
1989	Celtic v Rangers	1-0

TENNENTS SCOTTISH CUP

1990	Aberdeen v Celtic	0-0*
	Aberdeen won 9-8 on penalties.	
1991	Motherwell v Dundee U	4-3*
1992	Rangers v Airdrieonians	2-1
1993	Rangers v Aberdeen	2-1
1994	Dundee U v Rangers	1-0
1995	Celtic v Airdrieonians	1-0
1996	Rangers v Hearts	5-1
1997	Kilmarnock v Falkirk	1-0
1998	Hearts v Rangers	2-1
1999	Rangers v Celtic	1-0
2000	Rangers v Aberdeen	4-0
2001	Celtic v Hibernian	3-0
2002	Rangers v Celtic	3-2
2003	Rangers v Dundee	1-0
2004	Celtic v Dunfermline Ath	3-1
2005	Celtic v Dundee U	1-0
2006	Hearts v Gretna	1-1*
	Hearts won 4-2 on penalties.	
2007	Celtic v Dunfermline Ath	1-0

SCOTTISH CUP

2008	Rangers v Queen of the South	3-2

HOMECOMING SCOTTISH CUP

2009	Rangers v Falkirk	1-0

ACTIVE NATION SCOTTISH CUP

2010	Dundee U v Ross Co	3-0

SCOTTISH CUP

2011	Celtic v Motherwell	3-0

WILLIAM HILL SCOTTISH CUP

2012	Hearts v Hibernian	5-1
2013	Celtic v Hibernian	3-0
2014	St Johnstone v Dundee U	2-0
2015	Inverness CT v Falkirk	2-1
2016	Hibernian v Rangers	3-2
2017	Celtic v Aberdeen	2-1
2018	Celtic v Motherwell	2-0
2019	Celtic v Hearts	2-1
2020	Celtic v Hearts	3-3*
	Celtic won 4-3 on penalties.	

SCOTTISH CUP

2021	St Johnstone v Hibernian	1-0
2022	Rangers v Hearts	2-0*
2023	Celtic v Inverness CT	3-1

SCOTTISH GAS SCOTTISH CUP

2024	Celtic v Rangers	1-0
2025	Aberdeen v Celtic	1-1*
	Aberdeen won 4-3 on penalties.	

*After extra time.

SCOTTISH CUP WINS

Celtic 42†, Rangers 34†, Queen's Park 10, Aberdeen 8, Hearts 8, Clyde 3, Hibernian 3, Kilmarnock 3, St Mirren 3, Vale of Leven 3, Dundee U 2, Dunfermline Ath 2, Falkirk 2, Motherwell 2, Renton 2, St Johnstone 2, Third Lanark 2, Airdrieonians 1, Dumbarton 1, Dundee 1, East Fife 1, Inverness CT 1, Morton 1, Partick Thistle 1, St Bernard's 1.
†*The 1909 final between Celtic and Rangers is not included. Owing to a riot the cup was withheld.*

APPEARANCES IN FINAL

Celtic 62, Rangers 54, Aberdeen 17, Hearts 17, Hibernian 15, Queen's Park 12, Dundee U 10, Kilmarnock 8, Motherwell 8, Vale of Leven 7, Clyde 6, Dumbarton 6, St Mirren 6, Third Lanark 6, Dundee 5, Dunfermline Ath 5, Falkirk 5, Renton 5, Airdrieonians 4, East Fife 3, Hamilton A 2, Inverness CT 2, Morton 2, Partick Thistle 2, St Johnstone 2, Albion R 1, Cambuslang 1, Clydesdale 1, Gretna 1, Queen of the South 1, Raith R 1, Ross Co 1, St Bernard's 1, Thornliebank 1.

LEAGUE CHALLENGE FINALS 1990–2025

B&Q CENTENARY CUP

1990–91	Dundee v Ayr U	3-2*

B&Q CUP

1991–92	Hamilton A v Ayr U	1-0
1992–93	Hamilton A v Morton	3-2
1993–94	Falkirk v St Mirren	3-0
1994–95	Airdrieonians v Dundee	3-2*

SCOTTISH LEAGUE CHALLENGE CUP

1995–96	Stenhousemuir v Dundee U	0-0*
	Stenhousemuir won 5-4 on penalties.	
1996–97	Stranraer v St Johnstone	1-0
1997–98	Falkirk v Queen of the South	1-0
1998–99	*No competition.*	
	Suspended due to lack of sponsorship.	

BELL'S CHALLENGE CUP

1999–2000	Alloa Ath v Inverness CT	4-4*
	Alloa Ath won 5-4 on penalties.	
2000–01	Airdrieonians v Livingston	2-2*
	Airdrieonians won 3-2 on penalties.	
2001–02	Airdrieonians v Alloa Ath	2-1

BELL'S CUP

2002–03	Queen of the South v Brechin C	2-0
2003–04	Inverness CT v Airdrie U	2-0
2004–05	Falkirk v Ross Co	2-1
2005–06	St Mirren v Hamilton A	2-1

SCOTTISH LEAGUE CHALLENGE CUP

2006–07	Ross Co v Clyde	1-1*
	Ross Co won 5-4 on penalties.	
2007–08	St Johnstone v Dunfermline Ath	3-2

ALBA CHALLENGE CUP

2008–09	Airdrie U v Ross Co	2-2*
	Airdrie U won 3-2 on penalties.	
2009–10	Dundee v Inverness CT	3-2
2010–11	Ross Co v Queen of the South	2-0

RAMSDENS CUP

2011–12	Falkirk v Hamilton A	1-0
2012–13	Queen of the South v Partick Thistle	1-1*
	Queen of the South won 6-5 on penalties.	
2013–14	Raith R v Rangers	1-0*

PETROFAC TRAINING SCOTTISH LEAGUE CHALLENGE CUP

2014–15	Livingston v Alloa Ath	4-0
2015–16	Rangers v Peterhead	4-0

IRN-BRU SCOTTISH LEAGUE CHALLENGE CUP

2016–17	Dundee U v St Mirren	2-1
2017–18	Inverness CT v Dumbarton	1-0
2018–19	Ross Co v Connah's Quay Nomads	3-1

TUNNOCK'S CARAMEL WAFER SCOTTISH LEAGUE CHALLENGE CUP

2019–20†	Raith R v Inverness CT	Joint winners
2020–21	*No competition due to COVID-19 pandemic.*	

SPFL TRUST TROPHY

2021–22	Raith R v Queen of the South	3-1
2022–23	Hamilton A v Raith R	1-0
2023–24	Airdrieonians v The New Saints	2-1
2024–25	Livingston v Queen's Park	5-0

*After extra time. †Due to the COVID-19 pandemic, the final due to be played on Sunday 8 March 2020 was postponed.

SCOTTISH GAS SCOTTISH CUP 2024–25

*■ Denotes player sent off. *After extra time.*

PRELIMINARY ROUND 1

Bo'ness Ath v Beith Juniors	3-1
Culter v Invergordon	4-0

PRELIMINARY ROUND 2

Tynecastle v Glasgow University	4-0
Bo'ness Ath v Kilwinning Rangers	2-0
Glenafton Ath v Threave R	2-4
Coldstream v Camelon Juniors	0-6
Bonnyton Thistle v Dunbar U	0-1
Jeanfield Swifts v Newton Stewart	3-0
Lochee U v Hawick Royal Albert	4-0
Golspie Sutherland v Carluke R	0-2
Pollok v Darvel	1-3
Cupar Hearts v Wigtown & Bladnoch	4-0
Preston Ath v Irvine Meadow	2-3
Tayport v Dundee North End	1-3
Culter v Sauchie Juniors	1-2
Dundonald Bluebell v Edinburgh University	3-1
Fort William v Hill of Beath Hawthorn	0-8
Benburb v Vale of Leithen	0-3
Burntisland Shipyard v Dunipace	2-1
Haddington Ath v Auchinleck Talbot	1-4
Creetown v Cumnock Juniors	1-3
Girvan v St Cuthbert W	9-0
Penicuik Ath v Musselburgh Ath	0-1
Dalkeith Thistle v Blackburn U	0-4
Dalbeattie Star v Whitehill Welfare	1-2
Rutherglen Glencairn v Hutchison Vale	2-0
Clydebank v St Andrews U	7-0
Easthouses Lily Miners Welfare v Newtongrange Star	0-4

FIRST ROUND

Tynecastle v Hill of Beath Hawthorn	2-3
Dalkeith Thistle v Broxburn Ath	0-4
Forres Mechanics v Jeanfield Swifts	1-2
University of Stirling v Caledonian Braves	0-2
Brechin C v Newtongrange Star	1-0
Clachnacuddin v Nairn Co	3-1
Linlithgow Rose v Lossiemouth	3-1
Musselburgh Ath v Darvel	1-0*
Gala Fairydean R v Banks o' Dee	0-1
Broomhill v Turriff U	0-1
Cowdenbeath v Rutherglen Glencairn	3-2
East Stirlingshire v Lochee U	2-3
Cumbernauld Colts v Civil Service Strollers	0-3
Strathspey Thistle v Sauchie Juniors	0-6
Formartine U v Whitehill Welfare	2-0
Fraserburgh v Rothes	8-0
Threave R v Vale of Leithen	6-1
Brora Rangers v Cumnock Juniors	2-1
Buckie Thistle v Carluke R	2-1
Burntisland Shipyard v Irvine Meadow	1-4
Dundonald Bluebell v Inverurie Loco Works	1-1*
Inverurie Loco Works won 3-0 on penalties.	
Keith v Camelon Juniors	1-1*
Keith won 4-3 on penalties.	
Huntly v Wick Academy	2-2*
Huntly won 5-3 on penalties.	
Clydebank v Girvan	3-1
Dunbar U v Bo'ness Ath	1-4
East Kilbride v Gretna 2008	2-0
Albion R v Auchinleck Talbot	1-2
Dundee North End v Tranent	4-0
Berwick Rangers v Cupar Hearts	4-2
Deveronvale v Bo'ness U	2-4

SECOND ROUND

Threave R v Stranraer	2-3
Musselburgh Ath v Caledonian Braves	2-1
Sauchie Juniors v Buckie Thistle	0-2
Fraserburgh v Turriff U	3-1*
The Spartans v Cowdenbeath	1-2
Forfar Ath v Berwick Rangers	1-0
Keith v Clydebank	0-3
Peterhead v Lochee U	6-3
Elgin C v Clyde	1-1*
Elgin C won 8-7 on penalties.	
Irvine Meadow v Civil Service Strollers	3-0
Inverurie Loco Works v Dundee North End	1-3*

Hill of Beath Hawthorn v Bo'ness U	0-2
Brechin C v Huntly	3-2
Jeanfield Swifts v Edinburgh C	1-1*
Edinburgh C won 5-4 on penalties.	
Stirling Alb v Bo'ness Ath	6-0
Auchinleck Talbot v Broxburn Ath	0-1
Linlithgow Rose v Clachnacuddin	3-0
East Fife v Banks o' Dee	0-1
East Kilbride v Bonnyrigg Rose	3-1
Brora Rangers v Formartine U	2-1

THIRD ROUND

Friday, 29 November 2024

Dumbarton (3) 3 *(Niang 11, Hilton 13, Ruth 39)*

Alloa Ath (1) 2 *(Donnelly 43, Scougall 65)* 724

Dumbarton: (4231) Long; Pignatiello, Durnan, Brown, Clark; Gray, Niang; Orsi, Hilton (Mumbongo 80), McGuffie (Wallace 72); Ruth.
Alloa Ath: (41212) Morrison; Taggart, McKay, Neill, Waters; Hetherington; Cawley (McDonnell 59), Scougall; Donnelly; Rankin, Sammon.
Referee: Ryan Lee.

Saturday, 30 November 2024

Arbroath (0) 0

Queen of the South (0) 1 *(Doherty 81)* 818

Arbroath: (4231) McAdams; Wilkie, Watson, Smith, Bisland (Gold 85); Flynn (Murray 85), Slater (Reilly 66); Dow, Spalding, Stewart; Gallagher (Coulson 66).
Queen of the South: (352) Stewart; Douglas, Brydon (McKechnie 72), Hannah; Hewitt, O'Donnell (Doherty 46), Cochrane (Luissint 85), Lyon, Macintyre; McIntosh, Brooks (Walker 90).
Referee: Peter Stuart.

Ayr U (0) 2 *(Devlin 63, Murphy 89)*

Greenock Morton (0) 0 1775

Ayr U: (343) Russell; Stanger, Devlin, McMann; Watret (McAllister 82), Dempsey, Rus (Musonda 79), Reading; Henderson (Murphy 67), Oakley (Bavidge 83), McLennan.
Greenock Morton: (4231) Mullen; Ballantyne (Gillespie 74), Baird, Boyes, Delaney; Blues, Wilson; Moffat (McGinn 74), Lyall, Shaw (Garrity 61); Davies (Samuels 74).
Referee: Iain Snedden.

Banks o' Dee (0) 1 *(Philipson 62)*

Hamilton A (2) 2 *(Shaw 28, 45)* 350

Banks o' Dee: (4141) Hoban; Selbie, Cooney, Reynolds, Stark; Vigurs; Philipson (Alexander 70), Macleod (Hunter 65), Winton, Gilmour (Antoniazzi 81); Duell.
Hamilton A: (4312) Albinson; Tumilty, McGinty, McGowan (MacDonald 41), Hendrie; Bradley (Barjonas 62), Martin, Smith (Maguire 78); McKinstry (Henderson 62); O'Hara, Shaw.
Referee: Graham Grainger.

Clydebank (0) 2 *(Little 68, 73 (pen))*

Buckie Thistle (0) 0 924

Clydebank: (4231) Keaney; Grant (Hodge 86), Niven, Syme, McHugh; McGowan, Low; Gallacher (Truesdale 86), Little, McGonigle (Daramola 60); Mulcahy (Samson 70).
Buckie Thistle: (4231) Ridgers; Munro■, McKay, McHardy, Ramsay (Morrison 74); Pugh, Fraser (Keir 86); Wood■, MacAskill, Goodall; Harvey (Peters 70).
Referee: Alex Shepherd.

Cove Rangers (0) 2 *(Glass 89 (pen), McGrath 90)*

Inverness CT (0) 0 539

Cove Rangers: (352) Demus; Doyle, Gillingham, Harrington; Darge, McAllister, Yule, Scully, Emslie; Marshall (Glass 72), Megginson (McGrath 90).
Inverness CT: (4231) Dibaga; Nolan, Devine, Savage (MacKay 82), Strachan (Cairns 90); Gilmour, Allan; Thompson (Macleod 71), Mackinnon, Longstaff; McKay.
Referee: Steven Kirkland.

Cowdenbeath (0) 1 *(Sutherland 49)*
Brechin C (1) 4 *(McKay 31, 104, 120, Moreland 112)* 411
Cowdenbeath: (352) Lynch; Jordan, Hill (Walker 58), Newman; Mcpherson (McLean 109), Whyte, Swanson (Denham 103), McDonald, McNab; Docherty, Sutherland (Burke 70).
Brechin C: (4141) Wilson; Martin (Ferguson 114), Spark, McKay, McHattie; Moreland (Johnson 114); Scott (Logan 114), Macleod (Tosh 66), Patrick (Hunter 91), Loudon; Robertson (Milne R 66).
aet. Referee: Gary Hanvidge.

Edinburgh C (0) 1 *(Young 90 (pen))*
Dunfermline Ath (1) 2 *(Mebude 5, Todd 72)* 696
Edinburgh C: (4132) Weir; Robertson, Gormley (Wells 67), McArthur (Hamilton 82), Grigor; Jones; Stokes, Jarvis (Lynch 67), Mitchell (See 67); Lawson (Scally 88), Young.
Dunfermline Ath: (3421) Oluwayemi; Comrie, Benedictus, Otoo; Ritchie-Hosler, Todd, Chalmers (Hamilton 61), Ngwenya; Wotherspoon (Clay 88), Cooper (Sutherland T 59); Mebude.
Referee: Duncan Williams.

Elgin C (1) 3 *(Sargent 43, 83, Gavin 77)*
Kelty Hearts (0) 2 *(Flatman 58, Cunningham 86 (pen))* 716
Elgin C: (4231) Glavin; Cairns, Girvan, Murray, Booth; Cameron, Gallagher; Lesley (Gavin 73), Dingwall (Hyde 81), Sargent; Golding (McDonald 90).
Kelty Hearts: (433) Adamson; Mercer (Thomas 57), O'Ware, Flatman, Paterson; Allan C (Bryce 89), MacIntyre, Cunningham; Johnston, Williamson (Cole 78), Moore.
Referee: George Calder.

Forfar Ath (1) 3 *(McLean 39, 51, 102)*
Stirling Alb (2) 3 *(Brown 9, 107, Kerr 20)* 437
Forfar Ath: (4141) McCallum; Logan, Allan M, Morrison, Malcolm; Whatley; Skelly (Rodden 79), Robson, Inglis (Cannon 46), Taylor (Allan F 117); McLean.
Stirling Alb: (352) Gaston; Kerr, McGeachie, Sula; Harkness (Knox 91), Brown, Waugh (Cant 120), Wright (Davidson 46), Dall (Graham 46); Hilson (Roy 83), Carrick (McKinley 74).
aet; Forfar Ath won 4-2 on penalties.
Referee: Jordan Curran.

Fraserburgh (2) 2 *(Wood 39, Simpson 44)*
Annan Ath (0) 0 346
Fraserburgh: (4411) Barbour J; Aitken, Hay, Simpson, West (Sopel 10); Sweenie-Rowe, Young, Buchan, Wood (Bolton 76); Watt (Butcher 76); Barbour S (Hawkins 89).
Annan Ath: (4231) Smith J; Gibson, Muir T (Barnes 89), Kilsby, Lennon (Stevenson 46); Smith P, McGowan (Quigg 19); Todd, Fleming K, Dixon (Ross 46); Smith A.
Referee: Daniel Graves.

Irvine Meadow (0) 0
Stenhousemuir (1) 5 *(O'Reilly 43, 58, 90, Aitken M 48, Steele 66)* 281
Irvine Meadow: (4231) Barclay; McLennan, Kennedy, Currie, Gallagher; Anderson (McBryde 81), Davidson (Cruden 67); Sewell, Moore (Gilmour 73), Baird (Cree 80); Sharpe (Neilson 80).
Stenhousemuir: (4231) Jamieson D; Meechan, Buchanan (Banner 70), Steele, Bilham; Wedderburn (Berry 70), Andersen; Tomlinson (Cameron 76), Yates (Taylor 81), O'Reilly; Aitken M (O'Donnell 70).
Referee: Andy Gamble.

Linlithgow Rose (0) 0
Raith R (1) 4 *(Gibson 22, Easton 49 (pen), 58, Hamilton 85)* 1720
Linlithgow Rose: (4231) Binnie; Allen, McCracken, Skinner, Thomson; Maguire, McMullan; Paterson (Nicolson 73), Ogilvie (McMartin 66), Rae (Devine 54); Brown (Sneddon 66).
Raith R: (4231) Dabrowski; Dabo, Hanlon, Murray, Dick; Brown, Matthews (Montagu 68); Easton (Connolly 79), Stanton (Byrne 79), Gibson (Mullin 80); Adedoyin (Hamilton 61).
Referee: Alastair Grieve.

Livingston (2) 2 *(McAlear 20, Yengi 35)*
Brora Rangers (0) 0 799
Livingston: (433) Prior; Lawal (Jackson 54), Nottingham, McGowan, Clarke; Pitman (Sole 63), McAlear, Shinnie; Smith (Green 63), May (Winter 70), Yengi (Muirhead 70).
Brora Rangers: (4231) Mackay; Kelly, Gamble, Finnis, Williamson; MacLeod, Sutherland A; Ewan (Robesten 59), Dingwall, Mackenzie; Sutherland S (Wallace 70).
Referee: Colin Steven.

Musselburgh Ath (1) 3 *(Evans 11, Donaldson 61, Stevenson 87 (pen))*
Bo'ness U (1) 1 *(Stenhouse 27)* 1140
Musselburgh Ath: (352) Laing; O'Kane, Todd, Stevenson; Donaldson, Barfoot, Anderson, Khan, Auriemma (Myles 90); Evans, Reid (Court 59).
Bo'ness U: (433) Melrose; Masson, Hawkins (Osadolor 63), Travis, Macaulay; Stevenson (Duffy 63), Henderson, Gemmell (Johnston 63); Porteous, Stenhouse, Grant.
Referee: Joel Kennedy.

Peterhead (1) 2 *(Barry 39, Pawlett 90)*
Montrose (2) 3 *(Hester 9 (pen), 16, Lyons 84)* 599
Peterhead: (4231) McKenzie; Goldie, Jason Brown, Scott Ross, Dunne; McCarthy, Forrest; Barry (Duthie 90), Pawlett, Sebastian Ross (McAllister 76); Smith (Shanks 19).
Montrose: (4231) Gill; Dillon, Quinn, Mackenzie (Waddell 46), Steeves (Bertie 46); Masson (Machado 75), Gardyne (Watson 88); Webster, Brown, Lyons; Hester (MacIver-Redwood 68).
Referee: Colin Whyte.

Queen's Park (2) 2 *(Longridge 34, MacGregor 42)*
Partick Thistle (1) 2 *(Crawford 12, Tizzard 64 (og))* 1769
Queen's Park: (352) Ferrie; Kerr, Tizzard, Fieldson; Longridge, MacGregor (Hinds 72), Thomson, Turner (Hickey-Fugaccia 78), Duncan (Scott J 100); Rudden (McLeish 97), Thomas.
Partick Thistle: (4231) Roberts; Turner, Ashcroft, O'Reilly, Milne; Crawford (McBeth 90), Bannigan; Chalmers, Robinson (Diack 114), Fitzpatrick (Ablade 74); Graham (Lawless 96).
aet; Queen's Park won 7-6 on penalties.
Referee: Euan Anderson.

Stranraer (0) 1 *(Dunlop 82)*
Broxburn Ath (1) 2 *(Page J 31, Locke 97)* 707
Stranraer: (352) Pazikas; Ross, Robertson, Cummins; Grant, Gallagher, Hawkshaw (Dunlop 62), Russell, Ecrepont (Edgar 63); Guthrie (Brindley 62), Lang (McKnight 89).
Broxburn Ath: (4231) Watt; Smith, Page J, Page G, Rodden (Millar 15 (Ellis 119)); McCrory-Irving, Bell; Wardell, McLeod Kay (Mwangi 77), Jones (Locke 94); Brass (Downie 106).
aet.
Referee: Sean Murdoch.

Sunday, 1 December 2024
Dundee NE (0) 0
Airdrieonians (1) 1 *(McGregor 6)* 750
Dundee NE: (4141) Adam; Baird, Donald, Jamieson, Rice; Allan; Dow, Clark (Winter 56), Montgomery (Ferguson 56), Devine; Sludden (Blacklock 73).
Airdrieonians: (4141) Wright; Wilson B (Cooper 72), Graham, Watson, Hancock (Agyemang 54); Gallagher; McGrattan, Frizzell, Armstrong, McGregor (Mochrie 72); Duffy.
Referee: Duncan Nicolson.

Monday, 2 December 2024
East Kilbride (0) 1 *(Ferguson S 87)*
Falkirk (2) 3 *(Agyeman 20, Miller 37, Morrison 88)* 692
East Kilbride: (433) Connelly; Fagan, Hamilton, Spence, Lockie; Mimnaugh (Ferguson S 55), McShane, Balde; Robertson, Elliott, Flanagan (Livingstone 55).
Falkirk: (4231) Hogarth; Adams, Henderson, Mackie, McCann; Spencer, Tait (Yeats 85); Miller (Morrison 71), Nesbitt, Agyeman (McKenna 79); Oliver (MacIver 71).
Referee: Chris Graham.

FOURTH ROUND

Friday, 17 January 2025

Brechin C (1) 1 *(Bright 23)*

Hearts (1) 4 *(Dhanda 40, McHattie 52 (og),*
Kabangu 62, 79)   3650

Brechin C: (4141) Wilson; Martin, Spark (Bright 17), McKay, McHattie; Moreland; Scott (Ferguson 87), Macleod, Milne L (Tosh 61), Loudon (Logan 88); Robertson (Sheridan 61).
Hearts: (4231) Gordon; Forrester (Oyegoke 69), Halkett, McCart (Taylor 81), Penrice; Devlin (Forrest 87), Baningime; Vargas (Wilson 70), Grant, Dhanda (Spittal 69); Kabangu.
Referee: Grant Irvine.

Saturday, 18 January 2025

Broxburn Ath (0) 0

Ayr U (2) 8 *(Agbaire 16, Henderson 38 (pen), 52, 90,*
McKenzie 65, Oakley 69, Hastie 70, Watret 77)   2100

Broxburn Ath: (451) Watt; Ruari Ellis, Page J, Page G, Millar (Rodden 68); Wardell (Lorimer 72), Bell, Locke (Jones 63), McCrory-Irving, Mwangi (Turner 63); Brass (Douglas 63).
Ayr U: (352) Stone; Agbaire, Devlin (McAllister 73), McMann; Watret, McKenzie, McKinnon (Mitchell 72), Murphy, Reading (Hastie 54); Henderson, Oakley (Hislop 70).
Referee: Lloyd Wilson.

Celtic (1) 2 *(McGregor 12, Maeda 70)*

Kilmarnock (1) 1 *(Wales 45)*   40,916

Celtic: (433) Schmeichel; Johnston A, Carter-Vickers, Trusty, Taylor (Scales 83); Engels (Bernardo 68), McGregor, Hatate (McCowan 90); Kuhn, Furuhashi (Idah 83), Maeda.
Kilmarnock: (3421) McCrorie (O'Hara 4); Mayo, Wright, Deas; Lyons (Armstrong 40), Donnelly (McKenzie 66), Polworth (Watson 67), Ndaba; Murray, Wales (Anderson 87); Watkins.
Referee: Nick Walsh.

Cove Rangers (1) 2 *(Emslie 43, Gaffney 80)*

Forfar Ath (0) 0   578

Cove Rangers: (4132) Suman; Lobban, Doyle, Darge, Harrington; Marshall (McGrath 64); Fyvie, Glass (Gaffney 64), Scully; Megginson, Emslie.
Forfar Ath: (433) McCallum; Logan, Morrison, Hutchinson, Allan M; Robson, Rodden (MacLean 46), Whatley (Malcolm 67); Cannon, Skelly (Allan F 67), Inglis (Taylor 76).
Referee: Duncan Williams.

Dumbarton (0) 1 *(McGuffie 90)*

Airdrieonians (2) 5 *(McGrattan 4, Gallagher 11,*
Mochrie 74, Wilson B 76, Watson 86)   1113

Dumbarton: (433) Hayward; Pignatiello, Lynas (McGuffie 46), Durnan, Clark (Webster 77); Gray, Niang, Blair (Mumbongo 60); Orsi, Hilton (Wallace 78), Shiels.
Airdrieonians: (442) Wright; MacDonald, Watson, Graham, Hancock (Duffy 81); McGrattan (Cooper 75), McMaster, Gallagher (Armstrong 29), Frizzell; Wilson B, Mochrie (McGregor 75).
Referee: Colin Steven.

Dunfermline Ath (2) 3 *(Hamilton 16, Otoo 41, McCann 46)*

Stenhousemuir (0) 0   2353

Dunfermline Ath: (4231) Oluwayemi; Comrie, Fogarty, Benedictus, Otoo; Hamilton, Chalmers; Ritchie-Hosler (O'Halloran 79), Wotherspoon (Cooper 65), McCann (Mebude 79); Kane (Wighton 64).
Stenhousemuir: (4231) Jamieson D; Meechan (Ewen 80), Banner, Buchanan, Bilham; Wedderburn (Black 58), Jacobs (McGill 58), Alston (Taylor 65), Andersen, O'Reilly (Tomlinson 80); Yates.
Referee: Peter Stuart.

Elgin C (0) 0

Aberdeen (1) 3 *(Morris 21, Lopes 72, 90)*   4410

Elgin C: (4231) Glavin; Cairns, Girvan, Cameron, Booth*; Hyde, Gallagher; Lesley (Gavin 59 (MacDonald 86)), Dingwall, Sargent (McDonald 74); Golding.
Aberdeen: (4231) Doohan; Devlin, Rubezic, Tobers, Jensen; Palaversa (Shinnie 62), Nilsen (Clarkson 62); Morris, Polvara (Gueye 54), Lopes; Ambrose (Nisbet 62).
Referee: Calum Scott.

Hamilton A (1) 3 *(Hendrie 24, McGinty 89, Shaw 90)*

Musselburgh Ath (0) 1 *(Todd 49)*   1301

Hamilton A: (4231) Albinson; Tumilty, Maguire, McGinty, Hendrie (Longridge 90); Barjonas, Martin (MacDonald 46); O'Hara (Bradley 68), Smith, McKinstry (Henderson 69); Shaw.
Musselburgh Ath: (352) McCathie; Stevenson, Wilson, Todd; Dunsmore (Smith 90), Barfoot, Barker (Reid 90), Khan, Auriemma (Walsh 76); Evans, Court.
Referee: Graham Grainger.

Hibernian (1) 3 *(Boyle 2, 59, Molotnikov 46)*

Clydebank (0) 0   11,406

Hibernian: (3412) Smith; O'Hora, Bushiri (Cadden C 46), Iredale; Miller, Kwon (Gillie 72), Levitt (Amos 63), Molotnikov; Hoilett; Boyle (Bowie 63), Kukharevych (Campbell 46).
Clydebank: (4231) Leishman; Hodge (McGowan 36), Syme, Grant, McHugh (Darroch 78); Cairns, Low; Gallacher (McGonigle 78), Little, Truesdale (MacKenzie 68); Mulcahy (Samson 68).
Referee: Duncan Nicolson.

Queen of the South (0) 1 *(Dickenson 75)*

St Mirren (2) 3 *(Olusanya 10, 21, Boyd-Munce 90)*   2567

Queen of the South: (442) Stewart; Hewitt, Brydon, Douglas, Hannah (Cochrane 62); Doherty, Luissint (Bryden 80), Lyon, Macintyre; Brooks, Dickenson.
St Mirren: (352) Hemming; Fraser, Iacoviti (Taylor R 9), Gogic; Penman (John 82), Smyth, Phillips (Oseni 70), O'Hara, Tanser; Mandron, Olusanya (Boyd-Munce 70).
Referee: Ryan Lee.

Queen's Park (1) 3 *(McLeish 45, Rudden 90, Scott J 98)*

Montrose (0) 2 *(Lyons 56, 60)*   856

Queen's Park: (4231) Ferrie; Mauchin (Rudden 67), Ujdur, Tizzard, Scott J; Longridge, Welsh; Hickey-Fugaccia (Drozd 57), Turner, Duncan (Thompson 77); McLeish (Hinds 77).
Montrose: (433) Gill; Dillon, Quinn, Mackenzie, Bertie (Waddell 103); Machado (Shrive 80), Masson (Brown 72), Sandilands (Watson 86); Webster, Hester (Stirton 72), Lyons (MacIver-Redwood 86).
aet.
Referee: Dan McFarlane.

Ross Co (0) 2 *(White 56, Hale 73)*

Livingston (1) 3 *(Muirhead 45 (pen), Montano 62,*
Shinnie 119)   1802

Ross Co: (3142) Amissah; Wright, Lopata, Campbell (Grieves 46 (Telfer 105)); Kenneh (Allardice 106); Brown, Chilvers, Nisbet (Phillips 65), Harmon (Ashworth 46); White (Randall 80), Hale.
Livingston: (433) Prior; Finlayson, McGowan, Wilson, Fraser; Pitman (Winter 117), Brandon, McAlear; Muirhead, May (Shinnie 106), Montano (Ubochioma 106).
aet.
Referee: Chris Graham.

St Johnstone (1) 1 *(Kirk 9)*

Motherwell (0) 0   3892

St Johnstone: (4411) Fisher; Wright, Sanders, Mikulic, Douglas; Curtis, Sprangler, Griffith, Holt; Carey (Clark 66); Kirk (Mbunga-Kimpioka 66).
Motherwell: (3421) Mair; Blaney, Balmer, Casey (O'Donnell 46); Kaleta, Andrews (Sparrow 46), Halliday, Wilson; Nicholson (Slattery 68), Maswanhise (Ebiye 74); Vale (Watt 74).
Referee: John Beaton.

Sunday, 19 January 2025

Falkirk (0) 1 *(Morrison 79)*

Raith R (0) 2 *(Stanton 86, Easton 109 (pen))*   4557

Falkirk: (4231) Hogarth; Adams, Henderson, Donaldson, Mackie; Spencer, Tait (Oliver 112); Agyeman (Morrison 46), Nesbitt (Stewart 90), Ross (Miller 46); MacIver (McKenna 85).
Raith R: (3511) Dabrowski; Murray (Montagu 85), Hanlon, Dick; Doherty (Freeman 106), Brown (Stanton 72), Matthews, Pollock (Mullin 68), Stevenson; Easton (Gibson 114); Marsh (Connolly 85).
aet. Referee: Don Robertson.

Rangers (1) 5 *(Dessers 27, 57, 90, Nsiala-Makengo 52, McCausland 74)*

Fraserburgh (0) 0   36,276

Rangers: (4231) Munn; Tavernier (King 82), Propper (Yilmaz 62), Nsiala-Makengo, Jefte; Barron, Diomande (Rice 62); Lovelace (Curtis 62), Bajrami (Hagi 78), McCausland; Dessers.
Fraserburgh: (451) Barbour J; Aitken, Simpson (Watt 70), Hay, West (Hawkins 80); Wood (Strachan 79), Young, Beagrie, Buchan (McKay 86), Sweenie-Rowe; Barbour S (Butcher 70).
Referee: Iain Snedden.

Monday, 20 January 2025

Dundee (1) 1 *(Murray 1)*

Dundee U (0) 0   9294

Dundee: (343) Carson; Astley, Robertson C, Donnelly; Ingram, Sylla, Garza (Samuels 83), Robertson F; Cameron, Murray, Adewumi (Palmer-Houlden 66).
Dundee U: (3412) Walton; Graham (van der Sande 84), Gallagher, Holt; Strain (Trapanosvki 71), Adegboyega (Middleton 71), Sevelj, Ferry; Stephenson; Dalby, Moult (Paton 71).
Referee: Matthew MacDermid.

FIFTH ROUND

Friday, 7 February 2025

Ayr U (0) 0

Hibernian (0) 1 *(Bushiri 87)*   7364

Ayr U: (352) Stone; Stanger, Agbaire, McMann; McKenzie (McAllister 87), McLennan, Dempsey, McKinnon (Murphy 74), Reading; Henderson (Rus 74), Oakley (Main 87).
Hibernian: (3412) Smith; O'Hora, Bushiri, Iredale (Obita 90); Cadden C, Triantis, Levitt (Moriah-Welsh 74), Cadden N; Campbell; Boyle, Kukharevych (Bowie 62).
Referee: Kevin Clancy.

Saturday, 8 February 2025

Celtic (2) 5 *(Maeda 6, 45, 77, McCowan 47, Yang 56)*

Raith R (0) 0   39,207

Celtic: (433) Sinisalo; Ralston, Murray, Scales, Schlupp (Nawrocki 72); McCowan, McGregor (Engels 65), Bernardo (Hatate 37); Yang (Kenny 65), Maeda, Kuhn (Jota 65).
Raith R: (541) Rae; Doherty, Murray, Hanlon, Dick, Stevenson; Brown, Matthews, Mullin, Easton (Marsh 89); Gullan (Pollock 57).
Referee: Chris Graham.

Dundee (4) 4 *(Robertson C 13, Cameron 25, 44, Adewumi 40)*

Airdrieonians (0) 0   4335

Dundee: (343) McCracken; Donnelly, Robertson C (Shaughnessy 82), Portales; Mulligan, McGhee (Robertson F 72), Cameron (Sylla 71), Larkeche (Samuels 71); Tiffoney, Murray, Adewumi (Lopez 61).
Airdrieonians: (4231) Wright; MacDonald, Watson, Graham, Bruce (Hancock 66); Gallagher, McMaster (Armstrong 57); McGrattan (McGregor 57), Wilson B (Cooper 80), Frizzell; Mochrie (McStravick 66).
Referee: Euan Anderson.

Livingston (1) 3 *(McGowan 25, Yengi 81, 83)*

Cove Rangers (0) 0   1111

Livingston: (433) Prior; Finlayson, McGowan, Wilson, Fraser (Clarke 64); Brandon (Shinnie 64), Tait, McAlear (Pitman 56); Muirhead, May (Smith 79), Montano (Yengi 56).

Cove Rangers: (4312) Suman; Lobban, Darge, Doyle, Harrington; Marshall (Parker 78) Yule, Scully (Gaffney 78); Glass (Gillingham 78); Megginson (McGrath 84), Fyvie.
Referee: Matthew MacDermid.

St Johnstone (0) 1 *(Sidibeh 87)*

Hamilton A (0) 0   3095

St Johnstone: (3421) Fisher; Sprangler, Mikulic, Balodis; Curtis (Duke-Mckenna 46), Watt, Svedberg (Carey 65), Wright; Steven (Mitchell 89), Griffith (Clark 85); Kirk (Sidibeh 85).
Hamilton A: (352) Lyness; McGinty, McGowan, Lamie (Tumilty 59); Bradley (Henderson 84), Maguire, Smith, MacDonald, Hendrie (Longridge 59); O'Hara (Shaw 59), Todorov (McKinstry 59).
Referee: Nick Walsh.

Sunday, 9 February 2025

Aberdeen (1) 3 *(Gueye 45, Jensen 50, Nisbet 85)*

Dunfermline Ath (0) 0   9893

Aberdeen: (4231) Doohan; Jensen, Tobers, Knoester (Dorrington 68), MacKenzie; Nilsen (Shinnie 68), Palaversa (Clarkson 88); Keskinen, Gueye (Boyd 88), Okkels (Morris 61); Nisbet.
Dunfermline Ath: (4231) Oluwayemi; Comrie, Mullen, Benedictus, Chalmers (Ngwenya 55); Hamilton (Yeboah 55), Otoo; McCann, Wotherspoon (Hampson 88), Stevens (O'Halloran 67); Kane (Ritchie-Hosler 67).
Referee: Steven McLean.

Rangers (0) 0

Queen's Park (0) 1 *(Drozd 69)*   35,628

Rangers: (4231) Kelly; Tavernier, Fernandes (Souttar 60), Propper, Jefte; Diomande (Lawrence 86), Rice (Raskin 46); Cerny, Bajrami (Dessers 46), Hagi (Yilmaz 61); Igamane.
Queen's Park: (4231) Ferrie; Mauchin, Ujdur, Tizzard, Scott J (Montgomery 72); Longridge, Welsh; Hurst (Drozd 67), Turner, Duncan; Rudden.
Referee: Calum Scott.

Monday, 10 February 2025

St Mirren (1) 1 *(Mandron 23)*

Hearts (0) 1 *(Nieuwenhof 84)*   4611

St Mirren: (352) Hemming; Fraser, Gogic, Taylor R; Alebiosu (Bwomono 70), Phillips (Kenny 111), Boyd-Munce (Smyth 91), O'Hara (Kiltie 91), John; Mandron (Scott 110), Olusanya (Mooney 90).
Hearts: (4231) Gordon; Forrester (Taylor 83), Neilson (Steinwender 52), McCart, Penrice; Devlin (Wilson 63), Baningime; Forrest (Kartum 63), Shankland (Grant 106), Spittal (Nieuwenhof 83); Kabangu (Vargas 106).
aet; Hearts won 4-2 on penalties.
Referee: Don Robertson.

QUARTER-FINALS

Friday, 7 March 2025

Hearts (1) 3 *(Kartum 27, 68, Murray 63 (og))*

Dundee (0) 1 *(Shaughnessy 50)*   17,975

Hearts: (41212) Gordon; Forrester, Neilson, Steinwender, Penrice; Baningime; Kartum (Drammeh 86), Spittal (Forrest 77); Shankland; Vargas (Nieuwenhof 76), Kabangu (Wilson 86).
Dundee: (352) Carson; Astley, Shaughnessy, Donnelly; Mulligan, McGhee (Sylla 46), Garza (Reilly 82), Robertson F, Larkeche (Tiffoney 74); Adewumi, Murray.
Referee: Kevin Clancy.

Saturday, 8 March 2025

Aberdeen (3) 4 *(Nisbet 27, Dabbagh 28, 52, Shinnie 45)*

Queen's Park (0) 1 *(Rudden 68)*   10,705

Aberdeen: (4231) Mitov; Jensen, Dorrington (Milne 72), Knoester, Shinnie; Clarkson, Palaversa; Morris (Polvara 78), Nisbet (Gueye 58), Keskinen (Ambrose 58); Dabbagh (Boyd 58).
Queen's Park: (4231) Ferrie; Mauchin, Ujdur (Hinds 57), Tizzard, Devine (Raymond 46); Welsh (McGinlay 86), Longridge; Drozd (Hickey-Fugaccia 75), Hurst (MacGregor 75), Turner; Rudden.
Referee: David Dickinson.

Sunday, 9 March 2025

Celtic (1) 2 *(Maeda 39, Idah 90)*

Hibernian (0) 0 58,911

Celtic: (433) Schmeichel; Johnston A, Carter-Vickers, Trusty, Schlupp; Engels, McGregor (McCowan 75), Hatate; Kuhn (Idah 84), Maeda, Jota (Yang 75).
Hibernian: (352) Smith; Miller, Bushiri, Iredale; Cadden N (Obita 35), Triantis, Campbell (Hoilett 78), Moriah-Welsh (Levitt 64), Cadden C; Boyle (Youan 78), Bowie (Gayle 64).
Referee: Nick Walsh.

Monday, 10 March 2025

Livingston (0) 0

St Johnstone (0) 1 *(Carey 73)* 2603

Livingston: (442) Prior; Brandon (Ubochioma 85), McGowan, Wilson, Montano (Clarke 86); Pitman (Fraser 75), Tait, Kelly, Yengi; Shinnie (McAlear 85), Muirhead (Finlayson 71).
St Johnstone: (3412) Fisher; Balodis, Mitchell, Douglas; Curtis, Sprangler, Holt, Duke-Mckenna (Wright 46); Svedberg (Carey 69); Sidibeh, Kirk.
Referee: Don Robertson.

SEMI-FINALS (at Hampden Park)

SEMI-FINALS (at Hampden Park)

Saturday, 19 April 2025

Hearts (1) 1 *(Shankland 28)*

Aberdeen (1) 2 *(Gordon 18 (og), Dabbagh 118)* 39,836

Hearts: (41212) Gordon; Forrester (Kingsley 77), Steinwender*, McCart, Penrice; Baningime (Spittal 120); Devlin*, Grant (Kartum 86); Shankland (Drammeh 113); Wilson (Halkett 46), Kabangu (Kent 46).
Aberdeen: (4231) Mitov; Jensen (Boyd 117, Dorrington (Milne 108), Knoester, Shinnie; Clarkson, Palaversa (McGrath 69); Morris (Polvara 91), Gueye (Okkels 81), Keskinen (Dabbagh 81); Nisbet.
aet.
Referee: John Beaton.

Sunday, 20 April 2025

St Johnstone (0) 0

Celtic (4) 5 *(McGregor 34, Maeda 37, 45, Idah 45, Jota 67)* 43,632

St Johnstone: (4411) Fisher; Curtis, Balodis, Sprangler, Douglas (Steven 46); Carey (McPake 68), Holt, Griffith, Duke-Mckenna (Ikpeazu 75); Clark (Kirk 46); Sidibeh (Mbunga-Kimpioka 46).
Celtic: (433) Sinisalo; Johnston A (Ralston 77), Carter-Vickers, Scales, Taylor; Engels (McCowan 64), McGregor, Hatate (Bernardo 70); Forrest (Kuhn 64), Idah (Jota 63), Maeda.
Referee: Calum Scott.

SCOTTISH GAS SCOTTISH CUP FINAL 2024–25

Saturday, 24 May 2025

(at Hampden Park, attendance 49,545)

Aberdeen (0) 1   Celtic (1) 1

Aberdeen: (532) Mitov; Jensen, Dorrington (Morris 80), Milne (Tobers 94), Knoester, Devlin (MacKenzie 90); Palaversa, Shinnie, Clarkson (Polvara 79); Keskinen (Gueye 58), Nisbet (Dabbagh 79).
Scorer: Schmeichel 83 (og).

Celtic: (433) Schmeichel; Johnston A, Carter-Vickers, Scales, Taylor; Engels (McCowan 65), McGregor, Bernardo (Schlupp 99); Kuhn (Forrest 65 (Kenny 96)), Idah (Yang 66), Maeda.
Scorer: Dorrington 39 (og).

aet; Aberdeen won 4-3 on penalties.

Referee: Don Robertson.

Aberdeen's Dimitar Mitov makes a nice save in the penalty shootout during the Scottish Gas Scottish Cup final against Celtic at Hampden Park. (Rob Casey/SNS Group via Getty Images)

BARCLAYS WOMEN'S SUPER LEAGUE 2024–25

		P	W	D	L	F	A	W	D	L	F	A	W	D	L	F	A	GD	Pts
				Home						Away					Total				
1	Chelsea[1]	22	10	1	0	26	8	9	2	0	30	5	19	3	0	56	13	43	60
2	Arsenal[1]	22	8	2	1	39	11	7	1	3	23	15	15	3	4	62	26	36	48
3	Manchester U[2]	22	7	3	1	23	5	6	2	3	18	11	13	5	4	41	16	25	44
4	Manchester C	22	7	1	3	29	14	6	3	2	20	14	13	4	5	49	28	21	43
5	Brighton & HA	22	5	4	2	23	15	3	0	8	12	26	8	4	10	35	41	–6	28
6	Aston Villa	22	4	2	5	19	21	3	2	6	13	23	7	4	11	32	44	–12	25
7	Liverpool	22	3	3	5	12	16	4	1	6	10	21	7	4	11	22	37	–15	25
8	Everton	22	4	3	4	16	17	2	3	6	8	15	6	6	10	24	32	–8	24
9	West Ham U	22	5	3	3	17	15	1	2	8	19	26	6	5	11	36	41	–5	23
10	Leicester C	22	5	2	4	15	13	0	3	8	6	24	5	5	12	21	37	–16	20
11	Tottenham H	22	4	0	7	14	16	1	5	5	12	28	5	5	12	26	44	–18	20
12	Crystal Palace (P)	22	1	2	8	9	31	1	2	8	11	34	2	4	16	20	65	–45	10

[1]Chelsea and Arsenal (Champions League title holders) qualify for Women's Champions League league stage.
[2]Manchester U qualify for Champions League second round.

BARCLAYS WOMEN'S SUPER LEAGUE LEADING GOALSCORERS 2024–25

Player (Team)	Goals	Player (Team)	Goals
Alessia Russo (Arsenal)	12	Beth Mead (Arsenal)	7
Khadifa Shaw (Manchester C)	12	Vivianne Miedema (Manchester C)	7
Shekiera Martinez (West Ham U)	10	Nakita Parris (Brighton & HA)	7
Elisabeth Terland (Manchester U)	10	Olivia Smith (Liverpool)	7
Viviane Asseyi (West Ham U)	9	Caitlin Foord (Arsenal)	6
Agnes Beever-Jones (Chelsea)	9	Mary Fowler (Manchester C)	6
Mariona Caldentey (Arsenal)	9	Catarina Macario (Chelsea)	6
Grace Clinton (Manchester U)	8	Kiko Seike (Brighton & HA)	6
Rachel Daly (Aston Villa)	8	Stina Blackstenius (Arsenal)	5
Bethany England (Tottenham H)	8	Leah Galton (Manchester U)	5
Guro Reiten (Chelsea)	8	Jessica Park (Manchester C)	5
Fran Kirby (Brighton & HA)	7	Jill Roord (Manchester C)	5
Frida Maanum (Arsenal)	7	Ella Toone (Manchester U)	5

BARCLAYS WOMEN'S CHAMPIONSHIP 2024–25

		P	W	D	L	F	A	W	D	L	F	A	W	D	L	F	A	GD	Pts
				Home						Away					Total				
1	London City Lionesses	20	7	2	1	22	7	6	2	2	16	10	13	4	3	38	17	21	43
2	Birmingham C	20	6	2	2	20	9	6	3	1	14	6	12	5	3	34	15	19	41
3	Charlton Ath	20	4	4	2	18	11	6	3	1	20	10	10	7	3	38	21	17	37
4	Durham	20	8	0	2	23	10	3	3	4	12	17	11	3	6	35	27	8	36
5	Newcastle U (P)	20	5	3	2	21	12	4	4	2	17	12	9	7	4	38	24	14	34
6	Bristol C (R)	20	5	3	2	16	6	3	3	4	18	18	8	6	6	34	24	10	30
7	Sunderland	20	5	1	4	17	17	4	2	4	13	17	9	3	8	30	34	–4	30
8	Southampton	20	1	4	5	7	15	4	2	4	15	10	5	6	9	22	25	–3	21
9	Portsmouth (P)	20	2	2	6	9	22	1	2	7	7	26	3	4	13	16	48	–32	13
10	Blackburn R	20	2	2	6	10	18	1	1	8	6	23	3	3	14	16	41	–25	12
11	Sheffield U	20	0	3	7	7	16	1	1	8	5	21	1	4	15	12	37	–25	7

Reading withdrew pre-season, reducing relegation spots from two to one.

BARCLAYS WOMEN'S CHAMPIONSHIP LEADING GOALSCORERS 2024–25

Player (Team)	Goals	Player (Team)	Goals
Isobel Goodwin (London City Lionesses)	16	Aimee Claypole (Durham)	5
Shania Hayles (Newcastle U)	15	Rianna Dean (Southampton)	5
Lexi Lloyd-Smith (Bristol C)	10	Katie Kitching (Sunderland)	5
Ellie Brazil (Charlton Ath)	8	Simone Magill (Birmingham C)	5
Eleanor Dale (Sunderland)	8	Molly Pike (Southampton)	5
Katie Bradley (Charlton Ath)	7	Sophie Quirk (Portsmouth)	5
Jodie Hutton (Charlton Ath)	7	Kayleigh Barton (Charlton Ath)	4
Mollie Lambert (Durham)	7	Maria Farrugia (Sheffield U)	4
Beth Lumsden (Newcastle U)	7	Freya Gregory (Newcastle U)	4
Chantelle Boye-Hlorkah (London City Lionesses)	6	Lee Geum-Min (Birmingham C)	4
Beth Hepple (Durham)	6	Lucy Quinn (Birmingham C)	4
Ffion Morgan (Bristol C)	6	Tyler Toland (Blackburn R)	4
Kosovare Asllani (London City Lionesses)	5		

SUBWAY WOMEN'S LEAGUE CUP 2024–25

GROUP STAGE

Drawn games were decided by a penalty shoot-out.
WP = match won on penalties (2 pts);
LP = match lost on penalties (1 pt).

Chelsea, Manchester C and Arsenal competed in the
UEFA Women's Champions League group stage so
advanced directly to the Women's League Cup
knockout stage.

GROUP A

Manchester U v Liverpool	2-0
Newcastle U v Everton	1-1
Everton won 3-0 on penalties.	
Everton v Manchester U	0-2
Newcastle U v Liverpool	1-6
Liverpool v Everton	4-0
Manchester U v Newcastle U	5-3

Group A Table	P	W	PW	PL	L	F	A	GD	Pts
Manchester U	3	3	0	0	0	9	3	6	9
Liverpool	3	2	0	0	1	10	3	7	6
Everton	3	0	1	0	2	1	7	–6	2
Newcastle U	3	0	0	1	2	5	12	–7	1

GROUP B

Blackburn R v Durham	1-2
Sheffield U v Sunderland	1-2
Durham v Sheffield U	1-1
Durham won 4-3 on penalties.	
Sunderland v Blackburn R	1-3
Blackburn R v Sheffield U	4-2
Sunderland v Durham	1-2

Group B Table	P	W	PW	PL	L	F	A	GD	Pts
Durham	3	2	1	0	0	5	3	2	8
Blackburn R	3	2	0	0	1	8	5	3	6
Sunderland	3	1	0	0	2	4	6	–2	3
Sheffield U	3	0	0	1	2	4	7	–3	1

GROUP C

West Ham U v Portsmouth	6-1
Southampton v London City Lionesses	0-1
London City Lionesses v West Ham U	1-4
Portsmouth v Southampton	0-4
Portsmouth v London City Lionesses	2-5
West Ham U v Southampton	3-0

Group C Table	P	W	PW	PL	L	F	A	GD	Pts
West Ham U	3	3	0	0	0	13	2	11	9
London City Lionesses	3	2	0	0	1	7	6	1	6
Southampton	3	1	0	0	2	4	4	0	3
Portsmouth	3	0	0	0	3	3	15	–12	0

GROUP D

Birmingham C v Brighton & HA	0-3
Leicester C v Bristol C	1-1
Bristol C won 2-1 on penalties.	
Brighton & HA v Leicester C	0-0
Leicester C won 4-3 on penalties.	
Bristol C v Birmingham C	1-3
Brighton & HA v Bristol C	6-2
Leicester C v Birmingham C	5-2

Group D Table	P	W	PW	PL	L	F	A	GD	Pts
Brighton & HA	3	2	0	1	0	9	2	7	7
Leicester C	3	1	1	1	0	6	3	3	6
Birmingham C	3	1	0	0	2	5	9	–4	3
Bristol C	3	0	1	0	2	4	10	–6	2

GROUP E

Aston Villa v Crystal Palace	2-0
Charlton Ath v Tottenham H	1-2
Tottenham H v Aston Villa	1-0
Crystal Palace v Charlton Ath	2-0
Crystal Palace v Tottenham H	0-2
Aston Villa v Charlton Ath	4-1

Group D Table	P	W	PW	PL	L	F	A	GD	Pts
Tottenham H	3	3	0	0	0	5	1	4	9
Aston Villa	3	2	0	0	1	6	2	4	6
Crystal Palace	3	1	0	0	2	2	4	–2	3
Charlton Ath	3	0	0	0	3	2	8	–6	0

KNOCKOUT STAGE

QUARTER-FINALS

Chelsea v Durham	5-0
Manchester U v Manchester C	1-2
Brighton & HA v Arsenal	0-4
Tottenham H v West Ham U	1-2

SEMI-FINALS

Chelsea v West Ham U	2-0
Arsenal v Manchester C	1-2

SUBWAY WOMEN'S LEAGUE CUP FINAL 2024–25

Saturday, 15 March 2025

(at Pride Park Stadium, Derby, attendance 14,187)

Chelsea (1) 2   Manchester C (0) 1

Chelsea: (4231) Hampton; Bronze, Bright, Bjorn, Baltimore (Charles 87); Cuthbert, Nusken; Rytting Kaneryd (Beever-Jones 74), Macario (Hamano 74), James; Ramirez (Kaptein 79).
Scorers: Ramirez 8, Hasegawa 77 (og).

Manchester C: (433) Yamashita; Casparij, Prior, Aleixandri, Ouahabi; Roord, Hasegawa, Miedema; Fujino (Park 81), Shaw (Kerolin 81), Fowler.
Scorer: Fujino 64.

Referee: Emily Heaslip.

FA WOMEN'S NATIONAL LEAGUE 2024–25

FA WOMEN'S NATIONAL LEAGUE NORTHERN PREMIER DIVISION 2024–25

			Home				Away					Total						
		P	W	D	L	F	A	W	D	L	F	A	W	D	L	F	A	GD	Pts
1	Nottingham F	22	8	3	0	45	5	10	1	0	34	3	18	4	0	79	8	71	58
2	Wolverhampton W	22	10	0	1	41	7	7	4	0	38	14	17	4	1	79	21	58	55
3	Stoke C	22	7	1	3	33	15	9	0	2	33	15	16	1	5	66	30	36	49
4	Burnley	22	7	0	4	44	9	8	1	2	32	10	15	1	6	76	19	57	46
5	Rugby Bor	22	6	3	2	24	10	6	3	2	33	10	12	6	4	57	20	37	42
6	Liverpool Feds	22	5	2	4	16	21	5	0	6	19	32	10	2	10	35	53	–18	32
7	WBA	22	4	0	7	18	26	3	1	7	13	26	7	1	14	31	52	–21	22
8	Hull C (P)	22	2	3	6	14	24	4	1	6	13	31	6	4	12	27	55	–28	22
9	Derby Co	22	3	2	6	13	22	3	1	7	14	23	6	3	13	27	45	–18	21
10	Sporting Khalsa (P)	22	5	0	6	28	24	1	3	7	6	38	6	3	13	34	62	–28	21
11	Halifax	22	0	1	10	5	42	2	0	9	8	44	2	1	19	13	86	–73	7
12	Stourbridge*	22	1	0	10	10	42	1	0	10	4	45	2	0	20	14	87	–73	5

*Stourbridge deducted 1 point for failing to fulfil their fixture against Nottingham F on 2 March 2025. The fixture was rescheduled.

FA WOMEN'S NATIONAL LEAGUE SOUTHERN PREMIER DIVISION 2024–25

		P	W	D	L	F	A	W	D	L	F	A	W	D	L	F	A	GD	Pts
1	Ipswich T	22	10	1	0	49	4	7	2	2	40	6	17	3	2	89	10	79	54
2	Hashtag U	22	11	0	0	26	4	4	3	4	23	12	15	3	4	49	16	33	48
3	Watford (R)	22	8	0	3	31	8	5	5	1	26	9	13	5	4	57	17	40	44
4	Exeter C (P)	22	6	4	1	22	11	7	0	4	28	18	13	4	5	50	29	21	43
5	Oxford U	22	6	1	4	18	7	7	2	2	20	11	13	3	6	38	18	20	42
6	Lewes (R)	22	5	5	1	22	9	3	2	6	15	19	8	7	7	37	28	9	31
7	AFC Wimbledon (P)	22	4	3	4	18	13	5	1	5	14	15	9	4	9	32	28	4	31
8	Cheltenham T	22	4	2	5	19	21	3	0	8	13	26	7	2	13	32	47	–15	23
9	Gwalia U*†	22	4	2	5	11	14	1	3	7	9	24	6	4	12	20	38	–18	22
10	Plymouth Arg	22	3	2	6	14	31	3	0	8	11	22	6	2	14	25	53	–28	20
11	Billericay T*	22	6	0	5	18	25	0	3	8	7	31	5	2	15	25	56	–31	17
12	Milton Keynes D	22	0	1	10	7	62	0	0	11	3	62	0	1	21	10	124	–114	1

*Billericay T were deducted three points for fielding an ineligible player in their away fixture against Gwalia U on Sunday 17 November, which they won 1-0. The three points were transferred from Billericay T to Gwalia U. †Gwalia U rebranded from Cardiff C.

FA WOMEN'S NATIONAL LEAGUE DIVISION ONE NORTH 2024–25

		P	W	D	L	F	A	W	D	L	F	A	W	D	L	F	A	GD	Pts
1	Middlesbrough	22	10	1	0	32	4	5	5	1	13	9	15	6	1	45	13	32	51
2	Cheadle Town Stingers (P)	22	7	3	1	23	7	9	0	2	15	4	16	3	3	38	11	27	51
3	Chorley	22	8	1	2	27	15	5	3	3	20	15	13	4	5	47	30	17	43
4	Leeds U	22	7	0	4	24	13	6	2	3	29	19	13	2	7	53	32	21	41
5	Huddersfield T (R)	22	5	3	3	18	10	5	3	3	13	14	10	6	6	31	24	7	36
6	Durham Cestria	22	4	2	5	23	20	3	2	6	19	23	7	4	11	42	43	–1	25
7	Stockport Co	22	4	4	3	15	11	3	0	8	13	26	7	4	11	28	37	–9	25
8	Barnsley FC (P)	22	5	1	5	20	20	1	4	6	12	23	6	5	11	32	43	–11	23
9	Norton & Stockton Ancients	22	5	0	6	15	18	1	1	6	15	25	6	5	11	30	43	–13	23
10	York C	22	3	2	6	15	21	3	1	7	14	33	6	3	13	29	54	–25	21
11	Doncaster R Belles	22	3	3	5	23	25	1	2	8	11	29	4	5	13	34	54	–20	17
12	AFC Fylde (R)	22	2	2	7	11	20	1	3	7	10	26	3	5	14	21	46	–25	14

FA WOMEN'S NATIONAL LEAGUE DIVISION ONE MIDLANDS 2024–25

		P	W	D	L	F	A	W	D	L	F	A	W	D	L	F	A	GD	Pts
1	Loughborough Lightning	22	10	1	0	50	3	9	2	0	35	7	19	3	0	85	10	75	60
2	Northampton T	22	9	1	1	47	9	8	0	3	31	13	17	1	4	78	22	56	52
3	Peterborough U	22	9	1	1	34	8	7	2	2	28	13	16	3	3	62	21	41	51
4	Leafield Ath	22	10	0	1	37	11	6	0	5	22	11	16	0	6	59	22	37	48
5	Boldmere St Michaels	22	7	1	3	27	14	6	0	5	24	12	13	1	8	51	26	25	40
6	Barnsley Women's	22	5	1	5	22	18	5	2	4	23	18	10	3	9	45	36	9	33
7	Notts Co	22	4	2	5	23	24	6	0	5	20	29	10	2	10	43	53	–10	32
8	Sutton Coldfield T	22	4	1	6	22	19	4	0	7	13	27	8	1	13	35	46	–11	25
9	Lincoln U (P)	22	4	1	6	14	22	3	0	8	14	39	7	1	14	28	61	–33	22
10	Worcester C (P)	22	1	2	8	12	26	2	2	7	19	30	3	4	15	31	56	–25	13
11	Solihull Moors*	22	0	1	10	2	30	1	3	7	12	36	1	4	17	14	66	–52	6
12	Lincoln C	22	0	0	11	4	58	0	1	10	1	59	0	1	21	5	117	–112	1

*Solihull Moors were deducted 1 point for failing to fulfil their fixture against Loughborough Lightning on 13 November 2024. The game was rescheduled.

FA WOMEN'S NATIONAL LEAGUE DIVISION ONE SOUTH EAST 2024–25

		P	W	D	L	F	A	W	D	L	F	A	W	D	L	F	A	GD	Pts
1	Real Bedford (P)	22	7	4	0	44	8	7	3	1	22	7	14	7	1	66	15	51	49
2	Norwich C	22	9	1	1	28	4	5	4	2	22	13	14	5	3	50	17	33	47
3	Chatham T (R)	22	7	3	1	26	4	5	4	2	22	10	12	7	3	48	14	34	43
4	London Bees (R)	22	6	3	2	34	16	6	2	3	25	15	12	5	5	59	31	28	41
5	QPR	22	6	3	2	18	13	4	3	4	19	16	10	6	6	37	29	8	36
6	Actonians	22	6	1	4	22	13	4	3	4	18	11	10	4	8	40	24	16	34
7	AFC Sudbury	22	4	5	2	15	11	5	2	4	25	23	9	7	6	40	34	6	34
8	Dulwich Hamlet (P)	22	5	3	3	24	11	3	2	6	12	17	8	5	9	36	28	8	29
9	Cambridge U	22	3	2	6	15	21	4	2	5	22	19	7	4	11	37	40	–3	25
10	Chesham U	22	3	3	5	15	22	2	0	9	12	54	5	3	14	27	76	–49	18
11	Ashford T	22	1	0	10	13	48	1	2	8	11	35	2	2	18	24	83	–59	8
12	London Seaward	22	0	0	11	5	44	1	1	9	5	39	1	1	20	10	83	–73	4

FA WOMEN'S NATIONAL LEAGUE DIVISION ONE SOUTH WEST 2024–25

		P		Home				Away				Total				GD	Pts
			W	D	L	F	A	W	D	L	F	A	W	D	L	F	A		
1	Bournemouth	22	11	0	0	50	3	10	1	0	50	4	21	1	0	100	7	93	64
2	Moneyfields	22	7	2	2	34	11	8	1	2	29	14	15	3	4	63	25	38	48
3	Swindon T	22	6	3	2	38	16	7	2	2	25	10	13	5	4	63	26	37	44
4	Bristol R (P)	22	8	1	2	21	12	6	0	5	19	13	14	1	7	40	25	15	43
5	Worthing	22	7	1	3	29	19	5	1	5	22	22	12	2	8	51	41	10	38
6	Keynsham T	22	6	1	4	21	17	4	1	6	16	24	10	2	10	37	41	-4	32
7	Bridgwater U	22	5	0	6	19	18	3	3	5	12	24	8	3	11	31	42	-11	27
8	Maidenhead U	22	5	1	5	16	15	2	1	8	11	33	7	2	13	27	48	-21	23
9	Abingdon U	22	4	1	6	17	22	2	2	7	14	20	6	3	13	31	42	-11	21
10	Bournemouth Sports (P)	22	3	2	6	9	23	2	3	6	10	26	5	5	12	19	49	-30	20
11	Portishead T	22	2	3	6	10	27	1	1	9	9	33	3	4	15	19	60	-41	13
12	Southampton Women's*	22	2	1	8	6	38	0	0	11	4	47	2	1	19	10	85	-75	6

*Southampton Women's were deducted 1 point for failing to fulfil their fixture against Bristol R on 25 August 2024. The game was rescheduled.

FA WOMEN'S NATIONAL LEAGUE CUP 2024–25

*After extra time.

DETERMINING ROUND

AFC Sudbury v Billericay T	1-4
Hull C v Lincoln C	6-0
Northampton T v Cambridge U	3-2
Abingdon U v Oxford U	0-10
Barnsley v Barnsley Women's	1-0
Burnley v AFC Fylde	7-0
Chatham T v Hashtag U	0-2
Derby Co v Loughborough Lightning	2-1*
Exeter C v Portishead T	8-1
Gwalia U v Bristol R	2-0
Halifax v Leeds U	0-2
Lewes v Worthing	2-1*
Liverpool Feds v Stockport Co	3-2
Middlesbrough v Durham Cestria	4-1
QPR v AFC Wimbledon	1-0*
Real Bedford v Milton Keynes D	3-0
Solihull Moors v WBA (walkover)	
Sporting Khalsa v Sutton Coldfield T	1-2
Swindon T v Keynsham T	3-1
Wolverhampton W v Stoke C	1-3
York v Norton & Stockton Ancients	6-5
Boldmere St Michaels v Stourbridge	1-2
Chorley v Cheadle T Stingers	1-2
Huddersfield T v Doncaster R Belles	4-1
London Bees v Actonians	2-1
London Seaward v Dulwich Hamlet	0-4
Maidenhead U v Ashford T	4-2
Moneyfields v Bournemouth	4-3*
Norwich C v Ipswich T	0-4
Nottingham F v Notts Co	6-0
Peterborough U v Lincoln U	3-0
Plymouth Arg v Bridgwater U	4-2
Worcester C v Cheltenham T	1-0
Leafield Ath v Rugby Bor	0-7
Chesham U v Watford	1-7
Southampton Women's v Bournemouth Sports	1-0

PRELIMINARY ROUND

Plymouth Arg v London Bees	3-0
Southampton Women's v Moneyfields	0-3
Stourbridge v Middlesbrough	1-4
York C v Huddersfield T	1-3

FIRST ROUND

Barnsley v Stoke C	0-5
Billericay T v Oxford U	3-3*
Billericay T won 4-2 on penalties.	
Cheadle T Stingers v Nottingham F	0-1
Derby Co v Hashtag U	0-3
Exeter C v Ipswich T	1-3
Gwalia U v Real Bedford	1-2
Huddersfield T v Hull C	1-3
Lewes v Watford	0-1
Maidenhead U v Plymouth Arg	1-4
Middlesbrough v Leeds U	2-0
Moneyfields v Dulwich Hamlet	2-0
Peterborough U v Worcester C	3-0
QPR v Swindon T	2-0
Rugby Bor v Liverpool Feds	0-1
Sutton Coldfield T v Burnley	0-1
WBA v Northampton T	3-3*
WBA won 3-2 on penalties.	

SECOND ROUND

Hull C v Burnley	0-1
Ipswich T v Hashtag U	0-1
Middlesbrough v WBA	1-0
Moneyfields v Real Bedford	1-5
Nottingham F v Peterborough U	6-0
Plymouth Arg v Billericay T	2-1
Stoke C v Liverpool Feds	3-1*
Watford v QPR	6-1

QUARTER-FINALS

Hashtag U v Real Bedford	4-0
Plymouth Arg v Watford	1-0
Burnley v Stoke C	0-1
Middlesbrough v Nottingham F	1-2

SEMI-FINALS

Plymouth Arg v Stoke C	0-3
Hashtag U v Nottingham F	0-1

FA WOMEN'S NATIONAL LEAGUE CUP FINAL 2024–25

Saturday, 22 March 2025

(at Bescot Stadium, Walsall, attendance 1718)

Nottingham F (2) 3   Stoke C (0) 1

Nottingham F: Batty, Harkin, Johnson N, Longhurst, Domingo (Sims 87), Johnson M, Wellings (Hamilton 59), Olding, Green (Hennessy 90), Thomas, Chandarana (Manders 59).
Scorers: Wellings 29, 32, Johnson M 80.

Stoke C: Bracewell; Molinari, Cook, Suttie, Kivel, Reavill, Holder (Watson 74), Stamps, Ravening, Cole (Wilcock 71), Priestley (Nelson 87).
Scorer: Wilcock 72.

Referee: Francesca Catchpole.

THE ADOBE WOMEN'S FA CUP 2024–25

* After extra time.

FIRST ROUND QUALIFYING

Workington T v Gateshead	4-1
Gateshead Leam Rangers v Hartlepool U	2-0
Gateshead Rutherford v Berwick Rangers	3-2
Stockton T v Redcar T	2-0
Darlington v GT7	3-1
Bedlington Belles v Boldon CA	2-6
Washington (walkover) v i2i International	
Penrith v Carlisle U	18-2
Consett (walkover) v Stanwix	
Chester-le-Street U (walkover) v West Allotment Celtic	
Bishop Auckland v Thornaby	0-13
CLS Amazons v Birtley T	1-2
Hartlepool Pools Youth v Horden CW	3-1
Hessle Rangers v Handsworth	0-9
Guisborough T v Cramlington U	8-2
Sheffield Wed (walkover) v Millmoor Juniors	
Chesterfield Women v Grimsby Bor	3-0
Wyke W v Morley T	6-3
Oughtibridge War Memorial v Altofts	4-1
Mosborough v Beverley T (walkover)	
Farsley Celtic v Sheffield U Community	5-1
Brigg T v Brunsmeer Ath	1-13
Retford v Dronfield T	0-11
Gainsborough Trinity v Kiveton Park	6-1
Grimsby T v Lower Hopton	4-2
Leeds Modernians v Bottesford T	8-1
Forge Way v Cleethorpes T	8-0
Market Rasen T v Rossington Main	1-6
Buxton v Chester	2-6
Wirral Phoenix v Ellesmere Port T	3-1
Poulton Vic v Litherland REMYCA	1-0
FC St Helens v Rochdale	1-0
Penwortham T v Alder	1-0
Altrincham v Macclesfield	1-3
Silsden v Accrington S	0-7
Hindley Juniors v Mossley Hill (walkover)	

Tie awarded to Mossley Hill when Hindley Juniors had insufficient players to complete the match. The score at that time was 0-2.

Preston NE v Clitheroe Wolves	14-0
Runcorn Linnets v Skipton T	10-0
Blackpool v Atherton Laburnum R	2-1
Morecambe v Boltonians	1-0
Maghull Youth v Northwich Vixens	2-2

Maghull Youth won 5-4 on penalties.

AFC Crewe v Ashton T Lionesses	2-2

Ashton T Lionesses won 4-3 on penalties.

FC Northern v MSB Woolton	1-2
Pilkington v Radcliffe	5-3
Haslingden v Colne	8-0
Nantwich T v Fleetwood T Juniors	4-1
Sleaford T Rangers v Kirby Muxloe	4-2
Bugbrooke St Michaels v Rugby T	0-0

Bugbrooke St Michaels won 3-2 on penalties.

HBW U v Newark T	0-3
Ruston Sports v Arnold Eagles	0-3
Netherton U v Whittlesey Ath	3-0
River C v Allexton & New Parks	3-1
Moulton v Sherwood	1-5
Leicester C v Brookside Ath	5-3
Wellingborough T v Long Buckby A	6-0
Radcliffe Olympic v Asfordby Amateurs	1-4
AFC Rushden & Diamonds v Thrapston T	1-4
Birstall V v Beaumont Park	0-2
Cardea v Sleaford T	2-3
Long Eaton U (walkover) v Wyberton Wildcats	
Coventry C v Eccleshall	4-1
Walsall v Leamington Lions	2-1
Market Drayton T v Bromsgrove Sporting (walkover)	
Worthen Juniors v Hednesford T	0-7
Belper T v Albrighton	4-0
Droitwich Spa v Coton Green	1-3
Shrewsbury Up & Comers v Whitchurch Alport	1-3
AFC Telford U v Newcastle T	10-0
Redditch U v Crusaders	2-1
Halesowen T v Pride Park	9-0
Kingfisher v Lichfield C	1-6
Milton U (Staffordshire) v Nuneaton Bor	3-1
Borrowash Vic v Tamworth	2-1
Leafield Ath Lynx v Long Itchington	0-9

Mulbarton W v Stanway Pegasus	2-3
Fakenham T v Stanway R	5-1
Waterbeach Colts v Brantham Ath	1-4
Thetford T v Histon	2-6
Lawford v Newmarket T	0-5
Woodbridge T v Sprowston	4-1
Aylsham v Fulbourn Institute Bluebirds	1-1

Aylsham won 4-2 on penalties.

Bungay T v Cambridge Rangers	11-1
Frontiers v Toby	0-2
Hitchin Belles v Wormley R	0-2
Harpenden T v Biggleswade U	4-4

Biggleswade U won 4-1 on penalties.

Stotfold v Chelmsford C	0-10
Ware U v AFC Dunstable	0-6
Langford v Oaklands Wolves	1-3
Cheshunt v Leyton Orient (walkover)	
Hutton v Clapton Community	2-2

Hutton won 5-3 on penalties.

Hertford T v Islington Bor	3-2
Southminster U v Hackney	0-3
Richmond Park v Aylesford	0-5
Hammersmith v Bromley	4-0

Hammersmith expelled for fielding ineligible player.

Maidstone U v Tooting Bec	1-4
Kings Hill v Croydon	1-1

Croydon won 4-3 on penalties.

Tonbridge Angels v South London	0-4
Ashmount Leigh v Sevenoaks T	1-5
Herne Bay v Margate	2-2

Herne Bay won 5-4 on penalties.

AFC Whyteleafe v Tunbridge Wells Foresters	1-10
Bexhill U v Camden T	0-9
Soccer Elite Football Academy v Cray W	0-3
Denham U v Ruislip Rangers	8-0
Wallingford & Crowmarsh v Brackley T	1-3
Caversham U v Penn & Tylers Green	0-5
Milton U (Berks & Bucks) v Slough T	4-1
North Leigh v Brentford	1-18
Barton U v Camden & Islington U	0-2
Kidlington Youth v Headstone Manor	5-1
Tilehurst Panthers v Goring U	5-0
Newport Pagnell T v New Bradwell St Peter	2-1
Ashridge Park (walkover) v Banbury U	
Montpelier Villa v Bognor Regis T	4-4

Montpelier Villa won 4-1 on penalties.

Hassocks v Abbey Rangers	2-3
Fleet T v Rushmoor Community	4-0
East Preston v Leatherhead	0-9
Farnborough v Farnham T	0-6
Steyning T Community (walkover) v Eversley & California	
Horsham Sparrows v Horsham	1-5
Gosport Bor v Bursledon	0-1
Dorchester T v Shaftesbury	3-1
Merley Cobham Sports v Ridgeway	4-3
Havant & Waterlooville v United Services Portsmouth	10-0
Andover New Street v AFC Varsity	1-3
AFC Stoneham v Weymouth	4-1
Longfleet Lionesses v QK Southampton	1-4
Basingstoke T v Longham	1-2
Mangotsfield U v Hereford Pegasus	1-4
Paulton R v Weston-super-Mare	1-2
Bath C v Bitton	0-1
Cheltenham Saracens v Gloucester C	0-9
Cirencester T v Bishop's Cleeve	1-2
Bristol & West v Cheltenham Civil Service	2-4
Ross Juniors v Royal Wootton Bassett T	1-5
SGS Olveston U v Yeovil T	0-2
Frome T v FC Chippenham	10-0
Hereford v Corsham T	5-4
Signal Box Oak Villa v Helston Ath (walkover)	
Plympton v Bideford	6-0
Stoke Gabriel & Torbay Police v FXSU	21-0
Sticker v Saltash U	2-2

Saltash U won 4-2 on penalties.

RNAS Culdrose v Saltash Bor	0-4
Redruth U v Honiton T	1-1

Redruth U won 4-3 on penalties.

Bodmin v Feniton	0-1
Appledore v Westexe Park Rangers	4-2

SECOND QUALIFYING ROUND

Whitehaven v Darlington	3-3
Darlington won 3-2 on penalties.	
Hartlepool Pools Youth v Gateshead Leam Rangers	2-1
Thornaby v Guisborough T	9-0
Stockton T v Sunderland West End	0-6
Alnwick v Birtley T	2-1
Chester-le-Street T v Workington T	4-0
Ponteland U v South Shields	1-3
Washington A v Boldon CA	5-2
Wallsend BC v Penrith	2-3
Spennymoor T v Gateshead Rutherford	2-2
Spennymoor T won 3-1 on penalties.	
Consett v Chester-le-Street U	3-0
Rotherham U v Chesterfield Women	5-0
Oughtibridge War Memorial v Sheffield Wed	5-3
Gainsborough Trinity v Handsworth	2-4
Ilkley T v Chesterfield Ladies	0-3
Rossington Main v Beverley T	6-0
Bradford C v Farsley Celtic	4-3
Grimsby T v Ossett U	0-4
Wyke W v Sheffield	1-6
Dronfield T v Brunsmeer Ath	1-3
Harrogate T v Leeds Modernians	0-1
Hull U v Forge Way	3-0
St Joseph's Rockware of Worksop v	
York Railway Institute	3-2
Wigan Ath v Mancunian Unity	2-3
Preston NE v Maghull Youth	6-0
MSB Woolton v Wirral Phoenix	5-2
Pilkington v Chester	1-3
Tranmere R v Bolton W	3-1
Bury v Curzon Ashton	0-5
Wythenshawe v Salford C Lionesses	3-0
Warrington T v Accrington S	2-4
Haslingden v Darwen	1-4
West Didsbury & Chorlton v Morecambe	3-2
Macclesfield v Blackpool	3-2
Penwortham T v Crewe Alex	1-3
Nantwich T v Mossley Hill	3-2
FC St Helens v Poulton Vic	5-0
FC United of Manchester v Ashton T Lionesses	5-2
Fleetwood T Wrens v Runcorn Linnets	3-2
Wellingborough T v Netherton U	10-0
Long Eaton U v Bugbrooke St Michaels	2-2
Long Eaton U won 6-5 on penalties.	
Beaumont Park v Coalville T	2-1
Arnold Eagles v Stamford	0-7
Basford U v Sleaford T	0-0
Sleaford T won 3-0 on penalties.	
Dunton & Broughton U v Sleaford T Rangers	8-2
Mansfield T v Ilkeston T	0-1
Sherwood v River C	0-3
Nottingham Trent University v Leicester C	3-5
Anstey Nomads v Newark T	7-1
Asfordby Amateurs v Thrapston T	2-1
Alvechurch v Borrowash Vic	5-1
Inkberrow v Walsall	1-4
Bromsgrove Sporting v Knowle	1-2
Coventry C v Redditch Bor	2-3
Coton Green v Lye T	0-7
Coventry Sphinx v Burton Alb	3-4
Belper T v AFC Telford U	1-5
Whitchurch Alport v Long Itchington	1-2
Leek T v Coundon Court	4-0
Lichfield C v Shrewsbury T	0-1
Sedgley & Gornal U v Redditch U	0-10
Hednesford T v Doveridge	7-0
Shifnal T v Milton U (Staffordshire)	4-0
Solihull Sporting v Kidderminster H	0-9
Port Vale v Halesowen T	3-0
Needham Market v Histon	6-2
Dussindale & Hellesdon v King's Lynn T	7-0
Stanway Pegasus v Aylsham	4-2
Wroxham v Fakenham T	9-0
Brantham Ath v Long Stratton	0-0
Long Stratton won 4-3 on penalties.	
Woodbridge T v Cambridge C	0-3
Bungay T v Newmarket T	2-0
Stowupland Falcons v Costessey Sports (walkover)	
Hertford T v AFC Dunstable	3-0
St Margaretsbury v Wormley R	0-5
Chigwell v Luton T	0-11
Chelmsford C v Stevenage	0-5
Barking v Southend U Community SC	4-1
Bowers & Pitsea v Toby	3-0

Haringey Bor v Royston T	1-3
Leyton Orient v Oaklands Wolves	11-3
Enfield T v Hutton	0-1
St Albans C v Biggleswade U	3-0
Hackney v Wootton Blue Cross Lionesses	1-1
Hackney won 4-3 on penalties.	
Cray W v Comets	2-4
Aylesford v Tooting Bec	5-0
Herne Bay v Sutton U	1-1
Herne Bay won 5-4 on penalties.	
Croydon v Ashford U	1-2
Camden T v South London	2-3
Epsom & Ewell v Fulham	0-13
Richmond & Kew v Sevenoaks T	6-1
Millwall Lionesses v Ebbsfleet U	0-3
Dartford v Bromley	4-1
Tunbridge Wells Foresters v Sport London e Benfica	0-7
Brackley T v Reading	2-3
Haddenham v Camden & Islington U	0-1
Oxford C v Woodley U	1-2
Ascot U v Denham U	5-0
Penn & Tylers Green (walkover) v Long Crendon	
Kidlington Youth v Watford Development	0-3
Brentford v Tilehurst Panthers	12-1
Newport Pagnell T v Ashridge Park	5-2
Wycombe W v Milton U (Berks & Bucks)	13-1
Selsey v Leatherhead	1-1
Selsey won 4-3 on penalties.	
Newhaven v Farnham T	1-2
Montpelier Villa v Three Bridges	3-2
Saltdean U v Abbey Rangers	7-0
Fleet T v Badshot Lea	8-2
Horsham v Haywards Heath T	2-2
Horsham won 5-4 on penalties.	
Eastbourne T v Steyning T Community	0-15
Dorking W v Pagham	14-0
Warminster T v Havant & Waterlooville (walkover)	
Sholing v AFC Varsity	6-0
Bursledon v Longham	8-0
Winchester C Flyers v Dorchester T	14-0
Merley Cobham Sports v Poole T	1-7
QK Southampton v AFC Portchester	0-15
Shanklin v AFC Stoneham	1-5
Sherborne T v Bemerton Heath Harlequins	10-0
Hereford v Longlevens	4-0
Hereford Pegasus v Bitton	3-3
Bitton won 5-3 on penalties.	
Royal Wootton Bassett T v Ilminster T	2-2
Royal Wootton Bassett T won 5-4 on penalties.	
Gloucester C v Stockwood W	7-0
Frome T v Bishop's Cleeve	0-1
St Vallier v Bishops Lydeard	2-3
Downend Flyers v Cheltenham Civil Service	3-1
Frampton Rangers v Forest Green R	1-6
AEK Boco v Weston-super-Mare	2-0
Yeovil T v Pucklechurch Sports	1-1
Yeovil T won 4-3 on penalties.	
Stoke Gabriel & Torbay Police v Bradworthy	0-4
Saltash U v Teignmouth	5-1
Appledore v St Agnes	2-2
St Agnes won 4-2 on penalties.	
Marine Academy Plymouth v Feniton	6-0
AFC St Austell v Helston Ath	6-2
Saltash Bor v Redruth U	5-0
Torquay U v Plympton	5-2

THIRD QUALIFYING ROUND

Oughtibridge War Memorial v Sheffield	2-3
Huddersfield T (walkover) v Barnsley	
Accrington S v Macclesfield	5-2
Leeds Modernians v Norton & Stockton Ancients	3-5
Brunsmeer Ath v Handsworth	2-3
Preston NE v Hartlepool Pools Youth	5-0
AFC Fylde v Darlington	7-1
Washington v MSB Woolton	3-2
Rotherham U v Thornaby	1-1
Thornaby won 4-2 on penalties.	
Spennymoor T v St Joseph's Rockware of Worksop	4-0
South Shields v FC United of Manchester	3-1
Chorley v Stockport Co	2-3
Curzon Ashton v Sunderland West End	5-0
Darwen v Middlesbrough	1-2
West Didsbury & Chorlton v Rossington Main	1-2
Alnwick T v Durham Cestria	1-1
Durham Cestria won 4-2 on penalties.	
Cheadle T Stingers v Consett	7-0

Chesterfield Ladies v Bradford C — 1-2
Doncaster R Belles v Hull U — 4-0
Penrith v Tranmere R — 2-2
Penrith won 4-2 on penalties.
York C v Fleetwood T Wrens — 5-2
Mancunian Unity v Leeds U — 3-1
Wythenshawe v Barnsley — 7-0
Ossett U v Chester-le-Street T — 1-2
FC St Helens v Chester — 1-0
Peterborough U v Burton Alb — 5-0
Asfordby Amateurs v Walsall — 1-1
Asfordby Amateurs won 4-2 on penalties.
Hednesford T v Anstey Nomads — 2-0
Crewe Alex v Notts Co — 1-2
Kidderminster H v Redditch U — 4-0
Worcester C v Redditch Bor — 2-0
Dunton & Broughton U v Port Vale — 1-4
Leicester C v Lincoln C — 2-3
Nantwich T v Solihull Moors — 3-2
Leafield Ath v Lye T — 3-0
Shifnal T v Northampton T — 0-4
AFC Telford U v Ilkeston T — 3-2
Alvechurch v Sutton Coldfield T — 0-4
Sleaford T v Knowle — 0-7
Stamford v Long Eaton U — 4-0
Long Itchington v Beaumont Park — 5-1
Shrewsbury T v Lincoln U — 3-2
Loughborough Lightning v Wellingborough T — 5-0
Leek T v River C — 0-3
Boldmere St Michaels v Hereford — 3-0
Hutton v Leyton Orient — 3-1
Hertford T v Hackney — 2-3
London Seaward v Stanway Pegasus — 5-0
AFC Sudbury v Watford Development — 4-1
Cambridge U v Real Bedford — 3-1
Barking v Stevenage — 1-2
Wroxham v Long Stratton — 7-0
Wormley R v Cambridge C — 1-1
Cambridge C won 3-2 on penalties.
Dussindale & Hellesdon v Newport Pagnell T — 3-4
Bowers & Pitsea v Costessey Sports — 7-0
Luton T v St Albans C — 2-0
Norwich C v Needham Market — 5-0
Royston T v Bungay T — 6-0
Dorking W v Ashford T (Middlesex) — 2-1
Ascot U v Woodley U — 8-2
Penn & Tylers Green v Ashford U — 2-0
Steyning T Community v London Bees — 0-6
Actonians v Dartford — 2-0
Farnham T v Havant & Waterlooville — 5-3
Selsey v South London — 0-4
Chatham T v Horsham — 12-0
Richmond & Kew v Reading — 0-0
Reading won 3-2 on penalties.
Abingdon U v Worthing — 1-8
Ebbsfleet U v Saltdean U — 1-2
Brentford v Sport London e Benfica — 2-0
Chesham U v Montpelier Villa — 5-2
Fulham v Maidenhead U — 1-1
Fulham won 4-2 on penalties.
Wycombe W v Comets — 3-3
Comets won 3-1 on penalties.
Herne Bay v QPR — 1-2
Camden & Islington U v Aylesford — 0-8
Fleet T v Dulwich Hamlet — 0-7
Portishead T v AFC Portchester — 1-5
Forest Green R v Bridgwater U — 2-4
AFC St Austell v Sherborne T — 2-8
AFC Stoneham v Swindon T — 1-10
Bournemouth Sports v Bradworthy — 2-0
St Agnes v Saltash U — 1-7
Gloucester C v Marine Academy Plymouth — 1-3
Bursledon v Downend Flyers — 1-0
Bitton v Winchester C Flyers — 0-3
Yeovil T v Southampton — 1-1
Yeovil T won 4-2 on penalties.
Sholing v Bristol M — 1-2
Poole T v Bishop's Cleeve — 4-0
AEK Boco v Keynsham T — 1-8
Moneyfields v Saltash Bor — 14-0
Bournemouth v Bishops Lydeard — 5-3
Torquay U v Royal Wootton Bassett T — 3-1

FIRST ROUND

Cheadle Town Stingers v AFC Fylde — 2-0
FC St Helens v Doncaster R Belles — 2-1

Washington v Hull C — 0-7
Handsworth v York C — 2-0
Burnley v Spennymoor T — 12-0
Thornaby v Liverpool Feds — 2-7
Durham Cestria v Norton & Stockton Ancients — 4-0
Preston NE v Bradford C — 1-2
Huddersfield T v Nantwich T — 7-0
Curzon Ashton v Chester-le-Street T — 0-1
Rossington Main v Accrington S — 0-1
Wythenshawe v Middlesbrough — 0-3
Sheffield v Penrith — 2-1
Mancunian Unity v Stockport Co — 6-2
South Shields v Halifax — 3-3
South Shields won 4-3 on penalties.
Stamford v Worcester C — 2-3
Loughborough Lightning v Sutton Coldfield T — 2-1
Notts Co v Sporting Khalsa — 0-5
Boldmere St Michaels v Nottingham F — 1-3
Asfordby Amateurs v Wolverhampton W — 1-7
Kidderminster H v Port Vale — 3-1
Shrewsbury T v Northampton T — 3-2
Knowle v WBA — 1-7
AFC Telford U v Stourbridge — 1-5
River C v Long Itchington — 2-3
Stoke C v Hednesford T — 5-0
Derby Co v Leafield Ath — 1-3
Rugby Bor v Lincoln C — 7-0
Peterborough U v Billericay T — 2-2
Peterborough U won 4-2 on penalties.
London Seaward v Hackney — 3-1
Cambridge C v Stevenage — 2-2
Stevenage won 4-2 on penalties.
AFC Sudbury v Bowers & Pitsea — 3-0
Hashtag U v Wroxham — 6-0
Ipswich T v Milton Keynes D — 12-0
Royston T v Newport Pagnell T — 3-0
Cambridge U v Norwich C — 0-1
Hutton v Luton T — 2-4
Penn & Tylers Green v QPR — 0-3
Oxford U v Actonians — 5-0
Comets v Worthing — 2-5
AFC Wimbledon v Watford — 0-0
Watford won 4-2 on penalties.
Lewes v Dulwich Hamlet — 1-1
Lewes won 6-5 on penalties.
Fulham v Chesham U — 7-0
Aylesford v Reading — 3-1
Chatham T v Dorking W — 5-2
Farnham T v London Bees — 0-2
Saltdean U v South London — 2-1
Brentford v Ascot U — 4-2
Torquay U v Bridgwater U — 0-1
Cheltenham T v Yeovil T — 7-0
Bristol R v Sherborne T — 4-3
Plymouth Arg v Poole T — 6-0
Saltash U v Bournemouth — 0-6
Bournemouth Sports v Moneyfields — 0-1
Winchester C Flyers v AFC Portchester — 1-4
Bursledon v Marine Academy Plymouth — 0-4
Gwalia U v Swindon T — 4-1
Exeter C v Keynsham T — 4-0

SECOND ROUND

Hull C v Middlesbrough — 0-0
Middlesbrough won 5-4 on penalties.
Accrington S v Huddersfield T — 1-2
Durham Cestria v Chester-le-Street T — 1-1
Chester-le-Street T won 4-3 on penalties.
Mancunian Unity v Handsworth — 4-0
South Shields v Liverpool Feds — 0-11
Burnley v Bradford C — 11-0
FC St Helens v Cheadle Town Stingers — 0-4
Wolverhampton W v Sporting Khalsa — 8-1
Stoke C v Loughborough Lightning — 4-2
Norwich C v Leafield Ath — 1-0
Rugby Bor v Peterborough U — 7-1
Kidderminster H v Stourbridge — 1-1
Kidderminster H won 4-2 on penalties.
Shrewsbury T v Sheffield — 3-3
Shrewsbury T won 4-2 on penalties.
WBA v Worcester C — 6-0
Long Itchington v Nottingham F — 0-19
Brentford v London Seaward — 1-0
QPR v Saltdean U — 5-0
Hashtag U v Ipswich T — 2-2
Ipswich T won 4-1 on penalties.

| Oxford U v Watford | 1-0 |
| Aylesford v Worthing | 2-2 |

Worthing won 5-3 on penalties.

London Bees v Chatham T	3-2
Fulham v Royston T	4-3
Stevenage v Luton T	1-1

Luton T won 15-14 on penalties.

Lewes v AFC Sudbury	3-0
Plymouth Arg v Exeter C	1-5
Cheltenham T v Moneyfields	2-1
Marine Academy Plymouth v Bristol R	0-4
Gwalia U v Bridgwater U	4-0
AFC Portchester v Bournemouth	0-4

THIRD ROUND

Chester-le-Street T v Stoke C	1-2
Kidderminster H v Blackburn R	0-4
Wolverhampton W v Shrewsbury T	14-0
Liverpool Feds v Sheffield U	0-2
Newcastle U v Middlesbrough	2-0
WBA v Cheadle Town Stingers	2-0
Birmingham C v Durham	0-1
Sunderland v Huddersfield T	4-0
Rugby Bor v Mancunian Unity	3-0
Portsmouth v Luton T	5-0
Ipswich T v Bournemouth	1-0
London City Lionesses v Gwalia U	4-0
Brentford v Fulham	1-2
Oxford U v Bristol R	2-3
Charlton Ath v Lewes	4-0
Southampton v Bristol C	0-3
Cheltenham T v Norwich C	2-1*

1-1 at the end of normal time.

| Exeter C v Worthing | 3-1* |

1-1 at the end of normal time.

| London Bees v QPR | 6-3* |

2-2 at the end of normal time.

| Nottingham F v Burnley | 1-0* |

0-0 at the end of normal time.

FOURTH ROUND

London Bees v Rugby Bor	0-6
Leicester C v Stoke C	4-1
West Ham U v Liverpool	0-5
Arsenal v Bristol C	5-0
Chelsea v Charlton Ath	4-0
Exeter C v Sunderland	1-7
Cheltenham T v Wolverhampton W	0-2
Brighton & HA v Durham	4-1
Newcastle U v Nottingham F	1-0
Blackburn R v Portsmouth	1-3
Manchester U v Ipswich T	3-0
Aston Villa v Bristol R	9-0
Everton v Tottenham H	2-0
Manchester U v WBA	7-0
Crystal Palace v Sheffield U	6-1
Fulham v London City Lionesses	0-5

FIFTH ROUND

Wolverhampton W v Manchester U	0-6
Chelsea v Tottenham H	4-1
Portsmouth v Sunderland	0-2
Manchester C v Leicester C	3-1
Crystal Palace v Newcastle U	2-0
Aston Villa v Brighton & HA	3-2
Rugby Bor v Liverpool	0-2
Arsenal v London City Lionesses	2-0

QUARTER-FINALS

Manchester U v Sunderland	3-1
Manchester C v Aston Villa	2-0
Chelsea v Crystal Palace	1-0
Arsenal v Liverpool	0-1

SEMI-FINALS

| Chelsea v Liverpool | 2-1 |
| Manchester C v Manchester U | 0-2 |

ADOBE WOMEN'S FA CUP FINAL 2024–25

Sunday, 18 May 2025

(at Wembley Stadium, attendance 74,412)

Chelsea (1) 3　　Manchester U (0) 0

Chelsea: (541) Hampton; Bronze (Rytting Kaneryd 90), Bjorn, Bright, Girma, Charles; Beever-Jones (Kaptein 75), Walsh, Cuthbert (Nusken 90), Baltimore (Reiten 90); Ramirez (Macario 62).
Scorers: Baltimore 45 (pen), 90, Macario 84.

Manchester U: (4231) Tullis-Joyce; Mannion (Malard 70), Le Tissier, Turner (Toone 46), George (Sandberg 76); Miyazawa (Naalsund 81), Janssen; Bizet Ildhusoy (Williams 81), Clinton, Galton; Terland.

Referee: Stacey Fullicks.

Sandy Baltimore of Chelsea scores her team's first goal from the penalty spot during the Adobe Women's FA Cup final against Manchester United at Wembley Stadium. (Photo by Julian Finney/Getty Images)

WOMEN'S FA CUP FINALS 1970–71 to 2024–25

After extra time.

1970–71	Southampton v Stewarton Thistle	4-1
1971–72	Southampton v Lee's Ladies	3-2
1972–73	Southampton v Westthorn U	2-0
1973–74	Fodens v Southampton	2-1
1974–75	Southampton v Warminster	4-2
1975–76	Southampton v QPR	2-1*
1976–77	QPR v Southampton	1-0
1977–78	Southampton v QPR	8-2
1978–79	Southampton v Lowestoft	1-0
1979–80	St Helens v Preston NE	1-0
1980–81	Southampton v St Helens	4-2
1981–82	Lowestoft v Cleveland Spartans	2-0
1982–83	Doncaster Belles v St Helens	3-2
1983–84	Howbury Grange v Doncaster Belles	4-2
1984–85	Friends of Fulham v Doncaster Belles	2-0
1985–86	Norwich v Doncaster Belles	4-3
1986–87	Doncaster Belles v St Helens	2-0
1987–88	Doncaster Belles v Leasowe Pacific	3-1
1988–89	Leasowe Pacific v Friends of Fulham	3-2
1989–90	Doncaster Belles v Friends of Fulham	1-0
1990–91	Millwall Lionesses v Doncaster Belles	1-0
1991–92	Doncaster Belles v Red Star Southampton	4-0
1992–93	Arsenal v Doncaster Belles	3-0
1993–94	Doncaster Belles v Knowsley U	1-0
1994–95	Arsenal v Liverpool	3-2
1995–96	Croydon v Liverpool	1-1*
	Croydon won 3-2 on penalties.	
1996–97	Millwall Lionesses v Wembley	1-0
1997–98	Arsenal v Croydon	3-2
1998–99	Arsenal v Southampton Saints	2-0
1999–2000	Croydon v Doncaster Belles	2-1
2000–01	Arsenal v Fulham	1-0
2001–02	Fulham v Doncaster Belles	2-1
2002–03	Fulham v Charlton Ath	3-0
2003–04	Arsenal v Charlton Ath	3-0
2004–05	Charlton Ath v Everton	1-0
2005–06	Arsenal v Leeds U	5-0
2006–07	Arsenal v Charlton Ath	4-1
2007–08	Arsenal v Leeds U	4-1
2008–09	Arsenal v Sunderland	2-1
2009–10	Everton v Arsenal	3-2*
2010–11	Arsenal v Bristol Academy	2-0
2011–12	Birmingham C v Chelsea	2-2*
	Birmingham C won 3-2 on penalties.	
2012–13	Arsenal v Bristol Academy	3-0
2013–14	Arsenal v Everton	2-0
2014–15	Chelsea v Notts Co	1-0
2015–16	Arsenal v Chelsea	1-0
2016–17	Manchester C v Birmingham C	4-1
2017–18	Chelsea v Arsenal	3-1
2018–19	Manchester C v West Ham U	3-0
2019–20	Manchester C v Everton	3-1*
2020–21	Chelsea v Arsenal	3-0
2021–22	Chelsea v Manchester C	3-2*
2022–23	Chelsea v Manchester U	1-0
2023–24	Manchester U v Tottenham H	4-0
2024–25	Chelsea v Manchester U	3-0

UEFA WOMEN'S CHAMPIONS LEAGUE FINALS

After extra time.

EUROPEAN CUP FINALS

Year (leg)	Winners v Runners-up	Score (agg)	Venue	Attendance	Referee
2001–02	Frankfurt v Umea	2-0	Frankfurt	12,106	Katrina Elovirta (Finland)
2002–03 (1)	Umea v Fortuna Hjorring	4-1	Umea	7,648	Elke Gunthner (Germany)
2002–03 (2)	Fortuna Hjorring v Umea	0-3 (1-7)	Hjorring	2,119	Wendy Toms (England)
2003–04 (1)	Umea v Frankfurt	3-0	Stockholm	5,409	Floarea Ionescu (Romania)
2003–04 (2)	Frankfurt v Umea	0-5 (0-8)	Frankfurt	9,500	Claudine Brohet (Belgium)
2004–05 (1)	Djurgarden v Turbine Potsdam	0-2	Stockholm	1,382	Anna De Toni (Italy)
2004–05 (2)	Turbine Potsdam v Djurgarden	3-1 (5-1)	Potsdam	8,677	Lale Orta (Turkey)
2005–06 (1)	Turbine Potsdam v Frankfurt	0-4	Potsdam	4,431	Eva Oediun (Sweden)
2005–06 (2)	Frankfurt v Turbine Potsdam	3-2 (7-2)	Frankfurt	13,200	Dagmar Damkova (Czech Republic)
2006–07 (1)	Umea v Arsenal	0-1	Umea	6,265	Christine Beck (Germany)
2006–07 (2)	Arsenal v Umea	0-0 (1-0)	Borehamwood	3,467	Nicole Petignat (Switzerland)
2007–08 (1)	Umea v Frankfurt	1-1	Umea	4,128	Gyongyi Gaal (Hungary)
2007–08 (2)	Frankfurt v Umea	3-2 (4-3)	Frankfurt	27,640	Alexandra Ihringova (Slovakia)
2008–09 (1)	Zvezda Perm v Duisburg	0-6	Kazan	700	Claudine Brohet (Belgium)
2008–09 (2)	Duisburg v Zvezda Perm	1-1 (7-1)	Duisburg	28,112	Jenny Palmqvist (Sweden)

UEFA CHAMPIONS LEAGUE FINALS

2009–10	Turbine Potsdam v Lyon	0-0*	Getafe	10,372	Kirsi Heikkinen (Finland)
	Turbine Potsdam won 7-6 on penalties.				
2010–11	Lyon v Turbine Potsdam	2-0	Craven Cottage	14,303	Dagmar Damkova (Czech Republic)
2011–12	Lyon v Frankfurt	2-0	Munich	50,212	Jenny Palmqvist (Sweden)
2012–13	VfL Wolfsburg v Lyon	1-0	Stamford Bridge	19,278	Teodora Albon (Romania)
2013–14	VfL Wolfsburg v Tyreso	4-3	Lisbon	11,217	Kateryna Monzul (Ukraine)
2014–15	Frankfurt v Paris Saint-Germain	2-1	Berlin	17,147	Esther Staubli (Switzerland)
2015–16	Lyon v VfL Wolfsburg	1-1*	Reggio Emilia	15,117	Katalin Kulcsar (Hungary)
	Lyon won 4-3 on penalties.				
2016–17	Lyon v Paris Saint-Germain	0-0*	Cardiff	22,433	Bibiana Steinhaus (Germany)
	Lyon won 7-6 on penalties.				
2017–18	Lyon v VfL Wolfsburg	4-1*	Kyiv	14,237	Jane Adamkova (Czech Republic)
2018–19	Lyon v Barcelona	4-1	Budapest	19,487	Anastasia Pustovoitova (Russia)
2019–20	Lyon v VfL Wolfsburg	3-1	San Sebastian	0	Esther Staubli (Switzerland)
2020–21	Barcelona v Chelsea	4-0	Gothenburg	0	Riem Hussein (Germany)
2021–22	Lyon v Barcelona	3-1	Turin	32,257	Lina Lehtovaara (Finland)
2022–23	Barcelona v VfL Wolfsburg	3-2	Eindhoven	33,147	Cheryl Foster (Wales)
2023–24	Barcelona v Lyon	2-0	Bilbao	50,827	Rebecca Welsh (England)
2024–25	Arsenal v Barcelona	1-0	Lisbon	38,356	Ivana Martincic (Croatia)

UEFA WOMEN'S CHAMPIONS LEAGUE 2024–25

After extra time.

QUALIFYING STAGE

CHAMPIONS PATH

GROUP 1 SEMI-FINALS
SFK 2000 v KI	3-0
Benfica v Nordsjaelland	3-1

THIRD-PLACE PLAY-OFF
KI v Nordsjaelland	0-2

FINAL
Benfica v SFK 2000	4-0

GROUP 2 SEMI-FINALS
Vllaznia v Lanchkhuti	3-0
St Polten v Neftchi Baku	5-0

THIRD-PLACE PLAY-OFF
Lanchkhuti v Neftchi Baku	2-1

FINAL
St Polten v Vllaznia	1-0

GROUP 3 SEMI-FINALS
KuPS v Celtic	1-3*
Gintra v Agarista Anenii Noi	5-0

THIRD-PLACE PLAY-OFF
KuPS v Agarista Anenii Noi	6-0

FINAL
Gintra v Celtic	0-2

GROUP 4 SEMI-FINALS
Anderlecht v Red Star Belgrade	4-1
Breznica v Birkirkara	1-2*

THIRD-PLACE PLAY-OFF
Red Star Belgrade v Breznica	3-0

FINAL
Anderlecht v Birkirkara	5-0

GROUP 5 SEMI-FINALS
Valur v Ljuboten	10-0
FC Twente v Cardiff C	7-0

THIRD-PLACE PLAY-OFF
Ljuboten v Cardiff C	2-0

FINAL
FC Twente v Valur	5-0

GROUP 6 SEMI-FINALS
ZNK Mura v Glentoran	3-2
Apollon Ladies v FC Pyunik	3-0

THIRD-PLACE PLAY-OFF
Glentoran v FC Pyunik	1-0

FINAL
Apollon Ladies v ZNK Mura	2-3

GROUP 7 SEMI-FINALS
PAOK v Kiryat Gat	2-1*
Servette v Pogon Szczecin	1-0

THIRD-PLACE PLAY-OFF
Kiryat Gat v Pogon Szczecin	0-1

FINAL
Servette v PAOK	2-0

GROUP 8 SEMI-FINALS
BIIK Shymkent v NSA Sofia	3-0
Racing Union v Galatasaray	1-4

THIRD-PLACE PLAY-OFF
Racing Union v NSA Sofia	2-0

FINAL
BIIK Shymkent v Galatasaray	0-5

GROUP 9 SEMI-FINALS
Dinamo Minsk v Peamount	1-2*
Osijek v Spartak Myjava	2-0

THIRD-PLACE PLAY-OFF
Dinamo Minsk v Spartak Myjava	3-2

FINAL
Osijek v Peamount	2-1

GROUP 10 SEMI-FINALS
Vorskla Poltava v SFK Riga	5-0
Ferencvaros v Flora	2-1

THIRD-PLACE PLAY-OFF
SFK Riga v Flora	0-0*

Flora won 7-6 on penalties.

FINAL
Vorskla Poltava v Ferencvaros	2-0

GROUP 11 SEMI-FINAL
Mitrovica v Farul Constanta	0-4

FINAL
Valerenga v Farul Constanta	3-1

LEAGUE PATH

GROUP 1 SEMI-FINALS
Ajax v Kolos Kovalivka	4-1*
Brondby v Fiorentina	0-1

THIRD-PLACE PLAY-OFF
Brondby v Kolos Kovalivka	2-1

FINAL
Ajax v Fiorentina	0-1

GROUP 2 SEMI-FINALS
Paris FC v First Vienna	9-0
Sparta Prague v Linkoping	3-1*

THIRD-PLACE PLAY-OFF
Linkoping v First Vienna	8-0

FINAL
Paris FC v Sparta Prague	2-0

GROUP 3 SEMI-FINALS
Atletico Madrid v Rosenborg	2-2*

Rosenborg won 3-2 on penalties.
Arsenal v Rangers	6-0

THIRD-PLACE PLAY-OFF
Atletico Madrid v Rangers	3-0

FINAL
Arsenal v Rosenborg	1-0

GROUP 4 SEMI-FINALS
Eintracht Frankfurt v Sporting Lisbon	0-2
FC Minsk v Breidablik	1-6

THIRD-PLACE PLAY-OFF
Eintracht Frankfurt v FC Minsk	6-0

FINAL
Breidablik v Sporting Lisbon	0-2

ROUND 2 FIRST LEG

CHAMPIONS PATH – FIRST LEG
St Polten v ZNK Mura	3-0
Hammarby v Benfica	1-2
Osijek v FC Twente	1-4
Galatasaray v Slavia Prague	2-2
Roma v Servette	3-1
Anderlecht v Valerenga	1-2
Vorskla Poltava v Celtic	0-1

LEAGUE PATH – FIRST LEG
Sporting Lisbon v Real Madrid	1-2
Juventus v Paris Saint-Germain	3-1
Paris FC v Manchester C	0-5
Fiorentina v VfL Wolfsburg	0-7
Hacken v Arsenal	1-0

CHAMPIONS PATH – SECOND LEG

		(agg)
ZNK Mura v St Polten	0-5	0-8
Benfica v Hammarby	0-2	2-3
FC Twente v Osijek	4-0	8-1
Slavia Prague v Galatasaray	1-2*	3-4
Servette v Roma	2-7	3-10
Valerenga v Anderlecht	3-0	5-1
Celtic v Vorskla Poltava	2-0	3-0

LEAGUE PATH – SECOND LEG

		(agg)
Real Madrid v Sporting Lisbon	3-1	5-2
Paris Saint-Germain v Juventus	1-2	2-5
Manchester C v Paris FC	3-0	8-0
VfL Wolfsburg v Fiorentina	5-0	12-0
Arsenal v Hacken	4-0	4-1

GROUP STAGE

GROUP A

Lyon v Galatasaray	3-0
Roma v VfL Wolfsburg	1-0
Galatasaray v Roma	1-6
VfL Wolfsburg v Lyon	0-2
Galatasaray v VfL Wolfsburg	0-5
Roma v Lyon	0-3
VfL Wolfsburg v Galatasaray	5-0
Lyon v Roma	4-1
VfL Wolfsburg v Roma	6-1
Galatasaray v Lyon	0-6
Lyon v VfL Wolfsburg	1-0
Roma v Galatasaray	3-0

Group A Table	P	W	D	L	F	A	GD	Pts
Lyon	6	6	0	0	19	1	18	18
VfL Wolfsburg*	6	3	0	3	16	5	11	9
Roma*	6	3	0	3	12	14	−2	9
Galatasaray	6	0	0	6	1	28	−27	0

Ranking decided on head-to-head goal difference.

GROUP B

Chelsea v Real Madrid	3-2
Celtic v FC Twente	0-2
Real Madrid v Celtic	4-0
FC Twente v Chelsea	1-3
Real Madrid v FC Twente	7-0
Celtic v Chelsea	1-2
FC Twente v Real Madrid	2-3
Chelsea v Celtic	3-0
Chelsea v FC Twente	6-1
Celtic v Real Madrid	0-3
Real Madrid v Chelsea	1-2
FC Twente v Celtic	3-0

Group B Table	P	W	D	L	F	A	GD	Pts
Chelsea	6	6	0	0	19	6	13	18
Real Madrid	6	4	0	2	20	7	13	12
FC Twente	6	2	0	4	9	19	−10	6
Celtic	6	0	0	6	1	17	−16	0

GROUP C

Bayern Munich v Arsenal	5-2
Valerenga v Juventus	0-1
Juventus v Bayern Munich	0-2
Arsenal v Valerenga	4-1
Juventus v Arsenal	0-4
Bayern Munich v Valerenga	3-0
Valerenga v Bayern Munich	1-1
Arsenal v Juventus	1-0
Bayern Munich v Juventus	4-0
Valerenga v Arsenal	1-3
Arsenal v Bayern Munich	3-2
Juventus v Valerenga	3-0

Group C Table	P	W	D	L	F	A	GD	Pts
Arsenal	6	5	0	1	17	9	8	15
Bayern Munich	6	4	1	1	17	6	11	13
Juventus	6	2	0	4	4	11	−7	6
Valerenga	6	0	1	5	3	15	−12	1

GROUP D

Hammarby v St Polten	2-0
Manchester C v Barcelona	2-0
St Polten v Manchester C	2-3
Barcelona v Hammarby	9-0
Barcelona v St Polten	7-0
Manchester C v Hammarby	2-0
Hammarby v Manchester C	1-2
St Polten v Barcelona	1-4
Manchester C v St Polten	2-0
Hammarby v Barcelona	0-3
Barcelona v Manchester C	3-0
St Polten v Hammarby	1-2

Group D Table	P	W	D	L	F	A	GD	Pts
Barcelona*	6	5	0	1	26	3	23	15
Manchester C*	6	5	0	1	11	6	5	15
Hammarby	6	2	0	4	5	17	−12	6
St Polten	6	0	0	6	4	20	−16	0

Ranking decided on head-to-head goal difference.

KNOCKOUT STAGE

QUARTER-FINALS – FIRST LEG

Real Madrid v Arsenal	2-0
Bayern Munich v Lyon	0-2
VfL Wolfsburg v Barcelona	1-4
Manchester C v Chelsea	2-0

QUARTER-FINALS – SECOND LEG

		(agg)
Arsenal v Real Madrid	3-0	3-2
Lyon v Bayern Munich	4-1	6-1
Barcelona v VfL Wolfsburg	6-1	10-2
Chelsea v Manchester C	3-0	3-2

SEMI-FINALS – FIRST LEG

Barcelona v Chelsea	4-1
Arsenal v Lyon	1-2

SEMI-FINALS – SECOND LEG

		(agg)
Chelsea v Barcelona	1-4	2-8
Lyon v Arsenal	1-4	3-5

UEFA WOMEN'S CHAMPIONS LEAGUE FINAL 2024–25

Saturday, 24 May 2025

(at Estadio Jose Alvalade, Lisbon, attendance 38,356)

Arsenal (0) 1   Barcelona (0) 0

Arsenal: (4231) van Domselaar; Fox, Williamson, Catley, McCabe; Little, Caldenty; Kelly (Mead 67), Maanum (Blackstenius 67), Foord (Hurtig 86); Russo (Wubben-Moy 90).
Scorer: Blackstenius 74.

Barcelona: (433) Coll; Batlle, Paredes, Leon (Engen 79), Rolfo (Brugts 79); Bonmati, Guijarro, Putellas; Hansen, Pajor, Pina (Paralluelo 62).

Referee: Ivana Martincic (Croatia).

UEFA WOMEN'S EURO 2025 – QUALIFYING

Due to the continuing wars in Gaza and Ukraine, Israel, Belarus and Ukraine play home matches in neutral countries.

LEAGUE A

GROUP 1

Norway v Finland	4-0
Italy v Netherlands	2-0
Finland v Italy	2-1
Netherlands v Norway	1-0
Norway v Italy	0-0
Netherlands v Finland	1-0
Finland v Netherlands	1-1
Italy v Norway	1-1
Finland v Norway	1-1
Netherlands v Italy	0-0
Norway v Netherlands	1-1
Italy v Finland	4-0

Group 1 Table	P	W	D	L	F	A	GD	Pts
Italy*	6	2	3	1	8	3	5	9
Netherlands*	6	2	3	1	4	4	0	9
Norway	6	1	4	1	7	4	3	7
Finland	6	1	2	3	4	12	–8	5

Rankings on head-to-head points.

GROUP 2

Czech Republic v Denmark	1-3
Belgium v Spain	0-7
Denmark v Belgium	4-2
Spain v Czech Republic	3-1
Czech Republic v Belgium	1-2
Denmark v Spain	0-2
Belgium v Czech Republic	1-1
Spain v Denmark	3-2
Czech Republic v Spain	2-1
Belgium v Denmark	0-3
Spain v Belgium	2-0
Denmark v Czech Republic	2-0

Group 1 Table	P	W	D	L	F	A	GD	Pts
Spain	6	5	0	1	18	5	13	15
Denmark	6	4	0	2	14	8	6	12
Belgium*	6	1	1	4	5	18	–13	4
Czech Republic*	6	1	1	4	6	12	–6	4

Rankings on head-to-head points.

GROUP 3

England v Sweden	1-1
France v Republic of Ireland	1-0
Sweden v France	0-1
Republic of Ireland v England	0-2
Republic of Ireland v Sweden	0-3
England v France	1-2
Sweden v Republic of Ireland	1-0
France v England	1-2
England v Republic of Ireland	2-1
France v Sweden	2-1
Sweden v England	0-0
Republic of Ireland v France	3-1

Group 3 Table	P	W	D	L	F	A	GD	Pts
France	6	4	0	2	8	7	1	12
England	6	3	2	1	8	5	3	11
Sweden	6	2	2	2	6	4	2	8
Republic of Ireland	6	1	0	5	4	10	–6	3

GROUP 4

Iceland v Poland	3-0
Austria v Germany	2-3
Poland v Austria	1-3
Germany v Iceland	3-1
Austria v Iceland	1-1
Germany v Poland	4-1
Poland v Germany	1-3
Iceland v Austria	2-1
Austria v Poland	3-1
Iceland v Germany	3-0
Germany v Austria	4-0
Poland v Iceland	0-1

Group 4 Table	P	W	D	L	F	A	GD	Pts
Germany	6	5	0	1	17	8	9	15
Iceland	6	4	1	1	11	5	6	13
Austria	6	2	1	3	10	12	–2	7
Poland	6	0	0	6	4	17	–13	0

LEAGUE B

GROUP 1

Hungary v Azerbaijan	1-1
Switzerland v Turkey	3-1
Azerbaijan v Switzerland	0-4
Turkey v Hungary	2-1
Turkey v Azerbaijan	1-0
Switzerland v Hungary	2-1
Azerbaijan v Turkey	1-0
Hungary v Switzerland	1-0
Azerbaijan v Hungary	0-5
Turkey v Switzerland	0-2
Switzerland v Azerbaijan	3-0
Hungary v Turkey	1-4

Group 1 Table	P	W	D	L	F	A	GD	Pts
Switzerland	6	5	0	1	14	3	11	15
Turkey	6	3	0	3	8	8	0	9
Hungary	6	2	1	3	10	9	1	7
Azerbaijan	6	1	1	4	2	14	–12	4

GROUP 2

Slovakia v Israel	2-0
Serbia v Scotland	0-0
Israel v Serbia (in Hungary)	2-4
Scotland v Slovakia	1-0
Serbia v Slovakia	2-1
Scotland v Israel	4-1
Israel v Scotland (in Hungary)	0-5
Slovakia v Serbia	0-4
Slovakia v Scotland	0-2
Serbia v Israel	1-0
Scotland v Serbia	1-0
Israel v Slovakia (in Hungary)	2-2

Group 2 Table	P	W	D	L	F	A	GD	Pts
Scotland	6	5	1	0	13	1	12	16
Serbia	6	4	1	1	11	4	7	13
Slovakia	6	1	1	4	5	11	–6	4
Israel	6	0	1	5	5	18	–13	1

GROUP 3

Northern Ireland v Malta	0-0
Portugal v Bosnia and Herzegovina	3-0
Bosnia and Herzegovina v Northern Ireland	1-3
Malta v Portugal	0-2
Malta v Bosnia and Herzegovina	0-1
Portugal v Northern Ireland	4-0
Bosnia and Herzegovina v Malta	2-1
Northern Ireland v Portugal	1-2
Bosnia and Herzegovina v Portugal	0-0
Malta v Northern Ireland	0-2
Portugal v Malta	3-1
Northern Ireland v Bosnia and Herzegovina	2-0

Group 3 Table	P	W	D	L	F	A	GD	Pts
Portugal	6	5	1	0	14	2	12	16
Northern Ireland	6	3	1	2	8	7	1	10
Bosnia and Herzegovina	6	2	1	3	4	9	–5	7
Malta	6	0	1	5	2	10	–8	1

GROUP 4

Ukraine v Kosovo (in Turkey)	2-0
Wales v Croatia	4-0
Kosovo v Wales	0-6
Croatia v Ukraine	1-0
Kosovo v Croatia	0-1
Wales v Ukraine	1-1
Ukraine v Wales (in Poland)	2-2
Croatia v Kosovo	2-0
Kosovo v Ukraine	0-4
Croatia v Wales	0-3
Wales v Kosovo	2-0
Ukraine v Croatia (in North Macedonia)	2-0

Group 4 Table	P	W	D	L	F	A	GD	Pts
Wales	6	4	2	0	18	3	15	14
Ukraine	6	3	2	1	11	4	7	11
Croatia	6	3	0	3	4	9	–5	9
Kosovo	6	0	0	6	0	17	–17	0

LEAGUE C

GROUP 1

Cyprus v Belarus	0-3
Georgia v Lithuania	2-2
Belarus v Georgia (in Cyprus)	3-0
Lithuania v Cyprus	1-0
Lithuania v Belarus*	0-3
Cyprus v Georgia	0-2
Belarus v Lithuania*	3-0
Georgia v Cyprus	1-0
Georgia v Belarus	0-2
Cyprus v Lithuania	1-2
Belarus v Cyprus (in Georgia)	5-0
Lithuania v Georgia	0-1

Lithuania refused to play Belarus. Both games awarded 3-0 to Belarus by UEFA.

Group 1 Table	P	W	D	L	F	A	GD	Pts
Belarus	6	6	0	0	19	0	19	18
Georgia	6	3	1	2	6	7	–1	10
Lithuania	6	2	1	3	5	10	–5	7
Cyprus	6	0	0	6	1	14	–13	0

GROUP 2

Slovenia v Moldova	2-0
Latvia v North Macedonia	3-4
North Macedonia v Slovenia	0-5
Moldova v Latvia	0-1
North Macedonia v Moldova	1-1
Slovenia v Latvia	6-0
Latvia v Slovenia	0-4
Moldova v North Macedonia	2-4
North Macedonia v Latvia	1-2
Moldova v Slovenia	0-5
Slovenia v North Macedonia	4-0
Latvia v Moldova	2-1

Group 2 Table	P	W	D	L	F	A	GD	Pts
Slovenia	6	6	0	0	26	0	26	18
Latvia	6	3	0	3	8	16	–8	9
North Macedonia	6	2	1	3	10	17	–7	7
Moldova	6	0	1	5	4	15	–11	1

GROUP 3

Montenegro v Andorra	6-1
Greece v Faroe Islands	1-0
Montenegro v Faroe Islands	5-1
Andorra v Greece	0-3
Greece v Montenegro	2-2
Faroe Islands v Andorra	4-0
Faroe Islands v Greece	0-2
Andorra v Montenegro	1-5
Faroe Islands v Montenegro	2-1
Greece v Andorra	6-0
Montenegro v Greece	2-3
Andorra v Faroe Islands	0-4

Group 3 Table	P	W	D	L	F	A	GD	Pts
Greece	6	5	1	0	17	4	13	16
Montenegro	6	3	1	2	21	10	11	10
Faroe Islands	6	3	0	3	11	9	2	9
Andorra	6	0	0	6	2	28	–26	0

GROUP 4

Kazakhstan v Bulgaria	0-1
Armenia v Romania	0-5
Bulgaria v Armenia	2-3
Romania v Kazakhstan	1-0
Armenia v Kazakhstan	2-1
Romania v Bulgaria	1-0
Kazakhstan v Armenia	4-1
Bulgaria v Romania	0-3
Kazakhstan v Romania	0-3
Armenia v Bulgaria	1-3
Romania v Armenia	3-1
Bulgaria v Kazakhstan	0-0

Group 4 Table	P	W	D	L	F	A	GD	Pts
Romania	6	6	0	0	16	1	15	18
Bulgaria	6	2	1	3	6	8	–2	7
Armenia	6	2	0	4	8	18	–10	6
Kazakhstan	6	1	1	4	5	8	–3	4

GROUP 5

Luxembourg v Albania	2-1
Albania v Estonia	2-0
Estonia v Albania	1-2
Albania v Luxembourg	3-1
Luxembourg v Estonia	1-1
Estonia v Luxembourg	1-1

Group 5 Table	P	W	D	L	F	A	GD	Pts
Albania	4	3	0	1	8	4	4	9
Luxembourg	4	1	2	1	5	6	–1	5
Estonia	4	0	2	2	3	6	–3	2

PLAY-OFFS

After extra time.

ROUND 1: PATH 1 – FIRST LEG

Romania v Poland	1-2
Greece v Belgium	0-0
Montenegro v Finland	0-1
Georgia v Republic of Ireland	0-6
Slovenia v Austria	0-3
Luxembourg v Sweden	0-4
Belarus v Czech Republic	1-8
Albania v Norway	0-5

ROUND 1: PATH 1 – SECOND LEG

		(agg)
Romania v Poland	4-1	6-2
Greece v Belgium	5-0	5-0
Montenegro v Finland	5-0	6-0
Georgia v Republic of Ireland	3-0	9-0
Slovenia v Austria	2-1	5-1
Luxembourg v Sweden	8-0	12-0
Belarus v Czech Republic	0-0	8-1
Albania v Norway	9-0	14-0

ROUND 1: PATH 2 – FIRST LEG

Turkey v Ukraine	1-1
Croatia v Northern Ireland	1-1
Bosnia and Herzegovina v Serbia	2-2
Azerbaijan v Portugal	1-4
Hungary v Scotland	0-1
Slovakia v Wales	2-1

ROUND 1: PATH 2 – SECOND LEG

		(agg)
Ukraine v Turkey (in Moldova)	2-0	3-1
Northern Ireland v Croatia	1-0*	2-1
Serbia v Bosnia and Herzegovina	4-1	6-3
Portugal v Azerbaijan	4-0	8-1
Scotland v Hungary	4-0	5-0
Wales v Slovakia	2-0*	3-2

ROUND 2 – FIRST LEG

Portugal v Czech Republic	1-1
Scotland v Finland	0-0
Ukraine v Belgium (in Turkey)	0-2
Wales v Republic of Ireland	1-1
Poland v Austria	2-0
Northern Ireland v Norway	0-4
Serbia v Sweden	0-2

ROUND 2 – SECOND LEG

		(agg)
Czech Republic v Portugal	1-2	2-3
Finland v Scotland	2-0	2-0
Belgium v Ukraine	2-1	4-1
Republic of Ireland v Wales	1-2	2-3
Austria v Poland	0-1	0-2
Norway v Northern Ireland	3-0	7-0
Sweden v Serbia	6-0	8-0

QUALIFIED TEAMS

Switzerland	Netherlands
Germany	Portugal
Spain	Norway
Iceland	Finland
Denmark	Poland
France	Sweden
England	Belgium
Italy	Wales

Final competition in Switzerland 2–27 July 2025.

See Stop Press on page 1055 for group stage results and tables.

UEFA WOMEN'S NATIONS LEAGUE 2025

LEAGUE A

GROUP 1

Austria v Scotland	1-0
Netherlands v Germany	2-2
Germany v Austria	4-1
Scotland v Netherlands	1-2
Netherlands v Austria	3-1
Scotland v Germany	0-4
Austria v Netherlands	1-3
Germany v Scotland	6-1
Germany v Netherlands	4-0
Scotland v Austria	0-1
Austria v Germany	0-6
Netherlands v Scotland	1-1

Group 1 Table	P	W	D	L	F	A	GD	Pts
Germany	6	5	1	0	26	4	22	16
Netherlands	6	3	2	1	11	10	1	11
Austria	6	2	0	4	5	16	–11	6
Scotland	6	0	1	5	3	15	–12	1

GROUP 2

Switzerland v Iceland	0-0
France v Norway	1-0
Norway v Switzerland	2-1
France v Iceland	3-2
Iceland v Norway	0-0
Switzerland v France	0-2
Iceland v Switzerland	3-3
Norway v France	0-2
France v Switzerland	4-0
Norway v Iceland	1-1
Iceland v France	0-2
Switzerland v Norway	0-1

Group 2 Table	P	W	D	L	F	A	GD	Pts
France	6	6	0	0	14	2	12	18
Norway	6	2	2	2	4	5	–1	8
Iceland	6	0	4	2	6	9	–3	4
Switzerland	6	0	2	4	4	12	–8	2

GROUP 3

Spain v Belgium	3-2	Spain v Portugal	7-1
Portugal v England	1-1	Belgium v England	3-2
Belgium v Portugal	0-1	Belgium v Spain	1-5
England v Spain	1-0	England v Portugal	6-0
Portugal v Spain	2-4	Portugal v Belgium	0-3
England v Belgium	5-0	Spain v England	2-1

Group 3 Table	P	W	D	L	F	A	GD	Pts
Spain	6	5	0	1	21	8	13	15
England	6	3	1	2	16	6	10	10
Belgium	6	2	0	4	9	16	–7	6
Portugal	6	1	1	4	5	21	–16	4

GROUP 4

Italy v Wales	1-0	Denmark v Italy	0-3
Denmark v Sweden	1-2	Sweden v Wales	1-1
Italy v Denmark	1-3	Denmark v Wales	1-0
Wales v Sweden	1-1	Italy v Sweden	0-0
Sweden v Italy	3-2	Sweden v Denmark	6-1
Wales v Denmark	1-2	Wales v Italy	1-4

Group 4 Table	P	W	D	L	F	A	GD	Pts
Sweden	6	3	3	0	13	6	7	12
Italy	6	3	1	2	11	7	4	10
Denmark	6	3	0	3	8	13	–5	9
Wales	6	0	2	4	4	10	–6	2

LEAGUE B

GROUP 1

Bosnia & Herzegovina v Romania	4-0
Poland v Northern Ireland	2-0
Northern Ireland v Bosnia & Herzegovina	3-2
Romania v Poland	0-1
Poland v Bosnia & Herzegovina	5-1
Romania v Northern Ireland	1-1
Bosnia & Herzegovina v Poland	1-1
Northern Ireland v Romania	1-0
Northern Ireland v Poland	0-4
Romania v Bosnia & Herzegovina	2-0
Bosnia & Herzegovina v Northern Ireland	1-1
Poland v Romania	3-0

Group 1 Table	P	W	D	L	F	A	GD	Pts
Poland	6	5	1	0	16	2	14	16
Northern Ireland	6	2	2	2	6	10	–4	8
Bosnia & Herzegovina	6	1	2	3	9	12	–3	5
Romania	6	1	1	4	3	10	–7	4

GROUP 2

Greece v Slovenia	1-2
Republic of Ireland v Turkey	1-0
Slovenia v Republic of Ireland	4-0
Turkey v Greece	1-0
Greece v Republic of Ireland	0-4
Slovenia v Turkey	3-0
Republic of Ireland v Greece	2-1
Turkey v Slovenia	0-1
Slovenia v Greece	2-0
Turkey v Republic of Ireland	1-2
Greece v Turkey	0-1
Republic of Ireland v Slovenia	1-0

Group 2 Table	P	W	D	L	F	A	GD	Pts
Slovenia*	6	5	0	1	12	2	10	15
Republic of Ireland*	6	5	0	1	10	6	4	15
Turkey	6	2	0	4	3	7	–4	6
Greece	6	0	0	6	2	12	–10	0

Ranking decided on head-to-head goal difference.

GROUP 3

Belarus v Hungary	0-2	Belarus v Serbia	0-3
Serbia v Finland	1-0	Finland v Hungary	3-0
Hungary v Finland	0-1	Belarus v Finland	0-3
Serbia v Belarus	0-0	Serbia v Hungary	1-0
Finland v Belarus	0-0	Finland v Serbia	1-1
Hungary v Serbia	0-1	Hungary v Belarus	0-0

Group 3 Table	P	W	D	L	F	A	GD	Pts
Serbia	6	4	2	0	7	1	6	14
Finland	6	3	2	1	8	2	6	11
Hungary	6	1	1	4	2	6	–4	4
Belarus	6	0	3	3	0	8	–8	3

GROUP 4

Albania v Ukraine	1-2
Croatia v Czech Republic	0-4
Czech Republic v Albania	5-1
Ukraine v Croatia	2-1
Albania v Croatia	4-0
Ukraine v Czech Republic	1-0
Croatia v Albania	1-2
Czech Republic v Ukraine	1-1
Czech Republic v Croatia	5-0
Ukraine v Albania	2-1
Albania v Czech Republic	1-2
Croatia v Ukraine	2-0

Group 4 Table	P	W	D	L	F	A	GD	Pts
Ukraine*	6	4	1	1	8	6	2	13
Czech Republic*	6	4	1	1	17	4	13	13
Albania	6	2	0	4	10	12	–2	6
Croatia	6	1	0	5	4	17	–13	3

Ranking decided on head-to-head points.

LEAGUE C

GROUP 1

Moldova v Gibraltar	1-0
Slovakia v Faroe Islands	3-0
Gibraltar v Faroe Islands	0-1
Slovakia v Moldova	1-0
Faroe Islands v Moldova	2-0
Gibraltar v Slovakia	0-8
Faroe Islands v Gibraltar	5-0
Moldova v Slovakia	0-2
Moldova v Faroe Islands	1-1
Slovakia v Gibraltar	11-0
Faroe Islands v Slovakia	1-2
Gibraltar v Moldova	0-4

Group 1 Table	P	W	D	L	F	A	GD	Pts
Slovakia	6	6	0	0	27	1	26	18
Faroe Islands	6	3	1	2	10	6	4	10
Moldova	6	2	1	3	6	6	0	7
Gibraltar	6	0	0	6	0	30	–30	0

GROUP 2

Cyprus v Malta	2-1
Georgia v Andorra	2-1
Cyprus v Georgia	2-1
Malta v Andorra	1-0
Georgia v Malta	2-3
Cyprus v Andorra	2-2
Andorra v Cyprus	2-1
Malta v Georgia	2-1
Andorra v Georgia	1-2
Malta v Cyprus	1-0
Andorra v Malta	0-0
Georgia v Cyprus	1-2

Group 2 Table	P	W	D	L	F	A	GD	Pts
Malta	6	4	1	1	8	5	3	13
Cyprus	6	3	1	2	9	8	1	10
Georgia	6	2	0	4	9	11	-2	6
Andorra	6	1	2	3	6	8	-2	5

GROUP 3

Armenia v Liechtenstein	6-1
Luxembourg v Kazakhstan	2-2
Armenia v Kazakhstan	2-0
Luxembourg v Liechtenstein	7-0
Armenia v Luxembourg	1-3
Liechtenstein v Kazakhstan	0-4
Kazakhstan v Armenia	3-2
Liechtenstein v Luxembourg	2-3
Kazakhstan v Liechtenstein	4-0
Luxembourg v Armenia	2-0
Kazakhstan v Luxembourg	1-3
Liechtenstein v Armenia	2-2

Group 3 Table	P	W	D	L	F	A	GD	Pts
Luxembourg	6	5	1	0	20	6	14	16
Kazakhstan	6	3	1	2	14	9	5	10
Armenia	6	2	1	3	13	11	2	7
Liechtenstein	6	0	1	5	5	26	-21	1

GROUP 4

Azerbaijan v Montenegro	0-0
Montenegro v Lithuania	3-1
Lithuania v Azerbaijan	0-2
Montenegro v Azerbaijan	1-1
Azerbaijan v Lithuania	0-5
Lithuania v Montenegro	0-1

Group 4 Table	P	W	D	L	F	A	GD	Pts
Montenegro	4	2	2	0	5	2	3	8
Azerbaijan	4	1	2	1	3	6	-3	5
Lithuania	4	1	0	3	6	6	0	3

GROUP 5

Bulgaria v Israel	1-3
Israel v Estonia	3-1
Estonia v Bulgaria	0-0
Israel v Bulgaria	3-3
Estonia v Israel	0-3
Bulgaria v Estonia	0-1

Group 5 Table	P	W	D	L	F	A	GD	Pts
Israel	4	3	1	0	12	5	7	10
Estonia	4	1	1	2	2	6	-4	4
Bulgaria	4	0	2	2	4	7	-3	2

GROUP 6

North Macedonia v Kosovo	0-4
Kosovo v Latvia	0-1
North Macedonia v Latvia	1-2
Kosovo v North Macedonia	3-0
Latvia v North Macedonia	1-1
Latvia v Kosovo	2-2

Group 6 Table	P	W	D	L	F	A	GD	Pts
Latvia	4	2	2	0	6	4	2	8
Kosovo	4	2	1	1	9	3	6	7
North Macedonia	4	0	1	3	2	10	-8	1

WOMEN'S EUROPEAN CHAMPIONSHIP FINALS

UNOFFICIAL FINALS

Year (leg)	Winners v Runners-up	Score	Venue	Attendance	Referee
1969	Italy v Denmark	3-1	Turin	10,000	Nino Cosentino (Italy)
1979	Denmark v Italy	2-0	Naples	15,000	Anna Pancani (Italy)

OFFICIAL FINALS

Year	Winners v Runners-up	Score	Venue	Attendance	Referee
1984 (1)	Sweden v England	1-0	Gothenburg	5,662	Cees Bakker (Netherlands)
1984 (2)	Engand v Sweden	1-0	Luton	2,567	Ignace Gorice (Belgium)
	1-1 on aggregate; Sweden won 4-3 on penalties.				
1987	Norway v Sweden	2-1	Oslo	8,408	Eero Aho (Finland)
1989	West Germany v Norway	4-1	Osnabruck	22,000	Carlos Valente (Portugal)
1991	Germany v Norway	3-1*	Aalborg	6,000	James McCluskey (Scotland)
1993	Norway v Italy	1-0	Cesena	7,000	Alfred Woeser (Austria)
1995	Germany v Sweden	3-2	Kaiserslautern	8,500	Ilkka Koho (Finland)
1997	Germany v Italy	2-0	Oslo	2,221	Gitte Lyngo-Nielsen (Denmark)
2001	Germany v Sweden	1-0*	Ulm	18,000	Nicole Petignat (Switzerland)
	Golden goal				
2005	Germany v Norway	3-1	Blackburn	21,105	Alexandra Ihringova (Slovakia)
2009	Germany v England	6-2	Helsinki	15,877	Dagmar Damkova (Czech Republic)
2013	Germany v Norway	1-0	Solna	41,301	Cristina Dorcioman (Romania)
2017	Netherlands v Denmark	4-2	Enschede	28,182	Esther Staubli (Switzerland)
2022	England v Germany	2-1*	Wembley	87,192	Kateryna Monzul (Ukraine)

FIFA WOMEN'S WORLD CUP FINALS

Year	Winners v Runners-up	Score	Venue	Attendance	Referee
1991	USA v Norway	2-1	Guangzhou	63,000	Vadim Zhuk (Soviet Union)
1995	Norway v Germany	2-0	Stockholm	17,158	Ingrid Jonsson (Sweden)
1999	USA v China PR	0-0*	Pasadena	90,185	Nicole Petignat (Switzerland)
	USA won 5-4 on penalties.				
2003	Germany v Sweden	2-1*	Los Angeles	26,137	Cristina Ionescu (Romania)
2007	Germany v Brazil	2-0	Shanghai	31,000	Tammy Ogston (Australia)
2011	Japan v USA	2-2*	Frankfurt	48,817	Bibiana Steinhaus (Germany)
	Japan won 3-1 on penalties.				
2015	USA v Japan	5-2	Vancouver	53,341	Kateryna Monzul (Ukraine)
2019	USA v Netherlands	2-0	Lyon	57,900	Stephanie Frappart (France)
2023	Spain v England	1-0	Sydney	75,784	Tori Penso (USA)

ENGLAND WOMEN'S INTERNATIONALS 2024–25

FRIENDLIES
Wembley Stadium, Friday, 25 October 2024
England (2) 3 *(Stanway 33 (pen), 36, Bronze 81)*
Germany (3) 4 *(Gwinn 3 (pen) 11, Buhl 29,*
Dabritiz 72 (pen))   47,967
England: (4321) Hampton; Bronze (Le Tissier 81),
Bright, Williamson (Greenwood 61), Carter; Stanway,
Toone (Park 46), Walsh; Mead (Naz 81), Hemp; Russo
(Kelly 72).

Coventry, Tuesday, 29 October 2024
England (2) 2 *(Williamson 12, Clinton 23)*
South Africa (0) 1 *(Kgatlana 55)*   20,400
England: (4141) Earps; Le Tissier, Williamson (Bright
73), Greenwood, Morgan (Bronze 61); Stanway; Kelly,
Park (Kirby 62), Clinton (Toone 62), Mead (Hemp 73);
Naz (Russo 61).

Wembley Stadium, Saturday, 30 November 2024
England (0) 0
USA (0) 0   78,346
England: (4231) Earps; Bronze, Williamson, Carter,
Greenwood; Stanway, Walsh; Naz (Kelly 74), Park
(Kirby 75), Mead; Russo.

Bramall Lane, Sheffield, Tuesday, 3 December 2024
England (1) 1 *(Clinton 8)*
Switzerland (0) 0   23,870
England: (3142) Hampton; Morgan, Turner (Carter 84),
Bright; Mace (Walsh 63); Le Tissier, Clinton, Blindkilde-
Brown (Stanway 84), George (Mead 63); Park (Russo
46), Beever-Jones (Naz 84).

King Power Stadium, Leicester, Sunday, 29 June 2025
England (3) 7 *(Toone 10, 45, Bronze 32, Stanway 59,*
Russo 71, Beever-Jones 85, Mead 90)
Jamaica (0) 0   25,088
England: (4231) Hampton; Bronze (Charles 75),
Williamson, Greenwood (Morgan 63), Carter; Stanway,
Walsh (Clinton 75); Mead, Toone (James 63), Hemp
(Kelly 63); Russo (Beever-Jones 75).

UEFA NATIONS LEAGUE 2025-26
LEAGUE A
Algarve, Friday, 21 February 2025
Portugal (0) 1 *(Nazareth 75)*
England (1) 1 *(Russo 15)*   3221
England: (4321) Earps; Bronze (Carter 46), Williamson,
Bright, Charles; Toone, Walsh, Clinton (Beever-Jones
83); Park (Kelly 83), James; Russo.

Wembley Stadium, Wednesday, 26 February 2025
England (1) 1 *(Park 33)*
Spain (0) 0   46,550
England: (4321) Hampton; Bronze, Williamson, Bright,
Charles; Clinton, Walsh, Toone (Naz 83); Park (Kelly
64), James; Russo (Parris 64).

Ashton Gate, Bristol, Friday, 4 April 2025
England (2) 5 *(Bronze 21, Bright 45, Beever-Jones 67,*
Park 77, Walsh 88)
Belgium (0) 0   23,202
England: (4231) Hampton; Bronze, Williamson (Morgan
73), Bright (Carter 80), Charles; Clinton, Walsh; Mead,
Toone (Park 60), James (Beever-Jones 46); Russo (Parris
73).

Leuven, Tuesday, 8 April 2025
Belgium (3) 3 *(Wullaert 4, 29, Vanhaevermaet 16)*
England (1) 2 *(Mead 35 (pen), Agyemang 81)*   6253
England: (4231) Hampton; Bronze, Williamson, Bright
(Morgan 46), Charles (Carter 46); Clinton (Toone 60),
Walsh; Mead, Park (Agyemang 80), Beever-Jones; Parris
(Kirby 60).

Wembley Stadium, Friday, 30 May 2025
England (5) 6 *(Beever-Jones 3, 26, 33, Bronze 5, Mead 29,*
Kelly 62)
Portugal (0) 0   48,531
England: (4321) Hampton; Bronze (Le Tissier 57),
Williamson, Morgan (Greenwood 57); Carter; Clinton,
Walsh (Stanway 75), Park (Kirby 67); Mead, Hemp
(Kelly 57); Beever-Jones.

Barcelona, Tuesday, 3 June 2025
Spain (0) 2 *(Pina 60, 70)*
England (1) 1 *(Russo 22)*   14,107
England: (4231) Hampton; Bronze (Carter 56),
Williamson, Greenwood, Charles; Stanway (Bo Kearns
46), Walsh; Mead (Kelly 56), Park (Toone 75), Hemp;
Russo (Beever-Jones 87).

UEFA WOMEN'S EURO 2025 GROUP D
(IN SWITZERLAND)
Zurich, Saturday, 5 July 2025
France (2) 2 *(Katoto 36, Baltimore 39)*
England (0) 1 *(Walsh 87)*   22,542
England: (4231) Hampton; Bronze, Williamson,
Greenwood (Agyemang 86), Carter (Charles 60); Walsh,
Stanway (Clinton 77); Mead (Kelly 60), James (Toone
60), Hemp; Russo.

Zurich, Wednesday, 9 July 2025
England (2) 4 *(James 22, 60, Stanway 45, Toone 67)*
Netherlands (0) 0   22,600
England: (4231) Hampton; Bronze (Charles 84),
Williamson, Carter, Greenwood; Walsh, Stanway; James
(Kelly 69), Toone (Clinton 75), Hemp (Mead 75); Russo
(Beever-Jones 84).

St Gallen, Sunday, 13 July 2025
England (4) 6 *(Stanway 13 (pen), Toone 21, Hemp 30,*
Russo 44, Mead 73, Beever-Jones 89)
Wales (0) 1 *(Cain 76)*   15,953
England: (4231) Hampton; Bronze (Charles 79),
Williamson, Carter, Greenwood; Walsh, Stanway; James
(Kelly 57), Toone (Park 46), Hemp (Mead 46); Russo
(Beever-Jones 57).
Wales: (4231) Clark; Morgan E, Roberts, Evans,
Woodham (Green 46); James, Rowe (Ladd 65); Jones
(Barton 85), Fishlock, Holland (Cain 65); Morgan F
(Hughes 79).

QUARTER-FINALS
Zurich, Thursday, 17 July 2025
Sweden (2) 2 *(Asllani 2, Blackstenius 25)*
England (0) 2 *(Bronze 79, Agyemang 81)*   22,397
England: (433) Hampton; Bronze, Williamson (Charles
105), Carter (Morgan 70), Greenwood; Toone (Mead 70),
Walsh (Clinton 104), Stanway (Agyemang 70); James,
Hemp (Kelly 78), Russo.
aet; England won 3-2 on penalties.

ENGLAND WOMEN'S INTERNATIONAL MATCHES 1972–2025

Note: In the results that follow, WC = World Cup; EC = European (UEFA) Championships; NL = Nations League; M = Mundialito; CC = Cyprus Cup; AC = Algarve Cup. * = After extra time. Games were organised by the Women's Football Association from 1971 to 1992 and the Football Association from 1993 to date. **Bold type** indicates matches played in season 2024–25.

v ARGENTINA
wc2007	17 Sept	Chengdu	6-1
wc2019	14 June	Le Havre	1-0

v AUSTRALIA
2003	3 Sept	Burnley	1-0
cc2015	6 Mar	Nicosia	3-0
2015	27 Oct	Yongchuan	1-0
2018	9 Oct	Fulham	1-1
2023	11 Apr	Brentford	0-2
wc2023	16 Aug	Sydney	3-1

v AUSTRIA
wc2005	1 Sept	Amstetten	4-1
wc2006	20 Apr	Gillingham	4-0
wc2010	25 Mar	Queens Park Rangers	3-0
wc2010	21 Aug	Krems	4-0
2017	10 Apr	Milton Keynes	3-0
2018	8 Nov	Vienna	3-0
wc2021	27 Nov	Sunderland	1-0
EC2022	6 July	Manchester United	1-0
wc2022	3 Sept	Wiener Neustadt	2-0
2024	23 Feb	Algeciras	7-2

v BELARUS
EC2007	27 Oct	Walsall	4-0
EC2008	8 May	Minsk	6-1
wc2013	21 Sept	Bournemouth	6-0
wc2014	14 June	Minsk	3-0

v BELGIUM
1978	31 Oct	Southampton	3-0
1980	1 May	Ostend	1-2
M1984	20 Aug	Jesolo	1-1
M1984	25 Aug	Caorle	2-1
1989	14 May	Epinal	2-0
EC1990	17 Mar	Ypres	3-0
EC1990	7 Apr	Sheffield United	1-0
EC1993	6 Nov	Koksijde	3-0
EC1994	13 Mar	Nottingham Forest	6-0
EC2016	8 Apr	Rotherham	1-1
EC2016	20 Sept	Leuven	2-0
2019	29 Aug	Leuven	3-3
2022	16 June	Wolverhampton	3-0
2023	22 Feb	Bristol City	6-1
NL2023	27 Oct	Leicester	1-0
NL2023	31 Oct	Leuven	2-3
NL2025	**4 Apr**	**Bristol City**	**5-0**
NL2025	**8 Apr**	**Leuven**	**2-3**

v BOSNIA & HERZEGOVINA
EC2015	29 Nov	Bristol City	1-0
EC2016	12 Apr	Zenica	1-0
wc2017	24 Nov	Walsall	4-0
wc2018	10 Apr	Zenica	2-0

v BRAZIL
2018	6 Oct	Notts County	1-0
2019	27 Feb	Philadelphia	2-1
2019	5 Oct	Middlesbrough	1-2
2023	6 Apr	Wembley	1-1

v CAMEROON
wc2019	23 June	Valenciennes	3-0

v CANADA
wc1995	6 June	Helsingborg	3-2
2003	19 May	Montreal	0-4

2003	22 May	Ottawa	0-4
cc2009	12 Mar	Nicosia	3-1
cc2010	27 Feb	Nicosia	0-1
cc2011	7 Mar	Nicosia	0-2
cc2013	13 Mar	Nicosia	1-0
2013	7 Apr	Rotherham	1-0
cc2014	10 Mar	Nicosia	2-0
cc2015	11 Mar	Larnaca	1-0
2015	29 May	Hamilton	0-1
wc2015	27 June	Vancouver	2-1
2019	5 Apr	Manchester	0-1
2021	13 Apr	Stoke	0-2
2022	17 Feb	Middlesbrough	1-1

v CHINA PR
AC2005	15 Mar	Guia	0-0*
2007	26 Jan	Guangzhou	0-2
2015	9 Apr	Manchester	2-1
2015	23 Oct	Yongchuan	1-2
wc2023	1 Aug	Adelaide	6-1

v COLOMBIA
wc2015	17 June	Montreal	2-1
wc2023	12 Aug	Sydney	2-1

v CROATIA
EC1995	19 Nov	Charlton	5-0
EC1996	18 Apr	Osijek	2-0
EC2012	31 Mar	Vrbovec	6-0
EC2012	19 Sept	Walsall	3-0

v CZECH REPUBLIC
2005	26 May	Walsall	4-1
EC2008	20 Mar	Doncaster	0-0
EC2008	28 Sept	Prague	5-1
2019	12 Nov	Ceske Budejovice	3-2
2022	11 Oct	Brighton	2-1

v DENMARK
1979	19 May	Hvidovre	1-3
1979	13 Sept	Hull	2-2
1981	9 Sept	Tokyo	0-1
EC1984	8 Apr	Crewe	2-1
EC1984	28 Apr	Hjorring	1-0
M1985	19 Aug	Caorle	0-1
EC1987	8 Nov	Blackburn	2-1
EC1988	8 May	Herning	0-2
1991	28 June	Nordby	0-0
1991	30 June	Nordby	3-3
1999	22 Aug	Odense	1-0
2001	23 Aug	Northampton	0-3
2004	19 Feb	Portsmouth	2-0
EC2005	8 June	Blackburn	1-2
2009	22 July	Swindon	1-0
2017	1 July	Copenhagen	2-1
2019	25 May	Walsall	2-0
wc2023	28 July	Sydney	1-0

v ESTONIA
2015	21 Sept	Tallinn	8-0
EC2016	15 Sept	Notts County	5-0

v FINLAND
· 1979	19 July	Sorrento	3-1
EC1987	25 Oct	Kirkkonummi	2-1
EC1988	4 Sept	Millwall	1-1
EC1989	1 Oct	Brentford	0-0
EC1990	29 Sept	Tampere	0-0

2000	28 Sept	Leyton	2-1
EC2005	5 June	Manchester City	3-2
2009	9 Feb	Larnaca	2-2
2009	11 Feb	Larnaca	4-1
EC2009	3 Sept	Turku	3-2
cc2012	28 Feb	Nicosia	3-1
cc2014	7 Mar	Larnaca	3-0
cc2015	4 Mar	Larnaca	3-1

v FRANCE

1973	22 Apr	Brion	3-0
1974	7 Nov	Wimbledon	2-0
1977	26 Feb	Longjumeau	0-0
M1988	22 July	Riva del Garda	1-1
1998	15 Feb	Alencon	2-3
1999	15 Sept	Yeovil	0-1
2000	16 Aug	Marseilles	0-1
wc2002	17 Oct	Crystal Palace	0-1
wc2002	16 Nov	Saint-Etienne	0-1
wc2006	26 Mar	Blackburn	0-0
wc2006	30 Sept	Rennes	1-1
cc2009	7 Mar	Paralimni	2-2
wc2011	9 July	Leverkusen	1-1*
cc2012	4 Mar	Paralimni	0-3
2012	20 Oct	Paris	2-2
EC2013	18 July	Linkoping	0-3
cc2014	12 Mar	Nicosia	0-2
wc2015	9 June	Moncton	0-1
2016	9 Mar	Boca Raton	0-0
2016	21 Oct	Doncaster	0-0
2017	1 Mar	Chester (Pennsylvania)	1-2
2017	30 July	Deventer	1-0
2017	20 Oct	Valenciennes	0-1
2018	1 Mar	Columbus	4-1
2021	9 Apr	Caen	1-3
EC2024	31 May	Newcastle	1-2
EC2024	4 June	Saint-Etienne	2-1
EC2025	**5 July**	**Zurich**	**1-2**

v GERMANY

EC1990	25 Nov	High Wycombe	1-4
EC1990	16 Dec	Bochum	0-2
EC1994	11 Dec	Watford	1-4
EC1995	23 Feb	Bochum	1-2
wc1995	13 June	Vasteras	0-3
1997	27 Feb	Preston	4-6
wc1997	25 Sept	Dessau	0-3
wc1998	8 Mar	Millwall	0-1
EC2001	30 June	Jena	0-3
wc2001	27 Sept	Kassel	1-3
wc2002	19 May	Crystal Palace	0-1
2003	11 Sept	Darmstadt	0-4
2006	25 Oct	Aalen	1-5
2007	30 Jan	Guangzhou	0-0
wc2007	14 Sept	Shanghai	0-0
2008	17 July	Unterhaching	0-3
EC2009	10 Sept	Helsinki	2-6
2014	23 Nov	Wembley	0-3
wc2015	4 July	Vancouver	1-0*
2015	26 Nov	Duisburg	0-0
2016	6 Mar	Nashville	1-2
2017	7 Mar	Washington	0-1
2018	4 Mar	New Jersey	2-2
2019	9 Nov	Wembley	1-2
2022	23 Feb	Wolverhampton	3-1
EC2022	31 July	Wembley	2-1*
2024	**25 Oct**	**Wembley**	**3-4**

v HAITI

wc2023	22 July	Brisbane	1-0

v HUNGARY

wc2005	27 Oct	Tapolca	13-0
wc2006	11 May	Southampton	2-0

v ICELAND

EC1992	17 May	Yeovil	4-0
EC1992	19 July	Kopavogur	2-1
EC1994	8 Oct	Reykjavik	2-1

EC1994	30 Oct	Brighton	2-1
wc2002	16 Sept	Reykjavik	2-2
wc2002	22 Sept	Birmingham	1-0
2004	14 May	Peterborough	1-0
2006	9 Mar	Norwich	1-0
2007	17 May	Southend	4-0
2009	16 July	Colchester	0-2

v ITALY

1976	2 June	Rome	0-2
1976	4 June	Cesena	1-2
1977	15 Nov	Wimbledon	1-0
1979	25 July	Naples	1-3
1982	11 June	Pescara	0-2
M1984	24 Aug	Jesolo	1-1
M1985	20 Aug	Caorle	1-1
M1985	25 Aug	Caorle	3-2
EC1987	13 June	Drammen	1-2
M1988	30 July	Arco di Trento	2-1
1989	1 Nov	High Wycombe	1-1
1990	18 Aug	Wembley	1-4
EC1992	17 Oct	Solofra	2-3
EC1992	7 Nov	Rotherham	0-3
1995	25 Jan	Florence	1-1
EC1995	1 Nov	Sunderland	1-1
EC1996	16 Mar	Cosenza	1-2
1997	23 Apr	Turin	0-2
1998	21 Apr	West Bromwich	1-2
1999	26 May	Bologna	1-4
2003	25 Feb	Viareggio	0-1
2005	17 Feb	Milton Keynes	4-1
EC2009	25 Aug	Lahti	1-2
cc2010	3 Mar	Nicosia	3-2
cc2011	2 Mar	Larnaca	2-0
cc2012	6 Mar	Paralimni	1-3
cc2013	6 Mar	Nicosia	4-2
EC2014	5 Mar	Larnaca	2-0
2017	7 Apr	Port Vale	1-1
2023	19 Feb	Coventry	2-1
2024	27 Feb	Algeciras	5-1

v JAMAICA

2025	**29 June**	**Leicester**	**7-0**

v JAPAN

1981	6 Sept	Kobe	4-0
wc2007	11 Sept	Shanghai	2-2
wc2011	5 July	Augsburg	2-0
2013	26 June	Burton	1-1
wc2015	1 July	Edmonton	1-2
2019	5 Mar	Tampa	3-0
wc2019	19 June	Nice	2-0
2020	8 Mar	New Jersey	1-0
2022	11 Nov	San Pedro del Pinatar	4-0

v KAZAKHSTAN

wc2017	28 Nov	Colchester	5-0
wc2018	4 Sept	Pavlodar	6-0

v KOREA REPUBLIC

2010	19 Oct	Suwon	0-0
cc2011	9 Mar	Larnaca	2-0
2023	16 Feb	Milton Keynes	4-0

v LATVIA

wc2021	26 Oct	Liepaja	10-0
wc2021	30 Nov	Doncaster	20-0

v LUXEMBOURG

wc2021	21 Sept	Luxembourg	10-0
wc2022	6 Sept	Stoke	10-0

v MALTA

wc2009	25 Oct	Blackpool	8-0
wc2010	20 May	Ta'Qali	6-0

v MEXICO

AC2005	13 Mar	Lagos	5-0
wc2011	27 June	Wolfsburg	1-1
wc2015	13 June	Moncton	2-1

v MONTENEGRO

wc2014	5 Apr	Brighton	9-0
wc2014	17 Sept	Petrovac	10-0

v NETHERLANDS

1973	9 Nov	Reading	1-0
1974	31 May	Groningen	0-3
1976	2 May	Blackpool	2-0
1978	30 Sept	Vlissingen	1-3
1989	13 May	Epinal	0-0
wc1997	30 Oct	West Ham	1-0
wc1998	23 May	Waalwijk	1-2
wc2001	4 Nov	Grimsby	0-0
wc2002	23 Mar	Den Haag	4-1
2004	18 Sept	Heerhugowaard	2-1
2004	22 Sept	Tuitjenhoorn	1-0
wc2005	17 Nov	Zwolle	1-0
wc2006	31 Aug	Charlton	4-0
2007	14 Mar	Swindon	0-1
EC2009	6 Sept	Tampere	2-1*
EC2011	27 Oct	Zwolle	0-0
EC2012	17 June	Salford	1-0
CC2015	9 Mar	Nicosia	1-1
2016	29 Nov	Tilburg	1-0
2017	3 Aug	Enschede	0-3
2022	24 June	Leeds	5-1
NL2023	26 Sept	Utrecht	1-2
NL2023	1 Dec	Wembley	3-2
EC2025	**9 July**	**Zurich**	**4-0**

v NEW ZEALAND

2010	21 Oct	Suwon	0-0
wc2011	1 July	Dresden	2-1
CC2013	11 Mar	Larnaca	3-1
2019	1 June	Brighton	0-1

v NIGERIA

wc1995	10 June	Karlstad	3-2
2002	23 July	Norwich	0-1
2004	22 Apr	Reading	0-3
wc2023	7 Aug	Brisbane	0-0*

v NORTHERN IRELAND

1973	7 Sept	Bath	5-1
EC1982	19 Sept	Crewe	7-1
EC1983	14 May	Belfast	4-0
EC1985	25 May	Antrim	8-1
EC1986	16 Mar	Blackburn	10-0
1987	11 Apr	Leeds	6-0
AC2005	9 Mar	Paderne	4-0
EC2007	13 May	Gillingham	4-0
EC2008	6 Mar	Lurgan	2-0
2021	23 Feb	Burton	6-0
wc2021	23 Oct	Wembley	4-0
wc2022	12 Apr	Belfast	5-0
EC2022	15 July	Southampton	5-0

v NORTH MACEDONIA

wc2021	17 Sept	Southampton	8-0
wc2022	8 Apr	Skopje	10-0

v NORWAY

1981	25 Oct	Cambridge	0-3
EC1988	21 Aug	Kleppe	0-2
EC1988	18 Sept	Blackburn	1-3
EC1990	27 May	Kleppe	0-2
EC1990	2 Sept	Manchester United	0-0
wc1995	8 June	Karlstad	3-2
1997	8 June	Lillestrom	0-4
wc1998	14 May	Oldham	1-2
wc1998	15 Aug	Lillestrom	0-2
EC2000	7 Mar	Norwich	0-3
EC2000	4 June	Moss	0-8
AC2002	1 Mar	Albufeira	1-3

2005	6 May	Barnsley	1-0
2008	14 Feb	Larnaca	2-1
2009	23 Apr	Shrewsbury	3-0
2014	17 Jan	La Manga	1-1
wc2015	22 June	Ottawa	2-1
2017	22 Jan	La Manga	0-1
wc2019	27 June	Le Havre	3-0
2019	3 Sept	Bergen	1-2
EC2022	11 July	Brighton	8-0
2022	15 Nov	San Pedro del Pinatar	1-1

v PORTUGAL

EC1996	11 Feb	Benavente	5-0
EC1996	19 May	Brentford	3-0
EC2000	20 Feb	Barnsley	2-0
EC2000	22 Apr	Sacavem	2-2
wc2001	24 Nov	Gafanha da Nazare	1-1
wc2002	24 Feb	Portsmouth	3-0
AC2005	11 Mar	Faro	4-0
2017	27 July	Tilburg	2-1
2019	8 Oct	Setubal	1-0
2023	1 July	Milton Keynes	0-0
NL2025	21 Feb	**Portimao**	**1-1**
NL2025	30 May	**Wembley**	**6-0**

v REPUBLIC OF IRELAND

1978	2 May	Exeter	6-1
1981	2 May	Dublin	5-0
EC1982	7 Nov	Dublin	1-0
EC1983	11 Sept	Reading	6-0
EC1985	22 Sept	Cork	6-0
EC1986	27 Apr	Reading	4-0
1987	29 Mar	Dublin	1-0
EC2024	9 Apr	Dublin	2-0
EC2024	12 July	Norwich	2-1

v ROMANIA

EC1998	12 Sept	Campina	4-1
EC1998	11 Oct	High Wycombe	2-1

v RUSSIA

EC2001	24 June	Jena	1-1
2003	21 Oct	Moscow	2-2
2004	19 Aug	Bristol Rovers	1-2
2007	8 Mar	Milton Keynes	6-0
EC2009	28 Aug	Helsinki	3-2
EC2013	15 July	Linkoping	1-1
wc2017	19 Sept	Tranmere	6-0
wc2018	8 June	Moscow	3-1

v SCOTLAND

1972	18 Nov	Greenock	3-2
1973	23 June	Nuneaton	8-0
1976	23 May	Enfield	5-1
1977	29 May	Dundee	1-2
EC1982	3 Oct	Dumbarton	4-0
EC1983	22 May	Leeds	2-0
EC1985	17 Mar	Preston	4-0
EC1986	12 Oct	Kirkcaldy	3-1
1989	30 Apr	Kirkcaldy	3-0
1990	6 May	Paisley	4-0
1990	12 May	Wembley	4-0
1991	20 Apr	High Wycombe	5-0
EC1992	17 Apr	Walsall	1-0
EC1992	23 Aug	Perth	2-0
1997	9 Mar	Sheffield United	6-0
1997	23 Aug	Livingston	4-0
2001	27 May	Bolton	1-0
AC2002	7 Mar	Quarteira	4-1
2003	13 Nov	Preston	5-0
2005	21 Apr	Tranmere	2-1
2007	11 Mar	High Wycombe	1-0
CC2009	10 Mar	Larnaca	3-0
CC2011	4 Mar	Nicosia	0-2
CC2013	8 Mar	Larnaca	4-4
EC2017	19 July	Utrecht	6-0
wc2019	9 June	Nice	2-1
NL2023	22 Sept	Sunderland	2-1
NL2023	5 Dec	Glasgow	6-0

v SERBIA

EC2011	17 Sept	Belgrade	2-2
EC2011	23 Nov	Doncaster	2-0
EC2016	4 June	High Wycombe	7-0
EC2016	7 June	Stara Pazova	7-0

v SLOVENIA

EC1993	25 Sept	Ljubljana	10-0
EC1994	17 Apr	Brentford	10-0
EC2011	22 Sept	Swindon	4-0
EC2012	21 June	Velenje	4-0

v SOUTH AFRICA

cc2009	5 Mar	Larnaca	6-0
cc2010	24 Feb	Larnaca	1-0
2024	**29 Oct**	**Coventry**	**2-1**

v SPAIN

EC1993	19 Dec	Osuna	0-0
EC1994	20 Feb	Bradford	0-0
EC1996	8 Sept	Montilla	1-2
EC1996	29 Sept	Tranmere	1-1
2001	22 Mar	Luton	4-2
EC2007	25 Nov	Shrewsbury	1-0
EC2008	2 Oct	Zamora	2-2
wc2010	1 Apr	Millwall	1-0
wc2010	19 June	Aranda de Duero	2-2
EC2013	12 July	Linkoping	2-3
2016	25 Oct	Guadalajara	2-1
EC2017	23 July	Breda	2-0
2019	9 Apr	Swindon	2-1
2020	11 Mar	Frisco (Texas)	0-1
2022	20 Feb	Norwich	0-0
EC2022	20 July	Brighton	2-1*
wc2023	20 Aug	Sydney	0-1
NL2025	26 Feb	**Wembley**	**1-0**
NL2025	3 June	**Barcelona**	**1-2**

v SWEDEN

1975	15 June	Gothenburg	0-2
1975	7 Sept	Wimbledon	1-3
1979	27 July	Scafati	0-0*
1980	17 Sept	Leicester	1-1
1982	26 May	Kinna	1-1
1983	30 Oct	Charlton	2-2
EC1984	12 May	Gothenburg	0-1
EC1984	27 May	Luton	1-0
EC1987	11 June	Moss	2-3*
1989	23 May	Wembley	0-2
1995	13 May	Halmstad	0-4
1998	26 July	Dagenham	0-1
EC2001	27 June	Jena	0-4
2002	25 Jan	La Manga	0-5
AC2002	5 Mar	Lagos	3-6
EC2005	11 June	Blackburn	0-1
2006	7 Feb	Larnaca	0-0
2006	9 Feb	Achna	1-1
2008	12 Feb	Larnaca	0-2
EC2009	31 Aug	Turku	1-1
2011	17 May	Oxford	2-0
2013	4 July	Ljungskile	1-4
2014	3 Aug	Hartlepool	4-0
2017	24 Jan	La Manga	0-0
2018	11 Nov	Rotherham	0-2
wc2019	6 July	Nice	1-2
EC2022	26 July	Sheffield United	4-0
EC2024	5 Apr	Wembley	1-1
EC2024	16 July	Gothenburg	0-0
EC2025	**17 July**	**Zurich**	**2-2**

v SWITZERLAND

1975	19 Apr	Basel	3-1
1977	28 Apr	Hull	9-1
1979	23 July	Sorrento	2-0
EC1999	16 Oct	Zofingen	3-0

EC2000	13 May	Bristol Rovers	1-0
cc2010	1 Mar	Nicosia	2-2
wc2010	12 Sept	Shrewsbury	2-0
wc2010	16 Sept	Wohlen	3-2
cc2012	1 Mar	Larnaca	1-0
2017	10 June	Biel	4-0
2022	30 June	Zurich	4-0
2024	**3 Dec**	**Sheffield United**	**1-0**

v TURKEY

wc2009	26 Nov	Izmir	3-0
wc2010	29 July	Walsall	3-0
wc2013	26 Sept	Portsmouth	8-0
wc2013	31 Oct	Adana	4-0

v UKRAINE

EC2000	30 Oct	Kyiv	2-1
EC2000	28 Nov	Leyton	2-0
wc2014	8 May	Shrewsbury	4-0
wc2014	19 June	Lviv	2-1

v USA

M1985	23 Aug	Caorle	3-1
M1988	27 July	Riva del Garda	2-0
1990	9 Aug	Blaine	0-3
1991	25 May	Hirson	1-3
1997	9 May	San Jose	0-5
1997	11 May	Portland	0-6
AC2002	3 Mar	Ferreiras	0-2
2003	17 May	Birmingham (Alabama)	0-6
2007	28 Jan	Guangzhou	1-1
wc2007	22 Sept	Tianjin	0-3
2011	2 Apr	Leyton	2-1
2015	13 Feb	Milton Keynes	0-1
2016	4 Mar	Tampa	0-1
2017	4 Mar	New Jersey	1-0
2018	8 Mar	Orlando	0-1
2019	2 Mar	Nashville	2-2
wc2019	2 July	Lyon	1-2
2020	5 Mar	Orlando	0-2
2022	7 Oct	Wembley	2-1
2024	**30 Nov**	**Wembley**	**0-0**

v USSR

1990	11 Aug	Blaine	1-1
1991	20 July	Dmitrov	2-1
1991	21 July	Kashira	2-0
1991	7 Sept	Southampton	2-0
1991	8 Sept	Brighton	1-3

v WALES

1974	17 Mar	Slough	5-0
1976	22 May	Bedford	4-0
1976	17 Oct	Ebbw Vale	2-1
1977	18 Sept	Warminster	5-0
1980	1 June	Warminster	6-1
1985	17 Aug	Ramsey (Isle of Man)	6-0
wc2013	26 Oct	Millwall	2-0
wc2014	21 Aug	Cardiff	4-0
wc2018	6 Apr	Southampton	0-0
wc2018	31 Aug	Newport	3-0
EC2025	**13 July**	**St Gallen**	**6-1**

v WEST GERMANY

M1984	22 Aug	Jesolo	0-2
1990	5 Aug	Blaine	1-3

OTHER MATCHES

v ITALY B

1984	27 Aug	Monfalcone	3-1
M1988	20 July	Riva del Garda	3-0

v USA B

1990	7 Aug	Blaine	1-0

WELSH FOOTBALL 2024–25

JD CYMRU PREMIER TABLE 2024–25

	P	Home					Away					Total					GD	Pts
		W	D	L	F	A	W	D	L	F	A	W	D	L	F	A		
1 The New Saints[1]	32	14	0	2	47	15	12	0	4	42	16	26	0	6	89	31	58	78
2 Penybont[2]	32	10	5	1	28	11	9	2	5	28	21	19	7	6	56	32	24	64
3 Haverfordwest Co[3,5]	32	7	6	3	22	12	6	6	4	17	14	13	12	7	39	26	13	51
4 Caernarfon T[4]	32	7	2	7	30	30	7	4	5	23	21	14	6	12	53	51	2	48
5 Cardiff Met University[4]	32	7	5	4	25	25	5	3	8	18	21	12	8	12	43	46	-3	44
6 Bala T[4]	32	6	4	6	18	17	2	9	5	20	26	8	13	11	38	43	-5	37
7 Barry Town U[4]	32	9	3	4	30	22	6	4	6	25	29	15	7	10	55	51	4	52
8 Connah's Quay Nomads	32	7	2	7	25	16	5	4	7	22	19	12	6	14	47	35	12	42
9 Flint Town U (P)	32	9	1	6	28	19	4	2	10	20	43	13	3	16	48	62	-14	42
10 Briton Ferry Llansawel (P)	32	4	4	8	23	30	5	1	10	23	35	9	5	18	46	65	-19	32
11 Newtown	32	3	4	9	22	38	3	4	9	14	27	6	8	18	36	65	-29	26
12 Aberystwyth T	32	3	3	10	15	30	3	0	13	13	41	6	3	23	28	71	-43	21

Top 6 teams split after 22 games. [1]*The New Saints qualify for UEFA Champions League first qualifying round.* [2]*Penybont qualify for UEFA Conference League first qualifying round as runners-up after The New Saints won the Welsh FA Cup.* [3]*Haverfordwest Co qualify for Cymru Premier Conference League round play-off final.* [4]*Caernarfon T, Cardiff Met University, Bala T and Barry Town U qualify for Cymru Premier Conference League play-offs.* [5]*Haverfordwest Co qualify for UEFA Conference League first qualifying round after Cymru Premier Conference play-offs.*

PREVIOUS WELSH LEAGUE WINNERS

1993 Cwmbran Town	2002 Barry Town	2011 Bangor C	2020 Connah's Quay Nomads
1994 Bangor City	2003 Barry Town	2012 The New Saints	2021 Connah's Quay Nomads
1995 Bangor City	2004 Rhyl	2013 The New Saints	2022 The New Saints
1996 Barry Town	2005 TNS	2014 The New Saints	2023 The New Saints
1997 Barry Town	2006 TNS	2015 The New Saints	2024 The New Saints
1998 Barry Town	2007 TNS	2016 The New Saints	2025 The New Saints
1999 Barry Town	2008 Llanelli	2017 The New Saints	
2000 TNS	2009 Rhyl	2018 The New Saints	
2001 Barry Town	2010 The New Saints	2019 The New Saints	

JD CYMRU NORTH TABLE 2024–25

	P	Home					Away					Total					GD	Pts
		W	D	L	F	A	W	D	L	F	A	W	D	L	F	A		
1 Colwyn Bay (R)	30	13	1	1	49	13	13	2	0	39	9	26	3	1	88	22	66	81
2 Airbus UK Broughton	30	12	3	0	58	13	13	0	2	44	17	25	3	2	102	30	72	78
3 Holywell T	30	11	1	3	31	13	7	2	6	25	28	18	3	9	56	41	15	57
4 Llandudno	30	9	2	4	35	21	6	2	7	30	39	15	4	11	65	60	5	49
5 Buckley T	30	6	4	5	25	24	8	1	6	23	23	14	5	11	48	47	1	47
6 Guilsfield	30	8	3	4	33	25	5	3	7	26	27	13	6	11	59	52	7	45
7 Flint Mountain (P)	30	8	2	5	42	30	5	3	7	26	26	13	5	12	68	56	12	44
8 Mold Alexandra	30	8	1	6	35	21	5	4	6	17	27	13	5	12	52	48	4	44
9 Denbigh T	30	8	2	5	36	26	4	5	6	32	36	12	7	11	68	62	6	43
10 Penrhyncoch (P)	30	7	3	5	32	21	4	4	7	16	31	11	7	12	48	52	-4	40
11 Gresford Ath	30	6	4	5	27	32	5	1	9	17	35	11	5	14	44	67	-23	38
12 Caersws	30	6	2	7	29	22	4	2	9	18	33	10	4	16	47	55	-8	34
13 Ruthin T	30	6	3	6	25	14	2	2	11	15	45	8	5	17	40	59	-19	29
14 Bangor 1876	30	6	2	7	30	31	2	2	11	16	33	8	4	18	46	64	-18	28
15 Prestatyn T	30	4	0	11	18	33	0	1	14	20	72	4	1	25	38	105	-67	13
16 Llay Welfare* (P)	30	3	3	9	22	38	0	2	13	14	36	3	5	22	35	84	-49	11

Llay Welfare deducted 3 points for fielding an ineligible player.

JD CYMRU SOUTH TABLE 2024–25

	P	Home					Away					Total					GD	Pts
		W	D	L	F	A	W	D	L	F	A	W	D	L	F	A		
1 Llanelli T	30	9	4	2	37	11	9	6	0	27	14	18	10	2	64	25	39	64
2 Trethomas Bluebirds (P)	30	9	4	2	28	13	8	4	3	25	20	17	8	5	53	33	20	59
3 Newport C (P)	30	8	2	5	25	15	8	4	3	25	17	16	6	8	50	32	18	54
4 Trefelin BGC	30	9	3	3	30	19	6	5	4	24	22	15	8	7	54	41	13	53
5 Pontypridd U (R)	30	9	1	5	30	19	7	4	4	24	25	16	5	9	54	44	10	53
6 Cambrian U*	30	7	6	2	25	14	6	5	4	25	24	13	11	6	50	38	12	47
7 Carmarthen T	30	8	4	3	30	17	4	5	6	25	27	12	9	9	55	44	11	45
8 Baglan Dragons	30	5	5	3	29	21	6	5	4	15	13	11	10	9	44	34	10	43
9 Llantwit Major	30	6	6	3	21	15	5	4	6	16	19	11	10	9	37	34	3	43
10 Ammanford	30	6	1	8	32	25	5	2	8	15	25	11	3	16	47	50	-3	36
11 Afan Lido	30	6	4	5	24	20	2	6	7	20	31	8	10	12	44	51	-7	34
12 Caerau (Ely)	30	5	3	7	22	22	4	2	9	20	21	9	5	16	42	43	-1	32
13 Cwmbran Celtic	30	6	3	6	23	24	3	0	12	16	38	9	3	18	39	62	-23	30
14 Penrhiwceiber Rangers (P)	30	2	5	8	9	24	5	2	8	21	33	7	7	16	30	57	-27	28
15 Goytre U	30	3	2	10	19	31	3	3	9	22	41	6	5	19	41	72	-31	23
16 Taff's Well	30	2	3	10	23	39	1	3	11	9	37	3	6	21	32	76	-44	15

Cambrian U deducted 3 points for fielding an ineligible player.

JD WELSH FA CUP 2024–25

SECOND QUALIFYING ROUND NORTH

Rhostyllen v St Asaph C	2-3
NFA v Henllan	3-1
Rhyl 1879 v Glan Conwy	6-0
FC Queens Park v Blaenau Ffestiniog Amateur	3-1
Llansannan v Conwy Bor	2-2
Llansannan won 5-4 on penalties.	
Llannefydd v Penyffordd Lions	4-2
Llanrhaeadr v Llanystumdwy	3-1
Llanuwchllyn v Berriew	10-0
Montgomery T v Corwen	1-4
Connah's Quay T v Brickfield Rangers	2-4
Cerrigydrudion v Llansantffraid Village	3-1
Holyhead H v Bethesda Ath	4-2
Nefyn U v Menai Bridge Tigers	3-3
Menai Bridge Tigers won 4-2 on penalties.	
Talysarn Celts v Llandrindod Wells	1-0
Bro Cernyw v Llandudno Amateurs	0-3
Amlwch T v Porthmadog	0-5
Kinmel Bay v Bow	3-2
Llangollen T v Y Felinheli	2-0
Trearddur Bay v Llanfairfechan T	7-0
Carno v Penycae	2-1
Penmaenmawr Phoenix v Pwllheli	5-2
Cefn Alb v Penrhyndeudraeth	6-3
Llanberis v Bontnewydd	4-1
Rhos Aelwyd v Gaerwen	0-2
Cemaes Bay v Llanrwst U	0-3
Llangefni T v Chirk AAA	7-3
Rhydymwyn v Boded	3-1

SECOND QUALIFYING ROUND SOUTH

Blaenavon Blues v Cardiff Corinthians	1-4
Builth Wells v Cefn Cribwr	3-0
Goytre v Pontyclun	1-1
Goytre won 4-2 on penalties.	
Cardiff Draconians v Bettws	4-0
Aberdare T v Newport Corinthians	0-1
Rogerstone v Dafen Welfare	5-1
Clwb Cymric v Cwm W	2-1
Monmouth T v Seven Sisters Onllwyn	1-1
Monmouth T won 5-4 on penalties.	
Ffostrasol W v Pencoed Ath	1-2
Treherbert v Pantyscallog Village	3-2
Morriston T v Port Talbot T	1-0
Holton Road v Pill	3-6
Ely Rangers v Treforest	5-2
St Josephs v AFC Bargoed	13-0
FC Cwmaman v Cwmamman U	1-2
Clydach v West End	2-2
West End won 3-1 on penalties.	
New Inn v Evans & Williams	3-2
Abertillery Bluebirds v Cascade YC	3-2
Cardiff Bay Warriors v Cwrt Rawlin	7-3
Cwmbran T v Llangeinor	3-0
Penlan v Caldicot T	2-2
Caldicot T won 6-5 on penalties.	
Porthcawl Town Ath v Newport Saints	4-1
Risca U v Seaside	3-0
Ynysygerwn v Cardiff Airport	4-3
AFC Llwydcoed v Croesyceiliog	4-2
Pontardawe T v Aber Valley	3-4
Penydarren BGC v Canton	5-0
Bryn R v Chepstow T	3-5
Swansea University v Caerphilly Ath	1-1
Swansea University won 6-5 on penalties.	

FIRST ROUND NORTH

Byes: Airbus UK Broughton, Bangor 1876, Colwyn Bay, Denbigh T, Guilsfield, Holywell T, Mold Alex, and Ruthin T (Cymru North); Afan Lido, Ammanford, Caerau (Ely), Cambrian U, Carmarthen T, Goytre U, Llanelli T, and Pontypridd U (Cymru South).

Corwen v Llay Welfare	0-1
Llandudno v Llanberis	4-0
Llannefydd v Rhydymwyn	1-0

Penrhyncoch v Talysarn Celts	2-1
Llandudno Amateurs v Holyhead H	0-4
Buckley T v Builth Wells	7-2
St Asaph C v Llangollen T	0-2
Caersws v Cefn Alb	5-0
Llansannan v Cerrigydrudion	0-2
Carno v Llanrhaeadr	0-4
Llanrwst U v Menai Bridge Tigers	5-1
Gresford Ath v Prestatyn T	9-0
Kinmel Bay v Brickfield Rangers	3-1
FC Queens Park v Porthmadog	1-6
Trearddur Bay v NFA	2-1
Llangefni T v Gaerwen	7-1
Penmaenmawr Phoenix v Llanuwchllyn	1-2
Rhyl 1879 v Flint Mountain	1-1
Rhyl 1879 won 4-1 on penalties.	

FIRST ROUND SOUTH

Cardiff Corinthians v Risca U	4-1
Chepstow T v Pill	0-1
St Josephs v Cardiff Draconians	0-3
Goytre v Pencoed Ath	3-1
Newport Corinthians v AFC Llwydcoed	1-0
Penrhiwceiber Rangers v Cwmbran T	3-1
Cardiff Bay Warriors v West End	2-0
Taff's Well v Trethomas Bluebirds	0-1
Treherbert v Clwb Cymric	1-1
Clwb Cymric won 5-3 on penalties.	
Caldicot T v Morriston T	1-2
New Inn v Abertillery Bluebirds	1-1
New Inn won 4-2 on penalties.	
Aber Valley v Cwmamman U	1-3
Ynysygerwn v Rogerstone	1-3
Penydarren BGC v Porthcawl Town Ath	3-3
Penydarren BGC won 4-1 on penalties.	
Monmouth T v Newport C	2-0
Llantwit Major v Ely Rangers	3-2
Cwmbran Celtic v Trefelin BGC	3-4
Swansea University v Baglan Dragons	5-1

SECOND ROUND NORTH

Bangor 1876 v Llay Welfare	2-1
Bala T v Llanrhaeadr	3-1
Llannefydd v Trearddur Bay	1-2
Llanrwst U v Cerrigydrudion	2-1
Connah's Quay Nomads v Guilsfield	5-0
Denbigh T v Llangefni T	4-2
The New Saints v Llangollen T	16-0
Porthmadog v Airbus UK Broughton	0-2
Holywell T v Ruthin T	1-1
Ruthin T won 5-4 on penalties.	
Llanuwchllyn v Newtown	0-0
Llanuwchllyn won 5-3 on penalties.	
Caersws v Rhyl 1879	7-4
Holyhead H v Caernarfon T	0-0
Holyhead H won 6-5 on penalties.	
Buckley T v Colwyn Bay	2-2
Colwyn Bay won 6-5 on penalties.	
Penrhyncoch v Mold Alexandra	1-3
Flint Town U v Gresford Ath	5-1
Llandudno v Kinmel Bay	4-3

SECOND ROUND SOUTH

Barry Town U v Caerau (Ely)	3-3
Caerau (Ely) won 4-2 on penalties.	
Cardiff Bay Warriors v Rogerstone	2-4
Cardiff Corinthians v Afan Lido	3-3
Afan Lido won 4-2 on penalties.	
Penybont v Cardiff Metropolitan University	0-1
Goytre v Cardiff Draconians	1-0
Cambrian U v Goytre U	0-0
Cambrian U won 5-4 on penalties.	
Haverfordwest Co v Trethomas Bluebirds	2-2
Haverfordwest Co won 5-3 on penalties.	
Clwb Cymric v Llanelli T	0-3
Aberystwyth T v Ammanford	0-1

Penrhiwceiber Rangers v Carmarthen T	3-4
Penydarren BGC v Pontypridd U	2-0
Monmouth T v Pill	2-3
New Inn v Briton Ferry Llansawel	0-3
Trefelin BGC v Newport Corinthians	5-0
Llantwit Major v Morriston T	1-1

Morriston T won 6-5 on penalties.

Aber Valley v Swansea University	0-2

THIRD ROUND

Cardiff Metropolitan University v The New Saints	1-3
Caerau (Ely) v Rogerstone	8-1
Trefelin BGC v Connah's Quay Nomads	1-2
Colwyn Bay v Ruthin T	2-1
Caersws v Bangor 1876	2-1
Llanrwst U v Denbigh T	0-3
Penydarren BGC v Carmarthen T	2-2

Carmarthen T won 4-3 on penalties.

Airbus UK Broughton v Goytre	7-1
Flint T U v Bala T	2-2

Bala T won 4-2 on penalties.

Ammanford v Haverfordwest Co	1-1

Haverfordwest Co won 10-9 on penalties.

Mold Alexandra v Briton Ferry Llansawel	2-1
Cambrian U v Llandudno	3-2
Holyhead H v Trearddur Bay	0-0

Holyhead H won 5-4 on penalties.

Llanuwchllyn v Swansea University	3-0
Llanelli T v Pill	4-0
Afan Lido v Morriston T	1-1

Afan Lido won 6-5 on penalties.

FOURTH ROUND

Afan Lido v Cambrian U	0-0

Cambrian U won 3-1 on penalties.

The New Saints v Colwyn Bay	4-1
Haverfordwest Co v Llanelli T	0-2
Carmarthen T v Holyhead H	0-0

Carmarthen T won 4-3 on penalties.

Denbigh T v Llanuwchllyn	7-1
Caerau (Ely) v Bala T	1-0
Airbus UK Broughton v Caersws	2-0
Connah's Quay Nomads v Mold Alexandra	1-0

QUARTER-FINALS

Denbigh T v Llanelli T	0-1
Caerau (Ely) v Connah's Quay Nomads	0-2
The New Saints v Airbus UK Broughton	5-0
Cambrian U v Carmarthen T	3-1

SEMI-FINALS

Cambrian U v The New Saints	0-5
Connah's Quay Nomads v Llanelli T	2-1

JD WELSH FA CUP FINAL 2024–25

Sunday, 4 May 2025

(at Rodney Parade, Newport, attendance 1313)

The New Saints (1) 2   Connah's Quay Nomads (1) 1

The New Saints: (433) Roberts; Pask, McGahey, Bodenham, Redmond (Astles 90); Smith, Williams D, Holden (Clark 76); Wilson, Brobbell, Williams J.
Scorers: Holden 17, Williams J 54.

Connah's Quay Nomads: (352) Ratcliffe; Disney, Rushton (Marriott 1), Nash; Poole, Edwards, Hughes, Bratley, Owens (Durrant 57); Woodcock (Mwande 57), Kenny.
Scorer: Poole 7.

Referee: Tom Owen.

PREVIOUS WELSH CUP WINNERS

1878	Wrexham	1905	Wrexham	1938	Shrewsbury T	1973	Cardiff C	2002	Barry T
1879	Newtown White Stars	1906	Wellington T	1939	South Liverpool	1974	Cardiff C	2003	Barry T
		1907	Oswestry U	1940	Wellington T	1975	Wrexham	2004	Rhyl
1880	Druids	1908	Chester	1947	Chester	1976	Cardiff C	2005	TNS
1881	Druids	1909	Wrexham	1948	Lovell's Ath	1977	Shrewsbury T	2006	Rhyl
1882	Druids	1910	Wrexham	1949	Merthyr Tydfil	1978	Wrexham	2007	Carmarthen T
1883	Wrexham	1911	Wrexham	1950	Swansea T	1979	Shrewsbury T	2008	Bangor C
1884	Oswestry White Stars	1912	Cardiff C	1951	Merthyr Tydfil	1980	Newport Co	2009	Bangor C
		1913	Swansea T	1952	Rhyl	1981	Swansea C	2010	Bangor C
1885	Druids	1914	Wrexham	1953	Rhyl	1982	Swansea C	2011	Llanelli
1886	Druids	1915	Wrexham	1954	Flint Town U	1983	Swansea C	2012	The New Saints
1887	Chirk	1920	Cardiff C	1955	Barry T	1984	Shrewsbury T	2013	Prestatyn T
1888	Chirk	1921	Wrexham	1956	Cardiff C	1985	Shrewsbury T	2014	The New Saints
1889	Bangor	1922	Cardiff C	1957	Wrexham	1986	Wrexham	2015	The New Saints
1890	Chirk	1923	Cardiff C	1958	Wrexham	1987	Merthyr Tydfil	2016	The New Saints
1891	Shrewsbury T	1924	Wrexham	1959	Cardiff C	1988	Cardiff C	2017	Bala T
1892	Chirk	1925	Wrexham	1960	Wrexham	1989	Swansea C	2018	Connah's Quay Nomads
1893	Wrexham	1926	Ebbw Vale	1961	Swansea T	1990	Hereford U		
1894	Chirk	1927	Cardiff C	1962	Bangor C	1991	Swansea C	2019	The New Saints
1895	Newtown	1928	Cardiff C	1963	Borough U	1992	Cardiff C	2020	Not completed
1896	Bangor	1929	Connah's Quay	1964	Cardiff C	1993	Cardiff C	2021	Not completed
1897	Wrexham	1930	Cardiff C	1965	Cardiff C	1994	Barry T	2022	The New Saints
1898	Druids	1931	Wrexham	1966	Swansea T	1995	Wrexham	2023	The New Saints
1899	Druids	1932	Swansea T	1967	Cardiff C	1996	TNS	2024	Connah's Quay Nomads
1900	Aberystwyth T	1933	Chester	1968	Cardiff C	1997	Barry T		
1901	Oswestry U	1934	Bristol C	1969	Cardiff C	1998	Bangor C	2025	The New Saints
1902	Wellington T	1935	Tranmere R	1970	Cardiff C	1999	Inter Cable-Tel		
1903	Wrexham	1936	Crewe Alex	1971	Cardiff C	2000	Bangor C		
1904	Druids	1937	Crewe Alex	1972	Wrexham	2001	Barry T		

NATHANIEL MG WELSH LEAGUE CUP 2024–25

■ *Denotes player sent off.*

FIRST ROUND – NORTH

Llay Welfare v Denbigh T	3-1
Flint Mountain v Gresford Ath	0-3
Ruthin T v Bangor 1876	2-1
Penrhyncoch v Guilsfield	0-3
Caersws v Holywell T	0-1
Buckley T v Prestatyn T	5-1
Llandudno v Newport Co	3-0
Airbus UK Broughton v Mold Alexandra	3-2

FIRST ROUND – SOUTH

Taff's Well v Merthyr T	1-3
Afan Lido v Cardiff C U21	1-3
Cwmbran Celtic v Trethomas Bluebirds	2-3
Caerau (Ely) v Trefelin	2-1
Penrhiwceiber Rangers v Goytre U	1-4
Carmarthen T v Cambrian U	2-1
Llantwit Major v Newport C	2-0
Baglan Dragons v Swansea C U21	1-1
Baglan Dragons won 5-3 on penalties.	

SECOND ROUND – NORTH

Buckley T v Connah's Quay Nomads	0-3
The New Saints v Flint Town U	5-1
Llandudno v Guilsfield	2-2
Llandudno won 4-2 on penalties.	
Gresford Ath v Airbus UK Broughton	1-4
Ruthin T v Bala T	0-1
Colwyn Bay v Aberystwyth T	0-2
Newtown v Caernarfon T	2-2
Caernarfon T won 3-1 on penalties.	
Holywell T v Llay Welfare	3-1

SECOND ROUND – SOUTH

Briton Ferry Llansawel v Penybont	0-3
Cardiff C U21 v Pontypridd U	3-1
Trethomas Bluebirds v Baglan Dragons	3-1
Carmarthen T v Haverfordwest Co	0-5
Merthyr T v Ammanford	2-0
Goytre U v Caerau (Ely)	3-2
Llantwit Major v Cardiff Metropolitan University	2-3
Barry Town U v Llanelli T	1-1
Barry Town U won 5-3 on penalties.	

THIRD ROUND – NORTH

Connah's Quay Nomads v Caernarfon T	3-2
Airbus UK Broughton v The New Saints	0-1
Bala T v Holywell T	2-0
Aberystwyth T v Llandudno	3-2

THIRD ROUND – SOUTH

Cardiff C U21 v Merthyr T	2-1
Cardiff Metropolitan University v Goytre U	9-1
Penybont v Haverfordwest Co	1-0
Trethomas Bluebirds v Barry Town U	1-4

QUARTER-FINALS – NORTH

Connah's Quay Nomads v Aberystwyth T	1-2
The New Saints v Bala T	3-1

QUARTER-FINALS – SOUTH

Cardiff C U21 v Cardiff Met University	3-2
Barry Town U v Penybont	3-2

SEMI-FINALS

Aberystwyth T v Cardiff C U21	1-1
Aberystwyth T won 4-1 on penalties.	
Barry Town U v The New Saints	1-2

NATHANIEL MG WELSH LEAGUE CUP FINAL 2024–25

Friday, 28 February 2025

(at Latham Park, Newtown, attendance 813)

Aberystwyth T (0) 0   The New Saints (0) 1

Aberystwyth T: (4231) Jones; Davies B■, Scotcher, Bradford, Walsh; Thorn (Huxley 87), Patterson; Flint, Evans■, Sharif (Lewis 72); Owen (Darlington 76).

The New Saints: (4231) Roberts; Davies, McGahey, Bodenham, Marshall; Redmond■, Williams D; Wilson (Bradley 77), Smith (Clark 74), Williams J; Oteh (Brobbel 67).
Scorer: Oteh 49.

Referee: Aaron Wyn Jones.

WELSH LEAGUE CUP FINALS 1992–93 to 2024–25

*After extra time.

1992–93	Afan Lido v Caersws		1-1
	Afan Lido won 4-3 on penalties.		
1993–94	Afan Lido v Bangor C		1-0
1994–95	Llansantffraid v Ton Pentre		2-1
1995–96	Connah's Quay Nomads v Ebbw Vale		1-0
1996–97	Barry T v Bangor C		2-2
	Barry T won 4-2 on penalties.		
1997–98	Barry T v Bangor C		1-1
	Barry T won 5-4 on penalties.		
1998–99	Barry T v Caernarfon T		3-0
1999–2000	Barry T v Bangor C		6-0
2000–01	Caersws v Barry T		2-0
2001–02	Caersws v Cwmbran T		2-1
2002–03	Rhyl v Bangor C		2-2
	Rhyl won 4-3 on penalties.		
2003–04	Rhyl v Carmarthen T		4-0
2004–05	Carmarthen T v Rhyl		2-0*
2005–06	Total Network Solutions v Port Talbot T		4-0
2006–07	Caersws v Rhyl		1-1
	Caersws won 3-1 on penalties.		
2007–08	Llanelli v Rhyl		2-0
2008–09	The New Saints v Bangor C		2-0
2009–10	The New Saints v Rhyl		3-1
2010–11	The New Saints v Llanelli		4-3*
2011–12	Afan Lido v Newtown		1-1
	Afan Lido won 3–2 on penalties.		
2012–13	Carmarthen T v The New Saints		3-3
	Carmarthen T won 3-1 on penalties.		
2013–14	Carmarthen T v Bala T		0-0
	Carmarthen T won 3-1 on penalties.		
2014–15	The New Saints v Bala T		3-0
2015–16	The New Saints v Denbigh T		2-0
2016–17	The New Saints v Barry Town U		4-0
2017–18	The New Saints v Cardiff Met University		1-0
2018–19	Cardiff Met University v Cambrian & Clydach Vale		2-0
2019–20	Connah's Quay Nomads v STM Sports		3-0
2020–21	*Cancelled due to COVID-19 pandemic.*		
2021–22	Cardiff Met University v Connah's Quay Nomads		0-0
	Connah's Quay Nomads won 10-9 on penalties.		
2022–23	Bala T v Connah's Quay Nomads		0-0
	Bala T won 4-3 on penalties		
2023–24	The New Saints v Swansea C U21		5-1
2024–25	The New Saints v Aberystwyth T		1-0

DRAGON SIGNS FAW AMATEUR TROPHY 2024–25

SECOND ROUND – NORTH WEST

Bethesda Ath v CPD Cefni	4-1
CPD Pwllheli v CPD Llanberis	4-0
Holyhead Hotspur v Llanrwst U	0-0
Llanrwst U won 6-5 on penalties.	
Mochdre Sports v Bow Street	2-3
Nantlle Vale v CPD Cerrigydrudion	5-0
Trearddur Bay v Penmaenmawr Phoenix	5-0
Tywyn Bryncrug v Llanuwchllyn	1-3

SECOND ROUND – NORTH EAST

Berriew v Brickfield Rangers	0-4
Connah's Quay T v Kinmel Bay	3-2
CPD Llannefydd v Cefn Alb	3-2
CPD y Rhyl 1879 v Lex XI	1-2
Llanidloes T v Bow	2-1
Mynydd Isa Spartans v Four Crosses	2-0
Plas Madoc v Llanrhaeadr ym Mochnant	1-3

SECOND ROUND – SOUTH CENTRAL

Canton v AFC Wattstown	4-1
Cardiff Corinthians v Treharris Western Ath	2-2
Cardiff Corinthians won 6-5 on penalties.	
Cardiff Draconians v AFC Llwydcoed	2-1
FC Cwmaman v Holton Road	6-1
Penydarren v AFC Penrhiweceiber	1-0
Tata Steel U v Ynyshir Albions	1-1
Ynyshir Albions won 4-2 on penalties.	
Treforest v Llangeinor	1-3

SECOND ROUND – SOUTH WEST

Pontardawe v Giants Grave	2-3
Pontarddulais T v Port Talbot T	0-5
Rockspur v Penlan	0-1
Ynystawe Ath v St Josephs (Swansea)	0-4
Ynysygerwn v West End	2-2
West End won 4-2 on penalties.	

SECOND ROUND – SOUTH EAST

Abertillery Bluebirds v Abercarn U	2-3
Bridgend Street v Clydach Wasps	2-1
Goytre (Gwent) v Abergavenny T	2-0
Risca U v Newport Corinthians	3-1
Treowen Stars v Newbridge T	10-0

THIRD ROUND

Bethesda Ath v CPD Pwllheli	4-2
Llanrwst U v Nantlle Vale	4-0
Cardiff Draconians v Brickfield Rangers	0-1
Giants Grave v Canton	1-2
St Josephs (Swansea) v Connah's Quay T	2-2
Connah's Quay T won 4-2 on penalties.	
Llangeinor v Port Talbot T	0-2
FC Cwmaman v Llanrhaeadr ym Mochnant	3-2
Treowen Stars v Cardiff Corinthians	5-0
Risca U v Goytre (Gwent)	3-3
Goytre (Gwent) won 5-3 on penalties.	
Penydarren v Abercarn U	2-1
Lex XI v Llanidloes T	1-1
Lex XI won 5-4 on penalties.	
CPD Llannefydd v Bow Street	3-4
Trearddur Bay v Ynyshir Albions	3-1
Penlan v Llanuwchllyn	1-2
Mynydd Isa Spartans v West End	1-4
Bridgend Street v Penygraig U	0-4

FOURTH ROUND

Bethesda Ath v Llanrwst U	1-2
Brickfield Rangers v Canton	0-0
Brickfield Rangers won 4-1 on penalties.	
Connah's Quay T v Port Talbot T	0-0
Port Talbot T won 4-2 on penalties.	
FC Cwmaman v Treowen Stars	3-2
Goytre (Gwent) v Penydarren	4-3
Lex XI v Bow Street	2-3
Trearddur Bay v Llanuwchllyn	1-0
West End v Penygraig U	2-3

QUARTER-FINALS

Llanrwst U v Goytre (Gwent)	3-1
Trearddur Bay v Brickfield Rangers	7-2
Port Talbot T v FC Cwmaman	2-2
Port Talbot T won 4-2 on penalties.	
Bow Street v Penygraig U	1-1
Penygraig U won 4-2 on penalties.	

SEMI-FINALS

Penygraig U v Llanrwst U	1-0
Port Talbot T v Trearddur Bay	3-1

DRAGON SIGNS FAW AMATEUR TROPHY FINAL 2024–25

Saturday, 19 April 2025

(at Ynys Park, Trefelin, attendance 1213)

Port Talbot T (1) 2   Penygraig U (0) 1

Port Talbot T: Curtis; Baker, Saunders, Kostromin (Hayes K 90), Davies L, Davies A, Morris (Morgan 46), Hayes N, Edwards, Tomlinson, Allen (Chappell Smith 74).
Scorers: Davies 6, Edwards 52.

Penygraig U: Harrison; Simkiss (Garland 70), Davies, Crutch, Cooke, Smith, Edwards, Hathaway (James 62), Gould (Daye 70), Cicigoi, Watts.
Scorer: Smith 79.

Referee: Nicholas Pratt.

THE FAW TROPHY FINALS 1993–94 to 2024–25

1993–94	Barry T v Aberaman	2-1		2009–10	Glan Conwy v Clydach Wasps	5-1
1994–95	Rhydymwyn v Taffs Well	1-0		2010–11	Holywell T v Conwy U	3-2
1995–96	Rhydymwyn v Penrhyncoch	2-1		2011–12	Sully Sports v Holyhead Hotspur	2-1
1996–97	Cambrian U Sky Blues v Rhyl Delta	2-1		2012–13	Caernarfon T v Kilvey Fords	6-0
1997–98	Dinas Powys v Llanrwst	2-0		2013–14	Llanrug U v Chirk AAA	3-2
1998–99	Ragged School v Barry Ath	3-1		2014–15	Holywell T v Penrhyndeudraeth	4-2
1999-00	Trefelin BGC v Bryntirion Ath	6-2		2015-16	Abergavenny T v Sully Sports	1-0
2000–01	Ragged School v Gresford Ath	1-0		2016-17	Chirk AAA v Penlan Club	2-1
2001–02	Cefn U v Llangeinor	2-0		2017-18	Conwy Borough v Rhos Aelwyd	4-1
2002–03	Rhydyfelin Zenith v Tillery	4-1		2018-19	Cefn Albion v Pontardawe T	4-0
2003–04	Penycae v Llanrhaeadr	3-2		2019–20	*Cancelled due to COVID-19 pandemic.*	
2004–05	West End v Rhydymwyn	3-1		2020–21	*Cancelled due to COVID-19 pandemic.*	
2005–06	West End v Cefn U	4-2		2021–22	Mold Alex v Baglan Dragons	1-0
2006–07	Brymbo v Glan Conwy	6-2		2022–23	Trethomas Bluebirds v Denbigh T	2-1
2007–08	Rhos Aelwyd v Corwen	4-2		2023–24	Newport C v Penrhyncoch	5-4
2008–09	Ragged School v Penycae	1-0		2024–25	Port Talbot T v Penygraig U	2-1

NORTHERN IRISH FOOTBALL 2024–25

NIFL SPORTS DIRECT PREMIERSHIP TABLE 2024–25

		Home					Away					Total						
		P	W	D	L	F	A	W	D	L	F	A	W	D	L	F	A	GD	Pts
1	Linfield[1]	38	16	0	4	37	15	11	4	3	32	13	27	4	7	69	28	41	85
2	Larne[2]	38	6	7	5	17	15	11	5	4	29	18	17	12	9	46	33	13	63
3	Glentoran[4]	38	7	6	4	16	13	10	4	7	33	24	17	10	11	49	37	12	61
4	Dungannon Swifts[3]	38	10	3	7	27	25	7	3	8	24	23	17	6	15	51	48	3	57
5	Coleraine[4]	38	9	4	6	30	25	6	6	7	25	25	15	10	13	55	50	5	55
6	Crusaders[4]	38	8	4	8	30	36	8	2	8	17	17	16	6	16	47	53	−6	54
7	Cliftonville[4,5]	38	11	3	4	30	11	6	4	10	28	30	17	7	14	58	41	17	58
8	Portadown	38	11	5	4	28	19	5	3	10	20	26	16	8	14	48	45	3	56
9	Ballymena U	38	7	3	8	25	24	7	2	11	22	30	14	5	19	47	54	−7	47
10	Glenavon	38	6	5	8	22	24	6	5	8	20	23	12	10	16	42	47	−5	46
11	Carrick Rangers*	38	6	5	9	20	24	1	6	11	12	35	7	11	20	32	59	−27	32
12	Loughgall	38	3	3	13	22	45	2	4	13	14	40	5	7	26	36	85	−49	22

*Top 6 teams split after 33 games. [1]Linfield qualify for Champions League first qualifying round. [2]Larne qualify for UEFA Conference League first qualifying round. [3]Dungannon Swifts qualify for UEFA Conference League second qualifying round by winning the Irish Cup. [4]Glentoran, Coleraine, Crusaders and Cliftonville qualify for NIFL UEFA Conference League play-offs. [5]Cliftonville qualify for UEFA Conference League first qualifying round play-off after play-offs. *Carrick Rangers not relegated after play-offs: Carrick Rangers v Annagh U 8-3 on aggregate.*

UEFA CONFERENCE LEAGUE PLAY-OFFS SEMI-FINALS

| Glentoran v Cliftonville | 0-2 |
| Coleraine v Crusaders | 1-0 |

UEFA CONFERENCE LEAGUE PLAY-OFFS FINAL

| Coleraine v Cliftonville | 0-2 |

NIFL SPORTS DIRECT PREMIERSHIP PLAY-OFF FIRST LEG

| Annagh U v Carrick Rangers | 2-5 |

NIFL SPORTS DIRECT PREMIERSHIP PLAY-OFF SECOND LEG

| Carrick Rangers v Annagh U | 3-1 |

Carrick Rangers won 8-3 on aggregate.

NIFL SPORTS DIRECT PREMIERSHIP LEADING GOALSCORERS (League goals only)

Player (Club)	Goals	Player (Club)	Goals
Joe Gormley (Cliftonville)	20	David McDaid (Glenavon)	8
Matthew Shevlin (Coleraine)	20	Andrew Mitchell (Dungannon Swifts)	8
Joel Cooper (Linfield)	19	Paul O'Neill (Larne)	8
Ben Kennedy (Ballymena U)	13	Jay Boyd (Crusaders)	7
John McGovern (Dungannon Swifts)	13	*(includes 3 on loan at Loughgall)*	
Matthew Fitzpatrick (Linfield)	12	Peter Campbell (Glenavon)	7
Jordan Jenkins (Glentoran)	12	Nathaniel Ferris (Coleraine)	7
Kieran Offord (Linfield)	12	*(includes 6 at Loughgall)*	
(includes 10 at Crusaders on loan from St Mirren)		Kyle McClean (Linfield)	7
Andrew Ryan (Larne)	12	Christopher McKee (Linfield)	7
Ryan Curran (Cliftonville)	11	Tomas Galvin (Dungannon Swifts)	6
Rhyss Campbell (Coleraine)	9	Jamie Glackin (Coleraine)	6
Daniel Gibson (Carrick Rangers)	9	Paul Heatley (Carrick Rangers)	6
Ahu Obhakhan (Portadown)	9	Benjamin Magee (Larne)	6
Joshua Ukek (Portadown)	9	*(includes 4 on loan at Loughgall)*	
Ryan Mayse (Portadown)	8		

IRISH LEAGUE CHAMPIONSHIP WINNERS

1891	Linfield	1915	Belfast Celtic	1951	Glentoran	1976	Crusaders	2001	Linfield
1892	Linfield	1920	Belfast Celtic	1952	Glenavon	1977	Glentoran	2002	Portadown
1893	Linfield	1921	Glentoran	1953	Glentoran	1978	Linfield	2003	Glentoran
1894	Glentoran	1922	Linfield	1954	Linfield	1979	Linfield	2004	Linfield
1895	Linfield	1923	Linfield	1955	Linfield	1980	Linfield	2005	Glentoran
1896	Distillery	1924	Queen's Island	1956	Linfield	1981	Glentoran	2006	Linfield
1897	Glentoran	1925	Glentoran	1957	Glentoran	1982	Linfield	2007	Linfield
1898	Linfield	1926	Belfast Celtic	1958	Ards	1983	Linfield	2008	Linfield
1899	Distillery	1927	Belfast Celtic	1959	Linfield	1984	Linfield	2009	Glentoran
1900	Belfast Celtic	1928	Belfast Celtic	1960	Glenavon	1985	Linfield	2010	Linfield
1901	Distillery	1929	Belfast Celtic	1961	Linfield	1986	Linfield	2011	Linfield
1902	Linfield	1930	Linfield	1962	Linfield	1987	Linfield	2012	Linfield
1903	Distillery	1931	Glentoran	1963	Distillery	1988	Glentoran	2013	Cliftonville
1904	Linfield	1932	Linfield	1964	Glentoran	1989	Linfield	2014	Cliftonville
1905	Glentoran	1933	Belfast Celtic	1965	Derry City	1990	Portadown	2015	Crusaders
1906	Cliftonville/	1934	Linfield	1966	Linfield	1991	Portadown	2016	Crusaders
	Distillery (shared)	1935	Linfield	1967	Glentoran	1992	Glentoran	2017	Linfield
1907	Linfield	1936	Belfast Celtic	1968	Glentoran	1993	Linfield	2018	Crusaders
1908	Linfield	1937	Belfast Celtic	1969	Linfield	1994	Linfield	2019	Linfield
1909	Linfield	1938	Belfast Celtic	1970	Glentoran	1995	Crusaders	2020	Linfield
1910	Cliftonville	1939	Belfast Celtic	1971	Linfield	1996	Portadown	2021	Linfield
1911	Linfield	1940	Belfast Celtic	1972	Glentoran	1997	Crusaders	2022	Linfield
1912	Glentoran	1948	Belfast Celtic	1973	Crusaders	1998	Cliftonville	2023	Larne
1913	Glentoran	1949	Linfield	1974	Coleraine	1999	Glentoran	2024	Larne
1914	Linfield	1950	Linfield	1975	Linfield	2000	Linfield	2025	Linfield

NIFL PLAYR-FIT CHAMPIONSHIP TABLE 2024–25

			Home				Away					Total						
		P	W	D	L	F	A	W	D	L	F	A	W	D	L	F	A	GD	Pts
1	Bangor	38	12	4	3	44	22	11	3	5	38	24	23	7	8	82	46	36	76
2	Annagh U*	38	13	3	3	35	14	9	2	8	35	23	22	5	11	70	37	33	71
3	H&W Welders	38	12	0	7	40	22	8	6	5	39	31	20	6	12	79	53	26	66
4	Limavady U	38	10	3	6	31	22	8	9	2	36	22	18	12	8	67	44	23	66
5	Ards	38	7	5	7	26	27	7	5	7	28	29	14	10	14	55	57	–2	52
6	Dundela	38	8	2	9	29	31	7	5	7	29	31	15	7	16	58	62	–4	52
7	Institute	38	7	8	5	34	33	6	4	8	28	30	13	12	13	62	63	–1	51
8	Ballinamallard U	38	9	3	6	35	23	4	2	14	20	39	13	5	20	55	62	–7	44
9	Armagh C	38	5	6	9	38	45	5	6	7	23	32	10	12	16	62	78	–16	42
10	Newington	38	7	5	7	25	28	4	4	11	26	46	11	9	18	51	74	–23	42
11	Ballyclare Comrades†	38	4	6	8	28	45	7	1	12	24	40	11	7	20	52	85	–33	40
12	Newry C	38	6	6	7	28	32	1	4	14	18	46	7	10	21	46	78	–32	31

*Annagh U not promoted after play-offs. Championship Play-offs: Queen's University v Ballyclare Comrades 3-2 on aggregate. †Ballyclare Comrades relegated after play-offs.

NIFL CHAMPIONSHIP WINNERS

1996 Coleraine	2004 Loughgall	2012 Ballinamallard U	2020 Portadown
1997 Ballymena U	2005 Armagh C	2013 Ards	2021 No competition
1998 Newry T	2006 Crusaders	2014 Institute	2022 Newry C
1999 Distillery	2007 Institute	2015 Carrick Rangers	2023 Loughgall
2000 Omagh T	2008 Loughgall	2016 Ards	2024 Portadown
2001 Ards	2009 Portadown	2017 Warrenpoint T	2025 Bangor
2002 Lisburn Distillery	2010 Loughgall	2018 Institute	
2003 Dungannon Swifts	2011 Carrick Rangers	2019 Larne	

NIFL PLAYR-FIT PREMIER INTERMEDIATE LEAGUE 2024–25

			Home				Away					Total						
		P	W	D	L	F	A	W	D	L	F	A	W	D	L	F	A	GD	Pts
1	Warrenpoint T	26	12	1	0	33	10	7	1	5	19	17	19	2	5	52	27	25	59
2	Queen's University*	26	10	2	1	35	15	7	1	5	20	15	17	3	6	55	30	25	54
3	Rathfriland Rangers	26	7	1	5	26	16	9	0	4	33	14	16	1	9	59	30	29	49
4	Dollingstown	26	7	2	4	30	18	8	2	3	29	17	15	4	7	59	35	24	49
5	Ballymacash Rangers	26	3	3	7	13	20	8	3	2	31	17	11	6	9	44	37	7	39
6	Oxford Sunnyside	26	7	2	4	31	24	4	4	5	20	27	11	6	9	51	51	0	39
7	Moyola Park	26	5	4	4	29	22	6	1	6	19	22	11	5	10	48	44	4	38
8	Portstewart	26	4	1	8	16	31	6	3	4	17	17	10	4	12	33	48	–15	34
9	Knockbreda	26	3	3	7	17	25	5	4	4	26	27	8	7	11	43	52	–9	31
10	Lisburn Distillery	26	4	4	5	22	20	3	5	5	19	27	7	9	10	41	47	–6	30
11	Banbridge T	26	6	2	5	22	18	1	6	6	10	23	7	8	11	32	41	–9	29
12	Dergview	26	6	1	6	17	16	2	1	10	15	43	8	2	16	32	59	–27	26
13	Coagh U	26	5	3	5	23	23	1	0	12	12	36	6	3	17	35	59	–24	21
14	Tobermore U	26	3	3	7	18	24	1	1	11	12	30	4	4	18	30	54	–24	16

*Queen's University promoted after play-offs.

NIFL DEVELOPMENT LEAGUES 2024–25

PREMIERSHIP DEVELOPMENT LEAGUE 2024–25

	P	W	D	L	F	A	GD	Pts
Linfield Swifts	33	26	2	5	100	46	54	80
Larne Olympic	33	23	3	7	73	46	27	72
Crusaders	33	21	4	8	87	42	45	67
Glentoran	33	21	2	10	85	52	33	65
Cliftonville Olympic	33	19	3	11	81	56	25	60
Coleraine	33	13	6	14	74	62	12	45
Ballymena U	33	12	3	18	67	70	–3	39
Dungannon Swifts	33	12	0	21	56	84	–28	36
Glenavon	33	10	5	18	61	79	–18	35
Portadown	33	10	4	19	57	88	–31	34
Carrick Rangers*	33	9	0	24	39	91	–52	27
Loughgall	33	5	2	26	48	112	–64	17

*Carrick Rangers fielded an ineligible player in their match against Linfield Swifts (7/10/2024), Linfield Swifts were awarded the match 3-0.

PIL DEVELOPMENT LEAGUE 2024–25

	P	W	D	L	F	A	GD	Pts
Queen's University	21	14	4	3	70	31	39	46
Warrenpoint T	21	11	3	7	61	38	23	36
Knockbreda	21	11	3	7	44	49	–5	36
Ballymacash Rangers	21	11	2	8	55	38	17	35
Banbridge T	21	11	1	9	46	44	2	34
Lisburn Distillery	21	6	4	11	36	50	–14	22
Moyola Park Olympic	21	4	4	13	26	61	–35	16
Rathfriland	21	4	3	14	40	67	–27	15

CHAMPIONSHIP DEVELOPMENT LEAGUE 2024–25

	P	W	D	L	F	A	GD	Pts
Institute	27	21	4	2	91	25	66	67
Ards	27	17	5	5	80	44	36	56
Bangor	27	14	6	7	73	49	24	48
Limavady U	27	14	2	11	67	41	26	44
Dundela	27	14	1	12	60	57	3	43
Armagh City Olympic	27	10	7	10	49	52	–3	37
H&W Welders	27	9	5	13	63	72	–9	32
Newry C	27	8	6	13	44	59	–15	30
Ballyclare Comrades	27	6	4	17	54	79	–25	22
Newington	27	1	2	24	35	138	–103	5

IRISH CUP FINALS 1880–81 to 2024–25

After extra time.

Season	Match	Score
1880–81	Moyola Park v Cliftonville	1-0
1881–82	Queen's Island (1881) v Cliftonville	1-0
1882–83	Cliftonville v Ulster	5-0
1883–84	Distillery v Wellington Park	5-0
1884–85	Distillery v Limavady	3-0
1885–86	Distillery v Limavady	1-0
1886–87	Ulster v Cliftonville	3-0
1887–88	Cliftonville v Distillery	2-1
1888–89	Distillery v YMCA	5-4
1889–90	Gordon Highlanders v Cliftonville	2-2
Replay	Gordon Highlanders v Cliftonville	3-1
1890–91	Linfield v Ulster	4-2
1891–92	Linfield v The Black Watch	7-0
1892–93	Linfield v Cliftonville	5-1
1893–94	Distillery v Linfield	2-2
Replay	Distillery v Linfield	3-2
1894–95	Linfield v Bohemians	10-1
1895–96	Distillery v Glentoran	3-1
1896–97	Cliftonville v Sherwood Foresters	3-1
1897–98	Linfield v St Columb's Hall Celtic	2-0
1898–99	Linfield v Glentoran	2-1
1899–00	Cliftonville v Bohemians	2-1
1900–01	Cliftonville v Freebooters	1-0
1901–02	Linfield v Distillery	5-1
1902–03	Distillery v Bohemians	3-1
1903–04	Linfield v Derry Celtic	5-1
1904–05	Distillery v Shelbourne	3-0
1905–06	Shelbourne v Belfast Celtic	2-0
1906–07	Cliftonville v Shelbourne	0-0
Replay	Cliftonville v Shelbourne	1-0
1907–08	Bohemians v Shelbourne	1-1
Replay	Bohemians v Shelbourne	3-1
1908–09	Cliftonville v Bohemians	0-0
Replay	Cliftonville v Bohemians	2-1
1909–10	Distillery v Cliftonville	1-0
1910–11	Shelbourne v Bohemians	0-0
Replay	Shelbourne v Bohemians	2-1
1911–12	*Linfield were awarded the trophy after Cliftonville, Glentoran and Shelbourne resigned from the IFA at the semi-final stage.*	
1912–13	Linfield v Glentoran	2-0
1913–14	Glentoran v Linfield	3-1
1914–15	Linfield v Belfast Celtic	1-0
1915–16	Linfield v Glentoran	1-1
Replay	Linfield v Glentoran	1-0
1916–17	Glentoran v Belfast Celtic	2-0
1917–18	Belfast Celtic v Linfield	0-0
Replay	Belfast Celtic v Linfield	0-0
2nd replay	Belfast Celtic v Linfield	2-0
1918–19	Linfield v Glentoran	1-1
Replay	Linfield v Glentoran	0-0
2nd replay	Linfield v Glentoran	2-1
1919–20	*Shelbourne were awarded the trophy after Belfast Celtic and Glentoran were removed from the competition at the semi-final stage.*	
1920–21	Glentoran v Glenavon	2-0
1921–22	Linfield v Glenavon	2-0
1922–23	Linfield v Glentoran	2-0
1923–24	Queen's Island (1920) v Willowfield	1-0
1924–25	Distillery v Glentoran	2-1
1925–26	Belfast Celtic v Linfield	3-2
1926–27	Ards v Cliftonville	3-2
1927–28	Willowfield v Larne	1-0
1928–29	Ballymena v Belfast Celtic	2-1
1929–30	Linfield v Ballymena	4-3
1930–31	Linfield v Ballymena	3-0
1931–32	Glentoran v Linfield	2-1
1932–33	Glentoran v Distillery	1-1
Replay	Glentoran v Distillery	1-1
2nd replay	Glentoran v Distillery	3-1
1933–34	Linfield v Cliftonville	5-0
1934–35	Glentoran v Larne	0-0
Replay	Glentoran v Larne	1-0
2nd replay	Glentoran v Larne	1-0
1935–36	Linfield v Derry C	0-0
Replay	Linfield v Derry C	2-0
1936–37	Belfast Celtic v Linfield	3-0
1937–38	Belfast Celtic v Bangor	0-0
Replay	Belfast Celtic v Bangor	2-0
1938–39	Linfield v Ballymena U	2-0
1939–40	Ballymena U v Glenavon	2-0
1940–41	Belfast Celtic v Linfield	1-0
1941–42	Linfield v Glentoran	3-1
1942–43	Belfast Celtic v Glentoran	1-0
1943–44	Belfast Celtic v Linfield	3-1
1944–45	Linfield v Glentoran	4-2
1945–46	Linfield v Distillery	3-0
1946–47	Belfast Celtic v Glentoran	1-0
1947–48	Linfield v Coleraine	3-0
1948–49	Derry C v Glentoran	3-1
1949–50	Linfield v Distillery	2-1
1950–51	Glentoran v Ballymena U	3-1
1951–52	Ards v Glentoran	1-0
1952–53	Linfield v Coleraine	5-0
1953–54	Derry C v Glentoran	2-2
Replay	Derry C v Glentoran	0-0
2nd replay	Derry C v Glentoran	1-0
1954–55	Dundela v Glenavon	3-0
1955–56	Distillery v Glentoran	2-2
Replay	Distillery v Glentoran	0-0
2nd replay	Distillery v Glentoran	1-0
1956–57	Glenavon v Derry C	2-0
1957–58	Ballymena U v Linfield	2-0
1958–59	Glenavon v Ballymena U	1-1
Replay	Glenavon v Ballymena U	2-0
1959–60	Linfield v Ards	5-1
1960–61	Glenavon v Linfield	5-1
1961–62	Linfield v Portadown	4-0
1962–63	Linfield v Distillery	2-1
1963–64	Derry C v Glentoran	2-0
1964–65	Coleraine v Glenavon	2-1
1965–66	Glentoran v Linfield	2-0
1966–67	Crusaders v Glentoran	3-1
1967–68	Crusaders v Linfield	2-0
1968–69	Ards v Distillery	0-0
Replay	Ards v Distillery	4-2
1969–70	Linfield v Ballymena U	2-1
1970–71	Distillery v Derry C	3-0
1971–72	Coleraine v Portadown	2-1
1972–73	Glentoran v Linfield	3-2
1973–74	Ards v Ballymena U	2-1
1974–75	Coleraine v Linfield	1-1
Replay	Coleraine v Linfield	0-0
2nd replay	Coleraine v Linfield	1-0
1975–76	Carrick Rangers v Linfield	2-1
1976–77	Coleraine v Linfield	4-1
1977–78	Linfield v Ballymena U	3-1
1978–79	Cliftonville v Portadown	3-2
1979–80	Linfield v Crusaders	2-0
1980–81	Ballymena U v Glenavon	1-0
1981–82	Linfield v Coleraine	2-1
1982–83	Glentoran v Linfield	1-1
Replay	Glentoran v Linfield	2-1
1983–84	Ballymena U v Carrick Rangers	4-1
1984–85	Glentoran v Linfield	1-1
Replay	Glentoran v Linfield	1-0
1985–86	Glentoran v Coleraine	2-1
1986–87	Glentoran v Larne	1-0
1987–88	Glentoran v Glenavon	1-0
1988–89	Ballymena U v Larne	1-0
1989–90	Glentoran v Portadown	3-0
1990–91	Portadown v Glenavon	2-1
1991–92	Glenavon v Linfield	2-1
1992–93	Bangor v Ards	1-1*
Replay	Bangor v Ards	1-1*
2nd replay	Bangor v Ards	1-0
1993–94	Linfield v Bangor	2-0
1994–95	Linfield v Carrick Rangers	3-1
1995–96	Glentoran v Glenavon	1-0
1996–97	Glenavon v Cliftonville	1-0
1997–98	Glentoran v Glenavon	1-0*
1998–99	*Portadown awarded the trophy after Cliftonville were removed from the competition for fielding an ineligible player in the semi-final.*	
1999–2000	Glentoran v Portadown	1-0
2000–01	Glentoran v Linfield	1-0*
2001–02	Linfield v Portadown	2-1
2002–03	Coleraine v Glentoran	1-0
2003–04	Glentoran v Coleraine	1-0
2004–05	Portadown v Larne	5-1
2005–06	Linfield v Glentoran	2-1
2006–07	Linfield v Dungannon Swifts	2-2*
	Linfield won 3-2 on penalties.	
2007–08	Linfield v Coleraine	2-1
2008–09	Crusaders v Cliftonville	1-0
2009–10	Linfield v Portadown	2-1
2010–11	Linfield v Crusaders	2-1
2011–12	Linfield v Crusaders	4-1
2012–13	Glentoran v Cliftonville	3-1*
2013–14	Glenavon v Ballymena U	2-1
2014–15	Glentoran v Portadown	1-0
2015–16	Glenavon v Linfield	2-0
2016–17	Linfield v Coleraine	3-0
2017–18	Coleraine v Cliftonville	3-1
2018–19	Crusaders v Ballinamallard U	3-0
2019–20	Glentoran v Ballymena U	2-1*
2020–21	Linfield v Larne	2-1
2021–22	Crusaders v Ballymena U	2-1*
2022–23	Crusaders v Ballymena U	4-0
2023–24	Cliftonville v Linfield	3-1*
2024–25	Dungannon Swifts v Cliftonville	1-1*
	Dungannon Swifts won 4-3 on penalties.	

CLEARER WATER IRISH CUP 2024–25

■ *Denotes player sent off.* *After extra time.

FIRST ROUND

Byes: 18th Newtownabbey Old Boys, 1st Bangor Old Boys, Ards Rangers, Ballynahinch Olympic, Banbridge T, Belfast Celtic, Bloomfield, Bourneview Mill, Derriaghy Cricket Club, Desertmartin, Donegal Celtic, Dromara Village, Immaculata, Malachians, Moneyslane, Mossley, Oxford Sunnyside, Seagoe, Shankill U, Short Brothers, St Oliver Plunkett.

Aquinas v Wakehurst	2-3
Banbridge Rangers v Valley Rangers	2-0
Bryansburn Rangers v Coagh U	0-3
Castlewellan T v Tandragee R	3-0
Colin Valley v Islandmagee	1-2
Crewe U v Finaghy	2-0
Dollingstown (walkover) v Laurelvale	
Downshire Young Men v Greenisland	1-2
Dromore Amateurs v Wellington Recreation	0-3
Drumaness Mills v Crumlin U	0-2
Dundonald v Newbuildings U	1-2
Dunloy v Lisburn Rangers	3-1
Dunmurry Recreation v Albert Foundry	0-3
Dunmurry Young Men v Seapatrick	5-0
Fivemiletown U v Richhill	0-2
Grove U v Rosemount Rec (walkover)	
Hanover v Portadown BBOB	1-0
Heights v Rectory Rangers	7-0
Killyleagh Youth v Abbey Villa	0-4
Killymoon Rangers v Lurgan T	0-2
Kilmore Recreation v Newcastle	2-0
Knockbreda v Craigavon C	3-2
Larne Technical Old Boys v Comber Recreation	0-2
Maiden C v Woodvale	4-0
Markethill Swifts v Brantwood	2-3
Moyola Park v Lower Maze	9-0
Newtowne v Tullyvallen	5-0
Portaferry R v St Luke's	3-2
Portavogie Rangers v Newmills	2-2
Newmills won 5-4 on penalties.	
Portstewart (walkover) v Tullycarnet	
Queen's University v Ballymoney U	4-3
Rathfriland Rangers v Strabane Ath	2-1
Rosario Youth Club v Mindwell	6-1
Saintfield U v Cookstown Youth	3-2
Shamrock v Orangefield Old Boys	6-2
St James' Swifts v Lisburn Distillery	1-0
St Mary's Youth v Ballymacash Rangers	0-9
St Matthew's v Sirocco Works	0-6
Suffolk v Rathcoole	1-6
Tobermore U v Dergview	0-4
Warrenpoint T v Windmill Stars	1-2
Willowbank v Ballynahinch U	10-0
Glebe Rangers v PSNI	1-2

SECOND ROUND

Rathfriland Rangers v Windmill Stars	6-0
18th Newtownabbey Old Boys v Desertmartin	1-2
1st Bangor Old Boys v Dollingstown	2-4
Abbey Villa v Newmills	3-0
Ballymacash Rangers v Rathcoole	3-0
Ballynahinch Olympic v Richhill	1-2
Banbridge T v PSNI	3-0
Belfast Celtic v Saintfield U	2-1
Coagh U v Bourneview Mill	5-0
Dergview v Shamrock	4-0
Donegal Celtic v Bloomfield (walkover)	
Dromara Village v Crumlin U	4-1
Dunloy v Derriaghy Cricket Club	2-1
Dunmurry Young Men v Greenisland	5-0
Hanover v Newbuildings U	1-5
Islandmagee v Heights	2-2
Islandmagee won 4-3 on penalties.	
Kilmore Recreation v Seagoe	1-3
Knockbreda v Shankill U	1-0
Lurgan T v Short Brothers	6-3
Maiden C (walkover) v Malachians	
Moneyslane v Willowbank	2-3
Mossley v Rosemount Rec	4-0
Moyola Park v Immaculata	2-1

Newtowne v Queen's University	1-2
Oxford Sunnyside v Crewe U	1-0
Portaferry R v Ards Rangers	1-3
Portstewart v Brantwood	5-1
Rosario Youth Club (walkover) v Castlewellan T	
Sirocco Works v Banbridge Rangers	
St James' Swifts v Comber Recreation	1-5
St Oliver Plunkett v Wakehurst	2-1
St Oliver Plunkett v Wakehurst	2-2
Wakehurst won 4-2 on penalties.	
Wellington Recreation v Albert Foundry	3-3
Wellington Recreation won 4-3 on penalties.	

THIRD ROUND

Abbey Villa v Ballymacash Rangers	1-2
Ards Rangers v Queen's University	0-3
Banbridge T v Coagh U	3-0
Belfast Celtic v Oxford Sunnyside	2-1
Islandmagee v Desertmartin	4-3
Knockbreda v Bloomfield	5-1
Lurgan T v Seagoe	2-0
Maiden C v Rosario Youth Club	1-3
Mossley v St James' Swifts	1-1
St James' Swifts won 4-2 on penalties.	
Newbuildings U v Dollingstown	2-7
Portstewart v Dromara Village	
Rathfriland Rangers v Dunloy	2-0
Richhill v Wellington Recreation	1-4
Wakehurst v Banbridge Rangers	1-2
Dunmurry Young Men v Dergview	1-3
Willowbank v Moyola Park	4-5

FOURTH ROUND

Banbridge Rangers v Queen's University	1-1*
Banbridge Rangers on 3-2 on penalties.	
Lurgan T v Dollingstown	0-1
Moyola Park v St James' Swifts	1-0
Portstewart v Belfast Celtic	0-1
Rosario Youth Club v Rathfriland Rangers	2-4*
Knockbreda v Banbridge T	3-0
Islandmagee v Ballymacash Rangers	0-4
Wellington Recreation (walkover) v Dergview	

FIFTH ROUND

H&W Welders v Glentoran	2-4
Annagh U v Portadown	3-2
Ballymacash Rangers v Ballinamallard U	1-2
Ballymena U v Ards	1-2
Bangor v Newington	2-1*
Carrick Rangers v Newry C	4-3
Cliftonville v Banbridge Rangers	4-0
Coleraine v Armagh C	5-0
Crusaders v Knockbreda	3-0
Dungannon Swifts v Rathfriland Rangers	5-0
Limavady U v Larne	1-0*
Linfield v Wellington Recreation	4-0
Dollingstown v Ballyclare Comrades	1-0
Glenavon v Dundela	2-0
Institute v Loughgall	2-3
Moyola Park v Belfast Celtic	0-0
Moyola Park won 7-6 on penalties.	

SIXTH ROUND

Glentoran v Linfield	2-1*
Ballinamallard U v Carrick Rangers	0-3
Bangor v Annagh U	3-0
Cliftonville v Glenavon	3-2*
Crusaders v Limavady U	1-0
Dollingstown v Loughgall	0-3
Dungannon Swifts v Coleraine	2-1*
Moyola Park v Ards	1-3

QUARTER-FINALS

Bangor v Glentoran	3-1
Ards v Loughgall	2-0
Carrick Rangers v Dungannon Swifts	1-3
Crusaders v Cliftonville	1-2

SEMI-FINALS

Ards v Cliftonville	0-3
Bangor v Dungannon Swifts	0-2

CLEARER WATER IRISH CUP FINAL 2024–25

Saturday, 5 May 2025 (at Windsor Park, Belfast, attendance 12,786)

Dungannon Swifts (0) 1   Cliftonville (0) 1

Dungannon Swifts: (433) Dunne; Scott■, Wallace, Curry, Glenny; Dillon (Hutchinson 80 (Bermingham 120), Bigirimana, Knowles (McGinnty 73); Alves, McGovern (Boyd 91), Mitchell (Galvin 73).
Scorer: McGovern 24.

Cliftonville: (3412) Odumosu; Keaney, Addis, Casey (Peppper 106); Kearney, Gordon (Piesold 56), Wilson (Corrigan 70), Conlan; Hale; Curran (Parsons 56 (Glynn 87)), Gormley (McWoods 70).
Scorer: Kearney 90.

aet; Dungannon Swifts won 4-3 on penalties. Referee: Ian McNabb.

BETMcLEAN NORTHERN IRELAND FOOTBALL LEAGUE CUP 2024–25

After extra time.

PRELIMINARY ROUND

Ballymacash Rangers v Banbridge T	3-0
Dergview v Knockbreda	2-1
Moyola Park v Oxford Sunnyside	3-1
Rathfriland Rangers v Coagh U	2-1
Tobermore U v Queen's University	3-4*
Warrenpoint T v Lisburn Distillery	2-0*

FIRST ROUND

Ballinamallard U v Coleraine	0-4
Ballyclare Comrades v Crusaders	2-3
Ballymacash Rangers v Institute	0-1
Bangor v Warrenpoint T	4-0
Carrick Rangers v Queen's University	0-1
Dollingstown v Newry C	5-1
Dundela v Linfield	0-3
Dungannon Swifts v Portstewart	5-0
Glentoran v Dergview	2-0
H&W Welders v Larne	1-2
Limavady U v Cliftonville	0-2
Loughgall v Armagh C	2-3
Moyola Park v Annagh U	2-4*
Newington v Glenavon	2-3

Portadown v Ards — 0-1
Rathfriland Rangers v Ballymena U — 3-3*
Ballymena U won 5-4 on penalties.

SECOND ROUND

Annagh U v Queen's University	2-0
Armagh C v Glenavon	0-0*

Armagh C won 8-7 on penalties.

Ballymena U v Ards	1-0
Bangor v Cliftonville	0-1
Crusaders v Coleraine	2-1
Dungannon Swifts v Dollingstown	3-1
Institute v Larne	0-2
Linfield v Glentoran	0-1

QUARTER-FINALS

Annagh U v Larne	0-5
Armagh C v Cliftonville	0-3
Crusaders v Dungannon Swifts	4-2*
Glentoran v Ballymena U	2-0

SEMI-FINALS

Glentoran v Crusaders	4-2*
Larne v Cliftonville	0-1*

BETMcLEAN NORTHERN IRELAND FOOTBALL LEAGUE CUP FINAL 2024–25

Sunday, 9 March 2025 (at Windsor Park, Belfast, attendance 14,539)

Cliftonville (0) 1   Glentoran (0) 0

Cliftonville: (3412) Ridd; Casey, Addis, Kearney; Keaney, Gordon (Piesold 73), Wilson (Pepper 111), Conlan; Hale (Glynn, 114 mins); Parsons (Corrigan 97), Curran (Gormley 73).
Scorer: Gormley 99.

Glentoran: (433) Gyollai; Wightman (Pattisson 85), McEleney (Coll 98), Lyons-Foster, Amos; Palmer, Sule, Thorndike (Lindsay 60); Connolly (Russell 85 (Hvid 120)), Jenkins, Fisher (Ferris 60).

aet. Referee: Shane Andrews.

NIFWA AWARDS 2024–25

NIFWA PREMIERSHIP @SPORTSDIRECTUK PLAYER OF THE MONTH

Month	Player	Team
August	Joel Cooper	Linfield
September	Ben Kennedy	Ballymena U
October	Daniel Gyollai	Glentoran
November	Joe Gormley	Cliftonville
December	David Walsh	Linfield
January	Joel Cooper	Linfield
February	Jarlath O'Rourke	Crusaders
March	Charles Dunne	Coleraine
April	Danny Gibson	Carrick Rangers

NIFWA PREMIERSHIP MANAGER OF THE MONTH

Month	Manager	Team
August	David Healy	Linfield
September	Jim Ervin	Ballymena U
October	Declan Caddell	Crusaders
November	David Healy	Linfield
December	Declan Devine	Glentoran
January	Declan Devine	Glentoran
February	Declan Caddell	Crusaders
March	David Healy	Linfield
April	Gary Haveron	Larne

NIFWA CHAMPIONSHIP PLAYER OF THE MONTH

Month	Player	Team
August	Igor Rutkowski	Armagh C
September	Matthew Ferguson	Bangor
October	Shane Boyle	Institute

November	Michael McLellan	Dundela
December	Ryan Swan	Annagh U
January	Aiden Steele	Ards
February	Ben Arthurs	Bangor
March	Jay Donnelly	Newington
April	Stephen Murray	Annagh U

BELLEEK MANAGER OF THE YEAR
Rodney McAree (Dungannon Swifts)

SPORTS DIRECT PLAYER OF THE YEAR
Joel Cooper (Linfield)

CHAMPIONSHIP PLAYER OF THE YEAR
Ben Arthurs (Bangor)

YOUNG PLAYER OF THE YEAR
Matthew Orr (Linfield)

REAVEY AND CO INTERNATIONAL PERSONALITY OF THE YEAR
Conor Bradley (Liverpool and Northern Ireland)

SPORTS DIRECT WOMEN'S PREMIERSHIP PLAYER OF THE YEAR
Danielle Maxwell (Cliftonville, Burnley and Northern Ireland)

JUICE JAR MALCOLM BRODIE HALL OF FAME
Steven Davis and Stuart Dallas

NORTHERN IRELAND ROLL OF HONOUR SEASON 2024–25

NIFL Sports Direct Premiership: Linfield
Clearer Water Irish Cup: Dungannon Swifts
NIFL Playr-Fit Championship: Bangor
NIFL Playr-Fit Premier Intermediate: Warrenpoint T
BetMcLean Northern Ireland League Cup: Cliftonville
McComb's Coach Travel Intermediate Cup: Crumlin Star
NIFL Sports Direct Women's Premiership 2024: Cliftonville

Steel & Sons Cup: Derriaghy CC
Co Antrim Senior Shield: Glentoran
Co Antrim Junior Shield: St Marys
fonaCAB Irish Junior Cup: Ardmore
Mid Ulster Cup (Senior): Dungannon Swifts
Harry Cavan Youth Cup: Glentoran Colts
North West Senior Cup: Coleraine

EUROPEAN CUP FINALS 1956–1992

Year	Winners v Runners-up		Venue	Attendance	Referee
1956	Real Madrid v Reims	4-3	Paris	38,239	A. Ellis (England)
1957	Real Madrid v Fiorentina	2-0	Madrid	124,000	L. Horn (Netherlands)
1958	Real Madrid v AC Milan	3-2*	Brussels	67,000	A. Alsteen (Belgium)
1959	Real Madrid v Reims	2-0	Stuttgart	72,000	A. Dutsch (West Germany)
1960	Real Madrid v Eintracht Frankfurt	7-3	Glasgow	127,621	J. Mowat (Scotland)
1961	Benfica v Barcelona	3-2	Berne	26,732	G. Dienst (Switzerland)
1962	Benfica v Real Madrid	5-3	Amsterdam	61,257	L. Horn (Netherlands)
1963	AC Milan v Benfica	2-1	Wembley	45,715	A. Holland (England)
1964	Internazionale v Real Madrid	3-1	Vienna	71,333	J. Stoll (Austria)
1965	Internazionale v Benfica	1-0	Milan	89,000	G. Dienst (Switzerland)
1966	Real Madrid v Partizan Belgrade	2-1	Brussels	46,745	R. Kreitlein (West Germany)
1967	Celtic v Internazionale	2-1	Lisbon	45,000	K. Tschenscher (West Germany)
1968	Manchester U v Benfica	4-1*	Wembley	92,225	C. Lo Bello (Italy)
1969	AC Milan v Ajax	4-1	Madrid	31,782	J. Ortiz de Mendibil (Spain)
1970	Feyenoord v Celtic	2-1*	Milan	53,187	C. Lo Bello (Italy)
1971	Ajax v Panathinaikos	2-0	Wembley	90,000	J. Taylor (England)
1972	Ajax v Internazionale	2-0	Rotterdam	61,354	R. Helies (France)
1973	Ajax v Juventus	1-0	Belgrade	89,484	M. Guglovic (Yugoslavia)
1974	Bayern Munich v Atletico Madrid	1-1	Brussels	48,722	V. Loraux (Belgium)
Replay	Bayern Munich v Atletico Madrid	4-0	Brussels	23,325	A. Delcourt (Belgium)
1975	Bayern Munich v Leeds U	2-0	Paris	48,374	M. Kitabdjian (France)
1976	Bayern Munich v Saint-Etienne	1-0	Glasgow	54,864	K. Palotai (Hungary)
1977	Liverpool v Borussia Moenchengladbach	3-1	Rome	52,078	R. Wurtz (France)
1978	Liverpool v Club Brugge	1-0	Wembley	92,500	C. Corver (Netherlands)
1979	Nottingham F v Malmo	1-0	Munich	57,500	E. Linemayr (Austria)
1980	Nottingham F v Hamburg	1-0	Madrid	51,000	A. Garrido (Portugal)
1981	Liverpool v Real Madrid	1-0	Paris	48,360	K. Palotai (Hungary)
1982	Aston Villa v Bayern Munich	1-0	Rotterdam	46,000	G. Konrath (France)
1983	Hamburg v Juventus	1-0	Athens	73,500	N. Rainea (Romania)
1984	Liverpool v Roma	1-1*	Rome	69,693	E. Fredriksson (Sweden)
	Liverpool won 4-2 on penalties.				
1985	Juventus v Liverpool	1-0	Brussels	58,000	A. Daina (Switzerland)
1986	Steaua Bucharest v Barcelona	0-0*	Seville	70,000	M. Vautrot (France)
	Steaua won 2-0 on penalties.				
1987	FC Porto v Bayern Munich	2-1	Vienna	57,500	A. Ponnet (Belgium)
1988	PSV Eindhoven v Benfica	0-0*	Stuttgart	68,000	L. Agnolin (Italy)
	PSV Eindhoven won 6-5 on penalties.				
1989	AC Milan v Steaua Bucharest	4-0	Barcelona	97,000	K.-H. Tritschler (West Germany)
1990	AC Milan v Benfica	1-0	Vienna	57,500	H. Kohl (Austria)
1991	Red Star Belgrade v Marseille	0-0*	Bari	56,000	T. Lanese (Italy)
	Red Star Belgrade won 5-3 on penalties.				
1992	Barcelona v Sampdoria	1-0*	Wembley	70,827	A. Schmidhuber (Germany)

UEFA CHAMPIONS LEAGUE FINALS 1993–2025

Year	Winners v Runners-up		Venue	Attendance	Referee
1993	Marseille v AC Milan	1-0	Munich	64,400	K. Rothlisberger (Switzerland)
1994	AC Milan v Barcelona	4-0	Athens	70,000	P. Don (England)
1995	Ajax v AC Milan	1-0	Vienna	49,730	I. Craciunescu (Romania)
1996	Juventus v Ajax	1-1*	Rome	70,000	M. D. Vega (Spain)
	Juventus won 4-2 on penalties.				
1997	Borussia Dortmund v Juventus	3-1	Munich	59,000	S. Puhl (Hungary)
1998	Real Madrid v Juventus	1-0	Amsterdam	48,500	H. Krug (Germany)
1999	Manchester U v Bayern Munich	2-1	Barcelona	90,245	P. Collina (Italy)
2000	Real Madrid v Valencia	3-0	Paris	80,000	S. Braschi (Italy)
2001	Bayern Munich v Valencia	1-1*	Milan	79,000	D. Jol (Netherlands)
	Bayern Munich won 5-4 on penalties.				
2002	Real Madrid v Bayer Leverkusen	2-1	Glasgow	50,499	U. Meier (Switzerland)
2003	AC Milan v Juventus	0-0*	Manchester	62,315	M. Merk (Germany)
	AC Milan won 3-2 on penalties.				
2004	FC Porto v Monaco	3-0	Gelsenkirchen	53,053	K. M. Nielsen (Denmark)
2005	Liverpool v AC Milan	3-3*	Istanbul	65,000	M. M. González (Spain)
	Liverpool won 3-2 on penalties.				
2006	Barcelona v Arsenal	2-1	Paris	79,610	T. Hauge (Norway)
2007	AC Milan v Liverpool	2-1	Athens	74,000	H. Fandel (Germany)
2008	Manchester U v Chelsea	1-1*	Moscow	67,310	L. Michel (Slovakia)
	Manchester U won 6-5 on penalties.				
2009	Barcelona v Manchester U	2-0	Rome	62,467	M. Busacca (Switzerland)
2010	Internazionale v Bayern Munich	2-0	Madrid	73,490	H. Webb (England)
2011	Barcelona v Manchester U	3-1	Wembley	87,695	V. Kassai (Hungary)
2012	Chelsea v Bayern Munich	1-1*	Munich	62,500	P. Proença (Portugal)
	Chelsea won 4-3 on penalties.				
2013	Bayern Munich v Borussia Dortmund	2-1	Wembley	86,298	N. Rizzoli (Italy)
2014	Real Madrid v Atletico Madrid	4-1*	Lisbon	60,000	B. Kuipers (Netherlands)
2015	Barcelona v Juventus	3-1	Berlin	70,442	C. Cakir (Turkey)
2016	Real Madrid v Atletico Madrid	1-1*	Milan	71,942	M. Clattenburg (England)
	Real Madrid won 5-3 on penalties.				
2017	Real Madrid v Juventus	4-1	Cardiff	65,842	F. Brych (Germany)
2018	Real Madrid v Liverpool	3-1	Kyiv	61,561	M. Mazic (Serbia)
2019	Liverpool v Tottenham H	2-0	Madrid	63,272	D. Skomina (Slovenia)
2020	Bayern Munich v Paris Saint-Germain	1-0	Lisbon	0	D. Orsato (Italy)
2021	Chelsea v Manchester C	1-0	Porto	14,110	A. Lahoz (Spain)
2022	Real Madrid v Liverpool	1-0	Paris	73,000	C. Turpin (France)
2023	Manchester C v Internazionale	1-0	Istanbul	71,412	S. Marciniak (Poland)
2024	Real Madrid v Borussia Dortmund	2-0	Wembley	86,212	S. Vincic (Slovenia)
2025	Paris Saint-Germain v Internazionale	5-0	Munich	64,327	I. Kovacs (Romania)

UEFA CHAMPIONS LEAGUE 2024–25

After extra time. ■ Denotes player sent off. †Due to the war in Ukraine, Shakhtar Donetsk played home matches in Germany, Dynamo Kyiv in Poland and Dinamo Minsk in Hungary (behind closed doors). ‡Due to Israel's war in Gaza, Maccabi Tel Aviv played home matches in Hungary.

QUALIFYING PHASE

FIRST QUALIFYING ROUND – FIRST LEG

Tuesday, 9 July 2024

Hamrun Spartans v Lincoln Red Imps	0-1
Panevezys v HJK	3-0
The New Saints v Decic	3-0
UE Santa Coloma v Ballkani	1-2
Vikingur Reykjavik v Shamrock R	0-0
Virtus v FCSB	1-7

Wednesday, 10 July 2024

Borac Banja Luca v Egnatia	1-0
Dinamo Minsk† v Pyunik	0-0
FK RFS v Larne	3-0
Flora v Celje	0-5
KI v Differdange 03	2-0
Ludogorets Razgrad v Dinamo Batumi	3-1
Ordabasy v Petrocub Hincesti	0-0
Slovan Bratislava v Struga	4-2

Tuesday, 9 July 2024

The New Saints (3) 3 *(Young 4, 31, Davies 39)*

Decic (0) 0 810

The New Saints: (433) Roberts; Daniels, Pask, Bodenham, Davies; Clark (Holden 67), Redmond (Williams D 88), Smith; Brobbel (Bradley 88), Young (McManus 78), Williams J (Baker 78).
Decic: (4231) Nikic; Dresaj, Milic S (Sekulovic 74), Ujkaj, Malesevic; Chagas (Strikovic 81), Bozanovic; Stijepovic (Puleio 46), Bozovic (Kajevic 59), Masovic (Gjolaj 46); Matic.

Vikingur Reykjavik (0) 0

Shamrock R (0) 0 1108

Vikingur Reykjavik: (442) Jonsson; Gunnarsson, Vatnhamar, Ekroth, Fjoluson; Agnarsson, Punyed (Andrason 81), Gudjonsson (Sigurpalsson 66), Ingimundarson (Thordarson 81); Hansen (Vilhjalmsson 66), Djuric.
Shamrock R: (352) Pohls; Cleary, Lopes, Honohan; Nugent■, Watts (Towell 90), O'Neill, Clarke (Farrugia 73), Hoare; Greene (Kenny 66), Byrne (Burns 73).

Wednesday, 10 July 2024

FK RFS (1) 3 *(Kigurs 29, Balodis 48, Panic 60)*

Larne (0) 0 1700

FK RFS: (343) Ondoa; Balodis, Prenga, Lipuscek; Ikaunieks (Njie 78), Markhiyev (Lemajic 46); Panic, Mares; Diomande (Odisharia 77), Kigurs (Kouadio 69), Deocleciano (Ndjiki 86).
Larne: (433) Ferguson; Cosgrove, Altintop (Graham S 63), Bolger, Ives; Gallagher, Donnelly, Sloan (Thomson 63); Ryan (O'Neill 87), Bonis, McKendry (Lusty 69).

FIRST QUALIFYING ROUND – SECOND LEG *(agg)*

Tuesday, 16 July 2024

Ballkani v UE Santa Coloma	1-2*	3-3
UE Santa Coloma won 6-5 on penalties.		
Celje v Flora	2-1	7-1
Decic v The New Saints	1-1	1-4
FCSB v Virtus	4-0	11-1
HJK v Panevezys	1-1	1-4
Lincoln Red Imps v Hamrun Spartans	0-1*	1-1
Lincoln Red Imps won 5-4 on penalties.		
Pyunik v Dinamo Minsk	0-1	0-1
Shamrock R v Vikingur Reykjavik	2-1	2-1

Wednesday, 17 July 2024

Differdange 03 v KI	0-0	0-2
Dinamo Batumi v Ludogorets Razgrad	1-0	2-3
Egnatia v Borac Banja Luca	2-1*	2-2
Borac Banja Luca won 4-1 on penalties.		
Larne v FK RFS	0-4	0-7
Petrocub Hincesti v Ordabasy	1-0	1-0
Struga v Slovan Bratislava	1-2	3-6

Tuesday, 16 July 2024

Decic (0) 1 *(Kajevic 72)*

The New Saints (1) 1 *(Young 43 (pen))* 1400

Decic: (433) Nikic; Dresaj, Milic S (Ljuljduraj 46), Ujkaj, Malesevic; Bozovic, Bajovic (Sekulovic 46), Chagas (Kajevic 63); Puleio (Strikovic 46), Matic (Camaj 63), Masovic.
The New Saints: (433) Roberts; Daniels, Pask, Bodenham, Davies; Clark (Holden 62), Redmond (Williams D 75), Smith; Williams J (Bradley 84), Young (McManus 75), Brobbel (Baker 63).
The New Saints won 4-1 on aggregate.

Shamrock R (2) 2 *(Kenny 8, 20)*

Vikingur Reykjavik (0) 1 *(Hansen 60)* 7632

Shamrock R: (352) Pohls; Cleary, Lopes, Hoare; Honohan, O'Neill, Watts, Clarke (Farrugia 62), Byrne■; Kenny (Grace 80), Greene (Burns 66).
Vikingur Reykjavik: (442) Jonsson; Gunnarsson, Ekroth, Vatnhamar, Fjoluson; Agnarsson (Thrandarson 82), Punyed (Andrason 75), Sigurpalsson (Thordarson 75), Gudjonsson (Hansen 46); Ingimundarson, Djuric (Vilhjalmsson 46).
Shamrock R won 2-1 on aggregate.

Wednesday, 17 July 2024

Larne (0) 0

FK RFS (3) 4 *(Deocleciano 38, Lemajic 44, Ikaunieks 45, Diomande 56)* 2030

Larne: (433) Ferguson; Cosgrove, Bolger, Donnelly, Ives; Randall (Sloan 60), Gallagher (O'Neill 73), Graham S (Altintop 77); Lusty (Bonis 60), Ryan, McKendry (Thomson 73).
FK RFS: (343) Ondoa; Balodis, Prenga, Lipuscek; Ikaunieks (Kigurs 61), Markhiyev (Njie 46), Panic, Mares (Ndjiki 73); Diomande, Deocleciano (Odisharia 61), Lemajic (Kouadio 61).
FK RFS won 7-0 on aggregate.

SECOND QUALIFYING ROUND – FIRST LEG

Tuesday, 23 July 2024

APOEL v Petrocub Hincesti	1-0
Bodo/Glimt v FK RFS	4-0
Dynamo Kyiv† v Partizan Belgrade	6-2
FCSB v Maccabi Tel Aviv	1-1
Ferencvaros v The New Saints	5-0
Lincoln Red Imps v Qarabag	0-2
Lugano v Fenerbahce	3-4
Malmo v KI	4-1
Panevezys v Jagiellonia Bialystock	0-4
Shamrock R v Sparta Prague	0-2
UE Santa Coloma v Midtjylland	0-3

Wednesday, 24 July 2024

Celje v Slovan Bratislava	1-1
Ludogorets Razgrad v Dinamo Minsk	2-0
PAOK v Borac Banja Luca	3-2

Tuesday, 23 July 2024

Ferencvaros (3) 5 *(Traore 14, 21, 53, Zachariassen 24, Marquinhos 62 (pen))*

The New Saints (0) 0 16,231

Ferencvaros: (4231) Dibusz; Makreckis (Botka 77), Cisse, Raul Gustavo (Knoester 83), Ramirez; Maiga (Toth 77), Rommens; Traore, Zachariassen, Marquinhos (Kwabena 76); Pesic (Kady 76).
The New Saints: (4231) Roberts; Daniels, Pask, Bodenham, Davies (Baker 90); Smith, Redmond (Williams D 64); Williams J (Holden 64), Clark (Bradley 90), Brobbel; Young (McManus 76).

Shamrock R (0) 0

Sparta Prague (1) 2 (*Birmancevic 37, Wiesner 64*)   9684

Shamrock R: (352) Pohls; Honohan, Cleary, Lopes; Farrugia (Burns 65), Nugent, Clarke (Grace 84), O'Neill, Hoare; Watts, Kenny (Greene 66).
Sparta Prague: (343) Vindahl-Jensen; Vitik (Sorensen 46), Ross Jensen, Zeleny; Wiesner, Laci (Pavelka 62), Solbakken, Garcia de Albeniz; Tuci (Krasniqi 62), Kuchta (Olatunji 75), Birmancevic (Haraslin 46).

SECOND QUALIFYING ROUND – SECOND LEG (agg)
Tuesday, 30 July 2024

Fenerbahce v Lugano	2-1	6-4
KI v Malmo	3-2	4-6
Petrocub Hincesti v APOEL	1-1	1-2
Qarabag v Lincoln Red Imps	5-0	7-0
Slovan Bratislava v Celje	5-0	6-1
Sparta Prague v Shamrock R	4-2	6-2
The New Saints v Ferencvaros	1-2	1-7

Wednesday, 31 July 2024

Borac Banja Luca v PAOK	0-1	2-4
Dinamo Minsk† v Ludogorets Razgrad	1-0	1-2
FK RFS v Bodo/Glimt	1-3	1-7
Jagiellonia Bialystock v Panevezys	3-1	7-1
Maccabi Tel Aviv‡ v FCSB	0-1	1-2
Midtjylland v UE Santa Coloma	1-0	4-0
Partizan Belgrade v Dynamo Kyiv	0-3	2-9

Tuesday, 30 July 2024

Sparta Prague (2) 4 (*Olatunji 29, Ross Jensen 41, Sorensen 48, Tuci 70*)

Shamrock R (1) 2 (*Greene 32, 47*)   17,367

Sparta Prague: (343) Vindahl-Jensen; Ross Jensen, Pavelka, Sorensen (Solbakken 62); Wiesner (Suchomel 84), Sadilek, Laci (Zeleny 62), Garcia de Albeniz; Danek (Tuci 70), Olatunji (Kuchta 70), Krasniqi.
Shamrock R: (352) Pohls; Hoare (Cleary 24), Lopes, Grace; Honohan, Farrugia (Poom 63), O'Neill, Nugent, Clarke (Burns 63); Watts (Byrne 63), Greene (Burke 75).
Sparta Prague won 6-2 on aggregate.

The New Saints (0) 1 (*Daniels 90*)

Ferencvaros (1) 2 (*Zachariassen 43, Rommens 62 (pen)*)   1022

The New Saints: (442) Roberts; Daniels, Davies (Pask 63), Bodenham, Baker (Marshall 63); Holden (Clark 80), Redmond, Williams D, Brobbel (Bradley 63); Young, McManus (Williams J 75).
Ferencvaros: (4231) Dibusz; Makreckis, Cisse (Abena 72), Raul Gustavo, Ramirez; Maiga (Abu Fani 64), Rommens; Traore (Gruber 72), Zachariassen, Kehinde (Katona 85); Pesic (Kady 64).
Ferencvaros won 7-1 on aggregate.

THIRD QUALIFYING ROUND – FIRST LEG
Tuesday, 6 August 2024

Dynamo Kyiv† v Rangers	1-1
Lille v Fenerbahce	2-1
Malmo v PAOK	2-2
Midtjylland v Ferencvaros	2-0
Qarabag v Ludogorets Razgrad	1-2
Red Bull Salzburg v FC Twente	2-1
Sparta Prague v FCSB	1-1

Wednesday, 7 August 2024

Jagiellonia Bialystock v Bodo/Glimt	0-1
Slavia Prague v Union Saint-Gilloise	3-1
Slovan Bratislava v APOEL	2-0

Tuesday, 6 August 2024

Dynamo Kyiv† (1) 1 (*Yarmolenko 37*)

Rangers (0) 1 (*Dessers 90*)   8315

Dynamo Kyiv: (433) Bushchan; Karavaev, Popov, Mykhavko, Vivcharenko; Shaparenko (Lonwijk 69), Brazhko, Pikhalyonok (Buyalskyi 69); Yarmolenko (Voloshyn 77), Vanat, Kabayev (Braharu 77).
Rangers: (442) Butland; Tavernier, Souttar, Balogun, Yilmaz; McCausland (Cerny 60), Barron (Sterling 71), Diomande (Dowell 80), Wright (Jefte 46); Dessers, Lawrence.

THIRD QUALIFYING ROUND – SECOND LEG (agg)
Tuesday, 13 August 2024

APOEL v Slovan Bratislava	0-0	0-2
Bodo/Glimt v Jagiellonia Bialystock	4-1	5-1
FC Twente v Red Bull Salzburg	3-3	4-5
FCSB v Sparta Prague	2-3	3-4
Fenerbahce v Lille	1-1	2-3
Ferencvaros v Midtjylland	1-1	1-3
Ludogorets Razgrad v Qarabag	2-7	4-8
PAOK v Malmo	3-4	5-6
Rangers v Dynamo Kyiv	0-2	1-3
Union Saint-Gilloise v Slavia Prague	0-1	1-4

Tuesday, 13 August 2024

Rangers (0) 0

Dynamo Kyiv (0) 2 (*Pikhalyonok 82, Voloshyn 84*)   39,180

Rangers: (4231) Butland; Tavernier, Souttar, Propper, Yilmaz (Davies 77); Diomande (Sterling 68), Barron; McCausland (Cerny 46), Lawrence (Matondo 85), Jefte■; Dessers.
Dynamo Kyiv: (433) Bushchan; Karavaev (Bilovar 90), Popov, Mykhavko, Dubinchak; Buyalskyi (Pikhalyonok 75), Brazhko, Shaparenko (Lonwijk 90); Yarmolenko (Voloshyn 68), Vanat, Kabayev (Braharu 75).
Dynamo Kyiv won 3-1 on aggregate.

QUALIFYING PLAY-OFFS – FIRST LEG
Tuesday, 20 August 2024

Bodo/Glimt v Red Star Belgrade	2-1
Dinamo Zagreb v Qarabag	3-0
Lille v Slavia Prague	2-0

Wednesday, 21 August 2024

Dynamo Kyiv† v Red Bull Salzburg	0-2
Malmo v Sparta Prague	0-2
Midtjylland v Slovan Bratislava	1-1
Young Boys v Galatasaray	3-2

QUALIFYING PLAY-OFFS – SECOND LEG (agg)
Tuesday, 27 August 2024

Galatasaray v Young Boys	0-1	2-4
Red Bull Salzburg v Dynamo Kyiv	1-1	3-1
Sparta Prague v Malmo	2-0	4-0

Wednesday, 28 August 2024

Qarabag v Dinamo Zagreb	0-2	0-5
Red Star Belgrade v Bodo/Glimt	2-0	3-2
Slavia Prague v Lille	2-1	2-3
Slovan Bratislava v Midtjylland	3-2	4-3

LEAGUE PHASE

LEAGUE MATCHDAY 1
Tuesday, 17 September 2024

AC Milan v Liverpool	1-3
Bayern Munich v Dinamo Zagreb	9-2
Juventus v PSV Eindhoven	3-1
Real Madrid v VfB Stuttgart	3-1
Sporting Lisbon v Lille	2-0
Young Boys v Aston Villa	0-3

Wednesday, 18 September 2024

Bologna v Shakhtar Donetsk	0-0
Celtic v Slovan Bratislava	5-1
Club Brugge v Borussia Dortmund	0-3
Manchester C v Internazionale	0-0
Paris Saint-Germain v Girona	1-0
Sparta Prague v Red Bull Salzburg	3-0

Thursday, 19 September 2024

Atalanta v Arsenal	0-0
Atletico Madrid v RB Leipzig	2-1
Brest v Sturm Graz	2-1
Feyenoord v Bayer Leverkusen	0-4
Monaco v Barcelona	2-1
Red Star Belgrade v Benfica	1-2

Tuesday, 17 September 2024
AC Milan (1) 1 *(Pulisic 3)*
Liverpool (2) 3 *(Konate 23, van Dijk 41, Szoboszlai 67)*
59,826
AC Milan: (4231) Maignan (Torriani 51); Calabria (Emerson Royal 70), Tomori (Gabbia 84), Pavlovic, Hernandez; Fofana, Loftus-Cheek (Abraham 69); Pulisic, Reijnders, Leao; Morata (Okafor 84).
Liverpool: (4231) Alisson; Alexander-Arnold (Gomez 79), Konate, van Dijk, Tsimikas; Gravenberch, Mac Allister (Endo 90); Salah (Chiesa 90), Szoboszlai, Gakpo (Diaz 68); Jota (Nunez 68).

Young Boys (0) 0
Aston Villa (2) 3 *(Tielemans 27, Ramsey 38, Onana 86)*
31,500
Young Boys: (4231) von Ballmoos; Athekame, Camara, Zoukrou, Hadjam (Conte 63); Niasse (Elia 46), Lauper; Monteiro (Males 83), Ugrinic, Colley (Virginius 63); Ganvoula (Itten 83).
Aston Villa: (4231) Martinez; Bogarde (Diego Carlos 84), Konsa, Torres, Digne (Barkley 88); Onana, Tielemans (Maatsen 87); McGinn, Rogers (Buendia 88), Ramsey; Watkins (Duran 60).

Wednesday, 18 September 2024
Celtic (1) 5 *(Scales 17, Furuhashi 47, Engels 56 (pen), Maeda 70, Idah 86)*
Slovan Bratislava (0) 1 *(Wimmer 60)*
56,826
Celtic: (433) Schmeichel; Johnston A (Ralston 77), Carter-Vickers (Trusty 85), Scales, Taylor; Engels, McGregor, Hatate (Bernardo 77); Kuhn (Forrest 71), Furuhashi (Idah 77), Maeda.
Slovan Bratislava: (4231) Takac; Blackman, Kashia, Bajric, Wimmer; Kucka (Gajdos 85), Ignatenko (Savvidis 76); Barseghyan (Marcelli 76), Tolic, Weiss (Mak 76); Strelec (Metsoko 85).

Manchester C (0) 0
Internazionale (0) 0
50,992
Manchester C: (3241) Ederson; Akanji, Dias, Gvardiol; Lewis, Rodri; Savio (Foden 46), Bernardo Silva (Doku 80), De Bruyne (Gundogan 46), Grealish; Haaland.
Internazionale: (352) Sommer; Bisseck (Pavard 75), Acerbi, Bastoni; Darmian (Dumfries 75), Barella, Calhanoglu (Frattesi 82), Zielinski (Mkhitaryan 66), Carlos Augusto; Thuram (Martinez L 65), Taremi.

Thursday, 19 September 2024
Atalanta (0) 0
Arsenal (0) 0
22,858
Atalanta: (3421) Carnesecchi; Djimsiti, Hien, Kolasinac; Zappacosta (Bellanova 70), de Roon, Ederson Silva, Ruggeri (Pasalic 89); De Ketelaere (Cuadrado 60), Lookman (Samardzic 89); Retegui (Zaniolo 70).
Arsenal: (433) Raya; White, Saliba, Gabriel, Timber (Calafiori 73); Havertz, Partey (Jorginho 58) Rice; Saka (Sterling 73), Gabriel Jesus (Trossard 58), Martinelli.

LEAGUE MATCHDAY 2
Tuesday, 1 October 2024
Arsenal v Paris Saint-Germain	2-0
Barcelona v Young Boys	5-0
Bayer Leverkusen v AC Milan	1-0
Borussia Dortmund v Celtic	7-1
Internazionale v Red Star Belgrade	4-0
PSV Eindhoven v Sporting Lisbon	1-1
Red Bull Salzburg v Brest	0-4
Slovan Bratislava v Manchester C	0-4
VfB Stuttgart v Sparta Prague	1-1

Wednesday, 2 October 2024
Aston Villa v Bayern Munich	1-0
Benfica v Atletico Madrid	4-0
Dinamo Zagreb v Monaco	2-2
Girona v Feyenoord	2-3
Lille v Real Madrid	1-0
Liverpool v Bologna	2-0
RB Leipzig v Juventus	2-3
Shakhtar Donetsk† v Atalanta	0-3
Sturm Graz v Club Brugge	0-1

Tuesday, 1 October 2024
Arsenal (2) 2 *(Havertz 20, Saka 35)*
Paris Saint-Germain (0) 0
60,103
Arsenal: (442) Raya; Timber (Kiwior 46), Saliba, Gabriel, Calafiori; Saka (Lewis-Skelly 90), Partey (Merino 64), Rice, Martinelli; Havertz, Trossard (Gabriel Jesus 74).
Paris Saint-Germain: (433) Donnarumma; Hakimi, Marquinhos, Pacho, Nuno Mendes; Zaire-Emery, Vitinha (Fabian 64), Neves; Doue (Muani 64), Lee, Barcola.

Borussia Dortmund (5) 7 *(Can 7 (pen), Adeyemi 11, 29, 42, Guirassy 40 (pen), 66, Nmecha 79)*
Celtic (1) 1 *(Maeda 9)*
81,365
Borussia Dortmund: (4231) Kobel; Yan Couto (Bensebaini 62), Anton, Schlotterbeck, Ryerson; Can, Gross (Nmecha 61); Adeyemi (Duranville 48), Brandt (Beier 61), Bynoe-Gittens; Guirassy (Sabitzer 70).
Celtic: (433) Schmeichel; Johnston A (Ralston 86), Trusty, Scales, Taylor (Valle 46); Engels, McGregor, Bernardo (Hatate 46); Kuhn (Yang 63), Furuhashi (Idah 63), Maeda.

Slovan Bratislava (0) 0
Manchester C (2) 4 *(Gundogan 8, Foden 15, Haaland 58, McAtee 74)*
22,500
Slovan Bratislava: (4231) Takac; Blackman, Kashia, Bajric, Wimmer; Ignatenko (Szoke 63), Savvidis; Barseghyan (Mak 85), Tolic (Pauschek 78), Weiss (Zuberu 63); Strelec (Marcelli 78).
Manchester C: (4231) Ortega; Lewis, Akanji (Dias 61), Stones, Gvardiol (Walker 78); Matheus Luiz, Gundogan; Doku, Foden (Grealish 78), Savio (McAtee 60); Haaland (McAtee 60).

Wednesday, 2 October 2024
Aston Villa (0) 1 *(Duran 79)*
Bayern Munich (0) 0
38,991
Aston Villa: (4231) Martinez; Konsa, Diego Carlos, Torres, Digne; Onana (Barkley 60), Tielemans; Philogene-Bidace, Rogers, Ramsey (Bailey 27 (Maatsen 60)); Watkins (Duran 70).
Bayern Munich: (4231) Neuer; Laimer (Tel 86), Upamecano, Kim (Goretzka 86), Davies; Kimmich, Pavlovic (Joao Palhinha 76); Gnabry, Olise (Sane 66), Coman (Musiala 46); Kane.

Liverpool (1) 2 *(Mac Allister 11, Salah 75)*
Bologna (0) 0
59,816
Liverpool: (4231) Alisson; Alexander-Arnold (Bradley 85), Konate, van Dijk, Robertson (Tsimikas 72); Gravenberch, Mac Allister; Salah, Szoboszlai (Jones 86), Diaz (Gakpo 72); Nunez (Jota 61).
Bologna: (4141) Skorupski; Posch, Beukema (Casale 62), Lucumi, Miranda; Freuler (Fabbian 84); Orsolini, Urbanski (Aebischer 61), Moro, Ndoye (Iling-Junior 79); Dallinga (Castro 79).

LEAGUE MATCHDAY 3
Tuesday, 22 October 2024
AC Milan v Club Brugge	3-1
Arsenal v Shakhtar Donetsk	1-0
Aston Villa v Bologna	2-0
Girona v Slovan Bratislava	2-0
Juventus v VfB Stuttgart	0-1
Monaco v Red Star Belgrade	5-1
Paris Saint-Germain v PSV Eindhoven	1-1
Real Madrid v Borussia Dortmund	5-2
Sturm Graz v Sporting Lisbon	0-2

Wednesday, 23 October 2024
Atalanta v Celtic	0-0
Atletico Madrid v Lille	1-3
Barcelona v Bayern Munich	4-1
Benfica v Feyenoord	1-3
Brest v Bayer Leverkusen	1-1
Manchester C v Sparta Prague	5-0
RB Leipzig v Juventus	0-1
Red Bull Salzburg v Dinamo Zagreb	0-2
Young Boys v Internazionale	0-1

Tuesday, 22 October 2024

Arsenal (1) 1 *(Riznyk 29 (og))*

Shakhtar Donetsk (0) 0   59,594

Arsenal: (442) Raya; White (Merino 46), Saliba, Gabriel, Calafiori (Lewis-Skelly 72); Gabriel Jesus (Sterling 68), Partey, Rice, Martinelli; Havertz, Trossard (Jorginho 88).
Shakhtar Donetsk: (4231) Riznyk; Konoplya, Bondar, Matviyenko, Pedrinho P; Bondarenko (Marlon Gomes 87), Kryskiv; Zubkov (Pedrinho S 64), Sudakov, Eguinaldo (Traore 84); Sikan (Kevin 64).

Aston Villa (0) 2 *(McGinn 55, Duran 64)*

Bologna (0) 0   41,847

Aston Villa: (4231) Martinez; Konsa, Diego Carlos, Torres, Maatsen; Onana (Barkley 46), Tielemans (Kamara 78); Bailey (Ramsey 65), Rogers, McGinn (Philogene-Bidace 65); Duran (Watkins 65).
Bologna: (433) Skorupski; Posch, Beukema, Lucumi, Lykogiannis; Urbanski (Moro 66), Freuler, Fabbian; Orsolini (Odgaard 46), Dallinga (Castro 66), Ndoye (Iling-Junior 77).

Wednesday, 23 October 2024

Atalanta (0) 0

Celtic (0) 0   21,614

Atalanta: (3412) Carnesecchi; Djimsiti, Hien, Kolasinac (Ruggeri 78); Bellanova (Samardzic 58), de Roon, Ederson Silva, Zappacosta; Pasalic (Zaniolo 78); Retegui (De Ketelaere 59), Lookman (Cuadrado 69).
Celtic: (433) Schmeichel; Johnston A, Trusty, Scales, Valle; Engels (McCowan 75), McGregor, Hatate (Bernardo 68); Kuhn (Forrest 81), Idah (Furuhashi 68), Maeda (Palma 74).

Manchester C (1) 5 *(Foden 3, Haaland 58, 68, Stones 64, Matheus Luiz 88 (pen))*

Sparta Prague (0) 0   50,116

Manchester C: (4141) Ortega; Lewis, Stones (Dias 74), Akanji, Ake (Gvardiol 74); Gundogan (Kovacic 69); Savio, Foden, Bernardo Silva (McAtee 69), Matheus Luiz; Haaland (O'Reilly 81).
Sparta Prague: (343) Vindahl-Jensen; Vitik, Panak, Sorensen; Preciado, Kairinen (Solbakken 89), Laci, Rynes (Wiesner 89); Birmancevic (Danek 74), Olatunji (Rahmani 60), Haraslin (Krasniqi 46).

RB Leipzig (0) 0

Liverpool (1) 1 *(Nunez 27)*   45,228

RB Leipzig: (442) Gulacsi; Geertruida (Bitshiabu 76), Orban, Lukeba, Henrichs; Nusa, Vermeeren (Kampl 74), Haidara (Elmas 86), Simons (Poulsen 78); Sesko (Baumgartner 74), Openda.
Liverpool: (433) Kelleher; Alexander-Arnold (Gomez 75), Konate, van Dijk, Tsimikas (Robertson 75); Szoboszlai, Gravenberch, Mac Allister; Salah (Diaz 63), Nunez (Jones 74), Gakpo.

LEAGUE MATCHDAY 4

Tuesday, 5 November 2024

Bologna v Monaco	0-1
Borussia Dortmund v Sturm Graz	1-0
Celtic v RB Leipzig	3-1
Lille v Juventus	1-1
Liverpool v Bayer Leverkusen	4-0
PSV Eindhoven v Girona	4-0
Real Madrid v AC Milan	1-3
Slovan Bratislava v Dinamo Zagreb	1-4
Sporting Lisbon v Manchester C	4-1

Wednesday, 6 November 2024

Bayern Munich v Benfica	1-0
Club Brugge v Aston Villa	1-0
Feyenoord v Red Bull Salzburg	1-3
Internazionale v Arsenal	1-0
Paris Saint-Germain v Atletico Madrid	1-2
Red Star Belgrade v Barcelona	2-5
Shakhtar Donetsk† v Young Boys	2-1
Sparta Prague v Brest	1-2
VfB Stuttgart v Atalanta	0-2

Tuesday, 5 November 2024

Celtic (2) 3 *(Kuhn 35, 45, Hatate 72)*

RB Leipzig (1) 1 *(Baumgartner 23)*   57,551

Celtic: (433) Schmeichel; Johnston A, Carter-Vickers (Scales 74), Trusty, Taylor (Valle 68); Engels (Bernardo 68), McGregor, Hatate; Kuhn (Yang 74), Furuhashi (Idah 82), Maeda.
RB Leipzig: (442) Gulacsi; Geertruida, Orban, Bitshiabu, Henrichs; Baumgartner (Ouedraogo 76), Haidara (Seiwald 76), Kampl, Nusa (Elmas 68); Sesko (Poulsen 68), Openda (Andre Silva 81).

Liverpool (0) 4 *(Diaz 61, 83, 90, Gakpo 63)*

Bayer Leverkusen (0) 0   59,790

Liverpool: (433) Kelleher; Alexander-Arnold (Bradley 81), Konate (Quansah 88), van Dijk, Tsimikas (Robertson 80); Jones (Szoboszlai 73), Gravenberch, Mac Allister; Salah, Diaz, Gakpo (Nunez 80).
Bayer Leverkusen: (352) Hradecky; Tapsoba, Tah, Hincapie; Frimpong, Palacios (Hofmann 73), Xhaka, Garcia (Andrich 73), Grimaldo (Tella 81); Wirtz, Boniface (Schick 81).

Sporting Lisbon (1) 4 *(Gyokeres 38, 49 (pen), 80 (pen), Araujo 46)*

Manchester C (1) 1 *(Foden 4)*   47,453

Sporting Lisbon: (3421) Israel; Debast, Diomande, Matheus Reis (St Juste 75); Quenda (Quaresma 85), Morita (Braganca 75), Hjulmand, Araujo (Catamo 75); Trincao (Harder 88), Goncalves; Gyokeres.
Manchester C: (4141) Ederson; Lewis, Simpson-Pusey, Akanji, Gvardiol; Kovacic (De Bruyne 84); Savio (Doku 77), Foden, Bernardo Silva (Gundogan 77), Matheus Luiz; Haaland.

Wednesday, 6 November 2024

Club Brugge (1) 1 *(Vanaken 52 (pen))*

Aston Villa (0) 0   23,466

Club Brugge: (4231) Mignolet; Seys, Ordonez, Mechele, De Cuyper; Nielsen (Vetlesen 76), Jashari; Skov Olsen (Talbi 72), Vanaken, Tzolis (Meijer 75); Jutgla (Vermant 90).
Aston Villa: (4231) Martinez; Konsa, Diego Carlos (Nedeljkovic 80), Mings (Torres 66), Maatsen; Kamara, Tielemans; Bailey, McGinn (Duran 58), Rogers (Ramsey 66); Watkins (Buendia 80).

Internazionale (1) 1 *(Calhanoglu 45 (pen))*

Arsenal (0) 0   75,222

Internazionale: (352) Sommer; Pavard, de Vrij, Bisseck; Dumfries, Frattesi (Barella 62), Calhanoglu (Asllani 71), Zielinski (Mkhitaryan 62), Darmian; Taremi (Dimarco 79), Martinez L (Thuram 62).
Arsenal: (442) Raya; White, Saliba, Gabriel, Timber (Zinchenko 82); Saka, Partey, Merino (Gabriel Jesus 46), Martinelli; Trossard (Nwaneri 82), Havertz (Odegaard 90).

LEAGUE MATCHDAY 5

Tuesday, 26 November 2024

Barcelona v Brest	3-0
Bayer Leverkusen v Red Bull Salzburg	5-0
Bayern Munich v Paris Saint-Germain	1-0
Internazionale v RB Leipzig	1-0
Manchester C v Feyenoord	3-3
Slovan Bratislava v AC Milan	2-3
Sparta Prague v Atletico Madrid	0-6
Sporting Lisbon v Arsenal	1-5
Young Boys v Atalanta	1-6

Wednesday, 27 November 2024

Aston Villa v Juventus	0-0
Bologna v Lille	1-2
Celtic v Club Brugge	1-1
Dinamo Zagreb v Borussia Dortmund	0-3
Liverpool v Real Madrid	2-0
Monaco v Benfica	2-3
PSV Eindhoven v Shakhtar Donetsk	3-2
Red Star Belgrade v VfB Stuttgart	5-1
Sturm Graz v Girona	1-0

Tuesday, 26 November 2024

Manchester C (1) 3 *(Haaland 44 (pen), 53, Gundogan 50)*
Feyenoord (0) 3 *(Hadj Moussa 74, Gimenez 82, Hancko 89)*　　　　　　　　　　　　47,011
Manchester C: (4231) Ederson; Lewis, Akanji, Ake (Simpson-Pusey 69), Gvardiol; Matheus Luiz, Gundogan (De Bruyne 68); Bernardo Silva, Foden (McAtee 69), Grealish; Haaland.
Feyenoord: (433) Wellenreuther; Nieuwkoop (Lotomba 72), Trauner, Hancko, Smal (Beelen 68); Milambo (Zerrouki 68), Hwang (Gonzalez 90), Timber; Hadj Moussa, Carranza (Gimenez 72), Igor Paixao.

Sporting Lisbon (0) 1 *(Inacio 47)*
Arsenal (3) 5 *(Martinelli 7, Havertz 22, Gabriel 45, Saka 65 (pen), Trossard 82)*　　　　　　47,386
Sporting Lisbon: (3421) Israel; St Juste, Diomande, Inacio (Matheus Reis 88); Quenda, Hjulmund, Morita (Harder 78), Araujo (Catamo 68); Trincao (Simoes 88), Edwards (Braganca 68); Gyokeres.
Arsenal: (433) Raya; Timber, Saliba, Gabriel (Kiwior 84), Calafiori (Zinchenko 78); Odegaard (Nwaneri 78), Partey, Rice (Merino 70); Saka, Havertz, Martinelli (Trossard 70).

Wednesday, 27 November 2024

Aston Villa (0) 0
Juventus (0) 0　　　　　　　　　　　　　42,589
Aston Villa: (4231) Martinez; Cash, Diego Carlos, Torres, Digne; Kamara (Barkley 78), Tielemans; Bailey (Philogene-Bidace 86), McGinn, Rogers; Watkins (Duran 78).
Juventus: (4231) Di Gregorio; Savona (Danilo 66), Kalulu Kyatengwa, Gatti, Cambiaso; Locatelli, Thuram (Fagioli 86); Francisco Conceicao, Koopmeiners, Yildiz (Mbangula 82); Weah.

Celtic (0) 1 *(Maeda 60)*
Club Brugge (1) 1 *(Carter-Vickers 26 (og))*　　57,456
Celtic: (433) Schmeichel; Johnston A, Carter-Vickers, Trusty, Taylor (Valle 59); Engels (Bernardo 59), McGregor, Hatate; Kuhn (Yang 88), Furuhashi (Idah 76), Maeda (Forrest 76).
Club Brugge: (4231) Mignolet; Seys, Ordonez, Mechele, De Cuyper; Nwadike, Jashari, Skov Olsen (Talbi 77), Vanaken, Tzolis (Nielsen 90); Jutgla (Vermant 77).

Liverpool (0) 2 *(Mac Allister 52, Gakpo 76)*
Real Madrid (0) 0　　　　　　　　　　　59,546
Liverpool: (433) Kelleher; Bradley (Gomez 87), Konate, van Dijk, Robertson; Jones (Szoboszlai 83), Gravenberch, Mac Allister; Salah, Nunez (Gakpo 68), Diaz.
Real Madrid: (4222) Courtois; Valverde, Asencio, Rudiger, Mendy (Garcia 71); Camavinga (Ceballos 57), Modric (Endrick 79); Guler (Lucas 56), Bellingham; Diaz, Mbappe.

LEAGUE MATCHDAY 6

Tuesday, 10 December 2024

Atalanta v Real Madrid	2-3
Bayer Leverkusen v Internazionale	1-0
Brest v PSV Eindhoven	1-0
Club Brugge v Sporting Lisbon	2-1
Dinamo Zagreb v Celtic	0-0
Girona v Liverpool	0-1
RB Leipzig v Aston Villa	2-3
Red Bull Salzburg v Paris Saint-Germain	0-3
Shakhtar Donetsk† v Bayern Munich	1-5

Wednesday, 11 December 2024

AC Milan v Red Star Belgrade	2-1
Arsenal v Monaco	3-0
Atletico Madrid v Slovan Bratislava	3-1
Benfica v Bologna	0-0
Borussia Dortmund v Barcelona	2-3
Feyenoord v Sparta Prague	4-2
Juventus v Manchester C	2-0
Lille v Sturm Graz	3-2
VfB Stuttgart v Young Boys	5-1

Tuesday, 10 December 2024

Dinamo Zagreb (0) 0
Celtic (0) 0　　　　　　　　　　　　18,158
Dinamo Zagreb: (4231) Zagorac; Ristovski, Bernauer, Theophile-Catherine, Pierre Gabriel; Kacavenda, Rog; Spikic (Mbuku 73), Baturina (Stojkovic 82), Pjaca (Hoxha 82); Kulenovic.
Celtic: (433) Schmeichel; Johnston A (Ralston 46), Carter-Vickers, Trusty, Taylor; Bernardo (Engels 65), McGregor, Hatate (McCowan 65); Kuhn, Furuhashi (Idah 72), Maeda (Forrest 72).

Girona (0) 0
Liverpool (0) 1 *(Salah 63 (pen))*　　　　9241
Girona: (4231) Gazzaniga; Frances, Juanpe, Krejci, Blind (Solis 77); van de Beek (Martin 76); Romeu; Gil Salvatierra (Portu 71), Asprilla, Gutierrez; Danjuma (Stuani 72).
Liverpool: (433) Alisson; Alexander-Arnold, Gomez, van Dijk, Robertson; Szoboszlai, Gravenberch, Jones (Elliott 76); Salah, Nunez (Gakpo 71), Diaz (Endo 89).

RB Leipzig (1) 2 *(Openda 27, Baumgartner 62)*
Aston Villa (1) 3 *(McGinn 3, Duran 52, Barkley 85)* 40,406
RB Leipzig: (442) Gulacsi; Seiwald, Geertruida, Orban, Henrichs; Baumgartner, Vermeeren (Klostermann 84), Haidara (Kampl 46), Nusa; Sesko (Andre Silva 76), Openda.
Aston Villa: (4231) Martinez; Konsa, Diego Carlos, Torres, Digne (Maatsen 83); Tielemans (Barkley 83), Kamara; Cash (Nedeljkovic 71), Rogers, McGinn (Buendia 76); Watkins (Duran 46).

Wednesday, 11 December 2024

Arsenal (1) 3 *(Saka 34, 78, Havertz 88)*
Monaco (0) 0　　　　　　　　　　　　60,157
Arsenal: (433) Raya; Partey, Saliba, Kiwior, Lewis-Skelly (Timber 64); Odegaard (Nwaneri 79), Rice (Jorginho 64), Merino; Saka, Gabriel Jesus (Havertz 73), Martinelli (Trossard 64).
Monaco: (4231) Majecki; Vanderson (Teze 81), Kehrer, Salisu, Henrique; Camara (Matazo 81), Magassa (Minamino 46); Akliouche, Golovin, Ben Seghir; Embolo (Ilenikhena 81).

Juventus (0) 2 *(Vlahovic 53, McKennie 75)*
Manchester C (0) 0　　　　　　　　　　40,890
Juventus: (4231) Di Gregorio; Savona, Gatti, Kalulu Kyatengwa, Danilo; Locatelli, Thuram (McKennie 69); Francisco Conceicao (Weah 69), Koopmeiners, Yildiz (Mbangula 84); Vlahovic (Douglas Luiz 85).
Manchester C: (4231) Ederson; Walker, Dias, Gvardiol, Lewis; Gundogan, Grealish (Matheus Luiz 87); Bernardo Silva, De Bruyne, Doku (Savio 79); Haaland.

LEAGUE MATCHDAY 7

Tuesday, 21 January 2025

Atalanta v Sturm Graz	5-0
Atletico Madrid v Bayer Leverkusen	2-1
Benfica v Barcelona	4-5
Bologna v Borussia Dortmund	2-1
Club Brugge v Juventus	0-0
Liverpool v Lille	2-1
Monaco v Aston Villa	1-0
Red Star Belgrade v PSV Eindhoven	2-3
Slovan Bratislava v VfB Stuttgart	1-3

Wednesday, 22 January 2025

AC Milan v Girona	1-0
Arsenal v Dinamo Zagreb	3-0
Celtic v Young Boys	1-0
Feyenoord v Bayern Munich	3-0
Paris Saint-Germain v Manchester C	4-2
RB Leipzig v Sporting Lisbon	2-1
Real Madrid v Red Bull Salzburg	5-1
Shakhtar Donetsk† v Brest	2-0
Sparta Prague v Internazionale	0-1

Tuesday, 21 January 2025

Liverpool (1) 2 *(Salah 34, Elliott 67)*

Lille (0) 1 *(David 62)* 59,782

Liverpool: (433) Alisson; Bradley (Alexander-Arnold 86), Quansah, van Dijk, Tsimikas; Szoboszlai (Endo 63), Gravenberch (Mac Allister 46), Jones (Elliott 46); Salah, Nunez, Diaz (Chiesa 75).
Lille: (4231) Chevalier; Mandi■, Diakite, Alexsandro Victor, Gudmundsson (Ismaily 74); Mukau (Bouaddi 74), Andre; Bakker (Meunier 63), Arnar Haraldsson, Cabella (Sahraoui 63); David.

Monaco (1) 1 *(Singo 8)*

Aston Villa (0) 0 13,508

Monaco: (4231) Majecki; Vanderson, Singo, Kehrer, Mawissa Elebi; Camara (Magassa 65), Zakaria (Teze 79); Akliouche, Minamino (Michal 78), Ben Seghir (Golovin 66); Embolo.
Aston Villa: (4231) Martinez; Cash, Konsa, Mings, Digne (Maatsen 65); Kamara, Tielemans; Bailey (Duran 57), Rogers (Ramsey 86), Buendia (Bogarde 86); Watkins.

Wednesday, 22 January 2025

Arsenal (1) 3 *(Rice 2, Havertz 66, Odegaard 90)*

Dinamo Zagreb (0) 0 60,024

Arsenal: (433) Raya; Timber (Partey 59), Kiwior, Gabriel, Zinchenko (Tierney 74); Odegaard, Jorginho, Rice; Sterling (Nwaneri 58), Havertz (Trossard 74), Martinelli (Butler-Oyedeji 90).
Dinamo Zagreb: (541) Nevistic; Ristovski, Mmaee, Bernauer, Torrente, Pierre Gabriel (Hoxha 75); Stojkovic (Pjaca 74), Rog (Kacavenda 59), Ademi (Misic 59), Baturina (Spikic 87); Kulenovic.

Celtic (0) 1 *(Benito 86 (og))*

Young Boys (0) 0 56,544

Celtic: (433) Schmeichel; Johnston A, Carter-Vickers, Trusty, Taylor (Valle 69); Engels (Bernardo 69), McGregor, Hatate; Kuhn (Scales 90), Furuhashi (Idah 75), Maeda■.
Young Boys: (4231) Keller; Athekame (Blum 84), Camara, Benito, Hadjam; Niasse (Lauper 84), Lakomy; Males (Chaiwa 64), Ugrinic, Monteiro (Colley 72); Ganvoula (Itten 64).

Paris Saint-Germain (0) 4 *(Dembele 56, Barcola 60, Neves 78, Goncalo Ramos 90)*

Manchester C (0) 2 *(Grealish 50, Haaland 53)* 47,818

Paris Saint-Germain: (433) Donnarumma; Hakimi, Marquinhos, Pacho, Nuno Mendes; Neves, Vitinha, Fabian (Zaire-Emery 61); Doue (Goncalo Ramos 61), Lee (Dembele 46), Barcola (Hernandez 81).
Manchester C: (4231) Ederson; Matheus Luiz (Stones 78), Akanji, Dias (Lewis 46), Gvardiol; Bernardo Silva, Kovacic (Gundogan 70); Foden, De Bruyne (McAtee 70), Savio (Grealish 46); Haaland.

LEAGUE MATCHDAY 8

Wednesday, 29 January 2025

Aston Villa v Celtic	4-2
Barcelona v Atalanta	2-2
Bayer Leverkusen v Sparta Prague	2-0
Bayern Munich v Slovan Bratislava	3-1
Borussia Dortmund v Shakhtar Donetsk	3-1
Brest v Real Madrid	0-3
Dinamo Zagreb v AC Milan	2-1
Girona v Arsenal	1-2
Internazionale v Monaco	3-0
Juventus v Benfica	0-2
Lille v Feyenoord	6-1
Manchester C v Club Brugge	3-1
PSV Eindhoven v Liverpool	3-2
Red Bull Salzburg v Atletico Madrid	1-4
Sporting Lisbon v Bologna	1-1
Sturm Graz v RB Leipzig	1-0
VfB Stuttgart v Paris Saint-Germain	1-4
Young Boys v Red Star Belgrade	0-1

Wednesday, 29 January 2025

Aston Villa (2) 4 *(Rogers 3, 5, 90, Watkins 60)*

Celtic (2) 2 *(Idah 36, 38)* 42,824

Aston Villa: (4231) Martinez; Cash (McGinn 30), Konsa, Kamara, Digne (Maatsen 74); Bogarde, Tielemans; Bailey, Rogers, Ramsey; Watkins.
Celtic: (433) Schmeichel; Johnston A, Trusty, Scales (Murray 83), Taylor; Engels (Bernardo 73), McGregor, Hatate (McCowan 82); Kuhn, Idah (Cummings 79), Yang (Palma 73).

Girona (1) 1 *(Danjuma 28)*

Arsenal (2) 2 *(Jorginho 38 (pen), Nwaneri 42)* 9048

Girona: (4231) Pau Lopez; Martinez, Yaakobishvili, Juanpe, Frances; Romeu (Herrera 57), Martin (van de Beek 68); Tsygankov (Portu 68), Asprilla (Solis 57), Danjuma; Ruiz A (Stuani 57).
Arsenal: (433) Neto; Partey (Timber 46), Kiwior, Gabriel, Calafiori (Lewis-Skelly 70); Odegaard, Jorginho (Rice 82), Merino; Nwaneri (Martinelli 87), Trossard (Havertz 70), Sterling.

Manchester C (0) 3 *(Kovacic 53, Ordonez 62 (og), Savio 77)*

Club Brugge (1) 1 *(Nwadike 45)* 51,237

Manchester C: (4231) Ederson; Matheus Luiz, Stones, Akanji, Gvardiol; Kovacic, Gundogan (Savio 46); Bernardo Silva, De Bruyne (Lewis 81), Foden; Haaland.
Club Brugge: (4231) Mignolet; Seys, Ordonez, Mechele, De Cuyper; Nwadike, Jashari; Talbi (Skoras 70), Vanaken, Tzolis (Vetlesen 70); Jutgla (Vermant 70).

PSV Eindhoven (3) 3 *(Bakayoko 35, Saibari 45, Pepi 45)*

Liverpool (2) 2 *(Gakpo 28 (pen), Elliott 40)* 35,000

PSV Eindhoven: (442) Benitez; Karsdorp (Ledezma 66), Obispo (Nagalo 76), Boscagli, Junior; Bakayoko, Land, Veerman, Saibari (Driouech 76); Pepi (de Jong 76), Til (Babadi 90).
Liverpool: (433) Kelleher; Bradley, Quansah, Robertson (Nyoni 64), Tsimikas; Elliott, Endo, McConnell; Chiesa, Danns (Nallo■ 83), Gakpo (Morton 52).

UEFA Champions League – League Phase Final Table

		P	W	D	L	F	A	GD	Pts
1	Liverpool	8	7	0	1	17	5	12	21
2	Barcelona	8	6	1	1	28	13	15	19
3	Arsenal	8	6	1	1	16	3	13	19
4	Internazionale	8	6	1	1	11	1	10	19
5	Atletico Madrid	8	6	0	2	20	12	8	18
6	Bayer Leverkusen	8	5	1	2	15	7	8	16
7	Lille	8	5	1	2	17	10	7	16
8	Aston Villa	8	5	1	2	13	6	7	16
9	Atalanta	8	4	3	1	20	6	14	15
10	Borussia Dortmund	8	5	0	3	22	12	10	15
11	Real Madrid*	8	5	0	3	20	12	8	15
12	Bayern Munich*	8	5	0	3	20	12	8	15
13	AC Milan	8	5	0	3	14	11	3	15
14	PSV Eindhoven	8	4	2	2	16	12	4	14
15	Paris Saint-Germain	8	4	1	3	14	9	5	13
16	Benfica	8	4	1	3	16	12	4	13
17	Monaco	8	4	1	3	13	13	0	13
18	Brest	8	4	1	3	10	11	–1	13
19	Feyenoord	8	4	1	3	18	21	–3	13
20	Juventus	8	3	3	2	9	7	2	12
21	Celtic	8	3	3	2	13	14	–1	12
22	Manchester C	8	3	2	3	18	14	4	11
23	Sporting Lisbon	8	3	2	3	13	12	1	11
24	Club Brugge	8	3	2	3	7	11	–4	11
25	Dinamo Zagreb	8	3	2	3	12	19	–7	11
26	VfB Stuttgart	8	3	1	4	13	17	–4	10
27	Shakhtar Donetsk†	8	2	1	5	8	16	–8	7
28	Bologna	8	1	3	4	4	9	–5	6
29	Red Star Belgrade	8	2	0	6	13	22	–9	6
30	Sturm Graz	8	2	0	6	5	14	–9	6
31	Sparta Prague	8	1	1	6	7	21	–14	4
32	RB Leipzig	8	1	0	7	8	15	–7	3
33	Girona	8	1	0	7	5	13	–8	3
34	Red Bull Salzburg	8	1	0	7	6	19	–13	3
35	Slovan Bratislava	8	0	0	8	7	27	–20	0
36	Young Boys	8	0	0	8	3	24	–21	0

*Ranking decided on away wins. Real Madrid 2, Bayern Munich 1.
Positions 1–8 qualify for Round of 16;
Positions 9–24 qualify for League Phase Play-offs;
Positions 25–36 eliminated.*

LEAGUE PHASE PLAY-OFFS – FIRST LEG
Tuesday, 11 February 2025
Brest (0) 0
Paris Saint-Germain (2) 3 *(Vitinha 21 (pen),*
Dembele 45, 66)   15,831
Brest: (4312) Bizot; Lala, Chardonnet, Coulibaly, Haidara; Camara (Pereira Lage 83), Lees-Melou (Salah 83), Magnetti (Fernandes 64); Faivre (Doumbia 72); Ajorque, Sima (Balde 64).
Paris Saint-Germain: (433) Donnarumma; Hakimi, Marquinhos, Pacho, Nuno Mendes; Neves, Vitinha, Fabian; Doue (Kvaratskhelia 67), Dembele (Goncalo Ramos 82), Barcola (Lee 75).

Juventus (1) 2 *(McKennie 34, Mbangula 82)*
PSV Eindhoven (0) 1 *(Perisic 56)*
    39,886
Juventus: (4231) Di Gregorio; Weah, Gatti, Veiga, Kelly; Douglas Luiz, Locatelli (Thuram 68); Gonzalez (Francisco Conceicao 58), McKennie (Koopmeiners 68), Yildiz (Mbangula 46); Muani (Vlahovic 77).
PSV Eindhoven: (4231) Benitez; Ledezma, Flamingo, Obispo, Junior; Schouten, Veerman; Perisic, Saibari (Til 72), Lang (Bakayoko 72); de Jong.

Manchester C (1) 2 *(Haaland 19, 80 (pen))*
Real Madrid (0) 3 *(Mbappe 60, Diaz 86, Bellingham 90)*
    52,081
Manchester C: (4141) Ederson; Akanji (Lewis 46), Dias, Ake (Kovacic 61), Gvardiol; Stones; Savio (Marmoush 84), De Bruyne (Gundogan 84), Silva, Grealish (Foden 30); Haaland.
Real Madrid: (442) Courtois; Valverde, Tchouameni, Asencio, Mendy; Rodrygo (Diaz 84), Camavinga, Ceballos (Modric 81), Bellingham; Mbappe (Garcia 90), Vinicius Junior.

Sporting Lisbon (0) 0
Borussia Dortmund (0) 3 *(Guirassy 60, Gross 68,*
Adeyemi 82)   41,543
Sporting Lisbon: (4231) Rui Silva; Fresneda (Quaresma 73), Diomande, St Juste, Matheus Reis (Braganca 62); Debast (Gabriel Teixeira 73), Simoes (Morita 62); Quenda, Trincao, Araujo; Harder (Gyokeres 59).
Borussia Dortmund: (4231) Kobel; Ryerson, Can, Schlotterbeck, Svensson (Sule 90); Sabitzer, Gross (Ozcan 90); Adeyemi (Chukwuemeka 86), Brandt (Duranville 86), Bynoe-Gittens (Beier 65); Guirassy.

Wednesday, 12 February 2025
Celtic (0) 1 *(Maeda 79)*
Bayern Munich (1) 2 *(Olise 45, Kane 49)*   57,406
Celtic: (433) Schmeichel; Johnston, Carter-Vickers, Trusty, Taylor (Schlupp 65); Engels, McGregor, Hatate; Kuhn (Yang 77), Idah (Jota 65), Maeda.
Bayern Munich: (4231) Neuer; Laimer, Upamecano, Dier, Guerreiro (Ito 78); Kimmich, Goretzka; Olise (Gnabry 65), Musiala (Muller 87), Sane (Coman 65); Kane.

Club Brugge (1) 2 *(Jutgla 15, Nilsson 90 (pen))*
Atalanta (1) 1 *(Pasalic 41)*   24,242
Club Brugge: (4231) Mignolet; Seys, Ordonez, Mechele, De Cuyper; Nwadike, Jashari; Talbi (Siquet 86), Vanaken, Tzolis (Nilsson 70); Jutgla (Vetlesen 86).
Atalanta: (3412) Rui Patricio; Djimsiti, Hien, Posch (Toloi 71); Bellanova (Cuadrado 63), Ederson Silva, de Roon, Zappacosta (Palestra 86); Pasalic (Samardzic 63); De Ketelaere, Retegui (Brescianini 71).

Feyenoord (1) 1 *(Igor Paixao 3)*
AC Milan (0) 0   45,000
Feyenoord: (433) Wellenreuther; Read (Mitchell 79), Beelen, Hancko, Smal (Bueno 70); Moder, Milambo, Timber (Osman 79); Hadj Moussa, Ueda (Carranza 46), Igor Paixao (Ivanusec 85).
AC Milan: (4231) Maignan; Walker, Thiaw (Tomori 60), Pavlovic, Hernandez; Fofana, Reijnders; Pulisic (Chukwueze 60), Joao Felix, Leao (Camarda 83); Gimenez (Abraham 83).

Monaco (0) 0
Benfica (0) 1 *(Pavlidis 48)*   12,159
Monaco: (4231) Majecki; Vanderson, Kehrer, Salisu, Diatta; Zakaria, Al Musrati■; Akliouche (Minamino 68), Embolo, Golovin (Ben Seghir 67); Biereth (Magassa 57).
Benfica: (433) Trubin; Araujo (Di Maria 67 (Arthur Cabral 86)), Silva, Otamendi, Carreras; Aursnes, Florentino (Barreiro 67), Kokcu; Akturkoglu, Pavlidis (Belotti 78), Schjelderup (Amdouni 78).

LEAGUE PHASE PLAY-OFFS – SECOND LEG
Tuesday, 18 February 2025
AC Milan (1) 1 *(Gimenez 1)*
Feyenoord (0) 1 *(Carranza 73)*   54,749
AC Milan: (4231) Maignan; Walker, Thiaw, Pavlovic, Hernandez■; Musah (Chukwueze 82), Reijnders (Abraham 83); Pulisic (Bartesaghi 63), Joao Felix, Leao; Gimenez (Fofana 71).
Feyenoord: (433) Wellenreuther; Read■, Beelen, Hancko, Smal; Milambo, Moder, Bueno (Stengs 75); Hadj Moussa (Mitchell 87), Redmond (Carranza 64), Igor Paixao.
Feyenoord won 2-1 on aggregate.

Atalanta (0) 1 *(Lookman 46)*
Club Brugge (3) 3 *(Talbi 3, 27, Jutgla 45)*   21,727
Atalanta: (3412) Carnesecchi; Toloi■, Djimsiti, Kolasinac (Posch 77); Cuadrado (Bellanova 75), Ederson Silva (Brescianini 83), de Roon, Zappacosta; Pasalic (Lookman 46); De Ketelaere, Retegui (Samardzic 75).
Club Brugge: (4231) Mignolet; Seys, Ordonez, Mechele, De Cuyper; Nwadike, Jashari; Talbi (Siquet 54), Vanaken, Tzolis (Nielsen 75); Jutgla (Nilsson 86).
Club Brugge won 5-2 on aggregate.

Bayern Munich (0) 1 *(Davies 90)*
Celtic (0) 1 *(Kuhn 63)*   75,000
Bayern Munich: (4231) Neuer; Stanisic, Upamecano, Kim, Guerreiro (Davies 64); Kimmich, Goretzka; Olise, Musiala (Muller 90), Gnabry (Sane 64); Kane (Coman 46).
Celtic: (433) Schmeichel; Johnston, Carter-Vickers, Trusty, Schlupp; Engels, McGregor, Hatate; Kuhn (Yang 69), Maeda, Jota (Idah 60).
Bayern Munich won 3-2 on aggregate.

Benfica (1) 3 *(Akturkoglu 22, Pavlidis 76 (pen), Kokcu 84)*
Monaco (1) 3 *(Minamino 32, Ben Seghir 51,*
Ilenikhena 81)   60,776
Benfica: (433) Trubin; Araujo, Silva, Otamendi, Carreras; Aursnes, Barreiro, Kokcu (Rego 87); Akturkoglu (Amdouni 58), Pavlidis (Belotti 87), Schjelderup (Dahl 58).
Monaco: (532) Majecki; Diatta, Singo, Kehrer, Mawissa Elebi (Ilenikhena 80), Henrique (Ouattara 80); Akliouche, Camara, Ben Seghir; Minamino (Michal 87), Embolo (Biereth 65).
Benfica won 4-3 on aggregate.

Wednesday, 19 February 2025
Borussia Dortmund (0) 0
Sporting Lisbon (0) 0   80,300
Borussia Dortmund: (4231) Kobel; Ryerson, Can, Schlotterbeck, Svensson; Sabitzer (Anton 89), Gross; Adeyemi (Bensebaini 89), Brandt (Reyna 69), Bynoe-Gittens (Beier 46); Guirassy (Duranville 69).
Sporting Lisbon: (3421) Rui Silva; Quaresma, Diomande, Inacio (Afonso Moreira 56); Ricardo Esgaio, Hjulmand (Brito 46), Simoes (Debast 40), Matheus Reis; Quenda (Anjos 84), Gabriel Teixeira (Araujo 56); Harder.
Borussia Dortmund won 3-0 on aggregate.

Paris Saint-Germain (2) 7 *(Barcola 20, Kvaratskhelia 39,*
Vitinha 59, Doue 64, Nuno Mendes 69,
Goncalo Ramos 76, Mayulu 86)
Brest (0) 0   47,211
Paris Saint-Germain: (433) Donnarumma; Hakimi, Marquinhos, Pacho (Kimpembe 72), Nuno Mendes; Neves (Mayulu 72), Vitinha, Fabian (Lee 60); Kvaratskhelia, Dembele (Doue 60), Barcola (Goncalo Ramos 61).

Brest: (4411) Coudert; Zogbe, Chardonnet, Coulibaly, Haidara (Le Cardinal 70); Balde (Camara 60), Lees-Melou (Martin 82), Fernandes (Magnetti 60), Pereira Lage; Faivre (Doumbia 70); Sima.
Paris Saint-Germain won 10-0 on aggregate.

PSV Eindhoven (0) 3 *(Perisic 53, Saibari 74, Flamingo 98)*
Juventus (0) 1 *(Weah 63)* 35,000
PSV Eindhoven: (4231) Benitez; Ledezma (Malacia 78), Flamingo, Boscagli (Obispo 106), Junior; Schouten (Til 72), Veerman (Nagalo 116); Perisic (Bakayoko 85), Saibari, Lang (Driouech 115); de Jong.
Juventus: (4231) Di Gregorio; Weah, Gatti, Veiga (Cambiaso 12 (Mbangula 91)), Kelly; Koopmeiners (Savona 77), Locatelli (Thuram 77); Francisco Conceicao (Yildiz 77), McKennie, Gonzalez; Muani (Vlahovic 90).
aet; PSV Eindhoven won 4-3 on aggregate.

ROUND OF 16 – FIRST LEG
Tuesday, 4 March 2025

Borussia Dortmund (1) 1 *(Adeyemi 22)*
Lille (0) 1 *(Arnar Haraldsson 68)* 81,365
Borussia Dortmund: (4231) Kobel; Ryerson (Yan Couto 82), Can, Schlotterbeck, Svensson (Bensebaini 83); Sabitzer, Gross; Adeyemi, Brandt (Reyna 83), Bynoe-Gittens (Beier 66); Guirassy.
Lille: (4231) Chevalier; Meunier, Diakite, Alexsandro Victor, Ismaily (Bakker 77); Andre, Bouaddi; Mbappe (Fernandez 71), Mukau (Andre Gomes 77), Arnar Haraldsson; David.

Club Brugge (1) 1 *(De Cuyper 12)*
Aston Villa (1) 3 *(Bailey 3, Mechele 82 (og), Asensio 88 (pen))*
26,890
Club Brugge: (4231) Mignolet; Sabbe (Skoras 90), Ordonez, Mechele, De Cuyper; Nwadike (Vetlesen 90), Jashari; Talbi (Siquet 85), Vanaken, Tzolis; Jutgla (Nilsson 86).
Aston Villa: (4231) Martinez; Disasi (Cash 64), Konsa, Mings, Digne; McGinn (Ramsey 64), Tielemans; Bailey (Kamara 64), Rogers, Rashford (Asensio 64); Watkins (Bogarde 90).

PSV Eindhoven (1) 1 *(Lang 43 (pen))*
Arsenal (3) 7 *(Timber 18, Nwaneri 21, Merino 31, Odegaard 47, 73, Trossard 48, Calafiori 85)* 34,400
PSV Eindhoven: (4231) Benitez; Ledezma (Karsdorp 65), Flamingo (Nagalo 46), Boscagli (Obispo 82), Malacia; Schouten, Saibari (Veerman 82); Perisic, Til, Lang; de Jong (Bakayoko 65).
Arsenal: (433) Raya; Timber (White 77), Saliba, Gabriel, Lewis-Skelly (Calafiori 35); Odegaard, Partey (Zinchenko 71), Rice; Nwaneri (Sterling 71), Merino (Tierney 77), Trossard.

Real Madrid (1) 2 *(Rodrygo 4, Diaz 55)*
Atletico Madrid (1) 1 *(Alvarez 32)* 77,261
Real Madrid: (442) Courtois; Valverde (Lucas 82), Asencio, Rudiger, Mendy; Rodrygo, Tchouameni, Camavinga (Modric 62), Diaz (Endrick 89); Mbappe, Vinicius Junior.
Atletico Madrid: (442) Oblak; Llorente, Gimenez, Lenglet, Galan; Simeone (Molina 64), De Paul (Correa 75), Barrios (Sorloth 75), Samuel Dias (Gallagher 64); Alvarez, Griezmann (Le Normand 71).

Wednesday, 5 March 2025

Bayern Munich (1) 3 *(Kane 9, 75 (pen), Musiala 54)*
Bayer Leverkusen (0) 0 75,000
Bayern Munich: (4231) Neuer (Urbig 58); Laimer (Stanisic 68), Upamecano, Kim (Dier 89), Davies; Goretzka (Joao Palhinha 89), Kimmich; Olise, Musiala, Coman (Sane 68); Kane.
Bayer Leverkusen: (442) Kovar, Mukiele■, Tah, Hermoso, Hincapie; Frimpong (Arthur 81), Xhaka (Garcia 81), Palacios, Grimaldo (Buendia 87); Adli (Tapsoba 68), Wirtz (Schick 80).

Real Madrid (2) 3 *(Mbappe 4, 33, 61)*
Manchester C (0) 1 *(Gonzalez 90)* 77,023
Real Madrid: (442) Courtois; Valverde (Alaba 90), Asencio, Rudiger, Mendy; Rodrygo, Tchouameni (Modric 83), Ceballos (Camavinga 78), Bellingham; Mbappe (Diaz 78), Vinicius Junior (Endrick 90).
Manchester C: (41212) Ederson; Khusanov, Stones (Ake 8), Dias, Gvardiol, Gonzalez; Foden (McAtee 77), Silva; Gundogan (Kovacic 77); Savio, Marmoush.
Real Madrid won 6-3 on aggregate.

KNOCKOUT PHASE

Benfica (0) 0
Barcelona (0) 1 *(Raphinha 61)* 62,437
Benfica: (433) Trubin; Araujo (Dahl 57), Silva, Otamendi, Carreras; Barreiro (Belotti 70), Aursnes, Kokcu (Sanches 84); Akturkoglu, Pavlidis (Arthur Cabral 84), Schjelderup (Rego 70).
Barcelona: (4231) Szczesny; Kounde, Cubarsi■, Martinez, Balde; de Jong (Casado 79), Gonzalez; Yamal (Torres 56), Olmo (Araujo 28), Raphinha; Lewandowski (Gerard 78).

Feyenoord (0) 0
Internazionale (1) 2 *(Thuram 38, Martinez L 50)* 43,789
Feyenoord: (442) Wellenreuther; Mitchell, Beelen, Hancko, Bueno; Hadj Moussa, Moder, Smal, Osman; Igor Paixao, Carranza (Ueda 59).
Internazionale: (352) Martinez J; Pavard, de Vrij (Bisseck 72), Acerbi; Dumfries, Barella (Frattesi 72), Asllani (Calhanoglu 81), Zielinski, Bastoni; Martinez L (Arnautovic 81), Thuram (Taremi 62).

Paris Saint-Germain (0) 0
Liverpool (0) 1 *(Elliott 87)* 47,511
Paris Saint-Germain: (433) Donnarumma; Hakimi, Marquinhos, Pacho, Nuno Mendes; Neves, Vitinha, Fabian (Zaire-Emery 78); Kvaratskhelia (Goncalo Ramos 78), Dembele, Barcola (Doue 66).
Liverpool: (4231) Alisson; Alexander-Arnold, Konate, van Dijk, Robertson; Gravenberch (Endo 79), Mac Allister; Salah (Elliott 86), Szoboszlai, Diaz (Jones 67); Jota (Nunez 61).

ROUND OF 16 – SECOND LEG
Tuesday, 11 March 2025

Barcelona (3) 3 *(Raphinha 11, 42, Yamal 27)*
Benfica (1) 1 *(Otamendi 13)* 47,111
Barcelona: (4231) Szczesny; Kounde, Araujo, Martinez (Garcia 87), Balde; de Jong (Casado 81), Gonzalez; Yamal (Lopez 82), Olmo (Gavi 70), Raphinha; Lewandowski (Torres 70).
Benfica: (433) Trubin; Araujo (Rego 84), Silva, Otamendi, Dahl; Aursnes, Florentino (Barreiro 70), Kokcu (Belotti 70); Akturkoglu (Sanches 56), Pavlidis, Schjelderup (Amdouni 56).
Barcelona won 4-1 on aggregate.

Bayer Leverkusen (0) 0
Bayern Munich (0) 2 *(Kane 52, Davies 71)* 30,210
Bayer Leverkusen: (451) Hradecky; Arthur (Boniface 65), Tah, Hermoso (Andrich 38), Hincapie; Frimpong, Palacios, Xhaka, Garcia (Adli 66), Grimaldo (Buendia 84); Schick.
Bayern Munich: (4231) Urbig; Laimer (Stanisic 46), Upamecano, Kim, Davies; Goretzka (Joao Palhinha 84), Kimmich; Olise (Ito 69), Musiala, Coman (Gnabry 58); Kane (Muller 84).
Bayern Munich won 5-0 on aggregate.

Internazionale (1) 2 *(Thuram 8, Calhanoglu 51 (pen))*
Feyenoord (1) 1 *(Moder 42 (pen))* 55,536
Internazionale: (352) Sommer; Pavard, Acerbi (Cocchi 84), Bisseck; Dumfries, Frattesi (Berenbruch 84), Calhanoglu (Asllani 61), Mkhitaryan, Carlos Augusto (Bastoni 61); Thuram (Arnautovic 71), Taremi.
Feyenoord: (433) Wellenreuther; Read (Mitchell 75), Beelen, Hancko, Bueno; Moder, Smal, Ivanusec (Redmond 75); Hadj Moussa, Ueda (Carranza 63), Sliti (Trauner 63).
Internazionale won 4-1 on aggregate.

Liverpool (0) 0
Paris Saint-Germain (1) 1 *(Dembele 12)* 59,765
Liverpool: (4231) Alisson; Alexander-Arnold (Quansah 73), Konate (Endo 111), van Dijk, Robertson; Gravenberch, Mac Allister (Jones 91); Salah, Szoboszlai (Elliott 106), Diaz (Gakpo 102); Jota (Nunez 73).
Paris Saint-Germain: (433) Donnarumma; Hakimi, Marquinhos (Lucas Beraldo 90), Pacho, Nuno Mendes; Neves (Goncalo Ramos 120), Vitinha, Fabian (Zaire-Emery 91); Barcola (Doue 67), Dembele, Kvaratskhelia (Lee 101).
aet; Paris Saint-Germain won 4-1 on penalties.

Wednesday, 12 March 2025
Arsenal (2) 2 *(Zinchenko 6, Rice 37)*
PSV Eindhoven (1) 2 *(Perisic 18, Driouech 70)* 59,410
Arsenal: (433) Raya; White (Timber 79), Kiwior, Gabriel, Lewis-Skelly; Zinchenko (Odegaard 79), Jorginho, Rice (Calafiori 64); Sterling, Merino (Trossard 64), Tierney (Martinelli 79).
PSV Eindhoven: (433) Benitez; Ledezma, Nagalo (Flamingo 77), Obispo (Boscagli 69), Malacia; Til, Schouten (Veerman 46), Babadi; Bakayoko, Perisic (de Jong 68), Driouech (Bajraktarevic 80).
Arsenal won 9-3 on aggregate.

Aston Villa (0) 3 *(Asensio 50, 61, Maatsen 57)*
Club Brugge (0) 0 42,461
Aston Villa: (4231) Martinez; Cash (Disasi 73), Konsa, Mings (Torres 66), Maatsen; Kamara (Bailey 46), Tielemans; Rogers (Ramsey 66), McGinn, Rashford; Watkins (Asensio 46).
Club Brugge: (4231) Mignolet; Sabbe■, Ordonez (Romero 58), Mechele, De Cuyper; Nwadike, Jashari (Nielsen 58); Talbi (Skoras 58), Vanaken, Tzolis (Siquet 66); Jutgla (Nilsson 58).
Aston Villa won 6-1 on aggregate.

Atletico Madrid (1) 1 *(Gallagher 1)*
Real Madrid (0) 0 69,304
Atletico Madrid: (442) Oblak; Llorente, Gimenez, Lenglet (Le Normand 91), Mandava (Azpilicueta 58); Simeone (Correa 89), De Paul (Molina 90), Barrios, Gallagher (Samuel Dias 85); Griezmann (Sorloth 89), Alvarez.
Real Madrid: (442) Courtois; Valverde, Asencio, Rudiger, Mendy (Garcia 83); Rodrygo (Diaz 79), Modric (Lucas 65), Tchouameni (Camavinga 65), Bellingham; Mbappe, Vinicius Junior (Endrick 115).
aet; Real Madrid won 4-2 on penalties.

Lille (1) 1 *(David 5)*
Borussia Dortmund (0) 2 *(Can 54 (pen), Beier 65)* 48,042
Lille: (4231) Chevalier; Meunier, Diakite, Alexsandro Victor, Ismaily (Gudmundsson 67); Andre, Bouaddi (Fernandez 74); Cabella (Akpom 67), Mukau (Andre Gomes 83), Arnar Haraldsson (Sahraoui 83); David.
Borussia Dortmund: (4231) Kobel; Anton (Bensebaini 72), Can, Schlotterbeck, Ryerson; Sabitzer, Gross (Ozcan 86); Adeyemi (Bynoe-Gittens 79), Brandt (Chukwuemeka 85), Beier (Reyna 85); Guirassy.
Borussia Dortmund won 3-2 on aggregate.

QUARTER-FINALS – FIRST LEG
Tuesday, 8 April 2025
Arsenal (0) 3 *(Rice 58, 70, Merino 75)*
Real Madrid (0) 0 60,110
Arsenal: (433) Raya; Timber (White 90), Saliba, Kiwior, Lewis-Skelly; Odegaard, Partey, Rice (Tierney 80); Saka (Trossard 74), Merino, Martinelli.
Real Madrid: (442) Courtois; Valverde, Asencio, Rudiger, Alaba (Garcia 80); Rodrygo (Diaz 85), Modric (Lucas 71), Camavinga■, Bellingham; Mbappe, Vinicius Junior.

Bayern Munich (0) 1 *(Muller 85)*
Internazionale (1) 2 *(Martinez L 38, Frattesi 88)* 75,000
Bayern Munich: (4231) Urbig; Laimer, Dier, Kim (Boey 75), Stanisic; Kimmich, Goretzka; Olise, Guerreiro (Gnabry 74), Sane (Muller 74); Kane.
Internazionale: (352) Sommer; Pavard, Acerbi, Bastoni; Darmian (Bisseck 79), Barella, Calhanoglu, Mkhitaryan (Frattesi 74), Carlos Augusto; Thuram, Martinez L (Zalewski 90).

Wednesday, 9 April 2025
Barcelona (1) 4 *(Raphinha 25, Lewandowski 48, 66, Yamal 77)*
Borussia Dortmund (0) 0 49,760
Barcelona: (4231) Szczesny; Kounde, Cubarsi, Martinez (Araujo 81), Balde; de Jong, Gonzalez (Garcia 81); Yamal (Fati 86), Lopez (Gavi 74), Raphinha; Lewandowski (Torres 81).
Borussia Dortmund: (451) Kobel; Ryerson (Sule 79), Can, Anton, Bensebaini; Bynoe-Gittens (Duranville 79), Brandt, Nmecha (Ozcan 67), Chukwuemeka (Reyna 68), Adeyemi (Beier 46); Guirassy.

Paris Saint-Germain (1) 3 *(Doue 39, Kvaratskhelia 49, Nuno Mendes 90)*
Aston Villa (1) 1 *(Rogers 35)* 47,681
Paris Saint-Germain: (433) Donnarumma; Hakimi, Lucas Beraldo, Pacho, Nuno Mendes; Neves, Vitinha, Fabian (Zaire-Emery 72); Doue (Barcola 72), Dembele, Kvaratskhelia (Goncalo Ramos 90).
Aston Villa: (4231) Martinez; Cash (Disasi 46), Konsa, Torres, Digne; Kamara, Tielemans (Maatsen 80); Rogers, McGinn (Onana 80), Ramsey (Asensio 59); Rashford (Watkins 79).

QUARTER-FINALS – SECOND LEG
Tuesday, 15 April 2025
Aston Villa (1) 3 *(Tielemans 34, McGinn 55, Konsa 57)*
Paris Saint-Germain (2) 2 *(Hakimi 11, Nuno Mendes 27)* 42,535
Aston Villa: (4231) Martinez; Cash, Konsa, Torres, Digne (Maatsen 76); Kamara, Onana (Ramsey 67); Rogers, Tielemans (Barkley 88), McGinn (Asensio 66); Rashford (Watkins 76).
Paris Saint-Germain: (433) Donnarumma; Hakimi, Marquinhos, Pacho, Nuno Mendes; Neves, Vitinha, Fabian; Kvaratskhelia, Dembele, Barcola (Doue 58).
Paris Saint-Germain won 5-4 on aggregate.

Borussia Dortmund (1) 3 *(Guirassy 11 (pen), 49, 76)*
Barcelona (0) 1 *(Bensebaini 54 (og))* 81,365
Borussia Dortmund: (3421) Kobel; Sule, Anton, Bensebaini; Yan Couto (Brandt 77), Nmecha (Reyna 64), Gross, Svensson; Beier (Duranville 64), Adeyemi (Bynoe-Gittens 77); Guirassy.
Barcelona: (433) Szczesny; Kounde, Araujo, Cubarsi, Gerard; de Jong, Gavi (Gonzalez 59); Yamal (Torres 70), Lopez (Garcia 70), Raphinha; Lewandowski (Olmo 86).
Barcelona won 5-3 on aggregate.

Wednesday, 16 April 2025
Internazionale (0) 2 *(Martinez L 58, Pavard 61)*
Bayern Munich (0) 2 *(Kane 52, Dier 76)* 75,625
Internazionale: (352) Sommer; Pavard, Acerbi, Bastoni (Bisseck 87); Darmian, Barella (Frattesi 88), Calhanoglu, Mkhitaryan, Dimarco (Carlos Augusto 73); Thuram, Martinez L (Taremi 81).
Bayern Munich: (4231) Urbig; Laimer (Coman 83), Dier, Kim (Guerreiro 65); Stanisic; Goretzka (Pavlovic 83), Kimmich; Olise, Muller, Sane (Gnabry 65); Kane.
Internazionale won 4-3 on aggregate.

Real Madrid (0) 1 *(Vinicius Junior 67)*
Arsenal (0) 2 *(Saka 65, Martinelli 90)* 77,073
Real Madrid: (433) Courtois; Lucas (Endrick 61), Asencio (Modric 74), Rudiger, Alaba (Garcia 61); Valverde, Tchouameni, Bellingham; Rodrygo (Ceballos 61), Mbappe (Diaz 75), Vinicius Junior.
Arsenal: (433) Raya; Timber (White 90), Saliba, Kiwior, Lewis-Skelly; Odegaard, Partey, Rice (Zinchenko 90); Saka (Trossard 77), Merino, Martinelli (Tierney 90).
Arsenal won 5-1 on aggregate.

SEMI-FINALS – FIRST LEG

Tuesday, 29 April 2025

Arsenal (0) 0

Paris Saint-Germain (1) 1 *(Dembele 4)* 59,664

Arsenal: (433) Raya; Timber (White 83), Saliba, Kiwior, Lewis-Skelly; Odegaard (Nwaneri 90), Rice, Merino; Saka, Trossard, Martinelli.
Paris Saint-Germain: (433) Donnarumma; Hakimi, Marquinhos, Pacho, Nuno Mendes; Neves (Zaire-Emery 89), Vitinha, Fabian; Doue (Goncalo Ramos 76), Dembele (Barcola 70), Kvaratskhelia.

Wednesday, 30 April 2025

Barcelona (2) 3 *(Yamal 24, Torres 38, Sommer 65 (og))*

Internazionale (2) 3 *(Thuram 1, Dumfries 21, 63)* 50,314

Barcelona: (4231) Szczesny; Kounde (Garcia 42), Cubarsi (Christensen 83), Martinez, Gerard (Araujo 46); de Jong, Gonzalez (Gavi 83); Yamal, Olmo (Lopez 68), Raphinha; Torres.
Internazionale: (352) Sommer; Bisseck, Acerbi, Bastoni; Dumfries (Darmian 81), Barella, Calhanoglu (Frattesi 71), Mkhitaryan, Dimarco (Carlos Augusto 56); Thuram (Zielinski 81), Martinez L (Taremi 46).

SEMI-FINALS – SECOND LEG

Tuesday, 6 May 2025

Internazionale (2) 4 *(Martinez L 21, Calhanoglu 45 (pen), Acerbi 90, Frattesi 99)*

Barcelona (0) 3 *(Garcia 54, Olmo 60, Raphinha 87)* 75,504

Internazionale: (352) Sommer; Bisseck (Darmian 71), Acerbi, Bastoni; Dumfries (de Vrij 108), Barella, Calhanoglu (Zielinski 79), Mkhitaryan (Frattesi 79), Dimarco (Carlos Augusto 55); Martinez L (Taremi 71), Thuram.
Barcelona: (4231) Szczesny; Garcia (Fort 98), Cubarsi (Gavi 106), Martinez (Araujo 76), Gerard; de Jong, Gonzalez (Victor 106); Yamal, Olmo (Lopez 83), Raphinha; Torres (Lewandowski 90).
aet; Internazionale won 7-6 on aggregate.

Wednesday, 7 May 2025

Paris Saint-Germain (1) 2 *(Fabian 27, Hakimi 72)*

Arsenal (0) 1 *(Saka 76)* 47,511

Paris Saint-Germain: (433) Donnarumma; Hakimi, Marquinhos, Pacho, Nuno Mendes (Goncalo Ramos 88); Neves, Vitinha, Fabian; Doue (Hernandez 74), Barcola (Dembele 70), Kvaratskhelia.
Arsenal: (433) Raya; Timber (White 83), Saliba, Kiwior, Lewis-Skelly (Calafiori 68); Odegaard, Partey, Rice; Saka, Merino, Martinelli (Trossard 68).
Paris Saint-Germain won 3-1 on aggregate.

UEFA CHAMPIONS LEAGUE FINAL 2024–25

Saturday, 31 May 2025

(at Allianz Arena, Munich, attendance 64,327)

Paris Saint-Germain (2) 5   Internazionale (0) 0

Paris Saint-Germain: (433) Donnarumma; Hakimi, Marquinhos, Pacho, Nuno Mendes (Hernandez 78); Neves (Zaire-Emery 84), Vitinha, Fabian (Mayulu 84); Doue (Barcola 67), Dembele, Kvaratskhelia (Goncalo Ramos 84).
Scorers: Hakimi 12, Doue 20, 63, Kvaratskhelia 73, Mayulu 86.

Internazionale: (352) Sommer; Pavard (Bisseck 54 (Darmian 62)), Acerbi, Bastoni; Dumfries, Barella, Calhanoglu (Asllani 70), Mkhitaryan (Carlos Augusto 62), Dimarco (Zalewski 54); Thuram, Martinez L.

Referee: Istvan Kovacs.

Allez PSG! Désiré Doué scores his team's second goal during the UEFA Champions League final 2025 between Paris Saint-Germain and Internazionale at Munich's Allianz Arena. (Justin Setterfield/Getty Images)

EUROPEAN CUP-WINNERS' CUP FINALS 1961–99

Year	Winners v Runners-up		Venue	Attendance	Referee
1961	1st Leg Rangers v Fiorentina	0-2	Glasgow	80,000	C. E. Steiner (Austria)
	2nd Leg Fiorentina v Rangers	2-1	Florence	50,000	V. Hernadi (Hungary)
1962	Atletico Madrid v Fiorentina	1-1	Glasgow	27,389	T. Wharton (Scotland)
Replay	Atletico Madrid v Fiorentina	3-0	Stuttgart	38,000	K. Tschenscher (West Germany)
1963	Tottenham Hotspur v Atletico Madrid	5-1	Rotterdam	49,000	A. van Leuwen (Netherlands)
1964	Sporting Lisbon v MTK Budapest	3-3*	Brussels	3,208	L. van Nuffel (Belgium)
Replay	Sporting Lisbon v MTK Budapest	1-0	Antwerp	13,924	G. Versyp (Belgium)
1965	West Ham U v Munich 1860	2-0	Wembley	97,974	I. Zsolt (Hungary)
1966	Borussia Dortmund v Liverpool	2-1*	Glasgow	41,657	P. Schwinte (France)
1967	Bayern Munich v Rangers	1-0*	Nuremberg	69,480	C. Lo Bello (Italy)
1968	AC Milan v Hamburg	2-0	Rotterdam	53,000	J. Ortiz de Mendibil (Spain)
1969	Slovan Bratislava v Barcelona	3-2	Basel	19,000	L. van Ravens (Netherlands)
1970	Manchester C v Gornik Zabrze	2-1	Vienna	7,968	P. Schiller (Austria)
1971	Chelsea v Real Madrid	1-1*	Athens	45,000	R. Scheurer (Switzerland)
Replay	Chelsea v Real Madrid	2-1	Athens	19,917	R. Scheurer (Switzerland)
1972	Rangers v Dynamo Moscow	3-2	Barcelona	24,701	J. Ortiz de Mendibil (Spain)
1973	AC Milan v Leeds U	1-0	Salonika	40,154	C. Mihas (Greece)
1974	Magdeburg v AC Milan	2-0	Rotterdam	4,641	A. van Gemert (Netherlands)
1975	Dynamo Kyiv v Ferencvaros	3-0	Basel	13,000	R. Davidson (Scotland)
1976	Anderlecht v West Ham U	4-2	Brussels	51,296	R. Wurtz (France)
1977	Hamburg v Anderlecht	2-0	Amsterdam	66,000	P. Partridge (England)
1978	Anderlecht v Austria/WAC	4-0	Paris	48,679	H. Aldinger (West Germany)
1979	Barcelona v Fortuna Dusseldorf	4-3*	Basel	58,000	K. Palotai (Hungary)
1980	Valencia v Arsenal	0-0*	Brussels	40,000	V. Christov (Czechoslovakia)
	Valencia won 5-4 on penalties.				
1981	Dinamo Tbilisi v Carl Zeiss Jena	2-1	Dusseldorf	4,750	R. Lattanzi (Italy)
1982	Barcelona v Standard Liege	2-1	Barcelona	80,000	W. Eschweiler (West Germany)
1983	Aberdeen v Real Madrid	2-1*	Gothenburg	17,804	G. Menegali (Italy)
1984	Juventus v Porto	2-1	Basel	55,000	A. Prokop (Egypt)
1985	Everton v Rapid Vienna	3-1	Rotterdam	38,500	P. Casarin (Italy)
1986	Dynamo Kyiv v Atletico Madrid	3-0	Lyon	50,000	F. Wohrer (Austria)
1987	Ajax v Lokomotiv Leipzig	1-0	Athens	35,107	L. Agnolin (Italy)
1988	Mechelen v Ajax	1-0	Strasbourg	39,446	D. Pauly (West Germany)
1989	Barcelona v Sampdoria	2-0	Berne	42,707	G. Courtney (England)
1990	Sampdoria v Anderlecht	2-0*	Gothenburg	20,103	B. Galler (Switzerland)
1991	Manchester U v Barcelona	2-1	Rotterdam	43,500	B. Karlsson (Sweden)
1992	Werder Bremen v Monaco	2-0	Lisbon	16,000	P. D'Elia (Italy)
1993	Parma v Antwerp	3-1	Wembley	37,393	K.-J. Assenmacher (Germany)
1994	Arsenal v Parma	1-0	Copenhagen	33,765	V. Krondl (Czech Republic)
1995	Real Zaragoza v Arsenal	2-1	Paris	42,424	P. Ceccarini (Italy)
1996	Paris Saint-Germain v Rapid Vienna	1-0	Brussels	37,000	P. Pairetto (Italy)
1997	Barcelona v Paris Saint-Germain	1-0	Rotterdam	52,000	M. Merk (Germany)
1998	Chelsea v VfB Stuttgart	1-0	Stockholm	30,216	S. Braschi (Italy)
1999	Lazio v Mallorca	2-1	Villa Park	33,021	G. Benko (Austria)

INTER-CITIES FAIRS CUP FINALS 1958–71

Year	1st Leg		Attendance	2nd Leg	Attendance	Agg	Winner
1958	London XI v Barcelona	2-2	45,466	0-6	70,000	2-8	Barcelona
1960	Birmingham C v Barcelona	0-0	40,524	1-4	70,000	1-4	Barcelona
1961	Birmingham C v Roma	2-2	21,005	0-2	60,000	2-4	Roma
1962	Valencia v Barcelona	6-2	65,000	1-1	60,000	7-3	Valencia
1963	Dinamo Zagreb v Valencia	1-2	40,000	0-2	55,000	1-4	Valencia
1964	Real Zaragoza v Valencia	2-1	50,000	(in Barcelona, one match only)			Real Zaragoza
1965	Ferencvaros v Juventus	1-0	25,000	(in Turin, one match only)			Ferencvaros
1966	Barcelona v Real Zaragoza	0-1	70,000	4-2*	70,000	4-3	Barcelona
1967	Dinamo Zagreb v Leeds U	2-0	40,000	0-0	35,604	2-0	Dinamo Zagreb
1968	Leeds U v Ferencvaros	1-0	25,368	0-0	70,000	1-0	Leeds U
1969	Newcastle U v Ujpest Dozsa	3-0	60,000	3-2	37,000	6-2	Newcastle U
1970	Anderlecht v Arsenal	3-1	37,000	0-3	51,612	3-4	Arsenal
1971	Juventus v Leeds U	0-0	*(abandoned 51 minutes)*		42,000		
	Juventus v Leeds U	2-2	42,000	1-1	42,483	3-3	Leeds U
	Leeds U won on away goals rule.						

Trophy Play-Off – *between first and last winners to decide who would have possession of the original trophy*

1971	Barcelona v Leeds U	2-1	50,000 (in Barcelona, one match only)

*After extra time.

UEFA CUP FINALS 1972–97

Year	1st Leg		Attendance	2nd Leg	Attendance	Agg	Winner
1972	Wolverhampton W v Tottenham H	1-2	38,562	1-1	54,303	2-3	Tottenham H
1973	Liverpool v Moenchengladbach	0-0	*(abandoned after 27 minutes)*		44,967		
	Liverpool v Moenchengladbach	3-0	41,169	0-2	35,000	3-2	Liverpool
1974	Tottenham H v Feyenoord	2-2	46,281	0-2	59,317	2-4	Feyenoord
1975	Moenchengladbach v FC Twente	0-0	42,368	5-1	21,767	5-1	Moenchengladbach
1976	Liverpool v Club Brugge	3-2	49,981	1-1	29,423	4-3	Liverpool
1977	Juventus v Athletic Bilbao	1-0	66,000	1-2	39,700	2-2	Juventus
	Juventus won on away goals rule.						
1978	Bastia v PSV Eindhoven	0-0	8,006	0-3	28,000	0-3	PSV Eindhoven
1979	RS Belgrade v Moenchengladbach	1-1	65,000	0-1	45,000	1-2	Moenchengladbach
1980	Moenchengladbach v E. Frankfurt	3-2	25,000	0-1	59,000	3-3	E. Frankfurt
	Eintracht Frankfurt won on away goals rule.						
1981	Ipswich T v AZ 67 Alkmaar	3-0	27,532	2-4	22,291	5-4	Ipswich T
1982	IFK Gothenburg v Hamburg	1-0	42,548	3-0	57,312	4-0	IFK Gothenburg
1983	Anderlecht v Benfica	1-0	55,000	1-1	70,000	2-1	Anderlecht
1984	Anderlecht v Tottenham H	1-1	33,000	1-1*	46,258	2-2	Tottenham H
	Tottenham H won 4-3 on penalties.						
1985	Videoton v Real Madrid	0-3	30,000	1-0	80,000	1-3	Real Madrid
1986	Real Madrid v Cologne	5-1	60,000	0-2	22,000	5-3	Real Madrid
1987	IFK Gothenburg v Dundee U	1-0	48,614	1-1	20,900	2-1	IFK Gothenburg
1988	Espanol v Bayer Leverkusen	3-0	31,180	0-3*	21,600	3-3	Bayer Leverkusen
	Bayer Leverkusen won 3-2 on penalties.						
1989	Napoli v VfB Stuttgart	2-1	81,093	3-3	64,000	5-4	Napoli
1990	Juventus v Fiorentina	3-1	47,519	0-0	30,999	3-1	Juventus
1991	Internazionale v Roma	2-0	68,887	0-1	70,901	2-1	Internazionale
1992	Torino v Ajax	2-2	65,377	0-0	40,000	2-2	Ajax
	Ajax won on away goals rule.						
1993	Borussia Dortmund v Juventus	1-3	37,000	0-3	62,781	1-6	Juventus
1994	Salzburg v Internazionale	0-1	43,000	0-1	80,345	0-2	Internazionale
1995	Parma v Juventus	1-0	22,057	1-1	80,000	2-1	Parma
1996	Bayern Munich v Bordeaux	2-0	63,000	3-1	30,000	5-1	Bayern Munich
1997	Schalke 04 v Internazionale	1-0	57,000	0-1*	81,675	1-1	Schalke 04
	Schalke 04 won 4-1 on penalties.						

UEFA CUP FINALS 1998–2009

Year	Winners v Runners-up		Venue	Attendance	Referee
1998	Internazionale v Lazio	3-0	Paris	44,412	A. L. Nieto (Spain)
1999	Parma v Marseille	3-0	Moscow	61,000	H. Dallas (Scotland)
2000	Galatasaray v Arsenal	0-0*	Copenhagen	38,919	A. L. Nieto (Spain)
	Galatasaray won 4-1 on penalties.				
2001	Liverpool v Alaves	5-4*	Dortmund	48,050	G. Veissiere (France)
	Liverpool won on sudden death 'golden goal'.				
2002	Feyenoord v Borussia Dortmund	3-2	Rotterdam	45,611	V. M. M. Pereira (Portugal)
2003	FC Porto v Celtic	3-2*	Seville	52,140	L. Michel (Slovakia)
2004	Valencia v Marseille	2-0	Gothenburg	39,000	P. Collina (Italy)
2005	CSKA Moscow v Sporting Lisbon	3-1	Lisbon	47,085	G. Poll (England)
2006	Sevilla v Middlesbrough	4-0	Eindhoven	32,100	H. Fandel (Germany)
2007	Sevilla v Espanyol	2-2*	Glasgow	47,602	M. Busacca (Switzerland)
	Sevilla won 3-1 on penalties.				
2008	Zenit St Petersburg v Rangers	2-0	Manchester	43,878	P. Fröjdfeldt (Sweden)
2009	Shakhtar Donetsk v Werder Bremen	2-1*	Istanbul	37,357	L. M. Chantalejo (Spain)

UEFA EUROPA LEAGUE FINALS 2010–25

Year	Winners v Runners-up		Venue	Attendance	Referee
2010	Atletico Madrid v Fulham	2-1*	Hamburg	49,000	N. Rizzoli (Italy)
2011	FC Porto v Braga	1-0	Dublin	45,391	V. Carballo (Spain)
2012	Atletico Madrid v Athletic Bilbao	3-0	Bucharest	52,347	W. Stark (Germany)
2013	Chelsea v Benfica	2-1	Amsterdam	46,163	B. Kuipers (Netherlands)
2014	Sevilla v Benfica	0-0*	Turin	33,120	F. Brych (Germany)
	Sevilla won 4-2 on penalties.				
2015	Sevilla v Dnipro Dnipropetrovsk	3-2	Warsaw	45,000	M. Atkinson (England)
2016	Sevilla v Liverpool	3-1	Basel	34,429	J. Eriksson (Sweden)
2017	Manchester U v Ajax	2-0	Stockholm	46,961	D. Skomina (Slovenia)
2018	Atletico Madrid v Marseille	3-0	Lyon	55,768	B. Kuipers (Netherlands)
2019	Chelsea v Arsenal	4-1	Baku	51,370	G. Rocchi (Italy)
2020	Sevilla v Internazionale	3-2	Cologne	0	D. Makkelie (Netherlands)
2021	Villareal v Manchester U	1-1*	Gdansk	9,412	C. Turpin (France)
	Villareal won 11-10 on penalties.				
2022	Eintracht Frankfurt v Rangers	1-1*	Seville	38,842	S. Vincic (Slovenia)
	Eintracht Frankfurt won 5-4 on penalties.				
2023	Sevilla v Roma	1-1*	Budapest	61,476	A. Taylor (England)
	Sevilla won 4-1 on penalties.				
2024	Atalanta v Bayer Leverkusen	3-0	Dublin	47,135	I. Kovacs (Romania)
2025	Tottenham H v Manchester U	1-0	Bilbao	49,224	F. Zwayer (Germany)

After extra time.

UEFA EUROPA LEAGUE 2024–25

*After extra time. ■ Denotes player sent off. †Due to the war in Ukraine, Dynamo Kyiv played home matches in Germany, Kryvbas Kryvyi Rih in Slovakia and Dinamo Minsk in Hungary. ‡Due to Israel's war in Gaza, Maccabi Petah Tikva played home matches in Bulgaria; Maccabi Tel Aviv played in Hungary (qualifying phase) and Serbia (league phase).

QUALIFYING PHASE

FIRST QUALIFYING ROUND – FIRST LEG

Thursday, 11 July 2024

Botev Plovdiv v Maribor	2-1
Elfsborg v Pafos	3-0
Paks v Corvinul Hunedoara	0-4
Ruzomberok v Tobol	5-2
Sheriff v Zira	0-1
Wisla Krakow v Llapi	2-0

FIRST QUALIFYING ROUND – SECOND LEG *(agg)*

Thursday, 18 July 2024

Corvinul Hunedoara v Paks	0-2	4-2
Llapi v Wisla Krakow	1-2	1-4
Maribor v Botev Plovdiv	2-2	3-4
Pafos v Elfsborg	2-5	2-8
Tobol v Ruzomberok	1-0	3-5
Zira v Sheriff	1-2*	2-2
Sheriff won 5-4 on penalties.		

SECOND QUALIFYING ROUND – FIRST LEG

Thursday, 25 July 2024

Ajax v Vojvodina	1-0
Braga v Maccabi Petah Tikva	2-0
Corvinul Hunedoara v Rijeka	0-0
Kilmarnock v Cercle Brugge	1-1
Molde v Silkeborg	3-1
Panathinaikos v Botev Plovdiv	2-1
Ruzomberok v Trabzonspor	0-2
Sheriff v Elfsborg	0-1
Wisla Krakow v Rapid Vienna	1-2

Thursday, 25 July 2024

Kilmarnock (0) 1 *(Watson 70)*

Cercle Brugge (0) 1 *(Olaigbe 55)*   10,410

Kilmarnock: (433) McCrorie; Findlay, Wright, Mayo, Deas; Donnelly, Lyons, Watson (Polworth 77); Vassell, Kennedy (Murray 77), Armstrong (Anderson 77).
Cercle Brugge: (451) Warleson; Utkus, Daland, Nazinho (Miangue 76), Ravych; van der Bruggen, Francis, Somers, Olaigbe (Agyekum 76), Ouattara (Augusto 67); Denkey (Goncalves 89).

SECOND QUALIFYING ROUND – SECOND LEG *(agg)*

Thursday, 1 August 2024

Botev Plovdiv v Panathinaikos	0-4	1-6
Cercle Brugge v Kilmarnock	1-0	2-1
Elfsborg v Sheriff	2-0	3-0
Maccabi Petah Tikva‡ v Braga	0-5	0-7
Rapid Vienna v Wisla Krakow	6-1	8-2
Rijeka v Corvinul Hunedoara	1-0	1-0
Silkeborg v Molde	3-2	4-5
Trabzonspor v Ruzomberok	1-0	3-0
Vojvodina v Ajax	1-3	1-4

Thursday, 1 August 2024

Cercle Brugge (1) 1 *(Somers 21)*

Kilmarnock (0) 0   10,230

Cercle Brugge: (451) Warleson; Utkus, Daland, Nazinho (Miangue 87), Ravych; van der Bruggen (Agyekum 90), Francis, Somers, Olaigbe (Popovic 87), Ouattara (Bruninho 79); Denkey (Felipe Augusto 79).
Kilmarnock: (433) McCrorie; Findlay, Wright (Kennedy 46), Mayo, Deas (Anderson 90); McKenzie (Polworth 74), Donnelly, Lyons; Watkins, Vassell, Armstrong (Murray 74).
Cercle Brugge won 2-1 on aggregate.

THIRD QUALIFYING ROUND – FIRST LEG

Tuesday, 6 August 2024

Panevezys v Maccabi Tel Aviv	1-2
Petrocub Hincesti v The New Saints	1-0

Thursday, 8 August 2024

Braga v Servette	0-0
Celje v Shamrock R	1-0
Dinamo Minsk† v Lincoln Red Imps	2-0
KI v Borac Banja Luca	2-1
Kryvbas Kryvyi Rih† v Viktoria Plzen	1-2
Molde v Cercle Brugge	3-0
Panathinaikos v Ajax	0-1
Partizan Belgrade v Lugano	0-1
Rijeka v Elfsborg	1-1
Trabzonspor v Rapid Vienna	0-1
UE Santa Coloma v FK RFS	0-2

Tuesday, 6 August 2024

Petrocub Hincesti (1) 1 *(Davies 20 (og))*

The New Saints (0) 0   6272

Petrocub Hincesti: (343) Smalenea; Mudrac, Platica S, Bors; Jardan I, Douanla, Lungu (Jardan 84), Demian (Cotogoi 33); Ambros (Clescenco 84), Puscas (Sandu 72), Caruntu (Lupan 46).
The New Saints: (433) Roberts; Davies, Marshall (Baker 69), Daniels, Bodenham; Redmond (Clark 69), Smith, Williams D (Cieslewicz 77); Brobbel (Williams J 61), Holden (McManus 77), Young.

Thursday, 8 August 2024

Celje (1) 1 *(Menalo 34)*

Shamrock R (0) 0   2478

Celje: (343) Stubljar; Dulca (Kavcic 46), Zec, Nemanic; Kvesic (Edmilson 67), Menalo, Bobicanec, Brnic (Popovic 67); Matko (Kouter 67), Kucys (Aarons 46), Pisek.
Shamrock R: (352) Pohls; Lopes, Hoare, Cleary; O'Neill, Watts (Power 78), Clarke (Burns 57), Farrugia (Burke 78); Honohan; Greene, Nugent (McEneff 67).

THIRD QUALIFYING ROUND – SECOND LEG *(agg)*

Tuesday, 13 August 2024

The New Saints v Petrocub Hincesti	0-0	0-1

Wednesday, 14 August 2024

FK RFS v UE Santa Coloma	7-0	9-0

Thursday, 15 August 2024

Ajax v Panathinaikos	0-1*	1-1
Ajax won 13-12 on penalties.		
Borac Banja Luca v KI	3-1*	4-3
Cercle Brugge v Molde	1-0	1-3
Elfsborg v Rijeka	2-0	3-1
Lincoln Red Imps v Dinamo Minsk	2-1	2-3
Lugano v Partizan Belgrade	2-2*	3-2
Maccabi Tel Aviv‡ v Panevezys	3-0	5-1
Rapid Vienna v Trabzonspor	2-0	3-0
Servette v Braga	1-2	1-2
Shamrock R v Celje	3-1*	3-2
Viktoria Plzen v Kryvbas Kryvyi Rih	1-0	3-1

Tuesday, 13 August 2024

The New Saints (0) 0

Petrocub Hincesti (0) 0   851

The New Saints: (433) Roberts; Davies, Marshall (McManus 71), Daniels, Bodenham; Redmond (Williams D 90), Smith, Clark (Baker 61); Williams J■, Holden (Cieslewicz 61), Young.
Petrocub Hincesti: (343) Smalenea; Mudrac, Platica S, Bors; Jardan I, Douanla (Jardan V 67), Puscas■, Cotogoi (Diallo 59); Platica M, Ambros (Caruntu 75), Demian (Lungu 46).
Petrocub Hincesti won 1-0 on aggregate.

Thursday, 15 August 2024

Shamrock R (2) 3 *(Watts 37 (pen), Farrugia 40, Burke 96)*

Celje (0) 1 *(Karnicnik 83)*   6153

Shamrock R: (352) Pohls; Lopes, Hoare, Grace; O'Neill, Watts, Clarke (Cleary 80), Farrugia (Burke 88), Honohan (O'Sullivan C 110); Greene (Burns 91), Nugent (Towell 80).

Celje: (433) Stubljar; Vuklisevic, Zec, Nemanic (Karnicnik 46), Kavcic; Kvesic (Aarons 104), Bobicanec (Dulca 46), Pisek (Kouter 53); Matko (Edmilson 78), Brnic (Menalo 46), Kucys.
aet; Shamrock R won 3-2 on aggregate.

QUALIFYING PLAY-OFFS – FIRST LEG

Thursday, 22 August 2024

Braga v Rapid Vienna	2-1
Dinamo Minsk† v Anderlecht	0-1
Ferencvaros v Borac Banja Luca	0-0
FK RFS v APOEL	2-1
Jagiellonia Bialystock v Ajax	1-4
LASK v FCSB	1-1
Ludogorets Razgrad v Petrocub Hincesti	4-0
Lugano v Besiktas	3-3
Maccabi Tel Aviv‡ v TSC Backa Topola	3-0
Molde v Elfsborg	0-1
PAOK v Shamrock R	4-0
Viktoria Plzen v Hearts	1-0

Thursday, 22 August 2024

PAOK (1) 4 *(Cleary 45 (og), Taison 48, Konstantelias 67, Baba 90)*

Shamrock R (0) 0   13,871

PAOK: (451) Kotarski; Baba, Jonny Otto (Sastre 80), Kedziora, Koulierakis; Ozdoev, Taison, Schwab (Camara 80), Zivkovic (Despodov 80), Konstantelias (Murg 80); Thomas Llamas (Chalov 64).
Shamrock R: (352) Pohls; Hoare, Cleary, Grace; O'Neill, Watts (Byrne 73), Clarke (Lopez 27), Honohan■, Nugent (McEneff 73); Greene (Mandroiu 73), Farrugia (Burke 84).

Viktoria Plzen (0) 1 *(Oyegoke 90 (og))*

Hearts (0) 0   10,506

Viktoria Plzen: (352) Tvrdon; Jemelka, Dweh, Hranac; Kopic (Mosquera 74), Havel (Cadu 60), Kalvach, Sulc, Cerv; Jirka (Bello 60), Vasulin (Vydra 74).
Hearts: (541) Gordon; Kingsley, Kent, Penrice, Rowles, Taylor (Oyegoke 75); Grant (Spittal 75), Devlin, Boateng, Vargas (Oda 89); Shankland (Boyce 80).

LEAGUE PHASE

LEAGUE MATCHDAY 1

Wednesday, 25 September 2024

Anderlecht v Ferencvaros	2-1
AZ Alkmaar v Elfsborg	3-2
Bodo/Glimt v Porto	3-2
Dynamo Kyiv† v Lazio	0-3
Galatasaray v PAOK	3-1
Ludogorets Razgrad v Slavia Prague	0-2
Manchester U v FC Twente	1-1
Midtjylland v TSG 1899 Hoffenheim	1-1
Nice v Real Sociedad	1-1

Thursday, 26 September 2024

Ajax v Besiktas	4-0
Braga v Maccabi Tel Aviv	2-1
Eintracht Frankfurt v Viktoria Plzen	3-3
FCSB v FK RFS	4-1
Fenerbahce v Union Saint-Gilloise	2-1
Lyon v Olympiacos	2-0
Malmo v Rangers	0-2
Roma v Athletic Bilbao	1-1
Tottenham H v Qarabag	3-0

Wednesday, 25 September 2024

Manchester U (1) 1 *(Eriksen 35)*

FC Twente (0) 1 *(Lammers 68)*   73,069

Manchester U: (4231) Onana; Mazraoui, Maguire, Martinez, Dalot; Ugarte, Eriksen (Mainoo 79); Diallo (Garnacho 67), Fernandes, Rashford (Hojlund 79); Zirkzee (Mount 79).
FC Twente: (4231) Unnerstall; van Rooij, Hilgers, Bruns, Saleh-Eddine; Regeer (Lagerbielke 83), Vlap (Kjolo 61); van Wolfswinkel, Steijn (Rots D 60), van Bergen (Ltaief 74); Lammers (Besselink 83).

QUALIFYING PLAY-OFFS – SECOND LEG   *(agg)*

Thursday, 29 August 2024

Ajax v Jagiellonia Bialystock	3-0	7-1
Anderlecht v Dinamo Minsk	1-0	2-0
APOEL v FK RFS	2-1*	3-3
FK RFS won 4-2 on penalties.		
Besiktas v Lugano	5-1	8-4
Borac Banja Luca v Ferencvaros	1-1*	1-1
Ferencvaros won 3-2 on penalties.		
Elfsborg v Molde	0-1*	1-1
Elfsborg won 4-2 on penalties.		
FCSB v LASK	1-0	2-1
Hearts v Viktoria Plzen	0-1	0-2
Petrocub Hincesti v Ludogorets Razgrad	1-2	1-6
Rapid Vienna v Braga	2-2	3-4
Shamrock R v PAOK	0-2	0-6
TSC Backa Topola v Maccabi Tel Aviv	1-5	1-8

Thursday, 29 August 2024

Hearts (0) 0

Viktoria Plzen (0) 1 *(Cerv 76)*   18,164

Hearts: (352) Gordon; Kingsley, Kent, Rowles; Grant (Spittal 67), Penrice (Oda 67), Devlin (Forrest 82), Boateng, Taylor; Boyce (Dhanda 73), Vargas (Wilson 82).
Viktoria Plzen: (343) Tvrdon; Havel, Jemelka, Dweh; Kopic, Kalvach, Cerv, Cadu; Sulc (Sloncik 90), Vasulin (Hejda 88), Sojka (Vydra 58).
Viktoria Plzen won 2-0 on aggregate.

Shamrock R (0) 0

PAOK (0) 2 *(Ozdoev 64, Despodov 75)*   5079

Shamrock R: (343) Pohls; Lopes, Kavanagh (Grace 65), Cleary; Towell, O'Neill (Noonan C 65), McEneff, O'Sullivan C; McNulty (Mandroiu 65), Byrne (Burke 65), Burns (Farrugia 65).
PAOK: (451) Kotarski; Baba (Rafa Soares 76), Jonny Otto, Kedziora, Michailidis; Ozdoev (Schwab 72), Murg (Taison 72), Despodov, Zivkovic (Konstantelias 72), Camara; Tissoudali (Chalov 72).
PAOK won 6-0 on aggregate.

Tottenham H (1) 3 *(Johnson 12, Sarr 52, Solanke 68)*

Qarabag (0) 0   51,757

Tottenham H: (433) Vicario; Gray, Dragusin■, van de Ven, Davies; Sarr, Bissouma (Bentancur 71), Bergvall (Udogie 12); Johnson (Kulusevski 46), Solanke (Moore 85), Son (Werner 71).
Qarabag: (4231) Kochalski; Matheus Silva (Huseynov A 79), Mustafazade, Huseynov B, Cafarquliyev; Romao (Andrade L 68), Andrade P; Bayramov (Addai 67), Benzia, Zoubir (Jankovic 79); Juninho.

LEAGUE MATCHDAY 2

Thursday, 3 October 2024

Athletic Bilbao v AZ Alkmaar	2-0
Besiktas v Eintracht Frankfurt	1-3
Elfsborg v Roma	1-0
FC Twente v Fenerbahce	1-1
Ferencvaros v Tottenham H	1-2
FK RFS v Galatasaray	2-2
Lazio v Nice	4-1
Maccabi Tel Aviv‡ v Midtjylland	0-2
Olympiacos v Braga	3-0
PAOK v FCSB	0-1
Porto v Manchester U	3-3
Qarabag v Malmo	1-2
Rangers v Lyon	1-4

LEAGUE MATCHDAY 1

Thursday, 26 September 2024

Malmo (0) 0

Rangers (1) 2 *(Bajrami 1, McCausland 76)*   20,021

Malmo: (4231) Dahlin; Stryger Larsen, Rosler, Jansson, Busanello; Pena, Johnsen (Jorgensen 84); Christiansen (Botheim 61), Berg (Loukili 84), Bolin (Ali 69); Kiese Thelin (Rosengren 69).
Rangers: (4231) Butland; Tavernier, Souttar, Propper, Kasanwirjo; Diomande, Barron; Cerny (McCausland 69), Lawrence (Raskin 80), Bajrami (Sterling 84); Dessers.

Real Sociedad v Anderlecht	1-2
Slavia Prague v Ajax	1-1
TSG 1899 Hoffenheim v Dynamo Kyiv	2-0
Union Saint-Gilloise v Bodo/Glimt	0-0
Viktoria Plzen v Ludogorets Razgrad	0-0

Thursday, 3 October 2024

Ferencvaros (0) 1 *(Varga B 90)*

Tottenham H (1) 2 *(Sarr 23, Johnson 86)*   20,795

Ferencvaros: (4231) Dibusz; Gartenmann (Makreckis 77), Cisse, Raul Gustavo, Ramirez; Abu Fani (Pesic 84); Maiga; Traore (Kady 77), Saldanha (Zachariassen 60), Civic (Ben Romdhane 60); Varga B.
Tottenham H: (433) Vicario; Porro, Romero, Gray, Davies; Sarr (Solanke 81), Bissouma, Bergvall (Kulusevski 65); Moore, Lankshear (Maddison 66), Werner (Johnson 65).

Porto (2) 3 *(Pepe 27, Aghehowa 34, 50)*

Manchester U (2) 3 *(Rashford 7, Hojlund 20, Maguire 90)*   49,211

Porto: (433) Costa; Joao Mario (Gul 78), Ze Pedro, Perez N, Moura; Stephen Eustaquio (Vieira 78), Varela (Loader 90), Gonzalez; Pepe (Fernandes 68), Aghehowa (Grujic 78), Galeno.
Manchester U: (4231) Onana; Mazraoui, de Ligt (Evans 79), Martinez (Maguire 78), Dalot; Casemiro, Eriksen; Diallo (Antony 68), Fernandes■, Rashford (Garnacho 46); Hojlund (Zirkzee 68).

Rangers (1) 1 *(Lawrence 14)*

Lyon (3) 4 *(Fofana 10, 55, Lacazette 19, 45)*   41,981

Rangers: (4231) Butland; Tavernier (Kasanwirjo 61), Souttar, Propper, Jefte; Diomande, Barron (Raskin 69); Cerny (Sterling 69), Lawrence (Dowell 46), Bajrami (McCausland 81); Dessers.
Lyon: (433) Lucas Perri; Maitland-Niles, Mata (Niakhate 43), Caleta-Car, Tagliafico; Veretout (Diawara 75), Matic (Caqueret 28), Tolisso; Cherki (Nuamah 76), Lacazette, Fofana (Benrahma 75).

LEAGUE MATCHDAY 3

Wednesday, 23 October 2024

Braga v Bodo/Glimt	1-2
Galatasaray v Elfsborg	4-3

Thursday, 24 October 2024

Anderlecht v Ludogorets Razgrad	2-0
Athletic Bilbao v Slavia Prague	1-0
Eintracht Frankfurt v FK RFS	1-0
FC Twente v Lazio	0-2
Fenerbahce v Manchester U	1-1
Ferencvaros v Nice	1-0
Lyon v Besiktas	0-1
Maccabi Tel Aviv‡ v Real Sociedad	1-2
Malmo v Olympiacos	0-1
Midtjylland v Union Saint-Gilloise	1-0
PAOK v Viktoria Plzen	2-2
Porto v TSG 1899 Hoffenheim	2-0
Qarabag v Ajax	0-3
Rangers v FCSB	4-0
Roma v Dynamo Kyiv	1-0
Tottenham H v AZ Alkmaar	1-0

Thursday, 24 October 2024

Fenerbahce (0) 1 *(En-Nesyri 49)*

Manchester U (1) 1 *(Eriksen 15)*   41,443

Fenerbahce: (4231) Livakovic; Samuel (Rodrigo Becao 62), Soyuncu, Djiku, Muldur; Fred, Amrabat; Tadic (Dzeko 79), Szymanski (Yandas 90), Saint-Maximin (Yuksek 79); En-Nesyri (Kahveci 79).
Manchester U: (4231) Onana; Dalot, de Ligt, Lindelof (Casemiro 55), Martinez; Eriksen, Ugarte; Rashford (Antony 73 (Diallo 89)), Mazraoui, Garnacho; Zirkzee (Hojlund 55).

Rangers (2) 4 *(Lawrence 10, Cerny 31, 55, Igamane 71)*

FCSB (0) 0   41,191

Rangers: (4231) Butland; Tavernier, Souttar, Balogun (Propper 68), Jefte; Barron, Raskin; Cerny (Kasanwirjo 74), Lawrence (Diomande 46), Bajrami (Lovelace 74); Dessers (Igamane 57).

FCSB: (4231) Tarnovanu; Pantea (Radunovic 46), Ngezana, Dawa, Popescu M; Alhassan, Edjouma (Musi 60); Stefanescu (Baluta 46), Phelipe (Popescu O 46), Miculescu (Baeten 63); Birligea.

Tottenham H (0) 1 *(Richarlison 53 (pen))*

AZ Alkmaar (0) 0   53,438

Tottenham H: (433) Forster; Gray, Dragusin, Davies, Udogie; Bergvall (Kulusevski 73), Bentancur, Maddison (Sarr 73); Moore (Odobert 88), Richarlison (Solanke 64), Werner (Johnson 46).
AZ Alkmaar: (433) Owuso-Oduro; Maikuma (Lahdo 66), Penetra, Dekker (Meerdink 84), Wolfe■; Clasie, Mijnans (Kwakman 84), Belic (Koopmeiners 46); Poku, Parrott, van Bommel (Kasius 12).

LEAGUE MATCHDAY 4

Wednesday, 6 November 2024

Besiktas v Malmo	2-1

Thursday, 7 November 2024

Ajax v Maccabi Tel Aviv	5-0
AZ Alkmaar v Fenerbahce	3-1
Bodo/Glimt v Qarabag	1-2
Dynamo Kyiv† v Ferencvaros	0-4
Eintracht Frankfurt v Slavia Prague	1-0
Elfsborg v Braga	1-1
FCSB v Midtjylland	2-0
FK RFS v Anderlecht	1-1
Galatasaray v Tottenham H	3-2
Lazio v Porto	2-1
Ludogorets Razgrad v Athletic Bilbao	1-2
Manchester U v PAOK	2-0
Nice v FC Twente	2-2
Olympiacos v Rangers	1-1
TSG 1899 Hoffenheim v Lyon	2-2
Union Saint-Gilloise v Roma	1-1
Viktoria Plzen v Real Sociedad	2-1

Thursday, 7 November 2024

Galatasaray (3) 3 *(Akgun 6, Osimhen 31, 39)*

Tottenham H (1) 2 *(Lankshear 18, Solanke 69)*   51,739

Galatasaray: (3412) Muslera; Sanchez, Ayhan, Bardakci; Yilmaz, Torreira, Gabriel Sara (Kutlu 85), Akgun (Jelert 80); Mertens (Ziyech 73); Osimhen (Demirbay 80), Icardi (Batshuayi 85).
Tottenham H: (433) Forster; Porro, Dragusin, Davies, Gray; Bergvall (Solanke 66), Bissouma, Maddison (Sarr 66); Johnson (Bentancur 46), Lankshear■, Son (Kulusevski 46).

Manchester U (0) 2 *(Diallo 50, 77)*

PAOK (0) 0   73,174

Manchester U: (4231) Onana; Mazraoui, Lindelof, Evans, Dalot (Martinez 65); Ugarte (Eriksen 65), Casemiro; Diallo (Mount 81), Fernandes, Garnacho (Rashford 65); Hojlund (Zirkzee 90).
PAOK: (4231) Kotarski; Jonny Otto, Kedziora, Colley, Baba; Ozdoev, Schwab (Bakayoko 65); Zivkovic, Camara (Despodov 75), Taison (Shoretire 84); Tissoudali (Chalov 65).

Olympiacos (0) 1 *(El Kaabi 56)*

Rangers (0) 1 *(Dessers 64)*   31,795

Olympiacos: (4231) Tzolakis; Costinha (Pirola 77), Retsos, Carmo, Apostolopoulos (Velde 46); Mouzakitis (Kostoulas 86), Hezze; Rodinei, Chiquinho (Sergio Oliveira 77), Gelson Martins; El Kaabi.
Rangers: (4231) Butland; Sterling (Kasanwirjo 52), Souttar, Propper, Jefte; Barron, Raskin; Cerny (McCausland 85), Diomande, Bajrami (Tavernier 85); Dessers (Igamane 84).

LEAGUE MATCHDAY 5

Thursday, 28 November 2024

Anderlecht v Porto	2-2
Athletic Bilbao v Elfsborg	3-0
AZ Alkmaar v Galatasaray	1-1
Besiktas v Maccabi Tel Aviv	1-3
Braga v TSG 1899 Hoffenheim	3-0
Dynamo Kyiv† v Viktoria Plzen	1-2
FC Twente v Union Saint-Gilloise	0-1
FCSB v Olympiacos	0-0
Ferencvaros v Malmo	4-1

FK RFS v PAOK	0-2
Lazio v Ludogorets Razgrad	0-0
Manchester U v Bodo/Glimt	3-2
Midtjylland v Eintracht Frankfurt	1-2
Nice v Rangers	1-4
Qarabag v Lyon	1-4
Real Sociedad v Ajax	2-0
Slavia Prague v Fenerbahce	1-2
Tottenham H v Roma	2-2

Thursday, 28 November 2024

Manchester U (2) 3 *(Garnacho 1, Hojlund 45, 50)*

Bodo/Glimt (2) 2 *(Evjen 19, Zinckernagel 23)*   72,985

Manchester U: (3421) Onana; Mazraoui, de Ligt (Casemiro 66), Martinez (Shaw 60); Antony (Diallo 60), Ugarte, Fernandes, Malacia (Dalot 46); Mount (Rashford 59), Garnacho; Hojlund.
Bodo/Glimt: (433) Haikin; Wembangomo (Sjovold 63), Bjortuft, Gundersen, Bjorkan; Evjen (Auklend 83), Berg, Fet (Saltnes 72); Zinckernagel (Maatta 72), Helmersen (Hogh 63), Hauge.

Nice (0) 1 *(Bouanani 83)*

Rangers (3) 4 *(Cerny 35, Diomande 38, Igamane 45, 54)*   18,008

Nice: (3412) Bulka; Ndayishimiye (Nandjou 19), Rosario, Abdelmonem; Louchet, Boudaoui (Guessand 69), Camara (Salhi 69), Bard (Ndombele 46); Bouanani; Moukoko (Cho 69), Laborde.
Rangers: (4231) Butland; Sterling (Tavernier 62), Souttar, Propper, Jefte; Barron, Raskin; Cerny (McCausland 62), Diomande (Yilmaz 69), Bajrami (Rice 80); Igamane (Dessers 69).

Tottenham H (2) 2 *(Son 5 (pen), Johnson 33)*

Roma (1) 2 *(N'Dicka 20, Hummels 90)*   53,378

Tottenham H: (433) Forster; Porro, Dragusin, Davies, Gray; Kulusevski, Bentancur (Bergvall 77), Sarr (Bissouma 90); Johnson (Maddison 68), Solanke, Son (Werner 78).
Roma: (3421) Svilar; Mancini, Hummels, N'Dicka, Celik (Zalewski 65), Paredes, Kone, Angelino; Dybala (Soule 46), El Shaarawy (Saelemaekers 69); Dovbyk.

LEAGUE MATCHDAY 6

Wednesday, 11 December 2024
Fenerbahce v Athletic Bilbao	0-2

Thursday, 12 December 2024
Ajax v Lazio	1-3
Bodo/Glimt v Besiktas	2-1
Elfsborg v Qarabag	1-0
Ludogorets Razgrad v AZ Alkmaar	2-2
Lyon v Eintracht Frankfurt	3-2
Maccabi Tel Aviv‡ v FK RFS	2-1
Malmo v Galatasaray	2-2
Olympiacos v FC Twente	0-0
PAOK v Ferencvaros	5-0
Porto v Midtjylland	2-0
Rangers v Tottenham H	1-1
Real Sociedad v Dynamo Kyiv	3-0
Roma v Braga	3-0
Slavia Prague v Anderlecht	1-2
TSG 1899 Hoffenheim v FCSB	0-0
Union Saint-Gilloise v Nice	2-1
Viktoria Plzen v Manchester U	1-2

Thursday, 12 December 2024

Rangers (0) 1 *(Igamane 47)*

Tottenham H (0) 1 *(Kulusevski 75)*   48,064

Rangers: (4231) Butland; Tavernier, Souttar (Balogun 35), Propper, Jefte; Diomande, Raskin; Cerny (Sterling 69), Bajrami (Barron 68), Yilmaz (Fraser 80); Igamane (Dessers 80).
Tottenham H: (4231) Forster; Porro, Gray, Dragusin, Udogie; Bentancur (Sarr 61), Bissouma (Bergvall 61); Johnson (Solanke 60), Maddison, Werner (Kulusevski 46); Son.

Viktoria Plzen (0) 1 *(Vydra 48)*

Manchester U (0) 2 *(Hojlund 62, 88)*   11,320

Viktoria Plzen: (3421) Jedlicka; Dweh, Markovic, Jemelka; Cadu (Havel 78), Cerv, Kalvach, Souare; Vydra (Sojka 86), Sulc; Vasulin (Adu 71).
Manchester U: (3421) Onana; Mazraoui, de Ligt, Martinez; Dalot (Garnacho 81), Fernandes, Casemiro (Ugarte 81), Malacia (Antony 61); Diallo, Rashford (Hojlund 56); Zirkzee (Mount 61).

LEAGUE MATCHDAY 7

Tuesday, 21 January 2025
Galatasaray v Dynamo Kyiv	3-3

Wednesday, 22 January 2025
Besiktas v Athletic Bilbao	4-1

Thursday, 23 January 2025
AZ Alkmaar v Roma	1-0
Bodo/Glimt v Maccabi Tel Aviv	3-1
Eintracht Frankfurt v Ferencvaros	2-0
Elfsborg v Nice	1-0
Fenerbahce v Lyon	0-0
FK RFS v Ajax	1-0
Lazio v Real Sociedad	3-1
Ludogorets Razgrad v Midtjylland	0-2
Malmo v FC Twente	2-3
Manchester U v Rangers	2-1
PAOK v Slavia Prague	2-0
Porto v Olympiacos	0-1
Qarabag v FCSB	2-3
TSG 1899 Hoffenheim v Tottenham H	2-3
Union Saint-Gilloise v Braga	2-1
Viktoria Plzen v Anderlecht	2-0

Thursday, 23 January 2025

TSG 1899 Hoffenheim (0) 2 *(Stach 68, Mokwa 88)*

Tottenham H (2) 3 *(Maddison 3, Son 22, 77)*   30,150

TSG 1899 Hoffenheim: (4222) Baumann; Kaderabek, Akpoguma, N'Soki, Jurasek; Stach (Mokwa 79), Becker; Hlozek (Micheler 81), Bischof (Chaves 80); Kramaric, Moerstedt.
Tottenham H: (433) Austin; Porro, Dragusin, Davies, Gray; Bergvall, Bentancur, Maddison (Olusesi 89); Kulusevski, Richarlison (Moore 56), Son (Lankshear 78).

Manchester U (0) 2 *(Butland 52 (og), Fernandes 90)*

Rangers (0) 1 *(Dessers 88)*   73,288

Manchester U: (3421) Bayindir; Yoro (Malacia 55), de Ligt (Maguire 46), Martinez; Diallo, Collyer (Ugarte 73), Fernandes, Dalot; Eriksen (Mainoo 74), Garnacho; Zirkzee (Hojlund 82).
Rangers: (4231) Butland; Tavernier, Balogun (McCausland 46), Propper, Jefte; Barron (Rice 46), Raskin; Cerny (Curtis 60), Bajrami (Dessers 71), Yilmaz (King 90); Igamane.

LEAGUE MATCHDAY 8

Thursday, 30 January 2025
Ajax v Galatasaray	2-1
Anderlecht v TSG 1899 Hoffenheim	3-4
Athletic Bilbao v Viktoria Plzen	3-1
Braga v Lazio	1-0
Dynamo Kyiv† v FK RFS	1-0
FC Twente v Besiktas	1-0
FCSB v Manchester U	0-2
Ferencvaros v AZ Alkmaar	4-3
Lyon v Ludogorets Razgrad	1-1
Maccabi Tel Aviv† v Porto	0-1
Midtjylland v Fenerbahce	2-2
Nice v Bodo/Glimt	1-1
Olympiacos v Qarabag	3-0
Rangers v Union Saint-Gilloise	2-1
Real Sociedad v PAOK	2-0
Roma v Eintracht Frankfurt	2-0
Slavia Prague v Malmo	2-2
Tottenham H v Elfsborg	3-0

Thursday, 30 January 2025

FCSB (0) 0

Manchester U (0) 2 *(Dalot 60, Mainoo 68)*   50,128

FCSB: (532) Tarnovanu; Cretu (Baluta 66), Popescu M, Ngezana, Dawa, Radunovic; Edjouma (Alhassan 46), Sut, Miculescu (Musi 77); Tanase (Stefanescu 77); Birligea.
Manchester U: (3421) Bayindir; Mazraoui, de Ligt, Martinez (Yoro 71); Dalot, Collyer (Diallo 46), Fernandes, Malacia (Garnacho 46); Ériksen (Casemiro 72), Mainoo; Hojlund (Zirkzee 80).

Rangers (1) 2 *(Raskin 20, Cerny 55)*

Union Saint-Gilloise (0) 1 *(Mac Allister 83)*   46,993

Rangers: (433) Butland; King (McCausland 14), Tavernier, Propper, Jefte; Diomande, Raskin, Bajrami (Nsio 80); Cerny (Souttar 63), Dessers, Igamane (Lovelace 80).
Union-Saint Gilloise: (532) Moris; Khalaili, Mac Allister (Rasmussen 90), Leysen, Sykes, Niang; van de Perre (Ait El Hadj 30), Sadiki, Vanhoutte; Ivanovic, Fuseini (Rodriguez 69).

Tottenham H (0) 3 *(Scarlett 70, Ajayi 84, Moore 90)*

Elfsborg (0) 0   57,337

Tottenham H: (433) Austin; Porro, Gray, van de Ven (Dragusin 46 (Scarlett 66)), Davies; Sarr, Bentancur (Bissouma 46), Bergvall; Moore, Richarlison (Ajayi 81), Son (Kulusevski 46).
Elfsborg: (343) Pettersson; Holmen, Henriksson (Holten 86), Yegbe; Hedlund, Zeneli B, Thomasen (Kaib 81), Hult (Gudmundsson 86); Rapp (Richtner 81), Abdulai (Frick 80), Qasem.

UEFA Europa League – League Phase Final Table

		P	W	D	L	F	A	GD	Pts
1	Lazio	8	6	1	1	17	5	12	19
2	Athletic Bilbao	8	6	1	1	15	7	8	19
3	Manchester U	8	5	3	0	16	9	7	18
4	Tottenham H	8	5	2	1	17	9	8	17
5	Eintracht Frankfurt	8	5	1	2	14	10	4	16
6	Lyon	8	4	3	1	16	8	8	15
7	Olympiacos	8	4	3	1	9	3	6	15
8	Rangers	8	4	2	2	16	10	6	14
9	Bodo/Glimt	8	4	2	2	14	11	3	14
10	Anderlecht	8	4	2	2	14	12	2	14
11	FCSB	8	4	2	2	10	9	1	14
12	Ajax	8	4	1	3	16	8	8	13
13	Real Sociedad	8	4	1	3	13	9	4	13
14	Galatasaray	8	3	4	1	19	16	3	13
15	Roma	8	3	3	2	10	6	4	12
16	Viktoria Plzen	8	3	3	2	13	12	1	12
17	Ferencvaros	8	4	0	4	15	15	0	12
18	Porto	8	3	2	3	13	11	2	11
19	AZ Alkmaar	8	3	2	3	13	13	0	11
20	Midtjylland	8	3	2	3	9	9	0	11
21	Union Saint-Gilloise	8	3	2	3	8	8	0	11
22	PAOK	8	3	1	4	12	10	2	10
23	FC Twente	8	2	4	2	8	9	–1	10
24	Fenerbahce	8	2	4	2	9	11	–2	10
25	Braga	8	3	1	4	9	12	–3	10
26	Elfsborg	8	3	1	4	9	14	–5	10
27	TSG 1899 Hoffenheim	8	2	3	3	11	14	–3	9
28	Besiktas	8	3	0	5	10	15	–5	9
29	Maccabi Tel Aviv‡	8	2	0	6	8	17	–9	6
30	Slavia Prague	8	1	2	5	7	11	–4	5
31	Malmo	8	1	2	5	10	17	–7	5
32	FK RFS	8	1	2	5	6	13	–7	5
33	Ludogorets Razgrad	8	0	4	4	11	–7		4
34	Dynamo Kyiv†	8	1	1	6	5	18	–13	4
35	Nice	8	0	3	5	7	16	–9	3
36	Qarabag	8	1	0	7	6	20	–14	3

*Positions 1–8 qualify for Round of 16;
Positions 9–24 qualify for League Phase Play-offs;
Positions 25–36 eliminated.*

Thursday, 13 February 2025

AZ Alkmaar (2) 4 *(Mijnans 12, Parrott 37 (pen), Clasie 57, Wolfe 66)*

Galatasaray (1) 1 *(Sallai 20)*   14,092

AZ Alkmaar: (4231) Owuso-Oduro; Maikuma (Kasius 77), Goes, Penetra, Wolfe; Koopmeiners (Buurmeester 77), Clasie; Poku (Smit 83), Mijnans, Lahdo (Daal 83); Parrott (van Duijn 90).
Galatasaray: (3412) Muslera; Cuesta, Bardakci, Kutlu (Baltaci 71); Sallai, Ayhan■, Gabriel Sara (Lus 90), Jelert (Demir 71); Mertens (Demirbay 56); Morata (Akman 90), Yilmaz.
Referee: Joao Pedro Pinheiro.

FC Midtjylland (1) 1 *(Buksa 38)*

Real Sociedad (2) 2 *(Mendez 11 (pen), Kubo 31)*   9401

FC Midtjylland: (433) Lossl; Andersson, Diao, Sorensen M, Paulinho (Jensen 77); Castillo (Franculino 66), Daniel Silva (Bravo 46), Sorensen O (Andreasen 81); Osorio, Buksa, Simsir (Gogorza 66).
Real Sociedad: (4231) Marrero; Aramburu, Elustondo, Pacheco (Aguerd 46), Balda (Lopez 24); Olasagasti (Zubimendi 46), Marin; Kubo, Mendez, Barrenetxea (Gomez 46); Oskarsson (Oyarzabal 74).
Referee: Orel Grinfeeld.

FC Twente (1) 2 *(Ltaief 5, van Wolfswinkel 90 (pen))*

Bodo/Glimt (0) 1 *(Berg 85)*   29,500

FC Twente: (4231) Unnerstall; van Rooij, Hilgers, Lagerbielke, Kuipers; Vlap, Sadilek; Rots, Steijn (Verschueren 82), Ltaief (Unuvar 69); van Wolfswinkel.
Bodo/Glimt: (433) Haikin; Sjovold (Wembangomo 86), Nielsen, Gundersen, Bjorkan; Evjen, Berg, Saltnes (Fet 87); Blomberg, Hogh (Maatta 67), Hauge (Helmersen 87).
Referee: Sebastian Gishamer.

Fenerbahce (2) 3 *(Tadic 11, Dzeko 42, En-Nesyri 57)*

Anderlecht (0) 0   34,517

Fenerbahce: (3412) Egribayat; Skriniar, Amrabat, Akcicek; Samuel (Muldur 46), Fred, Szymanski, Kostic; Tadic (Yandas 86); En-Nesyri (Tosun 90), Dzeko (Talisca 75).
Anderlecht: (4231) Coosemans; Sardella, Adryelson, Hey, Augustinsson; Dendoncker, Leoni; Degreef (Angulo 86), Stroeykens (Hazard 63), Huerta (Edozie 73); Vazquez (Dolberg 63).
Referee: Nikola Dabanovic.

Ferencvaros (1) 1 *(Abu Fani 23)*

Viktoria Plzen (0) 0   18,519

Ferencvaros: (532) Grof; Makreckis, Gartenmann, Cisse, Raul Gustavo, Civic; Zachariassen (Ben Romdhane 59), Romao, Abu Fani (Rommens 81); Saldanha (Traore 64), Varga.
Viktoria Plzen: (3142) Jedlicka; Dweh, Markovic, Jemelka; Kalvach (Panos 76); Havel (Memic 56), Cerv, Sulc, Cadu (Doski 77); Vydra (Durosinmi 66), Adu.
Referee: Giorgi Kruashvili.

PAOK (1) 1 *(Samatta 21)*

FCSB (0) 2 *(Gheorghita 50, Dawa 60)*   18,343

PAOK: (4231) Kotarski; Jonny Otto, Kedziora, Michailidis (Colley 40), Baba; Meite (Ozdoev 69), Schwab (Camara 69); Pelkas (Despodov 61), Konstantelias, Taison■; Samatta (Thomas Llamas 61).
FCSB: (4231) Tarnovanu; Cretu, Ngezana (Dawa 46), Popescu, Radunovic, Chiriches (Edjouma 56); Sut; Miculescu (Gheorghita 46); Cisotti (Stefanescu 83); Tanase; Birligea (Alhassan 68).
Referee: Lawrence Visser.

Porto (0) 1 *(Moura 67)*

Roma (1) 1 *(Celik 45)*   37,129

Porto: (3421) Costa; Djalo, Perez N, Otavio (Loader 75); Joao Mario, Stephen Eustaquio, Varela (Vieira 63), Moura (Sanusi 85); Borges, Mora (Pepe 63), Aghehowa (Gul 85).
Roma: (352) Svilar; Celik, Mancini, N'Dicka; Saelemaekers (El Shaarawy 46), Kone (Pisilli 46), Cristante■, Pellegrini (Soule 68), Angelino; Dybala (Baldanzi 39), Dovbyk (Paredes 75).
Referee: Tobias Stieler.

Union Saint-Gilloise (0) 0

Ajax (0) 2 *(Rasmussen 59, Mokio 71)* 10,853

Union Saint-Gilloise: (3421) Moris; Mac Allister, Burgess, Leysen; Khalaili, Vanhoutte (Rasmussen 85), Sadiki, Niang; Ivanovic, Ait El Hadj (Fuseini 62); David (Rodriguez 63).

Ajax: (433) Pasveer; Rosa (Gaaei 72), Rugani (Sutalo 46), Baas, Hato; Mokio, Klaassen, Fitz-Jim (Taylor 72); Rasmussen (Godts 83), Berghuis (Traore 83), Edvardsen.

Referee: Donatas Rumsas.

LEAGUE STAGE PLAY-OFFS – SECOND LEG

Thursday, 20 February 2025

Ajax (0) 1 *(Taylor 93 (pen))*

Union Saint-Gilloise (2) 2 *(Mac Allister 16, David 28 (pen))* 51,835

Ajax: (4312) Pasveer; Rosa (Godts 61), Sutalo, Rugani (Kaplan 46), Hato; Mokio (Henderson 91), Klaassen■, Fitz-Jim; Berghuis (Gaaei 46); Rasmussen (Taylor 41), Edvardsen (Traore 46).

Union Saint-Gilloise: (3412) Moris; Mac Allister, Burgess (Sykes 106), Machida; Khalaili (Fuseini 94), Rasmussen (Van De Perre 94), Sadiki (Leysen 106), Niang; Boufal (Ait El Hadj 61); Ivanovic, David (Rodriguez 73).

aet; Ajax won 3-2 on aggregate.

Referee: Christopher Kavanagh.

Anderlecht (1) 2 *(Vazquez 19, 55)*

Fenerbahce (1) 2 *(En-Nesyri 4, Akcicek 63)* 13,724

Anderlecht: (3421) Coosemans; Adryelson, Hey (Vertonghen 66), N'Diaye (Augustinsson 82); Sardella, Leoni, Dendoncker, Maamar; Hazard (Goto 78), Huerta (Angulo 66); Vazquez (De Cat 82).

Fenerbahce: (3412) Egribayat; Skriniar, Amrabat, Akcicek; Samuel (Muldur 67), Szymanski (Yandas 84), Fred, Kostic; Tadic (Kahveci 78); En-Nesyri (Talisca 67), Dzeko (Tosun 84).

Fenerbahce won 5-2 on aggregate.

Referee: Sandro Scharer.

Bodo/Glimt (0) 5 *(Hogh 56 (pen), Hilgers 90 (og), Wembangomo 90, Fet 111, Verschueren 114 (og))*

FC Twente (1) 2 *(Sjovold 26 (og), Steijn 90)* 6417

Bodo/Glimt: (433) Haikin; Sjovold (Wembangomo 79), Nielsen (Bjortuft 79), Gundersen, Bjorkan; Evjen, Berg, Saltnes (Fet 72); Blomberg (Sorli 72 (Maatta 91)), Hogh (Helmersen 87), Hauge.

FC Twente: (4231) Unnerstall; van Rooij, Hilgers (Bruns 111), Lagerbielke, Kuipers; Vlap (Verschueren 102), Sadilek (Unuvar 91); Rots (Lammers 106), Steijn, Ltaief (Kjolo 91); van Wolfswinkel (Booth 106).

aet; Bodo/Glimt won 6-4 on aggregate.

Referee: Alejandro Hernandez.

FCSB (1) 2 *(Cisotti 30, Miculescu 81)*

PAOK (0) 0 50,248

FCSB: (4231) Tarnovanu; Cretu, Ngezana, Popescu, Radunovic; Chiriches (Alhassan 72), Sut; Miculescu (Baluta 78), Tanase (Edjouma 78), Cisotti; Birligea (Gheorghita 46).

PAOK: (4231) Kotarski; Jonny Otto, Kedziora, Michailidis, Baba; Meite (Camara 55), Ozdoev (Schwab 79); Zivkovic (Thomas Llamas 79), Pelkas (Despodov 63), Konstantelias; Samatta (Chalov 55).

FCSB won 4-1 on aggregate.

Referee: Matej Jug.

Galatasaray (0) 2 *(Osimhen 56, Sallai 70)*

AZ Alkmaar (1) 2 *(Maikuma 42, Kasius 55)* 37,343

Galatasaray: (442) Guvenc; Cuesta, Sanchez (Baltaci 46), Bardakci, Jelert; Yilmaz, Torreira (Kutlu 61), Gabriel Sara (Demir 73), Sallai; Mertens (Demirbay 46), Osimhen (Lus 80).

AZ Alkmaar: (4231) Owuso-Oduro; Maikuma, Goes, Penetra, Wolfe (de Wit 87); Koopmeiners, Belic (Smit 61); Poku, Mijnans (Buurmeester 12), Lahdo (Kasius 46); Parrott (Sadiq 87).

AZ Alkmaar won 6-3 on aggregate.

Referee: Anthony Taylor.

Real Sociedad (3) 5 *(Mendez 5, Sucic 18, 45, Oyarzabal 73 (pen), Oskarsson 90)*

FC Midtjylland (2) 2 *(Buksa 24 (pen), Osorio 38)* 27,728

Real Sociedad: (433) Remiro; Elustondo, Zubeldia, Aguerd, Munoz; Sucic (Marin 48), Olasagasti (Turrientes 67), Mendez; Kubo (Becker 67), Oyarzabal (Oskarsson 83), Barrenetxea (Zakharyan 83).

FC Midtjylland: (433) Lossl; Andersson (Mbabu 46), Diao, Sorensen M (Juninho 46), Paulinho (Jensen 60); Bravo, Daniel Silva■, Castillo; Osorio (Franculino 74), Buksa, Simsir (Andreasen 75).

Real Sociedad won 7-3 on aggregate.

Referee: Serdar Gozubuyuk.

Roma (2) 3 *(Dybala 35, 39, Pisilli 83)*

Porto (1) 2 *(Aghehowa 27, Rensch 90 (og))* 55,286

Roma: (3421) Svilar; Celik (Abdulhamid 90), Mancini, N'Dicka; El Shaarawy (Rensch 87), Kone, Paredes, Angelino; Dybala (Baldanzi 87), Pellegrini (Pisilli 78); Shomurodov (Soule 78).

Porto: (343) Costa; Djalo, Perez N, Otavio (Mora 65); Joao Mario, Varela (Perez T 82), Stephen Eustaquio■, Moura (Loader 82); Vieira (William 81), Aghehowa, Pepe (Borges 56).

Roma won 4-3 on aggregate.

Referee: Francois Letexier.

Viktoria Plzen (3) 3 *(Jemelka 27, Sulc 35, Durosinmi 38)*

Ferencvaros (0) 0 10,415

Viktoria Plzen: (3412) Jedlicka; Markovic, Dweh, Jemelka; Memic (Doski 70), Cerv, Kalvach, Cadu (Havel 83); Sulc; Vydra (Kopic 83), Durosinmi (Adu 55).

Ferencvaros: (532) Grof; Makreckis (Toth 78), Gartenmann, Cisse, Ramirez (Traore 46), Civic; Rommens (Ben Romdhane 78), Romao (Kehinde 46), Abu Fani; Zachariassen (Pesic 58), Saldanha.

Viktoria Plzen won 3-1 on aggregate.

Referee: Jerome Brisard.

KNOCKOUT PHASE

ROUND OF 16 – FIRST LEG
Thursday, 6 March 2025

Ajax (1) 1 *(Brobbey 10)*

Eintracht Frankfurt (1) 2 *(Larsson 27, Skhiri 70)*   52,641

Ajax: (433) Pasveer (Gorter 24); Gaaei, Sutalo, Baas, Hato; Mokio (Fitz-Jim 72), Henderson, Taylor; Traore (Konadu 71), Brobbey (Berghuis 64), Godts (Edvardsen 64).
Eintracht Frankfurt: (4231) Trapp; Kristensen, Collins, Tuta, Theate; Skhiri, Larsson; Knauff (Chaibi 82), Gotze (Uzun 90), Bahoya (Brown 73); Ekitike (Wahi 82).
Referee: Simone Sozza.

AZ Alkmaar (1) 1 *(Bergvall 18 (og))*

Tottenham H (0) 0   18,281

AZ Alkmaar: (4231) Owuso-Oduro; Maikuma, Goes, Penetra, Wolfe; Clasie, Koopmeiners; Poku (Belic 81), Buurmeester (Sadiq 81), Lahdo (Kasius 9 (Smit 66)); Parrott (van Duijn 81).
Tottenham H: (433) Vicario; Spence, Gray, Danso, Udogie (Porro 72); Bergvall, Bentancur, Maddison (Sarr 72); Johnson, Tel (Odobert 46), Son (Solanke 72 (Scarlett 90)).
Referee: Rade Obrenovic.

Bodo/Glimt (2) 3 *(Tzolakis 13 (og), Hogh 45, 55)*

Olympiacos (0) 0   8050

Bodo/Glimt: (433) Haikin; Sjovold, Bjortuft, Gundersen, Bjorkan; Evjen (Aukland 73), Berg, Fet (Saltnes 22); Blomberg (Maatta 74), Hogh (Helmersen 74), Hauge (Sorli 90).
Olympiacos: (4231) Tzolakis; Rodinei, Biancone, Carmo (Retsos 81), Ortega (Onyemaechi 81); Hezze, Mouzakitis (Costinha 59); Gelson Martins, Chiquinho, Palma (Velde 74); Yaremchuk (Kostoulas 59).
Referee: Mykola Balakin.

FCSB (0) 1 *(Baluta 68)*

Lyon (1) 3 *(Tagliafico 30, Fofana 86, 89)*   52,028

FCSB: (4231) Tarnovanu; Popescu, Ngezana, Dawa, Radunovic; Alhassan (Chiriches 46), Sut; Miculescu (Stefanescu 90), Edjouma (Baluta 46), Cisotti (Gheorghita 46); Tanase (Musi 77).
Lyon: (4231) Lucas Perri; Maitland-Niles, Mata, Niakhate, Tagliafico; Tessmann (Veretout 76), Matic (Almada 76); Cherki, Tolisso (Akouokou 90), Nuamah (Fofana 68); Mikautadze (Lacazette 68).
Referee: Tobias Stieler.

Fenerbahce (1) 1 *(Djiku 30)*

Rangers (2) 3 *(Dessers 6, Cerny 42, 81)*   42,090

Fenerbahce: (3412) Egribayat; Soyuncu (Djiku 16), Skriniar, Akcicek (Talisca 46); Muldur (Kahveci 79), Szymanski (Saint-Maximin 54); Amrabat, Kostic; Tadic; En-Nesyri, Dzeko.
Rangers: (3421) Butland; Tavernier, Souttar, Propper (Balogun 28); Yilmaz (Sterling 76), Barron, Raskin, Jefte; Cerny (Lawrence 88), Diomande (Hagi 76); Dessers (Igamane 88).
Referee: Alejandro Hernandez.

Real Sociedad (0) 1 *(Oyarzabal 70 (pen))*

Manchester U (0) 1 *(Zirkzee 57)*   34,391

Real Sociedad: (433) Remiro; Elustondo (Aramburu 63), Zubeldia, Aguerd, Munoz; Turrientes (Marin 63), Sucic (Olasagasti 88); Kubo (Becker 83), Oyarzabal, Barrenetxea (Oskarsson 63).
Manchester U: (343) Onana; Yoro (Lindelof 88), de Ligt, Mazraoui; Dalot, Fernandes, Casemiro, Dorgu; Garnacho (Eriksen 78), Hojlund, Zirkzee (Collyer 88).
Referee: Ivan Kruzliak.

Roma (0) 2 *(Angelino 56, Shomurodov 90)*

Athletic Bilbao (0) 1 *(Williams I 50)*   62,540

Roma: (3421) Svilar; Celik, Mancini, N'Dicka; Rensch (Saelemaekers 60), Pisilli (Kone 77), Cristante, Angelino; Dybala (Soule 71), Baldanzi (El Shaarawy 60); Dovbyk (Shomurodov 71).

Athletic Bilbao: (4231) Agirrezabala; De Marcos, Vivian (Paredes 23), Yeray■, Yuri; Jauregizar (Guruzeta 63), Ruiz de Galarreta; Williams I, Gomez (Vesga 77), Williams N (Berenguer 77); Sannadi (Prados 63).
Referee: Sandro Scharer.

Viktoria Plzen (0) 1 *(Durosinmi 53)*

Lazio (1) 2 *(Romagnoli 18, Isaksen 90)*   11,236

Viktoria Plzen: (3421) Jedlicka; Dweh, Markovic, Jemelka; Memic (Kopic 84), Cerv (Panos 80), Kalvach, Cadu; Sulc, Durosinmi (Adu 85); Vydra.
Lazio: (4231) Provedel; Marusic, Gigot■, Romagnoli, Tavares (Lazzari 55); Guendouzi, Rovella■; Isaksen, Dia (Patric Gil 82), Pedro (Vecino 62); Noslin (Tchaouna 62).
Referee: Donatas Rumsas.

ROUND OF 16 – SECOND LEG
Thursday, 13 March 2025

Athletic Bilbao (1) 3 *(Williams N 45, 82, Yuri 68)*

Roma (0) 1 *(Paredes 90 (pen))*   50,666

Athletic Bilbao: (4231) Agirrezabala; De Marcos, Nunez, Paredes (Lekue 69), Yuri; Jauregizar, Ruiz de Galarreta (Prados 88); Williams I (Gorosabel 88), Gomez (Berenguer 46), Williams N; Sannadi (Guruzeta 77).
Roma: (3421) Svilar; Mancini, Hummels■, N'Dicka; Rensch (El Shaarawy 84), Cristante (Saelemaekers 83), Paredes, Angelino; Dybala (Shomurodov 61), Baldanzi (Pisilli 61); Dovbyk (Soule 53).
Athletic Bilbao won 4-3 on aggregate.
Referee: Clement Turpin.

Eintracht Frankfurt (2) 4 *(Bahoya 7, Gotze 25, 82, Ekitike 67)*

Ajax (0) 1 *(Taylor 78)*   57,500

Eintracht Frankfurt: (4231) Santos; Kristensen (Amenda 85), Koch, Tuta, Brown; Skhiri (Dahoud 76), Larsson; Knauff, Gotze (Chaibi 85), Bahoya (Uzun 72); Ekitike (Batshuayi 77).
Ajax: (3421) Matheus Magalhaes; Rugani, Janse (Hato 78), Kaplan; Rosa (Gaaei 69), Mokio (Taylor 63), van den Boomen, Edvardsen; Berghuis (Godts 63), Klaassen; Konadu (Traore 63).
Eintracht Frankfurt won 6-2 on aggregate.
Referee: Irfan Peljto.

Lazio (0) 1 *(Romagnoli 77)*

Viktoria Plzen (0) 1 *(Sulc 52)*   39,547

Lazio: (4231) Provedel; Marusic, Patric Gil (Gila 79), Romagnoli, Tavares (Lazzari 67); Guendouzi, Vecino; Isaksen, Pedro (Dele-Bashiru 79), Zaccagni; Castellanos (Dia 67).
Viktoria Plzen: (532) Jedlicka; Memic (Kopic 86), Dweh, Markovic, Jemelka, Cadu (Doski 78); Cerv, Kalvach (Panos 86), Sulc; Durosinmi (Adu 72), Vydra (Sojka 78).
Lazio won 3-2 on aggregate. Referee: Danny Makkelie.

Lyon (2) 4 *(Mikautadze 14, 47, Nuamah 37, 88)*

FCSB (0) 0   37,322

Lyon: (4231) Lucas Perri; Maitland-Niles, Mata, Niakhate (Caleta-Car 46), Abner Vinicius (Kumbedi 75); Tessmann (Almada 54), Veretout; Nuamah, Cherki (Fofana 65), Tolisso (Matic 54); Mikautadze.
FCSB: (4231) Zima; Cretu (Popescu 46), Ngezana, Dawa, Radunovic (Miculescu 46); Chiriches, Sut (Musi 46); Stefanescu, Edjouma (Cisotti 46), Toma (Gheorghita 79); Baluta.
Lyon won 7-1 on aggregate. Referee: Anthony Taylor.

Manchester U (1) 4 *(Fernandes 16 (pen), 50 (pen), 87, Dalot 90)*

Real Sociedad (1) 1 *(Oyarzabal 10 (pen))*   73,189

Manchester U: (3421) Onana; Mazraoui, de Ligt, Heaven; Dalot, Casemiro (Collyer 79), Fernandes, Dorgu; Garnacho, Zirkzee (Eriksen 89); Hojlund.
Real Sociedad: (433) Remiro; Elustondo (Traore 80), Zubeldia (Aramburu■ 56), Aguerd, Munoz; Mendez, Zubimendi, Marin (Turrientes 56); Kubo (Oskarsson 76), Oyarzabal, Becker (Barrenetxea 55).
Manchester U won 5-2 on aggregate.
Referee: Benoit Bastien.

Olympiacos (0) 2 *(Yaremchuk 53, 65)*
Bodo/Glimt (1) 1 *(Hogh 36)* 31,850
Olympiacos: (4231) Tzolakis■; Costinha, Retsos, Pirola, Ortega (Onyemaechi 75); Hezze (Mouzakitis 46), Dani Garcia; Rodinei, Andre Horta (Yaremchuk 46), Chiquinho (Biancone 83); Gelson Martins (Palma 79).
Bodo/Glimt: (433) Haikin; Sjovold (Wembangomo 69), Bjortuft, Gundersen, Bjorkan; Evjen (Maatta 90), Berg, Saltnes (AukBlend 90); Blomberg, Hogh (Helmersen 69), Hauge (Nielsen 87).
Bodo/Glimt won 4-2 on aggregate.
Referee: Felix Zwayer.

Rangers (0) 0
Fenerbahce (1) 2 *(Szymanski 45, 73)* 50,061
Rangers: (3421) Butland; Tavernier, Souttar, Balogun; Sterling (Yilmaz 56), Raskin, Barron (Lawrence 95), Jefte (Hagi 85); Cerny, Diomande (Bajrami 68); Dessers (Igamane 68).
Fenerbahce: (3421) Egribayat; Muldur (Djiku 88), Skriniar, Akcicek; Samuel (Tadic 74), Amrabat, Fred, Kostic; Talisca (Dzeko 74), Szymanski (Yandas 106); En-Nesyri (Kahveci 106).
aet; Rangers won 3-2 on penalties.
Referee: Espen Eskas.

Tottenham H (1) 3 *(Odobert 26, 74, Maddison 48)*
AZ Alkmaar (0) 1 *(Koopmeiners 63)* 58,302
Tottenham H: (433) Vicario; Porro, Romero, van de Ven (Gray 61), Spence; Sarr, Bergvall (Davies 85), Maddison (Bissouma 77); Odobert (Johnson 78), Solanke, Son.
AZ Alkmaar: (4231) Owuso-Oduro; Maikuma (Meerdink 80), Goes (Belic 87), Penetra, Wolfe; Koopmeiners, Clasie; Sadiq (de Wit 46), Buurmeester (Smit 68), Poku; Parrott.
Tottenham H won 3-2 on aggregate.
Referee: Joao Pedro Pinheiro.

QUARTER-FINALS – FIRST LEG
Thursday, 10 April 2025
Bodo/Glimt (0) 2 *(Saltnes 47, 69)*
Lazio (0) 0 8124
Bodo/Glimt: (433) Haikin; Sjovold, Bjortuft, Gundersen, Bjorkan; Evjen, Berg, Saltnes (Fet 86); Blomberg (Maatta 87), Hogh (Helmersen 81), Hauge.
Lazio: (4231) Mandas; Hysaj (Lazzari 46), Gila, Romagnoli, Marusic; Guendouzi, Vecino; Isaksen (Tchaouna 81), Pedro (Castellanos 64), Zaccagni (Noslin 80); Dia (Dele-Bashiru 46).
Referee: Michael Oliver.

Lyon (1) 2 *(Almada 25, Cherki 90)*
Manchester U (1) 2 *(Yoro 45, Zirkzee 88)* 58,018
Lyon: (433) Lucas Perri; Maitland-Niles, Mata, Niakhate, Tagliafico; Veretout, Akouokou (Lacazette 51), Tolisso; Cherki, Mikautadze, Almada.
Manchester U: (343) Onana; Mazraoui, Maguire (Lindelof 83), Yoro; Dalot, Ugarte (Mount 73), Casemiro, Dorgu; Garnacho (Mainoo 83), Hojlund (Zirkzee 63), Fernandes.
Referee: Glenn Nyberg.

Rangers (0) 0
Athletic Bilbao (0) 0 49,922
Rangers: (343) Kelly; Sterling, Propper■, Balogun; Tavernier, Raskin, Rice (Barron 67), Yilmaz (Jefte 68); Cerny (McCausland 90), Dessers (Igamane 85), Hagi (Bajrami 90).
Athletic Bilbao: (4231) Agirrezabala; De Marcos (Gorosabel 90), Vivian, Yeray, Lekue; Ruiz de Galarreta (Prados 62), Jauregizar; Williams I, Sancet (Berenguer 74), Williams N; Sannadi (Guruzeta 62).
Referee: Istvan Kovacs.

Tottenham H (1) 1 *(Porro 26)*
Eintracht Frankfurt (1) 1 *(Ekitike 6)* 57,849
Tottenham H: (433) Vicario; Porro, Romero, van de Ven, Udogie (Spence 79); Bergvall, Bentancur, Maddison (Sarr 79); Johnson, Solanke (Richarlison 88), Son (Tel 80).

Eintracht Frankfurt: (4231) Santos; Kristensen, Tuta, Koch, Theate; Skhiri, Larsson; Bahoya (Chaibi 70), Gotze (Uzun 90), Brown (Nkounkou 90); Ekitike (Wahi 89).
Referee: Szymon Marciniak.

QUARTER-FINALS – SECOND LEG
Thursday, 17 April 2025
Athletic Bilbao (1) 2 *(Sancet 45 (pen), Williams N 80)*
Rangers (0) 0 52,114
Athletic Bilbao: (4231) Agirrezabala; De Marcos, Vivian, Yeray, Lekue; Jauregizar, Ruiz de Galarreta (Prados 75); Berenguer (Vesga 87), Sancet (Gomez 82), Williams N (Djalo 87); Sannadi (Guruzeta 74).
Rangers: (4231) Kelly; Tavernier, Souttar, Balogun (Igamane 50); Yilmaz (Barron 23), Diomande (Danilo 84), Raskin, Jefte; Cerny (Bajrami 84), Dessers, Hagi (Nsiala-Makengo 46).
Athletic Bilbao won 2-0 on aggregate.
Referee: Irfan Peljto.

Eintracht Frankfurt (0) 0
Tottenham H (1) 1 *(Solanke 43 (pen))* 57,500
Eintracht Frankfurt: (4231) Santos; Kristensen, Tuta, Koch, Theate; Skhiri, Larsson (Wahi 76); Bahoya (Uzun 58), Gotze (Chaibi 17), Brown (Knauff 77); Ekitike.
Tottenham H: (433) Vicario; Porro, Romero, van de Ven, Udogie; Bergvall, Bentancur, Maddison (Kulusevski 45); Johnson (Danso 85), Solanke, Tel (Sarr 79).
Tottenham H won 2-1 on aggregate.
Referee: Davide Massa.

Lazio (1) 3 *(Castellanos 21, Noslin 90, Dia 100)*
Bodo/Glimt (0) 1 *(Helmersen 109)* 54,873
Lazio: (4231) Mandas; Lazzari, Gila, Romagnoli, Marusic (Tavares 68 (Hysaj 94)); Rovella (Vecino 85), Guendouzi; Isaksen (Tchaouna 85), Pedro (Dia 68), Zaccagni (Noslin 88); Castellanos.
Bodo/Glimt: (433) Haikin; Sjovold, Bjortuft (Kjaer 106), Gundersen, Bjorkan (Sorli 103); Evjen (Moe 89), Berg, Saltnes (Fet 56); Blomberg (Maatta 76), Hogh (Helmersen■ 76), Hauge.
aet; Bodo/Glimt won 3-2 on penalties.
Referee: Daniel Siebert.

Manchester U (2) 5 *(Ugarte 10, Dalot 45, Fernandes 114 (pen), Mainoo 120, Maguire 120)*
Lyon (0) 4 *(Tolisso 71, Tagliafico 77, Cherki 104, Lacazette 109 (pen))* 73,228
Manchester U: (3421) Onana; Mazraoui (Shaw 46), Maguire, Yoro; Dalot, Casemiro, Ugarte (Mount 87), Dorgu (Amass 100); Fernandes, Garnacho (Eriksen 100); Hojlund (Mainoo 87).
Lyon: (4312) Lucas Perri; Maitland-Niles, Mata, Niakhate, Tagliafico (Caleta-Car 115); Veretout (Lacazette 55), Tolisso■, Akouokou (Tessman 55); Almada; Cherki (Abner Vinicius 107), Mikautadze (Fofana 64).
aet; Manchester U won 7-6 on aggregate.
Referee: Sandro Scharer.

SEMI-FINALS – FIRST LEG
Thursday, 1 May 2025
Athletic Bilbao (0) 0
Manchester U (3) 3 *(Casemiro 30, Fernandes 37 (pen), 45)* 51,980
Athletic Bilbao: (4231) Agirrezabala; De Marcos (Gorosabel 42), Vivian■, Yeray, Yuri; Ruiz de Galarreta (Prados 46), Jauregizar; Williams I (Djalo 87), Berenguer (Paredes 42), Williams N (Gomez 79); Sannadi.
Manchester U: (3421) Onana; Lindelof, Maguire (de Ligt 65), Yoro; Mazraoui (Shaw 74), Casemiro, Ugarte (Mount 65), Dorgu (Diallo 84); Garnacho (Mainoo 84), Fernandes; Hojlund.
Referee: Espen Eskas.

Tottenham H (2) 3 *(Johnson 1, Maddison 34, Solanke 61 (pen))*

Bodo/Glimt (0) 1 *(Saltnes 83)* 61,327

Tottenham H: (433) Vicario; Porro, Romero, van de Ven, Udogie; Bissouma, Bentancur, Maddison (Kulusevski 65); Johnson, Solanke (Odobert 75), Richarlison (Tel 46).
Bodo/Glimt: (433) Haikin; Sjovold, Nielsen (Moe 46), Gundersen, Bjorkan; Hauge, Fet (Kjaer 76), Saltnes; Maatta (Aukland 65), Hogh, Blomberg (Sorli 77).
Referee: Jose Maria Sanchez.

SEMI-FINALS – SECOND LEG

Thursday, 8 May 2025

Bodo/Glimt (0) 0

Tottenham H (0) 2 *(Solanke 63, Porro 69)* 8030

Bodo/Glimt: (433) Haikin; Sjovold, Nielsen (Nielsen 71), Gundersen, Bjorkan; Evjen, Berg, Saltnes (Aukland 72); Blomberg (Sorli 60), Hogh (Helmersen 60), Hauge (Maatta 84).
Tottenham H: (4231) Vicario; Porro, Romero, van de Ven, Udogie; Bentancur, Bissouma; Johnson (Sarr 68), Kulusevski, Richarlison (Tel 61); Solanke.
Tottenham H won 5-1 on aggregate.
Referee: Maurizio Mariani.

Manchester U (0) 4 *(Mount 72, 90, Casemiro 80, Hojlund 85)*

Athletic Bilbao (1) 1 *(Jauregizar 31)* 73,298

Manchester U: (3421) Onana; Lindelof (Amass 81), Maguire, Yoro; Mazraoui (Shaw 62), Ugarte (Mount 62), Casemiro (Mainoo 81), Dorgu; Garnacho (Diallo 63), Fernandes; Hojlund.
Athletic Bilbao: (4231) Agirrezabala; Gorosabel (De Marcos 61), Yeray, Nunez, Yuri; Ruiz de Galarreta (Prados 61 (Vesga 73)), Jauregizar; Djalo (Olabarrieta 62), Berenguer, Gomez (Guruzeta 67); Sannadi.
Manchester U won 7-1 on aggregate.
Referee: Daniel Siebert.

UEFA EUROPA LEAGUE FINAL 2024–25

Wednesday, 21 May 2025

(at Estadio de San Mames, Bilbao, attendance 49,224)

Tottenham H (1) 1   Manchester U (0) 0

Tottenham H: (433) Vicario; Porro, Romero, van de Ven, Udogie (Spence 90); Sarr (Gray 90), Bentancur, Bissouma; Johnson (Danso 79), Solanke, Richarlison (Son 67).
Scorer: Johnson 42.

Manchester U: (343) Onana; Yoro, Maguire, Shaw; Mazraoui (Dalot 85), Fernandes, Casemiro, Dorgu (Mainoo 90); Diallo, Hojlund (Zirkzee 71), Mount (Garnacho 71).

Referee: Felix Zwayer.

Smiles all round as captain Son Heung-Min finally lifts a trophy for Tottenham Hotspur after winning the UEFA Europa League final against Manchester United at Estadio de San Mames.
(Carl Recine/Getty Images)

UEFA CONFERENCE LEAGUE 2024–25

*After extra time. ■ Denotes player sent off. †Due to the war in Ukraine, Kryvbas Kryvyi Rih played home matches in Slovakia and Polissya Zhytomyr in Poland; Dinamo Minsk played in Azerbaijan (behind closed doors) and Neman Grodno, Torpedo-BelAZ Zhodino and Isloch Minsk Raion all in Hungary (behind closed doors). ‡Due to Israel's war in Gaza, Maccabi Haifa played home matches in Hungary; Maccabi Petah Tikva and Hapoel Be'er Sheva played in Bulgaria.

QUALIFYING PHASE

FIRST QUALIFYING ROUND – FIRST LEG

Wednesday, 10 July 2024

Auda v B36 Torshavn	2-0
Velez Mostar v Inter Club d'Escaldes	1-1

Thursday, 11 July 2024

Aktobe v Sarajevo	0-1
Atletic Club d'Escaldes v F91 Dudelange	0-1
Bala T v Paide Linnameeskond	1-2
Bravo v Connah's Quay Nomads	0-1
Caernarfon T v Crusaders	2-0
FCB Magpies v Derry C	2-0
FK Liepaja v Vikingur Gota	1-1
Floriana v Tre Penne	3-1
La Fiorita v Isloch Minsk Raion	0-1
Malisheva v Buducnost Podgorica	1-0
Mornar v Dinamo Tbilisi	2-1
Noah v Shkendija	2-0
Partizani Tirana v Marsaxlokk	1-1
Shelbourne v St Joseph's	2-1
Siauliai v FCI Levadia	0-2
Stjarnan v Linfield	2-0
Tallinna Kalev v Urartu	1-2
Tikvesh v Breidablik	3-2
Torpedo Kutaisi v KF Tirana	1-1
Torpedo-BelAZ Zhodino† v Milsami Orhei	2-4
UNA Strassen v KuPS	0-0
Valur v Vllaznia	2-2
VPS v Zalgiris Vilnius	1-2

Thursday, 11 July 2024

Bala T (0) 1 *(Ukek 90 (pen))*

Paide Linnameeskond (0) 2 *(Ceesay 64, Medic 90)*   476

Bala T: (442) Torrance; Downes, White, Harrison, Arsan (Kargbo 82); Edwards (Malkin 90), Peate, Robles (Abadaki 55), Newell (Ukek 82); Smith, Mendes.
Paide Linnameeskond: (442) Jarju; Lilander, Delevic, Juhkam, Saliste; Kristal, Medic, Luts S (Luts D 82), Saarma (Hoim 82); Henrik Ojamaa, Jepihhin (Ceesay 57).

Bravo (0) 0

Connah's Quay Nomads (0) 1 *(Maher 83)*   1100

Bravo: (442) Orbanic; Spanring, Jaksic, Miguel Rodrigues, Jovan; Pecar (Ivansek 83), Selan (Stravs 49), Trdin, Stankovic; Poplatnik, Tucic.
Connah's Quay Nomads: (442) Ratcliffe; Poole, Edwards K, Disney, Nash; Williams (Maher 72), Edwards N, Marriott, Bratley; Kenny (Dugan 72), Franklin.

Caernarfon T (2) 2 *(Owen 4, Clarke 37)*

Crusaders (0) 0   1088

Caernarfon T: (4231) McMullan; Owen, Sears, Mooney, Jones (John 11); Gossett, Mendes; Hill (Downey 71), Thomas D (Williams M 80), Lloyd; Clarke (Faux 80).
Crusaders: (433) Tuffey; Larmour, Weir, Blaney, Barr; Lowry, Clarke (Vance 71), Kennedy (Teelan 71); Offord (Lecky 46), Stewart (Nixon 46), O'Rourke.

FCB Magpies (0) 2 *(Taylor 49, Zuniga 82)*

Derry C (0) 0   725

FCB Magpies: (442) Coleing; Ronco (De Haro 82), Diaz, Taylor, Zuniga; Storer (Orihuela 64), Garcia (Coombes L 83), Carrascal, Bayode; Salles (Forjan 46), Arguez (Stevens 90).
Derry C: (442) Maher; Dummigan, Connolly, McEleney S (Todd 85), Doherty B; Diallo (Duffy 61), Patching, O'Reilly, Kelly (Whelan 85); Hoban (Mullen 79), McEleney P.

Shelbourne (1) 2 *(Coyle 1, Jarvis 58 (pen))*

St Joseph's (1) 1 *(Paul 40)*   3655

Shelbourne: (433) Kearns; Gannon, Barrett, Ledwidge, Wilson; Burt (Coote 59), Coyle (Caffrey 74), Lunney; Jarvis (Bone 89), Smith (Boyd 46), Martin (Wood 59).

St Joseph's: (541) Navas; Rey (Bautista 85), Paul (Pons 69), Jolley (Rosa 85), Cardozo, Alvarez (Aznar 63); Walker, Juanma, Sanchez Lopez, Olivero; Rodriguez (Juanfri 63).

Stjarnan (1) 2 *(Atlason 22, 60)*

Linfield (0) 0   682

Stjarnan: (541) Rosenorn; Omarsson, Aegisson, Kristjansson, Ingimarsson, Orvarsson; Thorkelsson, Ingason (Halldorsson 77), Kjartansson (Laxdal 66), Eggertsson (Brink 87); Atlason.
Linfield: (352) Johns; McKay, Roscoe, Whiteside; McGee, Ballantyne (Archer 77), Shields, McClean, Cooper; McKee (Fitzpatrick 73), Millar.

FIRST QUALIFYING ROUND – SECOND LEG   *(agg)*

Wednesday, 17 July 2024

B36 Torshavn v Auda	0-1	0-3
Crusaders v Caernarfon T	3-1*	3-3
Caernarfon T won 8-7 on penalties.		

Thursday, 18 July 2024

Breidablik v Tikvesh	3-1	5-4
Buducnost Podgorica v Malisheva	3-0	3-1
Connah's Quay Nomads v Bravo	0-2*	1-2
Derry C v FCB Magpies	2-1*	2-3
Dinamo Tbilisi v Mornar	1-1	2-3
F91 Dudelange v Atletic Club d'Escaldes	2-0	3-0
FCI Levadia v Siauliai	0-0	2-0
Inter Club d'Escaldes v Velez Mostar	5-1	6-2
Isloch Minsk Raion† v La Fiorita	0-1*	1-1
La Fiorita won 3-2 on penalties.		
KF Tirana v Torpedo-BelAZ Zhodino	0-1	1-2
KuPS v UNA Strassen	5-0	5-0
Linfield v Stjarnan	3-2	3-4
Marsaxlokk v Partizani Tirana	1-2	2-3
Milsami Orhei v Torpedo Kutaisi	0-0	4-2
Paide Linnameeskond v Bala T	1-1*	3-2
Sarajevo v Aktobe	2-3*	3-3
Sarajevo won 4-3 on penalties.		
Shkendija v Noah	1-2	1-4
St Joseph's v Shelbourne	1-1	2-3
Tre Penne v Floriana	1-1	2-4
Urartu v Tallinna Kalev	2-0	4-1
Vikingur Gota v FK Liepaja	2-0	3-1
Vllaznia v Valur	0-4	2-6
Zalgiris Vilnius v VPS	1-0	3-1

Wednesday, 17 July 2024

Crusaders (0) 3 *(Kennedy 47, Lecky 49, Lowry 72)*

Caernarfon T (1) 1 *(Hill 24)*   2184

Crusaders: (541) Tuffey; Offord (Boyd 78), Lowry, Clarke (Teelan 69), Barr, Larmour; Weir, Lecky (Owens 78), Blaney (Forsythe 35), O'Rourke; Nixon (Kennedy 46).
Caernarfon T: (4321) McMullan; Owen, John, Sears, Mooney (Downey 102); Mendes, Gossett, Lloyd (Evans 102); Thomas D (Williams M 102), Hill (Faux 55); Clarke.
aet; Caernarfon T won 8-7 on penalties.

Thursday, 18 July 2024

Connah's Quay Nomads (0) 0

Bravo (0) 2 *(Jaksic 88, Poplatnik 115)*   775

Connah's Quay Nomads: (433) Ratcliffe; Nash, Disney, Edwards K (Burman 116), Marriott; Williams (Roberts 77), Bratley (Maher 46), Edwards N; Poole, Franklin (Hogan 108), Kenny (Dugan 63).
Bravo: (442) Orbanic; Spanring, Jaksic, Miguel Rodrigues, Jovan; Pecar (Hribar 120), Trdin, Stravs (Sabotic 86), Stankovic (Ivansek 77); Poplatnik, Tucic (Selan 91).
aet; Bravo won 2-1 on aggregate.

Derry C (1) 2 *(Connolly 38, Hoban 57)*

FCB Magpies (0) 1 *(De Haro 111)*   2568

Derry C: (4321) Maher; Dummigan (Diallo 79), Connolly (Todd 91), Coll, Doherty B (Whelan 106); O'Reilly∎, Patching, Kelly (McEleney S 91); McMullan, Duffy (Mullen 81); Hoban.
FCB Magpies: (433) Coleing; Ronco (Orihuela 99), Diaz, Taylor, Zuniga (Coombes L 58); Carrascal, Storer (De Haro 46), Garcia (Del Rio 112); Bayode, Forjan, Arguez.
aet; FCB Magpies won 3-2 on aggregate.

Linfield (1) 3 *(Cooper 7, Orr 70, Fitzpatrick 76)*

Stjarnan (0) 2 *(Atlason 57, Halldorsson 88)*   3046

Linfield: (433) Johns; McGee (Orr 64), Whiteside, Roscoe, McKay (Annett 69); McClean, Shields∎, Cooper; Millar, Fitzpatrick, McKee (McBrien 64).
Stjarnan: (433) Rosenorn; Aegisson, Ingimarsson, Kristjansson, Orvarsson; Thorkelsson (Ingason 81), Laxdal, Kjartansson (Halldorsson 80); Eggertsson, Atlason, Omarsson (Brink 77).
Stjarnan won 4-3 on aggregate.

Paide Linnameeskond (0) 1 *(Hoim 120)*

Bala T (1) 1 *(Peate 12)*   1259

Paide Linnameeskond: (343) Jarju; Lilander, Juhkam, Saliste; Kristal, Delevic, Medic (Hoim 84), Henrik Ojamaa; Saarma (Jepihhin 74), Ceesay (Agyepong 46), Luts S (Luts D 84).
Bala T: (433) Torrance; White, Harrison, Peate∎, Downes; Abadaki, Edwards, Smith; Mendes (Ukek 80), Newell (Malkin 106), Robles (Arsan 87).
aet; Paide Linnameeskond won 3-2 on aggregate.

St Joseph's (1) 1 *(Walker 25)*

Shelbourne (1) 1 *(Bone 34)*   763

St Joseph's: (433) Navas; Barnett (Bautista 56), Cardozo, Paul, Pons; Walker, Juanma (Aznar 81), Sanchez Lopez; Alvarez (Juanfri 46), Rodriguez (Lucas Gaucho 56), Rey.
Shelbourne: (433) Kearns; Gannon∎, Bone, Barrett, Ledwidge (Wood 46); Lunney, Coyle (Smith 78), Wilson; Coote (Caffrey 46), Martin (Boyd 59 (O'Sullivan 90)), Jarvis (Griffin 86).
Shelbourne won 3-2 on aggregate.

SECOND QUALIFYING ROUND – FIRST LEG
Tuesday, 23 July 2024

Ballkani v Hamrun Spartans	0-0
Differdange 03 v Ordabasy	1-0
Virtus v Flora	0-0

Wednesday, 24 July 2024

AEK v Inter Club d'Escaldes	4-3
Cliftonville v Auda	1-2
Dinamo Batumi v Decic	0-2
Riga FC v Slask Wroclaw	1-0
Struga v Pyunik	2-1

Thursday, 25 July 2024

Banik Ostrava v Urartu	5-1
Breidablik v Drita	1-2
Brondby v Llapi	6-0
CFR Cluj v Neman Grodno	0-0
CSKA 1948 v Buducnost Podgorica	1-0
Djurgarden v Progres Niederkorn	3-0
F91 Dudelange v Hacken	2-6
FC Zurich v Shelbourne	3-0
FCB Magpies v FC Copenhagen	0-3
Floriana v Vitoria de Guimaraes	0-1
Gent v Vikingur	4-1
Go Ahead Eagles v Brann	0-0
Hajduk Split v B36 Torshavn	2-0
Hapoel Be'er Sheva‡ v Cherno More	0-0
Iberia 1999 v Partizani Tirana	2-0
Ilves v Austria Vienna	2-1
Istanbul Basaksehir v La Fiorita	6-1
KuPS v Tromso	0-1
Legia Warsaw v Caernarfon T	6-0
(played behind closed doors)	
Maccabi Haifa‡ v Sabah	0-3
Maribor v Universitatea Craiova	2-0
Milsami Orhei v Astana	1-1
Mlada Boleslav v TransINVEST	2-0
Noah v Sliema Wanderers	7-0

Olimpija Ljubljana v Polissya Zhytomyr	2-0
Omonia Nicosia v Torpedo-BelAZ Zhodino	3-1
Osijek v FCI Levadia	5-1
Paks v AEK Larnaca	3-0
Radnicki Nis v Mornar	1-0
Sarajevo v Spartak Trnava	0-0
St Gallen v Tobol	4-1
St Patrick's Ath v Vaduz	3-1
Stjarnan v Paide Linnameeskond	2-1
Sumqayit v Fehervar	1-2
Valur v St Mirren	0-0
Vikingur Reykjavik v Egnatia	0-1
Zalgiris Vilnius v Pafos	2-1
Zimbru Chisinau v Ararat-Armenia	0-3
Zira v DAC Dunajska Streda	4-0
Zrinjski Mostar v Bravo	0-1

Wednesday, 24 July 2024

Cliftonville (1) 1 *(Conlan 39)*

Auda (1) 2 *(Ogunniyi 32, Taiwo 76)*   2000

Cliftonville: (433) Odumosu; Pepper, Conlan, Addis, Stewart (Leppard 87); Gordon (Wylie 87), Newberry, Doherty; Kearney, Donnelly (Gormley 73), Curran (Corrigan 68).
Auda: (433) Zviedris; Hrvoj, Bosancic, Korotkovs, Tavares; Ogunniyi (Ramos 76), Talla, Melniks; Mane (Rubenis 90), Taiwo, Clemente (Isajevs 90).

Thursday, 25 July 2024

FC Zurich (2) 3 *(Matthew 1, Marchesano 29, 58)*

Shelbourne (0) 0   8676

FC Zurich: (442) Brecher; Katic, Gomez, Kryeziu, Wallner; Matthew, Conde, Marchesano (Okoflex 71), Krasniqi (Chouiar 59); Perea (Goure 71), Emmanuel (Ligue 82).
Shelbourne: (442) Kearns; Wilson (Boyd 46), Bone, Griffin, Ledwidge; Barrett, Lunney, Coyle (Caffrey 60), Jarvis (Tulloch 78); Wood (Coote 64), O'Sullivan (Smith 78).

Legia Warsaw (2) 6 *(Gual 22, 48, 53, Morishita 44, Kramer 71, Goncalves 90)*

Caernarfon T (0) 0   0

Legia Warsaw: (352) Tobiasz; Augustyniak, Jedrzejczyk, Kapuadi; Wszolek (Chodyna 64), Kapustka (Strzalek 64), Goncalves, Luquinhas (Szczepaniak 56), Morishita; Gual (Majchrzak 72), Kramer (Pekhart 72).
Caernarfon T: (541) McMullan; Owen, John, Sears (Faux 55), Mooney, Jones; Gossett, Thomas D (Davies 55), Mendes (Downey 78), Lloyd (Williams M 78); Clarke (Hill 68).
Played behind closed doors.

St Patrick's Ath (2) 3 *(Mulraney 6, 17, Redmond 77)*

Vaduz (0) 1 *(Del Toro 65)*   2388

St Patrick's Ath: (442) Anang; Sjoberg, Redmond, Grivosti, Breslin; Forrester (Nolan 87), Lennon, Mulraney (McClelland 76), Palmer (Bolger 76); Elbouzedi (Leavy 70), Melia (Kavanagh C 87).
Vaduz: (442) Buchel; Beeli, Simani, Berisha, Krauchi (Stober 86); Hasler (De Donno 82), Hammerich, Emini (Eberhard 46), Del Toro; Cavegn (Navarro 70), Schwizer.

Valur (0) 0

St Mirren (0) 0   1200

Valur: (433) Schram; Gunnarsson (Saevarsson 62), Palsson, Helgason, Larusson; Sigurdsson G, Antonsson Duffield, Sigurdsson K (Johannsson∎ 73); Haraldsson (Heimisson 73), Pedersen (Unnarsson 84), Jonsson J.
St Mirren: (451) Balcombe; Fraser, Gogic, Taylor R, Bwomono; Smyth, Boyd-Munce (Adeniran 16), O'Hara, Brown, Olusanya (Scott 68); Mandron (Ayunga 68).

SECOND QUALIFYING ROUND – SECOND LEG *(agg)*
Tuesday, 30 July 2024

Decic v Dinamo Batumi	0-0	2-0
Drita v Breidablik	1-0	3-1
Flora v Virtus	5-2*	5-2
Hamrun Spartans v Ballkani	0-2	0-2
Pyunik v Struga	3-1	4-3

Wednesday, 31 July 2024

Auda v Cliftonville	2-0	4-1
Austria Vienna v Ilves	4-3*	5-5

Ilves won 5-4 on penalties.

Fehervar v Sumqayit	0-0	2-1
Hacken v F91 Dudelange	6-1	12-3
Mornar v Radnicki Nis	2-1*	2-2

Mornar won 4-3 on penalties.

Spartak Trnava v Sarajevo	3-0	3-0

Thursday, August 1, 2024

AEK Larnaca v Paks	0-2	0-5
Ararat-Armenia v Zimbru Chisinau	3-1	6-1
Astana v Milsami Orhei	1-0	2-1
B36 Torshavn v Hajduk Split	0-0	0-2
Brann v Go Ahead Eagles	2-1	2-1
Bravo v Zrinjski Mostar	1-3	2-3
Buducnost Podgorica v CSKA 1948	1-1*	1-2
Caernarfon T v Legia Warsaw	0-5	0-11
Cherno More v Hapoel Be'er Sheva	1-2	1-2
DAC Dunajska Streda v Zira	1-2	1-6
Egnatia v Vikingur Reykjavik	0-2	1-2
FC Copenhagen v FCB Magpies	5-1	8-1
FCI Levadia v Osijek	0-1	1-6
Inter Club d'Escaldes v AEK	0-4	3-8
La Fiorita v Istanbul Basaksehir	0-4	1-10
Llapi v Brondby	2-2	2-8
Neman Grodno† v CFR Cluj	0-5	0-5
Ordabasy v Differdange 03	4-3*	4-4

Ordabasy won 4-3 on penalties.

Partizani Tirana v Iberia 1999	0-0	0-2
Paide Linnameeskond v Stjarnan	4-0	5-2
Pafos v Zalgiris Vilnius	3-0*	4-2
Polissya Zhytomyr† v Olimpija Ljubljana	1-2	1-4
Progres Niederkorn v Djurgarden	1-0	1-3
Sabah v Maccabi Haifa	3-6*	6-6

Sabah won 3-2 on penalties.

Shelbourne v FC Zurich	0-0	0-3
Slask Wroclaw v Riga FC	3-1	3-2
Sliema Wanderers v Noah	0-0	0-7
St Mirren v Valur	4-1	4-1
Tobol v St Gallen	0-1	1-5
Torpedo-BelAZ Zhodino† v Omonia Nicosia	1-2	2-5
Tromso v KuPS	1-0	2-0
TransINVEST v Mlada Boleslav	0-1	0-3
Tromso v KuPS	1-0	2-0
Universitatea Craiova v Maribor	3-2	3-4
Urartu v Banik Ostrava	0-2	1-7
Vaduz v St Patrick's Ath	2-2	3-5
Vikingur Gota v Gent	0-3	1-7
Vitoria de Guimaraes v Floriana	4-0	5-0
SC Dnipro-1 (withdrew) v Puskas Akademia (walkover)		

Wednesday, 31 July 2024

Auda (0) 2 *(Ogunniyi 51, Taiwo 61)*

Cliftonville (0) 0 1103

Auda: (433) Zviedris; Hrvoj, Ouedraogo, Bosancic, Tavares (Ogunji 85); Ogunniyi (Ramos 77), Melniks, Clemente (Kone 77); Mane (Camara 70), Taiwo, Talla (Traore 85).
Cliftonville: (433) Odumosu; Leppard (Stewart 64), Newberry, Addis, Conlan; Doherty (Wylie 80), Pepper (Gormley 63), Gordon; Kearney, Donnelly (Berry 80), Curran (Corrigan 73).
Auda won 4-1 on aggregate.

Thursday, 1 August 2024

Caernarfon T (0) 0

Legia Warsaw (0) 5 *(Kapustka 46, Jedrzejczyk 48, Pekhart 54, Nsame 72, Barcia 83)* 863

Caernarfon T: (442) McMullan; Owen, Sears■, John, Jones (Evans 74); Faux (Hill 61), Mendes (Downey 61), Gossett, Lloyd; Thomas D (Williams M 55), Clarke (Davies 55).
Legia Warsaw: (442) Kobylak; Pankov (Ziolkowski 57), Jedrzejczyk, Barcia, Chodyna; Kapustka (Urbanski 57), Celhaka (Adkonis 57), Morishita, Kun; Majchrzak (Zewlakow 74), Pekhart (Nsame 57).
Legia Warsaw won 11-0 on aggregate.

Shelbourne (0) 0   FC Zurich (0) 0 3655

Shelbourne: (442) Kearns; Wilson, Barrett, Griffin (Bone 46), Ledwidge; Coote (Lunney 72), O'Sullivan (Burt 63), Caffrey, Martin (Wood 64); Smith, Jarvis (Tulloch 63).
FC Zurich: (442) Brecher; Katic, Gomez, Kryeziu, Wallner; Krasniqi, Matthew (Tsawa 72), Marchesano, Chouiar (Conde 46); Emmanuel (Okoflex 80), Perea (Okita 81).
FC Zurich won 3-0 on aggregate.

St Mirren (1) 4 *(Rooney 16, Olusanya 52, O'Hara 65, Iacovitti 88)*

Valur (0) 1 *(Haraldsson 75)* 6715

St Mirren: (442) Balcombe; Fraser, Taylor R (Iacovitti 71), Brown, Adeniran (Smyth 70); Gogic, O'Hara, Ayunga, Olusanya (Scott 71); Idowu (Taylor F 89), Rooney (Bwomono 71).
Valur: (442) Schram; Gunnarsson, Palsson, Antonsson Duffield, Larusson (Unnarsson 62); Jonsson J, Heimisson, Sigurdsson K, Tryggvason (Saevarsson 32); Pedersen (Finsen 81), Haraldsson.
St Mirren won 4-1 on aggregate.

Vaduz (1) 2 *(Cavegn 22 (pen), 76)*

St Patrick's Ath (1) 2 *(Elbouzedi 28, Palmer 81)* 1405

Vaduz: (433) Schaffran; Beeli (Mertens 72), Simani, Berisha, Hasler (Hammerich 78); Del Toro, Wieser, Emini (Eberhard 78); Cavegn, Navarro (De Donno 67), Schwizer.
St Patrick's Ath: (433) Anang; Sjoberg, Redmond, Grivosti, Breslin; Lennon, Palmer (McClelland 85), Forrester (Bolger 50); Elbouzedi (Leavy 63), Melia (Kavanagh C 85), Mulraney (Kazeem 63).
St Patrick's Ath won 5-3 on aggregate.

THIRD QUALIFYING ROUND – FIRST LEG

Tuesday, 6 August 2024

Noah v AEK	3-1

Wednesday, 7 August 2024

FC Copenhagen v Banik Ostrava	1-0
Hacken v Paide Linnameeskond	6-1
Paks v Mornar	3-0
St Gallen v Slask Wroclaw	2-0

Thursday, 8 August 2024

Ararat-Armenia v Puskas Akademia	0-1
Auda v Drita	1-0
Ballkani v Larne	0-1
Botev Plovdiv v Zrinjski Mostar	2-1
Brondby v Legia Warsaw	2-3
Corvinul Hunedoara v Astana	1-2
CSKA 1948 v Pafos	2-1
FC Zurich v Vitoria de Guimaraes	0-3
HJK v Decic	1-0
Iberia 1999 v Istanbul Basaksehir	0-1
Ilves v Djurgarden	1-1
Kilmarnock v Tromso	2-2
Maccabi Petah Tikva‡ v CFR Cluj	0-1
Maribor v Vojvodina	2-1
Mlada Boleslav v Hapoel Be'er Sheva	1-1
Olimpija Ljubljana v Sheriff	3-0
Omonia Nicosia v Fehervar	1-0
Ordabasy v Pyunik	0-1
Osijek v Zira	1-1
Ruzomberok v Hajduk Split	2-2
Silkeborg v Gent	2-2
Spartak Trnava v Wisla Krakow	3-1
St Mirren v Brann	1-1
St Patrick's Ath v Sabah	1-0
Vikingur Reykjavik v Flora	1-1

Thursday, 8 August 2024

Ballkani (0) 0

Larne (0) 1 *(Donnelly 89)* 455

Ballkani: (352) Kolici; Halili (Smajli 22), Jashanica, Thaqi; Queven, Hamidi, Emerllahu, Ismajlgeci (Tolaj 64), Potoku; Karrica (Giovanni 74), Kryeziu.
Larne: (433) Ferguson; Cosgrove, Bolger, Donnelly, Ives; Sloan, Gallagher, Graham S (Want 81); Ryan (Lusty 81), Randall (Thomson 46), Bonis.

Kilmarnock (1) 2 *(Vassell 6, Wales 90)*

Tromso (0) 2 *(Romsaas 50, Nordas 64)* 6995

Kilmarnock: (442) McCrorie; Lyons, Wright, Mayo, Findlay; Armstrong (Wales 88), Donnelly (Watson 65), Polworth (McKenzie 65), Kennedy (Mackay-Steven 88); Vassell, Anderson (Murray 46).
Tromso: (352) Haugaard; Jenssen A (Barry 70), Guddall, Skjaervik; Paintsil (Nilsen 78), Antonsen (Winther 70), Jenssen R, Hjerto-Dahl, Norheim (Cornic 46); Romsaas, Nordas (Larsen 86).

St Mirren (0) 1 *(Olusanya 90)*

Brann (0) 1 *(Myhre 75)* 　　　　　　　　7023

St Mirren: (433) Balcombe; Fraser, Rooney, Taylor R (Iacovitti 69), Brown (Tanser 63); Smyth, Gogic, Boyd-Munce; Mandron (Olusanya 63), Ayunga (Scott 69), Idowu (Adeniran 63).
Brann: (433) Dyngeland; Pedersen, Knudsen, Kristiansen, Soltvedt; Kartum (Opsahl 89), Kornvig, Myhre; Blomberg (Mathisen 89), Finne (Heggebo 79), Castro (Sande 76).

St Patrick's Ath (1) 1 *(Palmer 35)*

Sabah (0) 0 　　　　　　　　　　　4352

St Patrick's Ath: (433) Anang; Sjoberg, Grivosti, Redmond, Breslin; Lennon (Bolger 88), Forrester, Palmer (McClelland 88); Mulraney (Leavy 71), Keena (Melia 46), Elbouzedi (Kavanagh B 79).
Sabah: (4231) Imanov; Seydiyev, Chakla, Irazabal, Letic; Lepinjica■, Camalov; Sekidika (Aliyev 82), Parris (Dashdamirov 72), Safranko (Kupusovic 82); Mickels (Alasgarov 72).

THIRD QUALIFYING ROUND – SECOND LEG 　*(agg)*

Tuesday, 13 August 2024

Mornar v Paks	2-2	2-5
Paide Linnameeskond v Hacken	1-1	2-7

Wednesday, 14 August 2024

Astana v Corvinul Hunedoara	6-1	8-2
Fehervar v Omonia Nicosia	0-2	0-3

Thursday, 15 August 2024

AEK v Noah	1-0	2-3
Banik Ostrava v FC Copenhagen	1-0*	1-1
Brann v St Mirren	3-1	4-2
CFR Cluj v Maccabi Petah Tikva	1-0	2-0
Decic v HJK	2-1	2-2
HJK won 4-3 on penalties.		
Djurgarden v Ilves	3-1	4-2
Drita v Auda	3-1*	3-2
Flora v Vikingur Reykjavik	1-2	2-3
Gent v Silkeborg	3-2*	5-4
Hajduk Split v Ruzomberok	0-1	0-1
Hapoel Be'er Sheva‡ v Mlada Boleslav	2-4	3-5
Istanbul Basaksehir v Iberia 1999	2-0	3-0
Larne v Ballkani	0-1	1-1
Larne won 4-1 on penalties.		
Legia Warsaw v Brondby	1-1	4-3
Pafos v CSKA 1948	4-0*	5-2
Puskas Akademia v Ararat-Armenia	3-3	4-3
Pyunik v Ordabasy	1-0	2-0
Sabah v St Patrick's Ath	0-1	0-2
Sheriff v Olimpija Ljubljana	0-1	0-4
Slask Wroclaw v St Gallen	3-2	3-4
Tromso v Kilmarnock	0-1	2-3
Vitoria de Guimaraes v FC Zurich	2-0	5-0
Vojvodina v Maribor	1-0*	2-2
Maribor won 4-2 on penalties.		
Wisla Krakow v Spartak Trnava	3-1*	4-4
Wisla Krakow won 12-11 on penalties.		
Zira v Osijek	2-2*	3-3
Zira won 2-1 on penalties.		
Zrinjski Mostar v Botev Plovdiv	2-0	3-2

Thursday, 15 August 2024

Brann (1) 3 *(Soltvedt 6, Myhre 85, Heggebo 88)*

St Mirren (0) 1 *(Iacovitti 74)* 　　　　14,500

Brann: (433) Dyngeland; Pedersen, Knudsen, Kristiansen, Soltvedt; Kartum (Sande 73), Kornvig, Myhre; Blomberg, Finne (Heggebo 78), Castro.
St Mirren: (4231) Balcombe; Idowu (Taylor F 71), Gogic, Taylor R (Iacovitti 71), Brown; Fraser, Boyd-Munce; Adeniran, Rooney, Olusanya; Ayunga (Mandron 71).
Brann won 4-2 on aggregate.

Larne (0) 0

Ballkani (1) 1 *(Hamidi 45 (pen))* 　　　2100

Larne: (433) Ferguson; Cosgrove, Bolger, Donnelly■, Ives (Want 110); Sloan (Randall 73), Gallagher, Graham S; Lusty (O'Neill 73), Thomson, Ryan.

Ballkani: (442) Kolici; Thaqi (Engjell 120), Jashanica, Potoku, Ismajlgeci■ (Sinani 108); Hamidi, Emerllahu, Queven (Dulaj 120), Smajli (Giovanni 101); Kryeziu (Tolaj 84). Adetunji.
aet; Larne won 4-1 on penalties. Donnelly and Ismajlgeci sent off after the end of the game.

Sabah (0) 0

St Patrick's Ath (0) 1 *(Elbouzedi 48)* 　　6132

Sabah: (4231) Imanov; Seydiyev, Chakla■, Irazabal, Letic; Khaybulaev (Dashdamirov 30), Camalov (Nuriyev 79); Parris (Alasgarov 58), Sekidika (Seyidov 79), Mickels; Safranko (Aliyev 58).
St Patrick's Ath: (433) Anang; Sjoberg, Redmond, Grivosti, Breslin; Forrester (Bolger 74), Palmer (Kazeem 90), Lennon; Elbouzedi (McClelland 90), Melia (Keena 74), Mulraney (Leavy 78).
St Patrick's Ath won 2-0 on aggregate.

Tromso (0) 0

Kilmarnock (1) 1 *(Skjaervik 11 (og))* 　5891

Tromso: (352) Haugaard; Barry (Larsen 89), Skjaervik (Jenssen A 69), Guddall; Cornic, Hjerto-Dahl, Jenssen R, Antonsen (Erlien 69), Paintsil (Norheim 46); Nordas, Romsaas.
Kilmarnock: (442) McCrorie; Mayo, Wright (McKenzie 90), Findlay, Bainbridge (Deas 70); Armstrong (Watson 70), Lyons, Donnelly, Kennedy; Vassell, Wales (Murray 70).
Kilmarnock won 3-2 on aggregate.

QUALIFYING PLAY-OFFS – FIRST LEG

Tuesday, 20 August 2024

Noah v Ruzomberok	3-0

Wednesday, 21 August 2024

Vitoria de Guimaraes v Zrinjski Mostar	3-0

Thursday, 22 August 2024

Brann v Astana	2-0
CFR Cluj v Pafos	1-0
Chelsea v Servette	2-0
Djurgarden v Maribor	1-0
FC Copenhagen v Kilmarnock	2-0
Fiorentina v Puskas Akademia	3-3
Hacken v 1. FC Heidenheim	1-2
KI v HJK	2-2
Kryvbas Kryvyi Rih† v Real Betis	0-2
Legia Warsaw v Drita	2-0
Lens v Panathinaikos	2-1
Lincoln Red Imps v Larne	2-1
Mlada Boleslav v Paks	2-2
Omonia Nicosia v Zira	6-0
Panevezys v The New Saints	0-3
Partizan Belgrade v Gent	0-1
Pyunik v Celje	1-0
Rijeka v Olimpija Ljubljana	1-1
St Gallen v Trabzonspor	0-0
St Patrick's Ath v Istanbul Basaksehir	0-0
Vikingur Reykjavik v UE Santa Coloma	5-0
Wisla Krakow v Cercle Brugge	1-6

Thursday, 22 August 2024

Chelsea (0) 2 *(Nkunku 50 (pen), Madueke 76)*

Servette (0) 0 　　　　　　　　　37,902

Chelsea: (442) Jorgensen; Veiga, Badiashile, Adarabioyo, Disasi (Gusto 78); Dewsbury-Hall, Caicedo (Lavia 84), Pedro Neto (Madueke 57); Nkunku (Fernandez 57); Guiu (Palmer 57), Mudryk.
Servette: (442) Frick; Tsunemoto, Rouiller, Severin, Mazikou; Douline (Magnin 69), Ondoua, Stevanovic (Antunes 61), Cognat (Ouattara 85); Kutesa (Von Moos 69), Crivelli (Guillemenot 61).

FC Copenhagen (0) 2 *(Diks 77 (pen), Jensen 90)*

Kilmarnock (0) 0 　　　　　　　　17,056

FC Copenhagen: (442) Trott; Gocholeishvili, Vavro, Diks, Meling (Gabriel Pereira 29); Lerager, Jensen, Elyounoussi, Froholdt (Mattsson 57); Oskarsson, Achouri (Robert 85).
Kilmarnock: (442) O'Hara; Mayo, Wright (Deas 66), Findlay, Burroughs (Bainbridge 71); Lyons, Donnelly, Watson, Kennedy (Armstrong 72); Vassell (Wales 72), Watkins (Cameron 87).

Lincoln Red Imps (2) 2 *(Gomez 23, Joe 42)*
Larne (1) 1 *(Lusty 16)* 220
Lincoln Red Imps: (433) Gomez (Villacanas 66); Joe, Santana, Nano, Torrilla; Munoz (Yahaya 82), Ayew, Lopes; Britto (Casciaro 82), Montero (Pozo 88), De Barr.
Larne: (433) Lusty (Magee 76); Ferguson, Cosgrove, Bolger, Want (McEneff 73); Ives, Thomson, Gallagher; Sloan (Glynn 90), Graham S, Ryan.

Panevezys (0) 0
The New Saints (0) 3 *(Davies 52, Williams D 64, Clark 90)* 1035
Panevezys: (442) Cerniauskas; Rasimavicius (Beneta 77), Dubra, Klimavicius, Mazan; Gorobsov (Cadjenovic 65), Benchaib, Veliulis (Sarpong 65), Palacios-Martinez (Vaickauskas 81); Dieng, Gussias (Mbo 65).
The New Saints: (442) Roberts; Daniels, Davies, Bodenham, Marshall (Pask 79); Smith, Williams D, Redmond, Cieslewicz (Wilson 79); Young (Bradley 87), Holden (Clark 79).

St Patrick's Ath (0) 0
Istanbul Basaksehir (0) 0 6219
St Patrick's Ath: (442) Anang; Sjoberg, Grivosti, Redmond, Breslin; Palmer (Leavy 45), Lennon, Forrester (Bolger 90), Elbouzedi; Melia (Keena 90), Mulraney (Kavanagh B 90).
Istanbul Basaksehir: (442) Sengezer; Leo Duarte, Gureler, Opoku, Sahiner (Lima 83); Pelkas (Gurler 83), Ergun, Ozcan (Ozdemir 90), Turuc; Piatek (Keny 90), Davidson (Joao Figueiredo 64).

QUALIFYING PLAY-OFFS – SECOND LEG *(agg)*

Wednesday, 28 August 2024

Gent v Partizan Belgrade	1-0	2-0
Istanbul Basaksehir v St Patrick's Ath	2-0	2-0

Thursday, 29 August 2024

1. FC Heidenheim v Hacken	3-2	5-3
Astana v Brann	3-0	3-2
Celje v Pyunik	4-1	4-2
Cercle Brugge v Wisla Krakow	1-4	7-5
Drita v Legia Warsaw	0-1	0-3
HJK v KI	2-1	4-3
Kilmarnock v FC Copenhagen	1-1	1-3
Larne v Lincoln Red Imps	3-1	4-3
Maribor v Djurgarden	0-1	0-2
Olimpija Ljubljana v Rijeka	5-0	6-1
Pafos v CFR Cluj	3-0	3-1
Paks v Mlada Boleslav	0-3	2-5
Panathinaikos v Lens	2-0	3-2
Puskas Akademia v Fiorentina	1-1*	4-4
Fiorentina won 5-4 on penalties.		
Real Betis v Kryvbas Kryvyi Rih	3-0	5-0
Ruzomberok v Noah	3-1	3-4
Servette v Chelsea	2-1	2-3
The New Saints v Panevezys	0-0	3-0
Trabzonspor v St Gallen	1-1*	1-1
St Gallen won 5-4 on penalties.		
UE Santa Coloma v Vikingur Reykjavik	0-0	0-5
Zira v Omonia Nicosia	1-0	1-6
Zrinjski Mostar v Vitoria de Guimaraes	0-4	0-7

LEAGUE MATCHDAY 1

Wednesday, 2 October 2024

Istanbul Basaksehir v Rapid Vienna	1-2
Vitoria de Guimaraes v Celje	3-1

Thursday, 3 October 2024

1. FC Heidenheim v Olimpija Ljubljana	2-1
Astana v TSC Backa Topola	1-0
Borac Banja Luca v Panathinaikos	1-1
Cercle Brugge v St Gallen	6-2
Chelsea v Gent	4-2
Dinamo Minsk† v Hearts	1-2
FC Copenhagen v Jagiellonia Bialystok	1-2
Fiorentina v The New Saints	2-0
LASK v Djurgarden	2-2
Legia Warsaw v Real Betis	1-0
Lugano v HJK	3-0

Wednesday, 28 August 2024
Istanbul Basaksehir (0) 2 *(Sahiner 64, Kemen 82)*
St Patrick's Ath (0) 0 6223
Istanbul Basaksehir: (433) Sengezer; Leo Duarte (Kemen 7), Gureler, Opoku, Sahiner (Ozdemir 76); Pelkas (Lima 76), Ergun, Ozcan; Turuc, Piatek (Keny 76), Davidson (Joao Figueiredo 70).
St Patrick's Ath: (433) Anang; Sjoberg, Redmond, Grivosti, Breslin; Forrester (Bolger▪ 77), Lennon, Leavy; Elbouzedi (Kazeem 88), Melia (Keena 68), Mulraney (Kavanagh B 77).
Istanbul Basaksehir won 2-0 on aggregate.

Thursday, 29 August 2024
Kilmarnock (1) 1 *(Watkins 16)*
FC Copenhagen (0) 1 *(Mayo 68 (og))* 8083
Kilmarnock: (442) O'Hara; Burroughs (Ndaba 83), Wright (Polworth 75), Mayo, Findlay; Armstrong (Mackay-Steven 83), Donnelly (Watson 25), Lyons, Kennedy; Vassell, Watkins (Wales 75).
FC Copenhagen: (433) Trott; Diks, Vavro, Gabriel Pereira, Lopez; Froholdt (Oskarsson 63), Lerager, Falk; Elyounoussi, Claesson (Mattsson 80), Achouri (Robert 77).
FC Copenhagen won 3-1 aggregate.

Larne (2) 3 *(Ryan 29 (pen), 42 (pen), 83)*
Lincoln Red Imps (1) 1 *(Lopes 20)* 2462
Larne: (433) Ferguson; Cosgrove, Want, Bolger (McEneff 46); Ives; Sloan, Thomson, Gallagher▪; Lusty (Magee 78), Ryan (Devlin 90), Graham S.
Lincoln Red Imps: (433) Santana; Nano, Munoz, Torrilla (Yahaya 56), Ayew (Casciaro 87); Britto, Lopes, Joe; Gomez, Montero (Villacanas 81), De Barr.
Larne won 4-3 on aggregate.

Servette (1) 2 *(Guillemenot 32, Crivelli 72)*
Chelsea (1) 1 *(Nkunku 14 (pen))* 28,000
Servette: (4411) Mall; Tsunemoto, Rouiller, Severin, Mazikou; Cognat, Ondoua, Douline (Ouattara 85), Kutesa (Von Moos 78); Antunes (Crivelli 62); Guillemenot (Stevanovic 62).
Chelsea: (4231) Jorgensen; Veiga, Badiashile, Adarabioyo, Disasi; Fernandez (Caicedo 63), Dewsbury-Hall; Madueke (George 62), Nkunku, Mudryk (Palmer 74); Guiu (Jackson 63).
Chelsea won 3-2 on aggregate.

The New Saints (0) 0
Panevezys (0) 0 1097
The New Saints: (433) Roberts; Daniels, Davies, Bodenham, Marshall (Pask 19); Smith, Redmond, Williams D (Hudson 89); Holden, Wilson (Clark 76), Cieslewicz (Bradley 89).
Panevezys: (4141) Timbur; Rasimavicius▪, Dubra, Klimavicius, Mazan; Cadjenovic; Dieng (Bosancic 89), Vaicekauskas, Benchaib, Veliulis (Sarpong 70); Gussias (Karvatskyi 78).
The New Saints won 3-0 on aggregate.

LEAGUE PHASE

Molde v Larne	3-0
Noah v Mlada Boleslav	2-0
Omonia Nicosia v Vikingur Reykjavik	4-0
Petrocub Hincesti v Pafos	1-4
Shamrock R v APOEL	1-1

Thursday, 3 October 2024
Chelsea (1) 4 *(Veiga 12, Pedro Neto 46, Nkunku 63, Dewsbury-Hall 70)*
Gent (0) 2 *(Watanabe 50, Gandelman 90)* 38,546
Chelsea: (4231) Jorgensen; Disasi, Adarabioyo, Badiashile, Veiga; Casadei, Dewsbury-Hall; Pedro Neto (George 80), Joao Felix (Mudryk; Nkunku (Guiu 80).
Gent: (343) Roef; Mitrovic, Watanabe, Torunarigha; Gambor (Samoise 89), Ito, Delorge-Knieper (Gandelman 78); Brown; Fadiga (Araujo 64), Gudjohnsen (Dean 64); Surdez (Kums 78).

Dinamo Minsk† (1) 1 *(Alfred 21)*

Hearts (1) 2 *(Politevich 37 (og), Dhanda 90)* 0

Dinamo Minsk: (4141) Lapoukhov; Pigas, Politevich, Sachivko, Rai (Selyava 30); Kalinin; Podstrelov (Adeola 72), Amian, Demchenko (Kulikov 72), Zherdev (Pedro Igor 46); Alfred (Melnichenko 85).
Hearts: (433) Gordon; Forrester, Kent, Rowles, Penrice; Devlin (Grant 74), Baningime (Tait 79), Spittal; Forrest (Vargas 56), Shankland, McKay (Dhanda 74).
Played behind closed doors.

Fiorentina (0) 2 *(Adli 65, Kean 68)*

The New Saints (0) 0 10,751

Fiorentina: (4231) Terracciano; Kayode (Dodo 58), Moreno, Biraghi, Parisi; Mandragora (Richardson 45), Adli (Cataldi 83); Ikone, Beltran (Gudmundsson 58), Sottil (Kean 58); Kouame.
The New Saints: (442) Roberts; Daniels, Davies, Bodenham, Redmond (Brobbel 82); Holden, Smith, Williams D, Bradley (Marshall 61); Wilson (Cieslewicz 82), Clark (McManus 67).

Molde (0) 3 *(Eikrem 51, Brynhildsen 78, Ihler 90)*

Larne (0) 0 3400

Molde: (352) Posiadata; Amundsen, Oyvann, Hagelskjaer; Linnes (Stenevik 45), Kaasa (Daehli 66), Enggard, Breivik (Eriksen 46), Lovik; Brynhildsen (Ihler 80), Eikrem (Hestad 80).
Larne: (541) Ferguson; Graham S, Cosgrove, Want, Todd, Ives; Sloan (Magee 86), Thomson, Marsh (Randall 79), McEneff (McKendry■ 79); Ryan (Lusty 86).

Shamrock R (0) 1 *(Watts 90)*

APOEL (0) 1 *(Laifis 58)* 7111

Shamrock R: (3421) Pohls; Cleary, Lopes, Grace; Farrugia■, Poom (O'Sullivan C 54), O'Neill (Towell 64), Honohan; Nugent (Byrne 77), Mandroiu (Greene 77); Kenny (Watts 77).
APOEL: (4231) Belec; Susic (Chebake 72), Petrovic, Laifis (Dvali 89), Quintilla; Kostadinov, Abagna (Kattirtzis 61); Ndongala (Corbu 89), Tejera, Marquinhos; El Arabi (Bah 72).

LEAGUE MATCHDAY 2

Thursday, 24 October 2024

APOEL v Borac Banja Luca	0-1
Celje v Istanbul Basaksehir	5-1
Djurgarden v Vitoria de Guimaraes	1-2
Gent v Molde	2-1
Hearts v Omonia Nicosia	2-0
HJK v Dinamo Minsk	1-0
Jagiellonia Bialystock v Petrocub Hincesti	2-0
Larne v Shamrock R	1-4
Mlada Boleslav v Lugano	0-1
Olimpija Ljubljana v LASK	2-0
Pafos v 1. FC Heidenheim	0-1
Panathinaikos v Chelsea	1-4
Rapid Vienna v Noah	1-0
Real Betis v FC Copenhagen	1-1
St Gallen v Fiorentina	2-4
The New Saints v Astana	2-0
TSC Backa Topola v Legia Warsaw	0-3
Vikingur Reykjavik v Cercle Brugge	3-1

Thursday, 24 October 2024

Hearts (2) 2 *(Forrest 16, Spittal 23)*

Omonia Nicosia (0) 0 17,178

Hearts: (442) Gordon; Forrester (Oyegoke 63), Kent, Rowles, Kingsley (McKay 84); Vargas (Grant 64), Boateng, Devlin, Forrest (Penrice 73); Shankland, Spittal (Dhanda 73).
Omonia Nicosia: (4141) Fabiano; Dionkou (Masouras 68), Coulibaly, Helander, Khammas (Kitsos 83); Maric; Simic (Loizou 53), Erakovic, Charalampous, Semedo (Alioum 68); Stepinski (Kakoullis 68).

Larne (0) 1 *(Gallagher 48)*

Shamrock R (3) 4 *(Honohan 3, Kenny 24, Cosgrove 30 (og), Burke 53)* 5439

Larne: (4231) Ferguson; Cosgrove (Want 90), Bolger, Todd, Ives; Gallagher, Thomson (McEneff 60); Magee (Lusty 74), Sloan (Randall 73), Graham S; Ryan.

Shamrock R: (3421) Pohls; Cleary, Lopes, Grace; Burns (Clarke 73), McEneff (Byrne 73), Poom (Watts 73), Honohan; Burke (Noonan C 66), Mandroiu (Nugent 60); Kenny.

Panathinaikos (0) 1 *(Pellistri 69)*

Chelsea (1) 4 *(Joao Felix 22, 55, Mudryk 48, Nkunku 59 (pen))* 59,742

Panathinaikos: (4231) Dragowski; Kotsiras, Schenkeveld, Jedvaj, Mladenovic (Vagiannidis 60); Maksimovic, Cerin; Mancini (Tete 60), Ounahi (Bakasetas 80), Pellistri (Djuricic 70); Jeremejeff (Sporar 70).
Chelsea: (4222) Jorgensen; Disasi, Badiashile, Veiga, Cucurella; Dewsbury-Hall (Chukwuemeka 77), Fernandez (Casadei 71); Pedro Neto (George 62), Mudryk; Nkunku (Guiu 61), Joao Felix.

The New Saints (1) 2 *(Holden 40, McManus 78 (pen))*

Astana (0) 0 2202

The New Saints: (433) Roberts; Daniels, Davies, Bodenham, Redmond; Smith, Williams D, Williams J (Cieslewicz 88); Holden (Clark 71), McManus (Canavan 90), Brobbel (Wilson 71).
Astana: (352) Zarutskiy; Beysebekov, Kalaica, Bystrov; Basmanov (Zhaksylyk 72), Osei, Kuat, Astanov, Dosmagambetov; Karimov, Ahanonu.

LEAGUE MATCHDAY 3

Thursday, 7 November 2024

APOEL v Fiorentina	2-1
Chelsea v Noah	8-0
Djurgarden v Panathinaikos	2-1
FC Copenhagen v Istanbul Basaksehir	2-2
Gent v Omonia Nicosia	1-0
Hearts v 1. FC Heidenheim	0-2
HJK v Olimpija Ljubljana	0-2
Jagiellonia Bialystock v Molde	3-0
Larne v St Gallen	1-2
LASK v Cercle Brugge	0-0
Legia Warsaw v Dinamo Minsk	4-0
Pafos v Astana	1-0
Petrocub Hincesti v Rapid Vienna	0-3
Real Betis v Celje	2-1
Shamrock R v The New Saints	2-1
TSC Backa Topola v Lugano	4-1
Vikingur Reykjavik v Borac Banja Luca	2-0
Vitoria de Guimaraes v Mlada Boleslav	2-1

Thursday, 7 November 2024

Chelsea (6) 8 *(Adarabioyo 12, Guiu 13, Disasi 18, Joao Felix 21, 41, Mudryk 39, Nkunku 69, 76 (pen))*

Noah (0) 0 38,305

Chelsea: (4141) Jorgensen; Disasi, Adarabioyo, Badiashile, Veiga; Fernandez (Casadei 46); George (Chukwuemeka 68), Nkunku (Rak-Sakyi 79), Joao Felix, Mudryk; Guiu (Dewsbury-Hall 46).
Noah: (4231) Cancarevic; Miljkovic (Mendoza 75), Goncalo Silva, Muradyan, Hambardzumyan (Avanesyan 62); Brice, Sangare (Pinson 62); Cinari, Manvelyan (Omar 46), Ferreira; Goncalo Gregorio (Aias 62).

Hearts (0) 0

1. FC Heidenheim (0) 2 *(Conteh 57, Schoppner 89)* 17,692

Hearts: (433) Gordon; Forrester (Oyegoke 77), Kent, Kingsley, Penrice; Boateng (Grant 77), Baningime (Devlin 64), Spittal; Forrest, Shankland, Dhanda (Vargas 64).
1. FC Heidenheim: (4141) Muller; Busch (Traore 37), Mainka, Siersleben, Theuerkauf; Maloney; Conteh (Wanner 64), Beck (Schoppner 83), Kerber, Kaufmann (Honsak 46); Breunig (Pieringer 83).

Larne (1) 1 *(Diaby 4 (og))*

St Gallen (1) 2 *(Gortler 29, Vandermersch 79)* 4448

Larne: (532) Ferguson; Seary, Want (Magee 90), Bolger, Todd, Ives; Sloan (Graham S 76), Gallagher (Donnelly 82), Thomson; Ryan (Randall 82), McEneff (Lusty 76).
St Gallen: (4312) Ati-Zigi; Vandermersch, Diaby, Vallci, Okoroji; Gortler, Stevanovic, Csoboth (Witzig 75); Toma (Konietzke 75); Geubbels (Faber 90), Akolo (Cisse 89).

Shamrock R (2) 2 *(Kenny 23, Watts 38)*
The New Saints (1) 1 *(Williams J 14)* 6108

Shamrock R: (352) Pohls; Cleary, Lopes, Grace; Burns (Byrne 70), Watts (Nugent 85), Poom (O'Neill 85), McEneff (Burke 70), Honohan; Farrugia, Kenny (Greene 79).
The New Saints: (442) Roberts; Daniels, Davies, Bodenham, Redmond; Brobbel, Smith, Williams D, Williams J (Wilson 83); McManus, Holden (Clark 75).

LEAGUE MATCHDAY 4

Wednesday, 27 November 2024
Istanbul Basaksehir v Petrocub Hincesti 1-1

Thursday, 28 November 2024
1. FC Heidenheim v Chelsea	0-2
Astana v Vitoria de Guimaraes	1-1
Borac Banja Luca v LASK	2-1
Celje v Jagiellonia Bialystock	3-3
Cercle Brugge v Hearts	2-0
Dinamo Minsk† v FC Copenhagen	1-2
Fiorentina v Pafos	3-2
Lugano v Gent	2-0
Mlada Boleslav v Real Betis	2-1
Molde v APOEL	0-1
Noah v Vikingur Reykjavik	0-0
Olimpija Ljubljana v Larne	1-0
Omonia Nicosia v Legia Warsaw	0-3
Panathinaikos v HJK	1-0
Rapid Vienna v Shamrock R	1-1
St Gallen v TSC Backa Topola	2-2
The New Saints v Djurgarden	0-1

Thursday, 28 November 2024

Cercle Brugge (1) 2 *(Efekele 40, Magnee 90)*
Hearts (0) 0 7722

Cercle Brugge: (3412) Delanghe; Diakite, Ravych (Utkus 61), Miangue; Efekele (Minda 62), De Wilde (Van der Bruggen 72), Francis, Magnee; Somers; Brunner (Olaigbe 85), Felipe Augusto (Agyekum 72).
Hearts: (4231) Gordon; Forrester (Oyegoke 60), Kent, Rowles, Penrice; Devlin, Boateng (McKay 75); Forrest (Boyce 87), Shankland, Dhanda (Spittal 60); Vargas (Wilson 75).

1. FC Heidenheim (0) 0

Chelsea (0) 2 *(Nkunku 51, Mudryk 86)* 15,000

1. FC Heidenheim: (4141) Muller; Traore (Breunig 68), Mainka, Siersleben, Theuerkauf; Maloney (Beck 68); Scienza, Wanner, Dorsch (Schoppner 57), Honsak (Conteh 56); Kaufmann (Gimber 77).
Chelsea: (4231) Jorgensen; Disasi, Adarabioyo, Badiashile, Veiga; Casadei■, Dewsbury-Hall (Rak-Sakyi 90); Sancho (George 90), Nkunku (Chukwuemeka 75), Mudryk; Guiu (Joao Felix 62).

Olimpija Ljubljana (0) 1 *(Durdov 67)*
Larne (0) 0 4954

Olimpija Ljubljana: (3142) Vidovsek; Pedreno (Diogo Pinto 46), Ratnik, Muhamedbegovic; Agba; Jorge Silva (Lasickas 88), Thalisson (Marin 46), Doffo, Sualehe; Florucz (Kojic 90), Brest (Durdov 65).
Larne: (541) Ferguson; Thomson (Magee 88), Want, Bolger, Donnelly, Graham S■; Sloan (McKendry 69), Randall (Todd 69), Gallagher, McEneff (Cosgrove 59); O'Neill (Lusty 69).

Rapid Vienna (1) 1 *(Cvetkovic 9)*
Shamrock R (0) 1 *(Kenny 55)* 20,700

Rapid Vienna: (4222) Hedl N; Bolla, Cvetkovic, Raux Yao, Auer; Sangare, Grgic; Schaub (Kaygin 67), Seidl (Wurmbrand 88); Beljo, Burgstaller (Bischof 67).
Shamrock R: (352) Pohls; Cleary, Lopes, Grace; Burns (Clarke 88), Watts (Byrne 88), O'Neill (Nugent 76), Poom, Honohan; Kenny, Farrugia.

The New Saints (0) 0

Djurgarden (1) 1 *(Gulliksen 41)* 3568

The New Saints: (442) Roberts; Baker (Wilson 69), Pask, McGahey, Davies; Daniels, Williams D (Smith 83), Redmond (Bradley 90), Williams J (Cieslewicz 83); Clark (Holden 69), McManus.

Djurgarden: (4231) Rinne; Stahl, Une Larsson, Danielson, Kosugi; Stensson (Schuller 70), Sabovic; Wikheim, Gulliksen (Aslund 90), Nguen (Haarala 90); Hummet.

LEAGUE MATCHDAY 5

Thursday, 12 December 2024
Astana v Chelsea	1-3
Dinamo Minsk† v Larne	2-0
FC Copenhagen v Hearts	2-0
Fiorentina v LASK	7-0
Gent v TSC Backa Topola	3-0
HJK v Molde	2-2
Istanbul Basaksehir v 1. FC Heidenheim	3-1
Legia Warsaw v Lugano	1-2
Mlada Boleslav v Jagiellonia Bialystock	1-0
Noah v APOEL	1-3
Olimpija Ljubljana v Cercle Brugge	1-4
Omonia Nicosia v Rapid Vienna	3-1
Pafos v Celje	2-0
Petrocub Hincesti v Real Betis	0-1
Shamrock R v Borac Banja Luca	3-0
St Gallen v Vitoria de Guimaraes	1-4
The New Saints v Panathinaikos	0-2
Vikingur Reykjavik v Djurgarden	1-2

Thursday, 12 December 2024

Astana (1) 1 *(Tomasov 45)*

Chelsea (3) 3 *(Guiu 14, 18, Veiga 39)* 20,982

Astana: (541) Seisen; Bartolec, Kazukolovas, Marochkin, Kalaica, Vorogovskiy; Tomasov (Gripshi 88), Ebong, Amanovic (Osei 46), Camara (Astanov 90); Geoffrey (Karimov 72).
Chelsea: (343) Jorgensen; Acheampong, Adarabioyo, Disasi; Dewsbury-Hall, Rak-Sakyi (Dyer 86), Chukwuemeka (Vale 67), Veiga; Pedro Neto (Ampah 46), Guiu (Mheuka 78), George.

Dinamo Minsk† (0) 2 *(Gavrilovich 67 (pen), Zherdev 73)*
Larne (0) 0 0

Dinamo Minsk: (433) Lapoukhov; Pigas, Begunov (Politevich 90), Gavrilovich, Rai; Kulikov (Amian 89), Kalinin, Demchenko; Sedko (Okoro 84), Adeola (Melnichenko 46), Podstrelov (Zherdev 46).
Larne: (532) Ferguson; Cosgrove, Want, Bolger■, Donnelly, Ives; Randall (Sloan 59), Gallagher, Thomson (Lusty 76); Ryan (McEneff 60), O'Neill (McKendry 76).
Played behind closed doors.

FC Copenhagen (0) 2 *(Chiakha 48, Diks 78 (pen))*
Hearts (0) 0 24,207

FC Copenhagen: (4231) Trott; Diks, Gabriel Pereira, Hatzidiakos, Lopez (Meling 90); Clem (Lerager 81), Delaney; Elyounoussi, Claesson (Mattsson 87), Robert (Froholdt 82); Chiakha (Cornelius 87).
Hearts: (442) Gordon; Oyegoke, Kent (Forrester 35), Rowles, Penrice; Vargas (Wilson 73), Devlin, Boateng, Forrest (Oda 73); Shankland, Spittal.

Shamrock R (1) 3 *(Kenny 12, 64, Farrugia 56)*
Borac Banja Luca (0) 0 7442

Shamrock R: (352) Pohls; Cleary, Lopes, Grace; Burns, Watts (Byrne 67), O'Neill, Poom (Noonan C 77), Honohan (Clarke 67); Kenny (Greene 66), Farrugia (Mandroiu 76).
Borac Banja Luca: (4231) Manojlovic; Vukcevic (Hrelja 70), Meijers, Carolina, Herrera; Grahovac, Skorup (Sreckovic 70); Kulasin, Ogrinec, Savic (Vranjes 79); Despotovic.

The New Saints (0) 0

Panathinaikos (1) 2 *(Djuricic 15, Ioannidis 61 (pen))* 5716

The New Saints: (442) Roberts; Baker (Daniels 11), McGahey, Pask, Davies; Brobbel (Bradley 78), Williams D (Smith 63), Redmond, Williams J (McManus 63); Holden, Clark (Wilson 78).
Panathinaikos: (4141) Dragowski; Vagiannidis (Kotsiras 89), Schenkeveld (Jedvaj 46), Ingason, Mladenovic (Max 73); Willian Arao; Tete, Bakasetas (Ounahi 89), Maksimovic, Djuricic (Mancini 73); Ioannidis.

LEAGUE MATCHDAY 6

Thursday, 19 December 2024

1. FC Heidenheim v St Gallen	1-1
APOEL v Astana	1-1
Borac Banja Luca v Omonia Nicosia	0-0
Celje v The New Saints	3-2
Cercle Brugge v Istanbul Basaksehir	1-1
Chelsea v Shamrock R	5-1
Djurgarden v Legia Warsaw	3-1
Hearts v Petrocub Hincesti	2-2
Jagiellonia Bialystock v Olimpija Ljubljana	0-0
Larne v Gent	1-0
LASK v Vikingur Reykjavik	1-1
Lugano v Pafos	2-2
Molde v Mlada Boleslav	4-3
Panathinaikos v Dinamo Minsk	4-0
Rapid Vienna v FC Copenhagen	3-0
Real Betis v HJK	1-0
TSC Backa Topola v Noah	4-3
Vitoria de Guimaraes v Fiorentina	1-1

Thursday, 19 December 2024

Celje (2) 3 *(Edmilson 20, 43, Zec 79)*

The New Saints (2) 2 *(Davies 19, Holden 42)*   2640

Celje: (4141) Rozman; Nieto, Zec, Nemanic (Vuklisevic 46), Karnicnik; Dulca (Brnic 46); Seslar, Lhernault (Kvesic 46), Svetlin (Kouter 74), Zabukovnik; Edmilson (Matko 59).
The New Saints: (532) Roberts; Daniels, Smith, Davies, Pask, Redmond (Williams J 67); Holden (Bradley 86), Williams D, Brobbel (Cieslewicz 61); McManus (Wilson 67), Clark (Marshall 61).

Chelsea (4) 5 *(Guiu 22, 34, 45, Dewsbury-Hall 40, Cucurella 58)*

Shamrock R (1) 1 *(Poom 26)*   38,467

Chelsea: (4231) Jorgensen; Acheampong, Disasi (Murray-Campbell 59), Veiga, Cucurella; Dewsbury-Hall (Rak-Sakyi 83), Casadei; Madueke (Vale 46), Nkunku, George; Guiu (Joao Felix 60).
Shamrock R: (352) Pohls; Cleary, Lopes, Grace; Burns, Watts (Byrne 67), O'Neill (Nugent 78), Poom (Mandroiu 68), Honohan; Kenny (Greene 73), Farrugia (Burke 73).

Hearts (0) 2 *(Wilson 64, Spittal 70)*

Petrocub Hincesti (1) 2 *(Platica S 20, Mudrac 83 (pen))*   17,103

Hearts: (442) Gordon; Oyegoke (Boyce 85), Halkett (Boateng 69), Rowles, Penrice; Forrest (Spittal 46), Devlin, Tait (Grant 69); Dhanda (Vargas 78); Shankland, Wilson.
Petrocub Hincesti: (343) Smalenea; Potirniche, Mudrac, Bors; Jardan I, Agyemang, Douanla (Diallo 78) Demian (Lupan 78); Ambros (Caruntu 60), Platica S, Puscas (Jardan V 89).

Larne (0) 1 *(Cosgrove 74)*

Gent (0) 0   2393

Larne: (532) Ferguson; Cosgrove, Want, Todd, Donnelly, Ives (McEneff 60); Randall (Thomson 55), Gallagher (Sloan 90), Graham S; Ryan (McKendry 90), Lusty (Magee 90).
Gent: (4231) Roef; Araujo (De Meyer 46), Watanabe, Mitrovic, Brown (Torunarigha 77); Ito, Kums (Delorge-Knieper 60); Surdez (Sonko 46), Gandelman, De Vlieger (Dean 60); Gudjohnsen.

UEFA Conference League – League Phase Final Table

		P	W	D	L	F	A	GD	Pts
1	Chelsea	6	6	0	0	26	5	21	18
2	Vitoria de Guimaraes	6	4	2	0	13	6	7	14
3	Fiorentina	6	4	1	1	18	7	11	13
4	Rapid Vienna	6	4	1	1	11	5	6	13
5	Djurgarden*	6	4	1	1	11	7	4	13
6	Lugano*	6	4	1	1	11	7	4	13
7	Legia Warsaw	6	4	0	2	13	5	8	12
8	Cercle Brugge	6	3	2	1	14	7	7	11
9	Jagiellonia Bialystock	6	3	2	1	10	5	5	11
10	Shamrock R	6	3	2	1	12	9	3	11
11	APOEL	6	3	2	1	8	5	3	11
12	Pafos	6	3	1	2	11	7	4	10
13	Panathinaikos	6	3	1	2	10	7	3	10
14	Olimpija Ljubljana	6	3	1	2	7	6	1	10
15	Real Betis	6	3	1	2	6	5	1	10
16	1. FC Heidenheim	6	3	1	2	7	7	0	10
17	Gent	6	3	0	3	8	8	0	9
18	FC Copenhagen	6	2	2	2	9	9	–1	8
19	Vikingur Reykjavik	6	2	2	2	7	8	–1	8
20	Borac Banja Luca	6	2	2	2	4	7	–3	8
21	Celje	6	2	1	3	13	13	0	7
22	Omonia Nicosia	6	2	1	3	7	7	0	7
23	Molde	6	2	1	3	10	11	–1	7
24	TSC Backa Topola	6	2	1	3	10	13	–3	7
25	Hearts	6	1	3	2	6	9	–3	7
26	Istanbul Basaksehir	6	1	3	2	9	12	–3	6
27	Mlada Boleslav	6	2	0	4	7	10	–3	6
28	Astana	6	1	2	3	4	8	–4	5
29	St Gallen	6	1	2	3	10	18	–8	5
30	HJK	6	1	1	4	3	9	–6	4
31	Noah	6	1	1	4	6	16	–10	4
32	The New Saints	6	1	0	5	5	10	–5	3
33	Dinamo Minsk†	6	1	0	5	4	13	–9	3
34	Larne	6	1	0	5	3	12	–9	3
35	LASK	6	0	3	3	4	14	–10	3
36	Petrocub Hincesti	6	0	2	4	4	13	–9	2

*Ranking decided on away goals scored:
Djurgarden 5, Lugano 4.
Positions 1–8 qualify for Round of 16;
Positions 9–24 qualify for League Phase Play-offs;
Positions 25–36 eliminated.*

LEAGUE PHASE PLAY-OFFS

LEAGUE PHASE PLAY-OFFS – FIRST LEG
Thursday, 13 February 2025

Borac Banja Luca (0) 1 *(Ogrinec 90)*

Olimpija Ljubljana (0) 0   8406

Borac Banja Luca: (4231) Manojlovic; Kvrzic (Cavic 66), Meijers, Carolina, Herrera; Nikolov (Vranjes 66), Zoric (Vukovic 23); Kulasin (Rogan 78), Ogrinec, Savic; Despotovic.
Olimpija Ljubljana: (442) Vidovsek; Jorge Silva, Ratnik, Muhamedbegovic, Sualehe (Lasickas 61); Blanco (Kojic 61), Celhaka, Doffo (Pedreno 90), Brest (Agba 88); Florucz■, Tamm (Durdov 90).

Celje (1) 2 *(Kucys 2, 59)*

APOEL (1) 2 *(Abagna 32, Laifis 70)*   4050

Celje: (4141) Silva; Nieto, Bejger (Vuklisevic 74), Nemanic, Karnicnik; Zabukovnik; Delaurier-Chaubet (Matko 74), Seslar (Edmilson 86), Kvesic (Lhernault 74), Svetlin; Kucys.
APOEL: (532) Belec; Chebake, Susic, Dvali■, Laifis, Quintilla; Abagna (Kattirtzis 83), Galanopoulos, Tejera; Drazic (El Arabi 61), Donis (Marquinhos 26 (Alejo 83)).

FC Copenhagen (1) 1 *(Larsson 45)*

1.FC Heidenheim (0) 2 *(Keller 59, Siersleben 85)*   22,789

FC Copenhagen: (442) Ramaj; Huescas (Clem 79), Gabriel Pereira, Hatzidiakos, Lopez; Larsson (Gocholeishvili 78), Delaney, Froholdt, Robert (Achouri 71); Mattsson (Chiakha 65), Claesson (Elyounoussi 71).
1.FC Heidenheim: (4141) Feller; Busch, Mainka, Siersleben, Theuerkauf (Traore 46); Keller; Conteh (Honsak 61), Wanner (Beck 84), Niehues (Schoppner 81), Scienza; Pieringer (Zivzivadze 61).

Gent (0) 0

Real Betis (0) 3 *(Antony 47, Bakambu 71, Altimira 84)*   11,051

Gent: (3412) Roef; Mitrovic, Watanabe, Torunarigha; Samoise, Ito, Da Silva Lopes (Delorge-Knieper 77), Araujo (Brown 71); Kums (De Vlieger 85); Vanzeir (Surdez 71); Gudjohnsen (Goore 77).
Real Betis: (4231) Vieites; Sabaly (Ortiz 90), Bartra, Natan, Perraud; Lo Celso (Flores 90), Roca (Altimira 81); Antony (Avila 74), Isco (Johnny 74), Ezzalzouli; Bakambu.

Molde (0) 0

Shamrock R (0) 1 *(Noonan 57)*   3051

Molde: (4231) Karlstrom; Stenevik, Amundsen, Lund■, Haugen (Linnes 72); Daehli, Breivik; Eriksen, Eikrem (Enggard 71), Kaasa (Hestad 46); Gulbrandsen (Haugan 44).
Shamrock R: (532) McGinty; Honohan, Cleary, Lopes, Grace, Grant; Watts (Burke 69), Healy (O'Neill 88), McEneff; Noonan M (Greene 82), Mandroiu.

Omonia Nicosia (0) 1 *(Semedo 51 (pen))*

Pafos (0) 1 *(Orsic 84)*   13,787

Omonia Nicosia: (433) Fabiano; Dionkou (Masouras 90), Coulibaly, Panagiotou, Khammas; Erakovic (Kousoulos 88), Maric, Jovetic; Loizou, Kakoullis, Semedo (Alioum 88).
Pafos: (442) Ivusic; Bruno, Sarlija, Goldar, Silva (Sema 75); Jaja (Orsic 63), Sunjic, Pepe, Tankovic; Jairo (Anderson Silva 75), Dragomir.

TSC Backa Topola (1) 1 *(Mboungou 28)*

Jagiellonia Bialystok (1) 3 *(Imaz 31, 89, Pululu 81)*   2550

TSC Backa Topola: (4321) Ilic; Djordjevic, Degenek, Capan, Radojevic; Milosavljevic (Pejic 90), Radin, Stanic; Jovanovic (Pantovic 84), Mboungou; Lazetic (Sos 76).
Jagiellonia Bialystok: (433) Abramowicz; Wojtuszek, Skrzypczak, Ebosse (Stojinovic 70), Moutinho; Villar (Pietuszewski 78), Kubicki, Flach (Romanchuk 78); Imaz, Pululu (Diaby-Fadiga 86), Churlinov (Hansen 70).

Vikingur Reykjavik (1) 2 *(Atlason 13, Vilhjalmsson 56)*

Panathinaikos (0) 1 *(Ioannidis 90 (pen))*   811

Vikingur Reykjavik: (352) Jonsson; Ibrahimagic (Andrason 84), Ekroth (Fjoluson 46), Thorkelsson; Atlason, Agnarsson (Djuric 71), Thrandarson (Vilhjalmsson 50), Hafsteinsson, Gudjonsson; Ingimundarson, Sigurpalsson.
Panathinaikos: (4231) Lodygin; Kotsiras, Palmer-Brown (Fikaj 37), Ingason, Mladenovic; Siopis (Cerin 66), Maksimovic; Mancini (Tete 66), Bakasetas (Swiderski 22), Djuricic; Jeremejeff (Ioannidis 66).

LEAGUE PHASE PLAY-OFFS – SECOND LEG

Thursday, 20 February 2025

1.FC Heidenheim (0) 1 *(Scienza 73)*

FC Copenhagen (1) 3 *(Chiakha 37, Diks 53 (pen), Huescas 113)*   12,336

1.FC Heidenheim: (3421) Feller; Keller (Pieringer 46), Mainka, Siersleben; Busch (Traore 74), Niehues (Schoppner 57), Kerber (Honsak 46), Fohrenbach (Scienza 57); Wanner (Theuerkauf 113), Beck; Zivzivadze.
FC Copenhagen: (4231) Ramaj; Diks, Gabriel Pereira, Garananga (Hatzidiakos 83), Meling; Clem (Delaney 71), Froholdt; Gocholeishvili (Huescas 106), Elyounoussi (Mattsson 64), Achouri (Robert 63); Chiakha (Larsson 83).
aet; FC Copenhagen won 4-3 on aggregate.

APOEL (0) 0

Celje (1) 2 *(Kucys 45, Svetlin 51)*   9108

APOEL: (442) Belec; Galanopoulos, Susic, Laifis, Quintilla; Abagna (Kattirtzis 31), Sarfo (Alejo 55 (Meyer 86)), Tejera, Satsias; El Arabi, Drazic.
Celje: (4141) Silva; Nieto, Bejger, Nemanic, Karnicnik; Zabukovnik (Dulca 80); Matko, Seslar, Delaurier-Chaubet (Kvesic 88), Svetlin; Kucys (Edmilson 73).
Celje won 4-2 on aggregate.

Jagiellonia Bialystok (1) 3 *(Hansen 8, Imaz 70, Radojevic 76 (og))*

TSC Backa Topola (1) 1 *(Lazetic 17)*   10,243

Jagiellonia Bialystok: (442) Abramowicz; Sacek (Wojtuszek 45), Skrzypczak, Ebosse, Moutinho; Villar (Churlinov 71), Flach, Kubicki, Hansen (Pietuszewski 71); Imaz (Romanchuk 80), Pululu (Diaby-Fadiga 80).
TSC Backa Topola: (433) Ilic; Jovanovic, Djordjevic, Degenek, Radojevic; Pejic (Pantovic 77), Radin, Stanic (Stancic 80); Milosavljevic (Savic 59), Lazetic, Mboungou (Sos 77).
Jagiellonia Bialystock won 6-2 on aggregate.

Olimpija Ljubljana (0) 0

Borac Banja Luca (0) 0   12,169

Olimpija Ljubljana: (3511) Vidovsek; Pedreno, Muhamedbegovic, Lasickas (Sualehe 46); Jorge Silva, Blanco (Diogo Pinto 46), Celhaka (Agba 82), Doffo, Brest (Marin 61); Kojic (Durdov 82); Tamm.
Borac Banja Luca: (4231) Manojlovic; Kvrzic, Meijers, Carolina, Herrera; Nikolov (Cavic 90), Ogrinec; Kulasin (Rogan 90), Savic (Vranjes 80), Vukovic (Celic 90); Despotovic.
Borac Banja Luca won 1-0 on aggregate.

Pafos (1) 2 *(Bruno 28, Silva 65)*

Omonia Nicosia (0) 1 *(Jovetic 60)*   5350

Pafos: (4231) Ivusic; Bruno (Sarlija 69), Luckassen, Goldar, Silva (Sema 84); Pepe, Sunjic, Correia (Orsic 69), Dragomir, Tankovic; Jairo (Anderson Silva 73).
Omonia Nicosia: (4411) Fabiano; Dionkou, Coulibaly, Panagiotou, Khammas; Loizou (Alioum 76), Erakovic, Maric (Stepinski 75), Semedo; Jovetic; Kakoullis.
Pafos won 3-2 on aggregate.

Panathinaikos (0) 2 *(Mladenovic 70, Tete 90)*

Vikingur Reykjavik (0) 0   8931

Panathinaikos: (433) Dragowski; Kotsiras (Vagiannidis 56), Maksimovic, Ingason, Mladenovic; Ounahi, Siopis, Cerin (Swiderski 57); Tete, Ioannidis, Djuricic (Willian Arao 90).
Vikingur Reykjavik: (541) Jonsson; Atlason (Gunnarsson 67), Ibrahimagic, Ekroth, Thorkelsson, Gudjonsson; Agnarsson (Hansen 66), Hafsteinsson (Vatnhamar 81), Thrandarson (Vilhjalmsson 55), Sigurpalsson; Ingimundarson.
Panathinaikos won 3-2 on aggregate.

Real Betis (0) 0

Gent (0) 1 *(Brown 87)*   51,510

Real Betis: (4231) Vieites; Sabaly (Ruibal 59), Llorente (Bartra 46), Natan, Perraud; Flores (Perez Guerrero 80), Altimira (Johnny 59); Antony (Isco 59), Avila, Ezzalzouli; Vitor Roque■.
Gent: (3412) Roef; Watanabe, Torunarigha, Brown; De Meyer, Ito (De Vlieger 74), Da Silva Lopes (Kums 61), Sonko (Araujo 88); Delorge-Knieper, Goore (Vanzeir 61), Surdez (Gudjohnsen 75).
Real Betis won 3-1 on aggregate.

Shamrock R (0) 0

Molde (1) 1 *(Eikrem 10)*   9533

Shamrock R: (352) McGinty; Honohan (Ozhianvuna 105), Lopes, Grace; Grant, Healy, O'Neill (O'Sullivan J 117), McEneff, O'Sullivan C; Burke (Greene 89), Noonan M.
Molde: (4231) Karlstrom; Linnes (Enggard 65), Amundsen■, Haugan, Stenevik; Daehli (Bjornbak 82), Breivik; Eriksen, Eikrem (Hestad 91), Kaasa (Daga 95); Gulbrandsen (Ihler 65).
aet; Molde won 5-4 on penalties.

KNOCKOUT PHASE

ROUND OF 16 – FIRST LEG

Thursday, 6 March 2025

Borac Banja Luca (0) 1 *(Vukovic 90 (pen))*
Rapid Vienna (1) 1 *(Beljo 34)* 9652

Borac Banja Luca: (4141) Manojlovic; Kvrzic (Vranjes 77), Meijers, Carolina, Rogan (Subic 67); Nikolov (Grahovac 59); Kulasin, Ogrinec, Savic (Cavic 77), Vukovic; Despotovic.
Rapid Vienna: (4231) Hedl N; Bolla (Oswald 74), Cvetkovic, Raux Yao, Auer (Scholler 46); Sangare, Grgic (Borkeeiet 74); Radulovic (Seidl 58), Schaub, Wurmbrand (Bischof 86); Beljo.

Celje (1) 1 *(Svetlin 23)*
Lugano (0) 0 5712

Celje: (4141) Silva; Nieto, Bejger (Vuklisevic 72), Nemanic, Karnicnik; Zabukovnik; Delaurier-Chaubet, Seslar, Kvesic (Dulca 46), Svetlin (Kouter 89); Kucys (Edmilson 84).
Lugano: (343) Saipi; Papadopoulos■, Mai, Hajdari; Zanotti, Belhadj Mahmoud, Grgic, Valenzuela (Daniel Correia 90); Steffen (El Wafi 90), Koutsias (Przybylko 62), Bottani (Cimignani 80).

FC Copenhagen (0) 1 *(Gabriel Pereira 79)*
Chelsea (0) 2 *(James 46, Fernandez 65)* 35,859

FC Copenhagen: (541) Ramaj; Gocholeishvili (Huescas 70), Gabriel Pereira, Diks (Garananga 79), Hatzidiakos, Meling (Lopez 70); Claesson (Mattsson 65), Clem, Froholdt, Achouri (Robert 65); Chiakha.
Chelsea: (4231) Sanchez; Chalobah, Adarabioyo, Badiashile (Colwill 46), Gusto (Cucurella 25); Caicedo (Fernandez 46), James; George, Palmer (Sancho 72), Dewsbury-Hall; Mheuka (Nkunku 46).

Jagiellonia Bialystok (0) 3 *(Pululu 69 (pen), 78, Romanchuk 75)*
Cercle Brugge (0) 0 17,221

Jagiellonia Bialystok: (433) Abramowicz; Wojtuszek (Stojinovic 11), Skrzypczak, Ebosse, Moutinho; Villar (Pietuszewski 85), Flach (Romanchuk 61); Kubicki (Tomas Silva 85); Imaz, Pululu, Churlinov (Hansen 62).
Cercle Brugge: (3421) Delanghe; Diakite, Perrin (Ravych 46), Utkus; Efekele, Francis■, Agyekum (De Wilde 76), Nazinho (Magnee 68); Somers, Minda (Erick 68); Felipe Augusto (Brunner 85).

Molde (3) 3 *(Hestad 11, Eriksen 17, Gulbrandsen 43)*
Legia Warsaw (0) 2 *(Chodyna 64, Luquinhas 67)* 4098

Molde: (4231) Karlstrom; Linnes, Haugan, Lund, Stenevik; Enggard, Breivik; Hestad (Ihler 72), Daehli, Eriksen; Gulbrandsen (Bjornbak 83).
Legia Warsaw: (4231) Kovacevic; Wszolek, Ziolkowski (Pankov 61), Kapuadi, Ruben Vinagre; Kapustka (Elitim 75), Oyedele (Augustyniak 61); Chodyna, Goncalves (Pekhart 75), Bichakhchyan (Luquinhas 66); Gual.

Pafos (0) 1 *(Tankovic 65)*
Djurgarden (0) 0 3809

Pafos: (4411) Ivusic; Bruno, Luckassen, Goldar (Sarlija 63), Silva (Pileas 86); Sema (Correia 64), Sunjic, Pepe, Tankovic (Orsic 80); Dragomir; Jairo (Anderson Silva 64).
Djurgarden: (433) Nilsson Safqvist; Stahl, Tenho (Danielson 74), Une Larsson, Kosugi; Aslund (Haarala 73), Schuller (Stensson 73), Gulliksen; Zugelj (Finndell 61), Nguen, Fallenius (Priske 83).

Panathinaikos (2) 3 *(Swiderski 5, Maksimovic 19, Tete 55)*
Fiorentina (2) 2 *(Beltran 20, Fagioli 23)* 26,849

Panathinaikos: (343) Dragowski; Willian Arao, Ingason, Mladenovic; Kotsiras (Vagiannidis 34), Ounahi, Siopis, Maksimovic (Cerin 76); Tete, Swiderski (Ioannidis 76), Djuricic (Mancini 90).
Fiorentina: (3511) Terracciano; Moreno, Comuzzo, Ranieri; Dodo, Fagioli (Parisi 76), Mandragora, Richardson (Cataldi 59), Gosens; Beltran (Gudmundsson 76); Kean.

Real Betis (0) 2 *(Bakambu 48, Isco 75)*
Vitoria de Guimaraes (0) 2 *(Joao Mendes 51, Oliveira 81)* 44,366

Real Betis: (4231) Vieites; Ruibal, Bartra, Natan, Perraud; Johnny (Flores 77), Altimira (Fornals 63); Antony, Isco, Rodriguez J (Ezzalzouli 77); Bakambu (Avila 80).
Vitoria de Guimaraes: (4231) Bruno Varela; Hevertton (Maga 67), Borevkovic, Villanueva, Teixeira Mendes; Tiago Silva, Handel; Embalo (Arcanjo 77), Joao Mendes (Samu 67), Nuno Santos; Oliveira (Michel 88).

ROUND OF 16 – SECOND LEG

Thursday, 13 March 2025

Cercle Brugge (1) 2 *(Van der Bruggen 8, Felipe Augusto 50)*
Jagiellonia Bialystok (0) 0 4646

Cercle Brugge: (3412) Warleson; Diakite (Jurado 80), Ravych, Utkus (Perrin 67); Efekele, Van der Bruggen (Erick 46), De Wilde, Nazinho (Magnee 46); Somers; Felipe Augusto, Bruninho (Brunner 67).
Jagiellonia Bialystok: (433) Abramowicz; Stojinovic (Tomas Silva 46); Skrzypczak, Ebosse, Moutinho; Imaz, Kubicki (Romanchuk 58), Flach; Villar (Churlinov 58), Pululu, Hansen.
Jagiellonia Bialystock won 3-2 on aggregate.

Chelsea (0) 1 *(Dewsbury-Hall 55)*
FC Copenhagen (0) 0 35,280

Chelsea: (4231) Jorgensen; Chalobah, Adarabioyo, Badiashile, Acheampong (Cucurella 46); Caicedo (James 79), Fernandez (Palmer 46); George, Dewsbury-Hall, Sancho (Nkunku 65); Pedro Neto (Antwi 90).
FC Copenhagen: (541) Ramaj; Huescas, Gabriel Pereira, Diks, Hatzidiakos, Meling; Elyounoussi (Larsson 60), Clem (Jensen 73), Froholdt (Mattsson 83), Achouri (Robert 76); Claesson (Chiakha 59).
Chelsea won 3-1 on aggregate.

Djurgarden (1) 3 *(Fallenius 35, Stensson 69, Nguen 86)*
Pafos (0) 0 17,653

Djurgarden: (4231) Nilsson Safqvist (Rinne 76); Stahl, Tenho, Une Larsson, Kosugi; Schuller (Finndell 83), Stensson; Aslund (Priske 83), Gulliksen, Fallenius; Nguen.
Pafos: (4231) Ivusic; Bruno (Sunjic 46), Luckassen, Sarlija, Silva; Pepe, Tankovic (Orsic 84); Correia, Dragomir (Jaja 74), Sema (Quina 74); Jairo (Anderson Silva 62).
Djurgarden won 3-1 on aggregate.

Fiorentina (2) 3 *(Mandragora 12, Gudmundsson 24, Kean 75)*
Panathinaikos (0) 1 *(Ioannidis 81 (pen))* 15,101

Fiorentina: (3511) de Gea; Pongracic, Comuzzo, Ranieri (Zaniolo 79); Dodo (Moreno 90), Mandragora (Adli 79), Cataldi (Folorunsho 61), Fagioli, Gosens; Gudmundsson (Beltran 60); Kean.
Panathinaikos: (433) Dragowski; Vagiannidis, Willian Arao (Cerin 87), Ingason, Mladenovic■; Ounahi, Siopis, Maksimovic; Tete (Pellistri 87), Swiderski (Jeremejeff 75), Djuricic (Ioannidis 57).
Fiorentina won 5-4 on aggregate.

Legia Warsaw (1) 2 *(Morishita 34, Gual 108)*
Molde (0) 0 26,153

Legia Warsaw: (433) Tobiasz; Wszolek, Jedrzejczyk■ (Ziolkowski 103), Kapuadi, Ruben Vinagre (Kun 103); Kapustka, Augustyniak (Oyedele 90), Elitim (Goncalves 84); Chodyna (Bichakhchyan 89), Gual, Morishita.
Molde: (4231) Karlstrom; Linnes (Haugen 61), Amundsen (Bjornbak 106), Lund (Nyheim 114), Stenevik; Breivik, Enggard (Daga 91); Daehli (Hestad 71), Eikrem, Eriksen■; Gulbrandsen (Ihler 90).
aet; Legia Warsaw won 4-3 on aggregate.

Lugano (3) 5 *(Belhadj Mahmoud 21, Koutsias 42, 80, Daniel Correia 44, Doumbia 118)*

Celje (1) 4 *(Seslar 40, Svetlin 68, Kucys 90 (pen), Nieto 97)* 1853

Lugano: (4231) Saipi; Zanotti, Mai, Hajdari■, Valenzuela (Marques 102); Grgic (Doumbia 102), Belhadj Mahmoud (El Wafi 90); Steffen, Bislimi, Daniel Correia (Cimignani 64); Koutsias (Przybylko 88).
Celje: (4411) Silva; Nieto, Vuklisevic, Bejger, Karnicnik; Delaurier-Chaubet (Matko 46), Zabukovnik, Dulca (Kvesic 46), Svetlin; Seslar; Kucys (Edmilson 115).
aet; Celje won 3-1 on penalties.

Rapid Vienna (0) 2 *(Beljo 70, Schaub 96)*

Borac Banja Luca (0) 1 *(Ogrinec 66)* 23,000

Rapid Vienna: (4222) Hedl N; Bolla, Cvetkovic, Raux Yao, Oswald (Bockle 103); Grgic (Seidl 67), Sangare (Borkeeiet 113); Schaub (Radulovic 103), Jansson (Bischof 103); Wurmbrand (Kara 82), Beljo.
Borac Banja Luca: (4231) Manojlovic; Rogan (Cavic 97), Meijers, Carolina, Herrera; Ogrinec, Grahovac (Djajic 102); Kulasin, Savic, Vukovic (Nikolov 74); Despotovic (Vranjes 86).
aet; Rapid Vienna won 3-2 on aggregate.

Vitoria de Guimaraes (0) 0

Real Betis (2) 4 *(Bakambu 5, 20, Antony 58, Isco 80)* 28,994

Vitoria de Guimaraes: (433) Bruno Varela; Hevertton (Maga 46), Borevkovic, Villanueva, Teixeira Mendes; Tiago Silva, Handel (Beni 74), Joao Mendes (Samu 60); Embalo (Arcanjo 46), Oliveira (Ramirez 76), Nuno Santos.
Real Betis: (4231) Vieites; Ruibal, Bartra, Llorente, Rodriguez R; Altimira (Natan 73), Fornals; Antony, Isco (Garcia 82), Rodriguez J (Ezzalzouli 60); Bakambu (Flores 82).
Real Betis won 6-2 on aggregate.

QUARTER-FINALS – FIRST LEG
Thursday, 10 April 2025

Celje (0) 1 *(Delaurier-Chaubet 68 (pen))*

Fiorentina (1) 2 *(Ranieri 27, Mandragora 62 (pen))* 12,512

Celje: (3421) Silva; Nieto, Vuklisevic, Nemanic; Matko, Zabukovnik, Svetlin, Karnicnik; Delaurier-Chaubet (Edmilson 89), Kvesic (Iosifov 83); Seslar.
Fiorentina: (352) de Gea; Pongracic, Comuzzo, Ranieri; Moreno (Parisi 46), Mandragora, Cataldi (Fagioli 63), Adli (Richardson 63), Folorunsho (Dodo 77); Beltran, Zaniolo (Kean 89).

Djurgarden (0) 0

Rapid Vienna (0) 1 *(Finndell 62 (og))* 23,531

Djurgarden: (433) Rinne; Stahl, Une Larsson, Danielson, Kosugi; Gulliksen (Bergh 83), Finndell, Haarala (Alemayehu 77); Zugelj (Tenho 89); Priske, Fallenius.
Rapid Vienna: (343) Hedl N; Bolla, Cvetkovic, Raux Yao; Schaub (Radulovic 85), Romeo (Bischof 62), Grgic (Borkeeiet 78), Oswald; Kara (Burgstaller 85), Beljo (Seidl 62), Jansson.

Legia Warsaw (0) 0

Chelsea (0) 3 *(George 49, Madueke 57, 74)* 29,055

Legia Warsaw: (541) Tobiasz; Wszolek (Kun 53), Pankov, Augustyniak, Kapuadi, Ruben Vinagre; Chodyna (Bichakhchyan 83), Oyedele (Szczepaniak 82), Elitim (Goncalves 75), Luquinhas (Pekhart 75); Morishita.
Chelsea: (4231) Jorgensen; Acheampong, Adarabioyo (Colwill 46), Badiashile, Gusto (Amougou 75); Dewsbury-Hall, James (Cucurella 58); Sancho, Palmer, Madueke 46), George (Mheuka 75); Nkunku.

Real Betis (2) 2 *(Bakambu 24, Rodriguez J 45)*

Jagiellonia Bialystok (0) 0 56,442

Real Betis: (4231) Vieites; Sabaly, Llorente (Bartra 46), Natan, Rodriguez R; Fornals (Altimira 85), Johnny; Antony (Avila 75), Isco (Lo Celso 46), Rodriguez J (Ruibal 57); Bakambu.

Jagiellonia Bialystok: (4231) Abramowicz; Stojinovic (Wojtuszek 61), Skrzypczak, Ebosse, Moutinho; Romanchuk, Flach (Tomas Silva 82); Villar (Hansen 61), Imaz (Kubicki 74), Churlinov; Pululu (Diaby-Fadiga 74).

QUARTER-FINALS – SECOND LEG
Thursday, 17 April 2025

Chelsea (1) 1 *(Cucurella 33)*

Legia Warsaw (1) 2 *(Pekhart 10 (pen), Kapuadi 53)* 32,549

Chelsea: (4231) Jorgensen; Acheampong, Adarabioyo, Badiashile, Cucurella (Gusto 58); Dewsbury-Hall, James; Sancho (Pedro Neto 83), Palmer (Madueke 58), Nkunku; Jackson (George 46).
Legia Warsaw: (4141) Kovacevic; Pankov, Ziolkowski (Jedrzejczyk 86), Kapuadi, Ruben Vinagre; Oyedele; Morishita, Elitim (Augustyniak 78), Goncalves (Bichakhchyan 86), Luquinhas (Szczepaniak 77); Pekhart (Chodyna 67).
Chelsea won 4-2 on aggregate.

Fiorentina (1) 2 *(Mandragora 37, Kean 67)*

Celje (0) 2 *(Matko 54, Nemanic 65)* 13,195

Fiorentina: (352) de Gea; Pongracic, Comuzzo, Ranieri; Folorunsho, Mandragora (Adli 90), Cataldi, Fagioli (Richardson 80), Parisi (Gosens 81); Kean, Gudmundsson (Beltran 90).
Celje: (3412) Silva; Nieto, Vuklisevic, Nemanic; Matko (Edmilson 90), Zabukovnik, Svetlin, Karnicnik; Seslar; Delaurier-Chaubet, Kvesic.
Fiorentina won 4-3 on aggregate.

Jagiellonia Bialystok (0) 1 *(Churlinov 81)*

Real Betis (1) 1 *(Bakambu 78)* 20,003

Jagiellonia Bialystok: (433) Abramowicz; Wojtuszek, Skrzypczak, Ebosse, Moutinho; Imaz, Romanchuk, Kubicki (Tomas Silva 71); Churlinov (Villar 89), Pululu (Diaby-Fadiga 79), Hansen (Pietuszewski 79).
Real Betis: (4231) Vieites; Sabaly, Bartra, Natan, Rodriguez R (Perraud 26); Fornals (Johnny 71), Altimira; Antony (Ezzalzouli 82), Lo Celso (Isco 82), Rodriguez J (Ruibal 71); Bakambu.
Real Betis won 3-1 on aggregate.

Rapid Vienna (1) 1 *(Une Larsson 45 (og))*

Djurgarden (1) 4 *(Danielson 42 (pen), Kosugi 77, Gulliksen 93, 105)* 25,600

Rapid Vienna: (442) Hedl; Oswald (Burgstaller 96), Cvetkovic (Groller 75), Raux Yao■, Auer (Bischof 96); Schaub (Jansson 67), Sangare■, Grgic, Seidl; Beljo (Bockle 75), Kara (Romeo 9).
Djurgarden: (4231) Rinne; Stahl, Une Larsson (Tenho 83), Danielson, Kosugi (Manneh 99); Stensson, Finndell (Alemayehu 83); Zugelj (Haarala 9 (Bergh 83)), Gulliksen, Fallenius (Priske 22); Nguen.
aet; Djurgarden won 4-2 on aggregate.

SEMI-FINALS – FIRST LEG
Thursday, 1 May 2025

Djurgarden (0) 1 *(Alemayehu 68)*

Chelsea (2) 4 *(Sancho 13, Madueke 43, Jackson 59, 65)* 26,703

Djurgarden: (4231) Rinne; Stahl, Une Larsson (Tenho 64), Kosugi (Bergh 80); Finndell, Stensson; Haarala (Alemayehu 63), Gulliksen, Priske; Nguen.
Chelsea: (4231) Jorgensen; Acheampong, Adarabioyo, Badiashile, Cucurella (Chalobah 46); Fernandez (Palmer 46), James (Caicedo 46); Madueke (Jackson 46), Dewsbury-Hall, Sancho; George (Walsh 88).

Real Betis (1) 2 *(Ezzalzouli 6, Antony 64)*

Fiorentina (0) 1 *(Ranieri 73)* 56,417

Real Betis: (4231) Vieites; Ruibal, Bartra, Natan, Perraud; Johnny, Fornals (Altimira 78); Antony, Isco, Ezzalzouli (Lo Celso 61); Bakambu.
Fiorentina: (352) de Gea; Pongracic, Comuzzo, Ranieri; Parisi (Folorunsho 69), Mandragora, Cataldi (Adli 29), Fagioli (Richardson 69), Gosens; Beltran (Kean 46), Gudmundsson (Zaniolo 85).

SEMI-FINALS – SECOND LEG
Thursday, 8 May 2025
Chelsea (1) 1 *(Dewsbury-Hall 38)*
Djurgarden (0) 0   32,464
Chelsea: (4411) Jorgensen; Gusto, Adarabioyo, Badiashile, Acheampong; Dewsbury-Hall, James (Chalobah 70), Cucurella (Mheuka 46), Sancho (Antwi 70); Walsh; George.
Djurgarden: (433) Rinne; Kosugi, Tenho, Une Larsson (Danielson 64), Bergh; Finndell (Selfven 86), Stensson (Persson 81), Gulliksen (Manneh 86); Priske, Haarala (Alemayehu 64), Nguen.
Chelsea won 5-1 on aggregate.

Fiorentina (2) 2 *(Gosens 34, 42)*
Real Betis (1) 2 *(Antony 30, Ezzalzouli 97)*   21,252
Fiorentina: (3511) de Gea; Pongracic (Zaniolo 106), Comuzzo, Ranieri; Dodo (Colpani 106), Mandragora, Adli (Richardson 46), Fagioli (Folorunsho 88), Gosens (Parisi 95); Gudmundsson (Beltran 95); Kean.
Real Betis: (4231) Vieites; Sabaly (Bellerin 87 (Garcia 114)), Bartra (Mendy 58), Natan, Rodriguez R; Johnny, Lo Celso (Ezzalzouli 58); Antony, Isco, Fornals (Ruibal 91); Bakambu (Altimira 91).
aet; Real Betis won 4-3 on aggregate.

UEFA EUROPA CONFERENCE LEAGUE FINAL 2024–25
Wednesday, 28 May 2025

(at Wroclaw Stadium, Wroclaw, attendance 39,754)

Real Betis (1) 1   **Chelsea (0) 4**

Real Betis: (4231) Adrian; Sabaly, Bartra, Natan, Rodriguez R (Perraud 46); Fornals (Altimira 85), Johnny (Lo Celso 85); Antony, Isco, Ezzalzouli (Rodriguez J 53); Bakambu (Ruibal 72).
Scorer: Ezzalzouli 9.

Chelsea: (4231) Jorgensen; Gusto (James 46), Chalobah, Badiashile (Colwill 61), Cucurella; Caicedo, Fernandez; Pedro Neto (Sancho 61), Palmer (Guiu 87), Madueke; Jackson (Dewsbury-Hall 80).
Scorers: Fernandez 65, Jackson 70, Sancho 83, Caicedo 90.

Referee: Irfan Peljto.

Chelsea's striker Nicolas Jackson (L) scores his side's second goal during the UEFA Conference League final against Real Betis in Wroclaw. (John Macdougall/AFP via Getty Images)

UEFA CONFERENCE LEAGUE FINALS 2022–25

Year	Winners v Runners-up		Venue	Attendance	Referee
2022	Roma v Feyenoord	1-0	Tirana	19,597	I. Kovacs (Romania)
2023	West Ham U v Fiorentina	2-1	Prague	17,363	C. Grande (Spain)
2024	Olympiacos v Fiorentina	1-0*	Athens	26,842	A. S. Dias (Portugal)
2025	Chelsea v Real Betis	4-1	Wroclaw	39,754	I. Peljto (Bosnia & Herzegovina)

After extra time.

BRITISH AND IRISH CLUBS IN EUROPE
SUMMARY OF APPEARANCES

EUROPEAN CUP AND CHAMPIONS LEAGUE 1955–2025
(Winners in brackets) (SE = seasons entered).

	SE	P	W	D	L	F	A
ENGLAND							
Manchester U (3)	31	299	161	70	68	545	299
Liverpool (6)	28	258	150	50	58	490	234
Arsenal	23	225	115	47	63	382	236
Chelsea (2)	19	201	104	53	44	342	181
Manchester C (1)	15	139	77	28	34	294	164
Tottenham H	7	63	28	13	22	116	90
Leeds U	4	40	22	6	12	76	41
Newcastle U	4	30	12	5	13	39	40
Aston Villa (1)	3	27	17	4	6	47	22
Nottingham F (2)	3	20	12	4	4	32	14
Everton	3	10	2	5	3	14	10
Derby Co	2	12	6	2	4	18	12
Wolverhampton W	2	8	2	2	4	12	16
Leicester C	1	10	5	2	3	11	10
Blackburn R	1	6	1	1	4	5	8
Ipswich T	1	4	3	0	1	16	5
Burnley	1	4	2	0	2	8	8
SCOTLAND							
Celtic (1)	39	238	105	44	89	357	302
Rangers	34	179	65	44	70	249	260
Aberdeen	3	12	5	4	3	14	12
Hearts	3	8	2	1	5	8	16
Dundee U	1	8	5	1	2	14	5
Dundee	1	8	5	0	3	20	14
Hibernian	1	6	3	1	2	9	5
Kilmarnock	1	4	1	2	1	4	7
Motherwell	1	2	0	0	2	0	5
WALES							
The New Saints	16	44	11	6	27	43	78
Barry Town U	6	14	4	1	9	11	38
Rhyl	2	4	0	0	4	1	19
Connah's Quay Nomads	2	3	0	1	2	2	5
Cwmbran T	1	2	1	0	1	4	4
Llanelli	1	2	1	0	1	1	4
Bangor C	1	2	0	0	2	0	13
NORTHERN IRELAND							
Linfield	32	77	10	23	44	63	139
Glentoran	12	28	3	7	18	20	59
Crusaders	6	14	1	2	11	7	52
Cliftonville	3	6	0	1	5	1	20
Portadown	3	6	0	1	5	3	24
Larne	2	4	0	1	3	3	15
Glenavon	1	2	0	1	1	0	3
Lisburn Distillery	1	2	0	1	1	3	8
Ards	1	2	0	0	2	3	10
Coleraine	1	2	0	0	2	1	11
REPUBLIC OF IRELAND							
Shamrock R	13	32	5	8	19	21	50
Dundalk	12	33	4	12	17	24	60
Shelbourne	6	20	4	8	8	21	31
Bohemians	6	18	4	4	10	13	29
Waterford U	6	14	3	0	11	15	47
Derry C	4	9	1	1	7	9	26
St Patrick's Ath	4	8	0	3	5	2	23
Cork C	3	10	2	1	7	7	16
Dublin C	3	6	1	0	5	3	25
Athlone T	2	4	0	2	2	7	14
Sligo R	2	4	0	0	4	0	9
Limerick	2	4	0	0	4	4	16
Drogheda U	1	4	2	1	1	6	5
Cork Hibernians	1	2	0	0	2	1	7
Cork Celtic	1	2	0	0	2	1	7

UEFA CUP AND EUROPA LEAGUE 1971–2025

	SE	P	W	D	L	F	A
ENGLAND							
Tottenham H (3)	17	168	98	40	30	343	147
Liverpool (3)	15	134	73	34	27	215	106
Aston Villa	13	56	24	14	18	77	60
Manchester U (1)	13	91	48	26	17	157	81
Arsenal	11	84	49	15	20	165	85
Ipswich T (1)	10	52	30	10	12	98	53
Everton	9	52	27	8	17	87	64
Newcastle U	8	72	42	17	13	123	60
Manchester C	8	52	28	13	11	84	51
Leeds U	8	46	20	10	16	66	48
Southampton	7	22	6	9	7	23	20
West Ham U	6	38	18	6	14	53	32
Blackburn R	6	22	7	8	7	27	26
Wolverhampton W	5	37	25	5	7	79	37
Chelsea (2)	5	32	22	5	5	64	30
Leicester C	4	18	6	5	7	29	26
Fulham	3	39	21	10	8	64	31
Nottingham F	3	20	10	5	5	18	16
Stoke C	3	16	8	4	4	21	16
WBA	3	12	5	2	5	15	13
Middlesbrough	2	25	13	4	8	36	24
Bolton W	2	18	6	10	2	18	14
QPR	2	12	8	1	3	39	18
Derby Co	2	10	5	2	3	32	17
Brighton & HA	1	8	5	1	3	11	9
Birmingham C	1	8	4	2	2	11	8
Burnley	1	6	2	3	1	7	6
Norwich C	1	6	2	2	2	6	4
Portsmouth	1	6	2	2	2	11	10
Watford	1	6	2	1	3	10	12
Wigan Ath	1	6	1	2	3	6	7
Sheffield Wed	1	4	2	1	1	13	7
Hull C	1	4	2	1	1	4	3
Millwall	1	2	0	1	1	2	4
SCOTLAND							
Celtic	24	139	60	29	50	219	176
Aberdeen	24	89	29	28	32	119	114
Rangers	23	160	71	49	40	237	193
Dundee U	19	82	33	25	24	134	89
Hearts	16	54	21	10	23	62	67
Hibernian	13	40	15	11	14	57	63
Motherwell	9	29	9	3	17	40	40
St Johnstone	8	26	7	8	11	28	35
Kilmarnock	5	16	5	3	8	10	19
Dundee	4	14	6	0	8	24	24
St Mirren	3	10	2	3	5	9	12
Dunfermline Ath	2	4	0	2	2	4	6
Raith R	1	6	2	1	3	10	8
Livingston	1	4	1	2	1	7	9
Falkirk	1	2	1	0	1	1	2
Inverness CT	1	2	0	1	1	0	1
Gretna	1	2	0	1	1	3	7
Queen of the South	1	2	0	0	2	2	4
Partick Thistle	1	2	0	0	2	0	4
WALES							
The New Saints	12	28	3	5	20	21	69
Bangor C	10	22	2	2	18	10	61
Bala T	6	12	4	0	8	8	21
Connah's Quay Nomads	5	13	3	1	9	7	18
Llanelli	5	12	3	3	6	12	24
Barry Town U	4	11	2	3	6	11	25
Cardiff Met Univ	3	8	2	0	6	3	20
Rhyl	3	8	2	1	5	9	12
Newtown	3	8	2	1	5	6	21
Air UK Broughton	3	6	0	4	2	6	9
Cwmbran T	3	6	0	0	6	0	21
Carmarthen T	2	6	1	0	5	8	21
Cefn Druids	2	4	0	2	2	1	7
Swansea C	1	12	4	4	4	17	10
Prestatyn T	1	4	1	0	3	3	11
Afan Lido	1	2	0	1	1	1	2
Haverfordwest Co	1	2	0	0	2	1	4
Neath	1	2	0	0	2	1	6
Port Talbot T	1	2	0	0	2	1	7
Llandudno T	1	2	0	0	2	1	7
Aberystwith T	1	2	0	0	2	0	9

NORTHERN IRELAND

Glentoran	19	42	4	8	30	24	102
Linfield	15	43	13	9	21	49	78
Portadown	11	28	3	7	18	16	62
Crusaders	11	26	6	4	16	27	62
Coleraine	10	21	2	7	12	13	49
Glenavon	9	20	2	2	16	10	49
Cliftonville	7	20	4	4	12	15	37
Ballymena U	3	8	2	1	5	4	20
Dungannon Swifts	1	2	1	0	1	1	4
Ards	1	2	1	0	1	4	8
Bangor	1	2	0	0	2	0	6
Lisburn Distillery	1	2	0	0	2	1	11

REPUBLIC OF IRELAND

Bohemians	15	31	3	10	18	17	57
Shamrock R	13	46	13	7	26	45	82
St Patrick's Ath	11	40	10	7	23	35	61
Cork C	11	32	7	7	18	23	46
Dundalk	10	37	9	5	23	34	73
Derry C	10	27	7	5	15	32	48
Shelbourne	6	12	0	2	10	8	28
Drogheda U	4	12	3	4	5	10	24
Sligo R	4	10	2	4	4	11	13
Longford T	3	6	1	1	4	6	12
Finn Harps	3	6	0	0	6	3	33
Athlone T	1	4	1	2	1	4	5
University College Dublin	1	4	1	0	3	3	8
Limerick	1	2	0	1	1	1	4
Sporting Fingal	1	2	0	0	2	4	6
Galway U	1	2	0	0	2	2	8
Bray W	1	2	0	0	2	0	8

UEFA CONFERENCE LEAGUE 2021–25

ENGLAND

	SE	P	W	D	L	F	A
West Ham U (1)	1	15	14	1	0	35	9
Chelsea (1)	1	13	12	0	1	42	10
Aston Villa	1	12	6	2	4	21	16
Leicester C	1	8	4	2	2	13	7
Tottenham H	1	7	3	1	3	14	9

SCOTLAND

Hearts	3	16	5	1	10	17	34
Aberdeen	2	12	4	3	5	21	20
Hibernian	2	10	4	2	4	19	20
St Mirren	1	4	1	2	1	6	5
Kilmarnock	1	4	1	2	1	4	5
St Johnstone	1	2	0	1	1	1	3
Motherwell	1	2	0	0	2	0	3
Celtic	1	2	0	0	2	1	5
Dundee U	1	2	1	0	1	1	7

WALES

The New Saints	4	18	6	4	8	29	23
Connah's Quay Nomads	3	6	3	0	3	7	9
Bala T	3	6	1	1	4	4	7

Newtown	2	6	1	0	5	4	13
Haverfordwest Co	1	4	1	1	2	3	4
Caernarfon T	1	4	1	0	3	3	14
Penybont	1	2	0	1	1	1	3

NORTHERN IRELAND

Larne	4	20	7	2	11	15	30
Linfield	4	12	3	3	6	19	21
Crusaders	3	10	3	3	4	15	16
Glentoran	2	4	0	3	1	4	6
Cliftonville	2	4	0	0	4	2	9
Coleraine	1	2	0	0	2	2	4

REPUBLIC OF IRELAND

Shamrock R	3	14	6	2	6	18	21
St Patrick's Ath	3	12	4	5	3	12	13
Derry C	3	10	4	2	4	9	12
Dundalk	2	10	4	4	2	18	13
Sligo R	1	8	4	0	4	8	11
Bohemians	1	6	4	1	1	10	4
Shelbourne	1	4	1	2	1	3	5

EUROPEAN CUP WINNERS' CUP 1960–1999

ENGLAND

	SE	P	W	D	L	F	A
Tottenham H (1)	6	33	20	5	8	65	34
Chelsea (2)	5	39	23	10	6	81	28
Liverpool	5	29	16	5	8	57	29
Manchester U (1)	5	31	16	9	6	55	35
West Ham U (1)	4	30	15	6	9	58	42
Arsenal (1)	3	27	15	10	2	48	20
Everton (1)	3	17	11	4	2	25	9
Manchester C (1)	2	18	11	2	5	32	13
Ipswich T	1	6	3	2	1	6	3
Leeds U	1	9	5	3	1	13	3
Leicester C	1	4	2	1	1	8	5
Newcastle U	1	2	1	0	1	2	2
Southampton	1	6	4	0	2	16	8
Sunderland	1	4	3	0	1	5	3
WBA	1	6	2	2	2	8	5
Wolverhampton W	1	4	1	1	2	6	5

SCOTLAND

Rangers (1)	10	54	27	11	16	100	62
Aberdeen (1)	8	39	22	5	12	79	37
Celtic	8	38	21	4	13	75	37
Dundee U	3	10	3	3	4	9	10
Hearts	3	10	3	3	4	16	14
Dunfermline Ath	2	14	7	2	5	34	14
Airdrieonians	1	2	0	0	2	1	3
Dundee	1	2	0	1	1	3	4
Hibernian	1	6	3	1	2	19	10
Kilmarnock	1	4	1	2	1	5	6
Motherwell	1	2	1	0	1	3	3
St Mirren	1	4	1	2	1	1	2

WALES

Cardiff C	14	49	16	14	19	67	61
Wrexham	8	28	10	8	10	34	35
Swansea C	7	18	3	4	11	32	37
Bangor C	3	9	1	2	6	5	12
Barry T	1	2	0	0	2	0	7
Borough U	1	4	1	1	2	2	4

Cwmbran T	1	2	0	0	2	2	12
Merthyr Tydfil	1	2	1	0	1	2	3
Newport Co	1	6	2	3	1	12	3
The New Saints	1	2	0	1	1	1	6
(Llansantffraid)							

NORTHERN IRELAND

Glentoran	9	22	3	7	12	18	46
Glenavon	5	10	1	3	6	11	25
Ballymena U	4	8	0	0	8	1	25
Coleraine	4	8	0	1	7	7	34
Crusaders	3	6	0	2	4	5	18
Derry C	3	6	1	1	4	1	11
Linfield	3	6	2	0	4	6	11
Ards	2	4	0	1	3	2	17
Bangor	2	4	0	1	3	2	8
Carrick Rangers	1	4	1	0	3	7	12
Cliftonville	1	2	0	0	2	0	8
Distillery	1	2	0	0	2	1	7
Portadown	1	2	1	0	1	4	7

REPUBLIC OF IRELAND

Shamrock R	6	16	5	2	9	19	27
Shelbourne	4	10	1	1	8	9	20
Bohemians	3	8	2	2	4	6	13
Dundalk	3	8	2	1	5	7	14
Limerick U	3	8	0	1	5	2	11
Waterford U	3	8	1	1	6	6	14
Cork C	2	4	1	0	3	2	9
Cork Hibernians	2	6	2	1	3	7	8
Galway U	2	4	0	0	4	2	11
Sligo R	2	6	1	1	4	5	11
Bray W	1	2	0	1	1	1	3
Cork Celtic	1	2	0	1	1	0	4
Finn Harps	1	2	0	1	1	2	4
Home Farm	1	2	0	1	1	1	7
St Patrick's Ath	1	2	0	0	2	1	8
University College Dublin	1	2	0	1	1	0	1

INTER-CITIES FAIRS CUP 1955–1970

	SE	P	W	D	L	F	A
ENGLAND							
Leeds U (2)	5	53	28	17	8	92	40
Birmingham C	4	25	14	6	5	51	38
Liverpool	4	22	12	4	6	46	15
Arsenal (1)	3	24	12	5	7	46	19
Chelsea	3	20	10	5	5	33	24
Everton	3	12	7	2	3	22	15
Newcastle U (1)	3	24	13	6	5	37	21
Nottingham F	2	6	3	0	3	8	9
Sheffield Wed	2	10	5	0	5	25	18
Burnley	1	8	4	3	1	16	5
Coventry C	1	4	3	0	1	9	8
London XI	1	8	4	1	3	14	13
Manchester U	1	11	6	3	2	29	10
Southampton	1	6	2	3	1	11	6
WBA	1	4	1	1	2	7	9
SCOTLAND							
Hibernian	7	36	18	5	13	66	60
Dunfermline Ath	5	28	16	3	9	49	31
Kilmarnock	4	20	8	3	9	34	32
Dundee U	3	10	5	1	4	11	12
Hearts	3	12	4	4	4	20	20
Rangers	3	18	8	4	6	27	17
Celtic	2	6	1	3	2	9	10
Aberdeen	1	4	2	1	1	4	4
Dundee	1	8	5	1	2	14	6
Morton	1	2	0	0	2	3	9
Partick Thistle	1	4	3	0	1	10	7
NORTHERN IRELAND							
Glentoran	4	8	1	1	6	7	22
Coleraine	2	8	2	1	5	15	23
Linfield	2	4	1	0	3	3	11
REPUBLIC OF IRELAND							
Drumcondra	2	6	2	0	4	8	19
Dundalk	2	6	1	1	4	4	25
Shamrock R	2	4	0	2	2	4	6
Cork Hibernians	1	2	0	0	2	1	6
Shelbourne	1	5	1	2	2	3	4
St Patrick's Ath	1	2	0	0	2	4	9

UEFA SUPER CUP 2024

Played annually between the winners of the European Champions' Cup and the European Cup-Winners' Cup (UEFA Cup from 2000; UEFA Europa League from 2010). AC Milan replaced Marseille in 1993–94. Match played in Monaco 1998–2012; various venues from 2013.

UEFA SUPER CUP 2024

Wednesday, 14 August 2024

(at Kazimierz Gorski National Stadium, Warsaw, attendance 56,042)

Real Madrid (0) 2   Atalanta (0) 0

Real Madrid: (4321) Courtois; Carvajal (Vasquez 89), Militao, Rudiger, Mendy; Valverde, Tchouameni, Bellingham (Ceballos 89); Rodrygo (Modric 76), Vinicius Junior (Guler 88); Mbappe (Diaz 83).
Scorers: Valverde 59, Mbappe 68.

Atalanta: (3412) Musso; Djimsiti, Hien (Palestra 90), Kolasinac (Bakker 71); Zappacosta (Godfrey 63), De Roon, Ederson, Ruggeri; Pasalic (Manzoni 90); De Ketelaere (Retegui 63), Lookman.

Referee: Sandro Scharer (Switzerland).

PREVIOUS MATCHES

1972 Ajax beat Rangers 3-1, 3-2
1973 Ajax beat AC Milan 0-1, 6-0
1974 Not contested
1975 Dynamo Kyiv beat Bayern Munich 1-0, 2-0
1976 Anderlecht beat Bayern Munich 4-1, 1-2
1977 Liverpool beat Hamburg 1-1, 6-0
1978 Anderlecht beat Liverpool 3-1, 1-2
1979 Nottingham F beat Barcelona 1-0, 1-1
1980 Valencia beat Nottingham F 1-0, 1-2
1981 Not contested
1982 Aston Villa beat Barcelona 0-1, 3-0
1983 Aberdeen beat Hamburg 0-0, 2-0
1984 Juventus beat Liverpool 2-0
1985 Juventus v Everton not contested due to UEFA ban on English clubs
1986 Steaua Bucharest beat Dynamo Kyiv 1-0
1987 FC Porto beat Ajax 1-0, 1-0
1988 KV Mechelen beat PSV Eindhoven 3-0, 0-1
1989 AC Milan beat Barcelona 1-1, 1-0
1990 AC Milan beat Sampdoria 1-1, 2-0
1991 Manchester U beat Red Star Belgrade 1-0
1992 Barcelona beat Werder Bremen 1-1, 2-1
1993 Parma beat AC Milan 0-1, 2-0
1994 AC Milan beat Arsenal 0-0, 2-0
1995 Ajax beat Real Zaragoza 1-1, 4-0
1996 Juventus beat Paris Saint-Germain 6-1, 3-1
1997 Barcelona beat Borussia Dortmund 2-0, 1-1
1998 Chelsea beat Real Madrid 1-0
1999 Lazio beat Manchester U 1-0
2000 Galatasaray beat Real Madrid 2-1

2001 Liverpool beat Bayern Munich 3-2
2002 Real Madrid beat Feyenoord 3-1
2003 AC Milan beat Porto 1-0
2004 Valencia beat Porto 2-1
2005 Liverpool beat CSKA Moscow 3-1
2006 Sevilla beat Barcelona 3-0
2007 AC Milan beat Sevilla 3-1
2008 Zenit St Petersburg beat Manchester U 2-1
2009 Barcelona beat Shakhtar Donetsk 1-0
2010 Atletico Madrid beat Internazionale 2-0
2011 Barcelona beat Porto 2-0
2012 Atletico Madrid beat Chelsea 4-1
2013 Bayern Munich beat Chelsea 5-4 on penalties after 2-2 draw
2014 Real Madrid beat Sevilla 2-0
2015 Barcelona beat Sevilla 5-4
2016 Real Madrid beat Sevilla 3-2
2017 Real Madrid beat Manchester U 2-1
2018 Atletico Madrid beat Real Madrid 4-2 after extra time
2019 Liverpool beat Chelsea 5-4 on penalties after 2-2 draw
2020 Bayern Munich beat Sevilla 2-1
2021 Chelsea beat Villarreal 6-5 on penalties after 1-1 draw
2022 Real Madrid beat Eintracht Frankfurt 2-0
2023 Manchester C beat Sevilla 5-4 on penalties after 1-1 draw
2024 Real Madrid beat Atalanta 2-0

FIFA CLUB WORLD CUP 2025

Formerly known as the FIFA Club World Championship, this tournament was played annually between 2000 and 2023 (with the exception of 2001–04 when it was not contested due to financial difficulties). It was held between the champion clubs from all 6 continental confederations, although between 2007 and 2023 the champions of Oceania played a qualifying play-off against the champion club of the host country.

The competition was expanded to 32 clubs for the 2025 edition with AFC having 4 clubs, CAF 4 clubs, CONCACAF 4 clubs, CONMEBOL 6 clubs, OFC 1 club, UEFA 12 clubs and the host nation USA 1 club.

PREVIOUS FINALS

2000	Corinthians beat Vasco da Gama 4-3 on penalties after 0-0 draw (aet)
2001–04	Not contested
2005	Sao Paulo beat Liverpool 1-0
2006	Internacional beat Barcelona 1-0
2007	AC Milan beat Boca Juniors 4-2
2008	Manchester U beat LDU Quito 1-0
2009	Barcelona beat Estudiantes 2-1 (aet)
2010	Internazionale beat TP Mazembe Englebert 3-0
2011	Barcelona beat Santos 4-0
2012	Corinthians beat Chelsea 1-0
2013	Bayern Munich beat Raja Casablanca 2-0
2014	Real Madrid beat San Lorenzo 2-0
2015	Barcelona beat River Plate 3-0
2016	Real Madrid beat Kashima Antlers 4-2 (aet)
2017	Real Madrid beat Gremio 1-0
2018	Real Madrid beat Al-Ain 4-1
2019	Liverpool beat Flamengo 1-0 (aet)
2020	Bayern Munich beat Tigres UANL 1-0
2021	Chelsea beat Palmeiras 2-1 (aet)
2022	Real Madrid beat Al Hilal 5-3
2023	Manchester C beat Fluminense 4-0
2025	Chelsea beat Paris Saint-Germain 3-0

After extra time. ■Denotes player sent off.

GROUP STAGE

GROUP A

Al Ahly v Inter Miami	0-0
Palmeiras v Porto	0-0
Palmeiras v Al Ahly	2-0
Inter Miami v Porto	2-1
Inter Miami v Palmeiras	2-2
Porto v Al Ahly	4-4

Group A Table	P	W	D	L	F	A	GD	Pts
Palmeiras	3	1	2	0	4	2	2	5
Inter Miami	3	1	2	0	4	3	1	5
Porto	3	0	2	1	5	6	–1	2
Al Ahly	3	0	2	1	4	6	–2	2

GROUP B

Paris Saint-Germain v Atletico Madrid	4-0
Botafogo v Seattle Sounders	2-1
Seattle Sounders v Atletico Madrid	1-3
Paris Saint-Germain v Botafogo	0-1
Seattle Sounders v Paris Saint-Germain	0-2
Atletico Madrid v Botafogo	1-0

Group B Table	P	W	D	L	F	A	GD	Pts
Paris Saint-Germain	3	2	0	1	6	1	5	6
Botafogo	3	2	0	1	3	2	1	6
Atletico Madrid	3	2	0	1	4	5	–1	6
Seattle Sounders	3	0	0	3	2	7	–5	0

GROUP C

Bayern Munich v Auckland C	10-0
Boca Juniors v Benfica	2-2
Benfica v Auckland C	6-0
Bayern Munich v Boca Juniors	2-1
Auckland C v Boca Juniors	1-1
Benfica v Bayern Munich	1-0

Group C Table	P	W	D	L	F	A	GD	Pts
Benfica	3	2	1	0	9	2	7	7
Bayern Munich	3	2	0	1	12	2	10	6
Boca Juniors	3	0	2	1	4	5	–1	2
Auckland C	3	0	1	2	1	17	–16	1

GROUP D

Chelsea v Los Angeles	2-0
Flamengo v Esperance de Tunis	2-0
Flamengo v Chelsea	3-1
Los Angeles v Esperance de Tunis	0-1
Los Angeles v Flamengo	1-1
Esperance de Tunis v Chelsea	0-3

Group D Table	P	W	D	L	F	A	GD	Pts
Flamengo	3	2	1	0	6	2	4	7
Chelsea	3	2	0	1	6	3	3	6
Esperance de Tunis	3	1	0	2	1	5	–4	3
Los Angeles	3	0	1	2	1	4	–3	1

Group E

River Plate v Urawa Red Diamonds	3-1
Monterrey v Internazionale	1-1
Internazionale v Urawa Red Diamonds	2-1
River Plate v Monterrey	0-0
Internazionale v River Plate	2-0
Urawa Red Diamonds v Monterrey	0-4

Group E Table	P	W	D	L	F	A	GD	Pts
Internazionale	3	2	1	0	5	2	3	7
Monterrey	3	1	2	0	5	1	4	5
River Plate	3	1	1	1	3	3	0	4
Urawa Red Diamonds	3	0	0	3	2	9	–7	0

GROUP F

Fluminense v Borussia Dortmund	0-0
Ulsan HD v Mamelodi Sundowns	0-1
Mamelodi Sundowns v Borussia Dortmund	3-4
Fluminense v Ulsan HD	4-2
Borussia Dortmund v Ulsan HD	1-0
Mamelodi Sundowns v Fluminense	0-0

Group F Table	P	W	D	L	F	A	GD	Pts
Borussia Dortmund	3	2	1	0	5	3	2	7
Fluminense	3	1	2	0	4	2	2	5
Mamelodi Sundowns	3	1	1	1	4	4	0	4
Ulsan HD	3	0	0	3	2	6	–4	0

GROUP G

Manchester C v Wydad AC	2-0
Al Ain v Juventus	0-5
Juventus v Wydad AC	4-1
Manchester C v Al Ain	6-0
Juventus v Manchester C	2-5
Wydad AC v Al Ain	1-2

Group G Table	P	W	D	L	F	A	GD	Pts
Manchester C	3	3	0	0	13	2	11	9
Juventus	3	2	0	1	11	6	5	6
Al Ain	3	1	0	2	2	12	–10	3
Wydad AC	3	0	0	3	2	8	–6	0

GROUP H

Real Madrid v Al-Hilal	1-1
Pachuca v Red Bull Salzburg	1-2
Real Madrid v Pachuca	3-1
Red Bull Salzburg v Al-Hilal	0-0
Al-Hilal v Pachuca	2-0
Red Bull Salzburg v Real Madrid	0-3

Group H Table	P	W	D	L	F	A	GD	Pts
Real Madrid	3	2	1	0	7	2	5	7
Al-Hilal	3	1	2	0	3	1	2	5
Red Bull Salzburg	3	1	1	1	2	4	–2	4
Pachuca	3	0	0	3	2	7	–5	0

KNOCKOUT STAGE

ROUND OF 16

Palmeiras v Botafogo	1-0*
Benfica v Chelsea	1-4*
Paris Saint-Germain v Inter Miami	4-0
Flamengo v Bayern Munich	2-4
Internazionale v Fluminense	0-2
Manchester C v Al-Hilal	3-4*
Real Madrid v Juventus	1-0
Borussia Dortmund v Monterrey	2-1

QUARTER-FINALS

Fluminense v Al-Hilal	2-1
Palmeiras v Chelsea	1-2
Paris Saint-Germain v Bayern Munich	2-0
Real Madrid v Borussia Dortmund	3-2

SEMI-FINALS

Fluminense v Chelsea	0-2
Paris Saint-Germain v Real Madrid	4-0

FIFA CLUB WORLD CUP FINAL 2025

Sunday, 13 July 2025 (at MetLife Stadium, New Jersey, attendance 81,118)

Chelsea (3) 3   Paris Saint-Germain (0) 0

Chelsea: (4231) Sanchez; Gusto, Chalobah, Colwill, Cucurella; James (Dewsbury-Hall 77), Caicedo; Palmer, Fernandez (Santos 61), Neto (Nkunku 77); Joao Pedro (Delap 67).
Scorers: Palmer 22, 30, Joao Pedro 43.

Paris Saint-Germain: (433) Donnarumma; Hakimi (Ramos 73), Marquinhos, Beraldo, Mendes; Ruiz (Zaire-Emery 73), Vitinha, Neves■; Doue (Mayulu 73), Dembele, Kvaratskhelia (Barcola 58).

Referee: Alireza Faghani (Australia).

CONCACAF GOLD CUP 2025

GROUP STAGE

GROUP A

Mexico v Dominican Republic	3-2
Costa Rica v Suriname	4-3
Costa Rica v Dominican Republic	2-1
Suriname v Mexico	0-2
Mexico v Costa Rica	0-0
Dominican Republic v Suriname	0-0

Group A Table	P	W	D	L	F	A	GD	Pts
Mexico	3	2	1	0	5	2	3	7
Costa Rica	3	2	1	0	6	4	2	7
Dominican Republic	3	0	1	2	3	5	-2	1
Suriname	3	0	1	2	3	6	-3	1

GROUP B

Curacao v El Salvador	0-0
Canada v Honduras	6-0
Curacao v Canada	1-1
Honduras v El Salvador	2-0
Honduras v Curacao	2-1
Canada v El Salvador	2-0

Group B Table	P	W	D	L	F	A	GD	Pts
Canada	3	2	1	0	9	1	8	7
Honduras	3	2	0	1	4	7	-3	6
Curacao	3	0	2	1	2	3	-1	2
El Salvador	3	0	1	2	0	4	-4	1

GROUP C

Panama v Guadeloupe	5-2
Jamaica v Guatemala	0-1
Jamaica v Guadeloupe	2-1
Guatemala v Panama	0-1
Panama v Jamaica	4-1
Guadeloupe v Guatemala	2-3

Group C Table	P	W	D	L	F	A	GD	Pts
Panama	3	3	0	0	10	3	7	9
Guatemala	3	2	0	1	4	3	1	6
Jamaica	3	1	0	2	3	6	-3	3
Guadeloupe	3	0	0	3	5	10	-5	0

GROUP D

USA v Trinidad & Tobago	5-0
Haiti v Saudi Arabia	0-1
Trinidad & Tobago v Haiti	1-1
Saudi Arabia v USA	0-1
Saudi Arabia v Trinidad & Tobago	1-1
USA v Haiti	2-1

Group D Table	P	W	D	L	F	A	GD	Pts
USA	3	3	0	0	8	1	7	9
Saudi Arabia	3	1	1	1	2	2	0	4
Trinidad & Tobago	3	0	2	1	2	7	-5	2
Haiti	3	0	1	2	2	4	-2	1

KNOCKOUT STAGE

QUARTER-FINALS

Panama v Honduras	1-1
Honduras won 5-4 on penalties.	
Mexico v Saudi Arabia	2-0
Canada v Guatemala	1-1
Guatemala won 6-5 on penalties.	
USA v Costa Rica	2-2
USA won 4-3 on penalties.	

SEMI-FINALS

USA v Guatemala	2-1
Mexico v Honduras	1-0

CONCACAF GOLD CUP FINAL 2025

Sunday, 6 July 2025

(at NRG Stadium, Houston, attendance 70,925)

USA (1) 1   Mexico (1) 2

USA: (442) Freese; Freeman, Richards, Ream, Arfsten (Tolken 86); Berhalter, Adams (McGlynn 82), Luna (Aaronson 86), de la Torre (Downs 69); Tillman, Agyemange.
Scorer: Richards 4.

Mexico: (433) Malagon; Sanchez (Reyes 86), Montes, Vasquez, Gallardo; Mora (Pineda 75), Edson Alvarez, Ruiz; Alvarado (Huerta 87), Jimenez (Gimenez 86), Vega.
Scorers: Jimenez 27, Edson Alvarez 77.

Referee: Mario Escobar (Guatemala).

INTERNATIONAL DIRECTORY

The directory provides the latest available information on international and club football in the 211 national associations in the six Confederations of FIFA, the world governing body. This includes addresses, foundation dates and national team colours. FIFA-recognised internationals played in season 2024–25 (i.e., *16 July 2024 to 15 July 2025*) are listed as well as league and cup champions at club level. In Europe, the latest league tables, cup winners and top scorers for the 55 UEFA nations are given, together with all-time league and cup honours.

The four home nations, England, Scotland, Northern Ireland and Wales, are dealt with elsewhere in the Yearbook, but basic details appear in this directory. Gozo is included here for its close links with Maltese football, the Channel Islands for their proximity to England. Northern Cyprus is not a member of either UEFA nor FIFA and is the subject of an international territorial dispute. Since the invasion of Ukraine in 2022, Russia's football federation has been suspended from FIFA and UEFA and its representative and club teams barred from all competitions. (In 2024–25 Russia played seven non-FIFA-sanctioned matches.) With the war ongoing, the national teams and club sides of Ukraine and Russia's ally Belarus competing in UEFA competitions continue to play 'home' matches at neutral venues. Since October 2023, 'home' representative matches of Israel and Palestine have been played at neutral venues; likewise, Israeli club sides play 'home' UEFA competition matches outside national borders.

International match venues are indicated as follows: home (h), away (a), neutral (n); in multi-nation tournaments the host nation is deemed to be playing at home and all others are on neutral territory; where a nation is unable to play a qualifier at home the neutral venue is stated in a note.

FIFA currently has 11 associate members who have affiliation to their Confederations: AFC: Northern Mariana Islands; CAF: Réunion, Zanzibar; CONCACAF: Bonaire, French Guiana, Guadeloupe, Martinique, Saint-Martin, Sint Maarten; OFC: Kiribati, Tuvalu. Matches involving associate members are indicated with †.

N.B. Final league rankings for clubs tied on points are decided on goal difference unless otherwise stated.

Key to table symbols used: (C) league champions; [1] UEFA Champions League qualifier; [2] UEFA Europa League qualifier; [3] UEFA Conference League qualifier; * team relegated; +* team relegated after play-offs; + team not relegated after play-offs.

EUROPE (UEFA)

ALBANIA
Football Association of Albania, Rr. Liman Kaba, Nd 5, 1019 Tirana.
Founded: 1930. *FIFA:* 1932; *UEFA:* 1954. *National Colours:* Red shirts with black trim, black shorts, black socks with red trim.

International matches 2024–25
Ukraine (a) 2-1*, Georgia (h) 0-1, Czech Republic (a) 0-2, Georgia (a) 1-0, Czech Republic (h) 0-0, Ukraine (h) 1-2, England (a) 0-2, Andorra (h) 3-0, Serbia (h) 0-0, Latvia (a) 1-1.
Match played in Czech Republic.

League Championship wins (1930–37; 1945–2025)
KF Tirana 26 (formerly SK Tirana; includes 17 Nentori 8); Dinamo City (formerly Dinamo Tirana) 18; Partizani (Tirana) 17; Vllaznia (Shkoder) 9; Skenderbeu (Korce) 8; Elbasani 2 (incl. Labinoti 1); Teuta 2; Egnatia (Rrogozhine) 2; Flamurtari (Vlore) 1; Kukesi 1.

Cup wins (1948–2025)
KF Tirana 16 (formerly SK Tirana; includes 17 Nentori 8); Partizani (Tirana) 15; Dinamo City (formerly Dinamo Tirana) 14; Vllaznia (Shkoder) 8; Flamurtari (Vlore) 4; Teuta 4; Elbasani 2 (incl. Labinoti 1); Besa 2; Laci 2; Kukesi 2; Egnatia (Rrogozhine) 2; Apolonia Fier 1; Skenderbeu (Korce) 1.

Albanian Kategoria Superiore 2024–25
	P	W	D	L	F	A	GD	Pts
Egnatia (C)†[1]	36	16	11	9	47	30	17	59
Vllaznia†[3]	36	15	12	9	54	39	15	57
Dinamo City†[3]	36	14	13	9	49	41	8	55
Partizani†	36	13	14	9	38	33	5	53
Elbasani	36	11	17	8	40	38	2	50
Teuta	36	10	14	12	29	42	–13	44
Bylis	36	11	9	16	33	50	–17	42
Tirana+	36	7	18	11	43	44	–1	39
Skenderbeu*	36	9	11	16	35	45	–10	38
Laci*	36	8	13	15	31	37	–6	37

†*Qualified for Final Four play-offs.*

Final Four Play-offs
Semi-finals
Vllaznia 2, Dinamo City 1
Egnatia 0, Partizani 0
Egnatia qualified for the final due to higher ranking in regular season.
Third-place Play-off
Dinamo City 1, Partizani 2
Final
Vllaznia 0, Egnatia 4
Top scorer: Bekim Balaj (Vllaznia) 19.
Cup Final: Dinamo City 2, Egnatia 2 *(aet; Dinamo City won 5-4 on penalties).*

ANDORRA
Federacio Andorrana de Futbol, C/ Batlle Tomas, 4 Baixos, AD 700, Escaldes-Engordany.
Founded: 1994. *FIFA:* 1996; *UEFA:* 1996. *National Colours:* Red shirts with blue and yellow trim, red shorts with blue trim, red socks with blue and yellow trim.

International matches 2024–25
Gibraltar (a) 0-1, Malta (h) 0-1, Moldova (a) 0-2, San Marino (h) 2-0, Moldova (h) 0-1, Malta (a) 0-0, Latvia (h) 0-1, Albania (a) 0-3, England (h) 0-1*, Serbia (a) 0-3.
Match played in Spain.

League Championship wins (1995–2025)
FC Santa Coloma 13; Inter Club d'Escaldes 4; Principat 3; FC Encamp 2; Sant Julia 2; Ranger's 2; Lusitanos 2; Constel-lacio Esportiva 1; Atletic Club d'Escaldes 1; UE Santa Coloma 1.

Cup wins (1991, 1994–2025)
FC Santa Coloma 10*; Principat 6*; Sant Julia 6; UE Santa Coloma 4; Inter Club d'Escaldes 3; Constel-lacio Esportiva 1; Lusitanos 1; UE Engordany 1; Atletic Club d'Escaldes 1.
Includes one unofficial title.

Andorran Primera Divisió 2024–25
	P	W	D	L	F	A	GD	Pts
Inter Club d'Escaldes (C)[1]	27	18	8	1	84	19	65	62
Atletic Club d'Escaldes[3]	27	16	7	4	70	25	45	55
FC Santa Coloma[3]	27	16	4	7	42	28	14	52
UE Santa Coloma	27	14	7	6	56	24	32	49
Ranger's	27	13	9	5	59	20	39	48
Ordino	27	9	6	12	32	48	–16	33
Penya Encarnada (–3)	27	9	6	12	32	46	–14	30
Pas de la Casa	27	8	5	14	35	36	–1	29
Esperança*	27	1	4	22	14	92	–78	7
La Massana*	27	1	2	24	10	102	–92	5

Penya Encarnada deducted 3pts.
Top scorer: Guillaume Lopez (Inter Club d'Escaldes) 14.
Cup Final: Inter Club d'Escaldes 1, Atletic Club d'Escaldes 0.

ARMENIA
Football Federation of Armenia, Khanjyan Street 27, 0010 Yerevan.
Founded: 1992. *FIFA:* 1992; *UEFA:* 1993. *National Colours:* All red.

International matches 2024–25
Latvia (h) 4-1, North Macedonia (a) 0-2, Faroe Islands (a) 2-2, North Macedonia (h) 0-2, Faroe Islands (h) 0-1, Latvia (a) 2-1, Georgia (h) 0-3, Georgia (a) 1-6, Kosovo (a) 2-5, Montenegro (a) 2-2.

League Championship wins (1992–2025)
Pyunik 16 (incl. Homenetmen 1*); Shirak 4*; Alashkert 4; Araks 2 (incl. Tsement 1); Urartu 2 (incl. Banants 1); Ararat-Armenia 2; Ararat Yerevan 1; FK Yerevan 1; Ulisses 1; Noah 1.
Includes one unofficial shared title.

Cup wins (1992–2025)
Pyunik (incl. Homenetmen 1) 8; Ararat Yerevan 6; Mika

6; Urartu 4 (incl. Banants 3); Tsement 2; Shirak 2; Noah 2; Gandzasar Kapan 1; Alashkert 1; Noravank 1; Ararat-Armenia 1.

See also Russia section for Armenian club honours in Soviet era 1936–91.

Armenian Premier League 2024–25

	P	W	D	L	F	A	GD	Pts
Noah (C)[1]	30	24	3	3	92	20	72	75
Ararat-Armenia[3]	30	21	3	6	75	28	47	66
Urartu[3]	30	19	5	6	64	31	33	62
Pyunik[3]	30	17	2	11	59	37	22	53
Van	30	15	7	8	56	36	20	52
BKMA†	30	10	6	14	44	54	–10	36
Shirak	30	10	5	15	30	50	–20	35
Ararat Yerevan	30	9	5	16	36	59	–23	32
Alashkert	30	6	8	16	24	52	–28	26
Gandzasar Kapan*	30	2	4	24	16	73	–57	10
West Armenia‡*	30	7	2	21	22	78	–56	23

†*BKMA reprieved from relegation in 2023–24.* ‡*West Armenia failed to fulfil fixture against Ararat-Armenia on 9 May 2025 and were expelled and their three remaining matches awarded as 3-0 wins to their opponents.*
Top scorer: Goncalo Gregorio (Noah) 20.
Cup Final: Noah 3, Ararat-Armenia 1.

AUSTRIA

Oesterreichischer Fussball-Bund, Ernst-Happel Stadion, Sektor A/F, Meiereistrasse 7, Postfach 340, 1021 Wien.
Founded: 1904. *FIFA:* 1905; *UEFA:* 1954. *National Colours:* Red shirts with white trim, red shorts, red socks.

International matches 2024–25
Slovenia (a) 1-1, Norway (a) 1-2, Kazakhstan (h) 4-0, Norway (h) 5-1, Kazakhstan (a) 2-0, Slovenia (a) 1-1, Serbia (h) 1-1, Serbia (a) 0-2, Romania (h) 2-1, San Marino (a) 4-0.

League Championship wins (1911–2025)
Rapid Vienna 32; Austria Vienna (formerly Amateure) 24; Red Bull Salzburg 17 (incl. Austria Salzburg 3); Wacker Innsbruck 10 (incl. Swarovski Tirol 2 [now WSG Tirol], Tirol Innsbruck 3); Admira Vienna (now Admira Wacker Modling) 9 (incl. Wacker Vienna 1); First Vienna 6; Sturm Graz 5; Wiener Sportklub 3; WAF 1; WAC 1; Floridsdorfer 1; Hakoah 1; LASK (Linz) 1; Voest Linz 1; GAK (Graz) 1.
Not completed in 1944–45.

Cup wins (1918–39; 1945–49; 1958–2025)
Austria Vienna (formerly Amateure) 27; Rapid Vienna 14; Red Bull Salzburg 9; Wacker Innsbruck 7 (incl. Swarovski Tirol 1); Admira Vienna (now Admira Wacker Modling) 6 (incl. Wacker Vienna 1); Sturm Graz 7; GAK Graz 4; First Vienna 3; WAC 3 (incl. Schwarz-Rot Wien 1); Ried 2; WAF 1; Wiener Sportklub 1; LASK (Linz) 1; Kremser 1; Stockerau 1; Karnten 1; Horn 1; Pasching 1; Wolfsberg 1.

Austrian Bundesliga Regular Season 2024–25

	P	W	D	L	F	A	GD	Pts
Sturm Graz†	22	14	4	4	51	28	23	46
Austria Vienna†	22	14	4	4	36	19	17	46
Red Bull Salzburg	22	10	8	4	33	22	11	38
Wolfsberg	22	11	3	8	44	30	14	36
Rapid Vienna	22	9	7	6	32	24	8	34
Blau-Weiss Linz	22	10	3	9	30	29	1	33
LASK	22	9	4	9	32	33	–1	31
Hartberg	22	6	8	8	24	31	–7	26
Austria Klagenfurt	22	5	6	11	22	44	–22	21
WSG Tirol	22	4	7	11	20	31	–11	19
Grazer AK‡	22	3	7	12	27	45	–18	16
SCR Altach‡	22	3	7	12	20	35	–15	16

†*Ranking decided on goals scored.* ‡*Ranking decided on head-to-head points.*
NB: *Points earned in regular season are halved and rounded down at start of Championship and Relegation rounds.*

Championship Round 2024–25

	P	W	D	L	F	A	GD	Pts
Sturm Graz (C)[1]	32	19	6	7	66	39	27	40
Red Bull Salzburg[1]	32	16	9	7	53	36	17	38
Austria Vienna†[3]	32	18	6	8	47	32	15	37
Wolfsberg†[2]	32	16	7	9	60	38	22	37
Rapid Vienna‡[3]	32	12	8	12	43	42	1	27
Blau-Weiss Linz	32	11	5	16	37	45	–8	21

†*Ranking decided on head-to-head points.* ‡*Qualified for UEFA Conference League Play-off final.*

Relegation Round 2024–25

	P	W	D	L	F	A	GD	Pts
LASK‡	32	16	6	10	51	36	15	38
Hartberg‡	32	11	11	10	40	40	0	31
WSG Tirol	32	7	9	16	35	50	–15	20
Grazer AK	32	5	13	14	34	54	–20	20
SCR Altach	32	5	11	16	29	46	–17	18
Austria Klagenfurt*	32	6	9	17	33	70	–37	16

‡*Qualified for UEFA Conference League Play-off semi-final.*
UEFA Conference League Play-off semi-final
LASK 2, Hartberg 0.
UEFA Conference League Play-off final first leg
LASK 3, Rapid Vienna 1.
UEFA Conference League Play-off final second leg
Rapid Vienna 3, LASK 0 *(Rapid Vienna won 4-3 on aggregate).*
Top scorer: Ronivaldo (Blau-Weiss Linz) 14.
Cup Final: Wolfsberg 1, Hartberg 0.

AZERBAIJAN

Association of Football Federations of Azerbaijan, 163, 8 November Avenue, 1025 Baku.
Founded: 1992. *FIFA:* 1994; *UEFA:* 1994. *National Colours:* All blue.

International matches 2024–25
Sweden (h) 1-3, Slovakia (a) 0-2, Estonia (a) 1-3, Slovakia (h) 1-3, Estonia (h) 0-0, Sweden (a) 0-6, Haiti (h) 0-3, Belarus (h) 0-2, Latvia (a) 0-0, Hungary (h) 1-2.

League Championship wins (1992–2025)
Qarabag 12; Neftci 9; Kapaz 3; Shamkir 3*; FK Baku 2; Inter Baku (renamed Keshla, now Shamakhi) 2; Turan Tovuz 1; Khazar Lankaran 1.
Includes one unofficial title.

Cup wins (1992–2025)
Qarabag 8; Neftci 7*; Kapaz 4; FK Baku 3; Khazar Lankaran 3; Keshla (formerly Inter Baku, now Shamakhi) 2; Gabala 2; Inshatchi 1; Shafa 1; Sabah 1.
No winner in 2019–20. *Includes one unofficial title.*

Azerbaijani Premyer Liqasi 2024–25

	P	W	D	L	F	A	GD	Pts
Qarabag (C)[1]	36	28	5	3	86	19	67	89
Zira[3]	36	23	5	8	59	27	32	74
Araz-Naxcivan[3]	36	15	13	8	34	29	5	58
Turan Tovuz	36	14	13	9	45	39	6	55
Sabah[2]	36	10	18	8	50	46	4	48
Neftci	36	10	13	13	39	49	–10	43
Shamakhi	36	9	9	18	32	46	–14	36
Sumgayit	36	9	6	21	31	53	–22	33
Kapaz	36	8	8	20	28	65	–37	32
Sabail*	36	4	10	22	28	59	–31	22

Top scorer: Leandro Andrade (Qarabag) 15.
Cup Final: Sabah 3, Qarabag 2 *(aet).*

BELARUS

Belarus Football Federation, Prospekt Pobeditelei 20/3, 220020 Minsk. (Due to Belarus's support for Russia's invasion of Ukraine, the national side plays home UEFA/FIFA matches at neutral venues behind closed doors.)
Founded: 1989. *FIFA:* 1992; *UEFA:* 1993. *National Colours:* All maroon with green trim.

International matches 2024–25
Bulgaria (h) 0-0*, Luxembourg (a) 1-0, Northern Ireland (h) 0-0*, Luxembourg (h) 1-1*, Northern Ireland (a) 0-2, Bulgaria (a) 1-1, Tajikistan (a) 5-0, Azerbaijan (a) 2-0, Kazakhstan (h) 4-1, Russia (h) 1-4‡.
Match played in Hungary. ‡*Match not sanctioned by FIFA due to Russia's invasion of Ukraine.*

League Championship wins (1992–2024)
BATE Borisov 15; Dinamo Minsk 9; Shakhtyor Soligorsk 3; Slavia Mozyr (incl. MPKC 1) 2; Dnepr Mogilev 1; Belshina Bobruisk 1; Gomel 1; Dinamo Brest 1.
No champion declared in 2022 following a match-fixing inquiry.

Cup wins (1992–2025)
BATE Borisov 5; Dinamo Minsk 3; Neman Grodno 3; Belshina Bobruisk 3; Gomel 3; Shakhtyor Soligorsk 3; Dinamo Brest 3; Slavia Mozyr (incl. MPKC 1) 2; MTZ-RIPA 2; Naftan Novopolotsk 2; Torpedo-BelAZ Zhodino 2; Dinamo 93 Minsk 1; Lokomotiv 96 1; FC Minsk 1.
See also Russia section for Belarusian club honours in Soviet era 1936–91.

Belarusian Vysheyshaya Liga 2024

	P	W	D	L	F	A	GD	Pts
Dinamo Minsk (C)[1]	30	20	8	2	50	13	37	68
Neman Grodno[3]	30	20	5	5	45	19	26	65
Torpedo-BelAZ Zhodino[3]	30	18	8	4	45	21	24	62
Dynamo Brest[3]	30	14	7	9	62	37	25	49
Vitebsk	30	14	5	11	33	25	8	47
Gomel	30	11	11	8	37	28	9	44
Isloch Minsk Raion	30	11	8	11	36	30	6	41
BATE Borisov	30	11	7	12	38	38	0	40
Slutsk	30	11	6	13	26	41	–15	39
Arsenal Dzerzhinsk	30	10	8	12	29	36	–7	38
Slavia Mozyr	30	8	11	11	28	33	–5	35
Smorgon	30	7	11	12	33	51	–18	32
Minsk	30	6	10	14	28	44	–16	28
Naftan Novopolotsk+	30	5	11	14	27	44	–17	26
Dnepr Mogilev*	30	3	9	18	27	53	–26	18
Shakhtyor Soligorsk* (–20)	30	5	7	18	19	45	–26	2

Shakhtyor Soligorsk deducted 20pts for match-fixing; at the end of the season they folded due to financial difficulties.
Top scorer: Junior Effaghe (Gomel) 17.
Cup Final: Neman Grodno 3, Torpedo-BelAZ Zhodino 0.

BELGIUM
Royale Belgian Football Association, Rue de Bruxelles 480, 1480 Tubize.
Founded: 1895. *FIFA:* 1904; *UEFA:* 1954. *National Colours:* Burgundy with black and yellow trim, black shorts with yellow trim, burgundy socks.
International matches 2024–25
Israel (h) 3-1*, France (a) 0-2, Italy (a) 2-2, France (h) 1-2, Italy (h) 0-1, Israel (a) 0-1†, Ukraine (a) 1-3§, Ukraine (h) 3-0, North Macedonia (a) 1-1, Wales (h) 4-3.
**Match played in Hungary due to protests against Israel's war in Gaza. †Match played in Hungary. §Match played in Spain.*
League Championship wins (1895–1914; 1919–39; 1941–44; 1945–2025)
Anderlecht 34; Club Brugge 19; Union Saint-Gilloise 12; Standard Liege 10; Beerschot VAC (became Germinal) 7; RC Brussels 6; RFC Liege 5; Daring Brussels 5; Antwerp 5; Lierse 4; Mechelen 4; Genk 4; Cercle Brugge 3; Beveren 2; RWD Molenbeek 1; Gent 1.
Cup wins (1912–14; 1927; 1935; 1953–63; 1963–2025)
Club Brugge 12; Anderlecht 9; Standard Liege 8; Genk 5; Antwerp 4; Gent 4; Union Saint-Gilloise 3; Cercle Brugge 2; Lierse 2; Beerschot VAC (became Germinal) 2; Beveren 2; Waterschei (became Racing Genk) 2; Mechelen 2; Beerschot Antwerpen Club (incl. Germinal Ekeren) 2; Zulte Waregem 2; Lokeren 2; Racing 1; Daring 1; Tournai 1; KFC Waregem 1; RFC Liege 1; Westerlo 1; La Louviere 1.
Belgian Pro League Regular Season 2024–25

	P	W	D	L	F	A	GD	Pts
Genk	30	21	5	4	55	33	22	68
Club Brugge	30	17	8	5	65	36	29	59
Union Saint-Gilloise	30	15	10	5	49	25	24	55
Anderlecht	30	15	6	9	50	27	23	51
Antwerp	30	12	10	8	47	32	15	46
Gent	30	11	12	7	41	33	8	45
Standard Liege	30	10	9	11	22	35	–13	39
Mechelen	30	10	8	12	45	40	5	38
Westerlo	30	10	7	13	50	49	1	37
Charleroi	30	10	7	13	36	36	0	37
Leuven	30	8	13	9	28	33	–5	37
Dender	30	8	8	14	33	51	–18	32
Cercle Brugge	30	7	11	12	29	44	–15	32
Sint-Truiden	30	7	10	13	41	56	–15	31
Kortrijk	30	7	5	18	28	55	–27	26
Beerschot	30	3	9	18	26	60	–34	18

NB: Points earned in regular season are halved and rounded up at start of Championship and Europe Play-offs phase; in the Relegation Play-offs phase full regular season points are retained.
Championship Play-offs 2024–25

	P	W	D	L	F	A	GD	Pts
Union Saint-Gilloise (C)[1]	10	9	1	0	22	3	19	56
Club Brugge[1]	10	7	2	1	21	6	15	53
Genk[2]	10	4	1	5	14	11	3	47
Anderlecht[2]	10	3	1	6	12	13	–1	36
Antwerp†	10	2	3	5	10	18	–8	32
Gent	10	1	0	9	4	32	–28	26

†*Qualified for UEFA Conference League Play-off.*

Europe Play-offs 2024–25

	P	W	D	L	F	A	GD	Pts
Charleroi†[3]	10	6	3	1	19	10	9	40
Westerlo	10	3	5	2	19	16	3	33
Mechelen	10	2	6	2	17	17	0	31
Dender	10	3	4	3	20	21	–1	29
Standard Liege	10	0	7	3	5	8	–3	27
Leuven	10	1	5	4	11	19	–8	27

†*Qualified for UEFA Conference League Play-off.*
Relegation Play-offs 2024–25

	P	W	D	L	F	A	GD	Pts
Sint-Truiden	6	3	1	2	9	10	–1	41
Cercle Brugge+	6	2	1	3	10	13	–3	39
Kortrijk*	6	3	2	1	12	8	4	37
Beerschot*	6	2	0	4	10	10	0	24

UEFA Conference League Play-off
Antwerp 1, Charleroi 2
Top scorers (joint): Tolu Arokodare (Genk), Adriano Bertaccini (Sint-Truiden) 21.
Cup Final: Club Brugge 2, Anderlecht 1.

BOSNIA & HERZEGOVINA
Football Federation of Bosnia & Herzegovina, Bulevar Mese Selimovica 95, 71000 Sarajevo.
Founded: 1992. *FIFA:* 1996; *UEFA:* 1998. *National Colours:* All blue with yellow trim.
International matches 2024–25
Netherlands (a) 2-5, Hungary (a) 0-0, Germany (h) 1-2, Hungary (h) 0-2, Germany (a) 0-7, Netherlands (h) 1-1, Romania (a) 1-0, Cyprus (h) 2-1, San Marino (h) 1-0, Slovenia (a) 1-2.
League Championship wins (1994–2025)
Zrinjski Mostar 9; Zeljeznicar 6; Sarajevo 5; Celik 3; Borac Banja Luka 3; Siroki Brijeg 2; Brotnjo 1; Leotar 1; Modrica 1.
Cup wins (1997–2025)
Sarajevo 8; Zeljeznicar 6; Siroki Brijeg 3; Zrinjski Mostar 3; Bosna Visoko 1; Modrica 1; Orasje 1; Slavija 1; Borac Banja Luka 1; Olimpik Sarajevo 1; Radnik Bijeljina 1; Velez Mostar 1.
No winner in 2019–20.
See also Serbia section for Bosnia & Herzegovina club honours in Yugoslav Republic era 1947–91.
Premijer Liga Bosne i Hercegovine 2024–25

	P	W	D	L	F	A	GD	Pts
Zrinjski Mostar (C)[1]	33	26	4	3	74	17	57	82
Borac Banja Luka[3]	33	26	3	4	58	13	45	81
Sarajevo[3]	33	18	11	4	59	24	35	65
Zeljeznicar[3]	33	20	5	8	55	38	17	65
Siroki Brijeg	33	13	7	13	43	46	–3	46
Sloga Meridian	33	13	5	15	35	45	–10	44
Velez Mostar	33	10	12	11	45	39	6	42
Radnik Bijeljina	33	12	4	17	44	52	–8	40
Posusje	33	10	7	16	36	41	–5	37
Igman Konjic*	33	8	5	20	30	66	–36	29
GOSK Gabela*	33	4	4	25	28	76	–48	16
Sloboda Tuzla* (–3)	33	1	7	25	21	71	–50	7

Sloboda Tuzla deducted 3pts after their players left the pitch in protest at the referee during the round 28 match against Posusje; Posusje awarded a 3-0 win. League reduced to 10 teams for 2025–26.
Top scorer: Mihael Mlinaric (Velez Mostar) 19.
Cup Final: Sarajevo 4, 1 Siroki Brijeg 0, 1 *(Sarajevo won 5-1 on aggregate).*

BULGARIA
Bulgarian Football Union, 18 Vitoshko Iale Str., Boyana, 1618 Sofia.
Founded: 1923. *FIFA:* 1992; *UEFA:* 1954. *National Colours:* White shirts with yellow trim, green shorts with yellow trim, white socks with yellow trim.
International matches 2024–25
Belarus (a) 0-0*, Northern Ireland (h) 1-0, Luxembourg (h) 0-0, Northern Ireland (a) 0-5, Luxembourg (a) 1-0, Belarus (h) 1-1, Republic of Ireland (h) 1-2, Republic of Ireland (a) 1-2, Cyprus (h) 2-2, Greece (a) 0-4.
**Match played in Hungary.*
League Championship wins (1925–2025)
CSKA Sofia 31; Levski Sofia 26; Ludogorets Razgrad 14; Slavia Sofia 7; Lokomotiv Sofia (renamed Lokomotiv 1929 Sofia) 4; Litex Lovech 4; Vladislav Varna (now Cherno More Varna) 3; Botev Plovdiv (includes Trakija) 2; Athletic Slava 1923 1; Sokol Varna (now Spartak Varna) 1; Sportklub Sofia (now Septemvri Sofia) 1; Ticha Varna (now Cherno More Varna) 1; Spartak Plovdiv 1;

Beroe (Stara Zagora) 1; Etar 1; Lokomotiv Plovdiv 1.
No winner in 1927, 1944.

Cup wins (1938–42; 1946–2025)
Levski Sofia (incl. Vitosha 1) 26; CSKA Sofia (incl.
Sredets 3) 21; Slavia Sofia 8; Lokomotiv Sofia (renamed
Lokomotiv 1929 Sofia) 4; Litex Lovech 4; Botev Plovdiv
(includes Trakija) 4; Ludogorets Razgrad 4; FK 13 Sofia
2; Beroe (Stara Zagora) 2; Lokomotiv Plovdiv 2; Shipka
Sofia 1; AS 23 Sofia 1; Spartak Plovdiv 1; Septemvri Sofia
1; Spartak Sofia 1; Marek Dupnitsa 1; Sliven 1; Cherno
More Varna 1.

Bulgarian First League Regular Season 2024–25

	P	W	D	L	F	A	GD	Pts
Ludogorets Razgrad	30	24	4	2	62	14	48	76
Levski Sofia	30	19	5	6	55	25	30	62
Arda†	30	15	8	7	49	33	16	53
Cherno More†	30	14	11	5	41	25	16	53
Botev Plovdiv	30	14	7	9	32	31	1	49
Spartak Varna	30	14	6	10	39	38	1	48
CSKA Sofia	30	13	8	9	40	27	13	47
Beroe‡	30	12	6	12	34	29	5	42
Slavia Sofia‡	30	12	6	12	43	42	1	42
CSKA 1948 Sofia	30	8	10	12	38	44	–6	34
Septemvri Sofia	30	10	3	17	32	47	–15	33
Lokomotiv Sofia†	30	8	6	16	29	49	–20	30
Krumovgrad†	30	7	9	14	16	31	–15	30
Lokomotiv Plovdiv	30	7	7	16	27	40	–13	28
Botev Vratsa	30	5	6	19	24	57	–33	21
Hebar 1918	30	3	8	19	23	52	–29	17

†*Ranking decided on head-to-head points.* ‡*Ranking decided on head-to-head away goals.*

Championship Round 2024–25

	P	W	D	L	F	A	GD	Pts
Ludogorets Razgrad (C)[1]	36	25	8	3	70	22	48	83
Levski Sofia[2]	36	21	9	6	64	29	35	72
Cherno More[3]	36	15	14	7	44	30	14	59
Arda[3]§	36	15	13	8	54	41	13	58

§*Qualified for UEFA Conference League Play-off.*

UEFA Conference League Round 2024–25

	P	W	D	L	F	A	GD	Pts
CSKA Sofia§	36	19	8	9	58	28	30	65
Botev Plovdiv	36	16	8	12	43	43	0	56
Spartak Varna	36	15	6	15	45	53	–8	51
Beroe	36	14	7	15	41	43	–2	49

§*Qualified for UEFA Conference League Play-off.*

Relegation Round 2024–25

	P	W	D	L	F	A	GD	Pts
Slavia Sofia	37	14	7	16	50	52	–2	49
Lokomotiv Sofia†	37	13	8	16	43	51	–8	47
CSKA 1948 Sofia†	37	12	11	14	45	47	–2	47
Septemvri Sofia	37	14	3	20	42	56	–14	45
Lokomotiv Plovdiv+	37	10	8	19	37	49	–12	38
Botev Vratsa+	37	10	6	21	34	65	–31	36
Krumovgrad*	37	8	9	20	20	45	–25	33
Hebar 1918*	37	4	9	24	28	64	–36	21

†*Ranking decided on head-to-head points.*

UEFA Conference League Play-off
Arda 1, CSKA Sofia 1 *(aet; Arda won 4-1 on penalties).*
Top scorer: Santiago Godoy (Beroe) 18.
Cup Final: Ludogorets Razgrad 1, CSKA Sofia 0.

CHANNEL ISLANDS

Guernsey
League Championship wins (1894–1939; 1946–2025)
Northerners 32; Guernsey Rangers 17; St Martin's 17;
Vale Recreation 16; Sylvans 10; Belgrave Wanderers 8;
2nd Bn Manchesters 3; Guernsey Rovers 3; 2nd Bn
Wiltshires 2; 2nd Bn Royal Irish Regt 2; Band Comp 2nd
Bn Royal Fusiliers 1; G&H Comp Royal Fusiliers 1; 10th
Comp W Div Royal Artillery 1; 2nd Bn PA Somerset
Light Infantry 1; Grange 1; 2nd Bn Leicesters 1; 2nd
Middlesex Regt 1; Yorkshire Regt (Green Howards);
Athletics 1.
No winner in 2019–20.

Guernsey Priaulx League 2024–25

	P	W	D	L	F	A	GD	Pts
St Martin's	18	14	2	2	54	12	42	44
Sylvans	18	11	1	6	46	19	27	34
Vale Recreation	18	11	1	6	51	30	21	34
Northerners	18	10	3	5	62	26	36	33
Rovers	18	8	3	7	32	30	2	27
Rangers	18	2	1	15	14	65	–51	7
Belgrave Wanderers	18	1	1	16	4	81	–77	4

Top scorer: Callum Le Lacheur (St Martin's) 13.

Jersey
League Championship wins (1904–1939; 1946–2025)
Jersey Wanderers 21; St Paul's 21; First Tower United 19;
Jersey Scottish 11; Beeches Old Boys 5; Magpies 4; St
Peter 4; 2nd Bn King's Own Regt 3; Oaklands 3; 1st Batt
Devon Regt 2; 1st Bn East Surrey Regt 2; Georgetown 2;
Mechanics 2; YMCA 2; St Clement 2; 2nd Bn East Surrey
Regt 1; 20th Comp Royal Garrison Artillery 1; National
Rovers 1; Sporting Academics 1; Trinity 1; Grouville 1.

Jersey Premiership 1 2024–25

	P	W	D	L	F	A	GD	Pts
Grouville	14	11	2	1	47	16	31	35
St Clement	14	10	1	3	47	15	32	31
St Paul's	14	8	1	5	47	29	18	25
St Brelade	14	6	2	6	41	41	0	20
Jersey Wanderers	14	5	1	8	34	38	–4	16
Madeira	14	3	5	6	26	45	–19	14
Sporting Academics*	14	3	2	9	19	46	–21	11
St Peter*	14	2	2	10	24	55	–31	8

Top scorer: Callum Gilroy (St Paul's) 14.

Upton Park Trophy 2025 (For Guernsey & Jersey League Champions)
Grouville 0, St Martin's 1.

Upton Park Trophy wins (1907–1939; 1947–2025)
Northerners 17 (incl. 1 shared); St Martin's 13; First
Tower United 12; St Paul's 12; Jersey Wanderers 11 (incl.
1 shared); Jersey Scottish 6; Guernsey Rangers 5; Vale
Recreation 5; Belgrave Wanderers 4; Old St Paul's 3;
Beeches Old Boys 3; Magpies 3; Sylvans 3; St Peter 3;
National Rovers 1; Jersey Mechanics 1; Jersey YMCA 1;
Sporting Academics 1; Trinity 1.
No winner in 2019–20, 2020–21.

CROATIA

Croatian Football Federation, Ulica grada Vukovara
269A, 10000 Zagreb.
Founded: 1912. *FIFA:* 1992; *UEFA:* 1993. *National
Colours:* Red and white check shirts, white shorts, white
socks.

International matches 2024–25
Portugal (a) 1-2, Poland (h) 1-0, Scotland (h) 2-1, Poland
(a) 3-3, Scotland (a) 0-1, Portugal (h) 1-1, France (h) 2-0,
France (a) 0-2 (4-5p), Gibraltar (a) 7-0*, Czech Republic
(h) 5-1.
**Match played in Portugal.*

League Championship wins (1992–2025)
Dinamo Zagreb (incl. Croatia Zagreb 3) 25; Hajduk Split
6; Rijeka 2; NK Zagreb 1.

Cup wins (1992–2025)
Dinamo Zagreb (incl. Croatia Zagreb 4) 17; Hajduk Split
8; Rijeka 7; Inter Zapresic 1; Osijek 1.
*See also Serbia section for Croatian club honours in
Yugoslav Republic era 1947–92.*

Croatian Hrvatska Nogometna Liga 2024–25

	P	W	D	L	F	A	GD	Pts
Rijeka (C)†[1]	36	18	11	7	49	21	28	65
Dinamo Zagreb†[2]	36	19	8	9	69	41	28	65
Hajduk Split[3]	36	17	12	7	49	34	15	63
Varazdin	36	11	16	9	28	24	4	49
Slaven Belupo‡	36	13	9	14	42	45	–3	48
Istra 1961‡	36	11	15	10	39	42	–3	48
Osijek	36	11	9	16	46	52	–6	42
Lokomotiva	36	10	9	17	45	54	–9	39
Gorica	36	9	10	17	29	51	–22	37
Sibenik*	36	7	9	20	28	60	–32	30

†*Ranking decided on head-to-head goal difference.*
‡*Ranking decided on goals scored.*
Top scorer: Marko Livaja (Hajduk Split) 19.
Cup Final: Slaven Belupo 1, 0, Rijeka 1, 1 *(Rijeka won
2-1 on aggregate).*

CYPRUS

Cyprus Football Association, 10 Achaion Street, 2413
Engomi, PO Box 25071, 1306 Nicosia.
Founded: 1934. *FIFA:* 1948; *UEFA:* 1962. *National
Colours:* All blue with white trim.

International matches 2024–25
Lithuania (a) 1-0, Kosovo (h) 0-4, Romania (h) 0-3,
Kosovo (a) 0-3, Lithuania (h) 2-1, Romania (a) 1-4, San
Marino (h) 2-0, Bosnia & Herzegovina (a) 1-2, Bulgaria
(a) 2-2, Romania (a) 0-2.

League Championship wins (1934–41; 1944–2025)
APOEL (Nicosia) 29; Omonia Nicosia 21; Anorthosis
Famagusta 13; AEL Limassol 6; Apollon Limassol 4;
EPA Larnaca 3; Olympiakos Nicosia 3; Pezoporikos

Larnaca 2; Trust 1; Cetinkaya 1; Aris Limassol 1; Pafos 1.
No winner in 1958–59, 1963–64, 2019–20.

Cup wins (1934–41; 1944–2025)
APOEL (Nicosia) 21; Omonia Nicosia 16; Anorthosis Famagusta 11; Apollon Limassol 9; AEL Limassol 7; EPA Larnaca 5; Trust 3; AEK Larnaca 3; Cetinkaya 2; Pezoporikos Larnaca 1; Olympiakos Nicosia 1; Nea Salamis Famagusta 1; APOP Kinyras 1; Pafos 1.
No winner in 1955–58, 1959–61, 2019–20.

Cypriot First Division Regular Season 2024–25
	P	W	D	L	F	A	GD	Pts
Pafos	26	20	2	4	50	12	38	62
Aris Limassol	26	18	7	1	53	15	38	61
AEK Larnaca	26	16	6	4	45	21	24	54
Omonia Nicosia	26	16	4	6	53	26	27	52
APOEL	26	12	7	7	52	25	27	43
Apollon Limassol	26	11	7	8	28	23	5	40
Anorthosis Famagusta	26	10	7	9	34	33	1	37
Ethnikos Achna	26	6	11	9	33	42	–9	29
Karmiotissa	26	7	6	13	26	51	–25	27
Omonia Aradippou	26	7	5	14	23	49	–26	26
AEL Limassol	26	6	6	14	26	46	–20	24
Enosis Neon Paralimni	26	5	4	17	18	41	–23	19
Nea Salamis Famagusta	26	4	5	17	22	52	–30	17
Omonia 29M	26	3	5	18	19	46	–27	14

Championship Round 2024–25
	P	W	D	L	F	A	GD	Pts
Pafos (C)[1]	36	26	4	6	67	21	46	82
Aris Limassol[3]	36	22	9	5	66	31	35	75
Omonia Nicosia†[3]	36	20	8	8	69	40	29	68
AEK Larnaca†[2]	36	19	11	6	58	30	28	68
APOEL	36	14	11	11	59	36	23	53
Apollon Limassol	36	10	12	14	37	39	–2	46

†Ranking decided on head-to-head points.

Relegation Round 2024–25
	P	W	D	L	F	A	GD	Pts
Anorthosis Famagusta	33	15	7	11	50	42	8	52
AEL Limassol‡	33	11	6	16	38	53	–15	39
Ethnikos Achna‡	33	9	12	12	44	53	–9	39
Omonia Aradippou†	33	10	5	18	32	58	–26	35
Enosis Neon Paralimni†	33	10	5	18	31	48	–17	35
Karmiotissa*	33	9	7	17	30	57	–27	34
Nea Salamis Famagusta*	33	6	8	19	31	62	–31	26
Omonia 29M*	33	3	5	25	23	65	–42	14

‡Ranking decided on head-to-head goals scored.
†Ranking decided on head-to-head points.
Top scorer: Youseff El-Arabi (APOEL) 13.
Cup Final: AEK Larnaca 0, Pafos 0 *(aet; AEK Larnaca won 5-4 on penalties).*

CZECH REPUBLIC (CZECHIA)
Fotbalova Asociace Ceske Republiky, Atletika 2474/8, PO Box 11, 169 00 Praha 6.
Founded: 1901. *FIFA:* 1907; *UEFA:* 1954. *National Colours:* Red shirts with blue and white trim, white shorts, blue socks with red and white trim.

International matches 2024–25
Georgia (a) 1-4, Ukraine (h) 3-2, Albania (h) 2-0, Ukraine (a) 1-1*, Albania (a) 0-0, Georgia (h) 2-1, Faroe Islands (h) 2-1, Gibraltar (a) 4-0‡, Montenegro (h) 2-0, Croatia (a) 1-5.
**Match played in Poland.* ‡*Match played in Portugal.*

League Championship wins – Czechoslovakia (1925–93)
Sparta Prague 21; Slavia Prague 13; Dukla Prague (prev. UDA, now Marila Pribram) 11; Slovan Bratislava (formerly NV Bratislava) 8; Spartak Trnava 5; Banik Ostrava 3; Viktoria Zizkov 1; Inter Bratislava 1; Spartak Hradec Kralove 1; Zbrojovka Brno 1; Bohemians 1; Vitkovice 1.
No winner in 1948.

League Championship wins – Czech Republic (1993–2025)
Sparta Prague 14; Slavia Prague 8; Viktoria Plzen 6; Slovan Liberec 3; Banik Ostrava 1.

Cup wins – Czechoslovakia (1961–93)
Dukla Prague 8; Sparta Prague 8; Slovan Bratislava 5; Spartak Trnava 4; Banik Ostrava 3; Lokomotiva Kosice 2; TJ Gottwaldov (now FC Zlin) 1; DAC 1904 Dunajska Streda 1; 1.FC Kosice 1.

Cup wins – Czech Republic (1993–2025)
Sparta Prague 8; Slavia Prague 7; Viktoria Zizkov 2; Jablonec 2; Slovan Liberec 2; Teplice 2; Mlada Boleslav 2; Sigma Olomouc 2; Hradec Kralove (formerly Spartak) 1; Banik Ostrava 1; Viktoria Plzen 1; FC Zlin 1; Slovacko 1.

Czech First League Regular Season 2024–25
	P	W	D	L	F	A	GD	Pts
Slavia Prague	30	25	3	2	61	11	50	78
Viktoria Plzen	30	20	5	5	59	28	31	65
Banik Ostrava	30	20	4	6	52	26	26	64
Sparta Prague	30	19	5	6	53	33	23	62
Jablonec	30	15	6	9	47	25	22	51
Sigma Olomouc	30	12	7	11	46	41	5	43
Slovan Liberec§	30	11	9	10	45	31	14	42
Karvina§	30	11	8	11	40	52	–12	41
Hradec Kralove§	30	11	7	12	33	31	2	40
Bohemians 1905§†	30	8	10	12	32	42	–10	34
Mlada Boleslav†	30	9	7	14	40	40	0	34
Teplice†	30	9	7	14	32	42	–10	34
Slovacko	30	7	9	14	25	51	–26	30
Dukla Prague	30	5	9	16	23	47	–24	24
Pardubice	30	4	7	19	22	49	–27	19
Ceske Budejovice	30	0	5	25	14	78	–64	5

†Ranking decided on head-to-head points. §Qualified for seventh to tenth place play-offs.

Championship Group 2024–25
	P	W	D	L	F	A	GD	Pts
Slavia Prague (C)[1]	35	29	3	3	77	18	59	90
Viktoria Plzen[1]	35	23	5	7	71	36	35	74
Banik Ostrava[2]	35	22	5	8	58	34	24	71
Sparta Prague[3]	35	19	6	10	61	44	17	63
Jablonec	35	19	6	10	60	33	27	63
Sigma Olomouc[2]	35	12	9	14	48	53	–5	45

Relegation Group 2024–25
	P	W	D	L	F	A	GD	Pts
Teplice	35	12	8	15	41	45	–4	44
Mlada Boleslav	35	11	8	16	48	48	0	41
Slovacko	35	9	11	15	31	56	–25	39
Dukla Prague+	35	8	10	17	34	55	–21	34
Pardubice+	35	6	7	22	25	56	–31	25
Ceske Budejovice*	35	0	6	29	16	86	–70	6

Seventh to Tenth Place Play-offs
Semi-finals
Bohemians 1905 4, 0, Slovan Liberec 1, 1 *(Bohemians 1905 won 4-2 on aggregate)*
Hradec Kralove 1, 4, Karvina 0, 0 *(Hradec Kralove won 5-0 on aggregate)*
Final
Bohemians 1905 1, 0, Hradec Kralove 0, 2 *(Hradec Kralove won 2-1 on aggregate)*
Top scorer: Jan Kliment (Sigma Olomouc) 18.
Cup Final: Sigma Olomouc 3, Sparta Prague 1.

DENMARK
Dansk Boldspil-Union, DBU Alle 1, 2605 Brondby.
Founded: 1889. *FIFA:* 1904; *UEFA:* 1954. *National Colours:* Red shirts with white trim, white shorts with red trim, red socks with white trim.

International matches 2024–25
Switzerland (h) 2-0, Serbia (h) 2-0, Spain (a) 0-1, Switzerland (a) 2-2, Spain (h) 1-2, Serbia (a) 0-0, Portugal (h) 1-0, Portugal (a) 2-5, Northern Ireland (h) 2-1, Lithuania (h) 5-0.

League Championship wins (1912–2025)
FC Copenhagen 16; KB (Copenhagen) 15; Brondby 11; B 93 (Copenhagen) 9; AB (Akademisk) 9; B 1903 (Copenhagen) 7; Frem 6; AGF (Aarhus) 5; Vejle 5; Esbjerg 5; AaB (Aalborg) 4; Midtjylland 4; Hvidovre 3; OB (Odense) 3; Koge 2; B 1909 (Odense) 2; Lyngby 2; Silkeborg 1; Herfolge 1; FC Nordsjaelland 1.
No winner in 1927–28.

Cup wins (1954–2025)
FC Copenhagen 10; AGF (Aarhus) 9; Brondby 7; Vejle 6; OB (Odense) 5; Esbjerg 3; AaB (Aalborg) 3; Randers Freja 3; Lyngby 3; Frem 2; B 1909 (Odense) 2; B 1903 (Copenhagen) 2; Silkeborg 2; Randers 2; Nordsjaelland 2; Midtjylland 2; B 1913 (Odense) 1; KB (Copenhagen) 1; Vanlose 1; Hvidovre 1; B 93 (Copenhagen) 1; AB (Akademisk) 1; Viborg 1; SonderjyskE 1.

Danish Superliga Regular Season 2024–25
	P	W	D	L	F	A	GD	Pts
Midtjylland	22	14	3	5	42	27	15	45
FC Copenhagen	22	11	8	3	38	24	14	41
AGF	22	9	9	4	42	23	19	36
Randers	22	9	8	5	39	28	11	35
Nordsjaelland	22	10	5	7	39	36	3	35
Brondby	22	8	9	5	42	32	10	33
Silkeborg	22	8	9	5	38	29	9	33
Viborg	22	7	7	8	38	39	–1	28
AaB	22	5	6	11	23	41	–18	21

Lyngby	22	3	9	10	15	26	−11	18
Sonderjyske	22	4	5	13	26	51	−25	17
Vejle	22	3	4	15	24	50	−26	13

Championship Round 2024–25

	P	W	D	L	F	A	GD	Pts
FC Copenhagen (C)[1]	32	18	9	5	60	33	27	63
Midtjylland[2]	32	19	5	8	64	42	22	62
Brondby[3]	32	13	12	7	58	46	12	51
Randers†	32	13	9	10	57	50	7	48
Nordsjaelland	32	13	7	12	53	56	−3	46
AGF	32	10	10	12	53	46	7	40

†*Qualified for UEFA Conference League Play-off.*

Relegation Round 2024–25

	P	W	D	L	F	A	GD	Pts
Silkeborg†[3]	32	13	10	9	56	41	15	49
Viborg	32	12	11	9	57	50	7	47
Sonderjyske	32	10	7	15	47	64	−17	37
Vejle	32	7	7	18	37	64	−27	28
Lyngby*	32	5	12	15	26	43	−17	27
AaB*	32	5	9	18	34	67	−33	24

†*Qualified for UEFA Conference League Play-off.*

UEFA Conference League Play-off
Randers 1, Silkeborg 3
Top scorer: Patrick Mortensen (AGF) 20.
Cup Final: Silkeborg 0, FC Copenhagen 3.

ENGLAND

The Football Association, Wembley Stadium, PO Box 1966, London SW1P 9EQ.
Founded: 1863. *FIFA:* 1905; *UEFA:* 1954. *National Colours:* White shirts with blue and red trim, navy shorts with white trim, white socks.

ESTONIA

Eesti Jalgpalli Liit, A. Le Coq Arena, Jalgpalli 21, 11312 Tallinn.
Founded: 1921. *FIFA:* 1923; *UEFA:* 1992. *National Colours:* Blue shirts with white trim, black shorts, white socks.

International matches 2024–25

Slovakia (h) 0-1, Sweden (a) 0-3, Azerbaijan (h) 3-1, Sweden (h) 0-3, Azerbaijan (a) 0-0, Slovakia (a) 0-1, Israel (a) 1-2*, Moldova (a) 3-2, Israel (h) 1-3, Norway (h) 0-1.
**Match played in Hungary.*

League Championship wins (1921–40; 1992–2024)

Flora 15; FCI Levadia (formerly Levadia Maardu) 11; Tallinna Sport 9; Estonia Tallinn 5; Tallinna Kalev 2; Tallinna JK 2; Norma 2; Lantana (formerly Nikol) 2; Nomme Kalju 2; Olimpia Tartu 1; TVMK Tallinn; FCI Tallinn 1.

Cup wins (1993–2025)

FCI Levadia (incl. Levadia Maardu 2) 11; Flora 8; Narva Trans 3; Tallinna Sadam 2; TVMK Tallinn 2; Nomme Kalju 2; Lantana (formerly Nikol) 1; Norma 1; Levadia Tallinn (pre-2004) 1; FCI Tallinn 1; Paide Linnameeskond 1.

Estonian Meistriliiga 2024

	P	W	D	L	F	A	GD	Pts
FCI Levadia (C)[1]	36	27	6	3	82	19	63	87
Nomme Kalju†[3]	36	21	9	6	79	44	35	72
Paide Linnameeskond†[3]	36	23	3	10	74	39	35	72
Flora[3]	36	21	7	8	69	43	26	70
Tammeka†	36	11	9	16	47	54	−7	42
Narva Trans†	36	10	12	14	48	63	−15	42
Vaprus	36	9	8	19	35	57	−22	35
Kuressaare	36	8	10	18	46	67	−21	34
Tallinna Kalev+	36	8	7	21	37	74	−37	31
Nomme United*	36	2	9	25	22	79	−57	15

†*Ranking decided on head-to-head points.*
Top scorer: Alex Tamm (Nomme Kalju) 28.
Cup Final: Nomme Kalju 3, FCI Levadia 3 *(aet; Nomme Kalju won 4-1 on penalties).*

FAROE ISLANDS

Fotboltssamband Foroya, Gundadalur, Postrum 3028, FO-110 Torshavn.
Founded: 1979. *FIFA:* 1988; *UEFA:* 1990. *National Colours:* White shirts with blue and red trim, blue shorts with red and white trim, white socks with blue and red trim.

International matches 2024–25

North Macedonia (h) 1-1, Latvia (a) 0-1, Armenia (h) 2-2, Latvia (h) 1-1, Armenia (a) 1-0, North Macedonia (a) 0-1, Czech Republic (a) 1-2, Montenegro (a) 0-1, Georgia (a) 0-1, Gibraltar (h) 2-1.

League Championship wins (1942–2024)

HB (Torshavn) 24; KI (Klaksvik) 21; B36 Torshavn 11; TB (Tvoroyri) (includes FC Suduroy and Royn) 7; GI (Gota) 6; B68 Toftir 3; Vikingur 3; EB/Streymur 2; SI (Sorvagur) 1; IF (Fuglafjordur) 1; B71 (Sandur) 1; VB Vagur 1; NSI Runavik 1.
No competition in 1944.

Cup wins (1955–2024)

HB (Torshavn) 30; B36 Torshavn 7; KI (Klaksvik) 6; GI (Gota) 6; Vikingur 6; TB (Tvoroyri) (includes FC Suduroy and Royn) 5; EB/Streymur 4; NSI Runavik 3; VB Vagur (now FC Suduroy) 1; B71 (Sandur) 1.
No winner in 1970.

Faroese Premier League 2024

	P	W	D	L	F	A	GD	Pts
Vikingur (C)[1]	27	24	1	2	79	14	65	73
KI[3]	27	22	1	4	58	24	34	67
HB[3]	27	19	2	6	55	23	32	59
NSI Runavik[3]	27	13	3	11	54	43	11	42
B36 Torshavn	27	11	8	8	56	42	14	41
07 Vestur	27	9	3	15	34	60	−26	30
EB/Streymur	27	9	1	17	35	49	−14	28
B68 Toftir	27	5	6	16	23	48	−25	21
Skala*	27	5	5	17	27	57	−30	20
IF*	27	1	4	22	24	85	−61	7

Top scorer: Pall Klettskard (KI) 23.
Cup Final: B36 Torshavn 2, HB 2 *(aet; HB won 4-3 on penalties).*

FINLAND

Suomen Palloliitto Finlands Bollfoerbund, Urheilukatu 5, PO Box 191, 00250 Helsinki.
Founded: 1907. *FIFA:* 1908; *UEFA:* 1954. *National Colours:* White shirts with blue trim, white shorts, white socks.

International matches 2024–25

Greece (a) 0-3, England (a) 0-2, Republic of Ireland (h) 1-2, England (h) 1-3, Republic of Ireland (a) 0-1, Greece (h) 0-2, Malta (a) 1-0, Lithuania (a) 2-2, Netherlands (h) 0-2, Poland (h) 2-1.

League Championship wins (1908–2024)

HJK (Helsinki) 33; HPS (Helsinki) 9; Haka (Valkeakoski) 9; TPS (Turku) 8; HIFK (Helsinki) 7; KuPS (Kuopio) 7; Kuusysi Lahti 5; KIF Helsinki 4; AIFK Turku 3; VIFK Vaasa 3; Reipas Lahti 3; Tampere United 3; VPS (Vaasa) 2; KTP (Kotka) 2; OPS Oulu 2; Jazz Pori 2; Unitas Helsinki 1; PUS Helsinki 1; Sudet Viipuri 1; Toverit (Helsinki) 1; Ilves-Kissat 1; Pyrkiva Turku 1; KPV (Kokkola) 1; Ilves (Tampere) 1; TPV Tampere 1; MyPa Anjalankoski (renamed MyPa-47) 1; Inter Turku 1; SJK (Seinajoki) 1; IFK Mariehamn 1.
No competition in 1914, 1943.

Cup wins (1955–2024)

HJK (Helsinki) 14; Haka (Valkeakoski) 12; Reipas Lahti 7; KuPS (Kuopio) 5; KTP (Kotka) 5; Tampere United 4; TPS (Turku) 3; MyPa Anjalankoski (renamed MyPa-47) 3; Mikkeli 2; Kuusysi Lahti 2; RoPS (Rovaniemi) 2; Inter Turku 2; Pallo-Pojat 1; Drott (renamed Jaro) 1; HPS (Helsinki) 1; AIFK Turku 1; Jokerit (formerly PK-35) 1; Atlantis 1; Tampere United 1; FC Honka 1; IFK Mariehamn 1; SJK (Seinajoki) 1.

Finnish Veikkausliiga Regular Season 2024

	P	W	D	L	F	A	GD	Pts
KuPS	22	13	5	4	39	22	17	44
HJK	22	13	4	5	41	21	20	43
Ilves	22	11	6	5	45	25	20	39
SJK	22	10	6	6	40	33	7	36
FC Haka	22	10	5	7	35	32	3	35
VPS	22	9	5	8	34	36	−2	32
Inter Turku	22	9	4	9	38	29	9	31
Gnistan	22	8	6	8	32	34	−2	30
Oulu	22	6	6	11	26	36	−10	24
IFK Mariehamn	22	5	5	12	20	38	−18	20
Lahti	22	3	10	9	26	38	−12	19
EIF	22	3	4	15	19	51	−32	13

Championship Round 2024

	P	W	D	L	F	A	GD	Pts
KuPS (C)[1]	27	17	5	5	46	24	22	56
Ilves[2]	27	16	6	5	56	27	29	54
HJK[3]	27	13	6	8	44	27	17	45
SJK†[3]	27	11	7	9	46	44	2	40
VPS‡	27	11	6	10	43	45	−2	39
FC Haka‡	27	11	5	11	40	43	−3	38

†*Qualified for UEFA Conference League Play-off final.*
‡*Qualified for UEFA Conference League Play-off quarter-finals.*

Relegation Round 2023

	P	W	D	L	F	A	GD	Pts
Inter Turku‡	27	12	5	10	46	34	12	41
Gnistan‡	27	10	7	10	40	43	–3	37
Oulu	27	7	7	13	32	40	–8	28
IFK Mariehamn	27	7	5	15	27	44	–17	26
Lahti+*	27	4	12	11	31	47	–16	24
EIF*	27	4	7	16	24	57	–33	19

‡*Qualified for UEFA Conference League Play-off quarter-finals.*

UEFA Conference League Play-offs
Quarter-finals
FC Haka 2, Inter Turku 1 *(aet)*.
VPS 0, Gnistan 1
Semi-final
FC Haka 3, Gnistan 3 *(aet; FC Haka won 4-3 on penalties)*.
Final
FC Haka 1, 2, SJK 2, 2 *(SJK won 4-3 on aggregate)*.
Top scorers (joint): Ashley Coffey (Oulu), Jaime Moreno (SJK) 12.
Cup Final: Inter Turku 1, KuPS 2 *(aet)*.

FRANCE
Federation Francaise de Football, 87 Boulevard de Grenelle, 75738 Paris Cedex 15.
Founded: 1904 (as USFSA), 1919 (FFF). *FIFA:* 1904; *UEFA:* 1954. *National Colours:* Blue shirts with red and white trim, white shorts with red and blue trim, red socks with blue trim.

International matches 2024–25
Italy (h) 1-3, Belgium (h) 2-0, Israel (a) 4-1*, Belgium (a) 2-1, Israel (h) 0-0, Italy (a) 3-1, Croatia (a) 0-2, Croatia (h) 2-0 (5-4p), Spain (n) 4-5, Germany (a) 2-0.
Match played in Hungary.

League Championship wins (1933–39; 1945–2025)
Paris Saint-Germain 13; Saint-Etienne 10; Olympique de Marseille 9; AS Monaco 8; Nantes 8; Olympique Lyonnais (Lyon) 7; Stade de Reims 6; Bordeaux 6; Lille Olympique SC 4; OGC Nice 4; FC Sete 2; Sochaux 2; Olympique Lillois 1; Racing Club Paris 1; Roubaix-Tourcoing 1; Strasbourg 1; AJ Auxerre 1; Lens 1; Montpellier 1.
No winner in 1992–93: Olympique de Marseille stripped of title.

Cup wins (1918–2025)
Paris Saint-Germain 16; Olympique de Marseille 10; Lille Olympique SC 6; Saint-Etienne 6; Red Star 5; Racing Club Paris 5; AS Monaco 5; Olympique Lyonnais (Lyon) 5; Bordeaux 4; Nantes 4; AJ Auxerre 4; Strasbourg 3; OGC Nice 3; Stade Rennais (Rennes) 3; CAS Genereaux 2; Montpellier 2; FC Sete 2; Sochaux 2; Stade de Reims 2; Sedan 2; Metz 2; Guingamp 2; Olympique de Pantin 1; CA Paris 1; Club Français 1; AS Cannes 1; Excelsior Roubaix 1; EF Nancy-Lorraine 1; Toulouse 1; Le Havre 1; AS Nancy 1; Bastia 1; Lorient 1; Toulouse 1.
No winner in 1991–92.

French Ligue 1 2024–25

	P	W	D	L	F	A	GD	Pts
Paris Saint-Germain (C)	34	26	6	2	92	35	57	84
Marseille[1]	34	20	5	9	74	47	27	65
Monaco[1]	34	18	7	9	63	41	22	61
Nice[1]	34	17	9	8	66	41	25	60
Lille[1]	34	17	9	8	52	36	16	60
Lyon[2]	34	17	6	11	65	46	19	57
Strasbourg[3]	34	16	9	9	56	44	12	57
Lens	34	15	7	12	42	39	3	52
Brest	34	15	5	14	52	59	–7	50
Toulouse	34	11	9	14	44	43	1	42
Auxerre	34	11	9	14	48	51	–3	42
Rennes	34	13	2	19	51	50	1	41
Nantes	34	8	12	14	39	52	–13	36
Angers	34	10	6	18	32	53	–21	36
Le Havre	34	10	4	20	40	71	–31	34
Reims+*	34	8	9	17	33	47	–14	33
Saint-Etienne*	34	8	6	20	39	77	–38	30
Montpellier*	34	4	4	26	23	79	–56	16

Top scorers (joint): Ousmane Dembele (Paris Saint-Germain), Mason Greenwood (Marseille) 21.
Cup Final: Paris Saint-Germain 3, Reims 0.

GEORGIA
Georgian Football Federation, 76a Chavchavadze Avenue, 0179 Tbilisi.
Founded: 1990. *FIFA:* 1992; *UEFA:* 1992. *National Colours:* White shirts with red trim, white shorts, white socks with red tops.

International matches 2024–25
Czech Republic (h) 4-1, Albania (a) 1-0, Ukraine (a) 0-1*, Albania (h) 0-1, Ukraine (h) 1-1, Czech Republic (a) 1-2, Armenia (a) 3-0, Armenia (h) 6-1, Faroe Islands (h) 1-0, Cape Verde (h) 1-1.
Match played in Poland.

League Championship wins (1990–2024)
Dinamo Tbilisi 19; Torpedo Kutaisi 4; WIT Georgia 2; Olimpi Rustavi 2; Zestaponi 2; Iberia 1999 (incl. Saburtalo 1) 2; Dinamo Batumi 2; Sioni Bolnisi 1; Dila Gori 1; Samtredia 1.

Cup wins (1990–2024)
Dinamo Tbilisi 13; Torpedo Kutaisi 5; Locomotivi Tbilisi 3; Saburtalo (now Iberia 1999) 3; Ameri Tbilisi 2; Gagra 2; Guria Lanchkhuti 1; Dinamo Batumi 1; Zestaponi 1; WIT Georgia 1; Dila Gori 1; Chikhura Sachkhere 1; Spaeri Tbilisi 1.
See also Russia section for Georgian club honours in Soviet era 1936–91.

Georgian Erovnuli Liga 2024

	P	W	D	L	F	A	GD	Pts
Iberia 1999 (C)[1]	36	23	6	7	74	46	28	75
Torpedo Kutaisi[3]	36	21	7	8	58	40	18	70
Dila Gori[3]	36	19	11	6	58	30	28	68
Dinamo Batumi	36	15	10	11	42	41	1	55
Samgurali Tsqaltubo	36	11	11	14	51	49	2	44
Kolkheti-1913	36	9	14	13	48	58	–10	41
Dinamo Tbilisi	36	9	12	15	33	44	–11	39
Gagra+	36	11	5	20	36	53	–17	38
Telavi+	36	8	10	18	32	43	–11	34
Samtredia*	36	5	12	19	33	61	–28	27

Top scorer: Bjorn Johnsen (Torpedo Kutaisi) 23.
Cup Final: Spaeri Tbilisi 2, Dinamo Tbilisi 2 *(aet; Spaeri Tbilisi won 5-4 on penalties)*.

GERMANY
Deutscher Fussball-Bund, DFB-Campus, Kennedyallee 274, 60528 Frankfurt am Main.
Founded: 1900. *FIFA:* 1904; *UEFA:* 1954. *National Colours:* All white with red and black trim.

International matches 2024–25
Hungary (h) 5-0, Netherlands (a) 2-2, Bosnia & Herzegovina (a) 2-1, Netherlands (h) 1-0, Bosnia & Herzegovina (h) 7-0, Hungary (a) 1-1, Italy (a) 2-1, Italy (h) 3-3, Portugal (h) 1-2, France (h) 0-2.

League Championship wins (1903–14; 1920–44; 1948–2025)
Bayern Munich 34; 1.FC Nuremberg 9; Borussia Dortmund 8; Schalke 04 7; Hamburger SV 6; VfB Stuttgart 5; Borussia Moenchengladbach 5; 1.FC Kaiserslautern 4; Werder Bremen 4; 1.FC Lokomotive Leipzig 3; SpVgg Greuther Furth 3; 1.FC Cologne 3; Viktoria Berlin 2; Hertha Berlin 2; Hannover 96 2; Dresden SC 2; Union Berlin 1; Freiburger FC 1; Phoenix Karlsruhe 1; Karlsruher FV 1; Holstein Kiel 1; Fortuna Dusseldorf 1; Rapid Vienna 1; VfR Mannheim 1; Rot-Weiss Essen 1; Eintracht Frankfurt 1; Munich 1860 1; Eintracht Braunschweig 1; VfL Wolfsburg 1; Bayer Leverkusen 1.
No winner in 1904, 1922, 1991–92.

Cup wins (1935–43; 1952–2025)
Bayern Munich 20; Werder Bremen 6; Schalke 04 5; Borussia Dortmund 5; Eintracht Frankfurt 5; 1.FC Nuremberg 4; VfB Stuttgart 4; 1.FC Cologne 4; Borussia Moenchengladbach 3; Hamburger SV 3; Dresden SC 2; Munich 1860 2; Karlsruhe SC 2; Fortuna Dusseldorf 2; 1.FC Kaiserslautern 2; Bayer Leverkusen 2; RB Leipzig 2; 1.FC Lokomotive Leipzig 1; Rapid Vienna 1; First Vienna 1; Rot-Weiss Essen 1; SW Essen 1; Kickers Offenbach 1; Bayer Uerdingen 1; Hannover 96 1; VfLWolfsburg 1.

German Bundesliga 2024–25

	P	W	D	L	F	A	GD	Pts
Bayern Munich (C)[1]	34	25	7	2	99	32	67	82
Bayer Leverkusen[1]	34	19	12	3	72	43	29	69
Eintracht Frankfurt[1]	34	17	9	8	68	46	22	60
Borussia Dortmund[1]	34	17	6	11	71	51	20	57
SC Freiburg	34	16	7	11	49	53	–4	55
Mainz 05[3]	34	14	10	10	55	43	12	52
RB Leipzig	34	13	12	9	53	48	5	51
Werder Bremen	34	14	9	11	54	57	–3	51
VfB Stuttgart[2]	34	14	8	12	57	51	6	50
Borussia M'gladbach	34	13	6	15	55	57	–2	45
VfL Wolfsburg	34	11	10	13	56	54	2	43
Augsburg	34	11	10	13	35	51	–16	43
Union Berlin	34	10	10	14	35	51	–16	40

St Pauli	34	8	8	18	28	41	–13	32
TSG 1899 Hoffenheim	34	7	11	16	46	68	–22	32
1.FC Heidenheim+	34	8	5	21	37	64	–27	29
Holstein Kiel*	34	6	7	21	49	80	–31	25
VfL Bochum*	34	6	7	21	33	67	–34	25

Top scorer: Harry Kane (Bayern Munich) 26.
Cup Final: Arminia Bielefeld 2, VfB Stuttgart 4.

GIBRALTAR

Gibraltar Football Association, 7.01b World Trade Center, Gibraltar GX11 1AA.
Founded: 1895. *FIFA:* 2016; *UEFA:* 2013. *National Colours:* All red with white trim.

International matches 2024–25
Andorra (h) 1-0, Liechtenstein (h) 2-2, San Marino (h) 1-0, Liechtenstein (a) 0-0, San Marino (a) 1-1, Moldova (h) 1-1, Montenegro (a) 1-3, Czech Republic (h) 0-4*, Croatia (h) 0-7*, Faroe Islands (a) 1-2.
**Match played in Portugal.*

League Championship wins (1907–2025)
Lincoln Red Imps (incl. Newcastle United 5; 1 title shared) 29; Glacis United 17 (incl. 1 shared); Prince of Wales 16; Britannia (now Britannia XI) 13; Gibraltar United 11; Europa 7; Manchester United (now Manchester 62) 7; St Theresa's 3; Chief Construction 2; South United 2; Gibraltar FC 1; Fortress Royal Engineers 1; Royal Sovereign 1; Commander of the Yard 1; St Joseph's 1.
No winner in 2019–20.

Cup wins (1895; 1897–1906; 1935–66; 1973–2025)
Lincoln Red Imps (incl. Newcastle United 4) 20; Europa 11; Gibraltar United 10; St Joseph's 10; Prince of Wales 6; Britannia (now Britannia XI) 6; Glacis United 4; Manchester United (now Manchester 62) 3; Jubilee 2; Exiles 2; FCB Magpies 2; Gibraltar FC 1; Albion 1; Athletic 1; Electricity Department 1; HMS Hood 1; 2nd Bn The King's Regt 1; Anti-Aircraft Section, RA 1; RAF New Camp 1; 4th Bn Royal Scots 1; Manchester United Reserves 1; 2nd Bn Royal Green Jackets 1; RAF Gibraltar 1; St Theresa's 1.
Not played in 1934–35; 1940–41; 1977–78. No winner in 2019–20.

Gibraltar Football League Regular Season 2024–25

	P	W	D	L	F	A	GD	Pts
St Joseph's	20	17	3	0	53	13	40	54
Lincoln Red Imps	20	16	3	1	57	7	50	51
Europa	20	13	4	3	49	19	30	43
FCB Magpies	20	11	1	8	48	28	20	34
Manchester 62	20	10	4	6	45	28	17	34
Lions Gibraltar	20	8	4	8	33	0	28	
Glacis United	20	6	1	13	29	52	–23	19
College 1975	20	5	3	12	18	39	–21	18
Lynx	20	5	2	13	25	51	–26	17
Mons Calpe	20	4	1	15	23	54	–31	13
Europa Point	20	0	4	16	14	70	–56	4

No relegation. The top six teams progress to the Championship Group and play a further five matches.

Championship Group 2024–25

	P	W	D	L	F	A	GD	Pts
Lincoln Red Imps (C)†[1]	25	21	3	1	68	7	61	66
St Joseph's†[3]	25	21	3	1	65	15	50	66
Europa	25	16	4	5	60	29	31	52
Manchester 62	25	12	4	9	49	34	15	40
FCB Magpies[3]‡	25	12	1	12	52	38	14	37
Lions Gibraltar	25	8	4	13	35	49	–14	28

†*Ranking decided on head-to-head points.* ‡*At the end of the season FCB Magpies merged with Calpe City to become Calpe City Magpies from 2026–27.*
Top scorer: Vittorio Vigolo (Europa) 15.
Cup Final: Lions Gibraltar 1, FCB Magpies 3.

GOZO

Gozo Football Association, GFA Headquarters, Mgarr Road, Xewkija, XWK 9014, Malta. (Not a member of FIFA or UEFA.)
Founded: 1936.

League Championship wins (1938–43; 1944–49; 1952–2025)
Nadur Youngsters 15; Victoria Hotspurs 13; Sannat Lions 10; Xewkija Tigers 8; Ghajnsielem 7; Xaghra United 6 (incl. Xaghra Blue Stars 3, Xaghra Young Stars 1); Salesian Youths (renamed Oratory Youths) 6; Victoria Athletics 4; Victoria Stars 1; Victoria City 1; Calypsians 1; Victoria United (renamed Victoria Wanderers) 1; Kercem Ajax 1; Zebbug Rovers 1; Qala Saints 1.
Competition not held in 1947, 1953, 1955. No winner in 1960–61, 2020–21.

Cup wins (1972–2025)
Xewkija Tigers 11; Nadur Youngsters 11; Sannat Lions 9; Ghajnsielem 6; Xaghra United 4; Victoria Hotspurs 2; Kercem Ajax 2; Qala Saints (incl. Qala Saint Joseph 1) 2; Calypsians 1; Calypsians Bosco Youths (renamed Oratory Youths) 1; Victoria Wanderers 1.
Competition not held in 1979–80, 2019–21.

Gozitan L-Ewwel Divizjoni 2024–25

	P	W	D	L	F	A	GD	Pts
Qala Saints (C)	18	15	0	3	54	14	40	45
Nadur Youngsters	18	11	2	5	39	22	17	35
Xewkija Tigers	18	9	3	6	33	24	9	30
Victoria Wanderers	18	8	3	7	43	31	12	27
Xaghra United	18	7	1	10	29	40	–11	22
Ghajnsielem	18	6	2	10	27	44	–17	20
Oratory Youths*	18	1	1	16	16	66	–50	4

Victoria Hotspurs withdrew pre-season.
Top scorer: Igor Henrique (Victoria Wanderers) 20.
Cup Final: Nadur Youngsters 3, Kercem Ajax 0.

GREECE

Hellenic Football Federation, Parko Goudi, PO Box 14161, 11510 Athens.
Founded: 1926. *FIFA:* 1927; *UEFA:* 1954. *National Colours:* All white with blue trim.

International matches 2024–25
Finland (h) 3-0, Republic of Ireland (a) 2-0, England (a) 2-1, Republic of Ireland (h) 2-0, England (h) 0-3, Finland (a) 2-0, Scotland (h) 0-1, Scotland (a) 3-0, Slovakia (h) 4-1, Bulgaria (h) 4-0.

League Championship wins (1927–2025)
Olympiacos 48; Panathinaikos 20; AEK (Athens) 13; PAOK (Thessaloniki) 4; Aris (Thessaloniki) 3; AEL (Larissa) 1.

Cup wins (1932–2025)
Olympiacos 29; Panathinaikos 20; AEK (Athens) 16; PAOK (Thessaloniki) 8; Panionios 2; AEL (Larissa) 2; Ethnikos 1; Aris (Thessaloniki) 1; Iraklis 1; Kastoria 1; OFI (Crete) 1.

Greek Super League Regular Season 2024–25

	P	W	D	L	F	A	GD	Pts
Olympiacos	26	18	6	2	45	16	29	60
AEK	26	16	5	5	44	16	28	53
Panathinaikos	26	14	8	4	31	22	9	50
PAOK	26	14	4	8	51	26	25	46
Aris	26	12	6	8	31	28	3	42
OFI	26	10	6	10	37	38	–1	36
Atromitos	26	10	5	11	32	32	0	35
Asteras Tripolis	26	10	5	11	27	29	–2	35
Panetolikos	26	9	6	11	20	22	–2	33
Levadiakos	26	6	10	10	30	34	–4	28
Panserraikos	26	8	4	14	30	47	–17	28
Volos	26	6	4	16	20	42	–22	22
Athens Kallithea	26	4	9	13	24	40	–16	21
Lamia	26	3	6	17	14	44	–30	15

Championship Round 2024–25

	P	W	D	L	F	A	GD	Pts
Olympiacos (C)[1]	32	23	6	3	58	22	36	75
Panathinaikos[1]	32	17	8	7	42	32	10	59
PAOK[2]	32	18	4	10	62	37	25	58
AEK[3]	32	16	5	11	48	28	20	53

European Qualification Round 2024–25

	P	W	D	L	F	A	GD	Pts
Aris[3]	32	16	8	8	42	32	10	35
Asteras Tripolis	32	13	5	14	35	40	–5	27
Atromitos	32	12	7	13	39	37	2	26
OFI	32	10	8	14	40	47	–7	20

Relegation Round 2024–25

	P	W	D	L	F	A	GD	Pts
Levadiakos	36	13	11	12	50	43	7	50
Panetolikos	36	13	9	14	29	31	–2	48
Volos	36	11	6	19	36	52	–16	39
Panserraikos	36	10	7	19	40	61	–21	37
Athens Kallithea*	36	8	12	16	36	52	–16	36
Lamia*	36	4	8	24	21	64	–43	20

Top scorer: Jefte Betancor (Panserraikos) 19.
Cup Final: OFI 0, Olympiacos 2.

HUNGARY

Magyar Labdarugo Szovetseg, Kanai ut 2.D, 1112 Budapest.
Founded: 1901. *FIFA:* 1907; *UEFA:* 1954. *National Colours:* Red shirts with white trim, white shorts with green trim, green socks.

International matches 2024–25

Germany (a) 0-5, Bosnia & Herzegovina (h) 0-0, Netherlands (h) 1-1, Bosnia & Herzegovina (a) 2-0, Netherlands (a) 0-4, Germany (h) 1-1, Turkey (a) 1-3, Turkey (h) 0-3, Sweden (h) 0-2, Azerbaijan (a) 2-1.

League Championship wins (1901–14; 1916–2025)

Ferencvaros 36; MTK Budapest 23; Ujpest 20; Budapest Honved 14 (incl. Kispest Honved); Debrecen 7; Vasas 6; Csepel 4; Gyor 4; Videoton (renamed Fehervar) 3; Budapesti TC 2; Nagyvarad 1; Vac 1; Dunaferr (renamed Dunaujvaros) 1; Zalaegerszeg 1.
No competition in 1956.

Cup wins (1909–14; 1921–44; 1951–2025)

Ferencvaros 24; MTK Budapest 12; Ujpest 11; Budapest Honved 8 (inc. Kispest Honved); Debrecen 6; Vasas 4; Gyor 4; Diosgyor 2; Fehervar (incl. Videoton 1, Vidi 1) 2; Paks 2; Bocskai 1; III Keruleti TUE 1; Soroksar 1; Szolnoki MAV 1; Siofoki Banyasz 1; Bekescsaba 1; Pecsi 1; Sopron 1; Kecskemet 1; Zalaegerszeg 1.
Cup not held regularly until 1964.

Hungarian Nemzeti Bajnoksag I 2024–25

	P	W	D	L	F	A	GD	Pts
Ferencvaros (C)[1]	33	20	9	4	64	31	33	69
Puskas Akademia[3]	33	20	6	7	58	38	20	66
Paks[2]	33	16	9	8	65	47	18	57
Gyor[3]	33	14	11	8	49	37	12	53
MTK Budapest	33	13	7	13	53	47	6	46
Diosgyor	33	11	11	11	43	51	–8	44
Ujpest	33	9	14	10	38	44	–6	41
Nyiregyhaza	33	9	9	15	31	52	–21	36
Debrecen†	33	9	7	17	52	59	–7	34
Zalaegerszeg†	33	7	13	13	35	42	–7	34
Fehervar*	33	8	7	18	34	52	–18	31
Kecskemet*	33	4	13	16	31	53	–22	25

†*Ranking decided on matches won.*
Top scorer: Daniel Bode (Paks) 15.
Cup Final: Ferencvaros 1, Paks 1 (aet; Paks won 4-3 on penalties).

ICELAND

Knattspyrnusamband Islands, Laugardal, 104 Reykjavik.
Founded: 1947. *FIFA:* 1947; *UEFA:* 1954. *National Colours:* All blue.

International matches 2024–25

Montenegro (h) 2-0, Turkey (a) 1-3, Wales (h) 1-3, Turkey (h) 2-4, Montenegro (a) 2-0, Wales (h) 1-4, Kosovo (a) 1-2, Kosovo (h) 1-3*, Scotland (a) 3-1, Northern Ireland (a) 0-1.
Match played in Spain due to construction work at Iceland's home stadium.

League Championship wins (1912–2024)

KR (Reykjavik) 27; Valur 23; Fram 18; IA (Akranes) 18; FH (Hafnarfjordur) 8; Vikingur Reykjavik 7; Keflavik 4; IBV (Vestmannaeyjar) 3; Breidablik 3; KA (Akureyri) 1; Stjarnan 1.

Cup wins (1960–2024)

KR (Reykjavik) 14; Valur 11; IA (Akranes) 9; Fram 8; IBV (Vestmannaeyjar) 5; Vikingur Reykjavik 5; Keflavik 4; Fylkir 2; FH (Hafnarfjordur) 2; IBA Akureyri 1; Breidablik 1; Stjarnan 1; KA (Akureyri) 1.
No winner in 2020.

Icelandic Besta deild karla Regular Season 2024

	P	W	D	L	F	A	GD	Pts
Vikingur Reykjavik	22	15	4	3	56	23	33	49
Breidablik	22	15	4	3	53	28	25	49
Valur	22	11	5	6	53	33	20	38
IA	22	10	4	8	41	31	10	34
Stjarnan	22	10	4	8	40	35	5	34
FH	22	9	6	7	39	38	1	33
Fram	22	7	6	9	31	32	–1	27
KA	22	7	6	9	32	38	–6	27
KR	22	5	6	11	35	46	–11	21
HK	22	6	2	14	26	56	–30	20
Vestri	22	4	6	12	22	43	–21	18
Fylkir	22	4	5	13	26	51	–25	17

Championship Round 2024

	P	W	D	L	F	A	GD	Pts
Breidablik (C)[1]	27	19	5	3	63	31	32	62
Vikingur Reykjavik[3]	27	18	5	4	68	33	35	59
Valur[3]	27	12	8	7	66	42	24	44
Stjarnan	27	12	6	9	51	43	8	42
IA	27	11	4	12	49	47	2	37
FH	27	9	7	11	43	50	–7	34

Relegation Round 2024

	P	W	D	L	F	A	GD	Pts
KA[3]	27	10	7	10	44	48	–4	37
KR	27	9	7	11	56	49	7	34
Fram	27	8	6	13	38	49	–11	30
Vestri	27	6	7	14	32	53	–21	25
HK*	27	7	4	16	34	71	–37	25
Fylkir*	27	5	6	16	32	60	–28	21

Top scorer: Benony Breki Andresson (KR) 21.
Cup Final: KA 2, Vikingur Reykjavik 0.

ISRAEL

Israel Football Association, Ramat Gan Stadium, 299 Aba Hilell Street, PO Box 3591, 52134 Ramat Gan. (Due to the ongoing war in Gaza, the Israel national side plays home matches at neutral venues.)
Founded: 1928. *FIFA:* 1929; *UEFA:* 1994. *National Colours:* Sky blue shirts with white trim, white shorts, sky blue socks.

International matches 2024–25

Belgium (a) 1-3*, Italy (h) 1-2*, France (h) 1-4*, Italy (a) 1-4, France (a) 0-0, Belgium (h) 1-0*, Estonia (h) 2-1*, Norway (h) 2-4*, Estonia (a) 3-1, Slovakia (n) 1-0.
Match played in Hungary.

League Championship wins (1932–2025)

Maccabi Tel Aviv 26 (incl. 1 regional title); Maccabi Haifa 15; Hapoel Tel Aviv 14 (incl. 1 shared); Hapoel Petah Tikva 6; Beitar Jerusalem 6; Maccabi Netanya 5; Hapoel Be'er Sheva 5; Hakoah Amidar Ramat Gan 2; British Police 1; Beitar Tel Aviv 1 (shared); Hapoel Ramat Gan 1; Hapoel Kfar Saba 1; Bnei Yehuda 1; Hapoel Haifa 1; Ironi Kiryat Shmona 1.
League not held regularly until 1955–56.

Cup wins (1928–2025)

Maccabi Tel Aviv 24; Hapoel Tel Aviv 16 (incl. 1 shared); Beitar Jerusalem 7; Maccabi Haifa 6; Hapoel Haifa 4; Bnei Yehuda 4; Hapoel Kfar Saba 3; Hapoel Be'er Sheva 3; Maccabi Petah Tikva 3; Beitar Tel Aviv 2; Hapoel Petah Tikva 2; Hakoah Amidar Ramat Gan 2; Hapoel Ramat Gan 2; Maccabi Hashmonai Jerusalem 1 (shared); British Police 1; Gunners 1; Hapoel Jerusalem 1; Maccabi Netanya 1; Hapoel Yehud 1; Hapoel Lod 1; Bnei Sakhnin 1; Ironi Kiryat Shmona 1.
Cup not held regularly until 1960–61.

Israeli Premier League Regular Season 2024–25

	P	W	D	L	F	A	GD	Pts
Hapoel Be'er Sheva (–2)	26	18	6	2	52	18	34	58
Maccabi Tel Aviv	26	17	6	3	56	27	29	57
Maccabi Haifa (–1)	26	14	6	6	54	32	22	47
Beitar Jerusalem	26	13	7	6	48	34	14	46
Hapoel Haifa	26	12	5	9	39	31	8	41
Hapoel Netanya	26	11	4	11	39	37	2	37
Ironi Kiryat Shmona	26	10	4	12	28	38	–10	34
Maccabi Bnei Reineh	26	9	4	13	27	35	–8	31
Hapoel Jerusalem	26	7	9	10	32	35	–3	30
Ironi Tiberias	26	9	1	11	20	36	–16	27
Maccabi Petah Tikva	26	6	6	14	22	44	–22	24
Bnei Sakhnin (–1)	26	6	6	14	37	37	–18	23
Ashdod	26	5	7	14	35	48	–13	22
Hapoel Hadera	26	5	4	17	26	49	–23	19

Points deductions: Round 2: Hapoel Be'er Sheva (2pts deducted) v Bnei Sakhnin (1pt deducted) was declared void after crowd trouble; Round 20: Maccabi Haifa deducted 1pt for crowd trouble.

Championship Round 2024–25

	P	W	D	L	F	A	GD	Pts
Maccabi Tel Aviv (C)[1]	36	24	8	4	86	36	50	80
Hapoel Be'er Sheva (–2)[1]	36	24	8	4	75	28	47	78
Maccabi Haifa (–1)[3]	36	18	8	10	68	54	14	61
Beitar Jerusalem (–1)[3]	36	15	9	12	58	54	4	53
Hapoel Haifa	36	15	7	14	51	50	1	52
Hapoel Netanya	36	13	6	17	51	58	–7	45

Round 32: Beitar Jerusalem deducted 1pt for crowd trouble.

Relegation Round 2024–25

	P	W	D	L	F	A	GD	Pts
Hapoel Jerusalem	33	11	11	11	47	42	5	44
Maccabi Bnei Reineh	33	12	5	16	36	43	–7	41
Ironi Kiryat Shmona	33	11	4	18	32	52	–20	37
Bnei Sakhnin (–1)	33	10	7	16	24	44	–18	36
Ashdod	33	8	11	14	48	55	–7	35
Ironi Tiberias	33	8	11	14	28	45	–17	35
Maccabi Petah Tikva*	33	8	9	16	31	50	–19	33
Hapoel Hadera*	33	5	12	16	31	57	–26	27

Top scorer: Guy Melamed (Maccabi Haifa) 21 (incl. 17 for Hapoel Haifa).
Cup Final: Beitar Jerusalem 0, Hapoel Be'er Sheva 2.

ITALY

Federazione Italiana Giuoco Calcio, Via Gregorio Allegri 14, 00198 Roma.
Founded: 1898. *FIFA:* 1905; *UEFA:* 1954. *National Colours:* Blue shirts with white trim, white shorts with blue trim, blue socks.

International matches 2024–25
France (a) 3-1, Israel (a) 2-1*, Belgium (h) 2-2, Israel (h) 4-1, Belgium (a) 1-0, France (h) 3-3, Germany (h) 1-2, Germany (h) 3-3, Norway (a) 0-3, Moldova (h) 2-0.
Match played in Hungary.

League Championship wins (1898–1915; 1919–43; 1945–2025)
Juventus 36 (excludes two titles revoked); Internazionale 20 (includes one title awarded); AC Milan 19; Genoa 9; Pro Vercelli 7; Bologna 7; Torino 7 (excludes one title revoked); Napoli 4; Roma 3; Fiorentina 2; Lazio 2; Casale 1; Novese 1; Cagliari 1; Hellas Verona 1; Sampdoria 1.
No winner in 1926–27, 2004–05.

Cup wins (1922; 1935–43; 1958–2025)
Juventus 15; Internazionale 9; Roma 9; Lazio 7; Fiorentina 6; Napoli 6; Torino 5; AC Milan 5; Sampdoria 4; Bologna 3; Parma 3; Vado 1; Genoa 1; Venezia 1; Atalanta 1; Vicenza 1.

Italian Serie A 2024–25
	P	W	D	L	F	A	GD	Pts
Napoli (C)[1]	38	24	10	4	59	27	32	82
Internazionale[1]	38	24	9	5	79	35	44	81
Atalanta[2]	38	22	8	8	78	37	41	74
Juventus[1]	38	18	16	4	58	35	23	70
Roma[2]	38	20	9	9	56	35	21	69
Fiorentina†[3]	38	19	8	11	60	41	19	65
Lazio†	38	18	11	9	61	49	12	65
AC Milan	38	18	9	11	61	43	18	63
Bologna[2]	38	16	14	8	57	47	10	62
Como	38	13	10	15	49	52	–3	49
Torino†	38	10	14	14	39	45	–6	44
Udinese†	38	12	8	18	41	56	–15	44
Genoa	38	10	13	15	37	49	–12	43
Hellas Verona	38	10	7	21	34	66	–32	37
Cagliari†	38	9	9	20	40	56	–16	36
Parma†	38	7	15	16	44	58	–14	36
Lecce	38	8	10	20	27	58	–31	34
Empoli*	38	6	13	19	33	59	–26	31
Venezia*	38	5	14	19	32	56	–24	29
Monza*	38	3	9	26	28	69	–41	18

†*Ranking decided on head-to-head points.*
Top scorer: Mateo Retegui (Atalanta) 25.
Cup Final: Bologna 1, AC Milan 0.

KAZAKHSTAN

Football Federation of Kazakhstan, Nur-Sultan City, B. Momyshuly Avenue 5A, 010000 Astana.
Founded: 1914. *FIFA:* 1994; *UEFA:* 2002. *National Colours:* All yellow with blue trim.

International matches 2024–25
Norway (h) 0-0, Slovenia (a) 0-3, Austria (a) 0-4, Slovenia (h) 0-1, Austria (h) 0-2, Norway (a) 0-5, North Korea (n) 0-2, Curacao (n) 2-0, Wales (a) 1-3, Liechtenstein (a) 2-0, Belarus (a) 1-4, North Macedonia (h) 0-1.

League Championship wins (1992–2024)
Astana 7; Irtysh Pavlodar (includes Ansat) 5; Aktobe 5; Kairat 4; Yelimay (renamed Spartak Semey) 3; FC Astana-64 (includes Zhenis) 3; Tobol 2; Shakhter Karagandy 2; Taraz 1; Ordabasy 1.

Cup wins (1992–2024)
Kairat 10; FC Astana-64 (incl. Zhenis) 3; Astana (incl. Lokomotiv) 3; Kaisar 2; Tobol 2; Aktobe 2; Ordabasy 2; Dostyk 1; Vostok 1; Yelimay (renamed Spartak Semey) 1; Irtysh Pavlodar 1; Taraz 1; Almaty 1; Atyrau 1; Shakhter Karagandy 1.
No winner in 2020.

Kazakh Premier Ligasy 2024
	P	W	D	L	F	A	GD	Pts
Kairat (C)[1]	24	14	5	5	39	21	18	47
Astana[3]	24	14	4	6	39	19	20	46
Aktobe[2]	24	12	7	5	39	26	13	43
Ordabasy[3]	24	12	6	6	36	24	12	42
Tobol	24	11	6	7	33	23	10	39
Elimai	24	10	7	7	35	32	3	37
Atyrau	24	9	8	7	28	20	8	35
Kaisar	24	9	7	8	28	29	–1	34
Kyzylzhar	24	8	5	11	29	26	3	29

Zhenis | 24 | 6 | 6 | 12 | 18 | 32 | –14 | 24

	P	W	D	L	F	A	GD	Pts
Zhenis	24	6	6	12	18	32	–14	24
Zhetysu	24	5	8	11	17	33	–16	23
Turan	24	5	5	14	16	39	–23	20
Shakhter*	24	2	4	18	12	45	–33	10

Top scorers (joint): Islam Chesnokov (Tobol), Joao Paulo (Kairat), Nikolay Signevich (Atyrau) 10.
Cup Final: Atyrau 1, Aktobe 2.

KOSOVO

Football Federation of Kosovo, 28 Nentori, Nr 171, 10000 Prishtina.
Founded: 1946. *FIFA:* 2016; *UEFA:* 2016. *National Colours:* Blue shirts with gold trim, black shorts with blue trim, blue socks with black trim.

International matches 2024–25
Romania (h) 0-3, Cyprus (a) 4-0, Lithuania (a) 2-1, Cyprus (h) 3-0, Romania (a) 0-3*, Lithuania (h) 1-0, Iceland (h) 2-1, Iceland (a) 3-1‡, Armenia (h) 5-2, Comoros (h) 4-0.

Match awarded to Romania after Kosovo team refused to resume playing at 0-0 following pro-Serb crowd chants.
‡*Match played in Spain due to construction work at Iceland's home stadium.*

League Championship wins (1945–97; 1999–2025)
Prishtina 15; Vellaznimi 9; KF Trepca 7; Liria 5; Budućnosti 4; Drita 4; Rudari 3; Red Star 3; Besa Peja 3; Feronikeli 3; Ballkani 3; Jedinstvo 2; Kosova Prishtina 2; Slloga 2; Obiliqi 2; Fushe-Kosova 2; Proleteri 1; KXEK Kosova 1; Rudniku 1; KNI Ramiz Sadiku 1; Dukagjini 1; Besiana 1; Hysi 1; Vushtrria 1; Trepca'89 1.
No competition in 1953.

Cup wins (1991–97; 1999–2025)
Prishtina 9; Besa Peja 3; Feronikeli 3; Flamurtari 2; Liria 2; Llapi 2; KF Trepca 1; KF 2 Korriku 1; Gjilani 1; Drita 1; Besiana 1; KEK-u 1; Kosova Prishtina 1; Vellaznimi 1; Hysi 1; Trepca'89 1; Ballkani 1.

Kosovar Superliga 2024–25
	P	W	D	L	F	A	GD	Pts
Drita (C)[1]	36	22	8	6	57	24	33	74
Ballkani[3]	36	17	11	8	61	39	22	62
Malisheva[3]	36	14	11	11	43	39	4	53
Gjilani	36	13	12	11	48	47	1	51
Ferizaj	36	14	8	14	42	47	–5	50
Prishtina†[2]	36	11	15	10	42	36	6	48
Dukagjini†	36	13	9	14	35	45	–10	48
Llapi+	36	12	11	13	42	41	1	47
Suhareka*	36	12	7	17	47	59	–12	43
Feronikeli*	36	3	6	27	24	64	–40	15

†*Ranking decided on head-to-head points.*
Top scorer: Mevlan Zeka (Suhareka) 14.
Cup Final: Prishtina 1, Llapi 0.

LATVIA

Latvijas Futbola Federacija, Olympic Sports Center, Grostonas Street 6b, 1013 Riga.
Founded: 1921. *FIFA:* 1922; *UEFA:* 1992. *National Colours:* Carmine shirts with orange and white trim, black shorts with orange trim, carmine socks.

International matches 2024–25
Armenia (a) 1-4, Faroe Islands (h) 1-0, North Macedonia (h) 0-3, Faroe Islands (a) 1-1, North Macedonia (a) 0-1, Armenia (h) 1-2, Andorra (a) 1-0, England (a) 0-3, Azerbaijan (h) 0-0, Albania (h) 1-1.

League Championship wins (1922–40; 1942–90; 1991–2024)
Skonto Riga 15; ASK Riga (incl. AVN 2) 11; Sarkanais Metalurgs Liepaja 9; RFK Riga 8; Olympija Liepaya 7; VEF Riga 6; Ventspils 6; Energija Riga (incl. ESR Riga 2) 4; Elektrons Riga (incl. Alfa 1) 4; Riga FC 3; Torpedo Riga 3; FK RFS 3; Keisermezhs (Kaiserwald) Riga 2; Khimikis Daugavpils 2; RAF Jelgava 2; Daugava Liepaja 2; Liepajas Metalurgs 2; JPFS/Spartaks Jurmala 2; Dinamo Riga 1; Zhmilyeva Team 1; Darba Rezervi 1; RER Riga 1; Starts Brotseni 1; Venta Ventspils 1; Jurnieks Riga 1; Gauja Valmiera 1; Daugava 1; FK Liepaja 1; Valmiera 1.
No competition in 1937, 1944.

Cup wins (1937–39; 1943; 1946–2024)
Skonto Riga 8; ASK Riga 7 (includes AVN 3); Elektrons Riga 7; Ventspils 7; Sarkanais Metalurgs Liepaja 4; Jelgava 4; VEF Riga 3; Tseltnieks Riga 3; RAF Jelgava 3; FK RFS 3; RFK Riga 2; Daugava Liepaja 2; Starts Brotseni 2; Selmash Liepaya 2; Jurnieks Riga 2; Khimikis Daugavpils 2; FK Liepaja 2; Rigas Vilki 1; Dinamo Liepaya 1; Dinamo Riga 1; RER Riga 1; Voulkan

Kouldiga 1; Baltika Liepaja 1; Venta Ventspils 1; Pilots Riga 1; Lielupe Yurmala 1; Energija Riga (formerly ESR Riga) 1; Torpedo Riga 1; Daugava SKIF Riga 1; Tseltnieks Daugavpils 1; Olympija Riga 1; FK Riga 1; Liepajas Metalurgs 1; Daugava 1; Riga FC 1; Auda 1.

Latvian Virsliga 2024

	P	W	D	L	F	A	GD	Pts
FK RFS (C)[1]	36	29	3	4	103	25	78	90
Riga FC[3]	36	27	6	3	99	23	76	87
Auda[3]	36	18	6	12	63	34	29	60
Valmiera (−3)[*]§	36	19	7	10	75	39	36	55
BFC Daugavpils[3]	36	11	9	16	43	60	−17	42
FK Liepaja	36	10	9	17	37	56	−19	39
Metta/LU	36	10	6	20	34	76	−42	36
Tukums 2000	36	9	8	19	38	81	−43	35
Grobina+	36	8	5	23	34	78	−44	29
Jelgava†	36	6	7	23	28	82	−54	25

Valmiera deducted 3pts. §Valmiera relegated at the end of the season for failing to gain League licences. †Jelgava reprieved from relegation.
Top scorer: Reginaldo Ramires (Riga FC) 25 (incl. 13 for Auda).
Cup Final: FK RFS 4, Auda 2 *(aet).*

LIECHTENSTEIN
Liechtensteiner Fussballverband, Landstrasse 149, 9494 Schaan.
Founded: 1934. *FIFA:* 1974; *UEFA:* 1974. *National Colours:* All blue with white trim.

International matches 2024–25
San Marino (a) 0-1, Gibraltar (a) 2-2, Hong Kong (h) 1-0, Gibraltar (h) 0-0, Malta (a) 0-2, San Marino (h) 1-3, North Macedonia (h) 0-3, Kazakhstan (h) 0-2, Wales (a) 0-3, Scotland (h) 0-4.
Liechtenstein has no national league. Teams compete in Swiss regional leagues.

Cup wins (1945–2025)
FC Vaduz 51; FC Balzers 11; FC Triesen 8; USV Eschen/Mauren 5; FC Schaan 3.
No winner in 2019–20, 2020–21.
Cup Final: FC Vaduz 3, FC Balzers 2.

LITHUANIA
Lietuvos Futbolo Federacija, Stadiono g. 2, 02106 Vilnius.
Founded: 1922. *FIFA:* 1923; *UEFA:* 1992. *National Colours:* All yellow with green trim.

International matches 2024–25
Cyprus (h) 0-1, Romania (a) 1-3, Kosovo (h) 1-2, Romania (h) 1-2, Cyprus (a) 1-2, Kosovo (a) 0-1, Poland (a) 0-1, Finland (h) 2-2, Malta (a) 0-5, Denmark (a) 0-5.

League Championship wins (1990–2024)
Zalgiris Vilnius 11; FBK Kaunas 8 (incl. Zalgiris Kaunas 1); Ekranas 7; Suduva (Marijampole) 3; Inkaras Kaunas 2; Kareda 2; Sirijus Klaipeda 1; ROMAR Mazeikiai 1; Panevezys 1.

Cup wins (1990–2024)
Zalgiris Vilnius 14; Ekranas 4; FBK Kaunas 4; Suduva (Marijampole) 3; Kareda 2; Atlantas 2; Sirijus Klaipeda 1; Lietuvos Makabi Vilnius (renamed Neris Vilnius) 1; Inkaras Kaunas 1; Stumbras 1; Panevezys 1; TransINVEST 1; Banga (Gargzdai) 1.

Lithuanian A Lyga 2024

	P	W	D	L	F	A	GD	Pts
Zalgiris Vilnius (C)[1]	36	24	7	5	76	31	45	79
Hegelmann[3]	36	19	10	7	60	40	20	67
Kauno Zalgiris[3]	36	15	9	12	43	40	3	54
Dainava	36	12	9	15	33	40	−7	45
Banga[3]	36	10	13	13	37	46	−9	43
Dziugas Telsani†	36	11	9	16	33	48	−15	42
Siauliai†	36	10	12	14	39	50	−11	42
Panevezys	36	9	14	13	34	40	−6	41
Suduva+	36	9	12	15	33	38	−5	39
TransINVEST*	36	11	5	20	35	50	−15	38

†Ranking decided on head-to-head points.
Top scorer: Liviu Antal (Zalgiris Vilnius) 20.
Cup Final: Banga 0, Hegelmann 0 *(aet; Banga won 4-1 on penalties).*

LUXEMBOURG
Federation Luxembourgeoise de Football, 148 Rue de Limpach, L-3932 Mondercange.
Founded: 1908. *FIFA:* 1910; *UEFA:* 1954. *National Colours:* All red with white and blue trim.

International matches 2024–25
Northern Ireland (a) 0-2, Belarus (h) 0-1, Bulgaria (a) 0-0, Belarus (a) 1-1*, Bulgaria (h) 0-1, Northern Ireland (h) 2-2, Sweden (h) 1-0, Switzerland (a) 1-3, Slovenia (h) 0-1, Republic of Ireland (h) 0-0.
**Match played in Hungary.*

League Championship wins (1909–40; 1944–2025)
Jeunesse Esch 28; F91 Dudelange 16; Spora Luxembourg 11; Stade Dudelange 10; Fola Esch 8; Red Boys Differdange 6; Union Luxembourg 6; Avenir Beggen 6; US Hollerich-Bonnevoie 5; Progres Niederkorn 3; Aris Bonnevoie 3; Sporting Club 2; FC Differdange 03 2; Racing Club 1; National Schifflange 1; Grevenmacher 1; Swift Hesperange 1.
No competition in 1912–13. No winner in 2019–20.

Cup wins (1921–1940; 1944–2025)
Red Boys Differdange 15; Jeunesse Esch 13; Union Luxembourg 10; Spora Luxembourg 8; F91 Dudelange 8; Avenir Beggen 7; FC Differdange 03 6; Progres Niederkorn 5; Stade Dudelange 4; Grevenmacher 4; Fola Esch 3; Alliance Dudelange 2; US Rumelange 2; Racing-Union 2; Racing Club 1; US Dudelange 1; SC Tetange 1; National Schifflange 1; Aris Bonnevoie 1; Jeunesse Hautcharage 1; Swift Hesperange 1; Etzella Ettelbruck 1; CS Petange (renamed Union Titus Petange) 1.
No winner in 2019–20, 2020–21.

Luxembourg Nationaldivisioun 2024–25

	P	W	D	L	F	A	GD	Pts
FC Differdange 03 (C)[1]	30	25	3	2	69	7	62	78
UNA Strassen[3]	30	18	6	6	62	23	39	60
F91 Dudelange[3]	30	17	6	7	67	34	33	57
Racing Union[3]	30	17	6	7	50	22	28	57
Progres Niederkorn	30	16	7	7	54	30	24	55
Swift Hesperange	30	16	6	8	56	34	22	54
Mondorf-les-Bains	30	16	5	9	53	39	14	53
Jeunesse Esch	30	11	9	10	41	48	−7	42
Union Titus Petange	30	11	8	11	41	32	9	41
Hostert	30	11	5	14	50	69	−19	38
Victoria Rosport	30	8	10	12	29	45	−16	34
Rodange	30	7	8	15	40	62	−22	29
Wiltz 71+*	30	8	5	17	37	61	−24	29
Bettembourg+*	30	7	2	21	29	59	−30	23
Fola Esch*	30	4	1	25	18	78	−60	13
Mondercange*	30	3	3	24	21	74	−53	12

Top scorer: Yann Mabella (Racing Union), Matheus (UNA Strassen) 22.
Cup Final: FC Differdange 03 2, F91 Dudelange 2 *(aet; FC Differdange 03 won 5-4 on penalties).*

MALTA
Malta Football Association, Millennium Stand, Floor 2, National Stadium, ATD 4000 Ta'Qali.
Founded: 1900. *FIFA:* 1959; *UEFA:* 1960. *National Colours:* All red with white trim.

International matches 2024–25
Moldova (a) 0-2, Andorra (a) 1-0, Moldova (h) 1-0, Liechtenstein (h) 2-0, Andorra (h) 0-0, Finland (h) 0-1, Poland (a) 0-2, Lithuania (h) 0-0, Netherlands (a) 0-8.

League Championship wins (1909–1940; 1944–2025)
Floriana 26; Sliema Wanderers 26; Valletta 25; Hibernians 13; Hamrun Spartans 13; Birkirkara 4; Rabat Ajax 2; St George's 1; King's Own Malta Regiment 1; Marsaxlokk 1.
No competition 1910–11, 1915–16.

Cup wins (1934–1940; 1944–2025)
Sliema Wanderers 22; Floriana 21; Valletta 14; Hibernians 11; Hamrun Spartans 6; Birkirkara 6; Melita 1; Gzira United 1; Zurrieq 1; Rabat Ajax 1; Balzan 1.
No winner in 2019–20, 2020–21.

Maltese Premier League Aggregate Table 2024–25

	P	W	D	L	F	A	GD	Pts
Floriana§[3]	32	17	11	4	48	23	25	62
Sliema Wanderers§	32	17	7	8	50	27	23	58
Birkirkara§[3]	32	16	8	8	45	28	17	56
Hamrun Spartans§ (C)[1]	32	15	7	10	48	28	20	52
Hibernians[3]	32	14	7	11	43	40	3	49
Marsaxlokk	32	13	8	11	47	39	8	47
Gzira United	32	11	9	12	34	42	−8	42
Mosta	32	12	2	18	35	53	−18	38
Zabbar St Patrick	32	10	6	16	45	50	−5	36
Naxxar Lions+	32	8	8	16	30	55	−25	32
Melita†+*	32	7	8	17	38	62	−24	29
Balzan†*	32	7	8	17	38	62	−24	29

§Qualification for final four play-off. †Ranking decided on head-to-head points.
The League is played over two rounds. After 11 matches in each round the table splits into mini leagues of the top

six and bottom six. Final rankings are decided on aggregate points totals from the two rounds. Play-offs then decide the champions and UEFA competition qualifiers.

Championship Play-offs
Semi-finals
Sliema Wanderers 0, Birkirkara 1 *(aet)*.
Floriana 0, Hamrun Spartans 0 *(aet; Hamrun Spartans won 4-2 on penalties)*.
Third Place Play-off
Sliema Wanderers 0, Floriana 4
Final
Birkirkara 0, Hamrun Spartans 1
Top scorer: Maxuell Samurai (Birkirkara) 22.
Cup Final: Birkirkara 1, Hibernians 2.

MOLDOVA

Federatia Moldoveneasca de Fotbal, Str. Tricolorului 39, 2012 Chisinau.
Founded: 1990. *FIFA:* 1994; *UEFA:* 1993. *National Colours:* All blue with white trim.

International matches 2024–25
Malta (h) 2-0, San Marino (h) 1-0, Andorra (h) 2-0, Malta (a) 0-1, Andorra (a) 1-0, Gibraltar (a) 1-1, Norway (h) 0-5, Estonia (h) 2-3, Poland (a) 0-2, Italy (a) 0-2.

League Championship wins (1992–2025)
Sheriff (Tiraspol) 21; Zimbru Chisinau 8; Milsami Orhei 2; Constructorul (renamed FC Tiraspol) 1; Dacia Chisinau 1; Petrocub Hincesti 1.

Cup wins (1992–2025)
Sheriff (Tiraspol) 13; Zimbru Chisinau 6; Tiligul-Tiras 3; FC Tiraspol 3 (incl. Constructorul 2); Milsami Orhei 2; Petrocub Hincesti 2; Bugeac Comrat 1; Nistru Otaci 1; Iskra-Stal 1; Zaria Balti (now Balti) 1; Sfintul Gheorghe 1.

Moldovan Super Liga 2024–25
Phase I

	P	W	D	L	F	A	GD	Pts
Sheriff	14	11	3	0	33	6	27	36
Zimbru Chisinau	14	8	1	5	32	16	16	25
Petrocub Hincesti†	14	6	5	3	20	9	11	23
Balti†	14	6	5	3	18	9	9	23
Milsami Orhei	14	6	3	5	30	18	12	21
Spartanii Sportul	14	3	5	6	12	17	−5	14
Dacia Buiucani	14	2	5	7	8	19	−11	11
Floresti	14	1	3	10	0	59	−59	1

†*Ranking decided on head-to-head goal difference. Top six qualify for Phase II.*

Phase II

	P	W	D	L	F	A	GD	Pts
Milsami Orhei (C)[1]	10	6	3	1	25	8	17	21
Sheriff†[2]	10	5	5	0	17	6	11	20
Zimbru Chisinau†[3]	10	6	2	2	22	9	13	20
Petrocub Hincesti[3]	10	4	2	4	20	17	3	14
Balti	10	1	2	7	9	24	−15	5
Spartanii Sportul	10	0	2	8	9	38	−29	2

†*Ranking decided on head-to-head away goals.*
Top scorer: Caio Martins (Balti) 12.
Cup Final: Sheriff 2, Milsami Orhei 1.

MONTENEGRO

Fudbalski savez Crne Gore, Bulevar Veljka Vlahovica bb, 81000 Podgorica.
Founded: 1931 *FIFA:* 2007; *UEFA:* 2007. *National Colours:* All red with gold trim.

International matches 2024–25
Iceland (a) 0-2, Wales (h) 1-2, Turkey (a) 0-1, Wales (a) 0-1, Iceland (h) 0-2, Turkey (h) 3-1, Gibraltar (h) 3-1, Faroe Islands (h) 1-0, Czech Republic (a) 0-2, Armenia (h) 2-2.

League Championship wins (2006–25)
Buducnost Podgorica 7; Sutjeska (Niksic) 5; Mogren (Budva) 2; Rudar Pljevlja 2; Zeta (Golubovci) 1; Mladost Podgorica (renamed OFK Titograd) 1; Decic (Tuzi) 1.

Cup wins (2006–25)
Buducnost Podgorica 5; Rudar Pljevlja 4; Mladost Podgorica (renamed OFK Titograd) 2; Sutjeska (Niksic) 2; Mogren (Budva) 1; OFK Petrovac 1; Celik (Niksic) 1; Lovcen (Cetinje) 1; Decic (Tuzi) 1.
No winner in 2019–20.

Montenegrin Prva CFL 2024–25

	P	W	D	L	F	A	GD	Pts
Buducnost Podgorica (C)‡[1]	35	26	6	3	90	29	61	84
Petrovac§	36	17	9	10	50	37	13	60
Sutjeska§[3]	36	14	9	13	40	38	2	51
Decic‡[3]	35	10	17	8	34	31	3	47
Mornar†	36	12	8	16	40	53	−13	44
Bokelj†	36	13	5	18	31	50	−19	44
Jedinstvo	36	11	10	15	45	58	−13	43
Arsenal Tivat+	36	10	12	14	32	47	−15	42
Jezero+	36	9	12	15	35	44	−9	39
Otrant-Olympic*	36	9	8	19	43	53	−10	35

†*Ranking decided on head-to-head points.* †*Round 36: Buducnost Podgorica v Decic abandoned due to crowd trouble and declared void.* §*Petrovac failed to obtain a licence for European competitions.*
Top scorer: Zarko Korac (Jedinstvo) 16.
Cup Final: Decic 1, Mornar 0.

NETHERLANDS

Koninklijke Nederlandse Voetbalbond, Woudenbergseweg 56–58, Postbus 515, 3707 HX Zeist.
Founded: 1889. *FIFA:* 1904; *UEFA:* 1954. *National Colours:* Orange shirts with royal blue trim, orange shorts with royal blue and white trim, orange socks.

International matches 2024–25
Bosnia & Herzegovina (h) 5-2, Germany (h) 2-2, Hungary (a) 1-1, Germany (a) 0-1, Hungary (h) 4-0, Bosnia & Herzegovina (a) 1-1, Spain (h) 2-2, Spain (a) 3-3 (4-5p), Finland (a) 2-0, Malta (h) 8-0.

League Championship wins (1888–2025)
Ajax 36; PSV Eindhoven 26; Feyenoord 16 (incl. 1 unofficial title); HVV Den Haag 10; Sparta Rotterdam 6; RAP Amsterdam 5; Go Ahead Eagles Deventer 4; HFC Haarlem 3; HBS Craeyenhout 3; Willem II 3; RCH Heemstede 2; Heracles 2; ADO Den Haag 2; AZ Alkmaar (formerly AZ 67) 2; VV Concordia 1; Quick Den Haag 1; Be Quick Groningen 1; NAC Breda 1; SC Enschede 1; Volewijckers Amsterdam 1; HFC Haarlem 1; BVV Den Bosch 1; Schiedam 1; Limburgia 1; EVV Eindhoven 1; SVV Rapid JC Den Heerlen (renamed Roda JC Kerkrade) 1; VV DOS (renamed FC Utrecht) 1; DWS Amsterdam 1; FC Twente 1.
No competition in 1944–45. No winner in 2019–20.

Cup wins (1898–2025)
Ajax 20; Feyenoord 14; PSV Eindhoven 11; Quick The Hague 4; AZ Alkmaar (formerly AZ 67) 4; HFC Haarlem 3; Sparta Rotterdam 3; FC Twente 3; FC Utrecht 3; Haarlem 2; VOC 2; HBS Craeyenhout 2; DFC 2; RCH Haarlem 2; Wageningen 2; Willem II 2; Fortuna 54 2; FC Den Haag (includes ADO) 2; Roda JC 2; RAP Amsterdam 1; Velocitas Breda 1; HVV Den Haag 1; Concordia Delft 1; CVV 1; Schoten 1; ZFC Zaandam 1; Longa 1; VUC 1; Velocitas Groningen 1; Roermond 1; FC Eindhoven 1; VSV 1; Quick 1888 Nijmegen 1; VVV Groningen 1; NAC Breda 1; Heerenveen 1; PEC Zwolle 1; FC Groningen 1; Vitesse 1; Go Ahead Eagles 1.
Cup not held regularly until 1960–61. No winner in 2019–20.

Dutch Eredivisie 2024–25

	P	W	D	L	F	A	GD	Pts
PSV Eindhoven (C)[1]	34	25	4	5	103	39	64	79
Ajax[1]	34	24	6	4	67	32	35	78
Feyenoord[1]	34	20	8	6	76	38	38	68
Utrecht[2]	34	18	10	6	62	45	17	64
AZ Alkmaar†[3]	34	16	9	9	58	37	21	57
FC Twente†	34	15	9	10	62	49	13	54
Go Ahead Eagles[2]	34	14	9	11	57	55	2	51
NEC†	34	12	7	15	51	46	5	43
Heerenveen†	34	12	7	15	42	57	−15	43
PEC Zwolle	34	10	11	13	43	51	−8	41
Fortuna Sittard	34	11	8	15	37	54	−17	41
Sparta Rotterdam	34	10	9	15	39	43	−4	39
Groningen	34	10	9	15	40	53	−13	39
Heracles Almelo	34	9	11	14	42	63	−21	38
NAC Breda	34	8	9	17	34	58	−24	33
Willem II+*	34	6	8	20	34	64	−30	26
RKC Waalwijk*	34	6	7	21	44	74	−30	25
Almere City*	34	4	10	20	23	64	−41	22

†*Qualified for UEFA Conference League Play-off Semi-finals.*

UEFA Conference League Play-off Semi-finals
AZ Alkmaar 4, Heerenveen 1
FC Twente 3, NEC 2 *(aet)*.
UEFA Conference League Play-off Final
AZ Alkmaar 3, FC Twente 2
Top scorer: Sem Steijn (FC Twente) 24.
Cup Final: AZ Alkmaar 1, Go Ahead Eagles 1 *(aet; Go Ahead Eagles won 4-2 on penalties)*.

NORTH MACEDONIA

Football Federation of North Macedonia, Bul. ASNOM br. 21, MK-1000 Skopje.
Founded: 1948. *FIFA:* 1994; *UEFA:* 1994. *National Colours:* All red with yellow trim.
International matches 2024–25
Faroe Islands (a) 1-1, Armenia (h) 2-0, Latvia (a) 3-0, Armenia (a) 2-0, Latvia (h) 1-0, Faroe Islands (h) 1-0, Liechtenstein (a) 3-0, Wales (h) 1-1, Belgium (h) 1-1, Kazakhstan (a) 1-0.
League Championship wins (1992–2025)
Vardar 11; Shkendija 5; Rabotnicki 4; Sileks 3; Sloga Jugomagnat 3; Pobeda 2; Struga 2; Makedonija GP 1; Renova 1; Shkupi 1.
Cup wins (1992–2025)
Vardar 6; Rabotnicki 4; Sileks 3; Sloga Jugomagnat 3; Makedonija GP 3; Pelister 2; Teteks 2; Shkendija 2; Pobeda 1; Cementarnica 55 1; Bashkimi 1; Metalurg 1; Renova 1; Akademija Pandev (now AP Brera Strumica) 1; Tikvesh 1.
No winner in 2019–20.
North Macedonian Prva Fudbalska Liga Table 2024–25

	P	W	D	L	F	A	GD	Pts
Shkendija (C)[1]	33	20	10	3	59	30	29	70
Sileks[3]	33	19	10	4	57	19	38	67
Rabotnichki[3]	33	15	11	7	38	21	17	56
Struga	33	13	12	8	41	37	4	51
Vardar[3]	33	12	9	12	39	37	2	45
Pelister	33	10	9	14	26	38	–12	39
Shkupi	33	10	8	15	47	47	0	38
Tikvesh	33	7	13	13	25	33	–8	34
AP Brera Strumica	33	9	7	17	41	56	–15	34
Besa*	33	9	6	18	34	53	–19	33
Gostivar (–18)†*	33	12	12	9	36	34	2	30
Voska Sport (–18)†*	33	5	7	21	25	63	–38	4

†*Gostivar and Voska Sport deducted 18pts and demoted to lowest tier.*
Top scorers (joint): Marko Gjorgjievski (Sileks), Besart Ibraimi (Shkendija) 15.
Cup Final: Vardar 2, Struga 0.

NORTHERN CYPRUS

Cyprus Turkish Football Federation, 7 Memduh Asaf Street, 107 Koskluciftlik, Lefkosa. (Not a member of FIFA or UEFA.)
Founded: 1955; *National Colours:* Red shirts with white trim, red shorts, red socks.
League Championship wins (1956–63; 1969–74; 1976–2025)
Cetinkaya 14; Magusa Turk Gucu 14; Yenicami Agdelen 9; Gonyeli 9; Dogan Turk Birligi 7; Baf Ulku Yurdu 4; Kucuk Kaymakli 4; Akincilar 1; Binatli 1.
No winner in 2020–21. Cetinkaya: 2 Cypriot League titles under Cyprus FA (until 1954).
Cup wins (1956–2025)
Cetinkaya 17; Yenicami Agdelen 8; Gonyeli 8; Magusa Turk Gucu 7; Kucuk Kaymakli 7; Turk Ocagi Limasol 6; Lefke 3; Dogan Turk Birligi 2; Genclik Gucu 1; Yalova 1; Binatli 1; Cihangir 1; Gocmenkoy 1.
No winner in 2020–21. Cetinkaya: 1 Cypriot Cup win under Cyprus FA (until 1954).
Northern Cyprus Super Lig Table 2024–25

	P	W	D	L	F	A	GD	Pts
Magusa Turk Gucu	30	22	6	2	91	30	61	72
Dogan Turk Birligi	30	21	7	2	67	25	42	70
Cihangir	30	18	4	8	65	40	25	58
Genclik Gucu†	30	16	3	11	53	41	12	51
Lefke†	30	16	3	11	49	45	4	51
Cetinkaya	30	14	5	11	62	46	16	47
Alsancak Yesilova	30	13	6	11	53	49	4	45
Mesarya	30	11	6	13	49	53	–4	39
Dumlupinar	30	12	2	16	47	55	–8	38
Esentepe	30	10	7	13	37	44	–7	37
Gocmenkoy+*	30	9	7	14	40	51	–11	34
Gonyeli†+	30	9	4	17	47	65	–18	31
Karsiyaka+	30	9	4	17	40	72	–32	31
Yenicami+	30	7	3	20	43	63	–20	24
Gencler Birligi*	30	5	5	20	27	64	–37	20
Degirmenlik (–36)‡*	30	12	0	18	26	53	–27	0

†*Ranking decided on head-to-head points.* ‡*Degirmenlik were expelled for failing to comply with registration regulations; all their 36 points from the first half of the season were deducted from their total, the three matches they played in rounds 16, 18 and 19 were awarded 0-3 losses against them, and all remaining matches were also awarded 3-0 wins to their opponents.*
Top scorer: Ussumane Djabi (Cetinkaya) 26.
Cup Final: Magusa Turk Gucu 1, Lefke 3.

NORTHERN IRELAND

Irish Football Association, National Football Stadium, Donegall Avenue, Belfast BT12 6LU.
Founded: 1880. *FIFA:* 1911; *UEFA:* 1954. *National Colours:* Emerald green shirts with white trim, emerald green shorts with white trim, white socks.

NORWAY

Norges Fotballforbund, Postboks 5000, Ullevaal Stadion, 0840 Oslo.
Founded: 1902. *FIFA:* 1908; *UEFA:* 1954. *National Colours:* Red shirts with blue and white trim, red shorts, dark blue socks.
International matches 2024–25
Kazakhstan (a) 0-0, Austria (h) 2-1, Slovenia (h) 3-0, Austria (a) 1-5, Slovenia (a) 4-1, Kazakhstan (h) 5-0, Moldova (a) 5-0, Israel (a) 4-2*, Italy (h) 3-0, Estonia (a) 1-0.
**Match played in Hungary.*
League Championship wins (1937–39; 1947– 2024)
Rosenborg 26; Fredrikstad 9; Viking Stavanger 8; Lillestrom 5; Valerenga 5; Molde 5; Bodo/Glimt 4; Larvik Turn 3; Brann 3; Lyn 2; Stromsgodset 2; IK Start 2; Freidig 1; Fram 1; Skeid 1; Moss 1; Stabaek 1.
Cup wins (1902–40; 1945–2024)
Odd Grenland 12; Fredrikstad 12; Rosenborg 12; Lyn 8; Skeid 8; Brann 7; Sarpsborg 6; Viking Stavanger 6; Lillestrom 6; Molde 6; Stromsgodset 5; Orn-Horten 4; Valerenga 4; Frigg 3; Mjondalen 3; Mercantile 2; Bodo/Glimt 2; Tromso 2; Aalesund 2; Grane Nordstrand 1; Kvik Halden 1; Sparta 1; Gjovik/Lyn 1; Moss 1; Bryne 1; Stabaek 1; Hodd 1.
(Known as the Norwegian Championship for HM The King's Trophy.)
No winner in 2020.
Norwegian Eliteserien 2024

	P	W	D	L	F	A	GD	Pts
Bodo/Glimt (C)[1]	30	18	8	4	71	31	40	62
Brann[1]	30	17	8	5	55	33	22	59
Viking[3]	30	16	9	5	61	39	22	57
Rosenborg[3]	30	16	5	9	52	39	13	53
Molde	30	15	7	8	64	36	28	52
Fredrikstad[2]	30	14	9	7	39	35	4	51
Stromsgodset	30	10	8	12	32	40	–8	38
KFUM	30	9	10	11	35	36	–1	37
Sarpsborg	30	10	7	13	43	55	–12	37
Sandefjord	30	9	7	14	41	46	–5	34
Kristiansund	30	8	10	12	32	45	–13	34
HamKam	30	8	9	13	34	39	–5	33
Tromso	30	9	6	15	34	44	–10	33
Haugesund+	30	9	6	15	29	46	–17	33
Lillestrom*	30	7	3	20	33	63	–30	24
Odd*	30	5	8	17	26	54	–28	23

Top scorer: Kristian Eriksen (Molde) 14.
Cup Final: Fredrikstad 0, Molde 0 *(aet; Fredrikstad won 5-4 on penalties).*

POLAND

Polski Zwiazek Pilki Noznej, ul. Bitwy Warszawskiej 1920 r. 7, 02-366 Warszawa.
Founded: 1919. *FIFA:* 1923; *UEFA:* 1954. *National Colours:* White shirts with red trim, red shorts with white trim, white socks.
International matches 2024–25
Scotland (a) 3-2, Croatia (a) 0-1, Portugal (h) 1-3, Croatia (h) 3-3, Portugal (a) 1-5, Scotland (h) 1-2, Lithuania (h) 1-0, Malta (h) 2-0, Moldova (h) 2-0, Finland (a) 1-2.
League Championship wins (1921–39; 1946–2025)
Legia Warsaw 15; Wisla Krakow 14; Gornik Zabrze 14; Ruch Chorzow 13; Lech Poznan 9; Cracovia 5; Pogon Lwow 4; Widzew Lodz 4; Warta Poznan 2; Polonia Warsaw 2; Polonia Bytom 2; LKS Lodz 2; Stal Mielec 2; Slask Wroclaw 2; Zaglebie Lubin 2; Garbarnia Krakow 1; Szombierki Bytom 1; Piast Gliwice 1; Rakow Czestochowa 1; Jagiellonia Bialystok 1.
No competition in 1939.
Cup wins (1925–26; 1950–57; 1961–2025)
Legia Warsaw 21; Gornik Zabrze 6; Wisla Krakow 5; Lech Poznan 5; Zaglebie Sosnowiec 4; Ruch Chorzow 3; GKS Katowice 3; Amica Wronki 3; Polonia Warsaw 2; Slask Wroclaw 2; Arka Gdynia 2; Lechia Gdansk 2; Dyskobolia Grodzisk 1 (excludes one title revoked); Rakow Czestochowa 2; Gwardia Warsaw 1; LKS Lodz 1; Stal Rzeszow 1; Widzew Lodz 1; Miedz Legnica 1; Wisla Plock 1; Jagiellonia Bialystok 1; Zawisza Bydgoszcz 1; Cracovia 1.
No winner in 2004–05.

Polish Ekstraklasa 2024–25

	P	W	D	L	F	A	GD	Pts
Lech Poznan (C)[1]	34	22	4	8	68	31	37	70
Rakow Czestochowa[3]	34	20	9	5	51	23	28	69
Jagiellonia Bialystok[3]	34	17	10	7	56	42	14	61
Pogon Szczecin	34	17	7	10	59	40	19	58
Legia Warsaw[2]	34	15	9	10	60	45	15	54
Cracovia	34	14	9	11	58	53	5	51
Motor Lublin†	34	14	7	13	48	59	–11	49
GKS Katowice†	34	14	7	13	49	47	2	49
Gornik Zabrze	34	13	8	13	43	39	4	47
Piast Gliwice†	34	11	12	11	37	36	1	45
Korona Kielce†	34	11	12	11	37	45	–8	45
Radomiak Radom	34	11	8	15	48	52	–4	41
Widzew Lodz	34	11	7	16	38	49	–11	40
Lechia Gdansk	34	10	7	17	44	59	–15	37
Zaglebie Lubin	34	10	6	18	33	51	–18	36
Stal Mielec*	34	7	10	17	39	56	–17	31
Slask Wroclaw*	34	6	12	16	38	53	–15	30
Puszcza Niepolomice*	34	6	10	18	37	63	–26	28

†*Ranking decided on head-to-head points.*
Top scorer: Efthymis Koulouris (Pogon Szczecin) 28.
Cup Final: Pogon Szczecin 3, Legia Warsaw 4.

PORTUGAL

Federacao Portuguesa de Futebol, Avenida das Selecoes, 1495-433 Cruz Quebrada-Dafundo.
Founded: 1914. *FIFA:* 1923; *UEFA:* 1954. *National Colours:* Carmine shirts with green trim, green shorts with carmine trim, carmine socks with green trim.

International matches 2024–25
Croatia (h) 2-1, Scotland (h) 2-1, Poland (a) 3-1, Scotland (a) 0-0, Poland (h) 5-1, Croatia (a) 1-1, Denmark (a) 0-1, Denmark (h) 5-2, Germany (a) 1-2, Spain (n) 2-2 (5-3p).

League Championship wins (1934–2025)
Benfica 38; Porto 30; Sporting Lisbon 21; Belenenses 1; Boavista 1.

Cup wins (1938–2025)
Benfica 26; Porto 20; Sporting Lisbon 18; Boavista 5; Belenenses 4; Vitoria de Setubal 3; Braga 3; Academica de Coimbra 2; Leixoes 1; Estrela da Amadora 1; Beira-Mar 1; Vitoria de Guimaraes 1; Desportivo das Aves 1.
No competition in 1946–47, 1949–50.

Portuguese Primeira Liga 2024–25

	P	W	D	L	F	A	GD	Pts
Sporting Lisbon (C)[1]	34	25	7	2	88	27	61	82
Benfica[1]	34	25	5	4	84	28	56	80
Porto[2]	34	22	5	7	65	30	35	71
Braga[2]	34	19	9	6	55	30	25	66
Santa Clara[3]	34	17	6	11	36	32	4	57
Vitoria de Guimaraes	34	14	12	8	47	37	10	54
Famalicao	34	12	11	11	44	39	5	47
Estoril	34	12	10	12	48	53	–5	46
Casa Pia	34	12	9	13	39	44	–5	45
Moreirense	34	10	10	14	42	50	–8	40
Rio Ave†	34	9	11	14	39	55	–16	38
Arouca†	34	9	11	14	35	49	–14	38
Gil Vicente†	34	8	10	16	34	47	–13	34
Nacional†	34	9	7	18	32	50	–18	34
Estrela da Amadora	34	7	8	19	24	50	–26	29
AVS†*	34	5	12	17	25	60	–35	27
Farense†*	34	6	9	19	25	46	–21	27
Boavista*	34	6	6	22	24	59	–35	24

†*Ranking decided on head-to-head points.*
Top scorer: Viktor Gyokeres (Sporting Lisbon) 39.
Cup Final: Benfica 1, Sporting Lisbon 3 (aet).

REPUBLIC OF IRELAND

Football Association of Ireland (Cumann Peile na hEireann), National Sports Campus, Abbotstown, Dublin 15.
Founded: 1921. *FIFA:* 1923; *UEFA:* 1954. *National Colours:* Green shirts with white trim, white shorts with green trim, green socks with orange and white trim.

League Championship wins (1921–2024)
Shamrock R 21; Dundalk 14; Shelbourne 14; Bohemians 11; St Patrick's Ath 8; Waterford U (renamed Waterford) 6; Cork U 5; Drumcondra 5; Sligo R 3; Cork C 3; St James's Gate 2; Cork Ath 2; Limerick 2; Athlone T 2; Derry C 2; Dolphin 1; Cork Hibernians 1; Cork Celtic 1; Drogheda U 1.

Cup wins (1921–2024)
Shamrock R 25; Dundalk 12; Bohemians 7; Shelbourne 7; Derry C 6; Drumcondra 5; St Patrick's Ath 5; Sligo R 5; Cork C 4; St James's Gate 2; Cork (incl. Fordsons 1) 2; Waterford U (renamed Waterford) 2; Cork U 2; Cork Ath 2; Limerick 2; Cork Hibernians 2; Bray W 2; Longford T 2; Drogheda U 2; Alton U 1; Athlone T 1; Transport 1; Finn Harps 1; Home Farm 1; University College Dublin (UCD) 1; Galway U 1; Sporting Fingal 1.

League of Ireland Premier Division 2024

	P	W	D	L	F	A	GD	Pts
Shelbourne (C)[1]	36	17	12	7	40	27	13	63
Shamrock R[3]	36	17	10	9	50	35	15	61
St Patrick's Ath[3]	36	17	8	11	51	37	14	59
Derry C	36	14	13	9	48	31	17	55
Galway U	36	13	13	10	33	29	4	52
Sligo R	36	13	10	13	40	51	–11	49
Waterford	36	13	6	17	43	47	–4	45
Bohemians	36	10	12	14	39	43	–4	42
Drogheda U[3]+	36	7	13	16	41	58	–17	34
Dundalk*	36	5	11	20	23	50	–27	26

Top scorers (joint): Padraig Amond (Waterford), Patrick Hoban (Derry C) 14.
Cup Final: Drogheda U 2, Derry C 0.

ROMANIA

Federatia Romana de Fotbal, House of Football, Str. Sergent Serbanica Vasile 12, 022186 Bucuresti.
Founded: 1909. *FIFA:* 1923; *UEFA:* 1954. *National Colours:* All yellow with red and blue trim.

International matches 2024–25
Kosovo (a) 3-0, Lithuania (h) 3-1, Cyprus (a) 3-0, Lithuania (a) 2-1, Kosovo (h) 3-0*, Cyprus (h) 4-1, Bosnia & Herzegovina (h) 0-1, San Marino (a) 5-1, Austria (a) 1-2, Cyprus (h) 2-0.
**Match awarded to Romania after Kosovo team refused to resume playing at 0-0 following pro-Serb crowd chants.*

League Championship wins (1909–16; 1919–41; 1946–2025)
FCSB (incl. CCA Bucharest 6, Steaua Bucharest 20)* 28; Dinamo Bucharest 18; CFR Cluj 8; Venus Bucharest 7†; Chinezul Timisoara 6; UTA Arad 6; Petrolul Ploiesti 4; Ripensia Timisoara 4; Universitatea Craiova 4; Rapid Bucharest 3; Olimpia Bucharest 2; United Ploiesti 2 (incl. Prahova Ploiesti 1); Colentina Bucharest 2; Arges Pitesti 2; Romano-Americana Bucharest 1; Coltea Brasov 1; Metalul Resita (renamed CSM Resita) 1; Unirea Tricolor 1; CA Oradea 1; Unirea Urziceni 1; Otelul Galati 1; Astra Giurgiu 1; Viitorul Constanta 1; Farul Constanta 1.
†*The validity of Venus Bucharest's first two titles is disputed.*

Cup wins (1933–43; 1947–2025)
FCSB (incl. CSCA Bucharest 1, CCA Bucharest 4, Steaua Bucharest 18)* 24; Rapid Bucharest 13; Dinamo Bucharest 13; Universitatea Craiova (incl. FC U Craiova 1948 1) 8; CFR Cluj 5; Petrolul Ploiesti 3; Ripensia Timisoara 2; UTA Arad 2; Politehnica Timisoara 2; Sepsi Sfantu Gheorghe 2; CFR Turnu Severin 1; Metalul Resita (renamed CSM Resita) 1; Progresul Oradea (formerly ICO) 1; Progresul Bucharest 1; Ariesul Turda 1; Universitatea Cluj (includes Stiinta) 1; Chimia Ramnicu Vilcea 1; Jiul Petrosani 1; Gloria Bistrita 1; Astra Giurgiu 1; Voluntari 1; Viitorul Constanta 1; Corvinul Hunedoara 1.
Club involved in protracted legal dispute about right to name, brand and historical honours; UEFA currently recognises FCSB as essentially the same entity as Steaua Bucharest.

Romanian Liga 1 Regular Season 2024–25

	P	W	D	L	F	A	GD	Pts
FCSB	30	15	11	4	43	24	19	56
CFR Cluj	30	14	12	4	56	32	24	54
Universitatea Craiova†	30	14	10	6	45	28	17	52
Universitatea Cluj†	30	14	10	6	43	27	16	52
Dinamo Bucharest	30	13	12	5	41	26	15	51
Rapid Bucharest	30	11	13	6	35	26	9	46
Sepsi Sfantu Gheorghe†	30	11	8	11	38	35	3	41
Hermannstadt†	30	11	8	11	34	40	–6	41
Petrolul Ploiesti	30	9	13	8	29	29	0	40
Farul Constanta	30	8	11	11	29	38	–9	35
UTA Arad	30	8	10	12	28	35	–7	34
Otelul Galati	30	7	11	12	24	32	–8	32
Politehnica Iasi†	30	8	7	15	29	46	–17	31
Botosani†	30	7	10	13	26	37	–11	31
Unirea Slobozia	30	7	5	18	28	47	–19	26
Gloria Buzau	30	5	5	20	25	51	–26	20

†*Rankings decided on head-to-head points.*
NB: Points earned in regular season are halved and rounded up at start of Championship and Relegation rounds.

Championship Round 2024–25

	P	W	D	L	F	A	GD	Pts
FCSB (C)[1]	10	7	3	0	18	9	9	52
CFR Cluj[2]	10	4	4	2	17	11	6	43
Universitatea Craiova[3]	10	4	2	4	13	11	2	40
Universitatea Cluj[3]	10	4	1	5	12	15	–3	39
Rapid Bucharest	10	2	4	4	12	17	–5	33
Dinamo Bucharest	10	1	2	7	10	19	–9	31

Relegation Round 2024–25

	P	W	D	L	F	A	GD	Pts
Hermannstadt	9	4	3	2	12	8	4	36
Otelul Galati	9	6	1	2	13	5	8	35
Petrolul Ploiesti†	9	3	2	4	10	10	0	31
UTA Arad†	9	4	2	3	9	11	–2	31
Farul Constanta†	9	3	4	2	12	9	3	31
Botosani	9	4	1	4	11	12	–1	29
Politehnica Iasi+*	9	3	3	3	9	5	4	28
Unirea Slobozia+	9	3	5	1	11	8	3	27
Sepsi Sfantu Gheorghe*	9	1	2	6	7	16	–9	26
Gloria Buzau*	9	2	1	6	4	14	–10	17

†*Rankings decided by whether or not team profited by half a point in rounding up after halving regular season points; if still tied, ranked by regular season points total.*
Top scorer: Louis Munteanu (CFR Cluj) 23.
Cup Final: CFR Cluj 3, Hermannstadt 2.

RUSSIA
Russian Football Union, Ulitsa Narodnaya 7, 115 172 Moscow. (Suspended from international competition by FIFA and UEFA on 28 February 2022 following Russia's invasion of Ukraine.)
Founded: 1912. *FIFA:* 1912; *UEFA:* 1954. *National Colours:* All brick red with white trim.

International matches 2024–25
Vietnam (a) 3-0*, Brunei (h) 11-0*, Syria (h) 4-0*, Grenada (h) 5-0*, Zambia (h) 5-0*, Nigeria (h) 1-1*, Belarus (a) 4-1*.
**Match not sanctioned by FIFA due to Russia's invasion of Ukraine.*

USSR League Championship wins (1936–41; 1945–91)
Dynamo Kyiv 13; Spartak Moscow 12; Dynamo Moscow 11; CSKA Moscow 7; Torpedo Moscow 3; Dinamo Tbilisi 2; Dnepr Dnepropetrovsk 2; Zorya Voroshilovgrad 1; Ararat Yerevan 1; Dynamo Minsk 1; Zenit Leningrad 1.
No winner in 1941. In 1936 and 1976 separate spring and autumn competitions were played.

Russian League Championship wins (1992–2025)
Spartak Moscow 10; Zenit St Petersburg 10; CSKA Moscow 6; Lokomotiv Moscow 3; Rubin Kazan 2; Spartak Vladikavkaz (formerly Alania) 1; Krasnodar 1.

USSR Cup wins (1936–39; 1944–92)
Spartak Moscow 10; Dynamo Kyiv 9; Dynamo Moscow 6; Torpedo Moscow 6; CSKA Moscow 5; Shakhtar Donetsk 4; Lokomotiv Moscow 2; Ararat Yerevan 2; Dinamo Tbilisi 2; Zenit Leningrad 2; Karpaty Lvov 1; SKA Rostov-on-Don 1; Metalist Kharkiv 1; Dnepr Dnepropetrovsk 1.

Russian Cup wins (1992–2025)
Lokomotiv Moscow 9; CSKA Moscow 9; Zenit St Petersburg 5; Spartak Moscow 4; Torpedo Moscow 3; Dynamo Moscow 1; Terek Grozny (renamed Akhmat Grozny) 1; Rubin Kazan 1; Rostov 1; Tosno 1.

Russian Premier Liga 2024–25

	P	W	D	L	F	A	GD	Pts
Krasnodar (C)	30	20	7	3	59	23	36	67
Zenit St Petersburg	30	20	6	4	58	18	40	66
CSKA Moscow	30	17	8	5	47	21	26	59
Spartak Moscow	30	17	6	7	56	25	31	57
Dynamo Moscow	30	16	8	6	61	35	26	56
Lokomotiv Moscow	30	15	8	7	51	41	10	53
Rubin Kazan	30	13	6	11	42	45	–3	45
Rostov	30	10	9	11	41	43	–2	39
Akron Tolyatti	30	10	5	15	39	55	–16	35
Krylia Sovetov Samara	30	8	7	15	36	51	–15	31
Dynamo Makhachkala†	30	6	11	13	27	35	–8	29
Khimki†*‡	30	6	11	13	35	56	–21	29
Pari Nizhny Novgorod+§	30	7	6	17	27	54	–27	27
Akhmat Grozny+	30	4	13	13	27	48	–21	25
Orenburg+	30	4	7	19	28	56	–28	19
Fakel Voronezh*	30	2	12	16	14	42	–28	18

Russian clubs excluded from international competitions until further notice.
†*Ranking decided on head-to-head points.* ‡*Khimki failed to gain licence and were relegated.* §*Pari Nizhny Novgorod reprieved from relegation.*

Top scorer: Manfred Ugalde (Spartak Moscow) 17.
Cup Final: Rostov 0, CSKA Moscow 0 *(aet; CSKA Moscow won 4-3 on penalties).*

SAN MARINO
Federazione Sammarinese Giuoco Calcio, Strada di Montecchio 17, 47890 San Marino.
Founded: 1931. *FIFA:* 1988; *UEFA:* 1988. *National Colours:* White shirts with cobalt blue trim, cobalt blue shorts with white trim, cobalt blue socks with white trim.

International matches 2024–25
Liechtenstein (h) 1-0, Moldova (a) 0-1, Gibraltar (a) 0-1, Andorra (a) 0-2, Gibraltar (h) 1-1, Liechtenstein (a) 3-1, Cyprus (a) 0-2, Romania (h) 1-5, Bosnia & Herzegovina (a) 0-1, Austria (h) 0-4.

League Championship wins (1985–2025)
Tre Fiori 8; La Fiorita 6; Folgore (Falciano) 5; Tre Penne 5; Domagnano 4; Faetano 3; Murata 3; Virtus 2; Montevito (renamed Fiorentino) 1; Libertas 1; Cosmos 1; Pennarossa 1.

Cup wins (1937–2025)
Libertas 11; Tre Fiori 8; Domagnano 8; La Fiorita 7; Tre Penne 6; Juvenes 5; Cosmos 4; Faetano 3; Murata 3; Dogana 2; Pennarossa 2; Juvenes/Dogana 2; Virtus 2; Folgore (Falciano) 1.
Competition not held regularly until 1965. No winner in 1969, 1973, 2019–20.

Campionato Sammarinese 2024–25
First Phase

	P	W	D	L	F	A	GD	Pts
Virtus (C)[1]	30	24	5	1	66	18	48	77
La Fiorita†[3]	30	22	7	1	74	19	55	73
Tre Fiori†[3]	30	17	5	8	61	28	33	56
Folgore†	30	15	8	7	41	31	10	53
Cosmos†	30	14	8	8	61	36	25	50
Tre Penne§†	30	12	13	5	48	33	15	49
San Giovanni§†	30	13	10	7	58	37	21	49
Fiorentino‡	30	13	6	11	33	34	–1	45
Murata‡	30	11	6	13	33	33	0	39
Faetano‡	30	9	4	17	32	62	–30	31
Juvenes/Dogana‡	30	8	6	16	24	35	–11	30
Domagnano	30	6	11	13	29	44	–15	29
Libertas	30	8	6	16	29	60	–31	26
Cailungo	30	6	5	19	35	66	–31	23
Pennarossa	30	3	8	19	26	76	–50	17
San Marino U22	30	4	4	22	30	68	–38	16

§*Ranking decided on head-to-head points.* †*Clubs placed second to seventh in the First Phase progress to the Second Phase quarter-finals.* ‡*Clubs placed eighth to eleventh contest the first round. Winners of drawn matches decided by head-to-head record in regular season. Winner of the Second Phase qualifies for the UEFA Conference League first qualifying round.*

Second Phase
First Round
Murata 0, Faetano 1
Fiorentino 1, Juvenes/Dogana 1 *(Fiorentino qualified on better regular season record).*
Quarter-finals First Leg
Folgore 0, San Giovanni 1; Tre Penne 1, Cosmos 1
La Fiorita 2, Faetano 1; Tre Fiori 3, Fiorentino 1
Quarter-finals Second Leg
San Giovanni 1, Folgore 1 *(San Giovanni won 2-1 on aggregate).*
Cosmos 1, Tre Penne 0 *(Cosmos won 2-1 on aggregate).*
Faetano 0, La Fiorita 2 *(La Fiorita won 4-1 on aggregate).*
Fiorentino 0, Tre Fiori 2 *(Tre Fiori won 5-1 on aggregate).*
Semi-finals First Leg
La Fiorita 0, Cosmos 0; San Giovanni 1, Tre Fiori 2
Semi-finals Second Leg
Cosmos 0, La Fiorita 0 *(La Fiorita qualified on better regular season record).*
Tre Fiori 1, San Giovanni 1 *(Tre Fiori won 3-2 on aggregate).*
Final
La Fiorita 1, Tre Fiori 0
Top scorer: Matteo Prandelli (Tre Fiori) 21.
Cup Final: Virtus 1, Tre Fiori 0.

SCOTLAND
Scottish Football Association, Hampden Park, Glasgow G42 9AY.
Founded: 1873. *FIFA:* 1910; *UEFA:* 1954. *National Colours:* Dark blue shirts with yellow and white trim, dark blue shorts with yellow trim, dark blue socks.

SERBIA

Futbalski svez Srbije, Terazije 35, PO Box 263, 11000 Beograd.
Founded: 1919. *FIFA:* 1921; *UEFA:* 1954. *National Colours:* Red shirts with blue and white trim, red shorts with blue trim, red socks.

International matches 2024–25
Spain (h) 0-0, Denmark (a) 0-2, Switzerland (h) 2-0, Spain (a) 0-3, Switzerland (a) 1-1, Denmark (h) 0-0, Austria (a) 1-1, Austria (h) 2-0, Albania (a) 0-0, Andorra (h) 3-0.

Yugoslav League Championship wins (1923–40; 1946–92)
Red Star Belgrade (Crvena zvezda) 19; Partizan Belgrade 11*; Hajduk Split 9; Gradjanski Zagreb 5; BSK Belgrade (renamed OFK) 5; Dinamo Zagreb 4; Jugoslavija Belgrade 2; Concordia Zagreb 2; Vojvodina Novi Sad 2; FK Sarajevo 1; HASK Zagreb 1; Zeljeznicar 1.
*No competition in 1934. *Total includes 1 League championship (1986–87) originally awarded to Macedonian club Vardar.*

Serbian League Championship wins (1991–2025)
Red Star Belgrade (Crvena zvezda) 17; Partizan Belgrade 16; Obilic 1.

Yugoslav Cup wins (1923–41; 1947–91)
Red Star Belgrade (Crvena zvezda) 12; Hajduk Split 9; Dinamo Zagreb 7; Partizan Belgrade 6; OFK Belgrade (incl. BSK 3) 5; Rijeka 2; Velez Mostar 2; HASK Zagreb 1; Jugoslavija Belgrade 1; Vardar Skopje 1; Borac Banjaluka 1.

Serbian and Serbia-Montenegro Cup wins (1991–2025)
Red Star Belgrade (Crvena zvezda) 17; Partizan Belgrade 11; Vojvodina 2; Sartid (now FK Smederevo 1924) 1; Zeleznik 1; Jagodina 1; Cukaricki 1.

Serbian SuperLiga Regular Season 2024–25

	P	W	D	L	F	A	GD	Pts
Red Star Belgrade	30	28	2	0	106	22	84	86
Partizan Belgrade	30	18	9	3	58	29	29	63
OFK Beograd	30	13	7	10	40	39	1	46
Radnicki 1923	30	13	6	11	47	40	7	45
Vojvodina†	30	11	9	10	48	40	8	42
Mladost Lucani†	30	11	9	10	32	35	–3	42
TSC Backa Topola	30	12	5	13	47	44	3	41
Novi Pazar	30	11	7	12	46	54	–8	40
Cukaricki	30	10	9	11	37	40	–3	39
IMT	30	10	7	13	37	46	–9	37
Zeleznicar†	30	9	8	13	37	37	0	35
Napredak Krusevac†	30	9	8	13	29	40	–11	35
Spartak Subotica	30	8	10	12	26	40	–14	34
Radnicki Nis	30	8	8	14	40	59	–19	32
Tekstilac Odzaci	30	9	4	17	25	52	–27	31
Jedinstvo Ub	30	4	4	22	22	60	–38	16

†Ranking decided on head-to-head goal difference.

Championship Round 2024–25

	P	W	D	L	F	A	GD	Pts
Red Star Belgrade (C)[1]	37	32	4	1	123	35	88	100
Partizan Belgrade[2]	37	21	10	6	73	40	33	73
Novi Pazar[3]	37	15	9	13	60	65	–5	54
OFK Beograd†§	37	15	8	14	53	54	–1	53
Radnicki 1923†[3]	37	15	8	14	60	53	7	53
Vojvodina†	37	14	11	12	57	49	8	53
Backa Topola	37	15	5	17	59	58	1	50
Mladost Lucani	37	12	11	14	38	48	–10	47

†Ranking decided on points in regular season. §OFK Beograd failed to obtain a UEFA competition licence.

Relegation Round 2024–25

	P	W	D	L	F	A	GD	Pts
Cukaricki†	37	12	13	12	47	49	–2	49
Zeleznicar†	37	13	10	14	49	43	6	49
IMT	37	13	9	15	49	55	–6	48
Spartak Subotica	37	11	11	15	35	51	–16	44
Radnicki Nis+	37	11	10	16	50	67	–17	43
Napredak Krusevac+	37	11	9	17	35	48	–13	42
Tekstilac Odzaci (–6)*	37	11	4	22	33	65	–32	31
Jedinstvo Ub*	37	7	4	26	32	73	–41	25

Tekstilac Odzaci deducted 6pts. †Ranking decided on points in regular season.
Top scorer: Cherif Ndiaye (Red Star Belgrade) 19.
Cup Final: Red Star Belgrade 3, Vojvodina 0.

SLOVAKIA

Slovensky Futbalovy Zvaz, Tomasikova 30C, 821 01 Bratislava.
Founded: 1938. *FIFA:* 1994; *UEFA:* 1993. *National Colours:* Royal blue shirts with black sleeves and white trim, royal blue shorts with black trim, royal blue socks with red and white trim.

International matches 2024–25
Estonia (a) 1-0, Azerbaijan (h) 2-0, Sweden (h) 2-2, Azerbaijan (a) 3-1, Sweden (a) 1-2, Estonia (h) 1-0, Slovenia (h) 0-0, Slovenia (a) 0-1, Greece (a) 1-4, Israel (n) 0-1.

League Championship wins (1938–44; 1993–2025)
Slovan Bratislava (incl. 4 as SK Bratislava) 19; Zilina 7; Kosice 2; Inter Bratislava 2; Artmedia Petrzalka 2; AS Trencin 2; Sparta Povazska Bystrica 1; OAP Bratislava 1; Ruzomberok 1; Spartak Trnava 1.

Cup wins (1961; 1969–93; 1993–2025)
Slovan Bratislava 17; Spartak Trnava 9; Inter Bratislava 6; VSS Kosice 5; Lokomotiva Kosice 3; Zilina 2; Dukla Banska Bystrica 2; Artmedia Petrzalka 2; AS Trencin 2; Ruzomberok 2; Jednota Trencin 1; DAC 1904 (Dunajska Streda) 1; Tatran Presov 1; Chemlon Humenne 1; Koba Senec 1; Matador Puchov 1; ViOn Zlate Moravce 1.
See also Czech Republic section for Slovak club honours in Czechoslovak era 1925–93.

Slovak Super Liga Qualifying Table 2024–25

	P	W	D	L	F	A	GD	Pts
Slovan Bratislava	22	15	4	3	48	25	23	49
Zilina	22	13	6	3	42	20	22	45
Spartak Trnava	22	12	8	2	34	17	17	44
DAC 1904	22	8	8	6	32	22	10	32
Podbrezova	22	7	9	6	31	29	2	30
Kosice	22	7	8	7	31	25	6	29
Zemplin Michalovce	22	6	9	7	28	34	–6	27
Komarno	22	6	4	12	24	38	–14	22
Ruzomberok†	22	5	5	12	22	39	–17	20
AS Trencin†	22	3	11	8	22	35	–13	20
Skalica	22	4	7	11	21	35	–14	19
Dukla Banska Bystrica	22	4	5	13	22	38	–16	17

†Ranking decided on head-to-head points.

Championship Round 2024–25

	P	W	D	L	F	A	GD	Pts
Slovan Bratislava (C)[1]	32	22	6	4	74	39	35	72
Zilina[3]	32	15	9	8	55	40	15	54
Spartak Trnava[2]	32	14	10	8	46	34	12	52
DAC 1904‡[3]	32	13	12	7	48	34	14	51
Kosice‡	32	11	11	10	45	38	7	44
Zeleziarne Podbrezova‡	32	8	13	11	40	43	–3	37

‡Qualified for UEFA Conference League Play-offs.

Relegation Round 2024–25

	P	W	D	L	F	A	GD	Pts
Zemplin Michalovce‡	32	10	10	12	48	56	–8	40
Komarno	32	11	6	15	36	48	–12	39
Skalica	32	10	8	14	36	45	–9	38
Ruzomberok	32	10	6	16	35	50	–15	36
AS Trencin+	32	7	14	11	37	48	–11	35
Dukla Banska Bystrica*	32	5	7	20	35	60	–25	22

‡Qualified for UEFA Conference League Play-offs.

UEFA Conference League Play-offs
Semi-finals
Kosice 2, Zeleziarne Podbrezova 2 *(aet; Zeleziarne Podbrezova won 5-4 on penalties).*
DAC 1904 2, Zemplin Michalovce 1.
Final
DAC 1904 3, Zeleziarne Podbrezova 2.
Top scorers (joint): Tigran Barseghyan (Slovan Bratislava), David Strelec (Slovan Bratislava) 20.
Cup Final: Ruzomberok 0, Spartak Trnava 1.

SLOVENIA

Nogometna Zveza Slovenije, Predoslje 41a, p.p. 130, Sl-4000 Kranj.
Founded: 1920. *FIFA:* 1992; *UEFA:* 1992. *National Colours:* White shirts with grey trim, white shorts, white socks.

International matches 2024–25
Austria (h) 1-1, Kazakhstan (h) 3-0, Norway (a) 0-3, Kazakhstan (a) 1-0, Norway (h) 1-4, Austria (a) 1-1, Slovakia (a) 0-0, Slovakia (h) 1-0, Luxembourg (a) 1-0, Bosnia & Herzegovina (h) 2-1.

League Championship wins (1991–2025)
Maribor 16; Olimpija (pre-2005) 4; Gorica 4; Olimpija Ljubljana (post-2005) 4; Domzale 2; Celje 1; Koper 1; Mura (post-2012) 1.

Cup wins (1991–2025)
Maribor 9; Olimpija (pre-2005) 4; Koper 4; Olimpija Ljubljana (post-2005) 4; Gorica 3; Celje 2; Interblock 2; Domzale 2; NK Mura (pre-2005) 1; Rudar Velenje 1; Mura (post-2012) 1; Rogaska 1.

Slovenian PrvaLiga 2024–25

	P	W	D	L	F	A	GD	Pts
Olimpija Ljubljana (C)[1]	36	21	11	4	63	20	43	74
Maribor[3]	36	19	10	7	64	32	32	67
Koper[3]	36	19	9	8	60	35	25	66
Celje[2]	36	17	10	9	76	51	25	61
Bravo	36	14	13	9	52	44	8	55
Primorje	36	11	10	15	41	61	–20	43
Mura†	36	9	8	19	37	51	–14	35
Radomlje†	36	10	5	21	37	69	–32	35
Domzale+	36	7	8	21	35	66	–31	29
Nafta 1903*	36	6	10	20	33	69	–36	28

†*Ranking decided on head-to-head points.*
Top scorer: Raul Florucz (Olimpija Ljubljana) 15.
Cup Final: Koper 0, Celje 4.

SPAIN

Real Federacion Espanola de Futbol, Plaza Luis Aragones s/n, 28232 Las Rozas.
Founded: 1913. *FIFA:* 1913; *UEFA:* 1954. *National Colours:* Red shirts with yellow trim, blue shorts with yellow trim, red socks with blue and yellow trim.

International matches 2024–25

Serbia (a) 0-0, Switzerland (a) 4-1, Denmark (h) 1-0, Serbia (h) 3-0, Denmark (a) 2-1, Switzerland (h) 3-2, Netherlands (a) 2-2, Netherlands (h) 3-3 (5-4p), France (n) 5-4, Portugal (n) 2-2 (3-5p).

League Championship wins (1929–36; 1939–2025)

Real Madrid 36; Barcelona 28; Atletico Madrid 11; Athletic Bilbao 8; Valencia 6; Real Sociedad 2; Real Betis 1; Sevilla 1; Deportivo La Coruna 1.

Cup wins (1903–36; 1939–2025)

Barcelona 32; Athletic Bilbao (includes Vizcaya Bilbao 1) 24; Real Madrid 20; Atletico Madrid 10; Valencia 8; Real Zaragoza 6; Sevilla 5; Espanyol 4; Real Union de Irun 3; Real Sociedad (includes Ciclista) 3; Real Betis 3; Deportivo La Coruna 2; Racing de Irun 1; Arenas 1; Mallorca 1.
No winner in 2019–20.

Spanish La Liga 2024–25

	P	W	D	L	F	A	GD	Pts
Barcelona (C)[1]	38	28	4	6	102	39	63	88
Real Madrid[1]	38	26	6	6	78	38	40	84
Atletico Madrid[1]	38	22	10	6	68	30	38	76
Athletic Bilbao†[1]	38	19	13	6	54	29	25	70
Villarreal†[1]	38	20	10	8	71	51	20	70
Real Betis[2]	38	16	12	10	57	50	7	60
Celta Vigo[2]	38	16	7	15	59	57	2	55
Rayo Vallecano†[3]	38	13	13	12	41	45	–4	52
Osasuna†	38	12	16	10	48	52	–4	52
Mallorca	38	13	9	16	35	44	–9	48
Real Sociedad‡	38	13	7	18	35	46	–11	46
Valencia‡	38	11	13	14	44	54	–10	46
Getafe†	38	11	9	18	34	39	–5	42
Espanyol†	38	11	9	18	40	51	–11	42
Alaves†	38	10	12	16	38	48	–10	42
Girona‡	38	11	8	19	44	60	–16	41
Sevilla‡	38	10	11	17	42	55	–13	41
Leganes*	38	9	13	16	39	56	–17	40
Las Palmas*	38	8	8	22	40	61	–21	32
Real Valladolid*	38	4	4	30	26	90	–64	16

†*Ranking decided on head-to-head points.* ‡*Ranking decided on head-to-head goal difference.*
Top scorer: Kylian Mbappe (Real Madrid) 31.
Cup Final: Barcelona 3, Real Madrid 2 (aet).

SWEDEN

Svenska Fotbollfoerbundet, Evenemangsgatan 31A, PO Box 1216, SE-171 23 Solna.
Founded: 1904. *FIFA:* 1904; *UEFA:* 1954. *National Colours:* Yellow shirts with light blue and dark blue trim, dark blue shorts with light blue trim, yellow socks.

International matches 2024–25

Azerbaijan (a) 3-1, Estonia (h) 3-0, Slovakia (a) 2-2, Estonia (a) 3-0, Slovakia (h) 2-1, Azerbaijan (h) 6-0, Luxembourg (a) 0-1, Northern Ireland (h) 5-1, Hungary (a) 2-0, Algeria (h) 4-3.

League Championship wins (1896–1925; 1930–2024)

Malmo 24; IFK Goteborg 18; IFK Norrkoping 13; Orgryte 12; AIK (Solna) 12; Djurgarden 12; Elfsborg 6; Helsingborg 5; GAIS (Gothenburg) 4; Oster Vaxjo 4; Halmstad 4; Atvidaberg 2; Goteborgs IF 1; IFK Eskilstuna 1; Fassberg 1; Brynas IF 1; IK Sleipner 1; Hammarby 1; Kalmar 1; Hacken 1.
Played in cup format 1896–1925.

Cup wins (1941–53; 1967–2025)

Malmo 16; AIK (Solna) 8; IFK Goteborg 8; IFK Norrkoping 6; Helsingborg 5; Djurgarden 5; Hacken 4; Kalmar 3; Elfsborg 3; Atvidaberg 2; GAIS (Gothenburg) 1; Raa IF 1; Landskrona 1; Oster Vaxjo 1; Degerfors 1; Halmstad 1; Orgryte 1; Ostersund 1; Hammarby 1.
No competition in 1968, 1991–92, 2012.

Allsvenskan 2024

	P	W	D	L	F	A	GD	Pts
Malmo (C)[1]	30	19	8	3	67	25	42	65
Hammarby[3]	30	16	6	8	48	25	23	54
AIK[3]	30	17	3	10	46	41	5	54
Djurgarden	30	16	5	9	45	35	10	53
Mjallby	30	14	8	8	44	35	9	50
GAIS	30	14	6	10	36	34	2	48
Elfsborg	30	13	6	11	52	44	8	45
Hacken[2]	30	12	6	12	54	51	3	42
Sirius	30	12	5	13	47	46	1	41
Brommapojkarna	30	8	10	12	46	53	–7	34
IFK Norrkoping	30	9	7	14	36	57	–21	34
Halmstads BK	30	10	3	17	32	50	–18	33
IFK Goteborg†	30	7	10	13	33	43	–10	31
Varnamo†+	30	7	10	13	30	40	–10	31
Kalmar*	30	8	6	16	38	58	–20	30
Vasteras*	30	6	5	19	26	43	–17	23

†*Ranking decided on goals scored.*
Top scorer: Nikola Vasic (Brommapojkarna) 17.
Cup Final: Malmo 0, Hacken 0 *(aet; Hacken won 4-2 on penalties).*

SWITZERLAND

Schweizerisher Fussballverband, Worbstrasse 48, 3074 Muri bei Bern.
Founded: 1895. *FIFA:* 1904; *UEFA:* 1954. *National Colours:* Red shirts with maroon and white trim, maroon shorts with red and white trim, red socks.

International matches 2024–25

Denmark (a) 0-2, Spain (h) 1-4, Serbia (a) 0-2, Denmark (h) 2-2, Serbia (h) 1-1, Spain (a) 2-3, Northern Ireland (a) 1-1, Luxembourg (h) 3-1, Mexico (n) 4-2, USA (a) 4-0.

League Championship wins (1898–2025)

Grasshopper 27; FC Basel 21; Servette 17; Young Boys 17; FC Zurich 13; Lausanne-Sport 7; Winterthur 3; Aarau 3; Lugano 3; La Chaux-de-Fonds 3; Neuchatel Xamax 2; Sion 2; Anglo-American Club 1; Brühl 1; Cantonal-Neuchatel 1; Etoile La Chaux-de-Fonds 1; Biel-Bienne 1; Bellinzona 1; Luzern 1.
No winner in 1922–03.

Cup wins (1925–2025)

Grasshopper 19; FC Basel 14; Sion 13; FC Zurich 10; Lausanne-Sport 9; Servette 8; Young Boys 8; La Chaux-de-Fonds 6; Lugano 4; Luzern 3; Urania Geneva Sport 1; Young Fellows Zurich (renamed Young Fellows Juventus) 1; FC Grenchen 1; St Gallen 1; Aarau 1; Wil 1.

Swiss Super League Regular Season 2024–25

	P	W	D	L	F	A	GD	Pts
FC Basel	33	18	7	8	72	32	40	61
Servette	33	15	10	8	52	43	9	55
Young Boys	33	15	8	10	49	42	7	53
Luzern	33	14	9	10	61	51	10	51
Lugano	33	14	7	12	48	47	1	49
Lausanne-Sport	33	13	8	12	52	44	8	47
St Gallen	33	12	11	10	46	43	3	47
FC Zurich	33	13	8	12	44	48	–4	47
Sion	33	9	9	15	41	51	–10	36
Grasshopper	33	7	12	14	35	46	–11	33
Yverdon-Sport	33	8	9	16	33	57	–14	33
Winterthur	33	8	6	19	32	61	–29	30

Championship Round 2024–25

	P	W	D	L	F	A	GD	Pts
FC Basel[1]	38	22	7	9	91	43	48	73
Servette[1]	38	17	12	9	64	55	9	63
Young Boys[2]	38	17	10	11	60	49	11	61
Lugano[2]	38	15	9	14	55	58	–3	54
Lausanne-Sport[3]	38	14	11	13	62	54	8	53
Luzern	38	14	10	14	66	64	2	52

Relegation Round 2024–25

	P	W	D	L	F	A	GD	Pts
FC Zurich	38	15	8	15	56	57	–1	53
St Gallen	38	13	13	12	52	53	–1	52
Sion	38	11	11	16	47	57	–10	44
Winterthur	38	11	7	20	43	68	–25	40
Grasshopper+	38	9	12	17	43	53	–10	39
Yverdon-Sport*	38	9	12	17	40	68	–28	39

Top scorer: Xherdan Shaqiri (FC Basel) 18.
Cup Final: Biel-Bienne 1, FC Basel 4.

TURKEY (TÜRKIYE)

Turkiye Futbol Federasyonu, Hasan Dogan Milli Takimlar, Kamp ve Egitim Tesisleri, Riva, Beykoz, Istanbul.
Founded: 1923. *FIFA:* 1923; *UEFA:* 1962. *National Colours:* All white with red trim.

International matches 2024–25

Wales (a) 0-0, Iceland (h) 3-1, Montenegro (h) 1-0, Iceland (a) 4-2, Wales (h) 0-0, Montenegro (a) 1-3, Hungary (h) 3-1, Hungary (a) 3-0, USA (a) 2-1, Mexico (n) 0-1.

League Championship wins (1959–2025)

Galatasaray 25; Fenerbahce 19; Besiktas 16*; Trabzonspor 7; Bursaspor 1; Istanbul Basaksehir 1.
*Includes two Federation Cup wins now regarded as national championships.

Cup wins (1962–2025)

Galatasaray 19; Besiktas 11; Trabzonspor 9; Fenerbahce 7; Altay Izmir 2; Goztepe Izmir 2; Ankaragucu 2; Genclerbirligi 2; Kocaelispor 2; Eskisehirspor 1; Bursaspor 1; Sakaryaspor 1; Kayseri 1; Konyaspor 1; Akhisar Belediyespor 1; Sivasspor 1.

Turkish Super Lig 2024–25

	P	W	D	L	F	A	GD	Pts
Galatasaray (C)[1]	36	30	5	1	91	31	60	95
Fenerbahce[1]	36	26	6	4	90	39	51	84
Samsunspor[2]	36	19	7	10	55	41	14	64
Besiktas[2]	36	17	11	8	59	36	23	62
Basaksehir[3]	36	16	6	14	60	56	4	54
Eyupspor	36	15	8	13	52	47	5	53
Trabzonspor	36	13	12	11	58	45	13	51
Goztepe	36	13	11	12	59	50	9	50
Rizespor	36	15	4	17	52	58	–6	49
Kasimpasa	36	11	14	11	62	63	–1	47
Konyaspor	36	13	7	16	45	50	–5	46
Alanyaspor†	36	12	9	15	43	50	–7	45
Kayserispor†	36	11	12	13	45	57	–12	45
Gaziantep†	36	12	9	15	45	50	–5	45
Antalyaspor	36	12	8	16	37	62	–25	44
Bodrum*	36	9	10	17	26	43	–17	37
Sivasspor*	36	9	8	19	44	60	–16	35
Hatayspor*	36	6	8	22	47	74	–27	26
Adana Demirspor* (–12)	36	3	5	28	34	92	–58	2
Galatasaray (C)[1]	36	30	5	1	91	31	60	95

Adana Demirspor deducted 12pts for a variety of infractions.
†Ranking decided on head-to-head points.
Top scorer: Victor Osimhen (Galatasaray) 26.
Cup Final: Trabzonspor 0, Galatasaray 3.

UKRAINE

Ukraine Association of Football, Provulok Laboratornyi 7-A, 01133 Kyiv. (Due to the ongoing invasion by Russia, the Ukraine national side plays home matches at neutral venues.)
Founded: 1991. *FIFA:* 1992; *UEFA:* 1992. *National Colours:* All yellow with blue trim.

International matches 2024–25

Albania (h) 1-2*, Czech Republic (a) 2-3, Georgia (h) 1-0‡, Czech Republic (h) 1-1‡, Georgia (a) 1-1, Albania (a) 2-1, Belgium (h) 3-1§, Belgium (a) 0-3, Canada (a) 2-4, New Zealand (n) 2-1.
*Match played in Czech Republic. ‡Match played in Poland. §Match played in Spain.

League Championship wins (1992–2025)

Dynamo Kyiv 16; Shakhtar Donetsk 14; Tavriya Simferopol 1.
No winner in 2021–22.

Cup wins (1992–2025)

Shakhtar Donetsk 15; Dynamo Kyiv 13; Chornomorets Odesa 2; Vorskla Poltava 1; Tavriya Simferopol 1.
No winner in 2021–22. No competition in 2022–23.
See also Russia section for Ukrainian club honours in Soviet era 1936–91.

Ukrainian Premier League 2024–25

	P	W	D	L	F	A	GD	Pts
Dynamo Kyiv (C)[1]	30	20	10	0	61	19	42	70
Oleksandriya[3]	30	20	7	3	46	22	24	67
Shakhtar Donetsk[2]	30	18	8	4	69	26	43	62
Polissya Zhytomyr[3]	30	12	12	6	38	28	10	48
Kryvbas Kryvyi Rih	30	13	9	8	34	26	8	47
Karpaty Lviv	30	13	7	10	42	36	6	46
Zorya Luhansk	30	12	4	14	34	39	–5	40
Rukh Lviv	30	9	11	10	30	27	3	38
Veres Rivne†	30	9	9	12	33	44	–11	36
Kolos Kovalivka†	30	8	12	10	27	25	2	36
Obolon Kyiv	30	8	8	14	19	43	–24	32
LNZ Cherkasy	30	7	10	13	25	37	–12	31
Vorskla Poltava+*	30	6	9	15	24	38	–14	27
Livyi Bereh Kyiv+*	30	7	5	18	18	39	–21	26
Inhulets Petrove*	30	5	9	16	21	47	–26	24
Chornomorets Odesa*	30	6	5	19	20	45	–25	23

SC Dnipro-1 folded before the season started and were replaced by Livyi Bereh Kyiv. †Ranking decided on head-to-head points.
Top scorer: Vladyslav Vanat (Dynamo Kyiv) 17.
Cup Final: Shakhtar Donetsk 1, Dynamo Kyiv 1 *(aet; Shakhtar Donetsk won 6-5 on penalties).*

WALES

Football Association of Wales, Hensol, Pontyclun, Vale of Glamorgan CF72 8JY.
Founded: 1876. *FIFA:* 1910; *UEFA:* 1954. *National Colours:* All red with green trim.

ASIA (AFC)

AFGHANISTAN

Afghanistan Football Federation, PO Box 128, Kabul. (Due to the ongoing security situation, the Afghanistan national team plays home matches at neutral venues.)
Founded: 1933. *FIFA:* 1948; *AFC:* 1954. *National Colours:* All red with white trim.

International matches 2024–25

Nepal (n) 0-2, Tajikistan (a) 1-3, Thailand (a) 0-2, Myanmar (a) 1-2, Syria (h) 0-1*.
*Match played in Saudi Arabia.
League champions 2024: Attack Energy; *2024–25:* Abu Muslim. *Cup winners:* No competition.

AUSTRALIA

Football Federation Australia Ltd, Locked Bag A4071, NSW 1235, Sydney South.
Founded: 1961. *FIFA:* 1963; *AFC:* 2006. *National Colours:* Gold and green patterned shirts with black trim, black shorts with gold trim, white socks green and black.
International matches 2024–25
Bahrain (h) 0-1, Indonesia (a) 0-0, China PR (h) 3-1, Japan (a) 1-1, Saudi Arabia (h) 0-0, Bahrain (a) 2-2, Indonesia (h) 5-1, China PR (a) 2-0, Japan (h) 1-0, Saudi Arabia (a) 2-1.
League champions 2024–25: Auckland FC. *Grand Final 2024:* Central Coast Mariners; *2025:* Melbourne City. *Cup winners 2024:* Macarthur FC; *2025:* Competition still being played.

BAHRAIN

Bahrain Football Association, Bahrain National Stadium, 26402 Manama.
Founded: 1957. *FIFA:* 1968; *AFC:* 1969. *National Colours:* All red.
International matches 2024–25
Australia (a) 1-0, Japan (h) 0-5, Indonesia (a) 2-2, Saudi Arabia (a) 0-0, China PR (h) 0-1, Australia (h) 2-2, Saudi Arabia (n) 3-2, Iraq (n) 2-0, Yemen (n) 1-2, Kuwait (a) 1-0, Oman (n) 2-1, Japan (a) 0-2, Indonesia (a) 0-1, Saudi Arabia (h) 0-2, China PR (a) 0-1.
League champions 2024–25: Al-Muharraq. *Cup winners 2023–24:* Al-Ahli; *2024–25:* Competition still being played.

BANGLADESH

Bangladesh Football Federation, BFF House, Motijheel Commercial Area, Dhaka 1000.
Founded: 1972. *FIFA:* 1976; *AFC:* 1974. *National Colours:* Green shirts with red trim, white shorts, white socks.
International matches 2024–25
Bhutan (a) 1-0, Bhutan (a) 0-1, Maldives (h) 0-1, Maldives (h) 2-1, India (a) 0-0, Bhutan (h) 2-0, Singapore (h) 1-2.
League champions 2024–25: Mohammedan. *Cup winners 2024–25:* Bashundhara Kings.

BHUTAN

Bhutan Football Federation, PO Box 365, Changlimthang, Thimphu 11001.
Founded: 1983. *FIFA:* 2000; *AFC:* 1993. *National Colours:* Orange shirts with yellow trim, yellow shorts, orange socks.
International matches 2024–25
Bangladesh (h) 0-1, Bangladesh (h) 1-0, Yemen (h) 0-0, Bangladesh (a) 0-2, Brunei (a) 1-2.
League champions 2024: Paro; *2025:* Competition still being played. *Cup winners:* No competition.

BRUNEI DARUSSALAM

Football Association of Brunei Darussalam, FABD House, Jalan Pusat Persidangan, BB4313 Bandar Seri Begawan. (Succeeded BAFA which was banned by FIFA and AFC in 2009.)
Founded: 2011 (BAFA 1952). *FIFA:* 2011 (BAFA 1969); *AFC:* 2011 (BAFA 1970). *National Colours:* Yellow shirts, white shorts, white socks.
International matches 2024–25
Macau (h) 3-0, Macau (a) 1-0, Timor-Leste (h) 0-1, Timor-Leste (a) 0-0*, Russia (a) 0-11‡, Lebanon (a) 0-5§, Sri Lanka (n) 0-1, Bhutan (h) 2-1.
*Match played in Thailand. ‡Match not sanctioned by FIFA due to Russia's invasion of Ukraine. §Match played in Qatar.
League champions 2024–25: Kasuka. *Cup winners 2025:* DPMM II.

CAMBODIA

Football Federation of Cambodia, National Football Centre, Road Kabsrov Sangkat Samrongkrom, Khan Dangkor, 2327 PPT3 Phnom Penh.
Founded: 1933. *FIFA:* 1954; *AFC:* 1954. *National Colours:* All black with blue trim.
International matches 2024–25
Sri Lanka (a) 0-0, Sri Lanka (h) 2-2 (2-4p), Chinese Taipei (h) 3-2, Hong Kong (a) 0-3, Malaysia (h) 2-2, Singapore (a) 1-2, Timor-Leste (h) 2-1, Thailand (a) 2-3, Vietnam (a) 1-2, Aruba (h) 1-2, Tajikistan (h) 1-2.
League champions 2024–25: Preah Khan Reach Svay Rieng. *Cup winners 2024–25:* Phnom Penh Crown.

CHINA PR

Chinese Football Association, Easton Centre Tower A (15F), 18 Guangqu Road, Chaoyang District, 100022 Beijing.
Founded: 1924. *FIFA:* 1931, withdrew 1958, rejoined 1980; *AFC:* 1974. *National Colours:* Red shirts with yellow and black trim, red shorts with black trim, red socks with yellow and black trim.
International matches 2024–25
Japan (a) 0-7, Saudi Arabia (h) 1-2, Australia (a) 1-3, Indonesia (h) 2-1, Bahrain (a) 1-0, Japan (h) 1-3, Kuwait (n) 3-1, Saudi Arabia (a) 0-1, Australia (h) 0-2, Indonesia (a) 0-1, Bahrain (h) 1-0, Korea Republic (a) 0-3, Japan (n) 0-2, Hong Kong (n) 1-0.
League champions 2024: Shanghai Port; *2025:* Competition still being played. *Cup winners 2024:* Shanghai Port; *2024:* Competition still being played.

CHINESE TAIPEI

Chinese Taipei Football Association, 2nd Floor, No. 730 Zhongyang Road, Xinzhuang District, 242030 New Taipei City.
Founded: 1924. *FIFA:* 1954; *AFC:* 1954. *National Colours:* All royal blue with light blue trim.
International matches 2024–25
Cambodia (a) 2-3, Singapore (a) 3-2, Mongolia (n) 4-0, Hong Kong (h) 1-2, Turkmenistan (h) 1-2, Sri Lanka (a) 1-3.
League champions 2024: Taiwan Steel (Tainan City); *2025:* Competition still being played. *Cup winners:* No competition.

GUAM

Guam Football Association, PO Box 20008, 96921 Barrigada.
Founded: 1975. *FIFA:* 1996; *AFC:* 1996. *National Colours:* Dark blue shirts with red trim, dark blue shorts, red socks.

International matches 2024–25
Northern Mariana Islands† (a) 2-2*, Northern Mariana Islands† (a) 1-2*, Macau (n) 2-1, Hong Kong (a) 0-5, Northern Mariana Islands† (a) 2-1, Northern Mariana Islands† (a) 8-0.
*Match played in April 2024; result omitted from previous edition.
League champions 2024: Wings; *2025:* Competition still being played. *Cup winners 2019:* Bank of Guam Strykers; *2020–:* Not contested.

HONG KONG

Hong Kong Football Association Ltd, 55 Fat Kwong Street, Homantin, Kowloon, Hong Kong.
Founded: 1914. *FIFA:* 1954; *AFC:* 1954. *National Colours:* Red shirts with black trim, black shorts with red trim, red socks.
International matches 2024–25
Solomon Islands (n) 3-0, Fiji (a) 1-1, Liechtenstein (a) 0-1, Cambodia (h) 3-0, Philippines (h) 3-1, Mauritius (h) 1-0, Mongolia (h) 3-0, Chinese Taipei (h) 2-1, Guam (h) 5-0, Macau (h) 2-0, Singapore (a) 0-0, Nepal (h) 0-0, India (h) 1-0, Japan (n) 1-6, Korea Republic (a) 0-2, China PR (n) 0-1.
League champions 2024–25: Wofoo Tai Po. *Cup winners 2023–24:* Eastern; *2024–25:* Eastern.

INDIA

All India Football Federation, Football House, Sector 19, Phase 1 Dwarka, 110075 New Delhi.
Founded: 1937. *FIFA:* 1948; *AFC:* 1954. *National Colours:* All light blue.
International matches 2024–25
Mauritius (h) 0-0, Syria (h) 0-3, Vietnam (a) 1-1, Malaysia (h) 1-1, Maldives (h) 3-0, Bangladesh (h) 0-0, Thailand (a) 0-2, Hong Kong (a) 0-1.
League champions 2024–25: Mohun Bagan. *Cup winners 2024:* NorthEast United; *2025:* Competition still being played.

INDONESIA

Football Association of Indonesia, GBK Arena 6th Floor, RT 01/RW 03, Kelurahan Gelora, Kecamatan Tanah Abang, 10270 Jakarta Pusat.
Founded: 1930. *FIFA:* 1952; *AFC:* 1954. *National Colours:* Red shirts with white trim, white shorts with red trim, red socks with white trim.
International matches 2024–25
Saudi Arabia (a) 1-1, Australia (h) 0-0, Bahrain (a) 2-2, China PR (a) 1-2, Japan (h) 0-4, Saudi Arabia (h) 2-0, Myanmar (a) 1-0, Laos (h) 3-3, Vietnam (a) 0-1, Philippines (h) 0-1, Australia (a) 1-5, Bahrain (h) 1-0, China PR (h) 1-0, Japan (a) 0-6.
League champions 2024–25: Persib (Bandung). *Cup winners 2018–19:* PSM (Makassar); *2020–:* Not contested.

IRAN

Football Federation of the Islamic Republic of Iran, No. 4 Third 12-meter St., Seoul Avenue, 19958-73781 Tehran.
Founded: 1920. *FIFA:* 1948; *AFC:* 1958. *National Colours:* All white.
International matches 2024–25
Kyrgyz Republic (h) 1-0, UAE (a) 1-0, Uzbekistan (a) 0-0, Qatar (h) 4-1*, Korea DPR (a) 3-2‡, Kyrgyz Republic (a) 3-2, UAE (h) 2-0, Uzbekistan (h) 2-2, Qatar (a) 0-1, Korea DPR (h) 3-0.
*Match played in UAE for security reasons. ‡Match played in Laos for security reasons.
League champions 2024–25: Tractor. *Cup winners 2024–25:* Esteghlal.

IRAQ

Iraq Football Association, Al-Shaab Stadium, PO Box 484, Baghdad.
Founded: 1948. *FIFA:* 1950; *AFC:* 1970. *National Colours:* Green shirts with white trim, green shorts, green socks with white trim.
International matches 2024–25
Oman (h) 1-0, Kuwait (a) 0-0, Palestine (h) 1-0, Korea Republic (a) 2-3, Jordan (h) 0-0, Oman (a) 1-0, Yemen (n) 1-0, Bahrain (n) 0-2, Saudi Arabia (n) 1-3, Kuwait (h) 2-2, Palestine (a) 1-2*, Korea Republic (h) 0-2, Jordan (a) 1-0.
*Match played in Jordan.

League champions 2024–25: Al-Shorta. *Cup winners 2023–24:* Al-Shorta; *2024–25:* Competition still being played.

JAPAN

Japan Football Association, Toyota Tokyo Bld., 1-4-18 Koraku, Bunkyo-ku, Tokyo 112-0004.
Founded: 1921. *FIFA:* 1929, rejoined 1950; *AFC:* 1954.
National Colours: All dark blue.
International matches 2024–25
China PR (h) 7-0, Bahrain (a) 5-0, Saudi Arabia (a) 2-0, Australia (h) 1-1, Indonesia (a) 4-0, China PR (a) 3-1, Bahrain (h) 2-0, Saudi Arabia (h) 0-0, Australia (a) 0-1, Indonesia (h) 6-0, Hong Kong (n) 6-1, China PR (n) 2-0, Korea Republic (a) 1-0.
League champions 2024: Vissel Kobe; *2025:* Competition still being played. *Cup winners 2024:* Vissel Kobe; *2025:* Competition still being played.

JORDAN

Jordan Football Association, Al-Hussein Youth City, PO Box 962024, 11196 Amman.
Founded: 1949. *FIFA:* 1956; *AFC:* 1975. *National Colours:* White shirts with red trim, white shorts, white socks.
International matches 2024–25
Korea DPR (h) 0-0, Korea DPR (h) 2-1, Kuwait (h) 1-1, Palestine (a) 3-1*, Korea Republic (h) 0-2, Oman (h) 4-0, Iraq (a) 0-0, Kuwait (a) 1-1, Uzbekistan (n) 0-0, Korea DPR (h) 1-1, Palestine (h) 3-1, Korea Republic (a) 1-1, Saudi Arabia (a) 0-2, Oman (a) 3-0, Iraq (h) 0-1.
*Match played in Malaysia.
League champions 2024–25: Al-Hussein. *Cup winners 2023–24:* Al-Wahdat; *2024–25:* Not contested.

KOREA DPR

DPR Korea Football Association, Kumsongdong, Kwangbok Street, Mangyongdae Dist., PO Box 818, Pyongyang.
Founded: 1945. *FIFA:* 1958; *AFC:* 1974. *National Colours:* All red with white trim.
International matches 2024–25
Jordan (a) 0-0, Jordan (a) 1-2, Uzbekistan (a) 0-1, Qatar (h) 2-2*, UAE (a) 1-1, Kyrgyz Republic (a) 0-1, Iran (h) 2-3*, Uzbekistan (h) 0-1*, Kazakhstan (n) 2-0, Jordan (a) 1-1, Qatar (a) 1-5, UAE (h) 1-2‡, Kyrgyz Republic (h) 2-2‡, Iran (a) 0-3.
*Match played in Laos for security reasons. ‡Match played in Saudi Arabia for security reasons.
League champions 2023–24: Ryomyong; *2024–25:* Competition still being played. *Cup winners 2024:* April 25.

KOREA REPUBLIC

Korea Football Association, KFA House, Gyeonghguigung-gil 46, Jongno-gu, 03175 Seoul.
Founded: 1933; reinstated 1948. *FIFA:* 1948; *AFC:* 1954.
National Colours: All red with black and white trim.
International matches 2024–25
Palestine (h) 0-0, Oman (a) 3-1, Jordan (a) 2-0, Iraq (h) 3-2, Kuwait (a) 3-1, Palestine (a)˙1-1*, Oman (h) 1-1, Jordan (h) 1-1, Iraq (a) 2-0, Kuwait (h) 4-0, China PR (h) 3-0, Hong Kong (h) 2-0, Japan (h) 0-1.
*Match played in Jordan.
League champions 2024: Ulsan HD (formerly Ulsan Hyundai); *2025:* Competition still being played. *Cup winners 2024:* Pohang Steelers; *2025:* Competition still being played.

KUWAIT

Kuwait Football Association, Udailiya, Block 4, Sami Ahmad Al-Munayes Street, PO Box 2029, Safat 13021 Kuwait City.
Founded: 1952. *FIFA:* 1964; *AFC:* 1964. *National Colours:* All blue with white trim.
International matches 2024–25
Jordan (a) 1-1, Iraq (h) 0-0, Oman (a) 0-4, Palestine (a) 2-2*, Korea Republic (h) 1-3, Jordan (h) 1-1, Yemen (n) 1-1, Lebanon (n) 1-2, Lebanon (n) 0-2, Oman (h) 1-1, UAE (h) 2-1, Qatar (h) 1-1, Bahrain (h) 0-1, China PR (n) 1-3, Iraq (a) 2-2, Oman (h) 0-1, Palestine (h) 0-2, Korea Republic (a) 0-4.
*Match played in Qatar.

League champions 2024–25: Al-Kuwait. *Cup winners 2025:* Al-Arabi.

KYRGYZ REPUBLIC

Football Federation of Kyrgyz Republic, Mederova Street 1 'B', PO Box 1484, 720082 Bishkek.
Founded: 1992. *FIFA:* 1994; *AFC:* 1994. *National Colours:* Red shirts with yellow trim, red shorts, red socks.
International matches 2024–25
Iran (a) 0-1, Uzbekistan (h) 2-3, Qatar (a) 1-3, Korea DPR (h) 1-0, UAE (a) 0-3, Iran (h) 2-3, Uzbekistan (a) 0-1, Qatar (h) 3-1, Korea DPR (a) 2-2‡, UAE (h) 1-1.
‡Match played in Saudi Arabia for security reasons.
League champions 2024: Abdysh-Ata Kant; *2025:* Competition still being played. *Cup winners 2024:* Muras United; *2025:* Competition still being played.

LAOS

Lao Football Federation, Ban Houayhong, Chanthabouly District, PO Box 1800, Vientiane.
Founded: 1951. *FIFA:* 1952; *AFC:* 1968. *National Colours:* Red shirts with white trim, red shorts, red socks.
International matches 2024–25
Malaysia (n) 1-3, Thailand (a) 3-3, Vietnam (h) 1-4, Indonesia (a) 3-3, Philippines (h) 1-1, Myanmar (a) 2-3, Sri Lanka (h) 1-2, Vietnam (a) 0-5, Nepal (h) 2-1.
League champions 2024–25: Ezra. *Cup winners 2022:* Young Elephants; *2023–:* Not contested.

LEBANON

Lebanese Football Association, Verdun Street, Bristol, Radwan Centre, PO Box 4732, Beirut.
Founded: 1933. *FIFA:* 1936; *AFC:* 1964. *National Colours:* All red with white trim.
International matches 2024–25
Tajikistan (n) 1-0, Malaysia (a) 0-1, Thailand (a) 0-0, Myanmar (a) 3-2, Kuwait (n) 2-1, Kuwait (n) 2-0, Timor-Leste (n) 4-0, Brunei (h) 5-0*, Oman (a) 0-1, Yemen (a) 0-0‡.
*Match played in Qatar. ‡Match played in Kuwait.
League champions 2023–24: Al-Nijmeh; *2024–25:* Competition still being played. *Cup winners 2023–24:* Al-Ansar; *2024–25:* Competition still being played.

MACAU

Associacao de Futebol de Macau, Avenida Olimpica, Olympic Sports Centre – Stadium (Room GS 10–11), Taipa.
Founded: 1939. *FIFA:* 1978; *AFC:* 1978. *National Colours:* All green with white trim.
International matches 2024–25
Brunei (a) 0-3, Brunei (h) 0-1, Guam (n) 1-2, Hong Kong (a) 0-2, Chinese Taipei (a) 0-2.
League champions 2024: Benfica de Macau; *2025:* Competition still being played. *Cup winners 2024:* Gala; *2025:* Competition still being played.

MALAYSIA

Football Association of Malaysia, Wisma FAM, Jalan SS5A/9, Kelana Jaya, 47301 Petaling Jaya, Selangor Darul Ehsan.
Founded: 1933. *FIFA:* 1954; *AFC:* 1954. *National Colours:* Yellow shirts with black trim, yellow shorts, yellow socks.
International matches 2024–25
Philippines (h) 2-1, Lebanon (h) 1-0, New Zealand (a) 0-4, Laos (n) 3-1, India (a) 1-1, Cambodia (a) 2-2, Timor-Leste (h) 3-2, Thailand (a) 0-1, Singapore (h) 0-0, Nepal (h) 2-0, Cape Verde (h) 1-1, Cape Verde (h) 0-3, Vietnam (h) 4-0.
League champions 2024–25: Johor Darul Ta'zim. *Cup winners 2024:* Johor Darul Ta'zim; *2025:* Competition still being played.

MALDIVES

Football Association of Maldives, FAM Office, National Stadium, VIP Entrance, 20102 Galolhu, Malé.
Founded: 1982. *FIFA:* 1986; *AFC:* 1986. *National Colours:* Red shirts with green trim, maroon shorts with green trim, red socks with green trim.

International matches 2024–25
Bangladesh (a) 1-0, Bangladesh (a) 1-2, India (a) 0-3, Philippines (a) 1-4, Singapore (a) 1-3, Timor-Leste (a) 0-1*.
**Match played in Australia.*
League champions 2023: Maziya; *2024–:* Not contested.
Cup winners 2022: Maziya; *2023–:* Not contested.

MONGOLIA

Mongolian Football Federation, Chinggis Avenue, PO Box 259, 210646 Ulaanbaatar.
Founded: 1959. *FIFA:* 1998; *AFC:* 1998. *National Colours:* All blue.
International matches 2024–25
Timor-Leste (a) 1-4*, Timor-Leste (h) 2-0, Hong Kong (a) 0-3, Chinese Taipei (n) 0-4.
**Match played in Indonesia.*
League champions 2023–24: SP Falcons; *2024–25:* Competition still being played. *Cup winners 2023–24:* SP Falcons; *2024–25:* Competition still being played.

MYANMAR

Myanmar Football Federation, National Football Training Centre, Waizayanta Road, Thuwunna, Thingankyun, 11072 Yangon.
Founded: 1947. *FIFA:* 1952; *AFC:* 1954. *National Colours:* Red shirts, burgundy shorts, burgundy socks.
International matches 2024–25
Sri Lanka (h) 2-0, Sri Lanka (h) 0-0, Singapore (h) 2-3, Lebanon (a) 2-3, Indonesia (h) 0-1, Philippines (a) 1-1, Laos (h) 3-2, Vietnam (a) 0-5, Afghanistan (h) 2-1, Pakistan (h) 1-0.
League champions 2024–25: Shan United. *Cup winners 2019:* Yangon United; *2020–:* Not contested.

NEPAL

All Nepal Football Association, ANFA House, Satdobato, Lalitpur-17, PO Box 12582, Kathmandu.
Founded: 1951. *FIFA:* 1972; *AFC:* 1954. *National Colours:* Red shirts with white and blue trim, red shorts, red socks.
International matches 2024–25
Tajikistan (a) 0-4, Afghanistan (n) 2-0, Singapore (a) 1-0, Malaysia (a) 0-2, Hong Kong (a) 0-0, Laos (a) 1-0.
League champions (A Division) 2023: Church Boys United; *2024–:* Not contested. *(Super League) 2025:* Lalitpur City. *Cup winners:* No competition.

NORTHERN MARIANA ISLANDS

Northern Mariana Islands Football Association, PMB 338 Box 10001, MP 96950 Saipan.
Founded: 2005. *FIFA:* Non-member. *AFC:* 2020. *National Colours:* Sky blue shirts with black trim, sky blue shorts, sky blue socks.
International matches 2024–25
Guam (h) 2-2*, Guam (h) 2-1*, Guam (a) 1-2, Guam (a) 0-8.
**Match played in April 2024; result omitted from previous edition.*
League champions 2024: Kanoa (Spring), Matansa (Fall); *2025:* Kanoa (Spring). *Cup winners:* No competition.

OMAN

Oman Football Association, Seeb Sports Complex, PO Box 1188, 132 Al Khoudh.
Founded: 1978. *FIFA:* 1980; *AFC:* 1980. *National Colours:* Red shirts with green trim, red shorts, red socks.
International matches 2024–25
Iraq (a) 0-1, Korea Republic (h) 1-3, Kuwait (h) 4-0, Jordan (a) 0-4, Palestine (h) 1-0, Iraq (h) 0-1, Yemen (h) 1-0, Kuwait (a) 1-1, Qatar (n) 2-1, UAE (n) 1-1, Saudi Arabia (n) 2-1, Bahrain (n) 1-2, Sudan (h) 0-0, Korea Republic (a) 1-1, Kuwait (a) 1-0, Jordan (h) 0-3, Palestine (a) 1-1*.
**Match played in Jordan.*
League champions 2024–25: Al-Seeb. *Cup winners 2023–24:* Dhofar; *2024–25:* Competition still being played.

PAKISTAN

Pakistan Football Federation, Football House, Ferozepur Road, Near Garden Town, 54600 Lahore.
Founded: 1947. *FIFA:* 1948; *AFC:* 1954. *National Colours:* Dark green shirts with light green trim, dark green shorts, dark green socks.

International matches 2024–25
Syria (a) 0-2*, Myanmar (a) 0-1.
**Match played in Saudi Arabia due to Syrian civil war.*
League champions 2018–19: Khan Research Laboratories; *2019–21:* Not contested; *2021–22:* Competition suspended; *2022–:* Not contested. *Cup winners 2023–24:* WAPDA; *2024–25:* Not contested.

PALESTINE

Palestinian Football Association, Nr. Faisal Al-Husseini Stadium, PO Box 4373, Jerusalem-al-Ram. (Due to the ongoing war in Gaza, the Palestine national team plays home matches at a neutral venue.)
Founded: 1928. *FIFA:* 1998; *AFC:* 1998. *National Colours:* Red shirts with green and white trim, red shorts, red socks.
International matches 2024–25
Korea Republic (a) 0-0, Jordan (h) 1-3*, Iraq (a) 0-1, Kuwait (h) 2-2‡, Oman (a) 0-1, Korea Republic (h) 1-1§, Jordan (a) 1-3, Iraq (h) 2-1§, Kuwait (a) 2-0, Oman (h) 1-1§.
**Match played in Malaysia. ‡Match played in Kuwait. §Match played in Jordan.*
West Bank League champions 2022–23: Jabal Mukabar; *2023–24:* Competition abandoned; *2024–:* Not contested. *West Bank Cup winners 2023:* Jabal Mukabar; *2024–:* Not contested.
Gaza Strip League champions 2022–23: Khadamat Rafah; *2023–24:* Competition abandoned; *2024–:* Not contested. *Gaza Strip Cup winners 2019–20:* Shabab Rafah; *2020–:* Not contested.

PHILIPPINES

Philippine Football Federation, 27 Danny Floro corner Capt. Henry Javier Streets, Oranbo, 1600 Pasig City.
Founded: 1907. *FIFA:* 1930; *AFC:* 1954. *National Colours:* Royal blue shirts with red and white trim, royal blue shorts, royal blue socks.
International matches 2024–25
Malaysia (a) 1-2, Tajikistan (n) 0-0 (3-4p), Thailand (a) 1-3, Tajikistan (n) 3-0, Hong Kong (a) 1-3, Myanmar (h) 1-1, Laos (a) 1-1, Vietnam (h) 1-1, Indonesia (a) 1-0, Thailand (n) 2-1, Thailand (a) 1-3, Maldives (h) 4-1, Tajikistan (h) 2-2.
League champions 2024–25: Kaya-Iloilo. *Cup winners 2023:* Kaya-Iloilo; *2024–:* Not contested.

QATAR

Qatar Football Association, 28th Floor, Al Bidda Tower, Corniche Street, West Bay, PO Box 5333, Doha.
Founded: 1960. *FIFA:* 1972; *AFC:* 1974. *National Colours:* All maroon with white trim.
International matches 2024–25
UAE (h) 1-3, Korea DPR (a) 2-2*, Kyrgyz Republic (h) 3-1, Iran (a) 1-4*, Uzbekistan (h) 3-2, UAE (a) 0-5, UAE (n) 1-1, Oman (n) 1-2, Kuwait (a) 1-1, Korea DPR (h) 5-1, Kyrgyz Republic (a) 1-3, Iran (h) 1-0, Uzbekistan (a) 0-3.
**Match played in UAE for security reasons.*
League champions 2024–25: Al-Sadd. *Cup winners 2025:* Al-Gharafa.

SAUDI ARABIA

Saudi Arabian Football Federation, Al Yasmin District, King Abdul Aziz Road, 13322 Riyadh.
Founded: 1956. *FIFA:* 1956; *AFC:* 1972. *National Colours:* Dark green shirts with light green and white trim, dark green shorts with white trim, dark green socks.
International matches 2024–25
Indonesia (h) 1-1, China PR (a) 2-1, Japan (h) 0-2, Bahrain (h) 0-0, Australia (a) 0-0, Indonesia (a) 0-2, Trinidad & Tobago (n) 3-1, Bahrain (n) 2-3, Yemen (n) 3-2, Iraq (n) 3-1, Oman (n) 1-2, China PR (h) 1-0, Japan (a) 0-0, Jordan (h) 2-0, Bahrain (a) 2-0, Australia (h) 1-2, Haiti (n) 1-0, USA (a) 0-1, Trinidad & Tobago (n) 1-1, Mexico (n) 0-2.
League champions 2024–25: Al-Ittihad. *Cup winners 2024–25:* Al-Ittihad.

SINGAPORE

Football Association of Singapore, Jalan Besar Stadium 01-02, 100 Tyrwhitt Road, 207542 Singapore.
Founded: 1892. *FIFA:* 1952; *AFC:* 1954. *National Colours:* All red with blue trim.
International matches 2024–25
Myanmar (h) 3-2, Chinese Taipei (h) 2-3, Cambodia (h) 2-1, Timor-Leste (a) 3-0*, Thailand (h) 2-4, Malaysia (a) 0-0, Vietnam (h) 0-2, Vietnam (a) 1-3, Nepal (h) 0-1, Hong Kong (h) 0-0, Maldives (h) 3-1, Bangladesh (a) 2-1.
*Match played in Vietnam.
League champions 2024–25: Lion City Sailors. *Cup winners 2024:* Not contested; *2025:* Lion City Sailors.

SRI LANKA

Football Federation of Sri Lanka, 100/9 Independence Avenue, 07 Colombo.
Founded: 1939. *FIFA:* 1952; *AFC:* 1954. *National Colours:* Yellow shirts, black shorts with yellow trim, yellow socks.
International matches 2024–25
Cambodia (h) 0-0, Cambodia (a) 2-2 (4-2p), Myanmar (a) 0-2, Myanmar (a) 0-0, Yemen (n) 1-0, Yemen (n) 0-2, Laos (a) 2-1, Thailand (a) 0-1, Brunei (a) 1-0, Chinese Taipei (h) 3-1.
League champions 2021–22: Blue Star; *2022–:* No competition. *Cup winners 2019–20:* Police; *2020–:* Not contested.

SYRIA

Syrian Arab Federation for Football, Al Faihaa Sports Complex, PO Box 421, 011 Damascus.
Founded: 1936. *FIFA:* 1937; *AFC:* 1970. *National Colours:* Green shirts with white trim, green shorts, green socks.
International matches 2024–25
Mauritius (n) 2-0, India (a) 3-0, Tajikistan (n) 1-0, Thailand (a) 1-2, Russia (a) 0-4*, Pakistan (h) 2-0‡, Afghanistan (h) 1-0‡.
*Match not sanctioned by FIFA due to Russia's invasion of Ukraine. ‡Match played in Saudi Arabia.
League champions 2023–24: Al-Fotuwa; *2024–25:* Competition suspended. *Cup winners 2023–24:* Al-Fotuwa; *2024–25:* Not contested.

TAJIKISTAN

Tajikistan Football Federation, 14/3 Ayni Street, 734 025 Dushanbe.
Founded: 1936. *FIFA:* 1994; *AFC:* 1994. *National Colours:* Red shirts with white trim, white shirts with red trim, green socks.
International matches 2024–25
Lebanon (n) 0-1, Philippines (n) 0-0 (4-3p), Syria (n) 0-1, Philippines (n) 0-3, Nepal (h) 4-0, Afghanistan (h) 3-1, Belarus (h) 0-5, Timor-Leste (h) 1-0, Cambodia (a) 2-1, Philippines (a) 2-2.
League champions 2024: Regar-TadAZ; *2025:* Competition still being played. *Cup winners 2024:* Regar-TadAZ; *2025:* Competition still being played.

THAILAND

Football Association of Thailand, 286 Ramkhamhaeng Road, Hua Mak, Bang Kapi, 10240 Bangkok.
Founded: 1916. *FIFA:* 1925; *AFC:* 1954. *National Colours:* All dark blue.
International matches 2024–25
Singapore (h) 3-1*, Vietnam (a) 2-1, Philippines (h) 3-1, Syria (a) 2-1, Lebanon (h) 0-0, Laos (h) 1-1, Timor-Leste (a) 10-0‡, Malaysia (h) 1-0, Singapore (a) 4-2, Cambodia (h) 3-2, Philippines (h) 1-2, Philippines (h) 3-1, Vietnam (a) 1-2, Vietnam (h) 2-3, Afghanistan (h) 2-0, Sri Lanka (h) 1-0, India (h) 2-0, Turkmenistan (a) 1-3.
*Match played 11.6.24; result omitted from previous edition. ‡Match played in Vietnam.
League champions 2024–25: Buriram United. *Cup winners 2023–24:* Bangkok United; *2024–25:* Buriram United.

TIMOR-LESTE

Federacao Futebol de Timor-Leste, Campo Democracia, Avenida Bairo Formosa, Dili.
Founded: 2002. *FIFA:* 2005; *AFC:* 2005. *National Colours:* Burgundy shirts with black and yellow trim, black shorts with burgundy and yellow trim, black socks with burgundy trim.

International matches 2024–25
Mongolia (h) 4-1*, Mongolia (a) 0-2, Brunei (a) 1-0, Brunei (h) 0-0‡, Thailand (h) 0-10§, Malaysia (a) 2-3, Singapore (h) 0-3§, Cambodia (a) 1-2, Lebanon (n) 0-4, Tajikistan (a) 0-1, Maldives (h) 1-0¶.
*Match played in Indonesia. ‡Match played in Thailand. §Match played in Vietnam. ¶Match played in Australia.
League champions 2023: Karketu Dili; *2024:* Not contested; *2025:* Competition still being played. *Cup winners 2020:* Lalenok United; *2021–:* Not contested.

TURKMENISTAN

Football Federation of Turkmenistan, G. Kuliyev Street 68, 744 001 Ashgabat.
Founded: 1992. *FIFA:* 1994; *AFC:* 1994. *National Colours:* Green shirts with red trim, green shorts with white trim, green socks.
International matches 2024–25
Chinese Taipei (a) 2-1, Thailand (h) 3-1.
League champions 2024: Arkadag; *2025:* Competition still being played. *Cup winners 2024:* Arkadag; *2024:* Competition still being played.

UNITED ARAB EMIRATES (UAE)

United Arab Emirates Football Association, Zayed Athletic City, PO Box 916, Abu Dhabi.
Founded: 1971. *FIFA:* 1974; *AFC:* 1974. *National Colours:* All white with red trim.
International matches 2024–25
Qatar (a) 3-1, Iran (h) 0-1, Korea DPR (h) 1-1, Uzbekistan (a) 0-1, Kyrgyz Republic (h) 3-0, Qatar (h) 5-0, Qatar (n) 1-1, Kuwait (a) 1-2, Oman (n) 1-1, Iran (a) 0-2, Korea DPR (a) 2-1*, Uzbekistan (h) 0-0, Kyrgyz Republic (a) 1-1.
*Match played in Saudi Arabia for security reasons.
League champions 2024–25: Shabab Al Ahli. *Cup winners 2024–25:* Shabab Al Ahli.

UZBEKISTAN

Uzbekistan Football Federation, Uzbekistanskaya Street 98/A, 100011 Tashkent.
Founded: 1946. *FIFA:* 1994; *AFC:* 1994. *National Colours:* All white.
International matches 2024–25
Korea DPR (h) 1-0, Kyrgyz Republic (a) 3-2, Iran (h) 0-0, UAE (h) 1-0, Qatar (a) 2-3, Korea DPR (a) 1-0*, Jordan (n) 0-0, Kyrgyz Republic (h) 1-0, Iran (a) 2-2, UAE (a) 0-0, Qatar (h) 3-0.
*Match played in Laos for security reasons.
League champions 2024: Nasaf Qarshi; *2025:* Competition still being played. *Cup winners 2024:* Nasaf Qarshi; *2025:* Competition still being played.

VIETNAM

Vietnam Football Federation, Le Quang Dao Street, Phu Do Ward, Nam Tu Liem District, 844 Hanoi.
Founded: 1960 (NV). *FIFA:* 1952 (SV), 1964 (NV); *AFC:* 1954 (SV), 1978 (SRV). *National Colours:* All red with yellow trim.
International matches 2024–25
Russia (h) 0-3*, Thailand (h) 1-2, India (h) 1-1, Laos (a) 4-1, Indonesia (h) 1-0, Philippines (a) 1-1, Myanmar (h) 5-0, Singapore (a) 2-0, Singapore (h) 3-1, Thailand (h) 2-1, Thailand (a) 3-2, Cambodia (h) 2-1, Laos (h) 5-0, Malaysia (a) 0-4.
*Match not sanctioned by FIFA due to Russia's invasion of Ukraine.
League champions 2024–25: Thep Xanh Nam Dinh. *Cup winners 2024–25:* Cong An Ha Noi.

YEMEN

Yemen Football Association, Quarter of Sport Al Jeraf (Ali Muhsen Al-Muraisi Stadium), PO Box 908, Al-Thawra City, Sana'a. (Due to the ongoing civil war, the Yemen national team plays home matches at a neutral venue.)
Founded: 1940 (SY), 1962 (NY). *FIFA:* 1967 (SY), 1980 (NY); *AFC:* 1972 (SY), 1980 (NY). *National Colours:* Red shirts with black and white trim, white shorts, black socks.

International matches 2024–25
Sri Lanka (n) 0-1, Sri Lanka (n) 2-0, Kuwait (n) 1-1, Oman (a) 0-1, Iraq (n) 0-1, Saudi Arabia (n) 2-3, Bahrain (n) 2-1, Bhutan (a) 0-0, Lebanon (h) 0-0*.
*Match played in Kuwait.
League champions 2023–24: Al-Ahli (Sanaa); *2024–:* Not contested. *Cup winners 2017:* Al-Wahda (Aden); *2018–:* Not contested.

AFRICA (CAF)

ALGERIA
Federation Algerienne De Football, Chemin Ahmed Ouaked, BP 39, Dely-Ibrahim, 16000 Algiers.
Founded: 1962. *FIFA:* 1963; *CAF:* 1964. *National Colours:* All white with green trim.
International matches 2024–25
Equatorial Guinea (h) 2-0, Liberia (a) 3-0, Togo (h) 5-1, Togo (a) 1-0, Equatorial Guinea (a) 0-0, Liberia (h) 5-1, Botswana (a) 3-1, Mozambique (h) 5-1, Rwanda (h) 2-0, Sweden (a) 3-4.
League champions 2024–25: MC Alger. *Cup winners 2024–25:* USM Alger.

ANGOLA
Federacao Angolana de Futebol, Avenida Pedro de Castro Van-Duném Loy, Urbanizacao Nova Vida No. 53, 3449 Luanda.
Founded: 1979. *FIFA:* 1980; *CAF:* 1980. *National Colours:* Red shirts with black and yellow trim, black shorts, red socks.
International matches 2024–25
Ghana (a) 1-0, Sudan (h) 2-1, Niger (h) 2-1, Niger (a) 1-0*, Ghana (h) 1-1, Sudan (a) 0-0‡, Libya (a) 1-1, Cape Verde (h) 1-2, Namibia (n) 1-1, Lesotho (n) 4-0, Malawi (n) 1-0, Madagascar (n) 4-1, South Africa (a) 3-0.
*Match played in Morocco. ‡Match played in Libya.
League champions 2024–25: Petro de Luanda. *Cup winners 2024–25:* Kabuscorp.

BENIN
Federation Beninoise de Football, Rue du boulevard Djassain, BP 112, 3ème Arrondissement 01, Porto-Novo.
Founded: 1962. *FIFA:* 1962; *CAF:* 1962. *National Colours:* All yellow with red and green trim.
International matches 2024–25
Nigeria (a) 0-3, Libya (a) 1-2*, Rwanda (h) 3-0*, Rwanda (a) 1-2, Togo (a) 0-2, Togo (h) 1-1*, Nigeria (h) 1-1*, Libya (a) 0-0, Zimbabwe (a) 2-2*, South Africa (h) 0-2*.
*Match played in Ivory Coast.
League champions 2024–25: Dadjè. *Cup winners 2019:* ESAE; *2020–:* Not contested.

BOTSWANA
Botswana Football Association, Plot 73281, Behind National Stadium, PO Box 1396, Gaborone.
Founded: 1970. *FIFA:* 1978; *CAF:* 1976. *National Colours:* Blue shirts with thin black stripes and white sleeves, blue shorts, blue socks with black trim.
International matches 2024–25
Libya (a) 0-1, Mauritania (a) 0-1, Egypt (h) 0-4, Cape Verde (a) 1-0, Cape Verde (h) 1-0, Mauritania (h) 1-1, Egypt (a) 1-1, Algeria (h) 1-3, Somalia (h) 2-0, Comoros (n) 0-0, Zambia (n) 3-3.
League champions 2024–25: Gaborone United. *Cup winners 2025:* Jwaneng Galaxy.

BURKINA FASO
Federation Burkinabe de Foot-Ball, Centre Technique National, Ouaga 2000, BP 57, 01 Ouagadougou.
Founded: 1960. *FIFA:* 1964; *CAF:* 1964. *National Colours:* All green with red trim.
International matches 2024–25
Senegal (a) 1-1, Malawi (h) 3-1*, Burundi (h) 4-1‡, Burundi (a) 2-0‡, Senegal (h) 0-1*, Malawi (a) 0-3, Ivory Coast (a) 0-2, Ivory Coast (a) 2-0 (4-2p)*, Kenya (n) 1-1, Tanzania (n) 2-0, Djibouti (h) 4-1§, Guinea-Bissau (n) 2-1, Tunisia (a) 0-2.
*Match played in Mali. ‡Match played in Ivory Coast. §Match played in Morocco.
League champions 2024–25: Rahimo. *Cup winners 2024:* Etoile Filante; *2025:* Rahimo.

BURUNDI
Federation de Football du Burundi, Avenue Muyinga, BP 3426, Bujumbura.
Founded: 1948. *FIFA:* 1972; *CAF:* 1972. *National Colours:* Red shirts with green trim, white shorts, green socks with red and white trim.
International matches 2024–25
Malawi (a) 3-2, Senegal (h) 0-1*, Burkina Faso (a) 1-4‡, Burkina Faso (h) 0-2‡, Malawi (h) 0-0‡, Senegal (a) 0-2, Uganda (h) 0-1§, Uganda (a) 0-1, Ivory Coast (h) 0-1¶, Seychelles (h) 5-0¶.
*Match played in Malawi. ‡Match played in Ivory Coast. §Match played in Uganda. ¶Match played in Morocco.
League champions 2024–25: Aigle Noir. *Cup winners 2025:* Flambeau du Centre.

CAMEROON
Federation Camerounaise de Football, Avenue du 27 aout 1940, Tsinga-Yaounde, BP 1116, 00237 Yaounde.
Founded: 1959. *FIFA:* 1962; *CAF:* 1963. *National Colours:* Green shirts with red and yellow trim, red shorts with green trim, yellow socks.
International matches 2024–25
Namibia (h) 1-0, Zimbabwe (a) 0-0*, Kenya (h) 4-1, Kenya (a) 1-0*, Namibia (a) 0-0‡, Zimbabwe (h) 2-1, Central African Republic (a) 1-0§, Central African Republic (h) 1-2*, Eswatini (a) 0-0‡, Libya (h) 3-1, Uganda (n) 3-0, Equatorial Guinea (n) 1-1.
*Match played in Uganda. ‡Match played in South Africa. §Match played in Ivory Coast.
League champions 2024–25: Colombe Sportive du Dja et Lobo. *Cup winners 2024:* Colombe Sportive du Dja et Lobo; *2025:* Competition still being played.

CAPE VERDE
Federacaò Caboverdiana de Futebol, Praia Cabo Verde, FCF CX, PO Box 234, Praia.
Founded: 1982. *FIFA:* 1986; *CAF:* 2000. *National Colours:* All dark blue with yellow trim.
International matches 2024–25
Egypt (a) 0-3, Mauritania (h) 2-0, Botswana (h) 0-1, Botswana (a) 0-1, Egypt (h) 1-1, Mauritania (a) 0-1, Mauritius (h) 1-0, Angola (a) 2-1, Malaysia (h) 3-0, Georgia (a) 1-1.
League champions 2024: FC Boavista (Santiago Sul); *2025:* GD Palmeira (Sal). *Cup winners 2025:* GD da Palmeira (Sal).

CENTRAL AFRICAN REPUBLIC
Federation Centrafricaine de Football, Avenue des Martyrs, BP 344, Bangui.
Founded: 1961. *FIFA:* 1964; *CAF:* 1965. *National Colours:* All blue with white trim.
International matches 2024–25
Lesotho (h) 3-1*, Gabon (a) 0-2, Morocco (a) 0-5, Morocco (h) 0-4*, Lesotho (a) 0-1‡, Gabon (h) 0-1‡, Cameroon (h) 0-1§, Cameroon (a) 2-1, Madagascar (h) 1-4*, Mali (h) 0-0*, Mauritania (n) 2-1.
*Match played in Morocco. ‡Match played in South Africa. §Match played in Ivory Coast.
League champions 2023–24: AS Tempête Mocaf; *2024–25:* Competition still being played. *Cup winners 2021:* Castel Foot; *2022–:* Not contested.

CHAD
Federation Tchadienne de Football, BP 886, N'Djamena.
Founded: 1962. *FIFA:* 1964; *CAF:* 1964. *National Colours:* Blue and black halved shirts with red and yellow trim, yellow shorts with black trim, blue socks with red and yellow trim.
International matches 2024–25
Sierra Leone (a) 0-0*, Ivory Coast (h) 0-2‡, Zambia (a) 0-0, Zambia (h) 0-1‡, Sierra Leone (h) 1-1§, Ivory Coast (a) 0-4, Congo DR (h) 1-1§, Congo DR (a) 1-3, Ghana (a) 0-5, Comoros (a) 0-1¶.
*Match played in Liberia. ‡Match played in Cameroon. §Match played in Ivory Coast. ¶Match played in Morocco.
League champions 2023: AS PSI; *2024:* Not contested; *2025:* Competition still being played. *Cup winners 2023:* Renaissance; *2024–:* Not contested.

COMOROS
Federation Comorienne de Football, Route d'Itsandra, BP 798, Moroni.
Founded: 1979. *FIFA:* 2005; *CAF:* 2003. *National Colours:* Emerald shirts with dark green sleeves, emerald shorts, emerald socks with dark green tops.
International matches 2024–25
Gambia (h) 1-1*, Madagascar (a) 1-1‡, Tunisia (a) 1-0, Tunisia (h) 1-1§, Gambia (a) 2-1*, Madagascar (h) 1-0*, Malawi (h) 0-2¶, Malawi (a) 0-2, Mali (h) 0-3*, Chad (a) 1-0*, Zambia (n) 1-0, Botswana (n) 0-0, Kosovo (a) 2-4, South Africa (a) 1-3, Madagascar (n) 1-0.
*Match played in Morocco. ‡Match played in Tunisia. §Match played in Ivory Coast. ¶Match played in Malawi.
League champions 2024–25: US Zilimadjou. *Cup winners 2025:* Djabal.

CONGO
Federation Congolaise de Football, 2 Rue de la Liberation de Paris, Arrondissement 3 Poto-Poto, Brazzaville. (FCF suspended by FIFA from 6 February to 14 May 2025 for government interference.)
Founded: 1962. *FIFA:* 1964; *CAF:* 1965. *National Colours:* All red with yellow and green trim.
International matches 2024–25
South Sudan (h) 1-0, Uganda (a) 0-2, South Africa (a) 0-5, South Africa (h) 1-1, South Sudan (a) 2-3, Uganda (h) 0-1, Equatorial Guinea (a) 0-3*, Equatorial Guinea (h) 0-3*, Tanzania (a) 0-3‡, Zambia (h) 0-3‡.
*Match awarded to Equatorial Guinea; Congo fielded ineligible player. ‡Match awarded due to Congo's suspension.
League champions 2023–24: AC Leopards de Dolisie; *2024–25 (competition not recognised by FCF, CAF or FIFA and not participated in by several first-tier clubs):* Still being played. *Cup winners 2023:* Diables Noirs; *2024:* Competition abandoned.

DR CONGO
Federation Congolaise de Football-Association, 31 Avenue de la Justice c/Gombe, BP 1284, 1 Kinshasa.
Founded: 1919. *FIFA:* 1964; *CAF:* 1964. *National Colours:* All blue with red trim.
International matches 2024–25
Guinea (h) 1-0, Ethiopia (a) 2-0*, Tanzania (h) 1-0, Tanzania (a) 2-0, Guinea (a) 0-1‡, Ethiopia (h) 1-2, Chad (a) 1-1§, Chad (h) 3-1, South Sudan (h) 1-0, Mauritania (a) 2-0, Mali (n) 1-0, Madagascar (n) 3-1.
*Match played in Tanzania. ‡Match played in Ivory Coast.
League champions 2024–25: Les Aigles du Congo. *Cup winners 2024:* AS Vita Club; *2024:* Competition still being played.

DJIBOUTI
Federation Djiboutienne de Football, Centre Technique National, BP 2694, Ville de Djibouti.
Founded: 1979. *FIFA:* 1994; *CAF:* 1994. *National Colours:* All sky blue with green and white trim.
International matches 2024–25
Rwanda (h) 1-0*, Rwanda (a) 0-3, Burkina Faso (h) 1-4‡, Ethiopia (a) 1-6‡.
*Match played in Rwanda. ‡Match played in Morocco.
League champions 2024–25: AS Ali Sabieh/Djibouti Telecom. *Cup winners 2024:* AS Port; *2025:* Competition still being played.

EGYPT
Egyptian Football Association, 5 Gabalaya Street, El Gezira, El Borg Post Office, Cairo.
Founded: 1921. *FIFA:* 1923; *CAF:* 1957. *National Colours:* Red shirts with black and white trim, white shorts, black socks.
International matches 2024–25
Cape Verde (h) 3-0, Botswana (a) 4-0, Mauritania (h) 2-0, Mauritania (a) 1-0, Cape Verde (a) 1-1, Botswana (h) 1-1, South Africa (a) 1-1, South Africa (h) 1-3, Ethiopia (a) 2-0*, Sierra Leone (h) 1-0.
*Match played in Morocco.
League champions 2023–24: Al-Ahly; *2024–25:* Al-Ahly. *Cup winners 2023–24:* Pyramids; *2024–25:* Zamalek.

EQUATORIAL GUINEA
Federacion Ecuatoguineana de Futbol, Avenida de Hassan II No. 1300, 1017 Malabo.
Founded: 1957. *FIFA:* 1986; *CAF:* 1986. *National Colours:* All red with white trim.
International matches 2024–25
Algeria (a) 0-2, Togo (h) 2-2, Liberia (h) 1-0, Liberia (a) 2-1, Algeria (h) 0-0, Togo (a) 0-3, Congo (h) 3-0*, Congo (a) 3-0*, Sao Tome & Principe (h) 2-0, Namibia (a) 1-1‡, Gambia (n) 1-2, Cameroon (n) 1-1.
*Match awarded to Equatorial Guinea; Congo fielded ineligible player. ‡Match played in South Africa.
League champions 2023–24: Deportivo Mongomo; *2024–25:* Competition still being played. *Cup winners 2025:* 15 de Agosto.

ERITREA
Eritrean National Football Federation, Sematat Avenue 29–31, PO Box 3665, Asmara.
Founded: 1996. *FIFA:* 1998; *CAF:* 1998. *National Colours:* All blue with red and dark blue trim.
International matches 2024–25
None played.
League champions 2020–22: Not contested; *2023:* Red Sea; *2024:* Denden. *Cup winners 2013:* Maitemanai; *2013–:* Not contested.

ESWATINI
Eswatini Football Association, Sigwaca House, Plot 582, Sheffield Road, PO Box 641, H100 Mbabane.
Founded: 1968. *FIFA:* 1978; *CAF:* 1976. *National Colours:* Blue shirts with yellow trim, blue shorts with yellow trim, yellow socks with blue tops.
International matches 2024–25
Guinea-Bissau (a) 0-1, Mali (h) 0-1*, Mozambique (a) 1-1, Mozambique (h) 0-3*, Zimbabwe (a) 3-0‡, Zimbabwe (h) 1-0*, Guinea-Bissau (h) 1-1*, Mali (a) 0-6, Madagascar (h) 0-2*, Madagascar (a) 1-0§, Cameroon (h) 0-0*, Mauritius (h) 3-3*.
*Match played in South Africa. ‡Match played in Botswana. §Match played in Mauritius.
League champions 2024–24: Nsingizini Hotspurs. *Cup winners 2019:* Young Buffaloes; *2020:* Competition abandoned; *2021–:* Not contested.

ETHIOPIA
Ethiopia Football Federation, Addis Ababa Stadium, PO Box 1080, 1000 Addis Ababa.
Founded: 1943. *FIFA:* 1952; *CAF:* 1957. *National Colours:* Green shirts with yellow and red trim, yellow shorts with green trim, red socks.
International matches 2024–25
Tanzania (a) 0-0, Congo DR (h) 0-2*, Guinea (a) 1-4‡, Guinea (h) 0-3‡, Tanzania (h) 0-2§, Congo DR (a) 2-1, Sudan (h) 0-2¶, Sudan (a) 1-2¶, Egypt (h) 0-2**, Djibouti (h) 6-1¶.
*Match played in Tanzania. ‡Match played in Ivory Coast. §Match played in DR Congo. ¶Match played in Libya. **Match played in Morocco.
League champions 2024–25: Ethiopia Medhin. *Cup winners 2024–25:* Sidama Bunna.

GABON
Federation Gabonaise de Football, BP 181, Libreville.
Founded: 1962. *FIFA:* 1966; *CAF:* 1967. *National Colours:* Yellow shirts with red trim, blue shorts, blue socks.
International matches 2024–25
Morocco (a) 1-4, Central African Republic (h) 2-0, Lesotho (h) 0-0, Lesotho (h) 2-0*, Morocco (h) 1-5, Central African Republic (a) 1-0*, Gambia (a) 0-0‡, Gambia (h) 0-0 (3-5p), Seychelles (h) 3-0, Kenya (a) 2-1.
*Match played in South Africa. ‡Match played in Senegal.
League champions 2023–24: Not contested; *2024–25:* AS Mangasport. *Cup winners: 2019 (League Cup):* Mangasport; *2020:* Competition abandoned; *2021–:* Not contested.

GAMBIA
Gambia Football Association, Kanifing Layout, 00220 Sere Kunda.

Founded: 1952. *FIFA:* 1968; *CAF:* 1966. *National Colours:* Red shirts with green, blue and white trim, blue shorts, green socks.
International matches 2024–25
Comoros (a) 1-1*, Tunisia (h) 1-2*, Madagascar (a) 1-1*, Madagascar (h) 1-0*, Comoros (h) 1-2*, Tunisia (a) 1-0, Gabon (h) 0-0‡, Gabon (a) 0-0 (5-3p), Kenya (h) 3-3§, Ivory Coast (a) 0-1, Equatorial Guinea (n) 2-1, Uganda (n) 1-1.
*Match played in Morocco. ‡Match played in Senegal. §Match played in Ivory Coast.
League champions 2024–25: Real de Banjul. Cup winners 2024: Medina United; 2025: Competition still being played.

GHANA

Ghana Football Association, General Secretariat, South East Ridge, PO Box AN 19338, Accra.
Founded: 1957 (dissolved 2018, reconvened 2019). *FIFA:* 1958; *CAF:* 1958. *National Colours:* White shirts with yellow trim, white shorts, white socks.
International matches 2024–25
Angola (h) 0-1, Niger (a) 1-1*, Sudan (h) 0-0, Sudan (a) 0-2‡, Angola (a) 1-1, Niger (h) 1-2, Nigeria (h) 0-0, Nigeria (a) 1-3, Chad (h) 5-0, Madagascar (a) 3-0*, Nigeria (n) 1-2, Trinidad & Tobago (n) 4-0.
*Match played in Morocco. ‡Match played in Libya.
League champions 2024–25: Bibiani Gold Stars. *Cup winners 2024–25:* Asante Kotoko.

GUINEA

Federation Guinéenne de Football, Temenetaye, Commune de Kaloum, GNF 3645 Conakry.
Founded: 1960. *FIFA:* 1962; *CAF:* 1963. *National Colours:* Red shirts with yellow trim, yellow shorts, green socks.
International matches 2024–25
DR Congo (a) 0-1, Tanzania (h) 1-2*, Ethiopia (h) 4-1*, Ethiopia (a) 3-0*, DR Congo (h) 1-0*, Tanzania (a) 0-1, Guinea-Bissau (h) 4-1*, Guinea-Bissau (a) 2-1, Somalia (h) 0-0*, Uganda (a) 0-1.
*Match played in Ivory Coast.
League champions 2024–25: Horoya. *Cup winners 2019:* Horoya; *2020–:* Not contested.

GUINEA-BISSAU

Federacao de Futebol da Guiné-Bissau, Alto Bandim Nova Sede, BP 375, 1035 Bissau.
Founded: 1974. *FIFA:* 1986; *CAF:* 1986. *National Colours:* All red with green and yellow trim.
International matches 2024–25
Eswatini (h) 1-0, Mozambique (a) 1-2, Mali (a) 0-1, Mali (h) 0-0, Eswatini (h) 1-1*, Mozambique (h) 1-2, Guinea (a) 1-4*, Guinea (h) 1-2, Sierra Leone (a) 1-3‡, Burkina Faso (h) 1-2, Burundi (n) 0-1, Gabon (n) 0-2.
*Match played in Ivory Coast. ‡Match played in Liberia.
League champions 2023–24: Benfica de Bissau; *2024–25:* Benfica de Bissau. *Cup winners 2024:* Uniao Desportiva Internacional de Bissau; *2025:* Competition still being played.

IVORY COAST

Federation Ivoirienne de Football, Treichville Avenue 1 – 01, BP 1202, 01 Abidjan.
Founded: 1960. *FIFA:* 1964; *CAF:* 1960. *National Colours:* All orange with green and white trim.
International matches 2024–25
Zambia (h) 2-0, Chad (a) 2-0*, Sierra Leone (h) 4-1, Sierra Leone (a) 0-1‡, Zambia (a) 0-1, Chad (h) 4-0, Burkina Faso (h) 2-0, Burkina Faso (a) 0-2 (2-4p)§, Burundi (a) 1-0¶, Gambia (h) 1-0, New Zealand (n) 0-1, Canada (a) 0-0 (5-4p).
*Match played in Cameroon. ‡Match played in Liberia. §Match played in Mali. ¶Match played in Morocco.
League champions 2024–25: Stade d'Abidjan. *Cup winners 2025:* FC San Pedro.

KENYA

Football Kenya Federation, Willmary Garden Estate, PO Box 12705-00400 NRB, Nairobi.
Founded: 1960 (KFF); 2011 (FKF). *FIFA:* 1960 (2012); *CAF:* 1968 (2012). *National Colours:* All red with black and white trim.

International matches 2024–25
Zimbabwe (h) 0-0*, Namibia (a) 2-1‡, Cameroon (a) 1-4, Cameroon (h) 0-1*, South Sudan (a) 0-2, South Sudan (h) 1-1*, Zimbabwe (a) 1-1‡, Namibia (h) 0-0‡, Burkina Faso (n) 1-1, Tanzania (n) 2-0, Gambia (a) 3-3, Gabon (h) 1-2.
*Match played in Uganda. ‡Match played in South Africa.
League champion 2024–25: Kenya Police. *Cup winners 2025:* Nairobi United.

LESOTHO

Lesotho Football Association, Bambatha Tsita Sports Arena, Old Polo Ground, PO Box 1879, 100 Maseru.
Founded: 1932. *FIFA:* 1964; *CAF:* 1964. *National Colours:* White shirts with blue sleeves and green trim, white shorts with green trim, white socks with blue trim.
International matches 2024–25
Central African Republic (a) 1-3*, Morocco (h) 0-1*, Gabon (a) 0-0, Gabon (h) 0-2‡, Namibia (h) 1-0‡, Namibia (h) 0-1 (4-3p)‡, Central African Republic (h) 1-0‡, Morocco (a) 0-7, Angola (h) 0-2‡, Angola (a) 1-0, South Africa (a) 0-2, Rwanda (a) 1-1, Malawi (n) 2-1, Angola (n) 0-4, Namibia (n) 0-3.
*Match played in Morocco. ‡Match played in South Africa.
League champion 2024–25: Lioli. *Cup winners 2019:* Matlama; *2020–:* Not contested.

LIBERIA

Liberia Football Association, Professional Building, Benson Street, PO Box 10-1066, Monrovia.
Founded: 1936. *FIFA:* 1964; *CAF:* 1962. *National Colours:* Red and white striped shirts with red sleeves, red shorts with white trim, red socks.
International matches 2024–25
Togo (a) 1-1, Algeria (h) 0-3, Equatorial Guinea (a) 0-1, Equatorial Guinea (h) 1-2, Sierra Leone (a) 2-1*, Sierra Leone (h) 1-1, Togo (h) 1-0, Algeria (a) 1-5, Senegal (h) 1-1, Senegal (a) 0-3, Tunisia (h) 0-1, Sao Tome & Principe (h) 2-1.
*Match played in Liberia.
League champions 2024–25: FC Fassell. *Cup winners 2024–25:* Black Man Warrior.

LIBYA

Libyan Football Federation, General Sports Federation Building, Sports City, Gorji, PO Box 5137, 02 Tripoli.
Founded: 1962. *FIFA:* 1964; *CAF:* 1965. *National Colours:* Red shirts with white trim, black shorts with white trim, black socks with white trim.
International matches 2024–25
Botswana (h) 1-0, Rwanda (h) 1-1, Benin (a) 1-2*, Nigeria (a) 0-1, Nigeria (h) 0-3‡, Rwanda (a) 1-0, Benin (h) 0-0, Angola (h) 1-1, Cameroon (a) 1-3.
*Match played in Ivory Coast. ‡Match awarded to Nigeria; Libya failed to fulfil fixture.
League champions 2023–24: Al-Nasr; *2024–25:* Competition still being played. *Cup winners 2022–23:* Al-Ahli Tripoli; *2023–:* Not contested.

MADAGASCAR

Federation Malagasy de Football, 29 Rue de Russie, Isoraka, PO Box 4409, 101 Antananarivo.
Founded: 1961. *FIFA:* 1964; *CAF:* 1963. *National Colours:* Green shirts with red trim, green shorts with white trim, green socks.
International matches 2024–25
Tunisia (a) 0-1, Comoros (h) 1-1*, Gambia (h) 1-1‡, Gambia (a) 0-1‡, Tunisia (h) 2-3§, Comoros (a) 0-1‡, Eswatini (a) 2-0§, Eswatini (h) 0-1¶, Central African Republic (a) 4-1‡, Ghana (h) 0-3‡.
*Match played in Tunisia. ‡Match played in Morocco. §Match played in South Africa. ¶Match played in Mauritius.
League champions 2024: Disciples; *2024–25:* Competition still being played. *Cup winners 2024:* ASSM Elgeco Plus; *2025:* Competition still being played.

MALAWI

Football Association of Malawi, Chiwembe Technical Centre, Off Chiwembe Road, PO Box 51657, Limbe.
Founded: 1966. *FIFA:* 1968; *CAF:* 1968. *National Colours:* All red with green trim.

International matches 2024–25
Burundi (h) 2-3, Burkina Faso (a) 1-3*, Senegal (a) 0-4, Senegal (h) 0-1, Burundi (h) 0-0‡, Burkina Faso (h) 3-0, Comoros (a) 2-0§, Comoros (h) 2-0, Namibia (h) 0-1, Tunisia (a) 0-2, South Africa (h) 1-0, South Africa (h) 0-2, Lesotho (n) 0-1, Namibia (n) 0-0, Angola (n) 0-1.
Match played in Mali. ‡Match played in Ivory Coast. §Match played in Malawi.
League champions 2024: Silver Strikers; *2025:* Competition still being played. *Cup winners 2024:* Blue Eagles; *2025:* Competition still being played.

MALI
Federation Malienne de Football, Avenue du Mali, Hamdallaye ACI 2000, BP 1020, 0000 Bamako.
Founded: 1960. *FIFA:* 1964; *CAF:* 1963. *National Colours:* Green shirts with red and yellow trim, yellow shorts, yellow socks.
International matches 2024–25
Mozambique (h) 1-1, Eswatini (a) 1-0*, Guinea-Bissau (h) 1-0, Guinea-Bissau (a) 0-0, Mozambique (a) 1-0, Eswatini (h) 6-0, Mauritania (a) 0-1, Mauritania (h) 0-0, Comoros (a) 3-0‡, Central African Republic (a) 0-0, DR Congo (n) 0-1.
Match played in South Africa. ‡Match played in Morocco.
League champions 2024–25: Stade Malien. *Cup winners 2025:* Stade Malien.

MAURITANIA
Federation de Foot-Ball de la Rep. Islamique de Mauritanie, Route de l'Espoire, BP 566, Nouakchott.
Founded: 1961. *FIFA:* 1970; *CAF:* 1968. *National Colours:* All green with yellow trim.
International matches 2024–25
Botswana (h) 1-0, Cape Verde (a) 0-2, Egypt (a) 0-2, Egypt (h) 0-1, Botswana (a) 1-1, Cape Verde (h) 1-0, Mali (h) 1-0, Mali (a) 0-0, Togo (a) 2-2, DR Congo (h) 0-2.
League champions 2024–25: FC Nouadhibou. *Cup winners 2024:* ASC SNIM; *2025:* Competition still being played.

MAURITIUS
Mauritius Football Association, Sepp Blatter House, Quatre Bornes, Trianon.
Founded: 1952. *FIFA:* 1964; *CAF:* 1963. *National Colours:* All red.
International matches 2024–25
India (a) 0-0, Syria (n) 0-2, Hong Kong (a) 0-1, Cape Verde (a) 0-1, Eswatini (a) 3-3*, Zimbabwe (n) 0-0, Mozambique (n) 0-0, South Africa (a) 0-0.
Match played in South Africa.
League champions 2024–25: Cercle de Joachim. *Cup winners 2023–24:* Pamplemousses; *2024–25:* Competition still being played.

MOROCCO
Federation Royale Marocaine de Football, Secteur 11, Angle Rue Arroz et Rue Arram, Hay Ryad, Rabat.
Founded: 1955. *FIFA:* 1960; *CAF:* 1959. *National Colours:* Red shirts with green trim, green shorts with red trim, red socks.
International matches 2024–25
Gabon (h) 4-1, Lesotho (a) 1-0*, Central African Republic (h) 5-0, Central African Republic (a) 4-0*, Gabon (a) 5-1, Lesotho (h) 7-0, Niger (a) 2-1*, Tanzania (h) 2-0, Tunisia (h) 2-0, Benin (h) 1-0.
Match played in Morocco.
League champions 2024–25: RS Berkane. *Cup winners 2024:* Raja Casablanca; *2025:* OC Safi.

MOZAMBIQUE
Federacao Mocambicana de Futebol, Avenida Agostinho Neto N°957, Caixa Postal 1467, Maputo.
Founded: 1976. *FIFA:* 1980; *CAF:* 1980. *National Colours:* Red shirts with black trim, black shorts, red socks.
International matches 2024–25
Mali (a) 1-1, Guinea-Bissau (h) 2-1, Eswatini (h) 1-1, Eswatini (a) 3-0*, Mali (h) 0-1, Guinea-Bissau (a) 2-1, Uganda (h) 3-1‡, Algeria (a) 1-5, South Africa (a) 1-0, Mauritius (n) 0-0, Zimbabwe (n) 1-3.

Match played in South Africa. ‡Match played in Egypt.
League champions 2024: Associacao Black Bulls; *2025:* Competition still being played. *Cup winners 2024:* Ferroviario; *2025:* Competition still being played.

NAMIBIA
Namibia Football Association, Richard Kamuhuka Street, Soccer House, Katutura, PO Box 1345, 9000 Windhoek.
Founded: 1990. *FIFA:* 1992; *CAF:* 1992. *National Colours:* Red patterned shirts, red shorts, red socks.
International matches 2024–25
Cameroon (a) 0-1, Kenya (h) 1-2*, Zimbabwe (h) 0-1*, Zimbabwe (a) 1-3*, Lesotho (a) 0-1*, Lesotho (h) 1-0 (3-4p), Cameroon (h) 0-0*, Kenya (h) 0-0*, Malawi (h) 1-0, Equatorial Guinea (h) 1-1*.
Match played in South Africa.
League champions 2024–25: African Stars. *Cup winners 2024:* African Stars; *2025:* Competition still being played.

NIGER
Federation Nigerienne de Football, Avenue Francois Mitterand, BP 10299, Niamey.
Founded: 1961. *FIFA:* 1964; *CAF:* 1965. *National Colours:* White shirts with orange, red and green trim, white shorts, white socks.
International matches 2024–25
Sudan (a) 0-1*, Ghana (h) 1-1‡, Angola (a) 0-2, Angola (h) 0-1‡, Sudan (h) 4-0§, Ghana (a) 2-1, Togo (a) 1-1, Togo (h) 0-0¶, Morocco (h) 1-2‡, Bonaire† (n) 6-0.
Match played in South Sudan. ‡Match played in Morocco. §Match played in Togo. ¶Match played in Mali.
League champions 2024–25: AS FAN (Armed Forces). *Cup winners 2025:* ASN NIGELEC.

NIGERIA
Nigeria Football Federation, Plot 2033, Olusegun Obasanjo Way, Zone 7, PO Box 5101, Garki, Abuja.
Founded: 1945. *FIFA:* 1960; *CAF:* 1960. *National Colours:* All white with green trim.
International matches 2024–25
Benin (h) 3-0, Rwanda (a) 0-0, Libya (h) 1-0, Libya (a) 3-0*, Benin (a) 1-1‡, Rwanda (h) 1-2, Ghana (a) 1-0, Ghana (h) 3-1, Rwanda (a) 2-0, Zimbabwe (h) 1-1, Ghana (n) 1-1, Jamaica (n) 2-2 (5-4p), Russia (a) 1-1§.
Match awarded to Nigeria; Libya failed to fulfil fixture. ‡Match played in Ivory Coast. §Match not sanctioned by FIFA due to Russia's invasion of Ukraine.
League champions 2024–25: Remo Stars. *Cup winners 2025:* Kwara United.

RWANDA
Federation Rwandaise de Football Association, BP 2000, Kigali.
Founded: 1972. *FIFA:* 1978; *CAF:* 1976. *National Colours:* Yellow shirts with blue and green trim, green shorts with blue and yellow trim, yellow socks with green and blue trim.
International matches 2024–25
Libya (a) 1-1, Nigeria (h) 0-0, Benin (a) 0-3*, Benin (h) 2-1, Djibouti (a) 0-1, Djibouti (h) 3-0, Libya (h) 2-1, Nigeria (a) 2-1, South Sudan (a) 2-3, South Sudan (h) 2-1, Nigeria (h) 0-2, Lesotho (h) 1-1, Algeria (a) 0-2.
Match played in Ivory Coast.
League champions 2024–25: APR FC. *Cup winners 2025:* APR FC.

SAO TOME & PRINCIPE
Federacao Santomense de Futebol, Rua Ex-Joao de Deus, CP 440, Sao Tome.
Founded: 1975. *FIFA:* 1986; *CAF:* 1986. *National Colours:* Green shirts with yellow and red trim, black shorts, green socks.
International matches 2024–25
Equatorial Guinea (a) 0-2, Liberia (a) 1-2.
League champions 2024: Agrosport; *2025:* Competition still being played. *Cup winners 2024:* GD Os Operarios; *2025:* Competition still being played.

SENEGAL
Federation Senegalaise de Football, VDN Ouest-Foire en face du CICES, BP 13021, Dakar.
Founded: 1960. *FIFA:* 1964; *CAF:* 1964. *National Colours:* All white with green, yellow and red trim.

International matches 2024–25
Burkina Faso (h) 1-1, Burundi (a) 1-0*, Malawi (h) 4-0, Malawi (a) 1-0, Burkina Faso (a) 1-0‡, Burundi (h) 2-0, Liberia (a) 1-1, Liberia (h) 3-0, Sudan (a) 0-0§, Togo (h) 2-0, Republic of Ireland (a) 1-1, England (a) 3-1.
*Match played in Malawi. ‡Match played in Mali. §Match played in Libya.
League champions 2024–25: ASC Jaraaf. *Cup winners 2023–24:* Mbour Petite Cote; *2024–25:* Competition still being played.

SEYCHELLES
Seychelles Football Federation, Maison Football, Roche Caiman, PO Box 843, Mahé.
Founded: 1979. *FIFA:* 1986; *CAF:* 1986. *National Colours:* Red shirts with maroon sleeves and white trim, maroon shorts with white trim, red socks.
International matches 2024–25
Gabon (a) 0-3, Burundi (a) 0-5*.
*Match played in Morocco.
League champion 2024–25: Cote d'Or. *Cup winners 2024–25:* Foresters.

SIERRA LEONE
Sierra Leone Football Association, 21 Battery Street, Kingtom, PO Box 672, Freetown.
Founded: 1960. *FIFA:* 1960; *CAF:* 1960. *National Colours:* All blue with white and green trim.
International matches 2024–25
Chad (h) 0-0*, Zambia (a) 2-3, Ivory Coast (a) 1-4, Ivory Coast (h) 1-0*, Liberia (h) 1-2*, Liberia (a) 1-1, Chad (a) 1-1‡, Zambia (h) 0-2*, Guinea-Bissau (h) 3-1*, Egypt (a) 0-1.
*Match played in Liberia. ‡Match played in Ivory Coast.
League champions 2023–24: Bo Rangers; *2024–25:* Competition still being played. *Cup winners: 2024:* Bo Rangers; *2025:* Competition still being played.

SOMALIA
Somali Football Federation, DHL Mogadishu, BN 03040 Mogadishu (DHL only).
Founded: 1951. *FIFA:* 1962; *CAF:* 1968. *National Colours:* Sky blue and white striped shirts, sky blue shorts, sky blue socks.
International matches 2024–25
Guinea (a) 0-0*, Botswana (a) 0-2.
*Match played in Ivory Coast.
League champions 2023–24: Dekedda; *2024–25:* Mogadishu City Club. *Cup winners 2024:* Dekedda; *2025:* Competition still being played.

SOUTH AFRICA
South African Football Association, 76 Nasrec Road, Nasrec Extension 3, PO Box 910, 2190 Johannesburg.
Founded: 1991. *FIFA:* 1992; *CAF:* 1992. *National Colours:* Yellow shirts with green trim, yellow shorts, yellow socks.
International matches 2024–25
Uganda (h) 2-2, South Sudan (a) 3-2, Congo (h) 5-0, Congo (a) 1-1, Uganda (a) 2-0, South Sudan (h) 3-0, Egypt (h) 1-1, Egypt (a) 3-1, Lesotho (h) 2-0, Benin (a) 2-0*, Malawi (a) 0-1, Malawi (h) 2-0, Mozambique (h) 0-1, Tanzania (h) 0-0, Zimbabwe (h) 2-0, Mauritius (h) 0-0, Mozambique (h) 2-0, Comoros (h) 3-1, Angola (h) 0-3.
*Match played in Ivory Coast.
League champions 2024–25: Mamelodi Sundowns. *Cup winners 2025:* Kaizer Chiefs.

SOUTH SUDAN
South Sudan Football Association, Nyakuron West, Plot No. 58B, Old Yei Road nr Hass Petroleum & Toyota House, Juba.
Founded: 2011. *FIFA:* 2012; *CAF:* 2012. *National Colours:* All white with red and green trim.
International matches 2024–25
Congo (a) 0-1, South Africa (h) 2-3, Uganda (a) 0-1, Uganda (h) 1-2, Kenya (h) 2-0, Kenya (a) 1-1*, Congo (h) 3-2, South Africa (a) 0-3, Rwanda (h) 3-2, Rwanda (a) 1-2, DR Congo (a) 0-1, Sudan (a) 1-1‡.
*Match played in Uganda. ‡Match played in Libya.
League champions 2025: Jamus. *Cup winners 2025:* Jamus.

SUDAN
Sudan Football Association, Baladia Street, PO Box 437, 11111 Khartoum.
Founded: 1936. *FIFA:* 1948; *CAF:* 1957. *National Colours:* All red with white trim.
International matches 2024–25
Niger (h) 1-0*, Angola (a) 1-2, Ghana (a) 0-0, Ghana (h) 2-0‡, Tanzania (h) 1-0§, Tanzania (a) 0-1 (6-5p), Niger (a) 0-4¶, Angola (h) 0-0¶, Ethiopia (a) 2-0‡, Ethiopia (h) 2-1‡, Oman (a) 0-0, Senegal (h) 0-0‡, South Sudan (h) 1-1.
*Match played in South Sudan. ‡Match played in Libya. §Match played in Mauritania. ¶Match played in Togo.
League champions 2024: Al-Hilal; *2025:* Competition still being played. *Cup winners 2022:* Al-Hilal; *2023–:* Not contested.

TANZANIA
Tanzania Football Federation, Karume Memorial Stadium, Uhuru/Shaurimoyo Road, Ilala, PO Box 1574, Dar es Salaam.
Founded: 1930. *FIFA:* 1964; *CAF:* 1964. *National Colours:* Blue shirts with yellow trim, blue shorts, blue socks.
International matches 2024–25
Ethiopia (h) 0-0, Guinea (a) 2-1*, DR Congo (a) 0-1, DR Congo (h) 0-2, Sudan (a) 0-1‡, Sudan (h) 1-0 (5-6p), Ethiopia (a) 2-0§, Guinea (h) 1-0, Kenya (n) 0-2, Burkina Faso (n) 0-2, Congo (h) 3-0¶, Morocco (a) 0-2.
*Match played in Ivory Coast. ‡Match played in Mauritania. §Match played in DR Congo. ¶Match awarded due to Congo's suspension.
League champions 2024–25: Young Africans. *Cup winners 2024–25:* Young Africans.

TOGO
Federation Togolaise de Football, Route de Kegué, BP 05, Lomé.
Founded: 1960. *FIFA:* 1964; *CAF:* 1963. *National Colours:* Yellow shirts with green trim, yellow shorts, yellow socks.
International matches 2024–25
Liberia (h) 1-1, Equatorial Guinea (a) 2-2, Algeria (a) 1-5, Algeria (h) 0-1, Benin (h) 2-0, Benin (a) 1-1*, Liberia (a) 0-1, Equatorial Guinea (h) 3-0, Niger (h) 1-1, Niger (a) 0-0‡, Mauritania (h) 2-2, Senegal (a) 0-2.
*Match played in Ivory Coast. ‡Match played in Mali.
League champions 2024–25: ASC de Kara. *Cup winners 2023–24:* ASC de Kara; *2024–25:* Competition still being played.

TUNISIA
Federation Tunisienne de Football, Stade Annexe d'El Menzah, Cité Olympique, 1003 El Menzah, Tunis.
Founded: 1957. *FIFA:* 1960; *CAF:* 1960. *National Colours:* All white with red trim.
International matches 2024–25
Madagascar (h) 1-0, Gambia (a) 2-1*, Comoros (h) 0-1, Comoros (a) 1-1‡, Madagascar (a) 3-2§, Gambia (h) 0-1, Liberia (a) 1-0, Malawi (h) 2-0, Burkina Faso (h) 1-0, Morocco (a) 0-2.
*Match played in Morocco. ‡Match played in Ivory Coast. §Match played in South Africa.
League champions 2024–25: Esperance de Tunis. *Cup winners 2024–25:* Esperance de Tunis.

UGANDA
Federation of Uganda Football Associations, FUFA House, Plot No. 879, Albert Cook Road, Road, Mengo, PO Box 22518, Kampala.
Founded: 1924. *FIFA:* 1960; *CAF:* 1960. *National Colours:* Yellow shirts with red and black trim, black shorts, yellow socks with red trim.
International matches 2024–25
South Africa (a) 2-2, Congo (h) 2-0, South Sudan (h) 1-0, South Sudan (a) 2-1, South Africa (h) 0-2, Congo (a) 1-0, Burundi (a) 1-0*, Burundi (h) 1-0, Mozambique (a) 1-3‡, Guinea (h) 1-0, Gambia (n) 1-1.
*Match played in Uganda. ‡Match played in Egypt.
League champions 2024–25: Vipers. *Cup winners 2024–25:* Vipers.

ZAMBIA

Football Association of Zambia, Football House, Alick Nkhata Road, Long Acres, PO Box 34751, Lusaka.
Founded: 1929. *FIFA:* 1964; *CAF:* 1964. *National Colours:* Gold shirts with black trim, black shorts with gold trim, gold socks.
International matches 2024–25
Ivory Coast (a) 0-2, Sierra Leone (h) 3-2, Chad (h) 0-0, Chad (a) 1-0*, Ivory Coast (h) 1-0, Sierra Leone (a) 2-0‡, Russia (a) 0-5§, Congo (a) 3-0¶, Comoros (n) 0-1, Botswana (n) 3-3.
**Match played in Ivory Coast.* ‡*Match played in Liberia.* §*Match not sanctioned by FIFA due to Russia's invasion of Ukraine.* ¶*Match awarded due to Congo's suspension.*
League champions 2024–25: Power Dynamos. *Cup winners 2025:* ZESCO United.

ZIMBABWE

Zimbabwe Football Association, 53 Livingston Avenue, Causeway, PO Box CY 114, Harare. ·
Founded: 1965. *FIFA:* 1965; *CAF:* 1980. *National Colours:* All gold with green, red and black trim.
International matches 2024–25
Kenya (a) 0-0*, Cameroon (h) 0-0*, Namibia (a) 1-0‡, Namibia (h) 3-1‡, Eswatini (h) 0-3§, Eswatini (a) 0-1§, Kenya (h) 1-1‡, Cameroon (a) 1-2, Benin (h) 2-2‡, Nigeria (a) 1-1, Mauritius (n) 0-0, South Africa (a) 0-2, Mozambique (n) 3-1.
**Match played in Uganda.* ‡*Match played in South Africa.* §*Match played in Botswana.*
League champions 2024: Simba Bora; *2025:* Competition still being played. *Cup winners 2024:* Dynamos; *2025:* Competition still being played.

NORTH AND CENTRAL AMERICA AND CARIBBEAN (CONCACAF)

ANGUILLA

Anguilla Football Association, 2 Queen Elizabeth Avenue, PO Box 1318, AI-2640 The Valley.
Founded: 1990. *FIFA:* 1996; *CONCACAF:* 1996. *National Colours:* Orange shirts with dark blue trim, dark blue shorts, dark blue socks.
International matches 2024–25
Turks & Caicos Islands (a) 2-0, Belize (h) 0-1, Belize (a) 0-1, Turks & Caicos Islands (n) 1-2, British Virgin Islands (h) 0-0, British Virgin Islands (a) 1-0, Saint-Martin† (a) 1-2, St Kitts & Nevis (n) 2-4, St Vincent/Grenadines (a) 0-6, El Salvador (h) 0-3.
League champions 2025: Roaring Lions. *Cup winners:* No competition.

ANTIGUA & BARBUDA

Antigua & Barbuda Football Association, ABFA HQ, Paynters, St George.
Founded: 1928. *FIFA:* 1970; *CONCACAF:* 1972. *National Colours:* Black shirts with yellow trim, yellow shorts, yellow socks.
International matches 2024–25
Dominica (h) 1-2, Bermuda (h) 0-1, Dominican Republic (n) 0-5, Dominican Republic (n) 0-5, Bermuda (n) 1-2, Dominica (n) 0-0, Cuba (h) 0-1, Honduras (a) 0-2.
League champions 2024–25: All Saints United. *Cup winners 2022* (new competition): Grenades; *2023–:* Not contested.

ARUBA

Arubaanse Voetbal Bond, Technical Centre Angel Botta, Shaba 24, PO Box 376, Noord.
Founded: 1932. *FIFA:* 1988; *CONCACAF:* 1986. *National Colours:* Yellow shirts with sky blue sleeves, yellow shorts with sky blue trim, yellow socks.
International matches 2024–25
Sint Maarten† (n) 0-2, Puerto Rico (a) 0-1, Haiti (h) 1-3, Haiti (h) 3-5, Puerto Rico (a) 1-5, Sint Maarten† (n) 0-1, Cambodia (a) 2-1, Barbados (a) 1-1, Haiti (h) 0-5.
League champions 2024–25: Britannia. *Cup winners 2024–25:* Dakota.

BAHAMAS

Bahamas Football Association, Rosetta Street, PO Box N-8434, NP Nassau.
Founded: 1967. *FIFA:* 1968; *CONCACAF:* 1981. *National Colours:* Yellow shirts with blue sash, black shorts with blue and yellow trim, black socks.
International matches 2024–25
US Virgin Islands (a) 3-3, Barbados (n) 2-3, US Virgin Islands (n) 3-1, Barbados (a) 2-6, Grenada (a) 0-6, Costa Rica (h) 0-8*.
**Match played in Barbados.*
League champions 2024–25: Western Warriors. *Cup winners 2023–24:* Not contested; *2024–25:* Western Warriors.

BARBADOS

Barbados Football Association, Sir Garfield Sobers Sports Complex, Wildey, St Michael, BB11000 Bridgetown.
Founded: 1910. *FIFA:* 1968; *CONCACAF:* 1967. *National Colours:* All gold with royal blue trim.
International matches 2024–25
Bahamas (n) 3-2, US Virgin Islands (a) 3-0, US Virgin Islands (h) 5-0, Bahamas (h) 6-2, Guyana (h) 1-4, Guyana (a) 3-5, Dominica (h) 0-0, Dominica (a) 0-0, Aruba (h) 1-1, St Lucia (a) 1-2.
League champions 2025: Weymouth Wales. *Cup winners 2023:* Weymouth Wales; *2024–:* Not contested.

BELIZE

Football Federation of Belize, 26 Hummingbird Highway, Belmopan, PO Box 1742, Belize City.
Founded: 1980. *FIFA:* 1986; *CONCACAF:* 1986. *National Colours:* White and grey hooped shirts with red trim and blue sleeves, white shorts with blue and red trim, white socks.
International matches 2024–25
Turks & Caicos Islands (a) 4-0, Anguilla (n) 1-0, Anguilla (h) 1-0, Turks & Caicos Islands (h) 3-0, French Guiana† (h) 2-1, French Guiana† (a) 2-2*, Costa Rica (h) 0-7, Costa Rica (a) 1-6, Montserrat (a) 0-1‡, Panama (h) 0-2.
**Match played in Suriname.* ‡*Match played in Trinidad & Tobago.*
League champions 2024–25: Port Layola (Opening), Verdes (Closing). *Cup winners:* No competition.

BERMUDA

Bermuda Football Association, 1 BFA Way, Devonshire DV 01, PO Box HM 745, HM CX Hamilton.
Founded: 1928. *FIFA:* 1962; *CONCACAF:* 1967. *National Colours:* Dark blue shirts with pink trim, white shorts with dark blue trim, dark blue socks.
International matches 2024–25
Dominican Republic (n) 2-3, Antigua & Barbuda (a) 0-1, Dominica (h) 6-1, Dominica (h) 3-2, Antigua & Barbuda (n) 2-1, Dominican Republic (a) 1-6, Honduras (h) 3-5, Honduras (a) 0-2, Cayman Islands (h) 5-0, Cuba (a) 2-1.
League champions 2024–25: North Village Rams. *Cup winners 2024–25:* North Village Rams.

BONAIRE

Federashon de Futbol Boneriano, Kaya Grandi 32B, Kralendijk.
Founded: 1960. *FIFA:* Non-member; *CONCACAF:* 2014. *National Colours:* Blue shirts with white trim, white shorts with blue trim, white socks.
International matches 2024–25
St Vincent/Grenadines (h) 1-1, El Salvador (h) 1-2, Montserrat (h) 0-1*, Montserrat (a) 1-0, El Salvador (a) 0-1, St Vincent/Grenadines (n) 1-3, Niger (n) 0-6.
**Match played in Montserrat.*
League champions 2023–24: Real Rincon; *2024–25:* Competition still being played. *Cup winners 2022* (new competition): Arriba Peru; *2023, 2024:* Not contested; *2025:* Competition still being played.

BRITISH VIRGIN ISLANDS

British Virgin Islands Football Association, Chapel Hill, East End, VG 1120 Tortola.
Founded: 1974. *FIFA:* 1996; *CONCACAF:* 1996. *National Colours:* Green shirts with black trim, black shorts, black socks.

International matches 2024–25
Cayman Islands (a) 0-1, St Kitts & Nevis (n) 0-2, St Kitts & Nevis (n) 1-3, Cayman Islands (n) 0-1, Anguilla (a) 0-0, Anguilla (a) 0-1, St Vincent/Grenadines (h) 1-1, Dominica (a) 0-3, Jamaica (h) 0-1.
League champions 2024–25: Virgin Gorda United. *Cup winners:* No competition.

CANADA

Canadian Soccer Association, Place Soccer Canada, 237 Metcalfe Street, Ottawa K2P 1R2, Ontario.
Founded: 1912. *FIFA:* 1912 (resigned 1926; rejoined 1948); *CONCACAF:* 1961. *National Colours:* Red shirts with burgundy sleeves, red shorts with burgundy and white trim, red socks with burgundy and white trim.
International matches 2024–25
USA (a) 2-1, Mexico (n) 0-0, Panama (h) 2-1, Suriname (a) 1-0, Suriname (h) 3-0, Mexico (n) 0-2, USA (a) 2-1, Ukraine (h) 4-2, Ivory Coast (h) 0-0 (4-5p), Netherlands (h) 6-0, Curacao (n) 1-1, El Salvador (n) 2-0, Guatemala (n) 1-1 (5-6p).
League champions 2024: Forge FC; *2025:* Competition still being played. *Cup winners 2024:* Vancouver Whitecaps; *2025:* Competition still being played. (N.B. Canadian teams also compete in MLS and USL.)

CAYMAN ISLANDS

Cayman Islands Football Association, 219 Poindexter Road, PO Box 178, Prospect, KY1-1104 Grand Cayman.
Founded: 1966. *FIFA:* 1992; *CONCACAF:* 1990. *National Colours:* All red with white trim.
International matches 2024–25
British Virgin Islands (n) 1-0, St Kitts & Nevis (h) 1-4, British Virgin Islands (n) 1-0, St Kitts & Nevis (a) 1-1, Guadeloupe† (h) 0-6, Guadeloupe† (a) 0-1, Bermuda (a) 0-5, Honduras (h) 0-1.
League champions 2023–24: Scholar's International; *2024–25:* Competition still being played. *Cup winners 2023–24:* Academy; *2024–25:* Competition still being played.

COSTA RICA

Federacion Costarricense de Futbol, 600 mts sur del Cruce de la Panasonic, San Rafael de Alajuela, Radial a Santa Ana, 670-1000 San Jose.
Founded: 1921. *FIFA:* 1927; *CONCACAF:* 1961. *National Colours:* Burgundy shirts with red sleeves and blue trim, blue shorts with red trim, red socks with blue trim.
International matches 2024–25
Guadeloupe† (h) 3-0, Guatemala (a) 0-0, Suriname (a) 1-1, Guatemala (h) 3-0, Panama (h) 0-1, Panama (a) 2-2, USA (a) 0-3, Belize (a) 7-0, Belize (h) 6-1, Bahamas (a) 8-0*, Trinidad & Tobago (h) 2-1, Suriname (n) 4-3, Dominican Republic (n) 2-1, Mexico (n) 0-0, USA (a) 2-2 (3-4p).
*Match played in Barbados.
League champions 2024–24: Herediano (Apertura), Herediano (Clausura). *Cup winners 2023:* Alajuelense; *2024–:* Not contested.

CUBA

Asociacion de Futbol de Cuba, Estadio Pedro Marrero, Escuela Nacional de Futbol, Avenida Avenida Mario Lopez 41, 44 y 46 Municipio Playa, Havana.
Founded: 1924. *FIFA:* 1932; *CONCACAF:* 1961. *National Colours:* Red shirts with dark blue and white trim, dark blue shorts with red trim, red socks.
International matches 2024–25
Jamaica (a) 0-0, Nicaragua (h) 1-1, Trinidad & Tobago (h) 2-2, Trinidad & Tobago (a) 1-3, St Kitts & Nevis (a) 1-2, St Kitts & Nevis (h) 4-0, Trinidad & Tobago (h) 1-2, Trinidad & Tobago (a) 0-4, Antigua & Barbuda (a) 1-0, Bermuda (h) 1-2.
League champions 2023: Cienfuegos; *2024:* Competition abandoned; *2025:* Competition still being played (Apertura). *Cup winners:* No competition.

CURACAO

Federashon Futbol Korsou, Kaya Andrew Jones #49, Willemstad.
Founded: 1921 (Netherlands Antilles); 2010. *FIFA:* 1932; 2010; *CONCACAF:* 1961; 2010. *National Colours:* All white.

International matches 2024–25
St Lucia (n) 1-2, Saint-Martin† (n) 4-0, Grenada (n) 0-0, Grenada (n) 1-0, Saint-Martin† (h) 5-0, St Lucia (h) 4-1, Kazakhstan (n) 0-2, St Lucia (h) 4-0, Haiti (a) 5-1*, El Salvador (n) 0-0, Canada (n) 1-1, Honduras (n) 1-2.
*Match played in Aruba.
League champions 2022: Jong Holland; *2023–:* Competition suspended due to legal dispute. *Cup winners 2025* (new competition): Jong Colombia.

DOMINICA

Dominica Football Association, Patrick John Football House, Bath Estate, PO Box 1080, Roseau.
Founded: 1970. *FIFA:* 1994; *CONCACAF:* 1994. *National Colours:* Emerald shirts with yellow sleeves, black shorts with yellow trim, emerald socks with yellow trim.
International matches 2024–25
Antigua & Barbuda (a) 2-1, Dominican Republic (n) 0-2, Bermuda (a) 1-6, Bermuda (a) 2-3, Dominican Republic (a) 1-6, Antigua & Barbuda (n) 0-0, Barbados (h) 0-0, Barbados (h) 0-0.
League champions 2024: Dublanc; *2025:* Competition still being played. *Cup winners 2022:* South East United; *2023–:* Not contested; *2024* (new competition): Dublanc.

DOMINICAN REPUBLIC

Federacion Dominicana de Futbol, Centro Olimpico Juan Pablo Duarte, Apartado Postal 1953, Santo Domingo.
Founded: 1953. *FIFA:* 1958; *CONCACAF:* 1964. *National Colours:* Blue shirts with red and white trim, blue shorts, blue socks.
International matches 2024–25
Bermuda (n) 3-2, Dominica (n) 2-0, Antigua & Barbuda (n) 5-0, Antigua & Barbuda (n) 5-0, Dominica (h) 6-1, Bermuda (h) 6-1, Puerto Rico (a) 2-2, Puerto Rico (h) 2-0, Guatemala (a) 2-4, Dominica (h) 5-0, Mexico (n) 2-3, Costa Rica (n) 1-2, Suriname (n) 0-0.
League champions 2024: Cibao; *2025* (transitional competition): Cibao. *Cup winners 2016:* Cibao; *2017–:* Not contested.

EL SALVADOR

Federacion Salvadorena de Futbol, Avenida Jose Matias Delgado, Frente al Centro Español, Colonia Escalon, Zona 10, 1029 San Salvador.
Founded: 1935. *FIFA:* 1938; *CONCACAF:* 1961. *National Colours:* Blue shirts with black trim, black shorts, blue socks.
International matches 2024–25
Guatemala (n) 1-0, Montserrat (n) 4-1, Bonaire† (n) 2-1, St Vincent/Grenadines (a) 3-2, St Vincent/Grenadines (a) 1-2, Bonaire† (h) 1-0, Montserrat (n) 1-0, Guatemala (n) 1-1, Anguilla (a) 3-0, Suriname (n) 1-1, Curacao (n) 0-0, Honduras (n) 0-2, Canada (n) 0-2.
League champions 2024–25: Once Deportivo (Apertura), Alianza (Clausura). *Cup winners: 2018–19:* Santa Tecla; *2019–:* Not contested.

FRENCH GUIANA

Ligue de Football de la Guyane, BP 765, Stade de Baduel, Cayenne 97322 CEDEX.
Founded: 1962. *FIFA:* Non-member; *CONCACAF:* 2013. *National Colours:* Yellow shirts, blue shorts, yellow socks.
International matches 2024–25
Haiti (h) 1-1*, Nicaragua (h) 0-1, Trinidad & Tobago (a) 0-0, Honduras (n) 2-3, Nicaragua (a) 2-3, Belize (a) 1-2, Belize (h) 2-2‡.
*Match played 23.3.24; result omitted from previous edition. ‡Match played in Suriname.
League champions 2024–25: US Sinnamary. *Cup winners 2024–25:* AS Etoile Matoury.

GRENADA

Grenada Football Association, National Stadium, Queens Park, PO Box 326, St George's.
Founded: 1924. *FIFA:* 1978; *CONCACAF:* 1978. *National Colours:* Red shirts with green trim, red shorts, red shorts, red socks.

International matches 2024–25
Saint-Martin† (h) 2-0, St Lucia (h) 1-2, Curacao (n) 0-0, Curacao (n) 0-1, St Lucia (n) 4-0, Saint-Martin† (n) 0-3, St Vincent/Grenadines (a) 1-1, St Vincent/Grenadines (a) 1-1, Russia (a) 0-5*, Anguilla (h) 2-0, Bahamas (h) 6-0, St Kitts & Nevis (a) 3-2.
*Match not sanctioned by FIFA due to Russia's invasion of Ukraine.
League champions 2024–25: Paradise. *Cup winners 2024:* Paradise.

GUADELOUPE

Ligue Guadeloupéenne de Football, Rue de la Ville d'Orly, Bergevin, 97110 Pointe-à-Pitre.
Founded: 1958. *FIFA:* Non-member; *CONCACAF:* 2013. *National Colours:* All red.
International matches 2024–25
Costa Rica (a) 0-3, Suriname (h) 1-0, Martinique† (h) 0-1, Martinique† (h) 0-0, Cayman Islands (a) 6-0, Cayman Islands (h) 1-0, Nicaragua (h) 1-0, Nicaragua (a) 1-0, Panama (n) 2-5, Jamaica (n) 1-2, Guatemala (n) 2-3.
League champions 2024–25: CS Moulien. *Cup winners 2021:* Amical Club; *2022, 2023:* Not contested; *2024:* AS Gosier; *2025:* Siroco.

GUATEMALA

Federacion Nacional de Futbol de Guatemala, 2a Calle 15-57, Zona 15, Boulevard Vista Hermosa, 01015 Guatemala City.
Founded: 1919. *FIFA:* 1946; *CONCACAF:* 1961. *National Colours:* White shirts with blue sash, white shorts with blue trim, white socks.
International matches 2024–25
El Salvador (n) 0-1, Martinique† (h) 3-1, Costa Rica (h) 0-0, Guyana (a) 3-1, Costa Rica (a) 0-3, Honduras (n) 2-1, Guyana (a) 2-3*, Guyana (h) 2-0, El Salvador (h) 1-1, Dominican Republic (h) 4-2, Jamaica (a) 0-3, Jamaica (n) 1-0, Panama (n) 0-1, Guadeloupe† (n) 3-2, Canada (n) 1-1 (6-5p), USA (a) 1-2.
*Match played in Barbados.
League champions 2024–25: Xelaju (Apertura), Antigua (Clausura). *Cup winners 2018–19:* Coban Imperial; *2019–:* Not contested.

GUYANA

Guyana Football Federation, Lot 17, Dadanawa Street, Section 'K' Campbellville, Georgetown.
Founded: 1902. *FIFA:* 1970; *CONCACAF:* 1969. *National Colours:* Yellow shirts with green and red trim, yellow shorts, red socks.
International matches 2024–25
Suriname (h) 1-3, Martinique† (a) 2-2, Guatemala (h) 1-3, Suriname (a) 1-5, Barbados (a) 4-1, Barbados (h) 5-3, Guatemala (h) 3-2*, Guatemala (a) 0-2, Nicaragua (a) 0-1, Montserrat (h) 3-0.
*Match played in Barbados.
League champions 2024: Guyana Defence Force; *2025:* Competition still being played. *Cup winners 2015:* Slingerz; *2016–:* Not contested.

HAITI

Federation Haitienne de Football, 26 Rue Mercier-Laham, Delmas 60, Port-au-Prince.
Founded: 1904. *FIFA:* 1934; *CONCACAF:* 1961. *National Colours:* Blue shirts with red trim, blue shorts, blue socks with red tops.
International matches 2024–25
French Guiana† (h) 1-1*, Puerto Rico (a) 4-1, Sint Maarten† (n) 6-0, Aruba (a) 3-1, Aruba (a) 5-3, Sint Maarten† (n) 8-0, Puerto Rico (a) 3-0, Azerbaijan (a) 3-0, Aruba (a) 5-0, Curacao (h) 1-5‡, Saudi Arabia (n) 0-1, Trinidad & Tobago (n) 1-1, USA (a) 1-2.
*Match played 23.3.24; result omitted from previous edition. ‡Match played in Aruba.
League champions 2025: Juventus. *Cup winners 2014:* America des Cayes; *2015–:* Not contested.

HONDURAS

Federacion Nacional Autonoma de Futbol de Honduras, Colonia Florencia Norte, Avenida Roble, Edificio Plaza America, PO Box 827, Tegucigalpa.
Founded: 1935. *FIFA:* 1946; *CONCACAF:* 1961. *National Colours:* All white with blue trim.

International matches 2024–25
Trinidad & Tobago (h) 4-0, Jamaica (h) 1-2, French Guiana† (a) 3-2, Jamaica (a) 0-0, Mexico (h) 2-0, Mexico (a) 0-4, Guatemala (n) 1-2, Bermuda (a) 5-3, Bermuda (h) 2-0, Cayman Islands (a) 1-0, Antigua & Barbuda (h) 2-0, Canada (n) 0-6, El Salvador (n) 2-0, Curacao (n) 2-1, Panama (n) 1-1 (5-4p), Mexico (n) 0-1.
League champions 2024–25: Motagua (Apertura), Olimpia (Clausura). *Cup winners 2018:* Platense; *2019–:* Not contested.

JAMAICA

Jamaica Football Federation Ltd, 20 St Lucia Crescent, Kingston 5.
Founded: 1910. *FIFA:* 1962; *CONCACAF:* 1963. *National Colours:* Gold shirts with green and black trim, gold shorts with green trim, gold socks.
International matches 2024–25
Cuba (h) 0-0, Honduras (a) 2-1, Nicaragua (a) 2-0, Honduras (h) 0-0, USA (h) 0-1, USA (a) 2-4, Trinidad & Tobago (h) 1-0, Trinidad & Tobago (h) 1-1, St Vincent/Grenadines (a) 1-1, St Vincent/Grenadines (h) 3-0, Trinidad & Tobago (n) 3-2, Nigeria (n) 2-2 (4-5p), British Virgin Islands (a) 1-0, Guatemala (h) 3-0, Guatemala (n) 0-1, Guadeloupe† (n) 2-1, Panama (n) 1-4.
League champions 2024–25: Cavalier. *Cup winners 2023:* Portmore United; *2024–:* Not contested.

MARTINIQUE

Ligue de Football de la Martinique, 2 rue Saint-John Perse, Boite Postale 307, Morne Tartenson, 97203 Fort-de-France.
Founded: 1953. *FIFA:* Non-member; *CONCACAF:* 2013. *National Colours:* White shirts with red and black trim, white shorts with red trim, white socks.
International matches 2024–25
Guatemala (a) 1-3, Guyana (h) 2-2, Guadeloupe† (a) 1-0, Guadeloupe† (h) 0-0, Guyana (a) 0-1, Suriname (h) 0-1.
League champions 2024–25: RC Saint-Joseph. *Cup winners 2023–24:* Club Franciscain; *2024–25:* Club Franciscain.

MEXICO

Federacion Mexicana de Futbol Asociacion, Avenida Arboleda 101, Ex Hacienda Santin, San Mateo Otzacatipan, CP 50210 Toluca, Estado de Mexico.
Founded: 1927. *FIFA:* 1929; *CONCACAF:* 1961. *National Colours:* Burgundy shirts with green trim, burgundy shorts with green trim, burgundy socks.
International matches 2024–25
New Zealand (n) 3-0, Canada (n) 0-0, USA (h) 2-0, Honduras (a) 0-2, Honduras (h) 4-0, Canada (n) 2-0, Panama (n) 2-1, Switzerland (n) 2-4, Turkey (n) 1-0, Dominican Republic (n) 3-2, Suriname (n) 2-0, Costa Rica (n) 0-0, Saudi Arabia (n) 2-0, Honduras (n) 1-0, USA (a) 2-1.
League champions 2024–25: América (Apertura), Toluca (Clausura). *Cup winners 2019–20:* Monterrey; *2020–:* Not contested.

MONTSERRAT

Montserrat Football Association Inc., PO Box 505, MSR 1250 Blakes, Plymouth.
Founded: 1994. *FIFA:* 1996; *CONCACAF:* 1996. *National Colours:* Green shirts with white trim, green shorts, green socks.
International matches 2024–25
El Salvador (n) 1-4, St Vincent/Grenadines (n) 0-2, Bonaire† (n) 1-0, Bonaire† (n) 0-1, St Vincent/Grenadines (n) 1-2, El Salvador (n) 0-1, Belize (h) 1-0*, Guyana (a) 0-3.
*Match played in Trinidad & Tobago.
League champions 2016: Royal Montserrat Police Force; *2017–:* Not contested. *Cup winners:* No competition.

NICARAGUA

Federacion Nicaraguense de Futbol, Porton Principal del Hospital Bautista 1 Cuadra Abajo, 1 Cuadra al Sur y 1/2 Cuadra Abajo, Apartado Postal 976, Managua.
Founded: 1931. *FIFA:* 1950; *CONCACAF:* 1961. *National Colours:* All blue with white trim.

International matches 2024–25
French Guiana† (a) 1-0, Cuba (a) 1-1, Jamaica (h) 0-2, French Guiana† (h) 3-2, Guadeloupe† (a) 0-1, Guadeloupe† (h) 0-1, Puerto Rico (n) 1-1, Guyana (h) 1-1, Panama (a) 0-3.
League champions 2024–25: Diriangen (Apertura), Managua (Clausura). *Cup winners 2024:* Diriangen; *2025:* Competition still being played.

PANAMA
Federacion Panamena de Futbol, Ciudad Deportiva Irving Saladino, Corregimiento de Juan Diaz, Apartado Postal 0835-394, Zona 10, Ciudad de Panama.
Founded: 1937. *FIFA:* 1938; *CONCACAF:* 1961. *National Colours:* All red with yellow trim.
International matches 2024–25
USA (a) 0-2, Canada (a) 1-2, Costa Rica (a) 1-0, Costa Rica (h) 2-2, Chile (a) 1-6, USA (a) 1-0, Mexico (n) 1-2, Belize (a) 2-0, Nicaragua (h) 3-0, Guadeloupe† (n) 5-2, Guatemala (n) 1-0, Jamaica (n) 4-1, Honduras (n) 1-1 (4-5p).
League champions 2024: Tauro (Apertura), CAI de La Chorrera (Clausura); *2025:* Plaza Amador (Apertura). *Cup winners 2018–19:* Costa del Este; *2019–:* Not contested.

PUERTO RICO
Federacion Puertorriquena de Futbol, PO Box 367567, PR 00936 San Juan.
Founded: 1940. *FIFA:* 1960; *CONCACAF:* 1964. *National Colours:* Red and white striped shirts with red sleeves, blue shorts with white trim, blue socks.
International matches 2024–25
Haiti (h) 1-4, Aruba (h) 1-0, Sint Maarten† (n) 2-3, Sint Maarten† (n) 2-1, Aruba (h) 5-1, Haiti (h) 0-3, Dominican Republic (h) 2-2, Dominican Republic (a) 0-2, Nicaragua (n) 1-1, Guyana (a) 0-1, St Vincent/Grenadines (h) 2-1.
League champions 2024–25: Metropolitan Football Academy. *Cup winners 2019:* Bayamon; *2020–:* Not contested.

SAINT-MARTIN
Saint-Martin Football Association, PO Box 811-97059, Sandy Ground, Saint-Martin CEDEX.
Founded: 1986. *FIFA:* Non-member; *CONCACAF:* 2013. *National Colours:* Red shirts with white trim, red shorts, white socks.
International matches 2024–25
Grenada (a) 0-2, Curacao (n) 0-4, St Lucia (a) 1-2, St Lucia (a) 4-0, Curacao (a) 0-5, Grenada (n) 3-0, Anguilla (h) 2-1, St Kitts & Nevis (h) 4-2.
League champions 2023–24: Junior Stars; *2024–25:* Junior Stars. *Cup winners:* No competition.

SINT MAARTEN
Sint Maarten Soccer Association, Airport Road 69, Philipsburg.
Founded: 1986. *FIFA:* Non-member; *CONCACAF:* 2013. *National Colours:* Red shirts with blue trim, red shorts, red socks.
International matches 2024–25
Aruba (n) 2-0, Haiti (n) 0-6, Puerto Rico (n) 3-2, Puerto Rico (n) 1-2, Haiti (n) 0-8, Aruba (n) 1-0.
League champions 2024–25: SCSA Eagles. *Cup winners:* No competition.

ST KITTS & NEVIS
St Kitts & Nevis Football Association, Lozack Road, PO Box 465, Basseterre.
Founded: 1932. *FIFA:* 1992; *CONCACAF:* 1992. *National Colours:* Green shirts with red trim, green shorts, green socks.
International matches 2024–25
Cayman Islands (a) 4-1, British Virgin Islands (n) 2-0, British Virgin Islands (h) 3-1, Cayman Islands (n) 1-0, Cuba (h) 2-1, Cuba (a) 0-4, St Vincent/Grenadines (h) 1-3, Anguilla (n) 4-2, Saint-Martin† (a) 1-4, St Vincent/Grenadines (a) 0-3, St Vincent/Grenadines (a) 1-1, Trinidad & Tobago (a) 2-6, Grenada (h) 2-3.
League champions 2024: St Paul's United Strikers; *2025:* Competition still being played. *Cup winners 2024:* United Old Road Jets; *2025:* Village Superstars.

ST LUCIA
St Lucia National Football Association, Barnard Hill, PO Box 255, Castries.
Founded: 1979. *FIFA:* 1988; *CONCACAF:* 1986. *National Colours:* All blue.
International matches 2024–25
Curacao (n) 2-1, Grenada (a) 2-1, Saint-Martin† (h) 2-1, Saint-Martin† (h) 0-4, Grenada (n) 0-4, Curacao (a) 1-4, Curacao (a) 0-4, Barbados (h) 2-1.
League champions 2023: Gros Islet; *2024:* La Clery; *2025:* Competition still being played. *Cup winners 2023:* Soufriere; *2024–:* Not contested.

ST VINCENT & THE GRENADINES
St Vincent & the Grenadines Football Federation, Corner of Grenville and Higginson Street, PO Box 1278, Kingstown.
Founded: 1979. *FIFA:* 1988; *CONCACAF:* 1986. *National Colours:* Yellow shirts with blue trim, yellow shorts, yellow socks.
International matches 2024–25
Bonaire† (a) 1-1, Montserrat (n) 2-0, El Salvador (n) 2-3, El Salvador (n) 2-1, Montserrat (n) 2-1, Bonaire† (n) 3-1, Grenada (h) 1-1, Grenada (h) 1-1, Jamaica (h) 1-1, Jamaica (a) 0-3, St Kitts & Nevis (a) 3-0, St Kitts & Nevis (a) 1-1, Anguilla (h) 6-0, Puerto Rico (a) 1-2.
League champions 2022–23: JeBelle; *2023–24:* Not contested; *2024–25:* North Leeward Predators. *Cup winners:* No competition.

SURINAME
Surinaamse Voetbal Bond, Letitia Vriesdelaan 7, PO Box 1223, Paramaribo.
Founded: 1920. *FIFA:* 1929; *CONCACAF:* 1961. *National Colours:* All red with green trim.
International matches 2024–25
Guyana (a) 3-1, Guadeloupe† (a) 0-1, Costa Rica (h) 1-1, Guyana (h) 5-1, Canada (h) 0-1, Canada (a) 0-3, Martinique† (h) 1-0, Martinique† (a) 1-0, Puerto Rico (h) 1-0, El Salvador (a) 1-1, Costa Rica (n) 3-4, Mexico (n) 0-2, Dominican Republic (n) 0-0.
League champions 2024: Robinhood; *2025:* Competition still being played. *Cup winners 2023–24:* Robinhood; *2024–25:* Competition still being played.

TRINIDAD & TOBAGO
Trinidad & Tobago Football Association, Ato Boldon Stadium, Couva, Trinidad.
Founded: 1908. *FIFA:* 1964; *CONCACAF:* 1964. *National Colours:* Red shirts with white trim, black shorts with white trim, red socks.
International matches 2024–25
Honduras (a) 0-4, French Guiana† (h) 0-0, Cuba (a) 2-2, Cuba (h) 3-1, Saudi Arabia (a) 1-3, Jamaica (a) 0-1, Jamaica (a) 1-1, Cuba (a) 2-1, Cuba (h) 4-0, Jamaica (n) 2-3, Ghana (n) 0-4, St Kitts & Nevis (h) 6-2, Costa Rica (a) 1-2, USA (a) 0-5, Haiti (n) 1-1, Saudi Arabia (n) 1-1.
League champions 2024–25: Defence Force. *Cup winners 2017:* Williams Connection; *2018–:* Not contested.

TURKS & CAICOS ISLANDS
Turks & Caicos Islands Football Association, TCIFA National Academy, Venetian Road, PO Box 626, Providenciales.
Founded: 1996. *FIFA:* 1998; *CONCACAF:* 1996. *National Colours:* All navy blue with yellow trim.
International matches 2024–25
Anguilla (h) 0-2, Belize (h) 0-4, Anguilla (n) 2-1, Belize (a) 0-3.
League champions 2024–25: SWA Sharks. *Cup winners 2024:* SWA Sharks; *2025:* Competition still being played.

UNITED STATES OF AMERICA (USA)
US Soccer Federation, 303 E Wacker Drive, Suite 1200, IL 60601 Chicago.
Founded: 1913. *FIFA:* 1914; *CONCACAF:* 1961. *National Colours:* White shirts with red and blue trim, blue shorts with red trim, white socks.
International matches 2024–25
Canada (h) 1-2, New Zealand (h) 1-1, Panama (h) 2-0, Mexico (a) 0-2, Jamaica (a) 1-0, Jamaica (a) 4-2, Venezuela (h) 3-1, Costa Rica (h) 3-0, Panama (h) 0-1, Canada (h) 1-2, Turkey (h) 1-2, Switzerland (h) 0-4,

Trinidad & Tobago (a) 5-0, Saudi Arabia (n) 1-0, Haiti (h) 2-1, Costa Rica (h) 2-2 (4-3p), Guatemala (h) 2-1, Mexico (h) 1-2.

MLS champions 2024: LA Galaxy; *2025:* Competition still being played. *Cup winners 2024:* Los Angeles; *2025:* Competition still being played.

(N.B. Teams from USA and Canada compete in MLS and USL.)

US VIRGIN ISLANDS

USVI Soccer Federation, 23-1 Bethlehem, PO Box 2346, 00851 Christiansted, St Croix.

Founded: 1987; constituted 1992. *FIFA:* 1998; *CONCACAF:* 1987. *National Colours:* Blue shirts with white sleeves and blue trim, blue shorts with white trim, blue socks.

International matches 2024–25

Bahamas (h) 3-3, Barbados (h) 0-3, Barbados (a) 0-5, Bahamas (n) 1-3.

League champions 2024: Rovers; *2025:* Competition still being played. *Cup winners:* No competition.

SOUTH AMERICA (CONMEBOL)

ARGENTINA

Asociacion del Futbol Argentina, Viamonte 1366/76, 1053 Buenos Aires.

Founded: 1893. *FIFA:* 1912; *CONMEBOL:* 1916. *National Colours:* Light blue and white striped shirts with white sleeves, white shorts with blue trim, white socks.

International matches 2024–25

Chile (h) 3-0, Colombia (a) 1-2, Venezuela (a) 1-1, Bolivia (h) 6-0, Paraguay (a) 1-2, Peru (h) 1-0, Uruguay (a) 1-0, Brazil (h) 4-1, Chile (a) 1-0, Colombia (h) 1-1.

League champions 2024: Velez Sarsfield; *2025:* Platense (Apertura). *Cup winners 2024:* Central Cordoba (SdE); *2025:* Competition still being played.

BOLIVIA

Federacion Boliviana de Futbol, Avenida Libertador Bolivar 1168, Casilla 484, Cochabamba.

Founded: 1925. *FIFA:* 1926; *CONMEBOL:* 1926. *National Colours:* Dark green shirts with white trim, white shorts with dark green trim, white socks with dark green trim.

International matches 2024–25

Venezuela (h) 4-0, Chile (a) 2-1, Colombia (h) 1-0, Argentina (a) 0-6, Ecuador (a) 0-4, Paraguay (h) 2-2, Peru (a) 1-3, Uruguay (h) 0-0, Venezuela (a) 0-2, Chile (h) 2-0.

League champions 2024: Bolivar; *2025:* Competition still being played. *Cup winners 2016:* Club Destroyers; *2017–24:* Not contested; *2025:* Resumed competition being played.

BRAZIL

Confederacao Brasileira de Futebol, Avenida Luis Carlos Prestes 130, Barra da Tijuca, 22775-055 Rio de Janeiro.

Founded: 1914. *FIFA:* 1923; *CONMEBOL:* 1916. *National Colours:* Yellow shirts with green trim, blue shorts with green trim, white socks with blue and green trim.

International matches 2024–25

Ecuador (h) 1-3, Paraguay (a) 0-1, Chile (a) 2-1, Peru (h) 4-0, Venezuela (h) 1-1, Uruguay (h) 1-1, Colombia (h) 2-1, Argentina (a) 1-4, Ecuador (a) 0-0, Paraguay (h) 1-0.

League champions 2024: Botafogo; *2025:* Competition still being played. *Cup winners 2024:* Flamengo; *2025:* Competition still being played.

CHILE

Federacion de Futbol de Chile, Avenida Quilin 5635, Comuna Penalolen, Santiago de Chile.

Founded: 1895. *FIFA:* 1913; *CONMEBOL:* 1916. *National Colours:* Red shirts with blue and white trim, blue shorts with white trim, red socks.

International matches 2024–25

Argentina (a) 0-3, Bolivia (h) 1-2, Brazil (h) 1-2, Colombia (a) 0-4, Peru (a) 0-0, Venezuela (h) 4-2, Panama (h) 6-1, Paraguay (a) 0-1, Ecuador (h) 0-0, Argentina (h) 0-1, Chile (a) 0-2.

League champions 2024: Colo-Colo; *2025:* Competition still being played. *Cup winners 2024:* Universidad de Chile; *2025:* Competition still being played.

COLOMBIA

Federacion Colombiana de Futbol, Carrera 45A No. 94-06, Pisos 6, 7 y 8, Bogota.

Founded: 1924. *FIFA:* 1936; *CONMEBOL:* 1936. *National Colours:* Yellow shirts with orange trim, blue shorts with orange trim, orange socks.

International matches 2024–25

Peru (a) 1-1, Argentina (h) 2-1, Bolivia (a) 0-1, Chile (h) 4-0, Uruguay (a) 2-3, Ecuador (h) 0-1, Brazil (a) 1-2, Paraguay (h) 2-2, Peru (h) 0-0, Argentina (a) 1-1.

League champions 2024: Atletico Bucaramanga (Apertura), Atletico Nacional (Finalizacion); *2025:* Santa Fe (Apertura). *Cup winners 2024:* Atletico Nacional; *2025:* Competition still being played.

ECUADOR

Federacion Ecuatoriana del Futbol, Avenida Las Aguas y Calle Alianza, PO Box 09-01-7447, 593 Guayaquil.

Founded: 1925. *FIFA:* 1926; *CONMEBOL:* 1927. *National Colours:* Yellow shirts with dark blue sash, dark blue shorts, dark blue socks.

International matches 2024–25

Brazil (a) 0-1, Peru (h) 1-0, Paraguay (h) 0-0, Uruguay (a) 0-0, Bolivia (h) 4-0, Colombia (a) 1-0, Venezuela (h) 2-1, Chile (a) 0-0, Brazil (h) 0-0, Peru (a) 0-0.

League champions 2024: LDU Quito; *2025:* Competition still being played. *Cup winners 2024:* El Nacional; *2025:* Competition still being played.

PARAGUAY

Asociacion Paraguaya de Futbol, Avenida Medallistas Olimpicos No.1, Parque Olimpico, Nu Guasu de la Ciudad de Luque, Asuncion.

Founded: 1906. *FIFA:* 1925; *CONMEBOL:* 1921. *National Colours:* Red and white striped shirts with blue trim, blue shorts with red trim, blue socks.

International matches 2024–25

Uruguay (a) 0-0, Brazil (h) 1-0, Ecuador (a) 0-0, Venezuela (h) 2-1, Argentina (h) 2-1, Bolivia (a) 2-2, Chile (h) 1-0, Colombia (a) 2-2, Uruguay (h) 2-0, Brazil (a) 0-1.

League champions 2024: Libertad (Apertura), Olimpia (Clausura); *2025:* Libertad (Apertura). *Cup winners 2024:* Libertad; *2025:* Competition still being played.

PERU

Federacion Peruana de Futbol, Avenida Aviacion 2085, RUC: 20156399036 San Luis, Lima.

Founded: 1922. *FIFA:* 1924; *CONMEBOL:* 1925. *National Colours:* White shirts with red sash, white shorts with red trim, white socks.

International matches 2024–25

Colombia (h) 1-1, Ecuador (a) 0-1, Uruguay (h) 1-0, Brazil (a) 0-4, Chile (h) 0-0, Argentina (h) 0-1, Bolivia (h) 3-1, Venezuela (a) 0-1, Colombia (a) 0-0, Ecuador (h) 0-0.

League champions 2024: Universitario; *2025:* Competition still being played. *Cup winners 2021:* Sporting Cristal; *2022–25:* Competition suspended pending league restructure.

URUGUAY

Asociacion Uruguaya de Futbol, Guayabo 1531, 11200 Montevideo.

Founded: 1900. *FIFA:* 1923; *CONMEBOL:* 1916. *National Colours:* Sky blue shirts with white and black trim, black shorts, black socks.

International matches 2024–25

Paraguay (h) 0-0, Venezuela (a) 0-0, Peru (a) 0-1, Ecuador (h) 0-0, Colombia (h) 3-2, Brazil (a) 1-1, Argentina (h) 0-1, Bolivia (a) 0-0, Paraguay (a) 0-2, Venezuela (h) 2-0.

League champions 2024: Penarol; *2025:* Competition still being played. *Cup winners 2024:* Defensor Sporting; *2025:* Competition still being played.

VENEZUELA

Federacion Venezolana de Futbol, Avenida Santos Erminy, 1a Calle las Delicias Torre Mega II, Sabana Grande, 1050 Caracas.

Founded: 1925. *FIFA:* 1952; *CONMEBOL:* 1953. *National Colours:* All burgundy with gold trim.

International matches 2024–25

Bolivia (a) 0-4, Uruguay (h) 0-0, Argentina (h) 1-1, Paraguay (a) 1-2, Brazil (h) 1-1, Chile (a) 2-4, USA (a) 1-3, Ecuador (a) 1-2, Peru (h) 1-0, Bolivia (h) 2-0, Uruguay (a) 0-2.

League champions 2024: Deportivo Tachira; *2025:* Competition still being played. *Cup winners 2024:* Deportivo La Guaira; *2025:* Competition still being played.

OCEANIA (OFC)

AMERICAN SAMOA

Football Federation American Samoa, Pago Park, PO Box 982413, AS 96799 Pago Pago.
Founded: 1984. *FIFA:* 1998; *OFC:* 1998. *National Colours:* All dark blue with white trim.
International matches 2024–25
Samoa (h) 0-2, Cook Islands (n) 2-1.
League champions 2024: Pago Youth; *2025:* Competition still being played. *Cup winners 2014:* Utelai Youth; *2015–:* Not contested.

COOK ISLANDS

Cook Islands Football Association, Matavera Main Road, PO Box 29, Avarua, Rarotonga.
Founded: 1971. *FIFA:* 1994; *OFC:* 1994. *National Colours:* All green.
International matches 2024–25
Tonga (n) 1-3, American Samoa (n) 1-2.
League champions 2024: Tupapa Maraerenga; *2025:* Competition still being played. *Cup winners 2024:* Tupapa Maraerenga; *2025:* Competition still being played.

FIJI

Fiji Football Association, Taramati Street, Vatuwaqa, PO Box 2514, Suva.
Founded: 1938. *FIFA:* 1964; *OFC:* 1966. *National Colours:* White shirts with black trim, black shorts with white trim, white socks.
International matches 2024–25
Solomon Islands (h) 1-0, Hong Kong (h) 1-1, Solomon Islands (h) 1-0, Papua New Guinea (a) 3-3, New Caledonia (n) 1-1, Vanuatu (n) 1-1, Papua New Guinea (n) 1-1, Solomon Islands (a) 3-1, New Zealand (a) 0-7.
League champions 2024: Rewa; *2025:* Competition still being played. *Cup winners 2023:* Labasa; *2024:* Lautoka; *2025:* Competition still being played.

KIRIBATI

Kiribati Islands Football Federation, PO Box 416, Betio, Tarawa.
Founded: 1980. *FIFA:* Non-member. *OFC:* Associate member. *National Colours:* Red shirts with yellow trim, red shorts with yellow trim, white socks with black trim.
International matches 2024–25
None played since 2011.
League champions 2023: Betio Town Council; *2024–:* Not contested. *Cup winners 2024:* Tekinati; 2025: Not contested.

NEW CALEDONIA

Federation Caledonienne de Football, 7 bis, Rue Suffren, Quartier Latin, BP 560, 99845 Noumea.
Founded: 1928. *FIFA:* 2004; *OFC:* 2004. *National Colours:* All white with grey trim.
International matches 2024–25
Papua New Guinea (n) 3-1, Solomon Islands (n) 3-2, Fiji (n) 1-1, Tahiti (n) 3-0, New Zealand (a) 0-3.
League champions 2023: AS Magenta; *2024:* Competition abandoned; *2025:* Competition still being played. *Cup winners 2023:* Hienghene Sport; *2024–:* Not contested.

NEW ZEALAND

New Zealand Football, Football House, North Harbour Stadium, Stadium Drive, PO Box 301-043, Albany, Auckland.
Founded: 1891. *FIFA:* 1948; *OFC:* 1966. *National Colours:* White shirts with light blue trim, white shorts, white socks.
International matches 2024–25
Mexico (n) 0-3, USA (a) 1-1, Tahiti (h) 3-0, Malaysia (h) 4-0, Vanuatu (h) 8-1, Samoa (h) 8-0, Fiji (h) 7-0, New Caledonia (h) 3-0, Ivory Coast (n) 1-0, Ukraine (n) 1-2.
League champions 2024: Auckland City; *2025:* Competition still being played. *Cup winners 2024:* Wellington Olympic; *2025:* Competition still being played.

PAPUA NEW GUINEA

Papua New Guinea Football Association, National Capital District, PO Box 371, Port Moresby.
Founded: 1962. *FIFA:* 1966. *OFC:* 1966. *National Colours:* Red shirts with black sleeves, red shorts, red socks.
International matches 2024–25
New Caledonia (n) 1-3, Fiji (h) 3-3, Solomon Islands (h) 1-2, Fiji (n) 1-1, Solomon Islands (a) 3-2, Vanuatu (n) 2-1.
League champions 2024: Hekari United; *2025:* Competition still being played. *Cup winners 2019:* Morobe; *2020–:* Not contested.

SAMOA

Football Federation Samoa, PO Box 1682, Tuana'imato, Apia.
Founded: 1968. *FIFA:* 1986; *OFC:* 1986. *National Colours:* All blue.
International matches 2024–25
American Samoa (h) 2-0, Tonga (h) 2-1, Vanuatu (a) 1-4, Tahiti (n) 0-3, New Zealand (a) 0-8.
League champions 2024: Vaipuna; *2025:* Competition still being played. *Cup winners 2018:* Manu-fili; *2019–:* Not contested.

SOLOMON ISLANDS

Solomon Islands Football Federation, Allan Boso Complex, Ranadi Highway, PO Box 854, Honiara.
Founded: 1978. *FIFA:* 1988; *OFC:* 1988. *National Colours:* Yellow shirts with blue trim, blue shorts, yellow socks.
International matches 2024–25
Fiji (a) 0-1, Hong Kong (n) 0-3, Fiji (a) 0-1, New Caledonia (n) 2-3, Papua New Guinea (a) 2-1, Vanuatu (h) 4-1, Papua New Guinea (h) 2-3, Fiji (h) 1-3.
League champions 2024: Central Coast; *2025:* Competition still being played. *Cup winners 2022:* Malaita Eagles; *2023–:* Not contested.

TAHITI

Federation Tahitienne de Football, 751 Rue Paul Berniere a Pirae, BP 50358, 98716 Pirae.
Founded: 1989. *FIFA:* 1990; *OFC:* 1990. *National Colours:* Red shirts with white patterned sleeves, red shorts, red socks.
International matches 2024–25
New Zealand (n) 0-3, Samoa (n) 3-0, Vanuatu (n) 2-0, New Caledonia (n) 0-3.
League champions 2024–25: AS Venus. *Cup winners 2024:* AS Dragon; *2025:* Competition still being played.

TONGA

Tonga Football Association, Loto-Tonga Soka Centre, Valungafulu Road, 'Atele, PO Box 852, Nuku'alofa.
Founded: 1965. *FIFA:* 1994; *OFC:* 1994. *National Colours:* All red with white trim.
International matches 2024–25
Cook Islands (n) 3-1, Samoa (a) 1-2.
League champions 2023: Veitongo; *2024–:* Not contested.
Cup winners 2020: Veitongo; *2021–:* Not contested.

TUVALU

Tuvalu Island Football Association, Tuvalu Sports Ground, Funafuti, tnfatu8@gmail.com.
Founded: 1979. *FIFA:* Non-member. *OFC:* Associate member. *National Colours:* Sky blue shirts with yellow trim, sky blue shorts, sky blue socks with yellow and white trim.
International matches 2024–25
None played.
League champions 2023: Nauti; *2024–:* Not contested. *Cup winners 2024:* Manu Laeva; *2025:* Competition still being played.

VANUATU

Vanuatu Football Federation, VFF House, Anabrou, PO Box 266, 678 Port Vila.
Founded: 1934. *FIFA:* 1988; *OFC:* 1988. *National Colours:* Yellow shirts with black trim, black shorts with yellow trim, yellow socks.
International matches 2024–25
Samoa (h) 4-1, New Zealand (a) 1-8, Tahiti (n) 0-2, Papua New Guinea (n) 1-2.
League champions 2023–24: Ifra Black Bird; *2024–25:* Galaxy. *Cup winners 2025:* Galaxy.

OLYMPIC FOOTBALL 2024 – PARIS

MEN'S COMPETITION

*After extra time.

GROUP A

Guinea v New Zealand		1-2
France v USA		3-0
New Zealand v USA		1-4
France v Guinea		1-0
New Zealand v France		0-3
USA v Guinea		3-0

Group A Table	P	W	D	L	F	A	GD	Pts
France	3	3	0	0	7	0	7	9
USA	3	2	0	1	7	4	3	6
New Zealand	3	1	0	2	3	8	–5	3
Guinea	3	0	0	3	1	6	–5	0

GROUP B

Argentina v Morocco	1-2
Iraq v Ukraine	2-1
Argentina v Iraq	3-1
Ukraine v Morocco	2-1
Ukraine v Argentina	0-2
Morocco v Iraq	3-0

Group B Table	P	W	D	L	F	A	GD	Pts
Morocco†	3	2	0	1	6	3	3	6
Argentina†	3	2	0	1	6	3	3	6
Ukraine	3	1	0	2	3	5	–2	3
Iraq	3	1	0	2	3	7	–4	3

†*Ranking decided on head-to-head result.*

GROUP C

Uzbekistan v Spain	1-2
Egypt v Dominican Republic	0-0
Dominican Republic v Spain	1-3
Uzbekistan v Egypt	0-1
Dominican Republic v Uzbekistan	1-1
Spain v Egypt	1-2

Group C Table	P	W	D	L	F	A	GD	Pts
Egypt	3	2	1	0	3	1	2	7
Spain	3	2	0	1	6	4	2	6
Dominican Republic	3	0	2	1	2	4	–2	2
Uzbekistan	3	0	1	2	2	4	–2	1

GROUP D

Japan v Paraguay	5-0
Mali v Israel	1-1
Israel v Paraguay	2-4
Japan v Mali	1-0
Israel v Japan	0-1
Paraguay v Mali	1-0

Group D Table	P	W	D	L	F	A	GD	Pts
Japan	3	3	0	0	7	0	7	9
Paraguay	3	2	0	1	5	7	–2	6
Mali	3	0	1	2	1	3	–2	1
Israel	3	0	1	2	3	6	–3	1

KNOCKOUT STAGE – QUARTER-FINALS

Morocco v USA	4-0
Japan v Spain	0-3
Egypt v Paraguay	1-1*
Egypt won 5-4 on penalties.	
France v Argentina	1-0

SEMI-FINALS

Morocco v Spain	1-2
France v Egypt	3-1*

BRONZE MEDAL MATCH

Egypt v Morocco	0-6

GOLD MEDAL MATCH

Parc des Princes, Paris, Friday, 9 August 2024   44,260

France (1) 3 *(Millot 11, Akliouche 79, Mateta 90 (pen))*

Spain (3) 5 *(Lopez F 18, 25, Baena 28, Camello 100, 120)*

France: (4312) Restes; Sildillia (Cherki 110), Bade, Lukeba, Truffert (Locko 90); Millot (Doue 78), Kone (Magassa 105), Chotard (Akliouche 52); Olise; Mateta, Lacazette (Kalimuendo 52).
Spain: (4231) Tenas; Pubill (Sanchez 73), Garcia E, Cubarsi, Miranda (Gutierrez 98); Barrios, Baena (Turrientes 83); Oroz (Pacheco 88), Lopez F (Bernabe 73), Gomez; Ruiz (Camello 83).
aet; 3-3 at end of normal time.
Referee: Ramon Abatti (Brazil).

WOMEN'S COMPETITION

GROUP A

Canada v New Zealand	2-1
France v Colombia	3-2
New Zealand v Colombia	0-2
France v Canada	1-2
New Zealand v France	1-2
Colombia v Canada	0-1

Group A Table	P	W	D	L	F	A	GD	Pts
France	3	2	0	1	6	5	1	6
Canada	3	3	0	0	5	2	3	3‡
Colombia	3	1	0	2	4	4	0	3
New Zealand	3	0	0	3	2	6	–4	0

‡*Canada deducted 6 points for involvement in illegal drone spying.*

GROUP B

Germany v Australia	3-0
USA v Zambia	3-0
Australia v Zambia	6-5
USA v Germany	4-1
Australia v USA	1-2
Zambia v Germany	1-4

Group B Table	P	W	D	L	F	A	GD	Pts
USA	3	3	0	0	9	2	7	9
Germany	3	2	0	1	8	5	3	6
Australia	3	1	0	2	7	10	–3	3
Zambia	3	0	0	3	6	13	–7	0

GROUP C

Spain v Japan	2-1
Nigeria v Brazil	0-1
Brazil v Japan	1-2
Spain v Nigeria	1-0
Brazil v Spain	0-2
Japan v Nigeria	3-1

Group C Table	P	W	D	L	F	A	GD	Pts
Spain	3	3	0	0	5	1	4	9
Japan	3	2	0	1	6	4	2	6
Brazil	3	1	0	2	2	4	–2	3
Nigeria	3	0	0	3	1	5	–4	0

KNOCKOUT STAGE – QUARTER-FINALS

USA v Japan	1-0*
Spain v Colombia	2-2*
Spain won 4-2 on penalties.	
Canada v Germany	0-0*
Germany won 4-2 on penalties.	
France v Brazil	0-1

SEMI-FINALS

USA v Germany	1-0*
Brazil v Spain	4-2

BRONZE MEDAL MATCH

Spain v Germany	0-1

GOLD MEDAL MATCH

Parc des Princes, Paris, Saturday, 10 August 2024

Brazil (0) 0

USA (0) 1 *(Swanson 57)*   43,813

Brazil: (3421) Lorena; Lauren (Souza 84), Tarciane, Ferreira; Adriana, Yaya (Vitoria 50), Sampaio (Angelina 61), Yasmim; Portilho, Ludmila (Marta 61); Jheniffer (Priscila 61).
USA: (4231) Naeher; Fox, Girma, Davidson (Sonnett 74), Dunn; Coffey, Albert, Rodman, Horan, Swanson (Krueger 74); Smith (Williams 84).
Referee: Tess Olofsson (Sweden).

MEN'S OLYMPIC FOOTBALL
PAST MEDALLISTS 1896–2024

* No official tournament. ** No official tournament but gold medal later awarded by IOC.

1896 Athens*
1 Denmark
2 Greece

1900 Paris*
1 Great Britain
2 France

1904 St Louis**
1 Canada
2 USA

1908 London
1 Great Britain
2 Denmark
3 Netherlands

1912 Stockholm
1 Great Britain†
2 Denmark
3 Netherlands
†England players only

1920 Antwerp
1 Belgium
2 Spain
3 Netherlands

1924 Paris
1 Uruguay
2 Switzerland
3 Sweden

1928 Amsterdam
1 Uruguay
2 Argentina
3 Italy

1932 Los Angeles
No tournament

1936 Berlin
1 Italy
2 Austria
3 Norway

1948 London
1 Sweden
2 Yugoslavia
3 Denmark

1952 Helsinki
1 Hungary
2 Yugoslavia
3 Sweden

1956 Melbourne
1 USSR
2 Yugoslavia
3 Bulgaria

1960 Rome
1 Yugoslavia
2 Denmark
3 Hungary

1964 Tokyo
1 Hungary
2 Czechoslovakia
3 East Germany

1968 Mexico City
1 Hungary
2 Bulgaria
3 Japan

1972 Munich
1 Poland
2 Hungary
3 E Germany/USSR

1976 Montreal
1 East Germany
2 Poland
3 USSR

1980 Moscow
1 Czechoslovakia
2 East Germany
3 USSR

1984 Los Angeles
1 France
2 Brazil
3 Yugoslavia

1988 Seoul
1 USSR
2 Brazil
3 West Germany

1992 Barcelona
1 Spain
2 Poland
3 Ghana

1996 Atlanta
1 Nigeria
2 Argentina
3 Brazil

2000 Sydney
1 Cameroon
2 Spain
3 Chile

2004 Athens
1 Argentina
2 Paraguay
3 Italy

2008 Beijing
1 Argentina
2 Nigeria
3 Brazil

2012 London
1 Mexico
2 Brazil
3 Korea Republic

2016 Rio
1 Brazil
2 Germany
3 Nigeria

2021 Tokyo
Postponed from 2020.
1 Brazil
2 Spain
3 Mexico

2024 Paris
1 Spain
2 France
3 Morocco

WOMEN'S OLYMPIC FOOTBALL
PAST MEDALLISTS 1996–2024

1996 Atlanta
1 USA
2 China
3 Norway

2000 Sydney
1 Norway
2 USA
3 Germany

2004 Athens
1 USA
2 Brazil
3 Germany

2008 Beijing
1 USA
2 Brazil
3 Germany

2012 London
1 USA
2 Japan
3 Canada

2016 Rio
1 Germany
2 Sweden
3 Canada

2021 Tokyo
Postponed from 2020.
1 Canada
2 Sweden
3 USA

2024 Paris
1 USA
2 Brazil
3 Germany

UEFA NATIONS LEAGUE 2024–25

■ *Denotes player sent off.*

GROUP A1

Thursday, 5 September 2024
Portugal (2) 2 *(Dalot 7, Ronaldo 34)*
Croatia (1) 1 *(Dalot 41 (og))*   57,675
Portugal: (433) Diogo Costa; Dalot, Dias, Inacio (Silva A 77), Nuno Mendes; Silva B, Vitinha (Goncalves 90), Fernandes; Pedro Neto (Nelson Semedo 46), Ronaldo (Jota 88), Leao (Neves J 46).
Croatia: (352) Livakovic; Sutalo, Pongracic (Caleta-Car 46), Gvardiol; Jakic (Perisic 76), Modric (Sucic P 77), Kovacic, Baturina (Matanovic 61), Sosa; Mario Pasalic (Sucic L 67), Kramaric.

Scotland (0) 2 *(Gilmour 46, McTominay 76)*
Poland (2) 3 *(Szymanski S 8, Lewandowski 44 (pen), Zalewski 90 (pen))*   46,356
Scotland: (4231) Gunn; Ralston, Hanley, McKenna, Robertson; Gilmour (Morgan 82), McLean (Doak 71); McGinn, McTominay, Christie (Gauld 71); Dykes (Shankland 71).
Poland: (352) Bulka; Bednarek, Dawidowicz, Kiwior (Walukiewicz 46); Frankowski, Szymanski S (Slisz 82), Zielinski (Moder 82), Urbanski, Zalewski; Piatek (Piotrowski 72), Lewandowski (Buksa 72).

Sunday, 8 September 2024
Croatia (0) 1 *(Modric 52)*
Poland (0) 0   12,612
Croatia: (352) Livakovic; Sutalo, Caleta-Car, Gvardiol; Pjaca, Sucic P (Sucic L 46), Modric, Kovacic (Mario Pasalic 79), Sosa (Perisic 90); Matanovic (Budimir 69), Petkovic (Kramaric 69).
Poland: (532) Skorupski; Kaminski (Frankowski 82), Walukiewicz, Bednarek, Dawidowicz, Zalewski; Szymanski S (Piotrowski 86), Zielinski (Slisz 62), Urbanski (Moder 62); Bogusz (Swiderski 62), Lewandowski.

Portugal (0) 2 *(Fernandes 54, Ronaldo 88)*
Scotland (1) 1 *(McTominay 7)*   59,894
Portugal: (433) Diogo Costa; Nelson Semedo (Dalot 76), Silva A, Dias, Nuno Mendes; Silva B (Neves J 68), Joao Palhinha (Neves R 46), Fernandes; Pedro Neto (Ronaldo 46), Jota, Leao (Joao Felix 68).
Scotland: (4231) Gunn; Ralston, Hanley, McKenna, Robertson; Gilmour, McLean (Gauld 74); Christie (Morgan 87), McTominay, McGinn (Doak 90); Dykes (Conway 74).

Saturday, 12 October 2024
Croatia (1) 2 *(Matanovic 36, Kramaric 70)*
Scotland (1) 1 *(Christie 32)*   21,702
Croatia: (3421) Livakovic; Sutalo, Caleta-Car, Gvardiol; Perisic (Jakic 90), Modric, Mario Pasalic (Sucic P 46), Sosa; Sucic L (Baturina 62), Kramaric (Petkovic 71); Matanovic (Budimir 71).
Scotland: (4231) Gordon; Ralston, Souttar, Hanley, Robertson; Gilmour, McLean; Doak (Gauld 77), McTominay, Christie; Dykes (Adams 77).

Poland (0) 1 *(Zielinski 78)*
Portugal (2) 3 *(Silva B 26, Ronaldo 37, Bednarek 88 (og))*   56,854
Poland: (352) Skorupski; Walukiewicz (Kiwior 46), Bednarek, Dawidowicz; Frankowski, Szymanski S (Piatek 84), Oyedele (Moder 66), Zielinski, Zalewski (Ameyaw 76); Lewandowski, Swiderski (Urbanski 76).
Portugal: (4231) Diogo Costa; Dalot, Dias, Veiga, Nuno Mendes; Neves R, Silva B (Samu 90); Pedro Neto (Nelson Semedo 82), Fernandes (Otavio 90), Leao (Trincao 64); Ronaldo (Jota 63).

Tuesday, 15 October 2024
Poland (2) 3 *(Zielinski 5, Zalewski 45, Szymanski S 68)*
Croatia (3) 3 *(Sosa 19, Sucic P 24, Baturina 26)*   56,103
Poland: (352) Bulka; Dawidowicz (Piatkowski 38), Bednarek, Kiwior; Kaminski (Ameyaw 62), Szymanski S, Moder (Oyedele 62), Zielinski (Kapustka 74), Zalewski; Swiderski (Lewandowski 62), Urbanski.
Croatia: (343) Livakovic■; Sutalo, Erlic (Labrovic 81), Gvardiol; Perisic, Modric, Sucic P, Sosa; Baturina (Sucic L 80), Matanovic (Budimir 61), Kramaric (Mario Pasalic 69).

Scotland (0) 0
Portugal (0) 0   49,057
Scotland: (4231) Gordon; Ralston (Devlin 89), Souttar, Hanley, Robertson; Gilmour, McLean; Christie (Gauld 68), McTominay, Doak (Morgan 67); Adams (Dykes 83).
Portugal: (433) Diogo Costa; Joao Cancelo (Nelson Semedo 88), Silva A, Dias, Nuno Mendes; Vitinha (Joao Felix 88), Joao Palhinha (Neves R 61), Fernandes; Francisco Conceicao (Silva B 61), Ronaldo, Jota (Leao 61).

Friday, 15 November 2024
Portugal (0) 5 *(Leao 59, Ronaldo 72 (pen), 87, Fernandes 80, Pedro Neto 83)*
Poland (0) 1 *(Marczuk 88)*   47,239
Portugal: (4231) Diogo Costa; Dalot, Silva A, Veiga, Nuno Mendes (Tavares 88); Neves J (Vitinha 46), Silva B (Samu 77); Pedro Neto (Trincao 84), Fernandes, Leao (Joao Felix 84); Ronaldo.
Poland: (352) Bulka; Piatkowski, Bednarek (Walukiewicz 46), Kiwior; Bereszynski (Kaminski 32), Urbanski (Buksa 73), Romanchuk, Zielinski, Zalewski; Bogusz (Marczuk 46), Piatek (Kozubal 81).

Scotland (0) 1 *(McGinn 86)*
Croatia (0) 0   48,810
Scotland: (4231) Gordon; Ralston, Souttar, Hanley (McKenna 46), Robertson; Gilmour, McLean (McGinn 67); Doak (Armstrong 90), McTominay, Christie (Gauld 67); Conway (Dykes 67).
Croatia: (4231) Kotarski; Jakic (Pjaca 82), Sutalo, Caleta-Car, Gvardiol; Modric, Kovacic; Sucic L (Perisic 65), Sucic P■, Baturina (Vlasic 75); Kramaric (Mario Pasalic 65).

Monday, 18 November 2024
Croatia (0) 1 *(Gvardiol 65)*
Portugal (1) 1 *(Joao Felix 33)*   33,386
Croatia: (541) Livakovic; Perisic (Sucic L 58), Sutalo, Caleta-Car, Gvardiol, Sosa (Jakic 46); Kramaric, Modric (Moro 78), Kovacic (Mario Pasalic 46), Baturina; Matanovic (Budimir 64).
Portugal: (352) Jose Sa; Araujo (Djalo 81), Veiga, Nuno Mendes (Dalot 81); Nelson Semedo, Otavio (Francisco Conceicao 71), Neves J, Vitinha, Joao Cancelo; Leao (Silva F 71), Joao Felix.

Poland (0) 1 *(Piatkowski 59)*
Scotland (1) 2 *(McGinn 3, Robertson 90)*   55,433
Poland: (352) Skorupski; Piatkowski, Walukiewicz, Kiwior; Kaminski (Puchacz 63), Szymanski S, Moder (Slisz 46), Zielinski, Zalewski; Buksa, Swiderski (Urbanski 75).
Scotland: (4231) Gordon; Ralston (Devlin 76), Souttar, Hanley, Robertson; Gilmour (Armstrong 87), McLean; Doak (Christie 66), McTominay (Gauld 76), McGinn; Dykes (Shankland 66).

Group A1 Table	P	W	D	L	F	A	GD	Pts
Portugal	6	4	2	0	13	5	8	14
Croatia	6	2	2	2	8	8	0	8
Scotland	6	2	1	3	7	8	–1	7
Poland	6	1	1	4	9	16	–7	4

GROUP A2

Due to their war in Gaza, Israel played home matches in Hungary.

Friday, 6 September 2024

Belgium (1) 3 *(De Bruyne 21, 52 (pen), Tielemans 48)*

Israel (1) 1 *(Castagne 36 (og))*   0

Belgium: (4231) Casteels; Castagne, Faes, Theate, De Cuyper (Debast 64); Onana, Tielemans (Engels 74); Lukebakio (Bakayoko 82), De Bruyne, Doku (Duranville 74); Openda (De Ketelaere 64).
Israel: (3421) Gerafi; Nachmias, Shlomo, Gandelman (Revivo 63); Yehezkel, Lavi, Abu Fani (Jaber 68), Gropper (David 64); Solomon (Biton 80), Gloukh (Dor Peretz 63); Khalaili.
Behind closed doors.

France (1) 1 *(Barcola 1)*

Italy (1) 3 *(Dimarco 30, Frattesi 51, Raspadori 74)* 44,956

France: (4231) Maignan; Clauss (Kounde 77), Konate, Saliba, Hernandez T; Fofana (Kone 58), Kante (Zaire-Emery 77), Olise (Dembele 58); Griezmann (Thuram 77), Barcola; Mbappe.
Italy: (3511) Donnarumma; Di Lorenzo, Bastoni, Calafiori (Buongiorno 71); Cambiaso, Frattesi (Udogie 62), Ricci, Tonali, Dimarco (Brescianini 81); Pellegrini (Raspadori 46); Retegui (Kean 81).

Monday, 9 September 2024

France (1) 2 *(Muani 29, Dembele 57)*

Belgium (0) 0   42,358

France: (433) Maignan; Kounde, Upamecano, Saliba, Digne; Kante (Fofana 90), Kone, Guendouzi (Griezmann 79); Dembele (Olise 80), Muani (Mbappe 67), Thuram (Barcola 67).
Belgium: (4231) Casteels; Castagne (Meunier 83), Faes, Debast, Theate; Tielemans (Mangala 60), Onana; Lukebakio (Bakayoko 60), De Bruyne, Doku (Duranville 83); Openda (De Ketelaere 69).

Israel (0) 1 *(Abu Fani 90)*

Italy (1) 2 *(Frattesi 38, Kean 62)*   2090

Israel: (4231) Gerafi; Yehezkel, Nachmias, Shlomo, Revivo; Lavi (Jaber 46), Kanichowsky (Abu Fani 67); Abada (David 78), Dor Peretz (Safouri 67), Solomon; Khalaili (Gloukh 46).
Italy: (3511) Donnarumma; Gatti, Buongiorno, Bastoni; Bellanova (Cambiaso 63), Frattesi, Ricci (Zaccagni 86), Tonali, Dimarco (Udogie 71); Raspadori (Brescianini 63); Kean (Retegui 86).

Thursday, 10 October 2024

Israel (1) 1 *(Gandelman 24)*

France (2) 4 *(Camavinga 6, Nkunku 28, Guendouzi 87, Barcola 89)*   2226

Israel: (3421) Glazer O; Feingold, Nachmias, Baltaxa; Abada, Jaber (Gropper 76), Abu Fani (Azulay 67), Haziza (Biton 76); Gandelman (Dor Peretz 62), Gloukh; Baribo (Khalaili 62).
France: (4231) Maignan; Kounde, Konate, Saliba, Hernandez T (Digne 90); Tchouameni (Zaire-Emery 90), Camavinga (Fofana 90); Dembele, Olise (Barcola 70), Nkunku (Guendouzi 77); Muani.

Italy (2) 2 *(Cambiaso 1, Retegui 24)*

Belgium (1) 2 *(De Cuyper 42, Trossard 61)*   44,297

Italy: (3511) Donnarumma; Di Lorenzo, Bastoni, Calafiori; Cambiaso, Frattesi (Bellanova 90), Ricci (Fagioli 70), Tonali (Pisilli 80), Dimarco (Udogie 70); Pellegrini**ᵇ**; Retegui (Raspadori 80).
Belgium: (4231) Casteels; Debast, Faes, Theate (Vranckx 69), De Cuyper; Tielemans, Mangala (Castagne 68); Doku (Fofana 87), De Ketelaere (Lukebakio 68), Trossard; Openda (Ngonge 87).

Monday, 14 October 2024

Belgium (1) 1 *(Openda 45)*

France (1) 2 *(Muani 35 (pen), 62)*   39,731

Belgium: (4141) Casteels; Debast, Faes, Theate, Castagne (De Cuyper 67); Mangala (Vranckx 67); Doku, De Ketelaere (Engels 81), Tielemans (Lukebakio 82), Trossard; Openda.
France: (433) Maignan; Kounde, Konate, Saliba, Digne; Kone, Tchouameni**ᵃ**, Guendouzi (Camavinga 74); Dembele (Fofana 79), Muani (Thuram 90), Barcola (Nkunku 74).

Italy (1) 4 *(Retegui 41 (pen), Di Lorenzo 54, 79, Frattesi 72)*

Israel (0) 1 *(Abu Fani 66)*   11,700

Italy: (3511) Vicario; Di Lorenzo, Bastoni, Calafiori; Cambiaso, Frattesi (Buongiorno 87), Fagioli (Ricci 46), Tonali, Dimarco (Udogie 73); Raspadori (Maldini 74); Retegui (Lucca 84).
Israel: (3421) Glazer O; Feingold, Nachmias, Baltaxa; Abada (Baribo 75), Abu Fani, Kanichowsky (Jaber 46), Haziza (Gropper 64); Dor Peretz (Safouri 81), Gloukh; Madmon (Khalaili 64).

Thursday, 14 November 2024

Belgium (0) 0

Italy (1) 1 *(Tonali 11)*   41,367

Belgium: (532) Casteels; Castagne (Bakayoko 86), Faes, Debast, Theate (Al Dakhil 71), De Cuyper (Lukebakio 79); Engels (Vermeeren 71), Onana, Trossard; Lukaku, Openda.
Italy: (3511) Donnarumma; Di Lorenzo, Buongiorno, Bastoni; Cambiaso (Gatti 82), Frattesi, Rovella (Locatelli 79), Tonali, Dimarco (Udogie 69); Barella (Raspadori 79); Retegui (Kean 69).

France (0) 0

Israel (0) 0   16,611

France: (4231) Maignan; Kounde, Konate, Upamecano, Hernandez; Kante, Camavinga (Rabiot 71); Olise (Coman 70), Zaire-Emery (Thuram 78), Barcola (Nkunku 71); Muani.
Israel: (541) Daniel Peretz; Yehezkel (Khalaili 84), Nachmias, Shlomo, Goldberg, Abada (Haziza 80); Solomon (Saba 72), Jaber, Abu Fani, Gloukh (Dor Peretz 84); Turgeman (David 73).

Sunday, 17 November 2024

Israel (0) 1 *(Shua 86)*

Belgium (0) 0   675

Israel: (541) Daniel Peretz; Dasa (Shua 74), Nachmias, Shlomo, Goldberg, Solomon; Dor Peretz (Haziza 74), Jaber, Abu Fani (Gandelman 61), Gloukh (Azulay 88); David (Saba 61).
Belgium: (4231) Casteels; Al Dakhil (Sardella 90), Faes, Debast (Smets 46), Castagne; Vermeeren (Sambi Lokonga 67), Mangala; Lukebakio, Engels (Bassette 90), Trossard (Bakayoko 37); Openda.
Due to the Israel-Hamas war the match was played in Hungary.

Italy (1) 1 *(Cambiaso 35)*

France (2) 3 *(Rabiot 2, 65, Vicario 33 (og))*   68,158

Italy: (3511) Vicario; Di Lorenzo, Buongiorno, Bastoni; Cambiaso (Maldini 78), Frattesi (Raspadori 67), Locatelli (Rovella 67), Tonali, Dimarco (Udogie 83); Barella; Retegui (Kean 66).
France: (4312) Maignan; Kounde (Pavard 82), Konate, Saliba, Digne; Guendouzi, Kone, Rabiot; Nkunku; Muani, Thuram (Barcola 78).

Group A2 Table	P	W	D	L	F	A	GD	Pts
France	6	4	1	1	12	6	6	13
Italy	6	4	1	1	13	5	8	13
Belgium	6	1	1	4	6	9	–3	4
Israel	6	1	1	4	5	13	–8	4

GROUP A3

Saturday, 7 September 2024

Germany (1) 5 *(Fullkrug 27, Musiala 58, Wirtz 66, Pavlovic 77, Havertz 81 (pen))*

Hungary (0) 0 49,235

Germany: (4231) ter Stegen; Kimmich, Tah, Schlotterbeck (Koch 69), Raum (Henrichs 69); Andrich (Stiller 82), Gross (Pavlovic 60); Wirtz, Havertz, Musiala; Fullkrug (Beier 60).
Hungary: (3421) Gulacsi; Balogh, Orban, Dardai M; Nego (Bolla 46), Schafer, Nagy A (Nikitscher 82), Kerkez (Nagy Z 66); Szoboszlai, Sallai (Csoboth 75); Varga (Adam 67).

Netherlands (2) 5 *(Zirkzee 13, Reijnders 45, Gakpo 56, Weghorst 88, Simons 90)*

Bosnia & Herzegovina (1) 2 *(Demirovic 27, Dzeko 73)*
31,139

Netherlands: (433) Verbruggen; Dumfries (Geertruida 67), de Ligt, van Dijk, Ake (Timber J 66); Schouten (Timber Q 83), Reijnders, Gravenberch; Simons, Zirkzee (Weghorst 74), Gakpo (Malen 66).
Bosnia & Herzegovina: (532) Vasilj; Gazibegovic, Barisic, Katic, Mujakic (Burnic 68), Dedic; Huseinbasic (Bajraktarevic 68), Tahirovic (Krunic 46); Gigovic (Saric 69); Dzeko, Demirovic (Tabakovic 83).

Tuesday, 10 September 2024

Hungary (0) 0

Bosnia & Herzegovina (0) 0 31,139

Hungary: (3421) Dibusz; Botka (Balogh 83), Orban, Dardai M; Bolla (Csoboth 75), Nikitscher, Schafer, Nagy Z (Kerkez 83); Sallai, Szoboszlai; Varga (Adam 82).
Bosnia & Herzegovina: (532) Vasilj; Gazibegovic, Bicakcic, Katic, Barisic, Dedic; Saric (Gigovic 60), Basic (Huseinbasic 61), Burnic (Tahirovic 46); Demirovic (Bajraktarevic 77), Dzeko.

Netherlands (1) 2 *(Reijnders 2, Dumfries 50)*

Germany (2) 2 *(Undav 38, Kimmich 45)* 50,109

Netherlands: (4231) Verbruggen; Dumfries, de Ligt (van Hecke 46), van Dijk, Ake (Timber J 45); Schouten (Timber Q 46), Gravenberch; Simons (Geertruida 74), Reijnders, Gakpo; Brobbey (Weghorst 82).
Germany: (4231) ter Stegen; Kimmich, Tah (Anton 46), Schlotterbeck, Raum; Andrich (Can 64), Gross (Pavlovic 63); Wirtz, Havertz, Musiala (Fuhrich 89); Undav 63).

Friday, 11 October 2024

Bosnia & Herzegovina (0) 1 *(Dzeko 70)*

Germany (2) 2 *(Undav 30, 36)* 11,000

Bosnia & Herzegovina: (532) Vasilj; Gazibegovic, Barisic, Katic, Kolasinac (Tabakovic 90), Burnic (Bajraktarevic 84); Gigovic (Saric 65), Basic (Tahirovic 46); Huseinbasic (Hajradinovic 65); Dzeko, Demirovic.
Germany: (4231) Nubel; Kimmich, Rudiger, Tah, Mittelstadt (Gosens 66); Andrich (Stiller 67), Gross (Anton 90); Gnabry (Fuhrich 82), Undav (Burkardt 67), Wirtz; Kleindienst.

Hungary (1) 1 *(Sallai 32)*

Netherlands (0) 1 *(Dumfries 83)* 55,300

Hungary: (3421) Dibusz; Fiola, Orban, Dardai M (Botka 46); Bolla (Gera 89), Nikitscher, Schafer, Nagy Z; Sallai (Csoboth 65), Szoboszlai; Varga (Nagy A 79).
Netherlands: (433) Verbruggen; Dumfries, de Vrij (Malen 75), van Dijk■, van de Ven; Gravenberch, Reijnders, Timber Q (Til 75); Simons (de Ligt 81), Zirkzee (Brobbey 76); Gakpo (Hato 89).

Monday, 14 October 2024

Bosnia & Herzegovina (0) 0

Hungary (1) 2 *(Szoboszlai 38, 50 (pen))* 8329

Bosnia & Herzegovina: (4231) Vasilj; Gazibegovic (Omerovic 46), Katic, Bicakcic, Kolasinac; Gigovic (Huseinbasic 64), Tahirovic (Skov Olsen 79); Bajraktarevic, Hajradinovic (Basic 79), Burnic (Tabakovic 64); Dzeko.
Hungary: (343) Dibusz; Kerkez (Willi 46), Orban, Fiola; Bolla (Gera 68), Nikitscher, Schafer (Nagy A 86), Nagy Z (Szucs 87); Sallai (Gazdag 68), Varga (Adam 78), Szoboszlai.

Germany (0) 1 *(Leweling 64)*

Netherlands (0) 0 68,367

Germany: (4231) Baumann; Kimmich, Rudiger, Schlotterbeck, Mittelstadt; Stiller (Anton 82), Pavlovic (Schade 77); Gnabry, Wirtz (Andrich 46), Leweling (Gosens 87); Kleindienst (Burkardt 82).
Netherlands: (4231) Verbruggen; Dumfries, de Vrij, van de Ven, Hato; Gravenberch (Geertruida 80), Timber Q (Wieffer 46); Simons, Reijnders (Malen 46), Gakpo (Frimpong 65); Brobbey (Zirkzee 75).

Saturday, 16 November 2024

Germany (3) 7 *(Musiala 2, Kleindienst 23, 79, Havertz 37, Wirtz 50, 57, Sane 66)*

Bosnia & Herzegovina (0) 0 28,143

Germany: (4231) Baumann; Kimmich (Koch 73), Rudiger, Tah, Mittelstadt (Henrichs 58); Andrich (Nmecha 58), Gross; Wirtz (Gnabry 58), Havertz, Musiala (Sane 58); Kleindienst.
Bosnia & Herzegovina: (532) Vasilj; Omerovic, Barisic, Bicakcic, Muharemovic, Burnic; Gigovic (Bajraktarevic 62), Sunjic (Huseinbasic 74), Tahirovic (Basic 63); Kulenovic (Bazdar 63), Demirovic (Hajradinovic 85).

Netherlands (2) 4 *(Weghorst 21 (pen), Gakpo 45 (pen), Dumfries 64, Koopmeiners 85)*

Hungary (0) 0 51,611

Netherlands: (433) Verbruggen; Dumfries, van Hecke, van Dijk, Timber J (Hato 68); Gravenberch (Wieffer 79), de Jong (Koopmeiners 68), Reijnders; Malen (Frimpong 84), Weghorst, Gakpo (Lang 79).
Hungary: (343) Dibusz; Balogh, Orban, Dardai M; Nego (Gera 74), Nikitscher, Schafer (Nagy A 74), Nagy Z; Sallai (Csoboth 80), Varga (Szabo 60), Szoboszlai.

Tuesday, 19 November 2024

Bosnia & Herzegovina (0) 1 *(Demirovic 67)*

Netherlands (1) 1 *(Brobbey 24)* 4134

Bosnia & Herzegovina: (442) Zlomislic; Bicakcic (Bazdar 63), Barisic, Muharemovic, Burnic; Dedic, Sunjic, Tahirovic (Basic 86); Gigovic (Bajraktarevic 63); Demirovic (Kulenovic 86), Dzeko (Djakovac 90).
Netherlands: (4231) Flekken; Frimpong (Rensch 66), de Vrij, de Ligt, Hato; Wieffer, Koopmeiners; Kluivert (Malen 66), Zirkzee (Weghorst 77), Lang (Gakpo 77); Brobbey (Gravenberch 71).

Hungary (0) 1 *(Szoboszlai 90 (pen))*

Germany (0) 1 *(Nmecha 76)* 53,212

Hungary: (3421) Dibusz; Fiola, Orban, Dardai M; Nego (Gera 65), Nikitscher (Kata 65), Schafer, Nagy Z (Schon 82); Sallai (Csoboth 82), Szoboszlai; Varga (Gruber 89).
Germany: (4231) Nubel; Kimmich (Gosens 46), Koch, Schlotterbeck, Henrichs; Andrich, Nmecha, Sane (Kleindienst 80), Brandt (Havertz 61), Fuhrich (Musiala 61); Gnabry (Wirtz 61).

Group A3 Table	P	W	D	L	F	A	GD	Pts
Germany	6	4	2	0	18	4	14	14
Netherlands	6	2	3	1	13	7	6	9
Hungary	6	1	3	2	4	11	–7	6
Bosnia & Herzegovina	6	0	2	4	4	17	–13	2

GROUP A4

Thursday, 5 September 2024

Denmark (0) 2 *(Dorgu 82, Hojbjerg 90)*

Switzerland (0) 0 26,024

Denmark: (3421) Schmeichel; Andersen, Vestergaard, Nelsson (Dorgu 81); Bah, Hojbjerg, Hjulmand (Norgaard 90), Kristiansen; Gronbaek (Skov Olsen 81), Eriksen (Damsgaard 62); Dolberg (Wind 62).
Switzerland: (343) Kobel; Elvedi■, Akanji, Rodriguez; Widmer (Omeragic 65), Freuler, Xhaka■, Aebischer (Amdouni 90); Rieder (Zakaria 65), Embolo (Duah 90), Vargas (Wuthrich 53).

Serbia (0) 0

Spain (0) 0   29,981

Serbia: (3421) Rajkovic; Erakovic (Simic 46), Milenkovic, Pavlovic; Nedeljkovic, Ilic I (Mitrovic S 85), Lukic, Birmancevic; Samardzic (Ratkov 74), Zivkovic A (Belic 62); Jovic (Grujic 74).
Spain: (4231) Raya; Carvajal, Le Normand, Laporte, Cucurella (Grimaldo 56); Zubimendi, Fabian (Gonzalez 76); Yamal, Olmo (Joselu 82), Williams (Torres F 82); Perez (Oyarzabal 57).

Sunday, 8 September 2024

Denmark (1) 2 *(Gronbaek 36, Poulsen 61)*

Serbia (0) 0   34,902

Denmark: (343) Schmeichel; Kristensen, Vestergaard, Andersen; Bah, Hojbjerg, Norgaard (Hjulmand 60), Kristiansen (Frendrup 82); Gronbaek (Isaksen 60), Poulsen (Wind 69), Eriksen (Dorgu 68).
Serbia: (3511) Rajkovic; Erakovic, Milenkovic, Pavlovic; Nedeljkovic (Mitrovic S 64), Ilic I, Grujic (Zivkovic A 46), Lukic (Belic 72), Birmancevic (Jovanovic D 80); Samardzic (Ratkov 64); Jovic.

Switzerland (1) 1 *(Amdouni 41)*

Spain (2) 4 *(Joselu 4, Fabian 13, 77, Torres F 80)*   26,265

Switzerland: (343) Kobel; Wuthrich, Akanji, Rodriguez (Rieder 62); Omeragic, Freuler, Zakaria (Sierro 62), Aebischer (Monteiro 76); Amdouni, Embolo (Duah 76), Vargas (Steffen 85).
Spain: (433) Raya; Carvajal, Le Normand[■], Laporte, Grimaldo; Gonzalez (Vivian 28), Rodri (Zubimendi 59), Fabian (Garcia A 81); Yamal (Torres F 46), Joselu, Williams (Pino 59).

Saturday, 12 October 2024

Serbia (1) 2 *(Elvedi 45 (og), Mitrovic A 61)*

Switzerland (0) 0   6383

Serbia: (3421) Rajkovic; Erakovic, Milenkovic, Pavlovic; Nedeljkovic (Simic 73), Maksimovic N, Grujic (Jovic 46), Birmancevic (Cumic 88); Samardzic, Lukic (Zdjelar 53); Mitrovic A (Maksimovic A 74).
Switzerland: (343) Kobel; Elvedi, Akanji, Rodriguez (Garcia 70); Widmer (Rieder 46), Freuler, Xhaka, Aebischer (Fernandes 70); Amdouni (Zeqiri 70), Embolo (Monteiro 86), Ndoye.

Spain (0) 1 *(Zubimendi 79)*

Denmark (0) 0   29,870

Spain: (4231) Raya; Porro, Vivian, Laporte, Grimaldo; Zubimendi, Fabian; Yamal (Gomez 90), Pedri (Merino 62), Oyarzabal (Baena 62); Morata (Joselu 78).
Denmark: (343) Schmeichel; Kristensen, Vestergaard, Nelsson; Bah, Hjulmand, Hojbjerg, Kristiansen; Eriksen (Isaksen 73), Dolberg (Poulsen 73), Gronbaek (Hojlund 78).

Tuesday, 15 October 2024

Spain (1) 3 *(Laporte 5, Morata 65, Baena 77)*

Serbia (0) 0   20,345

Spain: (4231) Raya; Porro, Vivian (Cubarsi 82), Laporte, Cucurella; Zubimendi, Fabian (Garcia 82); Oyarzabal, Merino (Pedri 65), Baena (Zaragoza 78); Morata (Joselu 78).
Serbia: (532) Rajkovic; Nedeljkovic (Cumic 64), Erakovic, Milenkovic, Pavlovic[■], Birmancevic; Samardzic (Grujic 46), Maksimovic N, Zdjelar (Maksimovic A 64); Mitrovic A (Simic 79), Joveljic (Jovic 46).

Switzerland (2) 2 *(Freuler 26, Amdouni 45 (pen))*

Denmark (1) 2 *(Isaksen 27, Eriksen 69)*   16,182

Switzerland: (4231) Kobel; Fernandes, Akanji, Elvedi, Garcia; Freuler (Aebischer 81), Xhaka; Amdouni (Witzig 89), Rieder (Ugrinic 67), Ndoye (Sierro 89); Embolo (Zeqiri 81).
Denmark: (3421) Schmeichel; Kristensen, Vestergaard, Nelsson (Dolberg 76); Bah, Eriksen, Hojbjerg, Dorgu (Maehle 86); Isaksen (Stage 76), Gronbaek (Wind 57); Hojlund (Skov Olsen 57).

Friday, 15 November 2024

Denmark (0) 1 *(Isaksen 84)*

Spain (1) 2 *(Oyarzabal 15, Perez 58)*   36,985

Denmark: (433) Schmeichel; Bah, Andersen, Vestergaard, Kristiansen (Dorgu 87); Hojbjerg, Norgaard (Damsgaard 61), Hjulmand; Eriksen (Skov Olsen 79), Hojlund (Dolberg 79), Gronbaek (Isaksen 61).
Spain: (4231) Raya; Porro, Vivian, Laporte, Cucurella; Zubimendi (Casado 70), Merino (Pedri 80); Oyarzabal, Olmo (Williams 70), Baena (Fabian 62); Perez (Morata 69).

Switzerland (0) 1 *(Amdouni 78)*

Serbia (0) 1 *(Terzic 88)*   21,115

Switzerland: (4231) Kobel; Fernandes (Mbabu 83), Comert, Amenda, Rodriguez (Garcia 89); Xhaka, Freuler; Rieder (Monteiro 66), Amdouni, Okafor (Kutesa 65); Embolo (Zeqiri 66).
Serbia: (3412) Petrovic; Veljkovic, Milenkovic, Babic (Stojic 46); Zivkovic A (Nedeljkovic 78), Maksimovic N, Gudelj, Terzic (Zdjelar 90); Samardzic (Topic 72); Vlahovic, Mitrovic A (Maksimovic A 90).

Monday, 18 November 2024

Serbia (0) 0

Denmark (0) 0   7295

Serbia: (352) Petrovic; Veljkovic, Milenkovic, Pavlovic[■]; Zivkovic A (Ivanovic 82), Samardzic (Maksimovic A 73), Gudelj (Zdjelar 72), Maksimovic N, Terzic; Vlahovic (Nedeljkovic 88), Mitrovic A.
Denmark: (433) Schmeichel; Roerslev, Nelsson, Vestergaard, Kristiansen; Eriksen, Hjulmand, Damsgaard (Gronbaek 71); Isaksen (Skov Olsen 81), Dolberg (Hojlund 70), Poulsen (Norgaard 53).

Spain (1) 3 *(Pino 32, Gil 68, Zaragoza 90 (pen))*

Switzerland (0) 2 *(Monteiro 63, Zeqiri 85 (pen))*   21,204

Spain: (433) Remiro (Sanchez 46); Mingueza, Cubarsi, Paredes, Grimaldo; Pedri (Barrios 79), Casado, Fabian; Pino (Zaragoza 69), Morata (Aghehowa 46), Williams (Gil 60).
Switzerland: (4231) Mvogo; Fernandes, Comert, Rodriguez, Muheim; Freuler, Xhaka (Sierro 60); Ugrinic (Monteiro 46), Sohm (Rieder 60), Kutesa (Okafor 72); Amdouni (Zeqiri 46).

Group A4 Table	P	W	D	L	F	A	GD	Pts
Spain	6	5	1	0	13	4	9	16
Denmark	6	2	2	2	7	5	2	8
Serbia	6	1	3	2	3	6	–3	6
Switzerland	6	0	2	4	6	14	–8	2

GROUP B1

Due to the continuing Russian invasion, Ukraine played home matches at neutral venues.

Saturday, 7 September 2024

Georgia (1) 4 *(Kvaratskhelia 33 (pen), Chakvetadze 53, Mikautadze 63, Kochorashvili 66)*

Czech Republic (0) 1 *(Kalvach 80)*   20,401

Georgia: (352) Mamardashvili; Gvelesiani (Goglichidze 88), Kashia, Dvali; Kakabadze (Gocholeishvili 75), Chakvetadze (Davitashvili 75), Kochorashvili, Kiteishvili (Nonikashvili 75), Lochoshvili; Mikautadze (Zivzivadze 75), Kvaratskhelia.
Czech Republic: (3421) Kovar; Zima, Hranac, Krejci; Coufal, Soucek, Kral (Kalvach 46), Rynes (Zeleny 26); Provod (Sulc 76), Cvancara (Lingr 46); Schick (Hlozek 68).

Ukraine (0) 1 *(Konoplya 49)*

Albania (0) 2 *(Ismajli 54, Asani 66)*   15,500

Ukraine: (4141) Trubin; Konoplya, Zabarnyi, Matviyenko, Mykolenko; Brazhko (Malinovsky 81); Tsygankov (Zinchenko 81), Sudakov (Yarmolenko 72), Shaparenko (Vanat 73), Kabayev (Pikhalyonok 72); Yaremchuk.
Albania: (4231) Strakosha; Hysaj, Ismajli, Kumbulla, Mitaj; Ramadani, Asllani; Asani, Laci (Berisha 73), Bajrami N (Hoxha 77); Manaj.
Match played in the Czech Republic.

Tuesday, 10 September 2024

Albania (0) 0

Georgia (0) 1 *(Kochorashvili 71)*   20,400

Albania: (4231) Strakosha; Hysaj, Ismajli, Kumbulla, Mitaj; Ramadani, Asllani; Asani (Spahiu 73), Bajrami N (Uzuni 81), Hoxha (Laci 61); Manaj (Seferi 72).
Georgia: (352) Mamardashvili; Gvelesiani, Kashia, Dvali; Kakabadze, Kochorashvili (Altunashvili 90), Chakvetadze, Kiteishvili, Lochoshvili; Mikautadze (Zivzivadze 86), Kvaratskhelia (Davitashvili 75).

Czech Republic (2) 3 *(Sulc 21, 45, Soucek 80 (pen))*

Ukraine (1) 2 *(Vanat 37, Sudakov 84)*   18,722

Czech Republic: (433) Kovar; Coufal, Vitik, Krejci, Zeleny; Sulc (Kusej 81), Soucek, Cerv (Kral 89); Cerny (Hlozek 66), Chory (Schick 81), Provod (Lingr 65).
Ukraine: (4141) Trubin; Tymchyk, Zabarnyi, Matviyenko, Mykolenko; Stepanenko (Malinovsky 79); Yarmolenko (Tsygankov 69), Shaparenko (Sudakov 69), Zinchenko (Pikhalyonok 85), Mudryk; Vanat (Yaremchuk 79).

Friday, 11 October 2024

Czech Republic (1) 2 *(Chory 3, 63)*

Albania (0) 0   17,823

Czech Republic: (4231) Kovar; Coufal, Vitik, Holes, Boril; Soucek, Cerv (Kral 90); Cerny (Hlozek 69), Sulc (Cvancara 90), Provod (Lingr 88); Chory (Kuchta 87).
Albania: (4231) Strakosha; Hysaj, Ismajli, Kumbulla, Mitaj; Laci (Seferi 79), Ramadani; Asani (Hoxha 65), Asllani, Bajrami N (Muci 88); Daku (Tuci 65).

Ukraine (1) 1 *(Mudryk 35)*

Georgia (0) 0   21,700

Ukraine: (4141) Trubin; Konoplya, Zabarnyi, Taloverov, Matviyenko, Kaliuzhnyi (Kryskiv 90); Gutsulyak (Zubkov 75), Shaparenko, Sudakov (Svatok 90), Mudryk (Nazarenko 86); Dovbyk (Yaremchuk 75).
Georgia: (352) Mamardashvili; Gvelesiani (Zivzivadze 82), Kashia, Dvali; Kakabadze, Kochorashvili (Davitashvili 71), Kiteishvili, Chakvetadze, Lochoshvili (Shengelia 60); Mikautadze, Kvaratskhelia.
Match played in Poland.

Monday, 14 October 2024

Georgia (0) 0

Albania (0) 1 *(Asllani 48)*   19,981

Georgia: (433) Mamardashvili; Kakabadze, Kashia, Dvali, Lochoshvili (Tsitaishvili 81); Davitashvili (Shengelia 90), Kiteishvili, Chakvetadze; Mikautadze, Zivzivadze, Kvaratskhelia.
Albania: (4231) Strakosha; Balliu, Ismajli, Ajeti, Mitaj; Ramadani, Asllani; Asani, Laci, Bajrami N (Seferi 77); Tuci (Daku 66).

Ukraine (0) 1 *(Dovbyk 52 (pen))*

Czech Republic (1) 1 *(Cerv 18)*   14,734

Ukraine: (4141) Trubin; Konoplya (Tymchyk 80), Zabarnyi, Taloverov, Matviyenko; Stepanenko (Kaliuzhnyi 64); Gutsulyak (Zubkov 22), Shaparenko (Kryskiv 64), Sudakov, Mudryk; Dovbyk (Yaremchuk 80).
Czech Republic: (4231) Kovar; Coufal, Vitik, Krejci, Boril (Zmrzly 70); Cerv, Soucek; Cerny (Lingr 58), Sulc (Kuchta 90), Provod (Hlozek 58); Chory (Kliment 70).
Match played in Poland.

Saturday, 16 November 2024

Albania (0) 0

Czech Republic (0) 0   20,800

Albania: (4141) Strakosha; Balliu, Ismajli, Ajeti, Mitaj; Ramadani; Asani (Seferi 30), Laci (Abrashi 85), Asllani, Bajrami N (Muci 72); Tuci (Uzuni 85).
Czech Republic: (4141) Kovar; Coufal, Holes, Jemelka, Boril; Cerv; Cerny (Kliment 65), Soucek, Sulc (Kuchta 83), Provod (Lingr 83); Chory (Hlozek 65).

Georgia (0) 1 *(Mikautadze 76)*

Ukraine (1) 1 *(Kvirkvelia 7 (og))*   19,120

Georgia: (3511) Mamardashvili; Kvirkvelia (Gocholeishvili 67), Kashia, Lochoshvili; Kakabadze, Chakvetadze (Davitashvili 46), Kiteishvili (Mekvabishvili 86), Kochorashvili, Shengelia (Tsitaishvili 67); Kvaratskhelia; Zivzivadze (Mikautadze 67).
Ukraine: (4141) Trubin; Konoplya, Zabarnyi, Matviyenko, Mykolenko; Brazhko (Kaliuzhnyi 80); Zubkov (Gutsulyak 64), Shaparenko (Kryskiv 64), Sudakov (Nazarenko 86), Mudryk; Dovbyk (Yaremchuk 80).

Tuesday, 19 November 2024

Albania (0) 1 *(Bajrami N 75 (pen))*

Ukraine (2) 2 *(Zinchenko 5, Yaremchuk 10)*   20,547

Albania: (433) Strakosha; Balliu, Ismajli, Ajeti, Mitaj; Laci (Seferi 90), Ramadani (Tuci 76), Asllani; Asani (Bajrami N 46), Daku (Uzuni 46), Muci (Hoxha 51).
Ukraine: (4141) Trubin; Konoplya (Sych 76), Zabarnyi, Matviyenko, Mykolenko; Kaliuzhnyi; Gutsulyak (Nazarenko 85), Zinchenko (Shaparenko 69), Sudakov, Mudryk (Taloverov 85); Yaremchuk (Dovbyk 76).

Czech Republic (2) 2 *(Sulc 3, Hlozek 24)*

Georgia (0) 1 *(Mikautadze 60)*   12,221

Czech Republic: (433) Kovar; Coufal, Holes, Jemelka, Boril; Sulc (Kuchta 88), Kral, Cerv; Cerny (Provod 57), Kliment (Chytil 57), Hlozek (Lingr 73).
Georgia: (352) Mamardashvili; Gvelesiani (Davitashvili 36), Kashia, Dvali; Kakabadze (Gocholeishvili 79), Chakvetadze (Zivzivadze 61), Kiteishvili (Mekvabishvili 60), Kochorashvili, Lochoshvili; Kvaratskhelia, Mikautadze (Lobjanidze 79).

Group B1 Table	P	W	D	L	F	A	GD	Pts
Czech Republic	6	3	2	1	9	8	1	11
Ukraine	6	2	2	2	8	8	0	8
Georgia	6	2	1	3	7	6	1	7
Albania	6	2	1	3	4	6	–2	7

GROUP B2

Saturday, 7 September 2024

Greece (2) 3 *(Ioannidis 23, 76, Kallman 37 (og))*

Finland (0) 0   17,293

Greece: (4231) Vlachodimos; Rota, Mavropanos, Koulierakis, Tsimikas; Mantalos (Siopis 65), Bouchalakis (Zafeiris 65); Chatzigiovanis (Konstantelias 46), Bakasetas (Pavlidis 77), Pelkas; Ioannidis (Vagiannidis 77).
Finland: (4231) Hradecky; Stahl, Hoskonen, Ivanov, Galvez; Peltola, Schuller (Nissila 44); Lod (Jensen F 62), Kamara (Walta 82), Antman (Keskinen 62); Kallman (Pohjanpalo 62).

Republic of Ireland (0) 0

England (2) 2 *(Rice 11, Grealish 26)*   50,359

Republic of Ireland: (3421) Kelleher; Coleman (O'Brien 57), Collins, O'Shea; Doherty (Knight 58), Molumby, Smallbone (Browne 75), Brady (Ferguson 82); Ogbene, Szmodics; Idah (McAteer 75).
England: (433) Pickford; Alexander-Arnold, Guehi, Maguire (Stones 85), Colwill; Mainoo (Gomes 77), Rice, Grealish (Gibbs-White 77); Saka, Kane (Bowen 84), Gordon (Eze 77).

Tuesday, 10 September 2024

England (0) 2 *(Kane 57, 76)*

Finland (0) 0   70,221

England: (4231) Pickford; Alexander-Arnold, Konsa (Colwill 61), Stones (Guehi 79), Lewis; Rice, Gomes; Saka (Madueke 66), Grealish, Gordon (Eze 66); Kane (Bowen 80).
Finland: (433) Hradecky; Stahl, Hoskonen, Ivanov, Uronen (Niskanen 46); Peltola, Schuller (Walta 84), Kamara; Jensen F (Lod 63), Pukki (Kallman 46), Keskinen (Antman 74).

Republic of Ireland (0) 0

Greece (0) 2 *(Ioannidis 50, Tzolis 87)*   37,274

Republic of Ireland: (4411) Kelleher; Omobamidele (Doherty 74), Collins, O'Shea, Brady; Ogbene (Robinson 84), Browne, Molumby (Ferguson 63), Knight (McAteer 74); Smallbone; Szmodics (Idah 84).
Greece: (4231) Vlachodimos; Rota, Mavropanos, Koulierakis, Tsimikas; Bouchalakis (Pelkas 68), Siopis (Ndoj 88); Chatzigiovanis (Zafeiris 67), Bakasetas, Tzolis (Vagiannidis 89); Ioannidis (Pavlidis 88).

Thursday, 10 October 2024

England (0) 1 *(Bellingham 87)*

Greece (0) 2 *(Pavlidis 49, 90)*   79,012

England: (442) Pickford; Alexander-Arnold, Stones, Colwill, Lewis; Saka (Madueke 61), Palmer, Rice, Gordon (Watkins 60); Foden (Solanke 72), Bellingham.
Greece: (4231) Vlachodimos; Rota, Mavropanos, Koulierakis, Giannoulis; Kourbelis (Mantalos 74), Siopis (Zafeiris 66); Masouras (Pelkas 66), Bakasetas (Vagiannidis 86), Tzolis (Konstantelias 86); Pavlidis.

Finland (1) 1 *(Pohjanpalo 17)*

Republic of Ireland (0) 2 *(Scales 57, Brady 88)*   16,105

Finland: (4231) Hradecky; Stahl, Hoskonen, Ivanov, Galvez; Walta (Pukki 78), Schuller (Antman 65); Lod, Kamara, Keskinen (Peltola 65); Pohjanpalo (Kallman 78).
Republic of Ireland: (4231) Kelleher; O'Shea, Collins, Scales, Brady; Cullen, Knight; Ogbene (Ebosele 80), Azaz (McGrath 71), Szmodics (Idah 80); Ferguson (Parrott 71).

Sunday, 13 October 2024

Finland (0) 1 *(Hoskonen 87)*

England (1) 3 *(Grealish 18, Alexander-Arnold 74, Rice 84)*   32,411

Finland: (541) Hradecky; Alho (Antman 82), Hoskonen, Ivanov, Peltola, Uronen; Jensen F (Lod 75), Kamara, Schuller (Walta 63), Keskinen (Pukki 75); Kallman (Pohjanpalo 63).
England: (4231) Henderson; Walker, Stones, Guehi, Alexander-Arnold; Gomes (Lewis 80), Rice (Gallagher 85); Palmer (Madueke 69), Bellingham (Foden 80), Grealish; Kane (Watkins 69).

Greece (0) 2 *(Bakasetas 48, Mantalos 90)*

Republic of Ireland (0) 0   30,253

Greece: (4231) Vlachodimos; Rota, Mavropanos, Hatzidiakos, Giannoulis; Kourbelis (Tsimikas 82), Siopis; Masouras (Pelkas 65), Bakasetas (Zafeiris 72), Tzolis (Mantalos 82); Pavlidis (Douvikas 72).
Republic of Ireland: (442) Kelleher; O'Shea (McAteer 82), Collins, Scales, Brady; Ogbene (Ebosele 57), Cullen, Knight (Molumby 72), Szmodics (Johnston 72); Ferguson (Taylor 57), Parrott.

Thursday, 14 November 2024

Greece (0) 0

England (1) 3 *(Watkins 7, Vlachodimos 77 (og), Jones 83)*   60,664

Greece: (4231) Vlachodimos; Rota, Mavropanos, Koulierakis, Tsimikas (Pelkas 57); Siopis (Mantalos 82), Zafeiris; Masouras (Konstantelias 70), Bakasetas (Ioannidis 57), Tzolis; Pavlidis (Giannoulis 56).
England: (4231) Pickford; Walker, Konsa (Hall 46), Guehi, Lewis; Gallagher (Gibbs-White 79), Jones; Madueke (Bowen 66), Bellingham, Gordon (Rogers 66); Watkins (Kane 66).

Republic of Ireland (1) 1 *(Ferguson 45)*

Finland (0) 0   39,163

Republic of Ireland: (442) Kelleher; Doherty (O'Shea 76), Collins, Scales, O'Dowda; Ebosele (Molumby 76), Cullen, Knight, Johnston (Manning 85); Szmodics (Cannon 85), Ferguson (Azaz 76).
Finland: (541) Hradecky; Alho (Niskanen 85), Hoskonen, Ivanov, Peltola (O'Shaughnessy 58), Uronen (Hakans 64); Lod, Kamara, Kairinen, Antman (Pohjanpalo 64); Kallman (Pukki 84).

Sunday, 17 November 2024

England (0) 5 *(Kane 53 (pen), Gordon 55, Gallagher 58, Bowen 76, Harwood-Bellis 79)*

Republic of Ireland (0) 0   79,969

England: (4231) Pickford; Livramento, Walker (Harwood-Bellis 62), Guehi, Hall; Gallagher (Solanke 75), Jones (Gomes 79); Madueke (Bowen 75), Bellingham, Gordon (Rogers 75); Kane.
Republic of Ireland: (4141) Kelleher; O'Shea, McGuinness, Scales■, O'Dowda (Azaz 67); Collins; Ebosele (Manning 67), Molumby, Cullen (Moran 76), Szmodics (McAteer 86); Ferguson (Parrott 67).

Finland (0) 0

Greece (0) 2 *(Bakasetas 52, Tzolis 56)*   17,661

Finland: (4231) Joronen; Alho (Niskanen 82), Hoskonen, Ivanov, Pikkarainen (Ollila 67); Hakans (Pukki 75); Lod, Kamara (Nissila 75), Kairinen, Kallman; Pohjanpalo (Antman 67).
Greece: (4231) Vlachodimos; Rota, Mavropanos, Koulierakis, Tsimikas; Kourbelis (Mouzakitis 90), Mantalos (Retsos 88); Masouras (Siopis 75), Bakasetas (Pelkas 74), Tzolis (Giannoulis 87); Pavlidis.

Group B2 Table	P	W	D	L	F	A	GD	Pts
England	6	5	0	1	16	3	13	15
Greece	6	5	0	1	11	4	7	15
Republic of Ireland	6	2	0	4	3	12	–9	6
Finland	6	0	0	6	2	13	–11	0

GROUP B3

Friday, 6 September 2024

Kazakhstan (0) 0

Norway (0) 0   23,173

Kazakhstan: (541) Shatski; Bystrov, Kasym, Marochkin, Alip, Vorogovskiy; Orazov (Abiken 58), Tagybergen, Zaynutdinov (Karimov 63), Chesnokov (Astanov E 80); Aymbetov (Samorodov 59).
Norway: (433) Nyland; Ryerson, Ostigard, Hanche-Olsen, Wolfe; Odegaard, Berg (Berge 70), Myhre (Larsen 70); Sorloth (Donnum 70), Haaland, Nusa (Walle 84).

Slovenia (1) 1 *(Sesko 16 (pen))*

Austria (1) 1 *(Laimer 28)*   14,834

Slovenia: (442) Vidovsek; Brekalo (Balkovec 86), Drkusic, Bijol, Janza; Stojanovic, Cerin, Elsnik, Lovric (Celar 63); Sesko, Sporar (Mlakar 63).
Austria: (4231) Pentz; Mwene, Posch, Wober, Prass; Laimer, Seiwald; Schmid (Stoger 82), Sabitzer, Wimmer (Baumgartner 46); Arnautovic (Adamu 82).

Monday, 9 September 2024

Norway (1) 2 *(Myhre 9, Haaland 80)*

Austria (1) 1 *(Sabitzer 37)*   23,171

Norway: (442) Nyland; Ryerson, Hanche-Olsen (Gundersen 28), Ostigard, Wolfe; Odegaard (Thorstvedt 67), Berge, Berg (Thorsby 46), Myhre (Nusa 46); Haaland, Sorloth (Langas 90).
Austria: (4231) Pentz; Mwene (Querfeld 57), Posch, Lienhart, Prass; Sabitzer, Seiwald; Schmid (Arnautovic 78), Wimmer (Stoger 78), Laimer; Baumgartner (Seidl 68).

Slovenia (2) 3 *(Sesko 23, 28, 63)*

Kazakhstan (0) 0   9814

Slovenia: (442) Oblak; Brekalo (Kurtic 87), Drkusic, Bijol, Janza; Stojanovic (Ilicic 78), Cerin, Elsnik, Mlakar (Stankovic 65); Sesko (Balkovec 87), Celar (Vipotnik 65).
Kazakhstan: (541) Shatski; Bystrov (Skvortsov 76), Maliy (Kasym 46), Marochkin, Alip, Vorogovskiy; Orazov (Astanov E 57), Tagybergen, Zaynutdinov, Samorodov (Chesnokov 46); Aymbetov (Zhaksylykov 76).

Thursday, 10 October 2024

Austria (1) 4 *(Baumgartner 10, Lienhart 53, Sabitzer 56, Seidl 79)*

Kazakhstan (0) 0 14,500

Austria: (4231) Schlager A; Posch, Trauner (Svoboda 62), Lienhart, Prass; Seiwald, Laimer (Grillitsch 76); Schmid (Wimmer 62), Baumgartner (Seidl 72), Sabitzer; Adamu (Arnautovic 62).
Kazakhstan: (442) Shatski; Astanov S, Kasym, Alip, Vorogovskiy; Zaynutdinov (Zhaksybaev 76), Tagybergen (Darabayev 67), Abiken (Orazov 46), Chesnokov; Islamkhan (Samorodov 46), Zhaksylykov (Shushenachev 59).

Norway (1) 3 *(Haaland 7, 62, Sorloth 52)*

Slovenia (0) 0 23,341

Norway: (442) Nyland; Ajer, Hanche-Olsen, Ostigard (Pedersen 46), Wolfe; Ryerson (Vetlesen 82), Berge, Thorsby (Berg 75), Nusa (Donnum 76); Sorloth (Larsen 76), Haaland.
Slovenia: (442) Oblak; Janza, Drkusic, Bijol, Balkovec (Vipotnik 57); Stojanovic, Cerin (Ilicic 79), Elsnik, Petrovic (Kurtic 73); Sporar (Celar 57), Sesko (Kramer 79).

Sunday, 13 October 2024

Austria (1) 5 *(Arnautovic 8, 49 (pen), Lienhart 58, Posch 62, Gregoritsch 71)*

Norway (1) 1 *(Sorloth 39)* 16,500

Austria: (4231) Pentz; Posch, Trauner (Svoboda 79), Lienhart, Mwene; Seiwald, Laimer (Grillitsch 84); Schmid (Wimmer 79), Baumgartner (Seidl 84), Sabitzer; Arnautovic (Gregoritsch 69).
Norway: (442) Nyland; Pedersen, Ajer, Hanche-Olsen, Wolfe (Heggem 79); Ryerson (Berg 63), Berge, Thorsby (Donnum 64), Nusa (Myhre 64); Sorloth (Larsen 84), Haaland.

Kazakhstan (0) 0

Slovenia (0) 1 *(Mlakar 55)* 19,783

Kazakhstan: (4231) Shatski; Bystrov, Marochkin, Alip, Vorogovskiy; Tagybergen (Skvortsov 69), Darabayev (Payruz 78); Zaynutdinov, Islamkhan, Chesnokov (Baltabekov 64); Aymbetov (Zhaksylykov 64).
Slovenia: (442) Oblak; Stojanovic, Drkusic (Bajric 47), Bijol, Janza; Ilicic (Petrovic 72), Cerin, Elsnik, Mlakar (Kurtic 87); Sporar (Vipotnik 71), Sesko.

Thursday, 14 November 2024

Kazakhstan (0) 0

Austria (2) 2 *(Baumgartner 15, Gregoritsch 25)* 9753

Kazakhstan: (4231) Pokatilov; Astanov S, Kasym, Marochkin█, Vorogovskiy; Darabayev (Tapalov 57), Tagybergen; Zaynutdinov (Payruz 69), Islamkhan (Zhumakhanov 26), Samorodov (Kenzhebek 68); Aymbetov (Karimov 46).
Austria: (4231) Schlager A; Posch (Mwene 64), Danso, Lienhart, Prass; Seiwald, Laimer (Seidl 64); Schmid (Weimann 77), Baumgartner (Adamu 72), Wimmer (Stoger 72); Gregoritsch.

Slovenia (1) 1 *(Sesko 21 (pen))*

Norway (2) 4 *(Nusa 4, 59, Haaland 45, Hauge 82)* 15,308

Slovenia: (442) Oblak; Karnicnik (Brekalo 72), Drkusic, Bijol, Janza; Stojanovic (Seslar 81), Cerin (Kurtic 81), Elsnik, Mlakar (Lovric 72); Vipotnik (Celar 72), Sesko.
Norway: (442) Selvik; Pedersen, Ostigard, Heggem (Gregersen 87), Ryerson; Donnum (Thorsby 46), Johnsen (Thorstvedt 60); Berge, Nusa (Hauge 70); Sorloth, Haaland (Larsen 87).

Sunday, 17 November 2024

Austria (1) 1 *(Schmid 27)*

Slovenia (0) 1 *(Cerin 81)* 46,000

Austria: (4231) Pentz; Posch, Lienhart, Wober, Mwene; Seiwald, Laimer (Grillitsch 90); Schmid (Gregoritsch 83), Baumgartner, Sabitzer; Arnautovic (Wimmer 90).
Slovenia: (442) Oblak; Karnicnik, Brekalo, Bijol, Janza; Stojanovic (Petrovic 65), Cerin, Elsnik (Lovric 81), Mlakar (Sporar 81); Vipotnik (Drkusic 90), Sesko.

Norway (3) 5 *(Haaland 23, 37, 71, Sorloth 41, Nusa 76)*

Kazakhstan (0) 0 23,458

Norway: (4231) Selvik; Pedersen (Heggem 63), Gregersen (Langas 73), Ostigard, Ryerson; Thorstvedt (Berg 63), Berge; Sorloth (Larsen 63), Thorsby, Nusa; Haaland (Rosler 86).
Kazakhstan: (442) Pokatilov; Astanov S, Kasym, Alip, Vorogovskiy; Chesnokov (Payruz 51), Tapalov (Islamkhan 46), Tagybergen (Baltabekov 90), Samorodov (Astanov E 68); Zaynutdinov, Aymbetov (Zhaksylykov 46).

Group B3 Table	P	W	D	L	F	A	GD	Pts
Norway	6	4	1	1	15	7	8	13
Austria	6	3	2	1	14	5	9	11
Slovenia	6	2	2	2	7	9	–2	8
Kazakhstan	6	0	1	5	0	15	–15	1

GROUP B4

Friday, 6 September 2024

Iceland (1) 2 *(Oskarsson 39, Thorsteinsson 58)*

Montenegro (0) 0 4683

Iceland: (4411) Valdimarsson; Sampsted, Hermannsson, Gretarsson, Tomasson; Anderson (Willumsson W 77), Gudmundsson J, Thordarson, Thorsteinsson (Sigurdsson A 65); Sigurdsson G (Gudjohnsen 65); Oskarsson (Johannesson 88).
Montenegro: (451) Mijatovic; Vukcevic M (Camaj 60), Tuci, Rubezic, Radunovic; Marusic, Erakovic, Brnovic, Jovovic, Osmajic (Jovetic 60); Krstovic (Mugosa 78).

Wales (0) 0

Turkey (0) 0 28,625

Wales: (433) Ward; Roberts, Rodon, Davies B, Williams; Wilson, Ampadu, James J (Cooper 88); Johnson, Ramsey (Moore 72), Thomas (Koumas 72).
Turkey: (541) Gunok; Celik (Topcu 90), Ayhan, Soyuncu, Bardakci, Muldur; Guler (Kahveci 90), Kokcu (Calhanoglu 64), Yuksek (Yokuslu 77), Yildiz (Akturkoglu 77); Yilmaz█.

Monday, 9 September 2024

Montenegro (0) 1 *(Camaj 73)*

Wales (2) 2 *(Moore 1, Wilson 3)* 3569

Montenegro: (4231) Mijatovic; Marusic (Vukcevic M 74), Rubezic, Sipcic, Vukcevic A (Radunovic 77); Brnovic (Osmajic 69), Jovovic; Camaj, Jovetic (Erakovic 74), Krstovic; Mugosa (Bakic 70).
Wales: (4411) Darlow; Roberts (Johnson 43), Mepham, Rodon, Davies B; Williams, Ampadu, Cooper (James J 61), Koumas (Thomas 46); Wilson (Ramsey 80); Moore (Harris 80).

Turkey (1) 3 *(Akturkoglu 2, 52, 88)*

Iceland (1) 1 *(Palsson 37)* 16,167

Turkey: (4231) Gunok; Muldur (Celik 74), Demiral, Bardakci, Elmali; Calhanoglu (Kokcu 46), Yuksek (Ayhan 87); Guler, Kahveci (Yildiz 74), Akturkoglu; Nayir (Yokuslu 81).
Iceland: (4411) Valdimarsson; Palsson (Fridriksson 59), Hermannsson, Gretarsson, Finnsson; Anderson (Willumsson W 46), Gudmundsson J, Thordarson, Thorsteinsson (Traustason 59); Sigurdsson G (Oskarsson 59); Gudjohnsen.

Friday, 11 October 2024

Iceland (0) 2 *(Tomasson 69, Ward 72 (og))*

Wales (2) 2 *(Johnson 11, Wilson 29)* 6141

Iceland: (442) Valdimarsson; Fridriksson, Ingason, Gretarsson, Finnsson (Tomasson 46); Willumsson W (Ellertsson 46), Gudmundsson J (Traustason 82), Thordarson, Thorsteinsson; Oskarsson, Gudjohnsen (Sigurdsson G 84).
Wales: (4231) Ward; Roberts (Cullen 76), Rodon, Davies B, Williams; James J, Cooper; Johnson (Burns 46), Wilson, Thomas (Cabango 76); Moore.

Turkey (0) 1 *(Kahveci 69)*

Montenegro (0) 0 28,829

Turkey: (4231) Cakir; Muldur (Celik 62), Demiral, Bardakci, Kadioglu; Calhanoglu, Kokcu; Akgun (Kahveci 63), Guler (Ayhan 83), Akturkoglu (Yildiz 69); Yilmaz (Yildirim 46).
Montenegro: (451) Nikic; Marusic, Vujacic, Sipcic, Vukcevic A, Camaj (Osmajic 61), Bakic (Vukotic M 90), Kuc (Jankovic 61), Jovovic (Brnovic 76), Krstovic; Jovetic (Mugosa 76).

Monday, 14 October 2024

Iceland (0) 2 *(Oskarsson 3, Gudjohnsen 83)*

Turkey (0) 4 *(Kahveci 62, Calhanoglu 67 (pen), Guler 88, Akturkoglu 90)* 5260

Iceland: (442) Valdimarsson; Fridriksson, Ingason, Gretarsson, Tomasson; Anderson (Johannesson 68), Traustason, Gudmundsson J, Ellertsson (Willumsson W 78); Oskarsson, Gudjohnsen.
Turkey: (4231) Cakir; Celik, Demiral, Bardakci, Kadioglu (Elmali 78); Kokcu (Akaydin 90), Calhanoglu; Kahveci (Akgun 78), Guler (Yokuslu 89), Yildiz (Yildirim 90); Akturkoglu.

Wales (1) 1 *(Wilson 36 (pen))*

Montenegro (0) 0 27,326

Wales: (4231) Darlow; Williams, Rodon, Cabango, Davies B; Wilson (Broadhead 69), Sheehan; Brooks (Allen 59), Cullen (Cooper 89), Burns (Thomas 69); Harris (Moore 89).
Montenegro: (4231) Nikic; Marusic (Vukcevic M 46), Vujacic, Sipcic, Vukcevic A (Radunovic 46); Jankovic (Kuc 82), Bakic; Camaj (Radulovic 46), Jovovic, Krstovic; Mugosa (Jovetic 46).

Saturday, 16 November 2024

Montenegro (0) 0

Iceland (0) 2 *(Oskarsson 74, Johannesson 88)* 2354

Montenegro: (4231) Nikic; Marusic, Vujacic, Sipcic, Radunovic; Jankovic, Bakic (Loncar 74); Radulovic (Kuc 46), Jovovic, Camaj (Mugosa 69); Krstovic.
Iceland: (442) Valdimarsson; Fridriksson, Ingason, Gunnarsson A (Palsson 20), Tomasson; Gudmundsson J, Thordarson (Johannesson 68), Traustason, Thorsteinsson (Ellertsson 68); Oskarsson (Willumsson W 90), Gudjohnsen.

Turkey (0) 0

Wales (0) 0 28,812

Turkey: (4411) Gunok; Muldur, Demiral, Bardakci, Elmali (Celik 75); Akgun, Kokcu, Calhanoglu (Yuksek 46), Yilmaz (Unal 65); Guler (Ayhan 86); Akturkoglu.
Wales: (4231) Darlow; Roberts, Rodon, Davies B, Williams; Sheehan, James J (Brooks 73); Johnson (Koumas 90), Wilson, Thomas (Cullen 72); Harris (James D 46).

Tuesday, 19 November 2024

Montenegro (2) 3 *(Krstovic 29, 45, 73)*

Turkey (1) 1 *(Yildiz 37)* 2579

Montenegro: (352) Nikic; Tuci, Vujacic, Sipcic; Vukcevic M, Vukotic M (Kuc 69), Jankovic, Loncar, Gasevic (Camaj 86); Krstovic, Jovetic (Brnovic 83).
Turkey: (4231) Gunok; Ayhan (Kilicsoy 82), Demiral, Topcu (Akaydin 46), Elmali (Muldur 46); Yokuslu (Yuksek 63), Kokcu; Akgun (Yilmaz 74), Guler, Yildiz; Akturkoglu.

Wales (2) 4 *(Cullen 32, 45, Johnson 65, Wilson 79)*

Iceland (1) 1 *(Gudjohnsen 7)* 28,240

Wales: (4231) Ward; Williams, Rodon, Cabango, Davies B; Wilson, Sheehan (James J 89); Johnson (Roberts 89), Cullen, James D (Thomas 73); Harris (Allen 65).
Iceland: (442) Valdimarsson; Sampsted (Thorhallsson 74), Ingason, Palsson, Fridriksson; Johannesson, Traustason, Gudmundsson J (Thordarson 46), Thorsteinsson (Willumsson W 74); Oskarsson (Ellertsson 25), Gudjohnsen.

Group B4 Table

	P	W	D	L	F	A	GD	Pts
Wales	6	3	3	0	9	4	5	12
Turkey	6	3	2	1	9	6	3	11
Iceland	6	2	1	3	10	13	–3	7
Montenegro	6	1	0	5	4	9	–5	3

GROUP C1

Thursday, 5 September 2024

Azerbaijan (0) 1 *(Dadashov 82)*

Sweden (0) 3 *(Isak 65, 71, Gyokeres 80 (pen))* 9450

Azerbaijan: (4231) Dzhenetov; Huseynov A (Seydiyev 84), Mustafazade, Huseynov B, Cafarquliyev; Diniyev (Kokcu 75), Isaev (Jamalov 83); Sheydayev (Akhundzade 83), Mahmudov (Nuriyev 69), Bayramov T; Dadashov.
Sweden: (4222) Johansson; Wahlqvist (Cajuste 72), Douglas (Bergvall 72), Hien, Augustinsson; Ayari (Starfelt 72), Svanberg (Saletros 64); Kulusevski, Elanga (Sema 46); Gyokeres, Isak.

Estonia (0) 0

Slovakia (0) 1 *(Suslov 70)* 6128

Estonia: (4411) Hein; Lilander, Tamm J, Mets, Schjonning-Larsen; Miller (Yakovlev 78), Ainsalu (Palumets 69), Shein, Sinyavskiy (Saarma 84); Sappinen; Tamm A (Vetkal 69).
Slovakia: (433) Dubravka; Pekarik (Gyomber 90), Skriniar, Obert (Vavro 65), Hancko; Duda (Rigo 83), Lobotka, Benes (Bero 83); Suslov, Bozenik (Strelec 65), Haraslin.

Sunday, 8 September 2024

Slovakia (2) 2 *(Duda 22 (pen), Strelec 26)*

Azerbaijan (0) 0 11,435

Slovakia: (433) Dubravka; Gyomber, Skriniar, Obert, Hancko (Kozlovsky 90); Kucka, Lobotka, Duda (Benes 71); Suslov (Duris 71), Strelec (Bozenik 84), Haraslin (Tupta 84).
Azerbaijan: (4231) Dzhenetov; Seydiyev (Huseynov A 37), Mammadov, Huseynov B (Aliyev S 70), Cafarquliyev; Jamalov (Diniyev 78), Isaev; Kokcu (Nuriyev 46), Mustafayev (Sheydayev 46), Bayramov T; Dadashov.

Sweden (3) 3 *(Gyokeres 30, 44, Isak 40)*

Estonia (0) 0 14,858

Sweden: (3412) Johansson; Douglas, Hien, Gudmundsson; Eliasson, Ayari (Nanasi 63), Saletros (Bergvall 84), Sema (Cajuste 63); Kulusevski; Gyokeres (Elanga 79), Isak (Nilsson 79).
Estonia: (4411) Hein; Paskotsi, Tamm J, Mets, Schjonning-Larsen (Peetson 59); Miller (Lilander 83), Palumets•, Shein (Poom 59), Sinyavskiy (Kristal 72); Vetkal; Sappinen (Tamm A 60).

Friday, 11 October 2024

Estonia (2) 3 *(Yakovlev 32, Sinyavskiy 45, Shein 71)*

Azerbaijan (1) 1 *(Bayramov T 45 (pen))* 6034

Estonia: (4231) Hein; Paskotsi (Peetson 29), Tamm J, Mets, Schjonning-Larsen; Ainsalu, Shein (Vetkal 84); Yakovlev (Zenjov 68) Kait (Poom 84), Sinyavskiy; Anier (Sorga 68).
Azerbaijan: (343) Dzhenetov; Mammadov, Huseynov B, Krivotsyuk; Huseynov A (Aliyev Q 77), Diniyev (Nuriyev 64), Isaev (Mahmudov 76), Cafarquliyev; Bayramov T (Emreli 64), Dadashov (Akhmedzade R 82), Sheydayev.

Slovakia (1) 2 *(Strelec 44, 72)*

Sweden (2) 2 *(Ayari 25, Sema 32)* 15,381

Slovakia: (433) Rodak; Pekarik (Gyomber 90), Vavro, Skriniar, Hancko; Duda (Bero 76), Lobotka, Benes; Suslov (Duris 90), Strelec (Bozenik 80), Haraslin (Tupta 90).
Sweden: (3412) Johansson; Douglas (Lindelof 62), Hien, Gudmundsson; Eliasson (Krafth 90), Karlstrom, Saletros, Sema; Ayari (Larsson 62); Kulusevski, Gyokeres.

Monday, 14 October 2024

Azerbaijan (1) 1 *(Bayramov T 38)*

Slovakia (1) 3 *(Mammadov 15 (og), Haraslin 75, Duris 86)*
4269

Azerbaijan: (343) Dzhenetov; Mammadov, Huseynov B, Krivotsyuk (Mahmudov 46); Aliyev Q (Huseynov A 84), Nuriyev (Abdullayev 88), Isaev (Dadashov 77), Cafarquliyev; Bayramov T, Emreli■, Sheydayev (Akhmedzade R 77).
Slovakia: (433) Rodak; Pekarik (Tomic 90), Satka, Skriniar, Hancko; Duda (Rigo 90), Lobotka (Hrosovsky 84), Benes; Suslov, Strelec (Tupta 84), Haraslin (Duris 83).

Estonia (0) 0

Sweden (2) 3 *(Nanasi 29, 37, Gyokeres 66)* 4706

Estonia: (4231) Hein; Peetson (Kuusk 83), Tamm J, Mets, Schjonning-Larsen; Ainsalu (Palumets 65), Kait; Yakovlev (Miller 54), Vetkal (Kristal 65), Sinyavskiy; Tamm A (Anier 83).
Sweden: (352) Johansson; Douglas (Eliasson 26), Hien, Gudmundsson; Krafth, Ayari (Svensson 89), Saletros (Larsson 83), Nanasi (Bolin 83), Sema; Gyokeres, Kulusevski.

Saturday, 16 November 2024

Azerbaijan (0) 0

Estonia (0) 0 1600

Azerbaijan: (4231) Jafarov; Huseynov A, Mammadov (Mustafazade 5), Huseynov B, Cafarquliyev; Diniyev, Isaev; Bayramov T (Akhundzade 70), Kokcu (Najafov 88), Sheydayev; Qurbanly.
Estonia: (4231) Hein; Paskotsi, Tamm J, Mets, Schjonning-Larsen; Palumets (Soomets 88), Poom; Miller (Yakovlev 64), Shein (Vetkal 68), Sinyavskiy; Anier (Tamm A 63).

Sweden (1) 2 *(Gyokeres 3, Isak 48)*

Slovakia (1) 1 *(Hancko 19)* 36,417

Sweden: (3412) Johansson; Lindelof (Starfelt 26), Hien, Gudmundsson; Eliasson (Holm 75), Ayari (Karlstrom 75), Saletros, Sema; Kulusevski; Isak, Gyokeres.
Slovakia: (433) Dubravka; Gyomber, Vavro (Obert 40), Skriniar■, Hancko; Duda (Rigo 67), Lobotka, Benes (Bero 58); Suslov, Strelec, Duris (Schranz 57).

Tuesday, 19 November 2024

Slovakia (0) 1 *(Strelec 72)*

Estonia (0) 0 4317

Slovakia: (433) Greif; Gyomber, Vavro, Obert, Hancko; Bero, Lobotka (Hrosovsky 60), Benes (Rigo 88); Suslov (Schranz 77), Bozenik (Strelec 46), Tupta (Sauer 60).
Estonia: (4231) Hein; Schjonning-Larsen, Paskotsi, Mets, Saliste (Peetson 71); Palumets (Tamm J 87), Poom (Shein 60); Yakovlev, Kristal (Vetkal 71), Sinyavskiy (Kuraksin 71); Tamm A.

Sweden (3) 6 *(Kulusevski 10, 57, Gyokeres 26, 37, 58, 70)*

Azerbaijan (0) 0 10,127

Sweden: (3412) Johansson; Starfelt, Gudmundsson (Zatterstrom 89), Sema; Ayari (Holm 51), Karlstrom (Bergvall 88), Saletros, Nanasi (Forsberg 66); Kulusevski; Gyokeres (Lidberg 89), Isak.
Azerbaijan: (433) Jafarov; Seydiyev (Huseynov A 56), Mustafazade, Huseynov B (Aliyev Z 46), Krivotsyuk; Diniyev, Kokcu (Nuriyev 46), Isaev (Qurbanly 64); Emreli, Akhundzade (Sheydayev 46), Bayramov T.

Group C1 Table	P	W	D	L	F	A	GD	Pts
Sweden	6	5	1	0	19	4	15	16
Slovakia	6	4	1	1	10	5	5	13
Estonia	6	1	1	4	3	9	–6	4
Azerbaijan	6	0	1	5	3	17	–14	1

GROUP C2

Friday, 6 September 2024

Kosovo (0) 0

Romania (1) 3 *(Man 40, Marin R 51 (pen), Dragus 82)*
12,872

Kosovo: (442) Muric; Vojvoda■, Amir Rrahmani, Aliti, Paqarada (Rrudhani 81); Zhegrova (Sahiti 81), Rexhbecaj, Berisha (Muslija 67), Rashica; Muriqi (Albion Rrahmani 66), Asllani (Krasniqi E 66).
Romania: (433) Nita; Ratiu, Dragusin, Burca, Bancu; Marin R (Olaru 86), Marin M, Stanciu (Mitrita 86); Man (Coman 78), Dragus (Puscas 83), Mihaila (Hagi 83).

Lithuania (0) 0

Cyprus (1) 1 *(Pittas 34)* 4905

Lithuania: (532) Gertmonas; Sirvys (Paulauskas G 70), Kazukolovas, Girdvainis, Tutyskinas, Lasickas; Slivka, Vorobjovas (Verbickas 86), Matulevicius (Kalinauskas 61); Kucys, Dolznikov (Paulauskas V 86).
Cyprus: (3421) Mall; Karo, Gogic, Kyprianou (Malekkides 46), Panayiotou (Andreou 46), Spoljaric (Chrysostomou 65), Artymatas, Ioannou; Kastanos, Tzionis (Anderson Correia 89); Pittas (Laifis 90).

Monday, 9 September 2024

Cyprus (0) 0

Kosovo (2) 4 *(Muriqi 9 (pen), 21, Albion Rrahmani 48, Dellova 55)* 2041

Cyprus: (3421) Mall; Karo, Gogic, Kyprianou (Laifis 46); Panayiotou (Andreou 46), Artymatas, Kastanos, Ioannou (Spoljaric 71); Tzionis (Loizou 65), Malekkides (Anderson Correia 58); Pittas.
Kosovo: (433) Bekaj; Hadergjonaj, Amir Rrahmani, Aliti (Dellova 46), Rrudhani; Rexhbecaj (Krasniqi I 70), Emerllahu (Bujupi 87), Berisha; Krasniqi E, Muriqi (Albion Rrahmani 66), Rashica (Sahiti 70).

Romania (1) 3 *(Mihaila 4, Marin R 87 (pen), Mitrita 90)*

Lithuania (1) 1 *(Kucys 34)* 28,168

Romania: (433) Tarnovanu; Ratiu, Dragusin, Burca, Bancu; Stanciu, Marin M (Olaru 56), Mihaila (Mitrita 70); Man (Hagi 70), Dragus (Alibec 88), Marin R.
Lithuania: (541) Gertmonas; Sirvys, Lekiatas, Girdvainis, Tutyskinas, Lasickas (Kazukolovas 90); Dolznikov (Kalinauskas 76), Matulevicius (Verbickas 66), Vorobjovas (Antanavicius 75), Slivka; Kucys (Paulauskas G 65).

Saturday, 12 October 2024

Cyprus (0) 0

Romania (3) 3 *(Man 16, Marin R 25 (pen), Dragusin 36)*
6092

Cyprus: (4231) Mall; Antoniou (Stylianou 33), Laifis, Panagiotou, Ioannou; Artymatas, Kousoulos (Charalampous 46); Loizou (Sotiriou P 46), Kastanos (Makris 75), Tzionis (Elia 46); Pittas.
Romania: (433) Nita; Ratiu, Dragusin (Olaru 63), Burca, Bancu (Chipciu 63); Marin R (Olaru 63), Marin M, Stanciu; Man (Hagi 72), Dragus (Puscas 72), Mihaila.

Lithuania (0) 0

Kosovo (1) 2 *(Zhegrova 20, Krasniqi E 65)* 7554

Lithuania: (3421) Gertmonas; Kazukolovas, Girdvainis, Tutyskinas; Sirvys, Vorobjovas (Golubickas 59), Gineitis, Slivka; Dolznikov (Paulauskas G 77), Lasickas (Cernych 59); Kucys (Matulevicius 78).
Kosovo: (4231) Saipi; Vojvoda, Amir Rrahmani, Dellova, Rrudhani (Hadergjonaj 59); Rexhbecaj, Berisha (Krasniqi I 75); Zhegrova, Muslija (Krasniqi E 59), Rashica (Jashari 88); Albion Rrahmani (Asllani 88).

Tuesday, 15 October 2024

Kosovo (1) 3 *(Amir Rrahmani 30, Krasniqi E 52, Sahiti 70)*

Cyprus (0) 0 12,863

Kosovo: (4231) Muric; Vojvoda, Amir Rrahmani (Aliti 77), Dellova, Rrudhani; Emerllahu, Jashari; Zhegrova (Sahiti 67), Rashica (Muslija 16), Krasniqi E; Albion Rrahmani (Asllani 78).
Cyprus: (4141) Dimitriou; Karo (Antoniou 72), Andreou, Laifis, Ioannou (Pileas 46); Artymatas; Loizou, Kastanos (Mamas 72), Charalampous, Makris (Tzionis 72); Pittas (Sotiriou P 77).

Lithuania (1) 1 *(Kucys 7 (pen))*
Romania (1) 2 *(Marin R 18 (pen), Dragus 65)*　　2585
Lithuania: (4231) Gertmonas; Sirvys (Cernych 75), Lekiatas, Girdvainis, Tutyskinas (Milasius 60); Vorobjovas (Matulevicius 80), Gineitis; Slivka, Golubickas (Dolznikov 59), Lasickas; Kucys (Paulauskas G 80).
Romania: (433) Nita; Ratiu, Dragusin, Burca, Sorescu; Marin R (Olaru 73), Marin M, Stanciu; Man (Hagi 84), Dragus, Mihaila (Coman 73).

Friday, 15 November 2024

Cyprus (1) 2 *(Kastanos 18, Tzionis 63)*
Lithuania (0) 1 *(Gineitis 47)*　　1733
Cyprus: (433) Dimitriou; Karo, Andreou, Panagiotou, Ioannou (Malekkidis 46); Kastanos (Satsias 81), Artymatas, Charalampous (Kousoulos 56); Loizou (Makris 76), Pittas, Kakoullis (Tzionis 56).
Lithuania: (451) Bertasius; Sirvys (Cernych 60), Kazukolovas, Girdvainis, Tutyskinas (Milasius 60); Dolznikov (Kalinauskas 46), Golubickas (Jansonas 80), Vorobjovas (Matulevicius 60), Gineitis, Lasickas; Paulauskas G.

Romania (0) 0
Kosovo (0) 0　　48,957
Romania: (433) Nita; Ratiu, Dragusin, Burca, Bancu; Marin R, Marin M (Sut 76), Stanciu (Olaru 46); Man (Alibec 64), Dragus (Hagi 89). Mihaila.
Kosovo: (4231) Muric; Hadergjonaj, Amir Rrahmani, Dellova, Vojvoda; Rexhbecaj, Berisha; Zhegrova, Muslija (Asllani 82), Jashari (Bytyqi 82); Muriqi (Albion Rrahmani 71).
Match abandoned after 90 minutes with the score at 0-0 due to Kosovo leaving the pitch after Romanian fans allegedly chanted anti-Kosovo and pro-Serbian slogans. Match awarded 3-0 to Romania.

Monday, 18 November 2024

Kosovo (1) 1 *(Jashari 5)*
Lithuania (0) 0　　12,856
Kosovo: (442) Muric; Hadergjonaj, Krasniqi I, Aliti, Vojvoda; Zhegrova (Hoti 79), Rexhbecaj, Berisha (Emerllahu 46), Jashari■; Albion Rrahmani (Bytyqi 46), Muriqi (Asllani 80).
Lithuania: (532) Gertmonas; Sirvys, Utkus, Girdvainis, Milasius, Lasickas; Cernych (Golubickas 60), Vorobjovas (Jansonas 80), Gineitis; Slivka, Paulauskas G.

Romania (2) 4 *(Birligea 2, Marin R 41, 80, Coman 83)*
Cyprus (0) 1 *(Pittas 52)*　　45,318
Romania: (433) Nita (Tarnovanu 67); Ratiu, Dragusin (Burca 68), Pascanu, Bancu; Marin R, Marin M (Coman 67), Olaru (Sut 66); Hagi, Birligea, Mihaila (Mitrita 84).
Cyprus: (442) Dimitriou; Karo (Antoniou 46), Andreou, Laifis■, Anderson Correia; Loizou, Spoljaric (Charalampous 46), Artymatas, Kakoullis (Pittas 46); Sotiriou P (Panagiotou 79), Tzionis (Makris 74).

Group C2 Table	P	W	D	L	F	A	GD	Pts
Romania	6	6	0	0	18	3	15	18
Kosovo	6	4	0	2	10	7	3	12
Cyprus	6	2	0	4	4	15	−11	6
Lithuania	6	0	0	6	4	11	−7	0

GROUP C3

Due to their support for the Russian invasion of Ukraine, Belarus's home matches were played behind closed doors in Hungary.

Thursday, 5 September 2024

Belarus (0) 0
Bulgaria (0) 0　　0
Belarus: (532) Lapoukhov; Kovalev (Karpovich 64), Volkov, Martynovich, Zabelin, Pechenin; Yablonskiy (Selyava 77), Kaplenko, Ebong (Klimovich 83); Shikavka (Melnichenko 83), Antilevskiy (Kireev 64).
Bulgaria: (4231) Mitov; Popov, Atanasov, Petkov A, Nurnberger; Antov (Minchev M 77), Gruev; Despodov (Ivanov 83), Krastev■, Kirilov (Minchev I 77); Kolev (Ahmedov 83).

Northern Ireland (2) 2 *(McNair 11, Ballard 16)*
Luxembourg (0) 0　　17,213
Northern Ireland: (343) Peacock-Farrell; Ballard (Smyth 83), McNair, Brown; Bradley, Charles S (McCann 83), Saville, Hume; Price (McCausland 74), Charles D (Magennis 46), Marshall (Lewis 57).
Luxembourg: (442) Moris; Jans (Dzogovic 74), Mahmutovic (Mica Pinto 46), Gerson, Carlson; Bohnert, Martins C, Barreiro, Veiga (Andrade Brites 74); Olesen (Thill S 85), Rodrigues (Muratovic 85).

Sunday, 8 September 2024

Bulgaria (1) 1 *(Despodov 40)*
Northern Ireland (0) 0　　14,300
Bulgaria: (4231) Mitov; Popov, Atanasov, Petkov A, Nurnberger; Kostadinov (Petrov S 78), Gruev; Despodov (Ivanov 78), Minchev M (Panayotov 72), Kirilov (Dimitrov 72); Kolev (Ahmedov 63).
Northern Ireland: (343) Peacock-Farrell; Ballard, McNair (Marshall 73), Brown; Hume (McCausland 83), Charles S, Saville (Smyth 73), Lewis; Bradley, Charles D (Lavery 59), Price (McCann 82).

Luxembourg (0) 0
Belarus (0) 1 *(Gromyko 76)*　　6820
Luxembourg: (4141) Moris; Dzogovic (Rupil 84), Chanot, Carlson, Jans (Mica Pinto 46); Martins C; Sinani, Olesen (Thill S 46), Barreiro, Bohnert (Mahmutovic 65); Muratovic.
Belarus: (343) Lapoukhov; Volkov, Martynovich, Zabelin; Karpovich (Kovalev 67), Selyava (Yablonskiy 46), Ebong, Pechenin; Bakhar (Kireev 42), Shikavka (Barkovsky 85), Antilevskiy (Gromyko 67).

Saturday, 12 October 2024

Belarus (0) 0
Northern Ireland (0) 0　　0
Belarus: (3421) Lapoukhov; Volkov, Politevich, Zabelin; Kovalev (Karpovich 64), Yablonskiy (Klimovich 75), Ebong, Pechenin; Antilevskiy (Kontsevoy 75), Korzun (Bocherov 90); Shikavka (Barkovsky 64).
Northern Ireland: (352) Charles P; Hume, McNair, Toal; Bradley, Price (Smyth 83), Charles S, Saville (McCann 83), Lewis (Spencer 67); Reid (Bonis 76), Marshall (Charles D 67).

Bulgaria (0) 0
Luxembourg (0) 0　　15,800
Bulgaria: (4231) Mitov; Popov, Atanasov, Petkov A, Nurnberger; Kostadinov (Chochev 83), Antov (Dimitrov 63); Despodov, Krastev, Kirilov (Minchev M 63); Kolev (Minchev G 76).
Luxembourg: (3142) Moris; Jans, Korac, Carlson (Martins M 90); Martins C; Bohnert, Barreiro, Olesen, Mica Pinto (D'Anzico 61); Sinani, Curci (Rodrigues 46).

Tuesday, 15 October 2024

Belarus (0) 1 *(Politevich 54)*
Luxembourg (0) 1 *(Rodrigues 78 (pen))*　　0
Belarus: (532) Lapoukhov; Pigas (Kovalev 89), Martynovich, Politevich, Zabelin, Pechenin; Gromyko (Korzun 61), Bocherov, Ebong (Klimovich 74); Barkovsky (Antilevskiy 74), Shikavka (Kontsevoy 89).
Luxembourg: (3412) Moris; D'Anzico (Martins M 46), Korac, Carlson; Jans, Olesen (Moreira 76), Barreiro, Mica Pinto; Sinani; Curci (Omosanya 63), Rodrigues.

Northern Ireland (3) 5 *(Price 15, 29, 81, Mitov 32 (og), Magennis 89)*
Bulgaria (0) 0　　17,891
Northern Ireland: (3421) Charles P; Hume, McNair, Toal (Brown 45); Bradley, McCann, Charles S (Magennis 85), Spencer; Price (Lyons 85), Marshall (Smyth 74); Charles D (Reid 74).
Bulgaria: (433) Mitov; Popov, Atanasov (Chochev 79), Petrov S, Petrov H; Krastev, Kostadinov, Yusein (Antov 46); Despodov (Iliev I 85), Minchev M (Minchev G 85), Kirilov (Dimitrov 46).

Friday, 15 November 2024

Luxembourg (0) 0

Bulgaria (1) 1 *(Kraev A 23)*   8371

Luxembourg: (4231) Pereira Cardoso; Jans, Korac, Carlson, Mica Pinto (Dzogovic 85); Martins C, Moreira; Sinani, Olesen (Rupil 77), Bohnert (Omosanya 62); Rodrigues.
Bulgaria: (442) Mitov; Popov, Petrov S, Petkov A, Nurnberger; Milanov (Atanasov 62), Panayotov, Kraev A (Antov 83), Despodov; Krastev (Ahmedov 78), Kolev (Kirilov 78).

Northern Ireland (0) 2 *(Ballard 50, Charles D 63 (pen))*

Belarus (0) 0   18,044

Northern Ireland: (3412) Charles P; Hume, Ballard (Saville 76), Brown; Bradley (Lyons 90), McCann, Charles S, Spencer; Price (McConville 86); Smyth (Reid 76), Charles D (Magennis 76).
Belarus: (532) Lapoukhov; Pigas, Martynovich, Politevich, Zabelin, Pechenin (Prishchepa 72); Yablonskiy (Klimovich 62), Selyava (Ebong 62); Gromyko (Demchenko 72); Barkovsky (Antilevskiy 62), Shikavka.

Monday, 18 November 2024

Bulgaria (1) 1 *(Panayotov 12)*

Belarus (0) 1 *(Kovalev 70)*   2200

Bulgaria: (4141) Mitov; Popov, Petrov S, Petkov A, Nurnberger; Kraev A; Petkov M (Atanasov 88), Panayotov (Antov 90), Milanov (Rusev 76), Kirilov (Krastev 76); Kolev (Ahmedov 76).
Belarus: (3421) Lapoukhov; Martynovich, Politevich, Polyakov (Zabelin 59); Karpovich, Bocherov (Yablonskiy 59), Ebong, Prishchepa (Kovalev 46); Gromyko (Antilevskiy 59), Lisakovich; Shikavka (Savitskiy 73).

Luxembourg (0) 2 *(Korac 72, Rodrigues 75)*

Northern Ireland (1) 2 *(Price 19, Bradley 50)*   6870

Luxembourg: (3421) Pereira Cardoso (Schon 74); Korac, Carlson (Martins M 82), Mica Pinto (Olesen 56); Jans, Barreiro (Mahmutovic 56), Martins C, Bohnert (Curci 74); Sinani, Moreira; Rodrigues.
Northern Ireland: (3421) Charles P; Hume, Ballard, McConville; Bradley, McCann (Saville 76), Charles S, Spencer; Galbraith (Smyth 89), Price (Devenny 90); Charles D (Reid 76).

Group C3 Table	P	W	D	L	F	A	GD	Pts
Northern Ireland	6	3	2	1	11	3	8	11
Bulgaria	6	2	3	1	3	6	–3	9
Belarus	6	1	4	1	3	4	–1	7
Luxembourg	6	0	3	3	7	–4	3

GROUP C4

Saturday, 7 September 2024

Armenia (2) 4 *(Bichakhchyan 6, Dubra 35 (og), Zelarrayan 48, Spertsyan 86)*

Latvia (1) 1 *(Harutyunyan G 9 (og))*   12,437

Armenia: (343) Cancarevic; Calisir (Muradyan 76), Haroyan, Harutyunyan G; Hovhannisyan, Spertsyan, Iwu, Tiknizyan; Bichakhchyan (Sevikyan 66), Zelarrayan (Ranos 84), Serobyan (Shaghoyan 66).
Latvia: (3412) Matrevics; Jurkovskis, Dubra (Balodis 63), Tobers, Jaunzems (Savalnieks 64), Saveljevs, Vapne (Zelenkovs 63), Ciganiks, Ikaunieks (Varslavans 82); Uldrikis, Daskevics (Gutkovskis 63).

Faroe Islands (1) 1 *(Davidsen 9 (pen))*

North Macedonia (0) 1 *(Bardhi 49 (pen))*   2057

Faroe Islands: (4141) Reynatrod; Danielsen, Chukwudi (Askham 46), Edmundsson A, Davidsen; Vatnhamar S; Joensen R (Mikkelsen 66), Vatnhamar S (Knudsen 84), Sorensen, Olsen M (Johannesen 84); Edmundsson J (Justinussen 66).
North Macedonia: (343) Dimitrievski, Iljazovski (Alioski 46); Serafimov, Musliu; Mitrovski (Qamili 46), Bardhi, Alimi, Dimoski; Miovski, Elmas, Churlinov (Ilievski M 77).

Tuesday, 10 September 2024

Latvia (0) 1 *(Varslavans 64)*

Faroe Islands (0) 0   5808

Latvia: (3412) Matrevics; Jurkovskis, Tobers, Balodis; Savalnieks, Zelenkovs (Vapne 80), Saveljevs, Ciganiks; Varslavans (Melniks 80); Gutkovskis (Uldrikis 72), Ikaunieks (Jaunzems 90).
Faroe Islands: (4141) Reynatrod; Danielsen (Knudsen 83), Chukwudi, Edmundsson A, Davidsen; Vatnhamar G; Joensen R (Olsen K 83), Vatnhamar S (Justinussen 46), Sorensen, Olsen M (Petersen 83); Edmundsson J (Mikkelsen 46).

North Macedonia (0) 2 *(Bardhi 70, Miovski 78)*

Armenia (0) 0   6829

North Macedonia: (4231) Dimitrievski; Askovski (Manev 83), Zajkov■, Musliu, Dimoski; Babunski (Serafimov 46), Alimi (Atanasov 59); Churlinov (Qamili 4), Bardhi, Elmas; Miovski.
Armenia: (3421) Cancarevic; Calisir (Manvelyan 86), Haroyan, Harutyunyan G; Hovhannisyan, Iwu, Spertsyan, Tiknizyan (Grigoryan E 66); Sevikyan (Bichakhchyan 66), Ranos (Serobyan 46); Zelarrayan (Harutyunyan H 74).

Thursday, 10 October 2024

Faroe Islands (1) 2 *(Benjaminsen 37, Bjartalid 85)*

Armenia (1) 2 *(Zelarrayan 44, Manvelyan 90)*   1852

Faroe Islands: (433) Reynatrod; Benjaminsen, Faero, Edmundsson A, Davidsen; Vatnhamar S (Hendriksson 61), Vatnhamar G, Sorensen (Joensen R 82); Agnarsson (Bjartalid 62), Edmundsson J (Knudsen 61), Olsen M (Justinussen 70).
Armenia: (532) Cancarevic; Hovhannisyan, Muradyan, Haroyan, Harutyunyan G, Tiknizyan; Bichakhchyan (Manvelyan 86), Iwu, Harutyunyan H (Sevikyan 67); Zelarrayan, Ranos (Miranyan 67).

Latvia (0) 0

North Macedonia (1) 3 *(Atanasov 35, Qamili 70, Elmas 90)*   5001

Latvia: (532) Matrevics; Jurkovskis, Balodis, Tobers, Jagodinskis (Uldrikis 71), Ciganiks; Zelenkovs (Daskevics 82), Saveljevs (Vapne 82), Varslavans; Ikaunieks, Gutkovskis (Sits 17).
North Macedonia: (4141) Dimitrievski; Babunski (Ristovski 66), Manev, Musliu (Kostadinov 55), Alioski (Qamili 66); Alimi; Askovski (Dimoski 55), Atanasov, Bardhi, Elmas; Miovski (Velkovski 85).

Sunday, 13 October 2024

Armenia (0) 0

North Macedonia (0) 2 *(Miovski 72, Alimi 85)*   14,371

Armenia: (3511) Cancarevic; Muradyan (Manvelyan 80), Haroyan, Calisir (Harutyunyan G 65); Hovhannisyan (Dashyan 74), Bichakhchyan (Sevikyan 74), Iwu, Spertsyan, Tiknizyan; Zelarrayan; Miranyan (Ranos 65).
North Macedonia: (3412) Dimitrievski; Manev (Velkovski 54), Serafimov, Zajkov; Dimoski (Qamili 54), Alimi, Atanasov (Kostadinov 54), Alioski; Bardhi (Askovski 87); Miovski (Ristovski 79), Elmas.

Faroe Islands (1) 1 *(Sorensen 40)*

Latvia (0) 1 *(Sits 69)*   2017

Faroe Islands: (4141) Reynatrod; Benjaminsen, Faero (Nattestad 78), Edmundsson A, Davidsen; Vatnhamar G; Joensen R (Bjartalid 57), Sorensen, Hendriksson (Vatnhamar S 58), Agnarsson (Justinussen 58); Olsen M (Edmundsson J 83).
Latvia: (352) Matrevics; Jurkovskis, Tobers, Balodis; Savalnieks (Cernomordijs 46), Zelenkovs, Saveljevs (Vapne 66), Varslavans (Melniks 90), Ciganiks; Ikaunieks (Sits 66), Uldrikis.

Thursday, 14 November 2024

Armenia (0) 0

Faroe Islands (1) 1 *(Davidsen 33 (pen))*   6043

Armenia: (451) Cancarevic; Hambardzumyan, Haroyan, Harutyunyan G (Manvelyan 85), Tiknizyan; Sevikyan (Shaghoyan 46), Bichakhchyan, Iwu, Spertsyan, Miranyan (Ranos 46); Zelarrayan.
Faroe Islands: (541) Gestsson; Danielsen, Faero, Vatnhamar G, Edmundsson A, Davidsen; Bjartalid (Vatnhamar S 76), Joensen R (Sorensen 62); Hendriksson (Mneney 76), Justinussen (Knudsen 68); Klettskard (Olsen M 68).

North Macedonia (0) 1 *(Serafimov 57)*

Latvia (0) 0   8851

North Macedonia: (4231) Dimitrievski; Dimoski (Mitrovski 59), Serafimov, Zajkov, Alioski (Askovski 78); Alimi, Bardhi; Churlinov (Ristovski 58), Trajkovski (Velkovski 78), Elmas (Qamili 24); Miovski.
Latvia: (541) Matrevics; Savalnieks (Tobers 64), Jurkovskis, Cernomordijs, Jagodinskis, Ciganiks; Jaunzems (Melniks 64), Vapne (Varslavans 64), Zelenkovs, Daskevics (Uldrikis 71); Sits (Gutkovskis 71).

Sunday, 17 November 2024

Latvia (0) 1 *(Uldriks 70)*

Armenia (0) 2 *(Spertsyan 48, Miranyan 74)*   5543

Latvia: (532) Matrevics; Jurkovskis (Krollis 76), Tobers (Vapne 82), Cernomordijs, Balodis, Ciganiks; Zelenkovs, Saveljevs (Savalnieks 67), Varslavans; Ikaunieks (Daskevics 67), Gutkovskis (Uldrikis 67).
Armenia: (433) Cancarevic; Harutyunyan G, Haroyan, Muradyan, Tiknizyan; Iwu, Udo (Manvelyan 46), Spertsyan; Bichakhchyan (Grigoryan N 63), Ranos (Miranyan 63), Zelarrayan (Calisir 84).

North Macedonia (0) 1 *(Miovski 62)*

Faroe Islands (0) 0   7450

North Macedonia: (4231) Dimitrievski; Ilievski B (Askovski 54), Serafimov, Zajkov, Alioski; Alimi, Atanasov; Churlinov (Qamili 54), Bardhi (Babunski 90), Trajkovski (Ristovski 54); Miovski (Velkovski 88).
Faroe Islands: (343) Reynatrod; Faero, Vatnhamar G, Edmundsson A; Benjaminsen, Hansson (Joensen R 58), Hendriksson (Justinussen 85), Davidsen; Sorensen (Vatnhamar S 85), Knudsen (Klettskard 79), Olsen M (Bjartalid 79).

Group C4 Table

	P	W	D	L	F	A	GD	Pts
North Macedonia	6	5	1	0	10	1	9	16
Armenia	6	2	1	3	8	9	–1	7
Faroe Islands	6	1	3	2	5	6	–1	6
Latvia	6	1	1	4	4	11	–7	4

GROUP D1

Thursday, 5 September 2024

San Marino (0) 1 *(Sensoli 53)*

Liechtenstein (0) 0   914

San Marino: (433) Colombo; Benvenuti G, Cevoli, Rossi, Tosi (Benvenuti T 71); Golinucci A (Battistini 62), Capicchioni (Mularoni 81), Casadei; Contadini, Nanni (Giacopetti 71), Sensoli (Zannoni 62).
Liechtenstein: (352) Buchel B; Beck N (Martin Marxer 62), Wieser, Goppel (Oberwaditzer 62); Wolfinger S, Hasler N, Sele (Luchinger 63), Buchel M, Zund (Meier 63); Notaro (Beck J 81), Saglam.

Sunday, 8 September 2024

Gibraltar (1) 2 *(Walker 8, Scanlon 90)*

Liechtenstein (0) 2 *(Saglam 53, Hasler N 90 (pen))*   681

Gibraltar: (4411) Banda; Jolley (Valarino 73), Lopes, Annesley, Olivero; Scanlon, Torrilla, Bent, Britto; Walker (Casciaro 90); De Barr (Bartolo 57).
Liechtenstein: (352) Buchel B; Beck N, Wieser, Goppel (Martin Marxer 87); Meier (Luchinger 90), Hasler N, Buchel M (Wolfinger F 87), Sele, Kindle (Marco Marxer 75); Notaro (Netzer 75), Saglam.

Thursday, 10 October 2024

Gibraltar (0) 1 *(Britto 62)*

San Marino (0) 0   677

Gibraltar: (4411) Banda; Jolley (Pozo 90), Lopes, Annesley, Olivero; Scanlon (Ronan 77), Torrilla, Bent, Britto; Walker; De Barr (Bartolo 88).
San Marino: (4141) Colombo; Benvenuti G (Fabbri 81), Cevoli, Rossi (Valentini 28), Tosi (Benvenuti T 81); Battistini; Contadini, Casadei, Zannoni (Lazzari 70); Berardi (Sensoli 69); Nanni.

Sunday, 13 October 2024

Liechtenstein (0) 0

Gibraltar (0) 0   1510

Liechtenstein: (352) Buchel B; Martin Marxer, Traber, Goppel; Hasler N, Luchinger (Kranz 90), Buchel M (Wolfinger F 83), Sele (Wolfinger S 64), Kindle (Meier 64); Saglam, Salanovic (Notaro 46).
Gibraltar: (4411) Banda; Jolley, Lopes, Annesley, Olivero; Scanlon, Pozo, Bent▪, Ronan (Casciaro 90); Walker; De Barr (Bartolo 90).

Friday, 15 November 2024

San Marino (0) 1 *(Nanni 90 (pen))*

Gibraltar (1) 1 *(Walker 11 (pen))*   1324

San Marino: (4141) Colombo; Benvenuti G (Fabbri 77), Cevoli, Rossi, Benvenuti T (Tosi 77); Golinucci A; Berardi (Sensoli 77), Casadei (Zannoni 61), Lazzari (Giacopetti 72), Contadini; Nanni.
Gibraltar: (4411) Banda; Jolley, Lopes, Annesley, Olivero; Scanlon (Mouelhi 78), Torrilla, Pozo, Britto (Ronan 89); Walker; De Barr.

Monday, 18 November 2024

Liechtenstein (1) 1 *(Sele 40)*

San Marino (0) 3 *(Lazzari 46, Nanni 66 (pen), Golinucci A 76)*   1157

Liechtenstein: (352) Buchel B; Martin Marxer (Schlegel 84), Wieser, Traber; Wolfinger S (Zund 78), Meier (Kindle 70), Buchel M (Kranz 71), Sele, Goppel; Saglam, Notaro (Ospelt 84).
San Marino: (451) Colombo; Fabbri, Valentini, Benvenuti T, Tosi; Contadini (Vitaioli 85), Zannoni (Golinucci A 62), Battistini, Lazzari (Mularoni 75), Berardi (Sensoli 61); Nanni (Giacopetti 85).

Group D1 Table

	P	W	D	L	F	A	GD	Pts
San Marino	4	2	1	1	5	3	2	7
Gibraltar	4	1	3	0	4	3	1	6
Liechtenstein	4	0	2	2	3	6	–3	2

GROUP D2

Saturday, 7 September 2024

Moldova (2) 2 *(Caimacov 32, Nicolaescu 45 (pen))*

Malta (0) 0   6142

Moldova: (541) Celeadnic; Platica S, Craciun, Mudrac, Marandici, Reabciuk; Caimacov (Cojocaru 85), Motpan (Bogaciuc 70), Rata, Ionita (Stina 75); Nicolaescu (Damascan 70).
Malta: (3412) Bonello; Muscat Z, Shaw, Borg; Mbong J, Yankam (Zammit Lonardelli 46), Guillaumier (Muscat N 85), Camenzuli; Pisani (Teuma 71); Reid (Montebello 46), Mbong P (Nwoko 70).

Tuesday, 10 September 2024

Andorra (0) 0

Malta (1) 1 *(Camenzuli 45)*   812

Andorra: (541) Alvarez; Borra (Fernandez R 64), Llovera, Vales M, Olivera, San Nicolas (de las Heras 81); Rubio (Alaez 64), Guillen (Teixeira 35), Vales E (Garcia C 81), Cervos; Rosas.
Malta: (3412) Bonello; Muscat Z, Shaw, Borg; Zammit Lonardelli, Mbong J, Guillaumier, Camenzuli; Teuma (Yankam 90); Nwoko (Mbong P 78), Montebello (Reid 60).

Thursday, 10 October 2024

Moldova (1) 2 *(Ionita 31, Cojocaru 90)*

Andorra (0) 0   6442

Moldova: (541) Celeadnic; Platica S, Craciun, Mudrac, Babohlo, Reabciuk; Caimacov (Stina 71), Motpan (Marandici 58), Rata (Mandricenco 82), Ionita (Cojocaru 71); Damascan (Postolachi 57).
Andorra: (541) Alvarez; San Nicolas, Llovera, Garcia C, Olivera, Garcia M (Sanchez 61); Martinez (Fernandez R 61), Teixeira (Vales E 71), Vales M (Pujol 84), Cervos; Rosas.

Sunday, 13 October 2024

Malta (0) 1 *(Teuma 87 (pen))*

Moldova (0) 0   5754

Malta: (3421) Bonello; Shaw (Tabone 90), Mentz Z 90), Borg; Mbong J, Guillaumier, Teuma, Camenzuli; Buhagiar (Tuma 46), Mbong P (Satariano 71); Montebello (Reid 46).
Moldova: (541) Celeadnic; Platica S, Craciun, Mudrac, Marandici (Cojocaru 46), Reabciuk; Caimacov, Babohlo, Rata (Postolachi 88), Ionita (Stina 77); Damascan (Mandricenco 56).

Saturday, 16 November 2024

Andorra (0) 0

Moldova (0) 1 *(Postolachi 90)*   984

Andorra: (541) Alvarez; Borra (Gomes 77), Llovera, Garcia C, Olivera (Pujol 89), San Nicolas; Fernandez R, Teixeira (de las Heras 60), Vales E (Guillen 59), Cervos; Sanchez (Fernandez I 77).
Moldova: (352) Celeadnic; Craciun, Babohlo, Mudrac; Platica S, Caimacov, Rata, Motpan (Cojocaru 77), Reabciuk; Nicolaescu, Postolachi.

Tuesday, 19 November 2024

Malta (0) 0

Andorra (0) 0   3142

Malta: (3421) Bonello; Shaw, Mentz*, Borg; Mbong J, Guillaumier, Teuma (Pisani 90), Camenzuli (Beerman 34); Buhagiar (Tuma 46), Mbong P (Satariano 46); Degabriele (Pepe 25).
Andorra: (541) Alvarez; Borra (Rubio 77), San Nicolas, Garcia C, Olivera (Pomares 86), Garcia M (Gomes 77); Fernandez I (Fernandez R 63), Teixeira (Babot 63), de las Heras, Cervos; Rosas.

Group D2 Table	P	W	D	L	F	A	GD	Pts
Moldova	4	3	0	1	5	1	4	9
Malta	4	2	1	1	2	2	0	7
Andorra	4	0	1	3	0	4	–4	1

UEFA NATIONS LEAGUE 2024–25 PROMOTION/RELEGATION PLAY-OFFS

LEAGUE A/B PLAY-OFF – FIRST LEG

Thursday, 20 March 2025

Austria (1) 1 *(Gregoritsch 37)*

Serbia (0) 1 *(Samardzic 61)*   46,400

Austria: (4231) Schlager A; Wimmer, Lienhart, Alaba, Mwene; Seiwald, Grillitsch (Schlager X 77); Schmid (Florucz 77), Gregoritsch (Stoger 89), Baumgartner (Saracevic 70); Arnautovic.
Serbia: (3412) Rajkovic; Erakovic, Gudelj (Simic 68), Babic; Mimovic, Maksimovic N, Lukic (Maksimovic A 82), Birmancevic (Mitrovic S 46); Samardzic (Cvetkovic 87); Vlahovic, Jovic (Topic 68).
Referee: Joao Pedro Pinheiro.

Greece (0) 0

Scotland (1) 1 *(McTominay 33 (pen))*   31,483

Greece: (4231) Tzolakis; Rota, Mavropanos, Koulierakis, Tsimikas; Siopis, Mantalos (Pelkas 72); Masouras (Karetsas 46), Konstantelias (Pavlidis 72), Tzolis (Zafeiris 72); Ioannidis (Fountas 81).
Scotland: (4231) Gordon; Ralston (Porteous 89), Souttar, Hanley, Robertson; Gilmour (Johnston 90), McLean (Tierney 76); McGinn, McTominay, Ferguson; Adams (Hirst 75).
Referee: Tobias Stieler.

Turkey (1) 3 *(Kokcu 9, Akturkoglu 69, Kahveci 73)*

Hungary (1) 1 *(Schafer 25)*   38,500

Turkey: (4231) Cakir; Ayhan (Muldur 27), Akaydin, Bardakci, Elmali; Kokcu (Yuksek 72), Calhanoglu; Aydin (Kahveci 72), Yildiz, Yilmaz (Gul 46); Akturkoglu (Uzun 85).
Hungary: (343) Dibusz; Fiola, Orban, Dardai M; Bolla (Osvath 90), Schafer (Kata 46), Nikitscher (Gazdag 90); Kerkez; Szoboszlai, Varga (Szabo 70), Nagy (Csoboth 77).
Referee: Ivan Kruzliak.

Ukraine (0) 3 *(Gutsulyak 66, Vanat 73, Zabarnyi 78)*

Belgium (1) 1 *(Lukaku 40)*   8767

Ukraine: (4141) Lunin; Konoplya (Sych 25 (Yarmolyuk 62)), Zabarnyi, Matviyenko, Mykolenko; Kaliuzhnyi (Nazaryna 88); Tsygankov, Zinchenko, Shaparenko (Vanat 62) Sudakov; Yaremchuk (Gutsulyak 63).
Belgium: (4231) Courtois; Meunier, De Winter (Raskin 80), Mechele, De Cuyper (Mokio 88); Debast, Tielemans; De Ketelaere (Lukebakio 70), De Bruyne (Vanaken 70), Trossard (Saelemaekers 80); Lukaku.
Match played in Spain. Referee: Sandro Scharer.

LEAGUE A/B PLAY-OFF – SECOND LEG

Sunday, 23 March 2025

Belgium (0) 3 *(De Cuyper 70, Lukaku 75, 86)*

Ukraine (0) 0   19,446

Belgium: (433) Sels; Meunier (De Cuyper 69), Faes, Debast, Castagne; De Bruyne, Raskin (Heynen 90), Vanaken; Trossard (Saelemaekers 69), Lukaku, Doku.
Ukraine: (3421) Lunin; Zabarnyi, Svatok (Yaremchuk 89), Matviyenko; Zinchenko, Kaliuzhnyi, Yarmolyuk, Mykolenko (Mykhaylichenko 69); Gutsulyak (Yarmolenko 89); Sudakov (Tsygankov 69); Vanat (Dovbyk 69).
Belgium won 4-3 on aggregate so both teams remain in their respective leagues.
Referee: Daniel Siebert.

Hungary (0) 0

Turkey (2) 3 *(Calhanoglu 37 (pen), Guler 39, Bardakci 90)*   57,861

Hungary: (3421) Dibusz; Fiola (Nego 46), Orban, Dardai M (Szalai A 60); Bolla, Dardai B (Nikitscher 46), Vecsei (Csoboth 74), Kerkez; Gazdag (Toth 60), Szoboszlai; Varga.
Turkey: (4231) Cakir; Muldur, Akaydin, Bardakci, Elmali; Calhanoglu, Yuksek (Ozcan 46); Aydin (Gul 71), Guler (Kahveci 64), Yildiz (Akcicek 82); Akturkoglu (Yilmaz 64).
Turkey won 6-1 on aggregate and are promoted to League A. Hungary are relegated to League B.
Referee: Felix Zwayer.

Scotland (0) 0

Greece (2) 3 *(Konstantelias 20, Karetsas 42, Tzolis 46)*   48,626

Scotland: (4231) Gordon; Ralston, Souttar, Hanley, Robertson (Wilson 73); Gilmour (Tierney 55), McLean (Ferguson 55); Christie (Conway 73), McTominay, McGinn; Adams (Hirst 55).
Greece: (4231) Tzolakis; Vagiannidis, Mavropanos, Koulierakis, Giannoulis; Zafeiris, Mouzakitis (Ioannidis 83); Karetsas (Masouras 73), Konstantelias (Pelkas 73), Tzolis (Retsos 90); Pavlidis (Galanopoulos 83).
Greece won 3-1 on aggregate and are promoted to League A. Scotland are relegated to League B.
Referee: Davide Massa.

Serbia (0) 2 *(Maksimovic N 56, Vlahovic 90)*

Austria (0) 0 22,112

Serbia: (3421) Rajkovic; Erakovic, Milenkovic, Pavlovic; Zivkovic A (Mimovic 90), Gudelj (Mitrovic S 46), Maksimovic N, Terzic (Jovic 46); Samardzic (Maksimovic A 83), Lukic (Topic 83); Vlahovic.

Austria: (4231) Schlager A; Wimmer, Trauner■, Lienhart, Mwene (Grull 46); Grillitsch (Alaba 75), Seiwald; Schmid, Laimer, Saracevic (Arnautovic 46); Gregoritsch (Stoger 75).

Serbia won 3-1 on aggregate so both teams remain in their respective leagues.

Referee: Jose Maria Sanchez.

LEAGUE B/C PLAY-OFF – FIRST LEG

Thursday, 20 March 2025

Armenia (0) 0

Georgia (2) 3 *(Kochorashvili 32, Mikautadze 37, 59)*

14,414

Armenia: (4231) Cancarevic; Harutyunyan G, Haroyan, Muradyan (Hambardzumyan 80), Tiknizyan; Iwu (Grigoryan N 65), Dashyan (Udo 46); Barseghyan, Sevikyan, Manvelyan (Bichakhchyan 46); Miranyan (Kaloukian 57).

Georgia: (4231) Mamardashvili; Kakabadze, Goglichidze, Lochoshvili (Dvali 70), Azarovi (Gocholeishvili 75); Kochorashvili, Kvekveskiri; Davitashvili, Chakvetadze (Tsitaishvili 66), Kiteishvili (Mekvabishvili 66); Mikautadze (Zivzivadze 66).

Referee: Radu Petrescu.

Bulgaria (1) 1 *(Petkov M 6)*

Republic of Ireland (2) 2 *(Azaz 21, Doherty 42)* 7835

Bulgaria: (442) Mitov; Nedyalkov, Atanasov, Petkov A, Nurnberger (Minkov 72); Petkov M, Kraev A (Nikolov 85), Gruev, Despodov; Krastev (Iliev I 85), Petkov L (Kraev B 72).

Republic of Ireland: (442) Kelleher; Doherty, Collins, O'Shea, Brady; Johnston (Sykes 76), Knight (Vata 79), Cullen, Manning (O'Brien 79); Azaz (Taylor 76), Parrott (Ferguson 76).

Referee: Benoit Bastien.

Kosovo (1) 2 *(Dellova 19, Rexhbecaj 58)*

Iceland (1) 1 *(Oskarsson 22)* 12,857

Kosovo: (4231) Muric; Vojvoda (Aliti 80), Amir Rrahmani, Dellova, Paqarada; Rexhbecaj, Berisha (Demaku 46); Krasniqi E, Rashica (Emerllahu 89), Rrudhani (Sahiti 46); Muriqi (Albion Rrahmani 89).

Iceland: (4411) Valdimarsson; Palsson, Gunnarsson A, Ingason, Tomasson (Thorsteinsson 65); Ellertsson (Helgason 89), Arnar Haraldsson, Johannesson (Thordarson 66), Gudjohnsen; Gudmundsson A (Traustason 65); Oskarsson.

Referee: Serdar Gozubuyuk.

Slovakia (0) 0

Slovenia (0) 0 12,545

Slovakia: (433) Dubravka; Gyomber, Vavro (Obert 11 (Mesik 46)), Skriniar, Hancko; Bero, Lobotka, Duda (Benes 84); Suslov, Bozenik (Mraz 78), Haraslin (Schranz 78).

Slovenia: (442) Oblak; Karnicnik, Drkusic, Bijol, Janza; Stojanovic (Horvat 79), Lovric (Zeljkovic 90), Elsnik (Stankovic 78), Mlakar (Vipotnik 31); Petrovic, Sesko (Kramer 90).

Referee: Maurizio Mariani.

LEAGUE B/C PLAY-OFF – SECOND LEG

Sunday, 23 March 2025

Georgia (5) 6 *(Haroyan 4 (og), Mikautadze 14, 35, Chakvetadze 23, Kiteishvili 27, Kvaratskhelia 62)*

Armenia (0) 1 *(Sevikyan 48)* 47,903

Georgia: (4231) Mamardashvili; Kakabadze, Kashia, Goglichidze (Dvali 69), Tsitaishvili (Guliashvili 70); Kochorashvili, Mekvabishvili; Chakvetadze (Shengelia 46), Kiteishvili (Zaria 77), Kvaratskhelia; Mikautadze (Zivzivadze 77).

Armenia: (541) Cancarevic; Hovhannisyan (Muradyan 39), Harutyunyan, Haroyan, Mkrtchyan, Tiknizyan; Barseghyan, Udo (Serobyan 40), Iwu (Grigoryan E 40), Sevikyan (Miranyan 70); Bichakhchyan (Grigoryan N 80).

Georgia won 9-1 on aggregate so both teams remain in their respective leagues.

Referee: Anthony Taylor.

Iceland (1) 1 *(Oskarsson 2)*

Kosovo (1) 3 *(Muriqi 35, 45, 79)* 1553

Iceland: (442) Valdimarsson; Fridriksson (Bjarkason 22), Thordarson, Ingason, Johannesson (Tomasson 46); Willumsson W (Hlynsson 65), Helgason, Traustason (Gunnarsson A■ 46), Thorsteinsson; Gudmundsson A, Oskarsson (Gudjohnsen 65).

Kosovo: (4231) Saipi; Vojvoda, Amir Rrahmani, Dellova, Paqarada; Demaku (Emerllahu 55), Rexhbecaj; Krasniqi E (Krasniqi I 78), Rashica (Sahiti 78), Muslija (Gallapeni 87); Muriqi (Albion Rrahmani 87).

Kosovo won 5-2 on aggregate and are promoted to League B. Iceland are relegated to League C.

Referee: Jesus Gil Manzano.

Republic of Ireland (0) 2 *(Ferguson 63, Idah 84)*

Bulgaria (1) 1 *(Antov 30)* 40,156

Republic of Ireland: (442) Kelleher; Doherty, Collins, O'Brien, Brady (Manning 66); Johnston (Idah 65), Cullen, Knight (Taylor 82), Azaz; Ferguson (Dunne 74), Parrott (Sykes 66).

Bulgaria: (541) Iliev P; Minkov, Antov, Petrov S, Nedyalkov, Nurnberger (Iliev I 89); Petkov M (Kirilov 75), Milanov (Krastev 75), Gruev (Shopov 89), Despodov; Kraev B (Nikolov 60).

Republic of Ireland won 4-2 on aggregate so both teams remain in their respective leagues.

Referee: Halil Meler.

Slovenia (0) 1 *(Cerin 95)*

Slovakia (0) 0 14,076

Slovenia: (433) Oblak; Karnicnik (Brekalo 120), Drkusic, Bijol, Janza; Lovric (Petrovic 67), Cerin (Zeljkovic 120), Elsnik (Kramer 90); Stojanovic, Sesko, Vipotnik (Stankovic 84).

Slovakia: (433) Dubravka; Gyomber, Skriniar, Mesik (Duris 118), Hancko; Bero (Tupta 106), Lobotka, Duda (Benes 99); Suslov, Bozenik (Mraz 75), Schranz (Haraslin 75).

aet; Slovenia won 1-0 on aggregate so both teams remain in their respective leagues.

Referee: Istvan Kovacs.

The League C/D play-offs are to be played on 26 and 31 March 2026.

UEFA NATIONS LEAGUE FINALS 2024–25

QUARTER-FINALS – FIRST LEG
Thursday, 20 March 2025
Croatia (2) 2 *(Budimir 26, Perisic 45)*
France (0) 0   30,551
Croatia: (4231) Livakovic; Stanisic, Sutalo, Caleta-Car, Gvardiol; Modric, Kovacic; Perisic (Vlasic 70), Baturina (Mario Pasalic 60), Kramaric (Sucic P 85); Budimir (Ivanovic 60).
France: (4312) Maignan; Kounde, Konate (Upamecano 46), Saliba, Digne; Guendouzi (Kone 84), Tchouameni, Rabiot (Camavinga 64); Dembele (Olise 84); Muani (Barcola 64), Mbappe.

Denmark (0) 1 *(Hojlund 78)*   **Portugal (0) 0**   36,322
Denmark: (4231) Schmeichel; Kristensen, Andersen, Vestergaard, Maehle; Hjulmand, Norgaard; Isaksen (Dorgu 87), Eriksen (Wind 86), Lindstrom (Skov Olsen 69); Biereth (Hojlund 69).
Portugal: (4231) Costa; Dalot (Nelson Semedo 66), Dias, Veiga (Inacio 76); Nuno Mendes; Vitinha, Neves J (Silva B 86); Pedro Neto, Fernandes, Leao (Neves R 76); Ronaldo.

Italy (1) 1 *(Tonali 9)*
Germany (0) 2 *(Kleindienst 49, Goretzka 76)*   60,334
Italy: (352) Donnarumma; Di Lorenzo, Bastoni, Calafiori; Politano (Bellanova 64), Barella (Frattesi 84), Rovella (Ricci 64), Tonali, Udogie; Kean (Lucca 83), Raspadori (Maldini 71).
Germany: (4231) Baumann; Kimmich, Tah, Rudiger, Raum (Schlotterbeck 90); Gross (Andrich 90), Goretzka; Amiri (Leweling 66), Sane (Adeyemi 82), Musiala; Burkardt (Kleindienst 46).

Netherlands (1) 2 *(Gakpo 28, Reijnders 46)*
Spain (1) 2 *(Williams 9, Merino 90)*
Netherlands: (4231) Verbruggen; Geertruida, van Hecke, van Dijk, Hato◼; de Jong (Koopmeiners 74), Reijnders (Wieffer 90); Frimpong, Kluivert (Simons 74), Gakpo; Depay (de Ligt 84).
Spain: (433) Simon; Porro, Le Normand, Cubarsi (Huijsen 41), Cucurella; Gonzalez (Olmo 66), Zubimendi, Fabian (Merino 84); Yamal (Oyarzabal 66), Morata (Perez 66), Williams.

QUARTER-FINALS – SECOND LEG
Sunday, 23 March 2025
France (0) 2 *(Olise 52, Dembele 80)*
Croatia (0) 0   77,502
France: (4231) Maignan; Kounde, Upamecano, Saliba, Hernandez T; Tchouameni, Kone (Zaire Emery 111); Dembele (Muani 99), Olise (Camavinga 106), Barcola (Doue 66); Mbappe.
Croatia: (4231) Livakovic; Stanisic, Sutalo, Caleta-Car, Gvardiol (Pongracic 106); Modric (Moro 82), Kovacic (Jakic 82); Perisic (Mario Pasalic 71), Sucic P, Kramaric (Baturina 71); Budimir (Ivanovic 60).
aet; France won 5-4 on penalties.

Germany (3) 3 *(Kimmich 30 (pen), Musiala 36, Kleindienst 45)*
Italy (0) 3 *(Kean 49, 69, Raspadori 90 (pen))*   64,762
Germany: (4231) Baumann; Kimmich, Rudiger (Bisseck 77), Tah, Schlotterbeck; Stiller (Gross 63), Goretzka (Amiri 63); Sane (Adeyemi 63), Musiala (Andrich 77), Mittelstadt; Kleindienst.
Italy: (352) Donnarumma; Gatti (Politano 46), Buongiorno, Bastoni; Di Lorenzo, Barella, Ricci (Zaccagni 85), Tonali (Raspadori 68), Udogie; Kean (Lucca 85), Maldini (Frattesi 46).
Germany won 5-4 on aggregate.

Portugal (1) 5 *(Andersen 38 (og), Ronaldo 72, Trincao 86, 91, Goncalo Ramos 115)*
Denmark (0) 2 *(Kristensen 56, Eriksen 76)*   47,123
Portugal: (433) Costa; Dalot (Trincao 81), Dias, Inacio, Nuno Mendes; Fernandes, Vitinha (Neves R 99), Silva B; Francisco Conceicao (Nelson Semedo 81), Ronaldo (Goncalo Ramos 90), Leao (Jota 62).

Denmark: (4231) Schmeichel; Kristensen, Andersen, Vestergaard, Dorgu (Harder 97); Norgaard (Froholdt 83), Hjulmand; Isaksen (Kristiansen 73), Eriksen (Frendrup 83), Lindstrom (Skov Olsen 65); Hojlund (Biereth 73).
aet; Portugal won 5-3 on aggregate.

Spain (1) 3 *(Oyarzabal 8 (pen), 67, Yamal 103)*
Netherlands (0) 3 *(Depay 54 (pen), Maatsen 79, Simons 109 (pen))*   48,082
Spain: (4231) Simon; Mingueza (Porro 94), Le Normand, Huijsen, Cucurella; Zubimendi (Garcia 106), Fabian (Merino 84); Yamal, Olmo (Gonzalez 84), Williams (Baena 117); Oyarzabal (Torres 69).
Netherlands: (4231) Verbruggen; Geertruida (Malen 78), van Hecke, van Dijk, Maatsen; Reijnders (Koopmeiners 110), de Jong (Taylor 106); Frimpong, Kluivert (Simons 78), Gakpo (Lang 77); Depay (Brobbey 101).
aet; Spain won 5-4 on penalties.

FINAL TOURNAMENT IN GERMANY

SEMI-FINALS
Wednesday, 4 June 2025
Germany (0) 1 *(Wirtz 48)*
Portugal (0) 2 *(Francisco Conceicao 63, Ronaldo 68)*   65,823
Germany: (3421) ter Stegen; Tah, Koch, Anton (Nmecha 71); Kimmich, Goretzka, Pavlovic (Adeyemi 71), Mittelstadt (Gosens 60); Sane (Gnabry 61), Wirtz; Woltemade (Fullkrug 61).
Portugal: (433) Costa; Neves J (Nelson Semedo 58), Dias, Inacio, Nuno Mendes; Silva, Neves R (Vitinha 58), Fernandes; Trincao (Francisco Conceicao 58), Ronaldo (Joao Palhinha 90), Pedro Neto (Jota 83).

Thursday, 5 June 2025
Spain (2) 5 *(Williams 22, Merino 25, Yamal 54 (pen), 67, Gonzalez 55)*
France (0) 4 *(Mbappe 59 (pen), Cherki 79, Vivian 84 (og), Muani 90)*   51,724
Spain: (433) Simon; Porro, Le Normand (Vivian 77), Huijsen, Cucurella; Gonzalez (Fabian 64), Zubimendi, Merino (Gavi 90); Yamal, Oyarzabal (Aghehowa 77), Williams (Olmo 64).
France: (4231) Maignan; Kalulu Kyatengwa (Gusto 63), Konate, Lenglet (Hernandez L 72); Hernandez T; Kone, Rabiot; Dembele (Muani 76), Olise (Cherki 63), Doue (Barcola 63); Mbappe.

THIRD PLACE PLAY-OFF
Sunday, 8 June 2025
Germany (0) 0
France (1) 2 *(Mbappe 45, Olise 84)*   51,313
Germany: (4132) ter Stegen; Kimmich, Koch, Tah, Raum (Mittelstadt 65); Gross (Kehrer 73); Adeyemi (Gnabry 78), Goretzka (Bischof 65), Wirtz; Woltemade (Undav 46), Fullkrug.
France: (4231) Maignan; Gusto, Bade, Hernandez L, Digne; Tchouameni (Kone 69), Rabiot; Muani (Doue 69), Cherki (Olise 69), Thuram (Guendouzi 90); Mbappe.

FINAL
Sunday, 8 June 2025
Portugal (1) 2 *(Nuno Mendes 26, Ronaldo 61)*
Spain (2) 2 *(Zubimendi 21, Oyarzabal 45)*   65,852
Portugal: (433) Costa; Neves J (Nelson Semedo 46), Dias, Inacio (Veiga 74), Nuno Mendes; Fernandes, Vitinha, Silva (Leao 74); Francisco Conceicao (Neves R 46), Ronaldo (Goncalo Ramos 88), Pedro Neto (Jota 106).
Spain: (433) Simon; Mingueza (Porro 93), Le Normand, Huijsen, Cucurella; Gonzalez (Isco 75), Zubimendi, Fabian (Merino 75); Yamal (Pino 106), Oyarzabal (Morata 111), Williams (Baena 92).
aet; Portugal won 5-3 on penalties.
Referee: Sandro Scharer.

FIFA WORLD CUP 2026 QUALIFYING – UEFA

■ *Denotes player sent off.*

GROUP G

Friday, 21 March 2025

Malta (0) 0

Finland (1) 1 *(Antman 38)* 5106

Malta: (352) Bonello; Muscat Z (Beerman 89), Carragher, Shaw■; Mbong J (Overend 83), Guillaumier, Satariano (Pepe 83), Chouaref, Camenzuli (Nwoko 71); Mbong P (Tuma 71), Teuma.
Finland: (433) Hradecky; Alho, Tenho, Ivanov, Uronen (Ollila 63); Jensen F, Peltola (Lod 46); Kairinen; Antman (Suhonen 82), Pohjanpalo (Hakans 63), Kallman (Pukki 71).

Poland (0) 1 *(Lewandowski 81)*

Lithuania (0) 0 55,738

Poland: (352) Skorupski; Piatkowski (Wieteska 77), Bednarek, Kiwior; Cash (Kaminski 68), Szymanski S, Moder, Piotrowski (Bogusz 77), Frankowski; Swiderski (Piatek 68), Lewandowski (Buksa 86).
Lithuania: (3421) Gertmonas; Kazukolovas, Utkus, Tutyskinas; Sirvys (Milasius 74), Antanavicius (Vareika 84), Gineitis, Lasickas; Golubickas (Matulevicius 61), Dolznikov (Cernych 62); Kucys (Paulauskas G 84).

Monday, 24 March 2025

Lithuania (1) 2 *(Kucys 39, Gineitis 69)*

Finland (2) 2 *(Kairinen 3, Pohjanpalo 17 (pen))* 10,421

Lithuania: (4231) Gertmonas; Sirvys, Kazukolovas, Girdvainis, Milasius; Matulevicius (Cernych 65), Utkus (Remeikis 77); Dolznikov (Golubickas 46), Gineitis, Lasickas; Kucys (Ruzgis 58).
Finland: (433) Hradecky; Alho, Tenho (Vaisanen 46), Ivanov, Uronen; Lod (Suhonen 61), Kairinen, Kamara (Peltola 77); Antman (Pukki 86), Pohjanpalo (Kallman 61), Hakans.

Poland (1) 2 *(Swiderski 27, 51)*

Malta (0) 0 45,872

Poland: (3142) Skorupski; Piatkowski, Bednarek (Wieteska 46), Kiwior; Moder; Frankowski (Cash 66), Szymanski S, Bogusz (Slisz 46), Kaminski (Bereszynski 87); Swiderski, Piatek (Lewandowski 66).
Malta: (352) Bonello; Muscat Z (Zammit Lonardelli 58), Carragher, Pepe (Borg 84); Mbong J (Overend 64), Guillaumier, Teuma, Satariano (Tuma 58), Camenzuli; Chouaref■, Mbong P (Nwoko 46).

Saturday, 7 June 2025

Finland (1) 2 *(Depay 6, Dumfries 23)*

Netherlands (2) 2 29,483

Finland: (343) Hradecky; Tenho (Kamara 70), Hoskonen, Ivanov (Valakari 76); Alho (Niskanen 70), Peltola, Kairinen, Uronen; Lod (Jensen F 55), Pohjanpalo (Kallman 55), Antman.
Netherlands: (433) Flekken; Dumfries, van Hecke (de Vrij 46), van Dijk, Ake (van de Ven 62); Gravenberch, de Jong, Reijnders (Kluivert 69); Frimpong, Depay (Weghorst 69), Gakpo (Simons 85).

Malta (0) 0

Lithuania (0) 0 2785

Malta: (4231) Bonello; Muscat Z (Corbalan 86), Carragher, Pepe, Camenzuli; Guillaumier, Satariano; Jones (Ewurum 81), Teuma, Mbong J (Nwoko 81); Mbong P (Tuma 74).
Lithuania: (4231) Gertmonas; Upstas (Golubickas 46 (Sesplaukis 74)), Kazukolovas, Utkus, Tutyskinas; Vorobjovas (Sirgedas 70), Gineitis, Lasickas, Slivka (Jansonas 81), Dolznikov (Cernych 70); Paulauskas G.

Tuesday, 10 June 2025

Finland (1) 2 *(Pohjanpalo 31 (pen), Kallman 64)*

Poland (0) 1 *(Kiwior 69)* 16,511

Finland: (3511) Hradecky; Peltola, Hoskonen, Uronen (Niskanen 71); Lod (Ivanov 86), Kairinen, Kamara, Tenho, Antman (Pukki 86); Jensen F (Alho 63); Pohjanpalo (Kallman 63).
Poland: (352) Skorupski; Skrzypczak, Bednarek, Kiwior; Cash, Szymanski S, Slisz, Moder (Piotrowski 87), Zalewski; Piatek (Buksa 86), Swiderski (Kaminski 58).

Netherlands (3) 8 *(Depay 9 (pen), 16, van Dijk 20, Simons 61, Malen 74, 80, Lang 78, van de Ven 90)*

Malta (0) 0 21,006

Netherlands: (4231) Flekken; Dumfries (Geertruida 79), de Vrij, van Dijk, van de Ven; Gravenberch (Wieffer 46); de Jong; Simons, Kluivert (Weghorst 62), Gakpo (Lang 46); Depay (Malen 72).
Malta: (4231) Bonello; Corbalan (Tuma 46), Mentz, Carragher, Camenzuli (Beerman 81); Guillaumier, Satariano (Azzopardi 81); Overend (Shaw 46), Teuma (Jones 60), Mbong J; Mbong P.

Group G Table	P	W	D	L	F	A	GD	Pts
Finland	4	2	1	1	5	5	0	7
Netherlands	2	2	0	0	10	0	10	6
Poland	3	2	0	1	4	2	2	6
Lithuania	3	0	2	1	2	3	–1	2
Malta	4	0	1	3	0	11	–11	1

GROUP H

Friday, 21 March 2025

Cyprus (0) 2 *(Pittas 55, Kakoullis 86)*

San Marino (0) 0 2336

Cyprus: (4231) Mall; Satsias, Sielis, Panagiotou, Anderson Correia (Malekkides 74); Kousoulos (Kyriakou 74), Kastanos; Loizou (Gavriel 89), Sotiriou P (Kakoullis 63), Tzionis (Kosti 63); Pittas.
San Marino: (433) Colombo; Fabbri (Benvenuti G 85), Cevoli, Benvenuti T, Tosi; Golinucci A, Capicchioni L (Casadei 64), Zannoni (Giacopetti 77); Contadini, Nanni, Berardi (Sensoli 63).

Romania (0) 0

Bosnia-Herzegovina (1) 1 *(Gigovic 14)* 49,413

Romania: (433) Nita; Ratiu, Popescu, Burca, Bancu; Marin R (Mitrita 74), Marin M (Sut 69), Stanciu; Man (Morutan 80), Dragus (Alibec 81), Tanase (Hagi 46).
Bosnia-Herzegovina: (442) Vasilj; Malic (Bicakcic 87), Barisic, Radeljic, Kolasinac; Gigovic (Memic 62), Sunjic, Tahirovic (Burnic 77), Dedic (Saric 77); Demirovic, Dzeko (Bazdar 46).

Monday, 24 March 2025

Bosnia-Herzegovina (1) 2 *(Demirovic 22, Hajradinovic 56)*

Cyprus (1) 1 *(Pittas 45)* 7464

Bosnia-Herzegovina: (4231) Vasilj; Malic (Burnic 72), Barisic (Katic 72), Radeljic, Kolasinac; Sunjic, Tahirovic (Saric 46); Hajradinovic (Basic 88), Gigovic (Bazdar 46), Dedic; Demirovic.
Cyprus: (4141) Mall; Satsias, Sielis, Laifis, Malekkides (Anderson Correia 88); Kousoulos (Tzionis 65); Loizou (Kyriakou 65), Kosti (Charalampous 72), Kastanos, Kakoullis (Sotiriou P 88); Pittas■.

San Marino (0) 1 *(Zannoni 67)*

Romania (2) 5 *(Cevoli 6 (og), Popescu 44, Marin R 55 (pen), Hagi 75 (pen), Alibec 90)* 3556

San Marino: (451) Amici; Benvenuti G, Cevoli, Benvenuti T, Tosi (Riccardi 62); Contadini (Sensoli 46), Golinucci, Capicchioni L (Casadei 46), Zannoni (Santi 76), Berardi (Giacopetti 46); Nanni.
Romania: (433) Moldovan; Ratiu, Popescu (Ciobotariu 61), Burca, Bancu; Marin R (Politic 80), Marin M (Mitrita 46), Stanciu (Dragomir 61); Man, Dragus (Alibec 80), Hagi.

Saturday, 7 June 2025

Austria (1) 2 *(Gregoritsch 42, Sabitzer 60)*
Romania (0) 1 *(Tanase 90)* 48,500
Austria: (4231) Pentz; Wimmer (Posch 61), Lienhart, Wober (Danso 69), Mwene; Seiwald, Laimer; Schmid (Grillitsch 82), Baumgartner (Schlager X 82), Sabitzer; Gregoritsch (Arnautovic 61).
Romania: (442) Moldovan; Ratiu, Popescu, Burca, Bancu; Man (Miculescu 78), Marin R (Sut 61), Chiriches, Stanciu (Tanase 85); Birligea (Alibec 78), Dragus (Mitrita 84).

Bosnia-Herzegovina (0) 1 *(Dzeko 66)*
San Marino (0) 0 11,828
Bosnia-Herzegovina: (4222) Vasilj; Malic (Dedic 46), Barisic (Muharemovic 46), Katic (Bicakcic 84), Burnic; Tahirovic, Sunjic; Hajradinovic, Gigovic (Memic 46), Demirovic, Bazdar (Dzeko 62).
San Marino: (433) Colombo; Fabbri, Cevoli, Benvenuti T, Riccardi (Mularoni 71); Golinucci, Capicchioni L (Casadei 46), Zannoni; Contadini (Benvenuti G 71), Nanni (Giacopetti 71), Lazzari (Sensoli 66).

Tuesday, 10 June 2025

Romania (2) 2 *(Tanase 43, Man 45)*
Cyprus (0) 0 45,324
Romania: (4231) Moldovan; Ratiu, Popescu, Burca (Ghita 73), Sorescu; Sut, Chiriches (Marin M 56); Man (Miculescu 82), Tanase (Alibec 73), Mihaila (Mitrita 56); Dragus.
Cyprus: (4231) Mall; Satsias, Sielis, Laifis, Malekkides; Kyriakou (Artymatas 81), Kastanos; Loizou (Ilia 46), Kosti (Charalampous 46), Anderson Correia (Tzionis 62); Kakoullis (Koutsakos 46).

San Marino (0) 0
Austria (4) 4 *(Arnautovic 3, 15, Gregoritsch 11, Baumgartner 27)* 3075
San Marino: (433) Colombo; Benvenuti G, Valentini, Benvenuti T, Riccardi; Golinucci, Capicchioni L (Casadei 63), Zannoni (Mularoni 72); Contadini (Sensoli 22), Nanni (Giacopetti 73), Lazzari (Capicchioni G 73).
Austria: (4231) Pentz (Lawal 46); Posch, Lienhart (Querfeld 46), Friedl, Honsak; Laimer (Schmid 46), Seiwald; Baumgartner (Grull 63), Sabitzer, Gregoritsch (Ballo 46); Arnautovic.

Group H Table	P	W	D	L	F	A	GD	Pts
Bosnia & Herzegovina	3	3	0	0	4	1	3	9
Austria	2	2	0	0	6	1	5	6
Romania	4	2	0	2	8	4	4	6
Cyprus	3	1	0	2	3	4	–1	3
San Marino	4	0	0	4	1	12	–11	0

GROUP I

Due to their war in Gaza, Israel played home matches in Hungary.

Saturday, 22 March 2025

Israel (1) 2 *(Hein 23 (og), Dasa 75)*
Estonia (1) 1 *(Paskotsi 10)* 270
Israel: (4231) Daniel Peretz; Dasa, Nachmias, Shlomo, Revivo; Jaber, Abu Fani (Dor Peretz 75); Biton (Peretz E 71), Gloukh (Shua 89), Solomon (Goldberg 89); David (Baribo 71).
Estonia: (4231) Hein (Igonen 46); Peetson (Tamm J 82), Paskotsi, Kuusk, Schjonning-Larsen; Soomets[■] (Poom (Anier 82); Yakovlev (Hussar 59), Kait, Sinyavskiy; Tamm A (Saarma 81).

Moldova (0) 0
Norway (4) 5 *(Ryerson 5, Haaland 23, Aasgaard 38, Sorloth 43, Donnum 69)* 9342
Moldova: (541) Celeadnic; Revenco (Cojocaru 46), Craciun, Baboblo, Mudrac, Reabciuk; Caimacov (Boicuic 87), Motpan (Stina 80), Rata (Posmac 81), Postolachi; Nicolaescu (Bodisteanu 65).
Norway: (4132) Nyland; Ryerson, Ajer, Ostigard (Heggem 37), Wolfe; Berge; Odegaard, Aasgaard (Berg 63), Schjelderup (Hauge 63); Sorloth (Donnum 63); Haaland (Botheim 78).
Referee: Matej Jug.

Tuesday, 25 March 2025

Israel (0) 2 *(Abu Fani 55, Turgeman 90)*
Norway (1) 4 *(Wolfe 39, Sorloth 59, Ajer 65, Haaland 83)* 1200
Israel: (4411) Daniel Peretz; Abada (Dasa 61), Nachmias, Shlomo, Goldberg (Revivo 46); Dor Peretz (Biton 61), Peretz E (Khalaili 78), Jaber (Abu Fani 46), Solomon; Gloukh; Turgeman.
Norway: (442) Nyland; Ryerson, Ajer, Heggem, Wolfe (Gregersen 90); Odegaard (Pedersen 90), Berge, Berg (Johnsen 75), Schjelderup (Donnum 61); Haaland, Sorloth (Hauge 74).

Moldova (0) 2 *(Nicolaescu 67, Caimacov 90)*
Estonia (2) 3 *(Peetson 19, Sappinen 30, Kait 70)* 6112
Moldova: (4231) Kozhukhar; Cojocaru[■], Craciun, Baboblo, Motpan (Platica S 78), Rata; Postolachi (Stina 78), Caimacov, Bodisteanu (Boicuic 85); Nicolaescu.
Estonia: (4231) Igonen; Peetson (Saliste 52), Paskotsi, Kuusk, Schjonning-Larsen; Palumets[■], Ainsalu; Yakovlev (Miller 87), Kait, Sinyavskiy; Sappinen (Tamm A 66).

Friday, 6 June 2025

Estonia (1) 1 *(Kait 31)*
Israel (1) 3 *(Biton 39, 49, Abu Fani 89 (pen))* 5967
Estonia: (4231) Hein; Schjonning-Larsen, Paskotsi, Kuusk, Saliste (Jepihhin 81); Soomets (Kristal 55); Shein; Yakovlev (Saarma 72), Kait (Ainsalu 81), Sinyavskiy; Tamm A (Anier 72).
Israel: (4231) Daniel Peretz; Dasa, Nachmias, Shlomo, Revivo; Peretz E (Jaber 67), Abu Fani (Abada 90); Biton (Dor Peretz 72), Gloukh, Solomon (Levi 90); Turgeman (Khalaili 67).

Norway (3) 3 *(Sorloth 14, Nusa 34, Haaland 42)*
Italy (0) 0 25,796
Norway: (433) Nyland; Ryerson, Ajer, Heggem (Ostigard 71), Wolfe (Pedersen 75); Odegaard, Berge, Thorsby (Berg 46); Sorloth (Larsen 83), Haaland, Nusa (Bobb 75).
Italy: (3511) Donnarumma; Di Lorenzo, Coppola, Bastoni; Zappacosta (Orsolini 71), Barella, Rovella (Frattesi 46), Tonali, Udogie (Dimarco 83); Raspadori (Ricci 83); Retegui (Lucca 72).

Monday, 9 June 2025

Estonia (0) 0
Norway (0) 1 *(Haaland 62)* 11,577
Estonia: (4411) Hein; Schjonning-Larsen, Paskotsi, Kuusk, Saliste (Saarma 84); Kait (Miller 46), Palumets (Poom 90), Shein, Sinyavskiy; Kristal (Anier 84); Sappinen (Tamm A 84).
Norway: (433) Nyland; Ryerson, Ajer, Heggem, Wolfe (Ostigard 90); Odegaard, Berge, Thorsby (Bobb 46 (Berg 90)); Sorloth (Larsen 82), Haaland, Nusa (Johnsen 68).

Italy (1) 2 *(Raspadori 40, Cambiaso 50)*
Moldova (0) 0 18,771
Italy: (3511) Donnarumma; Di Lorenzo, Bastoni, Ranieri (Coppola 83); Cambiaso, Frattesi, Ricci (Barella 46), Tonali, Dimarco (Orsolini 46); Raspadori (Maldini 77); Retegui (Lucca 71).
Moldova: (532) Avram; Platica S, Baboblo, Mudrac, Dumbravanu, Reabciuk; Caimacov (Stina 66), Ionita (Dros 72), Bodisteanu (Motpan 58); Nicolaescu (Damascan 72), Postolachi (Perciun 66).

Group I Table	P	W	D	L	F	A	GD	Pts
Norway	4	4	0	0	13	2	11	12
Israel	3	2	0	1	7	6	1	6
Italy	2	1	0	1	2	3	–1	3
Estonia	4	1	0	3	5	8	–3	3
Moldova	3	0	0	3	2	10	–8	0

GROUP J

Saturday, 22 March 2025

Liechtenstein (0) 0
North Macedonia (2) 3 *(Trajkovski 7, Musliu 42, Miovski 84)* 4094

Liechtenstein: (532) Buchel B; Wolfinger S (Zund 73), Traber, Wieser (Beck N 73), Goppel (Kindle 55); Hofer; Luchinger, Hasler N, Sele; Salanovic (Saglam 63), Pizzi (Notaro 63).
North Macedonia: (442) Dimitrievski; Zajkov, Serafimov (Ilievski 46), Musliu, Alioski (Dimoski 63); Churlinov (Trapanovski 80), Alimi (Atanasov 46), Bardhi, Elmas; Miovski, Trajkovski (Toshevski 63).

Wales (1) 3 *(James D 9, Davies B 47, Matondo 90)*
Kazakhstan (1) 1 *(Tagybergen 32 (pen))* 32,473

Wales: (4231) Darlow; Roberts, Rodon, Davies B, Williams; Sheehan, Cullen; James D (Matondo 86), Brooks (James J 62), Thomas; Johnson (Harris 62).
Kazakhstan: (541) Zarutskiy; Tapalov, Bystrov, Marochkin, Alip, Vorogovskiy; Chesnokov (Kenzhebek 86), Tagybergen, Muzhikov (Zhukov 62), Samorodov (Satpaev 74); Zhaksylykov (Aymbetov 74).

Tuesday, 25 March 2025

Liechtenstein (0) 0
Kazakhstan (2) 2 *(Samorodov 42, Marochkin 45)* 1123

Liechtenstein: (352) Buchel B; Traber, Wieser, Oberwaditzer, Kindle (Zund 46), Luchinger (Wolfinger F 77), Hasler N, Sele (Schlegel 82), Hofer (Notaro 68); Pizzi (Saglam 68), Salanovic.
Kazakhstan: (541) Seisen; Astanov S, Bystrov, Marochkin, Alip, Vorogovskiy (Zhagorov 72); Chesnokov (Zhaksylykov 72), Orazov (Tagybergen 65), Zhukov, Samorodov (Kenzhebek 65); Satpaev (Astanov E 77).

North Macedonia (0) 1 *(Miovski 90)*
Wales (0) 1 *(Brooks 90)* 23,114

North Macedonia: (3412) Dimitrievski; Zajkov (Atanasov 61), Serafimov, Musliu; Ilievski B (Dimoski 87), Alimi (Churlinov 61), Kostadinov, Alioski; Bardhi (Manev 90); Miovski (Trajkovski 90), Elmas.
Wales: (4231) Darlow; Williams, Rodon, Mepham, Davies B; Sheehan (Allen 84), James J; James D (Moore 64), Broadhead (Brooks 75), Thomas; Johnson (Matondo 84).

Friday, 6 June 2025

North Macedonia (0) 1 *(Alioski 86)*
Belgium (1) 1 *(De Cuyper 28)* 23,070

North Macedonia: (532) Dimitrievski; Ilievski B (Askovski 80), Stojchevski (Churlinov 57), Zajkov, Musliu, Alioski; Kostadinov (Mitrovski 80), Atanasov (Elezi 46), Elmas; Bardhi, Miovski (Ristovski 85).
Belgium: (433) Sels; Meunier (Tielemans 57), Faes, Debast, De Cuyper (Theate 78); Raskin, De Bruyne (De Winter 57), Vanaken (Onana 56); Saelemaekers, Lukaku (Openda 82), Doku.

Wales (1) 3 *(Rodon 39, Wilson 65, Moore 68)*
Liechtenstein (0) 0 30,646

Wales: (4231) Darlow; Roberts, Rodon, Davies B, Williams (Dasilva 24); Ampadu (Sheehan 64), Wilson (James J 74); Johnson (Brooks 64), Cullen, Thomas (Koumas 64); Moore.
Liechtenstein: (532) Buchel B; Meier (Kindle 46), Traber, Wieser, Hofer, Goppel; Luchinger (Netzer 73), Hasler N, Sele (Zund 90); Saglam (Pizzi 46), Notaro (Malin 70).

Monday, 9 June 2025

Belgium (3) 4 *(Lukaku 15 (pen), Tielemans 19, Doku 27, De Bruyne 88)*
Wales (1) 3 *(Wilson 45 (pen), Thomas 51, Johnson 69)* 33,653

Belgium: (4231) Sels; Meunier (De Winter 16), Debast, Faes, De Cuyper (Theate 46); Onana, Tielemans; Doku, De Bruyne (Saelemaekers 89), Trossard (Lukebakio 46 (Raskin 75)); Lukaku.
Wales: (541) Darlow; Roberts, Ampadu, Rodon, Mepham, Davies B; Brooks (Harris 63), James J (Cullen 63), Wilson, Thomas (Matondo 90); Johnson.

Kazakhstan (0) 0
North Macedonia (1) 1 *(Trajkovski 33)* 27,694

Kazakhstan: (541) Seisen; Astanov S, Bystrov (Mukhamed 81), Maliy, Alip, Vorogovskiy; Chesnokov (Zuev 85), Kuat, Tagybergen, Kenzhebek (Satpaev 59); Samorodov.
North Macedonia: (532) Dimitrievski; Churlinov (Mitrovski 53), Despotovski, Zajkov, Musliu, Alioski; Kostadinov (Elezi 53), Bardhi, Elmas (Askovski 67); Miovski (Ristovski 67), Trajkovski (Atanasov 84).

Group J Table	P	W	D	L	F	A	GD	Pts
North Macedonia	4	2	2	0	6	2	4	8
Wales	4	2	1	1	10	6	4	7
Belgium	2	1	1	0	5	4	1	4
Kazakhstan	3	1	0	2	3	4	−1	3
Liechtenstein	3	0	0	3	0	8	−8	0

GROUP K

Friday, 21 March 2025

Andorra (0) 0
Latvia (0) 1 *(Sits 58)* 957

Andorra: (541) Alvarez; Borra (Bernat 86), Llovera, Garcia C, Olivera, Cervos; Rodrigo Tapia (Fernandez R 65), Teixeira (Vales M 57), Babot (Rebes 86), Pujol (San Nicolas 57); Rosas.
Latvia: (3421) Zviedris; Balodis, Cernomordijs, Jurkovskis; Savalnieks (Jaunzems 78), Melniks (Sits 46), Saveljevs, Ciganiks (Jagodinskis 90); Zelenkovs, Ikaunieks; Gutkovskis (Krollis 74).

England (1) 2 *(Lewis-Skelly 20, Kane 77)*
Albania (0) 0 82,378

England: (4231) Pickford; Walker, Konsa, Burn, Lewis-Skelly (James 90); Jones (Rogers 74), Rice (Henderson 82); Foden (Bowen 74), Bellingham, Rashford (Gordon 74); Kane.
Albania: (4141) Strakosha (Kastrati 82); Balliu, Ajeti, Djimsiti, Aliji; Ramadani; Asani (Hoxha 78), Asllani, Laci (Pajaziti 78), Bajrami N (Broja 63); Uzuni.

Monday, 24 March 2025

Albania (2) 3 *(Manaj 9, 19, Uzuni 90)*
Andorra (0) 0 17,183

Albania: (4231) Strakosha; Balliu, Ajeti, Djimsiti (Kumbulla 67), Aliji; Shehu, Asllani; Broja (Uzuni 76), Laci (Pajaziti 75), Hoxha; Manaj.
Andorra: (541) Alvarez; Borra (Llovera 76), San Nicolas, Garcia C, Olivera, Garcia M; Rubio (Rodrigo Tapia 62), Rebes (Teixeira 62), Babot, Cervos (Lopez 87); Rosas (Fernandez R 62).

England (1) 3 *(James 38, Kane 68, Eze 76)*
Latvia (0) 0 79,572

England: (4231) Pickford; James, Konsa, Guehi, Lewis-Skelly (Walker 79); Bellingham (Foden 67), Rice (Henderson 79); Bowen (Eze 61), Rogers, Rashford (Jones 79); Kane.
Latvia: (541) Zviedris; Savalnieks (Jagodinskis 54), Jurkovskis (Daskevics 61), Cernomordijs, Balodis (Sliede 83), Ciganiks; Jaunzems, Saveljevs, Zelenkovs, Ikaunieks (Melniks 83); Gutkovskis (Sits 61).

Saturday, 7 June 2025

Albania (0) 0
Serbia (0) 0 20,427

Albania: (4231) Strakosha; Hysaj, Ajeti, Djimsiti, Mitaj; Asllani, Shehu (Ramadani 85); Broja (Uzuni 75), Laci, Hoxha (Bajrami N 63); Manaj (Daku 63).
Serbia: (3412) Petrovic; Erakovic, Milenkovic, Pavlovic; Zivkovic A (Nedeljkovic 88), Maksimovic N (Gudelj 88), Lukic, Terzic (Mitrovic S 69); Samardzic (Maksimovic A 69); Vlahovic, Mitrovic A (Jovic 76).

Andorra (0) 0
England (0) 1 *(Kane 50)* 8872
Andorra: (541) Alvarez; Borra (Rubio 75), Llovera, Garcia C, Olivera, San Nicolas; Rodrigo Tapia (Garcia M 65), Guillen (de las Heras 83), Babot (Vales M 75), Cervos; Fernandez R (Lopez 65).
England: (4231) Pickford; Jones (Rice 81), Konsa, Burn, James; Bellingham (Gibbs-White 90), Henderson (Eze 64); Rogers (Gordon 81), Palmer (Alexander-Arnold 64), Madueke; Kane.
Match played in Spain.

Tuesday, 10 June 2025
Latvia (1) 1 *(Cernomordijs 45)*
Albania (1) 1 *(Cernomordijs 29 (og))* 6083
Latvia: (541) Zviedris; Jaunzems, Balodis, Cernomordijs, Jurkovskis, Ciganiks; Varslavans (Tonisevs 90), Saveljevs (Vapne 82), Zelenkovs, Ikaunieks (Daskevics 75); Gutkovskis (Regza 75).
Albania: (4231) Strakosha; Balliu, Ismajli, Kumbulla, Mitaj; Shehu, Asllani; Broja (Uzuni 82), Laci (Bajrami N 69), Hoxha (Muci 60); Manaj (Daku 82).

Serbia (2) 3 *(Mitrovic A 12, 24, 53 (pen))*
Andorra (0) 0 7576
Serbia: (3142) Petrovic; Stojic (Simic 76), Milenkovic, Pavlovic; Gudelj (Maksimovic A 61); Zivkovic, Lukic, Katai (Racic 61), Terzic (Mitrovic S 60); Vlahovic, Mitrovic A (Stulic 83).
Andorra: (541) Alvarez; Borra, Llovera, Garcia C, Olivera, San Nicolas; Rodrigo Tapia (Garcia M 65), Vales E (de las Heras 66), Vales M (Teixeira 87), Cervos (Gomes 79); Lopez (Fernandez 67).

Group K Table	P	W	D	L	F	A	GD	Pts
England	3	3	0	0	6	0	6	9
Albania	4	1	2	1	4	3	1	5
Serbia	2	1	1	0	3	0	3	4
Latvia	3	1	1	1	2	4	-2	4
Andorra	4	0	0	4	0	8	-8	0

GROUP L

Saturday, 22 March 2025
Czech Republic (1) 2 *(Schick 25, 85)*
Faroe Islands (0) 1 *(Vatnhamar G 83)* 8978
Czech Republic: (442) Kovar; Coufal (Doudera 80), Holes (Zima 23), Krejci, Zeleny; Cerny (Sin 80), Soucek, Cerv (Cerv 62), Sulc (Provod 61); Schick, Chory.
Faroe Islands: (541) Reynatrod; Benjaminsen (Danielsen 39), Faero, Vatnhamar G, Edmundsson A, Davidsen; Frederiksberg (Justinussen 79), Hansson (Joensen R 64), Hendriksson (Klettskard 79), Sorensen; Knudsen (Olsen M 64).

Montenegro (1) 3 *(Jovetic 22, Tuci 70, Marusic 73)*
Gibraltar (1) 1 *(Bent 13)* 3021
Montenegro: (4231) Nikic; Vesovic, Tuci, Sipcic, Gasevic (Vukcevic A 76); Jankovic, Loncar (Kuc 59); Camaj (Vukotic M 76), Jovetic (Bakic 85), Krstovic; Mugosa (Marusic 59).
Gibraltar: (4141) Banda; Ronan, Lopes (McCafferty 83), Annesley, Britto, Bent (Pozo 82); Jessop (Valarino 65), De Barr, Scanlon (Walker 83), Richards; El Hmidi (Bartolo 72).

Tuesday, 25 March 2025
Gibraltar (0) 0
Czech Republic (1) 4 *(Cerny 21, Schick 50, Sulc 72, Kliment 90)* 583
Gibraltar: (433) Banda; Ronan, Lopes (McCafferty 25), Annesley, Britto (Mauro 52); De Barr (Bartolo 62), Bent, Scanlon; Jessop (Livingstone 62), El Hmidi (Pozo 62), Richards.
Czech Republic: (4231) Kovar; Coufal, Zima, Krejci, Zeleny (Jurasek 46); Cerv (Kral 63), Soucek; Cerny (Kuchta 79), Sulc (Sadilek 87), Provod; Schick (Kliment 62).
Match played in Portugal.

Montenegro (0) 1 *(Kuc 90)*
Faroe Islands (0) 0 3226
Montenegro: (4231) Popovic; Vesovic (Radulovic 70), Vujacic, Sipcic, Vukcevic A (Vukcevic M 77); Jankovic (Bakic 69), Loncar (Kuc 46); Marusic, Jovetic, Vukotic M (Camaj 46); Krstovic.
Faroe Islands: (541) Lamhauge; Danielsen, Faero, Vatnhamar G, Edmundsson A, Davidsen (Agnarsson 69); Sorensen (Frederiksberg 46), Hendriksson, Joensen R (Mneney 57), Olsen M (Justinussen 88); Knudsen (Klettskard 46).

Friday, 6 June 2025
Czech Republic (1) 2 *(Hlozek 23, Schick 65)*
Montenegro (0) 0 10,889
Czech Republic: (4231) Kovar; Coufal, Holes, Krejci, Zeleny; Soucek, Cerv (Sadilek 46); Cerny (Kusej 77), Sulc (Kral 90), Hlozek (Provod 28); Schick (Chory 77).
Montenegro: (3421) Nikic; Savic, Vujacic, Sipcic (Mugosa 84); Vesovic (Vukcevic M 84), Jankovic, Kuc (Loncar 62), Radunovic (Vukcevic A 63); Vukotic (Osmajic 62), Jovetic; Krstovic.

Gibraltar (0) 0
Croatia (2) 7 *(Mario Pasalic 28, Budimir 30, Ivanovic 60, 63, Perisic 73, Kramaric 77, 79)* 1516
Gibraltar: (433) Banda; Ronan (Valarino 62), Lopes, Annesley (Carrington 62), Mauro; Scanlon, Walker (Bent 86), De Barr (Torrilla 46); Jessop, Bartolo, Richards (Gibson 74).
Croatia: (4231) Livakovic; Stanisic (Marco Pasalic 64), Pongracic, Caleta-Car, Juranovic, Sucic P (Kramaric 46); Majer; Sucic L (Modric 64), Mario Pasalic (Baturina 71), Perisic; Budimir (Ivanovic 76).
Match played in Portugal.

Monday, 9 June 2025
Croatia (1) 5 *(Kramaric 42, 75, Modric 62 (pen), Perisic 68, Budimir 72 (pen))*
Czech Republic (0) 1 *(Soucek 58)* 12,207
Croatia: (4231) Livakovic; Stanisic, Sutalo, Caleta-Car (Vuskovic 88), Gvardiol; Modric (Moro 81), Sucic P; Perisic (Marco Pasalic 88) Kramaric (Jakic 81), Mario Pasalic; Budimir (Ivanovic 76).
Czech Republic: (4231) Kovar; Coufal, Holes, Krejci, Zeleny; Sadilek (Kral 77), Soucek; Cerny (Kusej 66), Sulc, Provod (Doudera 88); Schick (Chory 77).

Faroe Islands (0) 2 *(Frederiksberg 71, Johannesen 86)*
Gibraltar (1) 1 *(Scanlon 23)* 2632
Faroe Islands: (343) Reynatrod; Faero, Vatnhamar G, Edmundsson A (Johansen 64); Danielsen, Hansson, Hendriksson (Andreasen 90), Davidsen; Frederiksberg (Edmundsson J 74), Klettskard (Johannesen 64), Justinussen (Sorensen 64).
Gibraltar: (433) Banda; Ronan (Valarino 83), Lopes, Annesley, Britto; De Barr (Mauro 90), Walker (Jessop 69); Bent; Richards (Torrilla 83), El Hmidi (Bartolo 46), Scanlon.

Group L Table	P	W	D	L	F	A	GD	Pts
Czech Republic	4	3	0	1	9	6	3	9
Croatia	2	2	0	0	12	1	11	6
Montenegro	3	2	0	1	4	3	1	6
Faroe Islands	3	1	0	2	3	4	-1	3
Gibraltar	4	0	0	4	2	16	-14	0

OTHER BRITISH AND IRISH INTERNATIONAL MATCHES 2024–25

FRIENDLIES

**Denotes player sent off.*

ENGLAND

Nottingham, Tuesday, 10 June 2025

England (1) 1 *(Kane 8)*

Senegal (1) 3 *(Sarr 40, Diarra 62, Sabaly 90)*   26,322

England: (442) Henderson; Walker, Chalobah, Colwill, Lewis-Skelly (Toney 85); Saka (Madueke 71), Gallagher (Jones 59), Rice (Bellingham 71), Gordon (Gibbs-White 59); Eze, Kane (Rogers 59).

Senegal: (433) Mendy E; Diatta, Koulibaly, Niakhate, Diouf E; Diarra (Gueye P 70), Gueye I, Camara L; Sarr (Sabaly 70), Jackson (Dia 81), Ndiaye I.

Referee: Stephanie Frappart.

SCOTLAND

Hampden Park, Friday, 6 June 2025

Scotland (1) 1 *(Souttar 25)*

Iceland (2) 3 *(Gudjohnsen 8, Ferguson 45 (og), Palsson 52)*   32,797

Scotland: (541) Gunn (Slicker 7); Johnston (Patterson 80), Souttar, Hanley (McKenna 69), Tierney (Miller 68), Robertson; Ferguson, Gilmour, McGinn, McTominay (Conway 80); Hirst (Adams 68).

Iceland: (433) Olafsson; Palsson (Thorhallsson 60), Magnusson H (Gretarsson 46), Ingason (Gunnarsson A 77), Ellertsson; Thordarson (Anderson 72), Johannesson (Traustason 72), Arnar Haraldsson; Gudmundsson A, Thorsteinsson (Willumsson W 72), Gudjohnsen.

Referee: Granit Maqedonci.

Vaduz, Monday, 9 June 2025

Liechtenstein (0) 0

Scotland (2) 4 *(Adams 5, 26, 90, Hirst 49)*   4036

Liechtenstein: (352) Buchel B (Ospelt 46); Traber, Malin, Hofer; Kindle (Meier 52), Luchinger (Zund 80), Hasler N (Wolfinger F 65), Sele, Goppel; Saglam (Pizzi 81), Notaro (Netzer 51).

Scotland: (442) Doohan; Ralston (Patterson 68), Hendry, McKenna, Robertson (Doig 59); Ferguson (Bowie 78), Miller, Gilmour (Barron 78), McGinn (Irving 59); Adams, Hirst (Conway 68).

NORTHERN IRELAND

Belfast, Friday, 21 March 2025

Northern Ireland (1) 1 *(Price 17)*

Switzerland (1) 1 *(Sierro 29)*   17,862

Northern Ireland: (3412) Charles P; Hume, McNair, Brown; Spencer, Charles S, Saville (Devenny 69); Smyth (Donley 56); Galbraith (Devlin 75); Bonis (Taylor 56), Price.

Switzerland: (4231) Kobel; Gartenmann, Zesiger, Rodriguez, Schmidt (Blondel 68); Sierro (Sow 88), Zakaria; Ndoye (Sanches 68), Embolo (Monteiro 59), Vargas (Zeqiri 59); Aebischer (Rieder 59).

Referee: Mohammed Al-Hakim.

Solna, Tuesday, 25 March 2025

Sweden (2) 5 *(Holm 7, Nygren 33, Sema 59, Isak 64, Elanga 77)*

Northern Ireland (0) 1 *(Price 90)*   14,147

Sweden: (352) Johansson; Lindelof, Hien (Zeneli 80), Gudmundsson; Holm (Eliasson 71), Ayari (Lagerbielke 80), Saletros (Karlstrom 80), Nanasi (Elanga 71), Sema; Nygren (Widell 87), Isak.

Northern Ireland: (3412) Charles P; McNair, McConville, Brown; Devlin (Thompson 67), Charles S, Saville (Marshall 67), Spencer (Smyth 78); Devenny (Lyons 78); Price, Donley (Bonis 78).

Referee: Matthew MacDermid.

Copenhagen, Saturday, 7 June 2025

Denmark (1) 2 *(Isaksen 45, Eriksen 67)*

Northern Ireland (1) 1 *(Hojbjerg 6 (og))*   29,981

Denmark: (433) Jorgensen; Kristensen, Hogsberg, Andersen (Vestergaard 65), Maehle; Hojbjerg, Norgaard (Hjulmand 80), Eriksen (O'Riley 80); Isaksen (Dreyer 89), Hojlund (Biereth 65), Damsgaard (Kvistgaarden 65).

Northern Ireland: (3421) Hazard (Charles P 46); McConville, Ballard, Hume; Bradley (Spencer 73), Charles S, McCann (Saville 62), Devenny (Marshall 83); Price, Galbraith (Donley 62); Charles D (Smyth 73).

Referee: Menelaos Antoniou.

Belfast, Tuesday, 10 June 2025

Northern Ireland (1) 1 *(Price 37)*

Iceland (0) 0   18,021

Northern Ireland: (3421) Charles P; Spencer■, Ballard, Hume; Bradley (Devlin 90), Charles S, Saville (McConville 69), Devenny; Smyth (Galbraith 46), Price (Lyons 90); Hale (Bonis 68).

Iceland: (433) Valdimarsson; Palsson, Gretarsson (Helgason 62), Ingason, Tomasson (Thordarson 86); Gudmundsson A (Magnusson S 74), Traustason (Johannesson 46), Willumsson W (Anderson 62); Thorsteinsson (Hlynsson 62), Gudjohnsen, Arnar Haraldsson.

Referee: Morten Krogh.

REPUBLIC OF IRELAND

Dublin, Friday, 6 June 2025

Republic of Ireland (1) 1 *(McAteer 22)*

Senegal (0) 1 *(Sarr 83)*   32,478

Republic of Ireland: (343) Kelleher; O'Shea, Collins, Manning (O'Brien 67); Doherty (Phillips 66), Knight, Taylor (Ferguson 58), Brady (Scales 85); Smallbone (Moran 82), McAteer (Ebosele 80), Idah.

Senegal: (433) Diouf Y; Mendy A, Seck, Diallo, Jakobs (Diouf E 85); Diarra, Camara M (Sabaly 77), Diatta (Camara L 63); Sima (Sarr 63), Dia (Ndiaye C 77), Ndiaye I.

Luxembourg, Tuesday, 10 June 2025

Luxembourg (0) 0

Republic of Ireland (0) 0   6312

Luxembourg: (532) Pereira Cardoso; Dzogovic, Jans (Thill 62), Korac, Carlson (Gerson 89), Bohnert (Mica Pinto 62); Moreira (Duarte 89), Barreiro, Sinani; Rodrigues (Veiga 82), Dardari (Curci 76).

Republic of Ireland: (442) O'Leary; O'Brien, Brady (Manning 20), Knight (Patrick 90), O'Shea; Collins, McAteer (Doherty 76), Smallbone (Taylor 57), Ferguson (Idah 76); Parrott, Phillips (Ebosele 57).

Referee: Stefan Ebner.

BRITISH AND IRISH INTERNATIONAL RESULTS 1872–2025

Note: In the results that follow, wc = World Cup, ec = European Championship, nl = Nations League ui = Umbro International Trophy. tf = Tournoi de France. nc = Nations Cup. Northern Ireland played as Ireland before 1921. *After extra time.*

Bold type indicates matches played in season 2024–25.

ENGLAND v SCOTLAND

Played: 114; England won 48, Scotland won 41, Drawn 26. Goals: England 203, Scotland 174.

			E	S				E	S
1872	30 Nov	Glasgow	0	0	1935	6 Apr	Glasgow	0	2
1873	8 Mar	Kennington Oval	4	2	1936	4 Apr	Wembley	1	1
1874	7 Mar	Glasgow	1	2	1937	17 Apr	Glasgow	1	3
1875	6 Apr	Kennington Oval	2	2	1938	9 Apr	Wembley	0	1
1876	4 Mar	Glasgow	0	3	1939	15 Apr	Glasgow	2	1
1877	3 Mar	Kennington Oval	1	3	1947	12 Apr	Wembley	1	1
1878	2 Mar	Glasgow	2	7	1948	10 Apr	Glasgow	2	0
1879	5 Apr	Kennington Oval	5	4	1949	9 Apr	Wembley	1	3
1880	13 Mar	Glasgow	4	5	wc1950	15 Apr	Glasgow	1	0
1881	12 Mar	Kennington Oval	1	6	1951	14 Apr	Wembley	2	3
1882	11 Mar	Glasgow	1	5	1952	5 Apr	Glasgow	2	1
1883	10 Mar	Sheffield U	2	3	1953	18 Apr	Wembley	2	2
1884	15 Mar	Glasgow	0	1	wc1954	3 Apr	Glasgow	4	2
1885	21 Mar	Kennington Oval	1	1	1955	2 Apr	Wembley	7	2
1886	31 Mar	Glasgow	1	1	1956	14 Apr	Glasgow	1	1
1887	19 Mar	Blackburn	2	3	1957	6 Apr	Wembley	2	1
1888	17 Mar	Glasgow	5	0	1958	19 Apr	Glasgow	4	0
1889	13 Apr	Kennington Oval	2	3	1959	11 Apr	Wembley	1	0
1890	5 Apr	Glasgow	1	1	1960	9 Apr	Glasgow	1	1
1891	6 Apr	Blackburn	2	1	1961	15 Apr	Wembley	9	3
1892	2 Apr	Glasgow	4	1	1962	14 Apr	Glasgow	0	2
1893	1 Apr	Richmond	5	2	1963	6 Apr	Wembley	1	2
1894	7 Apr	Glasgow	2	2	1964	11 Apr	Glasgow	0	1
1895	6 Apr	Everton	3	0	1965	10 Apr	Wembley	2	2
1896	4 Apr	Glasgow	1	2	1966	2 Apr	Glasgow	4	3
1897	3 Apr	Crystal Palace	1	2	ec1967	15 Apr	Wembley	2	3
1898	2 Apr	Glasgow	3	1	ec1968	24 Jan	Glasgow	1	1
1899	8 Apr	Aston Villa	2	1	1969	10 May	Wembley	4	1
1900	7 Apr	Glasgow	1	4	1970	25 Apr	Glasgow	0	0
1901	30 Mar	Crystal Palace	2	2	1971	22 May	Wembley	3	1
1902	3 Mar	Aston Villa	2	2	1972	27 May	Glasgow	1	0
1903	4 Apr	Sheffield United	1	2	1973	14 Feb	Glasgow	5	0
1904	9 Apr	Glasgow	1	0	1973	19 May	Wembley	1	0
1905	1 Apr	Crystal Palace	1	0	1974	18 May	Glasgow	0	2
1906	7 Apr	Glasgow	1	2	1975	24 May	Wembley	5	1
1907	6 Apr	Newcastle	1	1	1976	15 May	Glasgow	1	2
1908	4 Apr	Glasgow	1	1	1977	4 June	Wembley	1	2
1909	3 Apr	Crystal Palace	2	0	1978	20 May	Glasgow	1	0
1910	2 Apr	Glasgow	0	2	1979	26 May	Wembley	3	1
1911	1 Apr	Everton	1	1	1980	24 May	Glasgow	2	0
1912	23 Mar	Glasgow	1	1	1981	23 May	Wembley	0	1
1913	5 Apr	Chelsea	1	0	1982	29 May	Glasgow	1	0
1914	14 Apr	Glasgow	1	3	1983	1 June	Wembley	2	0
1920	10 Apr	Sheffield Wednesday	5	4	1984	26 May	Glasgow	1	1
1921	9 Apr	Glasgow	0	3	1985	25 May	Glasgow	0	1
1922	8 Apr	Aston Villa	0	1	1986	23 Apr	Wembley	2	1
1923	14 Apr	Glasgow	2	2	1987	23 May	Glasgow	0	0
1924	12 Apr	Wembley	1	1	1988	21 May	Wembley	1	0
1925	4 Apr	Glasgow	0	2	1989	27 May	Glasgow	2	0
1926	17 Apr	Manchester United	0	1	ec1996	15 June	Wembley	2	0
1927	2 Apr	Glasgow	2	1	ec1999	13 Nov	Glasgow	2	0
1928	31 Mar	Wembley	1	5	ec1999	17 Nov	Wembley	0	1
1929	13 Apr	Glasgow	0	1	2013	14 Aug	Wembley	3	2
1930	5 Apr	Wembley	5	2	2014	18 Nov	Glasgow	3	1
1931	28 Mar	Glasgow	0	2	wc2016	11 Nov	Wembley	3	0
1932	9 Apr	Wembley	3	0	wc2017	10 June	Glasgow	2	2
1933	1 Apr	Glasgow	1	2	ec2021	18 June	Wembley	0	0
1934	14 Apr	Wembley	3	0	2023	12 Sept	Glasgow	3	1

ENGLAND v WALES

Played: 103; England won 69, Wales won 14, Drawn 21. Goals: England 253, Wales 91.

			E	W				E	W
1879	18 Jan	Kennington Oval	2	1	1885	14 Mar	Blackburn	1	1
1880	15 Mar	Wrexham	3	2	1886	29 Mar	Wrexham	3	1
1881	26 Feb	Blackburn	0	1	1887	26 Feb	Kennington Oval	4	0
1882	13 Mar	Wrexham	3	5	1888	4 Feb	Crewe	5	1
1883	3 Feb	Kennington Oval	5	0	1889	23 Feb	Stoke	4	1
1884	17 Mar	Wrexham	4	0	1890	15 Mar	Wrexham	3	1

			E	W
1891	7 May	Sunderland	4	1
1892	5 Mar	Wrexham	2	0
1893	13 Mar	Stoke	6	0
1894	12 Mar	Wrexham	5	1
1895	18 Mar	Queen's Club, Kensington	1	1
1896	16 Mar	Cardiff	9	1
1897	29 Mar	Sheffield United	4	0
1898	28 Mar	Wrexham	3	0
1899	20 Mar	Bristol City	4	0
1900	26 Mar	Cardiff	1	1
1901	18 Mar	Newcastle	6	0
1902	3 Mar	Wrexham	0	0
1903	2 Mar	Portsmouth	2	1
1904	29 Feb	Wrexham	2	2
1905	27 Mar	Liverpool	3	1
1906	19 Mar	Cardiff	1	0
1907	18 Mar	Fulham	1	1
1908	16 Mar	Wrexham	7	1
1909	15 Mar	Nottingham Forest	2	0
1910	14 Mar	Cardiff	1	0
1911	13 Mar	Millwall	3	0
1912	11 Mar	Wrexham	2	0
1913	17 Mar	Bristol City	4	3
1914	16 Mar	Cardiff	2	0
1920	15 Mar	Arsenal	1	2
1921	14 Mar	Cardiff	0	0
1922	13 Mar	Liverpool	1	0
1923	5 Mar	Cardiff	2	2
1924	3 Mar	Blackburn	1	2
1925	28 Feb	Swansea	2	1
1926	1 Mar	Crystal Palace	1	3
1927	12 Feb	Wrexham	3	3
1927	28 Nov	Burnley	1	2
1928	17 Nov	Swansea	3	2
1929	20 Nov	Chelsea	6	0
1930	22 Nov	Wrexham	4	0
1931	18 Nov	Liverpool	3	1
1932	16 Nov	Wrexham	0	0
1933	15 Nov	Newcastle	1	2
1934	29 Sept	Cardiff	4	0
1936	5 Feb	Wolverhampton	1	2
1936	17 Oct	Cardiff	1	2
1937	17 Nov	Middlesbrough	2	1
1938	22 Oct	Cardiff	2	4
1946	13 Nov	Manchester City	3	0
1947	18 Oct	Cardiff	3	0
1948	10 Nov	Aston Villa	1	0
wc1949	15 Oct	Cardiff	4	1
1950	15 Nov	Sunderland	4	2
1951	20 Oct	Cardiff	1	1
1952	12 Nov	Wembley	5	2
wc1953	10 Oct	Cardiff	4	1
1954	10 Nov	Wembley	3	2
1955	27 Oct	Cardiff	1	2
1956	14 Nov	Wembley	3	1
1957	19 Oct	Cardiff	4	0
1958	26 Nov	Aston Villa	2	2
1959	17 Oct	Cardiff	1	1
1960	23 Nov	Wembley	5	1
1961	14 Oct	Cardiff	1	1
1962	21 Oct	Wembley	4	0
1963	12 Oct	Cardiff	4	0
1964	18 Nov	Wembley	2	1
1965	2 Oct	Cardiff	0	0
EC1966	16 Nov	Wembley	5	1
EC1967	21 Oct	Cardiff	3	0
1969	7 May	Wembley	2	1
1970	18 Apr	Cardiff	1	1
1971	19 May	Wembley	0	0
1972	20 May	Cardiff	3	0
wc1972	15 Nov	Cardiff	1	0
wc1973	24 Jan	Wembley	1	1
1973	15 May	Wembley	3	0
1974	11 May	Cardiff	2	0
1975	21 May	Wembley	2	2
1976	24 Mar	Wrexham	2	1
1976	8 May	Cardiff	1	0
1977	31 May	Wembley	0	1
1978	3 May	Cardiff	3	1
1979	23 May	Wembley	0	0
1980	17 May	Wrexham	1	4
1981	20 May	Wembley	0	0
1982	27 Apr	Cardiff	1	0
1983	23 Feb	Wembley	2	1
1984	2 May	Wrexham	0	1
wc2004	9 Oct	Manchester United	2	0
wc2005	3 Sept	Cardiff	1	0
EC2011	26 Mar	Cardiff	2	0
EC2011	6 Sept	Wembley	1	0
EC2016	16 June	Lens	2	1
2020	8 Oct	Wembley	3	0
wc2022	29 Nov	Al Rayyan	3	0

ENGLAND v NORTHERN IRELAND

Played: 98; England won 75, Northern Ireland won 7, Drawn 16. Goals: England 323, Northern Ireland 81.

			E	NI
1882	18 Feb	Belfast	13	0
1883	24 Feb	Liverpool	7	0
1884	23 Feb	Belfast	8	1
1885	28 Feb	Manchester	4	0
1886	13 Mar	Belfast	6	1
1887	5 Feb	Sheffield United	7	0
1888	31 Mar	Belfast	5	1
1889	2 Mar	Everton	6	1
1890	15 Mar	Belfast	9	1
1891	7 Mar	Wolverhampton	6	1
1892	5 Mar	Belfast	2	0
1893	25 Feb	Birmingham	6	1
1894	3 Mar	Belfast	2	2
1895	9 Mar	Derby	9	0
1896	7 Mar	Belfast	2	0
1897	20 Feb	Nottingham	6	0
1898	5 Mar	Belfast	3	2
1899	18 Feb	Sunderland	13	2
1900	17 Mar	Dublin	2	0
1901	9 Mar	Southampton	3	0
1902	22 Mar	Belfast	1	0
1903	14 Feb	Wolverhampton	4	0
1904	12 Mar	Belfast	3	1
1905	25 Feb	Middlesbrough	1	1
1906	17 Feb	Belfast	5	0
1907	16 Feb	Everton	1	0
1908	15 Feb	Belfast	3	1
1909	13 Feb	Bradford	4	0
1910	12 Feb	Belfast	1	1
1911	11 Feb	Derby	2	1
1912	10 Feb	Dublin	6	1
1913	15 Feb	Belfast	1	2
1914	14 Feb	Middlesbrough	0	3
1919	25 Oct	Belfast	1	1
1920	23 Oct	Sunderland	2	0
1921	22 Oct	Belfast	1	1
1922	21 Oct	West Bromwich	2	0
1923	20 Oct	Belfast	1	2
1924	22 Oct	Everton	3	1
1925	24 Oct	Belfast	0	0
1926	20 Oct	Liverpool	3	3
1927	22 Oct	Belfast	0	2
1928	22 Oct	Everton	2	1
1929	19 Oct	Belfast	3	0
1930	20 Oct	Sheffield United	5	1
1931	17 Oct	Belfast	6	2
1932	17 Oct	Blackpool	1	0
1933	14 Oct	Belfast	3	0
1935	6 Feb	Everton	2	1
1935	19 Oct	Belfast	3	1
1936	18 Nov	Stoke	3	1
1937	23 Oct	Belfast	5	1
1938	16 Nov	Manchester United	7	0
1946	28 Sept	Belfast	7	2
1947	5 Nov	Everton	2	2
1948	9 Oct	Belfast	6	2
wc1949	16 Nov	Manchester City	9	2
1950	7 Oct	Belfast	4	1
1951	14 Nov	Aston Villa	2	0
1952	4 Oct	Belfast	2	2
wc1953	11 Nov	Everton	3	1
1954	2 Oct	Belfast	2	0
1955	2 Nov	Wembley	3	0
1956	10 Oct	Belfast	1	1

			E	NI					E	NI
1957	6 Nov	Wembley	2	3		1975	17 May	Belfast	0	0
1958	4 Oct	Belfast	3	3		1976	11 May	Wembley	4	0
1959	18 Nov	Wembley	2	1		1977	28 May	Belfast	2	1
1960	8 Oct	Belfast	5	2		1978	16 May	Wembley	1	0
1961	22 Nov	Wembley	1	1	EC1979	7 Feb	Wembley	4	0
1962	20 Oct	Belfast	3	1		1979	19 May	Belfast	2	0
1963	20 Nov	Wembley	8	3	EC1979	17 Oct	Belfast	5	1
1964	3 Oct	Belfast	4	3		1980	20 May	Wembley	1	1
1965	10 Nov	Wembley	2	1		1982	23 Feb	Wembley	4	0
EC1966	20 Oct	Belfast	2	0		1983	28 May	Belfast	0	0
EC1967	22 Nov	Wembley	2	0		1984	24 Apr	Wembley	1	0
1969	3 May	Belfast	3	1	WC1985	27 Feb	Belfast	1	0
1970	21 Apr	Wembley	3	1	WC1985	13 Nov	Wembley	0	0
1971	15 May	Belfast	1	0	EC1986	15 Oct	Wembley	3	0
1972	23 May	Wembley	0	1	EC1987	1 Apr	Belfast	2	0
1973	12 May	Everton	2	1	WC2005	26 Mar	Manchester United	4	0
1974	15 May	Wembley	1	0	WC2005	7 Sept	Belfast	0	0

SCOTLAND v WALES

Played: 107; Scotland won 61, Wales won 23, Drawn 23. Goals: Scotland 243, Wales 124.

			S	W					S	W
1876	25 Mar	Glasgow	4	0		1934	21 Nov	Aberdeen	3	2
1877	5 Mar	Wrexham	2	0		1935	5 Oct	Cardiff	1	1
1878	23 Mar	Glasgow	9	0		1936	2 Dec	Dundee	1	2
1879	7 Apr	Wrexham	3	0		1937	30 Oct	Cardiff	1	2
1880	3 Apr	Glasgow	5	1		1938	9 Nov	Hearts	3	2
1881	14 Mar	Wrexham	5	1		1946	19 Oct	Wrexham	1	3
1882	25 Mar	Glasgow	5	0		1947	12 Nov	Glasgow	1	2
1883	12 Mar	Wrexham	3	0		1948	23 Oct	Cardiff	3	1
1884	29 Mar	Glasgow	4	1	WC1949	9 Nov	Glasgow	2	0
1885	23 Mar	Wrexham	8	1		1950	21 Oct	Cardiff	3	1
1886	10 Apr	Glasgow	4	1		1951	14 Nov	Glasgow	0	1
1887	21 Mar	Wrexham	2	0		1952	18 Oct	Cardiff	2	1
1888	10 Mar	Hibernian	5	1	WC1953	4 Nov	Glasgow	3	3
1889	15 Apr	Wrexham	0	0		1954	16 Oct	Cardiff	1	0
1890	22 Mar	Paisley	5	0		1955	9 Nov	Glasgow	2	0
1891	21 Mar	Wrexham	4	3		1956	20 Oct	Cardiff	2	2
1892	26 Mar	Hearts	6	1		1957	13 Nov	Glasgow	1	1
1893	18 Mar	Wrexham	8	0		1958	18 Oct	Cardiff	3	0
1894	24 Mar	Kilmarnock	5	2		1959	4 Nov	Glasgow	1	1
1895	23 Mar	Wrexham	2	2		1960	20 Oct	Cardiff	0	2
1896	21 Mar	Dundee	4	0		1961	8 Nov	Glasgow	2	0
1897	20 Mar	Wrexham	2	2		1962	20 Oct	Cardiff	3	2
1898	19 Mar	Motherwell	5	2		1963	20 Nov	Glasgow	2	1
1899	18 Mar	Wrexham	6	0		1964	3 Oct	Cardiff	2	3
1900	3 Feb	Aberdeen	5	2	EC1965	24 Nov	Glasgow	4	1
1901	2 Mar	Wrexham	1	1	EC1966	22 Oct	Cardiff	1	1
1902	15 Mar	Morton	5	1		1967	22 Nov	Glasgow	3	2
1903	9 Mar	Cardiff	1	0		1969	3 May	Wrexham	5	3
1904	12 Mar	Dundee	1	1		1970	22 Apr	Glasgow	0	0
1905	6 Mar	Wrexham	1	3		1971	15 May	Cardiff	0	0
1906	3 Mar	Hearts	0	2		1972	24 May	Glasgow	1	0
1907	4 Mar	Wrexham	0	1		1973	12 May	Wrexham	2	0
1908	7 Mar	Dundee	2	1		1974	14 May	Glasgow	2	0
1909	1 Mar	Wrexham	2	3		1975	17 May	Cardiff	2	2
1910	5 Mar	Kilmarnock	1	0		1976	6 May	Glasgow	3	1
1911	6 Mar	Cardiff	2	2	WC1976	17 Nov	Glasgow	1	0
1912	2 Mar	Hearts	1	0		1977	28 May	Wrexham	0	0
1913	3 Mar	Wrexham	0	0	WC1977	12 Oct	Liverpool	2	0
1914	28 Feb	Glasgow	0	0		1978	17 May	Glasgow	1	1
1920	26 Feb	Cardiff	1	1		1979	19 May	Cardiff	0	3
1921	12 Feb	Aberdeen	2	1		1980	21 May	Glasgow	1	0
1922	4 Feb	Wrexham	1	2		1981	16 May	Swansea	0	2
1923	17 Mar	Paisley	2	0		1982	24 May	Glasgow	1	0
1924	16 Feb	Cardiff	0	2		1983	28 May	Cardiff	2	0
1925	14 Feb	Hearts	3	1		1984	28 Feb	Glasgow	2	1
1925	31 Oct	Cardiff	3	0	WC1985	27 Mar	Glasgow	0	1
1926	30 Oct	Glasgow	3	0	WC1985	10 Sept	Cardiff	1	1
1927	29 Oct	Wrexham	2	2		1997	27 May	Kilmarnock	0	1
1928	27 Oct	Glasgow	4	2		2004	18 Feb	Cardiff	0	4
1929	26 Oct	Cardiff	4	2		2009	14 Nov	Cardiff	0	3
1930	25 Oct	Glasgow	1	1	NC2011	25 May	Dublin	3	1
1931	31 Oct	Wrexham	3	2	WC2012	12 Oct	Cardiff	1	2
1932	26 Oct	Hearts	2	5	WC2013	22 Mar	Glasgow	1	2
1933	4 Oct	Cardiff	2	3						

SCOTLAND v NORTHERN IRELAND

Played: 96; Scotland won 64, Northern Ireland won 15, Drawn 17. Goals: Scotland 261, Northern Ireland 81.

			S	NI					S	NI
1884	26 Jan	Belfast	5	0		1888	24 Mar	Belfast	10	2
1885	14 Mar	Glasgow	8	2		1889	9 Mar	Glasgow	7	0
1886	20 Mar	Belfast	7	2		1890	29 Mar	Belfast	4	1
1887	19 Feb	Glasgow	4	1		1891	28 Mar	Glasgow	2	1

			S	NI				S	NI
1892	19 Mar	Belfast	3	2	1947	4 Oct	Belfast	0	2
1893	25 Mar	Glasgow	6	1	1948	17 Nov	Glasgow	3	2
1894	31 Mar	Belfast	2	1	wc1949	1 Oct	Belfast	8	2
1895	30 Mar	Glasgow	3	1	1950	1 Nov	Glasgow	6	1
1896	28 Mar	Belfast	3	3	1951	6 Oct	Belfast	3	0
1897	27 Mar	Glasgow	5	1	1952	5 Nov	Glasgow	1	1
1898	26 Mar	Belfast	3	0	wc1953	3 Oct	Belfast	3	1
1899	25 Mar	Glasgow	9	1	1954	3 Nov	Glasgow	2	2
1900	3 Mar	Belfast	3	0	1955	8 Oct	Belfast	1	2
1901	23 Feb	Glasgow	11	0	1956	7 Nov	Glasgow	1	0
1902	1 Mar	Belfast	5	1	1957	5 Oct	Belfast	1	1
1902	9 Aug	Belfast	3	0	1958	5 Nov	Glasgow	2	2
1903	21 Mar	Glasgow	0	2	1959	3 Oct	Belfast	4	0
1904	26 Mar	Dublin	1	1	1960	9 Nov	Glasgow	5	2
1905	18 Mar	Glasgow	4	0	1961	7 Oct	Belfast	6	1
1906	17 Mar	Dublin	1	0	1962	7 Nov	Glasgow	5	1
1907	16 Mar	Glasgow	3	0	1963	12 Oct	Belfast	1	2
1908	14 Mar	Dublin	5	0	1964	25 Nov	Glasgow	3	2
1909	15 Mar	Glasgow	5	0	1965	2 Oct	Belfast	2	3
1910	19 Mar	Belfast	0	1	1966	16 Nov	Glasgow	2	1
1911	18 Mar	Glasgow	2	0	1967	21 Oct	Belfast	0	1
1912	16 Mar	Belfast	4	1	1969	6 May	Glasgow	1	1
1913	15 Mar	Dublin	2	1	1970	18 Apr	Belfast	1	0
1914	14 Mar	Glasgow	1	1	1971	18 May	Glasgow	0	1
1920	13 Mar	Glasgow	3	0	1972	20 May	Glasgow	2	0
1921	26 Feb	Belfast	2	0	1973	16 May	Glasgow	1	2
1922	4 Mar	Glasgow	2	1	1974	11 May	Glasgow	0	1
1923	3 Mar	Belfast	1	0	1975	20 May	Glasgow	3	0
1924	1 Mar	Glasgow	2	0	1976	8 May	Glasgow	3	0
1925	28 Feb	Belfast	3	0	1977	1 June	Glasgow	3	0
1926	27 Feb	Glasgow	4	0	1978	13 May	Glasgow	1	1
1927	26 Feb	Belfast	2	0	1979	22 May	Glasgow	1	0
1928	25 Feb	Glasgow	0	1	1980	17 May	Belfast	0	1
1929	23 Feb	Belfast	7	3	wc1981	25 Mar	Glasgow	1	1
1930	22 Feb	Glasgow	3	1	1981	19 May	Glasgow	2	0
1931	21 Feb	Belfast	0	0	wc1981	14 Oct	Belfast	0	0
1931	19 Sept	Glasgow	3	1	1982	28 Apr	Belfast	1	1
1932	12 Sept	Belfast	4	0	1983	24 May	Glasgow	0	0
1933	16 Sept	Glasgow	1	2	1983	13 Dec	Belfast	0	2
1934	20 Oct	Belfast	1	2	1992	19 Feb	Glasgow	1	0
1935	13 Nov	Hearts	2	1	2008	20 Aug	Glasgow	0	0
1936	31 Oct	Belfast	3	1	NC2011	9 Feb	Dublin	3	0
1937	10 Nov	Aberdeen	1	1	2015	25 Mar	Glasgow	1	0
1938	8 Oct	Belfast	2	0	**2024**	**26 Mar**	**Glasgow**	**0**	**1**
1946	27 Nov	Glasgow	0	0					

WALES v NORTHERN IRELAND

Played: 96; Wales won 45, Northern Ireland won 27, Drawn 24. Goals: Wales 191, Northern Ireland 132.

			W	NI				W	NI
1882	25 Feb	Wrexham	7	1	1921	9 Apr	Swansea	2	1
1883	17 Mar	Belfast	1	1	1922	4 Apr	Belfast	1	1
1884	9 Feb	Wrexham	6	0	1923	14 Apr	Wrexham	0	3
1885	11 Apr	Belfast	8	2	1924	15 Mar	Belfast	1	0
1886	27 Feb	Wrexham	5	0	1925	18 Apr	Wrexham	0	0
1887	12 Mar	Belfast	1	4	1926	13 Feb	Belfast	0	3
1888	3 Mar	Wrexham	11	0	1927	9 Apr	Cardiff	2	2
1889	27 Apr	Belfast	3	1	1928	4 Feb	Belfast	2	1
1890	8 Feb	Shrewsbury	5	2	1929	2 Feb	Wrexham	2	2
1891	7 Feb	Belfast	2	7	1930	1 Feb	Belfast	0	7
1892	27 Feb	Bangor	1	1	1931	22 Apr	Wrexham	3	2
1893	8 Apr	Belfast	3	4	1931	5 Dec	Belfast	0	4
1894	24 Feb	Swansea	4	1	1932	7 Dec	Wrexham	4	1
1895	16 Mar	Belfast	2	2	1933	4 Nov	Belfast	1	1
1896	29 Feb	Wrexham	6	1	1935	27 Mar	Wrexham	3	1
1897	6 Mar	Belfast	3	4	1936	11 Mar	Belfast	2	3
1898	19 Feb	Llandudno	0	1	1937	17 Mar	Wrexham	4	1
1899	4 Mar	Belfast	0	1	1938	16 Mar	Belfast	0	1
1900	24 Feb	Llandudno	2	0	1939	15 Mar	Wrexham	3	1
1901	23 Mar	Belfast	1	0	1947	16 Apr	Belfast	1	2
1902	22 Mar	Cardiff	0	3	1948	10 Mar	Wrexham	2	0
1903	28 Mar	Belfast	0	2	1949	9 Apr	Belfast	2	0
1904	21 Mar	Bangor	0	1	wc1950	8 Mar	Wrexham	0	0
1905	18 Apr	Belfast	2	2	1951	7 Mar	Belfast	2	1
1906	2 Apr	Wrexham	4	4	1952	19 Mar	Swansea	3	0
1907	23 Feb	Belfast	3	2	1953	15 Apr	Belfast	3	2
1908	11 Apr	Aberdare	0	1	wc1954	31 Mar	Wrexham	1	2
1909	20 Mar	Belfast	3	2	1955	20 Apr	Belfast	3	2
1910	11 Apr	Wrexham	4	1	1956	11 Apr	Cardiff	1	1
1911	28 Jan	Belfast	2	1	1957	10 Apr	Belfast	0	0
1912	13 Apr	Cardiff	2	3	1958	16 Apr	Cardiff	1	1
1913	18 Jan	Belfast	1	0	1959	22 Apr	Belfast	1	4
1914	19 Jan	Wrexham	1	2	1960	6 Apr	Wrexham	3	2
1920	14 Feb	Belfast	2	2	1961	12 Apr	Belfast	5	1

			W	NI
1962	11 Apr	Cardiff	4	0
1963	3 Apr	Belfast	4	1
1964	15 Apr	Swansea	2	3
1965	31 Mar	Belfast	5	0
1966	30 Mar	Cardiff	1	4
EC1967	12 Apr	Belfast	0	0
EC1968	28 Feb	Wrexham	2	0
1969	10 May	Belfast	0	0
1970	25 Apr	Swansea	1	0
1971	22 May	Belfast	0	1
1972	27 May	Wrexham	0	0
1973	19 May	Everton	0	1
1974	18 May	Wrexham	1	0
1975	23 May	Belfast	0	1

			W	NI
1976	14 May	Swansea	1	0
1977	3 June	Belfast	1	1
1978	19 May	Wrexham	1	0
1979	25 May	Belfast	1	1
1980	23 May	Cardiff	0	1
1982	27 May	Wrexham	3	0
1983	31 May	Belfast	1	0
1984	22 May	Swansea	1	1
wc2004	8 Sept	Cardiff	2	2
wc2005	8 Oct	Belfast	3	2
2007	6 Feb	Belfast	0	0
NC2011	27 May	Dublin	2	0
2016	24 Mar	Cardiff	1	1
EC2016	25 June	Paris	1	0

OTHER BRITISH INTERNATIONAL RESULTS 1908–2025

ENGLAND

v ALBANIA

			E	A
wc1989	8 Mar	Tirana	2	0
wc1989	26 Apr	Wembley	5	0
wc2001	28 Mar	Tirana	3	1
wc2001	5 Sept	Newcastle	2	0
wc2021	28 Mar	Tirana	2	0
wc2021	12 Nov	Wembley	5	0
wc2025	**21 Mar**	**Wembley**	**2**	**0**

v ALGERIA

			E	A
wc2010	18 June	Cape Town	0	0

v ANDORRA

			E	A
EC2006	2 Sept	Manchester United	5	0
EC2007	28 Mar	Barcelona	3	0
wc2008	6 Sept	Barcelona	2	0
wc2009	10 June	Wembley	6	0
wc2021	5 Sept	Wembley	4	0
wc2021	9 Oct	Andorra La Vella	5	0
wc2025	**7 June**	**Barcelona**	**1**	**0**

v ARGENTINA

			E	A
1951	9 May	Wembley	2	1
1953	17 May	Buenos Aires	0	0
(abandoned after 21 mins)				
wc1962	2 June	Rancagua	3	1
1964	6 June	Rio de Janeiro	0	1
wc1966	23 July	Wembley	1	0
1974	22 May	Wembley	2	2
1977	12 June	Buenos Aires	1	1
1980	13 May	Wembley	3	1
wc1986	22 June	Mexico City	1	2
1991	25 May	Wembley	2	2
wc1998	30 June	Saint-Etienne	2	2
2000	23 Feb	Wembley	0	0
wc2002	7 June	Sapporo	1	0
2005	12 Nov	Geneva	3	2

v AUSTRALIA

			E	A
1980	31 May	Sydney	2	1
1983	11 June	Sydney	0	0
1983	15 June	Brisbane	1	0
1983	18 June	Melbourne	1	1
1991	1 June	Sydney	1	0
2003	12 Feb	West Ham	1	3
2016	27 May	Sunderland	2	1
2023	13 Oct	Wembley	1	0

v AUSTRIA

			E	A
1908	6 June	Vienna	6	1
1908	8 June	Vienna	11	1
1909	1 June	Vienna	8	1
1930	14 May	Vienna	0	0
1932	7 Dec	Chelsea	4	3
1936	6 May	Vienna	1	2
1951	28 Nov	Wembley	2	2
1952	25 May	Vienna	3	2
wc1958	15 June	Boras	2	2
1961	27 May	Vienna	1	3
1962	4 Apr	Wembley	3	1
1965	20 Oct	Wembley	2	3
1967	27 May	Vienna	1	0
1973	26 Sept	Wembley	7	0
1979	13 June	Vienna	3	4
wc2004	4 Sept	Vienna	2	2
wc2005	8 Oct	Manchester United	1	0
2007	16 Nov	Vienna	1	0
2021	2 June	Middlesbrough	1	0

v AZERBAIJAN

			E	A
wc2004	13 Oct	Baku	1	0
wc2005	30 Mar	Newcastle	2	0

v BELARUS

			E	B
wc2008	15 Oct	Minsk	3	1
wc2009	14 Oct	Wembley	3	0

v BELGIUM

			E	B
1921	21 May	Brussels	2	0
1923	19 Mar	Arsenal	6	1
1923	1 Nov	Antwerp	2	2
1924	8 Dec	West Bromwich	4	0
1926	24 May	Antwerp	5	3
1927	11 May	Brussels	9	1
1928	19 May	Antwerp	3	1
1929	11 May	Brussels	5	1
1931	16 May	Brussels	4	1
1936	9 May	Brussels	2	3
1947	21 Sept	Brussels	5	2
1950	18 May	Brussels	4	1
1952	26 Nov	Wembley	5	0
wc1954	17 June	Basel	4	4*
1964	21 Oct	Wembley	2	2
1970	25 Feb	Brussels	3	1
EC1980	12 June	Turin	1	1
wc1990	27 June	Bologna	1	0*
1998	29 May	Casablanca	0	0
1999	10 Oct	Sunderland	2	1
2012	2 June	Wembley	1	0
wc2018	28 June	Kaliningrad	0	1
wc2018	14 July	St Petersburg	0	2
NL2020	11 Oct	Wembley	2	1
NL2020	15 Nov	Leuven	0	2
2024	26 Mar	Wembley	2	2

v BOHEMIA

			E	B
1908	13 June	Prague	4	0

v BOSNIA & HERZEGOVINA

			E	BH
2024	3 June	Newcastle	3	0

v BRAZIL

			E	B
1956	9 May	Wembley	4	2
wc1958	11 June	Gothenburg	0	0
1959	13 May	Rio de Janeiro	0	2
wc1962	10 June	Vina del Mar	1	3
1963	8 May	Wembley	1	1
1964	30 May	Rio de Janeiro	1	5
1969	12 June	Rio de Janeiro	1	2
wc1970	7 June	Guadalajara	0	1
1976	23 May	Los Angeles	0	1
1977	8 June	Rio de Janeiro	0	0
1978	19 Apr	Wembley	1	1
1981	12 May	Wembley	0	1
1984	10 June	Rio de Janeiro	2	0
1987	19 May	Wembley	1	1
1990	28 Mar	Wembley	1	0
1992	17 May	Wembley	1	1
1993	13 June	Washington	1	1
U1995	11 June	Wembley	1	3
TF1997	10 June	Paris	0	1
2000	27 May	Wembley	1	1
wc2002	21 June	Shizuoka	1	2
2007	1 June	Wembley	1	1
2009	14 Nov	Doha	0	1
2013	6 Feb	Wembley	2	1
2013	2 June	Rio de Janeiro	2	2
2017	14 Nov	Wembley	0	0
2024	23 Mar	Wembley	0	1

v BULGARIA			E	B
wc1962	7 June	Rancagua	0	0
1968	11 Dec	Wembley	1	1
1974	1 June	Sofia	1	0
EC1979	6 June	Sofia	3	0
EC1979	22 Nov	Wembley	2	0
1996	27 Mar	Wembley	1	0
EC1998	10 Oct	Wembley	0	0
EC1999	9 June	Sofia	1	1
EC2010	3 Sept	Wembley	4	0
EC2011	2 Sept	Sofia	3	0
EC2019	7 Sept	Wembley	4	0
EC2019	14 Oct	Sofia	6	0

v CAMEROON			E	C
wc1990	1 July	Naples	3	2*
1991	6 Feb	Wembley	2	0
1997	15 Nov	Wembley	2	0
2002	26 May	Kobe	2	2

v CANADA			E	C
1986	24 May	Burnaby	1	0

v CHILE			E	C
wc1950	25 June	Rio de Janeiro	2	0
1953	24 May	Santiago	2	1
1984	17 June	Santiago	0	0
1989	23 May	Wembley	0	0
1998	11 Feb	Wembley	0	2
2013	15 Nov	Wembley	0	2

v CHINA PR			E	CPR
1996	23 May	Beijing	3	0

v CIS			E	C
1992	29 Apr	Moscow	2	2

v COLOMBIA			E	C
1970	20 May	Bogota	4	0
1988	24 May	Wembley	1	1
1995	6 Sept	Wembley	0	0
wc1998	26 June	Lens	2	0
2005	31 May	New Jersey	3	2
wc2018	3 July	Moscow	1	1

v COSTA RICA			E	C
wc2014	26 June	Belo Horizonte	0	0
2018	7 June	Leeds	2	0

v CROATIA			E	C
1996	24 Apr	Wembley	0	0
2003	20 Aug	Ipswich	3	1
EC2004	21 June	Lisbon	4	2
EC2006	11 Oct	Zagreb	0	2
EC2007	21 Nov	Wembley	2	3
EC2008	10 Sept	Zagreb	4	1
wc2009	9 Sept	Wembley	5	1
wc2018	11 July	Moscow	1	2*
NL2018	12 Oct	Rijeka	0	0
NL2018	18 Nov	Wembley	2	1
EC2021	13 June	Wembley	1	0

v CYPRUS			E	C
EC1975	16 Apr	Wembley	5	0
EC1975	11 May	Limassol	1	0

v CZECHOSLOVAKIA			E	C
1934	16 May	Prague	1	2
1937	1 Dec	Tottenham Hotspur	5	4
1963	29 May	Bratislava	4	2
1966	2 Nov	Wembley	0	0
wc1970	11 June	Guadalajara	1	0
1973	27 May	Prague	1	1
EC1974	30 Oct	Wembley	3	0
EC1975	30 Oct	Bratislava	1	2
1978	29 Nov	Wembley	1	0
wc1982	20 June	Bilbao	2	0
1990	25 Apr	Wembley	4	2
1992	25 Mar	Prague	2	2

v CZECH REPUBLIC			E	CR
1998	18 Nov	Wembley	2	0
2008	20 Aug	Wembley	2	2
EC2019	22 Mar	Wembley	5	0
EC2019	11 Oct	Prague	1	2
EC2021	22 June	Wembley	1	0

v DENMARK			E	D
1948	26 Sept	Copenhagen	0	0
1955	2 Oct	Copenhagen	5	1
wc1956	5 Dec	Wolverhampton	5	2
wc1957	15 May	Copenhagen	4	1
1966	3 July	Copenhagen	2	0
EC1978	20 Sept	Copenhagen	4	3
EC1979	12 Sept	Wembley	1	0
EC1982	22 Sept	Copenhagen	2	2
EC1983	21 Sept	Wembley	0	1
1988	14 Sept	Wembley	1	0
1989	7 June	Copenhagen	1	1
1990	15 May	Wembley	1	0
EC1992	11 June	Malmo	0	0
1994	9 Mar	Wembley	1	0
wc2002	15 June	Niigata	3	0
2003	16 Nov	Manchester United	2	3
2005	17 Aug	Copenhagen	1	4
2011	9 Feb	Copenhagen	2	1
2014	5 Mar	Wembley	1	0
NL2020	8 Sept	Copenhagen	0	0
NL2020	14 Oct	Wembley	0	1
EC2021	7 July	Wembley	2	1
EC2024	20 June	Frankfurt	1	1

v ECUADOR			E	Ec
1970	24 May	Quito	2	0
wc2006	25 June	Stuttgart	1	0
2014	4 June	Miami	2	2

v EGYPT			E	Eg
1986	29 Jan	Cairo	4	0
wc1990	21 June	Cagliari	1	0
2010	3 Mar	Wembley	3	1

v ESTONIA			E	Es
EC2007	6 June	Tallinn	3	0
EC2007	13 Oct	Wembley	3	0
EC2014	12 Oct	Tallinn	1	0
EC2015	9 Oct	Wembley	2	0

v FIFA			E	FIFA
1938	26 Oct	Arsenal	3	0
1953	21 Oct	Wembley	4	4
1963	23 Oct	Wembley	2	1

v FINLAND			E	F
1937	20 May	Helsinki	8	0
1956	20 May	Helsinki	5	1
1966	26 June	Helsinki	3	0
wc1976	13 June	Helsinki	4	1
wc1976	13 Oct	Wembley	2	1
1982	3 June	Helsinki	4	1
wc1984	17 Oct	Wembley	5	0
wc1985	22 May	Helsinki	1	1
1992	3 June	Helsinki	2	1
wc2000	11 Oct	Helsinki	0	0
wc2001	24 Mar	Liverpool	2	1
NL2024	10 Sept	Wembley	2	0
NL2024	13 Oct	Helsinki	3	1

v FRANCE			E	F
1923	10 May	Paris	4	1
1924	17 May	Paris	3	1
1925	21 May	Paris	3	2
1927	26 May	Paris	6	0
1928	17 May	Paris	5	1
1929	9 May	Paris	4	1
1931	14 May	Paris	2	5
1933	6 Dec	Tottenham Hotspur	4	1
1938	26 May	Paris	4	2
1947	3 May	Arsenal	3	0
1949	22 May	Paris	3	1
1951	3 Oct	Arsenal	2	2
1955	15 May	Paris	0	1
1957	27 Nov	Wembley	4	0
EC1962	3 Oct	Sheffield Wednesday	1	1
EC1963	27 Feb	Paris	2	5
wc1966	20 July	Wembley	2	0
1969	12 Mar	Wembley	5	0
wc1982	16 June	Bilbao	3	1
1984	29 Feb	Paris	0	2
1992	19 Feb	Wembley	2	0
EC1992	14 June	Malmo	0	0
TF1997	7 June	Montpellier	1	0
1999	10 Feb	Wembley	0	2
2000	2 Sept	Paris	1	1
EC2004	13 June	Lisbon	1	2
2008	26 Mar	Paris	0	1
2010	17 Nov	Wembley	1	2
EC2012	11 June	Donetsk	1	1
2015	17 Nov	Wembley	2	0
2017	13 June	Paris	2	3
wc2022	10 Dec	Al Khor	1	2

			E	G
v GEORGIA				
wc1996	9 Nov	Tbilisi	2	0
wc1997	30 Apr	Wembley	2	0

			E	G
v GERMANY				
1930	10 May	Berlin	3	3
1935	4 Dec	Tottenham Hotspur	3	0
1938	14 May	Berlin	6	3
1991	11 Sept	Wembley	0	1
1993	19 June	Detroit	1	2
EC1996	26 June	Wembley	1	1*
EC2000	17 June	Charleroi	1	0
wc2000	7 Oct	Wembley	0	1
wc2001	1 Sept	Munich	5	1
2007	22 Aug	Wembley	1	2
2008	19 Nov	Berlin	2	1
wc2010	27 June	Bloemfontein	1	4
2013	19 Nov	Wembley	0	1
2016	26 Mar	Berlin	3	2
2017	22 Mar	Dortmund	0	1
2017	10 Nov	Wembley	0	0
EC2021	29 June	Wembley	2	0
NL2022	7 June	Munich	1	1
NL2022	26 Sept	Wembley	3	3

			E	EG
v EAST GERMANY				
1963	2 June	Leipzig	2	1
1970	25 Nov	Wembley	3	1
1974	29 May	Leipzig	1	1
1984	12 Sept	Wembley	1	0

			E	WG
v WEST GERMANY				
1954	1 Dec	Wembley	3	1
1956	26 May	Berlin	3	1
1965	12 May	Nuremberg	1	0
1966	23 Feb	Wembley	1	0
wc1966	30 July	Wembley	4	2*
1968	1 June	Hanover	0	1
wc1970	14 June	Leon	2	3*
EC1972	29 Apr	Wembley	1	3
EC1972	13 May	Berlin	0	0
1975	12 Mar	Wembley	2	0
1978	22 Feb	Munich	1	2
wc1982	29 June	Madrid	0	0
1982	13 Oct	Wembley	1	2
1985	12 June	Mexico City	3	0
1987	9 Sept	Dusseldorf	1	3
wc1990	4 July	Turin	1	1*

			E	G
v GHANA				
2011	29 Mar	Wembley	1	1

			E	G
v GREECE				
EC1971	21 Apr	Wembley	3	0
EC1971	1 Dec	Piraeus	2	0
EC1982	17 Nov	Salonika	3	0
EC1983	30 Mar	Wembley	0	0
1989	8 Feb	Athens	2	1
1994	17 May	Wembley	5	0
wc2001	6 June	Athens	2	0
wc2001	6 Oct	Manchester United	2	2
2006	16 Aug	Manchester United	4	0
NL2024	**10 Oct**	**Wembley**	**1**	**2**
NL2024	**14 Nov**	**Athens**	**3**	**0**

			E	H
v HONDURAS				
2014	7 June	Miami	0	0

			E	H
v HUNGARY				
1908	10 June	Budapest	7	0
1909	29 May	Budapest	4	2
1909	31 May	Budapest	8	2
1934	10 May	Budapest	1	2
1936	2 Dec	Arsenal	6	2
1953	25 Nov	Wembley	3	6
1954	23 May	Budapest	1	7
1960	22 May	Budapest	0	2
wc1962	31 May	Rancagua	1	2
1965	5 May	Wembley	1	0
1978	24 May	Wembley	4	1
wc1981	6 June	Budapest	3	1
wc1981	18 Nov	Wembley	1	0
EC1983	27 Apr	Wembley	2	0
EC1983	12 Oct	Budapest	3	0
1988	27 Apr	Budapest	0	0
1990	12 Sept	Wembley	1	0
1992	12 May	Budapest	1	0
1996	18 May	Wembley	3	0
1999	28 Apr	Budapest	1	1

			E	H
2006	30 May	Manchester United	3	1
2010	11 Aug	Wembley	2	1
wc2021	2 Sept	Budapest	4	0
wc2021	12 Oct	Wembley	1	1
NL2022	4 June	Budapest	0	1
NL2022	14 June	Wolverhampton	0	4

			E	I
v ICELAND				
1982	2 June	Reykjavik	1	1
2004	5 June	Manchester City	6	1
EC2016	27 June	Nice	1	2
NL2020	5 Sept	Reykjavik	1	0
NL2020	18 Nov	Wembley	4	0
2024	7 June	Wembley	0	1

			E	I
v ISRAEL				
1986	26 Feb	Ramat Gan	2	1
1988	17 Feb	Tel Aviv	0	0
EC2007	24 Mar	Tel Aviv	0	0
EC2007	8 Sept	Wembley	3	0

			E	I
v IRAN				
wc2022	21 Nov	Al Rayyan	6	2

			E	I
v ITALY				
1933	13 May	Rome	1	1
1934	14 Nov	Arsenal	3	2
1939	13 May	Milan	2	2
1948	16 May	Turin	4	0
1949	30 Nov	Tottenham Hotspur	2	0
1952	18 May	Florence	1	1
1959	6 May	Wembley	2	2
1961	24 May	Rome	3	2
1973	14 June	Turin	0	2
1973	14 Nov	Wembley	0	1
1976	28 May	New York	3	2
wc1976	17 Nov	Rome	0	2
wc1977	16 Nov	Wembley	2	0
EC1980	15 June	Turin	0	1
1985	6 June	Mexico City	1	2
1989	15 Nov	Wembley	0	0
wc1990	7 July	Bari	1	2
wc1997	12 Feb	Wembley	0	1
TF1997	4 June	Nantes	2	0
wc1997	11 Oct	Rome	0	0
2000	15 Nov	Turin	0	1
2002	27 Mar	Leeds	1	2
EC2012	24 June	Kyiv	0	0
2012	15 Aug	Berne	2	1
wc2014	14 June	Manaus	1	2
2015	31 Mar	Turin	1	1
2018	27 Mar	Wembley	1	1
EC2021	11 July	Wembley	1	1*
NL2022	11 June	Wolverhampton	0	0
NL2022	23 Sept	Milan	0	1
EC2023	23 Mar	Naples	2	1
EC2023	17 Oct	Wembley	3	1

			E	IC
v IVORY COAST				
2022	29 Mar	Wembley	3	0

			E	J
v JAMAICA				
2006	3 June	Manchester United	6	0

			E	J
v JAPAN				
UI1995	3 June	Wembley	2	1
2004	1 June	Manchester City	1	1
2010	30 May	Graz	2	1

			E	K
v KAZAKHSTAN				
wc2008	11 Oct	Wembley	5	1
wc2009	6 June	Almaty	4	0

			E	KR
v KOREA REPUBLIC				
2002	21 May	Seoguipo	1	1

			E	K
v KOSOVO				
EC2019	10 Sept	Southampton	5	3
EC2019	17 Nov	Pristina	4	0

			E	K
v KUWAIT				
wc1982	25 June	Bilbao	1	0

			E	L
v LATVIA				
wc2025	**24 Mar**	**Wembley**	**3**	**0**

			E	L
v LIECHTENSTEIN				
EC2003	29 Mar	Vaduz	2	0
EC2003	10 Sept	Manchester United	2	0

		v LITHUANIA	E	L
EC2015	27 Mar	Wembley	4	0
EC2015	12 Oct	Vilnius	3	0
wc2017	26 Mar	Wembley	2	0
wc2017	8 Oct	Vilnius	1	0

		v LUXEMBOURG	E	L
1927	21 May	Esch-sur-Alzette	5	2
wc1960	19 Oct	Luxembourg	9	0
wc1961	28 Sept	Arsenal	4	1
wc1977	30 Mar	Wembley	5	0
wc1977	12 Oct	Luxembourg	2	0
EC1982	15 Dec	Wembley	9	0
EC1983	16 Nov	Luxembourg	4	0
EC1998	14 Oct	Luxembourg	3	0
EC1999	4 Sept	Wembley	6	0

		v MACEDONIA	E	M
EC2006	7 Oct	Manchester United	0	0

		v MALAYSIA	E	M
1991	12 June	Kuala Lumpur	4	2

		v MALTA	E	M
EC1971	3 Feb	Valletta	1	0
EC1971	12 May	Wembley	5	0
2000	3 June	Valletta	2	1
wc2016	8 Oct	Wembley	2	0
wc2017	1 Sept	Ta'Qali	4	0
EC2023	16 June	Ta'Qali	4	0
EC2023	17 Nov	Wembley	2	0

		v MEXICO	E	M
1959	24 May	Mexico City	1	2
1961	10 May	Wembley	8	0
wc1966	16 July	Wembley	2	0
1969	1 June	Mexico City	0	0
1985	9 June	Mexico City	0	1
1986	17 May	Los Angeles	3	0
1997	29 Mar	Wembley	2	0
2001	25 May	Derby	4	0
2010	24 May	Wembley	3	1

		v MOLDOVA	E	M
wc1996	1 Sept	Chisinau	3	0
wc1997	10 Sept	Wembley	4	0
wc2012	7 Sept	Chisinau	5	0
wc2013	6 Sept	Wembley	4	0

		v MONTENEGRO	E	M
2010	12 Oct	Wembley	0	0
EC2011	7 Oct	Podgorica	2	2
wc2013	26 Mar	Podgorica	1	1
wc2013	11 Oct	Wembley	4	1
EC2019	25 Mar	Podgorica	5	1
EC2019	14 Nov	Wembley	7	0

		v MOROCCO	E	M
wc1986	6 June	Monterrey	0	0
1998	27 May	Casablanca	1	0

		v NETHERLANDS	E	N
1935	18 May	Amsterdam	1	0
1946	27 Nov	Huddersfield	8	2
1964	9 Dec	Amsterdam	1	1
1969	5 Nov	Amsterdam	1	0
1970	14 June	Wembley	0	0
1977	9 Feb	Wembley	0	2
1982	25 May	Wembley	2	0
1988	23 Mar	Wembley	2	2
EC1988	15 June	Dusseldorf	1	3
wc1990	16 June	Cagliari	0	0
2005	9 Feb	Aston Villa	0	0
wc1993	28 Apr	Wembley	2	2
wc1993	13 Oct	Rotterdam	0	2
EC1996	18 June	Wembley	4	1
2001	15 Aug	Tottenham Hotspur	0	2
2002	13 Feb	Amsterdam	1	1
2006	15 Nov	Amsterdam	1	1
2009	12 Aug	Amsterdam	2	2
2012	29 Feb	Wembley	2	3
2016	29 Mar	Wembley	1	2
2018	23 Mar	Amsterdam	1	0
NL2019	6 June	Guimaraes	1	3
EC2024	10 July	Dortmund	2	1

		v NEW ZEALAND	E	NZ
1991	3 June	Auckland	1	0
1991	8 June	Wellington	2	0

		v NIGERIA	E	N
1994	16 Nov	Wembley	1	0
wc2002	12 June	Osaka	0	0
2018	2 June	Wembley	2	1

		v NORTH MACEDONIA	E	NM
EC2002	16 Oct	Southampton	2	2
EC2003	6 Sept	Skopje	2	1
EC2006	6 Sept	Skopje	1	0
EC2023	19 June	Manchester United	7	0
EC2023	20 Nov	Skopje	1	1

		v NORWAY	E	N
1937	14 May	Oslo	6	0
1938	9 Nov	Newcastle	4	0
1949	18 May	Oslo	4	1
1966	29 June	Oslo	6	1
wc1980	10 Sept	Wembley	4	0
wc1981	9 Sept	Oslo	1	2
wc1992	14 Oct	Wembley	1	1
wc1993	2 June	Oslo	0	2
1994	22 May	Wembley	0	0
1995	11 Oct	Oslo	0	0
2012	26 May	Oslo	1	0
2014	3 Sept	Wembley	1	0

		v PANAMA	E	P
wc2018	24 June	Nizhny Novgorod	6	1

		v PARAGUAY	E	P
wc1986	18 June	Mexico City	3	0
2002	17 Apr	Liverpool	4	0
wc2006	10 June	Frankfurt	1	0

		v PERU	E	P
1959	17 May	Lima	1	4
1962	20 May	Lima	4	0
2014	30 May	Wembley	3	0

		v POLAND	E	P
1966	5 Jan	Everton	1	1
1966	5 July	Chorzow	1	0
wc1973	6 June	Chorzow	0	2
wc1973	17 Oct	Wembley	1	1
wc1986	11 June	Monterrey	3	0
wc1989	3 June	Wembley	3	0
wc1989	11 Oct	Katowice	0	0
EC1990	17 Oct	Wembley	2	0
EC1991	13 Nov	Poznan	1	1
wc1993	29 May	Katowice	1	1
wc1993	8 Sept	Wembley	3	0
wc1996	9 Oct	Wembley	2	1
wc1997	31 May	Katowice	2	0
EC1999	27 Mar	Wembley	3	1
EC1999	8 Sept	Warsaw	0	0
wc2004	8 Sept	Katowice	2	1
wc2005	12 Oct	Manchester United	2	1
wc2012	17 Oct	Warsaw	1	1
wc2013	15 Oct	Wembley	2	0
wc2021	31 Mar	Wembley	2	1
wc2021	8 Sept	Warsaw	1	1

		v PORTUGAL	E	P
1947	25 May	Lisbon	10	0
1950	14 May	Lisbon	5	3
1951	19 May	Everton	5	2
1955	22 May	Oporto	1	3
1958	7 May	Wembley	2	1
wc1961	21 May	Lisbon	1	1
wc1961	25 Oct	Wembley	2	0
1964	17 May	Lisbon	4	3
1964	4 June	São Paulo	1	1
wc1966	26 July	Wembley	2	1
1969	10 Dec	Wembley	1	0
1974	3 Apr	Lisbon	0	0
EC1974	20 Nov	Wembley	0	0
EC1975	19 Nov	Lisbon	1	1
wc1986	3 June	Monterrey	0	1
1995	12 Dec	Wembley	1	1
1998	22 Apr	Wembley	3	0
EC2000	12 June	Eindhoven	2	3
2002	7 Sept	Aston Villa	1	1
2004	18 Feb	Faro	1	1
EC2004	24 June	Lisbon	2	2*
wc2006	1 July	Gelsenkirchen	0	0
2016	2 June	Wembley	1	0

		v REPUBLIC OF IRELAND	E	RI
1946	30 Sept	Dublin	1	0
1949	21 Sept	Everton	0	2
wc1957	8 May	Wembley	5	1

			E	RI
wc1957	19 May	Dublin	1	1
1964	24 May	Dublin	3	1
1976	8 Sept	Wembley	1	1
EC1978	25 Oct	Dublin	1	1
EC1980	6 Feb	Wembley	2	0
1985	26 Mar	Wembley	2	1
EC1988	12 June	Stuttgart	0	1
wc1990	11 June	Cagliari	1	1
EC1990	14 Nov	Dublin	1	1
EC1991	27 Mar	Wembley	1	1
1995	15 Feb	Dublin	0	1
	(abandoned after 27 mins)			
2013	29 May	Wembley	1	1
2015	7 June	Dublin	0	0
2020	12 Nov	Wembley	3	0
NL2024	**7 Sept**	**Dublin**	**2**	**0**
NL2024	**17 Nov**	**Wembley**	**5**	**0**

v ROMANIA			E	R
1939	24 May	Bucharest	2	0
1968	6 Nov	Bucharest	0	0
1969	15 Jan	Wembley	1	1
wc1970	2 June	Guadalajara	1	0
wc1980	15 Oct	Bucharest	1	2
wc1981	29 April	Wembley	0	0
wc1985	1 May	Bucharest	0	0
wc1985	11 Sept	Wembley	1	1
1994	12 Oct	Wembley	1	1
wc1998	22 June	Toulouse	1	2
EC2000	20 June	Charleroi	2	3
2021	6 June	Middlesbrough	1	0

v RUSSIA			E	R
EC2007	12 Sept	Wembley	3	0
EC2007	17 Oct	Moscow	1	2
EC2016	11 June	Marseille	1	1

v SAN MARINO			E	SM
wc1992	17 Feb	Wembley	6	0
wc1993	17 Nov	Bologna	7	1
wc2012	12 Oct	Wembley	5	0
wc2013	22 Mar	Serravalle	8	0
EC2014	9 Oct	Wembley	5	0
EC2015	5 Sept	Serravalle	6	0
wc2021	25 Mar	Wembley	5	0
wc2021	15 Nov	Serravalle	10	0

v SAUDI ARABIA			E	SA
1988	16 Nov	Riyadh	1	1
1998	23 May	Wembley	0	0

v SENEGAL			E	S
wc2022	4 Dec	Al Khor	3	0
2025	**10 June**	**Nottingham Forest**	**1**	**3**

v SERBIA			E	S
EC2024	16 June	Gelsenkirchen	1	0

v SERBIA-MONTENEGRO			E	SM
2003	3 June	Leicester	2	1

v SLOVAKIA			E	S
EC2002	12 Oct	Bratislava	2	1
EC2003	11 June	Middlesbrough	2	1
2009	28 Mar	Wembley	4	0
EC2016	20 June	Lille	0	0
wc2016	4 Sept	Trnava	1	0
wc2017	4 Sept	Wembley	2	1
EC2024	30 June	Gelsenkirchen	2	1

v SLOVENIA			E	S
2009	5 Sept	Wembley	2	1
wc2010	23 June	Port Elizabeth	1	0
EC2014	15 Nov	Wembley	3	1
EC2015	14 June	Ljubljana	3	2
wc2016	11 Oct	Ljubljana	0	0
wc2017	5 Oct	Wembley	1	0
EC2024	25 June	Cologne	0	0

v SOUTH AFRICA			E	SA
1997	24 May	Manchester United	2	1
2003	22 May	Durban	2	1

v SPAIN			E	S
1929	15 May	Madrid	3	4
1931	9 Dec	Arsenal	7	1
wc1950	2 July	Rio de Janeiro	0	1
1955	18 May	Madrid	1	1
1955	30 Nov	Wembley	4	1
1960	15 May	Madrid	0	3

			E	S
1960	26 Oct	Wembley	4	2
1965	8 Dec	Madrid	2	0
1967	24 May	Wembley	2	0
EC1968	3 Apr	Wembley	1	0
EC1968	8 May	Madrid	2	1
1980	26 Mar	Barcelona	2	0
EC1980	18 June	Naples	2	1
1981	25 Mar	Wembley	1	2
wc1982	5 July	Madrid	0	0
1987	18 Feb	Madrid	4	2
1992	9 Sept	Santander	0	1
EC 1996	22 June	Wembley	0	0*
2001	28 Feb	Aston Villa	3	0
2004	17 Nov	Madrid	0	1
2007	7 Feb	Manchester United	0	1
2009	11 Feb	Seville	0	2
2011	12 Nov	Wembley	1	0
2015	13 Nov	Alicante	0	2
2016	15 Nov	Wembley	2	2
NL2018	8 Sept	Wembley	1	2
NL2018	15 Oct	Seville	3	2
EC2024	14 July	Berlin	1	2

v SWEDEN			E	S
1923	21 May	Stockholm	4	2
1923	24 May	Stockholm	3	1
1937	17 May	Stockholm	4	0
1947	19 Nov	Arsenal	4	2
1949	13 May	Stockholm	1	3
1956	16 May	Stockholm	0	0
1959	28 Oct	Wembley	2	3
1965	16 May	Gothenburg	2	1
1968	22 May	Wembley	3	1
1979	10 June	Stockholm	0	0
1986	10 Sept	Stockholm	0	1
wc1988	19 Oct	Wembley	0	0
wc1989	6 Sept	Stockholm	0	0
EC1992	17 June	Stockholm	1	2
UI1995	8 June	Leeds	3	3
EC1998	5 Sept	Stockholm	1	2
EC1999	5 June	Wembley	0	0
2001	10 Nov	Manchester United	1	1
wc2002	2 June	Saitama	1	1
2004	31 Mar	Gothenburg	0	1
wc2006	20 June	Cologne	2	2
2011	15 Nov	Wembley	1	0
EC2012	15 June	Kyiv	3	2
2012	14 Nov	Stockholm	2	4
wc2018	7 July	Samara	2	0

v SWITZERLAND			E	S
1933	20 May	Berne	4	0
1938	21 May	Zurich	1	2
1947	18 May	Zurich	0	1
1948	2 Dec	Arsenal	6	0
1952	28 May	Zurich	3	0
wc1954	20 June	Berne	2	0
1962	9 May	Wembley	3	1
1963	5 June	Basel	8	1
EC1971	13 Oct	Basel	3	2
EC1971	10 Nov	Wembley	1	1
1975	3 Sept	Basel	2	1
1977	7 Sept	Wembley	0	0
wc1980	19 Nov	Wembley	2	1
wc1981	30 May	Basel	1	2
1988	28 May	Lausanne	1	0
1995	15 Nov	Wembley	3	1
EC1996	8 June	Wembley	1	1
1998	25 Mar	Berne	1	1
EC2004	17 June	Coimbra	3	0
2008	6 Feb	Wembley	2	1
EC1989	8 Mar	Tirana	2	0
EC2010	7 Sept	Basel	3	1
EC2011	4 June	Wembley	2	2
EC2014	8 Sept	Basel	2	0
EC2015	8 Sept	Wembley	2	0
2018	11 Sept	Leicester	1	0
NL2019	9 June	Guimaraes	0	0
2022	26 Mar	Wembley	2	1
EC2024	6 July	Dusseldorf	1	1*

v TRINIDAD & TOBAGO			E	TT
wc2006	15 June	Nuremberg	2	0
2008	2 June	Port of Spain	3	0

v TUNISIA			E	T
1990	2 June	Tunis	1	1
wc1998	15 June	Marseilles	2	0
wc2018	18 June	Volgograd	2	1

v TURKEY			E	T
wc1984	14 Nov	Istanbul	8	0
wc1985	16 Oct	Wembley	5	0
EC1987	29 Apr	Izmir	0	0
EC1987	14 Oct	Wembley	8	0
EC1991	1 May	Izmir	1	0
EC1991	16 Oct	Wembley	1	0
wc1992	18 Nov	Wembley	4	0
wc1993	31 Mar	Izmir	2	0
EC2003	2 Apr	Sunderland	2	0
EC2003	11 Oct	Istanbul	0	0
2016	22 May	Manchester City	2	1

v UKRAINE			E	U
2000	31 May	Wembley	2	0
2004	18 Aug	Newcastle	3	0
wc2009	1 Apr	Wembley	2	1
wc2009	10 Oct	Dnepr	0	1
EC2012	19 June	Donetsk	1	0
wc2012	11 Sept	Wembley	1	1
wc2013	10 Sept	Kyiv	0	0
EC2021	3 July	Rome	4	0
EC2023	26 Mar	Wembley	2	0
EC2023	9 Sept	Wroclaw	1	1

v URUGUAY			E	U
1953	31 May	Montevideo	1	2
wc1954	26 June	Basel	2	4
1964	6 May	Wembley	2	1
wc1966	11 July	Wembley	0	0
1969	8 June	Montevideo	2	1
1977	15 June	Montevideo	0	0
1984	13 June	Montevideo	0	2
1990	22 May	Wembley	1	2
1995	29 Mar	Wembley	0	0
2006	1 Mar	Liverpool	2	1
wc2014	19 June	Sao Paulo	1	2

v USA			E	USA
wc1950	29 June	Belo Horizonte	0	1
1953	8 June	New York	6	3
1959	28 May	Los Angeles	8	1
1964	27 May	New York	10	0
1985	16 June	Los Angeles	5	0
1993	9 June	Foxboro	0	2
1994	7 Sept	Wembley	2	0
2005	28 May	Chicago	2	1
2008	28 May	Wembley	2	0
wc2010	12 June	Rustenburg	1	1
2018	15 Nov	Wembley	3	0
wc2022	25 Nov	Al Khor	0	0

v USSR			E	USSR
1958	18 May	Moscow	1	1
wc1958	8 June	Gothenburg	2	2
wc1958	17 June	Gothenburg	0	1
1958	22 Oct	Wembley	5	0
1967	6 Dec	Wembley	2	2
EC1968	8 June	Rome	2	0
1973	10 June	Moscow	2	1
1984	2 June	Wembley	0	2
1986	26 Mar	Tbilisi	1	0
EC1988	18 June	Frankfurt	1	3
1991	21 May	Wembley	3	1

v YUGOSLAVIA			E	Y
1939	18 May	Belgrade	1	2
1950	22 Nov	Arsenal	2	2
1954	16 May	Belgrade	0	1
1956	28 Nov	Wembley	3	0
1958	11 May	Belgrade	0	5
1960	11 May	Wembley	3	3
1965	9 May	Belgrade	1	1
1966	4 May	Wembley	2	0
EC1968	5 June	Florence	0	1
1972	11 Oct	Wembley	1	1
1974	5 June	Belgrade	2	2
EC1986	12 Nov	Wembley	2	0
EC1987	11 Nov	Belgrade	4	1
1989	13 Dec	Wembley	2	1

SCOTLAND

v ALBANIA			S	A
NL2018	10 Sept	Glasgow	2	0
NL2018	17 Nov	Shkoder	4	0

v ARGENTINA			S	A
1977	18 June	Buenos Aires	1	1
1979	2 June	Glasgow	1	3
1990	28 Mar	Glasgow	1	0
2008	19 Nov	Glasgow	0	1

v ARMENIA			S	A
NL2022	8 June	Glasgow	2	0
NL2022	14 June	Yerevan	4	1

v AUSTRALIA			S	A
*1967	28 May	Sydney	1	0
*1967	31 May	Adelaide	2	1
*1967	3 June	Melbourne	2	0
wc1985	20 Nov	Glasgow	2	0
wc1985	4 Dec	Melbourne	0	0
1996	27 Mar	Glasgow	1	0
2000	15 Nov	Glasgow	0	2
2012	15 Aug	Hibernian	3	1

1967 tour upgraded to full internationals in October 2021.

v AUSTRIA			S	A
1931	16 May	Vienna	0	5
1933	29 Nov	Glasgow	2	2
1937	9 May	Vienna	1	1
1950	13 Dec	Glasgow	0	1
1951	27 May	Vienna	0	4
wc1954	16 June	Zurich	0	1
1955	19 May	Vienna	4	1
1956	2 May	Glasgow	1	1
1960	29 May	Vienna	1	4
1963	8 May	Glasgow	4	1
(abandoned after 79 mins)				
wc1968	6 Nov	Glasgow	2	1
wc1969	5 Nov	Vienna	0	2
EC1978	20 Sept	Vienna	2	3
EC1979	17 Oct	Glasgow	1	1
1994	20 Apr	Vienna	2	1
wc1996	31 Aug	Vienna	0	0
wc1997	2 Apr	Celtic Park	2	0
2003	30 Apr	Glasgow	0	2
2005	17 Aug	Graz	2	2
2007	30 May	Vienna	1	0
wc2021	25 Mar	Glasgow	2	2
wc2021	7 Sept	Vienna	1	0
2022	29 Mar	Vienna	2	2

v BELARUS			S	B
wc1997	8 June	Minsk	1	0
wc1997	7 Sept	Aberdeen	4	1
wc2005	8 June	Minsk	0	0
wc2005	8 Oct	Glasgow	0	1

v BELGIUM			S	B
1946	23 Jan	Glasgow	2	2
1947	18 May	Brussels	1	2
1948	28 Apr	Glasgow	2	0
1951	20 May	Brussels	5	0
EC1971	3 Feb	Liege	0	3
EC1971	10 Nov	Aberdeen	1	0
1974	1 June	Brussels	1	2
EC1979	21 Nov	Brussels	0	2
EC1979	19 Dec	Glasgow	1	3
EC1982	15 Dec	Brussels	2	3
EC1983	12 Oct	Glasgow	1	1
EC1987	1 Apr	Brussels	1	4
EC1987	14 Oct	Glasgow	2	0
wc2001	24 Mar	Glasgow	2	2
wc2001	5 Sept	Brussels	0	2
wc2012	16 Oct	Brussels	0	2
wc2013	6 Sept	Glasgow	0	2
2018	7 Sept	Glasgow	0	4
EC2019	11 June	Brussels	0	3
EC2019	9 Sept	Glasgow	0	4

v BOSNIA & HERZEGOVINA			S	BH
EC1999	4 Sept	Sarajevo	2	1
EC1999	5 Oct	Ibrox	1	0

v BRAZIL			S	B
1966	25 June	Glasgow	1	1
1972	5 July	Rio de Janeiro	0	1
1973	30 June	Glasgow	0	1
wc1974	18 June	Frankfurt	0	0

			S	B
1977	23 June	Rio de Janeiro	0	2
wc1982	18 June	Seville	1	4
1987	26 May	Glasgow	0	2
wc1990	20 June	Turin	0	1
wc1998	10 June	St Denis	1	2
2011	27 Mar	Arsenal	0	2

v BULGARIA

			S	B
1978	22 Feb	Glasgow	2	1
EC1986	10 Sept	Glasgow	0	0
EC1987	11 Nov	Sofia	1	0
EC1990	14 Nov	Sofia	1	1
EC1991	27 Mar	Glasgow	1	1
2006	11 May	Kobe	5	1

v CANADA

			S	C
*1967	13 June	Winnipeg	7	2
1983	12 June	Vancouver	2	0
1983	16 June	Edmonton	3	0
1983	20 June	Toronto	2	0
1992	21 May	Toronto	3	1
2002	15 Oct	Hibernian	3	1
2017	22 Mar	Hibernian	1	1

1967 tour upgraded to full internationals in October 2021.

v CHILE

			S	C
1977	15 June	Santiago	4	2
1989	30 May	Glasgow	2	0

v CIS

			S	C
EC1992	18 June	Norrkoping	3	0

v COLOMBIA

			S	C
1988	17 May	Glasgow	0	0
1996	29 May	Miami	0	1
1998	23 May	New York	2	2

v COSTA RICA

			S	CR
wc1990	11 June	Genoa	0	1
2018	23 Mar	Glasgow	0	1

v CROATIA

			S	C
wc2000	11 Oct	Zagreb	1	1
wc2001	1 Sept	Glasgow	0	0
2008	26 Mar	Glasgow	1	1
wc2013	7 June	Zagreb	1	0
wc2013	15 Oct	Glasgow	2	0
EC2021	22 June	Glasgow	1	3
NL2024	**12 Oct**	**Zagreb**	**1**	**2**
NL2024	**15 Nov**	**Glasgow**	**1**	**0**

v CYPRUS

			S	C
wc1968	11 Dec	Nicosia	5	0
wc1969	17 May	Glasgow	8	0
wc1989	8 Feb	Limassol	3	2
wc1989	26 Apr	Glasgow	2	1
2011	11 Nov	Larnaca	2	1
EC2019	8 June	Glasgow	2	1
EC2019	16 Nov	Nicosia	2	1
EC2023	25 Mar	Glasgow	3	0
EC2023	8 Sept	Larnaca	3	0

v CZECHOSLOVAKIA

			S	C
1937	15 May	Prague	3	1
1937	8 Dec	Glasgow	5	0
wc1961	14 May	Bratislava	0	4
wc1961	26 Sept	Glasgow	3	2
wc1961	29 Nov	Brussels	2	4*
1972	2 July	Porto Alegre	0	0
wc1973	26 Sept	Glasgow	2	1
wc1973	17 Oct	Bratislava	0	1
wc1976	13 Oct	Prague	0	2
wc1977	21 Sept	Glasgow	3	1

v CZECH REPUBLIC

			S	CR
EC1999	31 Mar	Glasgow	1	2
EC1999	9 June	Prague	2	3
2008	30 May	Prague	1	3
2010	3 Mar	Glasgow	1	0
EC2010	8 Oct	Prague	0	1
EC2011	3 Sept	Glasgow	2	2
2016	24 Mar	Prague	1	0
NL2020	7 Sept	Olomouc	2	1
NL2020	14 Oct	Glasgow	1	0
EC2021	14 June	Glasgow	0	2

v DENMARK

			S	D
1951	12 May	Glasgow	3	1
1952	25 May	Copenhagen	2	1
1968	16 Oct	Copenhagen	1	0
EC1970	11 Nov	Glasgow	1	0
EC1971	9 June	Copenhagen	0	1
wc1972	18 Oct	Copenhagen	4	1
wc1972	15 Nov	Glasgow	2	0
EC1975	3 Sept	Copenhagen	1	0
EC1975	29 Oct	Glasgow	3	1
wc1986	4 June	Nezahualcoyotl	0	1
1996	24 Apr	Copenhagen	0	2
1998	25 Mar	Ibrox	0	1
2002	21 Aug	Glasgow	0	1
2004	28 Apr	Copenhagen	0	1
2011	10 Aug	Glasgow	2	1
2016	29 Mar	Glasgow	1	0
wc2021	1 Sept	Copenhagen	0	2
wc2021	15 Nov	Glasgow	2	0

v ECUADOR

			S	E
1995	24 May	Toyama	2	1

v EGYPT

			S	E
1990	16 May	Aberdeen	1	3

v ESTONIA

			S	E
wc1993	19 May	Tallinn	3	0
wc1993	2 June	Aberdeen	3	1
wc1997	11 Feb	Monaco	0	0
wc1997	29 Mar	Kilmarnock	2	0
EC1998	10 Oct	Hearts	3	2
EC1999	8 Sept	Tallinn	0	0
2004	27 May	Tallinn	1	0
2013	6 Feb	Aberdeen	1	0

v FAROE ISLANDS

			S	F
EC1994	12 Oct	Glasgow	5	1
EC1995	7 June	Toftir	2	0
EC1998	14 Oct	Aberdeen	2	1
EC1999	5 June	Toftir	1	1
EC2002	7 Sept	Toftir	2	2
EC2003	6 Sept	Glasgow	3	1
EC2006	2 Sept	Celtic Park	6	0
EC2007	6 June	Toftir	2	0
2010	16 Nov	Aberdeen	3	0
wc2021	31 Mar	Glasgow	4	0
wc2021	12 Oct	Torshavn	1	0

v FINLAND

			S	F
1954	25 May	Helsinki	2	1
wc1964	21 Oct	Glasgow	3	1
wc1965	27 May	Helsinki	2	1
1976	8 Sept	Glasgow	6	0
1992	25 Mar	Glasgow	1	1
EC1994	7 Sept	Helsinki	2	0
EC1995	6 Sept	Glasgow	1	0
1998	22 Apr	Hibernian	1	1
2024	7 June	Glasgow	2	2

v FRANCE

			S	F
1930	18 May	Paris	2	0
1932	8 May	Paris	3	1
1948	23 May	Paris	0	3
1949	27 Apr	Glasgow	2	0
1950	27 May	Paris	1	0
1951	16 May	Glasgow	1	0
wc1958	15 June	Orebro	1	2
1984	1 June	Marseilles	0	2
wc1989	8 Mar	Glasgow	2	0
wc1989	11 Oct	Paris	0	3
1997	12 Nov	Saint-Etienne	1	2
2000	29 Mar	Glasgow	0	2
2002	27 Mar	Paris	0	5
EC2006	7 Oct	Glasgow	1	0
EC2007	12 Sept	Paris	1	0
2016	4 June	Metz	0	3
2023	17 Oct	Lille	1	4

v GEORGIA

			S	G
EC2007	24 Mar	Glasgow	2	1
EC2007	17 Oct	Tbilisi	0	2
EC2014	11 Oct	Ibrox	1	0
EC2015	4 Sept	Tblisi	0	1
EC2023	20 June	Glasgow	2	0
EC2023	16 Nov	Tbilisi	2	2

v GERMANY

			S	G
1929	1 June	Berlin	1	1
1936	14 Oct	Glasgow	2	0
EC1992	15 June	Norrkoping	0	2
1993	24 Mar	Glasgow	0	1

			S	G
1999	28 Apr	Bremen	1	0
EC2003	7 June	Glasgow	1	1
EC2003	10 Sept	Dortmund	1	2
EC2014	7 Sept	Dortmund	1	2
EC2015	7 Sept	Glasgow	2	3
EC2024	14 June	Munich	1	5

v EAST GERMANY			S	EG
1974	30 Oct	Glasgow	3	0
1977	7 Sept	East Berlin	0	1
EC1982	13 Oct	Glasgow	2	0
EC1983	16 Nov	Halle	1	2
1985	16 Oct	Glasgow	0	0
1990	25 Apr	Glasgow	0	1

v WEST GERMANY			S	WG
1957	22 May	Stuttgart	3	1
1959	6 May	Glasgow	3	2
1964	12 May	Hanover	2	2
wc1969	16 Apr	Glasgow	1	1
wc1969	22 Oct	Hamburg	2	3
1973	14 Nov	Glasgow	1	1
1974	27 Mar	Frankfurt	1	2
wc1986	8 June	Queretaro	1	2

v GIBRALTAR			S	G
EC2015	29 Mar	Glasgow	6	1
EC2015	11 Oct	Faro	6	0
2024	3 June	Faro	2	0

v GREECE			S	G
EC1994	18 Dec	Athens	0	1
EC1995	16 Aug	Glasgow	1	0
NL2025	20 Mar	Piraeus	1	0
NL2025	23 Mar	Glasgow	0	3

v HONG KONG XI			S	HK
†2002	23 May	Hong Kong	4	0

†*match not recognised by FIFA*

v HUNGARY			S	H
1938	7 Dec	Ibrox	3	1
1954	8 Dec	Glasgow	2	4
1955	29 May	Budapest	1	3
1958	7 May	Glasgow	1	1
1960	5 June	Budapest	3	3
1980	31 May	Budapest	1	3
1987	9 Sept	Glasgow	2	0
2004	18 Aug	Glasgow	0	3
2018	27 Mar	Budapest	1	0
EC2024	23 June	Stuttgart	0	1

v ICELAND			S	I
wc1984	17 Oct	Glasgow	3	0
wc1985	28 May	Reykjavik	1	0
EC2002	12 Oct	Reykjavik	2	0
EC2003	29 Mar	Glasgow	2	1
wc2008	10 Sept	Reykjavik	2	1
wc2009	1 Apr	Glasgow	2	1
NL2025	6 June	Glasgow	1	3

v IRAN			S	I
wc1978	7 June	Cordoba	1	1

v ISRAEL			S	I
*1967	16 May	Tel Aviv	2	1
wc1981	25 Feb	Tel Aviv	1	0
wc1981	28 Apr	Glasgow	3	1
1986	28 Jan	Tel Aviv	1	0
NL2018	11 Oct	Haifa	1	2
NL2018	20 Nov	Glasgow	3	2
NL2020	4 Sept	Glasgow	1	1
EC2020	8 Oct	Glasgow	0	0
NL2020	18 Nov	Netanya	0	1
wc2021	28 Mar	Tel Aviv	1	1
wc2021	9 Oct	Glasgow	3	2

*1967 tour upgraded to full internationals in October 2021.

v ITALY			S	I
1931	20 May	Rome	0	3
wc1965	9 Nov	Glasgow	1	0
wc1965	7 Dec	Naples	0	3
1988	22 Dec	Perugia	0	2
wc1992	18 Nov	Ibrox	0	0
wc1993	13 Oct	Rome	1	3
wc2005	26 Mar	Milan	0	2
wc2005	3 Sept	Glasgow	1	1
EC2007	28 Mar	Bari	0	2
EC2007	17 Nov	Glasgow	1	2
2016	29 May	Ta'Qali	0	1

v JAPAN			S	J
1995	21 May	Hiroshima	0	0
2006	13 May	Saitama	0	0
2009	10 Oct	Yokohama	0	2

v KAZAKHSTAN			S	K
EC2019	21 Mar	Astana	0	3
EC2019	19 Nov	Glasgow	3	1

v KOREA REPUBLIC			S	KR
2002	16 May	Busan	1	4

v LATVIA			S	L
wc1996	5 Oct	Riga	2	0
wc1997	11 Oct	Celtic Park	2	0
wc2000	2 Sept	Riga	1	0
wc2001	6 Oct	Glasgow	2	1

v LIECHTENSTEIN			S	L
EC2010	7 Sept	Glasgow	2	1
EC2011	8 Oct	Vaduz	1	0
NL2025	9 June	Vaduz	4	0

v LITHUANIA			S	L
EC1998	5 Sept	Vilnius	0	0
EC1999	9 Oct	Glasgow	3	0
EC2003	2 Apr	Kaunas	0	1
EC2003	11 Oct	Glasgow	1	0
EC2006	6 Sept	Kaunas	2	1
EC2007	8 Sept	Glasgow	3	1
EC2010	3 Sept	Kaunas	0	0
EC2011	6 Sept	Glasgow	1	0
EC2016	8 Oct	Glasgow	1	1
wc2017	1 Sept	Vilnius	3	0

v LUXEMBOURG			S	L
1947	24 May	Luxembourg	6	0
EC1986	12 Nov	Glasgow	3	0
EC1987	2 Dec	Esch	0	0
2012	14 Nov	Luxembourg	2	1
2021	6 June	Luxembourg	1	0

v MALTA			S	M
1988	22 Mar	Valletta	1	1
1990	28 May	Valletta	2	1
wc1993	17 Feb	Ibrox	3	0
wc1993	17 Nov	Valletta	2	0
1997	1 June	Valletta	3	2
wc2016	4 Sept	Ta'Qali	5	1
wc2017	4 Sept	Glasgow	2	0

v MEXICO			S	M
2018	3 June	Mexico City	0	1

v MOLDOVA			S	M
wc2004	13 Oct	Chisinau	1	1
wc2005	4 June	Glasgow	2	0
wc2021	4 Sept	Glasgow	1	0
wc2021	12 Nov	Chisinau	2	0

v MOROCCO			S	M
wc1998	23 June	Saint-Etienne	0	3

v NETHERLANDS			S	N
1929	4 June	Amsterdam	2	0
1938	21 May	Amsterdam	3	1
1959	27 May	Amsterdam	2	1
1966	11 May	Glasgow	0	3
1968	30 May	Amsterdam	0	0
1971	1 Dec	Amsterdam	1	2
wc1978	11 June	Mendoza	3	2
1982	23 Mar	Glasgow	2	1
1986	29 Apr	Eindhoven	0	0
EC1992	12 June	Gothenburg	0	1
1994	23 Mar	Glasgow	0	1
1994	27 May	Utrecht	1	3
EC1996	10 June	Aston Villa	0	0
2000	26 Apr	Arnhem	0	0
EC2003	15 Nov	Glasgow	1	0
EC2003	19 Nov	Amsterdam	0	6
EC2009	28 Mar	Amsterdam	0	3
wc2009	9 Sept	Glasgow	0	1
2017	9 Nov	Aberdeen	0	1
2021	2 June	Faro	2	2
2024	22 Mar	Amsterdam	0	4

v NEW ZEALAND			S	NZ
wc1982	15 June	Malaga	5	2
2003	27 May	Hearts	1	1

v NIGERIA			S	N
2002	17 Apr	Aberdeen	1	2
2014	28 May	Fulham	2	2

		v NORTH MACEDONIA	S	NM
wc2008	6 Sept	Skopje	0	1
wc2009	5 Sept	Glasgow	2	0
wc2012	11 Sept	Glasgow	1	1
wc2013	10 Sept	Skopje	2	1
		v NORWAY	S	N
1929	26 May	Oslo	7	3
1954	5 May	Glasgow	1	0
1954	19 May	Oslo	1	1
1963	4 June	Bergen	3	4
1963	7 Nov	Glasgow	6	1
1974	6 June	Oslo	2	1
EC1978	25 Oct	Glasgow	3	2
EC1979	7 June	Oslo	4	0
wc1988	14 Sept	Oslo	2	1
wc1989	15 Nov	Glasgow	1	1
1992	3 June	Oslo	0	0
wc1998	16 June	Bordeaux	1	1
2003	20 Aug	Oslo	0	0
wc2004	9 Oct	Glasgow	0	1
wc2005	7 Sept	Oslo	2	1
wc2008	11 Oct	Glasgow	0	0
wc2009	12 Aug	Oslo	0	4
2013	19 Nov	Molde	1	0
EC2023	17 June	Oslo	2	1
EC2023	19 Nov	Glasgow	3	3
		v PARAGUAY	S	P
wc1958	11 June	Norrkoping	2	3
		v PERU	S	P
1972	26 Apr	Glasgow	2	0
wc1978	3 June	Cordoba	1	3
1979	12 Sept	Glasgow	1	1
2018	30 May	Lima	0	2
		v POLAND	S	P
1958	1 June	Warsaw	2	1
1960	4 May	Glasgow	2	3
wc1965	23 May	Chorzow	1	1
wc1965	13 Oct	Glasgow	1	2
1980	28 May	Poznan	0	1
1990	19 May	Glasgow	1	1
2001	25 Apr	Bydgoszcz	1	1
2014	5 Mar	Warsaw	1	0
EC2014	14 Oct	Warsaw	2	2
EC2015	8 Oct	Glasgow	2	2
2022	24 Mar	Glasgow	1	1
NL2024	**5 Sept**	**Glasgow**	**2**	**3**
		v PORTUGAL	S	P
1950	21 May	Lisbon	2	2
1955	4 May	Glasgow	3	0
1959	3 June	Lisbon	0	1
1966	18 June	Glasgow	0	1
EC1971	21 Apr	Lisbon	0	2
EC1971	13 Oct	Glasgow	2	1
1975	13 May	Glasgow	1	0
EC1978	29 Nov	Lisbon	0	1
EC1980	26 Mar	Glasgow	4	1
wc1980	15 Oct	Glasgow	0	0
wc1981	18 Nov	Lisbon	1	2
wc1992	14 Oct	Ibrox	0	0
wc1993	28 Apr	Lisbon	0	5
2002	20 Nov	Braga	0	2
2018	14 Oct	Glasgow	1	3
NL2024	**8 Sept**	**Lisbon**	**1**	**2**
NL2024	**15 Oct**	**Glasgow**	**0**	**0**
		v QATAR	S	Q
2015	5 June	Hibernian	1	0
		v REPUBLIC OF IRELAND	S	RI
wc1961	3 May	Glasgow	4	1
wc1961	7 May	Dublin	3	0
1963	9 June	Dublin	0	1
1969	21 Sept	Dublin	1	1
EC1986	15 Oct	Dublin	0	0
EC1987	18 Feb	Glasgow	0	1
2000	30 May	Dublin	2	1
2003	12 Feb	Glasgow	0	2
NC2011	29 May	Dublin	0	1
EC2014	14 Nov	Glasgow	1	0
EC2015	13 June	Dublin	1	1
NL2022	11 June	Dublin	0	3

			S	
NL2022	24 Sept	Glasgow	2	1
		v ROMANIA	S	R
EC1975	1 June	Bucharest	1	1
EC1975	17 Dec	Glasgow	1	1
1986	26 Mar	Glasgow	3	0
EC1990	12 Sept	Glasgow	2	1
EC1991	16 Oct	Bucharest	0	1
2004	31 Mar	Glasgow	1	2
		v RUSSIA	S	R
EC1994	16 Nov	Glasgow	1	1
EC1995	29 Mar	Moscow	0	0
EC2019	6 Sept	Glasgow	1	2
EC2019	10 Oct	Moscow	0	4
		v SAN MARINO	S	SM
EC1991	1 May	Serravalle	2	0
EC1991	13 Nov	Glasgow	4	0
EC1995	26 Apr	Serravalle	2	0
EC1995	15 Nov	Glasgow	5	0
wc2000	7 Oct	Serravalle	2	0
wc2001	28 Mar	Glasgow	4	0
EC2019	24 Mar	Serravalle	2	0
EC2019	13 Oct	Glasgow	6	0
		v SAUDI ARABIA	S	SA
1988	17 Feb	Riyadh	2	2
		v SERBIA	S	Se
wc2012	8 Sept	Glasgow	0	0
wc2013	26 Mar	Novi Sad	0	2
EC2020	12 Nov	Belgrade	1	1
		v SLOVAKIA	S	Sl
wc2016	11 Oct	Trnava	0	3
wc2017	5 Oct	Glasgow	1	0
NL2020	11 Oct	Glasgow	1	0
NL2020	15 Nov	Trnava	0	1
		v SLOVENIA	S	Sl
wc2004	8 Sept	Glasgow	0	0
wc2005	12 Oct	Celje	3	0
2012	29 Feb	Koper	1	1
wc2017	26 Mar	Glasgow	1	0
wc2017	8 Oct	Ljubljana	2	2
		v SOUTH AFRICA	S	SA
2002	20 May	Hong Kong	0	2
2007	22 Aug	Aberdeen	1	0
		v SPAIN	S	S
wc1957	8 May	Glasgow	4	2
wc1957	26 May	Madrid	1	4
1963	13 June	Madrid	6	2
1965	8 May	Glasgow	0	0
EC1974	20 Nov	Glasgow	1	2
EC1975	5 Feb	Valencia	1	1
1982	24 Feb	Valencia	0	3
wc1984	14 Nov	Glasgow	3	1
wc1985	27 Feb	Seville	0	1
1988	27 Apr	Madrid	0	0
2004	3 Sept	Valencia	1	1

Match abandoned after 60 minutes; floodlight failure.

			S	
EC2010	12 Oct	Glasgow	2	3
EC2011	11 Oct	Alicante	1	3
EC2023	28 Mar	Glasgow	2	0
EC2023	12 Oct	Seville	0	2
		v SWEDEN	S	Sw
1952	30 May	Stockholm	1	3
1953	6 May	Glasgow	1	2
1975	16 Apr	Gothenburg	1	1
1977	27 Apr	Glasgow	3	1
wc1980	10 Sept	Stockholm	1	0
wc1981	9 Sept	Glasgow	2	0
wc1990	16 June	Genoa	2	1
1995	11 Oct	Stockholm	0	2
wc1996	10 Nov	Ibrox	1	0
wc1997	30 Apr	Gothenburg	1	2
2004	17 Nov	Hibernian	1	4
2010	11 Aug	Stockholm	0	3
		v SWITZERLAND	S	Sw
1931	24 May	Geneva	3	2
1946	15 May	Geneva	3	1
1948	17 May	Berne	1	2
1950	26 Apr	Glasgow	3	1
wc1957	19 May	Basel	2	1
wc1957	6 Nov	Glasgow	3	2
1973	22 June	Berne	0	1
1976	7 Apr	Glasgow	1	0

			S	Sw
EC1982	17 Nov	Berne	0	2
EC1983	30 May	Glasgow	2	2
EC1990	17 Oct	Glasgow	2	1
EC1991	11 Sept	Berne	2	2
wc1992	9 Sept	Berne	1	3
wc1993	8 Sept	Aberdeen	1	1
wc1996	18 June	Aston Villa	1	0
2006	1 Mar	Glasgow	1	3
EC2024	19 June	Cologne	1	1

v TRINIDAD & TOBAGO			S	TT
2004	30 May	Hibernian	4	1

v TURKEY			S	T
1960	8 June	Ankara	2	4
2022	16 Nov	Diyarbakir	1	2

v UKRAINE			S	U
EC2006	11 Oct	Kyiv	0	2
EC2007	13 Oct	Glasgow	3	1
wc2022	1 June	Glasgow	1	3
NL2022	21 Sept	Glasgow	3	0
NL2022	27 Sept	Krakow	0	0

v URUGUAY			S	U
wc1954	19 June	Basel	0	7
1962	2 May	Glasgow	2	3
1983	21 Sept	Glasgow	2	0
wc1986	13 June	Nezahualcoyotl	0	0

v USA			S	USA
1952	30 Apr	Glasgow	6	0
1992	17 May	Denver	1	0
1996	26 May	New Britain	1	2
1998	30 May	Washington	0	0
2005	12 Nov	Glasgow	1	1
2012	26 May	Jacksonville	1	5
2013	15 Nov	Glasgow	0	0

v USSR			S	USSR
1967	10 May	Glasgow	0	2
1971	14 June	Moscow	0	1
wc1982	22 June	Malaga	2	2
1991	6 Feb	Ibrox	0	1

v YUGOSLAVIA			S	Y
1955	15 May	Belgrade	2	2
1956	21 Nov	Glasgow	2	0
wc1958	8 June	Vasteras	1	1
1972	29 June	Belo Horizonte	2	2
wc1974	22 June	Frankfurt	1	1
1984	12 Sept	Glasgow	6	1
wc1988	19 Oct	Glasgow	1	1
wc1989	6 Sept	Zagreb	1	3

v ZAIRE			S	Z
wc1974	14 June	Dortmund	2	0

WALES

v ALBANIA			W	A
EC1994	7 Sept	Cardiff	2	0
EC1995	15 Nov	Tirana	1	1
2018	20 Nov	Elbasan	0	1
2021	5 June	Cardiff	0	0

v ANDORRA			W	A
EC2014	9 Sept	La Vella	2	1
EC2015	13 Oct	Cardiff	2	0

v ARGENTINA			W	A
1992	3 June	Tokyo	0	1
2002	13 Feb	Cardiff	1	1

v ARMENIA			W	A
wc2001	24 Mar	Yerevan	2	2
wc2001	1 Sept	Cardiff	0	0
EC2023	16 June	Cardiff	2	4
EC2023	18 Nov	Yerevan	1	1

v AUSTRALIA			W	A
2011	10 Aug	Cardiff	1	2

v AUSTRIA			W	A
1954	9 May	Vienna	0	2
1955	23 Nov	Wrexham	1	2
EC1974	4 Sept	Vienna	1	2
1975	19 Nov	Wrexham	1	0
1992	29 Apr	Vienna	1	1
EC2005	26 Mar	Cardiff	0	2
EC2005	30 Mar	Vienna	0	1
2013	6 Feb	Swansea	2	1
wc2016	6 Oct	Vienna	2	2
wc2017	2 Sept	Cardiff	1	0
wc2022	24 Mar	Cardiff	2	1

v AZERBAIJAN			W	A
EC2002	20 Nov	Baku	2	0
EC2003	29 Mar	Cardiff	4	0
wc2004	4 Sept	Baku	1	1
wc2005	12 Oct	Cardiff	2	0
wc2008	6 Sept	Cardiff	1	0
wc2009	6 June	Baku	1	0
EC2019	6 Sept	Cardiff	2	1
EC2019	16 Nov	Baku	2	0

v BELARUS			W	B
EC1998	14 Oct	Cardiff	3	2
EC1999	4 Sept	Minsk	2	1
wc2000	2 Sept	Minsk	1	2
wc2001	6 Oct	Cardiff	1	0
2019	9 Sept	Cardiff	1	0
wc2021	5 Sept	Kazan	3	2
wc2021	13 Nov	Cardiff	5	1

v BELGIUM			W	B
1949	22 May	Liege	1	3
1949	23 Nov	Cardiff	5	1
EC1990	17 Oct	Cardiff	3	1
EC1991	27 Mar	Brussels	1	1
wc1992	18 Nov	Brussels	0	2
wc1993	31 Mar	Cardiff	2	0
wc1997	29 Mar	Cardiff	1	2
wc1997	11 Oct	Brussels	2	3
wc2012	7 Sept	Cardiff	0	2
wc2013	15 Oct	Brussels	1	1
EC2014	16 Nov	Brussels	0	0
EC2015	12 June	Cardiff	1	0
EC2016	1 July	Lille	3	1
wc2021	24 Mar	Leuven	1	3
wc2021	16 Nov	Cardiff	1	1
NL2022	11 June	Cardiff	1	1
NL2022	22 Sept	Brussels	1	2
wc2025	**9 June**	**Brussels**	**3**	**4**

v BOSNIA & HERZEGOVINA			W	BH
2003	12 Feb	Cardiff	2	2
2012	15 Aug	Llanelli	0	2
EC2014	10 Oct	Cardiff	0	0
EC2015	10 Oct	Zenica	0	2

v BRAZIL			W	B
wc1958	19 June	Gothenburg	0	1
1962	12 May	Rio de Janeiro	1	3
1962	16 May	São Paulo	1	3
1966	14 May	Rio de Janeiro	1	3
1966	18 May	Belo Horizonte	0	1
1983	12 June	Cardiff	1	1
1991	11 Sept	Cardiff	0	3
1997	12 Nov	Brasilia	0	3
2000	23 May	Cardiff	0	3
2006	5 Sept	Cardiff	0	2

v BULGARIA			W	B
EC1983	27 Apr	Wrexham	1	0
EC1983	16 Nov	Sofia	0	1
EC1994	14 Dec	Cardiff	0	3
EC1995	29 Mar	Sofia	1	3
2006	15 Aug	Swansea	0	0
2007	22 Aug	Burgas	1	0
EC2010	8 Oct	Cardiff	0	1
EC2011	12 Oct	Sofia	1	0
NL2020	6 Sept	Cardiff	1	0
NL2020	14 Oct	Sofia	1	0

v CANADA			W	C
1986	10 May	Toronto	0	2
1986	20 May	Vancouver	3	0
2004	30 May	Wrexham	1	0

v CHILE			W	C
1966	22 May	Santiago	0	2
2014	4 June	Valparaiso	0	2

v CHINA

			W	C
2018	22 Mar	Nanning	6	0

v COSTA RICA

			W	CR
1990	20 May	Cardiff	1	0
2012	29 Feb	Cardiff	0	1

v CROATIA

			W	C
2002	21 Aug	Varazdin	1	1
2010	23 May	Osijek	0	2
wc2012	16 Oct	Osijek	0	2
wc2013	26 Mar	Swansea	1	2
EC2019	8 June	Osijek	1	2
EC2019	13 Oct	Cardiff	1	1
EC2023	25 Mar	Split	1	1
2023	15 Oct	Cardiff	2	1

v CYPRUS

			W	C
wc1992	14 Oct	Limassol	1	0
wc1993	13 Oct	Cardiff	2	0
2005	16 Nov	Limassol	0	1
EC2006	11 Oct	Cardiff	3	1
EC2007	13 Oct	Nicosia	1	3
EC2014	13 Oct	Cardiff	2	1
EC2015	3 Sept	Nicosia	1	0

v CZECHOSLOVAKIA

			W	C
wc1957	1 May	Cardiff	1	0
wc1957	26 May	Prague	0	2
EC1971	21 Apr	Swansea	1	3
EC1971	27 Oct	Prague	0	1
wc1977	30 Mar	Wrexham	3	0
wc1977	16 Nov	Prague	0	1
wc1980	19 Nov	Cardiff	1	0
wc1981	9 Sept	Prague	0	2
EC1987	29 Apr	Wrexham	1	1
EC1987	11 Nov	Prague	0	2
wc1993	28 Apr	Ostrava†	1	1
wc1993	8 Sept	Cardiff†	2	2

†*Czechoslovakia played as RCS (Republic of Czechs and Slovaks).*

v CZECH REPUBLIC

			W	CR
wc2021	30 Mar	Cardiff	1	0
wc2021	8 Oct	Prague	2	2
2022	29 Mar	Cardiff	1	1

v DENMARK

			W	D
wc1964	21 Oct	Copenhagen	0	1
wc1965	1 Dec	Wrexham	4	2
EC1987	9 Sept	Cardiff	1	0
EC1987	14 Oct	Copenhagen	0	1
1990	11 Sept	Copenhagen	0	1
EC1998	10 Oct	Copenhagen	2	1
EC1999	9 June	Liverpool	0	2
2008	19 Nov	Brondby	1	0
2018	9 Sept	Aarhus	0	2
NL2018	16 Nov	Cardiff	1	2
EC2021	26 June	Amsterdam	0	4

v ESTONIA

			W	E
1994	23 May	Tallinn	2	1
2009	29 May	Llanelli	1	0
wc2021	8 Sept	Cardiff	0	0
wc2021	11 Oct	Tallinn	1	0

v FAROE ISLANDS

			W	F
wc1992	9 Sept	Cardiff	6	0
wc1993	6 June	Toftir	3	0

v FINLAND

			W	F
EC1971	26 May	Helsinki	1	0
EC1971	13 Oct	Swansea	3	0
EC1987	10 Sept	Helsinki	1	1
NL2020	3 Sept	Helsinki	1	0
NL2020	18 Nov	Cardiff	3	1
EC1987	1 Apr	Wrexham	4	0
wc1988	19 Oct	Swansea	2	2
wc1989	6 Sept	Helsinki	0	1
2000	29 Mar	Cardiff	1	2
EC2002	7 Sept	Helsinki	2	0
EC2003	10 Sept	Cardiff	1	1
wc2009	28 Mar	Cardiff	0	2
wc2009	10 Oct	Helsinki	1	2
2013	16 Nov	Cardiff	1	1
2021	1 Sept	Helsinki	0	0
EC2023	21 Mar	Cardiff	4	1

v FRANCE

			W	F
1933	25 May	Paris	1	1
1939	20 May	Paris	1	2

			W	F
1953	14 May	Paris	1	6
1982	2 June	Toulouse	1	0
2017	10 Nov	Paris	0	2
2021	2 June	Nice	0	3

v GEORGIA

			W	G
EC1994	16 Nov	Tbilisi	0	5
EC1995	7 June	Cardiff	0	1
2008	20 Aug	Swansea	1	2
wc2016	9 Oct	Cardiff	1	1
wc2017	6 Oct	Tbilisi	1	0

v GERMANY

			W	G
EC1995	26 Apr	Dusseldorf	1	1
EC1995	11 Oct	Cardiff	1	2
2002	14 May	Cardiff	1	0
EC2007	8 Sept	Cardiff	0	2
EC2007	21 Nov	Frankfurt	0	0
wc2008	15 Oct	Moenchengladbach	0	1
wc2009	1 Apr	Cardiff	0	2

v GIBRALTAR

			W	G
2023	11 Oct	Wrexham	4	0
2024	6 June	Faro	0	0

v EAST GERMANY

			W	EG
wc1957	19 May	Leipzig	1	2
wc1957	25 Sept	Cardiff	4	1
wc1969	16 Apr	Dresden	1	2
wc1969	22 Oct	Cardiff	1	3

v WEST GERMANY

			W	WG
1968	8 May	Cardiff	1	1
1969	26 Mar	Frankfurt	1	1
1976	6 Oct	Cardiff	0	2
1977	14 Dec	Dortmund	1	1
EC1979	2 May	Wrexham	0	2
EC1979	17 Oct	Cologne	1	5
wc1989	31 May	Cardiff	0	0
wc1989	15 Nov	Cologne	1	2
EC1991	5 June	Cardiff	1	0
EC1991	16 Oct	Nuremberg	1	4

v GREECE

			W	G
wc1964	9 Dec	Athens	0	2
wc1965	17 Mar	Cardiff	4	1

v HUNGARY

			W	H
wc1958	8 June	Sanviken	1	1
wc1958	17 June	Stockholm	2	1
1961	28 May	Budapest	2	3
EC1962	7 Nov	Budapest	1	3
EC1963	20 Mar	Cardiff	1	1
EC1974	30 Oct	Cardiff	2	0
EC1975	16 Apr	Budapest	2	1
1985	16 Oct	Cardiff	0	3
2004	31 Mar	Budapest	2	1
2005	9 Feb	Cardiff	2	0
EC2019	11 June	Budapest	0	1
EC2019	19 Nov	Cardiff	2	0

v ICELAND

			W	I
wc1980	2 June	Reykjavik	4	0
wc1981	14 Oct	Swansea	2	2
wc1984	12 Sept	Reykjavik	0	1
wc1984	14 Nov	Cardiff	2	1
1991	1 May	Cardiff	1	0
2008	28 May	Reykjavik	1	0
2014	5 Mar	Cardiff	3	1
NL2024	**11 Oct**	**Reykjavik**	**2**	**2**
NL2024	**19 Nov**	**Cardiff**	**4**	**1**

v IRAN

			W	I
1978	18 Apr	Tehran	1	0
wc2022	25 Nov	Al Rayyan	0	2

v ISRAEL

			W	I
wc1958	15 Jan	Tel Aviv	2	0
wc1958	5 Feb	Cardiff	2	0
1984	10 June	Tel Aviv	0	0
1989	8 Feb	Tel Aviv	3	3
EC2015	28 Mar	Haifa	3	0
EC2015	6 Sept	Cardiff	0	0

v ITALY

			W	I
1965	1 May	Florence	1	4
wc1968	23 Oct	Cardiff	0	1
wc1969	4 Nov	Rome	1	4
1988	4 June	Brescia	1	0
1996	24 Jan	Terni	0	3

			W	I
EC1998	5 Sept	Liverpool	0	2
EC1999	5 June	Bologna	0	4
EC2002	16 Oct	Cardiff	2	1
EC2003	6 Sept	Milan	0	4
EC2021	20 June	Rome	0	1

v JAMAICA			W	J
1998	25 Mar	Cardiff	0	0

v JAPAN			W	J
1992	7 June	Matsuyama	1	0

v KAZAKHSTAN			W	K
wc2025	22 Mar	**Cardiff**	**3**	**1**

v KOREA REPUBLIC			W	KR
2023	7 Sept	Cardiff	0	0

v KUWAIT			W	K
1977	6 Sept	Wrexham	0	0
1977	20 Sept	Kuwait	0	0

v LATVIA			W	L
2004	18 Aug	Riga	2	0
EC2023	28 Mar	Cardiff	1	0
2023	11 Sept	Riga	2	0

v LIECHTENSTEIN			W	L
2006	14 Nov	Swansea	4	0
wc2008	11 Oct	Cardiff	2	0
wc2009	14 Oct	Vaduz	2	0
wc2025	6 June	**Cardiff**	**3**	**0**

v LUXEMBOURG			W	L
EC1974	20 Nov	Swansea	5	0
EC1975	1 May	Luxembourg	3	1
EC1990	14 Nov	Luxembourg	1	0
EC1991	13 Nov	Cardiff	1	0
2008	26 Mar	Luxembourg	2	0
2010	11 Aug	Llanelli	5	1

v MALTA			W	M
EC1978	25 Oct	Wrexham	7	0
EC1979	2 June	Valletta	2	0
1988	1 June	Valletta	3	2
1998	3 June	Valletta	3	0

v MEXICO			W	M
wc1958	11 June	Stockholm	1	1
1962	22 May	Mexico City	1	2
2012	27 May	New Jersey	0	2
2018	29 May	Pasadena	0	0
2021	27 Mar	Cardiff	1	0

v MOLDOVA			W	M
EC1994	12 Oct	Kishinev	2	3
EC1995	6 Sept	Cardiff	1	0
wc2016	5 Sept	Cardiff	4	0
wc2017	5 Sept	Chisinau	2	0

v MONTENEGRO			W	M
2009	12 Aug	Podgorica	1	2
EC2010	3 Sept	Podgorica	0	1
EC2011	2 Sept	Cardiff	2	1
NL2024	9 Sept	**Niksic**	**2**	**1**
NL2024	14 Oct	**Cardiff**	**1**	**0**

v NETHERLANDS			W	N
wc1988	14 Sept	Amsterdam	0	1
wc1989	11 Oct	Wrexham	1	2
1992	30 May	Utrecht	0	4
wc1996	5 Oct	Cardiff	1	3
wc1996	9 Nov	Eindhoven	1	7
2008	1 June	Rotterdam	0	2
2014	4 June	Amsterdam	0	2
2015	13 Nov	Cardiff	2	3
NL2022	8 June	Cardiff	1	2
NL2022	14 June	Feyenoord	2	3

v NEW ZEALAND			W	NZ
2007	26 May	Wrexham	2	2

v NORTH MACEDONIA			W	NM
wc2013	6 Sept	Skopje	1	2
wc2013	11 Oct	Cardiff	1	0
wc2025	25 Mar	**Skopje**	**1**	**1**

v NORWAY			W	N
EC1982	22 Sept	Swansea	1	0
EC1983	21 Sept	Oslo	0	0
1984	6 June	Trondheim	0	1
1985	26 Feb	Wrexham	1	1
1985	5 June	Bergen	2	4

			W	N
1994	9 Mar	Cardiff	1	3
wc2000	7 Oct	Cardiff	1	1
wc2001	5 Sept	Oslo	2	3
2004	27 May	Oslo	0	0
2008	6 Feb	Wrexham	3	0
2011	12 Nov	Cardiff	4	1

v PANAMA			W	P
2017	14 Nov	Cardiff	1	1

v PARAGUAY			W	P
2006	1 Mar	Cardiff	0	0

v POLAND			W	P
wc1973	28 Mar	Cardiff	2	0
wc1973	26 Sept	Katowice	0	3
1991	29 May	Radom	0	0
wc2000	11 Oct	Warsaw	0	0
wc2001	2 June	Cardiff	1	2
wc2004	13 Oct	Cardiff	2	3
wc2005	7 Sept	Warsaw	0	1
2009	11 Feb	Vila Real	0	1
NL2022	1 June	Wroclaw	1	2
NL2022	25 Sept	Cardiff	0	1
EC2024	26 Mar	Cardiff	0	0

v PORTUGAL			W	P
1949	15 May	Lisbon	2	3
1951	12 May	Cardiff	2	1
2000	2 June	Chaves	0	3
EC2016	6 July	Lille	0	2

v QATAR			W	Q
2000	23 Feb	Doha	1	0

v REPUBLIC OF IRELAND			W	RI
1960	28 Sept	Dublin	3	2
1979	11 Sept	Swansea	2	1
1981	24 Feb	Dublin	3	1
1986	26 Mar	Dublin	1	0
1990	28 Mar	Dublin	0	1
1991	6 Feb	Wrexham	0	3
1992	19 Feb	Dublin	1	0
1993	17 Feb	Dublin	1	2
1997	11 Feb	Cardiff	0	0
EC2007	24 Mar	Dublin	0	1
EC2007	17 Nov	Cardiff	2	2
NC2011	8 Feb	Dublin	0	3
2013	14 Aug	Cardiff	0	0
wc2017	24 Mar	Dublin	0	0
wc2017	9 Oct	Cardiff	0	1
NL2018	6 Sept	Cardiff	4	1
NL2018	16 Oct	Dublin	1	0
NL2020	11 Oct	Dublin	0	0
NL2020	15 Nov	Cardiff	1	0

v ROMANIA			W	R
EC1970	11 Nov	Cardiff	0	0
EC1971	24 Nov	Bucharest	0	2
1983	12 Oct	Wrexham	5	0
wc1992	20 May	Bucharest	1	5
wc1993	17 Nov	Cardiff	1	2

v RUSSIA			W	R
EC2003	15 Nov	Moscow	0	0
EC2003	19 Nov	Cardiff	0	1
wc2008	10 Sept	Moscow	1	2
wc2009	9 Sept	Cardiff	1	3
EC2016	20 June	Toulouse	3	0

v SAN MARINO			W	SM
wc1996	2 June	Serravalle	5	0
wc1996	31 Aug	Cardiff	6	0
EC2007	28 Mar	Cardiff	3	0
EC2007	17 Oct	Serravalle	2	1

v SAUDI ARABIA			W	SA
1986	25 Feb	Dahran	2	1

v SERBIA			W	S
wc2012	11 Sept	Novi Sad	1	6
wc2013	10 Sept	Cardiff	0	3
wc2016	12 Nov	Cardiff	1	1
wc2017	11 June	Belgrade	1	1

v SERBIA-MONTENEGRO			W	SM
EC2003	20 Aug	Belgrade	0	1
EC2003	11 Oct	Cardiff	2	3

v SLOVAKIA		W	S
EC2006	7 Oct	Cardiff	1	5
EC2007	12 Sept	Trnava	5	2
EC2016	11 June	Bordeaux	2	1
EC2019	24 Mar	Cardiff	1	0
EC2019	10 Oct	Trnava	1	1
2024	9 June	Trnava	0	4

v SLOVENIA		W	S
2005	17 Aug	Swansea	0	0

v SPAIN		W	S
wc1961	19 Apr	Cardiff	1	2
wc1961	18 May	Madrid	1	1
1982	24 Mar	Valencia	1	1
wc1984	17 Oct	Seville	0	3
wc1985	30 Apr	Wrexham	3	0
2018	11 Oct	Cardiff	1	4

v SWEDEN		W	S
wc1958	15 June	Stockholm	0	0
1988	27 Apr	Stockholm	1	4
1989	26 Apr	Wrexham	0	2
1990	25 Apr	Stockholm	2	4
1994	20 Apr	Wrexham	0	2
2010	3 Mar	Swansea	0	1
2016	5 June	Stockholm	0	3

v SWITZERLAND		W	S
1949	26 May	Berne	0	4
1951	16 May	Wrexham	3	2
1996	24 Apr	Lugano	0	2
EC1999	31 Mar	Zurich	0	2
EC1999	9 Oct	Wrexham	0	2
EC2010	12 Oct	Basel	1	4
EC2011	8 Oct	Swansea	2	0
EC2021	12 June	Baku	1	1

v TRINIDAD & TOBAGO		W	TT
2006	27 May	Graz	2	1
2019	20 Mar	Wrexham	1	0

v TUNISIA		W	T
1998	6 June	Tunis	0	4

v TURKEY		W	T
EC1978	29 Nov	Wrexham	1	0
EC1979	21 Nov	Izmir	0	1
wc1980	15 Oct	Cardiff	4	0
wc1981	25 Mar	Ankara	1	0
wc1996	14 Dec	Cardiff	0	0
wc1997	20 Aug	Istanbul	4	6
EC2021	16 June	Baku	2	0
EC2023	19 June	Samsun	0	2
EC2023	21 Nov	Cardiff	1	1
NL2024	**6 Sept**	**Cardiff**	**0**	**0**
NL2024	**16 Nov**	**Kayseri**	**0**	**0**

v UKRAINE		W	U
wc2001	28 Mar	Cardiff	1	1
wc2001	6 June	Kyiv	1	1
2016	28 Mar	Kyiv	0	1
wc2022	5 June	Cardiff	1	0

v REST OF UNITED KINGDOM		W	RUK
1951	5 Dec	Cardiff	3	2
1969	28 July	Cardiff	0	1

v URUGUAY		W	U
1986	21 Apr	Wrexham	0	0
2018	26 Mar	Nanning	0	1

v USA		W	USA
2003	27 May	San Jose	0	2
2020	12 Nov	Swansea	0	0
wc2022	21 Nov	Al Rayyan	1	1

v USSR		W	USSR
wc1965	30 May	Moscow	1	2
wc1965	27 Oct	Cardiff	2	1
wc1981	30 May	Wrexham	0	0
wc1981	18 Nov	Tbilisi	0	3
1987	18 Feb	Swansea	0	0

v YUGOSLAVIA		W	Y
1953	21 May	Belgrade	2	5
1954	22 Nov	Cardiff	1	3
EC1976	24 Apr	Zagreb	0	2
EC1976	22 May	Cardiff	1	1
EC1982	15 Dec	Titograd	4	4
EC1983	14 Dec	Cardiff	1	1
1988	23 Mar	Swansea	1	2

NORTHERN IRELAND

v ALBANIA		NI	A
wc1965	7 May	Belfast	4	1
wc1965	24 Nov	Tirana	1	1
EC1982	15 Dec	Tirana	0	0
EC1983	27 Apr	Belfast	1	0
wc1992	9 Sept	Belfast	3	0
wc1993	17 Feb	Tirana	2	1
wc1996	14 Dec	Belfast	2	0
wc1997	10 Sept	Zurich	0	1
2010	3 Mar	Tirana	0	1

v ALGERIA		NI	A
wc1986	3 June	Guadalajara	1	1

v ANDORRA		NI	A
2024	11 June	Murcia	2	0

v ARGENTINA		NI	A
wc1958	11 June	Halmstad	1	3

v ARMENIA		NI	A
wc1996	5 Oct	Belfast	1	1
wc1997	30 Apr	Yerevan	0	0
EC2003	29 Mar	Yerevan	0	1
EC2003	10 Sept	Belfast	0	1

v AUSTRALIA		NI	A
1980	11 June	Sydney	2	1
1980	15 June	Melbourne	1	1
1980	18 June	Adelaide	2	1

v AUSTRIA		NI	A
wc1982	1 July	Madrid	2	2
EC1982	13 Oct	Vienna	0	2
EC1983	21 Sept	Belfast	3	1
EC1990	14 Nov	Vienna	0	0
EC1991	16 Oct	Belfast	2	1
EC1994	12 Oct	Vienna	2	1
EC1995	15 Nov	Belfast	5	3
wc2004	13 Oct	Belfast	3	3
wc2005	12 Oct	Vienna	0	2
NL2018	12 Oct	Vienna	0	1

v AZERBAIJAN		NI	A
NL2018	18 Nov	Belfast	1	2
NL2020	11 Oct	Belfast	0	1
NL2020	15 Nov	Vienna	1	2

v AZERBAIJAN		NI	A
wc2004	9 Oct	Baku	0	0
wc2005	3 Sept	Belfast	2	0
wc2012	14 Nov	Belfast	1	1
wc2013	11 Oct	Baku	0	2
wc2016	11 Nov	Belfast	4	0
wc2017	10 June	Baku	1	0

v BARBADOS		NI	B
2004	30 May	Waterford	1	1

v BELARUS		NI	B
2016	27 May	Belfast	3	0
EC2019	24 Mar	Belfast	2	1
EC2019	11 June	Barysaw	1	0
NL2024	**12 Oct**	**Zalaegerszeg**	**0**	**0**
NL2024	**15 Nov**	**Belfast**	**2**	**0**

v BELGIUM		NI	B
wc1976	10 Nov	Liege	0	2
wc1977	16 Nov	Belfast	3	0
1997	11 Feb	Belfast	3	0

v BOSNIA & HERZEGOVINA		NI	BH
NL2018	8 Sept	Belfast	1	2
NL2018	15 Oct	Sarajevo	0	2
EC2020	8 Oct	Sarajevo	1	1

v BRAZIL		NI	B
wc1986	12 June	Guadalajara	0	3

v BULGARIA		NI	B
wc1972	18 Oct	Sofia	0	3
wc1973	26 Sept	Sheffield Wednesday	0	0
EC1978	29 Nov	Sofia	2	0
EC1979	2 May	Belfast	2	0
wc2001	28 Mar	Sofia	3	4

			NI	B
wc2001	2 June	Belfast	0	1
2008	6 Feb	Belfast	0	1
wc2021	31 Mar	Belfast	0	0
wc2021	12 Oct	Sofia	1	2
NL2024	**8 Sept**	**Plovdiv**	**0**	**1**
NL2024	**15 Oct**	**Belfast**	**5**	**0**

v CANADA

			NI	C
1995	22 May	Edmonton	0	2
1999	27 Apr	Belfast	1	1
2005	9 Feb	Belfast	0	1

v CHILE

			NI	C
1989	26 May	Belfast	0	1
1995	25 May	Edmonton	1	2
2010	30 May	Chillan	0	1
2014	4 June	Valparaiso	0	2

v COLOMBIA

			NI	C
1994	4 June	Boston	0	2

v COSTA RICA

			NI	CR
2018	3 June	San Jose	0	3

v CROATIA

			NI	C
2016	15 Nov	Belfast	0	3

v CYPRUS

			NI	C
EC1971	3 Feb	Nicosia	3	0
EC1971	21 Apr	Belfast	5	0
wc1973	14 Feb	Nicosia	0	1
wc1973	8 May	Fulham	3	0
2002	21 Aug	Belfast	0	0
2014	5 Mar	Nicosia	0	0
NL2022	5 June	Larnaca	0	0
NL2022	12 June	Belfast	2	2

v CZECHOSLOVAKIA

			NI	C
wc1958	8 June	Halmstad	1	0
wc1958	17 June	Malmo	2	1*

v CZECH REPUBLIC

			NI	CR
wc2001	24 Mar	Belfast	0	1
wc2001	6 June	Teplice	1	3
wc2008	10 Sept	Belfast	0	0
wc2009	14 Oct	Prague	0	0
wc2016	4 Sept	Prague	0	0
wc2017	4 Sept	Belfast	2	0
2019	14 Oct	Prague	3	2

v DENMARK

			NI	D
EC1978	25 Oct	Belfast	2	1
EC1979	6 June	Copenhagen	0	4
1986	26 Mar	Belfast	1	1
EC1990	17 Oct	Belfast	1	1
EC1991	13 Nov	Odense	1	2
wc1992	18 Nov	Belfast	0	1
wc1993	13 Oct	Copenhagen	0	1
wc2000	7 Oct	Belfast	1	1
wc2001	1 Sept	Copenhagen	1	1
EC2006	7 Oct	Copenhagen	0	0
EC2007	17 Nov	Belfast	2	1
EC2023	16 June	Copenhagen	0	1
EC2023	20 Nov	Belfast	2	0
2025	**8 June**	**Copenhagen**	**1**	**2**

v ESTONIA

			NI	E
2004	31 Mar	Tallinn	1	0
2006	1 Mar	Belfast	1	0
EC2011	6 Sept	Tallinn	1	4
EC2011	7 Oct	Belfast	1	2
EC2019	21 Mar	Belfast	2	0
EC2019	8 June	Tallinn	2	1
2021	5 Sept	Tallin	1	0

v FAROE ISLANDS

			NI	F
EC1991	1 May	Belfast	1	1
EC1991	11 Sept	Landskrona	5	0
EC2010	12 Oct	Toftir	1	1
EC2011	10 Aug	Belfast	4	0
EC2014	11 Oct	Belfast	2	0
EC2015	4 Sept	Torshavn	3	1

v FINLAND

			NI	F
wc1984	27 May	Pori	0	1
wc1984	14 Nov	Belfast	2	1
EC1998	10 Oct	Belfast	1	0
EC1998	9 Oct	Helsinki	1	4
2003	12 Feb	Belfast	0	1
2006	16 Aug	Helsinki	2	1

			NI	F
2012	15 Aug	Belfast	3	3
EC2015	29 Mar	Belfast	2	1
EC2015	11 Oct	Helsinki	1	1
EC2023	26 Mar	Belfast	0	1
EC2023	17 Nov	Helsinki	0	4

v FRANCE

			NI	F
1928	21 Feb	Paris	0	4
1951	12 May	Belfast	2	2
1952	11 Nov	Paris	1	3
wc1958	19 June	Norrkoping	0	4
1982	24 Mar	Paris	0	4
wc1982	4 July	Madrid	1	4
1986	26 Feb	Paris	0	0
1988	27 Apr	Belfast	0	0
1999	18 Aug	Belfast	0	1

v GEORGIA

			NI	G
2008	26 Mar	Belfast	4	1

v GERMANY

			NI	G
1992	2 June	Bremen	1	1
1996	29 May	Belfast	1	1
wc1996	9 Nov	Nuremberg	1	1
wc1997	20 Aug	Belfast	1	3
EC1999	27 Mar	Belfast	0	3
EC1999	8 Sept	Dortmund	0	4
2005	4 June	Belfast	1	4
EC2016	21 June	Paris	0	1
wc2016	11 Oct	Hanover	0	2
wc2017	5 Oct	Belfast	1	3
EC2019	9 Sept	Belfast	0	2
EC2019	19 Nov	Frankfurt	1	6

v WEST GERMANY

			NI	WG
wc1958	15 June	Malmo	2	2
wc1960	26 Oct	Belfast	3	4
wc1961	10 May	Hamburg	1	2
1966	7 May	Belfast	0	2
1977	27 Apr	Cologne	0	5
EC1982	17 Nov	Belfast	1	0
EC1983	16 Nov	Hamburg	1	0

v GREECE

			NI	G
wc1961	3 May	Athens	1	2
wc1961	17 Oct	Belfast	2	0
1988	17 Feb	Athens	2	3
EC2003	2 Apr	Belfast	0	2
EC2003	11 Oct	Athens	0	1
EC2014	14 Oct	Piraeus	2	0
EC2015	8 Oct	Belfast	3	1
NL2022	2 June	Belfast	0	1
NL2022	27 Sept	Athens	1	3

v HONDURAS

			NI	H
wc1982	21 June	Zaragoza	1	1

v HUNGARY

			NI	H
wc1988	19 Oct	Budapest	0	1
wc1989	6 Sept	Belfast	1	2
2000	26 Apr	Belfast	0	1
2008	19 Nov	Belfast	0	2
EC2014	7 Sept	Budapest	2	1
EC2015	7 Sept	Belfast	1	1
2022	29 Mar	Belfast	0	1

v ICELAND

			NI	I
wc1977	11 June	Reykjavik	0	1
wc1977	21 Sept	Belfast	2	0
wc2000	11 Oct	Reykjavik	0	1
wc2001	5 Sept	Belfast	3	0
EC2006	2 Sept	Belfast	0	3
EC2007	12 Sept	Reykjavik	1	2
2025	**10 June**	**Belfast**	**1**	**0**

v ISRAEL

			NI	I
1968	10 Sept	Jaffa	3	2
1976	3 Mar	Tel Aviv	1	1
wc1980	26 Mar	Tel Aviv	0	0
wc1981	18 Nov	Belfast	1	0
1984	16 Oct	Belfast	3	0
1987	18 Feb	Tel Aviv	1	1
2009	12 Aug	Belfast	1	1
wc2013	26 Mar	Belfast	0	2
wc2013	15 Oct	Tel Aviv	1	1
2018	11 Sept	Belfast	3	0

v ITALY		NI	I
wc1957	25 Apr Rome	0	1
1957	4 Dec Belfast	2	2
wc1958	15 Jan Belfast	2	1
1961	25 Apr Bologna	2	3
1997	22 Jan Palermo	0	2
2003	3 June Campobasso	0	2
2009	6 June Pisa	0	3
EC2010	8 Oct Belfast	0	0
EC2011	11 Oct Pescara	0	3
wc2021	25 Mar Parma	0	2
wc2021	15 Nov Belfast	0	0

v KAZAKHSTAN		NI	K
EC2023	19 June Belfast	0	1
EC2023	10 Sept Astana	0	1

v KOREA REPUBLIC		NI	KR
2018	24 Mar Belfast	2	1

v KOSOVO		NI	K
NL2022	9 June Prishtina	2	3
NL2022	24 Sept Belfast	1	1

v LATVIA		NI	L
wc1993	2 June Riga	2	1
wc1993	8 Sept Belfast	2	0
EC1995	26 Apr Riga	1	0
EC1995	7 June Belfast	1	2
EC2006	11 Oct Belfast	1	0
EC2007	8 Sept Riga	0	1
2015	13 Nov Belfast	1	0

v LIECHTENSTEIN		NI	L
EC1994	20 Apr Belfast	4	1
EC1995	11 Oct Eschen	4	0
2002	27 Mar Vaduz	0	0
EC2007	24 Mar Vaduz	4	1
EC2007	22 Aug Belfast	3	1

v LITHUANIA		NI	L
wc1992	28 Apr Belfast	2	2
wc1993	25 May Vilnius	1	0
wc2021	2 Sept Vilnius	4	1
wc2021	12 Nov Belfast	1	0

v LUXEMBOURG		NI	L
2000	23 Feb Luxembourg	3	1
wc2012	11 Sept Belfast	1	1
wc2013	10 Sept Luxembourg	2	3
2019	5 Sept Belfast	1	0
2022	25 Mar Luxembourg	3	1
NL2024	**5 Sept Belfast**	**2**	**0**
NL2024	**18 Nov Luxembourg**	**2**	**2**

v MALTA		NI	M
wc1988	21 May Belfast	3	0
wc1989	26 Apr Valletta	2	0
2000	28 Mar Valletta	3	0
wc2000	2 Sept Belfast	1	0
wc2001	6 Oct Valletta	1	0
2005	17 Aug Ta'Qali	1	1
2013	6 Feb Ta'Qali	0	0
2021	30 May Klagenfurt	3	0

v MEXICO		NI	M
1966	22 June Belfast	4	1
1994	11 June Miami	0	3

v MOLDOVA		NI	M
EC1998	18 Nov Belfast	2	2
EC1999	31 Mar Chisinau	0	0

v MONTENEGRO		NI	M
2010	11 Aug Podgorica	0	2

v MOROCCO		NI	M
1986	23 Apr Belfast	2	1
2010	17 Nov Belfast	1	1

v NETHERLANDS		NI	N
1962	9 May Rotterdam	0	4
wc1965	17 Mar Belfast	2	1
wc1965	7 Apr Rotterdam	0	0
wc1976	13 Oct Rotterdam	2	2
wc1977	12 Oct Belfast	0	1
2012	2 June Amsterdam	0	6
EC2019	10 Oct Rotterdam	1	3
EC2019	16 Nov Belfast	0	0

v NEW ZEALAND		NI	NZ
2017	2 June Belfast	1	0

v NORWAY		NI	N
1922	25 May Bergen	1	2
EC1974	4 Sept Oslo	1	2
EC1975	29 Oct Belfast	3	0
1990	27 Mar Belfast	2	3
1996	27 Mar Belfast	0	2
2001	28 Feb Belfast	0	4
2004	18 Feb Belfast	1	4
2012	29 Feb Belfast	0	3
wc2017	26 Mar Belfast	2	0
wc2017	8 Oct Oslo	0	1
NL2020	7 Sept Belfast	1	5
NL2020	14 Oct Oslo	0	1

v PANAMA		NI	P
2018	30 May Panama City	0	0

v POLAND		NI	P
EC1962	10 Oct Katowice	2	0
EC1962	28 Nov Belfast	2	0
1988	23 Mar Belfast	1	1
1991	5 Feb Belfast	3	1
2002	13 Feb Limassol	1	4
EC2004	4 Sept Belfast	0	3
EC2005	30 Mar Warsaw	0	1
wc2009	28 Mar Belfast	3	2
wc2009	5 Sept Chorzow	1	1
EC2016	12 June Nice	0	1

v PORTUGAL		NI	P
wc1957	16 Jan Lisbon	1	1
wc1957	1 May Belfast	3	0
wc1973	28 Mar Coventry	1	1
wc1973	14 Nov Lisbon	1	1
wc1980	19 Nov Lisbon	0	1
wc1981	29 Apr Belfast	1	0
EC1994	7 Sept Belfast	1	2
EC1995	3 Sept Lisbon	1	1
wc1997	29 Mar Belfast	0	0
wc1997	11 Oct Lisbon	0	1
2005	15 Nov Belfast	1	1
wc2012	16 Oct Porto	1	1
wc2013	6 Sept Belfast	2	4

v QATAR		NI	Q
2015	31 May Crewe	1	1

v REPUBLIC OF IRELAND		NI	RI
EC1978	20 Sept Dublin	0	0
EC1979	21 Nov Belfast	1	0
EC1988	14 Sept Belfast	0	0
wc1989	11 Oct Dublin	0	3
wc1993	31 Mar Dublin	0	3
wc1993	17 Nov Belfast	1	1
EC1994	16 Nov Belfast	0	4
EC1995	29 Mar Dublin	1	1
1999	29 May Dublin	1	0
NC2011	24 May Dublin	0	5
2018	15 Nov Dublin	0	0

v ROMANIA		NI	R
wc1984	12 Sept Belfast	3	2
wc1985	16 Oct Bucharest	1	0
1994	23 Mar Belfast	2	0
2006	27 May Chicago	0	2
EC2014	14 Nov Bucharest	0	2
EC2015	13 June Belfast	0	0
NL2020	4 Sept Bucharest	1	1
NL2020	18 Nov Belfast	1	1
2024	22 Mar Bucharest	1	1

v RUSSIA		NI	R
wc2012	7 Sept Moscow	0	2
wc2013	14 Aug Belfast	1	0

v ST KITTS & NEVIS		NI	SKN
2004	2 June Basseterre	2	0

v SAN MARINO		NI	SM
wc2008	15 Oct Belfast	4	0
wc2009	11 Feb Serravalle	3	0
wc2016	8 Oct Belfast	4	0
wc2017	1 Sept Serravalle	3	0
EC2023	23 Mar Serravalle	2	0
EC2023	14 Oct Belfast	3	0

v SERBIA		NI	S
2009	14 Nov Belfast	0	1
EC2011	25 Mar Belgrade	1	2
EC2011	2 Sept Belfast	0	1

v SERBIA-MONTENEGRO

			NI	SM
2004	28 Apr	Belfast	1	1

v SLOVAKIA

			NI	S
1998	25 Mar	Belfast	1	0
wc2008	6 Sept	Bratislava	1	2
wc2009	9 Sept	Belfast	0	2
2016	4 June	Trnava	0	0
ec2020	12 Nov	Belfast	1	2

v SLOVENIA

			NI	S
wc2008	11 Oct	Maribor	0	2
wc2009	1 Apr	Belfast	1	0
ec2010	3 Sept	Maribor	1	0
ec2011	29 Mar	Belfast	0	0
2016	28 Mar	Belfast	1	0
ec2023	7 Sept	Ljubljana	2	4
ec2023	17 Oct	Belfast	0	1

v SOUTH AFRICA

			NI	SA
1924	24 Sept	Belfast	1	2

v SPAIN

			NI	S
1958	15 Oct	Madrid	2	6
1963	30 May	Bilbao	1	1
1963	30 Oct	Belfast	0	1
ec1970	11 Nov	Seville	0	3
ec1972	16 Feb	Hull	1	1
wc1982	25 June	Valencia	1	0
1985	27 Mar	Palma	0	0
wc1986	7 June	Guadalajara	1	2
wc1988	21 Dec	Seville	0	4
wc1989	8 Feb	Belfast	0	2
wc1992	14 Oct	Belfast	0	0
wc1993	28 Apr	Seville	1	3
1998	2 June	Santander	1	4
2002	17 Apr	Belfast	0	5
ec2002	12 Oct	Albacete	0	3
ec2003	11 June	Belfast	0	0
ec2006	6 Sept	Belfast	3	2
ec2007	21 Nov	Las Palmas	0	1
2024	8 June	Palma	1	5

v SWEDEN

			NI	S
ec1974	30 Oct	Solna	2	0
ec1975	3 Sept	Belfast	1	2
wc1980	15 Oct	Belfast	3	0
wc1981	3 June	Solna	0	1
1996	24 Apr	Belfast	1	2
ec2007	28 Mar	Belfast	2	1
ec2007	17 Oct	Stockholm	1	1
2025	**25 Mar**	**Solna**	**1**	**5**

v SWITZERLAND

			NI	S
wc1964	14 Oct	Belfast	1	0
wc1964	14 Nov	Lausanne	1	2
1998	22 Apr	Belfast	1	0
2004	18 Aug	Zurich	0	0
wc2017	9 Nov	Belfast	0	1
wc2017	12 Nov	Basel	0	0
wc2021	8 Sept	Belfast	0	0
wc2021	9 Oct	Geneva	0	2
2025	**21 Mar**	**Belfast**	**1**	**1**

v THAILAND

			NI	T
1997	21 May	Bangkok	0	0

v TRINIDAD & TOBAGO

			NI	TT
2004	6 June	Bacolet	3	0

v TURKEY

			NI	T
wc1968	23 Oct	Belfast	4	1
wc1968	11 Dec	Istanbul	3	0
2013	15 Nov	Adana	0	1
ec1983	30 Mar	Belfast	2	1
ec1983	12 Oct	Ankara	0	1
ec1985	1 May	Belfast	2	0
wc1985	11 Sept	Izmir	0	0
ec1986	12 Nov	Izmir	0	0
ec1987	11 Nov	Belfast	1	0
ec1998	5 Sept	Istanbul	0	3
ec1999	4 Sept	Belfast	0	3
2010	26 May	New Britain, CT	0	2
2013	15 Nov	Adana	0	1

v UKRAINE

			NI	U
wc1996	31 Aug	Belfast	0	1
wc1997	2 Apr	Kyiv	1	2
ec2002	16 Oct	Belfast	0	0
ec2003	6 Sept	Donetsk	0	0
ec2016	16 June	Lyon	2	0
2021	3 June	Dnipro	0	1

v URUGUAY

			NI	U
1964	29 Apr	Belfast	3	0
1990	18 May	Belfast	1	0
2006	21 May	New Jersey	0	1
2014	30 May	Montevideo	0	1

v USA

			NI	USA
2021	28 Mar	Belfast	1	2

v USSR

			NI	USSR
wc1969	19 Sept	Belfast	0	0
wc1969	22 Oct	Moscow	0	2
ec1971	22 Sept	Moscow	0	1
ec1971	13 Oct	Belfast	1	1

v YUGOSLAVIA

			NI	Y
ec1975	16 Mar	Belfast	1	0
ec1975	19 Nov	Belgrade	0	1
wc1982	17 June	Zaragoza	0	0
ec1987	29 Apr	Belfast	1	2
ec1987	14 Oct	Sarajevo	0	3
ec1990	12 Sept	Belfast	0	2
ec1991	27 Mar	Belgrade	1	4
2000	16 Aug	Belfast	1	2

REPUBLIC OF IRELAND

v ALBANIA

			RI	A
wc1992	26 May	Dublin	2	0
wc1993	26 May	Tirana	2	1
ec2003	2 Apr	Tirana	0	0
ec2003	7 June	Dublin	2	1

v ALGERIA

			RI	A
1982	28 Apr	Algiers	0	2
2010	28 May	Dublin	3	0

v ANDORRA

			RI	A
wc2001	28 Mar	Barcelona	3	0
wc2001	25 Apr	Dublin	3	1
ec2010	7 Sept	Dublin	3	1
ec2011	7 Oct	Andorra La Vella	2	0
2021	3 June	Andorra La Vella	4	1

v ARGENTINA

			RI	A
1951	13 May	Dublin	0	1
†1979	29 May	Dublin	0	0
1980	16 May	Dublin	0	1
1998	22 Apr	Dublin	0	2
2010	11 Aug	Dublin	0	1

†Not considered a full international.

v ARMENIA

			RI	A
ec2010	3 Sept	Yerevan	1	0
ec2011	11 Oct	Dublin	2	1
nl2022	4 June	Yerevan	0	1
nl2022	27 Sept	Dublin	3	2

v AUSTRALIA

			RI	A
2003	19 Aug	Dublin	2	1
2009	12 Aug	Limerick	0	3

v AUSTRIA

			RI	A
1952	7 May	Vienna	0	6
1953	25 Mar	Dublin	4	0
1958	14 Mar	Vienna	1	3
wc2013	10 Sept	Vienna	0	1
1962	8 Apr	Dublin	2	3
ec1963	25 Sept	Vienna	0	0
ec1963	13 Oct	Dublin	3	2
1966	22 May	Vienna	0	1
1968	10 Nov	Dublin	2	2
ec1971	30 May	Dublin	1	4
ec1971	10 Oct	Linz	0	6
ec1995	11 June	Dublin	1	3
ec1995	6 Sept	Vienna	1	3
wc2013	26 Mar	Dublin	2	2
wc2013	10 Sept	Vienna	0	1
wc2016	12 Nov	Vienna	1	0
wc2017	11 June	Dublin	1	1

v AZERBAIJAN

			RI	A
wc2021	4 Sept	Dublin	1	1
wc2021	9 Oct	Baku	3	0

		v BELARUS	RI	B
2016	31 May	Cork	1	2

		v BELGIUM	RI	B
1928	12 Feb	Liege	4	2
1929	30 Apr	Dublin	4	0
1930	11 May	Brussels	3	1
wc1934	25 Feb	Dublin	4	4
1949	24 Apr	Dublin	0	2
1950	10 May	Brussels	1	5
1965	24 Mar	Dublin	0	2
1966	25 May	Liege	3	2
wc1980	15 Oct	Dublin	1	1
wc1981	25 Mar	Brussels	0	1
EC1986	10 Sept	Brussels	2	2
EC1987	29 Apr	Dublin	0	0
wc1997	29 Oct	Dublin	1	1
wc1997	16 Nov	Brussels	1	2
EC2016	18 June	Bordeaux	0	3
2022	26 Mar	Dublin	2	2
2024	23 Mar	Dublin	0	0

		v BOLIVIA	RI	B
1994	24 May	Dublin	1	0
1996	15 June	New Jersey	3	0
2007	26 May	Boston	1	1

		v BOSNIA & HERZEGOVINA	RI	BH
2012	26 May	Dublin	1	0
EC2015	13 Nov	Zenica	1	1
EC2015	16 Nov	Dublin	2	0

		v BRAZIL	RI	B
1974	5 May	Rio de Janeiro	1	2
1982	27 May	Uberlandia	0	7
1987	23 May	Dublin	1	0
2004	18 Feb	Dublin	0	0
2008	6 Feb	Dublin	0	1
2010	2 Mar	Arsenal	0	2

		v BULGARIA	RI	B
wc1977	1 June	Sofia	1	2
wc1977	12 Oct	Dublin	0	0
EC1979	19 May	Sofia	0	1
EC1979	17 Oct	Dublin	3	0
wc1987	1 Apr	Sofia	1	2
wc1987	14 Oct	Dublin	2	0
2004	18 Aug	Dublin	1	1
wc2009	28 Mar	Dublin	1	1
wc2009	6 June	Sofia	1	1
2019	10 Sept	Dublin	3	1
NL2020	3 Sept	Sofia	1	1
NL2020	18 Nov	Dublin	0	0
NL2025	**20 Mar**	**Plovdiv**	**2**	**1**
NL2025	**23 Mar**	**Dublin**	**2**	**1**

		v CAMEROON	RI	C
wc2002	1 June	Niigata	1	1

		v CANADA	RI	C
2003	18 Nov	Dublin	3	0

		v CHILE	RI	C
1960	30 Mar	Dublin	2	0
1972	21 June	Recife	1	2
1974	12 May	Santiago	2	1
1982	22 May	Santiago	0	1
1991	22 May	Dublin	1	1
2006	24 May	Dublin	0	1

		v CHINA PR	RI	CPR
1984	3 June	Sapporo	1	0
2005	29 Mar	Dublin	1	0

		v COLOMBIA	RI	C
2008	29 May	Fulham	1	0

		v COSTA RICA	RI	CR
2014	6 June	Philadelphia	1	1

		v CROATIA	RI	C
1996	2 June	Dublin	2	2
EC1998	5 Sept	Dublin	2	0
EC1999	4 Sept	Zagreb	0	1
2001	15 Aug	Dublin	2	2
2004	16 Nov	Dublin	1	0
2011	10 Aug	Dublin	0	0
EC2012	10 June	Poznan	1	3

		v CYPRUS	RI	C
wc1980	26 Mar	Nicosia	3	2
wc1980	19 Nov	Dublin	6	0
wc2001	24 Mar	Nicosia	4	0
wc2001	6 Oct	Dublin	4	0
wc2004	4 Sept	Dublin	3	0
wc2005	8 Oct	Nicosia	1	0
EC2006	7 Oct	Nicosia	2	5
EC2007	17 Oct	Dublin	1	1
2008	15 Oct	Dublin	1	0
wc2009	5 Sept	Nicosia	2	1

		v CZECHOSLOVAKIA	RI	C
1938	18 May	Prague	2	2
EC1959	5 Apr	Dublin	2	0
EC1959	10 May	Bratislava	0	4
wc1961	8 Oct	Dublin	1	3
wc1961	29 Oct	Prague	1	7
EC1967	21 May	Dublin	0	2
EC1967	22 Nov	Prague	2	1
wc1969	4 May	Dublin	1	2
wc1969	7 Oct	Prague	0	3
1979	26 Sept	Prague	1	4
1981	29 Apr	Dublin	3	1
1986	27 May	Reykjavik	1	0

		v CZECH REPUBLIC	RI	CR
1994	5 June	Dublin	1	3
1996	24 Apr	Prague	0	2
1998	25 Mar	Olomouc	1	2
2000	23 Feb	Dublin	3	2
2004	31 Mar	Dublin	2	1
EC2006	11 Oct	Dublin	1	1
EC2007	12 Sept	Prague	0	1
2012	29 Feb	Dublin	1	1

		v DENMARK	RI	D
wc1956	3 Oct	Dublin	2	1
wc1957	2 Oct	Copenhagen	2	0
wc1968	4 Dec	Dublin	1	1
(abandoned after 51 mins)				
wc1969	27 May	Copenhagen	0	2
wc1969	15 Oct	Dublin	1	1
EC1978	24 May	Copenhagen	3	3
EC1979	2 May	Dublin	2	0
wc1984	14 Nov	Copenhagen	0	3
wc1985	13 Nov	Dublin	1	4
wc1992	14 Oct	Copenhagen	0	0
wc1993	28 Apr	Dublin	1	1
2002	27 Mar	Dublin	3	0
2007	22 Aug	Copenhagen	4	0
wc2017	11 Nov	Copenhagen	0	0
wc2017	14 Nov	Dublin	1	5
NL2018	13 Oct	Dublin	0	0
NL2018	19 Nov	Aarhus	0	0
EC2019	7 June	Copenhagen	1	1
EC2019	18 Nov	Dublin	1	1

		v ECUADOR	RI	E
1972	19 June	Natal	3	2
2007	23 May	New Jersey	1	1

		v EGYPT	RI	E
wc1990	17 June	Palermo	0	0

		v ENGLAND	RI	E
1946	30 Sept	Dublin	0	1
1949	21 Sept	Everton	2	0
wc1957	8 May	Wembley	1	5
wc1957	19 May	Dublin	1	1
1964	24 May	Dublin	1	3
1976	8 Sept	Wembley	1	1
EC1978	25 Oct	Dublin	1	1
EC1980	6 Feb	Wembley	0	2
1985	26 Mar	Wembley	1	2
EC1988	12 June	Stuttgart	1	0
wc1990	11 June	Cagliari	1	1
EC1990	14 Nov	Dublin	1	1
EC1991	27 Mar	Wembley	1	1
1995	15 Feb	Dublin	1	0
(abandoned after 27 mins)				
2013	29 May	Wembley	1	1
2015	7 June	Dublin	0	0
2020	12 Nov	Wembley	0	3
NL2024	**7 Sept**	**Dublin**	**0**	**2**
NL2024	**17 Nov**	**Wembley**	**0**	**5**

	v ESTONIA		RI	E
wc2000	11 Oct	Dublin	2	0
wc2001	6 June	Tallinn	2	0
EC2011	11 Nov	Tallinn	4	0
EC2011	15 Nov	Dublin	1	1

	v FAROE ISLANDS		RI	F
EC2004	13 Oct	Dublin	2	0
EC2005	8 June	Toftir	2	0
wc2012	16 Oct	Torshavn	4	1
wc2013	7 June	Dublin	3	0

	v FINLAND		RI	F
wc1949	8 Sept	Dublin	3	0
wc1949	9 Oct	Helsinki	1	1
1990	16 May	Dublin	1	1
2000	15 Nov	Dublin	3	0
2002	21 Aug	Helsinki	3	0
NL2020	6 Sept	Dublin	0	1
NL2020	14 Oct	Helsinki	0	1
NL2024	**10 Oct**	**Helsinki**	**2**	**1**
NL2024	**14 Nov**	**Dublin**	**1**	**0**

	v FRANCE		RI	F
1937	23 May	Paris	2	0
1952	16 Nov	Dublin	1	1
wc1953	4 Oct	Dublin	3	5
wc1953	25 Nov	Paris	0	1
wc1972	15 Nov	Dublin	2	1
wc1973	19 May	Paris	1	1
wc1976	17 Nov	Paris	0	2
wc1977	30 Mar	Dublin	1	0
wc1980	28 Oct	Paris	0	2
wc1981	14 Oct	Dublin	3	2
1989	7 Feb	Dublin	0	0
wc2004	9 Oct	Paris	0	0
wc2005	7 Sept	Dublin	0	1
wc2009	14 Nov	Dublin	0	1
wc2009	18 Nov	Paris	1	1
EC2016	26 June	Lyon	1	2
2018	28 May	Paris	0	2
wc2023	27 Mar	Dublin	0	1
EC2023	7 Sept	Paris	0	2

	v GEORGIA		RI	G
EC2003	29 Mar	Tbilisi	2	1
EC2003	11 June	Dublin	2	0
wc2008	6 Sept	Mainz	2	1
wc2009	11 Feb	Dublin	2	1
2013	2 June	Dublin	3	0
EC2014	7 Sept	Tbilisi	2	1
EC2015	7 Sept	Dublin	1	0
EC2016	6 Oct	Dublin	1	0
wc2017	2 Sept	Tbilisi	1	1
EC2019	26 Mar	Dublin	1	0
EC2019	12 Oct	Tbilisi	0	0

	v GERMANY		RI	G
1935	8 May	Dortmund	1	3
1936	17 Oct	Dublin	5	2
1939	23 May	Bremen	1	1
1994	29 May	Hanover	2	0
wc2002	5 June	Ibaraki	1	1
EC2006	2 Sept	Stuttgart	0	1
EC2007	13 Oct	Dublin	0	0
wc2012	12 Oct	Dublin	1	6
wc2013	11 Oct	Cologne	0	3
EC2014	14 Oct	Gelsenkirchen	1	1
EC2015	8 Oct	Dublin	1	0

	v WEST GERMANY		RI	WG
1951	17 Oct	Dublin	3	2
1952	4 May	Cologne	0	3
1955	28 May	Hamburg	1	2
1956	25 Nov	Dublin	3	0
1960	11 May	Dusseldorf	1	0
1966	4 May	Dublin	0	4
1970	9 May	Berlin	1	2
1975	1 Mar	Dublin	1	0†
1979	22 May	Dublin	1	3
1981	21 May	Bremen	0	3†
1989	6 Sept	Dublin	1	1

†v West Germany 'B'

	v GIBRALTAR		RI	G
EC2014	11 Oct	Dublin	7	0
EC2015	4 Sept	Faro	4	0
EC2019	23 Mar	Gibraltar	1	0
EC2019	10 June	Dublin	2	0
wc2023	19 June	Dublin	3	0
EC2023	16 Oct	Faro	4	0

	v GREECE		RI	G
2000	26 Apr	Dublin	0	1
2002	20 Nov	Athens	0	0
2012	14 Nov	Dublin	0	1
wc2023	16 June	Athens	1	2
EC2023	13 Oct	Dublin	0	2
NL2024	**10 Sept**	**Dublin**	**0**	**2**
NL2024	**13 Oct**	**Piraeus**	**0**	**2**

	v HUNGARY		RI	H
1934	15 Dec	Dublin	2	4
1936	3 May	Budapest	3	3
1936	6 Dec	Dublin	2	3
1939	19 Mar	Cork	2	2
1939	18 May	Budapest	2	2
wc1969	8 June	Dublin	1	2
wc1969	5 Nov	Budapest	0	4
wc1989	8 Mar	Budapest	0	0
wc1989	4 June	Dublin	2	0
1991	11 Sept	Gyor	2	1
2012	4 June	Budapest	0	0
2021	8 June	Budapest	0	0
2024	4 June	Dublin	2	1

	v ICELAND		RI	I
EC1962	12 Aug	Dublin	4	2
EC1962	2 Sept	Reykjavik	1	1
EC1982	13 Oct	Dublin	2	0
EC1983	21 Sept	Reykjavik	3	0
1986	25 May	Reykjavik	2	1
wc1996	10 Nov	Dublin	0	0
wc1997	6 Sept	Reykjavik	4	2
2017	28 Mar	Dublin	0	1

	v IRAN		RI	I
1972	18 June	Recife	2	1
wc2001	10 Nov	Dublin	2	0
wc2001	15 Nov	Tehran	0	1

	v ISRAEL		RI	I
1984	4 Apr	Tel Aviv	0	3
1985	27 May	Tel Aviv	0	0
1987	10 Nov	Dublin	5	0
EC2005	26 Mar	Tel Aviv	1	1
EC2005	4 June	Dublin	2	2

	v ITALY		RI	I
1926	21 Mar	Turin	0	3
1927	23 Apr	Rome	1	2
EC1970	8 Dec	Rome	0	3
EC1971	10 May	Dublin	1	2
1985	5 Feb	Dublin	1	2
wc1990	30 June	Rome	0	1
1992	4 June	Foxboro	0	2
wc1994	18 June	New York	1	0
2005	17 Aug	Dublin	1	2
wc2009	1 Apr	Bari	1	1
wc2009	10 Oct	Dublin	2	2
2011	7 June	Liege	2	0
EC2012	18 June	Poznan	0	2
2014	31 May	Fulham	0	0
EC2016	22 June	Lille	1	0

	v JAMAICA		RI	J
2004	2 June	Charlton	1	0

	v KAZAKHSTAN		RI	K
wc2012	7 Sept	Astana	2	1
wc2013	15 Oct	Dublin	3	1

	v LATVIA		RI	L
wc1992	9 Sept	Dublin	4	0
wc1993	2 June	Riga	2	1
EC1994	7 Sept	Riga	3	0
EC1995	11 Oct	Dublin	2	1
2013	15 Nov	Dublin	3	0
2023	22 Mar	Dublin	3	2

	v LIECHTENSTEIN		RI	L
EC1994	12 Oct	Dublin	4	0
EC1995	3 June	Eschen	0	0
wc1996	31 Aug	Eschen	5	0
wc1997	21 May	Dublin	5	0

v LITHUANIA

			RI	L
wc1993	16 June	Vilnius	1	0
wc1993	8 Sept	Dublin	2	0
wc1997	20 Aug	Dublin	0	0
wc1997	10 Sept	Vilnius	2	1
2022	29 Mar	Dublin	1	0

v LUXEMBOURG

			RI	L
1936	9 May	Luxembourg	5	1
wc1953	28 Oct	Dublin	4	0
wc1954	7 Mar	Luxembourg	1	0
EC1987	28 May	Luxembourg	2	0
EC1987	9 Sept	Dublin	2	1
wc2021	27 Mar	Dublin	0	1
wc2021	14 Nov	Luxembourg	3	0
2025	**10 June**	**Luxembourg**	**0**	**0**

v MALTA

			RI	M
EC1983	30 Mar	Valletta	1	0
EC1983	16 Nov	Dublin	8	0
wc1989	28 May	Dublin	2	0
wc1989	15 Nov	Valletta	2	0
1990	2 June	Valletta	3	0
EC1998	14 Oct	Dublin	5	0
EC1999	8 Sept	Valletta	3	2
2022	20 Nov	Ta'Qali	1	0

v MEXICO

			RI	M
1984	8 Aug	Dublin	0	0
wc1994	24 June	Orlando	1	2
1996	13 June	New Jersey	2	2
1998	23 May	Dublin	0	0
2000	4 June	Chicago	2	2
2017	2 June	New Jersey	1	3

v MOLDOVA

			RI	M
wc2016	9 Oct	Chisinau	3	1
wc2017	6 Oct	Dublin	2	0

v MONTENEGRO

			RI	M
wc2008	10 Sept	Podgorica	0	0
wc2009	14 Oct	Dublin	0	0

v MOROCCO

			RI	M
1990	12 Sept	Dublin	1	0

v NETHERLANDS

			RI	N
1932	8 May	Amsterdam	2	0
1934	8 Apr	Amsterdam	2	5
1935	8 Dec	Dublin	3	5
1955	1 May	Dublin	1	0
1956	10 May	Rotterdam	4	1
wc1980	10 Sept	Dublin	2	1
wc1981	9 Sept	Rotterdam	2	2
EC1982	22 Sept	Rotterdam	1	2
EC1983	12 Oct	Dublin	2	3
EC1988	18 June	Gelsenkirchen	0	1
wc1990	21 June	Palermo	1	1
1994	20 Apr	Tilburg	1	0
wc1994	4 July	Orlando	0	2
EC1995	13 Dec	Liverpool	0	2
1996	4 June	Rotterdam	1	3
wc2000	2 Sept	Amsterdam	2	2
wc2001	1 Sept	Dublin	1	0
2004	5 June	Amsterdam	1	0
2006	16 Aug	Dublin	0	4
2016	27 May	Dublin	1	1
EC2023	10 Sept	Dublin	1	2
EC2023	18 Nov	Amsterdam	0	1

v NEW ZEALAND

			RI	NZ
2019	14 Nov	Dublin	3	1
2023	21 Nov	Dublin	1	1

v NIGERIA

			RI	N
2002	16 May	Dublin	1	2
2004	29 May	Charlton	0	3
2009	29 May	Fulham	1	1

v NORTHERN IRELAND

			RI	NI
EC1978	20 Sept	Dublin	0	0
EC1979	21 Nov	Belfast	0	1
wc1988	14 Sept	Dublin	0	0
wc1989	11 Oct	Dublin	3	0
wc1993	31 Mar	Dublin	3	0
wc1993	17 Nov	Belfast	1	1
EC1994	16 Nov	Belfast	4	0
EC1995	29 Mar	Dublin	1	1
1999	29 May	Dublin	0	1
NC2011	24 May	Dublin	5	0
2018	15 Nov	Dublin	0	0

v NORTH MACEDONIA

			RI	NM
wc1996	9 Oct	Dublin	3	0
wc1997	2 Apr	Skopje	2	3
EC1999	9 June	Dublin	1	0
EC1999	9 Oct	Skopje	1	1
EC2011	26 Mar	Dublin	2	1
EC2011	4 June	Podgorica	2	0

v NORWAY

			RI	N
wc1937	10 Oct	Oslo	2	3
wc1937	7 Nov	Dublin	3	3
1950	26 Nov	Dublin	2	2
1951	30 May	Oslo	3	2
1954	8 Nov	Dublin	2	1
1955	25 May	Oslo	3	1
1960	6 Nov	Dublin	3	1
1964	13 May	Oslo	4	1
1973	6 June	Oslo	1	1
1976	24 Mar	Dublin	3	0
1978	21 May	Oslo	0	0
wc1984	17 Oct	Oslo	0	1
wc1985	1 May	Dublin	0	0
1988	1 June	Oslo	0	0
wc1994	28 June	New York	0	0
2003	30 Apr	Dublin	1	0
2008	20 Aug	Oslo	1	1
2010	17 Nov	Dublin	1	2
2022	17 Nov	Dublin	1	2

v OMAN

			RI	O
2012	11 Sept	Fulham	4	1
2014	3 Sept	Dublin	2	0
2016	31 Aug	Dublin	4	0

v PARAGUAY

			RI	P
1999	10 Feb	Dublin	2	0
2010	25 May	Dublin	2	1

v POLAND

			RI	P
1938	22 May	Warsaw	0	6
1938	13 Nov	Dublin	3	2
1958	11 May	Katowice	2	2
1958	5 Oct	Dublin	2	2
1964	10 May	Kracow	1	3
1964	25 Oct	Dublin	3	2
1968	15 May	Dublin	2	2
1968	30 Oct	Katowice	0	1
1970	6 May	Dublin	1	2
1970	23 Sept	Dublin	0	2
1973	16 May	Wroclaw	0	2
1973	21 Oct	Dublin	1	0
1976	26 May	Poznan	2	0
1977	24 Apr	Dublin	0	0
1978	12 Apr	Lodz	0	3
1981	23 May	Bydgoszcz	0	3
1984	23 May	Dublin	0	0
1986	12 Nov	Warsaw	0	1
1988	22 May	Dublin	3	1
EC1991	1 May	Dublin	0	0
EC1991	16 Oct	Poznan	3	3
2004	28 Apr	Bydgoszcz	0	0
2013	19 Nov	Poznan	0	0
2008	19 Nov	Dublin	2	3
2013	6 Feb	Dublin	2	0
2013	19 Nov	Poznan	0	0
EC2015	29 Mar	Dublin	1	1
EC2015	11 Oct	Warsaw	1	2
2018	11 Sept	Wroclaw	1	1

v PORTUGAL

			RI	P
1946	16 June	Lisbon	1	3
1947	4 May	Dublin	0	2
1948	23 May	Lisbon	0	2
1949	22 May	Dublin	1	0
1972	25 June	Recife	1	2
1992	7 June	Boston	2	0
EC1995	26 Apr	Dublin	1	0
EC1995	15 Nov	Lisbon	0	3
1996	29 May	Dublin	0	1
wc2000	7 Oct	Lisbon	1	1
wc2001	2 June	Dublin	1	1
2005	9 Feb	Dublin	1	0
2014	10 June	New Jersey	1	5
wc2021	1 Sept	Algarve	1	2
wc2021	11 Nov	Dublin	0	0
2024	11 June	Aveiro	0	3

		v QATAR	RI	Q
2021	30 Mar	Dublin	1	1
2021	12 Oct	Dublin	4	0

		v ROMANIA	RI	R
1988	23 Mar	Dublin	2	0
wc1990	25 June	Genoa	0	0*
wc1997	30 Apr	Bucharest	0	1
wc1997	11 Oct	Dublin	1	1
2004	27 May	Dublin	1	0

		v RUSSIA	RI	R
1994	23 Mar	Dublin	0	0
1996	27 Mar	Dublin	0	2
2002	13 Feb	Dublin	2	0
EC2002	7 Sept	Moscow	2	4
EC2003	6 Sept	Dublin	1	1
EC2010	8 Oct	Dublin	2	3
EC2011	6 Sept	Moscow	0	0

		v SAN MARINO	RI	SM
EC2006	15 Nov	Dublin	5	0
EC2007	7 Feb	Serravalle	2	1

		v SAUDI ARABIA	RI	SA
wc2002	11 June	Yokohama	3	0

		v SCOTLAND	RI	S
wc1961	3 May	Glasgow	1	4
wc1961	7 May	Dublin	0	3
1963	9 June	Dublin	1	0
1969	21 Sept	Dublin	1	1
EC1986	15 Oct	Dublin	0	0
EC1987	18 Feb	Glasgow	1	0
2000	30 May	Dublin	1	2
2003	12 Feb	Glasgow	2	0
NC2011	29 May	Dublin	1	0
EC2014	14 Nov	Glasgow	0	1
EC2015	13 June	Dublin	1	1
NL2022	11 June	Dublin	3	0
NL2022	24 Sept	Glasgow	1	2

		v SENEGAL	RI	S
2025	**6 June**	**Dublin**	**1**	**1**

		v SERBIA	RI	S
2008	24 May	Dublin	1	1
2012	15 Aug	Belgrade	0	0
2014	5 Mar	Dublin	1	2
wc2016	5 Sept	Belgrade	2	2
wc2017	5 Sept	Dublin	0	1
wc2021	24 Mar	Belgrade	2	3
wc2021	7 Sept	Dublin	1	1

		v SLOVAKIA	RI	S
EC2007	28 Mar	Dublin	1	0
EC2007	8 Sept	Bratislava	2	2
EC2010	12 Oct	Zilina	1	1
EC2011	2 Sept	Dublin	0	0
2016	29 Mar	Dublin	2	2
EC2020	8 Oct	Bratislava	0	0

		v SOUTH AFRICA	RI	SA
2000	11 June	New Jersey	2	1
2009	8 Sept	Limerick	1	0

		v SPAIN	RI	S
1931	26 Apr	Barcelona	1	1
1931	13 Dec	Dublin	0	5
1946	23 June	Madrid	1	0
1947	2 Mar	Dublin	3	2
1948	30 May	Barcelona	1	2
1949	12 June	Dublin	1	4
1952	1 June	Madrid	0	6
1955	27 Nov	Dublin	2	2
EC1964	11 Mar	Seville	1	5
EC1964	8 Apr	Dublin	0	2
wc1965	5 May	Dublin	1	0
wc1965	27 Oct	Seville	1	4
wc1965	10 Nov	Paris	0	1
EC1966	23 Oct	Dublin	0	2
EC1966	7 Dec	Valencia	0	2
1977	9 Feb	Dublin	0	1
EC1982	17 Nov	Dublin	3	3
EC1983	27 Apr	Zaragoza	0	2
1985	26 May	Cork	0	0
wc1988	16 Nov	Seville	0	2
wc1989	26 Apr	Dublin	1	0
wc1992	18 Nov	Seville	0	0
wc1993	13 Oct	Dublin	1	3
wc2002	16 June	Suwon	1	1

		v SPAIN	RI	S
EC2012	14 June	Gdansk	0	4
2013	11 June	New York	0	2

		v SWEDEN	RI	S
wc1949	2 June	Stockholm	1	3
wc1949	13 Nov	Dublin	1	3
1959	1 Nov	Dublin	3	2
1960	18 May	Malmo	1	4
EC1970	14 Oct	Dublin	1	1
EC1970	28 Oct	Malmo	0	1
1999	28 Apr	Dublin	2	0
2006	1 Mar	Dublin	3	0
wc2013	22 Mar	Stockholm	0	0
wc2013	6 Sept	Dublin	1	2
EC2016	13 June	Paris	1	1

		v SWITZERLAND	RI	S
1935	5 May	Basel	0	1
1936	17 Mar	Dublin	1	0
1937	17 May	Berne	1	0
1938	18 Sept	Dublin	4	0
1948	5 Dec	Dublin	0	1
EC1975	11 May	Dublin	2	1
EC1975	21 May	Berne	0	1
1980	30 Apr	Dublin	2	0
EC1985	2 June	Dublin	3	0
EC1985	11 Sept	Berne	0	0
1992	25 Mar	Dublin	2	1
EC2002	16 Oct	Dublin	1	2
EC2003	11 Oct	Basel	0	2
wc2004	8 Sept	Basel	1	1
wc2005	12 Oct	Dublin	0	0
2016	25 Mar	Dublin	1	0
EC2019	5 Sept	Dublin	1	1
EC2019	15 Oct	Geneva	0	2
2024	26 Mar	Dublin	0	1

		v TRINIDAD & TOBAGO	RI	TT
1982	30 May	Port of Spain	1	2

		v TUNISIA	RI	T
1988	19 Oct	Dublin	4	0

		v TURKEY	RI	T
EC1966	16 Nov	Dublin	2	1
EC1967	22 Feb	Ankara	1	2
EC1974	20 Nov	Izmir	1	1
EC1975	29 Oct	Dublin	4	0
2014	25 May	Dublin	1	2
1976	13 Oct	Ankara	3	3
1978	5 Apr	Dublin	4	2
1990	26 May	Izmir	0	0
EC1990	17 Oct	Dublin	5	0
EC1991	13 Nov	Istanbul	3	1
EC1999	13 Nov	Dublin	1	1
EC1999	17 Nov	Bursa	0	0
2003	9 Sept	Dublin	2	2
2014	25 May	Dublin	1	2
2018	23 Mar	Antalya	0	1

		v UKRAINE	RI	U
NL2022	8 June	Dublin	0	1
NL2022	14 June	Lodz (Poland)	1	1

		v URUGUAY	RI	U
1974	8 May	Montevideo	0	2
1986	23 Apr	Dublin	1	1
2011	29 Mar	Dublin	2	3
2017	4 June	Dublin	3	1

		v USA	RI	USA
1979	29 Oct	Dublin	3	2
1991	1 June	Boston	1	1
1992	29 Apr	Dublin	4	1
1992	30 May	Washington	1	3
1996	9 June	Boston	1	2
2000	6 June	Boston	1	1
2002	17 Apr	Dublin	2	1
2014	18 Nov	Dublin	4	1
2018	2 June	Dublin	2	1

		v USSR	RI	USSR
wc1972	18 Oct	Dublin	1	2
wc1973	13 May	Moscow	0	1
EC1974	30 Oct	Dublin	3	0
EC1975	18 May	Kyiv	1	2
wc1984	12 Sept	Dublin	1	0
wc1985	16 Oct	Moscow	0	2
EC1988	15 June	Hanover	1	1
1990	25 Apr	Dublin	1	0

		v WALES	RI	W
1960	28 Sept	Dublin	2	3
1979	11 Sept	Swansea	1	2
1981	24 Feb	Dublin	1	3
1986	26 Mar	Dublin	0	1
1990	28 Mar	Dublin	1	0
1991	6 Feb	Wrexham	3	0
1992	19 Feb	Dublin	0	1
1993	17 Feb	Dublin	2	1
1997	11 Feb	Cardiff	0	0
EC2007	24 Mar	Dublin	1	0
EC2007	17 Nov	Cardiff	2	2
NC2011	8 Feb	Dublin	3	0
2013	14 Aug	Cardiff	0	0

			RI	W
wc2017	24 Mar	Dublin	0	0
wc2017	9 Oct	Cardiff	1	0
NL2018	6 Sept	Cardiff	1	4
NL2018	16 Oct	Dublin	0	1
NL2020	11 Oct	Dublin	0	0
NL2020	15 Nov	Cardiff	0	1

		v YUGOSLAVIA	RI	Y
1955	19 Sept	Dublin	1	4
1988	27 Apr	Dublin	2	0
EC1998	18 Nov	Belgrade	0	1
EC1999	1 Sept	Dublin	2	1

BRITISH AND IRISH INTERNATIONAL APPEARANCES 1872–2025

This is a list of full international appearances by Englishmen, Irishmen, Scotsmen and Welshmen in matches against the Home Countries and against foreign nations. It does not include unofficial matches against Commonwealth and Empire countries. The year indicated refers to the player's international debut season; i.e. 2025 is the 2024–25 season. **Bold** type indicates players who have made an international appearance in season 2024–25.

As at July 2025.

ENGLAND

Abbott, W. 1902 (Everton)	1
Abraham, K. O. T. (Tammy) 2018 (Chelsea, Roma)	11
A'Court, A. 1958 (Liverpool)	5
Adams, T. A. 1987 (Arsenal)	66
Adcock, H. 1929 (Leicester C)	5
Agbonlahor, G. 2009 (Aston Villa)	3
Alcock, C. W. 1875 (Wanderers)	1
Alderson, J. T. 1923 (Crystal Palace)	1
Aldridge, A. 1888 (WBA, Walsall Town Swifts)	2
Alexander-Arnold, T. J. 2018 (Liverpool)	34
Allen, A. 1888 (Aston Villa)	1
Allen, A. 1960 (Stoke C)	3
Allen, C. 1984 (QPR, Tottenham H)	5
Allen, H. 1888 (Wolverhampton W)	5
Allen, J. P. 1934 (Portsmouth)	2
Allen, R. 1952 (WBA)	5
Alli, B. J. (Dele) 2016 (Tottenham H)	37
Alsford, W. J. 1935 (Tottenham H)	1
Amos, A. 1885 (Old Carthusians)	2
Anderson, R. D. 1879 (Old Etonians)	1
Anderson, S. 1962 (Sunderland)	2
Anderson, V. A. 1979 (Nottingham F, Arsenal, Manchester U)	30
Anderton, D. R. 1994 (Tottenham H)	30
Angus, J. 1961 (Burnley)	1
Armfield, J. C. 1959 (Blackpool)	43
Armitage, G. H. 1926 (Charlton Ath)	1
Armstrong, D. 1980 (Middlesbrough, Southampton)	3
Armstrong, K. 1955 (Chelsea)	1
Arnold, J. 1933 (Fulham)	1
Arthur, J. W. H. 1885 (Blackburn R)	7
Ashcroft, J. 1906 (Woolwich Arsenal)	3
Ashmore, G. S. 1926 (WBA)	1
Ashton, C. T. 1926 (Corinthians)	1
Ashton, D. 2008 (West Ham U)	1
Ashurst, W. 1923 (Notts Co)	5
Astall, G. 1956 (Birmingham C)	2
Astle, J. 1969 (WBA)	5
Aston, J. 1949 (Manchester U)	17
Athersmith, W. C. 1892 (Aston Villa)	12
Atyeo, P. J. W. 1956 (Bristol C)	6
Austin, S. W. 1926 (Manchester C)	1
Bach, P. 1899 (Sunderland)	1
Bache, J. W. 1903 (Aston Villa)	7
Baddeley, T. 1903 (Wolverhampton W)	5
Bagshaw, J. J. 1920 (Derby Co)	1
Bailey, G. R. 1985 (Manchester U)	2
Bailey, H. P. 1908 (Leicester Fosse)	5
Bailey, M. A. 1964 (Charlton Ath)	2
Bailey, N. C. 1878 (Clapham R)	19
Baily, E. F. 1950 (Tottenham H)	9
Bain, J. 1877 (Oxford University)	1
Baines, L. J. 2010 (Everton)	30

Baker, A. 1928 (Arsenal)	1
Baker, B. H. 1921 (Everton, Chelsea)	2
Baker, J. H. 1960 (Hibernian, Arsenal)	8
Ball, A. J. 1965 (Blackpool, Everton, Arsenal)	72
Ball, J. 1928 (Bury)	1
Ball, M. J. 2001 (Everton)	1
Balmer, W. 1905 (Everton)	1
Bamber, J. 1921 (Liverpool)	1
Bambridge, A. L. 1881 (Swifts)	3
Bambridge, E. C. 1879 (Swifts)	18
Bambridge, E. H. 1876 (Swifts)	1
Bamford, P. J. 2022 (Leeds U)	1
Banks, G. 1963 (Leicester C, Stoke C)	73
Banks, H. E. 1901 (Millwall)	1
Banks, T. 1958 (Bolton W)	6
Bannister, W. 1901 (Burnley, Bolton W)	2
Barclay, R. 1932 (Sheffield U)	3
Bardsley, D. J. 1993 (QPR)	2
Barham, M. 1983 (Norwich C)	2
Barkas, S. 1936 (Manchester C)	5
Barker, J. 1935 (Derby Co)	11
Barker, R. 1872 (Hertfordshire Rangers)	1
Barker, R. R. 1895 (Casuals)	1
Barkley, R. 2013 (Everton, Chelsea)	33
Barlow, R. J. 1955 (WBA)	1
Barmby, N. J. 1995 (Tottenham H, Middlesbrough, Everton, Liverpool)	23
Barnes, H. L. 2021 (Leicester C)	1
Barnes, J. 1983 (Watford, Liverpool)	79
Barnes, P. S. 1978 (Manchester C, WBA, Leeds U)	22
Barnet, H. H. 1882 (Royal Engineers)	1
Barrass, M. W. 1952 (Bolton W)	3
Barrett, A. F. 1930 (Fulham)	1
Barrett, E. D. 1991 (Oldham Ath, Aston Villa)	3
Barrett, J. W. 1929 (West Ham U)	1
Barry, G. 2000 (Aston Villa, Manchester C)	53
Barry, L. 1928 (Leicester C)	5
Barson, F. 1920 (Aston Villa)	1
Barton, J. 1890 (Blackburn R)	1
Barton, J. A. 2007 (Manchester C)	1
Barton, P. H. 1921 (Birmingham)	7
Barton, W. D. 1995 (Wimbledon, Newcastle U)	3
Bassett, W. I. 1888 (WBA)	16
Bastard, S. R. 1880 (Upton Park)	1
Bastin, C. S. 1932 (Arsenal)	21
Batty, D. 1991 (Leeds U, Blackburn R, Newcastle U, Leeds U)	42
Baugh, R. 1886 (Stafford Road, Wolverhampton W)	2
Bayliss, A. E. J. M. 1891 (WBA)	1
Baynham, R. L. 1956 (Luton T)	3
Beardsley, P. A. 1986 (Newcastle U, Liverpool, Newcastle U)	59
Beasant, D. J. 1990 (Chelsea)	2
Beasley, A. 1939 (Huddersfield T)	1

Clayton, R. 1956 (Blackburn R)	35
Clegg, J. C. 1872 (Sheffield Wed)	1
Clegg, W. E. 1873 (Sheffield Wed, Sheffield Alb)	2
Clemence, R. N. 1973 (Liverpool, Tottenham H)	61
Clement, D. T. 1976 (QPR)	5
Cleverley, T. W. 2013 (Manchester U)	13
Clough, B. H. 1960 (Middlesbrough)	2
Clough, N. H. 1989 (Nottingham F)	14
Clyne, N. E. 2015 (Southampton, Liverpool)	14
Coady, C. D. 2021 (Wolverhampton W)	10
Coates, R. 1970 (Burnley, Tottenham H)	4
Cobbold, W. N. 1883 (Cambridge University, Old Carthusians)	9
Cock, J. G. 1920 (Huddersfield T, Chelsea)	2
Cockburn, H. 1947 (Manchester U)	13
Cohen, G. R. 1964 (Fulham)	37
Colclough, H. 1914 (Crystal Palace)	1
Cole, A. 2001 (Arsenal, Chelsea)	107
Cole, A. A. 1995 (Manchester U)	15
Cole, C. 2009 (West Ham U)	7
Cole, J. J. 2001 (West Ham U, Chelsea)	56
Coleman, E. H. 1921 (Dulwich Hamlet)	1
Coleman, J. 1907 (Woolwich Arsenal)	1
Collymore, S. V. 1995 (Nottingham F, Aston Villa)	3
Colwill, L. L. S. 2024 (Chelsea)	**5**
Common, A. 1904 (Sheffield U, Middlesbrough)	3
Compton, L. H. 1951 (Arsenal)	2
Conlin, J. 1906 (Bradford C)	1
Connelly, J. M. 1960 (Burnley, Manchester U)	20
Cook, L. J. 2018 (Bournemouth)	1
Cook, T. E. R. 1925 (Brighton)	1
Cooper, C. T. 1995 (Nottingham F)	2
Cooper, N. C. 1893 (Cambridge University)	1
Cooper, T. 1928 (Derby Co)	15
Cooper, T. 1969 (Leeds U)	20
Coppell, S. J. 1978 (Manchester U)	42
Copping, W. 1933 (Leeds U, Arsenal, Leeds U)	20
Corbett, B. O. 1901 (Corinthians)	1
Corbett, R. 1903 (Old Malvernians)	1
Corbett, W. S. 1908 (Birmingham)	3
Cork, J. F. P. 2018 (Burnley)	1
Corrigan, J. T. 1976 (Manchester C)	9
Cottee, A. R. 1987 (West Ham U, Everton)	7
Cotterill, G. H. 1891 (Cambridge University, Old Brightonians)	4
Cottle, J. R. 1909 (Bristol C)	1
Cowan, S. 1926 (Manchester C)	3
Cowans, G. S. 1983 (Aston Villa, Bari, Aston Villa)	10
Cowell, A. 1910 (Blackburn R)	1
Cox, J. 1901 (Liverpool)	3
Cox, J. D. 1892 (Derby Co)	1
Crabtree, J. W. 1894 (Burnley, Aston Villa)	14
Crawford, J. F. 1931 (Chelsea)	1
Crawford, R. 1962 (Ipswich T)	2
Crawshaw, T. H. 1895 (Sheffield Wed)	10
Crayston, W. J. 1936 (Arsenal)	8
Creek, F. N. S. 1923 (Corinthians)	1
Cresswell, A. W. 2017 (West Ham U)	3
Cresswell, W. 1921 (South Shields, Sunderland, Everton)	7
Crompton, R. 1902 (Blackburn R)	41
Crooks, S. D. 1930 (Derby Co)	26
Crouch, P. J. 2005 (Southampton, Liverpool, Portsmouth, Tottenham H)	42
Crowe, C. 1963 (Wolverhampton W)	1
Cuggy, F. 1913 (Sunderland)	2
Cullis, S. 1938 (Wolverhampton W)	12
Cunliffe, A. 1933 (Blackburn R)	2
Cunliffe, D. 1900 (Portsmouth)	1
Cunliffe, J. N. 1936 (Everton)	1
Cunningham, L. 1979 (WBA, Real Madrid)	6
Curle, K. 1992 (Manchester C)	3
Currey, E. S. 1890 (Oxford University)	2
Currie, A. W. 1972 (Sheffield U, Leeds U)	17
Cursham, A. W. 1876 (Notts Co)	6
Cursham, H. A. 1880 (Notts Co)	8
Daft, H. B. 1889 (Notts Co)	5
Daley, A. M. 1992 (Aston Villa)	7
Danks, T. 1885 (Nottingham F)	1
Davenport, P. 1985 (Nottingham F)	1
Davenport, J. K. 1885 (Bolton W)	2
Davies, K. C. 2011 (Bolton W)	1
Davis, G. 1904 (Derby Co)	2
Davis, H. 1903 (Sheffield Wed)	3

Davison, J. E. 1922 (Sheffield Wed)	1
Dawson, J. 1922 (Burnley)	2
Dawson, M. R. 2011 (Tottenham H)	4
Day, S. H. 1906 (Old Malvernians)	3
Dean, W. R. 1927 (Everton)	16
Deane, B. C. 1991 (Sheffield U)	3
Deeley, N. V. 1959 (Wolverhampton W)	2
Defoe, J. C. 2004 (Tottenham H, Portsmouth, Tottenham H, Sunderland)	57
Delph, F. 2015 (Aston Villa, Manchester C)	20
Devey, J. H. G. 1892 (Aston Villa)	2
Devonshire, A. 1980 (West Ham U)	8
Dewhurst, F. 1886 (Preston NE)	9
Dewhurst, G. P. 1895 (Liverpool Ramblers)	1
Dickinson, J. W. 1949 (Portsmouth)	48
Dier, E. J. E. 2016 (Tottenham H)	49
Dimmock, J. H. 1921 (Tottenham H)	3
Ditchburn, E. G. 1949 (Tottenham H)	6
Dix, R. W. 1939 (Derby Co)	1
Dixon, J. A. 1885 (Notts Co)	1
Dixon, K. M. 1985 (Chelsea)	8
Dixon, L. M. 1990 (Arsenal)	22
Dobson, A. T. C. 1882 (Notts Co)	4
Dobson, C. F. 1886 (Notts Co)	1
Dobson, J. M. 1974 (Burnley, Everton)	5
Doggart, A. G. 1924 (Corinthians)	1
Dorigo, A. R. 1990 (Chelsea, Leeds U)	15
Dorrell, A. R. 1925 (Aston Villa)	4
Douglas, B. 1958 (Blackburn R)	36
Downing, S. 2005 (Middlesbrough, Aston Villa, Liverpool, West Ham U)	35
Downs, R. W. 1921 (Everton)	1
Doyle, M. 1976 (Manchester C)	5
Drake, E. J. 1935 (Arsenal)	5
Drinkwater, D. N. 2016 (Leicester C)	3
Dublin, D. 1998 (Coventry C, Aston Villa)	4
Ducat, A. 1910 (Woolwich Arsenal, Aston Villa)	6
Dunk, L. C. 2019 (Brighton & HA)	6
Dunn, A. T. B. 1883 (Cambridge University, Old Etonians)	4
Dunn, D. J. I. 2003 (Blackburn R)	1
Duxbury, M. 1984 (Manchester U)	10
Dyer, K. C. 2000 (Newcastle U, West Ham U)	33
Earle, S. G. J. 1924 (Clapton, West Ham U)	2
Eastham, G. 1963 (Arsenal)	19
Eastham, G. R. 1935 (Bolton W)	1
Eckersley, W. 1950 (Blackburn R)	17
Edwards, D. 1955 (Manchester U)	18
Edwards, J. H. 1874 (Shropshire Wanderers)	1
Edwards, W. 1926 (Leeds U)	16
Ehiogu, U. 1996 (Aston Villa, Middlesbrough)	4
Ellerington, W. 1949 (Southampton)	2
Elliott, G. W. 1913 (Middlesbrough)	3
Elliott, W. H. 1952 (Burnley)	5
Evans, R. E. 1911 (Sheffield U)	4
Ewer, F. H. 1924 (Casuals)	2
Eze, E. O. 2023 (Crystal Palace)	**12**
Fairclough, P. 1878 (Old Foresters)	1
Fairhurst, D. 1934 (Newcastle U)	1
Fantham, J. 1962 (Sheffield Wed)	1
Fashanu, J. 1989 (Wimbledon)	2
Felton, W. 1925 (Sheffield Wed)	1
Fenton, M. 1938 (Middlesbrough)	1
Fenwick, T. W. 1984 (QPR, Tottenham H)	20
Ferdinand, L. 1993 (QPR, Newcastle U, Tottenham H)	17
Ferdinand, R. G. 1998 (West Ham U, Leeds U, Manchester U)	81
Field, E. 1876 (Clapham R)	2
Finney, T. 1947 (Preston NE)	76
Flanagan, J. P. 2014 (Liverpool)	1
Fleming, H. J. 1909 (Swindon T)	11
Fletcher, A. 1889 (Wolverhampton W)	2
Flowers, R. 1955 (Wolverhampton W)	49
Flowers, T. D. 1993 (Southampton, Blackburn R)	11
Foden, P. W. 2021 (Manchester C)	**45**
Forman, Frank 1898 (Nottingham F)	9
Forman, F. R. 1899 (Nottingham F)	3
Forrest, J. H. 1884 (Blackburn R)	11
Forster, F. G. 2013 (Celtic, Southampton)	6
Fort, J. 1921 (Millwall)	1
Foster, B. 2007 (Manchester U, Birmingham C, WBA)	8
Foster, R. E. 1900 (Oxford University, Corinthians)	5

Foster, S. 1982 (Brighton & HA) 3
Foulke, W. J. 1897 (Sheffield U) 1
Foulkes, W. A. 1955 (Manchester U) 1
Fowler, R. B. 1996 (Liverpool, Leeds U) 26
Fox, F. S. 1925 (Millwall) 1
Francis, G. C. J. 1975 (QPR) 12
Francis, T. 1977 (Birmingham C, Nottingham F,
   Manchester C, Sampdoria) 52
Franklin, C. F. 1947 (Stoke C) 27
Freeman, B. C. 1909 (Everton, Burnley) 5
Froggatt, J. 1950 (Portsmouth) 13
Froggatt, R. 1953 (Sheffield Wed) 4
Fry, C. B. 1901 (Corinthians) 1
Furness, W. I. 1933 (Leeds U) 1

Gallagher, C. J. 2022 (Chelsea) **22**
Galley, T. 1937 (Wolverhampton W) 2
Gardner, A. 2004 (Tottenham H) 1
Gardner, T. 1934 (Aston Villa) 2
Garfield, B. 1898 (WBA) 1
Garraty, W. 1903 (Aston Villa) 1
Garrett, T. 1952 (Blackpool) 3
Gascoigne, P. J. 1989 (Tottenham H, Lazio, Rangers,
   Middlesbrough) 57
Gates, E. 1981 (Ipswich T) 2
Gay, L. H. 1893 (Cambridge University,
   Old Brightonians) 3
Geary, F. 1890 (Everton) 2
Geaves, R. L. 1875 (Clapham R) 1
Gee, C. W. 1932 (Everton) 3
Geldard, A. 1933 (Everton) 4
George, C. 1977 (Derby Co) 1
George, W. 1902 (Aston Villa) 3
Gerrard, S. G. 2000 (Liverpool) 114
Gibbins, W. V. T. 1924 (Clapton) 2
Gibbs, K. J. R. 2011 (Arsenal) 10
Gibbs-White, M. A. 2025 (Nottingham F) **4**
Gidman, J. 1977 (Aston Villa) 1
Gillard, I. T. 1975 (QPR) 3
Gilliat, W. E. 1893 (Old Carthusians) 1
Godfrey, B. M. 2021 (Everton) 2
Goddard, P. 1982 (West Ham U) 1
Gomes, A. A. A. de A. (Lille) **4**
Gomez, J. D. 2018 (Liverpool) 15
Goodall, F. R. 1926 (Huddersfield T) 25
Goodall, J. 1888 (Preston NE, Derby Co) 14
Goodhart, H. C. 1883 (Old Etonians) 3
Goodwyn, A. G. 1873 (Royal Engineers) 1
Goodyer, A. C. 1879 (Nottingham F) 1
Gordon, A. M. 2024 (Newcastle U) **12**
Gosling, R. C. 1892 (Old Etonians) 5
Gosnell, A. A. 1906 (Newcastle U) 1
Gough, H. C. 1921 (Sheffield U) 1
Goulden, L. A. 1937 (West Ham U) 14
Graham, L. 1925 (Millwall) 2
Graham, T. 1931 (Nottingham F) 2
Grainger, C. 1956 (Sheffield U, Sunderland) 7
Gray, A. A. 1992 (Crystal Palace) 1
Gray, M. 1999 (Sunderland) 3
Grealish, J. P. 2021 (Aston Villa, Manchester C) **39**
Greaves, J. 1959 (Chelsea, Tottenham H) 57
Green, F. T. 1876 (Wanderers) 1
Green, G. H. 1925 (Sheffield U) 8
Green, R. P. 2005 (Norwich C, West Ham U) 12
Greenhalgh, E. H. 1872 (Notts Co) 2
Greenhoff, B. 1976 (Manchester U, Leeds U) 18
Greenwood, D. H. 1882 (Blackburn R) 2
Greenwood, M. W. J. 2021 (Manchester U) 1
Gregory, J. 1983 (QPR) 6
Grimsdell, A. 1920 (Tottenham H) 6
Grosvenor, A. T. 1934 (Birmingham) 3
Guehi, A. K. M.-I. 2022 (Crystal Palace) **23**
Gunn, W. 1884 (Notts Co) 2
Guppy, S. 2000 (Leicester C) 1
Gurney, R. 1935 (Sunderland) 1

Hacking, J. 1929 (Oldham Ath) 3
Hadley, H. 1903 (WBA) 1
Hagan, J. 1949 (Sheffield U) 1
Haines, J. T. W. 1949 (WBA) 1
Hall, A. E. 1910 (Aston Villa) 1
Hall, G. W. 1934 (Tottenham H) 10
Hall, J. 1956 (Birmingham C) 17
Hall, L. K. 2025 (Newcastle U) **2**

Halse, H. J. 1909 (Manchester U) 1
Hammond, H. E. D. 1889 (Oxford University) 1
Hampson, J. 1931 (Blackpool) 3
Hampton, H. 1913 (Aston Villa) 4
Hancocks, J. 1949 (Wolverhampton W) 3
Hapgood, E. 1933 (Arsenal) 30
Hardinge, H. T. W. 1910 (Sheffield U) 1
Hardman, H. P. 1905 (Everton) 4
Hardwick, G. F. M. 1947 (Middlesbrough) 13
Hardy, H. 1925 (Stockport Co) 1
Hardy, S. 1907 (Liverpool, Aston Villa) 21
Harford, M. G. 1988 (Luton T) 2
Hargreaves, F. W. 1880 (Blackburn R) 3
Hargreaves, J. 1881 (Blackburn R) 2
Hargreaves, O. 2002 (Bayern Munich, Manchester U) 42
Harper, E. C. 1926 (Blackburn R) 1
Harris, G. 1966 (Burnley) 1
Harris, P. P. 1950 (Portsmouth) 2
Harris, S. S. 1904 (Cambridge University,
   Old Westminsters) 6
Harrison, A. H. 1893 (Old Westminsters) 2
Harrison, G. 1921 (Everton) 2
Harrow, J. H. 1923 (Chelsea) 2
Hart, C. J. J. 2008 (Manchester C) 75
Hart, E. 1929 (Leeds U) 8
Hartley, F. 1923 (Oxford C) 1
Harvey, A. 1881 (Wednesbury Strollers) 1
Harvey, J. C. 1971 (Everton) 1
Harwood-Bellis, T. J. 2025 (Southampton) **1**
Hassall, H. W. 1951 (Huddersfield T, Bolton W) 5
Hateley, M. 1984 (Portsmouth, AC Milan, Monaco,
   Rangers) 32
Hawkes, R. M. 1907 (Luton T) 5
Haworth, G. 1887 (Accrington) 5
Hawtrey, J. P. 1881 (Old Etonians) 2
Haygarth, E. B. 1875 (Swifts) 1
Haynes, J. N. 1955 (Fulham) 56
Healless, H. 1925 (Blackburn R) 2
Heaton, T. 2016 (Burnley) 3
Hector, K. J. 1974 (Derby Co) 2
Hedley, G. A. 1901 (Sheffield U) 1
Hegan, K. E. 1923 (Corinthians) 4
Hellawell, M. S. 1963 (Birmingham C) 2
Henderson, D. B. 2021 (Manchester U, Crystal Palace) **3**
Henderson, J. B. 2011 (Sunderland, Liverpool,
   Al Ettifaq, Ajax) **84**
Hendrie, L. A. 1999 (Aston Villa) 1
Henfrey, A. G. 1891 (Cambridge University,
   Corinthians) 5
Henry, R. P. 1963 (Tottenham H) 1
Heron, F. 1876 (Wanderers) 1
Heron, G. H. H. 1873 (Uxbridge, Wanderers) 5
Heskey, E. W. I. 1999 (Leicester C, Liverpool,
   Birmingham C, Wigan Ath, Aston Villa) 62
Hibbert, W. 1910 (Bury) 1
Hibbs, H. E. 1930 (Birmingham) 25
Hill, F. 1963 (Bolton W) 2
Hill, G. A. 1976 (Manchester U) 6
Hill, J. H. 1925 (Burnley, Newcastle U) 11
Hill, R. 1983 (Luton T) 3
Hill, R. H. 1926 (Millwall) 1
Hillman, J. 1899 (Burnley) 1
Hills, A. F. 1879 (Old Harrovians) 1
Hilsdon, G. R. 1907 (Chelsea) 8
Hinchcliffe, A. G. 1997 (Everton, Sheffield Wed) 7
Hine, E. W. 1929 (Leicester C) 6
Hinton, A. T. 1963 (Wolverhampton W, Nottingham F) 3
Hirst, D. E. 1991 (Sheffield Wed) 3
Hitchens, G. A. 1961 (Aston Villa, Internazionale) 7
Hobbis, H. H. F. 1936 (Charlton Ath) 2
Hoddle, G. 1980 (Tottenham H, Monaco) 53
Hodge, S. B. 1986 (Aston Villa, Tottenham H,
   Nottingham F) 24
Hodgetts, D. 1888 (Aston Villa) 6
Hodgkinson, A. 1957 (Sheffield U) 5
Hodgson, G. 1931 (Liverpool) 3
Hodkinson, J. 1913 (Blackburn R) 3
Hogg, W. 1902 (Sunderland) 3
Holdcroft, G. H. 1937 (Preston NE) 2
Holden, A. D. 1959 (Bolton W) 5
Holden, G. H. 1881 (Wednesbury OA) 4
Holden-White, C. 1888 (Corinthians) 2
Holford, T. 1903 (Stoke) 1
Holley, G. H. 1909 (Sunderland) 10

Mainoo, K. B. 2024 (Manchester U) 10
Maitland Niles, A. C. 2021 (Arsenal) 5
Makepeace, H. 1906 (Everton) 4
Male, C. G. 1935 (Arsenal) 19
Mannion, W. J. 1947 (Middlesbrough) 26
Mariner, P. 1977 (Ipswich T, Arsenal) 35
Marsden, J. T. 1891 (Darwen) 1
Marsden, W. 1930 (Sheffield Wed) 3
Marsh, R. W. 1972 (QPR, Manchester C) 9
Marshall, T. 1880 (Darwen) 2
Martin, A. 1981 (West Ham U) 17
Martin, H. 1914 (Sunderland) 1
Martyn, A. N. 1992 (Crystal Palace, Leeds U) 23
Marwood, B. 1989 (Arsenal) 1
Maskrey, H. M. 1908 (Derby Co) 1
Mason, C. 1887 (Wolverhampton W) 3
Mason, R. G. 2015 (Tottenham H) 1
Matthews, R. D. 1956 (Coventry C) 5
Matthews, S. 1935 (Stoke C, Blackpool) 54
Matthews, V. 1928 (Sheffield U) 2
Maynard, W. J. 1872 (1st Surrey Rifles) 2
McCall, J. 1913 (Preston NE) 5
McCann, G. P. 2001 (Sunderland) 1
McCarthy, A. S. 2019 (Southampton) 1
McDermott, T. 1978 (Liverpool) 25
McDonald, C. A. 1958 (Burnley) 8
Macdonald, M. 1972 (Newcastle U) 14
McFarland, R. L. 1971 (Derby Co) 28
McGarry, W. H. 1954 (Huddersfield T) 4
McGuinness, W. 1959 (Manchester U) 2
McInroy, A. 1927 (Sunderland) 1
McMahon, S. 1988 (Liverpool) 17
McManaman, S. 1995 (Liverpool, Real Madrid) 37
McNab, R. 1969 (Arsenal) 4
McNeal, R. 1914 (WBA) 2
McNeil, M. 1961 (Middlesbrough) 9
Meadows, J. 1955 (Manchester C) 1
Medley, L. D. 1951 (Tottenham H) 6
Meehan, T. 1924 (Chelsea) 2
Melia, J. 1963 (Liverpool) 2
Mercer, D. W. 1923 (Sheffield U) 2
Mercer, J. 1939 (Everton) 5
Merrick, G. H. 1952 (Birmingham C) 23
Merson, P. C. 1992 (Arsenal, Middlesbrough,
  Aston Villa) 21
Metcalfe, V. 1951 (Huddersfield T) 2
Mew, J. W. 1921 (Manchester U) 1
Middleditch, B. 1897 (Corinthians) 1
Milburn, J. E. T. 1949 (Newcastle U) 13
Miller, B. G. 1961 (Burnley) 1
Miller, H. S. 1923 (Charlton Ath) 1
Mills, D. J. 2001 (Leeds U) 19
Mills, G. R. 1938 (Chelsea) 3
Mills, M. D. 1973 (Ipswich T) 42
Milne, G. 1963 (Liverpool) 14
Milner, J. P. 2010 (Aston Villa, Manchester C,
  Liverpool) 61
Milton, C. A. 1952 (Arsenal) 1
Milward, A. 1891 (Everton) 4
Mings, T. D. 2020 (Aston Villa) 18
Mitchell, C. 1880 (Upton Park) 5
Mitchell, J. F. 1925 (Manchester C) 1
Mitchell, T. K. 2022 (Crystal Palace) 2
Moffat, H. 1913 (Oldham Ath) 1
Molyneux, G. 1902 (Southampton) 4
Moon, W. R. 1888 (Old Westminsters) 7
Moore, H. T. 1883 (Notts Co) 2
Moore, J. 1923 (Derby Co) 1
Moore, R. F. 1962 (West Ham U) 108
Moore, W. G. B. 1923 (West Ham U) 1
Mordue, J. 1912 (Sunderland) 2
Morice, C. J. 1872 (Barnes) 1
Morley, A. 1982 (Aston Villa) 6
Morley, H. 1910 (Notts Co) 1
Morren, T. 1898 (Sheffield U) 1
Morris, F. 1920 (WBA) 2
Morris, J. 1949 (Derby Co) 3
Morris, W. W. 1939 (Wolverhampton W) 3
Morse, H. 1879 (Notts Co) 1
Mort, T. 1924 (Aston Villa) 3
Morten, A. 1873 (Crystal Palace) 1
Mortensen, S. H. 1947 (Blackpool) 25
Morton, J. R. 1938 (West Ham U) 1

Mosforth, W. 1877 (Sheffield Wed, Sheffield Alb,
  Sheffield W) 9
Moss, F. 1922 (Aston Villa) 5
Moss, F. 1934 (Arsenal) 4
Mosscrop, E. 1914 (Burnley) 2
Mount, M. T. 2020 (Chelsea) 36
Mozley, B. 1950 (Derby Co) 3
Mullen, J. 1947 (Wolverhampton W) 12
Mullery, A. P. 1965 (Tottenham H) 35
Murphy, D. B. 2002 (Liverpool) 9

Neal, P. G. 1976 (Liverpool) 50
Needham, E. 1894 (Sheffield U) 16
Neville, G. A. 1995 (Manchester U) 85
Neville, P. J. 1996 (Manchester U, Everton) 59
Newton, K. R. 1966 (Blackburn R, Everton) 27
Nicholls, J. 1954 (WBA) 2
Nicholson, W. E. 1951 (Tottenham H) 1
Nish, D. J. 1973 (Derby Co) 5
Nketiah, E. K. 2024 (Arsenal) 1
Norman, M. 1962 (Tottenham H) 23
Nugent, D. J. 2007 (Preston NE) 1
Nuttall, H. 1928 (Bolton W) 3

Oakley, W. J. 1895 (Oxford University, Corinthians) 16
O'Dowd, J. P. 1932 (Chelsea) 3
O'Grady, M. 1963 (Huddersfield T, Leeds U) 2
Ogilvie, R. A. M. M. 1874 (Clapham R) 1
Oliver, L. F. 1929 (Fulham) 1
Olney, B. A. 1928 (Aston Villa) 2
Osborne, F. R. 1923 (Fulham, Tottenham H) 4
Osborne, R. 1928 (Leicester C) 1
Osgood, P. L. 1970 (Chelsea) 4
Osman, L. 2013 (Everton) 2
Osman, R. 1980 (Ipswich T) 11
Ottaway, C. J. 1872 (Oxford University) 2
Owen, J. R. B. 1874 (Sheffield) 1
Owen, M. J. 1998 (Liverpool, Real Madrid,
  Newcastle U) 89
Owen, S. W. 1954 (Luton T) 3
Oxlade-Chamberlain, A. M. D. 2012 (Arsenal,
  Liverpool) 35

Page, L. A. 1927 (Burnley) 7
Paine, T. L. 1963 (Southampton) 19
Pallister, G. A. 1988 (Middlesbrough, Manchester U) 22
Palmer, C. J. 2024 (Chelsea) 12
Palmer, C. L. 1992 (Sheffield Wed) 18
Pantling, H. H. 1924 (Sheffield U) 1
Paravicini, P. J. de 1883 (Cambridge University) 3
Parker, P. A. 1989 (QPR, Manchester U) 19
Parker, S. M. 2004 (Charlton Ath, Chelsea,
  Newcastle U, West Ham U, Tottenham H) 18
Parker, T. R. 1925 (Southampton) 1
Parkes, P. B. 1974 (QPR) 1
Parkinson, J. 1910 (Liverpool) 2
Parlour, R. 1999 (Arsenal) 10
Parr, P. C. 1882 (Oxford University) 1
Parry, E. H. 1879 (Old Carthusians) 3
Parry, R. A. 1960 (Bolton W) 2
Patchitt, B. C. A. 1923 (Corinthians) 2
Pawson, F. W. 1883 (Cambridge University, Swifts) 2
Payne, J. 1937 (Luton T) 1
Peacock, A. 1962 (Middlesbrough, Leeds U) 6
Peacock, J. 1929 (Middlesbrough) 3
Pearce, S. 1987 (Nottingham F, West Ham U) 78
Pearson, H. F. 1932 (WBA) 1
Pearson, J. H. 1892 (Crewe Alex) 1
Pearson, J. S. 1976 (Manchester U) 15
Pearson, S. C. 1948 (Manchester U) 8
Pease, W. H. 1927 (Middlesbrough) 1
Pegg, D. 1957 (Manchester U) 1
Pejic, M. 1974 (Stoke C) 4
Pelly, F. R. 1893 (Old Foresters) 3
Pennington, J. 1907 (WBA) 25
Pentland, F. B. 1909 (Middlesbrough) 5
Perry, C. 1890 (WBA) 3
Perry, T. 1898 (WBA) 1
Perry, W. 1956 (Blackpool) 3
Perryman, S. 1982 (Tottenham H) 1
Peters, M. 1966 (West Ham U, Tottenham H) 67
Phelan, M. C. 1990 (Manchester U) 1
Phillips, K. 1999 (Sunderland) 8
Phillips, K. M. 2021 (Leeds U, Manchester C) 31

Phillips, L. H. 1952 (Portsmouth)	3
Pickering, F. 1964 (Everton)	3
Pickering, J. 1933 (Sheffield U)	1
Pickering, N. 1983 (Sunderland)	1
Pickford, J. L. 2018 (Everton)	**76**
Pike, T. M. 1886 (Cambridge University)	1
Pilkington, B. 1955 (Burnley)	1
Plant, J. 1900 (Bury)	1
Platt, D. 1990 (Aston Villa, Bari, Juventus, Sampdoria, Arsenal)	62
Plum, S. L. 1923 (Charlton Ath)	1
Pointer, R. 1962 (Burnley)	3
Pope, N. D. 2018 (Burnley, Newcastle U)	10
Porteous, T. S. 1891 (Sunderland)	1
Powell, C. G. 2001 (Charlton Ath)	5
Priest, A. E. 1900 (Sheffield U)	1
Prinsep, J. F. M. 1879 (Clapham R)	1
Puddefoot, S. C. 1926 (Blackburn R)	2
Pye, J. 1950 (Wolverhampton W)	1
Pym, R. H. 1925 (Bolton W)	3
Quantrill, A. 1920 (Derby Co)	4
Quixall, A. 1954 (Sheffield Wed)	5
Radford, J. 1969 (Arsenal)	2
Raikes, G. B. 1895 (Oxford University)	4
Ramsdale, A. C. 2022 (Arsenal)	5
Ramsey, A. E. 1949 (Southampton, Tottenham H)	32
Rashford, M. 2016 (Manchester U)	**62**
Rawlings, A. 1921 (Preston NE)	1
Rawlings, W. E. 1922 (Southampton)	2
Rawlinson, J. F. P. 1882 (Cambridge University)	1
Rawson, H. E. 1875 (Royal Engineers)	1
Rawson, W. S. 1875 (Oxford University)	2
Read, A. 1921 (Tufnell Park)	1
Reader, J. 1894 (WBA)	1
Reaney, P. 1969 (Leeds U)	3
Redknapp, J. F. 1996 (Liverpool)	17
Redmond, N. D. J. 2017 (Southampton)	1
Reeves, K. P. 1980 (Norwich C, Manchester C)	2
Regis, C. 1982 (WBA, Coventry C)	5
Reid, P. 1985 (Everton)	13
Revie, D. G. 1955 (Manchester C)	6
Reynolds, J. 1892 (WBA, Aston Villa)	8
Rice, D. 2019 (West Ham U, Arsenal)	**66**
Richards, C. H. 1898 (Nottingham F)	1
Richards, G. H. 1909 (Derby Co)	1
Richards, J. P. 1973 (Wolverhampton W)	1
Richards, M. 2007 (Manchester C)	13
Richardson, J. R. 1933 (Newcastle U)	2
Richardson, K. 1994 (Aston Villa)	1
Richardson, K. E. 2005 (Manchester U)	8
Richardson, W. G. 1935 (WBA)	1
Rickaby, S. 1954 (WBA)	1
Ricketts, M. B. 2002 (Bolton W)	1
Rigby, A. 1927 (Blackburn R)	5
Rimmer, E. J. 1930 (Sheffield Wed)	4
Rimmer, J. J. 1976 (Arsenal)	1
Ripley, S. E. 1994 (Blackburn R)	2
Rix, G. 1981 (Arsenal)	17
Robb, G. 1954 (Tottenham H)	1
Roberts, C. 1905 (Manchester U)	3
Roberts, F. 1925 (Manchester C)	4
Roberts, G. 1983 (Tottenham H)	6
Roberts, H. 1931 (Arsenal)	1
Roberts, H. 1931 (Millwall)	1
Roberts, R. 1887 (WBA)	3
Roberts, W. T. 1924 (Preston NE)	2
Robinson, J. 1937 (Sheffield Wed)	4
Robinson, J. W. 1897 (Derby Co, New Brighton Tower, Southampton)	11
Robinson, P. W. 2003 (Leeds U, Tottenham H, Blackburn R)	41
Robson, B. 1980 (WBA, Manchester U)	90
Robson, R. 1958 (WBA)	20
Rocastle, D. 1989 (Arsenal)	14
Rodgers, M. E. 2025 (Aston Villa)	**6**
Rodriguez, J. E. 2013 (Southampton)	1
Rodwell, J. 2012 (Everton)	3
Rooney, W. M. 2003 (Everton, Manchester U, D.C. United)	120
Rose, D. L. 2016 (Tottenham H)	29
Rose, W. C. 1884 (Swifts, Preston NE, Wolverhampton W)	5

Rostron, T. 1881 (Darwen)	2
Rowe, A. 1934 (Tottenham H)	1
Rowley, J. F. 1949 (Manchester U)	6
Rowley, W. 1889 (Stoke)	2
Royle, J. 1971 (Everton, Manchester C)	6
Ruddlesdin, H. 1904 (Sheffield Wed)	3
Ruddock, N. 1995 (Liverpool)	1
Ruddy, J. T. G. 2013 (Norwich C)	1
Ruffell, J. W. 1926 (West Ham U)	6
Russell, B. B. 1883 (Royal Engineers)	1
Rutherford, J. 1904 (Newcastle U)	11
Sadler, D. 1968 (Manchester U)	4
Sagar, C. 1900 (Bury)	2
Sagar, E. 1936 (Everton)	4
Saka, B. A. T. M. 2021 (Arsenal)	**44**
Salako, J. A. 1991 (Crystal Palace)	5
Sancho, J. M. 2019 (Borussia Dortmund, Manchester U)	23
Sandford, E. A. 1933 (WBA)	1
Sandilands, R. R. 1892 (Old Westminsters)	5
Sands, J. 1880 (Nottingham F)	1
Sansom, K. G. 1979 (Crystal Palace, Arsenal)	86
Saunders, F. E. 1888 (Swifts)	1
Savage, A. H. 1876 (Crystal Palace)	1
Sayer, J. 1887 (Stoke)	1
Scales, J. R. 1995 (Liverpool)	3
Scattergood, E. 1913 (Derby Co)	1
Schofield, J. 1892 (Stoke)	3
Scholes, P. 1997 (Manchester U)	66
Scott, L. 1947 (Arsenal)	17
Scott, W. R. 1937 (Brentford)	1
Seaman, D. A. 1989 (QPR, Arsenal)	75
Seddon, J. 1923 (Bolton W)	6
Seed, J. M. 1921 (Tottenham H)	5
Settle, J. 1899 (Bury, Everton)	6
Sewell, J. 1952 (Sheffield Wed)	6
Sewell, W. R. 1924 (Blackburn R)	1
Shackleton, L. F. 1949 (Sunderland)	5
Sharp, J. 1903 (Everton)	2
Sharpe, L. S. 1991 (Manchester U)	8
Shaw, G. E. 1932 (WBA)	1
Shaw, G. L. 1959 (Sheffield U)	5
Shaw, L. P. H. 2014 (Southampton, Manchester U)	34
Shawcross, R. J. 2013 (Stoke C)	1
Shea, D. 1914 (Blackburn R)	2
Shearer, A. 1992 (Southampton, Blackburn R, Newcastle U)	63
Shellito, K. J. 1963 (Chelsea)	1
Shelton A. 1889 (Notts Co)	6
Shelton, C. 1888 (Notts Rangers)	1
Shelvey, J. 2013 (Liverpool, Swansea C)	6
Shepherd, A. 1906 (Bolton W, Newcastle U)	2
Sheringham, E. P. 1993 (Tottenham H, Manchester U, Tottenham H)	51
Sherwood, T. A. 1999 (Tottenham H)	3
Shilton, P. L. 1971 (Leicester C, Stoke C, Nottingham F, Southampton, Derby Co)	125
Shimwell, E. 1949 (Blackpool)	1
Shorey, N. 2007 (Reading)	2
Shutt, G. 1886 (Stoke)	1
Silcock, J. 1921 (Manchester U)	3
Sillett, R. P. 1955 (Chelsea)	3
Simms, E. 1922 (Luton T)	1
Simpson, J. 1911 (Blackburn R)	8
Sinclair, T. 2002 (West Ham U, Manchester C)	12
Sinton, A. 1992 (QPR, Sheffield Wed)	12
Slater, W. J. 1955 (Wolverhampton W)	12
Smalley, T. 1937 (Wolverhampton W)	1
Smalling, C. L. 2012 (Manchester U)	31
Smart, T. 1921 (Aston Villa)	5
Smith, A. 1891 (Nottingham F)	3
Smith, A. 2001 (Leeds U, Manchester U, Newcastle U)	19
Smith, A. K. 1872 (Oxford University)	1
Smith, A. M. 1989 (Arsenal)	13
Smith, B. 1921 (Tottenham H)	2
Smith, C. E. 1876 (Crystal Palace)	1
Smith, G. O. 1893 (Oxford University, Old Carthusians, Corinthians)	20
Smith, H. 1905 (Reading)	4
Smith, J. 1920 (WBA)	2
Smith, Joe 1913 (Bolton W)	5
Smith, J. C. R. 1939 (Millwall)	2
Smith, J. W. 1932 (Portsmouth)	3

Smith, Leslie 1939 (Brentford)	1
Smith, Lionel 1951 (Arsenal)	6
Smith, R. A. 1961 (Tottenham H)	15
Smith, S. 1895 (Aston Villa)	1
Smith, S. C. 1936 (Leicester C)	1
Smith, T. 1960 (Birmingham C)	2
Smith, T. 1971 (Liverpool)	1
Smith, W. H. 1922 (Huddersfield T)	3
Smith Rowe, E. 2022 (Arsenal)	3
Solanke, D. A. 2018 (Liverpool, Tottenham H)	**3**
Sorby, T. H. 1879 (Thursday Wanderers, Sheffield)	1
Southgate, G. 1996 (Aston Villa, Middlesbrough)	57
Southworth, J. 1889 (Blackburn R)	3
Sparks, F. J. 1879 (Hertfordshire Rangers, Clapham R)	3
Spence, J. W. 1926 (Manchester U)	2
Spence, R. 1936 (Chelsea)	2
Spencer, C. W. 1924 (Newcastle U)	2
Spencer, H. 1897 (Aston Villa)	6
Spiksley, F. 1893 (Sheffield Wed)	7
Spilsbury, B. W. 1885 (Cambridge University)	3
Spink, N. 1983 (Aston Villa)	1
Spouncer, W. A. 1900 (Nottingham F)	1
Springett, R. D. G. 1960 (Sheffield Wed)	33
Sproston, B. 1937 (Leeds U, Tottenham H, Manchester C)	11
Squire, R. T. 1886 (Cambridge University)	3
Stanbrough, M. H. 1895 (Old Carthusians)	1
Staniforth, R. 1954 (Huddersfield T)	8
Starling, R. W. 1933 (Sheffield Wed, Aston Villa)	2
Statham, D. J. 1983 (WBA)	3
Steele, F. C. 1937 (Stoke C)	6
Stein, B. 1984 (Luton T)	1
Stephenson, C. 1924 (Huddersfield T)	1
Stephenson, G. T. 1928 (Derby Co, Sheffield Wed)	3
Stephenson, J. E. 1938 (Leeds U)	2
Stepney, A. C. 1968 (Manchester U)	1
Sterland, M. 1989 (Sheffield Wed)	1
Sterling, R. S. 2013 (Liverpool, Manchester C, Chelsea)	82
Steven, T. M. 1985 (Everton, Rangers, Marseille)	36
Stevens, G. A. 1985 (Tottenham H)	7
Stevens, M. G. 1985 (Everton, Rangers)	46
Stewart, J. 1907 (Sheffield Wed, Newcastle U)	3
Stewart, P. A. 1992 (Tottenham H)	3
Stiles, N. P. 1965 (Manchester U)	28
Stoker, J. 1933 (Birmingham)	3
Stone, S. B. 1996 (Nottingham F)	9
Stones, J. 2014 (Everton, Manchester C)	**83**
Storer, H. 1924 (Derby Co)	2
Storey, P. E. 1971 (Arsenal)	19
Storey-Moore, I. 1970 (Nottingham F)	1
Strange, A. H. 1930 (Sheffield Wed)	20
Stratford, A. H. 1874 (Wanderers)	1
Streten, B. 1950 (Luton T)	1
Sturgess, A. 1911 (Sheffield U)	2
Sturridge, D. A. 2012 (Chelsea, Liverpool)	26
Summerbee, M. G. 1968 (Manchester C)	8
Sunderland, A. 1980 (Arsenal)	1
Sutcliffe, J. W. 1893 (Bolton W, Millwall)	5
Sutton, C. R. 1998 (Blackburn R)	1
Swan, P. 1960 (Sheffield Wed)	19
Swepstone, H. A. 1880 (Pilgrims)	6
Swift, F. V. 1947 (Manchester C)	19
Tait, G. 1881 (Birmingham Excelsior)	1
Talbot, B. 1977 (Ipswich T, Arsenal)	6
Tambling, R. V. 1963 (Chelsea)	3
Tarkowski, J. A. 2018 (Burnley)	2
Tate, J. T. 1931 (Aston Villa)	3
Taylor, E. 1954 (Blackpool)	1
Taylor, E. H. 1923 (Huddersfield T)	8
Taylor, J. G. 1951 (Fulham)	2
Taylor, P. H. 1948 (Liverpool)	3
Taylor, P. J. 1976 (Crystal Palace)	4
Taylor, T. 1953 (Manchester U)	19
Temple, D. W. 1965 (Everton)	1
Terry, J. G. 2003 (Chelsea)	78
Thickett, H. 1899 (Sheffield U)	2
Thomas, D. 1975 (QPR)	8
Thomas, D. 1983 (Coventry C)	2
Thomas, G. R. 1991 (Crystal Palace)	9
Thomas, M. L. 1989 (Arsenal)	2
Thompson, A. 2004 (Celtic)	1
Thompson, P. 1964 (Liverpool)	16
Thompson, P. B. 1976 (Liverpool)	42

Thompson T. 1952 (Aston Villa, Preston NE)	2
Thomson, R. A. 1964 (Wolverhampton W)	8
Thornewell, G. 1923 (Derby Co)	4
Thornley, I. 1907 (Manchester C)	1
Tilson, S. F. 1934 (Manchester C)	4
Titmuss, F. 1922 (Southampton)	2
Todd, C. 1972 (Derby Co)	27
Tomori, O. O. (Fikayo) 2020 (Chelsea, AC Milan)	5
Toney, I. B. E. 2023 (Brentford, Al-Ahli)	**7**
Toone, G. 1892 (Notts Co)	2
Topham, A. G. 1894 (Casuals)	1
Topham, R. 1893 (Wolverhampton W, Casuals)	2
Towers, M. A. 1976 (Sunderland)	3
Townley, W. J. 1889 (Blackburn R)	2
Townrow, J. E. 1925 (Clapton Orient)	2
Townsend, A. D. 2013 (Tottenham H, Newcastle U, Crystal Palace)	13
Tremelling, D. R. 1928 (Birmingham)	1
Tresadern, J. 1923 (West Ham U)	2
Trippier, K. J. 2017 (Tottenham H, Atletico Madrid, Newcastle U)	54
Tueart, D. 1975 (Manchester C)	6
Tunstall, F. E. 1923 (Sheffield U)	7
Turnbull, R. J. 1920 (Bradford)	1
Turner, A. 1900 (Southampton)	2
Turner, H. 1931 (Huddersfield T)	2
Turner, J. A. 1893 (Bolton W, Stoke, Derby Co)	3
Tweedy, G. J. 1937 (Grimsby T)	1
Ufton, D. G. 1954 (Charlton Ath)	1
Underwood, A. 1891 (Stoke C)	2
Unsworth, D. G. 1995 (Everton)	1
Upson, M. J. 2003 (Birmingham C, West Ham U)	21
Urwin, T. 1923 (Middlesbrough, Newcastle U)	4
Utley, G. 1913 (Barnsley)	1
Vardy, J. R. 2015 (Leicester C)	26
Vassell, D. 2002 (Aston Villa)	22
Vaughton, O. H. 1882 (Aston Villa)	5
Veitch, C. C. M. 1906 (Newcastle U)	6
Veitch, J. G. 1894 (Old Westminsters)	1
Venables, T. F. 1965 (Chelsea)	2
Venison, B. 1995 (Newcastle U)	2
Vidal, R. W. S. 1873 (Oxford University)	1
Viljoen, C. 1975 (Ipswich T)	2
Viollet, D. S. 1960 (Manchester U)	2
Von Donop 1873 (Royal Engineers)	2
Wace, H. 1878 (Wanderers)	3
Waddle, C. R. 1985 (Newcastle U, Tottenham H, Marseille)	62
Wadsworth, S. J. 1922 (Huddersfield T)	9
Wainscoat, W. R. 1929 (Leeds U)	1
Waiters, A. K. 1964 (Blackpool)	5
Walcott, T. J. 2006 (Arsenal)	47
Walden, F. I. 1914 (Tottenham H)	2
Walker, D. S. 1989 (Nottingham F, Sampdoria, Sheffield W)	59
Walker, I. M. 1996 (Tottenham H, Leicester C)	4
Walker, K. A. 2012 (Tottenham H, Manchester C)	**96**
Walker, W. H. 1921 (Aston Villa)	18
Walker-Peters, K. L. 2022 (Southampton)	2
Wall, G. 1907 (Manchester U)	7
Wallace, C. W. 1913 (Aston Villa)	3
Wallace, D. L. 1986 (Southampton)	1
Walsh, P. A. 1983 (Luton T)	5
Walters, A. M. 1885 (Cambridge University, Old Carthusians)	9
Walters, K. M. 1991 (Rangers)	1
Walters, P. M. 1885 (Oxford University, Old Carthusians)	13
Walton, N. 1890 (Blackburn R)	1
Ward, J. T. 1885 (Blackburn Olympic)	1
Ward, P. 1980 (Brighton & HA)	1
Ward, T. V. 1948 (Derby Co)	2
Ward-Prowse, J. M. E. 2017 (Southampton)	11
Waring, T. 1931 (Aston Villa)	5
Warner, C. 1878 (Upton Park)	1
Warnock, S. 2008 (Blackburn R, Aston Villa)	2
Warren, B. 1906 (Derby Co, Chelsea)	22
Waterfield, G. S. 1927 (Burnley)	1
Watkins, O. G. A. 2021 (Aston Villa)	**18**
Watson, D. 1984 (Norwich C, Everton)	12

Watson, D. V. 1974 (Sunderland, Manchester C, Werder Bremen, Southampton, Stoke C)	65
Watson, V. M. 1923 (West Ham U)	5
Watson, W. 1913 (Burnley)	3
Watson, W. 1950 (Sunderland)	4
Weaver, S. 1932 (Newcastle U)	3
Webb, G. W. 1911 (West Ham U)	2
Webb, N. J. 1988 (Nottingham F, Manchester U)	26
Webster, M. 1930 (Middlesbrough)	3
Wedlock, W. J. 1907 (Bristol C)	26
Weir, D. 1889 (Bolton W)	2
Welbeck, D. N. T. M. 2011 (Manchester U, Arsenal)	42
Welch, R. de C. 1872 (Wanderers, Harrow Chequers)	2
Weller, K. 1974 (Leicester C)	4
Welsh, D. 1938 (Charlton Ath)	3
West, G. 1969 (Everton)	3
Westwood, R. W. 1935 (Bolton W)	6
Wharton, A. J. 2024 (Crystal Palace)	1
Whateley, O. 1883 (Aston Villa)	2
Wheeler, J. E. 1955 (Bolton W)	1
Wheldon, G. F. 1897 (Aston Villa)	4
White, B. W. 2021 (Brighton & HA, Arsenal)	4
White, D. 1993 (Manchester C)	1
White, T. A. 1933 (Everton)	1
Whitehead, J. 1893 (Accrington, Blackburn R)	2
Whitfeld, H. 1879 (Old Etonians)	1
Whitham, M. 1892 (Sheffield U)	1
Whitworth, S. 1975 (Leicester C)	7
Whymark, T. J. 1978 (Ipswich T)	1
Widdowson, S. W. 1880 (Nottingham F)	1
Wignall, F. 1965 (Nottingham F)	2
Wilcox, J. M. 1996 (Blackburn R, Leeds U)	3
Wilkes, A. 1901 (Aston Villa)	5
Wilkins, R. C. 1976 (Chelsea, Manchester U, AC Milan)	84
Wilkinson, B. 1904 (Sheffield U)	1
Wilkinson, L. R. 1891 (Oxford University)	1
Williams, B. F. 1949 (Wolverhampton W)	24
Williams, O. 1923 (Clapton Orient)	2
Williams, S. 1983 (Southampton)	6
Williams, W. 1897 (WBA)	6
Williamson, E. C. 1923 (Arsenal)	2
Williamson, R. G. 1905 (Middlesbrough)	7
Willingham, C. K. 1937 (Huddersfield T)	12
Willis, A. 1952 (Tottenham H)	1
Wilshaw, D. J. 1954 (Wolverhampton W)	12
Wilshere, J. A. 2011 (Arsenal)	34
Wilson, C. E. G. 2019 (Bournemouth, Newcastle U)	9
Wilson, C. P. 1884 (Hendon)	2
Wilson, C. W. 1879 (Oxford University)	2
Wilson, G. 1921 (Sheffield Wed)	12

Wilson, G. P. 1900 (Corinthians)	2
Wilson, R. 1960 (Huddersfield T, Everton)	63
Wilson, T. 1928 (Huddersfield T)	1
Winckworth, W. N. 1892 (Old Westminsters)	2
Windridge, J. E. 1908 (Chelsea)	8
Wingfield-Stratford, C. V. 1877 (Royal Engineers)	1
Winks, H. B. 2018 (Tottenham H)	10
Winterburn, N. 1990 (Arsenal)	2
Wise, D. F. 1991 (Chelsea)	21
Withe, P. 1981 (Aston Villa)	11
Wollaston, C. H. R. 1874 (Wanderers)	4
Wolstenholme, S. 1904 (Everton, Blackburn R)	3
Wood, H. 1890 (Wolverhampton W)	3
Wood, R. E. 1955 (Manchester U)	3
Woodcock, A. S. 1978 (Nottingham F, Cologne, Arsenal)	42
Woodgate, J. S. 1999 (Leeds U, Newcastle U, Real Madrid, Tottenham H)	8
Woodger, G. 1911 (Oldham Ath)	1
Woodhall, G. 1888 (WBA)	2
Woodley, V. R. 1937 (Chelsea)	19
Woods, C. C. E. 1985 (Norwich C, Rangers, Sheffield Wed)	43
Woodward, V. J. 1903 (Tottenham H, Chelsea)	23
Woosnam, M. 1922 (Manchester C)	1
Worrall, F. 1935 (Portsmouth)	2
Worthington, F. S. 1974 (Leicester C)	8
Wreford-Brown, C. 1889 (Oxford University, Old Carthusians)	4
Wright, E. G. D. 1906 (Cambridge University)	1
Wright, I. E. 1991 (Crystal Palace, Arsenal, West Ham U)	33
Wright, J. D. 1939 (Newcastle U)	1
Wright, M. 1984 (Southampton, Derby Co, Liverpool)	45
Wright, R. I. 2000 (Ipswich T, Arsenal)	2
Wright, T. J. 1968 (Everton)	11
Wright, W. A. 1947 (Wolverhampton W)	105
Wright-Phillips, S. C. 2005 (Manchester C, Chelsea, Manchester C)	36
Wylie, J. G. 1878 (Wanderers)	1
Yates, J. 1889 (Burnley)	1
York, R. E. 1922 (Aston Villa)	2
Young, A. 1933 (Huddersfield T)	9
Young, A. S. 2008 (Aston Villa, Manchester U)	39
Young, G. M. 1965 (Sheffield Wed)	1
Young, L. P. 2005 (Charlton Ath)	7
Zaha, D. W. A. 2013 (Manchester U)	2
Zamora, R. L. 2011 (Fulham)	2

NORTHERN IRELAND

Addis, D. J. 1922 (Cliftonville)	1
Aherne, T. 1947 (Belfast Celtic, Luton T)	4
Alexander, T. E. 1895 (Cliftonville)	1
Allan, C. 1936 (Cliftonville)	1
Allen, J. 1887 (Limavady)	1
Anderson, J. 1925 (Distillery)	1
Anderson, J. 1973 (Manchester U, Swindon T, Peterborough U)	22
Anderson, W. 1898 (Linfield, Cliftonville)	4
Andrews, W. 1908 (Glentoran, Grimsby T)	3
Armstrong, G. J. 1977 (Tottenham H, Watford, Real Mallorca, WBA, Chesterfield)	63
Baird, C. P. 2003 (Southampton, Fulham, Reading, Burnley, WBA, Derby Co)	79
Baird, G. 1896 (Distillery)	3
Baird, H. C. 1939 (Huddersfield T)	1
Balfe, J. 1909 (Shelbourne)	2
Ballard, D. G. 2021 (Arsenal, Sunderland)	**30**
Bambrick, J. 1929 (Linfield, Chelsea)	11
Banks, S. J. 1937 (Cliftonville)	1
Barr, H. H. 1962 (Linfield, Coventry C)	3
Barron, J. H. 1894 (Cliftonville)	7
Barry, J. 1888 (Cliftonville)	3
Barry, J. 1900 (Bohemians)	1
Barton, A. J. 2011 (Preston NE)	1
Baxter, R. A. 1887 (Distillery)	1
Baxter, S. N. 1887 (Cliftonville)	1
Bennett, L. V. 1889 (Dublin University)	1

Best, G. 1964 (Manchester U, Fulham)	37
Bingham, W. L. 1951 (Sunderland, Luton T, Everton, Port Vale)	56
Black, K. T. 1988 (Luton T, Nottingham F)	30
Black, T. 1901 (Glentoran)	1
Blair, H. 1928 (Portadown, Swansea T)	4
Blair, J. 1907 (Cliftonville)	5
Blair, R. V. 1975 (Oldham Ath)	5
Blanchflower, J. 1954 (Manchester U)	12
Blanchflower, R. D. 1950 (Barnsley, Aston Villa, Tottenham H)	56
Blayney, A. 2006 (Doncaster R, Linfield)	5
Bonis, L. 2025 (ADO Den Haag)	**4**
Bookman, L. J. O. 1914 (Bradford C, Luton T)	4
Bothwell, A. W. 1926 (Ards)	5
Bowler, G. C. 1950 (Hull C)	3
Boyce, L. 2011 (Werder Bremen, Ross Co, Burton Alb, Hearts)	28
Boyd-Munce, C. S. 2024 (St Mirren)	2
Boyle, P. 1901 (Sheffield U)	5
Bradley, C. 2021 (Liverpool)	**25**
Braithwaite, R. M. 1962 (Linfield, Middlesbrough)	10
Braniff, K. R. 2010 (Portadown)	2
Breen, T. 1935 (Belfast Celtic, Manchester U)	9
Brennan, B. 1912 (Bohemians)	1
Brennan, R. A. 1949 (Luton T, Birmingham C, Fulham)	5
Briggs, W. R. 1962 (Manchester U, Swansea T)	2
Brisby, D. 1891 (Distillery)	1
Brolly, T. H. 1937 (Millwall)	4

Brookes, E. A. 1920 (Shelbourne)   1
Brotherston, N. 1980 (Blackburn R)   27
Brown, C. M. 2020 (Cardiff C, Oxford U)   25
Brown, J. 1921 (Glenavon, Tranmere R)   3
Brown, J. 1935 (Wolverhampton W, Coventry C,
    Birmingham C)   10
Brown, N. M. 1887 (Limavady)   1
Brown, W. G. 1926 (Glenavon)   1
Browne, F. 1887 (Cliftonville)   5
Browne, R. J. 1936 (Leeds U)   6
Bruce, A. 1925 (Belfast Celtic)   1
Bruce, A. S. 2013 (Hull C)   2
Bruce, W. 1961 (Glentoran)   2
Brunt, C. 2005 (Sheffield Wed, WBA)   65
Bryan, M. A. 2010 (Watford)   2
Buckle, H. R. 1903 (Cliftonville, Sunderland, Bristol R)   3
Buckle, J. 1882 (Cliftonville)   1
Burnett, J. 1894 (Distillery, Glentoran)   5
Burnison, J. 1901 (Distillery)   2
Burnison, S. 1908 (Distillery, Bradford, Distillery)   8
Burns, J. 1923 (Glenavon)   1
Burns, W. 1925 (Glentoran)   1
Butler, M. P. 1939 (Blackpool)   1

Camp, L. M. J. 2011 (Nottingham F)   9
Campbell, A. C. 1963 (Crusaders)   2
Campbell, D. A. 1986 (Nottingham F, Charlton Ath)   10
Campbell, James 1897 (Cliftonville)   14
Campbell, John 1896 (Cliftonville)   1
Campbell, J. P. 1951 (Fulham)   2
Campbell, R. M. 1982 (Bradford C)   2
Campbell, W. G. 1968 (Dundee)   6
Capaldi, A. C. 2004 (Plymouth Arg, Cardiff C)   22
Carey, J. J. 1947 (Manchester U)   7
Carroll, E. 1925 (Glenavon)   1
Carroll, R. E. 1997 (Wigan Ath, Manchester U,
    West Ham U, Olympiacos, Notts Co, Linfield)   45
Carson, J. G. 2011 (Ipswich T)   4
Carson, S. 2009 (Coleraine)   1
Carson, T. 2018 (Motherwell, Dundee U)   8
Casement, C. 2009 (Ipswich T)   1
Casey, T. 1955 (Newcastle U, Portsmouth)   12
Caskey, W. 1979 (Derby Co, Tulsa Roughnecks)   7
Cassidy, T. 1971 (Newcastle U, Burnley)   24
Cathcart, C. G. 2011 (Blackpool, Watford)   73
Caughey, M. 1986 (Linfield)   2
Chambers, R. J. 1921 (Distillery, Bury, Nottingham F)   12
Charles, D. E. 2021 (Accrington S, Bolton W)   29
Charles, P. J. 2025 (Sheffield Wed)   8
Charles, S. E. 2022 (Manchester C, Southampton)   27
Chatton, H. A. 1925 (Partick Thistle)   3
Christian, J. 1889 (Linfield)   1
Clarke, C. J. 1986 (Bournemouth, Southampton,
    QPR, Portsmouth)   38
Clarke, R. 1901 (Belfast Celtic)   2
Cleary, J. 1982 (Glentoran)   5
Clements, D. 1965 (Coventry C, Sheffield Wed,
    Everton, New York Cosmos)   48
Clingan, S. G. 2006 (Nottingham F, Norwich C,
    Coventry C, Kilmarnock)   39
Clugston, J. 1888 (Cliftonville)   14
Clyde, M. G. 2005 (Wolverhampton W)   3
Coates, C. 2009 (Crusaders)   6
Cochrane, D. 1939 (Leeds U)   12
Cochrane, G. 1903 (Cliftonville)   1
Cochrane, G. T. 1976 (Coleraine, Burnley,
    Middlesbrough, Gillingham)   26
Cochrane, M. 1898 (Distillery, Leicester Fosse)   8
Collins, F. 1922 (Celtic)   1
Collins, R. 1922 (Cliftonville)   1
Condy, J. 1882 (Distillery)   3
Connell, T. E. 1978 (Coleraine)   1
Connor, J. 1901 (Glentoran, Belfast Celtic)   13
Connor, M. J. 1903 (Brentford, Fulham)   3
Cook, W. 1933 (Celtic, Everton)   15
Cooke, S. 1889 (Belfast YMCA, Cliftonville)   3
Coote, A. 1999 (Norwich C)   6
Coulter, J. 1934 (Belfast Celtic, Everton, Grimsby T,
    Chelmsford C)   11
Cowan, J. G. 1970 (Newcastle U)   1
Cowan, T. S. 1925 (Queen's Island)   1
Coyle, F. 1956 (Coleraine, Nottingham F)   4
Coyle, L. 1989 (Derry C)   1
Coyle, R. I. 1973 (Sheffield Wed)   5

Craig, A. B. 1908 (Rangers, Morton)   9
Craig, D. J. 1967 (Newcastle U)   25
Craigan, S. J. 2003 (Partick Thistle, Motherwell)   54
Crawford, A. 1889 (Distillery, Cliftonville)   7
Croft, T. 1922 (Queen's Island)   3
Crone, R. 1889 (Distillery)   4
Crone, W. 1882 (Distillery)   12
Crooks, W. J. 1922 (Manchester U)   1
Crossan, E. 1950 (Blackburn R)   3
Crossan, J. A. 1960 (Sparta-Rotterdam, Sunderland,
    Manchester C, Middlesbrough)   24
Crothers, C. 1907 (Distillery)   1
Cumming, L. 1929 (Huddersfield T, Oldham Ath)   3
Cunningham, W. 1892 (Ulster)   4
Cunningham, W. E. 1951 (St Mirren, Leicester C,
    Dunfermline Ath)   30
Curran, S. 1926 (Belfast Celtic)   4
Curran, J. J. 1922 (Glenavon, Pontypridd, Glenavon)   5
Cush, W. W. 1951 (Glenavon, Leeds U, Portadown)   26

Dallas, S. A. 2011 (Crusaders, Brentford, Leeds U)   62
Dalrymple, J. 1922 (Distillery)   1
Dalton, W. 1888 (YMCA, Linfield)   11
D'Arcy, S. D. 1952 (Chelsea, Brentford)   5
Darling, J. 1897 (Linfield)   22
Davey, H. H. 1926 (Reading, Portsmouth)   5
Davis, S. 2005 (Aston Villa, Fulham, Rangers,
    Southampton, Rangers)   140
Davis, T. L. 1937 (Oldham Ath)   1
Davison, A. J. 1996 (Bolton W, Bradford C, Grimsby T)   3
Davison, J. R. 1882 (Cliftonville)   8
Dennison, R. 1988 (Wolverhampton W)   18
Devenny, J. 2025 (Crystal Palace)   5
Devine, A. O. 1886 (Limavady)   4
Devine, J. 1990 (Glentoran)   1
Devlin, T. 2025 (Portsmouth)   3
Dickson, D. 1970 (Coleraine)   4
Dickson, T. A. 1957 (Linfield)   1
Dickson, W. 1951 (Chelsea, Arsenal)   12
Diffin, W. J. 1931 (Belfast Celtic)   1
Dill, A. H. 1882 (Knock, Down Ath, Cliftonville)   9
Doherty, I. 1901 (Belfast Celtic)   1
Doherty, J. 1928 (Portadown)   1
Doherty, J. 1933 (Cliftonville)   2
Doherty, L. 1985 (Linfield)   2
Doherty, M. 1938 (Derry C)   1
Doherty, P. D. 1935 (Blackpool, Manchester C,
    Derby Co, Huddersfield T, Doncaster R)   16
Doherty, T. E. 2003 (Bristol C)   9
Donaghy, B. 1903 (Belfast Celtic)   1
Donaghy, M. M. 1980 (Luton T, Manchester U,
    Chelsea)   91
Donley, J. P. 2025 (Tottenham H)   3
Donnelly, A. M. 2024 (Nottingham F)   1
Donnelly, L. 1913 (Distillery)   1
Donnelly, L. F. P. D. 2014 (Fulham, Motherwell)   4
Donnelly, M. 2009 (Crusaders)   1
Doran, J. F. 1921 (Brighton)   3
Dougan, A. D. 1958 (Portsmouth, Blackburn R,
    Aston Villa, Leicester C, Wolverhampton W)   43
Douglas, J. P. 1947 (Belfast Celtic)   1
Dowd, H. O. 1974 (Glenavon, Sheffield Wed)   3
Dowie, I. 1990 (Luton T, West Ham U, Southampton,
    C Palace, West Ham U, QPR)   59
Duff, M. J. 2002 (Cheltenham T, Burnley)   24
Duggan, H. A. 1930 (Leeds U)   8
Dunlop, G. 1985 (Linfield)   4
Dunne, J. 1928 (Sheffield U)   7

Eames, W. L. E. 1885 (Dublin University)   3
Eglington, T. J. 1947 (Everton)   6
Elder, A. R. 1960 (Burnley, Stoke C)   40
Elleman, A. R. 1889 (Cliftonville)   2
Elliott, S. 2001 (Motherwell, Hull C)   39
Elwood, J. H. 1929 (Bradford)   2
Emerson, W. 1920 (Glentoran, Burnley)   11
English, S. 1933 (Rangers)   2
Enright, J. 1912 (Leeds C)   1
Evans, C. J. 2009 (Manchester U, Hull C, Blackburn R,
    Sunderland)   72
Evans, J. G. 2007 (Manchester U, WBA, Leicester C,
    Manchester U)   107

Falloon, E. 1931 (Aberdeen)   2
Farquharson, T. G. 1923 (Cardiff C)   7

Farrell, P. 1901 (Distillery) 2
Farrell, P. 1938 (Hibernian) 1
Farrell, P. D. 1947 (Everton) 7
Feeney, J. M. 1947 (Linfield, Swansea T) 2
Feeney, W. 1976 (Glentoran) 1
Feeney, W. J. 2002 (Bournemouth, Luton T,
    Cardiff C, Oldham Ath, Plymouth Arg) 46
Ferguson, G. 1999 (Linfield) 5
Ferguson, S. K. 2009 (Newcastle U, Millwall,
    Rotherham U) 57
Ferguson, W. 1966 (Linfield) 2
Ferris, J. 1920 (Belfast Celtic, Chelsea, Belfast Celtic) 6
Ferris, R. O. 1950 (Birmingham C) 3
Fettis, A. W. 1992 (Hull C, Nottingham F,
    Blackburn R) 25
Finney, T. 1975 (Sunderland, Cambridge U) 14
Fitzpatrick, J. C. 1896 (Bohemians) 1
Flack, H. 1929 (Burnley) 2
Flanagan, T. M. 2017 (Burton Alb, Sunderland,
    Shrewsbury T) 15
Fleming, J. G. 1987 (Nottingham F, Manchester C,
    Barnsley) 31
Forbes, G. 1888 (Limavady, Distillery) 3
Forbes, M. 2024 (West Ham U) 1
Forde, J. T. 1959 (Ards) 4
Foreman, T. A. 1899 (Cliftonville) 1
Forsythe, J. 1888 (YMCA) 2
Fox, W. T. 1887 (Ulster) 2
Frame, T. 1925 (Linfield) 1
Fulton, R. P. 1928 (Larne, Belfast Celtic) 21

Gaffikin, G. 1890 (Linfield Ath) 15
Galbraith, E. S. W. 2020 (Manchester U, Leyton Orient) 7
Galbraith, W. 1890 (Distillery) 1
Gallagher, P. 1920 (Celtic, Falkirk) 11
Gallogly, C. 1951 (Huddersfield T) 2
Gara, A. 1902 (Preston NE) 3
Gardiner, A. 1930 (Cliftonville) 5
Garrett, J. 1925 (Distillery) 1
Garrett, R. 2009 (Linfield) 5
Gaston, R. 1969 (Oxford U) 1
Gaukrodger, G. 1895 (Linfield) 1
Gault, M. 2008 (Linfield) 1
Gaussen, A. D. 1884 (Moyola Park, Magherafelt) 6
Geary, J. 1931 (Glentoran) 2
Gibb, J. T. 1884 (Wellington Park, Cliftonville) 10
Gibb, T. J. 1936 (Cliftonville) 1
Gibson W. K. 1894 (Cliftonville) 14
Gillespie, K. R. 1995 (Manchester U, Newcastle U,
    Blackburn R, Leicester C, Sheffield U) 86
Gillespie, S. 1886 (Hertford) 6
Gillespie, W. 1889 (West Down) 1
Gillespie, W. 1913 (Sheffield U) 25
Goodall, A. L. 1899 (Derby Co, Glossop) 10
Goodbody, M. F. 1889 (Dublin University) 2
Gordon, H. 1895 (Linfield) 3
Gordon R. W. 1891 (Linfield) 7
Gordon, T. 1894 (Linfield) 2
Gorman, R. J. 2010 (Wolverhampton W) 9
Gorman, W. C. 1947 (Brentford) 4
Gough, J. 1925 (Queen's Island) 1
Gowdy, J. 1920 (Glentoran, Queen's Island, Falkirk) 6
Gowdy, W. A. 1932 (Hull C, Sheffield Wed, Linfield,
    Hibernian) 6
Graham, W. G. L. 1951 (Doncaster R) 14
Gray, P. 1993 (Luton T, Sunderland, Nancy, Luton T,
    Burnley, Oxford U) 26
Greer, W. 1909 (QPR) 3
Gregg, H. 1954 (Doncaster R, Manchester U) 25
Griffin, D. J. 1996 (St Johnstone, Dundee U,
    Stockport Co) 29
Grigg, W. D. 2012 (Walsall, Brentford,
    Milton Keynes D, Wigan Ath) 13

Hale, R. A. C. S. 2025 (Ross Co) 1
Hall, G. 1897 (Distillery) 1
Halligan, W. 1911 (Derby Co, Wolverhampton W) 2
Hamill, M. 1912 (Manchester U, Belfast Celtic,
    Manchester C) 7
Hamill, R. 1999 (Glentoran) 1
Hamilton, B. 1969 (Linfield, Ipswich T, Everton,
    Millwall, Swindon T) 50
Hamilton, G. 2003 (Portadown) 5
Hamilton, J. 1882 (Knock) 2

Hamilton, R. 1928 (Rangers) 5
Hamilton, W. D. 1885 (Dublin Association) 1
Hamilton, W. J. 1885 (Dublin Association) 1
Hamilton, W. J. 1908 (Distillery) 1
Hamilton, W. R. 1978 (QPR, Burnley, Oxford U) 41
Hampton, H. 1911 (Bradford C) 9
Hanna, J. 1912 (Nottingham F) 2
Hanna, J. D. 1899 (Royal Artillery, Portsmouth) 1
Hannon, D. J. 1908 (Bohemians) 6
Harkin, J. T. 1968 (Southport, Shrewsbury T) 5
Harland, A. I. 1922 (Linfield) 2
Harris, J. 1921 (Cliftonville, Glenavon) 3
Harris, V. 1906 (Shelbourne, Everton) 20
Harvey, M. 1961 (Sunderland) 34
Hastings, J. 1882 (Knock, Ulster) 7
Hatton, S. 1963 (Linfield) 2
Hayes, W. E. 1938 (Huddersfield T) 4
Hazard, C. W. 2018 (Celtic, Plymouth Arg) 9
Healy, D. J. 2000 (Manchester U, Preston NE,
    Leeds U, Fulham, Sunderland, Rangers, Bury) 95
Healy, P. J. 1982 (Coleraine, Glentoran) 4
Hegan, D. 1970 (WBA, Wolverhampton W) 7
Hehir, J. C. 1910 (Bohemians) 1
Henderson, J. 1885 (Ulster) 3
Hewison, G. 1885 (Moyola Park) 2
Hill, C. F. 1990 (Sheffield U, Leicester C, Trelleborg,
    Northampton T) 27
Hill, M. J. 1959 (Norwich C, Everton) 7
Hinton, E. 1947 (Fulham, Millwall) 7
Hodson, L. J. S. 2011 (Watford, Milton Keynes D,
    Rangers) 24
Holmes, S. P. 2002 (Wrexham) 1
Hopkins, J. 1926 (Brighton) 1
Horlock, K. 1995 (Swindon T, Manchester C) 32
Houston, J. 1912 (Linfield, Everton) 6
Houston, W. 1933 (Linfield) 1
Houston, W. J. 1885 (Moyola Park) 2
Hughes, A. W. 1998 (Newcastle U, Aston Villa,
    Fulham, QPR, Brighton & HA, Melbourne C,
    Kerala Blasters, Hearts) 112
Hughes, J. 2006 (Lincoln C) 2
Hughes, M. A. 2006 (Oldham Ath) 2
Hughes, M. E. 1992 (Manchester C, Strasbourg,
    West Ham U, Wimbledon, Crystal Palace) 71
Hughes, P. A. 1987 (Bury) 3
Hughes, W. 1951 (Bolton W) 1
Hume, T. 2021 (Sunderland) 22
Humphries, W. M. 1962 (Ards, Coventry C,
    Swansea T) 14
Hunter, A. 1905 (Distillery, Belfast Celtic) 8
Hunter, A. 1970 (Blackburn R, Ipswich T) 53
Hunter, B. V. 1995 (Wrexham, Reading) 15
Hunter, R. J. 1884 (Cliftonville) 3
Hunter, V. 1962 (Coleraine) 2

Ingham, M. G. 2005 (Sunderland, Wrexham) 3
Irvine, R. J. 1962 (Linfield, Stoke C) 8
Irvine, R. W. 1922 (Everton, Portsmouth,
    Connah's Quay, Derry C) 15
Irvine, W. J. 1963 (Burnley, Preston NE,
    Brighton & HA) 23
Irving, S. J. 1923 (Dundee, Cardiff C, Chelsea) 18

Jackson, T. A. 1969 (Everton, Nottingham F,
    Manchester U) 35
Jamison, J. 1976 (Glentoran) 1
Jenkins, I. 1997 (Chester C, Dundee U) 6
Jennings, P. A. 1964 (Watford, Tottenham H,
    Arsenal, Tottenham H) 119
Johnson, D. M. 1999 (Blackburn R, Birmingham C) 56
Johnston, H. 1927 (Portadown) 1
Johnston, R. S. 1882 (Distillery) 5
Johnston, R. S. 1905 (Distillery) 1
Johnston, S. 1890 (Linfield) 4
Johnston, W. 1885 (Oldpark) 2
Johnston, W. C. 1962 (Glenavon, Oldham Ath) 2
Jones, J. 1930 (Linfield, Hibernian, Glenavon) 23
Jones, J. 1956 (Glenavon) 3
Jones, J. L. 2018 (Kilmarnock, Rangers, Sunderland,
    Wigan Ath) 19
Jones, J. 1934 (Distillery, Blackpool) 2
Jones, S. G. 2003 (Crewe Alex, Burnley) 29
Jordan, T. 1895 (Linfield) 2

Kavanagh, P. J. 1930 (Celtic) 1
Keane, T. R. 1949 (Swansea T) 1
Kearns, A. 1900 (Distillery) 6
Kee, P. V. 1990 (Oxford U, Ards) 9
Keith, R. M. 1958 (Newcastle U) 23
Kelly, H. R. 1950 (Fulham, Southampton) 4
Kelly, J. 1896 (Glentoran) 1
Kelly, J. 1932 (Derry C) 11
Kelly, P. J. 1921 (Manchester C) 1
Kelly, P. M. 1950 (Barnsley) 1
Kennedy, A. L. 1923 (Arsenal) 2
Kennedy, M. 2021 (Aberdeen, Kilmarnock) 5
Kennedy, P. H. 1999 (Watford, Wigan Ath) 20
Kernaghan, N. 1936 (Belfast Celtic) 3
Kirk, A. R. 2000 (Hearts, Boston U, Northampton T, Dunfermline Ath) 11
Kirkwood, H. 1904 (Cliftonville) 1
Kirwan, J. 1900 (Tottenham H, Chelsea, Clyde) 17

Lacey, W. 1909 (Everton, Liverpool, New Brighton) 23
Lafferty, D. P. 2012 (Burnley) 13
Lafferty, K. 2006 (Burnley, Rangers, Sion, Palermo, Norwich C, Hearts, Rangers, Kilmarnock) 89
Lane, P. J. 2022 (Fleetwood T, Portsmouth) 4
Lavery, S. F. 2018 (Everton, Linfield, Blackpool, Cambridge U) **20**
Lawrie, J. 2009 (Port Vale) 3
Lawther, R. 1888 (Glentoran) 2
Lawther, W. I. 1960 (Sunderland, Blackburn R) 4
Leatham, J. 1939 (Belfast Celtic) 1
Ledwidge, J. J. 1906 (Shelbourne) 2
Lemon, J. 1886 (Glentoran, Belfast YMCA) 3
Lennon, N. F. 1994 (Crewe Alex, Leicester C, Celtic) 40
Leslie, W. 1887 (YMCA) 1
Lewis, J. 1899 (Glentoran, Distillery) 4
Lewis, J. P. 2018 (Norwich C, Newcastle U) **39**
Little, A. 2009 (Rangers) 9
Lockhart, H. 1884 (Rossall School) 1
Lockhart, N. H. 1947 (Linfield, Coventry C, Aston Villa) 8
Lomas, S. M. 1994 (Manchester C, West Ham U) 45
Loyal, J. 1891 (Clarence) 1
Lund, M. C. 2017 (Rochdale) 3
Lutton, R. J. 1970 (Wolverhampton W, West Ham U) 6
Lynas, R. 1925 (Cliftonville) 1
Lyner, D. R. 1920 (Glentoran, Manchester U, Kilmarnock) 6
Lyons, B. J. 2024 (Kilmarnock) **5**
Lytle, J. 1898 (Glentoran) 1

Mackie, J. A. 1923 (Arsenal, Portsmouth) 3
Madden, O. 1938 (Norwich C) 1
Magee, G. 1885 (Wellington Park) 3
Magennis, J. B. D. 2010 (Cardiff C, Aberdeen, St Mirren, Kilmarnock, Charlton Ath, Bolton W, Hull C, Wigan Ath, Exeter C) **82**
Magill, E. J. 1962 (Arsenal, Brighton & HA) 26
Magilton, J. 1991 (Oxford U, Southampton, Sheffield W, Ipswich T) 52
Maginnis, H. 1900 (Linfield) 8
Maguire, E. 1907 (Distillery) 1
Mahood, J. 1926 (Belfast Celtic, Ballymena) 9
Manderson, R. 1920 (Rangers) 5
Mannus, A. 2004 (Linfield, St Johnstone) 9
Mansfield, J. 1901 (Dublin Freebooters) 1
Marshall, C. 2023 (West Ham U) **10**
Martin, C. 1925 (Bo'ness) 1
Martin, C. J. 1947 (Glentoran, Leeds U, Aston Villa) 6
Martin, D. C. 1882 (Cliftonville) 3
Martin, D. K. 1934 (Belfast Celtic, Wolverhampton W, Nottingham F) 10
Mathieson, A. 1921 (Luton T) 2
Maxwell, J. 1902 (Linfield, Glentoran, Belfast Celtic) 7
McAdams, W. J. 1954 (Manchester C, Bolton W, Leeds U) 15
McAlery, J. M. 1882 (Cliftonville) 2
McAlinden, J. 1938 (Belfast Celtic, Portsmouth, Southend U) 4
McAllen, J. 1898 (Linfield) 9
McAlpine, S. 1901 (Cliftonville) 1
McArdle, R. A. 2010 (Rochdale, Aberdeen, Bradford C) 7
McArthur, A. 1886 (Distillery) 1
McAuley, G. 2005 (Lincoln C, Leicester C, Ipswich T, WBA, Rangers) 80
McAuley, J. L. 1911 (Huddersfield T) 6

McAuley, P. 1900 (Belfast Celtic) 1
McBride, S. D. 1991 (Glenavon) 4
McCabe, J. J. 1949 (Leeds U) 6
McCabe, W. 1891 (Ulster) 1
McCalmont, A. J. 2020 (Leeds U) 4
McCambridge, J. 1930 (Ballymena, Cardiff C) 4
McCandless, J. 1912 (Bradford) 5
McCandless, W. 1920 (Linfield, Rangers) 9
McCann, A. E. 2021 (St Johnstone, Preston NE) **29**
McCann, G. S. 2002 (West Ham U, Cheltenham T, Barnsley, Scunthorpe U, Peterborough U) 39
McCann, P. 1910 (Belfast Celtic, Glentoran) 7
McCartan, S. V. 2017 (Accrington S, Bradford C) 2
McCarthy, J. D. 1996 (Port Vale, Birmingham C) 18
McCartney, A. 1903 (Ulster, Linfield, Everton, Belfast Celtic, Glentoran) 15
McCartney, G. 2002 (Sunderland, West Ham U, Sunderland) 34
McCashin, J. W. 1896 (Cliftonville) 5
McCausland, R. 2024 (Rangers) **5**
McCavana, W. T. 1955 (Coleraine) 3
McCaw, J. H. 1927 (Linfield) 6
McClatchey, J. 1886 (Distillery) 3
McClatchey, T. 1895 (Distillery) 1
McCleary, J. W. 1955 (Cliftonville) 1
McCleery, W. 1922 (Cliftonville, Linfield) 10
McClelland, J. 1980 (Mansfield T, Rangers, Watford, Leeds U) 53
McClelland, J. T. 1961 (Arsenal, Fulham) 6
McClelland, S. 2021 (Chelsea) 1
McCluggage, A. 1922 (Cliftonville, Bradford, Burnley) 13
McClure, G. 1907 (Cliftonville, Distillery) 4
McConnell, E. 1904 (Cliftonville, Glentoran, Sunderland, Sheffield Wed) 12
McConnell, P. 1928 (Doncaster R, Southport) 2
McConnell, W. G. 1912 (Bohemians) 6
McConnell, W. H. 1925 (Reading) 8
McConville, R. 2025 (Norwich C) **5**
McCourt, F. J. 1952 (Manchester C) 6
McCourt, P. J. 2002 (Rochdale, Celtic, Barnsley, Brighton & HA, Luton T) 18
McCoy, R. K. 1987 (Coleraine) 1
McCoy, S. 1896 (Distillery) 1
McCracken, E. 1928 (Barking) 1
McCracken, R. 1921 (Crystal Palace) 4
McCracken, R. 1922 (Linfield) 1
McCracken, W. R. 1902 (Distillery, Newcastle U, Hull C) 16
McCreery, D. 1976 (Manchester U, QPR, Tulsa Roughnecks, Newcastle U, Hearts) 67
McCrory, S. 1958 (Southend U) 1
McCullough, K. 1935 (Belfast Celtic, Manchester C) 5
McCullough, L. 2014 (Doncaster R) 6
McCullough, W. J. 1961 (Arsenal, Millwall) 10
McCurdy, C. 1980 (Linfield) 1
McDonald, A. 1986 (QPR) 52
McDonald, R. 1930 (Rangers) 2
McDonnell, J. 1911 (Bohemians) 4
McElhinney, G. M. A. 1984 (Bolton W) 6
McEvilly, L. R. 2002 (Rochdale) 1
McFaul, W. S. 1967 (Linfield, Newcastle U) 6
McGarry, J. K. 1951 (Cliftonville) 3
McGaughey, M. 1985 (Linfield) 1
McGeehan, C. A. 2023 (Oostende) 1
McGibbon, P. C. G. 1995 (Manchester U, Wigan Ath) 7
McGinn, N. 2009 (Derry C, Celtic, Brentford, Aberdeen, Gwangju, Aberdeen, Dundee) 73
McGivern, R. 2009 (Manchester C, Hibernian, Port Vale, Shrewsbury) 24
McGovern, M. 2010 (Ross Co, Hamilton A, Norwich C) 33
McGrath, R. C. 1974 (Tottenham H, Manchester U) 21
McGregor, S. 1921 (Glentoran) 1
McGrillen, J. 1924 (Clyde, Belfast Celtic) 2
McGuire, J. 1928 (Linfield) 1
McIlroy, H. 1906 (Cliftonville) 1
McIlroy, J. 1952 (Burnley, Stoke C) 55
McIlroy, S. B. 1972 (Manchester U, Stoke C, Manchester C) 88
McIlvenny, P. 1924 (Distillery) 1
McIlvenny, R. 1890 (Distillery, Ulster) 2
McKay, W. R. 2013 (Inverness CT, Wigan Ath) 11
McKeag, W. 1968 (Glentoran) 2
McKeague, T. 1925 (Glentoran) 1

McKee, F. W. 1906 (Cliftonville, Belfast Celtic) 5
McKee, H. 1895 (Cliftonville) 3
McKelvey, H. 1901 (Glentoran) 2
McKenna, J. 1950 (Huddersfield T) 7
McKenzie, H. 1922 (Distillery) 2
McKenzie, R. 1967 (Airdrieonians) 1
McKeown, N. 1892 (Linfield) 7
McKinney, D. 1921 (Hull C, Bradford C) 2
McKinney, V. J. 1966 (Falkirk) 1
McKnight, A. D. 1988 (Celtic, West Ham U) 10
McKnight, J. 1912 (Preston NE, Glentoran) 2
McLaughlin, C. G. 2012 (Preston NE, Fleetwood T,
  Millwall, Sunderland) 43
McLaughlin, J. C. 1962 (Shrewsbury T, Swansea T) 12
McLaughlin, R. 2014 (Liverpool, Oldham Ath) 5
McLean, B. S. 2006 (Rangers) 1
McLean, T. 1885 (Limavady) 1
McMahon, G. J. 1995 (Tottenham H, Stoke C) 17
McMahon, J. 1934 (Bohemians) 1
McMaster, G. 1897 (Glentoran) 3
McMenamin, C. 2022 (Glentoran, St Mirren) 13
McMichael, A. 1950 (Newcastle U) 40
McMillan, G. 1903 (Distillery) 2
McMillan, S. T. 1963 (Manchester U) 2
McMillen, W. S. 1934 (Manchester U, Chesterfield) 7
McMordie, A. S. 1969 (Middlesbrough) 21
McMorran, E. J. 1947 (Belfast Celtic, Barnsley,
  Doncaster R) 15
McMullan, D. 1926 (Liverpool) 3
McNair, P. J. C. 2015 (Manchester U, Sunderland,
Middlesbrough, San Diego) **75**
McNally, B. A. 1986 (Shrewsbury T) 5
McNinch, J. 1931 (Ballymena) 3
McPake, J. 2012 (Coventry C) 1
McParland, P. J. 1954 (Aston Villa, Wolverhampton W) 34
McQuoid, J. J. B. 2011 (Millwall) 5
McShane, J. 1899 (Cliftonville) 4
McVeigh, P. M. 1999 (Tottenham H, Norwich C) 20
McVicker, J. 1888 (Linfield, Glentoran) 2
McWha, W. B. R. 1882 (Knock, Cliftonville) 7
Meek, H. L. 1925 (Glentoran) 1
Mehaffy, A. C. 1922 (Queen's Island) 1
Meldon, P. A. 1899 (Dublin Freebooters) 2
Mercer, H. V. A. 1908 (Linfield) 1
Mercer, J. T. 1898 (Distillery, Linfield, Distillery,
  Derby Co) 12
Millar, W. 1932 (Barrow) 2
Miller, J. 1929 (Middlesbrough) 3
Milligan, D. 1939 (Chesterfield) 1
Milne, R. G. 1894 (Linfield) 28
Mitchell, E. J. 1933 (Cliftonville, Glentoran) 2
Mitchell, W. 1932 (Distillery, Chelsea) 15
Molyneux, T. B. 1883 (Ligoniel, Cliftonville) 11
Montgomery, F. J. 1955 (Coleraine) 1
Moore, C. 1949 (Glentoran) 1
Moore, P. 1933 (Aberdeen) 1
Moore, R. 1891 (Linfield Ath) 3
Moore, R. L. 1887 (Ulster) 2
Moore, W. 1923 (Falkirk) 1
Moorhead, F. W. 1885 (Dublin University) 1
Moorhead, G. 1923 (Linfield) 4
Moran, J. 1912 (Leeds C) 1
Moreland, V. 1979 (Derby Co) 6
Morgan, G. F. 1922 (Linfield, Nottingham F) 8
Morgan, S. 1972 (Port Vale, Aston Villa,
  Brighton & HA, Sparta Rotterdam) 18
Morrison, R. 1891 (Linfield Ath) 2
Morrison, T. 1895 (Glentoran, Burnley) 7
Morrogh, D. 1896 (Bohemians) 1
Morrow, S. J. 1990 (Arsenal, QPR) 39
Morrow, W. J. 1883 (Moyola Park) 3
Muir, R. 1885 (Oldpark) 2
Mulgrew, J. 2010 (Linfield) 2
Mulholland, T. S. 1906 (Belfast Celtic) 2
Mullan, G. 1983 (Glentoran) 4
Mulligan, J. 1921 (Manchester C) 1
Mulryne, P. P. 1997 (Manchester U, Norwich C,
  Cardiff C) 27
Murdock, C. J. 2000 (Preston NE, Hibernian,
  Crewe Alex, Rotherham U) 34
Murphy, J. 1910 (Bradford C) 3
Murphy, N. 1905 (QPR) 3
Murray, J. M. 1910 (Motherwell, Sheffield Wed) 3

Napier, R. J. 1966 (Bolton W) 1
Neill, W. J. T. 1961 (Arsenal, Hull C) 59
Nelis, P. 1923 (Nottingham F) 1
Nelson, S. 1970 (Arsenal, Brighton & HA) 51
Nicholl, C. J. 1975 (Aston Villa, Southampton,
  Grimsby T) 51
Nicholl, H. 1902 (Belfast Celtic) 3
Nicholl, J. M. 1976 (Manchester U, Toronto Blizzard,
  Sunderland, Toronto Blizzard, Rangers,
  Toronto Blizzard, WBA) 73
Nicholson, J. J. 1961 (Manchester U, Huddersfield T) 41
Nixon, R. 1914 (Linfield) 1
Nolan, I. R. 1997 (Sheffield Wed, Bradford C,
  Wigan Ath) 18
Nolan-Whelan, J. V. 1901 (Dublin Freebooters) 5
Norwood, O. J. 2011 (Manchester U, Huddersfield T,
  Reading, Brighton & HA) 57
O'Boyle, G. 1994 (Dunfermline Ath, St Johnstone) 13
O'Brien, M. T. 1921 (QPR, Leicester C, Hull C,
  Derby Co) 10
O'Connell, P. 1912 (Sheffield Wed, Hull C) 5
O'Connor, M. J. 2008 (Crewe Alex, Scunthorpe U,
  Rotherham U) 11
O'Doherty, A. 1970 (Coleraine) 2
O'Driscoll, J. F. 1949 (Swansea T) 3
O'Hagan, C. 1905 (Tottenham H, Aberdeen) 11
O'Hagan, W. 1920 (St Mirren) 2
O'Kane, W. J. 1970 (Nottingham F) 20
O'Mahoney, M. T. 1939 (Bristol R) 1
O'Neill, C. 1989 (Motherwell) 3
O'Neill, J. 1962 (Sunderland) 1
O'Neill, J. P. 1980 (Leicester C) 39
O'Neill, M. A. M. 1988 (Newcastle U, Dundee U,
  Hibernian, Coventry C) 31
O'Neill, M. H. M. 1972 (Distillery, Nottingham F,
  Norwich C, Manchester C, Norwich C, Notts Co) 64
O'Reilly, H. 1901 (Dublin Freebooters) 3
Owens, J. 2011 (Crusaders) 1

Parke, J. 1964 (Linfield, Hibernian, Sunderland) 14
Paterson, M. A. 2008 (Scunthorpe U, Burnley,
  Huddersfield T) 22
Paton, P. R. 2014 (Dundee U) 4
Patterson, D. J. 1994 (Crystal Palace, Luton T,
  Dundee U) 17
Patterson, R. 2010 (Coleraine, Plymouth Arg) 5
Peacock, R. 1952 (Celtic, Coleraine) 31
Peacock-Farrell, B. 2018 (Leeds U, Burnley,
Sheffield Wed, Burnley, Aarhus, Birmingham C) **48**
Peden, J. 1887 (Linfield, Distillery) 24
Penney, S. 1985 (Brighton & HA) 17
Percy, J. C. 1889 (Belfast YMCA) 1
Platt, J. A. 1976 (Middlesbrough, Ballymena U,
  Coleraine) 23
Pollock, W. 1928 (Belfast Celtic) 1
Ponsonby, J. 1895 (Distillery) 9
Potts, R. M. C. 1883 (Cliftonville) 2
Price, I. J. 2023 (Everton, Standard Liege, WBA) **22**
Priestley, T. J. M. 1933 (Coleraine, Chelsea) 2
Pyper, Jas. 1897 (Cliftonville) 7
Pyper, John 1897 (Cliftonville) 9
Pyper, M. 1932 (Linfield) 1

Quinn, J. M. 1985 (Blackburn R, Swindon T,
  Leicester C, Bradford C, West Ham U,
  Bournemouth, Reading) 46
Quinn, S. J. 1996 (Blackpool, WBA, Willem II,
  Sheffield W, Peterborough U, Northampton T) 50

Rafferty, P. 1980 (Linfield) 1
Ramsey, P. C. 1984 (Leicester C) 14
Rankin, J. 1883 (Alexander) 2
Rattray, D. 1882 (Avoniel) 3
Rea, R. 1901 (Glentoran) 1
Redmond, R. 1884 (Cliftonville) 1
Reeves, B. N. 2015 (Milton Keynes D) 2
Reid, G. H. 1923 (Cardiff C) 1
Reid, J. 1883 (Ulster) 6
Reid, J. M. 2024 (Stevenage) **8**
Reid, S. E. 1934 (Derby Co) 3
Reid, W. 1931 (Hearts) 1
Reilly, M. M. 1900 (Portsmouth) 2
Renneville, W. T. J. 1910 (Leyton, Aston Villa) 4
Reynolds, J. 1890 (Distillery, Ulster) 5
Reynolds, R. 1905 (Bohemians) 1

Rice, P. J. 1969 (Arsenal) 49
Roberts, F. C. 1931 (Glentoran) 1
Robinson, P. 1920 (Distillery, Blackburn R) 2
Robinson, S. 1997 (Bournemouth, Luton T) 7
Rogan, A. 1988 (Celtic, Sunderland, Millwall) 18
Rollo, D. 1912 (Linfield, Blackburn R) 16
Roper, E. O. 1886 (Dublin University) 1
Rosbotham, A. 1887 (Cliftonville) 7
Ross, W. E. 1969 (Newcastle U) 1
Rowland, K. 1994 (West Ham U, QPR) 19
Rowley, R. W. M. 1929 (Southampton, Tottenham H) 6
Rushe, F. 1925 (Distillery) 1
Russell, A. 1947 (Linfield) 1
Russell, S. R. 1930 (Bradford C, Derry C) 3
Ryan, R. A. 1950 (WBA) 1

Sanchez, L. P. 1987 (Wimbledon) 3
Saville, G. A. 2018 (Millwall, Middlesbrough, Millwall) 60
Scott, E. 1920 (Liverpool, Belfast Celtic) 31
Scott, J. 1958 (Grimsby) 2
Scott, J. E. 1901 (Cliftonville) 1
Scott, L. J. 1895 (Dublin University) 1
Scott, P. W. 1975 (Everton, York C, Aldershot) 10
Scott, T. 1894 (Cliftonville) 13
Scott, W. 1903 (Linfield, Everton, Leeds C) 25
Scraggs, M. J. 1921 (Glentoran) 2
Seymour, H. C. 1914 (Bohemians) 1
Seymour, J. 1907 (Cliftonville) 2
Shanks, T. 1903 (Woolwich Arsenal, Brentford) 3
Sharkey, P. G. 1976 (Ipswich T) 1
Sheehan, Dr G. 1899 (Bohemians) 1
Sheridan, J. 1903 (Everton, Stoke C) 6
Sherrard, J. 1885 (Limavady) 3
Sherrard, W. C. 1895 (Cliftonville) 3
Sherry, J. J. 1906 (Bohemians) 2
Shields, R. J. 1957 (Southampton) 1
Shiels, D. 2006 (Hibernian, Doncaster R, Kilmarnock) 14
Silo, M. 1888 (Belfast YMCA) 1
Simpson, W. J. 1951 (Rangers) 12
Sinclair, J. 1882 (Knock) 2
Slemin, J. C. 1909 (Bohemians) 1
Sloan, A. S. 1925 (London Caledonians) 1
Sloan, D. 1969 (Oxford U) 2
Sloan, H. A. de B. 1903 (Bohemians) 8
Sloan, J. W. 1947 (Arsenal) 1
Sloan, T. 1926 (Cardiff C, Linfield) 11
Sloan, T. 1979 (Manchester U) 3
Small, J. M. 1887 (Clarence, Cliftonville) 4
Smith, A. W. 2003 (Glentoran, Preston NE) 18
Smith, E. E. 1921 (Cardiff C) 4
Smith, J. E. 1901 (Distillery) 2
Smith, M. 2016 (Peterborough U, Hearts) 19
Smyth, P. P. 2018 (QPR) 20
Smyth, R. H. 1886 (Dublin University) 1
Smyth, S. 1948 (Wolverhampton W, Stoke C) 9
Smyth, W. 1949 (Distillery) 1
Snape, A. 1920 (Airdrieonians) 1
Sonner, D. J. 1998 (Ipswich T, Sheffield Wed,
 Birmingham C, Nottingham F, Peterborough U) 13
Southwood, L. K. 2022 (Reading) 1
Spence, D. W. 1975 (Bury, Blackpool, Southend U) 29
Spencer, B. G. 2022 (Huddersfield T) 17
Spencer, S. 1890 (Distillery) 6
Spiller, E. A. 1883 (Cliftonville) 5
Sproule, I. 2006 (Hibernian, Bristol C) 11
Stanfield, O. M. 1887 (Distillery) 30
Steele, A. 1926 (Charlton Ath, Fulham) 4
Steele, J. 2013 (New York Red Bulls) 3
Stevenson, A. E. 1934 (Rangers, Everton) 17
Stewart, A. 1967 (Glentoran, Derby Co) 7
Stewart, D. C. 1978 (Hull C) 1
Stewart, I. 1982 (QPR, Newcastle U) 31
Stewart, R. K. 1890 (St Columb's Court, Cliftonville) 11
Stewart, T. C. 1961 (Linfield) 1
Swan, S. 1899 (Linfield) 1

Taggart, G. P. 1990 (Barnsley, Bolton W, Leicester C) 51
Taggart, J. 1899 (Walsall) 1
Taylor, D. 2022 (Nottingham F) 9
Taylor, M. S. 1999 (Fulham, Birmingham C, unattached) 88

Thompson, A. L. 2011 (Watford) 2
Thompson, F. W. 1910 (Cliftonville, Linfield,
 Bradford C, Clyde) 12
Thompson, J. 1897 (Distillery) 1
Thompson, J. A. 2018 (Rangers, Blackpool, Stoke C) 39
Thompson, P. 2006 (Linfield, Stockport Co) 8
Thompson, R. 1928 (Queen's Island) 1
Thompson, W. 1889 (Belfast Ath) 1
Thunder, P. J. 1911 (Bohemians) 1
Toal, E. 2024 (Bolton W) 8
Todd, S. J. 1966 (Burnley, Sheffield Wed) 11
Toner, C. 2003 (Leyton Orient) 2
Toner, J. 1922 (Arsenal, St Johnstone) 8
Torrans, R. 1893 (Linfield) 1
Torrans, S. 1889 (Linfield) 26
Trainor, D. 1967 (Crusaders) 1
Tuffey, J. 2009 (Partick Thistle, Inverness CT) 8
Tully, C. P. 1949 (Celtic) 10
Turner, A. 1896 (Cliftonville) 1
Turner, E. 1896 (Cliftonville) 1
Turner, W. 1886 (Cliftonville) 3
Twomey, J. F. 1938 (Leeds U) 2

Uprichard, W. N. M. C. 1952 (Swindon T, Portsmouth) 18

Vassell, K. T. 2019 (Rotherham U) 2
Vernon, J. 1947 (Belfast Celtic, WBA) 17

Waddell, T. M. R. 1906 (Cliftonville) 1
Walker, J. 1955 (Doncaster R) 1
Walker, T. 1911 (Bury) 1
Walsh, D. J. 1947 (WBA) 9
Walsh, W. 1948 (Manchester C) 5
Ward, J. J. 2012 (Derby Co, Nottingham F) 35
Waring, J. 1899 (Cliftonville) 1
Warren, P. 1913 (Shelbourne) 2
Washington, C. J. 2016 (QPR, Sheffield U, Hearts,
 Charlton Ath, Rotherham U, Derby Co) 43
Watson, J. 1883 (Ulster) 9
Watson, P. 1971 (Distillery) 1
Watson, T. 1926 (Cardiff C) 1
Wattie, J. 1899 (Distillery) 1
Webb, C. G. 1909 (Brighton & HA) 3
Webb, S. M. 2006 (Ross Co) 4
Weir, E. 1939 (Clyde) 1
Welsh, E. 1966 (Carlisle U) 4
Whiteside, N. 1982 (Manchester U, Everton) 38
Whiteside, T. 1891 (Distillery) 1
Whitfield, E. R. 1886 (Dublin University) 1
Whitley, Jeff 1997 (Manchester C, Sunderland,
 Cardiff C) 20
Whitley, Jim 1998 (Manchester C) 3
Whyte, G. 2019 (Oxford U, Cardiff C) 30
Williams, J. R. 1886 (Ulster) 2
Williams, M. S. 1999 (Chesterfield, Watford,
 Wimbledon, Stoke C, Wimbledon,
 Milton Keynes D) 36
Williams, P. A. 1991 (WBA) 1
Williamson, J. 1890 (Cliftonville) 3
Willighan, T. 1933 (Burnley) 2
Willis, G. 1906 (Linfield) 4
Wilson, D. J. 1987 (Brighton & HA, Luton T,
 Sheffield W) 24
Wilson, H. 1925 (Linfield) 2
Wilson, K. J. 1987 (Ipswich T, Chelsea, Notts Co,
 Walsall) 42
Wilson, M. 1884 (Distillery) 3
Wilson, R. 1888 (Cliftonville) 1
Wilson, S. J. 1962 (Glenavon, Falkirk, Dundee) 12
Wilton, J. M. 1888 (St Columb's Court, Cliftonville, St
 Columb's Court) 7
Winchester, C. 2011 (Oldham Ath) 1
Wood, T. J. 1996 (Walsall) 1
Worthington, N. 1984 (Sheffield Wed, Leeds U, Stoke C) 66
Wright, J. 1906 (Cliftonville) 6
Wright, T. J. 1989 (Newcastle U, Nottingham F,
 Manchester C) 31

Young, S. 1907 (Linfield, Airdrieonians, Linfield) 9

SCOTLAND

Scottish appearances and goals include those made on the Scottish tour of 1967. In October 2021, the following matches were upgraded to full internationals: v Israel (Tel Aviv, 16 May 1967); v Australia (Sydney, 28 May 1967); v Australia (Adelaide, 31 May 1967); v Australia (Melbourne, 3 June 1967); v Canada (Winnipeg, 13 June 1967).

Adam, C. G. 2007 (Rangers, Blackpool, Liverpool, Stoke C)	26
Adams, C. Z. E. F. 2021 (Southampton, Torino)	**39**
Adams, J. 1889 (Hearts)	3
Agnew, W. B. 1907 (Kilmarnock)	3
Aird, J. 1954 (Burnley)	4
Aitken, A. 1901 (Newcastle U, Middlesbrough, Leicester Fosse)	14
Aitken, G. G. 1949 (East Fife, Sunderland)	8
Aitken, R. 1886 (Dumbarton)	2
Aitken, R. 1980 (Celtic, Newcastle U, St Mirren)	57
Aitkenhead, W. A. C. 1912 (Blackburn R)	1
Albiston, A. 1982 (Manchester U)	14
Alexander, D. 1894 (East Stirlingshire)	2
Alexander, G. 2002 (Preston NE, Burnley)	40
Alexander, N. 2006 (Cardiff C)	3
Allan, D. S. 1885 (Queen's Park)	3
Allan, G. 1897 (Liverpool)	1
Allan, H. 1902 (Hearts)	1
Allan, J. 1887 (Queen's Park)	2
Allan, T. 1974 (Dundee)	2
Ancell, R. F. D. 1937 (Newcastle U)	2
Anderson, A. 1933 (Hearts)	28
Anderson, F. 1874 (Clydesdale)	1
Anderson, G. 1901 (Kilmarnock)	1
Anderson, H. A. 1914 (Raith R)	1
Anderson, J. 1954 (Leicester C)	1
Anderson, K. 1896 (Queen's Park)	3
Anderson, R. 2003 (Aberdeen, Sunderland)	11
Anderson, W. 1882 (Queen's Park)	6
Andrews, P. 1875 (Eastern)	1
Anya, I. 2013 (Watford, Derby Co)	29
Archer, J. G. 2018 (Millwall)	1
Archibald, A. 1921 (Rangers)	8
Archibald, S. 1980 (Aberdeen, Tottenham H, Barcelona)	27
Armstrong, M. W. 1936 (Aberdeen)	3
Armstrong, S. 2017 (Celtic, Southampton, Vancouver Whitecaps)	**53**
Arnott, W. 1883 (Queen's Park)	14
Auld, J. R. 1887 (Third Lanark)	3
Auld, R. 1959 (Celtic)	3
Bain, S. 2018 (Celtic)	3
Baird, A. 1892 (Queen's Park)	2
Baird, D. 1890 (Hearts)	3
Baird, H. 1956 (Airdrieonians)	1
Baird, J. C. 1876 (Vale of Leven)	3
Baird, S. 1957 (Rangers)	7
Baird, W. U. 1897 (St Bernard)	1
Bannan, B. 2011 (Aston Villa, Crystal Palace, Sheffield W)	27
Bannon, E. J. 1980 (Dundee U)	11
Barbour, A. 1885 (Renton)	1
Bardsley, P. A. 2011 (Sunderland)	13
Barker, J. B. 1893 (Rangers)	2
Barr, D. 2009 (Falkirk)	1
Barrett, F. 1894 (Dundee)	2
Barron, C. C. 2025 (Rangers)	**1**
Bates, D. 2019 (Hamburg)	4
Battles, B. 1901 (Celtic)	3
Battles, B. jun. 1931 (Hearts)	1
Bauld, W. 1950 (Hearts)	3
Baxter, J. C. 1961 (Rangers, Sunderland)	34
Baxter, R. D. 1939 (Middlesbrough)	3
Beattie, A. 1937 (Preston NE)	7
Beattie, C. 2006 (Celtic, WBA)	7
Beattie, R. 1939 (Preston NE)	1
Begbie, I. 1890 (Hearts)	4
Bell, A. 1912 (Manchester U)	1
Bell, C. 2011 (Kilmarnock)	1
Bell, J. 1890 (Dumbarton, Everton, Celtic)	10
Bell, M. 1901 (Hearts)	1
Bell, W. J. 1966 (Leeds U)	2
Bennett, A. 1904 (Celtic, Rangers)	11
Bennie, R. 1925 (Airdrieonians)	3
Bernard, P. R. J. 1995 (Oldham Ath)	2
Berra, C. D. 2008 (Hearts, Wolverhampton W, Ipswich T)	41
Berry, D. 1894 (Queen's Park)	3
Berry, W. H. 1888 (Queen's Park)	4
Bett, J. 1982 (Rangers, Lokeren, Aberdeen)	25
Beveridge, W. W. 1879 (Glasgow University)	3
Black, A. 1938 (Hearts)	3
Black, D. 1889 (Hurlford)	1
Black, E. 1988 (Metz)	2
Black, I. 2013 (Rangers)	1
Black, I. H. 1948 (Southampton)	1
Blackburn, J. E. 1873 (Royal Engineers)	1
Blacklaw, A. S. 1963 (Burnley)	3
Blackley, J. 1974 (Hibernian)	7
Blair, D. 1929 (Clyde, Aston Villa)	8
Blair, J. 1920 (Sheffield Wed, Cardiff C)	8
Blair, J. 1934 (Motherwell)	1
Blair, J. A. 1947 (Blackpool)	1
Blair, W. 1896 (Third Lanark)	1
Blessington, J. 1894 (Celtic)	4
Blyth, J. A. 1978 (Coventry C)	2
Bone, J. 1972 (Norwich C)	2
Booth, S. 1993 (Aberdeen, Borussia Dortmund, Twente)	21
Bowie, J. 1920 (Rangers)	2
Bowie, K. T. 2025 (Hibernian)	**1**
Bowie, W. 1891 (Linthouse)	1
Bowman, D. 1992 (Dundee U)	6
Bowman, G. A. 1892 (Montrose)	1
Boyd, G. I. 2013 (Peterborough U, Hull C)	1
Boyd, J. M. 1934 (Newcastle U)	1
Boyd, K. 2006 (Rangers, Middlesbrough)	18
Boyd, R. 1889 (Mossend Swifts)	2
Boyd, T. 1991 (Motherwell, Chelsea, Celtic)	72
Boyd, W. G. 1931 (Clyde)	2
Bradshaw, T. 1928 (Bury)	1
Brand, R. 1961 (Rangers)	8
Brandon, T. 1896 (Blackburn R)	1
Brazil, A. 1980 (Ipswich T, Tottenham H)	13
Breckenridge, T. 1888 (Hearts)	1
Bremner, D. 1976 (Hibernian)	1
Bremner, W. J. 1965 (Leeds U)	54
Brennan, F. 1947 (Newcastle U)	7
Breslin, B. 1897 (Hibernian)	1
Brewster, G. 1921 (Everton)	1
Bridcutt, L. 2013 (Brighton & HA, Sunderland)	2
Broadfoot, K. 2009 (Rangers)	4
Brogan, J. 1971 (Celtic)	4
Brophy, E. 2019 (Kilmarnock)	1
Brown, A. 1890 (St Mirren)	2
Brown, A. 1904 (Middlesbrough)	1
Brown, A. D. 1950 (East Fife, Blackpool)	14
Brown, G. C. P. 1931 (Rangers)	19
Brown, H. 1947 (Partick Thistle)	3
Brown, J. B. 1939 (Clyde)	1
Brown, J. G. 1975 (Sheffield U)	1
Brown, J. S. 2022 (Stoke C, Luton T)	8
Brown, R. 1884 (Dumbarton)	2
Brown, R. 1890 (Cambuslang)	1
Brown, R. 1947 (Rangers)	3
Brown, R. jun. 1885 (Dumbarton)	1
Brown, S. 2006 (Hibernian, Celtic)	55
Brown, W. D. F. 1958 (Dundee, Tottenham H)	28
Browning, J. 1914 (Celtic)	1
Brownlie, J. 1909 (Third Lanark)	16
Brownlie, J. 1971 (Hibernian)	7
Bruce, D. 1890 (Vale of Leven)	1
Bruce, R. F. 1934 (Middlesbrough)	1
Bryson, C. 2011 (Kilmarnock, Derby Co)	3
Buchan, M. M. 1972 (Aberdeen, Manchester U)	34
Buchanan, J. 1889 (Cambuslang)	1
Buchanan, J. 1929 (Rangers)	2
Buchanan, R. 1891 (Abercorn)	1
Buckley, P. 1954 (Aberdeen)	3
Buick, A. 1902 (Hearts)	2
Burchill, M. J. 2000 (Celtic)	6
Burke, C. 2006 (Rangers, Birmingham C)	7
Burke, O. J. 2016 (Nottingham F, RB Leipzig, WBA, Sheffield U)	13
Burley, C. W. 1995 (Chelsea, Celtic, Derby Co)	46
Burley, G. E. 1979 (Ipswich T)	11
Burns, F. 1970 (Manchester U)	1

Burns, K. 1974 (Birmingham C, Nottingham F)	20
Burns, T. 1981 (Celtic)	8
Busby, M. W. 1934 (Manchester C)	1
Cadden, C. 2018 (Motherwell)	2
Caddis, P. M. 2016 (Birmingham C)	1
Cairney, T. 2017 (Fulham)	2
Cairns, T. 1920 (Rangers)	8
Calderhead, D. 1889 (Q of S Wanderers)	1
Calderwood, C. 1995 (Tottenham H)	36
Calderwood, R. 1885 (Cartvale)	3
Caldow, E. 1957 (Rangers)	40
Caldwell, G. 2002 (Newcastle U, Hibernian, Celtic, Wigan Ath)	55
Caldwell, S. 2001 (Newcastle U, Sunderland, Burnley,Wigan Ath)	12
Callaghan, P. 1900 (Hibernian)	1
Callaghan, W. 1967 (Dunfermline Ath)	6
Cameron, C. 1999 (Hearts, Wolverhampton W)	28
Cameron, J. 1886 (Rangers)	1
Cameron, J. 1896 (Queen's Park)	1
Cameron, J. 1904 (St Mirren, Chelsea)	2
Campbell, A. 2022 (Luton T)	1
Campbell, C. 1874 (Queen's Park)	13
Campbell, H. 1889 (Renton)	1
Campbell, Jas 1913 (Sheffield Wed)	1
Campbell, J. 1880 (South Western)	1
Campbell, J. 1891 (Kilmarnock)	2
Campbell, John 1893 (Celtic)	12
Campbell, John 1899 (Rangers)	4
Campbell, K. 1920 (Liverpool, Partick Thistle)	8
Campbell, P. 1878 (Rangers)	2
Campbell, P. 1898 (Morton)	1
Campbell, R. 1947 (Falkirk, Chelsea)	5
Campbell, W. 1947 (Morton)	5
Canero, P. 2004 (Leicester C)	1
Carabine, J. 1938 (Third Lanark)	3
Carr, W. M. 1970 (Coventry C)	6
Cassidy, J. 1921 (Celtic)	4
Chalmers, S. 1965 (Celtic)	5
Chalmers, W. 1885 (Rangers)	1
Chalmers, W. S. 1929 (Queen's Park)	1
Chambers, T. 1894 (Hearts)	1
Chaplin, G. D. 1908 (Dundee)	1
Cheyne, A. G. 1929 (Aberdeen)	5
Christie, A. J. 1898 (Queen's Park)	3
Christie, R. 2018 (Celtic, Bournemouth)	**59**
Christie, R. M. 1884 (Queen's Park)	1
Clark, A. (Zander) 2024 (Hearts)	4
Clark, J. 1966 (Celtic)	4
Clark, R. B. 1968 (Aberdeen)	17
Clarke, S. 1988 (Chelsea)	6
Clarkson, D. 2008 (Motherwell)	2
Cleland, J. 1891 (Royal Albert)	1
Clements, R. 1891 (Leith Ath)	1
Clunas, W. L. 1924 (Sunderland)	2
Collier, W. 1922 (Raith R)	1
Collins, J. 1988 (Hibernian, Celtic, Monaco, Everton)	58
Collins, R. Y. 1951 (Celtic, Everton, Leeds U)	31
Collins, T. 1909 (Hearts)	1
Colman, D. 1911 (Aberdeen)	4
Colquhoun, E. P. 1967 (WBA, Sheffield U)	11
Colquhoun, J. 1988 (Hearts)	2
Combe, J. R. 1948 (Hibernian)	3
Commons, K. 2009 (Derby Co, Celtic)	12
Conn, A. 1956 (Hearts)	1
Conn, A. 1975 (Tottenham H)	2
Connachan, E. D. 1962 (Dunfermline Ath)	2
Connelly, G. 1974 (Celtic)	2
Connolly, J. 1973 (Everton)	1
Connor, J. 1886 (Airdrieonians)	1
Connor, J. 1930 (Sunderland)	4
Connor, R. 1986 (Dundee, Aberdeen)	4
Considine, A. 2021 (Aberdeen)	3
Conway, C. 2010 (Dundee U, Cardiff C)	7
Conway, T. D. J. 2024 (Bristol C, Middlesbrough)	**6**
Cook, W. L. 1934 (Bolton W)	3
Cooke, C. 1966 (Dundee, Chelsea)	16
Cooper, D. 1980 (Rangers, Motherwell)	22
Cooper, L. D. I. 2020 (Leeds U)	19
Cormack, P. B. 1966 (Hibernian, Nottingham F)	9
Cowan, J. 1896 (Aston Villa)	3
Cowan, J. 1948 (Morton)	25
Cowan, W, D. 1924 (Newcastle U)	1

Cowie, D. 1953 (Dundee)	20
Cowie, D. M. 2010 (Watford, Cardiff C)	10
Cox, C. J. 1948 (Hearts)	1
Cox, S. 1949 (Rangers)	24
Craig, A. 1929 (Motherwell)	3
Craig, J. 1977 (Celtic)	1
Craig, J. P. 1968 (Celtic)	1
Craig, T. 1927 (Rangers)	8
Craig, T. B. 1976 (Newcastle U)	1
Crainey, S. D. 2002 (Celtic, Southampton, Blackpool)	12
Crapnell, J. 1929 (Airdrieonians)	9
Crawford, D. 1894 (St Mirren, Rangers)	3
Crawford, J. 1932 (Queen's Park)	5
Crawford, S. 1995 (Raith R, Dunfermline Ath, Plymouth Arg)	25
Crerand, P. T. 1961 (Celtic, Manchester U)	16
Cringan, W. 1920 (Celtic)	5
Crosbie, J. A. 1920 (Ayr U, Birmingham)	2
Croal, J. A. 1913 (Falkirk)	3
Cropley, A. J. 1972 (Hibernian)	2
Cross, J. H. 1903 (Third Lanark)	1
Cruickshank, J. 1964 (Hearts)	9
Crum, J. 1936 (Celtic)	2
Cullen, M. J. 1956 (Luton T)	1
Cumming, D. S. 1938 (Middlesbrough)	1
Cumming, J. 1955 (Hearts)	9
Cummings, G. 1935 (Partick Thistle, Aston Villa)	9
Cummings, J. 2018 (Nottingham F)	2
Cummings, W. 2002 (Chelsea)	1
Cunningham, A. N. 1920 (Rangers)	12
Cunningham, W. C. 1954 (Preston NE)	8
Curran, H. P. 1970 (Wolverhampton W)	5
Dailly, C. 1997 (Derby Co, Blackburn R, West Ham U, Rangers)	67
Dalglish, K. 1972 (Celtic, Liverpool)	102
Davidson, C. I. 1999 (Blackburn R, Leicester C, Preston NE)	19
Davidson, D. 1878 (Queen's Park)	5
Davidson, J. A. 1954 (Partick Thistle)	8
Davidson, M. 2013 (St Johnstone)	1
Davidson, S. 1921 (Middlesbrough)	1
Dawson, A. 1980 (Rangers)	5
Dawson, J. 1935 (Rangers)	14
Deans, J. 1975 (Celtic)	2
Delaney, J. 1936 (Celtic, Manchester U)	13
Devine, A. 1910 (Falkirk)	1
Devlin, M. J. 2020 (Aberdeen)	3
Devlin, N. 2025 (Aberdeen)	**2**
Devlin, P. J. 2003 (Birmingham C)	10
Dewar, G. 1888 (Dumbarton)	2
Dewar, N. 1932 (Third Lanark)	3
Dick, J. 1959 (West Ham U)	1
Dickie, M. 1897 (Rangers)	3
Dickov, P. 2001 (Manchester C, Leicester C, Blackburn R)	10
Dickson, W. 1888 (Dundee Strathmore)	1
Dickson, W. 1970 (Kilmarnock)	5
Divers, J. 1895 (Celtic)	1
Divers, J. 1939 (Celtic)	1
Dixon, P. A. 2013 (Huddersfield T)	3
Doak, B. G. 2025 (Liverpool)	**6**
Dobie, R. S. 2002 (WBA)	6
Docherty, T. H. 1952 (Preston NE, Arsenal)	25
Dodds, D. 1984 (Dundee U)	2
Dodds, J. 1914 (Celtic)	3
Dodds, W. 1997 (Aberdeen, Dundee U, Rangers)	26
Doig, J. E. 1887 (Arbroath, Sunderland)	5
Doig, J. T. 2025 (Sassuolo)	**1**
Donachie, W. 1972 (Manchester C)	35
Donaldson, A. 1914 (Bolton W)	6
Donnachie, J. 1913 (Oldham Ath)	3
Donnelly, S. 1997 (Celtic)	10
Doohan, R. 2025 (Celtic)	**1**
Dorrans, G. 2010 (WBA, Norwich C)	12
Dougal, J. 1939 (Preston NE)	1
Dougall, C. 1947 (Birmingham C)	1
Dougan, R. 1950 (Hearts)	1
Douglas, A. 1911 (Chelsea)	1
Douglas, B. 2018 (Wolverhampton W)	1
Douglas, J. 1880 (Renfrew)	1
Douglas, R. 2002 (Celtic, Leicester C)	19
Dowds, P. 1892 (Celtic)	1
Downie, R. 1892 (Third Lanark)	1

Doyle, D. 1892 (Celtic)	8
Doyle, J. 1976 (Ayr U)	1
Drummond, J. 1892 (Falkirk, Rangers)	14
Dunbar, M. 1886 (Cartvale)	1
Duncan, A. 1975 (Hibernian)	6
Duncan, D. 1933 (Derby Co)	14
Duncan, D. M. 1948 (East Fife)	3
Duncan, J. 1878 (Alexandra Ath)	2
Duncan, J. 1926 (Leicester C)	1
Duncanson, J. 1947 (Rangers)	1
Dunlop, J. 1890 (St Mirren)	1
Dunlop, W. 1906 (Liverpool)	1
Dunn, J. 1925 (Hibernian, Everton)	6
Durie, G. S. 1988 (Chelsea, Tottenham H, Rangers)	43
Durrant, I. 1988 (Rangers, Kilmarnock)	20
Dykes, J. 1938 (Hearts)	2
Dykes, L. J. 2021 (QPR, Birmingham C)	**42**
Easson, J. F. 1931 (Portsmouth)	3
Elliott, M. S. 1998 (Leicester C)	18
Ellis, J. 1892 (Mossend Swifts)	1
Evans, A. 1982 (Aston Villa)	4
Evans, R. 1949 (Celtic, Chelsea)	48
Ewart, J. 1921 (Bradford C)	1
Ewing, T. 1958 (Partick Thistle)	2
Farm, G. N. 1953 (Blackpool)	10
Ferguson, A. 1967 (Dunfermline Ath)	4
Ferguson, B. 1999 (Rangers, Blackburn R, Rangers)	45
Ferguson, D. 1988 (Rangers)	2
Ferguson, D. 1992 (Dundee U, Everton)	7
Ferguson, I. 1989 (Rangers)	9
Ferguson, J. 1874 (Vale of Leven)	6
Ferguson, L. 2022 (Aberdeen, Bologna)	**16**
Ferguson, R. 1966 (Kilmarnock)	7
Fernie, W. 1954 (Celtic)	12
Findlay, R. 1898 (Kilmarnock)	1
Findlay, S. J. 2020 (Kilmarnock)	1
Fitchie, T. T. 1905 (Woolwich Arsenal, Queen's Park)	4
Flavell, R. 1947 (Airdrieonians)	2
Fleck, J. A. 2020 (Sheffield U)	5
Fleck, R. 1990 (Norwich C)	4
Fleming, C. 1954 (East Fife)	1
Fleming, J. W. 1929 (Rangers)	3
Fleming, R. 1886 (Morton)	1
Fletcher, D. B. 2004 (Manchester U, WBA, Stoke C)	80
Fletcher, S. K. 2008 (Hibernian, Burnley, Wolverhampton W, Sunderland, Sheffield Wed)	33
Forbes, A. R. 1947 (Sheffield U, Arsenal)	14
Forbes, J. 1884 (Vale of Leven)	5
Ford, D. 1974 (Hearts)	3
Forrest, J. 1958 (Motherwell)	1
Forrest, J. 1966 (Rangers, Aberdeen)	5
Forrest, J. 2011 (Celtic)	39
Forsyth, A. 1972 (Partick Thistle, Manchester U)	10
Forsyth, C. 2014 (Derby Co)	4
Forsyth, R. C. 1964 (Kilmarnock)	4
Forsyth, T. 1971 (Motherwell, Rangers)	22
Fox, D. J. 2010 (Burnley, Southampton)	4
Foyers, R. 1893 (St Bernards)	2
Fraser, D. M. 1967 (WBA)	7
Fraser, J. 1891 (Moffat)	1
Fraser, J. 1907 (Dundee)	1
Fraser, M. J. E. 1880 (Queen's Park)	5
Fraser, R. 2017 (Bournemouth, Newcastle U)	26
Fraser, W. 1955 (Sunderland)	2
Freedman, D. A. 2002 (Crystal Palace)	2
Fulton, W. 1884 (Abercorn)	1
Fyfe, J. H. 1895 (Third Lanark)	1
Gabriel, J. 1961 (Everton)	2
Gallacher, K. 1924 (Airdrieonians, Newcastle U, Chelsea, Derby Co)	20
Gallacher, K. W. 1988 (Dundee U, Coventry C, Blackburn R, Newcastle U)	53
Gallacher, P. 1935 (Sunderland)	1
Gallacher, P. 2002 (Dundee U)	8
Gallagher, D. P. 2020 (Motherwell)	9
Gallagher, P. 2004 (Blackburn R)	1
Galloway, M. 1992 (Celtic)	1
Galt, J. H. 1908 (Rangers)	2
Gardiner, I. 1958 (Motherwell)	1
Gardner, D. R. 1897 (Third Lanark)	1
Gardner, R. 1872 (Queen's Park, Clydesdale)	5

Gauld, R. S. 2025 (Vancouver Whitecaps)	**6**
Gemmell, T. 1955 (St Mirren)	2
Gemmell, T. 1966 (Celtic)	18
Gemmill, A. 1971 (Derby Co, Nottingham F, Birmingham C)	43
Gemmill, S. 1995 (Nottingham F, Everton)	26
Gibb, W. 1873 (Clydesdale)	1
Gibson, D. W. 1963 (Leicester C)	7
Gibson, J. D. 1926 (Partick Thistle, Aston Villa)	8
Gibson, N. 1895 (Rangers, Partick Thistle)	14
Gilchrist, J. E. 1922 (Celtic)	1
Gilhooley, M. 1922 (Hull C)	1
Gilks, M. 2013 (Blackpool)	3
Gillespie, G. 1880 (Rangers, Queen's Park)	7
Gillespie, G. T. 1988 (Liverpool)	13
Gillespie, Jas 1898 (Third Lanark)	1
Gillespie, John 1896 (Queen's Park)	1
Gillespie, R. 1927 (Queen's Park)	4
Gillick, T. 1937 (Everton)	5
Gilmour, B. C. 2021 (Chelsea, Brighton & HA, Napoli)	**40**
Gilmour, J. 1931 (Dundee)	1
Gilzean, A. J. 1964 (Dundee, Tottenham H)	22
Glass, S. 1999 (Newcastle U)	1
Glavin, R. 1977 (Celtic)	1
Glen, A. 1956 (Aberdeen)	2
Glen, R. 1895 (Renton, Hibernian)	3
Goodwillie, D. 2011 (Dundee U, Blackburn R)	3
Goram, A. L. 1986 (Oldham Ath, Hibernian, Rangers)	43
Gordon, C. A. 2004 (Hearts, Sunderland, Celtic, Hearts)	**81**
Gordon, J. E. 1912 (Rangers)	10
Gossland, J. 1884 (Rangers)	1
Goudie, J. 1884 (Abercorn)	1
Gough, C. R. 1983 (Dundee U, Tottenham H, Rangers)	61
Gould, J. 2000 (Celtic)	2
Gourlay, J. 1886 (Cambuslang)	2
Govan, J. 1948 (Hibernian)	6
Gow, D. R. 1888 (Rangers)	1
Gow, J. J. 1885 (Queen's Park)	1
Gow, J. R. 1888 (Rangers)	1
Graham, A. 1978 (Leeds U)	11
Graham, G. 1972 (Arsenal, Manchester U)	12
Graham, J. 1884 (Annbank)	1
Graham, J. A. 1921 (Arsenal)	1
Grant, J. 1959 (Hibernian)	2
Grant, P. 1989 (Celtic)	2
Gray, A. 1903 (Hibernian)	1
Gray, A. D. 2003 (Bradford C)	2
Gray, A. M. 1976 (Aston Villa, Wolverhampton W, Everton)	20
Gray, D. 1929 (Rangers)	10
Gray, E. 1969 (Leeds U)	12
Gray, F. T. 1976 (Leeds U, Nottingham F, Leeds U)	32
Gray, W. 1886 (Pollokshields Ath)	1
Green, A. 1971 (Blackpool, Newcastle U)	6
Greer, G. 2013 (Brighton & HA)	11
Greig, J. 1964 (Rangers)	44
Griffiths, L. 2013 (Hibernian, Celtic)	22
Groves, W. 1888 (Hibernian, Celtic)	3
Gulliland, W. 1891 (Queen's Park)	4
Gunn, A. F. J. 2023 (Norwich C)	**16**
Gunn, B. 1990 (Norwich C)	6
Haddock, H. 1955 (Clyde)	6
Haddow, D. 1894 (Rangers)	1
Haffey, F. 1960 (Celtic)	2
Hamilton, A. 1885 (Queen's Park)	4
Hamilton, A. W. 1962 (Dundee)	24
Hamilton, G. 1906 (Port Glasgow Ath)	1
Hamilton, G. 1947 (Aberdeen)	5
Hamilton, J. 1892 (Queen's Park)	3
Hamilton, J. 1924 (St Mirren)	1
Hamilton, R. C. 1899 (Rangers, Dundee)	11
Hamilton, T. 1891 (Hurlford)	1
Hamilton, T. 1932 (Rangers)	1
Hamilton, W. M. 1965 (Hibernian)	1
Hammell, S. 2005 (Motherwell)	1
Hanley, G. C. 2011 (Blackburn R, Newcastle U, Norwich C, Birmingham C)	**62**
Hanlon, P. T. 2021 (Hibernian)	1
Hannah, A. B. 1888 (Renton)	1
Hannah, J. 1889 (Third Lanark)	1
Hansen, A. D. 1979 (Liverpool)	26
Hansen, J. 1972 (Partick Thistle)	2
Harkness, J. D. 1927 (Queen's Park, Hearts)	12

Levein, C. 1990 (Hearts) 16
Liddell, W. 1947 (Liverpool) 28
Liddle, D. 1931 (East Fife) 3
Lindsay, D. 1903 (St Mirren) 1
Lindsay, J. 1880 (Dumbarton) 8
Lindsay, J. 1888 (Renton) 3
Linwood, A. B. 1950 (Clyde) 1
Little, R. J. 1953 (Rangers) 1
Livingstone, G. T. 1906 (Manchester C, Rangers) 2
Lochhead, A. 1889 (Third Lanark) 1
Logan, J. 1891 (Ayr) 1
Logan, T. 1913 (Falkirk) 1
Logie, J. T. 1953 (Arsenal) 1
Loney, W. 1910 (Celtic) 2
Long, H. 1947 (Clyde) 1
Longair, W. 1894 (Dundee) 1
Lorimer, P. 1970 (Leeds U) 21
Love, A. 1931 (Aberdeen) 3
Low, A. 1934 (Falkirk) 1
Low, J. 1891 (Cambuslang) 1
Low, T. P. 1897 (Rangers) 1
Low, W. L. 1911 (Newcastle U) 5
Lowe, J. 1887 (St Bernards) 1
Lundie, J. 1886 (Hibernian) 1
Lyall, J. 1905 (Sheffield Wed) 1

Macari, L. 1972 (Celtic, Manchester U) 24
Macauley, A. R. 1947 (Brentford, Arsenal) 7
MacDonald, A. 1976 (Rangers) 1
MacDougall, E. J. 1975 (Norwich C) 7
Macfarlane, A. 1904 (Dundee) 5
Macfarlane, W. 1947 (Hearts) 1
Mackail-Smith, C. 2011 (Peterborough U,
  Brighton & HA) 7
MacKay, D. 1959 (Celtic) 14
Mackay, D. C. 1957 (Hearts, Tottenham H) 22
Mackay, G. 1988 (Hearts) 4
Mackay, M. 2004 (Norwich C) 5
Mackay-Steven, G. 2013 (Dundee U, Aberdeen) 2
Mackenzie, J. A. 1954 (Partick Thistle) 9
Mackie, J. C. 2011 (QPR) 9
MacKinnon, W. 1883 (Dumbarton) 4
MacKinnon, W. W. 1872 (Queen's Park) 9
MacLeod, J. M. 1961 (Hibernian) 4
MacLeod, M. 1985 (Celtic, Borussia Dortmund,
  Hibernian) 20
Madden, J. 1893 (Celtic) 2
Maguire, C. 2011 (Aberdeen) 2
Main, F. R. 1938 (Rangers) 1
Main, J. 1909 (Hibernian) 1
Maley, W. 1893 (Celtic) 2
Maloney, S. R. 2006 (Celtic, Aston Villa, Celtic,
  Wigan Ath, Chicago Fire, Hull C) 47
Malpas, M. 1984 (Dundee U) 55
Marshall, D. J. 2005 (Celtic, Cardiff C, Hull C,
  Wigan Ath. Derby Co) 47
Marshall, G. 1992 (Celtic) 1
Marshall, H. 1899 (Celtic) 2
Marshall, J. 1885 (Third Lanark) 4
Marshall, J. 1921 (Middlesbrough, Llanelly) 7
Marshall, J. 1932 (Rangers) 3
Marshall, R. W. 1892 (Rangers) 2
Martin, B. 1995 (Motherwell) 2
Martin, C. H. 2014 (Derby Co) 17
Martin, F. 1954 (Aberdeen) 6
Martin, N. 1965 (Hibernian, Sunderland) 3
Martin, R. K. A. 2011 (Norwich C) 29
Martis, J. 1961 (Motherwell) 1
Mason, J. 1949 (Third Lanark) 7
Massie, A. 1932 (Hearts, Aston Villa) 18
Masson, D. S. 1976 (QPR, Derby Co) 17
Mathers, D. 1954 (Partick Thistle) 1
Matteo, D. 2001 (Leeds U) 6
Maxwell, W. S. 1898 (Stoke C) 1
May, J. 1906 (Rangers) 5
May, S. 2015 (Sheffield Wed) 1
McAdam, J. 1880 (Third Lanark) 1
McAllister, J. R. 2004 (Livingston) 1
McAllister, B. 1997 (Wimbledon) 3
McAllister, G. 1990 (Leicester C, Leeds U,
  Coventry C) 57
McArthur, D. 1895 (Celtic) 3
McArthur, J. 2011 (Wigan Ath, Crystal Palace) 32
McAtee, A. 1913 (Celtic) 1
McAulay, J. 1884 (Arthurlie) 1

McAulay, J. D. 1882 (Dumbarton) 9
McAulay, R. 1932 (Rangers) 2
McAvennie, F. 1986 (West Ham U, Celtic) 5
McBain, E. 1894 (St Mirren) 1
McBain, N. 1922 (Manchester U, Everton) 3
McBride, J. 1967 (Celtic) 2
McBride, P. 1904 (Preston NE) 6
McBurnie, O. R. 2018 (Swansea C, Sheffield U) 16
McCall, A. 1888 (Renton) 1
McCall, A. S. M. 1990 (Everton, Rangers) 40
McCall, J. 1886 (Renton) 5
McCalliog, J. 1967 (Sheffield Wed, Wolverhampton W) 10
McCallum, N. 1888 (Renton) 1
McCann, N. 1999 (Hearts, Rangers, Southampton) 26
McCann, R. J. 1959 (Motherwell) 5
McCartney, W. 1902 (Hibernian) 1
McClair, B. 1987 (Celtic, Manchester U) 30
McClory, A. 1927 (Motherwell) 3
McCloy, P. 1924 (Ayr U) 2
McCloy, P. 1973 (Rangers) 4
McCoist, A. 1986 (Rangers, Kilmarnock) 61
McColl, I. M. 1950 (Rangers) 14
McColl, R. S. 1896 (Queen's Park, Newcastle U,
  Queen's Park) 13
McColl, W. 1895 (Renton) 1
McCombie, A. 1903 (Sunderland, Newcastle U) 4
McCorkindale, J. 1891 (Partick Thistle) 1
McCormack, R. 2008 (Motherwell, Cardiff C,
  Leeds U, Fulham) 13
McCormick, R. 1886 (Abercorn) 1
McCrae, D. 1929 (St Mirren) 2
McCreadie, A. 1893 (Rangers) 2
McCreadie, E. G. 1965 (Chelsea) 23
McCrorie, Ross 2024 (Bristol C) 1
McCulloch, D. 1935 (Hearts, Brentford, Derby Co) 7
McCulloch, L. 2005 (Wigan Ath, Rangers) 18
McDonald, J. 1886 (Edinburgh University) 1
McDonald, J. 1956 (Sunderland) 2
McDonald, K. D. 2018 (Fulham) 5
McDougall, J. 1877 (Vale of Leven) 5
McDougall, J. 1926 (Airdrieonians) 1
McDougall, J. 1931 (Liverpool) 2
McEveley, J. 2008 (Derby Co) 3
McFadden, J. 2002 (Motherwell, Everton,
  Birmingham C) 48
McFadyen, W. 1934 (Motherwell) 2
McFarlane, R. 1896 (Greenock Morton) 1
McGarr, E. 1970 (Aberdeen) 2
McGarvey, F. P. 1979 (Liverpool, Celtic) 7
McGeoch, A. 1876 (Dumbreck) 4
McGeouch, D. 2018 (Hibernian) 2
McGhee, J. 1886 (Hibernian) 1
McGhee, M. 1983 (Aberdeen) 4
McGinlay, J. 1994 (Bolton W) 13
McGinn, J. 2016 (Hibernian, Aston Villa) 77
McGinn, P. 2022 (Hibernian) 1
McGonagle, W. 1933 (Celtic) 6
McGrain, D. 1973 (Celtic) 62
McGregor, A. J. 2007 (Rangers, Besiktas, Hull C,
  Rangers) 42
McGregor, C. W. 2018 (Celtic) 63
McGregor, J. C. 1877 (Vale of Leven) 4
McGrory, J. 1928 (Celtic) 7
McGrory, J. E. 1965 (Kilmarnock) 6
McGuire, W. 1881 (Beith) 2
McGurk, F. 1934 (Birmingham) 1
McHardy, H. 1885 (Rangers) 1
McInally, A. 1989 (Aston Villa, Bayern Munich) 8
McInally, J. 1987 (Dundee U) 10
McInally, T. B. 1926 (Celtic) 2
McInnes, D. 2003 (WBA) 2
McInnes, T. 1889 (Cowlairs) 1
McIntosh, W. 1905 (Third Lanark) 1
McIntyre, A. 1878 (Vale of Leven) 2
McIntyre, H. 1880 (Rangers) 1
McIntyre, J. 1884 (Rangers) 1
McKay, B. 2016 (Rangers) 1
McKay, J. 1924 (Blackburn R) 1
McKay, R. 1928 (Newcastle U) 1
McKean, R. 1976 (Rangers) 1
**McKenna, S. F. 2018 (Aberdeen, Nottingham F,
  FC Copenhagen, Las Palmas) 43**
McKenzie, D. 1938 (Brentford) 1
McKeown, M. 1889 (Celtic) 2

McKie, J. 1898 (East Stirling)	1
McKillop, T. R. 1938 (Rangers)	1
McKimmie, S. 1989 (Aberdeen)	40
McKinlay, D. 1922 (Liverpool)	2
McKinlay, T. 1996 (Celtic)	22
McKinlay, W. 1994 (Dundee U, Blackburn R)	29
McKinnon, A. 1874 (Queen's Park)	1
McKinnon, R. 1966 (Rangers)	28
McKinnon, R. 1994 (Motherwell)	3
McLaren, A. 1929 (St Johnstone)	5
McLaren, A. 1947 (Preston NE)	4
McLaren, A. 1992 (Hearts, Rangers)	24
McLaren, A. 2001 (Kilmarnock)	1
McLaren, J. 1888 (Hibernian, Celtic)	3
McLaughlin, J. P. 2018 (Hearts, Sunderland)	2
McLean, A. 1926 (Celtic)	4
McLean, D. 1896 (St Bernards)	2
McLean, D. 1912 (Sheffield Wed)	1
McLean, G. 1968 (Dundee)	1
McLean, K. 2016 (Aberdeen, Norwich C)	**50**
McLean, T. 1967 (Kilmarnock)	9
McLeish, A. 1980 (Aberdeen)	77
McLeod, D. 1905 (Celtic)	4
McLeod, J. 1888 (Dumbarton)	5
McLeod, W. 1886 (Cowlairs)	1
McLintock, A. 1875 (Vale of Leven)	3
McLintock, F. 1963 (Leicester C, Arsenal)	9
McLuckie, J. S. 1934 (Manchester C)	1
McMahon, A. 1892 (Celtic)	6
McManus, S. 2007 (Celtic, Middlesbrough)	26
McMenemy, J. 1905 (Celtic)	12
McMenemy, J. 1934 (Motherwell)	1
McMillan, I. L. 1952 (Airdrieonians, Rangers)	6
McMillan, J. 1897 (St Bernards)	1
McMillan, T. 1887 (Dumbarton)	1
McMullan, J. 1920 (Partick Thistle, Manchester C)	16
McNab, A. 1921 (Morton)	2
McNab, A. 1937 (Sunderland, WBA)	2
McNab, C. D. 1931 (Dundee)	6
McNab, J. S. 1923 (Liverpool)	1
McNair, A. 1906 (Celtic)	15
McNamara, J. 1997 (Celtic, Wolverhampton W)	33
McNamee, D. 2004 (Livingston)	4
McNaught, W. 1951 (Raith R)	5
McNaughton, K. 2002 (Aberdeen, Cardiff C)	4
McNeill, W. 1961 (Celtic)	29
McNiel, H. 1874 (Queen's Park)	10
McNiel, M. 1876 (Rangers)	2
McNulty, M. 2019 (Reading)	2
McPhail, J. 1950 (Celtic)	5
McPhail, R. 1927 (Airdrieonians, Rangers)	17
McPherson, D. 1892 (Kilmarnock)	1
McPherson, D. 1989 (Hearts, Rangers)	27
McPherson, J. 1875 (Clydesdale)	1
McPherson, J. 1879 (Vale of Leven)	8
McPherson, J. 1888 (Kilmarnock, Cowlairs, Rangers)	9
McPherson, J. 1891 (Hearts)	1
McPherson, R. 1882 (Arthurlie)	1
McQueen, G. 1974 (Leeds U, Manchester U)	30
McQueen, M. 1890 (Leith Ath)	2
McRorie, D. M. 1931 (Morton)	1
McSpadyen, A. 1939 (Partick Thistle)	2
McStay, P. 1984 (Celtic)	76
McStay, W. 1921 (Celtic)	13
McSwegan, G. 2000 (Hearts)	2
McTavish, J. 1910 (Falkirk)	1
McTominay, S. F. 2018 (Manchester U, Napoli)	**61**
McWattie, G. C. 1901 (Queen's Park)	2
McWilliam, P. 1905 (Newcastle U)	8
Meechan, P. 1896 (Celtic)	1
Meiklejohn, D. D. 1922 (Rangers)	15
Menzies, A. 1906 (Hearts)	1
Mercer, R. 1912 (Hearts)	2
Middleton, R. 1930 (Cowdenbeath)	1
Millar, J. 1897 (Rangers)	3
Millar, J. 1963 (Rangers)	2
Miller, A. 1939 (Hearts)	1
Miller, C. 2001 (Dundee U)	1
Miller, J. 1931 (St Mirren)	5
Miller, K. 2001 (Rangers, Wolverhampton W, Celtic, Derby Co, Rangers, Bursaspor, Cardiff C, Vancouver Whitecaps)	69
Miller, L. 2006 (Dundee U, Aberdeen)	3
Miller, L. L. 2025 (Motherwell)	**2**
Miller, P. 1882 (Dumbarton)	3
Miller, T. 1920 (Liverpool, Manchester U)	3
Miller, W. 1876 (Third Lanark)	1
Miller, W. 1947 (Celtic)	6
Miller, W. 1975 (Aberdeen)	65
Mills, W. 1936 (Aberdeen)	3
Milne, J. V. 1938 (Middlesbrough)	2
Mitchell, D. 1890 (Rangers)	5
Mitchell, J. 1908 (Kilmarnock)	3
Mitchell, R. C. 1951 (Newcastle U)	2
Mochan, N. 1954 (Celtic)	3
Moir, W. 1950 (Bolton W)	1
Moncur, R. 1968 (Newcastle U)	16
Morgan, H. 1898 (St Mirren, Liverpool)	2
Morgan, L. 2018 (St Mirren, New York Red Bulls)	**7**
Morgan, W. 1967 (Burnley, Manchester U)	26
Morris, D. 1923 (Raith R)	6
Morris, H. 1950 (East Fife)	1
Morrison, J. C. 2008 (WBA)	46
Morrison, T. 1927 (St Mirren)	1
Morton, A. L. 1920 (Queen's Park, Rangers)	31
Morton, H. A. 1929 (Kilmarnock)	2
Mudie, J. K. 1957 (Blackpool)	17
Muir, W. 1907 (Dundee)	1
Muirhead, T. A. 1922 (Rangers)	8
Mulgrew, C. P. 2012 (Celtic, Blackburn R)	44
Mulhall, G. 1960 (Aberdeen, Sunderland)	3
Munro, A. D. 1937 (Hearts, Blackpool)	3
Munro, F. M. 1971 (Wolverhampton W)	9
Munro, I. 1979 (St Mirren)	7
Munro, N. 1888 (Abercorn)	2
Murdoch, J. 1931 (Motherwell)	1
Murdoch, R. 1966 (Celtic)	12
Murphy, F. 1938 (Celtic)	1
Murphy, J. 2018 (Rangers)	1
Murray, I. 2003 (Hibernian, Rangers)	6
Murray, J. 1895 (Renton)	1
Murray, J. 1958 (Hearts)	5
Murray, J. W. 1890 (Vale of Leven)	1
Murray, P. 1896 (Hibernian)	2
Murray, S. 1972 (Aberdeen)	1
Murty, G. S. 2004 (Reading)	4
Mutch, G. 1938 (Preston NE)	1
Naismith, S. J. 2007 (Kilmarnock, Rangers, Everton, Norwich C, Hearts)	51
Napier, C. E. 1932 (Celtic, Derby Co)	5
Narey, D. 1977 (Dundee U)	35
Naysmith, G. A. 2000 (Hearts, Everton, Sheffield U)	46
Neil, R. G. 1896 (Hibernian, Rangers)	2
Neill, R. W. 1876 (Queen's Park)	5
Neilson, R. 2007 (Hearts)	1
Nellies, P. 1913 (Hearts)	2
Nelson, J. 1925 (Cardiff C)	4
Nevin, P. K. F. 1986 (Chelsea, Everton, Tranmere R)	28
Niblo, T. D. 1904 (Aston Villa)	1
Nibloe, J. 1929 (Kilmarnock)	11
Nicholas, C. 1983 (Celtic, Arsenal, Aberdeen)	20
Nicholson, B. 2001 (Dunfermline Ath)	3
Nicol, S. 1985 (Liverpool)	27
Nisbet, J. 1929 (Ayr U)	3
Nisbet, K. 2021 (Hibernian)	11
Niven, J. B. 1885 (Moffat)	1
O'Connor, G. 2002 (Hibernian, Lokomotiv Moscow, Birmingham C)	16
O'Donnell, F. 1937 (Preston NE, Blackpool)	6
O'Donnell, P. 1994 (Motherwell)	1
O'Donnell, S. G. 2018 (Kilmarnock, Motherwell)	26
Ogilvie, D. H. 1934 (Motherwell)	1
O'Hare, J. 1970 (Derby Co)	13
O'Neil, B. 1996 (Celtic, Wolfsburg, Derby Co, Preston NE)	7
O'Neil, J. 2001 (Hibernian)	1
Ormond, W. E. 1954 (Hibernian)	6
O'Rourke, F. 1907 (Airdrieonians)	1
Orr, J. 1892 (Kilmarnock)	1
Orr, R. 1902 (Newcastle U)	2
Orr, T. 1952 (Morton)	2
Orr, W. 1900 (Celtic)	3
Orrock, R. 1913 (Falkirk)	1
Oswald, J. 1889 (Third Lanark, St Bernards, Rangers)	3
Palmer, L. J. 2019 (Sheffield Wed)	8
Parker, A. H. 1955 (Falkirk, Everton)	15

Parlane, D. 1973 (Rangers) 12
Parlane, R. 1878 (Vale of Leven) 3
Paterson, C. T. O. 2016 (Hearts, Cardiff C,
   Sheffield Wed) 17
Paterson, G. D. 1939 (Celtic) 1
Paterson, J. 1920 (Leicester C) 1
Paterson, J. 1931 (Cowdenbeath) 3
Paton, A. 1952 (Motherwell) 2
Paton, D. 1896 (St Bernards) 1
Paton, M. 1883 (Dumbarton) 5
Paton, R. 1879 (Vale of Leven) 2
Patrick, J. 1897 (St Mirren) 2
Patterson, N. K. 2021 (Rangers, Everton) **23**
Paul, H. McD. 1909 (Queen's Park) 3
Paul, W. 1888 (Partick Thistle) 3
Paul, W. 1891 (Dykebar) 1
Pearson, S. P. 2004 (Motherwell, Celtic, Derby Co) 10
Pearson, T. 1947 (Newcastle U) 2
Penman, A. 1966 (Dundee, Rangers) 4
Pettigrew, W. 1976 (Motherwell) 5
Phillips, J. 1877 (Queen's Park) 3
Phillips, M. 2012 (Blackpool, QPR, WBA) 16
Plenderleith, J. B. 1961 (Manchester C) 1
Porteous, R. T. 2023 (Watford) **13**
Porteous, W. 1903 (Hearts) 1
Pressley, S. J. 2000 (Hearts) 32
Pringle, C. 1921 (St Mirren) 1
Provan, D. 1964 (Rangers) 5
Provan, D. 1980 (Celtic) 10
Pursell, P. 1914 (Queen's Park) 1

Quashie, N. F. 2004 (Portsmouth, Southampton, WBA) 14
Quinn, J. 1905 (Celtic) 11
Quinn, P. 1961 (Motherwell) 4

Rae, G. 2001 (Dundee, Rangers, Cardiff C) 14
Rae, J. 1889 (Third Lanark) 2
Raeside, J. S. 1906 (Third Lanark) 1
Raisbeck, A. G. 1900 (Liverpool) 8
Ralston, A. 2022 (Celtic) **21**
Ramsay, C. W. 2023 (Liverpool) 1
Rankin, G. 1890 (Vale of Leven) 3
Rankin, R. 1929 (St Mirren) 1
Redpath, W. 1949 (Motherwell) 9
Reid, J. G. 1914 (Airdrieonians) 3
Reid, R. 1938 (Brentford) 1
Reid, W. 1911 (Rangers) 9
Reilly, L. 1949 (Hibernian) 38
Rennie, H. G. 1900 (Hearts, Hibernian) 13
Renny-Tailyour, H. W. 1873 (Royal Engineers) 1
Rhind, A. 1872 (Queen's Park) 1
Rhodes, J. L. 2012 (Huddersfield T, Blackburn R,
   Sheffield Wed) 14
Richmond, A. 1906 (Queen's Park) 1
Richmond, J. T. 1877 (Clydesdale, Queen's Park) 3
Ring, T. 1953 (Clyde) 12
Rioch, B. D. 1975 (Derby Co, Everton, Derby Co) 24
Riordan, D. G. 2006 (Hibernian) 3
Ritchie, A. 1891 (East Stirlingshire) 1
Ritchie, H. 1923 (Hibernian) 2
Ritchie, J. 1897 (Queen's Park) 1
Ritchie, M. T. 2015 (Bournemouth, Newcastle U) 16
Ritchie, P. S. 1999 (Hearts, Bolton W, Walsall) 7
Ritchie, W. 1962 (Rangers) 1
Robb, D. T. 1971 (Aberdeen) 5
Robb, W. 1926 (Rangers, Hibernian) 2
Robertson, A. 1955 (Clyde) 5
Robertson, A. H. 2014 (Dundee U, Hull C, Liverpool) **84**
Robertson, D. 1992 (Rangers) 3
Robertson, G. 1910 (Motherwell, Sheffield Wed) 4
Robertson, G. 1938 (Kilmarnock) 1
Robertson, H. 1962 (Dundee) 1
Robertson, J. 1931 (Dundee) 2
Robertson, J. 1991 (Hearts) 16
Robertson, J. N. 1978 (Nottingham F, Derby Co) 28
Robertson, J. G. 1965 (Tottenham H) 1
Robertson, J. T. 1898 (Everton, Southampton, Rangers) 16
Robertson, P. 1903 (Dundee) 1
Robertson, S. 2009 (Dundee U) 1
Robertson, T. 1889 (Queen's Park) 4
Robertson, T. 1898 (Hearts) 1
Robertson, W. 1887 (Dumbarton) 2
Robinson, R. 1974 (Dundee) 4

Robson, B. G. G. 2008 (Dundee U, Celtic,
   Middlesbrough) 17
Ross, M. 2002 (Rangers) 13
Rough, A. 1976 (Partick Thistle, Hibernian) 53
Rougvie, D. 1984 (Aberdeen) 1
Rowan, A. 1880 (Caledonian, Queen's Park) 2
Russell, D. 1895 (Hearts, Celtic) 6
Russell, J. 1890 (Cambuslang) 1
Russell, J. S. S. 2015 (Derby Co, Kansas City) 14
Russell, W. F. 1924 (Airdrieonians) 2
Rutherford, E. 1948 (Rangers) 1

St John, I. 1959 (Motherwell, Liverpool) 21
Saunders, S. 2011 (Motherwell) 1
Sawers, W. 1895 (Dundee) 1
Scarff, P. 1931 (Celtic) 1
Schaedler, E. 1974 (Hibernian) 1
Scott, A. S. 1957 (Rangers, Everton) 16
Scott, J. 1966 (Hibernian) 1
Scott, J. 1971 (Dundee) 2
Scott, M. 1898 (Airdrieonians) 1
Scott, R. 1894 (Airdrieonians) 1
Scoular, J. 1951 (Portsmouth) 9
Sellar, W. 1885 (Battlefield, Queen's Park) 9
Semple, W. 1886 (Cambuslang) 1
Severin, S. D. 2002 (Hearts, Aberdeen) 15
Shankland, L. 2020 (Dundee U, Hearts) **16**
Shankly, W. 1938 (Preston NE) 5
Sharp, G. M. 1985 (Everton) 12
Sharp, J. 1904 (Dundee, Woolwich Arsenal, Fulham) 5
Shaw, D. 1947 (Hibernian) 8
Shaw, F. W. 1884 (Pollokshields Ath) 2
Shaw, J. 1947 (Rangers) 4
Shearer, D. 1994 (Aberdeen) 7
Shearer, R. 1961 (Rangers) 4
Shinnie, A. M. 2013 (Inverness CT) 1
Shinnie, G. 2018 (Aberdeen) 6
Sillars, D. C. 1891 (Queen's Park) 5
Simpson, J. 1895 (Third Lanark) 3
Simpson, J. 1935 (Rangers) 14
Simpson, N. 1983 (Aberdeen) 5
Simpson, R. C. 1967 (Celtic) 5
Sinclair, G. L. 1910 (Hearts) 3
Sinclair, J. W. E. 1966 (Leicester C) 1
Skene, L. H. 1904 (Queen's Park) 1
Slicker, C. P. 2025 (Ipswich T) **1**
Sloan, T. 1904 (Third Lanark) 1
Smellie, R. 1887 (Queen's Park) 6
Smith, A. 1898 (Rangers) 20
Smith, D. 1966 (Aberdeen, Rangers) 2
Smith, G. 1947 (Hibernian) 18
Smith, H. G. 1988 (Hearts) 3
Smith, J. 1924 (Ayr U) 1
Smith, J. 1935 (Rangers) 2
Smith, J. 1968 (Aberdeen, Newcastle U) 4
Smith, J. 2003 (Celtic) 2
Smith, J. E. 1959 (Celtic) 2
Smith, Jas 1872 (Queen's Park) 1
Smith, John 1877 (Mauchline, Edinburgh University,
   Queen's Park) 10
Smith, N. 1897 (Rangers) 12
Smith, R. 1872 (Queen's Park) 2
Smith, T. M. 1934 (Kilmarnock, Preston NE) 2
Snodgrass, R. 2011 (Leeds U, Norwich C, Hull C,
   West Ham U) 28
Somers, P. 1905 (Celtic) 4
Somers, W. S. 1879 (Third Lanark, Queen's Park) 3
Somerville, G. 1886 (Queen's Park) 1
Souness, G. J. 1975 (Middlesbrough, Liverpool,
   Sampdoria) 54
Souttar, J. 2019 (Hearts, Rangers) **16**
Speedie, D. R. 1985 (Chelsea, Coventry C) 10
Speedie, F. 1903 (Rangers) 3
Speirs, J. H. 1908 (Rangers) 1
Spencer, J. 1995 (Chelsea, QPR) 14
Stanton, P. 1966 (Hibernian) 16
Stark, J. 1909 (Rangers) 1
Steel, W. 1947 (Morton, Derby Co, Dundee) 30
Steele, D. M. 1923 (Huddersfield) 3
Stein, C. 1969 (Rangers, Coventry C) 21
Stephen, J. F. 1947 (Bradford) 2
Stevenson, G. 1928 (Motherwell) 12
Stevenson, L. 2018 (Hibernian) 1
Stewart, A. 1888 (Queen's Park) 2

WALES

Duffy, R. M. 2006 (Portsmouth) 13
Dummett, P. 2014 (Newcastle U) 5
Durban, A. 1966 (Derby Co) 27
Dwyer, P. J. 1978 (Cardiff C) 10

Eardley, N. 2008 (Oldham Ath, Blackpool) 16
Earnshaw, R. 2002 (Cardiff C, WBA, Norwich C,
  Derby Co, Nottingham F, Cardiff C) 59
Easter, J. M. 2007 (Wycombe W, Plymouth Arg,
  Milton Keynes D, Crystal Palace, Millwall) 12
Eastwood, F. 2008 (Wolverhampton W, Coventry C) 11
Edwards, C. 1878 (Wrexham) 1
Edwards, C. N. H. 1996 (Swansea C) 1
Edwards, D. A. 2008 (Luton T, Wolverhampton W,
  Reading) 43
Edwards, G. 1947 (Birmingham, Cardiff C) 12
Edwards, H. 1878 (Wrexham Civil Service, Wrexham) 8
Edwards, J. H. 1876 (Wanderers) 1
Edwards, J. H. 1895 (Oswestry) 3
Edwards, J. H. 1898 (Aberystwyth) 1
Edwards, L. T. 1957 (Charlton Ath) 2
Edwards, R. I. 1978 (Chester, Wrexham) 4
Edwards, R. O. 2003 (Aston Villa, Wolverhampton W) 15
Edwards, R. W. 1998 (Bristol C) 4
Edwards, T. 1932 (Linfield) 1
Egan, W. 1892 (Chirk) 1
Ellis, B. 1932 (Motherwell) 6
Ellis, E. 1931 (Nunhead, Oswestry) 3
Emanuel, W. J. 1973 (Bristol C) 2
England, H. M. 1962 (Blackburn R, Tottenham H) 44
Evans, B. 1972 (Swansea C, Hereford U) 7
Evans, C. M. 2008 (Manchester C, Sheffield U) 13
Evans, D. G. 1926 (Reading, Huddersfield T) 4
Evans, H. P. 1922 (Cardiff C) 6
Evans, I. 1976 (Crystal Palace) 13
Evans, J. 1893 (Oswestry) 3
Evans, J. 1912 (Cardiff C) 8
Evans, J. H. 1922 (Southend U) 4
Evans, L. 2018 (Wolverhampton W, Sheffield U,
  Wigan Ath) 4
Evans, Len 1927 (Aberdare Ath, Cardiff C,
  Birmingham) 4
Evans, M. 1884 (Oswestry) 1
Evans, P. S. 2002 (Brentford, Bradford C) 2
Evans, R. 1902 (Clapton) 1
Evans, R. E. 1906 (Wrexham, Aston Villa, Sheffield U) 10
Evans, R. O. 1902 (Wrexham, Blackburn R,
  Coventry C) 10
Evans, R. S. 1964 (Swansea T) 1
Evans, S. J. 2007 (Wrexham) 7
Evans, T. J. 1927 (Clapton Orient, Newcastle U) 1
Evans, W. 1933 (Tottenham H) 6
Evans, W. A. W. 1876 (Oxford University) 2
Evans, W. G. 1890 (Bootle, Aston Villa) 3
Evelyn, E. C. 1887 (Crusaders) 1
Eyton-Jones, J. A. 1883 (Wrexham) 4

Farmer, G. 1885 (Oswestry) 2
Felgate, D. 1984 (Lincoln C) 1
Finnigan, R. J. 1930 (Wrexham) 1
Fletcher, C. N. 2004 (Bournemouth, West Ham U,
  Crystal Palace) 36
Flynn, B. 1975 (Burnley, Leeds U, Burnley) 66
Fon Williams, O. 2016 (Inverness CT) 1
Ford, T. 1947 (Swansea T, Aston Villa, Sunderland,
  Cardiff C) 38
Foulkes, H. E. 1932 (WBA) 1
Foulkes, W. I. 1952 (Newcastle U) 11
Foulkes, W. T. 1884 (Oswestry) 2
Fowler, J. 1925 (Swansea T) 6
Freeman, K. S. 2019 (Sheffield U) 1
Freestone, R. 2000 (Swansea C) 1

Gabbidon, D. L. 2002 (Cardiff C, West Ham U,
  QPR, Crystal Palace) 49
Garner, G. 2006 (Leyton Orient) 1
Garner, J. 1896 (Aberystwyth) 2
Giggs, R. J. 1992 (Manchester U) 64
Giles, D. C. 1980 (Swansea C, Crystal Palace) 12
Gillam, S. 1889 (Wrexham, Shrewsbury, Clapton) 5
Glascodine, G. 1879 (Wrexham) 1
Glover, E. M. 1932 (Grimsby T) 7
Godding, G. 1923 (Wrexham) 2
Godfrey, B. C. 1964 (Preston NE) 3

Goodwin, U. 1881 (Ruthin) 1
Goss, J. 1991 (Norwich C) 9
Gough, R. T. 1883 (Oswestry White Star) 1
Gray, A. 1924 (Oldham Ath, Manchester C,
  Manchester Central, Tranmere R, Chester) 24
Green, A. W. 1901 (Aston Villa, Notts Co, Nottingham F) 8
Green, C. R. 1965 (Birmingham C) 15
Green, G. H. 1938 (Charlton Ath) 4
Green, R. M. 1998 (Wolverhampton W) 2
Grey, Dr D. 1876 (Druids) 2
Griffiths, A. T. 1971 (Wrexham) 17
Griffiths, F. J. 1900 (Blackpool) 2
Griffiths, G. 1887 (Chirk) 1
Griffiths, J. H. 1953 (Swansea T) 1
Griffiths, L. 1902 (Wrexham) 1
Griffiths, M. W. 1947 (Leicester C) 11
Griffiths, P. 1884 (Chirk) 6
Griffiths, P. H. 1932 (Everton) 1
Griffiths, T. P. 1927 (Everton, Bolton W,
  Middlesbrough, Aston Villa) 21
Gunter, C. R. 2007 (Cardiff C, Tottenham H,
  Nottingham F, Reading, Charlton Ath) 109

Hall, G. D. 1988 (Chelsea) 9
Hallam, J. 1889 (Oswestry) 1
Hanford, H. 1934 (Swansea T, Sheffield Wed) 7
Harrington, A. C. 1956 (Cardiff C) 11
Harris, C. S. 1976 (Leeds U) 24
Harris, T. M. 2022 (Cardiff C, Oxford U) 11
Harris, W. C. 1954 (Middlesbrough) 6
Harrison, W. C. 1899 (Wrexham) 5
Hartson, J. 1995 (Arsenal, West Ham U, Wimbledon,
  Coventry C, Celtic) 51
Haworth, S. O. 1997 (Cardiff C, Coventry C) 5
Hayes, A. 1890 (Wrexham) 2
Hedges, R. P. 2018 (Barnsley, Aberdeen) 3
Henley, A. D. 2016 (Blackburn R) 2
Hennessey, W. R. 2007 (Wolverhampton W,
  Crystal Palace, Burnley, Nottingham F) 109
Hersee, A. M. 1886 (Bangor) 2
Hersee, R. 1886 (Llandudno) 1
Hewitt, R. 1958 (Cardiff C) 5
Hewitt, T. J. 1911 (Wrexham, Chelsea,
  South Liverpool) 8
Heywood, D. 1879 (Druids) 1
Hibbott, H. 1880 (Newtown Excelsior, Newtown) 3
Higham, G. G. 1878 (Oswestry) 2
Hill, M. R. 1972 (Ipswich T) 2
Hockey, T. 1972 (Sheffield U, Norwich C, Aston Villa) 9
Hoddinott, T. F. 1921 (Watford) 2
Hodges, G. 1984 (Wimbledon, Newcastle U, Watford,
  Sheffield U) 18
Hodgkinson, A. V. 1908 (Southampton) 1
Holden, A. 1984 (Chester C) 1
Hole, B. G. 1963 (Cardiff C, Blackburn R,
  Aston Villa, Swansea C) 30
Hole, W. J. 1921 (Swansea T) 9
Hollins, D. M. 1962 (Newcastle U) 11
Hopkins, I. J. 1935 (Brentford) 12
Hopkins, J. 1983 (Fulham, Crystal Palace) 16
Hopkins, M. 1956 (Tottenham H) 34
Horne, B. 1988 (Portsmouth, Southampton, Everton,
  Birmingham C) 59
Howell, E. G. 1888 (Builth) 3
Howells, R. G. 1954 (Cardiff C) 2
Hugh, A. R. 1930 (Newport Co) 1
Hughes, A. 1894 (Rhos) 2
Hughes, A. 1907 (Chirk) 1
Hughes, C. M. 1992 (Luton T, Wimbledon) 8
Hughes, E. 1899 (Everton, Tottenham H) 14
Hughes, E. 1906 (Wrexham, Nottingham F,
  Wrexham, Manchester C) 16
Hughes, F. W. 1882 (Northwich Victoria) 6
Hughes, I. 1951 (Luton T) 4
Hughes, J. 1877 (Cambridge University, Aberystwyth) 2
Hughes, J. 1905 (Liverpool) 3
Hughes, J. 1935 (Blackburn R) 1
Hughes, L. M. 1984 (Manchester U, Barcelona,
  Manchester U, Chelsea, Southampton) 72
Hughes, P. W. 1887 (Bangor) 3
Hughes, W. 1891 (Bootle) 3
Hughes, W. A. 1949 (Blackburn R) 5
Hughes, W. M. 1938 (Birmingham) 10
Humphreys, J. V. 1947 (Everton) 1

Humphreys, R. 1888 (Druids)	1
Hunter, A. H. 1887 (FA of Wales Secretary)	1
Huws, E. W. 2014 (Manchester C, Wigan Ath, Cardiff C)	11
Isgrove, L. J. 2016 (Southampton)	1
Jackett, K. 1983 (Watford)	31
Jackson, W. 1899 (St Helens Rec)	1
James, D. O. 2019 (Swansea C, Manchester U, Leeds U)	**57**
James, E. 1893 (Chirk)	8
James, E. G. 1966 (Blackpool)	9
James, J. A. 2023 (Birmingham C, Rennes)	**20**
James, L. 1972 (Burnley, Derby Co, QPR, Burnley, Swansea C, Sunderland)	54
James, R. M. 1979 (Swansea C, Stoke C, QPR, Leicester C, Swansea C)	47
James, W. 1931 (West Ham U)	2
Jarrett, R. H. 1889 (Ruthin)	2
Jarvis, A. L. 1967 (Hull C)	3
Jenkins, E. 1925 (Lovell's Ath)	1
Jenkins, J. 1924 (Brighton & HA)	8
Jenkins, R. W. 1902 (Rhyl)	1
Jenkins, S. R. 1996 (Swansea C, Huddersfield T)	16
Jenkyns, C. A. L. 1892 (Small Heath, Woolwich Arsenal, Newton Heath, Walsall)	8
Jennings, W. 1914 (Bolton W)	11
John, D. C. 2013 (Cardiff C, Rangers, Swansea C)	7
John, R. F. 1923 (Arsenal)	15
John, W. R. 1931 (Walsall, Stoke C, Preston NE, Sheffield U, Swansea T)	14
Johnson, A. J. 1999 (Nottingham F, WBA)	15
Johnson, B. P. 2021 (Nottingham F, Tottenham H)	**37**
Johnson, M. G. 1964 (Swansea T)	1
Jones, A. 1987 (Port Vale, Charlton Ath)	6
Jones, A. F. 1877 (Oxford University)	1
Jones, A. T. 1905 (Nottingham F, Notts Co)	2
Jones, Bryn 1935 (Wolverhampton W, Arsenal)	17
Jones, B. S. 1963 (Swansea T, Plymouth Arg, Cardiff C)	15
Jones, Charlie 1926 (Nottingham F, Arsenal)	8
Jones, Cliff 1954 (Swansea T, Tottenham H, Fulham)	59
Jones, C. W. 1935 (Birmingham)	2
Jones, D. 1888 (Chirk, Bolton W, Manchester C)	14
Jones, D. E. 1976 (Norwich C)	8
Jones, D. O. 1934 (Leicester C)	7
Jones, Evan 1910 (Chelsea, Oldham Ath, Bolton W)	7
Jones, F. R. 1885 (Bangor)	3
Jones, F. W. 1893 (Small Heath)	1
Jones, G. P. 1907 (Wrexham)	2
Jones, H. 1902 (Aberaman)	1
Jones, Humphrey 1885 (Bangor, Queen's Park, East Stirlingshire, Queen's Park)	14
Jones, Ivor 1920 (Swansea T, WBA)	10
Jones, Jeffrey 1908 (Llandrindod Wells)	3
Jones, J. 1876 (Druids)	1
Jones, J. 1883 (Berwyn Rangers)	3
Jones, J. 1925 (Wrexham)	1
Jones, J. L. 1895 (Sheffield U, Tottenham H)	21
Jones, J. Love 1906 (Stoke, Middlesbrough)	2
Jones, J. O. 1901 (Bangor)	2
Jones, J. P. 1976 (Liverpool, Wrexham, Chelsea, Huddersfield T)	72
Jones, J. T. 1912 (Stoke, Crystal Palace)	15
Jones, K. 1950 (Aston Villa)	1
Jones, Leslie J. 1933 (Cardiff C, Coventry C, Arsenal	11
Jones, M. A. 2007 (Wrexham)	2
Jones, M. G. 2000 (Leeds U, Leicester C)	13
Jones, P. L. 1997 (Liverpool, Tranmere R)	2
Jones, P. S. 1997 (Stockport Co, Southampton, Wolverhampton W, QPR)	50
Jones, P. W. 1971 (Bristol R)	1
Jones, R. 1887 (Bangor, Crewe Alex)	3
Jones, R. 1898 (Leicester Fosse)	1
Jones, R. 1899 (Druids)	1
Jones, R. 1900 (Bangor)	2
Jones, R. 1906 (Millwall)	2
Jones, R. A. 1884 (Druids)	4
Jones, R. A. 1994 (Sheffield Wed)	1
Jones, R. S. 1894 (Everton)	1
Jones, S. 1887 (Wrexham, Chester)	2
Jones, S. 1893 (Wrexham, Burton Swifts, Druids)	6
Jones, T. 1926 (Manchester Utd)	4
Jones, T. D. 1908 (Aberdare)	1

Jones, T. G. 1938 (Everton)	17
Jones, T. J. 1932 (Sheffield Wed)	2
Jones, V. P. 1995 (Wimbledon)	9
Jones, W. E. A. 1947 (Swansea T, Tottenham H)	4
Jones, W. J. 1901 (Aberdare, West Ham U)	4
Jones, W. Lot 1905 (Manchester C, Southend U)	20
Jones, W. P. 1889 (Druids, Wynnstay)	4
Jones, W. R. 1897 (Aberystwyth)	1
Keenor, F. C. 1920 (Cardiff C, Crewe Alex)	32
Kelly, F. C. 1899 (Wrexham, Druids)	3
Kelsey, A. J. 1954 (Arsenal)	41
Kenrick, S. L. 1876 (Druids, Oswestry, Shropshire Wanderers)	5
Ketley, C. F. 1882 (Druids)	1
King, A. P. 2009 (Leicester C)	50
King, J. 1955 (Swansea T)	1
King, T. L. 2024 (Wolverhampton W)	1
Kinsey, N. 1951 (Norwich C, Birmingham C)	7
Knill, A. R. 1989 (Swansea C)	1
Koumas, J. 2001 (Tranmere R, WBA, Wigan Ath)	34
Koumas, L. T. 2024 (Liverpool)	**6**
Krzywicki, R. L. 1970 (WBA, Huddersfield T)	8
Lambert, R. 1947 (Liverpool)	5
Latham, G. 1905 (Liverpool, Southport Central, Cardiff C)	10
Law, B. J. 1990 (QPR)	1
Lawrence, E. 1930 (Clapton Orient, Notts Co)	2
Lawrence, J. A. 2019 (Anderlecht, St Pauli)	11
Lawrence, S. 1932 (Swansea T)	8
Lawrence, T. M. 2016 (Leicester C, Derby Co)	23
Lea, A. 1889 (Wrexham)	4
Lea, C. 1965 (Ipswich T)	2
Leary, P. 1889 (Bangor)	1
Ledley, J. C. 2006 (Cardiff C, Celtic, Crystal Palace, Derby Co)	77
Leek, K. 1961 (Leicester C, Newcastle U, Birmingham C, Northampton T)	13
Legg, A. 1996 (Birmingham C, Cardiff C)	6
Lever, A. R. 1953 (Leicester C)	1
Levitt, D. J. C. 2021 (Manchester U, Dundee U)	13
Lewis, B. 1891 (Chester, Wrexham, Middlesbrough, Wrexham)	10
Lewis, D. 1927 (Arsenal)	3
Lewis, D. 1983 (Swansea C)	1
Lewis, D. J. 1933 (Swansea T)	2
Lewis, D. M. 1890 (Bangor)	2
Lewis, J. 1906 (Bristol R)	1
Lewis, J. 1926 (Cardiff C)	1
Lewis, T. 1881 (Wrexham)	2
Lewis, W. 1885 (Bangor, Crewe Alex, Chester, Manchester C, Chester)	27
Lewis, W. L. 1927 (Swansea T, Huddersfield T)	6
Llewellyn, C. M. 1998 (Norwich C, Wrexham)	6
Lloyd, B. W. 1976 (Wrexham)	3
Lloyd, J. W. 1879 (Wrexham, Newtown)	2
Lloyd, R. A. 1891 (Ruthin)	2
Lockley, A. 1898 (Chirk)	1
Lockyer, T. A. 2018 (Bristol R, Charlton Ath, Luton T)	16
Lovell, S. 1982 (Crystal Palace, Millwall)	6
Low, J. D. 2024 (Wycombe W)	2
Lowndes, S. R. 1983 (Newport Co, Millwall, Barnsley)	10
Lowrie, G. 1948 (Coventry C, Newcastle U)	4
Lucas, P. M. 1962 (Leyton Orient)	4
Lucas, W. H. 1949 (Swansea T)	7
Lumber, A. 1929 (Wrexham, Wolverhampton W)	4
Lynch, J. J. 2013 (Huddersfield T)	1
MacDonald, S. B. 2011 (Swansea C, Bournemouth)	4
Maguire, G. T. 1990 (Portsmouth)	7
Mahoney, J. F. 1968 (Stoke C, Middlesbrough, Swansea C)	51
Mardon, P. J. 1996 (WBA)	1
Margetson, M. W. 2004 (Cardiff C)	1
Marriott, A. 1996 (Wrexham)	5
Martin, T. J. 1930 (Newport Co)	1
Marustik, C. 1982 (Swansea C)	6
Mates, J. 1891 (Chirk)	3
Matondo, R. 2019 (Manchester C, Schalke 04, Rangers)	**15**
Matthews, A. J. 2011 (Cardiff C, Celtic, Sunderland)	14
Matthews, R. W. 1921 (Liverpool, Bristol C, Bradford)	3
Matthews, W. 1905 (Chester)	2
Matthias, J. S. 1896 (Brymbo, Shrewsbury T, Wolverhampton W)	5

Matthias, T. J. 1914 (Wrexham) 12
Mays, A. W. 1929 (Wrexham) 1
McCarthy, T. P. 1889 (Wrexham) 1
McMillan, R. 1881 (Shrewsbury Engineers) 2
Medwin, T. C. 1953 (Swansea T, Tottenham H) 30
Melville, A. K. 1990 (Swansea C, Oxford U,
    Sunderland, Fulham, West Ham U) 65
Mepham, C. J. 2018 (Brentford, Bournemouth) 49
Meredith, S. 1900 (Chirk, Stoke, Leyton) 8
Meredith, W. H. 1895 (Manchester C, Manchester U) 48
Mielczarek, R. 1971 (Rotherham U) 1
Millership, H. 1920 (Rotherham Co) 6
Millington, A. H. 1963 (WBA, Crystal Palace,
    Peterborough U, Swansea C) 21
Mills, T. J. 1934 (Clapton Orient, Leicester C) 4
Mills-Roberts, R. H. 1885 (St Thomas' Hospital,
    Preston NE, Llanberis) 8
Moore, G. 1960 (Cardiff C, Chelsea, Manchester U,
    Northampton T, Charlton Ath) 21
**Moore, K. R. F. 2020 (Wigan Ath, Cardiff C,
    Bournemouth, Sheffield U)** 49
Morgan, C. 2007 (Milton Keynes D, Peterborough U,
    Preston NE) 23
Morgan, J. R. 1877 (Cambridge University,
    Derby School Staff) 10
Morgan, J. T. 1905 (Wrexham) 1
Morgan-Owen, H. 1902 (Oxford University, Corinthians) 5
Morgan-Owen, M. M. 1897 (Oxford University,
    Corinthians) 12
Morison, S. W. 2011 (Millwall, Norwich C) 20
Morley, E. J. 1925 (Swansea T, Clapton Orient) 4
Morrell, J. 2. 2020 (Bristol C, Luton T, Portsmouth) 37
Morris, A. G. 1896 (Aberystwyth, Swindon T,
    Nottingham F) 21
Morris, C. 1900 (Chirk, Derby Co, Huddersfield T) 27
Morris, E. 1893 (Chirk) 3
Morris, H. 1894 (Sheffield U, Manchester C,
    Grimsby T) 3
Morris, J. 1887 (Oswestry) 1
Morris, J. 1898 (Chirk) 1
Morris, R. 1900 (Chirk, Shrewsbury T) 6
Morris, R. 1902 (Newtown, Druids, Liverpool,
    Leeds C, Grimsby T, Plymouth Arg) 11
Morris, S. 1937 (Birmingham) 5
Morris, W. 1947 (Burnley) 5
Moulsdale, J. R. B. 1925 (Corinthians) 1
Murphy, J. P. 1933 (WBA) 15
Myhill, G. O. 2008 (Hull C, WBA) 19

Nardiello, D. 1978 (Coventry C) 2
Nardiello, D. A. 2007 (Barnsley, QPR) 3
Neal, J. E. 1931 (Colwyn Bay) 2
Neilson, A. B. 1992 (Newcastle U, Southampton) 5
Newnes, J. 1926 (Nelson) 1
Newton, L. F. 1912 (Cardiff Corinthians) 1
Nicholas, D. S. 1923 (Stoke, Swansea T) 3
Nicholas, P. 1979 (Crystal Palace, Arsenal, Crystal
    Palace, Luton T, Aberdeen, Chelsea, Watford) 73
Nicholls, J. 1924 (Newport Co, Cardiff C) 4
Niedzwiecki, E. A. 1985 (Chelsea) 2
Nock, W. 1897 (Newtown) 1
Nogan, L. M. 1992 (Watford, Reading) 2
Norman, A. J. 1986 (Hull C) 5
Norrington-Davies, R. L. 2021 (Sheffield U) 13
Nurse, M. T. G. 1960 (Swansea T, Middlesbrough) 12
Nyatanga, L. J. 2006 (Derby Co, Bristol C) 34

O'Callaghan, E. 1929 (Tottenham H) 11
Oliver, A. 1905 (Bangor, Blackburn R) 2
Oster, J. M. 1998 (Everton, Sunderland) 13
O'Sullivan, P. A. 1973 (Brighton & HA) 3
Owen, D. 1879 (Oswestry) 1
Owen, E. 1884 (Ruthin Grammar School) 3
Owen, G. 1888 (Chirk, Newton Heath, Chirk) 4
Owen, J. 1892 (Newton Heath) 1
Owen, T. 1879 (Oswestry) 1
Owen, Trevor 1899 (Crewe Alex) 2
Owen, W. 1884 (Chirk) 16
Owen, W. P. 1880 (Ruthin) 12
Owens, J. 1902 (Wrexham) 1

Page, M. E. 1971 (Birmingham C) 28
Page, R. J. 1997 (Watford, Sheffield U, Cardiff C,
    Coventry C) 41

Palmer, D. 1957 (Swansea T) 3
Parris, J. E. 1932 (Bradford) 1
Parry, B. J. 1951 (Swansea T) 1
Parry, C. 1891 (Everton, Newtown) 13
Parry, E. 1922 (Liverpool) 5
Parry, M. 1901 (Liverpool) 16
Parry, P. I. 2004 (Cardiff C) 12
Parry, T. D. 1900 (Oswestry) 7
Parry, W. 1895 (Newtown) 1
Partridge, D. W. 2005 (Motherwell, Bristol C) 7
Pascoe, C. 1984 (Swansea C, Sunderland) 10
Paul, R. 1949 (Swansea T, Manchester C) 33
Peake, E. 1908 (Aberystwyth, Liverpool) 11
Peers, E. J. 1914 (Wolverhampton W, Port Vale) 12
Pembridge, M. A. 1992 (Luton T, Derby Co,
    Sheffield W, Benfica, Everton, Fulham) 54
Perry, E. 1938 (Doncaster R) 3
Perry, J. 1994 (Cardiff C) 1
Phennah, E. 1878 (Civil Service) 1
Phillips, C. 1931 (Wolverhampton W, Aston Villa) 13
Phillips, D. 1984 (Plymouth Arg, Manchester C,
    Coventry C, Norwich C, Nottingham F) 62
Phillips, L. 1971 (Cardiff C, Aston Villa, Swansea C,
    Charlton Ath) 58
Phillips, T. J. S. 1973 (Chelsea) 4
Phoenix, H. 1882 (Wrexham) 1
Pipe, D. R. 2003 (Coventry C) 1
Poland, G. 1939 (Wrexham) 2
Pontin, K. 1980 (Cardiff C) 2
Poole, R. L. 2024 (Portsmouth) 1
Powell, A. 1947 (Leeds U, Everton, Birmingham C) 8
Powell, D. 1968 (Wrexham, Sheffield U) 11
Powell, I. V. 1947 (QPR, Aston Villa) 8
Powell, J. 1878 (Druids, Bolton W, Newton Heath) 15
Powell, Seth 1885 (Oswestry, WBA) 7
Price, H. 1907 (Aston Villa, Burton U, Wrexham) 5
Price, J. 1877 (Wrexham) 12
Price, L. P. 2006 (Ipswich T, Derby Co,
    Crystal Palace) 11
Price, P. 1980 (Luton T, Tottenham H) 25
Pring, K. D. 1966 (Rotherham U) 3
Pritchard, H. K. 1985 (Bristol C) 1
Pryce-Jones, A. W. 1895 (Newtown) 1
Pryce-Jones, W. E. 1887 (Cambridge University) 5
Pugh, A. 1889 (Rhostyllen) 1
Pugh, D. H. 1896 (Wrexham, Lincoln C) 7
Pugsley, J. 1930 (Charlton Ath) 1
Pullen, W. J. 1926 (Plymouth Arg) 1

**Ramsey, A. J. 2009 (Arsenal, Juventus, Rangers, Nice,
    Cardiff C)** 86
Rankmore, F. E. J. 1966 (Peterborough U) 1
Ratcliffe, K. 1981 (Everton, Cardiff C) 59
Rea, J. C. 1894 (Aberystwyth) 9
Ready, K. 1997 (QPR) 5
Reece, G. I. 1966 (Sheffield U, Cardiff C) 29
Reed, W. G. 1955 (Ipswich T) 2
Rees, A. 1984 (Birmingham C) 1
Rees, J. M. 1992 (Luton T) 1
Rees, R. R. 1965 (Coventry C, WBA, Nottingham F) 39
Rees, W. 1949 (Cardiff C, Tottenham H) 4
Ribeiro, C. M. 2010 (Bristol C) 2
Richards, A. 1932 (Barnsley) 1
Richards, A. D. J. (Jazz) 2012 (Swansea C, Cardiff C) 14
Richards, D. 1931 (Wolverhampton W, Brentford,
    Birmingham) 21
Richards, G. 1899 (Druids, Oswestry, Shrewsbury T) 6
Richards, R. W. 1920 (Wolverhampton W,
    West Ham U, Mold) 9
Richards, S. V. 1947 (Cardiff C) 1
Richards, W. E. 1933 (Fulham) 1
Ricketts, S. D. 2005 (Swansea C, Hull C, Bolton W,
    Wolverhampton W) 52
Roach, J. 1885 (Oswestry) 1
Robbins, W. W. 1931 (Cardiff C, WBA) 11
Roberts, A. M. 1993 (QPR) 2
Roberts, C. R. J. 2018 (Swansea C, Burnley) 63
Roberts, D. F. 1973 (Oxford U, Hull C) 17
Roberts, G. W. 2000 (Tranmere R) 9
Roberts, I. W. 1990 (Watford, Huddersfield T,
    Leicester C, Norwich C) 15
Roberts, Jas 1913 (Wrexham) 2
Roberts, J. 1879 (Corwen, Berwyn R) 7
Roberts, J. 1881 (Ruthin) 2

Williams, N. S. 2021 (Liverpool, Nottingham F) — 47
Williams, R. 1935 (Newcastle U) — 2
Williams, R. P. 1886 (Caernarvon) — 1
Williams, S. G. 1954 (WBA, Southampton) — 43
Williams, W. 1876 (Druids, Oswestry, Druids) — 11
Williams, W. 1925 (Northampton T) — 1
Wilson, H. M. 2013 (Liverpool, Fulham) — 62
Wilson, J. S. 2013 (Bristol C) — 1
Witcomb, D. F. 1947 (WBA, Sheffield Wed) — 3
Woodburn, B. 2018 (Liverpool) — 11

Woosnam, A. P. 1959 (Leyton Orient, West Ham U,
 Aston Villa) — 17
Woosnam, G. 1879 (Newtown Excelsior) — 1
Worthington, T. 1894 (Newtown) — 1
Wynn, G. A. 1909 (Wrexham, Manchester C) — 11
Wynn, W. 1903 (Chirk) — 1

Yorath, T. C. 1970 (Leeds U, Coventry C,
 Tottenham H, Vancouver Whitecaps) — 59
Young, E. 1990 (Wimbledon, Crystal Palace,
 Wolverhampton W) — 21

REPUBLIC OF IRELAND

Aherne, T. 1946 (Belfast Celtic, Luton T) — 16
Aldridge, J. W. 1986 (Oxford U, Liverpool,
 Real Sociedad, Tranmere R) — 69
Ambrose, P. 1955 (Shamrock R) — 5
Anderson, J. 1980 (Preston NE, Newcastle U) — 16
Andrews, K. J. 2009 (Blackburn R, WBA) — 35
Andrews, P. 1936 (Bohemians) — 1
Armstrong, S. N. 2024 (QPR) — 1
Arrigan, T. 1938 (Waterford) — 1
Arter, H. N. 2015 (Bournemouth) — 19
Azaz, F. I. 2024 (Middlesbrough) — 7

Babb, P. A. 1994 (Coventry C, Liverpool, Sunderland) — 35
Bailham, E. 1964 (Shamrock R) — 1
Barber, E. 1966 (Shelbourne, Birmingham C) — 2
Barrett, G. 2003 (Arsenal, Coventry C) — 6
Barry, P. 1928 (Fordsons) — 2
Bazunu, G. O. 2021 (Manchester C, Southampton) — 22
Beglin, J. 1984 (Liverpool) — 15
Bennett, A. J. 2007 (Reading) — 1
Bermingham, J. 1929 (Bohemians) — 1
Bermingham, P. 1935 (St James' Gate) — 1
Best, L. J. B. 2009 (Coventry C, Newcastle U) — 7
Bonner, P. 1981 (Celtic) — 80
Boyle, A. 2017 (Preston NE) — 1
Braddish, S. 1978 (Dundalk) — 2
Bradshaw, P. 1939 (St James' Gate) — 5
Brady, F. 1926 (Fordsons) — 2
**Brady, R. 2013 (Hull C, Norwich C, Burnley,
 Preston NE)** — 72
Brady, T. R. 1964 (QPR) — 6
Brady, W. L. 1975 (Arsenal, Juventus, Sampdoria,
 Internazionale, Ascoli, West Ham U) — 72
Branagan, K. G. 1997 (Bolton W) — 1
Breen, G. 1996 (Birmingham C, Coventry C,
 West Ham U, Sunderland) — 63
Breen, T. 1937 (Manchester U, Shamrock R) — 5
Brennan, F. 1965 (Drumcondra) — 1
Brennan, S. A. 1965 (Manchester U, Waterford) — 19
Brown, J. 1937 (Coventry C) — 2
Browne, A. J. 2017 (Preston NE, Sunderland) — 37
Browne, W. 1964 (Bohemians) — 3
Bruce, A. S. 2007 (Ipswich T) — 2
Buckley, L. 1984 (Shamrock R, Waregem) — 2
Burke, F. 1952 (Cork Ath) — 1
Burke, G. D. 2018 (Shamrock R, Preston NE) — 1
Burke, J. 1929 (Shamrock R) — 1
Burke, J. 1934 (Cork) — 1
Butler, P. J. 2000 (Sunderland) — 1
Butler, T. 2003 (Sunderland) — 2
Byrne, A. B. 1970 (Southampton) — 14
Byrne, D. 1929 (Shelbourne, Shamrock R, Coleraine) — 3
Byrne, J. 1928 (Bray Unknowns) — 1
Byrne, J. 1985 (QPR, Le Havre, Brighton & HA,
 Sunderland, Millwall) — 23
Byrne, J. 2004 (Shelbourne) — 2
Byrne, J. 2020 (Shamrock R) — 4
Byrne, P. 1931 (Dolphin, Shelbourne, Drumcondra) — 3
Byrne, P. 1984 (Shamrock R) — 8
Byrne, S. 1931 (Bohemians) — 1

Campbell, A. 1985 (Santander) — 3
Campbell, N. 1971 (St Patrick's Ath, Fortuna Cologne) — 11
Cannon, H. 1926 (Bohemians) — 2
Cannon, T. C. 2024 (Leicester C) — 2
Cantwell, N. 1954 (West Ham U, Manchester U) — 36
Carey, B. P. 1992 (Manchester U, Leicester C) — 3
Carey, J. J. 1938 (Manchester U) — 29
Carolan, J. 1960 (Manchester U) — 2
Carr, S. 1999 (Tottenham H, Newcastle U) — 44

Carroll, B. 1949 (Shelbourne) — 2
Carroll, T. R. 1968 (Ipswich T, Birmingham C) — 17
Carsley, L. K. 1998 (Derby Co, Blackburn R,
 Coventry C, Everton) — 39
Cascarino, A. G. 1986 (Gillingham, Millwall,
 Aston Villa, Celtic, Chelsea, Marseille, Nancy) — 88
Chandler, J. 1980 (Leeds U) — 2
Chatton, H. A. 1931 (Shelbourne, Dumbarton, Cork) — 3
Christie, C. S. F. 2015 (Derby Co, Middlesbrough,
 Fulham) — 30
Clark, C. 2011 (Aston Villa, Newcastle U) — 36
Clarke, C. R. 2004 (Stoke C) — 2
Clarke, J. 1978 (Drogheda U) — 1
Clarke, K. 1948 (Drumcondra) — 2
Clarke, M. 1950 (Shamrock R) — 1
Clinton, T. J. 1951 (Everton) — 3
Coad, P. 1947 (Shamrock R) — 11
Coffey, T. 1950 (Drumcondra) — 1
Coleman, S. 2011 (Everton) — 73
Colfer, M. D. 1950 (Shelbourne) — 2
Colgan, N. 2002 (Hibernian, Barnsley) — 9
Collins, F. 1927 (Jacobs) — 1
Collins, J. S. 2020 (Luton T, Cardiff C) — 14
**Collins, N. M. 2022 (Burnley, Wolverhampton W,
 Brentford)** — 30
Conmy, O. M. 1965 (Peterborough U) — 5
Connolly, A. A. 2020 (Brighton & HA, Hull C) — 9
Connolly, D. J. 1996 (Watford, Feyenoord,
 Wolverhampton W, Excelsior, Feyenoord,
 Wimbledon, West Ham U, Wigan Ath) — 41
Connolly, H. 1937 (Cork) — 1
Connolly, J. 1926 (Fordsons) — 1
Conroy, G. A. 1970 (Stoke C) — 27
Conway, J. P. 1967 (Fulham, Manchester C) — 20
Corr, P. J. 1949 (Everton) — 4
Courtney, E. 1946 (Cork U) — 1
Cox, S. R. 2011 (WBA, Nottingham F) — 30
Coyle, O. C. 1994 (Bolton W) — 1
Coyne, T. 1992 (Celtic, Tranmere R, Motherwell) — 22
Crowe, G. 2003 (Bohemians) — 2
Cullen, J. J. 2020 (West Ham U, Anderlecht, Burnley) — 42
Cummins, G. P. 1954 (Luton T) — 19
Cuneen, T. 1951 (Limerick) — 1
Cunningham, G. R. 2010 (Manchester C, Bristol C) — 4
Cunningham, K. 1996 (Wimbledon, Birmingham C) — 72
Curtis, D. P. 1957 (Shelbourne, Bristol C, Ipswich T,
 Exeter C) — 17
Curtis, R. 2019 (Portsmouth) — 7
Cusack, S. 1953 (Limerick) — 1

Daish, L. S. 1992 (Cambridge U, Coventry C) — 5
Daly, G. A. 1973 (Manchester U, Derby Co,
 Coventry C, Birmingham C, Shrewsbury T) — 48
Daly, J. 1932 (Shamrock R) — 2
Daly, M. 1978 (Wolverhampton W) — 2
Daly, P. 1950 (Shamrock R) — 1
Davis, T. L. 1937 (Oldham Ath, Tranmere R) — 4
Deacy, E. 1982 (Aston Villa) — 4
Delaney, D. F. 2008 (QPR, Ipswich T, Crystal Palace) — 9
Delap, R. J. 1998 (Derby Co, Southampton) — 11
De Mange, K. J. P. P. 1987 (Liverpool, Hull C) — 2
Dempsey, J. T. 1967 (Fulham, Chelsea) — 19
Dennehy, J. 1972 (Cork Hibernians, Nottingham F,
 Walsall) — 11
Desmond, P. 1950 (Middlesbrough) — 4
Devine, J. 1980 (Arsenal, Norwich C) — 13
Doherty, G. M. T. 2000 (Luton T, Tottenham H,
 Norwich C) — 34
**Doherty, M. J. 2018 (Wolverhampton W, Tottenham H,
 Atletico Madrid, Wolverhampton W)** — 52

Donnelly, J. 1935 (Dundalk)	10
Donnelly, T. 1938 (Drumcondra, Shamrock R)	2
Donovan, D. C. 1955 (Everton)	5
Donovan, T. 1980 (Aston Villa)	2
Douglas, J. 2004 (Blackburn R, Leeds U)	8
Dowdall, C. 1928 (Fordsons, Barnsley, Cork)	3
Doyle, C. 1959 (Shelbourne)	1
Doyle, C. A. 2007 (Birmingham C, Bradford C)	4
Doyle, D. 1926 (Shamrock R)	1
Doyle, K. E. 2006 (Reading, Wolverhampton W, Colorado Rapids)	63
Doyle, L. 1932 (Dolphin)	1
Doyle, M. P. 2004 (Coventry C)	1
Duff, D. A. 1998 (Blackburn R, Chelsea, Newcastle U, Fulham)	100
Duffy, B. 1950 (Shamrock R)	1
Duffy, S. P. M. 2014 (Everton, Blackburn R, Brighton & HA, Norwich C)	61
Duggan, H. A. 1927 (Leeds U, Newport Co)	5
Dunne, P. 1962 (Manchester U, Bolton W)	33
Dunne, J. 1930 (Sheffield U, Arsenal, Southampton, Shamrock R)	15
Dunne, J. C. 1971 (Fulham)	1
Dunne, J. D. G. 2025 (QPR)	**1**
Dunne, L. 1935 (Manchester C)	2
Dunne, P. A. J. 1965 (Manchester U)	5
Dunne, R. P. 2000 (Everton, Manchester C, Aston Villa, QPR)	80
Dunne, S. 1953 (Luton T)	15
Dunne, T. 1956 (St Patrick's Ath)	3
Dunning, P. 1971 (Shelbourne)	2
Dunphy, E. M. 1966 (York C, Millwall)	23
Dwyer, N. M. 1960 (West Ham U, Swansea T)	14
Ebosele, F. O. 2024 (Udinese)	**9**
Eccles, P. 1986 (Shamrock R)	1
Egan, J. 2017 (Brentford, Sheffield U)	36
Egan, R. 1929 (Dundalk)	1
Eglington, T. J. 1946 (Shamrock R, Everton)	24
Elliot, R. 2014 (Newcastle U)	4
Elliott, S. W. 2005 (Sunderland)	9
Ellis, P. 1935 (Bohemians)	7
Evans, M. J. 1998 (Southampton)	1
Fagan, E. 1973 (Shamrock R)	1
Fagan, F. 1955 (Manchester C, Derby Co)	8
Fagan, J. 1926 (Shamrock R)	1
Fahey, K. D. 2010 (Birmingham C)	16
Fairclough, M. 1982 (Dundalk)	2
Fallon, S. 1951 (Celtic)	8
Fallon, W. J. 1935 (Notts Co, Sheffield Wed)	9
Farquharson, T. G. 1929 (Cardiff C)	4
Farrell, P. 1937 (Hibernian)	2
Farrell, P. D. 1946 (Shamrock R, Everton)	28
Farrelly, G. 1996 (Aston Villa, Everton, Bolton W)	6
Feenan, J. 1937 (Sunderland)	2
Ferguson, E. J. 2023 (Brighton & HA)	**22**
Finnan, S. 2000 (Fulham, Liverpool, Espanyol)	53
Finucane, A. 1967 (Limerick)	11
Fitzgerald, F. J. 1955 (Waterford)	2
Fitzgerald, P. J. 1961 (Leeds U, Chester)	5
Fitzpatrick, K. 1970 (Limerick)	1
Fitzsimons, A. G. 1950 (Middlesbrough, Lincoln C)	26
Fleming, C. 1996 (Middlesbrough)	10
Flood, J. J. 1926 (Shamrock R)	5
Fogarty, A. 1960 (Sunderland, Hartlepools U)	11
Folan, C. C. 2009 (Hull C)	7
Foley, D. J. 2000 (Watford)	6
Foley, J. 1934 (Cork, Celtic)	7
Foley, K. P. 2009 (Wolverhampton W)	8
Foley, M. 1926 (Shelbourne)	1
Foley, T. C. 1964 (Northampton T)	9
Forde, D. 2011 (Millwall)	24
Foy, T. 1938 (Shamrock R)	2
Fullam, J. 1961 (Preston NE, Shamrock R)	11
Fullam, R. 1926 (Shamrock R)	2
Gallagher, C. 1967 (Celtic)	2
Gallagher, M. 1954 (Hibernian)	1
Gallagher, P. 1932 (Falkirk)	1
Galvin, A. 1983 (Tottenham H, Sheffield Wed, Swindon T)	29
Gamble, J. 2007 (Cork C)	2
Gannon, E. 1949 (Notts Co, Sheffield Wed, Shelbourne)	14

Gannon, M. 1972 (Shelbourne)	1
Gaskins, P. 1934 (Shamrock R, St James' Gate)	7
Gavin, J. T. 1950 (Norwich C, Tottenham H, Norwich C)	7
Geoghegan, M. 1937 (St James' Gate)	2
Gibbons, A. 1952 (St Patrick's Ath)	4
Gibson, D. T. D. 2008 (Manchester U, Everton)	27
Gilbert, R. 1966 (Shamrock R)	1
Giles, C. 1951 (Doncaster R)	1
Giles, M. J. 1960 (Manchester U, Leeds U, WBA, Shamrock R)	59
Given, S. J. J. 1996 (Blackburn R, Newcastle U, Manchester C, Aston Villa, Stoke C)	134
Givens, D. J. 1969 (Manchester U, Luton T, QPR, Birmingham C, Neuchatel X)	56
Gleeson, S. M. 2007 (Wolverhampton W, Birmingham C)	4
Glen, W. 1927 (Shamrock R)	8
Glynn, D. 1952 (Drumcondra)	2
Godwin, T. F. 1949 (Shamrock R, Leicester C, Bournemouth)	13
Golding, J. 1928 (Shamrock R)	2
Goodman, J. 1997 (Wimbledon)	4
Goodwin, J. 2003 (Stockport Co)	1
Gorman, W. C. 1936 (Bury, Brentford)	13
Grace, J. 1926 (Drumcondra)	1
Grealish, A. 1976 (Orient, Luton T, Brighton & HA, WBA)	45
Green, P. J. 2010 (Derby Co, Leeds U)	20
Gregg, E. 1978 (Bohemians)	8
Griffith, R. 1935 (Walsall)	1
Grimes, A. A. 1978 (Manchester U, Coventry C, Luton T)	18
Hale, A. 1962 (Aston Villa, Doncaster R, Waterford)	14
Hamilton, C. N. 2022 (Blackpool)	1
Hamilton, T. 1959 (Shamrock R)	2
Hand, E. K. 1969 (Portsmouth)	20
Harrington, W. 1936 (Cork)	5
Harte, I. P. 1996 (Leeds U, Levante)	64
Hartnett, J. B. 1949 (Middlesbrough)	2
Haverty, J. 1956 (Arsenal, Blackburn R, Millwall, Celtic, Bristol R, Shelbourne)	32
Hayes, A. W. P. 1979 (Southampton)	1
Hayes, J. 2016 (Aberdeen)	4
Hayes, W. E. 1947 (Huddersfield T)	2
Hayes, W. J. 1949 (Limerick)	1
Healey, R. 1977 (Cardiff C)	2
Healy, C. 2002 (Celtic, Sunderland)	13
Heighway, S. D. 1971 (Liverpool, Minnesota K)	34
Henderson, B. 1948 (Drumcondra)	2
Henderson, W. C. P. 2006 (Brighton & HA, Preston NE)	6
Hendrick, J. P. 2013 (Derby Co, Burnley, Newcastle U)	79
Hennessy, J. 1965 (Shelbourne, St Patrick's Ath)	5
Herrick, J. 1972 (Cork Hibernians, Shamrock R)	3
Higgins, J. 1951 (Birmingham C)	1
Hogan, S. A. 2018 (Aston Villa, Birmingham C)	12
Holland, M. R. 2000 (Ipswich T, Charlton Ath)	49
Holmes, J. 1971 (Coventry C, Tottenham H, Vancouver Whitecaps)	30
Hoolahan, W. 2008 (Blackpool, Norwich C)	43
Horgan, D. J. 2017 (Preston NE, Hibernian, Wycombe W)	17
Horlacher, A. F. 1930 (Bohemians)	7
Houghton, R. J. 1986 (Oxford U, Liverpool, Aston Villa, Crystal Palace, Reading)	73
Hourihane, C. 2017 (Aston Villa, Derby Co)	36
Howlett, G. 1984 (Brighton & HA)	1
Hoy, M. 1938 (Dundalk)	6
Hughton, C. 1980 (Tottenham H, West Ham U)	53
Hunt, N. 2009 (Reading)	3
Hunt, S. P. 2007 (Reading, Hull C, Wolverhampton W)	39
Hurley, C. J. 1957 (Millwall, Sunderland, Bolton W)	40
Hutchinson, F. 1935 (Drumcondra)	2
Idah, A. U. 2021 (Norwich C, Celtic)	**32**
Ireland S. J. 2006 (Manchester C)	6
Irwin, D. J. 1991 (Manchester U)	56
Johnston, M. A. 2023 (Celtic, WBA)	**15**
Jordan, D. 1937 (Wolverhampton W)	2
Jordan, W. 1934 (Bohemians)	2
Judge, A. C. 2016 (Brentford, Ipswich T)	9

Obafemi, M. O. 2019 (Southampton, Swansea C,
  Burnley) — 12
O'Brien, A. 2007 (Newcastle U) — 5
O'Brien, A. 2019 (Millwall) — 5
O'Brien, A. J. 2001 (Newcastle U, Portsmouth) — 26
O'Brien, F. 1980 (Philadelphia F) — 3
O'Brien, J. 2024 (Lyon, Everton) — **7**
O'Brien J. M. 2006 (Bolton W, West Ham U) — 5
O'Brien, L. 1986 (Shamrock R, Manchester U,
  Newcastle U, Tranmere R) — 16
O'Brien, M. T. 1927 (Derby Co, Walsall, Norwich C,
  Watford) — 4
O'Brien, R. 1976 (Notts Co) — 5
O'Byrne, L. B. 1949 (Shamrock R) — 1
O'Callaghan, B. R. 1979 (Stoke C) — 6
O'Callaghan, K. 1981 (Ipswich T, Portsmouth) — 21
O'Cearuill, J. 2007 (Arsenal) — 2
O'Connell, A. 1967 (Dundalk, Bohemians) — 2
O'Connor, L. P. 2020 (Celtic) — 1
O'Connor, T. 1950 (Shamrock R) — 4
O'Connor, T. 1968 (Fulham, Dundalk, Bohemians) — 7
O'Dea, D. 2010 (Celtic, Toronto, Metalurh Donetsk) — 20
O'Dowda, C. J. R. 2016 (Oxford U, Bristol C,
  Cardiff C) — **32**
O'Driscoll, J. F. 1949 (Swansea T) — 3
O'Driscoll, S. 1982 (Fulham) — 3
O'Farrell, F. 1952 (West Ham U, Preston NE) — 9
O'Flanagan, K. P. 1938 (Bohemians, Arsenal) — 10
O'Flanagan, M. 1947 (Bohemians) — 1
Ogbene, C. S. 2021 (Rotherham U, Luton T) — **24**
O'Halloran, S. E. 2007 (Aston Villa) — 2
O'Hanlon, K. G. 1988 (Rotherham U) — 1
O'Hara, K. M. 2020 (Manchester U) — 2
O'Kane, E. C. 2016 (Bournemouth, Leeds U) — 7
O'Kane, P. 1935 (Bohemians) — 3
O'Keefe, E. 1981 (Everton, Port Vale) — 5
O'Keefe, T. 1934 (Cork, Waterford) — 3
O'Leary, D. 1977 (Arsenal) — 68
O'Leary, M. E. 2025 (Bristol C) — **1**
O'Leary, P. 1980 (Shamrock R) — 7
O'Mahoney, M. T. 1938 (Bristol R) — 6
Omobamidele, A. A. 2022 (Norwich C, Nottingham F) — **10**
O'Neill, F. S. 1962 (Shamrock R) — 20
O'Neill, J. 1952 (Everton) — 17
O'Neill, J. 1961 (Preston NE) — 1
O'Neill, K. P. 1996 (Norwich C, Middlesbrough) — 13
O'Neill, W. 1936 (Dundalk) — 11
O'Regan, K. 1984 (Brighton & HA) — 4
O'Reilly, J. 1932 (Brideville, Aberdeen, Brideville,
  St James' Gate) — 20
O'Reilly, J. 1946 (Cork U) — 2
O'Shea, D. J. 2021 (WBA, Burnley, Ipswich T) — **35**
O'Shea, J. F. 2002 (Manchester U, Sunderland) — 118

Parrott, T. D. 2020 (Tottenham H, AZ Alkmaar) — **29**
Patrick, J. J. P. F. 2025 (Reims) — **1**
Pearce, A. J. 2013 (Reading, Derby Co) — 9
Peyton, G. 1977 (Fulham, Bournemouth, Everton) — 33
Peyton, N. 1957 (Shamrock R, Leeds U) — 6
Phillips, K. 2025 (St Mirren) — **2**
Phelan, T. 1992 (Wimbledon, Manchester C, Chelsea,
  Everton, Fulham) — 42
Pilkington, A. N. J. 2013 (Norwich C, Cardiff C) — 9
Potter, D. M. 2007 (Wolverhampton W) — 5

Quinn, A. 2003 (Sheffield Wed, Sheffield U) — 8
Quinn, B. S. 2000 (Coventry C) — 4
Quinn, N. J. 1986 (Arsenal, Manchester C,
  Sunderland) — 91
Quinn, S. 2013 (Hull C, Reading) — 18

Randolph, D. E. 2013 (Motherwell, West Ham U,
  Middlesbrough) — 50
Reid, A. M. 2004 (Nottingham F, Tottenham H,
  Charlton Ath, Sunderland, Nottingham F) — 29
Reid, C. 1931 (Brideville) — 1
Reid, S. J. 2002 (Millwall, Blackburn R) — 23
Rice, D. 2018 (West Ham U) — 3
Richardson, D. J. 1972 (Shamrock R, Gillingham) — 3
Rigby, A. 1935 (St James' Gate) — 3
Ringstead, A. 1951 (Sheffield U) — 20
Robinson, C. J. 2019 (Preston NE, Sheffield U, WBA,
  Cardiff C) — **38**

Robinson, J. 1928 (Bohemians, Dolphin) — 2
Robinson, M. 1981 (Brighton & HA, Liverpool, QPR) — 24
Roche, P. J. 1972 (Shelbourne, Manchester U) — 8
Rogers, E. 1968 (Blackburn R, Charlton Ath) — 19
Rowlands, M. C. 2004 (QPR) — 5
Ryan, G. 1978 (Derby Co, Brighton & HA) — 18
Ryan, R. A. 1950 (WBA, Derby Co) — 16

Sadlier, R. T. 2002 (Millwall) — 1
Sammon, C. 2013 (Derby Co) — 9
Savage, D. P. T. 1996 (Millwall) — 5
Saward, P. 1954 (Millwall, Aston Villa,
  Huddersfield T) — 18
Scales, L. 2024 (Celtic) — **10**
Scannell, T. 1954 (Southend U) — 1
Scully, P. J. 1989 (Arsenal) — 1
Sheedy, K. 1984 (Everton, Newcastle U) — 46
Sheridan, C. 2010 (Celtic, CSKA Sofia) — 3
Sheridan, J. J. 1988 (Leeds U, Sheffield Wed) — 34
Slaven, B. 1990 (Middlesbrough) — 7
Sloan, J. W. 1946 (Arsenal) — 2
Smallbone, W. A. P. 2023 (Southampton) — **13**
Smyth, M. 1969 (Shamrock R) — 1
Squires, J. 1934 (Shelbourne) — 1
Stapleton, F. 1977 (Arsenal, Manchester U, Ajax,
  Le Havre, Blackburn R) — 71
Staunton, S. 1989 (Liverpool, Aston Villa, Liverpool,
  Aston Villa) — 102
St Ledger-Hall, S. P. 2009 (Preston NE, Leicester C) — 37
Stevens, E. J. 2018 (Sheffield U, Stoke C) — 26
Stevenson, A. E. 1932 (Dolphin, Everton) — 7
Stokes, A. 2007 (Sunderland, Celtic) — 9
Strahan, F. 1964 (Shelbourne) — 5
Sullivan, J. 1928 (Fordsons) — 1
Swan, M. M. G. 1960 (Drumcondra) — 1
Sykes, M. 2023 (Bristol C) — **7**
Synnott, N. 1978 (Shamrock R) — 3
Szmodics, S. J. 2024 (Blackburn R, Ipswich T) — **10**

Taylor, J. H. P. 2025 (Ipswich T) — **5**
Taylor, T. 1959 (Waterford) — 1
Thomas, P. 1974 (Waterford) — 2
Thompson, J. 2004 (Nottingham F) — 1
Townsend, A. D. 1989 (Norwich C, Chelsea,
  Aston Villa, Middlesbrough) — 70
Travers, M. 2020 (Bournemouth) — 4
Traynor, T. J. 1954 (Southampton) — 8
Treacy, K. 2011 (Preston NE, Burnley) — 6
Treacy, R. C. P. 1966 (WBA, Charlton Ath,
  Swindon T, Preston NE, WBA, Shamrock R) — 42
Tuohy, L. 1956 (Shamrock R, Newcastle U,
  Shamrock R) — 8
Turner, C. J. 1936 (Southend U, West Ham U) — 10
Turner, P. 1963 (Celtic) — 2

Vata, R. 2025 (Watford) — **1**
Vernon, J. 1946 (Belfast Celtic) — 2

Waddock, G. 1980 (QPR, Millwall) — 21
Walsh, D. J. 1946 (Linfield, WBA, Aston Villa) — 20
Walsh, J. 1982 (Limerick) — 1
Walsh, M. 1976 (Blackpool, Everton, QPR, Porto) — 21
Walsh, M. 1982 (Everton) — 4
Walsh, W. 1947 (Manchester C) — 9
Walters, J. R. 2011 (Stoke C, Burnley) — 54
Ward, S. R. 2011 (Wolverhampton W, Burnley) — 50
Waters, J. 1977 (Grimsby T) — 2
Watters, F. 1926 (Shelbourne) — 1
Weir, I. 1939 (Clyde) — 3
Westwood, K. 2009 (Coventry C, Sunderland,
  Sheffield W) — 21
Whelan, G. D. 2008 (Stoke C, Aston Villa, Hearts) — 91
Whelan, R. 1964 (St Patrick's Ath) — 2
Whelan, R. 1981 (Liverpool, Southend U) — 53
Whelan, W. 1956 (Manchester U) — 4
White, J. J. 1928 (Bohemians) — 1
Whittaker, R. 1959 (Chelsea) — 1
Williams, D. S. 2018 (Blackburn R) — 3
Williams, J. 1938 (Shamrock R) — 1
Williams, S. 2018 (Millwall) — 3
Wilson, M. D. 2011 (Stoke C, Bournemouth) — 25

BRITISH AND IRISH INTERNATIONAL GOALSCORERS 1872–2025

Where two players with the same surname and initials have appeared for the same country, and one or both have scored, they have been distinguished by reference to the club which appears *first* against their name in the international appearances section.

Bold type indicates players who have scored international goals in season 2024–25.

ENGLAND

Name	
Abraham, K. O. T. (Tammy)	3
A'Court, A.	1
Adams, T. A.	5
Adcock, H.	1
Alcock, C. W.	1
Alexander-Arnold, T. J.	**4**
Allen, A.	3
Allen, R.	2
Alli, B. J. (Dele)	3
Amos, A.	1
Anderson, V.	2
Anderton, D. R.	7
Astall, G.	1
Athersmith, W. C.	3
Atyeo, P. J. W.	5
Bache, J. W.	4
Bailey, N. C.	2
Baily, E. F.	5
Baines, L. J.	1
Baker, J. H.	3
Ball, A. J.	8
Bambridge, A. L.	1
Bambridge, E. C.	11
Barclay, R.	2
Barkley, R.	6
Barmby, N. J.	4
Barnes, J.	11
Barnes, P. S.	4
Barry, G.	3
Barton, J.	1
Bassett, W. I.	8
Bastin, C. S.	12
Beardsley, P. A.	9
Beasley, A.	1
Beattie, T. K.	1
Beckham, D. R. J.	17
Becton, F.	2
Bedford, H.	1
Bell, C.	9
Bellingham, J. V. W.	**6**
Bent, D. A.	4
Bentley, R. T. F.	9
Bertrand, R.	1
Bishop, S. M.	1
Blackburn, F.	1
Blissett, L.	3
Bloomer, S.	28
Bond, R.	2
Bonsor, A. G.	1
Bowden, E. R.	1
Bowen, J.	**1**
Bowers, J. W.	2
Bowles, S.	1
Bradford, G. R. W.	1
Bradford, J.	7
Bradley, W.	2
Bradshaw, F.	3
Brann, G.	1
Bridge, W. M.	1
Bridges, B. J.	1
Bridgett, A.	3
Brindle, T.	1
Britton, C. S.	1
Broadbent, P. F.	2
Broadis, I. A.	8
Brodie, J. B.	1
Bromley-Davenport, W.	2
Brook, E. F.	10
Brooking, T. D.	5
Brooks, J.	2
Broome, F. H.	3
Brown, A.	4
Brown, A. S.	1
Brown, G.	5
Brown, J.	3
Brown, W.	1
Brown, W. M.	1
Buchan, C. M.	4
Bull, S. G.	4
Bullock, N.	2
Burgess, H.	4
Butcher, T.	3
Byrne, J. J.	8
Cahill, G. J.	5
Calvert-Lewin, D. N.	4
Campbell, S. J.	1
Camsell, G. H.	18
Carroll, A. T.	2
Carter, H. S.	7
Carter, J. H.	4
Caulker, S. A.	1
Chadwick, E.	3
Chamberlain, M.	1
Chambers, H.	5
Channon, M. R.	21
Charlton, J.	6
Charlton, R.	49
Chenery, C. J.	1
Chilwell, B. J.	1
Chivers, M.	13
Clarke, A. J.	10
Coady, C. D.	1
Cobbold, W. N.	6
Cock, J. G.	2
Cole, A.	1
Cole, J. J.	10
Common, A.	2
Connelly, J. M.	7
Coppell, S. J.	7
Cotterill, G. H.	2
Cowans, G.	2
Crawford, R.	1
Crawshaw, T. H.	1
Crayston, W. J.	1
Creek, F. N. S.	1
Crooks, S. D.	7
Crouch, P. J.	22
Currey, E. S.	2
Currie, A. W.	3
Cursham, A. W.	2
Cursham, H. A.	5
Daft, H. B.	3
Davenport, J. K.	2
Davis, G.	1
Davis, H.	1
Day, S. H.	2
Dean, W. R.	18
Defoe, J. C.	20
Devey, J. H. G.	1
Dewhurst, F.	11
Dier, E. J. E.	3
Dix, W. R.	1
Dixon, K. M.	4
Dixon, L. M.	1
Dorrell, A. R.	1
Douglas, B.	11
Drake, E. J.	6
Ducat, A.	1
Dunn, A. T. B.	2
Eastham, G.	2
Edwards, D.	5
Ehiogu, U.	1
Elliott, W. H.	3
Evans, R. E.	1
Eze, E. O.	**1**
Ferdinand, L.	5
Ferdinand, R. G.	3
Finney, T.	30
Fleming, H. J.	9
Flowers, R.	10
Foden, P. W.	4
Forman, Frank	1
Forman, Fred	3
Foster, R. E.	3
Fowler, R. B.	7
Francis, G. C. J.	3
Francis, T.	12
Freeman, B. C.	3
Froggatt, J.	2
Froggatt, R.	2
Gallagher, C. J.	**1**
Galley, T.	1
Gascoigne, P. J.	10
Geary, F.	3
Gerrard, S. G.	21
Gibbins, W. V. T.	3
Gilliatt, W. E.	3
Goddard, P.	1
Goodall, J.	12
Goodyer, A. C.	1
Gordon, A. M.	**1**
Gosling, R. C.	2
Goulden, L. A.	4
Grainger, C.	3
Grealish, J. P.	**4**
Greaves, J.	44
Grovesnor, A. T.	2
Gunn, W.	1
Haines, J. T. W.	2
Hall, G. W.	9
Halse, H. J.	2
Hampson, J.	5
Hampton, H.	2
Hancocks, J.	2
Hardman, H. P.	1
Harris, S. S.	2
Harwood-Bellis, T. J.	**1**
Hassall, H. W.	4
Hateley, M.	9
Haynes, J. N.	18
Hegan, K. E.	4
Henderson, J. B.	3
Henfrey, A. G.	2
Heskey, E. W.	7
Hilsdon, G. R.	14
Hine, E. W.	4
Hinton, A. T.	1
Hirst, D. E.	1
Hitchens, G. A.	5
Hobbis, H. H. F.	1
Hoddle, G.	8
Hodgetts, D.	1
Hodgson, G.	1
Holley, G. H.	8
Houghton, W. E.	5
Howell, R.	1
Hughes, E. W.	1
Hulme, J. H. A.	4
Hunt, G. S.	1
Hunt, R.	18
Hunter, N.	2
Hurst, G. C.	24
Ince, P. E. C.	2
Ings, D.	1
Jack, D. N. B.	3
Jagielka, P. N.	3
James, R. L.	**1**
Jeffers, F.	1
Jenas, J. A.	1
Johnson, A.	2
Johnson, D. E.	6
Johnson, E.	2
Johnson, G. M. C.	1
Johnson, J. A.	2
Johnson, T. C. F.	5
Johnson, W. H.	1
Jones, C. L.	**1**
Kail, E. I. L.	2
Kane, H. E.	**73**
Kay, A. H.	1
Keane, M. V.	1
Keegan, J. K.	21
Kelly, R.	8
Kennedy, R.	3
Kenyon-Slaney, W. S.	2
Keown, M. R.	2
Kevan, D. T.	8
Kidd, B.	1
King, L. B.	1
Kingsford, R. K.	1
Kirchen, A. J.	2
Kirton, W. J.	1
Lallana, A. D.	3
Lambert, R. L.	3
Lampard, F. J.	29
Langton, R.	1
Latchford, R. D.	5
Latheron, E. G.	1
Lawler, C.	1
Lawton, T.	22
Lee, F.	10
Lee, J.	1
Lee, R. M.	2
Lee, S.	2
Lescott, J.	1
Le Saux, G. P.	1
Lewis-Skelly, M. A.	**1**
Lindley, T.	14
Lineker, G.	48

Jones, S. (Distillery)	1
Jones, S. (Crewe Alex)	1
Jones, J.	1
Jones, J. L.	1
Kelly, J.	4
Kernaghan, N.	2
Kirwan, J.	2
Lacey, W.	3
Lafferty, K.	20
Lavery, S. F.	3
Lemon, J.	2
Lennon, N. F.	2
Lockhart, N.	3
Lomas, S. M.	3
Magennis, J. B. D.	**12**
Magilton, J.	5
Mahood, J.	2
Martin, D. K.	3
Maxwell, J.	2
McAdams, W. J.	7
McAllen, J.	1
McAuley, G.	9
McAuley, J. L.	1
McCann, A.	1
McCann, G. S.	4
McCartney, G.	1
McCandless, J.	2
McCandless, W.	1
McCaw, J. H.	1
McClelland, J.	1
McCluggage, A.	2
McCourt, P.	2
McCracken, W.	1
McCrory, S.	1
McCurdy, C.	1
McDonald, A.	3
McGarry, J. K.	1
McGrath, R. C.	4
McGinn, N.	6
McIlroy, J.	10
McIlroy, S. B.	5
McKenzie, H	1
McKnight, J.	2
McLaughlin, C. G.	1
McLaughlin, J. C.	6
McMahon, G. J.	2
McMenamin, C.	1
McMordie, A. S.	3
McMorran, E. J.	4
McNair, P. J. C.	**7**
McParland, P. J.	10
McWha, W. B. R.	1
Meldon, P. A	1
Mercer, J. T.	1
Millar, W.	1
Milligan, D.	1
Milne, R. G.	2
Molyneux, T. B.	1
Moreland, V.	1
Morgan, S.	3
Morrow, S. J.	1
Morrow, W. J.	1
Mulryne, P. P.	3
Murdock, C. J.	1
Murphy, N.	1
Neill, W. J. T.	2
Nelson, S.	1
Nicholl, C. J.	3
Nicholl, J. M.	1
Nicholson, J. J.	6
O'Boyle, G.	1
O'Hagan, C.	2
O'Kane, W. J.	1
O'Neill, J.	2
O'Neill, M. A.	4

O'Neill, M. H.	8
Own goals	10
Paterson, M. A.	3
Patterson, D. J.	1
Patterson, R.	1
Peacock, R.	2
Peden, J.	7
Penney, S.	2
Price, I. J.	**9**
Pyper, James	2
Pyper, John	1
Quinn, J. M.	12
Quinn, S. J.	4
Reid, J. M.	1
Reynolds, J.	1
Rowland, K.	1
Rowley, R. W. M.	2
Rushe, F.	1
Sheridan, J.	2
Sherrard, J.	1
Sherrard, W. C.	2
Shields, D.	1
Simpson, W. J.	5
Sloan, H. A. de B.	4
Smith, M.	1
Smyth, P. P.	2
Smyth, S.	5
Spence, D. W.	3
Sproule, I.	1
Stanfield, O. M.	11
Stevenson, A. E.	5
Stewart, I.	2
Taggart, G. P.	7
Thompson, F. W.	2
Torrans, S.	1
Tully, C. P.	3
Turner, A.	1
Walker, J.	1
Walsh, D. J.	5
Ward, J. J.	4
Washington, C. J.	6
Welsh, E.	1
Whiteside, N.	9
Whiteside, T.	1
Whitley, Jeff	2
Whyte, G.	5
Williams, J. R.	1
Williams, M. S.	1
Williamson, J.	1
Wilson, D. J.	1
Wilson, K. J.	6
Wilson, S. J.	7
Wilton, J. M.	2
Young, S.	1

N.B. In 1914 Young goal should be credited to Gillespie W v Wales

SCOTLAND

Adams, C. Z. E. F.	**9**
Aitken, R. (Celtic)	1
Aitken, R. (Dumbarton)	1
Aitkenhead, W. A. C.	2
Alexander, D.	1
Allan, D. S.	4
Allan, J.	2
Anderson, F.	1
Anderson, W.	4
Andrews, P.	1
Anya, S.	3
Archibald, A.	1
Archibald, S.	4
Armstrong, S.	5

Baird, D.	2
Baird, J. C.	2
Baird, S.	2
Bannon, E.	1
Barbour, A.	1
Barker, J. B.	4
Battles, B, Jr	1
Bauld, W.	2
Baxter, J. C.	3
Beattie, C.	1
Bell, J.	5
Bennett, A.	2
Berra, C. D.	4
Berry, D.	1
Bett, J.	1
Beveridge, W. W.	1
Black, A.	3
Black, D.	1
Bone, J.	1
Booth, S.	6
Boyd, K	7
Boyd, R.	2
Boyd, T.	1
Boyd, W. G.	1
Brackenridge, T.	1
Brand, R.	8
Brazil, A.	1
Bremner, W. J.	3
Broadfoot, K.	1
Brown, A. D.	6
Brown, S.	4
Buchanan, P. S.	1
Buchanan, R.	1
Buckley, P.	1
Buick, A.	2
Burke, C.	2
Burke, O. J.	1
Burley, C. W.	3
Burns, K.	1
Cairns, T.	1
Caldwell, G.	2
Calderwood, C.	1
Calderwood, R.	2
Caldow, E.	4
Cameron, C.	2
Campbell, C.	1
Campbell, John (Celtic)	5
Campbell, John (Rangers)	4
Campbell, J. (South Western)	1
Campbell, P.	2
Campbell, R.	1
Cassidy, J.	1
Chalmers, S.	3
Chambers, T.	1
Cheyne, A. G.	4
Christie, A. J.	1
Christie, R.	**7**
Clarkson, D.	1
Clunas, W. L.	1
Collins, J.	12
Collins, R. Y.	10
Combe, J. R.	1
Commons, K.	2
Conn, A.	1
Cooper, D.	6
Craig, J.	1
Craig, T.	1
Crawford, S.	4
Cunningham, A. N.	5
Curran, H. P.	1
Dailly, C.	6
Dalglish, K.	30
Davidson, D.	1
Davidson, J. A.	1
Delaney, J.	3
Devine, A.	1

Dewar, G.	1
Dewar, N.	4
Dickov, P.	1
Dickson, W.	4
Divers, J.	1
Dobie, R. S.	1
Docherty, T. H.	1
Dodds, D.	1
Dodds, W.	7
Donaldson, A.	1
Donnachie, J.	1
Dougall, J.	1
Drummond, J.	2
Dunbar, M.	1
Duncan, D.	7
Duncan, D. M.	1
Duncan, J.	1
Dunn, J.	2
Durie, G. S.	7
Dykes, L. J.	9
Easson, J. F.	1
Elliott, M. S.	1
Ellis, J.	1
Ferguson, A.	4
Ferguson, B.	3
Ferguson, J.	6
Fernie, W.	1
Findlay, S. J.	1
Fitchie, T. T.	1
Flavell, R.	2
Fleming, C.	2
Fleming, J. W.	3
Fletcher, D.	5
Fletcher, S. K.	10
Forrest, J.	5
Fraser, M. J. E.	3
Fraser, R.	4
Freedman, D. A.	1
Gallacher, H. K.	23
Gallacher, K. W.	9
Gallacher, P.	1
Galt, J. H.	1
Gemmell, T. (St Mirren)	1
Gemmell, T. (Celtic)	
Gemmill, A.	8
Gemmill, S.	1
Gibb, W.	1
Gibson, D. W.	3
Gibson, J. D.	1
Gibson, N.	1
Gillespie, Jas.	3
Gillick, T.	3
Gilmour, B. C.	**2**
Gilzean, A. J.	12
Goodwillie, D.	1
Gossland, J.	2
Goudie, J.	1
Gough, C. R.	6
Gourlay, J.	1
Graham, A.	2
Graham, G.	3
Gray, A.	7
Gray, E.	3
Gray, F.	1
Greig, J.	3
Griffiths, L.	4
Groves, W.	1
Hamilton, G.	4
Hamilton, J. (Queen's Park)	3
Hamilton, R. C.	15
Hanley, G. C.	2
Harper, J. M.	7
Hartley, P. J.	1
Harrower, W.	5
Hartford, R. A.	4

Name	Goals
Heggie, C. W	4
Henderson, J. G.	1
Henderson, W.	5
Hendry, E. C. J.	3
Hendry, J. W.	3
Herd, D. G.	3
Herd, G.	1
Hewie, J. D.	2
Higgins, A. (Newcastle U)	1
Higgins, A. (Kilmarnock)	4
Highet, T. C.	1
Hirst, G. D. E.	**1**
Holt, G.J.	1
Holton, J. A.	2
Hope, R.	1
Hopkin, D.	2
Houliston, W.	2
Howie, H.	1
Howie, J.	2
Hughes, J.	1
Hunter, W.	1
Hutchison, D.	6
Hutchison, T.	1
Hutton, J.	1
Hyslop, T.	1
Imrie, W. N.	1
Jackson, A.	8
Jackson, C.	1
Jackson, D.	4
James, A. W.	4
Jardine, A.	1
Jenkinson, T.	1
Jess, E.	2
Johnston, A.	2
Johnston, L. H.	1
Johnston, M.	14
Johnstone, D.	2
Johnstone, J.	4
Johnstone, Jas.	1
Johnstone, R.	10
Johnstone, W.	1
Jordan, J.	11
Kay, J. L.	5
Keillor, A.	3
Kelly, J.	1
Kelso, R.	1
Ker, G.	10
King, A.	1
King, J.	1
Kinnear, D.	1
Kyle, K.	1
Lambert, P.	1
Lambie, J.	1
Lambie, W. A.	5
Lang, J. J.	2
Latta, A.	2
Law, D.	30
Leggat, G.	8
Lennie, W.	1
Lennox, R.	3
Liddell, W.	6
Lindsay, J.	6
Linwood, A. B.	1
Logan, J.	1
Lorimer, P.	4
Love, A.	1
Low, J. (Cambuslang)	1
Lowe, J. (St Bernards)	1
Macari, L.	5
MacDougall, E. J.	3
MacFarlane, A.	1
MacLeod, M.	1
Mackay, D. C.	4
Mackay, G.	1
MacKenzie, J. A.	1
Mackail-Smith, C.	1
Mackie, J. C.	2
MacKinnon, W. W.	5
Madden, J.	5
Maloney, S. R.	7
Marshall, H.	1
Marshall, J.	1
Martin, C. H.	3
Mason, J.	4
Massie, A.	1
Masson, D. S.	5
McAdam, J.	1
McAllister, G.	5
McArthur, J.	4
McAulay, J. D.	1
McAvennie, F.	1
McCall, J.	1
McCall, S. M.	1
McCalliog, J.	1
McCallum, N.	1
McCann, N.	3
McClair, B. J.	2
McCoist, A.	19
McColl, R. S.	13
McCormack, R.	2
McCulloch, D.	3
McCulloch, L.	1
McDougall, J.	4
McFadden, J.*	15
McFadyen, W.	2
McGhee, M.	2
McGinlay, J.	4
McGinn, J.	**20**
McGregor, C. W.	3
McGregor, J.	1
McGrory, J.	6
McGuire, W.	1
McInally, A.	3
McInnes, T.	2
McKenna, S. F.	1
McKie, J.	2
McKimmie, S.	1
McKinlay, W.	4
McKinnon, A.	1
McKinnon, R.	1
McLaren, A.	4
McLaren, J.	1
McLean, A.	1
McLean, K.	2
McLean, T.	1
McLintock, F.	1
McMahon, A.	6
McManus, S.	2
McMenemy, J.	5
McMillan, I. L.	2
McNeill, W.	3
McNiel, H.	5
McPhail, J.	3
McPhail, R.	7
McPherson, J. (Kilmarnock)	7
McPherson, J. (Vale of Leven)	1
McPherson, R.	1
McQueen, G.	5
McStay, P.	9
McSwegan, G.	1
McTominay, S. F.	**12**
Meiklejohn, D. D.	3
Millar, J.	2
Miller, K.	18
Miller, T.	2
Miller, W.	1
Mitchell, R. C.	1
Morgan, W.	4
Morris, D.	1
Morris, H.	3
Morrison, J. C.	3
Morton, A. L.	5
Mudie, J. K.	9
Mulgrew, C. P.	3
Mulhall, G.	1
Munro, A. D.	1
Munro, N.	2
Murdoch, R.	5
Murphy, F.	1
Murray, J.	1
Napier, C. E.	3
Narey, D.	1
Naismith, S. J.	10
Naysmith, G. A.	1
Neil, R. G.	2
Nevin, P. K. F.	5
Nicholas, C.	5
Nisbet, J.	2
Nisbet, K.	1
O'Connor, G.	4
O'Donnell, F.	2
O'Hare, J.	5
Ormond, W. E.	2
O'Rourke, F.	1
Orr, R.	1
Orr, T.	1
Oswald, J.	1
Own goals	21
Parlane, D.	1
Patterson, N. K.	1
Paul, H. McD.	2
Paul, W.	5
Pettigrew, W.	2
Phillips, M.	1
Porteous, R. T.	1
Provan, D.	1
Quashie, N. F.	1
Quinn, J.	7
Quinn, P.	1
Ralston, A.	1
Rankin, G.	2
Rankin, R.	2
Reid, W.	4
Reilly, L.	22
Renny-Tailyour, H. W.	1
Rhodes, J. L.	3
Richmond, J. T.	1
Ring, T.	2
Rioch, B. D.	6
Ritchie, H.	1
Ritchie, M. T.	3
Ritchie, P. S.	1
Robertson, A. (Clyde)	2
Robertson, A. H.	**4**
Robertson, J.	3
Robertson, J. N.	8
Robertson, J. T.	2
Robertson, T.	1
Robertson, W.	1
Russell, D.	1
Russell, J. S. S.	1
Scott, A. S.	5
Sellar, W.	4
Shankland, L.	3
Sharp, G.	1
Shaw, F. W.	1
Shearer, D.	2
Simpson, J.	1
Smith, A.	5
Smith, G.	4
Smith, J.	1
Smith, John	13
Snodgrass, R.	7
Somerville, G.	1
Souness, G. J.	4
Souttar, J.	**2**
Speedie, F.	2
St John, I.	9
Steel, W.	12
Stein, C.	10
Stevenson, G.	4
Stewart, A.	1
Stewart, R.	1
Stewart, W. E.	1
Strachan, G.	5
Sturrock, P.	3
Taylor, J. D.	1
Templeton, R.	1
Thompson, S.	3
Thomson, A.	1
Thomson, C.	4
Thomson, R.	1
Thomson, W.	1
Thornton, W.	1
Tierney, K.	1
Townsend, J.	1
Waddell, T. S.	1
Waddell, W.	6
Walker, J.	2
Walker, R.	7
Walker, T.	9
Wallace, I. A.	1
Wark, J.	7
Watson, J. A. K.	1
Watt, F.	2
Watt, W. W.	1
Webster, A.	1
Weir, A.	1
Weir, D.	1
Weir, J. B.	2
White, J. A.	3
Wilkie, L.	1
Wilson, A. (Sheffield Wed)	2
Wilson, A. N. (Dunfermline Ath)	13
Wilson, D. (Liverpool)	1
Wilson, D. (Queen's Park)	2
Wilson, D. (Rangers)	9
Wilson, H.	1
Wylie, T. G.	1
Young, A.	5

WALES

Name	Goals
Allchurch, I. J.	23
Allen, J. M.	2
Allen, M.	3
Astley, D. J.	12
Atherton, R. W.	2
Bale, G. F.	41
Bamford, T.	1
Barnes, W.	1
Bellamy, C. D.	19
Blackmore, C. G.	1
Blake, D.	1
Blake, N. A.	4
Bodin, P. J.	3
Boulter, L. M.	1
Bowdler, J. C. H.	3
Bowen, D. L.	1
Bowen, M.	3
Boyle, T.	1

* The Scottish FA officially changed Robson's goal against Iceland on 10 September 2008 to McFadden.

BRITISH AND IRISH INTERNATIONAL MANAGERS

ENGLAND
Walter Winterbottom 1946–1962 (after period as coach); Alf Ramsey 1963–1974; Joe Mercer (caretaker) 1974; Don Revie 1974–1977; Ron Greenwood 1977–1982; Bobby Robson 1982–1990; Graham Taylor 1990–1993; Terry Venables (coach) 1994–1996; Glenn Hoddle 1996–1999; Kevin Keegan 1999–2000; Sven-Goran Eriksson 2001–2006; Steve McClaren 2006–2007; Fabio Capello 2008–2012; Roy Hodgson 2012–2016; Sam Allardyce 2016 for one match; Gareth Southgate 2016–24; Lee Carsley (interim) 2024; Thomas Tuchel from January 2025.

NORTHERN IRELAND
Peter Doherty 1951–1952; Bertie Peacock 1962–1967; Billy Bingham 1967–1971; Terry Neill 1971–1975; Dave Clements (player-manager) 1975–1976; Danny Blanchflower 1976–1979; Billy Bingham 1980–1994; Bryan Hamilton 1994–1998; Lawrie McMenemy 1998–1999; Sammy McIlroy 2000–2003; Lawrie Sanchez 2004–2007; Nigel Worthington 2007–2011; Michael O'Neill 2011–2020; Ian Baraclough 2020–2022; Michael O'Neill from December 2022.

SCOTLAND (since 1967)
Bobby Brown 1967–1971; Tommy Docherty 1971–1972; Willie Ormond 1973–1977; Ally MacLeod 1977–1978; Jock Stein 1978–1985; Alex Ferguson (caretaker) 1985–1986 Andy Roxburgh (coach) 1986–1993; Craig Brown 1993–2001; Berti Vogts 2002–2004; Walter Smith 2004–2007; Alex McLeish 2007; George Burley 2008–2009; Craig Levein 2009–2012; Gordon Strachan 2013–2017; Alex McLeish 2018–2019; Steve Clarke from May 2019.

WALES (since 1974)
Mike Smith 1974–1979; Mike England 1980–1988; David Williams (caretaker) 1988; Terry Yorath 1988–1993; John Toshack 1994 for one match; Mike Smith 1994–1995; Bobby Gould 1995–1999; Mark Hughes 1999–2004; John Toshack 2004–2010; Gary Speed 2010–2011; Chris Coleman 2012–2017; Ryan Giggs from January 2018; Robert Page (caretaker) from November 2020, (permanent) 2022–24. Craig Bellamy from July 2024.

REPUBLIC OF IRELAND
Liam Tuohy 1971–1972; Johnny Giles 1973–1980 (after period as player-manager); Eoin Hand 1980–1985; Jack Charlton 1986–1996; Mick McCarthy 1996–2002; Brian Kerr 2003–2006; Steve Staunton 2006–2007; Giovanni Trapattoni 2008–2013; Martin O'Neill 2013–2018; Mick McCarthy 2018–2020; Stephen Kenny 2020–2023; John O'Shea (interim) February–July 2024; Heimir Hallgrimsson from July 2024.

SOUTH AMERICA

* After extra time.   ▪ *Denotes player sent off.*

COPA AMERICA 2024 – USA

GROUP STAGE

GROUP A
Argentina v Canada	2-0
Peru v Chile	0-0
Peru v Canada	0-1
Chile v Argentina	0-1
Argentina v Peru	2-0
Canada v Chile	0-0

Group A Table	P	W	D	L	F	A	GD	Pts
Argentina	3	3	0	0	5	0	5	9
Canada	3	1	1	1	2	-1	4
Chile	3	0	2	1	0	1	-1	2
Peru	3	0	1	2	0	3	-3	1

GROUP B
Ecuador v Venezuela	1-2
Mexico v Jamaica	1-0
Ecuador v Jamaica	3-1
Venezuela v Mexico	1-0
Mexico v Ecuador	0-0
Jamaica v Venezuela	0-3

Group B Table	P	W	D	L	F	A	GD	Pts
Venezuela	3	3	0	0	6	1	5	9
Ecuador	3	1	1	1	4	3	1	4
Mexico	3	1	1	1	1	1	0	4
Jamaica	3	0	0	3	1	7	-6	0

GROUP C
United States v Bolivia	2-0
Uruguay v Panama	3-1
Panama v United States	2-1
Uruguay v Bolivia	5-0
United States v Uruguay	0-1
Bolivia v Panama	1-3

Group C Table	P	W	D	L	F	A	GD	Pts
Uruguay	3	3	0	0	9	1	8	9
Panama	3	2	0	1	6	5	1	6
United States	3	1	0	2	3	3	0	3
Bolivia	3	0	0	3	1	10	-9	0

GROUP D
Colombia v Paraguay	2-1
Brazil v Costa Rica	0-0
Colombia v Costa Rica	3-0
Paraguay v Brazil	1-4
Brazil v Colombia	1-1
Costa Rica v Paraguay	2-1

Group D Table	P	W	D	L	F	A	GD	Pts
Colombia	3	2	1	0	6	2	4	7
Brazil	3	1	2	0	5	2	3	5
Costa Rica	3	1	1	1	2	4	-2	4
Paraguay	3	0	0	3	3	8	-5	0

KNOCKOUT STAGE

QUARTER-FINALS
Argentina v Ecuador	1-1
Argentina won 4-2 on penalties.	
Venezuela v Canada	1-1
Canada won 4-3 on penalties.	
Colombia v Panama	5-0
Uruguay v Brazil	0-0
Uruguay won 4-2 on penalties.	

SEMI-FINALS
| Argentina v Canada | 2-0 |
| Uruguay v Colombia | 0-1 |

THIRD PLACE PLAY-OFF
| Canada v Uruguay | 2-2 |
| *Uruguay won 4-3 on penalties.* | |

COPA AMERICA FINAL 2024

Hard Rock Stadium, Miami, Florida,
Sunday, 14 July 2024

Argentina (0) 1 *(Lautaro Martinez 112)*
Colombia (0) 0   65,300

Argentina: (442) Martinez E; Montiel (Molina 72), Romero, Lisandro Martinez, Tagliafico; Di Maria (Otamendi 117), De Paul, Fernandez (Lo Celso 97), Mac Allister (Paredes 97); Messi (Gonzalez 66), Alvarez (Lautaro Martinez 97).

Colombia: (4321) Vargas; Arias S, Sanchez, Cuesta, Mojica; Rios (Castano 89), Lerma (Uribe 105), Arias J (Carrascal 105); Rodriguez (Quintero 90), Diaz (Borja 105); Cordoba (Borre 89).

aet; 0-0 at end of normal time.

Referee: Raphael Claus (Brazil).

COPA LIBERTADORES 2024

QUALIFYING STAGE

FIRST STAGE – FIRST LEG
Academia Puerto Cabello v Defensor Sporting	3-2
Aurora v Melgar	1-0
Aucas v Nacional	1-0

FIRST STAGE – SECOND LEG
		(agg)
Defensor Sporting v Academia Puerto Cabello 1-0		3-3
Academia Puerto Cabello won 4-2 on penalties.		
Melgar v Aurora	1-1	1-2
Nacional v Aucas	3-0	3-1

SECOND STAGE – FIRST LEG
Aguilas Doradas v Red Bull Bragantino	0-0
Nacional v Atletico Nacional	1-0
Always Ready v Sporting Cristal	6-1
Godoy Cruz v Colo-Colo	0-1
Sportivo Trinidense v El Nacional	1-1
Academia Puerto Cabello v Nacional	0-2
Portuguesa v Palestino	1-2
Aurora v Botafogo	1-1

SECOND STAGE – SECOND LEG
		(agg)
Red Bull Bragantino v Aguilas Doradas	0-0	0-0
Red Bull Bragantino won 4-3 on penalties.		
Atletico Nacional v Nacional	0-3	0-4
Sporting Cristal v Always Ready	3-1	4-7
Colo-Colo v Godoy Cruz	0-0	1-0
El Nacional v Sportivo Trinidense	0-1	1-2
Nacional v Academia Puerto Cabello	2-0	4-0
Palestino v Portuguesa	2-1	4-2
Botafogo v Aurora	6-0	7-1

THIRD STAGE – FIRST LEG
Botafogo v Red Bull Bragantino	2-1
Nacional v Palestino	0-2
Always Ready v Nacional	1-0
Sportivo Trinidense v Colo-Colo	1-1

THIRD STAGE – SECOND LEG
		(agg)
Red Bull Bragantino v Botafogo	1-1	2-1
Palestino v Nacional	1-3	3-3
Palestino won 3-1 on penalties.		
Nacional v Always Ready	2-1	2-2
Nacional won 5-4 on penalties.		
Colo-Colo v Sportivo Trinidense	2-1	3-2

GROUP STAGE

GROUP A

Colo-Colo v Cerro Porteno	1-0
Alianza Lima v Fluminense	1-1
Fluminense v Colo-Colo	2-1
Cerro Porteno v Alianza Lima	1-0
Colo-Colo v Alianza Lima	0-0
Cerro Porteno v Fluminense	0-0
Alianza Lima v Cerro Porteno	1-1
Colo-Colo v Fluminense	0-1
Alianza Lima v Colo-Colo	1-1
Fluminense v Cerro Porteno	2-1
Fluminense v Alianza Lima	3-2
Cerro Porteno v Colo-Colo	1-1

Group A Table	P	W	D	L	F	A	GD	Pts
Fluminense	6	4	2	0	9	5	4	14
Colo-Colo†	6	1	3	2	4	5	−1	6
Cerro Porteno†	6	1	3	2	4	5	−1	6
Alianza Lima	6	0	4	2	5	7	−2	4

†*Ranking decided on away goals scored.*

GROUP B

Cobresal v Barcelona	1-1
Talleres v Sao Paulo	2-1
Sao Paulo v Cobresal	2-0
Barcelona v Talleres	2-2
Cobresal v Talleres	0-2
Barcelona v Sao Paulo	0-2
Talleres v Barcelona	3-1
Cobresal v Sao Paulo	1-3
Talleres v Cobresal	1-0
Sao Paulo v Barcelona	0-0
Sao Paulo v Talleres	2-0
Barcelona v Cobresal	2-1

Group B Table	P	W	D	L	F	A	GD	Pts
Sao Paulo	6	4	1	1	10	3	7	13
Talleres	6	4	1	1	10	6	4	13
Barcelona	6	1	3	2	6	9	−3	6
Cobresal	6	0	1	5	3	11	−8	1

GROUP C

The Strongest v Gremio	2-0
Huachipato v Estudiantes	1-1
Estudiantes v The Strongest	2-1
Gremio v Huachipato	0-2
Estudiantes v Gremio	0-1
Huachipato v The Strongest	0-0
The Strongest v Estudiantes	1-0
The Strongest v Huachipato	4-0
Gremio v The Strongest	4-0
Estudiantes v Huachipato	3-4
Huachipato v Gremio	0-1
Gremio v Estudiantes	1-1

Group C Table	P	W	D	L	F	A	GD	Pts
The Strongest	6	3	1	2	8	6	2	10
Gremio	6	3	1	2	7	5	2	10
Huachipato	6	2	2	2	7	9	−2	8
Estudiantes	6	1	2	3	7	9	−2	5

GROUP D

Universitario v LDU Quito	2-1
Botafogo v Junior	1-3
Junior v Universitario	1-1
LDU Quito v Botafogo	1-0
Junior v LDU Quito	1-1
Botafogo v Universitario	3-1
Universitario v Junior	1-1
Botafogo v LDU Quito	2-1
LDU Quito v Junior	0-1
Universitario v Botafogo	0-1
LDU Quito v Universitario	2-0
Junior v Botafogo	0-0

Group D Table	P	W	D	L	F	A	GD	Pts
Junior	6	2	4	0	7	4	3	10
Botafogo	6	3	1	2	7	6	1	10
LDU Quito	6	2	1	3	6	6	0	7
Universitario	6	1	2	3	5	9	−4	5

GROUP E

Millonarios v Flamengo	1-1
Palestino v Bolivar	0-4
Flamengo v Palestino	2-0
Bolivar v Millonarios	3-2
Bolivar v Flamengo	2-1
Palestino v Millonarios	3-1
Palestino v Flamengo	1-0
Millonarios v Bolivar	1-1
Millonarios v Palestino	1-1
Flamengo v Bolivar	4-0
Flamengo v Millonarios	3-0
Bolivar v Palestino	3-1

Group E Table	P	W	D	L	F	A	GD	Pts
Bolivar	6	4	1	1	13	9	4	13
Flamengo	6	3	1	2	11	4	7	10
Palestino	6	2	1	3	6	11	−5	7
Millonarios	6	0	3	3	6	12	−6	3

GROUP F

San Lorenzo v Palmeiras	1-1
Liverpool v Independiente del Valle	1-1
Independiente del Valle v San Lorenzo	2-0
Palmeiras v Liverpool	3-1
Liverpool v San Lorenzo	1-0
Independiente del Valle v Palmeiras	2-3
San Lorenzo v Independiente del Valle	2-0
Liverpool v Palmeiras	0-5
Palmeiras v Independiente del Valle	2-1
San Lorenzo v Liverpool	3-2
Palmeiras v San Lorenzo	0-0
Independiente del Valle v Liverpool	2-1

Group F Table	P	W	D	L	F	A	GD	Pts
Palmeiras	6	4	2	0	14	5	9	14
San Lorenzo	6	2	2	2	6	6	0	8
Independiente del Valle	6	2	1	3	8	9	−1	7
Liverpool	6	1	1	4	6	14	−8	4

GROUP G

Caracas v Atletico Mineiro	1-4
Rosario Central v Penarol	1-0
Atletico Mineiro v Rosario Central	2-1
Penarol v Caracas	5-0
Caracas v Rosario Central	1-1
Atletico Mineiro v Penarol	3-2
Rosario Central v Atletico Mineiro	0-1
Caracas v Penarol	0-1
Penarol v Atletico Mineiro	2-0
Rosario Central v Caracas	4-1
Penarol v Rosario Central	2-1
Atletico Mineiro v Caracas	4-0

Group G Table	P	W	D	L	F	A	GD	Pts
Atletico Mineiro	6	5	0	1	14	6	8	15
Penarol	6	4	0	2	12	5	7	12
Rosario Central	6	2	1	3	8	7	1	7
Caracas	6	0	1	5	3	19	−16	1

GROUP H

Deportivo Tachira v River Plate	0-2
Nacional v Libertad	2-0
Libertad v Deportivo Tachira	3-0
River Plate v Nacional	2-0
Nacional v Deportivo Tachira	2-1
Libertad v River Plate	1-2
Deportivo Tachira v Libertad	1-1
Nacional v River Plate	2-2
River Plate v Libertad	2-0
Deportivo Tachira v Nacional	0-1
River Plate v Deportivo Tachira	2-0
Libertad v Nacional	2-1

Group H Table	P	W	D	L	F	A	GD	Pts
River Plate	6	5	1	0	12	3	9	16
Nacional	6	3	1	2	8	7	1	10
Libertad	6	2	1	3	7	8	−1	7
Deportivo Tachira	6	0	1	5	2	11	−9	1

KNOCKOUT STAGE

ROUND OF 16 – FIRST LEG

San Lorenzo v Atletico Mineiro	1-1
Nacional v Sao Paulo	0-0
Flamengo v Bolivar	2-0
Colo-Colo v Junior	1-0
Talleres v River Plate	0-1
Penarol v The Strongest	4-0
Botafogo v Palmeiras	2-1
Gremio v Fluminense	2-1

ROUND OF 16 – SECOND LEG

		(agg)
Atletico Mineiro v San Lorenzo	1-0	2-1
Sao Paulo v Nacional	2-0	2-0
Bolivar v Flamengo	1-0	1-2
Junior v Colo-Colo	1-2	1-3
River Plate v Talleres	2-1	3-1
The Strongest v Penarol	1-0	1-4
Palmeiras v Botafogo	2-2	3-4
Fluminense v Gremio	2-1	3-3
Fluminense won 4-2 on penalties.		

QUARTER-FINALS – FIRST LEG

Fluminense v Atletico Mineiro	1-0
Botafogo v Sao Paulo	0-0
Flamengo v Penarol	0-1
Colo-Colo v River Plate	1-1

QUARTER-FINALS – SECOND LEG

		(agg)
Atletico Mineiro v Fluminense	2-0	2-1
Sao Paulo v Botafogo	1-1	1-1
Botafogo won 5-4 on penalties.		
Penarol v Flamengo	0-0	1-0
River Plate v Colo-Colo	1-0	2-1

SEMI-FINALS – FIRST LEG

Atletico Mineiro v River Plate	3-0
Botafogo v Penarol	5-0

SEMI-FINALS – SECOND LEG

		(agg)
River Plate v Atletico Mineiro	0-0	0-3
Penarol v Botafogo	3-1	3-6

COPA LIBERTADORES FINAL 2024

Estadio Monumental, Buenos Aires,
Saturday, 30 November 2024

Atletico Mineiro (0) 1 *(Vargas 47)*

Botafogo (2) 3 *(Luiz Henrique 35, Telles 44 (pen),
Santos 90)*   69,803

Atletico Mineiro: (3421) Everson; Lyanco (Mariano 46),
Battaglia, Alonso; Scarpa (Vargas 46), Vera (Bernard
46), Franco, Arana; Hulk, Paulinho; Deyverson (Kardec
76).
Botafogo: (4231) John; Vitinho, Adryelson, Barboza,
Telles (Marcal 58); Freitas, Gregore■; Luiz Henrique
(Martins 79), Savarino (Barbosa 58), Almada (Santos
79); Jesus (Allan 90).
Referee: Facundo Tello (Argentina).

COPA SUDAMERICANA 2024

QUALIFYING STAGE

FIRST STAGE

Universitario de Vinto v Nacional Potosi	0-2
Real Tomayapo v Jorge Wilstermann	0-0
Real Tomayapo won 4-3 on penalties.	
Everton v Union La Calera	0-1
Universidad Catolica v Coquimbo Unido	0-2
Deportes Tolima v Independiente Medellin	0-0
Independiente Medellin won 4-2 on penalties.	
Alianza v America de Cali	2-1
Deportivo Cuenca v Delfin	2-5
Tecnico Universitario v Universidad Catolica	0-3
Guarani v Sportivo Luqueno	0-1
Sportivo Ameliano v Olimpia	2-0
Deportivo Garcilaso v ADT	0-0
Deportivo Garcilaso won 4-3 on penalties.	
Universidad Cesar Vallejo v Sport Huancayo	2-0
Montevideo Wanderers v Danubio	0-1
Racing v Cerro Largo	2-0
Carabobo v Metropolitanos	1-1
Metropolitanos won 5-4 on penalties.	
Rayo Zuliano v Deportivo La Guaira	0-0
Rayo Zuliano won 4-2 on penalties.	

GROUP STAGE

GROUP A

Universidad Cesar Vallejo v Defensa y Justicia	0-1
Always Ready v Independiente Medellin	2-0
Defensa y Justicia v Always Ready	1-1
Independiente Medellin v Universidad Cesar Vallejo	4-2
Always Ready v Universidad Cesar Vallejo	2-0
Independiente Medellin v Defensa y Justicia	2-1
Universidad Cesar Vallejo v Independiente Medellin	1-5
Always Ready v Defensa y Justicia	3-0
Defensa y Justicia v Independiente Medellin	1-1
Universidad Cesar Vallejo v Always Ready	2-2
Defensa y Justicia v Universidad Cesar Vallejo	0-1
Independiente Medellin v Always Ready	4-0

Group A Table	P	W	D	L	F	A	GD	Pts
Independiente Medellin	6	4	1	1	16	7	9	13
Always Ready	6	3	2	1	10	7	3	11
Defensa y Justicia	6	1	2	3	4	8	–4	5
Universidad Cesar Vallejo	6	1	1	4	6	14	–8	4

GROUP B

Alianza v Union La Calera	0-1
Universidad Catolica v Cruzeiro	0-0
Union La Calera v Universidad Catolica	0-1
Cruzeiro v Alianza	3-3
Union La Calera v Cruzeiro	0-0
Alianza v Universidad Catolica	1-3
Alianza v Cruzeiro	0-3
Universidad Catolica v Union La Calera	4-0
Cruzeiro v Union La Calera	1-0
Universidad Catolica v Alianza	0-0
Cruzeiro v Universidad Catolica	1-0
Union La Calera v Alianza	0-1

Group B Table	P	W	D	L	F	A	GD	Pts
Cruzeiro	6	3	3	0	8	3	5	12
Universidad Catolica	6	3	2	1	8	2	6	11
Alianza	6	1	2	3	5	10	–5	5
Union La Calera	6	1	1	4	1	7	–6	4

GROUP C

Belgrano v Internacional	0-0
Real Tomayapo v Delfin	0-2
Internacional v Real Tomayapo	0-0
Delfin v Belgrano	1-1
Real Tomayapo v Belgrano	0-2
Delfin v Internacional	1-2
Belgrano v Delfin	1-1
Belgrano v Real Tomayapo	1-0
Internacional v Belgrano	1-2
Delfin v Real Tomayapo	4-3
Real Tomayapo v Internacional	0-2
Internacional v Delfin	1-0

Group C Table	P	W	D	L	F	A	GD	Pts
Belgrano	6	3	3	0	7	3	4	12
Internacional	6	3	2	1	6	3	3	11
Delfin	6	2	2	2	9	8	1	8
Real Tomayapo	6	0	1	5	3	11	–8	1

GROUP D

Sportivo Trinidense v Fortaleza	0-2
Nacional Potosi v Boca Juniors	0-0
Boca Juniors v Sportivo Trinidense	1-0
Fortaleza v Nacional Potosi	5-0
Sportivo Trinidense v Nacional Potosi	2-0
Fortaleza v Boca Juniors	4-2
Nacional Potosi v Fortaleza	4-1
Sportivo Trinidense v Boca Juniors	1-2
Nacional Potosi v Sportivo Trinidense	2-1
Boca Juniors v Fortaleza	1-1
Boca Juniors v Nacional Potosi	4-0
Fortaleza v Sportivo Trinidense	2-1

Group D Table	P	W	D	L	F	A	GD	Pts
Fortaleza	6	4	1	1	15	8	7	13
Boca Juniors	6	3	2	1	10	6	4	11
Nacional Potosi	6	2	1	3	6	13	–7	7
Sportivo Trinidense	6	1	0	5	5	9	–4	3

GROUP E

Sportivo Ameliano v Athletico Paranaense	1-4
Rayo Zuliano v Danubio	0-2
Danubio v Sportivo Ameliano	0-0
Athletico Paranaense v Rayo Zuliano	6-0

Danubio v Athletico Paranaense	0-1
Rayo Zuliano v Sportivo Ameliano	0-4
Sportivo Ameliano v Danubio	2-1
Rayo Zuliano v Athletico Paranaense	1-5
Sportivo Ameliano v Rayo Zuliano	1-0
Athletico Paranaense v Danubio	1-2
Athletico Paranaense v Sportivo Ameliano	0-1
Danubio v Rayo Zuliano	0-0

Group E Table	P	W	D	L	F	A	GD	Pts
Sportivo Ameliano	6	4	1	1	9	5	4	13
Athletico Paranaense	6	4	0	2	17	5	12	12
Danubio	6	2	2	2	5	4	1	8
Rayo Zuliano	6	0	1	5	1	18	–17	1

GROUP F

Nacional v Argentinos Juniors	2-3
Racing v Corinthians	1-1
Argentinos Juniors v Racing	0-3
Corinthians v Nacional	4-0
Argentinos Juniors v Corinthians	1-0
Nacional v Racing	2-2
Racing v Argentinos Juniors	2-1
Nacional v Corinthians	0-2
Racing v Nacional	2-1
Corinthians v Argentinos Juniors	4-0
Corinthians v Racing	3-0
Argentinos Juniors v Nacional	2-1

Group F Table	P	W	D	L	F	A	GD	Pts
Corinthians	6	4	1	1	14	2	12	13
Racing	6	3	2	1	10	8	2	11
Argentinos Juniors	6	3	0	3	7	12	–5	9
Nacional	6	0	1	5	6	15	–9	1

GROUP G

Cuiaba v Lanus	1-1
Deportivo Garcilaso v Metropolitanos	3-2
Metropolitanos v Cuiaba	0-2
Lanus v Deportivo Garcilaso	2-1
Deportivo Garcilaso v Cuiaba	1-1
Metropolitanos v Lanus	0-2
Cuiaba v Metropolitanos	3-0
Deportivo Garcilaso v Lanus	0-2
Lanus v Metropolitanos	5-0
Cuiaba v Deportivo Garcilaso	1-1
Lanus v Cuiaba	0-1
Metropolitanos v Deportivo Garcilaso	1-1

Group G Table	P	W	D	L	F	A	GD	Pts
Lanus	6	4	1	1	12	3	9	13
Cuiaba	6	3	3	0	9	3	6	12
Deportivo Garcilaso	6	1	3	2	7	9	–2	6
Metropolitanos	6	0	1	5	3	16	–13	1

GROUP H

Red Bull Bragantino v Coquimbo Unido	1-0
Sportivo Luqueno v Racing	0-2
Racing v Red Bull Bragantino	3-0
Coquimbo Unido v Sportivo Luqueno	1-0
Coquimbo Unido v Racing	1-2
Red Bull Bragantino v Sportivo Luqueno	2-1
Sportivo Luqueno v Coquimbo Unido	0-0
Red Bull Bragantino v Racing	2-1
Racing v Coquimbo Unido	3-0
Sportivo Luqueno v Red Bull Bragantino	2-3
Racing v Sportivo Luqueno	3-0
Coquimbo Unido v Red Bull Bragantino	1-1

Group H Table	P	W	D	L	F	A	GD	Pts
Racing	6	5	0	1	14	3	11	15
Red Bull Bragantino	6	4	1	1	9	8	1	13
Coquimbo Unido	6	1	2	3	3	7	–4	5
Sportivo Luqueno	6	0	1	5	3	11	–8	1

KNOCKOUT STAGE

KNOCKOUT ROUND PLAY-OFFS – FIRST LEG

Barcelona v Red Bull Bragantino	1-1
Cerro Porteno v Athletico Paranaense	1-1

KNOCKOUT ROUND PLAY-OFFS – SECOND LEG

		(agg)
Red Bull Bragantino v Barcelona	3-2	4-3
Athletico Paranaense v Cerro Porteno	2-1	3-2
Cuiaba v Palestino	1-2	2-3
Universidad Catolica v Libertad	1-1	1-3
Boca Juniors v Independiente del Valle	1-0	1-0
Always Ready v LDU Quito	3-1	3-4
Internacional v Rosario Central	1-1	1-2
Racing v Huachipato	0-1	3-3

Huachipato won 3-0 on penalties.

ROUND OF 16 – FIRST LEG

Rosario Central v Fortaleza	1-1
Libertad v Sportivo Ameliano	1-1
LDU Quito v Lanus	1-2
Huachipato v Racing	0-2
Athletico Paranaense v Belgrano	2-1
Palestino v Independiente Medellin	2-2
Boca Juniors v Cruzeiro	1-0
Red Bull Bragantino v Corinthians	1-2

ROUND OF 16 – SECOND LEG

		(agg)
Fortaleza v Rosario Central	3-1	4-2
Sportivo Ameliano v Libertad	0-0	1-1

Libertad won 4-3 on penalties.

Lanus v LDU Quito	3-1	5-2
Racing v Huachipato	6-1	8-1
Belgrano v Athletico Paranaense	0-2	1-4
Independiente Medellin v Palestino	4-0	6-2
Cruzeiro v Boca Juniors	2-1	2-2

Cruzeiro won 5-4 on penalties.

Corinthians v Red Bull Bragantino	1-2	3-3

Corinthians won 5-4 on penalties.

QUARTER-FINALS – FIRST LEG

Fortaleza v Corinthians	0-2
Libertad v Cruzeiro	0-2
Lanus v Independiente Medellin	0-0
Athletico Paranaense v Racing	1-0

QUARTER-FINALS – SECOND LEG

		(agg)
Corinthians v Fortaleza	3-0	5-0
Cruzeiro v Libertad	1-1	3-1
Independiente Medellin v Lanus	1-1	1-1

Lanus won 6-5 on penalties.

Racing v Athletico Paranaense	4-1	4-2

SEMI-FINALS – FIRST LEG

Corinthians v Racing	2-2
Cruzeiro v Lanus	1-1

SEMI-FINALS – SECOND LEG

		(agg)
Racing v Corinthians	2-1	4-3
Lanus v Cruzeiro	0-1	1-2

COPA SUDAMERICANA 2024 FINAL

Estadio General Pablo Rojas, Asuncion,
Saturday, 23 November 2024

Racing (2) 3 *(Martirena 15, Martinez A 20, Martinez R 90)*

Cruzeiro (0) 1 *(Jorge 52)* 43,828

Racing: (3421) Arias; Di Cesare, Sosa, Basso; Martirena, Nardoni, Almendra (Zuculina 56), Rojas; Quintero (Solari 87), Salas; Martinez A (Martinez R).
Cruzeiro: (4231) Cassio; William, Marcelo, Villalba, Marlon (Kenji 85); Romero (Barreal 78), Walace (Silva 30); Veron (Diaz 78), Pereira, Henrique; Jorge.
Referee: Esteban Ostojich (Uruguay).

RECOPA SUDAMERICANA 2025

FINAL – FIRST LEG

Racing v Botafogo	2-0

FINAL – SECOND LEG

Botafogo v Racing	0-2

Racing won 4-0 on aggregate.

NORTH AMERICA

MAJOR LEAGUE SOCCER 2024

After extra time.

EASTERN CONFERENCE

	P	W	D	L	F	A	GD	Pts
Inter Miami	34	22	4	8	79	49	30	74
Columbus Crew	34	19	6	9	72	40	32	66
FC Cincinnati	34	18	11	5	58	48	10	59
Orlando C	34	15	12	7	59	50	9	52
Charlotte	34	14	11	9	46	37	9	51
New York City	34	14	12	8	54	49	5	50
New York Red Bulls	34	11	9	14	55	50	5	47
CF Montreal	34	11	13	10	48	64	–16	43
Atlanta U	34	10	14	10	46	49	–3	40
DC United	34	10	14	10	52	70	–18	40
Toronto	34	11	19	4	40	61	–21	37
Philadelphia Union	34	9	15	10	62	55	7	37
Nashville	34	9	16	9	38	54	–16	36
New England Revolution	34	9	21	4	37	74	–37	31
Chicago Fire	34	7	18	9	40	62	–22	30

WESTERN CONFERENCE

	P	W	D	L	F	A	GD	Pts
Los Angeles	34	19	8	7	63	43	20	64
LA Galaxy	34	19	8	7	69	50	19	64
Real Salt Lake	34	16	7	11	65	48	17	59
Seattle Sounders	34	16	9	9	51	35	16	57
Houston Dynamo	34	15	10	9	47	39	8	54
Minnesota U	34	15	12	7	58	49	9	52
Colorado Rapids	34	15	14	5	61	60	1	50
Vancouver Whitecaps	34	13	13	8	52	49	3	47
Portland Timbers	34	12	11	11	65	56	9	47
Austin	34	11	14	9	39	48	–9	42
FC Dallas	34	11	15	8	54	56	–2	41
St Louis C	34	8	13	13	50	63	–13	37
Sporting Kansas City	34	8	19	7	51	66	–15	31
San Jose Earthquakes	34	6	25	3	41	78	–37	21

EASTERN CONFERENCE WILD CARD ROUND
CF Montreal v Atlanta U   2-2
Atlanta U won 5-4 on penalties.

WESTERN CONFERENCE WILD CARD ROUND
Vancouver Whitecaps v Portland Timbers   5-0

FIRST ROUND – BEST OF THREE SERIES

EASTERN CONFERENCE FIRST ROUND – MATCH 1
Inter Miami v Atlanta U   2-1
Columbus Crew v New York Red Bulls   0-1
FC Cincinnati v New York City   1-0
Orlando C v Charlotte   2-0

EASTERN CONFERENCE FIRST ROUND – MATCH 2
Atlanta U v Inter Miami   2-1
New York Red Bulls v Columbus Crew   2-2
New York Red Bulls won 5-4 on penalties and won the series 2-0.
New York City v FC Cincinnati   3-1
Charlotte v Orlando C   0-0
Charlotte won 3-1 on penalties.

EASTERN CONFERENCE FIRST ROUND – MATCH 3
Inter Miami v Atlanta U   2-3
Atlanta U won the series 2-1.
FC Cincinnati v New York City   0-0
New York City won 6-5 on penalties and won the series 2-1.
Orlando C v Charlotte   1-1
Orlando C won 4-1 on penalties and won the series 2-1.

WESTERN CONFERENCE FIRST ROUND – MATCH 1
Los Angeles v Vancouver Whitecaps   2-1
LA Galaxy v Colorado Rapids   5-0
Real Salt Lake v Minnesota U   0-0
Minnesota U won 5-4 on penalties.
Seattle Sounders v Houston Dynamo   0-0
Seattle Sounders won 5-4 on penalties.

WESTERN CONFERENCE FIRST ROUND – MATCH 2
Vancouver Whitecaps v Los Angeles   3-0
Colorado Rapids v LA Galaxy   1-4
La Galaxy won the series 2-0.
Minnesota U v Real Salt Lake   1-1
Minnesota U won 3-1 on penalties and won the series 2-0.
Houston Dynamo v Seattle Sounders   1-1
Seattle Sounders won 7-6 on penalties and won the series 2-0.

WESTERN CONFERENCE FIRST ROUND – MATCH 3
Los Angeles v Vancouver Whitecaps   1-0
Los Angeles won the series 2-1.

EASTERN CONFERENCE SEMI-FINALS
New York City v New York Red Bulls   0-2
Orlando C v Atlanta U   1-0

WESTERN CONFERENCE SEMI-FINALS
Los Angeles v Seattle Sounders   1-2
aet.
LA Galaxy v Minnesota U   6-2

EASTERN CONFERENCE FINAL
Orlando C v New York Red Bulls   0-1

WESTERN CONFERENCE FINAL
LA Galaxy v Seattle Sounders   1-0

MLS CUP FINAL 2024

Carson, California, Saturday, 7 December 2024

LA Galaxy (2) 2 *(Paintsil 9, Joveljic 13)*

New York Red Bulls (1) 1 *(Nealis S 28)*   26,812

LA Galaxy: (433) McCarthy; Yamane, Garces, Yoshida, Nelson; Delgado, Cerrillo, Brugman (Reus 75); Pec, Joveljic (Fagundez 78), Paintsil (Neal 90).
New York Red Bulls: (3412) Coronel; Nealis D (Burke 84), Eile; Nealis S; Harper, Stroud (Donkor 65), Edelman (Carmona 84), Tolkin; Vanzeir (Manoel 65), Fosberg; Morgan.
Referee: Guido Gonzales Jr.

UEFA YOUTH LEAGUE 2024–25

†*Due to the war in Ukraine, teams from Ukraine and Belarus played home games at a neutral venue.*

UEFA CHAMPIONS LEAGUE PATH LEAGUE PHASE

MATCHDAY 1

Young Boys v Aston Villa	2-1
Juventus v PSV Eindhoven	1-0
AC Milan v Liverpool	0-0
Bayern Munich v Dinamo Zagreb	2-1
Real Madrid v VfB Stuttgart	1-0
Sporting Lisbon v Lille	2-2
Sparta Prague v Red Bull Salzburg	2-3
Bologna v Shakhtar Donetsk	3-4
Celtic v Slovan Bratislava	4-0
Club Brugge v Borussia Dortmund	1-1
Manchester C v Internazionale	2-4
Paris Saint-Germain v Girona	0-2
Feyenoord v Bayer Leverkusen	1-2
Red Star Belgrade v Benfica	1-2
Monaco v Barcelona	4-3
Atalanta v Arsenal	4-1
Atletico Madrid v RB Leipzig	4-0
Brest v Sturm Graz	1-4

MATCHDAY 2

Red Bull Salzburg v Brest	5-1
VfB Stuttgart v Sparta Prague	3-0
Arsenal v Paris Saint-Germain	1-0
Bayer Leverkusen v AC Milan	3-1
Borussia Dortmund v Celtic	4-0
Barcelona v Young Boys	4-2
Internazionale v Red Star Belgrade	4-0
PSV Eindhoven v Sporting Lisbon	0-2
Slovan Bratislava v Manchester C	0-4
Shakhtar Donetsk v Atalanta	0-3
Girona v Feyenoord	2-0
Aston Villa v Bayern Munich	0-1
Dinamo Zagreb v Monaco	1-0
Liverpool v Bologna	2-1
Lille v Real Madrid	2-1
RB Leipzig v Juventus	0-3
Sturm Graz v Club Brugge	1-1
Benfica v Atletico Madrid	2-2

MATCHDAY 3

AC Milan v Club Brugge	1-1
Monaco v Red Star Belgrade	1-1
Arsenal v Shakhtar Donetsk	0-1
Aston Villa v Bologna	3-1
Girona v Slovan Bratislava	2-2
Juventus v VfB Stuttgart	2-3
Paris Saint-Germain v PSV Eindhoven	3-3
Real Madrid v Borussia Dortmund	1-2
Sturm Graz v Sporting Lisbon	1-3
Atalanta v Celtic	2-1
Brest v Bayer Leverkusen	1-1
Atletico Madrid v Lille	1-1
Young Boys v Internazionale	2-3
Barcelona v Bayern Munich	3-1
Red Bull Salzburg v Dinamo Zagreb	3-2
Manchester C v Sparta Prague	3-0
RB Leipzig v Liverpool	3-1
Benfica v Feyenoord	2-0

MATCHDAY 4

PSV Eindhoven v Girona	1-1
Slovan Bratislava v Dinamo Zagreb	2-2
Bologna v Monaco	0-0
Borussia Dortmund v Sturm Graz	2-3
Celtic v RB Leipzig	3-2
Liverpool v Bayer Leverkusen	4-1
Lille v Juventus	0-0
Real Madrid v AC Milan	2-1
Sporting Lisbon v Manchester C	2-0
Club Brugge v Aston Villa	2-6
Shakhtar Donetsk v Young Boys	3-2
Sparta Prague v Brest	1-1
Bayern Munich v Benfica	3-3
Internazionale v Arsenal	4-1
Feyenoord v Red Bull Salzburg	2-2
Red Star Belgrade v Barcelona	1-2
Paris Saint-Germain v Atletico Madrid	4-2
VfB Stuttgart v Atalanta	4-1

MATCHDAY 5

Sparta Prague v Atletico Madrid	1-2
Slovan Bratislava v AC Milan	2-3
Bayer Leverkusen v Red Bull Salzburg	0-1
Young Boys v Atalanta	2-4
Barcelona v Brest	2-0
Bayern Munich v Paris Saint-Germain	2-5
Internazionale v RB Leipzig	3-2
Manchester C v Feyenoord	6-1
Sporting Lisbon v Arsenal	3-0
Red Star Belgrade v VfB Stuttgart	1-1
Sturm Graz v Girona	0-0
Monaco v Benfica	1-0
Aston Villa v Juventus	0-2
Bologna v Lille	2-2
Celtic v Club Brugge	1-0
Dinamo Zagreb v Borussia Dortmund	0-0
Liverpool v Real Madrid	0-1
PSV Eindhoven v Shakhtar Donetsk	1-1

MATCHDAY 6

Girona v Liverpool	2-2
Dinamo Zagreb v Celtic	2-1
Atalanta v Real Madrid	0-4
Bayer Leverkusen v Internazionale	0-1
Club Brugge v Sporting Lisbon	0-1
Red Bull Salzburg v Paris Saint-Germain	3-2
Shakhtar Donetsk v Bayern Munich	0-2
RB Leipzig v Aston Villa	3-4
Brest v PSV Eindhoven	1-3
Atletico Madrid v Slovan Bratislava	5-0
Lille v Sturm Graz	1-1
AC Milan v Red Star Belgrade	1-3
Arsenal v Monaco	2-0
Borussia Dortmund v Barcelona	2-3
Feyenoord v Sparta Prague	3-0
Juventus v Manchester C	1-1
Benfica v Bologna	3-0
VfB Stuttgart v Young Boys	2-1

League Phase Table	P	W	D	L	F	A	GD	Pts
Internazionale	6	6	0	0	19	7	12	18
Sporting Lisbon	6	5	1	0	13	3	10	16
Red Bull Salzburg	6	5	1	0	17	9	8	16
Barcelona	6	5	0	1	17	10	7	15
VfB Stuttgart	6	4	1	1	13	6	7	13
Real Madrid	6	4	0	2	10	5	5	12
Atalanta	6	4	0	2	14	12	2	12
Atletico Madrid	6	3	2	1	16	8	8	11
Benfica	6	3	2	1	12	7	5	11
Juventus	6	3	2	1	9	4	5	11
Manchester C	6	3	1	2	16	8	8	10
Girona	6	2	4	0	9	5	4	10
Bayern Munich	6	3	1	2	11	12	−1	10
Shakhtar Donetsk	6	3	1	2	9	11	−2	10
Aston Villa	6	3	0	3	14	11	3	9
Sturm Graz	6	2	3	1	10	8	2	9
Celtic	6	3	0	3	10	10	0	9
Borussia Dortmund	6	2	2	2	11	8	3	8
Liverpool	6	2	2	2	9	8	1	8
Lille	6	1	5	0	8	7	1	8
Dinamo Zagreb	6	2	2	2	8	8	0	8
Monaco	6	2	2	2	6	7	−1	8
Paris Saint-Germain	6	2	1	3	14	13	1	7
Bayer Leverkusen	6	2	1	3	7	9	−2	7
PSV Eindhoven	6	1	3	2	8	9	−1	6
Arsenal	6	2	0	4	5	12	−7	6
AC Milan*	6	1	2	3	7	11	−4	5
Red Star Belgrade*	6	1	2	3	7	11	−4	5
Feyenoord	6	1	1	4	7	14	−7	4
Young Boys	6	1	0	5	11	17	−6	3
Club Brugge	6	0	3	3	5	11	−6	3
RB Leipzig	6	1	0	5	10	18	−8	3
Bologna	6	0	2	4	7	14	−7	2
Brest	6	0	2	4	5	16	−11	2
Slovan Bratislava	6	0	2	4	6	20	−14	2
Sparta Prague	6	0	1	5	4	15	−11	1

Top 22 qualify for knockout phase.
Ranking decided on away goals scored
(AC Milan 5, Red Star Belgrade 4).

DOMESTIC CHAMPIONS PATH

FIRST ROUND – FIRST LEG

HB v Progres Niederkorn	1-2
UCD v Stjarnan	3-0
Bylis v 2 Korriku	1-2
Lincoln Red Imps v Maribor	0-6
Kauno Zalgiris v The New Saints	3-2
FC Honka v Valletta	1-0
BFC Daugavpils v Cliftonville	1-0
Tallinna Kalev v FC Santa Coloma	7-0
AP Brera Strumica v Sarajevo	2-2
Dinamo Minsk v Pyunik	4-2
Kairat v Academia Rebeja	2-1
Dinamo Tbilisi v Buducnost Podgorica	3-2

FIRST ROUND – SECOND LEG

		(agg)
Progres Niederkorn v HB	3-0	5-1
Stjarnan v UCD	3-2	3-5
2 Korriku v Bylis	2-1	4-2
Maribor v Lincoln Red Imps	2-0	8-0
The New Saints v Kauno Zalgiris	0-4	2-7
Valletta v FC Honka	3-2	3-3
Valletta won 3-0 on penalties.		
Cliftonville v BFC Daugavpils	2-1	2-2
BFC Daugavpils won 4-2 on penalties.		
FC Santa Coloma v Tallinna Kalev	0-4	0-11
Sarajevo v AP Brera Strumica	2-0	4-2
Pyunik v Dinamo Minsk	1-2	3-6
Academia Rebeja v Kairat	1-4	2-6
Buducnost Podgorica v Dinamo Tbilisi	4-1	6-4

SECOND ROUND – FIRST LEG

IFK Goteborg v TSG Hoffenheim	0-3
Aberdeen v Puskas Akademia	1-5
Stromsgodset v AZ Alkmaar	1-4
2 Korriku v UCD	2-1
Progres Niederkorn v Midtjylland	0-4
Kauno Zalgiris v Manchester U	2-5
Dynamo Kyiv v Maribor	1-1
Genk v CSKA Sofia	3-1
Legia Warsaw v Pafos	3-0
Auxerre v Valletta	5-0
BFC Daugavpils v Sassuolo	0-5
Farul Constanta v IMT	2-0
Olympiacos v Tallinna Kalev	5-0
FC Basel v Sabah	6-0
Maccabi Petah Tikva v Sarajevo*	0-3
Trabzonspor v Buducnost Podgorica	3-1
Braga v Rapid Vienna	0-0
Real Betis v Kairat	6-1
Trencin v Zbrojovka Brno	3-2
Lokomotiva Zagreb v Dinamo Minsk	2-1

SECOND ROUND – SECOND LEG

		(agg)
TSG Hoffenheim v IFK Goteborg	4-1	7-1
Puskas Akademia v Aberdeen	3-0	8-1
AZ Alkmaar v Stromsgodset	4-1	8-2
UCD v 2 Korriku	1-3	2-5
Midtjylland v Progres Niederkorn	5-0	9-0
Manchester U v Kauno Zalgiris	6-0	11-2
Maribor v Dynamo Kyiv	1-3	2-4
CSKA Sofia v Genk	1-3	2-6
Pafos v Legia Warsaw	0-3	0-6
Valletta v Auxerre	0-2	0-7
Sassuolo v BFC Daugavpils	4-0	9-0
IMT v Farul Constanta	1-0	1-2
Tallinna Kalev v Olympiacos	1-2	1-7
Sabah v FC Basel	1-2	1-8
Sarajevo v Maccabi Petah Tikva*	3-0	6-0
Buducnost Podgorica v Trabzonspor	2-5	3-8
Rapid Vienna v Braga	3-2	3-2
Kairat v Real Betis	0-5	1-11
Zbrojovka Brno v Trencin	1-3	3-6
Dinamo Minsk v Lokomotiva Zagreb	0-0	1-2

*Match awarded to Sarajevo; Maccabi Petah Tikva failed to fulfil fixture.

THIRD ROUND – FIRST LEG

Dynamo Kyiv v 2 Korriku	5-0
AZ Alkmaar v Manchester U	2-1
Puskas Akademia v Genk	1-0
Auxerre v TSG Hoffenheim	1-2
Legia Warsaw v Midtjylland	0-2
Real Betis v Sassuolo	3-1

Farul Constanta v Lokomotiva Zagreb	0-2
Trencin v Olympiacos	1-1
FC Basel v Rapid Vienna	1-2
Sarajevo v Trabzonspor	2-2

THIRD ROUND – SECOND LEG

		(agg)
2 Korriku v Dynamo Kyiv	1-4	1-9
Manchester U v AZ Alkmaar	0-0	1-2
Genk v Puskas Akademia	2-1	2-2
Puskas Akademia won 6-5 on penalties.		
TSG Hoffenheim v Auxerre	1-0	3-1
Midtjylland v Legia Warsaw	7-0	9-0
Sassuolo v Real Betis	1-1	2-4
Lokomotiva Zagreb v Farul Constanta	4-1	6-1
Olympiacos v Trencin	4-1	5-2
Rapid Vienna v FC Basel	3-0	5-1
Trabzonspor v Sarajevo	6-1	8-3

KNOCKOUT PHASE

ROUND OF 32

Internazionale v Lille	3-1
Sporting Lisbon v Monaco	4-0
Red Bull Salzburg v Celtic	1-1
Red Bull Salzburg won 4-2 on penalties.	
Barcelona v Dinamo Zagreb	2-2
Barcelona won 5-3 on penalties.	
VfB Stuttgart v Liverpool	2-2
VfB Stuttgart won 5-3 on penalties.	
Real Madrid v Borussia Dortmund	2-0
Dynamo Kyiv v Atalanta	3-3
Atalanta won 7-6 on penalties.	
Rapid Vienna v Atletico Madrid	1-2
AZ Alkmaar v Benfica	2-2
AZ Alkmaar won 4-3 on penalties.	
Trabzonspor v Juventus	1-0
Midtjylland v Manchester C	2-2
Manchester C won 5-4 on penalties.	
Olympiacos v Girona	1-0
Real Betis v Bayern Munich	0-1
TSG Hoffenheim v Shakhtar Donetsk	5-1
Puskas Akademia v Aston Villa	1-2
Lokomotiva Zagreb v Sturm Graz	1-1
Sturm Graz won 5-3 on penalties.	

ROUND OF 16

Trabzonspor v Atalanta	0-0
Trabzonspor won 5-3 on penalties.	
Sturm Graz v Olympiacos	1-1
Olympiacos won 5-4 on penalties.	
Bayern Munich v Internazionale	1-1
Internazionale won 5-4 on penalties.	
Red Bull Salzburg v Atletico Madrid	2-1
Real Madrid v AZ Alkmaar	0-2
Sporting Lisbon v VfB Stuttgart	2-3
TSG Hoffenheim v Manchester C	1-2
Aston Villa v Barcelona	1-3

QUARTER-FINALS

AZ Alkmaar v Manchester C	1-0
VfB Stuttgart v Barcelona	1-2
Red Bull Salzburg v Olympiacos	1-0
Trabzonspor v Internazionale	1-0

SEMI-FINALS

AZ Alkmaar v Barcelona	0-1
Red Bull Salzburg v Trabzonspor	1-2

UEFA YOUTH LEAGUE FINAL 2024–25

Colovray Stadium, Nyon, Monday, 28 April 2025

Barcelona (2) 4 *(Diarra 11, 68, Cuenca 18, Alba 57)*

Trabzonspor (0) 1 *(Tibukoglu 88)*   3081

Barcelona: (4321) Yaakobishvili; Espart (Walton 79), Kospo, Cuenca, Farre; Diarra (Rodriguez 80), Farinas, Junyent (Virgili 59); Pradas (Fernandez 79), Hernandez (Marques 71); Alba.
Trabzonspor: (4321) Colak; Yilmaz, Ince, Ozturk, Tibukoglu; Erdogan (Terzi 46), Malkocoglu (Ozcan 78), Baskan; Turan (Duymaz 46), Bayram (Tuncer 89); Cakiroglu (Alkurt 73).
Referee: Andrea Colombo (Italy).

UEFA UNDER-17 CHAMPIONSHIP 2024–25

ROUND 1

GROUP 1 (MALTA)

England v Malta	4-0	Sweden v Malta	5-0
Latvia v Sweden	1-2	Malta v Latvia	1-4
England v Latvia	4-0	Sweden v England	2-4

Group 1 Table	P	W	D	L	F	A	GD	Pts
England	3	3	0	0	12	2	10	9
Sweden	3	2	0	1	9	5	4	6
Latvia	3	1	0	2	5	7	–2	3
Malta	3	0	0	3	1	13	–12	0

GROUP 2 (SLOVENIA)

Poland v Armenia	8-0	Slovenia v Armenia	1-0
Georgia v Slovenia	1-2	Slovenia v Poland	2-2
Poland v Georgia	3-0	Armenia v Georgia	1-3

Group 2 Table	P	W	D	L	F	A	GD	Pts
Poland	3	2	1	0	13	2	11	7
Slovenia	3	2	1	0	5	3	2	7
Georgia	3	1	0	2	4	6	–2	3
Armenia	3	0	0	3	1	12	–11	0

GROUP 3 (ALBANIA)

Netherlands v Faroe Islands	6-0
Albania v Croatia	1-1
Croatia v Faroe Islands	7-0
Netherlands v Albania	5-0
Croatia v Netherlands	3-1
Faroe Islands v Albania	0-1

Group 3 Table	P	W	D	L	F	A	GD	Pts
Croatia	3	2	1	0	11	2	9	7
Netherlands	3	2	0	1	12	3	9	6
Albania	3	1	1	1	2	6	–4	4
Faroe Islands	3	0	0	3	0	14	–14	0

GROUP 4 (BELGIUM)

Kosovo v Ukraine	2-4	Belgium v Kosovo	2-1
Belgium v Kazakhstan	3-1	Ukraine v Belgium	1-2
Ukraine v Kazakhstan	3-0	Kazakhstan v Kosovo	4-4

Group 4 Table	P	W	D	L	F	A	GD	Pts
Belgium	3	3	0	0	7	3	4	9
Ukraine	3	2	0	1	8	4	4	6
Kosovo	3	0	1	2	7	10	–3	1
Kazakhstan	3	0	1	2	5	10	–5	1

GROUP 5 (PORTUGAL)

Portugal v Liechtenstein	10-0
Finland v Bosnia & Herzegovina	2-2
Portugal v Finland	5-1
Bosnia & Herzegovina v Liechtenstein	6-0
Bosnia & Herzegovina v Portugal	2-4
Liechtenstein v Finland	0-8

Group 5 Table	P	W	D	L	F	A	GD	Pts
Portugal	3	3	0	0	19	3	16	9
Finland	3	1	1	1	11	7	4	4
Bosnia & Herzegovina	3	1	1	1	10	6	4	4
Liechtenstein	3	0	0	3	0	24	–24	0

GROUP 6 (ROMANIA)

Hungary v Azerbaijan	4-0	Greece v Azerbaijan	3-0
Romania v Greece	0-3	Greece v Hungary	2-2
Hungary v Romania	0-0	Azerbaijan v Romania	1-1

Group 6 Table	P	W	D	L	F	A	GD	Pts
Greece	3	2	1	0	8	2	6	7
Hungary	3	1	2	0	6	2	4	5
Romania	3	0	2	1	1	4	–3	2
Azerbaijan	3	0	1	2	1	8	–7	1

GROUP 7 (GERMANY)

Germany v Andorra	4-0
Belarus v Czech Republic	0-3
Germany v Belarus	8-2
Czech Republic v Andorra	8-0
Czech Republic v Germany	3-3
Andorra v Belarus	1-3

Group 7 Table	P	W	D	L	F	A	GD	Pts
Czech Republic	3	2	1	0	14	3	11	7
Germany	3	2	1	0	15	5	10	7
Belarus	3	1	0	2	5	12	–7	3
Andorra	3	0	0	3	1	15	–14	0

GROUP 8 (NORTHERN IRELAND)

Republic of Ireland v Lithuania	2-2
Northern Ireland v Scotland	3-1
Scotland v Lithuania	2-1
Republic of Ireland v Northern Ireland	1-3
Scotland v Republic of Ireland	0-3
Lithuania v Northern Ireland	3-1

Group 8 Table	P	W	D	L	F	A	GD	Pts
Northern Ireland	3	2	0	1	7	5	2	6
Republic of Ireland†	3	1	1	1	6	5	1	4
Lithuania†	3	1	1	1	6	5	1	4
Scotland	3	1	0	2	3	7	–4	3

†Ranking decided on disciplinary points.

GROUP 9 (SAN MARINO)

Italy v San Marino	5-0	Norway v San Marino	3-0
Wales v Norway	3-4	Norway v Italy	0-7
Italy v Wales	4-0	San Marino v Wales	0-6

Group 9 Table	P	W	D	L	F	A	GD	Pts
Italy	3	3	0	0	16	0	16	9
Norway	3	2	0	1	7	10	–3	6
Wales	3	1	0	2	9	8	1	3
San Marino	3	0	0	3	0	14	–14	0

GROUP 10 (MOLDOVA)

Montenegro v Israel	1-1
Switzerland v Moldova	4-0
Switzerland v Montenegro	3-0
Israel v Moldova	4-0
Israel v Switzerland	2-2
Moldova v Montenegro	0-3

Group 10 Table	P	W	D	L	F	A	GD	Pts
Switzerland	3	2	1	0	9	2	7	7
Israel	3	1	2	0	7	3	4	5
Montenegro	3	1	1	1	4	4	0	4
Moldova	3	0	0	3	0	11	–11	0

GROUP 11 (CYPRUS)

France v Gibraltar	6-0	France v Cyprus	2-0
Cyprus v Slovakia	2-3	Slovakia v France	0-1
Slovakia v Gibraltar	7-0	Gibraltar v Cyprus	0-6

Group 11 Table	P	W	D	L	F	A	GD	Pts
France	3	3	0	0	9	0	9	9
Slovakia	3	2	0	1	10	3	7	6
Cyprus	3	1	0	2	8	5	3	3
Gibraltar	3	0	0	3	0	19	–19	0

GROUP 12 (ICELAND)

Spain v Estonia	4-0
North Macedonia v Iceland	1-4
Spain v North Macedonia	5-0
Iceland v Estonia	3-1
Estonia v North Macedonia	2-4
Iceland v Spain	2-2

Group 12 Table	P	W	D	L	F	A	GD	Pts
Spain	3	2	1	0	11	2	9	7
Iceland	3	2	1	0	9	4	5	7
North Macedonia	3	1	0	2	5	11	–6	3
Estonia	3	0	0	3	3	11	–8	0

GROUP 13 (SERBIA)

Bulgaria v Serbia	0-2
Turkey v Bulgaria	1-0
Serbia v Turkey	1-1

Group 13 Table	P	W	D	L	F	A	GD	Pts
Serbia	2	1	1	0	3	1	2	4
Turkey	2	1	1	0	2	1	1	4
Bulgaria	2	0	0	2	0	3	–3	0

GROUP 14 (DENMARK)

Luxembourg v Denmark	0-3
Austria v Luxembourg	1-1
Denmark v Austria	0-1

Group 14 Table	P	W	D	L	F	A	GD	Pts
Austria	2	1	1	0	2	1	1	4
Denmark	2	1	0	1	3	1	2	3
Luxembourg	2	0	1	1	1	4	–3	1

ROUND 2
LEAGUE A

GROUP A1 (CROATIA)

Ukraine v Croatia	1-2	Croatia v Slovakia	2-1
Italy v Slovakia	1-0	Slovakia v Ukraine	0-1
Italy v Ukraine	2-1	Croatia v Italy	1-2

Group A1 Table	P	W	D	L	F	A	GD	Pts
Italy	3	3	0	0	5	2	3	9
Croatia	3	2	0	1	5	4	1	6
Ukraine	3	1	0	2	3	4	–1	3
Slovakia	3	0	0	3	1	4	–3	0

GROUP A2 (SPAIN)

Germany v Austria	2-2	Spain v Germany	2-3
Spain v Norway	2-1	Austria v Spain	3-3
Austria v Norway	2-1	Norway v Germany	1-4

Group A2 Table	P	W	D	L	F	A	GD	Pts
Germany	3	2	1	0	9	5	4	7
Austria	3	1	2	0	7	6	1	5
Spain	3	1	1	1	7	7	0	4
Norway	3	0	0	3	3	8	–5	0

GROUP A3 (FRANCE)

France v Finland	4-0	Greece v Finland	3-1
Denmark v Greece	3-1	Greece v France	1-5
France v Denmark	4-1	Finland v Denmark	5-2

Group A3 Table	P	W	D	L	F	A	GD	Pts
France	3	3	0	0	13	2	11	9
Finland	3	1	0	2	6	9	–3	3
Greece*	3	1	0	2	5	9	–4	3
Denmark*	3	1	0	2	6	10	–4	3

Rankings decided on head-to-head goal difference.

GROUP A4 (PORTUGAL)

Netherlands v Serbia	0-1	Portugal v Netherlands	3-1
Portugal v Hungary	2-0	Serbia v Portugal	1-3
Serbia v Hungary	1-1	Hungary v Netherlands	2-2

Group A4 Table	P	W	D	L	F	A	GD	Pts
Portugal	3	3	0	0	8	2	6	9
Serbia	3	1	1	1	3	4	–1	4
Hungary	3	0	2	1	3	5	–2	2
Netherlands	3	0	1	2	3	6	–3	1

GROUP A5 (SWITZERLAND)

Turkey v Switzerland	2-3
Czech Republic v Sweden	3-2
Czech Republic v Turkey	1-1
Switzerland v Sweden	1-0
Switzerland v Czech Republic	1-3
Sweden v Turkey	4-0

Group A5 Table	P	W	D	L	F	A	GD	Pts
Czech Republic	3	2	1	0	7	4	3	7
Switzerland	3	2	0	1	5	5	0	6
Sweden	3	1	0	2	6	4	2	3
Turkey	3	0	1	2	3	8	–5	1

GROUP A6 (POLAND)

Belgium v Republic of Ireland	1-0
Iceland v Poland	1-1
Belgium v Iceland	2-1
Poland v Republic of Ireland	0-2
Poland v Belgium	2-2
Republic of Ireland v Iceland	5-0

Group A6 Table	P	W	D	L	F	A	GD	Pts
Belgium	3	2	1	0	5	3	2	7
Republic of Ireland	3	2	0	1	7	1	6	6
Poland	3	0	2	1	3	5	–2	2
Iceland	3	0	1	2	2	8	–6	1

GROUP A7 (ENGLAND)

England v Israel	2-0
Slovenia v Northern Ireland	1-1
England v Slovenia	3-2
Northern Ireland v Israel	0-1
Northern Ireland v England	0-5
Israel v Slovenia	0-1

Group A7 Table	P	W	D	L	F	A	GD	Pts
England	3	3	0	0	10	2	8	9
Slovenia	3	1	1	1	4	4	0	4
Israel	3	1	0	2	1	3	–2	3
Northern Ireland	3	0	1	2	1	7	–6	1

LEAGUE B

GROUP B1 (SCOTLAND)

Romania v Liechtenstein	10-0
Scotland v North Macedonia	2-2
North Macedonia v Liechtenstein	1-0
Romania v Scotland	0-2
North Macedonia v Romania	0-3
Liechtenstein v Scotland	0-8

Group B1 Table	P	W	D	L	F	A	GD	Pts
Scotland	3	2	1	0	12	2	10	7
Romania	3	2	0	1	13	2	11	6
North Macedonia	3	1	1	1	3	5	–2	4
Liechtenstein	3	0	0	3	19	–19	0

GROUP B2 (BOSNIA & HERZEGOVINA)

Bosnia & Herzegovina v San Marino	5-0
Belarus v Armenia	4-0
Bosnia & Herzegovina v Armenia	3-0
Belarus v San Marino	1-0
Belarus v Bosnia & Herzegovina	1-2
San Marino v Armenia	0-1

Group B2 Table	P	W	D	L	F	A	GD	Pts
Bosnia & Herzegovina	3	3	0	0	10	1	9	9
Belarus	3	2	0	1	6	2	4	6
Armenia	3	1	0	2	1	7	–6	3
San Marino	3	0	0	3	0	7	–7	0

GROUP B3 (MONTENEGRO)

Estonia v Montenegro	3-1
Latvia v Estonia	0-1
Montenegro v Latvia	3-0

Group B3 Table	P	W	D	L	F	A	GD	Pts
Estonia	2	2	0	0	4	1	3	6
Montenegro	2	1	0	1	4	3	1	3
Latvia	2	0	0	2	0	4	–4	0
Gibraltar*	0	0	0	0	0	0	0	0

Gibraltar withdrew.

GROUP B4 (CYPRUS)

Kosovo v Andorra	0-0	Cyprus v Andorra	1-0
Cyprus v Moldova	2-0	Cyprus v Kosovo	0-0
Kosovo v Moldova	1-0	Andorra v Moldova	1-0

Group B4 Table	P	W	D	L	F	A	GD	Pts
Cyprus	3	2	1	0	3	0	3	7
Kosovo	3	1	2	0	1	0	1	5
Andorra	3	1	1	1	1	1	0	4
Moldova	3	0	0	3	0	4	–4	0

GROUP B5 (MALTA)

Bulgaria v Malta	3-0
Luxembourg v Faroe Islands	0-0
Luxembourg v Malta	2-1
Bulgaria v Faroe Islands	1-0
Faroe Islands v Malta	2-1
Bulgaria v Luxembourg	2-0

Group B5 Table	P	W	D	L	F	A	GD	Pts
Bulgaria	3	3	0	0	6	0	6	9
Faroe Islands	3	1	1	1	2	2	0	4
Luxembourg	3	1	1	1	2	3	–1	4
Malta	3	0	0	3	2	7	–5	0

GROUP B6 (ALBANIA)

Azerbaijan v Albania	1-4
Wales v Azerbaijan	0-0
Albania v Wales	1-2

Group B6 Table	P	W	D	L	F	A	GD	Pts
Wales	2	1	1	0	2	1	1	4
Albania	2	1	0	1	5	3	2	3
Azerbaijan	2	0	1	1	1	4	–3	1

GROUP B7 (KAZAKHSTAN)

Georgia v Kazakhstan	0-3
Lithuania v Georgia	3-0
Kazakhstan v Lithuania	5-2

Group B7 Table	P	W	D	L	F	A	GD	Pts
Kazakhstan	2	2	0	0	8	2	6	6
Lithuania	2	1	0	1	5	5	0	3
Georgia	2	0	0	2	0	6	–6	0

UEFA UNDER-17 FINAL TOURNAMENT (ALBANIA)

GROUP A

Albania v Portugal	0-4
Germany v France	0-3
Albania v Germany	0-4
France v Portugal	0-0
France v Albania	4-0
Portugal v Germany	2-1

Group A Table	P	W	D	L	F	A	GD	Pts
France	3	2	1	0	7	0	7	7
Portugal	3	2	1	0	6	1	5	7
Germany	3	1	0	2	5	5	0	3
Albania	3	0	0	3	0	12	–12	0

GROUP B

England v Belgium	1-1
Italy v Czech Republic	2-1
Belgium v Czech Republic	3-1
Italy v England	4-2
Belgium v Italy	1-2
Czech Republic v England	2-4

Group B Table	P	W	D	L	F	A	GD	Pts
Italy	3	3	0	0	8	4	4	9
Belgium	3	1	1	1	5	4	1	4
England	3	1	1	1	7	7	0	4
Czech Republic	3	0	0	3	4	9	–5	0

SEMI-FINALS

| France v Belgium | 3-2 |
| Italy v Portugal | 2-2 |

Portugal won 4-3 on penalties.

UEFA UNDER-17 CHAMPIONSHIP FINAL 2024–25

Sunday, 1 June 2025

(at Arena Kombetare, Tirana)

France (0) 0   Portugal (2) 3

France: (442) Jourdren; Antonio, Diandaga, Mbemba, Batbedat (Raiani 84); Matondo (Camara S 77), Camara A (Munongo 61), Eymard, Coulibaly (Azizi 61); Himbert (Batola 77), N'Guessan.

Portugal: (433) Cunha R; Danjaqui, Chelmik, Furtado, Neto J; Mide (Neves 58), Quintas, Lima (Verdi 77); Cunha D (Neto R), Cabral (Soares 58), Manuel (Pereira 58).
Scorers: Cabral 30, Cunha D 38, Neves 60.

Referee: Oleski Derevinskyi (Ukraine).

UEFA UNDER-19 CHAMPIONSHIP 2023–24

FINAL TOURNAMENT (NORTHERN IRELAND)

■ *Denotes player sent off.* **After extra time.*

GROUP STAGE

GROUP A

Italy v Norway	2-1
Northern Ireland v Ukraine	0-0
Norway v Ukraine	0-0
Northern Ireland v Italy	0-3
Norway v Northern Ireland	2-0
Ukraine v Italy	3-2

Group A Table	P	W	D	L	F	A	GD	Pts
Italy	3	2	0	1	7	4	3	6
Ukraine	3	1	2	0	3	2	1	5
Norway	3	1	1	1	3	2	1	4
Northern Ireland	3	0	1	2	0	5	–5	1

GROUP B

Denmark v Spain	1-2
France v Turkey	2-1
Denmark v France	2-4
Turkey v Spain	1-1
Turkey v Denmark	3-3
Spain v France	2-2

Group B Table	P	W	D	L	F	A	GD	Pts
France	3	2	1	0	8	5	3	7
Spain	3	1	2	0	5	4	1	5
Turkey	3	0	2	1	5	6	–1	2
Denmark	3	0	1	2	6	9	–3	1

KNOCKOUT STAGE

FIFA U-20 WORLD CUP PLAY-OFF

| Norway v Turkey | 1-1* |

Norway won 10-9 on penalties.
Five teams from UEFA qualified for the 2025 FIFA Under-20 World Cup in Chile.
Italy, France, Ukraine, Spain, Norway.

SEMI-FINALS

| Italy v Spain | 0-1* |
| France v Ukraine | 1-0 |

UEFA UNDER-19 CHAMPIONSHIP FINAL 2023–24

Thursday, 25 July 2024

(at Windsor Park, Belfast, attendance 8358)

Spain (1) 2   France (0) 0

Spain: (4321) Jimenez; Perea, Simo, Gasiorowski, Diaz; Belaid (Senhadji 81), Andres, Hernandez; Rodriguez D (Diao 68), Mella (Rodriguez J 81); Bravo.
Scorers: Bravo 41, Jacquet (og) 69.

France: (4231) Bengui-Joao; Kumbedi (Sarr 81), Jacquet, Gomis■, Soumahoro; Benama (Amougou 73), Atangana Edoa; Assoumani (Michal 62), Bahoya (Mayulu 62), Bouabre (Ngoura 62); Kroupi.

Referee: Vassilis Fotias (Greece).

UEFA UNDER-19 CHAMPIONSHIP 2024–25

GROUP STAGE

NB: Tied teams ranked on head-to-head results; goal difference; goals scored; disciplinary points.

GROUP 1 (NETHERLANDS)

Ukraine v Kazakhstan		1-2
Slovenia v Netherlands		0-2
Ukraine v Slovenia		0-1
Netherlands v Kazakhstan		2-0
Netherlands v Ukraine		1-0
Kazakhstan v Slovenia		1-2

Group 1 Table	P	W	D	L	F	A	GD	Pts
Netherlands	3	3	0	0	5	0	5	9
Slovenia	3	2	0	1	3	0	3	6
Kazakhstan	3	1	0	2	3	5	–2	3
Ukraine	3	0	0	3	1	4	–3	0

GROUP 2 (ANDORRA)

Cyprus v Hungary	1-3	Hungary v Andorra	1-0
Germany v Andorra	2-0	Hungary v Germany	1-2
Germany v Cyprus	3-1	Andorra v Cyprus	0-1

Group 2 Table	P	W	D	L	F	A	GD	Pts
Germany	3	3	0	0	7	2	5	9
Hungary	3	2	0	1	5	3	2	6
Cyprus	3	1	0	2	3	6	–3	3
Andorra	3	0	0	3	0	4	–4	0

GROUP 3 (BULGARIA)

England v Lithuania	1-0	England v Bulgaria	2-1
Bulgaria v Belgium	1-1	Belgium v England	0-0
Belgium v Lithuania	4-1	Lithuania v Bulgaria	0-2

Group 3 Table	P	W	D	L	F	A	GD	Pts
England	3	2	1	0	3	1	2	7
Belgium	3	1	2	0	5	2	3	5
Bulgaria	3	1	1	1	4	3	1	4
Lithuania	3	0	0	3	1	7	–6	0

GROUP 4 (POLAND)

Turkey v Gibraltar	7-0	Poland v Gibraltar	4-0
Malta v Poland	0-6	Poland v Turkey	3-0
Turkey v Malta	2-0	Gibraltar v Malta	1-2

Group 4 Table	P	W	D	L	F	A	GD	Pts
Poland	3	3	0	0	13	0	13	9
Turkey	3	2	0	1	9	3	6	6
Malta	3	1	0	2	2	9	–7	3
Gibraltar	3	0	0	3	1	13	–12	0

GROUP 5 (SCOTLAND)

Wales v Scotland		1-0
France v Liechtenstein		7-0
Scotland v Liechtenstein		4-0
France v Wales		2-1
Liechtenstein v Wales		0-5
Scotland v France		0-0

Group 5 Table	P	W	D	L	F	A	GD	Pts
France	3	2	1	0	9	1	8	7
Wales	3	2	0	1	7	2	5	6
Scotland	3	1	1	1	4	1	3	4
Liechtenstein	3	0	0	3	0	16	–16	0

GROUP 6 (FINLAND)

Czech Republic v San Marino		2-0
Switzerland v Finland		0-1
Finland v San Marino		5-0
Czech Republic v Switzerland		0-1
Finland v Czech Republic		2-3
San Marino v Switzerland		0-4

Group 6 Table	P	W	D	L	F	A	GD	Pts
Czech Republic†	3	2	0	1	5	3	2	6
Finland†	3	2	0	1	8	3	5	6
Switzerland†	3	2	0	1	5	1	4	6
San Marino	3	0	0	3	0	11	–11	0

GROUP 7 (MOLDOVA)

Azerbaijan v Iceland		0-2
Republic of Ireland v Moldova		0-0
Republic of Ireland v Azerbaijan		4-0
Iceland v Moldova		1-0
Iceland v Republic of Ireland		1-2
Moldova v Azerbaijan		2-2

Group 7 Table	P	W	D	L	F	A	GD	Pts
Republic of Ireland	3	2	1	0	6	1	5	7
Iceland	3	2	0	1	4	2	2	6
Moldova	3	0	2	1	2	3	–1	2
Azerbaijan	3	0	1	2	2	8	–6	1

GROUP 8 (GREECE)

Italy v Montenegro	3-0
Bosnia & Herzegovina v Greece	2-5
Italy v Bosnia & Herzegovina	3-0
Greece v Montenegro	0-3
Greece v Italy	0-1
Montenegro v Bosnia & Herzegovina	3-2

Group 8 Table	P	W	D	L	F	A	GD	Pts
Italy	3	3	0	0	7	0	7	9
Montenegro	3	2	0	1	6	5	1	6
Greece	3	1	0	2	5	6	–1	3
Bosnia & Herzegovina	3	0	0	3	4	11	–7	0

GROUP 9 (SWEDEN)

Norway v Estonia	2-1	Sweden v Estonia	1-2
Georgia v Sweden	2-1	Sweden v Norway	1-2
Norway v Georgia	3-2	Estonia v Georgia	1-1

Group 9 Table	P	W	D	L	F	A	GD	Pts
Norway	3	3	0	0	7	4	3	9
Georgia	3	1	1	1	5	5	0	4
Estonia	3	1	1	1	4	4	0	4
Sweden	3	0	0	3	6	6	–3	0

GROUP 10 (KOSOVO)

Spain v Faroe Islands	3-0	Spain v Kosovo	3-4
Kosovo v Austria	0-4	Austria v Spain	0-1
Austria v Faroe Islands	4-0	Faroe Islands v Kosovo	0-2

Group 10 Table	P	W	D	L	F	A	GD	Pts
Austria†	3	2	0	1	8	1	7	6
Spain†	3	2	0	1	7	4	3	6
Kosovo†	3	2	0	1	6	7	–1	6
Faroe Islands	3	0	0	3	0	9	–9	0

GROUP 11 (ALBANIA)

Northern Ireland v Denmark	0-4
Israel v Albania	6-0
Israel v Northern Ireland	3-1
Denmark v Albania	1-0
Denmark v Israel	3-2
Albania v Northern Ireland	0-1

Group 11 Table	P	W	D	L	F	A	GD	Pts
Denmark	3	3	0	0	8	2	6	9
Israel	3	2	0	1	11	4	7	6
Northern Ireland	3	1	0	2	2	7	–5	3
Albania	3	0	0	3	0	8	–8	0

GROUP 12 (LUXEMBOURG)

Slovakia v Luxembourg	2-1
North Macedonia v Latvia	1-1
Slovakia v North Macedonia	3-0
Latvia v Luxembourg	2-3
Latvia v Slovakia	2-0
Luxembourg v North Macedonia	1-1

Group 12 Table	P	W	D	L	F	A	GD	Pts
Slovakia	3	2	0	1	5	3	2	6
Luxembourg†	3	1	1	1	5	5	0	4
Latvia†	3	1	1	1	5	4	1	4
North Macedonia	3	0	2	1	2	5	–3	2

GROUP 13 (CROATIA)

Serbia v Belarus	2-2
Armenia v Croatia	0-4
Serbia v Armenia	2-0
Croatia v Belarus	2-0
Croatia v Serbia	0-3
Belarus v Armenia	3-1

Group 13 Table	P	W	D	L	F	A	GD	Pts
Serbia	3	2	1	0	7	2	5	7
Croatia	3	2	0	1	6	3	3	6
Belarus	3	1	1	1	5	5	0	4
Armenia	3	0	0	3	1	9	–8	0

UEFA UNDER-19 ELITE ROUND 2024–25

GROUP 1 (HUNGARY)

Denmark v Iceland	2-0	Denmark v Hungary	1-0
Hungary v Austria	1-3	Austria v Denmark	1-2
Austria v Iceland	3-1	Iceland v Hungary	0-1

Group 1 Table	P	W	D	L	F	A	GD	Pts
Denmark	3	3	0	0	5	1	4	9
Austria	3	2	0	1	7	4	3	6
Hungary	3	1	0	2	2	4	–2	3
Iceland	3	0	0	3	1	6	–5	0

GROUP 2 (GEORGIA)

Montenegro v Slovakia	1-1
Poland v Georgia	3-0
Poland v Montenegro	0-1
Slovakia v Georgia	0-2
Slovakia v Poland	0-2
Georgia v Montenegro	1-3

Group 2 Table	P	W	D	L	F	A	GD	Pts
Montenegro	3	2	1	0	5	2	3	7
Poland	3	2	0	1	5	1	4	6
Georgia	3	1	0	2	3	6	–3	3
Slovakia	3	0	1	2	1	5	–4	1

GROUP 3 (CZECH REPUBLIC)

Netherlands v Croatia	2-1
Luxembourg v Czech Republic	0-2
Netherlands v Luxembourg	0-0
Czech Republic v Croatia	1-0
Czech Republic v Netherlands	0-4
Croatia v Luxembourg	1-2

Group 3 Table	P	W	D	L	F	A	GD	Pts
Netherlands	3	2	1	0	6	1	5	7
Czech Republic	3	2	0	1	3	4	–1	6
Luxembourg	3	1	1	1	2	3	–1	4
Croatia	3	0	0	3	2	5	–3	0

GROUP 4 (SERBIA)

Norway v Belgium	2-0	Serbia v Belgium	1-1
Israel v Serbia	2-3	Serbia v Norway	1-2
Norway v Israel	2-1	Belgium v Israel	3-2

Group 4 Table	P	W	D	L	F	A	GD	Pts
Norway	3	3	0	0	6	2	4	9
Serbia	3	1	1	1	5	5	0	4
Belgium	3	1	1	1	4	5	–1	4
Israel	3	0	0	3	5	8	–3	0

GROUP 5 (ITALY)

Spain v France	2-1	Italy v Spain	2-2
Italy v Latvia	1-1	France v Italy	0-2
France v Latvia	2-1	Latvia v Spain	1-4

Group 5 Table	P	W	D	L	F	A	GD	Pts
Spain	3	2	1	0	8	4	4	7
Italy	3	1	2	0	5	3	2	5
France	3	1	0	2	3	5	–2	3
Latvia	3	0	1	2	3	7	–4	1

GROUP 6 (GERMANY)

Finland v Republic of Ireland	3-0
Germany v Slovenia	2-0
Republic of Ireland v Slovenia	1-1
Germany v Finland	2-1
Republic of Ireland v Germany	0-1
Slovenia v Finland	2-1

Group 6 Table	P	W	D	L	F	A	GD	Pts
Germany	3	3	0	0	5	1	4	9
Slovenia	3	1	1	1	3	4	–1	4
Finland	3	1	0	2	5	4	1	3
Republic of Ireland	3	0	1	2	1	5	–4	1

GROUP 7 (WALES)

Portugal v Turkey	2-2	Portugal v Wales	1-0
Wales v England	0-2	England v Portugal	1-0
England v Turkey	0-0	Turkey v Wales	1-3

Group 7 Table	P	W	D	L	F	A	GD	Pts
England	3	2	1	0	3	0	3	7
Portugal	3	1	1	1	3	3	0	4
Wales	3	1	0	2	3	4	–1	3
Turkey	3	0	2	1	3	5	–2	2

UEFA UNDER-19 FINAL TOURNAMENT (ROMANIA)

GROUP STAGE

GROUP A

Spain v Denmark	1-0
Romania v Montenegro	2-1
Denmark v Montenegro	5-0
Romania v Spain	1-3
Denmark v Romania	0-3
Montenegro v Spain	0-5

Group A Table	P	W	D	L	F	A	GD	Pts
Spain	3	3	0	0	9	1	8	9
Romania	3	2	0	1	6	4	2	6
Denmark	3	1	0	2	5	4	1	3
Montenegro	3	0	0	3	1	12	–11	0

GROUP B

England v Norway	2-2
Germany v Netherlands	0-3
Norway v Netherlands	0-2
Germany v England	5-5
Norway v Germany	1-2
Netherlands v England	4-2

Group B Table	P	W	D	L	F	A	GD	Pts
Netherlands	3	3	0	0	9	2	7	9
Germany	3	1	1	1	7	9	–2	4
England	3	0	2	1	9	11	–2	2
Norway	3	0	1	2	3	6	–3	1

KNOCKOUT STAGE

SEMI-FINALS

Spain v Germany	6-5*
Netherlands v Romania	3-1

UEFA UNDER-19 CHAMPIONSHIP FINAL 2024–25

Thursday, 26 June 2025

(at Rapid-Giulesti Stadium, Bucharest, attendance 6159)

Spain (0) 0   Netherlands (0) 1

Spain: (433) Raul Jimenez; Olmedo, Martin J, Cuenca (Granados 84), Munoz; Marcos (Junyent 66), Merino, Monserrate (Huestamendia 77); Pablo Garcia, Janneh (Diaz 66), Cordero (Virgili 77).

Netherlands: (433) Heerkens; Read, Ugwu, Janse, Dijkstra; Land (Boogaard 77), Smit, Verkuijl (Rots 81); Oufkir, Konadu (Panneflek 90) Sliti.
Scorer: Raul Jimenez 63 (og).

Referee: Rob Hennessy (Ireland).

UEFA UNDER-21 CHAMPIONSHIP 2025

QUALIFYING RESULTS 2024–25 – continued from previous edition

GROUP A

Latvia v Norway	0-1
Italy v San Marino	7-0
Turkey v Republic of Ireland	0-1
Republic of Ireland v Latvia	2-2
Norway v Italy	0-3
San Marino v Turkey	1-6
Turkey v Latvia	3-0
Republic of Ireland v Norway	1-1
San Marino v Latvia	0-3
Norway v Turkey	5-1
Italy v Republic of Ireland	1-1

Group A Table	P	W	D	L	F	A	GD	Pts
Italy	10	6	4	0	27	4	23	22
Norway†	10	6	1	3	28	11	17	19
Republic of Ireland†	10	5	4	1	24	12	12	19
Turkey	10	4	1	5	21	15	6	13
Latvia	10	3	2	5	10	18	–8	11
San Marino	10	0	0	10	1	51	–50	0

†Rankings decided on head-to-head points.

GROUP B

Kazakhstan v Malta	4-1
Scotland v Spain	1-2
Kazakhstan v Belgium	0-3
Hungary v Spain	0-1
Malta v Scotland	0-5
Hungary v Malta	2-1
Spain v Kazakhstan	4-3
Scotland v Belgium	0-2
Spain v Malta	6-0
Belgium v Hungary	0-1
Kazakhstan v Scotland	3-2

Group B Table	P	W	D	L	F	A	GD	Pts
Spain	10	9	1	0	28	5	23	28
Belgium	10	6	1	3	13	6	7	19
Scotland†	10	5	1	4	19	11	8	16
Hungary†	10	5	1	4	12	8	4	16
Kazakhstan	10	3	0	7	13	24	–11	9
Malta	10	0	0	10	4	35	–31	0

†Rankings decided on head-to-head points.

GROUP C

Georgia v Moldova	3-0
Netherlands v North Macedonia	5-0
Sweden v Gibraltar	9-0
Gibraltar v North Macedonia	0-2
Netherlands v Georgia	3-1
Moldova v Sweden	0-0
Sweden v Georgia	3-2
North Macedonia v Moldova	2-1
Netherlands v Sweden	3-0
Georgia v North Macedonia	2-1

Group C Table	P	W	D	L	F	A	GD	Pts
Netherlands	10	10	0	0	32	3	29	30
Georgia	10	6	1	3	14	10	4	19
Sweden	10	5	2	3	25	10	15	17
North Macedonia	10	4	0	6	8	15	–7	12
Moldova	10	2	1	7	7	20	–13	7
Gibraltar	10	1	0	9	3	31	–28	3

GROUP D

Israel* v Germany	1-5
Israel* v Estonia	1-0
Estonia v Germany	1-10
Bulgaria v Poland	1-3
Israel* v Kosovo	0-1
Estonia v Israel	1-0
Germany v Bulgaria	2-1
Kosovo v Poland	0-4
Estonia v Kosovo	3-1
Poland v Germany	3-3
Israel* v Bulgaria	0-1

Group D Table	P	W	D	L	F	A	GD	Pts
Germany	10	8	2	0	35	10	25	26
Poland	10	7	1	2	24	10	14	22
Bulgaria	10	4	3	3	17	12	5	15
Kosovo	10	3	3	4	10	17	–7	12
Estonia	10	2	1	7	7	31	–24	7
Israel	10	1	0	9	5	18	–13	3

*Match played in Hungary.

GROUP E

Armenia v Finland	1-3
Romania v Montenegro	1-0
Switzerland v Albania	1-2
Finland v Romania	2-0
Montenegro v Switzerland	0-2
Montenegro v Romania	2-6
Switzerland v Finland	1-1
Albania v Armenia	1-0
Romania v Switzerland	3-1
Finland v Montenegro	2-1

Group E Table	P	W	D	L	F	A	GD	Pts
Romania	10	7	1	2	23	10	13	22
Finland	10	6	2	2	21	8	13	20
Switzerland	10	5	3	2	21	12	9	18
Albania	10	5	1	4	12	17	–5	16
Montenegro	10	2	1	7	8	19	–11	7
Armenia	10	0	2	8	2	21	–19	2

GROUP F

Ukraine* v Serbia	2-1
Luxembourg v Azerbaijan	2-0
Northern Ireland v England	0-0
Azerbaijan v Serbia	0-2
Northern Ireland v Ukraine	1-2
England v Ukraine	2-1
Northern Ireland v Azerbaijan	5-0
Serbia v Ukraine	1-0
England v Azerbaijan	7-0
Luxembourg v Northern Ireland	0-0

Group F Table	P	W	D	L	F	A	GD	Pts
England	10	8	1	1	41	6	35	25
Ukraine	10	8	0	2	20	7	13	24
Serbia	10	5	1	4	13	18	–5	16
Northern Ireland	10	3	2	5	10	10	0	11
Luxembourg	10	2	2	6	6	23	–17	8
Azerbaijan	10	1	0	9	4	30	–26	3

*Match played in Latvia.

GROUP G

Croatia v Faroe Islands	2-1
Faroe Islands v Greece	0-4
Croatia v Portugal	0-2
Faroe Islands v Portugal	1-3
Croatia v Andorra	2-0
Andorra v Portugal	1-2
Croatia v Greece	3-2
Faroe Islands v Belarus	1-0

Group G Table	P	W	D	L	F	A	GD	Pts
Portugal	10	9	0	1	33	6	27	27
Croatia	10	7	1	2	20	14	6	22
Greece	10	5	2	3	16	10	6	17
Faroe Islands	10	3	1	6	11	24	–13	10
Belarus	10	1	3	6	6	20	–14	6
Andorra	10	0	3	7	4	16	–12	3

GROUP H

Bosnia & Herzegovina v Austria	0-2
France v Slovenia	1-1
Slovenia v Cyprus	2-0
France v Bosnia & Herzegovina	2-0
Cyprus v France	0-3
Austria v Slovenia	1-1
Bosnia & Herzegovina v Cyprus	1-3
France v Austria	1-2

Group H Table

	P	W	D	L	F	A	GD	Pts
Slovenia	8	5	2	1	13	7	6	17
France	8	5	1	2	22	6	16	16
Austria	8	4	3	1	12	6	6	15
Cyprus	8	1	2	5	7	23	−16	5
Bosnia & Herzegovina	8	1	0	7	5	17	−12	3

GROUP I

Lithuania v Czech Republic	1-2
Iceland v Denmark	4-2
Iceland v Wales	1-2
Denmark v Czech Republic	5-0
Iceland v Lithuania	0-2
Wales v Czech Republic	1-2
Czech Republic v Lithuania	3-0
Denmark v Iceland	2-0

Group I Table

	P	W	D	L	F	A	GD	Pts
Denmark	8	5	2	1	18	8	10	17
Czech Republic†	8	4	2	2	13	11	2	14
Wales†	8	4	2	2	13	11	2	14
Iceland	8	3	0	5	9	14	−5	9
Lithuania	8	1	0	7	7	16	−9	3

†Rankings on head-to-head points.

PLAY-OFFS FIRST LEG

Finland v Norway	5-1
Belgium v Czech Republic	0-2
Georgia v Croatia	1-0

PLAY-OFFS SECOND LEG *(agg)*

Norway v Finland	2-1	3-6
Czech Republic v Belgium	1-1	3-1
Croatia v Georgia	3-2*	3-3

aet; Georgia won 7-6 on penalties.

QUALIFIED TEAMS

Czech Republic, Denmark, England, Finland, France, Georgia, Germany, Italy, Netherlands, Poland, Portugal, Romania, Slovakia (hosts), Slovenia, Spain, Ukraine.

UEFA UNDER-21 CHAMPIONSHIP 2025

FINALS IN SLOVAKIA

*After extra time.

GROUP A

Slovakia v Spain	2-3
Italy v Romania	1-0
Spain v Romania	2-1
Slovakia v Italy	0-1
Romania v Slovakia	1-2
Spain v Italy	1-1

Group A Table

	P	W	D	L	F	A	GD	Pts
Spain†	3	2	1	0	6	4	2	7
Italy†	3	2	1	0	3	1	2	7
Slovakia	3	1	0	2	4	5	−1	3
Romania	3	0	0	3	2	5	−3	0

†Rankings decided on goals scored.

GROUP B

Czech Republic v England	1-3
Germany v Slovenia	3-0
England v Slovenia	0-0
Czech Republic v Germany	2-4
Slovenia v Czech Republic	0-2
England v Germany	1-2

Group B Table

	P	W	D	L	F	A	GD	Pts
Germany	3	3	0	0	9	3	6	9
England	3	1	1	1	4	3	1	4
Czech Republic	3	1	0	2	5	7	−2	3
Slovenia	3	0	1	2	0	5	−5	1

GROUP C

Portugal v France	0-0
Poland v Georgia	1-2
Portugal v Poland	5-0
France v Georgia	3-2
Georgia v Portugal	0-4
France v Poland	4-1

Group C Table

	P	W	D	L	F	A	GD	Pts
Portugal	3	2	1	0	9	0	9	7
France	3	2	1	0	7	3	4	7
Georgia	3	1	0	2	4	8	−4	3
Poland	3	0	0	3	2	11	−9	0

GROUP D

Ukraine v Denmark	2-3
Finland v Netherlands	2-2
Finland v Ukraine	0-2
Netherlands v Denmark	1-2
Denmark v Finland	2-2
Netherlands v Ukraine	2-0

Group D Table

	P	W	D	L	F	A	GD	Pts
Denmark	3	2	1	0	7	5	2	7
Netherlands	3	1	1	1	5	4	1	4
Ukraine	3	1	0	2	4	5	−1	3
Finland	3	0	2	1	4	6	−2	2

QUARTER-FINALS

Portugal v Netherlands	0-1
Spain v England	1-3
Denmark v France	2-3
Germany v Italy	3-2*

SEMI-FINALS

England v Netherlands	2-1
Germany v France	3-0

UEFA UNDER-21 CHAMPIONSHIP FINAL 2025

Saturday, 28 June 2025

(at Tehelne pole, Bratislava, attendance 19,153)

England (2) 3   Germany (1) 2

England: (4411) Beadle; Livramento, Hinshelwood, Cresswell, Quansah; Anderson (Egan-Riley 99), Elliott (Rowe 91), Scott (Morton 44), Hutchinson (Iling-Junior 98); McAtee (Nwaneri 91); Stansfield (Norton-Cuffy 62).
Scorers: Elliott 5, Hutchinson 24, Rowe 92.

Germany: (433) Atubolu; Collins, Arrey-Mbi, Oermann (Wanner 106), Brown (Ullrich 86); Martel (Tresoldi 98), Gruda (Knauff 73), Reitz; Nebel, Woltemade (Weiper 80).
Scorers: Weiper 45, Nebel 61.

aet. Referee: Sander van der Eijk (Netherlands).

ENGLAND UNDER-21 RESULTS 1976–2025

EC *UEFA Competition for Under-21 Teams*

Bold type indicates matches played in season 2024–25.

Year	Date		Venue	Eng	Alb
			v ALBANIA	Eng	Alb
EC1989	Mar	7	Shkoder	2	1
EC1989	April	25	Ipswich	2	0
EC2001	Mar	27	Tirana	1	0
EC2001	Sept	4	Middlesbrough	5	0
EC2019	Nov	15	Shkoder	3	0
EC2020	Nov	17	Wolverhampton	5	0
EC2022	Mar	29	Elbasan	3	0
EC2022	June	7	Chesterfield	3	0

			v ANDORRA	Eng	And
EC2017	Oct	10	Andorra la Vella	1	0
ec2018	Oct	11	Chesterfield	7	0
EC2020	Oct	7	Andorra la Vella	3	3
EC2020	Nov	13	Wolverhampton	3	1
EC2021	Oct	11	Andorra la Vella	1	0
EC2022	Mar	25	Bournemouth	4	1

			v ANGOLA	Eng	Ang
1995	June	10	Toulon	1	0
1996	May	28	Toulon	0	2

			v ARGENTINA	Eng	Arg
1998	May	18	Toulon	0	2
2000	Feb	22	Fulham	1	0

			v AUSTRIA	Eng	Aus
1994	Oct	11	Kapfenberg	3	1
1995	Nov	14	Middlesbrough	2	1
EC2004	Sept	3	Krems	2	0
EC2005	Oct	7	Leeds	1	2
2013	June	26	Brighton	4	0
EC2019	Oct	15	Milton Keynes	5	1
EC2020	Sept	9	Reid	2	1
2024	**Sept**	**9**	**Luton**	**4**	**1**

			v AZERBAIJAN	Eng	Az
EC2004	Oct	12	Baku	0	0
EC2005	Mar	29	Middlesbrough	2	0
2009	June	8	Milton Keynes	7	0
EC2011	Sept	1	Watford	6	0
EC2012	Sept	6	Baku	2	0
EC2024	Mar	22	Baku	5	1
EC2024	**Oct**	**15**	**Bristol City**	**7**	**0**

			v BELARUS	Eng	Bel
2015	June	11	Barnsley	1	0

			v BELGIUM	Eng	Belg
1994	June	5	Marseille	2	1
1996	May	24	Toulon	1	0
EC2011	Nov	14	Mons	1	2
EC2012	Feb	29	Middlesbrough	4	0

			v BOSNIA & HERZEGOVINA	Eng	BH
EC2015	Nov	12	Sarajevo Canton	0	0
EC2016	Oct	11	Walsall	5	0

			v BRAZIL	Eng	Bra
1993	June	11	Toulon	0	0
1995	June	6	Toulon	0	2
1996	June	1	Toulon	1	2

			v BULGARIA	Eng	Bul
EC1979	June	5	Pernik	3	1
EC1979	Nov	20	Leicester	5	0
1989	June	5	Toulon	2	3
EC1998	Oct	9	West Ham	1	0
EC1999	June	8	Vratsa	1	0
EC2007	Sept	11	Sofia	2	0
EC2007	Nov	16	Milton Keynes	2	0

			v CHINA PR	Eng	CPR
2018	May	26	Toulon	2	1

			v CROATIA	Eng	Cro
1996	Apr	23	Sunderland	0	1
2003	Aug	19	West Ham	0	3
EC2014	Oct	10	Wolverhampton	2	1
EC2014	Oct	14	Vinkovci	2	1
EC2019	June	24	Serravalle	3	3
EC2021	Mar	31	Koper	2	1
2023	Mar	28	Fulham	1	2

			v CZECHOSLOVAKIA	Eng	Cz
1990	May	28	Toulon	2	1
1992	May	26	Toulon	1	2
1993	June	9	Toulon	1	1

			v CZECH REPUBLIC	Eng	CzR
1998	Nov	17	Ipswich	0	1
EC2007	June	11	Arnhem	0	0
2008	Nov	18	Sheffield United	2	0
EC2011	June	19	Viborg	1	2
2015	Mar	27	Prague	1	0
EC2021	Nov	11	Burnley	3	1
EC2022	June	3	Ceske Budejovice	2	1
EC2023	June	22	Batumi	2	0
EC2025	**June**	**12**	**Dunajska**	**3**	**1**

			v DENMARK	Eng	Den
EC1978	Sept	19	Hvidovre	2	1
EC1979	Sept	11	Watford	1	0
EC1982	Sept	21	Hvidovre	4	1
EC1983	Sept	20	Norwich	4	1
EC1986	Mar	12	Copenhagen	1	0
EC1986	Mar	26	Manchester City	1	1
1988	Sept	13	Watford	0	0
1994	Mar	8	Brentford	1	0
1999	Oct	8	Bradford	4	1
2005	Aug	16	Herning	1	0
2011	Mar	24	Viborg	4	0
2017	Mar	27	Randers	4	0
2018	Nov	20	Esbjerg	5	1

			v ECUADOR	Eng	Ec
2009	Feb	10	Malaga	2	3

			v FINLAND	Eng	Fin
EC1977	May	26	Helsinki	1	0
EC1977	Oct	12	Hull	8	1
EC1984	Oct	16	Southampton	2	0
EC1985	May	21	Mikkeli	1	3
EC2000	Oct	10	Valkeakoski	2	2
EC2001	Mar	23	Barnsley	4	0
EC2009	June	15	Halmstad	2	1
EC2013	Sept	9	Tampere	1	1
EC2013	Nov	14	Milton Keynes	3	0

			v FRANCE	Eng	Fra
EC1984	Feb	28	Sheffield Wednesday	6	1
EC1984	Mar	28	Rouen	1	0
1987	June	11	Toulon	0	2
EC1988	April	13	Besancon	2	4
EC1988	April	27	Arsenal	2	2

				Eng	Fra
1988	June	12	Toulon	2	4
1990	May	23	Toulon	7	3
1991	June	3	Toulon	1	0
1992	May	28	Toulon	0	0
1993	June	15	Toulon	1	0
1994	May	31	Aubagne	0	3
1995	June	10	Toulon	0	2
1998	May	14	Toulon	1	1
1999	Feb	9	Derby	2	1
EC2005	Nov	11	Tottenham Hotspur	1	1
EC2005	Nov	15	Nancy	1	2
2009	Mar	31	Nottingham Forest	0	2
2014	Nov	17	Paris	2	3
2016	May	29	Toulon	2	1
2016	Nov	14	Bondoufle	2	3
EC2019	June	18	Cesena	1	2
2023	Mar	25	Leicester	4	0
2025	**Mar**	**21**	**Lorient**	**3**	**5**

v GEORGIA				Eng	Geo
EC1996	Nov	8	Batumi	1	0
EC1997	April	29	Charlton	0	0
2000	Aug	31	Middlesbrough	6	1
2021	Nov	16	Batumi	2	3

v GERMANY				Eng	Ger
1991	Sept	10	Scunthorpe	2	1
EC2000	Oct	6	Derby	1	1
EC2001	Aug	31	Freiburg	2	1
2005	Mar	25	Hull	2	2
2005	Sept	6	Mainz	1	1
EC2006	Oct	6	Coventry	1	0
EC2006	Oct	10	Leverkusen	2	0
EC2009	June	22	Halmstad	1	1
EC2009	June	29	Malmo	0	4
2010	Nov	16	Wiesbaden	0	2
2015	Mar	30	Middlesbrough	3	2
2017	Mar	24	Wiesbaden	0	1
EC2017	June	27	Tychy	2	2
2019	Mar	26	Bournemouth	1	2
2022	Sept	27	Sheffield United	3	1
EC2023	June	28	Batumi	2	0
EC2025	**June**	**18**	**Nitra**	**1**	**2**
EC2025	**June**	**28**	**Bratislava**	**3**	**2**

v EAST GERMANY				Eng	EG
EC1980	April	16	Sheffield United	1	2
EC1980	April	23	Jena	0	1

v WEST GERMANY				Eng	WG
EC1982	Sept	21	Sheffield United	3	1
EC1982	Oct	12	Bremen	2	3
1987	Sept	8	Ludenscheid	0	2

v GREECE				Eng	Gre
EC1982	Nov	16	Piraeus	0	1
EC1983	Mar	29	Portsmouth	2	1
1989	Feb	7	Patras	0	1
EC1997	Nov	13	Heraklion	0	2
EC1997	Dec	17	Norwich	4	2
EC2001	June	5	Athens	1	3
EC2001	Oct	5	Blackburn	2	1
EC2009	Sept	8	Tripoli	1	1
EC2010	Mar	3	Doncaster	1	2

v GUINEA				Eng	Gui
2016	May	23	Toulon	7	1

v HUNGARY				Eng	Hun
EC1981	June	5	Keszthely	2	1
EC1981	Nov	17	Nottingham Forest	2	0
EC1983	April	26	Newcastle	1	0
EC1983	Oct	11	Nyiregyhaza	2	0

				Eng	Hun
1990	Sept	11	Southampton	3	1
1992	May	12	Budapest	2	2
1999	April	27	Budapest	2	2

v ICELAND				Eng	Ice
2011	Mar	28	Preston	1	2
EC2011	Oct	6	Reykjavik	3	0
EC2011	Nov	10	Colchester	5	0

v ISRAEL				Eng	Isr
1985	Feb	27	Tel Aviv	2	1
2011	Sept	5	Barnsley	4	1
EC2013	June	11	Jerusalem	0	1
EC2023	June	25	Kutaisi	2	0
EC2023	July	5	Batumi	3	0

v ITALY				Eng	Ita
EC1978	Mar	8	Manchester City	2	1
EC1978	April	5	Rome	0	0
EC1984	April	18	Manchester City	3	1
EC1984	May	2	Florence	0	1
EC1986	April	9	Pisa	0	2
EC1986	April	23	Swindon	1	1
EC1997	Feb	12	Bristol City	1	0
EC1997	Oct	10	Rieti	1	0
EC2000	May	27	Bratislava	0	2
2000	Nov	14	Monza*	0	0
Abandoned 11 mins; fog.					
2002	Mar	26	Bradford	1	1
EC2002	May	20	Basle	1	2
2003	Feb	11	Pisa	0	1
2007	Mar	24	Wembley	3	3
EC2007	June	14	Arnhem	2	2
2011	Feb	8	Empoli	0	1
EC2013	June	5	Tel Aviv	0	1
EC2015	June	24	Olomouc	1	3
2016	Nov	10	Southampton	3	2
2018	Nov	15	Ferrara	2	1
2022	Sept	22	Pescara	2	0

v JAPAN				Eng	Jap
2016	May	27	Toulon	1	0

v KAZAKHSTAN				Eng	Kaz
EC2015	Oct	13	Coventry	3	0
EC2016	Oct	6	Aktobe	1	0

v KOSOVO				Eng	Kos
EC2019	Sept	9	Hull	2	0
EC2020	Sept	4	Prishtina	6	0
EC2021	Sept	7	Milton Keynes	2	0
EC2022	June	10	Prishtina	5	0

v LATVIA				Eng	Lat
1995	April	25	Riga	1	0
1995	June	7	Burnley	4	0
EC2017	Sept	5	Bournemouth	3	0
EC2018	Sept	11	Jelgava	2	1

v LITHUANIA				Eng	Lit
EC2009	Nov	17	Vilnius	0	0
EC2010	Sept	7	Colchester	3	0
EC2013	Oct	15	Ipswich	5	0
EC2014	Sept	5	Zaliakalnis	1	0

v LUXEMBOURG				Eng	Lux
EC1998	Oct	13	Grevenmacher	5	0
EC1999	Sept	3	Reading	5	0
EC2023	Sept	11	Differdange	3	0
EC2024	Mar	26	Bolton	7	0

v MALAYSIA				Eng	Mal
1995	June	8	Toulon	2	0

v MEXICO

				Eng	Mex
1988	June	5	Toulon	2	1
1991	May	29	Toulon	6	0
1992	May	25	Toulon	1	1
2001	May	24	Leicester	3	0
2018	May	29	Toulon	0	0
2018	June	9	Toulon	2	1

v MOLDOVA

				Eng	Mol
EC1996	Aug	31	Chisinau	2	0
EC1997	Sept	9	Wycombe	1	0
EC2006	Aug	15	Ipswich	2	2
EC2013	Sept	5	Reading	1	0
EC2014	Sept	9	Tiraspol	3	0

v MONTENEGRO

				Eng	Mon
EC2007	Sept	7	Podgorica	3	0
EC2007	Oct	12	Leicester	1	0

v MOROCCO

				Eng	Mor
1987	June	7	Toulon	2	0
1988	June	9	Toulon	1	0

v NETHERLANDS

				Eng	N
EC1993	April	27	Portsmouth	3	0
EC1993	Oct	12	Utrecht	1	1
2001	Aug	14	Reading	4	0
EC2001	Nov	9	Utrecht	2	2
EC2001	Nov	13	Derby	1	0
2004	Feb	17	Hull	3	2
2005	Feb	8	Derby	1	2
2006	Nov	14	Alkmaar	1	0
EC2007	June	20	Heerenveen	1	1
2009	Aug	11	Groningen	0	0
EC2017	Sept	1	Doetinchem	1	1
EC2018	Sept	6	Norwich	0	0
2019	Nov	19	Doetinchem	1	2
2024	**Nov**	**18**	**Almere**	**1**	**1**
EC2025	**June**	**25**	**Bratislava**	**2**	**1**

v NORTHERN IRELAND

				Eng	NI
2012	Nov	13	Blackpool	2	0
EC2023	Nov	21	Everton	3	0
EC2024	**Sept**	**6**	**Ballymena**	**0**	**0**

v NORTH MACEDONIA

				Eng	M
EC2002	Oct	15	Reading	3	1
EC2003	Sept	5	Skopje	1	1
EC2009	Sept	4	Prilep	2	1
EC2009	Oct	9	Coventry	6	3

v NORWAY

				Eng	Nor
EC1977	June	1	Bergen	2	1
EC1977	Sept	6	Brighton	6	0
1980	Sept	9	Southampton	3	0
1981	Sept	8	Drammen	0	0
EC1992	Oct	13	Peterborough	0	2
EC1993	June	1	Stavanger	1	1
1995	Oct	10	Stavanger	2	2
2006	Feb	28	Reading	3	1
2009	Mar	27	Sandefjord	5	0
2011	June	5	Southampton	2	0
EC2011	Oct	10	Drammen	2	1
EC2012	Sept	10	Chesterfield	1	0
EC2013	June	8	Petah Tikva	1	3
EC2015	Sept	7	Drammen	1	0
EC2016	Sept	6	Colchester	6	1

v PARAGUAY

				Eng	Par
2016	May	25	Toulon	4	0

v POLAND

				Eng	Pol
EC1982	Mar	17	Warsaw	2	1
EC1982	April	7	West Ham	2	2
EC1989	June	2	Plymouth	2	1
EC1989	Oct	10	Jastrzebie	3	1
EC1990	Oct	16	Tottenham Hotspur	0	1
EC1991	Nov	12	Pila	1	2
EC1993	May	28	Zdroj	4	1
EC1993	Sept	7	Millwall	1	2
EC1996	Oct	8	Wolverhampton	0	0
EC1997	May	30	Katowice	1	1
EC1999	Mar	26	Southampton	5	0
EC1999	Sept	7	Plock	1	3
EC2004	Sept	7	Rybnik	3	1
EC2005	Oct	11	Sheffield Wednesday	4	1

v POLAND

				Eng	Pol
2008	Mar	25	Wolverhampton	0	0
EC2017	June	22	Kielce	3	0
2019	Mar	21	Bristol City	1	1

v PORTUGAL

				Eng	Por
1987	June	13	Toulon	0	0
1990	May	21	Toulon	0	1
1993	June	7	Toulon	2	0
1994	June	7	Toulon	2	0
EC1994	Sept	6	Leicester	0	0
1995	Sept	2	Lisbon	0	2
1996	May	30	Toulon	1	3
2000	Apr	16	Stoke	0	1
EC2002	May	22	Zurich	1	3
EC2003	Mar	28	Rio Major	2	4
EC2003	Sept	9	Everton	1	2
EC2008	Nov	20	Agueda	1	1
2008	Sept	5	Wembley	2	0
EC2009	Nov	14	Wembley	1	0
EC2010	Sept	3	Barcelos	1	0
2014	Nov	13	Burnley	3	1
EC2015	June	18	Uherske Hradiste	0	1
2016	May	19	Toulon	1	0
EC2021	Mar	28	Ljubljana	0	2
EC2023	July	2	Kutaisi	1	0
2025	**Mar**	**24**	**West Bromwich**	**4**	**2**

v QATAR

				Eng	Qat
2018	June	1	Toulon	4	0

v REPUBLIC OF IRELAND

				Eng	RoI
1981	Feb	25	Liverpool	1	0
1985	Mar	25	Portsmouth	3	2
1989	June	9	Toulon	0	0
EC1990	Nov	13	Cork	3	0
EC1991	Mar	26	Brentford	3	0
1994	Nov	15	Newcastle	1	0
1995	Mar	27	Dublin	2	0
EC2007	Oct	16	Cork	3	0
EC2008	Feb	5	Southampton	3	0

v ROMANIA

				Eng	Rom
EC1980	Oct	14	Ploesti	0	4
EC1981	April	28	Swindon	3	0
EC1985	April	30	Brasov	0	0
EC1985	Sept	10	Ipswich	3	0
2007	Aug	21	Bristol City	1	1
EC2010	Oct	8	Norwich	2	1
EC2010	Oct	12	Botosani	0	0
2013	Mar	21	Wycombe	3	0
2018	Mar	24	Wolverhampton	2	1
EC2019	June	21	Cesena	2	4

v RUSSIA

				Eng	Rus
1994	May	30	Bandol	2	0

v SAN MARINO

				Eng	SM
EC1993	Feb	16	Luton	6	0
EC1993	Nov	17	Serravalle	4	0
EC2013	Oct	10	Serravalle	4	0
EC2013	Nov	19	Shrewsbury	9	0

v SCOTLAND

				Eng	Sco
1977	April	27	Sheffield United	1	0
EC1980	Feb	12	Coventry	2	1
EC1980	Mar	4	Aberdeen	0	0
EC1982	April	19	Hampden Park	1	0
EC1982	April	28	Manchester City	1	1
EC1988	Feb	16	Aberdeen	1	0
EC1988	Mar	22	Nottingham	1	0
1993	June	13	Toulon	1	0
2013	Aug	13	Sheffield United	6	0
EC2017	Oct	6	Middlesbrough	3	1
2018	June	6	Toulon	3	1
EC2018	Oct	16	Hearts	2	0

v SENEGAL

				Eng	Sen
1989	June	7	Toulon	6	1
1991	May	27	Toulon	2	1

v SERBIA

				Eng	Ser
EC2007	June	17	Nijmegen	2	0
EC2012	Oct	12	Norwich	1	0
EC2012	Oct	16	Krusevac	1	0
EC2023	Oct	12	Nottingham Forest	9	1
EC2023	Nov	18	Backa Topola	3	0

v SERBIA-MONTENEGRO

				Eng	SM
2003	June	2	Hull	3	2

v SLOVAKIA

				Eng	Slo
EC2002	June	1	Bratislava	0	2
EC2002	Oct	11	Trnava	4	0
EC2003	June	10	Sunderland	2	0
2007	June	5	Norwich	5	0
EC2017	June	19	Kielce	2	1
EC2021	Oct	7	Celje	2	2
EC2022	June	13	Huddersfield	1	2

v SLOVENIA

				Eng	Slo
2000	Feb	12	Nova Gorica	1	0
2008	Aug	19	Hull	2	1
2019	Oct	11	Maribor	2	2
EC2025	**June**	**15**	**Nitra**	**0**	**0**

v SOUTH AFRICA

				Eng	SA
1998	May	16	Toulon	3	1

v SPAIN

				Eng	Spa
EC1984	May	17	Seville	1	0
EC1984	May	24	Sheffield United	2	0
1987	Feb	18	Burgos	2	1
1992	Sept	8	Burgos	1	0
2001	Feb	27	Birmingham City	0	4
2004	Nov	16	Alcala	0	1
2007	Feb	6	Derby	2	2
EC2009	June	18	Gothenburg	2	0
EC2011	June	12	Herning	1	1
EC2023	July	8	Batumi	1	0
2024	**Nov**	**15**	**La Linea**	**0**	**1**
EC2025	**June**	**21**	**Trnava**	**3**	**1**

v SWEDEN

				Eng	Swe
1979	June	9	Vasteras	2	1
1986	Sept	9	Ostersund	1	1
EC1988	Oct	18	Coventry	1	1
EC1989	Sept	5	Uppsala	0	1
EC1998	Sept	4	Sundvall	2	0
EC1999	June	4	Huddersfield	3	0
2004	Mar	30	Kristiansund	2	2
EC2009	June	26	Gothenburg	3	3
2013	Feb	5	Walsall	4	0
EC2015	Jun	21	Olomouc	1	0
EC2017	June	16	Kielce	0	0

v SWITZERLAND

				Eng	Swi
EC1980	Nov	18	Ipswich	5	0
EC1981	May	31	Neuenburg	0	0
1988	May	28	Lausanne	1	1
1996	April	1	Swindon	0	0
1998	Mar	24	Brugglifeld	0	2
EC2002	May	17	Zurich	2	1
EC2006	Sept	6	Lucerne	3	2
EC2015	Nov	16	Brighton	3	1
EC2016	Mar	26	Thun	1	1
EC2021	Mar	25	Koper	0	1

v TURKEY

				Eng	Tur
EC1984	Nov	13	Bursa	0	0
EC1985	Oct	15	Bristol City	3	0
EC1987	April	28	Izmir	0	0
EC1987	Oct	13	Sheffield United	1	1
EC1991	April	30	Izmir	2	2
1991	Oct	15	Reading	2	0
EC1992	Nov	17	Leyton	0	1
EC1993	Mar	30	Izmir	0	0
EC2000	May	29	Bratislava	6	0
EC2003	April	1	Newcastle	1	1
EC2003	Oct	10	Istanbul	0	1
EC2019	Sept	6	Izmir	3	2
EC2020	Oct	13	Wolverhampton	2	1

v UKRAINE

				Eng	Ukr
2004	Aug	17	Middlesbrough	3	1
EC2011	June	15	Herning	0	0
EC2017	Nov	10	Kyiv	2	0
EC2018	Mar	27	Sheffield United	2	1
EC2023	Oct	16	Kosice	2	3
EC2024	**Oct**	**11**	**Bournemouth**	**2**	**1**

v USA

				Eng	USA
1989	June	11	Toulon	0	2
1994	June	2	Toulon	3	0
2015	Sept	3	Preston	1	0

v USSR

				Eng	USSR
1987	June	9	Toulon	0	0
1988	June	7	Toulon	1	0
1990	May	25	Toulon	2	1
1991	May	31	Toulon	2	1

v UZBEKISTAN

				Eng	Uzb
2010	Aug	10	Bristol City	2	0

v WALES

				Eng	Wal
1976	Dec	15	Wolverhampton	0	0
1979	Feb	6	Swansea	1	0
1990	Dec	5	Tranmere	0	0
EC2004	Oct	8	Blackburn	2	0
EC2005	Sept	2	Wrexham	4	0
2008	May	5	Wrexham	2	0
EC2008	Oct	10	Cardiff	3	2
EC2008	Oct	14	Aston Villa	2	2
EC2013	Mar	5	Derby	1	0
EC2013	May	19	Swansea	3	1

v YUGOSLAVIA

				Eng	Yug
EC1978	April	19	Novi Sad	1	2
EC1978	May	2	Manchester City	1	1
EC1986	Nov	11	Peterborough	1	1
EC1987	Nov	10	Zemun	5	1
EC2000	Mar	29	Barcelona	3	0
2002	Sept	6	Bolton	1	1

BRITISH AND IRISH UNDER-21 TEAMS 2024–25

■ *Denotes player sent off.*

ENGLAND

UEFA UNDER-21 CHAMPIONSHIP 2025 QUALIFYING GROUP F

Friday, 6 September 2024
Northern Ireland U21 (0) 0
England U21 (0) 0 3237
Northern Ireland U21: (352) Charles; Fogarty, Donnelly, Forbes; Devlin (Kearney 84), Kelly, Robinson (Baggley 84), Devenny, Stewart (Russell 84); McKiernan (Kirk 64), Taylor (Allen 79).
England U21: (3412) Trafford; Harwood-Bellis, Quansah, Doyle (Hall 69); Gray, Anderson (Fellows 88), Hackney, Bynoe-Gittens (Iling-Junior 69); McAtee; Rogers, Rowe (Delap 60).

Friday, 11 October 2024
England U21 (0) 2 *(McAtee 88, 90)*
Ukraine U21 (0) 1 *(Mykhavko 70)* 9858
England U21: (532) Trafford; Gray (Rogers 64), Harwood-Bellis, Quansah, Hall, Philogene-Bidace (Iling-Junior 84); McAtee, Morton (Anderson 78), Hinshelwood (Scarlett 84); Hutchinson (Bynoe-Gittens 64), Delap.
Ukraine U21: (433) Neshcheret; Krupskyi (Braharu 46), Melnychenko, Mykhavko, Vivcharenko; Ocheretko, Fedor (Yatsyk 72), Yarmolyuk; Voloshyn (Kvasnytsya 84), Krasnopir (Gorbach 57), Khlan (Smolyakov 57).

Tuesday, 15 October 2024
England U21 (2) 7 *(Cresswell 2, Doyle 27, McAtee 55, Huseynov 70 (og), Anderson 72, Scarlett 85, Hutchinson 90)*
Azerbaijan U21 (0) 0 14,974
England U21: (3421) Beadle; Quansah, Cresswell, Doyle (Hall 71); Iling-Junior, Gray (Hinshelwood 71), Anderson, Bynoe-Gittens (Scarlett 60); Scott (Morton 71), Rogers (Hutchinson 61); McAtee.
Azerbaijan U21: (3412) Farzullayev; Hasanov, Huseynov, Damadayev; Rzayev (Safarov Q 86), Abdurahmanov, Aliyev (Abdullayev 76), Abbasov (Ahmadov 76); Yusifli; Akhundzade (Velijev 81), Qurbanly (Salyanskiy 76).

UEFA UNDER-21 CHAMPIONSHIP 2025 FINALS GROUP B

Thursday, 12 June 2025
Czech Republic U21 (0) 1 *(Fila 51)*
England U21 (1) 3 *(Elliott 39, Rowe 48, Cresswell 76)* 8087
Czech Republic U21: (3412) Hornicek; Spacil, Prebsl, Chaloupek; Hadas (Kozeluh 86), Suchomel, Stransky (Sojka 81), Vydra (Kricfalusi 87); Danek (Vecheta 81); Fila (Karabec 64), Sejk.
England U21: (4231) Beadle; Gray, Livramento, Cresswell, Quansah; Scott (Morton 84), Anderson (Hackney 84); Elliott, McAtee (Stansfield 69), Hutchinson (Iling-Junior 78); Rowe (Nwaneri 69).

Sunday, 15 June 2025
England U21 (0) 0
Slovenia U21 (0) 0 5217
England U21: (4231) Beadle; Gray (Norton-Cuffy 64), Livramento, Cresswell, Quansah; Hackney (Morton 72), Anderson (Hinshelwood 64); Elliott, McAtee, Nwaneri (Stansfield 72); Rowe (Hutchinson 65).
Slovenia U21: (343) Turk; Jevsenak, Golic (Topalovic 87), Kuzmic; Ilenic, Brest, Zeljkovic, Ostrc (Pisek 66); Cipot (Kojic 75), Seslar, Begic (Cuber Potocnik 76).

Wednesday, 18 June 2025
England U21 (0) 1 *(Scott 76)*
Germany U21 (2) 2 *(Knauff 3, Weiper 33)* 5624
England U21: (4231) Beadle; Hinshelwood, Iling-Junior (Norton-Cuffy 46), Cresswell, Quansah; Anderson (Morton 63), Scott; Nwaneri (Fellows 63), Elliott (McAtee 46), Hutchinson; Rowe (Stansfield 46).

Germany U21: (433) Ernst; Baum (Collins 88), Ullrich, Oermann, Siebert; Jander, Rohl (Tresoldi 77), Wanner (Martel 88); Thielmann, Weiper (Arrey-Mbi 85), Knauff (Nebel 77).

QUARTER-FINAL

Saturday, 21 June 2025
Spain U21 (1) 1 *(Guerra 39 (pen))*
England U21 (2) 3 *(McAtee 10, Elliott 15, Anderson 90 (pen))* 8247
Spain U21: (4231) Iturbe; Pubill, Bueno, Tarrega, Mosquera; Guerra, Turrientes (Moro 57); Sanchez (Jauregizar 57), Moleiro (Rodriguez 78), Lopez D (Fernandez R 71); Fernandez M (Torre 71).
England U21: (4231) Beadle; Livramento, Hinshelwood, Cresswell, Quansah; Scott (Anderson 51), Morton; Elliott (Norton-Cuffy 71), McAtee (Hackney 72), Hutchinson (Rowe 52); Stansfield (Nwaneri 81).

SEMI-FINAL

Wednesday, 25 June 2025
England U21 (0) 2 *(Elliott 62, 85)*
Netherlands U21 (0) 1 *(Ohio 72)* 14,719
England U21: (4411) Beadle; Livramento, Hinshelwood, Cresswell, Quansah; Scott (Hackney 84), Elliott (Gray 90), Anderson, Hutchinson (Norton-Cuffy 78); McAtee (Rowe 78); Stansfield (Nwaneri 84).
Netherlands U21: (433) Roefs; Kasanwirjo (Goes 46), Maatsen, van den Berg, Hato; Flamingo, Valente (Meijer 76), Milambo (Ohio 69); van Bergen (Regeer 87), Manhoef (van Brederode 87), Poku.

FINAL

Saturday, 28 June 2025
England U21 (2) 3 *(Elliott 5, Hutchinson 24, Rowe 92)*
Germany U21 (1) 2 *(Weiper 45, Nebel 61)* 19,153
England U21: (4411) Beadle; Livramento, Hinshelwood, Cresswell, Quansah; Anderson (Egan-Riley 99), Elliott (Rowe 91), Scott (Morton 44), Hutchinson (Iling-Junior 98); McAtee (Nwaneri 91); Stansfield (Norton-Cuffy 62).
Germany U21: (442) Atubolu; Collins, Brown (Ullrich 86), Oermann (Wanner 106), Arrey-Mbi; Martel (Tresoldi 98), Gruda (Knauff 73), Reitz, Nebel; Woltemade, Weiper (Rohl 80).
aet.

FRIENDLIES

Monday, 9 September 2024
England U21 (1) 4 *(Rogers 25 (pen), 49, McAtee 59, Fellows 81)*
Austria U21 (1) 1 *(Ballo 35)*
England U21: (433) Beadle; Hinshelwood, Harwood-Bellis (Cresswell 46), Quansah (Wood-Gordon 81); Hall; Morton (Gray 72), Scott (Hackney 59), McAtee (Anderson 72); Rogers (Bynoe-Gittens 59), Delap (Rowe 72), Iling-Junior (Fellows 72).
Austria U21: (433) Polster (Jungwirth 82); Baidoo, Bockle (Omoregie 82), Estrada (Koller 46), Wohlmuth (Gattermayer 64); Ballo, Seidl (Oswald 64), Briedl (Sattlberger 54); Micheler (Braunoder 46), Lang (Reischl 82), Grgic (Adewumi 64).

Friday, 15 November 2024
Spain U21 (0) 0
England U21 (0) 0
Spain U21: (442) Iturbe; Huijsen (Sanchez 88), Lopez J (Bueno 64), Mosquera (Marin 72), Pubill (Salas 88); Barrios (Bajcetic 46), Guerra (Sotelo 88), Navarro (Moro 46), Veiga (Torre 63); Fernandez M (Bravo 63), Lopez D (Moleiro 72).

England U21: (433) Beadle; Humphreys, Cresswell, Dibling (Rak-Sakyi 68), Gray; Bellingham (Miley 68), McAtee (Chrisene 90), Morton (Gyabi 78); Iling-Junior (Mengi 78), Delap (Scarlett 68), Philogene-Bidace (Earthy 78).

Monday, 18 November 2024
Netherlands U21 (0) 1 *(van Bergen 82)*
England U21 (1) 1 *(Scarlett 5)*
Netherlands U21: (4231) Roefs; Asante, Meijer (Kasanwirjo 13 (Kasius 80)), Baas (Bruns 66), Flamingo; Banzuzi (Fitz-Jim 80), Saleh-Eddine; Manhoef, Zechel (van Bergen 74), van Brederode (Hansen 66); Ohio.
England U21: (4231) Beadle; Gray, Cresswell (Mengi 56), Humphreys, Iling-Junior; Morton (Gyabi 78), Bellingham; Dibling (Philogene-Bidace 56), McAtee (Earthy 90), Miley (Rak-Sakyi 56); Scarlett (Delap 57).

Friday, 21 March 2025
France U21 (3) 5 *(Merlin 4, Ekitike 7, 34, 55, Cherki 76)*
England U21 (2) 3 *(McAtee 2, Elliott 38, Delap 61)* 15,271
France U21: (433) Nkambadio; Doukoure (Jacquet 90), Matsima, Lukeba, Agoume (Lepenant 67); Millot (Bouaddi 90), Akliouche (Bakwa 83), Merlin; Cherki (Barry 86), Odobert (Diouf 85), Ekitike (Tel 66).
England U21: (352) Beadle; Lewis (Branthwaite 73), Harwood-Bellis (Cresswell 62), Egan-Riley (Gray 78); Anderson (Bellingham 73), McAtee (Nwaneri 89), Scott (Hinshelwood 73), Elliott (Edwards 78), Wharton (Hackney 78); Philogene-Bidace (Iling-Junior 73), Delap (Hutchinson■ 78).

Monday, 24 March 2025
England U21 (2) 4 *(Hackney 7, Nwaneri 10, Hutchinson 76, Philogene-Bidace 90)*
Portugal U21 (1) 2 *(Silva 22, Forbs 85)* 14,773
England U21: (442) Beadle (Sharman-Lowe 46); Gray (Lewis 71), Branthwaite (Egan-Riley 61), Cresswell (Edwards 71), Iling-Junior (Philogene-Bidace 72); Bellingham (Anderson 70), Hackney (Wharton 71), Hinshelwood (Scott 61), Elliott (McAtee 62); Nwaneri (Delap 71), Hutchinson.
Portugal U21: (4312) Joao Carvalho (Pinto 61); Pinheiro, Quaresma (Marques C 46), Muniz, Nazinho (Chissumba 46); Santos (Moreira 77), Sa (Marques J 46), Nascimento (Nogueira 46); Fernandes M (Fernandes J 46); Silva (Araujo 46), Tomas (Forbs 46).

NORTHERN IRELAND

UEFA UNDER-21 CHAMPIONSHIP 2025 QUALIFYING GROUP F

Tuesday, 10 September 2024
Northern Ireland U21 (0) 1 *(Allen 81 (pen))*
Ukraine U21 (2) 2 *(Voloshyn 10, Braharu 30)* 697
Northern Ireland U21: (343) Charles; Fogarty, Donnelly, Forbes; Devlin, Robinson (Magee 46), Devenny, Stewart (McKiernan 46); Taylor (Lusty 73), Kelly (Baggley 62), Allen.
Ukraine U21: (433) Neshcheret; Krupskyi, Salyuk, Batagov■, Smolyakov (Roman 85); Ocheretko, Varfolomeyev (Rubchynskyi 55), Yarmolyuk (Melnychenko 73); Braharu, Krasnopir (Gorbach 72), Voloshyn (Kvasnytsya 85).

Saturday, 12 October 2024
Northern Ireland U21 (1) 5 *(Allen 11 (pen), McKiernan 56, Kelly 64, Devenny 67, Samiqullin 80 (og))*
Azerbaijan U21 (0) 0 440
Northern Ireland U21: (532) McMullan; Johnston (Kearney 80), Fogarty, McConville (Robinson 80), Donnelly, Stewart; McKiernan, Devenny, Kelly (Devlin 73); Allen (Kirk 74); Taylor (Lusty 74).
Azerbaijan U21: (343) Samiqullin; Hasanov, Huseynov, Damadasov; Safarov Q (Rzayev 46), Rustamli, Safarov E (Yusifli 70); Abbasov; Velijev (Akhundzade 46), Qurbanly (Salyanskiy 62), Abdullayev (Aliyev 62).

Tuesday, 15 October 2024
Luxembourg U21 (0) 0
Northern Ireland U21 (0) 0 257
Luxembourg U21: (442) Latik; Torres, Agostinelli, Fernandes, Sinner; Irigoyen, Ikene (Flick 90), Englaro, Lohei (Djabi Embalo 85); Jonathans (Dardari 85), Videira (Elshan 69).
Northern Ireland U21: (442) McMullan; Fogarty, McConville, Forbes, Donnelly; Johnston, Devenny (Sloan 84), McKiernan (Devlin 71), Kelly (Robinson 84); Allen■, Taylor (Kirk 84).

FRIENDLIES
Thursday, 20 March 2025
Moldova U21 (1) 1 *(Rotaru 9)*
Northern Ireland U21 (0) 1 *(Oudnie-Morgan 69 (pen))*
Moldova U21: (433) Nazarciuc; Gherasimencov, Costin, Colis, Dijinari; Perciun, Pascaluta (David 66), Lupan; Cozma (Radu 66), Forov, Rotaru.
Northern Ireland: (541) Barnsley; Kearney, Fogarty, Carson, Orr, Inwood; Turley, Kelly, Oudnie-Morgan, McDonnell (McMullan); Kirk.
Reported substitutes: Doherty, Falls, McCann.

Saturday, 22 March 2025
Ukraine U20 (1) 1 *(Chaban 51)*
Northern Ireland U21 (0) 0
Ukraine: (4141) Voloshyn (Voronov 46); Gusev (Drozd 46), Kyrychok (Yermachkov 61), Ogarkov (Zakharchenko 46), Digtyar (Vernattus 46); Chaban (Salenko 61); Shakh (Godya 61), Budko (Karaman 46), Melnychenko (Vashchenko 46), Gadzhyev (Matkevych 46); Zadorozhnyi (Ponomarenko 46).
Northern Ireland U21: (433) McMullan; Barr, Robinson, Fogarty, McCann; Kelly, McDonnell, Doherty; Falls, McStravick, Glenfield.
Reported substitutes: Oudnie-Morgan, Kirk.

Tuesday, 25 March 2025
Northern Ireland U21 (0) 1 *(Turley 57)*
Uzbekistan U21 (0) 0
Northern Ireland U21: Munn; Kearney, Carson, Orr, Atcheson, Robinson, Oudnie-Morgan, Kelly, Kirk, Wilson, Turley.
Reported substitutes: Barr, Doherty.

SCOTLAND

UEFA UNDER-21 CHAMPIONSHIP 2025 QUALIFYING GROUP B

Friday, 6 September 2024
Scotland U21 (0) 1 *(Mebude 62)*
Spain U21 (0) 2 *(Huijsen 59, Fernandez M 69)* 2558
Scotland U21: (433) Slicker; Mullen, Murray, Neilson, Anderson; Mulligan (Apter 76), King (Watson 66), Kelly; Ramsay (Milne 56), Bowie (Mebude 56), Cameron (Wilson E 76).
Spain U21: (4231) Iturbe; Sanchez, Cubarsi, Huijsen, Carreras; Gonzalez (Guerra 76), Turrientes; Novoa (Frances 90), Torre (Veiga 76), Lopez D (Moleiro 66); Aghehowa (Fernandez M 66).

Tuesday, 10 September 2024
Malta U21 (0) 0
Scotland U21 (3) 5 *(Matthew Ellul 3 (og), Murray 9, Mulligan 17, Miller 56, Neilson 82)* 238
Malta U21: (532) Debono; Micallef J, Xerri, Matthew Ellul (Vella 76), Leonardi (Gambin 88), Micallef N (Mohnani 76); Borg A, Zammit, Scicluna D; Vesleji (Chukunyere 58), Tuma (Letherby 76).
Scotland U21: (433) Slicker; Neilson, Murray (Watson 46), Mullen, Johnston; Wilson E, Miller, Cameron (Thomson 86); Bowie (Kelly 36), Mebude (Wales 76), Mulligan (Ramsay 76).

Friday, 11 October 2024
Scotland U21 (0) 0
Belgium U21 (0) 2 *(Stassin 72, 90)* 2103
Scotland U21: (532) Budinauckas; Johnston (Ramsay 83), Mullen (Milne 90), Murray, Neilson, Doig; Miller, Barron, Cameron (Kelly 82); Mebude (Fiorini 77), Mulligan (One 77).
Belgium U21: (4411) Lammens; Sardella, Van Den Bosch, Spileers, Rommens; Steuckers (Siquet 82), Keita, Vermeeren, Mbangula (Stassin 71); Stroeykens; Sylla (Olaigbe 70).

Tuesday, 15 October 2024
Kazakhstan U21 (1) 2 *(Abdulla 30, Zhumakhanov 66 (pen), Trufanov 74)*
Scotland U21 (0) 2 *(Miller 61, Mullen 85)* 578
Kazakhstan U21: (451) Anarbekov; Kasabulat, Shirobokov, Zhumakhanov, Kurgin; Aymanov (Mrynskiy 59), Kalmyrza (Serikkul 86), Abdulla (Trufanov 59), Nazymkhanov (Kaldybekov 73), Kenzhebek (Ensebaev 73); Sviridov.
Scotland U21: (343) Budinauckas; Mullen, Murray*, Neilson; Johnston (Apter 62), Cameron, Miller, Doig (Wilson E 90); Mulligan, One (Mebude 46), Kelly.

FRIENDLIES
Friday, 21 March 2025
Republic of Ireland U21 (0) 0
Scotland U21 (1) 2 *(Wales 5, Bonnar 77)*
Republic of Ireland U21: (442) Maguire (Walsh 84); Alex Murphy, O'Brien, Grehan (Barrett 84), Slater; Mullins (Adam Murphy 84), Moorhouse (Maher 63), O'Brien-Whitmarsh (Lipsiuc 78), Umeh (Vaughan 63); O'Mahony (Gardner 63), Hakiki.
Scotland U21: (442) Johnson (Adams 46); Forrester, Anderson (Wilson E 58), Graham (McArthur 46), Donovan (Smith 86); Mullen, Kelly (Bragg 46), Watson, Mebude (One 58); Wales (Bonnar 58), Lawrence (Rice 63).

Tuesday, 25 March 2025
Scotland U21 (0) 1 *(One 50)*
Iceland U21 (3) 6 *(Andresson 24, 45, Gudmundsson E 40, Haraldsson 58, Mikaelsson 78, Bjarnason 81)*
Scotland U21: (442) McFarlane (Mahady 46); Wilson E (Anderson 46), McArthur (Smith 46), Cleall-Harding (Donovan 46), Agbaire (Mullen 46); Bonnar (Watson 46), Bragg (Forrester 46), Pollock*, Rice; Thomson, One (Wales 60).
Iceland U21: (433) Georgsson (Johannesson 61); Thorkelsson, Robertsson, Orrason (Berndsen 61), Kristjansson; Bjarnason (Karlsson 83), Gudmundsson E (Nokkvason 61), Haraldsson (Ingason 71); Birgisson (Fjeldsted 61), Andresson (Mikaelsson 71), Hardarson (Thorsteinsson 71).

WALES

UEFA UNDER-21 CHAMPIONSHIP 2025 QUALIFYING GROUP I
Tuesday, 10 September 2024
Iceland U21 (0) 1 *(Borgthorsson 90)*
Wales U21 (0) 2 *(Cotterill 47, 72)* 265
Iceland U21: (433) Petersson; Karlsson, Robertsson (Valgeirsson 76), Thorkelsson (Andresson 65), Kristjansson; Sigurpalsson (Borgthorsson 88), Baldursson, Ingason; Sigurgeirsson (Gudmundsson O 65), Mikaelsson, Gudmundsson E (Thordarson 88).
Wales U21: (433) Beach; Stevens F, Low, Baker, Hoole; Savage, Ashworth, King; Colwill (Popov 88), Cotterill (Hammond 90), Thomas (Ashford 90).

Friday, 11 October 2024
Wales U21 (0) 1 *(Hoole 90)*
Czech Republic U21 (1) 2 *(Baker 27 (og), Sejk 50)* 2386
Wales U21: (433) Watts E; Stevens F, Hoole, Baker, Davies; King, Savage (Popov 54), Ashworth (Congreve 75); Colwill (Hammond O 61), Thomas (Ashford 62), Cotterill.

Czech Republic U21: (3421) Hornicek; Vydra, Prebsl, Chaloupek; Hadas, Danek (Langhamer 77), Harustak, Icha; Jurasek (Kricfalusi 90), Karabec (Sin 67); Sejk.

FRIENDLIES
Tuesday, 15 October 2024
Slovakia U21 (2) 4 *(Ujlaky 23, Cerepkai 45, Hajovsky 54, Marcelli 74)*
Wales U21 (1) 2 *(Hammond O 15, Farrell 60)*
Slovakia U21: (433) Danko; Jakubko (Selecky 88), Sikula (Kosa 62), Veselovsky (Marcelli 69), Ujlaky (Javorcek 62); Spacil (Holly 62), Hajovsky (Nebyla 62), Svidersky; Tucny (Hranica 46), Cerepkai (Gajdos 68), Griger.
Wales U21: (433) Benjamin (Watts E 62); Williams A (Stevens F 62), Baker, Turns (Hoole 62), Ashworth (Davies T 46); Hammond O (King 73), Crew, Colwill (Cotterill 46); Popov (Farrell 46), Congreve, Hampson (Thomas 73).

Thursday, 20 March 2025
Wales U21 (1) 1 *(Popov 24)*
Andorra U21 (0) 0
Wales U21: (442) Watts E (Hollinshead 46); Williams A (Hammond B 46), Katsukunya (Dabrowski 46), Williams Z (Harris L 46), Harris A (Cotterill 46); Watts D (Briggs 46), Hampson (Congreve 46), Tweedy (Roberts 46), Ashford (Tripp 46); Lloyd (James 46), Popov (Agius 46).
Andorra U21: (433) de Castro; Rodriguez, Vieira (Torne), Acosta, Linares; Simonet, Santaella (Estrada 82), Bienert (Sanchez 65); Agharbi (Dominguez), Rodriguez (Meireles 65), Sola.

Sunday, 23 March 2025
Wales U21 (0) 1 *(Ashford 78)*
Sweden U21 (1) 1 *(Agbonifo 45)*
Wales U21: (451) Watts E; James, Williams Z (Katsukunya 88), Harris A (Tweedy 84), Williams A; Cotterill, Congreve (Lloyd 84), Harris -L, Colwill, Ashford; Popov (Roberts 90).
Sweden U21: Viktor Andersson (Picornell 79), Mellberg (Vinlof 84), Skoglund, Rouhi, Jeng, Bjorklund (Loukili 46), Kjellnas (Karlsson 64), Odefalk (Dahbo 79), Sonko (Pihlstrom 46), Kusi-Asare (Rapp 64), Agbonifo (Omorova 64).

Friday, 6 June 2025
Norway (2) 4 *(Egeli S 15, Broholm 32, Skogvold 84, Hegland 90)*
Wales (0) 0
Norway: (4231) Borsheim (Ree 46); Brewery, Helland, Hopland (Gjengaar 62), Egeli V (Odegard 62); Hjerto-Dahl (Romsaas 82), Roaldsoy (Holten 46); Broholm (Skogvold 43), Nypan (Sivertsen 62), Austbo (Halvorsen 62); Egeli S (Hegland 82).
Wales: (4231) Benjamin (Watts E 46); Williams A, Lawlor, Hammond B, Harris A (Parker 62), Andrews, Cotterill (Perrett 82); Congreve (Nyakuhwa 62), Colwill (Bland 62), Ashford; Popov.

REPUBLIC OF IRELAND

UEFA UNDER-21 CHAMPIONSHIP 2025 QUALIFYING
GROUP A

Friday, 6 September 2024

Turkey U21 (0) 0

Republic of Ireland U21 (0) 1 *(Curtis 84)*   2188

Turkey U21: (532) Bilgin; Yildiz, Baltaci, Saatci (Gureler 65), Altikardes (Altunbas 79), Ozcan; Konak (Akman 71), Elmaz, Burcu (Onal 62); Canak (Ince 71), Hekimoglu.
Republic of Ireland U21: (541) Keeley; Curtis, Abankwah, O'Riordan, Garcia MacNulty, Roughan; Emakhu (Adeeko 68), Healy, Hodge, Moran; Armstrong (O'Mahony 77).

Tuesday, 10 September 2024

Republic of Ireland U21 (1) 2 *(Armstrong 16, Roughan 65)*

Latvia U21 (1) 2 *(Anmanis 42, Patrikejevs 63)*   953

Republic of Ireland U21: (433) Keeley; Curtis, Abankwah, Garcia MacNulty, Roughan; Hodge, Healy, Moran; O'Neill (Emakhu 64), Armstrong (Kenny 79), Vata (Okoflex 79).
Latvia U21: (442) Beks; Rascevskis (Druzinins 58), Vientiess, Reingolcs, Maslovs; Kauselis (Rekis 67), Anmanis, Penkevics, Melkis; Patika, Melnis (Patrikejevs 46).

Friday, 11 October 2024

Republic of Ireland U21 (0) 1 *(Roughan 75)*

Norway U21 (0) 1 *(Schjelderup 90)*   5754

Republic of Ireland U21: (532) Brooks; Curtis, Adegboyega, Abankwah, Garcia MacNulty, Roughan; Phillips (Adeeko 77), Healy, Moran; Kenny (O'Mahony 77), Emakhu (Vata 77).
Norway U21: (343) Tangvik; Helland, Guddall, Ostrom (Nypan 90); Braude (Walle 81), Arnstad, Hansen-Aaroen (Aasgaard 81), Lovik; Mvuka, Nordas (Melkersen 81), Schjelderup (Skaret 90).

Tuesday, 15 October 2024

Italy U21 (1) 1 *(Casadei 23)*

Republic of Ireland U21 (0) 1 *(Moran 66)*   1730

Italy U21: (4321) Desplanches; Savona, Ghilardi, Bertola, Zanotti (Turicchia 77); Casadei, Prati, Ndour; Baldanzi (Bonfanti 90), Gnonto (Koleosho 77); Esposito (Fabbian 54).
Republic of Ireland U21: (532) Brooks; Curtis (O'Brien 46), Adegboyega, Abankwah, Garcia MacNulty, Roughan (Adaramola 46); Adeeko (O'Mahony 81), Healy, Moran; Kenny (Emakhu 59), Armstrong.

FRIENDLIES

Thursday, 14 November 2024

Sweden U21 (0) 2 *(Skoglund 48, Omorowa 87)*

Republic of Ireland U21 (0) 0

Sweden U21: (433) Viktor Andersson; Skoglund (Skogmar 72), Makolli (Amoran 88), Jeng (Dahbo 88), Rouhi; Bjorklund (Boudri 88), Odefalk (Karlsson 72), Rafferty (Hodzic 56); Victor Andersson (Agbonifo 57), Rapp (Omorowa 56), Sonko (Ljungberg 72).
Republic of Ireland U21: (442) Jauny; O'Brien, Abankwah, Grehan, Alex Murphy; McJannet (Mullins 66), Nzingo, O'Brien-Whitmarsh, Vata; O'Mahony (Lonergan 66), Moore.

Sunday, 17 November 2024

Republic of Ireland U21 (1) 3 *(Mullins 15, Vata 48, O'Mahony 50)*

Sweden U21 (1) 2 *(Amoran 35, Bjorklund 58)*

Republic of Ireland U21: (442) Maguire (Walsh 61); Slater, Alex Murphy, Okagbue, O'Brien (Abankwah 78); Vata (Moore 61), Mullins (Thibaut 71), Nzingo (Quinn 61), O'Brien-Whitmarsh (Lipsiuc 61); O'Mahony (Lonergan 61), Hakiki (Zefi 71).
Sweden U21: (433) Sidklev (Bishesari 46); Skoglund (Skogmar 46), Amoran, Rouhi (Victor Andersson 72), Vinlof (Makolli 61); Karlsson, Odefalk (Hodzic 46), Bjorklund (Raffert 83); Dahbo (Agbonifo 46), Omorowa (Rapp 61), Boudri.

Monday, 24 March 2025

Hungary U21 (1) 1 *(Jurek 33)*

Republic of Ireland U21 (1) 3 *(Mason Melia 16 (pen), McManus 79, 84)*

Hungary U21: Toth B (Dala 46); Yaakobishvili, Markgraf, Banati (Bakti 68), Csoka (Kajan 68), Denes A, Okeke, Peto (Vansca 46), Toth R (Babos 46), Vingler (Rabb 75), Jurek (Denes C 75).
Republic of Ireland U21: Jauny; O'Brien (Barratt 88), Okagbue, McManus, Mullins (Adam Murphy 46), Vaughan (Gardner 88), Otegbayo (Alex Murphy 68), Hakiki (Umeh 68), Melia, Lipsiuc, Maher (O'Mahony 46).

Friday, 6 June 2025

Croatia U21 (0) 1 *(Krivak 52)*

Republic of Ireland U21 (0) 0

Croatia U21: (532) Sajko; Barisic, Zivkovic, Damjanic, Hrgovic (Tunjic 62); Vrbancic, Krivak (Kavelj 75), Jagusic (Brajkovic 75); Durdov, Topic (Rukavina 62), Soticek (Kulusic 82).
Republic of Ireland U21: (532) Maguire (Jauny 46); Curtis (O'Sullivan 89), Okagbue, Grehan, Alex Murphy, Slater; Lipsiuc, (Vaughan 66), Mullins (Devaney 82), Adam Murphy (McJannet 66); O'Mahony (Dillon 46), Gardner (Davis 46).

Tuesday, 10 June 2025

Republic of Ireland U21 (0) 0

Qatar U23 (0) 0

Republic of Ireland U21: (442) Wogan; Slater, Otegbayo (Alex Murphy 74), Grehan, Mullins; McJannet (O'Brien-Whitmarsh 46), Vaughan (Davis 74), Devaney, O'Sullivan (Slater 46); Dillon (O'Mahony 74), Hakiki.
Qatar U23: (442) Mohammed; Chasar, Al Oui, Reyad, Hagana; Said, Salem, Surag (Gouda 56), Al Sharshani (Shahabi 56); Hussain (Gamer 79), Jamshid.

BRITISH UNDER-21 APPEARANCES 1976–2025

Bold type indicates players who made an international appearance in season 2024–25.

ENGLAND

Aarons, M. J. 2020 (Norwich C) 26
Ablett, G. 1988 (Liverpool) 1
Abraham, K. O. T. (Tammy) 2017 (Chelsea) 26
Akpom, C. A. 2015 (Arsenal) 5
Adams, N. 1987 (Everton) 1
Adams, T. A. 1985 (Arsenal) 5
Addison, M. 2010 (Derby Co) 1
Afobe, B. T. 2012 (Arsenal) 2
Agbonlahor, G. 2007 (Aston Villa) 16
Albrighton, M. K. 2011 (Aston Villa) 8
Alexander-Arnold, T. J. 2018 (Liverpool) 3
Alli, B. J. (Dele) 2015 (Tottenham H) 2
Allen, B. 1992 (QPR) 8
Allen, C. 1980 (QPR, Crystal Palace) 3
Allen, C. A. 1995 (Oxford U) 2
Allen, M. 1987 (QPR) 2
Allen, P. 1985 (West Ham U, Tottenham H) 3
Allen, R. W. 1998 (Tottenham H) 3
Alnwick, B. R. 2008 (Tottenham H) 1
Ambrose, D. P. F. 2003 (Ipswich T, Newcastle U,
  Charlton Ath) 10
Ameobi, F. 2001 (Newcastle U) 19
Ameobi, S. 2012 (Newcastle U) 5
Amos, B. P. 2012 (Manchester U) 3
Anderson, E. J. 2025 (Nottingham F) 12
Anderson, V. A. 1978 (Nottingham F) 1
Anderton, D. R. 1993 (Tottenham H) 12
Andrews, I. 1987 (Leicester C) 1
Archer, C. D. 2022 (Aston Villa) 10
Ardley, N. C. 1993 (Wimbledon) 10
Armstrong, A. J. 2018 (Newcastle U) 5
Ashcroft, L. 1992 (Preston NE) 1
Ashton, D. 2004 (Crewe Alex, Norwich C) 9
Atherton, P. 1992 (Coventry C) 1
Atkinson, B. 1991 (Sunderland) 6
Awford, A. T. 1993 (Portsmouth) 9

Bailey, G. R. 1979 (Manchester U) 14
Baines, L. J. 2005 (Wigan Ath) 16
Baker, G. E. 1981 (Southampton) 2
Baker, L. R. 2015 (Chelsea) 17
Baker, N. L. 2011 (Aston Villa) 3
Ball, M. J. 1999 (Everton) 7
Balogun, F. J. 2022 (Arsenal) 13
Bamford, P. J. 2013 (Chelsea) 2
Bannister, G. 1982 (Sheffield Wed) 1
Barker, S. 1985 (Blackburn R) 4
Barkley, R. 2012 (Everton) 5
Barmby, N. J. 1994 (Tottenham H, Everton) 4
Barnes, H. L. 2019 (Leicester C) 4
Barnes, J. 1983 (Watford) 2
Barnes, P. S. 1977 (Manchester C) 9
Barrett, E. D. 1990 (Oldham Ath) 4
Barry, G. 1999 (Aston Villa) 27
Barton, J. 2004 (Manchester C) 2
Bart-Williams, C. G. 1993 (Sheffield Wed) 16
Batty, D. 1988 (Leeds U) 7
Bazeley, D. S. 1992 (Watford) 1
Beadle, J. G. 2025 (Brighton & HA) 12
Beagrie, P. 1988 (Sheffield U) 2
Beardsmore, R. 1989 (Manchester U) 5
Beattie, J. S. 1999 (Southampton) 5
Beckham, D. R. J. 1995 (Manchester U) 9
Bellingham, J. S. P. 2024 (Sunderland) 6
Bellingham, J. V. W. 2021 (Borussia Dortmund) 4
Berahino, S. 2013 (WBA) 11
Bennett, J. 2011 (Middlesbrough) 3
Bennett, R. 2012 (Norwich City) 2
Bent, D. A. 2003 (Ipswich T, Charlton Ath) 14
Bent, M. N. 1998 (Crystal Palace) 2
Bentley, D. M. 2004 (Arsenal, Blackburn R) 8
Beeston, C 1988 (Stoke C) 1
Benjamin, T. J. 2001 (Leicester C) 1
Bertrand, R. 2009 (Chelsea) 16
Bertschin, K. E. 1977 (Birmingham C) 3
Bettinelli, M. 2015 (Fulham) 1
Birtles, G. 1980 (Nottingham F) 2
Blackett, T. N. 2014 (Manchester U) 1

Blackstock, D. A. 2008 (QPR) 2
Blackwell, D. R. 1991 (Wimbledon) 6
Blake, M. A. 1990 (Aston Villa) 8
Blissett, L. L. 1979 (Watford) 4
Bond, J. H. 2013 (Watford) 5
Booth, A. D. 1995 (Huddersfield T) 3
Bothroyd, J. 2001 (Coventry C) 1
Bowyer, L. D. 1996 (Charlton Ath, Leeds U) 13
Bracewell, P. 1983 (Stoke C) 13
Bradbury, L. M. 1997 (Portsmouth, Manchester C) 3
Bradshaw, P. W. 1977 (Wolverhampton W) 4
Bramble, T. M. 2001 (Ipswich T, Newcastle U) 10
Branch, P. M. 1997 (Everton) 1
Branthwaite, J. P. 2023 (Everton) 7
Breacker, T. 1986 (Luton T) 2
Brennan, M. 1987 (Ipswich T) 5
Brewster, R. J. 2020 (Liverpool, Sheffield U) 18
Bridge, W. M. 1999 (Southampton) 8
Bridges, M. 1997 (Sunderland, Leeds U) 3
Briggs, M. 2012 (Fulham) 2
Brightwell, I. 1989 (Manchester C) 4
Briscoe, L. S. 1996 (Sheffield Wed) 5
Brock, K. 1984 (Oxford U) 4
Broomes, M. C. 1997 (Blackburn R) 2
Brown, M. R. 1996 (Manchester C) 4
Brown, W. M. 1999 (Manchester U) 8
Buchanan, L. D. 2021 (Derby Co) 2
Bull, S. G. 1989 (Wolverhampton W) 5
Bullock, M. J. 1998 (Barnsley) 1
Burrows, D. 1989 (WBA, Liverpool) 7
Bursik, J. J. 2021 (Stoke C, Club Brugge) 10
Butcher, T. I. 1979 (Ipswich T) 7
Butland, J. 2012 (Birmingham C, Stoke C) 28
Butt, N. 1995 (Manchester U) 7
Butters, G. 1989 (Tottenham H) 3
Butterworth, I. 1985 (Coventry C, Nottingham F) 8
Bynoe-Gittens, J. J. 2024 (Borussia Dortmund) 11
Bywater, S. 2001 (West Ham U) 6

Cadamarteri, D. L. 1999 (Everton) 3
Caesar, G. 1987 (Arsenal) 3
Cahill, G. J. 2007 (Aston Villa) 3
Callaghan, N. 1983 (Watford) 9
Calvert-Lewin, D. N. 2018 (Everton) 17
Camp, L. M. J. 2005 (Derby Co) 5
Campbell, A. P. 2000 (Middlesbrough) 4
Campbell, F. L. 2008 (Manchester U) 14
Campbell, K. J. 1991 (Arsenal) 4
Campbell, S. 1994 (Tottenham) 11
Cantwell, T. P. 2020 (Norwich C) 4
Carbon, M. P. 1996 (Derby Co) 4
Carr, C. 1985 (Fulham) 1
Carr, F. 1987 (Nottingham F) 9
Carragher, J. L. 1997 (Liverpool) 27
Carroll, A. T. 2010 (Newcastle U) 5
Carroll, T. J. 2013 (Tottenham H) 17
Carlisle, C. J. 2001 (QPR) 3
Carrick, M. 2001 (West Ham U) 14
Carson, S. P. 2004 (Leeds U, Liverpool) 29
Casper, C. M. 1995 (Manchester U) 1
Caton, T. 1982 (Manchester C) 14
Cattermole, L. B. 2008 (Middlesbrough, Wigan Ath,
  Sunderland) 16
Caulker, S. R. 2011 (Tottenham H) 10
Chadwick, L. H. 2000 (Manchester U) 13
Challis, T. M. 1996 (QPR) 2
Chalobah, N. N. 2012 (Chelsea) 40
Chalobah, T. T. 2020 (Chelsea) 3
Chamberlain, M. 1983 (Stoke C) 4
Chambers, C. 2015 (Arsenal) 22
Chaplow, R. D. 2004 (Burnley) 1
Chapman, L. 1981 (Stoke C) 1
Charles, G. A. 1991 (Nottingham F) 4
Chettle, S. 1988 (Nottingham F) 12
Chilwell, B. J. 2016 (Leicester C) 10
Chopra, R. M. 2004 (Newcastle U) 1
Choudhury, H. D. 2018 (Leicester C) 7
Chrisene, B. J. 2024 (Norwich C) 3

Clark, L. R. 1992 (Newcastle U)	11
Clarke, P. M. 2003 (Everton)	8
Clarke-Salter, J. L. 2018 (Chelsea)	12
Christie, M. N. 2001 (Derby Co)	11
Clegg, M. J. 1998 (Manchester U)	2
Clemence, S. N. 1999 (Tottenham H)	1
Cleverley, T. W. 2010 (Manchester U)	16
Clough, N. H. 1986 (Nottingham F)	15
Clyne, N. E. 2012 (Crystal Palace)	8
Cole, A. 2001 (Arsenal)	4
Cole, A. A. 1992 (Arsenal, Bristol C, Newcastle U)	8
Cole, C. 2003 (Chelsea)	19
Cole, J. J. 2000 (West Ham U)	8
Colwill, L. S 2022 (Chelsea)	10
Coney, D. 1985 (Fulham)	4
Connolly, C. A. 2018 (Everton)	1
Connor, T. 1987 (Brighton & HA)	1
Cook, L. J. 2018 (Bournemouth)	14
Cooke, R. 1986 (Tottenham H)	1
Cooke, T. J. 1996 (Manchester U)	4
Cooper, C. T. 1988 (Middlesbrough)	8
Cork, J. F. P. 2009 (Chelsea)	13
Corrigan, J. T. 1978 (Manchester C)	3
Cort, C. E. R. 1999 (Wimbledon)	12
Cottee, A. R. 1985 (West Ham U)	8
Couzens, A. J. 1995 (Leeds U)	3
Cowans, G. S. 1979 (Aston Villa)	5
Cox, N. J. 1993 (Aston Villa)	6
Cranie, M. J. 2008 (Portsmouth)	16
Cranson, I. 1985 (Ipswich T)	5
Cresswell, C. R. 2022 (Leeds U, Toulouse)	**25**
Cresswell, R. P. W. 1999 (York C, Sheffield Wed)	4
Croft, G. 1995 (Grimsby T)	4
Crooks, G. 1980 (Stoke C)	4
Crossley, M. G. 1990 (Nottingham F)	3
Crouch, P. J. 2002 (Portsmouth, Aston Villa)	5
Cundy, J. V. 1991 (Chelsea)	3
Cunningham, L. 1977 (WBA)	6
Curbishley, L. C. 1981 (Birmingham C)	1
Curtis, J. C. K. 1998 (Manchester U)	16
Daniel, P. W. 1977 (Hull C)	7
Dann, S. 2008 (Coventry C)	2
Dasilva, J. R. 2018 (Chelsea)	13
Dasilva, P. J. T. 2021 (Brentford)	5
Davenport, C. R. P. 2005 (Tottenham H)	8
Davies, A. J. 2004 (Middlesbrough)	1
Davies, C. E. 2006 (WBA)	3
Davies, K. C. 1998 (Southampton, Blackburn R, Southampton)	3
Davies, T. 2018 (Everton)	23
Davis, K. G. 1995 (Luton T)	3
Davis, P. 1982 (Arsenal)	11
Davis, S. 2001 (Fulham)	11
Dawson, C. 2012 (WBA)	15
Dawson, M. R. 2003 (Nottingham F, Tottenham H)	13
Day, C. N. 1996 (Tottenham H, Crystal Palace)	6
D'Avray, M. 1984 (Ipswich T)	2
Deehan, J. M. 1977 (Aston Villa)	7
Defoe, J. C. 2001 (West Ham U)	23
Delap, L. R. 2024 (Manchester C, Ipswich T)	**12**
Delfouneso, N. 2010 (Aston Villa)	17
Delph, F. 2009 (Leeds U, Aston Villa)	4
Dennis, M. E. 1980 (Birmingham C)	3
Derbyshire, M. A. 2007 (Blackburn R)	14
Diangana, G. G. 2020 (West Ham U)	1
Dibling, T.-J. R. 2025 (Southampton)	**2**
Dichio, D. S. E. 1996 (QPR)	1
Dickens, A. 1985 (West Ham U)	1
Dicks, J. 1988 (West Ham U)	4
Dier, E. J. E. 2013 (Sporting Lisbon, Tottenham H)	9
Digby, F. 1987 (Swindon T)	5
Dillon, K. P. 1981 (Birmingham C)	1
Dixon, M. K. 1985 (Chelsea)	1
Dobson, A. 1989 (Coventry C)	4
Dodd, J. R. 1991 (Southampton)	8
Donowa, L. 1985 (Norwich C)	3
Dorigo, A. R. 1987 (Aston Villa)	11
Dowell, K. O. 2018 (Everton)	17
Downing, S. 2004 (Middlesbrough)	8
Doyle, C. C. 2024 (Manchester C)	**5**
Doyle, T. G. 2022 (Manchester C)	12
Dozzell, J. 1987 (Ipswich T)	9
Draper, M. A. 1991 (Notts Co)	3
Drameh, C. C. P. (Leeds U)	1

Driver, A. 2009 (Hearts)	1
Duberry, M. W. 1997 (Chelsea)	5
Dunn, D. J. I. 1999 (Blackburn R)	20
Duxbury, M. 1981 (Manchester U)	7
Dyer, B. A. 1994 (Crystal Palace)	10
Dyer, K. C. 1998 (Ipswich T, Newcastle U)	11
Dyson, P. I. 1981 (Coventry C)	4
Eadie, D. M. 1994 (Norwich C)	7
Earthy, G. R. 2024 (West Ham U)	**4**
Ebanks-Blake, S. 2009 (Wolverhampton W)	1
Ebbrell, J. 1989 (Everton)	14
Edghill, R. A. 1994 (Manchester C)	3
Edwards, R. L. 2025 (Southampton)	**2**
Egan-Riley, C. J. 2025 (Burnley)	**3**
Ehiogu, U. 1992 (Aston Villa)	15
Ejaria, O. D. 2018 (Liverpool)	1
Elliott, H. D. J. 2022 (Liverpool)	**27**
Elliott, P. 1985 (Luton T)	3
Elliott, R. J. 1996 (Newcastle U)	2
Elliott, S. W. 1998 (Derby Co)	3
Etherington, N, 2002 (Tottenham H)	3
Euell, J. J. 1998 (Wimbledon)	6
Evans, R. 2003 (Chelsea)	2
Eze, E. O. 2020 (QPR, Crystal Palace)	8
Fairclough, C. 1985 (Nottingham F, Tottenham H)	7
Fairclough, D. 1977 (Liverpool)	1
Fashanu, J. 1980 (Norwich C, Nottingham F)	11
Fear, P. 1994 (Wimbledon)	3
Fellows, T. A. 2025 (WBA)	**3**
Fenton, G. A. 1995 (Aston Villa)	1
Fenwick, T. W. 1981 (Crystal Palace, QPR)	11
Ferdinand, A. J. 2005 (West Ham U)	17
Ferdinand, R. G. 1997 (West Ham U)	5
Fereday, W. 1985 (QPR)	5
Fielding, F. D. 2009 (Blackburn R)	12
Fisher, K. L. 2024 (Norwich C)	**2**
Flanagan, J. 2012 (Liverpool)	3
Flitcroft, G. W. 1993 (Manchester C)	10
Flowers, T. D. 1987 (Southampton)	3
Foden, P. W. 2019 (Manchester C)	15
Ford, M. 1996 (Leeds U)	2
Forster, N. M. 1995 (Brentford)	4
Forsyth, M. 1988 (Derby Co)	1
Forster-Caskey, J. D. 2014 (Brighton & HA)	14
Foster, S. 1980 (Brighton & HA)	1
Fowler, R. B. 1994 (Liverpool)	8
Fox, D. J. 2008 (Coventry C)	1
Froggatt, S. J. 1993 (Aston Villa)	2
Fry, D. J. 2018 (Middlesbrough)	11
Futcher, P. 1977 (Luton T, Manchester C)	11
Gabbiadini, M. 1989 (Sunderland)	2
Gale, A. 1982 (Fulham)	1
Gallagher, C. J. 2020 (Chelsea)	15
Gallen, K. A. 1995 (QPR)	4
Galloway, B. J. 2017 (Everton)	3
Garbutt, L. S. 2014 (Everton)	11
Gardner, A. 2002 (Tottenham H)	1
Gardner, C. 2008 (Aston Villa)	14
Gardner, G. 2012 (Aston Villa)	5
Garner, J. D. 2022 (Manchester U, Everton)	17
Gascoigne, P. J. 1987 (Newcastle U)	13
Gayle, H. 1984 (Birmingham C)	3
Gernon, T. 1983 (Ipswich T)	1
Gerrard, P. W. 1993 (Oldham Ath)	18
Gerrard, S. G. 2000 (Liverpool)	4
Gibbs, K. J. R. 2009 (Arsenal)	15
Gibbs, N. 1987 (Watford)	5
Gibbs-White, M. A. 2019 (Wolverhampton W, Nottingham F)	17
Gibson, B. J. 2014 (Middlesbrough)	10
Gibson, C. 1982 (Aston Villa)	1
Gilbert, W. A. 1979 (Crystal Palace)	11
Goddard, P. 1981 (West Ham U)	8
Godfrey, B. M. 2020 (Norwich C, Everton)	9
Gomes, A. A. A. de A. 2022 (Lille)	18
Gomez, J. D. 2015 (Liverpool)	7
Gordon, A. M. 2022 (Everton, Newcastle U)	15
Gordon, D. 1987 (Norwich C)	4
Gordon, D. D. 1994 (Crystal Palace)	13
Gosling, D. 2010 (Everton, Newcastle U)	3
Grant, A. J. 1996 (Everton)	1
Grant, L. A. 2003 (Derby Co)	4
Granville, D. P. 1997 (Chelsea)	3

Gray, A. 1988 (Aston Villa) 2
Gray, A. J. F. 2024 (Leeds U, Tottenham H) 13
Gray, D. R. 2016 (Leicester C) 26
Grealish, J. 2016 (Aston Villa) 7
Green, E. 2022 (Saint-Etienne) 2
Greening, J. 1999 (Manchester U, Middlesbrough) 18
Greenwood, M. W. J. 2020 (Manchester U) 4
Greenwood, S. 2022 (Leeds U) 1
Griffin, A. 1999 (Newcastle U) 3
Griffiths, J. J. 2023 (WBA) 1
Grimes, M. J. 2016 (Swansea C) 4
Guehi, A. K. M.-I. (Marc) 2020 (Chelsea,
  Crystal Palace) 16
Gunn, A. 2015 (Manchester C, Southampton) 12
Guppy, S. A. 1998 (Leicester C) 1
Gyabi, D. B. 2025 (Leeds U) 2

Hackney, H. R. 2024 (Middlesbrough) 13
Haigh, P. 1977 (Hull C) 1
Hall, L. K. 2025 (Newcastle U) 4
Hall, M. T. J. 1997 (Coventry C) 8
Hall, R. A. 1992 (Southampton) 11
Hamilton, D. V. 1997 (Newcastle U) 1
Hammill, A. 2010 (Wolverhampton W) 1
Harding, D. A. 2005 (Brighton & HA) 4
Hardyman, P. 1985 (Portsmouth) 2
Hargreaves, O. 2001 (Bayern Munich) 3
Harley, J. 2000 (Chelsea) 3
Harrison, J. D. 2018 (Manchester C) 2
Hart, C. J. J. (Joe) 2007 (Manchester C) 21
**Harwood-Bellis, T. J. 2022 (Manchester C,
  Southampton)** 26
Hateley, M. 1982 (Coventry C, Portsmouth) 10
Hause, K. P. D. 2015 (Wolverhampton W) 10
Hayden, I. 2017 (Newcastle U) 3
Hayes, M. 1987 (Arsenal) 3
Hazell, R. J. 1979 (Wolverhampton W) 1
Heaney, N. A. 1992 (Arsenal) 6
Heath, A. 1981 (Stoke C, Everton) 8
Heaton, T. D. 2008 (Manchester U) 3
Henderson, D. B. 2018 (Manchester U) 11
Henderson, J. B. 2011 (Sunderland, Liverpool) 27
Hendon, I. M. 1992 (Tottenham H) 7
Hendrie, L. A. 1996 (Aston Villa) 13
Hesford, I. 1981 (Blackpool) 7
Heskey, E. W. I. 1997 (Leicester C, Liverpool) 16
Hilaire, V. 1980 (Crystal Palace) 9
Hill, D. R. L. 1995 (Tottenham H) 4
Hill, J. C. 2022 (Bournemouth) 1
Hillier, D. 1991 (Arsenal) 1
Hinchcliffe, A. 1989 (Manchester C) 1
Hines, Z. 2010 (West Ham U) 2
Hinshelwood, J. L. 2025 (Brighton & HA) 10
Hinshelwood, P. A. 1978 (Crystal Palace) 2
Hirst, D. E. 1988 (Sheffield Wed) 7
Hislop, N. S. 1998 (Newcastle U) 1
Hoddle, G. 1977 (Tottenham H) 12
Hodge, S. B. 1983 (Nottingham F, Aston Villa) 8
Hodgson, D. J. 1981 (Middlesbrough) 6
Holding, R. S. 2016 (Bolton W, Arsenal) 5
Holdsworth, D. 1989 (Watford) 1
Holgate, M. 2017 (Everton) 6
Holland, C. J. 1995 (Newcastle U) 10
Holland, P. 1995 (Mansfield T) 4
Holloway, D. 1998 (Sunderland) 1
Horne, B. 1989 (Millwall) 5
Howe, E. J. F. 1998 (Bournemouth) 2
Howson, J. M. 2011 (Leeds U) 5
Hoyte, J. R. 2004 (Arsenal) 18
Hucker, P. 1984 (QPR) 2
Huckerby, D. 1997 (Coventry C) 4
Huddlestone, T. A. 2005 (Derby Co,
  Tottenham H) 33
Hudson-Odoi, C. J. 2020 (Chelsea) 9
Hughes, S. J. 1997 (Arsenal) 8
Hughes, W. J. 2012 (Derby Co) 22
Humphreys, B. 2024 (Chelsea) 5
Humphreys, R. J. 1997 (Sheffield Wed) 3
Hunt, N. B. 2004 (Bolton W) 10
Hutchinson, O. E. 2025 (Ipswich T) 10

Ibe, J. A. F. 2015 (Liverpool) 4
Iling-Junior, S. 2024 (Juventus, Aston Villa) 16
Impey, A. R. 1993 (QPR) 1
Ince, P. E. C. 1989 (West Ham U) 1
Ince, T. C. 2012 (Blackpool, Hull C) 18

Ings, D. W. J. 2013 (Burnley) 13
Iorfa, D. 2016 (Wolverhampton W) 13

Jackson, M. A. 1992 (Everton) 10
Jagielka, P. N. 2003 (Sheffield U) 6
James, D. B. 1991 (Watford) 10
James, J. C. 1990 (Luton T) 2
James, R. 2020 (Chelsea) 2
Jansen, M. B. 1999 (Crystal Palace, Blackburn R) 6
Jeffers, F. 2000 (Everton, Arsenal) 16
Jemson, N. B. 1991 (Nottingham F) 1
Jenas, J. A. 2002 (Newcastle U) 9
Jenkinson, C. D. 2013 (Arsenal) 14
Jerome, C. 2006 (Cardiff C, Birmingham C) 10
Joachim, J. K. 1994 (Leicester C) 9
John-Jules, T. R. 2022 (Arsenal) 2
Johnson, A. 2008 (Middlesbrough) 19
Johnson, B. A. 2022 (West Ham U) 10
Johnson, G. M. C. 2003 (West Ham U, Chelsea) 14
Johnson, M. 2008 (Manchester C) 2
Johnson, S. A. M. 1999 (Crewe Alex, Derby Co,
  Leeds U) 15
Johnson, T. 1991 (Notts Co, Derby Co) 7
Johnston, C. P. 1981 (Middlesbrough) 2
Jones, C. J. 2021 (Liverpool) 19
Jones, D. R. 1977 (Everton) 1
Jones, C. H. 1978 (Tottenham H) 1
Jones, D. F. L. 2004 (Manchester U) 1
Jones, P. A. 2011 (Blackburn R) 9
Jones, R. 1993 (Liverpool) 2
Justin, J. M. 2020 (Leicester C) 8

Kane, H. E. 2013 (Tottenham H) 14
Keane, M. V. 2013 (Manchester U, Burnley) 16
Keane, W. D. 2012 (Manchester U) 3
Keegan, G. A. 1977 (Manchester C) 1
Kelly, L. C. 2019 (Bournemouth) 10
Kelly, M. R. 2011 (Liverpool) 8
Kenny, J. 2018 (Everton) 16
Kenny, W. 1993 (Everton) 1
Keown, M. R. 1987 (Aston Villa) 8
Kerslake, D. 1986 (QPR) 1
Kightly, M. J. 2008 (Wolverhampton W) 7
Kilcline, B. 1983 (Notts C) 2
Kilgallon, M. 2004 (Leeds U) 5
King, A. E. 1977 (Everton) 2
King, L. B. 2000 (Tottenham H) 12
Kirkland, C. E. 2001 (Coventry C, Liverpool) 8
Kitson, P. 1991 (Leicester C, Derby Co) 7
Knight, A. 1983 (Portsmouth) 2
Knight, I. 1987 (Sheffield Wed) 2
Knight, Z. 2002 (Fulham) 4
Konchesky, P. M. 2002 (Charlton Ath) 15
Konsa, E. 2018 (Charlton Ath, Brentford) 7
Kozluk, R. 1998 (Derby Co) 2

Lake, P. 1989 (Manchester C) 5
Lallana, A. D. 2009 (Southampton) 1
Lampard, F. J. 1998 (West Ham U) 19
Lamptey, T. K. N.-L. 2021 (Brighton & HA) 2
Langley, T. W. 1978 (Chelsea) 1
Lansbury, H. G. 2010 (Arsenal, Nottingham F) 16
Lascelles, J. 2014 (Newcastle U) 2
Leadbitter, G. 2008 (Sunderland) 3
Lee, D. J. 1990 (Chelsea) 10
Lee, R. M. 1986 (Charlton Ath) 1
Lee, S. 1981 (Liverpool) 6
Lees, T. J. 2012 (Leeds U) 6
Lennon, A. J. 2006 (Tottenham H) 5
Le Saux, G. P. 1990 (Chelsea) 4
Lescott, J. P. 2003 (Wolverhampton W) 2
Lewis, J. P. 2008 (Peterborough U) 5
Lewis, R. M. 2023 (Manchester C) 7
Lewis-Potter, K. W. 2022 (Hull C) 4
Lingard, J. E. 2013 (Manchester U) 11
Lita, L. H. 2005 (Bristol C, Reading) 9
**Livramento, V. F. (Tino) 2022 (Southampton,
  Newcastle U)** 14
Loach, S. J. 2009 (Watford) 14
Loftus-Cheek, R. I. 2015 (Chelsea) 17
Lookman, A. 2018 (Everton) 11
Lowe, D. 1988 (Ipswich T) 2
Lowe, J. J. 2012 (Blackburn R) 11
Lukic, J. 1981 (Leeds U) 7
Lund, G. 1985 (Grimsby T) 3

Mabbutt, G. 1982 (Bristol R, Tottenham H)	7
Maddison, J. D. 2018 (Norwich C, Leicester C)	9
Madueke, C. T. (Noni) 2021 (PSV Eindhoven, Chelsea)	**19**
Maguire, J. H. 2012 (Sheffield U)	1
Maitland-Niles, A. C. 2018 (Arsenal)	4
Makin, C. 1994 (Oldham Ath)	5
Mancienne, M. I. 2008 (Chelsea)	30
March, S. B. 2015 (Brighton & HA)	3
Marney, D. E. 2005 (Tottenham H)	1
Marriott, A. 1992 (Nottingham F)	1
Marsh, S. T. 1998 (Oxford U)	1
Marshall, A. J. 1995 (Norwich C)	4
Marshall, B. 2012 (Leicester C)	2
Marshall, L. K. 1999 (Norwich C)	1
Martin, L. 1989 (Manchester U)	1
Martyn, A. N. 1988 (Bristol R)	11
Matteo, D. 1994 (Liverpool)	4
Mattock, J. W. 2008 (Leicester C)	5
Matthew, D. 1990 (Chelsea)	9
Mawson, A. R. J. 2017 (Swansea C)	6
May, A. 1986 (Manchester C)	1
Mbete, L. 2023 (Manchester C)	2
McAtee, J. J. 2022 (Manchester C)	**24**
McCall, S. H. 1981 (Ipswich T)	6
McCarthy, A. S. 2011 (Reading)	3
McDonald, N. 1987 (Newcastle U)	5
McEachran, J. M. 2011 (Chelsea)	13
McEveley, J. 2003 (Blackburn R)	1
McGrath, L. 1986 (Coventry C)	1
MacKenzie, S. 1982 (WBA)	3
McLeary, A. 1988 (Millwall)	1
McLeod, I. M. 2006 (Milton Keynes D)	1
McMahon, S. 1981 (Everton, Aston Villa)	6
McManaman, S. 1991 (Liverpool)	7
McNeil, D. J. M. 2020 (Burnley)	10
McQueen, S. J. 2017 (Southampton)	1
Mee, B. 2011 (Manchester C)	2
Mengi, T. M. 2024 (Luton T)	**3**
Merson, P. C. 1989 (Arsenal)	4
Middleton, J. 1977 (Nottingham F, Derby Co)	3
Miley, L. 2025 (Newcastle U)	**2**
Miller, A. 1988 (Arsenal)	4
Mills, D. J. 1999 (Charlton Ath, Leeds U)	14
Mills, G. R. 1981 (Nottingham F)	2
Milner, J. P. 2004 (Leeds U, Newcastle U, Aston Villa)	46
Mimms, R. 1985 (Rotherham U, Everton)	3
Minto, S. C. 1991 (Charlton Ath)	6
Mitchell, J. 2017 (Derby Co)	1
Mola, C. 2022 (VfB Stuttgart)	1
Moore, I. 1996 (Tranmere R, Nottingham F)	1
Moore, L. 2012 (Leicester C)	10
Moore, L. I. 2006 (Aston Villa)	5
Moran, S. 1982 (Southampton)	2
Morgan, S. 1987 (Leicester C)	2
Morris, J. 1997 (Chelsea)	2
Morrison, R. R. 2013 (West Ham U)	4
Mortimer, P. 1989 (Charlton Ath)	1
Morton, T. S. 2024 (Liverpool)	**13**
Moses, A. P. 1997 (Barnsley)	2
Moses, R. M. 1981 (WBA, Manchester U)	8
Moses, V. 2011 (Wigan Ath)	1
Mount, M. T. 2019 (Chelsea)	4
Mountfield, D. 1984 (Everton)	1
Muamba, F. N. 2008 (Birmingham C, Bolton W)	33
Muggleton, C. D. 1990 (Leicester C)	1
Mullins, H. I. 1999 (Crystal Palace)	3
Murphy, D. B. 1998 (Liverpool)	4
Murphy, Jacob K. 2017 (Norwich C)	6
Murray, P. 1997 (QPR)	1
Murray, M. W. 2003 (Wolverhampton W)	5
Musiala, J. 2021 (Bayern Munich)	2
Mutch, A. 1989 (Wolverhampton W)	1
Mutch, J. J. E. S. 2011 (Birmingham C)	1
Myers. A. 1995 (Chelsea)	4
Naughton, K. 2009 (Sheffield U, Tottenham H)	9
Naylor, L. M. 2000 (Wolverhampton W)	1
Nelson, R. L. 2019 (Arsenal)	12
Nethercott, S. H. 1994 (Tottenham H)	8
Neville, P. J. 1995 (Manchester U)	7
Newell, M. 1986 (Luton T)	4
Newton, A. L. 2001 (West Ham U)	1
Newton, E. J. I. 1993 (Chelsea)	2
Newton, S. O. 1997 (Charlton Ath)	3
Nicholls, A. 1994 (Plymouth Arg)	1
Nketiah, E. K. 2018 (Arsenal)	17

Nmecha, L. 2018 (Manchester C)	3
Noble, M. J. 2007 (West Ham U)	20
Nolan, K. A. J. 2003 (Bolton W)	1
Norton-Cuffy, B. D. N. 2024 (Arsenal)	**9**
Nugent, D. J. 2006 (Preston NE)	14
Nwaneri, E. C. 2025 (Arsenal)	**8**
Oakes, M. C. 1994 (Aston Villa)	6
Oakes, S. J. 1993 (Luton T)	1
Oakley, M. 1997 (Southampton)	4
O'Brien, A. J. 1999 (Bradford C)	1
O'Connor, J. 1996 (Everton)	3
O'Hara, J. D. 2008 (Tottenham H)	7
Ojo, O. B. (Sheyi) 2018 (Liverpool)	1
Oldfield, D. 1989 (Luton T)	1
Olney, I. A. 1990 (Aston Villa)	10
O'Neil, G. P. 2005 (Portsmouth)	9
Onomah, J. O. P. 2017 (Tottenham H)	8
Onuoha, C. 2006 (Manchester C)	21
Ord, R. J. 1991 (Sunderland)	3
Osman, R. C. 1979 (Ipswich T)	7
Owen, G. A. 1977 (Manchester C, WBA)	22
Owen, M. J. 1998 (Liverpool)	1
Oxlade-Chamberlain, A. M. D. 2011 (Southampton, Arsenal)	8
Painter, I. 1986 (Stoke C)	1
Palmer, C. J. 2022 (Manchester C)	15
Palmer, C. L. 1989 (Sheffield Wed)	4
Palmer, K. R. 2016 (Chelsea)	6
Panzo, J. W. 2020 (Monaco)	5
Parker, G. 1986 (Hull C, Nottingham F)	6
Parker, P. A. 1985 (Fulham)	8
Parker, S. M. 2001 (Charlton Ath)	12
Parkes, P. B. F. 1979 (QPR)	1
Parkin, S. 1987 (Stoke C)	5
Parlour, R. 1992 (Arsenal)	12
Parnaby, S. 2003 (Middlesbrough)	4
Patino, C. M. 2024 (Arsenal)	2
Peach, D. S. 1977 (Southampton)	6
Peake, A. 1982 (Leicester C)	1
Pearce, I. A. 1995 (Blackburn R)	3
Pearce, S. 1987 (Nottingham F)	1
Pearce, T. M. 2018 (Leeds U)	2
Pennant, J. 2001 (Arsenal)	24
Philogene-Bidace, J. R. 2024 (Hull C, Ipswich T)	**9**
Pickering N. 1983 (Sunderland, Coventry C)	15
Pickford, J. L. 2015 (Sunderland)	14
Platt, D. 1988 (Aston Villa)	3
Plummer, C. S. 1996 (QPR)	5
Pollock, J. 1995 (Middlesbrough)	3
Porter, G. 1987 (Watford)	12
Potter, G. S. 1997 (Southampton)	1
Powell, N. E. 2012 (Manchester U)	2
Pressman, K. 1989 (Sheffield Wed)	1
Pritchard, A. D. 2014 (Tottenham H)	9
Proctor, M. 1981 (Middlesbrough, Nottingham F)	4
Prutton, D. T. 2001 (Nottingham F, Southampton)	25
Purse, D. J. 1998 (Birmingham C)	2
Quansah, J. A. 2024 (Liverpool)	**14**
Quashie, N. F. 1997 (QPR)	4
Quinn, W. R. 1998 (Sheffield U)	2
Rak-Sakyi, J. 2025 (Crystal Palace)	**2**
Ramage, C. D. 1991 (Derby Co)	3
Ramsdale, A. C. 2018 (Bournemouth)	15
Ramsey, J. M. 2022 (Aston Villa)	15
Ranson, R. 1980 (Manchester C)	10
Rashford, M. 2017 (Manchester U)	1
Redknapp, J. F. 1993 (Liverpool)	19
Redmond, N. D. J. 2013 (Birmingham C, Norwich C, Southampton)	38
Redmond, S. 1988 (Manchester C)	14
Reeves, K. P. 1978 (Norwich C, Manchester C)	10
Regis, C. 1979 (WBA)	6
Reid, N. S. 1981 (Manchester C)	6
Reid, P. 1977 (Bolton W)	6
Reo-Coker, N. S. A. 2004 (Wimbledon, West Ham U)	23
Richards, D. I. 1995 (Wolverhampton W)	4
Richards, J. P. 1977 (Wolverhampton W)	2
Richards, M. 2007 (Manchester C)	15
Richards, M. L. 2005 (Ipswich T)	1
Richards, O. T. C. 2020 (Reading)	1
Richardson, K. E. 2005 (Manchester U)	12
Rideout, P. 1985 (Aston Villa, Bari)	5

Ridgewell, L. M. 2004 (Aston Villa) 8
Riggott, C. M. 2001 (Derby Co) 8
Ripley, S. E. 1988 (Middlesbrough) 8
Ritchie, A. 1982 (Brighton & HA) 1
Rix, G. 1978 (Arsenal) 7
Roberts, A. J. 1995 (Millwall, Crystal Palace) 5
Roberts, B. J. 1997 (Middlesbrough) 1
Robins, M. G. 1990 (Manchester U) 6
Robinson, J. 2012 (Liverpool, QPR) 10
Robinson, P. P. 1999 (Watford) 3
Robinson, P. W. 2000 (Leeds U) 11
Robson, B. 1979 (WBA) 7
Robson, S. 1984 (Arsenal, West Ham U) 8
Rocastle, D. 1987 (Arsenal) 14
Roche, L. P. 2001 (Manchester U) 1
Rodger, G. 1987 (Coventry C) 4
Rodriguez, J. E. 2011 (Burnley) 1
Rodwell, J. 2009 (Everton) 21
Rogers, A. 1998 (Nottingham F) 3
Rogers, M. E. 2024 (Aston Villa) **6**
Rosario, R. 1987 (Norwich C) 4
Rose, D. L. 2009 (Tottenham H) 29
Rose, M. 1997 (Arsenal) 4
Rosenior, L. J. 2005 (Fulham) 7
Routledge, W. 2005 (Crystal Palace, Tottenham H) 12
Rowe, J. D. H. 2024 (Norwich C) **10**
Rowell, G. 1977 (Sunderland) 1
Rudd, D. T. 2013 (Norwich C) 1
Ruddock, N. 1989 (Southampton) 4
Rufus, R. R. 1996 (Charlton Ath) 6
Ryan, J. 1983 (Oldham Ath) 1
Ryder, S. H. 1995 (Walsall) 3

Saka, B. A. T. M. 2021 (Arsenal) 1
Samuel, J. 2002 (Aston Villa) 7
Samways, V. 1988 (Tottenham H) 5
Sansom, K. G. 1979 (Crystal Palace) 8
Scarlett, D. F. 2024 (Tottenham H) **7**
Scimeca, R. 1996 (Aston Villa) 9
Scott, A. J. 2024 (Bournemouth) **11**
Scowcroft, J. B. 1997 (Ipswich T) 5
Seaman, D. A. 1985 (Birmingham C) 10
Sears, F. D. 2010 (West Ham U) 3
Sedgley, S. 1987 (Coventry C, Tottenham H) 11
Sellars, S. 1988 (Blackburn R) 3
Selley, I. 1994 (Arsenal) 3
Serrant, C. 1998 (Oldham Ath) 2
Sessegnon, K. R. (Ryan) 2018 (Fulham, Tottenham H) 20
Sessegnon, Z. S. (Steven) 2020 (Fulham) 5
Sharman-Low, T. S. 2025 (Chelsea) **1**
Sharpe, L. S. 1989 (Manchester U) 8
Shaw, L. P. H. 2013 (Southampton, Manchester U) 5
Shaw, G. R. 1981 (Aston Villa) 7
Shawcross, R. J. 2008 (Stoke C) 2
Shearer, A. 1991 (Southampton) 11
Shelton, G. 1985 (Sheffield Wed) 1
Shelvey, J. 2012 (Liverpool, Swansea C) 13
Sheringham, E. P. 1988 (Millwall) 1
Sheron, M. N. 1992 (Manchester U) 16
Sherwood, T. A. 1990 (Norwich C) 4
Shipperley, N. J. 1994 (Chelsea, Southampton) 7
Sidwell, S. J. 2003 (Reading) 5
Simonsen, S. P. A. 1998 (Tranmere R, Everton) 1
Simpson, J. B. 2019 (Bournemouth) 1
Simpson, P. 1986 (Manchester C) 5
Sims, S. 2010 (Leicester C) 10
Sinclair, S. A. 2011 (Swansea C) 7
Sinclair, T. 1994 (QPR, West Ham U) 5
Sinnott, L. 1985 (Watford) 1
Skipp, O. W. 2020 (Tottenham H) 23
Slade, S. A. 1996 (Tottenham H) 4
Slater, S. I. 1990 (West Ham U) 3
Small, B. 1993 (Aston Villa) 12
Smalling, C. L. 2010 (Fulham, Manchester U) 14
Smith, A. 2000 (Leeds U) 10
Smith, A. J. 2012 (Tottenham H) 11
Smith, D. 1988 (Coventry C) 10
Smith, M. 1981 (Sheffield Wed) 5
Smith, M. 1995 (Sunderland) 1
Smith, T. W. 2001 (Watford) 1
Smith Rowe, E. 2021 (Arsenal) 15
Snodin, I. 1985 (Doncaster R) 4
Soares, T. J. 2006 (Crystal Palace) 4
Solanke, D. A. 2015 (Chelsea, Liverpool,
Bournemouth) 18

Sordell, M. A. 2012 (Watford, Bolton W) 14
Spence, D. T. D.-H. 2022 (Middlesbrough, Tottenham H) 6
Spence, J. 2011 (West Ham U) 1
Stansfield, J. 2024 (Fulham, Birmingham C) **9**
Stanislaus, F. J. 2010 (West Ham U) 2
Statham, B. 1988 (Tottenham H) 3
Statham, D. J. 1978 (WBA) 6
Stead, J. G. 2004 (Blackburn R, Sunderland) 11
Stearman, R. J. 2009 (Wolverhampton W) 4
Steele, J. 2011 (Middlesbrough) 7
Stein, B. 1984 (Luton T) 3
Stephens, J. 2015 (Southampton) 8
Sterland, M. 1984 (Sheffield Wed) 7
Sterling, R. S. 2012 (Liverpool) 8
Steven, T. M. 1985 (Everton) 2
Stevens, G. A. 1983 (Brighton & HA, Tottenham H) 8
Stewart, J. 2003 (Leicester C) 1
Stewart, P. 1988 (Manchester C) 1
Stockdale, R. K. 2001 (Middlesbrough) 1
Stones, J. 2013 (Everton) 12
Stuart, G. C. 1990 (Chelsea) 5
Stuart, J. C. 1996 (Charlton Ath) 4
Sturridge, D. A. 2010 (Chelsea) 15
Suckling, P. 1986 (Coventry C, Manchester C,
Crystal Palace) 10
Summerbee, N. J. 1993 (Swindon T) 3
Sunderland, A. 1977 (Wolverhampton W) 1
Surman, A. R. E. 2008 (Bournemouth) 4
Surridge, S. W. 2020 (Bournemouth) 3
Sutch, D. 1992 (Norwich C) 4
Sutton, C. R. 1993 (Norwich C) 13
Swift, J. D. 2015 (Chelsea, Reading) 13
Swindlehurst, D. 1977 (Crystal Palace) 1

Talbot, B. 1977 (Ipswich T) 1
Tangana, J. M. 2021 (Tottenham H) 2
Targett, M. R. 2015 (Southampton) 12
Taylor, A. D. 2007 (Middlesbrough) 13
Taylor, M. 2001 (Blackburn R) 1
Taylor, M. S. 2003 (Portsmouth) 4
Taylor, R. A. 2006 (Wigan Ath) 3
Taylor, S. J. 2002 (Arsenal) 3
Taylor, S. V. 2004 (Newcastle U) 29
Terry, J. G. 2001 (Chelsea) 9
Thatcher, B. D. 1996 (Millwall, Wimbledon) 4
Thelwell, A. A. 2001 (Tottenham H) 1
Thirlwell, P. 2001 (Sunderland) 1
Thomas, D. 1981 (Coventry C, Tottenham H) 7
Thomas, J. W. 2006 (Charlton Ath) 2
Thomas, L. J. 2022 (Leicester C) 14
Thomas, M. 1986 (Luton T) 3
Thomas, M. L. 1988 (Arsenal) 12
Thomas, R. E. 1990 (Watford) 1
Thompson, A. 1995 (Bolton W) 2
Thompson, D. A. 1997 (Liverpool) 7
Thompson, G. L. 1981 (Coventry C) 6
Thorn, A. 1988 (Wimbledon) 5
Thornley, B. L. 1996 (Manchester U) 3
Thorpe, T. J. 2013 (Manchester U) 1
Tickle, S. L. 2024 (Wigan Ath) 1
Tiler, C. 1990 (Barnsley, Nottingham F) 13
Tomkins, J. O. C. 2009 (West Ham U) 10
Tomori, O. O. (Fikayo) 2018 (Chelsea) 15
Tonge, M. W. E. 2004 (Sheffield U) 2
Townsend, A. D. 2012 (Tottenham H) 3
Trafford, J. 2022 (Manchester C, Burnley) **18**
Trippier, K. J. 2011 (Manchester C) 2
Tuanzebe, A. 2018 (Manchester U) 1

Unsworth, D. G. 1995 (Everton) 6
Upson, M. J. 1999 (Arsenal) 11

Vassell, D. 1999 (Aston Villa) 11
Vaughan, J. O. 2007 (Everton) 4
Venison, B. 1983 (Sunderland) 10
Vernazza, P. A. P. 2001 (Arsenal, Watford) 2
Vieira, R. A. 2018 (Leeds U) 3
Vinnicombe, C. 1991 (Rangers) 12

Waddle, C. R. 1985 (Newcastle U) 1
Waghorn, M. T. 2012 (Leicester C) 5
Walcott, T. J. 2007 (Arsenal) 21
Wallace, D. L. 1983 (Southampton) 14
Wallace, Ray 1989 (Southampton) 4
Wallace, Rod 1989 (Southampton) 11

Walker, D. 1985 (Nottingham F)	7
Walker, I. M. 1991 (Tottenham H)	9
Walker, K. 2010 (Tottenham H)	7
Walker-Peters, K. L. 2018 (Tottenham H)	11
Walsh, G. 1988 (Manchester U)	2
Walsh, P. A. 1983 (Luton T)	4
Walters, K. 1984 (Aston Villa)	9
Walton, C. T. 2017 (Brighton & HA)	1
Wan Bissaka, A. 2019 (Crystal Palace)	3
Ward, P. 1978 (Brighton & HA)	2
Ward-Prowse, J. M. E. 2013 (Southampton)	31
Warhurst, P. 1991 (Oldham Ath, Sheffield Wed)	8
Watmore, D. I. 2015 (Sunderland)	13
Watson, B. 2007 (Crystal Palace)	1
Watson, D. 1984 (Norwich C)	7
Watson, D. N. 1994 (Barnsley)	5
Watson, G. 1991 (Sheffield Wed)	2
Watson, S. C. 1993 (Newcastle U)	12
Weaver, N. J. 2000 (Manchester C)	10
Webb, N. J. 1985 (Portsmouth, Nottingham F)	3
Welbeck, D. 2009 (Manchester U)	14
Welsh, J. J. 2004 (Liverpool, Hull C)	8
Wharton, A. J. 2024 (Crystal Palace)	**3**
Wheater, D. J. 2008 (Middlesbrough)	11
Whelan, P. J. 1993 (Ipswich T)	3
Whelan, N. 1995 (Leeds U)	2
Whittingham, P. 2004 (Aston Villa, Cardiff C)	17
White, D. 1988 (Manchester C)	6
Whyte, C. 1982 (Arsenal)	4
Wickham, C. N. R. 2011 (Ipswich T, Sunderland)	17
Wicks, S. 1982 (QPR)	1
Wilkins, R. C. 1977 (Chelsea)	1
Wilkinson, P. 1985 (Grimsby T, Everton)	4
Williams, B. P. B. 2021 (Manchester U)	1
Williams, D. 1998 (Sunderland)	2
Williams, P. 1989 (Charlton Ath)	4

Williams, P. D. 1991 (Derby Co)	6
Williams, R. 2021 (Liverpool)	2
Williams, S. C. 1977 (Southampton)	14
Willock, J. G. 2020 (Arsenal)	4
Wilmot, B. L. 2020 (Watford)	4
Wilshere, J. A. 2010 (Arsenal)	7
Wilson, C. E. G. 2014 (Bournemouth)	1
Wilson, J. A. 2015 (Manchester U)	1
Wilson, M. A. 2001 (Manchester U, Middlesbrough)	6
Wilson-Esbrand, J. D. K. 2024 (Manchester C)	2
Winks, H. 2017 (Tottenham H)	2
Winterburn, N. 1986 (Wimbledon)	1
Wisdom, A. 2012 (Liverpool)	10
Wise, D. F. 1988 (Wimbledon)	1
Wood-Gordon, N. D. J. 2023 (Swansea C, Southampton)	**4**
Woodcook, A. S. 1978 (Nottingham F)	2
Woodgate, J. S. 2000 (Leeds U)	1
Woodhouse, C. 1999 (Sheffield U)	4
Woodman, F. J. 2017 (Newcastle U)	6
Woodrow, C. 2014 (Fulham)	9
Woods, C. C. E. 1979 (Nottingham F, QPR, Norwich C)	6
Worrall, J. A. 2018 (Nottingham F)	3
Wright, A. G. 1993 (Blackburn R)	2
Wright, M. 1983 (Southampton)	4
Wright, R. I. 1997 (Ipswich T)	15
Wright, S. J. 2001 (Liverpool)	10
Wright, W. 1979 (Everton)	6
Wright-Phillips, S. C. 2002 (Manchester C)	6
Yates, D. 1989 (Notts Co)	5
Young, A. S. 2007 (Watford, Aston Villa)	10
Young, L. P. 1999 (Tottenham H, Charlton Ath)	12
Zaha, D. W. A. 2012 (Crystal Palace, Manchester U)	13
Zamora, R. L. 2002 (Brighton & HA)	6

NORTHERN IRELAND

Allen, C. 2009 (Lisburn Distillery)	1
Allen, C. S. 2022 (Leeds U, Linfield)	**14**
Amos, D. 2019 (Doncaster R)	7
Anderson, H. 2022 (Portadown)	1
Annett, R. 2024 (Linfield)	1
Archer, J. 2024 (Linfield)	1
Armstrong, D. T. 2007 (Hearts)	1
Atcheson, T. J. 2025 (Blackburn R)	**1**
Baggley (Crowe), B. T. 2021 (Fleetwood T)	**9**
Bagnall, L. 2011 (Sunderland)	1
Bailie, N. 1990 (Linfield)	2
Baird, C. P. 2002 (Southampton)	6
Ball, D. 2013 (Tottenham H)	2
Ball, M. J. 2011 (Norwich C)	5
Ballard, D. G. 2019 (Arsenal)	3
Balmer, K. 2019 (Ballymena U, Larne)	20
Bansal-McNulty, A. P. S. 2021 (QPR)	2
Barnsley, F. 2024 (Everton)	**2**
Barr, C. 2025 (Ballymena U)	**1**
Beatty, S. 1990 (Chelsea, Linfield)	2
Berry, D. 2022 (Norwich C)	2
Bird, P. M. 2019 (Notts Co)	4
Black, J. 2003 (Tottenham H)	1
Black, K. T. 1990 (Luton T)	1
Black, R. Z. 2002 (Morecambe)	1
Blackledge, G. 1978 (Portadown)	1
Blake, R. G. 2011 (Brentford)	2
Blayney, A. 2003 (Southampton)	4
Bonis, L. 2021 (Portadown)	2
Boyd-Munce, C. S. 2019 (Birmingham C, St Mirren)	21
Boyce, L. 2010 (Cliftonville, Werder Bremen)	8
Boyle, D. M. 2021 (Fleetwood T)	5
Boyle, W. S. 1998 (Leeds U)	7
Braniff, K. R. 2002 (Millwall)	11
Breeze, J. 2011 (Wigan Ath)	4
Brennan, C. 2013 (Kilmarnock)	13
Brobbel, R. 2013 (Middlesbrough)	9
Brotherston, N. 1978 (Blackburn R)	1
Brown, C. M. 2020 (Cardiff C)	4
Browne, G. 2003 (Manchester C)	5
Brunt, C. 2005 (Sheffield Wed)	2
Bryan, M. A. 2010 (Watford)	4
Buchanan, D. T. H. 2006 (Bury)	15
Buchanan, W. B. 2002 (Bolton W, Lisburn Distillery)	5
Burns, A. 2014 (Linfield)	1

Burns, R. (Bobby) 2018 (Glenavon, Hearts, Barrow)	12
Burns, L. 1998 (Port Vale)	13
Callaghan, A. 2006 (Limavady U, Ballymena U, Derry C)	15
Campbell, S. 2003 (Ballymena U)	1
Camps, C. 2015 (Rochdale)	1
Capaldi, A. C. 2002 (Birmingham C, Plymouth Arg)	14
Carlisle, W. T. 2000 (Crystal Palace)	9
Carroll, R. E. 1998 (Wigan Ath)	11
Carson, J. G. 2011 (Ipswich T, York C)	12
Carson, M. 2025 (Torquay U)	**2**
Carson, S. 2000 (Rangers, Dundee U)	2
Carson, T. 2007 (Sunderland)	15
Carvill, M. D. 2008 (Wrexham, Linfield)	8
Casement, C. 2007 (Ipswich T, Dundee)	18
Casey, O. 2024 (Cliftonville)	2
Cathcart, C. 2007 (Manchester U)	15
Catney, R. 2007 (Lisburn Distillery)	1
Chapman, A. 2008 (Sheffield U, Oxford U)	7
Charles, D. 2017 (Fleetwood T)	3
Charles, P. J. 2024 (Sheffield Wed)	**4**
Charles, S. E. 2022 (Manchester C)	3
Clarke, J. 2024 (Celtic)	1
Clarke, L. 2003 (Peterborough U)	4
Clarke, R. 2006 (Newry C)	7
Clarke, R. D. J. 1999 (Portadown)	7
Clingan, S. G. 2003 (Wolverhampton W, Nottingham F)	11
Close, B. 2002 (Middlesbrough)	10
Clucas, M. S. 2011 (Preston NE, Bristol R)	11
Clyde, M. G. 2002 (Wolverhampton W)	5
Colligan, L. 2009 (Ballymena U)	1
Conlan, L. 2013 (Burnley, Morecambe)	11
Conn-Clarke, C. S. M. 2021 (Fleetwood T)	6
Connell, T. E. 1978 (Coleraine)	1
Cooper, J. 2015 (Glenavon)	5
Coote, A. 1998 (Norwich C)	12
Convery, J. 2000 (Celtic)	4
Cousin-Dawson, F. 2021 (Bradford C)	7
Dallas, S. 2012 (Crusaders, Brentford)	2
Davey, H. 2010 (UCD)	3
Davis, S. 2004 (Aston Villa)	3
Daws, M. 2022 (Bournemouth)	1
Devenny, J. 2024 (Crystal Palace)	**8**

Devine, D. 1994 (Omagh T) | 1
Devine, D. G. 2011 (Preston NE) | 2
Devine, J. 1990 (Glentoran) | 1
Devlin, C. 2011 (Manchester U, unattached, Cliftonville) | 11
Devlin, T. 2022 (Dungannon Swifts, Portsmouth) | **14**
Dickson, H. 2002 (Wigan Ath) | 1
Doherty, A. P. 2025 (Blackburn R) | **2**
Doherty, B. 2018 (Derry C) | 4
Doherty, J. E. 2014 (Watford, Leyton O, Crawley T) | 6
Doherty, M. 2007 (Hearts) | 2
Dolan, J. 2000 (Millwall) | 6
Donaghy, M. M. 1978 (Larne) | 1
Donnelly, A. 2021 (Larne) | 5
Donnelly, A. M. 2021 (Nottingham F) | **15**
Donnelly, L. F. P. 2012 (Fulham, Hartlepool U, Motherwell) | 23
Donnelly, M. 2007 (Sheffield U, Crusaders) | 5
Donnelly, R. 2013 (Swansea C) | 1
Dowie, I. 1990 (Luton T) | 1
Drummond, W. 2011 (Rangers) | 2
Dudgeon, J. P. 2010 (Manchester U) | 4
Duff, S. 2003 (Cheltenham T) | 1
Duffy, M. 2014 (Derry C, Celtic) | 9
Duffy, S. P. M. 2010 (Everton) | 3
Dummigan, C. 2014 (Burnley, Oldham Ath) | 18
Dunne, D. 2019 (Cliftonville) | 1
Dunwoody, J. 2017 (Stoke C, Derry C, Helsinki IFK) | 16

Elliott, S. 1999 (Glentoran) | 1
Ervin, J. 2005 (Linfield) | 2
Evans, C. J. 2009 (Manchester U) | 10
Evans, J. 2006 (Manchester U) | 3

Falls, C. N. 2024 (Huddersfield T) | **3**
Farquhar, C. 2024 (Crystal Palace) | 1
Feeney, L. 1998 (Linfield, Rangers) | 8
Feeney, W. 2002 (Bournemouth) | 8
Ferguson, M. 2000 (Glentoran) | 2
Ferguson, S. 2009 (Newcastle U) | 11
Ferris, C. 2020 (Portadown) | 1
Finlayson, D. 2019 (Rangers) | 3
Fitzgerald, D. 1998 (Rangers) | 4
Flanagan, T. M. 2012 (Milton Keynes D) | 1
Flynn, J. J. 2009 (Blackburn R, Ross Co) | 11
Fogarty, T. P. 2024 (Birmingham C) | **12**
Forbes, M. 2024 (West Ham U) | **8**
Fordyce, D. T. 2007 (Portsmouth, Glentoran) | 12
Friars, E. C. 2005 (Notts Co) | 7
Friars, S. M. 1998 (Liverpool, Ipswich T) | 21

Galbraith, E. S. W. 2019 (Manchester U) | 20
Gallagher, C. 2019 (Glentoran) | 5
Garrett, R. 2007 (Stoke C, Linfield) | 14
Gartside, N. J. 2020 (Derry C) | 2
Gault, M. 2005 (Linfield) | 2
Gibb, S. 2009 (Falkirk, Drogheda U) | 2
Gilfillan, B. J. 2005 (Gretna, Peterhead) | 9
Gillespie, K. R. 1994 (Manchester U) | 1
Glendinning, M. 1994 (Bangor) | 1
Glendinning, R. 2012 (Linfield) | 3
Glenfield, S. C. 2025 (Waterford) | **1**
Glynn, M. 2024 (Larne) | 3
Gordon, S. M. 2017 (Motherwell, Partick Thistle) | 9
Gorman, D. A. 2015 (Stevenage, Leyton Orient) | 13
Gorman, R. J. 2012 (Wolverhampton W, Leyton Orient) | 4
Graham, G. L. 1999 (Crystal Palace) | 5
Graham, R. S. 1999 (QPR) | 15
Graham, S. 2020 (Blackpool) | 2
Gray, J. P. 2012 (Accrington S) | 11
Gray, P. 1990 (Luton T) | 2
Griffin, D. J. 1998 (St Johnstone) | 10
Grigg, W. D. 2011 (Walsall) | 10

Hall, B. 2018 (Notts Co) | 3
Hamilton, G. 2000 (Blackburn R, Portadown) | 12
Hamilton, W. R. 1978 (Linfield) | 1
Hanley, N. 2011 (Linfield) | 1
Harkin, M. P. 2000 (Wycombe W) | 9
Harney, J. J. 2014 (West Ham U) | 1
Harvey, J. 1978 (Arsenal) | 1
Hawe, S. 2001 (Blackburn R) | 2
Hayes, T. 1978 (Luton T) | 1
Hazard, C. 2019 (Celtic) | 12
Hazley, M. 2007 (Stoke C) | 3

Healy, D. J. 1999 (Manchester U) | 8
Hegarty, C. 2011 (Rangers) | 7
Herron, C. J. 2003 (QPR) | 2
Higgins, R. 2006 (Derry C) | 1
Hodson, L. J. S. 2010 (Watford) | 10
Holden, R. 2019 (Bristol C) | 2
Holmes, S. 2000 (Manchester C, Wrexham) | 13
Howland, D. 2007 (Birmingham C) | 4
Hughes, J. 2006 (Lincoln C) | 7
Hughes, L. 2020 (Celtic, Liverpool) | 6
Hughes, M. A. 2003 (Tottenham H, Oldham Ath) | 12
Hughes, M. E. 1990 (Manchester C) | 1
Hume, T. 2021 (Linfield, Sunderland) | 11
Hunter, M. 2002 (Glentoran) | 1

Ingham, M. G. 2001 (Sunderland) | 4
Inwood, S. L. 2025 (Bolton W) | **1**

Jarvis, D. 2010 (Aberdeen) | 2
Johns, C. 2014 (Southampton) | 1
Johnson, D. M. 1998 (Blackburn R) | 11
Johnson, R. A. 2015 (Stevenage) | 13
Johnston, B. 1978 (Cliftonville) | 1
Johnston, C. R. 2021 (Fleetwood T) | **17**
Julian, A. A. 2005 (Brentford) | 1

Kane, A. M. 2008 (Blackburn R) | 5
Kane, M. 2012 (Glentoran) | 1
Kearney, S. 2025 (Cliftonville) | **4**
Kee, B. R. 2010 (Leicester C, Torquay U, Burton Alb) | 10
Kee, P. V. 1990 (Oxford U) | 1
Kelly, D. 2000 (Derry C) | 11
Kelly, J. 2019 (Maidenhead U) | 2
Kelly, N. 1990 (Oldham Ath) | 1
Kelly, P. 2024 (West Ham U) | **13**
Kennedy, B. J. 2017 (Stevenage) | 8
Kennedy, M. C. P. 2015 (Charlton Ath) | 7
Kerr, N. 2019 (Glentoran, Portadown) | 6
Kirk, A. R. 1999 (Hearts) | 9
Kirk, M. 2025 (St Johnstone) | **6**
Knowles, J. 2012 (Blackburn R) | 2

Lafferty, D. 2009 (Celtic) | 6
Lafferty, K. 2006 (Burnley) | 2
Lane, P. J. 2022 (Fleetwood T) | 6
Larkin, R. 2021 (Linfield) | 2
Lavery, C. 2011 (Ipswich T, Sheffield Wed) | 7
Lavery, S. 2017 (Everton, Linfield) | 13
Lawrie, J. 2009 (Port Vale, AFC Telford U) | 9
Lennon, N. F. 1990 (Manchester C, Crewe Alex) | 2
Lester, C. 2013 (Bolton W) | 1
Lewis, J. 2017 (Norwich C) | 1
Lindsay, J. C. S. 2024 (Derby Co) | 2
Lindsay, K. 2006 (Larne) | 1
Little, A. 2009 (Rangers) | 6
Lowry, P. 2009 (Institute, Linfield) | 6
Lund, M. 2011 (Stoke C) | 6
Lusty, M. 2023 (Larne) | **3**
Lyttle, G. 1998 (Celtic, Peterborough U) | 8

MacKinnon, L. 2023 (Rangers) | 3
Magee, B. 2024 (Loughgall) | **3**
Magee, J. 1994 (Bangor) | 1
Magee, J. 2009 (Lisburn Distillery) | 1
Magennis, J. B. D. 2010 (Cardiff C, Aberdeen) | 16
Magilton, J. 1990 (Liverpool) | 1
Magnay, C. 2010 (Chelsea) | 1
Maloney, L. 2015 (Middlesbrough) | 6
Marron, C. 2020 (Glenavon) | 9
Marshall, C. 2024 (West Ham U) | 2
Marshall, R. 2017 (Glenavon) | 1
Matthews, N. P. 1990 (Blackpool) | 1
McAlinden, L. J. 2012 (Wolverhampton W) | 3
McAllister, M. 2007 (Dungannon Swifts) | 4
McArdle, R. A. 2006 (Sheffield Wed, Rochdale) | 19
McAreavey, P. 2000 (Swindon T) | 7
McBride, J. 1994 (Glentoran) | 1
McCaffrey, D. 2006 (Hibernian) | 8
McCallion, E. 1998 (Coleraine) | 1
McAlmont, A. J. 2019 (Leeds U) | 18
McCann, A. 2020 (St Johnstone) | 6
McCann, B. 2025 (Barnsley) | **2**
McCann, C. L. 2022 (Rangers) | 7
McCann, G. S. 2000 (West Ham U) | 11
McCann, L. 2020 (Dunfermline Ath) | 5
McCann, P. 2003 (Portadown) | 1

McCann, R. 2002 (Rangers, Linfield)	2
McCartan, S. V. 2013 (Accrington S)	9
McCartney, G. 2001 (Sunderland)	5
McCashin, S. 2011 (Jerez Industrial, unattached)	2
McCausland, R. 2022 (Rangers)	6
McChrystal, M. 2005 (Derry C)	9
McClean, J. 2010 (Derry C)	3
McClean, K. 2019 (St Johnstone, Linfield)	7
McClelland, K. 2022 (Rangers)	2
McClelland, S. 2022 (Chelsea, St Johnstone)	13
McClure, M. 2012 (Wycombe W)	1
McConville, R. 2024 (Brighton & HA)	**5**
McCourt, P. J. 2002 (Rochdale, Derry C)	8
McCoy, R. K. 1990 (Coleraine)	1
McCreery, D. 1978 (Manchester U)	1
McCullough, D. 2023 (Burnley)	1
McCullough, L. 2013 (Doncaster R)	8
McDaid, R. 2015 (Leeds U)	5
McDermott, C. 2017 (Derry C)	4
McDonagh, J. D. C. 2015 (Sheffield U, Derry C)	9
McDonnell, J. C. 2024 (Nottingham F)	**7**
McEleney, S. 2012 (Derry C)	2
McElroy, P. 2013 (Hull C)	1
McEvilly, L. R. 2003 (Rochdale)	9
McFlynn, T. M. 2000 (QPR, Woking, Margate)	19
McGee, E. 2024 (Linfield)	2
McGeehan, C. 2013 (Norwich C)	3
McGibbon, P. C. G. 1994 (Manchester U)	1
McGivern, R. 2010 (Manchester C)	6
McGlinchey, B. 1998 (Manchester C, Port Vale, Gillingham)	14
McGonigle, J. 2017 (Coleraine)	4
McGovern, J. 2022 (Newry C)	8
McGovern, M. 2005 (Celtic)	10
McGowan, M. V. 2006 (Clyde)	2
McGuckin, C. R. 2022 (Rotherham U)	9
McGurk, A. 2010 (Aston Villa)	1
McIlroy, T. 1994 (Linfield)	1
McKay, W. 2009 (Leicester C, Northampton T)	7
McKee, C. 2022 (Linfield)	10
McKenna, K. 2007 (Tottenham H)	6
McKeown, R. 2012 (Kilmarnock)	12
McKiernan, J. J. 2021 (Watford, Morecambe, Lincoln C)	**11**
McKnight, D. 2015 (Shrewsbury T, Stalybridge Celtic)	5
McKnight, P. 1998 (Rangers)	3
McLaughlin, C. G. 2010 (Preston NE, Fleetwood T)	7
McLaughlin, P. 2010 (Newcastle U, York C)	10
McLaughlin, R. 2012 (Liverpool, Oldham Ath)	6
McLean, B. S. 2006 (Rangers)	1
McLean, J. 2009 (Derry C)	4
McLellan, M. 2012 (Preston NE)	1
McMahon, G. J. 2002 (Tottenham H)	1
McMenamin, L. A. 2009 (Sheffield Wed)	4
McMullan, S. D. S. 2024 (Fleetwood T)	**8**
McNair, P. J. C. 2014 (Manchester U)	2
McNally, P. 2013 (Celtic)	1
McQuilken, J. 2009 (Tescoma Zlin)	1
McQuoid, J. J. B. 2009 (Bournemouth)	8
McStravick, L. 2025 (Airdrieonians)	**1**
McVeigh, A. 2002 (Ayr U)	1
McVeigh, P. M. 1998 (Tottenham H)	11
McVey, K. 2006 (Coleraine)	8
Mee, D. 2021 (Manchester U)	5
Meenan, D. 2007 (Finn Harps, Monaghan U)	3
Melaugh, G. M. 2002 (Aston Villa, Glentoran)	11
Millar, K. S. 2011 (Oldham Ath, Linfield)	11
Millar, W. P. 1990 (Port Vale)	1
Miskelly, D. T. 2000 (Oldham Ath)	10
Mitchell, A. 2012 (Rangers)	3
Mitchell, C. 2017 (Burnley)	10
Moreland, V. 1978 (Glentoran)	1
Morgan, D. 2012 (Nottingham F)	4
Morgan, M. P. T. 1999 (Preston NE)	1
Morris, E. J. 2002 (WBA, Glentoran)	8
Morrison, O. 2001 (Sheffield Wed, Sheffield U)	7
Morrow, A. 2001 (Northampton T)	1
Morrow, S. 2005 (Hibernian)	4
Mulgrew, J. 2007 (Linfield)	10
Mulryne, P. P. 1999 (Manchester U, Norwich C)	5
Munn, M. F. 2025 (Rangers)	**2**
Murray, W. 1978 (Linfield)	1
Murtagh, C. 2005 (Hearts)	1
Nicholl, J. M. 1978 (Manchester U)	1
Nixon, C. 2000 (Glentoran)	1

Nolan, L. J. 2014 (Crewe Alex, Southport)	4
Norwood, O. J. 2010 (Manchester U)	11
O'Connor, M. J. 2008 (Crewe Alex)	3
O'Hara, G. 1994 (Leeds U)	1
O'Kane, E. 2009 (Everton, Torquay U)	4
O'Mahony, J. 2020 (Glenavon)	1
O'Neill, J. P. 1978 (Leicester C)	1
O'Neill, M. A. M. 1994 (Hibernian)	1
O'Neill, P. 2020 (Glentoran, Cliftonville)	10
O'Neill, S. 2009 (Ballymena U)	4
Orr, M. 2025 (Linfield)	**2**
Oudnie-Morgan, R. M. 2025 (Ipswich T)	**3**
Owens, C. 2018 (QPR)	2
Palmer, C. 2019 (Rangers, Linfield)	10
Parkhouse, D. 2017 (Sheffield U)	16
Paterson, M. A. 2007 (Stoke C)	2
Patterson, D. J. 1994 (Crystal Palace)	1
Paul, C. D. 2017 (QPR)	3
Peacock-Farrell, B. 2018 (Leeds U)	1
Price, I. J. 2022 (Everton)	3
Quigley, C. 2017 (Dundee)	2
Quinn, S. J. 1994 (Blackpool)	1
Ramsey, C. 2011 (Portadown)	3
Ramsey, K. 2006 (Institute)	1
Reid, J. T. 2013 (Exeter C)	2
Robinson, D. R. R. 2024 (Derby Co)	**9**
Robinson, H. D. 2020 (Motherwell)	1
Robinson, S. 1994 (Tottenham H)	1
Rooney, L. J. 2017 (Plymouth Arg)	1
Roy, A. 2019 (Derry C)	2
Russell, J. 2024 (Glentoran)	**2**
Scott, A. 2021 (Larne)	1
Scott, J. 2020 (Wolverhampton W)	14
Scullion, D. 2006 (Dungannon Swifts)	8
Sendles-White J. 2013 (QPR, Hamilton A)	12
Sharpe, R. 2013 (Derby Co, Notts Co)	6
Shiels, D. 2005 (Hibernian)	6
Shields, S. P. 2013 (Dagenham & Red)	2
Shroot, R. 2009 (Harrow B, Birmingham C)	4
Simms, G. 2001 (Hartlepool U)	14
Singleton, J. 2015 (Glenavon)	2
Skates, G. 2000 (Blackburn R)	4
Sloan, D. 2024 (Larne)	**2**
Sloan, T. 1978 (Ballymena U)	1
Smylie, D. 2006 (Newcastle U, Livingston)	6
Smyth, O. 2021 (Dunganon Swifts, Oxford U)	9
Smyth, P. 2017 (Linfield, QPR)	12
Stewart, J. 2015 (Swindon T)	2
Stewart, S. 2009 (Aberdeen)	1
Stewart, S. 2021 (Norwich C, Cliftonville)	**14**
Stewart, T. 2006 (Wolverhampton W, Linfield)	19
Sykes, M. 2017 (Glenavon)	10
Taylor, D. 2021 (Nottingham F)	**15**
Taylor, J. 2007 (Hearts, Glentoran)	10
Taylor, M. S. 1998 (Fuham)	1
Teggart, N. 2005 (Sunderland)	2
Tempest, G. 2013 (Notts Co)	6
Thompson, A. L. 2011 (Watford)	11
Thompson, J. 2017 (Rangers, Blackpool)	13
Thompson, L. 2020 (Blackburn R)	6
Thompson, P. 2006 (Linfield)	4
Toal, E. 2019 (Derry C)	13
Toner, C. 2000 (Tottenham H, Leyton Orient)	17
Tuffey, J. 2007 (Partick Thistle)	13
Turley, F. 2025 (Celtic)	**2**
Turner, C. 2007 (Sligo R, Bohemians)	12
Waide, R. 2021 (Ballymena U)	7
Ward, J. J. 2006 (Aston Villa, Chesterfield)	7
Ward, M. 2006 (Dungannon Swifts)	1
Ward, S. 2005 (Glentoran)	10
Waterman, D. G. 1998 (Portsmouth)	14
Waterworth, A. 2008 (Lisburn Distillery, Hamilton A)	7
Webb, S. M. 2004 (Ross Co, St Johnstone, Ross Co)	6
Webber, O. H. 2021 (Crystal Palace, Portsmouth)	4
Weir, R. J. 2009 (Sunderland)	8
Wells, D. P. 1999 (Barry T)	1
Whitley, J. 1998 (Manchester C)	17
Whyte, G. 2015 (Crusaders)	7

SCOTLAND

Doak, B. G. 2023 (Liverpool) 7
Docherty, G. 2017 (Hamilton A) 4
Dodds, D. 1978 (Dundee U) 1
Dods, D. 1997 (Hibernian) 5
Doig, C. R. 2000 (Nottingham F) 13
Doig, J. T. 2022 (Hibernian, Verona, Sassuolo) **12**
Donald, G. S. 1992 (Hibernian) 3
Donnelly, S. 1994 (Celtic) 11
Donovan, C. 2025 (Celtic) **2**
Doohan, R. 2018 (Celtic) 13
Dorrans, G. 2007 (Livingston) 6
Dow, A. 1993 (Dundee, Chelsea) 3
Dowie, A. J. 2003 (Rangers, Partick Thistle) 14
Duff, J. 2009 (Inverness CT) 1
Duff, S. 2003 (Dundee U) 9
Duffie, K. 2011 (Falkirk) 6
Duffy, D. A. 2005 (Falkirk, Hull C) 8
Duffy, J. 1987 (Dundee) 1
Duncan, R. A. 2023 (Aberdeen) 5
Durie, G. S. 1987 (Chelsea) 4
Durrant, I. 1987 (Rangers) 4
Doyle, J. 1981 (Partick Thistle) 2

Easton, B. 2009 (Hamilton A) 3
Easton, C. 1997 (Dundee U) 21
Edwards, M. 2012 (Rochdale) 1
Elliot, B. 1998 (Celtic) 2
Elliot, C. 2006 (Hearts) 9
Erhahon, E. 2021 (St Mirren) 2
Esson, R. 2000 (Aberdeen) 7

Fagan, S. M. 2005 (Motherwell) 1
Ferguson, B. 1997 (Rangers) 12
Ferguson, D. 1987 (Rangers) 5
Ferguson, D. 1992 (Dundee U) 7
Ferguson, D. 1992 (Manchester U) 5
Ferguson, I. 1983 (Dundee) 4
Ferguson, I. 1987 (Clyde, St Mirren, Rangers) 6
Ferguson, L. 2019 (Aberdeen) 11
Ferguson, R. 1977 (Hamilton A) 1
Feruz, I. 2012 (Chelsea) 4
Findlay, S. 2012 (Celtic) 13
Findlay, W. 1991 (Hibernian) 5
Fiorini, L. P. 2021 (Manchester C, Stockport Co) **13**
Fitzpatrick, A. 1977 (St Mirren) 5
Fitzpatrick, M. 2007 (Motherwell) 4
Flannigan, C. 1993 (Clydebank) 1
Fleck, J. 2009 (Rangers) 5
Fleck, R. 1987 (Rangers, Norwich C) 6
Fleming, J. 2008 (Gretna) 1
Fletcher, D. B. 2003 (Manchester U) 2
Fletcher, S. 2007 (Hibernian) 7
Forrest, A. 2017 (Ayr U) 1
Forrest, J. 2011 (Celtic) 4
Forrester, A. 2025 (Hearts) **2**
Foster, R. M. 2005 (Aberdeen) 5
Fotheringham, K. C. (Dundee U) 1
Fotheringham, M. M. 2004 (Dundee) 3
Fowler, J. 2002 (Kilmarnock) 5
Foy, R. A. 2004 (Liverpool) 3
Fraser, M. 2012 (Celtic) 5
Fraser, R. 2013 (Aberdeen, Bournemouth) 10
Fraser, R. 2023 (Rangers) 2
Fraser, S. T. 2000 (Luton T) 4
Freedman, D. A. 1995 (Barnet, Crystal Palace) 8
Freeman, K. E. 2022 (Dundee U) 2
Fridge, L. 1989 (St Mirren) 2
Fullarton, J. 1993 (St Mirren) 17
Fulton, J. 2014 (Swansea C) 2
Fulton, R. 2017 (Liverpool, Hamilton A) 11
Fulton, M. 1980 (St Mirren) 5
Fulton, S. 1991 (Celtic) 7
Fyvie, F. 2012 (Wigan Ath) 8

Gallacher, K. W. 1987 (Dundee U) 7
Gallacher, P. 1999 (Dundee U) 7
Gallacher, S. 2009 (Rangers) 2
Gallagher, P. 2003 (Blackburn R) 11
Galloway, M. 1989 (Hearts, Celtic) 2
Gardiner, J. 1993 (Hibernian) 1
Gauld, R. 2013 (Dundee U, Sporting Lisbon) 11
Geddes, R. 1982 (Dundee) 5
Gemmill, S. 1992 (Nottingham F) 4
Germaine, G. 1997 (WBA) 1
Gilles, R. 1997 (St Mirren) 7

Gillespie, G. T. 1979 (Coventry C) 8
Gilmour, B. C. 2019 (Chelsea) 13
Glass, S. 1995 (Aberdeen) 11
Glover, L. 1988 (Nottingham F) 3
Goodwillie, D. 2009 (Dundee U) 9
Goram, A. L. 1987 (Oldham Ath) 1
Gordon, C. S. 2003 (Hearts) 5
Gough, C. R. 1983 (Dundee U) 5
Graham, D. 1998 (Rangers) 8
Graham, L. 2025 (Dundee) **1**
Graham, R. J. 2022 (Dundee U) 3
Grant, P. 1985 (Celtic) 10
Gray, D. P. 2009 (Manchester U) 2
Gray, S. 1987 (Aberdeen) 1
Gray S. 1995 (Celtic) 7
Griffiths, L. 2010 (Dundee, Wolverhampton W) 11
Grimmer, J. 2014 (Fulham) 1
Gunn, B. 1984 (Aberdeen) 9

Hackney, H. R. 2023 (Middlesbrough) 2
Hagen, D. 1992 (Rangers) 8
Hamill, J. 2008 (Kilmarnock) 11
Hamilton, B. 1989 (St Mirren) 4
Hamilton, C. 2018 (Hearts) 3
Hamilton, J. 1995 (Dundee, Hearts) 14
Hamilton, J. 2014 (Hearts) 8
Hammell, S. 2001 (Motherwell) 11
Handling, D. 2014 (Hibernian) 3
Handyside, P. 1993 (Grimsby T) 7
Hanley, G. 2011 (Blackburn R) 1
Hanlon, P. 2009 (Hibernian) 23
Hannah, D. 1993 (Dundee U) 16
Hardie, R. 2017 (Rangers) 8
Harper, C. 2021 (Inverness CT) 1
Harper, K. 1995 (Hibernian) 7
Hartford, R. A. 1977 (Manchester C) 1
Hartley, P. J. 1997 (Millwall) 1
Harvie, D. W. 2018 (Aberdeen, Ayr U) 15
Hastie, J. 2019 (Motherwell) 1
Hegarty, P. 1987 (Dundee U) 1
Henderson, E. 2020 (Celtic) 6
Henderson, J. 2022 (St Mirren) 2
Henderson, L. 2015 (Celtic) 9
Hendrie, S. 2014 (West Ham U) 3
Hendry, J. 1992 (Tottenham H) 1
Henly, J. 2014 (Reading) 1
Herron, J. 2012 (Celtic) 2
Hetherston, B. 1997 (St Mirren) 1
Hewitt, J. 1982 (Aberdeen) 6
High, S. J. 2022 (Huddersfield T) 7
Hogarth, J. 2023 (Rangers) 2
Hogg, G. 1984 (Manchester U) 4
Holsgrove, J. 2019 (Reading) 5
Holt, J. 2012 (Hearts) 7
Hood, G. 1993 (Ayr U) 3
Horn, R. 1997 (Hearts) 6
Hornby, F. D. I. 2018 (Everton, Reims) 18
House, B. 2019 (Reading) 1
Howie, S. 1993 (Cowdenbeath) 5
Hughes, R. D. 1999 (Bournemouth) 9
Hughes, S. 2002 (Rangers) 12
Hunter, G. 1987 (Hibernian) 3
Hunter, P. 1989 (East Fife) 3
Hutton, A. 2004 (Rangers) 7
Hutton, K. 2011 (Rangers) 1
Hyam, D. J. 2014 (Reading) 5

Iacovitti, A. 2017 (Nottingham F) 4
Inman, B. 2011 (Newcastle U) 2
Irving, A. 2021 (Hearts) 1
Irvine, G. 2006 (Celtic) 2

Jack, R. 2012 (Aberdeen) 19
James, K. F. 1997 (Falkirk) 1
Jardine, I. 1979 (Kilmarnock) 1
Jess, E. 1990 (Aberdeen) 14
Johnson, G. I. 1992 (Dundee U) 6
Johnson, M. 2025 (Hibernian) **1**
Johnston, A. 1994 (Hearts) 1
Johnston, F. 1993 (Falkirk) 1
Johnston, G. 2019 (Liverpool, Feyenoord) 10
Johnston, M. A. 2018 (Celtic) 7
Johnston, M. 1984 (Partick Thistle, Watford) 3
Johnston, M. 2023 (Motherwell, Sturm Graz) **10**
Jones, J. C. 2017 (Crewe Alex) 4

Jordan, A. J. 2000 (Bristol C)	3
Joseph, K. A. 2021 (Wigan Ath)	1
Jules, Z. K. 2017 (Reading)	3
Jupp, D. A. 1995 (Fulham)	9
Kelly, D. 2025 (Millwall)	**5**
Kelly, L. A. 2017 (Reading)	11
Kelly, S. 2014 (St Mirren)	1
Kelly, S. 2020 (Rangers)	1
Kennedy, J. 2003 (Celtic)	15
Kennedy, K. A. 2022 (Rangers)	1
Kennedy, M. 2012 (Kilmarnock)	1
Kenneth, G. 2008 (Dundee U)	8
Kerr, B. 2003 (Newcastle U)	14
Kerr, F. 2012 (Birmingham C)	3
Kerr, J. 2018 (St Johnstone)	6
Kerr, M. 2001 (Kilmarnock)	1
Kerr, S. 1993 (Celtic)	10
Kettings, C. D. 2012 (Blackpool)	3
King, A. 2014 (Swansea C)	1
King, C. M. 2014 (Norwich C)	1
King, L. T. 2022 (Rangers)	**12**
King, W. 2015 (Hearts)	8
Kingsley, S. 2015 (Swansea C)	6
Kinnear, B. 2021 (Rangers)	2
Kinniburgh, W. D. 2004 (Motherwell)	3
Kirkwood, D. 1990 (Hearts)	1
Kyle, K. 2001 (Sunderland)	12
Lambert, P. 1991 (St Mirren)	11
Langfield, J. 2000 (Dundee)	2
Lappin, S. 2004 (St Mirren)	10
Lauchlan, J. 1998 (Kilmarnock)	11
Lavety, B. 1993 (St Mirren)	9
Lavin, G. 1993 (Watford)	7
Lawrence, E. 2025 (Manchester C)	**1**
Lawson, P. 2004 (Celtic)	10
Leighton, J. 1982 (Aberdeen)	1
Lennon, S. 2008 (Rangers)	6
Leonard, M. H. 2022 (Brighton & HA)	7
Levein, C. 1985 (Hearts)	2
Leven, P. 2005 (Kilmarnock)	2
Liddell, A. M. 1994 (Barnsley)	12
Lindsey, J. 1979 (Motherwell)	1
Locke, G. 1994 (Hearts)	10
Love, D. 2015 (Manchester U)	5
Love, G. 1995 (Hibernian)	1
Lowry, A. 2023 (Rangers)	2
Loy, R. 2009 (Dunfermline Ath, Rangers)	5
Lynch, S. 2003 (Celtic, Preston NE)	13
MacGregor, R. 2021 (Inverness CT)	1
Mackay, D. 2021 (Inverness CT, Hibernian)	2
Mackay-Steven, G. 2012 (Dundee U)	3
Mackie, S. 2019 (Hibernian)	1
Magennis, K. 2019 (St Mirren)	5
Maguire, B. 2019 (Motherwell)	10
Maguire, C. 2009 (Aberdeen)	12
Mahady, R. 2025 (Leeds U)	**1**
Main, A. 1988 (Dundee U)	3
Mair, A. 2021 (Norwich C)	2
Malcolm, R. 2001 (Rangers)	1
Mallan, S. 2017 (St Mirren, Barnsley, St Mirren)	9
Maloney, S. 2002 (Celtic)	21
Malpas, M. 1983 (Dundee U)	8
Marr, B. 2011 (Ross Co)	1
Marshall, D. J. 2004 (Celtic)	10
Marshall, S. R. 1995 (Arsenal)	5
Martin, A. 2009 (Leeds U, Ayr U)	12
Mason, G. R. 1999 (Manchester C, Dunfermline Ath)	2
Mathieson, D. 1997 (Queen of the South)	3
May, E. 1989 (Hibernian)	4
May, S. 2013 (St Johnstone, Sheffield Wed)	8
Mayo, L. 2021 (Rangers)	12
McAllister, G. 1990 (Leicester C)	1
McAllister, K. 2019 (Derby Co, St Mirren)	2
McAllister, R. 2008 (Inverness CT)	2
McAlpine, H. 1983 (Dundee U)	5
McAnespie, K. 1998 (St Johnstone)	4
McArthur, C. W. 2025 (Newcastle U)	**2**
McArthur, J. 2008 (Hamilton A)	1
McAuley, S. 1993 (St Johnstone)	1
McAvennie, F. 1982 (St Mirren)	5
McAvoy, C. 2023 (Fulham)	1
McBride, J. 1981 (Everton)	1

McBride, J. P. 1998 (Celtic)	2
McBurnie, O. 2015 (Swansea C)	12
McCabe, R. 2012 (Rangers, Sheffield Wed)	3
McCall, A. S. M. 1988 (Bradford C, Everton)	2
McCann, K. 2008 (Hibernian)	4
McCann, N. 1994 (Dundee)	9
McCart, J. 2017 (Celtic)	1
McClair, B. 1984 (Celtic)	8
McCluskey, G. 1979 (Celtic)	6
McCluskey, S. 1997 (St Johnstone)	14
McCoist, A. 1984 (Rangers)	1
McConnell, I. 1997 (Clyde)	1
McCormack, D. 2008 (Hibernian)	1
McCormack, R. 2006 (Rangers, Motherwell, Cardiff C)	13
McCracken, D. 2002 (Dundee U)	5
McCrorie, Robby 2018 (Rangers)	7
McCrorie, Ross 2017 (Rangers)	20
McCulloch, A. 1981 (Kilmarnock)	1
McCulloch, I. 1982 (Notts Co)	2
McCulloch, L. 1997 (Motherwell)	14
McCunnie, J. 2001 (Dundee U, Ross Co, Dunfermline Ath)	20
MacDonald, A. 2011 (Burnley)	6
MacDonald, C. 2017 (Derby Co)	2
MacDonald, J. 1980 (Rangers)	8
MacDonald, J. 2007 (Hearts)	11
McDonald, C. 1995 (Falkirk)	5
McDonald, K. 2008 (Dundee, Burnley)	14
McEwan, C. 1997 (Clyde, Raith R)	17
McEwan, D. 2003 (Livingston)	2
McFadden, J. 2003 (Motherwell)	7
McFadzean C. 2015 (Sheffield U)	3
McFarlane, D. 1997 (Hamilton A)	3
McFarlane, L. 2025 (Hearts)	**1**
McGarry, S. 1997 (St Mirren)	3
McGarvey, F. P. 1977 (St Mirren, Celtic)	3
McGarvey, S. 1982 (Manchester U)	4
McGeough, D. 2012 (Celtic)	10
McGhee, J. 2013 (Hearts)	20
McGhee, M. 1981 (Aberdeen)	1
McGinn, J. 2014 (St Mirren, Hibernian)	9
McGinn, S. 2009 (St Mirren, Watford)	8
McGinnis, G. 1985 (Dundee U)	1
McGlinchey, M. R. 2007 (Celtic)	1
McGregor, A. 2003 (Rangers)	6
McGregor, C. W. 2013 (Celtic)	5
McGrillen, P. 1994 (Motherwell)	2
McGuire, D. 2002 (Aberdeen)	2
McHattie, K. 2012 (Hearts)	6
McInally, J. 1989 (Dundee U)	1
McInroy, K. 2021 (Celtic)	1
McIntyre, T. P. 2019 (Reading)	3
McKay, B. 2012 (Rangers)	4
McKay, B. 2013 (Hearts)	1
McKean, K. 2011 (St Mirren)	1
McKenna, S. 2018 (Aberdeen)	5
McKenzie, R. 2013 (Kilmarnock)	4
McKenzie, R. 1997 (Hearts)	2
McKimmie, S. 1985 (Aberdeen)	1
McKinlay, T. 1984 (Dundee)	6
McKinlay, W. 1989 (Dundee U)	6
McKinnon, C. 2023 (Rangers)	3
McKinnon, R. 1991 (Dundee U)	6
McLaren, A, 1989 (Hearts)	11
McLaren, A. 1993 (Dundee U)	4
McLaughlin, B. 1995 (Celtic)	1
McLaughlin, J. 1981 (Morton)	10
McLean, E. 2008 (Dundee U, St Johnstone)	2
McLean, S. 2003 (Rangers)	4
McLeish, A. 1978 (Aberdeen)	6
McLean, K. 2012 (St Mirren)	11
McLennon, C. 2020 (Aberdeen)	9
MacLeod, A. 1979 (Hibernian)	3
McLeod, J. 1989 (Dundee U)	2
MacLeod, L. 2012 (Rangers)	8
MacLeod, M. 1979 (Dumbarton, Celtic)	5
McManus, D. J. 2014 (Aberdeen, Fleetwood T)	4
McManus, T. 2001 (Hibernian)	14
McMillan, S. 1997 (Motherwell)	4
McMullan, P. 2017 (Celtic)	1
McNab, N. 1978 (Tottenham H)	1
McNally, M. 1991 (Celtic)	2
McNamara, J. 1994 (Dunfermline Ath, Celtic)	12
McNaughton, K. 2002 (Aberdeen)	1
McNeil, A. 2007 (Hibernian)	1
McNichol, J. 1979 (Brentford)	7

McNiven, D. 1977 (Leeds U) 3
McNiven, S. A. 1996 (Oldham Ath) 1
McPake, J. 2021 (Rangers) 1
McParland, A. 2003 (Celtic) 1
McPhee, S. 2002 (Port Vale) 1
McPherson, B. 2023 (Celtic) 5
McPherson, D. 1984 (Rangers, Hearts) 4
McQuilken, J. 1993 (Celtic) 2
McStay, P. 1983 (Celtic) 5
McWhirter, N. 1991 (St Mirren) 1
Mebude, A. E. A. (Dire) 2023 (Manchester C,
Westerlo, Hamburg) **14**
Mebude, A. P. O. A. (Dapo) 2022 (Watford) 5
Meekison, A. A. 2023 (Dundee U) 2
Meldrum, C. 1996 (Kilmarnock) 6
Mellon, M. J. D. 2024 (Burnley) 3
Melrose, J. 1977 (Partick Thistle) 8
Middleton, G. B. D. 2018 (Rangers) 23
Millar, M, 2009 (Celtic) 1
Miller, C. 1995 (Rangers) 8
Miller, J. 1987 (Aberdeen, Celtic) 7
Miller, K. 2000 (Hibernian, Rangers) 7
Miller, L. L. 2024 (Motherwell) **5**
Miller, W. 1991 (Hibernian) 7
Miller, W. F. 1978 (Aberdeen) 2
Milne, J. 2024 (Aberdeen) **3**
Milne, K. 2000 (Hearts) 1
Milne, R. 1982 (Dundee U) 3
Mitchell, C. 2008 (Falkirk) 7
Mochrie, C. R. 2023 (Dundee U) 2
Money, I. C. 1987 (St Mirren) 3
Montgomery, A. 2022 (Celtic) 4
Montgomery, N. A. 2003 (Sheffield U) 2
Morgan, L. 2017 (Celtic) 9
Morrison, L. 2023 (Bayern Munich) 1
Morrison, S. A. 2004 (Aberdeen, Dunfermline Ath) 12
Muir, L. 1977 (Hibernian) 1
Mulgrew, C. P. 2006 (Celtic, Wolverhampton W,
Aberdeen) 14
Mullen, J. 2023 (Leeds U) **15**
Mulligan, J. 2022 (Dundee) **16**
Murphy J. 2009 (Motherwell) 13
Murray, D. 2025 (Celtic) **4**
Murray, H. 2000 (St Mirren) 3
Murray, I. 2001 (Hibernian) 15
Murray, N. 1993 (Rangers) 16
Murray, R. 1993 (Bournemouth) 1
Murray, S. 2004 (Kilmarnock) 2

Narey, D. 1977 (Dundee U) 4
Naismith, J. 2014 (St Mirren) 1
Naismith, S. J. 2006 (Kilmarnock, Rangers) 15
Naysmith, G. A. 1997 (Hearts) 22
Neilson, L. 2023 (Hearts) **12**
Neilson, R. 2000 (Hearts) 1
Nesbitt, A. 2017 (Celtic) 2
Ness, J, 2011 (Rangers) 2
Nevin, P. 1985 (Chelsea) 5
Newman, J. C. 2023 (Dundee U) 2
Nicholas, C. 1981 (Celtic, Arsenal) 6
Nicholson, B. 1999 (Rangers) 7
Nicholson, S. 2015 (Hearts) 8
Nicol, S. 1981 (Ayr U, Liverpool) 14
Nisbet, S. 1989 (Rangers) 5
Noble, D. J. 2003 (West Ham U) 2
Notman, A. M. 1999 (Manchester U) 10

O'Brien, B. 1999 (Blackburn R, Livingston) 6
O'Connor, G. 2003 (Hibernian) 8
O'Donnell, P. 1992 (Motherwell) 8
O'Donnell, S. 2013 (Partick Thistle) 1
O'Halloran, M. 2012 (Bolton W) 2
O'Hara, M. 2015 (Kilmarnock, Dundee) 2
O'Leary, R. 2008 (Kilmarnock) 2
O'Neil, B. 1992 (Celtic) 7
O'Neil, J. 1991 (Dundee U) 1
O'Neill, M. 1995 (Clyde) 6
One, R. 2025 (Sheffield U) **4**
Orr, N. 1978 (Morton) 7

Palmer, L. J. 2011 (Sheffield Wed) 8
Park, C. 2012 (Middlesbrough) 1
Parker, K. 2001 (St Johnstone) 1
Parlane, D. 1977 (Rangers) 1
Paterson, C. 1981 (Hibernian) 2
Paterson, C. 2012 (Hearts) 12

Paterson, J. 1997 (Dundee U) 9
Patterson, N. K. 2021 (Rangers) 4
Pawlett, P. 2012 (Aberdeen) 7
Payne, P. 1978 (Dundee U) 3
Peacock, L. A. 1997 (Carlisle U) 1
Pearce, A. J. 2008 (Reading) 2
Pearson, S. P. 2003 (Motherwell) 8
Perry, R. 2010 (Rangers, Falkirk, Rangers) 16
Pollock, F. 2025 (Hearts) **1**
Polworth, L. 2016 (Inverness CT) 1
Porteous, R. 2018 (Hibernian) 14
Pressley, S. J. 1993 (Rangers, Coventry C, Dundee U) 26
Provan, D. 1977 (Kilmarnock) 1
Prunty, B. 2004 (Aberdeen) 6

Quinn, P. C. 2004 (Motherwell) 3
Quinn, R. 2006 (Celtic) 9
Quitongo, J. 2017 (Hamilton A) 1

Rae, A. 1991 (Millwall) 8
Rae, G. 1999 (Dundee) 6
Ralston, A. 2018 (Celtic) 5
Ramsay, C. W. 2022 (Liverpool) **6**
Reading, P. J. 2020 (Stevenage) 6
Redford, I. 1981 (Rangers) 6
Reid, B. 1991 (Rangers) 4
Reid, C. 1993 (Hibernian) 3
Reid, J. K. 2023 (Coventry C) 3
Reid, M. 1982 (Celtic) 2
Reid, R. 1977 (St Mirren) 3
Reilly, A. 2004 (Wycombe W) 1
Renicks, S. 1997 (Hamilton A) -1
Reynolds, M. 2007 (Motherwell) 1
Rhodes, J. L. 2011 (Huddersfield T) 8
Rice, B. 1985 (Hibernian) 1
Richardson, L. 1980 (St Mirren) 2
Ridgers, M. 2012 (Hearts) 5
Rice, B. 2025 (Rangers) **2**
Riordan, D. G. 2004 (Hibernian) 5
Ritchie, A. 1980 (Morton) 1
Ritchie, P. S. 1996 (Hearts) 7
Robertson, A. 1991 (Rangers) 1
Robertson, A. 2013 (Dundee U, Hull C) 4
Robertson, C. 1977 (Rangers) 1
Robertson, C. 2012 (Aberdeen) 10
Robertson, D. 2007 (Dundee U) 4
Robertson, D. A. 1987 (Aberdeen) 7
Robertson, F. 2024 (Dundee) 1
Robertson, G. A. 2004 (Nottingham F, Rotherham U) 15
Robertson, H. 1994 (Aberdeen) 2
Robertson, J. 1985 (Hearts) 2
Robertson, L. 1993 (Rangers) 3
Robertson, S. 1998 (St Johnstone) 2
Roddie, A. 1992 (Aberdeen) 5
Ross, G. 2007 (Dunfermline Ath) 1
Ross, N. 2011 (Inverness CT) 2
Ross, T. W. 1977 (Arsenal) 1
Rowson, D. 1997 (Aberdeen) 5
Rudden, Z. A. 2022 (Partick Thistle) 3
Ruddy, J. 2017 (Wolverhampton W) 1
Russell, J. 2011 (Dundee U) 11
Russell, R. 1978 (Rangers) 3

Salton, D. B. 1992 (Luton T) 6
Sammut, R. A. M. 2017 (Chelsea) 3
Samson, C. I. 2004 (Kilmarnock) 6
Saunders, S. 2011 (Motherwell) 2
Scobbie, T. 2008 (Falkirk) 12
Scott, J. R. 2020 (Motherwell, Hull C) 3
Scott, M. 2006 (Livingston) 1
Scott, P. 1994 (St Johnstone) 4
Scougall, S. 2012 (Livingston, Sheffield U) 7
Scrimgour, D. 1997 (St Mirren) 3
Seaton, A. 1998 (Falkirk) 1
Severin, S. D. 2000 (Hearts) 10
Shankland, L. 2015 (Aberdeen) 4
Shannon, R. 1987 (Dundee) 7
Sharp, G. M. 1982 (Everton) 1
Sharp, R. 1990 (Dunfermline Ath) 4
Shaw, O. 2019 (Hibernian) 2
Sheerin, P. 1996 (Southampton) 1
Sheppard, J. 2017 (Reading) 2
Shields, G. 1997 (Rangers) 2
Shinnie, A. 2009 (Dundee, Rangers) 3
Shinnie, G. 2012 (Inverness CT) 2
Simmons, S. 2003 (Hearts) 1

Simpson, N. 1982 (Aberdeen)	11
Sinclair, G. 1977 (Dumbarton)	1
Sinclair, R. 2022 (St Johnstone)	3
Skilling, M. 1993 (Kilmarnock)	2
Slater, C. 2014 (Kilmarnock, Colchester U)	9
Slicker, C. P. 2021 (Manchester C, Ipswich T)	**19**
Smith, B. M. 1992 (Celtic)	5
Smith, C. 2008 (St Mirren)	2
Smith, C. 2015 (Aberdeen)	1
Smith, C. 2022 (Hearts)	9
Smith, D. 2012 (Hearts)	4
Smith, D. 2025 (Ross Co)	**2**
Smith, D. L. 2006 (Motherwell)	2
Smith, G. 1978 (Rangers)	1
Smith, G. 2004 (Rangers)	8
Smith, H. G. 1987 (Hearts)	2
Smith, J. 2023 (Newcastle U)	1
Smith, L. 2017 (Hearts, Ayr U)	12
Smith, L. 2020 (Hamilton A)	1
Smith, L. K. 2023 (Swansea C)	2
Smith, S. 2007 (Rangers)	1
Sneddon, A. 1979 (Celtic)	1
Snodgrass, R. 2008 (Livingston)	2
Soutar, D. 2003 (Dundee)	11
Souttar, J. 2016 (Dundee U, Hearts)	11
Speedie, D. R. 1985 (Chelsea)	1
Spencer, J. 1991 (Rangers)	3
Stanton, P. 1977 (Hibernian)	1
Stanton, S. 2014 (Hibernian)	1
Stark, W. 1985 (Aberdeen)	1
St Clair, H. 2018 (Chelsea)	3
Stephen, R. 1983 (Dundee)	1
Stevens, G. 1977 (Motherwell)	1
Stevenson, L. 2008 (Hibernian)	8
Stewart, C. 2002 (Kilmarnock)	1
Stewart, J. 1978 (Kilmarnock, Middlesbrough)	3
Stewart, M. J. 2000 (Manchester U)	17
Stewart, R. 1979 (Dundee U, West Ham U)	12
Stillie, D. 1995 (Aberdeen)	14
Storie, C. 2017 (Aberdeen)	2
Strachan, G. D. 1998 (Coventry C)	7
Sturrock, P. 1977 (Dundee U)	9
Summers, B. 2023 (Celtic)	5
Sweeney, P. H. 2004 (Millwall)	8
Sweeney, S. 1991 (Clydebank)	7
Tapping, C. 2013 (Hearts)	1
Tarrant, N. K. 1999 (Aston Villa)	5
Taylor, G. J. 2017 (Kilmarnock)	14
Teale, G. 1997 (Clydebank, Ayr U)	6
Telfer, P. N. 1993 (Luton T)	3
Templeton, D. 2011 (Hearts)	2
Thomas, D. 2017 (Motherwell)	6
Thomas, K. 1993 (Hearts)	8
Thompson, S. 1997 (Dundee U)	12
Thomson, C. 2011 (Hearts)	2
Thomson, J. A. 2017 (Celtic)	1
Thomson, K. 2005 (Hibernian)	6
Thomson, M. 2025 (Dundee U)	**2**

Thomson, W. 1977 (Partick Thistle, St Mirren)	10
Tolmie, J. 1980 (Morton)	1
Tortolano, J. 1987 (Hibernian)	2
Toshney, L. 2012 (Celtic)	5
Turnbull, D. 2019 (Motherwell)	4
Turner, I. 2005 (Everton)	6
Tweed, S. 1993 (Hibernian)	3
Urain, E. R. 2021 (Athletic Bilbao)	2
Wales, B. (Kilmarnock)	**3**
Wales, G. 2000 (Hearts)	1
Walker, A. 1988 (Celtic)	1
Walker, J. 2013 (Hearts)	1
Wallace, I. A. 1978 (Coventry C)	1
Wallace, L. 2007 (Hearts)	10
Wallace, M. 2012 (Huddersfield T)	4
Wallace, R. 2004 (Celtic, Sunderland)	4
Walsh, C. 1984 (Nottingham F)	5
Wark, J. 1977 (Ipswich T)	8
Watson, A. 1981 (Aberdeen)	4
Watson, D. S. 2024 (Kilmarnock)	**6**
Watson, K. 1977 (Rangers)	2
Watt, A. 2012 (Celtic)	9
Watt, E. 2018 (Wolverhampton W)	3
Watt, M. 1991 (Aberdeen)	12
Watt. S. M. 2005 (Chelsea)	5
Webster, A. 2003 (Hearts)	2
Welsh, S. 2021 (Celtic)	10
Whiteford, A. 1997 (St Johnstone)	1
Whittaker, S. G. 2005 (Hibernian)	18
Whyte, D. 1987 (Celtic)	9
Wighton, C. R. 2017 (Dundee)	6
Wilkie, L. 2000 (Dundee)	6
Will, J. A. 1992 (Arsenal)	3
Williams, G. 2002 (Nottingham F)	9
Williamson, B. 2021 (Rangers)	6
Williamson, R. 2018 (Dunfermline)	4
Wilson, D. 2011 (Liverpool, Hearts)	13
Wilson, E. 2025 (Motherwell)	**5**
Wilson, I. 2018 (Kilmarnock)	7
Wilson, M. 2004 (Dundee U, Celtic)	19
Wilson, R. 2023 (Aston Villa)	2
Wilson, S. 1999 (Rangers)	7
Wilson, T. 1983 (St Mirren)	1
Wilson, T. 1988 (Nottingham F)	4
Winnie, D. 1988 (St Mirren)	1
Woods, M. 2006 (Sunderland)	2
Wotherspoon, D. 2011 (Hibernian)	16
Wright, K. 2021 (Rangers)	1
Wright, P. 1989 (Aberdeen, QPR)	3
Wright, Stephen 1991 (Aberdeen)	14
Wright, Scott 2018 (Aberdeen)	5
Wright, T. 1987 (Oldham Ath)	1
Wylde, G. 2011 (Rangers)	7
Young, Darren 1997 (Aberdeen)	8
Young, Derek 2000 (Aberdeen)	5

WALES

Abbruzzese, R. 2018 (Cardiff C)	3
Absolom, K. 2019 (Ostersund)	1
Adams, J. A. 2021 (Brentford, Dundalk)	10
Adams, N. W. 2008 (Bury, Leicester C)	5
Agius, C. S. 2025 (Crewe Alex)	**1**
Alfei, D. M. 2010 (Swansea C)	13
Aizlewood, M. 1979 (Luton T)	4
Allen, J. M. 2008 (Swansea C)	13
Andrews, K. B. J. 2025 (Coventry C)	**1**
Anthony, B. 2005 (Cardiff C)	8
Ashford, C. 2024 (Cardiff C)	**8**
Ashworth, Z. 2022 (WBA, Blackpool)	**10**
Astley, R. 2021 (Everton)	7
Babos, A. 2018 (Derby Co)	7
Baddeley, L. M. 1996 (Cardiff C)	2
Baker, A. T. 2019 (Sheffield Wed)	4
Baker, M. 2023 (Stoke C, Newport Co)	**10**
Balcombe, S. 1982 (Leeds U)	1
Bale, G. 2006 (Southampton, Tottenham H)	4
Barden, D. J. 2021 (Norwich C)	2
Barnhouse, D. J. 1995 (Swansea C)	3
Basey, G. W. 2009 (Charlton Ath)	1

Bater, P. T. 1977 (Bristol R)	2
Beach, E. J. 2023 (Chelsea)	**8**
Beck, O. M. 2022 (Liverpool)	14
Beevers, L. J. 2005 (Boston U, Lincoln C)	7
Bellamy, C. D. 1996 (Norwich C)	8
Bender, T. J. 2011 (Colchester U)	4
Benjamin, L. J. 2025 (Wolverhampton W)	**2**
Bevan, O. L. 2023 (Bournemouth)	5
Birchall, A. S. 2003 (Arsenal, Mansfield T)	12
Bird, A. 1993 (Cardiff C)	6
Blackmore, C. 1984 (Manchester U)	3
Blake, D. J. 2007 (Cardiff C)	14
Blake, N. A. 1991 (Cardiff C)	5
Blaney, S. D. 1997 (West Ham U)	3
Bland, J. P. R. 2025 (Barnsley)	**1**
Bloom, J. 2011 (Falkirk)	1
Bodin, B. P. 2010 (Swindon T, Torquay U)	21
Bodin, P. J. 1983 (Cardiff C)	1
Bond, J. H. 2011 (Watford)	1
Bowen, J. P. 1993 (Swansea C)	5
Bowen, M. R. 1983 (Tottenham H)	3
Bowen, S. L. 2021 (Cardiff C)	4
Boyes, M. M. 2021 (Liverpool, Livingston)	11

Boyle, T. 1982 (Crystal Palace)	1
Brace, D. P. 1995 (Wrexham)	6
Bradley, M. S. 2007 (Walsall)	17
Bradshaw, T. 2012 (Shrewsbury T)	8
Briggs, L. 2025 (Leicester C)	**1**
Broadhead, N. P. 2018 (Everton)	17
Brooks, D. R. 2018 (Sheffield U)	3
Brough, M. 2003 (Notts Co)	3
Brown, J. D. 2008 (Cardiff C)	6
Brown, J. R. 2003 (Gillingham)	7
Brown, T. A. F. 2011 (Ipswich T, Rotherham U, Aldershot T)	10
Burns, W. J. 2013 (Bristol C)	18
Burton, R. L. 2018 (Arsenal)	9
Byrne, M. T. 2003 (Bolton W)	1
Cabango, B. 2019 (Swansea C)	5
Calliste, R. T. 2005 (Manchester U, Liverpool)	15
Carpenter, R. E. 2005 (Burnley)	1
Cassidy, J. A. 2011 (Wolverhampton W)	8
Cegielski, W. 1977 (Wrexham)	2
Chamberlain, E. C. 2010 (Leicester C)	9
Chapple, S. R. 1992 (Swansea C)	8
Charles, J. D. 2016 (Huddersfield T, Barnsley)	9
Charles, J. M. 1979 (Swansea C)	2
Christie-Davies, I. 2018 (Chelsea, Liverpool)	4
Church, S. R. 2008 (Reading)	15
Clark, J. 1978 (Manchester U, Derby Co)	2
Clifton, H. L. 2019 (Grimsby T)	6
Coates, J. S. 1996 (Swansea C)	5
Coleman, C. 1990 (Swansea C)	3
Collins, J. M. 2003 (Cardiff C)	7
Collins, L. R. 2021 (Newport Co)	2
Collins, M. J. 2007 (Fulham, Swansea C)	2
Collison, J. D. 2008 (West Ham U)	7
Colwill, J. W. 2024 (Cardiff C)	**7**
Colwill, R. J. 2021 (Cardiff C)	9
Congreve, C. M. 2023 (Swansea C)	**7**
Connolly, J. 2022 (Cardiff C)	1
Cooper, B. J. 2019 (Swansea C)	14
Cooper, O. J. 2020 (Swansea C)	3
Cornell, D. J. 2010 (Swansea C)	4
Cotterill, D. R. G. B. 2005 (Bristol C, Wigan Ath)	11
Cotterill, J. A. 2023 (Swansea C)	**13**
Coyne, D. 1992 (Tranmere R)	7
Coxe, C. T. 2018 (Cardiff C, Solihull Moors)	16
Craig, N. L. 2009 (Everton)	4
Critchell, K. A. R. 2005 (Southampton)	3
Crofts, A. L. 2005 (Gillingham)	10
Crew, C. 2024 (Leeds U)	**4**
Crowe, M. T. T. 2017 (Ipswich T)	1
Crowell, M. T. 2004 (Wrexham)	7
Cullen, L. J. 2018 (Swansea C)	12
Curtis, A. T. 1977 (Swansea C)	1
Dabrowski, S. 2025 (Swansea C)	**1**
Dasilva, C. P. 2018 (Chelsea, Brentford)	3
Davies, A. 1982 (Manchester U)	6
Davies, A. G. 2006 (Cambridge U)	6
Davies, A. R. 2005 (Southampton, Yeovil T)	14
Davies, C. M. 2005 (Oxford U, Verona, Oldham Ath)	9
Davies, D. 1999 (Barry T)	1
Davies, G. M. 1993 (Hereford U, Crystal Palace)	7
Davies, I. C. 1978 (Norwich C)	1
Davies, I. J. 2022 (Cardiff C)	5
Davies, K. E. 2019 (Swansea C)	1
Davies, L. 2005 (Bangor C)	1
Davies, R. J. 2006 (WBA)	4
Davies, S. 1999 (Peterborough U, Tottenham H)	10
Davies, T. A. 2024 (Cardiff C, Newport Co)	**4**
Dawson, C. 2013 (Leeds U)	2
Day, R. 2000 (Manchester C, Mansfield T)	11
Deacy, N. 1977 (PSV Eindhoven)	1
De-Vulgt, L. S. 2002 (Swansea C)	2
Dibble, A. 1983 (Cardiff C)	3
Dibble, C. 2014 (Barnsley)	1
Doble, R. A. 2010 (Southampton)	10
Doughty, M. E. 2012 (QPR)	1
Doyle, S. C. 1979 (Preston NE, Huddersfield T)	2
Duffy, R. M. 2005 (Portsmouth)	7
Dummett, P. 2011 (Newcastle U)	3
Dwyer, P. J. 1979 (Cardiff C)	1
Eardley, N. 2007 (Oldham Ath, Blackpool)	11
Earnshaw, R. 1999 (Cardiff C)	10

Easter, D. J. 2006 (Cardiff C)	1
Ebdon, M. 1990 (Everton)	2
Edwards, C. N. H. 1996 (Swansea C)	7
Edwards, D. A. 2006 (Shrewsbury T, Luton T, Wolverhampton W)	9
Edwards, G. D. R. 2012 (Swansea C)	6
Edwards, R. I. 1977 (Chester)	2
Edwards, R. W. 1991 (Bristol C)	13
Evans, A. 1977 (Bristol R)	1
Evans, C. 2007 (Manchester C, Sheffield U)	13
Evans, J. A. J. 2014 (Fulham, Wrexham)	6
Evans, J. M. 2018 (Swansea C)	13
Evans, K. 1999 (Leeds U, Cardiff C)	4
Evans, K. G. 2019 (Swansea C)	2
Evans, L. 2013 (Wolverhampton W)	13
Evans, O. R. 2018 (Wigan Ath)	3
Evans, P. S. 1996 (Shrewsbury T)	1
Evans, S. J. 2001 (Crystal Palace)	2
Evans, T. 1995 (Cardiff C)	3
Ewing, O. J. 2024 (Leicester C)	2
Farrell, J. 2023 (Granada, Villanovense)	**5**
Fish, N. 2005 (Cardiff C)	2
Fleetwood, S. 2005 (Cardiff C)	5
Flynn, C. P. 2007 (Crewe Alex)	1
Folland, R. W. 2000 (Oxford U)	1
Foster, M. G. 1993 (Tranmere R)	1
Fowler, L. A. 2003 (Coventry C, Huddersfield T)	9
Fox, M. A. 2013 (Charlton Ath)	6
Freeman, K. 2012 (Nottingham F, Derby Co)	15
Freestone, R. 1990 (Chelsea)	1
Gabbidon, D. L. 1999 (WBA, Cardiff C)	17
Gale, D. 1983 (Swansea C)	2
Gall, K. A. 2002 (Bristol R, Yeovil T)	8
Gibson, N. D. 1999 (Tranmere R, Sheffield Wed)	11
Giggs, R. J. 1991 (Manchester U)	1
Gilbert, P. 2005 (Plymouth Arg)	12
Giles, D. C. 1977 (Cardiff C, Swansea C, Crystal Palace)	4
Giles, P. 1982 (Cardiff C)	3
Graham, D. 1991 (Manchester U)	1
Green, R. M. 1998 (Wolverhampton W)	16
Griffith, C. 1990 (Cardiff C)	1
Griffiths, C. 1991 (Shrewsbury T)	1
Grubb, D. 2007 (Bristol C)	1
Gunter, C. 2006 (Cardiff C, Tottenham H)	8
Haldane, L. O. 2007 (Bristol R)	1
Hall, G. D. 1990 (Chelsea)	1
Hammond, B. 2025 (Nottingham F)	**2**
Hammond, O. J. 2022 (Nottingham F)	**13**
Hamson, O. 2025 (Sheffield U)	**2**
Harries, C. W. T. 2018 (Swansea C)	7
Harris, A. A. P. 2025 (Bournemouth)	**3**
Harris, L. B. 2024 (Fulham)	**8**
Harris, M. T. 2018 (Cardiff C)	20
Harrison, E. W. 2013 (Bristol R)	14
Hartson, J. 1994 (Luton T, Arsenal)	9
Haworth, S. O. 1997 (Cardiff C, Coventry C, Wigan Ath)	12
Hedges, R. P. 2014 (Swansea C)	11
Henley, A. 2012 (Blackburn R)	3
Hennessey, W. R. 2006 (Wolverhampton W)	6
Hesketh, O. J. M. 2023 (Wolverhampton W)	1
Hewitt, E. J. 2012 (Macclesfield T, Ipswich T)	10
Hill, T. D. 2024 (Liverpool)	1
Hillier, I. M. 2001 (Tottenham H, Luton T)	5
Hodges, G. 1983 (Wimbledon)	5
Holden, A. 1984 (Chester C)	1
Hollingshead, R. 2024 (WBA)	**2**
Holloway, C. D. 1999 (Exeter C)	2
Hoole, L. A. 2022 (Bristol R, Shrewsbury T)	**12**
Hopkins, J. 1982 (Fulham)	5
Hopkins, S. A. 1999 (Wrexham)	1
Howells, J. 2012 (Luton T)	5
Howley, R. O. 2023 (Coventry C)	1
Huggins, D. S. 1996 (Bristol C)	1
Huggins, N. J. 2019 (Leeds U, Sunderland)	4
Hughes, B. 2024 (Swansea C)	1
Hughes, D. 2005 (Kaiserslautern, Regensburg)	2
Hughes, D. R. 1994 (Southampton)	1
Hughes, I. 1992 (Bury)	11
Hughes, I. T. 2023 (Leicester C)	1
Hughes, L. M. 1983 (Manchester U)	5

Hughes, R. 2022 (Everton) 9
Hughes, R. D. 1996 (Aston Villa, Shrewsbury T) 13
Hughes, W. 1977 (WBA) 3
Huws, E. W. 2012 (Manchester C) 6

Isgrove, L. J. 2013 (Southampton) 6

Jackett, K. 1981 (Watford) 2
Jacobson, J. M. 2006 (Cardiff C, Bristol R) 15
James, D. O. 2017 (Swansea C) 11
James, E. G. M. 2025 (Exeter C) **2**
James, L. R. S. 2006 (Southampton) 10
James, R. M. 1977 (Swansea C) 3
Jarman, L. 1996 (Cardiff C) 10
Jeanne, L. C. 1999 (QPR) 8
Jelleyman, G. A. 1999 (Peterborough U) 1
Jenkins, L. D. 1998 (Swansea C) 9
Jenkins, S. R. 1993 (Swansea C) 2
Jephcott, L. O. 2021 (Plymouth Arg) 12
John, D. C. 2014 (Cardiff C) 9
Johnson, B. P. 2020 (Nottingham F) 4
Jones, C. T. 2007 (Swansea C) 1
Jones, E. 2021 (Stoke C) 7
Jones, E. P. 2000 (Blackpool) 1
Jones, F. 1981 (Wrexham) 1
Jones, G. W. 2014 (Everton) 9
Jones, J. A. 2001 (Swansea C) 3
Jones, L. 1982 (Cardiff C) 3
Jones, M. A. 2004 (Wrexham) 4
Jones, M. G. 1998 (Leeds U) 7
Jones, O. R. 2015 (Swansea C) 1
Jones, P. L. 1992 (Liverpool) 12
Jones, P. S. 2022 (Huddersfield T) 7
Jones, R. 2011 (AFC Wimbledon) 1
Jones, R. A. 1994 (Sheffield Wed) 3
Jones, S. J. 2005 (Swansea C) 1
Jones, V. 1979 (Bristol R) 2

Katsukunya, T. 2025 (Aston Villa) **2**
Kendall, L. M. 2001 (Crystal Palace) 2
Kendall, M. 1978 (Tottenham H) 1
Kenworthy, J. R. 1994 (Tranmere R) 3
King, A. 2008 (Leicester C) 11
King, E. J. 2022 (Cardiff C) **15**
Knott, G. R. 1996 (Tottenham H) 1
Koumas, L. T. 2024 (Liverpool) 2

Law, B. J. 1990 (QPR) 2
Lawless, A. 2006 (Torquay U) 1
Lawlor, D. R. 2025 (Cardiff C) **1**
Lawrence, T. 2013 (Manchester U) 8
Ledley, J. C. 2005 (Cardiff C) 5
Leeson, H. R. 2024 (Bristol C) 1
Lemonheigh-Evans, C. 2019 (Bristol C) 3
Letheran, G. 1977 (Leeds U) 2
Letheran, K. C. 2006 (Swansea C) 1
Levitt, D. J. C. 2020 (Manchester U) 1
Lewis, A. 2018 (Swansea C, Lincoln C) 12
Lewis, D. 1982 (Swansea C) 9
Lewis, J. 1983 (Cardiff C) 1
Lewis, J. C. 2020 (Swansea C) 2
Llewellyn, C. M. 1998 (Norwich C) 14
Lloyd, B. 2025 (Swansea C) **1**
Lockyer, T. A. 2015 (Bristol R) 7
Loveridge, J. 1982 (Swansea C) 3
Low, Joe D. 2023 (Bristol C, Wycombe W) **7**
Low, Josh D. 1999 (Bristol R, Cardiff C) 1
Lowndes, S. R. 1979 (Newport Co, Millwall) 4
Lucas, L. P. 2011 (Swansea C) 19

MacDonald, S. B. 2006 (Swansea C) 25
McCarthy, A. J. 1994 (QPR) 3
McDonald, C. 2006 (Cardiff C) 3
McLaughlin-Miles, T. 2024 (Liverpool) 1
Mackin, L. 2006 (Wrexham) 1
Maddy, P. 1982 (Cardiff C) 2
Malone, D. E. 2023 (Stoke C) 1
Margetson, M. W. 1992 (Manchester C) 7
Martin, A. P. 1999 (Crystal Palace) 1
Martin, D. A. 2006 (Notts Co) 1
Marustik, C. 1982 (Swansea C) 7
Matondo, R. 2018 (Manchester C) 8
Matthews, A. J. 2010 (Cardiff C) 5
Maxwell, C. 2009 (Wrexham) 16
Maxwell, L. J. 1999 (Liverpool, Cardiff C) 14
Meades, J. 2012 (Cardiff C) 4

Meaker, M. J. 1994 (QPR) 2
Melville, A. K. 1990 (Swansea C, Oxford U) 2
Mepham, C. J. 2018 (Brentford) 4
Micallef, C. 1982 (Cardiff C) 3
Mooney, D. 2019 (Fleetwood T) 4
Morgan, A. M. 1995 (Tranmere R) 4
Morgan, C. 2004 (Wrexham, Milton Keynes D) 12
Morrell, J. J. 2018 (Bristol C) 8
Morris, A. J. 2009 (Cardiff C, Aldershot T) 8
Moss, D. M. 2003 (Shrewsbury T) 6
Mountain, P. D. 1997 (Cardiff C) 2
Mumford, A. O. 2003 (Swansea C) 4

Nardiello, D. 1978 (Coventry C) 1
Neilson, A. B. 1993 (Newcastle U) 7
Nicholas, P. 1978 (Crystal Palace, Arsenal) 3
Nogan, K. 1990 (Luton T) 2
Nogan, L. M. 1991 (Oxford U) 1
Norrington-Davies, R. L. 2018 (Sheffield U) 14
Norton, C. A. 2021 (Stoke C) 1
Nyakuhwa, T. (Cardiff C) **1**
Nyatanga, L. J. 2005 (Derby Co) 10

Oakley, A. 2013 (Swindon T) 1
O'Brien, B. T. 2015 (Manchester C) 8
Ogleby, R. 2011 (Hearts, Wrexham) 12
Oster, J. M. 1997 (Grimsby T, Everton) 9
O'Sullivan, T. P. 2013 (Cardiff C) 15
Owen, G. 1991 (Wrexham) 8

Page, R. J. 1995 (Watford) 4
Parker, S. D. 2025 (Swansea C) **1**
Parslow, D. 2005 (Cardiff C) 4
Partington, J. M. 2009 (Bournemouth) 8
Partridge, D. W. 1997 (West Ham U) 1
Pascoe, C. 1983 (Swansea C) 4
Pearce, S. 2006 (Bristol C) 3
Pearson, S. 2021 (Bristol C) 12
Pejic, S. M. 2003 (Wrexham) 6
Pembridge, M. A. 1991 (Luton T) 1
Peniket, R. 2012 (Fulham) 1
Perrett, T. R. 2025 (Cardiff C) **1**
Perry, J. 1990 (Cardiff C) 3
Peters, M. 1992 (Manchester C, Norwich C) 3
Phillips, D. 1984 (Plymouth Arg) 3
Phillips, G. R. 2001 (Swansea C) 3
Phillips, L. 1979 (Swansea C, Charlton Ath) 2
Pilling, L. 2018 (Tranmere R) 9
Pipe, D. R. 2003 (Coventry C, Notts Co) 12
Pontin, K. 1978 (Cardiff C) 1
Poole, R. L. 2017 (Manchester C, Milton Keynes D) 23
Popov, C. P. 2022 (Leicester C) **13**
Powell, L. 1991 (Southampton) 4
Powell, L. 2004 (Leicester C) 3
Powell, R. 2006 (Bolton W) 1
Price, J. J. 1998 (Swansea C) 7
Price, L. P. 2005 (Ipswich T) 10
Price, M. D. 2001 (Everton, Hull C, Scarborough) 13
Price, P. 1981 (Luton T) 1
Price, T. O. 2019 (Swansea C) 1
Pritchard, J. P. 2013 (Fulham) 2
Pritchard, M. O. 2006 (Swansea C) 4
Pugh, D. 1982 (Doncaster R) 2
Pugh, S. 1993 (Wrexham) 2
Pugh, T. 2019 (Scunthorpe U) 2
Pulis, A. J. 2006 (Stoke C) 5
Przybek, A. 2020 (Ipswich T) 3

Ramasut, M. W. T. 1997 (Bristol R) 4
Ramsey, A. J. 2008, (Cardiff C, Arsenal) 12
Ratcliffe, G. 2019 (Cardiff C) 10
Ratcliffe, K. 1981 (Everton) 2
Ray, G. E. 2013 (Crewe Alex) 5
Raymond, J. 2023 (Crystal Palace) 2
Ready, K. 1992 (QPR) 5
Rees, A. 1984 (Birmingham C) 1
Rees, J. M. 1990 (Luton T) 3
Rees, M. R. 2003 (Millwall) 4
Reid, B. 2014 (Wolverhampton W) 1
Ribeiro, C. M. 2008 (Bristol C) 8
Richards, A. D. J. 2010 (Swansea C) 16
Richards, E. A. 2012 (Bristol R) 1
Roberts, A. 2025 (Norwich C) **2**
Roberts, A. M. 1991 (QPR) 2
Roberts, C. 2013 (Cheltenham T) 6
Roberts, C. J. 1999 (Cardiff C) 1

Roberts, C. R. J. 2016 (Swansea C) 2
Roberts, G. 1983 (Hull C) 1
Roberts, G. W. 1997 (Liverpool, Panionios,
  Tranmere R) 11
Roberts, J. G. 1977 (Wrexham) 1
Roberts, N. W. 1999 (Wrexham) 3
Roberts, P. 1997 (Porthmadog) 1
Roberts, S. I. 1999 (Swansea C) 13
Roberts, S. W. 2000 (Wrexham) 3
Roberts, T. W. 2018 (Leeds U) 5
Robinson, C. P. 1996 (Wolverhampton W) 6
Robinson, J. R. C. 1992 (Brighton & HA, Charlton Ath) 5
Robson, D. L. 2023 (Hull C) 1
Robson-Kanu, K. H. 2010 (Reading) 4
Rodon, J. P. 2017 (Swansea C) 9
Rowlands, A. J. R. 1996 (Manchester C) 5
Rush, I. 1981 (Liverpool) 2

Sass-Davies, W. J. 2021 (Crewe Alex) 7
Savage, C. W. H. 2023 (Manchester U, Reading) **8**
Savage, R. W. 1995 (Crewe Alex) 3
Saunders, C. L. 2015 (Crewe Alex) 1
Sayer, P. A. 1977 (Cardiff C) 2
Searle, D. 1991 (Cardiff C) 6
Sheehan, J. L. 2014 (Swansea C) 12
Shephard, L. 2015 (Swansea C) 2
Shepperd, N. 2021 (Brentford, Dundalk) 4
Slatter, D. 2000 (Chelsea) 6
Slatter, N. 1983 (Bristol R) 6
Smith, D. 2014 (Shrewsbury T) 3
Smith, M. 2018 (Manchester C) 5
Somner, M. J. 2004 (Brentford) 2
Sparrow, T. L. 2022 (Stoke C) 3
Speed, G. A. 1990 (Leeds U) 2
Spence, S. 2021 (Cardiff C, Crystal Palace) 6
Spender, S. 2005 (Wrexham) 6
Stephens, D. 2011 (Hibernian) 7
Stevens, F. J. 2021 (Brentford, St Pauli) **21**
Stevenson, N. 1982 (Swansea C) 2
Stevenson, W. B. 1977 (Leeds U) 3
Stirk, R. W. 2020 (Birmingham C) 7
Stock, B. B. 2003 (Bournemouth) 4
Symons, C. J. 1991 (Portsmouth) 2

Tancock, S. 2013 (Swansea C) 6
Taylor, A. J. 2012 (Tranmere R) 3
Taylor, G. K. 1995 (Bristol R) 4
Taylor, J. W. J. 2023 (Luton T) 3
Taylor, J. W. T. 2010 (Reading) 12
Taylor, N. J. 2008 (Wrexham, Swansea C) 13
Taylor, R. F. 2008 (Chelsea) 5
Taylor, T. 2020 (Wolverhampton W, Burton Alb) 12
Thomas, C. E. 2010 (Swansea C) 3
Thomas, D. G. 1977 (Leeds U) 3
Thomas, D. J. 1998 (Watford) 2
Thomas, G. S. 2018 (Leicester C) 8
Thomas, J. A. 1996 (Blackburn R) 21
Thomas, J. J. 2023 (Swansea C) **10**
Thomas, Martin R. 1979 (Bristol R) 2
Thomas, Mickey R. 1977 (Wrexham) 2
Thomas, S. 2001 (Wrexham) 5
Thompson, L. C. W. 2015 (Norwich C) 2
Thorpe E. 2022 (Luton T) 2

Tibbott, L. 1977 (Ipswich T) 2
Tipton, M. J. 1998 (Oldham Ath) 6
Tolley, J. C. 2001 (Shrewsbury T) 12
Touray, M. 2019 (Newport Co, Salford C) 6
Tripp, C. M. 2025 (Milton Keynes D) **1**
Tudur-Jones, O. 2006 (Swansea C) 3
Turns, E. J. 2022 (Brighton & HA) **4**
Tweedy, T. M. 2025 (Burnley) **2**
Twiddy, C. 1995 (Plymouth Arg) 3
Tyler, C. L. 2023 (Coventry C) 1

Vale, J. R. 2020 (Blackburn R) 8
Valentine, R. D. 2001 (Everton, Darlington) 8
Vaughan, D. O. 2003 (Crewe Alex) 8
Vaughan, N. 1982 (Newport Co) 2
Vokes, S. M. 2007 (Bournemouth,
  Wolverhampton W) 14

Waite, J. 2021 (Cardiff C) 2
Walsh, D. 2000 (Wrexham) 8
Walsh, I. P. 1979 (Crystal Palace, Swansea C) 2
Walsh, J. 2012 (Swansea C, Crawley T) 11
Walton, M. 1991 (Norwich C.) 1
Ward, D. 1996 (Notts Co) 2
Ward, D. 2013 (Liverpool) 6
Warlow, O. J. 2007 (Lincoln C) 2
Watts, D. 2025 (Swansea C) **1**
Watts, E. 2024 (Swansea C) **6**
Webb, L. 2021 (Swansea C) 2
Weeks, D. L. 2014 (Wolverhampton W) 2
Weston, R. D. 2001 (Arsenal, Cardiff C) 4
Wharton, T. J. 2014 (Cardiff C) 1
Whitfield, P. M. 2003 (Wrexham) 1
Wiggins, R. 2006 (Crystal Palace) 9
Williams, A. D. 2024 (WBA) **5**
Williams, A. P. 1998 (Southampton) 9
Williams, A. S. 1996 (Blackburn R) 16
Williams, D. 1983 (Bristol R) 1
Williams, D. I. L. 1998 (Liverpool, Wrexham) 9
Williams, D. P. 2021 (Swansea C) 8
Williams, D. T. 2006 (Yeovil T) 1
Williams, E. 1997 (Caernarfon T) 2
Williams, G. 1983 (Bristol R) 2
Williams, G. A. 2003 (Crystal Palace) 5
Williams, G. C. 2014 (Fulham) 3
Williams, J. P. 2011 (Crystal Palace) 8
Williams, J. T. 2023 (Fulham) 1
Williams, M. 2001 (Manchester U) 10
Williams, M. I. (Zac) 2025 (Crewe Alex) **2**
Williams, M. P. 2006 (Wrexham) 14
Williams, M. J. 2014 (Notts Co) 2
Williams, M. R. 2006 (Wrexham) 6
Williams, O. fon 2007 (Crewe Alex, Stockport Co) 11
Williams, R. 2007 (Middlesbrough) 10
Williams, S. J. 1995 (Wrexham) 4
Wilmot, R. 1982 (Arsenal) 6
Wilson, H. 2014 (Liverpool) 10
Wilson, J. S. 2009 (Bristol C) 3
Worgan, L. J. 2005 (Milton Keynes D, Rushden & D) 5
Wright, A. A. 1998 (Oxford U) 3
Wright, J. 2014 (Huddersfield T) 2

Yorwerth, J. 2014 (Cardiff C) 7
Young, S. 1996 (Cardiff C) 5

ENGLAND C 2024–25

INTERNATIONAL CHALLENGE MATCH 2024

Monday, 6 May 2024

(at Aldershot, attendance 5560)

England C (2) 2   Nepal (0) 0

England C: Ashmore (Justham 46); Chapman (Scott 58), Harfield, Collinge, Ellison (Barnham 58), Kensdale, Payne, Edser, Kabamba, Stead (Asare 58), Goddard (Frost 58).
Scorers: Kabamba 7, Stead 13.

Referee: Tom Owen (Wales).

ENGLAND YOUTH GAMES 2024–25

■ *Denotes player sent off.*

ENGLAND UNDER-16

FRIENDLIES

Rome, Tuesday, 27 August 2024

Italy (1) 2 *(Fustini 4, Fugazzola 54)*

England (1) 3 *(Kavuma-McQueen 6, 71, Wilkinson 50)*

England: (4231) Hardy; Ebho (Sambou 80), Lawrie, Wilkinson, Watson (Diakite 51); Holland, Wilkes (De Lisle 51); Monga (Rabbaj 67), Alabi (Vidal-Philbert 51), Kavuma-McQueen; Boast (Tavares 67).

Rome, Thursday, 29 August 2024

Italy (4) 5 *(Giammattei 18, 32, Paonessa 26, 35, Fustini 72)*

England (0) 0

England: (4231) Collinson; Da Silva (Ebho 41), Sambou (Wilkinson 41), Hamilton-Forsyth (Lawrie 41), Diakite (Watson 68); De Lisle (Holland 53), Philogene (Wilkes 70); Rabbaj (Alabi 70), Alker (Monga 53), Vidal-Philbert (Kavuma-McQueen 41); Tavares (Boast 53).

Burton, Sunday, 15 December 2024

England (1) 2 *(Olayiwola 36 (pen), Lawrie 90)*

Netherlands (1) 1 *(Simeon 24)*

England: (343) Mair; Ebho (Howard 76), Wilkinson (Taylor 76), Barrett; Nicol-Jazuli (Holland 73), Gueke, Olayiwola (Alabi 73), Lawrie; Cadarmateri (Boast 60), Tavares (Kavuma-McQueen 60), Mills (Higgins 60).

Burton, Tuesday, 17 December 2024

England (2) 3 *(Kavuma-McQueen 42, 45, Boast 62)*

Netherlands (0) 2 *(Abdalla 70, Simeon 81)*

England: (334) Bell (Doyle 63); Diakite, Howard, Taylor; Lawrie, Holland (Gueke 64), Alabi (Olayiwola 63); Boast (Mills 63), Kavuma-McQueen (Nicol-Jazuli 63), Monga (Cadarmateri 74), Higgins (Tavares 73).

PINATAR ARENA TOURNAMENT 2024

Pinatar, Thursday, 26 September 2024

England (1) 3 *(Samba 7, Monga 52, Tavares 86)*

Ukraine (0) 0

England: (4231) Hardy; Ebho (Chadwick 76), Lawrie (Thornton 76), Wilkinson (Barrett 87), Stachow; Monga (Olayiwola 62), Samba; Monga (Tavares 76), Kavuma-McQueen (Mills 62), Eboue (De Lisle 76); Boast (Parsons 62).

San Pedro del Pinatar, Saturday, 28 September 2024

Israel (1) 1 *(Janah 45)*

England (1) 2 *(Mills 18, Thornton 90)*

England: (4231) Streets; Chadwick (Ebho 71), Barrett, Thornton, Alabi (Stachow 71); Olayiwola (Holland 65), De Lisle (Samba 72); Tavares (Eboue 60), Rabbaj (Monga 65), Mills (Kavuma-McQueen 65); Parsons (Boast 60).

San Pedro del Pinatar, Tuesday, 1 October 2024

England (1) 1 *(Eboue 22)*

France (0) 0 *(Decrenisse■)*

England: (343) Bell; Ebho, Wilkinson, Stachow; Olayiwola (Alabi 67), Eboue (Tavares 79), Lawrie (Thornton 67), Boast (de Lisle 67), Mills (Kavuma-McQueen 46), Monga (Parsons 79).

UEFA DEVELOPMENT TOURNAMENT AT PINATAR ARENA 2025

San Pedro del Pinatar, Friday, 22 February 2025

Colombia (0) 0

England (2) 4 *(Kavuma-McQueen 12, 32, Greenwood 85, Monga 90)*

England: (4231) Mair; Ebho (Taylor 86), Lawrie (Howard 86), Thornton, Diakite (Barrett 68); Holland (Nicoll-Jazuli 68), Alabi (Olayiwola 68); Mills (Boast 78), Kavuma-McQueen (Drakes-Thomas 78), Monga; Higgins (Greenwood 68).

San Pedro del Pinatar, Sunday, 2 March 2025

England (3) 7 *(Greenwood 6, 51, Nicoll-Jazuli 9, Monga 20 (pen), Boast 55, 74, Mills 90)*

Denmark (1) 3 *(Chukwuani 23, Thomsen 80, Khattar 81)*

England: (433) Hardy; Taylor, Howard, Diakite (Alabi 46), Barrett; Olayiwola (Holland 70), Nicoll-Jazuli, Drakes-Thomas (Thornton 78); Boast (Mills 78), Monga (Kavuma-McQueen 46), Greenwood (Higgins 70).

San Pedro del Pinatar, Wednesday, 5 March 2025

England (0) 1 *(Monga 84 (pen))*

France (1) 2 *(Merrifield 16, Batola 54 (pen))*

England: (4231) Mair (Hardy 46); Ebho (Taylor 82), Lawrie (Howard 83), Barrett (Thornton 83), Diakite; Olayiwola (Holland 36), Nicoll-Jazuli (Boast 73); Mills (Alabi 60), Monga, Kavuma-McQueen (Drakes-Thomas 60); Higgins (Greenwood 60).

TOURNOI DE MONTAIGU 2025

Les Herbiers, Tuesday, 15 April 2025

Japan (1) 2 *(Takaki 40, Satomi 45)*

England (1) 3 *(Kavuma-McQueen 36, 70, Nicoll-Jazuli 53)*

England: (4231) Mair; King (Ebho 59), Barrett, Thornton, Stachow (Diakite 59); Olayiwola (Watson 60), Samba (Alabi 77); Kavuma-McQueen (Adediran 77), Nicoll-Jazuli, Greenwood (Parsons 78); Higgins (Grant 51).

La-Chataigneraie, Thursday, 17 April 2025

England (0) 0

Mexico (1) 3 *(Mota 19, Kimbrough 62, Perez 69)*

England: (433) Hardy; Ebho (King 56), Lawrie, Wilkinson (Barrett 68), Diakite; Alabi (Nicoll-Jazuli 57), Watson, Farkas; Adediran (Kavuma-McQueen 57), Parsons (Greenwood 57), Grant (Higgins 68).

La-Chataigneraie, Saturday, 19 April 2025

Portugal (2) 3 *(Semedo 2, 78 Rodrigues 40)*

England (1) 1 *(Kavuma-McQueen 14)*

England: (532) Mair; King, Thornton, Barrett, Stachow, Diakite (Watson 50); Olayiwola (Grant 50), Nicoll-Jazuli, Samba (Farkas 70); Kavuma-McQueen, Greenwood (Higgins 62).

ENGLAND UNDER-17

FRIENDLIES

Dusseldorf, Wednesday, 4 September 2024

England (2) 5 *(Dowman 22 (pen), Dike 39 (pen), Howell 50 (pen), 60, Jenner 90)*

Mexico (0) 0

England: (4231) Awesu; Okoduwa (Julienne 69), Hardy (Simmonds 61), Byfield (Headley 69), Mantato (Braithwaite 46); Ridgeon (Jenner 61), Nwosu (Rawlings 61); Howell (Heskey 69), Dowman (Gorman 61), Dike (Williams-Barnett 61); Tyjon (Ezenwata 61).

Duisburg, Saturday, 7 September 2024

England (0) 0

Israel (0) 0

England: (4231) Bernal; Julienne (Byfield 76), Simmonds (Nwosu 65), Braithwaite (Hardy 65), Headley (Mantato 65); Jenner (Gorman 64), Rawlings (Dike 76); Heskey (Howell 76), Williams-Barnett (Dowman 65), McAdoo (Ridgeon 65); Ezenwata (Tyjon 64).

Duisburg, Tuesday, 10 September 2024

Germany (1) 1 *(Staff 8)*

England (0) 3 *(Braithwaite 50, Ridgeon 53, Heskey 75)* 634

England: (4231) Porter; Okoduwa (Jenner 90), Hardy, Byfield (Simmonds 72), Braithwaite (Mantato 80); Nwosu (Rawlings 58); Ridgeon (Julienne 80), Howell (Headley 80), Gorman (Williams-Barnett 65), Dowman (McAdoo 72); Tyjon (Heskey 65).

Tubize, Friday, 15 November 2024

Belgium (0) 1 *(Murenzi 58 (pen))*

England (0) 1 *(McAidoo 73)*

England: (4411) Asemota (Awesu 62); Okoduwa (Julienne 74), Simmonds (Nwosu 74), Ngwashi (Hardy 62), Braithwaite (Mantato 74); Burrowes (McAidoo 62), Miles (Emenalo 74), Palmer (Page 62), Ngumoha (Heskey 74); Dowman (McGrath 74); Rodriguez (Tyjon 74).

Tubize, Monday, 18 November 2024

Belgium (1) 2 *(Murenzi 22, Camara 67)*

England (1) 1 *(McAidoo 34)*

England: (4231) Stokes; Julienne (Okoduwa 62), Hardy (Ngwashi 68), Page (Miles 68), Mantato (Braithwaite 68); Nwosu (Palmer 81), Emenalo (Simmonds 62); McAidoo (Burrowes 64), McGrath (Dowman 62), Heskey (Rodriguez 68); Tyjon (Ngumoha 69).

Vila Real de Santo Antonio, Thursday, 20 February 2025

Netherlands (1) 2 *(Ouarghi 26, Duah 47)*

England (1) 3 *(Nijstad 19 (og), Nwosu 46, Page 59)*

England: (442) Awesu (Bernal 68); Okoduwa (Ford 74), Ngwashi (Ridgeon 74), Simmonds, Kukonki; Howell, Nwosu (Benamar 60), Page (Rodriguez 60), Ngumoha (Miles 60); Dowman (Palmer 68), Gray (Burrows 74).

Vila Real de Santo Antonio, Sunday, 23 February 2025

Netherlands (0) 0

England (3) 4 *(Benamar 6, Rodriguez 23 (pen), 29, Williams-Barnett 90)*

England: (343) Bernal (Moses 62); Ford (Ngumoha 61), Hardy, Byfield (Kukonki 82); Burrowes (Ngwashi 72), Ridgeon (Nwosu 62), Miles (Page 62), Benamar (Okoduwa 72); Palmer (Dowman 62), Rodriguez (Gray 72), Williams-Barnett.

UEFA UNDER-17 CHAMPIONSHIP QUALIFICATION ROUND 1, GROUP 1

Ta'Qali, Thursday, 24 October 2024

England (1) 4 *(Ezenwata 12, 53, Dowman 68, Tyjon 90)*

Malta (0) 0 407

England: (442) Porter; Byfield (Richards 71), Hardy, Simmonds, Mantato (Dike 79); Howell (Dowman 56), Emenalo, Nwosu, Ngumoha (Williams-Barnett 56); Ezenwata (Tyjon 71), Gorman.

Ta'Qali, Sunday, 27 October 2024

England (3) 4 *(Rawlings 17, Williams-Barnett 30, Tyjon 34, Howell 57)*

Latvia (0) 0 120

England: (442) Asemota; Richards, Simmonds, Byfield (Palmer 61), Mantato (Emenalo 46); Howell (Dike 61), Rawlings, Nwosu (Walsh 46), Williams-Barnett; Tyjon, Dowman (Ngumoha 69).

Ta'Qali, Wednesday, 30 October 2024

Sweden (1) 2 *(Saeed 26, Hedlof 90)*

England (1) 4 *(Walsh, 40, Dike 47, Gorman 74 (pen), Dowman 90)* 116

England: (442) Porter; Richards (Rawlings 75), Hardy, Byfield (Simmonds 75), Dike; Ngumoha (Howell 61), Emenalo, Walsh (Palmer 68), Dowman; Ezenwata (Tyjon 61), Gorman.

UEFA UNDER-17 CHAMPIONSHIP QUALIFICATION ROUND 2, GROUP A7

Burton, Wednesday, 19 March 2025

England (1) 2 *(Rodriguez 25, 60)*

Israel (0) 0 285

England: (442) Porter; Headley (Benamar 77), Hardy, Byfield, Braithwaite; Howell, Ridgeon, Nwosu (Page 52), Heskey (Ngumoha 77); Dowman (Gorman 85), Rodriguez (Burrowes 85).

Burton, Saturday, 22 March 2025

England (2) 3 *(Simmonds 3, McAidoo 10, Rodriguez 84)*

Slovenia (1) 2 *(Kozar 16, Videnovic 75)* 312

England: (442) Porter; Headley, Simmonds (Byfield 65), Hardy, Braithwaite; McAidoo (Burrowes 64), Ridgeon, Page, Ngumoha (Howell 64); Dowman (Gorman 64), Rodriguez (Heskey 85).

Burton, Wednesday, 19 March 2025

England (4) 5 *(Gorman 7, 26, Ngumoha 19, 64, Dowman 31)*

Northern Ireland (0) 0 282

England: (442) Awesu; Byfield, Nwosu (Braithwaite 46), Simmonds, Benamar; McAidoo (Rodriguez 73), Gorman, Dowman (Page 46), Ngumoha; Burrowes (Howell 74), Heskey.

Northern Ireland: (433) McDonnell F; Anderson, Leacock (Faloona 46), McDonnell N, Wilson; Walker, Savage, Burns (Gamble 46); Kerr (Atherton 65), McGovern (Downey 46), Feeney (Thompson 65).

UEFA UNDER-17 CHAMPIONSHIP FINALS IN ALBANIA GROUP B

Rrogozhine, Tuesday, 20 May 2025

England (1) 1 *(Rodriguez 12)*

Belgium (0) 1 *(Fernandez 49)* 1688

England: (4231) Porter; Burrowes, Braithwaite, Byfield, Benamar; Page (Williams-Barnett 84), Ridgeon (Emenalo 64); McAidoo (Heskey 64), Dowman, Ngumoha (Gray 77); Rodriguez (Gorman 84).

Rrogozhine, Friday, 23 May 2025

Italy (2) 4 *(Inacio 10, De Paoli 37, Campaniello 67, Luongo 77)*

England (1) 2 *(Rodriguez 23, 49)* 3074

England: (442) Porter; Byfield, Hardy, Braithwaite, Benamar; Burrowes (McAidoo 70), Page (Gray 77), Ridgeon, Ngumoha (Heskey 63); Dowman (Gorman 70), Rodriguez.

Rrogozhine, Monday, 26 May 2025

Czech Republic (0) 2 *(Palascak 59, Sochurek 89)*

England (4) 4 *(Dowman 5, Rodriguez 15, Howell 37, Gray 40)* 1513

England: (442) Porter; Hardy, Simmonds, Braithwaite (Byfield 86), Benamar (McAidoo 90); Howell, Gorman, Ridgeon (Page 61), Dowman (Williams Barnett 61); Gray, Rodriguez (Heskey 86).

ENGLAND UNDER-18

LAFARGE INTERNATIONAL TOURNAMENT

Limoges, Wednesday, 4 September 2024

England (1) 2 *(Derry 8, Nyoni 51)*

Portugal (0) 2 *(Patrao 54, Camacho 82)*

England: (4321) Whatmuff; Dixon, Pinnington, Amissah, Amass (McFarlane 77); King (Rigg 77), Sidibe, Nyoni (Fletcher 63); Mane (Mukasa 86), Derry (Sanusi 63); Dipepa (Mheuka 63).

A penalty shoot-out finished 4-4.

Limoges, Friday, 6 September 2024

Switzerland (0) 1 *(Cakolli 90 (pen))*

England (1) 1 *(Sanusi 42)*

England: (343) Brits; Amass (Dixon 46), Golambeckis, Olagunku; Shahar, Rigg (King 66), Harrison, Fletcher (Sidibe 71); Mukasa (Mane 71), Sanusi (Derry 66), Mhueka (Rodrigez 71).

A penalty shoot-out finished 5-5.

Limoges, Sunday, 8 September 2024

France (0) 1 *(Molebe 69)*

England (0) 1 *(Nyoni 67)*

England: (4321) Lukjanciks; Shahar (Dixon 56), Golambeckis (Sidibe 46), Pinnington, Amissah; King (Rigg 46), Harrison (Amass 46), Nyoni (Fletcher 87); Mukasa (Mane 46), Derry (Sanusi 46); Rodriguez (Dipepa 56).

A penalty shoot-out finished 2-0 to England.

MARBELLA INTERNATIONAL TOURNAMENT
Marbella, Friday, 11 October 2024
Sweden (2) 2 *(Redkin 30, Jonsson 35)*
England (0) 0
England: (4321) Whatmuff; Shahar (Dixon 68); Subuloye, Pinnington (Golambeckis 68), Adiele (Amass 78); Rigg (Olusesi 78), Harrison (Sidibe 59), Armstrong (Nyoni 60); Runham (Sanusi 69), Derry (Broggio78); Mane (Dipepa 59).

Marbella, Monday, 14 October 2024
Ukraine (1) 1 *(Synchuk 36)*
England (2) 3 *(Olusesi 7, 30, Golambeckis 86)*
England: (4231) Lukjanciks (Michalski 46); Shahar (Pinnington 61), Dixon, Golambeckis, Amass; Olusesi (Rigg 73), Sidibe (Harrison 84); Nyoni (Armstrong 84), Sanusi (Runham 84), Broggio (Derry 73); Dipepa.

FRIENDLIES
Valencia, Friday, 15 November 2024
England (1) 1 *(Broggio 16)*
Poland (1) 3 *(Monka 25, Basse 49, Falowski 63)*
England: (4321) Lukjanciks (Michalski 61); Dixon (Noble 61), Amissah (Olagunju 69), Routh (Mfuni 61), McFarlane; Fletcher (Hemmings 62), Sidibe (Harrison 69), Armstrong (Olusesi 69); Sanusi, Broggio (Adiele 69); Dipepa (Neave 69).

Valencia, Monday, 18 November 2024
England (0) 0
Germany (1) 1 *(Culbreath 14)* 189
England: (3412) Whatmuff (Michalski 68); Olagunju (Amissah 56), Noble (Dixon 68), Mfuni; Shahar, Harrison, Hemmings, Adiele (Sanusi 68); Olusesi (Sidibe 78); Armstrong (Fletcher 69), Neave (Dipepa 56).

FRIENDLIES
Ponta Delgarda, Thursday, 20 March 2025
England (0) 2 *(Sesay 49, Dipepa 75)*
Czech Republic (1) 2 *(Ruzicka 44, Pavlo 89)*
England: (433) Whatmuff; Dixon, Routh, Noble, Amass; Sesay (Harrison 69), Hemmings, Fletcher (Dipepa 62 (Garcia 90)); Mukasa (Golambeckis 62), Mane (Adiele 90), Derry (Sonni-Lambie 69).

Freamunde, Saturday, 22 March 2025
France (0) 2 *(Molebe 72 (pen), 77)*
England (2) 2 *(Shahar 3, Sonni-Lambie 16)*
England: (4231) Austin (Ranson 46); Shahar, Golambeckis, Amissah, Garcia (Amass 32); Armstrong (Hemmings 81), Harrison; Robinson (Derry 61), Mukasa (Fletcher 61), Adiele; Sonni-Lambie (Mane 61).

Porto, Tuesday, 25 March 2025
Portugal (0) 0
England (1) 1 *(Derry 12)*
England: (4231) Whatmuff; Shahar (Dixon 85), Noble, Golambeckis, Amass; Armstrong, Hemmings; Derry (Adiele 55), Fletcher (Mane 70), Sesay (Harrison 70); Sonni-Lambie.

Sale, Morocco, Sunday, 25 May 2025
Morocco (0) 1 *(Hamdaoua 85)*
England (2) 3 *(Derry 6, 41, Sonni-Lambie 69)*
England: (4231) Whatmuff; Noble (Golambeckis 85), Garcia (Harrison 60), Sidibe (Okoduwa 60), Dixon; Amissah (Sesay 85), Armstrong; Nyoni, Sonni-Lambie (Harriman-Annous75), Derry (Oyekunle 75); Nabizada (Dipepa 75).

Sale, Morocco, Wednesday, 28 May 2025
Morocco (1) 2 *(Benachour 28, Hamdaoua 49 (pen))*
England (1) 1 *(Nyoni 32)*
England: (4231) Ransom; Okoduwa (Amissah 46), Noble, Golambeckis (Dixon 52), Sesay (Sonni-Lambie 62); Armstrong, Harrison (Garcia 52); Derry (Sidibe 52), Nyoni, Harriman-Annous (Nabizada 75).

ENGLAND UNDER-19

FRIENDLIES
Koprivnica, Wednesday, 4 September 2024
Italy (2) 2 *(Fini 4, Sia 40)*
England (1) 2 *(Nwaneri 44, Black 86))*
England: (4321) Herrick; Henderson-Hall (Black 76), Acheampong (Murray-Campbell 67), Johnson (Heaven 77), Samuels-Smith (Meghoma 76); Nwaneri (Dibling 77), Lewis-Skelly (Dyer 77), Russell-Denny (Golding 68); Donovan (Amo-Ameyaw 68), George (Moore 68); Wheatley (Ajala 68).

Nedelisce, Saturday, 7 September 2024
Croatia (0) 1 *(Lukic 73 (pen))*
England (0) 0 *(George 76)*
England: (4321) Setford (Proctor 77); Black (Henderson-Hall 78), Murray-Campbell, Heaven (Johnson 68), Meghoma (Acheampong 78); Dibling (Nwaneri 68), Dyer (Lewis-Skelly 77), Golding (Russell-Denny 78); Amo-Ameyaw (Donovan 68), Moore (George 68); Ajala (Wheatley 68).

Koprivnica, Tuesday, 10 September 2024
Germany (1) 3 *(Moerstedt 19, El Mala 78, 83)*
England (0) 2 *(Nwaneri 58, Dibling 85)*
England: (4321) Setford; Black (Henderson-Hall 75), Acheampong, Murray-Campbell (Johnson 68), Meghoma; Nwaneri, Dyer, Russell-Denny (Dibling 76); Amo-Ameyaw (George 75), Moore; Wheatley (Ajala 68).

MARBELLA INTERNATIONAL TOURNAMENT
Marbella, Wednesday, 9 October 2024
Portugal (2) 2 *(Simoes 22, Martins 41)*
England (0) 1 *(Nwaneri 73 (pen))*
England: (4321) Curd; Rowe (Black 66), Murray-Campbell (Abbott 74), Nallo (Mfuni 66), Meghoma (Johnson 74); Nwaneri (George 74), Dyer (Orford 67), Russell-Denny (King 74); Amo-Ameyaw (Young 67), Moore (Ndala 74); Wheeldon (Mheuka 66).

Marbella, Saturday, 12 October 2024
Netherlands (0) 1 *(Bergraaf 54)*
England (2) 4 *(Young 39, Mheuka 45, Orford 72, Moore 90)*
England: (4321) Herrick; Black (Rowe 66), Abbott (Nwaneri 66), Mfuni (Nallo 73), Johnson (Dyer 73); King (Meghoma 74), Orford (Amo-Ameyaw 73), George (Moore 65); Young (Russell-Denny 73), Ndala (Wheeldon 66); Mheuka (Murray-Campbell 65).

Marbella, Tuesday, 15 October 2024
France (2) 2 *(Diliwidi 21, 27 (pen))*
England (3) 4 *(Nwaneri 8, King 12, Mheuka 42, Wheeldon 69)*
England: (4321) Young; Black (Meghoma 62), Nallo (Murray-Campbell 46), Mfuni (Abbott 46), Johnson (Rowe 62); Nwaneri (George 69), Orford (Russell-Denny 68), King (Dyer 62); Young (Amo-Ameyaw 68), Moore (Ndala 62); Mheuka (Wheeldon 69).

UEFA UNDER-19 EUROPEAN CHAMPIONSHIP 2025 QUALIFYING ROUND GROUP 3
Pazardjik, Wednesday, 13 November 2024
England (1) 1 *(Nwaneri 7)*
Lithuania (0) 0 75
England: (3421) Herrick; Johnson, Murray-Campbell, Meghoma; Young (Amo-Ameyaw 90), Black (Acheampong 90), Dyer, King (Lewis-Skelly 71); Nwaneri, George (Derry 71); Mheuka (Wheatley 71).

Plovdiv, Saturday, 16 November 2024
England (2) 2 *(Nwaneri 27, Orford 45)*
Bulgaria (1) 1 *(Raychev 4)* 600
England: (352) Setford; Acheampong (Black 90), Abbott, Johnson; Derry (George 86), Lewis-Skelly, Nwaneri, Orford (Nyoni 87), Meghoma; Amo-Ameyaw (Young 72), Wheatley (Mheuka 72).

Plovdiv, Tuesday, 19 November 2024

Belgium (0) 0

England (0) 0   75

England: (3421) Setford; Lewis-Skelly, Abbott, Acheampong (Murray-Campbell 63); Black, Dyer, Nyoni (Orford 90), King (Nwaneri 73); Young (Amo-Ameyaw 63), George (Derry 63); Mheuka.

UEFA UNDER-19 EUROPEAN CHAMPIONSHIP 2025 ELITE ROUND GROUP B7

Bangor, Wednesday, 19 March 2025

Wales (0) 0

England (0) 2 *(Wheatley 57, Mheuka 84)*   2541

Wales: (433) Benjamin; Parker, Lawlor, Clarke, Giles; Yoganathan (Morgan 80), Crew (Mafico 85), Perrett (Tuck 67); Issaka (Allen 67), Biancheri, Myles (Twose 80).
England: (4231) Setford; Rowe, Acheampong, Abbott, Johnson; Dyer (Orford 90), Miley; Dibling (Young 68), King (Rigg 68), George (Moore 72); Wheatley (Mheuka 68).

Connah's Quay, Saturday, 22 March 2025

England (0) 0

Turkey (0) 0   742

England: (3421) Herrick; Murray-Campbell, Abbott, Mfuni; Kporha, Miley, Orford, Rigg (King 75); Young (George 79), Moore; Mheuka (Dibling 75).

Connah's Quay, Tuesday, 25 March 2025

England (1) 1 *(Rigg 9)*

Portugal (0) 0   1009

England: (4231) Setford; Rowe, Acheampong, Abbott, Mfuni; Rigg (King 79), Miley; Dibling (Dyer 90), Moore, George; Mheuka (Young 87).

UEFA UNDER-19 CHAMPIONSHIP FINALS IN ROMANIA

GROUP B

Ploiesti, Saturday, 14 June 2025

England (1) 2 *(Watson 11, Moore 80 (pen))*

Norway (2) 2 *(Rossing-Lelesiit 18, Granaas 45)*   1433

England: (442) Setford; Rowe (Kporha 46), Murray-Campbell, Mfuni, Meghoma (Johnson 87); Young (Amo-Ameyaw 76), Dyer, King (Wheatley 82), Watson (Derry 75); Moore, Mheuka.

Bucharest, Tuesday, 17 June 2025

Germany (4) 5 *(Darvich 7, El Mala 31, 48, Moerstedt 41, Wurm 44)*

England (1) 5 *(King 35, Wheatley 52, Russell-Denny 55, Abbott 60, Derry 63)*   1104

England: (3412) Setford; Kporha, Abbott (Oboavwoduo 89), Mfuni; Russell-Denny (Murray-Campbell 89), Dyer, King (Mheuka 77), Meghoma; Amo-Ameyaw (Young 46); Derry (Watson 77), Wheatley.

Bucharest, Friday, 20 June 2025

Netherlands (3) 4 *(Smit 22, Redmond 35, 69, Vennegor of Hesselink 42)*

England (0) 2 *(Wheatley 52, Derry 90)*   738

England: (352) Setford; Kporha, Abbott, Mfuni; Young, Watson (Derry 77), Dyer, Russell-Denny, Meghoma; Mheuka, Wheatley (Oboavwoduo 84).

ENGLAND UNDER-20

EUROPEAN ELITE LEAGUE

Istanbul, Friday, 6 September 2024

Turkey (1) 1 *(Yildirim 20 (pen))*

England (0) 1 *(Ballard 89)*

England: (4321) Simkin; Walters (Fisher 63), Phillips, Nelson, Chambers; O'Reilly (Ballard 63), Wright, Bellingham; Esse (Gordon 77), Alves (Tezgel 77); Scarlett (Marsh 90).

Stockport, Tuesday, 10 September 2024

England (1) 2 *(Scarlett 30, Marsh 76)*

Romania (0) 0   2527

England: (4321) Simkin; Fisher, Casey, Scanlon (Chambers 76), Alleyne; Nelson, Wright, Ballard (Marsh 70); Gordon (Cozier-Duberry 70), Tezgel (Esse 60); Scarlett (Braybrooke 76).

Frosinone, Thursday, 10 October 2024

Italy (1) 1 *(Ebone 39)*

England (0) 2 *(Gyabi 58, Dean 90)*

England: (4321) Simkin; Fisher (Acheampong 80), Casey (Hills 80), Phillips (Alleyne 64), Chrisene (Campbell 80); Collyer, Gyabi, Nelson; Esse (Ballard 69), Earthy (Gordon 69); Lankshear (Dean 64).

Doncaster, Monday, 14 October 2024

England (1) 3 *(Dean 45, 58, Gordon 62)*

Czech Republic (0) 0   2670

England: (4321) Simkin (Merrick 79); Acheampong (Fisher 65), Phillips (Casey 74), Alleyne (Hills 79), Chrisene (Campbell 74); Collyer (Esse 74), Braybrooke, Gyabi (Nelson 65); Gordon, Ballard (Lankshear 65); Dean.

Chesterfield, Friday, 15 November 2024

England (2) 4 *(Esse 15, Dean 40, Peck 56, Lankshear 73)*

Germany (0) 0   3311

England: (451) Simkin; Andrews (Dornelly 83), Casey (Small 83), Alleyne, Campbell; Gordon (Ballard 60), Peck (Nelson 85), Wright, Braybrooke (Doyle 60), Esse; Dean (Lankshear 60).

Pulawy, Tuesday, 19 November 2024

Poland (1) 1 *(Luberecki 39)*

England (0) 1 *(Ballard 50)*

England: (442) Young; Dornelly (Andrews 61), Casey, Alleyne, Campbell; Gordon, Wright, Peck (Nelson 74), Ballard (Esse 74); Doyle (Dean 61), Lankshear.

Leiria, Friday, 21 March 2025

Portugal (1) 1 *(Monteiro 32)*

England (1) 1 *(Scarlett 7)*

England: (4231) Young; Norton-Cuffy (Fisher 60), Phillips, Nelson, Scarles; Gyabi, Peck (McConnell); Esse (Bangura-Williams 72), O'Reilly (Wright 60), Cozier-Duberry (Nyoni 72); Scarlett (Mubama 60).

FRIENDLY

Marbella, Monday, 24 March 2025

England (1) 2 *(Mubama 15, Peck 89)*

Switzerland (0) 2 *(Ouattara 68, Manzambi 72 (pen))*

England: (442) Harrison; Fisher (Norton-Cuffy 59), Casey (Phillips 79), Alleyne, O'Reilly (Scarles 66); Nyoni (Bangura-Williams 59), Wright, McConnell (Peck 59), Cozier-Duberry (Esse 46); Mubama (Scarlett 59), Collyer (Gyabi 59).

SCHOOLS FOOTBALL 2024–25

BOODLES INDEPENDENT SCHOOLS FA CUP 2024–25

*After extra time.

PRELIMINARY ROUND
ACS Hillingdon v Reddam House (walkover)

Gosfield v St Columba's College	0-10
Gresham's v New Hall (Essex)	9-4
King's Bruton v Claycsmore	5-3
Loughborough GS v Trent College	2-4

St Edward's, Oxford (walkover) v Cokethorpe

Stamford v Stephen Perse	3-1

FIRST ROUND

Abingdon v Highgate	2-3
Ackworth v Bolton	3-2
ACS Cobham v Chigwell	1-2
American School in London v St Dunstan's	3-1
Bede's v Buckswood	4-0
Brighton College v King Edward's, Witley	0-2
Bryanston v Bedales	3-4
Bury GS v Grammar School at Leeds	0-4
City of London v KCS Wimbledon	1-3
Clifton College v Reading Blue Coat	2-3
Dame Allan's v RGS Newcastle	5-1
Denstone v Wolverhampton GS	7-0
Eastbourne v Tonbridge	0-7
Ellesmere v Stockport GS	1-6

Haberdashers' (walkover) v Reddam House

Haileybury v Lingfield College	6-1
Harrodian v Kingston GS	9-0
Hulme GS v St Bede's College	1-2
John Lyon v Epsom	0-4
King's Bruton v Marlborough	0-15
King's Chester v Merchant Taylors' Crosby	5-3*
King's Worcester v St Edward's, Oxford	3-2
Lancing v Ibstock Place	1-2
Latymer Upper v Dulwich College	1-2
Malvern v Bristol GS	4-2*
Merchant Taylors', Northwd v University Col. Sch.	2-4
Mill Hill v Harrow	1-7
Princethorpe v Trent College	1-4
QEGS Wakefield v Bootham	4-3
Reigate GS v Wellington	1-2
RGS Guildford v St Paul's	0-8
Sevenoaks v Claremont Fan Court	4-1
Sherborne v Bournemouth Collegiate	4-3
St Columba's College v Gresham's	3-5
Stamford v Norwich	0-1
The Grange v Oswestry	0-9
Trinity v St John's, Leatherhead	3-1
Westminster v Whitgift	3-4

SECOND ROUND

Aldenham v Whitgift	5-1
American School in London v Alleyn's	0-4
Ardingly v Berkhamsted	1-3
Bedales v Marlborough	1-7
Dame Allan's v Manchester GS	5-2
Denstone v QEGS Wakefield	3-0
Dulwich College v Chigwell	5-0
Epsom v Forest	2-2*

Epsom won 4-2 on penalties.

Grammar School at Leeds v Trent College	4-3
Gresham's v Kimbolton	1-4
Haberdashers' v King's Worcester	6-2
Haileybury v Norwich	4-1
Harrodian v Brentwood	3-1
Harrow v University Col. Sch.	12-1
Highgate v Trinity	3-2
KCS Wimbledon v Bede's	1-4
Malvern v Eton	1-7
Oswestry v Cheadle Hulme	0-6
Queen Ethelburga's v King's Chester	2-1
Reading Blue Coat v Wellington	5-0

ISFA U15 CUP FINAL

Aldenham v Hampton	3-2

at Burton Alb

Sevenoaks v King Edward's, Witley	6-0
St Bede's College v Ackworth	1-5
St Paul's v Charterhouse	2-5
Stockport GS v Rossall	5-0
Tonbridge v Ibstock Place	0-0*

Ibstock Place won 6-5 on penalties.

Winchester v Sherborne	6-1

THIRD ROUND

Ackworth v Millfield	3-5
Alleyn's v Eton	0-0*

Eton won 4-2 on penalties.

Berkhamsted v Haileybury	2-0
Bradfield v Denstone	3-1
Charterhouse v Harrow	1-2
Dame Allan's v Dulwich College	0-5
Epsom v Royal Russell	2-2*

Epsom won 4-3 on penalties.

Grammar School at Leeds v Cheadle Hulme	2-4
Harrodian v Highgate	5-1
Hampton v Ibstock Place	5-3
Kimbolton v Bede's	2-3
Marlborough v Shrewsbury	0-1
Queen Ethelburga's v Repton	0-1
Sevenoaks v Haberdashers'	3-2
Stockport GS v Reading Blue Coat	0-0*

Reading Blue Coat won 6-5 on penalties.

Winchester v Aldenham	1-2

FOURTH ROUND

Berkhamsted v Repton	1-3
Dulwich College v Bede's	2-3
Epsom v Harrodian	3-1
Eton v Bradfield	2-2*

Bradfield won 4-3 on penalties.

Harrow v Cheadle Hulme	1-0
Millfield v Reading Blue Coat	2-1
Sevenoaks v Hampton	0-7
Shrewsbury v Aldenham	1-0

QUARTER-FINALS

Bede's v Shrewsbury	4-5
Epsom v Repton	1-5
Hampton v Harrow	2-2*

Hampton won 4-1 on penalties.

Millfield v Bradfield	1-1*

Bradfield won 3-2 on penalties.

SEMI-FINALS

Hampton v Bradfield	0-4
Repton v Shrewsbury	0-1

BOODLES INDEPENDENT SCHOOLS
FA CUP FINAL 2024–25

Stadium MK, Milton Keynes

Monday, 17 March 2025

Bradfield (1) 2 *(John, Robinson)*

Shrewsbury (0) 0

Bradfield: G. Sapsford; J. Gerrard, T. Paice, A. Huntley, A. Lee, S. Willis, C.-B. Bowdery, D. Mihaylov, R. Bartley, M. John, S. Robinson.
Substitutes: R. Yeoman, A. Costaroudas, A. Hume, C. Astor, K. Evans.

Shrewsbury: B. Duplessis; M. Woodhouse, L. Querfurth, T. Bolinbroke, L. Bergin, H. Vaughan, I. England, W. Eyer, T. Barrow, S. Bowen, R. Carsen.
Substitutes: F. Dale, D. Samson, J. Van Cutsem, S. Spiby, Y. Lok Mak.

Referee: Darren England.

ISFA U13 CUP FINAL

St John's, Leatherhead v Dulwich College	4-1

at Burton Alb

NATIONAL LEAGUE SYSTEM STEP 3 2024–25

PITCHING IN NORTHERN PREMIER LEAGUE – PREMIER DIVISION

			Home				Away					Total						
		P	W	D	L	F	A	W	D	L	F	A	W	D	L	F	A	GD	Pts
1	Macclesfield	42	19	1	1	57	12	16	3	2	52	18	35	4	3	109	30	79	109
2	Worksop T¶	42	13	2	6	57	26	13	3	5	39	25	26	5	11	96	51	45	83
3	Stockton T† (P)	42	12	4	5	34	20	11	2	8	32	27	23	6	13	66	47	19	75
4	Guiseley	42	10	7	4	35	22	10	7	4	32	23	20	14	8	67	45	22	74
5	Ashton U	42	11	4	6	38	26	9	5	7	34	32	20	9	13	72	58	14	69
6	Ilkeston T	42	12	7	2	45	21	6	5	10	24	35	18	12	12	69	56	13	66
7	Gainsborough Trinity	42	9	4	8	30	28	9	6	6	28	25	18	10	14	58	53	5	64
8	Morpeth T	42	6	8	7	25	31	10	6	5	32	30	16	14	12	57	61	-4	62
9	Hyde U	42	7	8	6	31	33	7	7	7	28	30	14	15	13	59	63	-4	57
10	Prescot Cables (P)	42	11	4	6	26	16	5	3	13	23	38	16	9	17	49	54	-5	57
11	Warrington Rylands 1906	42	6	6	9	27	31	8	8	5	33	22	14	14	14	60	53	7	56
12	Workington	42	11	5	5	38	23	4	2	15	23	42	15	7	20	61	65	-4	52
13	Bamber Bridge	42	9	2	10	36	35	6	5	10	29	35	15	7	20	65	70	-5	52
14	Hebburn T (P)	42	8	5	8	32	30	5	8	8	28	35	13	13	16	60	65	-5	52
15	Leek T (P)	42	7	4	10	27	33	7	6	8	20	22	14	10	18	47	55	-8	52
16	Whitby T	42	6	5	10	21	26	9	2	10	34	45	15	7	20	55	71	-16	52
17	FC United of Manchester	42	5	7	9	33	34	7	8	6	22	28	12	15	15	55	62	-7	51
18	Lancaster C	42	5	10	6	25	29	7	5	9	27	34	12	15	15	52	63	-11	51
19	Matlock T*	42	7	6	8	32	32	3	9	9	27	37	10	15	17	59	69	-10	42
20	Mickleover	42	8	2	11	24	29	2	7	12	17	46	10	9	23	41	75	-34	39
21	Basford U	42	7	4	10	31	39	3	3	15	19	40	10	7	25	50	79	-29	37
22	Blyth Spartans (R)	42	2	6	13	20	45	1	3	17	18	55	3	9	30	38	100	-62	18

¶Worksop T promoted via play-offs. *Matlock T deducted 3 points for fielding an ineligible player in the game against Hyde U. †Stockton T disqualified from play-off final after fielding an ineligible player in their play-off semi-final against Guiseley.

PITCHING IN SOUTHERN FOOTBALL LEAGUE – PREMIER DIVISION CENTRAL

		P	W	D	L	F	A	W	D	L	F	A	W	D	L	F	A	GD	Pts
1	Bedford T (P)	42	14	3	4	46	31	11	4	6	33	27	25	7	10	79	58	21	82
2	Kettering T	42	12	7	2	42	21	10	4	7	31	23	22	11	9	73	44	29	77
3	AFC Telford U¶	42	13	6	2	50	26	6	11	4	32	34	19	17	6	82	60	22	74
4	Halesowen T	42	13	4	4	36	25	8	7	6	29	21	21	11	10	65	46	19	74
5	Harborough T (P)	42	12	2	7	32	19	8	9	4	33	23	20	11	11	65	42	23	71
6	Stamford	42	12	4	5	33	24	8	5	8	20	27	20	9	13	53	51	2	69
7	Spalding U (P)	42	12	4	5	35	23	8	4	9	35	31	20	8	14	70	54	16	68
8	Stratford T	42	9	8	4	34	18	9	5	7	27	26	18	13	11	61	44	17	67
9	Stourbridge	42	8	7	6	25	21	10	2	9	35	29	18	9	15	60	50	10	63
10	Leiston	42	9	5	7	33	30	7	7	7	23	28	16	12	14	56	58	-2	60
11	Royston T	42	9	4	8	28	24	5	7	9	23	25	14	11	17	51	49	2	57
12	Banbury U (R)	42	8	8	5	18	13	6	7	8	22	27	14	15	13	40	40	0	57
13	Alvechurch	42	10	3	8	26	22	6	5	10	23	24	16	8	18	49	46	3	56
14	Bromsgrove Sporting	42	7	3	11	30	29	8	3	10	27	32	15	6	21	57	61	-4	51
15	Bishop's Stortford (R)	42	8	4	9	29	29	6	5	10	23	33	14	9	19	52	62	-10	51
16	St Ives T	42	8	5	8	36	32	5	6	10	22	28	13	11	18	58	60	-2	50
17	AFC Sudbury	42	7	8	6	30	22	6	3	12	22	35	13	11	18	52	57	-5	50
18	Redditch U	42	7	8	6	30	26	6	2	13	20	32	13	10	19	50	58	-8	49
19	Barwell*	42	9	2	10	34	38	4	5	12	22	37	13	7	22	56	75	-19	46
20	Lowestoft T (P)	42	6	4	11	23	42	4	3	14	32	64	10	7	25	55	106	-51	37
21	Hitchin T	42	4	4	11	27	37	2	6	13	27	47	8	10	24	54	84	-30	34
22	Biggleswade T (P)	42	2	8	11	18	35	3	5	13	26	42	5	13	24	44	77	-33	28

¶AFC Telford U promoted via play-offs. *Barwell reprieved from relegation.

PITCHING IN SOUTHERN FOOTBALL LEAGUE – PREMIER DIVISION SOUTH

		P	W	D	L	F	A	W	D	L	F	A	W	D	L	F	A	GD	Pts
1	Merthyr T	42	14	6	1	58	17	13	4	4	47	29	27	10	5	105	46	60	91
2	AFC Totton¶	42	15	6	0	51	16	10	7	4	34	19	25	13	4	85	35	50	88
3	Walton & Hersham	42	13	7	1	50	26	11	4	6	40	28	24	11	7	90	54	36	83
4	Gloucester C (R)	42	14	5	2	53	22	7	9	5	28	31	21	14	7	81	53	28	77
5	Dorchester T	42	14	5	2	46	21	5	13	3	29	27	19	18	5	75	48	27	75
6	Havant & Waterlooville (R)	42	14	4	3	54	18	7	7	7	30	31	21	11	10	84	49	35	74
7	Hungerford T	42	10	5	6	37	24	6	6	9	26	31	16	11	15	63	55	8	59
8	Hanwell T	42	7	9	5	28	24	8	4	9	30	38	15	13	14	58	62	-4	58
9	Taunton T (R)	42	6	11	4	38	30	7	7	7	26	28	13	18	11	64	58	6	57
10	Wimborne T (P)	42	11	5	5	29	22	4	7	10	20	34	15	12	15	49	56	-7	57
11	Sholing	42	8	5	8	30	29	6	5	10	29	39	14	10	18	59	68	-9	52
12	Gosport Bor	42	7	5	9	31	32	6	7	8	22	29	13	12	17	53	61	-8	51
13	Plymouth Parkway	42	8	3	10	38	36	6	5	10	25	41	14	8	20	63	77	-14	50
14	Poole T	42	9	4	8	24	22	4	6	11	24	40	13	10	19	48	62	-14	49
15	Basingstoke T	42	6	6	9	26	28	5	9	7	36	36	11	15	16	62	64	-2	48
16	Chertsey T (P)	42	6	4	11	36	40	8	1	12	31	42	14	5	23	67	82	-15	47
17	Tiverton T	42	8	6	7	23	28	4	5	12	16	43	12	11	19	39	71	-32	47
18	Bracknell T	42	6	7	8	32	34	5	6	10	25	38	11	13	18	57	72	-15	46
19	Winchester C	42	4	6	11	25	40	8	4	9	29	34	12	10	20	54	74	-20	46
20	Swindon Supermarine	42	7	7	7	31	29	5	1	15	29	49	12	8	22	60	78	-18	44
21	Frome T (P)	42	3	6	12	22	32	6	7	8	17	28	9	13	20	39	60	-21	40
22	Marlow (P)	42	3	4	14	23	45	2	2	17	22	70	5	6	31	45	115	-70	21

¶AFC Totton promoted via play-offs.

PITCHING IN ISTHMIAN LEAGUE – PREMIER DIVISION

			Home				Away				Total					
		P	W	D	L	F	A	W	D	L	F	A	W	D	L	F	A	GD	Pts
1	Horsham	42	16	1	4	46	17	12	2	7	36	23	28	3	11	82	40	42	87
2	Billericay T	42	15	3	3	44	20	11	6	4	39	22	26	9	7	83	42	41	87
3	Dartford (R)	42	12	5	4	40	20	13	4	4	37	29	25	9	8	77	49	28	84
4	Cray Valley (PM)* (P)	42	12	6	3	42	26	11	5	5	38	30	23	11	8	80	56	24	77
5	Dover Ath¶ (R)	42	10	3	8	39	29	13	4	4	44	19	23	7	12	83	48	35	76
6	Chichester C (P)	42	11	5	5	35	27	11	2	8	37	32	22	7	13	72	59	13	73
7	Carshalton Ath	42	11	6	4	43	30	9	4	8	29	24	20	10	12	72	54	18	70
8	Hashtag U	42	11	3	7	44	36	7	7	7	38	35	18	10	14	82	71	11	64
9	Chatham T	42	9	6	6	39	25	8	6	7	35	28	17	12	13	74	53	21	63
10	Cray W	42	10	7	4	31	21	8	0	13	27	31	18	7	17	58	52	6	61
11	Wingate & Finchley	42	8	7	6	33	28	9	2	10	43	39	17	9	16	76	67	9	60
12	Folkestone Invicta	42	10	3	8	30	29	7	4	10	31	37	17	7	18	61	66	–5	58
13	Lewes	42	9	7	5	38	31	6	6	9	21	33	15	13	14	59	64	–5	58
14	Potters Bar T	42	9	3	9	29	41	8	3	10	28	34	17	6	19	57	75	–18	57
15	Cheshunt	42	6	4	11	30	34	8	3	10	31	35	14	7	21	61	69	–8	49
16	Whitehawk	42	10	3	8	26	19	4	4	13	23	47	14	7	21	49	66	–17	49
17	Canvey Island	42	7	3	11	26	30	6	2	13	22	36	13	5	24	48	66	–18	44
18	Dulwich Hamlet	42	10	2	9	38	37	2	6	13	20	43	12	8	22	58	80	–22	44
19	Hendon	42	9	3	9	40	40	0	9	12	21	39	9	12	21	61	79	–18	39
20	Hastings U	42	4	5	12	22	36	4	5	12	15	39	8	10	24	37	75	–38	34
21	Bognor Regis T	42	5	3	13	23	44	3	5	13	28	56	8	8	26	51	100	–49	32
22	Bowers & Pitsea (P)	42	4	3	14	18	39	3	2	16	16	45	7	5	30	34	84	–50	26

¶*Dover Ath promoted via play-offs.* *Cray Valley (PM) deducted 3 points.*

NATIONAL LEAGUE SYSTEM STEP 4 2024–25

PITCHING IN NORTHERN PREMIER LEAGUE – DIVISION ONE EAST

		P	W	D	L	F	A	W	D	L	F	A	W	D	L	F	A	GD	Pts
1	Cleethorpes T	42	13	6	2	45	20	15	3	3	46	15	28	9	5	91	35	56	93
2	Dunston UTS	42	14	3	4	48	26	10	6	5	34	21	24	9	9	82	47	35	81
3	Stocksbridge Park Steels¶	42	12	4	5	34	14	11	5	5	30	23	23	9	10	64	37	27	78
4	Belper T	42	12	2	7	38	26	11	7	3	35	25	23	9	10	73	51	22	78
5	Emley	42	13	4	4	34	20	10	4	7	24	15	23	8	11	58	35	23	77
6	Newton Aycliffe	42	12	5	4	53	27	9	7	5	40	33	21	12	9	93	60	33	75
7	Carlton T	42	11	6	4	40	25	9	7	5	29	30	20	11	11	69	55	14	71
8	North Ferriby	42	10	5	6	29	24	10	3	8	26	22	20	8	14	55	46	9	68
9	Garforth T (P)	42	7	7	7	22	17	9	4	8	31	32	16	11	15	53	49	4	59
10	Bradford Park Avenue (R)	42	9	6	6	35	27	7	3	11	27	31	16	9	17	62	58	4	57
11	Bishop Auckland (P)	42	7	5	9	36	33	6	8	7	24	32	13	13	16	60	65	–5	52
12	Heaton Stannington (P)	42	9	3	9	31	30	5	6	10	23	37	14	9	19	54	67	–13	51
13	Pontefract Collieries	42	6	7	8	28	35	7	5	9	27	35	13	12	17	55	70	–15	51
14	Consett	42	6	8	7	28	34	6	5	10	31	44	12	13	17	59	78	–19	49
15	Ossett U	42	5	7	9	21	28	8	2	11	26	33	13	9	20	47	61	–14	48
16	Ashington	42	5	4	12	26	40	8	5	8	24	27	13	9	20	50	67	–17	48
17	Grimsby Bor*	42	6	4	11	23	27	7	7	7	23	22	13	11	18	46	49	–3	47
18	Bridlington T	42	6	2	13	18	34	8	2	11	32	41	14	4	24	50	75	–25	46
19	Brighouse T*	42	5	8	8	22	33	6	6	9	25	40	11	14	17	47	73	–26	44
20	Sherwood Colliery (P)	42	5	5	11	18	34	5	1	15	25	50	10	6	26	43	84	–41	36
21	Liversedge	42	3	5	13	24	36	4	8	9	25	33	7	13	22	49	69	–20	34
22	Sheffield	42	5	2	14	29	39	2	6	13	22	41	7	8	27	51	80	–29	29

¶*Stocksbridge Park Steels promoted via play-offs.* *Grimsby Bor deducted 3 points. Brighouse T deducted 3 points but reprieved from relegation.*

PITCHING IN NORTHERN PREMIER LEAGUE – DIVISION ONE WEST

		P	W	D	L	F	A	W	D	L	F	A	W	D	L	F	A	GD	Pts
1	Widnes	42	13	4	4	40	18	12	6	3	39	20	25	10	7	79	38	41	85
2	Hednesford T¶	42	11	6	4	40	20	13	4	4	41	20	24	10	8	81	40	41	82
3	Congleton T (P)	42	14	3	4	41	20	10	3	8	41	36	24	6	12	82	56	26	78
4	Chasetown	42	15	2	4	53	23	7	6	8	31	30	22	8	12	84	53	31	74
5	Vauxhall Motors	42	10	4	7	38	30	12	4	5	35	25	22	8	12	73	55	18	74
6	Stalybridge Celtic	42	13	2	6	35	26	8	5	8	37	40	21	7	14	72	66	6	70
7	Avro	42	10	7	4	33	24	7	6	8	20	22	17	13	12	53	46	7	64
8	Nantwich T	42	10	5	6	45	24	8	3	10	29	32	18	8	15	74	56	18	63
9	Trafford	42	7	5	9	26	29	10	6	5	28	27	17	11	14	54	56	–2	62
10	Clitheroe	42	10	7	4	47	27	7	3	11	32	45	17	10	15	79	72	7	61
11	Runcorn Linnets	42	9	3	9	32	38	8	7	6	22	32	17	10	15	54	70	–16	61
12	Stafford Rangers (R)	42	9	5	7	35	29	7	5	9	31	31	16	10	16	66	60	6	58
13	Mossley	42	8	7	6	24	18	7	5	9	25	28	15	12	15	49	46	3	57
14	Bootle	42	8	5	8	33	30	8	3	10	34	37	16	8	18	67	67	0	56
15	Atherton Collieries (R)	42	8	5	8	31	31	8	3	10	25	31	16	8	18	56	62	–6	56
16	Newcastle T	42	8	5	8	26	23	6	7	8	23	27	14	12	16	49	50	–1	54
17	Witton Alb	42	9	3	9	30	26	7	3	11	24	37	16	6	20	54	63	–9	54
18	Kidsgrove Ath	42	8	9	4	27	27	5	7	9	26	36	13	11	13	53	63	–10	50
19	Wythenshawe T* (P)	42	5	6	10	30	33	6	8	7	26	26	11	13	18	56	59	–3	46
20	Wythenshawe (P)	42	3	7	11	22	36	7	1	13	23	39	10	8	24	45	75	–30	38
21	Hanley T	42	2	2	17	15	42	3	8	10	22	41	5	10	27	37	83	–46	25
22	City of Liverpool	42	0	5	16	17	60	3	1	17	20	58	3	6	33	37	118	–81	15

¶*Hednesford T promoted via play-offs.* *Wythenshawe T reprieved from relegation.*

PITCHING IN NORTHERN PREMIER LEAGUE – DIVISION ONE MIDLANDS

	P	Home					Away					Total					GD	Pts
		W	D	L	F	A	W	D	L	F	A	W	D	L	F	A		
1 Quorn	40	15	4	1	56	16	17	3	0	48	9	32	7	1	104	25	79	103
2 Corby T	40	14	2	4	45	18	13	2	5	39	22	27	4	9	84	40	44	85
3 Anstey Nomads	40	13	4	3	40	20	11	4	5	43	25	24	8	8	83	45	38	80
4 Worcester C¶ (P)	40	15	1	4	49	21	8	3	9	34	31	23	4	13	83	52	31	73
5 Long Eaton U (R)	40	11	5	4	45	23	11	1	8	47	31	22	6	12	92	54	38	72
6 Sporting Khalsa	40	10	3	7	39	32	10	4	6	35	28	20	7	13	74	60	14	67
7 Darlaston T (1874) (P)	40	8	5	7	27	26	9	5	6	30	23	17	10	13	57	49	8	61
8 Wellingborough T (P)	40	10	5	5	30	19	6	5	9	27	33	16	10	14	57	52	5	58
9 Coleshill T	40	9	4	7	35	28	7	4	9	26	28	16	8	16	61	56	5	56
10 Hinckley LR	40	8	4	8	26	22	7	6	7	28	28	15	10	15	54	50	4	55
11 Racing Club Warwick (P)	40	9	3	8	36	32	6	4	10	25	33	15	7	18	61	65	-4	52
12 Sutton Coldfield T	40	9	2	9	26	28	6	3	11	25	32	15	5	20	51	60	-9	50
13 Shepshed Dynamo	40	7	6	7	20	23	6	5	9	27	35	13	11	16	47	58	-11	50
14 AFC Rushden & Diamonds	40	8	5	7	29	31	5	5	10	15	30	13	10	17	44	61	-17	49
15 Loughborough Students (P)	40	8	4	8	27	29	5	5	10	26	40	13	9	18	53	69	-16	48
16 Boldmere St Michaels	40	8	3	9	27	32	5	5	10	18	37	13	8	19	45	69	-24	47
17 Coventry Sphinx	40	5	6	9	23	33	6	7	7	27	32	11	13	16	50	65	-15	46
18 Bedworth U	40	5	5	10	27	38	4	7	9	27	34	9	12	19	54	72	-18	39
19 Rugby T	40	5	6	9	20	38	3	5	12	16	38	8	11	21	36	76	-40	35
20 Lye T	40	4	5	11	19	44	2	4	14	14	40	6	9	25	33	84	-51	27
21 Grantham T	40	2	8	10	17	37	0	3	17	13	54	2	11	27	30	91	-61	17
22 Walsall Wood*	0	0	0	0	0	0	0	0	0	0	0	0	0	0	0	0	0	0

¶Worcester C promoted via play-offs. *Walsall Wood resigned from the league, record expunged.

PITCHING IN SOUTHERN FOOTBALL LEAGUE – DIVISION ONE CENTRAL

	P	Home					Away					Total					GD	Pts
		W	D	L	F	A	W	D	L	F	A	W	D	L	F	A		
1 Real Bedford (P)	40	15	4	1	77	22	18	1	1	52	11	33	5	2	129	33	96	104
2 Berkhamsted¶ (R)	40	14	4	2	45	18	13	4	3	49	29	27	8	5	94	47	47	89
3 Flackwell Heath (P)	40	14	3	3	46	16	12	3	5	43	29	26	6	8	89	45	44	84
4 Barton R	40	13	5	2	37	19	9	6	5	35	28	22	11	7	72	47	25	77
5 Hadley	40	15	2	3	45	16	7	7	7	36	33	22	9	9	81	49	32	75
6 Thame U	40	11	3	6	48	28	11	3	6	29	30	22	6	12	77	58	19	72
7 Leighton T	40	11	4	5	35	24	7	5	8	28	28	18	9	13	63	52	11	63
8 Biggleswade	40	9	4	7	33	34	7	6	7	29	38	16	10	14	62	72	-10	58
9 Welwyn Garden C	40	9	4	7	28	20	7	5	8	30	33	16	9	15	58	53	5	57
10 Ware	40	8	8	4	35	26	5	9	6	29	25	13	17	10	64	51	13	56
11 Beaconsfield T (R)	40	6	5	9	33	34	7	6	7	25	28	13	11	16	58	62	-4	50
12 Enfield	40	9	3	8	37	37	3	9	8	25	35	12	12	16	62	72	-6	48
13 Hertford T	40	7	8	5	37	35	5	4	11	22	32	12	12	16	59	67	-8	48
14 AFC Dunstable	40	8	5	7	26	25	5	3	12	24	43	13	8	19	50	68	-18	47
15 Aylesbury U	40	6	3	11	19	31	8	0	12	27	39	14	3	23	46	70	-24	45
16 Northwood	40	7	2	11	30	31	5	2	13	28	48	12	4	24	58	79	-21	40
17 Stotfold	40	7	3	10	27	37	4	4	12	25	49	11	7	22	52	86	-34	40
18 Leverstock Green (P)	40	5	6	9	20	24	4	6	10	26	39	9	12	19	46	63	-17	39
19 Kings Langley	40	4	7	9	34	37	5	4	11	18	27	9	11	20	52	64	-12	38
20 Kidlington	40	3	4	13	22	43	4	3	13	17	47	7	7	26	39	90	-51	28
21 North Leigh	40	1	3	16	14	49	1	2	17	9	61	2	5	33	23	110	-87	11

¶Berkhamsted promoted via play-offs.

PITCHING IN SOUTHERN FOOTBALL LEAGUE – DIVISION ONE SOUTH

	P	Home					Away					Total					GD	Pts
		W	D	L	F	A	W	D	L	F	A	W	D	L	F	A		
1 Yate T	42	13	6	2	34	19	13	4	4	38	19	26	10	6	72	38	34	88
2 Evesham U¶	42	15	2	4	41	20	10	5	6	25	16	25	7	10	66	36	30	82
3 Bishop's Cleeve	42	13	5	3	47	18	11	1	9	29	16	24	6	12	76	34	42	78
4 Malvern T	42	14	4	3	57	28	7	8	6	39	34	21	12	9	96	62	34	75
5 Exmouth T	42	11	4	6	36	21	11	4	6	33	18	22	8	12	69	39	30	74
6 Mousehole	42	15	2	4	50	19	5	10	6	32	35	20	12	10	82	54	28	72
7 Bemerton Heath Harlequins†	42	14	5	2	50	22	7	4	10	29	36	21	9	12	79	58	21	72
8 Melksham T	42	11	4	6	40	23	6	8	7	32	31	17	12	13	72	54	18	63
9 Falmouth T (P)	42	9	5	7	30	24	8	2	11	32	37	17	7	18	62	61	1	58
10 Bideford	42	10	5	6	30	24	5	8	8	34	41	15	13	14	64	65	-1	58
11 Didcot T (R)	42	11	6	4	28	20	4	6	11	27	43	15	12	15	55	63	-8	57
12 Bristol Manor Farm	42	7	8	6	33	30	6	8	7	40	40	13	16	13	73	70	3	55
13 Westbury U	42	8	6	7	33	28	7	4	10	25	29	15	10	17	58	57	1	55
14 Bashley	42	8	7	6	31	32	6	6	9	23	34	14	13	15	54	66	-12	55
15 Willand R	42	9	6	6	35	24	4	7	10	26	38	13	13	16	61	62	-1	52
16 Tavistock*	42	8	3	10	28	25	6	5	10	27	33	14	8	20	55	58	-3	49
17 Shaftesbury (P)	42	9	5	7	41	39	4	2	15	23	47	13	7	22	64	86	-22	46
18 Larkhall Ath	42	7	8	6	37	37	4	2	15	19	42	11	10	21	56	79	-23	43
19 Helston Ath (P)	42	6	8	7	34	43	4	3	14	20	57	10	11	21	54	100	-46	41
20 Thatcham T (R)	42	10	3	8	29	31	0	6	15	17	47	10	9	23	46	78	-32	39
21 Cribbs	42	3	4	14	17	40	6	2	13	18	46	9	6	27	35	86	-51	33
22 Cinderford T (P)	42	3	3	15	27	50	5	4	12	29	49	8	7	27	56	99	-43	31

¶Evesham U promoted via play-offs. *Tavistock deducted 1 point. †Bemerton Heath Harlequins resigned from the league and demoted to the ninth tier.

PITCHING IN ISTHMIAN LEAGUE – DIVISION ONE NORTH

			Home				Away					Total						
		P	W	D	L	F	A	W	D	L	F	A	W	D	L	F	A	GD	Pts
1	Brentwood T	42	15	3	3	63	23	13	2	6	34	23	28	5	9	97	46	51	89
2	Felixstowe & Walton U	42	16	3	2	50	23	10	4	7	42	25	26	7	9	92	48	44	85
3	Bury T¶	42	14	4	3	37	20	11	6	4	38	25	25	10	7	75	45	30	85
4	Waltham Abbey	42	11	6	4	50	22	12	4	5	30	22	23	10	9	80	44	36	79
5	Brightlingsea Regent	42	10	6	5	31	24	12	4	5	38	26	22	10	10	69	50	19	76
6	Tilbury (P)	42	14	4	3	37	18	7	4	10	24	35	21	8	13	61	53	8	71
7	Witham T	42	12	2	7	43	31	9	4	8	29	30	21	6	15	72	61	11	69
8	Gorleston	42	12	4	5	40	21	7	7	7	26	27	19	11	12	66	48	18	68
9	Grays Ath	42	10	4	7	25	25	10	4	7	37	24	20	8	14	62	49	13	68
10	Walthamstow	42	12	2	7	38	27	8	5	8	36	29	20	7	15	74	56	18	67
11	Cambridge C	42	9	4	8	27	25	8	5	8	37	37	17	9	16	64	62	2	60
12	Redbridge	42	11	2	8	48	33	5	8	8	29	36	16	10	16	77	69	8	58
13	Maldon & Tiptree	42	8	5	8	26	23	5	7	9	23	28	13	12	17	49	51	-2	51
14	Heybridge Swifts	42	3	8	10	22	38	10	4	7	37	33	13	12	17	59	71	-12	51
15	Mildenhall T (P)	42	7	5	9	19	22	6	5	10	22	31	13	10	19	41	53	-12	49
16	Concord Rangers (R)	42	9	2	10	32	34	4	7	10	26	38	13	9	20	58	72	-14	48
17	Wroxham	42	3	10	8	23	33	7	4	10	27	32	10	14	18	50	65	-15	44
18	Newmarket T (P)	42	6	6	9	31	39	5	4	12	24	45	11	10	21	55	84	-29	43
19	Haringey Bor (R)	42	5	8	8	32	38	4	7	10	26	35	9	15	18	58	73	-15	42
20	Ipswich W	42	3	6	12	16	32	4	2	15	18	47	7	8	27	34	79	-45	29
21	Basildon U	42	5	4	12	23	36	2	2	17	16	51	7	6	29	39	87	-48	27
22	Sporting Bengal U (P)	42	5	4	12	19	49	1	3	17	17	53	6	7	29	36	102	-66	25

¶*Bury T promoted via play-offs.*

PITCHING IN ISTHMIAN LEAGUE – DIVISION ONE SOUTH CENTRAL

			Home				Away					Total						
		P	W	D	L	F	A	W	D	L	F	A	W	D	L	F	A	GD	Pts
1	Farnham T (P)	42	15	4	2	52	15	17	2	2	68	17	32	6	4	120	32	88	102
2	Uxbridge¶	42	13	3	5	56	30	12	4	5	34	26	25	7	10	90	56	34	82
3	Hanworth Villa	42	12	5	4	40	24	12	2	7	33	27	24	7	11	73	51	22	79
4	Ascot U	42	11	5	5	38	25	11	6	4	41	30	22	11	9	79	55	24	77
5	Kingstonian (R)	42	12	3	6	45	30	11	4	6	41	28	23	7	12	86	58	28	76
6	Hayes & Yeading U (R)	42	13	5	3	44	27	8	7	6	33	26	21	12	9	77	53	24	75
7	Moneyfields (P)	42	14	3	4	57	36	8	5	8	33	34	22	8	12	90	70	20	74
8	Leatherhead	42	15	0	6	46	22	6	9	6	34	37	21	9	12	80	59	21	72
9	Raynes Park Vale	42	8	6	7	44	32	11	4	6	39	32	19	10	13	83	64	19	67
10	Hartley Wintney	42	11	1	9	37	25	10	2	9	33	33	21	3	18	70	58	12	66
11	Rayners Lane (P)	42	11	3	7	48	40	6	7	8	41	48	17	10	15	89	88	1	61
12	Westfield	42	9	6	6	36	35	6	4	11	26	42	15	10	17	62	77	-15	55
13	Southall	42	9	5	7	36	38	5	4	12	27	32	14	9	19	63	70	-7	51
14	Harrow Bor (R)	42	10	5	6	31	24	4	4	13	25	43	14	9	19	56	67	-11	51
15	South Park	42	9	6	6	37	37	3	4	14	19	34	12	10	20	56	71	-15	46
16	Metropolitan Police	42	7	5	9	27	34	5	3	13	25	40	12	8	22	52	74	-22	44
17	Horndean	42	7	7	7	33	34	4	3	14	29	63	11	10	21	62	97	-35	43
18	Binfield	42	5	5	11	17	31	7	2	12	35	57	12	7	23	52	88	-36	43
19	Guernsey	42	6	4	11	31	48	5	5	11	30	47	11	9	22	61	95	-34	42
20	Ashford T	42	6	3	12	38	46	4	4	13	21	41	10	7	25	59	87	-28	37
21	Sutton Common R	42	4	3	14	16	41	6	1	14	32	39	10	4	28	48	80	-32	34
22	Badshot Lea	42	2	4	15	20	50	1	5	15	25	53	3	9	30	45	103	-58	18

¶*Uxbridge promoted via play-offs.*

PITCHING IN ISTHMIAN LEAGUE – DIVISION ONE SOUTH EAST

			Home				Away					Total						
		P	W	D	L	F	A	W	D	L	F	A	W	D	L	F	A	GD	Pts
1	Ramsgate	42	19	1	1	75	16	16	3	2	52	22	35	4	3	127	38	89	109
2	Sittingbourne	42	18	3	0	73	9	13	5	3	44	20	31	8	3	117	29	88	101
3	Burgess Hill T¶	42	16	3	2	47	16	11	6	4	40	26	27	9	6	87	42	45	90
4	Margate (R)	42	10	9	2	42	22	15	3	3	47	28	25	12	5	89	50	39	87
5	Merstham	42	11	7	3	53	31	11	5	5	39	31	22	12	8	92	62	30	78
6	Beckenham T	42	11	5	5	49	27	11	3	7	40	38	22	8	12	89	65	24	74
7	Deal T (P)	42	12	1	8	48	33	9	1	11	44	48	21	2	19	92	81	11	65
8	Three Bridges	42	9	4	8	43	36	10	3	8	36	40	19	7	16	79	76	3	64
9	Sevenoaks T	42	9	7	5	36	34	8	4	9	45	47	17	11	14	81	81	0	62
10	Sheppey U	42	12	3	6	39	27	6	4	11	30	38	18	7	17	69	65	4	61
11	Ashford U	42	9	4	8	41	39	7	4	10	34	39	16	8	18	75	78	-3	56
12	AFC Croydon Ath (P)	42	10	6	5	39	26	4	7	10	24	36	14	13	15	63	62	1	55
13	Broadbridge Heath	42	5	5	11	37	44	10	5	6	31	29	15	10	17	68	73	-5	55
14	Erith T (P)	42	9	5	7	41	28	5	6	10	31	36	14	11	17	72	64	8	53
15	Eastbourne T (P)	42	7	5	9	28	30	8	3	10	28	36	15	8	19	56	66	-10	53
16	Herne Bay	42	8	4	9	39	39	4	5	12	23	40	12	9	21	62	79	-17	45
17	East Grinstead T	42	6	0	15	22	49	7	5	9	27	42	13	5	24	49	91	-42	44
18	Littlehampton T	42	7	3	11	38	40	5	4	12	27	48	12	7	23	66	88	-21	43
19	Phoenix Sports	42	7	3	11	23	37	3	3	15	18	49	10	6	26	41	86	-45	36
20	Steyning T (P)	42	3	3	15	25	46	4	2	15	29	56	7	5	30	54	102	-48	26
21	Hythe T	42	5	2	14	26	50	1	2	18	13	59	6	4	32	39	109	-70	22
22	Lancing	42	5	2	14	20	41	1	2	18	17	77	6	4	32	37	118	-81	22

¶*Burgess Hill T promoted via play-offs.*

THE ISUZU FA TROPHY 2024–25

PRELIMINARY ROUND

Congleton T v Ashington	4-1
City of Liverpool v Bootle	3-3
City of Liverpool won 5-4 on penalties.	
Lye T v Anstey Nomads	0-1
Long Eaton U v Stafford Rangers	2-2
Long Eaton won 4-3 on penalties. Original match	
which finished 1-2 was ordered to be replayed after	
Stafford Rangers fielded an ineligible player.	
AFC Dunstable v Concord Rangers	2-0
Biggleswade v Hertford T	2-2
Biggleswade won 5-4 on penalties.	
Littlehampton T v Rayners Lane	2-2
Littlehampton T won 5-4 on penalties.	
Moneyfields v Hayes & Yeading U	0-2
Ashford T (Middlesex) v Ascot U	1-1
Ascot U won 4-3 on penalties.	
South Park (Reigate) v Steyning Town Community	0-0
Steyning Town Community won 4-2 on penalties.	
Lancing v Southall	0-4
Original match which finished 0-1 was ordered to be	
replayed after Southall fielded two ineligible players.	
Farnham T v Erith T	3-0
Cribbs v Thatcham T	0-1
Didcot T v Helston Ath	1-3

FIRST QUALIFYING ROUND

Heaton Stannington v North Ferriby	1-0
Congleton T v Wythenshawe	1-0
Bishop Auckland v Nantwich T	1-2
Stalybridge Celtic v Ossett U	1-1
Ossett U won 7-6 on penalties.	
Liversedge v Avro	1-2
Garforth T v Wythenshawe T	0-1
City of Liverpool v Mossley	2-2
City of Liverpool won 4-2 on penalties.	
Emley v Dunston UTS	2-0
Bridlington T v Trafford	0-1
Runcorn Linnets v Pontefract Collieries	1-2
Brighouse T v Clitheroe	1-1
Clitheroe won 5-3 on penalties.	
Consett v Atherton Collieries	1-1
Atherton Collieries won 5-4 on penalties.	
Vauxhall Motors v Newton Aycliffe	1-1
Newton Aycliffe won 3-2 on penalties.	
Stocksbridge Park Steels v Widnes	3-0
Witton Alb v Bradford (Park Avenue)	1-3
Hednesford T v Quorn	4-1
Kidsgrove Ath v AFC Rushden & Diamonds	3-1
Grantham T v Coleshill T	0-2
Sutton Coldfield T v Newcastle T	3-1
Sheffield v Loughborough Students	2-3
Original match which finished 0-1 was ordered to be	
replayed after Loughborough Students fielded an	
ineligible player.	
Grimsby Bor v Chasetown	2-2
Chasetown won 3-2 on penalties.	
Bedworth U v Sherwood Colliery	1-3
Darlaston T v Cleethorpes T	0-2
Belper T v Boldmere St Michaels	2-1
Rugby v Carlton T	0-0
Carlton T won 5-4 on penalties.	
Racing Club Warwick v Hanley T	2-3
Anstey Nomads v Shepshed Dynamo	6-1
Coventry Sphinx v Sporting Khalsa	0-2
Worcester C v Hinckley LR	1-4
Wellingborough T v Corby T	2-3
Walsall Wood v Stafford Rangers	2-1
Felixstowe & Walton U v Basildon U	4-2
Tilbury v Welwyn Garden City	1-1
Tilbury won 6-5 on penalties.	
Leighton v Stotfold	0-0
Leighton T won 4-3 on penalties.	
Enfield v Biggleswade	2-0
Heybridge Swifts v Maldon & Tiptree	0-1

Wroxham v Aylesbury U	0-0
Wroxham won 4-3 on penalties.	
Hadley v Grays Ath	2-1
Walthamstow v Real Bedford	1-2
Redbridge v Haringey Bor	1-3
Leverstock Green v Bury T	1-0
Barton R v Waltham Abbey	1-1
Barton R won 4-2 on penalties.	
Mildenhall T v Brightlingsea Regent	2-4
AFC Dunstable v Berkhamsted	2-2
Berkhamsted won 3-2 on penalties.	
Ware v Newmarket T	2-2
Newmarket T won 4-2 on penalties.	
Brentwood T v Witham T	3-2
Cambridge C v Kings Langley	1-0
Ipswich W v Gorleston	2-0
Uxbridge v Phoenix Sports	6-0
Hartley Wintney v East Grinstead T	2-1
Sheppey U v Ramsgate	2-3
Raynes Park Vale v Beckenham T	4-3
Badshot Lea v Broadbridge Heath	0-4
Horndean v Binfield	3-0
Deal T v Ashford U	0-1
Hanworth Villa v Margate	0-5
Three Bridges v Hythe T	2-1
Westfield v Metropolitan Police	4-0
Littlehampton T v Sporting Bengal U	3-2
Ascot U v Merstham	5-0
Sevenoaks T v Harrow Bor	3-0
Farnham T v Flackwell Heath	1-2
Steyning Town Community v Thame U	0-5
Kingstonian v Eastbourne T	3-0
Herne Bay v Northwood	1-0
Southall v Burgess Hill T	0-2
AFC Croydon Ath v Beaconsfield T	1-0
Hayes & Yeading U v Leatherhead	0-1
Sittingbourne v Sutton Common R	2-0
Willand R v Bishop's Cleeve	0-2
Mousehole v Bashley	4-0
Original match at Bashley which finished 1-1 and a	
7-6 win on penalties to Bashley was ordered to be	
replayed at Mousehole after Bashley fielded an	
ineligible player.	
Helston Ath v Melksham T	1-1
Melksham T won 3-2 on penalties.	
Shaftesbury v North Leigh	0-1
Exmouth T v Kidlington	4-1
Bemerton Heath Harlequins v Yate T	1-3
Original match which finished 0-5 was ordered to be	
replayed after Yate T fielded an ineligible player.	
Bideford v Malvern T	2-0
Falmouth T v Cinderford T	3-0
Thatcham T v Evesham U	1-2
Original match which finished 2-4 was ordered to be	
replayed after Evesham fielded an ineligible player.	
Bristol Manor Farm v Westbury U	2-0
Tavistock v Larkhall Ath	3-2

SECOND QUALIFYING ROUND

Trafford v Atherton Collieries	3-1
Ossett U v Bradford (Park Avenue)	2-1
City of Liverpool v Pontefract Collieries	4-0
Emley v Newton Aycliffe	0-3
Clitheroe v Heaton Stannington	3-1
Wythenshawe T v Stocksbridge Park Steels	2-2
Stocksbridge Park Steels won 4-3 on penalties.	
Avro v Congleton T	0-1
Hanley T v Sherwood Colliery	1-0
Sporting Khalsa v Nantwich T	4-3
Hednesford T v Chasetown	1-2
Anstey Nomads v Sutton Coldfield T	2-0
Coleshill T v Carlton T	3-2
Walsall Wood v Cleethorpes T	1-1
Cleethorpes T won 5-4 on penalties.	
Kidsgrove Ath v Belper T	1-2

Loughborough Students v Hinckley LR	1-1
Hinckley LR won 3-2 on penalties.	
Maldon & Tiptree v Corby T	2-2
Maldon & Tiptree won 4-2 on penalties.	
Felixstowe & Walton U v Enfield	2-1
Hadley v Ipswich W	4-1
Leverstock Green v Barton R	3-4
Newmarket T v Cambridge C	1-3
Real Bedford v Leighton T	4-0
Berkhamsted v Tilbury	4-0
Brightlingsea Regent v Brentwood T	1-2
Wroxham v Haringey Bor	1-3
Sittingbourne v Kingstonian	4-1
Ashford U v Hartley Wintney	2-1
Westfield v Thame U	1-3
Three Bridges v Herne Bay	0-3
Uxbridge v AFC Croydon Ath	2-1
Littlehampton T v Burgess Hill T	0-0
Littlehampton T won 5-4 on penalties.	
Ramsgate v Raynes Park Vale	2-1
Ascot U v Margate	1-0
Flackwell Heath v Broadbridge Heath	6-1
Sevenoaks T v Leatherhead	1-2
Tavistock v North Leigh	3-0
Exmouth T v Horndean	1-2
Mousehole v Falmouth T	3-1
Melksham T v Bishop's Cleeve	2-0
Evesham U v Bristol Manor Farm	2-2
Bristol Manor Farm won 5-4 on penalties.	
Yate T v Bideford	2-0

THIRD QUALIFYING ROUND

Workington v Morpeth T	3-1
Blyth Spartans v Stockton T	0-2
City of Liverpool v Macclesfield	0-3
Whitby T v Newton Aycliffe	0-1
Ossett U v Prescot Cables	2-0
Congleton T v Hyde U	1-0
Trafford v Ashton U	2-5
Stocksbridge Park Steels v Warrington Rylands	1-1
Warrington Rylands won 3-1 on penalties.	
Guiseley v Bamber Bridge	0-1
Hebburn T v FC United of Manchester	0-3
Clitheroe v Lancaster C	2-0
Stourbridge v Matlock T	3-0
Kettering T v Gainsborough Trinity	0-2
Stamford v Anstey Nomads	1-5
Belper T v Hinckley LR	3-1
Chasetown v Bromsgrove Sporting	1-0
Sporting Khalsa v Harborough T	5-2
Redditch U v Halesowen T	0-3
Basford U v Hanley T	2-2
Basford U won 4-1 on penalties.	
Barwell v Stratford T	1-0
AFC Telford U v Cleethorpes T	1-1
AFC Telford U won 5-4 on penalties.	
Ilkeston T v Coleshill T	2-3
Worksop T v St Ives T	2-1
Leek T v Mickleover	0-1
Spalding U v Alvechurch	1-2
Ramsgate v Cray Valley (PM)	1-3
Bowers & Pitsea v Real Bedford	3-0
Sittingbourne v Bognor Regis T	2-1
Potters Bar T v Whitehawk	2-1
Uxbridge v Thame U	3-2
Ashford U v Walton & Hersham	1-0
Felixstowe & Walton v Haringey Borough	4-0
Hanwell T v Berkhamsted	1-1
Hanwell T won 3-1 on penalties.	
AFC Sudbury v Cambridge C	0-1
Leatherhead v Hastings U	1-2
Folkestone Invicta v Ascot U	8-1
Lewes v Bracknell T	6-3
Leiston v Horsham	1-1
Horsham won 4-3 on penalties.	
Bedford T v Hendon	1-5
Maldon & Tiptree v Canvey Island	1-2
Flackwell Heath v Bishop's Stortford	1-1
Bishop's Stortford won 4-1 on penalties.	
Dover Ath v Cheshunt	3-0

Brentwood T v Cray W	1-1
Brentwood T won 4-3 on penalties.	
Lowestoft T v Royston T	2-3
Marlow v Biggleswade T	0-1
Littlehampton T v Barton R	0-1
Chichester C v Herne Bay	2-0
Chertsey T v Billericay T	1-1
Chertsey T won 6-5 on penalties.	
Chatham T v Wingate & Finchley	1-0
Dartford v Dulwich Hamlet	0-1
Hashtag U v Hitchin T	1-0
Hadley v Carshalton Ath	3-1
Mousehole v Bristol Manor Farm	0-2
Gloucester C v Wimborne T	2-2
Gloucester C won 8-7 on penalties.	
Frome T v Havant & Waterlooville	1-1
Havant & Waterlooville won 5-4 on penalties.	
Taunton T v Basingstoke T	1-0
AFC Totton v Merthyr T	1-0
Hungerford T v Sholing	3-1
Tiverton T v Dorchester T	0-0
Dorchester T won 5-4 on penalties.	
Plymouth Parkway v Banbury U	3-2
Poole T v Gosport Bor	1-1
Gosport Bor won 4-3 on penalties.	
Yate T v Melksham T	3-0
Winchester C v Swindon Supermarine	5-2
Tavistock v Horndean	3-1

FIRST ROUND

Worksop T v FC United of Manchester	2-0
Warrington Rylands v Ossett U	4-0
Macclesfield v Ashton U	7-1
Clitheroe v Gainsborough Trinity	1-4
Workington v Bamber Bridge	2-3
Stockton T v Newton Aycliffe	2-1
Mickleover v AFC Telford U	1-2
Basford U v Anstey Nomads	1-1
Basford U won 5-3 on penalties.	
Barwell v Sporting Khalsa	0-2
Chasetown v Belper T	1-1
Chasetown won 5-4 on penalties.	
Halesowen T v Congleton T	4-1
Stourbridge v Alvechurch	0-1
Gloucester C v Coleshill T	2-3
Dulwich Hamlet v Hashtag U	1-1
Hashtag U won 5-3 on penalties.	
Lewes v Ashford U	2-2
Lewes won 8-7 on penalties.	
Bishop's Stortford v Felixstowe & Walton U	1-6
Dover Ath v Sittingbourne	0-2
Cambridge C v Royston T	1-2
Uxbridge v Chertsey T	0-3
Brentwood T v Cray Valley (PM)	4-3
Biggleswade T v Potters Bar T	2-0
Barton R v Folkestone Invicta	0-3
Bowers & Pitsea v Chatham T	0-1
Hanwell T v Hendon	5-0
Hadley v Hastings U	4-3
Canvey Island v Horsham	0-2
Gosport Bor v Taunton T	5-1
Hungerford T v Yate T	2-3
Bristol Manor Farm v Havant & Waterlooville	1-1
Havant & Waterlooville won 4-2 on penalties.	
AFC Totton v Dorchester T	1-0
Tavistock v Winchester C	0-4
Plymouth Parkway v Chichester C	0-4

SECOND ROUND

Southport v Warrington T	3-0
Scunthorpe U v Warrington Rylands	1-2
Gainsborough Trinity v Chester	1-0
Bamber Bridge v Farsley Celtic	0-1
Spennymoor T v South Shields	2-1
Darlington v Buxton	1-0
Stockton T v Scarborough Ath	3-1
Curzon Ashton v Macclesfield	2-2
Macclesfield won 5-3 on penalties.	
Chorley v Marine	3-1
Radcliffe v Worksop T	3-2

Coleshill T v Biggleswade T	4-5
Alfreton T v Needham Market	3-2
Aveley v Hemel Hempstead T	2-1
Hashtag U v Brackley T	3-2
Oxford C v Sporting Khalsa	5-0
Enfield T v Hornchurch	1-1
Enfield T won 8-7 on penalties.	
Alvechurch v Chasetown	0-0
Alvechurch won 5-4 on penalties.	
Leamington v King's Lynn T	2-1
Hereford v Brentwood T	0-1
Royston T v Rushall Olympic	0-1
Kidderminster H v Halesowen T	2-1
Boreham Wood v Felixstowe & Walton U	1-1
Boreham Wood won 5-4 on penalties.	
Peterborough Sports v Chelmsford C	2-0
Hadley v AFC Telford U	1-0
St Albans C v Basford U	1-2
Lewes v AFC Totton	0-2
Salisbury v Farnborough	3-0
Yate T v Hampton & Richmond Bor	0-2
Folkestone Invicta v Hanwell T	0-2
Horsham v Maidstone U	2-1
Gosport Bor v Tonbridge Angels	1-0
Welling U v Havant & Waterlooville	1-2
Slough T v Chatham T	1-1
Slough T won 4-2 on penalties.	
Chesham U v Chippenham T	2-0
Chichester C v Worthing	2-3
Winchester C v Sittingbourne	1-1
Sittingbourne won 5-4 on penalties.	
Torquay U v Truro C	1-0
Bath C v Chertsey T	2-3
Weston-super-Mare v Weymouth	2-3
Dorking W v Eastbourne Bor	1-1
Eastbourne Bor won 4-2 on penalties.	

THIRD ROUND

Basford U v FC Halifax T	2-2
Basford U won 6-5 on penalties.	
Hartlepool U v Tamworth	1-1
Tamworth won 3-0 on penalties.	
AFC Fylde v Kidderminster H	2-2
Kidderminster H won 3-0 on penalties.	
Gateshead v Farsley Celtic	8-1
Stockton T v Oldham Ath	2-0
Southport v Peterborough Sports	2-1
Solihull Moors v Radcliffe	1-2
Boston U v Alvechurch	1-0
Altrincham v Macclesfield	0-0
Altrincham won 4-2 on penalties.	
Leamington v Rochdale	0-2
York C v Darlington	3-1
Gainsborough Trinity v Rushall Olympic	2-1
Chorley v Warrington Rylands	3-2
Alfreton T v Spennymoor T	0-1
Chertsey T v Dagenham & Red	1-0
Braintree T v Forest Green R	1-1
Forest Green R won 5-3 on penalties.	
Barnet v Aveley	2-0
Sutton U v Ebbsfleet U	3-3
Sutton U won 4-2 on penalties.	

Boreham Wood v Eastbourne Bor	1-0
Aldershot T v Wealdstone	3-1
Oxford C v Hadley	2-1
Woking v Havant & Waterlooville	3-3
Woking won 4-2 on penalties.	
Sittingbourne v Enfield T	4-2
Torquay U v Horsham	2-0
Yeovil T v Weymouth	1-2
Chesham U v Salisbury	2-3
Biggleswade T v AFC Totton	1-1
Biggleswade T won 3-2 on penalties.	
Hanwell T v Eastleigh	1-2
Brentwood T v Southend U	3-5
Slough T v Maidenhead U	2-1
Worthing v Gosport Bor	1-1
Gosport Bor won 3-2 on penalties. Gosport Bor were	
subsequently removed after fielding an ineligible player	
in their Second Round match against Tonbridge Angels.	
Hampton & Richmond Bor v Hashtag U	3-0

FOURTH ROUND

Aldershot T v Chertsey T	8-0
Kidderminster H v Slough T	4-0
Rochdale v Stockton T	0-0
Rochdale won 4-3 on penalties.	
Altrincham v Barnet	3-1
Worthing v Torquay U	5-1
Biggleswade T v Oxford C	0-3
Sittingbourne v Salisbury	2-1
Forest Green R v Chorley	2-0
Woking v Radcliffe	4-0
Sutton U v Tamworth	1-0
Gainsborough Trinity v York C	1-0
Basford U v Eastleigh	1-4
Weymouth v Boreham Wood	1-2
Gateshead v Boston U	1-3
Hampton & Richmond Bor v Spennymoor T	0-2
Southend U v Southport	1-0

FIFTH ROUND

Gainsborough Trinity v Woking	0-3
Southend U v Sittingbourne	0-1
Spennymoor T v Boston U	2-2
Spennymoor T won 3-1 on penalties.	
Oxford C v Forest Green R	1-0
Aldershot T v Boreham Wood	2-0
Kidderminster H v Sutton U	0-1
Worthing v Rochdale	1-2
Altrincham v Eastleigh	1-0

QUARTER-FINALS

Sittingbourne v Aldershot T	0-3
Oxford C v Woking	2-2
Woking won 2-1 on penalties.	
Sutton U v Spennymoor T	0-2
Rochdale v Altrincham	2-0

SEMI-FINALS

Aldershot v Woking	2-1
Rochdale v Spennymoor T	2-2
Spennymoor T won 5-4 on penalties	

THE ISUZU FA TROPHY FINAL 2024–25

Sunday, 11 May 2025

(at Wembley Stadium, attendance combined with Isuzu FA Vase 38,600)

Aldershot T (0) 3   Spennymoor T (0) 0

Aldershot: Dewhurst (Van Stappershoef 90); Jones A, Woodhouse, Ellison, Armitage, Frost (Scott 90), Tetek (Corbett 57), Widdrington, Henry (Mullins 82), Barham (Thomas 75), Barrett.
Scorers: Barham 48, Ellison 71, Barrett 87.

Spennymoor T: James (Johnson 90); Dyson, Ledger, Beals (Rowe 84), Staunton, Dolan (Ross 84), Shrimpton, Mondal (Rutledge 69), Ramshaw, McKeown (Harris 75), Taylor.

Referee: Lewis Smith.

THE ISUZU FA VASE 2024–25

FIRST QUALIFYING ROUND

Longridge v Whitley Bay	2-3
Newcastle Blue Star v Easington Colliery	0-1
Sunderland RCA v FC Hartlepool	0-4
Ilkley T v Penrith	1-2
Tow Law T v Kendal T	2-5
Thackley v Colne	1-3
Shildon v Yarm & Eaglescliffe	2-0
Alnwick T v Billingham Synthonia	1-1
Billingham Synthonia won 3-2 on penalties.	
Birtley T v Horden Community Welfare	0-2
Jarrow v Sunderland West End	3-2
Pickering T v Newcastle Benfield	2-3
Chester-le-Street T v Billingham T	0-1
Thornaby v Padiham	1-2
Northallerton T (walkover) v Route One R	
Boldon CA v Seaham Red Star	2-3
Redcar T v North Shields	0-4
Parkgate v Sandbach U	0-2
Horbury T v Ashton T	2-2
Ashton T won 5-4 on penalties.	
Runcorn T v Handsworth	1-3
Wombwell T v Nostell MW	4-0
Athersley Recreation v Retford U	0-2
Dearne & District v Darwen	0-1
FC St Helens v Cheadle Heath Nomads	2-1
Winsford U v Litherland Remyca	4-0
Eccleshill U v Chadderton	3-7
Wakefield v 1874 Northwich	2-0
Golcar U v New Mills	2-2
New Mills won 6-5 on penalties.	
Burscough v Droylsden	2-1
Ashton Ath v Stockport Georgians	2-1
Euxton Villa v Squires Gate	2-1
Bottesford T v Barnton	1-5
Maghull v Bury	1-3
Worsbrough Bridge Ath v Prestwich Heys	3-2
Selby T v Skelmersdale U	1-0
Rossington Main v Retford	1-3
Dronfield T v Beverley T	1-3
Glasshoughton Welfare v Cheadle T	1-3
Brigg T v Winterton Rangers	1-1
Winterton Rangers won 3-2 on penalties.	
AFC Liverpool v Northwich Vic	3-1
Cammell Laird 1907 v Armthorpe Welfare	1-4
Barton T v Stockport T	1-2
Chelmsley T v Allscott Heath	2-3
Stapenhill v Pershore T	2-1
Southam U v Wolverhampton Casuals	0-3
Bilston T v Stafford T	1-4
Shifnal T v Cradley T	3-0
Market Drayton T v Studley	1-0
Wednesfield v Atherstone T	2-9
Droitwich Spa v Nuneaton Griff	6-2
Alsager T v Heather St Johns	2-2
Heather St Johns won 3-1 on penalties.	
Worcester Raiders v Eccleshall	1-0
Westfields v AFC Wulfrunians	0-4
Brocton v OJM Black Country	2-0
Rugby Bor v Gresley R	4-1
Bewdley T v AFC Bridgnorth	4-0
Allexton & New Parks v Clipstone	1-3
Bourne T v Harrowby U	3-2
Birstall U v Dunkirk	1-1
Dunkirk won 3-2 on penalties.	
Clifton All Whites v Deeping Rangers	1-1
Deeping Rangers won 4-1 on penalties.	
Blackstones v Saffron Dynamo	3-2
Newark T v AFC Mansfield	4-3
Lutterworth T v Pinchbeck U	6-1
GNG Oadby T v Radford	1-2
Sandiacre T v Newark & Sherwood U	0-5
Leicester Nirvana v Aylestone Park	0-2
Gedling MW v Sleaford T	0-2
Louth T v Heanor T	0-2
Holwell Sports v Kimberley MW	0-3
Ingles v Melton T	0-4
Clay Cross T v Selston	7-1
Harleston T v Wisbech T	0-0
Harleston T won 4-3 on penalties.	
March Town U v Dussindale & Hellesdon R	5-2
Great Yarmouth T v Soham Town Rangers	3-0

St Neots T v Sheringham	5-0
Dereham T v FC Peterborough	4-1
Mulbarton W v Godmanchester R	8-0
Stowmarket T v Huntingdon T	2-1
Framlingham T v Ely C	3-0
Eynesbury R v Lakenheath	2-0
Diss T v Heacham	1-2
Haverhill R v Baldock T	1-2
Long Melford v Hullbridge Sports	0-2
Brimsdown v Hackney Wick	1-1
Brimsdown won 4-2 on penalties.	
Newbury Forest v Cannons Wood	2-1
Takeley v Hutton	3-0
Coggeshall T v May & Baker Eastbrook Community	3-1
Harlow T v Ilford	2-0
Colney Heath v Wivenhoe T	4-0
Buckhurst Hill v Cockfosters	3-1
St Margaretsbury v Haverhill Bor	1-3
Hadleigh U v Woodford T	0-0
Hadleigh U won 4-3 on penalties.	
Basildon T v Rayleigh T	2-4
Potton U v Little Oakley	2-2
Potton U won 3-2 on penalties.	
Barking v FC Baresi	4-0
West Essex v Southend Manor	3-1
Halstead T v Langford	3-3
Halstead T won 6-5 on penalties.	
Risborough Rangers v Ardley U	1-0
Bedfont Sports Club v Langley	5-0
Holyport v Hillingdon Bor	5-0
Rising Ballers Kensington v Bugbrooke St Michaels	0-0
Bugbrooke St Michaels won 4-3 on penalties.	
Desborough T v Aylesbury Vale Dynamos	3-2
Raunds T v Penn & Tylers Green	2-4
Holmer Green v Rothwell Corinthians	2-3
Wellingborough Whitworths v Milton Keynes Irish	1-3
Kempston R v Spartans Youth	3-2
Oxhey Jets v Ampthill T	1-1
Ampthill T won 3-2 on penalties.	
London Colney v Winslow U	0-1
Amersham T v Staines Lammas	1-2
Northampton Sileby Rangers v Northampton ON Chenecks	1-1
Northampton ON Chenecks won 4-2 on penalties.	
NW London v Wembley	0-2
Clanfield 85 v Tadley Calleva	1-4
Sandhurst T v Nailsea & Tickenham	4-1
Milton U v Woodley U	2-1
Stonehouse T v Corsham T	0-0
Stonehouse T won 3-1 on penalties.	
Brimscombe & Thrupp v Roman Glass St George	1-2
Oldland Abbotonians v Cirencester T	1-0
Malmesbury Vic v Longlevens	3-0
Hallen v Portishead T	2-2
Portishead T won 3-1 on penalties.	
Berks Co v Calne T	6-1
Tytherington Rocks v Keynsham T	5-1
Reading C v Abingdon U	3-2
Hengrove Ath v Shirehampton	1-1
Hengrove Ath won 4-3 on penalties.	
Wantage T v Bitton	2-4
Wokingham & Emmbrook v Cheltenham Saracens	3-3
Cheltenham Saracens won 4-3 on penalties.	
Newent T v Cadbury Heath	1-3
Odd Down v Brislington	0-2
Westside v VCD Ath	1-4
Redhill v Billingshurst	2-3
Selsey v Larkfield & New Hythe	1-1
Selsey won 5-4 on penalties.	
Mile Oak v Glebe	2-4
Ash U v Crawley Down Gatwick	2-3
FC Elmstead v Frimley Green	0-3
Abbey Rangers v Rochester U	2-3
Montpelier Villa v Haywards Heath T	0-3
Meridian v Lewisham Bor (Community)	2-2
Meridian won 5-3 on penalties.	
Balham v Punjab U	1-1
Balham won 4-2 on penalties.	
Sheppey Sports v Reigate Priory	4-0
Peacehaven & Telscombe v Snodland T	1-0
Sporting Club Thamesmead v Little Common	1-1
Little Common won 4-3 on penalties.	

Rusthall v Soul Tower Hamlets	2-3
Midhurst & Easebourne v Sutton Ath	3-3
Sutton Ath won 5-4 on penalties.	
Hollands & Blair v AFC Varndeanians	3-0
Banstead Ath v Lordswood	2-4
Fisher v Faversham T	0-1
Corinthian v Tooting & Mitcham U	1-1
Tooting & Mitcham U won 5-4 on penalties.	
Oakwood v Alfold	2-2
Alfold won 5-4 on penalties.	
Tooting Bec v Newhaven (walkover)	
Faversham Strike Force v AFC Uckfield T	4-3
Godalming T v Erith & Belvedere	0-0
Erith & Belvedere won 4-3 on penalties.	
Corinthian Casuals v Whitstable T	1-4
Chipstead v Chessington & Hook U	3-1
Forest Row v Staplehurst Monarchs U	3-5
Kennington v Loxwood	2-0
Horsham YMCA v East Preston	4-2
Hassocks v Storrington Community	6-0
Bearsted v Bexhill U	5-2
Crowborough Ath v Wick	1-3
Bridon Ropes v Lydd T	0-3
Guildford C v Worthing U	3-1
Bournemouth v Cowes Sports	0-5
Andover New Street v Lymington T	6-1
Ringwood T v Petersfield T	2-2
Petersfield T won 9-8 on penalties.	
Folland Sports v Sturminster Newton U	2-3
Whitchurch U v Portland U	1-0
Hythe & Dibden v Brockenhurst	2-6
Sherborne T v Alresford T	1-1
Sherborne T won 4-2 on penalties.	
Hamworthy v Warminster T	3-1
Totton & Eling v Verwood T	1-2
Baffins Milton R v AFC Portchester	6-2
Clanfield v Laverstock & Ford	0-6
Fawley v Christchurch	1-2
Millbrook (Hampshire) v New Milton T	4-0
Blackfield & Langley v United Services Portsmouth	1-0
Fleetlands v Romsey T	4-1
Callington T v Shepton Mallet	1-1
Callington T won 5-4 on penalties.	
Newton Abbot Spurs v Ivybridge T	0-2
St Blazey v Saltash U	3-1
Wendron U v Dobwalls	5-0
Sidmouth T v Torrington	3-1
Bovey Tracey v Liskeard Ath	2-1
Camelford v Bishops Lydeard	0-1
Torridgeside v Newquay	2-1
Middlezoy R v Okehampton Arg	1-2
Launceston v Millbrook (Cornwall)	2-3
Street v Elburton Villa	2-3
Crediton U v Buckland Ath	1-3
Wadebridge T v Cheddar	5-1

SECOND QUALIFYING ROUND

North Shields v Billingham T	3-0
Crook T v Holker Old Boys	0-0
Crook T won 4-2 on penalties.	
Guisborough T v Shildon	2-1
Prudhoe Youth Club v West Allotment Celtic	6-1
Horden Community Welfare v Kendal T	1-0
Ryton & Crawcrook Alb v Garstang	5-2
Easington Colliery v Boro Rangers	1-3
Campion v Billingham Synthonia	2-0
Albion Sports v Tadcaster Alb	1-1
Albion Sports won 5-4 on penalties.	
Esh Winning v Marske U	0-1
Barnoldswick T v Steeton	3-1
Harrogate Railway Ath v Whitley Bay	2-2
Harrogate Railway Ath won 4-3 on penalties.	
Jarrow v Seaham Red Star	2-2
Jarrow won 3-2 on penalties.	
Northallerton T (walkover) v Bedlington Terriers	
Yorkshire Amateur v Newcastle Benfield	3-1
Redcar Ath v West Auckland T	1-1
Redcar Ath won 5-4 on penalties.	
Colne v Knaresborough T	2-1
Chester-le-Street U v FC Hartlepool	0-3
Penrith v Padiham	1-2
Bury v Burscough	3-0
Selby T v AFC Liverpool	1-3
Stockport T v FC St Helens	2-1
Daisy Hill v Lower Breck	1-0
Chadderton v Retford U	8-4

Beverley T v Winterton Rangers	5-0
Ashton T v Armthorpe Welfare	1-0
Maine Road v Winsford U	1-3
Pilkington v Staveley MW	2-3
Retford v Glossop North End	0-1
Abbey Hey v Penistone Church	4-2
Frickley Ath v Sandbach U	2-2
Sandbach U won 5-4 on penalties.	
Wakefield v Barnton	2-1
Euxton Villa v Bacup Bor	2-0
Goole v New Mills	1-3
Atherton LR v Cheadle T	3-1
Darwen v Maltby Main	3-1
Worsbrough Bridge Ath v Handsworth	0-2
Wombwell T v Ashton Ath	3-0
Abbey Hulton U v Worcester Raiders	1-1
Abbey Hulton U won 6-5 on penalties.	
Romulus v Wolverhampton Casuals	3-0
Shawbury U v Market Drayton T	0-1
Coton Green v Foley Meir	4-4
Foley Meir won 4-3 on penalties.	
Dudley T v Stone Old Alleynians	4-0
Atherstone T v Shifnal T	1-1
Atherstone T won 3-1 on penalties.	
Sutton U (Birmingham) v Stafford T	1-1
Sutton U (Birmingham) won 5-3 on penalties.	
FC Stratford v Hinckley	2-1
Heather St Johns v Sporting Club Inkberrow	2-0
Brocton v Allscott Heath	1-4
Paget Rangers v Rugby Bor	1-4
Coventry Copsewood v Stapenhill	1-1
Stapenhill won 3-2 on penalties.	
Uttoxeter T v Hereford Pegasus	2-3
AFC Wulfrunians v Coventry U	5-4
Bewdley T v Droitwich Spa	3-6
Kimberley MW v Skegness T	0-3
Sleaford T v Kirby Muxloe	0-3
Aylestone Park v Clay Cross T	6-6
Clay Cross T won 4-3 on penalties.	
Newark v Southwell C	4-3
Belper U v Deeping Rangers	2-0
Blackstones v Bourne T	2-4
Coalville v Lutterworth T	4-0
Radford v Newark & Sherwood U	2-4
Heanor T v Dunkirk	4-0
Lutterworth Ath v Hucknall T	1-6
Pinxton v Leicester St Andrews	3-2
Shirebrook T v Holbeach U	1-1
Holbeach U won 4-1 on penalties.	
Melton T v Clipstone	2-1
Thetford T v Swaffham T	3-1
Great Yarmouth T v Eynesbury R	3-0
Harleston T v Heacham	3-0
Stowmarket T v Histon	1-4
Yaxley v Kirkley & Pakefield	4-3
March Town U v Mulbarton W	3-0
St Neots T v Downham T	0-1
Framlingham T v Dereham T	0-4
Woodbridge T v Whittlesey Ath	5-1
FC Romania v Cornard U	1-2
Brantham Ath v Sawbridgeworth T	4-1
Letchworth Garden City Eagles v FC Clacton	5-0
Benfleet v Baldock T	3-1
Potton U v Hullbridge Sports	4-1
Enfield Bor v Frenford	2-3
Hadleigh U v Harlow T	3-1
Halstead T v Haverhill Bor	4-3
Stansted v Burnham Ramblers	2-0
Brimsdown v Wormley R	1-0
Shefford T & Campton v West Essex	1-2
Clapton Community v Hoddesdon T	2-2
Clapton Community won 5-4 on penalties.	
Harwich & Parkeston v Rayleigh T	4-4
Rayleigh T won 7-6 on penalties.	
Colney Heath v Stanway R	0-0
Colney Heath won 4-3 on penalties.	
Barking v Takeley	0-3
AFC Welwyn Romans v Arlesey T	0-1
Coggeshall T v Barkingside	5-2
Buckhurst Hill v Newbury Forest	0-2
Cranfield U v Staines Lammas	2-2
Cranfield U won 5-3 on penalties.	
Dunstable T v Tring Ath	2-5
Broadfields U v Rothwell Corinthians	1-1
Rothwell Corinthians won 4-2 on penalties.	

London Samurai R v Spelthorne Sports — 1-1
Spelthorne Sports won 4-2 on penalties.
Kempston R v Desborough T — 1-0
Chalfont St Peter v Harpenden T — 0-4
Bedfont Sports Club v Bedfont — 3-0
Irchester U v Milton Keynes Irish — 1-2
Windsor & Eton v Easington Sports — 3-0
Buckingham v Brook House — 0-3
Daventry T v Rushden & Higham U — 7-0
Long Buckby v Risborough Rangers — 4-2
Ampthill T v British Airways — 1-3
Wembley v FC Deportivo Galicia — 3-0
Virginia Water v Winslow U — 1-0
Edgware & Kingsbury v Newport Pagnell T — 1-2
Penn & Tylers Green v Moulton — 4-1
Crawley Green v Holyport — 1-4
Bugbrooke St Michaels v Northampton ON Chenecks — 0-1
Cheltenham Saracens v Roman Glass St George — 0-5
Bristol Telephones v Tadley Calleva — 1-5
Tytherington Rocks v Chipping Sodbury T — 0-2
Lydney T v Oldland Abbotonians — 2-2
Lydney T won 4-3 on penalties.
Fairford T v Reading C — 4-1
Mangotsfield U v Stonehouse T — 2-2
Stonehouse T won 4-3 on penalties.
Eversley & California v Yateley U — 0-2
Wallingford & Crowmarsh v Sandhurst T — 2-0
Bitton v Tuffley R — 3-1
AFC Aldermaston v Bradford T — 1-3
Longwell Green Sports v Portishead T — 0-3
Milton U v Hengrove Ath — 4-1
Berks Co v Brislington — 3-0
Shortwood U v Cadbury Heath — 2-3
Thornbury T v Malmesbury Vic — 2-0
Devizes T v Slimbridge — 2-1
Horley T v Hassocks — 1-2
Chipstead v VCD Ath — 0-3
Camberley T v Horsham YMCA — 3-1
Meridian v Haywards Heath T — 0-2
Molesey v Crawley Down Gatwick — 1-1
Crawley Down Gatwick won 4-2 on penalties.
Wick v Alfold — 5-1
Tunbridge Wells v Glebe — 2-0
Sheerwater v Faversham T — 0-6
Faversham Strike Force v Selsey — 3-0
Billingshurst v Knaphill — 1-1
Sheppey Sports v Stansfeld — 1-1
Stansfeld won 4-2 on penalties.
Guildford C v Tooting & Mitcham U — 1-0
Rochester U v Welling T — 4-0
Newhaven v Lydd T — 2-2
Lydd T won 4-2 on penalties.
Canterbury C v Lordswood — 0-0
Lordswood won 3-1 on penalties.
Balham v Arundel — 0-3
AFC Whyteleafe v Soul Tower Hamlets — 1-0
Bearsted v Kennington — 1-1
Bearsted won 5-4 on penalties.
Copthorne v Sutton Ath — 1-4
Erith & Belvedere v Frimley Green — 1-0
Staplehurst Monarchs U v Pagham — 0-1
Saltdean U v Shoreham — 3-1
Little Common v Peacehaven & Telscombe — 0-1
Whitstable T v Hollands & Blair — 1-0
Epsom & Ewell v Seaford T — 3-2
Greenways v Colliers Wood U — 1-3
Newport (IW) v Verwood T — 0-1
Fareham T v Cowes Sports — 4-0
Baffins Milton R v Andover New Street — 2-2
Andover New Street won 4-3 on penalties.
Bridport v Brockenhurst — 3-1
Blackfield & Langley v East Cowes Vic Ath — 2-3
Christchurch v AFC Stoneham — 0-2
Millbrook (Hampshire) v Alton — 3-0
Fleet T v Hamworthy U — 6-2
Whitchurch U v Sherborne T — 0-4
Sturminster Newton U v Infinity — 5-0
Petersfield T v Wincanton T — 7-0
Fleetlands v Laverstock & Ford — 3-1
Wadebridge T v Bodmin T — 0-1
Wendron U v St Blazey — 4-4
Wendron U won 4-2 on penalties.
Welton R v Ivybridge T — 2-6
Buckland Ath v Callington T — 2-2
Buckland Ath won 3-1 on penalties.
Okehampton Arg v Millbrook (Cornwall) — 4-0

Elburton Villa (walkover) v Axminster T
Paulton R v Torridgeside — 3-0
Bishops Lydeard v Radstock T — 2-3
Ilfracombe T v Bovey Tracey — 2-2
Ilfracombe T won 5-4 on penalties.
Honiton T v Torpoint Ath — 0-2
Wellington v Sidmouth T — 1-3

FIRST ROUND

Wombwell T v Handsworth — 3-2
West Didsbury & Chorlton v Stockport T — 2-0
Guisborough T v Carlisle C — 0-1
Crook T v Newcastle University — 5-2
Prudhoe Youth Club v Redcar Ath — 2-5
Ramsbottom U v Euxton Villa — 2-0
Yorkshire Amateur v New Mills — 0-2
Atherton LR v Colne — 2-1
Daisy Hill v Ashton T — 3-4
Padiham v Horden Community Welfare — 5-0
Ashville v Marske U — 2-1
Northallerton T v Campion — 2-0
Glossop North End v Sandbach U — 1-2
Chadderton v Bury — 1-1
Chadderton won 4-3 on penalties.
Darwen v Harrogate Railway Ath — 3-0
Beverley T v Abbey Hey — 1-3
Ryton & Crawcrook Alb v Barnoldswick T — 3-0
Staveley MW v Irlam — 1-1
Staveley MW won 4-2 on penalties.
Albion Sports v Boro Rangers — 3-3
Albion Sports won 5-3 on penalties.
Jarrow v FC Hartlepool — 0-1
Winsford U v AFC Liverpool — 4-0
Wakefield v North Shields — 0-1
Rothwell Corinthians v Abbey Hulton U — 2-5
Belper U v Newark T — 1-2
AFC Wulfrunians v Sutton U (Birmingham) — 1-3
Holbeach U v Droitwich Spa — 0-3
Hucknall T v Heanor T — 1-1
Heanor T won 5-3 on penalties.
Newark & Sherwood U v Clay Cross T — 2-2
Clay Cross T won 5-4 on penalties.
Newport Pagnell T v Milton Keynes Irish — 0-0
Newport Pagnell T won 6-5 on penalties.
Kirby Muxloe v FC Stratford — 3-1
Foley Meir v Yaxley — 2-4
Skegness T v Allscott Heath — 4-0
Highgate U v Daventry T — 1-2
Tividale v Cranfield U — 3-2
Coalville T v Romulus — 3-1
Long Buckby v Bourne T — 1-4
Northampton ON Chenecks v Heather St Johns — 2-1
Boston T v Atherstone T — 1-3
Rugby Bor v Dudley T — 4-0
Pinxton v Melton T — 1-2
Market Drayton T v Hereford Pegasus — 4-0
Stapenhill v Eastwood Community — 0-2
Hadleigh U v London Lions — 0-2
Stansted v Clapton Community — 1-2
Colney Heath v Potton U — 1-1
Potton U won 4-3 on penalties.
Woodbridge T v Takeley — 2-2
Takeley won 6-5 on penalties.
Halstead T v Harleston T — 0-3
Thetford T v Cornard U — 6-1
Great Yarmouth T v Histon — 2-0
Downham T v Brantham Ath — 0-2
Coggeshall T v March Town U — 2-4
Letchworth Garden City Eagles v Biggleswade U — 0-1
Harpenden T v Fakenham T — 2-1
Brimsdown v West Essex — 0-2
Arlesey T v Rayleigh T — 0-1
Frenford v Dereham T — 0-3
Kempston R v White Ensign — 1-2
Saffron Walden T v Tring Ath — 0-3
Benfleet v Newbury Forest — 1-1
Benfleet won 7-6 on penalties.
Faversham T v British Airways — 1-0
Camberley T v Hassocks — 0-2
Yateley U v Bearsted — 2-4
Stansfeld v Peacehaven & Telscombe — 1-1
Peacehaven & Telscombe won 4-1 on penalties.
Lingfield v Billingshurst — 0-1
Guildford C v Arundel — 0-0
Arundel won 4-3 on penalties.
Epsom & Ewell v Berks Co — 3-1

Lordswood v Rochester U	4-4
Rochester U won 4-3 on penalties.	
Egham T v Colliers Wood U	4-1
Athletic Newham v Lydd T	2-3
Burnham v Eastbourne U	0-0
Burnham won 5-3 on penalties.	
Windsor & Eton v Brook House	3-1
Tunbridge Wells v Pagham	3-1
Wick v Harefield U	0-3
AFC Whyteleafe v Saltdean U	4-0
Spelthorne Sports v Holyport	1-1
Spelthorne Sports won 4-3 on penalties.	
Erith & Belvedere v Wallingford & Crowmarsh	1-1
Erith & Belvedere won 2-0 on penalties.	
VCD Ath v Roffey	1-1
VCD Ath won 5-3 on penalties.	
Whitstable T v Virginia Water	1-0
Sutton Ath v Fleet T	1-1
Fleet T won 5-3 on penalties.	
Penn & Tylers Green v Bedfont Sports Club	0-2
Wembley v Crawley Down Gatwick	0-2
Faversham Strike Force v Haywards Heath T	1-2
Torpoint Ath v Thornbury T	0-1
Paulton R v Radstock T	5-0
AFC St Austell v Cadbury Heath	3-1
Tadley Calleva v Ivybridge T	3-1
AFC Stoneham v Royal Wootton Bassett T	3-0
Elburton Villa v Petersfield T	2-1
Sturminster Newton U v Okehampton Arg	0-1
Verwood T v Sherborne T	0-5
Milton U v Chipping Sodbury T	3-0
Buckland Ath v Millbrook (Hampshire)	1-0
Devizes v Wells C	1-1
Wells C won 5-4 on penalties.	
Portishead T v Fleetlands	3-0
Bridport v Hamble Club	0-2
Fairford T v East Cowes Vic Ath	0-2
Sidmouth T v Barnstaple T	1-3
Downton v Stonehouse T	1-1
Downton won 4-2 on penalties.	
Bradford v Andover New Street	1-2
Bodmin T v Lydney T	3-2
Clevedon T v Wendron U	5-1
Fareham T v Bitton	3-0
Ilfracombe T v Roman Glass St George	0-4

SECOND ROUND

Northallerton T v Crook T	1-2
Hallam v New Mills	1-0
Ryton & Crawcrook Alb v West Didsbury & Chorlton	0-2
Abbey Hey v Atherton LR	1-4
Winsford U v Darwen	6-1
Ashton T v FC Hartlepool	1-0
Silsden v Ramsbottom U	2-0
North Shields v Charnock Richard	3-1
Ashville v Wombwell T	1-2
Whickham v Redcar Ath	0-1
Carlisle C v Blyth T	2-0
Albion Sports v Padiham	5-5
Albion Sports won 5-3 on penalties.	
South Liverpool v Chadderton	2-0
Tividale v Sutton U (Birmingham)	0-2
Stourport Swifts v Clay Cross T	3-4
Atherstone T v Abbey Hulton U	0-2
Northampton ON Chenecks v Kirby Muxloe	2-0
Market Drayton T v Bourne T	1-3
Yaxley v Melton T	1-2
Sandbach U v Heanor T	2-3
Eastwood Community v Lincoln U	2-2
Lincoln U won 3-2 on penalties.	
Daventry T v Staveley MW	1-0
Ashby Ivanhoe v Droitwich Spa	1-3
Newark T v Lichfield C	1-1
Newark T won 4-3 on penalties.	
Rugby Bor v Skegness T	3-2
Whitchurch Alport v Coalville T	2-2
Whitchurch Alport won 4-2 on penalties.	
Walsham Le Willows v Potton U	3-0
Newport Pagnell T v Dereham T	1-2
Clapton Community v Thetford T	0-0
Thetford T won 8-7 on penalties.	
Biggleswade U v March Town U	2-3
White Ensign v West Essex	2-0
Great Wakering R v Great Yarmouth T	2-2
Great Yarmouth T won 4-3 on penalties.	
London Lions v Stanway Pegasus	10-2

Tring Ath v Harleston T	4-1
Brantham Ath v Benfleet	2-1
Rayleigh T v Harpenden T	2-4
Takeley v Romford	3-2
Rochester U v Fleet T	0-1
Windsor & Eton v Hilltop	5-0
Epsom & Ewell v North Greenford U	2-0
Tunbridge Wells v Hassocks	1-1
Tunbridge Wells won 3-0 on penalties.	
Bedfont Sports Club v Jersey Bulls	0-2
Egham T v Haywards Heath T	2-1
Faversham T v Billingshurst	4-1
Whitstable T v Lydd T	2-1
Peacehaven & Telscombe v Crawley Down Gatwick	0-8
Bearsted v Erith & Belvedere	0-0
Erith & Belvedere won 4-2 on penalties.	
VCD Ath v Arundel	2-0
Spelthorne Sports v Holmesdale	1-1
Spelthorne Sports won 4-3 on penalties.	
Burnham v Cobham	1-0
AFC Whyteleafe v Harefield U	3-1
Hamble Club v AFC Stoneham	0-2
Highworth T v Sherborne T	2-0
Andover New Street v AFC St Austell	2-2
Andover New Street won 5-4 on penalties.	
Downton v Milton U	1-1
Downton won 5-3 on penalties.	
Fareham T v Barnstaple T	0-0
Fareham T won 2-0 on penalties.	
Buckland Ath v Clevedon T	0-3
Thornbury T v Okehampton Arg	0-2
Roman Glass St George v Hamworthy Recreation	3-0
Portishead T v Paulton R	4-2
Brixham v Elburton Villa	3-0
Tadley Calleva v Bridgwater U	4-1
Bodmin T v Wells C	2-5
Hartpury University v East Cowes Vic Ath	1-0

THIRD ROUND

Crook T v Carlisle C	2-0
Atherton LR v Ashton T	1-1
Atherton LR won 7-6 on penalties.	
South Liverpool v Albion Sports	0-2
West Didsbury & Chorlton v Silsden	5-1
Wombwell T v Hallam	0-4
Redcar Ath v North Shields	1-2
Clay Cross T v Melton T	1-0
Whitchurch Alport v Lincoln U	3-1
Rugby Bor v Heanor T	0-5
Newark T v Daventry T	1-1
Daventry T won 11-10 on penalties.	
Abbey Hulton U v Droitwich Spa	4-2
Winsford U v Sutton U (Birmingham)	1-2
Northampton ON Chenecks v Bourne T	1-2
Dereham T v Harpenden T	2-2
Dereham T won 7-6 on penalties.	
London Lions v Great Yarmouth T	5-0
Walsham Le Willows v Brantham Ath	2-1
March Town U v Takeley	1-0
White Ensign v Thetford T	4-3
Tunbridge Wells v Crawley Down Gatwick	2-2
Crawley Down Gatwick won 5-4 on penalties.	
Spelthorne Sports v Egham T	0-5
VCD Ath v Windsor & Eton	2-0
AFC Whyteleafe v Tadley Calleva	3-1
Tring Ath v Fleet T	2-2
Fleet T won 4-2 on penalties.	
Whitstable T v Jersey Bulls	2-1
Epsom & Ewell v Burnham	2-1
Faversham T v Erith & Belvedere	0-1
AFC Stoneham v Brixham	4-0
Downton v Fareham T	0-2
Hartpury University v Wells C	1-0
Andover New Street v Clevedon T	1-1
Andover New Street won 4-2 on penalties.	
Roman Glass St George v Highworth T	2-0
Portishead T v Okehampton Arg	6-1

FOURTH ROUND

Albion Sports v Crook T	0-2
Atherton LR v Hallam	3-2
North Shields v West Didsbury & Chorlton	2-1
Sutton U (Birmingham) v Bourne T	2-4
Clay Cross T v Whitchurch Alport	1-5
March Town U v Daventry T	0-1
Abbey Hulton U v Heanor T	0-2

VCD Ath v Epsom & Ewell	1-0
Walsham Le Willows v Whitstable T	1-1
Whistable T won 3-2 on penalties.	
Crawley Down Gatwick v Fleet T	1-2
Egham T v London Lions	3-1
AFC Whyteleafe v Dereham T	5-0
White Ensign v Erith & Belvedere	1-1
Erith & Belvedere won 4-2 on penalties.	
Portishead T v AFC Stoneham	0-4
Hartpury University v Fareham T	1-0
Roman Glass St George v Andover New Street	1-0
Roman Glass St George subsequently removed after fielding an ineligible player. Andover New Street progress.	

FIFTH ROUND

North Shields v Whitchurch Alport	1-2
Atherton LR v Bourne T	2-2
Bourne T won 5-4 on penalties.	
Heanor T v Crook T	2-0
VCD Ath v Hartpury University	0-1

Andover New Street v AFC Stoneham	1-1
Andover New Street won 6-5 on penalties.	
AFC Whyteleafe v Egham T	1-0
Erith & Belvedere v Daventry T	2-2
Erith & Belvedere won 4-2 on penalties.	
Whitstable T v Fleet T	2-1

QUARTER-FINAL

Whitstable T v Whitchurch Alport	3-2
Hartpury University v Erith & Belvedere	2-1
Andover New Street v Heanor T	1-0
AFC Whyteleafe v Bourne T	1-0

SEMI-FINAL – FIRST LEG

AFC Whyteleafe v Andover New Street	3-1
Whitstable T v Hartpury University	2-0

SEMI-FINAL – SECOND LEG

Andover New Street v AFC Whyteleafe	0-1
AFC Whyteleafe won 4-1 on aggregate	
Hartpury University v Whitstable T	0-0
Whitstable T won 2-0 on aggregate	

THE ISUZU FA VASE FINAL 2024–25

Sunday, 11 May 2025

(at Wembley Stadium, attendance combined with Isuzu FA Trophy 38,600)

AFC Whyteleafe (1) 1　　　　　Whitstable T (0) 2

AFC Whyteleafe: Hill; Orome (De Melo 79), Bennett (Ansah 90), Holder, Mico (Mascoll 72), Watson (Eruotor 85), Leeward (Teodorescu 90), Braham-Barrett, Gondoh, Goode, Johnson-Palmer.
Scorer: Bennett 17.

Whitstable T: Colmer; Thompson, Coyle, Smith (Thomas 116), Sithole, Jeche (O'Mara-Knapp 85), Cotton, O'Mara, Dalton (Healy 105), McIntyre (Aboagye 70), Wilkins (Rees 45).
Scorers: Smith 51, Sithole 99.

aet. Referee: Ruebyn Ricard.

THE FA YOUTH CUP 2024–25

*After extra time.

PRELIMINARY ROUND

Billingham T v Whickham	1-3
Blyth Spartans v Hebburn T	4-2
Chester-le-Street U v Newcastle Benfield	5-1
Heaton Stannington (walkover) v Carlisle C	
Consett v Stockton T	0-11
Morpeth T v Whitby T	5-0
Newcastle Blue Star v Boro Rangers	3-3
Newcastle Blue Star won 5-3 on penalties.	
Avro v Wythenshawe	3-3
Wythenshawe won 5-4 on penalties.	
Hyde U v Macclesfield	2-2
Macclesfield won 3-1 on penalties.	
Lancaster C v Trafford	2-2
Trafford won 6-5 on penalties.	
FC United of Manchester v Atherton LR	3-4
Warrington Rylands v Nantwich T	5-1
AFC Liverpool v Clitheroe	2-1
Vauxhall Motors v Ramsbottom U	4-1
Squires Gate v Stalybridge Celtic	3-0
South Liverpool v Congleton T	3-2
Pilkington v Bootle	5-0
Atherton Collieries v Stockport Georgians	2-2
Stockport Georgians won 5-4 on penalties.	
Burscough v Irlam	2-8
Ashton T v Runcorn Linnets	6-1
Ashton U v Skelmersdale U	0-2
Emley v Tadcaster Alb	1-1
Tadcaster Alb won 5-4 on penalties.	
Garforth T v Bottesford T	1-8
Handsworth v Cleethorpes T	7-1
Goole v Staveley MW	2-5
Grimsby Bor v Retford	5-1
Pontefract Collieries v Sheffield	2-0
Penistone Church (walkover) v Silsden	
Yorkshire Amateur v Guiseley	0-7
Stocksbridge Park Steels v Bradford (Park Avenue)	2-2
Bradford (Park Avenue) won 2-1 on penalties.	
Golcar U v Brighouse T	2-3
Basford U v Lutterworth Ath	3-3
Basford U won 3-1 on penalties.	
Matlock T v Mickleover	3-2

Kirby Muxloe v Kimberley MW	7-0
Clifton All Whites v Harborough T	1-2
Sherwood Colliery (walkover) v Stapenhill	
Quorn v Heather St Johns	2-0
Coalville T v Hinckley	2-2
Coalville T won 5-4 on penalties.	
Leicester St Andrews v Aylestone Park	0-3
Gresley R v Long Eaton U	4-3
Grantham T v Blackstones	1-5
GNG Oadby T v Birstall U	1-2
Deeping Rangers v Eastwood Community	0-5
Saffron Dynamo v Anstey Nomads	2-4
Stamford v Ashby Ivanhoe	2-1
Coventry Sphinx v Nuneaton Griff	2-3
Sutton Coldfield T v Chasetown	0-0
Chasetown won 4-3 on penalties.	
Paget Rangers v Coton Green	0-10
Bilston T (walkover) v Evesham U	
Rugby Bor v Lichfield C	1-3
Lye T v AFC Telford U	1-1
Lye T won 8-7 on penalties.	
Stratford T v Newcastle T	0-2
AFC Bridgnorth v Worcester Raiders	0-6
Stourport Swifts v Bedworth U	1-3
Worcester C v Coventry Copsewood	4-4
Coventry Copsewood won 5-4 on penalties.	
Alvechurch v Allscott Heath	2-2
Allscott Heath won 4-2 on penalties.	
Malvern T v Brocton	1-1
Brocton won 9-8 on penalties.	
Pershore T v Boldmere St Michaels	1-0
Atherstone T v Racing Club Warwick	0-2
Tividale v Wolverhampton Casuals	0-6
Walsall Wood v AFC Wulfrunians	0-6
Leighton T v St Neots T	6-3
Buckingham v Bugbrooke St Michaels	0-4
Ampthill T v Godmanchester R	4-2
Daventry T v AFC Rushden & Diamonds	0-1
St Ives T v Royston T	4-1
Cranfield U v AFC Dunstable	1-2
Desborough T v Corby T	2-3
Hitchin T v Dunstable T	2-5
Arlesey T v Wellingborough T	8-0
Winslow U v Kempston R	0-3

Harpenden T (walkover) v Baldock T

Wellingborough Whitworths v Raunds T — 7-0

Huntingdon T v Newport Pagnell T — 4-2

Histon v Rothwell Corinthians — 9-0

Shefford T & Campton v Biggleswade T — 9-1

Cambridge C v Brantham Ath — 1-1
Brantham Ath won 4-3 on penalties.

Cornard U v Haverhill R — 1-2

Ipswich T v Ely C — 6-2

Framlingham T v Lakenheath — 4-1

Lowestoft T v Wroxham — 6-2

Bury T v Mulbarton W — 4-0

Walsham Le Willows v Dereham T — 3-3
Dereham T won 5-4 on penalties.

Newmarket T v Gorleston — 5-1

Leiston v Hadleigh U — 4-2

AFC Sudbury v Felixstowe & Walton U — 3-0

Thetford v Diss T — 0-12

Sheringham v Fakenham T — 1-0

Witham T v Bowers & Pitsea — 1-13

Concord Rangers v Barking — 1-2

Colney Heath v Bishop's Stortford — 3-1

Grays Ath v Hackney Wick — 1-4

Stanway R v Ilford — 1-1
Stanway R won 4-3 on penalties.

Ware v St Margaretsbury — 12-1

Buckhurst Hill v Woodford T — 4-3

Hullbridge Sports v Heybridge Swifts — 0-1

Cheshunt v Hertford T — 0-3

FC Clacton v Redbridge — 0-6

Wingate & Finchley (walkover) v Romford

Hashtag U v Barkingside — 1-2

May & Baker Eastbrook Community (walkover) v
Great Wakering R

Saffron Walden T v Haringey Bor — 1-8

Takeley v Cockfosters — 5-1

Enfield Bor v Tilbury — 6-2

FC Baresi v Billericay T — 0-3

Berkhamsted v Oxhey Jets — 2-4

Hanwell T v Hillingdon Bor — 0-2

Northwood v Kings Langley — 2-2
Northwood won 4-3 on penalties.

Harrow Bor v Rayners Lane — 1-2

Southall v Penn & Tylers Green — 2-2
Southall won 3-1 on penalties.

Edgware & Kingsbury v Chalfont St Peter — 3-4

Uxbridge v Tring Ath — 1-2

Leverstock Green v Beaconsfield T — 1-5

Rising Ballers Kensington v Hayes & Yeading U — 2-0

Bedfont Sports Club v Hanworth Villa — 3-3
Bedfont Sports Club won 8-7 on penalties.

Langley v Hilltop — 4-1

Flackwell Heath v Amersham T (walkover)

AFC Croydon Ath v Hollands & Blair — 0-2

Margate v Rusthall — 1-2

Sutton Common R v Balham — 6-1

Punjab U v Erith & Belvedere — 1-9

Stansfeld v Folkestone Invicta — 6-2

Holmesdale v Deal T (walkover)

Whitstable T v Lewisham Bor (Community) — 1-1
Whitstable T won 4-1 on penalties.

Erith T v Cray W — 2-1

Sittingbourne v Ramsgate — 0-1

Herne Bay v Dartford — 2-2
Dartford won 5-3 on penalties.

Faversham T v Ashford U — 2-1

Dover Ath v Chatham T — 2-3

Chichester C v Worthing U — 1-1
Chichester C won 5-4 on penalties.

Broadbridge Heath v Burgess Hill T — 0-10

Hastings U v Newhaven — 3-0

Haywards Heath T (walkover) v Wick

Tooting Bec v Eastbourne T — 2-0

Knaphill v AFC Whyteleafe — 0-8

Whitehawk v Chipstead — 1-1
Whitehawk won 5-4 on penalties.

Cobham v Abbey Rangers — 0-3

Corinthian Casuals v Shoreham — 0-1

Westside v Three Bridges — 2-3

Lewes v Kingstonian — 0-2

Chessington & Hook U v Leatherhead — 0-2

Peacehaven & Telscombe v Colliers Wood U — 2-3

Bexhill U v Pagham — 1-6

Jersey Bulls v Metropolitan Police — 4-1

Farnham T v Merstham — 0-7

Lancing v Tooting & Mitcham U (walkover)

Carshalton Ath v Walton & Hersham — 0-3

Loxwood (walkover) v Crowborough Ath

Eastbourne U v East Grinstead T — 2-1

South Park (Reigate) v Badshot Lea — 3-3
Badshot Lea won 4-3 on penalties.

Horsham YMCA v AFC Uckfield T — 6-1

Camberley T v Eversley & California — 6-0

Risborough Rangers v Wokingham & Emmbrook — 1-2

Clanfield 85 v Windsor & Eton — 3-1

Ascot U (walkover) v Bracknell T

Thatcham T v Wallingford & Crowmarsh — 5-2

Banbury U v Basingstoke T — 1-2

North Leigh v Hartley Wintney — 5-2

Easington Sports v Reading C — 2-4

Binfield v Didcot T — 1-3

Sandhurst T v Yateley U — 2-0

Aylesbury Vale Dynamos v Wantage T — 5-2

Gosport Bor v AFC Totton — 7-1

Millbrook (Hampshire) v Poole T — 2-8

Alton v Portland U — 0-0
Portland U won 4-2 on penalties.

Moneyfields v Christchurch — 4-0

Wimborne T v AFC Portchester — 4-0

Sholing v Brockenhurst — 0-2

Bournemouth v Winchester C — 0-5

Swindon Supermarine (walkover) v Hamworthy U

Folland Sports v Hamble Club — 0-3

AFC Stoneham v Havant & Waterlooville — 2-2
Havant & Waterlooville won 5-3 on penalties.

Radstock T v Tuffley R — 5-0

Cheltenham Saracens v Cinderford T — 2-3

Oldland Abbotonians v Welton R — 2-0

Shepton Mallet v Longwell Green Sports (walkover)

Paulton R v Cirencester T — 1-3

Bristol Manor Farm v Lydney T — 7-1

Hartpury University v Mangotsfield U — 4-0

Slimbridge v Gloucester T — 3-2

Bishop's Cleeve v Bristol Telephones — 2-0

Frome T v Brislington — 0-10

Longlevens v Hallen — 2-2
Hallen won 5-4 on penalties.

Clevedon T v Street — 1-3

Bridgwater U v Cribbs — 8-1

Portishead T v Fairford T — 1-4

Callington T v Elburton Villa — 3-1

Barnstaple T v AFC St Austell (walkover)

Saltash U v Bishops Lydeard — 3-1

Mousehole v Helston Ath (walkover)

Brixham (walkover) v Bideford

FIRST QUALIFYING ROUND

South Shields v Stockton T — 2-1

Darlington v Heaton Stannington — 2-3

Chester-le-Street U v Whickham — 1-0

Newcastle Blue Star v Blyth Spartans — 1-5

Morpeth T v Spennymoor T — 1-2

Chester v South Liverpool — 1-0

Atherton LR v AFC Liverpool — 1-2

Marine v Trafford — 0-3

Curzon Ashton v Chorley — 5-0

Warrington Rylands v Macclesfield — 1-5

Warrington T v Radcliffe — 6-0

Skelmersdale U v Irlam — 0-2

Pilkington v Stockport Georgians — 1-3

Wythenshawe v Ashton T — 5-2

Squires Gate v Buxton — 1-3

Vauxhall Motors v Southport — 1-2

Handsworth v Bradford (Park Avenue) — 5-2

Grimsby Bor v Scarborough Ath — 7-0

Penistone Church v Staveley MW — 3-2

Tadcaster Alb v Pontefract Collieries — 1-0

Bottesford T v Farsley Celtic — 1-3

Guiseley v Brighouse T — 7-1

Basford U v Corby T — 3-1

Sherwood Colliery v Anstey Nomads — 9-1

Matlock T v Blackstones — 1-4

Coalville T v Stamford — 4-0

Aylestone Park v Quorn — 4-1

Eastwood Community v Alfreton T — 2-0

Birstall U v Gresley R — 0-7

Harborough T v Kirby Muxloe — 2-1

Leamington v Allscott Heath — 4-0

Lichfield C v Rushall Olympic — 2-1

Coventry Copsewood v Bilston T — 0-1

Nuneaton Griff v Wolverhampton Casuals — 2-1

Coton Green v Kidderminster H — 0-6

Brocton v Pershore T	2-0
Worcester Raiders v Chasetown	0-2
Hereford v Lye T	0-1
Racing Club Warwick v Newcastle T	2-3
AFC Wulfrunians v Bedworth U	4-2
AFC Dunstable v AFC Rushden & Diamonds	4-1
Shefford T & Campton v Histon	0-4
Bugbrooke St Michaels v Leighton T	3-3

Bugbrooke St Michaels won 4-2 on penalties.

St Ives T v Huntingdon T	5-4
Kempston R v Ampthill T	2-0
Brackley T v Wellingborough Whitworths	0-17
Arlesey T v Dunstable T	0-1
Lowestoft T v Ipswich W	3-0
Sheringham v Diss T	5-1
Brantham Ath v Needham Market	0-3
Framlingham T v AFC Sudbury	0-7
Newmarket T v Haverhill R	1-6
King's Lynn T v Leiston	2-0
Dereham T v Bury T	1-1

Bury T won 4-3 on penalties.

Aveley v Billericay T	1-2
Colney Heath v Enfield Bor	4-0
Stanway R v Hornchurch	5-0
Bowers & Pitsea v Takeley	3-0
May & Baker Eastbrook Community v Haringey Bor	0-2
Barking v Ware	4-0
Chelmsford C v Harpenden T	1-5
Enfield T v St Albans C	2-5
Boreham Wood v Hertford T	1-3
Buckhurst Hill v Hackney Wick	0-1
Barkingside v Redbridge	3-3

Redbridge won 7-6 on penalties.

Heybridge Swifts v Wingate & Finchley	1-1

Heybridge Swifts won 3-2 on penalties.

Southall v Northwood	2-1
Amersham T v Langley	2-4
Oxhey Jets v Hemel Hempstead T	1-4
Rayners Lane v Bedfont Sports Club	2-3
Beaconsfield T v Hillingdon Bor	4-1
Slough T v Rising Ballers Kensington	1-2
Tring Ath v Chalfont St Peter	7-0
Tonbridge Angels v Hastings U	1-2
Erith & Belvedere v Chatham T	1-7
Hollands & Blair v Ramsgate	0-4
Deal T v Burgess Hill T	3-8
Whitstable T v Stansfeld	0-2
Faversham T v Maidstone U	0-3
Dartford v Erith T	3-3

Erith T won 4-3 on penalties.

Sutton Common R v Rusthall	1-0
Hampton & Richmond Bor v Badshot Lea	3-4
Chichester C v Eastbourne U	2-3
Shoreham v Eastbourne Bor	0-5
AFC Whyteleafe v Loxwood	5-0
Tooting & Mitcham U v Walton & Hersham	0-5
Whitehawk v Three Bridges	4-1
Dorking W v Horsham YMCA	9-0
Tooting Bec v Haywards Heath T	6-0
Worthing v Colliers Wood U	3-1
Kingstonian v Abbey Rangers	4-2
Merstham v Pagham	17-0
Leatherhead v Jersey Bulls	1-4
Ascot U v Aylesbury Vale Dynamos	2-1
Basingstoke T v Oxford C	2-0
Reading C v Thatcham T	4-0
Wokingham & Emmbrook v North Leigh	3-3

North Leigh won 4-3 on penalties.

Clanfield 85 v Camberley T	0-4
Didcot T v Sandhurst T	4-3
Gosport Bor v Winchester C	3-2
Salisbury v Brockenhurst	1-1

Brockenhurst won 6-5 on penalties.

Wimborne T v Portland U	1-1

Wimborne T won 4-3 on penalties.

Havant & Waterlooville v Moneyfields	6-1
Hamble Club v Poole T	1-2
Weston-super-Mare v Street	0-0

Street won 4-2 on penalties.

Cinderford T v Brislington	0-3
Chippenham T v Hartpury University	0-2
Longwell Green Sports v Hallen	1-2
Cirencester T v Oldland Abbotonians	2-0
Bishop's Cleeve v Bath C	0-2
Slimbridge v Bristol Manor Farm	3-2
Radstock T v Swindon Supermarine	1-2

Torquay U v Saltash U	2-0
Truro C v AFC St Austell	10-0
Callington T v Bridgwater U	3-3

Bridgwater U won 7-6 on penalties.

Brixham v Fairford T	1-4
Helston Ath v Weymouth	6-1

SECOND QUALIFYING ROUND

Hartlepool U v Blyth Spartans	0-5
Heaton Stannington v Gateshead	0-4
South Shields v Tadcaster Alb	4-1
Chester-le-Street U v Spennymoor T	3-3

Spennymoor T won 5-3 on penalties.

Chester v Irlam	1-0
Southport v Trafford	3-3

Trafford won 4-3 on penalties.

Stockport Georgians v Macclesfield	0-2
Altrincham v Warrington T	2-1
AFC Liverpool v Oldham Ath	2-2

Oldham Ath won 4-2 on penalties.

Rochdale v Buxton	4-0
Curzon Ashton v AFC Fylde	2-3
FC Halifax T v Wythenshawe	6-2
Penistone Church v Farsley Celtic	0-7
Guiseley v York C	2-1
Handsworth v Grimsby Bor	4-2
Sherwood Colliery v Boston U	1-5
Eastwood Community v Gresley R	1-2
Aylestone Park v Harborough T	2-0
Blackstones v Coalville T	2-2

Coalville T won 5-4 on penalties.

Wellingborough Whitworths v Basford U	4-2
Newcastle T v Kidderminster H	3-2
Lichfield C v Chasetown	1-1

Lichfield C won 4-3 on penalties.

Leamington v AFC Wulfrunians	1-2
Tamworth v Lye T	5-2
Nuneaton Griff v Brocton	2-4
Bilston T v Solihull Moors	0-3
St Ives T v Kempston R	2-3
Dunstable T v AFC Dunstable	1-1

AFC Dunstable won 4-2 on penalties.

Histon v Bugbrooke St Michaels	4-2
Sheringham v King's Lynn T	5-0
AFC Sudbury v Lowestoft T	2-0
Needham Market v Stanway R	4-2
Haverhill R v Bury T	2-3
Hertford T v Colney Heath	6-0
Bowers & Pitsea v Barking	0-3
Billericay T v Redbridge	1-0
Southend U v Harpenden T	1-2
Heybridge Swifts v Haringey Bor	4-0
Hackney Wick v Dagenham & Red	5-0
Wealdstone v Maidenhead U	3-4
Bedfont Sports Club v Beaconsfield T	0-3
Hemel Hempstead T v Rising Ballers Kensington	1-6
St Albans C v Langley	6-2
Tring Ath v Barnet	2-1
Hastings U v Stansfeld	0-4
Ramsgate v Ebbsfleet U	3-0
Chatham T v Erith T	0-2
Burgess Hill T v Maidstone U	1-0
Eastbourne U v Tooting Bec	1-0
Jersey Bulls v AFC Whyteleafe	3-2
Worthing v Whitehawk	0-2
Aldershot T v Dorking W	1-1

Aldershot T won 5-4 on penalties.

Eastbourne Bor v Woking	0-2
Sutton Common R v Merstham	0-3
Walton & Hersham v Sutton U	1-3
Southall v Kingstonian	1-3
Camberley T v Didcot T	7-1
Hartpury University v Ascot U	8-1
Reading C v North Leigh	2-0
Badshot Lea v Havant & Waterlooville	5-1
Brockenhurst v Eastleigh	2-3
Gosport Bor v Basingstoke T	2-1
Wimborne T v Poole T	1-0
Street v Bath C	2-1
Hallen v Forest Green R	3-4
Brislington v Swindon Supermarine	2-0
Cirencester T v Slimbridge	3-2
Bridgwater U v Fairford T	2-1
Helston Ath v Yeovil T	1-4
Torquay U v Truro C	4-1

THIRD QUALIFYING ROUND

Rochdale v Blyth Spartans	1-1
Blyth Spartans won 7-6 on penalties.	
Macclesfield v Guiseley	0-3
Oldham Ath v South Shields	2-1
Gateshead v Trafford	2-3
FC Halifax T v Farsley Celtic	0-1
Spennymoor T v AFC Fylde	0-2
Altrincham v Chester	1-0
AFC Wulfrunians v Lichfield C	0-1
Coalville T v Brocton	2-1
Newcastle T v Gresley R	5-0
Boston U v Solihull Moors	0-2
Wellingborough Whitworths v Handsworth	1-0
Aylestone Park v Tamworth	0-3
Billericay T v Kempston R	0-1
Bury T v St Albans C	2-3
Barking v Histon	5-2
AFC Dunstable v Needham Market	2-0
Heybridge Swifts v Hackney Wick	3-3
Hackney Wick won 4-2 on penalties.	
Sheringham v Harpenden T	2-0
Hertford T v AFC Sudbury	3-0
Whitehawk v Kingstonian	2-1
Rising Ballers Kensington v Jersey Bulls	6-1
Ramsgate v Woking	0-4
Stansfeld v Sutton U	0-5
Burgess Hill T v Erith T	2-1
Beaconsfield T v Merstham	0-1
Tring Ath v Aldershot T	1-1
Aldershot T won 6-5 on penalties.	
Eastbourne U v Maidenhead U	0-3
Brislington v Camberley T	1-2
Wimborne T v Torquay U	2-4
Forest Green R v Reading C	3-0
Hartpury University v Gosport Bor	9-2
Bridgwater U v Yeovil T	2-1
Badshot Lea v Cirencester T	4-0
Street v Eastleigh	1-2

FIRST ROUND

Rotherham U v Bolton W	2-6
Accrington S v Farsley Celtic	2-1
Oldham Ath v Barnsley	0-6
Stockport Co v Blackpool	0-3
Blyth Spartans v Bradford C	1-1*
Bradford C won 4-3 on penalties. Match ordered to be replayed due to Bradford C making too many substitutions.	
Replay: Bradford C v Blyth Spartans	1-1*
Blyth Spartans won 9-8 on penalties.	
Wrexham v Morecambe	1-0*
(0-0 at the end of normal time)	
Altrincham v Carlisle U	1-4*
(1-1 at the end of normal time)	
AFC Fylde v Doncaster R	3-0
Harrogate T v Guiseley	2-0
Fleetwood T v Wigan Ath	4-1
Trafford v Tranmere R	0-1
Salford C v Huddersfield T	2-1
Lichfield C v Lincoln C	0-5
Shrewsbury T v Coalville T	9-0
Kempston R v Notts Co	1-2
Mansfield T v Grimsby T	1-2
Peterborough U v Northampton T	1-2
Solihull Moors v Crewe Alex	1-2
Chesterfield v Walsall	1-0*
(0-0 at the end of normal time)	
Port Vale v Burton Alb	0-4
Tamworth v Wellingborough Whitworths	2-1
Newcastle T v Birmingham C	2-4
Woking v Bromley	2-4*
Match ordered to be replayed due to Bromley making too many substitutions.	
Replay: Bromley v Woking	1-2*
Colchester U v Hackney Wick	4-2
Barking v Whitehawk	2-3
Milton Keynes D v Stevenage	0-4
Maidenhead U v Burgess Hill T	2-2*
Burgess Hill T won 3-2 on penalties.	
Sutton U v AFC Wimbledon	0-1
Hertford T v Cambridge U	3-2
Sheringham v Rising Ballers Kensington	0-1
Merstham v St Albans C	4-0
Gillingham v Charlton Ath	4-3*
(3-3 at the end of normal time)	

AFC Dunstable v Reading ... 2-1

AFC Dunstable v Reading	2-1
Leyton Orient v Aldershot T	1-0
Exeter C v Bridgwater U	2-0
Hartpury University v Cheltenham T	1-3
Swindon T v Newport Co	3-1
Bristol R v Badshot Lea	3-1*
(1-1 at the end of normal time)	
Camberley T v Forest Green R	0-2
Eastleigh v Torquay U	5-2

SECOND ROUND

Chesterfield v Shrewsbury T	2-2*
Chesterfield won 4-2 on penalties.	
Harrogate T v Birmingham C	3-1
Burton Alb v Notts Co	1-2
AFC Fylde v Northampton T	3-3
AFC Fylde won 4-3 on penalties.	
Barnsley v Carlisle U	0-1
Tranmere R v Wrexham	1-3
Fleetwood T v Tamworth	7-0
Accrington S v Blyth Spartans	6-1
Crewe Alex v Blackpool	2-0
Grimsby T v Salford C	3-2
Bolton W v Lincoln C	2-3
Hertford T v Bristol R	4-3*
(3-3 at the end of normal time)	
Leyton Orient v Whitehawk	6-0
Eastleigh v AFC Wimbledon	0-6
Woking v Rising Ballers Kensington	3-2
Burgess Hill T v Colchester U	2-2
Burgess Hill T won 5-4 on penalties.	
Gillingham v Swindon T	1-2
Exeter C v AFC Dunstable	4-0
Merstham v Forest Green R	3-0
Stevenage v Cheltenham T	4-1*
(1-1 at the end of normal time)	

THIRD ROUND

Watford v Oxford U	2-1
Millwall v Hull C	2-2
Millwall won 5-4 on penalties.	
Leyton Orient v AFC Fylde	1-2
Hertford T v Arsenal	3-4
Bournemouth v Ipswich T	3-2
Harrogate T v WBA	4-6*
(4-4 at the end of normal time)	
QPR v Swindon T	3-1
Derby Co v Sunderland	4-1
Notts Co v Fulham	0-4
Leicester C v Chelsea	2-3
Stoke C v Woking	3-0
Cardiff C v Chesterfield	3-2
Bristol C v Sheffield Wed	3-1
Portsmouth v Leeds U	2-3*
(2-2 at the end of normal time)	
AFC Wimbledon v Wolverhampton W	1-2
Tottenham H v Middlesbrough	3-2
Norwich C v Brentford	4-3
Fleetwood T v Burnley	1-0
Aston Villa v Accrington S	6-0
Sheffield U v Blackburn R	3-2
Merstham v Burgess Hill T	3-1
Luton T v Crewe Alex	2-2
Crewe Alex won 4-3 on penalties.	
Grimsby T v West Ham U	1-0
Everton v Nottingham F	7-0
Preston NE v Liverpool	4-1
Manchester U v Coventry C	5-0
Swansea C v Southampton	0-2
Stevenage v Exeter C	0-1
Manchester C v Crystal Palace	1-0
Lincoln C v Wrexham	4-2
Carlisle U v Plymouth Arg	2-4*
(2-2 at the end of normal time)	
Newcastle U v Brighton & HA	2-1

FOURTH ROUND

AFC Fylde v Leeds U	2-3
Bournemouth v Norwich C	1-3
Sheffield U v Derby Co	1-3
Grimsby T v Tottenham H	3-5*
(3-3 at the end of normal time)	
Chelsea v Merstham	7-1
Stoke C v WBA	0-2
Cardiff C v Bristol C	1-2
Manchester U v Preston NE	5-2

Fleetwood T v Southampton	0-3
Arsenal v QPR	3-3*
Arsenal won 4-2 on penalties.	
Watford v Crewe Alex	4-1
Newcastle U v Aston Villa	0-4
Plymouth Arg v Lincoln C	2-2*
Plymouth Arg won 5-4 on penalties.	
Exeter C v Fulham	1-4
Everton v Wolverhampton W	3-1
Manchester C v Millwall	5-1

FIFTH ROUND

Watford v Tottenham H	4-2
Everton v Plymouth Arg	0-1
Manchester U v Chelsea	5-1
Norwich C v WBA	2-4

Southampton v Derby Co	4-1
Aston Villa v Bristol C	3-2
Fulham v Arsenal	1-2
Leeds U v Manchester C	1-6

QUARTER-FINALS

Arsenal v Manchester U	2-3*
(2-2 at the end of normal time)	
WBA v Manchester C	0-6
Aston Villa v Plymouth Arg	3-0
Watford v Southampton	2-1

SEMI-FINALS

Aston Villa v Manchester U	1-1*
Aston Villa won 3-1 on penalties.	
Watford v Manchester C	0-1

THE FA YOUTH CUP FINAL 2024–25

Monday, 5 May 2025

(at Villa Park, attendance 23,989)

Aston Villa (2) 3   Manchester C 1) 1

Aston Villa: Proctor; Rowe, Fortes (Bloomfield 76), Carroll, Routh, Borland, Burrowes (Mulley 90), Hemmings, Cotcher (Jenner 86), Jimoh-Aloba (McWilliams 76), Brannigan (Quinn 72).
Scorers: Carroll 4, Brannigan 31, Jimoh-Aloba 67.

Manchester C: Whatmuff; Parker, Noble, Mfuni, Braithwaite (Fletcher 76), Miles (Thomas 72), Dunbar-McDonald (Henderson-Hall 46), Gorman (Samba 66), Warhurst, Mukasa, Heskey.
Scorer: Warhurst 2.

Referee: Gavin Ward.

THE FA SUNDAY CUP 2024–25

FIRST ROUND

Hartlepool Supporters v Fox Cover Ashington	4-1
The Lansdowne v Marley Pots	1-1
Marley Pots won 4-2 on penalties.	
Carpet Centres Sky Lounge Elite v Ferryhill Dynamos	9-0
Norton George & Dragon v Newton Aycliffe WMC	1-1
Norton George & Dragon won 3-2 on penalties.	
Sunderland Southwick v Belle Vue R	3-0
AFC West Hull Gunners v Thorpe U Sunday Red	4-0
Westville v Olympic	4-0
Chapeltown v LIV Supplies	4-1
Seven Seas v North Ferriby Sporting	4-1
Quarry Green v Rochdalians	2-2
Rochdalians won 6-5 on penalties.	
Queens Park v Canada	1-1
Queens Park won 5-4 on penalties.	
The Molly v Aigburth Arms	1-3
Mackenzies v Custys	1-1
Mackenzies won 5-4 on penalties.	
Pineapple v Sefton Young Boys	5-0
The George & Dragon v Brow	3-3
The George & Dragon won 8-7 on penalties.	
Black Bull v Mayfair	0-0
Mayfair won 4-3 on penalties.	
Dock (walkover) v Dovecot	
Halton Sports v Woodchurch Hotel	2-2
Woodchurch Hotel won 4-2 on penalties.	
AFC Prestbury v AFC Preston (walkover)	
Rubery Athletico v Rednal Bilbao	1-0
GXNG v The Queens Head (walkover)	
Long Itchington v Bulls Head	0-0
Bulls Head won 5-4 on penalties.	
Littleton Arms v Athletic Midlands	1-1
Littleton Arms won 4-3 on penalties.	
Rose & Crown v Hazelwell	4-0
Oldfields v North Solihull Ath	1-1
North Solihull Ath won 4-3 on penalties.	
Water Orton U v Greenhoffs	0-5
Stourport Swifts (Sunday) v VIP International	4-2
Shire Ath v ANP Internazionale	2-3
Long Whatton v Poet Young Boys	3-1
North Kilworth v Fulhurst Rangers	1-1
North Kilworth won 4-3 on penalties.	
Showtime Mash v West End	1-1
West End won 4-2 on penalties.	

Vale v Sporting Dynamo	1-2
FC Monday v CFA	0-3
Braunstone Ath v Birstall Stamford	2-4
St Josephs (Luton) v Sileby Ath	4-1
NEBA Seniors v Shepshed Oaks	10-0
Moreton Hall Ferals v Acle Rangers	4-1
Priory Sports v The Middle Green	4-0
FC Steamers (walkover) v Long Stratton Sunday	
East London Ballers (walkover) v Olympia	
Hatch Lane (walkover) v Frontiers	
Aveley U v Brook Ath	0-5
Baddoo v AC Milano	1-7
Baiteze v Heavy Hitters	5-1
Denham U v ECS Classic XI	0-3
Jam v Broadfields U (Sunday)	1-2
Under The Radar v WD Bushey	6-0
Clapham R v AFC Hammersmith T	1-2
St Josephs (South Oxhey) v Ebony	1-2
Highgate Alb v Cassiobury Rangers	8-0
Club Lewsey v Phoenix	3-2
North Watford v Flaunden	3-1
FC LM v Brewster Plumbing	2-0
Squirrel Tavern v Strafford Arms	1-5
Hatcham v Hassocks Fatboys	2-3
Wandgas Rangers v BN Dons	3-0
AS Crawley v Market Hotel	3-0
AFC Southborough v SAHA	1-3
Tidworth T v FC Bapco	2-2
FC Bapco won 4-3 on penalties.	
Burghfield v East Christchurch SSC	3-0
Tilehurst El Patrons v East Christchurch Ath	6-2
Godolphin Atlantic Legion v Bristol Academia	1-6
Kraken Sports v Speak Out U Mental Health	9-0

SECOND ROUND

Carpet Centres Sky Lounge Elite v Marley Pots	1-1
Marley Pots won 5-3 on penalties.	
Sunderland Southwick v Chapeltown	3-1
Norton George & Dragon v Hartlepool Supporters	1-3
Dock v Mackenzies	0-2
Aigburth Arms v The George & Dragon	6-1
AFC Preston v Woodchurch Hotel	0-5
Mayfair v Queens Park	9-0
Pineapple v Home Bargains	1-2

Seven Seas v AFC West Hull Gunners	3-3
Seven Seas won 5-3 on penalties.	
Rochdalians v Westville	1-0
Rubery Athletico v The Queens Head	5-1
Stourport Swifts (Sunday) v Littleton Arms	0-6
Bulls Head v North Solihull Ath	1-2
Greenhoffs v Rose & Crown	5-3
ANP Internazionale v Long Whatton	0-4
NEBA Seniors v West End	0-2
North Kilworth v CFA	0-6
Birstall Stamford v Sporting Dynamo	2-2
Birstall Stamford won 5-4 on penalties.	
Moreton Hall Ferals v Priory Sports	3-2
Brook Ath v Hatch Lane	3-7
FC Steamers v AC Milano	0-1
East London Ballers v Baiteze	5-4
St Josephs (Luton) v Ebony	1-0
Highgate Alb (walkover) v North Watford	
Strafford Arms v Club Lewsey	3-1
ECS Classic XI v Broadfields U (Sunday)	5-2
SAHA v AFC Hammersmith T	1-5
Under The Radar v Wandgas Rangers	5-4
AS Crawley v Hassocks Fatboys	5-1
Burghfield v FC Bapco	0-1
Bristol Academia v Kraken Sports	1-5
Tilehurst El Patrons v FC LM	4-1

THIRD ROUND

Rochdalians v Seven Seas	2-5
Hartlepool Supporters v Aigburth Arms	2-1
Marley Pots v Mackenzies	1-1
Marley Pots won 7-6 on penalties.	
Woodchurch Hotel v Mayfair	1-2
Sunderland Southwick v Home Bargains	2-2
Home Bargains won 5-4 on penalties.	

West End v Long Whatton	1-2
North Solihull Ath v CFA	2-0
Rubery Athletico v Birstall Stamford	6-2
Greenhoffs v Littleton Arms	5-2
East London Ballers v Moreton Hall Ferals	4-0
St Josephs (Luton) v Hatch Lane	2-0
Strafford Arms v AC Milano	1-1
AC Milano won 5-3 on penalties.	
FC Bapco v AS Crawley	5-2
AFC Hammersmith T v Kraken Sports	2-0
Highgate Alb v Tilehurst El Patrons	9-0
Under The Radar v ECS Classic XI	4-0

FOURTH ROUND

Seven Seas v Marley Pots	0-6
Hartlepool Supporters v Greenhoffs	3-1
Mayfair v Home Bargains	1-0
AC Milano v East London Ballers	0-4
Rubery Athletico v North Solihull Ath	1-2
St Josephs (Luton) v Long Whatton	5-0
FC Bapco v Under The Radar	3-3
Under The Radar won 7-6 on penalties.	
Highgate Alb v AFC Hammersmith T	2-1

QUARTER-FINALS

North Solihull Ath v Hartlepool Supporters	2-0
Marley Pots v Mayfair	2-4
Under The Radar v East London Ballers	1-5
St Josephs (Luton) v Highgate Alb	1-3

SEMI-FINALS

Highgate Alb v Mayfair	1-0
East London Ballers v North Solihull Ath	1-1
North Solihull Ath won 4-3 on penalties.	

THE FA SUNDAY CUP FINAL 2024–25

Sunday, 4 May 2025

(at Stadium MK, Milton Keynes, attendance 516)

Highgate Alb (2) 3   North Solihull Ath (0) 0

Highgate Alb: Gavriloaia; Kyeremeh, Sterling, Stacey, Talla, Kandola, Kennedy, Stones (Ofori T 76), Riley (Hayes 83), Muhemba, Semakula (Ofori S 90).
Scorers: Stones 33, Semakula 34, Muhemba 90.

North Solihull Ath: Allsop; Savery (Moulton 57), Morris, Dudley, Caines-Powell (Perkins 88), Mohammed (Baker 65), George, Kyle Burke, Kory Burke, Eliss (Copeland 46), Walters (Mendes 71).

Referee: George Laflin.

UNIVERSITY FOOTBALL 2024–25

THE 140TH UNIVERSITY MATCH

Friday, 21 March 2025

(at Abbey Stadium, Cambridge, attendance 2000+)

Cambridge (2) 4   Oxford (0) 1

Cambridge: Aram Sarkissian* (Trinity Hall), Makaful Avevor* (Robinson), Oli Johnson (Sidney Sussex), Patrick Brownlow* (Fitzwilliam), Josh Hickingbotham (Girton), Aaran Mehmood* (Emmanuel), Jesse Tapnack (Trinity), Harry Antill (Trinity), Deniz Ozer* (Trinity Hall), Thomas Musie (Hughes Hall), Cai La Trobe-Roberts* (Jesus), Tom Willock (Fitzwilliam), Asa Campbell* (Fitzwilliam), Josiah Riley (St Edmund's), Ben Pearce (St John's), Alex Durrani (Queens'), Reece Linney* (Girton), Aaron Kay* (Clare).
Scorers: La Trobe-Roberts 38, 45 (pen), 52 (pen), Campbell 48.

Oxford: Chris Gregory (New), Ed Routh (Brasenose), Nick Tredre (Keble), Will Hawkins (Christ Church), Marcel Tenkorang (St Hilda's), Will Rawlings (St Catherine's), Nick Lai* (Mansfield), Brian Kot* (St Antony's), Gonzo Castellano (Jesus), Tom Deighton (Regent's Park), Noah Fletcher* (Keble), Ryan Smalley (Keble), Zac Gunaratnum-Bailey (Jesus), Jonny Evans-Hutchinson* (St Peter's), Rob Dowsett (St Hilda's), Gus Woods (Keble), Karlton Charles (Balliol), Sasha Gorin-Delmas (Lincoln).
Scorer: Fletcher 60 (pen).

*Returning blue.

Oxford have won 59 games (3 on penalties), Cambridge 54 games (4 on penalties) and 27 games have been drawn. Oxford have scored 222 goals, Cambridge 213 goals.

PREMIER LEAGUE 2 2024–25

After extra time.

U21 PREMIER LEAGUE 2 DIVISION ONE 2024–25

	P	W	D	L	F	A	GD	Pts
Manchester C	20	15	2	3	61	23	38	47
Fulham	20	14	3	3	49	30	19	45
Chelsea	20	12	2	6	51	30	21	38
West Ham U	20	12	2	6	30	24	6	38
Manchester U	20	11	3	6	45	31	14	36
Crystal Palace	20	10	5	5	44	35	9	35
Southampton	20	10	4	6	38	31	7	34
Arsenal	20	10	3	7	44	38	6	33
Newcastle U	20	10	2	8	39	37	2	32
Leicester C	20	9	4	7	39	30	9	31
Brighton & HA	20	8	6	6	39	22	17	30
Everton	20	8	5	7	41	43	−2	29
Sunderland	20	8	4	8	48	35	13	28
Wolverhampton W	20	8	4	8	30	36	−6	28
Nottingham F	20	8	3	9	32	28	4	27
Liverpool	20	7	6	7	29	31	−2	27
Leeds U	20	6	7	7	27	32	−5	25
WBA	20	7	4	9	33	42	−9	25
Middlesbrough	20	7	1	12	27	43	−16	22
Reading	20	6	3	11	26	45	−19	21
Blackburn R	20	6	2	12	31	47	−16	20
Tottenham H	20	6	1	13	35	47	−12	19
Derby C	20	5	4	11	27	43	−16	19
Norwich C	20	5	3	12	29	49	−20	18
Stoke C	20	4	3	13	26	43	−17	15
Aston Villa	20	2	6	12	26	51	−25	12

Top 16 qualify for knockout stage.

KNOCKOUT STAGE

ROUND OF 16

Arsenal v Newcastle U	2-1
Manchester C v Liverpool	2-1*
Manchester U v Everton	4-2
West Ham U v Sunderland	3-1
Chelsea v Wolverhampton W	4-0
Southampton v Leicester C	5-3*
Crystal Palace v Brighton & HA	3-1
Fulham v Nottingham F	1-0*

QUARTER-FINALS

Crystal Palace v Chelsea	6-0
Southampton v Fulham	5-2
Manchester C v Arsenal	3-2*
Manchester U v West Ham U	4-1

SEMI-FINALS

Manchester C v Manchester U	2-0
Crystal Palace v Southampton	1-2*

FINAL

Manchester C v Southampton	2-1

U21 PREMIER LEAGUE 2 LEAGUE CUP

GROUP STAGE

Group A Table	P	W	D	L	F	A	GD	Pts
Exeter C	6	5	1	0	14	6	8	16
Bromley	6	3	0	3	10	11	−1	9
Bristol C	6	1	3	2	8	9	−1	6
Norwich C	6	0	2	4	6	12	−6	2

Group B Table	P	W	D	L	F	A	GD	Pts
Nottingham F	6	4	1	1	11	4	7	13
Leicester C	6	3	1	2	9	7	2	10
Hull C	6	2	0	4	7	9	−2	6
Coventry C	6	1	2	3	4	11	−7	5

Group C Table	P	W	D	L	F	A	GD	Pts
WBA	6	2	3	1	12	9	3	9
Southampton	6	2	3	1	12	10	2	9
Swansea C	6	2	2	2	14	9	5	8
Fleetwood T	6	2	0	4	8	18	−10	6

Group D Table	P	W	D	L	F	A	GD	Pts
Sheffield U	6	5	0	1	17	7	10	15
Sunderland	6	3	1	2	15	7	8	10
Wolverhampton W	6	2	1	3	8	9	−1	7
Huddersfield T	6	1	0	5	7	24	−17	3

Group E Table	P	W	D	L	F	A	GD	Pts
QPR	6	3	1	2	12	5	7	10
Blackburn R	6	2	3	1	10	9	1	9
Colchester U	6	2	2	2	7	7	0	8
Preston NE	6	1	2	3	9	17	−8	5

Group F Table	P	W	D	L	F	A	GD	Pts
Cardiff C	6	3	2	1	12	9	3	11
Ipswich T	6	2	3	1	11	9	2	9
Everton	6	1	3	2	9	10	−1	6
Watford	6	2	0	4	7	11	−4	6

Group G Table	P	W	D	L	F	A	GD	Pts
Burnley	6	5	1	0	18	3	15	16
Luton T	6	3	1	2	10	13	−3	10
Brighton & HA	6	2	1	3	8	9	−1	7
Reading	6	0	1	5	7	18	−11	1

Group H Table	P	W	D	L	F	A	GD	Pts
Charlton Ath	6	4	2	0	17	6	11	14
Stockport Co	6	3	0	3	15	15	0	9
Leeds U	6	2	1	3	11	12	−1	7
Birmingham C	6	1	1	4	8	18	−10	4

Group I Table	P	W	D	L	F	A	GD	Pts
Chelsea	6	4	1	1	19	12	7	13
Brentford	6	3	1	2	14	12	2	10
Derby Co	6	3	0	3	12	12	0	9
Bournemouth	6	1	0	5	7	16	−9	3

KNOCKOUT STAGE

ROUND OF 16

QPR v Leicester C	2-0
Chelsea v Ipswich T	2-1
Cardiff C v WBA	1-1*
WBA won 5-4 on penalties.	
Nottingham F v Luton T	2-0
Burnley v Sunderland	1-0
Charlton Ath v Blackburn R	7-0
Sheffield U v Southampton	1-4
Exeter C v Brentford	0-1

QUARTER-FINALS

Brentford v Nottingham F	1-0
Southampton v Charlton Ath	5-3*
WBA v QPR	2-3
Burnley v Chelsea	2-0

SEMI-FINALS

QPR v Burnley	2-0
Southampton v Brentford	0-2

FINAL

QPR v Brentford	3-1

PREMIER LEAGUE 2
INTERNATIONAL CUP 2024–25

*After extra time.

GROUP STAGE

GROUP A

Tottenham H v Valencia	1-3
Reading v Ajax	2-1
Nottingham F v Dinamo Zagreb	3-0
Wolverhampton W v Monaco	1-1
Nottingham F v Valencia	0-1
Reading v Monaco	1-4
Wolverhampton W v Dinamo Zagreb	3-3
Nottingham F v Ajax	1-0
Reading v Dinamo Zagreb	2-3
Wolverhampton W v Ajax	0-3
Tottenham H v Monaco	0-4
Wolverhampton W v Valencia	0-1
Tottenham H v Ajax	1-5
Nottingham F v Monaco	3-1
Reading v Valencia	1-1
Tottenham H v Dinamo Zagreb	2-1

Group A Table	P	W	D	L	F	A	GD	Pts
Valencia	4	3	1	0	6	2	4	10
Nottingham F	4	3	0	1	7	2	5	9
Monaco	4	2	1	1	10	5	5	7
Ajax	4	2	0	2	9	4	5	6
Dinamo Zagreb	4	1	1	2	7	10	–3	4
Reading	4	1	1	2	6	9	–3	4
Tottenham H	4	1	0	3	4	13	–9	3
Wolverhampton W	4	0	2	2	4	8	–4	2

GROUP B

Sunderland v Athletic Bilbao	2-2
Blackburn R v Lyon	0-2
Sunderland v Borussia Moenchengladbach	0-3
West Ham U v Benfica	2-2
Sunderland v Lyon	2-0
West Ham U v Athletic Bilbao	2-2
Blackburn R v Benfica	1-1
Blackburn R v Borussia Moenchengladbach	3-1
Middlesbrough v Lyon	0-1
Middlesbrough v Borussia Moenchengladbach	3-2
West Ham U v Lyon	0-2
West Ham U v Borussia Moenchengladbach	3-1
Middlesbrough v Benfica	0-1
Middlesbrough v Athletic Bilbao	0-4
Sunderland v Benfica	2-1
Blackburn R v Athletic Bilbao	1-2

Group B Table	P	W	D	L	F	A	GD	Pts
Lyon	4	3	0	1	5	2	3	9
Athletic Bilbao	4	2	2	0	10	5	5	8
Sunderland	4	2	1	1	6	6	0	7
West Ham U	4	1	2	1	7	7	0	5
Benfica	4	1	2	1	5	5	0	5
Blackburn R	4	1	1	2	5	6	–1	4
Borussia M'gladbach	4	1	0	3	7	9	–2	3
Middlesbrough	4	1	0	3	3	8	–5	3

GROUP C

Liverpool v PSV Eindhoven	0-4
Fulham v PSV Eindhoven	4-4
Norwich C v Sparta Prague	2-1
Manchester U v Hertha Berlin	1-1
Liverpool v Hertha Berlin	3-4
Manchester U v PSV Eindhoven	1-1
Norwich C v Nordsjaelland	0-2
Fulham v Sparta Prague	3-1
Liverpool v Nordsjaelland	3-4
Norwich C v PSV Eindhoven	2-0
Manchester U v Sparta Prague	1-3
Fulham v Hertha Berlin	5-3
Liverpool v Sparta Prague	1-3
Manchester U v Nordsjaelland	1-3
Norwich C v Hertha Berlin	2-4
Fulham v Nordsjaelland	1-1

Group C Table	P	W	D	L	F	A	GD	Pts
Nordsjaelland	4	3	1	0	7	4	3	10
Fulham	4	2	2	0	13	9	4	8
Hertha Berlin	4	2	1	1	12	11	1	7
Sparta Prague	4	2	0	2	8	7	1	6
Norwich C	4	2	0	2	9	8	1	6
PSV Eindhoven	4	1	2	1	9	7	2	5
Manchester U	4	0	2	2	4	8	–4	2
Liverpool	4	0	0	4	7	15	–8	0

GROUP D

Chelsea v RB Leipzig	2-4
Crystal Palace v Real Sociedad	2-2
Chelsea v Anderlecht	4-0
Brighton & HA v RB Leipzig	3-0
Crystal Palace v Sporting Lisbon	1-2
Brighton & HA v Real Sociedad	1-0
Southampton v RB Leipzig	4-1
Chelsea v Real Sociedad	2-1
Brighton & HA v Anderlecht	2-0
Crystal Palace v Anderlecht	3-1
Southampton v Real Sociedad	3-4
Southampton v Sporting Lisbon	0-5
Brighton & HA v Sporting Lisbon	2-0
Chelsea v Sporting Lisbon	1-2
Crystal Palace v RB Leipzig	1-2
Southampton v Anderlecht	3-1

Group D Table	P	W	D	L	F	A	GD	Pts
Brighton & HA	4	4	0	0	8	0	8	12
Sporting Lisbon	4	3	0	1	9	4	5	9
Chelsea	4	2	0	2	9	7	2	6
Southampton	4	2	0	2	10	11	–1	6
RB Leipzig	4	2	0	2	7	10	–3	6
Crystal Palace	4	1	1	2	7	7	0	4
Real Sociedad	4	1	1	2	7	8	–1	4
Anderlecht	4	0	0	4	2	12	–10	0

KNOCKOUT STAGE

QUARTER-FINALS

Brighton & HA v Athletic Bilbao	1-5
Lyon v Valencia	3-0
Nottingham F v Nordsjaelland	2-1
Fulham v Sporting Lisbon	2-1

SEMI-FINALS

Nottingham F v Athletic Bilbao	2-0*
Fulham v Lyon	0-2

PREMIER LEAGUE 2 INTERNATIONAL CUP FINAL 2024–25
Wednesday, 7 May 2025
(at City Ground, Nottingham, attendance 2642)
Nottingham F (0) 0   Lyon (0) 0

Nottingham F: (433) Murray-Jones; Hammond, Thompson, Abbott, Powell (Newton 101); Nadin (Blake 72), Perry (Hanks 85), McAdam; Sinclair (Whitehall 101), Gardner (Berry 76), Perkins.

Lyon: (433) Konan; Kango (Alamine Ali 80), Mbatshi Mukuba, Mounsesse (Fall 105), Chaib; Fall, de Carvalho (Lomami 90), Merah (Bossiwa 63); Coponat, Rodriguez (Benlahlou 104), Garnier (Gueye 63).

aet; Nottingham F won 5-4 on penalties.

Referee: Thomas Parsons.

UNDER-18 PROFESSIONAL DEVELOPMENT LEAGUE 2024–25

U18 PREMIER LEAGUE 2024–25

NORTH

	P	W	D	L	F	A	GD	Pts
Manchester C	24	21	2	1	90	20	70	65
Manchester U	24	20	3	1	90	24	66	63
Everton	24	14	4	6	55	47	8	46
Derby Co	24	14	2	8	73	44	29	44
Newcastle U	24	10	5	9	55	57	–2	35
Sunderland	24	10	2	12	57	52	5	32
Blackburn R	24	9	5	10	49	63	–14	32
Stoke C	24	7	6	11	47	59	–12	27
Wolverhampton W	24	7	3	14	36	49	–13	24
Middlesbrough	24	7	3	14	45	74	–29	24
Liverpool	24	5	4	15	42	71	–29	19
Nottingham F	24	5	3	16	33	65	–32	18
Leeds U	24	3	6	15	36	83	–47	15

SOUTH

	P	W	D	L	F	A	GD	Pts
Aston Villa	24	15	2	7	47	37	10	47
Southampton	24	13	6	5	68	41	27	45
Arsenal	24	13	5	6	68	53	15	44
Chelsea	24	13	3	8	58	46	12	42
Fulham	24	12	3	9	44	37	7	39
Crystal Palace	24	10	8	6	48	39	9	38
Tottenham H	24	10	7	7	64	48	16	37
Reading	24	9	5	10	30	42	–12	32
West Ham U	24	6	7	11	40	53	–13	25
Brighton & HA	24	6	6	12	45	54	–9	24
Norwich C	24	6	5	13	44	60	–16	23
Leicester C	24	6	5	13	51	70	–19	23
WBA	24	3	6	15	34	61	–27	15

U18 PREMIER LEAGUE PLAY-OFF FINAL

Aston Villa v Manchester C	1-0

U18 PREMIER LEAGUE CUP

Group A Table

	P	W	D	L	F	A	GD	Pts
Derby Co	3	2	0	1	10	10	0	6
Manchester C	3	1	1	1	8	6	2	4
Norwich C	3	1	1	1	6	6	0	4
Brighton & HA	3	1	0	2	9	11	–2	3

Group B Table

	P	W	D	L	F	A	GD	Pts
Manchester U	3	2	0	1	8	5	3	6
Leeds U	3	2	0	1	7	5	2	6
Tottenham H	3	2	0	1	7	6	1	6
Leicester C	3	0	0	3	2	8	–6	0

Group C Table

	P	W	D	L	F	A	GD	Pts
Reading	3	2	0	1	8	5	3	6
Sunderland	3	2	0	1	7	4	3	6
Blackburn R	3	1	0	2	6	8	–2	3
WBA	3	1	0	2	4	8	–4	3

Group D Table

	P	W	D	L	F	A	GD	Pts
West Ham U	3	2	1	0	9	5	4	7
Everton	3	2	1	0	10	7	3	7
Southampton	3	1	0	2	9	9	0	3
Nottingham F	3	0	0	3	3	10	–7	0

Group E Table

	P	W	D	L	F	A	GD	Pts
Fulham	3	2	1	0	5	1	4	7
Aston Villa	3	1	2	0	3	2	1	5
Middlesbrough	3	1	0	2	3	4	–1	3
Wolverhampton W	3	0	1	2	0	4	–4	1

Group F Table

	P	W	D	L	F	A	GD	Pts
Chelsea	3	3	0	0	11	4	7	9
Newcastle U	3	1	1	1	6	7	–1	4
Millwall	3	1	1	1	5	7	–2	4
Stoke C	3	0	0	3	6	10	–4	0

Group G Table

	P	W	D	L	F	A	GD	Pts
Liverpool	3	2	0	1	11	8	3	6
Crystal Palace	3	2	0	1	7	5	2	6
Arsenal	3	2	0	1	8	7	1	6
Birmingham C	3	0	0	3	3	9	–6	0

QUARTER-FINALS

Chelsea v Liverpool	2-3
West Ham U v Manchester U	2-2
aet; West Ham U won 5-4 on penalties.	
Derby Co v Fulham	4-0
Reading v Everton	2-1

SEMI-FINALS

Derby Co v West Ham U	1-3
Liverpool v Reading	0-3

FINAL

Reading v West Ham U	1-2

U18 DEVELOPMENT LEAGUE 2024–25

NORTH

	P	W	D	L	F	A	GD	Pts
Burnley	31	22	3	6	88	26	62	69
Sheffield Wed	31	20	5	6	86	45	41	65
Coventry C	31	17	4	10	59	50	9	55
Sheffield U	31	15	5	11	65	61	4	50
Wigan Ath	31	15	3	13	69	46	23	48
Barnsley	31	14	5	12	54	48	6	47
Crewe Alex	31	13	5	13	58	54	4	44
Hull C	31	12	5	14	46	60	–14	41
Birmingham C	31	11	3	17	47	65	–18	36
Peterborough U	31	8	3	20	49	77	–28	27
Fleetwood T	31	7	3	21	42	91	–49	24

SOUTH

	P	W	D	L	F	A	GD	Pts
Bristol C	31	20	6	5	73	45	28	66
Watford	31	19	3	9	67	45	22	60
Cardiff C	31	16	4	11	75	59	16	52
Millwall	31	14	5	12	72	48	24	47
Bournemouth	31	14	2	15	75	64	11	44
Brentford	31	13	5	13	67	67	0	44
Swansea C	31	13	4	14	64	63	1	43
Charlton Ath	31	10	4	17	62	69	–7	34
Ipswich T	31	8	5	18	58	91	–33	29
QPR	31	7	6	18	50	106	–56	27
Colchester U	31	7	4	20	50	96	–46	25

SEMI-FINALS

Bristol C v Sheffield W	2-0
Burnley v Watford	1-2

FINAL

Bristol C v Watford	2-1

U18 DEVELOPMENT LEAGUE CUP

Group A Table

	P	W	D	L	F	A	GD	Pts
Swindon T	3	2	0	1	10	5	5	6
Bournemouth	3	2	0	1	7	4	3	6
Portsmouth	3	1	1	1	7	7	0	4
Cardiff C	3	0	1	2	4	12	–8	1

Group B Table

	P	W	D	L	F	A	GD	Pts
Bolton W	3	2	1	0	8	5	3	7
Wrexham	3	2	0	1	11	7	4	6
Fleetwood T	3	0	2	1	8	9	–1	2
Crewe Alex	3	0	1	2	5	11	–6	1

Group C Table

	P	W	D	L	F	A	GD	Pts
Barnsley	3	3	0	0	10	2	8	9
Doncaster R	3	2	0	1	3	6	–3	6
Bradford C	3	1	0	2	2	4	–2	3
Hull C	3	0	0	3	4	7	–3	0

Group D Table

	P	W	D	L	F	A	GD	Pts
Sheffield U	3	3	0	0	6	2	4	9
Preston NE	3	2	0	1	7	7	0	6
Burnley	3	1	0	2	5	3	2	3
Wigan Ath	3	0	0	3	2	8	–6	0

Group E Table

	P	W	D	L	F	A	GD	Pts
Colchester U	3	3	0	0	8	1	7	9
Stevenage	3	2	0	1	6	4	2	6
Charlton Ath	3	0	1	2	4	7	–3	1
QPR	3	0	1	2	1	7	–6	1

Group F Table

	P	W	D	L	F	A	GD	Pts
Brentford	3	2	0	1	4	2	2	6
Coventry C	3	1	1	1	5	4	1	4
AFC Wimbledon	3	1	1	1	4	4	0	4
Watford	3	0	2	1	2	5	–3	2

Group G Table

	P	W	D	L	F	A	GD	Pts
Cheltenham T	3	3	0	0	12	3	9	9
Swansea C	3	1	1	1	8	10	–2	4
Bristol C	3	0	2	1	7	8	–1	2
Plymouth Arg	3	0	1	2	5	11	–6	1

Group H Table

	P	W	D	L	F	A	GD	Pts
Peterborough U	3	2	1	0	7	3	4	7
Luton T	3	2	0	1	11	8	3	6
Mansfield T	3	1	1	1	3	3	0	4
Ipswich T	3	0	0	3	5	12	–7	0

QUARTER-FINALS

Cheltenham T v Barnsley	2-1
Peterborough U v Swindon T	4-2
Sheffield U v Brentford	6-1
Colchester U v Bolton W	2-1

SEMI-FINALS

Peterborough U v Cheltenham T	6-1
Sheffield U v Colchester U	4-2

FINAL

Sheffield U v Peterborough U	0-1

CENTRAL LEAGUE 2024–25

CENTRAL LEAGUE TABLES 2024–25

		Home					Away					Total					
		P	W	D	L	F	A	W	D	L	F	A	W	D	L	F	A	GD	Pts
1	Derby Co	9	4	0	1	12	4	3	0	1	10	1	7	0	2	22	5	17	21
2	Stoke C	9	2	1	1	17	8	4	0	1	10	4	6	1	2	27	12	15	19
3	Salford C	9	3	0	1	8	6	3	1	1	11	6	6	1	2	19	12	7	19
4	Mansfield T	9	3	0	2	10	5	2	0	2	5	6	5	0	4	15	11	4	15
5	Bolton W	9	3	0	2	13	4	1	2	1	3	5	4	2	3	16	9	7	14
6	Chesterfield	9	2	1	2	6	5	1	1	2	5	10	3	2	4	11	15	–4	11
7	Wrexham	9	1	2	2	7	9	2	0	2	9	12	3	2	4	16	21	–5	11
8	Huddersfield	9	3	0	1	16	5	0	1	4	4	13	3	1	5	20	18	2	10
9	Preston NE	9	1	1	2	4	8	1	0	4	7	19	2	1	6	11	27	–16	7
10	Notts Co	9	0	0	4	5	13	1	0	4	3	19	1	0	8	5	32	–27	3

CENTRAL LEAGUE CUP 2024–25

GROUP 1

Carlisle U v Blackburn R	0-5
Burnley v Carlisle U	5-0
Blackburn R v Burnley	1-3
Morecambe v Blackburn R	0-1
Carlisle U v Morecambe	0-8
Burnley v Morecambe	0-2

Group 1 Table	P	W	D	L	F	A	GD	Pts
Morecambe	3	2	0	1	10	1	9	6
Burnley	3	2	0	1	8	3	5	6
Blackburn R	3	2	0	1	7	3	4	6
Carlisle U	3	0	0	3	18	–18	0

Barrow withdrew from the competition.

GROUP 2

Preston NE v Stoke C	3-4
Stoke C v Stockport Co	1-1
Stoke C v Wigan Ath	2-2
Wigan Ath v Preston NE	4-8
Wigan Ath v Stockport Co	8-1
Stockport Co v Preston NE	2-3

Group 2 Table	P	W	D	L	F	A	GD	Pts
Preston NE	3	2	0	1	14	10	4	6
Stoke C	3	1	2	0	7	6	1	5
Wigan Ath	3	1	1	1	14	11	3	4
Stockport Co	3	0	1	2	4	12	–8	1

GROUP 3

Accrington S v Bolton W	1-1
Salford C v Accrington S	1-3
Bolton W v Salford C	3-1
Huddersfield T v Salford C	4-0

Bolton W v Huddersfield T	2-5
Accrington S v Rotherham U	2-5
Rotherham U v Bolton W	4-0
Rotherham U v Huddersfield T	2-8
Huddersfield T v Accrington S	5-2
Salford C v Rotherham U	0-2

Group 3 Table	P	W	D	L	F	A	GD	Pts
Huddersfield T	4	4	0	0	22	6	16	12
Rotherham U	4	3	0	1	13	10	3	9
Accrington S	4	1	1	2	8	12	–4	4
Bolton W	4	1	1	2	6	11	–5	4
Salford C	4	0	0	4	2	12	–10	0

GROUP 4

Chesterfield v Grimsby T	0-2
Mansfield T v Notts Co	1-0
Notts Co v Chesterfield	0-2
Mansfield T v Chesterfield	4-0
Grimsby T v Notts Co	3-0
Grimsby T v Mansfield T	1-2

Group 4 Table	P	W	D	L	F	A	GD	Pts
Mansfield T	3	3	0	0	7	1	6	9
Grimsby T	3	2	0	1	6	2	4	6
Chesterfield	3	1	0	2	2	6	–4	3
Notts Co	3	0	0	3	0	6	–6	0

SEMI-FINALS

Huddersfield T v Morecambe	3-2
Mansfield T v Preston NE	2-0

FINAL

Huddersfield T v Mansfield T	1-2

YOUTH ALLIANCE LEAGUE 2024–25

NORTH	P	W	D	L	F	A	GD	Pts
Bolton W	24	19	3	2	83	25	58	60
Wrexham	24	18	4	2	74	27	47	58
Rotherham U	24	13	5	6	52	39	13	44
Preston NE	24	14	2	8	65	53	12	44
Lincoln C	24	12	5	7	46	36	10	41
Blackpool	24	11	7	6	52	41	11	40
Burton Alb	24	11	6	7	51	37	14	39
Chesterfield	24	12	3	9	41	38	3	39
Port Vale	24	10	5	9	47	42	5	35
Stockport Co	24	10	4	10	45	40	5	34
Bradford C	24	9	7	8	45	42	3	34
Grimsby T	24	9	7	8	42	41	1	34
Mansfield T	24	11	1	12	36	40	–4	34
Accrington S	24	9	5	10	52	60	–8	32
Doncaster R	24	9	5	10	32	40	–8	32
Rochdale	24	8	6	10	53	55	–2	30
Morecambe	24	8	6	10	44	47	–3	30
Harrogate T	24	8	6	10	49	54	–5	30
Shrewsbury T	24	6	8	10	37	46	–9	26
Walsall	24	7	5	12	35	47	–12	26
Salford C	24	7	4	13	51	69	–18	25
Carlisle U	24	6	6	12	28	39	–11	24
Hartlepool U	24	4	6	14	38	59	–21	18
Notts Co	24	4	5	15	29	70	–41	17
Huddersfield T	24	4	1	19	31	71	–40	13

SOUTH	P	W	D	L	F	A	GD	Pts
Luton T	27	22	2	3	85	36	49	68
Oxford U	26	20	2	4	72	32	40	62
AFC Wimbledon	27	18	3	6	75	43	32	57
Gillingham	27	17	3	7	73	47	26	54
Plymouth Arg	26	14	4	8	59	36	23	46
Leyton Orient	27	14	4	9	59	39	20	46
Swindon T	26	12	3	11	56	50	6	39
Stevenage	27	11	6	10	43	43	0	39
Sutton U	27	11	6	10	41	51	–10	39
Portsmouth	26	12	1	13	45	54	–9	37
Bromley	27	10	7	10	50	51	–1	37
Cheltenham T	26	10	4	12	49	60	–11	34
Forest Green R	26	10	1	15	50	58	–8	31
Milton Keynes D	27	9	4	14	47	54	–7	31
Cambridge U	27	7	6	14	50	65	–15	27
Bristol R	26	6	3	17	42	72	–30	21
Newport Co	26	6	2	18	49	75	–26	20
Northampton T	27	6	2	19	39	81	–42	20
Exeter C	26	5	1	20	38	75	–37	16

**YOUTH ALLIANCE CHAMPIONSHIP
PLAY-OFF FINAL**

Bolton W v Luton T	7-2

YOUTH ALLIANCE LEAGUE CUP 2024–25

GROUP 1

Morecambe 2 Blackpool 5, Preston NE 1 Bolton W 1,
Carlisle U 4 Accrington S 1, Carlisle U 3 Preston NE 2,
Bolton W 1 Morecambe 0, Blackpool 3 Accrington S 2,
Morecambe 2 Carlisle U 3, Bolton W 3 Blackpool 2,
Preston NE 5 Accrington S 1, Accrington S 3
Morecambe 0, Blackpool 2 Preston NE 1, Carlisle U 0
Bolton W 4, Preston NE 1 Morecambe 5, Blackpool 3
Carlisle U 5, Accrington S 2 Bolton W 1.

Group 1 Table	P	W	D	L	F	A	GD	Pts
Carlisle U	5	4	0	1	15	12	3	12
Bolton W	5	3	1	1	10	5	5	10
Blackpool	5	3	0	2	15	13	2	9
Accrington S	5	2	0	3	9	13	–4	6
Preston NE	5	1	1	3	10	12	–2	4
Morecambe	5	1	0	4	9	13	–4	3

GROUP 2

Salford C 6 Stockport Co 1, Port Vale 0 Wrexham 3,
Rochdale 5 Stockport Co 3, Shrewsbury T 0 Wrexham 1,
Port Vale 0 Salford C 3, Rochdale 1 Wrexham 2,
Port Vale 1 Stockport Co 3, Shrewsbury T 1 Rochdale 3,
Salford C 1 Wrexham 4, Stockport Co 1 Shrewsbury T 0,
Shrewsbury T 3 Salford C 1, Stockport Co 3 Wrexham 2,
Shrewsbury T PP Port Vale, Port Vale 0 Rochdale 3,
Rochdale 1 Salford C 2.

Group 2 Table	P	W	D	L	F	A	GD	Pts
Wrexham	5	4	0	1	12	5	7	12
Rochdale	5	3	0	2	13	8	5	9
Salford C	5	3	0	2	13	10	3	9
Stockport Co	5	3	0	2	11	14	–3	9
Shrewsbury T	4	1	0	3	4	6	–2	3
Port Vale	4	0	0	4	2	12	–10	0

GROUP 3

Bradford C 0 Harrogate T 1, Hartlepool U 0
Doncaster R 5, Huddersfield T 3 Grimsby T 2,
Harrogate T 5 Huddersfield T 3, Grimsby T 7
Doncaster R 1, Hartlepool U 1 Bradford C 1,
Grimsby T 3 Bradford C 1, Doncaster R 4
Huddersfield T 4, Harrogate T 1 Grimsby T 2,
Doncaster R 2 Harrogate T 7, Hartlepool U 3
Harrogate T 1, Bradford C 1 Huddersfield T 1,
Bradford C 3 Doncaster R 5, Huddersfield T 3
Hartlepool U 2, Grimsby T 2 Hartlepool U 1.

Group 3 Table	P	W	D	L	F	A	GD	Pts
Grimsby T	5	4	0	1	16	7	9	12
Harrogate T	5	3	0	2	15	10	5	9
Huddersfield T	5	2	2	1	14	14	0	8
Doncaster R	5	2	1	2	17	21	–4	7
Hartlepool U	5	1	1	3	7	12	–5	4
Bradford C	5	0	2	3	6	11	–5	2

GROUP 4

Rotherham U 0 Chesterfield 0, Mansfield T 0
Lincoln C 0, Notts Co 2 Burton Alb 2, Chesterfield 1
Lincoln C 0, Notts Co 1 Rotherham U 3, Mansfield T 1
Burton Alb 5, Rotherham U 0 Burton Alb 3, Mansfield T 0
Chesterfield 1, Notts Co 1 Lincoln C 3, Mansfield T 1
Rotherham 5, Burton Alb 1 Lincoln C 1, Notts Co 1
Chesterfield 1, Burton Alb 1 Chesterfield 1,
Mansfield T 3 Notts Co 2, Rotherham 5 Lincoln C 1.

Group 4 Table	P	W	D	L	F	A	GD	Pts
Rotherham U	5	3	1	1	13	6	7	10
Burton Alb	5	2	3	0	12	5	7	9
Chesterfield	5	2	3	0	4	2	2	9
Lincoln C	5	1	2	2	5	8	–3	5
Mansfield T	5	1	1	3	5	13	–8	4
Notts Co	5	0	2	3	7	12	–5	2

GROUP 5

Forest Green R 1 Cheltenham T 4, Swindon T 3
Walsall 0, Oxford U 1 Swindon T 3, Walsall 2
Forest Green R 3, Cheltenham T 1 Oxford U 1,
Forest Green R 1 Swindon T 3, Cheltenham T 6
Walsall 1, Oxford U 4 Forest Green R 1, Swindon T 6
Cheltenham T 0, Walsall 0 Oxford U 2.

Group 5 Table	P	W	D	L	F	A	GD	Pts
Swindon T	4	4	0	0	15	2	13	12
Oxford U	4	2	1	1	8	5	3	7
Cheltenham T	4	2	1	1	11	9	2	7
Forest Green R	4	1	0	3	6	13	–7	3
Walsall	4	0	0	4	3	14	–11	0

GROUP 6

Bristol R 2 Newport Co 5, Exeter C 1 Plymouth Arg 3,
Plymouth Arg 5 Bristol R 0, Newport Co 1 Portsmouth 0,
Plymouth Arg 1 Newport Co 1, Bristol R 1 Portsmouth 4,
Portsmouth 3 Exeter C 5, Portsmouth 1 Plymouth Arg 0,
Exeter C PP Bristol R, Newport Co 5 Exeter C 1.

Group 6 Table	P	W	D	L	F	A	GD	Pts
Newport Co	4	3	1	0	12	4	8	10
Plymouth Arg	4	2	1	1	9	3	6	7
Portsmouth	4	2	0	2	8	7	1	6
Exeter C	3	1	0	2	7	11	–4	3
Bristol R	3	0	0	3	3	14	–11	0

GROUP 7

Stevenage 2 Luton T 1, Milton Keynes D 5
Northampton T 0, Northampton T 3 Luton T 3,
Cambridge U 3 Stevenage 4, Stevenage 5
Milton Keynes D 2, Luton T 3 Cambridge U 0, Luton T 6
Milton Keynes D 1, Northampton T 4 Stevenage 0,
Milton Keynes D 1 Cambridge U 5, Cambridge U 4
Northampton T 2.

Group 7 Table	P	W	D	L	F	A	GD	Pts
Stevenage	4	3	0	1	11	10	1	9
Luton T	4	2	1	1	13	6	7	7
Cambridge U	4	2	0	2	12	10	2	6
Northampton T	4	1	1	2	9	12	–3	4
Milton Keynes D	4	1	0	3	9	16	–7	3

GROUP 8

Leyton Orient 1 AFC Wimbledon 0, Bromley 0
Gillingham 2, Gillingham 2 Leyton Orient 2,
AFC Wimbledon 0 Sutton U 2, Gillingham 3
AFC Wimbledon 2, Sutton U 2 Bromley 3,
AFC Wimbledon 1 Bromley 2, Leyton Orient 0
Sutton U 0, Bromley 3 Leyton Orient 0, Sutton U 3
Gillingham 1.

Group 8 Table	P	W	D	L	F	A	GD	Pts
Bromley	4	3	0	1	8	5	3	9
Sutton U	4	2	1	1	7	4	3	7
Gillingham	4	2	1	1	8	7	1	7
Leyton Orient	4	1	2	1	3	5	–2	5
AFC Wimbledon	4	0	0	4	3	8	–5	0

ROUND OF 16

Bolton W v Rochdale	PP
Burton Alb v Rotherham U	5-0
Harrogate T v Grimsby T	3-2
Wrexham v Carlisle U	4-0
Plymouth Arg v Newport Co	7-1
Sutton U v Bromley	2-3
Stevenage v Oxford U	1-3
Swindon T v Luton T	0-1

QUARTER-FINALS

Bolton W v Harrogate T	3-2
Bromley v Luton T	0-0
Bromley won 4-2 on penalties.	
Oxford U v Plymouth Arg	1-1
Oxford U won 4-3 on penalties.	
Wrexham v Burton Alb	0-3

SEMI-FINALS

Oxford U v Bromley	0-0
Bromley won 5-4 on penalties.	
Bolton W v Burton Alb	0-2

YOUTH ALLIANCE LEAGUE CUP FINAL

Burton Alb v Bromley	1-0

IMPORTANT ADDRESSES

The Football Association: Wembley Stadium, Empire Way, Wembley, Brent HA9 0WS. *0800 093 0824*

Scotland (SFA): Hampden Park, Glasgow G42 9AY. *0141 616 6000*

Northern Ireland (IFA): Donegal Avenue, Belfast, Northern Ireland BT12 6LU. *028 9066 9458*

Wales (FAW): 11/12 Neptune Court, Vanguard Way, Cardiff CF24 5PJ. *029 2043 5830*

Republic of Ireland (FAI): National Sports Campus, Abbotstown, Dublin D15 X8PD. *353 1 8999 500*

International Federation (FIFA): Strasse 20, P.O. Box 8044, Zurich, Switzerland. *00 41 43 222 7277.*

Union of European Football Associations (UEFA): Secretary, Route de Geneve 46, P.O. Box 1260, Nyon 2, Switzerland. *+41(0) 848 00 2727*

THE LEAGUES

The Premier League: Brunel Building, 57 North Wharf Road, London W2 1HQ. *0207 864 9000*

English Football League: EFL House, 10–12 West Cuff, Preston PR1 8HU. *01772 325 800.*

The National League: 4th Floor, Waterloo House, 20 Waterloo Street, Birmingham B2 5TB. *0121 643 3143*

Women's Professional Leagues: Wembley Stadium, Wembley, London HA9 0WS. *0844 980 8200*

Scottish Professional Football League: Hampden Park, Glasgow G42 9DE. *0141 620 4140*

Cymru Premier League: 11/12 Neptune Court, Vanguard Way, Cardiff CF24 5PJ. *029 2043 5830*

Northern Ireland Football League: Mervyn Brown Suite, National Stadium at Windsor Park, Donegal Avenue, Belfast BT12 6LW. *028 9560 7150*

Football League of Ireland: National Sports Campus, Abbotstown, Dublin 15. *00 353 1 8999 500*

Southern League: Messenger House, 35 St Michael's Square, Gloucester GL1 1HX.

Northern Premier League: Ms A. Firth, 23 High Lane, Norton Tower, Halifax, W. Yorkshire HX2 0NW. *01422 410 691*

Isthmian League: Enterprise House, Essex Road, Suite 8, Dartford, Kent DA1 2AU. *07432 600 964*

Combined Counties League: A. Constable, 3 Craigwell Close, Chertsey Lane, Staines, Middlesex TW18 3NP. *01784 440 613*

Eastern Counties League: Kevin Lorkins, 9 Ashes Road, Stondon Massey, Brentwood CM15 0ER. *07485 150 640*

Essex Senior League: Secretary: Ms M. Dorling, 39 Milwards, Harlow, Essex CM19 4SG. *07939 850 627*

Hellenic League: John Ostinelli, 2 Wynn Grove, Hazlemere HP15 7LY. *07900 081 814*

Midland League: N. Wood, PO Box 18402, Sutton Coldfield B73 9WE. *07967 440 007*

North West Counties League: J. Deal, 24 The Pastures, Crossens, Southport PR9 8RH. *01704 212 917*

Northern Counties East: Matt Jones, 346 Heneage Road, Grimsby DN32 9NJ. *07415 068 996*

Northern League: K. Hewitt, 55 Greens Lane, Hartburn, Stockton-on-Tees TS28 5JA. *07897 611 640*

South Midlands League: Louise Condon, Century House, Skimpot Lane, Dunstable LU5 4JU. *01582 567 714*

Southern Combination League: Unit 43, Newhaven Enterprise Centre, Newhaven, East Sussex BN9 9BA. *01323 764 218*

Southern Counties East League: Andy Short, secretary@scefl.com

United Counties League: Ms W. Newey, Nene Valley Community Centre, Candy Street, Peterborough PE2 9RE. *07980 518 457*

Wessex League: Ian Craig, 7 Old River, Denmead PO7 6UX. *023 9225 0980*

Western League: Malcolm Price, 18 Hayes Park Road, Midsomer Norton, Radstock, Somerset BA3 2EW. *07872 818 868*

OTHER USEFUL ADDRESSES

Amateur Football Alliance: Unit 3, 7 Wenlock Road, London N1 7SL. *0208 122 0147*

Association of Football Badge Collectors: K. Wilkinson, 18 Hinton St, Fairfield, Liverpool L6 3AR. *0151 260 0554*

British Blind Sport (including football): 19 Coventry Road, Cubbington, Leamington Spa CV32 7JN. *01926 424 247*

British Olympic Association: 101 New Cavendish Street, London W1W 6XH. *0207 842 5700*

British Universities and Colleges Sports Association: BUCSA, 20–24 King's Bench Street, London SE1 0QX. *0207 633 5080*

England Amputee Football Association: 363 Liverpool Road, Southport PR8 3BT. *01704 576 676*

England Supporters Club: Wembley Stadium, London HA9 0WS. *0800 389 1966*

English Schools FA: 4 Parker Court, Staffordshire Technology Park, Stafford ST18 0WP. *01785 785 970*

Football Foundation: Wembley Stadium, Wembley Park, London HA9 0WS. *0345 345 4555*

Football Postcard Collectors Club: PRO: John Farrelly, 163 Collingwood Road, Hillingdon UB8 3EW. Web: www.hobbyist.co.uk/fpcc

Football Safety Officers Association: Suite 309A, Regus Manchester Business Park, 3000 Aviator Way, Manchester M22 5TG. *0161 521 9987.*

The Football Supporters' Association: PO Box 1449, Sunderland, Tyne and Wear SR5 9UW.

Grassroots Football Limited: Unit 5, St Hilda's Industrial Estate, Station Road, South Shields, Tyne and Wear NE33 1RA. *0191 447 5250*

Institute of Groundsmanship: 28 Stratford Office Village, Walker Avenue, Wolverton, Milton Keynes MK12 5TW. *01908 312 511*

League Managers Association: St George's Park, Newborough Road, Needwood, Burton on Trent DE13 9PD. *0128 357 6350*

National Football Museum: Urbis Building, Cathedral Gardens, Todd Street, Manchester M4 3BG. *0161 605 8200*

The Ninety-Two Club: Mr M. Kimberley, The Ninety-Two Club, 153 Hayes Lane, Kenley, Surrey CR8 5HP.

Professional Footballers' Association: 20 Oxford Court, Bishopsgate, Off Lower Moseley Street, Manchester M2 3WQ. *0161 236 0575*

Programme Monthly & Football Collectable Magazine: R. P. Matz, 11 Tannington Terrace, London N5 1LE. *020 7359 8687*

Programme Promotions: 21 Roughwood Close, Watford WD17 3HN. *01923 861 468*

Referees' Association: 1C Bagshaw Close, Ryton-on-Dunsmore, Coventry CV8 3EX. *024 7642 0360*

Scottish Football Museum: Hampden Park, Glasgow G42 9BA. *0141 616 6139*

Soccer Aid For Unicef: 1 Westfield Avenue, London E20 1HZ. *0300 330 5580*

Sport England: 10 South Colonnade, Canary Wharf, London E14 4PU. *0345 8508 508*

Sports Grounds Safety Authority: 10 South Colonnade, Canary Wharf, London E14 4PU. *0207 930 6693*

Sports Turf Research Institute: St Ives Grove, Harden, Bingley, West Yorkshire BD16 1AU. *01274 565 131*

Walking Football Association: Kemp House, 160 City Road, London EC1V 2NX. *07517 033248*

Wheelchair Football Association: c/o Birmingham County FA, Ray Hall Lane, Birmingham B43 6JF.

FOOTBALL CLUB CHAPLAINCY

CHAPLAINS IN FOOTBALL

'It's an absolute no brainer that every football club should have a chaplain.' Those were the words of a club staff member when speaking of chaplaincy. Amid the noise and pressure of the football calendar, it is the quiet, consistent presence of the club chaplain that can make the difference. The chaplain doesn't come with all the answers, but simply offers time, space, and understanding – without judgement, without agenda.

It's this kind of impact – often unseen and uncelebrated – that shows the true value of chaplaincy in football. Week in, week out, chaplains across the country quietly walk the corridors of stadiums and training grounds, building relationships and offering confidential, independent support to players and staff alike. Some have no particular faith and may never step foot in a church, yet still find themselves drawn to the care and presence of their chaplain.

Chaplaincy continues to flourish in the game today. Sports Chaplaincy UK (SCUK) – the charity recognised by football's governing bodies as the lead provider of chaplaincy – continues to train, appoint and support chaplains across all levels of the game. Their emphasis is that chaplains are to be pastorally proactive and spiritually reactive. That means they don't wait in an office for people to come to them – they're out and about, visible and available. And while they're not there to push faith, they are ready to respond sensitively when spiritual questions or personal struggles arise.

Over the past decade, there's been a marked increase in spiritual curiosity, particularly among players. Whether it's a quiet conversation in the gym, a prayer before kick-off, or a group Bible study during the week, chaplains are creating space for those who want to explore life's bigger questions. Many clubs now provide multi-faith spaces, supported by chaplains, recognising the diverse spiritual needs of their communities.

Football is more than a game – it's a culture, a family, and for many, a place of belonging. That's why the presence of a chaplain remains so important. They bring a calm voice into a pressured environment, a listening ear when it's most needed, and a reminder that every individual – no matter their faith, background, or role in the club – is seen and valued.

THE REV
football@sportschaplaincy.org.uk

OFFICIAL CHAPLAINS TO FA PREMIER LEAGUE AND FOOTBALL LEAGUE CLUBS

Accrington S – Debra Phillips
Aston Villa – Jon Grant
Barnsley – Zac Zachariah
Birmingham C (Stadium) – Kirk McAtear
Birmingham C (First team) – Matt Atkins
Birmingham C (Academy) – Tim Atkins
Blackburn R – Ken Howles
Blackpool – David O'Brien
Bolton W – Philip Mason
Bournemouth – Adam Parrett
Bradford C – Oliver Evans
Brentford – Sarah Guinness (not SCUK)
Bristol C – Derek Cleave
Bristol R – Wayne Massey
Burton Alb – Phil Pusey
Cambridge U – Ben Barton
Cambridge U – Stuart Wood
Cardiff C (Academy) – James Roach
Charlton Ath – Matt Baker
Charlton Ath (Academy) – Gareth Morgan
Chelsea – Martin Swan (not SCUK)
Cheltenham T – Malcolm Allen
Chesterfield – Paul Hollingworth
Crawley T – Steve Alliston
Crewe Alex – Phil Howell
Crystal Palace (Academy) – Julian Powell
Derby Co – Tony Luke
Doncaster R – Barry Miller
Everton – Henry Corbett
Fleetwood T – George Ayoma
Fulham – Gary Piper
Gillingham – Richard Hayton
Harrogate T – Rob Brett
Huddersfield T – Phil Gedye
Huddersfield T – Dudley Martin
Ipswich T – Kevan McCormack
Leyton Orient – Steve Opie
Lincoln C – Andrew Vaughan

Liverpool – Bill Bygroves
Manchester C – Pete Horlock
Millwall – Owen Beament
Millwall – Dom Toms
Milton Keynes D – Tim Cutting
Newport Co – Keith Beardmore
Northampton T – Haydon Spenceley
Norwich C – Jon Norman
Norwich C (Academy) – James Cowell
Notts Co – Liam O'Boyle
Notts Co – Jacob Tyers
Oldham Ath – Daniel Burton
Peterborough U – Richard Longfoot
Plymouth Arg – Arthur Goode
Preston NE – Chris Nelson
QPR – Denis Adide
Reading – Steven Prince
Rotherham U – Baz Gascoyne
Sheffield Wed – Baz Gascoyne
Sheffield Wed (Wise Old Owls) – David Jeans
Shrewsbury T – Alastair Bissell
Southampton – Jonny Goodchild
Stevenage – Phil Weston
Stockport Co – Billy Montgomery
Sunderland – Marc Lyden-Smith
Swansea C – Eirian Wyn
Swindon T – Simon Stevenette
Tranmere R – Buddy Owen
Tranmere R (Stadium) – Matt Graham
Walsall – Joe Clark
Watford – Clive Ross
WBA – Christian Wienkamp
West Ham U – Philip Wright
Wigan Ath – Ben Tarbuck
Wolverhampton W (Academy) – Steve Davies
Wrexham – Sarah Sankey
Wrexham – Josh Smith
Wycombe W – Benedict Musola

CURRENT CHAPLAINS IN WOMEN'S FOOTBALL

Aston Villa – Jon Grant
Birmingham C – Sophie Hardwick
Bristol C – Esther Legg-Bagg
Charlton Ath – Kathryn Sales
Crystal Palace – Dotha Blackwood
Derby Co – Sarah Crathorne
Ipswich T – Kevan McCormack
Lewes – Kirsty Langsford

Lewes (Academy) – Sharon Phillips
London Lionesses – Jane Branagan
Oxford U – Deborah Rooke
Portsmouth – Debs Smart
Reading – Angy King
Watford – Melanie Sills
West Ham U – Jane Quinton

The chaplains hope that those who read this page will see the value and benefit of chaplaincy work in football and will take appropriate steps to spread the word where this is possible. They would also like to thank the editors of the Football Yearbook *for their continued support for this specialist and growing area of work.*

For further information, please contact: Sports Chaplaincy UK, Odsal Stadium, Bradford BD6 1BS. Telephone: 0800 181 4051 or email: football@sportschaplaincy.org.uk. Website: www.sportschaplaincy.org.uk

OBITUARIES

Billy Abercrom (Born: Ruchill, Paisley, 14 September 1958. Died: June 2024.) A product of the St Mirren Boys' Club, Billy Abercromby developed into a hard-tackling midfield player and went on to make more than 350 appearances during a 13-year spell with St Mirren. He captained the team that won the Scottish Cup in 1987, also helping them win the First Division title in 1976–77 and the Anglo-Scottish Cup in 1979–80. He left in December 1988 to join Partick Thistle as a player-coach and later had brief associations with Dunfermline Athletic, Cowdenbeath, East Stirlingshire and Inverness Thistle. He won a single cap for Scotland U21s.

Wayne Addicoat (Born: 17 June 1979. Died: Elgin, 15 April 2025.) Wayne Addicoat was a winger who spent three years on the books of Inverness Caledonian Thistle in the 1990s, making 53 appearances during his stay. Later he continued his career in the Highland League with Huntly, Elgin City and Forres Mechanics.

Kenny Aird (Born: Glasgow, 13 April 1947. Died: 22 November 2024.) Kenny Aird was a pacy winger who joined Celtic from Drumchapel Amateurs in June 1964, but he was unable to break into the first team at Parkhead before moving on to St Mirren. He did well in two seasons with the Buddies before moving on to St Johnstone. He became a key player in six years at Muirton Park, making over 200 appearances and appearing in the team defeated by Celtic in the 1969–70 Scottish League Cup final. He went on to spend four years with Hearts then wound down his career with brief spells at Toronto Metros-Croatia and Arbroath.

Terry Allcock (Born: Leeds, 10 December 1935. Died: 11 June 2024.) Inside-forward Terry Allcock joined Bolton Wanderers from junior football in the Blackpool area, signing professional forms at the age of 17. He was unable to break into the side on a regular basis and in March 1958 he signed for Norwich City. He helped the Canaries reach the FA Cup semi-finals in 1958–59 and then win promotion to the Second Division the following season. He stayed at Carrow Road until the end of the 1968–69 season, latterly appearing in the half-back line, and finished with a total of 106 goals from 339 Football League appearances. He was also a talented cricketer, playing as a wicketkeeper/batsman for Norfolk in the Minor Counties Championship between 1959 and 1975.

Bill Asprey (Born: Wolverhampton, 11 September 1936. Died: Jersey, 25 May 2025.) Bill Asprey was a product of Wolverhampton schools' football who went on to sign professional forms for Stoke City at the age of 17. He established himself in the first team at the Victoria Ground and went to make over 300 first-team appearances. He played every match in 1962–63 when the Potters won the Second Division title and gained a League Cup runners-up prize the following season after they were defeated by Leicester City in the final. After leaving in January 1966 he continued his career with Oldham Athletic and Port Vale before turning to coaching and management. Later he had spells as manager of both Oxford United and Stoke City.

Graham Bailey (Born: Old Park, Dawley, Shropshire, 22 March 1920. Died: Falmouth, Cornwall, 15 November 2024.) Defender Graham Bailey joined the groundstaff at Huddersfield Town in August 1936, signing professional forms when he reached the age of 17. He made his debut for the Terriers in May 1940 and went on to play more than 200 games in the wartime emergency competitions, remaining at Leeds Road for the 1946–47 season when he was a regular in the team playing in the First Division. Later he spent two seasons with Sheffield United before retiring to focus on his business interests. At the time of his death he was believed to be the oldest living former Football League player.

George Baldock (Born: Buckingham, 9 March 1993. Died: Glyfada, South Athens, Greece, 9 October 2024.) Defender George Baldock was a product of the Milton Keynes Dons Academy and made his senior debut at the age of 17. He developed in a series of loans elsewhere, notably with Oxford United in the 2015–16 season when he helped the U's win promotion from League Two and was named in the PFA divisional Team of the Year. In June 2017 he signed for Sheffield United where he spent seven years, twice winning promotion to the Premier League and making over 200 appearances. After his contract expired he signed for Panathinaikos where he was playing at the time of his sudden death. He won 12 caps for Greece between 2022 and 2024.

Sol Bamba (Born: Ivry-sur-Seine, France, 13 January 1985. Died: Manisa, Turkey, 31 August 2024.) Sol Bamba was a quick and powerful central defender who developed in the youth set-up at Paris Saint-Germain before joining Dunfermline Athletic in July 2006. He won a Scottish Cup runners-up medal in 2006–07 and later moved on to Hibernian and then Leicester City. This was followed by spells with Trabzonspor and Palermo, before he signed for Leeds United, initially arriving on loan. He later spent five years with Cardiff City where he made over 100 appearances and was a regular in the team that won promotion to the Premier League in 2017–18. He concluded his playing career at Middlesbrough before turning to coaching and at the time of his death he was head coach of Turkish club Adnansport. He was capped 48 times by Ivory Coast between 2008 and 2014.

Tommy Banks (Born: Farnworth, Lancashire,10 November 1929. Died: Bolton, 13 June 2024.) Full-back Tommy Banks won representative honours for the England Boys' Club team before signing for Bolton Wanderers in October 1947. He was mostly a reserve in his early days with the Trotters, and it was not until the 1953–54 season that he won a regular place in the line-up. His career peaked in 1958 when he gained an FA Cup winners' medal, as well as appearing for England in the World Cup finals in Sweden and winning representative honours for the Football League. He made a total of more than 250 appearances during his stay at Burnden Park and later played in non-league for Altrincham and Bangor City. He won six full caps for England.

Chris Barnard (Born: Cardiff, 1 August 1947. Died: 13 January 2025.) Midfielder Chris Barnard developed in the Southend United youth set-up and went on to score two goals on his debut in a League Cup tie at Newport County in September 1965. The following summer he signed for Ipswich Town, but in four seasons at Portman Road he received few first-team opportunities and in October 1970 he was on his way to Torquay United. He stayed 14 months at Plainmoor, making 36 appearances, then after a very brief spell with Charlton Athletic he joined Chelmsford City.

Tony Bartley (Born: Stalybridge, Cheshire, 8 March 1938. Died: September 2024.) Winger Tony Bartley joined Bury from Stalybridge Celtic in November 1958 but although he made his first-team debut shortly afterwards it was not until towards the end of the 1961–62 campaign that he won a regular place in the side. After making 132 appearances for the Shakers he was sold to Oldham Athletic in September 1964 where he spent two seasons before concluding his senior career at Chesterfield. Later he was player-coach of Sligo Rovers.

Per Bartram (Born: Odense, Denmark, 8 January 1944. Died: 12 May 2025.) Per Bartram was a tall, athletic forward who scored at a prolific rate in Denmark with Odense BK, helping them win promotion to the top flight in the 1966 season. In January 1967 he signed for Morton, but injuries initially hampered his progress. He did well in 1968–69, scoring regularly and registering a hat-trick against Celtic in the first 10 minutes of the last match of the campaign. He moved on to Crystal Palace in August 1969 but made few appearances during his time at Selhurst Park. He spent the second half of the 1970–71 campaign back at Morton before returning to Denmark to conclude his career with Odense. He won a single cap for Denmark, appearing against Sweden in September 1975.

Anthony Basso (Born: Besançon, France, 4 July 1979. Died: Besançon, France, 23 January 2025.) Goalkeeper Anthony Basso began his career with Auxerre and Udinese before enjoying a productive spell with Viking in Norway. He signed for Heart of Midlothian at the start of the 2007–08 season and spent 18 months on the books at Tynecastle where he made eight first-team appearances before being released.

Chic Bates (Born: West Bromwich, 28 November 1949. Died: May 2025.) Striker Chic Bates was a prolific scorer in non-league football for Stourbridge and was a member of the Glassboys team defeated by Cardiff City in the 1973–74 Welsh Cup final. He signed for Shrewsbury Town in May 1974 and in his first season as a professional scored 17 goals as the Shrews won promotion to Division Three. He then went on to play for Swindon Town and Bristol Rovers before returning to Gay Meadow in December 1980. He continued to feature regularly before becoming player-manager in July 1984, taking

the club to eighth place in the Division Two table in 1984–85, their best-ever League placing. Later he worked in the backroom staff at Swindon Town, Stoke City, and Celtic, also having a spell as manager of Stoke before returning to work as assistant-manager at Shrewsbury until his retirement from football in 2004.

Tony Bedeau (Born: Hammersmith, London, 24 March 1979. Died: London, 11 February 2025.) Striker Tony Bedeau joined Torquay United as a trainee on leaving school and went on to make his debut at the age of 16. He spent nine seasons with the Gulls, finishing as the club's top scorer in 1999–2000 and helping them to win promotion from the Third Division in 2003–04. He joined Walsall for the 2006–07 campaign before returning to Torquay, although he did not add further first-team appearances during his second spell. He was capped by Grenada.

Tony Bentley (Born: Stoke-on-Trent, 20 December 1939. Died: Kentville, Nova Scotia, Canada, 18 December 2024.) Tony Bentley came up through the ranks with Stoke City, where he played on the wing and at centre-forward. In the summer of 1961 he signed for Southend United where he was converted to a defensive role. He was a near ever-present in his first six seasons at Roots Hall and by the time he left at the end of the 1970–71 season had played 419 games, the fourth highest total in the history of the club. He later played for Folkestone Town and Ashford Town before emigrating to Canada.

Russell Blake (Born: Colchester, 24 July 1935. Died: Colchester, 5 August 2024.) Winger Russell Blake was on the books of Colchester United as an amateur when he made his Football League debut in September 1955, signing professional forms the following summer. He remained at Layer Road until the end of the 1960–61 season, making 61 appearances before joining non-league Sudbury Town.

Norman Bodell (Born: Manchester, 29 January 1938. Died: 22 November 2024.) Defender Norman Bodell came up through the ranks with Rochdale, breaking into the first team in February 1959. He saw plenty of action during a lengthy spell at Spotland before leaving to sign for Crewe Alexandra in May 1963. He went on to make over 100 Football League appearances for the Alex before concluding his playing career with Halifax Town and Altrincham. He was later manager of Barrow and then worked for many years as a coach and scout.

Dennis Bond (Born: Walthamstow, London, 17 March 1947. Died: 2 March 2025.) Dennis Bond was a winger who was capped for England Schoolboys prior to becoming an apprentice at Watford. He went on to win Youth international honours and made over 100 appearances as a teenager for the Hornets before being sold to Tottenham Hotspur in March 1967. However, he was never able to establish himself at White Hart Lane and it was only when he moved on to Charlton Athletic that he played regular first-team football again. Later he returned to Vicarage Road to conclude his senior career, adding a further 200-odd appearances before switching to non-league football with Dagenham.

Tony Book (Born: Bath, 4 September 1934. Died: 13 January 2025.) Full-back Tony Book came to prominence with Bath City where he captained the team that won the Southern League title in 1959–60 and reached the FA Cup third round in 1963–64. Thereafter his career was closely linked to manager Malcolm Allison, following him to Toronto City, Plymouth Argyle and finally Manchester City. He was 31 when he made his debut for City and captained their successful team of the late 1960s, winning the Football League title in 1967–68, the FA Cup the following season and the European Cup Winners' Cup and Football League Cup in 1969–70. He retired as a player in November 1973 and joined the backroom staff at Maine Road, going on to serve as manager from April 1974 to July 1979, with his team winning the League Cup in 1975–76. He then continued to work for City in various roles through until 1997 apart from a brief spell assisting Cardiff City. He was joint Footballer of the Year in 1968–69.

Colin Booth (Born: Middleton, Lancashire, 30 December 1934. Died: 11 May 2025.) Inside-forward Colin Booth progressed through the ranks with Wolverhampton Wanderers before making his debut in April 1955. He spent just over five seasons as a professional at Molineux, where he contributed to two Football League title winning teams, while in November 1956 he scored four goals in a 5-2 win over Arsenal. In October 1959 he moved on to Nottingham Forest where he featured regularly in three seasons in the top flight. He later wound down his career with spells at Doncaster Rovers and Oxford United, where he was a member of the team that won the Fourth Division title in 1964–65, before joining Southern League club Cambridge United. He was capped for England U23s against France in October 1956.

Ronnie Boyce (Born: East Ham, London, 6 January 1943. Died: Norfolk, 13 February 2025.) Inside-forward Ronnie Boyce was capped for England Schoolboys before joining the groundstaff at West Ham United and went on to work for the club as a player and member of the backroom staff for more than 35 years. He gained England Youth international honours and made his debut in October 1960, becoming a regular in the first team from the start of the 1962–63 campaign. He featured in the club's successes in winning the FA Cup in 1963–64 (when he scored the decisive goal) and the European Cup Winners' Cup the following season and went on to make a total of 341 appearances. When his playing days were over he joined the coaching staff, and was later chief scout before retiring in 1995.

Alec Brader, MBE (Born: Horncastle, Lincolnshire, 6 October 1942. Died: Lincoln, 27 October 2024.) Alec Brader made two appearances for Grimsby Town in the 1960–61 season while still a pupil at Horncastle Grammar School. He went on to sign a professional contract but did not add to his experience of senior football with the Mariners. He later played in non-league football with several teams including Skegness Town and Boston United. He was a key figure in Lincolnshire schools' football for many years and in 2009 he was awarded an MBE for services to young people in the New Year's Honours List.

Alex Brash (Born: Dundee, 21 February 1955. Died: Dundee, 15 January 2025.) Alex Brash was a big, no-nonsense central defender who joined Forfar Athletic from Dundee Elmwood shortly after the start of the 1974–75 campaign. He stayed 12 years at Station Park, making almost 450 appearances, with the highlights including appearing in the Scottish Cup semi-final and replay against Rangers in April 1982 and winning the Division Two title in 1983–84. He went on to play for Raith Rovers and Brechin City, where he was a member of the team that won Division Two in 1989–90, eventually retiring after 17 years in senior football and having played just short of 600 games.

Gerry Bright (Born: Northampton, 2 December 1954. Died: 5 November 2024.) Centre-forward Gerry Bright came up through the ranks with Northampton Town and was still an amateur when he made his Football League debut in the final game of the 1956–57 season. He made three further appearances before joining Central Alliance club Wellingborough Town for the 1958–59 campaign.

Garry Brooke (Born: Bethnal Green, London, 24 November 1960. Died: 18 January 2025.) Midfielder Garry Brooke developed in the youth set-up at Tottenham Hotspur before making his senior debut at the age of 20. He gained FA Cup winners' medals as a substitute in both the 1981 and 1982 finals, and began to establish himself in 1982–83, featuring regularly and scoring a hat-trick against Coventry City. However, in February 1983 he was seriously injured in a car accident, and never hit the same levels of form afterwards. He moved on to Norwich City in July 1985 then played in the Netherlands for Groningen, and later for Wimbledon, Brentford and Reading before leaving senior football.

Alec Brown (Born: Methil, Fife, 15 August 1937. Died: 22 December 2024.) Goalkeeper Alec Brown joined Dundee United from Lochgelly Albert in September 1958 and made 90 League and Cup appearances over the next four seasons, being a regular in 1959–60 when the club won promotion to the top flight. He followed this with two seasons at Morton, contributing to the club's successes in winning the Second Division title and losing out to Rangers in the 1963–64 League Cup final.

Jimmy Brown (Born: Circa 1936. Died: July 2024.) Wing-half Jimmy Brown spent his formative years playing in Scottish Junior football, joining Dundee United from Glencraig Colliery towards the end of the 1956–57 season. He was a regular at Tannadice throughout the following campaign before dropping back to the Juniors with Thornton Hibs. Later he had a short spell with East Fife in the second half of 1959–60.

Alex Bryce (Born: Airdrie, 22 April 1944. Died: April 2025.) Alex Bryce was a skilful inside-forward who developed in local amateur football with Hozier Thistle before signing for Third Lanark in the summer of 1961. After breaking into the first team he moved on to Clyde where he had two seasons as a regular in the line-up. In June 1966 he signed for Dundee where he made 150 appearances and played in the defeat to Celtic in the 1967–68 League Cup final. Later he wound down his career with spells at Falkirk and Cowdenbeath.

Mickey Bullock (Born: Stoke-on-Trent, 2 October 1946. Died: December 2024.) Mickey Bullock captained the Stoke-on-Trent team that won the English Schools' Shield in 1961–62 and was capped by England Schoolboys before joining Birmingham City as an apprentice. He scored the winner at Old Trafford on his first-team debut but was never able to establish himself at St Andrew's. A move to Oxford United saw him top the club's scoring charts in 1967–68 when they won the Division Three title, then he spent seven years at Orient, making over 300 appearances and winning the Division Three title once again. He wound down his career with Halifax Town, staying on to join the coaching staff and then serving as manager between July 1981 and October 1984.

Ronnie Burbeck (Born: Leicester, 27 February 1934. Died: Leicester, 31 January 2025.) Ronnie Burbeck was a winger who signed professional forms for Leicester City in May 1952. He received few opportunities at Filbert Street but fared much better after signing for Middlesbrough in October 1956. He made 152 appearances during his time at Ayresome Park then ended his senior career with a season at Darlington. He subsequently linked up with former colleague Bob Dennison at Hereford United, where he continued to play until the end of the 1966–67 campaign. He won England Youth international honours and represented Leicestershire Seconds at cricket in the Minor Counties Championship.

Jim Burns (Born: Stirling, 10 August 1943. Died: Stirling, 11 May 2025.) Jim Burns was a busy midfielder and later a defender who joined Cowdenbeath from Dunipace Juniors in June 1962. He went on to become one of the most consistent players in the lower divisions of Scottish football, playing over 500 League games in a career that spanned more than 15 years. He set a club record of 144 consecutive League appearances for Cowdenbeath, going on to better that with 179 consecutive games for Clyde between April 1968 and April 1972. He was a member of two Second Division title winning teams (Clyde in 1972–73 and Stirling Albion in 1976–77) and later worked with the coaching staff at both Stirling and Cowdenbeath.

Peter Burridge (Born: Harlow, Essex, 30 December 1933. Died: April 2025.) Peter Burridge was an inside-forward who helped Barnet reach the semi-finals of the FA Amateur Cup in 1957–58 before signing for Leyton Orient. He made little impact at Brisbane Road but did much better in a two-year spell with Millwall, rarely missing a match and contributing to their success in winning the Fourth Division title in 1961–62. A move to Crystal Palace saw him gain another promotion in 1963–64 before he ended his senior career with Charlton Athletic. Later he played in the Southern League for Bedford Town.

Barry Butler (Born: Farnworth, Lancashire, 4 June 1962. Died: Leigh, Lancashire, 10 June 2024.) Barry Butler signed for Chester City in December 1985 after having spent several years developing in the North West Counties League. He went on to make over 300 appearances during his time, mostly playing in midfield or defence. He left the club at the end of the 1992–93 campaign and later played in non-league with Barrow and Altrincham.

Fabian Caballero (Born: Misiones, Argentina, 31 January 1978. Died: Asunción, Paraguay, 27 September 2024.) Fabian Caballero was a striker who played his early football in Argentina and Paraguay. In October 1998 he joined Arsenal on loan from Cerro Porteño until the end of the season, however, he mostly played reserve-team football at Highbury where he made just three appearances from the bench. He returned to South America then in July 2000 signed for Dundee, initially arriving on loan before signing a longer agreement for what remains a club-record transfer fee. He became something of a cult figure for the Dens Park fans, making 142 appearances in two spells and featuring in the 2002–03 Scottish Cup final defeat to Rangers. He departed in May 2005, continuing his career back in Paraguay with Olimpia Asunción.

Jimmy Calderwood (Born: Govan, Glasgow, 28 February 1955. Died: Glasgow, 19 January 2025.) Jimmy Calderwood joined Birmingham City as an apprentice and went on to make his debut at the age of 17. He developed into a useful full-back who made over 150 appearances during his time at St Andrew's before moving to play in the Netherlands in the summer of 1980. He stayed abroad for almost 20 years as a player, notably in a lengthy spell with Roda JC, and then as a coach with Willem II and NEC Nijmegen. In November 1999 he returned to Scotland as manager of Dunfermline Athletic, gaining promotion to the top flight in his first season and then taking the Pars to the Scottish Cup final in 2004. He went on to spend five years in charge of Aberdeen, then had brief spells with Kilmarnock and Ross County, where he won the Scottish League Challenge Cup in 2010–11. He was capped for Scotland U23s against England in March 1974.

Tommy Callaghan (Born: Cowdenbeath, Fife, 6 December 1944. Died: 25 October 2024.) Tommy Callaghan developed with Cowdenbeath Royals, and then briefly with Lochore Welfare before signing for Dunfermline Athletic in September 1962. Although initially a winger he switched to wing-half at East End Park, but after establishing himself in the team he suffered a broken leg in November 1966. He made a full recovery and went on to win a Scottish Cup winners' medal for the Pars in 1968 before being sold to Celtic the following November. During his time at Parkhead he was a member of the team that won the Scottish League title every season between 1968–69 and 1973–74 and won three Scottish Cups as well as the League Cup on one occasion. Later he played a few games in the NASL for San Antonio Thunder then concluded his career with spells at Clydebank and Galway Rovers, where he was player-manager. He won two caps for the Scottish League representative side.

Charlie Calow (Born: Belfast, 30 September 1931. Died: Bangor, Co Down, 31 December 2024.) Goalkeeper Charlie Calow developed in the Irish League with Cliftonville and was capped for Northern Ireland Amateurs against Scotland in April 1952. Soon afterwards he signed professional forms for Bradford Park Avenue where he spent the 1952–53 campaign, making a solitary Football League appearance before continuing his career back in Ireland with Distillery.

Kevin Campbell (Born: Lambeth, London, 4 February 1970. Died: Manchester, 15 June 2024.) Kevin Campbell was a striker who developed in the youth set-up at Arsenal with whom he was an FA Youth Cup winner in 1987–88. He made his senior debut shortly afterwards and went on to establish himself in the first team towards the end of the 1990–91 campaign as the Gunners won the Football League title. He remained at Highbury until the summer of 1995, gaining an FA Cup winners' medal in 1992–93. Moving on to Nottingham Forest he scored 23 goals when they won the Division Two title in 1997–98, then had a short spell in Turkey with Trabzonspor, before joining Everton, initially on loan, in March 1999. He spent six years at Goodison and was the top scorer in his first three seasons at the club, before finishing his career with spells at West Bromwich Albion and Cardiff City. He won international honours for England B and U21s.

Roy Campbell (Born: Congleton, Cheshire, 19 October 1934. Died: Macclesfield, 16 January 2025.) Wing-half Roy Campbell spent three seasons as a professional with Crewe Alexandra in the late 1950s making 14 Football League appearances. He moved on to Congleton Town in the summer of 1958 where he spent a decade as a player and then served as manager from 1968 to 1981.

Ralph Cann (Born: Sheffield, 17 November 1934. Died: Rotherham, 22 September 2024.) Centre-half Ralph Cann developed with Norton Woodseats and Sheffield FC before signing for Mansfield Town in May 1957. He spent two seasons on the books at Field Mill, with his only senior appearance coming in the game at Darlington in February 1958.

Willie Carlin (Born: Liverpool, 6 October 1940. Died: June 2024.) Inside-forward Willie Carlin was a member of the Liverpool Boys' team that won the English Schools Shield in 1955–56 and was capped for England Schoolboys and Youth teams. He signed professional forms for Liverpool in May 1958 and but made just one appearance during his time at Anfield and after four years he joined Halifax Town. He topped the scoring charts for the Shaymen in 1963–64 then had a four-year spell with Carlisle United before moving on to Sheffield United and then Derby County. He was a regular for the Rams when they won the Second Division title in 1968–69, going on to gain a second title with Leicester City two years later. He concluded his career with spells at Notts County and Cardiff City before retiring from senior football having scored 81 goals from 489 appearances.

Ally Carrie (Born: Woodville Feus, nr. Arbroath, 17 November 1944. Died: Arbroath, 2 January 2025.) Ally Carrie was an attacking full-back who signed for Forfar Athletic shortly after the start of the 1964–65 campaign. He remained at Station Park until the summer of 1970, making 162 appearances before moving on to Arbroath Victoria.

Tommy Cassidy (Born: Belfast, 18 November 1950. Died: 1 August 2024.) Tommy Cassidy was a skilful midfield player who developed with Irish League club Glentoran. He signed for Newcastle United in October 1970 and stayed for a decade at St James' Park, making over 200 appearances. He featured in the sides that lost out in the 1974 FA Cup final and the League

Cup final two years later. He went on to spend three seasons at Burnley, where he was a prominent member of the team that won the Division Three title in 1981–82, then played for and later managed the Cypriot club APOEL. He also had spells as manager of Glentoran, Ards and Sligo Rovers, as well as several non-league clubs.

Dennis Churms (Born: Rotherham, 8 May 1931. Died: Folkestone, 22 September 2024.) Inside-forward Dennis Churms signed professional forms for Rotherham United and went on to make his League debut in February 1954. He was mostly a reserve for the Millers and in a part-season with Coventry City but featured regularly in a 15-month spell with Exeter City for whom he scored eight goals in 45 appearances. He subsequently moved to Folkestone Town, where he featured in the team that reached the third round of the FA Cup in 1965–66.

Tommy Clish (Born. Wheatley Hill, Co Durham, 19 October 1932. Died: Co Durham, 30 July 1924.) Goalkeeper Tommy Clish was playing in County Durham junior football when he signed for West Ham United in September 1953. However, in two seasons at the Boleyn Ground he was unable to break into the first team and after being released on a free transfer he returned to the North East to sign for Darlington. Although mostly a back-up for the Quakers he made 58 first-team appearances before leaving to join the police with Durham Constabulary.

Dave Clunie (Born: Edinburgh, 16 March 1948. Died: Edinburgh, 22 April 2025.) Dave Clunie was a reliable defender who was capped for Scotland Schoolboys. After a spell with Salveson Boys' Club he signed for Heart of Midlothian, making his debut in October 1966. He went on to spend 11 years on the books at Tynecastle, making over 300 League and Cup appearances and winning representative honours for Scotland U23s and the Scottish League XI. After moving on in the summer of 1977 he made a single appearance as a triallist for Berwick Rangers, then spent the remainder of 1977–78 with St Johnstone before retiring from senior football.

David Cobb (Born: 1944. Died: 6 September 2024.) David Cobb was a goalkeeper who won a single cap for England Amateurs, appearing against Greece in June 1973. He twice played in the Varsity match for Cambridge University and enjoyed a lengthy career in club football, notably in spells at Tooting & Mitcham United and Croydon.

Tony Connell (Born: Govan, Glasgow, 27 January 1944. Died: 30 December 2024.) Defender Tony Connell played in the Juniors with Strathclyde and after signing for Third Lanark he made his senior debut in January 1964. He went on to feature in almost 100 Scottish League games before the club folded in the summer of 1967. He then enjoyed a four-year stay at St Mirren, helping them to win the Second Division title in 1967–68, before concluding his senior career with Queen of the South.

Stevie Convery (Born: Glasgow, 27 October 1972. Died: 10 November 2024.) Stevie Convery was a striker who gained Scotland Junior international honours and was a member of the Arthurlie team that won the Scottish Junior Cup in 1998. In July 1998 he signed for Clyde where he finished his first season as the team's top scorer with 14 League and Cup goals. He remained another four years although his appearances were often restricted by injuries. He finished his senior career with Hamilton Academical before returning to the Juniors to sign for Beith.

Peter Cormack (Born: Edinburgh, 17 July 1946. Died: Leith, 10 October 2024.) Peter Cormack was a skilful, creative midfield player who was briefly on the groundstaff at Heart of Midlothian before signing for Hibernian. He made his League debut at 16 and was capped for Scotland Amateurs shortly afterwards. He went on to make 291 appearances during his time at Easter Road, scoring 106 goals. In March 1970 he was sold to Nottingham Forest, but it was not until the summer of 1972 when he signed for Liverpool that his career blossomed. He was a Football League and UEFA Cup winner in his first season, then won the FA Cup in 1973–74. He finished his career with spells at Bristol City and back at Hibs before being appointed player-manager of Partick Thistle in December 1980. He spent four years with the Jags and then had short spells in charge of Cowdenbeath and Morton. He won nine full caps for Scotland and also appeared for the U23s and the Scottish League representative team.

Colin Court (Born: Ebbw Vale, 3 September 1937. Died: 3 February 2025.) Colin Court was an outside-right who was capped by Wales Schoolboys before joining the groundstaff at Chelsea in July 1953. He graduated to the professional ranks 12 months later, but his only first-team appearance during his time at Stamford Bridge came in an Inter Cities Fairs Cup tie in September 1958. He subsequently moved on to Torquay United where he contributed to their success in winning promotion from the Fourth Division in 1959–60. He then dropped into the Southern League, signing for Weymouth where he featured in the team that reached the FA Cup fourth round in 1961–62.

Doug Coutts (Born: Aberdeen, 3 March 1942. Died: 25 April 2025.) Central defender Doug Coutts was capped for Scotland Schoolboys and went on to progress from Banks o'Dee to sign for Aberdeen in February 1960. It was not until the 1962–63 campaign that he featured regularly in the side and after making over 100 appearances he moved on to Berwick Rangers in the summer of 1965. Here he captained the team that knocked Rangers out of the Scottish Cup in January 1967. He later moved south, spending three seasons with Wigan Athletic, before concluding his career with Altrincham and, briefly, Skelmersdale United.

Don Cowan (Born: Sherburn, Co Durham, 17 August 1931. Died: Bishop Auckland, 19 November 2024.) Goalkeeper Don Cowan was a member of the Bowburn CW team that won the Durham and District League title in 1951–52 before signing professional forms for Darlington in November 1952. He spent three seasons at Feethams, making 17 appearances, and then moved on to South Shields in the summer of 1955.

Graeme Crawford (Born: Falkirk, 7 August 1947. Died: York, 27 May 2025.) Goalkeeper Graeme Crawford developed with Bo'ness United before joining East Stirlingshire in the summer of 1968 but stayed just a few months before being sold to Sheffield United. He had few chances for the Blades and moved on to York City in October 1971. He spent six years at Bootham Crescent, making 280 appearances and establishing himself as one of the best goalkeepers in the lower divisions. He was a regular in 1973–74 when the club won promotion from the Third Division, equalling a then Football League record by keeping a clean sheet in 11 consecutive games. In August 1977 he signed for Scunthorpe United where he made 115 consecutive League and Cup appearances before being dropped. He briefly returned to York then played for Rochdale and Scarborough.

Mick Cullen (Born: Glasgow, 3 July 1931. Died: Luton, 2 September 2024.) Mick Cullen played just a handful of games for Douglasdale Juniors before signing for Luton Town in August 1949. After waiting until April 1952 for his League debut he developed into a clever winger at Kenilworth Road. He moved on to Grimsby Town for the 1958–59 campaign and he was a near ever-present throughout his time at Blundell Park, making 188 appearances and assisting in their promotion campaign to Division Two in 1961–62. He concluded his senior career with Derby County before joining non-league Wellington Town in February 1965. He won a single cap for Scotland in May 1956.

Jack Currie (Born: Motherwell, 19 March 1935. Died: Rishton, Lancashire, 25 January 2024.) Inside-forward Jack Currie played in the Juniors for Bellshill Athletic and Cleland, then made a single Scottish League appearance as a triallist for Alloa Athletic before signing for Accrington Stanley in November 1953. He spent 18 months on the books at Peel Park making 17 first-team appearances before leaving senior football.

Frank D'Arcy (Born: Liverpool, 8 December 1946. Died: 14 June 2024.) Full-back Frank D'Arcy was an apprentice with Everton and a member of the Toffees team that won the FA Youth Cup in 1965. He remained at Goodison until the summer of 1972 but was mostly a reserve during his stay, making a total of 16 first-team appearances. He moved on to Tranmere Rovers, but his career was cut short after he suffered a knee injury in February 1973.

George Davies (Born: Rednal, Shropshire, 1 March 1927. Died: 9 February 2025.) George Davies was a wing-half who joined Sheffield Wednesday from Birmingham League club Oswestry Town in June 1950. He made his debut towards the end of the 1950–51 campaign and went on to spend six seasons at Hillsborough, making over 100 appearances. He signed for Chester in the summer of 1956 where he was a regular in his first season only to lose his place in the side shortly after the start of 1957–58, moving on to non-league Wellington Town soon afterwards.

Ray De Gruchy (Born: Guernsey, 18 May 1932. Died: 2 March 2025.) Ray De Gruchy appeared for Jersey in their Muratti Vase fixture against rivals Guernsey in 1953 and soon afterwards signed professional forms for Nottingham Forest. He spent 12 months at the City Ground without progressing beyond the reserve team, then signed for Grimsby Town in May 1954.

He was a near ever-present for the Mariners in 1955–56 when they won the Division Three North title and in total made 78 appearances during a four-year spell at Blundell Park. Later he had a season with Chesterfield before returning to Jersey where he played for St Ouen.

David Demaine (Born: Cleveleys, Lancashire, 7 May 1942. Died: 19 May 2025.) David Demaine was a pacy winger who was on the books of Blackpool as a youngster. He went on to make his Football League debut for Tranmere Rovers in March 1962 but after one further appearance moved on to sign for Southport. He played six first-team games for the Sandgrounders at the beginning of 1962–63 and then played in non-league football before emigrating to Canada in April 1965. He continued to play for clubs in North America, including a season with Toronto Falcons in the National Professional Soccer League.

John Dempsey (Born: Hampstead, London, 15 March 1946. Died: November 2024.) Centre-half John Dempsey joined Fulham as an apprentice in November 1962 and went on to become an established first-team player in the 1965–66 season. He made a total of more than 150 appearances during his time at Craven Cottage before moving to Chelsea in January 1969. He was a regular in the successful Blues team of the 1970s, gaining an FA Cup winners' medal in 1970 while 12 months later he was a European Cup Winners' Cup winner, scoring the opening goal in the replayed final when Chelsea beat Real Madrid 2-1. He later played for Philadelphia Fury in the NASL and had spells as player-manager of Maidenhead United and Dundalk. He won 19 caps for the Republic of Ireland between 1966 and 1972.

Shaun Dennis (Born: Kirkcaldy, Fife, 20 December 1969. Died: Methil, Fife, 16 May 2025.) Shaun Dennis was a tall, powerful central defender who signed for Raith Rovers in the summer of 1988. He spent most of his career at Stark's Park, making over 350 League appearances before joining the coaching staff at the club. Highlights included featuring in First Division title winning teams in 1992–93 and 1994–95 and being a member of the side that beat Celtic on penalties to win the League Cup in November 1994. In between his spells at Raith he played for Hibernian between January 1997 and September 2000, winning promotion back to the top flight with them in 1998–99. He also played a few games for Brechin City. He was capped for Scotland U21s against Switzerland in September 1991.

Cecil Dixon (Born: Trowbridge, 28 March 1935. Died: Melbourne, Australia, 5 September 2024.) Outside-right Cecil Dixon played Western League football for Trowbridge Town as a teenager before signing professional forms for Cardiff City in July 1954. He was mostly a back-up player during his time at Ninian Park but after moving on to Newport County he enjoyed four seasons of regular first-team football, making over 100 Football League appearances. He later had a season each with Northampton Town and Southern League Wisbech Town before emigrating to Australia in 1963, where he played for Latrobe (Queensland League) and JUST (Victoria State League).

Martin Doak (Born: Greenock, 11 May 1964. Died: 19 August 2024.) Martin Doak was a powerful defender or central midfield player who joined Morton from local team Shamrock Boys' Club, making his senior debut in November 1982. With the exception of a two-year spell in Australia's National Soccer League with West Adelaide he remained at Cappielow until his career was ended by injury in February 1994. He made more than 300 appearances for the club and was twice a member of teams that won the First Division title.

John Docherty (Born: Glasgow, 29 April 1940. Died: 4 December 2024.) Winger John Docherty joined Brentford from Junior club St Roch's in July 1959 and went on to make over 250 appearances for the club in three separate spells, helping them win promotion to the Third Division in 1971–72. His early promise earned him a move to Sheffield United, but he was never really able to establish himself and returned to Griffin Park. He also spent a couple of years at Reading before returning to the Bees for a third spell. Later he had a successful career in management with Brentford, Cambridge United (where he won promotion from the Third Division in 1977–78), Millwall on two occasions, and Bradford City. His first spell at The Den saw him take the club to the top flight for the first time in their history in 1987–88 and the following season's 10th place in the First Division remains their best-ever in the Football League.

Lawrence Docherty (Born: 14 December 1957. Died: 13 January 2025.) Lawrence Docherty was a striker who was a member of the Cumnock Juniors team that won the Scottish Junior Cup in 1979. The following season he had a spell with Hamilton Academical, before quickly returning to Cumnock. Later he made several senior appearances for Stranraer in the 1983–84 season.

Jim Doherty (Born: Irvine, Ayrshire, 13 September 1958. Died: 4 August 2024.) Jim Doherty was a versatile player who appeared in midfield, defence and attack at various times in his career. After starting out at Kilmarnock he enjoyed the best years of his career with Clyde where he was a regular in 1981–82 when they won the First Division title and made over 200 senior appearances. Later he had spells with Queen of the South and, briefly, Stranraer before retiring through injury.

Les Dolphin (Born: Birmingham, 20 February 1922. Died: October 2024.) Les Dolphin was a defender who made a handful of appearances as an amateur for Birmingham City in the emergency competitions in World War Two after being spotted playing in Works' League football. He continued to appear for Blues' reserve team for a while after the war ended, then enjoyed a lengthy career in local football as a player and manager.

Derek Draper (Born: Swansea, 11 May 1943. Died: Chester, 29 August 2024.) Inside-forward Derek Draper came up through the ranks with Swansea Town and went on to establish himself in the line-up, featuring in the team that reached the FA Cup semi-finals in 1963–64. In April 1966 he was sold to Derby County but made little impact at the Baseball Ground, then spent two seasons with struggling Bradford Park Avenue before signing for Chester in January 1969. He made over 350 appearances during his stay at Sealand Road and was a key figure in the team that won promotion from Division Four and reached the League Cup semi-finals in 1974–75. He was capped for Wales U23s in November 1964.

Charlie Drummond (Born: Larbert, Stirlingshire, 8 May 1930. Died: Larbert, Stirlingshire, 14 March 2025.) Goalkeeper Charlie Drummond joined Raith Rovers from Lochore Welfare in March 1952 and spent nine seasons at Stark's Park. He played 141 League games during his stay and featured in the team that reached the semi-finals of the Scottish Cup in 1956–57. After a season with Cowdenbeath he played for Gala Fairydean, where he was a member of the team that reached the last 16 of the Scottish Cup in 1962–63.

Mick Dunlop (Born: Govan, 12 January 1957. Died: 16 December 2024.) Striker Mick Dunlop was on Clyde's books as a youngster before developing in Junior football. In September 1981 he joined Dumbarton from Benburb and played regularly in two seasons at Boghead Park before continuing his career with Queen of the South and Stenhousemuir. He was later manager of the Renfrew team that won the Scottish Junior Cup in 2001.

Jon Durham (Born: Greasbrough, Rotherham, 12 June 1965. Died: March 2025.) Striker Jon Durham developed in the youth set-up at Rotherham United and progressed to a professional contract in June 1983. He made a handful of first-team appearances for the Millers in 1983–84 then signed for Torquay United where he played in 28 first-team games before switching to non-league football. He was later a member of the Taunton Town team who were losing finalists in the FA Vase in 1994.

George Eastham, OBE (Born: Blackpool, 23 September 1936. Died: Berea, Johannesburg, South Africa, 20 December 2024.) George Eastham was a clever inside-forward who made his debut for Ards in the Irish League as a 16-year-old, playing alongside his father who was the club's player-manager. In May 1956 he was sold to Newcastle United where he won representative honours for England U23s. After four years at St James' Park he wanted a move. However, the restraints of the retain and transfer system required Newcastle to approve his transfer request, but they refused. The case went to Court and although the verdict was not announced until 1963 its success proved to be a major step forward for English players on the road to freedom of contract. In the meantime George moved on to Arsenal, where he made over 200 appearances, before joining Stoke City in August 1966. He thrived at the Victoria Ground and in March 1972 scored the winner when the Potters defeated Chelsea to win the League Cup final. He won 19 caps for England and appeared for the Irish League and Football League representative sides. He was awarded the OBE for services to football in the Queen's Birthday Honours List in 1973.

Joe Eaton (Born: Cuckney, Nottinghamshire, 16 May 1931. Died: April 2025.) Inside-forward Joe Eaton joined Mansfield Town as an amateur in 1948 before becoming a part-time professional in August 1951. He remained on the club's books as a player for five seasons, making four first-team appearances. In September 1953 he was appointed as assistant-secretary for the Stags, and after a lengthy period when he held the post on a temporary basis he served as secretary from 1956 until 1993. He received a long-service award from the Football League in 1976.

Alex Edwards (Born: Dunfermline, 14 February 1946. Died: 11 December 2024.) Alex Edwards was a fiery winger who joined the groundstaff at Dunfermline Athletic on leaving school and went on to make his debut shortly after his 16th birthday. He was capped for Scotland Amateur and Youth teams the following year, turning professional after reaching the age of 17. He was a regular for the Pars, gaining a Scottish Cup runners-up medal in 1965 while still a teenager, and then appearing for the team that defeated Hearts to lift the trophy in 1968. In October 1971 he was transferred to Hibernian where he was a Scottish League Cup winner in 1972–73. He finished his senior career with a spell at Arbroath. He won a single cap for Scotland U23s.

Len Edwards (Born: Wrexham, 30 May 1930. Died: Sheffield, 15 October 2024.) Wing-half Len Edwards signed for Sheffield Wednesday in January 1951, but he was mostly a reserve at Hillsborough, making two first-team appearances in December 1951. He moved on to Brighton & Hove Albion in March 1954 where he was again a back-up player. A later spell at Crewe Alexandra was more productive and he played 40 games for the Alex before leaving senior football to sign for Macclesfield Town in the summer of 1957.

Christy Egan (Born: Limerick, 6 August 1953. Died: 16 February 2025.) Winger Christy Egan developed in the League of Ireland with Cork City before joining Derby County in October 1973. He spent three seasons at the Baseball Ground without managing to break into the first team. After being released at the end of the 1975–76 campaign he signed for Newport County where he made seven Football League appearances before moving on in November 1976. Later he played in East Midlands non-league football starting with a spell at Eastwood Town.

Joe Elwood (Born: Belfast, 26 October 1939. Died: London, 14 July 2024.) Winger Joe Elwood played in the Irish League as a teenager and came to the attention of Leyton Orient after scoring two goals for the Northern Ireland Youth team against England at Brisbane Road in May 1957. He signed for the O's 12 months later and went on to spend eight seasons with the club, making over 100 League appearances. Highlights included scoring all four goals in a home win over Bristol City in November 1958 and becoming the club's first used substitute in a League match in September 1965. He returned to Ireland to play for Ards in the summer of 1966. He won a single cap for Northern Ireland U23s.

Sven-Göran Eriksson (Born: Sunne, Sweden, 5 February 1948. Died: Sunne, Sweden, 26 August 2024.) Sven-Göran Eriksson played in the lower divisions in Sweden before turning to coaching. He came to wider notice as the coach of IFK Göteborg, where his team won a domestic double in 1982 as well as the UEFA Cup in 1981–82. He moved to Benfica soon afterwards and this was the start of a coaching career that took him around the world. He achieved notable success with Lazio, where his team won the European Cup Winners' Cup in 1998–99, and in January 2001 he was appointed as manager of the England national team. He won the first five games of his reign and reached the quarter-finals of Euro 2004 and the 2006 World Cup, before departing in July 2006. Later he had spells in charge of Manchester City and Leicester City and was briefly director of football at Notts County. He also managed the national teams of Mexico, Ivory Coast and the Philippines.

Keith Etheridge (Born: Ivybridge, Devon, 14 May 1944. Died: 20 January 2025.) Keith Etheridge developed in the South Western League with St Blazey, signing amateur forms for Plymouth Argyle in January 1966. The following summer he turned professional and spent two seasons at Home Park, where he proved to be a versatile forward, scoring five goals from 32 appearances. He continued his career with Weymouth and Falmouth Town.

Carlton Fairweather (Born: Camberwell, London, 22 September 1961. Died: April 2025.) Carlton Fairweather was a winger who developed in non-league football before joining Wimbledon from Tooting & Mitcham midway through the 1984–85 campaign. He helped the Dons win promotion to the First Division in 1985–86 and went on to make over 150 appearances during his stay. Later he had a season with Carlisle United then played in Hong Kong and the USA. After retiring as a player he became youth team coach at Wimbledon and then worked as a coach with Sunderland for over 20 years.

Alec Farrall (Born: West Kirby, Cheshire, 3 March 1936. Died: Prenton, Birkenhead, 19 May 2025.) Alec Farrall was a skilful midfield player who won representative honours for England Schoolboys, then came up through the ranks with Everton, making his first-team debut shortly after his 17th birthday. However, he had few first-team opportunities at Goodison and in March 1957 he moved on to Preston North End, but here too he was mostly a reserve. The best years of his career were spent with Gillingham where he made over 200 appearances in a five-year spell, missing only one game in the 1963–64 campaign when they won the Fourth Division title. He later wound down his career with spells at Lincoln City and Watford.

Gerry Fell (Born: Newark, Nottinghamshire, 1 March 1951. Died: Collingham, Nottinghamshire, 13 May 2025.) Gerry Fell was a winger who played in non-league football for Stamford and Long Eaton United before joining Brighton & Hove Albion in November 1974. He stayed four years with the Seagulls, assisting in their promotion campaign from the Third Division in 1976–77. Later he appeared for Southend United (where he again won promotion in 1977–78), Torquay United, and, briefly, York City, before leaving senior football.

Jake Findlay (Born: Blairgowrie, Perthshire, 13 July 1954. Died: 3 May 2025.) Goalkeeper Jake Findlay joined Aston Villa as an apprentice and was a member of the team that won the FA Youth Cup in 1971–72. He then spent six years as a professional at Villa Park, but he was mostly in the reserves and made just 18 first-team appearances. In November 1978 he was sold to Luton Town where he almost immediately became first choice and retained the jersey until March 1983 when he suffered a broken thumb. He made a total of 187 appearances for the Hatters, winning the Division Two title in 1981–82. He later played a few games for Swindon Town before retiring as a player.

Steve Fleet (Born: Urmston, Manchester, 2 July 1937. Died: 1 March 2025.) Goalkeeper Steve Fleet came up through the ranks with Manchester City, signing professional forms in February 1955. He stayed with the club until the summer of 1963, making six first-team appearances before joining Wrexham where he had three seasons of regular first-team football and played in close on 100 games. He concluded his senior career with Stockport County where he played enough games to win a Fourth Division champions' medal in 1966–67. Later he had further spells back at Maine Road as youth team coach, Sports Development Officer and manager of the Platt Lane complex.

Neil Fleming (Born: Felixstowe, Suffolk, 9 January 1950. Died: Lincoln, 13 May 2025.) Neil Fleming was a centre-half who was an amateur with Lincoln City for three seasons in the early 1970s. He played regularly for the reserves and made a single first-team appearance in April 1974. He later continued his career with spells at Grantham United and Grantham.

Joe Forte (Born: Northumberland, 18 November 1958. Died: Haddington, East Lothian, 2 September 2024.) Joe Forte played for Haddington United as a youngster then had a season with Hibernian before joining Berwick Rangers, for whom he made three appearances as a substitute in the 1977–78 season. He went on to spend the 1979–80 campaign with Meadowbank Thistle before concluding his career at Ormiston Primrose.

Gerry Francis (Born: Johannesburg, South Africa, 6 December 1933. Died: Ontario, Canada, 10 May 2025.) Winger Gerry Francis was playing for the Johannesburg club Blackpool United when he came to England for a trial with Leeds United. He was initially an amateur at Elland Road before signing professional forms in the summer of 1957 and went on to make his Football League debut against Birmingham City in November of that year, becoming the first black player to appear for the club. He waited two years for his next opportunity but eventually made 52 appearances then had a spell with York City before winding down his career with a three-year stay in the Southern League with Tonbridge.

John Fraser (Born: Portobello, Edinburgh, 1936. Died: March 2025.) John Fraser was an outside-right who joined Hibernian from Edinburgh Thistle in August 1954 and made his first-team debut three months later. He took some time to win a regular place in the line-up but in 1957–58 he gained a Scottish Cup runners-up medal. He went on to make over 250 appearances during his time at Easter Road, then after a season as player-coach at Stenhousemuir he returned to join the backroom staff.

Clive Freeman (Born: Leeds, 12 September 1962. Died: 3 September 2024.) Clive Freeman was a defender who came to prominence as a member of the Bridlington Town team that were runners-up in the 1989–90 FA Vase final. Shortly afterwards he signed for Swansea City, making his Football League debut at the age of 28, but he was unable to establish himself at the Vetch Field. He spent the 1992–93 season with Altrincham then returned to the League with Doncaster Rovers the following summer where he added further senior appearances before continuing his career with non-league Emley.

Mick Gannon (Born: Liverpool, 2 February 1943. Died: 13 June 2024.) Defender Mick Gannon joined Everton on leaving school and was a member of the team that were beaten finalists in the 1960–61 FA Youth Cup. He made three first-team appearances during his time at Goodison then had two seasons with Scunthorpe United where he was mainly a reserve. His best seasons were spent with Crewe Alexandra for whom he made over 200 Football League appearances and was an ever-present in the team that won promotion from Division Four in 1967–68. Later he played in non-league for Altrincham and Holyhead Town.

Bobby Gardner (Born: Circa 1944. Died: Kirkcaldy, Fife, 18 July 2024.) Winger Bobby Gardner was playing in the Juniors with Blairgowrie before stepping up to sign for Stirling Albion in April 1964. He spent two seasons at Annfield then had brief spells with Raith Rovers and Montrose before leaving senior football.

David Gaskell (Born: Wigan, 5 October 1940. Died: 24 January 2025.) Goalkeeper David Gaskell was capped for England Schoolboys before joining the groundstaff at Manchester United. He became the club's youngest-ever player when coming on as a substitute for Ray Wood during the 1956–57 FA Charity Shield match aged 16 years and 19 days. Later that season he won an FA Youth Cup winners' medal, and he went on to sign professional forms when he turned 17. He spent a decade on the books at Old Trafford and although rarely first choice he made 120 appearances, gaining an FA Cup winners' medal in 1963. He spent the 1968–69 campaign with Wigan Athletic then joined Wrexham, where he missed just one match as they finished as runners-up in Division Four in 1969–70. He concluded his career playing in South Africa with Arcadia Shepherds.

Don Gibson (Born: Manchester, 12 May 1929. Died: 16 September 2024.) Wing-half Don Gibson was a product of Manchester schools' football, signing as an amateur for Manchester United at the age of 15. He progressed to the professional ranks and made his debut shortly after the start of the 1950–51 season. He went on to make over 100 appearances for United before being sold to Sheffield Wednesday in June 1955. He stayed five years at Hillsborough, and although he was often affected by injuries he was a member of two promotion teams (1955–56 and 1958–59). He finished his senior career with Leyton Orient then had a short spell as player-manager of Buxton before leaving football to focus on his business interests.

Bobby Gillon (Born: Cupar, Fife, 4 November 1932. Died: Falkland, Cupar, Fife, 25 September 2024.) Inside-forward Bobby Gillon developed with Kemback Youth Club and Luthrie Amateurs before joining East Fife at the age of 18. His early career was disrupted by National Service, and although he was a regular scorer for the reserves he was a rarely a first-team regular, making 26 appearances during his time with the club.

Brian Glanville (Born: Hendon, Middlesex, 24 September 1931. Died: 16 May 2025.) Brian Glanville was a prolific journalist, author, playwright and scriptwriter who was football correspondent for the *Sunday Times* for 33 years and a contributor to *World Soccer* magazine for over 50 years. He worked for many other publications, including *The Times* and *The People*, and also wrote novels and short stories with a football theme. He covered every World Cup finals tournament from 1958 to 2006 as a journalist.

Vic Gomersall (Born: Manchester, 17 June 1942. Died: Treboeth, Swansea, 12 December 2024.) Vic Gomersall was a hard-tackling full-back who came up through the ranks with Manchester City, making his First Division debut as a teenager. However, he struggled to establish himself in the line-up and eventually moved on to sign for Swansea Town, as the club was then known, in the summer of 1966. He spent five seasons at the Vetch Field and was a member of the team that won promotion from Division Four in 1969–70. Later he helped Chelmsford City win the Southern League title in 1971–72.

Roy Greaves (Born: Farnworth, Lancashire, 4 April 1947. Died: August 2024.) Roy Greaves joined Bolton Wanderers as a 15-year-old centre-forward, going on to make his first-team debut in October 1965. He established himself as a regular in the side in 1967–68 and retained his place through until his departure in February 1980, dropping to play further back as time progressed. He won the Third Division title with Bolton in 1972–73 then captained the side that won the Second Division in 1978–79. He made a total of 590 appearances, just three short of the club record, and was top scorer in 1967–68 and 1968–69. Later he played for NASL club Seattle Sounders and had a spell as player-coach of Rochdale.

Len Green (Born: Middleton St George, Co Durham, 2 October 1936. Died: 2 November 2024.) Full-back Len Green joined Darlington from local junior football in October 1955 and went on to make his debut the following March. He spent six years with the Quakers, making 56 appearances and featuring in the team that defeated Chelsea to reach the fifth round of the FA Cup in 1957–58. He later played for Horden Colliery Welfare.

John Gregson (Born: Skelmersdale, Lancashire, 17 May 1939. Died: 27 April 2025.) John Gregson was a winger who joined Blackpool from Skelmersdale United in the summer of 1957 and spent five years on the books at Bloomfield Road, making three senior appearances. In May 1962 he signed for Chester and from then onwards he played regular first-team football in a career that also saw him play for Shrewsbury Town, Mansfield Town, Lincoln City and Cambridge United. He was a member of the U's team that won two successive Southern League titles in the late 1960s and continued to play in their first season in the Football League before suffering a badly broken leg in April 1971 that ended his career.

Keith Hague (Born: Hull, 25 May 1946. Died: 19 May 2025.) Centre-half Keith Hague played for Bridlington Trinity and Chilton Amateurs before joining York City in October 1965. He appeared regularly for the reserves and made a single first-team appearance as a substitute, coming off the bench for the last 15 minutes of the home game with Brentford in March 1966. He later spent a decade with non-league Goole Town, making over 400 appearances for them.

Jan Halup (Born: Alloa, Stirlingshire, 28 February 1950. Died: 29 January 2025.) Outside-left Jan Halup played in the Juniors for Sauchie and Clackmannan before spending the second half of the 1968–69 campaign with Alloa Athletic. He made 11 first-team appearances for the Wasps then returned to Clackmannan.

Ken Hancock (Born: Stoke-on-Trent, 25 November 1937. Died: 27 April 2025.) Goalkeeper Ken Hancock signed for Port Vale shortly after the start of the 1958–59 season. He was promoted to the first team after just three reserve games and kept his place throughout the second half of the campaign as Vale won the Fourth Division title. Barring injuries he remained first choice until he was sold to Ipswich Town in December 1964. He was in similar form at Portman Road, adding a further 190 appearances and being ever-present in 1967–68 when they won the Second Division championship. Later he spent two seasons as understudy to Pat Jennings at Tottenham Hotspur before concluding his senior career at Bury.

John Hardie (Born: Edinburgh, 7 February 1938. Died: Edinburgh, 18 December 2024.) Goalkeeper John Hardie was a product of Edinburgh Thistle Juveniles and then became a provisional signing for Hibernian. He made no first-team appearances at Easter Road then played two games for Falkirk before signing for Oldham Athletic in July 1960. He spent a season at Boundary Park then moved on to Chester where he was first choice for two seasons before losing his place. In December 1963 he signed for Bradford Park Avenue, very quickly establishing himself and rarely missing a match as he went on to make 279 appearances. After Park Avenue were voted out of the League he had a spell as back-up keeper with Crystal Palace without adding to his appearances before leaving senior football.

Steve Hardwick (Born: Mansfield, 6 September 1956. Died: 16 September 2024.) Goalkeeper Steve Hardwick joined Chesterfield on amateur forms before signing as a professional in July 1974. An England Youth international, he established himself for the Spireites towards the end of the 1975–76 campaign and was then sold to Newcastle United in December 1976. He was a regular at St James' Park for two seasons before eventually moving on to Oxford United in February 1983. He enjoyed the best period of his career at the Manor Ground where he was a key member of the team that won successive promotions to take them from the Third Division to the top flight in the 1980s. He finished his career with Huddersfield Town, retiring at the end of the 1990–91 season having made nearly 500 senior appearances.

Colin Harrington (Born: Bicester, Oxfordshire, 3 April 1943. Died: Oxford, 24 December 2024.) Colin Harrington was a tall, quick outside-left who spent two years on the books of Wolverhampton Wanderers before signing professional forms for Oxford United soon after their elevation to the Football League. He won a regular place in the U's line-up in the closing stages of the 1962–63 season and went on to make over 250 appearances, appearing in two promotion teams during his stay at the Manor Ground. He concluded his career with spells at Mansfield Town and Kettering Town.

Barry Hartle (Born: Salford, 8 August 1939. Died: 29 January 2025.) Winger Barry Hartle joined Watford in August 1956 after impressing in junior football in Salford and went on to assist the Hornets to their first-ever promotion as they gained a top-four position in Division Four in 1959–60. In the summer of 1960 he was sold to Sheffield United, and enjoyed the best years of his career at Bramall Lane, making over 100 First Division appearances in a six-year stay. He continued with spells at Carlisle United, Stockport County, Oldham Athletic and Southport before leaving senior football at the end of the 1971–72 campaign having made a total of more than 300 League and Cup appearances.

John Hawksby (Born: York, 12 June 1942. Died: Kettering, 13 June 2024.) Winger John Hawksby joined the groundstaff at Leeds United on leaving school and went on to gain England Youth international honours before signing professional terms. He broke into the first team at the start of the 1960–61 season, scoring on his debut against Rotherham United, but he was mostly a reserve during his time at Elland Road. In the summer of 1964 he moved on to Lincoln City where he was a first-team regular, and then York City in March 1966. He made just short of 200 senior appearances in total before continuing his career in non-league football, later helping Kettering Town win the Southern League title in 1972–73.

George Herd (Born: Gartcosh, Lanarkshire, 6 May 1936. Died: Sunderland, 5 August 2024.) George Herd was a centre- or inside-forward who played as a youngster for Gartcosh Thistle in the local amateur league. He linked up with Inverness Thistle during his National Service then spent the 1956–57 season with Queen's Park, winning Amateur international honours for Scotland. In May 1957 he signed as a professional for Clyde where he enjoyed four successful years, gaining a Scottish Cup winners' medal in 1958 and five full caps for Scotland, as well as appearing for the Scottish League representative side. In April 1961 he became Sunderland's most expensive signing, and made over 300 first-team appearances during his time at Roker Park, helping the Black Cats win promotion back to the top flight in 1963–64. Later he had a spell with Hartlepools United and then enjoyed a lengthy career in coaching, also serving Queen of the South as manager between June and December 1980.

John Herrick (Born: Cork, 26 July 1946. Died: Galway, 26 March 2025.) Defender John Herrick was a key figure in the successful Cork Hibs team of the early 1970s, helping them win the League of Ireland in 1970–71 and the FAI Cup the following season. He also had spells with Shamrock Rovers, Limerick, Drogheda United and Galway Rovers. He was capped on three occasions by the Republic of Ireland and won representative honours for the League of Ireland team.

Jim Herriot (Born: Chapelhall, Airdrie, 20 December 1939. Died: 23 April 2025.) Jim Herriot was a goalkeeper who joined Dunfermline Athletic from Douglasdale Juniors in October 1958. He made his first-team debut in October 1960, but it was not until the 1963–64 season that he became the undisputed first choice at East End Park. After gaining a Scottish Cup runners-up medal in 1965 he was sold to Birmingham City where he made over 200 appearances. After a brief spell in South Africa he returned to Scotland, signing for Hibernian in August 1971. He was a member of the team that won both the League Cup and the Drybrough Cup in 1972–73 and later played for St Mirren and Partick Thistle before ending his career back at Dunfermline. He won eight caps for Scotland and also appeared twice for the Scottish League representative side.

Jack Hobbs (Born: Swanage, Dorset, 17 April 1930. Died: New Westminster, British Columbia, Canada, 11 June 2024.) Centre-forward Jack Hobbs joined Bournemouth in October 1952 and stayed three years at Dean Court, making six Football League appearances. He emigrated to Canada in 1956 where he continued his career in the Pacific Coast League with Westminster Royals, North Shore Carlings and Vancouver Columbus.

Alex Hodge (Born: Lochgelly, Fife, 7 July 1941. Died: Lochgelly, Fife, 18 January 2025.) Full-back Alex Hodge developed in the Secondary Juveniles with Ballingry Rovers and then in the Juniors with Blairhall Colliery before signing for Alloa Athletic in February 1962. He was a regular for the Wasps over the next nine seasons, making 286 senior appearances before leaving senior football.

Alan Holt (Born: Edinburgh, 21 August 1956. Died: Livingston, February 2025.) Alan Holt joined Falkirk from Juvenile outfit Edinburgh Thistle and was still a teenager when he established himself as a central defender at Brockville. In March 1978 he was allowed to leave for Alloa Athletic where he made 192 appearances over the next five years, featuring in the team that won promotion from the Second Division in 1981–82. He later spent a season with Meadowbank Thistle before moving into the Juniors with Tranent.

Ray Holt (Born: Thorne, Yorkshire, 29 October 1939. Died: 7 December 2024.) Centre-half Ray Holt was on the books of Huddersfield Town as an amateur before signing a professional contract in August 1958 but was mostly a reserve during his time at Leeds Road. In the summer of 1965 he moved on to Oldham Athletic and, the following year, Halifax Town. He was a regular in two seasons at The Shay then had a spell with Scunthorpe United before switching to non-league with Worksop Town.

Niall Hopper (Born: Cambuslang, Lanarkshire, 9 September 1935. Died: Rutherglen, Lanarkshire, 11 July 2024.) Niall Hopper was a winger who came to prominence with Rutherglen St Andrew's, with whom he won youth international honours, and Cambuslang Rangers before signing for Queen's Park in September 1955. He went on to make over 350 appearances during a 14-year spell with the Spiders, also winning 27 caps for Scotland Amateurs and appearing on three occasions for the Great Britain Olympic team. He scored Scotland's goal in their 2-1 defeat by Austria in the final of the UEFA Amateur Nations Cup in June 1967.

Roly Horrey (Born: Bishop Auckland, 7 March 1943. Died: 4 December 2024.) Roly Horrey was an outside-right who played for Bishop Auckland and Ferryhill Athletic, before signing professional forms for Blackburn Rovers in December 1963. He made three top-flight appearances during his time at Ewood Park and after being made available for transfer he moved to York City in July 1966. He was a regular for the Minstermen for two seasons then signed for Cambridge United, at the time a non-league club. He was a member of the U's team that won consecutive Southern League titles before being elected to the Football League for the 1970–71 campaign, when he featured regularly. He lost his place the following season and moved on to Chelmsford City in December 1972.

Charles Hughes (Born: Clitheroe, Lancashire, 28 July 1933. Died: August 2024.) Charles Hughes was a schoolteacher and FA staff coach when he was appointed as manager of the England Amateur and Great Britain Olympic teams in November 1963, remaining in both positions until amateur status was abolished in 1974. He also took on the role of assistant director of coaching of the FA, and then, from 1990 until he retired in 1997, was director of coaching. He is credited with establishing the FA Centres of Excellence, the FA's medical and rehab centre and the FA National School, while he was also involved with the setting up of the Football in the Community programme.

Norrie Innes (Born: Baillieston, Lanarkshire, 20 December 1934. Died: 28 August 2024.) Norrie Innes was a ball-playing inside-forward who signed for Clyde in August 1954 after a brief spell with Ashfield Juniors. He had to wait until January 1956 for his first-team debut but the following season he scored 22 goals as the Bully Wee won the Second Division title. He left Clyde in the summer of 1959, spending a few months with Stirling Albion then signing for St Johnstone, where he contributed to their success in winning promotion to the top flight in 1959–60. He had two seasons as a regular at Muirton Park before concluding his career with spells at Falkirk and Albion Rovers.

Roy Ironside (Born: Sheffield, 28 May 1935. Died: 8 June 2024.) Goalkeeper Roy Ironside signed professional forms for Rotherham United in July 1954 but had to wait almost three years for his first-team debut. He then went on to make over 250 appearances for the Millers and was a member of the team defeated by Aston Villa in the first-ever Football League Cup final in 1960–61. He moved on to Barnsley in July 1965, where he spent a further four seasons and was a regular in the side that won promotion from the Fourth Division in 1967–68.

Cecil Irwin (Born: Ellington, Northumberland, 8 April 1942. Died: 21 April 2025.) Full-back Cecil Irwin came up through the ranks with Sunderland, receiving his first-team debut in September 1958 making him, at the time, the club's youngest-

ever Football League player. He won England Youth international honours and went on to establish himself as a first-team regular during the 1961–62 season. He held his place in the side for a decade, helping the Black Cats gain promotion from the Second Division in 1963–64 and making a total of 353 first-team appearances. He later had a spell as manager of Yeovil Town.

George Jagger (Born: Great Houghton, South Yorkshire, 30 September 1941. Died: Telford, 26 August 2024.) George Jagger was a winger who developed in local youth football before signing for Barnsley in the summer of 1960. He spent three years at Oakwell, making a total of 49 appearances before dropping into the Southern League with Corby Town. In the summer of 1966 he signed for Wellington Town, soon to become Telford United, where he played over 400 games and featured in two FA Trophy finals, gaining a winners' medal in 1971.

Ken Jenkin (Born: Grimsby, 27 November 1931. Died: 15 July 2024.) Winger Ken Jenkin was a product of the Grimsby Schoolboys team then signed for Grimsby Town as a part-time professional in the summer of 1950. He went on to score six goals from 23 appearances for the Mariners before he suffered a knee injury shortly after the start of the 1953–54 season, which effectively ended his career.

Bryn Jones (Born: Bagilit, Flintshire, 26 May 1939. Died: Prestatyn, 21 January 2025.) Full-back Bryn Jones won seven caps for Wales Amateurs with Holywell Town and Bangor City before signing professional forms for Watford in January 1963. He played a couple of games for the Hornets before moving on to Chester in August 1964. He was a regular at Sealand Road at the start of 1965–66 before suffering a broken leg that sidelined him for many months. Soon after his return to action a further leg injury effectively ended his senior career.

Geir Karlsen (Born: Skien, Norway, 18 September 1948. Died: 26 July 2024.) Goalkeeper Geir Karlsen started out with his local club Odd before moving on to Rosenborg BK with whom he won a domestic double in the 1971 season. In November 1973 he signed for Dunfermline Athletic, and he was a regular with the Pars throughout his stay, making 55 League appearances before returning to Scandinavia to sign for Vålerengen. He gained 31 caps for Norway between 1969 and 1977.

Allan Kell (Born: Spennymoor, Co Durham, 9 April 1949. Died: 11 August 2024.) Right-half Allan Kell made two appearances as a substitute for Darlington during the 1967–68 season when he also featured for the Quakers' reserve team. He later had a lengthy spell with Spennymoor United before moving on to Whitby Town.

Scott Kemlo (Born: Dundee, 8 July 1974. Died: 18 April 2025.) Defender Scott Kemlo joined Brechin City in March 1994 and made 17 appearances before switching to Junior club Dundee North End where his career was ended after he suffered a badly broken leg in April 1998. His premature death came following a heart attack while working on an oil rig in the North Sea.

Jimmy Kemp (Born: Durris, Aberdeenshire, 13 February 1940. Died: Kingsmuir, Angus, 29 September 2024.) Jimmy Kemp was a goalscoring inside-forward whose tally of 164 goals in two spells made him the second-highest scorer in the history of Montrose. He joined the club from Forfar West End in May 1959 and, apart from a spell with East Stirlingshire, where his goals helped free them to promotion to the top flight in 1962–63, remained until January 1971. He concluded his senior career with Brechin City.

Bobby Kennedy (Born: Motherwell, 23 June 1937. Died: 11 January 2025.) Wing-half Bobby Kennedy developed with Wishaw YMCA and Coltness United before signing for Kilmarnock in March 1957. After establishing himself in the first team he was sidelined for several months due to a bout of tuberculosis but returned to full health and appeared in the teams that lost out in the Scottish Cup final in 1959–60 and the League Cup final the following season. He was sold to Manchester City in August 1961, where he made over 250 appearances in an eight-year spell, helping them win the Second Division title in 1965–66. He moved on to become player-manager of Grimsby Town, and later he was manager of Bradford City, taking them to the sixth round of the FA Cup in 1975–66 and promotion from the Fourth Division the following season. He was capped for Scotland U23s.

Mike Kenning (Born: Erdington, Birmingham, 18 August 1940. Died: Johannesburg, South Africa, 15 March 2025.) Mike Kenning was a winger who developed with Aston Villa where he made three first-team appearances before being sold to Shrewsbury Town in May 1961. He was rarely absent during his time with the Shrews but after 14 months he moved on to Charlton Athletic. He went on to enjoy the best years of his career with the Addicks, playing a total of more than 200 games in two separate spells with the club. In between he played for Norwich City and in the First Division with Wolverhampton Wanderers. After concluding his career at Watford he emigrated to South Africa where he played for Port Elizabeth City before joining Germiston Callies as player-manager.

Don Kichenbrand (Born: Germiston, South Africa, 13 August 1933. Died: Benoni, Gauteng, South Africa, 16 March 2025.) Don Kichenbrand was a powerful, bustling centre-forward who signed for Rangers in September 1955 having previously played in Transvaal for Delfos. He enjoyed a tremendous first season at Ibrox, finishing as the team's top scorer as they won the Scottish League title, and netting five goals in an 8-0 win over Queen of the South in March 1956. He rarely appeared afterwards and in March 1958 he was sold to Sunderland. He netted on his debut and scored regularly during his time at Roker Park, ending with a tally of 28 goals from 54 appearances. He played his last game for the Black Cats in August 1959 and later returned to South Africa. He came back to Scotland in June 1962, going on to play for Forfar Athletic, Montrose (very briefly), and in the Highland League for Keith.

Adam King (Born: Hillingdon, Middlesex, 4 October 1969. Died: February 2025.) Midfielder Adam King was a product of the FA School of Excellence, winning caps for England at U16 and U17 levels. He became a trainee with West Ham United then spent a further two seasons as a professional without making a senior appearance. In March 1990 he signed for Plymouth Argyle where he featured regularly in the closing stages of the 1989–90 campaign. He added further appearances the following season before dropping into non-league to play for Hendon.

Johnny King (Born: Wrenbury, Cheshire, 9 August 1932. Died: April 2025.) Centre-forward Johnny King developed as a junior with Crewe Alexandra, making his Football League debut on Boxing Day 1950. He became a regular for the Alex in the 1952–53 campaign and the following September was sold to Stoke City. He spent eight seasons with the Potters, scoring 105 goals in 284 League appearances. Later he had a season at Cardiff before returning to Crewe, where he helped fire the team to promotion from Division Four in 1962–63. He remained at Gresty Road until being released at the end of the 1966–67 season.

Alex Kinninmonth (Born: Methil, Fife, 26 September 1941. Died: Kirkcaldy, Fife, 8 August 2024.) Alex Kinninmonth was a midfield player who developed with St Andrew's Swifts and Blairgowrie Juniors before signing provisional forms for Dundee in November 1960. He was called up for his debut in May 1964 and remained at Dens Park until the end of the 1971–72 campaign. Although rarely a regular in the line-up he played a total of 167 games. After moving on to Dunfermline Athletic he made 152 consecutive appearances through until December 1975 assisting the Pars to promotion to the top flight in 1972–73. Later he briefly played for Forfar Athletic before joining the coaching staff at Raith Rovers.

Denis Law, CBE (Born: Aberdeen, 24 February 1940. Died: 17 January 2025.) Denis Law was one of the most talented forwards in British football in the 1960s. A product of Aberdeen schools' football, he joined the groundstaff at Huddersfield Town before progressing to a professional contract. Manager Bill Shankly had already introduced him to first-team football, and he remains the youngest ever to play in the Football League for the Terriers. He was sold to Manchester City in March 1960, where he scored six goals in an FA Cup tie at Luton in January 1961 only for the game to be abandoned. He briefly joined the mini-exodus of British players to Italy in 1961, spending a season with Torino, before returning to sign for Manchester United. He spent 11 years at Old Trafford where the legendary trio of Best, Law and Charlton guided the club to success at home and in Europe. Denis was an FA Cup winner in 1963 and a member of two Football League title winning teams with the Reds, and when he left in July 1973 he had scored 239 goals from just over 400 appearances. He concluded his career back at Manchester City before retiring as a player. He won 55 caps for Scotland between 1958 and 1974, scoring 30 goals, making him his country's joint top scorer. He was European Footballer of the Year in 1964 and won representative honours for both the Football League and the Italian League. He was awarded the CBE for services to football and charity in the 2016 New Year's Honours List.

Glan Letheren (Born: Dafen, Llanelli, 1 May 1956. Died: 6 June 2024.) Goalkeeper Glan Letheren joined Leeds United as a teenager and was just 17 when he made his senior debut, coming on as a substitute in the UEFA Cup tie at Hibernian in November 1973. However, he made just one further appearance during his time at Elland Road, and after a successful loan spell with Scunthorpe United was sold to Chesterfield in December 1977. He was the Spireites' first-choice keeper for 18 months then had a spell with Swansea City before dropping into non-league football. He later spent time in charge of the Wales national women's team. He was capped for Wales at U18, U21 and U23 levels.

Jim Liddle (Born: Edinburgh, 9 April 1958. Died: Edinburgh, 13 October 2024.) Centre-forward Jim Liddle joined Cowdenbeath from Whitehill Welfare in September 1978 and after establishing himself in the line-up became a regular goalscorer. In February 1983 he was sold to Forfar Athletic for what was a record fee for the Station Park club. He enjoyed a fine season in 1983–84 when he led the club's scoring charts with 22 goals as they won the Division Two title with Jim selected as the divisional Player of the Year. He had a brief spell in the Premier League with Hamilton Academical before winding down his career with Meadowbank Thistle and in Belgium with FC Jeunesse Lorraine Arlonaise.

Alan Little (Born: Horden, Co Durham, 5 February 1955. Died: 5 August 2024.) Alan Little was a hard-tackling midfield player who became an apprentice with Aston Villa and was a member of the team that won the FA Youth Cup in 1971–72. He made little impact at first-team level, however, and in December 1974 was sold to Southend United where he was immediately installed in the first team. He went on to spend a dozen years playing in the lower divisions, also appearing for Barnsley, Doncaster Rovers, Torquay United, Halifax Town and Hartlepool United, accumulating more than 450 senior appearances. Highlights included winning promotion from the Fourth Division with Barnsley and Doncaster. Later he served York City, Southend United and Halifax Town as manager, leading York to promotion with a play-off final victory over Crewe Alexandra in May 1993.

Barry Lloyd (Born: Hillingdon, Middlesex, 19 February 1949. Died: 28 September 2024.) Midfielder Barry Lloyd developed with Chelsea as a youngster and was capped for the England Youth team. He made his debut as an 18-year-old but struggled to make any significant breakthrough at Stamford Bridge and in December 1968 was sold to Fulham. He proved a key figure at Craven Cottage over the next six years, captaining the team that won promotion from Division Three in 1970–71 and playing just over 300 first-team games. He later had spells with Hereford United, Brentford and NASL club Houston Hurricane before becoming player-manager of Yeovil Town. Following a further spell in management with Worthing he took over at Brighton & Hove Albion in January 1987. He remained in post until March 1993, gaining promotion as Third Division runners-up in 1987–88.

Jack Lovatt (Born: Burton upon Trent, 23 August 1941. Died: Netherseal, Swadlincote, Derbyshire, 3 March 2025.) Centre-forward Jack Lovatt developed with Erdington Albion, a nursery team for West Bromwich Albion, before signing a professional contract with the Baggies in December 1958. He scored on his first-team debut at West Ham in March 1961 but was mostly a back-up player during his time at The Hawthorns, making 18 appearances before departing to join Nuneaton Borough in November 1963.

Simon Lowe (Born: Westminster, London, 26 December 1962. Died: August 2024.) Simon Lowe was a hard-working striker who was an apprentice with York City then moved into non-league football with Ossett Town. He returned to senior football with Barnsley in December 1983, but he was generally a reserve at Oakwell. He subsequently spent two seasons with Halifax Town, where he topped the club's scoring charts in 1984–85, before concluding his career with spells at Hartlepool United, Colchester United and Scarborough.

Roy McCarthy (Born: Barugh Green, Barnsley, 17 January 1945. Died: 24 August 2024.) Roy McCarthy was a tricky winger who joined the groundstaff at Barnsley on leaving school and then signed a professional contract at the age of 17. However, he made few appearances for the team at Oakwell before being released and signing for Barrow. He enjoyed five seasons of regular first-team football at Holker Street, making over 200 appearances and helping the Bluebirds win promotion from Division Four in 1966–67. He concluded his senior career with a season at Southport.

John McClelland (Born: Bradford, 5 March 1939. Died: 15 June 2024.) John McClelland was on the books of Manchester City as an amateur before turning professional in March 1957. He made his first-team debut at the start of the 1956–57 season, but was only a fringe player at Maine Road, and it was not until signing for Lincoln City in September 1958 that he experienced regular first-team football. A pacy winger, he led the Imps' scoring charts in 1959–60 and made over 100 League appearances before moving on for a two-year stay at Queens Park Rangers. In May 1963 he signed for Portsmouth and over the next three seasons was a regular for the Division Two club. Later he had a season with Newport County before retiring from football.

Steve McCormick (Born: Seafield, West Lothian, 19 March 1965. Died: 10 May 2025.) Steve McCormick was a striker who joined Stenhousemuir from Whitburn Juniors in the summer of 1989 and quickly established himself, finishing his first season as the club's top scorer. After three years at Ochilview he continued his career with spells at Alloa Athletic, Forfar Athletic (where he was a member of the team that won the Third Division title in 1994–95), and Arbroath before leaving senior football.

Colin McCullie (Born: Bellshill, Lanarkshire, 12 May 1951. Died: 3 November 2024.) Colin McCullie was a pacy forward who joined Cowdenbeath from Gairdoch United and featured as a teenager for the club in their last season of top-flight football in 1970–71. He continued his career with spells at Stranraer (where he made over 100 League appearances) and Raith Rovers, switching to play as an attacking full-back.

Mick McGrath (Born: Dublin, 7 April 1936. Died: Blackburn, 18 April 2025.) Wing-half Mick McGrath joined Blackburn Rovers from Home Farm, where he won youth international honours for the Republic of Ireland. He gained a regular place in the line-up towards the end of the 1956–57 season and went on to make over 300 appearances during his time at Ewood Park, helping Rovers win promotion to the top flight in 1957–58 and gaining an FA Cup runners-up medal in 1960. He concluded his senior career at Bradford Park Avenue before being appointed as player-manager of Cheshire League club Bangor City. He won 22 full caps for the Republic of Ireland between 1958 and 1967 and appeared for the Football League representative team.

Willie McInnes (Born: Douglas Water, Lanarkshire, 20 May 1931. Died: Accrington, 15 October 2024.) Goalkeeper Willie McInnes played a few games for Falkirk in the early 1950s and appeared fairly regularly for Alloa Athletic in 1954–55 before joining Accrington Stanley in October 1955. He was mostly a first choice during six seasons at Peel Park, making 168 appearances before concluding his senior career with a two-year spell at Southport.

Ronnie McIntosh (Born: Circa 1935. Died: Perth, Scotland, 8 April 2025.) Centre-forward Ronnie McIntosh made his senior debut as a triallist for Forfar Athletic in November 1957. Later that month he signed for Brechin City where his goalscoring exploits earned him a transfer to Arbroath shortly after the start of the following season. He was released in the summer of 1959 and returned to Brechin where his tally of 26 League goals in the 1959–60 season established a club record that stood for more than 60 years. He later played briefly for Forfar again before returning to the Juniors with St Johnstone YM.

Ian McKinlay (Born: Huyton, Liverpool, 21 June 1949. Died: Liverpool, 28 August 2024.) Outside-right Ian McKinlay was an apprentice at Wrexham before joining Southport for the 1966–67 campaign. He was just 17 when he made his Football League debut for the Sandgrounders but after making 13 appearances over two seasons he moved on to Wigan Athletic, then a non-league club. Soon afterwards he suffered a bad knee injury, and this effectively ended his career.

Jim McLaughlin (Born: Derry, Co Londonderry, 22 December 1940. Died: Blackrock, Co Louth, Republic of Ireland, 15 August 2024.) Outside-left Jim McLaughlin won youth international honours for Northern Ireland before moving from Derry City to Birmingham City in June 1958. However, he was unable to break into the first-team at St Andrew's and two years later was sold to Shrewsbury Town. He was a near ever-present for the next three seasons then joined Swansea Town, helping them reach the semi-final of the FA Cup in 1963–64. A brief spell with Peterborough United was then followed by returns to both Shrewsbury and Swansea before he retired having scored 163 goals in 527 senior

appearances. Later he was a successful manager in the League of Ireland, winning the title with three different clubs including a domestic treble with Derry City in 1988–89. He won 12 caps for Northern Ireland between 1961 and 1966.

Derek McLean (Born: Brotton, North Yorkshire, 21 December 1932. Died: Middlesbrough, 1 February 2025.) Inside-forward Derek McLean was playing in the Teesside League for North Skelton Athletic when he signed for Middlesbrough in August 1952. He had to wait almost four years for his senior debut but then went on to score 30 goals from 121 appearances for Boro' before he was sold to Hartlepools United in October 1961. He was rarely absent in three seasons with Pools, finishing as joint-top scorer in 1962–63, before concluding his career with Scarborough.

John McNamee (Born: Coatbridge, Lanarkshire, 11 June 1941. Died: 28 November 2024.) John McNamee was a rugged centre-half who joined Celtic from Bellshill Athletic in August 1959 and went on to make his debut in February 1961. He was rarely a first-team regular at Parkhead but won a Scottish Cup runners-up medal in 1963 before moving on to Hibernian in April 1964. He was a member of the Hibs team that won the Summer Cup in 1964 and made over 100 appearances but was then sold to Newcastle United in December 1966. He was a key player during his five years at St James' Park and gained an Inter Cities Fairs Cup winners' medal in 1968–69 when he featured as an unused substitute in the final. He wound down his career with spells at Blackburn Rovers, Morton and Hartlepool United before finishing off as player-manager at Workington.

Peter McParland (Born: Newry, Co Down, 25 April 1934. Died: Bournemouth, 4 May 2025.) Peter McParland was a tall, powerful winger who was playing first-team football for Dundalk at the age of 16. In September 1952 he signed for Aston Villa where he became a regular in the line-up, scoring 120 goals from 341 games, reaching his peak in the 1957 FA Cup final when he netted twice as Villa defeated Manchester United to win the trophy. He was a regular in the team that won the Second Division title and the inaugural Football League Cup in 1960–61, before going on to play for Wolverhampton Wanderers and Plymouth Argyle. He won 34 caps for Northern Ireland between 1954 and 1962 and was the last surviving member of the team that reached the quarter-finals of the World Cup in 1958. He also won representative honours for the Football League XI.

John McTavish (Born: Glasgow, 2 February 1932. Died: Glasgow, 3 March 2025.) Wing-half John McTavish developed with Glentyan Thistle before joining Manchester City in the summer of 1952. He spent eight years on the books at Maine Road, but it was only in 1959–60 that he was a regular in the first team. In November 1960 he moved to St Mirren as part of the deal that saw Gerry Baker join City and spent four seasons at Love Street, making over 90 League appearances before finishing his career with Stranraer.

Gerry McWilliam (Born: Gartcosh, Lanarkshire, 26 April 1933. Died: 2 August 2024.) Centre-forward Gerry McWilliam progressed from Cleland Juniors to Airdrieonians in September 1952 but was unable to break into the first team at Broomfield Park and in the summer of 1956 he signed for Dunfermline Athletic. Although he scored in his first four League appearances for the Pars it was not until 1957–58 that he became a first-team regular and he contributed 26 goals as the club won promotion back to the top flight. In December 1959 he moved on to Stirling Albion then had brief spells with Cowdenbeath and Portadown before leaving senior football.

Tony Macedo (Born: Gibraltar, 22 February 1938. Died: June 2024.) Goalkeeper Tony Macedo joined the groundstaff at Fulham on leaving school and went on to make his first-team debut in December 1957. He was first choice in 1958–59 when the Cottagers won promotion to the top flight, appeared in two FA Cup semi-finals, and in total made just short of 400 appearances before concluding his career with a season at Colchester United. He later moved to South Africa where he played for Durban City and Highlands Park. He won 10 caps for England U23s.

Brian Makepeace (Born: Rossington, nr. Doncaster, 6 October 1931. Died: June 2024.) Brian Makepeace joined Doncaster Rovers as a centre-half from Rossington Youth Club in March 1949 but played most of his senior career at right-back. He broke into the first team at Belle Vue towards the end of the 1950–51 campaign and was a regular in the line-up for the next nine seasons, making a total of 378 appearances without scoring. After leaving Doncaster in the summer of 1962 he went on to play in the Midland League for Boston United and Worksop Town.

Sam Malcolmson (Born: Dumfries, 2 April 1947. Died: Auckland, New Zealand, 18 September 2024.) Central defender Sam Malcolmson won representative honours for the Royal Navy and Combined Services before leaving the Navy in 1971. He later had a season with Airdrieonians without breaking into the first team, then had spells with Queen of the South and Albion Rovers, making senior appearances for both clubs before emigrating to New Zealand in 1974. He became a New Zealand citizen and won 15 caps for the All Whites, appearing for them in the 1982 World Cup finals.

Brian Marjoribanks (Born: Falkirk, 22 July 1942. Died: Palma de Mallorca, Spain, 9 August 2024.) Centre-forward Brian Marjoribanks was a member of the Kilmarnock Amateurs team that won the Scottish Amateur U18 Youth Cup in 1958–59 and went on to join Hibernian in July 1961. He scored on his debut for Hibs at Tynecastle but received few first-team opportunities at Easter Road. He spent the 1963–64 season with Hearts without breaking into the first team and subsequently retired from football to focus on a career in acting. He was later a sports presenter for BBC Radio and Television in Scotland for 17 years until 1983.

Gordon Marshall (Born: Farnham, Surrey, 2 July 1939. Died: 6 February 2025.) Goalkeeper Gordon Marshall played for more than 20 years in senior football. A product of Juvenile club Balgreen Rovers, he signed for Heart of Midlothian in July 1956 and made his debut the following November. He enjoyed success at Tynecastle, where he won the League title in 1957–58 and 1959–60, and three League Cup winners' prizes. He was sold to Newcastle United in the summer of 1963 where he spent five seasons as a first-team regular and was ever-present in the team that won the Second Division title in 1964–65. He later played for Nottingham Forest, Hibernian, Celtic and Aberdeen before concluding his senior career at Arbroath, where he added a further 187 appearances.

Bob Massey (Born: Marylebone, London, 6 April 1940. Died: 5 September 2024.) Defender Bob Massey came up through the ranks at Bournemouth before signing as a professional in May 1958. He made five appearances for the Cherries before he moved on to Guildford City where he was a Southern League Cup winner in 1962–63 and a member of the team that knocked Brentford out of the FA Cup in 1967–68.

Jeff Miles (Born: Caldicot, Monmouthshire, 17 January 1949. Died: 10 August 2024.) Goalkeeper Jeff Miles was on the books of Newport County as an amateur in the mid-1960s and during this time made four Football League appearances. He also spent time with Southern League clubs Cheltenham Town, Gloucester City and Hereford United.

Grenville Millington (Born: Queensferry, Flintshire, 10 December 1951. Died: May 2025.) Goalkeeper Grenville Millington was capped for Wales Youths and played as an amateur for Chester and Rhyl, making his Football League debut as a 17-year-old. He went on to win amateur international honours for Wales before eventually signing professional forms for Chester in September 1973. He made 334 appearances during his time at Sealand Road and played in every match in 1974–75 when the team reached the semi-finals of the League Cup and won promotion to Division Three. Later he had a brief spell with Oswestry Town before adding further appearances for Wrexham in 1983–84 as cover for injuries.

John Moore (Born: Liverpool, 9 September 1945. Died: Bishopston, West Glamorgan, 26 December 2024.) Wing-half John Moore was an apprentice at Everton before signing for Stoke City in July 1963 but in five seasons at the Victoria Ground he made just 13 appearances. His best years were spent at Shrewsbury Town where he played over 150 games before following manager Harry Gregg to Swansea City in January 1973. He suffered a knee injury shortly afterwards, which effectively ended his career.

Liam Munroe (Born: Dublin, 28 November 1933. Died: Dublin, 9 August 2024.) Inside-forward Liam Munroe developed with Shamrock Rovers and Ards before signing for Bristol City in December 1957. He made just one appearance during his time at Ashton Gate, then had a brief spell at Scunthorpe United without adding to his senior experience before returning to Ireland where he played with some success for Distillery, Dundalk and Ards. He was capped for the Republic of Ireland against Luxembourg in October 1953 and played for the League of Ireland representative side.

Cammy Murray (Born: Bellshill, Lanarkshire, 20 June 1944. Died: Kirkfieldbank, Lanarkshire, 19 February 2025.) Centre-half Cammy Murray won Scotland Youth international honours while with Drumchapel Amateurs before joining St Mirren shortly afterwards. He quickly became a fixture in the line-up and established a new club record of 170 consecutive League appearances between August 1962 and April 1967. He went on to play over 400 senior games for the Buddies, helping them to win the Second Division title in 1967–68. After a relatively unproductive season with Motherwell he concluded his career with a five-year spell at Arbroath.

Landry Nguémo (Born: Yaoundé, Cameroon, 28 November 1985. Died: Obala, Cameroon, 27 June 2024.) Landry Nguémo was a defensive midfielder who played most of his career in France, notably with AS Nancy and Bordeaux. He spent the 2009–10 season on loan to Celtic from Nancy, featuring regularly in the line-up. He won 41 caps for Cameroon between 2006 and 2014. His premature death was a result of a road traffic accident.

David Parry (Born: Southport, 11 February 1948. Died: 25 August 2024.) David Parry was a pacy winger who joined Blackpool as an apprentice, but he was unable to break into the first team and in the summer of 1967 moved on to Tranmere Rovers. Here too he found it difficult to get in the line-up, making three appearances during his season at Prenton Park, then a couple the following season during a brief association with Halifax Town. He then moved into non-league football with Wigan Athletic.

Paul Petts (Born: Hackney, London, 27 September 1961. Died: 24 March 2025.) Winger Paul Petts made his debut for Bristol Rovers at the age of 17 and went on to gain England Youth international honours but he received few first-team opportunities and in July 1980 signed for Shrewsbury Town. He spent five seasons at Gay Meadow where he made 181 appearances, and in October 1983 he scored a hat-trick in a seven-minute spell in a 5-1 win against Leeds United. Later he played in non-league with Merthyr Tydfil and Newport AFC.

Gary Pierce (Born: Bury, Lancashire, 2 March 1951. Died: Bury, Lancashire, 24 May 2025.) Goalkeeper Gary Pierce came to prominence at Mossley, and within a few months he was transferred to Huddersfield Town, then members of the First Division. He made his debut at Newcastle in August 1971 and featured regularly in two seasons with the Terriers before moving on to Wolverhampton Wanderers in August 1973. He spent six years at Molineux, playing over 100 games including every match when Wolves won the Second Division title in 1976–77. The highlight of his career came in March 1974 when he stepped in to produce a tremendous performance as Wolves beat Manchester City to win the League Cup final. He later had spells with Barnsley and Blackpool before returning to play in non-league football with Chorley.

Billy Pirie (Born: Aberdeen, 2 April 1949. Died: Brechin, 2 February 2025.) Billy Pirie was a striker who scored prolifically throughout his career, netting 135 goals from 218 Scottish League appearances between 1972 and 1980. A product of Junior outfit Banks o'Dee, he then played two seasons in South Africa for Arcadia Shepherds, where he led the scoring charts in the 1970 campaign. He subsequently had a brief spell in the Highland League with Huntly, then signed for Arbroath in February 1972, helping them win promotion to the top flight in his first season. He moved on to Aberdeen and then Dundee, where his scoring exploits continued as he set a new club record of 44 goals from 45 League and Cup appearances in 1976–77 and was chosen as the First Division Player of the Year.

Peter Popely (Born: York, 7 April 1943. Died: 3 August 2024.) Full-back Peter Popely joined York City from local junior club Cliftonville in August 1962 and spent several years with the Minstermen. He made a total of 26 appearances before retiring from football.

Fred Potter (Born: Cradley Heath, Staffordshire, 29 November 1940. Died: Stourbridge, 23 July 2024.) Fred Potter signed amateur forms for Aston Villa as a goalscoring inside-forward from Codsall Villa before turning professional in July 1949. He made little progress until he made the switch to playing in goal and his career then blossomed. Although he made only six first-team appearances at Villa Park he was a regular with Doncaster Rovers for three-and-a-half seasons. He then dropped into the Southern League firstly with Burton Albion and then with Hereford United where he was a member of the team that knocked Newcastle United out of the FA Cup in 1971–72, then played a few games for them in their early Football League days.

John Pratt (Born: Atherstone, Warwickshire, 1 March 1943. Died: 2 July 2024.) Goalkeeper John Pratt joined Reading from Wycombe Wanderers in July 1969 and spent three years on the books at Elm Park. He was mostly a back-up for Steve Death during this time but made a total of 29 appearances before dropping into the Southern League to play for Bath City.

Gordon Pulley (Born: Stourbridge, 18 September 1936. Died: 23 December 2024.) Winger Gordon Pulley developed with Stourbridge and, briefly, Oswestry Town before signing for Millwall in September 1956. He went straight in the first team at The Den, featuring regularly before being placed on the transfer list at the end of 1957–58. He signed for Gillingham where he went on to make over 200 Football League appearances and was a member of the team that won the Fourth Division title in 1963–64. He wound down his senior career with Peterborough United before joining Southern League club Chelmsford City. He was also a talented cricketer and played for Worcestershire Second XI as a youngster.

Chris Rabjohn (Born: Sheffield, 10 March 1945. Died: 7 May 2025.) Chris Rabjohn was a midfield player who won representative honours for the England Boys' Club team before going on to join Rotherham United. He never quite established himself at Millmoor before moving on to Doncaster Rovers as part of a multiple player-exchange deal in February 1968. He spent the next five years at Belle Vue, making over 150 appearances and contributing to the team that won the Division Four title in 1968–69 before being released on a free transfer in the summer of 1973.

Terry Reardon (Born: 23 November 1944. Died: 1 June 2024.) Midfielder Terry Reardon spent most of his career with Slough Town, making a club record 475 appearances for them and appearing in the team that lost out to Walton & Hersham in the 1973 FA Amateur Cup final. He won a single cap for England Amateurs, appearing in the final amateur international against England in April 1974.

Billy Rees (Born: Swansea, 30 September 1937. Died: January 2025.) Winger Billy Rees was a member of the Swansea Boys' team that won the English Schools Shield in 1952–53 and was capped for Wales Schoolboys. He joined Swansea Town, but in five seasons at the Vetch Field made just six first-team appearances. He spent the 1958–59 campaign with Midland League club Peterborough United, before adding further senior appearances for Crystal Palace the following season. He later played in non-league football for Ashford Town, Merthyr Tydfil and Haverfordwest.

Gordon Revel (Born: Mansfield, 1 October 1957. Died: 29 September 2024.) Centre-half Gordon Revel was on Mansfield Town's books as an amateur before signing professional terms in May 1950. He made a solitary first-team appearance for the Stags in September 1952 before moving on to Worksop Town two years later.

Tony Rhodes (Born: Dover, 17 September 1946. Died: Halifax, December 2024.) Centre-half Tony Rhodes joined Derby County on amateur terms on leaving school, but although he progressed to become a professional was mostly a reserve during his time at the Baseball Ground. In November 1970 he was sold to Halifax Town where he became club captain and made over 250 appearances. In the summer of 1976 he moved on to Southport, but injuries restricted his opportunities. He stayed just a season before concluding his career with Burton Albion.

Hughen Riley (Born: Accrington, 12 June 1947. Died: Salisbury, 19 February 2025.) Hughen Riley joined Rochdale as a winger at the age of 19 and spent five years on the books at Spotland. He developed into a hard-tackling central midfielder and enjoyed a career in the lower divisions lasting more than a decade with Dale, Crewe Alexandra, Bury and AFC Bournemouth. He retired from senior football in 1978 after making over 350 appearances, including more than 100 for both Rochdale and Crewe.

Dudley Roberts (Born: Derby, 16 October 1945. Died: 4 July 2024.) Dudley Roberts developed in junior football in Coventry before joining Coventry City as an apprentice. He went on to make his first-team debut shortly before his 20th birthday but struggled to get in the line-up at Highfield Road and in March 1968 he moved on to sign for Mansfield Town. He had a good six-year spell with the Stags, playing in the team that reached the FA Cup quarter-finals in 1968–69 and making a total of more than 200 appearances. He later played for Scunthorpe United, Burton Albion and Sutton Town before injury ended his career in January 1978.

Len Roe (Born: Hayes, Middlesex, 11 January 1932. Died: 24 June 2024.) Wing-half Len Roe signed professional forms for Brentford in May 1951 and went on to spend seven years at Griffin Park, mostly featuring in the reserves. He made his senior debut in the final game of the 1954–55 season and made eight first-team appearances during his stay before later playing in the Southern League for Yiewsley.

Drew Rogerson (Born: Whins of Milton, Stirlingshire, 7 February 1941. Died: 9 December 2024.) Drew Rogerson was a reliable centre-half who joined Alloa Athletic from Alva Albion Rangers shortly after the start of the 1959–60 season. He stayed with the Wasps for six years, making almost 200 League appearances, before moving on to Stirling Albion where he played regularly in their First Division team and went on the historic tour of Japan in the summer of 1966. He continued his career with spells at Albion Rovers, Stenhousemuir, Ayr United, St Mirren and Raith Rovers, taking his total of League appearances beyond the 400-mark.

Paul Round (Born: Blackburn, 22 June 1959. Died: 10 February 2025.) Paul Round was a striker who joined Blackburn Rovers as an apprentice and made his first-team debut at the age of 17, scoring against Millwall in March 1977. He signed professional forms shortly afterwards but in four seasons at Ewood Park he was never a first-team regular although he made a total of 66 appearances. After leaving he had a brief and unproductive spell with Bury and then moved into non-league football, signing for Altrincham in February 1982.

Andy Rowland (Born: Derby, 8 September 1954. Died: Swindon, 20 June 2024.) Striker Andy Rowland was on the books of Derby County as a youngster and scored a hat-trick for England Youths against Scotland in January 1973. The following month he signed professional forms for the Rams but was unable to get into the first team and in the summer of 1974 moved on to Bury. He spent four years at Gigg Lane, rarely missing a match during his time at the club. In September 1978 he signed for Swindon Town and went on to make almost 350 appearances during his time at the County Ground. When he retired as a player he stayed on the coaching staff, remaining at the club until October 1996.

Ian Sandiford (Born: Chorley, Lancashire, 26 February 1946. Died: Chorley, Lancashire, 24 March 2025.) Forward Ian Sandiford was an apprentice at Blackburn Rovers and, briefly, a professional before being released at the end of the 1963–64 campaign. He signed for Stockport County where he featured regularly the following season only to lose his place and in January 1966 he was sold to Crewe Alexandra. He scored 10 goals from 24 appearances in his first season at Gresty Road and continued to contribute in 1966–67 before moving on to Wigan Athletic, then members of the Cheshire League, in November 1967.

Matija Sarkic (Born: Grimsby, 23 July 1997. Died: Budva, Montenegro, 15 June 2024.) Goalkeeper Matija Sarkic developed as a youngster with Anderlecht before joining Aston Villa at the age of 18, but his only experience of senior football during his time at Villa Park came in loan spells elsewhere. He signed for Wolverhampton Wanderers in July 2020 and spent three years at Molineux, but again he was mostly out on loan, notably with Shrewsbury Town and Birmingham City. In August 2023 he moved on to Millwall where he became the club's first-choice keeper, making 32 EFL appearances in the 2023–24 campaign. He won nine full caps for Montenegro. His early death was reportedly due to sudden heart failure.

Tony Screen (Born: Swansea, 9 May 1952. Died: Ammanford, 11 April 2025.) Tony Screen joined Swansea Town, as the club was then known, as an apprentice and made his Football League debut at the age of 16. He signed professional forms in May 1970 and went on to spend five seasons on the books at the Vetch Field, making over 150 first-team appearances before moving on to Ammanford. He played mainly at full-back but switched to a more advanced role in 1973–74 when he finished as the club's top scorer.

Bobby Scrugham (Born: Cleator Moor, Cumberland, 15 May 1932. Died: Cockermouth, Cumbria, October 2024.) Bobby Scrugham was a goalkeeper who signed for Workington from Cleator Moor Celtic in August 1953, and although third-choice, he stepped in to make three Football League appearances as cover for injuries in September 1953. He stayed at Borough Park until the end of the 1956–57 season without gaining further opportunities and later returned to play in local football.

Gordon Seaton (Born: Wick, 1 September 1945. Died: Strathpeffer, Ross & Cromarty, 2 January 2025.) Gordon Seaton was a wing-half or inside-forward who developed with Tynecastle Athletic and Hibernian before signing for Berwick Rangers in January 1964. He made 28 appearances during an 18-month stay at Shielfield Park then headed to Wales to play for Rhyl Athletic. Later he spent a season-and-a-half with Chester playing more than 50 senior games before moving back into North West non-league football. He eventually returned to Scotland where he played in the Highland League for Ross County and Inverness Clachnacuddin.

Eric Sellars (Born: Dundee, 28 November 1954. Died: Dundee, 22 December 2024.) Winger Eric Sellars joined Arbroath from Carnoustie Panmure in the summer of 1966 and was a regular for the best part of nine seasons, making over 350 appearances and scoring 93 goals; he was a member of the teams that won promotion to the top flight in both 1967–68 and 1971–72. He wound down his career with brief spells at St Johnstone and Brechin City.

Ronnie Selway (Born: Dundee, 19 March 1946. Died: Forfar, 26 October 2024.) Wing-half Ronnie Selway developed with Butterburn Juveniles and Dundee St Joseph's before moving south to sign for Preston North End. He featured regularly in the reserve team at Deepdale before returning to Scotland in the summer of 1966 when he signed for Dundee. He went on to make 79 appearances during an injury-hit six-year stay at Dens Park before concluding his senior career at Raith Rovers.

Craig Shakespeare (Born: Birmingham, 26 October 1963. Died: 1 August 2024.) Craig Shakespeare was a versatile midfield player who joined Walsall as an apprentice. He broke into the Saddlers' first team in September 1982 and quickly established himself in the side, going on to make over 350 appearances. A highlight came as the member of the team that defeated Bristol City in the 1987–88 Division Three play-off final. He continued with spells at Sheffield Wednesday, West Bromwich Albion, Grimsby Town and Scunthorpe United, finishing with a career total of more than 600 appearances. Later he worked as a coach for several clubs and briefly had a spell as manager of Leicester City.

Joe Sharman (Born: Rothwell, Northamptonshire, 2 February 1932. Died: 6 February 2025.) Goalkeeper Joe Sharman was playing for United Counties League club Symington's when he signed for Derby County in February 1949. He went on to make two First Division appearances for the Rams in April 1951 then played in non-league football for Ilkeston Town and Gresley Rovers. Later he spent two seasons on the books of Bradford City without adding to his appearances.

Gary Shaw (Born: Birmingham, 21 January 1961. Died: Birmingham, 16 September 2024.) Gary Shaw was a nippy striker with an eye for goal who joined Aston Villa as an apprentice. He went on to form a productive striking partnership with Peter Withe and was a regular as Villa won the League title in 1980–81. In May 1982 he was a member of the team that defeated Bayern Munich to win the European Cup and in 1982–83 he appeared in the side that won the European Super Cup. He suffered a knee injury in January 1983 and this became progressively worse, restricting his appearances. He eventually left the club at the end of the 1987–88 campaign and continued his career with spells in Denmark and Austria, also playing briefly with Walsall, Kilmarnock and Shrewsbury Town before retiring in September 1993. He won seven caps for England U21s and in 1980–81 was chosen as the PFA Young Player of the Year.

Malcolm Shaw (Born: Circa 1939. Died: November 2024.) Goalkeeper Malcolm Shaw played in amateur football for Grays Athletic, Walthamstow Avenue and Tilbury during the 1960s. He was capped for England Amateurs against Wales in November 1963.

Lex Shields (Born: Edinburgh, 27 February 1958. Died: 23 October 2024.) Winger Lex Shields spent most of his career in the Juniors notably in two spells with Bo'ness United for whom he made more than 300 appearances and scored both their goals in the 1984 Scottish Junior Cup final victory over Baillieston. He was also capped for Scotland Juniors. He was on the books of Alloa Athletic between December 1979 and May 1981, playing 55 games during his stay.

Alan Shoulder (Born: Bishop Auckland, Co Durham, 4 February 1953. Died: 2 February 2025.) Alan Shoulder was a busy striker who was a member of the Blyth Spartans team that reached the fifth round of the FA Cup in 1977–78. He signed for Newcastle United in December 1978 and was a regular in his first two-and-a-half seasons at St James' Park, finishing the 1979–80 campaign as the club's leading scorer with 20 League goals. He moved on to Carlisle United in the summer of 1982 and then Hartlepool United, where injuries ended his senior career in March 1988.

John Simpson (Born: Circa 1942. Died: Tullibody, Clackmannanshire, 6 September 2024.) John Simpson was a full-back who made his senior debut as a triallist for Alloa Athletic in February 1965. In November of the same year he joined East Stirlingshire from Clackmannan Juniors and made 28 appearances over the next two seasons before leaving senior football. He later worked as a journalist, covering Alloa Athletic for the *Alloa Advertiser* for several years.

Granville Smith (Born: Penrhiwceiber, Glamorgan, 4 February 1937. Died: August 2024.) Granville Smith was a versatile winger who came up through the ranks with Bristol Rovers, signing professional forms in May 1957. Although only a fringe player in three seasons at Eastville, he prospered on moving to Newport County where he made over 250 appearances. After a spell with Bath City he returned to Somerton Park as reserve-team coach.

Ray Smith (Born: Hull, 13 September 1934. Died: Peterborough, 21 November 2024.) Ray Smith began his career as a winger with Hull City, for whom he signed professional forms in August 1952. He never really established himself at Boothferry Park and in the summer of 1956 he signed for Peterborough United, going on to help them win four consecutive Midland League titles before they were elected to the Football League in 1960. He was a regular in the team that won the Fourth Division title in 1961–62 before moving on to Northampton Town in October 1962. He later had a spell with Luton Town before leaving senior football.

Rodney Smithson (Born: Leicester, 9 October 1943. Died: 21 August 2024.) Rodney Smithson was capped for England Schoolboys and then joined the groundstaff at Arsenal. He went on to win England Youth international honours and made his first-team debut at the age of 18 but found few opportunities at Highbury. In July 1964 he signed for Oxford United where he made over 150 appearances and played a prominent role in the team that won the Third Division title in 1967–68. In January 1975 he departed to become player-manager of Witney Town.

Ray Snowball (Born: Sunderland, 10 March 1932. Died: 6 March 2025.) Goalkeeper Ray Snowball was best known for his performances for Crook Town for whom he made over 300 appearances and gained three FA Amateur Cup winners' medals. He signed amateur forms for Darlington in 1964–65 and had a short run in the line-up in the closing stages of the campaign, later returning to Feethams to add a further appearance as an emergency stand-in in December 1966.

Cecil Steeds (Born: Bristol, 11 January 1929. Died: 30 December 2024.) Inside-forward Cecil Steeds developed with Bedminster Down Lads' Club before signing amateur forms for Bristol City in May 1946. He became a professional the following year but was generally a reserve at Ashton Gate, making nine first-team appearances. In May 1952 he signed for local rivals Bristol Rovers, adding two more appearances in a six-year stay before switching to the Southern League with Bath City.

Billy Steel (Born: Circa 1936. Died: Edinburgh, 25 February 2025.) Billy Steel was a tricky inside-forward who joined St Johnstone from Junior club Edinburgh City towards the end of the 1952–53 campaign. He went on to spend five years on the staff at Muirton Park scoring 35 goals from 83 appearances before moving on to Eyemouth United.

Robin Stenhouse (Born: Edinburgh, 29 March 1942. Died: 17 July 2024.) Robin Stenhouse was a powerful forward who signed for Heart of Midlothian from Edina Boys' Club. He was subsequently 'farmed out' to Loanhead Mayflower before being called up to Tynecastle for the 1961–62 season. He scored four goals in five appearances for the Jambos, then after a spell in Canada with Hamilton Steelers he joined Third Lanark, where he scored regularly. A season with Crewe Alexandra yielded just one first-team outing then he returned to Scotland to play for Duns. Later he appeared for Penicuik in the 1970 Scottish Junior Cup final.

Willie Stevenson (Born: Leith, 26 October 1939. Died: Congleton, Cheshire, 26 May 2025.) Willie Stevenson was a left-half who was capped by Scotland Schools and Youth teams. He was a provisional signing for Rangers, going on to make his first-team debut in October 1958. He made over 100 appearances during his time at Ibrox, gaining a League championship medal in his first season, and appearing in the team that won the Scottish Cup and reached the European Cup semi-finals in 1959–60. He then lost his place in the side and in October 1962 he was sold to Liverpool. In five years at Anfield he helped them win two League titles, gained an FA Cup winners' medal in 1964 and was a member of the team defeated in the final of the European Cup Winners' Cup in May 1966. In December 1967 he signed for Stoke City where he featured regularly until suffering a broken leg, then wound down his career with spells at Tranmere Rovers, Limerick and Vancouver Whitecaps in the NASL. He was capped for the Scottish League and appeared for Scotland in an unofficial international against Jutland in May 1959.

Ron Stockin (Born: Birmingham, 27 June 1931. Died: West Bromwich, July 2024.) Inside-forward Ron Stockin signed professional forms for Walsall shortly after completing his National Service and after playing just five first-team games he was sold to Wolverhampton Wanderers in February 1952. He enjoyed a useful scoring record at Molineux with seven goals from 21 appearances but was mostly a reserve during his stay. He moved on to Cardiff City, where he played over 50 games in the top flight then wound down his senior career with Grimsby Town.

Freddie Strahan (Born: Dublin, 21 December 1938. Died: Dublin, 13 December 2024.) Defender Freddie Strahan spent 12 years with Shelbourne with whom he won the FAI Cup on two occasions and the League of Ireland once. He won five full caps for the Republic of Ireland between 1964 and 1966 and played eight times for the League of Ireland representative side.

Richard Symonds (Born: Langham, Norfolk, 21 November 1959. Died: 10 September 2024.) Richard Symonds was a defender who was regularly used as a specialist man-to-man marker during his career. He developed in the youth set-up at Norwich City then spent five years as a professional on the club's books, making 70 appearances before switching to playing in local football.

Tibor Szabo (Born: Wibsey, Bradford, 28 October 1959. Died: 5 August 2024.) Tibor Szabo was a lively attacking player who made 13 appearances, scoring one goal for Bradford City in the 1978–79 season. He was then released and signed for Macclesfield Town in the summer of 1979.

Bobby Tebbutt (Born: Irchester, Northamptonshire,10 November 1934. Died: Northampton, 23 June 2024.) Inside-forward Bobby Tebbutt played for Irchester United as a youngster before joining Northampton Town on amateur forms, but it was not until October 1956 that he signed a professional contract. He went on to make 60 appearances during his time at the County Ground, scoring the opening goal in the 3-1 FA Cup win over Arsenal in January 1958. He suffered a broken leg in March 1960, which effectively ended his senior career although he later played in the Southern League for Bedford Town and Kettering Town.

Brian Third (Born: Aberdeenshire, 1945. Died: Aberdeen, 30 March 2025.) Brian Third was a big, powerful centre-forward who netted close on 200 goals for Highland League club Peterhead before joining Montrose in March 1971. He continued his scoring feats at Links Park, hitting a club record six goals in the 6-3 win away to Stranraer in September 1972 and finishing the 1972–73 campaign with 28 League goals, an all-time record for the Gable Endies. In June 1973 he was transferred to St Mirren where he added further appearances over the next two seasons before returning to Peterhead.

Joe Thompson (Born: Bath, 5 March 1989. Died: 17 April 2025.) Joe Thompson was a right-sided midfield player who developed in the Manchester United Academy before joining Rochdale as a youth trainee. He made his debut for Dale as a 17-year-old and established himself as a regular in the line-up while still a teenager. He continued to add to his appearances before moving on to Tranmere Rovers and later played for Bury and Carlisle United before returning to Spotland, where injuries led to his retirement from football in February 2019. His premature death was due to cancer.

Peter Thompson (Born: Blackhall, Co Durham, 16 February 1935. Died: March 2025.) Centre-forward Peter Thompson was serving as a PT Instructor at RAF Cosford when he signed amateur forms for Wrexham and he became a regular goalscorer at the Racecourse Ground, also gaining four caps for England Amateurs. After buying himself out of the RAF he signed for Hartlepools United where he was top scorer in 1957–58 before turning professional in the summer of 1958. Soon afterwards he was sold to Derby County, then in the Second Division, and he went on to play for Bournemouth before returning to play for Pools. He left senior football in the 1966 close season having scored 122 career goals from 289 appearances.

Bobby Thomson (Born: Dundee, 21 March 1937. Died: 6 August 2024.) Inside-forward Bobby Thomson made his senior debut for Albion Rovers in September 1952 as a 15-year-old and added further appearances that season before joining Airdrieonians for the 1953–54 campaign. In August 1954 he signed as a professional for Wolverhampton Wanderers, but made just one appearance in five seasons at Molineux. In June 1959 he was transferred to Aston Villa and scored 20 goals in his first season as Villa won the Division Two title. He remained a regular during his time at the club and featured in the team that won the inaugural Football League Cup in 1960–61. In September 1963 he moved on to Birmingham City where he continued to play regularly before winding down his senior career with Stockport County.

Bobby Thomson (Born: Kirkcaldy, Fife, 1 December 1946. Died: January 2025.) Wing-half Bobby Thomson had a spell on the books of Stoke City as a youngster before returning to Scotland to sign for Nairn Thistle Juniors. In August 1965 he returned to the seniors, signing for Montrose. This was the start of a six-year career in Scottish League football during which he also played for Cowdenbeath and Stenhousemuir, accumulating more than 200 appearances.

David Thomson (Born: Kirkcaldy, Fife, 22 July 1958. Died: 2 June 2024.) Defender David Thomson joined Raith Rovers from Juvenile outfit Warout Thistle in March 1976. He went on to make over 150 Scottish League appearances during his time at Stark's Park and was a prominent member of the team that won promotion from the Second Division in 1977–78.

Eddie Thomson (Born: 1947. Died: Dunfermline, 4 January 2025.) Eddie Thomson was a winger who joined East Fife from Frances Colliery in August 1969. He spent a season with the Leven club, scoring three goals from 13 appearances before returning to the Juniors with Newburgh.

Colin Toon (Born: New Houghton, Derbyshire, 26 April 1940. Died: 18 June 2024.) Right-back Colin Toon joined Mansfield Town from local football in July 1957 and was just 17 when he made his Football League debut. He went on to make over 200 appearances for the Stags and was a regular in the team that won promotion from the Fourth Division in 1962–63. He later had a couple of seasons with Cambridge United, then in the Southern League, before signing for Worksop Town.

John Tudor (Born: Ilkeston, 24 June 1946. Died: Minnetonka, Minnesota, USA, 9 February 2025.) Centre-forward John Tudor played for Ilkeston Town before signing professional forms for Coventry City in January 1966. He made his debut the following season and was a regular in the Sky Blues' first campaign in the top flight before being sold to Sheffield United in November 1968. He scored two goals in each of his first two matches for the Blades and featured regularly before moving to Newcastle United in a player-exchange deal. After a slow start on Tyneside he flourished following the arrival of Malcolm MacDonald in the summer of 1971, with the two forming a productive partnership up front as the club reached the FA Cup final in 1973–74 and won the Anglo Italian Cup (1973) and the Texaco Cup (1974 and 1975). Injuries took their toll, and he left in October 1976 for Stoke City before finishing his career in Belgium with KAA Gent.

Brian Usher (Born: Durham, 11 March 1944. Died: 3 January 2025.) Brian Usher was a winger who joined Sunderland as a 15-year-old and burst on the scene in the 1963–64 campaign when the Black Cats won promotion to the top flight. He lost his place midway through the following season and was transferred to Sheffield Wednesday in June 1965. He spent three years at Hillsborough then concluded his senior career with Doncaster Rovers, helping them win promotion from the Fourth Division in 1968–69. He was capped for England U23s against France in April 1964.

Albert Uytenbogaardt (Born: Cape Town, South Africa, 5 March 1930. Died: 25 October 2024.) Albert Uytenbogaardt was a tall, well-built goalkeeper who joined Charlton Athletic from Cape Town club Tramway in October 1948. He spent five seasons on the books at The Valley where he was back-up to Sam Bartram, making six appearances during his stay. He later returned to South Africa where he played for Tramway, Cape Town City and Hellenic, winning five caps for his country.

Steve Uzelac (Born: Doncaster, 12 March 1953. Died: 3 May 2025.) Centre-half Steve Uzelac developed in the Doncaster Rovers junior teams before signing professional terms in June 1971. A hard and committed defender, he went on to make over 200 appearances at Belle Vue before moving on to sign for Preston North End in May 1977. However, a constant stream of injuries affected his time both at Deepdale and when he moved on to Stockport County, with these eventually leading to his retirement at the end of the 1981–82 campaign.

Mick Walker (Born: Belper, Derbyshire, 27 November 1940. Died: Leeds, February 2025.) Mick Walker played as a winger and was capped by England Schoolboys. He had a spell as an amateur with Nottingham Forest and then played in the Midland League while pursuing a career in teaching. He entered senior football in September 1978 when he joined the Notts County coaching staff and then managed the Magpies between January 1993 and September 1994 before working in the Leeds United Academy.

Peter Wall (Born: Westbury, Shropshire, 13 September 1944. Died: 30 October 2024.) Defender Peter Wall joined Shrewsbury Town as an apprentice and made his debut in December 1963 but was unable to make a mark at Gay Meadow. In November 1965 he signed for Wrexham and just as he began to establish himself was sold to Liverpool. He was mostly a fringe player at Anfield apart from enjoying a short run in the line-up at the start of 1968–69 and in the summer of 1970 he signed for Crystal Palace. He enjoyed the best seasons of his career at Selhurst Park where he made over 200 appearances. Later he played in the NASL with St Louis Stars and California Surf, then coached California Surf and Los Angeles Lazers.

Bernard Wallbank (Born: Preston, 11 November 1943. Died: 17 December 2024.) Centre-forward Bernard Wallbank developed in local football in Preston before joining Southport as an amateur in September 1960. He made his debut in April 1962 and signed professional forms shortly afterwards. He added no further senior appearances during his stay before moving on to Lancashire Combination club Clitheroe in October 1962.

Ernie Walley (Born: Caernarvon, 19 April 1933. Died: February 2025.) Wing-half Ernie Walley developed with Caernarvon Town as a youngster before joining Tottenham Hotspur. He spent seven years as a professional at White Hart Lane, making five first-team appearances and also appeared in the Football League for Middlesbrough. Later he was a member of the Gravesend & Northfleet team that reached the FA Cup fourth round in 1962–63. After turning to coaching he led Arsenal to success in the FA Youth Cup in 1965–66 then moved to Crystal Palace where he spent 13 years including a spell as care-taker-manager.

Davie Watkins (Born: Duns, Berwickshire, 17 July 1944. Died: Melrose, Roxburghshire, 2 July 2024.) Winger Davie Watkins spent most of his playing career in the East of Scotland League, gaining a cap for Scotland Amateurs against the Netherlands in April 1969. He made two appearances on trial with Berwick Rangers in March 1972, scoring with his first touch in the opening minute of his debut against Alloa Athletic.

Bernard Weakley (Born: Rotherham, 20 December 1932. Died: 18 January 2025.) Winger Bernard Weakley joined Rotherham United from Denaby United in August 1955 and spent 18 months on the books at Millmoor, making two appearances. In January 1957 he moved on for a brief association with Goole Town before joining Grantham.

Allan Westwater (Born: Bridge of Allan, Stirlingshire, 26 March 1946. Died: Denny, Stirlingshire, 27 June 2024.) Although born in Scotland, Allan Westwater emigrated to Australia with his family at an early age and played for New South Wales club Bankstown as a schoolboy. In the summer of 1963 he signed for Stirling Albion where he was quickly promoted to the first team only to break his ankle on his debut. He spent three seasons at Annfield, making a contribution to the club's promotion campaign in 1964–65. He subsequently returned to Australia, signing for Sydney club Pan Hellenic and winning 14 full caps for his adopted country.

Andy Wharton (Born: Whitewell Bottom, Lancashire, 21 December 1961. Died: 3 April 2025.) Defender Andy Wharton was an apprentice with Burnley before signing professional forms in December 1979. He was a regular for the Clarets in 1981–82 when they won the Third Division title and made over 75 appearances for the club during his stay. Later he had a short spell with Chester City then continued his career in non-league football.

Jeff Whitefoot (Born: Cheadle, Cheshire, 31 December 1933. Died: 24 June 2024.) Wing-half Jeff Whitefoot was capped for England Schools and went on to sign for Manchester United, making his senior debut at the age of 16. He won a regular place in the line-up in 1953–54 but competition was fierce at Old Trafford, and he later lost out to the emerging talent of Eddie Colman. He moved on to a brief period with Grimsby Town before spending a decade with Nottingham Forest, for whom he made over 250 League appearances, all in the top flight. He won a single cap for England U23s.

Gordon Whitelaw (Born: Glasgow, 13 October 1938. Died: Bearsden, East Renfrewshire, 31 May 2025.) Gordon Whitelaw began his career as a forward with Partick Thistle, making his debut as a triallist towards the end of the 1960–61 season then signing on amateur forms shortly afterwards. He was capped for Scotland Amateurs in 1961–62 and toured East Africa with Middlesex Wanderers before signing professional forms on his return. He went on to spend the 1963–64 campaign with Airdrieonians then joined St Johnstone in July 1964. His career blossomed at Muirton Park, and he finished as top scorer in 1966–67 and 1967–68 while in 1969–70 he won a League Cup runners-up prize. He scored a total of 69 goals from 224 appearances for the club before ending his senior career with Raith Rovers. As a youngster he captained the Scotland U20 basketball team and also appeared for the full international side.

Trevor Whymark (Born: Burston, Norfolk, 4 May 1950. Died: Harleston, Norfolk, 31 October 2024.) Striker Trevor Whymark was playing for Diss Town in the Anglian Combination as a 15-year-old before signing for Ipswich Town in May 1969. He became a regular in the first team in 1972–73 and retained his place for the next four seasons, eventually leaving Portman Road with a total of 104 League and Cup goals, the sixth highest in the club's history. He later spent four years with Grimsby Town before finishing his career with spells at Southend United, Peterborough United and, briefly, Colchester United. He was capped for England against Luxembourg in October 1977 and also appeared six times for the U23s.

Allan Whyte (Born: Perth, Scotland, 1935. Died: Perth, Scotland, 15 February 2025.) Allan Whyte played as an inside-forward with Jeanfield Swifts as a youngster and made one Scottish League appearance on trial for Alloa Athletic in the 1955–56 season. He went on to sign for St Johnstone in January 1957 where he switched to playing at full-back and featured regularly in the 1957–58 campaign but then lost his place in the side.

Roy Wilkinson (Born: Hindley Green, Wigan, 17 September 1941. Died: March 2025.) Wing-half Roy Wilkinson joined Bolton Wanderers from local junior football in July 1960 and spent four seasons on the books at Burnden Park, making four first-team appearances. He moved on to Wigan Athletic in the summer of 1964.

Len Willett (Born: Ruabon, Denbighshire, 17 September 1940. Died: Wrexham, 11 August 2024.) Wing-half Len Willett was capped for Wales Schoolboys and signed amateur forms for Wolverhampton Wanderers in the summer of 1956. He made little progress at Molineux and moved on to Wrexham in May 1958. He made a single Football League appearance during his stay before joining Winsford United in August 1961.

Evan Williams (Born: Dumbarton, 15 July 1943. Died: Helensburgh, Dunbartonshire, 20 February 2025.) Goalkeeper Evan Williams played two games as a triallist for East Fife in the 1963–64 season while with Vale of Leven Juniors before going on to sign for Third Lanark in October 1964. He featured regularly for Thirds then moved on to Wolverhampton Wanderers, but in over three years at Molineux he was mostly second choice. In November 1969 he joined Celtic where he enjoyed the best seasons of his career. He made close on 150 appearances during his time at Parkhead, featuring in the team that lost to Feyenoord in the 1970 European Cup final. He was a member of four Scottish League title winning sides and won two Scottish Cup winners' medals. Later he played for Clyde and, briefly, Stranraer.

Kenny Wilson (Born: Dumbarton, 15 September 1946. Died: 16 January 2025.) Kenny Wilson was an inside- or centre-forward who was a consistent scorer for Beith in the Juniors. He made his debut in senior football as a triallist for Arbroath in April 1966 and was capped for Scotland Juniors, scoring a hat-trick on his debut against Wales. After a spell with St Johnstone he joined Dumbarton in July 1970. He topped the club's scoring charts in his first two seasons, with his tally of 38 League goals in 1971–72, including five against Raith Rovers, establishing a new club record as they won the Division Two title. However, a move to Carlisle United proved to be unproductive and he finished his senior career with spells at Hamilton Academical and in Australia for APIA.

Padi Wilson (Born: Manchester, 9 November 1971. Died: 21 December 2024.) Padi Wilson was a powerful striker who joined Plymouth Argyle from non-league Ashton United in the summer of 1997. Although he scored in his first start he struggled to make an impact at Home Park and in January 1998 moved on to sign for Doncaster Rovers. He was a regular during his time at Belle Vue but was unable to help them avoid relegation out of the League before moving on to Hyde United.

David Woodfield (Born: Leamington Spa, 11 October 1943. Died: April 2025.) David Woodfield was a rugged, no-nonsense centre-half who joined the groundstaff at Wolverhampton Wanderers at the age of 15 and went on to spend more than a decade as a professional at Molineux. He was a regular in the line-up from the start of the 1962–63 campaign and was a key figure in the team that won promotion back to the First Division in 1966–67. After making more than 250 appearances for Wolves he moved on to Watford where injuries restricted his availability and he turned to coaching.

Charlie Wright (Born: Glasgow, 11 December 1938. Died: 27 December 2024.) Goalkeeper Charlie Wright was playing for Glentyan Thistle when he made his senior debut as a triallist for Morton in April 1956. He moved on to Rutherglen Glencairn, then spent two seasons with Rangers without making the first team. In June 1958 he moved south to sign for Workington. After establishing himself as first choice in the 1960–61 season, he went on to play regular first-team football for more than a decade with spells at Grimsby Town, Charlton Athletic and Bolton Wanderers. He made over 600 appearances and was a member of the Bolton team that won the Division Three title in 1972–73, retiring shortly afterwards through injury. He later had spells as manager of York City and Bolton.

Jimmy Wright (Born: Lochgelly, 1 November 1957. Died: Cramlington, Northumberland, 27 February 2025.) Jimmy Wright was a winger who joined Leeds United as an apprentice on leaving school but did not break into the first team and returned to Scotland to sign for St Johnstone where he made 30 League appearances in the late 1970s. He had a brief association with Heart of Midlothian then played for Sydney club West Adelaide. In 1990 he gained a Scottish Junior Cup winners' medal Hill of Beath Hawthorn. He later became a leading figure in British greyhound racing.

Ron Yeats (Born: Aberdeen, 15 November 1937. Died: 6 September 2024.) Ron Yeats was a powerful centre-half who developed in local youth football with ALC Thistle and Aberdeen Lads' Club, winning representative honours for Scotland in the Boys' Club internationals. He joined Dundee United and quickly established himself in the line-up, going on to become a key figure in the team that won promotion from the Second Division in 1959–60. In July 1961 he was sold to Liverpool where he was appointed captain and became one of the cornerstones of the club's successful period during the 1960s. He led the Reds to promotion to the top flight in his first season, won two Football League titles, and then the FA Cup in 1964–65, while he was also a European Cup Winners' Cup runner-up in 1965–66. He was later player-manager of Tranmere Rovers and Barrow, and then returned to Anfield as a scout, a role he performed for 20 years. He won two full caps for Scotland.

Tony Young (Born: Urmston, 24 December 1952. Died: December 2024.) Defender Tony Young progressed through the youth set-up with Manchester United and went on to make over 100 appearances during his time at Old Trafford before moving to Charlton Athletic in January 1976. He stayed only briefly at The Valley then signed for York City, linking up with the former United manager Wilf McGuinness. He had two seasons of regular first-team football at Bootham Crescent then continued his career in non-league with Runcorn and Bangor City, separated by a spell in Australia.

Tom Youngs (Born: Bury St Edmunds, Suffolk, 31 August 1979. Died: Bury St Edmunds, Suffolk, 4 May 2025.) Tom Youngs was a busy, intelligent forward who developed in the youth set-up at Cambridge United before signing a professional contract in July 1997. He established himself as a regular for the U's in 1999–2000 then topped the club's scoring charts in the next two seasons before departing to Northampton Town in March 2003. He was increasingly affected by injuries from then onwards, although he later played for Leyton Orient and Bury before retiring from full-time football at the end of the 2006–07 season.

Ian Nannestad

THE FOOTBALL RECORDS

ALL-TIME PREMIER LEAGUE CHAMPIONSHIP SEASONS ON POINTS AVERAGE

	Team	Season	P	W	D	L	F	A	Pts	Pts Av
1	Manchester C	2017–18	38	32	4	2	106	27	100	2.63
2	Liverpool	2019–20	38	32	3	3	85	33	99	2.61
3	Manchester C	2018–19	38	32	2	4	95	23	98	2.58
4	Chelsea	2004–05	38	29	8	1	72	15	95	2.50
5	Chelsea	2016–17	38	30	3	5	85	33	93	2.45
6	Manchester C	2021–22	38	29	6	3	99	26	93	2.45
7	Manchester C	2023–24	38	28	7	3	96	34	91	2.39
	Manchester U	1999–2000	38	28	7	3	97	45	91	2.39
9	Chelsea	2005–06	38	29	4	5	72	22	91	2.39
10	Arsenal	2003–04	38	26	12	0	73	26	90	2.36
	Manchester U	2008–09	38	28	6	4	68	24	90	2.36
12	Manchester C	2022–23	38	28	5	5	94	33	89	2.34
	Manchester C	2011–12	38	28	5	5	93	29	89	2.34
	Manchester U	2006–07	38	28	5	5	83	27	89	2.34
	Manchester U	2012–13	38	28	5	5	86	43	89	2.34
16	Arsenal	2001–02	38	26	9	3	79	36	87	2.28
	Manchester U	2007–08	38	27	6	5	80	22	87	2.28
	Chelsea	2014–15	38	26	9	3	73	32	87	2.28
19	Chelsea	2009–10	38	27	5	6	103	32	86	2.26
	Manchester C	2013–14	38	27	5	6	102	37	86	2.26
	Manchester C	2020–21	38	27	5	6	83	32	86	2.26
22	Liverpool	2024–25	38	25	9	4	86	41	84	2.21
23	Manchester U	1993–94	42	27	11	4	80	38	92	2.19
24	Manchester U	2002–03	38	25	8	5	74	34	83	2.18
25	Manchester U	1995–96	38	25	7	6	73	35	82	2.15
26	Leicester C	2015–16	38	23	12	3	68	36	81	2.13
27	Blackburn R	1994–95	42	27	8	7	80	39	89	2.11
28	Manchester U	2000–01	38	24	8	6	79	31	80	2.10
	Manchester U	2010–11	38	23	11	4	78	37	80	2.10
30	Manchester U	1998–99	38	22	13	3	80	37	79	2.07
31	Arsenal	1997–98	38	23	9	6	68	33	78	2.05
32	Manchester U	1992–93	42	24	12	6	67	31	84	2.00
33	Manchester U	1996–97	38	21	12	5	76	44	75	1.97

PREMIER LEAGUE EVER-PRESENT CLUBS

	P	W	D	L	F	A	Pts
Manchester U	1266	755	278	233	2300	1167	2543
Arsenal	1266	693	309	264	2196	1220	2388
Liverpool	1266	677	311	278	2182	1235	2342
Chelsea	1266	667	313	286	2088	1235	2314
Tottenham H	1266	551	298	417	1889	1562	1951
Everton*	1266	450	356	460	1565	1589	1698

Everton deducted 8pts in 2023–24.

TOP TEN PREMIER LEAGUE APPEARANCES

1	Barry, Gareth	653	6	Speed, Gary	535
2	Milner, James	638	7	Heskey, Emile	516
3	Giggs, Ryan	632	8	Schwarzer, Mark	514
4	Lampard, Frank	609	9	Carragher, Jamie	508
5	James, David	572	10	Neville, Phil	505

TOP TEN PREMIER LEAGUE GOALSCORERS

1	Shearer, Alan	260	6	Aguero, Sergio	184
2	Kane, Harry	213	7	Lampard, Frank	177
3	Rooney, Wayne	208	8	Henry, Thierry	175
4	Cole, Andrew	187	9	Fowler, Robbie	163
5	Salah, Mohamed	186	10	Defoe, Jermain	162

SCOTTISH PREMIERSHIP SINCE 1998–99

	P	W	D	L	F	A	GD	Pts
Celtic	1014	750	154	110	2419	756	1663	2404
Rangers*	861	585	155	121	1833	712	1121	1900
Aberdeen	1014	401	234	379	1279	1313	−34	1437
Hearts*	938	367	232	339	1227	1158	69	1318
Motherwell	1014	356	221	437	1269	1526	−257	1289
Kilmarnock	976	320	244	412	1152	1399	−247	1204
Hibernian	864	302	234	328	1155	1191	−36	1140
Dundee U*	756	239	206	311	919	1125	−206	920

Rangers deducted 10pts in 2011–12; Hearts deducted 15pts in 2013–14; Dundee U deducted 3pts in 2015–16.

DOMESTIC LANDMARKS 2024–25

SEPTEMBER 2024

10   Harry Kane made his 100th international appearance for England in the Nations League match against Finland at Wembley. Kane scored both England's goals in the 2-0 victory. Kane's goalscoring record increased to 68 goals in 100 appearances.

28   Brentford became the first team in Premier League history to score in the first minute of three consecutive matches. Yoane Wissa scored after 22 seconds against Manchester C at the Etihad Stadium on 14 September; Bryan Mbeumo after 23 seconds v Tottenham H at the Tottenham Hotspur Stadium on 21 September and Bryan Mbeumo on 37 seconds in the home game against West Ham U on 28 September. Unfortunately, Brentford failed to win any of the matches, losing 2-1 to Manchester C and 3-1 to Tottenham before drawing 1-1 with West Ham U.

OCTOBER 2024

19   Southampton set a new unwanted record for their longest sequence without a top-flight league win in the Premier League match against Leicester C at St Mary's. It was their 21st consecutive top-flight match without a win when Leicester C came from 0-2 behind to win 3-2.

26   Manchester C set a new record for unbeaten European Cup/Champions League games in their 5-0 victory over Sparta Prague at the Etihad Stadium. It was their 26th match without defeat stretching back to September 2022, breaking the record set by Manchester U in 2009.

NOVEMBER 2024

9   Manchester C manager Pep Guardiola lost his fourth game in a row for the first time in his managerial career. Brighton & HA defeated City with two late goals after Erling Haaland had given City a first-half lead.

30   Justin Kluivert became the first player to score a hat-trick of penalties in the same match in Premier League history. He scored the first two from the spot in the first half and completed his hat-trick in the 74th minute of Bournemouth's 4-2 victory over Wolverhampton W at Molineux.

DECEMBER 2024

11   Bernardo Silva became the all-time Champions League appearance holder for Manchester C with his 74th game in the competition. Juventus ran out 2-0 winners in Turin.

29   Pep Guardiola took charge of his 500th game as Manchester C manager when his side won 2-0 at Leicester C in the Premier League.

JANUARY 2025

25   David Moyes took charge of his 700th game in the Premier League when Everton played Brighton & HA at the Amex Stadium. The Toffees took the spoils, winning 1-0 with an Iliman Ndiaye penalty just before half time.

30   Mikey Moore became the youngest English player to score in a major European match at 17 years and 172 days in the Europa League win over Elfsborg. His injury-time goal was the third for Tottenham in a 3-0 victory.

FEBRUARY 2025

16   Trent Alexander-Arnold made his 250th Premier League appearance for Liverpool in their home win over Wolverhampton W. He became the youngest Liverpool player at 26 years and 132 days to reach 250 Premier League appearances.

21   Leicester C lost their sixth consecutive home game without scoring a goal in the Premier League when defeated 4-0 by Brentford at the King Power Stadium. This was the longest goalless run by a club at home in the history of the top-flight in English football.

MARCH 2025

21   Myles Lewis-Skelly became the youngest player to score on his full debut for England at 18 years and 176 days. He scored the first goal in the 20th minute of England's 2-0 victory over Albania in the 2026 FIFA World Cup Group K match.

APRIL 2025

6   Southampton became the first club in Premier League history to be relegated with seven games still to play.

20   Leicester C lost 1-0 at home to Liverpool to become the first team in England's top-flight history to lose nine successive home league games without scoring.

27   Liverpool became only the second team to have won the English top-flight league title 20 times. A 5-1 victory over Tottenham H at Anfield secured the title with four matches left to play.

MAY 2025

4   Chido Obi became the youngest player to start for Manchester U in the Premier League at 17 years 156 days, Obi made his debut against Brentford in a 4-3 defeat at the Gtech Community Stadium

18   Jamie Vardie scored his 200th goal for Leicester C on his 500th appearance for the club. He scored Leicester's first on 28 minutes in the 2-0 victory over Ipswich T at the King Power Stadium.

EUROPEAN CUP AND CHAMPIONS LEAGUE RECORDS

MOST WINS BY CLUB

Real Madrid	15	1956, 1957, 1958, 1959, 1960, 1966, 1998, 2000, 2002, 2014, 2016, 2017, 2018, 2022, 2024.
AC Milan	7	1963, 1969, 1989, 1990, 1994, 2003, 2007.
Liverpool	6	1977, 1978, 1981, 1984, 2005, 2019.
Bayern Munich	6	1974, 1975, 1976, 2001, 2013, 2020.
Barcelona	5	1992, 2006, 2009, 2011, 2015.

MOST APPEARANCES IN FINAL
Real Madrid 18; AC Milan 11; Bayern Munich 11.

MOST FINAL APPEARANCES PER COUNTRY
Spain 31 (20 wins, 11 defeats)
Italy 30 (12 wins, 18 defeats)
England 26 (15 wins, 11 defeats)
Germany 19 (8 wins, 11 defeats)

MOST CHAMPIONS LEAGUE/EUROPEAN CUP APPEARANCES
187 Cristiano Ronaldo (Manchester U, Real Madrid, Juventus, Manchester U)
181 Iker Casillas (Real Madrid, Porto)
165 Thomas Muller (Bayern Munich)
163 Lionel Messi (Barcelona, Paris Saint-Germain)
157 Xavi (Barcelona)
153 Toni Kroos (Bayern Munich, Real Madrid)
152 Karim Benzema (Lyon, Real Madrid)
152 Manuel Neuer (Schalke 04, Bayern Munich)
151 Ryan Giggs (Manchester U)
144 Raul (Real Madrid, Schalke)
142 Sergio Ramos (Real Madrid, Paris Saint-Germain, Sevilla)
142 Luka Modric (Tottenham H, Real Madrid)
139 Paolo Maldini (AC Milan)
132 Andreas Iniesta (Barcelona)
132 Gianluigi Buffon (Parma, Juventus, Paris Saint-Germain)
131 Clarence Seedorf (Ajax, Real Madrid, Internazionale, AC Milan)
130 Paul Scholes (Manchester U)

MOST WINS WITH DIFFERENT CLUBS
Toni Kroos 6, (Bayern Munich) 2013; (Real Madrid) 2016, 2017, 2018, 2022, 2024.

MOST WINNERS MEDALS
6 Francisco Gento (Real Madrid) 1956, 1957, 1958, 1959, 1960, 1966; Dani Carvajal and Luka Modric (Real Madrid) 2014, 2016, 2017, 2018, 2022, 2024.

BIGGEST WINS
European Cup
Real Madrid 8, Sevilla 0, 21.1.1958.
Champions League
HJK Helsinki 10, Bangor C 0, 19.7.2011 *(qualifier)*.
Liverpool 8, Besiktas 0, 6.11.2007.
Real Madrid 8, Malmo 0, 8.12.2015.

MOST SUCCESSIVE APPEARANCES
Champions League
Real Madrid (Spain) 28: 1997–98 to 2024-25.
European Cup
Real Madrid (Spain) 15: 1955–56 to 1969–70.

MOST SUCCESSIVE WINS IN THE CHAMPIONS LEAGUE
Bayern Munich (Germany) 15: 18.9.2019 to 25.11.2020.

LONGEST UNBEATEN RUN IN THE CHAMPIONS LEAGUE
Manchester U (England) 25: 2007–08 to 2009 (Final).

MOST GOALS OVERALL
141 Cristiano Ronaldo (Manchester U, Real Madrid, Juventus, Manchester U).
129 Lionel Messi (Barcelona, Paris Saint-Germain).
105 Robert Lewandowski (Borussia Dortmund, Bayern Munich, Barcelona).
90 Karim Benzema (Lyon, Real Madrid).
71 Raul (Real Madrid, Schalke).
60 Ruud van Nistelrooy (PSV Eindhoven, Manchester U, Real Madrid).

59 Andriy Shevchenko (Dynamo Kyiv, AC Milan, Chelsea, Dynamo Kyiv).
57 Thomas Muller (Bayern Munich).
55 Kylian Mbappe (Monaco, Paris Saint-Germain).
51 Thierry Henry (Monaco, Arsenal, Barcelona).
50 Filippo Inzaghi (Juventus, AC Milan).
49 Alfredo Di Stefano (Real Madrid).
49 Zlatan Ibrahimovic (Ajax, Juventus, Internazionale, AC Milan, Paris Saint-Germain).
49 Erling Haaland (RB Slazburg, Borussia Dortmund, Manchester C).
47 Eusebio (Benfica).

MOST GOALS IN CHAMPIONS LEAGUE MATCH
5 Lionel Messi, Barcelona v Bayer Leverkusen (25, 42, 49, 58, 84 mins) (7-1), 7.3.2012.
5 Luiz Adriano, Shaktar Donetsk v BATE (28, 36, 40, 44, 82 mins) (0-7), 21.10.2014.
5 Erling Haaland, Manchester C v RB Leipzig (22 (p), 24, 45, 53, 57 mins) (7-0), 14.3.2023.

MOST GOALS IN ONE SEASON
17 Cristiano Ronaldo 2013–14
16 Cristiano Ronaldo 2015–16
15 Cristiano Ronaldo 2017–18
15 Robert Lewandowski 2019–20
15 Karim Benzema 2021–22
14 Jose Altafini 1962–63
14 Ruud van Nistelrooy 2002–03
14 Lionel Messi 2011–12

MOST GOALS SCORED IN FINALS
7 Alfredo Di Stefano (Real Madrid), 1956 (1), 1957 (1 pen), 1958 (1), 1959 (1), 1960 (3).
7 Ferenc Puskas (Real Madrid), 1960 (4), 1962 (3).

HIGHEST SCORE IN A MATCH
European Cup
14 KR Reykjavik (Iceland) 2 Feyenoord (Netherlands) 12 *(First Round First Leg 1969–70)*
Champions League
12 Borussia Dortmund 8, Legia Warsaw 4 *(Group Stage 2016–17)*

HIGHEST AGGREGATE IN A MATCH
European Cup
Benfica (Portugal) 18, Stade Dudelange (Luxembourg) 0 – 8-0 (h), 10-0 (a) *(Preliminary Round 1965–66)*
Champions League
Bayern Munich (Germany) 12, Sporting Lisbon (Portugal) 1 – 7-1 (h), 5-0 (a) *(Round of 16 2008–09)*

FASTEST GOALS SCORED IN CHAMPIONS LEAGUE

10.12 sec	Roy Makaay for Bayern Munich v Real Madrid, 7.3.2007.
10.96 sec	Jonas for Valencia v Bayer Leverkusen, 1.11.2011.
20.07 sec	Gilberto Silva for Arsenal at PSV Eindhoven, 25.9.2002.
20.12 sec	Alessandro Del Piero for Juventus at Manchester U, 1.10.1997.

YOUNGEST CHAMPIONS LEAGUE GOALSCORER
Ansu Fati for Barcelona v Internazionale 17 years 40 days in 2019–20.

OLDEST CHAMPIONS LEAGUE GOALSCORER
Pepe for Porto v Shakhtar Donetsk 40 years 290 days in 2023–24.

FASTEST HAT-TRICK SCORED IN CHAMPIONS LEAGUE
Mohamed Salah, 6 mins 12 sec for Liverpool v Rangers (1-7) 12.10.2022.

MOST GOALS BY A GOALKEEPER
Hans-Jorg Butt (for three different clubs)
Hamburg 13.9.2000, Bayer Leverkusen 12.5.2002, Bayern Munich 8.12.2009 – all achieved against Juventus.

EUROPEAN CUP AND CHAMPIONS LEAGUE RECORDS – continued

LANDMARK GOALS CHAMPIONS LEAGUE
1st Daniel Amokachi, Club Brugge v CSKA Moscow
17 minutes 25.11.1992
1,000th Dmitri Khokhlov, PSV Eindhoven v Benfica
41 minutes 9.12.1998
5,000th Luisao, Benfica v Hapoel Tel Aviv 21 minutes
14.9.2010
10,000th Bruno Fernandes, Galatasaray v Manchester U
18 minutes 29.11.2023

HIGHEST SCORING DRAW
Vorus Lobogo 4, Reims 4, 28.12.1955
Hamburg 4, Juventus 4, 13.9.2000
Chelsea 4, Liverpool 4, 14.4.2009
Bayer Leverkusen 4, Roma 4, 20.10.2015
Chelsea 4, Ajax 4, 5.11.2019

MOST CLUB CLEAN SHEETS IN ONE SEASON
10: Arsenal 2005–06 (995 minutes with two
goalkeepers Manuel Almunia 347 minutes and Jens
Lehmann 648 minutes).

CHAMPIONS LEAGUE ATTENDANCES AND GOALS FROM GROUP/LEAGUE STAGES ONWARDS

Season	Attendances	Average	Goals	Games
1992–93	873,251	34,930	56	25
1993–94	1,202,289	44,529	71	27
1994–95	2,328,515	38,172	140	61
1995–96	1,874,316	30,726	159	61
1996–97	2,093,228	34,315	161	61
1997–98	2,868,271	33,744	239	85
1998–99	3,608,331	42,451	238	85
1999–2000	5,490,709	34,973	442	157
2000–01	5,773,486	36,774	449	157
2001–02	5,417,716	34,508	393	157
2002–03	6,461,112	41,154	431	157
2003–04	4,611,214	36,890	309	125
2004–05	4,946,820	39,575	331	125
2005–06	5,291,187	42,330	285	125
2006–07	5,591,463	44,732	309	125
2007–08	5,454,718	43,638	330	125
2008–09	5,003,754	40,030	329	125
2009–10	5,295,708	42,366	320	125
2010–11	5,474,654	43,797	355	125
2011–12	5,225,363	41,803	345	125
2012–13	5,773,366	46,187	368	125
2013–14	5,713,049	45,704	362	125
2014–15	5,207,592	42,685	361	125
2015–16	5,116,690	40,934	347	125
2016–17	5,398,851	43,191	380	125
2017–18	5,744,918	45,959	401	125
2018–19	5,746,629	45,973	366	125
2019–20	4,757,233	44,048	386	119
2020–21	No attendances published		366	125
2021–22	4,394,473	35,439	380	125
2022–23	6,197,200	49,578	372	125
2023–24	6,515,017	52,120	375	125
2024–25	8,373,025	44,302	618	189

HIGHEST AVERAGE ATTENDANCE IN ONE EUROPEAN CUP/CHAMPIONS LEAGUE SEASON
2023–24   52,120 from a total attendance of 6,515,017.

GREATEST COMEBACKS
Werder Bremen beat Anderlecht 5-3 after being three goals down in 33 minutes on 8.12.1993. They scored five goals in 23 second-half minutes.
Deportivo La Coruna beat Paris Saint-Germain 4-3 after being three goals down in 55 minutes on 7.3.2001. They scored four goals in 27 second-half minutes.
Liverpool three goals down to FC Basel in 29 minutes on 12.11.2002. They scored three second half goals in 24 minutes to draw 3-3.
Liverpool after being three goals down to AC Milan in the first half on 25.5.2005 in the Champions League Final. They scored three goals in five second-half minutes and won the penalty shoot-out after extra time 3-2.

MOST SUCCESSFUL MANAGER
Carlo Ancelotti 5 wins, 2002–03, 2006–07 (AC Milan), 2013–14, 2021–22, 2023–24 (Real Madrid).

REINSTATED WINNERS EXCLUDED FROM NEXT COMPETITION
Marseille were originally stripped of the title in 1993. This was rescinded but they were not allowed to compete the following season.

INTERNATIONAL LANDMARKS 2024–25

SEPTEMBER 2024
5 Cristiano Ronaldo scored his 900th career goal when scoring for Portugal in their Nations League Group A1 game against Croatia in Lisbon. His 34th minute goal helped his country to a 2-1 victory.
10 Mo Salah made his 100th international appearance for Egypt in the Africa Cup of Nations Group C match in Botswana. Salah scored Egypt's third goal in Egypt's 4-0 victory.

OCTOBER 2024
15 Andrej Kramaric made his 100th international appearance for Croatia in their Nations League Group A1 game against Poland in Warsaw. After leading 3-1 Croatia then drew 3-3.
22 Francesco Camarda became AC Milan and Italy's youngest player in the Champions League at 16 years 226 days. Camarda was a 73rd minute substitute for Alvaro Morata in AC Milan's 3-1 victory over Club Brugge at the San Siro.

NOVEMBER 2024
19 Karol Mets made his 100th international appearance for Estonia in their Nations League Group B1 1-0 defeat to Slovakia in Trnava.
26 Barcelona's Robert Lewandowski became the third player to score 100 goals in the Champions League. A 10th-minute penalty and an injury time strike in the Champions League league phase match against Brest were his 100th and 101st goals in the competition.

DECEMBER 2024
13 VfL Wolfsburg's Sveindis Jonsdottir became the first substitute to score four goals in a Women's Champions League match with her four goals against Roma in Group A.

FEBRUARY 2025
1 Harry Kane set a new Bundesliga record with two goals for Bayern Munich against Holstein Kiel at the Allianz Arena. His record of 55 goals in his first 50 appearances beat the record held by Erling Haaland with 50 goals in 50 appearances.

MARCH 2025
21 Riyad Mahrez made his 100th international appearance for Algeria in their FIFA World Cup 2026 qualifying group G match against Botswana in Francistown. Algeria won the match 3-1.
22 Henri Anier made his 100th international appearance for Estonia in their FIFA World Cup 2026 qualifying group I match against Israel in Debrecen, Hungary. Israel ran out 2-1 winners.

23 Bernardo Silva made his 100th international appearance for Portugal in their Nations League quarter-final second leg match against Denmark in Lisbon. After a 1-0 defeat in the first leg, Portugal's 3-2 victory in normal time sent the tie into extra time where Portugal ran out 5-2 winners to secure a semi-final spot with an aggregate win of 5-3.

23 Mephis Depay made his 100th international appearance for Netherlands in their Nations League quarter-final against Spain in Valencia. The first leg was a 2-2 draw and in the second leg Depay scored a penalty in a 3-3 draw after extra time, making the aggregate score 5-5. Spain went on to win the penalty shoot-out 5-4.

APRIL 2025

26 Thomas Muller made his 500th appearance for Bayern Munich in the 3-0 home win over Mainz 05. He came on as a substitute for Leroy Sane in the 84th minute.

30 Marcus Thuram scored the fastest goal of any semi-final of the UEFA Champions League. His goal in 30 seconds for Internazionale at Barcelona was the first of a six-goal thriller with the score ending 3-3. In the same game Lamine Yamal became the youngest player to score in a UEFA Champions League semi-final with his 24th minute equaliser to make it 1-1.

MAY 2025

10 Alexander Sorloth broke the record for the fastest hat-trick in La Liga history with his treble for Atletico Madrid against Real Sociedad. He achieved the feat in 3 minutes 47 seconds. He would add a fourth within 30 minutes as Atletico won 4-0 in Madrid.

15 Barcelona became the first club to ever win the 'pure' domestic treble in Spain by winning all three of La Liga, Copa del Rey and Supercopa de Espana in the same season. Their 2-0 away win at rivals Espanyol secured the La Liga title with two games to spare.

31 Paris Saint-Germain become the first team to win a Champions League or European Cup final by a 5-goal margin when beating Internazionale 5-0 in the Champions League final in Munich.

JUNE 2025

4 Joshua Kimmic made his 100th international appearance for Germany in their Nations League semi-final match against Portugal in Munich. Kimmich captained his country but although they led early in the second half, Portugal secured a 2-1 victory with goals from Francisco Conceicao and Cristiano Ronaldo.

7 Fedor Cernych made his 100th international appearance for Lithuania in the 2026 World Cup qualifying group G 0-0 draw with Malta in Ta'Qali.

7 Lukas Hradecky made his 100th international appearance for Finland in the 2026 World Cup qualifying group G 0-2 defeat to Netherlands in Helsinki.

TOP TEN AVERAGE ATTENDANCES

1	Manchester U	2006–07	75,826
2	Manchester U	2007–08	75,691
3	Manchester U	2012–13	75,530
4	Manchester U	2011–12	75,387
5	Manchester U	2014–15	75,335
6	Manchester U	2008–09	75,308
7	Manchester U	2016–17	75,290
8	Manchester U	2015–16	75,279
9	Manchester U	2013–14	75,207
10	Manchester U	2010–11	75,109

TOP TEN AVERAGE WORLD CUP FINALS CROWDS

1	In USA	1994	68,991
2	In Qatar	2022	53,191
3	In Brazil	2014	52,621
4	In Germany	2006	52,491
5	In Mexico	1970	50,124
6	In South Africa	2010	49,669
7	In West Germany	1974	49,098
8	In England	1966	48,847
9	In Italy	1990	48,388
10	In Brazil	1950	47,511

TOP TEN ALL-TIME ENGLAND CAPS

1	Peter Shilton	125
2	Wayne Rooney	120
3	David Beckham	115
4	Steven Gerrard	114
5	Bobby Moore	108
6	Ashley Cole	107
	Harry Kane	107
8	Bobby Charlton	106
	Frank Lampard	106
10	Billy Wright	105

TOP TEN ALL-TIME ENGLAND GOALSCORERS

1	Harry Kane	73
2	Wayne Rooney	53
3	Bobby Charlton	49
4	Gary Lineker	48
5	Jimmy Greaves	44
6	Michael Owen	40
	Tom Finney	30
7	Nat Lofthouse	30
	Alan Shearer	30
8	Vivian Woodward	29
	Frank Lampard	29

GOALKEEPING RECORDS
(without conceding a goal)

FA PREMIER LEAGUE
Edwin van der Sar (Manchester U) in 1,311 minutes during the 2008–09 season.

FOOTBALL LEAGUE
Steve Death (Reading) 1,103 minutes from 24 March to 18 August 1979.

SCOTTISH PREMIER LEAGUE
Fraser Forster (Celtic) in 1,215 minutes from 6 December 2013 to 25 February 2014.

MOST CLEAN SHEETS IN A SEASON
Petr Cech (Chelsea) 24, 2004–05

MOST CLEAN SHEETS OVERALL IN PREMIER LEAGUE
Petr Cech (Chelsea and Arsenal) 202 games.

MOST GOALS FOR IN A SEASON

FA PREMIER LEAGUE

		Goals	Games
2017–18	Manchester C	106	38

FOOTBALL LEAGUE
Division 4

1960–61	Peterborough U	134	46

SCOTTISH PREMIER LEAGUE

2022–23	Celtic	114	38

SCOTTISH LEAGUE
Division 2

1937–38	Raith R	142	34

MOST GOALS AGAINST IN A SEASON

FA PREMIER LEAGUE

		Goals	Games
2023–24	Sheffield U	104	38

FOOTBALL LEAGUE
Division 2

1898–99	Darwen	141	34

SCOTTISH PREMIER LEAGUE

1999–2000	Aberdeen	83	36
2007–08	Gretna	83	38

SCOTTISH LEAGUE
Division 2

1931–32	Edinburgh C	146	38

MOST LEAGUE GOALS IN A SEASON

FA PREMIER LEAGUE

		Goals	Games
2022–23	Erling Haaland (Manchester C)	36	35
1993–94	Andrew Cole (Newcastle U)	34	40
1994–95	Alan Shearer (Blackburn R)	34	42
2017–18	Mohamed Salah (Liverpool)	32	38

FOOTBALL LEAGUE
Division 1

1927–28	Dixie Dean (Everton)	60	39

Division 2

1926–27	George Camsell (Middlesbrough)	59	37

Division 3(S)

1936–37	Joe Payne (Luton T)	55	39

Division 3(N)

1936–37	Ted Harston (Mansfield T)	55	41

Division 3

1959–60	Derek Reeves (Southampton)	39	46

Division 4

1960–61	Terry Bly (Peterborough U)	52	46

FA CUP

1887–88	Jimmy Ross (Preston NE)	20	8

LEAGUE CUP

1986–87	Clive Allen (Tottenham H)	12	9

SCOTTISH PREMIER LEAGUE

2000–01	Henrik Larsson (Celtic)	35	37

SCOTTISH LEAGUE
Division 1

1931–32	William McFadyen (Motherwell)	52	34

Division 2

1927–28	Jim Smith (Ayr U)	66	38

MOST FA CUP FINAL GOALS

Ian Rush (Liverpool) 5: 1986(2), 1989(2), 1992(1)

SCORED IN EVERY PREMIERSHIP GAME

Arsenal 2001–02: 38 matches

FEWEST GOALS FOR IN A SEASON

FA PREMIER LEAGUE

		Goals	Games
2007–08	Derby Co	20	38
2023–24	Sheffield U	20	38

FOOTBALL LEAGUE
Division 2

1899–1900	Loughborough T	18	34

SCOTTISH PREMIERSHIP

2010–11	St Johnstone	23	38

SCOTTISH LEAGUE
New Division 1

1980–81	Stirling Alb	18	39

FEWEST GOALS AGAINST IN A SEASON

FA PREMIER LEAGUE

	Goals	Games
2004–05 Chelsea	15	38

FOOTBALL LEAGUE
Championship

2024–25 Burnley	16	46

SCOTTISH PREMIERSHIP

2020–21 Rangers	13	38

SCOTTISH LEAGUE
Division 2

1914–15 Cowdenbeath	17	26

MOST LEAGUE GOALS IN A CAREER

FOOTBALL LEAGUE

Arthur Rowley	Goals	Games	Season
WBA	4	24	1946–48
Fulham	27	56	1948–50
Leicester C	251	303	1950–58
Shrewsbury T	152	236	1958–65
	434	619	

SCOTTISH LEAGUE

Jimmy McGrory			
Celtic	1	3	1922–23
Clydebank	13	30	1923–24
Celtic	396	375	1924–38
	410	408	

MOST HAT-TRICKS

Career
37: Dixie Dean (Tranmere R, Everton, Notts Co, England)

Division 1 (one season post-war)
6: Jimmy Greaves (Chelsea), 1960–61

Three for one team in one match
West, Spouncer, Hooper, Nottingham F v Leicester Fosse, Division 1, 21 April 1909
Loasby, Smith, Wells, Northampton T v Walsall, Division 3S, 5 Nov 1927
Bowater, Hoyland, Readman, Mansfield T v Rotherham U, Division 3N, 27 Dec 1932
Barnes, Ambler, Davies, Wrexham v Hartlepools U, Division 4, 3 March 1962
Adcock, Stewart, White, Manchester C v Huddersfield T, Division 2, 7 Nov 1987

MOST CUP GOALS IN A CAREER

FA CUP (pre-Second World War)
Henry Cursham   48   (Notts Co)

FA CUP (post-war)
Ian Rush   43   (Chester, Liverpool)

LEAGUE CUP
Geoff Hurst   49   (West Ham U, Stoke C)
Ian Rush   49   (Chester, Liverpool, Newcastle U)

GOALS PER GAME (Football League to 1991–92)

Goals per game	Division 1		Division 2		Division 3		Division 4		Division 3(S)		Division 3(N)	
	Games	Goals	Games	Goals	Games	Goals	Games	Goals	Games	Goals	Games	Goals
0	2465	0	2665	0	1446	0	1438	0	997	0	803	0
1	5606	5606	5836	5836	3225	3225	3106	3106	2073	2073	1914	1914
2	8275	16550	8609	17218	4569	9138	4441	8882	3314	6628	2939	5878
3	7731	23193	7842	23526	3784	11352	4041	12123	2996	8988	2922	8766
4	6229	24920	5897	23588	2837	11348	2784	11136	2445	9780	2410	9640
5	3752	18755	3634	18170	1566	7830	1506	7530	1554	7770	1599	7995
6	2137	12822	2007	12042	769	4614	786	4716	870	5220	930	5580
7	1092	7644	1001	7007	357	2499	336	2352	451	3157	461	3227
8	542	4336	376	3008	135	1080	143	1144	209	1672	221	1768
9	197	1773	164	1476	64	576	35	315	76	684	102	918
10	83	830	68	680	13	130	8	80	33	330	45	450
11	37	407	19	209	2	22	7	77	15	165	15	165
12	12	144	17	204	1	12	0	0	7	84	8	96
13	4	52	4	52	0	0	0	0	2	26	4	52
14	2	28	1	14	0	0	0	0	0	0	0	0
17	0	0	0	0	0	0	0	0	0	0	1	17
	38164	117060	38140	113030	18768	51826	18631	51461	15042	46577	14374	46466

Extensive research by statisticians has unearthed seven results from the early years of the Football League which differ from the original scores. These are 26 January 1889 Wolverhampton W 5 Everton 0 (not 4-0), 16 March 1889 Notts Co 3 Derby Co 5 (not 2-5), 4 January 1896 Arsenal 5 Loughborough 0 (not 6-0), 28 November 1896 Leicester Fosse 4 Walsall 2 (not 4-1), 21 April 1900 Burslem Port Vale 2 Lincoln C 1 (not 2-0), 25 December 1902 Glossop NE 3 Stockport Co 0 (not 3-1), 26 April 1913 Hull C 2 Leicester C 0 (not 2-1).

GOALS PER GAME (from 1992–93)

Goals per game	Premier		Championship/Div 1		League One/Div 2		League Two/Div 3	
	Games	Goals	Games	Goals	Games	Goals	Games	Goals
0	1005	0	1475	0	1397	0	1455	0
1	2262	2262	3464	3464	3380	3380	3482	3482
2	3082	6164	4615	9230	4560	9120	4518	9036
3	2725	8175	3977	11931	4008	12024	3904	11712
4	1945	7780	2500	10000	2483	9932	2391	9564
5	1001	5005	1325	6625	1362	6810	1258	6290
6	461	2766	572	3432	563	3378	515	3090
7	197	1379	202	1414	218	1526	208	1456
8	77	616	66	528	66	528	65	520
9	25	225	11	99	21	189	25	225
10	5	50	7	70	6	60	9	90
11	1	11	2	22	0	0	4	44
	12786	34433	18216	46815	18064	46947	17834	45509

New Overall Totals (since 1992)		Totals (up to 1991–92)		Complete Overall Totals (since 1888–89)	
Games	66900	Games	143119	Games	210019
Goals	173704	Goals	426420	Goals	600124
Goals per game	2.60		2.98		2.86

A CENTURY OF LEAGUE AND CUP GOALS IN CONSECUTIVE SEASONS

George Camsell	League	Cup	Season
Middlesbrough	59	5	1926–27
(101 goals)	33	4	1927–28

(Camsell's cup goals were all scored in the FA Cup.)

Steve Bull			
Wolverhampton W	34	18	1987–88
(102 goals)	37	13	1988–89

(Bull had 12 in the Sherpa Van Trophy, 3 Littlewoods Cup, 3 FA Cup in 1987–88; 11 Sherpa Van Trophy, 2 Littlewoods Cup in 1988–89.)

PENALTIES

Most in a season (individual)

Division 1	Goals	Season
Francis Lee (Manchester C)	13	1971–72

Also scored 2 cup goals.

Most awarded in one game

5	Crystal Palace (1 scored, 3 missed)	
	v Brighton & HA (1 scored), Div 2	1988–89

Most saved in a season

Division 1		
Paul Cooper (Ipswich T)	8 (of 10)	1979–80

MOST GOALS IN A GAME

FA PREMIER LEAGUE
4 Mar 1995 Andrew Cole (Manchester U)
5 goals v Ipswich T
19 Sept 1999 Alan Shearer (Newcastle U)
5 goals v Sheffield Wed
22 Nov 2009 Jermain Defoe (Tottenham H)
5 goals v Wigan Ath
27 Nov 2010 Dimitar Berbatov (Manchester U)
5 goals v Blackburn R
3 Oct 2015 Sergio Aguero (Manchester C)
5 goals v Newcastle U

FOOTBALL LEAGUE
Division 1
14 Dec 1935 Ted Drake (Arsenal) 7 goals v Aston Villa
Division 2
5 Feb 1955 Tommy Briggs (Blackburn R)
7 goals v Bristol R
23 Feb 1957 Neville Coleman (Stoke C) 7 goals v
Lincoln C
Division 3(S)
13 Apr 1936 Joe Payne (Luton T) 10 goals v Bristol R
Division 3(N)
26 Dec 1935 Bunny Bell (Tranmere R)
9 goals v Oldham Ath
Division 3
24 Apr 1965 Barrie Thomas (Scunthorpe U)
5 goals v Luton T
20 Nov 1965 Keith East (Swindon T)
5 goals v Mansfield T
16 Sept 1969 Steve Earle (Fulham) 5 goals v Halifax T
2 Oct 1971 Alf Wood (Shrewsbury T)
5 goals v Blackburn R
10 Sept 1983 Tony Caldwell (Bolton W)
5 goals v Walsall
4 May 1987 Andy Jones (Port Vale)
5 goals v Newport Co
3 Apr 1990 Steve Wilkinson (Mansfield T)
5 goals v Birmingham C
5 Sept 1998 Giuliano Grazioli (Peterborough U)
5 goals v Barnet
6 Apr 2002 Lee Jones (Wrexham)
5 goals v Cambridge U
Division 4
26 Dec 1962 Bert Lister (Oldham Ath)
6 goals v Southport

FA CUP
20 Nov 1971 Ted MacDougall (Bournemouth)
9 goals v Margate (*1st Round*)

LEAGUE CUP
25 Oct 1989 Frankie Bunn (Oldham Ath)
6 goals v Scarborough

SCOTTISH LEAGUE
Premier Division
17 Nov 1984 Paul Sturrock (Dundee U)
5 goals v Morton
Premier League
23 Aug 1996 Marco Negri (Rangers) 5 goals v
Dundee U
4 Nov 2000 Kenny Miller (Rangers) 5 goals v
St Mirren
25 Sept 2004 Kris Boyd (Kilmarnock) 5 goals v
Dundee U
30 Dec 2009 Kris Boyd (Rangers) 5 goals v
Dundee U
13 May 2012 Gary Hooper (Celtic) 5 goals v Hearts
Division 1
14 Sept 1928 Jimmy McGrory (Celtic)
8 goals v Dunfermline Ath
Division 2
1 Oct 1927 Owen McNally (Arthurlie)
8 goals v Armadale
2 Jan 1930 Jim Dyet (King's Park)
8 goals v Forfar Ath
18 Apr 1936 John Calder (Morton)
8 goals v Raith R
20 Aug 1937 Norman Hayward (Raith R)
8 goals v Brechin C

SCOTTISH CUP
12 Sept 1885 John Petrie (Arbroath)
13 goals v Bon Accord (*1st Round*)

LONGEST SEQUENCE OF CONSECUTIVE DEFEATS

	Team	Games
FOOTBALL LEAGUE **Division 2**		
1898–99	Darwen	18

LONGEST UNBEATEN SEQUENCE

	Team	Games
FA PREMIER LEAGUE		
May 2003–Oct 2004	Arsenal	49
FOOTBALL LEAGUE – League 1		
Jan 2011–Nov 2011	Huddersfield T	43

LONGEST UNBEATEN CUP SEQUENCE

Liverpool	25 rounds	League Cup	1980–84

LONGEST UNBEATEN SEQUENCE IN A SEASON

	Team	Games
FA PREMIER LEAGUE		
2003–04	Arsenal	38
FOOTBALL LEAGUE – Championship		
2024–25	Burnley	33
SCOTTISH PREMIERSHIP		
2016–17	Celtic	38

LONGEST UNBEATEN START TO A SEASON

	Team	Games
FA PREMIER LEAGUE		
2003–04	Arsenal	38
FOOTBALL LEAGUE – Division 1		
1973–74	Leeds U	29
1987–88	Liverpool	29

LONGEST SEQUENCE WITHOUT A WIN IN A SEASON

	Team	Games
FA PREMIER LEAGUE		
2007–08	Derby Co	32
FOOTBALL LEAGUE **Division 2**		
1983–84	Cambridge U	31

LONGEST SEQUENCE WITHOUT A WIN FROM SEASON'S START

	Team	Games
FOOTBALL LEAGUE **Division 4**		
1970–71	Newport Co	25

LONGEST SEQUENCE OF CONSECUTIVE SCORING (individual)

FA PREMIER LEAGUE
Jamie Vardy (Leicester C) 13 in 11 games   2015–16
FOOTBALL LEAGUE RECORD
Tom Phillipson
(Wolverhampton W)   23 in 13 games   1926–27

LONGEST WINNING SEQUENCE

	Team	Games
FA PREMIER LEAGUE		
2017–18	Manchester C	18
2019–20	Liverpool	18
FOOTBALL LEAGUE – Division 2		
1904–05	Manchester U	14
1905–06	Bristol C	14
1950–51	Preston NE	14
FROM SEASON'S START – Division 3		
1985–86	Reading	13
SCOTTISH PREMIER LEAGUE		
2003–04	Celtic	25

HIGHEST WINS

Highest win in a First-Class Match
(*Scottish Cup 1st Round*)
Arbroath   36 Bon Accord   0   12 Sept 1885

Highest win in an International Match
England   13 Ireland   0   18 Feb 1882

Highest win in an FA Cup Match
Preston NE   26 Hyde U   0   15 Oct 1887
(*1st Round*)

Highest win in a League Cup Match
West Ham U   10 Bury   0   25 Oct 1983
(*2nd Round, 2nd Leg*)
Liverpool   10 Fulham   0   23 Sept 1986
(*2nd Round, 1st Leg*)

Highest win in an FA Premier League Match
Manchester U   9 Ipswich T   0   4 Mar 1995
Manchester U   9 Southampton   0   2 Jan 2021
Southampton   0 Leicester C   9   25 Oct 2019
Tottenham H   9 Wigan Ath   1   22 Nov 2009
Liverpool   9 Bournemouth   0   27 Aug 2022

Highest win in a Football League Match
Division 2 – highest home win
Newcastle U   13 Newport Co   0   5 Oct 1946
Division 3(N) – highest home win
Stockport Co   13 Halifax T   0   6 Jan 1934
Division 2 – highest away win
Burslem Port Vale 0 Sheffield U   10   10 Dec 1892

Highest wins in a Scottish League Match
Scottish Premiership – highest home win
Celtic   9 Aberdeen   0   6 Nov 2010
Scottish Division 2 – highest home win
Airdrieonians   15 Dundee W   1   1 Dec 1894
Scottish Premiership – highest away win
Dundee U   0 Celtic   9   27 Aug 2022

MOST HOME WINS IN A SEASON

Brentford won all 21 games in Division 3(S), 1929–30

RECORD AWAY WINS IN A SEASON

Doncaster R won 18 of 21 games in Division 3(N), 1946–47

CONSECUTIVE AWAY WINS

FA PREMIER LEAGUE
Manchester C 12 games (2020–21)

FOOTBALL LEAGUE
Division 1
Tottenham H 10 games (1959–60 (2), 1960–61 (8))

HIGHEST AGGREGATE SCORES

FA PREMIER LEAGUE
Portsmouth   7 Reading   4   29 Sept 2007

Highest Aggregate Score England
Division 3(N)
Tranmere R   13 Oldham Ath   4   26 Dec 1935

Highest Aggregate Score Scotland
Division 2
Airdrieonians   15 Dundee Wanderers 1   1 Dec 1894

FEWEST WINS IN A SEASON

FA PREMIER LEAGUE		Wins	Games
2007–08	Derby Co	1	38
FOOTBALL LEAGUE			
Division 2			
1899–1900	Loughborough T	1	34
SCOTTISH PREMIER LEAGUE			
1998–99	Dunfermline Ath	4	36
SCOTTISH LEAGUE			
Division 1			
1891–92	Vale of Leven	0	22

MOST WINS IN A SEASON

FA PREMIER LEAGUE		Wins	Games
2017–18	Manchester C	32	38
2018–19	Manchester C	32	38
2019–20	Liverpool	32	38
FOOTBALL LEAGUE			
Division 3(N)			
1946–47	Doncaster R	33	42
SCOTTISH PREMIERSHIP			
2016–17	Celtic	34	38
SCOTTISH LEAGUE			
Division 1			
1920–21	Rangers	35	42

UNDEFEATED AT HOME OVERALL

Liverpool 85 games (63 League, 9 League Cup, 7 European, 6 FA Cup), Jan 1978–Jan 1981

UNDEFEATED AT HOME LEAGUE

Chelsea 86 games, Mar 2004–Oct 2008

UNDEFEATED AWAY

Arsenal 19 games, FA Premier League 2001–02 and 2003–04 (only Preston NE with 11 in 1888–89 had previously remained unbeaten away) in the top flight.

MOST POINTS IN A SEASON
(three points for a win)

FA PREMIER LEAGUE		Points	Games
2017–18	Manchester C	100	38
FOOTBALL LEAGUE			
Championship			
2005–06	Reading	106	46
SCOTTISH PREMIER LEAGUE			
2001–02	Celtic	103	38
SCOTTISH LEAGUE			
League One			
2013–14	Rangers	102	36

MOST POINTS IN A SEASON
(under old system of two points for a win)

FOOTBALL LEAGUE		Points	Games
Division 4			
1975–76	Lincoln C	74	46
SCOTTISH LEAGUE			
Division 1			
1920–21	Rangers	76	42

FEWEST POINTS IN A SEASON

FA PREMIER LEAGUE		Points	Games
2007–08	Derby Co	11	38
FOOTBALL LEAGUE			
Division 2			
1904–05	Doncaster R	8	34
1899–1900	Loughborough T	8	34
SCOTTISH PREMIER LEAGUE			
2007–08	Gretna	13	38
SCOTTISH LEAGUE			
Division 1			
1954–55	Stirling Alb	6	30

NO DEFEATS IN A SEASON

FA PREMIER LEAGUE
2003–04   Arsenal   won 26, drew 12

FOOTBALL LEAGUE
Division 1
1888–89   Preston NE   won 18, drew 4
Division 2
1893–94   Liverpool   won 22, drew 6

SCOTTISH LEAGUE
Premiership
2016–17   Celtic   won 34, drew 4
2020–21   Rangers   won 32, drew 6
Division 1
1898–99   Rangers   won 18
League One
2013–14   Rangers   won 33, drew 3

ONE DEFEAT IN A SEASON

FA PREMIER LEAGUE		Defeats	Games
2004–05	Chelsea	1	38
2018–19	Liverpool	1	38

FOOTBALL LEAGUE			
Division 1			
1990–91	Arsenal	1	38

SCOTTISH PREMIERSHIP			
2001–02	Celtic	1	38
2013–14	Celtic	1	38

SCOTTISH LEAGUE			
Division 1			
1920–21	Rangers	1	42
Division 2			
1956–57	Clyde	1	36
1962–63	Morton	1	36
1967–68	St Mirren	1	36
New Division 1			
2011–12	Ross Co	1	36
2022–23	Dunfermline Ath	1	36
New Division 2			
1975–76	Raith R	1	26

MOST DEFEATS IN A SEASON

FA PREMIER LEAGUE		Defeats	Games
2024–25	Southampton	30	38

FOOTBALL LEAGUE			
Division 3			
1997–98	Doncaster R	34	46

SCOTTISH PREMIERSHIP			
2005–06	Livingston	28	38

SCOTTISH LEAGUE			
New Division 1			
1992–93	Cowdenbeath	34	44

MOST DRAWN GAMES IN A SEASON

FA PREMIER LEAGUE		Draws	Games
1993–94	Manchester C	18	42
1993–94	Sheffield U	18	42
1994–95	Southampton	18	42

FOOTBALL LEAGUE			
Division 1			
1978–79	Norwich C	23	42
Division 3			
1997–98	Cardiff C	23	46
1997–98	Hartlepool U	23	46
Division 4			
1986–87	Exeter C	23	46

SCOTTISH PREMIER LEAGUE			
1998–99	Dunfermline Ath	16	38

SCOTTISH LEAGUE			
Premier Division			
1993–94	Aberdeen	21	44
New Division 1			
1986–87	East Fife	21	44

SENDINGS-OFF

SEASON
451 (League alone)   2003–04
(Before rescinded cards taken into account)

DAY
19 (League)   13 Dec 2003

FA CUP FINAL
Kevin Moran, Manchester U v Everton   1985
Jose Antonio Reyes, Arsenal v Manchester U   2005
Pablo Zabaleta, Manchester C v Wigan Ath   2013
Chris Smalling, Manchester U v Crystal Palace   2016
Victor Moses, Chelsea v Arsenal   2017
Mateo Kovacic, Chelsea v Arsenal   2020

QUICKEST
FA Premier League
Andreas Johansson, Wigan Ath v Arsenal (7 May 2006) and Keith Gillespie, Sheffield U v Reading (20 January 2007) both in 10 seconds
Football League
Walter Boyd, Swansea C v Darlington, Div 3 as substitute in zero seconds   23 Nov 1999

MOST IN ONE GAME
Five: Chesterfield (2) v Plymouth Arg (3)   22 Feb 1997
Five: Wigan Ath (1) v Bristol R (4)   2 Dec 1997
Five: Exeter C (3) v Cambridge U (2)   23 Nov 2002
Five: Bradford C (3) v Crawley T (2)*   27 Mar 2012
All five sent off after final whistle for fighting

MOST IN ONE TEAM
Wigan Ath (1) v Bristol R (4)   2 Dec 1997
Hereford U (4) v Northampton T (0)   6 Sept 1992

MOST SUCCESSFUL MANAGERS

Sir Alex Ferguson CBE
Manchester U
1986–2013, 25 major trophies:
13 Premier League, 5 FA Cup, 4 League Cup, 2 Champions League, 1 Cup-Winners' Cup.

Aberdeen
1976–86, 9 major trophies:
3 League, 4 Scottish Cup, 1 League Cup, 1 Cup Winners' Cup.

Bob Paisley – Liverpool
1974–83, 13 major trophies:
6 League, 3 European Cup, 3 League Cup, 1 UEFA Cup.

Bill Struth – Rangers
1920–54, 30 major trophies:
18 League, 10 Scottish Cup, 2 League Cup.

CONSECUTIVE LEAGUE TITLES

4   Manchester C   2020–21 to 2023–24

MOST FA CUP WINNERS MEDALS

Ashley Cole 7 (Arsenal 2002, 2003, 2005; Chelsea 2007, 2009, 2010, 2012).

MOST LEAGUE WINNERS MEDALS

Ryan Giggs (Manchester U) 13: 1993, 1994, 1996, 1997, 1999, 2000, 2001, 2003, 2007, 2008, 2009, 2011 and 2013.

MOST SENIOR MATCHES

1,390 Peter Shilton (1,005 League, 86 FA Cup, 102 League Cup, 125 Internationals, 13 Under-23, 4 Football League XI, 20 European Cup, 7 Texaco Cup, 5 Simod Cup, 4 European Super Cup, 4 UEFA Cup, 3 Screen Sport Super Cup, 3 Zenith Data Systems Cup, 2 Autoglass Trophy, 2 Charity Shield, 2 Full Members Cup, 1 Anglo-Italian Cup, 1 Football League play-offs, 1 World Club Championship)

MOST LEAGUE APPEARANCES (750+)

1,005 Peter Shilton (286 Leicester C, 110 Stoke C, 202 Nottingham F, 188 Southampton, 175 Derby Co, 34 Plymouth Arg, 1 Bolton W, 9 Leyton Orient) 1966–97

931 Tony Ford (355 Grimsby T, 9 Sunderland (loan), 112 Stoke C, 114 WBA, 68 Grimsby T, 5 Bradford C (loan), 76 Scunthorpe U, 103 Mansfield T, 89 Rochdale) 1975–2002

909 Graeme Armstrong (204 Stirling A, 83 Berwick Rangers, 353 Meadowbank Thistle, 268 Stenhousemuir, 1 Alloa Ath) 1975–2001

863 Tommy Hutchison (165 Blackpool, 314 Coventry C, 46 Manchester C, 92 Burnley, 178 Swansea C, 68 Alloa Ath) 1965–91

833 Graham Alexander (33 Scunthorpe U, 150 Luton T, 370 Preston NE, 154 Burnley) 1990–2012

824 Terry Paine (713 Southampton, 111 Hereford U) 1957–77

820 Dean Lewington (29 Wimbledon, 791 Milton Keynes D) 2002–25

791 Luke Chambers (124 Northampton T, 205 Nottingham F, 376 Ipswich T, 86 Colchester U) 2002–23

790 Neil Redfearn (35 Bolton W, 10 Lincoln C (loan), 90 Lincoln C, 46 Doncaster R, 57 Crystal Palace, 24 Watford, 62 Oldham Ath, 292 Barnsley, 30 Charlton Ath, 17 Bradford C, 22 Wigan Ath, 42 Halifax T, 54 Boston U, 9 Rochdale) 1982–2004

788 David James (89 Watford, 214 Liverpool, 67 Aston Villa, 91 West Ham U, 93 Manchester C, 134 Portsmouth, 81 Bristol C, 19 Bournemouth) 1988–2013

782 Robbie James (484 Swansea C, 48 Stoke C, 87 QPR, 23 Leicester C, 89 Bradford C, 51 Cardiff C) 1973–94

778 Peter Clarke (9 Everton, 13 Port Vale (loan), 139 Blackpool, 5 Coventry C (loan), 126 Southend U, 192 Huddersfield T, 63 Bury, 107 Oldham Ath, 12 Fleetwood T, 98 Tranmere R, 14 Walsall) 1998–2023

777 Alan Oakes (565 Manchester C, 211 Chester C, 1 Port Vale) 1959–84

774 Dave Beasant (340 Wimbledon, 20 Newcastle U, 133 Chelsea, 6 Grimsby T (loan), 4 Wolverhampton W (loan), 88 Southampton, 139 Nottingham F, 27 Portsmouth, 1 Portsmouth H (loan), 16 Brighton & HA) 1979–2003

771 John Burridge (27 Workington, 134 Blackpool, 65 Aston Villa, 6 Southend U (loan), 88 Crystal Palace, 39 QPR, 74 Wolverhampton W, 6 Derby Co (loan), 109 Sheffield U, 62 Southampton, 67 Newcastle U, 65 Hibernian, 3 Scarborough, 4 Lincoln C, 3 Aberdeen, 3 Dumbarton, 3 Falkirk, 4 Manchester C, 3 Darlington, 6 Queen of the S) 1968–96

770 John Trollope (all for Swindon T) 1960–80†

764 Jimmy Dickinson (all for Portsmouth) 1946–65

763 Stuart McCall (395 Bradford C, 103 Everton, 194 Rangers, 71 Sheffield U) 1982–2004

761 Roy Sproson (all for Port Vale) 1950–72

760 Mick Tait (64 Oxford U, 106 Carlisle U, 33 Hull C, 240 Portsmouth, 99 Reading, 79 Darlington, 139 Hartlepool U) 1975–97

758 Ray Clemence (48 Scunthorpe U, 470 Liverpool, 240 Tottenham H) 1966–87

758 Billy Bonds (95 Charlton Ath, 663 West Ham U) 1964–88

757 Pat Jennings (48 Watford, 472 Tottenham H, 237 Arsenal) 1963–86

757 Frank Worthington (171 Huddersfield T, 210 Leicester C, 84 Bolton W, 75 Birmingham C, 32 Leeds U, 19 Sunderland, 34 Southampton, 31 Brighton & HA, 59 Tranmere R, 23 Preston NE, 19 Stockport Co) 1966–88

755 Jamie Cureton (98 Norwich C, 5 Bournemouth (loan), 174 Bristol R, 108 Reading, 43 QPR, 30 Swindon T, 52 Colchester U, 8 Barnsley (loan), 12 Shrewsbury T (loan), 88 Exeter C, 19 Leyton Orient, 35 Cheltenham T, 83 Dagenham & Red) 1992–2016

753 Andy Millen (71 St Johnstone, 111 Alloa Ath, 119 Hamilton A, 57 Kilmarnock, 51, Hibernian, 18 Raith R, 60 Ayr U, 44 Greenock Morton, 89 Clyde, 114 St Mirren, 19 Queen's Park) 1986–2012

752 Wayne Allison (84 Halifax T, 7 Watford, 195 Bristol C, 101 Swindon T, 74 Huddersfield T, 103 Tranmere R, 73 Sheffield U, 115 Chesterfield) 1987–2008

† *record for one club*

CONSECUTIVE
401 Harold Bell (401 Tranmere R; 459 in all games) 1946–55

YOUNGEST PLAYERS

FA Premier League appearance
Ethan Nwaneri, 15 years 181 days, Arsenal v Brentford, 19.9.2022

FA Premier League scorer
James Vaughan, 16 years 271 days, Everton v Crystal Palace 10.4.2005

Football League appearance
Reuben Noble-Lazarus, 15 years 45 days, Barnsley v Ipswich T, FL Championship 30.9.2008

Football League scorer
Ronnie Dix, 15 years 180 days, Bristol Rovers v Norwich C, Division 3S, 3.3.1928

FA Cup appearance (any round)
Andy Awford, 15 years 88 days as substitute Worcester City v Boreham Wood, 3rd Qual. rd, 10.10.1987

FA Cup goalscorer
Finn Smith, 16 years 0 days, Newport (IoW) v Fleet T (Extra Preliminary Round), 6.8.2022

FA Cup appearance (competition rounds)
Chris Rigg, 15 years 203 days, Sunderland v Shrewsbury T, (Third Round) 7.2.2023

FA Cup Final appearance
Curtis Weston, 17 years 119 days, Millwall v Manchester U, 22.5.2004

FA Cup Final scorer
Norman Whiteside, 18 years 18 days, Manchester United v Brighton & HA, 1983

FA Cup Final captain
David Nish, 21 years 212 days, Leicester C v Manchester U, 1969

League Cup appearance
Harvey Elliott, 15 years and 174 days, Millwall v Fulham (Third Round), 25.9.18

League Cup goalscorer
Connor Wickham, 16 years 133 days, Ipswich T v Shrewsbury T, 11.8.2009

League Cup Final scorer
Norman Whiteside, 17 years 324 days, Manchester U v Liverpool, 1983

League Cup Final captain
Barry Venison, 20 years 7 months 8 days, Sunderland v Norwich C, 1985

Scottish Premiership appearance
Dylan Reid, 16 years 5 days, St Mirren v Rangers, 6.3.2021

Scottish Football League appearance
Jordan Allan, 14 years 189 days, Airdrie U v Livingston, 26.4.2013

Scottish Premiership scorer
Fraser Fyvie, 16 years 306 days, Aberdeen v Hearts, 27.1.2010

OLDEST PLAYERS

FA Premier League appearance
John Burridge, 43 years 162 days, Manchester C v QPR, 14.5.95

Football League appearance
Neil McBain, 52 years 4 months, New Brighton v Hartlepools U, Div 3N, 15.3.47 (McBain was New Brighton's manager and had to play in an emergency)

Division 1 appearance
Stanley Matthews, 50 years 5 days, Stoke C v Fulham, 6.2.65

INTERNATIONAL RECORDS

MOST GOALS IN AN INTERNATIONAL

Record/World Cup (13 goals)   Archie Thompson (Australia) v American Samoa (11.4.2001)

England (5 goals)   Howard Vaughton (Aston Villa) v Ireland, at Belfast (18.2.1882); Steve Bloomer (Derby Co) v Wales, at Cardiff (16.3.1896); Willie Hall (Tottenham H) v N. Ireland, at Old Trafford (16.11.1938); Malcolm Macdonald (Newcastle U) v Cyprus, at Wembley (16.4.1975)

Scotland (4 goals)   Alexander Higgins (Kilmarnock) v Ireland, at Hampden Park (14.3.1885); Charles Heggie (Rangers) v Ireland, at Belfast (20.3.1886); William Dickson (Dundee Strathmore) v Ireland, at Belfast (24.3.1888); William Paul (Partick Thistle) v Wales, at Paisley (22.3.1890); Jake Madden (Celtic) v Wales, at Wrexham (18.3.1893); Duke McMahon (Celtic) v Ireland, at Celtic Park (23.2.1901); Bob Hamilton (Rangers) v Ireland, at Celtic Park (23.2.1901); Jimmy Quinn (Celtic) v Ireland, at Dublin (14.3.1908); Hughie Gallacher (Newcastle U) v N. Ireland, at Belfast (23.2.1929); Billy Steel (Dundee) v N. Ireland, at Hampden Park (1.11.1950); Denis Law (Manchester U) v N. Ireland, at Hampden Park (7.11.1962); Denis Law (Manchester U) v Norway, at Hampden Park (7.11.1963); Colin Stein (Rangers) v Cyprus, at Hampden Park (17.5.1969)

Wales (4 goals)   John Price (Wrexham) v Ireland, at Wrexham (25.2.1882); John Doughty (Newton Heath) v Ireland, at Wrexham (3.3.1888); Mel Charles (Cardiff C) v N. Ireland, at Cardiff (11.4.1962); Ian Edwards (Chester) v Malta, at Wrexham (25.10.1978)

Northern Ireland (6 goals)   Joe Bambrick (Linfield) v Wales, at Belfast (1.2.1930)

Republic of Ireland (4 goals)   Paddy Moore (Aberdeen) v Belguim, at Dublin (25.2.1934); Don Givens (QPR) v Turkey, at Dublin (29.10.1975)

MOST GOALS IN AN INTERNATIONAL CAREER

		Goals	Games
England	Harry Kane (Tottenham H, Bayern Munich)	73	107
Scotland	Denis Law (Huddersfield T, Manchester C, Torino, Manchester U)	30	55
	Kenny Dalglish (Celtic, Liverpool)	30	102
Northern Ireland	David Healy (Manchester U, Preston NE, Leeds U, Fulham, Sunderland, Rangers, Bury)	36	95
Wales	Gareth Bale (Southampton, Tottenham H, Real Madrid)	41	111
Republic of Ireland	Robbie Keane (Wolverhampton W, Coventry C, Internazionale, Leeds U, Tottenham H, Liverpool, Tottenham H, LA Galaxy)	68	146

HIGHEST SCORES

World Cup Match	Australia	31	American Samoa	0	2001
European Championship	San Marino	0	Germany	13	2006
Olympic Games	Denmark	17	France	1	1908
	Germany	16	Russia	0	1912
Olympic Qualifying Tournament	Vanuatu	46	Micronesia	0	2015
Other International Match	Libya	21	Oman	0	1966
	Abandoned after 80 minutes as Oman refused to play on.				
European Cup	KR Reykjavik	2	Feyenoord	12	1969
European Cup-Winners' Cup	Sporting Lisbon	16	Apoel Nicosia	1	1963
Fairs & UEFA Cups	Ajax	14	Red Boys Differdange	0	1984

GOALSCORING RECORDS

World Cup Final	Geoff Hurst (England) 3 goals v West Germany	1966
	Kylian Mbappe (France) 3 goals v Argentina	2022
World Cup Final tournament	Just Fontaine (France) 13 goals	1958
World Cup career	Miroslav Klose (Germany) 16 goals	2002, 2006, 2010, 2014
Career	Artur Friedenreich (Brazil) 1,329 goals	1910–30
	Pele (Brazil) 1,281 goals	*1956–78
	Franz 'Bimbo' Binder (Austria, Germany) 1,006 goals	1930–50
World Cup Finals fastest	Hakan Sukur (Turkey) 10.8 secs v South Korea	2002
International Career	Cristiano Ronaldo (Portugal) 138 goals	2003–25

Pele subsequently scored two goals in Testimonial matches making his total 1,283.

MOST CAPPED INTERNATIONALS IN BRITAIN AND IRELAND

Republic of Ireland	Robbie Keane	146 appearances	1998–2016
Northern Ireland	Steven Davis	140 appearances	2005–2022
England	Peter Shilton	125 appearances	1970–1990
Wales	Gareth Bale	111 appearances	2007–2023
Scotland	Kenny Dalglish	102 appearances	1971–1986

THE PREMIER LEAGUE AND FOOTBALL LEAGUE FIXTURES
2025–26

All fixtures subject to change.
Fixtures may not take place on the designated date due to the involvement of one or both clubs in European competition.

Community Shield

Sunday, 10 August 2025
Crystal Palace v Liverpool

Premier League

Friday, 15 August 2025
Liverpool v Bournemouth

Saturday, 16 August 2025
Aston Villa v Newcastle U
Brighton & HA v Fulham
Nottingham F v Brentford
Sunderland v West Ham U
Tottenham H v Burnley
Wolverhampton W v Manchester C

Sunday, 17 August 2025
Chelsea v Crystal Palace
Manchester U v Arsenal

Monday, 18 August 2025
Leeds U v Everton

Saturday, 23 August 2025
Bournemouth v Wolverhampton W
Arsenal v Leeds U
Brentford v Aston Villa
Burnley v Sunderland
Crystal Palace v Nottingham F
Everton v Brighton & HA
Fulham v Manchester U
Manchester C v Tottenham H
Newcastle U v Liverpool
West Ham U v Chelsea

Saturday, 30 August 2025
Aston Villa v Crystal Palace
Brighton & HA v Manchester C
Chelsea v Fulham
Leeds U v Newcastle U
Liverpool v Arsenal
Manchester U v Burnley
Nottingham F v West Ham U
Sunderland v Brentford
Tottenham H v Bournemouth
Wolverhampton W v Everton

Saturday, 13 September 2025
Bournemouth v Brighton & HA
Arsenal v Nottingham F
Brentford v Chelsea
Burnley v Liverpool
Crystal Palace v Sunderland
Everton v Aston Villa
Fulham v Leeds U
Manchester C v Manchester U
Newcastle U v Wolverhampton W
West Ham U v Tottenham H

Saturday, 20 September 2025
Bournemouth v Newcastle U
Arsenal v Manchester C
Brighton & HA v Tottenham H
Burnley v Nottingham F
Fulham v Brentford
Liverpool v Everton
Manchester U v Chelsea
Sunderland v Aston Villa

West Ham U v Crystal Palace
Wolverhampton W v Leeds U

Saturday, 27 September 2025
Aston Villa v Fulham
Brentford v Manchester U
Chelsea v Brighton & HA
Crystal Palace v Liverpool
Everton v West Ham U
Leeds U v Bournemouth
Manchester C v Burnley
Newcastle U v Arsenal
Nottingham F v Sunderland
Tottenham H v Wolverhampton W

Saturday, 4 October 2025
Bournemouth v Fulham
Arsenal v West Ham U
Aston Villa v Burnley
Brentford v Manchester C
Chelsea v Liverpool
Everton v Crystal Palace
Leeds U v Tottenham H
Manchester U v Sunderland
Newcastle U v Nottingham F
Wolverhampton W v Brighton & HA

Saturday, 18 October 2025
Brighton & HA v Newcastle U
Burnley v Leeds U
Crystal Palace v Bournemouth
Fulham v Arsenal
Liverpool v Manchester U
Manchester C v Everton
Nottingham F v Chelsea
Sunderland v Wolverhampton W
Tottenham H v Aston Villa
West Ham U v Brentford

Saturday, 25 October 2025
Bournemouth v Nottingham F
Arsenal v Crystal Palace
Aston Villa v Manchester C
Brentford v Liverpool
Chelsea v Sunderland
Everton v Tottenham H
Leeds U v West Ham U
Manchester U v Brighton & HA
Newcastle U v Fulham
Wolverhampton W v Burnley

Saturday, 1 November 2025
Brighton & HA v Leeds U
Burnley v Arsenal
Crystal Palace v Brentford
Fulham v Wolverhampton W
Liverpool v Aston Villa
Manchester C v Bournemouth
Nottingham F v Manchester U
Sunderland v Everton
Tottenham H v Chelsea
West Ham U v Newcastle U

Saturday, 8 November 2025
Aston Villa v Bournemouth
Brentford v Newcastle U
Chelsea v Wolverhampton W
Crystal Palace v Brighton & HA
Everton v Fulham
Manchester C v Liverpool

Nottingham F v Leeds U
Sunderland v Arsenal
Tottenham H v Manchester U
West Ham U v Burnley

Saturday, 22 November 2025
Bournemouth v West Ham U
Arsenal v Tottenham H
Brighton & HA v Brentford
Burnley v Chelsea
Fulham v Sunderland
Leeds U v Aston Villa
Liverpool v Nottingham F
Manchester U v Everton
Newcastle U v Manchester C
Wolverhampton W v Crystal Palace

Saturday, 29 November 2025
Aston Villa v Wolverhampton W
Brentford v Burnley
Chelsea v Arsenal
Crystal Palace v Manchester U
Everton v Newcastle U
Manchester C v Leeds U
Nottingham F v Brighton & HA
Sunderland v Bournemouth
Tottenham H v Fulham
West Ham U v Liverpool

Wednesday, 3 December 2025
Bournemouth v Everton
Arsenal v Brentford
Brighton & HA v Aston Villa
Burnley v Crystal Palace
Fulham v Manchester C
Leeds U v Chelsea
Liverpool v Sunderland
Manchester U v West Ham U
Newcastle U v Tottenham H
Wolverhampton W v Nottingham F

Saturday, 6 December 2025
Bournemouth v Chelsea
Aston Villa v Arsenal
Brighton & HA v West Ham U
Everton v Nottingham F
Fulham v Crystal Palace
Leeds U v Liverpool
Manchester C v Sunderland
Newcastle U v Burnley
Tottenham H v Brentford
Wolverhampton W v Manchester U

Saturday, 13 December 2025
Arsenal v Wolverhampton W
Brentford v Leeds U
Burnley v Fulham
Chelsea v Everton
Crystal Palace v Manchester C
Liverpool v Brighton & HA
Manchester U v Bournemouth
Nottingham F v Tottenham H
Sunderland v Newcastle U
West Ham U v Aston Villa

Saturday, 20 December 2025
Bournemouth v Burnley
Aston Villa v Manchester U
Brighton & HA v Sunderland
Everton v Arsenal

Fulham v Nottingham F
Leeds U v Crystal Palace
Manchester C v West Ham U
Newcastle U v Chelsea
Tottenham H v Liverpool
Wolverhampton W v Brentford

Saturday, 27 December 2025
Arsenal v Brighton & HA
Brentford v Bournemouth
Burnley v Everton
Chelsea v Aston Villa
Crystal Palace v Tottenham H
Liverpool v Wolverhampton W
Manchester U v Newcastle U
Nottingham F v Manchester C
Sunderland v Leeds U
West Ham U v Fulham

Tuesday, 30 December 2025
Arsenal v Aston Villa
Brentford v Tottenham H
Burnley v Newcastle U
Chelsea v Bournemouth
Crystal Palace v Fulham
Liverpool v Leeds U
Manchester U v Wolverhampton W
Nottingham F v Everton
Sunderland v Manchester C
West Ham U v Brighton & HA

Saturday, 3 January 2026
Bournemouth v Arsenal
Aston Villa v Nottingham F
Brighton & HA v Burnley
Everton v Brentford
Fulham v Liverpool
Leeds U v Manchester U
Manchester C v Chelsea
Newcastle U v Crystal Palace
Tottenham H v Sunderland
Wolverhampton W v West Ham U

Wednesday, 7 January 2026
Bournemouth v Tottenham H
Arsenal v Liverpool
Brentford v Sunderland
Burnley v Manchester U
Crystal Palace v Aston Villa
Everton v Wolverhampton W
Fulham v Chelsea
Manchester C v Brighton & HA
Newcastle U v Leeds U
West Ham U v Nottingham F

Saturday, 17 January 2026
Aston Villa v Everton
Brighton & HA v Bournemouth
Chelsea v Brentford
Leeds U v Fulham
Liverpool v Burnley
Manchester U v Manchester C
Nottingham F v Arsenal
Sunderland v Crystal Palace
Tottenham H v West Ham U
Wolverhampton W v Newcastle U

Saturday, 24 January 2026
Bournemouth v Liverpool
Arsenal v Manchester U
Brentford v Nottingham F
Burnley v Tottenham H
Crystal Palace v Chelsea
Everton v Leeds U
Fulham v Brighton & HA
Manchester C v Wolverhampton W
Newcastle U v Aston Villa
West Ham U v Sunderland

Saturday, 31 January 2026
Aston Villa v Brentford
Brighton & HA v Everton

Chelsea v West Ham U
Leeds U v Arsenal
Liverpool v Newcastle U
Manchester U v Fulham
Nottingham F v Crystal Palace
Sunderland v Burnley
Tottenham H v Manchester C
Wolverhampton W v Bournemouth

Saturday, 7 February 2026
Bournemouth v Aston Villa
Arsenal v Sunderland
Brighton & HA v Crystal Palace
Burnley v West Ham U
Fulham v Everton
Leeds U v Nottingham F
Liverpool v Manchester C
Manchester U v Tottenham H
Newcastle U v Brentford
Wolverhampton W v Chelsea

Wednesday, 11 February 2026
Aston Villa v Brighton & HA
Brentford v Arsenal
Chelsea v Leeds U
Crystal Palace v Burnley
Everton v Bournemouth
Manchester C v Fulham
Nottingham F v Wolverhampton W
Sunderland v Liverpool
Tottenham H v Newcastle U
West Ham U v Manchester U

Saturday, 21 February 2026
Aston Villa v Leeds U
Brentford v Brighton & HA
Chelsea v Burnley
Crystal Palace v Wolverhampton W
Everton v Manchester U
Manchester C v Newcastle U
Nottingham F v Liverpool
Sunderland v Fulham
Tottenham H v Arsenal
West Ham U v Bournemouth

Saturday, 28 February 2026
Bournemouth v Sunderland
Arsenal v Chelsea
Brighton & HA v Nottingham F
Burnley v Brentford
Fulham v Tottenham H
Leeds U v Manchester C
Liverpool v West Ham U
Manchester U v Crystal Palace
Newcastle U v Everton
Wolverhampton W v Aston Villa

Wednesday, 4 March 2026
Bournemouth v Brentford
Aston Villa v Chelsea
Brighton & HA v Arsenal
Everton v Burnley
Fulham v West Ham U
Leeds U v Sunderland
Manchester C v Nottingham F
Newcastle U v Manchester U
Tottenham H v Crystal Palace
Wolverhampton W v Liverpool

Saturday, 14 March 2026
Arsenal v Everton
Brentford v Wolverhampton W
Burnley v Bournemouth
Chelsea v Newcastle U
Crystal Palace v Leeds U
Liverpool v Tottenham H
Manchester U v Aston Villa
Nottingham F v Fulham
Sunderland v Brighton & HA
West Ham U v Manchester C

Saturday, 21 March 2026
Bournemouth v Manchester U
Aston Villa v West Ham U
Brighton & HA v Liverpool
Everton v Chelsea
Fulham v Burnley
Leeds U v Brentford
Manchester C v Crystal Palace
Newcastle U v Sunderland
Tottenham H v Nottingham F
Wolverhampton W v Arsenal

Saturday, 11 April 2026
Arsenal v Bournemouth
Brentford v Everton
Burnley v Brighton & HA
Chelsea v Manchester C
Crystal Palace v Newcastle U
Liverpool v Fulham
Manchester U v Leeds U
Nottingham F v Aston Villa
Sunderland v Tottenham H
West Ham U v Wolverhampton W

Saturday, 18 April 2026
Aston Villa v Sunderland
Brentford v Fulham
Chelsea v Manchester U
Crystal Palace v West Ham U
Everton v Liverpool
Leeds U v Wolverhampton W
Manchester C v Arsenal
Newcastle U v Bournemouth
Nottingham F v Burnley
Tottenham H v Brighton & HA

Saturday, 25 April 2026
Bournemouth v Leeds U
Arsenal v Newcastle U
Brighton & HA v Chelsea
Burnley v Manchester C
Fulham v Aston Villa
Liverpool v Crystal Palace
Manchester U v Brentford
Sunderland v Nottingham F
West Ham U v Everton
Wolverhampton W v Tottenham H

Saturday, 2 May 2026
Bournemouth v Crystal Palace
Arsenal v Fulham
Aston Villa v Tottenham H
Brentford v West Ham U
Chelsea v Nottingham F
Everton v Manchester C
Leeds U v Burnley
Manchester U v Liverpool
Newcastle U v Brighton & HA
Wolverhampton W v Sunderland

Saturday, 9 May 2026
Brighton & HA v Wolverhampton W
Burnley v Aston Villa
Crystal Palace v Everton
Fulham v Bournemouth
Liverpool v Chelsea
Manchester C v Brentford
Nottingham F v Newcastle U
Sunderland v Manchester U
Tottenham H v Leeds U
West Ham U v Arsenal

Sunday, 17 May 2026
Bournemouth v Manchester C
Arsenal v Burnley
Aston Villa v Liverpool
Brentford v Crystal Palace
Chelsea v Tottenham H
Everton v Sunderland
Leeds U v Brighton & HA
Manchester U v Nottingham F
Newcastle U v West Ham U
Wolverhampton W v Fulham

Sunday, 24 May 2026
Brighton & HA v Manchester U
Burnley v Wolverhampton W
Crystal Palace v Arsenal
Fulham v Newcastle U
Liverpool v Brentford
Manchester C v Aston Villa
Nottingham F v Bournemouth
Sunderland v Chelsea
Tottenham H v Everton
West Ham U v Leeds U

EFL Championship

Friday, 8 August 2025
Birmingham C v Ipswich T

Saturday, 9 August 2025
Charlton Ath v Watford
Coventry C v Hull C
Middlesbrough v Swansea C
Norwich C v Millwall
Oxford U v Portsmouth
QPR v Preston NE
Sheffield U v Bristol C
Southampton v Wrexham
Stoke C v Derby Co
WBA v Blackburn R

Sunday, 10 August 2025
Leicester C v Sheffield Wed

Saturday, 16 August 2025
Blackburn R v Birmingham C
Bristol C v Charlton Ath
Derby Co v Coventry C
Hull C v Oxford U
Ipswich T v Southampton
Millwall v Middlesbrough
Portsmouth v Norwich C
Preston NE v Leicester C
Sheffield Wed v Stoke C
Swansea C v Sheffield U
Watford v QPR
Wrexham v WBA

Saturday, 23 August 2025
Birmingham C v Oxford U
Charlton Ath v Leicester C
Coventry C v QPR
Derby Co v Bristol C
Hull C v Blackburn R
Norwich C v Middlesbrough
Preston NE v Ipswich T
Sheffield U v Millwall
Southampton v Stoke C
Swansea C v Watford
WBA v Portsmouth
Wrexham v Sheffield Wed

Saturday, 30 August 2025
Blackburn R v Norwich C
Bristol C v Hull C
Ipswich T v Derby Co
Leicester C v Birmingham C
Middlesbrough v Sheffield U
Millwall v Wrexham
Oxford U v Coventry C
Portsmouth v Preston NE
QPR v Charlton Ath
Sheffield Wed v Swansea C
Stoke C v WBA
Watford v Southampton

Saturday, 13 September 2025
Charlton Ath v Millwall
Coventry C v Norwich C
Ipswich T v Sheffield U
Oxford U v Leicester C
Preston NE v Middlesbrough
Sheffield Wed v Bristol C
Southampton v Portsmouth

Stoke C v Birmingham C
Swansea C v Hull C
Watford v Blackburn R
WBA v Derby Co
Wrexham v QPR

Saturday, 20 September 2025
Birmingham C v Swansea C
Blackburn R v Ipswich T
Bristol C v Oxford U
Derby Co v Preston NE
Hull C v Southampton
Leicester C v Coventry C
Middlesbrough v WBA
Millwall v Watford
Norwich C v Wrexham
Portsmouth v Sheffield Wed
QPR v Stoke C
Sheffield U v Charlton Ath

Saturday, 27 September 2025
Charlton Ath v Blackburn R
Coventry C v Birmingham C
Ipswich T v Portsmouth
Oxford U v Sheffield U
Preston NE v Bristol C
Sheffield Wed v QPR
Southampton v Middlesbrough
Stoke C v Norwich C
Swansea C v Millwall
Watford v Hull C
WBA v Leicester C
Wrexham v Derby Co

Tuesday, 30 September 2025
Birmingham C v Sheffield Wed
Blackburn R v Swansea C
Bristol C v Ipswich T
Derby Co v Charlton Ath
Hull C v Preston NE
Leicester C v Wrexham
Middlesbrough v Stoke C
Sheffield U v Southampton

Wednesday, 1 October 2025
Millwall v Coventry C
Norwich C v WBA
Portsmouth v Watford
QPR v Oxford U

Saturday, 4 October 2025
Blackburn R v Stoke C
Bristol C v QPR
Derby Co v Southampton
Hull C v Sheffield U
Ipswich T v Norwich C
Millwall v WBA
Portsmouth v Middlesbrough
Preston NE v Charlton Ath
Sheffield Wed v Coventry C
Swansea C v Leicester C
Watford v Oxford U
Wrexham v Birmingham C

Saturday, 18 October 2025
Birmingham C v Hull C
Charlton Ath v Sheffield Wed
Coventry C v Blackburn R
Leicester C v Portsmouth
Middlesbrough v Ipswich T
Norwich C v Bristol C
Oxford U v Derby Co
QPR v Millwall
Sheffield U v Watford
Southampton v Swansea C
Stoke C v Wrexham
WBA v Preston NE

Tuesday, 21 October 2025
Blackburn R v Sheffield U
Bristol C v Southampton
Derby Co v Norwich C
Hull C v Leicester C

Ipswich T v Charlton Ath
Millwall v Stoke C
Portsmouth v Coventry C
Preston NE v Birmingham C

Wednesday, 22 October 2025
Sheffield Wed v Middlesbrough
Swansea C v QPR
Watford v WBA
Wrexham v Oxford U

Saturday, 25 October 2025
Blackburn R v Southampton
Bristol C v Birmingham C
Coventry C v Watford
Derby Co v QPR
Hull C v Charlton Ath
Ipswich T v WBA
Middlesbrough v Wrexham
Millwall v Leicester C
Portsmouth v Stoke C
Preston NE v Sheffield U
Sheffield Wed v Oxford U
Swansea C v Norwich C

Tuesday, 11 November 2025
Birmingham C v Portsmouth
Charlton Ath v Swansea C
Leicester C v Blackburn R
Norwich C v Hull C
Oxford U v Millwall
QPR v Ipswich T
Sheffield U v Derby Co
Southampton v Preston NE
Stoke C v Bristol C
Watford v Middlesbrough
WBA v Sheffield Wed
Wrexham v Coventry C

Tuesday, 4 November 2025
Birmingham C v Millwall
Bristol C v Blackburn R
Charlton Ath v WBA
Coventry C v Sheffield U
Derby Co v Hull C
Ipswich T v Watford
Leicester C v Middlesbrough
Oxford U v Stoke C

Wednesday, 5 November 2025
Portsmouth v Wrexham
Preston NE v Swansea C
QPR v Southampton
Sheffield Wed v Norwich C

Saturday, 8 November 2025
Blackburn R v Derby Co
Hull C v Portsmouth
Middlesbrough v Birmingham C
Millwall v Preston NE
Norwich C v Leicester C
Sheffield U v QPR
Southampton v Sheffield Wed
Stoke C v Coventry C
Swansea C v Ipswich T
Watford v Bristol C
WBA v Oxford U
Wrexham v Charlton Ath

Saturday, 22 November 2025
Birmingham C v Norwich C
Bristol C v Swansea C
Charlton Ath v Southampton
Coventry C v WBA
Derby Co v Watford
Ipswich T v Wrexham
Leicester C v Stoke C
Oxford U v Middlesbrough
Portsmouth v Millwall
Preston NE v Blackburn R
QPR v Hull C
Sheffield Wed v Sheffield U

Tuesday, 25 November 2025
Hull C v Ipswich T
Middlesbrough v Coventry C
Millwall v Sheffield Wed
Sheffield U v Portsmouth
Southampton v Leicester C
Stoke C v Charlton Ath
Swansea C v Derby Co
Watford v Preston NE

Wednesday, 26 November 2025
Blackburn R v QPR
Norwich C v Oxford U
WBA v Birmingham C
Wrexham v Bristol C

Saturday, 29 November 2025
Birmingham C v Watford
Coventry C v Charlton Ath
Leicester C v Sheffield U
Middlesbrough v Derby Co
Millwall v Southampton
Norwich C v QPR
Oxford U v Ipswich T
Portsmouth v Bristol C
Sheffield Wed v Preston NE
Stoke C v Hull C
WBA v Swansea C
Wrexham v Blackburn R

Saturday, 6 December 2025
Blackburn R v Sheffield Wed
Bristol C v Millwall
Charlton Ath v Portsmouth
Derby Co v Leicester C
Hull C v Middlesbrough
Ipswich T v Coventry C
Preston NE v Wrexham
QPR v WBA
Sheffield U v Stoke C
Southampton v Birmingham C
Swansea C v Oxford U
Watford v Norwich C

Tuesday, 9 December 2025
Blackburn R v Oxford U
Charlton Ath v Middlesbrough
Preston NE v Coventry C
QPR v Birmingham C
Sheffield U v Norwich C
Southampton v WBA
Swansea C v Portsmouth
Watford v Sheffield Wed

Wednesday, 10 December 2025
Bristol C v Leicester C
Derby Co v Millwall
Hull C v Wrexham
Ipswich T v Stoke C

Saturday, 13 December 2025
Birmingham C v Charlton Ath
Coventry C v Bristol C
Leicester C v Ipswich T
Middlesbrough v QPR
Millwall v Hull C
Norwich C v Southampton
Oxford U v Preston NE
Portsmouth v Blackburn R
Sheffield Wed v Derby Co
Stoke C v Swansea C
WBA v Sheffield U
Wrexham v Watford

Saturday, 20 December 2025
Blackburn R v Millwall
Bristol C v Middlesbrough
Charlton Ath v Oxford U
Derby Co v Portsmouth
Hull C v WBA
Ipswich T v Sheffield Wed
Preston NE v Norwich C
QPR v Leicester C

Sheffield U v Birmingham C
Southampton v Coventry C
Swansea C v Wrexham
Watford v Stoke C

Friday, 26 December 2025
Birmingham C v Derby Co
Coventry C v Swansea C
Leicester C v Watford
Middlesbrough v Blackburn R
Millwall v Ipswich T
Norwich C v Charlton Ath
Oxford U v Southampton
Portsmouth v QPR
Sheffield Wed v Hull C
Stoke C v Preston NE
WBA v Bristol C
Wrexham v Sheffield U

Monday, 29 December 2025
Birmingham C v Southampton
Coventry C v Ipswich T
Leicester C v Derby Co
Middlesbrough v Hull C
Millwall v Bristol C
Norwich C v Watford
Oxford U v Swansea C
Portsmouth v Charlton Ath
Sheffield Wed v Blackburn R
Stoke C v Sheffield U
WBA v QPR
Wrexham v Preston NE

Thursday, 1 January 2026
Blackburn R v Wrexham
Bristol C v Portsmouth
Charlton Ath v Coventry C
Derby Co v Middlesbrough
Hull C v Stoke C
Ipswich T v Oxford U
Preston NE v Sheffield Wed
QPR v Norwich C
Sheffield U v Leicester C
Southampton v Millwall
Swansea C v WBA
Watford v Birmingham C

Sunday, 4 January 2026
Birmingham C v Coventry C
Blackburn R v Charlton Ath
Bristol C v Preston NE
Derby Co v Wrexham
Hull C v Watford
Leicester C v WBA
Middlesbrough v Southampton
Millwall v Swansea C
Norwich C v Stoke C
Portsmouth v Ipswich T
QPR v Sheffield Wed
Sheffield U v Oxford U

Saturday, 17 January 2026
Charlton Ath v Sheffield U
Coventry C v Leicester C
Ipswich T v Blackburn R
Oxford U v Bristol C
Preston NE v Derby Co
Sheffield Wed v Portsmouth
Southampton v Hull C
Stoke C v QPR
Swansea C v Birmingham C
Watford v Millwall
WBA v Middlesbrough
Wrexham v Norwich C

Tuesday, 20 January 2026
Coventry C v Millwall
Ipswich T v Bristol C
Oxford U v QPR
Preston NE v Hull C
Sheffield Wed v Birmingham C
Swansea C v Blackburn R

WBA v Norwich C
Wrexham v Leicester C

Wednesday, 21 January 2026
Charlton Ath v Derby Co
Southampton v Sheffield U
Stoke C v Middlesbrough
Watford v Portsmouth

Saturday, 24 January 2026
Birmingham C v Stoke C
Blackburn R v Watford
Bristol C v Sheffield Wed
Derby Co v WBA
Hull C v Swansea C
Leicester C v Oxford U
Middlesbrough v Preston NE
Millwall v Charlton Ath
Norwich C v Coventry C
Portsmouth v Southampton
QPR v Wrexham
Sheffield U v Ipswich T

Saturday, 31 January 2026
Blackburn R v Hull C
Bristol C v Derby Co
Ipswich T v Preston NE
Leicester C v Charlton Ath
Middlesbrough v Norwich C
Millwall v Sheffield U
Oxford U v Birmingham C
Portsmouth v WBA
QPR v Coventry C
Sheffield Wed v Wrexham
Stoke C v Southampton
Watford v Swansea C

Saturday, 7 February 2026
Birmingham C v Leicester C
Charlton Ath v QPR
Coventry C v Oxford U
Derby Co v Ipswich T
Hull C v Bristol C
Norwich C v Blackburn R
Preston NE v Portsmouth
Sheffield U v Middlesbrough
Southampton v Watford
Swansea C v Sheffield Wed
WBA v Stoke C
Wrexham v Millwall

Saturday, 14 February 2026
Birmingham C v WBA
Bristol C v Wrexham
Charlton Ath v Stoke C
Coventry C v Middlesbrough
Derby Co v Swansea C
Ipswich T v Hull C
Leicester C v Southampton
Oxford U v Norwich C
Portsmouth v Sheffield U
Preston NE v Watford
QPR v Blackburn R
Sheffield Wed v Millwall

Saturday, 21 February 2026
Blackburn R v Preston NE
Hull C v QPR
Middlesbrough v Oxford U
Millwall v Portsmouth
Norwich C v Birmingham C
Sheffield U v Sheffield Wed
Southampton v Charlton Ath
Stoke C v Leicester C
Swansea C v Bristol C
Watford v Derby Co
WBA v Coventry C
Wrexham v Ipswich T

Tuesday, 24 February 2026
Hull C v Derby Co
Middlesbrough v Leicester C
Southampton v QPR

Stoke C v Oxford U
Swansea C v Preston NE
Watford v Ipswich T
WBA v Charlton Ath
Wrexham v Portsmouth

Wednesday, 25 February 2026
Blackburn R v Bristol C
Millwall v Birmingham C
Norwich C v Sheffield Wed
Sheffield U v Coventry C

Saturday, 28 February 2026
Birmingham C v Middlesbrough
Bristol C v Watford
Charlton Ath v Wrexham
Coventry C v Stoke C
Derby Co v Blackburn R
Ipswich T v Swansea C
Leicester C v Norwich C
Oxford U v WBA
Portsmouth v Hull C
Preston NE v Millwall
QPR v Sheffield U
Sheffield Wed v Southampton

Saturday, 7 March 2026
Blackburn R v Portsmouth
Bristol C v Coventry C
Charlton Ath v Birmingham C
Derby Co v Sheffield Wed
Hull C v Millwall
Ipswich T v Leicester C
Preston NE v Oxford U
QPR v Middlesbrough
Sheffield U v WBA
Southampton v Norwich C
Swansea C v Stoke C
Watford v Wrexham

Tuesday, 10 March 2026
Birmingham C v QPR
Leicester C v Bristol C
Millwall v Derby Co
Norwich C v Sheffield U
Portsmouth v Swansea C
Sheffield Wed v Watford
Stoke C v Ipswich T
Wrexham v Hull C

Wednesday, 11 March 2026
Coventry C v Preston NE
Middlesbrough v Charlton Ath
Oxford U v Blackburn R
WBA v Southampton

Saturday, 14 March 2026
Birmingham C v Sheffield U
Coventry C v Southampton
Leicester C v QPR
Middlesbrough v Bristol C
Millwall v Blackburn R
Norwich C v Preston NE
Oxford U v Charlton Ath
Portsmouth v Derby Co
Sheffield Wed v Ipswich T
Stoke C v Watford
WBA v Hull C
Wrexham v Swansea C

Saturday, 21 March 2026
Blackburn R v Middlesbrough
Bristol C v WBA
Charlton Ath v Norwich C
Derby Co v Birmingham C
Hull C v Sheffield Wed
Ipswich T v Millwall
Preston NE v Stoke C
QPR v Portsmouth
Sheffield U v Wrexham
Southampton v Oxford U
Swansea C v Coventry C
Watford v Leicester C

Friday, 3 April 2026
Birmingham C v Blackburn R
Charlton Ath v Bristol C
Coventry C v Derby Co
Leicester C v Preston NE
Middlesbrough v Millwall
Norwich C v Portsmouth
Oxford U v Hull C
QPR v Watford
Sheffield U v Swansea C
Southampton v Ipswich T
Stoke C v Sheffield Wed
WBA v Wrexham

Monday, 6 April 2026
Blackburn R v WBA
Bristol C v Sheffield U
Derby Co v Stoke C
Hull C v Coventry C
Ipswich T v Birmingham C
Millwall v Norwich C
Portsmouth v Oxford U
Preston NE v QPR
Sheffield Wed v Leicester C
Swansea C v Middlesbrough
Watford v Charlton Ath
Wrexham v Southampton

Saturday, 11 April 2026
Birmingham C v Wrexham
Charlton Ath v Preston NE
Coventry C v Sheffield Wed
Leicester C v Swansea C
Middlesbrough v Portsmouth
Norwich C v Ipswich T
Oxford U v Watford
QPR v Bristol C
Sheffield U v Hull C
Southampton v Derby Co
Stoke C v Blackburn R
WBA v Millwall

Saturday, 18 April 2026
Blackburn R v Coventry C
Bristol C v Norwich C
Derby Co v Oxford U
Hull C v Birmingham C
Ipswich T v Middlesbrough
Millwall v QPR
Portsmouth v Leicester C
Preston NE v WBA
Sheffield Wed v Charlton Ath
Swansea C v Southampton
Watford v Sheffield U
Wrexham v Stoke C

Tuesday, 21 April 2026
Coventry C v Portsmouth
Middlesbrough v Sheffield Wed
Norwich C v Derby Co
Oxford U v Wrexham
QPR v Swansea C
Southampton v Bristol C
Stoke C v Millwall
WBA v Watford

Wednesday, 22 April 2026
Birmingham C v Preston NE
Charlton Ath v Ipswich T
Leicester C v Hull C
Sheffield U v Blackburn R

Saturday, 25 April 2026
Birmingham C v Bristol C
Charlton Ath v Hull C
Coventry C v Wrexham
Leicester C v Millwall
Middlesbrough v Watford
Norwich C v Swansea C
Oxford U v Sheffield Wed
QPR v Derby Co
Sheffield U v Preston NE
Southampton v Blackburn R

Stoke C v Portsmouth
WBA v Ipswich T

Saturday, 2 May 2026
Blackburn R v Leicester C
Bristol C v Stoke C
Derby Co v Sheffield U
Hull C v Norwich C
Ipswich T v QPR
Millwall v Oxford U
Portsmouth v Birmingham C
Preston NE v Southampton
Sheffield Wed v WBA
Swansea C v Charlton Ath
Watford v Coventry C
Wrexham v Middlesbrough

EFL League One

Friday, 1 August 2025
Luton T v AFC Wimbledon

Saturday, 2 August 2025
Blackpool v Stevenage
Bradford C v Wycombe W
Burton Alb v Mansfield T
Cardiff C v Peterborough U
Doncaster R v Exeter C
Huddersfield T v Leyton Orient
Lincoln C v Reading
Plymouth Arg v Barnsley
Rotherham U v Port Vale
Wigan Ath v Northampton T

Sunday, 3 August 2025
Stockport Co v Bolton W

Saturday, 9 August 2025
AFC Wimbledon v Lincoln C
Barnsley v Burton Alb
Bolton W v Plymouth Arg
Exeter C v Blackpool
Leyton Orient v Wigan Ath
Mansfield T v Doncaster R
Northampton T v Bradford C
Peterborough U v Luton T
Port Vale v Cardiff C
Reading v Huddersfield T
Stevenage v Rotherham U
Wycombe W v Stockport Co

Saturday, 16 August 2025
Barnsley v Bolton W
Blackpool v Huddersfield T
Bradford C v Luton T
Burton Alb v Port Vale
Cardiff C v Rotherham U
Doncaster R v Wycombe W
Exeter C v Mansfield T
Leyton Orient v Stockport Co
Lincoln C v Plymouth Arg
Reading v AFC Wimbledon
Stevenage v Northampton T
Wigan Ath v Peterborough U

Tuesday, 19 August 2025
AFC Wimbledon v Cardiff C
Bolton W v Reading
Huddersfield T v Doncaster R
Luton T v Wigan Ath
Mansfield T v Blackpool
Northampton T v Lincoln C
Peterborough U v Barnsley
Plymouth Arg v Leyton Orient
Port Vale v Stevenage
Rotherham U v Burton Alb
Stockport Co v Bradford C
Wycombe W v Exeter C

Saturday, 23 August 2025
AFC Wimbledon v Barnsley
Bolton W v Lincoln C
Huddersfield T v Stevenage

Luton T v Cardiff C
Mansfield T v Leyton Orient
Northampton T v Exeter C
Peterborough U v Bradford C
Plymouth Arg v Blackpool
Port Vale v Doncaster R
Rotherham U v Wigan Ath
Stockport Co v Burton Alb
Wycombe W v Reading

Saturday, 30 August 2025
Barnsley v Huddersfield T
Blackpool v Bolton W
Bradford C v AFC Wimbledon
Burton Alb v Luton T
Cardiff C v Plymouth Arg
Doncaster R v Rotherham U
Exeter C v Peterborough U
Leyton Orient v Northampton T
Lincoln C v Mansfield T
Reading v Port Vale
Stevenage v Wycombe W
Wigan Ath v Stockport Co

Saturday, 6 September 2025
Blackpool v Luton T
Bolton W v AFC Wimbledon
Cardiff C v Burton Alb
Doncaster R v Bradford C
Huddersfield T v Peterborough U
Lincoln C v Wigan Ath
Plymouth Arg v Stockport Co
Port Vale v Leyton Orient
Reading v Northampton T
Rotherham U v Exeter C
Stevenage v Barnsley
Wycombe W v Mansfield T

Saturday, 13 September 2025
AFC Wimbledon v Rotherham U
Barnsley v Reading
Bradford C v Huddersfield T
Burton Alb v Lincoln C
Exeter C v Port Vale
Leyton Orient v Bolton W
Luton T v Plymouth Arg
Mansfield T v Stevenage
Northampton T v Blackpool
Peterborough U v Wycombe W
Stockport Co v Cardiff C
Wigan Ath v Doncaster R

Saturday, 20 September 2025
Blackpool v Barnsley
Bolton W v Wigan Ath
Cardiff C v Bradford C
Doncaster R v AFC Wimbledon
Huddersfield T v Burton Alb
Lincoln C v Luton T
Plymouth Arg v Peterborough U
Port Vale v Mansfield T
Reading v Leyton Orient
Rotherham U v Stockport Co
Stevenage v Exeter C
Wycombe W v Northampton T

Saturday, 27 September 2025
AFC Wimbledon v Wycombe W
Barnsley v Port Vale
Bradford C v Blackpool
Burton Alb v Plymouth Arg
Exeter C v Huddersfield T
Leyton Orient v Stevenage
Luton T v Doncaster R
Mansfield T v Rotherham U
Northampton T v Bolton W
Peterborough U v Lincoln C
Stockport Co v Reading
Wigan Ath v Cardiff C

Saturday, 4 October 2025
Blackpool v AFC Wimbledon
Bolton W v Peterborough U

Cardiff C v Leyton Orient
Doncaster R v Burton Alb
Huddersfield T v Stockport Co
Lincoln C v Exeter C
Plymouth Arg v Wigan Ath
Port Vale v Northampton T
Reading v Mansfield T
Rotherham U v Bradford C
Stevenage v Luton T
Wycombe W v Barnsley

Saturday, 11 October 2025
AFC Wimbledon v Port Vale
Barnsley v Cardiff C
Bradford C v Lincoln C
Burton Alb v Bolton W
Exeter C v Reading
Leyton Orient v Doncaster R
Luton T v Huddersfield T
Mansfield T v Plymouth Arg
Northampton T v Rotherham U
Peterborough U v Stevenage
Stockport Co v Blackpool
Wigan Ath v Wycombe W

Saturday, 18 October 2025
Blackpool v Wycombe W
Bradford C v Barnsley
Burton Alb v Peterborough U
Cardiff C v Reading
Doncaster R v Northampton T
Huddersfield T v Bolton W
Lincoln C v Stevenage
Luton T v Mansfield T
Plymouth Arg v AFC Wimbledon
Rotherham U v Leyton Orient
Stockport Co v Exeter C
Wigan Ath v Port Vale

Saturday, 25 October 2025
AFC Wimbledon v Burton Alb
Barnsley v Rotherham U
Bolton W v Cardiff C
Exeter C v Plymouth Arg
Leyton Orient v Lincoln C
Mansfield T v Wigan Ath
Northampton T v Luton T
Peterborough U v Blackpool
Port Vale v Stockport Co
Reading v Doncaster R
Stevenage v Bradford C
Wycombe W v Huddersfield T

Saturday, 8 November 2025
Blackpool v Cardiff C
Bolton W v Port Vale
Bradford C v Burton Alb
Doncaster R v Barnsley
Exeter C v Wigan Ath
Huddersfield T v Plymouth Arg
Northampton T v Mansfield T
Peterborough U v AFC Wimbledon
Reading v Stevenage
Rotherham U v Lincoln C
Stockport Co v Luton T
Wycombe W v Leyton Orient

Saturday, 15 November 2025
AFC Wimbledon v Stockport Co
Barnsley v Northampton T
Burton Alb v Blackpool
Cardiff C v Huddersfield T
Leyton Orient v Exeter C
Lincoln C v Doncaster R
Luton T v Rotherham U
Mansfield T v Peterborough U
Plymouth Arg v Bradford C
Port Vale v Wycombe W
Stevenage v Bolton W
Wigan Ath v Reading

Saturday, 22 November 2025
AFC Wimbledon v Wigan Ath
Barnsley v Luton T
Bolton W v Bradford C
Exeter C v Burton Alb
Leyton Orient v Blackpool
Mansfield T v Huddersfield T
Northampton T v Cardiff C
Peterborough U v Stockport Co
Port Vale v Plymouth Arg
Reading v Rotherham U
Stevenage v Doncaster R
Wycombe W v Lincoln C

Saturday, 29 November 2025
Blackpool v Reading
Bradford C v Exeter C
Burton Alb v Leyton Orient
Cardiff C v Mansfield T
Doncaster R v Peterborough U
Huddersfield T v AFC Wimbledon
Lincoln C v Port Vale
Luton T v Bolton W
Plymouth Arg v Northampton T
Rotherham U v Wycombe W
Stockport Co v Barnsley
Wigan Ath v Stevenage

Tuesday, 9 December 2025
Doncaster R v Stockport Co
Exeter C v AFC Wimbledon
Leyton Orient v Luton T
Lincoln C v Barnsley
Mansfield T v Bolton W
Northampton T v Huddersfield T
Port Vale v Bradford C
Reading v Peterborough U
Rotherham U v Blackpool
Stevenage v Cardiff C
Wigan Ath v Burton Alb
Wycombe W v Plymouth Arg

Saturday, 13 December 2025
AFC Wimbledon v Mansfield T
Barnsley v Leyton Orient
Blackpool v Lincoln C
Bolton W v Exeter C
Bradford C v Reading
Burton Alb v Wycombe W
Cardiff C v Doncaster R
Huddersfield T v Wigan Ath
Luton T v Port Vale
Peterborough U v Northampton T
Plymouth Arg v Rotherham U
Stockport Co v Stevenage

Saturday, 20 December 2025
Doncaster R v Plymouth Arg
Exeter C v Barnsley
Leyton Orient v Bradford C
Lincoln C v Cardiff C
Mansfield T v Stockport Co
Northampton T v AFC Wimbledon
Port Vale v Peterborough U
Reading v Luton T
Rotherham U v Huddersfield T
Stevenage v Burton Alb
Wigan Ath v Blackpool
Wycombe W v Bolton W

Friday, 26 December 2025
AFC Wimbledon v Stevenage
Barnsley v Mansfield T
Blackpool v Doncaster R
Bolton W v Rotherham U
Bradford C v Wigan Ath
Burton Alb v Northampton T
Cardiff C v Exeter C
Huddersfield T v Port Vale
Luton T v Wycombe W
Peterborough U v Leyton Orient

Plymouth Arg v Reading
Stockport Co v Lincoln C

Monday, 29 December 2025
AFC Wimbledon v Exeter C
Barnsley v Lincoln C
Blackpool v Rotherham U
Bolton W v Mansfield T
Bradford C v Port Vale
Burton Alb v Wigan Ath
Cardiff C v Stevenage
Huddersfield T v Northampton T
Luton T v Leyton Orient
Peterborough U v Reading
Plymouth Arg v Wycombe W
Stockport Co v Doncaster R

Thursday, 1 January 2026
Doncaster R v Bolton W
Exeter C v Luton T
Leyton Orient v AFC Wimbledon
Lincoln C v Huddersfield T
Mansfield T v Bradford C
Northampton T v Stockport Co
Port Vale v Blackpool
Reading v Burton Alb
Rotherham U v Peterborough U
Stevenage v Plymouth Arg
Wigan Ath v Barnsley
Wycombe W v Cardiff C

Sunday, 4 January 2026
Blackpool v Bradford C
Bolton W v Northampton T
Cardiff C v Wigan Ath
Doncaster R v Luton T
Huddersfield T v Exeter C
Lincoln C v Peterborough U
Plymouth Arg v Burton Alb
Port Vale v Barnsley
Reading v Stockport Co
Rotherham U v Mansfield T
Stevenage v Leyton Orient
Wycombe W v AFC Wimbledon

Saturday, 10 January 2026
AFC Wimbledon v Blackpool
Barnsley v Wycombe W
Bradford C v Rotherham U
Burton Alb v Doncaster R
Exeter C v Lincoln C
Leyton Orient v Cardiff C
Luton T v Stevenage
Mansfield T v Reading
Northampton T v Port Vale
Peterborough U v Bolton W
Stockport Co v Huddersfield T
Wigan Ath v Plymouth Arg

Saturday, 17 January 2026
AFC Wimbledon v Doncaster R
Barnsley v Blackpool
Bradford C v Cardiff C
Burton Alb v Huddersfield T
Exeter C v Stevenage
Leyton Orient v Reading
Luton T v Lincoln C
Mansfield T v Port Vale
Northampton T v Wycombe W
Peterborough U v Plymouth Arg
Stockport Co v Rotherham U
Wigan Ath v Bolton W

Saturday, 24 January 2026
Blackpool v Northampton T
Bolton W v Leyton Orient
Cardiff C v Stockport Co
Doncaster R v Wigan Ath
Huddersfield T v Bradford C
Lincoln C v Burton Alb
Plymouth Arg v Luton T
Port Vale v Exeter C
Reading v Barnsley

Rotherham U v AFC Wimbledon
Stevenage v Mansfield T
Wycombe W v Peterborough U

Tuesday, 27 January 2026
Blackpool v Stockport Co
Bolton W v Burton Alb
Cardiff C v Barnsley
Doncaster R v Leyton Orient
Huddersfield T v Luton T
Lincoln C v Bradford C
Plymouth Arg v Mansfield T
Port Vale v AFC Wimbledon
Reading v Exeter C
Rotherham U v Northampton T
Stevenage v Peterborough U
Wycombe W v Wigan Ath

Saturday, 31 January 2026
AFC Wimbledon v Bolton W
Barnsley v Stevenage
Bradford C v Doncaster R
Burton Alb v Cardiff C
Exeter C v Rotherham U
Leyton Orient v Port Vale
Luton T v Blackpool
Mansfield T v Wycombe W
Northampton T v Reading
Peterborough U v Huddersfield T
Stockport Co v Plymouth Arg
Wigan Ath v Lincoln C

Saturday, 7 February 2026
AFC Wimbledon v Reading
Bolton W v Barnsley
Huddersfield T v Blackpool
Luton T v Bradford C
Mansfield T v Exeter C
Northampton T v Stevenage
Peterborough U v Wigan Ath
Plymouth Arg v Lincoln C
Port Vale v Burton Alb
Rotherham U v Cardiff C
Stockport Co v Leyton Orient
Wycombe W v Doncaster R

Saturday, 14 February 2026
Barnsley v AFC Wimbledon
Blackpool v Plymouth Arg
Bradford C v Peterborough U
Burton Alb v Stockport Co
Cardiff C v Luton T
Doncaster R v Port Vale
Exeter C v Northampton T
Leyton Orient v Mansfield T
Lincoln C v Bolton W
Reading v Wycombe W
Stevenage v Huddersfield T
Wigan Ath v Rotherham U

Tuesday, 17 February 2026
Barnsley v Peterborough U
Blackpool v Mansfield T
Bradford C v Stockport Co
Burton Alb v Rotherham U
Cardiff C v AFC Wimbledon
Doncaster R v Huddersfield T
Exeter C v Wycombe W
Leyton Orient v Plymouth Arg
Lincoln C v Northampton T
Reading v Bolton W
Stevenage v Port Vale
Wigan Ath v Luton T

Saturday, 21 February 2026
AFC Wimbledon v Bradford C
Bolton W v Blackpool
Huddersfield T v Barnsley
Luton T v Burton Alb
Mansfield T v Lincoln C
Northampton T v Leyton Orient
Peterborough U v Exeter C
Plymouth Arg v Cardiff C

Port Vale v Reading
Rotherham U v Doncaster R
Stockport Co v Wigan Ath
Wycombe W v Stevenage

Saturday, 28 February 2026
Doncaster R v Cardiff C
Exeter C v Bolton W
Leyton Orient v Barnsley
Lincoln C v Blackpool
Mansfield T v AFC Wimbledon
Northampton T v Peterborough U
Port Vale v Luton T
Reading v Bradford C
Rotherham U v Plymouth Arg
Stevenage v Stockport Co
Wigan Ath v Huddersfield T
Wycombe W v Burton Alb

Saturday, 7 March 2026
AFC Wimbledon v Northampton T
Barnsley v Exeter C
Blackpool v Wigan Ath
Bolton W v Wycombe W
Bradford C v Leyton Orient
Burton Alb v Stevenage
Cardiff C v Lincoln C
Huddersfield T v Rotherham U
Luton T v Reading
Peterborough U v Port Vale
Plymouth Arg v Doncaster R
Stockport Co v Mansfield T

Saturday, 14 March 2026
Doncaster R v Blackpool
19 Exeter C v Cardiff C17/03/2026:45
Leyton Orient v Peterborough U
Lincoln C v Stockport Co
Mansfield T v Barnsley
Northampton T v Burton Alb
Port Vale v Huddersfield T
Reading v Plymouth Arg
Rotherham U v Bolton W
Stevenage v AFC Wimbledon
Wigan Ath v Bradford C
Wycombe W v Luton T

Tuesday, 17 March 2026
AFC Wimbledon v Leyton Orient
Barnsley v Wigan Ath
Blackpool v Port Vale
Bolton W v Doncaster R
Bradford C v Mansfield T
Burton Alb v Reading
Cardiff C v Wycombe W
Huddersfield T v Lincoln C
Luton T v Exeter C
Peterborough U v Rotherham U
Plymouth Arg v Stevenage
Stockport Co v Northampton T

Saturday, 21 March 2026
AFC Wimbledon v Peterborough U
Barnsley v Doncaster R
Burton Alb v Bradford C
Cardiff C v Blackpool
Leyton Orient v Wycombe W
Lincoln C v Rotherham U
Luton T v Stockport Co
Mansfield T v Northampton T
Plymouth Arg v Huddersfield T
Port Vale v Bolton W
Stevenage v Reading
Wigan Ath v Exeter C

Saturday, 28 March 2026
Blackpool v Burton Alb
Bolton W v Stevenage
Bradford C v Plymouth Arg
Doncaster R v Lincoln C
Exeter C v Leyton Orient
Huddersfield T v Cardiff C
Northampton T v Barnsley

Peterborough U v Mansfield T
Reading v Wigan Ath
Rotherham U v Luton T
Stockport Co v AFC Wimbledon
Wycombe W v Port Vale

Friday, 3 April 2026
Blackpool v Exeter C
Bradford C v Northampton T
Burton Alb v Barnsley
Cardiff C v Port Vale
Doncaster R v Mansfield T
Huddersfield T v Reading
Lincoln C v AFC Wimbledon
Luton T v Peterborough U
Plymouth Arg v Bolton W
Rotherham U v Stevenage
Stockport Co v Wycombe W
Wigan Ath v Leyton Orient

Monday, 6 April 2026
AFC Wimbledon v Luton T
Barnsley v Plymouth Arg
Bolton W v Stockport Co
Exeter C v Doncaster R
Leyton Orient v Huddersfield T
Mansfield T v Burton Alb
Northampton T v Wigan Ath
Peterborough U v Cardiff C
Port Vale v Rotherham U
Reading v Lincoln C
Stevenage v Blackpool
Wycombe W v Bradford C

Saturday, 11 April 2026
Blackpool v Peterborough U
Bradford C v Stevenage
Burton Alb v AFC Wimbledon
Cardiff C v Bolton W
Doncaster R v Reading
Huddersfield T v Wycombe W
Lincoln C v Leyton Orient
Luton T v Northampton T
Plymouth Arg v Exeter C
Rotherham U v Barnsley
Stockport Co v Port Vale
Wigan Ath v Mansfield T

Saturday, 18 April 2026
AFC Wimbledon v Plymouth Arg
Barnsley v Bradford C
Bolton W v Huddersfield T
Exeter C v Stockport Co
Leyton Orient v Rotherham U
Mansfield T v Luton T
Northampton T v Doncaster R
Peterborough U v Burton Alb
Port Vale v Wigan Ath
Reading v Cardiff C
Stevenage v Lincoln C
Wycombe W v Blackpool

Saturday, 25 April 2026
Blackpool v Leyton Orient
Bradford C v Bolton W
Burton Alb v Exeter C
Cardiff C v Northampton T
Doncaster R v Stevenage
Huddersfield T v Mansfield T
Lincoln C v Wycombe W
Luton T v Barnsley
Plymouth Arg v Port Vale
Rotherham U v Reading
Stockport Co v Peterborough U
Wigan Ath v AFC Wimbledon

Saturday, 2 May 2026
AFC Wimbledon v Huddersfield T
Barnsley v Stockport Co
Bolton W v Luton T
Exeter C v Bradford C
Leyton Orient v Burton Alb
Mansfield T v Cardiff C

Northampton T v Plymouth Arg
Peterborough U v Doncaster R
Port Vale v Lincoln C
Reading v Blackpool
Stevenage v Wigan Ath
Wycombe W v Rotherham U

EFL League Two

Saturday, 2 August 2025
Accrington S v Gillingham
Barnet v Fleetwood T
Bristol R v Harrogate T
Cambridge U v Cheltenham T
Chesterfield v Barrow
Colchester U v Tranmere R
Grimsby T v Crawley T
Milton Keynes D v Oldham Ath
Newport Co v Notts Co
Salford C v Crewe Alex
Shrewsbury T v Bromley
Walsall v Swindon T

Saturday, 9 August 2025
Barrow v Milton Keynes D
Bromley v Barnet
Cheltenham T v Chesterfield
Crawley T v Newport Co
Crewe Alex v Accrington S
Fleetwood T v Bristol R
Gillingham v Walsall
Harrogate T v Grimsby T
Notts Co v Salford C
Oldham Ath v Colchester U
Swindon T v Cambridge U
Tranmere R v Shrewsbury T

Saturday, 16 August 2025
Barnet v Walsall
Barrow v Notts Co
Bromley v Fleetwood T
Cambridge U v Harrogate T
Chesterfield v Bristol R
Crewe Alex v Crawley T
Grimsby T v Newport Co
Milton Keynes D v Cheltenham T
Oldham Ath v Swindon T
Salford C v Accrington S
Shrewsbury T v Colchester U
Tranmere R v Gillingham

Tuesday, 19 August 2025
Accrington S v Tranmere R
Bristol R v Oldham Ath
Cheltenham T v Bromley
Colchester U v Cambridge U
Crawley T v Milton Keynes D
Fleetwood T v Crewe Alex
Gillingham v Chesterfield
Harrogate T v Barrow
Newport Co v Salford C
Notts Co v Shrewsbury T
Swindon T v Barnet
Walsall v Grimsby T

Saturday, 23 August 2025
Accrington S v Grimsby T
Bristol R v Cambridge U
Cheltenham T v Barnet
Colchester U v Barrow
Crawley T v Tranmere R
Fleetwood T v Oldham Ath
Gillingham v Crewe Alex
Harrogate T v Chesterfield
Newport Co v Milton Keynes D
Notts Co v Bromley
Swindon T v Shrewsbury T
Walsall v Salford C

Saturday, 30 August 2025
Barnet v Colchester U
Barrow v Fleetwood T

Bromley v Harrogate T
Cambridge U v Newport Co
Chesterfield v Crawley T
Crewe Alex v Swindon T
Grimsby T v Bristol R
Milton Keynes D v Walsall
Oldham Ath v Gillingham
Salford C v Cheltenham T
Shrewsbury T v Accrington S
Tranmere R v Notts Co

Saturday, 6 September 2025
Barnet v Shrewsbury T
Barrow v Swindon T
Bromley v Gillingham
Cambridge U v Oldham Ath
Cheltenham T v Accrington S
Colchester U v Crewe Alex
Harrogate T v Crawley T
Milton Keynes D v Grimsby T
Newport Co v Bristol R
Notts Co v Fleetwood T
Salford C v Tranmere R
Walsall v Chesterfield

Saturday, 13 September 2025
Accrington S v Colchester U
Bristol R v Barrow
Chesterfield v Milton Keynes D
Crawley T v Cheltenham T
Crewe Alex v Barnet
Fleetwood T v Walsall
Gillingham v Notts Co
Grimsby T v Cambridge U
Oldham Ath v Bromley
Shrewsbury T v Salford C
Swindon T v Harrogate T
Tranmere R v Newport Co

Saturday, 20 September 2025
Barnet v Grimsby T
Barrow v Crewe Alex
Bromley v Chesterfield
Cambridge U v Fleetwood T
Cheltenham T v Oldham Ath
Colchester U v Bristol R
Harrogate T v Shrewsbury T
Milton Keynes D v Accrington S
Newport Co v Gillingham
Notts Co v Crawley T
Salford C v Swindon T
Walsall v Tranmere R

Saturday, 27 September 2025
Accrington S v Walsall
Bristol R v Salford C
Chesterfield v Newport Co
Crawley T v Barrow
Crewe Alex v Notts Co
Fleetwood T v Colchester U
Gillingham v Harrogate T
Grimsby T v Cheltenham T
Oldham Ath v Barnet
Shrewsbury T v Milton Keynes D
Swindon T v Bromley
Tranmere R v Cambridge U

Saturday, 4 October 2025
Barnet v Accrington S
Barrow v Shrewsbury T
Bromley v Tranmere R
Cambridge U v Crawley T
Cheltenham T v Fleetwood T
Colchester U v Chesterfield
Harrogate T v Crewe Alex
Milton Keynes D v Gillingham
Newport Co v Swindon T
Notts Co v Oldham Ath
Salford C v Grimsby T
Walsall v Bristol R

Saturday, 11 October 2025
Accrington S v Newport Co
Bristol R v Milton Keynes D
Chesterfield v Salford C
Crawley T v Walsall
Crewe Alex v Bromley
Fleetwood T v Harrogate T
Gillingham v Cheltenham T
Grimsby T v Colchester U
Oldham Ath v Barrow
Shrewsbury T v Cambridge U
Swindon T v Notts Co
Tranmere R v Barnet

Saturday, 18 October 2025
Accrington S v Swindon T
Barnet v Notts Co
Bristol R v Tranmere R
Cambridge U v Bromley
Chesterfield v Fleetwood T
Colchester U v Harrogate T
Grimsby T v Gillingham
Milton Keynes D v Crewe Alex
Newport Co v Cheltenham T
Salford C v Oldham Ath
Shrewsbury T v Crawley T
Walsall v Barrow

Saturday, 25 October 2025
Barrow v Barnet
Bromley v Milton Keynes D
Cheltenham T v Walsall
Crawley T v Bristol R
Crewe Alex v Grimsby T
Fleetwood T v Accrington S
Gillingham v Salford C
Harrogate T v Newport Co
Notts Co v Cambridge U
Oldham Ath v Shrewsbury T
Swindon T v Colchester U
Tranmere R v Chesterfield

Tuesday, 11 November 2025
Barnet v Milton Keynes D
Barrow v Grimsby T
Bristol R v Gillingham
Cheltenham T v Notts Co
Chesterfield v Accrington S
Colchester U v Bromley
Crawley T v Fleetwood T
Crewe Alex v Shrewsbury T
Harrogate T v Oldham Ath
Newport Co v Walsall
Salford C v Cambridge U
Swindon T v Tranmere R

Saturday, 15 November 2025
Accrington S v Bristol R
Bromley v Barrow
Cambridge U v Barnet
Fleetwood T v Swindon T
Gillingham v Crawley T
Grimsby T v Chesterfield
Milton Keynes D v Salford C
Notts Co v Harrogate T
Oldham Ath v Crewe Alex
Shrewsbury T v Newport Co
Tranmere R v Cheltenham T
Walsall v Colchester U

Saturday, 22 November 2025
Barrow v Cambridge U
Bromley v Salford C
Cheltenham T v Bristol R
Crawley T v Accrington S
Crewe Alex v Chesterfield
Fleetwood T v Shrewsbury T
Gillingham v Barnet
Harrogate T v Walsall
Notts Co v Colchester U
Oldham Ath v Newport Co

Swindon T v Grimsby T
Tranmere R v Milton Keynes D

Saturday, 29 November 2025
Accrington S v Oldham Ath
Barnet v Harrogate T
Bristol R v Notts Co
Cambridge U v Crewe Alex
Chesterfield v Swindon T
Colchester U v Cheltenham T
Grimsby T v Tranmere R
Milton Keynes D v Fleetwood T
Newport Co v Barrow
Salford C v Crawley T
Shrewsbury T v Gillingham
Walsall v Bromley

Tuesday, 9 December 2025
Barnet v Bristol R
Barrow v Tranmere R
Bromley v Crawley T
Cambridge U v Chesterfield
Colchester U v Gillingham
Crewe Alex v Newport Co
Fleetwood T v Salford C
Harrogate T v Accrington S
Notts Co v Milton Keynes D
Oldham Ath v Walsall
Shrewsbury T v Grimsby T
Swindon T v Cheltenham T

Saturday, 13 December 2025
Accrington S v Bromley
Bristol R v Swindon T
Cheltenham T v Harrogate T
Chesterfield v Barnet
Crawley T v Oldham Ath
Gillingham v Barrow
Grimsby T v Notts Co
Milton Keynes D v Cambridge U
Newport Co v Fleetwood T
Salford C v Colchester U
Tranmere R v Crewe Alex
Walsall v Shrewsbury T

Saturday, 20 December 2025
Barnet v Salford C
Barrow v Cheltenham T
Bromley v Grimsby T
Cambridge U v Accrington S
Colchester U v Newport Co
Crewe Alex v Bristol R
Fleetwood T v Gillingham
Harrogate T v Milton Keynes D
Notts Co v Walsall
Oldham Ath v Tranmere R
Shrewsbury T v Chesterfield
Swindon T v Crawley T

Friday, 26 December 2025
Accrington S v Barrow
Bristol R v Bromley
Cheltenham T v Shrewsbury T
Chesterfield v Notts Co
Crawley T v Colchester U
Gillingham v Cambridge U
Grimsby T v Oldham Ath
Milton Keynes D v Swindon T
Newport Co v Barnet
Salford C v Harrogate T
Tranmere R v Fleetwood T
Walsall v Crewe Alex

Monday, 29 December 2025
Accrington S v Harrogate T
Bristol R v Barnet
Cheltenham T v Swindon T
Chesterfield v Cambridge U
Crawley T v Bromley
Gillingham v Colchester U
Grimsby T v Shrewsbury T
Milton Keynes D v Notts Co
Newport Co v Crewe Alex

Salford C v Fleetwood T
Tranmere R v Barrow
Walsall v Oldham Ath

Thursday, 1 January 2026
Barnet v Crawley T
Barrow v Salford C
Bromley v Newport Co
Cambridge U v Walsall
Colchester U v Milton Keynes D
Crewe Alex v Cheltenham T
Fleetwood T v Grimsby T
Harrogate T v Tranmere R
Notts Co v Accrington S
Oldham Ath v Chesterfield
Shrewsbury T v Bristol R
Swindon T v Gillingham

Sunday, 4 January 2026
Barnet v Crewe Alex
Barrow v Bristol R
Bromley v Oldham Ath
Cambridge U v Grimsby T
Cheltenham T v Crawley T
Colchester U v Accrington S
Harrogate T v Swindon T
Milton Keynes D v Chesterfield
Newport Co v Tranmere R
Notts Co v Gillingham
Salford C v Shrewsbury T
Walsall v Fleetwood T

Saturday, 10 January 2026
Accrington S v Barnet
Bristol R v Walsall
Chesterfield v Colchester U
Crawley T v Cambridge U
Crewe Alex v Harrogate T
Fleetwood T v Cheltenham T
Gillingham v Milton Keynes D
Grimsby T v Salford C
Oldham Ath v Notts Co
Shrewsbury T v Barrow
Swindon T v Newport Co
Tranmere R v Bromley

Saturday, 17 January 2026
Accrington S v Milton Keynes D
Bristol R v Colchester U
Chesterfield v Bromley
Crawley T v Notts Co
Crewe Alex v Barrow
Fleetwood T v Cambridge U
Gillingham v Newport Co
Grimsby T v Barnet
Oldham Ath v Cheltenham T
Shrewsbury T v Harrogate T
Swindon T v Salford C
Tranmere R v Walsall

Saturday, 24 January 2026
Barnet v Oldham Ath
Barrow v Crawley T
Bromley v Swindon T
Cambridge U v Tranmere R
Cheltenham T v Grimsby T
Colchester U v Fleetwood T
Harrogate T v Gillingham
Milton Keynes D v Shrewsbury T
Newport Co v Chesterfield
Notts Co v Crewe Alex
Salford C v Bristol R
Walsall v Accrington S

Tuesday, 27 January 2026
Barnet v Tranmere R
Barrow v Oldham Ath
Bromley v Crewe Alex
Cambridge U v Shrewsbury T
Cheltenham T v Gillingham
Colchester U v Grimsby T
Harrogate T v Fleetwood T
Milton Keynes D v Bristol R

Newport Co v Accrington S
Notts Co v Swindon T
Salford C v Chesterfield
Walsall v Crawley T

Saturday, 31 January 2026
Accrington S v Cheltenham T
Bristol R v Newport Co
Chesterfield v Walsall
Crawley T v Harrogate T
Crewe Alex v Colchester U
Fleetwood T v Notts Co
Gillingham v Bromley
Grimsby T v Milton Keynes D
Oldham Ath v Cambridge U
Shrewsbury T v Barnet
Swindon T v Barrow
Tranmere R v Salford C

Saturday, 7 February 2026
Accrington S v Salford C
Bristol R v Chesterfield
Cheltenham T v Milton Keynes D
Colchester U v Shrewsbury T
Crawley T v Crewe Alex
Fleetwood T v Bromley
Gillingham v Tranmere R
Harrogate T v Cambridge U
Newport Co v Grimsby T
Notts Co v Barrow
Swindon T v Oldham Ath
Walsall v Barnet

Saturday, 14 February 2026
Barnet v Cheltenham T
Barrow v Colchester U
Bromley v Notts Co
Cambridge U v Bristol R
Chesterfield v Harrogate T
Crewe Alex v Gillingham
Grimsby T v Accrington S
Milton Keynes D v Newport Co
Oldham Ath v Fleetwood T
Salford C v Walsall
Shrewsbury T v Swindon T
Tranmere R v Crawley T

Tuesday, 17 February 2026
Barnet v Swindon T
Barrow v Harrogate T
Bromley v Cheltenham T
Cambridge U v Colchester U
Chesterfield v Gillingham
Crewe Alex v Fleetwood T
Grimsby T v Walsall
Milton Keynes D v Crawley T
Oldham Ath v Bristol R
Salford C v Newport Co
Shrewsbury T v Notts Co
Tranmere R v Accrington S

Saturday, 21 February 2026
Accrington S v Shrewsbury T
Bristol R v Grimsby T
Cheltenham T v Salford C
Colchester U v Barnet
Crawley T v Chesterfield
Fleetwood T v Barrow
Gillingham v Oldham Ath
Harrogate T v Bromley
Newport Co v Cambridge U
Notts Co v Tranmere R
Swindon T v Crewe Alex
Walsall v Milton Keynes D

Saturday, 28 February 2026
Barnet v Chesterfield
Barrow v Gillingham
Bromley v Accrington S
Cambridge U v Milton Keynes D
Colchester U v Salford C

Crewe Alex v Tranmere R
Fleetwood T v Newport Co
Harrogate T v Cheltenham T
Notts Co v Grimsby T
Oldham Ath v Crawley T
Shrewsbury T v Walsall
Swindon T v Bristol R

Saturday, 7 March 2026
Accrington S v Cambridge U
Bristol R v Crewe Alex
Cheltenham T v Barrow
Chesterfield v Shrewsbury T
Crawley T v Swindon T
Gillingham v Fleetwood T
Grimsby T v Bromley
Milton Keynes D v Harrogate T
Newport Co v Colchester U
Salford C v Barnet
Tranmere R v Oldham Ath
Walsall v Notts Co

Saturday, 14 March 2026
Barnet v Newport Co
Barrow v Accrington S
Bromley v Bristol R
Cambridge U v Gillingham
Colchester U v Crawley T
Crewe Alex v Walsall
Fleetwood T v Tranmere R
Harrogate T v Salford C
Notts Co v Chesterfield
Oldham Ath v Grimsby T
Shrewsbury T v Cheltenham T
Swindon T v Milton Keynes D

Tuesday, 17 March 2026
Accrington S v Notts Co
Bristol R v Shrewsbury T
Cheltenham T v Crewe Alex
Chesterfield v Oldham Ath
Crawley T v Barnet
Gillingham v Swindon T
Grimsby T v Fleetwood T
Milton Keynes D v Colchester U
Newport Co v Bromley
Salford C v Barrow
Tranmere R v Harrogate T
Walsall v Cambridge U

Saturday, 21 March 2026
Accrington S v Chesterfield
Bromley v Colchester U
Cambridge U v Salford C
Fleetwood T v Crawley T
Gillingham v Bristol R
Grimsby T v Barrow
Milton Keynes D v Barnet
Notts Co v Cheltenham T
Oldham Ath v Harrogate T
Shrewsbury T v Crewe Alex
Tranmere R v Swindon T
Walsall v Newport Co

Saturday, 28 March 2026
Barnet v Cambridge U
Barrow v Bromley
Bristol R v Accrington S
Cheltenham T v Tranmere R
Chesterfield v Grimsby T
Colchester U v Walsall
Crawley T v Gillingham
Crewe Alex v Oldham Ath
Harrogate T v Notts Co
Newport Co v Shrewsbury T
Salford C v Milton Keynes D
Swindon T v Fleetwood T

Friday, 3 April 2026
Accrington S v Crewe Alex
Barnet v Bromley

Bristol R v Fleetwood T
Cambridge U v Swindon T
Chesterfield v Cheltenham T
Colchester U v Oldham Ath
Grimsby T v Harrogate T
Milton Keynes D v Barrow
Newport Co v Crawley T
Salford C v Notts Co
Shrewsbury T v Tranmere R
Walsall v Gillingham

Monday, 6 April 2026
Barrow v Chesterfield
Bromley v Shrewsbury T
Cheltenham T v Cambridge U
Crawley T v Grimsby T
Crewe Alex v Salford C
Fleetwood T v Barnet
Gillingham v Accrington S
Harrogate T v Bristol R
Notts Co v Newport Co
Oldham Ath v Milton Keynes D
Swindon T v Walsall
Tranmere R v Colchester U

Saturday, 11 April 2026
Accrington S v Fleetwood T
Barnet v Barrow
Bristol R v Crawley T
Cambridge U v Notts Co
Chesterfield v Tranmere R
Colchester U v Swindon T
Grimsby T v Crewe Alex
Milton Keynes D v Bromley
Newport Co v Harrogate T
Salford C v Gillingham
Shrewsbury T v Oldham Ath
Walsall v Cheltenham T

Saturday, 18 April 2026
Barrow v Walsall
Bromley v Cambridge U
Cheltenham T v Newport Co
Crawley T v Shrewsbury T
Crewe Alex v Milton Keynes D
Fleetwood T v Chesterfield
Gillingham v Grimsby T
Harrogate T v Colchester U
Notts Co v Barnet
Oldham Ath v Salford C
Swindon T v Accrington S
Tranmere R v Bristol R

Saturday, 25 April 2026
Accrington S v Crawley T
Barnet v Gillingham
Bristol R v Cheltenham T
Cambridge U v Barrow
Chesterfield v Crewe Alex
Colchester U v Notts Co
Grimsby T v Swindon T
Milton Keynes D v Tranmere R
Newport Co v Oldham Ath
Salford C v Bromley
Shrewsbury T v Fleetwood T
Walsall v Harrogate T

Saturday, 2 May 2026
Barrow v Newport Co
Bromley v Walsall
Cheltenham T v Colchester U
Crawley T v Salford C
Crewe Alex v Cambridge U
Fleetwood T v Milton Keynes D
Gillingham v Shrewsbury T
Harrogate T v Barnet
Notts Co v Bristol R
Oldham Ath v Accrington S
Swindon T v Chesterfield
Tranmere R v Grimsby T

NATIONAL LEAGUE
FIXTURES 2025–26

All fixtures subject to change.

Saturday, 9 August 2025
Altrincham v Aldershot T
Boreham Wood v Rochdale
Boston U v Morecambe
Brackley T v Eastleigh
Braintree T v FC Halifax T
Gateshead v Southend U
Solihull Moors v Forest Green R
Tamworth v Scunthorpe U
Wealdstone v Truro C
Woking v Carlisle U
Yeovil T v Hartlepool U
York C v Sutton U

Saturday, 16 August 2025
Aldershot T v Boston U
Carlisle U v Boreham Wood
Eastleigh v Gateshead
FC Halifax T v Wealdstone
Forest Green R v Yeovil T
Hartlepool U v Braintree T
Morecambe v Brackley T
Rochdale v Altrincham
Scunthorpe U v Woking
Southend U v Tamworth
Sutton U v Solihull Moors
Truro C v York C

Tuesday, 19 August 2025
Altrincham v Hartlepool U
Boston U v FC Halifax T
Carlisle U v Solihull Moors
Scunthorpe U v Morecambe
Tamworth v Truro C
Woking v Wealdstone

Wednesday, 20 August 2025
Aldershot T v Eastleigh
Boreham Wood v Braintree T
Forest Green R v Sutton U
Rochdale v Gateshead
Southend U v York C
Yeovil T v Brackley T

Saturday, 23 August 2025
Brackley T v Rochdale
Braintree T v Yeovil T
Eastleigh v Boston U
FC Halifax T v Forest Green R
Gateshead v Tamworth
Hartlepool U v Woking
Morecambe v Altrincham
Solihull Moors v Aldershot T
Sutton U v Scunthorpe U
Truro C v Southend U
Wealdstone v Carlisle U

Monday, 25 August 2025
Aldershot T v Morecambe
Altrincham v Solihull Moors
Boreham Wood v Truro C
Boston U v Wealdstone
Carlisle U v Braintree T
Forest Green R v Eastleigh
Rochdale v Sutton U
Scunthorpe U v FC Halifax T
Southend U v Hartlepool U
Tamworth v Brackley T

Woking v York C
Yeovil T v Gateshead

Saturday, 30 August 2025
Brackley T v Scunthorpe U
Braintree T v Forest Green R
Eastleigh v Altrincham
FC Halifax T v Yeovil T
Gateshead v Aldershot T
Hartlepool U v Boreham Wood
Morecambe v Woking
Solihull Moors v Southend U
Sutton U v Carlisle U
Truro C v Boston U
Wealdstone v Rochdale

Tuesday, 2 September 2025
Braintree T v Tamworth
Eastleigh v Scunthorpe U
Morecambe v Forest Green R
Solihull Moors v Yeovil T
Wealdstone v Southend U
York C v Rochdale

Wednesday, 3 September 2025
Brackley T v Carlisle U
FC Halifax T v Woking
Gateshead v Altrincham
Hartlepool U v Boston U
Sutton U v Boreham Wood
Truro C v Aldershot T

Saturday, 6 September 2025
Aldershot T v Brackley T
Altrincham v Sutton U
Boreham Wood v Morecambe
Boston U v Solihull Moors
Carlisle U v Truro C
Forest Green R v Hartlepool U
Rochdale v Braintree T
Scunthorpe U v Wealdstone
Southend U v FC Halifax T
Tamworth v Eastleigh
Woking v Gateshead
Yeovil T v York C

Tuesday, 9 September 2025
York C v Tamworth

Saturday, 13 September 2025
Boreham Wood v Altrincham
Braintree T v York C
Carlisle U v Aldershot T
FC Halifax T v Eastleigh
Forest Green R v Scunthorpe U
Hartlepool U v Brackley T
Solihull Moors v Morecambe
Southend U v Boston U
Sutton U v Tamworth
Truro C v Rochdale
Wealdstone v Gateshead
Yeovil T v Woking

Saturday, 20 September 2025
Aldershot T v Hartlepool U
Altrincham v Carlisle U
Boston U v Boreham Wood
Brackley T v Sutton U
Eastleigh v Braintree T
Gateshead v FC Halifax T

Morecambe v Wealdstone
Rochdale v Southend U
Scunthorpe U v Truro C
Tamworth v Yeovil T
Woking v Forest Green R
York C v Solihull Moors

Tuesday, 23 September 2025
Altrincham v Forest Green R
Brackley T v Truro C
Gateshead v Hartlepool U
Rochdale v Solihull Moors
Woking v Sutton U
York C v Carlisle U

Wednesday, 24 September 2025
Aldershot T v Yeovil T
Boston U v Braintree T
Eastleigh v Southend U
Morecambe v FC Halifax T
Scunthorpe U v Boreham Wood
Tamworth v Wealdstone

Saturday, 27 September 2025
Boreham Wood v Woking
Braintree T v Gateshead
Carlisle U v Rochdale
FC Halifax T v Aldershot T
Forest Green R v York C
Hartlepool U v Tamworth
Solihull Moors v Brackley T
Southend U v Scunthorpe U
Sutton U v Boston U
Truro C v Morecambe
Wealdstone v Eastleigh
Yeovil T v Altrincham

Tuesday, 30 September 2025
Aldershot T v Braintree T
Boreham Wood v Southend U
Morecambe v Gateshead
Solihull Moors v Woking
Sutton U v Yeovil T
Truro C v Eastleigh

Wednesday, 1 October 2025
Altrincham v Tamworth
Boston U v Forest Green R
Brackley T v Wealdstone
Carlisle U v Hartlepool U
Rochdale v FC Halifax T
York C v Scunthorpe U

Saturday, 4 October 2025
Braintree T v Sutton U
Eastleigh v Solihull Moors
FC Halifax T v Brackley T
Forest Green R v Rochdale
Gateshead v Boston U
Hartlepool U v York C
Scunthorpe U v Carlisle U
Southend U v Aldershot T
Tamworth v Morecambe
Wealdstone v Altrincham
Woking v Truro C
Yeovil T v Boreham Wood

Saturday, 18 October 2025
Aldershot T v Tamworth
Altrincham v Woking

Boreham Wood v Eastleigh
Boston U v Scunthorpe U
Brackley T v Gateshead
Carlisle U v Forest Green R
Morecambe v Southend U
Rochdale v Yeovil T
Solihull Moors v Braintree T
Sutton U v Hartlepool U
Truro C v FC Halifax T
York C v Wealdstone

Tuesday, 21 October 2025
York C v Boreham Wood

Saturday, 25 October 2025
Braintree T v Altrincham
Eastleigh v Morecambe
FC Halifax T v York C
Forest Green R v Boreham Wood
Gateshead v Truro C
Hartlepool U v Solihull Moors
Scunthorpe U v Aldershot T
Southend U v Brackley T
Tamworth v Boston U
Wealdstone v Sutton U
Woking v Rochdale
Yeovil T v Carlisle U

Tuesday, 4 November 2025
Boreham Wood v Aldershot T
Carlisle U v FC Halifax T
Forest Green R v Tamworth
Hartlepool U v Morecambe
Rochdale v Scunthorpe U
Yeovil T v Wealdstone

Wednesday, 5 November 2025
Altrincham v Boston U
Braintree T v Brackley T
Solihull Moors v Truro C
Sutton U v Eastleigh
Woking v Southend U
York C v Gateshead

Saturday, 8 November 2025
Aldershot T v Forest Green R
Boston U v Rochdale
Brackley T v Boreham Wood
Eastleigh v York C
FC Halifax T v Hartlepool U
Gateshead v Solihull Moors
Morecambe v Sutton U
Scunthorpe U v Yeovil T
Southend U v Carlisle U
Tamworth v Woking
Truro C v Altrincham
Wealdstone v Braintree T

Saturday, 15 November 2025
Altrincham v Brackley T
Boreham Wood v Tamworth
Braintree T v Truro C
Carlisle U v Eastleigh
Forest Green R v Gateshead
Hartlepool U v Wealdstone
Rochdale v Aldershot T
Solihull Moors v Scunthorpe U
Sutton U v FC Halifax T
Woking v Boston U
Yeovil T v Southend U
York C v Morecambe

Saturday, 22 November 2025
Aldershot T v Woking
Boston U v Carlisle U
Brackley T v York C
Eastleigh v Hartlepool U

FC Halifax T v Solihull Moors
Gateshead v Boreham Wood
Morecambe v Yeovil T
Scunthorpe U v Braintree T
Southend U v Altrincham
Tamworth v Rochdale
Truro C v Sutton U
Wealdstone v Forest Green R

Saturday, 29 November 2025
Altrincham v Scunthorpe U
Boreham Wood v FC Halifax T
Braintree T v Morecambe
Carlisle U v Tamworth
Forest Green R v Southend U
Hartlepool U v Truro C
Rochdale v Eastleigh
Solihull Moors v Wealdstone
Sutton U v Gateshead
Woking v Brackley T
Yeovil T v Boston U
York C v Aldershot T

Saturday, 6 December 2025
Aldershot T v Altrincham
Carlisle U v Woking
Eastleigh v Brackley T
FC Halifax T v Braintree T
Forest Green R v Solihull Moors
Hartlepool U v Yeovil T
Morecambe v Boston U
Rochdale v Boreham Wood
Scunthorpe U v Tamworth
Southend U v Gateshead
Sutton U v York C
Truro C v Wealdstone

Saturday, 20 December 2025
Altrincham v Rochdale
Boreham Wood v Carlisle U
Boston U v Aldershot T
Brackley T v Morecambe
Braintree T v Hartlepool U
Gateshead v Eastleigh
Solihull Moors v Sutton U
Tamworth v Southend U
Wealdstone v FC Halifax T
Woking v Scunthorpe U
Yeovil T v Forest Green R
York C v Truro C

Friday, 26 December 2025
Brackley T v Forest Green R
Braintree T v Southend U
Eastleigh v Woking
FC Halifax T v Altrincham
Gateshead v Carlisle U
Hartlepool U v Scunthorpe U
Morecambe v Rochdale
Solihull Moors v Tamworth
Sutton U v Aldershot T
Truro C v Yeovil T
Wealdstone v Boreham Wood
York C v Boston U

Tuesday, 30 December 2025
Aldershot T v Wealdstone
Altrincham v York C
Boreham Wood v Solihull Moors
Boston U v Brackley T
Carlisle U v Morecambe
Forest Green R v Truro C
Rochdale v Hartlepool U
Scunthorpe U v Gateshead
Southend U v Sutton U
Tamworth v FC Halifax T

Woking v Braintree T
Yeovil T v Eastleigh

Saturday, 3 January 2026
Aldershot T v Solihull Moors
Altrincham v Morecambe
Boreham Wood v York C
Boston U v Eastleigh
Carlisle U v Wealdstone
Forest Green R v FC Halifax T
Rochdale v Brackley T
Scunthorpe U v Sutton U
Southend U v Truro C
Tamworth v Gateshead
Woking v Hartlepool U
Yeovil T v Braintree T

Saturday, 17 January 2026
Brackley T v Yeovil T
Braintree T v Boreham Wood
Eastleigh v Aldershot T
FC Halifax T v Boston U
Gateshead v Rochdale
Hartlepool U v Altrincham
Morecambe v Scunthorpe U
Solihull Moors v Carlisle U
Sutton U v Forest Green R
Truro C v Tamworth
Wealdstone v Woking
York C v Southend U

Tuesday, 20 January 2026
Braintree T v Boston U
Hartlepool U v Gateshead
Southend U v Eastleigh
Sutton U v Woking
Truro C v Brackley T
Yeovil T v Aldershot T

Wednesday, 21 January 2026
Boreham Wood v Scunthorpe U
Carlisle U v York C
FC Halifax T v Morecambe
Forest Green R v Altrincham
Solihull Moors v Rochdale
Wealdstone v Tamworth

Saturday, 24 January 2026
Aldershot T v Carlisle U
Altrincham v Boreham Wood
Boston U v Southend U
Brackley T v Hartlepool U
Eastleigh v FC Halifax T
Gateshead v Wealdstone
Morecambe v Solihull Moors
Rochdale v Truro C
Scunthorpe U v Forest Green R
Tamworth v Sutton U
Woking v Yeovil T
York C v Braintree T

Saturday, 31 January 2026
Boreham Wood v Boston U
Braintree T v Eastleigh
Carlisle U v Altrincham
FC Halifax T v Gateshead
Forest Green R v Woking
Hartlepool U v Aldershot T
Solihull Moors v York C
Southend U v Rochdale
Sutton U v Brackley T
Truro C v Scunthorpe U
Wealdstone v Morecambe
Yeovil T v Tamworth

Saturday, 7 February 2026
Aldershot T v FC Halifax T
Altrincham v Yeovil T
Boston U v Sutton U
Brackley T v Solihull Moors
Eastleigh v Wealdstone
Gateshead v Braintree T
Morecambe v Truro C
Rochdale v Carlisle U
Scunthorpe U v Southend U
Tamworth v Hartlepool U
Woking v Boreham Wood
York C v Forest Green R

Tuesday, 10 February 2026
Altrincham v Wealdstone
Boston U v Gateshead
Carlisle U v Scunthorpe U
Morecambe v Tamworth
Solihull Moors v Eastleigh
Truro C v Woking

Wednesday, 11 February 2026
Aldershot T v Southend U
Boreham Wood v Yeovil T
Brackley T v FC Halifax T
Rochdale v Forest Green R
Sutton U v Braintree T
York C v Hartlepool U

Saturday, 14 February 2026
Braintree T v Solihull Moors
Eastleigh v Boreham Wood
FC Halifax T v Truro C
Forest Green R v Carlisle U
Gateshead v Brackley T
Hartlepool U v Sutton U
Scunthorpe U v Boston U
Southend U v Morecambe
Tamworth v Aldershot T
Wealdstone v York C
Woking v Altrincham
Yeovil T v Rochdale

Saturday, 21 February 2026
Aldershot T v Scunthorpe U
Altrincham v Braintree T
Boreham Wood v Forest Green R
Boston U v Tamworth
Brackley T v Southend U
Carlisle U v Yeovil T
Morecambe v Eastleigh
Rochdale v Woking
Solihull Moors v Hartlepool U
Sutton U v Wealdstone
Truro C v Gateshead
York C v FC Halifax T

Tuesday, 24 February 2026
FC Halifax T v Rochdale
Forest Green R v Boston U
Scunthorpe U v York C
Southend U v Boreham Wood
Tamworth v Altrincham
Wealdstone v Brackley T

Wednesday, 25 February 2026
Braintree T v Aldershot T
Eastleigh v Truro C
Gateshead v Morecambe
Hartlepool U v Carlisle U
Woking v Solihull Moors
Yeovil T v Sutton U

Saturday, 28 February 2026
Aldershot T v Rochdale
Boston U v Woking

Brackley T v Altrincham
Eastleigh v Carlisle U
FC Halifax T v Sutton U
Gateshead v Forest Green R
Morecambe v York C
Scunthorpe U v Solihull Moors
Southend U v Yeovil T
Tamworth v Boreham Wood
Truro C v Braintree T
Wealdstone v Hartlepool U

Saturday, 7 March 2026
Altrincham v Truro C
Boreham Wood v Brackley T
Braintree T v Wealdstone
Carlisle U v Southend U
Forest Green R v Aldershot T
Hartlepool U v FC Halifax T
Rochdale v Boston U
Solihull Moors v Gateshead
Sutton U v Morecambe
Woking v Tamworth
Yeovil T v Scunthorpe U
York C v Eastleigh

Saturday, 14 March 2026
Aldershot T v York C
Boston U v Yeovil T
Brackley T v Woking
Eastleigh v Rochdale
FC Halifax T v Boreham Wood
Gateshead v Sutton U
Morecambe v Braintree T
Scunthorpe U v Altrincham
Southend U v Forest Green R
Tamworth v Carlisle U
Truro C v Hartlepool U
Wealdstone v Solihull Moors

Saturday, 21 March 2026
Altrincham v Southend U
Boreham Wood v Gateshead
Braintree T v Scunthorpe U
Carlisle U v Boston U
Forest Green R v Wealdstone
Hartlepool U v Eastleigh
Rochdale v Tamworth
Solihull Moors v FC Halifax T
Sutton U v Truro C
Woking v Aldershot T
Yeovil T v Morecambe
York C v Brackley T

Tuesday, 24 March 2026
Aldershot T v Boreham Wood
Boston U v Altrincham
Brackley T v Braintree T
Eastleigh v Sutton U
FC Halifax T v Carlisle U
Gateshead v York C

Wednesday, 25 March 2026
Morecambe v Hartlepool U
Scunthorpe U v Rochdale
Southend U v Woking
Tamworth v Forest Green R
Truro C v Solihull Moors
Wealdstone v Yeovil T

Saturday, 28 March 2026
Brackley T v Tamworth
Braintree T v Carlisle U
Eastleigh v Forest Green R
FC Halifax T v Scunthorpe U
Gateshead v Yeovil T
Hartlepool U v Southend U
Morecambe v Aldershot T

Solihull Moors v Altrincham
Sutton U v Rochdale
Truro C v Boreham Wood
Wealdstone v Boston U
York C v Woking

Friday, 3 April 2026
Aldershot T v Sutton U
Altrincham v FC Halifax T
Boreham Wood v Wealdstone
Boston U v York C
Carlisle U v Gateshead
Forest Green R v Brackley T
Rochdale v Morecambe
Scunthorpe U v Hartlepool U
Southend U v Braintree T
Tamworth v Solihull Moors
Woking v Eastleigh
Yeovil T v Truro C

Monday, 6 April 2026
Brackley T v Boston U
Braintree T v Woking
Eastleigh v Yeovil T
FC Halifax T v Tamworth
Gateshead v Scunthorpe U
Hartlepool U v Rochdale
Morecambe v Carlisle U
Solihull Moors v Boreham Wood
Sutton U v Southend U
Truro C v Forest Green R
Wealdstone v Aldershot T
York C v Altrincham

Saturday, 11 April 2026
Aldershot T v Gateshead
Altrincham v Eastleigh
Boreham Wood v Hartlepool U
Boston U v Truro C
Carlisle U v Sutton U
Forest Green R v Braintree T
Rochdale v Wealdstone
Scunthorpe U v Brackley T
Southend U v Solihull Moors
Tamworth v York C
Woking v Morecambe
Yeovil T v FC Halifax T

Saturday, 18 April 2026
Brackley T v Aldershot T
Braintree T v Rochdale
Eastleigh v Tamworth
FC Halifax T v Southend U
Gateshead v Woking
Hartlepool U v Forest Green R
Morecambe v Boreham Wood
Solihull Moors v Boston U
Sutton U v Altrincham
Truro C v Carlisle U
Wealdstone v Scunthorpe U
York C v Yeovil T

Saturday, 25 April 2026
Aldershot T v Truro C
Altrincham v Gateshead
Boreham Wood v Sutton U
Boston U v Hartlepool U
Carlisle U v Brackley T
Forest Green R v Morecambe
Rochdale v York C
Scunthorpe U v Eastleigh
Southend U v Wealdstone
Tamworth v Braintree T
Woking v FC Halifax T
Yeovil T v Solihull Moors

THE SCOTTISH PREMIERSHIP AND SCOTTISH LEAGUE FIXTURES 2025–26

All fixtures subject to change.

Scottish Premiership

Saturday, 2 August 2025
Kilmarnock v Livingston
Motherwell v Rangers

Sunday, 3 August 2025
Falkirk v Dundee U
Dundee v Hibernian
Celtic v St Mirren

Monday, 4 August 2025
Hearts v Aberdeen

Saturday, 9 August 2025
Dundee U v Hearts
Hibernian v Kilmarnock
Livingston v Falkirk
St Mirren v Motherwell
Rangers v Dundee

Sunday, 10 August 2025
Aberdeen v Celtic

Saturday, 23 August 2025
Celtic v Livingston
Dundee U v Aberdeen
Falkirk v Hibernian
Hearts v Motherwell
Kilmarnock v Dundee
St Mirren v Rangers

Saturday, 30 August 2025
Aberdeen v Falkirk
Dundee v Dundee U
Hibernian v St Mirren
Livingston v Hearts
Motherwell v Kilmarnock

Sunday, 31 August 2025
Rangers v Celtic

Saturday, 13 September 2025
Aberdeen v Livingston
Dundee v Motherwell
Falkirk v St Mirren
Hibernian v Dundee U
Kilmarnock v Celtic
Rangers v Hearts

Saturday, 27 September 2025
Celtic v Hibernian
Dundee U v Kilmarnock
Hearts v Falkirk
Livingston v Rangers
Motherwell v Aberdeen
St Mirren v Dundee

Saturday, 4 October 2025
Aberdeen v Dundee
Celtic v Motherwell
Dundee U v Livingston
Falkirk v Rangers
Hearts v Hibernian
Kilmarnock v St Mirren

Saturday, 18 October 2025
Dundee v Celtic
Hibernian v Livingston
Kilmarnock v Hearts
Motherwell v Falkirk
Rangers v Dundee U
St Mirren v Aberdeen

Saturday, 25 October 2025
Aberdeen v Hibernian
Dundee U v St Mirren
Falkirk v Dundee
Hearts v Celtic

Livingston v Motherwell
Rangers v Kilmarnock

Wednesday, 29 October 2025
Celtic v Falkirk
Dundee v Livingston
Hibernian v Rangers
Kilmarnock v Aberdeen
Motherwell v Dundee U
St Mirren v Hearts

Saturday, 1 November 2025
Dundee U v Celtic
Falkirk v Kilmarnock
Hearts v Dundee
Livingston v St Mirren
Motherwell v Hibernian
Rangers v Aberdeen

Saturday, 8 November 2025
Aberdeen v Motherwell
Celtic v Kilmarnock
Dundee v Rangers
Falkirk v Livingston
St Mirren v Hibernian

Sunday, 9 November 2025
Hearts v Dundee U

Saturday, 22 November 2025
Aberdeen v Hearts
Dundee U v Falkirk
Hibernian v Dundee
Kilmarnock v Motherwell
Rangers v Livingston
St Mirren v Celtic

Saturday, 29 November 2025
Dundee v St Mirren
Hibernian v Celtic
Kilmarnock v Dundee U
Livingston v Aberdeen
Motherwell v Hearts
Rangers v Falkirk

Wednesday, 3 December 2025
Aberdeen v St Mirren
Celtic v Dundee
Dundee U v Rangers
Falkirk v Motherwell
Hearts v Kilmarnock
Livingston v Hibernian

Saturday, 6 December 2025
Celtic v Hearts
Dundee v Aberdeen
Hibernian v Falkirk
Kilmarnock v Rangers
Motherwell v Livingston
St Mirren v Dundee U

Saturday, 13 December 2025
Aberdeen v Kilmarnock
Dundee U v Motherwell
Falkirk v Celtic
Hearts v St Mirren
Livingston v Dundee
Rangers v Hibernian

Saturday, 20 December 2025
Celtic v Aberdeen
Dundee U v Hibernian
Hearts v Rangers
Kilmarnock v Falkirk
Motherwell v Dundee
St Mirren v Livingston

Saturday, 27 December 2025
Hibernian v Hearts
Aberdeen v Dundee U

Dundee v Falkirk
Livingston v Celtic
Rangers v Motherwell
St Mirren v Kilmarnock

Tuesday, 30 December 2025
Dundee v Kilmarnock
Falkirk v Hearts
Hibernian v Aberdeen
Livingston v Dundee U
Motherwell v Celtic
Rangers v St Mirren

Saturday, 3 January 2026
Celtic v Rangers
Dundee U v Dundee
Falkirk v Aberdeen
Hearts v Livingston
Kilmarnock v Hibernian
Motherwell v St Mirren

Saturday, 10 January 2026
Aberdeen v Rangers
Celtic v Dundee U
Dundee v Hearts
Hibernian v Motherwell
Livingston v Kilmarnock
St Mirren v Falkirk

Saturday, 24 January 2026
Aberdeen v Livingston
Dundee U v St Mirren
Falkirk v Hibernian
Hearts v Celtic
Motherwell v Kilmarnock
Rangers v Dundee

Saturday, 31 January 2026
Celtic v Falkirk
Dundee U v Hearts
Hibernian v Rangers
Kilmarnock v Aberdeen
Livingston v Motherwell
St Mirren v Dundee

Wednesday, 4 February 2026
Aberdeen v Celtic
Dundee v Motherwell
Hibernian v Dundee U
Livingston v Falkirk
Rangers v Kilmarnock
St Mirren v Hearts

Wednesday, 11 February 2026
Celtic v Livingston
Dundee U v Aberdeen
Falkirk v Dundee
Hearts v Hibernian
Kilmarnock v St Mirren
Motherwell v Rangers

Saturday, 14 February 2026
Dundee v Livingston
Falkirk v Dundee U
Hibernian v St Mirren
Kilmarnock v Celtic
Motherwell v Aberdeen
Rangers v Hearts

Saturday, 21 February 2026
Aberdeen v Dundee
Celtic v Hibernian
Dundee U v Kilmarnock
Hearts v Falkirk
Livingston v Rangers
St Mirren v Motherwell

Saturday, 28 February 2026
Dundee v Hibernian
Falkirk v Kilmarnock

Hearts v Aberdeen
Livingston v St Mirren
Motherwell v Dundee U
Rangers v Celtic

Saturday, 14 March 2026
Aberdeen v Falkirk
Celtic v Motherwell
Dundee v Dundee U
Hibernian v Livingston
Kilmarnock v Hearts
St Mirren v Rangers

Saturday, 21 March 2026
Dundee U v Celtic
Falkirk v St Mirren
Hearts v Dundee
Kilmarnock v Livingston
Motherwell v Hibernian
Rangers v Aberdeen

Saturday, 4 April 2026
Dundee v Celtic
Hibernian v Kilmarnock
Livingston v Hearts
Motherwell v Falkirk
Rangers v Dundee U
St Mirren v Aberdeen

Saturday, 11 April 2026
Aberdeen v Hibernian
Celtic v St Mirren
Dundee U v Livingston
Falkirk v Rangers
Hearts v Motherwell
Kilmarnock v Dundee

Scottish Championship

Friday, 1 August 2025
Arbroath v Ayr U

Saturday, 2 August 2025
Airdrieonians v Ross Co
Greenock Morton v Dunfermline Ath
Raith R v Queen's Park
St Johnstone v Partick Thistle

Saturday, 9 August 2025
Ayr U v Raith R
Dunfermline Ath v Airdrieonians
Partick Thistle v Greenock Morton
Queen's Park v Arbroath
Ross Co v St Johnstone

Saturday, 23 August 2025
Airdrieonians v Queen's Park
Greenock Morton v Ayr U
Raith R v Dunfermline Ath
Ross Co v Partick Thistle
St Johnstone v Arbroath

Saturday, 30 August 2025
Arbroath v Airdrieonians
Ayr U v Queen's Park
Dunfermline Ath v Ross Co
Partick Thistle v Raith R
St Johnstone v Greenock Morton

Saturday, 6 September 2025
Airdrieonians v St Johnstone
Dunfermline Ath v Ayr U
Greenock Morton v Raith R
Queen's Park v Partick Thistle
Ross Co v Arbroath

Saturday, 13 September 2025
Arbroath v Dunfermline Ath
Ayr U v Ross Co
Partick Thistle v Airdrieonians
Queen's Park v Greenock Morton
Raith R v St Johnstone

Saturday, 20 September 2025
Airdrieonians v Raith R
Arbroath v Greenock Morton
Partick Thistle v Ayr U

Ross Co v Queen's Park
St Johnstone v Dunfermline Ath

Saturday, 27 September 2025
Ayr U v Airdrieonians
Dunfermline Ath v Partick Thistle
Greenock Morton v Ross Co
Queen's Park v St Johnstone
Raith R v Arbroath

Saturday, 4 October 2025
Airdrieonians v Greenock Morton
Dunfermline Ath v Queen's Park
Partick Thistle v Arbroath
Ross Co v Raith R
St Johnstone v Ayr U

Saturday, 11 October 2025
Airdrieonians v Dunfermline Ath
Arbroath v Queen's Park
Greenock Morton v Partick Thistle
Raith R v Ayr U
St Johnstone v Ross Co

Saturday, 18 October 2025
Arbroath v St Johnstone
Ayr U v Greenock Morton
Dunfermline Ath v Raith R
Partick Thistle v Ross Co
Queen's Park v Airdrieonians

Saturday, 25 October 2025
Airdrieonians v Arbroath
Greenock Morton v St Johnstone
Queen's Park v Ayr U
Raith R v Partick Thistle
Ross Co v Dunfermline Ath

Saturday, 1 November 2025
Arbroath v Ross Co
Ayr U v Dunfermline Ath
Partick Thistle v Queen's Park
Raith R v Greenock Morton
St Johnstone v Airdrieonians

Saturday, 8 November 2025
Airdrieonians v Partick Thistle
Dunfermline Ath v St Johnstone
Greenock Morton v Arbroath
Queen's Park v Raith R
Ross Co v Ayr U

Saturday, 15 November 2025
Ayr U v Arbroath
Partick Thistle v Dunfermline Ath
Raith R v Airdrieonians
Ross Co v Greenock Morton
St Johnstone v Queen's Park

Saturday, 22 November 2025
Airdrieonians v Ayr U
Arbroath v Raith R
Dunfermline Ath v Greenock Morton
Partick Thistle v St Johnstone
Queen's Park v Ross Co

Saturday, 6 December 2025
Ayr U v Partick Thistle
Dunfermline Ath v Arbroath
Greenock Morton v Queen's Park
Ross Co v Airdrieonians
St Johnstone v Raith R

Saturday, 13 December 2025
Arbroath v Partick Thistle
Ayr U v St Johnstone
Greenock Morton v Airdrieonians
Queen's Park v Dunfermline Ath
Raith R v Ross Co

Saturday, 20 December 2025
Airdrieonians v Queen's Park
Dunfermline Ath v Ayr U
Partick Thistle v Raith R
Ross Co v Arbroath
St Johnstone v Greenock Morton

Saturday, 27 December 2025
Arbroath v Airdrieonians
Greenock Morton v Ayr U

Queen's Park v Partick Thistle
Raith R v Dunfermline Ath
Ross Co v St Johnstone

Saturday, 3 January 2026
Airdrieonians v Raith R
Ayr U v Queen's Park
Dunfermline Ath v Ross Co
Partick Thistle v Greenock Morton
St Johnstone v Arbroath

Saturday, 10 January 2026
Ayr U v Airdrieonians
Greenock Morton v Dunfermline Ath
Queen's Park v St Johnstone
Raith R v Arbroath
Ross Co v Partick Thistle

Saturday, 24 January 2026
Airdrieonians v Ross Co
Arbroath v Greenock Morton
Partick Thistle v Ayr U
Raith R v Queen's Park
St Johnstone v Dunfermline Ath

Saturday, 31 January 2026
Ayr U v Raith R
Dunfermline Ath v Airdrieonians
Greenock Morton v Ross Co
Queen's Park v Arbroath
St Johnstone v Partick Thistle

Saturday, 14 February 2026
Airdrieonians v St Johnstone
Arbroath v Ayr U
Dunfermline Ath v Partick Thistle
Greenock Morton v Raith R
Ross Co v Queen's Park

Saturday, 21 February 2026
Arbroath v Dunfermline Ath
Ayr U v Ross Co
Partick Thistle v Airdrieonians
Queen's Park v Greenock Morton
Raith R v St Johnstone

Saturday, 28 February 2026
Airdrieonians v Greenock Morton
Dunfermline Ath v Queen's Park
Partick Thistle v Arbroath
Ross Co v Raith R
St Johnstone v Ayr U

Saturday, 7 March 2026
Arbroath v Ross Co
Ayr U v Dunfermline Ath
Greenock Morton v St Johnstone
Queen's Park v Airdrieonians
Raith R v Partick Thistle

Saturday, 14 March 2026
Airdrieonians v Arbroath
Dunfermline Ath v Raith R
Greenock Morton v Partick Thistle
Queen's Park v Ayr U
St Johnstone v Ross Co

Saturday, 21 March 2026
Arbroath v Queen's Park
Ayr U v Greenock Morton
Partick Thistle v St Johnstone
Raith R v Airdrieonians
Ross Co v Dunfermline Ath

Saturday, 28 March 2026
Airdrieonians v Dunfermline Ath
Greenock Morton v Arbroath
Partick Thistle v Ross Co
Raith R v Ayr U
St Johnstone v Queen's Park

Saturday, 4 April 2026
Arbroath v St Johnstone
Ayr U v Partick Thistle
Dunfermline Ath v Greenock Morton
Queen's Park v Raith R
Ross Co v Airdrieonians

Saturday, 11 April 2026
Ayr U v Arbroath
Partick Thistle v Dunfermline Ath
Queen's Park v Ross Co
Raith R v Greenock Morton
St Johnstone v Airdrieonians

Saturday, 18 April 2026
Airdrieonians v Partick Thistle
Arbroath v Raith R
Dunfermline Ath v St Johnstone
Greenock Morton v Queen's Park
Ross Co v Ayr U

Saturday, 25 April 2026
Airdrieonians v Ayr U
Arbroath v Partick Thistle
Queen's Park v Dunfermline Ath
Ross Co v Greenock Morton
St Johnstone v Raith R

Friday, 1 May 2026
Ayr U v St Johnstone
Dunfermline Ath v Arbroath
Greenock Morton v Airdrieonians
Partick Thistle v Queen's Park
Raith R v Ross Co

Scottish League One

Saturday, 2 August 2025
Alloa Ath v Stenhousemuir
Cove Rangers v Queen of the South
Hamilton A v Montrose
Kelty Hearts v Inverness CT
Peterhead v East Fife

Saturday, 9 August 2025
East Fife v Alloa Ath
Inverness CT v Peterhead
Montrose v Kelty Hearts
Queen of the South v Hamilton A
Stenhousemuir v Cove Rangers

Saturday, 16 August 2025
Cove Rangers v Montrose
Hamilton A v East Fife
Inverness CT v Stenhousemuir
Kelty Hearts v Alloa Ath
Queen of the South v Peterhead

Saturday, 23 August 2025
Alloa Ath v Hamilton A
East Fife v Kelty Hearts
Montrose v Inverness CT
Peterhead v Cove Rangers
Stenhousemuir v Queen of the South

Saturday, 30 August 2025
Hamilton A v Cove Rangers
Inverness CT v Alloa Ath
Montrose v Peterhead
Queen of the South v Kelty Hearts
Stenhousemuir v East Fife

Saturday, 13 September 2025
Alloa Ath v Montrose
Cove Rangers v Inverness CT
East Fife v Queen of the South
Kelty Hearts v Stenhousemuir
Peterhead v Hamilton A

Saturday, 20 September 2025
Alloa Ath v Cove Rangers
East Fife v Montrose
Kelty Hearts v Hamilton A
Queen of the South v Inverness CT
Stenhousemuir v Peterhead

Saturday, 27 September 2025
Cove Rangers v Kelty Hearts
Hamilton A v Stenhousemuir
Inverness CT v East Fife
Montrose v Queen of the South
Peterhead v Alloa Ath

Saturday, 4 October 2025
East Fife v Cove Rangers
Hamilton A v Inverness CT

Kelty Hearts v Peterhead
Queen of the South v Alloa Ath
Stenhousemuir v Montrose

Saturday, 18 October 2025
Alloa Ath v East Fife
Cove Rangers v Stenhousemuir
Inverness CT v Kelty Hearts
Montrose v Hamilton A
Peterhead v Queen of the South

Saturday, 25 October 2025
Hamilton A v Queen of the South
Kelty Hearts v East Fife
Montrose v Cove Rangers
Peterhead v Inverness CT
Stenhousemuir v Alloa Ath

Saturday, 1 November 2025
Alloa Ath v Kelty Hearts
Cove Rangers v Peterhead
East Fife v Hamilton A
Inverness CT v Montrose
Queen of the South v Stenhousemuir

Saturday, 8 November 2025
Hamilton A v Peterhead
Inverness CT v Cove Rangers
Montrose v Alloa Ath
Queen of the South v East Fife
Stenhousemuir v Kelty Hearts

Saturday, 15 November 2025
Alloa Ath v Inverness CT
Cove Rangers v Hamilton A
East Fife v Stenhousemuir
Kelty Hearts v Queen of the South
Peterhead v Montrose

Saturday, 22 November 2025
Cove Rangers v Alloa Ath
Hamilton A v Kelty Hearts
Inverness CT v Queen of the South
Montrose v East Fife
Peterhead v Stenhousemuir

Saturday, 6 December 2025
Alloa Ath v Peterhead
East Fife v Inverness CT
Kelty Hearts v Montrose
Queen of the South v Cove Rangers
Stenhousemuir v Hamilton A

Saturday, 13 December 2025
Alloa Ath v Queen of the South
Cove Rangers v East Fife
Inverness CT v Hamilton A
Montrose v Stenhousemuir
Peterhead v Kelty Hearts

Saturday, 20 December 2025
East Fife v Peterhead
Hamilton A v Alloa Ath
Kelty Hearts v Cove Rangers
Queen of the South v Montrose
Stenhousemuir v Inverness CT

Saturday, 27 December 2025
Alloa Ath v Stenhousemuir
East Fife v Kelty Hearts
Montrose v Inverness CT
Peterhead v Cove Rangers
Queen of the South v Hamilton A

Saturday, 3 January 2026
Cove Rangers v Montrose
Hamilton A v East Fife
Inverness CT v Peterhead
Kelty Hearts v Alloa Ath
Stenhousemuir v Queen of the South

Saturday, 10 January 2026
Alloa Ath v Montrose
Cove Rangers v Inverness CT
Peterhead v Hamilton A
Queen of the South v Kelty Hearts
Stenhousemuir v East Fife

Saturday, 24 January 2026
East Fife v Queen of the South
Hamilton A v Cove Rangers

Inverness CT v Alloa Ath
Kelty Hearts v Stenhousemuir
Montrose v Peterhead

Saturday, 31 January 2026
Alloa Ath v Cove Rangers
East Fife v Montrose
Kelty Hearts v Hamilton A
Queen of the South v Inverness CT
Stenhousemuir v Peterhead

Saturday, 7 February 2026
Cove Rangers v Queen of the South
Hamilton A v Stenhousemuir
Inverness CT v East Fife
Montrose v Kelty Hearts
Peterhead v Alloa Ath

Saturday, 14 February 2026
East Fife v Cove Rangers
Hamilton A v Inverness CT
Kelty Hearts v Peterhead
Queen of the South v Alloa Ath
Stenhousemuir v Montrose

Saturday, 21 February 2026
Alloa Ath v Hamilton A
Cove Rangers v Kelty Hearts
Inverness CT v Stenhousemuir
Montrose v Queen of the South
Peterhead v East Fife

Saturday, 28 February 2026
East Fife v Alloa Ath
Hamilton A v Montrose
Kelty Hearts v Inverness CT
Queen of the South v Peterhead
Stenhousemuir v Cove Rangers

Saturday, 7 March 2026
Alloa Ath v Kelty Hearts
Cove Rangers v Peterhead
East Fife v Hamilton A
Inverness CT v Montrose
Queen of the South v Stenhousemuir

Saturday, 14 March 2026
Hamilton A v Queen of the South
Inverness CT v Cove Rangers
Kelty Hearts v East Fife
Montrose v Alloa Ath
Peterhead v Stenhousemuir

Saturday, 21 March 2026
Alloa Ath v Inverness CT
Cove Rangers v Hamilton A
Peterhead v Montrose
Queen of the South v East Fife
Stenhousemuir v Kelty Hearts

Saturday, 28 March 2026
Alloa Ath v Peterhead
East Fife v Stenhousemuir
Hamilton A v Kelty Hearts
Inverness CT v Queen of the South
Montrose v Cove Rangers

Saturday, 4 April 2026
Cove Rangers v Alloa Ath
Kelty Hearts v Queen of the South
Montrose v East Fife
Peterhead v Inverness CT
Stenhousemuir v Hamilton A

Saturday, 11 April 2026
East Fife v Peterhead
Hamilton A v Alloa Ath
Kelty Hearts v Montrose
Queen of the South v Cove Rangers
Stenhousemuir v Inverness CT

Saturday, 18 April 2026
Alloa Ath v East Fife
Cove Rangers v Stenhousemuir
Inverness CT v Kelty Hearts
Montrose v Hamilton A
Peterhead v Queen of the South

Saturday, 25 April 2026
East Fife v Inverness CT
Hamilton A v Peterhead
Kelty Hearts v Cove Rangers
Queen of the South v Montrose
Stenhousemuir v Alloa Ath

Saturday, 2 May 2026
Alloa Ath v Queen of the South
Cove Rangers v East Fife
Inverness CT v Hamilton A
Montrose v Stenhousemuir
Peterhead v Kelty Hearts

Scottish League Two

Saturday, 2 August 2025
Annan Ath v Elgin C
Dumbarton v Clyde
East Kilbride v The Spartans
Edinburgh C v Stirling Alb
Forfar Ath v Stranraer

Saturday, 9 August 2025
Clyde v Forfar Ath
Elgin C v East Kilbride
Stirling Alb v Annan Ath
Stranraer v Edinburgh C
The Spartans v Dumbarton

Saturday, 16 August 2025
Clyde v The Spartans
Dumbarton v Elgin C
East Kilbride v Stranraer
Edinburgh C v Annan Ath
Forfar Ath v Stirling Alb

Saturday, 23 August 2025
Annan Ath v Dumbarton
Elgin C v Edinburgh C
Stirling Alb v East Kilbride
Stranraer v Clyde
The Spartans v Forfar Ath

Saturday, 30 August 2025
Clyde v Elgin C
Dumbarton v Edinburgh C
East Kilbride v Forfar Ath
Stirling Alb v Stranraer
The Spartans v Annan Ath

Saturday, 13 September 2025
Annan Ath v Clyde
Edinburgh C v East Kilbride
Elgin C v Stirling Alb
Forfar Ath v Dumbarton
Stranraer v The Spartans

Saturday, 20 September 2025
Clyde v Edinburgh C
East Kilbride v Dumbarton
Forfar Ath v Annan Ath
Stranraer v Elgin C
The Spartans v Stirling Alb

Saturday, 27 September 2025
Annan Ath v East Kilbride
Dumbarton v Stranraer
Edinburgh C v Forfar Ath
Elgin C v The Spartans
Stirling Alb v Clyde

Saturday, 4 October 2025
Clyde v East Kilbride
Elgin C v Forfar Ath
Stirling Alb v Dumbarton
Stranraer v Annan Ath
The Spartans v Edinburgh C

Saturday, 18 October 2025
Annan Ath v Stirling Alb
Dumbarton v The Spartans
East Kilbride v Elgin C
Edinburgh C v Stranraer
Forfar Ath v Clyde

Saturday, 1 November 2025
Clyde v Dumbarton
Elgin C v Annan Ath

Stirling Alb v Edinburgh C
Stranraer v Forfar Ath
The Spartans v East Kilbride

Saturday, 8 November 2025
Clyde v Stranraer
Dumbarton v Annan Ath
East Kilbride v Stirling Alb
Edinburgh C v Elgin C
Forfar Ath v The Spartans

Saturday, 15 November 2025
Annan Ath v Edinburgh C
Elgin C v Dumbarton
Stirling Alb v Forfar Ath
Stranraer v East Kilbride
The Spartans v Clyde

Saturday, 22 November 2025
Clyde v Annan Ath
Dumbarton v Forfar Ath
East Kilbride v Edinburgh C
Stirling Alb v Elgin C
The Spartans v Stranraer

Saturday, 6 December 2025
Annan Ath v The Spartans
Edinburgh C v Dumbarton
Elgin C v Clyde
Forfar Ath v East Kilbride
Stranraer v Stirling Alb

Saturday, 13 December 2025
Annan Ath v Forfar Ath
Dumbarton v East Kilbride
Edinburgh C v Clyde
Elgin C v Stranraer
Stirling Alb v The Spartans

Saturday, 20 December 2025
Clyde v Stirling Alb
East Kilbride v Annan Ath
Forfar Ath v Edinburgh C
Stranraer v Dumbarton
The Spartans v Elgin C

Saturday, 27 December 2025
Annan Ath v Stranraer
Dumbarton v Stirling Alb
East Kilbride v Clyde
Edinburgh C v The Spartans
Forfar Ath v Elgin C

Saturday, 3 January 2026
Clyde v Forfar Ath
Elgin C v East Kilbride
Stirling Alb v Annan Ath
Stranraer v Edinburgh C
The Spartans v Dumbarton

Saturday, 10 January 2026
Annan Ath v Elgin C
Dumbarton v Clyde
East Kilbride v The Spartans
Edinburgh C v Stirling Alb
Forfar Ath v Stranraer

Saturday, 17 January 2026
Annan Ath v Dumbarton
Elgin C v Edinburgh C
Stirling Alb v East Kilbride
Stranraer v Clyde
The Spartans v Forfar Ath

Saturday, 24 January 2026
Clyde v The Spartans
Dumbarton v Elgin C
East Kilbride v Stranraer
Edinburgh C v Annan Ath
Forfar Ath v Stirling Alb

Saturday, 31 January 2026
Annan Ath v Clyde
Dumbarton v Edinburgh C
East Kilbride v Forfar Ath
Elgin C v The Spartans
Stirling Alb v Stranraer

Saturday, 7 February 2026
Clyde v Elgin C
Edinburgh C v East Kilbride

Forfar Ath v Dumbarton
Stranraer v Annan Ath
The Spartans v Stirling Alb

Saturday, 14 February 2026
Annan Ath v East Kilbride
Dumbarton v Stranraer
Elgin C v Forfar Ath
Stirling Alb v Clyde
The Spartans v Edinburgh C

Saturday, 21 February 2026
Clyde v Edinburgh C
East Kilbride v Dumbarton
Elgin C v Stirling Alb
Forfar Ath v Annan Ath
Stranraer v The Spartans

Saturday, 28 February 2026
Clyde v East Kilbride
Edinburgh C v Forfar Ath
Stirling Alb v Dumbarton
Stranraer v Elgin C
The Spartans v Annan Ath

Saturday, 7 March 2026
Annan Ath v Stirling Alb
Dumbarton v The Spartans
East Kilbride v Elgin C
Edinburgh C v Stranraer
Forfar Ath v Clyde

Saturday, 14 March 2026
Annan Ath v Edinburgh C
Elgin C v Dumbarton
Stirling Alb v Forfar Ath
Stranraer v East Kilbride
The Spartans v Clyde

Saturday, 21 March 2026
Clyde v Stranraer
Dumbarton v Annan Ath
East Kilbride v Stirling Alb
Edinburgh C v Elgin C
Forfar Ath v The Spartans

Saturday, 28 March 2026
Annan Ath v Stranraer
Dumbarton v Forfar Ath
Elgin C v Clyde
Stirling Alb v Edinburgh C
The Spartans v East Kilbride

Saturday, 4 April 2026
Clyde v Stirling Alb
East Kilbride v Annan Ath
Edinburgh C v The Spartans
Forfar Ath v Elgin C
Stranraer v Dumbarton

Saturday, 11 April 2026
Dumbarton v Stirling Alb
Edinburgh C v Clyde
Elgin C v Annan Ath
Forfar Ath v East Kilbride
The Spartans v Stranraer

Saturday, 18 April 2026
Annan Ath v The Spartans
Clyde v Dumbarton
East Kilbride v Edinburgh C
Stirling Alb v Elgin C
Stranraer v Forfar Ath

Saturday, 25 April 2026
Clyde v Annan Ath
Dumbarton v East Kilbride
Forfar Ath v Edinburgh C
Stranraer v Stirling Alb
The Spartans v Elgin C

Saturday, 2 May 2026
Annan Ath v Forfar Ath
East Kilbride v Clyde
Edinburgh C v Dumbarton
Elgin C v Stranraer
Stirling Alb v The Spartans

STOP PRESS

England U21s win UEFA Championship for second tournament running ... Tottenham sack Ange and appoint Frank ... Liverpool break club transfer record signing Wirtz for £116m and in negotiations to sign Ekiteke ... Chelsea thrash favourites Paris Saint-Germain and become World champions ... Another Bellingham signs for Borussia Dortmund as Jobe moves from Sunderland ... Delap chooses Chelsea, as does Joao Pedro ... Jordan Henderson signs for Brentford ... Luka Modric joins AC Milan after 13 seasons at Real Madrid ... Arsenal women sign Olivia Smith from Liverpool in first £1m women's transfer ... England women through to semi-finals in Euro 2025.

SELECTED SUMMER TRANSFERS 2025

1 June: Matheus Cunha Wolverhampton W to Manchester U £62.5m.

2 June: Nathan Baxter Bolton W to Watford; Romelle Donovan Birmingham C to Brentford; Dario Essugo Sporting Lisbon to Chelsea £18m; Marcus Harness Ipswich T to Huddersfield T.

3 June: Mark Flekken Brentford to Bayer Leverkusen £8m; Caoimhin Kelleher Liverpool to Brentford £12.5m; Pol Valentin Sheffield Wed to Preston NE.

4 June: Liam Delap Ipswich T to Chelsea £30m; Michael Ihiekwe Sheffield Wed to Blackpool.

5 June: Antonio Cordero Malaga to Newcastle U; Nuno Taveres Arsenal to Lazio.

6 June: Marc Bola Samsunspor to Watford; Sonny Carey Blackpool to Charlton Ath; Dan Grimshaw Plymouth Arg to Norwich C; Jorginho Arsenal to Flamengo; Lloyd Kelly Newcastle U to Juventus £20m; Thierry Small Charlton Ath to Preston NE; Jean-Clair Todibo Nice to West Ham U.

7 June: Armin Pecsi Puskas Akademia to Liverpool; Sorba Thomas Huddersfield T to Stoke C.

9 June: Rayan Ait-Nouri Wolverhampton W to Manchester C £31m; Sam Dalby Wrexham to Bolton W; Marquinhos Arsenal to Cruzeiro; Mamadou Sarr Strasbourg to Chelsea £12m.

10 June: Jobe Bellingham Sunderland to Borussia Dortmund £31m; Marcus Bettinelli Chelsea to Manchester C; Chem Campbell Wolverhampton W to Stevenage; Rayan Cherki Lyon to Manchester C £30.45m; Filozofe Mabete Wolverhampton W to Swindon T; Kal Naismith Bristol C to Luton T; Dion de Neve KV Kortrijk to Blackburn R; Rico Richards Aston Villa to Port Vale; Joe Snowdon Leeds U to Swindon T; Kieran Tierney Arsenal to Celtic.

11 June: Tijjani Reijnders AC Milan to Manchester C £46.5m; George Saville Millwall to Luton T; Ehije Ukaki Botev Plovdiv to Sheffield U.

12 June: Charalampos Kostoulas Olympiakos to Brighton & HA £29.78m; Reda Laalaoui Fath Union Sport to Hull C; Xavier Simons Hull C to Bolton W.

14 June: Cameron Burgess Ipswich T to Swansea C; CJ Egan-Riley Burnley to Marseille.

15 June: Lukas Nmecha Wolfsburg to Leeds U; Mathys Tel Bayern Munich to Tottenham H £30m.

16 June: Harry Darling Swansea C to Norwich C; Ryan Hardie Plymouth Arg to Wrexham; Dillon Phillips Rotherham U to Hull C.

17 June: Diego Coppola Verona to Brighton & HA; Mykola Kuharevich Swansea C to Slovan Bratislava; Dilan Markanday Blackburn R to Chesterfield.

18 June: Louie Moulden Crystal Palace to Norwich C; Adrian Segecic Sydney FC to Portsmouth; Murray Wallace Millwall to Huddersfield T.

19 June: Semi Ajayi WBA to Hull C; Miguel Angel Brau Granada to Coventry C; Christian Saydee Portsmouth to Wigan Ath; Francisco Sierralta Watford to Auxerre.

20 June: Sonny Bradley Derby Co to Lincoln C; Zach Hemming Middlesbrough to Chesterfield; Ben Hughes Swansea C to Cambridge U; Fer Lopez Celta Vigo to Wolverhampton W £19m; Adam Randell Plymouth Arg to Bristol C; Sidnei Taveres Moreirense to Blackburn R; Jaden Williams Tottenham H to Colchester U; Ben Winterbottom Brentford to Barrow; Florian Wirtz Bayer Leverkusen to Liverpool £116m.

23 June: Walter Benitez PSV Eindhoven to Crystal Palace; Jaka Bijol Udinese to Leeds U; Nat Phillips Liverpool to WBA.

24 June: Killian Cahill Brighton & HA to Leyton Orient; Ted Cann WBA to Rotherham U; Max Crocombe Burton Alb to Millwall; Sean Grehan Crystal Palace to Doncaster R; Andrew Omobamidele Nottingham F to Strasbourg.

25 June: Niall Ennis Stoke C to Blackpool; Tyrese Fornah Derby Co to Northampton T; George Honeyman Millwall to Blackpool; Brandon Khela Birmingham C to Peterborough U; Joe Lumley Southampton to Bristol C; Jakov Medic Ajax to Norwich C; Anthony Racioppi, external Hull C to FC Sion; Andy Smith Hull C to Gillingham; Max Weiss Karlsruher to Burnley £4.3m; Ayumu Yokoyama Birmingham C to KRC Genk.

26 June: Will Boyle Wrexham to Shrewsbury T; Josh Coburn Millwall to Middlesbrough; Dara Costelloe Burnley to Wigan Ath; Milos Kerkez Bournemouth to Liverpool £40m; Vladan Kovacevic Sporting Lisbon to Norwich C; Amadou Mbengue Reading to QPR; Carlton Morris Luton T to Derby Co; Paul Onuachu Southampton to Trabzonspor; Ruben Rodrigues Oxford U to EC Vitoria; Axel Tuanzebe Ipswich T to Burnley; Brad Young Leicester C to Bristol R.

27 June: Kealey Adamson Macarthur to QPR; Daiki Hashioka Luton T to Slavia Prague; Lewis Shipley Norwich C to Barrow.

28 June: Kwame Poku Peterborough U to QPR.

30 June: Reyes Cleary WBA to Barnsley; Emil Riis Jakobsen Preston NE to Bristol C; Josh McEachran Oxford U to Bristol R; Callum Osmand Fulham to Celtic.

1 July: Kepa Arrizabalaga Chelsea to Arsenal £5m; Danny Batth Blackburn R to Derby Co; Nathan Bishop Sunderland to AFC Wimbledon; Sebastiaan Bornauw Wolfsburg to Leeds U £5.1m; Habib Diarra Strasbourg to Sunderland £30m; Brian De Keersmaecker Heracles to Oxford U; Kaine Kesler-Hayden Aston Villa to Coventry C;

Jorgen Strand Larsen Celta Vigo to Wolverhampton W £23m; Delano McCoy-Splatt Fulham to AFC Wimbledon; Richard O'Donnell Blackpool to Derby Co; Zepiqueno Redmond Feyenoord to Aston Villa; Danny Ward Leicester C to Wrexham; Andreas Weimann Blackburn R to Derby Co.

2 July: Valentin Barco Brighton & HA to Strasbourg; Olivier Boscagli PSV Eindhoven to Brighton & HA; Jack Bray Harrogate T to WBA; Zak Gilsenan Blackburn R to Grimsby T; Tanto Olaofe Stockport Co to Charlton Ath; Joao Pedro Brighton & HA to Chelsea £60m; Jarell Quansah Liverpool to Bayer Leverkusen £35m; Kamaldeen Sulemana Southampton to Atalanta £18m; Loum Tchaouna Lazio to Burnley.

3 July: Demarai Gray Al-Ettifaq to Birmingham C; Antoni Milambo Feyenoord to Brentford; Amari'i Bell Luton T to Charlton Ath; Philippe Coutinho Aston Villa to Vasco da Gama; Jonathan David Lille to Juventus; Idris El Mizouni Oxford U to Leyton Orient; Louis Flower Brighton & HA to Crawley T; Ethan Galbraith Leyton Orient to Swansea C; Bright Osayi-Samuel Fenerbahce to Birmingham C; Bim Pepple Luton T to Plymouth Arg; Dion Pereira Luton T to Crawley T; Noah Sadiki Union Saint-Gilloise to Sunderland £15m.

5 July: Maxim de Cuyper Club Brugge to Brighton & HA; Kyogo Furuhashi Rennes to Birmingham C; Jamie Gittens Borussia Dortmund to Chelsea £48.5m; Igor Jesus Botafogo to Nottingham F £10m; Diego Leon Cerro Porteno to Manchester U; Odel Offiah Brighton & HA to Preston NE; Vivaldo Semedo Udinese to Watford; Vinicius Souza Sheffield U to Wolfsburg; Maksym Talovierov Plymouth Arg to Stoke C; Kyle Walker Manchester C to Burnley £5m.

6 July: Kanya Fujimoto Gil Vicente to Birmingham C; Martin Zubimendi Real Sociedad to Arsenal £60m.

7 July: Aaron Connolly Millwall to Leyton Orient; Aune Heggebo SK Brann to WBA; Ryley Towler Portsmouth to Lincoln C.

8 July: Ayman Benarous Bristol C to Plymouth Arg; Gabriel Gudmundsson Lille to Leeds U £10m; Ryan Howley Coventry C to Bristol R; Mathias Kvistgaarden Brondby to Norwich C £6.9m; Reinildo Mandava Atletico Madrid to Sunderland; Kota Takai Kawasaki Frontale to Tottenham H £5m.

9 July: Thierno Barry Villarreal to Everton £27m; Reece Burke Luton T to Charlton Ath; Damion Downs Cologne to Southampton £7m; Ben Perry Nottingham F to Colchester U; Ramon Sosa Nottingham F to Palmeiras £10m; Chemsdine Talbi Club Brugge to Sunderland; Jack Whatmough Preston NE to Huddersfield T.

10 July: Simon Adingra Brighton & HA to Sunderland £21m; Ryan Alebiosu KV Kortrijk to Blackburn R; Aaron Cresswell West Ham U to Stoke C; Mohammed Kudus West Ham U to Tottenham H £55m; Emmanuel Longelo Birmingham C to Motherwell; Christian Norgaard Brentford to Arsenal £15m; Brodie Spencer Huddersfield T to Oxford U; Nahki Wells Bristol C to Luton T; Mallik Wilks Sheffield Wed to Pendikspor.

11 July: Jacob Bruun Larsen Stuttgart to Burnley; Jair Cunha Botafogo to Nottingham F; Anthony Elanga Nottingham F to Newcastle U £55m; Othmane Maamma Montpellier to Watford; Joe Rankin-Costello Blackburn R to Charlton Ath; Borna Sosa Ajax to Crystal Palace.

13 July: Azor Matusiwa Rennes to Ipswich T; Borja Sainz Norwich C to FC Porto £14.25m.

14 July: Zak Sturge Chelsea to Millwall.

15 July: Marco Bizot Brest to Aston Villa; El Hadji Malick Diouf Slavia Prague to West Ham U £19m; Lyndon Gooch Stoke C to Huddersfield T; Jordan Henderson Ajax to Brentford; Jamie Mullins Brighton & HA to Wycombe W; John Swift WBA to Portsmouth; Mark Travers Bournemouth to Everton.

16 July: Djordje Petrovic Chelsea to Bournemouth £25m.

WOMEN'S EURO 2025 FINALS

IN SWITZERLAND

GROUP STAGE

GROUP A

Iceland v Finland	0-1
Switzerland v Norway	1-2
Norway v Finland	2-1
Switzerland v Iceland	2-0
Finland v Switzerland	1-1
Norway v Iceland	4-3

Group A Table	P	W	D	L	F	A	GD	Pts
Norway	3	3	0	0	8	5	3	9
Switzerland	3	1	1	1	4	3	1	4
Finland	3	1	1	1	3	3	0	4
Iceland	3	0	0	3	3	7	–4	0

GROUP B

Belgium v Italy	0-1
Spain v Portugal	5-0
Spain v Belgium	6-2
Portugal v Italy	1-1
Italy v Spain	1-3
Portugal v Belgium	1-2

Group B Table	P	W	D	L	F	A	GD	Pts
Spain	3	3	0	0	14	3	11	9
Italy	3	1	1	1	3	4	–1	4
Belgium	3	1	0	2	4	8	–4	3
Portugal	3	0	1	2	2	8	–6	1

Competion still being played.

GROUP C

Denmark v Sweden	0-1
Germany v Poland	2-0
Germany v Denmark	2-1
Poland v Sweden	0-3
Sweden v Germany	4-1
Poland v Denmark	3-2

Group C Table	P	W	D	L	F	A	GD	Pts
Sweden	3	3	0	0	8	1	7	9
Germany	3	2	0	1	5	5	0	6
Poland	3	1	0	2	3	7	–4	3
Denmark	3	0	0	3	3	6	–3	0

GROUP D

Wales v Netherlands	0-3
France v England	2-1
England v Netherlands	4-0
France v Wales	4-1
Netherlands v France	2-5
England v Wales	6-1

Group D Table	P	W	D	L	F	A	GD	Pts
France	3	3	0	0	11	4	7	9
England	3	2	0	1	11	3	8	6
Netherlands	3	1	0	2	5	9	–4	3
Wales	3	0	0	3	2	13	–11	0

Now you can buy any of these other football titles from your normal retailer or direct from the publisher.

FREE P&P AND UK DELIVERY
(Overseas and Ireland £3.50 per book)

Tinseltown: Hollywood and the Beautiful Game – A Match Made in Wrexham	Ian Herbert	£12.99
How to Be a Football Manager	Ian Holloway	£12.99
Not for Me, Clive: Stories from the Voice of Football	Clive Tyldesley	£12.99
Hooked: Addiction and the Long Road to Recovery	Paul Merson	£12.99
Whistle Blower: My Autobiography	Mark Clattenburg	£10.99
Toxic: Tackling 'Razor' and Finding the Real Me	Neil Ruddock	£12.99
I've Got Mail: The Soccer Saturday Letters	Jeff Stelling	£12.99
Extra Time Beckons, Penalties Loom: How to Use (and Abuse) The Language of Football	Adam Hurrey	£20.00
Me, Family and the Making of a Footballer	Jamie Redknapp	£9.99
Old Too Soon, Smart Too Late	Kieron Dyer	£12.99
Football: My Life, My Passion	Graeme Souness	£10.99
Fearless	Jonathan Northcroft	£10.99
Saturday Afternoon Fever: The Autobiography	Jeff Stelling	£12.99
Football Clichés	Adam Hurrey	£10.99
I Believe in Miracles	Daniel Taylor	£10.99
Big Sam: My Autobiography	Sam Allardyce	£10.99
Bend it Like Bullard	Jimmy Bullard	£10.99
Hammer Time: Me, West Ham, and a Passion for the Shirt	Julian Dicks	£12.99
Angeball: The Definitive Biography of Ange Postecoglou	Vince Rugari	£14.99

TO ORDER SIMPLY CALL THIS NUMBER
01235 759555

or visit our website:
www.headline.co.uk

Prices and availability subject to change without notice.